BUTTERWORTHS
COMPANY LAW
HANDBOOK

EDITOR'S INTRODUCTION TO THE THIRTY-SIXTH EDITION

As ever, our aim in this edition is to provide as comprehensive a collection of company law materials, including the most recent developments, as is possible within the physical constraints of a single volume work.

While the Queen's Speech of 10 May 2022 promised a number of measures of interest to company lawyers in 2022–2023 (notably, a further Economic Crime and Corporate Transparency Bill which will make significant changes to the role and powers of the registrar of companies), the Parliamentary session 2021–2022 yielded only one significant new measure of primary legislation, namely the Economic Crime (Transparency and Enforcement) Act 2022.

Part 1 of the ECTEA 2022, which was brought into force (almost entirely) by the ECTEA (Commencement No 3) Regulations 2022 on 1 August 2022, provides for the establishment of a register of overseas entities (including information on their beneficial owners) which is maintained by the registrar of companies. Much of the implementation of that Part is dependent on supporting statutory instruments, see the Register of Overseas Entities (Verification and Provision of Information) Regulations 2022, SI 2022/725 and the Register of Overseas Entities (Delivery, Protection and Trust Services) Regulations 2022, SI 2022/870, which are included in Part 10 at **[10.1363]** and **[10.1376]** respectively.

A limited primary legislation measure provided for the disqualification of directors of dissolved companies. This measure was contained in the Rating (Coronavirus) and Directors Disqualification (Dissolved Companies) Act 2021, and the necessary amendments are incorporated into the Company Directors Disqualification Act 1986 at **[5.76]** et seq.

Statutory instruments of particular note in recent months include:

— Four sets of Regulations giving effect to the National Security and Investment Act 2021 (NSIA 2021) which came fully into force on 4 January 2022 (all of which are included in Part 10 of this Handbook). Given the significance of this legislation, readers may be interested to know that the Department for Business, Energy and Industrial Strategy has published the first annual review of the legislation, see *BEIS, National Security and Investment Act 2021, Annual Report 2022 (June 2022)*. This initial report only covers the period 4 January 2022 (commencement) to 31 March 2022, subsequent reports will cover a twelve-month period.

— The Companies (Strategic Report) (Climate-related Financial Disclosure) Regulations 2022, SI 2022/31 and the Limited Liability Partnerships (Climate-related Financial Disclosure) Regulations 2022, SI 2022/46. These Regulations are reflected in amendments to the relevant provisions of the CA 2006 and, for LLPs, in amendments to the Limited Liability Partnerships Regulations 2001 and the Limited Liability Partnerships (Accounts and Audit) (Application of Companies Act 2006) Regulations 2008. They provide for mandatory climate-related disclosures by a range of large publicly traded companies – but also other large public and private companies, and limited liability partnerships, with more than 500 employees and a turnover of more than £500m. The Regulations make provision for a non-financial and sustainability information statement in the strategic report, and this requirement applies to financial years commencing on or after 6 April 2022.

In this edition, the Commencement Orders made under the Companies Act 2006 have been moved from Part 2 to an online Appendix, but the 'at a glance' table of commencement information for all provisions of the 2006 Act – including sections and Schedules added to the Act since 2006 – remains. The table (which is at paragraph **[2.1]**) also contains detailed footnotes and cross-references to all applicable transitional provisions and savings in connection with the commencement of the 2006 Act.

In Part 11, there are included relevant EU Directives and Regulations pertaining to company law. Of course, those EU Directives which were adopted prior to Brexit were transposed by the UK and are embedded in the Companies Act 2006 and related statutory instruments. As such, they formed part of domestic law before Implementation Period Completion Day (11pm on 31 December 2020 – see the European Union (Withdrawal) Act 2018, s 39(1)) and, thereafter, they continue to have effect in domestic law (see the European Union (Withdrawal) Act 2018, s 2) with any modifications. Those modifications were effected in many instances by the EU-Exit Regulations which are included in Part 12.

There are only a small number of EU Regulations of relevance to this volume, mainly the Insolvency Regulation (2015/848/EU) and the Prospectus Regulation (2017/1129/EU) which, pursuant to the European Union (Withdrawal) Act 2018, s 3, now form part of domestic law – as modified by domestic law from time to time. Again, such modifications as have been made have been effected by a number of the EU-Exit Regulations. By these mechanisms, therefore, company law derived from Directives, and Regulations adopted and in force prior to Brexit, are retained law and, as such, continue to be (in the case of Directives), or now form part of domestic law (in the case of Regulations) – see the European Union (Withdrawal) Act 2018, s 6(7). See also the explanatory notes to the European Union (Withdrawal) Act 2018, paras 23, 48, 75 and 83.

Part 11 reflects these EU company law measures as they stand at the date of publication of this edition – while the Notes make clear the extent to which the measures apply in the UK as domestic law. The EU measures are set out as currently adopted by the EU – as these provisions are of continuing relevance to those UK businesses active in Europe, depending on the scope of the relevant measure and the business structure adopted by the UK business. Additionally, Part 11 includes various EU measures which have no application in the UK – for example, Regulation 2019/2088/EU on sustainability-related disclosures in the financial services sector, known as SFDR, which only applied from 10 March 2021. Such measures are included because the broader picture of EU regulation of company law remains of interest and importance to our users, especially those advising companies operating within the EU.

This, the thirty-sixth edition of Butterworths Company Law Handbook, follows the same format of its predecessors. In relation to the Companies Act 1985 material, the Handbook now only includes (in Part 5) those provisions that remain in force. Users needing access to the full 1985 Act materials, prior to the 2006 Act related repeals (eg, when dealing with corporate events occurring prior to 1 October 2009) should either consult the special one-off archival edition of the Handbook published in 2010 (*Butterworths Company Law Handbook: The Companies Act 1985 Regime*), or view those provisions via the online or CD versions of this Handbook (as to which, see below).

As before, this year's print edition does not include the explanatory notes to the Companies Act 2006, nor the Insolvency Rules 1986. The 1986 Rules were revoked by the Insolvency (England and Wales) Rules 2016, SI 2016/1024 (which are included) with effect from 6 April 2017. The 1986 Rules remain relevant in cases where an application to court was filed, or a petition was presented, under the Insolvency Act 1986 or the 1986 Rules before 6 April 2017. In light of the above, it is recommended that users of this Handbook retain the thirtieth edition of this work in order to refer to the 2006 Act's explanatory notes or the 1986 Rules as needed. The 1986 Rules (and related materials) also continue to be included in this Handbook's companion publication – *Butterworths Insolvency Law Handbook* – which is published annually.

The contents are reproduced as amended to include all materials published at 1 August 2022.

Professor Brenda Hannigan,
August 2022.

If you have any comments regarding this Handbook, please email the in-house editor at: robin.mitchell@lexisnexis.co.uk.

Contents of this Handbook

The aim of this annual Handbook is to make available, in a convenient and up-to-date form, the full text of the most important company law statutes, statutory instruments, European legislation, and Retained European Regulations.

The Handbook is divided into 12 main Parts together with four related Appendices. Within each Part, the contents are printed in chronological order. A list of all the amending provisions is provided at the beginning of each Act, statutory instrument, European Regulation/Directive, and Retained European Regulation. A purely amending or repealing provision is not normally reproduced; instead, the amendments, etc, are incorporated into the affected provision (see further the note on house style of amendments below). Appendix 4 does, however, provide a comprehensive list of *all* statutory instruments made under the Companies Act 2006, including a summary of their effect.

An index and glossary are also provided in this Handbook. References in the index and glossary are to the unique paragraph number given to each provision – not its page number.

The main Parts of the Handbook are as follows—

Companies Act 2006 (Part 1). This Part contains the complete and fully-updated version of the 2006 Act.

Companies Act 2006 – Commencement (Part 2). Contains a fully-updated table of commencements for the 2006 Act with commencement details for all of the original provisions plus details for all added, substituted and repealed provisions. Note that the 2006 Act commencement orders (which were previously included in this Part) have been removed from the 2022 edition in order to create space for newer and more relevant legislation. The commencement orders are, however, included in a new online Appendix (Appendix 10). Appendix 10 is also included in the CD version of this Handbook.

Companies Act 2006 Supporting Materials, etc (Part 3). This Part contains the UK Corporate Governance Code 2018, the table of origins for the 2006 Act, the tables of destinations for the Companies Acts 1985 and 1989, and the Ministerial statements on duties of directors.

Companies Act 2006 Statutory Instruments (Part 4). This Part contains the substantive companies statutory instruments made under the 2006 Act (with the exception of the commencement orders). Note also, that where an instrument is made under the authority of more than one Act, the instrument will be included in its most appropriate Part. See, for example, the Limited Liability Partnerships (Accounts and Audit) (Application of Companies Act 2006) Regulations 2008. The 2008 Regulations were made under the Companies Act 2006, ss 1210(1)(h), 1292(2), and the Limited Liability Partnerships Act 2000, ss 15, 17. Even though the Regulations were partly made under CA 2006, the subject matter of the Regulations, and the fact that their main authority is the Limited Liability Partnerships Act 2000, means that they are included in Part 10 of this Handbook, and not Part 4.

Other companies Primary Legislation (Part 5). This Part contains the Companies Act 1985 (as remaining in force at 1 August 2022). Repealed provisions are not reproduced but details of the repeal are given, together with details of any relevant savings or transitional provisions and cross-references to the relevant savings provision. It also contains the Company Directors Disqualification Act 1986, the unrepealed provisions of the Companies Act 1989, the relevant provisions of the Criminal Justice Act 1993, and the Companies (Audit, Investigations and Community Enterprise) Act 2004.

Other Companies Statutory instruments (Part 6). This Part contains the statutory instruments made under the primary legislation contained in Part 5. Again, it should be noted that where an instrument is made under the authority of more than one Act, the instrument will be included in its most appropriate Part (see the example given in the entry relating to Part 4 above).

Financial Services Primary Legislation (Part 7). Selected provisions of the Financial Services and Markets Act 2000, the Financial Services Act 2012, and the Financial Services Act 2021 are reproduced in Part 7. It should be emphasised that this edition of *Butterworths Company Law Handbook* (unlike some of its predecessors) does not contain the full text of FSMA 2000. It is felt that, because of the pressure on space in this work, such material is more appropriately contained in volumes dealing with financial services law, as opposed to company law. Where a provision has been omitted due to space considerations, a note is included to that effect. Those users of this work who need such material are referred to this Handbook's companion works, such as *Butterworths Securities & Financial Services Law Handbook* (which is published annually).

Financial Services Statutory Instruments (Part 8). This Part includes the texts of those statutory instruments made under financial services primary legislation that are most relevant to company lawyers.

Miscellaneous other Primary Legislation (Part 9). This Part includes a variety of other primary legislation covering such subject areas as partnerships, limited liability partnerships, insolvency, and economic crime.

Miscellaneous other Statutory Instruments (Part 10). The most relevant statutory instruments made under the Acts included in Part 9 are set out here.

Selected EU Legislation & Retained EU Legislation (Part 11). Part 11 contains a selection of European Regulations and Directives. This Part sets out EU Regulations both as they apply in the EU at the date of publication, and as they apply in the UK as retained domestic law under the European Union (Withdrawal) Act 2018. The main version of the text is that applicable in the EU, and all amendments that apply to the UK are set out in the Notes to the affected provision. See further, the note "General Note – General Scheme of Legislation Contained in this Part" at the beginning of Part 11 *post*.

Exiting the EU Materials (Part 12). This Part contains the European Union (Withdrawal) Act 2018 and the European Union (Withdrawal Agreement) Act 2020, as well as the relevant 'Exiting the EU' Regulations made under the 2018 Act.

Appendices. Appendix 1 contains the Companies Act 2006 Model Articles. The text of the Companies Act 1948 Table A is reproduced because this version of Table A continues to apply to many companies incorporated prior to 1 July 1985 (Appendix 3). For convenience, the Companies Act 1985 Table A is set out in Appendix 2. Appendix 4 contains a complete list and summaries of all statutory instruments made under the Companies Act 2006.

House style for amendments

Amendments are indicated using the house style of the Handbooks series as follows: In force repeals/revocations are indicated by an ellipsis. Insertions and in force substitutions are in square brackets. Prospective repeals/revocations or substitutions are in italics with, in the case of substitutions, the text to be substituted set out in the notes (note that this also applies to prospective substitutions that have been brought into force for some, but not all, purposes). Details of the provenance of changes are given in the notes, together with the effective date. Text that has been repealed or revoked with savings in relation to its continued application is also in italics (with full details of the relevant savings or transitional provisions set out in the notes). A summary follows—

— **insertion (in force and prospective):** [text in square brackets]

— **in force substitution:** [text in square brackets]

— **prospective substitution:** *text in italics* (with new text set out in notes)

— **in force repeal or revocation:** . . . (an ellipsis)

— **prospective repeal or revocation:** *text in italics*

— **repealed/revoked with savings or transitional provisions:** *text in italics* (with details of savings, etc, set out in notes)

In the case of amendments made by statutory instruments, the full name and number of the instrument is cited in the notes to a provision in the first amendment note to that provision.

If there are other amendments made by the instrument to the same provision, then only the SI number is given in those subsequent amendment notes.

Commencement information is given at provision level for Acts and statutory instruments in cases where the provision came into force on or after 1 July 2019, or where it is not yet in force for all or some purposes. If no commencement information is given at provision level, then the provision in question was brought into force for all purposes before 1 July 2019.

Electronic versions of this Handbook

Butterworths Company Law Handbook is included as part of the Lexis®Library service (at www.lexisnexis.com/uk/legal). The Handbook is updated fortnightly on this service.

There is also a CD version of this work that is updated monthly and which can be ordered from the LexisNexis Customer Services Department.

Note that both electronic versions of the Handbook contain certain extra material that has not been included in the hardcopy version simply because there is not the space to fit it all into a one volume work. This material is as follows:

- Appendix 5 — Summaries of all statutory instruments made under the Financial Services and Markets Act 2000
- Appendix 6 — Summaries of all statutory instruments made under the Financial Services Act 2012
- Appendix 7 — Companies Act 1985 (at 7 November 2006)
- Appendix 8 — Companies Act 1985 (at 1 October 2010)
- Appendix 9 — Companies Act 2006 (as at 1 October 2009)
- Appendix 10 — Companies Act 2006 Commencement Orders.

CONTENTS

PART 5 — OTHER COMPANIES PRIMARY LEGISLATION

PART 6 — OTHER COMPANIES STATUTORY INSTRUMENTS

PART 7 — FINANCIAL SERVICES PRIMARY LEGISLATION

PART 8 — FINANCIAL SERVICES STATUTORY INSTRUMENTS

PART 9 — MISCELLANEOUS OTHER PRIMARY LEGISLATION

PART 10 — MISCELLANEOUS OTHER STATUTORY INSTRUMENTS

PART 11 — SELECTED EU LEGISLATION & RETAINED EU LEGISLATION

Chronological list

List of common names of main Directives & Regulations

PART 12 — EXITING THE EU MATERIALS

APPENDICES

Glossary of Words and Phrases

accounting documents, **[4.217]**

accounting standards, **[1.529]**

acquirer, **[9.572]**

act as insolvency practitioner, **[9.400]**

administrative receiver, **[9.396]**

affiliated undertakings, **[11.154]**

ancillary document, **[5.58]**

annual accounts, **[1.536]**

annuities on human life, **[8.3]**

applicant, **[7.588]**

application, **[7.588]**

appropriate audit authority, **[1.606]**

appropriate rate, **[1.675]**, **[1.692]**, **[9.463]**

approved exchange, **[8.438]**

arrangement, **[1.1034]**, **[1.1042]**

Article 21 relief application, **[10.184]**

Article 21 remedy application, **[10.196]**

associate, **[1.390]**, **[1.1457]**, **[9.463]**

associated pension scheme, **[4.117]**

associated undertaking, **[11.154]**

auction platform, **[8.3]**

audit committee, **[1.573]**

Audit Directive, **[1.573]**

Auditor General, **[1.573]**

audit working papers, **[1.1458]**

authorised building society, **[8.556]**

authorised deposit-taker, **[10.482]**

authorised insurance company, **[10.257]**

authorised unit trust scheme, **[7.438]**

bank, **[10.36]**

banking company, **[1.1334]**, **[10.257]**

banking group, **[1.1334]**

banking LLP, **[10.257]**

beneficial owner, **[9.678]**

body corporate, **[7.699]**

borrower, **[8.155]**

borrower-lender agreement, **[8.155]**

borrower-lender-supplier agreement, **[8.155]**

building, **[9.197]**

building operations, **[9.197]**

business, **[9.44]**

business day, **[9.396]**, **[10.482]**, **[6.33]**

called-up share capital, **[1.629]**

cash balance benefit, **[8.129]**

central bank, **[10.62]**

central counterparty, **[7.588]**, **[10.62]**

central counterparty recognition order, **[7.588]**

central securities depository, **[7.699]**

certified sophisticated investor, **[8.498]**

charge, **[1.982]**, **[4.332]**, **[10.62]**,

chattel leasing agreement, **[9.396]**

chief executive, **[7.699]**

clearing, **[7.588]**

clearing house, **[10.62]**

close relative, **[8.3]**

collateral security, **[10.62]**

collateral security charge, **[10.62]**

collective investment scheme, **[7.434]**

communications, **[8.279]**

Companies Acts, **[1.2]**

Companies House Direct, **[4.471]**

company, **[1.1]**

company (disqualification of directors), **[5.120]**

company (insider dealing), **[5.201]**

company contributions, **[4.111]**

company limited by guarantee, **[1.3]**

company limited by shares, **[1.3]**

company records, **[1.1304]**, **[4.542]**

conditional sale agreement, **[8.155]**

connected with company, **[9.394]**

consumers, **[7.7]**, **[7.715]**, **[7.716]**, **[8.81]**, **[8.156]**, **[8.164]**

contract of employment, **[10.153]**

contract of insurance, **[8.3]**
contractually-based investment, **[8.3]**
contributory, **[1.1342]**, **[9.208]**
controller, **[7.708]**
convertible securities, **[1.1151]**
core investment service, **[8.4]**
coronavirus, **[9.548]**
corporate governance statement, **[1.538]**, **[1.620]**
corporate insolvency or governance legislation, **[9.548]**
corporate insolvency or restructuring procedure, **[9.548]**
court, **[1.1326]**, **[1.1354]**, **[9.44]**
credit institution, **[1.1345]**, **[7.8]**, **[10.62]**
credit-related regulated activity, **[7.699]**
credit union, **[8.155]**, **[9.511]**
creditor's voluntary winding-up resolution, **[10.62]**
current assets, **[4.59]**, **[4.114]**
CVA, **[10.482]**
daily default fine, **[1.1295]**
data protection legislation, **[7.699]**
date of the original directors' remuneration report, **[4.22]**
date of the original directors' report, **[4.22]**
date of revision, **[4.22]**
dealing in securities, **[5.196]**
debenture, **[1.823]**
debt, **[10.482]**
default arrangements, **[10.62]**
default rules, **[5.185]**
dematerialised instructions, **[6.42]**
dematerialised loan instrument, **[6.42]**
deposit, **[8.155]**
derivatives, **[4.59]**, **[4.114]**
designated disadvantaged area, **[9.197]**
designated professional body, **[8.253]**
designated system, **[10.62]**
direct EU legislation, **[12.5]**
director, **[5.120]**, **[1.278]**, **[7.699]**, **[9.396]**
directors' remuneration policy, **[1.249]**
director's service contract, **[1.256]**
distributable profits, **[1.766]**

distributions, **[1.947]**

division, **[1.1077]**

document, **[7.699]**

domestic property, **[8.157]**

dormant, **[1.1339]**

e-money issuer, **[10.257]**, **[10.275]**

EEA company, **[1.1340]**

EEA state, **[1.1340]**

EEA undertaking, **[1.1340]**

EEIG establishment, **[10.14]**

eligible debt security, **[6.42]**

eligible Northern Ireland Treasury Bill, **[6.42]**

eligible Treasury Bill, **[6.42]**

e-money issuer, **[1.540]**, **[1.621]**, **[7.8]**

EMIR regulation, **[7.588]**

emission allowance auctioning regulation, **[8.3]**

emission allowance trading directive, **[8.3]**

emoluments, **[4.111]**

employee, **[10.153]**

employee liability information, **[10.163]**

employees' share scheme, **[1.1336]**

engineering operations, **[9.197]**

environmentally sustainable investment, **[11.790]**

equity security, **[1.642]**

equity share capital, **[1.630]**

equity shares, **[1.699]**

ESMA, **[7.699]**

establishment, **[4.327]**

EU tertiary legislation, **[12.28]**

exempt consumer buy-to-let mortgage contract, **[8.166]**

exempt person (regulated activities), **[7.699]**

exit day, **[12.28]**

expedited petition, **[9.100]**

Extranet, **[4.471]**

fellow subsidiary undertaking, **[1.1331]**

financial assistance, **[1.760]**

financial crime, **[7.8]**

financial institution, **[1.863]**, **[1.1345]**, **[9.511]**

financial instrument, **[7.279]**

financial holding undertakings, **[11.154]**

firm, **[1.1345]**, **[9.4]**

fixed assets, **[4.59]**, **[4.114]**, **[11.154]**

fixed security, **[5.58]**, **[9.190]**

fixed sum credit, **[8.155]**

flexible benefit, **[8.129]**

floating charge, **[9.396]**

former Companies Acts, **[1.1343]**

former name, **[4.191]**

full accounts and reports, **[4.495]**

funeral plan contract, **[8.138]**

fungible assets, **[4.114]**

Gazette, **[1.1345]**

general local authority security, **[6.42]**

general partner, **[9.56]**

general public sector security, **[6.42]**

general UK Government security, **[6.42]**

go into liquidation, **[9.391]**

government, **[11.194]**

green deal credit agreement, **[8.157]**

greenhouse gas emissions allowances, **[8.3]**

group, **[1.540]**, **[7.705]**, **[11.154]**

group undertaking, **[1.1331]**

hire-purchase agreement, **[8.155]**

IAS Regulation, **[1.540]**

immediate group, **[7.706]**

improver, **[8.157]**

information made public, **[5.199]**

inside information, **[5.197]**

insiders, **[5.198]**

insolvency, **[9.391]**, **[9.511]**

inspection place, **[4.542]**

insurance company, **[1.1335]**

insurance mediation activity, **[8.253]**

insurer, **[9.511]**

interest in a security, **[6.42]**

interim relief application, **[10.184]**

international accounting standards, **[1.540]**

investment company, **[1.951]**, **[10.257]**

investment firm, **[7.713]**, **[8.4]**

investment professional, **[8.290]**

investment property loan, **[8.166]**

investment service, **[8.3]**

investment undertakings, **[11.154]**

issuer, **[1.573]**, **[8.437]**, **[7.279]**

issuer-instruction, **[6.42]**

issuer register of securities, **[6.42]**

joint enterprise, **[8.3]**

joint stock company, **[1.1204]**

land of freehold tenure, **[4.114]**

lease, **[4.114]**

lender, **[8.155]**

liability limitation agreement, **[1.615]**

limited company, **[1.3]**

limited interest second charge credit union loan, **[8.166]**

limited liability partnership, **[4.471]**

limited liability partnership agreement, **[10.100]**

limited partnership, **[4.471]**

limited payment second charge bridging loan, **[8.166]**

liquidation committee, **[10.36]**

listed instruments, **[4.114]**

listed investment, **[4.59]**

loans, **[4.59]**, **[4.114]**

local authority, **[1.55]**, **[9.77]**, **[8.3]**, **[8.327]**, **[6.42]**

local authority security, **[6.42]**

local bank, **[10.36]**

local bank account, **[10.36]**

long lease, **[4.114]**

main proceedings, **[10.482]**

major audit **[1.606]**

manager, **[7.710]**

managing agent, **[8.3]**

market charges, **[5.169]**

market contracts, **[5.150]**

materiality, **[4.59]**, **[4.114]**

member of company, **[9.395]**

merger, **[1.1056]**

micro business, **[9.516]**

MiFID investment firm, **[1.540]**, **[1.621]**, **[10.257]**, **[10.275]**

modification or termination order, **[10.184]**, **[10.196]**

name, **[4.191]**

moratorium debt, **[9.133]**

net assets, **[1.93]**, **[1.949]**

net turnover, **[11.154]**

netting, **[10.62]**

network, **[1.573]**

non-cash asset, **[1.1333]**

non-public interest company, **[1.600]**

occupational pension scheme, **[8.3]**

notifiable acquisition, **[9.573]**

offer period, **[1.1133]**

offer to the public, **[1.841]**

offeror, **[1.1133]**

office-holder, **[10.482]**

officer, **[1.1345]**

official list, **[7.234]**

old public company, **[4.428]**

open-ended investment company, **[7.436]**, **[8.340]**

operator-instruction, **[6.42]**

operator register of securities, **[6.42]**

operator-system, **[6.42]**

operator (uncertificated securities), **[6.42]**

opted-out creditor, **[9.393]**

ordinary shares, **[1.642]**

original, **[4.22]**

overseas applicant, **[7.588]**

overseas company, **[1.1207]**

overseas clearing house, **[7.588]**

overseas entity, **[9.635]**

overseas investment exchange, **[7.588]**

overseas person, **[8.3]**

parent company, **[1.1345]**

parent law, **[4.217]**

parent undertaking, **[1.1332]**, **[7.704]**, **[11.154]**

participating interests in, **[4.59]**, **[4.114]**, **[7.707]**

participating security, **[6.42]**

partnership, **[9.1]**

partnership property, **[9.20]**
payment for loss of office, **[1.238]**
pension costs, **[4.59]**, **[4.114]**
pension fund management contract, **[8.3]**
pension scheme, **[4.111]**, **[8.129]**
performance measure, **[4.111]**
police force, **[4.191]**
political donation, **[1.414]**
political expenditure, **[1.415]**
PRA-regulated person, **[7.634]**
pre-1982 pre-emption requirement, **[1.659]**
pre-moratorium creditor, **[9.92]**
pre-moratorium debt, **[9.133]**
prescribed, **[1.1337]**
primary information provider, **[7.212]**
private company, **[1.4]**
processor, **[4.210]**
production cost, **[11.154]**
professional intermediary, **[5.200]**
profit and loss account, **[1.540]**
property, **[9.464]**
protected items, **[7.694]**
public authority, **[1.55]**
public company, **[1.4]**
public function, **[4.210]**
public interest company, **[1.573]**, **[1.600]**
public-interest entities, **[11.154]**
public sector body, **[5.201]**
public servant, **[5.37]**
purchase price, **[4.59]**, **[4.114]**, **[11.154]**
qualifying asset, **[9.574]**
qualifying entity, **[9.574]**
qualifying authorised person, **[7.401]**
qualifying contract of insurance, **[8.3]**
qualifying provision, **[7.717]**
qualifying parent undertaking, **[7.402]**
qualifying partnership, **[10.204]**
qualifying services, **[4.111]**
quasi-loan, **[1.222]**

quoted company, **[1.437]**, **[1.612]**

real time communications, **[8.280]**

realised profit and losses, **[4.59]**, **[4.114]**

receiver, **[9.190]**, **[9.396]**

recognised CSD, **[7.699]**

recognised clearing house, **[7.536]**

recognised investment exchange, **[7.536]**

recognition application, **[10.184]**, **[10.196]**

recognition order, **[10.184]**, **[10.196]**

recorded insurance intermediary, **[8.254]**

register, **[1.1245]**

register of overseas entities, **[9.636]**

registered securities, **[9.77]**

registered third country auditor, **[1.1426]**

registrar of companies, **[1.1224]**

register of securities, **[6.33]**

regulated activity, **[1.540]**

regulated benchmark, **[7.8]**

regulated claims management activity, **[7.699]**

regulated financial services, **[7.8]**

regulated home purchase plan, **[8.174]**

regulated home reversion plan, **[8.170]**

regulated market, **[1.573]**, **[5.201]**

regulator, **[7.38]**, **[7.699]**

regulatory functions, **[5.135]**

relevant friendly society, **[8.556]**

relevant markets, **[7.6]**

relevant office-holder, **[5.186]**

relevant recipient of credit, **[8.155]**

relevant transfer, **[10.154]**

relevant UK authorised person, **[8.556]**

remuneration committee, **[4.111]**

remuneration payment, **[1.249]**

restricted use credit agreement, **[8.155]**

retained direct EU legislation, **[12.28]**

retained EU law, **[12.9]**

retention of title agreement, **[9.396]**

retirement benefits, **[4.111]**

revised accounts, **[4.22]**

revised report, **[4.22]**

revision by replacement, **[4.22]**

revision by supplementary note, **[4.22]**

running account credit, **[8.155]**

safeguarded benefits, **[8.129]**

scheme, **[4.111]**

scheme interest, **[4.111]**

scheme property, **[8.340]**

second charge business loan, **[8.166]**

secondary proceedings, **[10.184]**, **[10.482]**

section 243 applicant, **[4.191]**

section 243 application, **[4.191]**

section 243 beneficiary, **[4.191]**

section 243 decision, **[4.191]**

section 1088 application, **[4.191]**

section 1088 beneficiary, **[4.191]**

section 1088 decision, **[4.191]**

secured creditor, **[9.392]**

secured debenture, **[9.190]**

securities, **[9.77]**, **[1.867]**, **[6.42]**

security, **[8.155]**, **[9.77]**

senior management function, **[7.119]**, **[7.146]**, **[9.511]**

senior manager, **[7.145]**, **[7.146]**, **[9.511]**

series of secured debentures, **[9.190]**

settlement, **[6.42]**

settlement account, **[10.62]**

settlement agent, **[10.62]**

settlement bank, **[6.33]**, **[6.42]**

shadow director, **[5.120]**, **[1.279]**

share, **[1.622]**

share option, **[4.111]**

shares, **[4.111]**

short lease, **[4.114]**

short selling regulation, **[7.699]**

significant control, **[1.877]**

small business, **[9.516]**

social security costs, **[4.59]**, **[4.114]**

solicited and non-solicited real time communications, **[8.281]**

state within the European Economic Area, **[6.22]**

statutory auditor, **[1.1381]**

stock exchange, **[9.77]**

stock exchange transaction, **[9.77]**

sub-fund, **[8.340]**

subsidiary, **[1.1329]**, **[1.1330]**

subsidiary undertaking, **[1.1332]**, **[7.704]**, **[11.154]**

substantial non-cash asset, **[1.214]**

supervisory body, **[1.1388]**

survivor, **[8.129]**

sustainability factors, **[11.766]**

sustainable investment, **[11.766]**

system-beneficiary, **[6.33]**

system-charge, **[6.33]**

system-member, **[6.42]**, **[6.33]**

system-member instruction, **[6.42]**

system-participant, **[6.42]**

system-user, **[6.42]**

takeover bid, **[1.1116]**, **[1.1133]**

takeover offer, **[1.1136]**

territorial proceedings, **[10.184]**, **[10.482]**

total price, **[8.155]**

third country, **[10.62]**

trade repository, **[8.3]**

traded company, **[1.406]**, **[1.540]**

transfer, **[5.187]**

transfer order, **[10.62]**

transferable securities, **[1.1426]**, **[1.573]**

trigger event, **[9.572]**

trustees or managers, **[8.129]**

turnover, **[1.540]**, **[1.621]**

UCITS management company, **[1.540]**

UK company, **[1.1354]**

UK establishment, **[4.327]**

UK financial system, **[7.9]**

UK institution, **[9.511]**

UK registered company, **[1.1328]**

UK Societas, **[4.471]**

UK-traded non-EEA company, **[1.1426]**

UKEIG, **[10.14]**

umbrella company, **[8.340]**

uncalled share capital, **[1.629]**

uncertificated, **[6.42]**

uncertificated unit of a security, **[6.42]**

uncrystallised funds pension lump sum, **[8.129]**

undertaking, **[1.1331]**

undertaking active in the extractive industry, **[11.194]**

undertaking active in the logging of primary forests, **[11.194]**

unit of a security, **[6.42]**

unit trust scheme, **[7.438]**

unlimited company, **[1.3]**

unqualified report, **[1.93]**

unquoted company, **[1.437]**

unregistered company, **[9.351]**, **[4.390]**

value, **[4.111]**

value adjustment, **[11.154]**

voteholder information, **[7.198]**

voting shares, **[8.3]**

waste, **[9.197]**

Welsh company, **[1.89]**

wholly dematerialised security, **[6.42]**

winding up by the court, **[10.482]**

withdrawal agreement, **[12.28]**

working days, **[1.1345]**

written resolution, **[1.324]**

XML, **[4.471]**

XML Gateway, **[4.471]**

undertaking, [1.1334]

unlimited company, [1.9]

voting shares, [6.3]

PART 1
COMPANIES ACT 2006

COMPANIES ACT 2006

(2006 c 46)

NOTES

Commencement: the commencement of this Act is provided for by s 1300 at **[1.1497]** and the Orders made under that section. For a summary of all commencement information, see the Table of commencements for the Companies Act 2006 at **[2.1]**.

Commencement (transitional adaptations): various commencement Orders made under s 1300 provided that the provisions brought into force by those Orders shall have effect subject to any specified transitional adaptations. In so far as these transitional adaptations had not been revoked (subject to certain savings) by earlier Orders, they were fully revoked by the Companies Act 2006 (Commencement No 8, Transitional Provisions and Savings) Order 2008, SI 2008/2860, art 6. The commencement orders containing the transitional adaptations are no longer reproduced in this Handbook due to space considerations. All the commencement orders are, however, included in full in the (online only) Appendix 10 to this Handbook.

General saving for existing companies etc: the Companies Act 2006 (Commencement No 8, Transitional Provisions and Savings) Order 2008, SI 2008/2860, Sch 2, para 1(1) provides that nothing in this Act affects: (a) the registration or re-registration of a company under the former Companies Acts, or the continued existence of a company by virtue of such registration or re-registration, or (b) the application in relation to an existing company of (i) Table B in the Joint Stock Companies Act 1856, (ii) Table A in any of the former Companies Acts, or the Companies (Tables A to F) Regulations 1985 or the Companies (Tables A to F) Regulations (Northern Ireland) 1986.

Application of this Act to old public companies:

See the Companies Act 2006 (Consequential Amendments and Transitional Provisions) Order 2011, SI 2011/1265, Sch 1 at **[4.428]**. Note that for these purposes, an "old public company" is a company limited by shares, or a company limited by guarantee and having a share capital, in respect of which the following conditions are met: (a) the company either existed on 22 December 1980 or was incorporated after that date pursuant to an application made before that date; (b) on that date or, if later, on the day of the company's incorporation, the company was not or (as the case may be) would not have been a private company within the meaning of the Companies Act 1948, s 28; and (c) the company has not since that date or the day of the company's incorporation (as the case may be) either been re-registered as a public company within the meaning of the Companies Act 1985, s 1(3) or the Companies Act 2006, s 4(2) or become a private company within the meaning of s 1(3) of the 1985 Act or s 4(1) of the 2006 Act. See also, in relation to companies incorporated under Northern Ireland legislation, the Companies Act 2006 (Consequential Amendments, Transitional Provisions and Savings) Order 2009, SI 2009/1941, Sch 3 at **[4.368]**.

Offences under the Companies Acts: see, generally, Part 36 of this Act at **[1.1291]** et seq. As to offences under the Companies Act 1985, see also the Companies Act 2006 (Commencement No 8, Transitional Provisions and Savings) Order 2008, SI 2008/2860, Sch 2, para 116 to the 2008 Order (savings for provisions relating to offences).

Application to limited liability partnerships: as to the application of this Act to LLPs, see:

- (i) the Limited Liability Partnerships (Accounts and Audit) (Application of Companies Act 2006) Regulations 2008, SI 2008/1911 at **[10.223]**; (ii) the Limited Liability Partnerships (Application of Companies Act 2006) Regulations 2009, SI 2009/1804 at **[10.319]**. The 2008 Regulations apply provisions on the accounts and audit of companies contained in this Act to LLPs, with modifications. The 2009 Regulations apply the remaining provisions of this Act (in so far as appropriate) to LLPs with modifications. Both sets of Regulations replace certain provisions in the Limited Liability Partnerships Regulations 2001, SI 2001/1090 (which applied the Companies Act 1985 to LLPs). Both sets of Regulations also set out, in full, the applied provisions of this Act in so far as they apply to LLPs.
- As to LLPs, see also the Small Limited Liability Partnerships (Accounts) Regulations 2008, SI 2008/1912 at **[10.288]**, and the Large and Medium-sized Limited Liability Partnerships (Accounts) Regulations 2008, SI 2008/1913 at **[10.302]**. These Regulations specify the form and content of the accounts of LLPs by applying, with modifications, provisions of the Small Companies and Groups (Accounts and Directors' Report) Regulations 2008 (SI 2008/409) and the Large and Medium-sized Companies and Groups (Accounts and Reports) Regulations 2008 (SI 2008/410).

Application to overseas companies: as to the application of this Act to overseas companies, see the Overseas Companies Regulations 2009, SI 2009/1801 at **[10.318]**, and the Overseas Companies (Execution of Documents and Registration of Charges) Regulations 2009, SI 2009/1917 at **[4.326]**.

Application to unregistered companies: as to the application of certain parts of this Act to unregistered companies, see the Unregistered Companies Regulations 2009, SI 2009/2436 at **[4.389]** et seq.

Application to partnerships: as to the application of the accounts and audit provisions of this Act to partnerships, see the Partnerships (Accounts) Regulations 2008, SI 2008/569 at **[10.202]**.

Application to UK Economic Interest Groupings (UKEIGs) and EEIG establishments: certain provisions of this Act are applied with modifications to UKEIGs and EEIG establishments; see the European Economic Interest Grouping Regulations 1989, SI 1989/638, reg 18, Sch 4 at **[10.13]** et seq (as amended by the European Economic Interest Grouping (Amendment) Regulations 2009, SI 2009/2399, and the European Economic Interest Grouping (Amendment) (EU Exit) Regulations 2018, SI 2018/1299).

Application to UK Societas (formerly Societas Europaea): as to the application of certain provisions of this Act to a UK Societas, see the European Public Limited-Liability Company Regulations 2004, SI 2004/2326 (as amended by the European Public Limited-Liability Company (Amendment) Regulations 2009, SI 2009/2400, and the European Public Limited-Liability Company (Amendment etc) (EU Exit) Regulations 2018, SI 2018/1298). See in particular, Sch 2 (provisions of this Act applying to the registration of UK Societas), and Sch 4 (modifications of this Act and the Insolvency Act 1986). See also (i) the European Public Limited-Liability Company (Register of People with Significant Control) Regulations 2016, SI 2016/375; and (ii) the International Accounting Standards and European Public Limited-Liability Company (Amendment etc) (EU Exit) Regulations 2019, SI 2019/685, Sch 3, Pt 1.

Application to insurance undertakings: as to the application of the accounts and audit provisions of this Act to specified insurance undertakings, see the Insurance Accounts Directive (Miscellaneous Insurance Undertakings) Regulations 2008, SI 2008/565. See also, the Insurance Accounts Directive (Lloyd's Syndicate and Aggregate Accounts) Regulations 2008, SI 2008/1950.

Application to banks: as to the application of this Act to bank insolvency and administration, see the Banking Act 2009 and the Orders etc made under that Act. As to the application of certain provisions of this Act to particular banks, see also the Banking (Special Provisions) Act 2008 and the Banking Act 2009, and the Orders made under those Acts.

Application to credit institutions, investment firms and companies in the same group as a credit institution or investment firm: see the Bank Recovery and Resolution (No 2) Order 2014, SI 2014/3348 at **[8.564]**. The Order modifies the application of this Act (and the Companies Act 2006 (Commencement No 8, Transitional Provisions and Savings) Order 2008) in relation to a company under resolution.

Application to miscellaneous other bodies: as to the application of this Act to logging undertakings and mining or quarrying undertakings, see the Reports on Payments to Governments Regulations 2014, SI 2014/3209 (see the note at **[A4]**). As to the application of this Act to further education bodies that are companies or statutory corporations, see the Technical and Further Education Act 2017 and the Further Education Bodies (Insolvency) Regulations 2019, SI 2019/138. As to the application to protected cell companies, see the Risk Transformation Regulations 2017, SI 2017/1212. As to the application of this Act to payment institutions and electronic money institutions, see the Payment and Electronic Money Institution Insolvency Regulations 2021, SI 2021/716.

Application to bodies considered to be outside the scope of this work: note that the application of this Act to certain other bodies (*eg* charities, co-operative and community benefit societies, and building societies) is not noted as it is considered outside the scope of this work.

Civil Procedure Rules: the Civil Procedure Rules 1998, SI 1998/3132, r 49, states that those Rules apply to proceedings under (a) the Companies Act 1985; (b) the Companies Act 2006; and (c) other legislation relating to companies and limited liability partnerships, subject to the provision of the relevant practice direction which applies to those proceedings.

This Act is reproduced as amended by the following Acts:

2008	Charities Act (Northern Ireland) 2008.
2010	Corporation Tax Act 2010.
2011	Budget Responsibility and National Audit Act 2011; Damages (Scotland) Act 2011; Charities Act 2011.
2012	Land Registration etc (Scotland) Act 2012; Financial Services Act 2012.
2013	Crime and Courts Act 2013; Enterprise and Regulatory Reform Act 2013; Public Audit (Wales) Act 2013.
2014	Local Audit and Accountability Act 2014; Co-operative and Community Benefit Societies Act 2014; Pensions Act 2014.
2015	Deregulation Act 2015; Consumer Rights Act 2015; Small Business, Enterprise and Employment Act 2015.
2018	Data Protection Act 2018.
2020	Corporate Insolvency and Governance Act 2020.
2022	Charities Act 2022.

This Act is reproduced as amended by the following SIs:

1991	High Court and County Courts Jurisdiction Order 1991, SI 1991/724 (as amended by SI 2014/821).
2007	Companies (EEA State) Regulations 2007, SI 2007/732; Government of Wales Act 2006 (Consequential Modifications and Transitional Provisions) Order 2007, SI 2007/1388; Markets in Financial Instruments Directive (Consequential Amendments) Regulations 2007, SI 2007/2932; Reinsurance Directive Regulations 2007, SI 2007/3253; Statutory Auditors and Third Country Auditors Regulations 2007, SI 2007/3494.
2008	Companies Act 2006 (Amendment) (Accounts and Reports) Regulations 2008, SI 2008/393; Insurance Accounts Directive (Miscellaneous Insurance Undertakings) Regulations 2008, SI 2008/565; Bank Accounts Directive (Miscellaneous Banks) Regulations 2008, SI 2008/567; Companies (Mergers and Divisions of Public Companies) (Amendment) Regulations 2008, SI 2008/690; Companies Act 2006 (Consequential Amendments etc) Order 2008, SI 2008/948; Insurance Accounts Directive (Lloyd's Syndicate and Aggregate Accounts) Regulations 2008, SI 2008/1950; Companies Act 2006 (Annual Return and Service Addresses) Regulations 2008, SI 2008/3000.
2009	Companies Act 2006 (Amendment of Schedule 2) (No 2) Order 2009, SI 2009/1208; Financial Services and Markets Act 2000 (Regulated Activities) (Amendment) Order 2009, SI 2009/1342; Companies Act 2006 (Accounts, Reports and Audit) Regulations 2009, SI 2009/1581; Companies (Shareholders' Rights) Regulations 2009, SI 2009/1632; Companies Act 2006 (Part 35) (Consequential Amendments, Transitional Provisions and Savings) Order 2009, SI 2009/1802; Companies Act 2006 (Consequential Amendments, Transitional Provisions and Savings) Order 2009, SI 2009/1941; Companies (Share Capital and Acquisition by Company of its Own Shares) Regulations 2009, SI 2009/2022; Companies Act 2006 (Allotment of Shares and Right of Pre-emption) (Amendment) Regulations 2009, SI 2009/2561; Government of Wales Act 2006 (Consequential Modifications, Transitional Provisions and Saving) Order 2009, SI 2009/2958; Companies Act 2006 (Amendment of Section 413) Regulations 2009, SI 2009/3022; Companies Act 2006 (Substitution of Section 1201) Regulations 2009, SI 2009/3182.
2010	Transfer of Tribunal Functions Order 2010, SI 2010/22; Companies Act 2006 (Transfer of Audit Working Papers to Third Countries) Regulations 2010, SI 2010/2537.
2011	Companies Act 2006 (Consequential Amendments and Transitional Provisions) Order 2011, SI 2011/1265; Companies Act 2006 (Annual Returns) Regulations 2011, SI 2011/1487; Companies (Reporting Requirements in Mergers and Divisions) Regulations 2011, SI 2011/1606; Statutory Auditors and Third Country Auditors (Amendment) Regulations 2011, SI 2011/1856.
2012	Companies Act 2006 (Amendment of Part 23) (Investment Companies) Regulations 2012, SI 2012/952; Supervision of Accounts and Reports (Prescribed Body) and Companies (Defective Accounts and Directors' Reports) (Authorised Person) Order 2012, SI 2012/1439; Statutory Auditors (Amendment of Companies Act 2006 and Delegation of Functions etc) Order 2012, SI 2012/1741; Treaty of Lisbon (Changes in Terminology or Numbering) Order 2012, SI 2012/1809; Companies and Limited Liability Partnerships (Accounts and Audit Exemptions and Change of Accounting Framework) Regulations 2012, SI 2012/2301.
2013	Companies Act 2006 (Amendment of Part 25) Regulations 2013, SI 2013/600; Financial Services Act 2012 (Consequential Amendments) Order 2013, SI 2013/636; Companies Act 2006 (Amendment of Part 18) Regulations 2013, SI 2013/999; Statutory Auditors and Third Country Auditors Regulations 2013, SI 2013/1672; Alternative Investment Fund Managers Regulations 2013, SI 2013/1773; Financial Services and Markets Act 2000 (Regulated Activities) (Amendment) (No 2) Order 2013, SI 2013/1881; Financial Services Act 2012 (Consumer Credit) Order 2013, SI 2013/1882; Companies Act 2006 (Strategic Report

	and Directors' Report) Regulations 2013, SI 2013/1970; Companies and Partnerships (Accounts and Audit) Regulations 2013, SI 2013/2005; Public Bodies (Merger of the Gambling Commission and the National Lottery Commission) Order 2013, SI 2013/2329; Small Companies (Micro-Entities' Accounts) Regulations 2013, SI 2013/3008; Capital Requirements Regulations 2013, SI 2013/3115; Consumer Contracts (Information, Cancellation and Additional Charges) Regulations 2013, SI 2013/3134.
2014	Enterprise and Regulatory Reform Act 2013 (Competition) (Consequential, Transitional and Saving Provisions) Order 2014, SI 2014/892; Public Bodies (Abolition of the National Consumer Council and Transfer of the Office of Fair Trading's Functions in relation to Estate Agents etc) Order 2014, SI 2014/631; Companies Act 2006 (Interconnection of Registers) Order 2014, SI 2014/1557; Companies (Striking Off) (Electronic Communications) Order 2014, SI 2014/1602; Reports on Payments to Governments Regulations 2014, SI 2014/3209.
2015	Companies Act 2006 (Amendment of Part 17) Regulations 2015, SI 2015/472; Companies Act 2006 (Amendment of Part 18) Regulations 2015, SI 2015/532; Solvency 2 Regulations 2015, SI 2015/575; Legal Aid, Sentencing and Punishment of Offenders Act 2012 (Fines on Summary Conviction) Regulations 2015, SI 2015/664; Companies, Partnerships and Groups (Accounts and Reports) Regulations 2015, SI 2015/980.
2016	Companies Act 2006 (Amendment of Part 21A) Regulations 2016, SI 2016/136; Statutory Auditors and Third Country Auditors Regulations 2016, SI 2016/649; Bankruptcy (Scotland) Act 2016 (Consequential Provisions and Modifications) Order 2016, SI 2016/1034; Companies Act 2006 (Distributions of Insurance Companies) Regulations 2016, SI 2016/1194; Companies, Partnerships and Groups (Accounts and Non-Financial Reporting) Regulations 2016, SI 2016/1245.
2017	Bank of England and Financial Services (Consequential Amendments) Regulations 2017, SI 2017/80; Statutory Auditors and Third Country Auditors Regulations 2017, SI 2017/516; Information about People with Significant Control (Amendment) Regulations 2017, SI 2017/693; Scottish Partnerships (Register of People with Significant Control) Regulations 2017, SI 2017/694; Financial Services and Markets Act 2000 (Markets in Financial Instruments) Regulations 2017, SI 2017/701; Central Securities Depositories Regulations 2017, SI 2017/1064; Statutory Auditors Regulations 2017, SI 2017/1164; Risk Transformation Regulations 2017, SI 2017/1212; Company Names (Listed Bodies) Order 2017, SI 2017/1233; Financial Services and Markets Act 2000 (Markets in Financial Instruments) (No 2) Regulations 2017, SI 2017/1255.
2018	Financial Services and Markets Act 2000 (Prospectus and Markets in Financial Instruments) Regulations 2018, SI 2018/786; Companies (Miscellaneous Reporting) Regulations 2018, SI 2018/860; Occupational Pension Schemes (Master Trusts) Regulations 2018, SI 2018/1030; Third Parties (Rights Against Insurers) Act 2010 (Consequential Amendment of Companies Act 2006) Regulations 2018, SI 2018/1162; European Economic Interest Grouping (Amendment) (EU Exit) Regulations 2018, SI 2018/1299.
2019	Accounts and Reports (Amendment) (EU Exit) Regulations 2019, SI 2019/145; Statutory Auditors and Third Country Auditors (Amendment) (EU Exit) Regulations 2019, SI 2019/177; Takeovers (Amendment) (EU Exit) Regulations 2019, SI 2019/217; Companies, Limited Liability Partnerships and Partnerships (Amendment etc) (EU Exit) Regulations 2019, SI 2019/348; International Accounting Standards and European Public Limited-Liability Company (Amendment etc) (EU Exit) Regulations 2019, SI 2019/685; the Uncertificated Securities (Amendment and EU Exit) Regulations 2019, SI 2019/679; Official Listing of Securities, Prospectus and Transparency (Amendment etc) (EU Exit) Regulations 2019, SI 2019/707; Companies (Directors' Remuneration Policy and Directors' Remuneration Report) Regulations 2019, SI 2019/970; Money Laundering and Terrorist Financing (Amendment) Regulations 2019, SI 2019/1511.
2020	Statutory Auditors and Third Country Auditors (Amendment) (EU Exit) Regulations 2020, SI 2020/108; Companies (Shareholders' Rights to Voting Confirmations) Regulations 2020, SI 2020/717.
2022	Companies (Strategic Report) (Climate-related Financial Disclosure) Regulations 2022, SI 2022/31; the Criminal Justice Act 2003 (Commencement No 33) and Sentencing Act 2020 (Commencement No 2) Regulations 2022, SI 2022/500; Money Laundering and Terrorist Financing (Amendment) (No 2) Regulations 2022 SI 2022/860.

ARRANGEMENT OF SECTIONS

PART 1
GENERAL INTRODUCTORY PROVISIONS

Companies and Companies Acts

Types of company

PART 2
COMPANY FORMATION

General

Requirements for registration

Registration and its effect

PART 3
A COMPANY'S CONSTITUTION

CHAPTER 1 INTRODUCTORY

CHAPTER 2 ARTICLES OF ASSOCIATION

General

Alteration of articles

Supplementary

CHAPTER 3 RESOLUTIONS AND AGREEMENTS AFFECTING A COMPANY'S CONSTITUTION

CHAPTER 4 MISCELLANEOUS AND SUPPLEMENTARY PROVISIONS

Statement of company's objects

Other provisions with respect to a company's constitution

Supplementary provisions

PART 4
A COMPANY'S CAPACITY AND RELATED MATTERS

Capacity of company and power of directors to bind it

Formalities of doing business under the law of England and Wales or Northern Ireland

PART 6
A COMPANY'S REGISTERED OFFICE

General

PART 7
RE-REGISTRATION AS A MEANS OF ALTERING A COMPANY'S STATUS

Introductory

PART 8
A COMPANY'S MEMBERS

CHAPTER 1 THE MEMBERS OF A COMPANY

CHAPTER 2 REGISTER OF MEMBERS

General

PART 10
A COMPANY'S DIRECTORS

CHAPTER 1 APPOINTMENT AND REMOVAL OF DIRECTORS

Requirement to have directors

Appointment

Register of directors, etc

Option to keep information on the central register

Removal

CHAPTER 2 GENERAL DUTIES OF DIRECTORS

Introductory

The general duties

Supplementary provisions

CHAPTER 3 DECLARATION OF INTEREST IN EXISTING TRANSACTION OR ARRANGEMENT

CHAPTER 4 TRANSACTIONS WITH DIRECTORS REQUIRING APPROVAL OF MEMBERS

CHAPTER 4A DIRECTORS OF QUOTED COMPANIES AND TRADED COMPANIES: SPECIAL PROVISION

CHAPTER 5 DIRECTORS' SERVICE CONTRACTS

PART 12
COMPANY SECRETARIES

Private companies

Public companies

Provisions applying to private companies with a secretary and to public companies

Option to keep information on the central register

PART 13
RESOLUTIONS AND MEETINGS

CHAPTER 1 GENERAL PROVISIONS ABOUT RESOLUTIONS

CHAPTER 2 WRITTEN RESOLUTIONS

General provisions about written resolutions

Circulation of written resolutions

Agreeing to written resolutions

Supplementary

CHAPTER 3 RESOLUTIONS AT MEETINGS

General provisions about resolutions at meetings

Calling meetings

CHAPTER 5 ADDITIONAL REQUIREMENTS FOR QUOTED COMPANIES AND TRADED COMPANIES

PART 15
ACCOUNTS AND REPORTS

CHAPTER 1 INTRODUCTION

General

Companies subject to the small companies regime

Quoted and unquoted companies

CHAPTER 2 ACCOUNTING RECORDS

CHAPTER 3 A COMPANY'S FINANCIAL YEAR

CHAPTER 4 ANNUAL ACCOUNTS

General

Individual accounts

Group accounts: other companies

Group accounts: general

Information to be given in notes to the accounts

Approval and signing of accounts

CHAPTER 4A STRATEGIC REPORT

CHAPTER 5 DIRECTORS' REPORT

Directors' report

CHAPTER 6 QUOTED COMPANIES AND TRADED COMPANIES: DIRECTORS' REMUNERATION REPORT

CHAPTER 7 PUBLICATION OF ACCOUNTS AND REPORTS

Duty to circulate copies of accounts and reports

Option to provide strategic report with supplementary material

Section 172(1) statement: requirements as to website publication

Quoted companies and traded companies: requirements as to website publication

Right of member or debenture holder to demand copies of accounts and reports

Requirements in connection with publication of accounts and reports

CHAPTER 8 PUBLIC COMPANIES: LAYING OF ACCOUNTS AND REPORTS BEFORE GENERAL MEETING

CHAPTER 9 QUOTED COMPANIES AND TRADED COMPANIES: MEMBERS' APPROVAL OF DIRECTORS' REMUNERATION REPORT

CHAPTER 10 FILING OF ACCOUNTS AND REPORTS

Duty to file accounts and reports

Requirements applicable in relation to relevant accounts

Application of provisions to successive distributions etc

CHAPTER 3 SUPPLEMENTARY PROVISIONS

Accounting matters

Distributions in kind

Consequences of unlawful distribution

Other matters

PART 24

ANNUAL CONFIRMATION OF ACCURACY OF INFORMATION ON REGISTER

PART 25

COMPANY CHARGES

CHAPTER A1 REGISTRATION OF COMPANY CHARGES

Company charges

Consequence of non-delivery

The register

PART 26
ARRANGEMENTS AND RECONSTRUCTIONS: GENERAL

PART 26A
ARRANGEMENTS AND RECONSTRUCTIONS: COMPANIES IN FINANCIAL DIFFICULTY

PART 27
MERGERS AND DIVISIONS OF PUBLIC COMPANIES

CHAPTER 1 INTRODUCTORY

CHAPTER 2 MERGER

PART 28
TAKEOVERS ETC

CHAPTER 1 THE TAKEOVER PANEL

The Panel and its rules

"Sell-out"

PART 35
THE REGISTRAR OF COMPANIES

Scheme of this Part

CHAPTER 5 REGISTERED THIRD COUNTRY AUDITORS

CHAPTER 6 SUPPLEMENTARY AND GENERAL

PART 43
TRANSPARENCY OBLIGATIONS AND RELATED MATTERS

Introductory

Transparency obligations

Other matters

PART 44
MISCELLANEOUS PROVISIONS

Regulation of actuaries etc

Information as to exercise of voting rights by institutional investors

Disclosure of information under the Enterprise Act 2002

Expenses of winding up

Commonhold associations

PART 45
NORTHERN IRELAND

PART 46
GENERAL SUPPLEMENTARY PROVISIONS

Regulations and orders

Bank of England

Meaning of "enactment"

Consequential and transitional provisions

PART 47
FINAL PROVISIONS

SCHEDULES

An Act to reform company law and restate the greater part of the enactments relating to companies; to make other provision relating to companies and other forms of business organisation; to make provision about directors' disqualification, business names, auditors and actuaries; to amend Part 9 of the Enterprise Act 2002; and for connected purposes

[8 November 2006]

PART 1 GENERAL INTRODUCTORY PROVISIONS

Companies and Companies Acts

[1.1]

1 Companies

(1) In the Companies Acts, unless the context otherwise requires—

"company" means a company formed and registered under this Act, that is—

(a) a company so formed and registered after the commencement of this Part, or

(b) a company that immediately before the commencement of this Part—

(i) was formed and registered under the Companies Act 1985 (c 6) or the Companies (Northern Ireland) Order 1986 (SI 1986/1032 (NI 6)), or

(ii) was an existing company for the purposes of that Act or that Order, (which is to be treated on commencement as if formed and registered under this Act).

(2) Certain provisions of the Companies Acts apply to—

(a) companies registered, but not formed, under this Act (see Chapter 1 of Part 33), and

(b) bodies incorporated in the United Kingdom but not registered under this Act (see Chapter 2 of that Part).

(3) For provisions applying to companies incorporated outside the United Kingdom, see Part 34 (overseas companies).

[1.2]

2 The Companies Acts

(1) In this Act "the Companies Acts" means—

(a) the company law provisions of this Act,

(b) Part 2 of the Companies (Audit, Investigations and Community Enterprise) Act 2004 (c 27) (community interest companies), and

(c) the provisions of the Companies Act 1985 (c 6) and the Companies Consolidation (Consequential Provisions) Act 1985 (c 9) that remain in force.

(2) The company law provisions of this Act are—

(a) the provisions of Parts 1 to 39 of this Act, and

(b) the provisions of Parts 45 to 47 of this Act so far as they apply for the purposes of those Parts.

Types of company

[1.3]

3 Limited and unlimited companies

(1) A company is a "limited company" if the liability of its members is limited by its constitution.

It may be limited by shares or limited by guarantee.

(2) If their liability is limited to the amount, if any, unpaid on the shares held by them, the company is "limited by shares".

(3) If their liability is limited to such amount as the members undertake to contribute to the assets of the company in the event of its being wound up, the company is "limited by guarantee".

(4) If there is no limit on the liability of its members, the company is an "unlimited company".

[1.4]

4 Private and public companies

(1) A "private company" is any company that is not a public company.

(2) A "public company" is a company limited by shares or limited by guarantee and having a share capital—

(a) whose certificate of incorporation states that it is a public company, and

(b) in relation to which the requirements of this Act, or the former Companies Acts, as to registration or re-registration as a public company have been complied with on or after the relevant date.

(3) For the purposes of subsection (2)(b) the relevant date is—

(a) in relation to registration or re-registration in Great Britain, 22nd December 1980;

(b) in relation to registration or re-registration in Northern Ireland, 1st July 1983.

(4) For the two major differences between private and public companies, see Part 20.

[1.5]

5 Companies limited by guarantee and having share capital

(1) A company cannot be formed as, or become, a company limited by guarantee with a share capital.

(2) Provision to this effect has been in force—

(a) in Great Britain since 22nd December 1980, and

(b) in Northern Ireland since 1st July 1983.

(3) Any provision in the constitution of a company limited by guarantee that purports to divide the company's undertaking into shares or interests is a provision for a share capital.

This applies whether or not the nominal value or number of the shares or interests is specified by the provision.

[1.6]

6 Community interest companies

(1) In accordance with Part 2 of the Companies (Audit, Investigations and Community Enterprise) Act 2004 (c 27)—

(a) a company limited by shares or a company limited by guarantee and not having a share capital may be formed as or become a community interest company, and

(b) a company limited by guarantee and having a share capital may become a community interest company.

(2) The other provisions of the Companies Acts have effect subject to that Part.

PART 2 COMPANY FORMATION

General

[1.7]

7 Method of forming company

(1) A company is formed under this Act by one or more persons—

(a) subscribing their names to a memorandum of association (see section 8), and

(b) complying with the requirements of this Act as to registration (see sections 9 to 13).

(2) A company may not be so formed for an unlawful purpose.

[1.8]

8 Memorandum of association

(1) A memorandum of association is a memorandum stating that the subscribers—

(a) wish to form a company under this Act, and

(b) agree to become members of the company and, in the case of a company that is to have a share capital, to take at least one share each.

(2) The memorandum must be in the prescribed form and must be authenticated by each subscriber.

NOTES

Regulations: the Companies (Registration) Regulations 2008, SI 2008/3014 at **[4.179]**. For a summary of all statutory instruments made under this Act, see Appendix 4 at **[A4]**.

Requirements for registration

[1.9]

9 Registration documents

(1) The memorandum of association must be delivered to the registrar together with an application for registration of the company, the documents required by this section and a statement of compliance.

(2) The application for registration must state—

(a) the company's proposed name,

(b) whether the company's registered office is to be situated in England and Wales (or in Wales), in Scotland or in Northern Ireland,

(c) whether the liability of the members of the company is to be limited, and if so whether it is to be limited by shares or by guarantee, and

(d) whether the company is to be a private or a public company.

(3) If the application is delivered by a person as agent for the subscribers to the memorandum of association, it must state his name and address.

(4) The application must contain—

(a) in the case of a company that is to have a share capital, a statement of capital and initial shareholdings (see section 10);

(b) in the case of a company that is to be limited by guarantee, a statement of guarantee (see section 11);

(c) a statement of the company's proposed officers (see section 12);

[(d) a statement of initial significant control (see section 12A).]

(5) The application must also contain—

(a) a statement of the intended address of the company's registered office; . . .

(b) a copy of any proposed articles of association (to the extent that these are not supplied by the default application of model articles: see section 20)[; and

(c) a statement of the type of company it is to be and its intended principal business activities].

[(5A) The information as to the company's type must be given by reference to the classification scheme prescribed for the purposes of this section.

(5B) The information as to the company's intended principal business activities may be given by reference to one or more categories of any prescribed system of classifying business activities.]

(6) The application must be delivered—

(a) to the registrar of companies for England and Wales, if the registered office of the company is to be situated in England and Wales (or in Wales);

(b) to the registrar of companies for Scotland, if the registered office of the company is to be situated in Scotland;

(c) to the registrar of companies for Northern Ireland, if the registered office of the company is to be situated in Northern Ireland.

NOTES

Sub-s (4): para (d) inserted by the Small Business, Enterprise and Employment Act 2015, s 81, Sch 3, Pt 2, paras 3, 4, as from 30 June 2016.

Word omitted from sub-s (5)(a) repealed, and sub-s (5)(c) (and the preceding word) inserted, by the Small Business, Enterprise and Employment Act 2015, s 93(1), (2), as from 30 June 2016.

Sub-ss (5A), (5B) inserted by the Small Business, Enterprise and Employment Act 2015, s 93(1), (3), as from 1 January 2016 (for the purposes of enabling the exercise of any power to make provision by regulations, rules or order made by statutory instrument), and as from 30 June 2016 (otherwise).

Classification scheme prescribed for the purposes of sub-s (5A) above: see the Companies and Limited Liability Partnerships (Filing Requirements) Regulations 2016, SI 2016/599, reg 6 and Sch 4 at **[4.644]**, **[4.648]**.

The Standard Industrial Classification 2007 is prescribed for the purposes of sub-s (5B) above (and s 853C(3) *post*), with the addition of the following codes and designations, see the Companies and Limited Liability Partnerships (Filing Requirements) Regulations 2016, SI 2016/599, reg 7 and Sch 5 at **[4.645]**, **[4.649]**:

- 74990 non-trading company
- 98000 residents' property management company.
- 99999 dormant company.

Regulations: the Companies and Limited Liability Partnerships (Filing Requirements) Regulations 2016, SI 2016/599 at **[4.640]**. For a summary of all statutory instruments made under this Act, see Appendix 4 at **[A4]**.

[1.10]

10 Statement of capital and initial shareholdings

(1) The statement of capital and initial shareholdings required to be delivered in the case of a company that is to have a share capital must comply with this section.

(2) It must state—

(a) the total number of shares of the company to be taken on formation by the subscribers to the memorandum of association,

(b) the aggregate nominal value of those shares,

[(ba) the aggregate amount (if any) to be unpaid on those shares (whether on account of their nominal value or by way of premium), and]

(c) for each class of shares—

(i) prescribed particulars of the rights attached to the shares,

(ii) the total number of shares of that class, and

(iii) the aggregate nominal value of shares of that class, . . .

(d) . . .

(3) It must contain such information as may be prescribed for the purpose of identifying the subscribers to the memorandum of association.

(4) It must state, with respect to each subscriber to the memorandum—

(a) the number, nominal value (of each share) and class of shares to be taken by him on formation, and

(b) the amount to be paid up and the amount (if any) to be unpaid on each share (whether on account of the nominal value of the share or by way of premium).

(5) Where a subscriber to the memorandum is to take shares of more than one class, the information required under subsection (4)(a) is required for each class.

NOTES

Sub-s (2): para (ba) inserted, and para (d) and the preceding word repealed, by the Small Business, Enterprise and Employment Act 2015, s 97, Sch 6, paras 1, 2, as from 30 June 2016.

Regulations and Orders: the Companies (Registration) Regulations 2008, SI 2008/3014 at **[4.179]**; the Companies (Shares and Share Capital) Order 2009, SI 2009/388. For a summary of all statutory instruments made under this Act, see Appendix 4 at **[A4]**.

[1.11]

11 Statement of guarantee

(1) The statement of guarantee required to be delivered in the case of a company that is to be limited by guarantee must comply with this section.

(2) It must contain such information as may be prescribed for the purpose of identifying the subscribers to the memorandum of association.

(3) It must state that each member undertakes that, if the company is wound up while he is a member, or within one year after he ceases to be a member, he will contribute to the assets of the company such amount as may be required for—

(a) payment of the debts and liabilities of the company contracted before he ceases to be a member,

(b) payment of the costs, charges and expenses of winding up, and

(c) adjustment of the rights of the contributories among themselves,

not exceeding a specified amount.

NOTES

Regulations: the Companies (Registration) Regulations 2008, SI 2008/3014 at **[4.179]**. For a summary of all statutory instruments made under this Act, see Appendix 4 at **[A4]**.

[1.12]

12 Statement of proposed officers

(1) The statement of the company's proposed officers required to be delivered to the registrar must contain the required particulars of—

(a) the person who is, or persons who are, to be the first director or directors of the company;

(b) in the case of a company that is to be a private company, any person who is (or any persons who are) to be the first secretary (or joint secretaries) of the company;

(c) in the case of a company that is to be a public company, the person who is (or the persons who are) to be the first secretary (or joint secretaries) of the company.

(2) The required particulars are the particulars that will be required [(or, in the absence of an election under section 167A or 279A, would be required)] to be stated—

(a) in the case of a director, in the company's register of directors and register of directors' residential addresses (see sections 162 to 166);

(b) in the case of a secretary, in the company's register of secretaries (see sections 277 to 279).

(3) [The statement must also include a statement by the subscribers to the memorandum of association that each of the persons named as a director, as secretary or as one of the joint secretaries has consented to act in the relevant capacity].

If all the partners in a firm are to be joint secretaries, consent may be given by one partner on behalf of all of them.

NOTES

Sub-s (2): words in square brackets inserted by the Small Business, Enterprise and Employment Act 2015, s 94, Sch 5, Pt 2, paras 11, 12, as from 30 June 2016.

Sub-s (3): words in square brackets substituted by the Small Business, Enterprise and Employment Act 2015, s 100(1), (2), as from 10 October 2015 (for transitional provision, see the note below).

Transitional provisions: the amendments made by the Small Business, Enterprise and Employment Act 2015, s 100 do not apply if the statement of proposed officers, statement of the company's proposed secretary or notice under ss 167 or 276 of this Act was received by the registrar before s 100 comes into force, ie, 10 October 2015 (see s 100(6)).

[1.13]

[12A Statement of initial significant control

(1) The statement of initial significant control required to be delivered to the registrar must—

(a) state whether, on incorporation, there will be anyone who will count for the purposes of section 790M (register of people with significant control over a company) as either a registrable person or a registrable relevant legal entity in relation to the company,

(b) include the required particulars of anyone who will count as such, and

(c) include any other matters that on incorporation will be required (or, in the absence of an election under section 790X, would be required) to be entered in the company's PSC register by virtue of section 790M.

(2) It is not necessary to include under subsection (1)(b) the date on which someone becomes a registrable person or a registrable relevant legal entity in relation to the company.

(3) If the statement includes required particulars of an individual, it must also contain a statement that those particulars are included with the knowledge of that individual.

(4) "Registrable person", "registrable relevant legal entity" and "required particulars" have the meanings given in Part 21A (see sections 790C and 790K).]

NOTES

Inserted by the Small Business, Enterprise and Employment Act 2015, s 81, Sch 3, Pt 2, paras 3, 5, as from 30 June 2016.

[1.14]

13 Statement of compliance

(1) The statement of compliance required to be delivered to the registrar is a statement that the requirements of this Act as to registration have been complied with.

(2) The registrar may accept the statement of compliance as sufficient evidence of compliance.

Registration and its effect

[1.15]

14 Registration

If the registrar is satisfied that the requirements of this Act as to registration are complied with, he shall register the documents delivered to him.

[1.16]

15 Issue of certificate of incorporation

(1) On the registration of a company, the registrar of companies shall give a certificate that the company is incorporated.

(2) The certificate must state—

(a) the name and registered number of the company,
(b) the date of its incorporation,
(c) whether it is a limited or unlimited company, and if it is limited whether it is limited by shares or limited by guarantee,
(d) whether it is a private or a public company, and
(e) whether the company's registered office is situated in England and Wales (or in Wales), in Scotland or in Northern Ireland.

(3) The certificate must be signed by the registrar or authenticated by the registrar's official seal.

(4) The certificate is conclusive evidence that the requirements of this Act as to registration have been complied with and that the company is duly registered under this Act.

[1.17]

16 Effect of registration

(1) The registration of a company has the following effects as from the date of incorporation.

(2) The subscribers to the memorandum, together with such other persons as may from time to time become members of the company, are a body corporate by the name stated in the certificate of incorporation.

(3) That body corporate is capable of exercising all the functions of an incorporated company.

(4) The status and registered office of the company are as stated in, or in connection with, the application for registration.

(5) In the case of a company having a share capital, the subscribers to the memorandum become holders of the shares specified in the statement of capital and initial shareholdings.

(6) The persons named in the statement of proposed officers—

(a) as director, or
(b) as secretary or joint secretary of the company,

are deemed to have been appointed to that office.

PART 3 A COMPANY'S CONSTITUTION

CHAPTER 1 INTRODUCTORY

[1.18]

17 A company's constitution

Unless the context otherwise requires, references in the Companies Acts to a company's constitution include—

(a) the company's articles, and
(b) any resolutions and agreements to which Chapter 3 applies (see section 29).

CHAPTER 2 ARTICLES OF ASSOCIATION

General

[1.19]

18 Articles of association

(1) A company must have articles of association prescribing regulations for the company.

(2) Unless it is a company to which model articles apply by virtue of section 20 (default application of model articles in case of limited company), it must register articles of association.

(3) Articles of association registered by a company must—

(a) be contained in a single document, and
(b) be divided into paragraphs numbered consecutively.

(4) References in the Companies Acts to a company's "articles" are to its articles of association.

[1.20]

19 Power of Secretary of State to prescribe model articles

(1) The Secretary of State may by regulations prescribe model articles of association for companies.

(2) Different model articles may be prescribed for different descriptions of company.

(3) A company may adopt all or any of the provisions of model articles.

(4) Any amendment of model articles by regulations under this section does not affect a company registered before the amendment takes effect.

"Amendment" here includes addition, alteration or repeal.

(5) Regulations under this section are subject to negative resolution procedure.

NOTES

Regulations: the Companies (Model Articles) Regulations 2008, SI 2008/3229 at **[4.187]**. For a summary of all statutory instruments made under this Act, see Appendix 4 at **[A4]**.

[1.21]

20 Default application of model articles

(1) On the formation of a limited company—

(a) if articles are not registered, or

(b) if articles are registered, in so far as they do not exclude or modify the relevant model articles,

the relevant model articles (so far as applicable) form part of the company's articles in the same manner and to the same extent as if articles in the form of those articles had been duly registered.

(2) The "relevant model articles" means the model articles prescribed for a company of that description as in force at the date on which the company is registered.

Alteration of articles

[1.22]

21 Amendment of articles

(1) A company may amend its articles by special resolution.

(2) In the case of a company that is a charity, this is subject to—

(a) in England and Wales, [sections 197 and 198 of the Charities Act 2011];

(b) in Northern Ireland, [section 96 of the Charities Act (Northern Ireland) 2008]).

(3) In the case of a company that is registered in the Scottish Charity Register, this is subject to—

(a) section 112 of the Companies Act 1989 (c 40), and

(b) section 16 of the Charities and Trustee Investment (Scotland) Act 2005 (asp 10).

NOTES

Sub-s (2): words in first pair of square brackets substituted by the Charities Act 2011, s 354, Sch 7, Pt 2, para 113, as from 14 March 2012. Words in second pair of square brackets substituted by the Charities Act (Northern Ireland) 2008, s 183, Sch 8, para 13(1), as from 24 June 2013.

[1.23]

22 Entrenched provisions of the articles

(1) A company's articles may contain provision ("provision for entrenchment") to the effect that specified provisions of the articles may be amended or repealed only if conditions are met, or procedures are complied with, that are more restrictive than those applicable in the case of a special resolution.

(2) Provision for entrenchment may only be made—

(a) in the company's articles on formation, or

(b) by an amendment of the company's articles agreed to by all the members of the company.

(3) Provision for entrenchment does not prevent amendment of the company's articles—

(a) by agreement of all the members of the company, or

(b) by order of a court or other authority having power to alter the company's articles.

(4) Nothing in this section affects any power of a court or other authority to alter a company's articles.

NOTES

Commencement: 1 October 2009 (sub-ss (1), (3), (4)); to be appointed (sub-s (2)).

Note: the Companies Act 2006 (Commencement No 8, Transitional Provisions and Savings) Order 2008, SI 2008/2860, art 3(c) originally provided that this section would come into force for all purposes on 1 October 2009. That article was subsequently amended by the Companies Act 2006 and Limited Liability Partnerships (Transitional Provisions and Savings) (Amendment) Regulations 2009, SI 2009/2476, art 2(1), (2) which substituted the words "sections 18 to 21, 22(1), (3) and (4) and 23 to 28" for the original words "sections 18 to 28" in art 3(c) (as from 30 September 2009). The effect of this amendment was to prevent sub-s (2) above coming into force on 1 October 2009.

[1.24]

23 Notice to registrar of existence of restriction on amendment of articles

(1) Where a company's articles—

(a) on formation contain provision for entrenchment,

(b) are amended so as to include such provision, or

(c) are altered by order of a court or other authority so as to restrict or exclude the power of the company to amend its articles,

the company must give notice of that fact to the registrar.

(2) Where a company's articles—

(a) are amended so as to remove provision for entrenchment, or

(b) are altered by order of a court or other authority—

(i) so as to remove such provision, or

(ii) so as to remove any other restriction on, or any exclusion of, the power of the company to amend its articles,

the company must give notice of that fact to the registrar.

[1.25]

24 Statement of compliance where amendment of articles restricted

(1) This section applies where a company's articles are subject—

(a) to provision for entrenchment, or
(b) to an order of a court or other authority restricting or excluding the company's power to amend the articles.

(2) If the company—
(a) amends its articles, and
(b) is required to send to the registrar a document making or evidencing the amendment,

the company must deliver with that document a statement of compliance.

(3) The statement of compliance required is a statement certifying that the amendment has been made in accordance with the company's articles and, where relevant, any applicable order of a court or other authority.

(4) The registrar may rely on the statement of compliance as sufficient evidence of the matters stated in it.

[1.26]

25 Effect of alteration of articles on company's members

(1) A member of a company is not bound by an alteration to its articles after the date on which he became a member, if and so far as the alteration—
(a) requires him to take or subscribe for more shares than the number held by him at the date on which the alteration is made, or
(b) in any way increases his liability as at that date to contribute to the company's share capital or otherwise to pay money to the company.

(2) Subsection (1) does not apply in a case where the member agrees in writing, either before or after the alteration is made, to be bound by the alteration.

[1.27]

26 Registrar to be sent copy of amended articles

(1) Where a company amends its articles it must send to the registrar a copy of the articles as amended not later than 15 days after the amendment takes effect.

(2) This section does not require a company to set out in its articles any provisions of model articles that—
(a) are applied by the articles, or
(b) apply by virtue of section 20 (default application of model articles).

(3) If a company fails to comply with this section an offence is committed by—
(a) the company, and
(b) every officer of the company who is in default.

(4) A person guilty of an offence under this section is liable on summary conviction to a fine not exceeding level 3 on the standard scale and, for continued contravention, a daily default fine not exceeding one-tenth of level 3 on the standard scale.

[1.28]

27 Registrar's notice to comply in case of failure with respect to amended articles

(1) If it appears to the registrar that a company has failed to comply with any enactment requiring it—
(a) to send to the registrar a document making or evidencing an alteration in the company's articles, or
(b) to send to the registrar a copy of the company's articles as amended,

the registrar may give notice to the company requiring it to comply.

(2) The notice must—
(a) state the date on which it is issued, and
(b) require the company to comply within 28 days from that date.

(3) If the company complies with the notice within the specified time, no criminal proceedings may be brought in respect of the failure to comply with the enactment mentioned in subsection (1).

(4) If the company does not comply with the notice within the specified time, it is liable to a civil penalty of £200.

This is in addition to any liability to criminal proceedings in respect of the failure mentioned in subsection (1).

(5) The penalty may be recovered by the registrar and is to be paid into the Consolidated Fund.

Supplementary

[1.29]

28 Existing companies: provisions of memorandum treated as provisions of articles

(1) Provisions that immediately before the commencement of this Part were contained in a company's memorandum but are not provisions of the kind mentioned in section 8 (provisions of new-style memorandum) are to be treated after the commencement of this Part as provisions of the company's articles.

(2) This applies not only to substantive provisions but also to provision for entrenchment (as defined in section 22).

(3) The provisions of this Part about provision for entrenchment apply to such provision as they apply to provision made on the company's formation, except that the duty under section 23(1)(a) to give notice to the registrar does not apply.

NOTES

Transitional provisions: for transitional provisions where, in the case of an existing or transitional company, the company's articles are deemed to contain a statement of its name by virtue of this section, and the company changes its name (by any means) on or after 1 October 2009, see the Companies Act 2006 (Consequential Amendments, Transitional Provisions and Savings) Order 2009, SI 2009/1941, art 5 (at **[4.359]**).

CHAPTER 3 RESOLUTIONS AND AGREEMENTS AFFECTING A COMPANY'S CONSTITUTION

[1.30]

29 Resolutions and agreements affecting a company's constitution

(1) This Chapter applies to—
(a) any special resolution;
(b) any resolution or agreement agreed to by all the members of a company that, if not so agreed to, would not have been effective for its purpose unless passed as a special resolution;

(c) any resolution or agreement agreed to by all the members of a class of shareholders that, if not so agreed to, would not have been effective for its purpose unless passed by some particular majority or otherwise in some particular manner;

(d) any resolution or agreement that effectively binds all members of a class of shareholders though not agreed to by all those members;

(e) any other resolution or agreement to which this Chapter applies by virtue of any enactment.

(2) References in subsection (1) to a member of a company, or of a class of members of a company, do not include the company itself where it is such a member by virtue only of its holding shares as treasury shares.

[1.31]

30 Copies of resolutions or agreements to be forwarded to registrar

(1) A copy of every resolution or agreement to which this Chapter applies, or (in the case of a resolution or agreement that is not in writing) a written memorandum setting out its terms, must be forwarded to the registrar within 15 days after it is passed or made.

(2) If a company fails to comply with this section, an offence is committed by—

(a) the company, and

(b) every officer of it who is in default.

(3) A person guilty of an offence under this section is liable on summary conviction to a fine not exceeding level 3 on the standard scale and, for continued contravention, a daily default fine not exceeding one-tenth of level 3 on the standard scale.

(4) For the purposes of this section, a liquidator of the company is treated as an officer of it.

CHAPTER 4 MISCELLANEOUS AND SUPPLEMENTARY PROVISIONS

Statement of company's objects

[1.32]

31 Statement of company's objects

(1) Unless a company's articles specifically restrict the objects of the company, its objects are unrestricted.

(2) Where a company amends its articles so as to add, remove or alter a statement of the company's objects—

(a) it must give notice to the registrar,

(b) on receipt of the notice, the registrar shall register it, and

(c) the amendment is not effective until entry of that notice on the register.

(3) Any such amendment does not affect any rights or obligations of the company or render defective any legal proceedings by or against it.

(4) In the case of a company that is a charity, the provisions of this section have effect subject to—

(a) in England and Wales, [sections 197 and 198 of the Charities Act 2011];

(b) in Northern Ireland, [section 96 of the Charities Act (Northern Ireland) 2008].

(5) In the case of a company that is entered in the Scottish Charity Register, the provisions of this section have effect subject to the provisions of the Charities and Trustee Investment (Scotland) Act 2005 (asp 10).

NOTES

Sub-s (4): words in square brackets in para (a) substituted by the Charities Act 2011, s 354, Sch 7, Pt 2, para 114, as from 14 March 2012. Words in square brackets in para (b) substituted by the Charities Act (Northern Ireland) 2008, s 183, Sch 8, para 13(2), as from 24 June 2013.

Other provisions with respect to a company's constitution

[1.33]

32 Constitutional documents to be provided to members

(1) A company must, on request by any member, send to him the following documents—

(a) an up-to-date copy of the company's articles;

(b) a copy of any resolution or agreement relating to the company to which Chapter 3 applies (resolutions and agreements affecting a company's constitution) and that is for the time being in force;

(c) a copy of any document required to be sent to the registrar under—

(i) section 34(2) (notice where company's constitution altered by enactment), or

(ii) section 35(2)(a) (notice where order of court or other authority alters company's constitution);

(d) a copy of any court order under section 899 (order sanctioning compromise or arrangement) or section 900 (order facilitating reconstruction or amalgamation);

[(da) a copy of any court order under section 901F (order sanctioning compromise or arrangement for company in financial difficulty) or section 901J (order facilitating reconstruction or amalgamation);]

(e) a copy of any court order under section 996 (protection of members against unfair prejudice: powers of the court) that alters the company's constitution;

(f) a copy of the company's current certificate of incorporation, and of any past certificates of incorporation;

(g) in the case of a company with a share capital, a current statement of capital;

(h) in the case of a company limited by guarantee, a copy of the statement of guarantee.

(2) The statement of capital required by subsection (1)(g) is a statement of—

(a) the total number of shares of the company,

(b) the aggregate nominal value of those shares,

[(ba) the aggregate amount (if any) unpaid on those shares (whether on account of their nominal value or by way of premium), and]

(c) for each class of shares—

(i) prescribed particulars of the rights attached to the shares,

(ii) the total number of shares of that class, and

(iii) the aggregate nominal value of shares of that class, . . .

(d) . . .

(3) If a company makes default in complying with this section, an offence is committed by every officer of the company who is in default.

(4) A person guilty of an offence under this section is liable on summary conviction to a fine not exceeding level 3 on the standard scale.

NOTES

Sub-s (1): para (da) inserted by the Corporate Insolvency and Governance Act 2020, s 7, Sch 9, Pt 2, paras 30, 32, as from 26 June 2020.

Sub-s (2): para (ba) inserted, and para (d) and the preceding word repealed, by the Small Business, Enterprise and Employment Act 2015, s 97, Sch 6, paras 1, 3, as from 30 June 2016.

Orders: the Companies (Shares and Share Capital) Order 2009, SI 2009/388 at **[4.211]**. For a summary of all statutory instruments made under this Act, see Appendix 4 at **[A4]**.

[1.34]

33 Effect of company's constitution

(1) The provisions of a company's constitution bind the company and its members to the same extent as if there were covenants on the part of the company and of each member to observe those provisions.

(2) Money payable by a member to the company under its constitution is a debt due from him to the company.

In England and Wales and Northern Ireland it is of the nature of an ordinary contract debt.

NOTES

Contractual rights of third parties: the Contracts (Rights of Third Parties) Act 1999, s 1, confers no rights on a third party in the case of any contract binding on a company and its members under this section; see s 6(2) of the 1999 Act (as amended).

[1.35]

34 Notice to registrar where company's constitution altered by enactment

(1) This section applies where a company's constitution is altered by an enactment, other than an enactment amending the general law.

(2) The company must give notice of the alteration to the registrar, specifying the enactment, not later than 15 days after the enactment comes into force.

In the case of a special enactment the notice must be accompanied by a copy of the enactment.

(3) If the enactment amends—

(a) the company's articles, or

(b) a resolution or agreement to which Chapter 3 applies (resolutions and agreements affecting a company's constitution),

the notice must be accompanied by a copy of the company's articles, or the resolution or agreement in question, as amended.

(4) A "special enactment" means an enactment that is not a public general enactment, and includes—

(a) an Act for confirming a provisional order,

(b) any provision of a public general Act in relation to the passing of which any of the standing orders of the House of Lords or the House of Commons relating to Private Business applied, or

(c) any enactment to the extent that it is incorporated in or applied for the purposes of a special enactment.

(5) If a company fails to comply with this section an offence is committed by—

(a) the company, and

(b) every officer of the company who is in default.

(6) A person guilty of an offence under this section is liable on summary conviction to a fine not exceeding level 3 on the standard scale and, for continued contravention, a daily default fine not exceeding one-tenth of level 3 on the standard scale.

[1.36]

35 Notice to registrar where company's constitution altered by order

(1) Where a company's constitution is altered by an order of a court or other authority, the company must give notice to the registrar of the alteration not later than 15 days after the alteration takes effect.

(2) The notice must be accompanied by—

(a) a copy of the order, and

(b) if the order amends—

(i) the company's articles, or

(ii) a resolution or agreement to which Chapter 3 applies (resolutions and agreements affecting the company's constitution),

a copy of the company's articles, or the resolution or agreement in question, as amended.

(3) If a company fails to comply with this section an offence is committed by—

(a) the company, and

(b) every officer of the company who is in default.

(4) A person guilty of an offence under this section is liable on summary conviction to a fine not exceeding level 3 on the standard scale and, for continued contravention, a daily default fine not exceeding one-tenth of level 3 on the standard scale.

(5) This section does not apply where provision is made by another enactment for the delivery to the registrar of a copy of the order in question.

[1.37]

36 Documents to be incorporated in or accompany copies of articles issued by company

(1) Every copy of a company's articles issued by the company must be accompanied by—

(a) a copy of any resolution or agreement relating to the company to which Chapter 3 applies (resolutions and agreements affecting a company's constitution),

(b) where the company has been required to give notice to the registrar under section 34(2) (notice where company's constitution altered by enactment), a statement that the enactment in question alters the effect of the company's constitution,

(c) where the company's constitution is altered by a special enactment (see section 34(4)), a copy of the enactment, and

(d) a copy of any order required to be sent to the registrar under section 35(2)(a) (order of court or other authority altering company's constitution).

(2) This does not require the articles to be accompanied by a copy of a document or by a statement if—

(a) the effect of the resolution, agreement, enactment or order (as the case may be) on the company's constitution has been incorporated into the articles by amendment, or

(b) the resolution, agreement, enactment or order (as the case may be) is not for the time being in force.

(3) If the company fails to comply with this section, an offence is committed by every officer of the company who is in default.

(4) A person guilty of an offence under this section is liable on summary conviction to a fine not exceeding level 3 on the standard scale for each occasion on which copies are issued, or, as the case may be, requested.

(5) For the purposes of this section, a liquidator of the company is treated as an officer of it.

Supplementary provisions

[1.38]
37 Right to participate in profits otherwise than as member void

In the case of a company limited by guarantee and not having a share capital any provision in the company's articles, or in any resolution of the company, purporting to give a person a right to participate in the divisible profits of the company otherwise than as a member is void.

[1.39]
38 Application to single member companies of enactments and rules of law

Any enactment or rule of law applicable to companies formed by two or more persons or having two or more members applies with any necessary modification in relation to a company formed by one person or having only one person as a member.

PART 4 A COMPANY'S CAPACITY AND RELATED MATTERS

Capacity of company and power of directors to bind it

[1.40]
39 A company's capacity

(1) The validity of an act done by a company shall not be called into question on the ground of lack of capacity by reason of anything in the company's constitution.

(2) This section has effect subject to section 42 (companies that are charities).

[1.41]
40 Power of directors to bind the company

(1) In favour of a person dealing with a company in good faith, the power of the directors to bind the company, or authorise others to do so, is deemed to be free of any limitation under the company's constitution.

(2) For this purpose—

(a) a person "deals with" a company if he is a party to any transaction or other act to which the company is a party,

(b) a person dealing with a company—

(i) is not bound to enquire as to any limitation on the powers of the directors to bind the company or authorise others to do so,

(ii) is presumed to have acted in good faith unless the contrary is proved, and

(iii) is not to be regarded as acting in bad faith by reason only of his knowing that an act is beyond the powers of the directors under the company's constitution.

(3) The references above to limitations on the directors' powers under the company's constitution include limitations deriving—

(a) from a resolution of the company or of any class of shareholders, or

(b) from any agreement between the members of the company or of any class of shareholders.

(4) This section does not affect any right of a member of the company to bring proceedings to restrain the doing of an action that is beyond the powers of the directors.

But no such proceedings lie in respect of an act to be done in fulfilment of a legal obligation arising from a previous act of the company.

(5) This section does not affect any liability incurred by the directors, or any other person, by reason of the directors' exceeding their powers.

(6) This section has effect subject to—

section 41 (transactions with directors or their associates), and

section 42 (companies that are charities).

[1.42]
41 Constitutional limitations: transactions involving directors or their associates

(1) This section applies to a transaction if or to the extent that its validity depends on section 40 (power of directors deemed to be free of limitations under company's constitution in favour of person dealing with company in good faith).

Nothing in this section shall be read as excluding the operation of any other enactment or rule of law by virtue of which the transaction may be called in question or any liability to the company may arise.

(2) Where—

(a) a company enters into such a transaction, and

(b) the parties to the transaction include—

(i) a director of the company or of its holding company, or
(ii) a person connected with any such director,

the transaction is voidable at the instance of the company.

(3) Whether or not it is avoided, any such party to the transaction as is mentioned in subsection (2)(b)(i) or (ii), and any director of the company who authorised the transaction, is liable—

(a) to account to the company for any gain he has made directly or indirectly by the transaction, and
(b) to indemnify the company for any loss or damage resulting from the transaction.

(4) The transaction ceases to be voidable if—

(a) restitution of any money or other asset which was the subject matter of the transaction is no longer possible, or
(b) the company is indemnified for any loss or damage resulting from the transaction, or
(c) rights acquired bona fide for value and without actual notice of the directors' exceeding their powers by a person who is not party to the transaction would be affected by the avoidance, or
(d) the transaction is affirmed by the company.

(5) A person other than a director of the company is not liable under subsection (3) if he shows that at the time the transaction was entered into he did not know that the directors were exceeding their powers.

(6) Nothing in the preceding provisions of this section affects the rights of any party to the transaction not within subsection (2)(b)(i) or (ii).

But the court may, on the application of the company or any such party, make an order affirming, severing or setting aside the transaction on such terms as appear to the court to be just.

(7) In this section—

(a) "transaction" includes any act; and
(b) the reference to a person connected with a director has the same meaning as in Part 10 (company directors).

[1.43]
42 Constitutional limitations: companies that are charities

(1) Sections 39 and 40 (company's capacity and power of directors to bind company) do not apply to the acts of a company that is a charity except in favour of a person who—

(a) does not know at the time the act is done that the company is a charity, or
(b) gives full consideration in money or money's worth in relation to the act in question and does not know (as the case may be)—
    (i) that the act is not permitted by the company's constitution, or
    (ii) that the act is beyond the powers of the directors.

(2) Where a company that is a charity purports to transfer or grant an interest in property, the fact that (as the case may be)—

(a) the act was not permitted by the company's constitution, or
(b) the directors in connection with the act exceeded any limitation on their powers under the company's constitution,

does not affect the title of a person who subsequently acquires the property or any interest in it for full consideration without actual notice of any such circumstances affecting the validity of the company's act.

(3) In any proceedings arising out of subsection (1) or (2) the burden of proving—

(a) that a person knew that the company was a charity, or
(b) that a person knew that an act was not permitted by the company's constitution or was beyond the powers of the directors,

lies on the person asserting that fact.

(4) In the case of a company that is a charity the affirmation of a transaction to which section 41 applies (transactions with directors or their associates) is ineffective without the prior written consent of—

(a) in England and Wales, the Charity Commission;
(b) in Northern Ireland, the Department for Social Development.

(5) This section does not extend to Scotland (but see section 112 of the Companies Act 1989 (c 40)).

Formalities of doing business under the law of England and Wales or Northern Ireland

[1.44]
43 Company contracts

(1) Under the law of England and Wales or Northern Ireland a contract may be made—

(a) by a company, by writing under its common seal, or
(b) on behalf of a company, by a person acting under its authority, express or implied.

(2) Any formalities required by law in the case of a contract made by an individual also apply, unless a contrary intention appears, to a contract made by or on behalf of a company.

[1.45]
44 Execution of documents

(1) Under the law of England and Wales or Northern Ireland a document is executed by a company—

(a) by the affixing of its common seal, or
(b) by signature in accordance with the following provisions.

(2) A document is validly executed by a company if it is signed on behalf of the company—

(a) by two authorised signatories, or
(b) by a director of the company in the presence of a witness who attests the signature.

(3) The following are "authorised signatories" for the purposes of subsection (2)—

(a) every director of the company, and
(b) in the case of a private company with a secretary or a public company, the secretary (or any joint secretary) of the company.

(4) A document signed in accordance with subsection (2) and expressed, in whatever words, to be executed by the company has the same effect as if executed under the common seal of the company.

(5) In favour of a purchaser a document is deemed to have been duly executed by a company if it purports to be signed in accordance with subsection (2).

A "purchaser" means a purchaser in good faith for valuable consideration and includes a lessee, mortgagee or other person who for valuable consideration acquires an interest in property.

(6) Where a document is to be signed by a person on behalf of more than one company, it is not duly signed by that person for the purposes of this section unless he signs it separately in each capacity.

(7) References in this section to a document being (or purporting to be) signed by a director or secretary are to be read, in a case where that office is held by a firm, as references to its being (or purporting to be) signed by an individual authorised by the firm to sign on its behalf.

(8) This section applies to a document that is (or purports to be) executed by a company in the name of or on behalf of another person whether or not that person is also a company.

[1.46]

45 Common seal

(1) A company may have a common seal, but need not have one.

(2) A company which has a common seal shall have its name engraved in legible characters on the seal.

(3) If a company fails to comply with subsection (2) an offence is committed by—

(a) the company, and

(b) every officer of the company who is in default.

(4) An officer of a company, or a person acting on behalf of a company, commits an offence if he uses, or authorises the use of, a seal purporting to be a seal of the company on which its name is not engraved as required by subsection (2).

(5) A person guilty of an offence under this section is liable on summary conviction to a fine not exceeding level 3 on the standard scale.

(6) This section does not form part of the law of Scotland.

[1.47]

46 Execution of deeds

(1) A document is validly executed by a company as a deed for the purposes of section 1(2)(b) of the Law of Property (Miscellaneous Provisions) Act 1989 (c 34) and for the purposes of the law of Northern Ireland if, and only if—

(a) it is duly executed by the company, and

(b) it is delivered as a deed.

(2) For the purposes of subsection (1)(b) a document is presumed to be delivered upon its being executed, unless a contrary intention is proved.

[1.48]

47 Execution of deeds or other documents by attorney

(1) Under the law of England and Wales or Northern Ireland a company may, by instrument executed as a deed, empower a person, either generally or in respect of specified matters, as its attorney to execute deeds or other documents on its behalf.

(2) A deed or other document so executed, whether in the United Kingdom or elsewhere, has effect as if executed by the company.

Formalities of doing business under the law of Scotland

[1.49]

48 Execution of documents by companies

(1) The following provisions form part of the law of Scotland only.

(2) Notwithstanding the provisions of any enactment, a company need not have a company seal.

(3) For the purposes of any enactment—

(a) providing for a document to be executed by a company by affixing its common seal, or

(b) referring (in whatever terms) to a document so executed,

a document signed or subscribed [(or, in the case of an electronic document, authenticated)] by or on behalf of the company in accordance with the provisions of the Requirements of Writing (Scotland) Act 1995 (c 7) has effect as if so executed.

NOTES

Sub-s (3): words in square brackets inserted by the Land Registration etc (Scotland) Act 2012, s 119, Sch 5, para 50(1), (2), as from 8 December 2014.

Other matters

[1.50]

49 Official seal for use abroad

(1) A company that has a common seal may have an official seal for use outside the United Kingdom.

(2) The official seal must be a facsimile of the company's common seal, with the addition on its face of the place or places where it is to be used.

(3) The official seal when duly affixed to a document has the same effect as the company's common seal.

This subsection does not extend to Scotland.

(4) A company having an official seal for use outside the United Kingdom may—

(a) by writing under its common seal, or

(b) as respects Scotland, by writing subscribed [or authenticated] in accordance with the Requirements of Writing (Scotland) Act 1995,

authorise any person appointed for the purpose to affix the official seal to any deed or other document to which the company is party.

(5) As between the company and a person dealing with such an agent, the agent's authority continues—

(a) during the period mentioned in the instrument conferring the authority, or

(b) if no period is mentioned, until notice of the revocation or termination of the agent's authority has been given to the person dealing with him.

(6) The person affixing the official seal must certify in writing on the deed or other document to which the seal is affixed the date on which, and place at which, it is affixed.

NOTES

Sub-s (4): words in square brackets in para (b) inserted by the Land Registration etc (Scotland) Act 2012, s 119, Sch 5, para 50(1), (3), as from 8 December 2014.

[1.51]

50 Official seal for share certificates etc

(1) A company that has a common seal may have an official seal for use—

(a) for sealing securities issued by the company, or

(b) for sealing documents creating or evidencing securities so issued.

(2) The official seal—

(a) must be a facsimile of the company's common seal, with the addition on its face of the word "Securities", and

(b) when duly affixed to the document has the same effect as the company's common seal.

[1.52]

51 Pre-incorporation contracts, deeds and obligations

(1) A contract that purports to be made by or on behalf of a company at a time when the company has not been formed has effect, subject to any agreement to the contrary, as one made with the person purporting to act for the company or as agent for it, and he is personally liable on the contract accordingly.

(2) Subsection (1) applies—

(a) to the making of a deed under the law of England and Wales or Northern Ireland, and

(b) to the undertaking of an obligation under the law of Scotland,

as it applies to the making of a contract.

[1.53]

52 Bills of exchange and promissory notes

A bill of exchange or promissory note is deemed to have been made, accepted or endorsed on behalf of a company if made, accepted or endorsed in the name of, or by or on behalf or on account of, the company by a person acting under its authority.

PART 5 A COMPANY'S NAME

CHAPTER 1 GENERAL REQUIREMENTS

Prohibited names

[1.54]

53 Prohibited names

A company must not be registered under this Act by a name if, in the opinion of the Secretary of State—

(a) its use by the company would constitute an offence, or

(b) it is offensive.

Sensitive words and expressions

[1.55]

54 Names suggesting connection with government or public authority

(1) The approval of the Secretary of State is required for a company to be registered under this Act by a name that would be likely to give the impression that the company is connected with—

(a) Her Majesty's Government, any part of the Scottish administration[, the Welsh Assembly Government] or Her Majesty's Government in Northern Ireland,

(b) a local authority, or

(c) any public authority specified for the purposes of this section by regulations made by the Secretary of State.

(2) For the purposes of this section—

"local authority" means—

(a) a local authority within the meaning of the Local Government Act 1972 (c 70), the Common Council of the City of London or the Council of the Isles of Scilly,

(b) a council constituted under section 2 of the Local Government etc (Scotland) Act 1994 (c 39), or

(c) a district council in Northern Ireland;

"public authority" includes any person or body having functions of a public nature.

(3) Regulations under this section are subject to affirmative resolution procedure.

NOTES

Sub-s (1): words in square brackets inserted by the Government of Wales Act 2006 (Consequential Modifications, Transitional Provisions and Saving) Order 2009, SI 2009/2958, arts 8, 9, as from 6 November 2009.

National Assembly for Wales: see further, in relation to the renaming of the National Assembly for Wales as the Senedd Cymru or the Welsh Parliament, the Senedd and Elections (Wales) Act 2020, s 2 (with effect from 6 May 2020). See also ss 3–9 of the 2020 Act in relation to the renaming of Acts of the National Assembly for Wales, Members of the National Assembly for Wales, etc.

Regulations: the Company, Limited Liability Partnership and Business (Names and Trading Disclosures) Regulations 2015, SI 2015/17 at **[4.514]**. For a summary of all statutory instruments made under this Act, see Appendix 4 at **[A4]**.

[1.56]

55 Other sensitive words or expressions

(1) The approval of the Secretary of State is required for a company to be registered under this Act by a name that includes a word or expression for the time being specified in regulations made by the Secretary of State under this section.

(2) Regulations under this section are subject to approval after being made.

NOTES

Chamber of commerce: by the Company and Business Names (Chamber of Commerce, etc) Act 1999, s 1 (as amended), the Secretary of State is required to include the title "chamber of commerce" (and its Welsh equivalent "siambr fasnach") in the list of controlled titles maintained in accordance with regulations made under this section.

Regulations: the Company, Limited Liability Partnership and Business Names (Sensitive Words and Expressions) Regulations 2014, SI 2014/3140 at **[4.503]**. For a summary of all statutory instruments made under this Act, see Appendix 4 at **[A4]**.

[1.57]

56 Duty to seek comments of government department or other specified body

(1) The Secretary of State may by regulations under—

(a) section 54 (name suggesting connection with government or public authority), or

(b) section 55 (other sensitive words or expressions),

require that, in connection with an application for the approval of the Secretary of State under that section, the applicant must seek the view of a specified Government department or other body.

(2) Where such a requirement applies, the applicant must request the specified department or other body (in writing) to indicate whether (and if so why) it has any objections to the proposed name.

(3) Where a request under this section is made in connection with an application for the registration of a company under this Act, the application must—

(a) include a statement that a request under this section has been made, and

(b) be accompanied by a copy of any response received.

(4) Where a request under this section is made in connection with a change in a company's name, the notice of the change sent to the registrar must be accompanied by—

(a) a statement by a director or secretary of the company that a request under this section has been made, and

(b) a copy of any response received.

(5) In this section "specified" means specified in the regulations.

NOTES

Regulations under ss 54, 55: see the notes to those sections *ante*.

Permitted characters etc

[1.58]

57 Permitted characters etc

(1) The Secretary of State may make provision by regulations—

(a) as to the letters or other characters, signs or symbols (including accents and other diacritical marks) and punctuation that may be used in the name of a company registered under this Act; and

(b) specifying a standard style or format for the name of a company for the purposes of registration.

(2) The regulations may prohibit the use of specified characters, signs or symbols when appearing in a specified position (in particular, at the beginning of a name).

(3) A company may not be registered under this Act by a name that consists of or includes anything that is not permitted in accordance with regulations under this section.

(4) Regulations under this section are subject to negative resolution procedure.

(5) In this section "specified" means specified in the regulations.

NOTES

Regulations: the Company, Limited Liability Partnership and Business (Names and Trading Disclosures) Regulations 2015, SI 2015/17 at **[4.514]**. For a summary of all statutory instruments made under this Act, see Appendix 4 at **[A4]**.

CHAPTER 2 INDICATIONS OF COMPANY TYPE OR LEGAL FORM

Required indications for limited companies

[1.59]

58 Public limited companies

(1) The name of a limited company that is a public company must end with "public limited company" or "p.l.c.".

(2) In the case of a Welsh company, its name may instead end with "cwmni cyfyngedig cyhoeddus" or "c.c.c.".

(3) This section does not apply to community interest companies (but see section 33(3) and (4) of the Companies (Audit, Investigations and Community Enterprise) Act 2004 (c 27)).

[1.60]

59 Private limited companies

(1) The name of a limited company that is a private company must end with "limited" or "ltd.".

(2) In the case of a Welsh company, its name may instead end with "cyfyngedig" or "cyf.".

(3) Certain companies are exempt from this requirement (see section 60).

(4) This section does not apply to community interest companies (but see section 33(1) and (2) of the Companies (Audit, Investigations and Community Enterprise) Act 2004).

[1.61]

60 Exemption from requirement as to use of "limited"

(1) A private company is exempt from section 59 (requirement to have name ending with "limited" or permitted alternative) if—

(a) it is a charity,

(b) it is exempted from the requirement of that section by regulations made by the Secretary of State, or

(c) it meets the conditions specified in—

section 61 (continuation of existing exemption: companies limited by shares), or

section 62 (continuation of existing exemption: companies limited by guarantee).

(2) The registrar may refuse to register a private limited company by a name that does not include the word "limited" (or a permitted alternative) unless a statement has been delivered to him that the company meets the conditions for exemption.

(3) The registrar may accept the statement as sufficient evidence of the matters stated in it.

(4) Regulations under this section are subject to negative resolution procedure.

NOTES

Regulations: the Company, Limited Liability Partnership and Business (Names and Trading Disclosures) Regulations 2015, SI 2015/17 at **[4.514]**. For a summary of all statutory instruments made under this Act, see Appendix 4 at **[A4]**.

[1.62]

61 Continuation of existing exemption: companies limited by shares

(1) This section applies to a private company limited by shares—

(a) that on 25th February 1982—

(i) was registered in Great Britain, and

(ii) had a name that, by virtue of a licence under section 19 of the Companies Act 1948 (c 38) (or corresponding earlier legislation), did not include the word "limited" or any of the permitted alternatives, or

(b) that on 30th June 1983—

(i) was registered in Northern Ireland, and

(ii) had a name that, by virtue of a licence under section 19 of the Companies Act (Northern Ireland) 1960 (c 22 (NI)) (or corresponding earlier legislation), did not include the word "limited" or any of the permitted alternatives.

(2) A company to which this section applies is exempt from section 59 (requirement to have name ending with "limited" or permitted alternative) so long as—

(a) it continues to meet the following two conditions, and

(b) it does not change its name.

(3) The first condition is that the objects of the company are the promotion of commerce, art, science, education, religion, charity or any profession, and anything incidental or conducive to any of those objects.

(4) The second condition is that the company's articles—

(a) require its income to be applied in promoting its objects,

(b) prohibit the payment of dividends, or any return of capital, to its members, and

(c) require all the assets that would otherwise be available to its members generally to be transferred on its winding up either—

(i) to another body with objects similar to its own, or

(ii) to another body the objects of which are the promotion of charity and anything incidental or conducive thereto,

(whether or not the body is a member of the company).

[1.63]

62 Continuation of existing exemption: companies limited by guarantee

(1) A private company limited by guarantee that immediately before the commencement of this Part—

(a) was exempt by virtue of section 30 of the Companies Act 1985 (c 6) or Article 40 of the Companies (Northern Ireland) Order 1986 (SI 1986/ 1032 (NI 6)) from the requirement to have a name including the word "limited" or a permitted alternative, and

(b) had a name that did not include the word "limited" or any of the permitted alternatives,

is exempt from section 59 (requirement to have name ending with "limited" or permitted alternative) so long as it continues to meet the following two conditions and does not change its name.

(2) The first condition is that the objects of the company are the promotion of commerce, art, science, education, religion, charity or any profession, and anything incidental or conducive to any of those objects.

(3) The second condition is that the company's articles—

(a) require its income to be applied in promoting its objects,

(b) prohibit the payment of dividends to its members, and

(c) require all the assets that would otherwise be available to its members generally to be transferred on its winding up either—

(i) to another body with objects similar to its own, or

(ii) to another body the objects of which are the promotion of charity and anything incidental or conducive thereto,

(whether or not the body is a member of the company).

[1.64]

63 Exempt company: restriction on amendment of articles

(1) A private company—

(a) that is exempt under section 61 or 62 from the requirement to use "limited" (or a permitted alternative) as part of its name, and

(b) whose name does not include "limited" or any of the permitted alternatives,

must not amend its articles so that it ceases to comply with the conditions for exemption under that section.

(2) If subsection (1) above is contravened an offence is committed by—

(a) the company, and

(b) every officer of the company who is in default.

For this purpose a shadow director is treated as an officer of the company.

(3) A person guilty of an offence under this section is liable on summary conviction to a fine not exceeding level 5 on the standard scale and, for continued contravention, a daily default fine not exceeding [one-tenth of the greater of £5,000 or level 4 on the standard scale].

(4) Where immediately before the commencement of this section—

(a) a company was exempt by virtue of section 30 of the Companies Act 1985 (c 6) or Article 40 of the Companies (Northern Ireland) Order 1986 (SI 1986/1032 (NI 6)) from the requirement to have a name including the word "limited" (or a permitted alternative), and

(b) the company's memorandum or articles contained provision preventing an alteration of them without the approval of—

(i) the Board of Trade or a Northern Ireland department (or any other department or Minister), or

(ii) the Charity Commission,

that provision, and any condition of any such licence as is mentioned in section 61(1)(a)(ii) or (b)(ii) requiring such provision, shall cease to have effect.

This does not apply if, or to the extent that, the provision is required by or under any other enactment.

(5) It is hereby declared that any such provision as is mentioned in subsection (4)(b) formerly contained in a company's memorandum was at all material times capable, with the appropriate approval, of being altered or removed under section 17 of the Companies Act 1985 or Article 28 of the Companies (Northern Ireland) Order 1986 (SI 1986/1032 (NI 6)) (or corresponding earlier enactments).

NOTES

Sub-s (3): words in square brackets substituted (for the original words "one-tenth of level 5 on the standard scale") by the Legal Aid, Sentencing and Punishment of Offenders Act 2012 (Fines on Summary Conviction) Regulations 2015, SI 2015/664, regs 3, 5, Sch 3, Pt 1, para 9(1), (2), as from 12 March 2015, in relation to England and Wales only (except in relation to (a) fines for offences committed before 12 March 2015, (b) the operation of restrictions on fines that may be imposed on a person aged under 18, or (c) fines that may be imposed on a person convicted by a magistrates' court who is to be sentenced as if convicted on indictment).

[1.65]

64 Power to direct change of name in case of company ceasing to be entitled to exemption

(1) If it appears to the Secretary of State that a company whose name does not include "limited" or any of the permitted alternatives—

(a) has ceased to be entitled to exemption under section 60(1)(a) or (b), or

(b) in the case of a company within section 61 or 62 (which impose conditions as to the objects and articles of the company)—

(i) has carried on any business other than the promotion of any of the objects mentioned in subsection (3) of section 61 or, as the case may be, subsection (2) of section 62, or

(ii) has acted inconsistently with the provision required by subsection (4)(a) or (b) of section 61 or, as the case may be, subsection (3)(a) or (b) of section 62,

the Secretary of State may direct the company to change its name so that it ends with "limited" or one of the permitted alternatives.

(2) The direction must be in writing and must specify the period within which the company is to change its name.

(3) A change of name in order to comply with a direction under this section may be made by resolution of the directors.

This is without prejudice to any other method of changing the company's name.

(4) Where a resolution of the directors is passed in accordance with subsection (3), the company must give notice to the registrar of the change.

Sections 80 and 81 apply as regards the registration and effect of the change.

(5) If the company fails to comply with a direction under this section an offence is committed by—

(a) the company, and

(b) every officer of the company who is in default.

(6) A person guilty of an offence under this section is liable on summary conviction to a fine not exceeding level 5 on the standard scale and, for continued contravention, a daily default fine not exceeding [one-tenth of the greater of £5,000 or level 4 on the standard scale].

(7) A company that has been directed to change its name under this section may not, without the approval of the Secretary of State, subsequently change its name so that it does not include "limited" or one of the permitted alternatives. This does not apply to a change of name on re-registration or on conversion to a community interest company.

NOTES

Sub-s (6): words in square brackets substituted (for the original words "one-tenth of level 5 on the standard scale") by the Legal Aid, Sentencing and Punishment of Offenders Act 2012 (Fines on Summary Conviction) Regulations 2015, SI 2015/664, regs 3, 5, Sch 3, Pt 1, para 9(1), (3), as from 12 March 2015, in relation to England and Wales only (except in relation to (a) fines for offences committed before 12 March 2015, (b) the operation of restrictions on fines that may be imposed on a person aged under 18, or (c) fines that may be imposed on a person convicted by a magistrates' court who is to be sentenced as if convicted on indictment).

Inappropriate use of indications of company type or legal form

[1.66]

65 Inappropriate use of indications of company type or legal form

(1) The Secretary of State may make provision by regulations prohibiting the use in a company name of specified words, expressions or other indications —

(a) that are associated with a particular type of company or form of organisation, or

(b) that are similar to words, expressions or other indications associated with a particular type of company or form of organisation.

(2) The regulations may prohibit the use of words, expressions or other indications—

(a) in a specified part, or otherwise than in a specified part, of a company's name;

(b) in conjunction with, or otherwise than in conjunction with, such other words, expressions or indications as may be specified.

(3) A company must not be registered under this Act by a name that consists of or includes anything prohibited by regulations under this section.
(4) In this section "specified" means specified in the regulations.
(5) Regulations under this section are subject to negative resolution procedure.

NOTES

Regulations: the Company, Limited Liability Partnership and Business (Names and Trading Disclosures) Regulations 2015, SI 2015/17 at **[4.514]**. For a summary of all statutory instruments made under this Act, see Appendix 4 at **[A4]**.

CHAPTER 3 SIMILARITY TO OTHER NAMES

Similarity to other name on registrar's index

[1.67]

66 Name not to be the same as another in the index

(1) A company must not be registered under this Act by a name that is the same as another name appearing in the registrar's index of company names.
(2) The Secretary of State may make provision by regulations supplementing this section.
(3) The regulations may make provision—
- (a) as to matters that are to be disregarded, and
- (b) as to words, expressions, signs or symbols that are, or are not, to be regarded as the same,

for the purposes of this section.
(4) The regulations may provide—
- (a) that registration by a name that would otherwise be prohibited under this section is permitted—
  - (i) in specified circumstances, or
  - (ii) with specified consent, and
- (b) that if those circumstances obtain or that consent is given at the time a company is registered by a name, a subsequent change of circumstances or withdrawal of consent does not affect the registration.

(5) Regulations under this section are subject to negative resolution procedure.
(6) In this section "specified" means specified in the regulations.

NOTES

Regulations: the Company, Limited Liability Partnership and Business (Names and Trading Disclosures) Regulations 2015, SI 2015/17 at **[4.514]**. For a summary of all statutory instruments made under this Act, see Appendix 4 at **[A4]**.

[1.68]

67 Power to direct change of name in case of similarity to existing name

(1) The Secretary of State may direct a company to change its name if it has been registered in a name that is the same as or, in the opinion of the Secretary of State, too like—
- (a) a name appearing at the time of the registration in the registrar's index of company names, or
- (b) a name that should have appeared in that index at that time.

(2) The Secretary of State may make provision by regulations supplementing this section.
(3) The regulations may make provision—
- (a) as to matters that are to be disregarded, and
- (b) as to words, expressions, signs or symbols that are, or are not, to be regarded as the same,

for the purposes of this section.
(4) The regulations may provide—
- (a) that no direction is to be given under this section in respect of a name—
  - (i) in specified circumstances, or
  - (ii) if specified consent is given, and
- (b) that a subsequent change of circumstances or withdrawal of consent does not give rise to grounds for a direction under this section.

(5) Regulations under this section are subject to negative resolution procedure.
(6) In this section "specified" means specified in the regulations.

NOTES

Regulations: no Regulations have been made under this section.

[1.69]

68 Direction to change name: supplementary provisions

(1) The following provisions have effect in relation to a direction under section 67 (power to direct change of name in case of similarity to existing name).
(2) Any such direction—
- (a) must be given within twelve months of the company's registration by the name in question, and
- (b) must specify the period within which the company is to change its name.

(3) The Secretary of State may by a further direction extend that period.

Any such direction must be given before the end of the period for the time being specified.

(4) A direction under section 67 or this section must be in writing.
(5) If a company fails to comply with the direction, an offence is committed by—
- (a) the company, and
- (b) every officer of the company who is in default.

For this purpose a shadow director is treated as an officer of the company.

(6) A person guilty of an offence under this section is liable on summary conviction to a fine not exceeding level 3 on the standard scale and, for continued contravention, a daily default fine not exceeding one-tenth of level 3 on the standard scale.

Similarity to other name in which person has goodwill

[1.70]

69 Objection to company's registered name

(1) A person ("the applicant") may object to a company's registered name on the ground—

(a) that it is the same as a name associated with the applicant in which he has goodwill, or

(b) that it is sufficiently similar to such a name that its use in the United Kingdom would be likely to mislead by suggesting a connection between the company and the applicant.

(2) The objection must be made by application to a company names adjudicator (see section 70).

(3) The company concerned shall be the primary respondent to the application. Any of its members or directors may be joined as respondents.

(4) If the ground specified in subsection (1)(a) or (b) is established, it is for the respondents to show—

(a) that the name was registered before the commencement of the activities on which the applicant relies to show goodwill; or

(b) that the company—

(i) is operating under the name, or

(ii) is proposing to do so and has incurred substantial start-up costs in preparation, or

(iii) was formerly operating under the name and is now dormant;

or

(c) that the name was registered in the ordinary course of a company formation business and the company is available for sale to the applicant on the standard terms of that business; or

(d) that the name was adopted in good faith; or

(e) that the interests of the applicant are not adversely affected to any significant extent.

If none of those is shown, the objection shall be upheld.

(5) If the facts mentioned in subsection (4)(a), (b) or (c) are established, the objection shall nevertheless be upheld if the applicant shows that the main purpose of the respondents (or any of them) in registering the name was to obtain money (or other consideration) from the applicant or prevent him from registering the name.

(6) If the objection is not upheld under subsection (4) or (5), it shall be dismissed.

(7) In this section "goodwill" includes reputation of any description.

[1.71]

70 Company names adjudicators

(1) The Secretary of State shall appoint persons to be company names adjudicators.

(2) The persons appointed must have such legal or other experience as, in the Secretary of State's opinion, makes them suitable for appointment.

(3) An adjudicator—

(a) holds office in accordance with the terms of his appointment,

(b) is eligible for re-appointment when his term of office ends,

(c) may resign at any time by notice in writing given to the Secretary of State, and

(d) may be dismissed by the Secretary of State on the ground of incapacity or misconduct.

(4) One of the adjudicators shall be appointed Chief Adjudicator.

He shall perform such functions as the Secretary of State may assign to him.

(5) The other adjudicators shall undertake such duties as the Chief Adjudicator may determine.

(6) The Secretary of State may—

(a) appoint staff for the adjudicators;

(b) pay remuneration and expenses to the adjudicators and their staff;

(c) defray other costs arising in relation to the performance by the adjudicators of their functions;

(d) compensate persons for ceasing to be adjudicators.

[1.72]

71 Procedural rules

(1) The Secretary of State may make rules about proceedings before a company names adjudicator.

(2) The rules may, in particular, make provision—

(a) as to how an application is to be made and the form and content of an application or other documents;

(b) for fees to be charged;

(c) about the service of documents and the consequences of failure to serve them;

(d) as to the form and manner in which evidence is to be given;

(e) for circumstances in which hearings are required and those in which they are not;

(f) for cases to be heard by more than one adjudicator;

(g) setting time limits for anything required to be done in connection with the proceedings (and allowing for such limits to be extended, even if they have expired);

(h) enabling the adjudicator to strike out an application, or any defence, in whole or in part—

(i) on the ground that it is vexatious, has no reasonable prospect of success or is otherwise misconceived, or

(ii) for failure to comply with the requirements of the rules;

(i) conferring power to order security for costs (in Scotland, caution for expenses);

(j) as to how far proceedings are to be held in public;

(k) requiring one party to bear the costs (in Scotland, expenses) of another and as to the taxing (or settling) the amount of such costs (or expenses).

(3) The rules may confer on the Chief Adjudicator power to determine any matter that could be the subject of provision in the rules.

(4) Rules under this section shall be made by statutory instrument which shall be subject to annulment in pursuance of a resolution of either House of Parliament.

NOTES

Rules: the Company Names Adjudicator Rules 2008, SI 2008/1738 at **[4.148]**. For a summary of all statutory instruments made under this Act, see Appendix 4 at **[A4]**.

[1.73]

72 Decision of adjudicator to be made available to public

(1) A company names adjudicator must, within 90 days of determining an application under section 69, make his decision and his reasons for it available to the public.

(2) He may do so by means of a website or by such other means as appear to him to be appropriate.

[1.74]

73 Order requiring name to be changed

(1) If an application under section 69 is upheld, the adjudicator shall make an order—

(a) requiring the respondent company to change its name to one that is not an offending name, and

(b) requiring all the respondents—

(i) to take all such steps as are within their power to make, or facilitate the making, of that change, and

(ii) not to cause or permit any steps to be taken calculated to result in another company being registered with a name that is an offending name.

(2) An "offending name" means a name that, by reason of its similarity to the name associated with the applicant in which he claims goodwill, would be likely—

(a) to be the subject of a direction under section 67 (power of Secretary of State to direct change of name), or

(b) to give rise to a further application under section 69.

(3) The order must specify a date by which the respondent company's name is to be changed and may be enforced—

(a) in England and Wales or Northern Ireland, in the same way as an order of the High Court;

(b) in Scotland, in the same way as a decree of the Court of Session.

(4) If the respondent company's name is not changed in accordance with the order by the specified date, the adjudicator may determine a new name for the company.

(5) If the adjudicator determines a new name for the respondent company he must give notice of his determination—

(a) to the applicant,

(b) to the respondents, and

(c) to the registrar.

(6) For the purposes of this section a company's name is changed when the change takes effect in accordance with section 81(1) (on the issue of the new certification of incorporation).

[1.75]

74 Appeal from adjudicator's decision

(1) An appeal lies to the court from any decision of a company names adjudicator to uphold or dismiss an application under section 69.

(2) Notice of appeal against a decision upholding an application must be given before the date specified in the adjudicator's order by which the respondent company's name is to be changed.

(3) If notice of appeal is given against a decision upholding an application, the effect of the adjudicator's order is suspended.

(4) If on appeal the court—

(a) affirms the decision of the adjudicator to uphold the application, or

(b) reverses the decision of the adjudicator to dismiss the application,

the court may (as the case may require) specify the date by which the adjudicator's order is to be complied with, remit the matter to the adjudicator or make any order or determination that the adjudicator might have made.

(5) If the court determines a new name for the company it must give notice of the determination—

(a) to the parties to the appeal, and

(b) to the registrar.

CHAPTER 4 OTHER POWERS OF THE SECRETARY OF STATE

[1.76]

75 Provision of misleading information etc

(1) If it appears to the Secretary of State—

(a) that misleading information has been given for the purposes of a company's registration by a particular name, or

(b) that an undertaking or assurance has been given for that purpose and has not been fulfilled,

the Secretary of State may direct the company to change its name.

(2) Any such direction—

(a) must be given within five years of the company's registration by that name, and

(b) must specify the period within which the company is to change its name.

(3) The Secretary of State may by a further direction extend the period within which the company is to change its name.

Any such direction must be given before the end of the period for the time being specified.

(4) A direction under this section must be in writing.

(5) If a company fails to comply with a direction under this section, an offence is committed by—

(a) the company, and

(b) every officer of the company who is in default.

For this purpose a shadow director is treated as an officer of the company.

(6) A person guilty of an offence under this section is liable on summary conviction to a fine not exceeding level 3 on the standard scale and, for continued contravention, a daily default fine not exceeding one-tenth of level 3 on the standard scale.

[1.77]
76 Misleading indication of activities
(1) If in the opinion of the Secretary of State the name by which a company is registered gives so misleading an indication of the nature of its activities as to be likely to cause harm to the public, the Secretary of State may direct the company to change its name.
(2) The direction must be in writing.
(3) The direction must be complied with within a period of six weeks from the date of the direction or such longer period as the Secretary of State may think fit to allow.
This does not apply if an application is duly made to the court under the following provisions.
(4) The company may apply to the court to set the direction aside.
The application must be made within the period of three weeks from the date of the direction.
(5) The court may set the direction aside or confirm it.
If the direction is confirmed, the court shall specify the period within which the direction is to be complied with.
(6) If a company fails to comply with a direction under this section, an offence is committed by—
(a) the company, and
(b) every officer of the company who is in default.
For this purpose a shadow director is treated as an officer of the company.
(7) A person guilty of an offence under this section is liable on summary conviction to a fine not exceeding level 3 on the standard scale and, for continued contravention, a daily default fine not exceeding one-tenth of level 3 on the standard scale.

CHAPTER 5 CHANGE OF NAME

[1.78]
77 Change of name
(1) A company may change its name—
(a) by special resolution (see section 78), or
(b) by other means provided for by the company's articles (see section 79).
(2) The name of a company may also be changed—
(a) by resolution of the directors acting under section 64 (change of name to comply with direction of Secretary of State under that section);
(b) on the determination of a new name by a company names adjudicator under section 73 (powers of adjudicator on upholding objection to company name);
(c) on the determination of a new name by the court under section 74 (appeal against decision of company names adjudicator);
(d) under section 1033 (company's name on restoration to the register);
[(e) by resolution of the directors acting under section 45(3) of the Charities Act 2011 (change of name to comply with direction of Charity Commission)].

NOTES
Sub-s (2): para (e) inserted by the Charities Act 2022, s 40, Sch 2, Pt 5, para 46, as from a day to be appointed.

[1.79]
78 Change of name by special resolution
(1) Where a change of name has been agreed to by a company by special resolution, the company must give notice to the registrar.
This is in addition to the obligation to forward a copy of the resolution to the registrar.
(2) Where a change of name by special resolution is conditional on the occurrence of an event, the notice given to the registrar of the change must—
(a) specify that the change is conditional, and
(b) state whether the event has occurred.
(3) If the notice states that the event has not occurred—
(a) the registrar is not required to act under section 80 (registration and issue of new certificate of incorporation) until further notice,
(b) when the event occurs, the company must give notice to the registrar stating that it has occurred, and
(c) the registrar may rely on the statement as sufficient evidence of the matters stated in it.

[1.80]
79 Change of name by means provided for in company's articles
(1) Where a change of a company's name has been made by other means provided for by its articles—
(a) the company must give notice to the registrar, and
(b) the notice must be accompanied by a statement that the change of name has been made by means provided for by the company's articles.
(2) The registrar may rely on the statement as sufficient evidence of the matters stated in it.

[1.81]
80 Change of name: registration and issue of new certificate of incorporation
(1) This section applies where the registrar receives notice of a change of a company's name.
(2) If the registrar is satisfied—
(a) that the new name complies with the requirements of this Part, and
(b) that the requirements of the Companies Acts, and any relevant requirements of the company's articles, with respect to a change of name are complied with,
the registrar must enter the new name on the register in place of the former name.
(3) On the registration of the new name, the registrar must issue a certificate of incorporation altered to meet the circumstances of the case.

[1.82]

81 Change of name: effect

(1) A change of a company's name has effect from the date on which the new certificate of incorporation is issued.

(2) The change does not affect any rights or obligations of the company or render defective any legal proceedings by or against it.

(3) Any legal proceedings that might have been continued or commenced against it by its former name may be continued or commenced against it by its new name.

CHAPTER 6 TRADING DISCLOSURES

[1.83]

82 Requirement to disclose company name etc

(1) The Secretary of State may by regulations make provision requiring companies—

(a) to display specified information in specified locations,

(b) to state specified information in specified descriptions of document or communication, and

(c) to provide specified information on request to those they deal with in the course of their business.

(2) The regulations—

(a) must in every case require disclosure of the name of the company, and

(b) may make provision as to the manner in which any specified information is to be displayed, stated or provided.

(3) The regulations may provide that, for the purposes of any requirement to disclose a company's name, any variation between a word or words required to be part of the name and a permitted abbreviation of that word or those words (or vice versa) shall be disregarded.

(4) In this section "specified" means specified in the regulations.

(5) Regulations under this section are subject to affirmative resolution procedure.

NOTES

Regulations: the Company, Limited Liability Partnership and Business (Names and Trading Disclosures) Regulations 2015, SI 2015/17 at **[4.514]**. For a summary of all statutory instruments made under this Act, see Appendix 4 at **[A4]**.

[1.84]

83 Civil consequences of failure to make required disclosure

(1) This section applies to any legal proceedings brought by a company to which section 82 applies (requirement to disclose company name etc) to enforce a right arising out of a contract made in the course of a business in respect of which the company was, at the time the contract was made, in breach of regulations under that section.

(2) The proceedings shall be dismissed if the defendant (in Scotland, the defender) to the proceedings shows—

(a) that he has a claim against the claimant (pursuer) arising out of the contract that he has been unable to pursue by reason of the latter's breach of the regulations, or

(b) that he has suffered some financial loss in connection with the contract by reason of the claimant's (pursuer's) breach of the regulations,

unless the court before which the proceedings are brought is satisfied that it is just and equitable to permit the proceedings to continue.

(3) This section does not affect the right of any person to enforce such rights as he may have against another person in any proceedings brought by that person.

[1.85]

84 Criminal consequences of failure to make required disclosures

(1) Regulations under section 82 may provide—

(a) that where a company fails, without reasonable excuse, to comply with any specified requirement of regulations under that section an offence is committed by—

(i) the company, and

(ii) every officer of the company who is in default;

(b) that a person guilty of such an offence is liable on summary conviction to a fine not exceeding level 3 on the standard scale and, for continued contravention, a daily default fine not exceeding one-tenth of level 3 on the standard scale.

(2) The regulations may provide that, for the purposes of any provision made under subsection (1), a shadow director of the company is to be treated as an officer of the company.

(3) In subsection (1)(a) "specified" means specified in the regulations.

NOTES

Regulations under section 82: see the notes to that section at **[1.83]**.

[1.86]

85 Minor variations in form of name to be left out of account

(1) For the purposes of this Chapter, in considering a company's name no account is to be taken of—

(a) whether upper or lower case characters (or a combination of the two) are used,

(b) whether diacritical marks or punctuation are present or absent,

(c) whether the name is in the same format or style as is specified under section 57(1)(b) for the purposes of registration,

provided there is no real likelihood of names differing only in those respects being taken to be different names.

(2) This does not affect the operation of regulations under section 57(1)(a) permitting only specified characters, diacritical marks or punctuation.

PART 6 A COMPANY'S REGISTERED OFFICE

General

[1.87]

86 A company's registered office

A company must at all times have a registered office to which all communications and notices may be addressed.

[1.88]

87 Change of address of registered office

(1) A company may change the address of its registered office by giving notice to the registrar.

(2) The change takes effect upon the notice being registered by the registrar, but until the end of the period of 14 days beginning with the date on which it is registered a person may validly serve any document on the company at the address previously registered.

(3) For the purposes of any duty of a company—

(a) to keep available for inspection at its registered office any register, index or other document, or

(b) to mention the address of its registered office in any document,

a company that has given notice to the registrar of a change in the address of its registered office may act on the change as from such date, not more than 14 days after the notice is given, as it may determine.

(4) Where a company unavoidably ceases to perform at its registered office any such duty as is mentioned in subsection (3)(a) in circumstances in which it was not practicable to give prior notice to the registrar of a change in the address of its registered office, but—

(a) resumes performance of that duty at other premises as soon as practicable, and

(b) gives notice accordingly to the registrar of a change in the situation of its registered office within 14 days of doing so,

it is not to be treated as having failed to comply with that duty.

NOTES

Temporary modification: this section was modified by the Companies etc (Filing Requirements) (Temporary Modifications) Regulations 2020, SI 2020/645, reg 4. By virtue of the Corporate Insolvency and Governance Act 2020, s 39(8), the modification applied from 27 June 2020 to the end of the day on 5 April 2021 (subject to the saving provision in s 39(9) which provides that the expiry of s 39 on 5 April 2021 does not affect the continued operation of any Regulations made under that section for the purpose of determining the length of any period that began before the expiry). As modified, sub-s (4) above had effect as if for the reference to "14 days" there were substituted a reference to "42 days".

Welsh companies

[1.89]

88 Welsh companies

(1) In the Companies Acts a "Welsh company" means a company as to which it is stated in the register that its registered office is to be situated in Wales.

(2) A company—

(a) whose registered office is in Wales, and

(b) as to which it is stated in the register that its registered office is to be situated in England and Wales,

may by special resolution require the register to be amended so that it states that the company's registered office is to be situated in Wales.

(3) A company—

(a) whose registered office is in Wales, and

(b) as to which it is stated in the register that its registered office is to be situated in Wales,

may by special resolution require the register to be amended so that it states that the company's registered office is to be situated in England and Wales.

(4) Where a company passes a resolution under this section it must give notice to the registrar, who shall—

(a) amend the register accordingly, and

(b) issue a new certificate of incorporation altered to meet the circumstances of the case.

PART 7 RE-REGISTRATION AS A MEANS OF ALTERING A COMPANY'S STATUS

Introductory

[1.90]

89 Alteration of status by re-registration

A company may by re-registration under this Part alter its status—

(a) from a private company to a public company (see sections 90 to 96);

(b) from a public company to a private company (see sections 97 to 101);

(c) from a private limited company to an unlimited company (see sections 102 to 104);

(d) from an unlimited private company to a limited company (see sections 105 to 108);

(e) from a public company to an unlimited private company (see sections 109 to 111).

Private company becoming public

[1.91]

90 Re-registration of private company as public

(1) A private company (whether limited or unlimited) may be re-registered as a public company limited by shares if—

(a) a special resolution that it should be so re-registered is passed,

(b) the conditions specified below are met, and

(c) an application for re-registration is delivered to the registrar in accordance with section 94, together with—

(i) the other documents required by that section, and

(ii) a statement of compliance.

(2) The conditions are—

(a) that the company has a share capital;
(b) that the requirements of section 91 are met as regards its share capital;
(c) that the requirements of section 92 are met as regards its net assets;
(d) if section 93 applies (recent allotment of shares for non-cash consideration), that the requirements of that section are met; and
(e) that the company has not previously been re-registered as unlimited.

(3) The company must make such changes—
(a) in its name, and
(b) in its articles,

as are necessary in connection with its becoming a public company.

(4) If the company is unlimited it must also make such changes in its articles as are necessary in connection with its becoming a company limited by shares.

[1.92]
91 Requirements as to share capital

(1) The following requirements must be met at the time the special resolution is passed that the company should be re-registered as a public company—
(a) the nominal value of the company's allotted share capital must be not less than the authorised minimum;
(b) each of the company's allotted shares must be paid up at least as to one-quarter of the nominal value of that share and the whole of any premium on it;
(c) if any shares in the company or any premium on them have been fully or partly paid up by an undertaking given by any person that he or another should do work or perform services (whether for the company or any other person), the undertaking must have been performed or otherwise discharged;
(d) if shares have been allotted as fully or partly paid up as to their nominal value or any premium on them otherwise than in cash, and the consideration for the allotment consists of or includes an undertaking to the company (other than one to which paragraph (c) applies), then either—
  (i) the undertaking must have been performed or otherwise discharged, or
  (ii) there must be a contract between the company and some person pursuant to which the undertaking is to be performed within five years from the time the special resolution is passed.

(2) For the purpose of determining whether the requirements in subsection (1)(b), (c) and (d) are met, the following may be disregarded—
(a) shares allotted—
  (i) before 22nd June 1982 in the case of a company then registered in Great Britain, or
  (ii) before 31st December 1984 in the case of a company then registered in Northern Ireland;
(b) shares allotted in pursuance of an employees' share scheme by reason of which the company would, but for this subsection, be precluded under subsection (1)(b) (but not otherwise) from being re-registered as a public company.

(3) No more than one-tenth of the nominal value of the company's allotted share capital is to be disregarded under subsection (2)(a).

For this purpose the allotted share capital is treated as not including shares disregarded under subsection (2)(b).

(4) Shares disregarded under subsection (2) are treated as not forming part of the allotted share capital for the purposes of subsection (1)(a).

(5) A company must not be re-registered as a public company if it appears to the registrar that—
(a) the company has resolved to reduce its share capital,
(b) the reduction—
  (i) is made under section 626 (reduction in connection with redenomination of share capital),
  (ii) is supported by a solvency statement in accordance with section 643, or
  (iii) has been confirmed by an order of the court under section 648, and
(c) the effect of the reduction is, or will be, that the nominal value of the company's allotted share capital is below the authorised minimum.

[1.93]
92 Requirements as to net assets

(1) A company applying to re-register as a public company must obtain—
(a) a balance sheet prepared as at a date not more than seven months before the date on which the application is delivered to the registrar,
(b) an unqualified report by the company's auditor on that balance sheet, and
(c) a written statement by the company's auditor that in his opinion at the balance sheet date the amount of the company's net assets was not less than the aggregate of its called-up share capital and undistributable reserves.

(2) Between the balance sheet date and the date on which the application for re-registration is delivered to the registrar, there must be no change in the company's financial position that results in the amount of its net assets becoming less than the aggregate of its called-up share capital and undistributable reserves.

(3) In subsection (1)(b) an "unqualified report" means—
(a) if the balance sheet was prepared for a financial year of the company, a report stating without material qualification the auditor's opinion that the balance sheet has been properly prepared in accordance with the requirements of this Act;
(b) if the balance sheet was not prepared for a financial year of the company, a report stating without material qualification the auditor's opinion that the balance sheet has been properly prepared in accordance with the provisions of this Act which would have applied if it had been prepared for a financial year of the company.

(4) For the purposes of an auditor's report on a balance sheet that was not prepared for a financial year of the company, the provisions of this Act apply with such modifications as are necessary by reason of that fact.

(5) For the purposes of subsection (3) a qualification is material unless the auditor states in his report that the matter giving rise to the qualification is not material for the purpose of determining (by reference to the company's balance sheet) whether at the balance sheet date the amount of the company's net assets was not less than the aggregate of its called-up share capital and undistributable reserves.

(6) In this Part "net assets" and "undistributable reserves" have the same meaning as in section 831 (net asset restriction on distributions by public companies).

[1.94]

93 Recent allotment of shares for non-cash consideration

(1) This section applies where—

(a) shares are allotted by the company in the period between the date as at which the balance sheet required by section 92 is prepared and the passing of the resolution that the company should re-register as a public company, and

(b) the shares are allotted as fully or partly paid up as to their nominal value or any premium on them otherwise than in cash.

(2) The registrar shall not entertain an application by the company for re-registration as a public company unless—

(a) the requirements of section 593(1)(a) and (b) have been complied with (independent valuation of non-cash consideration; valuer's report to company not more than six months before allotment), or

(b) the allotment is in connection with—

(i) a share exchange (see subsections (3) to (5) below), or

(ii) a proposed merger with another company (see subsection (6) below).

(3) An allotment is in connection with a share exchange if—

(a) the shares are allotted in connection with an arrangement under which the whole or part of the consideration for the shares allotted is provided by—

(i) the transfer to the company allotting the shares of shares (or shares of a particular class) in another company, or

(ii) the cancellation of shares (or shares of a particular class) in another company; and

(b) the allotment is open to all the holders of the shares of the other company in question (or, where the arrangement applies only to shares of a particular class, to all the holders of the company's shares of that class) to take part in the arrangement in connection with which the shares are allotted.

(4) In determining whether a person is a holder of shares for the purposes of subsection (3), there shall be disregarded—

(a) shares held by, or by a nominee of, the company allotting the shares;

(b) shares held by, or by a nominee of—

(i) the holding company of the company allotting the shares,

(ii) a subsidiary of the company allotting the shares, or

(iii) a subsidiary of the holding company of the company allotting the shares.

(5) It is immaterial, for the purposes of deciding whether an allotment is in connection with a share exchange, whether or not the arrangement in connection with which the shares are allotted involves the issue to the company allotting the shares of shares (or shares of a particular class) in the other company.

(6) There is a proposed merger with another company if one of the companies concerned proposes to acquire all the assets and liabilities of the other in exchange for the issue of its shares or other securities to shareholders of the other (whether or not accompanied by a cash payment).

"Another company" includes any body corporate.

(7) For the purposes of this section—

(a) the consideration for an allotment does not include any amount standing to the credit of any of the company's reserve accounts, or of its profit and loss account, that has been applied in paying up (to any extent) any of the shares allotted or any premium on those shares; and

(b) "arrangement" means any agreement, scheme or arrangement, (including an arrangement sanctioned in accordance with—

(i) Part 26 [or 26A] of this Act (arrangements and reconstructions), or

(ii) section 110 of the Insolvency Act 1986 (c 45) or Article 96 of the Insolvency (Northern Ireland) Order 1989 (SI 1989/2405 (NI 19)) (liquidator in winding up accepting shares as consideration for sale of company's property)).

NOTES

Sub-s (7): words in square brackets inserted by the Corporate Insolvency and Governance Act 2020, s 7, Sch 9, Pt 2, paras 30, 32, as from 26 June 2020.

[1.95]

94 Application and accompanying documents

(1) An application for re-registration as a public company must contain—

(a) a statement of the company's proposed name on re-registration; and

(b) in the case of a company without a secretary, a statement of the company's proposed secretary (see section 95).

(2) The application must be accompanied by—

(a) a copy of the special resolution that the company should re-register as a public company (unless a copy has already been forwarded to the registrar under Chapter 3 of Part 3);

(b) a copy of the company's articles as proposed to be amended;

(c) a copy of the balance sheet and other documents referred to in section 92(1); . . .

(d) if section 93 applies (recent allotment of shares for non-cash consideration), a copy of the valuation report (if any) under subsection (2)(a) of that section[; and

(e) a statement of the aggregate amount paid up on the shares of the company on account of their nominal value].

(3) The statement of compliance required to be delivered together with the application is a statement that the requirements of this Part as to re-registration as a public company have been complied with.
(4) The registrar may accept the statement of compliance as sufficient evidence that the company is entitled to be re-registered as a public company.

NOTES

Sub-s (3): word omitted from para (c) repealed, and para (e) (and the preceding word) inserted, by the Small Business, Enterprise and Employment Act 2015, s 98(1), (2), as from 30 June 2016.

[1.96]
95 Statement of proposed secretary

(1) The statement of the company's proposed secretary must contain the required particulars of the person who is or the persons who are to be the secretary or joint secretaries of the company.
(2) The required particulars are the particulars that will be required to be stated in the company's register of secretaries (see sections 277 to 279).
(3) [The statement must also include a statement by the company that the person named as secretary, or each of the persons named as joint secretaries, has consented to act in the relevant capacity]. If all the partners in a firm are to be joint secretaries, consent may be given by one partner on behalf of all of them.

NOTES

Sub-s (3): words in square brackets substituted by the Small Business, Enterprise and Employment Act 2015, s 100(1), (3), as from 10 October 2015 (for transitional provisions see the note to s 12 at **[1.12]**).

[1.97]
96 Issue of certificate of incorporation on re-registration

(1) If on an application for re-registration as a public company the registrar is satisfied that the company is entitled to be so re-registered, the company shall be re-registered accordingly.
(2) The registrar must issue a certificate of incorporation altered to meet the circumstances of the case.
(3) The certificate must state that it is issued on re-registration and the date on which it is issued.
(4) On the issue of the certificate—
- (a) the company by virtue of the issue of the certificate becomes a public company,
- (b) the changes in the company's name and articles take effect, and
- (c) where the application contained a statement under section 95 (statement of proposed secretary), the person or persons named in the statement as secretary or joint secretary of the company are deemed to have been appointed to that office.

(5) The certificate is conclusive evidence that the requirements of this Act as to re-registration have been complied with.

Public company becoming private

[1.98]
97 Re-registration of public company as private limited company

(1) A public company may be re-registered as a private limited company if—
- (a) a special resolution that it should be so re-registered is passed,
- (b) the conditions specified below are met, and
- (c) an application for re-registration is delivered to the registrar in accordance with section 100, together with—
  - (i) the other documents required by that section, and
  - (ii) a statement of compliance.

(2) The conditions are that—
- (a) where no application under section 98 for cancellation of the resolution has been made—
  - (i) having regard to the number of members who consented to or voted in favour of the resolution, no such application may be made, or
  - (ii) the period within which such an application could be made has expired, or
- (b) where such an application has been made—
  - (i) the application has been withdrawn, or
  - (ii) an order has been made confirming the resolution and a copy of that order has been delivered to the registrar.

(3) The company must make such changes—
- (a) in its name, and
- (b) in its articles,

as are necessary in connection with its becoming a private company limited by shares or, as the case may be, by guarantee.

[1.99]
98 Application to court to cancel resolution

(1) Where a special resolution by a public company to be re-registered as a private limited company has been passed, an application to the court for the cancellation of the resolution may be made—
- (a) by the holders of not less in the aggregate than 5% in nominal value of the company's issued share capital or any class of the company's issued share capital (disregarding any shares held by the company as treasury shares);
- (b) if the company is not limited by shares, by not less than 5% of its members; or
- (c) by not less than 50 of the company's members;

but not by a person who has consented to or voted in favour of the resolution.
(2) The application must be made within 28 days after the passing of the resolution and may be made on behalf of the persons entitled to make it by such one or more of their number as they may appoint for the purpose.
(3) On the hearing of the application the court shall make an order either cancelling or confirming the resolution.

(4) The court may—

(a) make that order on such terms and conditions as it thinks fit,

(b) if it thinks fit adjourn the proceedings in order that an arrangement may be made to the satisfaction of the court for the purchase of the interests of dissentient members, and

(c) give such directions, and make such orders, as it thinks expedient for facilitating or carrying into effect any such arrangement.

(5) The court's order may, if the court thinks fit—

(a) provide for the purchase by the company of the shares of any of its members and for the reduction accordingly of the company's capital; and

(b) make such alteration in the company's articles as may be required in consequence of that provision.

(6) The court's order may, if the court thinks fit, require the company not to make any, or any specified, amendments to its articles without the leave of the court.

[(7) In this section and section 99(3) "the court", in England and Wales, means the High Court.]

NOTES

Sub-s (7): added by the High Court and County Courts Jurisdiction Order 1991, SI 1991/724, art 6F, Schedule, Pt I (as amended by SI 2014/821), as from 22 April 2014 (except in relation to proceedings commenced before that date).

[1.100]

99 Notice to registrar of court application or order

(1) On making an application under section 98 (application to court to cancel resolution) the applicants, or the person making the application on their behalf, must immediately give notice to the registrar.

This is without prejudice to any provision of rules of court as to service of notice of the application.

(2) On being served with notice of any such application, the company must immediately give notice to the registrar.

(3) Within 15 days of the making of the court's order on the application, or such longer period as the court may at any time direct, the company must deliver to the registrar a copy of the order.

(4) If a company fails to comply with subsection (2) or (3) an offence is committed by—

(a) the company, and

(b) every officer of the company who is in default.

(5) A person guilty of an offence under this section is liable on summary conviction to a fine not exceeding level 3 on the standard scale and, for continued contravention, a daily default fine not exceeding one-tenth of level 3 on the standard scale.

[1.101]

100 Application and accompanying documents

(1) An application for re-registration as a private limited company must contain a statement of the company's proposed name on re-registration.

(2) The application must be accompanied by—

(a) a copy of the resolution that the company should re-register as a private limited company (unless a copy has already been forwarded to the registrar under Chapter 3 of Part 3); and

(b) a copy of the company's articles as proposed to be amended.

(3) The statement of compliance required to be delivered together with the application is a statement that the requirements of this Part as to re-registration as a private limited company have been complied with.

(4) The registrar may accept the statement of compliance as sufficient evidence that the company is entitled to be re-registered as a private limited company.

[1.102]

101 Issue of certificate of incorporation on re-registration

(1) If on an application for re-registration as a private limited company the registrar is satisfied that the company is entitled to be so re-registered, the company shall be re-registered accordingly.

(2) The registrar must issue a certificate of incorporation altered to meet the circumstances of the case.

(3) The certificate must state that it is issued on re-registration and the date on which it is issued.

(4) On the issue of the certificate—

(a) the company by virtue of the issue of the certificate becomes a private limited company, and

(b) the changes in the company's name and articles take effect.

(5) The certificate is conclusive evidence that the requirements of this Act as to re-registration have been complied with.

Private limited company becoming unlimited

[1.103]

102 Re-registration of private limited company as unlimited

(1) A private limited company may be re-registered as an unlimited company if—

(a) all the members of the company have assented to its being so re-registered,

(b) the condition specified below is met, and

(c) an application for re-registration is delivered to the registrar in accordance with section 103, together with—

(i) the other documents required by that section, and

(ii) a statement of compliance.

(2) The condition is that the company has not previously been re-registered as limited.

(3) The company must make such changes in its name and its articles—

(a) as are necessary in connection with its becoming an unlimited company; and

(b) if it is to have a share capital, as are necessary in connection with its becoming an unlimited company having a share capital.

(4) For the purposes of this section—

(a) a trustee in bankruptcy of a member of the company is entitled, to the exclusion of the member, to assent to the company's becoming unlimited; and

(b) the personal representative of a deceased member of the company may assent on behalf of the deceased.

(5) In subsection (4)(a), "a trustee in bankruptcy of a member of the company" includes—

[(a) a trustee or interim trustee in the sequestration under the Bankruptcy (Scotland) Act 2016 of the estate of a member of the company;]

(b) a trustee under a protected trustee deed (within the meaning of the Bankruptcy (Scotland) Act [2016]) granted by a member of the company.

NOTES

Sub-s (5): para (a) was substituted, and in para (b) the year "2016" in square brackets was substituted, by the Bankruptcy (Scotland) Act 2016 (Consequential Provisions and Modifications) Order 2016, SI 2016/1034, art 7(1), (3), Sch 1, para 29(1), (2), as from 30 November 2016 (except in relation to (i) a sequestration as regards which the petition is presented, or the debtor application is made before that date; or (ii) a trust deed executed before that date).

[1.104]

103 Application and accompanying documents

(1) An application for re-registration as an unlimited company must contain a statement of the company's proposed name on re-registration.

(2) The application must be accompanied by—

(a) the prescribed form of assent to the company's being registered as an unlimited company, authenticated by or on behalf of all the members of the company;

(b) a copy of the company's articles as proposed to be amended.

(3) The statement of compliance required to be delivered together with the application is a statement that the requirements of this Part as to re-registration as an unlimited company have been complied with.

(4) The statement must contain a statement by the directors of the company—

(a) that the persons by whom or on whose behalf the form of assent is authenticated constitute the whole membership of the company, and

(b) if any of the members have not authenticated that form themselves, that the directors have taken all reasonable steps to satisfy themselves that each person who authenticated it on behalf of a member was lawfully empowered to do so.

(5) The registrar may accept the statement of compliance as sufficient evidence that the company is entitled to be re-registered as an unlimited company.

NOTES

Regulations: the Companies (Registration) Regulations 2008, SI 2008/3014 at **[4.179]**. For a summary of all statutory instruments made under this Act, see Appendix 4 at **[A4]**.

[1.105]

104 Issue of certificate of incorporation on re-registration

(1) If on an application for re-registration of a private limited company as an unlimited company the registrar is satisfied that the company is entitled to be so re-registered, the company shall be re-registered accordingly.

(2) The registrar must issue a certificate of incorporation altered to meet the circumstances of the case.

(3) The certificate must state that it is issued on re-registration and the date on which it is issued.

(4) On the issue of the certificate—

(a) the company by virtue of the issue of the certificate becomes an unlimited company, and

(b) the changes in the company's name and articles take effect.

(5) The certificate is conclusive evidence that the requirements of this Act as to re-registration have been complied with.

Unlimited private company becoming limited

[1.106]

105 Re-registration of unlimited company as limited

(1) An unlimited company may be re-registered as a private limited company if—

(a) a special resolution that it should be so re-registered is passed,

(b) the condition specified below is met, and

(c) an application for re-registration is delivered to the registrar in accordance with section 106, together with—

(i) the other documents required by that section, and

(ii) a statement of compliance.

(2) The condition is that the company has not previously been re-registered as unlimited.

(3) The special resolution must state whether the company is to be limited by shares or by guarantee.

(4) The company must make such changes—

(a) in its name, and

(b) in its articles,

as are necessary in connection with its becoming a company limited by shares or, as the case may be, by guarantee.

[1.107]

106 Application and accompanying documents

(1) An application for re-registration as a limited company must contain a statement of the company's proposed name on re-registration.

(2) The application must be accompanied by—

(a) a copy of the resolution that the company should re-register as a private limited company (unless a copy has already been forwarded to the registrar under Chapter 3 of Part 3);

(b) if the company is to be limited by guarantee, a statement of guarantee;

(c) a copy of the company's articles as proposed to be amended.

(3) The statement of guarantee required to be delivered in the case of a company that is to be limited by guarantee must state that each member undertakes that, if the company is wound up while he is a member, or within one year after he ceases to be a member, he will contribute to the assets of the company such amount as may be required for—

(a) payment of the debts and liabilities of the company contracted before he ceases to be a member,

(b) payment of the costs, charges and expenses of winding up, and

(c) adjustment of the rights of the contributories among themselves,

not exceeding a specified amount.

(4) The statement of compliance required to be delivered together with the application is a statement that the requirements of this Part as to re-registration as a limited company have been complied with.

(5) The registrar may accept the statement of compliance as sufficient evidence that the company is entitled to be re-registered as a limited company.

[1.108]

107 Issue of certificate of incorporation on re-registration

(1) If on an application for re-registration of an unlimited company as a limited company the registrar is satisfied that the company is entitled to be so re-registered, the company shall be re-registered accordingly.

(2) The registrar must issue a certificate of incorporation altered to meet the circumstances of the case.

(3) The certificate must state that it is issued on re-registration and the date on which it is so issued.

(4) On the issue of the certificate—

(a) the company by virtue of the issue of the certificate becomes a limited company, and

(b) the changes in the company's name and articles take effect.

(5) The certificate is conclusive evidence that the requirements of this Act as to re-registration have been complied with.

[1.109]

108 Statement of capital required where company already has share capital

(1) A company which on re-registration under section 107 already has allotted share capital must within 15 days after the re-registration deliver a statement of capital to the registrar.

(2) This does not apply if the information which would be included in the statement has already been sent to the registrar in—

(a) a statement of capital and initial shareholdings (see section 10), or

[(b) (if different) the last statement of capital sent by the company].

(3) The statement of capital must state with respect to the company's share capital on re-registration—

(a) the total number of shares of the company,

(b) the aggregate nominal value of those shares,

[(ba) the aggregate amount (if any) unpaid on those shares (whether on account of their nominal value or by way of premium), and]

(c) for each class of shares—

(i) prescribed particulars of the rights attached to the shares,

(ii) the total number of shares of that class, and

(iii) the aggregate nominal value of shares of that class, . . .

(d) . . .

(4) If default is made in complying with this section, an offence is committed by—

(a) the company, and

(b) every officer of the company who is in default.

(5) A person guilty of an offence under this section is liable on summary conviction to a fine not exceeding level 3 on the standard scale and, for continued contravention, a daily default fine not exceeding one-tenth of level 3 on the standard scale.

NOTES

Sub-s (2): para (b) substituted by the Small Business, Enterprise and Employment Act 2015, s 93(1), (4), as from 30 June 2016.

Sub-s (3): para (ba) inserted, and para (d) and the preceding word repealed, by the Small Business, Enterprise and Employment Act 2015, s 97, Sch 6, paras 1, 4, as from 30 June 2016.

Orders: the Companies (Shares and Share Capital) Order 2009, SI 2009/388 at **[4.211]**. For a summary of all statutory instruments made under this Act, see Appendix 4 at **[A4]**.

Public company becoming private and unlimited

[1.110]

109 Re-registration of public company as private and unlimited

(1) A public company limited by shares may be re-registered as an unlimited private company with a share capital if—

(a) all the members of the company have assented to its being so re-registered,

(b) the condition specified below is met, and

(c) an application for re-registration is delivered to the registrar in accordance with section 110, together with—

(i) the other documents required by that section, and

(ii) a statement of compliance.

(2) The condition is that the company has not previously been re-registered—

(a) as limited, or

(b) as unlimited.

(3) The company must make such changes—

(a) in its name, and

(b) in its articles,

as are necessary in connection with its becoming an unlimited private company.

(4) For the purposes of this section—

(a) a trustee in bankruptcy of a member of the company is entitled, to the exclusion of the member, to assent to the company's re-registration; and

(b) the personal representative of a deceased member of the company may assent on behalf of the deceased.

(5) In subsection (4)(a), "a trustee in bankruptcy of a member of the company" includes—

[(a) a trustee or interim trustee in the sequestration under the Bankruptcy (Scotland) Act 2016 of the estate of a member of the company;]

(b) a trustee under a protected trustee deed (within the meaning of the Bankruptcy (Scotland) Act [2016]) granted by a member of the company.

NOTES

Sub-s (5): para (a) was substituted, and in para (b) the year "2016" in square brackets was substituted, by the Bankruptcy (Scotland) Act 2016 (Consequential Provisions and Modifications) Order 2016, SI 2016/1034, art 7(1), (3), Sch 1, para 29(1), (3), as from 30 November 2016 (except in relation to (i) a sequestration as regards which the petition is presented, or the debtor application is made before that date; or (ii) a trust deed executed before that date).

[1.111]

110 Application and accompanying documents

(1) An application for re-registration of a public company as an unlimited private company must contain a statement of the company's proposed name on re-registration.

(2) The application must be accompanied by—

(a) the prescribed form of assent to the company's being registered as an unlimited company, authenticated by or on behalf of all the members of the company, and

(b) a copy of the company's articles as proposed to be amended.

(3) The statement of compliance required to be delivered together with the application is a statement that the requirements of this Part as to re-registration as an unlimited private company have been complied with.

(4) The statement must contain a statement by the directors of the company—

(a) that the persons by whom or on whose behalf the form of assent is authenticated constitute the whole membership of the company, and

(b) if any of the members have not authenticated that form themselves, that the directors have taken all reasonable steps to satisfy themselves that each person who authenticated it on behalf of a member was lawfully empowered to do so.

(5) The registrar may accept the statement of compliance as sufficient evidence that the company is entitled to be re-registered as an unlimited private company.

NOTES

Regulations: the Companies (Registration) Regulations 2008, SI 2008/3014 at **[4.179]**. For a summary of all statutory instruments made under this Act, see Appendix 4 at **[A4]**.

[1.112]

111 Issue of certificate of incorporation on re-registration

(1) If on an application for re-registration of a public company as an unlimited private company the registrar is satisfied that the company is entitled to be so re-registered, the company shall be re-registered accordingly.

(2) The registrar must issue a certificate of incorporation altered to meet the circumstances of the case.

(3) The certificate must state that it is issued on re-registration and the date on which it is so issued.

(4) On the issue of the certificate—

(a) the company by virtue of the issue of the certificate becomes an unlimited private company, and

(b) the changes in the company's name and articles take effect.

(5) The certificate is conclusive evidence that the requirements of this Act as to re-registration have been complied with.

PART 8 A COMPANY'S MEMBERS

CHAPTER 1 THE MEMBERS OF A COMPANY

[1.113]

112 The members of a company

(1) The subscribers of a company's memorandum are deemed to have agreed to become members of the company, and on its registration become members and must be entered as such in its register of members.

(2) Every other person who agrees to become a member of a company, and whose name is entered in its register of members, is a member of the company.

[(3) Where an election under section 128B is in force in respect of a company—

(a) the requirement in subsection (1) to enter particulars of members in the company's register of members does not apply, and

(b) subsection (2) has effect as if the reference to a person whose name is entered in the company's register of members were a reference to a person with respect to whom the following steps have been taken—

(i) the person's name has been delivered to the registrar under section 128E, and

(ii) the document containing that information has been registered by the registrar.]

NOTES

Sub-s (3): added by the Small Business, Enterprise and Employment Act 2015, s 94, Sch 5, Pt 2, paras 11, 13, as from 30 June 2016.

CHAPTER 2 REGISTER OF MEMBERS

General

[1.114]

[112A Alternative method of record-keeping

This Chapter must be read with Chapter 2A (which allows for an alternative method of record-keeping in the case of private companies).]

NOTES

Inserted by the Small Business, Enterprise and Employment Act 2015, s 94, Sch 5, Pt 1, paras 1, 2, as from 30 June 2016.

[1.115]

113 Register of members

(1) Every company must keep a register of its members.

(2) There must be entered in the register—

(a) the names and addresses of the members,

(b) the date on which each person was registered as a member, and

(c) the date at which any person ceased to be a member.

(3) In the case of a company having a share capital, there must be entered in the register, with the names and addresses of the members, a statement of—

(a) the shares held by each member, distinguishing each share—

(i) by its number (so long as the share has a number), and

(ii) where the company has more than one class of issued shares, by its class, and

(b) the amount paid or agreed to be considered as paid on the shares of each member.

(4) If the company has converted any of its shares into stock, and given notice of the conversion to the registrar, the register of members must show the amount and class of stock held by each member instead of the amount of shares and the particulars relating to shares specified above.

(5) In the case of joint holders of shares or stock in a company, the company's register of members must state the names of each joint holder.

In other respects joint holders are regarded for the purposes of this Chapter as a single member (so that the register must show a single address).

(6) In the case of a company that does not have a share capital but has more than one class of members, there must be entered in the register, with the names and addresses of the members, a statement of the class to which each member belongs.

(7) If a company makes default in complying with this section an offence is committed by—

(a) the company, and

(b) every officer of the company who is in default.

(8) A person guilty of an offence under this section is liable on summary conviction to a fine not exceeding level 3 on the standard scale and, for continued contravention, a daily default fine not exceeding one-tenth of level 3 on the standard scale.

[1.116]

114 Register to be kept available for inspection

(1) A company's register of members must be kept available for inspection—

(a) at its registered office, or

(b) at a place specified in regulations under section 1136.

(2) A company must give notice to the registrar of the place where its register of members is kept available for inspection and of any change in that place.

(3) No such notice is required if the register has, at all times since it came into existence (or, in the case of a register in existence on the relevant date, at all times since then) been kept available for inspection at the company's registered office.

(4) The relevant date for the purposes of subsection (3) is—

(a) 1st July 1948 in the case of a company registered in Great Britain, and

(b) 1st April 1961 in the case of a company registered in Northern Ireland.

(5) If a company makes default for 14 days in complying with subsection (2), an offence is committed by—

(a) the company, and

(b) every officer of the company who is in default.

(6) A person guilty of an offence under this section is liable on summary conviction to a fine not exceeding level 3 on the standard scale and, for continued contravention, a daily default fine not exceeding one-tenth of level 3 on the standard scale.

NOTES

Temporary modification: this section was modified by the Companies etc (Filing Requirements) (Temporary Modifications) Regulations 2020, SI 2020/645, reg 6. By virtue of the Corporate Insolvency and Governance Act 2020, s 39(8), the modification applied from 27 June 2020 to the end of the day on 5 April 2021 (subject to the saving provision in s 39(9) which provides that the expiry of s 39 on 5 April 2021 does not affect the continued operation of any Regulations made under that section for the purpose of determining the length of any period that began before the expiry). As modified, sub-s (5) above had effect as if for the reference to "14 days" there were substituted a reference to "42 days".

[1.117]

115 Index of members

(1) Every company having more than 50 members must keep an index of the names of the members of the company, unless the register of members is in such a form as to constitute in itself an index.

(2) The company must make any necessary alteration in the index within 14 days after the date on which any alteration is made in the register of members.

(3) The index must contain, in respect of each member, a sufficient indication to enable the account of that member in the register to be readily found.

(4) The index must be at all times kept available for inspection at the same place as the register of members.

(5) If default is made in complying with this section, an offence is committed by—

(a) the company, and

(b) every officer of the company who is in default.

(6) A person guilty of an offence under this section is liable on summary conviction to a fine not exceeding level 3 on the standard scale and, for continued contravention, a daily default fine not exceeding one-tenth of level 3 on the standard scale.

[1.118]

116 Rights to inspect and require copies

(1) The register and the index of members' names must be open to the inspection—

(a) of any member of the company without charge, and

(b) of any other person on payment of such fee as may be prescribed.

(2) Any person may require a copy of a company's register of members, or of any part of it, on payment of such fee as may be prescribed.

(3) A person seeking to exercise either of the rights conferred by this section must make a request to the company to that effect.

(4) The request must contain the following information—

(a) in the case of an individual, his name and address;

(b) in the case of an organisation, the name and address of an individual responsible for making the request on behalf of the organisation;

(c) the purpose for which the information is to be used; and

(d) whether the information will be disclosed to any other person, and if so—

(i) where that person is an individual, his name and address,

(ii) where that person is an organisation, the name and address of an individual responsible for receiving the information on its behalf, and

(iii) the purpose for which the information is to be used by that person.

NOTES

Regulations: the Companies (Fees for Inspection and Copying of Company Records) Regulations 2007, SI 2007/2612 at **[4.11]**. For a summary of all statutory instruments made under this Act, see Appendix 4 at **[A4]**.

[1.119]

117 Register of members: response to request for inspection or copy

(1) Where a company receives a request under section 116 (register of members: right to inspect and require copy), it must within five working days either—

(a) comply with the request, or

(b) apply to the court.

(2) If it applies to the court it must notify the person making the request.

(3) If on an application under this section the court is satisfied that the inspection or copy is not sought for a proper purpose—

(a) it shall direct the company not to comply with the request, and

(b) it may further order that the company's costs (in Scotland, expenses) on the application be paid in whole or in part by the person who made the request, even if he is not a party to the application.

(4) If the court makes such a direction and it appears to the court that the company is or may be subject to other requests made for a similar purpose (whether made by the same person or different persons), it may direct that the company is not to comply with any such request.

The order must contain such provision as appears to the court appropriate to identify the requests to which it applies.

(5) If on an application under this section the court does not direct the company not to comply with the request, the company must comply with the request immediately upon the court giving its decision or, as the case may be, the proceedings being discontinued.

[1.120]

118 Register of members: refusal of inspection or default in providing copy

(1) If an inspection required under section 116 (register of members: right to inspect and require copy) is refused or default is made in providing a copy required under that section, otherwise than in accordance with an order of the court, an offence is committed by—

(a) the company, and

(b) every officer of the company who is in default.

(2) A person guilty of an offence under this section is liable on summary conviction to a fine not exceeding level 3 on the standard scale and, for continued contravention, a daily default fine not exceeding one-tenth of level 3 on the standard scale.

(3) In the case of any such refusal or default the court may by order compel an immediate inspection or, as the case may be, direct that the copy required be sent to the person requesting it.

[1.121]

119 Register of members: offences in connection with request for or disclosure of information

(1) It is an offence for a person knowingly or recklessly to make in a request under section 116 (register of members: right to inspect or require copy) a statement that is misleading, false or deceptive in a material particular.

(2) It is an offence for a person in possession of information obtained by exercise of either of the rights conferred by that section—

(a) to do anything that results in the information being disclosed to another person, or

(b) to fail to do anything with the result that the information is disclosed to another person, knowing, or having reason to suspect, that person may use the information for a purpose that is not a proper purpose.

(3) A person guilty of an offence under this section is liable—

(a) on conviction on indictment, to imprisonment for a term not exceeding two years or a fine (or both);

(b) on summary conviction—

(i) in England and Wales, to imprisonment for a term not exceeding twelve months or to a fine not exceeding the statutory maximum (or both);

(ii) in Scotland or Northern Ireland, to imprisonment for a term not exceeding six months, or to a fine not exceeding the statutory maximum (or both).

NOTES

Offences under this section: see further s 1131 at **[1.1301]**.

[1.122]

120 Information as to state of register and index

(1) When a person inspects the register, or the company provides him with a copy of the register or any part of it, the company must inform him of the most recent date (if any) on which alterations were made to the register and [whether there are] further alterations to be made.

(2) When a person inspects the index of members' names, the company must inform him whether there is any alteration to the register that is not reflected in the index.

(3) If a company fails to provide the information required under subsection (1) or (2), an offence is committed by—

(a) the company, and

(b) every officer of the company who is in default.

(4) A person guilty of an offence under this section is liable on summary conviction to a fine not exceeding level 3 on the standard scale.

NOTES

Sub-s (1): words in square brackets substituted by the Small Business, Enterprise and Employment Act 2015, s 81, Sch 3, Pt 2, paras 3, 6, as from 6 April 2016.

[1.123]

121 Removal of entries relating to former members

An entry relating to a former member of the company may be removed from the register after the expiration of ten years from the date on which he ceased to be a member.

Special cases

[1.124]

122 Share warrants

[(1) Until a share warrant issued by a company is surrendered the following are deemed to be the particulars required to be entered in the register of members in respect of the warrant—

(a) the fact of the issue of the warrant,

(b) a statement of the shares included in the warrant, distinguishing each share by its number so long as the share has a number, and

(c) the date of the issue of the warrant.]

(3) The bearer of a share warrant may, if the articles of the company so provide, be deemed a member of the company within the meaning of this Act, either to the full extent or for any purposes defined in the articles.

(4) . . .

(5) The company is responsible for any loss incurred by any person by reason of the company entering in the register the name of a bearer of a share warrant in respect of the shares specified in it without the warrant being surrendered and cancelled.

(6) On the surrender of a share warrant, the date of the surrender must be entered in the register.

NOTES

Sub-s (1): substituted (for the original sub-ss (1), (2)) by the Small Business, Enterprise and Employment Act 2015, s 84, Sch 4, Pt 2, paras 22, 23(a), as from 26 May 2015.

Sub-s (4): repealed by the Small Business, Enterprise and Employment Act 2015, s 84, Sch 4, Pt 2, paras 22, 23(b), as from 26 May 2015.

[1.125]

123 Single member companies

(1) If a limited company is formed under this Act with only one member there shall be entered in the company's register of members, with the name and address of the sole member, a statement that the company has only one member.

(2) If the number of members of a limited company falls to one, or if an unlimited company with only one member becomes a limited company on re-registration, there shall upon the occurrence of that event be entered in the company's register of members, with the name and address of the sole member—

(a) a statement that the company has only one member, and

(b) the date on which the company became a company having only one member.

(3) If the membership of a limited company increases from one to two or more members, there shall upon the occurrence of that event be entered in the company's register of members, with the name and address of the person who was formerly the sole member—

(a) a statement that the company has ceased to have only one member, and

(b) the date on which that event occurred.

(4) If a company makes default in complying with this section, an offence is committed by—

(a) the company, and

(b) every officer of the company who is in default.

(5) A person guilty of an offence under this section is liable on summary conviction to a fine not exceeding level 3 on the standard scale and, for continued contravention, a daily default fine not exceeding one-tenth of level 3 on the standard scale.

[1.126]

124 Company holding its own shares as treasury shares

(1) Where a company purchases its own shares in circumstances in which section 724 (treasury shares) applies—

(a) the requirements of section 113 (register of members) need not be complied with if the company cancels all of the shares forthwith after the purchase, and

(b) if the company does not cancel all of the shares forthwith after the purchase, any share that is so cancelled shall be disregarded for the purposes of that section.

(2) Subject to subsection (1), where a company holds shares as treasury shares the company must be entered in the register as the member holding those shares.

Supplementary

[1.127]

125 Power of court to rectify register

(1) If—

(a) the name of any person is, without sufficient cause, entered in or omitted from a company's register of members, or

(b) default is made or unnecessary delay takes place in entering on the register the fact of any person having ceased to be a member,

the person aggrieved, or any member of the company, or the company, may apply to the court for rectification of the register.

(2) The court may either refuse the application or may order rectification of the register and payment by the company of any damages sustained by any party aggrieved.

(3) On such an application the court may decide any question relating to the title of a person who is a party to the application to have his name entered in or omitted from the register, whether the question arises between members or alleged members, or between members or alleged members on the one hand and the company on the other hand, and generally may decide any question necessary or expedient to be decided for rectification of the register.

(4) In the case of a company required by this Act to send a list of its members to the registrar of companies, the court, when making an order for rectification of the register, shall by its order direct notice of the rectification to be given to the registrar.

[1.128]

126 Trusts not to be entered on register

No notice of any trust, expressed, implied or constructive, shall be entered on the register of members of a company registered in England and Wales or Northern Ireland, or be receivable by the registrar.

[1.129]

127 Register to be evidence

The register of members is prima facie evidence of any matters which are by this Act directed or authorised to be inserted in it[, except for any matters of which the central register is prima facie evidence by virtue of section 128H].

NOTES

Words in square brackets inserted by the Small Business, Enterprise and Employment Act 2015, s 94, Sch 5, Pt 2, paras 11, 14, as from 30 June 2016.

[1.130]

128 Time limit for claims arising from entry in register

(1) Liability incurred by a company—

(a) from the making or deletion of an entry in the register of members, or

(b) from a failure to make or delete any such entry,

is not enforceable more than ten years after the date on which the entry was made or deleted or, as the case may be, the failure first occurred.

(2) This is without prejudice to any lesser period of limitation (and, in Scotland, to any rule that the obligation giving rise to the liability prescribes before the expiry of that period).

[CHAPTER 2A OPTION TO KEEP INFORMATION ON CENTRAL REGISTER

[1.131]

128A Introduction

(1) This Chapter sets out rules allowing private companies to keep information on the register kept by the registrar instead of entering it in their register of members.

(2) The register kept by the registrar (see section 1080) is referred to in this Chapter as "the central register".]

NOTES

Chapter 2A (ss 128A–128K) inserted by the Small Business, Enterprise and Employment Act 2015, s 94, Sch 5, Pt 1, paras 1, 3, as from 30 June 2016.

[1.132]

[128B Right to make an election

(1) An election may be made under this section—

(a) by the subscribers wishing to form a private company under this Act, or

(b) by the private company itself once it is formed and registered.

(2) In the latter case, the election is of no effect unless, before it is made—

(a) all the members of the company have assented to the making of the election, and

(b) any overseas branch registers that the company was keeping under Chapter 3 have been discontinued and all the entries in those registers transferred to the company's register of members in accordance with section 135.

(3) An election under this section is made by giving notice of election to the registrar.

(4) If the notice is given by subscribers wishing to form a private company—

(a) it must be given when the documents required to be delivered under section 9 are delivered to the registrar, and

(b) it must be accompanied by a statement containing all the information that—

(i) would be required (in the absence of the notice) to be entered in the company's register of members on incorporation of the company, and

(ii) is not otherwise included in the documents delivered under section 9.

(5) If the notice is given by the company, it must be accompanied by—

(a) a statement by the company—

(i) that all the members of the company have assented to the making of the election, and

(ii) if the company was keeping any overseas branch registers, that all such registers have been discontinued and all the entries in them transferred to the company's register of members in accordance with section 135, and

(b) a statement containing all the information that is required to be contained in the company's register of members as at the date of the notice in respect of matters that are current as at that date.

(6) The company must where necessary update the statement sent under subsection (5)(b) to ensure that the final version delivered to the registrar contains all the information that is required to be contained in the company's register of members as at the time immediately before the election takes effect (see section 128C) in respect of matters that are current as at that time.

(7) The obligation in subsection (6) to update the statement includes an obligation to rectify it (where necessary) in consequence of the company's register of members being rectified (whether before or after the election takes effect).

(8) If default is made in complying with subsection (6), an offence is committed by—

(a) the company, and

(b) every officer of the company who is in default.

For this purpose a shadow director is treated as an officer of the company.

(9) A person guilty of an offence under this section is liable on summary conviction to a fine not exceeding level 3 on the standard scale and, for continued contravention, a daily default fine not exceeding one-tenth of level 3 on the standard scale.

(10) A reference in this Chapter to matters that are current as at a given date or time is a reference to—

(a) persons who are members of the company as at that date or time, and

(b) any other matters that are current as at that date or time.]

NOTES

Inserted as noted to s 128A at **[1.131]**.

[1.133]

[128C Effective date of election

(1) An election made under section 128B takes effect when the notice of election is registered by the registrar.

(2) The election remains in force until either—

(a) the company ceases to be a private company, or

(b) a notice of withdrawal sent by the company under section 128J is registered by the registrar,

whichever occurs first.]

NOTES

Inserted as noted to s 128A at **[1.131]**.

[1.134]

[128D Effect of election on obligations under Chapter 2

(1) The effect of an election under section 128B on a company's obligations under Chapter 2 is as follows.

(2) The company's obligation to maintain a register of members does not apply with respect to the period when the election is in force.

(3) This means that, during that period—

(a) the company must continue to keep a register of members in accordance with Chapter 2 (a "historic" register) containing all the information that was required to be stated in that register as at the time immediately before the election took effect, but

(b) the company does not have to update that register to reflect any changes that occur after that time.

(4) Subsections (2) and (3) apply to the index of members (if the company is obliged to keep an index of members) as they apply to the register of members.

(5) The provisions of Chapter 2 (including the rights to inspect or require copies of the register and to inspect the index) continue to apply to the historic register and, if applicable, the historic index during the period when the election is in force.

(6) The company must place a note in its historic register—

(a) stating that an election under section 128B is in force,

(b) recording when that election took effect, and

(c) indicating that up-to-date information about its members is available for public inspection on the central register.

(7) Subsections (7) and (8) of section 113 apply if a company makes default in complying with subsection (6) as they apply if a company makes default in complying with that section.

(8) The obligations under this section with respect to a historic register and historic index do not apply in a case where the election was made by subscribers wishing to form a private company.]

NOTES

Inserted as noted to s 128A at **[1.131]**.

[1.135]

[128E Duty to notify registrar of changes

(1) The duty under subsection (2) applies during the period when an election under section 128B is in force.

(2) The company must deliver to the registrar any relevant information that the company would during that period have been obliged under this Act to enter in its register of members, had the election not been in force.

(3) "Relevant information" means information other than—

- (a) the date mentioned in section 113(2)(b) (date when person registered as member),
- (b) the date mentioned in section 123(3)(b) (date when membership of limited company increases from one to two or more members), and
- (c) the dates mentioned in the following provisions, but only in cases where the date to be recorded in the central register is to be the date on which the document containing information of the relevant change is registered by the registrar—
  - (i) section 113(2)(c) (date when person ceases to be member),
  - (ii) section 123(2)(b) (date when company becomes single member company).

(4) The relevant information must be delivered as soon as reasonably practicable after the company becomes aware of it and, in any event, no later than the time by which the company would have been required to enter the information in its register of members.

(5) In a case of the kind described in subsection (3)(c), the company must, when it delivers information under subsection (2) of the relevant change, indicate to the registrar that, in accordance with section 1081(1A), the date to be recorded in the central register is to be the date on which the document containing that information is registered by the registrar.

(6) If default is made in complying with this section, an offence is committed by—

- (a) the company, and
- (b) every officer of the company who is in default.

For this purpose a shadow director is treated as an officer of the company.

(7) A person guilty of an offence under this section is liable on summary conviction to a fine not exceeding level 3 on the standard scale and, for continued contravention, a daily default fine not exceeding one-tenth of level 3 on the standard scale.]

NOTES

Inserted as noted to s 128A at **[1.131]**.

[1.136]

[128F Information as to state of central register

(1) When a person inspects or requests a copy of material on the central register relating to a company in respect of which an election under section 128B is in force, the person may ask the company to confirm that all information that the company is required to deliver to the registrar under this Chapter has been delivered.

(2) If a company fails to respond to a request under subsection (1), an offence is committed by—

- (a) the company, and
- (b) every officer of the company who is in default.

(3) A person guilty of an offence under this section is liable on summary conviction to a fine not exceeding level 3 on the standard scale.]

NOTES

Inserted as noted to s 128A at **[1.131]**.

[1.137]

[128G Power of court to order company to remedy default or delay

(1) This section applies if—

- (a) the name of a person is without sufficient cause included in, or omitted from, information that a company delivers to the registrar under this Chapter concerning its members, or
- (b) default is made or unnecessary delay takes place in informing the registrar under this Chapter of—
  - (i) the name of a person who is to be a member of the company, or
  - (ii) the fact that a person has ceased or is to cease to be a member of the company.

(2) The person aggrieved, or any member of the company, or the company, may apply to the court for an order—

- (a) requiring the company to deliver to the registrar the information (or statements) necessary to rectify the position, and
- (b) where applicable, requiring the registrar to record under section 1081(1A) the date determined by the court.

(3) The court may either refuse the application or may make the order and order the company to pay any damages sustained by any party aggrieved.

(4) On such an application the court may decide—

- (a) any question relating to the title of a person who is a party to the application to have the person's name included in or omitted from information delivered to the registrar under this Chapter about the company's members, whether the question arises between members or alleged members, or between members or alleged members on the one hand and the company on the other hand, and
- (b) any question necessary or expedient to be decided for rectifying the position.

(5) Nothing in this section affects a person's rights under section 1095 or 1096 (rectification of register on application to registrar or under court order).]

NOTES

Inserted as noted to s 128A at **[1.131]**.

[1.138]

[128H Central register to be evidence

(1) The central register is prima facie evidence of any matters about which a company is required to deliver information to the registrar under this Chapter.

(2) Subsection (1) does not apply to information to be included in a statement under section 128B(5)(b) or in any updated statement under section 128B(6).]

NOTES

Inserted as noted to s 128A at **[1.131]**.

[1.139]

[128I Time limits for claims arising from delivery to registrar

(1) Liability incurred by a company—

(a) from the delivery to the registrar of information under this Chapter, or

(b) from a failure to deliver any such information,

is not enforceable more than 10 years after the date on which the information was delivered or, as the case may be, the failure first occurred.

(2) This is without prejudice to any lesser period of limitation (and, in Scotland, to any rule that the obligation giving rise to the liability prescribes before the expiry of that period).]

NOTES

Inserted as noted to s 128A at **[1.131]**.

[1.140]

[128J Withdrawing the election

(1) A company may withdraw an election made by or in respect of it under section 128B.

(2) Withdrawal is achieved by giving notice of withdrawal to the registrar.

(3) The withdrawal takes effect when the notice is registered by the registrar.

(4) The effect of withdrawal is that the company's obligation under Chapter 2 to maintain a register of members applies from then on with respect to the period going forward.

(5) This means that, when the withdrawal takes effect—

(a) the company must enter in its register of members all the information that is required to be contained in that register in respect of matters that are current as at that time,

(b) the company must also retain in its register all the information that it was required under section 128D(3)(a) to keep in a historic register while the election was in force, but

(c) the company is not required to enter in its register information relating to the period when the election was in force that is no longer current.

(6) The company must place a note in its register of members—

(a) stating that the election under section 128B has been withdrawn,

(b) recording when that withdrawal took effect, and

(c) indicating that information about its members relating to the period when the election was in force that is no longer current is available for public inspection on the central register.

(7) Subsections (7) and (8) of section 113 apply if a company makes default in complying with subsection (6) as they apply if a company makes default in complying with that section.]

NOTES

Inserted as noted to s 128A at **[1.131]**.

[1.141]

[128K Power to extend option to public companies

(1) The Secretary of State may by regulations amend this Act—

(a) to extend sections 128A to 128J (with or without modification) to public companies or public companies of a class specified in the regulations, and

(b) to make such other amendments as the Secretary of State thinks fit in consequence of that extension.

(2) Regulations under this section are subject to affirmative resolution procedure.]

NOTES

Inserted as noted to s 128A at **[1.131]**.

CHAPTER 3 OVERSEAS BRANCH REGISTERS

[1.142]

129 Overseas branch registers

(1) A company having a share capital may, if it transacts business in a country or territory to which this Chapter applies, cause to be kept there a branch register of members resident there (an "overseas branch register").

(2) This Chapter applies to—

(a) any part of Her Majesty's dominions outside the United Kingdom, the Channel Islands and the Isle of Man, and

(b) the countries or territories listed below.

Bangladesh
Cyprus
Dominica
The Gambia
Ghana
Guyana
The Hong Kong Special Administrative Region of the People's Republic of China
India
Ireland

Kenya
Kiribati
Lesotho
Malawi
Malaysia
Malta
Nigeria
Pakistan
Seychelles
Sierra Leone
Singapore
South Africa
Sri Lanka
Swaziland
Trinidad and Tobago
Uganda
Zimbabwe

(3) The Secretary of State may make provision by regulations as to the circumstances in which a company is to be regarded as keeping a register in a particular country or territory.

(4) Regulations under this section are subject to negative resolution procedure.

(5) References—

(a) in any Act or instrument (including, in particular, a company's articles) to a dominion register, or

(b) in articles registered before 1st November 1929 to a colonial register,

are to be read (unless the context otherwise requires) as a reference to an overseas branch register kept under this section.

[(6) A company's right under subsection (1) to keep an overseas branch register does not apply during or with respect to any period when an election is in force in respect of the company under section 128B.]

NOTES

Sub-s (6): added by the Small Business, Enterprise and Employment Act 2015, s 94, Sch 5, Pt 1, paras 1, 4, as from 30 June 2016.

Regulations: no Regulations have been made under this section.

[1.143]

130 Notice of opening of overseas branch register

(1) A company that begins to keep an overseas branch register must give notice to the registrar within 14 days of doing so, stating the country or territory in which the register is kept.

(2) If default is made in complying with subsection (1), an offence is committed by—

(a) the company, and

(b) every officer of the company who is in default.

(3) A person guilty of an offence under subsection (2) is liable on summary conviction to a fine not exceeding level 3 on the standard scale and, for continued contravention, a daily default fine not exceeding one-tenth of level 3 on the standard scale.

[1.144]

131 Keeping of overseas branch register

(1) An overseas branch register is regarded as part of the company's register of members ("the main register").

(2) The Secretary of State may make provision by regulations modifying any provision of Chapter 2 (register of members) as it applies in relation to an overseas branch register.

(3) Regulations under this section are subject to negative resolution procedure.

(4) Subject to the provisions of this Act, a company may by its articles make such provision as it thinks fit as to the keeping of overseas branch registers.

NOTES

Regulations: no Regulations have been made under this section.

[1.145]

132 Register or duplicate to be kept available for inspection in UK

(1) A company that keeps an overseas branch register must keep available for inspection—

(a) the register, or

(b) a duplicate of the register duly entered up from time to time,

at the place in the United Kingdom where the company's main register is kept available for inspection.

(2) Any such duplicate is treated for all purposes of this Act as part of the main register.

(3) If default is made in complying with subsection (1), an offence is committed by—

(a) the company, and

(b) every officer of the company who is in default.

(4) A person guilty of an offence under subsection (3) is liable on summary conviction to a fine not exceeding level 3 on the standard scale and, for continued contravention, a daily default fine not exceeding one-tenth of level 3 on the standard scale.

[1.146]

133 Transactions in shares registered in overseas branch register

(1) Shares registered in an overseas branch register must be distinguished from those registered in the main register.

(2) No transaction with respect to shares registered in an overseas branch register may be registered in any other register.

(3) An instrument of transfer of a share registered in an overseas branch register—

(a) is regarded as a transfer of property situated outside the United Kingdom, and

(b) unless executed in a part of the United Kingdom, is exempt from stamp duty.

[1.147]

134 Jurisdiction of local courts

(1) A competent court in a country or territory where an overseas branch register is kept may exercise the same jurisdiction as is exercisable by a court in the United Kingdom—

(a) to rectify the register (see section 125), or

(b) in relation to a request for inspection or a copy of the register (see section 117).

(2) The offences—

(a) of refusing inspection or failing to provide a copy of the register (see section 118), and

(b) of making a false, misleading or deceptive statement in a request for inspection or a copy (see section 119),

may be prosecuted summarily before any tribunal having summary criminal jurisdiction in the country or territory where the register is kept.

(3) This section extends only to those countries and territories to which paragraph 3 of Schedule 14 to the Companies Act 1985 (c 6) (which made similar provision) extended immediately before the coming into force of this Chapter.

[1.148]

135 Discontinuance of overseas branch register

(1) A company may discontinue an overseas branch register.

(2) If it does so all the entries in that register must be transferred—

(a) to some other overseas branch register kept in the same country or territory, or

(b) to the main register.

(3) The company must give notice to the registrar within 14 days of the discontinuance.

(4) If default is made in complying with subsection (3), an offence is committed by—

(a) the company, and

(b) every officer of the company who is in default.

(5) A person guilty of an offence under subsection (4) is liable on summary conviction to a fine not exceeding level 3 on the standard scale and, for continued contravention, a daily default fine not exceeding one-tenth of level 3 on the standard scale.

CHAPTER 4 PROHIBITION ON SUBSIDIARY BEING MEMBER OF ITS HOLDING COMPANY

General prohibition

[1.149]

136 Prohibition on subsidiary being a member of its holding company

(1) Except as provided by this Chapter—

(a) a body corporate cannot be a member of a company that is its holding company, and

(b) any allotment or transfer of shares in a company to its subsidiary is void.

(2) The exceptions are provided for in—

section 138 (subsidiary acting as personal representative or trustee), and

section 141 (subsidiary acting as authorised dealer in securities).

[1.150]

137 Shares acquired before prohibition became applicable

(1) Where a body corporate became a holder of shares in a company—

(a) before the relevant date, or

(b) on or after that date and before the commencement of this Chapter in circumstances in which the prohibition in section 23(1) of the Companies Act 1985 or Article 33(1) of the Companies (Northern Ireland) Order 1986 (SI 1986/1032 (NI 6)) (or any corresponding earlier enactment), as it then had effect, did not apply, or

(c) on or after the commencement of this Chapter in circumstances in which the prohibition in section 136 did not apply,

it may continue to be a member of the company.

(2) The relevant date for the purposes of subsection (1)(a) is—

(a) 1st July 1948 in the case of a company registered in Great Britain, and

(b) 1st April 1961 in the case of a company registered in Northern Ireland.

(3) So long as it is permitted to continue as a member of a company by virtue of this section, an allotment to it of fully paid shares in the company may be validly made by way of capitalisation of reserves of the company.

(4) But, so long as the prohibition in section 136 would (apart from this section) apply, it has no right to vote in respect of the shares mentioned in subsection (1) above, or any shares allotted as mentioned in subsection (3) above, on a written resolution or at meetings of the company or of any class of its members.

Subsidiary acting as personal representative or trustee

[1.151]

138 Subsidiary acting as personal representative or trustee

(1) The prohibition in section 136 (prohibition on subsidiary being a member of its holding company) does not apply where the subsidiary is concerned only—

(a) as personal representative, or

(b) as trustee,

unless, in the latter case, the holding company or a subsidiary of it is beneficially interested under the trust.

(2) For the purpose of ascertaining whether the holding company or a subsidiary is so interested, there shall be disregarded—

(a) any interest held only by way of security for the purposes of a transaction entered into by the holding company or subsidiary in the ordinary course of a business that includes the lending of money;

(b) any interest within—

section 139 (interests to be disregarded: residual interest under pension scheme or employees' share scheme), or section 140 (interests to be disregarded: employer's rights of recovery under pension scheme or employees' share scheme);

(c) any rights that the company or subsidiary has in its capacity as trustee, including in particular—
   (i) any right to recover its expenses or be remunerated out of the trust property, and
   (ii) any right to be indemnified out of the trust property for any liability incurred by reason of any act or omission in the performance of its duties as trustee.

[1.152]

139 Interests to be disregarded: residual interest under pension scheme or employees' share scheme

(1) Where shares in a company are held on trust for the purposes of a pension scheme or employees' share scheme, there shall be disregarded for the purposes of section 138 any residual interest that has not vested in possession.

(2) A "residual interest" means a right of the company or subsidiary ("the residual beneficiary") to receive any of the trust property in the event of—

(a) all the liabilities arising under the scheme having been satisfied or provided for, or
(b) the residual beneficiary ceasing to participate in the scheme, or
(c) the trust property at any time exceeding what is necessary for satisfying the liabilities arising or expected to arise under the scheme.

(3) In subsection (2)—

(a) the reference to a right includes a right dependent on the exercise of a discretion vested by the scheme in the trustee or another person, and
(b) the reference to liabilities arising under a scheme includes liabilities that have resulted, or may result, from the exercise of any such discretion.

(4) For the purposes of this section a residual interest vests in possession—

(a) in a case within subsection (2)(a), on the occurrence of the event mentioned there (whether or not the amount of the property receivable pursuant to the right is ascertained);
(b) in a case within subsection (2)(b) or (c), when the residual beneficiary becomes entitled to require the trustee to transfer to him any of the property receivable pursuant to the right.

(5) In this section "pension scheme" means a scheme for the provision of benefits consisting of or including relevant benefits for or in respect of employees or former employees.

(6) In subsection (5)—

(a) "relevant benefits" means any pension, lump sum, gratuity or other like benefit given or to be given on retirement or on death or in anticipation of retirement or, in connection with past service, after retirement or death; and
(b) "employee" shall be read as if a director of a company were employed by it.

[1.153]

140 Interests to be disregarded: employer's rights of recovery under pension scheme or employees' share scheme

(1) Where shares in a company are held on trust for the purposes of a pension scheme or employees' share scheme, there shall be disregarded for the purposes of section 138 any charge or lien on, or set-off against, any benefit or other right or interest under the scheme for the purpose of enabling the employer or former employer of a member of the scheme to obtain the discharge of a monetary obligation due to him from the member.

(2) In the case of a trust for the purposes of a pension scheme there shall also be disregarded any right to receive from the trustee of the scheme, or as trustee of the scheme to retain, an amount that can be recovered or retained, under . . . section 57 of the Pension Schemes (Northern Ireland) Act 1993 (c 49) (deduction of contributions equivalent premium from refund of scheme contributions) or otherwise, as reimbursement or partial reimbursement for any contributions equivalent premium paid in connection with the scheme under Part 3 of that Act.

(3) In this section "pension scheme" means a scheme for the provision of benefits consisting of or including relevant benefits for or in respect of employees or former employees.

"Relevant benefits" here means any pension, lump sum, gratuity or other like benefit given or to be given on retirement or on death or in anticipation of retirement or, in connection with past service, after retirement or death.

(4) In this section "employer" and "employee" shall be read as if a director of a company were employed by it.

NOTES

Sub-s (2): words omitted repealed by the Pensions Act 2014, s 24, Sch 13, Pt 2, paras 74, 75, as from 6 April 2016.

Subsidiary acting as dealer in securities

[1.154]

141 Subsidiary acting as authorised dealer in securities

(1) The prohibition in section 136 (prohibition on subsidiary being a member of its holding company) does not apply where the shares are held by the subsidiary in the ordinary course of its business as an intermediary.

(2) For this purpose a person is an intermediary if he—

(a) carries on a bona fide business of dealing in securities,
(b) is a member of or has access to a [UK regulated market], and
(c) does not carry on an excluded business.

(3) The following are excluded businesses—

(a) a business that consists wholly or mainly in the making or managing of investments;
(b) a business that consists wholly or mainly in, or is carried on wholly or mainly for the purposes of, providing services to persons who are connected with the person carrying on the business;
(c) a business that consists in insurance business;
(d) a business that consists in managing or acting as trustee in relation to a pension scheme, or that is carried on by the manager or trustee of such a scheme in connection with or for the purposes of the scheme;

(e) a business that consists in operating or acting as trustee in relation to a collective investment scheme, or that is carried on by the operator or trustee of such a scheme in connection with and for the purposes of the scheme.

(4) For the purposes of this section—

(a) the question whether a person is connected with another shall be determined in accordance with [section 1122 of the Corporation Tax Act 2010];

(b) "collective investment scheme" has the meaning given in section 235 of the Financial Services and Markets Act 2000 (c 8);

(c) "insurance business" means business that consists in the effecting or carrying out of contracts of insurance;

(d) "securities" includes—

(i) options,

(ii) futures, and

(iii) contracts for differences,

and rights or interests in those investments;

(e) "trustee" and "the operator" in relation to a collective investment scheme shall be construed in accordance with section 237(2) of the Financial Services and Markets Act 2000 (c 8).

(5) Expressions used in this section that are also used in the provisions regulating activities under the Financial Services and Markets Act 2000 have the same meaning here as they do in those provisions.

See section 22 of that Act, orders made under that section and Schedule 2 to that Act.

NOTES

Sub-s (2): words in square brackets substituted by the Companies, Limited Liability Partnerships and Partnerships (Amendment etc) (EU Exit) Regulations 2019, SI 2019/348, reg 6, Sch 1, paras 1, 2, as from IP completion day (as defined in the European Union (Withdrawal Agreement) Act 2020, s 39) (for transitional provisions see Sch 4, para 1 to the 2019 Regulations at **[12.105]**).

Sub-s (4): words in square brackets in para (a) substituted by the Corporation Tax Act 2010, s 1177, Sch 1, Pt 2, paras 487, 488 (note that the 2010 Act comes into force on 1 April 2010 and has effect, for corporation tax purposes for accounting periods ending on or after that day, and for income tax and capital gains tax purposes for the tax year 2010–11 and subsequent tax years; see s 1184(1) of the 2010 Act).

[1.155]

142 Protection of third parties in other cases where subsidiary acting as dealer in securities

(1) This section applies where—

(a) a subsidiary that is a dealer in securities has purportedly acquired shares in its holding company in contravention of the prohibition in section 136, and

(b) a person acting in good faith has agreed, for value and without notice of the contravention, to acquire shares in the holding company—

(i) from the subsidiary, or

(ii) from someone who has purportedly acquired the shares after their disposal by the subsidiary.

(2) A transfer to that person of the shares mentioned in subsection (1)(a) has the same effect as it would have had if their original acquisition by the subsidiary had not been in contravention of the prohibition.

Supplementary

[1.156]

143 Application of provisions to companies not limited by shares

In relation to a company other than a company limited by shares, the references in this Chapter to shares shall be read as references to the interest of its members as such, whatever the form of that interest.

[1.157]

144 Application of provisions to nominees

The provisions of this Chapter apply to a nominee acting on behalf of a subsidiary as to the subsidiary itself.

PART 9 EXERCISE OF MEMBERS' RIGHTS

Effect of provisions in company's articles

[1.158]

145 Effect of provisions of articles as to enjoyment or exercise of members' rights

(1) This section applies where provision is made by a company's articles enabling a member to nominate another person or persons as entitled to enjoy or exercise all or any specified rights of the member in relation to the company.

(2) So far as is necessary to give effect to that provision, anything required or authorised by any provision of the Companies Acts to be done by or in relation to the member shall instead be done, or (as the case may be) may instead be done, by or in relation to the nominated person (or each of them) as if he were a member of the company.

(3) This applies, in particular, to the rights conferred by—

(a) sections 291 and 293 (right to be sent proposed written resolution);

(b) section 292 (right to require circulation of written resolution);

(c) section 303 (right to require directors to call general meeting);

(d) section 310 (right to notice of general meetings);

(e) section 314 (right to require circulation of a statement);

[(ea) section 319A (right to ask question at meeting of traded company);]

(f) section 324 (right to appoint proxy to act at meeting);

(g) section 338 (right to require circulation of resolution for AGM of public company); and

[(ga) section 338A (traded companies: members' power to include matters in business dealt with at AGM);]

[(gb) 360AA (traded companies: confirmation of receipt of electronic voting);]

[(gc) 360BA (traded companies: right to confirmation of vote after a general meeting);]

(h) section 423 (right to be sent a copy of annual accounts and reports).

(4) This section and any such provision as is mentioned in subsection (1)—

(a) do not confer rights enforceable against the company by anyone other than the member, and

(b) do not affect the requirements for an effective transfer or other disposition of the whole or part of a member's interest in the company.

NOTES

Sub-s (3) is amended as follows:

Paras (ea), (ga) inserted by the Companies (Shareholders' Rights) Regulations 2009, SI 2009/1632, regs 12(2), 17(2), as from 3 August 2009, in relation to meetings of which notice is given, or first given, on or after that date.

Para (gb) inserted by the Companies (Shareholders' Rights to Voting Confirmations) Regulations 2020, SI 2020/717, reg 4(2), as from 3 September 2020, in relation to votes cast on or after that date (see reg 2 of those Regulations).

Para (gc) inserted by SI 2020/717, reg 5(2), as from 3 September 2020, in relation to votes cast at a general meeting which takes place on or after that date (see reg 3 of those Regulations).

Information rights

[1.159]

146 Traded companies: nomination of persons to enjoy information rights

(1) This section applies to a company whose shares are admitted to trading on a [UK regulated market or an EU regulated market].

(2) A member of such a company who holds shares on behalf of another person may nominate that person to enjoy information rights.

(3) "Information rights" means—

(a) the right to receive a copy of all communications that the company sends to its members generally or to any class of its members that includes the person making the nomination, and

(b) the rights conferred by—

(i) section 431 or 432 (right to require copies of accounts and reports), and

(ii) section 1145 (right to require hard copy version of document or information provided in another form).

(4) The reference in subsection (3)(a) to communications that a company sends to its members generally includes the company's annual accounts and reports. For the application of section 426 (option to provide [strategic report with supplementary material]) in relation to a person nominated to enjoy information rights, see subsection (5) of that section.

(5) A company need not act on a nomination purporting to relate to certain information rights only.

NOTES

Sub-s (1): words in square brackets substituted by the Companies, Limited Liability Partnerships and Partnerships (Amendment etc) (EU Exit) Regulations 2019, SI 2019/348, reg 6, Sch 1, paras 1, 3, as from IP completion day (as defined in the European Union (Withdrawal Agreement) Act 2020, s 39).

Sub-s (4): words in square brackets substituted by the Companies Act 2006 (Strategic Report and Directors' Report) Regulations 2013, SI 2013/1970, reg 14, Schedule, paras 1, 2, in respect of financial years ending on or after 30 September 2013.

[1.160]

147 Information rights: form in which copies to be provided

(1) This section applies as regards the form in which copies are to be provided to a person nominated under section 146 (nomination of person to enjoy information rights).

(2) If the person to be nominated wishes to receive hard copy communications, he must—

(a) request the person making the nomination to notify the company of that fact, and

(b) provide an address to which such copies may be sent.

This must be done before the nomination is made.

(3) If having received such a request the person making the nomination—

(a) notifies the company that the nominated person wishes to receive hard copy communications, and

(b) provides the company with that address,

the right of the nominated person is to receive hard copy communications accordingly.

(4) This is subject to the provisions of Parts 3 and 4 of Schedule 5 (communications by company) under which the company may take steps to enable it to communicate in electronic form or by means of a website.

(5) If no such notification is given (or no address is provided), the nominated person is taken to have agreed that documents or information may be sent or supplied to him by the company by means of a website.

(6) That agreement—

(a) may be revoked by the nominated person, and

(b) does not affect his right under section 1145 to require a hard copy version of a document or information provided in any other form.

[1.161]

148 Termination or suspension of nomination

(1) The following provisions have effect in relation to a nomination under section 146 (nomination of person to enjoy information rights).

(2) The nomination may be terminated at the request of the member or of the nominated person.

(3) The nomination ceases to have effect on the occurrence in relation to the member or the nominated person of any of the following—

(a) in the case of an individual, death or bankruptcy;

(b) in the case of a body corporate, dissolution or the making of an order for the winding up of the body otherwise than for the purposes of reconstruction.

(4) In subsection (3)—

(a) the reference to bankruptcy includes—

(i) the sequestration of a person's estate, and

(ii) a person's estate being the subject of a protected trust deed (within the meaning of the Bankruptcy (Scotland) Act [2016]); and

(b) the reference to the making of an order for winding up is to—

(i) the making of such an order under the Insolvency Act 1986 (c 45) or the Insolvency (Northern Ireland) Order 1989 (SI 1989/2405 (NI 19)), or

(ii) any corresponding proceeding under the law of a country or territory outside the United Kingdom.

(5) The effect of any nominations made by a member is suspended at any time when there are more nominated persons than the member has shares in the company.

(6) Where—

(a) the member holds different classes of shares with different information rights, and

(b) there are more nominated persons than he has shares conferring a particular right,

the effect of any nominations made by him is suspended to the extent that they confer that right.

(7) Where the company—

(a) enquires of a nominated person whether he wishes to retain information rights, and

(b) does not receive a response within the period of 28 days beginning with the date on which the company's enquiry was sent,

the nomination ceases to have effect at the end of that period.

Such an enquiry is not to be made of a person more than once in any twelve-month period.

(8) The termination or suspension of a nomination means that the company is not required to act on it.

It does not prevent the company from continuing to do so, to such extent or for such period as it thinks fit.

NOTES

Sub-s (4): year "2016" in square brackets substituted by the Bankruptcy (Scotland) Act 2016 (Consequential Provisions and Modifications) Order 2016, SI 2016/1034, art 7(1), (3), Sch 1, para 29(1), (4), as from 30 November 2016 (except in relation to (i) a sequestration as regards which the petition is presented, or the debtor application is made before that date; or (ii) a trust deed executed before that date).

[1.162]

149 Information as to possible rights in relation to voting

(1) This section applies where a company sends a copy of a notice of a meeting to a person nominated under section 146 (nomination of person to enjoy information rights).

(2) The copy of the notice must be accompanied by a statement that—

(a) he may have a right under an agreement between him and the member by whom he was nominated to be appointed, or to have someone else appointed, as a proxy for the meeting, and

(b) if he has no such right or does not wish to exercise it, he may have a right under such an agreement to give instructions to the member as to the exercise of voting rights.

(3) Section 325 (notice of meeting to contain statement of member's rights in relation to appointment of proxy) does not apply to the copy, and the company must either—

(a) omit the notice required by that section, or

(b) include it but state that it does not apply to the nominated person.

[1.163]

150 Information rights: status of rights

(1) This section has effect as regards the rights conferred by a nomination under section 146 (nomination of person to enjoy information rights).

(2) Enjoyment by the nominated person of the rights conferred by the nomination is enforceable against the company by the member as if they were rights conferred by the company's articles.

(3) Any enactment, and any provision of the company's articles, having effect in relation to communications with members has a corresponding effect (subject to any necessary adaptations) in relation to communications with the nominated person.

(4) In particular—

(a) where under any enactment, or any provision of the company's articles, the members of a company entitled to receive a document or information are determined as at a date or time before it is sent or supplied, the company need not send or supply it to a nominated person—

(i) whose nomination was received by the company after that date or time, or

(ii) if that date or time falls in a period of suspension of his nomination; and

(b) where under any enactment, or any provision of the company's articles, the right of a member to receive a document or information depends on the company having a current address for him, the same applies to any person nominated by him.

(5) The rights conferred by the nomination—

(a) are in addition to the rights of the member himself, and

(b) do not affect any rights exercisable by virtue of any such provision as is mentioned in section 145 (provisions of company's articles as to enjoyment or exercise of members' rights).

(6) A failure to give effect to the rights conferred by the nomination does not affect the validity of anything done by or on behalf of the company.

(7) References in this section to the rights conferred by the nomination are to—

(a) the rights referred to in section 146(3) (information rights), and

(b) where applicable, the rights conferred by section 147(3) (right to hard copy communications) and section 149 (information as to possible voting rights).

[1.164]

151 Information rights: power to amend

(1) The Secretary of State may by regulations amend the provisions of sections 146 to 150 (information rights) so as to—

(a) extend or restrict the classes of companies to which section 146 applies,

(b) make other provision as to the circumstances in which a nomination may be made under that section, or

(c) extend or restrict the rights conferred by such a nomination.

(2) The regulations may make such consequential modifications of any other provisions of this Part, or of any other enactment, as appear to the Secretary of State to be necessary.

(3) Regulations under this section are subject to affirmative resolution procedure.

NOTES

Regulations: no Regulations have been made under this section.

Exercise of rights where shares held on behalf of others

[1.165]

152 Exercise of rights where shares held on behalf of others: exercise in different ways

(1) Where a member holds shares in a company on behalf of more than one person—

(a) rights attached to the shares, and

(b) rights under any enactment exercisable by virtue of holding the shares,

need not all be exercised, and if exercised, need not all be exercised in the same way.

(2) A member who exercises such rights but does not exercise all his rights, must inform the company to what extent he is exercising the rights.

(3) A member who exercises such rights in different ways must inform the company of the ways in which he is exercising them and to what extent they are exercised in each way.

(4) If a member exercises such rights without informing the company—

(a) that he is not exercising all his rights, or

(b) that he is exercising his rights in different ways,

the company is entitled to assume that he is exercising all his rights and is exercising them in the same way.

[1.166]

153 Exercise of rights where shares held on behalf of others: members' requests

(1) This section applies for the purposes of—

(a) section 314 (power to require circulation of statement),

(b) section 338 (public companies: power to require circulation of resolution for AGM),

[(ba) section 338A (traded companies: members' power to include matters in business dealt with at AGM),]

(c) section 342 (power to require independent report on poll), and

(d) section 527 (power to require website publication of audit concerns).

(2) A company is required to act under any of those sections if it receives a request in relation to which the following conditions are met—

(a) it is made by at least 100 persons;

(b) it is authenticated by all the persons making it;

(c) in the case of any of those persons who is not a member of the company, it is accompanied by a statement—

(i) of the full name and address of a person ("the member") who is a member of the company and holds shares on behalf of that person,

(ii) that the member is holding those shares on behalf of that person in the course of a business,

(iii) of the number of shares in the company that the member holds on behalf of that person,

(iv) of the total amount paid up on those shares,

(v) that those shares are not held on behalf of anyone else or, if they are, that the other person or persons are not among the other persons making the request,

(vi) that some or all of those shares confer voting rights that are relevant for the purposes of making a request under the section in question, and

(vii) that the person has the right to instruct the member how to exercise those rights;

(d) in the case of any of those persons who is a member of the company, it is accompanied by a statement—

(i) that he holds shares otherwise than on behalf of another person, or

(ii) that he holds shares on behalf of one or more other persons but those persons are not among the other persons making the request;

(e) it is accompanied by such evidence as the company may reasonably require of the matters mentioned in paragraph (c) and (d);

(f) the total amount of the sums paid up on—

(i) shares held as mentioned in paragraph (c), and

(ii) shares held as mentioned in paragraph (d),

divided by the number of persons making the request, is not less than £100;

(g) the request complies with any other requirements of the section in question as to contents, timing and otherwise.

NOTES

Sub-s (1): para (ba) inserted by the Companies (Shareholders' Rights) Regulations 2009, SI 2009/1632, reg 17(3), as from 3 August 2009, in relation to meetings of which notice is given, or first given, on or after that date.

PART 10 A COMPANY'S DIRECTORS

CHAPTER 1 APPOINTMENT AND REMOVAL OF DIRECTORS

Requirement to have directors

[1.167]

154 Companies required to have directors

(1) A private company must have at least one director.

(2) A public company must have at least two directors.

[1.168]

155 Companies required to have at least one director who is a natural person

(1) A company must have at least one director who is a natural person.

(2) This requirement is met if the office of director is held by a natural person as a corporation sole or otherwise by virtue of an office.

NOTES

Repealed by the Small Business, Enterprise and Employment Act 2015, s 87(1), (2), as from a day to be appointed.

As to the duty of the Secretary of State to carry out a review of the Small Business, Enterprise and Employment Act 2015, s 87, see s 88 of that Act at **[9.522]**.

[1.169]

156 Direction requiring company to make appointment

(1) If it appears to the Secretary of State that a company is in breach of—

section 154 (requirements as to number of directors), or

section 155 (requirement to have at least one director who is a natural person),

the Secretary of State may give the company a direction under this section.

(2) The direction must specify—

(a) the statutory requirement the company appears to be in breach of,

(b) what the company must do in order to comply with the direction, and

(c) the period within which it must do so.

That period must be not less than one month or more than three months after the date on which the direction is given.

(3) The direction must also inform the company of the consequences of failing to comply.

(4) Where the company is in breach *of section 154 or 155* it must comply with the direction by—

(a) making the necessary appointment or appointments, and

(b) giving notice of them under section 167,

before the end of the period specified in the direction.

(5) If the company has already made the necessary appointment or appointments (or so far as it has done so), it must comply with the direction by giving notice of them under section 167 before the end of the period specified in the direction.

(6) If a company fails to comply with a direction under this section, an offence is committed by—

(a) the company, and

(b) every officer of the company who is in default.

For this purpose a shadow director is treated as an officer of the company.

(7) A person guilty of an offence under this section is liable on summary conviction to a fine not exceeding level 5 on the standard scale and, for continued contravention, a daily default fine not exceeding [one-tenth of the greater of £5,000 or level 4 on the standard scale].

NOTES

Sub-s (1): for the words in italics there are substituted the words "provision by virtue of section 156B(4)" by the Small Business, Enterprise and Employment Act 2015, s 87(1), (3)(a), as from a day to be appointed.

Sub-s (4): for the words in italics there are substituted the words "as mentioned in subsection (1)" by the Small Business, Enterprise and Employment Act 2015, s 87(1), (3)(b), as from a day to be appointed.

Sub-s (7): words in square brackets substituted (for the original words "one-tenth of level 5 on the standard scale") by the Legal Aid, Sentencing and Punishment of Offenders Act 2012 (Fines on Summary Conviction) Regulations 2015, SI 2015/664, regs 3, 5, Sch 3, Pt 1, para 9(1), (4), as from 12 March 2015, in relation to England and Wales only (except in relation to (a) fines for offences committed before 12 March 2015, (b) the operation of restrictions on fines that may be imposed on a person aged under 18, or (c) fines that may be imposed on a person convicted by a magistrates' court who is to be sentenced as if convicted on indictment).

As to the duty of the Secretary of State to carry out a review of the Small Business, Enterprise and Employment Act 2015, s 87, see s 88 of that Act at **[9.522]**.

Appointment

[1.170]

[156A Each director to be a natural person

(1) A person may not be appointed a director of a company unless the person is a natural person.

(2) Subsection (1) does not prohibit the holding of the office of director by a natural person as a corporation sole or otherwise by virtue of an office.

(3) An appointment made in contravention of this section is void.

(4) Nothing in this section affects any liability of a person under any provision of the Companies Acts or any other enactment if the person—

(a) purports to act as director, or

(b) acts as shadow director,

although the person could not, by virtue of this section, be validly appointed as a director.

(5) This section has effect subject to section 156B (power to provide for exceptions from requirement that each director be a natural person).

(6) If a purported appointment is made in contravention of this section, an offence is committed by—

(a) the company purporting to make the appointment,

(b) where the purported appointment is of a body corporate or a firm that is a legal person under the law by which it is governed, that body corporate or firm, and

(c) every officer of a person falling within paragraph (a) or (b) who is in default.

For this purpose a shadow director is treated as an officer of a company.

(7) A person guilty of an offence under this section is liable on summary conviction—

(a) in England and Wales, to a fine;

(b) in Scotland or Northern Ireland, to a fine not exceeding level 5 on the standard scale.]

NOTES

Commencement: to be appointed.

Inserted, together with ss 156B, 156C, by the Small Business, Enterprise and Employment Act 2015, s 87(1), (4), as from a day to be appointed.

As to the duty of the Secretary of State to carry out a review of the Small Business, Enterprise and Employment Act 2015, s 87, see s 88 of that Act at **[9.522]**.

[1.171]

[156B Power to provide for exceptions from requirement that each director be a natural person

(1) The Secretary of State may make provision by regulations for cases in which a person who is not a natural person may be appointed a director of a company.

(2) The regulations must specify the circumstances in which, and any conditions subject to which, the appointment may be made.

(3) Provision made by virtue of subsection (2) may in particular include provision that an appointment may be made only with the approval of a regulatory body specified in the regulations.

(4) The regulations must include provision that a company must have at least one director who is a natural person (and for this purpose the requirement is met if the office of director is held by a natural person as a corporation sole or otherwise by virtue of an office).

(5) Regulations under this section may amend section 164 so as to require particulars relating to exceptions to be contained in a company's register of directors.

(6) The regulations may make different provision for different parts of the United Kingdom.
This is without prejudice to the general power to make different provision for different cases.

(7) Regulations under this section are subject to affirmative resolution procedure.]

NOTES

Commencement: to be appointed.

Inserted as noted to s 156A at **[1.170]**.

[1.172]

[156C Existing director who is not a natural person

(1) In this section "the relevant day" is the day after the end of the period of 12 months beginning with the day on which section 156A comes into force.

(2) Where—

(a) a person appointed a director of a company before section 156A comes into force is not a natural person, and

(b) the case is not one excepted from that section by regulations under section 156B,

that person ceases to be a director on the relevant day.

(3) The company must—

(a) make the necessary consequential alteration in its register of directors, and

(b) give notice to the registrar of the change in accordance with section 167.

(4) If an election is in force under section 167A in respect of the company, the company must, in place of doing the things required by subsection (3), deliver to the registrar in accordance with section 167D the information of which the company would otherwise have been obliged to give notice under subsection (3).

(5) If it appears to the registrar that—

(a) a notice should have, but has not, been given in accordance with subsection (3)(b), or

(b) information should have, but has not, been delivered in accordance with subsection (4),

the registrar must place a note in the register recording the fact.]

NOTES

Commencement: to be appointed.

Inserted as noted to s 156A at **[1.170]**.

[1.173]

157 Minimum age for appointment as director

(1) A person may not be appointed a director of a company unless he has attained the age of 16 years.

(2) This does not affect the validity of an appointment that is not to take effect until the person appointed attains that age.

(3) Where the office of director of a company is held by a corporation sole, or otherwise by virtue of another office, the appointment to that other office of a person who has not attained the age of 16 years is not effective also to make him a director of the company until he attains the age of 16 years.

(4) An appointment made in contravention of this section is void.

(5) Nothing in this section affects any liability of a person under any provision of the Companies Acts if he—

(a) purports to act as director, or

(b) acts as a shadow director,

although he could not, by virtue of this section, be validly appointed as a director.

(6) This section has effect subject to section 158 (power to provide for exceptions from minimum age requirement).

[1.174]

158 Power to provide for exceptions from minimum age requirement

(1) The Secretary of State may make provision by regulations for cases in which a person who has not attained the age of 16 years may be appointed a director of a company.

(2) The regulations must specify the circumstances in which, and any conditions subject to which, the appointment may be made.

(3) If the specified circumstances cease to obtain, or any specified conditions cease to be met, a person who was appointed by virtue of the regulations and who has not since attained the age of 16 years ceases to hold office.

(4) The regulations may make different provision for different parts of the United Kingdom.

This is without prejudice to the general power to make different provision for different cases.

(5) Regulations under this section are subject to negative resolution procedure.

NOTES

Regulations: no Regulations have been made under this section.

[1.175]

159 Existing under-age directors

(1) This section applies where—

(a) a person appointed a director of a company before section 157 (minimum age for appointment as director) comes into force has not attained the age of 16 when that section comes into force, or

(b) the office of director of a company is held by a corporation sole, or otherwise by virtue of another office, and the person appointed to that other office has not attained the age of 16 years when that section comes into force,

and the case is not one excepted from that section by regulations under section 158.

(2) That person ceases to be a director on section 157 coming into force.

(3) The company must make the necessary consequential alteration in its register of directors but need not give notice to the registrar of the change.

(4) If it appears to the registrar (from other information) that a person has ceased by virtue of this section to be a director of a company, the registrar shall note that fact on the register.

[1.176]

160 Appointment of directors of public company to be voted on individually

(1) At a general meeting of a public company a motion for the appointment of two or more persons as directors of the company by a single resolution must not be made unless a resolution that it should be so made has first been agreed to by the meeting without any vote being given against it.

(2) A resolution moved in contravention of this section is void, whether or not its being so moved was objected to at the time.

But where a resolution so moved is passed, no provision for the automatic reappointment of retiring directors in default of another appointment applies.

(3) For the purposes of this section a motion for approving a person's appointment, or for nominating a person for appointment, is treated as a motion for his appointment.

(4) Nothing in this section applies to a resolution amending the company's articles.

[1.177]

161 Validity of acts of directors

(1) The acts of a person acting as a director are valid notwithstanding that it is afterwards discovered—

(a) that there was a defect in his appointment;

(b) that he was disqualified from holding office;

(c) that he had ceased to hold office;

(d) that he was not entitled to vote on the matter in question.

(2) This applies even if the resolution for his appointment is void under section 160 (appointment of directors of public company to be voted on individually).

Register of directors, etc

[1.178]

[161A Alternative method of record-keeping

Sections 162 to 167 must be read with sections 167A to 167E (which allow for an alternative method of record-keeping in the case of private companies).]

NOTES

Inserted by the Small Business, Enterprise and Employment Act 2015, s 94, Sch 5, Pt 1, paras 5, 6, as from 30 June 2016.

[1.179]

162 Register of directors

(1) Every company must keep a register of its directors.

(2) The register must contain the required particulars (see sections 163, 164 and 166) of each person who is a director of the company.

(3) The register must be kept available for inspection—

(a) at the company's registered office, or

(b) at a place specified in regulations under section 1136.

(4) The company must give notice to the registrar—

(a) of the place at which the register is kept available for inspection, and

(b) of any change in that place,

unless it has at all times been kept at the company's registered office.

(5) The register must be open to the inspection—

(a) of any member of the company without charge, and

(b) of any other person on payment of such fee as may be prescribed.

(6) If default is made in complying with subsection (1), (2) or (3) or if default is made for 14 days in complying with subsection (4), or if an inspection required under subsection (5) is refused, an offence is committed by—

(a) the company, and

(b) every officer of the company who is in default.

For this purpose a shadow director is treated as an officer of the company.

(7) A person guilty of an offence under this section is liable on summary conviction to a fine not exceeding level 5 on the standard scale and, for continued contravention, a daily default fine not exceeding [one-tenth of the greater of £5,000 or level 4 on the standard scale].

(8) In the case of a refusal of inspection of the register, the court may by order compel an immediate inspection of it.

NOTES

Sub-s (7): words in square brackets substituted (for the original words "one-tenth of level 5 on the standard scale") by the Legal Aid, Sentencing and Punishment of Offenders Act 2012 (Fines on Summary Conviction) Regulations 2015, SI 2015/664, regs 3, 5, Sch 3, Pt 1, para 9(1), (5), as from 12 March 2015, in relation to England and Wales only (except in relation to (a) fines for offences committed before 12 March 2015, (b) the operation of restrictions on fines that may be imposed on a person aged under 18, or (c) fines that may be imposed on a person convicted by a magistrates' court who is to be sentenced as if convicted on indictment).

Temporary modification: this section was modified by the Companies etc (Filing Requirements) (Temporary Modifications) Regulations 2020, SI 2020/645, reg 7. By virtue of the Corporate Insolvency and Governance Act 2020, s 39(8), the modification applied from 27 June 2020 to the end of the day on 5 April 2021 (subject to the saving provision in s 39(9) which provides that the expiry of s 39 on 5 April 2021 does not affect the continued operation of any Regulations made under that section for the purpose of determining the length of any period that began before the expiry). As modified, sub-s (6) above had effect as if for the reference to "14 days" there were substituted a reference to "42 days".

Regulations: the Companies (Fees for Inspection of Company Records) Regulations 2008, SI 2008/3007 at **[4.177]**. For a summary of all statutory instruments made under this Act, see Appendix 4 at **[A4]**.

[1.180]

163 Particulars of directors to be registered: individuals

(1) A company's register of directors must contain the following particulars in the case of an individual—

(a) name and any former name;
(b) a service address;
(c) the country or state (or part of the United Kingdom) in which he is usually resident;
(d) nationality;
(e) business occupation (if any);
(f) date of birth.

(2) For the purposes of this section "name" means a person's Christian name (or other forename) and surname, except that in the case of—

(a) a peer, or
(b) an individual usually known by a title,

the title may be stated instead of his Christian name (or other forename) and surname or in addition to either or both of them.

(3) For the purposes of this section a "former name" means a name by which the individual was formerly known for business purposes.

Where a person is or was formerly known by more than one such name, each of them must be stated.

(4) It is not necessary for the register to contain particulars of a former name in the following cases—

(a) in the case of a peer or an individual normally known by a British title, where the name is one by which the person was known previous to the adoption of or succession to the title;
(b) in the case of any person, where the former name—
   (i) was changed or disused before the person attained the age of 16 years, or
   (ii) has been changed or disused for 20 years or more.

(5) A person's service address may be stated to be "The company's registered office".

[1.181]

164 Particulars of directors to be registered: corporate directors and firms

A company's register of directors must contain the following particulars in the case of a body corporate, or a firm that is a legal person under the law by which it is governed—

(a) corporate or firm name;
(b) registered or principal office;
[(c) in the case of a limited company that is a UK-registered company, the registered number;]
(d) in any other case, particulars of—
   (i) the legal form of the company or firm and the law by which it is governed, and
   (ii) if applicable, the register in which it is entered (including details of the state) and its registration number in that register.

NOTES

Para (c) was substituted by the Companies, Limited Liability Partnerships and Partnerships (Amendment etc) (EU Exit) Regulations 2019, SI 2019/348, reg 6, Sch 1, paras 1, 4, as from IP completion day (as defined in the European Union (Withdrawal Agreement) Act 2020, s 39) (for transitional provisions see Sch 4, para 2 to the 2019 Regulations at **[12.105]**).

[1.182]

165 Register of directors' residential addresses

(1) Every company must keep a register of directors' residential addresses.

(2) The register must state the usual residential address of each of the company's directors.

(3) If a director's usual residential address is the same as his service address (as stated in the company's register of directors), the register of directors' residential addresses need only contain an entry to that effect.

This does not apply if his service address is stated to be "The company's registered office".

(4) If default is made in complying with this section, an offence is committed by—

(a) the company, and
(b) every officer of the company who is in default.

For this purpose a shadow director is treated as an officer of the company.

(5) A person guilty of an offence under this section is liable on summary conviction to a fine not exceeding level 5 on the standard scale and, for continued contravention, a daily default fine not exceeding [one-tenth of the greater of £5,000 or level 4 on the standard scale].

(6) This section applies only to directors who are individuals, not where the director is a body corporate or a firm that is a legal person under the law by which it is governed.

NOTES

Sub-s (5): words in square brackets substituted (for the original words "one-tenth of level 5 on the standard scale") by the Legal Aid, Sentencing and Punishment of Offenders Act 2012 (Fines on Summary Conviction) Regulations 2015, SI 2015/664, regs 3, 5, Sch 3, Pt 1, para 9(1), (6), as from 12 March 2015, in relation to England and Wales only (except in relation to (a) fines for offences committed before 12 March 2015, (b) the operation of restrictions on fines that may be imposed on a person aged under 18, or (c) fines that may be imposed on a person convicted by a magistrates' court who is to be sentenced as if convicted on indictment).

[1.183]

166 Particulars of directors to be registered: power to make regulations

(1) The Secretary of State may make provision by regulations amending—

section 163 (particulars of directors to be registered: individuals),

section 164 (particulars of directors to be registered: corporate directors and firms), or

section 165 (register of directors' residential addresses),

so as to add to or remove items from the particulars required to be contained in a company's register of directors or register of directors' residential addresses.

(2) Regulations under this section are subject to affirmative resolution procedure.

NOTES

Regulations: no Regulations have been made under this section.

[1.184]

167 Duty to notify registrar of changes

(1) A company must, within the period of 14 days from—

(a) a person becoming or ceasing to be a director, or

(b) the occurrence of any change in the particulars contained in its register of directors or its register of directors' residential addresses,

give notice to the registrar of the change and of the date on which it occurred.

(2) Notice of a person having become a director of the company must—

(a) contain a statement of the particulars of the new director that are required to be included in the company's register of directors and its register of directors' residential addresses, and

[(b) be accompanied by a statement by the company that the person has consented to act in that capacity.]

(3) Where—

(a) a company gives notice of a change of a director's service address as stated in the company's register of directors, and

(b) the notice is not accompanied by notice of any resulting change in the particulars contained in the company's register of directors' residential addresses,

the notice must be accompanied by a statement that no such change is required.

(4) If default is made in complying with this section, an offence is committed by—

(a) the company, and

(b) every officer of the company who is in default.

For this purpose a shadow director is treated as an officer of the company.

(5) A person guilty of an offence under this section is liable on summary conviction to a fine not exceeding level 5 on the standard scale and, for continued contravention, a daily default fine not exceeding [one-tenth of the greater of £5,000 or level 4 on the standard scale].

NOTES

Sub-s (2): para (b) substituted by the Small Business, Enterprise and Employment Act 2015, s 100(1), (4), as from 10 October 2015 (for transitional provisions see the note to s 12 of this Act at **[1.12]**).

Sub-s (5): words in square brackets substituted (for the original words "one-tenth of level 5 on the standard scale") by the Legal Aid, Sentencing and Punishment of Offenders Act 2012 (Fines on Summary Conviction) Regulations 2015, SI 2015/664, regs 3, 5, Sch 3, Pt 1, para 9(1), (7), as from 12 March 2015, in relation to England and Wales only (except in relation to (a) fines for offences committed before 12 March 2015, (b) the operation of restrictions on fines that may be imposed on a person aged under 18, or (c) fines that may be imposed on a person convicted by a magistrates' court who is to be sentenced as if convicted on indictment).

Temporary modification: this section was modified by the Companies etc (Filing Requirements) (Temporary Modifications) Regulations 2020, SI 2020/645, reg 8. By virtue of the Corporate Insolvency and Governance Act 2020, s 39(8), the modification applied from 27 June 2020 to the end of the day on 5 April 2021 (subject to the saving provision in s 39(9) which provides that the expiry of s 39 on 5 April 2021 does not affect the continued operation of any Regulations made under that section for the purpose of determining the length of any period that began before the expiry). As modified, sub-s (1) above had effect as if for the reference to "14 days" there were substituted a reference to "42 days".

[Option to keep information on the central register

[1.185]

167A Right to make an election

(1) An election may be made under this section in respect of a register of directors or a register of directors' residential addresses (or both).

(2) The election may be made—

(a) by the subscribers wishing to form a private company under this Act, or

(b) by the private company itself once it is formed and registered.

(3) The election is made by giving notice of election to the registrar.

(4) If the notice is given by subscribers wishing to form a private company, it must be given when the documents required to be delivered under section 9 are delivered to the registrar.]

NOTES

Inserted, together with the preceding heading and ss 167B–167F, by the Small Business, Enterprise and Employment Act 2015, s 94, Sch 5, Pt 1, paras 5, 7, as from 30 June 2016.

[1.186]

[167B Effective date of election

(1) An election made under section 167A takes effect when the notice of election is registered by the registrar.

(2) The election remains in force until either—

(a) the company ceases to be a private company, or

(b) a notice of withdrawal sent by the company under section 167E is registered by the registrar,

whichever occurs first.]

NOTES

Inserted as noted to s 167A at **[1.185]**.

[1.187]

[167C Effect of election on obligations under sections 162 to 167

(1) If an election is in force under section 167A with respect to a company, the company's obligations under sections 162 to 167—

(a) to keep and maintain a register of the relevant kind, and

(b) to notify the registrar of changes to it,

do not apply with respect to the period when the election is in force.

(2) The reference in subsection (1) to a register "of the relevant kind" is to a register (whether a register of directors or a register of directors' residential addresses) of the kind in respect of which the election is made.]

NOTES

Inserted as noted to s 167A at **[1.185]**.

[1.188]

[167D Duty to notify registrar of changes

(1) The duty under subsection (2) applies during the period when an election under section 167A is in force.

(2) The company must deliver to the registrar—

(a) any information of which the company would during that period have been obliged to give notice under section 167, had the election not been in force, and

(b) any statement that would have had to accompany such a notice.

(3) The information (and any accompanying statement) must be delivered as soon as reasonably practicable after the company becomes aware of the information and, in any event, no later than the time by which the company would have been required under section 167 to give notice of the information.

(4) If default is made in complying with this section, an offence is committed by—

(a) the company, and

(b) every officer of the company who is in default.

For this purpose a shadow director is treated as an officer of the company.

(5) A person guilty of an offence under this section is liable on summary conviction—

(a) in England and Wales, to a fine and, for continued contravention, a daily default fine not exceeding the greater of £500 and one-tenth of level 4 on the standard scale;

(b) in Scotland or Northern Ireland, to a fine not exceeding level 5 on the standard scale and, for continued contravention, a daily default fine not exceeding one-tenth of level 5 on the standard scale.]

NOTES

Inserted as noted to s 167A at **[1.185]**.

[1.189]

[167E Withdrawing the election

(1) A company may withdraw an election made by or in respect of it under section 167A.

(2) Withdrawal is achieved by giving notice of withdrawal to the registrar.

(3) The withdrawal takes effect when the notice is registered by the registrar.

(4) The effect of withdrawal is that the company's obligation under section 162 or (as the case may be) 165 to keep and maintain a register of the relevant kind, and its obligation under section 167 to notify the registrar of changes to that register, apply from then on with respect to the period going forward.

(5) This means that, when the withdrawal takes effect—

(a) the company must enter in that register all the information that is required to be contained in that register in respect of matters that are current as at that time, but

(b) the company is not required to enter in its register information relating to the period when the election was in force that is no longer current.]

NOTES

Inserted as noted to s 167A at **[1.185]**.

[1.190]

[167F Power to extend option to public companies

(1) The Secretary of State may by regulations amend this Act—

(a) to extend sections 167A to 167E (with or without modification) to public companies or public companies of a class specified in the regulations, and

(b) to make such other amendments as the Secretary of State thinks fit in consequence of that extension.

(2) Regulations under this section are subject to affirmative resolution procedure.]

NOTES

Inserted as noted to s 167A at **[1.185]**.

Removal

[1.191]

168 Resolution to remove director

(1) A company may by ordinary resolution at a meeting remove a director before the expiration of his period of office, notwithstanding anything in any agreement between it and him.

(2) Special notice is required of a resolution to remove a director under this section or to appoint somebody instead of a director so removed at the meeting at which he is removed.

(3) A vacancy created by the removal of a director under this section, if not filled at the meeting at which he is removed, may be filled as a casual vacancy.

(4) A person appointed director in place of a person removed under this section is treated, for the purpose of determining the time at which he or any other director is to retire, as if he had become director on the day on which the person in whose place he is appointed was last appointed a director.

(5) This section is not to be taken—

(a) as depriving a person removed under it of compensation or damages payable to him in respect of the termination of his appointment as director or of any appointment terminating with that as director, or

(b) as derogating from any power to remove a director that may exist apart from this section.

[1.192]

169 Director's right to protest against removal

(1) On receipt of notice of an intended resolution to remove a director under section 168, the company must forthwith send a copy of the notice to the director concerned.

(2) The director (whether or not a member of the company) is entitled to be heard on the resolution at the meeting.

(3) Where notice is given of an intended resolution to remove a director under that section, and the director concerned makes with respect to it representations in writing to the company (not exceeding a reasonable length) and requests their notification to members of the company, the company shall, unless the representations are received by it too late for it to do so—

(a) in any notice of the resolution given to members of the company state the fact of the representations having been made; and

(b) send a copy of the representations to every member of the company to whom notice of the meeting is sent (whether before or after receipt of the representations by the company).

(4) If a copy of the representations is not sent as required by subsection (3) because received too late or because of the company's default, the director may (without prejudice to his right to be heard orally) require that the representations shall be read out at the meeting.

(5) Copies of the representations need not be sent out and the representations need not be read out at the meeting if, on the application either of the company or of any other person who claims to be aggrieved, the court is satisfied that the rights conferred by this section are being abused.

(6) The court may order the company's costs (in Scotland, expenses) on an application under subsection (5) to be paid in whole or in part by the director, notwithstanding that he is not a party to the application.

CHAPTER 2 GENERAL DUTIES OF DIRECTORS

Introductory

[1.193]

170 Scope and nature of general duties

(1) The general duties specified in sections 171 to 177 are owed by a director of a company to the company.

(2) A person who ceases to be a director continues to be subject—

(a) to the duty in section 175 (duty to avoid conflicts of interest) as regards the exploitation of any property, information or opportunity of which he became aware at a time when he was a director, and

(b) to the duty in section 176 (duty not to accept benefits from third parties) as regards things done or omitted by him before he ceased to be a director.

To that extent those duties apply to a former director as to a director, subject to any necessary adaptations.

(3) The general duties are based on certain common law rules and equitable principles as they apply in relation to directors and have effect in place of those rules and principles as regards the duties owed to a company by a director.

(4) The general duties shall be interpreted and applied in the same way as common law rules or equitable principles, and regard shall be had to the corresponding common law rules and equitable principles in interpreting and applying the general duties.

[(5) The general duties apply to a shadow director of a company where and to the extent that they are capable of so applying.]

NOTES

Sub-s (5): substituted by the Small Business, Enterprise and Employment Act 2015, s 89(1), as from 26 May 2015 (see further s 89(2) of the 2015 Act at **[9.523]**).

The general duties

[1.194]

171 Duty to act within powers

A director of a company must—

(a) act in accordance with the company's constitution, and

(b) only exercise powers for the purposes for which they are conferred.

[1.195]

172 Duty to promote the success of the company

(1) A director of a company must act in the way he considers, in good faith, would be most likely to promote the success of the company for the benefit of its members as a whole, and in doing so have regard (amongst other matters) to—

(a) the likely consequences of any decision in the long term,
(b) the interests of the company's employees,
(c) the need to foster the company's business relationships with suppliers, customers and others,
(d) the impact of the company's operations on the community and the environment,
(e) the desirability of the company maintaining a reputation for high standards of business conduct, and
(f) the need to act fairly as between members of the company.

(2) Where or to the extent that the purposes of the company consist of or include purposes other than the benefit of its members, subsection (1) has effect as if the reference to promoting the success of the company for the benefit of its members were to achieving those purposes.

(3) The duty imposed by this section has effect subject to any enactment or rule of law requiring directors, in certain circumstances, to consider or act in the interests of creditors of the company.

[1.196]

173 Duty to exercise independent judgment

(1) A director of a company must exercise independent judgment.

(2) This duty is not infringed by his acting—

(a) in accordance with an agreement duly entered into by the company that restricts the future exercise of discretion by its directors, or
(b) in a way authorised by the company's constitution.

[1.197]

174 Duty to exercise reasonable care, skill and diligence

(1) A director of a company must exercise reasonable care, skill and diligence.

(2) This means the care, skill and diligence that would be exercised by a reasonably diligent person with—

(a) the general knowledge, skill and experience that may reasonably be expected of a person carrying out the functions carried out by the director in relation to the company, and
(b) the general knowledge, skill and experience that the director has.

[1.198]

175 Duty to avoid conflicts of interest

(1) A director of a company must avoid a situation in which he has, or can have, a direct or indirect interest that conflicts, or possibly may conflict, with the interests of the company.

(2) This applies in particular to the exploitation of any property, information or opportunity (and it is immaterial whether the company could take advantage of the property, information or opportunity).

(3) This duty does not apply to a conflict of interest arising in relation to a transaction or arrangement with the company.

(4) This duty is not infringed—

(a) if the situation cannot reasonably be regarded as likely to give rise to a conflict of interest; or
(b) if the matter has been authorised by the directors.

(5) Authorisation may be given by the directors—

(a) where the company is a private company and nothing in the company's constitution invalidates such authorisation, by the matter being proposed to and authorised by the directors; or
(b) where the company is a public company and its constitution includes provision enabling the directors to authorise the matter, by the matter being proposed to and authorised by them in accordance with the constitution.

(6) The authorisation is effective only if—

(a) any requirement as to the quorum at the meeting at which the matter is considered is met without counting the director in question or any other interested director, and
(b) the matter was agreed to without their voting or would have been agreed to if their votes had not been counted.

(7) Any reference in this section to a conflict of interest includes a conflict of interest and duty and a conflict of duties.

[1.199]

176 Duty not to accept benefits from third parties

(1) A director of a company must not accept a benefit from a third party conferred by reason of—

(a) his being a director, or
(b) his doing (or not doing) anything as director.

(2) A "third party" means a person other than the company, an associated body corporate or a person acting on behalf of the company or an associated body corporate.

(3) Benefits received by a director from a person by whom his services (as a director or otherwise) are provided to the company are not regarded as conferred by a third party.

(4) This duty is not infringed if the acceptance of the benefit cannot reasonably be regarded as likely to give rise to a conflict of interest.

(5) Any reference in this section to a conflict of interest includes a conflict of interest and duty and a conflict of duties.

[1.200]

177 Duty to declare interest in proposed transaction or arrangement

(1) If a director of a company is in any way, directly or indirectly, interested in a proposed transaction or arrangement with the company, he must declare the nature and extent of that interest to the other directors.

(2) The declaration may (but need not) be made—

(a) at a meeting of the directors, or

(b) by notice to the directors in accordance with—

(i) section 184 (notice in writing), or

(ii) section 185 (general notice).

(3) If a declaration of interest under this section proves to be, or becomes, inaccurate or incomplete, a further declaration must be made.

(4) Any declaration required by this section must be made before the company enters into the transaction or arrangement.

(5) This section does not require a declaration of an interest of which the director is not aware or where the director is not aware of the transaction or arrangement in question.

For this purpose a director is treated as being aware of matters of which he ought reasonably to be aware.

(6) A director need not declare an interest—

(a) if it cannot reasonably be regarded as likely to give rise to a conflict of interest;

(b) if, or to the extent that, the other directors are already aware of it (and for this purpose the other directors are treated as aware of anything of which they ought reasonably to be aware); or

(c) if, or to the extent that, it concerns terms of his service contract that have been or are to be considered—

(i) by a meeting of the directors, or

(ii) by a committee of the directors appointed for the purpose under the company's constitution.

Supplementary provisions

[1.201]

178 Civil consequences of breach of general duties

(1) The consequences of breach (or threatened breach) of sections 171 to 177 are the same as would apply if the corresponding common law rule or equitable principle applied.

(2) The duties in those sections (with the exception of section 174 (duty to exercise reasonable care, skill and diligence)) are, accordingly, enforceable in the same way as any other fiduciary duty owed to a company by its directors.

[1.202]

179 Cases within more than one of the general duties

Except as otherwise provided, more than one of the general duties may apply in any given case.

[1.203]

180 Consent, approval or authorisation by members

(1) In a case where—

(a) section 175 (duty to avoid conflicts of interest) is complied with by authorisation by the directors, or

(b) section 177 (duty to declare interest in proposed transaction or arrangement) is complied with,

the transaction or arrangement is not liable to be set aside by virtue of any common law rule or equitable principle requiring the consent or approval of the members of the company.

This is without prejudice to any enactment, or provision of the company's constitution, requiring such consent or approval.

(2) The application of the general duties is not affected by the fact that the case also falls within Chapter 4 [or 4A] (transactions requiring approval of members), except that where [either of those Chapters] applies and—

(a) approval is given under [the Chapter concerned], or

(b) the matter is one as to which it is provided that approval is not needed,

it is not necessary also to comply with section 175 (duty to avoid conflicts of interest) or section 176 (duty not to accept benefits from third parties).

(3) Compliance with the general duties does not remove the need for approval under any applicable provision of Chapter 4 [or 4A] (transactions requiring approval of members).

(4) The general duties—

(a) have effect subject to any rule of law enabling the company to give authority, specifically or generally, for anything to be done (or omitted) by the directors, or any of them, that would otherwise be a breach of duty, and

(b) where the company's articles contain provisions for dealing with conflicts of interest, are not infringed by anything done (or omitted) by the directors, or any of them, in accordance with those provisions.

(5) Otherwise, the general duties have effect (except as otherwise provided or the context otherwise requires) notwithstanding any enactment or rule of law.

NOTES

Words in first and third pairs of square brackets in sub-s (2) substituted, and words "or 4A" in square brackets in sub-ss (2) and (3) inserted, by the Enterprise and Regulatory Reform Act 2013, s 81(1), (2), as from 1 October 2013.

[1.204]

181 Modification of provisions in relation to charitable companies

(1) In their application to a company that is a charity, the provisions of this Chapter have effect subject to this section.

(2) Section 175 (duty to avoid conflicts of interest) has effect as if—

(a) for subsection (3) (which disapplies the duty to avoid conflicts of interest in the case of a transaction or arrangement with the company) there were substituted—

"(3) This duty does not apply to a conflict of interest arising in relation to a transaction or arrangement with the company if or to the extent that the company's articles allow that duty to be so disapplied, which they may do only in relation to descriptions of transaction or arrangement specified in the company's articles.";

(b) for subsection (5) (which specifies how directors of a company may give authority under that section for a transaction or arrangement) there were substituted—

"(5) Authorisation may be given by the directors where the company's constitution includes provision enabling them to authorise the matter, by the matter being proposed to and authorised by them in accordance with the constitution.".

(3) Section 180(2)(b) (which disapplies certain duties under this Chapter in relation to cases excepted from requirement to obtain approval by members under Chapter 4) applies only if or to the extent that the company's articles allow those duties to be so disapplied, which they may do only in relation to descriptions of transaction or arrangement specified in the company's articles.

(4) *(Inserted the Charities Act 1993, s 26(5A), and was repealed by the Charities Act 2011, s 354, Sch 10, as from 14 March 2012.)*

(5) This section does not extend to Scotland.

CHAPTER 3 DECLARATION OF INTEREST IN EXISTING TRANSACTION OR ARRANGEMENT

[1.205]

182 Declaration of interest in existing transaction or arrangement

(1) Where a director of a company is in any way, directly or indirectly, interested in a transaction or arrangement that has been entered into by the company, he must declare the nature and extent of the interest to the other directors in accordance with this section.

This section does not apply if or to the extent that the interest has been declared under section 177 (duty to declare interest in proposed transaction or arrangement).

(2) The declaration must be made—

(a) at a meeting of the directors, or

(b) by notice in writing (see section 184), or

(c) by general notice (see section 185).

(3) If a declaration of interest under this section proves to be, or becomes, inaccurate or incomplete, a further declaration must be made.

(4) Any declaration required by this section must be made as soon as is reasonably practicable.

Failure to comply with this requirement does not affect the underlying duty to make the declaration.

(5) This section does not require a declaration of an interest of which the director is not aware or where the director is not aware of the transaction or arrangement in question.

For this purpose a director is treated as being aware of matters of which he ought reasonably to be aware.

(6) A director need not declare an interest under this section—

(a) if it cannot reasonably be regarded as likely to give rise to a conflict of interest;

(b) if, or to the extent that, the other directors are already aware of it (and for this purpose the other directors are treated as aware of anything of which they ought reasonably to be aware); or

(c) if, or to the extent that, it concerns terms of his service contract that have been or are to be considered—

(i) by a meeting of the directors, or

(ii) by a committee of the directors appointed for the purpose under the company's constitution.

[1.206]

183 Offence of failure to declare interest

(1) A director who fails to comply with the requirements of section 182 (declaration of interest in existing transaction or arrangement) commits an offence.

(2) A person guilty of an offence under this section is liable—

(a) on conviction on indictment, to a fine;

(b) on summary conviction, to a fine not exceeding the statutory maximum.

[1.207]

184 Declaration made by notice in writing

(1) This section applies to a declaration of interest made by notice in writing.

(2) The director must send the notice to the other directors.

(3) The notice may be sent in hard copy form or, if the recipient has agreed to receive it in electronic form, in an agreed electronic form.

(4) The notice may be sent—

(a) by hand or by post, or

(b) if the recipient has agreed to receive it by electronic means, by agreed electronic means.

(5) Where a director declares an interest by notice in writing in accordance with this section—

(a) the making of the declaration is deemed to form part of the proceedings at the next meeting of the directors after the notice is given, and

(b) the provisions of section 248 (minutes of meetings of directors) apply as if the declaration had been made at that meeting.

[1.208]

185 General notice treated as sufficient declaration

(1) General notice in accordance with this section is a sufficient declaration of interest in relation to the matters to which it relates.

(2) General notice is notice given to the directors of a company to the effect that the director—

(a) has an interest (as member, officer, employee or otherwise) in a specified body corporate or firm and is to be regarded as interested in any transaction or arrangement that may, after the date of the notice, be made with that body corporate or firm, or

(b) is connected with a specified person (other than a body corporate or firm) and is to be regarded as interested in any transaction or arrangement that may, after the date of the notice, be made with that person.

(3) The notice must state the nature and extent of the director's interest in the body corporate or firm or, as the case may be, the nature of his connection with the person.

(4) General notice is not effective unless—

(a) it is given at a meeting of the directors, or

(b) the director takes reasonable steps to secure that it is brought up and read at the next meeting of the directors after it is given.

[1.209]
186 Declaration of interest in case of company with sole director

(1) Where a declaration of interest under section 182 (duty to declare interest in existing transaction or arrangement) is required of a sole director of a company that is required to have more than one director—

(a) the declaration must be recorded in writing,

(b) the making of the declaration is deemed to form part of the proceedings at the next meeting of the directors after the notice is given, and

(c) the provisions of section 248 (minutes of meetings of directors) apply as if the declaration had been made at that meeting.

(2) Nothing in this section affects the operation of section 231 (contract with sole member who is also a director: terms to be set out in writing or recorded in minutes).

[1.210]
187 Declaration of interest in existing transaction by shadow director

(1) The provisions of this Chapter relating to the duty under section 182 (duty to declare interest in existing transaction or arrangement) apply to a shadow director as to a director, but with the following adaptations.

(2) Subsection (2)(a) of that section (declaration at meeting of directors) does not apply.

(3) In section 185 (general notice treated as sufficient declaration), subsection (4) (notice to be given at or brought up and read at meeting of directors) does not apply.

(4) General notice by a shadow director is not effective unless given by notice in writing in accordance with section 184.

CHAPTER 4 TRANSACTIONS WITH DIRECTORS REQUIRING APPROVAL OF MEMBERS

Service contracts

[1.211]
188 Directors' long-term service contracts: requirement of members' approval

(1) This section applies to provision under which the guaranteed term of a director's employment—

(a) with the company of which he is a director, or

(b) where he is the director of a holding company, within the group consisting of that company and its subsidiaries,

is, or may be, longer than two years.

(2) A company may not agree to such provision unless it has been approved—

(a) by resolution of the members of the company, and

(b) in the case of a director of a holding company, by resolution of the members of that company.

(3) The guaranteed term of a director's employment is—

(a) the period (if any) during which the director's employment—

(i) is to continue, or may be continued otherwise than at the instance of the company (whether under the original agreement or under a new agreement entered into in pursuance of it), and

(ii) cannot be terminated by the company by notice, or can be so terminated only in specified circumstances, or

(b) in the case of employment terminable by the company by notice, the period of notice required to be given,

or, in the case of employment having a period within paragraph (a) and a period within paragraph (b), the aggregate of those periods.

(4) If more than six months before the end of the guaranteed term of a director's employment the company enters into a further service contract (otherwise than in pursuance of a right conferred, by or under the original contract, on the other party to it), this section applies as if there were added to the guaranteed term of the new contract the unexpired period of the guaranteed term of the original contract.

(5) A resolution approving provision to which this section applies must not be passed unless a memorandum setting out the proposed contract incorporating the provision is made available to members—

(a) in the case of a written resolution, by being sent or submitted to every eligible member at or before the time at which the proposed resolution is sent or submitted to him;

(b) in the case of a resolution at a meeting, by being made available for inspection by members of the company both—

(i) at the company's registered office for not less than 15 days ending with the date of the meeting, and

(ii) at the meeting itself.

(6) No approval is required under this section on the part of the members of a body corporate that—

(a) is not a UK-registered company, or

(b) is a wholly-owned subsidiary of another body corporate.

(7) In this section "employment" means any employment under a director's service contract.

[1.212]

189 Directors' long-term service contracts: civil consequences of contravention

If a company agrees to provision in contravention of section 188 (directors' long-term service contracts: requirement of members' approval)—

(a) the provision is void, to the extent of the contravention, and

(b) the contract is deemed to contain a term entitling the company to terminate it at any time by the giving of reasonable notice.

Substantial property transactions

[1.213]

190 Substantial property transactions: requirement of members' approval

(1) A company may not enter into an arrangement under which—

(a) a director of the company or of its holding company, or a person connected with such a director, acquires or is to acquire from the company (directly or indirectly) a substantial non-cash asset, or

(b) the company acquires or is to acquire a substantial non-cash asset (directly or indirectly) from such a director or a person so connected,

unless the arrangement has been approved by a resolution of the members of the company or is conditional on such approval being obtained.

For the meaning of "substantial non-cash asset" see section 191.

(2) If the director or connected person is a director of the company's holding company or a person connected with such a director, the arrangement must also have been approved by a resolution of the members of the holding company or be conditional on such approval being obtained.

(3) A company shall not be subject to any liability by reason of a failure to obtain approval required by this section.

(4) No approval is required under this section on the part of the members of a body corporate that—

(a) is not a UK-registered company, or

(b) is a wholly-owned subsidiary of another body corporate.

(5) For the purposes of this section—

(a) an arrangement involving more than one non-cash asset, or

(b) an arrangement that is one of a series involving non-cash assets,

shall be treated as if they involved a non-cash asset of a value equal to the aggregate value of all the non-cash assets involved in the arrangement or, as the case may be, the series.

(6) This section does not apply to a transaction so far as it relates—

(a) to anything to which a director of a company is entitled under his service contract, or

(b) to payment for loss of office as defined in section 215 [(payments to which the requirements of Chapter 4 or 4A apply)].

NOTES

Sub-s (6): words in square brackets substituted by the Enterprise and Regulatory Reform Act 2013, s 81(1), (3), as from 1 October 2013.

[1.214]

191 Meaning of "substantial"

(1) This section explains what is meant in section 190 (requirement of approval for substantial property transactions) by a "substantial" non-cash asset.

(2) An asset is a substantial asset in relation to a company if its value—

(a) exceeds 10% of the company's asset value and is more than £5,000, or

(b) exceeds £100,000.

(3) For this purpose a company's "asset value" at any time is—

(a) the value of the company's net assets determined by reference to its most recent statutory accounts, or

(b) if no statutory accounts have been prepared, the amount of the company's called-up share capital.

(4) A company's "statutory accounts" means its annual accounts prepared in accordance with Part 15, and its "most recent" statutory accounts means those in relation to which the time for sending them out to members (see section 424) is most recent.

(5) Whether an asset is a substantial asset shall be determined as at the time the arrangement is entered into.

[1.215]

192 Exception for transactions with members or other group companies

Approval is not required under section 190 (requirement of members' approval for substantial property transactions)—

(a) for a transaction between a company and a person in his character as a member of that company, or

(b) for a transaction between—

(i) a holding company and its wholly-owned subsidiary, or

(ii) two wholly-owned subsidiaries of the same holding company.

[1.216]

193 Exception in case of company in winding up or administration

(1) This section applies to a company—

(a) that is being wound up (unless the winding up is a members' voluntary winding up), or

(b) that is in administration within the meaning of Schedule B1 to the Insolvency Act 1986 (c 45) or the Insolvency (Northern Ireland) Order 1989 (SI 1989/2405 (NI 19)).

(2) Approval is not required under section 190 (requirement of members' approval for substantial property transactions)—

(a) on the part of the members of a company to which this section applies, or

(b) for an arrangement entered into by a company to which this section applies.

[1.217]

194 Exception for transactions on recognised investment exchange

(1) Approval is not required under section 190 (requirement of members' approval for substantial property transactions) for a transaction on a recognised investment exchange effected by a director, or a person connected with him, through the agency of a person who in relation to the transaction acts as an independent broker.

(2) For this purpose—

(a) "independent broker" means a person who, independently of the director or any person connected with him, selects the person with whom the transaction is to be effected; and

(b) "recognised investment exchange" has the same meaning as in Part 18 of the Financial Services and Markets Act 2000 (c 8).

[1.218]

195 Property transactions: civil consequences of contravention

(1) This section applies where a company enters into an arrangement in contravention of section 190 (requirement of members' approval for substantial property transactions).

(2) The arrangement, and any transaction entered into in pursuance of the arrangement (whether by the company or any other person), is voidable at the instance of the company, unless—

(a) restitution of any money or other asset that was the subject matter of the arrangement or transaction is no longer possible,

(b) the company has been indemnified in pursuance of this section by any other persons for the loss or damage suffered by it, or

(c) rights acquired in good faith, for value and without actual notice of the contravention by a person who is not a party to the arrangement or transaction would be affected by the avoidance.

(3) Whether or not the arrangement or any such transaction has been avoided, each of the persons specified in subsection (4) is liable—

(a) to account to the company for any gain that he has made directly or indirectly by the arrangement or transaction, and

(b) (jointly and severally with any other person so liable under this section) to indemnify the company for any loss or damage resulting from the arrangement or transaction.

(4) The persons so liable are—

(a) any director of the company or of its holding company with whom the company entered into the arrangement in contravention of section 190,

(b) any person with whom the company entered into the arrangement in contravention of that section who is connected with a director of the company or of its holding company,

(c) the director of the company or of its holding company with whom any such person is connected, and

(d) any other director of the company who authorised the arrangement or any transaction entered into in pursuance of such an arrangement.

(5) Subsections (3) and (4) are subject to the following two subsections.

(6) In the case of an arrangement entered into by a company in contravention of section 190 with a person connected with a director of the company or of its holding company, that director is not liable by virtue of subsection (4)(c) if he shows that he took all reasonable steps to secure the company's compliance with that section.

(7) In any case—

(a) a person so connected is not liable by virtue of subsection (4)(b), and

(b) a director is not liable by virtue of subsection (4)(d),

if he shows that, at the time the arrangement was entered into, he did not know the relevant circumstances constituting the contravention.

(8) Nothing in this section shall be read as excluding the operation of any other enactment or rule of law by virtue of which the arrangement or transaction may be called in question or any liability to the company may arise.

[1.219]

196 Property transactions: effect of subsequent affirmation

Where a transaction or arrangement is entered into by a company in contravention of section 190 (requirement of members' approval) but, within a reasonable period, it is affirmed—

(a) in the case of a contravention of subsection (1) of that section, by resolution of the members of the company, and

(b) in the case of a contravention of subsection (2) of that section, by resolution of the members of the holding company,

the transaction or arrangement may no longer be avoided under section 195.

Loans, quasi-loans and credit transactions

[1.220]

197 Loans to directors: requirement of members' approval

(1) A company may not—

(a) make a loan to a director of the company or of its holding company, or

(b) give a guarantee or provide security in connection with a loan made by any person to such a director,

unless the transaction has been approved by a resolution of the members of the company.

(2) If the director is a director of the company's holding company, the transaction must also have been approved by a resolution of the members of the holding company.

(3) A resolution approving a transaction to which this section applies must not be passed unless a memorandum setting out the matters mentioned in subsection (4) is made available to members—

(a) in the case of a written resolution, by being sent or submitted to every eligible member at or before the time at which the proposed resolution is sent or submitted to him;

(b) in the case of a resolution at a meeting, by being made available for inspection by members of the company both—

(i) at the company's registered office for not less than 15 days ending with the date of the meeting, and
(ii) at the meeting itself.

(4) The matters to be disclosed are—
(a) the nature of the transaction,
(b) the amount of the loan and the purpose for which it is required, and
(c) the extent of the company's liability under any transaction connected with the loan.

(5) No approval is required under this section on the part of the members of a body corporate that—
(a) is not a UK-registered company, or
(b) is a wholly-owned subsidiary of another body corporate.

[1.221]
198 Quasi-loans to directors: requirement of members' approval

(1) This section applies to a company if it is—
(a) a public company, or
(b) a company associated with a public company.

(2) A company to which this section applies may not—
(a) make a quasi-loan to a director of the company or of its holding company, or
(b) give a guarantee or provide security in connection with a quasi-loan made by any person to such a director,

unless the transaction has been approved by a resolution of the members of the company.

(3) If the director is a director of the company's holding company, the transaction must also have been approved by a resolution of the members of the holding company.

(4) A resolution approving a transaction to which this section applies must not be passed unless a memorandum setting out the matters mentioned in subsection (5) is made available to members—
(a) in the case of a written resolution, by being sent or submitted to every eligible member at or before the time at which the proposed resolution is sent or submitted to him;
(b) in the case of a resolution at a meeting, by being made available for inspection by members of the company both—
(i) at the company's registered office for not less than 15 days ending with the date of the meeting, and
(ii) at the meeting itself.

(5) The matters to be disclosed are—
(a) the nature of the transaction,
(b) the amount of the quasi-loan and the purpose for which it is required, and
(c) the extent of the company's liability under any transaction connected with the quasi-loan.

(6) No approval is required under this section on the part of the members of a body corporate that—
(a) is not a UK-registered company, or
(b) is a wholly-owned subsidiary of another body corporate.

[1.222]
199 Meaning of "quasi-loan" and related expressions

(1) A "quasi-loan" is a transaction under which one party ("the creditor") agrees to pay, or pays otherwise than in pursuance of an agreement, a sum for another ("the borrower") or agrees to reimburse, or reimburses otherwise than in pursuance of an agreement, expenditure incurred by another party for another ("the borrower")—
(a) on terms that the borrower (or a person on his behalf) will reimburse the creditor; or
(b) in circumstances giving rise to a liability on the borrower to reimburse the creditor.

(2) Any reference to the person to whom a quasi-loan is made is a reference to the borrower.

(3) The liabilities of the borrower under a quasi-loan include the liabilities of any person who has agreed to reimburse the creditor on behalf of the borrower.

[1.223]
200 Loans or quasi-loans to persons connected with directors: requirement of members' approval

(1) This section applies to a company if it is—
(a) a public company, or
(b) a company associated with a public company.

(2) A company to which this section applies may not—
(a) make a loan or quasi-loan to a person connected with a director of the company or of its holding company, or
(b) give a guarantee or provide security in connection with a loan or quasi-loan made by any person to a person connected with such a director,

unless the transaction has been approved by a resolution of the members of the company.

(3) If the connected person is a person connected with a director of the company's holding company, the transaction must also have been approved by a resolution of the members of the holding company.

(4) A resolution approving a transaction to which this section applies must not be passed unless a memorandum setting out the matters mentioned in subsection (5) is made available to members—
(a) in the case of a written resolution, by being sent or submitted to every eligible member at or before the time at which the proposed resolution is sent or submitted to him;
(b) in the case of a resolution at a meeting, by being made available for inspection by members of the company both—
(i) at the company's registered office for not less than 15 days ending with the date of the meeting, and
(ii) at the meeting itself.

(5) The matters to be disclosed are—
(a) the nature of the transaction,
(b) the amount of the loan or quasi-loan and the purpose for which it is required, and
(c) the extent of the company's liability under any transaction connected with the loan or quasi-loan.

(6) No approval is required under this section on the part of the members of a body corporate that—
(a) is not a UK-registered company, or

(b) is a wholly-owned subsidiary of another body corporate.

[1.224]
201 Credit transactions: requirement of members' approval

(1) This section applies to a company if it is—
  (a) a public company, or
  (b) a company associated with a public company.
(2) A company to which this section applies may not—
  (a) enter into a credit transaction as creditor for the benefit of a director of the company or of its holding company, or a person connected with such a director, or
  (b) give a guarantee or provide security in connection with a credit transaction entered into by any person for the benefit of such a director, or a person connected with such a director,

unless the transaction (that is, the credit transaction, the giving of the guarantee or the provision of security, as the case may be) has been approved by a resolution of the members of the company.

(3) If the director or connected person is a director of its holding company or a person connected with such a director, the transaction must also have been approved by a resolution of the members of the holding company.
(4) A resolution approving a transaction to which this section applies must not be passed unless a memorandum setting out the matters mentioned in subsection (5) is made available to members—
  (a) in the case of a written resolution, by being sent or submitted to every eligible member at or before the time at which the proposed resolution is sent or submitted to him;
  (b) in the case of a resolution at a meeting, by being made available for inspection by members of the company both—
    (i) at the company's registered office for not less than 15 days ending with the date of the meeting, and
    (ii) at the meeting itself.
(5) The matters to be disclosed are—
  (a) the nature of the transaction,
  (b) the value of the credit transaction and the purpose for which the land, goods or services sold or otherwise disposed of, leased, hired or supplied under the credit transaction are required, and
  (c) the extent of the company's liability under any transaction connected with the credit transaction.
(6) No approval is required under this section on the part of the members of a body corporate that—
  (a) is not a UK-registered company, or
  (b) is a wholly-owned subsidiary of another body corporate.

[1.225]
202 Meaning of "credit transaction"

(1) A "credit transaction" is a transaction under which one party ("the creditor")—
  (a) supplies any goods or sells any land under a hire-purchase agreement or a conditional sale agreement,
  (b) leases or hires any land or goods in return for periodical payments, or
  (c) otherwise disposes of land or supplies goods or services on the understanding that payment (whether in a lump sum or instalments or by way of periodical payments or otherwise) is to be deferred.
(2) Any reference to the person for whose benefit a credit transaction is entered into is to the person to whom goods, land or services are supplied, sold, leased, hired or otherwise disposed of under the transaction.
(3) In this section—
  "conditional sale agreement" has the same meaning as in the Consumer Credit Act 1974 (c 39); and
  "services" means anything other than goods or land.

[1.226]
203 Related arrangements: requirement of members' approval

(1) A company may not—
  (a) take part in an arrangement under which—
    (i) another person enters into a transaction that, if it had been entered into by the company, would have required approval under section 197, 198, 200 or 201, and
    (ii) that person, in pursuance of the arrangement, obtains a benefit from the company or a body corporate associated with it, or
  (b) arrange for the assignment to it, or assumption by it, of any rights, obligations or liabilities under a transaction that, if it had been entered into by the company, would have required such approval,

unless the arrangement in question has been approved by a resolution of the members of the company.

(2) If the director or connected person for whom the transaction is entered into is a director of its holding company or a person connected with such a director, the arrangement must also have been approved by a resolution of the members of the holding company.
(3) A resolution approving an arrangement to which this section applies must not be passed unless a memorandum setting out the matters mentioned in subsection (4) is made available to members—
  (a) in the case of a written resolution, by being sent or submitted to every eligible member at or before the time at which the proposed resolution is sent or submitted to him;
  (b) in the case of a resolution at a meeting, by being made available for inspection by members of the company both—
    (i) at the company's registered office for not less than 15 days ending with the date of the meeting, and
    (ii) at the meeting itself.
(4) The matters to be disclosed are—
  (a) the matters that would have to be disclosed if the company were seeking approval of the transaction to which the arrangement relates,
  (b) the nature of the arrangement, and
  (c) the extent of the company's liability under the arrangement or any transaction connected with it.
(5) No approval is required under this section on the part of the members of a body corporate that—

(a) is not a UK-registered company, or
(b) is a wholly-owned subsidiary of another body corporate.

(6) In determining for the purposes of this section whether a transaction is one that would have required approval under section 197, 198, 200 or 201 if it had been entered into by the company, the transaction shall be treated as having been entered into on the date of the arrangement.

[1.227]
204 Exception for expenditure on company business

(1) Approval is not required under section 197, 198, 200 or 201 (requirement of members' approval for loans etc) for anything done by a company—

(a) to provide a director of the company or of its holding company, or a person connected with any such director, with funds to meet expenditure incurred or to be incurred by him—
   (i) for the purposes of the company, or
   (ii) for the purpose of enabling him properly to perform his duties as an officer of the company, or
(b) to enable any such person to avoid incurring such expenditure.

(2) This section does not authorise a company to enter into a transaction if the aggregate of—

(a) the value of the transaction in question, and
(b) the value of any other relevant transactions or arrangements,

exceeds £50,000.

[1.228]
205 Exception for expenditure on defending proceedings etc

(1) Approval is not required under section 197, 198, 200 or 201 (requirement of members' approval for loans etc) for anything done by a company—

(a) to provide a director of the company or of its holding company with funds to meet expenditure incurred or to be incurred by him—
   (i) in defending any criminal or civil proceedings in connection with any alleged negligence, default, breach of duty or breach of trust by him in relation to the company or an associated company, or
   (ii) in connection with an application for relief (see subsection (5)), or
(b) to enable any such director to avoid incurring such expenditure,

if it is done on the following terms.

(2) The terms are—

(a) that the loan is to be repaid, or (as the case may be) any liability of the company incurred under any transaction connected with the thing done is to be discharged, in the event of—
   (i) the director being convicted in the proceedings,
   (ii) judgment being given against him in the proceedings, or
   (iii) the court refusing to grant him relief on the application; and
(b) that it is to be so repaid or discharged not later than—
   (i) the date when the conviction becomes final,
   (ii) the date when the judgment becomes final, or
   (iii) the date when the refusal of relief becomes final.

(3) For this purpose a conviction, judgment or refusal of relief becomes final—

(a) if not appealed against, at the end of the period for bringing an appeal;
(b) if appealed against, when the appeal (or any further appeal) is disposed of.

(4) An appeal is disposed of—

(a) if it is determined and the period for bringing any further appeal has ended, or
(b) if it is abandoned or otherwise ceases to have effect.

(5) The reference in subsection (1)(a)(ii) to an application for relief is to an application for relief under—

section 661(3) or (4) (power of court to grant relief in case of acquisition of shares by innocent nominee), or
section 1157 (general power of court to grant relief in case of honest and reasonable conduct).

[1.229]
206 Exception for expenditure in connection with regulatory action or investigation

Approval is not required under section 197, 198, 200 or 201 (requirement of members' approval for loans etc) for anything done by a company—

(a) to provide a director of the company or of its holding company with funds to meet expenditure incurred or to be incurred by him in defending himself—
   (i) in an investigation by a regulatory authority, or
   (ii) against action proposed to be taken by a regulatory authority,

   in connection with any alleged negligence, default, breach of duty or breach of trust by him in relation to the company or an associated company, or
(b) to enable any such director to avoid incurring such expenditure.

[1.230]
207 Exceptions for minor and business transactions

(1) Approval is not required under section 197, 198 or 200 for a company to make a loan or quasi-loan, or to give a guarantee or provide security in connection with a loan or quasi-loan, if the aggregate of—

(a) the value of the transaction, and
(b) the value of any other relevant transactions or arrangements,

does not exceed £10,000.

(2) Approval is not required under section 201 for a company to enter into a credit transaction, or to give a guarantee or provide security in connection with a credit transaction, if the aggregate of—

(a) the value of the transaction (that is, of the credit transaction, guarantee or security), and
(b) the value of any other relevant transactions or arrangements,

does not exceed £15,000.

(3) Approval is not required under section 201 for a company to enter into a credit transaction, or to give a guarantee or provide security in connection with a credit transaction, if—

(a) the transaction is entered into by the company in the ordinary course of the company's business, and

(b) the value of the transaction is not greater, and the terms on which it is entered into are not more favourable, than it is reasonable to expect the company would have offered to, or in respect of, a person of the same financial standing but unconnected with the company.

[1.231]

208 Exceptions for intra-group transactions

(1) Approval is not required under section 197, 198 or 200 for—

(a) the making of a loan or quasi-loan to an associated body corporate, or

(b) the giving of a guarantee or provision of security in connection with a loan or quasi-loan made to an associated body corporate.

(2) Approval is not required under section 201—

(a) to enter into a credit transaction as creditor for the benefit of an associated body corporate, or

(b) to give a guarantee or provide security in connection with a credit transaction entered into by any person for the benefit of an associated body corporate.

[1.232]

209 Exceptions for money-lending companies

(1) Approval is not required under section 197, 198 or 200 for the making of a loan or quasi-loan, or the giving of a guarantee or provision of security in connection with a loan or quasi-loan, by a money-lending company if—

(a) the transaction (that is, the loan, quasi-loan, guarantee or security) is entered into by the company in the ordinary course of the company's business, and

(b) the value of the transaction is not greater, and its terms are not more favourable, than it is reasonable to expect the company would have offered to a person of the same financial standing but unconnected with the company.

(2) A "money-lending company" means a company whose ordinary business includes the making of loans or quasi-loans, or the giving of guarantees or provision of security in connection with loans or quasi-loans.

(3) The condition specified in subsection (1)(b) does not of itself prevent a company from making a home loan—

(a) to a director of the company or of its holding company, or

(b) to an employee of the company,

if loans of that description are ordinarily made by the company to its employees and the terms of the loan in question are no more favourable than those on which such loans are ordinarily made.

(4) For the purposes of subsection (3) a "home loan" means a loan—

(a) for the purpose of facilitating the purchase, for use as the only or main residence of the person to whom the loan is made, of the whole or part of any dwelling-house together with any land to be occupied and enjoyed with it,

(b) for the purpose of improving a dwelling-house or part of a dwelling-house so used or any land occupied and enjoyed with it, or

(c) in substitution for any loan made by any person and falling within paragraph (a) or (b).

[1.233]

210 Other relevant transactions or arrangements

(1) This section has effect for determining what are "other relevant transactions or arrangements" for the purposes of any exception to section 197, 198, 200 or 201. In the following provisions "the relevant exception" means the exception for the purposes of which that falls to be determined.

(2) Other relevant transactions or arrangements are those previously entered into, or entered into at the same time as the transaction or arrangement in question in relation to which the following conditions are met.

(3) Where the transaction or arrangement in question is entered into—

(a) for a director of the company entering into it, or

(b) for a person connected with such a director,

the conditions are that the transaction or arrangement was (or is) entered into for that director, or a person connected with him, by virtue of the relevant exception by that company or by any of its subsidiaries.

(4) Where the transaction or arrangement in question is entered into—

(a) for a director of the holding company of the company entering into it, or

(b) for a person connected with such a director,

the conditions are that the transaction or arrangement was (or is) entered into for that director, or a person connected with him, by virtue of the relevant exception by the holding company or by any of its subsidiaries.

(5) A transaction or arrangement entered into by a company that at the time it was entered into—

(a) was a subsidiary of the company entering into the transaction or arrangement in question, or

(b) was a subsidiary of that company's holding company,

is not a relevant transaction or arrangement if, at the time the question arises whether the transaction or arrangement in question falls within a relevant exception, it is no longer such a subsidiary.

[1.234]

211 The value of transactions and arrangements

(1) For the purposes of sections 197 to 214 (loans etc)—

(a) the value of a transaction or arrangement is determined as follows, and

(b) the value of any other relevant transaction or arrangement is taken to be the value so determined reduced by any amount by which the liabilities of the person for whom the transaction or arrangement was made have been reduced.

(2) The value of a loan is the amount of its principal.

(3) The value of a quasi-loan is the amount, or maximum amount, that the person to whom the quasi-loan is made is liable to reimburse the creditor.

(4) The value of a credit transaction is the price that it is reasonable to expect could be obtained for the goods, services or land to which the transaction relates if they had been supplied (at the time the transaction is entered into) in the ordinary course of business and on the same terms (apart from price) as they have been supplied, or are to be supplied, under the transaction in question.
(5) The value of a guarantee or security is the amount guaranteed or secured.
(6) The value of an arrangement to which section 203 (related arrangements) applies is the value of the transaction to which the arrangement relates.
(7) If the value of a transaction or arrangement is not capable of being expressed as a specific sum of money—
- (a) whether because the amount of any liability arising under the transaction or arrangement is unascertainable, or for any other reason, and
- (b) whether or not any liability under the transaction or arrangement has been reduced,

its value is deemed to exceed £50,000.

[1.235]
212 The person for whom a transaction or arrangement is entered into
For the purposes of sections 197 to 214 (loans etc) the person for whom a transaction or arrangement is entered into is—
- (a) in the case of a loan or quasi-loan, the person to whom it is made;
- (b) in the case of a credit transaction, the person to whom goods, land or services are supplied, sold, hired, leased or otherwise disposed of under the transaction;
- (c) in the case of a guarantee or security, the person for whom the transaction is made in connection with which the guarantee or security is entered into;
- (d) in the case of an arrangement within section 203 (related arrangements), the person for whom the transaction is made to which the arrangement relates.

[1.236]
213 Loans etc: civil consequences of contravention
(1) This section applies where a company enters into a transaction or arrangement in contravention of section 197, 198, 200, 201 or 203 (requirement of members' approval for loans etc).
(2) The transaction or arrangement is voidable at the instance of the company, unless—
- (a) restitution of any money or other asset that was the subject matter of the transaction or arrangement is no longer possible,
- (b) the company has been indemnified for any loss or damage resulting from the transaction or arrangement, or
- (c) rights acquired in good faith, for value and without actual notice of the contravention by a person who is not a party to the transaction or arrangement would be affected by the avoidance.

(3) Whether or not the transaction or arrangement has been avoided, each of the persons specified in subsection (4) is liable—
- (a) to account to the company for any gain that he has made directly or indirectly by the transaction or arrangement, and
- (b) (jointly and severally with any other person so liable under this section) to indemnify the company for any loss or damage resulting from the transaction or arrangement.

(4) The persons so liable are—
- (a) any director of the company or of its holding company with whom the company entered into the transaction or arrangement in contravention of section 197, 198, 201 or 203,
- (b) any person with whom the company entered into the transaction or arrangement in contravention of any of those sections who is connected with a director of the company or of its holding company,
- (c) the director of the company or of its holding company with whom any such person is connected, and
- (d) any other director of the company who authorised the transaction or arrangement.

(5) Subsections (3) and (4) are subject to the following two subsections.
(6) In the case of a transaction or arrangement entered into by a company in contravention of section 200, 201 or 203 with a person connected with a director of the company or of its holding company, that director is not liable by virtue of subsection (4)(c) if he shows that he took all reasonable steps to secure the company's compliance with the section concerned.
(7) In any case—
- (a) a person so connected is not liable by virtue of subsection (4)(b), and
- (b) a director is not liable by virtue of subsection (4)(d),

if he shows that, at the time the transaction or arrangement was entered into, he did not know the relevant circumstances constituting the contravention.
(8) Nothing in this section shall be read as excluding the operation of any other enactment or rule of law by virtue of which the transaction or arrangement may be called in question or any liability to the company may arise.

[1.237]
214 Loans etc: effect of subsequent affirmation
Where a transaction or arrangement is entered into by a company in contravention of section 197, 198, 200, 201 or 203 (requirement of members' approval for loans etc) but, within a reasonable period, it is affirmed—
- (a) in the case of a contravention of the requirement for a resolution of the members of the company, by a resolution of the members of the company, and
- (b) in the case of a contravention of the requirement for a resolution of the members of the company's holding company, by a resolution of the members of the holding company,

the transaction or arrangement may no longer be avoided under section 213.

[1.238]

215 Payments for loss of office

(1) In this Chapter a "payment for loss of office" means a payment made to a director or past director of a company—

(a) by way of compensation for loss of office as director of the company,

(b) by way of compensation for loss, while director of the company or in connection with his ceasing to be a director of it, of—

(i) any other office or employment in connection with the management of the affairs of the company, or

(ii) any office (as director or otherwise) or employment in connection with the management of the affairs of any subsidiary undertaking of the company,

(c) as consideration for or in connection with his retirement from his office as director of the company, or

(d) as consideration for or in connection with his retirement, while director of the company or in connection with his ceasing to be a director of it, from—

(i) any other office or employment in connection with the management of the affairs of the company, or

(ii) any office (as director or otherwise) or employment in connection with the management of the affairs of any subsidiary undertaking of the company.

(2) The references to compensation and consideration include benefits otherwise than in cash and references in this Chapter to payment have a corresponding meaning.

(3) For the purposes of sections 217 to 221 (payments requiring members' approval)—

(a) payment to a person connected with a director, or

(b) payment to any person at the direction of, or for the benefit of, a director or a person connected with him,

is treated as payment to the director.

(4) References in those sections to payment by a person include payment by another person at the direction of, or on behalf of, the person referred to.

[(5) Nothing in this section or sections 216 to 222 applies in relation to a payment for loss of office to a director of a quoted company [or unquoted traded company] other than a payment to which section 226C does not apply by virtue of section 226D(6).]

[(6) "Unquoted traded company" means a traded company (as defined by section 360C) that is not a quoted company.]

NOTES

Sub-s (5): added by the Enterprise and Regulatory Reform Act 2013, s 81(1), (4), as from 1 October 2013; for transitional provisions see s 82(3)–(5) of the 2013 Act at **[1.238]**. Words in square brackets inserted by the Companies (Directors' Remuneration Policy and Directors' Remuneration Report) Regulations 2019, SI 2019/970, regs 3, 4(a), as from 10 June 2019 (for transitional provisions, etc, see reg 2 of the 2019 Regulations at **[4.680]**).

Sub-s (6): added by SI 2019/970, regs 3, 4(b), as from 10 June 2019 (for transitional provisions, etc, see reg 2 of the 2019 Regulations at **[4.680]**).

[1.239]

216 Amounts taken to be payments for loss of office

(1) This section applies where in connection with any such transfer as is mentioned in section 218 or 219 (payment in connection with transfer of undertaking, property or shares) a director of the company—

(a) is to cease to hold office, or

(b) is to cease to be the holder of—

(i) any other office or employment in connection with the management of the affairs of the company, or

(ii) any office (as director or otherwise) or employment in connection with the management of the affairs of any subsidiary undertaking of the company.

(2) If in connection with any such transfer—

(a) the price to be paid to the director for any shares in the company held by him is in excess of the price which could at the time have been obtained by other holders of like shares, or

(b) any valuable consideration is given to the director by a person other than the company,

the excess or, as the case may be, the money value of the consideration is taken for the purposes of those sections to have been a payment for loss of office.

[1.240]

217 Payment by company: requirement of members' approval

(1) A company may not make a payment for loss of office to a director of the company unless the payment has been approved by a resolution of the members of the company.

(2) A company may not make a payment for loss of office to a director of its holding company unless the payment has been approved by a resolution of the members of each of those companies.

(3) A resolution approving a payment to which this section applies must not be passed unless a memorandum setting out particulars of the proposed payment (including its amount) is made available to the members of the company whose approval is sought—

(a) in the case of a written resolution, by being sent or submitted to every eligible member at or before the time at which the proposed resolution is sent or submitted to him;

(b) in the case of a resolution at a meeting, by being made available for inspection by the members both—

(i) at the company's registered office for not less than 15 days ending with the date of the meeting, and

(ii) at the meeting itself.

(4) No approval is required under this section on the part of the members of a body corporate that—

(a) is not a UK-registered company, or

(b) is a wholly-owned subsidiary of another body corporate.

[1.241]

218 Payment in connection with transfer of undertaking etc: requirement of members' approval

(1) No payment for loss of office may be made by any person to a director of a company in connection with the transfer of the whole or any part of the undertaking or property of the company unless the payment has been approved by a resolution of the members of the company.

(2) No payment for loss of office may be made by any person to a director of a company in connection with the transfer of the whole or any part of the undertaking or property of a subsidiary of the company unless the payment has been approved by a resolution of the members of each of the companies.

(3) A resolution approving a payment to which this section applies must not be passed unless a memorandum setting out particulars of the proposed payment (including its amount) is made available to the members of the company whose approval is sought—

- (a) in the case of a written resolution, by being sent or submitted to every eligible member at or before the time at which the proposed resolution is sent or submitted to him;
- (b) in the case of a resolution at a meeting, by being made available for inspection by the members both—
  - (i) at the company's registered office for not less than 15 days ending with the date of the meeting, and
  - (ii) at the meeting itself.

(4) No approval is required under this section on the part of the members of a body corporate that—

- (a) is not a UK-registered company, or
- (b) is a wholly-owned subsidiary of another body corporate.

(5) A payment made in pursuance of an arrangement—

- (a) entered into as part of the agreement for the transfer in question, or within one year before or two years after that agreement, and
- (b) to which the company whose undertaking or property is transferred, or any person to whom the transfer is made, is privy,

is presumed, except in so far as the contrary is shown, to be a payment to which this section applies.

[1.242]

219 Payment in connection with share transfer: requirement of members' approval

(1) No payment for loss of office may be made by any person to a director of a company in connection with a transfer of shares in the company, or in a subsidiary of the company, resulting from a takeover bid unless the payment has been approved by a resolution of the relevant shareholders.

(2) The relevant shareholders are the holders of the shares to which the bid relates and any holders of shares of the same class as any of those shares.

(3) A resolution approving a payment to which this section applies must not be passed unless a memorandum setting out particulars of the proposed payment (including its amount) is made available to the members of the company whose approval is sought—

- (a) in the case of a written resolution, by being sent or submitted to every eligible member at or before the time at which the proposed resolution is sent or submitted to him;
- (b) in the case of a resolution at a meeting, by being made available for inspection by the members both—
  - (i) at the company's registered office for not less than 15 days ending with the date of the meeting, and
  - (ii) at the meeting itself.

(4) Neither the person making the offer, nor any associate of his (as defined in section 988), is entitled to vote on the resolution, but—

- (a) where the resolution is proposed as a written resolution, they are entitled (if they would otherwise be so entitled) to be sent a copy of it, and
- (b) at any meeting to consider the resolution they are entitled (if they would otherwise be so entitled) to be given notice of the meeting, to attend and speak and if present (in person or by proxy) to count towards the quorum.

(5) If at a meeting to consider the resolution a quorum is not present, and after the meeting has been adjourned to a later date a quorum is again not present, the payment is (for the purposes of this section) deemed to have been approved.

(6) No approval is required under this section on the part of shareholders in a body corporate that—

- (a) is not a UK-registered company, or
- (b) is a wholly-owned subsidiary of another body corporate.

(7) A payment made in pursuance of an arrangement—

- (a) entered into as part of the agreement for the transfer in question, or within one year before or two years after that agreement, and
- (b) to which the company whose shares are the subject of the bid, or any person to whom the transfer is made, is privy,

is presumed, except in so far as the contrary is shown, to be a payment to which this section applies.

[1.243]

220 Exception for payments in discharge of legal obligations etc

(1) Approval is not required under section 217, 218 or 219 (payments requiring members' approval) for a payment made in good faith—

- (a) in discharge of an existing legal obligation (as defined below),
- (b) by way of damages for breach of such an obligation,
- (c) by way of settlement or compromise of any claim arising in connection with the termination of a person's office or employment, or
- (d) by way of pension in respect of past services.

(2) In relation to a payment within section 217 (payment by company) an existing legal obligation means an obligation of the company, or any body corporate associated with it, that was not entered into in connection with, or in consequence of, the event giving rise to the payment for loss of office.

(3) In relation to a payment within section 218 or 219 (payment in connection with transfer of undertaking, property or shares) an existing legal obligation means an obligation of the person making the payment that was not entered into for the purposes of, in connection with or in consequence of, the transfer in question.

(4) In the case of a payment within both section 217 and section 218, or within both section 217 and section 219, subsection (2) above applies and not subsection (3).

(5) A payment part of which falls within subsection (1) above and part of which does not is treated as if the parts were separate payments.

[1.244]

221 Exception for small payments

(1) Approval is not required under section 217, 218 or 219 (payments requiring members' approval) if—

(a) the payment in question is made by the company or any of its subsidiaries, and

(b) the amount or value of the payment, together with the amount or value of any other relevant payments, does not exceed £200.

(2) For this purpose "other relevant payments" are payments for loss of office in relation to which the following conditions are met.

(3) Where the payment in question is one to which section 217 (payment by company) applies, the conditions are that the other payment was or is paid—

(a) by the company making the payment in question or any of its subsidiaries,

(b) to the director to whom that payment is made, and

(c) in connection with the same event.

(4) Where the payment in question is one to which section 218 or 219 applies (payment in connection with transfer of undertaking, property or shares), the conditions are that the other payment was (or is) paid in connection with the same transfer—

(a) to the director to whom the payment in question was made, and

(b) by the company making the payment or any of its subsidiaries.

[1.245]

222 Payments made without approval: civil consequences

(1) If a payment is made in contravention of section 217 (payment by company)—

(a) it is held by the recipient on trust for the company making the payment, and

(b) any director who authorised the payment is jointly and severally liable to indemnify the company that made the payment for any loss resulting from it.

(2) If a payment is made in contravention of section 218 (payment in connection with transfer of undertaking etc), it is held by the recipient on trust for the company whose undertaking or property is or is proposed to be transferred.

(3) If a payment is made in contravention of section 219 (payment in connection with share transfer)—

(a) it is held by the recipient on trust for persons who have sold their shares as a result of the offer made, and

(b) the expenses incurred by the recipient in distributing that sum amongst those persons shall be borne by him and not retained out of that sum.

(4) If a payment is in contravention of section 217 and section 218, subsection (2) of this section applies rather than subsection (1).

(5) If a payment is in contravention of section 217 and section 219, subsection (3) of this section applies rather than subsection (1), unless the court directs otherwise.

Supplementary

[1.246]

223 Transactions requiring members' approval: application of provisions to shadow directors

(1) For the purposes of—

(a) sections 188 and 189 (directors' service contracts),

(b) sections 190 to 196 (property transactions),

(c) sections 197 to 214 (loans etc), and

(d) sections 215 to 222 (payments for loss of office),

a shadow director is treated as a director.

(2) Any reference in those provisions to loss of office as a director does not apply in relation to loss of a person's status as a shadow director.

[1.247]

224 Approval by written resolution: accidental failure to send memorandum

(1) Where—

(a) approval under this Chapter is sought by written resolution, and

(b) a memorandum is required under this Chapter to be sent or submitted to every eligible member before the resolution is passed,

any accidental failure to send or submit the memorandum to one or more members shall be disregarded for the purpose of determining whether the requirement has been met.

(2) Subsection (1) has effect subject to any provision of the company's articles.

[1.248]

225 Cases where approval is required under more than one provision

(1) Approval may be required under more than one provision of this Chapter.

(2) If so, the requirements of each applicable provision must be met.

(3) This does not require a separate resolution for the purposes of each provision.

226 (*This section substituted the Charities Act 1993, ss 66, 66A (for the original s 66), and was repealed by the Charities Act 2011, s 354, Sch 10, as from 14 March 2012.*)

[CHAPTER 4A DIRECTORS OF QUOTED COMPANIES [AND TRADED COMPANIES]: SPECIAL PROVISION

NOTES

Words in square brackets in the preceding Chapter heading inserted by the Companies (Directors' Remuneration Policy and Directors' Remuneration Report) Regulations 2019, SI 2019/970, regs 3, 5, as from 10 June 2019 (for transitional provisions, etc, see reg 2 of the 2019 Regulations at **[4.680]**).

Interpretation

[1.249]

226A Key definitions

(1) In this Chapter—

"directors' remuneration policy" means the policy of a quoted company[, or of an unquoted traded company,] with respect to the making of remuneration payments and payments for loss of office;

"quoted company" has the same meaning as in Part 15 of this Act;

"remuneration payment" means any form of payment or other benefit made to or otherwise conferred on a person as consideration for the person—

(a) holding, agreeing to hold or having held office as director of a company, or

(b) holding, agreeing to hold or having held, during a period when the person is or was such a director—

(i) any other office or employment in connection with the management of the affairs of the company, or

(ii) any office (as director or otherwise) or employment in connection with the management of the affairs of any subsidiary undertaking of the company,

other than a payment for loss of office;

"payment for loss of office" has the same meaning as in Chapter 4 of this Part;

["unquoted traded company" means a traded company (as defined by section 360C) that is not a quoted company].

(2) Subsection (3) applies where, in connection with a relevant transfer, a director of a quoted company [or unquoted traded company] is—

(a) to cease to hold office as director, or

(b) to cease to be the holder of—

(i) any other office or employment in connection with the management of the affairs of the company, or

(ii) any office (as director or otherwise) or employment in connection with the management of the affairs of any subsidiary undertaking of the company.

(3) If in connection with the transfer—

(a) the price to be paid to the director for any shares in the company held by the director is in excess of the price which could at the time have been obtained by other holders of like shares, or

(b) any valuable consideration is given to the director by a person other than the company,

the excess or, as the case may be, the money value of the consideration is taken for the purposes of section 226C to have been a payment for loss of office.

(4) In subsection (2), "relevant transfer" means—

(a) a transfer of the whole or any part of the undertaking or property of the company or a subsidiary of the company;

(b) a transfer of shares in the company, or in a subsidiary of the company, resulting from a takeover bid.

(5) References in this Chapter to the making of a remuneration payment or to the making of a payment for loss of office are to be read in accordance with this section.

(6) References in this Chapter to a payment by a company include a payment by another person at the direction of, or on behalf of, the company.

(7) References in this Chapter to a payment to a person ("B") who is, has been or is to be a director of a company include—

(a) a payment to a person connected with B, or

(b) a payment to a person at the direction of, or for the benefit of, B or a person connected with B.

(8) Section 252 applies for the purposes of determining whether a person is connected with a person who has been, or is to be, a director of a company as it applies for the purposes of determining whether a person is connected with a director.

(9) References in this Chapter to a director include a shadow director but references to loss of office as a director do not include loss of a person's status as a shadow director.

[(10) References in this Chapter (other than sections 226E(2)(b) and (5)) to a director of a company include a person who is not a director of the company but who is—

(a) its chief executive officer (however described), or

(b) where such a function exists in the company, its deputy chief executive officer (however described).]]

NOTES

Chapter 4A (ss 226A–226F) was inserted by the Enterprise and Regulatory Reform Act 2013, s 80, as from 1 October 2013; for transitional provisions see the note below.

The definition "unquoted traded company", the words in square brackets in the definition "directors' remuneration policy" in sub-s (1), and the words in square brackets in sub-s (2) were inserted, and sub-s (10) was added, by the Companies (Directors' Remuneration Policy and Directors' Remuneration Report) Regulations 2019, SI 2019/970, regs 3, 6 (the amendments apply to a quoted company from the first date on or after 10 June 2019 on which a relevant directors' remuneration policy for the company approved under s 439A of this Act takes effect – see reg 2 of the 2019 Regulations at **[4.680]**).

Transitional provisions: the Enterprise and Regulatory Reform Act 2013, s 82(3) and (4) provide that Chapter 4A of Part 10 does not apply in relation to remuneration payments or payments for loss of office that are required to be made under an agreement entered into before 27 June 2012 or in consequence of any other obligation arising before that date. Furthermore, an agreement entered into, or any other obligation arising, before 27 June 2012 that is modified or renewed on or after that date is to be treated for the purposes of the previous sentence as having been entered into or (as the case may be) as having arisen on the date on which it was modified or renewed.

[Restrictions relating to remuneration or loss of office payments

[1.250]
226B Remuneration payments
(1) A quoted company [or unquoted traded company] may not make a remuneration payment to a person who is, or is to be or has been, a director of the company unless—
(a) the payment is consistent with the approved directors' remuneration policy, or
[(b) an amendment to that policy authorising the company to make the payment has been approved by resolution of the members of the company.]
(2) The approved directors' remuneration policy is the most recent remuneration policy to have been approved by a resolution passed by the members of the company in general meeting.]

NOTES
Chapter 4A (ss 226A–226F) was inserted as noted to s 226A at **[1.249]**.
Sub-s (1): the words in the first pair of square brackets were inserted, and para (b) was substituted, by the Companies (Directors' Remuneration Policy and Directors' Remuneration Report) Regulations 2019, SI 2019/970, regs 3, 7 (the amendments apply to a quoted company from the first date on or after 10 June 2019 on which a relevant directors' remuneration policy for the company approved under s 439A of this Act takes effect – see reg 2 of the 2019 Regulations at **[4.680]**).

[1.251]
[226C Loss of office payments
(1) No payment for loss of office may be made by any person to a person who is, or has been, a director of a quoted company [or of an unquoted traded company] unless—
(a) the payment is consistent with the approved directors' remuneration policy, or
[(b) an amendment to that policy authorising the company to make the payment has been approved by resolution of the members of the company.]
(2) The approved directors' remuneration policy is the most recent remuneration policy to have been approved by a resolution passed by the members of the company in general meeting.]

NOTES
Chapter 4A (ss 226A–226F) was inserted as noted to s 226A at **[1.249]**.
Sub-s (1): the words in the first pair of square brackets were inserted, and para (b) was substituted, by the Companies (Directors' Remuneration Policy and Directors' Remuneration Report) Regulations 2019, SI 2019/970, regs 3, 8 (the amendments apply to a quoted company from the first date on or after 10 June 2019 on which a relevant directors' remuneration policy for the company approved under s 439A of this Act takes effect – see reg 2 of the 2019 Regulations at **[4.680]**).

[1.252]
[226D Sections 226B and 226C: supplementary
(1) A resolution approving [an amendment] for the purposes of section 226B(1)(b) or 226C(1)(b) must not be passed unless a memorandum setting out particulars of the proposed payment [to which the amendment relates] (including its amount) is made available for inspection by the members of the company—
(a) at the company's registered office for not less than 15 days ending with the date of the meeting at which the resolution is to be considered, and
(b) at that meeting itself.
[(2) The memorandum must explain the ways in which the payment would be inconsistent with the approved directors' remuneration policy (within the meaning of the section in question) but for the amendment.]
(3) The company must ensure that the memorandum is made available on the company's website from the first day on which the memorandum is made available for inspection under subsection (1) until its next accounts meeting.
(4) Failure to comply with subsection (3) does not affect the validity of the meeting at which a resolution is passed approving [the amendment] to which the memorandum relates or the validity of anything done at the meeting.
(5) Nothing in section 226B or 226C authorises the making of a remuneration payment or (as the case may be) a payment for loss of office in contravention of the articles of the company concerned.
(6) Nothing in section 226B or 226C applies in relation to a remuneration payment or (as the case may be) a payment for loss of office made to a person who is, or is to be or has been, a director of a quoted company [or of an unquoted traded company] before the earlier of—
(a) the end of the first financial year of the company to begin on or after the day on which it becomes a quoted company [or (as the case may be) an unquoted traded company], and
(b) the date from which the company's first directors' remuneration policy to be approved under section 439A takes effect.
(7) In this section the "company's website" is the website on which the company makes material available under section 430.]

NOTES
Chapter 4A (ss 226A–226F) was inserted as noted to s 226A at **[1.249]**.
All amendments to this section were made by the Companies (Directors' Remuneration Policy and Directors' Remuneration Report) Regulations 2019, SI 2019/970, regs 3, 9 (these amendments apply to a quoted company from the first date on or after 10 June 2019 on which a relevant directors' remuneration policy for the company approved under s 439A of this Act takes effect – see reg 2 of the 2019 Regulations at **[4.680]**).

[Supplementary

[1.253]
226E Payments made without approval: civil consequences
(1) An obligation (however arising) to make a payment which would be in contravention of section 226B or 226C has no effect.

(2) If a payment is made in contravention of section 226B or 226C—

(a) it is held by the recipient on trust for the company or other person making the payment, and

(b) in the case of a payment by a company, any director who authorised the payment is jointly and severally liable to indemnify the company that made the payment for any loss resulting from it.

(3) If a payment for loss of office is made in contravention of section 226C to a director of a quoted company [or of an unquoted traded company] in connection with the transfer of the whole or any part of the undertaking or property of the company or a subsidiary of the company—

(a) subsection (2) does not apply, and

(b) the payment is held by the recipient on trust for the company whose undertaking or property is or is proposed to be transferred.

(4) If a payment for loss of office is made in contravention of section 226C to a director of a quoted company [or of an unquoted traded company] in connection with a transfer of shares in the company, or in a subsidiary of the company, resulting from a takeover bid—

(a) subsection (2) does not apply,

(b) the payment is held by the recipient on trust for persons who have sold their shares as a result of the offer made, and

(c) the expenses incurred by the recipient in distributing that sum amongst those persons shall be borne by the recipient and not retained out of that sum.

(5) If in proceedings against a director for the enforcement of a liability under subsection (2)(b)—

(a) the director shows that he or she has acted honestly and reasonably, and

(b) the court considers that, having regard to all the circumstances of the case, the director ought to be relieved of liability,

the court may relieve the director, either wholly or in part, from liability on such terms as the court thinks fit.]

NOTES

Chapter 4A (ss 226A–226F) was inserted as noted to s 226A at **[1.249]**.

Sub-ss (3), (4): words in square brackets inserted by the Companies (Directors' Remuneration Policy and Directors' Remuneration Report) Regulations 2019, SI 2019/970, regs 3, 10 (the amendments apply to a quoted company from the first date on or after 10 June 2019 on which a relevant directors' remuneration policy for the company approved under s 439A of this Act takes effect – see reg 2 of the 2019 Regulations at **[4.680]**).

[1.254]

[226F Relationship with requirements under Chapter 4

(1) This Chapter does not affect any requirement for approval by a resolution of the members of a company which applies in relation to the company under Chapter 4.

(2) Where the making of a payment to which section 226B or 226C applies requires approval by a resolution of the members of the company concerned under Chapter 4, approval obtained for the purposes of that Chapter is to be treated as satisfying the requirements of section 226B(1)(b) or (as the case may be) 226C(1)(b).]

NOTES

Chapter 4A (ss 226A–226F) was inserted as noted to s 226A at **[1.249]**.

CHAPTER 5 DIRECTORS' SERVICE CONTRACTS

[1.255]

227 Directors' service contracts

(1) For the purposes of this Part a director's "service contract", in relation to a company, means a contract under which—

(a) a director of the company undertakes personally to perform services (as director or otherwise) for the company, or for a subsidiary of the company, or

(b) services (as director or otherwise) that a director of the company undertakes personally to perform are made available by a third party to the company, or to a subsidiary of the company.

(2) The provisions of this Part relating to directors' service contracts apply to the terms of a person's appointment as a director of a company.

They are not restricted to contracts for the performance of services outside the scope of the ordinary duties of a director.

[1.256]

228 Copy of contract or memorandum of terms to be available for inspection

(1) A company must keep available for inspection—

(a) a copy of every director's service contract with the company or with a subsidiary of the company, or

(b) if the contract is not in writing, a written memorandum setting out the terms of the contract.

(2) All the copies and memoranda must be kept available for inspection at—

(a) the company's registered office, or

(b) a place specified in regulations under section 1136.

(3) The copies and memoranda must be retained by the company for at least one year from the date of termination or expiry of the contract and must be kept available for inspection during that time.

(4) The company must give notice to the registrar—

(a) of the place at which the copies and memoranda are kept available for inspection, and

(b) of any change in that place,

unless they have at all times been kept at the company's registered office.

(5) If default is made in complying with subsection (1), (2) or (3), or default is made for 14 days in complying with subsection (4), an offence is committed by every officer of the company who is in default.

(6) A person guilty of an offence under this section is liable on summary conviction to a fine not exceeding level 3 on the standard scale and, for continued contravention, a daily default fine not exceeding one-tenth of level 3 on the standard scale.

(7) The provisions of this section apply to a variation of a director's service contract as they apply to the original contract.

[1.257]

229 Right of member to inspect and request copy

(1) Every copy or memorandum required to be kept under section 228 must be open to inspection by any member of the company without charge.

(2) Any member of the company is entitled, on request and on payment of such fee as may be prescribed, to be provided with a copy of any such copy or memorandum.

The copy must be provided within seven days after the request is received by the company.

(3) If an inspection required under subsection (1) is refused, or default is made in complying with subsection (2), an offence is committed by every officer of the company who is in default.

(4) A person guilty of an offence under this section is liable on summary conviction to a fine not exceeding level 3 on the standard scale and, for continued contravention, a daily default fine not exceeding one-tenth of level 3 on the standard scale.

(5) In the case of any such refusal or default the court may by order compel an immediate inspection or, as the case may be, direct that the copy required be sent to the person requiring it.

NOTES

Regulations: the Companies (Fees for Inspection and Copying of Company Records) Regulations 2007, SI 2007/2612 at **[4.11]**. For a summary of all statutory instruments made under this Act, see Appendix 4 at **[A4]**.

[1.258]

230 Directors' service contracts: application of provisions to shadow directors

A shadow director is treated as a director for the purposes of the provisions of this Chapter.

CHAPTER 6 CONTRACTS WITH SOLE MEMBERS WHO ARE DIRECTORS

[1.259]

231 Contract with sole member who is also a director

(1) This section applies where—

(a) a limited company having only one member enters into a contract with the sole member,
(b) the sole member is also a director of the company, and
(c) the contract is not entered into in the ordinary course of the company's business.

(2) The company must, unless the contract is in writing, ensure that the terms of the contract are either—

(a) set out in a written memorandum, or
(b) recorded in the minutes of the first meeting of the directors of the company following the making of the contract.

(3) If a company fails to comply with this section an offence is committed by every officer of the company who is in default.

(4) A person guilty of an offence under this section is liable on summary conviction to a fine not exceeding level 5 on the standard scale.

(5) For the purposes of this section a shadow director is treated as a director.

(6) Failure to comply with this section in relation to a contract does not affect the validity of the contract.

(7) Nothing in this section shall be read as excluding the operation of any other enactment or rule of law applying to contracts between a company and a director of the company.

CHAPTER 7 DIRECTORS' LIABILITIES

Provision protecting directors from liability

[1.260]

232 Provisions protecting directors from liability

(1) Any provision that purports to exempt a director of a company (to any extent) from any liability that would otherwise attach to him in connection with any negligence, default, breach of duty or breach of trust in relation to the company is void.

(2) Any provision by which a company directly or indirectly provides an indemnity (to any extent) for a director of the company, or of an associated company, against any liability attaching to him in connection with any negligence, default, breach of duty or breach of trust in relation to the company of which he is a director is void, except as permitted by—

(a) section 233 (provision of insurance),
(b) section 234 (qualifying third party indemnity provision), or
(c) section 235 (qualifying pension scheme indemnity provision).

(3) This section applies to any provision, whether contained in a company's articles or in any contract with the company or otherwise.

(4) Nothing in this section prevents a company's articles from making such provision as has previously been lawful for dealing with conflicts of interest.

[1.261]

233 Provision of insurance

Section 232(2) (voidness of provisions for indemnifying directors) does not prevent a company from purchasing and maintaining for a director of the company, or of an associated company, insurance against any such liability as is mentioned in that subsection.

[1.262]

234 Qualifying third party indemnity provision

(1) Section 232(2) (voidness of provisions for indemnifying directors) does not apply to qualifying third party indemnity provision.

(a) information as to his usual residential address;
(b) the information that his service address is his usual residential address.

(2) That information is referred to in this Chapter as "protected information".

(3) Information does not cease to be protected information on the individual ceasing to be a director of the company. References in this Chapter to a director include, to that extent, a former director.

[1.269]

241 Protected information: restriction on use or disclosure by company

(1) A company must not use or disclose protected information about any of its directors, except—
(a) for communicating with the director concerned,
(b) in order to comply with any requirement of the Companies Acts as to particulars to be sent to the registrar, or
(c) in accordance with section 244 (disclosure under court order).

(2) Subsection (1) does not prohibit any use or disclosure of protected information with the consent of the director concerned.

[1.270]

242 Protected information: restriction on use or disclosure by registrar

(1) The registrar must omit protected information from the material on the register that is available for inspection where—
(a) it is contained in a document delivered to him in which such information is required to be stated, and
(b) in the case of a document having more than one part, it is contained in a part of the document in which such information is required to be stated.

(2) The registrar is not obliged—
(a) to check other documents or (as the case may be) other parts of the document to ensure the absence of protected information, or
(b) to omit from the material that is available for public inspection anything registered before this Chapter comes into force.

(3) The registrar must not use or disclose protected information except—
(a) as permitted by section 243 (permitted use or disclosure by registrar), or
(b) in accordance with section 244 (disclosure under court order).

[1.271]

243 Permitted use or disclosure by the registrar

(1) The registrar may use protected information for communicating with the director in question.

(2) The registrar may disclose protected information—
(a) to a public authority specified for the purposes of this section by regulations made by the Secretary of State, or
(b) to a credit reference agency.

(3) The Secretary of State may make provision by regulations—
(a) specifying conditions for the disclosure of protected information in accordance with this section, and
(b) providing for the charging of fees.

(4) The Secretary of State may make provision by regulations requiring the registrar, on application, to refrain from disclosing protected information relating to a director to a credit reference agency.

(5) Regulations under subsection (4) may make provision as to—
(a) who may make an application,
(b) the grounds on which an application may be made,
(c) the information to be included in and documents to accompany an application, and
(d) how an application is to be determined.

(6) Provision under subsection (5)(d) may in particular—
(a) confer a discretion on the registrar;
(b) provide for a question to be referred to a person other than the registrar for the purposes of determining the application.

(7) In this section—

"credit reference agency" means a person carrying on a business comprising the furnishing of information relevant to the financial standing of individuals, being information collected by the agency for that purpose; and

"public authority" includes any person or body having functions of a public nature.

(8) Regulations under this section are subject to negative resolution procedure.

NOTES

Regulations: the Companies (Disclosure of Address) Regulations 2009, SI 2009/214 at **[4.191]**; the Companies (Disclosure of Address) (Amendment) Regulations 2010, SI 2010/2156; the Registrar of Companies (Fees) (Companies, Overseas Companies and Limited Liability Partnerships) Regulations 2012, SI 2012/1907 at **[4.452]**; the Companies (Disclosure of Address) (Amendment) Regulations 2015, SI 2015/842; the Companies (Disclosure of Date of Birth Information) Regulations 2015, SI 2015/1694 at **[4.552]**; the Register of People with Significant Control Regulations 2016, SI 2016/339 at **[4.559]**; the Companies and Limited Liability Partnerships (Filing Requirements) Regulations 2016, SI 2016/599 at **[4.640]**; the Registrar of Companies (Fees) (Amendment) Regulations 2016, SI 2016/621; the Companies (Disclosure of Address) (Amendment) Regulations 2018, SI 2018/528. For a summary of all statutory instruments made under this Act, see Appendix 4 at **[A4]**.

[1.272]

244 Disclosure under court order

(1) The court may make an order for the disclosure of protected information by the company or by the registrar if—
(a) there is evidence that service of documents at a service address other than the director's usual residential address is not effective to bring them to the notice of the director, or

(b) it is necessary or expedient for the information to be provided in connection with the enforcement of an order or decree of the court,

and the court is otherwise satisfied that it is appropriate to make the order.

(2) An order for disclosure by the registrar is to be made only if the company—

(a) does not have the director's usual residential address, or

(b) has been dissolved.

(3) The order may be made on the application of a liquidator, creditor or member of the company, or any other person appearing to the court to have a sufficient interest.

(4) The order must specify the persons to whom, and purposes for which, disclosure is authorised.

[1.273]

245 Circumstances in which registrar may put address on the public record

(1) The registrar may put a director's usual residential address on the public record if—

(a) communications sent by the registrar to the director and requiring a response within a specified period remain unanswered, or

(b) there is evidence that service of documents at a service address provided in place of the director's usual residential address is not effective to bring them to the notice of the director.

(2) The registrar must give notice of the proposal—

(a) to the director, and

(b) to every company of which the registrar has been notified that the individual is a director.

(3) The notice must—

(a) state the grounds on which it is proposed to put the director's usual residential address on the public record, and

(b) specify a period within which representations may be made before that is done.

(4) It must be sent to the director at his usual residential address, unless it appears to the registrar that service at that address may be ineffective to bring it to the individual's notice, in which case it may be sent to any service address provided in place of that address.

(5) The registrar must take account of any representations received within the specified period.

(6) What is meant by putting the address on the public record is explained in section 246.

[1.274]

246 Putting the address on the public record

(1) The registrar, on deciding in accordance with section 245 that a director's usual residential address is to be put on the public record, shall proceed as if notice of a change of registered particulars had been given—

(a) stating that address as the director's service address, and

(b) stating that the director's usual residential address is the same as his service address.

(2) The registrar must give notice of having done so—

(a) to the director, and

(b) to the company.

(3) On receipt of the notice the company must—

(a) enter the director's usual residential address in its register of directors as his service address, and

(b) state in its register of directors' residential addresses that his usual residential address is the same as his service address.

[(3A) But—

(a) subsection (3)(a) does not apply if an election under section 167A is in force in respect of the company's register of directors, and

(b) subsection (3)(b) does not apply if an election under section 167A is in force in respect of the company's register of directors' residential addresses.]

(4) If the company has been notified by the director in question of a more recent address as his usual residential address, it must—

(a) enter that address in its register of directors as the director's service address, and

(b) give notice to the registrar as on a change of registered particulars.

[(4A) If an election under section 167A is in force in respect of the company's register of directors, the company must, in place of doing the things mentioned in subsection (4)(a) and (b), deliver the particulars to the registrar in accordance with section 167D.]

(5) If a company fails to comply with subsection (3)[, (4) or (4A)], an offence is committed by—

(a) the company, and

(b) every officer of the company who is in default.

(6) A person guilty of an offence under subsection (5) is liable on summary conviction to a fine not exceeding level 5 on the standard scale and, for continued contravention, a daily default fine not exceeding [one-tenth of the greater of £5,000 or level 4 on the standard scale].

(7) A director whose usual residential address has been put on the public record by the registrar under this section may not register a service address other than his usual residential address for a period of five years from the date of the registrar's decision.

NOTES

Sub-ss (3A), (4A): inserted by the Small Business, Enterprise and Employment Act 2015, s 94, Sch 5, Pt 2, paras 11, 15(a), (b), as from 30 June 2016.

Sub-s (5): words in square brackets substituted by the Small Business, Enterprise and Employment Act 2015, s 94, Sch 5, Pt 2, paras 11, 15(c), as from 30 June 2016.

Sub-s (6): words in square brackets substituted (for the original words "one-tenth of level 5 on the standard scale") by the Legal Aid, Sentencing and Punishment of Offenders Act 2012 (Fines on Summary Conviction) Regulations 2015, SI 2015/664, regs 3, 5, Sch 3, Pt 1, para 9(1), (8), as from 12 March 2015, in relation to England and Wales only (except in relation to (a) fines for offences committed before 12 March 2015, (b) the operation of restrictions on fines that may be imposed on a person aged under 18, or (c) fines that may be imposed on a person convicted by a magistrates' court who is to be sentenced as if convicted on indictment).

CHAPTER 9 SUPPLEMENTARY PROVISIONS

Provision for employees on cessation or transfer of business

[1.275]

247 Power to make provision for employees on cessation or transfer of business

(1) The powers of the directors of a company include (if they would not otherwise do so) power to make provision for the benefit of persons employed or formerly employed by the company, or any of its subsidiaries, in connection with the cessation or the transfer to any person of the whole or part of the undertaking of the company or that subsidiary.

(2) This power is exercisable notwithstanding the general duty imposed by section 172 (duty to promote the success of the company).

(3) In the case of a company that is a charity it is exercisable notwithstanding any restrictions on the directors' powers (or the company's capacity) flowing from the objects of the company.

(4) The power may only be exercised if sanctioned—

(a) by a resolution of the company, or

(b) by a resolution of the directors,

in accordance with the following provisions.

(5) A resolution of the directors—

(a) must be authorised by the company's articles, and

(b) is not sufficient sanction for payments to or for the benefit of directors, former directors or shadow directors.

(6) Any other requirements of the company's articles as to the exercise of the power conferred by this section must be complied with.

(7) Any payment under this section must be made—

(a) before the commencement of any winding up of the company, and

(b) out of profits of the company that are available for dividend.

Records of meetings of directors

[1.276]

248 Minutes of directors' meetings

(1) Every company must cause minutes of all proceedings at meetings of its directors to be recorded.

(2) The records must be kept for at least ten years from the date of the meeting.

(3) If a company fails to comply with this section, an offence is committed by every officer of the company who is in default.

(4) A person guilty of an offence under this section is liable on summary conviction to a fine not exceeding level 3 on the standard scale and, for continued contravention, a daily default fine not exceeding one-tenth of level 3 on the standard scale.

[1.277]

249 Minutes as evidence

(1) Minutes recorded in accordance with section 248, if purporting to be authenticated by the chairman of the meeting or by the chairman of the next directors' meeting, are evidence (in Scotland, sufficient evidence) of the proceedings at the meeting.

(2) Where minutes have been made in accordance with that section of the proceedings of a meeting of directors, then, until the contrary is proved—

(a) the meeting is deemed duly held and convened,

(b) all proceedings at the meeting are deemed to have duly taken place, and

(c) all appointments at the meeting are deemed valid.

Meaning of "director" and "shadow director"

[1.278]

250 "Director"

In the Companies Acts "director" includes any person occupying the position of director, by whatever name called.

[1.279]

251 "Shadow director"

(1) In the Companies Acts "shadow director", in relation to a company, means a person in accordance with whose directions or instructions the directors of the company are accustomed to act.

(2) A person is not to be regarded as a shadow director by reason only that the directors act[—

(a) on advice given by that person in a professional capacity;

(b) in accordance with instructions, a direction, guidance or advice given by that person in the exercise of a function conferred by or under an enactment;

(c) in accordance with guidance or advice given by that person in that person's capacity as a Minister of the Crown (within the meaning of the Ministers of the Crown Act 1975)].

(3) A body corporate is not to be regarded as a shadow director of any of its subsidiary companies for the purposes of—

Chapter 2 (general duties of directors),

Chapter 4 (transactions requiring members' approval), or

Chapter 6 (contract with sole member who is also a director),

by reason only that the directors of the subsidiary are accustomed to act in accordance with its directions or instructions.

NOTES

Sub-s (2): words in square brackets substituted by the Small Business, Enterprise and Employment Act 2015, s 90(3), as from 26 May 2015.

Other definitions

[1.280]

252 Persons connected with a director

(1) This section defines what is meant by references in this Part to a person being "connected" with a director of a company (or a director being "connected" with a person).

(2) The following persons (and only those persons) are connected with a director of a company—

(a) members of the director's family (see section 253);

(b) a body corporate with which the director is connected (as defined in section 254);

(c) a person acting in his capacity as trustee of a trust—

(i) the beneficiaries of which include the director or a person who by virtue of paragraph (a) or (b) is connected with him, or

(ii) the terms of which confer a power on the trustees that may be exercised for the benefit of the director or any such person,

other than a trust for the purposes of an employees' share scheme or a pension scheme;

(d) a person acting in his capacity as partner—

(i) of the director, or

(ii) of a person who, by virtue of paragraph (a), (b) or (c), is connected with that director;

(e) a firm that is a legal person under the law by which it is governed and in which—

(i) the director is a partner,

(ii) a partner is a person who, by virtue of paragraph (a), (b) or (c) is connected with the director, or

(iii) a partner is a firm in which the director is a partner or in which there is a partner who, by virtue of paragraph (a), (b) or (c), is connected with the director.

(3) References in this Part to a person connected with a director of a company do not include a person who is himself a director of the company.

[1.281]

253 Members of a director's family

(1) This section defines what is meant by references in this Part to members of a director's family.

(2) For the purposes of this Part the members of a director's family are—

(a) the director's spouse or civil partner;

(b) any other person (whether of a different sex or the same sex) with whom the director lives as partner in an enduring family relationship;

(c) the director's children or step-children;

(d) any children or step-children of a person within paragraph (b) (and who are not children or step-children of the director) who live with the director and have not attained the age of 18;

(e) the director's parents.

(3) Subsection (2)(b) does not apply if the other person is the director's grandparent or grandchild, sister, brother, aunt or uncle, or nephew or niece.

[1.282]

254 Director "connected with" a body corporate

(1) This section defines what is meant by references in this Part to a director being "connected with" a body corporate.

(2) A director is connected with a body corporate if, but only if, he and the persons connected with him together—

(a) are interested in shares comprised in the equity share capital of that body corporate of a nominal value equal to at least 20% of that share capital, or

(b) are entitled to exercise or control the exercise of more than 20% of the voting power at any general meeting of that body.

(3) The rules set out in Schedule 1 (references to interest in shares or debentures) apply for the purposes of this section.

(4) References in this section to voting power the exercise of which is controlled by a director include voting power whose exercise is controlled by a body corporate controlled by him.

(5) Shares in a company held as treasury shares, and any voting rights attached to such shares, are disregarded for the purposes of this section.

(6) For the avoidance of circularity in the application of section 252 (meaning of "connected person") —

(a) a body corporate with which a director is connected is not treated for the purposes of this section as connected with him unless it is also connected with him by virtue of subsection (2)(c) or (d) of that section (connection as trustee or partner); and

(b) a trustee of a trust the beneficiaries of which include (or may include) a body corporate with which a director is connected is not treated for the purposes of this section as connected with a director by reason only of that fact.

[1.283]

255 Director "controlling" a body corporate

(1) This section defines what is meant by references in this Part to a director "controlling" a body corporate.

(2) A director of a company is taken to control a body corporate if, but only if—

(a) he or any person connected with him—

(i) is interested in any part of the equity share capital of that body, or

(ii) is entitled to exercise or control the exercise of any part of the voting power at any general meeting of that body, and

(b) he, the persons connected with him and the other directors of that company, together—
   (i) are interested in more than 50% of that share capital, or
   (ii) are entitled to exercise or control the exercise of more than 50% of that voting power.

(3) The rules set out in Schedule 1 (references to interest in shares or debentures) apply for the purposes of this section.

(4) References in this section to voting power the exercise of which is controlled by a director include voting power whose exercise is controlled by a body corporate controlled by him.

(5) Shares in a company held as treasury shares, and any voting rights attached to such shares, are disregarded for the purposes of this section.

(6) For the avoidance of circularity in the application of section 252 (meaning of "connected person")—
(a) a body corporate with which a director is connected is not treated for the purposes of this section as connected with him unless it is also connected with him by virtue of subsection (2)(c) or (d) of that section (connection as trustee or partner); and
(b) a trustee of a trust the beneficiaries of which include (or may include) a body corporate with which a director is connected is not treated for the purposes of this section as connected with a director by reason only of that fact.

[1.284]
256 Associated bodies corporate

For the purposes of this Part—
(a) bodies corporate are associated if one is a subsidiary of the other or both are subsidiaries of the same body corporate, and
(b) companies are associated if one is a subsidiary of the other or both are subsidiaries of the same body corporate.

[1.285]
257 References to company's constitution

(1) References in this Part to a company's constitution include—
(a) any resolution or other decision come to in accordance with the constitution, and
(b) any decision by the members of the company, or a class of members, that is treated by virtue of any enactment or rule of law as equivalent to a decision by the company.

(2) This is in addition to the matters mentioned in section 17 (general provision as to matters contained in company's constitution).

General

[1.286]
258 Power to increase financial limits

(1) The Secretary of State may by order substitute for any sum of money specified in this Part a larger sum specified in the order.

(2) An order under this section is subject to negative resolution procedure.

(3) An order does not have effect in relation to anything done or not done before it comes into force.

Accordingly, proceedings in respect of any liability incurred before that time may be continued or instituted as if the order had not been made.

NOTES

Orders: no Orders have been made under this section.

[1.287]
259 Transactions under foreign law

For the purposes of this Part it is immaterial whether the law that (apart from this Act) governs an arrangement or transaction is the law of the United Kingdom, or a part of it, or not.

PART 11 DERIVATIVE CLAIMS AND PROCEEDINGS BY MEMBERS

CHAPTER 1 DERIVATIVE CLAIMS IN ENGLAND AND WALES OR NORTHERN IRELAND

[1.288]
260 Derivative claims

(1) This Chapter applies to proceedings in England and Wales or Northern Ireland by a member of a company—
(a) in respect of a cause of action vested in the company, and
(b) seeking relief on behalf of the company.

This is referred to in this Chapter as a "derivative claim".

(2) A derivative claim may only be brought—
(a) under this Chapter, or
(b) in pursuance of an order of the court in proceedings under section 994 (proceedings for protection of members against unfair prejudice).

(3) A derivative claim under this Chapter may be brought only in respect of a cause of action arising from an actual or proposed act or omission involving negligence, default, breach of duty or breach of trust by a director of the company.

The cause of action may be against the director or another person (or both).

(4) It is immaterial whether the cause of action arose before or after the person seeking to bring or continue the derivative claim became a member of the company.

(5) For the purposes of this Chapter—
(a) "director" includes a former director;
(b) a shadow director is treated as a director; and

(c) references to a member of a company include a person who is not a member but to whom shares in the company have been transferred or transmitted by operation of law.

[1.289]
261 Application for permission to continue derivative claim

(1) A member of a company who brings a derivative claim under this Chapter must apply to the court for permission (in Northern Ireland, leave) to continue it.

(2) If it appears to the court that the application and the evidence filed by the applicant in support of it do not disclose a prima facie case for giving permission (or leave), the court—

(a) must dismiss the application, and
(b) may make any consequential order it considers appropriate.

(3) If the application is not dismissed under subsection (2), the court—

(a) may give directions as to the evidence to be provided by the company, and
(b) may adjourn the proceedings to enable the evidence to be obtained.

(4) On hearing the application, the court may—

(a) give permission (or leave) to continue the claim on such terms as it thinks fit,
(b) refuse permission (or leave) and dismiss the claim, or
(c) adjourn the proceedings on the application and give such directions as it thinks fit.

[1.290]
262 Application for permission to continue claim as a derivative claim

(1) This section applies where—

(a) a company has brought a claim, and
(b) the cause of action on which the claim is based could be pursued as a derivative claim under this Chapter.

(2) A member of the company may apply to the court for permission (in Northern Ireland, leave) to continue the claim as a derivative claim on the ground that—

(a) the manner in which the company commenced or continued the claim amounts to an abuse of the process of the court,
(b) the company has failed to prosecute the claim diligently, and
(c) it is appropriate for the member to continue the claim as a derivative claim.

(3) If it appears to the court that the application and the evidence filed by the applicant in support of it do not disclose a prima facie case for giving permission (or leave), the court—

(a) must dismiss the application, and
(b) may make any consequential order it considers appropriate.

(4) If the application is not dismissed under subsection (3), the court—

(a) may give directions as to the evidence to be provided by the company, and
(b) may adjourn the proceedings to enable the evidence to be obtained.

(5) On hearing the application, the court may—

(a) give permission (or leave) to continue the claim as a derivative claim on such terms as it thinks fit,
(b) refuse permission (or leave) and dismiss the application, or
(c) adjourn the proceedings on the application and give such directions as it thinks fit.

[1.291]
263 Whether permission to be given

(1) The following provisions have effect where a member of a company applies for permission (in Northern Ireland, leave) under section 261 or 262.

(2) Permission (or leave) must be refused if the court is satisfied—

(a) that a person acting in accordance with section 172 (duty to promote the success of the company) would not seek to continue the claim, or
(b) where the cause of action arises from an act or omission that is yet to occur, that the act or omission has been authorised by the company, or
(c) where the cause of action arises from an act or omission that has already occurred, that the act or omission—
    (i) was authorised by the company before it occurred, or
    (ii) has been ratified by the company since it occurred.

(3) In considering whether to give permission (or leave) the court must take into account, in particular—

(a) whether the member is acting in good faith in seeking to continue the claim;
(b) the importance that a person acting in accordance with section 172 (duty to promote the success of the company) would attach to continuing it;
(c) where the cause of action results from an act or omission that is yet to occur, whether the act or omission could be, and in the circumstances would be likely to be—
    (i) authorised by the company before it occurs, or
    (ii) ratified by the company after it occurs;
(d) where the cause of action arises from an act or omission that has already occurred, whether the act or omission could be, and in the circumstances would be likely to be, ratified by the company;
(e) whether the company has decided not to pursue the claim;
(f) whether the act or omission in respect of which the claim is brought gives rise to a cause of action that the member could pursue in his own right rather than on behalf of the company.

(4) In considering whether to give permission (or leave) the court shall have particular regard to any evidence before it as to the views of members of the company who have no personal interest, direct or indirect, in the matter.

(5) The Secretary of State may by regulations—

(a) amend subsection (2) so as to alter or add to the circumstances in which permission (or leave) is to be refused;
(b) amend subsection (3) so as to alter or add to the matters that the court is required to take into account in considering whether to give permission (or leave).

(6) Before making any such regulations the Secretary of State shall consult such persons as he considers appropriate.

(7) Regulations under this section are subject to affirmative resolution procedure.

NOTES

Regulations: no Regulations have been made under this section.

[1.292]

264 Application for permission to continue derivative claim brought by another member

(1) This section applies where a member of a company ("the claimant")—

(a) has brought a derivative claim,

(b) has continued as a derivative claim a claim brought by the company, or

(c) has continued a derivative claim under this section.

(2) Another member of the company ("the applicant") may apply to the court for permission (in Northern Ireland, leave) to continue the claim on the ground that—

(a) the manner in which the proceedings have been commenced or continued by the claimant amounts to an abuse of the process of the court,

(b) the claimant has failed to prosecute the claim diligently, and

(c) it is appropriate for the applicant to continue the claim as a derivative claim.

(3) If it appears to the court that the application and the evidence filed by the applicant in support of it do not disclose a prima facie case for giving permission (or leave), the court—

(a) must dismiss the application, and

(b) may make any consequential order it considers appropriate.

(4) If the application is not dismissed under subsection (3), the court—

(a) may give directions as to the evidence to be provided by the company, and

(b) may adjourn the proceedings to enable the evidence to be obtained.

(5) On hearing the application, the court may—

(a) give permission (or leave) to continue the claim on such terms as it thinks fit,

(b) refuse permission (or leave) and dismiss the application, or

(c) adjourn the proceedings on the application and give such directions as it thinks fit.

CHAPTER 2 DERIVATIVE PROCEEDINGS IN SCOTLAND

[1.293]

265 Derivative proceedings

(1) In Scotland, a member of a company may raise proceedings in respect of an act or omission specified in subsection (3) in order to protect the interests of the company and obtain a remedy on its behalf.

(2) A member of a company may raise such proceedings only under subsection (1).

(3) The act or omission referred to in subsection (1) is any actual or proposed act or omission involving negligence, default, breach of duty or breach of trust by a director of the company.

(4) Proceedings may be raised under subsection (1) against (either or both)—

(a) the director referred to in subsection (3), or

(b) another person.

(5) It is immaterial whether the act or omission in respect of which the proceedings are to be raised or, in the case of continuing proceedings under section 267 or 269, are raised, arose before or after the person seeking to raise or continue them became a member of the company.

(6) This section does not affect—

(a) any right of a member of a company to raise proceedings in respect of an act or omission specified in subsection (3) in order to protect his own interests and obtain a remedy on his own behalf, or

(b) the court's power to make an order under section 996(2)(c) or anything done under such an order.

(7) In this Chapter—

(a) proceedings raised under subsection (1) are referred to as "derivative proceedings",

(b) the act or omission in respect of which they are raised is referred to as the "cause of action",

(c) "director" includes a former director,

(d) references to a director include a shadow director, and

(e) references to a member of a company include a person who is not a member but to whom shares in the company have been transferred or transmitted by operation of law.

[1.294]

266 Requirement for leave and notice

(1) Derivative proceedings may be raised by a member of a company only with the leave of the court.

(2) An application for leave must—

(a) specify the cause of action, and

(b) summarise the facts on which the derivative proceedings are to be based.

(3) If it appears to the court that the application and the evidence produced by the applicant in support of it do not disclose a prima facie case for granting it, the court—

(a) must refuse the application, and

(b) may make any consequential order it considers appropriate.

(4) If the application is not refused under subsection (3)—

(a) the applicant must serve the application on the company,

(b) the court—

(i) may make an order requiring evidence to be produced by the company, and

(ii) may adjourn the proceedings on the application to enable the evidence to be obtained, and

(c) the company is entitled to take part in the further proceedings on the application.

(5) On hearing the application, the court may—

(a) grant the application on such terms as it thinks fit,

(b) refuse the application, or

(c) adjourn the proceedings on the application and make such order as to further procedure as it thinks fit.

[1.295]

267 Application to continue proceedings as derivative proceedings

(1) This section applies where—

(a) a company has raised proceedings, and

(b) the proceedings are in respect of an act or omission which could be the basis for derivative proceedings.

(2) A member of the company may apply to the court to be substituted for the company in the proceedings, and for the proceedings to continue in consequence as derivative proceedings, on the ground that—

(a) the manner in which the company commenced or continued the proceedings amounts to an abuse of the process of the court,

(b) the company has failed to prosecute the proceedings diligently, and

(c) it is appropriate for the member to be substituted for the company in the proceedings.

(3) If it appears to the court that the application and the evidence produced by the applicant in support of it do not disclose a prima facie case for granting it, the court—

(a) must refuse the application, and

(b) may make any consequential order it considers appropriate.

(4) If the application is not refused under subsection (3)—

(a) the applicant must serve the application on the company,

(b) the court—

(i) may make an order requiring evidence to be produced by the company, and

(ii) may adjourn the proceedings on the application to enable the evidence to be obtained, and

(c) the company is entitled to take part in the further proceedings on the application.

(5) On hearing the application, the court may—

(a) grant the application on such terms as it thinks fit,

(b) refuse the application, or

(c) adjourn the proceedings on the application and make such order as to further procedure as it thinks fit.

[1.296]

268 Granting of leave

(1) The court must refuse leave to raise derivative proceedings or an application under section 267 if satisfied—

(a) that a person acting in accordance with section 172 (duty to promote the success of the company) would not seek to raise or continue the proceedings (as the case may be), or

(b) where the cause of action is an act or omission that is yet to occur, that the act or omission has been authorised by the company, or

(c) where the cause of action is an act or omission that has already occurred, that the act or omission—

(i) was authorised by the company before it occurred, or

(ii) has been ratified by the company since it occurred.

(2) In considering whether to grant leave to raise derivative proceedings or an application under section 267, the court must take into account, in particular—

(a) whether the member is acting in good faith in seeking to raise or continue the proceedings (as the case may be),

(b) the importance that a person acting in accordance with section 172 (duty to promote the success of the company) would attach to raising or continuing them (as the case may be),

(c) where the cause of action is an act or omission that is yet to occur, whether the act or omission could be, and in the circumstances would be likely to be—

(i) authorised by the company before it occurs, or

(ii) ratified by the company after it occurs,

(d) where the cause of action is an act or omission that has already occurred, whether the act or omission could be, and in the circumstances would be likely to be, ratified by the company,

(e) whether the company has decided not to raise proceedings in respect of the same cause of action or to persist in the proceedings (as the case may be),

(f) whether the cause of action is one which the member could pursue in his own right rather than on behalf of the company.

(3) In considering whether to grant leave to raise derivative proceedings or an application under section 267, the court shall have particular regard to any evidence before it as to the views of members of the company who have no personal interest, direct or indirect, in the matter.

(4) The Secretary of State may by regulations—

(a) amend subsection (1) so as to alter or add to the circumstances in which leave or an application is to be refused,

(b) amend subsection (2) so as to alter or add to the matters that the court is required to take into account in considering whether to grant leave or an application.

(5) Before making any such regulations the Secretary of State shall consult such persons as he considers appropriate.

(6) Regulations under this section are subject to affirmative resolution procedure.

[1.297]

269 Application by member to be substituted for member pursuing derivative proceedings

(1) This section applies where a member of a company ("the claimant")—

(a) has raised derivative proceedings,

(b) has continued as derivative proceedings raised by the company, or

(c) has continued derivative proceedings under this section.

(2) Another member of the company ("the applicant") may apply to the court to be substituted for the claimant in the action on the ground that—

(a) the manner in which the proceedings have been commenced or continued by the claimant amounts to an abuse of the process of the court,

(b) the claimant has failed to prosecute the proceedings diligently, and

(c) it is appropriate for the applicant to be substituted for the claimant in the proceedings.

(3) If it appears to the court that the application and the evidence produced by the applicant in support of it do not disclose a prima facie case for granting it, the court—

(a) must refuse the application, and

(b) may make any consequential order it considers appropriate.

(4) If the application is not refused under subsection (3)—

(a) the applicant must serve the application on the company,

(b) the court—

(i) may make an order requiring evidence to be produced by the company, and

(ii) may adjourn the proceedings on the application to enable the evidence to be obtained, and

(c) the company is entitled to take part in the further proceedings on the application.

(5) On hearing the application, the court may—

(a) grant the application on such terms as it thinks fit,

(b) refuse the application, or

(c) adjourn the proceedings on the application and make such order as to further procedure as it thinks fit.

PART 12 COMPANY SECRETARIES

Private companies

[1.298]

270 Private company not required to have secretary

(1) A private company is not required to have a secretary.

(2) References in the Companies Acts to a private company "without a secretary" are to a private company that for the time being is taking advantage of the exemption in subsection (1); and references to a private company "with a secretary" shall be construed accordingly.

(3) In the case of a private company without a secretary—

(a) anything authorised or required to be given or sent to, or served on, the company by being sent to its secretary—

(i) may be given or sent to, or served on, the company itself, and

(ii) if addressed to the secretary shall be treated as addressed to the company; and

(b) anything else required or authorised to be done by or to the secretary of the company may be done by or to—

(i) a director, or

(ii) a person authorised generally or specifically in that behalf by the directors.

Public companies

[1.299]

271 Public company required to have secretary

A public company must have a secretary.

[1.300]

272 Direction requiring public company to appoint secretary

(1) If it appears to the Secretary of State that a public company is in breach of section 271 (requirement to have secretary), the Secretary of State may give the company a direction under this section.

(2) The direction must state that the company appears to be in breach of that section and specify—

(a) what the company must do in order to comply with the direction, and

(b) the period within which it must do so.

That period must be not less than one month or more than three months after the date on which the direction is given.

(3) The direction must also inform the company of the consequences of failing to comply.

(4) Where the company is in breach of section 271 it must comply with the direction by—

(a) making the necessary appointment, and

(b) giving notice of it under section 276,

before the end of the period specified in the direction.

(5) If the company has already made the necessary appointment, it must comply with the direction by giving notice of it under section 276 before the end of the period specified in the direction.

(6) If a company fails to comply with a direction under this section, an offence is committed by—

(a) the company, and

(b) every officer of the company who is in default.

For this purpose a shadow director is treated as an officer of the company.

(7) A person guilty of an offence under this section is liable on summary conviction to a fine not exceeding level 5 on the standard scale and, for continued contravention, a daily default fine not exceeding [one-tenth of the greater of £5,000 or level 4 on the standard scale].

NOTES

Sub-s (7): words in square brackets substituted (for the original words "one-tenth of level 5 on the standard scale") by the Legal Aid, Sentencing and Punishment of Offenders Act 2012 (Fines on Summary Conviction) Regulations 2015, SI 2015/664, regs 3, 5, Sch 3, Pt 1, para 9(1), (9), as from 12 March 2015, in relation to England and Wales only (except in relation to (a) fines for offences committed before 12 March 2015, (b) the operation of restrictions on fines that may be imposed on a person aged under 18, or (c) fines that may be imposed on a person convicted by a magistrates' court who is to be sentenced as if convicted on indictment).

[1.301]
273 Qualifications of secretaries of public companies
(1) It is the duty of the directors of a public company to take all reasonable steps to secure that the secretary (or each joint secretary) of the company—
(a) is a person who appears to them to have the requisite knowledge and experience to discharge the functions of secretary of the company, and
(b) has one or more of the following qualifications.
(2) The qualifications are—
(a) that he has held the office of secretary of a public company for at least three of the five years immediately preceding his appointment as secretary;
(b) that he is a member of any of the bodies specified in subsection (3);
(c) that he is a barrister, advocate or solicitor called or admitted in any part of the United Kingdom;
(d) that he is a person who, by virtue of his holding or having held any other position or his being a member of any other body, appears to the directors to be capable of discharging the functions of secretary of the company.
(3) The bodies referred to in subsection (2)(b) are—
(a) the Institute of Chartered Accountants in England and Wales;
(b) the Institute of Chartered Accountants of Scotland;
(c) the Association of Chartered Certified Accountants;
(d) the Institute of Chartered Accountants in Ireland;
(e) the Institute of Chartered Secretaries and Administrators;
(f) the Chartered Institute of Management Accountants;
(g) the Chartered Institute of Public Finance and Accountancy.

Provisions applying to private companies with a secretary and to public companies

[1.302]
274 Discharge of functions where office vacant or secretary unable to act
Where in the case of any company the office of secretary is vacant, or there is for any other reason no secretary capable of acting, anything required or authorised to be done by or to the secretary may be done—
(a) by or to an assistant or deputy secretary (if any), or
(b) if there is no assistant or deputy secretary or none capable of acting, by or to any person authorised generally or specifically in that behalf by the directors.

[1.303]
[274A Alternative method of record-keeping
Sections 275 and 276 must be read with sections 279A to 279E (which allow for an alternative method of record-keeping in the case of private companies).]

NOTES
Inserted by the Small Business, Enterprise and Employment Act 2015, s 94, Sch 5, Pt 1, paras 8, 9, as from 30 June 2016.

[1.304]
275 Duty to keep register of secretaries
(1) A company must keep a register of its secretaries.
(2) The register must contain the required particulars (see sections 277 to 279) of the person who is, or persons who are, the secretary or joint secretaries of the company.
(3) The register must be kept available for inspection—
(a) at the company's registered office, or
(b) at a place specified in regulations under section 1136.
(4) The company must give notice to the registrar—
(a) of the place at which the register is kept available for inspection, and
(b) of any change in that place,
unless it has at all times been kept at the company's registered office.
(5) The register must be open to the inspection—
(a) of any member of the company without charge, and
(b) of any other person on payment of such fee as may be prescribed.
(6) If default is made in complying with subsection (1), (2) or (3), or if default is made for 14 days in complying with subsection (4), or if an inspection required under subsection (5) is refused, an offence is committed by—
(a) the company, and
(b) every officer of the company who is in default.
For this purpose a shadow director is treated as an officer of the company.
(7) A person guilty of an offence under this section is liable on summary conviction to a fine not exceeding level 5 on the standard scale and, for continued contravention, a daily default fine not exceeding [one-tenth of the greater of £5,000 or level 4 on the standard scale].
(8) In the case of a refusal of inspection of the register, the court may by order compel an immediate inspection of it.

NOTES
Sub-s (7): words in square brackets substituted (for the original words "one-tenth of level 5 on the standard scale") by the Legal Aid, Sentencing and Punishment of Offenders Act 2012 (Fines on Summary Conviction) Regulations 2015, SI 2015/664, regs 3, 5, Sch 3, Pt 1, para 9(1), (10), as from 12 March 2015, in relation to England and Wales only (except in relation to (a) fines for offences committed before 12 March 2015, (b) the operation of restrictions on fines that may be imposed on a person aged under 18, or (c) fines that may be imposed on a person convicted by a magistrates' court who is to be sentenced as if convicted on indictment).

Temporary modification: this section was modified by the Companies etc (Filing Requirements) (Temporary Modifications) Regulations 2020, SI 2020/645, reg 9. By virtue of the Corporate Insolvency and Governance Act 2020, s 39(8), the modification applied from 27 June 2020 to the end of the day on 5 April 2021 (subject to the saving provision in s 39(9) which provides that the expiry of s 39 on 5 April 2021 does not affect the continued operation of any Regulations made under that section for the purpose of determining the length of any period that began before the expiry). As modified, sub-s (6) above had effect as if for the reference to "14 days" there were substituted a reference to "42 days".

Regulations: the Companies (Fees for Inspection of Company Records) Regulations 2008, SI 2008/3007 at **[4.177]**. For a summary of all statutory instruments made under this Act, see Appendix 4 at **[A4]**.

[1.305]

276 Duty to notify registrar of changes

(1) A company must, within the period of 14 days from—

(a) a person becoming or ceasing to be its secretary or one of its joint secretaries, or

(b) the occurrence of any change in the particulars contained in its register of secretaries,

give notice to the registrar of the change and of the date on which it occurred.

(2) Notice of a person having become secretary, or one of joint secretaries, of the company must be accompanied by a [statement by the company that the person has consented] to act in the relevant capacity.

(3) If default is made in complying with this section, an offence is committed by every officer of the company who is in default.

For this purpose a shadow director is treated as an officer of the company.

(4) A person guilty of an offence under this section is liable on summary conviction to a fine not exceeding level 5 on the standard scale and, for continued contravention, a daily default fine not exceeding [one-tenth of the greater of £5,000 or level 4 on the standard scale].

NOTES

Sub-s (2): words in square brackets substituted by the Small Business, Enterprise and Employment Act 2015, s 100(1), (5), as from 10 October 2015 (for savings provisions see the note to s 12 of this Act at **[1.12]**).

Sub-s (4): words in square brackets substituted (for the original words "one-tenth of level 5 on the standard scale") by the Legal Aid, Sentencing and Punishment of Offenders Act 2012 (Fines on Summary Conviction) Regulations 2015, SI 2015/664, regs 3, 5, Sch 3, Pt 1, para 9(1), (11), as from 12 March 2015, in relation to England and Wales only (except in relation to (a) fines for offences committed before 12 March 2015, (b) the operation of restrictions on fines that may be imposed on a person aged under 18, or (c) fines that may be imposed on a person convicted by a magistrates' court who is to be sentenced as if convicted on indictment).

Temporary modification: this section was modified by the Companies etc (Filing Requirements) (Temporary Modifications) Regulations 2020, SI 2020/645, reg 10. By virtue of the Corporate Insolvency and Governance Act 2020, s 39(8), the modification applied from 27 June 2020 to the end of the day on 5 April 2021 (subject to the saving provision in s 39(9) which provides that the expiry of s 39 on 5 April 2021 does not affect the continued operation of any Regulations made under that section for the purpose of determining the length of any period that began before the expiry). As modified, sub-s (1) above had effect as if for the reference to "14 days" there were substituted a reference to "42 days".

[1.306]

277 Particulars of secretaries to be registered: individuals

(1) A company's register of secretaries must contain the following particulars in the case of an individual—

(a) name and any former name;

(b) address.

(2) For the purposes of this section "name" means a person's Christian name (or other forename) and surname, except that in the case of—

(a) a peer, or

(b) an individual usually known by a title,

the title may be stated instead of his Christian name (or other forename) and surname or in addition to either or both of them.

(3) For the purposes of this section a "former name" means a name by which the individual was formerly known for business purposes.

Where a person is or was formerly known by more than one such name, each of them must be stated.

(4) It is not necessary for the register to contain particulars of a former name in the following cases—

(a) in the case of a peer or an individual normally known by a British title, where the name is one by which the person was known previous to the adoption of or succession to the title;

(b) in the case of any person, where the former name—

(i) was changed or disused before the person attained the age of 16 years, or

(ii) has been changed or disused for 20 years or more.

(5) The address required to be stated in the register is a service address. This may be stated to be "The company's registered office".

[1.307]

278 Particulars of secretaries to be registered: corporate secretaries and firms

(1) A company's register of secretaries must contain the following particulars in the case of a body corporate, or a firm that is a legal person under the law by which it is governed—

(a) corporate or firm name;

(b) registered or principal office;

[(c) in the case of a limited company that is a UK-registered company, the registered number;]

(d) in any other case, particulars of—

(i) the legal form of the company or firm and the law by which it is governed, and

(ii) if applicable, the register in which it is entered (including details of the state) and its registration number in that register.

(2) If all the partners in a firm are joint secretaries it is sufficient to state the particulars that would be required if the firm were a legal person and the firm had been appointed secretary.

NOTES

Para (c) was substituted by the Companies, Limited Liability Partnerships and Partnerships (Amendment etc) (EU Exit) Regulations 2019, SI 2019/348, reg 6, Sch 1, paras 1, 5, as from IP completion day (as defined in the European Union (Withdrawal Agreement) Act 2020, s 39) (for transitional provisions see Sch 4, para 2 to the 2019 Regulations at **[12.105]**).

[1.308]

279 Particulars of secretaries to be registered: power to make regulations

(1) The Secretary of State may make provision by regulations amending—

section 277 (particulars of secretaries to be registered: individuals), or

section 278 (particulars of secretaries to be registered: corporate secretaries and firms),

so as to add to or remove items from the particulars required to be contained in a company's register of secretaries.

(2) Regulations under this section are subject to affirmative resolution procedure.

[Option to keep information on the central register

[1.309]

279A Right to make an election

(1) An election may be made under this section—

(a) by the subscribers wishing to form a private company under this Act, or

(b) by the private company itself once it is formed and registered.

(2) The election is made by giving notice of election to the registrar.

(3) If the notice is given by subscribers wishing to form a private company, it must be given when the documents required to be delivered under section 9 are delivered to the registrar.]

NOTES

Inserted, together with the preceding heading and ss 279B–279F, by the Small Business, Enterprise and Employment Act 2015, s 94, Sch 5, Pt 1, paras 8, 10, as from 30 June 2016.

[1.310]

[279B Effective date of election

(1) An election made under section 279A takes effect when the notice of election is registered by the registrar.

(2) The election remains in force until either—

(a) the company ceases to be a private company, or

(b) a notice of withdrawal sent by the company under section 279E is registered by the registrar,

whichever occurs first.]

NOTES

Inserted as noted to s 279A at **[1.309]**.

[1.311]

[279C Effect of election on obligations under sections 275 and 276

If an election is in force under section 279A in respect of a company, the company's obligations—

(a) to keep and maintain a register of secretaries under section 275, and

(b) to notify the registrar of changes to it under section 276,

do not apply with respect to the period when the election is in force.]

NOTES

Inserted as noted to s 279A at **[1.309]**.

[1.312]

[279D Duty to notify registrar of changes

(1) The duty under subsection (2) applies during the period when an election under section 279A is in force.

(2) The company must deliver to the registrar—

(a) any information of which the company would during that period have been obliged to give notice under section 276, had the election not been in force, and

(b) any statement that would have had to accompany such a notice.

(3) The information (and any accompanying statement) must be delivered as soon as reasonably practicable after the company becomes aware of the information and, in any event, no later than the time by which the company would have been obliged under section 276 to give notice of the information.

(4) If default is made in complying with this section, an offence is committed by—

(a) the company, and

(b) every officer of the company who is in default.

For this purpose a shadow director is treated as an officer of the company.

(5) A person guilty of an offence under this section is liable on summary conviction—

(a) in England and Wales, to a fine and, for continued contravention, a daily default fine not exceeding the greater of £500 and one-tenth of level 4 on the standard scale;

(b) in Scotland or Northern Ireland, to a fine not exceeding level 5 on the standard scale and, for continued contravention, a daily default fine not exceeding one-tenth of level 5 on the standard scale.]

NOTES

Inserted as noted to s 279A at **[1.309]**.

[1.313]

[279E Withdrawing the election

(1) A company may withdraw an election made by or in respect of it under section 279A.

(2) Withdrawal is achieved by giving notice of withdrawal to the registrar.

(3) The withdrawal takes effect when the notice is registered by the registrar.

(4) The effect of withdrawal is that the company's obligation under section 275 to keep and maintain a register of secretaries, and its obligation under section 276 to notify the registrar of changes to that register, apply from then on with respect to the period going forward.

(5) This means that, when the withdrawal takes effect—

(a) the company must enter in its register of secretaries all the information that is required to be contained in that register in respect of matters that are current as at that time, but

(b) the company is not required to enter in its register information relating to the period when the election was in force that is no longer current.]

NOTES

Inserted as noted to s 279A at **[1.309]**.

[1.314]

[279F Power to extend option to public companies

(1) The Secretary of State may by regulations amend this Act—

(a) to extend sections 279A to 279E (with or without modification) to public companies or public companies of a class specified in the regulations, and

(b) to make such other amendments as the Secretary of State thinks fit in consequence of that extension.

(2) Regulations under this section are subject to affirmative resolution procedure.]

NOTES

Inserted as noted to s 279A at **[1.309]**.

[1.315]

280 Acts done by person in dual capacity

A provision requiring or authorising a thing to be done by or to a director and the secretary of a company is not satisfied by its being done by or to the same person acting both as director and as, or in place of, the secretary.

PART 13 RESOLUTIONS AND MEETINGS

CHAPTER 1 GENERAL PROVISIONS ABOUT RESOLUTIONS

[1.316]

281 Resolutions

(1) A resolution of the members (or of a class of members) of a private company must be passed—

(a) as a written resolution in accordance with Chapter 2, or

(b) at a meeting of the members (to which the provisions of Chapter 3 apply).

(2) A resolution of the members (or of a class of members) of a public company must be passed at a meeting of the members (to which the provisions of Chapter 3 and, where relevant, Chapter 4 apply).

(3) Where a provision of the Companies Acts—

(a) requires a resolution of a company, or of the members (or a class of members) of a company, and

(b) does not specify what kind of resolution is required,

what is required is an ordinary resolution unless the company's articles require a higher majority (or unanimity).

(4) Nothing in this Part affects any enactment or rule of law as to—

(a) things done otherwise than by passing a resolution,

(b) circumstances in which a resolution is or is not treated as having been passed, or

(c) cases in which a person is precluded from alleging that a resolution has not been duly passed.

[1.317]

282 Ordinary resolutions

(1) An ordinary resolution of the members (or of a class of members) of a company means a resolution that is passed by a simple majority.

(2) A written resolution is passed by a simple majority if it is passed by members representing a simple majority of the total voting rights of eligible members (see Chapter 2).

(3) A resolution passed at a meeting on a show of hands is passed by a simple majority if it is passed by [a simple majority of the votes cast by those entitled to vote].

(4) A resolution passed on a poll taken at a meeting is passed by a simple majority if it is passed by members representing a simple majority of the total voting rights of members who (being entitled to do so) vote [in person, by proxy or in advance (see section 322A)] on the resolution.

(5) Anything that may be done by ordinary resolution may also be done by special resolution.

NOTES

Sub-ss (3), (4): words in square brackets substituted by the Companies (Shareholders' Rights) Regulations 2009, SI 2009/1632, regs 2(1), 5(2), as from 3 August 2009, in relation to meetings of which notice is given, or first given, on or after that date.

[1.318]

283 Special resolutions

(1) A special resolution of the members (or of a class of members) of a company means a resolution passed by a majority of not less than 75%.

(2) A written resolution is passed by a majority of not less than 75% if it is passed by members representing not less than 75% of the total voting rights of eligible members (see Chapter 2).

(3) Where a resolution of a private company is passed as a written resolution—

(a) the resolution is not a special resolution unless it stated that it was proposed as a special resolution, and

(b) if the resolution so stated, it may only be passed as a special resolution.

(4) A resolution passed at a meeting on a show of hands is passed by a majority of not less than 75% if it is passed by [not less than 75% of the votes cast by those entitled to vote]

(5) A resolution passed on a poll taken at a meeting is passed by a majority of not less than 75% if it is passed by members representing not less than 75% of the total voting rights of the members who (being entitled to do so) vote [in person, by proxy or in advance (see section 322A)] on the resolution.

(6) Where a resolution is passed at a meeting—

(a) the resolution is not a special resolution unless the notice of the meeting included the text of the resolution and specified the intention to propose the resolution as a special resolution, and

(b) if the notice of the meeting so specified, the resolution may only be passed as a special resolution.

NOTES

Sub-ss (4), (5): words in square brackets substituted by the Companies (Shareholders' Rights) Regulations 2009, SI 2009/1632, reg 2(2), 5(2), as from 3 August 2009, in relation to meetings of which notice is given, or first given, on or after that date.

[1.319]

284 Votes: general rules

(1) On a vote on a written resolution—

(a) in the case of a company having a share capital, every member has one vote in respect of each share or each £10 of stock held by him, and

(b) in any other case, every member has one vote.

[(2) On a vote on a resolution on a show of hands at a meeting, each member present in person has one vote.]

(3) On a vote on a resolution on a poll taken at a meeting—

(a) in the case of a company having a share capital, every member has one vote in respect of each share or each £10 of stock held by him, and

(b) in any other case, every member has one vote.

(4) The provisions of this section have effect subject to any provision of the company's articles.

[(5) Nothing in this section is to be read as restricting the effect of—

section 152 (exercise of rights by nominees),
section 285 (voting by proxy),
section 322 (exercise of voting rights on poll),
section 322A (voting on a poll: votes cast in advance), or
section 323 (representation of corporations at meetings).]

NOTES

Sub-s (2) substituted, and sub-s (5) added, by the Companies (Shareholders' Rights) Regulations 2009, SI 2009/1632, reg 2(3), (4), as from 3 August 2009, in relation to meetings of which notice is given, or first given, on or after that date.

[1.320]

[285 Voting by proxy

(1) On a vote on a resolution on a show of hands at a meeting, every proxy present who has been duly appointed by one or more members entitled to vote on the resolution has one vote.

This is subject to subsection (2).

(2) On a vote on a resolution on a show of hands at a meeting, a proxy has one vote for and one vote against the resolution if—

(a) the proxy has been duly appointed by more than one member entitled to vote on the resolution, and

(b) the proxy has been instructed by one or more of those members to vote for the resolution and by one or more other of those members to vote against it.

(3) On a poll taken at a meeting of a company all or any of the voting rights of a member may be exercised by one or more duly appointed proxies.

(4) Where a member appoints more than one proxy, subsection (3) does not authorise the exercise by the proxies taken together of more extensive voting rights than could be exercised by the member in person.

(5) Subsections (1) and (2) have effect subject to any provision of the company's articles.]

NOTES

Substituted, together with s 285A (for the original s 285), by the Companies (Shareholders' Rights) Regulations 2009, SI 2009/1632, reg 3, as from 3 August 2009, in relation to meetings of which notice is given, or first given, on or after that date.

[1.321]

[285A Voting rights on poll or written resolution

In relation to a resolution required or authorised by an enactment, if a private company's articles provide that a member has a different number of votes in relation to a resolution when it is passed as a written resolution and when it is passed on a poll taken at a meeting—

(a) the provision about how many votes a member has in relation to the resolution passed on a poll is void, and

(b) a member has the same number of votes in relation to the resolution when it is passed on a poll as the member has when it is passed as a written resolution.]

NOTES

Substituted as noted to s 285 at **[1.320]**.

[1.322]

286 Votes of joint holders of shares

(1) In the case of joint holders of shares of a company, only the vote of the senior holder who votes (and any proxies duly authorised by him) may be counted by the company.

(2) For the purposes of this section, the senior holder of a share is determined by the order in which the names of the joint holders appear in the register of members [(or, if an election under section 128B is in force in respect of the company, in the register kept by the registrar under section 1080)].

(3) Subsections (1) and (2) have effect subject to any provision of the company's articles.

NOTES

Sub-s (2): words in square brackets inserted by the Small Business, Enterprise and Employment Act 2015, s 94, Sch 5, Pt 2, paras 11, 16, as from 30 June 2016.

[1.323]

287 Saving for provisions of articles as to determination of entitlement to vote

Nothing in this Chapter affects—

(a) any provision of a company's articles—

(i) requiring an objection to a person's entitlement to vote on a resolution to be made in accordance with the articles, and

(ii) for the determination of any such objection to be final and conclusive, or

(b) the grounds on which such a determination may be questioned in legal proceedings.

CHAPTER 2 WRITTEN RESOLUTIONS

General provisions about written resolutions

[1.324]

288 Written resolutions of private companies

(1) In the Companies Acts a "written resolution" means a resolution of a private company proposed and passed in accordance with this Chapter.

(2) The following may not be passed as a written resolution—

(a) a resolution under section 168 removing a director before the expiration of his period of office;

(b) a resolution under section 510 removing an auditor before the expiration of his term of office.

(3) A resolution may be proposed as a written resolution—

(a) by the directors of a private company (see section 291), or

(b) by the members of a private company (see sections 292 to 295).

(4) References in enactments passed or made before this Chapter comes into force to—

(a) a resolution of a company in general meeting, or

(b) a resolution of a meeting of a class of members of the company,

have effect as if they included references to a written resolution of the members, or of a class of members, of a private company (as appropriate).

(5) A written resolution of a private company has effect as if passed (as the case may be)—

(a) by the company in general meeting, or

(b) by a meeting of a class of members of the company,

and references in enactments passed or made before this section comes into force to a meeting at which a resolution is passed or to members voting in favour of a resolution shall be construed accordingly.

[1.325]

289 Eligible members

(1) In relation to a resolution proposed as a written resolution of a private company, the eligible members are the members who would have been entitled to vote on the resolution on the circulation date of the resolution (see section 290).

(2) If the persons entitled to vote on a written resolution change during the course of the day that is the circulation date of the resolution, the eligible members are the persons entitled to vote on the resolution at the time that the first copy of the resolution is sent or submitted to a member for his agreement.

Circulation of written resolutions

[1.326]

290 Circulation date

References in this Part to the circulation date of a written resolution are to the date on which copies of it are sent or submitted to members in accordance with this Chapter (or if copies are sent or submitted to members on different days, to the first of those days).

[1.327]

291 Circulation of written resolutions proposed by directors

(1) This section applies to a resolution proposed as a written resolution by the directors of the company.

(2) The company must send or submit a copy of the resolution to every eligible member.

(3) The company must do so—

(a) by sending copies at the same time (so far as reasonably practicable) to all eligible members in hard copy form, in electronic form or by means of a website, or

(b) if it is possible to do so without undue delay, by submitting the same copy to each eligible member in turn (or different copies to each of a number of eligible members in turn),

or by sending copies to some members in accordance with paragraph (a) and submitting a copy or copies to other members in accordance with paragraph (b).

(4) The copy of the resolution must be accompanied by a statement informing the member—

(a) how to signify agreement to the resolution (see section 296), and

(b) as to the date by which the resolution must be passed if it is not to lapse (see section 297).

(5) In the event of default in complying with this section, an offence is committed by every officer of the company who is in default.

(6) A person guilty of an offence under this section is liable—

(a) on conviction on indictment, to a fine;

(b) on summary conviction, to a fine not exceeding the statutory maximum.

(7) The validity of the resolution, if passed, is not affected by a failure to comply with this section.

[1.328]

292 Members' power to require circulation of written resolution

(1) The members of a private company may require the company to circulate a resolution that may properly be moved and is proposed to be moved as a written resolution.

(2) Any resolution may properly be moved as a written resolution unless—

(a) it would, if passed, be ineffective (whether by reason of inconsistency with any enactment or the company's constitution or otherwise),

(b) it is defamatory of any person, or

(c) it is frivolous or vexatious.

(3) Where the members require a company to circulate a resolution they may require the company to circulate with it a statement of not more than 1,000 words on the subject matter of the resolution.

(4) A company is required to circulate the resolution and any accompanying statement once it has received requests that it do so from members representing not less than the requisite percentage of the total voting rights of all members entitled to vote on the resolution.

(5) The "requisite percentage" is 5% or such lower percentage as is specified for this purpose in the company's articles.

(6) A request—

(a) may be in hard copy form or in electronic form,

(b) must identify the resolution and any accompanying statement, and

(c) must be authenticated by the person or persons making it.

[1.329]

293 Circulation of written resolution proposed by members

(1) A company that is required under section 292 to circulate a resolution must send or submit to every eligible member—

(a) a copy of the resolution, and

(b) a copy of any accompanying statement.

This is subject to section 294(2) (deposit or tender of sum in respect of expenses of circulation) and section 295 (application not to circulate members' statement).

(2) The company must do so—

(a) by sending copies at the same time (so far as reasonably practicable) to all eligible members in hard copy form, in electronic form or by means of a website, or

(b) if it is possible to do so without undue delay, by submitting the same copy to each eligible member in turn (or different copies to each of a number of eligible members in turn),

or by sending copies to some members in accordance with paragraph (a) and submitting a copy or copies to other members in accordance with paragraph (b).

(3) The company must send or submit the copies (or, if copies are sent or submitted to members on different days, the first of those copies) not more than 21 days after it becomes subject to the requirement under section 292 to circulate the resolution.

(4) The copy of the resolution must be accompanied by guidance as to—

(a) how to signify agreement to the resolution (see section 296), and

(b) the date by which the resolution must be passed if it is not to lapse (see section 297).

(5) In the event of default in complying with this section, an offence is committed by every officer of the company who is in default.

(6) A person guilty of an offence under this section is liable—

(a) on conviction on indictment, to a fine;

(b) on summary conviction, to a fine not exceeding the statutory maximum.

(7) The validity of the resolution, if passed, is not affected by a failure to comply with this section.

[1.330]

294 Expenses of circulation

(1) The expenses of the company in complying with section 293 must be paid by the members who requested the circulation of the resolution unless the company resolves otherwise.

(2) Unless the company has previously so resolved, it is not bound to comply with that section unless there is deposited with or tendered to it a sum reasonably sufficient to meet its expenses in doing so.

[1.331]

295 Application not to circulate members' statement

(1) A company is not required to circulate a members' statement under section 293 if, on an application by the company or another person who claims to be aggrieved, the court is satisfied that the rights conferred by section 292 and that section are being abused.

(2) The court may order the members who requested the circulation of the statement to pay the whole or part of the company's costs (in Scotland, expenses) on such an application, even if they are not parties to the application.

Agreeing to written resolutions

[1.332]

296 Procedure for signifying agreement to written resolution

(1) A member signifies his agreement to a proposed written resolution when the company receives from him (or from someone acting on his behalf) an authenticated document—

(a) identifying the resolution to which it relates, and

(b) indicating his agreement to the resolution.

(2) The document must be sent to the company in hard copy form or in electronic form.

(3) A member's agreement to a written resolution, once signified, may not be revoked.

(4) A written resolution is passed when the required majority of eligible members have signified their agreement to it.

[1.333]

297 Period for agreeing to written resolution

(1) A proposed written resolution lapses if it is not passed before the end of—

(a) the period specified for this purpose in the company's articles, or

(b) if none is specified, the period of 28 days beginning with the circulation date.

(2) The agreement of a member to a written resolution is ineffective if signified after the expiry of that period.

Supplementary

[1.334]

298 Sending documents relating to written resolutions by electronic means

(1) Where a company has given an electronic address in any document containing or accompanying a proposed written resolution, it is deemed to have agreed that any document or information relating to that resolution may be sent by electronic means to that address (subject to any conditions or limitations specified in the document).

(2) In this section "electronic address" means any address or number used for the purposes of sending or receiving documents or information by electronic means.

[1.335]

299 Publication of written resolution on website

(1) This section applies where a company sends—

(a) a written resolution, or

(b) a statement relating to a written resolution,

to a person by means of a website.

(2) The resolution or statement is not validly sent for the purposes of this Chapter unless the resolution is available on the website throughout the period beginning with the circulation date and ending on the date on which the resolution lapses under section 297.

[1.336]

300 Relationship between this Chapter and provisions of company's articles

A provision of the articles of a private company is void in so far as it would have the effect that a resolution that is required by or otherwise provided for in an enactment could not be proposed and passed as a written resolution.

CHAPTER 3 RESOLUTIONS AT MEETINGS

General provisions about resolutions at meetings

[1.337]

301 Resolutions at general meetings

A resolution of the members of a company is validly passed at a general meeting if—

(a) notice of the meeting and of the resolution is given, and

(b) the meeting is held and conducted,

in accordance with the provisions of this Chapter (and, where relevant, Chapter 4) and the company's articles.

Calling meetings

[1.338]

302 Directors' power to call general meetings

The directors of a company may call a general meeting of the company.

[1.339]

303 Members' power to require directors to call general meeting

(1) The members of a company may require the directors to call a general meeting of the company.

(2) The directors are required to call a general meeting once the company has received requests to do so from—

(a) members representing at least [5%] of such of the paid-up capital of the company as carries the right of voting at general meetings of the company (excluding any paid-up capital held as treasury shares); or

(b) in the case of a company not having a share capital, members who represent at least [5%] of the total voting rights of all the members having a right to vote at general meetings.

(3) . . .

(4) A request—

(a) must state the general nature of the business to be dealt with at the meeting, and

(b) may include the text of a resolution that may properly be moved and is intended to be moved at the meeting.

(5) A resolution may properly be moved at a meeting unless—

(a) it would, if passed, be ineffective (whether by reason of inconsistency with any enactment or the company's constitution or otherwise),

(b) it is defamatory of any person, or

(c) it is frivolous or vexatious.

(6) A request—

(a) may be in hard copy form or in electronic form, and

(b) must be authenticated by the person or persons making it.

NOTES

The figures in square brackets in sub-s (2) were substituted, and sub-s (3) was repealed, by the Companies (Shareholders' Rights) Regulations 2009, SI 2009/1632, reg 4, as from 3 August 2009, in relation to meetings of which notice is given, or first given, on or after that date.

[1.340]

304 Directors' duty to call meetings required by members

(1) Directors required under section 303 to call a general meeting of the company must call a meeting—

(a) within 21 days from the date on which they become subject to the requirement, and

(b) to be held on a date not more than 28 days after the date of the notice convening the meeting.

(2) If the requests received by the company identify a resolution intended to be moved at the meeting, the notice of the meeting must include notice of the resolution.

(3) The business that may be dealt with at the meeting includes a resolution of which notice is given in accordance with this section.

(4) If the resolution is to be proposed as a special resolution, the directors are treated as not having duly called the meeting if they do not give the required notice of the resolution in accordance with section 283.

[1.341]

305 Power of members to call meeting at company's expense

(1) If the directors—

(a) are required under section 303 to call a meeting, and

(b) do not do so in accordance with section 304,

the members who requested the meeting, or any of them representing more than one half of the total voting rights of all of them, may themselves call a general meeting.

(2) Where the requests received by the company included the text of a resolution intended to be moved at the meeting, the notice of the meeting must include notice of the resolution.

(3) The meeting must be called for a date not more than three months after the date on which the directors become subject to the requirement to call a meeting.

(4) The meeting must be called in the same manner, as nearly as possible, as that in which meetings are required to be called by directors of the company.

(5) The business which may be dealt with at the meeting includes a resolution of which notice is given in accordance with this section.

(6) Any reasonable expenses incurred by the members requesting the meeting by reason of the failure of the directors duly to call a meeting must be reimbursed by the company.

(7) Any sum so reimbursed shall be retained by the company out of any sums due or to become due from the company by way of fees or other remuneration in respect of the services of such of the directors as were in default.

[1.342]

306 Power of court to order meeting

(1) This section applies if for any reason it is impracticable—

(a) to call a meeting of a company in any manner in which meetings of that company may be called, or

(b) to conduct the meeting in the manner prescribed by the company's articles or this Act.

(2) The court may, either of its own motion or on the application—

(a) of a director of the company, or

(b) of a member of the company who would be entitled to vote at the meeting,

order a meeting to be called, held and conducted in any manner the court thinks fit.

(3) Where such an order is made, the court may give such ancillary or consequential directions as it thinks expedient.

(4) Such directions may include a direction that one member of the company present at the meeting be deemed to constitute a quorum.

(5) A meeting called, held and conducted in accordance with an order under this section is deemed for all purposes to be a meeting of the company duly called, held and conducted.

Notice of meetings

[1.343]

307 Notice required of general meeting

[(A1) This section applies to—

(a) a general meeting of a company that is not a traded company; and

(b) a general meeting of a traded company that is an opted-in company (as defined by section 971(1)), where—

(i) the meeting is held to decide whether to take any action that might result in the frustration of a takeover bid for the company; or

(ii) the meeting is held by virtue of section 969 (power of offeror to require general meeting to be held).

(A2) For corresponding provision in relation to general meetings of traded companies (other than meetings within subsection (A1)(b)), see section 307A.]

(1) A general meeting of a private company (other than an adjourned meeting) must be called by notice of at least 14 days.

(2) A general meeting of a public company (other than an adjourned meeting) must be called by notice of—

(a) in the case of an annual general meeting, at least 21 days, and

(b) in any other case, at least 14 days.

(3) The company's articles may require a longer period of notice than that specified in subsection (1) or (2).

(4) A general meeting may be called by shorter notice than that otherwise required if shorter notice is agreed by the members.

(5) The shorter notice must be agreed to by a majority in number of the members having a right to attend and vote at the meeting, being a majority who—

(a) together hold not less than the requisite percentage in nominal value of the shares giving a right to attend and vote at the meeting (excluding any shares in the company held as treasury shares), or

(b) in the case of a company not having a share capital, together represent not less than the requisite percentage of the total voting rights at that meeting of all the members.

(6) The requisite percentage is—

(a) in the case of a private company, 90% or such higher percentage (not exceeding 95%) as may be specified in the company's articles;

(b) in the case of a public company, 95%.

(7) Subsections (5) and (6) do not apply to an annual general meeting of a public company (see instead section 337(2)).

NOTES

Sub-ss (A1), (A2): inserted by the Companies (Shareholders' Rights) Regulations 2009, SI 2009/1632, reg 9(1), as from 3 August 2009, in relation to meetings of which notice is given, or first given, on or after that date.

[1.344]

[307A Notice required of general meeting: certain meetings of traded companies

(1) A general meeting of a traded company must be called by notice of—

(a) in a case where conditions A to C (set out below) are met, at least 14 days;

(b) in any other case, at least 21 days.

(2) Condition A is that the general meeting is not an annual general meeting.

(3) Condition B is that the company offers the facility for members to vote by electronic means accessible to all members who hold shares that carry rights to vote at general meetings.

This condition is met if there is a facility, offered by the company and accessible to all such members, to appoint a proxy by means of a website.

(4) Condition C is that a special resolution reducing the period of notice to not less than 14 days has been passed—

(a) at the immediately preceding annual general meeting, or

(b) at a general meeting held since that annual general meeting.

(5) In the case of a company which has not yet held an annual general meeting, condition C is that a special resolution reducing the period of notice to not less than 14 days has been passed at a general meeting.

(6) The company's articles may require a longer period of notice than that specified in subsection (1).

(7) Where a general meeting is adjourned, the adjourned meeting may be called by shorter notice than required by subsection (1).

But in the case of an adjournment for lack of a quorum this subsection applies only if—

(a) no business is to be dealt with at the adjourned meeting the general nature of which was not stated in the notice of the original meeting, and

(b) the adjourned meeting is to be held at least 10 days after the original meeting.

(8) Nothing in this section applies in relation to a general meeting of a kind mentioned in section 307(A1)(b) (certain meetings regarding takeover of opted-in company).]

NOTES

Inserted by the Companies (Shareholders' Rights) Regulations 2009, SI 2009/1632, reg 9(2), as from 3 August 2009, in relation to meetings of which notice is given, or first given, on or after that date (note that in sub-ss (4) and (5) above, references to annual general meetings and general meetings include ones held before 3 August 2009 (see reg 23 of the 2009 Regulations)).

[1.345]

308 Manner in which notice to be given

Notice of a general meeting of a company must be given—

(a) in hard copy form,

(b) in electronic form, or

(c) by means of a website (see section 309),

or partly by one such means and partly by another.

[1.346]

309 Publication of notice of meeting on website

(1) Notice of a meeting is not validly given by a company by means of a website unless it is given in accordance with this section.

(2) When the company notifies a member of the presence of the notice on the website the notification must—

(a) state that it concerns a notice of a company meeting,

(b) specify the place, date and time of the meeting, and

(c) in the case of a public company, state whether the meeting will be an annual general meeting.

(3) The notice must be available on the website throughout the period beginning with the date of that notification and ending with the conclusion of the meeting.

[1.347]

310 Persons entitled to receive notice of meetings

(1) Notice of a general meeting of a company must be sent to—

(a) every member of the company, and

(b) every director.

(2) In subsection (1), the reference to members includes any person who is entitled to a share in consequence of the death or bankruptcy of a member, if the company has been notified of their entitlement.

(3) In subsection (2), the reference to the bankruptcy of a member includes—

(a) the sequestration of the estate of a member;

(b) a member's estate being the subject of a protected trust deed (within the meaning of the Bankruptcy (Scotland) Act [2016]).

(4) This section has effect subject to—

(a) any enactment, and

(b) any provision of the company's articles.

NOTES

Sub-s (3): year "2016" in square brackets substituted by the Bankruptcy (Scotland) Act 2016 (Consequential Provisions and Modifications) Order 2016, SI 2016/1034, art 7(1), (3), Sch 1, para 29(1), (5), as from 30 November 2016 (except in relation to (i) a sequestration as regards which the petition is presented, or the debtor application is made before that date; or (ii) a trust deed executed before that date).

[1.348]

311 Contents of notices of meetings

(1) Notice of a general meeting of a company must state—

(a) the time and date of the meeting, and

(b) the place of the meeting.

(2) Notice of a general meeting of a company must state the general nature of the business to be dealt with at the meeting.

[In relation to a company other than a traded company, this subsection has effect subject to any provision of the company's articles].

[(3) Notice of a general meeting of a traded company must also include—

(a) a statement giving the address of the website on which the information required by section 311A (traded companies: publication of information in advance of general meeting) is published;

(b) a statement—

(i) that the right to vote at the meeting is determined by reference to the register of members [(or, if an election under section 128B is in force in respect of the company, by reference to the register kept by the registrar under section 1080)], and

(ii) of the time when that right will be determined in accordance with section 360B(2) (traded companies: share dealings before general meetings);

(c) a statement of the procedures with which members must comply in order to be able to attend and vote at the meeting (including the date by which they must comply);

(d) a statement giving details of any forms to be used for the appointment of a proxy;

(e) where the company offers the facility for members to vote in advance (see section 322A) or by electronic means (see section 360A), a statement of the procedure for doing so (including the date by which it must be done, and details of any forms to be used); and

(f) a statement of the right of members to ask questions in accordance with section 319A (traded companies: questions at meetings).]

NOTES

Sub-s (2): words in square brackets substituted by the Companies (Shareholders' Rights) Regulations 2009, SI 2009/1632, reg 10(1), (2), as from 3 August 2009, in relation to meetings of which notice is given, or first given, on or after that date.

Sub-s (3): added by SI 2009/1632, reg 10(1), (3), as from 3 August 2009, in relation to meetings of which notice is given, or first given, on or after that date. Words in square brackets inserted by the Small Business, Enterprise and Employment Act 2015, s 94, Sch 5, Pt 2, paras 11, 17, as from 30 June 2016.

[1.349]

[311A Traded companies: publication of information in advance of general meeting

(1) A traded company must ensure that the following information relating to a general meeting of the company is made available on a website—

(a) the matters set out in the notice of the meeting;

(b) the total numbers of—

(i) shares in the company, and

(ii) shares of each class,

in respect of which members are entitled to exercise voting rights at the meeting;

(c) the totals of the voting rights that members are entitled to exercise at the meeting in respect of the shares of each class;

(d) members' statements, members' resolutions and members' matters of business received by the company after the first date on which notice of the meeting is given.

(2) The information must be made available on a website that—

(a) is maintained by or on behalf of the company, and

(b) identifies the company.

(3) Access to the information on the website, and the ability to obtain a hard copy of the information from the website, must not be conditional on payment of a fee or otherwise restricted.

(4) The information—

(a) must be made available—

(i) in the case of information required by subsection (1)(a) to (c), on or before the first date on which notice of the meeting is given, and

(ii) in the case of information required by subsection (1)(d), as soon as reasonably practicable, and

(b) must be kept available throughout the period of two years beginning with the date on which it is first made available on a website in accordance with this section.

(5) A failure to make information available throughout the period specified in subsection (4)(b) is disregarded if—

(a) the information is made available on the website for part of that period, and

(b) the failure is wholly attributable to circumstances that it would not be reasonable to have expected the company to prevent or avoid.

(6) The amounts mentioned in subsection (1)(b) and (c) must be ascertained at the latest practicable time before the first date on which notice of the meeting is given.

(7) Failure to comply with this section does not affect the validity of the meeting or of anything done at the meeting.

(8) If this section is not complied with as respects any meeting, an offence is committed by every officer of the company who is in default.

(9) A person guilty of an offence under this section is liable on summary conviction to a fine not exceeding level 3 on the standard scale.]

NOTES

Inserted by the Companies (Shareholders' Rights) Regulations 2009, SI 2009/1632, reg 11, as from 3 August 2009, in relation to meetings of which notice is given, or first given, on or after that date.

[1.350]

312 Resolution requiring special notice

(1) Where by any provision of the Companies Acts special notice is required of a resolution, the resolution is not effective unless notice of the intention to move it has been given to the company at least 28 days before the meeting at which it is moved.

(2) The company must, where practicable, give its members notice of any such resolution in the same manner and at the same time as it gives notice of the meeting.

(3) Where that is not practicable, the company must give its members notice at least 14 days before the meeting—

(a) by advertisement in a newspaper having an appropriate circulation, or

(b) in any other manner allowed by the company's articles.

(4) If, after notice of the intention to move such a resolution has been given to the company, a meeting is called for a date 28 days or less after the notice has been given, the notice is deemed to have been properly given, though not given within the time required.

[1.351]

313 Accidental failure to give notice of resolution or meeting

(1) Where a company gives notice of—

(a) a general meeting, or

(b) a resolution intended to be moved at a general meeting,

any accidental failure to give notice to one or more persons shall be disregarded for the purpose of determining whether notice of the meeting or resolution (as the case may be) is duly given.

(2) Except in relation to notice given under—

(a) section 304 (notice of meetings required by members),

(b) section 305 (notice of meetings called by members), or

(c) section 339 (notice of resolutions at AGMs proposed by members),

subsection (1) has effect subject to any provision of the company's articles.

Members' statements

[1.352]

314 Members' power to require circulation of statements

(1) The members of a company may require the company to circulate, to members of the company entitled to receive notice of a general meeting, a statement of not more than 1,000 words with respect to—

(a) a matter referred to in a proposed resolution to be dealt with at that meeting, or

(b) other business to be dealt with at that meeting.

(2) A company is required to circulate a statement once it has received requests to do so from—

(a) members representing at least 5% of the total voting rights of all the members who have a relevant right to vote (excluding any voting rights attached to any shares in the company held as treasury shares), or

(b) at least 100 members who have a relevant right to vote and hold shares in the company on which there has been paid up an average sum, per member, of at least £100.

See also section 153 (exercise of rights where shares held on behalf of others).

(3) In subsection (2), a "relevant right to vote" means—

(a) in relation to a statement with respect to a matter referred to in a proposed resolution, a right to vote on that resolution at the meeting to which the requests relate, and

(b) in relation to any other statement, a right to vote at the meeting to which the requests relate.

(4) A request—

(a) may be in hard copy form or in electronic form,

(b) must identify the statement to be circulated,

(c) must be authenticated by the person or persons making it, and

(d) must be received by the company at least one week before the meeting to which it relates.

[1.353]

315 Company's duty to circulate members' statement

(1) A company that is required under section 314, to circulate a statement must send a copy of it to each member of the company entitled to receive notice of the meeting—

(a) in the same manner as the notice of the meeting, and

(b) at the same time as, or as soon as reasonably practicable after, it gives notice of the meeting.

(2) Subsection (1) has effect subject to section 316(2) (deposit or tender of sum in respect of expenses of circulation) and section 317 (application not to circulate members' statement).

(3) In the event of default in complying with this section, an offence is committed by every officer of the company who is in default.

(4) A person guilty of an offence under this section is liable—

(a) on conviction on indictment, to a fine;

(b) on summary conviction, to a fine not exceeding the statutory maximum.

[1.354]

316 Expenses of circulating members' statement

(1) The expenses of the company in complying with section 315 need not be paid by the members who requested the circulation of the statement if—

- (a) the meeting to which the requests relate is an annual general meeting of a public company, and
- (b) requests sufficient to require the company to circulate the statement are received before the end of the financial year preceding the meeting.

(2) Otherwise—

- (a) the expenses of the company in complying with that section must be paid by the members who requested the circulation of the statement unless the company resolves otherwise, and
- (b) unless the company has previously so resolved, it is not bound to comply with that section unless there is deposited with or tendered to it, not later than one week before the meeting, a sum reasonably sufficient to meet its expenses in doing so.

[1.355]

317 Application not to circulate members' statement

(1) A company is not required to circulate a members' statement under section 315 if, on an application by the company or another person who claims to be aggrieved, the court is satisfied that the rights conferred by section 314 and that section are being abused.

(2) The court may order the members who requested the circulation of the statement to pay the whole or part of the company's costs (in Scotland, expenses) on such an application, even if they are not parties to the application.

Procedure at meetings

[1.356]

318 Quorum at meetings

(1) In the case of a company limited by shares or guarantee and having only one member, one qualifying person present at a meeting is a quorum.

(2) In any other case, subject to the provisions of the company's articles, two qualifying persons present at a meeting are a quorum, unless—

- (a) each is a qualifying person only because he is authorised under section 323 to act as the representative of a corporation in relation to the meeting, and they are representatives of the same corporation; or
- (b) each is a qualifying person only because he is appointed as proxy of a member in relation to the meeting, and they are proxies of the same member.

(3) For the purposes of this section a "qualifying person" means—

- (a) an individual who is a member of the company,
- (b) a person authorised under section 323 (representation of corporations at meetings) to act as the representative of a corporation in relation to the meeting, or
- (c) a person appointed as proxy of a member in relation to the meeting.

[1.357]

319 Chairman of meeting

(1) A member may be elected to be the chairman of a general meeting by a resolution of the company passed at the meeting.

(2) Subsection (1) is subject to any provision of the company's articles that states who may or may not be chairman.

[1.358]

[319A Traded companies: questions at meetings

(1) At a general meeting of a traded company, the company must cause to be answered any question relating to the business being dealt with at the meeting put by a member attending the meeting.

(2) No such answer need be given—

- (a) if to do so would—
  - (i) interfere unduly with the preparation for the meeting, or
  - (ii) involve the disclosure of confidential information;
- (b) if the answer has already been given on a website in the form of an answer to a question; or
- (c) if it is undesirable in the interests of the company or the good order of the meeting that the question be answered.]

NOTES

Inserted by the Companies (Shareholders' Rights) Regulations 2009, SI 2009/1632, reg 12(1), as from 3 August 2009, in relation to meetings of which notice is given, or first given, on or after that date.

[1.359]

320 Declaration by chairman on a show of hands

(1) On a vote on a resolution at a meeting on a show of hands, a declaration by the chairman that the resolution—

- (a) has or has not been passed, or
- (b) passed with a particular majority,

is conclusive evidence of that fact without proof of the number or proportion of the votes recorded in favour of or against the resolution.

(2) An entry in respect of such a declaration in minutes of the meeting recorded in accordance with section 355 is also conclusive evidence of that fact without such proof.

(3) This section does not have effect if a poll is demanded in respect of the resolution (and the demand is not subsequently withdrawn).

[1.360]
321 Right to demand a poll

(1) A provision of a company's articles is void in so far as it would have the effect of excluding the right to demand a poll at a general meeting on any question other than—

(a) the election of the chairman of the meeting, or

(b) the adjournment of the meeting.

(2) A provision of a company's articles is void in so far as it would have the effect of making ineffective a demand for a poll on any such question which is made—

(a) by not less than 5 members having the right to vote on the resolution; or

(b) by a member or members representing not less than 10% of the total voting rights of all the members having the right to vote on the resolution (excluding any voting rights attached to any shares in the company held as treasury shares); or

(c) by a member or members holding shares in the company conferring a right to vote on the resolution, being shares on which an aggregate sum has been paid up equal to not less than 10% of the total sum paid up on all the shares conferring that right (excluding shares in the company conferring a right to vote on the resolution which are held as treasury shares).

[1.361]
322 Voting on a poll

On a poll taken at a general meeting of a company, a member entitled to more than one vote need not, if he votes, use all his votes or cast all the votes he uses in the same way.

[1.362]
[322A Voting on a poll: votes cast in advance

(1) A company's articles may contain provision to the effect that on a vote on a resolution on a poll taken at a meeting, the votes may include votes cast in advance.

(2) In the case of a traded company any such provision in relation to voting at a general meeting may be made subject only to such requirements and restrictions as are—

(a) necessary to ensure the identification of the person voting, and

(b) proportionate to the achievement of that objective.

Nothing in this subsection affects any power of a company to require reasonable evidence of the entitlement of any person who is not a member to vote.

(3) Any provision of a company's articles is void in so far as it would have the effect of requiring any document casting a vote in advance to be received by the company or another person earlier than the following time—

(a) in the case of a poll taken more than 48 hours after it was demanded, 24 hours before the time appointed for the taking of the poll;

(b) in the case of any other poll, 48 hours before the time for holding the meeting or adjourned meeting.

(4) In calculating the periods mentioned in subsection (3), no account is to be taken of any part of a day that is not a working day.]

NOTES

Inserted by the Companies (Shareholders' Rights) Regulations 2009, SI 2009/1632, reg 5(1), as from 3 August 2009, in relation to meetings of which notice is given, or first given, on or after that date.

[1.363]
323 Representation of corporations at meetings

(1) If a corporation (whether or not a company within the meaning of this Act) is a member of a company, it may by resolution of its directors or other governing body authorise a person or persons to act as its representative or representatives at any meeting of the company.

[(2) A person authorised by a corporation is entitled to exercise (on behalf of the corporation) the same powers as the corporation could exercise if it were an individual member of the company.

Where a corporation authorises more than one person, this subsection is subject to subsections (3) and (4).

(3) On a vote on a resolution on a show of hands at a meeting of the company, each authorised person has the same voting rights as the corporation would be entitled to.

(4) Where subsection (3) does not apply and more than one authorised person purport to exercise a power under subsection (2) in respect of the same shares—

(a) if they purport to exercise the power in the same way as each other, the power is treated as exercised in that way;

(b) if they do not purport to exercise the power in the same way as each other, the power is treated as not exercised.]

NOTES

Sub-ss (2)–(4): substituted by the Companies (Shareholders' Rights) Regulations 2009, SI 2009/1632, reg 6, as from 3 August 2009, in relation to meetings of which notice is given, or first given, on or after that date.

Proxies

[1.364]
324 Rights to appoint proxies

(1) A member of a company is entitled to appoint another person as his proxy to exercise all or any of his rights to attend and to speak and vote at a meeting of the company.

(2) In the case of a company having a share capital, a member may appoint more than one proxy in relation to a meeting, provided that each proxy is appointed to exercise the rights attached to a different share or shares held by him, or (as the case may be) to a different £10, or multiple of £10, of stock held by him.

[1.365]
[324A Obligation of proxy to vote in accordance with instructions
A proxy must vote in accordance with any instructions given by the member by whom the proxy is appointed.]

NOTES
Inserted by the Companies (Shareholders' Rights) Regulations 2009, SI 2009/1632, reg 7, as from 3 August 2009, in relation to meetings of which notice is given, or first given, on or after that date.

[1.366]
325 Notice of meeting to contain statement of rights
(1) In every notice calling a meeting of a company there must appear, with reasonable prominence, a statement informing the member of—
(a) his rights under section 324, and
(b) any more extensive rights conferred by the company's articles to appoint more than one proxy.
(2) Failure to comply with this section does not affect the validity of the meeting or of anything done at the meeting.
(3) If this section is not complied with as respects any meeting, an offence is committed by every officer of the company who is in default.
(4) A person guilty of an offence under this section is liable on summary conviction to a fine not exceeding level 3 on the standard scale.

[1.367]
326 Company-sponsored invitations to appoint proxies
(1) If for the purposes of a meeting there are issued at the company's expense invitations to members to appoint as proxy a specified person or a number of specified persons, the invitations must be issued to all members entitled to vote at the meeting.
(2) Subsection (1) is not contravened if—
(a) there is issued to a member at his request a form of appointment naming the proxy or a list of persons willing to act as proxy, and
(b) the form or list is available on request to all members entitled to vote at the meeting.
(3) If subsection (1) is contravened as respects a meeting, an offence is committed by every officer of the company who is in default.
(4) A person guilty of an offence under this section is liable on summary conviction to a fine not exceeding level 3 on the standard scale.

[1.368]
327 Notice required of appointment of proxy etc
[(A1) In the case of a traded company—
(a) the appointment of a person as proxy for a member must be notified to the company in writing;
(b) where such an appointment is made, the company may require reasonable evidence of—
(i) the identity of the member and of the proxy,
(ii) the member's instructions (if any) as to how the proxy is to vote, and
(iii) where the proxy is appointed by a person acting on behalf of the member, authority of that person to make the appointment;
but may not require to be provided with anything else relating to the appointment.]
(1) [The following provisions apply in the case of traded companies and other companies as regards]—
(a) the appointment of a proxy, and
(b) any document necessary to show the validity of, or otherwise relating to, the appointment of a proxy.
(2) Any provision of the company's articles is void in so far as it would have the effect of requiring any such appointment or document to be received by the company or another person earlier than the following time—
(a) in the case of a meeting or adjourned meeting, 48 hours before the time for holding the meeting or adjourned meeting;
(b) in the case of a poll taken more than 48 hours after it was demanded, 24 hours before the time appointed for the taking of the poll;
(c) . . .
(3) In calculating the periods mentioned in subsection (2) no account shall be taken of any part of a day that is not a working day.

NOTES
Sub-s (A1): inserted by the Companies (Shareholders' Rights) Regulations 2009, SI 2009/1632, reg 13(1), as from 3 August 2009, in relation to meetings of which notice is given, or first given, on or after that date.
Sub-s (1): words in square brackets substituted by SI 2009/1632, reg 13(2), as from 3 August 2009, in relation to meetings of which notice is given, or first given, on or after that date.
Sub-s (2): para (c) repealed by the Deregulation Act 2015, s 19, Sch 6, Pt 8, para 29, as from 26 May 2015 (without ever coming into force).

[1.369]
328 Chairing meetings
(1) A proxy may be elected to be the chairman of a general meeting by a resolution of the company passed at the meeting.
(2) Subsection (1) is subject to any provision of the company's articles that states who may or who may not be chairman.

[1.370]
329 Right of proxy to demand a poll
(1) The appointment of a proxy to vote on a matter at a meeting of a company authorises the proxy to demand, or join in demanding, a poll on that matter.

(2) In applying the provisions of section 321(2) (requirements for effective demand), a demand by a proxy counts—

(a) for the purposes of paragraph (a), as a demand by the member;

(b) for the purposes of paragraph (b), as a demand by a member representing the voting rights that the proxy is authorised to exercise;

(c) for the purposes of paragraph (c), as a demand by a member holding the shares to which those rights are attached.

[1.371]

330 Notice required of termination of proxy's authority

[(A1) In the case of a traded company the termination of the authority of a person to act as proxy must be notified to the company in writing.]

(1) [The following provisions apply in the case of traded companies and other companies as regards] notice that the authority of a person to act as proxy is terminated ("notice of termination").

(2) The termination of the authority of a person to act as proxy does not affect—

(a) whether he counts in deciding whether there is a quorum at a meeting,

(b) the validity of anything he does as chairman of a meeting, or

(c) the validity of a poll demanded by him at a meeting,

unless the company receives notice of the termination before the commencement of the meeting.

(3) The termination of the authority of a person to act as proxy does not affect the validity of a vote given by that person unless the company receives notice of the termination—

(a) before the commencement of the meeting or adjourned meeting at which the vote is given, or

(b) in the case of a poll taken more than 48 hours after it is demanded, before the time appointed for taking the poll.

(4) If the company's articles require or permit members to give notice of termination to a person other than the company, the references above to the company receiving notice have effect as if they were or (as the case may be) included a reference to that person.

(5) Subsections (2) and (3) have effect subject to any provision of the company's articles which has the effect of requiring notice of termination to be received by the company or another person at a time earlier than that specified in those subsections.

This is subject to subsection (6).

(6) Any provision of the company's articles is void in so far as it would have the effect of requiring notice of termination to be received by the company or another person earlier than the following time—

(a) in the case of a meeting or adjourned meeting, 48 hours before the time for holding the meeting or adjourned meeting;

(b) in the case of a poll taken more than 48 hours after it was demanded, 24 hours before the time appointed for the taking of the poll;

(c) . . .

(7) In calculating the periods mentioned in subsections (3)(b) and (6) no account shall be taken of any part of a day that is not a working day.

NOTES

Sub-s (A1): inserted by the Companies (Shareholders' Rights) Regulations 2009, SI 2009/1632, reg 13(3)(a), as from 3 August 2009, in relation to meetings of which notice is given, or first given, on or after that date.

Sub-s (1): words in square brackets substituted by SI 2009/1632, reg 13(3)(b), as from 3 August 2009, in relation to meetings of which notice is given, or first given, on or after that date.

Sub-s (6): para (c) repealed by the Deregulation Act 2015, s 19, Sch 6, Pt 8, para 30, as from 26 May 2015 (without ever coming into force).

[1.372]

331 Saving for more extensive rights conferred by articles

Nothing in sections 324 to 330 (proxies) prevents a company's articles from conferring more extensive rights on members or proxies than are conferred by those sections.

Adjourned meetings

[1.373]

332 Resolution passed at adjourned meeting

Where a resolution is passed at an adjourned meeting of a company, the resolution is for all purposes to be treated as having been passed on the date on which it was in fact passed, and is not to be deemed passed on any earlier date.

Electronic communications

[1.374]

333 Sending documents relating to meetings etc in electronic form

(1) Where a company has given an electronic address in a notice calling a meeting, it is deemed to have agreed that any document or information relating to proceedings at the meeting may be sent by electronic means to that address (subject to any conditions or limitations specified in the notice).

(2) Where a company has given an electronic address—

(a) in an instrument of proxy sent out by the company in relation to the meeting, or

(b) in an invitation to appoint a proxy issued by the company in relation to the meeting,

it is deemed to have agreed that any document or information relating to proxies for that meeting may be sent by electronic means to that address (subject to any conditions or limitations specified in the notice).

(3) In subsection (2), documents relating to proxies include—

(a) the appointment of a proxy in relation to a meeting,

(b) any document necessary to show the validity of, or otherwise relating to, the appointment of a proxy, and

(c) notice of the termination of the authority of a proxy.

(4) In this section "electronic address" means any address or number used for the purposes of sending or receiving documents or information by electronic means.

[1.375]

[333A Traded company: duty to provide electronic address for receipt of proxies etc

(1) A traded company must provide an electronic address for the receipt of any document or information relating to proxies for a general meeting.

(2) The company must provide the address either—

- (a) by giving it when sending out an instrument of proxy for the purposes of the meeting or issuing an invitation to appoint a proxy for those purposes; or
- (b) by ensuring that it is made available, throughout the period beginning with the first date on which notice of the meeting is given and ending with the conclusion of the meeting, on the website on which the information required by section 311A(1) is made available.

(3) The company is deemed to have agreed that any document or information relating to proxies for the meeting may be sent by electronic means to the address provided (subject to any limitations specified by the company when providing the address).

(4) In this section—

- (a) documents relating to proxies include—
  - (i) the appointment of a proxy for a meeting,
  - (ii) any document necessary to show the validity of, or otherwise relating to, the appointment of a proxy, and
  - (iii) notice of the termination of the authority of a proxy;
- (b) "electronic address" has the meaning given by section 333(4).]

NOTES

Inserted by the Companies (Shareholders' Rights) Regulations 2009, SI 2009/1632, reg 13(4), as from 3 August 2009, in relation to meetings of which notice is given, or first given, on or after that date.

Application to class meetings

[1.376]

334 Application to class meetings

(1) The provisions of this Chapter apply (with necessary modifications) in relation to a meeting of holders of a class of shares as they apply in relation to a general meeting.

This is subject to subsections [(2) to (3)].

(2) The following provisions of this Chapter do not apply in relation to a meeting of holders of a class of shares—

- (a) sections 303 to 305 (members' power to require directors to call general meeting), . . .
- (b) section 306 (power of court to order meeting)[, and
- (c) sections 311(3), 311A, 319A, 327(A1), 330(A1) and 333A (additional requirements relating to traded companies)].

[(2A) Section 307(1) to (6) apply in relation to a meeting of holders of a class of shares in a traded company as they apply in relation to a meeting of holders of a class of shares in a company other than a traded company (and, accordingly, section 307A does not apply in relation to such a meeting).]

(3) The following provisions (in addition to those mentioned in subsection (2)) do not apply in relation to a meeting in connection with the variation of rights attached to a class of shares (a "variation of class rights meeting")—

- (a) section 318 (quorum), and
- (b) section 321 (right to demand a poll).

(4) The quorum for a variation of class rights meeting is—

- (a) for a meeting other than an adjourned meeting, two persons present holding at least one-third in nominal value of the issued shares of the class in question (excluding any shares of that class held as treasury shares);
- (b) for an adjourned meeting, one person present holding shares of the class in question.

(5) For the purposes of subsection (4), where a person is present by proxy or proxies, he is treated as holding only the shares in respect of which those proxies are authorised to exercise voting rights.

(6) At a variation of class rights meeting, any holder of shares of the class in question present may demand a poll.

(7) For the purposes of this section—

- (a) any amendment of a provision contained in a company's articles for the variation of the rights attached to a class of shares, or the insertion of any such provision into the articles, is itself to be treated as a variation of those rights, and
- (b) references to the variation of rights attached to a class of shares include references to their abrogation.

NOTES

Sub-s (1): words in square brackets substituted by the Companies (Shareholders' Rights) Regulations 2009, SI 2009/1632, reg 14(1), (2), as from 3 August 2009, in relation to meetings of which notice is given, or first given, on or after that date.

Sub-s (2): the word omitted from para (a) was repealed, and para (c) (and the preceding word) was inserted, by SI 2009/1632, reg 14(1), (3), as from 3 August 2009, in relation to meetings of which notice is given, or first given, on or after that date.

Sub-s (2A): inserted by SI 2009/1632, reg 14(1), (4), as from 3 August 2009, in relation to meetings of which notice is given, or first given, on or after that date.

[1.377]

335 Application to class meetings: companies without a share capital

(1) The provisions of this Chapter apply (with necessary modifications) in relation to a meeting of a class of members of a company without a share capital as they apply in relation to a general meeting.

This is subject to subsections (2) and (3).

(2) The following provisions of this Chapter do not apply in relation to a meeting of a class of members—

- (a) sections 303 to 305 (members' power to require directors to call general meeting), and
- (b) section 306 (power of court to order meeting).

(3) The following provisions (in addition to those mentioned in subsection (2)) do not apply in relation to a meeting in connection with the variation of the rights of a class of members (a "variation of class rights meeting")—

(a) section 318 (quorum), and

(b) section 321 (right to demand a poll).

(4) The quorum for a variation of class rights meeting is—

(a) for a meeting other than an adjourned meeting, two members of the class present (in person or by proxy) who together represent at least one-third of the voting rights of the class;

(b) for an adjourned meeting, one member of the class present (in person or by proxy).

(5) At a variation of class rights meeting, any member present (in person or by proxy) may demand a poll.

(6) For the purposes of this section—

(a) any amendment of a provision contained in a company's articles for the variation of the rights of a class of members, or the insertion of any such provision into the articles, is itself to be treated as a variation of those rights, and

(b) references to the variation of rights of a class of members include references to their abrogation.

CHAPTER 4 PUBLIC COMPANIES [AND TRADED COMPANIES]: ADDITIONAL REQUIREMENTS FOR AGMS

NOTES

Words in square brackets in the preceding Chapter heading inserted by the Companies (Shareholders' Rights) Regulations 2009, SI 2009/1632, reg 15(5), as from 3 August 2009, in relation to meetings of which notice is given, or first given, on or after that date.

[1.378]

336 Public companies [and traded companies]: annual general meeting

(1) Every public company must hold a general meeting as its annual general meeting in each period of 6 months beginning with the day following its accounting reference date (in addition to any other meetings held during that period).

[(1A) Every private company that is a traded company must hold a general meeting as its annual general meeting in each period of 9 months beginning with the day following its accounting reference date (in addition to any other meetings held during that period).]

(2) A company that fails to comply with subsection (1) [or (1A)] as a result of giving notice under section 392 (alteration of accounting reference date)—

(a) specifying a new accounting reference date, and

(b) stating that the current accounting reference period or the previous accounting reference period is to be shortened,

shall be treated as if it had complied with subsection (1) [or (1A)] if it holds a general meeting as its annual general meeting within 3 months of giving that notice.

(3) If a company fails to comply with subsection (1) [or (1A)], an offence is committed by every officer of the company who is in default.

(4) A person guilty of an offence under this section is liable—

(a) on conviction on indictment, to a fine;

(b) on summary conviction, to a fine not exceeding the statutory maximum.

NOTES

All words in square brackets in this section were inserted by the Companies (Shareholders' Rights) Regulations 2009, SI 2009/1632, reg 15(1)–(4), as from 3 August 2009, in relation to meetings of which notice is given, or first given, on or after that date.

[1.379]

337 Public companies [and traded companies]: notice of AGM

(1) A notice calling an annual general meeting of a public company [or a private company that is a traded company] must state that the meeting is an annual general meeting.

(2) An annual general meeting [of a public company that is not a traded company] may be called by shorter notice than that required by section 307(2) or by the company's articles (as the case may be), if all the members entitled to attend and vote at the meeting agree to the shorter notice.

[(3) Where a notice calling an annual general meeting of a traded company is given more than 6 weeks before the meeting, the notice must include—

(a) if the company is a public company, a statement of the right under section 338 to require the company to give notice of a resolution to be moved at the meeting, and

(b) whether or not the company is a public company, a statement of the right under section 338A to require the company to include a matter in the business to be dealt with at the meeting.]

NOTES

Words in square brackets in the section heading and sub-ss (1), (2) inserted, and sub-s (3) added, by the Companies (Shareholders' Rights) Regulations 2009, SI 2009/1632, reg 16(1)–(5), as from 3 August 2009, in relation to meetings of which notice is given, or first given, on or after that date.

[1.380]

338 Public companies: members' power to require circulation of resolutions for AGMs

(1) The members of a public company may require the company to give, to members of the company entitled to receive notice of the next annual general meeting, notice of a resolution which may properly be moved and is intended to be moved at that meeting.

(2) A resolution may properly be moved at an annual general meeting unless—

(a) it would, if passed, be ineffective (whether by reason of inconsistency with any enactment or the company's constitution or otherwise),

(b) it is defamatory of any person, or
(c) it is frivolous or vexatious.
(3) A company is required to give notice of a resolution once it has received requests that it do so from—
(a) members representing at least 5% of the total voting rights of all the members who have a right to vote on the resolution at the annual general meeting to which the requests relate (excluding any voting rights attached to any shares in the company held as treasury shares), or
(b) at least 100 members who have a right to vote on the resolution at the annual general meeting to which the requests relate and hold shares in the company on which there has been paid up an average sum, per member, of at least £100.

See also section 153 (exercise of rights where shares held on behalf of others).

(4) A request—
(a) may be in hard copy form or in electronic form,
(b) must identify the resolution of which notice is to be given,
(c) must be authenticated by the person or persons making it, and
(d) must be received by the company not later than—
(i) 6 weeks before the annual general meeting to which the requests relate, or
(ii) if later, the time at which notice is given of that meeting.

[1.381]

[338A Traded companies: members' power to include other matters in business dealt with at AGM

(1) The members of a traded company may request the company to include in the business to be dealt with at an annual general meeting any matter (other than a proposed resolution) which may properly be included in the business.
(2) A matter may properly be included in the business at an annual general meeting unless—
(a) it is defamatory of any person, or
(b) it is frivolous or vexatious.
(3) A company is required to include such a matter once it has received requests that it do so from—
(a) members representing at least 5% of the total voting rights of all the members who have a right to vote at the meeting, or
(b) at least 100 members who have a right to vote at the meeting and hold shares in the company on which there has been paid up an average sum, per member, of at least £100.

See also section 153 (exercise of rights where shares held on behalf of others).

(4) A request—
(a) may be in hard copy form or in electronic form,
(b) must identify the matter to be included in the business,
(c) must be accompanied by a statement setting out the grounds for the request, and
(d) must be authenticated by the person or persons making it.
(5) A request must be received by the company not later than—
(a) 6 weeks before the meeting, or
(b) if later, the time at which notice is given of the meeting.]

NOTES

Inserted by the Companies (Shareholders' Rights) Regulations 2009, SI 2009/1632, reg 17(1), as from 3 August 2009, in relation to meetings of which notice is given, or first given, on or after that date.

[1.382]

339 Public companies: company's duty to circulate members' resolutions for AGMs

(1) A company that is required under section 338 to give notice of a resolution must send a copy of it to each member of the company entitled to receive notice of the annual general meeting—
(a) in the same manner as notice of the meeting, and
(b) at the same time as, or as soon as reasonably practicable after, it gives notice of the meeting.
(2) Subsection (1) has effect subject to section 340(2) (deposit or tender of sum in respect of expenses of circulation).
(3) The business which may be dealt with at an annual general meeting includes a resolution of which notice is given in accordance with this section.
(4) In the event of default in complying with this section, an offence is committed by every officer of the company who is in default.
(5) A person guilty of an offence under this section is liable—
(a) on conviction on indictment, to a fine;
(b) on summary conviction, to a fine not exceeding the statutory maximum.

[1.383]

340 Public companies: expenses of circulating members' resolutions for AGM

(1) The expenses of the company in complying with section 339 need not be paid by the members who requested the circulation of the resolution if requests sufficient to require the company to circulate it are received before the end of the financial year preceding the meeting.
(2) Otherwise—
(a) the expenses of the company in complying with that section must be paid by the members who requested the circulation of the resolution unless the company resolves otherwise, and
(b) unless the company has previously so resolved, it is not bound to comply with that section unless there is deposited with or tendered to it, not later than—
(i) six weeks before the annual general meeting to which the requests relate, or
(ii) if later, the time at which notice is given of that meeting,

a sum reasonably sufficient to meet its expenses in complying with that section.

[1.384]

[340A Traded companies: duty to circulate members' matters for AGM

(1) A company that is required under section 338A to include any matter in the business to be dealt with at an annual general meeting must—

(a) give notice of it to each member of the company entitled to receive notice of the annual general meeting—

(i) in the same manner as notice of the meeting, and

(ii) at the same time as, or as soon as reasonably practicable after, it gives notice of the meeting, and

(b) publish it on the same website as that on which the company published the information required by section 311A.

(2) Subsection (1) has effect subject to section 340B(2) (deposit or tender of sum in respect of expenses of circulation).

(3) In the event of default in complying with this section, an offence is committed by every officer of the company who is in default.

(4) A person guilty of an offence under this section is liable—

(a) on conviction on indictment, to a fine;

(b) on summary conviction, to a fine not exceeding the statutory maximum.]

NOTES

Inserted, together with s 340B, by the Companies (Shareholders' Rights) Regulations 2009, SI 2009/1632, reg 18(1), as from 3 August 2009, in relation to meetings of which notice is given, or first given, on or after that date.

[1.385]

[340B Traded companies: expenses of circulating members' matters to be dealt with at AGM

(1) The expenses of the company in complying with section 340A need not be paid by the members who requested the inclusion of the matter in the business to be dealt with at the annual general meeting if requests sufficient to require the company to include the matter are received before the end of the financial year preceding the meeting.

(2) Otherwise—

(a) the expenses of the company in complying with that section must be paid by the members who requested the inclusion of the matter unless the company resolves otherwise, and

(b) unless the company has previously so resolved, it is not bound to comply with that section unless there is deposited with or tendered to it, not later than—

(i) six weeks before the annual general meeting to which the requests relate, or

(ii) if later, the time at which notice is given of that meeting,

a sum reasonably sufficient to meet its expenses in complying with that section.]

NOTES

Inserted as noted to s 340A at **[1.384]**.

CHAPTER 5 ADDITIONAL REQUIREMENTS FOR QUOTED COMPANIES [AND TRADED COMPANIES]

NOTES

Words in square brackets in the preceding Chapter heading inserted by the Companies (Shareholders' Rights) Regulations 2009, SI 2009/1632, reg 19(5), as from 3 August 2009, in relation to meetings of which notice is given, or first given, on or after that date.

Website publication of poll results

[1.386]

341 Results of poll to be made available on website

(1) Where a poll is taken at a general meeting of a quoted company [that is not a traded company], the company must ensure that the following information is made available on a website—

(a) the date of the meeting,

(b) the text of the resolution or, as the case may be, a description of the subject matter of the poll,

(c) the number of votes cast in favour, and

(d) the number of votes cast against.

[(1A) Where a poll is taken at a general meeting of a traded company, the company must ensure that the following information is made available on a website—

(a) the date of the meeting,

(b) the text of the resolution or, as the case may be, a description of the subject matter of the poll,

(c) the number of votes validly cast,

(d) the proportion of the company's issued share capital (determined at the time at which the right to vote is determined under section 360B(2)) represented by those votes,

(e) the number of votes cast in favour,

(f) the number of votes cast against, and

(g) the number of abstentions (if counted).

(1B) A traded company must comply with subsection (1A) by—

(a) the end of 16 days beginning with the day of the meeting, or

(b) if later, the end of the first working day after the day on which the result of the poll is declared.]

(2) The provisions of section 353 (requirements as to website availability) apply.

(3) In the event of default in complying with this section (or with the requirements of section 353 as it applies for the purposes of this section), an offence is committed by every officer of the company who is in default.

(4) A person guilty of an offence under subsection (3) is liable on summary conviction to a fine not exceeding level 3 on the standard scale.

(5) Failure to comply with this section (or the requirements of section 353) does not affect the validity of—

(a) the poll, or

(b) the resolution or other business (if passed or agreed to) to which the poll relates.

(6) This section only applies to polls taken after this section comes into force.

NOTES

Sub-s (1): words in square brackets inserted by the Companies (Shareholders' Rights) Regulations 2009, SI 2009/1632, reg 19(1), (2), as from 3 August 2009, in relation to meetings of which notice is given, or first given, on or after that date.

Sub-ss (1A), (1B): inserted by SI 2009/1632, reg 19(1), (3), as from 3 August 2009, in relation to meetings of which notice is given, or first given, on or after that date.

Independent report on poll

[1.387]

342 Members' power to require independent report on poll

(1) The members of a quoted company may require the directors to obtain an independent report on any poll taken, or to be taken, at a general meeting of the company.

(2) The directors are required to obtain an independent report if they receive requests to do so from—

(a) members representing not less than 5% of the total voting rights of all the members who have a right to vote on the matter to which the poll relates (excluding any voting rights attached to any shares in the company held as treasury shares), or

(b) not less than 100 members who have a right to vote on the matter to which the poll relates and hold shares in the company on which there has been paid up an average sum, per member, of not less than £100.

See also section 153 (exercise of rights where shares held on behalf of others).

(3) Where the requests relate to more than one poll, subsection (2) must be satisfied in relation to each of them.

(4) A request—

(a) may be in hard copy form or in electronic form,

(b) must identify the poll or polls to which it relates,

(c) must be authenticated by the person or persons making it, and

(d) must be received by the company not later than one week after the date on which the poll is taken.

[1.388]

343 Appointment of independent assessor

(1) Directors who are required under section 342 to obtain an independent report on a poll or polls must appoint a person they consider to be appropriate (an "independent assessor") to prepare a report for the company on it or them.

(2) The appointment must be made within one week after the company being required to obtain the report.

(3) The directors must not appoint a person who—

(a) does not meet the independence requirement in section 344, or

(b) has another role in relation to any poll on which he is to report (including, in particular, a role in connection with collecting or counting votes or with the appointment of proxies).

(4) In the event of default in complying with this section, an offence is committed by every officer of the company who is in default.

(5) A person guilty of an offence under this section is liable on summary conviction to a fine not exceeding level 5 on the standard scale.

(6) If at the meeting no poll on which a report is required is taken—

(a) the directors are not required to obtain a report from the independent assessor, and

(b) his appointment ceases (but without prejudice to any right to be paid for work done before the appointment ceased).

[1.389]

344 Independence requirement

(1) A person may not be appointed as an independent assessor—

(a) if he is—

(i) an officer or employee of the company, or

(ii) a partner or employee of such a person, or a partnership of which such a person is a partner;

(b) if he is—

(i) an officer or employee of an associated undertaking of the company, or

(ii) a partner or employee of such a person, or a partnership of which such a person is a partner;

(c) if there exists between— (i) the person or an associate of his, and (ii) the company or an associated undertaking of the company, a connection of any such description as may be specified by regulations made by the Secretary of State.

(2) An auditor of the company is not regarded as an officer or employee of the company for this purpose.

(3) In this section—

"associated undertaking" means—

(a) a parent undertaking or subsidiary undertaking of the company, or

(b) a subsidiary undertaking of a parent undertaking of the company; and

"associate" has the meaning given by section 345.

(4) Regulations under this section are subject to negative resolution procedure.

[1.390]

345 Meaning of "associate"

(1) This section defines "associate" for the purposes of section 344 (independence requirement).

(2) In relation to an individual, "associate" means—

(a) that individual's spouse or civil partner or minor child or step-child,

(b) any body corporate of which that individual is a director, and

(c) any employee or partner of that individual.

(3) In relation to a body corporate, "associate" means—

(a) any body corporate of which that body is a director,

(b) any body corporate in the same group as that body, and
(c) any employee or partner of that body or of any body corporate in the same group.

(4) In relation to a partnership that is a legal person under the law by which it is governed, "associate" means—
(a) any body corporate of which that partnership is a director,
(b) any employee of or partner in that partnership, and
(c) any person who is an associate of a partner in that partnership.

(5) In relation to a partnership that is not a legal person under the law by which it is governed, "associate" means any person who is an associate of any of the partners.

(6) In this section, in relation to a limited liability partnership, for "director" read "member".

[1.391]
346 Effect of appointment of a partnership

(1) This section applies where a partnership that is not a legal person under the law by which it is governed is appointed as an independent assessor.

(2) Unless a contrary intention appears, the appointment is of the partnership as such and not of the partners.

(3) Where the partnership ceases, the appointment is to be treated as extending to—
(a) any partnership that succeeds to the practice of that partnership, or
(b) any other person who succeeds to that practice having previously carried it on in partnership.

(4) For the purposes of subsection (3)—
(a) a partnership is regarded as succeeding to the practice of another partnership only if the members of the successor partnership are substantially the same as those of the former partnership, and
(b) a partnership or other person is regarded as succeeding to the practice of a partnership only if it or he succeeds to the whole or substantially the whole of the business of the former partnership.

(5) Where the partnership ceases and the appointment is not treated under subsection (3) as extending to any partnership or other person, the appointment may with the consent of the company be treated as extending to a partnership, or other person, who succeeds to—
(a) the business of the former partnership, or
(b) such part of it as is agreed by the company is to be treated as comprising the appointment.

[1.392]
347 The independent assessor's report

(1) The report of the independent assessor must state his opinion whether—
(a) the procedures adopted in connection with the poll or polls were adequate;
(b) the votes cast (including proxy votes) were fairly and accurately recorded and counted;
(c) the validity of members' appointments of proxies was fairly assessed;
(d) the notice of the meeting complied with section 325 (notice of meeting to contain statement of rights to appoint proxy);
(e) section 326 (company-sponsored invitations to appoint proxies) was complied with in relation to the meeting.

(2) The report must give his reasons for the opinions stated.

(3) If he is unable to form an opinion on any of those matters, the report must record that fact and state the reasons for it.

(4) The report must state the name of the independent assessor.

[1.393]
348 Rights of independent assessor: right to attend meeting etc

(1) Where an independent assessor has been appointed to report on a poll, he is entitled to attend—
(a) the meeting at which the poll may be taken, and
(b) any subsequent proceedings in connection with the poll.

(2) He is also entitled to be provided by the company with a copy of—
(a) the notice of the meeting, and
(b) any other communication provided by the company in connection with the meeting to persons who have a right to vote on the matter to which the poll relates.

(3) The rights conferred by this section are only to be exercised to the extent that the independent assessor considers necessary for the preparation of his report.

(4) If the independent assessor is a firm, the right under subsection (1) to attend the meeting and any subsequent proceedings in connection with the poll is exercisable by an individual authorised by the firm in writing to act as its representative for that purpose.

[1.394]
349 Rights of independent assessor: right to information

(1) The independent assessor is entitled to access to the company's records relating to—
(a) any poll on which he is to report;
(b) the meeting at which the poll or polls may be, or were, taken.

(2) The independent assessor may require anyone who at any material time was—
(a) a director or secretary of the company,
(b) an employee of the company,
(c) a person holding or accountable for any of the company's records,
(d) a member of the company, or
(e) an agent of the company,

to provide him with information or explanations for the purpose of preparing his report.

(3) For this purpose "agent" includes the company's bankers, solicitors and auditor.

(4) A statement made by a person in response to a requirement under this section may not be used in evidence against him in criminal proceedings except proceedings for an offence under section 350 (offences relating to provision of information).

(5) A person is not required by this section to disclose information in respect of which a claim to legal professional privilege (in Scotland, to confidentiality of communications) could be maintained in legal proceedings.

[1.395]
350 Offences relating to provision of information

(1) A person who fails to comply with a requirement under section 349 without delay commits an offence unless it was not reasonably practicable for him to provide the required information or explanation.
(2) A person guilty of an offence under subsection (1) is liable on summary conviction to a fine not exceeding level 3 on the standard scale.
(3) A person commits an offence who knowingly or recklessly makes to an independent assessor a statement (oral or written) that—
 (a) conveys or purports to convey any information or explanations which the independent assessor requires, or is entitled to require, under section 349, and
 (b) is misleading, false or deceptive in a material particular.
(4) A person guilty of an offence under subsection (3) is liable—
 (a) on conviction on indictment, to imprisonment for a term not exceeding two years or a fine (or both);
 (b) on summary conviction—
  (i) in England and Wales, to imprisonment for a term not exceeding twelve months or to a fine not exceeding the statutory maximum (or both);
  (ii) in Scotland or Northern Ireland, to imprisonment for a term not exceeding six months, or to a fine not exceeding the statutory maximum (or both).
(5) Nothing in this section affects any right of an independent assessor to apply for an injunction (in Scotland, an interdict or an order for specific performance) to enforce any of his rights under section 348 or 349.

[1.396]
351 Information to be made available on website

(1) Where an independent assessor has been appointed to report on a poll, the company must ensure that the following information is made available on a website—
 (a) the fact of his appointment,
 (b) his identity,
 (c) the text of the resolution or, as the case may be, a description of the subject matter of the poll to which his appointment relates, and
 (d) a copy of a report by him which complies with section 347.
(2) The provisions of section 353 (requirements as to website availability) apply.
(3) In the event of default in complying with this section (or with the requirements of section 353 as it applies for the purposes of this section), an offence is committed by every officer of the company who is in default.
(4) A person guilty of an offence under subsection (3) is liable on summary conviction to a fine not exceeding level 3 on the standard scale.
(5) Failure to comply with this section (or the requirements of section 353) does not affect the validity of—
 (a) the poll, or
 (b) the resolution or other business (if passed or agreed to) to which the poll relates.

Supplementary

[1.397]
352 Application of provisions to class meetings

[(1) The provisions of section 341 (results of poll to be made available on website) apply (with any necessary modifications) in relation to a meeting of holders of a class of shares of a quoted company or traded company in connection with the variation of the rights attached to such shares as they apply in relation to a general meeting of the company.
(1A) The provisions of section 342 to 351 (independent report on poll) apply (with any necessary modifications) in relation to a meeting of holders of a class of shares of a quoted company in connection with the variation of the rights attached to such shares as they apply in relation to a general meeting of the company.]
(2) For the purposes of this section—
 (a) any amendment of a provision contained in a company's articles for the variation of the rights attached to a class of shares, or the insertion of any such provision into the articles, is itself to be treated as a variation of those rights, and
 (b) references to the variation of rights attached to a class of shares include references to their abrogation.

NOTES

Sub-ss (1), (1A): substituted, for the original sub-s (1), by the Companies (Shareholders' Rights) Regulations 2009, SI 2009/1632, reg 19(4), as from 3 August 2009, in relation to meetings of which notice is given, or first given, on or after that date.

[1.398]
353 Requirements as to website availability

(1) The following provisions apply for the purposes of—
 section 341 (results of poll to be made available on website), and
 section 351 (report of independent observer to be made available on website).
(2) The information must be made available on a website that—
 (a) is maintained by or on behalf of the company, and
 (b) identifies the company in question.
(3) Access to the information on the website, and the ability to obtain a hard copy of the information from the website, must not be conditional on the payment of a fee or otherwise restricted.
(4) The information—
 (a) must be made available as soon as reasonably practicable, and

(b) must be kept available throughout the period of two years beginning with the date on which it is first made available on a website in accordance with this section.

(5) A failure to make information available on a website throughout the period specified in subsection (4)(b) is disregarded if—

(a) the information is made available on the website for part of that period, and

(b) the failure is wholly attributable to circumstances that it would not be reasonable to have expected the company to prevent or avoid.

[1.399]

354 Power to limit or extend the types of company to which provisions of this Chapter apply

(1) The Secretary of State may by regulations—

(a) limit the types of company to which some or all of the provisions of this Chapter apply, or

(b) extend some or all of the provisions of this Chapter to additional types of company.

(2) Regulations under this section extending the application of any provision of this Chapter are subject to affirmative resolution procedure.

(3) Any other regulations under this section are subject to negative resolution procedure.

(4) Regulations under this section may—

(a) amend the provisions of this Chapter (apart from this section);

(b) repeal and re-enact provisions of this Chapter with modifications of form or arrangement, whether or not they are modified in substance;

(c) contain such consequential, incidental and supplementary provisions (including provisions amending, repealing or revoking enactments) as the Secretary of State thinks fit.

NOTES

Regulations: no Regulations have been made under this section.

CHAPTER 6 RECORDS OF RESOLUTIONS AND MEETINGS

[1.400]

355 Records of resolutions and meetings etc

(1) Every company must keep records comprising—

(a) copies of all resolutions of members passed otherwise than at general meetings,

(b) minutes of all proceedings of general meetings, and

(c) details provided to the company in accordance with section 357 (decisions of sole member).

(2) The records must be kept for at least ten years from the date of the resolution, meeting or decision (as appropriate).

(3) If a company fails to comply with this section, an offence is committed by every officer of the company who is in default.

(4) A person guilty of an offence under this section is liable on summary conviction to a fine not exceeding level 3 on the standard scale and, for continued contravention, a daily default fine not exceeding one-tenth of level 3 on the standard scale.

[1.401]

356 Records as evidence of resolutions etc

(1) This section applies to the records kept in accordance with section 355.

(2) The record of a resolution passed otherwise than at a general meeting, if purporting to be signed by a director of the company or by the company secretary, is evidence (in Scotland, sufficient evidence) of the passing of the resolution.

(3) Where there is a record of a written resolution of a private company, the requirements of this Act with respect to the passing of the resolution are deemed to be complied with unless the contrary is proved.

(4) The minutes of proceedings of a general meeting, if purporting to be signed by the chairman of that meeting or by the chairman of the next general meeting, are evidence (in Scotland, sufficient evidence) of the proceedings at the meeting.

(5) Where there is a record of proceedings of a general meeting of a company, then, until the contrary is proved—

(a) the meeting is deemed duly held and convened,

(b) all proceedings at the meeting are deemed to have duly taken place, and

(c) all appointments at the meeting are deemed valid.

[1.402]

357 Records of decisions by sole member

(1) This section applies to a company limited by shares or by guarantee that has only one member.

(2) Where the member takes any decision that—

(a) may be taken by the company in general meeting, and

(b) has effect as if agreed by the company in general meeting,

he must (unless that decision is taken by way of a written resolution) provide the company with details of that decision.

(3) If a person fails to comply with this section he commits an offence.

(4) A person guilty of an offence under this section is liable on summary conviction to a fine not exceeding level 2 on the standard scale.

(5) Failure to comply with this section does not affect the validity of any decision referred to in subsection (2).

[1.403]

358 Inspection of records of resolutions and meetings

(1) The records referred to in section 355 (records of resolutions etc) relating to the previous ten years must be kept available for inspection—

(a) at the company's registered office, or

(b) at a place specified in regulations under section 1136.

(2) The company must give notice to the registrar—

(a) of the place at which the records are kept available for inspection, and

(b) of any change in that place,

unless they have at all times been kept at the company's registered office.

(3) The records must be open to the inspection of any member of the company without charge.

(4) Any member may require a copy of any of the records on payment of such fee as may be prescribed.

(5) If default is made for 14 days in complying with subsection (2) or an inspection required under subsection (3) is refused, or a copy requested under subsection (4) is not sent, an offence is committed by every officer of the company who is in default.

(6) A person guilty of an offence under this section is liable on summary conviction to a fine not exceeding level 3 on the standard scale and, for continued contravention, a daily default fine not exceeding one-tenth of level 3 on the standard scale.

(7) In a case in which an inspection required under subsection (3) is refused or a copy requested under subsection (4) is not sent, the court may by order compel an immediate inspection of the records or direct that the copies required be sent to the persons who requested them.

NOTES

Regulations: the Companies (Fees for Inspection and Copying of Company Records) Regulations 2007, SI 2007/2612 at **[4.11]**. For a summary of all statutory instruments made under this Act, see Appendix 4 at **[A4]**.

[1.404]

359 Records of resolutions and meetings of class of members

The provisions of this Chapter apply (with necessary modifications) in relation to resolutions and meetings of—

(a) holders of a class of shares, and

(b) in the case of a company without a share capital, a class of members,

as they apply in relation to resolutions of members generally and to general meetings.

CHAPTER 7 SUPPLEMENTARY PROVISIONS

[1.405]

360 Computation of periods of notice etc: clear day rule

(1) This section applies for the purposes of the following provisions of this Part—

section 307(1) and (2) (notice required of general meeting),

[section 307A(1), (4), (5) and (7)(b) (notice required of general meeting of traded company),]

section 312(1) and (3) (resolution requiring special notice),

section 314(4)(d) (request to circulate members' statement),

section 316(2)(b) (expenses of circulating statement to be deposited or tendered before meeting),

[section 337(3) (contents of notice of AGM of traded company),]

section 338(4)(d)(i) (request to circulate member's resolution at AGM of public company), . . .

[section 338A(5) (request to include matter in the business to be dealt with at AGM of traded company),]

section 340(2)(b)(i) (expenses of circulating statement to be deposited or tendered before meeting),

[section 340B(2)(b) (traded companies: duty to circulate members' matters for AGM)].

(2) Any reference in those provisions to a period of notice, or to a period before a meeting by which a request must be received or sum deposited or tendered, is to a period of the specified length excluding—

(a) the day of the meeting, and

(b) the day on which the notice is given, the request received or the sum deposited or tendered.

NOTES

Sub-s (1): words in square brackets inserted, and word omitted repealed, by the Companies (Shareholders' Rights) Regulations 2009, SI 2009/1632, regs 9(3), 16(6), 17(4), 18(2), as from 3 August 2009, in relation to meetings of which notice is given, or first given, on or after that date.

[1.406]

[360A Electronic meetings and voting

(1) Nothing in this Part is to be taken to preclude the holding and conducting of a meeting in such a way that persons who are not present together at the same place may by electronic means attend and speak and vote at it.

(2) In the case of a traded company the use of electronic means for the purpose of enabling members to participate in a general meeting may be made subject only to such requirements and restrictions as are—

(a) necessary to ensure the identification of those taking part and the security of the electronic communication, and

(b) proportionate to the achievement of those objectives.

(3) Nothing in subsection (2) affects any power of a company to require reasonable evidence of the entitlement of any person who is not a member to participate in the meeting.]

NOTES

Inserted by the Companies (Shareholders' Rights) Regulations 2009, SI 2009/1632, reg 8, as from 3 August 2009, in relation to meetings of which notice is given, or first given, on or after that date.

[1.407]

[360AA Traded companies: confirmation of receipt of electronic voting

(1) In the case of a traded company, where a vote is cast on a poll by electronic means the company must ensure that, as soon as reasonably practicable after the vote has been received, confirmation of receipt of the vote is sent by electronic means to—

(a) the member, where that person cast the vote,

(b) the proxy, where the vote was cast by proxy, or

(c) the representative, where the vote was cast by a person authorised to act as a representative of a corporation in accordance with section 323(1).

(2) A vote under subsection (1) includes any vote cast—

(a) at a meeting;

(b) at an electronic meeting conducted in accordance with section 360A;

(c) in advance of a meeting or electronic meeting (see section 322A).]

NOTES

Commencement: 3 September 2020.

Inserted by the Companies (Shareholders' Rights to Voting Confirmations) Regulations 2020, SI 2020/717, reg 4(1), as from 3 September 2020, in relation to votes cast on or after that date (see reg 2 of those Regulations).

[1.408]

[360B Traded companies: requirements for participating in and voting at general meetings

(1) Any provision of a traded company's articles is void in so far as it would have the effect of—

(a) imposing a restriction on a right of a member to participate in and vote at a general meeting of the company unless the member's shares have (after having been acquired by the member and before the meeting) been deposited with, or transferred to, or registered in the name of another person, or

(b) imposing a restriction on the right of a member to transfer shares in the company during the period of 48 hours before the time for the holding of a general meeting of the company if that right would not otherwise be subject to that restriction.

(2) A traded company must determine the right to vote at a general meeting of the company by reference to the register of members as at a time (determined by the company) that is not more than 48 hours before the time for the holding of the meeting.

(3) In calculating the period mentioned in subsection (1)(b) or (2), no account is to be taken of any part of a day that is not a working day.

(4) Nothing in this section affects—

(a) the operation of—

(i) Part 22 of this Act (information about interests in a company's shares),

(ii) Part 15 of the Companies Act 1985 (orders imposing restrictions on shares), or

(iii) any provision in a company's articles relating to the application of any provision of either of those Parts; or

(b) the validity of articles prescribed, or to the same effect as articles prescribed, under section 19 of this Act (power of Secretary of State to prescribe model articles).

[(5) If an election is in force under section 128B in respect of a company, the reference in subsection (2) to the register of members is to be read as a reference to the register kept by the registrar under section 1080.]]

NOTES

Inserted by the Companies (Shareholders' Rights) Regulations 2009, SI 2009/1632, reg 20, as from 3 August 2009, in relation to meetings of which notice is given, or first given, on or after that date.

Sub-s (5): added by the Small Business, Enterprise and Employment Act 2015, s 94, Sch 5, Pt 2, paras 11, 18, as from 30 June 2016.

[1.409]

[360BA Traded companies: right to confirmation of vote after a general meeting

(1) Where the conditions in subsection (2) are met, a traded company must provide information to a member which enables the member to confirm that their vote on a resolution at a general meeting where a poll has been taken has been validly recorded and counted.

(2) The conditions are that—

(a) the member makes a request for the information, which request is received by the company no later than 30 days from the date of that general meeting, and

(b) the member does not have any other reasonable means by which to determine that their vote has been validly recorded and counted by the company.

(3) The information under subsection (1) must be provided to the member as soon as reasonably practicable and in any event by the end of the period of 15 days beginning with whichever is the later of the first working day after the day on which—

(a) the result of the poll is declared for that resolution; or

(b) the request for information under subsection (2)(a) is received by the company.]

NOTES

Commencement: 3 September 2020.

Inserted by the Companies (Shareholders' Rights to Voting Confirmations) Regulations 2020, SI 2020/717, reg 5(1), as from 3 September 2020, in relation to votes cast at a general meeting which takes place on or after that date (see reg 3 of those Regulations).

[1.410]

[360C Meaning of "traded company"

In this Part, "traded company" means a company any shares of which—

(a) carry rights to vote at general meetings, and

(b) are admitted to trading on a [UK regulated market or an EU regulated market] by or with the consent of the company.]

NOTES

Inserted by the Companies (Shareholders' Rights) Regulations 2009, SI 2009/1632, reg 21(1), as from 3 August 2009, in relation to meetings of which notice is given, or first given, on or after that date.

Words in square brackets substituted by the Companies, Limited Liability Partnerships and Partnerships (Amendment etc) (EU Exit) Regulations 2019, SI 2019/348, reg 6, Sch 1, paras 1, 6, as from IP completion day (as defined in the European Union (Withdrawal Agreement) Act 2020, s 39).

[1.411]

361 Meaning of "quoted company"

In this Part "quoted company" has the same meaning as in Part 15 of this Act.

PART 14 CONTROL OF POLITICAL DONATIONS AND EXPENDITURE

Introductory

[1.412]

362 Introductory

This Part has effect for controlling—

(a) political donations made by companies to political parties, to other political organisations and to independent election candidates, and

(b) political expenditure incurred by companies.

Donations and expenditure to which this Part applies

[1.413]

363 Political parties, organisations etc to which this Part applies

[(1) This Part applies to a political party if it is registered under Part 2 of the Political Parties, Elections and Referendums Act 2000 (c 41).]

(2) This Part applies to an organisation (a "political organisation") if it carries on, or proposes to carry on, activities that are capable of being reasonably regarded as intended—

(a) to affect public support for a political party to which, or an independent election candidate to whom, this Part applies, or

(b) to influence voters in relation to any national or regional referendum held under the law of the United Kingdom . . .

(3) This Part applies to an independent election candidate at any election to public office held in the United Kingdom . . .

(4) Any reference in the following provisions of this Part to a political party, political organisation or independent election candidate, or to political expenditure, is to a party, organisation, independent candidate or expenditure to which this Part applies.

NOTES

Sub-s (1) was substituted, and the words omitted from sub-ss (2) and (3) were repealed, by the Companies, Limited Liability Partnerships and Partnerships (Amendment etc) (EU Exit) Regulations 2019, SI 2019/348, reg 6, Sch 1, paras 1, 7, as from IP completion day (as defined in the European Union (Withdrawal Agreement) Act 2020, s 39).

[1.414]

364 Meaning of "political donation"

(1) The following provisions have effect for the purposes of this Part as regards the meaning of "political donation".

(2) In relation to a political party or other political organisation—

(a) "political donation" means anything that in accordance with sections 50 to 52 of the Political Parties, Elections and Referendums Act 2000—

(i) constitutes a donation for the purposes of Chapter 1 of Part 4 of that Act (control of donations to registered parties), or

(ii) would constitute such a donation reading references in those sections to a registered party as references to any political party or other political organisation,

and

(b) section 53 of that Act applies, in the same way, for the purpose of determining the value of a donation.

(3) In relation to an independent election candidate—

(a) "political donation" means anything that, in accordance with sections 50 to 52 of that Act, would constitute a donation for the purposes of Chapter 1 of Part 4 of that Act (control of donations to registered parties) reading references in those sections to a registered party as references to the independent election candidate, and

(b) section 53 of that Act applies, in the same way, for the purpose of determining the value of a donation.

(4) For the purposes of this section, sections 50 and 53 of the Political Parties, Elections and Referendums Act 2000 (c 41) (definition of "donation" and value of donations) shall be treated as if the amendments to those sections made by the Electoral Administration Act 2006 (which remove from the definition of "donation" loans made otherwise than on commercial terms) had not been made.

[1.415]

365 Meaning of "political expenditure"

(1) In this Part "political expenditure", in relation to a company, means expenditure incurred by the company on—

(a) the preparation, publication or dissemination of advertising or other promotional or publicity material—

(i) of whatever nature, and

(ii) however published or otherwise disseminated,

that, at the time of publication or dissemination, is capable of being reasonably regarded as intended to affect public support for a political party or other political organisation, or an independent election candidate, or

(b) activities on the part of the company that are capable of being reasonably regarded as intended—

(i) to affect public support for a political party or other political organisation, or an independent election candidate, or

(ii) to influence voters in relation to any national or regional referendum held under the law of [the United Kingdom].

(2) For the purposes of this Part a political donation does not count as political expenditure.

NOTES

Sub-s (1): words in square brackets in sub-para (b)(ii) substituted by the Companies, Limited Liability Partnerships and Partnerships (Amendment etc) (EU Exit) Regulations 2019, SI 2019/348, reg 6, Sch 1, paras 1, 8, as from IP completion day (as defined in the European Union (Withdrawal Agreement) Act 2020, s 39).

Authorisation required for donations or expenditure

[1.416]

366 Authorisation required for donations or expenditure

(1) A company must not—

(a) make a political donation to a political party or other political organisation, or to an independent election candidate, or

(b) incur any political expenditure,

unless the donation or expenditure is authorised in accordance with the following provisions.

(2) The donation or expenditure must be authorised—

(a) in the case of a company that is not a subsidiary of another company, by a resolution of the members of the company;

(b) in the case of a company that is a subsidiary of another company by—

(i) a resolution of the members of the company, and

(ii) a resolution of the members of any relevant holding company.

(3) No resolution is required on the part of a company that is a wholly-owned subsidiary of a UK-registered company.

(4) For the purposes of subsection (2)(b)(ii) a "relevant holding company" means a company that, at the time the donation was made or the expenditure was incurred—

(a) was a holding company of the company by which the donation was made or the expenditure was incurred,

(b) was a UK-registered company, and

(c) was not a subsidiary of another UK-registered company.

(5) The resolution or resolutions required by this section—

(a) must comply with section 367 (form of authorising resolution), and

(b) must be passed before the donation is made or the expenditure incurred.

(6) Nothing in this section enables a company to be authorised to do anything that it could not lawfully do apart from this section.

[1.417]

367 Form of authorising resolution

(1) A resolution conferring authorisation for the purposes of this Part may relate to—

(a) the company passing the resolution,

(b) one or more subsidiaries of that company, or

(c) the company passing the resolution and one or more subsidiaries of that company.

(2) A resolution may be expressed to relate to all companies that are subsidiaries of the company passing the resolution—

(a) at the time the resolution is passed, or

(b) at any time during the period for which the resolution has effect,

without identifying them individually.

(3) The resolution may authorise donations or expenditure under one or more of the following heads—

(a) donations to political parties or independent election candidates;

(b) donations to political organisations other than political parties;

(c) political expenditure.

(4) The resolution must specify a head or heads—

(a) in the case of a resolution under subsection (2), for all of the companies to which it relates taken together;

(b) in the case of any other resolution, for each company to which it relates.

(5) The resolution must be expressed in general terms conforming with [subsection (3)] and must not purport to authorise particular donations or expenditure.

(6) For each of the specified heads the resolution must authorise donations or, as the case may be, expenditure up to a specified amount in the period for which the resolution has effect (see section 368).

(7) The resolution must specify such amounts—

(a) in the case of a resolution under subsection (2), for all of the companies to which it relates taken together;

(b) in the case of any other resolution, for each company to which it relates.

NOTES

Sub-s (5): words in square brackets substituted by the Companies Act 2006 (Consequential Amendments, Transitional Provisions and Savings) Order 2009, SI 2009/1941, art 2(1), Sch 1, para 260(1), (2), as from 1 October 2009.

[1.418]

368 Period for which resolution has effect

(1) A resolution conferring authorisation for the purposes of this Part has effect for a period of four years beginning with the date on which it is passed unless the directors determine, or the articles require, that it is to have effect for a shorter period beginning with that date.

(2) The power of the directors to make a determination under this section is subject to any provision of the articles that operates to prevent them from doing so.

Remedies in case of unauthorised donations or expenditure

[1.419]

369 Liability of directors in case of unauthorised donation or expenditure

(1) This section applies where a company has made a political donation or incurred political expenditure without the authorisation required by this Part.

(2) The directors in default are jointly and severally liable—

(a) to make good to the company the amount of the unauthorised donation or expenditure, with interest, and

(b) to compensate the company for any loss or damage sustained by it as a result of the unauthorised donation or expenditure having been made.

(3) The directors in default are—

(a) those who, at the time the unauthorised donation was made or the unauthorised expenditure was incurred, were directors of the company by which the donation was made or the expenditure was incurred, and

(b) where—

(i) that company was a subsidiary of a relevant holding company, and

(ii) the directors of the relevant holding company failed to take all reasonable steps to prevent the donation being made or the expenditure being incurred,

the directors of the relevant holding company.

(4) For the purposes of subsection (3)(b) a "relevant holding company" means a company that, at the time the donation was made or the expenditure was incurred—

(a) was a holding company of the company by which the donation was made or the expenditure was incurred,

(b) was a UK-registered company, and

(c) was not a subsidiary of another UK-registered company.

(5) The interest referred to in subsection (2)(a) is interest on the amount of the unauthorised donation or expenditure, so far as not made good to the company—

(a) in respect of the period beginning with the date when the donation was made or the expenditure was incurred, and

(b) at such rate as the Secretary of State may prescribe by regulations.

Section 379(2) (construction of references to date when donation made or expenditure incurred) does not apply for the purposes of this subsection.

(6) Where only part of a donation or expenditure was unauthorised, this section applies only to so much of it as was unauthorised.

NOTES

Regulations: the Companies (Interest Rate for Unauthorised Political Donation or Expenditure) Regulations 2007, SI 2007/2242 at **[4.10]**. For a summary of all statutory instruments made under this Act, see Appendix 4 at **[A4]**.

[1.420]

370 Enforcement of directors' liabilities by shareholder action

(1) Any liability of a director under section 369 is enforceable—

(a) in the case of a liability of a director of a company to that company, by proceedings brought under this section in the name of the company by an authorised group of its members;

(b) in the case of a liability of a director of a holding company to a subsidiary, by proceedings brought under this section in the name of the subsidiary by—

(i) an authorised group of members of the subsidiary, or

(ii) an authorised group of members of the holding company.

(2) This is in addition to the right of the company to which the liability is owed to bring proceedings itself to enforce the liability.

(3) An "authorised group" of members of a company means—

(a) the holders of not less than 5% in nominal value of the company's issued share capital,

(b) if the company is not limited by shares, not less than 5% of its members, or

(c) not less than 50 of the company's members.

(4) The right to bring proceedings under this section is subject to the provisions of section 371.

(5) Nothing in this section affects any right of a member of a company to bring or continue proceedings under Part 11 (derivative claims or proceedings).

[1.421]

371 Enforcement of directors' liabilities by shareholder action: supplementary

(1) A group of members may not bring proceedings under section 370 in the name of a company unless—

(a) the group has given written notice to the company stating—

(i) the cause of action and a summary of the facts on which the proceedings are to be based,

(ii) the names and addresses of the members comprising the group, and

(iii) the grounds on which it is alleged that those members constitute an authorised group; and

(b) not less than 28 days have elapsed between the date of the giving of the notice to the company and the bringing of the proceedings.

(2) Where such a notice is given to a company, any director of the company may apply to the court within the period of 28 days beginning with the date of the giving of the notice for an order directing that the proposed proceedings shall not be brought, on one or more of the following grounds—

(a) that the unauthorised amount has been made good to the company;

(b) that proceedings to enforce the liability have been brought, and are being pursued with due diligence, by the company;

(c) that the members proposing to bring proceedings under this section do not constitute an authorised group.

(3) Where an application is made on the ground mentioned in subsection (2)(b), the court may as an alternative to directing that the proposed proceedings under section 370 are not to be brought, direct—

(a) that such proceedings may be brought on such terms and conditions as the court thinks fit, and

(b) that the proceedings brought by the company—
  (i) shall be discontinued, or
  (ii) may be continued on such terms and conditions as the court thinks fit.

(4) The members by whom proceedings are brought under section 370 owe to the company in whose name they are brought the same duties in relation to the proceedings as would be owed by the company's directors if the proceedings were being brought by the company.

But proceedings to enforce any such duty may be brought by the company only with the permission of the court.

(5) Proceedings brought under section 370 may not be discontinued or settled by the group except with the permission of the court, which may be given on such terms as the court thinks fit.

[1.422]
372 Costs of shareholder action

(1) This section applies in relation to proceedings brought under section 370 in the name of a company ("the company") by an authorised group ("the group").

(2) The group may apply to the court for an order directing the company to indemnify the group in respect of costs incurred or to be incurred by the group in connection with the proceedings.

The court may make such an order on such terms as it thinks fit.

(3) The group is not entitled to be paid any such costs out of the assets of the company except by virtue of such an order.

(4) If no such order has been made with respect to the proceedings, then—
(a) if the company is awarded costs in connection with the proceedings, or it is agreed that costs incurred by the company in connection with the proceedings should be paid by any defendant, the costs shall be paid to the group; and
(b) if any defendant is awarded costs in connection with the proceedings, or it is agreed that any defendant should be paid costs incurred by him in connection with the proceedings, the costs shall be paid by the group.

(5) In the application of this section to Scotland for "costs" read "expenses" and for "defendant" read "defender".

[1.423]
373 Information for purposes of shareholder action

(1) Where proceedings have been brought under section 370 in the name of a company by an authorised group, the group is entitled to require the company to provide it with all information relating to the subject matter of the proceedings that is in the company's possession or under its control or which is reasonably obtainable by it.

(2) If the company, having been required by the group to do so, refuses to provide the group with all or any of that information, the court may, on an application made by the group, make an order directing—
(a) the company, and
(b) any of its officers or employees specified in the application,
to provide the group with the information in question in such form and by such means as the court may direct.

Exemptions

[1.424]
374 Trade unions

(1) A donation to a trade union, other than a contribution to the union's political fund, is not a political donation for the purposes of this Part.

(2) A trade union is not a political organisation for the purposes of section 365 (meaning of "political expenditure").

(3) In this section—
"trade union" has the meaning given by section 1 of Trade Union and Labour Relations (Consolidation) Act 1992 (c 52) or Article 3 of the Industrial Relations (Northern Ireland) Order 1992 (SI 1992/807 (NI 5));
"political fund" means the fund from which payments by a trade union in the furtherance of political objects are required to be made by virtue of section 82(1)(a) of that Act or Article 57(2)(a) of that Order.

[1.425]
375 Subscription for membership of trade association

(1) A subscription paid to a trade association for membership of the association is not a political donation for the purposes of this Part.

(2) For this purpose—
"trade association" means an organisation formed for the purpose of furthering the trade interests of its members, or of persons represented by its members, and
"subscription" does not include a payment to the association to the extent that it is made for the purpose of financing any particular activity of the association.

[1.426]
376 All-party parliamentary groups

(1) An all-party parliamentary group is not a political organisation for the purposes of this Part.

(2) An "all-party parliamentary group" means an all-party group composed of members of one or both of the Houses of Parliament (or of such members and other persons).

[1.427]
377 Political expenditure exempted by order

(1) Authorisation under this Part is not needed for political expenditure that is exempt by virtue of an order of the Secretary of State under this section.

(2) An order may confer an exemption in relation to—
(a) companies of any description or category specified in the order, or
(b) expenditure of any description or category so specified (whether framed by reference to goods, services or other matters in respect of which such expenditure is incurred or otherwise),
or both.

(3) If or to the extent that expenditure is exempt from the requirement of authorisation under this Part by virtue of an order under this section, it shall be disregarded in determining what donations are authorised by any resolution of the company passed for the purposes of this Part.

(4) An order under this section is subject to affirmative resolution procedure.

NOTES

Orders: the Companies (Political Expenditure Exemption) Order 2007, SI 2007/2081 at **[4.6]**. For a summary of all statutory instruments made under this Act, see Appendix 4 at **[A4]**.

[1.428]

378 Donations not amounting to more than £5,000 in any twelve month period

(1) Authorisation under this Part is not needed for a donation except to the extent that the total amount of—

(a) that donation, and

(b) other relevant donations made in the period of 12 months ending with the date on which that donation is made,

exceeds £5,000.

(2) In this section—

"donation" means a donation to a political party or other political organisation or to an independent election candidate; and

"other relevant donations" means—

(a) in relation to a donation made by a company that is not a subsidiary, any other donations made by that company or by any of its subsidiaries;

(b) in relation to a donation made by a company that is a subsidiary, any other donations made by that company, by any holding company of that company or by any other subsidiary of any such holding company.

(3) If or to the extent that a donation is exempt by virtue of this section from the requirement of authorisation under this Part, it shall be disregarded in determining what donations are authorised by any resolution passed for the purposes of this Part.

Supplementary provisions

[1.429]

379 Minor definitions

(1) In this Part—

"director" includes shadow director; and

"organisation" includes any body corporate or unincorporated association and any combination of persons.

(2) Except as otherwise provided, any reference in this Part to the time at which a donation is made or expenditure is incurred is, in a case where the donation is made or expenditure incurred in pursuance of a contract, any earlier time at which that contract is entered into by the company.

PART 15 ACCOUNTS AND REPORTS

NOTES

See further, the Finance Act 2009, s 93, Sch 46 in relation to the duty of the senior accounting officer of a qualifying company to take reasonable steps to ensure that the company establishes and maintains appropriate tax accounting arrangements. A company is a "qualifying company" for these purposes if the company's turnover exceeds £200 million or if the company's balance sheet total exceeds £2 billion (or both) (see Sch 46, para 15).

CHAPTER 1 INTRODUCTION

General

[1.430]

380 Scheme of this Part

(1) The requirements of this Part as to accounts and reports apply in relation to each financial year of a company.

(2) In certain respects different provisions apply to different kinds of company.

(3), (4) . . .

NOTES

Sub-ss (3), (4): repealed by the Companies, Partnerships and Groups (Accounts and Reports) Regulations 2015, SI 2015/980, reg 4(1), (2), in relation to (a) financial years beginning on or after 1 January 2016, and (b) a financial year of a company beginning on or after 1 January 2015, but before 1 January 2016, if the directors of the company so decide (subject to transitional provisions, etc, in regs 2, 3 of the 2015 Regulations as noted below).

Application and transitional provisions etc: the Companies, Partnerships and Groups (Accounts and Reports) Regulations 2015, SI 2015/980, regs 2, 3 (as amended by the Companies, Partnerships and Groups (Accounts and Reports) (No 2) Regulations 2015, SI 2015/1672, reg 5, as from 1 October 2015) provide as follows—

"2 Commencement and Application

(1) These Regulations come into force on 6th April 2015.

(2) Subject to paragraph (3) and regulation 3, the amendments made by these Regulations have effect in relation to—

(a) financial years beginning on or after 1st January 2016, and

(b) a financial year of a company beginning on or after 1st January 2015, but before 1st January 2016, if the directors of the company so decide.

(3) Where—

(a) [by virtue of paragraph (2)(b) above and regulation 2(2)(b) of the Companies, Partnerships and Groups (Accounts and Reports) (No 2) Regulations 2015 ("the No 2 Regulations"), the amendments made by these Regulations and by regulations 3 and 4 of the No 2 Regulations] have effect in relation to a financial year beginning on or after 1st January 2015, but before 1st January 2016, and

(b) as a result the company qualifies as a small company in relation to that year,

the company is not exempt from the requirements of the Act relating to the audit of annual accounts for that year if the company would not have been so exempt had the amendments not had effect in relation to that year.

(4) In determining whether a company or group qualifies as small or medium-sized under section 382(2), 383(3), 465(2) or 466(3) of the Act (qualification in relation to subsequent financial year by reference to circumstances in preceding financial years) in relation to a financial year in relation to which the amendments made by these Regulations [and by regulations 3 and 4 of the No 2 Regulations] have effect, the company or group is to be treated as having qualified as small or medium-sized (as the case may be) in any previous year in which it would have so qualified if amendments to the same effect as the amendments made by these Regulations [and by regulations 3 and 4 of the No 2 Regulations] had had effect in relation to that previous year.

(5) Notwithstanding paragraph (2), the directors of a company cannot take advantage of subsection (2) of section 410 of the Act (information about related undertakings: alternative compliance) in relation to annual accounts of the company approved, pursuant to section 414 of the Act, on or after 1st July 2015.

3 Disapplication of these Regulations to Limited Liability Partnerships

The amendments made by these Regulations to the Act, the Small Companies Accounts Regulations or the Large and Medium-sized Companies Accounts Regulations do not have effect in relation to the application of any provision of the Act or those regulations—

(a) to limited liability partnerships by the Limited Liability Partnerships (Accounts and Audit) (Application of Companies Act 2006) Regulations 2008, . . .

(b) to limited liability partnerships by the Small Limited Liability Partnerships (Accounts) Regulations 2008[; or

(c) to limited liability partnerships by the Large and Medium-sized Limited Liability Partnerships (Accounts) Regulations 2008].

Note for these purposes that "the No 2 Regulations" are the Companies, Partnerships and Groups (Accounts and Reports) (No 2) Regulations 2015, SI 2015/1672.

Companies subject to the small companies regime

[1.431]

381 Companies subject to the small companies regime

The small companies regime . . . applies to a company for a financial year in relation to which the company—

(a) qualifies as small (see sections 382 and 383), and

(b) is not excluded from the regime (see section 384).

NOTES

Words omitted repealed by the Companies Act 2006 (Amendment) (Accounts and Reports) Regulations 2008, SI 2008/393, reg 6(1), as from 6 April 2008, in relation to financial years beginning on or after that date.

[1.432]

382 Companies qualifying as small: general

(1) A company qualifies as small in relation to its first financial year if the qualifying conditions are met in that year.

[(1A) Subject to subsection (2), a company qualifies as small in relation to a subsequent financial year if the qualifying conditions are met in that year.]

[(2) In relation to a subsequent financial year, where on its balance sheet date a company meets or ceases to meet the qualifying conditions, that affects its qualification as a small company only if it occurs in two consecutive financial years.]

(3) The qualifying conditions are met by a company in a year in which it satisfies two or more of the following requirements—

1 Turnover	[Not more than £10.2 million]
2 Balance sheet total	[Not more than £5.1 million]
3 Number of employees	Not more than 50

(4) For a period that is a company's financial year but not in fact a year the maximum figures for turnover must be proportionately adjusted.

(5) The balance sheet total means the aggregate of the amounts shown as assets in the company's balance sheet.

(6) The number of employees means the average number of persons employed by the company in the year, determined as follows—

(a) find for each month in the financial year the number of persons employed under contracts of service by the company in that month (whether throughout the month or not),

(b) add together the monthly totals, and

(c) divide by the number of months in the financial year.

(7) This section is subject to section 383 (companies qualifying as small: parent companies).

NOTES

Sub-s (1A): inserted by the Small Companies (Micro-Entities' Accounts) Regulations 2013, SI 2013/3008, reg 4(1), (2)(a), in relation to (a) financial years ending on or after 30 September 2013, and (b) companies which deliver the accounts required by s 444 of this Act to the registrar on or after 1 December 2013 (as to application of this amendment, see the note below).

Sub-s (2): substituted by SI 2013/3008, reg 4(1), (2)(b), in relation to (a) financial years ending on or after 30 September 2013, and (b) companies which deliver the accounts required by s 444 of this Act to the registrar on or after 1 December 2013 (as to application of this amendment, see the note below).

Sub-s (3): words in square brackets substituted by the Companies, Partnerships and Groups (Accounts and Reports) Regulations 2015, SI 2015/980, reg 4(1), (3), in relation to (a) financial years beginning on or after 1 January 2016, and (b) a financial year of a company beginning on or after 1 January 2015, but before 1 January 2016, if the directors of the company so decide (subject to transitional provisions, etc, in regs 2, 3 of the 2015 Regulations as noted to s 380 at **[1.430]**).

See also, as to whether a company qualifies as small for the purposes of sub-s (2), the Companies, Partnerships and Groups (Accounts and Reports) Regulations 2015, SI 2015/980, reg 2(4) (see the note to s 380 at **[1.430]**).

Note that the Small Companies (Micro-Entities' Accounts) Regulations 2013, SI 2013/3008, reg 3 provides as follows (note that para (a) below was revoked by the Limited Liability Partnerships, Partnerships and Groups (Accounts and Audit) Regulations 2016, SI 2016/575, reg 63, as from 17 May 2016, in relation to (a) financial years beginning on or after 1 January 2016; and (b) a financial year of a qualifying partnership (within the meaning given by reg 3 of the Partnerships (Accounts)

Regulations 2008) beginning on or after 1 January 2015, but before 1 January 2016, if: (i) the partners so decide; and (ii) no copy of the qualifying partnership's accounts for that financial year has been delivered to the registrar in accordance with reg 5(1) of those Regulations)—

"(1) The amendments made by these Regulations to any provision of the 2006 Act or the 2008 Regulations do not have effect in relation to the application of any such provision—

(a) . . .

(b) to limited liability partnerships by the Limited Liability Partnerships (Accounts and Audit) (Application of Companies Act 2006) Regulations 2008;

(c) to limited liability partnerships by the Small Limited Liability Partnerships (Accounts) Regulations 2008;

(d) to overseas companies by Chapter 3 of Part 5 or Chapter 3 of Part 6 of the Overseas Companies Regulations 2009;

(e) to unregistered companies by regulation 3 of and Schedule 1 to the Unregistered Companies Regulations 2009; or

(f) to companies registered pursuant to section 1040 of the 2006 Act by regulation 18 of the Companies (Companies Authorised to Register) Regulations 2009.

(2) Any new provision of the 2006 Act or the 2008 Regulations inserted by these Regulations is not, by virtue of any provision mentioned in sub-paragraphs (a) to (f) of paragraph (1), applied to the entities mentioned in those sub-paragraphs.".

[1.433]

383 Companies qualifying as small: parent companies

(1) A parent company qualifies as a small company in relation to a financial year only if the group headed by it qualifies as a small group.

(2) A group qualifies as small in relation to the parent company's first financial year if the qualifying conditions are met in that year.

[(2A) Subject to subsection (3), a group qualifies as small in relation to a subsequent financial year of the parent company if the qualifying conditions are met in that year.]

[(3) In relation to a subsequent financial year of the parent company, where on the parent company's balance sheet date the group meets or ceases to meet the qualifying conditions, that affects the group's qualification as a small group only if it occurs in two consecutive financial years.]

(4) The qualifying conditions are met by a group in a year in which it satisfies two or more of the following requirements—

1. Aggregate turnover	[Not more than £10.2 million net (or £12.2 million gross)]
2. Aggregate balance sheet total	[Not more than £5.1 million net (or £6.1 million gross)]
3. Aggregate number of employees	Not more than 50

(5) The aggregate figures are ascertained by aggregating the relevant figures determined in accordance with section 382 for each member of the group.

(6) In relation to the aggregate figures for turnover and balance sheet total—

"net" means after any set-offs and other adjustments made to eliminate group transactions—

(a) in the case of Companies Act accounts, in accordance with regulations under section 404,

(b) in the case of IAS accounts, in accordance with [UK-adopted international accounting standards]; and

"gross" means without those set-offs and other adjustments.

A company may satisfy any relevant requirement on the basis of either the net or the gross figure.

(7) The figures for each subsidiary undertaking shall be those included in its individual accounts for the relevant financial year, that is—

(a) if its financial year ends with that of the parent company, that financial year, and

(b) if not, its financial year ending last before the end of the financial year of the parent company.

If those figures cannot be obtained without disproportionate expense or undue delay, the latest available figures shall be taken.

NOTES

Sub-s (2A): inserted by the Small Companies (Micro-Entities' Accounts) Regulations 2013, SI 2013/3008, reg 4(1), (3)(a), in relation to (a) financial years ending on or after 30 September 2013, and (b) companies which deliver the accounts required by s 444 of this Act to the registrar on or after 1 December 2013 (as to application of this amendment, see the note at **[1.432]**).

Sub-s (3): substituted by SI 2013/3008, reg 4(1), (3)(b), in relation to (a) financial years ending on or after 30 September 2013, and (b) companies which deliver the accounts required by s 444 of this Act to the registrar on or after 1 December 2013 (as to application of this amendment, see the note at **[1.432]**).

Sub-s (4): words in square brackets substituted by the Companies, Partnerships and Groups (Accounts and Reports) Regulations 2015, SI 2015/980, reg 4(1), (4), in relation to (a) financial years beginning on or after 1 January 2016, and (b) a financial year of a company beginning on or after 1 January 2015, but before 1 January 2016, if the directors of the company so decide (subject to transitional provisions, etc, in regs 2, 3 of the 2015 Regulations as noted to s 380 at **[1.430]**).

Sub-s (6): words in square brackets in the definition "net" substituted by the International Accounting Standards and European Public Limited-Liability Company (Amendment etc) (EU Exit) Regulations 2019, SI 2019/685, reg 19, Sch 1, Pt 1, paras 1, 2, in relation to accounts for financial years beginning on or after IP completion day (as defined in the European Union (Withdrawal Agreement) Act 2020, s 39) (note also that in relation to accounts for financial years which begin before but end on or after IP completion day, the enactments amended by Parts 1–3 of Sch 1 to the 2019 Regulations have effect as if the UK were a member State until the end of the financial year in question (for transitional provisions see reg 1 of, and Sch 1, Pt 4 to, the 2019 Regulations at **[12.130]** and **[12.151]** respectively)).

See also, as to whether a group qualifies as small for the purposes of sub-s (3), the Companies, Partnerships and Groups (Accounts and Reports) Regulations 2015, SI 2015/980, reg 2(4) (see the note to s 380 at **[1.430]**).

[1.434]

384 Companies excluded from the small companies regime

(1) The small companies regime does not apply to a company that . . . was at any time within the financial year to which the accounts relate—

(a) a public company,

(b) a company that—

(i) is an authorised insurance company, a banking company, an e-money issuer, [a MiFID investment firm] or a UCITS management company, . . .

(ii) carries on insurance market activity, or

[(iii) is a scheme funder of a Master Trust scheme within the meanings given by section 39(1) of the Pension Schemes Act 2017 (interpretation of Part 1), or]

(c) a member of an ineligible group.

(2) A group is ineligible if any of its members is—

[(a) a traded company,]

(b) a body corporate (other than a company) whose shares are admitted to trading on a [UK regulated market],

(c) a person (other than a small company) who has permission under [Part 4A] of the Financial Services and Markets Act 2000 (c 8) to carry on a regulated activity,

[(ca) an e-money issuer,]

(d) a small company that is an authorised insurance company, a banking company, . . . [a MiFID investment firm] or a UCITS management company, . . .

(e) a person who carries on insurance market activity, [or]

[(f) a scheme funder of a Master Trust scheme within the meanings given by section 39(1) of the Pension Schemes Act 2017 (interpretation of Part 1)].

(3) A company is a small company for the purposes of subsection (2) if it qualified as small in relation to its last financial year ending on or before the end of the financial year to which the accounts relate.

NOTES

Sub-s (1): first words omitted repealed by the Companies, Partnerships and Groups (Accounts and Reports) Regulations 2015, SI 2015/980, reg 4(1), (5)(a), in relation to (a) financial years beginning on or after 1 January 2016, and (b) a financial year of a company beginning on or after 1 January 2015, but before 1 January 2016, if the directors of the company so decide (subject to transitional provisions, etc, in regs 2, 3 of the 2015 Regulations as noted to s 380 at **[1.430]**). Words in square brackets in sub-para (b)(i) substituted by the Markets in Financial Instruments Directive (Consequential Amendments) Regulations 2007, SI 2007/2932, reg 3(1), (2)(a), as from 1 November 2007. Word omitted from sub-para (b)(i) repealed, and sub-para (b)(iii) inserted, by the Occupational Pension Schemes (Master Trusts) Regulations 2018, SI 2018/1030, reg 30(1), (2)(a), as from 1 October 2018.

Sub-s (2) is amended as follows:

Para (a) substituted by SI 2015/980, reg 4(1), (5)(b), as from the same dates and for the same purposes as specified in the first note relating to the 2015 Regulations above.

Words in square brackets in para (b) substituted by the Accounts and Reports (Amendment) (EU Exit) Regulations 2019, SI 2019/145, reg 5, Sch 2, Pt 1, paras 1, 2, in relation to financial years beginning on or after IP completion day (as defined in the European Union (Withdrawal Agreement) Act 2020, s 39) (for transitional provisions see reg 7 of the 2019 Regulations at **[12.79]**).

Words in square brackets in para (c) substituted by the Financial Services Act 2012, s 114(1), Sch 18, Pt 2, paras 110, 111, as from 1 April 2013.

Para (ca) inserted, and first words omitted from para (d) repealed, by the Companies and Partnerships (Accounts and Audit) Regulations 2013, SI 2013/2005, reg 2(1), (2), in relation to a financial year of a company beginning on or after 1 October 2013.

Words in square brackets in para (d) substituted by SI 2007/2932, reg 3(1), (2)(b), as from 1 November 2007.

Word omitted from the end of para (d) repealed, word in square brackets in para (e) inserted, and para (f) added, by SI 2018/1030, reg 30(1), (2)(b), as from 1 October 2018.

[1.435]

[384A Companies qualifying as micro-entities

(1) A company qualifies as a micro-entity in relation to its first financial year if the qualifying conditions are met in that year.

(2) Subject to subsection (3), a company qualifies as a micro-entity in relation to a subsequent financial year if the qualifying conditions are met in that year.

(3) In relation to a subsequent financial year, where on its balance sheet date a company meets or ceases to meet the qualifying conditions, that affects its qualification as a micro-entity only if it occurs in two consecutive financial years.

(4) The qualifying conditions are met by a company in a year in which it satisfies two or more of the following requirements—

1. Turnover	Not more than £632,000
2. Balance sheet total	Not more than £316,000
3. Number of employees	Not more than 10

(5) For a period that is a company's financial year but not in fact a year the maximum figures for turnover must be proportionately adjusted.

(6) The balance sheet total means the aggregate of the amounts shown as assets in the company's balance sheet.

(7) The number of employees means the average number of persons employed by the company in the year, determined as follows—

(a) find for each month in the financial year the number of persons employed under contracts of service by the company in that month (whether throughout the month or not),

(b) add together the monthly totals, and

(c) divide by the number of months in the financial year.

(8) In the case of a company which is a parent company, the company qualifies as a micro-entity in relation to a financial year only if—

(a) the company qualifies as a micro-entity in relation to that year, as determined by subsections (1) to (7), and

(b) the group headed by the company qualifies as a small group, as determined by section 383(2) to (7).]

NOTES

Inserted, together with s 384B, by the Small Companies (Micro-Entities' Accounts) Regulations 2013, SI 2013/3008, reg 4(1), (4), in relation to (a) financial years ending on or after 30 September 2013, and (b) companies which deliver the accounts required by s 444 of this Act to the registrar on or after 1 December 2013 (as to application of this section, see the note at **[1.432]**).

[1.436]

[384B Companies excluded from being treated as micro-entities

(1) The micro-entity provisions do not apply in relation to a company's accounts for a particular financial year if the company . . . at any time within that year—

(a) [was] a company excluded from the small companies regime by virtue of section 384,

(b) [would have been] an investment undertaking as defined in Article 2(14) of Directive 2013/34/EU of 26 June 2013 on the annual financial statements etc of certain types of undertakings [were the United Kingdom a member State],

(c) [would have been] a financial holding undertaking as defined in Article 2(15) of that Directive [were the United Kingdom a member State],

[(d) a credit institution within the meaning given by Article 4(1)(1) of Regulation (EU) No 575/2013 of the European Parliament and of the Council, [which is a CRR firm within the meaning of Article 4(1)(2A) of that Regulation,]]

(e) [would have been] an insurance undertaking as defined in Article 2(1) of Council Directive 91/674/EEC of 19 December 1991 on the annual accounts of insurance undertakings [were the United Kingdom a member State], or

(f) [was] a charity.

(2) The micro-entity provisions also do not apply in relation to a company's accounts for a financial year if—

(a) the company is a parent company which prepares group accounts for that year as permitted by section [399(4)], or

(b) the company is not a parent company but its accounts are included in consolidated group accounts for that year.]

NOTES

Inserted as noted to s 384A at **[1.435]**.

Sub-s (1) is amended as follows:

The word omitted was repealed, all words in square brackets (with the exception of para (d) and the words in square brackets in that paragraph) were inserted, and the words in square brackets in para (d) were substituted, by the Accounts and Reports (Amendment) (EU Exit) Regulations 2019, SI 2019/145, reg 5, Sch 2, Pt 1, paras 1, 3, in relation to financial years beginning on or after IP completion day (as defined in the European Union (Withdrawal Agreement) Act 2020, s 39) (for transitional provisions see reg 7 of the 2019 Regulations at **[12.79]**).

Para (d) was previously substituted by SI 2019/145, reg 4, Sch 1, para 1, as from 6 February 2019.

Sub-s (2): number in square brackets substituted by the Companies, Partnerships and Groups (Accounts and Non-Financial Reporting) Regulations 2016, SI 2016/1245, regs 2, 3(1), in relation to the financial years of companies and qualifying partnerships beginning on or after 1 January 2017 (and only in relation to companies (as defined by s 1 *ante*) and qualifying partnerships (as defined in the Partnerships (Accounts) Regulations 2008, reg 3)).

Quoted and unquoted companies

[1.437]

385 Quoted and unquoted companies

(1) For the purposes of this Part a company is a quoted company in relation to a financial year if it is a quoted company immediately before the end of the accounting reference period by reference to which that financial year was determined.

(2) A "quoted company" means a company whose equity share capital—

(a) has been included in the official list in accordance with the provisions of Part 6 of the Financial Services and Markets Act 2000 (c 8), or

(b) is officially listed in an EEA State, or

(c) is admitted to dealing on either the New York Stock Exchange or the exchange known as Nasdaq.

In paragraph (a) "the official list" has the meaning given by section 103(1) of the Financial Services and Markets Act 2000.

(3) An "unquoted company" means a company that is not a quoted company.

(4) The Secretary of State may by regulations amend or replace the provisions of subsections (1) to (2) so as to limit or extend the application of some or all of the provisions of this Part that are expressed to apply to quoted companies.

(5) Regulations under this section extending the application of any such provision of this Part are subject to affirmative resolution procedure.

(6) Any other regulations under this section are subject to negative resolution procedure.

NOTES

Regulations: no Regulations have been made under this section.

CHAPTER 2 ACCOUNTING RECORDS

[1.438]

386 Duty to keep accounting records

(1) Every company must keep adequate accounting records.

(2) Adequate accounting records means records that are sufficient—

(a) to show and explain the company's transactions,

(b) to disclose with reasonable accuracy, at any time, the financial position of the company at that time, and

(c) to enable the directors to ensure that any accounts required to be prepared comply with the requirements of this Act . . .

(3) Accounting records must, in particular, contain—

(a) entries from day to day of all sums of money received and expended by the company and the matters in respect of which the receipt and expenditure takes place, and

(b) a record of the assets and liabilities of the company.

(4) If the company's business involves dealing in goods, the accounting records must contain—

(a) statements of stock held by the company at the end of each financial year of the company,

(b) all statements of stocktakings from which any statement of stock as is mentioned in paragraph (a) has been or is to be prepared, and

(c) except in the case of goods sold by way of ordinary retail trade, statements of all goods sold and purchased, showing the goods and the buyers and sellers in sufficient detail to enable all these to be identified.

(5) A parent company that has a subsidiary undertaking in relation to which the above requirements do not apply must take reasonable steps to secure that the undertaking keeps such accounting records as to enable the directors of the parent company to ensure that any accounts required to be prepared under this Part comply with the requirements of this Act . . .

NOTES

Sub-ss (2), (5): words omitted repealed by the International Accounting Standards and European Public Limited-Liability Company (Amendment etc) (EU Exit) Regulations 2019, SI 2019/685, reg 19, Sch 1, Pt 1, paras 1, 3, in relation to accounts for financial years beginning on or after IP completion day (as defined in the European Union (Withdrawal Agreement) Act 2020, s 39) (note also that in relation to accounts for financial years which begin before but end on or after IP completion day, the enactments amended by Parts 1–3 of Sch 1 to the 2019 Regulations have effect as if the UK were a member State until the end of the financial year in question (for transitional provisions see reg 1 of, and Sch 1, Pt 4 to, the 2019 Regulations at **[12.130]** and **[12.151]** respectively)).

[1.439]

387 Duty to keep accounting records: offence

(1) If a company fails to comply with any provision of section 386 (duty to keep accounting records), an offence is committed by every officer of the company who is in default.

(2) It is a defence for a person charged with such an offence to show that he acted honestly and that in the circumstances in which the company's business was carried on the default was excusable.

(3) A person guilty of an offence under this section is liable—

(a) on conviction on indictment, to imprisonment for a term not exceeding two years or a fine (or both);

(b) on summary conviction—

(i) in England and Wales, to imprisonment for a term not exceeding twelve months or to a fine not exceeding the statutory maximum (or both);

(ii) in Scotland or Northern Ireland, to imprisonment for a term not exceeding six months, or to a fine not exceeding the statutory maximum (or both).

NOTES

Offences under this section: see further s 1131 at **[1.1301]**.

[1.440]

388 Where and for how long records to be kept

(1) A company's accounting records—

(a) must be kept at its registered office or such other place as the directors think fit, and

(b) must at all times be open to inspection by the company's officers.

(2) If accounting records are kept at a place outside the United Kingdom, accounts and returns with respect to the business dealt with in the accounting records so kept must be sent to, and kept at, a place in the United Kingdom, and must at all times be open to such inspection.

(3) The accounts and returns to be sent to the United Kingdom must be such as to—

(a) disclose with reasonable accuracy the financial position of the business in question at intervals of not more than six months, and

(b) enable the directors to ensure that the accounts required to be prepared under this Part comply with the requirements of this Act . . .

(4) Accounting records that a company is required by section 386 to keep must be preserved by it—

(a) in the case of a private company, for three years from the date on which they are made;

(b) in the case of a public company, for six years from the date on which they are made.

(5) Subsection (4) is subject to any provision contained in rules made under section 411 of the Insolvency Act 1986 (c 45) (company insolvency rules) or Article 359 of the Insolvency (Northern Ireland) Order 1989 (SI 1989/2405 (NI 19)).

NOTES

Sub-s (3): words omitted repealed by the International Accounting Standards and European Public Limited-Liability Company (Amendment etc) (EU Exit) Regulations 2019, SI 2019/685, reg 19, Sch 1, Pt 1, paras 1, 4, in relation to accounts for financial years beginning on or after IP completion day (as defined in the European Union (Withdrawal Agreement) Act 2020, s 39) (note also that in relation to accounts for financial years which begin before but end on or after IP completion day, the enactments amended by Parts 1–3 of Sch 1 to the 2019 Regulations have effect as if the UK were a member State until the end of the financial year in question (for transitional provisions see reg 1 of, and Sch 1, Pt 4 to, the 2019 Regulations at **[12.130]** and **[12.151]** respectively)).

[1.441]

389 Where and for how long records to be kept: offences

(1) If a company fails to comply with any provision of subsections (1) to (3) of section 388 (requirements as to keeping of accounting records), an offence is committed by every officer of the company who is in default.

(2) It is a defence for a person charged with such an offence to show that he acted honestly and that in the circumstances in which the company's business was carried on the default was excusable.

(3) An officer of a company commits an offence if he—

- (a) fails to take all reasonable steps for securing compliance by the company with subsection (4) of that section (period for which records to be preserved), or
- (b) intentionally causes any default by the company under that subsection.

(4) A person guilty of an offence under this section is liable—

- (a) on conviction on indictment, to imprisonment for a term not exceeding two years or a fine (or both);
- (b) on summary conviction—
  - (i) in England and Wales, to imprisonment for a term not exceeding twelve months or to a fine not exceeding the statutory maximum (or both);
  - (ii) in Scotland or Northern Ireland, to imprisonment for a term not exceeding six months, or to a fine not exceeding the statutory maximum (or both).

NOTES

Offences under this section: see further s 1131 at **[1.1301]**.

CHAPTER 3 A COMPANY'S FINANCIAL YEAR

[1.442]

390 A company's financial year

(1) A company's financial year is determined as follows.

(2) Its first financial year—

- (a) begins with the first day of its first accounting reference period, and
- (b) ends with the last day of that period or such other date, not more than seven days before or after the end of that period, as the directors may determine.

(3) Subsequent financial years—

- (a) begin with the day immediately following the end of the company's previous financial year, and
- (b) end with the last day of its next accounting reference period or such other date, not more than seven days before or after the end of that period, as the directors may determine.

(4) In relation to an undertaking that is not a company, references in this Act to its financial year are to any period in respect of which a profit and loss account of the undertaking is required to be made up (by its constitution or by the law under which it is established), whether that period is a year or not.

(5) The directors of a parent company must secure that, except where in their opinion there are good reasons against it, the financial year of each of its subsidiary undertakings coincides with the company's own financial year.

[1.443]

391 Accounting reference periods and accounting reference date

(1) A company's accounting reference periods are determined according to its accounting reference date in each calendar year.

(2) The accounting reference date of a company incorporated in Great Britain before 1st April 1996 is—

- (a) the date specified by notice to the registrar in accordance with section 224(2) of the Companies Act 1985 (c 6) (notice specifying accounting reference date given within nine months of incorporation), or
- (b) failing such notice—
  - (i) in the case of a company incorporated before 1st April 1990, 31st March, and
  - (ii) in the case of a company incorporated on or after 1st April 1990, the last day of the month in which the anniversary of its incorporation falls.

(3) The accounting reference date of a company incorporated in Northern Ireland before 22nd August 1997 is—

- (a) the date specified by notice to the registrar in accordance with article 232(2) of the Companies (Northern Ireland) Order 1986 (SI 1986/1032 (NI 6)) (notice specifying accounting reference date given within nine months of incorporation), or
- (b) failing such notice—
  - (i) in the case of a company incorporated before the coming into operation of Article 5 of the Companies (Northern Ireland) Order 1990 (SI 1990/593 (NI 5)), 31st March, and
  - (ii) in the case of a company incorporated after the coming into operation of that Article, the last day of the month in which the anniversary of its incorporation falls.

(4) The accounting reference date of a company incorporated—

- (a) in Great Britain on or after 1st April 1996 and before the commencement of this Act,
- (b) in Northern Ireland on or after 22nd August 1997 and before the commencement of this Act, or
- (c) after the commencement of this Act,

is the last day of the month in which the anniversary of its incorporation falls.

(5) A company's first accounting reference period is the period of more than six months, but not more than 18 months, beginning with the date of its incorporation and ending with its accounting reference date.

(6) Its subsequent accounting reference periods are successive periods of twelve months beginning immediately after the end of the previous accounting reference period and ending with its accounting reference date.

(7) This section has effect subject to the provisions of section 392 (alteration of accounting reference date).

[1.444]

392 Alteration of accounting reference date

(1) A company may by notice given to the registrar specify a new accounting reference date having effect in relation to—

(a) the company's current accounting reference period and subsequent periods, or

(b) the company's previous accounting reference period and subsequent periods.

A company's "previous accounting reference period" means the one immediately preceding its current accounting reference period.

(2) The notice must state whether the current or previous accounting reference period—

(a) is to be shortened, so as to come to an end on the first occasion on which the new accounting reference date falls or fell after the beginning of the period, or

(b) is to be extended, so as to come to an end on the second occasion on which that date falls or fell after the beginning of the period.

(3) A notice extending a company's current or previous accounting reference period is not effective if given less than five years after the end of an earlier accounting reference period of the company that was extended under this section.

This does not apply—

(a) to a notice given by a company that is a subsidiary undertaking or parent undertaking of another [UK] undertaking if the new accounting reference date coincides with that of the other [UK] undertaking or, where that undertaking is not a company, with the last day of its financial year, or

(b) where the company is in administration under Part 2 of the Insolvency Act 1986 (c 45) or Part 3 of the Insolvency (Northern Ireland) Order 1989 (SI 1989/2405 (NI 19)), or

(c) where the Secretary of State directs that it should not apply, which he may do with respect to a notice that has been given or that may be given.

(4) A notice under this section may not be given in respect of a previous accounting reference period if the period for filing accounts and reports for the financial year determined by reference to that accounting reference period has already expired.

(5) An accounting reference period may not be extended so as to exceed 18 months and a notice under this section is ineffective if the current or previous accounting reference period as extended in accordance with the notice would exceed that limit.

This does not apply where the company is in administration under Part 2 of the Insolvency Act 1986 (c 45) or Part 3 of the Insolvency (Northern Ireland) Order 1989 (SI 1989/2405 (NI 19)).

(6) In this section "[UK undertaking]" means an undertaking established under the law of any part of the United Kingdom . . .

NOTES

Sub-s (3): words in square brackets substituted by the Accounts and Reports (Amendment) (EU Exit) Regulations 2019, SI 2019/145, reg 5, Sch 2, Pt 1, paras 1, 4(a), as from IP completion day (as defined in the European Union (Withdrawal Agreement) Act 2020, s 39).

Sub-s (6): words in square brackets substituted, and words omitted repealed, by SI 2019/145, reg 5, Sch 2, Pt 1, paras 1, 4(b), as from IP completion day (as defined in the European Union (Withdrawal Agreement) Act 2020, s 39).

CHAPTER 4 ANNUAL ACCOUNTS

General

[1.445]

393 Accounts to give true and fair view

(1) The directors of a company must not approve accounts for the purposes of this Chapter unless they are satisfied that they give a true and fair view of the assets, liabilities, financial position and profit or loss—

(a) in the case of the company's individual accounts, of the company;

(b) in the case of the company's group accounts, of the undertakings included in the consolidation as a whole, so far as concerns members of the company.

[(1A) The following provisions apply to the directors of a company which qualifies as a micro-entity in relation to a financial year (see sections 384A and 384B) in their consideration of whether the Companies Act individual accounts of the company for that year give a true and fair view as required by subsection (1)(a)—

(a) where the accounts comprise only micro-entity minimum accounting items, the directors must disregard any provision of an accounting standard which would require the accounts to contain information additional to those items,

(b) in relation to a micro-entity minimum accounting item contained in the accounts, the directors must disregard any provision of an accounting standard which would require the accounts to contain further information in relation to that item, and

(c) where the accounts contain an item of information additional to the micro-entity minimum accounting items, the directors must have regard to any provision of an accounting standard which relates to that item.]

(2) The auditor of a company in carrying out his functions under this Act in relation to the company's annual accounts must have regard to the directors' duty under subsection (1).

NOTES

Sub-s (1A): inserted by the Small Companies (Micro-Entities' Accounts) Regulations 2013, SI 2013/3008, reg 5(1), (2), in relation to (a) financial years ending on or after 30 September 2013, and (b) companies which deliver the accounts required by s 444 of this Act to the registrar on or after 1 December 2013 (as to application of this amendment, see the note at **[1.432]**).

Individual accounts

[1.446]

394 Duty to prepare individual accounts

The directors of every company must prepare accounts for the company for each of its financial years [unless the company is exempt from that requirement under section 394A].

Those accounts are referred to as the company's "individual accounts".

NOTES

Words in square brackets inserted by the Companies and Limited Liability Partnerships (Accounts and Audit Exemptions and Change of Accounting Framework) Regulations 2012, SI 2012/2301, regs 2, 8, as from 1 October 2012 (in relation to accounts for financial years ending on or after that date).

[1.447]

[394A Individual accounts: exemption for dormant subsidiaries

(1) A company is exempt from the requirement to prepare individual accounts for a financial year if—

(a) it is itself a subsidiary undertaking,

(b) it has been dormant throughout the whole of that year, and

(c) its parent undertaking is established under the law of [any part of the United Kingdom].

(2) Exemption is conditional upon compliance with all of the following conditions—

(a) all members of the company must agree to the exemption in respect of the financial year in question,

(b) the parent undertaking must give a guarantee under section 394C in respect of that year,

(c) the company must be included in the consolidated accounts drawn up for that year or to an earlier date in that year by the parent undertaking in accordance with—

[(i) if the undertaking is a company, the requirements of this Part of this Act, or, if the undertaking is not a company, the legal requirements which apply to the drawing up of consolidated accounts for that undertaking, or]

(ii) [UK-adopted international accounting standards],

(d) the parent undertaking must disclose in the notes to the consolidated accounts that the company is exempt from the requirement to prepare individual accounts by virtue of this section, and

(e) the directors of the company must deliver to the registrar within the period for filing the company's accounts and reports for that year—

(i) a written notice of the agreement referred to in subsection (2)(a),

(ii) the statement referred to in section 394C(1),

(iii) a copy of the consolidated accounts referred to in subsection (2)(c),

(iv) a copy of the auditor's report on those accounts, and

(v) a copy of the consolidated annual report drawn up by the parent undertaking.]

NOTES

Inserted, together with ss 394B, 394C, by the Companies and Limited Liability Partnerships (Accounts and Audit Exemptions and Change of Accounting Framework) Regulations 2012, SI 2012/2301, regs 2, 9, as from 1 October 2012 (in relation to accounts for financial years ending on or after that date).

Sub-s (1): words in square brackets in para (c) substituted by the Accounts and Reports (Amendment) (EU Exit) Regulations 2019, SI 2019/145, reg 5, Sch 2, Pt 1, paras 1, 5(a), in relation to financial years beginning on or after IP completion day (as defined in the European Union (Withdrawal Agreement) Act 2020, s 39) (for transitional provisions see reg 7 of the 2019 Regulations at **[12.79]**).

Sub-s (2) is amended as follows:

Sub-para (c)(i) originally substituted by the Companies, Partnerships and Groups (Accounts and Reports) Regulations 2015, SI 2015/980, reg 5(1), (2), in relation to (a) financial years beginning on or after 1 January 2016, and (b) a financial year of a company beginning on or after 1 January 2015, but before 1 January 2016, if the directors of the company so decide (subject to transitional provisions, etc, in regs 2, 3 of the 2015 Regulations as noted to s 380 at **[1.430]**). Further substituted by SI 2019/145, reg 5, Sch 2, Pt 1, paras 1, 5(b), in relation to financial years beginning on or after IP completion day (as defined in the European Union (Withdrawal Agreement) Act 2020, s 39) (for transitional provisions see reg 7 of the 2019 Regulations at **[12.79]**).

Words in square brackets in sub-para (c)(ii) substituted by the International Accounting Standards and European Public Limited-Liability Company (Amendment etc) (EU Exit) Regulations 2019, SI 2019/685, reg 19, Sch 1, Pt 1, paras 1, 5, in relation to accounts for financial years beginning on or after IP completion day (as defined in the European Union (Withdrawal Agreement) Act 2020, s 39) (note also that in relation to accounts for financial years which begin before but end on or after IP completion day, the enactments amended by Parts 1–3 of Sch 1 to the 2019 Regulations have effect as if the UK were a member State until the end of the financial year in question (for transitional provisions see reg 1 of, and Sch 1, Pt 4 to, the 2019 Regulations at **[12.130]** and **[12.151]** respectively)).

[1.448]

[394B Companies excluded from the dormant subsidiaries exemption

A company is not entitled to the exemption conferred by section 394A (dormant subsidiaries) if it was at any time within the financial year in question—

[(a) a traded company,]

(b) a company that—

(i) is an authorised insurance company, a banking company, an e-money issuer, a MiFID investment firm or a UCITS management company, or

(ii) carries on insurance market activity, or

(c) a special register body as defined in section 117(1) of the Trade Union and Labour Relations (Consolidation) Act 1992 (c 52) or an employers' association as defined in section 122 of that Act or Article 4 of the Industrial Relations (Northern Ireland) Order 1992 (SI 1992/807) (NI 5).]

NOTES

Inserted as noted to s 394A at **[1.447]**.

Para (a) substituted by the Companies, Partnerships and Groups (Accounts and Reports) Regulations 2015, SI 2015/980, reg 5(1), (3), in relation to (a) financial years beginning on or after 1 January 2016, and (b) a financial year of a company beginning on or after 1 January 2015, but before 1 January 2016, if the directors of the company so decide (subject to transitional provisions, etc, in regs 2, 3 of the 2015 Regulations as noted to s 380 at **[1.430]**).

[1.449]

[394C Dormant subsidiaries exemption: parent undertaking declaration of guarantee

(1) A guarantee is given by a parent undertaking under this section when the directors of the subsidiary company deliver to the registrar a statement by the parent undertaking that it guarantees the subsidiary company under this section.

(2) The statement under subsection (1) must be authenticated by the parent undertaking and must specify—

(a) the name of the parent undertaking,

[(b) the registered number (if any) of the parent undertaking,]

(c) . . .

(d) the name and registered number of the subsidiary company in respect of which the guarantee is being given,

(e) the date of the statement, and

(f) the financial year to which the guarantee relates.

(3) A guarantee given under this section has the effect that—

(a) the parent undertaking guarantees all outstanding liabilities to which the subsidiary company is subject at the end of the financial year to which the guarantee relates, until they are satisfied in full, and

(b) the guarantee is enforceable against the parent undertaking by any person to whom the subsidiary company is liable in respect of those liabilities.]

NOTES

Inserted as noted to s 394A at **[1.447]**.

Sub-s (2): para (b) was substituted, and para (c) was repealed, by the Accounts and Reports (Amendment) (EU Exit) Regulations 2019, SI 2019/145, reg 5, Sch 2, Pt 1, paras 1, 6, in relation to financial years beginning on or after IP completion day (as defined in the European Union (Withdrawal Agreement) Act 2020, s 39) (for transitional provisions see reg 7 of the 2019 Regulations at **[12.79]**). Note that SI 2019/145, Sch 2, Pt 1, para 6 was amended by the Statutory Auditors, Third Country Auditors and International Accounting Standards (Amendment) (EU Exit) Regulations 2019, SI 2019/1392, regs 9, 10, with effect from immediately before IP completion day and that the effect of that amendment has been incorporated above.

[1.450]

395 Individual accounts: applicable accounting framework

(1) A company's individual accounts may be prepared—

(a) in accordance with section 396 ("Companies Act individual accounts"), or

(b) in accordance with [UK-adopted international accounting standards] ("IAS individual accounts").

This is subject to the following provisions of this section and to section 407 (consistency of financial reporting within group).

(2) The individual accounts of a company that is a charity must be Companies Act individual accounts.

(3) After the first financial year in which the directors of a company prepare IAS individual accounts ("the first IAS year"), all subsequent individual accounts of the company must be prepared in accordance with [UK-adopted international accounting standards] unless there is a relevant change of circumstance. [This is subject to subsection (4A)].

(4) There is a relevant change of circumstance if, at any time during or after the first IAS year—

(a) the company becomes a subsidiary undertaking of another undertaking that does not prepare IAS individual accounts,

[(aa) the company ceases to be a subsidiary undertaking,]

(b) the company ceases to be a company with securities admitted to trading on a [UK regulated market], or

(c) a parent undertaking of the company ceases to be an undertaking with securities admitted to trading on a [UK regulated market].

[(4A) After a financial year in which the directors of a company prepare IAS individual accounts for the company, the directors may change to preparing Companies Act individual accounts for a reason other than a relevant change of circumstance provided they have not changed to Companies Act individual accounts in the period of five years preceding the first day of that financial year.

(4B) In calculating the five year period for the purpose of subsection (4A), no account should be taken of a change due to a relevant change of circumstance.]

(5) If, having changed to preparing Companies Act individual accounts . . . , the directors again prepare IAS individual accounts for the company, subsections (3) and (4) apply again as if the first financial year for which such accounts are again prepared were the first IAS year.

NOTES

Sub-s (1): words in square brackets in sub-para (b) substituted by the International Accounting Standards and European Public Limited-Liability Company (Amendment etc) (EU Exit) Regulations 2019, SI 2019/685, reg 19, Sch 1, Pt 1, paras 1, 6, in relation to accounts for financial years beginning on or after IP completion day (as defined in the European Union (Withdrawal Agreement) Act 2020, s 39) (note also that in relation to accounts for financial years which begin before but end on or after IP completion day, the enactments amended by Parts 1–3 of Sch 1 to the 2019 Regulations have effect as if the UK were a member State until the end of the financial year in question (for transitional provisions see reg 1 of, and Sch 1, Pt 4 to, the 2019 Regulations at **[12.130]** and **[12.151]** respectively)).

Sub-s (3): words in first pair of square brackets substituted by SI 2019/685, reg 19, Sch 1, Pt 1, paras 1, 6, in relation to accounts for financial years beginning on or after IP completion day (see also the first note relating to the 2019 Regulations above). Words in second pair of square brackets inserted by the Companies and Limited Liability Partnerships (Accounts and Audit Exemptions and Change of Accounting Framework) Regulations 2012, SI 2012/2301, regs 2, 12, as from 1 October 2012 (in relation to accounts for financial years ending on or after that date).

Sub-s (4): para (aa) inserted by the Companies Act 2006 (Amendment) (Accounts and Reports) Regulations 2008, SI 2008/393, reg 9, as from 6 April 2008, in relation to financial years beginning on or after that date. Words in square brackets in paras (b), (c) substituted by the Accounts and Reports (Amendment) (EU Exit) Regulations 2019, SI 2019/145, reg 5, Sch 2, Pt 1, paras 1, 7, in relation to financial years beginning on or after IP completion day (as defined in the European Union (Withdrawal Agreement) Act 2020, s 39) (for transitional provisions see reg 7 of the 2019 Regulations at **[12.79]**).

Sub-ss (4A), (4B): inserted by SI 2012/2301, regs 2, 13, as from 1 October 2012 (in relation to accounts for financial years ending on or after that date).

Sub-s (5): words omitted repealed by SI 2012/2301, regs 2, 14, as from 1 October 2012 (in relation to accounts for financial years ending on or after that date).

[1.451]

396 Companies Act individual accounts

[(A1) Companies Act individual accounts must state—

(a) the part of the United Kingdom in which the company is registered,

(b) the company's registered number,

(c) whether the company is a public or a private company and whether it is limited by shares or by guarantee,

(d) the address of the company's registered office, and

(e) where appropriate, the fact that the company is being wound-up.]

(1) Companies Act individual accounts must comprise—

(a) a balance sheet as at the last day of the financial year, and

(b) a profit and loss account.

(2) The accounts must—

(a) in the case of the balance sheet, give a true and fair view of the state of affairs of the company as at the end of the financial year, and

(b) in the case of the profit and loss account, give a true and fair view of the profit or loss of the company for the financial year.

[(2A) In the case of the individual accounts of a company which qualifies as a micro-entity in relation to the financial year (see sections 384A and 384B), the micro-entity minimum accounting items included in the company's accounts for the year are presumed to give the true and fair view required by subsection (2).]

(3) The accounts must comply with provision made by the Secretary of State by regulations as to—

(a) the form and content of the balance sheet and profit and loss account, and

(b) additional information to be provided by way of notes to the accounts.

(4) If compliance with the regulations, and any other provision made by or under this Act as to the matters to be included in a company's individual accounts or in notes to those accounts, would not be sufficient to give a true and fair view, the necessary additional information must be given in the accounts or in a note to them.

(5) If in special circumstances compliance with any of those provisions is inconsistent with the requirement to give a true and fair view, the directors must depart from that provision to the extent necessary to give a true and fair view.

Particulars of any such departure, the reasons for it and its effect must be given in a note to the accounts.

[(6) Subsections (4) and (5) do not apply in relation to the micro-entity minimum accounting items included in the individual accounts of a company for a financial year in relation to which the company qualifies as a micro-entity.]

NOTES

Sub-s (A1): inserted by the Companies, Partnerships and Groups (Accounts and Reports) Regulations 2015, SI 2015/980, reg 5(1), (4), in relation to (a) financial years beginning on or after 1 January 2016, and (b) a financial year of a company beginning on or after 1 January 2015, but before 1 January 2016, if the directors of the company so decide (subject to transitional provisions, etc, in regs 2, 3 of the 2015 Regulations as noted to s 380 at **[1.430]**).

Sub-ss (2A), (6): inserted and added respectively by the Small Companies (Micro-Entities' Accounts) Regulations 2013, SI 2013/3008, reg 5(1), (3), in relation to (a) financial years ending on or after 30 September 2013, and (b) companies which deliver the accounts required by s 444 of this Act to the registrar on or after 1 December 2013 (as to application of this amendment, see the note at **[1.432]**).

Regulations: the Small Companies and Groups (Accounts and Directors' Report) Regulations 2008, SI 2008/409 at **[4.41]**; the Large and Medium-sized Companies and Groups (Accounts and Reports) Regulations 2008, SI 2008/410 at **[4.60]**; the Small Companies (Micro-Entities' Accounts) Regulations 2013, SI 2013/3008; the Companies, Partnerships and Groups (Accounts and Reports) Regulations 2015, SI 2015/980; the Companies, Partnerships and Groups (Accounts and Reports) (No 2) Regulations 2015, SI 2015/1672; the Limited Liability Partnerships, Partnerships and Groups (Accounts and Audit) Regulations 2016, SI 2016/575; the Companies (Miscellaneous Reporting) Regulations 2018, SI 2018/860 (see the note at **[4.674]**). For a summary of all statutory instruments made under this Act, see Appendix 4 at **[A4]**.

[1.452]

[397 IAS individual accounts

(1) IAS individual accounts must state—

(a) the part of the United Kingdom in which the company is registered,

(b) the company's registered number,

(c) whether the company is a public or a private company and whether it is limited by shares or by guarantee,

(d) the address of the company's registered office, and

(e) where appropriate, the fact that the company is being wound-up.

(2) The notes to the accounts must state that the accounts have been prepared in accordance with [UK-adopted international accounting standards].]

NOTES

Substituted by the Companies, Partnerships and Groups (Accounts and Reports) Regulations 2015, SI 2015/980, reg 5(1), (5), in relation to (a) financial years beginning on or after 1 January 2016, and (b) a financial year of a company beginning on or after 1 January 2015, but before 1 January 2016, if the directors of the company so decide (subject to transitional provisions, etc, in regs 2, 3 of the 2015 Regulations as noted to s 380 at **[1.430]**).

Sub-s (2): words in square brackets substituted by the International Accounting Standards and European Public Limited-Liability Company (Amendment etc) (EU Exit) Regulations 2019, SI 2019/685, reg 19, Sch 1, Pt 1, paras 1, 7, in relation to accounts for financial years beginning on or after IP completion day (as defined in the European Union (Withdrawal Agreement) Act 2020, s 39) (note also that in relation to accounts for financial years which begin before but end on or after IP completion day, the enactments amended by Parts 1–3 of Sch 1 to the 2019 Regulations have effect as if the UK were a member State until the end of the financial year in question (for transitional provisions see reg 1 of, and Sch 1, Pt 4 to, the 2019 Regulations at **[12.130]** and **[12.151]** respectively)).

. . .

398 (*Repealed, together with the preceding heading, by the Companies, Partnerships and Groups (Accounts and Non-Financial Reporting) Regulations 2016, SI 2016/1245, regs 2, 3(2), in relation to the financial years of companies and qualifying partnerships beginning on or after 1 January 2017 (and only in relation to companies (as defined by s 1 ante) and qualifying partnerships (as defined in the Partnerships (Accounts) Regulations 2008, reg 3)).*)

Group accounts: . . .

[1.453]
399 Duty to prepare group accounts
(1) . . .
(2) If at the end of a financial year [a company] is a parent company the directors, as well as preparing individual accounts for the year, must prepare group accounts for the year unless the company is exempt from that requirement.
[(2A) A company is exempt from the requirement to prepare group accounts if—
(a) at the end of the financial year, the company—
(i) is subject to the small companies regime, or
(ii) would be subject to the small companies regime but for being a public company, and
(b) is not a member of a group which, at any time during the financial year, has an undertaking falling within subsection (2B) as a member.
(2B) An undertaking falls within this subsection if—
(a) it is established under the law of [any part of the United Kingdom],
(b) it has to prepare accounts in accordance with [the requirements of this Part of this Act, and]
[(c) it—
(i) is an undertaking whose transferable securities are admitted to trading on a UK regulated market,
(ii) is a credit institution within the meaning given by Article 4(1)(1) of Regulation (EU) No 575/2013 of the European Parliament and of the Council, which is a CRR firm within the meaning of Article 4(1)(2A) of that Regulation, or
(iii) would be an insurance undertaking within the meaning given by Article 2(1) of Council Directive 91/674/EEC of the European Parliament and of the Council on the annual accounts of insurance undertakings were the United Kingdom a member State].]
(3) There are [further] exemptions under—
section 400 (company included in [UK] accounts of larger group),
section 401 (company included in [non-UK] accounts of larger group), and
section 402 (company none of whose subsidiary undertakings need be included in the consolidation).
(4) A company . . . which is exempt from the requirement to prepare group accounts, may do so.

NOTES

The words omitted from the heading preceding this section, and the words omitted from sub-s (4) were repealed, sub-s (1) was repealed, the words in square brackets in sub-s (2) were substituted, and sub-ss (2A), (2B) were substituted (for the original sub-s (2A)), by the Companies, Partnerships and Groups (Accounts and Non-Financial Reporting) Regulations 2016, SI 2016/1245, regs 2, 3(3), (4), in relation to the financial years of companies and qualifying partnerships beginning on or after 1 January 2017 (and only in relation to companies (as defined by s 1 *ante*) and qualifying partnerships (as defined in the Partnerships (Accounts) Regulations 2008, reg 3)).

The original sub-s (2A) was inserted, and the word "further" in square brackets in sub-s (3) was inserted, by the Companies, Partnerships and Groups (Accounts and Reports) Regulations 2015, SI 2015/980, reg 5(1), (6), in relation to (a) financial years beginning on or after 1 January 2016, and (b) a financial year of a company beginning on or after 1 January 2015, but before 1 January 2016, if the directors of the company so decide (subject to transitional provisions, etc, in regs 2, 3 of the 2015 Regulations as noted to s 380 at **[1.430]**).

Sub-ss (2B), (3): words in square brackets substituted by the Accounts and Reports (Amendment) (EU Exit) Regulations 2019, SI 2019/145, reg 5, Sch 2, Pt 1, paras 1, 8, in relation to financial years beginning on or after IP completion day (as defined in the European Union (Withdrawal Agreement) Act 2020, s 39) (for transitional provisions see reg 7 of the 2019 Regulations at **[12.79]**).

[1.454]
400 Exemption for company included in [UK] group accounts of larger group
(1) A company is exempt from the requirement to prepare group accounts if it is itself a subsidiary undertaking and its immediate parent undertaking is established under the law of [any part of the United Kingdom], in the following cases—
(a) where the company is a wholly-owned subsidiary of that parent undertaking;
[(b) where that parent undertaking holds 90% or more of the allotted shares in the company and the remaining shareholders have approved the exemption;
(c) where that parent undertaking holds more than 50% (but less than 90%) of the allotted shares in the company and notice requesting the preparation of group accounts has not been served on the company by the shareholders holding in aggregate at least 5% of the allotted shares in the company.
Such notice must be served at least six months before the end of the financial year to which it relates.]
(2) Exemption is conditional upon compliance with all of the following conditions—
(a) the company must be included in consolidated accounts for a larger group drawn up to the same date, or to an earlier date in the same financial year, by a parent undertaking established under the law of [any part of the United Kingdom];
(b) those accounts must be drawn up and audited, and that parent undertaking's annual report must be drawn up . . . —
[(i) if the undertaking is a company, in accordance with the requirements of this Part of this Act, or, if the undertaking is not a company, the legal requirements which apply to the drawing up of consolidated accounts for that undertaking, or]
(ii) in accordance with [UK-adopted international accounting standards];

(c) the company must disclose in [the notes to] its individual accounts that it is exempt from the obligation to prepare and deliver group accounts;

(d) the company must state in its individual accounts the name of the parent undertaking that draws up the group accounts referred to above and—

[(i) the address of the undertaking's registered office . . . , or]

(ii) if it is unincorporated, the address of its principal place of business;

(e) the company must deliver to the registrar, within the period for filing its accounts and reports for the financial year in question, copies of—

(i) those group accounts, and

(ii) the parent undertaking's annual report,

together with the auditor's report on them;

(f) any requirement of Part 35 of this Act as to the delivery to the registrar of a certified translation into English must be met in relation to any document comprised in the accounts and reports delivered in accordance with paragraph (e).

(3) For the purposes of subsection (1)(b) [and (c)] shares held by a wholly-owned subsidiary of the parent undertaking, or held on behalf of the parent undertaking or a wholly-owned subsidiary, shall be attributed to the parent undertaking.

(4) The exemption does not apply to a company [which is a traded company].

(5) Shares held by directors of a company for the purpose of complying with any share qualification requirement shall be disregarded in determining for the purposes of this section whether the company is a wholly-owned subsidiary.

(6) . . .

NOTES

Section heading: the word "UK" in square brackets was substituted by the Accounts and Reports (Amendment) (EU Exit) Regulations 2019, SI 2019/145, reg 5, Sch 2, Pt 1, paras 1, 9(a), in relation to financial years beginning on or after IP completion day (as defined in the European Union (Withdrawal Agreement) Act 2020, s 39) (for transitional provisions see reg 7 of the 2019 Regulations at **[12.79]**).

Sub-s (1): words in first pair of square brackets substituted by SI 2019/145, reg 5, Sch 2, Pt 1, paras 1, 9(b), in relation to financial years beginning on or after IP completion day (see also the first note relating to the 2019 Regulations above). Paras (b), (c) substituted (for the original para (b)) by the Companies, Partnerships and Groups (Accounts and Reports) Regulations 2015, SI 2015/980, reg 5(1), (7)(a), in relation to (a) financial years beginning on or after 1 January 2016, and (b) a financial year of a company beginning on or after 1 January 2015, but before 1 January 2016, if the directors of the company so decide (subject to transitional provisions, etc, in regs 2, 3 of the 2015 Regulations as noted to s 380 at **[1.430]**).

Sub-s (2) is amended as follows:

Words in square brackets in para (a) substituted, words omitted from sub-paras (b) and (d)(i) repealed, and sub-para (b)(i) substituted, by SI 2019/145, reg 5, Sch 2, Pt 1, paras 1, 9(c), in relation to financial years beginning on or after IP completion day (as defined in the European Union (Withdrawal Agreement) Act 2020, s 39) (for transitional provisions see reg 7 of the 2019 Regulations at **[12.79]**).

Sub-para (d)(i) substituted, and words in square brackets in para (c) inserted, by SI 2015/980, reg 5(1), (7)(b), as from the same dates and for the same purposes as specified in the first note relating to the 2015 Regulations above.

Words in square brackets in sub-para (b)(ii) substituted by the International Accounting Standards and European Public Limited-Liability Company (Amendment etc) (EU Exit) Regulations 2019, SI 2019/685, reg 19, Sch 1, Pt 1, paras 1, 8, in relation to accounts for financial years beginning on or after IP completion day (as defined in the European Union (Withdrawal Agreement) Act 2020, s 39) (note also that in relation to accounts for financial years which begin before but end on or after IP completion day, the enactments amended by Parts 1–3 of Sch 1 to the 2019 Regulations have effect as if the UK were a member State until the end of the financial year in question (for transitional provisions see reg 1 of, and Sch 1, Pt 4 to, the 2019 Regulations at **[12.130]** and **[12.151]** respectively)).

Sub-s (3): words in square brackets inserted by SI 2015/980, reg 5(1), (7)(c), as from the same dates and for the same purposes as specified in the first note relating to the 2015 Regulations above.

Sub-s (4): words in square brackets substituted by SI 2015/980, reg 5(1), (7)(d), as from the same dates and for the same purposes as specified in the first note relating to the 2015 Regulations above.

Sub-s (6): repealed by SI 2015/980, reg 5(1), (7)(e), as from the same dates and for the same purposes as specified in the first note relating to the 2015 Regulations above.

[1.455]

401 Exemption for company included in [non-UK] group accounts of larger group

(1) A company is exempt from the requirement to prepare group accounts if it is itself a subsidiary undertaking and its parent undertaking is not established under the law of [any part of the United Kingdom], in the following cases—

(a) where the company is a wholly-owned subsidiary of that parent undertaking;

[(b) where that parent undertaking holds 90% or more of the allotted shares in the company and the remaining shareholders have approved the exemption; or

(c) where that parent undertaking holds more than 50% (but less than 90%) of the allotted shares in the company and notice requesting the preparation of group accounts has not been served on the company by the shareholders holding in aggregate at least 5% of the allotted shares in the company.

Such notice must be served at least six months before the end of the financial year to which it relates.]

(2) Exemption is conditional upon compliance with all of the following conditions—

(a) the company and all of its subsidiary undertakings must be included in consolidated accounts for a larger group drawn up to the same date, or to an earlier date in the same financial year, by a parent undertaking;

[(b) those accounts and, where appropriate, the group's annual report, must be drawn up—

(i) . . .

(ii) in a manner equivalent to consolidated accounts and consolidated reports [drawn up in accordance with the requirements of this Part of this Act],

(iii) in accordance with [UK-adopted international accounting standards], or

(iv) in accordance with accounting standards which are equivalent to such international accounting standards, as determined pursuant to Commission Regulation (EC) No 1569/2007 of 21 December 2007 establishing a mechanism for the determination of equivalence of accounting standards applied by third country issuers of securities pursuant to Directives 2003/71/EC and 2004/109/EC of the European Parliament and of the Council;]

(c) the group accounts must be audited by one or more persons authorised to audit accounts under the law under which the parent undertaking which draws them up is established;

(d) the company must disclose in its individual accounts that it is exempt from the obligation to prepare and deliver group accounts;

(e) the company must state in its individual accounts the name of the parent undertaking which draws up the group accounts referred to above and—

[(i) the address of the undertaking's registered office (whether in or outside the United Kingdom), or;]

(ii) if it is unincorporated, the address of its principal place of business;

(f) the company must deliver to the registrar, within the period for filing its accounts and reports for the financial year in question, copies of—

(i) the group accounts, and

(ii) where appropriate, the consolidated annual report,

together with the auditor's report on them;

(g) any requirement of Part 35 of this Act as to the delivery to the registrar of a certified translation into English must be met in relation to any document comprised in the accounts and reports delivered in accordance with paragraph (f).

(3) For the purposes of subsection (1)(b) [and (c)], shares held by a wholly-owned subsidiary of the parent undertaking, or held on behalf of the parent undertaking or a wholly-owned subsidiary, are attributed to the parent undertaking.

(4) The exemption does not apply to a company [which is a traded company].

(5) Shares held by directors of a company for the purpose of complying with any share qualification requirement shall be disregarded in determining for the purposes of this section whether the company is a wholly-owned subsidiary.

(6) . . .

NOTES

Section heading: words in square brackets substituted by the Accounts and Reports (Amendment) (EU Exit) Regulations 2019, SI 2019/145, reg 5, Sch 2, Pt 1, paras 1, 10(a), in relation to financial years beginning on or after IP completion day (as defined in the European Union (Withdrawal Agreement) Act 2020, s 39) (for transitional provisions see reg 7 of the 2019 Regulations at **[12.79]**).

Sub-s (1): words in first pair of square brackets substituted by SI 2019/145, reg 5, Sch 2, Pt 1, paras 1, 10(b), in relation to financial years beginning on or after IP completion day (see also the first note relating to the 2019 Regulations above). Paras (b), (c) substituted (for the original para (b)) by the Companies, Partnerships and Groups (Accounts and Reports) Regulations 2015, SI 2015/980, reg 5(1), (8)(a), in relation to (a) financial years beginning on or after 1 January 2016, and (b) a financial year of a company beginning on or after 1 January 2015, but before 1 January 2016, if the directors of the company so decide (subject to transitional provisions, etc, in regs 2, 3 of the 2015 Regulations as noted to s 380 at **[1.430]**).

Sub-s (2): para (b) and sub-para (e)(i) were substituted by SI 2015/980, reg 5(1), (8)(b), (c), as from the same dates and for the same purposes as specified in the first note relating to the 2015 Regulations above. Sub-para (b)(i) was repealed, and the words in square brackets in sub-para (b)(ii) were substituted, by SI 2019/145, reg 5, Sch 2, Pt 1, paras 1, 10(c), in relation to financial years beginning on or after IP completion day (see also the first note relating to the 2019 Regulations above). Words in square brackets in sub-para (b)(iii) substituted by the International Accounting Standards and European Public Limited-Liability Company (Amendment etc) (EU Exit) Regulations 2019, SI 2019/685, reg 19, Sch 1, Pt 1, paras 1, 9, in relation to accounts for financial years beginning on or after IP completion day (as defined in the European Union (Withdrawal Agreement) Act 2020, s 39) (note also that in relation to accounts for financial years which begin before but end on or after IP completion day, the enactments amended by Parts 1–3 of Sch 1 to the 2019 Regulations have effect as if the UK were a member State until the end of the financial year in question (for transitional provisions see reg 1 of, and Sch 1, Pt 4 to, the 2019 Regulations at **[12.130]** and **[12.151]** respectively)).

Sub-s (3): words in square brackets inserted by SI 2015/980, reg 5(1), (8)(d), as from the same dates and for the same purposes as specified in the first note relating to the 2015 Regulations above.

Sub-s (4): words in square brackets substituted by SI 2015/980, reg 5(1), (8)(e), as from the same dates and for the same purposes as specified in the first note relating to the 2015 Regulations above.

Sub-s (6): repealed by SI 2015/980, reg 5(1), (8)(f), as from the same dates and for the same purposes as specified in the first note relating to the 2015 Regulations above.

[1.456]

402 Exemption if no subsidiary undertakings need be included in the consolidation

A parent company is exempt from the requirement to prepare group accounts if under section 405 all of its subsidiary undertakings could be excluded from consolidation in Companies Act group accounts.

Group accounts: general

[1.457]

403 Group accounts: applicable accounting framework

[(1) The group accounts of a parent company whose securities are, on its balance sheet date, admitted to trading on a UK regulated market must be prepared in accordance with UK-adopted international accounting standards ("IAS group accounts").]

(2) The group accounts of other companies may be prepared—

(a) in accordance with section 404 ("Companies Act group accounts"), or

(b) in accordance with [UK-adopted international accounting standards] ("IAS group accounts").

This is subject to the following provisions of this section.

(3) The group accounts of a parent company that is a charity must be Companies Act group accounts.

(4) After the first financial year in which the directors of a parent company prepare IAS group accounts ("the first IAS year"), all subsequent group accounts of the company must be prepared in accordance with [UK-adopted international accounting standards] unless there is a relevant change of circumstance. [This is subject to subsection (5A).]

(5) There is a relevant change of circumstance if, at any time during or after the first IAS year—

(a) the company becomes a subsidiary undertaking of another undertaking that does not prepare IAS group accounts,

(b) the company ceases to be a company with securities admitted to trading on a [UK regulated market], or

(c) a parent undertaking of the company ceases to be an undertaking with securities admitted to trading on a [UK regulated market].

[(5A) After a financial year in which the directors of a parent company prepare IAS group accounts for the company, the directors may change to preparing Companies Act group accounts for a reason other than a relevant change of circumstance provided they have not changed to Companies Act group accounts in the period of five years preceding the first day of that financial year.

(5B) In calculating the five year period for the purpose of subsection (5A), no account should be taken of a change due to a relevant change of circumstance.]

(6) If, having changed to preparing Companies Act group accounts . . . , the directors again prepare IAS group accounts for the company, subsections (4) and (5) apply again as if the first financial year for which such accounts are again prepared were the first IAS year.

NOTES

Sub-s (1): substituted by the International Accounting Standards and European Public Limited-Liability Company (Amendment etc) (EU Exit) Regulations 2019, SI 2019/685, reg 19, Sch 1, Pt 1, paras 1, 10(a), in relation to accounts for financial years beginning on or after IP completion day (as defined in the European Union (Withdrawal Agreement) Act 2020, s 39) (note also that in relation to accounts for financial years which begin before but end on or after IP completion day, the enactments amended by Parts 1–3 of Sch 1 to the 2019 Regulations have effect as if the UK were a member State until the end of the financial year in question (for transitional provisions see reg 1 of, and Sch 1, Pt 4 to, the 2019 Regulations at **[12.130]** and **[12.151]** respectively)).

Sub-s (2): words in square brackets substituted by SI 2019/685, reg 19, Sch 1, Pt 1, paras 1, 10(b), in relation to accounts for financial years beginning on or after IP completion day (see also the first note relating to the 2019 Regulations above).

Sub-s (4): words in first pair of square brackets substituted by SI 2019/685, reg 19, Sch 1, Pt 1, paras 1, 10(b), in relation to accounts for financial years beginning on or after IP completion day (see also the first note relating to the 2019 Regulations above). Words in second pair of square brackets inserted by the Companies and Limited Liability Partnerships (Accounts and Audit Exemptions and Change of Accounting Framework) Regulations 2012, SI 2012/2301, regs 2, 15, as from 1 October 2012 (in relation to accounts for financial years ending on or after that date).

Sub-s (5): words in square brackets in paras (b) and (c) substituted by the Accounts and Reports (Amendment) (EU Exit) Regulations 2019, SI 2019/145, reg 5, Sch 2, Pt 1, paras 1, 11, in relation to financial years beginning on or after IP completion day (as defined in the European Union (Withdrawal Agreement) Act 2020, s 39) (for transitional provisions see reg 7 of the 2019 Regulations at **[12.79]**).

Sub-ss (5A), (5B): inserted by SI 2012/2301, regs 2, 16, as from 1 October 2012 (in relation to accounts for financial years ending on or after that date).

Sub-s (6): words omitted repealed by SI 2012/2301, regs 2, 17, as from 1 October 2012 (in relation to accounts for financial years ending on or after that date).

[1.458]

404 Companies Act group accounts

[(A1) Companies Act group accounts must state, in respect of the parent company—

(a) the part of the United Kingdom in which the company is registered,

(b) the company's registered number,

(c) whether the company is a public or a private company and whether it is limited by shares or by guarantee,

(d) the address of the company's registered office, and

(e) where appropriate, the fact that the company is being wound-up.]

(1) Companies Act group accounts must comprise—

(a) a consolidated balance sheet dealing with the state of affairs of the parent company and its subsidiary undertakings, and

(b) a consolidated profit and loss account dealing with the profit or loss of the parent company and its subsidiary undertakings.

(2) The accounts must give a true and fair view of the state of affairs as at the end of the financial year, and the profit or loss for the financial year, of the undertakings included in the consolidation as a whole, so far as concerns members of the company.

(3) The accounts must comply with provision made by the Secretary of State by regulations as to—

(a) the form and content of the consolidated balance sheet and consolidated profit and loss account, and

(b) additional information to be provided by way of notes to the accounts.

(4) If compliance with the regulations, and any other provision made by or under this Act as to the matters to be included in a company's group accounts or in notes to those accounts, would not be sufficient to give a true and fair view, the necessary additional information must be given in the accounts or in a note to them.

(5) If in special circumstances compliance with any of those provisions is inconsistent with the requirement to give a true and fair view, the directors must depart from that provision to the extent necessary to give a true and fair view.

Particulars of any such departure, the reasons for it and its effect must be given in a note to the accounts.

NOTES

Sub-s (A1): inserted by the Companies, Partnerships and Groups (Accounts and Reports) Regulations 2015, SI 2015/980, reg 5(1), (9), in relation to (a) financial years beginning on or after 1 January 2016, and (b) a financial year of a company beginning on or after 1 January 2015, but before 1 January 2016, if the directors of the company so decide (subject to transitional provisions, etc, in regs 2, 3 of the 2015 Regulations as noted to s 380 at **[1.430]**).

Regulations: the Small Companies and Groups (Accounts and Directors' Report) Regulations 2008, SI 2008/409 at **[4.41]**; the Large and Medium-sized Companies and Groups (Accounts and Reports) Regulations 2008, SI 2008/410 at **[4.60]**; the Companies, Partnerships and Groups (Accounts and Reports) Regulations 2015, SI 2015/980; the Companies (Miscellaneous Reporting) Regulations 2018, SI 2018/860 (see the note at **[4.674]**). For a summary of all statutory instruments made under this Act, see Appendix 4 at **[A4]**.

[1.459]

405 Companies Act group accounts: subsidiary undertakings included in the consolidation

(1) Where a parent company prepares Companies Act group accounts, all the subsidiary undertakings of the company must be included in the consolidation, subject to the following exceptions.

(2) A subsidiary undertaking may be excluded from consolidation if its inclusion is not material for the purpose of giving a true and fair view (but two or more undertakings may be excluded only if they are not material taken together).

(3) A subsidiary undertaking may be excluded from consolidation where—

- (a) severe long-term restrictions substantially hinder the exercise of the rights of the parent company over the assets or management of that undertaking, or
- (b) [extremely rare circumstances mean that] the information necessary for the preparation of group accounts cannot be obtained without disproportionate expense or undue delay, or
- (c) the interest of the parent company is held exclusively with a view to subsequent resale.

(4) The reference in subsection (3)(a) to the rights of the parent company and the reference in subsection (3)(c) to the interest of the parent company are, respectively, to rights and interests held by or attributed to the company for the purposes of the definition of "parent undertaking" (see section 1162) in the absence of which it would not be the parent company.

NOTES

Sub-s (3): words in square brackets in para (b) inserted by the Companies, Partnerships and Groups (Accounts and Reports) Regulations 2015, SI 2015/980, reg 5(1), (10), in relation to (a) financial years beginning on or after 1 January 2016, and (b) a financial year of a company beginning on or after 1 January 2015, but before 1 January 2016, if the directors of the company so decide (subject to transitional provisions, etc, in regs 2, 3 of the 2015 Regulations as noted to s 380 at **[1.430]**).

[1.460]

[406 IAS group accounts

(1) IAS group accounts must state—

- (a) the part of the United Kingdom in which the company is registered,
- (b) the company's registered number,
- (c) whether the company is a public or a private company and whether it is limited by shares or by guarantee,
- (d) the address of the company's registered office, and
- (e) where appropriate, the fact that the company is being wound-up.

(2) The notes to the accounts must state that the accounts have been prepared in accordance with [UK-adopted international accounting standards].]

NOTES

Substituted by the Companies, Partnerships and Groups (Accounts and Reports) Regulations 2015, SI 2015/980, reg 5(1), (11), in relation to (a) financial years beginning on or after 1 January 2016, and (b) a financial year of a company beginning on or after 1 January 2015, but before 1 January 2016, if the directors of the company so decide (subject to transitional provisions, etc, in regs 2, 3 of the 2015 Regulations as noted to s 380 at **[1.430]**).

Sub-s (2): words in square brackets substituted by the International Accounting Standards and European Public Limited-Liability Company (Amendment etc) (EU Exit) Regulations 2019, SI 2019/685, reg 19, Sch 1, Pt 1, paras 1, 11, in relation to accounts for financial years beginning on or after IP completion day (as defined in the European Union (Withdrawal Agreement) Act 2020, s 39) (note also that in relation to accounts for financial years which begin before but end on or after IP completion day, the enactments amended by Parts 1–3 of Sch 1 to the 2019 Regulations have effect as if the UK were a member State until the end of the financial year in question (for transitional provisions see reg 1 of, and Sch 1, Pt 4 to, the 2019 Regulations at **[12.130]** and **[12.151]** respectively)).

[1.461]

407 Consistency of financial reporting within group

(1) The directors of a parent company must secure that the individual accounts of—

- (a) the parent company, and
- (b) each of its subsidiary undertakings,

are all prepared using the same financial reporting framework, except to the extent that in their opinion there are good reasons for not doing so.

(2) Subsection (1) does not apply if the directors do not prepare group accounts for the parent company.

(3) Subsection (1) only applies to accounts of subsidiary undertakings that are required to be prepared under this Part.

(4) Subsection (1) does not require accounts of undertakings that are charities to be prepared using the same financial reporting framework as accounts of undertakings which are not charities.

(5) Subsection (1)(a) does not apply where the directors of a parent company prepare IAS group accounts and IAS individual accounts.

[1.462]

408 Individual profit and loss account where group accounts prepared

(1) This section applies where—

- (a) a company prepares group accounts in accordance with this Act, and
- [(b) the company's individual balance sheet shows the company's profit and loss for the financial year determined in accordance with this Act.]

(2) . . .

(3) The company's individual profit and loss account must be approved in accordance with section 414(1) (approval by directors) but may be omitted from the company's annual accounts for the purposes of the other provisions of the Companies Acts.

(4) The exemption conferred by this section is conditional upon its being disclosed in the company's annual accounts that the exemption applies.

NOTES

Sub-s (1): para (b) substituted by the Companies, Partnerships and Groups (Accounts and Reports) Regulations 2015, SI 2015/980, reg 5(1), (12)(a), in relation to (a) financial years beginning on or after 1 January 2016, and (b) a financial year of a company beginning on or after 1 January 2015, but before 1 January 2016, if the directors of the company so decide (subject to transitional provisions, etc, in regs 2, 3 of the 2015 Regulations as noted to s 380 at **[1.430]**).

Sub-s (2): repealed by SI 2015/980, reg 5(1), (12)(b), as from 6 April 2015, as from the same dates and for the same purposes as specified in the first note relating to the 2015 Regulations above.

Information to be given in notes to the accounts

[1.463]

409 Information about related undertakings

(1) The Secretary of State may make provision by regulations requiring information about related undertakings to be given in notes to a company's annual accounts.

(2) The regulations—

- (a) may make different provision according to whether or not the company prepares group accounts, and
- (b) may specify the descriptions of undertaking in relation to which they apply, and make different provision in relation to different descriptions of related undertaking.

(3) The regulations may provide that information need not be disclosed with respect to an undertaking that—

- (a) is established under the law of a country outside the United Kingdom, or
- (b) carries on business outside the United Kingdom,

if the following conditions are met.

(4) The conditions are—

- (a) that in the opinion of the directors of the company the disclosure would be seriously prejudicial to the business of—
  - (i) that undertaking,
  - (ii) the company,
  - (iii) any of the company's subsidiary undertakings, or
  - (iv) any other undertaking which is included in the consolidation;
- (b) that the Secretary of State agrees that the information need not be disclosed.

(5) Where advantage is taken of any such exemption, that fact must be stated in a note to the company's annual accounts.

NOTES

Regulations: the Small Companies and Groups (Accounts and Directors' Report) Regulations 2008, SI 2008/409 at **[4.41]**; the Large and Medium-sized Companies and Groups (Accounts and Reports) Regulations 2008, SI 2008/410 at **[4.60]**; the Companies and Partnerships (Accounts and Audit) Regulations 2013, SI 2013/2005; the Companies, Partnerships and Groups (Accounts and Reports) Regulations 2015, SI 2015/980. For a summary of all statutory instruments made under this Act, see Appendix 4 at **[A4]**.

410 (*Repealed by the Companies, Partnerships and Groups (Accounts and Reports) Regulations 2015, SI 2015/980, reg 5(1), (13), in relation to (a) financial years beginning on or after 1 January 2016, and (b) a financial year of a company beginning on or after 1 January 2015, but before 1 January 2016, if the directors of the company so decide (subject to transitional provisions, etc, in regs 2, 3 of the 2015 Regulations as noted to s 380 at* **[1.430]**.)

[1.464]

[410A Information about off-balance sheet arrangements

[(1) If in any financial year—

- (a) a company is or has been party to arrangements that are not reflected in its balance sheet, and
- (b) at the balance sheet date the risks or benefits arising from those arrangements are material,

the information required by this section must be given in the notes to the company's annual accounts.]

(2) The information required is—

- (a) the nature and business purpose of the arrangements, and
- (b) the financial impact of the arrangements on the company.

(3) The information need only be given to the extent necessary for enabling the financial position of the company to be assessed.

[(4) If the company is subject to the small companies regime in relation to the financial year (see section 381), it need not comply with subsection (2)(b).]

(5) This section applies in relation to group accounts as if the undertakings included in the consolidation were a single company.]

NOTES

Inserted by the Companies Act 2006 (Amendment) (Accounts and Reports) Regulations 2008, SI 2008/393, reg 8, as from 6 April 2008, in relation to financial years beginning on or after that date.

Sub-s (1): substituted by the Companies, Partnerships and Groups (Accounts and Reports) Regulations 2015, SI 2015/980, reg 5(1), (14)(a), in relation to (a) financial years beginning on or after 1 January 2016, and (b) a financial year of a company beginning on or after 1 January 2015, but before 1 January 2016, if the directors of the company so decide (subject to transitional provisions, etc, in regs 2, 3 of the 2015 Regulations as noted to s 380 at **[1.430]**).

Sub-s (4): substituted by SI 2015/980, reg 5(1), (14)(b), as from 6 April 2015, as from the same dates and for the same purposes as specified in the first note relating to the 2015 Regulations above.

[1.465]

411 Information about employee numbers and costs

[(1) The notes to a company's annual accounts must disclose the average number of persons employed by the company in the financial year.

(1A) In the case of a company not subject to the small companies regime, the notes to the company's accounts must also disclose the average number of persons within each category of persons so employed.]

(2) The categories by reference to which the number required to be disclosed by [subsection (1A)] is to be determined must be such as the directors may select having regard to the manner in which the company's activities are organised.

(3) The average number required by [subsection (1) or (1A)] is determined by dividing the relevant annual number by the number of months in the financial year.

(4) The relevant annual number is determined by ascertaining for each month in the financial year—

(a) for the purposes of [subsection (1)], the number of persons employed under contracts of service by the company in that month (whether throughout the month or not);

(b) for the purposes of [subsection (1A)], the number of persons in the category in question of persons so employed;

and adding together all the monthly numbers.

[(5) Except in the case of a company subject to the small companies regime, the notes to the company's annual accounts or the profit and loss account must disclose, with reference to all persons employed by the company during the financial year, the total staff costs of the company relating to the financial year broken down between—

(a) wages and salaries paid or payable in respect of that year to those persons,

(b) social security costs incurred by the company on their behalf, and

(c) other pension costs so incurred.]

(6) In subsection (5)—

"pension costs" includes any costs incurred by the company in respect of—

(a) any pension scheme established for the purpose of providing pensions for persons currently or formerly employed by the company,

(b) any sums set aside for the future payment of pensions directly by the company to current or former employees, and

(c) any pensions paid directly to such persons without having first been set aside;

"social security costs" means any contributions by the company to any state social security or pension scheme, fund or arrangement.

[(7) This section applies in relation to group accounts as if the undertakings included in the consolidation were a single company.]

NOTES

Sub-ss (1), (1A): substituted (for the original sub-s (1)) by the Companies, Partnerships and Groups (Accounts and Reports) Regulations 2015, SI 2015/980, reg 5(1), (15)(a), in relation to (a) financial years beginning on or after 1 January 2016, and (b) a financial year of a company beginning on or after 1 January 2015, but before 1 January 2016, if the directors of the company so decide (subject to transitional provisions, etc, in regs 2, 3 of the 2015 Regulations as noted to s 380 at **[1.430]**).

Sub-ss (2)–(4): words in square brackets substituted by SI 2015/980, reg 5(1), (15)(b)–(d), as from the same dates and for the same purposes as specified in the first note relating to the 2015 Regulations above.

Sub-s (5): substituted by SI 2015/980, reg 5(1), (15)(e), as from the same dates and for the same purposes as specified in the first note relating to the 2015 Regulations above.

Sub-s (7): substituted by the Companies Act 2006 (Amendment) (Accounts and Reports) Regulations 2008, SI 2008/393, reg 11, as from 6 April 2008, in relation to financial years beginning on or after that date.

[1.466]

412 Information about directors' benefits: remuneration

(1) The Secretary of State may make provision by regulations requiring information to be given in notes to a company's annual accounts about directors' remuneration.

(2) The matters about which information may be required include—

(a) gains made by directors on the exercise of share options;

(b) benefits received or receivable by directors under long-term incentive schemes;

(c) payments for loss of office (as defined in section 215);

(d) benefits receivable, and contributions for the purpose of providing benefits, in respect of past services of a person as director or in any other capacity while director;

(e) consideration paid to or receivable by third parties for making available the services of a person as director or in any other capacity while director.

(3) Without prejudice to the generality of subsection (1), regulations under this section may make any such provision as was made immediately before the commencement of this Part by Part 1 of Schedule 6 to the Companies Act 1985 (c 6).

(4) For the purposes of this section, and regulations made under it, amounts paid to or receivable by—

(a) a person connected with a director, or

(b) a body corporate controlled by a director,

are treated as paid to or receivable by the director.

The expressions "connected with" and "controlled by" in this subsection have the same meaning as in Part 10 (company directors).

(5) It is the duty of—

(a) any director of a company, and

(b) any person who is or has at any time in the preceding five years been a director of the company,

to give notice to the company of such matters relating to himself as may be necessary for the purposes of regulations under this section.

(6) A person who makes default in complying with subsection (5) commits an offence and is liable on summary conviction to a fine not exceeding level 3 on the standard scale.

NOTES

Regulations: the Small Companies and Groups (Accounts and Directors' Report) Regulations 2008, SI 2008/409 at **[4.41]**; the Large and Medium-sized Companies and Groups (Accounts and Reports) Regulations 2008, SI 2008/410 at **[4.60]**; the Companies, Partnerships and Groups (Accounts and Reports) Regulations 2015, SI 2015/980. For a summary of all statutory instruments made under this Act, see Appendix 4 at **[A4]**.

[1.467]

413 Information about directors' benefits: advances, credit and guarantees

(1) In the case of a company that does not prepare group accounts, details of—

(a) advances and credits granted by the company to its directors, and

(b) guarantees of any kind entered into by the company on behalf of its directors,

must be shown in the notes to its individual accounts.

(2) In the case of a parent company that prepares group accounts, details of—

(a) advances and credits granted to the directors of the parent company, by that company or by any of its subsidiary undertakings, and

(b) guarantees of any kind entered into on behalf of the directors of the parent company, by that company or by any of its subsidiary undertakings,

must be shown in the notes to the group accounts.

(3) The details required of an advance or credit are—

(a) its amount,

(b) an indication of the interest rate,

(c) its main conditions, . . .

(d) any amounts repaid,

[(e) any amounts written off, and

(f) any amounts waived].

(4) The details required of a guarantee are—

(a) its main terms,

(b) the amount of the maximum liability that may be incurred by the company (or its subsidiary), and

(c) any amount paid and any liability incurred by the company (or its subsidiary) for the purpose of fulfilling the guarantee (including any loss incurred by reason of enforcement of the guarantee).

(5) There must also be stated in the notes to the accounts the totals—

(a) of amounts stated under subsection (3)(a),

(b) of amounts stated under subsection (3)(d),

[(ba) of amounts stated under subsection 3(e),

(bb) of amounts stated under subsection 3(f),]

(c) of amounts stated under subsection (4)(b), and

(d) of amounts stated under subsection (4)(c).

(6) References in this section to the directors of a company are to the persons who were [directors] at any time in the financial year to which the accounts relate.

(7) The requirements of this section apply in relation to every advance, credit or guarantee subsisting at any time in the financial year to which the accounts relate—

(a) whenever it was entered into,

(b) whether or not the person concerned was a director of the company in question at the time it was entered into, and

(c) in the case of an advance, credit or guarantee involving a subsidiary undertaking of that company, whether or not that undertaking was such a subsidiary undertaking at the time it was entered into.

(8) Banking companies and the holding companies of credit institutions need only state the details required by [subsection (5)(a) and (c)].

NOTES

Sub-s (3): word omitted from para (c) repealed, and paras (e), (f) added, by the Companies, Partnerships and Groups (Accounts and Reports) Regulations 2015, SI 2015/980, reg 5(1), (16)(a), in relation to (a) financial years beginning on or after 1 January 2016, and (b) a financial year of a company beginning on or after 1 January 2015, but before 1 January 2016, if the directors of the company so decide (subject to transitional provisions, etc, in regs 2, 3 of the 2015 Regulations as noted to s 380 at **[1.430]**).

Sub-s (5): paras (ba), (bb) inserted by SI 2015/980, reg 5(1), (16)(b), as from 6 April 2015, as from the same dates and for the same purposes as specified in the first note relating to the 2015 Regulations above.

Sub-s (6): word in square brackets substituted by SI 2015/980, reg 5(1), (16)(c), as from 6 April 2015, as from the same dates and for the same purposes as specified in the first note relating to the 2015 Regulations above.

Sub-s (8): words in square brackets substituted by the Companies Act 2006 (Amendment of Section 413) Regulations 2009, SI 2009/3022, reg 2, as from 23 December 2009, with effect in relation to financial years which end on or after that date.

Approval and signing of accounts

[1.468]

414 Approval and signing of accounts

(1) A company's annual accounts must be approved by the board of directors and signed on behalf of the board by a director of the company.

(2) The signature must be on the company's balance sheet.

[(3) If the accounts are prepared in accordance with the small companies regime, the balance sheet must contain, in a prominent position above the signature—

(a) in the case of individual accounts prepared in accordance with the micro-entity provisions, a statement to that effect, or

(b) in the case of accounts not prepared as mentioned in paragraph (a), a statement to the effect that the accounts have been prepared in accordance with the provisions applicable to companies subject to the small companies regime.]

(4) If annual accounts are approved that do not comply with the requirements of this Act . . . , every director of the company who—

(a) knew that they did not comply, or was reckless as to whether they complied, and

(b) failed to take reasonable steps to secure compliance with those requirements or, as the case may be, to prevent the accounts from being approved,

commits an offence.

(5) A person guilty of an offence under this section is liable—

(a) on conviction on indictment, to a fine;

(b) on summary conviction, to a fine not exceeding the statutory maximum.

NOTES

Sub-s (3): substituted by the Small Companies (Micro-Entities' Accounts) Regulations 2013, SI 2013/3008, reg 5(1), (4), in relation to (a) financial years ending on or after 30 September 2013, and (b) companies which deliver the accounts required by s 444 of this Act to the registrar on or after 1 December 2013 (as to application of this amendment, see the note at **[1.432]**).

Sub-s (4): words omitted repealed by the International Accounting Standards and European Public Limited-Liability Company (Amendment etc) (EU Exit) Regulations 2019, SI 2019/685, reg 19, Sch 1, Pt 1, paras 1, 12, in relation to accounts for financial years beginning on or after IP completion day (as defined in the European Union (Withdrawal Agreement) Act 2020, s 39) (note also that in relation to accounts for financial years which begin before but end on or after IP completion day, the enactments amended by Parts 1–3 of Sch 1 to the 2019 Regulations have effect as if the UK were a member State until the end of the financial year in question (for transitional provisions see reg 1 of, and Sch 1, Pt 4 to, the 2019 Regulations at **[12.130]** and **[12.151]** respectively)).

[CHAPTER 4A STRATEGIC REPORT

[1.469]

414A Duty to prepare strategic report

(1) The directors of a company must prepare a strategic report for each financial year of the company.

(2) Subsection (1) does not apply if the company is entitled to the small companies exemption.

(3) For a financial year in which—

(a) the company is a parent company, and

(b) the directors of the company prepare group accounts,

the strategic report must be a consolidated report (a "group strategic report") relating to the undertakings included in the consolidation.

(4) A group strategic report may, where appropriate, give greater emphasis to the matters that are significant to the undertakings included in the consolidation, taken as a whole.

(5) In the case of failure to comply with the requirement to prepare a strategic report, an offence is committed by every person who—

(a) was a director of the company immediately before the end of the period for filing accounts and reports for the financial year in question, and

(b) failed to take all reasonable steps for securing compliance with that requirement.

(6) A person guilty of an offence under this section is liable—

(a) on conviction on indictment, to a fine;

(b) on summary conviction, to a fine not exceeding the statutory maximum.]

NOTES

Inserted, together with ss 414B, 414C, 414D, by the Companies Act 2006 (Strategic Report and Directors' Report) Regulations 2013, SI 2013/1970, regs 2, 3, in respect of financial years ending on or after 30 September 2013.

[1.470]

[414B Strategic report: small companies exemption

A company is entitled to [the] small companies exemption in relation to the strategic report for a financial year if—

(a) it is entitled to prepare accounts for the year in accordance with the small companies regime, or

(b) it would be so entitled but for being or having been a member of an ineligible group.]

NOTES

Inserted as noted to s 414A at **[1.469]**.

Word in square brackets inserted by the Companies, Partnerships and Groups (Accounts and Reports) Regulations 2015, SI 2015/980, reg 6, as from 6 April 2015 (note that this amendment corrects an error in the original 2013 Regulations).

[1.471]

[414C Contents of strategic report

(1) The purpose of the strategic report is to inform members of the company and help them assess how the directors have performed their duty under section 172 (duty to promote the success of the company).

(2) The strategic report must contain—

(a) a fair review of the company's business, and

(b) a description of the principal risks and uncertainties facing the company.

[Section 414CZA (section 172(1) statement) and sections 414CA and 414CB (non-financial [and sustainability] information statement) make further provision about the contents of a strategic report.]

(3) The review required is a balanced and comprehensive analysis of—

(a) the development and performance of the company's business during the financial year, and

(b) the position of the company's business at the end of that year,

consistent with the size and complexity of the business.

(4) The review must, to the extent necessary for an understanding of the development, performance or position of the company's business, include—

(a) analysis using financial key performance indicators, and

(b) where appropriate, analysis using other key performance indicators, including information relating to environmental matters and employee matters.

(5) In subsection (4), "key performance indicators" means factors by reference to which the development, performance or position of the company's business can be measured effectively.

(6) Where a company qualifies as medium-sized in relation to a financial year (see sections 465 to 467), the review for the year need not comply with the requirements of subsection (4) so far as they relate to non-financial information.

(7) In the case of a quoted company the strategic report must, to the extent necessary for an understanding of the development, performance or position of the company's business, include—

(a) the main trends and factors likely to affect the future development, performance and position of the company's business, and

(b) information about—

(i) environmental matters (including the impact of the company's business on the environment),

(ii) the company's employees, and

(iii) social, community and human rights issues,

including information about any policies of the company in relation to those matters and the effectiveness of those policies.

If the report does not contain information of each kind mentioned in paragraphs (b)(i), (ii) and (iii), it must state which of those kinds of information it does not contain.

(8) In the case of a quoted company the strategic report must include—

(a) a description of the company's strategy,

(b) a description of the company's business model,

(c) a breakdown showing at the end of the financial year—

(i) the number of persons of each sex who were directors of the company;

(ii) the number of persons of each sex who were senior managers of the company (other than persons falling within sub-paragraph (i)); and

(iii) the number of persons of each sex who were employees of the company.

(9) In subsection (8), "senior manager" means a person who—

(a) has responsibility for planning, directing or controlling the activities of the company, or a strategically significant part of the company, and

(b) is an employee of the company.

(10) In relation to a group strategic report—

(a) the reference to the company in subsection (8)(c)(i) is to the parent company; and

(b) the breakdown required by subsection (8)(c)(ii) must include the number of persons of each sex who were the directors of the undertakings included in the consolidation.

(11) The strategic report may also contain such of the matters otherwise required by regulations made under section 416(4) to be disclosed in the directors' report as the directors consider are of strategic importance to the company.

(12) The report must, where appropriate, include references to, and additional explanations of, amounts included in the company's annual accounts.

(13) Subject to paragraph (10), in relation to a group strategic report this section has effect as if the references to the company were references to the undertakings included in the consolidation.

(14) Nothing in this section requires the disclosure of information about impending developments or matters in the course of negotiation if the disclosure would, in the opinion of the directors, be seriously prejudicial to the interests of the company.]

NOTES

Inserted as noted to s 414A at **[1.469]**.

Sub-s (2): words in first (outer) pair of square brackets added by the Companies (Miscellaneous Reporting) Regulations 2018, SI 2018/860, regs 2, 3, in relation to the financial years of companies beginning on or after 1 January 2019. Words in second (inner) pair of square brackets inserted by the Companies (Strategic Report) (Climate-related Financial Disclosure) Regulations 2022, SI 2022/31, reg 2, as from 6 April 2022, in respect of any financial year of a company which commences on or after that date.

[1.472]

[414CZA Section 172(1) statement

(1) A strategic report for a financial year of a company must include a statement (a "section 172(1) statement") which describes how the directors have had regard to the matters set out in section 172(1)(a) to (f) when performing their duty under section 172.

(2) Subsection (1) does not apply if the company qualifies as medium-sized in relation to that financial year (see sections 465 to 467).]

NOTES

Inserted by the Companies (Miscellaneous Reporting) Regulations 2018, SI 2018/860, regs 2, 4, in relation to the financial years of companies beginning on or after 1 January 2019.

[1.473]

[414CA Non-financial [and sustainability] information statement

[(A1) A strategic report of a company to which this subsection applies must include a non-financial and sustainability information statement.]

(1) [Subsection (A1) applies to a company if it] was at any time within the financial year to which the report relates—

(a) a traded company,
(b) a banking company,
(c) an authorised insurance company, *or*
(d) a company carrying on insurance market activity[, or
(e) a company any securities of which are admitted to trading on the market known as the Alternative Investment Market].

[(1A) Subsection (A1) also applies to a company if it was a high turnover company in relation to that financial year.
(1B) Subsections (1) and (1A) are subject to subsections (3) to (7).]

(2) If the company's strategic report is a group strategic report, the non-financial [and sustainability] information statement to be included in the report under [subsection (A1)] must be a consolidated statement (a "group non-financial [and sustainability] information statement") relating to the undertakings included in the consolidation.

[(2A) A company is a "high turnover company" in relation to a financial year—
(a) where the company was not a parent company in that financial year, if in that year the company's turnover was more than £500 million;
(b) where the company was a parent company at any time within that financial year, if in that year a group headed by the company had an aggregate turnover of more than £500 million net.

(2B) For a period that is a company's financial year but not in fact a year the figures for turnover given by subsection (2A) must be proportionately adjusted.

(2C) For the purposes of subsection (2A)(b)—
(a) aggregate turnover is ascertained by aggregating the relevant figures determined for each member of the group;
(b) "net", in relation to aggregate turnover, is to be interpreted in accordance with section 383(6).

(2D) Section 383(7) applies for the purposes of subsection (2A)(b) of this section as it applies for the purposes of section 383.]

(3) [Subsection (A1) does not apply to a company if]—
(a) the company is subject to the small companies regime in relation to that financial year (see sections 382 to 384), or
(b) the company qualifies as medium-sized in relation to that financial year (see sections 465 to 467).

(4) [Subsection (A1) does not apply—
(a) to a company which was not a parent company in that financial year, if] the company had no more than 500 employees in that financial year, or
(b) [to a company which was a parent company at any time within that financial year, if] the aggregate number of employees for a group headed by that company in that financial year was no more than 500.

(5) The number of employees means the average number of persons employed by the company in the year, determined as follows—
(a) find for each month in the financial year the number of persons employed under contracts of service by the company in that month (whether throughout the month or not),
(b) add together the monthly totals, and
(c) divide by the number of months in the financial year.

(6) The aggregate number of employees for a group is ascertained by aggregating the relevant figures determined in accordance with subsection (5) for each member of the group.

(7) [Subsection (A1) does not apply to a company if] the company is a subsidiary undertaking at the end of that financial year and is included in—
(a) a group strategic report of a parent undertaking of the company that satisfies the requirements in subsection (8) . . .
(b) . . .

(8) The requirements in this subsection are that—
(a) the group strategic report relates to undertakings that include the company and its subsidiary undertakings (if any),
(b) the report is prepared for a financial year of the parent undertaking that ends at the same time as, or before the end of, the company's financial year, and
(c) the report includes a group non-financial [and sustainability] information statement in respect of all the undertakings included in the consolidation.

(9) . . .

(10) A company to which subsection [(A1)] does not apply may include a non-financial [and sustainability] information statement in its strategic report or, as the case may be, a group non-financial [and sustainability] information statement in its group strategic report.]

NOTES

Inserted, together with s 414CB, by the Companies, Partnerships and Groups (Accounts and Non-Financial Reporting) Regulations 2016, SI 2016/1245, regs 2, 4, in relation to the financial years of companies and qualifying partnerships beginning on or after 1 January 2017 (and only in relation to companies (as defined by s 1 *ante*) and qualifying partnerships (as defined in the Partnerships (Accounts) Regulations 2008, reg 3)).

Section heading: words in square brackets inserted by the Companies (Strategic Report) (Climate-related Financial Disclosure) Regulations 2022, SI 2022/31, reg 3, as from 6 April 2022, in respect of any financial year of a company which commences on or after that date.

Sub-s (A1): inserted by SI 2022/31, reg 3, as from 6 April 2022, in respect of any financial year of a company which commences on or after that date.

Sub-s (1): the words in the first pair of square brackets were substituted (for the original words "A strategic report of a company must include a non-financial information statement if the company"), the word in italics in para (c) was repealed, and para (e) and the preceding word were inserted, by SI 2022/31, reg 3, as from 6 April 2022, in respect of any financial year of a company which commences on or after that date.

Sub-ss (1A), (1B): inserted by SI 2022/31, reg 3, as from 6 April 2022, in respect of any financial year of a company which commences on or after that date.

Sub-s (2): the words in the first and third pairs of square brackets were inserted, and the words in the second pair of square brackets were substituted (for the original words "subsection (A1)"), by SI 2022/31, reg 3, as from 6 April 2022, in respect of any financial year of a company which commences on or after that date.

Sub-ss (2A)–(2D): inserted by SI 2022/31, reg 3, as from 6 April 2022, in respect of any financial year of a company which commences on or after that date.

Sub-s (3): words in square brackets substituted (for the original words "Subsection (1) does not apply if") by SI 2022/31, reg 3, as from 6 April 2022, in respect of any financial year of a company which commences on or after that date.

Sub-s (4): all words in square brackets were substituted by SI 2022/31, reg 3, as from 6 April 2022, in respect of any financial year of a company which commences on or after that date. Prior to its amendment, sub-s (4) read as follows—

"(4) Subsection (1) does not apply if—

(a) where the company was not a parent company in that financial year, the company had no more than 500 employees in that financial year, or

(b) where the company was a parent company at any time within that financial year, the aggregate number of employees for a group headed by that company in that financial year was no more than 500.".

Sub-s (7): the words in square brackets were substituted (for the original words "Subsection (1) does not apply if") by SI 2022/31, reg 3, as from 6 April 2022, in respect of any financial year of a company which commences on or after that date. Para (b) and the preceding word were repealed by the Accounts and Reports (Amendment) (EU Exit) Regulations 2019, SI 2019/145, reg 5, Sch 2, Pt 1, paras 1, 12, in relation to financial years beginning on or after IP completion day (as defined in the European Union (Withdrawal Agreement) Act 2020, s 39) (for transitional provisions see reg 7 of the 2019 Regulations at **[12.79]**).

Sub-s (8): words in square brackets in para (c) inserted by SI 2022/31, reg 3, as from 6 April 2022, in respect of any financial year of a company which commences on or after that date.

Sub-s (9): repealed by SI 2019/145, reg 5, Sch 2, Pt 1, paras 1, 12, in relation to financial years beginning on or after IP completion day (as defined in the European Union (Withdrawal Agreement) Act 2020, s 39) (for transitional provisions see reg 7 of the 2019 Regulations at **[12.79]**).

Sub-s (10): the figure "(A1)" in square brackets was substituted (for the original figure "(1)"), and the words in square brackets were inserted, by SI 2022/31, reg 3, as from 6 April 2022, in respect of any financial year of a company which commences on or after that date.

[1.474]

[414CB Contents of non-financial [and sustainability] information statement

[(A1) The non-financial and sustainability information statement must contain the climate-related financial disclosures of the company.]

(1) [If the company is of a kind described in section 414CA(1)(a), (b), (c) or (d), the non-financial and sustainability information statement must] contain information, to the extent necessary for an understanding of the company's development, performance and position and the impact of its activity, relating to, as a minimum—

(a) environmental matters (including the impact of the company's business on the environment),

(b) the company's employees,

(c) social matters,

(d) respect for human rights, and

(e) anti-corruption and anti-bribery matters.

(2) The information [required by subsection (1)] must include—

(a) a brief description of the company's business model,

(b) a description of the policies pursued by the company in relation to the matters mentioned in subsection (1)(a) to (e) and any due diligence processes implemented by the company in pursuance of those policies,

(c) a description of the outcome of those policies,

(d) a description of the principal risks relating to the matters mentioned in subsection (1)(a) to (e) arising in connection with the company's operations and, where relevant and proportionate—

(i) a description of its business relationships, products and services which are likely to cause adverse impacts in those areas of risk, and

(ii) a description of how it manages the principal risks, and

(e) a description of the non-financial key performance indicators relevant to the company's business.

[(2A) In this section, "climate-related financial disclosures" mean—

(a) a description of the company's governance arrangements in relation to assessing and managing climate-related risks and opportunities;

(b) a description of how the company identifies, assesses, and manages climate-related risks and opportunities;

(c) a description of how processes for identifying, assessing, and managing climate-related risks are integrated into the company's overall risk management process;

(d) a description of—

(i) the principal climate-related risks and opportunities arising in connection with the company's operations, and

(ii) the time periods by reference to which those risks and opportunities are assessed;

(e) a description of the actual and potential impacts of the principal climate-related risks and opportunities on the company's business model and strategy;

(f) an analysis of the resilience of the company's business model and strategy, taking into consideration different climate-related scenarios;

(g) a description of the targets used by the company to manage climate-related risks and to realise climate-related opportunities and of performance against those targets; and

(h) a description of the key performance indicators used to assess progress against targets used to manage climate-related risks and realise climate-related opportunities and of the calculations on which those key performance indicators are based.]

(3) In subsection (2)(e), "key performance indicators" means factors by reference to which the development, performance or position of the company's business, or the impact of the company's activity, can be measured effectively.

(4) If the company does not pursue policies in relation to one or more of the matters mentioned in subsection (1)(a) to (e), the statement must provide a clear and reasoned explanation for the company's not doing so.

[(4A) Where the directors of a company reasonably believe that, having regard to the nature of the company's business, and the manner in which it is carried on, the whole or a part of a climate-related financial disclosure required by subsection (2A)(e), (f), (g) or (h) is not necessary for an understanding of the company's business, the directors may omit the whole or (as the case requires) the relevant part of that climate-related financial disclosure.

(4B) Where the directors omit the whole or part of a climate-related financial disclosure in reliance on subsection (4A) the non-financial and sustainability information statement must provide a clear and reasoned explanation of the directors' reasonable belief mentioned in that subsection.]

(5) The statement must, where appropriate, include references to, and additional explanations of, amounts included in the company's annual accounts.

(6) If information required by subsections (1) to (5) to be included in the statement is published by the company by means of a national, EU-based or international reporting framework, the statement must specify the framework or frameworks used, instead of including that information.

(7) If a non-financial [and sustainability] information statement complies with subsections (1) to (6), the strategic report of which it is part is to be treated as complying with the requirements in—

(a) section 414C(4)(b),
(b) section 414C(7), except as it relates to community issues,
(c) section 414C(8)(b), and
(d) section 414C(12), so far as relating to the provisions mentioned in paragraphs (a) to (c).

(8) In relation to a group non-financial [and sustainability] information statement, this section has effect as if the references to the company were references to the undertakings included in the consolidation.

(9) Nothing in this section requires the disclosure of information about impending developments or matters in the course of negotiation if the disclosure would, in the opinion of the directors, be seriously prejudicial to the commercial interests of the company, provided that the non-disclosure does not prevent a fair and balanced understanding of the company's development, performance or position or the impact of the company's activity.

[(10) The Secretary of State may issue guidance on the climate-related financial disclosures, which are described in subsection (2A), and otherwise in connection with the requirements of this section and section 414CA.]]

NOTES

Inserted as noted to s 414CA at **[1.473]**.

Section heading: words in square brackets inserted by the Companies (Strategic Report) (Climate-related Financial Disclosure) Regulations 2022, SI 2022/31, reg 4, as from 6 April 2022, in respect of any financial year of a company which commences on or after that date.

Sub-s (A1): inserted by SI 2022/31, reg 4, as from 6 April 2022, in respect of any financial year of a company which commences on or after that date.

Sub-s (1): words in square brackets substituted (for the original words "The non-financial information statement must") by SI 2022/31, reg 4, as from 6 April 2022, in respect of any financial year of a company which commences on or after that date.

Sub-s (2): words in square brackets inserted by SI 2022/31, reg 4, as from 6 April 2022, in respect of any financial year of a company which commences on or after that date.

Sub-ss (2A), (4A), (4B): inserted by SI 2022/31, reg 4, as from 6 April 2022, in respect of any financial year of a company which commences on or after that date.

Sub-ss (7), (8): words in square brackets inserted by SI 2022/31, reg 4, as from 6 April 2022, in respect of any financial year of a company which commences on or after that date.

Sub-s (10): added by SI 2022/31, reg 4, as from 6 April 2022, in respect of any financial year of a company which commences on or after that date.

Guidance under sub-s (10): the Department for Business, Energy & Industrial Strategy issued the relevant guidance on 23 February 2022. The guidance (*Mandatory climate-related financial disclosures by publicly quoted companies, large private companies and LLPs – Non-binding guidance*) aims to help in-scope companies and limited liability partnerships understand how to meet new mandatory climate-related financial disclosure requirements under the Companies (Strategic Report) (Climate-related Financial Disclosure) Regulations 2022, and the Limited Liability Partnerships (Climate-related Financial Disclosure) Regulations 2022. The Regulations apply to reporting for financial years starting on or after 6 April 2022. See www.gov.uk/government/publications/climate-related-financial-disclosures-for-companies-and-limited-liability-partnerships-llps.

[1.475]

[414D Approval and signing of strategic report

(1) The strategic report must be approved by the board of directors and signed on behalf of the board by a director or the secretary of the company.

(2) If a strategic report is approved that does not comply with the requirements of this Act, every director of the company who—

(a) knew that it did not comply, or was reckless as to whether it complied, and
(b) failed to take reasonable steps to secure compliance with those requirements or, as the case may be, to prevent the report from being approved,

commits an offence.

(3) A person guilty of an offence under this section is liable—

(a) on conviction on indictment, to a fine;
(b) on summary conviction, to a fine not exceeding the statutory maximum.]

NOTES

Inserted as noted to s 414A at **[1.469]**.

CHAPTER 5 DIRECTORS' REPORT

Directors' report

[1.476]

415 Duty to prepare directors' report

(1) The directors of a company must prepare a directors' report for each financial year of the company.

[(1A) Subsection (1) does not apply if the company qualifies as a micro-entity (see sections 384A and 384B).]

(2) For a financial year in which—

(a) the company is a parent company, and

(b) the directors of the company prepare group accounts,

the directors' report must be a consolidated report (a "group directors' report") relating to the undertakings included in the consolidation.

(3) A group directors' report may, where appropriate, give greater emphasis to the matters that are significant to the undertakings included in the consolidation, taken as a whole.

(4) In the case of failure to comply with the requirement to prepare a directors' report, an offence is committed by every person who—

(a) was a director of the company immediately before the end of the period for filing accounts and reports for the financial year in question, and

(b) failed to take all reasonable steps for securing compliance with that requirement.

(5) A person guilty of an offence under this section is liable—

(a) on conviction on indictment, to a fine;

(b) on summary conviction, to a fine not exceeding the statutory maximum.

NOTES

Sub-s (1A): inserted by the Companies, Partnerships and Groups (Accounts and Reports) Regulations 2015, SI 2015/980, reg 7, in relation to (a) financial years beginning on or after 1 January 2016, and (b) a financial year of a company beginning on or after 1 January 2015, but before 1 January 2016, if the directors of the company so decide (subject to transitional provisions, etc, in regs 2, 3 of the 2015 Regulations as noted to s 380 at **[1.430]**).

Transfer of money held in dormant bank accounts: where (a) directors of a company that is a bank are required by sub-s (1) above to prepare a report for a particular financial year, and (b) in that year the company made transfers in relation to which the Dormant Bank and Building Society Accounts Act 2008, s 2 applied (or a transfer required by s 2A(8) of that Act) the report must identify each of the charities concerned and specify the amount transferred to each of them. See s 13 of the 2008 Act.

[1.477]

[415A Directors' report: small companies exemption

(1) A company is entitled to small companies exemption in relation to the directors' report for a financial year if—

(a) it is entitled to prepare accounts for the year in accordance with the small companies regime, or

(b) it would be so entitled but for being or having been a member of an ineligible group.

(2) The exemption is relevant to—

section 416(3) (contents of report: statement of amount recommended by way of dividend), [and]

. . .

sections 444 to 446 (filing obligations of different descriptions of company).]

NOTES

Inserted by the Companies Act 2006 (Amendment) (Accounts and Reports) Regulations 2008, SI 2008/393, reg 6(2), as from 6 April 2008, in relation to financial years beginning on or after that date.

Sub-s (2): word in square brackets added, and words omitted repealed, by the Companies Act 2006 (Strategic Report and Directors' Report) Regulations 2013, SI 2013/1970, regs 2, 4, in respect of financial years ending on or after 30 September 2013.

[1.478]

416 Contents of directors' report: general

(1) The directors' report for a financial year must state—

(a) the names of the persons who, at any time during the financial year, were directors of the company, . . .

(b) . . .

(2) . . .

(3) Except in the case of a company [entitled to the small companies exemption], the report must state the amount (if any) that the directors recommend should be paid by way of dividend.

(4) The Secretary of State may make provision by regulations as to other matters that must be disclosed in a directors' report.

Without prejudice to the generality of this power, the regulations may make any such provision as was formerly made by Schedule 7 to the Companies Act 1985.

NOTES

Sub-s (1)(b) (and the word immediately preceding it) and sub-s (2) were repealed by the Companies Act 2006 (Strategic Report and Directors' Report) Regulations 2013, SI 2013/1970, reg 6, in respect of financial years ending on or after 30 September 2013.

The words in square brackets in sub-s (3) were substituted by the Companies Act 2006 (Amendment) (Accounts and Reports) Regulations 2008, SI 2008/393, reg 6(3), as from 6 April 2008, in relation to financial years beginning on or after that date.

Regulations: the Small Companies and Groups (Accounts and Directors' Report) Regulations 2008, SI 2008/409 at **[4.41]**; the Large and Medium-sized Companies and Groups (Accounts and Reports) Regulations 2008, SI 2008/410 at **[4.60]**; the Companies Act 2006 (Strategic Report and Directors' Report) Regulations 2013, SI 2013/1970; the Companies (Miscellaneous Reporting) Regulations 2018, SI 2018/860 (see the note at **[4.674]**); the Companies (Directors' Report) and Limited Liability Partnerships (Energy and Carbon Report) Regulations 2018, SI 2018/1155. For a summary of all statutory instruments made under this Act, see Appendix 4 at **[A4]**.

417 (*Repealed by the Companies Act 2006 (Strategic Report and Directors' Report) Regulations 2013, SI 2013/1970, regs 2, 5, in respect of financial years ending on or after 30 September 2013.*)

[1.479]

418 Contents of directors' report: statement as to disclosure to auditors

(1) This section applies to a company unless—

(a) it is exempt for the financial year in question from the requirements of Part 16 as to audit of accounts, and

(b) the directors take advantage of that exemption.

(2) The directors' report must contain a statement to the effect that, in the case of each of the persons who are directors at the time the report is approved—

(a) so far as the director is aware, there is no relevant audit information of which the company's auditor is unaware, and

(b) he has taken all the steps that he ought to have taken as a director in order to make himself aware of any relevant audit information and to establish that the company's auditor is aware of that information.

(3) "Relevant audit information" means information needed by the company's auditor in connection with preparing his report.

(4) A director is regarded as having taken all the steps that he ought to have taken as a director in order to do the things mentioned in subsection (2)(b) if he has—

(a) made such enquiries of his fellow directors and of the company's auditors for that purpose, and

(b) taken such other steps (if any) for that purpose,

as are required by his duty as a director of the company to exercise reasonable care, skill and diligence.

(5) Where a directors' report containing the statement required by this section is approved but the statement is false, every director of the company who—

(a) knew that the statement was false, or was reckless as to whether it was false, and

(b) failed to take reasonable steps to prevent the report from being approved,

commits an offence.

(6) A person guilty of an offence under subsection (5) is liable—

(a) on conviction on indictment, to imprisonment for a term not exceeding two years or a fine (or both);

(b) on summary conviction—

(i) in England and Wales, to imprisonment for a term not exceeding twelve months or to a fine not exceeding the statutory maximum (or both);

(ii) in Scotland or Northern Ireland, to imprisonment for a term not exceeding six months, or to a fine not exceeding the statutory maximum (or both).

NOTES

Offences under this section: see further s 1131 at **[1.1301]**.

[1.480]

419 Approval and signing of directors' report

(1) The directors' report must be approved by the board of directors and signed on behalf of the board by a director or the secretary of the company.

(2) [If in preparing the report advantage is taken of the small companies exemption,] it must contain a statement to that effect in a prominent position above the signature.

(3) If a directors' report is approved that does not comply with the requirements of this Act, every director of the company who—

(a) knew that it did not comply, or was reckless as to whether it complied, and

(b) failed to take reasonable steps to secure compliance with those requirements or, as the case may be, to prevent the report from being approved,

commits an offence.

(4) A person guilty of an offence under this section is liable—

(a) on conviction on indictment, to a fine;

(b) on summary conviction, to a fine not exceeding the statutory maximum.

NOTES

Sub-s (2): words in square brackets substituted by the Companies Act 2006 (Amendment) (Accounts and Reports) Regulations 2008, SI 2008/393, reg 6(5), as from 6 April 2008, in relation to financial years beginning on or after that date.

[1.481]

[419A Approval and signing of separate corporate governance statement

Any separate corporate governance statement must be approved by the board of directors and signed on behalf of the board by a director or the secretary of the company.]

NOTES

Inserted by the Companies Act 2006 (Accounts, Reports and Audit) Regulations 2009, SI 2009/1581, reg 2, in relation to financial years beginning on or after 29 June 2008 which have not ended before 27 June 2009.

CHAPTER 6 QUOTED COMPANIES [AND TRADED COMPANIES]: DIRECTORS' REMUNERATION REPORT

NOTES

Words in square brackets in the preceding Chapter heading inserted by the Companies (Directors' Remuneration Policy and Directors' Remuneration Report) Regulations 2019, SI 2019/970, regs 3, 11, as from 10 June 2019 (for transitional provisions, etc, see reg 2 of the 2019 Regulations at **[4.680]**).

[1.482]

420 Duty to prepare directors' remuneration report

(1) The directors of a quoted company[, or of a traded company (as defined by section 360C) that is not a quoted company,] must prepare a directors' remuneration report for each financial year of the company.

(2) In the case of failure to comply with the requirement to prepare a directors' remuneration report, every person who—

- (a) was a director of the company immediately before the end of the period for filing accounts and reports for the financial year in question, and
- (b) failed to take all reasonable steps for securing compliance with that requirement,

commits an offence.

(3) A person guilty of an offence under this section is liable—

- (a) on conviction on indictment, to a fine;
- (b) on summary conviction, to a fine not exceeding the statutory maximum.

NOTES

Sub-s (1): words in square brackets inserted by the Companies (Directors' Remuneration Policy and Directors' Remuneration Report) Regulations 2019, SI 2019/970, regs 3, 12, as from 10 June 2019 (for transitional provisions, etc, see reg 2 of the 2019 Regulations at **[4.680]**).

Executives' remuneration reports: the Financial Services Act 2010, s 4 provides that the Treasury may make provision by Regulations about the preparation, approval and disclosure of executives' remuneration reports. Section 5(4) of the 2010 Act provides that Regulations under s 4 may apply any provision made by or under this Act relating to directors' remuneration reports, subject to such exceptions, adaptations and modifications as the Treasury consider appropriate.

[1.483]

421 Contents of directors' remuneration report

(1) The Secretary of State may make provision by regulations as to—

- (a) the information that must be contained in a directors' remuneration report,
- (b) how information is to be set out in the report, and
- (c) what is to be the auditable part of the report.

(2) Without prejudice to the generality of this power, the regulations may make any such provision as was made, immediately before the commencement of this Part, by Schedule 7A to the Companies Act 1985 (c 6).

[(2A) The regulations must provide that any information required to be included in the report as to the policy of the company with respect to the making of remuneration payments and payments for loss of office (within the meaning of Chapter 4A of Part 10) is to be set out in a separate part of the report.]

(3) It is the duty of—

- (a) any director of a company, and
- (b) any person who is or has at any time in the preceding five years been a director of the company,

to give notice to the company of such matters relating to himself as may be necessary for the purposes of regulations under this section.

(4) A person who makes default in complying with subsection (3) commits an offence and is liable on summary conviction to a fine not exceeding level 3 on the standard scale.

NOTES

Sub-s (2A): inserted by the Enterprise and Regulatory Reform Act 2013, s 79(1), as from 25 April 2013 (so far as is necessary for enabling the exercise of any power to make regulations) and as from 1 October 2013 (otherwise).

Executives' remuneration reports: see the note to s 420 at **[1.482]**.

Regulations: the Large and Medium-sized Companies and Groups (Accounts and Reports) Regulations 2008, SI 2008/410 at **[4.60]**; the Large and Medium-sized Companies and Groups (Accounts and Reports) (Amendment) Regulations 2013, SI 2013/1981; the Companies (Miscellaneous Reporting) Regulations 2018, SI 2018/860 (see the note at **[4.674]**); the Companies (Directors' Remuneration Policy and Directors' Remuneration Report) Regulations 2019, SI 2019/970 at **[4.679]**. For a summary of all statutory instruments made under this Act, see Appendix 4 at **[A4]**.

[1.484]

422 Approval and signing of directors' remuneration report

(1) The directors' remuneration report must be approved by the board of directors and signed on behalf of the board by a director or the secretary of the company.

(2) If a directors' remuneration report is approved that does not comply with the requirements of this Act, every director of the company who—

- (a) knew that it did not comply, or was reckless as to whether it complied, and
- (b) failed to take reasonable steps to secure compliance with those requirements or, as the case may be, to prevent the report from being approved,

commits an offence.

(3) A person guilty of an offence under this section is liable—

- (a) on conviction on indictment, to a fine;
- (b) on summary conviction, to a fine not exceeding the statutory maximum.

NOTES

Executives' remuneration reports: see the note to s 420 at **[1.482]**.

[1.485]

[422A Revisions to directors' remuneration policy

(1) The directors' remuneration policy contained in a company's directors' remuneration report may be revised.

(2) Any such revision must be approved by the board of directors.

(3) The policy as so revised must be set out in a document signed on behalf of the board by a director or the secretary of the company.

(4) Regulations under section 421(1) may make provision as to—

(a) the information that must be contained in a document setting out a revised directors' remuneration policy, and
(b) how information is to be set out in the document.

(5) Sections 422(2) and (3), 454, 456 and 463 apply in relation to such a document as they apply in relation to a directors' remuneration report.

(6) In this section, "directors' remuneration policy" means the policy of a company with respect to the matters mentioned in section 421(2A).]

NOTES

Inserted by the Enterprise and Regulatory Reform Act 2013, s 79(2), as from 25 April 2013 (for the purposes of enabling the exercise of any power to make provision by regulations), and as from 1 October 2013 (otherwise).

Regulations under s 421(1): see that section *ante*. For a summary of all statutory instruments made under this Act, see Appendix 4 at **[A4]**.

CHAPTER 7 PUBLICATION OF ACCOUNTS AND REPORTS

Duty to circulate copies of accounts and reports

[1.486]

423 Duty to circulate copies of annual accounts and reports

(1) Every company must send a copy of its annual accounts and reports for each financial year to—
(a) every member of the company,
(b) every holder of the company's debentures, and
(c) every person who is entitled to receive notice of general meetings.

(2) Copies need not be sent to a person for whom the company does not have a current address.

(3) A company has a "current address" for a person if—
(a) an address has been notified to the company by the person as one at which documents may be sent to him, and
(b) the company has no reason to believe that documents sent to him at that address will not reach him.

(4) In the case of a company not having a share capital, copies need not be sent to anyone who is not entitled to receive notices of general meetings of the company.

(5) Where copies are sent out over a period of days, references in the Companies Acts to the day on which copies are sent out shall be read as references to the last day of that period.

(6) This section has effect subject to section 426 (option to provide [strategic report with supplementary material]).

NOTES

Sub-s (6): words in square brackets substituted by the Companies Act 2006 (Strategic Report and Directors' Report) Regulations 2013, SI 2013/1970, reg 14, Schedule, paras 1, 3, in respect of financial years ending on or after 30 September 2013.

[1.487]

424 Time allowed for sending out copies of accounts and reports

(1) The time allowed for sending out copies of the company's annual accounts and reports is as follows.

(2) A private company must comply with section 423 not later than—
(a) the end of the period for filing accounts and reports, or
(b) if earlier, the date on which it actually delivers its accounts and reports to the registrar.

(3) A public company must comply with section 423 at least 21 days before the date of the relevant accounts meeting.

(4) If in the case of a public company copies are sent out later than is required by subsection (3), they shall, despite that, be deemed to have been duly sent if it is so agreed by all the members entitled to attend and vote at the relevant accounts meeting.

(5) Whether the time allowed is that for a private company or a public company is determined by reference to the company's status immediately before the end of the accounting reference period by reference to which the financial year for the accounts in question was determined.

(6) In this section the "relevant accounts meeting" means the accounts meeting of the company at which the accounts and reports in question are to be laid.

[1.488]

425 Default in sending out copies of accounts and reports: offences

(1) If default is made in complying with section 423 or 424, an offence is committed by—
(a) the company, and
(b) every officer of the company who is in default.

(2) A person guilty of an offence under this section is liable—
(a) on conviction on indictment, to a fine;
(b) on summary conviction, to a fine not exceeding the statutory maximum.

Option to provide [strategic report with supplementary material]

[1.489]

426 Option to provide [strategic report with supplementary material]

(1) A company may—
(a) in such cases as may be specified by regulations made by the Secretary of State, and
(b) provided any conditions so specified are complied with,

provide a [copy of the strategic report together with the supplementary material described in section 426A] instead of copies of the accounts and reports required to be sent out in accordance with section 423.

(2) Copies of those accounts and reports must, however, be sent to any person entitled to be sent them in accordance with that section and who wishes to receive them.

(3) The Secretary of State may make provision by regulations as to the manner in which it is to be ascertained, whether before or after a person becomes entitled to be sent a copy of those accounts and reports, whether he wishes to receive them.

(4) . . .

(5) This section applies to copies of accounts and reports required to be sent out by virtue of section 146 to a person nominated to enjoy information rights as it applies to copies of accounts and reports required to be sent out in accordance with section 423 to a member of the company.

(6) Regulations under this section are subject to negative resolution procedure.

NOTES

The words in square brackets in the section heading, in the heading preceding this section, and in sub-s (1) were substituted, and sub-s (4) was repealed, by the Companies Act 2006 (Strategic Report and Directors' Report) Regulations 2013, SI 2013/1970, regs 9, 10, as from 6 August 2013 (for the purposes only of the exercise of the powers to make regulations), and as from 1 October 2013 (otherwise, in respect of financial years ending on or after 30 September 2013).

Regulations: the Companies (Receipt of Accounts and Reports) Regulations 2013, SI 2013/1973 at **[4.494]**. For a summary of all statutory instruments made under this Act, see Appendix 4 at **[A4]**.

[1.490]

[426A Supplementary material

(1) The supplementary material referred to in section 426 must be prepared in accordance with this section.

(2) The supplementary material must—

(a) contain a statement that the strategic report is only part of the company's annual accounts and reports;

(b) state how a person entitled to them can obtain a full copy of the company's annual accounts and reports;

(c) state whether the auditor's report on the annual accounts was unqualified or qualified and, if it was qualified, set out the report in full together with any further material needed to understand the qualification;

(d) state whether, in that report, the auditor's statement under section 496 (whether strategic report and directors' report consistent with the accounts) was unqualified or qualified and, if it was qualified, set out the qualified statement in full together with any further material needed to understand the qualification;

(e) in the case of a quoted company [or of a traded company (as defined by section 360C) that is not a quoted company], contain a copy of that part of the directors' remuneration report which sets out the single total figure table in respect of the company's directors' remuneration in accordance with the requirements of Schedule 8 to the Large and Medium-sized Companies (Accounts and Reports) Regulations 2008 (SI 2008/410).]

NOTES

Inserted by the Companies Act 2006 (Strategic Report and Directors' Report) Regulations 2013, SI 2013/1970, regs 9, 12, in respect of financial years ending on or after 30 September 2013.

Sub-s (2): words in square brackets in para (e) inserted by the Companies (Directors' Remuneration Policy and Directors' Remuneration Report) Regulations 2019, SI 2019/970, regs 3, 13, as from 10 June 2019 (for transitional provisions, etc, see reg 2 of the 2019 Regulations at **[4.680]**).

[Section 172(1) statement: requirements as to website publication

[1.491]

426B Section 172(1) statement to be made available on website

(1) This section applies if—

(a) a company is required by section 414CZA to include a section 172(1) statement in its strategic report for a financial year, and

(b) the company is an unquoted company in relation to that financial year.

(2) The company must ensure that the section 172(1) statement—

(a) is made available on a website, and

(b) remains so available until—

(i) the section 172(1) statement for the company's next financial year is made available in accordance with this section, or

(ii) if the obligation under this section to make a section 172(1) statement available does not arise in relation to the company's next financial year, the end of the company's next financial year.

(3) The section 172(1) statement must be made available on a website that—

(a) is maintained by or on behalf of the company, and

(b) identifies the company in question.

(4) Access to the section 172(1) statement made available on the website under subsection (2), and the ability to obtain a hard copy of the statement from the website, must not be—

(a) conditional on the payment of a fee, or

(b) otherwise restricted, except so far as necessary to comply with any enactment or regulatory requirement (in the United Kingdom or elsewhere).

(5) The section 172(1) statement—

(a) must be made available on a website as soon as reasonably practicable, and

(b) must be kept available throughout the period specified in subsection (2)(b)(i) or (as the case may be) (ii).

(6) A failure to make the section 172(1) statement available on a website throughout the period specified in subsection (2)(b)(i) or (as the case may be) (ii) is disregarded if—

(a) the statement is made available on the website for part of that period, and

(b) the failure is wholly attributable to circumstances that it would not be reasonable to have expected the company to prevent or avoid.

(7) In the event of default in complying with this section, an offence is committed by every officer of the company who is in default.

(8) A person guilty of an offence under subsection (7) is liable on summary conviction to a fine not exceeding level 3 on the standard scale.]

NOTES

Inserted, together with the preceding heading, by the Companies (Miscellaneous Reporting) Regulations 2018, SI 2018/860, regs 2, 5, in relation to the financial years of companies beginning on or after 1 January 2019.

427–429 (*Repealed by the Companies Act 2006 (Strategic Report and Directors' Report) Regulations 2013, SI 2013/1970, regs 9, 11, in respect of financial years ending on or after 30 September 2013.*)

Quoted companies [and traded companies]: requirements as to website publication

NOTES

Words in square brackets in the preceding heading inserted by the Companies (Directors' Remuneration Policy and Directors' Remuneration Report) Regulations 2019, SI 2019/970, regs 3, 14, as from 10 June 2019 (for transitional provisions, etc, see reg 2 of the 2019 Regulations at **[4.680]**).

[1.492]

430 Quoted companies [and traded companies]: annual accounts and reports to be made available on website

(1) A quoted company [or unquoted traded company] must ensure that its annual accounts and reports—

(a) are made available on a website, and

(b) [subject to subsection (4ZA),] remain so available until the annual accounts and reports for the company's next financial year are made available in accordance with this section.

(2) The annual accounts and reports must be made available on a website that—

(a) is maintained by or on behalf of the company, and

(b) identifies the company in question.

[(2A) If the directors' remuneration policy of a quoted company [or unquoted traded company] is revised in accordance with section 422A, [or amended as mentioned in section 226B(1)(b) or section 226C(1)(b),] the company must ensure that the revised [or amended] policy is made available on the website on which its annual accounts and reports are made available.

(2B) If a person ceases to be a director of a quoted company [or of an unquoted traded company], the company must ensure that the following information is made available on the website on which its annual accounts and reports are made available—

(a) the name of the person concerned,

(b) particulars of any remuneration payment (within the meaning of Chapter 4A of Part 10) made or to be made to the person after ceasing to be a director, including its amount and how it was calculated, and

(c) particulars of any payment for loss of office (within the meaning of that Chapter) made or to be made to the person, including its amount and how it was calculated.]

[(2C) Where the members of a quoted company or of an unquoted traded company have passed a resolution approving the relevant directors' remuneration policy (within the meaning of section 439A(7))—

(a) the company must ensure that the following information is made available on the website on which its remuneration policy is made available as soon as reasonably practicable, and kept available for as long as that information is applicable —

(i) the date of the resolution,

(ii) the number of votes validly cast,

(iii) the proportion of the company's issued share capital represented by those votes,

(iv) the number of votes cast in favour,

(v) the number of votes cast against, and

(vi) the number of abstentions; and

(b) for the purposes of paragraph (a)(iii), the proportion of the issued share capital must be determined by reference to the register of members as at a time (determined by the company) that is not more than 48 hours before the time for the holding of the meeting at which the resolution was passed.]

(3) Access to [the material made available on the website under subsections (1) to [(2C)]], and the ability to obtain a hard copy of [such material from] the website, must not be—

(a) conditional on the payment of a fee, or

(b) otherwise restricted, except so far as necessary to comply with any enactment or regulatory requirement (in the United Kingdom or elsewhere).

(4) The annual accounts and reports—

(a) must be made available as soon as reasonably practicable, and

(b) [subject to subsection (4ZA),] must be kept available throughout the period specified in subsection (1)(b).

[(4ZA) The directors' remuneration report—

(a) must be kept available for a period of ten years beginning with the date it is first made available in accordance with this section, and

(b) may be kept available for a longer period if it does not contain personal data within the meaning of the Data Protection Act 2018 (see section 3(2) of that Act).]

[(4A) Where subsection (2A) or (2B) applies, the material in question—

(a) must be made available as soon as reasonably practicable, . . .

(b) must be kept available until the next directors' remuneration report of the company is made available on the website[, and]

[(c) in a subsection (2A) case, must be kept available for at least as long as it is applicable.]]

(5) A failure to make [material available on a website throughout the period mentioned in subsection (4) or (as the case may be) [(4ZA) or] (4A)] is disregarded if—

(a) [the material is] made available on the website for part of that period, and

(b) the failure is wholly attributable to circumstances that it would not be reasonable to have expected the company to prevent or avoid.

(6) In the event of default in complying with this section, an offence is committed by every officer of the company who is in default.

(7) A person guilty of an offence under subsection (6) is liable on summary conviction to a fine not exceeding level 3 on the standard scale.

[(8) In this section "unquoted traded company" means a traded company (as defined by section 360C) that is not a quoted company.]

NOTES

Section heading, sub-ss (1), (4): words in square brackets inserted by the Companies (Directors' Remuneration Policy and Directors' Remuneration Report) Regulations 2019, SI 2019/970, regs 3, 15(a)–(c), (h) (these amendments apply in relation to (i) a directors' remuneration report or directors' remuneration policy of a quoted company first required to be made available under this section on or after 10 June 2019, (ii) annual accounts and reports of an unquoted traded company for a financial year of the company beginning on or after the same date – see further reg 2 of the 2019 Regulations at **[4.680]**).

Sub-ss (2A), (2B): inserted by the Enterprise and Regulatory Reform Act 2013, s 81(6), as from 1 October 2013. Words in square brackets inserted by SI 2019/970, regs 3, 15(d), (e) (as to the commencement and application of these amendments, see the first note relating to the 2019 Regulations above).

Sub-ss (2C), (4ZA), (8): inserted and added respectively by SI 2019/970, regs 3, 15(f), (i), (l) (as to the commencement and application of these amendments, see the first note relating to the 2019 Regulations above).

Sub-s (3): words in first (outer) pair of square brackets and words in third pair of square brackets substituted by the Enterprise and Regulatory Reform Act 2013, s 81(7), as from 1 October 2013. Figure "(2C)" in square brackets substituted by SI 2019/970, regs 3, 15(g) (as to the commencement and application of this amendment, see the first note relating to the 2019 Regulations above).

Sub-s (4A): inserted by the Enterprise and Regulatory Reform Act 2013, s 81(8), as from 1 October 2013. The word omitted from para (a) was repealed, and para (c) and the preceding word were inserted, by SI 2019/970, regs 3, 15(j) (as to the commencement and application of these amendments, see the first note relating to the 2019 Regulations above).

Sub-s (5): words in first (outer) pair of square brackets and words in square brackets in para (a) substituted by the Enterprise and Regulatory Reform Act 2013, s 81(9), as from 1 October 2013. Words "(4ZA) or" in square brackets inserted by SI 2019/970, regs 3, 15(k) (as to the commencement and application of this amendment, see the first note relating to the 2019 Regulations above).

Right of member or debenture holder to demand copies of accounts and reports

[1.493]

431 Right of member or debenture holder to copies of accounts and reports: unquoted companies

(1) A member of, or holder of debentures of, an unquoted company is entitled to be provided, on demand and without charge, with a copy of—

(a) the company's last annual accounts,

[(aa) the strategic report (if any) for the last financial year,]

(b) the last directors' report, . . .

[(ba) the last directors' remuneration report (if any), and]

(c) the auditor's report on those accounts (including the statement on that report [and (where applicable) on the strategic report] [and on the directors' remuneration report]).

(2) The entitlement under this section is to a single copy of those documents, but that is in addition to any copy to which a person may be entitled under section 423.

(3) If a demand made under this section is not complied with within seven days of receipt by the company, an offence is committed by—

(a) the company, and

(b) every officer of the company who is in default.

(4) A person guilty of an offence under this section is liable on summary conviction to a fine not exceeding level 3 on the standard scale and, for continued contravention, a daily default fine not exceeding one-tenth of level 3 on the standard scale.

NOTES

Sub-s (1): para (aa) and the words in the first pair of square brackets in para (c) were inserted by the Companies Act 2006 (Strategic Report and Directors' Report) Regulations 2013, SI 2013/1970, reg 14, Schedule, paras 1, 4, in respect of financial years ending on or after 30 September 2013. The word omitted from para (b) was repealed, and para (ba) and the words in the second pair of square brackets in para (c) were inserted, by the Companies (Directors' Remuneration Policy and Directors' Remuneration Report) Regulations 2019, SI 2019/970, regs 3, 16, as from 10 June 2019 (for transitional provisions, etc, see reg 2 of the 2019 Regulations at **[4.680]**).

[1.494]

432 Right of member or debenture holder to copies of accounts and reports: quoted companies

(1) A member of, or holder of debentures of, a quoted company is entitled to be provided, on demand and without charge, with a copy of—

(a) the company's last annual accounts,

(b) the last directors' remuneration report,

[(ba) the strategic report (if any) for the last financial year,]

(c) the last directors' report, and

(d) the auditor's report on those accounts (including the report on the directors' remuneration report[, on the strategic report (where this is covered by the auditor's report)] and on the directors' report).

(2) The entitlement under this section is to a single copy of those documents, but that is in addition to any copy to which a person may be entitled under section 423.

(3) If a demand made under this section is not complied with within seven days of receipt by the company, an offence is committed by—

(a) the company, and

(b) every officer of the company who is in default.

(4) A person guilty of an offence under this section is liable on summary conviction to a fine not exceeding level 3 on the standard scale and, for continued contravention, a daily default fine not exceeding one-tenth of level 3 on the standard scale.

NOTES

Sub-s (1): words in square brackets inserted by the Companies Act 2006 (Strategic Report and Directors' Report) Regulations 2013, SI 2013/1970, reg 14, Schedule, paras 1, 5, in respect of financial years ending on or after 30 September 2013.

Requirements in connection with publication of accounts and reports

[1.495]

433 Name of signatory to be stated in published copies of accounts and reports

(1) Every copy of a document to which this section applies that is published by or on behalf of the company must state the name of the person who signed it on behalf of the board.

(2) In the case of an unquoted company [that is not a traded company], this section applies to copies of—

(a) the company's balance sheet, . . .

[(aa) the strategic report, and]

(b) the directors' report.

(3) In the case of a quoted company [or of a traded company (as defined by section 360C) that is not a quoted company], this section applies to copies of—

(a) the company's balance sheet,

(b) the directors' remuneration report, . . .

[(ba) the strategic report, and]

(c) the directors' report.

(4) If a copy is published without the required statement of the signatory's name, an offence is committed by—

(a) the company, and

(b) every officer of the company who is in default.

(5) A person guilty of an offence under this section is liable on summary conviction to a fine not exceeding level 3 on the standard scale.

NOTES

The words "that is not a traded company" in sub-s (2) and "or of a traded company (as defined by section 360C) that is not a quoted company" in sub-s (3) were inserted by the Companies (Directors' Remuneration Policy and Directors' Remuneration Report) Regulations 2019, SI 2019/970, regs 3, 17, as from 10 June 2019 (for transitional provisions, etc, see reg 2 of the 2019 Regulations at **[4.680]**).

Words omitted repealed, and sub-ss (2)(aa), (3)(ba) inserted, by the Companies Act 2006 (Strategic Report and Directors' Report) Regulations 2013, SI 2013/1970, reg 14, Schedule, paras 1, 6, in respect of financial years ending on or after 30 September 2013.

[1.496]

434 Requirements in connection with publication of statutory accounts

(1) If a company publishes any of its statutory accounts, they must be accompanied by the auditor's report on those accounts (unless the company is exempt from audit and the directors have taken advantage of that exemption).

(2) A company that prepares statutory group accounts for a financial year must not publish its statutory individual accounts for that year without also publishing with them its statutory group accounts.

(3) A company's "statutory accounts" are its accounts for a financial year as required to be delivered to the registrar under section 441.

(4) If a company contravenes any provision of this section, an offence is committed by—

(a) the company, and

(b) every officer of the company who is in default.

(5) A person guilty of an offence under this section is liable on summary conviction to a fine not exceeding level 3 on the standard scale.

(6) . . .

NOTES

Sub-s (6): repealed by the Companies Act 2006 (Strategic Report and Directors' Report) Regulations 2013, SI 2013/1970, reg 14, Schedule, paras 1, 7, in respect of financial years ending on or after 30 September 2013.

[1.497]

435 Requirements in connection with publication of non-statutory accounts

(1) If a company publishes non-statutory accounts, it must publish with them a statement indicating—

(a) that they are not the company's statutory accounts,

(b) whether statutory accounts dealing with any financial year with which the non-statutory accounts purport to deal have been delivered to the registrar, and

(c) whether an auditor's report has been made on the company's statutory accounts for any such financial year, and if so whether the report—

(i) was qualified or unqualified, or included a reference to any matters to which the auditor drew attention by way of emphasis without qualifying the report, or

(ii) contained a statement under section 498(2) (accounting records or returns inadequate or accounts or directors' remuneration report not agreeing with records and returns), or section 498(3) (failure to obtain necessary information and explanations).

(2) The company must not publish with non-statutory accounts the auditor's report on the company's statutory accounts.

(3) References in this section to the publication by a company of "non-statutory accounts" are to the publication of—

(a) any balance sheet or profit and loss account relating to, or purporting to deal with, a financial year of the company, or

(b) an account in any form purporting to be a balance sheet or profit and loss account for a group headed by the company relating to, or purporting to deal with, a financial year of the company,

otherwise than as part of the company's statutory accounts.

(4) In subsection (3)(b) "a group headed by the company" means a group consisting of the company and any other undertaking (regardless of whether it is a subsidiary undertaking of the company) other than a parent undertaking of the company.

(5) If a company contravenes any provision of this section, an offence is committed by—

(a) the company, and

(b) every officer of the company who is in default.

(6) A person guilty of an offence under this section is liable on summary conviction to a fine not exceeding level 3 on the standard scale.

(7) . . .

NOTES

Sub-s (7): repealed by the Companies Act 2006 (Strategic Report and Directors' Report) Regulations 2013, SI 2013/1970, reg 14, Schedule, paras 1, 8, in respect of financial years ending on or after 30 September 2013.

[1.498]

436 Meaning of "publication" in relation to accounts and reports

(1) This section has effect for the purposes of—

section 433 (name of signatory to be stated in published copies of accounts and reports),

section 434 (requirements in connection with publication of statutory accounts), and

section 435 (requirements in connection with publication of non-statutory accounts).

(2) For the purposes of those sections a company is regarded as publishing a document if it publishes, issues or circulates it or otherwise makes it available for public inspection in a manner calculated to invite members of the public generally, or any class of members of the public, to read it.

CHAPTER 8 PUBLIC COMPANIES: LAYING OF ACCOUNTS AND REPORTS BEFORE GENERAL MEETING

[1.499]

437 Public companies: laying of accounts and reports before general meeting

(1) The directors of a public company must lay before the company in general meeting copies of its annual accounts and reports.

(2) This section must be complied with not later than the end of the period for filing the accounts and reports in question.

(3) In the Companies Acts "accounts meeting", in relation to a public company, means a general meeting of the company at which the company's annual accounts and reports are (or are to be) laid in accordance with this section.

[1.500]

438 Public companies: offence of failure to lay accounts and reports

(1) If the requirements of section 437 (public companies: laying of accounts and reports before general meeting) are not complied with before the end of the period allowed, every person who immediately before the end of that period was a director of the company commits an offence.

(2) It is a defence for a person charged with such an offence to prove that he took all reasonable steps for securing that those requirements would be complied with before the end of that period.

(3) It is not a defence to prove that the documents in question were not in fact prepared as required by this Part.

(4) A person guilty of an offence under this section is liable on summary conviction to a fine not exceeding level 5 on the standard scale and, for continued contravention, a daily default fine not exceeding [one-tenth of the greater of £5,000 or level 4 on the standard scale].

NOTES

Sub-s (4): words in square brackets substituted (for the original words "one-tenth of level 5 on the standard scale") by the Legal Aid, Sentencing and Punishment of Offenders Act 2012 (Fines on Summary Conviction) Regulations 2015, SI 2015/664, regs 3, 5, Sch 3, Pt 1, para 9(1), (12), as from 12 March 2015, in relation to England and Wales only (except in relation to (a) fines for offences committed before 12 March 2015, (b) the operation of restrictions on fines that may be imposed on a person aged under 18, or (c) fines that may be imposed on a person convicted by a magistrates' court who is to be sentenced as if convicted on indictment).

CHAPTER 9 QUOTED COMPANIES [AND TRADED COMPANIES]: MEMBERS' APPROVAL OF DIRECTORS' REMUNERATION REPORT

NOTES

Words in square brackets in the preceding Chapter heading inserted by the Companies (Directors' Remuneration Policy and Directors' Remuneration Report) Regulations 2019, SI 2019/970, regs 3, 18, as from 10 June 2019 (for transitional provisions, etc, see reg 2 of the 2019 Regulations at **[4.680]**).

[1.501]

439 Quoted companies [and traded companies]: members' approval of directors' remuneration report

(1) A [company to which this section applies] must, prior to the accounts meeting, give to the members of the company entitled to be sent notice of the meeting notice of the intention to move at the meeting, as an ordinary resolution, a resolution approving the directors' remuneration report for the financial year [other than the part containing the directors' remuneration policy (as to which see section 439A)].

[(1A) This section applies to—

(a) a quoted company, and

(b) a traded company (as defined by section 360C) that is not a quoted company.]

(2) The notice may be given in any manner permitted for the service on the member of notice of the meeting.

(3) The business that may be dealt with at the accounts meeting includes the resolution.

This is so notwithstanding any default in complying with subsection (1) or (2).

(4) The existing directors must ensure that the resolution is put to the vote of the meeting.

(5) No entitlement of a person to remuneration is made conditional on the resolution being passed by reason only of the provision made by this section.

(6) In this section—

"the accounts meeting" means the general meeting of the company before which the company's annual accounts for the financial year are to be laid; and

"existing director" means a person who is a director of the company immediately before that meeting.

NOTES

The words in square brackets in the section heading, and sub-s (1A), were inserted, and the words in the first pair of square brackets in subs (1) were substituted, by the Companies (Directors' Remuneration Policy and Directors' Remuneration Report) Regulations 2019, SI 2019/970, regs 3, 19, as from 10 June 2019 (for transitional provisions, etc, see reg 2 of the 2019 Regulations at **[4.680]**).

The words in the second pair of square brackets in sub-s (1) were inserted by the Enterprise and Regulatory Reform Act 2013, s 79(3), as from 1 October 2013.

[1.502]

[439A Quoted companies [and traded companies]: members' approval of directors' remuneration policy

(1) A quoted company [or unquoted traded company] must give notice of the intention to move, as an ordinary resolution, a resolution approving the relevant directors' remuneration policy—

(a) at the accounts meeting held in the first financial year which begins on or after the day on which the company becomes a quoted company [or (as the case may be) an unquoted traded company], and

(b) at an accounts or other general meeting held no later than the end of the period of three financial years beginning with the first financial year after the last accounts or other general meeting in relation to which notice is given under this subsection.

(2) A quoted company [or unquoted traded company] must give notice of the intention to move at an accounts meeting, as an ordinary resolution, a resolution approving the relevant directors' remuneration policy if—

(a) a resolution required to be put to the vote under section 439 was not passed at the last accounts meeting of the company, and

(b) no notice under this section was given in relation to that meeting or any other general meeting held before the next accounts meeting.

[(2A) A quoted company or unquoted traded company must give notice of the intention to move at an accounts or other general meeting, as an ordinary resolution, a resolution approving the relevant directors' remuneration policy if—

(a) a resolution required to be put to the vote under subsection (1) or (2) or this subsection was not passed at the last accounts or other general meeting of the company, and

(b) no notice under this section was given in relation to any other general meeting held before the next accounts meeting.]

(3) Subsection (2) does not apply in relation to a quoted company [or unquoted traded company] before the first meeting in relation to which it gives notice under subsection (1).

(4) A notice given under subsection (2) [or (2A)] is to be treated as given under subsection (1) for the purpose of determining the period within which the next notice under subsection (1) must be given.

(5) Notice of the intention to move a resolution to which this section applies must be given, prior to the meeting in question, to the members of the company entitled to be sent notice of the meeting.

(6) Subsections (2) to (4) of section 439 apply for the purposes of a resolution to which this section applies as they apply for the purposes of a resolution to which section 439 applies, with the modification that, for the purposes of a resolution relating to a general meeting other than an accounts meeting, subsection (3) applies as if for "accounts meeting" there were substituted "general meeting".

(7) For the purposes of this section, the relevant directors' remuneration policy is—

(a) in a case where notice is given in relation to an accounts meeting, the remuneration policy contained in the directors' remuneration report in respect of which a resolution under section 439 is required to be put to the vote at that accounts meeting;

(b) in a case where notice is given in relation to a general meeting other than an accounts meeting—

(i) the remuneration policy contained in the directors' remuneration report in respect of which such a resolution was required to be put to the vote at the last accounts meeting to be held before that other general meeting, or

(ii) where that policy has been revised in accordance with section 422A, the policy as so revised.

(8) In this section—

(a) "accounts meeting" means a general meeting of the company before which the company's annual accounts for a financial year are to be laid;

(b) "directors' remuneration policy" means the policy of the company with respect to the matters mentioned in section 421(2A);

[(c) "unquoted traded company" means a traded company (as defined by section 360C) that is not a quoted company.]]

NOTES

Inserted by the Enterprise and Regulatory Reform Act 2013, s 79(4), as from 1 October 2013 (subject to transitional provisions in s 82 of that Act in relation to a company that was a quoted company immediately before that date).

All words in square brackets in this section were inserted by the Companies (Directors' Remuneration Policy and Directors' Remuneration Report) Regulations 2019, SI 2019/970, regs 3, 20, as from 10 June 2019 (for transitional provisions, etc, see reg 2 of the 2019 Regulations at **[4.680]**).

[1.503]

440 Quoted companies [and traded companies]: offences in connection with procedure for approval

(1) In the event of default in complying with section 439(1) [or 439A(1)[, (2) or (2A)]] (notice to be given of resolution for approval of directors' remuneration report [or policy]), an offence is committed by every officer of the company who is in default.

(2) If the resolution is not put to the vote of [the meeting to which it relates], an offence is committed by each existing director.

(3) It is a defence for a person charged with an offence under subsection (2) to prove that he took all reasonable steps for securing that the resolution was put to the vote of the meeting.

(4) A person guilty of an offence under this section is liable on summary conviction to a fine not exceeding level 3 on the standard scale.

(5) In this section—

. . .

"existing director" means a person who is a director of the company immediately before that meeting.

NOTES

The words in square brackets in the section heading were inserted, and the words ", (2) or (2A)" in square brackets in sub-s (1) were substituted, by the Companies (Directors' Remuneration Policy and Directors' Remuneration Report) Regulations 2019, SI 2019/970, regs 3, 21, as from 10 June 2019 (for transitional provisions, etc, see reg 2 of the 2019 Regulations at **[4.680]**).

The words in the first (outer) and third pairs of square brackets in sub-s (1) were inserted, the words in square brackets in sub-s (2) were substituted, and in sub-s (5) the definition "the accounts meeting" (omitted) was repealed, by the Enterprise and Regulatory Reform Act 2013, s 81(1), (5), (10), as from 1 October 2013.

CHAPTER 10 FILING OF ACCOUNTS AND REPORTS

Duty to file accounts and reports

[1.504]

441 Duty to file accounts and reports with the registrar

(1) The directors of a company must deliver to the registrar for each financial year the accounts and reports required by—

section 444 (filing obligations of companies subject to small companies regime),
[section 444A (filing obligations of companies entitled to small companies exemption in relation to directors' report),]
section 445 (filing obligations of medium-sized companies),
section 446 (filing obligations of unquoted companies), or
section 447 (filing obligations of quoted companies).

[(2) This is subject to—

section 448 (unlimited companies exempt from filing obligations), and
section 448A (dormant subsidiaries exempt from filing obligations).]

NOTES

Sub-s (1): words in square brackets inserted by the Companies Act 2006 (Amendment) (Accounts and Reports) Regulations 2008, SI 2008/393, reg 6(6), as from 6 April 2008, in relation to financial years beginning on or after that date.

Sub-s (2): substituted by the Companies and Limited Liability Partnerships (Accounts and Audit Exemptions and Change of Accounting Framework) Regulations 2012, SI 2012/2301, regs 2, 10, as from 1 October 2012 (in relation to accounts for financial years ending on or after that date).

[1.505]

442 Period allowed for filing accounts

(1) This section specifies the period allowed for the directors of a company to comply with their obligation under section 441 to deliver accounts and reports for a financial year to the registrar.

This is referred to in the Companies Acts as the "period for filing" those accounts and reports.

(2) The period is—

(a) for a private company, nine months after the end of the relevant accounting reference period, and
(b) for a public company, six months after the end of that period.

This is subject to the following provisions of this section.

(3) If the relevant accounting reference period is the company's first and is a period of more than twelve months, the period is—

(a) nine months or six months, as the case may be, from the first anniversary of the incorporation of the company, or
(b) three months after the end of the accounting reference period,

whichever last expires.

(4) If the relevant accounting reference period is treated as shortened by virtue of a notice given by the company under section 392 (alteration of accounting reference date), the period is—

(a) that applicable in accordance with the above provisions, or
(b) three months from the date of the notice under that section,

whichever last expires.

(5) [Subject to subsection (5A),] if for any special reason the Secretary of State thinks fit he may, on an application made before the expiry of the period otherwise allowed, by notice in writing to a company extend that period by such further period as may be specified in the notice.

[(5A) Any such extension must not have the effect of extending the period for filing to more than twelve months after the end of the relevant accounting reference period.]

(6) Whether the period allowed is that for a private company or a public company is determined by reference to the company's status immediately before the end of the relevant accounting reference period.

(7) In this section "the relevant accounting reference period" means the accounting reference period by reference to which the financial year for the accounts in question was determined.

NOTES

Words in square brackets in sub-s (5) inserted, and sub-s (5A) inserted, by the Companies, Partnerships and Groups (Accounts and Reports) Regulations 2015, SI 2015/980, reg 8(1), (2), in relation to (a) financial years beginning on or after 1 January 2016, and (b) a financial year of a company beginning on or after 1 January 2015, but before 1 January 2016, if the directors of the company so decide (subject to transitional provisions, etc, in regs 2, 3 of the 2015 Regulations as noted to s 380 at **[1.430]**).

Temporary modification: the Companies etc (Filing Requirements) (Temporary Modifications) Regulations 2020, SI 2020/645, reg 11 provided for the following temporary modifications of this section. By virtue of the Corporate Insolvency and Governance Act 2020, s 39(8), the modifications applied from 27 June 2020 to the end of the day on 5 April 2021 (subject to the saving provision in s 39(9) which provides that the expiry of s 39 on 5 April 2021 does not affect the continued operation of any Regulations made under that section for the purpose of determining the length of any period that begins before the expiry):

Section 442 (period allowed for filing accounts) is to have effect as if—
- (a) in subsection (2)—
  - (i) in paragraph (a) for the reference to "nine months" there were substituted a reference to "twelve months";
  - (i) in paragraph (b) for the reference to "six months" there were substituted a reference to "nine months";
- (b) in subsection (3), in paragraph (a), for the reference to "nine months or six months" there were substituted a reference to "twelve months or nine months".

See also the Corporate Insolvency and Governance Act 2020, s 38 at **[9.550]** (temporary extension of period for public company to file accounts). It provides that where the period allowed for the directors of a public company to comply with their obligation under s 441 to deliver accounts and reports for a financial year to the registrar would end (a) after 25 March 2020, and (b) before the relevant day; the period allowed for the directors to comply with that obligation is to be taken to be a period that ends with the relevant day. For these purposes, the relevant day is whichever is the earlier of (a) 30 September 2020, and (b) the last day of the period of 12 months immediately following the end of the relevant accounting reference period.

[1.506]

443 Calculation of period allowed

(1) This section applies for the purposes of calculating the period for filing a company's accounts and reports which is expressed as a specified number of months from a specified date or after the end of a specified previous period.

(2) Subject to the following provisions, the period ends with the date in the appropriate month corresponding to the specified date or the last day of the specified previous period.

(3) If the specified date, or the last day of the specified previous period, is the last day of a month, the period ends with the last day of the appropriate month (whether or not that is the corresponding date).

(4) If—
- (a) the specified date, or the last day of the specified previous period, is not the last day of a month but is the 29th or 30th, and
- (b) the appropriate month is February,

the period ends with the last day of February.

(5) "The appropriate month" means the month that is the specified number of months after the month in which the specified date, or the end of the specified previous period, falls.

Filing obligations of different descriptions of company

[1.507]

444 Filing obligations of companies subject to small companies regime

(1) The directors of a company subject to the small companies regime—
- (a) must deliver to the registrar for each financial year a copy of [the balance sheet] drawn up as at the last day of that year, and
- (b) may also deliver to the registrar—
  - (i) a copy of the company's profit and loss account for that year, and
  - (ii) a copy of the directors' report for that year.

(2) [Where the directors deliver to the registrar a copy of the company's profit and loss account under subsection (1)(b)(i),] the directors must also deliver to the registrar a copy of the auditor's report on [the accounts (and any directors' report) that it delivers].

This does not apply if the company is exempt from audit and the directors have taken advantage of that exemption.

[(2A) Where the balance sheet or profit and loss account is abridged pursuant to paragraph 1A of Schedule 1 to the Small Companies and Groups (Accounts and Directors' Report) Regulations (SI 2008/409), the directors must also deliver to the registrar a statement by the company that all the members of the company have consented to the abridgement.]

[(3) . . . the copies of accounts and reports delivered to the registrar must be copies of the company's annual accounts and reports.]

[(3A), (3B) . . .]

(4) . . .

(5) Where the directors of a company subject to the small companies regime . . . —
- (a) do not deliver to the registrar a copy of the company's profit and loss account, or
- (b) do not deliver to the registrar a copy of the directors' report,

the copy of the balance sheet delivered to the registrar must contain in a prominent position a statement that the company's annual accounts and reports have been delivered in accordance with the provisions applicable to companies subject to the small companies regime.

[(5A) Subject to subsection (5C), where the directors of a company subject to the small companies regime do not deliver to the registrar a copy of the company's profit and loss account—
- (a) the copy of the balance sheet delivered to the registrar must disclose that fact, and
- (b) unless the company is exempt from audit and the directors have taken advantage of that exemption, the notes to the balance sheet delivered must satisfy the requirements in subsection (5B).

(5B) Those requirements are that the notes to the balance sheet must—

(a) state whether the auditor's report was qualified or unqualified,

(b) where that report was qualified, disclose the basis of the qualification (reproducing any statement under section 498(2)(a) or (b) or section 498(3), if applicable),

(c) where that report was unqualified, include a reference to any matters to which the auditor drew attention by way of emphasis, and

(d) state—

(i) the name of the auditor and (where the auditor is a firm) the name of the person who signed the auditor's report as senior statutory auditor, or

(ii) if the conditions in section 506 (circumstances in which names may be omitted) are met, that a resolution has been passed and notified to the Secretary of State in accordance with that section.

(5C) Subsection (5A) does not apply in relation to a company if—

(a) the company qualifies as a micro-entity (see sections 384A and 384B) in relation to a financial year, and

(b) the company's accounts are prepared for that year in accordance with any of the micro-entity provisions.]

(6) The copies of the balance sheet and any directors' report delivered to the registrar under this section must state the name of the person who signed it on behalf of the board.

(7) The copy of the auditor's report delivered to the registrar under this section must—

(a) state the name of the auditor and (where the auditor is a firm) the name of the person who signed it as senior statutory auditor, or

(b) if the conditions in section 506 (circumstances in which names may be omitted) are met, state that a resolution has been passed and notified to the Secretary of State in accordance with that section.

[(8) If more than one person is appointed as auditor, the references in subsections (5B)(d)(i) and (7)(a) to the name of the auditor are to be read as references to the names of all the auditors.]

NOTES

Sub-s (1): words in square brackets substituted by the Companies, Partnerships and Groups (Accounts and Reports) Regulations 2015, SI 2015/980, reg 8(1), (3)(a), in relation to (a) financial years beginning on or after 1 January 2016, and (b) a financial year of a company beginning on or after 1 January 2015, but before 1 January 2016, if the directors of the company so decide (subject to transitional provisions, etc, in regs 2, 3 of the 2015 Regulations as noted to s 380 at **[1.430]**).

Sub-s (2): words in first pair of square brackets inserted by SI 2015/980, reg 8(1), (3)(b), as from the same dates and for the same purposes as specified in the first note relating to the 2015 Regulations above. Words in second pair of square brackets substituted by the Companies Act 2006 (Amendment) (Accounts and Reports) Regulations 2008, SI 2008/393, reg 12, as from 6 April 2008, in relation to financial years beginning on or after that date.

Sub-s (2A): inserted by SI 2015/980, reg 8(1), (3)(c), as from the same dates and for the same purposes as specified in the first note relating to the 2015 Regulations above.

Sub-s (3): substituted by the Small Companies (Micro-Entities' Accounts) Regulations 2013, SI 2013/3008, reg 6(a), in relation to (a) financial years ending on or after 30 September 2013, and (b) companies which deliver the accounts required by s 444 of this Act to the registrar on or after 1 December 2013 (as to application of this amendment, see the note at **[1.432]**). Words omitted repealed by SI 2015/980, reg 8(1), (3)(d), as from the same dates and for the same purposes as specified in the first note relating to the 2015 Regulations above.

Sub-ss (3A), (3B): originally inserted by SI 2013/3008, reg 6(b), in relation to (a) financial years ending on or after 30 September 2013, and (b) companies which deliver the accounts required by s 444 of this Act to the registrar on or after 1 December 2013 (as to application of this amendment, see the note at **[1.432]**). Subsequently repealed by SI 2015/980, reg 8(1), (3)(e), as from the same dates and for the same purposes as specified in the first note relating to the 2015 Regulations above.

Sub-s (4): repealed by SI 2015/980, reg 8(1), (3)(e), as from the same dates and for the same purposes as specified in the first note relating to the 2015 Regulations above.

Sub-s (5): words omitted repealed by SI 2015/980, reg 8(1), (3)(f), as from the same dates and for the same purposes as specified in the first note relating to the 2015 Regulations above.

Sub-ss (5A)–(5C): inserted by SI 2015/980, reg 8(1), (3)(g), as from the same dates and for the same purposes as specified in the first note relating to the 2015 Regulations above.

Sub-s (8): added by the Statutory Auditors Regulations 2017, SI 2017/1164, reg 3, Sch 1, paras 7, 8, in relation to financial years of companies beginning on or after 17 June 2016 (see**[4.671]** et seq).

Regulations: the Small Companies and Groups (Accounts and Directors' Report) Regulations 2008, SI 2008/409 at **[4.41]**. For a summary of all statutory instruments made under this Act, see Appendix 4 at **[A4]**.

[1.508]

[444A Filing obligations of companies entitled to small companies exemption in relation to directors' report

(1) The directors of a company that is entitled to small companies exemption in relation to the directors' report for a financial year—

(a) must deliver to the registrar a copy of the company's annual accounts for that year, and

(b) may also deliver to the registrar a copy of the directors' report.

(2) The directors must also deliver to the registrar a copy of the auditor's report on the accounts (and any directors' report) that it delivers.

This does not apply if the company is exempt from audit and the directors have taken advantage of that exception.

(3) The copies of the balance sheet and directors' report delivered to the registrar under this section must state the name of the person who signed it on behalf of the board.

[(4) The copy of the auditor's report delivered to the registrar under this section must—

(a) state the name of the auditor and (where the auditor is a firm) the name of the person who signed it as senior statutory auditor, or

(b) if the conditions in section 506 (circumstances in which names may be omitted) are met, state that a resolution has been passed and notified to the Secretary of State in accordance with that section.]

[(4A) If more than one person is appointed as auditor, the reference in subsection (4)(a) to the name of the auditor is to be read as a reference to the names of all the auditors.]

(5) This section does not apply to companies within section 444 (filing obligations of companies subject to the small companies regime).]

NOTES

Inserted by the Companies Act 2006 (Amendment) (Accounts and Reports) Regulations 2008, SI 2008/393, reg 6(7), as from 6 April 2008, in relation to financial years beginning on or after that date.

Sub-s (4): substituted by the Companies Act 2006 (Accounts, Reports and Audit) Regulations 2009, SI 2009/1581, reg 10, as from 1 October 2009.

Sub-s (4A): inserted by the Statutory Auditors Regulations 2017, SI 2017/1164, reg 3, Sch 1, paras 7, 9, in relation to financial years of companies beginning on or after 17 June 2016 (see **[4.671]** et seq).

[1.509]

445 Filing obligations of medium-sized companies

(1) The directors of a company that qualifies as a medium-sized company in relation to a financial year (see sections 465 to 467) must deliver to the registrar a copy of—

(a) the company's annual accounts, . . .

[(aa) the strategic report, and]

(b) the directors' report.

(2) They must also deliver to the registrar a copy of the auditor's report on those accounts (and on [the strategic report and] the directors' report).

This does not apply if the company is exempt from audit and the directors have taken advantage of that exemption.

(3), (4) . . .

(5) The copies of the balance sheet[, strategic report] and directors' report delivered to the registrar under this section must state the name of the person who signed it on behalf of the board.

(6) The copy of the auditor's report delivered to the registrar under this section must—

(a) state the name of the auditor and (where the auditor is a firm) the name of the person who signed it as senior statutory auditor, or

(b) if the conditions in section 506 (circumstances in which names may be omitted) are met, state that a resolution has been passed and notified to the Secretary of State in accordance with that section.

[(6A) If more than one person is appointed as auditor, the reference in subsection (6)(a) to the name of the auditor is to be read as a reference to the names of all the auditors.]

[(7) This section does not apply to companies within—

(a) section 444 (filing obligations of companies subject to the small companies regime), or

(b) section 444A (filing obligations of companies entitled to small companies exemption in relation to directors' report).]

NOTES

The word omitted from para (a) of sub-s (1) was repealed, para (aa) of that subsection was inserted, and the words in square brackets in sub-ss (2), (5), were inserted, by the Companies Act 2006 (Strategic Report and Directors' Report) Regulations 2013, SI 2013/1970, reg 14, Schedule, paras 1, 9, in respect of financial years ending on or after 30 September 2013.

Sub-ss (3), (4) were repealed by the Companies, Partnerships and Groups (Accounts and Reports) Regulations 2015, SI 2015/980, reg 8(1), (4), (5), in relation to (a) financial years beginning on or after 1 January 2016, and (b) a financial year of a company beginning on or after 1 January 2015, but before 1 January 2016, if the directors of the company so decide (subject to transitional provisions, etc, in regs 2, 3 of the 2015 Regulations as noted to s 380 at **[1.430]**).

Sub-s (6A): inserted by the Statutory Auditors Regulations 2017, SI 2017/1164, reg 3, Sch 1, paras 7, 10, in relation to financial years of companies beginning on or after 17 June 2016 (see **[4.671]** et seq).

Sub-s (7) was substituted by the Companies Act 2006 (Amendment) (Accounts and Reports) Regulations 2008, SI 2008/393, reg 6(8), as from 6 April 2008, in relation to financial years beginning on or after that date.

Regulations: the Large and Medium-sized Companies and Groups (Accounts and Reports) Regulations 2008, SI 2008/410 at **[4.60]**. For a summary of all statutory instruments made under this Act, see Appendix 4 at **[A4]**.

[1.510]

446 Filing obligations of unquoted companies

(1) The directors of an unquoted company must deliver to the registrar for each financial year of the company a copy of—

(a) the company's annual accounts, . . .

[(aa) the strategic report,]

(b) the directors' report[, . . .

[(ba) any directors' remuneration report, and]

(c) any separate corporate governance statement].

(2) The directors must also deliver to the registrar a copy of the auditor's report on those accounts (and [the strategic report (where this is covered by the auditor's report),] the directors' report[, any directors' remuneration report] [and any separate corporate governance statement]).

This does not apply if the company is exempt from audit and the directors have taken advantage of that exemption.

(3) The copies of the balance sheet[, strategic report][, directors' report[, any directors' remuneration report] and any separate corporate governance statement] delivered to the registrar under this section must state the name of the person who signed it on behalf of the board.

(4) The copy of the auditor's report delivered to the registrar under this section must—

(a) state the name of the auditor and (where the auditor is a firm) the name of the person who signed it as senior statutory auditor, or

(b) if the conditions in section 506 (circumstances in which names may be omitted) are met, state that a resolution has been passed and notified to the Secretary of State in accordance with that section.

[(4A) If more than one person is appointed as auditor, the reference in subsection (4)(a) to the name of the auditor is to be read as a reference to the names of all the auditors.]

(5) This section does not apply to companies within—

(a) section 444 (filing obligations of companies subject to the small companies regime), . . .

[(aa) section 444A (filing obligations of companies entitled to small companies exemption in relation to directors' report), or]

(b) section 445 (filing obligations of medium-sized companies).

NOTES

Sub-s (1): the word omitted from para (a) was repealed, and para (c) (and the word preceding it) was added by the Companies Act 2006 (Accounts, Reports and Audit) Regulations 2009, SI 2009/1581, reg 3(1), (2), in relation to financial years beginning on or after 29 June 2008 which have not ended before 27 June 2009. Para was (aa) inserted by the Companies Act 2006 (Strategic Report and Directors' Report) Regulations 2013, SI 2013/1970, reg 14, Schedule, paras 1, 10(a), in respect of financial years ending on or after 30 September 2013. The word omitted from para (b) was repealed, and para (ba) was inserted, by the Companies (Directors' Remuneration Policy and Directors' Remuneration Report) Regulations 2019, SI 2019/970, regs 3, 22(a), as from 10 June 2019 (for transitional provisions, etc, see reg 2 of the 2019 Regulations at **[4.680]**).

Sub-s (2): words in first pair of square brackets inserted by SI 2013/1970, reg 14, Schedule, paras 1, 10(b), in respect of financial years ending on or after 30 September 2013. Words in second pair of square brackets inserted by SI 2019/970, regs 3, 22(b), as from 10 June 2019 (for transitional provisions, etc, see reg 2 of the 2019 Regulations at **[4.680]**). Words in third pair of square brackets inserted by SI 2009/1581, reg 3(1), (3), in relation to financial years beginning on or after 29 June 2008 which have not ended before 27 June 2009.

Sub-s (3): words in first pair of square brackets inserted by SI 2013/1970, reg 14, Schedule, paras 1, 10(c), in respect of financial years ending on or after 30 September 2013. Words in second (outer) pair of square brackets substituted by SI 2009/1581, reg 3(1), (6), in relation to financial years beginning on or after 29 June 2008 which have not ended before 27 June 2009. Words in third (inner) pair of square brackets inserted by SI 2019/970, regs 3, 22(c), as from 10 June 2019 (for transitional provisions, etc, see reg 2 of the 2019 Regulations at **[4.680]**).

Sub-s (4A): inserted by the Statutory Auditors Regulations 2017, SI 2017/1164, reg 3, Sch 1, paras 7, 11, in relation to financial years of companies beginning on or after 17 June 2016 (see**[4.671]** et seq).

Sub-s (5): word omitted from para (a) repealed, and para (aa) inserted, by the Companies Act 2006 (Amendment) (Accounts and Reports) Regulations 2008, SI 2008/393, reg 6(9), as from 6 April 2008, in relation to financial years beginning on or after that date.

[1.511]

447 Filing obligations of quoted companies

(1) The directors of a quoted company must deliver to the registrar for each financial year of the company a copy of—

(a) the company's annual accounts,

(b) the directors' remuneration report, . . .

[(ba) the strategic report,]

(c) the directors' report[, and

(d) any separate corporate governance statement].

(2) They must also deliver a copy of the auditor's report on those accounts (and on the directors' remuneration report [the strategic report (where this is covered by the auditor's report),] [the directors' report and any separate corporate governance statement]).

(3) The copies of the balance sheet, the directors' remuneration report[, the strategic report][, the directors' report and any separate corporate governance statement] delivered to the registrar under this section must state the name of the person who signed it on behalf of the board.

(4) The copy of the auditor's report delivered to the registrar under this section must—

(a) state the name of the auditor and (where the auditor is a firm) the name of the person who signed it as senior statutory auditor, or

(b) if the conditions in section 506 (circumstances in which names may be omitted) are met, state that a resolution has been passed and notified to the Secretary of State in accordance with that section.

[(5) If more than one person is appointed as auditor, the reference in subsection (4)(a) to the name of the auditor is to be read as a reference to the names of all the auditors.]

NOTES

Sub-s (1): the word omitted from para (b) was repealed, and para (d) (and the word preceding it) was added by the Companies Act 2006 (Accounts, Reports and Audit) Regulations 2009, SI 2009/1581, reg 4(1), (2), in relation to financial years beginning on or after 29 June 2008 which have not ended before 27 June 2009. Para (ba) was inserted by the Companies Act 2006 (Strategic Report and Directors' Report) Regulations 2013, SI 2013/1970, reg 14, Schedule, paras 1, 11(a), in respect of financial years ending on or after 30 September 2013.

Sub-ss (2), (3): words in first pair of square brackets inserted by SI 2013/1970, reg 14, Schedule, paras 1, 11(b), (c), in respect of financial years ending on or after 30 September 2013. Words in second pair of square brackets substituted by SI 2009/1581, reg 4(1), (3), (6), in relation to financial years beginning on or after 29 June 2008 which have not ended before 27 June 2009.

Sub-s (5): added by the Statutory Auditors Regulations 2017, SI 2017/1164, reg 3, Sch 1, paras 7, 12, in relation to financial years of companies beginning on or after 17 June 2016 (see**[4.671]** et seq).

[1.512]

448 Unlimited companies exempt from obligation to file accounts

(1) The directors of an unlimited company are not required to deliver accounts and reports to the registrar in respect of a financial year if the following conditions are met.

(2) The conditions are that at no time during the relevant accounting reference period—

(a) has the company been, to its knowledge, a subsidiary undertaking of an undertaking which was then limited, or

(b) have there been, to its knowledge, exercisable by or on behalf of two or more undertakings which were then limited, rights which if exercisable by one of them would have made the company a subsidiary undertaking of it, or

(c) has the company been a parent company of an undertaking which was then limited.

The references above to an undertaking being limited at a particular time are to an undertaking (under whatever law established) the liability of whose members is at that time limited.

(3) The exemption conferred by this section does not apply if—

(a) the company is a banking or insurance company or the parent company of a banking or insurance group, or

[(b) each of the members of the company is—

(i) a limited company,

(ii) another unlimited company each of whose members is a limited company, . . .

(iii) a Scottish partnership [which is not a limited partnership,] each of whose members is a limited company][, or

(iv) a Scottish partnership which is a limited partnership, each of whose general partners is a limited company.]

[The references in paragraph (b) to a limited company, another unlimited company[, a Scottish partnership which is not a limited partnership or a Scottish partnership which is a limited partnership] include a comparable undertaking incorporated in or formed under the law of a country or territory outside the United Kingdom.]

(4) Where a company is exempt by virtue of this section from the obligation to deliver accounts—

(a) section 434(3) (requirements in connection with publication of statutory accounts: meaning of "statutory accounts") has effect with the substitution for the words "as required to be delivered to the registrar under section 441" of the words "as prepared in accordance with this Part and approved by the board of directors"; and

(b) section 435(1)(b) (requirements in connection with publication of non-statutory accounts: statement whether statutory accounts delivered) has effect with the substitution for the words from "whether statutory accounts" to "have been delivered to the registrar" of the words "that the company is exempt from the requirement to deliver statutory accounts".

[(5) In this section—

"general partner" means—

(a) in relation to a Scottish partnership which is a limited partnership, a person who is a general partner within the meaning of the Limited Partnerships Act 1907; and

(b) in relation to an undertaking incorporated in or formed under the law of any country or territory outside the United Kingdom and which is comparable to a Scottish partnership which is a limited partnership, a person comparable to such a general partner;

"limited partnership" means a partnership registered under the Limited Partnerships Act 1907; and

the "relevant accounting reference period", in relation to a financial year, means the accounting reference period by reference to which that financial year was determined.]

NOTES

Sub-s (3) is amended as follows:

Para (b) was substituted, and the words in square brackets beginning with the words "The references in paragraph (b)" were inserted, by the Companies Act 2006 (Amendment) (Accounts and Reports) Regulations 2008, SI 2008/393, reg 13, as from 6 April 2008, in relation to financial years beginning on or after that date.

The word omitted from sub-para (b)(ii) was repealed, the words in square brackets in sub-para (b)(iii) were inserted, sub-para (b)(iv) (and the preceding word) was inserted, and the words in square brackets beginning with the words ", a Scottish partnership" were substituted, by the Companies and Partnerships (Accounts and Audit) Regulations 2013, SI 2013/2005, reg 2(1), (3)–(5), in relation to a financial year of a company beginning on or after 1 October 2013.

Sub-s (5) was substituted by SI 2013/2005, reg 2(1), (3), (6), in relation to a financial year of a company beginning on or after 1 October 2013.

[1.513]

[448A Dormant subsidiaries exempt from obligation to file accounts

(1) The directors of a company are not required to deliver a copy of the company's individual accounts to the registrar in respect of a financial year if—

(a) the company is a subsidiary undertaking,

(b) it has been dormant throughout the whole of that year, and

(c) its parent undertaking is established under the law of [any part of the United Kingdom].

(2) Exemption is conditional upon compliance with all of the following conditions—

(a) all members of the company must agree to the exemption in respect of the financial year in question,

(b) the parent undertaking must give a guarantee under section 448C in respect of that year,

(c) the company must be included in the consolidated accounts drawn up for that year or to an earlier date in that year by the parent undertaking in accordance with—

[(i) if the undertaking is a company, the requirements of this Part of this Act, or, if the undertaking is not a company, the legal requirements which apply to the drawing up of consolidated accounts for that undertaking, or]

(ii) [UK-adopted international accounting standards],

(d) the parent undertaking must disclose in the notes to the consolidated accounts that the directors of the company are exempt from the requirement to deliver a copy of the company's individual accounts to the registrar by virtue of this section, and

(e) the directors of the company must deliver to the registrar within the period for filing the company's accounts and reports for that year—

(i) a written notice of the agreement referred to in subsection (2)(a),

(ii) the statement referred to in section 448C(1),

(iii) a copy of the consolidated accounts referred to in subsection (2)(c),

(iv) a copy of the auditor's report on those accounts, and

(v) a copy of the consolidated annual report drawn up by the parent undertaking.]

NOTES

Inserted, together with ss 448B, 448C, by the Companies and Limited Liability Partnerships (Accounts and Audit Exemptions and Change of Accounting Framework) Regulations 2012, SI 2012/2301, regs 2, 11, as from 1 October 2012 (in relation to accounts for financial years ending on or after that date).

Sub-s (1): words in square brackets substituted by the Accounts and Reports (Amendment) (EU Exit) Regulations 2019, SI 2019/145, reg 5, Sch 2, Pt 1, paras 1, 13(a), in relation to financial years beginning on or after IP completion day (as defined in the European Union (Withdrawal Agreement) Act 2020, s 39) (for transitional provisions see reg 7 of the 2019 Regulations at **[12.79]**).

Sub-s (2) is amended as follows:

Sub-para (c)(i) substituted by SI 2019/145, reg 5, Sch 2, Pt 1, paras 1, 13(b), in relation to financial years beginning on or after IP completion day (as defined in the European Union (Withdrawal Agreement) Act 2020, s 39) (for transitional provisions see reg 7 of the 2019 Regulations at **[12.79]**).

Words in square brackets in sub-para (c)(ii) substituted by the International Accounting Standards and European Public Limited-Liability Company (Amendment etc) (EU Exit) Regulations 2019, SI 2019/685, reg 19, Sch 1, Pt 1, paras 1, 13, in relation to accounts for financial years beginning on or after IP completion day (as defined in the European Union (Withdrawal Agreement) Act 2020, s 39) (note also that in relation to accounts for financial years which begin before but end on or after IP completion day, the enactments amended by Parts 1–3 of Sch 1 to the 2019 Regulations have effect as if the UK were a member State until the end of the financial year in question (for transitional provisions see reg 1 of, and Sch 1, Pt 4 to, the 2019 Regulations at **[12.130]** and **[12.151]** respectively)).

[1.514]

[448B Companies excluded from the dormant subsidiaries exemption

The directors of a company are not entitled to the exemption conferred by section 448A (dormant subsidiaries) if the company was at any time within the financial year in question—

[(a) a traded company,]

(b) a company that—

(i) is an authorised insurance company, a banking company, an e-Money issuer, a MiFID investment firm or a UCITS management company, or

(ii) carries on insurance market activity, or

(c) a special register body as defined in section 117(1) of the Trade Union and Labour Relations (Consolidation) Act 1992 (c 52) or an employers' association as defined in section 122 of that Act or Article 4 of the Industrial Relations (Northern Ireland) Order 1992 (SI 1992/807) (NI 5).]

NOTES

Inserted as noted to s 448A at **[1.513]**.

Para (a) substituted by the Companies, Partnerships and Groups (Accounts and Reports) Regulations 2015, SI 2015/980, reg 8(1), (7), in relation to (a) financial years beginning on or after 1 January 2016, and (b) a financial year of a company beginning on or after 1 January 2015, but before 1 January 2016, if the directors of the company so decide (subject to transitional provisions, etc, in regs 2, 3 of the 2015 Regulations as noted to s 380 at **[1.430]**).

[1.515]

[448C Dormant subsidiaries filing exemption: parent undertaking declaration of guarantee

(1) A guarantee is given by a parent undertaking under this section when the directors of the subsidiary company deliver to the registrar a statement by the parent undertaking that it guarantees the subsidiary company under this section.

(2) The statement under subsection (1) must be authenticated by the parent undertaking and must specify—

(a) the name of the parent undertaking,

[(b) the registered number (if any) of the parent undertaking,]

(c) . . .

(d) the name and registered number of the subsidiary company in respect of which the guarantee is being given,

(e) the date of the statement, and

(f) the financial year to which the guarantee relates.

(3) A guarantee given under this section has the effect that—

(a) the parent undertaking guarantees all outstanding liabilities to which the subsidiary company is subject at the end of the financial year to which the guarantee relates, until they are satisfied in full, and

(b) the guarantee is enforceable against the parent undertaking by any person to whom the subsidiary company is liable in respect of those liabilities.]

NOTES

Inserted as noted to s 448A at **[1.513]**.

Sub-s (2): para (b) was substituted, and para (c) was repealed, by the Accounts and Reports (Amendment) (EU Exit) Regulations 2019, SI 2019/145, reg 5, Sch 2, Pt 1, paras 1, 14, in relation to financial years beginning on or after IP completion day (as defined in the European Union (Withdrawal Agreement) Act 2020, s 39) (for transitional provisions see reg 7 of the 2019 Regulations at **[12.79]**). Note that SI 2019/145, Sch 2, Pt 1, para 14 was amended by the Statutory Auditors, Third Country Auditors and International Accounting Standards (Amendment) (EU Exit) Regulations 2019, SI 2019/1392, regs 9, 10, with effect from immediately before IP completion day and that the effect of that amendment has been incorporated above.

449, 450 (*Repealed by the Companies, Partnerships and Groups (Accounts and Reports) Regulations 2015, SI 2015/980, reg 8(1), (8), (9), in relation to (a) financial years beginning on or after 1 January 2016, and (b) a financial year of a company beginning on or after 1 January 2015, but before 1 January 2016, if the directors of the company so decide (subject to transitional provisions, etc, in regs 2, 3 of the 2015 Regulations as noted to s 380 at* **[1.430]**).)

Failure to file accounts and reports

[1.516]

451 Default in filing accounts and reports: offences

(1) If the requirements of section 441 (duty to file accounts and reports) are not complied with in relation to a company's accounts and reports for a financial year before the end of the period for filing those accounts and reports, every person who immediately before the end of that period was a director of the company commits an offence.

(2) It is a defence for a person charged with such an offence to prove that he took all reasonable steps for securing that those requirements would be complied with before the end of that period.

(3) It is not a defence to prove that the documents in question were not in fact prepared as required by this Part.

(4) A person guilty of an offence under this section is liable on summary conviction to a fine not exceeding level 5 on the standard scale and, for continued contravention, a daily default fine not exceeding [one-tenth of the greater of £5,000 or level 4 on the standard scale].

NOTES

Sub-s (4): words in square brackets substituted (for the original words "one-tenth of level 5 on the standard scale") by the Legal Aid, Sentencing and Punishment of Offenders Act 2012 (Fines on Summary Conviction) Regulations 2015, SI 2015/664, regs 3, 5, Sch 3, Pt 1, para 9(1), (13), as from 12 March 2015, in relation to England and Wales only (except in relation to (a) fines for offences committed before 12 March 2015, (b) the operation of restrictions on fines that may be imposed on a person aged under 18, or (c) fines that may be imposed on a person convicted by a magistrates' court who is to be sentenced as if convicted on indictment).

[1.517]

452 Default in filing accounts and reports: court order

(1) If—

(a) the requirements of section 441 (duty to file accounts and reports) are not complied with in relation to a company's accounts and reports for a financial year before the end of the period for filing those accounts and reports, and

(b) the directors of the company fail to make good the default within 14 days after the service of a notice on them requiring compliance,

the court may, on the application of any member or creditor of the company or of the registrar, make an order directing the directors (or any of them) to make good the default within such time as may be specified in the order.

(2) The court's order may provide that all costs (in Scotland, expenses) of and incidental to the application are to be borne by the directors.

[1.518]

453 Civil penalty for failure to file accounts and reports

(1) Where the requirements of section 441 are not complied with in relation to a company's accounts and reports for a financial year before the end of the period for filing those accounts and reports, the company is liable to a civil penalty.

This is in addition to any liability of the directors under section 451.

(2) The amount of the penalty shall be determined in accordance with regulations made by the Secretary of State by reference to—

(a) the length of the period between the end of the period for filing the accounts and reports in question and the day on which the requirements are complied with, and

(b) whether the company is a private or public company.

(3) The penalty may be recovered by the registrar and is to be paid into the Consolidated Fund.

(4) It is not a defence in proceedings under this section to prove that the documents in question were not in fact prepared as required by this Part.

(5) Regulations under this section having the effect of increasing the penalty payable in any case are subject to affirmative resolution procedure. Otherwise, the regulations are subject to negative resolution procedure.

NOTES

Regulations: the Companies (Late Filing Penalties) and Limited Liability Partnerships (Filing Periods and Late Filing Penalties) Regulations 2008, SI 2008/497 at **[4.125]**. For a summary of all statutory instruments made under this Act, see Appendix 4 at **[A4]**.

CHAPTER 11 REVISION OF DEFECTIVE ACCOUNTS AND REPORTS

Voluntary revision

[1.519]

454 Voluntary revision of accounts etc

(1) If it appears to the directors of a company that—

(a) the company's annual accounts,

(b) the directors' remuneration report or the directors' report, or

[(c) a strategic report of the company,]

did not comply with the requirements of this Act . . . , they may prepare revised accounts or a revised report or statement.

(2) Where copies of the previous accounts or report have been sent out to members, delivered to the registrar or (in the case of a public company) laid before the company in general meeting, the revisions must be confined to—

(a) the correction of those respects in which the previous accounts or report did not comply with the requirements of this Act . . . , and

(b) the making of any necessary consequential alterations.

(3) The Secretary of State may make provision by regulations as to the application of the provisions of this Act in relation to—

(a) revised annual accounts,

(b) a revised directors' remuneration report or directors' report, or

[(c) a revised strategic report of the company].

(4) The regulations may, in particular—

(a) make different provision according to whether the previous accounts [or report] are replaced or are supplemented by a document indicating the corrections to be made;

(b) make provision with respect to the functions of the company's auditor in relation to the revised accounts [or report];

(c) require the directors to take such steps as may be specified in the regulations where the previous accounts or report have been—

(i) sent out to members and others under section 423,

(ii) laid before the company in general meeting, or

(iii) delivered to the registrar,

or where a [strategic report and supplementary material] containing information derived from the previous accounts or report [have] been sent to members under section 426;

(d) apply the provisions of this Act (including those creating criminal offences) subject to such additions, exceptions and modifications as are specified in the regulations.

(5) Regulations under this section are subject to negative resolution procedure.

NOTES

Sub-s (1): para (c) substituted by the Companies Act 2006 (Strategic Report and Directors' Report) Regulations 2013, SI 2013/1970, reg 14, Schedule, paras 1, 12(a), in respect of financial years ending on or after 30 September 2013. The words omitted were repealed by the International Accounting Standards and European Public Limited-Liability Company (Amendment etc) (EU Exit) Regulations 2019, SI 2019/685, reg 19, Sch 1, Pt 1, paras 1, 14, in relation to accounts for financial years beginning on or after IP completion day (as defined in the European Union (Withdrawal Agreement) Act 2020, s 39) (note also that in relation to accounts for financial years which begin before but end on or after IP completion day, the enactments amended by Parts 1–3 of Sch 1 to the 2019 Regulations have effect as if the UK were a member State until the end of the financial year in question (for transitional provisions see reg 1 of, and Sch 1, Pt 4 to, the 2019 Regulations at **[12.130]** and **[12.151]** respectively)).

Sub-s (2): the words omitted were repealed by SI 2019/685, reg 19, Sch 1, Pt 1, paras 1, 14, in relation to accounts for financial years beginning on or after IP completion day (see also the first note relating to the 2019 Regulations above).

Sub-s (3): para (c) substituted by SI 2013/1970, reg 14, Schedule, paras 1, 12(b), as from 6 August 2013 (in respect of financial years ending on or after 30 September 2013).

Sub-s (4): words in square brackets substituted by SI 2013/1970, reg 14, Schedule, paras 1, 12(c), as from 6 August 2013 (for the purposes only of the exercise of the powers to make regulations), and as from 1 October 2013 (otherwise) in respect of financial years ending on or after 30 September 2013).

Regulations: the Companies (Revision of Defective Accounts and Reports) Regulations 2008, SI 2008/373 at **[4.21]**; the Companies (Revision of Defective Accounts and Reports) (Amendment) (No 2) Regulations 2013, SI 2013/2224; the Statutory Auditors Regulations 2017, SI 2017/1164 at **[4.671]**. For a summary of all statutory instruments made under this Act, see Appendix 4 at **[A4]**.

Secretary of State's notice

[1.520]

455 Secretary of State's notice in respect of accounts or reports

(1) This section applies where—

(a) copies of a company's annual accounts[, strategic report or directors' report] have been sent out under section 423, or

(b) a copy of a company's annual accounts[, strategic report or directors' report] has been delivered to the registrar or (in the case of a public company) laid before the company in general meeting,

and it appears to the Secretary of State that there is, or may be, a question whether the accounts or report comply with the requirements of this Act . . .

(2) The Secretary of State may give notice to the directors of the company indicating the respects in which it appears that such a question arises or may arise.

(3) The notice must specify a period of not less than one month for the directors to give an explanation of the accounts or report or prepare revised accounts or a revised report.

(4) If at the end of the specified period, or such longer period as the Secretary of State may allow, it appears to the Secretary of State that the directors have not—

(a) given a satisfactory explanation of the accounts or report, or

(b) revised the accounts or report so as to comply with the requirements of this Act . . . ,

the Secretary of State may apply to the court.

(5) The provisions of this section apply equally to revised annual accounts[, revised strategic reports and revised directors' reports], in which case they have effect as if the references to revised accounts or reports were references to further revised accounts or reports.

NOTES

Sub-s (1): words in square brackets substituted by the Companies Act 2006 (Strategic Report and Directors' Report) Regulations 2013, SI 2013/1970, reg 14, Schedule, paras 1, 13, in respect of financial years ending on or after 30 September 2013. The words omitted were repealed by the International Accounting Standards and European Public Limited-Liability Company (Amendment etc) (EU Exit) Regulations 2019, SI 2019/685, reg 19, Sch 1, Pt 1, paras 1, 15, in relation to accounts for financial years beginning on or after IP completion day (as defined in the European Union (Withdrawal Agreement) Act 2020, s 39) (note also that in relation to accounts for financial years which begin before but end on or after IP completion day, the enactments amended by Parts 1–3 of Sch 1 to the 2019 Regulations have effect as if the UK were a member State until the end of the financial year in question (for transitional provisions see reg 1 of, and Sch 1, Pt 4 to, the 2019 Regulations at **[12.130]** and **[12.151]** respectively)).

Sub-s (4): the words omitted were repealed by SI 2019/685, reg 19, Sch 1, Pt 1, paras 1, 15, in relation to accounts for financial years beginning on or after IP completion day (see also the first note relating to the 2019 Regulations above).

Sub-s (5): words in square brackets substituted by SI 2013/1970, reg 14, Schedule, paras 1, 13, in respect of financial years ending on or after 30 September 2013.

Application to court

[1.521]

456 Application to court in respect of defective accounts or reports

(1) An application may be made to the court—

(a) by the Secretary of State, after having complied with section 455, or

(b) by a person authorised by the Secretary of State for the purposes of this section,

for a declaration (in Scotland, a declarator) that the annual accounts of a company do not comply, [or a strategic report] or a directors' report does not comply, with the requirements of this Act . . . and for an order requiring the directors of the company to prepare revised accounts or a revised report.

(2) Notice of the application, together with a general statement of the matters at issue in the proceedings, shall be given by the applicant to the registrar for registration.

(3) If the court orders the preparation of revised accounts, it may give directions as to—

(a) the auditing of the accounts,

(b) the revision of any directors' remuneration report, [strategic report and supplementary material or,] directors' report . . . , and

(c) the taking of steps by the directors to bring the making of the order to the notice of persons likely to rely on the previous accounts,

and such other matters as the court thinks fit.

(4) If the court orders the preparation of a revised [strategic report or] directors' report it may give directions as to—

(a) the review of the report by the auditors,

(b) . . .

(c) the taking of steps by the directors to bring the making of the order to the notice of persons likely to rely on the previous report, and

(d) such other matters as the court thinks fit.

(5) If the court finds that the accounts or report did not comply with the requirements of this Act . . . it may order that all or part of—

(a) the costs (in Scotland, expenses) of and incidental to the application, and

(b) any reasonable expenses incurred by the company in connection with or in consequence of the preparation of revised accounts or a revised report,

are to be borne by such of the directors as were party to the approval of the defective accounts or report.

For this purpose every director of the company at the time of the approval of the accounts or report shall be taken to have been a party to the approval unless he shows that he took all reasonable steps to prevent that approval.

(6) Where the court makes an order under subsection (5) it shall have regard to whether the directors party to the approval of the defective accounts or report knew or ought to have known that the accounts or report did not comply with the requirements of this Act . . . , and it may exclude one or more directors from the order or order the payment of different amounts by different directors.

(7) On the conclusion of proceedings on an application under this section, the applicant must send to the registrar for registration a copy of the court order or, as the case may be, give notice to the registrar that the application has failed or been withdrawn.

(8) The provisions of this section apply equally to revised annual accounts[, revised strategic reports and revised directors' reports], in which case they have effect as if the references to revised accounts or reports were references to further revised accounts or reports.

NOTES

The words in square brackets in sub-ss (1), (3), (4) were inserted, the words omitted from sub-ss (3), (4) were repealed, and the words in square brackets in sub-s (8) were substituted, by the Companies Act 2006 (Strategic Report and Directors' Report) Regulations 2013, SI 2013/1970, reg 14, Schedule, paras 1, 14, in respect of financial years ending on or after 30 September 2013.

The words omitted from sub-ss (1), (5) and (6) were repealed by the International Accounting Standards and European Public Limited-Liability Company (Amendment etc) (EU Exit) Regulations 2019, SI 2019/685, reg 19, Sch 1, Pt 1, paras 1, 16, in relation to accounts for financial years beginning on or after IP completion day (as defined in the European Union (Withdrawal Agreement) Act 2020, s 39) (note also that in relation to accounts for financial years which begin before but end on or after IP completion day, the enactments amended by Parts 1–3 of Sch 1 to the 2019 Regulations have effect as if the UK were a member State until the end of the financial year in question (for transitional provisions see reg 1 of, and Sch 1, Pt 4 to, the 2019 Regulations at **[12.130]** and **[12.151]** respectively)).

The Financial Reporting Council Limited is authorised for the purposes of this section (see further, the Supervision of Accounts and Reports (Prescribed Body) and Companies (Defective Accounts and Reports) (Authorised Person) Order 2021, SI 2021/465 at **[4.722]**).

[1.522]

457 Other persons authorised to apply to the court

(1) The Secretary of State may by order (an "authorisation order") authorise for the purposes of section 456 any person appearing to him—

(a) to have an interest in, and to have satisfactory procedures directed to securing, compliance by companies with the requirements of this Act . . . relating to accounts[, strategic reports and directors' reports],

(b) to have satisfactory procedures for receiving and investigating complaints about companies' annual accounts[, strategic reports and directors' reports], and

(c) otherwise to be a fit and proper person to be authorised.

(2) A person may be authorised generally or in respect of particular classes of case, and different persons may be authorised in respect of different classes of case.

(3) The Secretary of State may refuse to authorise a person if he considers that his authorisation is unnecessary having regard to the fact that there are one or more other persons who have been or are likely to be authorised.

(4) If the authorised person is an unincorporated association, proceedings brought in, or in connection with, the exercise of any function by the association as an authorised person may be brought by or against the association in the name of a body corporate whose constitution provides for the establishment of the association.

(5) An authorisation order may contain such requirements or other provisions relating to the exercise of functions by the authorised person as appear to the Secretary of State to be appropriate.

No such order is to be made unless it appears to the Secretary of State that the person would, if authorised, exercise his functions as an authorised person in accordance with the provisions proposed.

(6) Where authorisation is revoked, the revoking order may make such provision as the Secretary of State thinks fit with respect to pending proceedings.

(7) An order under this section is subject to negative resolution procedure.

NOTES

Sub-s (1): the words omitted were repealed by the International Accounting Standards and European Public Limited-Liability Company (Amendment etc) (EU Exit) Regulations 2019, SI 2019/685, reg 19, Sch 1, Pt 1, paras 1, 17, in relation to accounts for financial years beginning on or after IP completion day (as defined in the European Union (Withdrawal Agreement) Act 2020, s 39) (note also that in relation to accounts for financial years which begin before but end on or after IP completion day, the enactments amended by Parts 1–3 of Sch 1 to the 2019 Regulations have effect as if the UK were a member State until the end of the financial year in question (for transitional provisions see reg 1 of, and Sch 1, Pt 4 to, the 2019 Regulations at **[12.130]** and **[12.151]** respectively)). The words in square brackets were substituted by the Companies Act 2006 (Strategic Report and Directors' Report) Regulations 2013, SI 2013/1970, reg 14, Schedule, paras 1, 15, in respect of financial years ending on or after 30 September 2013.

Orders: the Supervision of Accounts and Reports (Prescribed Body) and Companies (Defective Accounts and Directors' Reports) (Authorised Person) Order 2012, SI 2012/1439 (at **[4.429]**); the Supervision of Accounts and Reports (Prescribed Body) and Companies (Defective Accounts and Reports) (Authorised Person) Order 2021, SI 2021/465 at **[4.722]**. Note that the 2021 Order largely revokes the 2012 Order. For a summary of all statutory instruments made under this Act, see Appendix 4 at **[A4]**.

[1.523]

458 Disclosure of information by tax authorities

(1) The Commissioners for Her Majesty's Revenue and Customs may disclose information to a person authorised under section 457 for the purpose of facilitating—

(a) the taking of steps by that person to discover whether there are grounds for an application to the court under section 456 (application in respect of defective accounts etc), or

(b) a decision by the authorised person whether to make such an application.

(2) This section applies despite any statutory or other restriction on the disclosure of information.

Provided that, in the case of personal data [within the meaning of Parts 5 to 7 of the Data Protection Act 2018 (see section 3(2) and (14) of that Act)], information is not to be disclosed in contravention of [the data protection legislation].

(3) Information disclosed to an authorised person under this section—

(a) may not be used except in or in connection with—

(i) taking steps to discover whether there are grounds for an application to the court under section 456, or

(ii) deciding whether or not to make such an application,

or in, or in connection with, proceedings on such an application; and

(b) must not be further disclosed except—

(i) to the person to whom the information relates, or

(ii) in, or in connection with, proceedings on any such application to the court.

(4) A person who contravenes subsection (3) commits an offence unless—

(a) he did not know, and had no reason to suspect, that the information had been disclosed under this section, or

(b) he took all reasonable steps and exercised all due diligence to avoid the commission of the offence.

(5) A person guilty of an offence under subsection (4) is liable—

(a) on conviction on indictment, to imprisonment for a term not exceeding two years or a fine (or both);

(b) on summary conviction—

(i) in England and Wales, to imprisonment for a term not exceeding twelve months or to a fine not exceeding the statutory maximum (or both);

(ii) in Scotland or Northern Ireland, to imprisonment for a term not exceeding six months, or to a fine not exceeding the statutory maximum (or both).

[(6) Where an offence under this section is committed by a body corporate, every officer of the body who is in default also commits the offence.

For this purpose—

(a) any person who purports to act as director, manager or secretary of the body is treated as an officer of the body, and

(b) if the body is a company, any shadow director is treated as an officer of the company.]

NOTES

Sub-s (2): words in square brackets substituted by the Data Protection Act 2018, s 211, Sch 19, Pt 1, paras 120, 121, as from 25 May 2018 (for transitional provisions and savings relating to the repeal of the Data Protection Act 1998, see Sch 20 to the 2018 Act).

Sub-s (6): added by the Companies Act 2006 (Consequential Amendments etc) Order 2008, SI 2008/948, art 3(1), Sch 1, Pt 2, para 244, as from 6 April 2008.

Offences under this section: see further s 1131 at **[1.1301]**.

Power of authorised person to require documents etc

[1.524]

459 Power of authorised person to require documents, information and explanations

(1) This section applies where it appears to a person who is authorised under section 457 that there is, or may be, a question whether a company's annual accounts[, strategic report or directors' report complies] with the requirements of this Act . . .

(2) The authorised person may require any of the persons mentioned in subsection (3) to produce any document, or to provide him with any information or explanations, that he may reasonably require for the purpose of—

(a) discovering whether there are grounds for an application to the court under section 456, or

(b) deciding whether to make such an application.

(3) Those persons are—

(a) the company;

(b) any officer, employee, or auditor of the company;

(c) any persons who fell within paragraph (b) at a time to which the document or information required by the authorised person relates.

(4) If a person fails to comply with such a requirement, the authorised person may apply to the court.

(5) If it appears to the court that the person has failed to comply with a requirement under subsection (2), it may order the person to take such steps as it directs for securing that the documents are produced or the information or explanations are provided.

(6) A statement made by a person in response to a requirement under subsection (2) or an order under subsection (5) may not be used in evidence against him in any criminal proceedings.

(7) Nothing in this section compels any person to disclose documents or information in respect of which a claim to legal professional privilege (in Scotland, to confidentiality of communications) could be maintained in legal proceedings.

(8) In this section "document" includes information recorded in any form.

NOTES

Sub-s (1): words in square brackets substituted by the Companies Act 2006 (Strategic Report and Directors' Report) Regulations 2013, SI 2013/1970, reg 14, Schedule, paras 1, 16, in respect of financial years ending on or after 30 September 2013. The words omitted were repealed by the International Accounting Standards and European Public Limited-Liability Company (Amendment etc) (EU Exit) Regulations 2019, SI 2019/685, reg 19, Sch 1, Pt 1, paras 1, 18, in relation to accounts for financial years beginning on or after IP completion day (as defined in the European Union (Withdrawal Agreement) Act 2020, s 39) (note also that in relation to accounts for financial years which begin before but end on or after IP completion day, the enactments amended by Parts 1–3 of Sch 1 to the 2019 Regulations have effect as if the UK were a member State until the end of the financial year in question (for transitional provisions see reg 1 of, and Sch 1, Pt 4 to, the 2019 Regulations at **[12.130]** and **[12.151]** respectively)).

[1.525]

460 Restrictions on disclosure of information obtained under compulsory powers

(1) This section applies to information (in whatever form) obtained in pursuance of a requirement or order under section 459 (power of authorised person to require documents etc) that relates to the private affairs of an individual or to any particular business.

(2) No such information may, during the lifetime of that individual or so long as that business continues to be carried on, be disclosed without the consent of that individual or the person for the time being carrying on that business.

(3) This does not apply—

(a) to disclosure permitted by section 461 (permitted disclosure of information obtained under compulsory powers), or

(b) to the disclosure of information that is or has been available to the public from another source.

(4) A person who discloses information in contravention of this section commits an offence, unless—

(a) he did not know, and had no reason to suspect, that the information had been disclosed under section 459, or

(b) he took all reasonable steps and exercised all due diligence to avoid the commission of the offence.

(5) A person guilty of an offence under this section is liable—

(a) on conviction on indictment, to imprisonment for a term not exceeding two years or a fine (or both);

(b) on summary conviction—

(i) in England and Wales, to imprisonment for a term not exceeding twelve months or to a fine not exceeding the statutory maximum (or both);

(ii) in Scotland or Northern Ireland, to imprisonment for a term not exceeding six months, or to a fine not exceeding the statutory maximum (or both).

[(6) Where an offence under this section is committed by a body corporate, every officer of the body who is in default also commits the offence.

For this purpose—

(a) any person who purports to act as director, manager or secretary of the body is treated as an officer of the body, and

(b) if the body is a company, any shadow director is treated as an officer of the company.]

NOTES

Sub-s (6): added by the Companies Act 2006 (Consequential Amendments etc) Order 2008, SI 2008/948, art 3(1), Sch 1, Pt 2, para 245, as from 6 April 2008.

Offences under this section: see further s 1131 at **[1.1301]**.

[1.526]

461 Permitted disclosure of information obtained under compulsory powers

(1) The prohibition in section 460 of the disclosure of information obtained in pursuance of a requirement or order under section 459 (power of authorised person to require documents etc) that relates to the private affairs of an individual or to any particular business has effect subject to the following exceptions.

(2) It does not apply to the disclosure of information for the purpose of facilitating the carrying out by the authorised person of his functions under section 456.

(3) It does not apply to disclosure to—

(a) the Secretary of State,

(b) the Department of Enterprise, Trade and Investment for Northern Ireland,

(c) the Treasury,

(d) the Bank of England,

[(e) the Financial Conduct Authority,

(ea) the Prudential Regulation Authority, or]

(f) the Commissioners for Her Majesty's Revenue and Customs.

(4) It does not apply to disclosure—

(a) for the purpose of assisting a body designated by an order under [section 1252] (delegation of functions of the Secretary of State) to exercise its functions under [Part 42];

[(aa) for the purpose of assisting the competent authority to exercise its functions under the Statutory Auditors and Third Country Auditors Regulations 2016 and under the Audit Regulation;]

(b) with a view to the institution of, or otherwise for the purposes of, disciplinary proceedings relating to the performance by an accountant or auditor of his professional duties;

(c) for the purpose of enabling or assisting the Secretary of State or the Treasury to exercise any of their functions under any of the following—

(i) the Companies Acts,

(ii) Part 5 of the Criminal Justice Act 1993 (c 36) (insider dealing),

(iii) the Insolvency Act 1986 (c 45) or the Insolvency (Northern Ireland) Order 1989 (SI 1989/2405 (NI 19)),

(iv) the Company Directors Disqualification Act 1986 (c 46) or the Company Directors Disqualification (Northern Ireland) Order 2002 (SI 2002/3150 (NI 4)),

(v) the Financial Services and Markets Act 2000 (c 8);

(d) for the purpose of enabling or assisting the Department of Enterprise, Trade and Investment for Northern Ireland to exercise any powers conferred on it by the enactments relating to companies, directors' disqualification or insolvency;

(e) for the purpose of enabling or assisting the Bank of England to exercise its functions;

(f) for the purpose of enabling or assisting the Commissioners for Her Majesty's Revenue and Customs to exercise their functions;

(g) for the purpose of enabling or assisting the [Financial Conduct Authority or the Prudential Regulation Authority] to exercise its functions under any of the following—

(i) the legislation relating to friendly societies . . . ,

[(ia) the Credit Unions Act 1979,]

(ii) the Building Societies Act 1986 (c 53),

(iii) Part 7 of the Companies Act 1989 (c 40),

(iv) the Financial Services and Markets Act 2000,

[(v) the Co-operative and Community Benefit Societies Act 2014;] or

(h) in pursuance of any [retained] [EU] obligation.

(5) It does not apply to disclosure to a body exercising functions of a public nature under legislation in any country or territory outside the United Kingdom that appear to the authorised person to be similar to his functions under section 456 for the purpose of enabling or assisting that body to exercise those functions.

(6) In determining whether to disclose information to a body in accordance with subsection (5), the authorised person must have regard to the following considerations—

(a) whether the use which the body is likely to make of the information is sufficiently important to justify making the disclosure;

(b) whether the body has adequate arrangements to prevent the information from being used or further disclosed other than—

(i) for the purposes of carrying out the functions mentioned in that subsection, or

(ii) for other purposes substantially similar to those for which information disclosed to the authorised person could be used or further disclosed.

(7) Nothing in this section authorises the making of a disclosure in contravention of [the data protection legislation].

NOTES

Sub-s (3): paras (e), (ea) substituted (for the original para (e)) by the Financial Services Act 2012, s 114(1), Sch 18, Pt 2, paras 110, 112(1), (2), as from 1 April 2013.

Sub-s (4) is amended as follows:

Words in square brackets in para (a) substituted by the Companies Act 2006 (Consequential Amendments etc) Order 2008, SI 2008/948, art 3(1), Sch 1, Pt 2, para 246, as from 6 April 2008.

Para (aa) originally inserted by the Supervision of Accounts and Reports (Prescribed Body) and Companies (Defective Accounts and Directors' Reports) (Authorised Person) Order 2012, SI 2012/1439, art 6(2), as from 2 July 2012. Subsequently substituted by the Statutory Auditors and Third Country Auditors Regulations 2016, SI 2016/649, reg 15, Sch 3, Pt 2, para 3, as from 17 June 2016 (note that this amendment does not apply where Sch 10, para 23 to this Act continues to apply by virtue of reg 1(9) of the 2016 Regulations (see reg 1(10) of the 2016 Regulations at **[4.650]**)).

Words in first pair of square brackets in para (g) substituted by the Financial Services Act 2012, s 114(1), Sch 18, Pt 2, paras 110, 112(1), (3), as from 1 April 2013.

Words omitted from sub-para (g)(i) repealed, and sub-paras (g)(ia), (v) inserted, by the Co-operative and Community Benefit Societies Act 2014, s 151, Sch 4, Pt 2, paras 99, 100, as from 1 August 2014.

Word in first pair of square brackets in para (h) inserted by the Accounts and Reports (Amendment) (EU Exit) Regulations 2019, SI 2019/145, reg 5, Sch 2, Pt 1, paras 1, 15, as from IP completion day (as defined in the European Union (Withdrawal Agreement) Act 2020, s 39). Word "EU" in square brackets in para (h) substituted by virtue of the Treaty of Lisbon (Changes in Terminology) Order 2011, SI 2011/1043, art 6(1)(e), as from 22 April 2011.

Sub-s (7): words in square brackets substituted by the Data Protection Act 2018, s 211, Sch 19, Pt 1, paras 120, 122, as from 25 May 2018 (for transitional provisions and savings relating to the repeal of the Data Protection Act 1998, see Sch 20 to the 2018 Act).

[1.527]

462 Power to amend categories of permitted disclosure

(1) The Secretary of State may by order amend section 461(3), (4) and (5).

(2) An order under this section must not—

(a) amend subsection (3) of that section (UK public authorities) by specifying a person unless the person exercises functions of a public nature (whether or not he exercises any other function);

(b) amend subsection (4) of that section (purposes for which disclosure permitted) by adding or modifying a description of disclosure unless the purpose for which the disclosure is permitted is likely to facilitate the exercise of a function of a public nature;

(c) amend subsection (5) of that section (overseas regulatory authorities) so as to have the effect of permitting disclosures to be made to a body other than one that exercises functions of a public nature in a country or territory outside the United Kingdom.

(3) An order under this section is subject to negative resolution procedure.

NOTES

Orders: the Supervision of Accounts and Reports (Prescribed Body) and Companies (Defective Accounts and Directors' Reports) (Authorised Person) Order 2012, SI 2012/1439 at **[4.429]**. Note that the 2012 Order is largely revoked by the Supervision of Accounts and Reports (Prescribed Body) and Companies (Defective Accounts and Reports) (Authorised Person) Order 2021, SI 2021/465 at **[4.722]**. For a summary of all statutory instruments made under this Act, see Appendix 4 at **[A4]**.

CHAPTER 12 SUPPLEMENTARY PROVISIONS

Liability for false or misleading statements in reports [and statements]

[1.528]

463 Liability for false or misleading statements in reports [and statements]

(1) The reports [and statements] to which this section applies are—

[(za) the strategic report,]

(a) the directors' report,

(b) the directors' remuneration report, . . .

(c) . . .

[(d) any separate corporate governance statement.]

(2) A director of a company is liable to compensate the company for any loss suffered by it as a result of—

(a) any untrue or misleading statement in a report [or statement] to which this section applies, or

(b) the omission from a report [or statement] to which this section applies of anything required to be included in it.

(3) He is so liable only if—

(a) he knew the statement to be untrue or misleading or was reckless as to whether it was untrue or misleading, or

(b) he knew the omission to be dishonest concealment of a material fact.

(4) No person shall be subject to any liability to a person other than the company resulting from reliance, by that person or another, on information in a report [or statement] to which this section applies.

(5) The reference in subsection (4) to a person being subject to a liability includes a reference to another person being entitled as against him to be granted any civil remedy or to rescind or repudiate an agreement.

(6) This section does not affect—

(a) liability for a civil penalty, or

(b) liability for a criminal offence.

NOTES

Sub-s (1)(za) inserted, and sub-s (1)(c) (and the preceding word) repealed, by the Companies Act 2006 (Strategic Report and Directors' Report) Regulations 2013, SI 2013/1970, reg 14, Schedule, paras 1, 16, in respect of financial years ending on or after 30 September 2013.

All other words in square brackets in this section (and those in the heading preceding this section) were inserted by the Statutory Auditors Regulations 2017, SI 2017/1164, reg 3, Sch 1, paras 7, 13, in relation to financial years of companies beginning on or after 17 June 2016 (see**[4.671]** et seq).

Accounting and reporting standards

[1.529]

464 Accounting standards

(1) In this Part "accounting standards" means statements of standard accounting practice issued by such body or bodies as may be prescribed by regulations.

(2) References in this Part to accounting standards applicable to a company's annual accounts are to such standards as are, in accordance with their terms, relevant to the company's circumstances and to the accounts.

(3) Regulations under this section may contain such transitional and other supplementary and incidental provisions as appear to the Secretary of State to be appropriate.

NOTES

Orders: the Statutory Auditors (Amendment of Companies Act 2006 and Delegation of Functions etc) Order 2012, SI 2012/1741 at **[4.430]**; the Accounting Standards (Prescribed Bodies) (United States of America and Japan) Regulations 2015, SI 2015/1675 (note that the 2016 Regulations cease to have effect on 30 September 2022). For a summary of all statutory instruments made under this Act, see Appendix 4 at **[A4]**.

Companies qualifying as medium-sized

[1.530]

465 Companies qualifying as medium-sized: general

(1) A company qualifies as medium-sized in relation to its first financial year if the qualifying conditions are met in that year.

(2) A company qualifies as medium-sized in relation to a subsequent financial year—

(a) if the qualifying conditions are met in that year and the preceding financial year;

(b) if the qualifying conditions are met in that year and the company qualified as medium-sized in relation to the preceding financial year;

(c) if the qualifying conditions were met in the preceding financial year and the company qualified as medium-sized in relation to that year.

(3) The qualifying conditions are met by a company in a year in which it satisfies two or more of the following requirements—

1 Turnover	[Not more than £36 million]
2 Balance sheet total	[Not more than £18 million]
3 Number of employees	Not more than 250

(4) For a period that is a company's financial year but not in fact a year the maximum figures for turnover must be proportionately adjusted.

(5) The balance sheet total means the aggregate of the amounts shown as assets in the company's balance sheet.

(6) The number of employees means the average number of persons employed by the company in the year, determined as follows—

(a) find for each month in the financial year the number of persons employed under contracts of service by the company in that month (whether throughout the month or not),

(b) add together the monthly totals, and

(c) divide by the number of months in the financial year.

(7) This section is subject to section 466 (companies qualifying as medium-sized: parent companies).

NOTES

Sub-s (3): words in square brackets substituted by the Companies, Partnerships and Groups (Accounts and Reports) Regulations 2015, SI 2015/980, reg 9(1), (2), in relation to (a) financial years beginning on or after 1 January 2016, and (b) a financial year of a company beginning on or after 1 January 2015, but before 1 January 2016, if the directors of the company so decide (subject to transitional provisions, etc, in regs 2, 3 of the 2015 Regulations as noted to s 380 at **[1.430]**).

See also, as to whether a company qualifies as medium-sized for the purposes of sub-s (2), the Companies, Partnerships and Groups (Accounts and Reports) Regulations 2015, SI 2015/980, reg 2(4) (see the note to s 380 at **[1.430]**).

[1.531]

466 Companies qualifying as medium-sized: parent companies

(1) A parent company qualifies as a medium-sized company in relation to a financial year only if the group headed by it qualifies as a medium-sized group.

(2) A group qualifies as medium-sized in relation to the parent company's first financial year if the qualifying conditions are met in that year.

(3) A group qualifies as medium-sized in relation to a subsequent financial year of the parent company—

(a) if the qualifying conditions are met in that year and the preceding financial year;

(b) if the qualifying conditions are met in that year and the group qualified as medium-sized in relation to the preceding financial year;

(c) if the qualifying conditions were met in the preceding financial year and the group qualified as medium-sized in relation to that year.

(4) The qualifying conditions are met by a group in a year in which it satisfies two or more of the following requirements—

1 Aggregate turnover	[Not more than £36 million net (or £43.2 million gross)]
2 Aggregate balance sheet total	[Not more than £18 million net (or £21.6 million gross)]
3 Aggregate number of employees	Not more than 250

(5) The aggregate figures are ascertained by aggregating the relevant figures determined in accordance with section 465 for each member of the group.

(6) In relation to the aggregate figures for turnover and balance sheet total—

"net" means after any set-offs and other adjustments made to eliminate group transactions—

(a) in the case of Companies Act accounts, in accordance with regulations under section 404,

(b) in the case of IAS accounts, in accordance with [UK-adopted international accounting standards]; and

"gross" means without those set-offs and other adjustments.

A company may satisfy any relevant requirement on the basis of either the net or the gross figure.

(7) The figures for each subsidiary undertaking shall be those included in its individual accounts for the relevant financial year, that is—

(a) if its financial year ends with that of the parent company, that financial year, and

(b) if not, its financial year ending last before the end of the financial year of the parent company.

If those figures cannot be obtained without disproportionate expense or undue delay, the latest available figures shall be taken.

NOTES

Sub-s (4): words in square brackets substituted by the Companies, Partnerships and Groups (Accounts and Reports) Regulations 2015, SI 2015/980, reg 9(1), (3), in relation to (a) financial years beginning on or after 1 January 2016, and (b) a financial year of a company beginning on or after 1 January 2015, but before 1 January 2016, if the directors of the company so decide (subject to transitional provisions, etc, in regs 2, 3 of the 2015 Regulations as noted to s 380 at **[1.430]**).

Sub-s (6): words in square brackets substituted by the International Accounting Standards and European Public Limited-Liability Company (Amendment etc) (EU Exit) Regulations 2019, SI 2019/685, reg 19, Sch 1, Pt 1, paras 1, 19, in relation to accounts for financial years beginning on or after IP completion day (as defined in the European Union (Withdrawal Agreement) Act 2020, s 39) (note also that in relation to accounts for financial years which begin before but end on or after IP completion day, the enactments amended by Parts 1–3 of Sch 1 to the 2019 Regulations have effect as if the UK were a member State until the end of the financial year in question (for transitional provisions see reg 1 of, and Sch 1, Pt 4 to, the 2019 Regulations at **[12.130]** and **[12.151]** respectively)).

See also, as to whether a group qualifies as medium-sized for the purposes of sub-s (3), the Companies, Partnerships and Groups (Accounts and Reports) Regulations 2015, SI 2015/980, reg 2(4) (see the note to s 380 at **[1.430]**).

[1.532]

467 Companies excluded from being treated as medium-sized

(1) A company is not entitled to take advantage of any of the provisions of this Part relating to companies qualifying as medium-sized if it was at any time within the financial year in question—

- (a) a public company,
- (b) a company that—
  - (i) has permission under [Part 4A] of the Financial Services and Markets Act 2000 (c 8) to carry on a regulated activity, . . .
  - (ii) carries on insurance market activity, [or]
  - [(iii) is a scheme funder of a Master Trust scheme within the meanings given by section 39(1) of the Pension Schemes Act 2017 (interpretation of Part 1), or]
- [(ba) an e-money issuer,] or
- (c) a member of an ineligible group.

(2) A group is ineligible if any of its members is—

- [(a) a traded company,]
- (b) a body corporate (other than a company) whose shares are admitted to trading on a [UK] regulated market,
- (c) a person (other than a small company) who has permission under [Part 4A] of the Financial Services and Markets Act 2000 to carry on a regulated activity,
- [(ca) an e-money issuer,]
- (d) a small company that is an authorised insurance company, a banking company, . . . [a MiFID investment firm] or a UCITS management company, . . .
- (e) a person who carries on insurance market activity, [or]
- [(f) a scheme funder of a Master Trust scheme within the meanings given by section 39(1) of the Pension Schemes Act 2017 (interpretation of Part 1)].

(3) A company is a small company for the purposes of subsection (2) if it qualified as small in relation to its last financial year ending on or before the end of the financial year in question.

[(4) This section does not prevent a company from taking advantage of section 417(7) (business review: non-financial information) by reason only of its having been a member of an ineligible group at any time within the financial year in question.]

NOTES

Sub-s (1): words in square brackets in sub-para (b)(i) substituted by the Financial Services Act 2012, s 114(1), Sch 18, Pt 2, paras 110, 113, as from 1 April 2013. Word omitted from sub-para (b)(i) repealed, word in square brackets in sub-para (b)(ii) inserted, and sub-para (b)(iii) inserted, by the Occupational Pension Schemes (Master Trusts) Regulations 2018, SI 2018/1030, reg 30(1), (3)(a), as from 1 October 2018. Para (ba) inserted by the Companies and Partnerships (Accounts and Audit) Regulations 2013, SI 2013/2005, reg 2(1), (7)(a), in relation to a financial year of a company beginning on or after 1 October 2013.

Sub-s (2) is amended as follows:

Para (a) substituted by the Companies, Partnerships and Groups (Accounts and Reports) Regulations 2015, SI 2015/980, reg 9(1), (4), in relation to (a) financial years beginning on or after 1 January 2016, and (b) a financial year of a company beginning on or after 1 January 2015, but before 1 January 2016, if the directors of the company so decide (subject to transitional provisions, etc, in regs 2, 3 of the 2015 Regulations as noted to s 380 at **[1.430]**).

Word in square brackets in para (b) inserted by the Accounts and Reports (Amendment) (EU Exit) Regulations 2019, SI 2019/145, reg 5, Sch 2, Pt 1, paras 1, 16, in relation to financial years beginning on or after IP completion day (as defined in the European Union (Withdrawal Agreement) Act 2020, s 39) (for transitional provisions see reg 7 of the 2019 Regulations at **[12.79]**).

Words in square brackets in para (c) substituted by the Financial Services Act 2012, s 114(1), Sch 18, Pt 2, paras 110, 113, as from 1 April 2013.

Para (ca) inserted, and first words omitted from para (d) repealed, by SI 2013/2005, reg 2(1), (7)(b), (c), in relation to a financial year of a company beginning on or after 1 October 2013.

Words in square brackets in para (d) substituted by the Markets in Financial Instruments Directive (Consequential Amendments) Regulations 2007, SI 2007/2932, reg 3(1), (3), as from 1 November 2007.

Word omitted from the end of para (d) repealed, word in square brackets in para (e) inserted, and para (f) added, by SI 2018/1030, reg 30(1), (3)(b), as from 1 October 2018.

Sub-s (4): added by the Companies Act 2006 (Amendment) (Accounts and Reports) Regulations 2008, SI 2008/393, reg 7, as from 6 April 2008, in relation to financial years beginning on or after that date.

General power to make further provision about accounts and reports

[1.533]

468 General power to make further provision about accounts and reports

(1) The Secretary of State may make provision by regulations about—

- (a) the accounts and reports that companies are required to prepare;
- (b) the categories of companies required to prepare accounts and reports of any description;
- (c) the form and content of the accounts and reports that companies are required to prepare;

(d) the obligations of companies and others as regards—
   (i) the approval of accounts and reports,
   (ii) the sending of accounts and reports to members and others,
   (iii) the laying of accounts and reports before the company in general meeting,
   (iv) the delivery of copies of accounts and reports to the registrar, and
   (v) the publication of accounts and reports.

(2) The regulations may amend this Part by adding, altering or repealing provisions.

(3) But they must not amend (other than consequentially)—
   (a) section 393 (accounts to give true and fair view), or
   (b) the provisions of Chapter 11 (revision of defective accounts and reports).

(4) The regulations may create criminal offences in cases corresponding to those in which an offence is created by an existing provision of this Part.

The maximum penalty for any such offence may not be greater than is provided in relation to an offence under the existing provision.

(5) The regulations may provide for civil penalties in circumstances corresponding to those within section 453(1) (civil penalty for failure to file accounts and reports).

The provisions of section 453(2) to (5) apply in relation to any such penalty.

NOTES

Regulations: the Companies Act 2006 (Amendment) (Accounts and Reports) Regulations 2008, SI 2008/393; the Companies Act 2006 (Accounts, Reports and Audit) Regulations 2009, SI 2009/1581; the Companies Act 2006 (Amendment of Section 413) Regulations 2009, SI 2009/3022; the Companies and Limited Liability Partnerships (Accounts and Audit Exemptions and Change of Accounting Framework) Regulations 2012, SI 2012/2301; the Companies Act 2006 (Strategic Report and Directors' Report) Regulations 2013, SI 2013/1970; the Companies and Partnerships (Accounts and Audit) Regulations 2013, SI 2013/2005; the Small Companies (Micro-Entities' Accounts) Regulations 2013, SI 2013/3008; the Reports on Payments to Governments Regulations 2014, SI 2014/3209; the Companies, Partnerships and Groups (Accounts and Reports) Regulations 2015, SI 2015/980; the Companies, Partnerships and Groups (Accounts and Non-Financial Reporting) Regulations 2016, SI 2016/1245; the Companies (Miscellaneous Reporting) Regulations 2018, SI 2018/860 (see the note at **[4.674]**); the Companies (Directors' Remuneration Policy and Directors' Remuneration Report) Regulations 2019, SI 2019/970 at **[4.679]**; the Companies (Strategic Report) (Climate-related Financial Disclosure) Regulations 2022, SI 2022/31. For a summary of all statutory instruments made under this Act, see Appendix 4 at **[A4]**.

Other supplementary provisions

[1.534]

469 Preparation and filing of accounts in euros

(1) The amounts set out in the annual accounts of a company may also be shown in the same accounts translated into euros.

(2) When complying with section 441 (duty to file accounts and reports), the directors of a company may deliver to the registrar an additional copy of the company's annual accounts in which the amounts have been translated into euros.

(3) In both cases—
   (a) the amounts must have been translated at the exchange rate prevailing on the date to which the balance sheet is made up, and
   (b) that rate must be disclosed in the notes to the accounts.

[(3A) Subsection (3)(b) does not apply to the Companies Act individual accounts of a company for a financial year in which the company qualifies as a micro-entity (see sections 384A and 384B).]

(4) For the purposes of sections 434 and 435 (requirements in connection with published accounts) any additional copy of the company's annual accounts delivered to the registrar under subsection (2) above shall be treated as statutory accounts of the company.

In the case of such a copy, references in those sections to the auditor's report on the company's annual accounts shall be read as references to the auditor's report on the annual accounts of which it is a copy.

NOTES

Sub-s (3A): inserted by the Small Companies (Micro-Entities' Accounts) Regulations 2013, SI 2013/3008, reg 7(1), (2), in relation to (a) financial years ending on or after 30 September 2013, and (b) companies which deliver the accounts required by s 444 of this Act to the registrar on or after 1 December 2013 (as to application of this amendment, see the note at **[1.432]**).

[1.535]

470 Power to apply provisions to banking partnerships

(1) The Secretary of State may by regulations apply to banking partnerships, subject to such exceptions, adaptations and modifications as he considers appropriate, the provisions of this Part (and of regulations made under this Part) applying to banking companies.

(2) A "banking partnership" means a partnership which has permission under [Part 4A] of the Financial Services and Markets Act 2000 (c 8).

But a partnership is not a banking partnership if it has permission to accept deposits only for the purpose of carrying on another regulated activity in accordance with that permission.

(3) Expressions used in this section that are also used in the provisions regulating activities under the Financial Services and Markets Act 2000 have the same meaning here as they do in those provisions.

See section 22 of that Act, orders made under that section and Schedule 2 to that Act.

(4) Regulations under this section are subject to affirmative resolution procedure.

NOTES

Sub-s (2): words in square brackets substituted by the Financial Services Act 2012, s 114(1), Sch 18, Pt 2, paras 110, 114, as from 1 April 2013.

Regulations: no Regulations have been made under this section.

[1.536]

471 Meaning of "annual accounts" and related expressions

(1) In this Part a company's "annual accounts", in relation to a financial year, means—

[(a) any individual accounts prepared by the company for that year (see section 394), and]

(b) any group accounts prepared by the company for that year (see [section] 399).

This is subject to section 408 (option to omit individual profit and loss account from annual accounts where information given in [notes to the individual balance sheet]).

(2) In the case of an unquoted company, its "annual accounts and reports" for a financial year are—

(a) its annual accounts,

[(aa) the strategic report (if any),]

[(ab) the directors' remuneration report (if any),]

(b) the directors' report, and

(c) the auditor's report on those accounts[, the strategic report (where this is covered by the auditor's report)] and the directors' report (unless the company is exempt from audit).

(3) In the case of a quoted company, its "annual accounts and reports" for a financial year are—

(a) its annual accounts,

(b) the directors' remuneration report,

[(ba) the strategic report (if any),]

(c) the directors' report, and

(d) the auditor's report on those accounts, on the auditable part of the directors' remuneration report[, on the strategic report (where this is covered by the auditor's report)] and on the directors' report.

NOTES

Sub-s (1): para (a) substituted by the Companies and Limited Liability Partnerships (Accounts and Audit Exemptions and Change of Accounting Framework) Regulations 2012, SI 2012/2301, regs 2, 18, as from 1 October 2012 (in relation to accounts for financial years ending on or after that date). Word in square brackets in para (b) substituted by the Companies, Partnerships and Groups (Accounts and Non-Financial Reporting) Regulations 2016, SI 2016/1245, regs 2, 3(5), in relation to the financial years of companies and qualifying partnerships beginning on or after 1 January 2017 (and only in relation to companies (as defined by s 1 *ante*) and qualifying partnerships (as defined in the Partnerships (Accounts) Regulations 2008, reg 3)). Words in final pair of square brackets substituted by the Small Companies (Micro-Entities' Accounts) Regulations 2013, SI 2013/3008, reg 7(1), (3), in relation to (a) financial years ending on or after 30 September 2013, and (b) companies which deliver the accounts required by s 444 of this Act to the registrar on or after 1 December 2013 (as to application of this amendment, see the note at **[1.432]**).

Sub-s (2): para (aa) and the words in square brackets in para (c) were inserted by the Companies Act 2006 (Strategic Report and Directors' Report) Regulations 2013, SI 2013/1970, reg 14, Schedule, paras 1, 18, in respect of financial years ending on or after 30 September 2013. Para (ab) was inserted by the Companies (Directors' Remuneration Policy and Directors' Remuneration Report) Regulations 2019, SI 2019/970, regs 3, 23, as from 10 June 2019 (for transitional provisions, etc, see reg 2 of the 2019 Regulations at **[4.680]**).

Sub-s (3): words in square brackets inserted by SI 2013/1970, reg 14, Schedule, paras 1, 18, in respect of financial years ending on or after 30 September 2013.

[1.537]

472 Notes to the accounts

(1) . . .

[(1A) . . . in the case of a company which qualifies as a micro-entity in relation to a financial year (see sections 384A and 384B), the notes to the accounts for that year required by section 413 of this Act and regulation 5A of, and paragraph 57 of Part 3 of Schedule 1 to, the Small Companies and Groups (Accounts and Directors' Report) Regulations 2008 (SI 2008/409) must be included at the foot of the balance sheet.]

(2) References in this Part to a company's annual accounts, or to a balance sheet or profit and loss account, include notes to the accounts giving information which is required by any provision of this Act or [UK-adopted international accounting standards], and required or allowed by any such provision to be given in a note to company accounts.

NOTES

Sub-s (1): repealed by the Companies, Partnerships and Groups (Accounts and Reports) Regulations 2015, SI 2015/980, reg 9(1), (5)(a), in relation to (a) financial years beginning on or after 1 January 2016, and (b) a financial year of a company beginning on or after 1 January 2015, but before 1 January 2016, if the directors of the company so decide (subject to transitional provisions, etc, in regs 2, 3 of the 2015 Regulations as noted to s 380 at **[1.430]**).

Sub-s (1A): inserted by the Small Companies (Micro-Entities' Accounts) Regulations 2013, SI 2013/3008, reg 7(1), (4), in relation to (a) financial years ending on or after 30 September 2013, and (b) companies which deliver the accounts required by s 444 of this Act to the registrar on or after 1 December 2013 (as to application of this amendment, see the note at **[1.432]**). Word omitted repealed by SI 2015/980, reg 9(1), (5)(b), as from 6 April 2015, as from the same dates and for the same purposes as specified in the first note relating to the 2015 Regulations above.

Sub-s (2): words in square brackets substituted by the International Accounting Standards and European Public Limited-Liability Company (Amendment etc) (EU Exit) Regulations 2019, SI 2019/685, reg 19, Sch 1, Pt 1, paras 1, 20, in relation to accounts for financial years beginning on or after IP completion day (as defined in the European Union (Withdrawal Agreement) Act 2020, s 39) (note also that in relation to accounts for financial years which begin before but end on or after IP completion day, the enactments amended by Parts 1–3 of Sch 1 to the 2019 Regulations have effect as if the UK were a member State until the end of the financial year in question (for transitional provisions see reg 1 of, and Sch 1, Pt 4 to, the 2019 Regulations at **[12.130]** and **[12.151]** respectively)).

[1.538]

[472A Meaning of "corporate governance statement" etc

(1) In this Part "corporate governance statement" means the statement required by rules 7.2.1 to 7.2.11 in the Disclosure Rules and Transparency Rules sourcebook [made by the Financial Conduct Authority].

(2) Those rules were inserted by Annex C of the Disclosure Rules and Transparency Rules Sourcebook (Corporate Governance Rules) Instrument 2008 made by the Authority on 26th June 2008 (FSA 2008/32).

(3) A "separate" corporate governance statement means one that is not included in the directors' report.]

NOTES

Inserted by the Companies Act 2006 (Accounts, Reports and Audit) Regulations 2009, SI 2009/1581, reg 5, in relation to financial years beginning on or after 29 June 2008 which have not ended before 27 June 2009.

Para (1): words in square brackets substituted by the Financial Services Act 2012 (Consequential Amendments) Order 2013, SI 2013/636, art 2, Schedule, para 9(1), (2), as from 1 April 2013.

[1.539]

473 Parliamentary procedure for certain regulations under this Part

(1) This section applies to regulations under the following provisions of this Part—

section 396 (Companies Act individual accounts),
section 404 (Companies Act group accounts),
section 409 (information about related undertakings),
section 412 (information about directors' benefits: remuneration, pensions and compensation for loss of office),
section 416 (contents of directors' report: general),
section 421 (contents of directors' remuneration report),
section 444 (filing obligations of companies subject to small companies regime),
section 445 (filing obligations of medium-sized companies),
section 468 (general power to make further provision about accounts and reports).

(2) Any such regulations may make consequential amendments or repeals in other provisions of this Act, or in other enactments.

(3) Regulations that—

(a) restrict the classes of company which have the benefit of any exemption, exception or special provision,
(b) require additional matter to be included in a document of any class, or
(c) otherwise render the requirements of this Part more onerous,

are subject to affirmative resolution procedure.

(4) Otherwise, the regulations are subject to negative resolution procedure.

NOTES

As to Regulations made under the sections listed in sub-s (1), see the notes to those sections *ante*.

[1.540]

474 Minor definitions

(1) In this Part—

"e-money issuer" [means—

(a) an electronic money institution, within the meaning of the Electronic Money Regulations 2011 (SI 2011/99), or
(b)] a person who has permission under [Part 4A] of the Financial Services and Markets Act 2000 (c 8) to carry on the activity of issuing electronic money within the meaning of article 9B of the Financial Services and Markets Act 2000 (Regulated Activities) Order 2001 (SI 2001/544);

"group" means a parent undertaking and its subsidiary undertakings;

. . .

"included in the consolidation", in relation to group accounts, or "included in consolidated group accounts", means that the undertaking is included in the accounts by the method of full (and not proportional) consolidation, and references to an undertaking excluded from consolidation shall be construed accordingly;

"international accounting standards" means the international accounting standards, within the meaning of [Article 2 of Regulation (EC) No 1606/2002 of the European Parliament and of the Council of 19 July 2002 on the application of international accounting standards];

. . .

["micro-entity minimum accounting item" means an item of information required by this Part or by regulations under this Part to be contained in the Companies Act individual accounts of a company for a financial year in relation to which it qualifies as a micro-entity (see sections 384A and 384B);

"micro-entity provisions" means any provisions of this Part, Part 16 or regulations under this Part relating specifically to the individual accounts of a company which qualifies as a micro-entity;]

["MiFID investment firm" means an investment firm within the meaning of [Article 2.1A of Regulation (EU) No 600/2014] [of the European Parliament and of the Council of 15 May 2014] on markets in financial instruments, other than—

(a) a company [which is exempted from the definition of "investment firm" by Schedule 3 to the Financial Services and Markets Act 2000 (Regulated Activities) Order 2001 (SI 2001/544),]
[(b) a company which is an exempt investment firm as defined by regulation 8 (meaning of "exempt investment firm") of the Financial Services and Markets Act 2000 (Markets in Financial Instruments) Regulations 2017 (SI 2017/701);]
(c) any other company which fulfils all the requirements set out in regulation [6(3)] of those Regulations;]

"profit and loss account", in relation to a company that prepares IAS accounts, includes an income statement or other equivalent financial statement required to be prepared by [UK-adopted international accounting standard];

["qualified", in relation to an auditor's report, means that the report does not state the auditor's unqualified opinion that the accounts have been properly prepared in accordance with this Act;]

"regulated activity" has the meaning given in section 22 of the Financial Services and Markets Act 2000, except that it does not include activities of the kind specified in any of the following provisions of the Financial Services and Markets Act 2000 (Regulated Activities) Order 2001 (SI 2001/544)—

(a) article 25A (arranging regulated mortgage contracts),

(b) article 25B (arranging regulated home reversion plans),
(c) article 25C (arranging regulated home purchase plans),
[(ca) article 25E (arranging regulated sale and rent back agreements),]
(d) article 39A (assisting administration and performance of a contract of insurance),
(e) article 53A (advising on regulated mortgage contracts),
(f) article 53B (advising on regulated home reversion plans),
(g) article 53C (advising on regulated home purchase plans),
[(ga) article 53D (advising on regulated sale and rent back agreements),]
(h) article 21 (dealing as agent), article 25 (arranging deals in investments) or article 53 (advising on investments) where the activity concerns relevant investments that are not contractually based investments (within the meaning of article 3 of that Order), or
(i) article 64 (agreeing to carry on a regulated activity of the kind mentioned in paragraphs (a) to (h));

["traded company"[, unless the context otherwise requires,] means a company any of whose transferable securities are admitted to trading on a [UK] regulated market;]

"turnover", in relation to a company, means the amounts derived from the provision of goods and services . . . , after deduction of—
(a) trade discounts,
(b) value added tax, and
(c) any other taxes based on the amounts so derived;

"UCITS management company" has the meaning given by the Glossary forming part of the Handbook made by the [Financial Conduct Authority] under the Financial Services and Markets Act 2000 (c 8);

["UK-adopted international accounting standards" means the international accounting standards which are adopted for use within the United Kingdom by virtue of Chapter 2 or 3 of Part 2 of the International Accounting Standards and European Public Limited-Liability Company (Amendment etc) (EU Exit) Regulations 2019].

(2) In the case of an undertaking not trading for profit, any reference in this Part to a profit and loss account is to an income and expenditure account. References to profit and loss and, in relation to group accounts, to a consolidated profit and loss account shall be construed accordingly.

NOTES

Sub-s (1) is amended as follows:

The words in the first pair of square brackets in the definition "e-money issuer" were substituted by the Companies and Partnerships (Accounts and Audit) Regulations 2013, SI 2013/2005, reg 2(1), (8), in relation to a financial year of a company beginning on or after 1 October 2013.

The words in the second pair of square brackets in the definition "e-money issuer" were substituted by the Financial Services Act 2012, s 114(1), Sch 18, Pt 2, paras 110, 115, as from 1 April 2013.

Definition "IAS Regulation" (omitted) repealed by the International Accounting Standards and European Public Limited-Liability Company (Amendment etc) (EU Exit) Regulations 2019, SI 2019/685, reg 19, Sch 1, Pt 1, paras 1, 21(a), in relation to accounts for financial years beginning on or after IP completion day (as defined in the European Union (Withdrawal Agreement) Act 2020, s 39) (note also that in relation to accounts for financial years which begin before but end on or after IP completion day, the enactments amended by Parts 1–3 of Sch 1 to the 2019 Regulations have effect as if the UK were a member State until the end of the financial year in question (for transitional provisions see reg 1 of, and Sch 1, Pt 4 to, the 2019 Regulations at **[12.130]** and **[12.151]** respectively)).

Words in square brackets in the definition "international accounting standards" substituted by SI 2019/685, reg 19, Sch 1, Pt 1, paras 1, 21(b), in relation to accounts for financial years beginning on or after IP completion day (see also the first note relating to the 2019 Regulations above).

Definition "ISD investment firm" (omitted) repealed by the Markets in Financial Instruments Directive (Consequential Amendments) Regulations 2007, SI 2007/2932, reg 3(4), as from 1 November 2007.

Definitions "micro-entity minimum accounting item" and "micro-entity provisions" inserted by the Small Companies (Micro-Entities' Accounts) Regulations 2013, SI 2013/3008, reg 7(1), (5), in relation to (a) financial years ending on or after 30 September 2013, and (b) companies which deliver the accounts required by s 444 of this Act to the registrar on or after 1 December 2013 (as to application of this amendment, see the note at **[1.432]**).

Definition "MiFID investment firm" inserted by SI 2007/2932, reg 3(4), as from 1 November 2007. Words in first pair of square brackets substituted, and words in square brackets in para (a) substituted, by the Accounts and Reports (Amendment) (EU Exit) Regulations 2019, SI 2019/145, reg 5, Sch 2, Pt 1, paras 1, 17(a), in relation to financial years beginning on or after IP completion day (as defined in the European Union (Withdrawal Agreement) Act 2020, s 39) (for transitional provisions see reg 7 of the 2019 Regulations at **[12.79]**). Words in second pair of square brackets substituted by virtue of the Financial Services and Markets Act 2000 (Markets in Financial Instruments) Regulations 2017, SI 2017/701, reg 50(3), Sch 4, para 9(1), (2)(a), as from 3 January 2018. Para (b) substituted, and figure in square brackets in para (c) substituted, by the Financial Services and Markets Act 2000 (Markets in Financial Instruments) (No 2) Regulations 2017, SI 2017/1255, reg 7, as from 3 January 2018.

Words in square brackets in the definition "profit and loss account" substituted by SI 2019/685, reg 19, Sch 1, Pt 1, paras 1, 21(c), in relation to accounts for financial years beginning on or after IP completion day (as defined in the European Union (Withdrawal Agreement) Act 2020, s 39) (as to the effect of this amendment, see the first note relating to the 2019 Regulations above).

In the definition "regulated activity", paras (ca), (ga) were inserted by the Financial Services and Markets Act 2000 (Regulated Activities) (Amendment) Order 2009, SI 2009/1342, art 26, as from 1 July 2009.

Definitions "qualified" and "traded company" inserted, and words omitted from the definition "turnover" repealed, by the Companies, Partnerships and Groups (Accounts and Reports) Regulations 2015, SI 2015/980, reg 9(1), (6), in relation to (a) financial years beginning on or after 1 January 2016, and (b) a financial year of a company beginning on or after 1 January 2015, but before 1 January 2016, if the directors of the company so decide (subject to transitional provisions, etc, in regs 2, 3 of the 2015 Regulations as noted to s 380 at **[1.430]**).

Words ", unless the context otherwise requires," in square brackets in the definition "traded company" inserted by the Companies (Directors' Remuneration Policy and Directors' Remuneration Report) Regulations 2019, SI 2019/970, regs 3, 24, as from 10 June 2019 (for transitional provisions, etc, see reg 2 of the 2019 Regulations at **[4.680]**).

Word "UK" in square brackets in the definition "traded company" inserted by SI 2019/145, reg 5, Sch 2, Pt 1, paras 1, 17(b), in relation to financial years beginning on or after IP completion day (see also the first note relating to the 2019 Regulations above).

Words in square brackets in the definition "UCITS management company" substituted by the Financial Services Act 2012 (Consequential Amendments) Order 2013, SI 2013/636, art 2, Schedule, para 9(1), (3), as from 1 April 2013.

Definition "UK-adopted international accounting standards" inserted by SI 2019/685, reg 19, Sch 1, Pt 1, paras 1, 21(d), in relation to accounts for financial years beginning on or after IP completion day (see also the first note relating to the 2019 Regulations above).

PART 16 AUDIT

CHAPTER 1 REQUIREMENT FOR AUDITED ACCOUNTS

Requirement for audited accounts

[1.541]

475 Requirement for audited accounts

(1) A company's annual accounts for a financial year must be audited in accordance with this Part unless the company—

(a) is exempt from audit under—
section 477 (small companies),
[section 479A (subsidiary companies)] or
section 480 (dormant companies);
or

(b) is exempt from the requirements of this Part under section 482 (non-profit-making companies subject to public sector audit).

(2) A company is not entitled to any such exemption unless its balance sheet contains a statement by the directors to that effect.

(3) A company is not entitled to exemption under any of the provisions mentioned in subsection (1)(a) unless its balance sheet contains a statement by the directors to the effect that—

(a) the members have not required the company to obtain an audit of its accounts for the year in question in accordance with section 476, and

(b) the directors acknowledge their responsibilities for complying with the requirements of this Act with respect to accounting records and the preparation of accounts.

(4) The statement required by subsection (2) or (3) must appear on the balance sheet above the signature required by section 414.

NOTES

Sub-s (1): words in square brackets inserted by the Companies and Limited Liability Partnerships (Accounts and Audit Exemptions and Change of Accounting Framework) Regulations 2012, SI 2012/2301, regs 2, 6, as from 1 October 2012 (in relation to accounts for financial years ending on or after that date).

[1.542]

476 Right of members to require audit

(1) The members of a company that would otherwise be entitled to exemption from audit under any of the provisions mentioned in section 475(1)(a) may by notice under this section require it to obtain an audit of its accounts for a financial year.

(2) The notice must be given by—

(a) members representing not less in total than 10% in nominal value of the company's issued share capital, or any class of it, or

(b) if the company does not have a share capital, not less than 10% in number of the members of the company.

(3) The notice may not be given before the financial year to which it relates and must be given not later than one month before the end of that year.

Exemption from audit: small companies

[1.543]

477 Small companies: conditions for exemption from audit

(1) A company that [qualifies as a small company in relation to] a financial year is exempt from the requirements of this Act relating to the audit of accounts for that year.

(2), (3) . . .

(4) For the purposes of this section—

(a) whether a company qualifies as a small company shall be determined in accordance with section 382(1) to (6), . . .

(b) . . .

(5) This section has effect subject to—
section 475(2) and (3) (requirements as to statements to be contained in balance sheet),
section 476 (right of members to require audit),
section 478 (companies excluded from small companies exemption), and
section 479 (availability of small companies exemption in case of group company).

NOTES

The words in square brackets in sub-s (1) were substituted, and sub-ss (2), (3), (4)(b) (and the word preceding sub-s (4)(b)) were repealed, by the Companies and Limited Liability Partnerships (Accounts and Audit Exemptions and Change of Accounting Framework) Regulations 2012, SI 2012/2301, regs 2, 4, as from 1 October 2012 (in relation to accounts for financial years ending on or after that date).

[1.544]

478 Companies excluded from small companies exemption

A company is not entitled to the exemption conferred by section 477 (small companies) if it was at any time within the financial year in question—

(a) a public company,

(b) a company that—

(i) is an authorised insurance company, a banking company, an e-money issuer, [a MiFID investment firm] or a UCITS management company, . . .

(ii) carries on insurance market activity, or

[(iii) is a scheme funder of a Master Trust scheme within the meanings given by section 39(1) of the Pension Schemes Act 2017 (interpretation of Part 1), or]

(c) a special register body as defined in section 117(1) of the Trade Union and Labour Relations (Consolidation) Act 1992 (c 52) or an employers' association as defined in section 122 of that Act or Article 4 of the Industrial Relations (Northern Ireland) Order 1992 (SI 1992/807 (NI 5)).

NOTES

Words in square brackets in sub-para (b)(i) substituted by the Markets in Financial Instruments Directive (Consequential Amendments) Regulations 2007, SI 2007/2932, reg 3(5), as from 1 November 2007.

Word omitted from sub-para (b)(i) repealed, and sub-para (b)(iii) inserted, by the Occupational Pension Schemes (Master Trusts) Regulations 2018, SI 2018/1030, reg 30(1), (4), as from 1 October 2018.

[1.545]

479 Availability of small companies exemption in case of group company

(1) A company is not entitled to the exemption conferred by section 477 (small companies) in respect of a financial year during any part of which it was a group company unless—

[(a) the group—

(i) qualifies as a small group in relation to that financial year, and

(ii) was not at any time in that year an ineligible group, or]

(b) subsection (3) applies.

(2) . . .

(3) A company is not excluded by subsection (1) if, throughout the whole of the period or periods during the financial year when it was a group company, it was both a subsidiary undertaking and dormant.

(4) In this section—

(a) "group company" means a company that is a parent company or a subsidiary undertaking, and

(b) "the group", in relation to a group company, means that company together with all its associated undertakings.

For this purpose undertakings are associated if one is a subsidiary undertaking of the other or both are subsidiary undertakings of a third undertaking.

(5) For the purposes of this section—

(a) whether a group qualifies as small shall be determined in accordance with section 383 (companies qualifying as small: parent companies);

(b) "ineligible group" has the meaning given by section 384(2) and (3);

(c)–(e) . . .

(6) The provisions mentioned in subsection (5) apply for the purposes of this section as if all the bodies corporate in the group were companies.

NOTES

Sub-s (1)(a) was substituted, and sub-ss (2) and (5)(c)–(e) were repealed, by the Companies and Limited Liability Partnerships (Accounts and Audit Exemptions and Change of Accounting Framework) Regulations 2012, SI 2012/2301, regs 2, 5(a), as from 1 October 2012 (in relation to accounts for financial years ending on or after that date).

[Exemption from audit: qualifying subsidiaries

[1.546]

479A Subsidiary companies: conditions for exemption from audit

(1) A company is exempt from the requirements of this Act relating to the audit of individual accounts for a financial year if—

(a) it is itself a subsidiary undertaking, and

(b) its parent undertaking is established under the law of [any part of the United Kingdom].

(2) Exemption is conditional upon compliance with all of the following conditions—

(a) all members of the company must agree to the exemption in respect of the financial year in question,

(b) the parent undertaking must give a guarantee under section 479C in respect of that year,

(c) the company must be included in the consolidated accounts drawn up for that year or to an earlier date in that year by the parent undertaking in accordance with—

[(i) if the undertaking is a company, the requirements of Part 15 of this Act, or, if the undertaking is not a company, the legal requirements which apply to the drawing up of consolidated accounts for that undertaking, or]

(ii) [UK-adopted international accounting standards],

(d) the parent undertaking must disclose in the notes to the consolidated accounts that the company is exempt from the requirements of this Act relating to the audit of individual accounts by virtue of this section, and

(e) the directors of the company must deliver to the registrar on or before the date that they file the accounts for that year—

(i) a written notice of the agreement referred to in subsection (2)(a),

(ii) the statement referred to in section 479C(1),

(iii) a copy of the consolidated accounts referred to in subsection (2)(c),

(iv) a copy of the auditor's report on those accounts, and

(v) a copy of the consolidated annual report drawn up by the parent undertaking.

(3) This section has effect subject to—

section 475(2) and (3) (requirements as to statements contained in balance sheet), and

section 476 (right of members to require audit).]

NOTES

Inserted, together with the preceding heading and ss 479B, 479C, by the Companies and Limited Liability Partnerships (Accounts and Audit Exemptions and Change of Accounting Framework) Regulations 2012, SI 2012/2301, regs 2, 7, as from 1 October 2012 (in relation to accounts for financial years ending on or after that date).

Sub-s (1): words in square brackets in para (b) substituted by the Statutory Auditors and Third Country Auditors (Amendment) (EU Exit) Regulations 2019, SI 2019/177, regs 3, 4(a), as from IP completion day (as defined in the European Union (Withdrawal Agreement) Act 2020, s 39) (for transitional provisions in relation to audits of accounts for financial years that begin before IP completion day, see Sch 4 to the 2019 Regulations at **[12.88]**). Note that SI 2019/177, reg 4 was substituted by the Statutory Auditors, Third Country Auditors and International Accounting Standards (Amendment) (EU Exit) Regulations 2019, SI 2019/1392, regs 2, 4, with effect from immediately before IP completion day (and that the effect of that substitution has been incorporated).

Sub-s (2) is amended as follows:

Sub-para (c)(i) substituted by SI 2019/177, regs 3, 4(b), as from IP completion day (see also the first note relating to the 2019 Regulations above).

Words in square brackets in sub-para (c)(ii) substituted by the International Accounting Standards and European Public Limited-Liability Company (Amendment etc) (EU Exit) Regulations 2019, SI 2019/685, reg 19, Sch 1, Pt 1, paras 1, 22, in relation to accounts for financial years beginning on or after IP completion day (as defined in the European Union (Withdrawal Agreement) Act 2020, s 39) (note also that in relation to accounts for financial years which begin before but end on or after IP completion day, the enactments amended by Parts 1–3 of Sch 1 to the 2019 Regulations have effect as if the UK were a member State until the end of the financial year in question).

[1.547]

[479B Companies excluded from the subsidiary companies audit exemption

A company is not entitled to the exemption conferred by section 479A (subsidiary companies) if it was at any time within the financial year in question—

[(a) a traded company as defined in section 474(1),]

(b) a company that—

(i) is an authorised insurance company, a banking company, an e-money issuer, a MiFID investment firm or a UCITS management company, . . .

(ii) carries on insurance market activity, or

[(iii) is a scheme funder of a Master Trust scheme within the meanings given by section 39(1) of the Pension Schemes Act 2017 (interpretation of Part 1), or]

(c) a special register body as defined in section 117(1) of the Trade Union and Labour Relations (Consolidation) Act 1992 (c 52) or an employers' association as defined in section 122 of that Act or Article 4 of the Industrial Relations (Northern Ireland) Order 1992 (SI 1992/807) (NI 5).]

NOTES

Inserted as noted to s 479A at **[1.546]**.

Para (a) substituted by the Companies, Partnerships and Groups (Accounts and Reports) Regulations 2015, SI 2015/980, reg 10(1), (3), in relation to (a) financial years beginning on or after 1 January 2016, and (b) a financial year of a company beginning on or after 1 January 2015, but before 1 January 2016, if the directors of the company so decide (subject to transitional provisions, etc, in regs 2, 3 of the 2015 Regulations as noted to s 380 at **[1.430]**).

Word omitted from sub-para (b)(i) repealed, and sub-para (b)(iii) inserted, by the Occupational Pension Schemes (Master Trusts) Regulations 2018, SI 2018/1030, reg 30(1), (5), as from 1 October 2018.

[1.548]

[479C Subsidiary companies audit exemption: parent undertaking declaration of guarantee

(1) A guarantee is given by a parent undertaking under this section when the directors of the subsidiary company deliver to the registrar a statement by the parent undertaking that it guarantees the subsidiary company under this section.

(2) The statement under subsection (1) must be authenticated by the parent undertaking and must specify—

(a) the name of the parent undertaking,

[(b) the registered number (if any) of the parent undertaking,]

(c) . . .

(d) the name and registered number of the subsidiary company in respect of which the guarantee is being given,

(e) the date of the statement, and

(f) the financial year to which the guarantee relates.

(3) A guarantee given under this section has the effect that—

(a) the parent undertaking guarantees all outstanding liabilities to which the subsidiary company is subject at the end of the financial year to which the guarantee relates, until they are satisfied in full, and

(b) the guarantee is enforceable against the parent undertaking by any person to whom the subsidiary company is liable in respect of those liabilities.]

NOTES

Inserted as noted to s 479A at **[1.546]**.

Sub-s (2): para (b) was substituted, and para (c) was repealed, by the Statutory Auditors and Third Country Auditors (Amendment) (EU Exit) Regulations 2019, SI 2019/177, regs 3, 4A, as from IP completion day (as defined in the European Union (Withdrawal Agreement) Act 2020, s 39) (for transitional provisions in relation to audits of accounts for financial years that begin before IP completion day, see Sch 4 to the 2019 Regulations at **[12.88]**). Note that the original SI 2019/177, reg 4 was substituted (by new regs 4, 4A) with effect from immediately before IP completion day.

Exemption from audit: dormant companies

[1.549]
480 Dormant companies: conditions for exemption from audit

(1) A company is exempt from the requirements of this Act relating to the audit of accounts in respect of a financial year if—
- (a) it has been dormant since its formation, or
- (b) it has been dormant since the end of the previous financial year and the following conditions are met.

(2) The conditions are that the company—
- (a) as regards its individual accounts for the financial year in question—
  - (i) is entitled to prepare accounts in accordance with the small companies regime (see sections 381 to 384), or
  - (ii) would be so entitled but for having been a public company or a member of an ineligible group, and
- (b) is not required to prepare group accounts for that year.

(3) This section has effect subject to—

section 475(2) and (3) (requirements as to statements to be contained in balance sheet),
section 476 (right of members to require audit), and
section 481 (companies excluded from dormant companies exemption).

[1.550]
481 Companies excluded from dormant companies exemption

A company is not entitled to the exemption conferred by section 480 (dormant companies) if it was at any time within the financial year in question a company that—
- [(za) is a traded company as defined in section 474(1),]
- (a) is an authorised insurance company, a banking company, an e-money issuer, [a MiFID investment firm] or a UCITS management company, or
- (b) carries on insurance market activity.

NOTES

Para (za) inserted by the Companies, Partnerships and Groups (Accounts and Reports) Regulations 2015, SI 2015/980, reg 10(1), (4), in relation to (a) financial years beginning on or after 1 January 2016, and (b) a financial year of a company beginning on or after 1 January 2015, but before 1 January 2016, if the directors of the company so decide (subject to transitional provisions, etc, in regs 2, 3 of the 2015 Regulations as noted to s 380 at **[1.430]**).

Words in square brackets in para (a) substituted by the Markets in Financial Instruments Directive (Consequential Amendments) Regulations 2007, SI 2007/2932, reg 3(6), as from 1 November 2007.

Companies subject to public sector audit

[1.551]
482 Non-profit-making companies subject to public sector audit

(1) The requirements of this Part as to audit of accounts do not apply to a company for a financial year if it is non-profit-making and its accounts—
- [(a) are subject to audit by the Comptroller and Auditor General by virtue of an order under section 25(6) of the Government Resources and Accounts Act 2000;
- (ab) are subject to audit by the Auditor General for Wales by virtue of—
  - (i) an order under section 144 of the Government of Wales Act 1998, or
  - (ii) paragraph 18 of Schedule 8 to the Government of Wales Act 2006;]
- (b) are accounts—
  - (i) in relation to which section 21 of the Public Finance and Accountability (Scotland) Act 2000 (asp 1) (audit of accounts: Auditor General for Scotland) applies, or
  - (ii) that are subject to audit by the Auditor General for Scotland by virtue of an order under section 483 (Scottish public sector companies: audit by Auditor General for Scotland); or
- (c) are subject to audit by the Comptroller and Auditor General for Northern Ireland by virtue of an order under Article 5(3) of the Audit and Accountability (Northern Ireland) Order 2003 (SI 2003/418 (NI 5)).

(2) In the case of a company that is a parent company or a subsidiary undertaking, subsection (1) applies only if every group undertaking is non-profit-making.

(3) In this section "non-profit-making" has the same meaning as in [Article 54 of the Treaty on the Functioning of the European Union].

(4) This section has effect subject to section 475(2) (balance sheet to contain statement that company entitled to exemption under this section).

NOTES

Sub-s (1): paras (a), (ab) substituted, for the original para (a), by the Government of Wales Act 2006 (Consequential Modifications, Transitional Provisions and Saving) Order 2009, SI 2009/2958, arts 8, 10, as from 6 November 2009.

Sub-s (3): words in square brackets substituted by the Treaty of Lisbon (Changes in Terminology or Numbering) Order 2012, SI 2012/1809, art 3, Schedule, Pt 1, as from 1 August 2012 (except in relation to things done before 1 December 2009).

[1.552]
483 Scottish public sector companies: audit by Auditor General for Scotland

(1) The Scottish Ministers may by order provide for the accounts of a company having its registered office in Scotland to be audited by the Auditor General for Scotland.

(2) An order under subsection (1) may be made in relation to a company only if it appears to the Scottish Ministers that the company—
- (a) exercises in or as regards Scotland functions of a public nature none of which relate to reserved matters (within the meaning of the Scotland Act 1998 (c 46)), or
- (b) is entirely or substantially funded from a body having accounts falling within paragraph (a) or (b) of subsection (3).

(3) Those accounts are—

(a) accounts in relation to which section 21 of the Public Finance and Accountability (Scotland) Act 2000 (asp 1) (audit of accounts: Auditor General for Scotland) applies,

(b) accounts which are subject to audit by the Auditor General for Scotland by virtue of an order under this section.

(4) An order under subsection (1) may make such supplementary or consequential provision (including provision amending an enactment) as the Scottish Ministers think expedient.

(5) An order under subsection (1) shall not be made unless a draft of the statutory instrument containing it has been laid before, and approved by resolution of, the Scottish Parliament.

NOTES

Orders: the Companies Act 2006 (Scottish public sector companies to be audited by the Auditor General for Scotland) Order 2008, SSI 2008/144; the Companies Act 2006 (Scottish public sector companies to be audited by the Auditor General for Scotland) Order 2019, SSI 2019/180; the Companies Act 2006 (Scottish public sector companies to be audited by the Auditor General for Scotland) Order 2020, SSI 2020/402; the Companies Act 2006 (Scottish public sector companies to be audited by the Auditor General for Scotland) Order 2021, SSI 2021/129; the Companies Act 2006 (Scottish public sector companies to be audited by the Auditor General for Scotland) Order 2022, SSI 2022/207. For a summary of all statutory instruments made under this Act, see Appendix 4 at **[A4]**.

General power of amendment by regulations

[1.553]

484 General power of amendment by regulations

(1) The Secretary of State may by regulations amend this Chapter or section 539 (minor definitions) so far as applying to this Chapter by adding, altering or repealing provisions.

(2) The regulations may make consequential amendments or repeals in other provisions of this Act, or in other enactments.

(3) Regulations under this section imposing new requirements, or rendering existing requirements more onerous, are subject to affirmative resolution procedure.

(4) Other regulations under this section are subject to negative resolution procedure.

NOTES

Regulations: the Companies Act 2006 (Amendment) (Accounts and Reports) Regulations 2008, SI 2008/393; the Companies and Limited Liability Partnerships (Accounts and Audit Exemptions and Change of Accounting Framework) Regulations 2012, SI 2012/2301; the Companies and Partnerships (Accounts and Audit) Regulations 2013, SI 2013/2005; the Companies, Partnerships and Groups (Accounts and Reports) Regulations 2015, SI 2015/980; the Statutory Auditors and Third Country Auditors (Amendment) (EU Exit) Regulations 2019, SI 2019/177 at **[12.83]**; the Statutory Auditors, Third Country Auditors and International Accounting Standards (Amendment) (EU Exit) Regulations 2019, SI 2019/1392; the Statutory Auditors and Third Country Auditors (Amendment) (EU Exit) Regulations 2020, SI 2020/108 at **[12.171]**. For a summary of all statutory instruments made under this Act, see Appendix 4 at **[A4]**.

CHAPTER 2 APPOINTMENT OF AUDITORS

Private companies

[1.554]

485 Appointment of auditors of private company: general

(1) An auditor or auditors of a private company must be appointed for each financial year of the company, unless the directors reasonably resolve otherwise on the ground that audited accounts are unlikely to be required.

(2) For each financial year for which an auditor or auditors is or are to be appointed (other than the company's first financial year), the appointment must be made before the end of the period of 28 days beginning with—

(a) the end of the time allowed for sending out copies of the company's annual accounts and reports for the previous financial year (see section 424), or

(b) if earlier, the day on which copies of the company's annual accounts and reports for the previous financial year are sent out under section 423.

This is the "period for appointing auditors".

(3) The directors may appoint an auditor or auditors of the company—

(a) at any time before the company's first period for appointing auditors,

(b) following a period during which the company (being exempt from audit) did not have any auditor, at any time before the company's next period for appointing auditors, or

(c) to fill a casual vacancy in the office of auditor.

(4) The members may appoint an auditor or auditors by ordinary resolution—

(a) during a period for appointing auditors,

(b) if the company should have appointed an auditor or auditors during a period for appointing auditors but failed to do so, or

(c) where the directors had power to appoint under subsection (3) but have failed to make an appointment.

(5) An auditor or auditors of a private company may only be appointed—

(a) in accordance with this section, or

(b) in accordance with section 486 [or 486A] (default power of Secretary of State).

This is without prejudice to any deemed re-appointment under section 487.

NOTES

Sub-s (5): words in square brackets inserted by the Statutory Auditors Regulations 2017, SI 2017/1164, reg 3, Sch 1, paras 7, 14, in relation to financial years of companies beginning on or after 17 June 2016 (see**[4.671]** et seq).

[1.555]

[485A Appointment of auditors of private company: additional requirements for public interest entities with audit committees

(1) This section applies to the appointment under section 485(4) of an auditor or auditors of a private company—

(a) which is also a public interest entity; and

(b) which has an audit committee.

(2) But it does not apply to the appointment of an Auditor General as auditor or one of the auditors of the company.

(3) Before an appointment to which this section applies is made—

(a) the audit committee of the company must make a recommendation to the directors in connection with the appointment, and

(b) the directors must propose an auditor or auditors for appointment . . .

(4) Before the audit committee makes a recommendation or the directors make a proposal under subsection (3), the committee . . . must carry out a selection procedure in accordance with Article 16(3) of the Audit Regulation, unless the company is a small or medium sized enterprise within the meaning in Article 2(1)(f) of Directive 2003/71/EC.

(5) The audit committee must in its recommendation—

(a) identify its first and second choice candidates for appointment [drawn from those auditors who have participated in a selection procedure under subsection (4)],

(b) give reasons for the choices so identified,

(c) state that—

(i) the recommendation is free from influence by a third party, and

(ii) no contractual term of the kind mentioned in Article 16(6) of the Audit Regulation has been imposed on the company.

[(6) The directors must include in their proposal—

(a) the recommendation made by the audit committee in connection with the appointment, and

(b) if the proposal of the directors departs from the preference of the audit committee—

(i) a recommendation for a candidate or candidates for appointment drawn from those auditors who have participated in a selection procedure under subsection (4), and

(ii) the reasons for not following the audit committee's recommendation.

(7) Where the audit committee recommends re-appointment of the company's existing auditor or auditors, and the directors are in agreement, subsections (4) and (5)(a) and (b) do not apply.]]

NOTES

Inserted, together with s 485B, by the Statutory Auditors and Third Country Auditors Regulations 2016, SI 2016/649, reg 15, Sch 3, Pt 3, para 4, as from 17 June 2016, in relation to financial years beginning on or after that date.

The words omitted from sub-ss (3) and (4) were repealed, the words in square brackets in sub-s (5) were inserted, and sub-ss (6) and (7) were substituted (for the original sub-ss (6)–(8)), by the Statutory Auditors and Third Country Auditors Regulations 2017, SI 2017/516, reg 12(1), (2), in relation to financial years of companies beginning on or after 17 June 2016.

[1.556]

[485B Appointment of auditors of private company: additional requirements for public interest entities without audit committees

(1) This section applies to the appointment under section 485(4) of an auditor or auditors of a private company—

(a) which is also a public interest entity; and

(b) which does not have an audit committee.

(2) But it does not apply to the appointment of an Auditor General as auditor or one of the auditors of the company.

(3) Before an appointment to which this section applies is made the directors must propose an auditor or auditors for appointment.

(4) Before the directors make a proposal under subsection (3), they must carry out a selection procedure in accordance with Article 16(3) of the Audit Regulation, [from which their proposed auditor or auditors must be drawn,] unless the company is a small or medium sized enterprise within the meaning in Article 2(1)(f) of Directive 2003/71/EC.

[(5) Subsection (4) does not apply in relation to a proposal to re-appoint the company's existing auditor or auditors.]]

NOTES

Inserted as noted to s 485A at **[1.555]**.

The words in square brackets in sub-s (4) were inserted, and sub-s (5) was substituted (for the original sub-ss (5)–(7)), by the Statutory Auditors and Third Country Auditors Regulations 2017, SI 2017/516, reg 12(1), (3), in relation to financial years of companies beginning on or after 17 June 2016.

[1.557]

[485C Restriction on appointment of auditor of private company which is a public interest entity

(1) A person who has been, or will have been, auditor of a private company which is a public interest entity for every financial year comprised in the maximum engagement period (see section 494ZA) may not be appointed as auditor of the company for any financial year which begins within the period of 4 years beginning with the day after the last day of the last financial year of the maximum engagement period.

(2) A person who is a member of the same network as the auditor mentioned in subsection (1) may not be appointed as auditor of the company for any financial year which begins within the period of 4 years mentioned in that subsection.

(3) This section does not apply in relation to an Auditor General.]

NOTES

Inserted by the Statutory Auditors and Third Country Auditors Regulations 2017, SI 2017/516, reg 12(1), (4), in relation to financial years of companies beginning on or after 17 June 2016.

[1.558]

486 Appointment of auditors of private company: default power of Secretary of State

(1) If a private company fails to appoint an auditor or auditors in accordance with section 485 . . . the Secretary of State may appoint one or more persons to fill the vacancy.

(2) Where subsection (2) of [section 485] applies and the company fails to make the necessary appointment before the end of the period for appointing auditors, the company must within one week of the end of that period give notice to the Secretary of State of his power having become exercisable.

(3) If a company fails to give the notice required by this section, an offence is committed by—

(a) the company, and

(b) every officer of the company who is in default.

(4) A person guilty of an offence under this section is liable on summary conviction to a fine not exceeding level 3 on the standard scale and, for continued contravention, a daily default fine not exceeding one-tenth of level 3 on the standard scale.

NOTES

Sub-s (1): words omitted repealed by the Statutory Auditors Regulations 2017, SI 2017/1164, reg 3, Sch 1, paras 7, 15, in relation to financial years of companies beginning on or after 17 June 2016 (see**[4.671]** et seq).

Sub-s (2): words in square brackets substituted by the Statutory Auditors and Third Country Auditors Regulations 2017, SI 2017/516, reg 12(1), (5), in relation to financial years of companies beginning on or after 17 June 2016.

[1.559]

[486A Defective appointments: default power of Secretary of State

(1) If—

(a) a private company appoints, or purports to appoint, an auditor or auditors, and

(b) the appointment or purported appointment is made in breach of section 485A, 485B or 485C (requirements applying to appointment of auditors by public interest entities),

the Secretary of State may appoint another auditor or auditors in place of the auditor or auditors referred to in paragraph (a).

(2) The breach of section 485A, 485B or 485C does not invalidate any report made under Chapter 3 of this Part by the auditor or auditors on the company's annual reports or accounts before the auditor or auditors are replaced under subsection (1) of this section.

(3) But where the breach in question is a breach of section 485C, sections 1248 and 1249 (Secretary of State's power to require second audit) apply as if the auditor was not an appropriate person, or the auditors were not appropriate persons, for the period during which the audit was conducted.

(4) Within one week of becoming aware of the breach of section 485A, 485B or 485C, the company must give notice to the Secretary of State that the power under subsection (1) of this section has become exercisable.

(5) If the company fails to give the notice required by subsection (4), an offence is committed by—

(a) the company, and

(b) every officer of the company who is in default.

(6) A person guilty of an offence under this section is liable on summary conviction to a fine not exceeding level 3 on the standard scale and, for continued contravention, a daily default fine not exceeding one-tenth of level 3 on the standard scale.]

NOTES

Inserted by the Statutory Auditors Regulations 2017, SI 2017/1164, reg 3, Sch 1, paras 7, 16, in relation to financial years of companies beginning on or after 17 June 2016 (see**[4.671]** et seq).

[1.560]

487 Term of office of auditors of private company

(1) An auditor or auditors of a private company hold office in accordance with the terms of their appointment, subject to the requirements that—

(a) they do not take office until any previous auditor or auditors cease to hold office, and

(b) they cease to hold office at the end of the next period for appointing auditors unless re-appointed.

[(1A)–(1E) . . .]

(2) Where no auditor has been appointed by the end of the next period for appointing auditors, any auditor in office immediately before that time is deemed to be re-appointed at that time, unless—

(a) he was appointed by the directors, or

(b) the company's articles require actual re-appointment, or

(c) the deemed re-appointment is prevented by the members under section 488, or

(d) the members have resolved that he should not be re-appointed, or

(e) the directors have resolved that no auditor or auditors should be appointed for the financial year in question[, or

[(f) the auditor's appointment would be in breach of section 485C]].

(3) This is without prejudice to the provisions of this Part as to removal and resignation of auditors.

(4) No account shall be taken of any loss of the opportunity of deemed re-appointment under this section in ascertaining the amount of any compensation or damages payable to an auditor on his ceasing to hold office for any reason.

NOTES

Sub-ss (1A)–(1E) originally inserted, and sub-s (2)(f) (and the preceding word) inserted, by the Statutory Auditors and Third Country Auditors Regulations 2016, SI 2016/649, reg 15, Sch 3, Pt 3, para 6, as from 17 June 2016, in relation to financial years beginning on or after that date.

Sub-ss (1A)–(1E) subsequently repealed, and sub-s (2)(f) substituted, by the Statutory Auditors and Third Country Auditors Regulations 2017, SI 2017/516, reg 12(1), (6), in relation to financial years of companies beginning on or after 17 June 2016.

487A (*Inserted by the Statutory Auditors and Third Country Auditors Regulations 2016, SI 2016/649, reg 15, Sch 3, Pt 3, para 7, as from 17 June 2016, in relation to financial years beginning on or after that date. Subsequently repealed by the Statutory Auditors and Third Country Auditors Regulations 2017, SI 2017/516, reg 12(1), (7), in relation to financial years of companies beginning on or after 17 June 2016.*)

[1.561]

488 Prevention by members of deemed re-appointment of auditor

(1) An auditor of a private company is not deemed to be re-appointed under section 487(2) if the company has received notices under this section from members representing at least the requisite percentage of the total voting rights of all members who would be entitled to vote on a resolution that the auditor should not be re-appointed.

(2) The "requisite percentage" is 5%, or such lower percentage as is specified for this purpose in the company's articles.

(3) A notice under this section—

- (a) may be in hard copy or electronic form,
- (b) must be authenticated by the person or persons giving it, and
- (c) must be received by the company before the end of the accounting reference period immediately preceding the time when the deemed re-appointment would have effect.

Public companies

[1.562]

489 Appointment of auditors of public company: general

(1) An auditor or auditors of a public company must be appointed for each financial year of the company, unless the directors reasonably resolve otherwise on the ground that audited accounts are unlikely to be required.

(2) For each financial year for which an auditor or auditors is or are to be appointed (other than the company's first financial year), the appointment must be made before the end of the accounts meeting of the company at which the company's annual accounts and reports for the previous financial year are laid.

(3) The directors may appoint an auditor or auditors of the company—

- (a) at any time before the company's first accounts meeting;
- (b) following a period during which the company (being exempt from audit) did not have any auditor, at any time before the company's next accounts meeting;
- (c) to fill a casual vacancy in the office of auditor.

(4) The members may appoint an auditor or auditors by ordinary resolution—

- (a) at an accounts meeting;
- (b) if the company should have appointed an auditor or auditors at an accounts meeting but failed to do so;
- (c) where the directors had power to appoint under subsection (3) but have failed to make an appointment.

(5) An auditor or auditors of a public company may only be appointed—

- (a) in accordance with this section, or
- (b) in accordance with section 490 [or 490A] (default power of Secretary of State).

NOTES

Sub-s (5): words in square brackets inserted by the Statutory Auditors Regulations 2017, SI 2017/1164, reg 3, Sch 1, paras 7, 17, in relation to financial years of companies beginning on or after 17 June 2016 (see **[4.671]** et seq).

[1.563]

[489A Appointment of auditors of public company: additional requirements for public interest entities with audit committees

(1) This section applies to the appointment under section 489(4) of an auditor or auditors of a public company—

- (a) which is also a public interest entity; and
- (b) which has an audit committee.

(2) But it does not apply to the appointment of an Auditor General as auditor or one of the auditors of the company.

(3) Before an appointment to which this section applies is made—

- (a) the audit committee of the company must make a recommendation to the directors in connection with the appointment, and
- (b) the directors must propose an auditor or auditors for appointment . . .

(4) Before the audit committee makes a recommendation or the directors make a proposal under subsection (3), the committee . . . must carry out a selection procedure in accordance with Article 16(3) of the Audit Regulation, unless the company is—

- (a) a small or medium sized enterprise within the meaning in Article 2(1)(f) of Directive 2003/71/EC; or
- (b) a company with reduced market capitalisation within the meaning in Article 2(1)(t) of that Directive.

(5) The audit committee must in its recommendation—

- (a) identify its first and second choice candidates for appointment, [drawn from those auditors who have participated in a selection procedure under subsection (4)]
- (b) give reasons for the choices so identified,
- (c) state that—
  - (i) the recommendation is free from influence by a third party, and
  - (ii) no contractual term of the kind mentioned in Article 16(6) of the Audit Regulation has been imposed on the company.

[(6) The directors must include in their proposal—

- (a) the recommendation made by the audit committee in connection with the appointment, and
- (b) if the proposal of the directors departs from the preference of the audit committee—
  - (i) a recommendation for a candidate or candidates for appointment drawn from those auditors who have participated in a selection procedure under subsection (4), and
  - (ii) the reasons for not following the audit committee's recommendation.

(7) Where the audit committee recommends re-appointment of the company's existing auditor or auditors, and the directors are in agreement, subsections (4) and (5)(a) and (b) do not apply.]]

NOTES

Inserted, together with s 489B, by the Statutory Auditors and Third Country Auditors Regulations 2016, SI 2016/649, reg 15, Sch 3, Pt 3, para 8, as from 17 June 2016, in relation to financial years beginning on or after that date.

The words omitted from sub-ss (3) and (4) were repealed, the words in square brackets in sub-s (5) were inserted, and sub-ss (6) and (7) were substituted (for the original sub-ss (6)–(8)), by the Statutory Auditors and Third Country Auditors Regulations 2017, SI 2017/516, reg 12(1), (8), in relation to financial years of companies beginning on or after 17 June 2016.

[1.564]

[489B Appointment of auditors of public company: additional requirements for public interest entities without audit committees

(1) This section applies to the appointment under section 489(4) of an auditor or auditors of a public company—

(a) which is also a public interest entity; and

(b) which does not have an audit committee.

(2) But it does not apply to the appointment of an Auditor General as auditor or one of the auditors of the company.

(3) Before an appointment to which this section applies is made the directors must propose an auditor or auditors for appointment.

(4) Before the directors make a proposal under subsection (3), the directors must carry out a selection procedure in accordance with Article 16(3) of the Audit Regulation, [from which their proposed auditor or auditors must be drawn,] unless the company is—

(a) a small or medium sized enterprise within the meaning in Article 2(1)(f) of Directive 2003/71/EU; or

(b) a company with reduced market capitalisation within the meaning in Article 2(1)(t) of that Directive.

[(5) Subsection (4) does not apply in relation to a proposal to re-appoint the company's existing auditor or auditors.]]

NOTES

Inserted as noted to s 489A at **[1.563]**.

The words in square brackets in sub-s (4) were inserted, and sub-s (5) was substituted (for the original sub-ss (5)–(7)), by the Statutory Auditors and Third Country Auditors Regulations 2017, SI 2017/516, reg 12(1), (9), in relation to financial years of companies beginning on or after 17 June 2016.

[1.565]

[489C Restriction on appointment of auditor of public company which is a public interest entity

(1) A person who has been, or will have been, auditor of a public company which is a public interest entity for every financial year comprised in the maximum engagement period (see section 494ZA) may not be appointed as auditor of the company for any financial year which begins within the period of 4 years beginning with the day after the last day of the last financial year of the maximum engagement period.

(2) A person who is a member of the same network as the auditor mentioned in subsection (1) may not be appointed as auditor of the company for any financial year which begins within the period of 4 years mentioned in that subsection.

(3) This section does not apply in relation to an Auditor General.]

NOTES

Inserted by the Statutory Auditors and Third Country Auditors Regulations 2017, SI 2017/516, reg 12(1), (10), in relation to financial years of companies beginning on or after 17 June 2016.

[1.566]

490 Appointment of auditors of public company: default power of Secretary of State

(1) If a public company fails to appoint an auditor or auditors in accordance with section 489 . . . the Secretary of State may appoint one or more persons to fill the vacancy.

(2) Where subsection (2) of [section 489] applies and the company fails to make the necessary appointment before the end of the accounts meeting, the company must within one week of the end of that meeting give notice to the Secretary of State of his power having become exercisable.

(3) If a company fails to give the notice required by this section, an offence is committed by—

(a) the company, and

(b) every officer of the company who is in default.

(4) A person guilty of an offence under this section is liable on summary conviction to a fine not exceeding level 3 on the standard scale and, for continued contravention, a daily default fine not exceeding one-tenth of level 3 on the standard scale.

NOTES

Sub-s (1): words omitted repealed by the Statutory Auditors Regulations 2017, SI 2017/1164, reg 3, Sch 1, paras 7, 18, in relation to financial years of companies beginning on or after 17 June 2016 (see **[4.671]** et seq).

Sub-s (2): words in square brackets substituted by the Statutory Auditors and Third Country Auditors Regulations 2017, SI 2017/516, reg 12(1), (11), in relation to financial years of companies beginning on or after 17 June 2016.

[1.567]

[490A Defective appointments: default power of Secretary of State

(1) If—

(a) a public company appoints, or purports to appoint, an auditor or auditors, and

(b) the appointment or purported appointment is made in breach of section 489A, 489B or 489C (requirements applying to appointment of auditors by public interest entities),

the Secretary of State may appoint another auditor or auditors in place of the auditor or auditors referred to in paragraph (a).

(2) The breach of section 489A, 489B or 489C does not invalidate any report made under Chapter 3 of this Part by the auditor or auditors on the company's annual reports or accounts before the auditor or auditors are replaced under subsection (1) of this section.

(3) But where the breach in question is a breach of section 489C, sections 1248 and 1249 (Secretary of State's power to require second audit) apply as if the auditor was not an appropriate person, or the auditors were not appropriate persons, for the period during which the audit was conducted.

(4) Within one week of becoming aware of the breach of section 489A, 489B or 489C, the company must give notice to the Secretary of State that the power under subsection (1) of this section has become exercisable.

(5) If the company fails to give the notice required by subsection (4), an offence is committed by—

- (a) the company, and
- (b) every officer of the company who is in default.

(6) A person guilty of an offence under this section is liable on summary conviction to a fine not exceeding level 3 on the standard scale and, for continued contravention, a daily default fine not exceeding one-tenth of level 3 on the standard scale.]

NOTES

Inserted by the Statutory Auditors Regulations 2017, SI 2017/1164, reg 3, Sch 1, paras 7, 19, in relation to financial years of companies beginning on or after 17 June 2016 (see **[4.671]** et seq).

[1.568]
491 Term of office of auditors of public company

(1) The auditor or auditors of a public company hold office in accordance with the terms of their appointment, subject to the requirements that—

- (a) they do not take office until the previous auditor or auditors have ceased to hold office, and
- (b) they cease to hold office at the conclusion of the accounts meeting next following their appointment, unless re-appointed.

[(1A)–(1E) . . .]

(2) This is without prejudice to the provisions of this Part as to removal and resignation of auditors.

NOTES

Sub-ss (1A)–(1E): originally inserted by the Statutory Auditors and Third Country Auditors Regulations 2016, SI 2016/649, reg 15, Sch 3, Pt 3, para 10, as from 17 June 2016, in relation to financial years beginning on or after that date. Subsequently repealed by the Statutory Auditors and Third Country Auditors Regulations 2017, SI 2017/516, reg 12(1), (12), in relation to financial years of companies beginning on or after 17 June 2016.

491A (*Inserted by the Statutory Auditors and Third Country Auditors Regulations 2016, SI 2016/649, reg 15, Sch 3, Pt 3, para 11, as from 17 June 2016, in relation to financial years beginning on or after that date. Subsequently repealed by the Statutory Auditors and Third Country Auditors Regulations 2017, SI 2017/516, reg 12(1), (13), in relation to financial years of companies beginning on or after 17 June 2016.*)

General provisions

[1.569]
492 Fixing of auditor's remuneration

(1) The remuneration of an auditor appointed by the members of a company must be fixed by the members by ordinary resolution or in such manner as the members may by ordinary resolution determine.

(2) The remuneration of an auditor appointed by the directors of a company must be fixed by the directors.

(3) The remuneration of an auditor appointed by the Secretary of State must be fixed by the Secretary of State.

(4) For the purposes of this section "remuneration" includes sums paid in respect of expenses.

(5) This section applies in relation to benefits in kind as to payments of money.

[1.570]
493 Disclosure of terms of audit appointment

(1) The Secretary of State may make provision by regulations for securing the disclosure of the terms on which a company's auditor is appointed, remunerated or performs his duties.

Nothing in the following provisions of this section affects the generality of this power.

(2) The regulations may—

- (a) require disclosure of—
  - (i) a copy of any terms that are in writing, and
  - (ii) a written memorandum setting out any terms that are not in writing;
- (b) require disclosure to be at such times, in such places and by such means as are specified in the regulations;
- (c) require the place and means of disclosure to be stated—
  - (i) in a note to the company's annual accounts (in the case of its individual accounts) or in such manner as is specified in the regulations (in the case of group accounts),
  - (ii) in [the strategic report or] the directors' report, or
  - (iii) in the auditor's report on the company's annual accounts.

(3) The provisions of this section apply to a variation of the terms mentioned in subsection (1) as they apply to the original terms.

(4) Regulations under this section are subject to affirmative resolution procedure.

NOTES

Sub-s (2): words in square brackets in sub-para (c)(ii) inserted by the Companies Act 2006 (Strategic Report and Directors' Report) Regulations 2013, SI 2013/1970, reg 14, Schedule, paras 1, 19, in respect of financial years ending on or after 30 September 2013.

Regulations: no Regulations have been made under this section.

[1.571]
494 Disclosure of services provided by auditor or associates and related remuneration

(1) The Secretary of State may make provision by regulations for securing the disclosure of—

(a) the nature of any services provided for a company by the company's auditor (whether in his capacity as auditor or otherwise) or by his associates;

(b) the amount of any remuneration received or receivable by a company's auditor, or his associates, in respect of any such services.

Nothing in the following provisions of this section affects the generality of this power.

(2) The regulations may provide—

(a) for disclosure of the nature of any services provided to be made by reference to any class or description of services specified in the regulations (or any combination of services, however described);

(b) for the disclosure of amounts of remuneration received or receivable in respect of services of any class or description specified in the regulations (or any combination of services, however described);

(c) for the disclosure of separate amounts so received or receivable by the company's auditor or any of his associates, or of aggregate amounts so received or receivable by all or any of those persons.

(3) The regulations may—

(a) provide that "remuneration" includes sums paid in respect of expenses;

(b) apply to benefits in kind as well as to payments of money, and require the disclosure of the nature of any such benefits and their estimated money value;

(c) apply to services provided for associates of a company as well as to those provided for a company;

(d) define "associate" in relation to an auditor and a company respectively.

(4) The regulations may provide that any disclosure required by the regulations is to be made—

(a) in a note to the company's annual accounts (in the case of its individual accounts) or in such manner as is specified in the regulations (in the case of group accounts),

(b) in [the strategic report or] the directors' report, or

(c) in the auditor's report on the company's annual accounts.

(5) If the regulations provide that any such disclosure is to be made as mentioned in subsection (4)(a) or (b), the regulations may require the auditor to supply the directors of the company with any information necessary to enable the disclosure to be made.

(6) Regulations under this section are subject to negative resolution procedure.

NOTES

Sub-s (4): words in square brackets in para (b) inserted by the Companies Act 2006 (Strategic Report and Directors' Report) Regulations 2013, SI 2013/1970, reg 14, Schedule, paras 1, 20, in respect of financial years ending on or after 30 September 2013.

Regulations: the Companies (Disclosure of Auditor Remuneration and Liability Limitation Agreements) Regulations 2008, SI 2008/489 at **[4.115]**; the Companies (Disclosure of Auditor Remuneration and Liability Limitation Agreements) (Amendment) Regulations 2011, SI 2011/2198; the Statutory Auditors and Third Country Auditors Regulations 2016, SI 2016/649 at **[4.650]**. For a summary of all statutory instruments made under this Act, see Appendix 4 at **[A4]**.

[1.572]

[494ZA The maximum engagement period

(1) Where a person is auditor of a company for consecutive financial years, the maximum engagement period of the person as auditor of the company—

(a) begins with the first of those years (see the appropriate entry in the first column of the following Table), and

(b) ends with the financial year specified in the corresponding entry in the second column of the Table:

First financial year of the maximum engagement period	*Last financial year of the maximum engagement period*
A financial year of the company beginning before 17 June 1994	The last financial year of the company to begin before 17 June 2020.
A financial year of the company beginning— (a) on or after 17 June 1994, and (b) before 17 June 2003	The last financial year of the company to begin before 17 June 2023.
A financial year of the company beginning— (a) on or after 17 June 2003, and (b) before 17 June 2016	*No qualifying selection procedure* Where neither the first financial year of the maximum engagement period nor any subsequent financial year is one for which the auditor has been appointed following the carrying out of a qualifying selection procedure, the later of— (a) the last financial year of the company to begin before 17 June 2016, and (b) the last financial year of the company to begin within the period of 10 years beginning with the first day of the first financial year of the maximum engagement period. *No qualifying selection procedure within 10 years* Where the last day of the last financial year of the company to begin within the period of 10 years beginning with the first day of the last financial year of the company for which the auditor was appointed following a qualifying selection procedure is before 17 June 2016— (a) the last financial year of the company to begin before 17 June 2016, unless (b) the auditor is appointed following a qualifying selection procedure for the first financial year of the company to begin on or after 17 June 2016, in which case it is the last financial year of the company to begin within the period of 20 years beginning with the first day of the first financial year of the maximum engagement period.

First financial year of the maximum engagement period	*Last financial year of the maximum engagement period*
	Qualifying selection procedure within 10 years In any other case, the earlier of— (a) the last financial year of the company to begin within the period of 10 years beginning with the first day of the last financial year of the company for which the auditor was appointed following a qualifying selection procedure, and (b) the last financial year of the company to begin within the period of 20 years beginning with the first day of the first financial year of the maximum engagement period.
A financial year of the company beginning on or after 17 June 2016	The earlier of— (a) the last financial year of the company to begin within the period of 10 years beginning with the first day of the last financial year of the company for which the auditor was appointed following a qualifying selection procedure, and (b) the last financial year of the company to begin within the period of 20 years beginning with the first day of the first financial year of the maximum engagement period.

(2) Where the first financial year of the maximum engagement period begins on or after 17 June 2003, the maximum engagement period may be extended by a period of no more than 2 years with the approval of the competent authority.

(3) Such approval may be given by the competent authority only if it is satisfied that exceptional circumstances exist.

(4) Where the competent authority gives its approval as mentioned in subsection (2)—

(a) the second column of the Table in subsection (1) has effect with the necessary modifications, and

(b) the first appointment to be made after the end of the period as so extended must be made following a qualifying selection procedure.

(5) [In this section] "qualifying selection procedure" means—

(a) in the case of an appointment for a financial year beginning on or after 17 June 2016 made after the Statutory Auditors and Third Country Auditors Regulations 2017 come into force—

(i) if the company is a private company and has an audit committee, a selection procedure that complies with the requirements of section 485A(4) and (5)(a) and (b),

(ii) if the company is a public company and has an audit committee, a selection procedure that complies with the requirements of subsections 489A(4) and (5)(a) and (b), . . .

[(iii) if the company is a private company and does not have an audit committee, a selection procedure that complies with the requirements of section 485B(4),

(iv) if the company is a public company and does not have an audit committee, a selection procedure that complies with the requirements of section 489B(4),]

(b) in any other case, a selection procedure that substantially meets the requirements of Article 16(2) to (5) of the Audit Regulation [as it had effect immediately before IP completion day], having regard to the circumstances at the time (including whether the company had an audit committee).]

NOTES

Inserted by the Statutory Auditors and Third Country Auditors Regulations 2017, SI 2017/516, reg 12(1), (14), in relation to financial years of companies beginning on or after 17 June 2016.

Sub-s (5) is amended as follows:

Words in first pair of square brackets substituted by the Statutory Auditors Regulations 2017, SI 2017/1164, reg 3, Sch 1, paras 7, 20, as from 1 January 2018.

The word omitted from sub-para (a)(ii) was repealed, sub-paras (a)(iii), (iv) were substituted (for the original sub-para (a)(iii)), and the words in square brackets in sub-para (b) were inserted, by the Statutory Auditors and Third Country Auditors (Amendment) (EU Exit) Regulations 2019, SI 2019/177, regs 3, 5, as from IP completion day (as defined in the European Union (Withdrawal Agreement) Act 2020, s 39) (for transitional provisions in relation to audits of accounts for financial years that begin before IP completion day, see Sch 4 to the 2019 Regulations at **[12.88]**).

Note that reg 5 of the 2019 Regulations was amended by the Companies and Statutory Auditors etc (Consequential Amendments) (EU Exit) Regulations 2020, SI 2020/523, reg 14(a), with effect from immediately before IP completion day (and that the effect of this amendment has been incorporated into the text above).

[1.573]

[494A Interpretation

In this Chapter—

["audit committee" means a body which performs—

(a) the functions referred to in—

(i) rule 7.1.3 of the Disclosure Guidance and Transparency Rules sourcebook made by the Financial Conduct Authority (audit committees and their functions) under the Financial Services and Markets Act 2000, or

(ii) rule 2.4 of the Audit Committee Part of the Rulebook made by the Prudential Regulation Authority (audit committee) under that Act,

as they have effect on IP completion day, or

(b) equivalent functions;]

. . .

"Auditor General" means—

(a) the Comptroller and Auditor General,

(b) the Auditor General for Scotland,

(c) the Auditor General for Wales, or

(d) the Comptroller and Auditor General for Northern Ireland;

"issuer" has the same meaning as in Part 6 of the Financial Services and Markets Act 2000 (see section 102A(6));

"network" means an association of persons other than a firm co-operating in audit work by way of—

(a) profit-sharing;

(b) cost sharing;

(c) common ownership, control or management;

(d) common quality control policies and procedures;

(e) common business strategy; or

(f) use of a common name;

"public interest [entity]" means—

(a) an issuer whose transferable securities are admitted to trading on a [UK regulated market];

(b) a credit institution within the meaning given by Article 4(1)(1) of Regulation (EU) No 575/2013 of the European Parliament and of the Council, [which is a CRR firm within the meaning of Article 4(1)(2A) of that Regulation];

[(c) a person who would be an insurance undertaking as defined in Article 2(1) of Council Directive 91/674/EEC of 19 December 1991 of the European Parliament and of the Council on the annual accounts and consolidated accounts of insurance undertakings as that Article had effect immediately before IP completion day, were the United Kingdom a member State;]

. . .

. . .

NOTES

Inserted by the Statutory Auditors and Third Country Auditors Regulations 2016, SI 2016/649, reg 15, Sch 3, Pt 3, para 12, as from 17 June 2016, in relation to financial years beginning on or after that date.

Definition "audit committee" substituted by the Statutory Auditors and Third Country Auditors (Amendment) (EU Exit) Regulations 2019, SI 2019/177, regs 3, 6(a), as from IP completion day (as defined in the European Union (Withdrawal Agreement) Act 2020, s 39) (for transitional provisions in relation to audits of accounts for financial years that begin before IP completion day, see Sch 4 to the 2019 Regulations at **[12.88]**). Note that reg 6 of the 2019 Regulations was amended by the Companies and Statutory Auditors etc (Consequential Amendments) (EU Exit) Regulations 2020, SI 2020/523, reg 14(b), with effect from immediately before IP completion day (and that the effect of the amendment has been incorporated in the text set out above).

Definitions "Audit Directive", "regulated market" and "transferable securities (all omitted) repealed by SI 2019/177, regs 3, 6(b), (d), as from IP completion day (see also the first note relating to the 2019 Regulations above).

Word "entity" in square brackets in the definition "public interest entity" substituted by the Statutory Auditors and Third Country Auditors Regulations 2017, SI 2017/516, reg 12(1), (15), in relation to financial years of companies beginning on or after 17 June 2016. All the other words in square brackets in this definition were substituted by SI 2019/177, regs 3, 6(c), as from IP completion day (see also the first note relating to the 2019 Regulations above).

CHAPTER 3 FUNCTIONS OF AUDITOR

Auditor's report

[1.574]

495 Auditor's report on company's annual accounts

(1) A company's auditor must make a report to the company's members on all annual accounts of the company of which copies are, during his tenure of office—

(a) in the case of a private company, to be sent out to members under section 423;

(b) in the case of a public company, to be laid before the company in general meeting under section 437.

[(2) The auditor's report must include—

(a) the identity of the company whose annual accounts are the subject of the audit,

(b) a description of the annual accounts that are the subject of the audit (including the period covered by those accounts),

(c) a description of the financial reporting framework that has been applied in the preparation of those accounts, and

(d) a description of the scope of the audit identifying the auditing standards in accordance with which the audit was conducted.]

(3) The report must state clearly whether, in the auditor's opinion, the annual accounts—

(a) give a true and fair view—

(i) in the case of an individual balance sheet, of the state of affairs of the company as at the end of the financial year,

(ii) in the case of an individual profit and loss account, of the profit or loss of the company for the financial year,

(iii) in the case of group accounts, of the state of affairs as at the end of the financial year and of the profit or loss for the financial year of the undertakings included in the consolidation as a whole, so far as concerns members of the company;

(b) have been properly prepared in accordance with the relevant financial reporting framework; and

(c) have been prepared in accordance with the requirements of this Act . . .

Expressions used in this subsection [or subsection (3A)] that are defined for the purposes of Part 15 (see [sections 464, 471 and 474]) have the same meaning as in that Part.

[(3A) The following provisions apply to the auditors of a company which qualifies as a micro-entity in relation to a financial year (see sections 384A and 384B) in their consideration of whether the Companies Act individual accounts of the company for that year give a true and fair view as mentioned in subsection (3)(a)—

(a) where the accounts comprise only micro-entity minimum accounting items, the auditors must disregard any provision of an accounting standard which would require the accounts to contain information additional to those items,

(b) in relation to a micro-entity minimum accounting item contained in the accounts, the auditors must disregard any provision of an accounting standard which would require the accounts to contain further information in relation to that item, and

(c) where the accounts contain an item of information additional to the micro-entity minimum accounting items, the auditors must have regard to any provision of an accounting standard which relates to that item.]

[(4) The auditor's report—

(a) must be either unqualified or qualified,

(b) must include a reference to any matters to which the auditor wishes to draw attention by way of emphasis without qualifying the report,

(c) must include a statement on any material uncertainty relating to events [or conditions] that may cast significant doubt about the company's ability to continue to adopt the going concern basis of accounting, and

(d) must identify the auditor's place of establishment.]

[(5) Where more than one person is appointed as an auditor—

(a) all the persons appointed must jointly make a report under this section and the report must include a statement as to whether all the persons appointed agree on the matters contained in the report, and

(b) if all the persons appointed cannot agree on the matters contained in the report, the report must include the opinions of each person appointed and give reasons for the disagreement.]

NOTES

Sub-s (2): substituted by the Statutory Auditors and Third Country Auditors Regulations 2016, SI 2016/649, reg 15, Sch 3, Pt 3, para 13(1), (2), as from 17 June 2016, in relation to financial years beginning on or after that date.

Sub-s (3): words omitted from sub-para (c) repealed by the International Accounting Standards and European Public Limited-Liability Company (Amendment etc) (EU Exit) Regulations 2019, SI 2019/685, reg 19, Sch 1, Pt 1, paras 1, 23, in relation to accounts for financial years beginning on or after IP completion day (as defined in the European Union (Withdrawal Agreement) Act 2020, s 39) (note also that in relation to accounts for financial years which begin before but end on or after IP completion day, the enactments amended by Parts 1–3 of Sch 1 to the 2019 Regulations have effect as if the UK were a member State until the end of the financial year in question). Words in the first pair of square brackets inserted, and words in second pair of square brackets substituted, by the Small Companies (Micro-Entities' Accounts) Regulations 2013, SI 2013/3008, reg 8(1), (2), in relation to (a) financial years ending on or after 30 September 2013, and (b) companies which deliver the accounts required by s 444 of this Act to the registrar on or after 1 December 2013 (as to application of these amendments, see the note at **[1.432]**).

Sub-s (3A): inserted by SI 2013/3008, reg 8(1), (3), in relation to (a) financial years ending on or after 30 September 2013, and (b) companies which deliver the accounts required by s 444 of this Act to the registrar on or after 1 December 2013 (as to application of these amendments, see the note at **[1.432]**).

Sub-s (4): substituted by SI 2016/649, reg 15, Sch 3, Pt 3, para 13(1), (3), as from 17 June 2016, in relation to financial years beginning on or after that date. Words in square brackets in para (c) inserted by the Statutory Auditors and Third Country Auditors Regulations 2017, SI 2017/516, reg 12(1), (16), in relation to financial years of companies beginning on or after 17 June 2016.

Sub-s (5): added by SI 2016/649, reg 15, Sch 3, Pt 3, para 13(1), (4), as from 17 June 2016, in relation to financial years beginning on or after that date.

Audit of companies connected with local authorities in England and Wales: see the Local Democracy, Economic Development and Construction Act 2009, s 44(2) in relation to the application of sub-ss (2)–(4) of this section and ss 496–501 of this Act where a person is appointed under the Local Democracy, Economic Development and Construction Act 2009, Pt 2, Chapter 3 (audit of entities connected with local authorities). Note that as of 1 August 2022, s 44 of the 2009 Act had not been brought into force.

[1.575]

[496 Auditor's report on strategic report and director's report

[(1)] In his report on the company's annual accounts, the auditor must—

(a) state whether, in his opinion, based on the work undertaken in the course of the audit—

(i) the information given in the strategic report (if any) and the directors' report for the financial year for which the accounts are prepared is consistent with those accounts, and

(ii) any such strategic report and the directors' report have been prepared in accordance with applicable legal requirements,

(b) state whether, in the light of the knowledge and understanding of the company and its environment obtained in the course of the audit, he has identified material misstatements in the strategic report (if any) and the directors' report, and

(c) if applicable, give an indication of the nature of each of the misstatements referred to in paragraph (b).

[(2) Where more than one person is appointed as auditor, the report must include a statement as to whether all the persons appointed agree on the statements and indications given under subsection (1) and, if they cannot agree on those statements and indications, the report must include the opinions of each person appointed and give reasons for the disagreement.]]

NOTES

Substituted by the Companies, Partnerships and Groups (Accounts and Reports) Regulations 2015, SI 2015/980, reg 11(1), (2), in relation to (a) financial years beginning on or after 1 January 2016, and (b) a financial year of a company beginning on or after 1 January 2015, but before 1 January 2016, if the directors of the company so decide (subject to transitional provisions, etc, in regs 2, 3 of the 2015 Regulations as noted to s 380 at **[1.430]**).

Sub-s (1) numbered as such, and sub-s (2) added, by the Statutory Auditors and Third Country Auditors Regulations 2016, SI 2016/649, reg 15, Sch 3, Pt 3, para 14, as from 17 June 2016, in relation to financial years beginning on or after that date.

Audit of companies connected with local authorities in England and Wales: see the note to s 495 at **[1.574]**.

[1.576]

497 Auditor's report on auditable part of directors' remuneration report

(1) If the company is a quoted company [or unquoted traded company], the auditor, in his report on the company's annual accounts for the financial year, must—

(a) report to the company's members on the auditable part of the directors' remuneration report, and

(b) state whether in his opinion that part of the directors' remuneration report has been properly prepared in accordance with this Act.

(2) For the purposes of this Part, "the auditable part" of a directors' remuneration report is the part identified as such by regulations under section 421.

[(3) In this section "unquoted traded company" means a traded company (as defined by section 360C) that is not a quoted company.]

NOTES

Words in square brackets in sub-s (1) inserted, and sub-s (3) added, by the Companies (Directors' Remuneration Policy and Directors' Remuneration Report) Regulations 2019, SI 2019/970, regs 3, 25, as from 10 June 2019 (for transitional provisions, etc, see reg 2 of the 2019 Regulations at **[4.680]**).

Audit of companies connected with local authorities in England and Wales: see the note to s 495 at **[1.574]**.

[1.577]

[497A Auditor's report on separate corporate governance statement

[(1)] Where the company prepares a separate corporate governance statement in respect of a financial year, the auditor must, in his report of the company's annual accounts for that year—

(a) state whether, in his opinion, based on the work undertaken in the course of the audit, the information given in the statement in compliance with rules 7.2.5 and 7.2.6 in the Disclosure Rules and Transparency Rules sourcebook made by the Financial Conduct Authority (information about internal control and risk management systems in relation to financial reporting processes and about share capital structures)—

(i) is consistent with those accounts, and

(ii) has been prepared in accordance with applicable legal requirements,

(b) state whether, in the light of the knowledge and understanding of the company and its environment obtained in the course of the audit, he has identified material misstatements in the information in the statement referred to in paragraph (a),

(c) if applicable, give an indication of the nature of each of the misstatements referred to in paragraph (b), and

(d) state whether, in his opinion, based on the work undertaken in the course of the audit, rules 7.2.2, 7.2.3 and 7.2.7 in the Disclosure Rules and Transparency Rules sourcebook made by the Financial Conduct Authority (information about the company's corporate governance code and practices and about its administrative, management and supervisory bodies and their committees) have been complied with, if applicable.

[(2) Where more than one person is appointed as auditor, the report must include a statement as to whether all the persons appointed agree on the statements and indications given under subsection (1) and, if they cannot agree on those statements and indications, the report must include the opinions of each person appointed and give reasons for the disagreement.]]

NOTES

Originally inserted by the Companies Act 2006 (Accounts, Reports and Audit) Regulations 2009, SI 2009/1581, reg 6, in relation to financial years beginning on or after 29 June 2008 which have not ended before 27 June 2009.

Subsequently substituted by the Companies, Partnerships and Groups (Accounts and Reports) Regulations 2015, SI 2015/980, reg 11(1), (3), in relation to (a) financial years beginning on or after 1 January 2016, and (b) a financial year of a company beginning on or after 1 January 2015, but before 1 January 2016, if the directors of the company so decide (subject to transitional provisions, etc, in regs 2, 3 of the 2015 Regulations as noted to s 380 at **[1.430]**).

Sub-s (1) numbered as such, and sub-s (2) added, by the Statutory Auditors and Third Country Auditors Regulations 2016, SI 2016/649, reg 15, Sch 3, Pt 3, para 15, as from 17 June 2016, in relation to financial years beginning on or after that date.

Audit of companies connected with local authorities in England and Wales: see the note to s 495 at **[1.574]**.

Duties and rights of auditors

[1.578]

498 Duties of auditor

(1) A company's auditor, in preparing his report, must carry out such investigations as will enable him to form an opinion as to—

(a) whether adequate accounting records have been kept by the company and returns adequate for their audit have been received from branches not visited by him, and

(b) whether the company's individual accounts are in agreement with the accounting records and returns, and

(c) in the case of a quoted company [or unquoted traded company], whether the auditable part of the company's directors' remuneration report is in agreement with the accounting records and returns.

(2) If the auditor is of the opinion—

(a) that adequate accounting records have not been kept, or that returns adequate for their audit have not been received from branches not visited by him, or

(b) that the company's individual accounts are not in agreement with the accounting records and returns, or

(c) in the case of a quoted company [or unquoted traded company], that the auditable part of its directors' remuneration report is not in agreement with the accounting records and returns,

the auditor shall state that fact in his report.

(3) If the auditor fails to obtain all the information and explanations which, to the best of his knowledge and belief, are necessary for the purposes of his audit, he shall state that fact in his report.

(4) If—

(a) the requirements of regulations under section 412 (disclosure of directors' benefits: remuneration, pensions and compensation for loss of office) are not complied with in the annual accounts, or

(b) in the case of a quoted company, the requirements of regulations under section 421 as to information forming the auditable part of the directors' remuneration report are not complied with in that report,

the auditor must include in his report, so far as he is reasonably able to do so, a statement giving the required particulars.

[(5) If the directors of the company—

(a) have prepared accounts in accordance with the small companies regime, or

(b) have taken advantage of small companies exemption [from the requirement to prepare a strategic report or] in preparing the directors' report,

and in the auditor's opinion they were not entitled to do so, the auditor shall state that fact in his report.]

[(6) Where more than one person is appointed as auditor, the report must include a statement as to whether all the persons appointed agree on the statements given under subsections (2) to (5) and, if they cannot agree on those statements, the report must include the opinions of each person appointed and give reasons for the disagreement.]

[(7) In this section "unquoted traded company" means a traded company (as defined by section 360C) that is not a quoted company.]

NOTES

Sub-ss (1), (2): words in square brackets in para (c) inserted by the Companies (Directors' Remuneration Policy and Directors' Remuneration Report) Regulations 2019, SI 2019/970, regs 3, 26(a), as from 10 June 2019 (for transitional provisions, etc, see reg 2 of the 2019 Regulations at **[4.680]**).

Sub-s (5): substituted by the Companies Act 2006 (Amendment) (Accounts and Reports) Regulations 2008, SI 2008/393, reg 6(10), as from 6 April 2008, in relation to financial years beginning on or after that date. Words in square brackets inserted by the Companies Act 2006 (Strategic Report and Directors' Report) Regulations 2013, SI 2013/1970, reg 14, Schedule, paras 1, 22, in respect of financial years ending on or after 30 September 2013.

Sub-s (6): added by the Statutory Auditors and Third Country Auditors Regulations 2016, SI 2016/649, reg 15, Sch 3, Pt 3, para 16, as from 17 June 2016, in relation to financial years beginning on or after that date.

Sub-s (7): added by SI 2019/970, regs 3, 26(b), as from 10 June 2019 (for transitional provisions, etc, see reg 2 of the 2019 Regulations at **[4.680]**).

Audit of companies connected with local authorities in England and Wales: see the note to s 495 at **[1.574]**.

[1.579]

[498A Auditor's duties in relation to separate corporate governance statement

Where the company is required to prepare a corporate governance statement in respect of a financial year and no such statement is included in the directors' report—

(a) the company's auditor, in preparing his report on the company's annual accounts for that year, must ascertain whether a corporate governance statement has been prepared, and

(b) if it appears to the auditor that no such statement has been prepared, he must state that fact in his report.]

NOTES

Inserted by the Companies Act 2006 (Accounts, Reports and Audit) Regulations 2009, SI 2009/1581, reg 7, in relation to financial years beginning on or after 29 June 2008 which have not ended before 27 June 2009.

Audit of companies connected with local authorities in England and Wales: see the note to s 495 at **[1.574]**.

[1.580]

499 Auditor's general right to information

(1) An auditor of a company—

(a) has a right of access at all times to the company's books, accounts and vouchers (in whatever form they are held), and

(b) may require any of the following persons to provide him with such information or explanations as he thinks necessary for the performance of his duties as auditor.

(2) Those persons are—

(a) any officer or employee of the company;

(b) any person holding or accountable for any of the company's books, accounts or vouchers;

(c) any subsidiary undertaking of the company which is a body corporate incorporated in the United Kingdom;

(d) any officer, employee or auditor of any such subsidiary undertaking or any person holding or accountable for any books, accounts or vouchers of any such subsidiary undertaking;

(e) any person who fell within any of paragraphs (a) to (d) at a time to which the information or explanations required by the auditor relates or relate.

(3) A statement made by a person in response to a requirement under this section may not be used in evidence against him in criminal proceedings except proceedings for an offence under section 501.

(4) Nothing in this section compels a person to disclose information in respect of which a claim to legal professional privilege (in Scotland, to confidentiality of communications) could be maintained in legal proceedings.

NOTES

Audit of companies connected with local authorities in England and Wales: see the note to s 495 at **[1.574]**.

[1.581]

500 Auditor's right to information from overseas subsidiaries

(1) Where a parent company has a subsidiary undertaking that is not a body corporate incorporated in the United Kingdom, the auditor of the parent company may require it to obtain from any of the following persons such information or explanations as he may reasonably require for the purposes of his duties as auditor.

(2) Those persons are—

(a) the undertaking;

(b) any officer, employee or auditor of the undertaking;

(c) any person holding or accountable for any of the undertaking's books, accounts or vouchers;

(d) any person who fell within paragraph (b) or (c) at a time to which the information or explanations relates or relate.

(3) If so required, the parent company must take all such steps as are reasonably open to it to obtain the information or explanations from the person concerned.

(4) A statement made by a person in response to a requirement under this section may not be used in evidence against him in criminal proceedings except proceedings for an offence under section 501.

(5) Nothing in this section compels a person to disclose information in respect of which a claim to legal professional privilege (in Scotland, to confidentiality of communications) could be maintained in legal proceedings.

NOTES

Audit of companies connected with local authorities in England and Wales: see the note to s 495 at **[1.574]**.

[1.582]

501 Auditor's rights to information: offences

(1) A person commits an offence who knowingly or recklessly makes to an auditor of a company a statement (oral or written) that—

(a) conveys or purports to convey any information or explanations which the auditor requires, or is entitled to require, under section 499, and

(b) is misleading, false or deceptive in a material particular.

(2) A person guilty of an offence under subsection (1) is liable—

(a) on conviction on indictment, to imprisonment for a term not exceeding two years or a fine (or both);

(b) on summary conviction—

(i) in England and Wales, to imprisonment for a term not exceeding twelve months or to a fine not exceeding the statutory maximum (or both);

(ii) in Scotland or Northern Ireland, to imprisonment for a term not exceeding six months or to a fine not exceeding the statutory maximum (or both).

(3) A person who fails to comply with a requirement under section 499 without delay commits an offence unless it was not reasonably practicable for him to provide the required information or explanations.

(4) If a parent company fails to comply with section 500, an offence is committed by—

(a) the company, and

(b) every officer of the company who is in default.

(5) A person guilty of an offence under subsection (3) or (4) is liable on summary conviction to a fine not exceeding level 3 on the standard scale.

(6) Nothing in this section affects any right of an auditor to apply for an injunction (in Scotland, an interdict or an order for specific performance) to enforce any of his rights under section 499 or 500.

NOTES

Audit of companies connected with local authorities in England and Wales: see the note to s 495 at **[1.574]**.

Offences under this section: see further s 1131 at **[1.1301]**.

[1.583]

502 Auditor's rights in relation to resolutions and meetings

(1) In relation to a written resolution proposed to be agreed to by a private company, the company's auditor is entitled to receive all such communications relating to the resolution as, by virtue of any provision of Chapter 2 of Part 13 of this Act, are required to be supplied to a member of the company.

(2) A company's auditor is entitled—

(a) to receive all notices of, and other communications relating to, any general meeting which a member of the company is entitled to receive,

(b) to attend any general meeting of the company, and

(c) to be heard at any general meeting which he attends on any part of the business of the meeting which concerns him as auditor.

(3) Where the auditor is a firm, the right to attend or be heard at a meeting is exercisable by an individual authorised by the firm in writing to act as its representative at the meeting.

Signature of auditor's report

[1.584]

503 Signature of auditor's report

(1) The auditor's report must state the name of the auditor and be signed and dated.

(2) Where the auditor is an individual, the report must be signed by him.

(3) Where the auditor is a firm, the report must be signed by the senior statutory auditor in his own name, for and on behalf of the auditor.

[(4) Where more than one person is appointed as auditor, the report must be signed by all those appointed.]

NOTES

Sub-s (4): added by the Statutory Auditors and Third Country Auditors Regulations 2016, SI 2016/649, reg 15, Sch 3, Pt 3, para 17, as from 17 June 2016, in relation to financial years beginning on or after that date.

[1.585]

504 Senior statutory auditor

(1) The senior statutory auditor means the individual identified by the firm as senior statutory auditor in relation to the audit in accordance with—

(a) . . .

(b) . . . any relevant guidance issued by—

(i) the Secretary of State, or

(ii) a body appointed by order of the Secretary of State.

(2) The person identified as senior statutory auditor must be eligible for appointment as auditor of the company in question (see Chapter 2 of Part 42 of this Act).

(3) The senior statutory auditor is not, by reason of being named or identified as senior statutory auditor or by reason of his having signed the auditor's report, subject to any civil liability to which he would not otherwise be subject.

(4) An order appointing a body for the purpose of subsection (1)(b)(ii) is subject to negative resolution procedure.

NOTES

Sub-s (1): para (a) and the words omitted from in para (b) were repealed by the Statutory Auditors and Third Country Auditors (Amendment) (EU Exit) Regulations 2019, SI 2019/177, regs 3, 7, as from IP completion day (as defined in the

European Union (Withdrawal Agreement) Act 2020, s 39) (for transitional provisions in relation to audits of accounts for financial years that begin before IP completion day, see Sch 4 to the 2019 Regulations at **[12.88]**).

Orders: the Statutory Auditors (Amendment of Companies Act 2006 and Delegation of Functions etc) Order 2012, SI 2012/1741 at **[4.430]** (see art 15 which appoints the Financial Reporting Council Limited for the purposes of sub-s (1)(b)(ii) above). For a summary of all statutory instruments made under this Act, see Appendix 4 at **[A4]**.

[1.586]

505 Names to be stated in published copies of auditor's report

(1) Every copy of the auditor's report that is published by or on behalf of the company must—

- (a) state the name of the auditor and (where the auditor is a firm) the name of the person who signed it as senior statutory auditor, or
- (b) if the conditions in section 506 (circumstances in which names may be omitted) are met, state that a resolution has been passed and notified to the Secretary of State in accordance with that section.

[(1A) If more than one person is appointed as auditor, the reference in subsection (1)(a) to the name of the auditor is to be read as a reference to the names of all the auditors.]

(2) For the purposes of this section a company is regarded as publishing the report if it publishes, issues or circulates it or otherwise makes it available for public inspection in a manner calculated to invite members of the public generally, or any class of members of the public, to read it.

(3) If a copy of the auditor's report is published without the statement required by this section, an offence is committed by—

- (a) the company, and
- (b) every officer of the company who is in default.

(4) A person guilty of an offence under this section is liable on summary conviction to a fine not exceeding level 3 on the standard scale.

NOTES

Sub-s (1A): inserted by the Statutory Auditors and Third Country Auditors Regulations 2016, SI 2016/649, reg 15, Sch 3, Pt 3, para 18, as from 17 June 2016, in relation to financial years beginning on or after that date.

[1.587]

506 Circumstances in which names may be omitted

(1) [An auditor's] name and, where the auditor is a firm, the name of the person who signed the report as senior statutory auditor, may be omitted from—

- (a) published copies of the report, and
- (b) the copy of the report delivered to the registrar under Chapter 10 of Part 15 (filing of accounts and reports),

if the following conditions are met.

(2) The conditions are that the company—

- (a) considering on reasonable grounds that statement of the name would create or be likely to create a serious risk that the auditor or senior statutory auditor, or any other person, would be subject to violence or intimidation, has resolved that the name should not be stated, and
- (b) has given notice of the resolution to the Secretary of State, stating—
  - (i) the name and registered number of the company,
  - (ii) the financial year of the company to which the report relates, and
  - (iii) the name of the auditor and (where the auditor is a firm) the name of the person who signed the report as senior statutory auditor.

NOTES

Sub-s (1): words in square brackets substituted by the Statutory Auditors and Third Country Auditors Regulations 2017, SI 2017/516, reg 12(1), (17), in relation to financial years of companies beginning on or after 17 June 2016.

Offences in connection with auditor's report

[1.588]

507 Offences in connection with auditor's report

(1) A person to whom this section applies commits an offence if he knowingly or recklessly causes a report under section 495 (auditor's report on company's annual accounts) to include any matter that is misleading, false or deceptive in a material particular.

(2) A person to whom this section applies commits an offence if he knowingly or recklessly causes such a report to omit a statement required by—

- (a) section 498(2)(b) (statement that company's accounts do not agree with accounting records and returns),
- (b) section 498(3) (statement that necessary information and explanations not obtained), or
- (c) section 498(5) (statement that directors wrongly took advantage of exemption from obligation to prepare group accounts).

(3) This section applies to—

- (a) where the auditor is an individual, that individual and any employee or agent of his who is eligible for appointment as auditor of the company;
- (b) where the auditor is a firm, any director, member, employee or agent of the firm who is eligible for appointment as auditor of the company.

(4) A person guilty of an offence under this section is liable—

- (a) on conviction on indictment, to a fine;
- (b) on summary conviction, to a fine not exceeding the statutory maximum.

[1.589]

508 Guidance for regulatory and prosecuting authorities: England, Wales and Northern Ireland

(1) The Secretary of State may issue guidance for the purpose of helping relevant regulatory and prosecuting authorities to determine how they should carry out their functions in cases where behaviour occurs that—

(a) appears to involve the commission of an offence under section 507 (offences in connection with auditor's report), and

[(b) has been, is being or may be investigated—

(i) pursuant to arrangements under paragraph 15 of Schedule 10 (investigation of complaints against auditors and supervisory bodies), or

(ii) by the competent authority under the Statutory Auditors and Third Country Auditors Regulations 2016.]

(2) The Secretary of State must obtain the consent of the Attorney General before issuing any such guidance.

(3) In this section "relevant regulatory and prosecuting authorities" means—

(a) supervisory bodies within the meaning of Part 42 of this Act,

(b) bodies to which the Secretary of State may make grants under section 16(1) of the Companies (Audit, Investigations and Community Enterprise) Act 2004 (c 27) (bodies concerned with accounting standards etc),

(c) the Director of the Serious Fraud Office,

(d) the Director of Public Prosecutions or the Director of Public Prosecutions for Northern Ireland, and

(e) the Secretary of State.

(4) This section does not apply to Scotland.

NOTES

Sub-s (1): para (b) substituted by the Statutory Auditors and Third Country Auditors Regulations 2016, SI 2016/649, reg 15, Sch 3, Pt 3, para 19, as from 17 June 2016, in relation to financial years beginning on or after that date.

[1.590]

509 Guidance for regulatory authorities: Scotland

(1) The Lord Advocate may issue guidance for the purpose of helping relevant regulatory authorities to determine how they should carry out their functions in cases where behaviour occurs that—

(a) appears to involve the commission of an offence under section 507 (offences in connection with auditor's report), and

[(b) has been, is being or may be investigated—

(i) pursuant to arrangements under paragraph 15 of Schedule 10 (investigation of complaints against auditors and supervisory bodies), or

(ii) by the competent authority under the Statutory Auditors and Third Country Auditors Regulations 2016.]

(2) The Lord Advocate must consult the Secretary of State before issuing any such guidance.

(3) In this section "relevant regulatory authorities" means—

(a) supervisory bodies within the meaning of Part 42 of this Act,

(b) bodies to which the Secretary of State may make grants under section 16(1) of the Companies (Audit, Investigations and Community Enterprise) Act 2004 (c 27) (bodies concerned with accounting standards etc), and

(c) the Secretary of State.

(4) This section applies only to Scotland.

NOTES

Sub-s (1): para (b) substituted by the Statutory Auditors and Third Country Auditors Regulations 2016, SI 2016/649, reg 15, Sch 3, Pt 3, para 20, as from 17 June 2016, in relation to financial years beginning on or after that date.

CHAPTER 4 REMOVAL, RESIGNATION, ETC OF AUDITORS

Removal of auditor

[1.591]

510 Resolution removing auditor from office

(1) The members of a company may remove an auditor from office at any time.

(2) This power is exercisable only—

(a) by ordinary resolution at a meeting, and

(b) in accordance with section 511 (special notice of resolution to remove auditor).

(3) Nothing in this section is to be taken as depriving the person removed of compensation or damages payable to him in respect of the termination—

(a) of his appointment as auditor, or

(b) of any appointment terminating with that as auditor.

[(4) An auditor may not be removed from office before the expiration of his term of office except—

(a) by resolution under this section, or

(b) in accordance with section 511A.]

NOTES

Sub-s (4): substituted by the Statutory Auditors and Third Country Auditors Regulations 2016, SI 2016/649, reg 15, Sch 3, Pt 3, para 21, as from 17 June 2016, in relation to financial years beginning on or after that date.

[1.592]

511 Special notice required for resolution removing auditor from office

(1) Special notice is required for a resolution at a general meeting of a company removing an auditor from office.

(2) On receipt of notice of such an intended resolution the company must immediately send a copy of it to the auditor proposed to be removed.

(3) The auditor proposed to be removed may make with respect to the intended resolution representations in writing to the company (not exceeding a reasonable length) and request their notification to members of the company.

(4) The company must (unless the representations are received by it too late for it to do so)—

(a) in any notice of the resolution given to members of the company, state the fact of the representations having been made, and

(b) send a copy of the representations to every member of the company to whom notice of the meeting is or has been sent.

(5) If a copy of any such representations is not sent out as required because received too late or because of the company's default, the auditor may (without prejudice to his right to be heard orally) require that the representations be read out at the meeting.

(6) Copies of the representations need not be sent out and the representations need not be read at the meeting if, on the application either of the company or of any other person claiming to be aggrieved, the court is satisfied that the auditor is using the provisions of this section to secure needless publicity for defamatory matter.

The court may order the company's costs (in Scotland, expenses) on the application to be paid in whole or in part by the auditor, notwithstanding that he is not a party to the application.

[1.593]

[511A Public interest companies: application to court to remove auditor from office

(1) This section applies only to a public interest company.

(2) The competent authority may apply to the court for an order removing an auditor of a company from office if the authority considers that there are proper grounds for removing the auditor from office.

(3) The members of a company may apply to the court for an order removing an auditor of the company from office if the applicant or applicants consider that there are proper grounds for removing the auditor from office.

(4) If the court is satisfied, on hearing an application under subsection (2), that there are proper grounds for removing the auditor from office, it may make an order removing the auditor from office.

(5) If the court is satisfied, on hearing an application under subsection (3), that—

(a) the applicants represent in total—

(i) not less than 5% of the voting rights of all the members having a right to vote at a general meeting of the company, or

(ii) not less than 5% in nominal value of the company's share capital, and

(b) there are proper grounds for removing the auditor from office,

the court may make an order removing the auditor from office.

(6) For the purposes of this section, divergence of opinions on accounting treatments or audit procedures are not to be taken to be proper grounds for removing an auditor from office.

(7) . . .]

NOTES

Inserted by the Statutory Auditors and Third Country Auditors Regulations 2016, SI 2016/649, reg 15, Sch 3, Pt 3, para 22, as from 17 June 2016, in relation to financial years beginning on or after that date.

Sub-s (7): repealed by the Statutory Auditors and Third Country Auditors Regulations 2017, SI 2017/516, reg 12(1), (18), in relation to financial years of companies beginning on or after 17 June 2016.

512 *(Repealed by the Deregulation Act 2015, s 18(5), Sch 5, Pt 1, paras 1, 2, as from 1 October 2015, in relation to financial years beginning on or after that date.)*

[1.594]

513 Rights of auditor who has been removed from office

(1) An auditor who has been removed by resolution under section 510 [or by order of the court under section 511A] has, notwithstanding his removal, the rights conferred by section 502(2) in relation to any general meeting of the company—

(a) at which his term of office would otherwise have expired, or

(b) at which it is proposed to fill the vacancy caused by his removal.

(2) In such a case the references in that section to matters concerning the auditor as auditor shall be construed as references to matters concerning him as a former auditor.

NOTES

Sub-s (1): words in square brackets inserted by the Statutory Auditors and Third Country Auditors Regulations 2016, SI 2016/649, reg 15, Sch 3, Pt 3, para 23, as from 17 June 2016, in relation to financial years beginning on or after that date.

Failure to re-appoint auditor

[1.595]

514 Failure to re-appoint auditor: special procedure required for written resolution

[(1) This section applies where a resolution is proposed as a written resolution of a private company whose effect would be to appoint a person as auditor in place of a person (the "outgoing auditor") who, at the time the resolution is proposed, is an auditor of the company and who is to cease to hold office at the end of a period for appointing auditors.

But this section does not apply if the auditor is to cease to hold office by virtue of section 510[, 511A] or 516.

(2) This section also applies where a resolution is proposed as a written resolution of a private company whose effect would be to appoint a person as auditor where, at the time the resolution is proposed, the company does not have an auditor and the person proposed to be appointed is not a person (the "outgoing auditor") who was an auditor of the company when the company last had an auditor.

But this is subject to subsection (2A).

(2A) This section does not apply (by virtue of subsection (2)) if—

(a) a period for appointing auditors has ended since the outgoing auditor ceased to hold office,

(b) the outgoing auditor ceased to hold office by virtue of section 510[, 511A] or 516, or

(c) the outgoing auditor has previously had the opportunity to make representations with respect to a proposed resolution under subsection (4) of this section or an intended resolution under section 515(4).]

(3) [Where this section applies, the] company must send a copy of the proposed resolution to the person proposed to be appointed and to the outgoing auditor.

(4) The outgoing auditor may, within 14 days after receiving the notice, make with respect to the proposed resolution representations in writing to the company (not exceeding a reasonable length) and request their circulation to members of the company.

(5) The company must circulate the representations together with the copy or copies of the resolution circulated in accordance with section 291 (resolution proposed by directors) or section 293 (resolution proposed by members).

(6) Where subsection (5) applies—

(a) the period allowed under section 293(3) for service of copies of the proposed resolution is 28 days instead of 21 days, and

(b) the provisions of section 293(5) and (6) (offences) apply in relation to a failure to comply with that subsection as in relation to a default in complying with that section.

(7) Copies of the representations need not be circulated if, on the application either of the company or of any other person claiming to be aggrieved, the court is satisfied that the auditor is using the provisions of this section to secure needless publicity for defamatory matter.

The court may order the company's costs (in Scotland, expenses) on the application to be paid in whole or in part by the auditor, notwithstanding that he is not a party to the application.

(8) If any requirement of this section is not complied with, the resolution is ineffective.

NOTES

Sub-ss (1), (2), (2A): substituted (for the original sub-ss (1), (2)) by the Deregulation Act 2015, s 18(5), Sch 5, Pt 2, paras 13, 14(1), (2), as from 1 October 2015, in relation to financial years beginning on or after that date.

Figures in square brackets in sub-ss (1), (2A) inserted by the Statutory Auditors and Third Country Auditors Regulations 2016, SI 2016/649, reg 15, Sch 3, Pt 3, para 24, as from 17 June 2016, in relation to financial years beginning on or after that date.

Sub-s (3): words in square brackets substituted by the Deregulation Act 2015, s 18(5), Sch 5, Pt 2, paras 13, 14(1), (3), as from 1 October 2015, in relation to financial years beginning on or after that date.

[1.596]

515 Failure to re-appoint auditor: special notice required for resolution at general meeting

[(1) Special notice is required for a resolution at a general meeting of a private company whose effect would be to appoint a person as auditor in place of a person (the "outgoing auditor") who, at the time the notice is given, is an auditor of the company and who is to cease to hold office at the end of a period for appointing auditors.

But special notice is not required under this subsection if the auditor is to cease to hold office by virtue of section 510[, 511A] or 516.

(1A) Special notice is required for a resolution at a general meeting of a public company whose effect would be to appoint a person as auditor in place of a person (the "outgoing auditor") who, at the time the notice is given, is an auditor of the company and who is to cease to hold office at the end of an accounts meeting.

But special notice is not required under this subsection if the auditor is to cease to hold office by virtue of section 510[, 511A] or 516.

(2) Special notice is required for a resolution at a general meeting of a company whose effect would be to appoint a person as auditor where, at the time the notice is given, the company does not have an auditor and the person proposed to be appointed is not a person (the "outgoing auditor") who was an auditor of the company when the company last had an auditor.

But this is subject to subsection (2A).

(2A) Special notice is not required under subsection (2) if—

(a) a period for appointing auditors has ended or (as the case may be) an accounts meeting of the company has been held since the outgoing auditor ceased to hold office,

(b) the outgoing auditor ceased to hold office by virtue of section 510[, 511A] or 516, or

(c) the outgoing auditor has previously had the opportunity to make representations with respect to an intended resolution under subsection (4) of this section or a proposed resolution under section 514(4).]

(3) On receipt of notice of . . . an intended resolution [mentioned in subsection (1), (1A) or (2)] the company shall forthwith send a copy of it to the person proposed to be appointed and to the outgoing auditor.

(4) The outgoing auditor may make with respect to the intended resolution representations in writing to the company (not exceeding a reasonable length) and request their notification to members of the company.

(5) The company must (unless the representations are received by it too late for it to do so)—

(a) in any notice of the resolution given to members of the company, state the fact of the representations having been made, and

(b) send a copy of the representations to every member of the company to whom notice of the meeting is or has been sent.

(6) If a copy of any such representations is not sent out as required because received too late or because of the company's default, the outgoing auditor may (without prejudice to his right to be heard orally) require that the representations be read out at the meeting.

(7) Copies of the representations need not be sent out and the representations need not be read at the meeting if, on the application either of the company or of any other person claiming to be aggrieved, the court is satisfied that the auditor is using the provisions of this section to secure needless publicity for defamatory matter.

The court may order the company's costs (in Scotland, expenses) on the application to be paid in whole or in part by the outgoing auditor, notwithstanding that he is not a party to the application.

NOTES

Sub-ss (1)–(2A): substituted (for the original sub-ss (1), (2)) by the Deregulation Act 2015, s 18(5), Sch 5, Pt 2, paras 13, 15(1), (2), as from 1 October 2015, in relation to financial years beginning on or after that date.

Figures in square brackets in sub-ss (1), (1A), (2A) inserted by the Statutory Auditors and Third Country Auditors Regulations 2016, SI 2016/649, reg 15, Sch 3, Pt 3, para 25, as from 17 June 2016, in relation to financial years beginning on or after that date.

Sub-s (3): word omitted repealed, and words in square brackets inserted, by the Deregulation Act 2015, s 18(5), Sch 5, Pt 2, paras 13, 15(1), (3), as from 1 October 2015, in relation to financial years beginning on or after that date.

Resignation of auditor

[1.597]

516 Resignation of auditor

(1) An auditor of a company may resign his office by [sending a notice to that effect to the company].

(2) [Where the company is a public interest company, the] notice is not effective unless it is accompanied by the statement required by section 519.

(3) An effective notice of resignation operates to bring the auditor's term of office to an end as of the date on which the notice is [received] or on such later date as may be specified in it.

NOTES

Sub-ss (1), (3): words in square brackets substituted by the Deregulation Act 2015, s 18(5), Sch 5, Pt 2, paras 13, 16, as from 1 October 2015, in relation to financial years beginning on or after that date.

Sub-s (2): words in square brackets substituted by the Deregulation Act 2015, s 18(5), Sch 5, Pt 1, paras 1, 3, as from 1 October 2015, in relation to financial years beginning on or after that date.

517 *(Repealed by the Deregulation Act 2015, s 18(5), Sch 5, Pt 1, paras 1, 4, as from 1 October 2015, in relation to financial years beginning on or after that date.)*

[1.598]

518 Rights of resigning auditor

(1) This section applies where an [auditor's (A's) notice of resignation is accompanied by a statement under section 519 except where—

(a) the company is a non-public interest company, and

(b) the statement includes a statement to the effect that A considers that none of the reasons for A's ceasing to hold office, and no matters (if any) connected with A's ceasing to hold office, need to be brought to the attention of members or creditors of the company (as required by section 519(3B)).]

(2) He may [send] with the notice [an authenticated] requisition calling on the directors of the company forthwith duly to convene a general meeting of the company for the purpose of receiving and considering such explanation of the [reasons for, and matters connected with,] his resignation as he may wish to place before the meeting.

(3) He may request the company to circulate to its members—

(a) before the meeting convened on his requisition, or

(b) before any general meeting at which his term of office would otherwise have expired or at which it is proposed to fill the vacancy caused by his resignation,

a statement in writing (not exceeding a reasonable length) of the [reasons for, and matters connected with,] his resignation.

(4) The company must (unless the statement is received too late for it to comply)—

(a) in any notice of the meeting given to members of the company, state the fact of the statement having been made, and

(b) send a copy of the statement to every member of the company to whom notice of the meeting is or has been sent.

(5) The directors must within 21 days from the date [on which the company receives] a requisition under this section proceed duly to convene a meeting for a day not more than 28 days after the date on which the notice convening the meeting is given.

(6) If default is made in complying with subsection (5), every director who failed to take all reasonable steps to secure that a meeting was convened commits an offence.

(7) A person guilty of an offence under this section is liable—

(a) on conviction on indictment, to a fine;

(b) on summary conviction to a fine not exceeding the statutory maximum.

(8) If a copy of the statement mentioned above is not sent out as required because received too late or because of the company's default, the auditor may (without prejudice to his right to be heard orally) require that the statement be read out at the meeting.

(9) Copies of a statement need not be sent out and the statement need not be read out at the meeting if, on the application either of the company or of any other person who claims to be aggrieved, the court is satisfied that the auditor is using the provisions of this section to secure needless publicity for defamatory matter.

The court may order the company's costs (in Scotland, expenses) on such an application to be paid in whole or in part by the auditor, notwithstanding that he is not a party to the application.

(10) An auditor who has resigned has, notwithstanding his resignation, the rights conferred by section 502(2) in relation to any such general meeting of the company as is mentioned in subsection (3)(a) or (b) above.

In such a case the references in that section to matters concerning the auditor as auditor shall be construed as references to matters concerning him as a former auditor.

NOTES

All words in square brackets in this section were substituted by the Deregulation Act 2015, s 18(5), Sch 5, Pt 1, paras 1, 5 and Sch 5, Pt 2, paras 13, 17, as from 1 October 2015, in relation to financial years beginning on or after that date.

Statement by auditor on ceasing to hold office

[1.599]

519 Statement by auditor to be [sent to] company

[(1) An auditor of a public interest company who is ceasing to hold office (at any time and for any reason) must send to the company a statement of the reasons for doing so.

(2) An auditor ("A") of a non-public interest company who is ceasing to hold office must send to the company a statement of the reasons for doing so unless A satisfies the first or second condition.

(2A) The first condition is that A is ceasing to hold office—

(a) in the case of a private company, at the end of a period for appointing auditors;

(b) in the case of a public company, at the end of an accounts meeting.

(2B) The second condition is that—

(a) A's reasons for ceasing to hold office are all exempt reasons (as to which see section 519A(3)), and

(b) there are no matters connected with A's ceasing to hold office that A considers need to be brought to the attention of members or creditors of the company.

(3) A statement under this section must include—

(a) the auditor's name and address;

(b) the number allocated to the auditor on being entered in the register of auditors kept under section 1239;

(c) the company's name and registered number.

(3A) Where there are matters connected with an auditor's ceasing to hold office that the auditor considers need to be brought to the attention of members or creditors of the company, the statement under this section must include details of those matters.

(3B) Where—

(a) an auditor ("A") of a non-public interest company is required by subsection (2) to send a statement, and

(b) A considers that none of the reasons for A's ceasing to hold office, and no matters (if any) connected with A's ceasing to hold office, need to be brought to the attention of members or creditors of the company,

A's statement under this section must include a statement to that effect.]

(4) [A statement under this section] must be [sent]—

(a) in the case of resignation, along with the notice of resignation;

(b) in the case of failure to seek re-appointment, not less than 14 days before the end of the time allowed for next appointing an auditor;

(c) in any other case, not later than the end of the period of 14 days beginning with the date on which he ceases to hold office.

(5) A person ceasing to hold office as auditor who fails to comply with this section commits an offence.

(6) In proceedings for such an offence it is a defence for the person charged to show that he took all reasonable steps and exercised all due diligence to avoid the commission of the offence.

(7) A person guilty of an offence under this section is liable—

(a) on conviction on indictment, to a fine;

(b) on summary conviction, to a fine not exceeding the statutory maximum.

[(8) Where an offence under this section is committed by a body corporate, every officer of the body who is in default also commits the offence.

For this purpose—

(a) any person who purports to act as director, manager or secretary of the body is treated as an officer of the body, and

(b) if the body is a company, any shadow director is treated as an officer of the company.]

NOTES

Section heading: words in square brackets substituted by the Deregulation Act 2015, s 18(5), Sch 5, Pt 2, paras 13, 18(1), (3), as from 1 October 2015, in relation to financial years beginning on or after that date.

Sub-ss (1)–(3B): substituted (for the original sub-ss (1)–(3)) by the Deregulation Act 2015, s 18(1), (2), as from 1 October 2015, in relation to financial years beginning on or after that date.

Sub-s (4): words in square brackets substituted by the Deregulation Act 2015, s 18(5), Sch 5, paras 1, 6, 13, 18(1), (2), as from 1 October 2015, in relation to financial years beginning on or after that date.

Sub-s (8): added by the Companies Act 2006 (Consequential Amendments etc) Order 2008, SI 2008/948, art 3(1), Sch 1, Pt 2, para 247, as from 6 April 2008.

[1.600]

[519A Meaning of "public interest company", "non-public interest company" and "exempt reasons"

(1) In this Chapter—

["public interest company" means a company which is—

(a) an issuer whose transferable securities are admitted to trading on a [UK regulated market];

(b) a credit institution within the meaning given by Article 4(1)(1) of Regulation (EU) No 575/2013 of the European Parliament and of the Council, [which is a CRR firm within the meaning of Article 4(1)(2A) of that Regulation]; or

[(c) a person who would be an insurance undertaking as defined in Article 2(1) of Council Directive 91/674/EEC of 19 December 1991 of the European Parliament and of the Council on the annual accounts and consolidated accounts of insurance undertakings as that Article had effect immediately before IP completion day, were the United Kingdom a member State;]

"non-public interest company" means a company that is not a public interest company.

[(2) For the purposes of the definition of "public interest company"—

"issuer" has the same meaning as in Part 6 of the Financial Services and Markets Act 2000 (see section 102A(6));

. . .

. . .

(3) In the application of this Chapter to an auditor ("A") of a company ceasing to hold office, the following are "exempt reasons"—

(a) A is no longer to carry out statutory audit work within the meaning of Part 42 (see section 1210(1));

(b) the company is, or is to become, exempt from audit under section 477, 479A or 480, or from the requirements of this Part under section 482, and intends to include in its balance sheet a statement of the type described in section 475(2);

(c) the company is a subsidiary undertaking of a parent undertaking that is incorporated in the United Kingdom and—

(i) the parent undertaking prepares group accounts, and

(ii) A is being replaced as auditor of the company by the auditor who is conducting, or is to conduct, an audit of the group accounts;

(d) the company is being wound up under Part 4 of the Insolvency Act 1986 or Part 5 of the Insolvency (Northern Ireland) Order 1989 (SI 1989/2405 (NI 19)), whether voluntarily or by the court, or a petition under Part 4 of that Act or Part 5 of that Order for the winding up of the company has been presented and not finally dealt with or withdrawn.

(4) But the reason described in subsection (3)(c) is only an exempt reason if the auditor who is conducting, or is to conduct, an audit of the group accounts is also conducting, or is also to conduct, the audit (if any) of the accounts of each of the subsidiary undertakings (of the parent undertaking) that is incorporated in the United Kingdom and included in the consolidation.

(5) The Secretary of State may by order amend the definition of "public interest company" in subsection (1).

(6) An order under subsection (5) is subject to negative resolution procedure.]

NOTES

Inserted by the Deregulation Act 2015, s 18(1), (3), as from 1 October 2015, in relation to financial years beginning on or after that date.

Sub-s (1) is amended as follows:

Definition "public interest company" substituted by the Statutory Auditors and Third Country Auditors Regulations 2016, SI 2016/649, reg 15, Sch 3, Pt 3, para 26(1), (2), as from 17 June 2016, in relation to financial years beginning on or after that date.

Words in square brackets in paras (a) and (b) of the definition "public interest company" substituted, and para (c) of that definition substituted, by the Statutory Auditors and Third Country Auditors (Amendment) (EU Exit) Regulations 2019, SI 2019/177, regs 3, 8(a), as from IP completion day (as defined in the European Union (Withdrawal Agreement) Act 2020, s 39) (for transitional provisions in relation to audits of accounts for financial years that begin before IP completion day, see Sch 4 to the 2019 Regulations at **[12.88]**). Note that reg 8(a) of the 2019 Regulations was amended by the Companies and Statutory Auditors etc (Consequential Amendments) (EU Exit) Regulations 2020, SI 2020/523, reg 14(c), with effect from immediately before IP completion day (and that the effect of the amendment has been incorporated in the text set out above).

Sub-s (2): substituted by SI 2016/649, reg 15, Sch 3, Pt 3, para 26(1), (3), as from 17 June 2016, in relation to financial years beginning on or after that date. Definitions "regulated market" and "transferable securities" (omitted) repealed by SI 2019/177, regs 3, 8(b), as from IP completion day (see also the first note relating to the 2019 Regulations above).

Regulations: the Statutory Auditors and Third Country Auditors Regulations 2016, SI 2016/649 at **[4.650]**; the Statutory Auditors and Third Country Auditors (Amendment) (EU Exit) Regulations 2019, SI 2019/177 at **[12.83]**. For a summary of all statutory instruments made under this Act, see Appendix 4 at **[A4]**

[1.601]

520 Company's duties in relation to statement

(1) This section applies where [a company receives from an auditor ("A") who is ceasing to hold office a statement under section 519 except where—

(a) the company is a non-public interest company, and

(b) the statement includes a statement to the effect that A considers that none of the reasons for A's ceasing to hold office, and no matters (if any) connected with A's ceasing to hold office, need to be brought to the attention of members or creditors of the company (as required by section 519(3B)).]

(2) [Where this section applies, the] company must within 14 days of the [receipt] of the statement either—

(a) send a copy of it to every person who under section 423 is entitled to be sent copies of the accounts, or

(b) apply to the court.

(3) If it applies to the court, the company must notify the auditor of the application.

(4) If the court is satisfied that the auditor is using the provisions of section 519 to secure needless publicity for defamatory matter—

(a) it shall direct that copies of the statement need not be sent out, and

(b) it may further order the company's costs (in Scotland, expenses) on the application to be paid in whole or in part by the auditor, even if he is not a party to the application.

The company must within 14 days of the court's decision send to the persons mentioned in subsection (2)(a) a statement setting out the effect of the order.

(5) If no such direction is made the company must send copies of the statement to the persons mentioned in subsection (2)(a) within 14 days of the court's decision or, as the case may be, of the discontinuance of the proceedings.

(6) In the event of default in complying with this section an offence is committed by every officer of the company who is in default.

(7) In proceedings for such an offence it is a defence for the person charged to show that he took all reasonable steps and exercised all due diligence to avoid the commission of the offence.

(8) A person guilty of an offence under this section is liable—

(a) on conviction on indictment, to a fine;

(b) on summary conviction, to a fine not exceeding the statutory maximum.

NOTES

Sub-ss (1), (2): the words in square brackets were substituted by the Deregulation Act 2015, s 18(5), Sch 5, Pt 1, paras 1, 7 and Sch 5, Pt 2, paras 13, 19, as from 1 October 2015, in relation to financial years beginning on or after that date.

[1.602]

521 Copy of statement to be sent to registrar

[(A1) This section applies where an auditor ("A") of a company sends a statement to the company under section 519 except where—

(a) the company is a non-public interest company, and

(b) the statement includes a statement to the effect that A considers that none of the reasons for A's ceasing to hold office, and no matters (if any) connected with A's ceasing to hold office, need to be brought to the attention of members or creditors of the company (as required by section 519(3B)).]

(1) [Where this section applies, unless] within 21 days beginning with the day on which he [sent] the statement under section 519 the auditor receives notice of an application to the court under section 520, he must within a further seven days send a copy of the statement to the registrar.

(2) If an application to the court is made under section 520 and the auditor subsequently receives notice under subsection (5) of that section, he must within seven days of receiving the notice send a copy of the statement to the registrar.

(3) An auditor who fails to comply with subsection (1) or (2) commits an offence.

(4) In proceedings for such an offence it is a defence for the person charged to show that he took all reasonable steps and exercised all due diligence to avoid the commission of the offence.

(5) A person guilty of an offence under this section is liable—

(a) on conviction on indictment, to a fine;

(b) on summary conviction, to a fine not exceeding the statutory maximum.

[(6) Where an offence under this section is committed by a body corporate, every officer of the body who is in default also commits the offence.

For this purpose—

(a) any person who purports to act as director, manager or secretary of the body is treated as an officer of the body, and

(b) if the body is a company, any shadow director is treated as an officer of the company.]

NOTES

Sub-s (A1): inserted by the Deregulation Act 2015, s 18(5), Sch 5, Pt 1, paras 1, 8(1), (2), as from 1 October 2015, in relation to financial years beginning on or after that date.

Sub-s (1): words in first pair of square brackets substituted by the Deregulation Act 2015, s 18(5), Sch 5, Pt 1, paras 1, 8(1), (3), as from 1 October 2015, in relation to financial years beginning on or after that date. Word in second pair of square brackets substituted by s 18(5) of, and Sch 5, Pt 2, paras 13, 20, to the 2015 Act, as from the same date.

Sub-s (6): added by the Companies Act 2006 (Consequential Amendments etc) Order 2008, SI 2008/948, art 3(1), Sch 1, Pt 2, para 248, as from 6 April 2008.

[1.603]

522 Duty of auditor to [send statement to] appropriate audit authority

[(1) Where an auditor of a company sends a statement under section 519, the auditor must at the same time send a copy of the statement to the appropriate audit authority.]

(5) A person ceasing to hold office as auditor who fails to comply with this section commits an offence.

(6) If that person is a firm an offence is committed by—

(a) the firm, and

(b) every officer of the firm who is in default.

(7) In proceedings for an offence under this section it is a defence for the person charged to show that he took all reasonable steps and exercised all due diligence to avoid the commission of the offence.

(8) A person guilty of an offence under this section is liable—

(a) on conviction on indictment, to a fine;

(b) on summary conviction, to a fine not exceeding the statutory maximum.

NOTES

Section heading: words in square brackets substituted by the Deregulation Act 2015, s 18(5), Sch 5, Pt 1, paras 1, 9(1), (3), as from 1 October 2015, in relation to financial years beginning on or after that date.

Sub-s (1): substituted (for the original sub-ss (1)–(4)) by the Deregulation Act 2015, s 18(5), Sch 5, Pt 1, paras 1, 9(1), (2), as1 October 2015, in relation to financial years beginning on or after that date.

[1.604]

523 Duty of company to notify appropriate audit authority

[(1) This section applies if an auditor is ceasing to hold office—

(a) in the case of a private company, at any time other than at the end of a period for appointing auditors;

(b) in the case of a public company, at any time other than at the end of an accounts meeting.

(1A) But this section does not apply if the company reasonably believes that the only reasons for the auditor's ceasing to hold office are exempt reasons (as to which see section 519A(3)).

(2) Where this section applies, the company must give notice to the appropriate audit authority that the auditor is ceasing to hold office.

(2A) The notice is to take the form of a statement by the company of what the company believes to be the reasons for the auditor's ceasing to hold office and must include the information listed in section 519(3).

This is subject to subsection (2C).

(2B) Subsection (2C) applies where—

(a) the company receives a statement from the auditor under section 519,

(b) the statement is sent at the time required by section 519(4), and

(c) the company agrees with the contents of the statement.

(2C) Where this subsection applies, the notice may instead take the form of a copy of the statement endorsed by the company to the effect that it agrees with the contents of the statement.

(3) A notice under this section must be given within the period of 28 days beginning with the day on which the auditor ceases to hold office.]

(4) If a company fails to comply with this section, an offence is committed by—

(a) the company, and

(b) every officer of the company who is in default.

(5) In proceedings for such an offence it is a defence for the person charged to show that he took all reasonable steps and exercised all due diligence to avoid the commission of the offence.

(6) A person guilty of an offence under this section is liable—

(a) on conviction on indictment, to a fine;

(b) on summary conviction, to a fine not exceeding the statutory maximum.

NOTES

Sub-ss (1), (1A), (2)–(2C), (3): substituted (for the original sub-ss (1)–(3)) by the Deregulation Act 2015, s 18(1), (4), as from 1 October 2015, in relation to financial years beginning on or after that date.

[1.605]

524 [Provision of information] to accounting authorities

[(1) Where the appropriate audit authority receives a statement under section 522 or a notice under section 523, the authority may forward to the accounting authorities—

(a) a copy of the statement or notice, and

(b) any other information the authority has received from the auditor or the company concerned in connection with the auditor's ceasing to hold office.]

(2) The accounting authorities are—

(a) the Secretary of State, and

(b) any person authorised by the Secretary of State for the purposes of section 456 (revision of defective accounts: persons authorised to apply to court).

(3) . . .

(4) If the court has made an order under section 520(4) directing that copies of the statement need not be sent out by the company, sections 460 and 461 (restriction on further disclosure) apply in relation to the copies sent to the accounting authorities as they apply to information obtained under section 459 (power to require documents etc).

NOTES

All amendments to this section were made by the Deregulation Act 2015, s 18(5), Sch 5, Pt 1, paras 1, 10, as from 1 October 2015, in relation to financial years beginning on or after that date.

[1.606]

525 Meaning of "appropriate audit authority" . . .

(1) In sections 522, 523 and 524 "appropriate audit authority" means—

(a) [in relation to an auditor of a public interest company (other than an Auditor General)]—

(i) the Secretary of State, or

(ii) if the Secretary of State has delegated functions under section 1252 to a body whose functions include receiving the [statement or] notice in question, that body;

(b) [in relation to an auditor of a non-public interest company (other than an Auditor General)], the relevant supervisory body;

[(c) [in relation to] an Auditor General, the Independent Supervisor.]

["Supervisory body" and "Independent Supervisor" have the same meaning] as in Part 42 (statutory auditors) (see [sections 1217 and 1228]).

(2), (3) . . .

NOTES

Section heading: words omitted repealed by the Deregulation Act 2015, s 18(5), Sch 5, Pt 1, paras 1, 11(1), (4), as from 1 October 2015, in relation to financial years beginning on or after that date.

Sub-s (1) is amended as follows:

The words in the first pair of square brackets in para (a) were substituted, the words "statement or" in square brackets sub-para (a)(ii) were inserted, the words in square brackets in para (b) were substituted, and the words "in relation to" in square brackets in para (c) were substituted, by the Deregulation Act 2015, s 18(5), Sch 5, Pt 1, paras 1, 11(1), (2), as from 1 October 2015, in relation to financial years beginning on or after that date.

Other words in square brackets inserted or substituted by the Statutory Auditors and Third Country Auditors Regulations 2007, SI 2007/3494, reg 41, as from 6 April 2008.

Sub-ss (2), (3): repealed by the Deregulation Act 2015, s 18(5), Sch 5, Pt 1, paras 1, 11(1), (3), as from 1 October 2015, in relation to financial years beginning on or after that date.

Orders: the Statutory Auditors (Amendment of Companies Act 2006 and Delegation of Functions etc) Order 2012, SI 2012/1741 at **[4.430]**. Article 8 of that Order provides that the functions of the Financial Reporting Council Limited include the receipt of notices under ss 522 and 523 of this Act and, accordingly, that body is the appropriate audit authority under sub-s (1)(a)(ii) above. For a summary of all statutory instruments made under this Act, see Appendix 4 at **[A4]**.

Supplementary

[1.607]

526 Effect of casual vacancies

If an auditor ceases to hold office for any reason, any surviving or continuing auditor or auditors may continue to act.

CHAPTER 5 QUOTED COMPANIES: RIGHT OF MEMBERS TO RAISE AUDIT CONCERNS AT ACCOUNTS MEETING

[1.608]

527 Members' power to require website publication of audit concerns

(1) The members of a quoted company may require the company to publish on a website a statement setting out any matter relating to—

(a) the audit of the company's accounts (including the auditor's report and the conduct of the audit) that are to be laid before the next accounts meeting, or

(b) any circumstances connected with an auditor of the company ceasing to hold office since the previous accounts meeting,

that the members propose to raise at the next accounts meeting of the company.

(2) A company is required to do so once it has received requests to that effect from—

(a) members representing at least 5% of the total voting rights of all the members who have a relevant right to vote (excluding any voting rights attached to any shares in the company held as treasury shares), or

(b) at least 100 members who have a relevant right to vote and hold shares in the company on which there has been paid up an average sum, per member, of at least £100.

See also section 153 (exercise of rights where shares held on behalf of others).

(3) In subsection (2) a "relevant right to vote" means a right to vote at the accounts meeting.

(4) A request—

(a) may be sent to the company in hard copy or electronic form,

(b) must identify the statement to which it relates,

(c) must be authenticated by the person or persons making it, and

(d) must be received by the company at least one week before the meeting to which it relates.

(5) A quoted company is not required to place on a website a statement under this section if, on an application by the company or another person who claims to be aggrieved, the court is satisfied that the rights conferred by this section are being abused.

(6) The court may order the members requesting website publication to pay the whole or part of the company's costs (in Scotland, expenses) on such an application, even if they are not parties to the application.

[1.609]

528 Requirements as to website availability

(1) The following provisions apply for the purposes of section 527 (website publication of members' statement of audit concerns).

(2) The information must be made available on a website that—

(a) is maintained by or on behalf of the company, and

(b) identifies the company in question.

(3) Access to the information on the website, and the ability to obtain a hard copy of the information from the website, must not be conditional on the payment of a fee or otherwise restricted.

(4) The statement—

(a) must be made available within three working days of the company being required to publish it on a website, and

(b) must be kept available until after the meeting to which it relates.

(5) A failure to make information available on a website throughout the period specified in subsection (4)(b) is disregarded if—

(a) the information is made available on the website for part of that period, and

(b) the failure is wholly attributable to circumstances that it would not be reasonable to have expected the company to prevent or avoid.

[1.610]

529 Website publication: company's supplementary duties

(1) A quoted company must in the notice it gives of the accounts meeting draw attention to—

(a) the possibility of a statement being placed on a website in pursuance of members' requests under section 527, and

(b) the effect of the following provisions of this section.

(2) A company may not require the members requesting website publication to pay its expenses in complying with that section or section 528 (requirements in connection with website publication).

(3) Where a company is required to place a statement on a website under section 527 it must forward the statement to the company's auditor not later than the time when it makes the statement available on the website.

(4) The business which may be dealt with at the accounts meeting includes any statement that the company has been required under section 527 to publish on a website.

[1.611]

530 Website publication: offences

(1) In the event of default in complying with

(a) section 528 (requirements as to website publication), or

(b) section 529 (companies' supplementary duties in relation to request for website publication),

an offence is committed by every officer of the company who is in default.

(2) A person guilty of an offence under this section is liable—

(a) on conviction on indictment, to a fine;

(b) on summary conviction, to a fine not exceeding the statutory maximum.

[1.612]

531 Meaning of "quoted company"

(1) For the purposes of this Chapter a company is a quoted company if it is a quoted company in accordance with section 385 (quoted and unquoted companies for the purposes of Part 15) in relation to the financial year to which the accounts to be laid at the next accounts meeting relate.

(2) The provisions of subsections (4) to (6) of that section (power to amend definition by regulations) apply in relation to the provisions of this Chapter as in relation to the provisions of that Part.

CHAPTER 6 AUDITORS' LIABILITY

Voidness of provisions protecting auditors from liability

[1.613]

532 Voidness of provisions protecting auditors from liability

(1) This section applies to any provision—

(a) for exempting an auditor of a company (to any extent) from any liability that would otherwise attach to him in connection with any negligence, default, breach of duty or breach of trust in relation to the company occurring in the course of the audit of accounts, or

(b) by which a company directly or indirectly provides an indemnity (to any extent) for an auditor of the company, or of an associated company, against any liability attaching to him in connection with any negligence, default, breach of duty or breach of trust in relation to the company of which he is auditor occurring in the course of the audit of accounts.

(2) Any such provision is void, except as permitted by—

(a) section 533 (indemnity for costs of successfully defending proceedings), or

(b) sections 534 to 536 (liability limitation agreements).

(3) This section applies to any provision, whether contained in a company's articles or in any contract with the company or otherwise.

(4) For the purposes of this section companies are associated if one is a subsidiary of the other or both are subsidiaries of the same body corporate.

Indemnity for costs of defending proceedings

[1.614]

533 Indemnity for costs of successfully defending proceedings

Section 532 (general voidness of provisions protecting auditors from liability) does not prevent a company from indemnifying an auditor against any liability incurred by him—

(a) in defending proceedings (whether civil or criminal) in which judgment is given in his favour or he is acquitted, or

(b) in connection with an application under section 1157 (power of court to grant relief in case of honest and reasonable conduct) in which relief is granted to him by the court.

Liability limitation agreements

[1.615]

534 Liability limitation agreements

(1) A "liability limitation agreement" is an agreement that purports to limit the amount of a liability owed to a company by its auditor in respect of any negligence, default, breach of duty or breach of trust, occurring in the course of the audit of accounts, of which the auditor may be guilty in relation to the company.

(2) Section 532 (general voidness of provisions protecting auditors from liability) does not affect the validity of a liability limitation agreement that—

(a) complies with section 535 (terms of liability limitation agreement) and of any regulations under that section, and

(b) is authorised by the members of the company (see section 536).

(3) Such an agreement—

(a) is effective to the extent provided by section 537, and

(b) is not subject—

(i) in England and Wales or Northern Ireland, to section 2(2) or 3(2)(a) of the Unfair Contract Terms Act 1977 (c 50);

(ii) in Scotland, to section 16(1)(b) or 17(1)(a) of that Act.

[1.616]

535 Terms of liability limitation agreement

(1) A liability limitation agreement—

(a) must not apply in respect of acts or omissions occurring in the course of the audit of accounts for more than one financial year, and

(b) must specify the financial year in relation to which it applies.

(2) The Secretary of State may by regulations—

(a) require liability limitation agreements to contain specified provisions or provisions of a specified description;

(b) prohibit liability limitation agreements from containing specified provisions or provisions of a specified description.

"Specified" here means specified in the regulations.

(3) Without prejudice to the generality of the power conferred by subsection (2), that power may be exercised with a view to preventing adverse effects on competition.

(4) Subject to the preceding provisions of this section, it is immaterial how a liability limitation agreement is framed.

In particular, the limit on the amount of the auditor's liability need not be a sum of money, or a formula, specified in the agreement.

(5) Regulations under this section are subject to negative resolution procedure.

NOTES

Regulations: no Regulations have been made under this section.

[1.617]

536 Authorisation of agreement by members of the company

(1) A liability limitation agreement is authorised by the members of the company if it has been authorised under this section and that authorisation has not been withdrawn.

(2) A liability limitation agreement between a private company and its auditor may be authorised—

(a) by the company passing a resolution, before it enters into the agreement, waiving the need for approval,

(b) by the company passing a resolution, before it enters into the agreement, approving the agreement's principal terms, or

(c) by the company passing a resolution, after it enters into the agreement, approving the agreement.

(3) A liability limitation agreement between a public company and its auditor may be authorised—

(a) by the company passing a resolution in general meeting, before it enters into the agreement, approving the agreement's principal terms, or

(b) by the company passing a resolution in general meeting, after it enters into the agreement, approving the agreement.

(4) The "principal terms" of an agreement are terms specifying, or relevant to the determination of—

(a) the kind (or kinds) of acts or omissions covered,

(b) the financial year to which the agreement relates, or

(c) the limit to which the auditor's liability is subject.

(5) Authorisation under this section may be withdrawn by the company passing an ordinary resolution to that effect—

(a) at any time before the company enters into the agreement, or

(b) if the company has already entered into the agreement, before the beginning of the financial year to which the agreement relates.

Paragraph (b) has effect notwithstanding anything in the agreement.

[1.618]
537 Effect of liability limitation agreement

(1) A liability limitation agreement is not effective to limit the auditor's liability to less than such amount as is fair and reasonable in all the circumstances of the case having regard (in particular) to—

(a) the auditor's responsibilities under this Part,

(b) the nature and purpose of the auditor's contractual obligations to the company, and

(c) the professional standards expected of him.

(2) A liability limitation agreement that purports to limit the auditor's liability to less than the amount mentioned in subsection (1) shall have effect as if it limited his liability to that amount.

(3) In determining what is fair and reasonable in all the circumstances of the case no account is to be taken of—

(a) matters arising after the loss or damage in question has been incurred, or

(b) matters (whenever arising) affecting the possibility of recovering compensation from other persons liable in respect of the same loss or damage.

[1.619]
538 Disclosure of agreement by company

(1) A company which has entered into a liability limitation agreement must make such disclosure in connection with the agreement as the Secretary of State may require by regulations.

(2) The regulations may provide, in particular, that any disclosure required by the regulations shall be made—

(a) in a note to the company's annual accounts (in the case of its individual accounts) or in such manner as is specified in the regulations (in the case of group accounts), or

(b) in the directors' report.

(3) Regulations under this section are subject to negative resolution procedure.

NOTES

Regulations: the Companies (Disclosure of Auditor Remuneration and Liability Limitation Agreements) Regulations 2008, SI 2008/489 at **[4.115]**. For a summary of all statutory instruments made under this Act, see Appendix 4 at **[A4]**.

CHAPTER 7 SUPPLEMENTARY PROVISIONS

[1.620]
[538A Meaning of "corporate governance statement" etc

(1) In this Part "corporate governance statement" means the statement required by rules 7.2.1 to 7.2.11 in the Disclosure Rules and Transparency Rules sourcebook [made by the Financial Conduct Authority].

(2) . . .

(3) A "separate" corporate governance statement means one that is not included in the directors' report.]

NOTES

Inserted by the Companies Act 2006 (Accounts, Reports and Audit) Regulations 2009, SI 2009/1581, reg 8, in relation to financial years beginning on or after 29 June 2008 which have not ended before 27 June 2009.

Words in square brackets in sub-s (1) substituted, and sub-s (2) repealed, by the Financial Services Act 2012 (Consequential Amendments) Order 2013, SI 2013/636, art 2, Schedule, para 9(1), (5), as from 1 April 2013.

[1.621]
539 Minor definitions

In this Part—

"e-money issuer" [means—

(a) an electronic money institution, within the meaning of the Electronic Money Regulations 2011 (SI 2011/99), or

(b)] a person who has permission under [Part 4A] of the Financial Services and Markets Act 2000 (c 8) to carry on the activity of issuing electronic money within the meaning of article 9B of the Financial Services and Markets Act 2000 (Regulated Activities) Order 2001 (SI 2001/544);

["MiFID investment firm" means an investment firm within the meaning of [Article 2(1A) of Regulation (EU) No 600/2014 of the European Parliament and of the Council of 15 May 2014 on markets in financial instruments and amending Regulation (EU) No 648/2012] other than—

(a) a company [which is exempted from the definition of "investment firm" by Schedule 3 to the Financial Services and Markets Act 2000 (Regulated Activities) Order 2001 (SI 2001/544)], [. . .]

[(b) a company which is an exempt investment firm as defined by regulation 8 (Meaning of "exempt investment firm" in Chapter 1) of the Financial Services and Markets Act 2000 (Markets in Financial Instruments) Regulations 2017 [(SI 2017/701), and];

[(c) any other company which fulfils all the requirements set out in regulation 6(3) of those Regulations;]]

"qualified", in relation to an auditor's report (or a statement contained in an auditor's report), means that the report or statement does not state the auditor's unqualified opinion that the accounts have been properly prepared in accordance with this Act or, in the case of an undertaking not required to prepare accounts in accordance with this Act, under any corresponding legislation under which it is required to prepare accounts;

"turnover", in relation to a company, means the amounts derived from the provision of goods and services falling within the company's ordinary activities, after deduction of—

- (a) trade discounts,
- (b) value added tax, and
- (c) any other taxes based on the amounts so derived;

"UCITS management company" has the meaning given by the Glossary forming part of the Handbook made by the [Financial Conduct Authority] under the Financial Services and Markets Act 2000.

NOTES

Words in first pair of square brackets in the definition "e-money issuer" substituted by the Companies and Partnerships (Accounts and Audit) Regulations 2013, SI 2013/2005, reg 2(1), (9), in relation to a financial year of a company beginning on or after 1 October 2013.

Words in second pair of square brackets in the definition "e-money issuer" substituted by the Financial Services Act 2012, s 114(1), Sch 18, Pt 2, paras 110, 116, as from 1 April 2013.

Definition "ISD investment firm" (omitted) repealed by the Markets in Financial Instruments Directive (Consequential Amendments) Regulations 2007, SI 2007/2932, reg 3(7), as from 1 November 2007.

The Definition "MiFID investment firm" was inserted by SI 2007/2932, reg 3(7), as from 1 November 2007, and has been amended as follows:

The words in the first pair of square brackets and the words in square brackets in para (a) were substituted by the Statutory Auditors and Third Country Auditors (Amendment) (EU Exit) Regulations 2019, SI 2019/177, regs 3, 9, as from IP completion day (as defined in the European Union (Withdrawal Agreement) Act 2020, s 39) (for transitional provisions in relation to audits of accounts for financial years that begin before IP completion day, see Sch 4 to the 2019 Regulations at **[12.88]**).

The word omitted from para (a) was originally inserted, and para (b) was substituted (for the original paras (b), (c)), by the Financial Services and Markets Act 2000 (Markets in Financial Instruments) Regulations 2017, SI 2017/701, reg 50(3), Sch 4, para 9(1), (5), as from 3 January 2018.

The word omitted from para (a) was repealed, the words in square brackets in para (b) were substituted, and para (c) was added, by the Financial Services and Markets Act 2000 (Prospectus and Markets in Financial Instruments) Regulations 2018, SI 2018/786, reg 3, as from 21 July 2018.

Words in square brackets in the definition "UCITS management company" substituted by the Financial Services Act 2012 (Consequential Amendments) Order 2013, SI 2013/636, art 2, Schedule, para 9(1), (6), as from 1 April 2013.

PART 17 A COMPANY'S SHARE CAPITAL

CHAPTER 1 SHARES AND SHARE CAPITAL OF A COMPANY

Shares

[1.622]

540 Shares

(1) In the Companies Acts "share", in relation to a company, means share in the company's share capital.

(2) A company's shares may no longer be converted into stock.

(3) Stock created before the commencement of this Part may be reconverted into shares in accordance with section 620.

(4) In the Companies Acts—

- (a) references to shares include stock except where a distinction between share and stock is express or implied, and
- (b) references to a number of shares include an amount of stock where the context admits of the reference to shares being read as including stock.

[1.623]

541 Nature of shares

The shares or other interest of a member in a company are personal property (or, in Scotland, moveable property) and are not in the nature of real estate (or heritage).

[1.624]

542 Nominal value of shares

(1) Shares in a limited company having a share capital must each have a fixed nominal value.

(2) An allotment of a share that does not have a fixed nominal value is void.

(3) Shares in a limited company having a share capital may be denominated in any currency, and different classes of shares may be denominated in different currencies.

But see section 765 (initial authorised minimum share capital requirement for public company to be met by reference to share capital denominated in sterling or euros).

(4) If a company purports to allot shares in contravention of this section, an offence is committed by every officer of the company who is in default.

(5) A person guilty of an offence under this section is liable—

- (a) on conviction on indictment, to a fine;
- (b) on summary conviction, to a fine not exceeding the statutory maximum.

[1.625]

543 Numbering of shares

(1) Each share in a company having a share capital must be distinguished by its appropriate number, except in the following circumstances.

(2) If at any time—

- (a) all the issued shares in a company are fully paid up and rank *pari passu* for all purposes, or

(b) all the issued shares of a particular class in a company are fully paid up and rank *pari passu* for all purposes, none of those shares need thereafter have a distinguishing number so long as it remains fully paid up and ranks *pari passu* for all purposes with all shares of the same class for the time being issued and fully paid up.

[1.626]
544 Transferability of shares

(1) The shares or other interest of any member in a company are transferable in accordance with the company's articles.

(2) This is subject to—

(a) the Stock Transfer Act 1963 (c 18) or the Stock Transfer Act (Northern Ireland) 1963 (c 24 (NI)) (which enables securities of certain descriptions to be transferred by a simplified process), and

(b) regulations under Chapter 2 of Part 21 of this Act (which enable title to securities to be evidenced and transferred without a written instrument).

(3) See Part 21 of this Act generally as regards share transfers.

[1.627]
545 Companies having a share capital

References in the Companies Acts to a company having a share capital are to a company that has power under its constitution to issue shares.

[1.628]
546 Issued and allotted share capital

(1) References in the Companies Acts—

(a) to "issued share capital" are to shares of a company that have been issued;

(b) to "allotted share capital" are to shares of a company that have been allotted.

(2) References in the Companies Acts to issued or allotted shares, or to issued or allotted share capital, include shares taken on the formation of the company by the subscribers to the company's memorandum.

Share capital

[1.629]
547 Called-up share capital

In the Companies Acts—

"called-up share capital", in relation to a company, means so much of its share capital as equals the aggregate amount of the calls made on its shares (whether or not those calls have been paid), together with—

(a) any share capital paid up without being called, and

(b) any share capital to be paid on a specified future date under the articles, the terms of allotment of the relevant shares or any other arrangements for payment of those shares; and

"uncalled share capital" is to be construed accordingly.

[1.630]
548 Equity share capital

In the Companies Acts "equity share capital", in relation to a company, means its issued share capital excluding any part of that capital that, neither as respects dividends nor as respects capital, carries any right to participate beyond a specified amount in a distribution.

CHAPTER 2 ALLOTMENT OF SHARES: GENERAL PROVISIONS

Power of directors to allot shares

[1.631]
549 Exercise by directors of power to allot shares etc

(1) The directors of a company must not exercise any power of the company—

(a) to allot shares in the company, or

(b) to grant rights to subscribe for, or to convert any security into, shares in the company,

except in accordance with section 550 (private company with single class of shares) or section 551 (authorisation by company).

(2) Subsection (1) does not apply—

(a) to the allotment of shares in pursuance of an employees' share scheme, or

(b) to the grant of a right to subscribe for, or to convert any security into, shares so allotted.

[(3) Subsection (1) does not apply to the allotment of shares pursuant to a right to subscribe for, or to convert any security into, shares in the company.]

[(3A) Subsection (1) does not apply to anything done for the purposes of a compromise or arrangement sanctioned in accordance with Part 26A (arrangements and reconstructions: companies in financial difficulty).]

(4) A director who knowingly contravenes, or permits or authorises a contravention of, this section commits an offence.

(5) A person guilty of an offence under this section is liable—

(a) on conviction on indictment, to a fine;

(b) on summary conviction, to a fine not exceeding the statutory maximum.

(6) Nothing in this section affects the validity of an allotment or other transaction.

NOTES

Sub-s (3): substituted by the Companies Act 2006 (Allotment of Shares and Right of Pre-emption) (Amendment) Regulations 2009, SI 2009/2561, reg 2(1), as from 1 October 2009.

Sub-s (3A): inserted by the Corporate Insolvency and Governance Act 2020, s 7, Sch 9, Pt 2, paras 30, 33(1), (2), as from 26 June 2020.

[1.632]

550 Power of directors to allot shares etc: private company with only one class of shares

Where a private company has only one class of shares, the directors may exercise any power of the company—

(a) to allot shares of that class, or

(b) to grant rights to subscribe for or to convert any security into such shares,

except to the extent that they are prohibited from doing so by the company's articles.

[1.633]

551 Power of directors to allot shares etc: authorisation by company

(1) The directors of a company may exercise a power of the company—

(a) to allot shares in the company, or

(b) to grant rights to subscribe for or to convert any security into shares in the company,

if they are authorised to do so by the company's articles or by resolution of the company.

(2) Authorisation may be given for a particular exercise of the power or for its exercise generally, and may be unconditional or subject to conditions.

(3) Authorisation must—

(a) state the maximum amount of shares that may be allotted under it, and

(b) specify the date on which it will expire, which must be not more than five years from—

(i) in the case of authorisation contained in the company's articles at the time of its original incorporation, the date of that incorporation;

(ii) in any other case, the date on which the resolution is passed by virtue of which the authorisation is given.

(4) Authorisation may—

(a) be renewed or further renewed by resolution of the company for a further period not exceeding five years, and

(b) be revoked or varied at any time by resolution of the company.

(5) A resolution renewing authorisation must—

(a) state (or restate) the maximum amount of shares that may be allotted under the authorisation or, as the case may be, the amount remaining to be allotted under it, and

(b) specify the date on which the renewed authorisation will expire.

(6) In relation to rights to subscribe for or to convert any security into shares in the company, references in this section to the maximum amount of shares that may be allotted under the authorisation are to the maximum amount of shares that may be allotted pursuant to the rights.

(7) The directors may allot shares, or grant rights to subscribe for or to convert any security into shares, after authorisation has expired if—

(a) the shares are allotted, or the rights are granted, in pursuance of an offer or agreement made by the company before the authorisation expired, and

(b) the authorisation allowed the company to make an offer or agreement which would or might require shares to be allotted, or rights to be granted, after the authorisation had expired.

(8) A resolution of a company to give, vary, revoke or renew authorisation under this section may be an ordinary resolution, even though it amends the company's articles.

(9) Chapter 3 of Part 3 (resolutions affecting a company's constitution) applies to a resolution under this section.

Prohibition of commissions, discounts and allowances

[1.634]

552 General prohibition of commissions, discounts and allowances

(1) Except as permitted by section 553 (permitted commission), a company must not apply any of its shares or capital money, either directly or indirectly, in payment of any commission, discount or allowance to any person in consideration of his—

(a) subscribing or agreeing to subscribe (whether absolutely or conditionally) for shares in the company, or

(b) procuring or agreeing to procure subscriptions (whether absolute or conditional) for shares in the company.

(2) It is immaterial how the shares or money are so applied, whether by being added to the purchase money of property acquired by the company or to the contract price of work to be executed for the company, or being paid out of the nominal purchase money or contract price, or otherwise.

(3) Nothing in this section affects the payment of such brokerage as has previously been lawful.

[1.635]

553 Permitted commission

(1) A company may, if the following conditions are satisfied, pay a commission to a person in consideration of his subscribing or agreeing to subscribe (whether absolutely or conditionally) for shares in the company, or procuring or agreeing to procure subscriptions (whether absolute or conditional) for shares in the company.

(2) The conditions are that—

(a) the payment of the commission is authorised by the company's articles; and

(b) the commission paid or agreed to be paid does not exceed—

(i) 10% of the price at which the shares are issued, or

(ii) the amount or rate authorised by the articles,

whichever is the less.

(3) A vendor to, or promoter of, or other person who receives payment in money or shares from, a company may apply any part of the money or shares so received in payment of any commission the payment of which directly by the company would be permitted by this section.

Registration of allotment

[1.636]

554 Registration of allotment

(1) A company must register an allotment of shares as soon as practicable and in any event within two months after the date of the allotment.

(2) This does not apply if the company has issued a share warrant in respect of the shares (see section 779).

[(2A) If an election is in force under Chapter 2A of Part 8, the obligation under subsection (1) to register the allotment of shares is replaced by an obligation to deliver particulars of the allotment of shares to the registrar in accordance with that Chapter.]

(3) If a company fails to comply with this section, an offence is committed by—

(a) the company, and

(b) every officer of the company who is in default.

(4) A person guilty of an offence under this section is liable on summary conviction to a fine not exceeding level 3 on the standard scale and, for continued contravention, a daily default fine not exceeding one-tenth of level 3 on the standard scale.

(5) For the company's duties as to the issue of share certificates etc, see Part 21 (certification and transfer of securities).

NOTES

Sub-s (2A): inserted by the Small Business, Enterprise and Employment Act 2015, s 94, Sch 5, Pt 2, paras 11, 19, as from 30 June 2016.

Return of allotment

[1.637]

555 Return of allotment by limited company

(1) This section applies to a company limited by shares and to a company limited by guarantee and having a share capital.

(2) The company must, within one month of making an allotment of shares, deliver to the registrar for registration a return of the allotment.

(3) The return must—

(a) contain the prescribed information, and

(b) be accompanied by a statement of capital.

(4) The statement of capital must state with respect to the company's share capital at the date to which the return is made up—

(a) the total number of shares of the company,

(b) the aggregate nominal value of those shares,

[(ba) the aggregate amount (if any) unpaid on those shares (whether on account of their nominal value or by way of premium), and]

(c) for each class of shares—

(i) prescribed particulars of the rights attached to the shares,

(ii) the total number of shares of that class, and

(iii) the aggregate nominal value of shares of that class, . . .

(d) . . .

NOTES

Sub-s (4): para (ba) inserted, and para (d) and the preceding word repealed, by the Small Business, Enterprise and Employment Act 2015, s 97, Sch 6, paras 1, 5, as from 30 June 2016.

Orders: the Companies (Shares and Share Capital) Order 2009, SI 2009/388 at **[4.211]**. For a summary of all statutory instruments made under this Act, see Appendix 4 at **[A4]**.

[1.638]

556 Return of allotment by unlimited company allotting new class of shares

(1) This section applies to an unlimited company that allots shares of a class with rights that are not in all respects uniform with shares previously allotted.

(2) The company must, within one month of making such an allotment, deliver to the registrar for registration a return of the allotment.

(3) The return must contain the prescribed particulars of the rights attached to the shares.

(4) For the purposes of this section shares are not to be treated as different from shares previously allotted by reason only that the former do not carry the same rights to dividends as the latter during the twelve months immediately following the former's allotment.

NOTES

Orders: the Companies (Shares and Share Capital) Order 2009, SI 2009/388 at **[4.211]**. For a summary of all statutory instruments made under this Act, see Appendix 4 at **[A4]**.

[1.639]

557 Offence of failure to make return

(1) If a company makes default in complying with—

section 555 (return of allotment of shares by limited company), or

section 556 (return of allotment of new class of shares by unlimited company),

an offence is committed by every officer of the company who is in default.

(2) A person guilty of an offence under this section is liable—

(a) on conviction on indictment, to a fine;

(b) on summary conviction, to a fine not exceeding the statutory maximum and, for continued contravention, a daily default fine not exceeding [one-tenth of the greater of £5,000 or the amount corresponding to level 4 on the standard scale for summary offences].

(3) In the case of default in delivering to the registrar within one month after the allotment the return required by section 555 or 556—

(a) any person liable for the default may apply to the court for relief, and

(b) the court, if satisfied—

(i) that the omission to deliver the document was accidental or due to inadvertence, or
(ii) that it is just and equitable to grant relief,

may make an order extending the time for delivery of the document for such period as the court thinks proper.

NOTES

Sub-s (2): words in square brackets substituted (for the original words "one-tenth of the statutory maximum") by the Legal Aid, Sentencing and Punishment of Offenders Act 2012 (Fines on Summary Conviction) Regulations 2015, SI 2015/664, regs 3, 5, Sch 3, Pt 1, para 9(1), (15), as from 12 March 2015, in relation to England and Wales only (except in relation to (a) fines for offences committed before 12 March 2015, (b) the operation of restrictions on fines that may be imposed on a person aged under 18, or (c) fines that may be imposed on a person convicted by a magistrates' court who is to be sentenced as if convicted on indictment).

Supplementary provisions

[1.640]

558 When shares are allotted

For the purposes of the Companies Acts shares in a company are taken to be allotted when a person acquires the unconditional right to be included in the company's register of members [(or, as the case may be, to have the person's name and other particulars delivered to the registrar under Chapter 2A of Part 8 and registered by the registrar)] in respect of the shares.

NOTES

Words in square brackets inserted by the Small Business, Enterprise and Employment Act 2015, s 94, Sch 5, Pt 2, paras 11, 20, as from 30 June 2016.

[1.641]

559 Provisions about allotment not applicable to shares taken on formation

The provisions of this Chapter have no application in relation to the taking of shares by the subscribers to the memorandum on the formation of the company.

CHAPTER 3 ALLOTMENT OF EQUITY SECURITIES:
EXISTING SHAREHOLDERS' RIGHT OF PRE-EMPTION

Introductory

[1.642]

560 Meaning of "equity securities" and related expressions

(1) In this Chapter—

"equity securities" means—

(a) ordinary shares in the company, or
(b) rights to subscribe for, or to convert securities into, ordinary shares in the company;

"ordinary shares" means shares other than shares that as respects dividends and capital carry a right to participate only up to a specified amount in a distribution.

[(2) References in this Chapter to the allotment of equity securities—

(a) include the grant of a right to subscribe for, or to convert any securities into, ordinary shares in the company, and
(b) do not include the allotment of shares pursuant to such a right.

(3) References in this Chapter to the allotment of equity securities include the sale of ordinary shares in the company that immediately before the sale were held by the company as treasury shares.]

NOTES

Sub-ss (2), (3): substituted, for the original sub-s (2), by the Companies Act 2006 (Allotment of Shares and Right of Pre-emption) (Amendment) Regulations 2009, SI 2009/2561, reg 2(2), as from 1 October 2009.

Existing shareholders' right of pre-emption

[1.643]

561 Existing shareholders' right of pre-emption

(1) A company must not allot equity securities to a person on any terms unless—

(a) it has made an offer to each person who holds ordinary shares in the company to allot to him on the same or more favourable terms a proportion of those securities that is as nearly as practicable equal to the proportion in nominal value held by him of the ordinary share capital of the company, and
(b) the period during which any such offer may be accepted has expired or the company has received notice of the acceptance or refusal of every offer so made.

(2) Securities that a company has offered to allot to a holder of ordinary shares may be allotted to him, or anyone in whose favour he has renounced his right to their allotment, without contravening subsection (1)(b).

(3) . . .

(4) Shares held by the company as treasury shares are disregarded for the purposes of this section, so that—

(a) the company is not treated as a person who holds ordinary shares, and
(b) the shares are not treated as forming part of the ordinary share capital of the company.

(5) This section is subject to—

(a) sections 564 to [566A] (exceptions to pre-emption right),
(b) sections 567 and 568 (exclusion of rights of pre-emption),
(c) sections 569 to 573 (disapplication of pre-emption rights), and
(d) section 576 (saving for certain older pre-emption procedures).

NOTES

Sub-s (3): repealed by the Companies Act 2006 (Allotment of Shares and Right of Pre-emption) (Amendment) Regulations 2009, SI 2009/2561, reg 2(3), as from 1 October 2009.

Sub-s (5): number in square brackets substituted by the Corporate Insolvency and Governance Act 2020, s 7, Sch 9, Pt 2, paras 30, 33(1), (3)(a), as from 26 June 2020.

[1.644]

562 Communication of pre-emption offers to shareholders

(1) This section has effect as to the manner in which offers required by section 561 are to be made to holders of a company's shares.

(2) The offer may be made in hard copy or electronic form.

(3) If the holder—

(a) has no registered address in [the United Kingdom or an EEA State] and has not given to the company an address in [the United Kingdom or an EEA State] for the service of notices on him, or

(b) is the holder of a share warrant,

the offer may be made by causing it, or a notice specifying where a copy of it can be obtained or inspected, to be published in the Gazette.

(4) The offer must state a period during which it may be accepted and the offer shall not be withdrawn before the end of that period.

(5) The period must be a period of at least [14 days] beginning—

(a) in the case of an offer made in hard copy form, with the date on which the offer is sent or supplied;

(b) in the case of an offer made in electronic form, with the date on which the offer is sent;

(c) in the case of an offer made by publication in the Gazette, with the date of publication.

(6) The Secretary of State may by regulations made by statutory instrument—

(a) reduce the period specified in subsection (5) (but not to less than 14 days), or

(b) increase that period.

(7) A statutory instrument containing regulations made under subsection (6) is subject to affirmative resolution procedure.

NOTES

Sub-s (3): words in square brackets substituted by the Companies, Limited Liability Partnerships and Partnerships (Amendment etc) (EU Exit) Regulations 2019, SI 2019/348, reg 6, Sch 1, paras 1, 9, as from IP completion day (as defined in the European Union (Withdrawal Agreement) Act 2020, s 39).

Sub-s (5): words in square brackets substituted by the Companies (Share Capital and Acquisition by Company of its Own Shares) Regulations 2009, SI 2009/2022, reg 2, as from 1 October 2009.

Regulations: the Companies (Share Capital and Acquisition by Company of its Own Shares) Regulations 2009, SI 2009/2022 at **[4.369]**. For a summary of all statutory instruments made under this Act, see Appendix 4 at **[A4]**.

[1.645]

563 Liability of company and officers in case of contravention

(1) This section applies where there is a contravention of—

section 561 (existing shareholders' right of pre-emption), or

section 562 (communication of pre-emption offers to shareholders).

(2) The company and every officer of it who knowingly authorised or permitted the contravention are jointly and severally liable to compensate any person to whom an offer should have been made in accordance with those provisions for any loss, damage, costs or expenses which the person has sustained or incurred by reason of the contravention.

(3) No proceedings to recover any such loss, damage, costs or expenses shall be commenced after the expiration of two years—

(a) from the delivery to the registrar of companies of the return of allotment, or

(b) where equity securities other than shares are granted, from the date of the grant.

Exceptions to right of pre-emption

[1.646]

564 Exception to pre-emption right: bonus shares

Section 561(1) (existing shareholders' right of pre-emption) does not apply in relation to the allotment of bonus shares.

[1.647]

565 Exception to pre-emption right: issue for non-cash consideration

Section 561(1) (existing shareholders' right of pre-emption) does not apply to a particular allotment of equity securities if these are, or are to be, wholly or partly paid up otherwise than in cash.

[1.648]

[566 Exceptions to pre-emption right: employees' share schemes

Section 561 (existing shareholders' right of pre-emption) does not apply to the allotment of equity securities that would, apart from any renunciation or assignment of the right to their allotment, be held under or allotted or transferred pursuant to an employees' share scheme.]

NOTES

Substituted by the Companies Act 2006 (Allotment of Shares and Right of Pre-emption) (Amendment) Regulations 2009, SI 2009/2561, reg 2(4), as from 1 October 2009.

[1.649]

[566A Exception to pre-emption right: companies in financial difficulty

Section 561(1) (existing shareholders' right of pre-emption) does not apply to an allotment of equity securities that is carried out as part of a compromise or arrangement sanctioned in accordance with Part 26A (arrangements and reconstructions: companies in financial difficulty).]

NOTES

Commencement: 26 June 2020.

Inserted by the Corporate Insolvency and Governance Act 2020, s 7, Sch 9, Pt 2, paras 30, 33(1), (3)(b), as from 26 June 2020.

Exclusion of right of pre-emption

[1.650]

567 Exclusion of requirements by private companies

(1) All or any of the requirements of—

(a) section 561 (existing shareholders' right of pre-emption), or

(b) section 562 (communication of pre-emption offers to shareholders)

may be excluded by provision contained in the articles of a private company.

(2) They may be excluded—

(a) generally in relation to the allotment by the company of equity securities, or

(b) in relation to allotments of a particular description.

(3) Any requirement or authorisation contained in the articles of a private company that is inconsistent with either of those sections is treated for the purposes of this section as a provision excluding that section.

(4) A provision to which section 568 applies (exclusion of pre-emption right: corresponding right conferred by articles) is not to be treated as inconsistent with section 561.

[1.651]

568 Exclusion of pre-emption right: articles conferring corresponding right

(1) The provisions of this section apply where, in a case in which section 561 (existing shareholders' right of pre-emption) would otherwise apply—

(a) a company's articles contain provision ("pre-emption provision") prohibiting the company from allotting ordinary shares of a particular class unless it has complied with the condition that it makes such an offer as is described in section 561(1) to each person who holds ordinary shares of that class, and

(b) in accordance with that provision—

(i) the company makes an offer to allot shares to such a holder, and

(ii) he or anyone in whose favour he has renounced his right to their allotment accepts the offer.

(2) In that case, section 561 does not apply to the allotment of those shares and the company may allot them accordingly.

(3) The provisions of section 562 (communication of pre-emption offers to shareholders) apply in relation to offers made in pursuance of the pre-emption provision of the company's articles.

This is subject to section 567 (exclusion of requirements by private companies).

(4) If there is a contravention of the pre-emption provision of the company's articles, the company, and every officer of it who knowingly authorised or permitted the contravention, are jointly and severally liable to compensate any person to whom an offer should have been made under the provision for any loss, damage, costs or expenses which the person has sustained or incurred by reason of the contravention.

(5) No proceedings to recover any such loss, damage, costs or expenses may be commenced after the expiration of two years—

(a) from the delivery to the registrar of companies of the return of allotment, or

(b) where equity securities other than shares are granted, from the date of the grant.

Disapplication of pre-emption rights

[1.652]

569 Disapplication of pre-emption rights: private company with only one class of shares

(1) The directors of a private company that has only one class of shares may be given power by the articles, or by a special resolution of the company, to allot equity securities of that class as if section 561 (existing shareholders' right of pre-emption)—

(a) did not apply to the allotment, or

(b) applied to the allotment with such modifications as the directors may determine.

(2) Where the directors make an allotment under this section, the provisions of this Chapter have effect accordingly.

[1.653]

570 Disapplication of pre-emption rights: directors acting under general authorisation

(1) Where the directors of a company are generally authorised for the purposes of section 551 (power of directors to allot shares etc: authorisation by company), they may be given power by the articles, or by a special resolution of the company, to allot equity securities pursuant to that authorisation as if section 561 (existing shareholders' right of pre-emption)—

(a) did not apply to the allotment, or

(b) applied to the allotment with such modifications as the directors may determine.

(2) Where the directors make an allotment under this section, the provisions of this Chapter have effect accordingly.

(3) The power conferred by this section ceases to have effect when the authorisation to which it relates—

(a) is revoked, or

(b) would (if not renewed) expire.

But if the authorisation is renewed the power may also be renewed, for a period not longer than that for which the authorisation is renewed, by a special resolution of the company.

(4) Notwithstanding that the power conferred by this section has expired, the directors may allot equity securities in pursuance of an offer or agreement previously made by the company if the power enabled the company to make an offer or agreement that would or might require equity securities to be allotted after it expired.

[1.654]

571 Disapplication of pre-emption rights by special resolution

(1) Where the directors of a company are authorised for the purposes of section 551 (power of directors to allot shares etc: authorisation by company), whether generally or otherwise, the company may by special resolution resolve that section 561 (existing shareholders' right of pre-emption)—

(a) does not apply to a specified allotment of equity securities to be made pursuant to that authorisation, or

(b) applies to such an allotment with such modifications as may be specified in the resolution.

(2) Where such a resolution is passed the provisions of this Chapter have effect accordingly.

(3) A special resolution under this section ceases to have effect when the authorisation to which it relates—

(a) is revoked, or

(b) would (if not renewed) expire.

But if the authorisation is renewed the resolution may also be renewed, for a period not longer than that for which the authorisation is renewed, by a special resolution of the company.

(4) Notwithstanding that any such resolution has expired, the directors may allot equity securities in pursuance of an offer or agreement previously made by the company if the resolution enabled the company to make an offer or agreement that would or might require equity securities to be allotted after it expired.

(5) A special resolution under this section, or a special resolution to renew such a resolution, must not be proposed unless—

(a) it is recommended by the directors, and

(b) the directors have complied with the following provisions.

(6) Before such a resolution is proposed, the directors must make a written statement setting out—

(a) their reasons for making the recommendation,

(b) the amount to be paid to the company in respect of the equity securities to be allotted, and

(c) the directors' justification of that amount.

(7) The directors' statement must—

(a) if the resolution is proposed as a written resolution, be sent or submitted to every eligible member at or before the time at which the proposed resolution is sent or submitted to him;

(b) if the resolution is proposed at a general meeting, be circulated to the members entitled to notice of the meeting with that notice.

[1.655]

572 Liability for false statement in directors' statement

(1) This section applies in relation to a directors' statement under section 571 (special resolution disapplying pre-emption rights) that is sent, submitted or circulated under subsection (7) of that section.

(2) A person who knowingly or recklessly authorises or permits the inclusion of any matter that is misleading, false or deceptive in a material particular in such a statement commits an offence.

(3) A person guilty of an offence under this section is liable—

(a) on conviction on indictment, to imprisonment for a term not exceeding two years or a fine (or both);

(b) on summary conviction—

(i) in England and Wales, to imprisonment for a term not exceeding twelve months or to a fine not exceeding the statutory maximum (or both);

(ii) in Scotland or Northern Ireland, to imprisonment for a term not exceeding six months, or to a fine not exceeding the statutory maximum (or both).

NOTES

Offences under this section: see further s 1131 at **[1.1301]**.

[1.656]

573 Disapplication of pre-emption rights: sale of treasury shares

(1) This section applies in relation to a sale of shares that is an allotment of equity securities by virtue of [section 560(3)] (sale of shares held by company as treasury shares).

(2) The directors of a company may be given power by the articles, or by a special resolution of the company, to allot equity securities as if section 561 (existing shareholders' right of pre-emption)—

(a) did not apply to the allotment, or

(b) applied to the allotment with such modifications as the directors may determine.

(3) The provisions of section 570(2) and (4) apply in that case as they apply to a case within subsection (1) of that section.

(4) The company may by special resolution resolve that section 561—

(a) shall not apply to a specified allotment of securities, or

(b) shall apply to the allotment with such modifications as may be specified in the resolution.

(5) The provisions of section 571(2) and (4) to (7) apply in that case as they apply to a case within subsection (1) of that section.

NOTES

Sub-s (1): words in square brackets substituted by the Companies Act 2006 (Allotment of Shares and Right of Pre-emption) (Amendment) Regulations 2009, SI 2009/2561, reg 2(5), as from 1 October 2009.

Supplementary

[1.657]

574 References to holder of shares in relation to offer

(1) In this Chapter, in relation to an offer to allot securities required by—

(a) section 561 (existing shareholders' right of pre-emption), or

(b) any provision to which section 568 applies (articles conferring corresponding right),

a reference (however expressed) to the holder of shares of any description is to whoever was the holder of shares of that description at the close of business on a date to be specified in the offer.

(2) The specified date must fall within the period of 28 days immediately before the date of the offer.

[1.658]
575 Saving for other restrictions on offer or allotment

(1) The provisions of this Chapter are without prejudice to any other enactment by virtue of which a company is prohibited (whether generally or in specified circumstances) from offering or allotting equity securities to any person.

(2) Where a company cannot by virtue of such an enactment offer or allot equity securities to a holder of ordinary shares of the company, those shares are disregarded for the purposes of section 561 (existing shareholders' right of pre-emption), so that—

(a) the person is not treated as a person who holds ordinary shares, and
(b) the shares are not treated as forming part of the ordinary share capital of the company.

[1.659]
576 Saving for certain older pre-emption requirements

(1) In the case of a public company the provisions of this Chapter do not apply to an allotment of equity securities that are subject to a pre-emption requirement in relation to which section 96(1) of the Companies Act 1985 (c 6) or Article 106(1) of the Companies (Northern Ireland) Order 1986 (SI 1986/1032 (NI 6)) applied immediately before the commencement of this Chapter.

(2) In the case of a private company a pre-emption requirement to which section 96(3) of the Companies Act 1985 or Article 106(3) of the Companies (Northern Ireland) Order 1986 applied immediately before the commencement of this Chapter shall have effect, so long as the company remains a private company, as if it were contained in the company's articles.

(3) A pre-emption requirement to which section 96(4) of the Companies Act 1985 or Article 106(4) of the Companies (Northern Ireland) Order 1986 applied immediately before the commencement of this section shall be treated for the purposes of this Chapter as if it were contained in the company's articles.

[1.660]
577 Provisions about pre-emption not applicable to shares taken on formation

The provisions of this Chapter have no application in relation to the taking of shares by the subscribers to the memorandum on the formation of the company.

CHAPTER 4 PUBLIC COMPANIES: ALLOTMENT WHERE ISSUE NOT FULLY SUBSCRIBED

[1.661]
578 Public companies: allotment where issue not fully subscribed

(1) No allotment shall be made of shares of a public company offered for subscription unless—

(a) the issue is subscribed for in full, or
(b) the offer is made on terms that the shares subscribed for may be allotted—
    (i) in any event, or
    (ii) if specified conditions are met (and those conditions are met).

(2) If shares are prohibited from being allotted by subsection (1) and 40 days have elapsed after the first making of the offer, all money received from applicants for shares must be repaid to them forthwith, without interest.

(3) If any of the money is not repaid within 48 days after the first making of the offer, the directors of the company are jointly and severally liable to repay it, with interest at the rate for the time being specified under section 17 of the Judgments Act 1838 (c 110) from the expiration of the 48th day.

A director is not so liable if he proves that the default in the repayment of the money was not due to any misconduct or negligence on his part.

(4) This section applies in the case of shares offered as wholly or partly payable otherwise than in cash as it applies in the case of shares offered for subscription.

(5) In that case—

(a) the references in subsection (1) to subscription shall be construed accordingly;
(b) references in subsections (2) and (3) to the repayment of money received from applicants for shares include—
    (i) the return of any other consideration so received (including, if the case so requires, the release of the applicant from any undertaking), or
    (ii) if it is not reasonably practicable to return the consideration, the payment of money equal to its value at the time it was so received;
(c) references to interest apply accordingly.

(6) Any condition requiring or binding an applicant for shares to waive compliance with any requirement of this section is void.

[1.662]
579 Public companies: effect of irregular allotment where issue not fully subscribed

(1) An allotment made by a public company to an applicant in contravention of section 578 (public companies: allotment where issue not fully subscribed) is voidable at the instance of the applicant within one month after the date of the allotment, and not later.

(2) It is so voidable even if the company is in the course of being wound up.

(3) A director of a public company who knowingly contravenes, or permits or authorises the contravention of, any provision of section 578 with respect to allotment is liable to compensate the company and the allottee respectively for any loss, damages, costs or expenses that the company or allottee may have sustained or incurred by the contravention.

(4) Proceedings to recover any such loss, damages, costs or expenses may not be brought more than two years after the date of the allotment.

CHAPTER 5 PAYMENT FOR SHARES

General rules

[1.663]
580 Shares not to be allotted at a discount
(1) A company's shares must not be allotted at a discount.
(2) If shares are allotted in contravention of this section, the allottee is liable to pay the company an amount equal to the amount of the discount, with interest at the appropriate rate.

[1.664]
581 Provision for different amounts to be paid on shares
A company, if so authorised by its articles, may—
(a) make arrangements on the issue of shares for a difference between the shareholders in the amounts and times of payment of calls on their shares;
(b) accept from any member the whole or part of the amount remaining unpaid on any shares held by him, although no part of that amount has been called up;
(c) pay a dividend in proportion to the amount paid up on each share where a larger amount is paid up on some shares than on others.

[1.665]
582 General rule as to means of payment
(1) Shares allotted by a company, and any premium on them, may be paid up in money or money's worth (including goodwill and know-how).
(2) This section does not prevent a company—
(a) from allotting bonus shares to its members, or
(b) from paying up, with sums available for the purpose, any amounts for the time being unpaid on any of its shares (whether on account of the nominal value of the shares or by way of premium).
(3) This section has effect subject to the following provisions of this Chapter (additional rules for public companies).

[1.666]
583 Meaning of payment in cash
(1) The following provisions have effect for the purposes of the Companies Acts.
(2) A share in a company is deemed paid up (as to its nominal value or any premium on it) in cash, or allotted for cash, if the consideration received for the allotment or payment up is a cash consideration.
(3) A "cash consideration" means—
(a) cash received by the company,
(b) a cheque received by the company in good faith that the directors have no reason for suspecting will not be paid,
(c) a release of a liability of the company for a liquidated sum,
(d) an undertaking to pay cash to the company at a future date, or
(e) payment by any other means giving rise to a present or future entitlement (of the company or a person acting on the company's behalf) to a payment, or credit equivalent to payment, in cash.
(4) The Secretary of State may by order provide that particular means of payment specified in the order are to be regarded as falling within subsection (3)(e).
(5) In relation to the allotment or payment up of shares in a company—
(a) the payment of cash to a person other than the company, or
(b) an undertaking to pay cash to a person other than the company,
counts as consideration other than cash.
This does not apply for the purposes of Chapter 3 (allotment of equity securities: existing shareholders' right of pre-emption).
(6) For the purpose of determining whether a share is or is to be allotted for cash, or paid up in cash, "cash" includes foreign currency.
(7) An order under this section is subject to negative resolution procedure.

NOTES
Orders: the Companies (Shares and Share Capital) Order 2009, SI 2009/388 at **[4.211]**. For a summary of all statutory instruments made under this Act, see Appendix 4 at **[A4]**.

Additional rules for public companies

[1.667]
584 Public companies: shares taken by subscribers of memorandum
Shares taken by a subscriber to the memorandum of a public company in pursuance of an undertaking of his in the memorandum, and any premium on the shares, must be paid up in cash.

[1.668]
585 Public companies: must not accept undertaking to do work or perform services
(1) A public company must not accept at any time, in payment up of its shares or any premium on them, an undertaking given by any person that he or another should do work or perform services for the company or any other person.
(2) If a public company accepts such an undertaking in payment up of its shares or any premium on them, the holder of the shares when they or the premium are treated as paid up (in whole or in part) by the undertaking is liable—
(a) to pay the company in respect of those shares an amount equal to their nominal value, together with the whole of any premium or, if the case so requires, such proportion of that amount as is treated as paid up by the undertaking; and
(b) to pay interest at the appropriate rate on the amount payable under paragraph (a).
(3) The reference in subsection (2) to the holder of shares includes a person who has an unconditional right—

(a) to be included in the company's register of members in respect of those shares, or
(b) to have an instrument of transfer of them executed in his favour.

[1.669]
586 Public companies: shares must be at least one-quarter paid up

(1) A public company must not allot a share except as paid up at least as to one-quarter of its nominal value and the whole of any premium on it.
(2) This does not apply to shares allotted in pursuance of an employees' share scheme.
(3) If a company allots a share in contravention of this section—
(a) the share is to be treated as if one-quarter of its nominal value, together with the whole of any premium on it, had been received, and
(b) the allottee is liable to pay the company the minimum amount which should have been received in respect of the share under subsection (1) (less the value of any consideration actually applied in payment up, to any extent, of the share and any premium on it), with interest at the appropriate rate.
(4) Subsection (3) does not apply to the allotment of bonus shares, unless the allottee knew or ought to have known the shares were allotted in contravention of this section.

[1.670]
587 Public companies: payment by long-term undertaking

(1) A public company must not allot shares as fully or partly paid up (as to their nominal value or any premium on them) otherwise than in cash if the consideration for the allotment is or includes an undertaking which is to be, or may be, performed more than five years after the date of the allotment.
(2) If a company allots shares in contravention of subsection (1), the allottee is liable to pay the company an amount equal to the aggregate of their nominal value and the whole of any premium (or, if the case so requires, so much of that aggregate as is treated as paid up by the undertaking), with interest at the appropriate rate.
(3) Where a contract for the allotment of shares does not contravene subsection (1), any variation of the contract that has the effect that the contract would have contravened the subsection, if the terms of the contract as varied had been its original terms, is void.

This applies also to the variation by a public company of the terms of a contract entered into before the company was re-registered as a public company.
(4) Where—
(a) a public company allots shares for a consideration which consists of or includes (in accordance with subsection (1)) an undertaking that is to be performed within five years of the allotment, and
(b) the undertaking is not performed within the period allowed by the contract for the allotment of the shares,
the allottee is liable to pay the company, at the end of the period so allowed, an amount equal to the aggregate of the nominal value of the shares and the whole of any premium (or, if the case so requires, so much of that aggregate as is treated as paid up by the undertaking), with interest at the appropriate rate.
(5) References in this section to a contract for the allotment of shares include an ancillary contract relating to payment in respect of them.

Supplementary provisions

[1.671]
588 Liability of subsequent holders of shares

(1) If a person becomes a holder of shares in respect of which—
(a) there has been a contravention of any provision of this Chapter, and
(b) by virtue of that contravention another is liable to pay any amount under the provision contravened,
that person is also liable to pay that amount (jointly and severally with any other person so liable), subject as follows.
(2) A person otherwise liable under subsection (1) is exempted from that liability if either—
(a) he is a purchaser for value and, at the time of the purchase, he did not have actual notice of the contravention concerned, or
(b) he derived title to the shares (directly or indirectly) from a person who became a holder of them after the contravention and was not liable under subsection (1).
(3) References in this section to a holder, in relation to shares in a company, include any person who has an unconditional right—
(a) to be included in the company's register of members [(or, as the case may be, to have his name and other particulars delivered to the registrar under Chapter 2A of Part 8 and registered by the registrar)] in respect of those shares, or
(b) to have an instrument of transfer of the shares executed in his favour.
(4) This section applies in relation to a failure to carry out a term of a contract as mentioned in section 587(4) (public companies: payment by long-term undertaking) as it applies in relation to a contravention of a provision of this Chapter.

NOTES

Sub-s (3): words in square brackets inserted by the Small Business, Enterprise and Employment Act 2015, s 94, Sch 5, Pt 2, paras 11, 21, as from 30 June 2016.

[1.672]
589 Power of court to grant relief

(1) This section applies in relation to liability under—
section 585(2) (liability of allottee in case of breach by public company of prohibition on accepting undertaking to do work or perform services),
section 587(2) or (4) (liability of allottee in case of breach by public company of prohibition on payment by long-term undertaking), or
section 588 (liability of subsequent holders of shares),
as it applies in relation to a contravention of those sections.

(2) A person who—

(a) is subject to any such liability to a company in relation to payment in respect of shares in the company, or

(b) is subject to any such liability to a company by virtue of an undertaking given to it in, or in connection with, payment for shares in the company,

may apply to the court to be exempted in whole or in part from the liability.

(3) In the case of a liability within subsection (2)(a), the court may exempt the applicant from the liability only if and to the extent that it appears to the court just and equitable to do so having regard to—

(a) whether the applicant has paid, or is liable to pay, any amount in respect of—

(i) any other liability arising in relation to those shares under any provision of this Chapter or Chapter 6, or

(ii) any liability arising by virtue of any undertaking given in or in connection with payment for those shares;

(b) whether any person other than the applicant has paid or is likely to pay, whether in pursuance of any order of the court or otherwise, any such amount;

(c) whether the applicant or any other person—

(i) has performed in whole or in part, or is likely so to perform any such undertaking, or

(ii) has done or is likely to do any other thing in payment or part payment for the shares.

(4) In the case of a liability within subsection (2)(b), the court may exempt the applicant from the liability only if and to the extent that it appears to the court just and equitable to do so having regard to—

(a) whether the applicant has paid or is liable to pay any amount in respect of liability arising in relation to the shares under any provision of this Chapter or Chapter 6;

(b) whether any person other than the applicant has paid or is likely to pay, whether in pursuance of any order of the court or otherwise, any such amount.

(5) In determining whether it should exempt the applicant in whole or in part from any liability, the court must have regard to the following overriding principles—

(a) a company that has allotted shares should receive money or money's worth at least equal in value to the aggregate of the nominal value of those shares and the whole of any premium or, if the case so requires, so much of that aggregate as is treated as paid up;

(b) subject to that, where a company would, if the court did not grant the exemption, have more than one remedy against a particular person, it should be for the company to decide which remedy it should remain entitled to pursue.

(6) If a person brings proceedings against another ("the contributor") for a contribution in respect of liability to a company arising under any provision of this Chapter or Chapter 6 and it appears to the court that the contributor is liable to make such a contribution, the court may, if and to the extent that it appears to it just and equitable to do so having regard to the respective culpability (in respect of the liability to the company) of the contributor and the person bringing the proceedings—

(a) exempt the contributor in whole or in part from his liability to make such a contribution, or

(b) order the contributor to make a larger contribution than, but for this subsection, he would be liable to make.

[1.673]

590 Penalty for contravention of this Chapter

(1) If a company contravenes any of the provisions of this Chapter, an offence is committed by—

(a) the company, and

(b) every officer of the company who is in default.

(2) A person guilty of an offence under this section is liable—

(a) on conviction on indictment, to a fine;

(b) on summary conviction, to a fine not exceeding the statutory maximum.

[1.674]

591 Enforceability of undertakings to do work etc

(1) An undertaking given by any person, in or in connection with payment for shares in a company, to do work or perform services or to do any other thing, if it is enforceable by the company apart from this Chapter, is so enforceable notwithstanding that there has been a contravention in relation to it of a provision of this Chapter or Chapter 6.

(2) This is without prejudice to section 589 (power of court to grant relief etc in respect of liabilities).

[1.675]

592 The appropriate rate of interest

(1) For the purposes of this Chapter the "appropriate rate" of interest is 5% per annum or such other rate as may be specified by order made by the Secretary of State.

(2) An order under this section is subject to negative resolution procedure.

NOTES

Orders: no Orders have been made under this section.

CHAPTER 6 PUBLIC COMPANIES: INDEPENDENT VALUATION OF NON-CASH CONSIDERATION

Non-cash consideration for shares

[1.676]

593 Public company: valuation of non-cash consideration for shares

(1) A public company must not allot shares as fully or partly paid up (as to their nominal value or any premium on them) otherwise than in cash unless—

(a) the consideration for the allotment has been independently valued in accordance with the provisions of this Chapter,

(b) the valuer's report has been made to the company during the six months immediately preceding the allotment of the shares, and

(c) a copy of the report has been sent to the proposed allottee.

(2) For this purpose the application of an amount standing to the credit of—

(a) any of a company's reserve accounts, or

(b) its profit and loss account,

in paying up (to any extent) shares allotted to members of the company, or premiums on shares so allotted, does not count as consideration for the allotment.

Accordingly, subsection (1) does not apply in that case.

(3) If a company allots shares in contravention of subsection (1) and either—

(a) the allottee has not received the valuer's report required to be sent to him, or

(b) there has been some other contravention of the requirements of this section or section 596 that the allottee knew or ought to have known amounted to a contravention,

the allottee is liable to pay the company an amount equal to the aggregate of the nominal value of the shares and the whole of any premium (or, if the case so requires, so much of that aggregate as is treated as paid up by the consideration), with interest at the appropriate rate.

(4) This section has effect subject to—

section 594 (exception to valuation requirement: arrangement with another company), and

section 595 (exception to valuation requirement: merger [or division]).

NOTES

Sub-s (4): words in square brackets inserted by the Companies (Reporting Requirements in Mergers and Divisions) Regulations 2011, SI 2011/1606, reg 2(4)(b), as from 1 August 2011 (except in relation to any merger or division the draft terms of which were adopted before that date).

[1.677]

594 Exception to valuation requirement: arrangement with another company

(1) Section 593 (valuation of non-cash consideration) does not apply to the allotment of shares by a company ("company A") in connection with an arrangement to which this section applies.

(2) This section applies to an arrangement for the allotment of shares in company A on terms that the whole or part of the consideration for the shares allotted is to be provided by—

(a) the transfer to that company, or

(b) the cancellation,

of all or some of the shares, or of all or some of the shares of a particular class, in another company ("company B").

(3) It is immaterial whether the arrangement provides for the issue to company A of shares, or shares of any particular class, in company B.

(4) This section applies to an arrangement only if under the arrangement it is open to all the holders of the shares in company B (or, where the arrangement applies only to shares of a particular class, to all the holders of shares of that class) to take part in the arrangement.

(5) In determining whether that is the case, the following shall be disregarded—

(a) shares held by or by a nominee of company A;

(b) shares held by or by a nominee of a company which is—

(i) the holding company, or a subsidiary, of company A, or

(ii) a subsidiary of such a holding company;

(c) shares held as treasury shares by company B.

(6) In this section—

(a) "arrangement" means any agreement, scheme or arrangement (including an arrangement sanctioned in accordance with—

(i) Part 26 [or 26A] (arrangements and reconstructions), or

(ii) section 110 of the Insolvency Act 1986 (c 45) or Article 96 of the Insolvency (Northern Ireland) Order 1989 (SI 1989/2405 (NI 19)) (liquidator in winding up accepting shares as consideration for sale of company property)), and

(b) "company", except in reference to company A, includes any body corporate.

NOTES

Sub-s (6): words in square brackets inserted by the Corporate Insolvency and Governance Act 2020, s 7, Sch 9, Pt 2, paras 30, 33(1), (4), as from 26 June 2020.

[1.678]

595 Exception to valuation requirement: merger [or division]

(1) Section 593 (valuation of non-cash consideration) does not apply to the allotment of shares by a company [as part of a scheme to which Part 27 (mergers and divisions of public companies) applies if—

(a) in the case of a scheme involving a merger, an expert's report is drawn up as required by section 909, or

(b) in the case of a scheme involving a division, an expert's report is drawn up as required by section 924.]

(2), (3) . . .

NOTES

The words in square brackets in the section heading were added, the words in square brackets in sub-s (1) were substituted, and sub-ss (2), (3) were repealed, by the Companies (Reporting Requirements in Mergers and Divisions) Regulations 2011, SI 2011/1606, reg 2(1)–(4)(a), as from 1 August 2011 (except in relation to any merger or division the draft terms of which were adopted before that date)

[1.679]

596 Non-cash consideration for shares: requirements as to valuation and report

(1) The provisions of sections 1150 to 1153 (general provisions as to independent valuation and report) apply to the valuation and report required by section 593 (public company: valuation of non-cash consideration for shares).

(2) The valuer's report must state—

(a) the nominal value of the shares to be wholly or partly paid for by the consideration in question;
(b) the amount of any premium payable on the shares;
(c) the description of the consideration and, as respects so much of the consideration as he himself has valued, a description of that part of the consideration, the method used to value it and the date of the valuation;
(d) the extent to which the nominal value of the shares and any premium are to be treated as paid up—
(i) by the consideration;
(ii) in cash.

(3) The valuer's report must contain or be accompanied by a note by him—
(a) in the case of a valuation made by a person other than himself, that it appeared to himself reasonable to arrange for it to be so made or to accept a valuation so made,
(b) whoever made the valuation, that the method of valuation was reasonable in all the circumstances,
(c) that it appears to the valuer that there has been no material change in the value of the consideration in question since the valuation, and
(d) that, on the basis of the valuation, the value of the consideration, together with any cash by which the nominal value of the shares or any premium payable on them is to be paid up, is not less than so much of the aggregate of the nominal value and the whole of any such premium as is treated as paid up by the consideration and any such cash.

(4) Where the consideration to be valued is accepted partly in payment up of the nominal value of the shares and any premium and partly for some other consideration given by the company, section 593 and the preceding provisions of this section apply as if references to the consideration accepted by the company included the proportion of that consideration that is properly attributable to the payment up of that value and any premium.

(5) In such a case—
(a) the valuer must carry out, or arrange for, such other valuations as will enable him to determine that proportion, and
(b) his report must state what valuations have been made under this subsection and also the reason for, and method and date of, any such valuation and any other matters which may be relevant to that determination.

[1.680]
597 Copy of report to be delivered to registrar

(1) A company to which a report is made under section 593 as to the value of any consideration for which, or partly for which, it proposes to allot shares must deliver a copy of the report to the registrar for registration.

(2) The copy must be delivered at the same time that the company files the return of the allotment of those shares under section 555 (return of allotment by limited company).

(3) If default is made in complying with subsection (1) or (2), an offence is committed by every officer of the company who is in default.

(4) A person guilty of an offence under this section is liable—
(a) on conviction on indictment, to a fine;
(b) on summary conviction, to a fine not exceeding the statutory maximum and, for continued contravention, a daily default fine not exceeding [one-tenth of the greater of £5,000 or the amount corresponding to level 4 on the standard scale for summary offences].

(5) In the case of default in delivering to the registrar any document as required by this section, any person liable for the default may apply to the court for relief.

(6) The court, if satisfied—
(a) that the omission to deliver the document was accidental or due to inadvertence, or
(b) that it is just and equitable to grant relief,

may make an order extending the time for delivery of the document for such period as the court thinks proper.

NOTES

Sub-s (4): words in square brackets substituted (for the original words "one-tenth of the statutory maximum") by the Legal Aid, Sentencing and Punishment of Offenders Act 2012 (Fines on Summary Conviction) Regulations 2015, SI 2015/664, regs 3, 5, Sch 3, Pt 1, para 9(1), (16), as from 12 March 2015, in relation to England and Wales only (except in relation to (a) fines for offences committed before 12 March 2015, (b) the operation of restrictions on fines that may be imposed on a person aged under 18, or (c) fines that may be imposed on a person convicted by a magistrates' court who is to be sentenced as if convicted on indictment).

Transfer of non-cash asset in initial period

[1.681]
598 Public company: agreement for transfer of non-cash asset in initial period

(1) A public company formed as such must not enter into an agreement—
(a) with a person who is a subscriber to the company's memorandum,
(b) for the transfer by him to the company, or another, before the end of the company's initial period of one or more non-cash assets, and
(c) under which the consideration for the transfer to be given by the company is at the time of the agreement equal in value to one-tenth or more of the company's issued share capital,

unless the conditions referred to below have been complied with.

(2) The company's "initial period" means the period of two years beginning with the date of the company being issued with a certificate under section 761 (trading certificate).

(3) The conditions are those specified in—
section 599 (requirement of independent valuation), and
section 601 (requirement of approval by members).

(4) This section does not apply where—
(a) it is part of the company's ordinary business to acquire, or arrange for other persons to acquire, assets of a particular description, and
(b) the agreement is entered into by the company in the ordinary course of that business.

(5) This section does not apply to an agreement entered into by the company under the supervision of the court or of an officer authorised by the court for the purpose.

[1.682]

599 Agreement for transfer of non-cash asset: requirement of independent valuation

(1) The following conditions must have been complied with—

(a) the consideration to be received by the company, and any consideration other than cash to be given by the company, must have been independently valued in accordance with the provisions of this Chapter,

(b) the valuer's report must have been made to the company during the six months immediately preceding the date of the agreement, and

(c) a copy of the report must have been sent to the other party to the proposed agreement not later than the date on which copies have to be circulated to members under section 601(3).

(2) The reference in subsection (1)(a) to the consideration to be received by the company is to the asset to be transferred to it or, as the case may be, to the advantage to the company of the asset's transfer to another person.

(3) The reference in subsection (1)(c) to the other party to the proposed agreement is to the person referred to in section 598(1)(a).

If he has received a copy of the report under section 601 in his capacity as a member of the company, it is not necessary to send another copy under this section.

(4) This section does not affect any requirement to value any consideration for purposes of section 593 (valuation of non-cash consideration for shares).

[1.683]

600 Agreement for transfer of non-cash asset: requirements as to valuation and report

(1) The provisions of sections 1150 to 1153 (general provisions as to independent valuation and report) apply to the valuation and report required by section 599 (public company: transfer of non-cash asset).

(2) The valuer's report must state—

(a) the consideration to be received by the company, describing the asset in question (specifying the amount to be received in cash) and the consideration to be given by the company (specifying the amount to be given in cash), and

(b) the method and date of valuation.

(3) The valuer's report must contain or be accompanied by a note by him—

(a) in the case of a valuation made by a person other than himself, that it appeared to himself reasonable to arrange for it to be so made or to accept a valuation so made,

(b) whoever made the valuation, that the method of valuation was reasonable in all the circumstances,

(c) that it appears to the valuer that there has been no material change in the value of the consideration in question since the valuation, and

(d) that, on the basis of the valuation, the value of the consideration to be received by the company is not less than the value of the consideration to be given by it.

(4) Any reference in section 599 or this section to consideration given for the transfer of an asset includes consideration given partly for its transfer.

(5) In such a case—

(a) the value of any consideration partly so given is to be taken as the proportion of the consideration properly attributable to its transfer,

(b) the valuer must carry out or arrange for such valuations of anything else as will enable him to determine that proportion, and

(c) his report must state what valuations have been made for that purpose and also the reason for and method and date of any such valuation and any other matters which may be relevant to that determination.

[1.684]

601 Agreement for transfer of non-cash asset: requirement of approval by members

(1) The following conditions must have been complied with—

(a) the terms of the agreement must have been approved by an ordinary resolution of the company,

[(b) copies of the valuer's report must have been circulated to the members entitled to notice of the meeting at which the resolution is proposed, not later than the date on which notice of the meeting is given, and]

(c) a copy of the proposed resolution must have been sent to the other party to the proposed agreement.

(2) The reference in subsection (1)(c) to the other party to the proposed agreement is to the person referred to in section 598(1)(a).

(3) . . .

NOTES

Sub-s (1): para (b) substituted by the Companies Act 2006 (Consequential Amendments, Transitional Provisions and Savings) Order 2009, SI 2009/1941, art 2(1), Sch 1, para 260(1), (3)(a), as from 1 October 2009.

Sub-s (3): repealed by SI 2009/1941, art 2(1), Sch 1, para 260(1), (3)(b), as from 1 October 2009.

[1.685]

602 Copy of resolution to be delivered to registrar

(1) A company that has passed a resolution under section 601 with respect to the transfer of an asset must, within 15 days of doing so, deliver to the registrar a copy of the resolution together with the valuer's report required by that section.

(2) If a company fails to comply with subsection (1), an offence is committed by—

(a) the company, and

(b) every officer of the company who is in default.

(3) A person guilty of an offence under this section is liable on summary conviction to a fine not exceeding level 3 on the standard scale and, for continued contravention, to a daily default fine not exceeding one-tenth of level 3 on the standard scale.

[1.686]

603 Adaptation of provisions in relation to company re-registering as public

The provisions of sections 598 to 602 (public companies: transfer of non-cash assets) apply with the following adaptations in relation to a company re-registered as a public company—

(a) the reference in section 598(1)(a) to a person who is a subscriber to the company's memorandum shall be read as a reference to a person who is a member of the company on the date of re-registration;

(b) the reference in section 598(2) to the date of the company being issued with a certificate under section 761 (trading certificate) shall be read as a reference to the date of re-registration.

[1.687]

604 Agreement for transfer of non-cash asset: effect of contravention

(1) This section applies where a public company enters into an agreement in contravention of section 598 and either—

(a) the other party to the agreement has not received the valuer's report required to be sent to him, or

(b) there has been some other contravention of the requirements of this Chapter that the other party to the agreement knew or ought to have known amounted to a contravention.

(2) In those circumstances—

(a) the company is entitled to recover from that person any consideration given by it under the agreement, or an amount equal to the value of the consideration at the time of the agreement, and

(b) the agreement, so far as not carried out, is void.

(3) If the agreement is or includes an agreement for the allotment of shares in the company, then—

(a) whether or not the agreement also contravenes section 593 (valuation of non-cash consideration for shares), this section does not apply to it in so far as it is for the allotment of shares, and

(b) the allottee is liable to pay the company an amount equal to the aggregate of the nominal value of the shares and the whole of any premium (or, if the case so requires, so much of that aggregate as is treated as paid up by the consideration), with interest at the appropriate rate.

Supplementary provisions

[1.688]

605 Liability of subsequent holders of shares

(1) If a person becomes a holder of shares in respect of which—

(a) there has been a contravention of section 593 (public company: valuation of non-cash consideration for shares), and

(b) by virtue of that contravention another is liable to pay any amount under the provision contravened,

that person is also liable to pay that amount (jointly and severally with any other person so liable), unless he is exempted from liability under subsection (3) below.

(2) If a company enters into an agreement in contravention of section 598 (public company: agreement for transfer of non-cash asset in initial period) and—

(a) the agreement is or includes an agreement for the allotment of shares in the company,

(b) a person becomes a holder of shares allotted under the agreement, and

(c) by virtue of the agreement and allotment under it another person is liable to pay an amount under section 604,

the person who becomes the holder of the shares is also liable to pay that amount (jointly and severally with any other person so liable), unless he is exempted from liability under subsection (3) below.

This applies whether or not the agreement also contravenes section 593.

(3) A person otherwise liable under subsection (1) or (2) is exempted from that liability if either—

(a) he is a purchaser for value and, at the time of the purchase, he did not have actual notice of the contravention concerned, or

(b) he derived title to the shares (directly or indirectly) from a person who became a holder of them after the contravention and was not liable under subsection (1) or (2).

(4) References in this section to a holder, in relation to shares in a company, include any person who has an unconditional right—

(a) to be included in the company's register of members [(or, as the case may be, to have his name and other particulars delivered to the registrar under Chapter 2A of Part 8 and registered by the registrar)] in respect of those shares, or

(b) to have an instrument of transfer of the shares executed in his favour.

NOTES

Sub-s (4): words in square brackets inserted by the Small Business, Enterprise and Employment Act 2015, s 94, Sch 5, Pt 2, paras 11, 22, as from 30 June 2016.

[1.689]

606 Power of court to grant relief

(1) A person who—

(a) is liable to a company under any provision of this Chapter in relation to payment in respect of any shares in the company, or

(b) is liable to a company by virtue of an undertaking given to it in, or in connection with, payment for any shares in the company,

may apply to the court to be exempted in whole or in part from the liability.

(2) In the case of a liability within subsection (1)(a), the court may exempt the applicant from the liability only if and to the extent that it appears to the court just and equitable to do so having regard to—

(a) whether the applicant has paid, or is liable to pay, any amount in respect of—

(i) any other liability arising in relation to those shares under any provision of this Chapter or Chapter 5, or

(ii) any liability arising by virtue of any undertaking given in or in connection with payment for those shares;

(b) whether any person other than the applicant has paid or is likely to pay, whether in pursuance of any order of the court or otherwise, any such amount;

(c) whether the applicant or any other person—

(i) has performed in whole or in part, or is likely so to perform any such undertaking, or

(ii) has done or is likely to do any other thing in payment or part payment for the shares.

(3) In the case of a liability within subsection (1)(b), the court may exempt the applicant from the liability only if and to the extent that it appears to the court just and equitable to do so having regard to—

(a) whether the applicant has paid or is liable to pay any amount in respect of liability arising in relation to the shares under any provision of this Chapter or Chapter 5;

(b) whether any person other than the applicant has paid or is likely to pay, whether in pursuance of any order of the court or otherwise, any such amount.

(4) In determining whether it should exempt the applicant in whole or in part from any liability, the court must have regard to the following overriding principles—

(a) that a company that has allotted shares should receive money or money's worth at least equal in value to the aggregate of the nominal value of those shares and the whole of any premium or, if the case so requires, so much of that aggregate as is treated as paid up;

(b) subject to this, that where such a company would, if the court did not grant the exemption, have more than one remedy against a particular person, it should be for the company to decide which remedy it should remain entitled to pursue.

(5) If a person brings proceedings against another ("the contributor") for a contribution in respect of liability to a company arising under any provision of this Chapter or Chapter 5 and it appears to the court that the contributor is liable to make such a contribution, the court may, if and to the extent that it appears to it, just and equitable to do so having regard to the respective culpability (in respect of the liability to the company) of the contributor and the person bringing the proceedings—

(a) exempt the contributor in whole or in part from his liability to make such a contribution, or

(b) order the contributor to make a larger contribution than, but for this subsection, he would be liable to make.

(6) Where a person is liable to a company under section 604(2) (agreement for transfer of non-cash asset: effect of contravention), the court may, on application, exempt him in whole or in part from that liability if and to the extent that it appears to the court to be just and equitable to do so having regard to any benefit accruing to the company by virtue of anything done by him towards the carrying out of the agreement mentioned in that subsection.

[1.690]

607 Penalty for contravention of this Chapter

(1) This section applies where a company contravenes—

section 593 (public company allotting shares for non-cash consideration), or

section 598 (public company entering into agreement for transfer of non-cash asset).

(2) An offence is committed by—

(a) the company, and

(b) every officer of the company who is in default.

(3) A person guilty of an offence under this section is liable—

(a) on conviction on indictment, to a fine;

(b) on summary conviction, to a fine not exceeding the statutory maximum.

[1.691]

608 Enforceability of undertakings to do work etc

(1) An undertaking given by any person, in or in connection with payment for shares in a company, to do work or perform services or to do any other thing, if it is enforceable by the company apart from this Chapter, is so enforceable notwithstanding that there has been a contravention in relation to it of a provision of this Chapter or Chapter 5.

(2) This is without prejudice to section 606 (power of court to grant relief etc in respect of liabilities).

[1.692]

609 The appropriate rate of interest

(1) For the purposes of this Chapter the "appropriate rate" of interest is 5% per annum or such other rate as may be specified by order made by the Secretary of State.

(2) An order under this section is subject to negative resolution procedure.

NOTES

Orders: no Orders have been made under this section.

CHAPTER 7 SHARE PREMIUMS

The share premium account

[1.693]

610 Application of share premiums

(1) If a company issues shares at a premium, whether for cash or otherwise, a sum equal to the aggregate amount or value of the premiums on those shares must be transferred to an account called "the share premium account".

(2) Where, on issuing shares, a company has transferred a sum to the share premium account, it may use that sum to write off—

(a) the expenses of the issue of those shares;

(b) any commission paid on the issue of those shares.

(3) The company may use the share premium account to pay up new shares to be allotted to members as fully paid bonus shares.

(4) Subject to subsections (2) and (3), the provisions of the Companies Acts relating to the reduction of a company's share capital apply as if the share premium account were part of its paid up share capital.

(5) This section has effect subject to—

section 611 (group reconstruction relief);
section 612 (merger relief);
section 614 (power to make further provisions by regulations).

(6) In this Chapter "the issuing company" means the company issuing shares as mentioned in subsection (1) above.

Relief from requirements as to share premiums

[1.694]

611 Group reconstruction relief

(1) This section applies where the issuing company—

(a) is a wholly-owned subsidiary of another company ("the holding company"), and
(b) allots shares—
  (i) to the holding company, or
  (ii) to another wholly-owned subsidiary of the holding company,
 in consideration for the transfer to the issuing company of non-cash assets of a company ("the transferor company") that is a member of the group of companies that comprises the holding company and all its wholly-owned subsidiaries.

(2) Where the shares in the issuing company allotted in consideration for the transfer are issued at a premium, the issuing company is not required by section 610 to transfer any amount in excess of the minimum premium value to the share premium account.

(3) The minimum premium value means the amount (if any) by which the base value of the consideration for the shares allotted exceeds the aggregate nominal value of the shares.

(4) The base value of the consideration for the shares allotted is the amount by which the base value of the assets transferred exceeds the base value of any liabilities of the transferor company assumed by the issuing company as part of the consideration for the assets transferred.

(5) For the purposes of this section—

(a) the base value of assets transferred is taken as—
  (i) the cost of those assets to the transferor company, or
  (ii) if less, the amount at which those assets are stated in the transferor company's accounting records immediately before the transfer;
(b) the base value of the liabilities assumed is taken as the amount at which they are stated in the transferor company's accounting records immediately before the transfer.

[1.695]

612 Merger relief

(1) This section applies where the issuing company has secured at least a 90% equity holding in another company in pursuance of an arrangement providing for the allotment of equity shares in the issuing company on terms that the consideration for the shares allotted is to be provided—

(a) by the issue or transfer to the issuing company of equity shares in the other company, or
(b) by the cancellation of any such shares not held by the issuing company.

(2) If the equity shares in the issuing company allotted in pursuance of the arrangement in consideration for the acquisition or cancellation of equity shares in the other company are issued at a premium, section 610 does not apply to the premiums on those shares.

(3) Where the arrangement also provides for the allotment of any shares in the issuing company on terms that the consideration for those shares is to be provided—

(a) by the issue or transfer to the issuing company of non-equity shares in the other company, or
(b) by the cancellation of any such shares in that company not held by the issuing company,

relief under subsection (2) extends to any shares in the issuing company allotted on those terms in pursuance of the arrangement.

(4) This section does not apply in a case falling within section 611 (group reconstruction relief).

[1.696]

613 Merger relief: meaning of 90% equity holding

(1) The following provisions have effect to determine for the purposes of section 612 (merger relief) whether a company ("company A") has secured at least a 90% equity holding in another company ("company B") in pursuance of such an arrangement as is mentioned in subsection (1) of that section.

(2) Company A has secured at least a 90% equity holding in company B if in consequence of an acquisition or cancellation of equity shares in company B (in pursuance of that arrangement) it holds equity shares in company B of an aggregate amount equal to 90% or more of the nominal value of that company's equity share capital.

(3) For this purpose—

(a) it is immaterial whether any of those shares were acquired in pursuance of the arrangement; and
(b) shares in company B held by the company as treasury shares are excluded in determining the nominal value of company B's share capital.

(4) Where the equity share capital of company B is divided into different classes of shares, company A is not regarded as having secured at least a 90% equity holding in company B unless the requirements of subsection (2) are met in relation to each of those classes of shares taken separately.

(5) For the purposes of this section shares held by—

(a) a company that is company A's holding company or subsidiary, or
(b) a subsidiary of company A's holding company, or
(c) its or their nominees,

are treated as held by company A.

[1.697]

614 Power to make further provision by regulations

(1) The Secretary of State may by regulations make such provision as he thinks appropriate—

(a) for relieving companies from the requirements of section 610 (application of share premiums) in relation to premiums other than cash premiums;

(b) for restricting or otherwise modifying any relief from those requirements provided by this Chapter.

(2) Regulations under this section are subject to affirmative resolution procedure.

NOTES

Regulations: no Regulations have been made under this section.

[1.698]

615 Relief may be reflected in company's balance sheet

An amount corresponding to the amount representing the premiums, or part of the premiums, on shares issued by a company that by virtue of any relief under this Chapter is not included in the company's share premium account may also be disregarded in determining the amount at which any shares or other consideration provided for the shares issued is to be included in the company's balance sheet.

Supplementary provisions

[1.699]

616 Interpretation of this Chapter

(1) In this Chapter—

"arrangement" means any agreement, scheme or arrangement (including an arrangement sanctioned in accordance with—

(a) Part 26 [or 26A] (arrangements and reconstructions), or

(b) section 110 of the Insolvency Act 1986 (c 45) or Article 96 of the Insolvency (Northern Ireland) Order 1989 (SI 1989/2405 (NI 19)) (liquidator in winding up accepting shares as consideration for sale of company property));

"company", except in reference to the issuing company, includes any body corporate;

"equity shares" means shares comprised in a company's equity share capital, and "non-equity shares" means shares (of any class) that are not so comprised;

"the issuing company" has the meaning given by section 610(6).

(2) References in this Chapter (however expressed) to—

(a) the acquisition by a company of shares in another company, and

(b) the issue or allotment of shares to, or the transfer of shares to or by, a company,

include (respectively) the acquisition of shares by, and the issue or allotment or transfer of shares to or by, a nominee of that company.

The reference in section 611 to the transferor company shall be read accordingly.

(3) References in this Chapter to the transfer of shares in a company include the transfer of a right to be included in the company's register of members [(or, as the case may be, have your name and other particulars delivered to the registrar under Chapter 2A of Part 8 and registered by the registrar)] in respect of those shares.

NOTES

Sub-s (1): words in square brackets in the definition "arrangement" inserted by the Corporate Insolvency and Governance Act 2020, s 7, Sch 9, Pt 2, paras 30, 33(1), (5), as from 26 June 2020.

Sub-s (3): words in square brackets inserted by the Small Business, Enterprise and Employment Act 2015, s 94, Sch 5, Pt 2, paras 11, 23, as from 30 June 2016.

CHAPTER 8 ALTERATION OF SHARE CAPITAL

How share capital may be altered

[1.700]

617 Alteration of share capital of limited company

(1) A limited company having a share capital may not alter its share capital except in the following ways.

(2) The company may—

(a) increase its share capital by allotting new shares in accordance with this Part, or

(b) reduce its share capital in accordance with Chapter 10.

(3) The company may—

(a) sub-divide or consolidate all or any of its share capital in accordance with section 618, or

(b) reconvert stock into shares in accordance with section 620.

(4) The company may redenominate all or any of its shares in accordance with section 622, and may reduce its share capital in accordance with section 626 in connection with such a redenomination.

(5) Nothing in this section affects—

(a) the power of a company to purchase its own shares, or to redeem shares, in accordance with Part 18;

(b) the power of a company to purchase its own shares in pursuance of an order of the court under—

(i) section 98 (application to court to cancel resolution for re-registration as a private company),

(ii) section 721(6) (powers of court on objection to redemption or purchase of shares out of capital),

(iii) section 759 (remedial order in case of breach of prohibition of public offers by private company), or

(iv) Part 30 (protection of members against unfair prejudice);

(c) the forfeiture of shares, or the acceptance of shares surrendered in lieu, in pursuance of the company's articles, for failure to pay any sum payable in respect of the shares;

(d) the cancellation of shares under section 662 (duty to cancel shares held by or for a public company);

(e) the power of a company—

(i) to enter into a compromise or arrangement in accordance with Part 26 [or 26A] (arrangements and reconstructions), or

(ii) to do anything required to comply with an order of the court on an application under that Part;

[(f) the cancellation of a share warrant issued by the company and of the shares specified in it by a cancellation order or suspended cancellation order made under paragraph 6 of Schedule 4 to the Small Business, Enterprise and Employment Act 2015 (cancellation where share warrants not surrendered in accordance with that Schedule);

(g) the cancellation of a share warrant issued by the company and of the shares specified in it pursuant to section 1028A(2) or 1032A(2) (cancellation of share warrants on restoration of a company).]

NOTES

Sub-s (5): words in square brackets in sub-para (e)(i) inserted by the Corporate Insolvency and Governance Act 2020, s 7, Sch 9, Pt 2, paras 30, 33(1), (6), as from 26 June 2020. Paras (f), (g) added by the Small Business, Enterprise and Employment Act 2015, s 84, Sch 4, Pt 2, paras 22, 24, as from 26 May 2015.

Subdivision or consolidation of shares

[1.701]

618 Sub-division or consolidation of shares

(1) A limited company having a share capital may—

(a) sub-divide its shares, or any of them, into shares of a smaller nominal amount than its existing shares, or

(b) consolidate and divide all or any of its share capital into shares of a larger nominal amount than its existing shares.

(2) In any sub-division, consolidation or division of shares under this section, the proportion between the amount paid and the amount (if any) unpaid on each resulting share must be the same as it was in the case of the share from which that share is derived.

(3) A company may exercise a power conferred by this section only if its members have passed a resolution authorising it to do so.

(4) A resolution under subsection (3) may authorise a company—

(a) to exercise more than one of the powers conferred by this section;

(b) to exercise a power on more than one occasion;

(c) to exercise a power at a specified time or in specified circumstances.

(5) The company's articles may exclude or restrict the exercise of any power conferred by this section.

[1.702]

619 Notice to registrar of sub-division or consolidation

(1) If a company exercises the power conferred by section 618 (sub-division or consolidation of shares) it must within one month after doing so give notice to the registrar, specifying the shares affected.

(2) The notice must be accompanied by a statement of capital.

(3) The statement of capital must state with respect to the company's share capital immediately following the exercise of the power—

(a) the total number of shares of the company,

(b) the aggregate nominal value of those shares,

[(ba) the aggregate amount (if any) unpaid on those shares (whether on account of their nominal value or by way of premium), and]

(c) for each class of shares—

(i) prescribed particulars of the rights attached to the shares,

(ii) the total number of shares of that class, and

(iii) the aggregate nominal value of shares of that class, . . .

(d) . . .

(4) If default is made in complying with this section, an offence is committed by—

(a) the company, and

(b) every officer of the company who is in default.

(5) A person guilty of an offence under this section is liable on summary conviction to a fine not exceeding level 3 on the standard scale and, for continued contravention, a daily default fine not exceeding one-tenth of level 3 on the standard scale.

NOTES

Sub-s (3): para (ba) inserted, and para (d) and the preceding word repealed, by the Small Business, Enterprise and Employment Act 2015, s 97, Sch 6, paras 1, 6, as from 30 June 2016.

Orders: the Companies (Shares and Share Capital) Order 2009, SI 2009/388 at **[4.211]**. For a summary of all statutory instruments made under this Act, see Appendix 4 at **[A4]**.

Reconversion of stock into shares

[1.703]

620 Reconversion of stock into shares

(1) A limited company that has converted paid-up shares into stock (before the repeal by this Act of the power to do so) may reconvert that stock into paid-up shares of any nominal value.

(2) A company may exercise the power conferred by this section only if its members have passed an ordinary resolution authorising it to do so.

(3) A resolution under subsection (2) may authorise a company to exercise the power conferred by this section—

(a) on more than one occasion;

(b) at a specified time or in specified circumstances.

[1.704]

621 Notice to registrar of reconversion of stock into shares

(1) If a company exercises a power conferred by section 620 (reconversion of stock into shares) it must within one month after doing so give notice to the registrar, specifying the stock affected.

(2) The notice must be accompanied by a statement of capital.

(3) The statement of capital must state with respect to the company's share capital immediately following the exercise of the power—

(a) the total number of shares of the company,

(b) the aggregate nominal value of those shares,

[(ba) the aggregate amount (if any) unpaid on those shares (whether on account of their nominal value or by way of premium), and]

(c) for each class of shares—

(i) prescribed particulars of the rights attached to the shares,

(ii) the total number of shares of that class, and

(iii) the aggregate nominal value of shares of that class, . . .

(d) . . .

(4) If default is made in complying with this section, an offence is committed by—

(a) the company, and

(b) every officer of the company who is in default.

(5) A person guilty of an offence under this section is liable on summary conviction to a fine not exceeding level 3 on the standard scale and, for continued contravention, a daily default fine not exceeding one-tenth of level 3 on the standard scale.

NOTES

Sub-s (3): para (ba) inserted, and para (d) and the preceding word repealed, by the Small Business, Enterprise and Employment Act 2015, s 97, Sch 6, paras 1, 7, as from 30 June 2016.

Orders: the Companies (Shares and Share Capital) Order 2009, SI 2009/388 at **[4.211]**. For a summary of all statutory instruments made under this Act, see Appendix 4 at **[A4]**.

Redenomination of share capital

[1.705]

622 Redenomination of share capital

(1) A limited company having a share capital may by resolution redenominate its share capital or any class of its share capital.

"Redenominate" means convert shares from having a fixed nominal value in one currency to having a fixed nominal value in another currency.

(2) The conversion must be made at an appropriate spot rate of exchange specified in the resolution.

(3) The rate must be either—

(a) a rate prevailing on a day specified in the resolution, or

(b) a rate determined by taking the average of rates prevailing on each consecutive day of a period specified in the resolution.

The day or period specified for the purposes of paragraph (a) or (b) must be within the period of 28 days ending on the day before the resolution is passed.

(4) A resolution under this section may specify conditions which must be met before the redenomination takes effect.

(5) Redenomination in accordance with a resolution under this section takes effect—

(a) on the day on which the resolution is passed, or

(b) on such later day as may be determined in accordance with the resolution.

(6) A resolution under this section lapses if the redenomination for which it provides has not taken effect at the end of the period of 28 days beginning on the date on which it is passed.

(7) A company's articles may prohibit or restrict the exercise of the power conferred by this section.

(8) Chapter 3 of Part 3 (resolutions affecting a company's constitution) applies to a resolution under this section.

[1.706]

623 Calculation of new nominal values

For each class of share the new nominal value of each share is calculated as follows:

Step One

Take the aggregate of the old nominal values of all the shares of that class.

Step Two

Translate that amount into the new currency at the rate of exchange specified in the resolution.

Step Three

Divide that amount by the number of shares in the class.

[1.707]

624 Effect of redenomination

(1) The redenomination of shares does not affect any rights or obligations of members under the company's constitution, or any restrictions affecting members under the company's constitution.

In particular, it does not affect entitlement to dividends (including entitlement to dividends in a particular currency), voting rights or any liability in respect of amounts unpaid on shares.

(2) For this purpose the company's constitution includes the terms on which any shares of the company are allotted or held.

(3) Subject to subsection (1), references to the old nominal value of the shares in any agreement or statement, or in any deed, instrument or document, shall (unless the context otherwise requires) be read after the resolution takes effect as references to the new nominal value of the shares.

[1.708]

625 Notice to registrar of redenomination

(1) If a limited company having a share capital redenominates any of its share capital, it must within one month after doing so give notice to the registrar, specifying the shares redenominated.

(2) The notice must—

(a) state the date on which the resolution was passed, and

(b) be accompanied by a statement of capital.

(3) The statement of capital must state with respect to the company's share capital as redenominated by the resolution—

(a) the total number of shares of the company,

(b) the aggregate nominal value of those shares,

[(ba) the aggregate amount (if any) unpaid on those shares (whether on account of their nominal value or by way of premium), and]

(c) for each class of shares—

(i) prescribed particulars of the rights attached to the shares,

(ii) the total number of shares of that class, and

(iii) the aggregate nominal value of shares of that class, . . .

(d) . . .

(4) If default is made in complying with this section, an offence is committed by—

(a) the company, and

(b) every officer of the company who is in default.

(5) A person guilty of an offence under this section is liable on summary conviction to a fine not exceeding level 3 on the standard scale and, for continued contravention, a daily default fine not exceeding one-tenth of level 3 on the standard scale.

NOTES

Sub-s (3): para (ba) inserted, and para (d) and the preceding word repealed, by the Small Business, Enterprise and Employment Act 2015, s 97, Sch 6, paras 1, 8, as from 30 June 2016.

Orders: the Companies (Shares and Share Capital) Order 2009, SI 2009/388 at **[4.211]**. For a summary of all statutory instruments made under this Act, see Appendix 4 at **[A4]**.

[1.709]

626 Reduction of capital in connection with redenomination

(1) A limited company that passes a resolution redenominating some or all of its shares may, for the purpose of adjusting the nominal values of the redenominated shares to obtain values that are, in the opinion of the company, more suitable, reduce its share capital under this section.

(2) A reduction of capital under this section requires a special resolution of the company.

(3) Any such resolution must be passed within three months of the resolution effecting the redenomination.

(4) The amount by which a company's share capital is reduced under this section must not exceed 10% of the nominal value of the company's allotted share capital immediately after the reduction.

(5) A reduction of capital under this section does not extinguish or reduce any liability in respect of share capital not paid up.

(6) Nothing in Chapter 10 applies to a reduction of capital under this section.

[1.710]

627 Notice to registrar of reduction of capital in connection with redenomination

(1) A company that passes a resolution under section 626 (reduction of capital in connection with redenomination) must within 15 days after the resolution is passed give notice to the registrar stating—

(a) the date of the resolution, and

(b) the date of the resolution under section 622 in connection with which it was passed.

This is in addition to the copies of the resolutions themselves that are required to be delivered to the registrar under Chapter 3 of Part 3.

(2) The notice must be accompanied by a statement of capital.

(3) The statement of capital must state with respect to the company's share capital as reduced by the resolution—

(a) the total number of shares of the company,

(b) the aggregate nominal value of those shares,

[(ba) the aggregate amount (if any) unpaid on those shares (whether on account of their nominal value or by way of premium), and]

(c) for each class of shares—

(i) prescribed particulars of the rights attached to the shares,

(ii) the total number of shares of that class, and

(iii) the aggregate nominal value of shares of that class, . . .

(d) . . .

(4) The registrar must register the notice and the statement on receipt.

(5) The reduction of capital is not effective until those documents are registered.

(6) The company must also deliver to the registrar, within 15 days after the resolution is passed, a statement by the directors confirming that the reduction in share capital is in accordance with section 626(4) (reduction of capital not to exceed 10% of nominal value of allotted shares immediately after reduction).

(7) If default is made in complying with this section, an offence is committed by—

(a) the company, and

(b) every officer of the company who is in default.

(8) A person guilty of an offence under this section is liable—

(a) on conviction on indictment to a fine, and

(b) on summary conviction to a fine not exceeding the statutory maximum.

NOTES

Sub-s (3): para (ba) inserted, and para (d) and the preceding word repealed, by the Small Business, Enterprise and Employment Act 2015, s 97, Sch 6, paras 1, 9, as from 30 June 2016.

Orders: the Companies (Shares and Share Capital) Order 2009, SI 2009/388 at **[4.211]**. For a summary of all statutory instruments made under this Act, see Appendix 4 at **[A4]**.

[1.711]

628 Redenomination reserve

(1) The amount by which a company's share capital is reduced under section 626 (reduction of capital in connection with redenomination) must be transferred to a reserve, called "the redenomination reserve".

(2) The redenomination reserve may be applied by the company in paying up shares to be allotted to members as fully paid bonus shares.

(3) Subject to that, the provisions of the Companies Acts relating to the reduction of a company's share capital apply as if the redenomination reserve were paid-up share capital of the company.

CHAPTER 9 CLASSES OF SHARE AND CLASS RIGHTS

Introductory

[1.712]

629 Classes of shares

(1) For the purposes of the Companies Acts shares are of one class if the rights attached to them are in all respects uniform.

(2) For this purpose the rights attached to shares are not regarded as different from those attached to other shares by reason only that they do not carry the same rights to dividends in the twelve months immediately following their allotment.

Variation of class rights

[1.713]

630 Variation of class rights: companies having a share capital

(1) This section is concerned with the variation of the rights attached to a class of shares in a company having a share capital.

(2) Rights attached to a class of a company's shares may only be varied—

(a) in accordance with provision in the company's articles for the variation of those rights, or

(b) where the company's articles contain no such provision, if the holders of shares of that class consent to the variation in accordance with this section.

(3) This is without prejudice to any other restrictions on the variation of the rights.

(4) The consent required for the purposes of this section on the part of the holders of a class of a company's shares is—

(a) consent in writing from the holders of at least three-quarters in nominal value of the issued shares of that class (excluding any shares held as treasury shares), or

(b) a special resolution passed at a separate general meeting of the holders of that class sanctioning the variation.

(5) Any amendment of a provision contained in a company's articles for the variation of the rights attached to a class of shares, or the insertion of any such provision into the articles, is itself to be treated as a variation of those rights.

(6) In this section, and (except where the context otherwise requires) in any provision in a company's articles for the variation of the rights attached to a class of shares, references to the variation of those rights include references to their abrogation.

[1.714]

631 Variation of class rights: companies without a share capital

(1) This section is concerned with the variation of the rights of a class of members of a company where the company does not have a share capital.

(2) Rights of a class of members may only be varied—

(a) in accordance with provision in the company's articles for the variation of those rights, or

(b) where the company's articles contain no such provision, if the members of that class consent to the variation in accordance with this section.

(3) This is without prejudice to any other restrictions on the variation of the rights.

(4) The consent required for the purposes of this section on the part of the members of a class is—

(a) consent in writing from at least three-quarters of the members of the class, or

(b) a special resolution passed at a separate general meeting of the members of that class sanctioning the variation.

(5) Any amendment of a provision contained in a company's articles for the variation of the rights of a class of members, or the insertion of any such provision into the articles, is itself to be treated as a variation of those rights.

(6) In this section, and (except where the context otherwise requires) in any provision in a company's articles for the variation of the rights of a class of members, references to the variation of those rights include references to their abrogation.

[1.715]

632 Variation of class rights: saving for court's powers under other provisions

Nothing in section 630 or 631 (variation of class rights) affects the power of the court under—

section 98 (application to cancel resolution for public company to be re-registered as private),

Part 26 (arrangements and reconstructions[: general]),

[Part 26A (arrangements and reconstructions: companies in financial difficulty),] or

Part 30 (protection of members against unfair prejudice).

NOTES

Words in square brackets inserted by the Corporate Insolvency and Governance Act 2020, s 7, Sch 9, Pt 2, paras 30, 33(1), (7), as from 26 June 2020.

[1.716]

633 Right to object to variation: companies having a share capital

(1) This section applies where the rights attached to any class of shares in a company are varied under section 630 (variation of class rights: companies having a share capital).

(2) The holders of not less in the aggregate than 15% of the issued shares of the class in question (being persons who did not consent to or vote in favour of the resolution for the variation) may apply to the court to have the variation cancelled.

For this purpose any of the company's share capital held as treasury shares is disregarded.

(3) If such an application is made, the variation has no effect unless and until it is confirmed by the court.

(4) Application to the court—

- (a) must be made within 21 days after the date on which the consent was given or the resolution was passed (as the case may be), and
- (b) may be made on behalf of the shareholders entitled to make the application by such one or more of their number as they may appoint in writing for the purpose.

(5) The court, after hearing the applicant and any other persons who apply to the court to be heard and appear to the court to be interested in the application, may, if satisfied having regard to all the circumstances of the case that the variation would unfairly prejudice the shareholders of the class represented by the applicant, disallow the variation, and shall if not so satisfied confirm it. The decision of the court on any such application is final.

(6) References in this section to the variation of the rights of holders of a class of shares include references to their abrogation.

[1.717]

634 Right to object to variation: companies without a share capital

(1) This section applies where the rights of any class of members of a company are varied under section 631 (variation of class rights: companies without a share capital).

(2) Members amounting to not less than 15% of the members of the class in question (being persons who did not consent to or vote in favour of the resolution for the variation) may apply to the court to have the variation cancelled.

(3) If such an application is made, the variation has no effect unless and until it is confirmed by the court.

(4) Application to the court must be made within 21 days after the date on which the consent was given or the resolution was passed (as the case may be) and may be made on behalf of the members entitled to make the application by such one or more of their number as they may appoint in writing for the purpose.

(5) The court, after hearing the applicant and any other persons who apply to the court to be heard and appear to the court to be interested in the application, may, if satisfied having regard to all the circumstances of the case that the variation would unfairly prejudice the members of the class represented by the applicant, disallow the variation, and shall if not so satisfied confirm it.

The decision of the court on any such application is final.

(6) References in this section to the variation of the rights of a class of members include references to their abrogation.

[1.718]

635 Copy of court order to be forwarded to the registrar

(1) The company must within 15 days after the making of an order by the court on an application under section 633 or 634 (objection to variation of class rights) forward a copy of the order to the registrar.

(2) If default is made in complying with this section an offence is committed by—

- (a) the company, and
- (b) every officer of the company who is in default.

(3) A person guilty of an offence under this section is liable on summary conviction to a fine not exceeding level 3 on the standard scale and, for continued contravention, a daily default fine not exceeding one-tenth of level 3 on the standard scale.

Matters to be notified to the registrar

[1.719]

636 Notice of name or other designation of class of shares

(1) Where a company assigns a name or other designation, or a new name or other designation, to any class or description of its shares, it must within one month from doing so deliver to the registrar a notice giving particulars of the name or designation so assigned.

(2) If default is made in complying with this section, an offence is committed by—

- (a) the company, and
- (b) every officer of the company who is in default.

(3) A person guilty of an offence under this section is liable on summary conviction to a fine not exceeding level 3 on the standard scale and, for continued contravention, a daily default fine not exceeding one-tenth of level 3 on the standard scale.

[1.720]

637 Notice of particulars of variation of rights attached to shares

(1) Where the rights attached to any shares of a company are varied, the company must within one month from the date on which the variation is made deliver to the registrar a notice giving particulars of the variation.

(2) If default is made in complying with this section, an offence is committed by—

- (a) the company, and
- (b) every officer of the company who is in default.

(3) A person guilty of an offence under this section is liable on summary conviction to a fine not exceeding level 3 on the standard scale and, for continued contravention, a daily default fine not exceeding one-tenth of level 3 on the standard scale.

[1.721]

638 Notice of new class of members

(1) If a company not having a share capital creates a new class of members, the company must within one month from the date on which the new class is created deliver to the registrar a notice containing particulars of the rights attached to that class.

(2) If default is made in complying with this section, an offence is committed by—
  (a) the company, and
  (b) every officer of the company who is in default.

(3) A person guilty of an offence under this section is liable on summary conviction to a fine not exceeding level 3 on the standard scale and, for continued contravention, a daily default fine not exceeding one-tenth of level 3 on the standard scale.

[1.722]

639 Notice of name or other designation of class of members

(1) Where a company not having a share capital assigns a name or other designation, or a new name or other designation, to any class of its members, it must within one month from doing so deliver to the registrar a notice giving particulars of the name or designation so assigned.

(2) If default is made in complying with this section, an offence is committed by—
  (a) the company, and
  (b) every officer of the company who is in default.

(3) A person guilty of an offence under this section is liable on summary conviction to a fine not exceeding level 3 on the standard scale and, for continued contravention, a daily default fine not exceeding one-tenth of level 3 on the standard scale.

[1.723]

640 Notice of particulars of variation of class rights

(1) If the rights of any class of members of a company not having a share capital are varied, the company must within one month from the date on which the variation is made deliver to the registrar a notice containing particulars of the variation.

(2) If default is made in complying with this section, an offence is committed by—
  (a) the company, and
  (b) every officer of the company who is in default.

(3) A person guilty of an offence under this section is liable on summary conviction to a fine not exceeding level 3 on the standard scale and, for continued contravention, a daily default fine not exceeding one-tenth of level 3 on the standard scale.

CHAPTER 10 REDUCTION OF SHARE CAPITAL

Introductory

[1.724]

641 Circumstances in which a company may reduce its share capital

(1) A limited company having a share capital may reduce its share capital—
  (a) in the case of a private company limited by shares, by special resolution supported by a solvency statement (see sections 642 to 644);
  (b) in any case, by special resolution confirmed by the court (see sections 645 to 651).

(2) A company may not reduce its capital under subsection (1)(a) if as a result of the reduction there would no longer be any member of the company holding shares other than redeemable shares.

[(2A) A company may not reduce its share capital under subsection (1)(a) or (b) as part of a scheme by virtue of which a person, or a person together with its associates, is to acquire all the shares in the company or (where there is more than one class of shares in a company) all the shares of one or more classes, in each case other than shares that are already held by that person or its associates.

(2B) Subsection (2A) does not apply to a scheme under which—
  (a) the company is to have a new parent undertaking,
  (b) all or substantially all of the members of the company become members of the parent undertaking, and
  (c) the members of the company are to hold proportions of the equity share capital of the parent undertaking in the same or substantially the same proportions as they hold the equity share capital of the company.

(2C) In this section—

"associate" has the meaning given by section 988 (meaning of "associate"), reading references in that section to an offeror as references to the person acquiring the shares in the company;

"scheme" means a compromise or arrangement sanctioned by the court under Part 26 [or 26A] (arrangements and reconstructions).]

(3) [Subject to subsections (2) to (2B)], a company may reduce its share capital under this section in any way.

(4) In particular, a company may—
  (a) extinguish or reduce the liability on any of its shares in respect of share capital not paid up, or
  (b) either with or without extinguishing or reducing liability on any of its shares—
    (i) cancel any paid-up share capital that is lost or unrepresented by available assets, or
    (ii) repay any paid-up share capital in excess of the company's wants.

(5) A special resolution under this section may not provide for a reduction of share capital to take effect later than the date on which the resolution has effect in accordance with this Chapter.

(6) This Chapter (apart from subsection (5) above) has effect subject to any provision of the company's articles restricting or prohibiting the reduction of the company's share capital.

[(7) In subsection (1)(b), section 91(5)(b)(iii), sections 645 to 651 (except in [the phrases "sanctioned by the court under Part 26" and "sanctioned by the court under Part 26A"]) and 653(1) "the court" means, in England and Wales, the High Court.]

NOTES

Sub-ss (2A)–(2C): inserted by the Companies Act 2006 (Amendment of Part 17) Regulations 2015, SI 2015/472, reg 3(1), (2), as from 4 March 2015; for effect, see the final note below. Words in square brackets in the definition "scheme" in sub-s (2C) inserted by the Corporate Insolvency and Governance Act 2020, s 7, Sch 9, Pt 2, paras 30, 33(1), (8)(a), as from 26 June 2020.

Sub-s (3): words in square brackets substituted by SI 2015/472, reg 3(1), (3), as from 4 March 2015; for effect, see the final note below.

Sub-s (7): added by the High Court and County Courts Jurisdiction Order 1991, SI 1991/724, art 6F, Schedule, Pt I (as amended by SI 2014/821), as from 22 April 2014 (except in relation to proceedings commenced before that date). Words in square brackets substituted by the Corporate Insolvency and Governance Act 2020, s 7, Sch 9, Pt 2, paras 30, 33(1), (8)(b), as from 26 June 2020.

Note: the Companies Act 2006 (Amendment of Part 17) Regulations 2015, SI 2015/472, reg 2(2), (3) provide as follows—

"(2) These Regulations do not apply in relation to a scheme that—

(a) gives effect to, or is proposed in connection with, a takeover announcement made in relation to a company before the day on which these Regulations come into force, or

(b) gives effect to, or is proposed in connection with, a pre-commencement offer to acquire all the shares in a company that is not subject to the rules or (where there is more than one class of shares in a company) all the shares of one or more classes, in each case other than shares that on the date that the terms of the offer were agreed were already held by the person making the offer or its associates.

(3) In this Regulation—

"pre-commencement offer" means an offer the terms of which (including the fact that the offer will be implemented by a scheme) have been agreed between the company concerned and the person making the offer before the day on which these Regulations come into force; and

"takeover announcement" means a public announcement that—

(a) concerns a firm intention to acquire all the shares in a company or (where there is more than one class of shares in a company) all the shares of one or more classes, in each case other than shares that on the date of the announcement were already held by the person making the announcement or its associates, and

(b) on the date of the announcement, was made under rules made by the Panel.".

Private companies: reduction of capital supported by solvency statement

[1.725]

642 Reduction of capital supported by solvency statement

(1) A resolution for reducing share capital of a private company limited by shares is supported by a solvency statement if—

(a) the directors of the company make a statement of the solvency of the company in accordance with section 643 (a "solvency statement") not more than 15 days before the date on which the resolution is passed, and

(b) the resolution and solvency statement are registered in accordance with section 644.

(2) Where the resolution is proposed as a written resolution, a copy of the solvency statement must be sent or submitted to every eligible member at or before the time at which the proposed resolution is sent or submitted to him.

(3) Where the resolution is proposed at a general meeting, a copy of the solvency statement must be made available for inspection by members of the company throughout that meeting.

(4) The validity of a resolution is not affected by a failure to comply with subsection (2) or (3).

[1.726]

643 Solvency statement

(1) A solvency statement is a statement that each of the directors—

(a) has formed the opinion, as regards the company's situation at the date of the statement, that there is no ground on which the company could then be found to be unable to pay (or otherwise discharge) its debts; and

(b) has also formed the opinion—

(i) if it is intended to commence the winding up of the company within twelve months of that date, that the company will be able to pay (or otherwise discharge) its debts in full within twelve months of the commencement of the winding up; or

(ii) in any other case, that the company will be able to pay (or otherwise discharge) its debts as they fall due during the year immediately following that date.

(2) In forming those opinions, the directors must take into account all of the company's liabilities (including any contingent or prospective liabilities).

(3) The solvency statement must be in the prescribed form and must state—

(a) the date on which it is made, and

(b) the name of each director of the company.

(4) If the directors make a solvency statement without having reasonable grounds for the opinions expressed in it, and the statement is delivered to the registrar, an offence is committed by every director who is in default.

(5) A person guilty of an offence under subsection (4) is liable—

(a) on conviction on indictment, to imprisonment for a term not exceeding two years or a fine (or both);

(b) on summary conviction—

(i) in England and Wales, to imprisonment for a term not exceeding twelve months or to a fine not exceeding the statutory maximum (or both);

(ii) in Scotland or Northern Ireland, to imprisonment for a term not exceeding six months, or to a fine not exceeding the statutory maximum (or both).

NOTES

Offences under this section: see further s 1131 at **[1.1301]**.

Orders: the Companies (Reduction of Share Capital) Order 2008, SI 2008/1915 at **[4.164]**. For a summary of all statutory instruments made under this Act, see Appendix 4 at **[A4]**.

[1.727]

644 Registration of resolution and supporting documents

(1) Within 15 days after the resolution for reducing share capital is passed the company must deliver to the registrar—

(a) a copy of the solvency statement, and

(b) a statement of capital.

This is in addition to the copy of the resolution itself that is required to be delivered to the registrar under Chapter 3 of Part 3.

(2) The statement of capital must state with respect to the company's share capital as reduced by the resolution—

(a) the total number of shares of the company,

(b) the aggregate nominal value of those shares,

[(ba) the aggregate amount (if any) unpaid on those shares (whether on account of their nominal value or by way of premium), and]

(c) for each class of shares—

(i) prescribed particulars of the rights attached to the shares,

(ii) the total number of shares of that class, and

(iii) the aggregate nominal value of shares of that class, . . .

(d) . . .

(3) The registrar must register the documents delivered to him under subsection (1) on receipt.

(4) The resolution does not take effect until those documents are registered.

(5) The company must also deliver to the registrar, within 15 days after the resolution is passed, a statement by the directors confirming that the solvency statement was—

(a) made not more than 15 days before the date on which the resolution was passed, and

(b) provided to members in accordance with section 642(2) or (3).

(6) The validity of a resolution is not affected by—

(a) a failure to deliver the documents required to be delivered to the registrar under subsection (1) within the time specified in that subsection, or

(b) a failure to comply with subsection (5).

(7) If the company delivers to the registrar a solvency statement that was not provided to members in accordance with section 642(2) or (3), an offence is committed by every officer of the company who is in default.

(8) If default is made in complying with this section, an offence is committed by—

(a) the company, and

(b) every officer of the company who is in default.

(9) A person guilty of an offence under subsection (7) or (8) is liable—

(a) on conviction on indictment, to a fine;

(b) on summary conviction, to a fine not exceeding the statutory maximum.

NOTES

Sub-s (2): para (ba) inserted, and para (d) and the preceding word repealed, by the Small Business, Enterprise and Employment Act 2015, s 97, Sch 6, paras 1, 10, as from 30 June 2016.

Orders: the Companies (Shares and Share Capital) Order 2009, SI 2009/388 at **[4.211]**. For a summary of all statutory instruments made under this Act, see Appendix 4 at **[A4]**.

Reduction of capital confirmed by the court

[1.728]

645 Application to court for order of confirmation

(1) Where a company has passed a resolution for reducing share capital, it may apply to the court for an order confirming the reduction.

(2) If the proposed reduction of capital involves either—

(a) diminution of liability in respect of unpaid share capital, or

(b) the payment to a shareholder of any paid-up share capital,

section 646 (creditors entitled to object to reduction) applies unless the court directs otherwise.

(3) The court may, if having regard to any special circumstances of the case it thinks proper to do so, direct that section 646 is not to apply as regards any class or classes of creditors.

(4) The court may direct that section 646 is to apply in any other case.

[1.729]

646 Creditors entitled to object to reduction

(1) Where this section applies (see section 645(2) and (4)), every creditor of the company who[—

(a)] at the date fixed by the court is entitled to any debt or claim that, if that date were the commencement of the winding up of the company would be admissible in proof against the company, [and

(b) can show that there is a real likelihood that the reduction would result in the company being unable to discharge his debt or claim when it fell due,]

is entitled to object to the reduction of capital.

(2) The court shall settle a list of creditors entitled to object.

(3) For that purpose the court—

(a) shall ascertain, as far as possible without requiring an application from any creditor, the names of those creditors and the nature and amount of their debts or claims, and

(b) may publish notices fixing a day or days within which creditors not entered on the list are to claim to be so entered or are to be excluded from the right of objecting to the reduction of capital.

(4) If a creditor entered on the list whose debt or claim is not discharged or has not determined does not consent to the reduction, the court may, if it thinks fit, dispense with the consent of that creditor on the company securing payment of his debt or claim.

(5) For this purpose the debt or claim must be secured by appropriating (as the court may direct) the following amount—

(a) if the company admits the full amount of the debt or claim or, though not admitting it, is willing to provide for it, the full amount of the debt or claim;

(b) if the company does not admit, and is not willing to provide for, the full amount of the debt or claim, or if the amount is contingent or not ascertained, an amount fixed by the court after the like enquiry and adjudication as if the company were being wound up by the court.

NOTES

Sub-s (1): words in square brackets inserted by the Companies (Share Capital and Acquisition by Company of its Own Shares) Regulations 2009, SI 2009/2022, reg 3, as from 1 October 2009.

[1.730]

647 Offences in connection with list of creditors

(1) If an officer of the company—
- (a) intentionally or recklessly—
  - (i) conceals the name of a creditor entitled to object to the reduction of capital, or
  - (ii) misrepresents the nature or amount of the debt or claim of a creditor, or
- (b) is knowingly concerned in any such concealment or misrepresentation,

he commits an offence.

(2) A person guilty of an offence under this section is liable—
- (a) on conviction on indictment, to a fine;
- (b) on summary conviction, to a fine not exceeding the statutory maximum.

[1.731]

648 Court order confirming reduction

(1) The court may make an order confirming the reduction of capital on such terms and conditions as it thinks fit.

(2) The court must not confirm the reduction unless it is satisfied, with respect to every creditor of the company who is entitled to object to the reduction of capital that either—
- (a) his consent to the reduction has been obtained, or
- (b) his debt or claim has been discharged, or has determined or has been secured.

(3) Where the court confirms the reduction, it may order the company to publish (as the court directs) the reasons for reduction of capital, or such other information in regard to it as the court thinks expedient with a view to giving proper information to the public, and (if the court thinks fit) the causes that led to the reduction.

(4) The court may, if for any special reason it thinks proper to do so, make an order directing that the company must, during such period (commencing on or at any time after the date of the order) as is specified in the order, add to its name as its last words the words "and reduced".

If such an order is made, those words are, until the end of the period specified in the order, deemed to be part of the company's name.

[1.732]

649 Registration of order and statement of capital

(1) The registrar, on production of an order of the court confirming the reduction of a company's share capital and the delivery of a copy of the order and of a statement of capital (approved by the court), shall register the order and statement.

This is subject to section 650 (public company reducing capital below authorised minimum).

(2) The statement of capital must state with respect to the company's share capital as altered by the order—
- (a) the total number of shares of the company,
- (b) the aggregate nominal value of those shares,
- [(ba) the aggregate amount (if any) unpaid on those shares (whether on account of their nominal value or by way of premium), and]
- (c) for each class of shares—
  - (i) prescribed particulars of the rights attached to the shares,
  - (ii) the total number of shares of that class, and
  - (iii) the aggregate nominal value of shares of that class, . . .
- (d) . . .

(3) The resolution for reducing share capital, as confirmed by the court's order, takes effect—
- (a) in the case of a reduction of share capital that forms part of a compromise or arrangement sanctioned by the court under Part 26 (arrangements and reconstructions[: general])—
  - (i) on delivery of the order and statement of capital to the registrar, or
  - (ii) if the court so orders, on the registration of the order and statement of capital;
- [(aa) in the case of a reduction of share capital that forms part of a compromise or arrangement sanctioned by the court under Part 26A (arrangements and reconstructions: companies in financial difficulty)—
  - (i) in the case of any company other than one to which sub-paragraph (ii) applies, on delivery of the order and statement of capital to the registrar;
  - (ii) in the case of an overseas company that is not required to register particulars under section 1046, on publication of the order and statement of capital in the Gazette;
  - (iii) in either case, if the court so orders, on the registration of the order and statement of capital;]
- (b) in [any case not falling within paragraph (a) or (aa)], on the registration of the order and statement of capital.

(4) Notice of the registration of the order and statement of capital must be published in such manner as the court may direct.

(5) The registrar must certify the registration of the order and statement of capital.

(6) The certificate—
- (a) must be signed by the registrar or authenticated by the registrar's official seal, and
- (b) is conclusive evidence—
  - (i) that the requirements of this Act with respect to the reduction of share capital have been complied with, and
  - (ii) that the company's share capital is as stated in the statement of capital.

NOTES

Sub-s (2): para (ba) inserted, and para (d) and the preceding word repealed, by the Small Business, Enterprise and Employment Act 2015, s 97, Sch 6, paras 1, 11, as from 30 June 2016.

Sub-s (3): words in square brackets in para (a) inserted, para (aa) inserted, and words in square brackets in para (b) substituted, by the Corporate Insolvency and Governance Act 2020, s 7, Sch 9, Pt 2, paras 30, 33(1), (9), as from 26 June 2020.

See further the Companies (Authorised Minimum) Regulations 2009, SI 2009/2425, reg 5 at **[4.385]** (Registration of a court order confirming a capital reduction: assumptions which may be made by the registrar).

Orders: the Companies (Shares and Share Capital) Order 2009, SI 2009/388 at **[4.211]**. For a summary of all statutory instruments made under this Act, see Appendix 4 at **[A4]**.

Public company reducing capital below authorised minimum

[1.733]

650 Public company reducing capital below authorised minimum

(1) This section applies where the court makes an order confirming a reduction of a public company's capital that has the effect of bringing the nominal value of its allotted share capital below the authorised minimum.

(2) The registrar must not register the order unless either—

(a) the court so directs, or

(b) the company is first re-registered as a private company.

(3) Section 651 provides an expedited procedure for re-registration in these circumstances.

NOTES

See further the Companies (Authorised Minimum) Regulations 2009, SI 2009/2425, reg 3 (Application of the authorised minimum requirement for certain purposes), and reg 5 (Registration of a court order confirming a capital reduction: assumptions which may be made by the registrar) at **[4.383]** and **[4.385]**.

[1.734]

651 Expedited procedure for re-registration as a private company

(1) The court may authorise the company to be re-registered as a private company without its having passed the special resolution required by section 97.

(2) If it does so, the court must specify in the order the changes to the company's name and articles to be made in connection with the re-registration.

(3) The company may then be re-registered as a private company if an application to that effect is delivered to the registrar together with—

(a) a copy of the court's order, and

(b) notice of the company's name, and a copy of the company's articles, as altered by the court's order.

(4) On receipt of such an application the registrar must issue a certificate of incorporation altered to meet the circumstances of the case.

(5) The certificate must state that it is issued on re-registration and the date on which it is issued.

(6) On the issue of the certificate—

(a) the company by virtue of the issue of the certificate becomes a private company, and

(b) the changes in the company's name and articles take effect.

(7) The certificate is conclusive evidence that the requirements of this Act as to re-registration have been complied with.

Effect of reduction of capital

[1.735]

652 Liability of members following reduction of capital

(1) Where a company's share capital is reduced a member of the company (past or present) is not liable in respect of any share to any call or contribution exceeding in amount the difference (if any) between—

(a) the nominal amount of the share as notified to the registrar in the statement of capital delivered under section 644[, 649, 1028A or 1032A of this Act or paragraph 7 of Schedule 4 to the Small Business, Enterprise and Employment Act 2015], and

(b) the amount paid on the share or the reduced amount (if any) which is deemed to have been paid on it, as the case may be.

(2) This is subject to section 653 (liability to creditor in case of omission from list).

(3) Nothing in this section affects the rights of the contributories among themselves.

NOTES

Sub-s (1): words in square brackets substituted by the Small Business, Enterprise and Employment Act 2015, s 84, Sch 4, Pt 2, paras 22, 25, as from 26 May 2015.

[1.736]

653 Liability to creditor in case of omission from list of creditors

(1) This section applies where, in the case of a reduction of capital confirmed by the court—

(a) a creditor entitled to object to the reduction of share capital is by reason of his ignorance—

(i) of the proceedings for reduction of share capital, or

(ii) of their nature and effect with respect to his debt or claim,

not entered on the list of creditors, and

(b) after the reduction of capital the company is unable to pay the amount of his debt or claim.

(2) Every person who was a member of the company at the date on which the resolution for reducing capital took effect under section 649(3) is liable to contribute for the payment of the debt or claim an amount not exceeding that which he would have been liable to contribute if the company had commenced to be wound up on the day before that date.

(3) If the company is wound up, the court on the application of the creditor in question, and proof of ignorance as mentioned in subsection (1)(a), may if it thinks fit—

(a) settle accordingly a list of persons liable to contribute under this section, and

(b) make and enforce calls and orders on them as if they were ordinary contributories in a winding up.

(4) The reference in subsection (1)(b) to a company being unable to pay the amount of a debt or claim has the same meaning as in section 123 of the Insolvency Act 1986 (c 45) or Article 103 of the Insolvency (Northern Ireland) Order 1989 (SI 1989/2405 (NI 19)).

CHAPTER 11 MISCELLANEOUS AND SUPPLEMENTARY PROVISIONS

[1.737]

654 Treatment of reserve arising from reduction of capital

(1) A reserve arising from the reduction of a company's share capital is not distributable, subject to any provision made by order under this section.

(2) The Secretary of State may by order specify cases in which—

(a) the prohibition in subsection (1) does not apply, and

(b) the reserve is to be treated for the purposes of Part 23 (distributions) as a realised profit.

(3) An order under this section is subject to affirmative resolution procedure.

NOTES

Orders: the Companies (Reduction of Share Capital) Order 2008, SI 2008/1915 at **[4.164]**. For a summary of all statutory instruments made under this Act, see Appendix 4 at **[A4]**.

[1.738]

655 Shares no bar to damages against company

A person is not debarred from obtaining damages or other compensation from a company by reason only of his holding or having held shares in the company or any right to apply or subscribe for shares or to be included in the company's register of members [(or have his name and other particulars delivered to the registrar under Chapter 2A of Part 8 and registered by the registrar)] in respect of shares.

NOTES

Words in square brackets inserted by the Small Business, Enterprise and Employment Act 2015, s 94, Sch 5, Pt 2, paras 11, 24, as from 30 June 2016.

[1.739]

656 Public companies: duty of directors to call meeting on serious loss of capital

(1) Where the net assets of a public company are half or less of its called-up share capital, the directors must call a general meeting of the company to consider whether any, and if so what, steps should be taken to deal with the situation.

(2) They must do so not later than 28 days from the earliest day on which that fact is known to a director of the company.

(3) The meeting must be convened for a date not later than 56 days from that day.

(4) If there is a failure to convene a meeting as required by this section, each of the directors of the company who—

(a) knowingly authorises or permits the failure, or

(b) after the period during which the meeting should have been convened, knowingly authorises or permits the failure to continue,

commits an offence.

(5) A person guilty of an offence under this section is liable—

(a) on conviction on indictment, to a fine;

(b) on summary conviction, to a fine not exceeding the statutory maximum.

(6) Nothing in this section authorises the consideration at a meeting convened in pursuance of subsection (1) of any matter that could not have been considered at that meeting apart from this section.

[1.740]

657 General power to make further provision by regulations

(1) The Secretary of State may by regulations modify the following provisions of this Part—

sections 552 and 553 (prohibited commissions, discounts and allowances),

Chapter 5 (payment for shares),

Chapter 6 (public companies: independent valuation of non-cash consideration),

Chapter 7 (share premiums),

sections 622 to 628 (redenomination of share capital),

Chapter 10 (reduction of capital), and

section 656 (public companies: duty of directors to call meeting on serious loss of capital).

(2) The regulations may—

(a) amend or repeal any of those provisions, or

(b) make such other provision as appears to the Secretary of State appropriate in place of any of those provisions.

(3) Regulations under this section may make consequential amendments or repeals in other provisions of this Act, or in other enactments.

(4) Regulations under this section are subject to affirmative resolution procedure.

NOTES

Orders and Regulations: the Companies Act 2006 (Consequential Amendments, Transitional Provisions and Savings) Order 2009, SI 2009/1941 at **[4.355]**; the Companies (Share Capital and Acquisition by Company of its Own Shares) Regulations 2009, SI 2009/2022 at **[4.369]**; the Companies Act 2006 (Amendment of Part 17) Regulations 2015, SI 2015/472. For a summary of all statutory instruments made under this Act, see Appendix 4 at **[A4]**.

PART 18 ACQUISITION BY LIMITED COMPANY OF ITS OWN SHARES

CHAPTER 1 GENERAL PROVISIONS

Introductory

[1.741]

658 General rule against limited company acquiring its own shares

(1) A limited company must not acquire its own shares, whether by purchase, subscription or otherwise, except in accordance with the provisions of this Part.

(2) If a company purports to act in contravention of this section—

(a) an offence is committed by—

(i) the company, and

(ii) every officer of the company who is in default, and

(b) the purported acquisition is void.

(3) A person guilty of an offence under this section is liable—

(a) on conviction on indictment, to imprisonment for a term not exceeding two years or a fine (or both);

(b) on summary conviction—

(i) in England and Wales, to imprisonment for a term not exceeding twelve months or a fine not exceeding the statutory maximum (or both);

(ii) in Scotland or Northern Ireland, to imprisonment for a term not exceeding six months or a fine not exceeding the statutory maximum (or both).

NOTES

Offences under this section: see further s 1131 at **[1.1301]**.

Deferred Prosecution Agreements: as to the application of Deferred Prosecution Agreements to an offence under this section (ie, an agreement between a designated prosecutor and a person accused of a crime (P) whereby proceedings against P in respect of the alleged offence are automatically suspended as soon as they are instituted if P agrees to comply with certain requirements), see s 45 of, and Sch 17, Pt 1 and Sch 17, Pt 2, para 24 to, the Crime and Courts Act 2013.

[1.742]

659 Exceptions to general rule

(1) A limited company may acquire any of its own fully paid shares otherwise than for valuable consideration.

(2) Section 658 does not prohibit—

(a) the acquisition of shares in a reduction of capital duly made;

(b) the purchase of shares in pursuance of an order of the court under—

(i) section 98 (application to court to cancel resolution for re-registration as a private company),

(ii) section 721(6) (powers of court on objection to redemption or purchase of shares out of capital),

(iii) section 759 (remedial order in case of breach of prohibition of public offers by private company), or

(iv) Part 30 (protection of members against unfair prejudice);

(c) the forfeiture of shares, or the acceptance of shares surrendered in lieu, in pursuance of the company's articles, for failure to pay any sum payable in respect of the shares.

Shares held by company's nominee

[1.743]

660 Treatment of shares held by nominee

(1) This section applies where shares in a limited company—

(a) are taken by a subscriber to the memorandum as nominee of the company,

(b) are issued to a nominee of the company, or

(c) are acquired by a nominee of the company, partly paid up, from a third person.

(2) For all purposes—

(a) the shares are to be treated as held by the nominee on his own account, and

(b) the company is to be regarded as having no beneficial interest in them.

(3) This section does not apply—

(a) to shares acquired otherwise than by subscription by a nominee of a public company, where—

(i) a person acquires shares in the company with financial assistance given to him, directly or indirectly, by the company for the purpose of or in connection with the acquisition, and

(ii) the company has a beneficial interest in the shares;

(b) to shares acquired by a nominee of the company when the company has no beneficial interest in the shares.

[1.744]

661 Liability of others where nominee fails to make payment in respect of shares

(1) This section applies where shares in a limited company—

(a) are taken by a subscriber to the memorandum as nominee of the company,

(b) are issued to a nominee of the company, or

(c) are acquired by a nominee of the company, partly paid up, from a third person.

(2) If the nominee, having been called on to pay any amount for the purposes of paying up, or paying any premium on, the shares, fails to pay that amount within 21 days from being called on to do so, then—

(a) in the case of shares that he agreed to take as subscriber to the memorandum, the other subscribers to the memorandum, and

(b) in any other case, the directors of the company when the shares were issued to or acquired by him,

are jointly and severally liable with him to pay that amount.

(3) If in proceedings for the recovery of an amount under subsection (2) it appears to the court that the subscriber or director—

(a) has acted honestly and reasonably, and

(b) having regard to all the circumstances of the case, ought fairly to be relieved from liability,

the court may relieve him, either wholly or in part, from his liability on such terms as the court thinks fit.

(4) If a subscriber to a company's memorandum or a director of a company has reason to apprehend that a claim will or might be made for the recovery of any such amount from him—

(a) he may apply to the court for relief, and

(b) the court has the same power to relieve him as it would have had in proceedings for recovery of that amount.

(5) This section does not apply to shares acquired by a nominee of the company when the company has no beneficial interest in the shares.

Shares held by or for public company

[1.745]

662 Duty to cancel shares in public company held by or for the company

(1) This section applies in the case of a public company—

(a) where shares in the company are forfeited, or surrendered to the company in lieu of forfeiture, in pursuance of the articles, for failure to pay any sum payable in respect of the shares;

(b) where shares in the company are surrendered to the company in pursuance of section 102C(1)(b) of the Building Societies Act 1986 (c 53);

(c) where shares in the company are acquired by it (otherwise than in accordance with this Part or Part 30 (protection of members against unfair prejudice)) and the company has a beneficial interest in the shares;

(d) where a nominee of the company acquires shares in the company from a third party without financial assistance being given directly or indirectly by the company and the company has a beneficial interest in the shares; or

(e) where a person acquires shares in the company, with financial assistance given to him, directly or indirectly, by the company for the purpose of or in connection with the acquisition, and the company has a beneficial interest in the shares.

(2) Unless the shares or any interest of the company in them are previously disposed of, the company must—

(a) cancel the shares and diminish the amount of the company's share capital by the nominal value of the shares cancelled, and

(b) where the effect is that the nominal value of the company's allotted share capital is brought below the authorised minimum, apply for re-registration as a private company, stating the effect of the cancellation.

(3) It must do so no later than—

(a) in a case within subsection (1)(a) or (b), three years from the date of the forfeiture or surrender;

(b) in a case within subsection (1)(c) or (d), three years from the date of the acquisition;

(c) in a case within subsection (1)(e), one year from the date of the acquisition.

(4) The directors of the company may take any steps necessary to enable the company to comply with this section, and may do so without complying with the provisions of Chapter 10 of Part 17 (reduction of capital).

See also section 664 (re-registration as private company in consequence of cancellation).

(5) Neither the company nor, in a case within subsection (1)(d) or (e), the nominee or other shareholder may exercise any voting rights in respect of the shares.

(6) Any purported exercise of those rights is void.

NOTES

See further the Companies (Authorised Minimum) Regulations 2009, SI 2009/2425, reg 3 at **[4.383]** (Application of the authorised minimum requirement for certain purposes).

[1.746]

663 Notice of cancellation of shares

(1) Where a company cancels shares in order to comply with section 662, it must within one month after the shares are cancelled give notice to the registrar, specifying the shares cancelled.

(2) The notice must be accompanied by a statement of capital.

(3) The statement of capital must state with respect to the company's share capital immediately following the cancellation—

(a) the total number of shares of the company,

(b) the aggregate nominal value of those shares,

[(ba) the aggregate amount (if any) unpaid on those shares (whether on account of their nominal value or by way of premium), and]

(c) for each class of shares—

(i) prescribed particulars of the rights attached to the shares,

(ii) the total number of shares of that class, and

(iii) the aggregate nominal value of shares of that class, . . .

(d) . . .

(4) If default is made in complying with this section, an offence is committed by—

(a) the company, and

(b) every officer of the company who is in default.

(5) A person guilty of an offence under this section is liable on summary conviction to a fine not exceeding level 3 on the standard scale and, for continued contravention, a daily default fine not exceeding one-tenth of level 3 on the standard scale.

NOTES

Sub-s (3): para (ba) inserted, and para (d) and the preceding word repealed, by the Small Business, Enterprise and Employment Act 2015, s 97, Sch 6, paras 1, 12, as from 30 June 2016.

Orders: the Companies (Shares and Share Capital) Order 2009, SI 2009/388 at **[4.211]**. For a summary of all statutory instruments made under this Act, see Appendix 4 at **[A4]**.

[1.747]

664 Re-registration as private company in consequence of cancellation

(1) Where a company is obliged to re-register as a private company to comply with section 662, the directors may resolve that the company should be so re-registered.

Chapter 3 of Part 3 (resolutions affecting a company's constitution) applies to any such resolution.

(2) The resolution may make such changes—

(a) in the company's name, and

(b) in the company's articles,

as are necessary in connection with its becoming a private company.

(3) The application for re-registration must contain a statement of the company's proposed name on re-registration.

(4) The application must be accompanied by—

(a) a copy of the resolution (unless a copy has already been forwarded under Chapter 3 of Part 3),

(b) a copy of the company's articles as amended by the resolution, and

(c) a statement of compliance.

(5) The statement of compliance required is a statement that the requirements of this section as to re-registration as a private company have been complied with.

(6) The registrar may accept the statement of compliance as sufficient evidence that the company is entitled to be re-registered as a private company.

[1.748]

665 Issue of certificate of incorporation on re-registration

(1) If on an application under section 664 the registrar is satisfied that the company is entitled to be re-registered as a private company, the company shall be re-registered accordingly.

(2) The registrar must issue a certificate of incorporation altered to meet the circumstances of the case.

(3) The certificate must state that it is issued on re-registration and the date on which it is issued.

(4) On the issue of the certificate—

(a) the company by virtue of the issue of the certificate becomes a private company, and

(b) the changes in the company's name and articles take effect.

(5) The certificate is conclusive evidence that the requirements of this Act as to re-registration have been complied with.

[1.749]

666 Effect of failure to re-register

(1) If a public company that is required by section 662 to apply to be re-registered as a private company fails to do so before the end of the period specified in subsection (3) of that section, Chapter 1 of Part 20 (prohibition of public offers by private company) applies to it as if it were a private company.

(2) Subject to that, the company continues to be treated as a public company until it is so re-registered.

[1.750]

667 Offence in case of failure to cancel shares or re-register

(1) This section applies where a company, when required to do by section 662—

(a) fails to cancel any shares, or

(b) fails to make an application for re-registration as a private company,

within the time specified in subsection (3) of that section.

(2) An offence is committed by—

(a) the company, and

(b) every officer of the company who is in default.

(3) A person guilty of an offence under this section is liable on summary conviction to a fine not exceeding level 3 on the standard scale and, for continued contravention, a daily default fine not exceeding one-tenth of level 3 on the standard scale.

NOTES

See further the Companies (Authorised Minimum) Regulations 2009, SI 2009/2425, reg 6 at **[4.386]** (Determination of exchange rates by the court in certain proceedings).

[1.751]

668 Application of provisions to company re-registering as public company

(1) This section applies where, after shares in a private company—

(a) are forfeited in pursuance of the company's articles or are surrendered to the company in lieu of forfeiture,

(b) are acquired by the company (otherwise than by any of the methods permitted by this Part or Part 30 (protection of members against unfair prejudice)), the company having a beneficial interest in the shares,

(c) are acquired by a nominee of the company from a third party without financial assistance being given directly or indirectly by the company, the company having a beneficial interest in the shares, or

(d) are acquired by a person with financial assistance given to him, directly or indirectly, by the company for the purpose of or in connection with the acquisition, the company having a beneficial interest in the shares,

the company is re-registered as a public company.

(2) In that case the provisions of sections 662 to 667 apply to the company as if it had been a public company at the time of the forfeiture, surrender or acquisition, subject to the following modification.

(3) The modification is that the period specified in section 662(3)(a), (b) or (c) (period for complying with obligations under that section) runs from the date of the re-registration of the company as a public company.

[1.752]

669 Transfer to reserve on acquisition of shares by public company or nominee

(1) Where—

(a) a public company, or a nominee of a public company, acquires shares in the company, and

(b) those shares are shown in a balance sheet of the company as an asset,

an amount equal to the value of the shares must be transferred out of profits available for dividend to a reserve fund and is not then available for distribution.

(2) Subsection (1) applies to an interest in shares as it applies to shares.

As it so applies the reference to the value of the shares shall be read as a reference to the value to the company of its interest in the shares.

Charges of public company on own shares

[1.753]

670 Public companies: general rule against lien or charge on own shares

(1) A lien or other charge of a public company on its own shares (whether taken expressly or otherwise) is void, except as permitted by this section.

(2) In the case of any description of company, a charge is permitted if the shares are not fully paid up and the charge is for an amount payable in respect of the shares.

(3) In the case of a company whose ordinary business—

(a) includes the lending of money, or

(b) consists of the provision of credit or the bailment (in Scotland, hiring) of goods under a hire-purchase agreement, or both,

a charge is permitted (whether the shares are fully paid or not) if it arises in connection with a transaction entered into by the company in the ordinary course of that business.

(4) In the case of a company that has been re-registered as a public company, a charge is permitted if it was in existence immediately before the application for re-registration.

Supplementary provisions

[1.754]

671 Interests to be disregarded in determining whether company has beneficial interest

In determining for the purposes of this Chapter whether a company has a beneficial interest in shares, there shall be disregarded any such interest as is mentioned in—

section 672 (residual interest under pension scheme or employees' share scheme),

section 673 (employer's charges and other rights of recovery), or

section 674 (rights as personal representative or trustee).

[1.755]

672 Residual interest under pension scheme or employees' share scheme

(1) Where the shares are held on trust for the purposes of a pension scheme or employees' share scheme, there shall be disregarded any residual interest of the company that has not vested in possession.

(2) A "residual interest" means a right of the company to receive any of the trust property in the event of—

(a) all the liabilities arising under the scheme having been satisfied or provided for, or

(b) the company ceasing to participate in the scheme, or

(c) the trust property at any time exceeding what is necessary for satisfying the liabilities arising or expected to arise under the scheme.

(3) In subsection (2)—

(a) the reference to a right includes a right dependent on the exercise of a discretion vested by the scheme in the trustee or another person, and

(b) the reference to liabilities arising under a scheme includes liabilities that have resulted, or may result, from the exercise of any such discretion.

(4) For the purposes of this section a residual interest vests in possession—

(a) in a case within subsection (2)(a), on the occurrence of the event mentioned there (whether or not the amount of the property receivable pursuant to the right is ascertained);

(b) in a case within subsection (2)(b) or (c), when the company becomes entitled to require the trustee to transfer to it any of the property receivable pursuant to that right.

(5) Where by virtue of this section shares are exempt from section 660 or 661 (shares held by company's nominee) at the time they are taken, issued or acquired but the residual interest in question vests in possession before they are disposed of or fully paid up, those sections apply to the shares as if they had been taken, issued or acquired on the date on which that interest vests in possession.

(6) Where by virtue of this section shares are exempt from sections 662 to 668 (shares held by or for public company) at the time they are acquired but the residual interest in question vests in possession before they are disposed of, those sections apply to the shares as if they had been acquired on the date on which the interest vests in possession.

[1.756]

673 Employer's charges and other rights of recovery

(1) Where the shares are held on trust for the purposes of a pension scheme there shall be disregarded—

(a) any charge or lien on, or set-off against, any benefit or other right or interest under the scheme for the purpose of enabling the employer or former employer of a member of the scheme to obtain the discharge of a monetary obligation due to him from the member;

(b) any right to receive from the trustee of the scheme, or as trustee of the scheme to retain, an amount that can be recovered or retained—

(i) . . .

(ii) under section 57 of the Pension Schemes (Northern Ireland) Act 1993 (c 49), or otherwise, as reimbursement or partial reimbursement for any contributions equivalent premium paid in connection with the scheme under Part 3 of that Act.

(2) Where the shares are held on trust for the purposes of an employees' share scheme, there shall be disregarded any charge or lien on, or set-off against, any benefit or other right or interest under the scheme for the purpose of enabling the employer or former employer of a member of the scheme to obtain the discharge of a monetary obligation due to him from the member.

NOTES

Sub-s (1): sub-para (b)(i) repealed by the Pensions Act 2014, s 24, Sch 13, Pt 2, paras 74, 76, as from 6 April 2016.

[1.757]

674 Rights as personal representative or trustee

Where the company is a personal representative or trustee, there shall be disregarded any rights that the company has in that capacity including, in particular—

(a) any right to recover its expenses or be remunerated out of the estate or trust property, and

(b) any right to be indemnified out of that property for any liability incurred by reason of any act or omission of the company in the performance of its duties as personal representative or trustee.

[1.758]

675 Meaning of "pension scheme"

(1) In this Chapter "pension scheme" means a scheme for the provision of benefits consisting of or including relevant benefits for or in respect of employees or former employees.

(2) In subsection (1) "relevant benefits" means any pension, lump sum, gratuity or other like benefit given or to be given on retirement or on death or in anticipation of retirement or, in connection with past service, after retirement or death.

[1.759]

676 Application of provisions to directors

For the purposes of this Chapter references to "employer" and "employee", in the context of a pension scheme or employees' share scheme, shall be read as if a director of a company were employed by it.

CHAPTER 2 FINANCIAL ASSISTANCE FOR PURCHASE OF OWN SHARES

Introductory

[1.760]

677 Meaning of "financial assistance"

(1) In this Chapter "financial assistance" means—

(a) financial assistance given by way of gift,

(b) financial assistance given—

(i) by way of guarantee, security or indemnity (other than an indemnity in respect of the indemnifier's own neglect or default), or

(ii) by way of release or waiver,

(c) financial assistance given—

(i) by way of a loan or any other agreement under which any of the obligations of the person giving the assistance are to be fulfilled at a time when in accordance with the agreement any obligation of another party to the agreement remains unfulfilled, or

(ii) by way of the novation of, or the assignment (in Scotland, assignation) of rights arising under, a loan or such other agreement, or

(d) any other financial assistance given by a company where—

(i) the net assets of the company are reduced to a material extent by the giving of the assistance, or

(ii) the company has no net assets.

(2) "Net assets" here means the aggregate amount of the company's assets less the aggregate amount of its liabilities.

(3) For this purpose a company's liabilities include—

(a) where the company draws up Companies Act individual accounts, any provision of a kind specified for the purposes of this subsection by regulations under section 396, and

(b) where the company draws up IAS individual accounts, any provision made in those accounts.

NOTES

Regulations under section 396: see the notes to that section at **[1.451]**. See also the Small Companies and Groups (Accounts and Directors' Report) Regulations 2008, SI 2008/409, reg 12 (at **[4.49]**), and the Large and Medium-sized Companies and Groups (Accounts and Reports) Regulations 2008, SI 2008/410, reg 12 (at **[4.71]**) which provide that Sch 7 to SI 2008/409 (at **[4.57]**, **[4.58]**) and Sch 9 to SI 2008/410 (at **[4.112]**, **[4.113]**) define "provisions" for the purpose of those Regulations and for the purposes of sub-s (3)(a) above.

Circumstances in which financial assistance prohibited

[1.761]

678 Assistance for acquisition of shares in public company

(1) Where a person is acquiring or proposing to acquire shares in a public company, it is not lawful for that company, or a company that is a subsidiary of that company, to give financial assistance directly or indirectly for the purpose of the acquisition before or at the same time as the acquisition takes place.

(2) Subsection (1) does not prohibit a company from giving financial assistance for the acquisition of shares in it or its holding company if—

(a) the company's principal purpose in giving the assistance is not to give it for the purpose of any such acquisition, or

(b) the giving of the assistance for that purpose is only an incidental part of some larger purpose of the company,

and the assistance is given in good faith in the interests of the company.

(3) Where—

(a) a person has acquired shares in a company, and

(b) a liability has been incurred (by that or another person) for the purpose of the acquisition,

it is not lawful for that company, or a company that is a subsidiary of that company, to give financial assistance directly or indirectly for the purpose of reducing or discharging the liability if, at the time the assistance is given, the company in which the shares were acquired is a public company.

(4) Subsection (3) does not prohibit a company from giving financial assistance if—

(a) the company's principal purpose in giving the assistance is not to reduce or discharge any liability incurred by a person for the purpose of the acquisition of shares in the company or its holding company, or

(b) the reduction or discharge of any such liability is only an incidental part of some larger purpose of the company,

and the assistance is given in good faith in the interests of the company.

(5) This section has effect subject to sections 681 and 682 (unconditional and conditional exceptions to prohibition).

[1.762]

679 Assistance by public company for acquisition of shares in its private holding company

(1) Where a person is acquiring or proposing to acquire shares in a private company, it is not lawful for a public company that is a subsidiary of that company to give financial assistance directly or indirectly for the purpose of the acquisition before or at the same time as the acquisition takes place.

(2) Subsection (1) does not prohibit a company from giving financial assistance for the acquisition of shares in its holding company if—

(a) the company's principal purpose in giving the assistance is not to give it for the purpose of any such acquisition, or

(b) the giving of the assistance for that purpose is only an incidental part of some larger purpose of the company,

and the assistance is given in good faith in the interests of the company.

(3) Where—

(a) a person has acquired shares in a private company, and

(b) a liability has been incurred (by that or another person) for the purpose of the acquisition,

it is not lawful for a public company that is a subsidiary of that company to give financial assistance directly or indirectly for the purpose of reducing or discharging the liability.

(4) Subsection (3) does not prohibit a company from giving financial assistance if—

(a) the company's principal purpose in giving the assistance is not to reduce or discharge any liability incurred by a person for the purpose of the acquisition of shares in its holding company, or

(b) the reduction or discharge of any such liability is only an incidental part of some larger purpose of the company,

and the assistance is given in good faith in the interests of the company.

(5) This section has effect subject to sections 681 and 682 (unconditional and conditional exceptions to prohibition).

[1.763]

680 Prohibited financial assistance an offence

(1) If a company contravenes section 678(1) or (3) or section 679(1) or (3) (prohibited financial assistance) an offence is committed by—

(a) the company, and

(b) every officer of the company who is in default.

(2) A person guilty of an offence under this section is liable—

(a) on conviction on indictment, to imprisonment for a term not exceeding two years or a fine (or both);

(b) on summary conviction—

(i) in England and Wales, to imprisonment for a term not exceeding twelve months or to a fine not exceeding the statutory maximum (or both);

(ii) in Scotland or Northern Ireland, to imprisonment for a term not exceeding six months, or to a fine not exceeding the statutory maximum (or both).

NOTES

Offences under this section: see further s 1131 at **[1.1301]**.

Deferred Prosecution Agreements: as to the application of Deferred Prosecution Agreements to an offence under this section (ie, an agreement between a designated prosecutor and a person accused of a crime (P) whereby proceedings against P in respect of the alleged offence are automatically suspended as soon as they are instituted if P agrees to comply with certain requirements), see s 45 of, and Sch 17, Pt 1 and Sch 17, Pt 2, para 24 to, the Crime and Courts Act 2013.

Exceptions from prohibition

[1.764]

681 Unconditional exceptions

(1) Neither section 678 nor section 679 prohibits a transaction to which this section applies.

(2) Those transactions are—

(a) a distribution of the company's assets by way of—

(i) dividend lawfully made, or

(ii) distribution in the course of a company's winding up;

(b) an allotment of bonus shares;

(c) a reduction of capital under Chapter 10 of Part 17;

(d) a redemption of shares under Chapter 3 or a purchase of shares under Chapter 4 of this Part;

(e) anything done in pursuance of an order of the court under Part 26 [or 26A] (order sanctioning compromise or arrangement with members or creditors);

(f) anything done under an arrangement made in pursuance of section 110 of the Insolvency Act 1986 (c 45) or Article 96 of the Insolvency (Northern Ireland) Order 1989 (SI 1989/2405 (NI 19)) (liquidator in winding up accepting shares as consideration for sale of company's property);

(g) anything done under an arrangement made between a company and its creditors that is binding on the creditors by virtue of Part 1 of the Insolvency Act 1986 or Part 2 of the Insolvency (Northern Ireland) Order 1989 (SI 1989/2405 (NI 19)).

NOTES

Sub-s (2): words in square brackets in para (e) inserted by the Corporate Insolvency and Governance Act 2020, s 7, Sch 9, Pt 2, paras 30, 34, as from 26 June 2020.

[1.765]
682 Conditional exceptions

(1) Neither section 678 nor section 679 prohibits a transaction to which this section applies—

- (a) if the company giving the assistance is a private company, or
- (b) if the company giving the assistance is a public company and—
  - (i) the company has net assets that are not reduced by the giving of the assistance, or
  - (ii) to the extent that those assets are so reduced, the assistance is provided out of distributable profits.

(2) The transactions to which this section applies are—

- (a) where the lending of money is part of the ordinary business of the company, the lending of money in the ordinary course of the company's business;
- (b) the provision by the company, in good faith in the interests of the company or its holding company, of financial assistance for the purposes of an employees' share scheme;
- (c) the provision of financial assistance by the company for the purposes of or in connection with anything done by the company (or another company in the same group) for the purpose of enabling or facilitating transactions in shares in the first-mentioned company or its holding company between, and involving the acquisition of beneficial ownership of those shares by—
  - (i) bona fide employees or former employees of that company (or another company in the same group), or
  - (ii) spouses or civil partners, widows, widowers or surviving civil partners, or minor children or step-children of any such employees or former employees;
- (d) the making by the company of loans to persons (other than directors) employed in good faith by the company with a view to enabling those persons to acquire fully paid shares in the company or its holding company to be held by them by way of beneficial ownership.

(3) The references in this section to "net assets" are to the amount by which the aggregate of the company's assets exceeds the aggregate of its liabilities.

(4) For this purpose—

- (a) the amount of both assets and liabilities shall be taken to be as stated in the company's accounting records immediately before the financial assistance is given, and
- (b) "liabilities" includes any amount retained as reasonably necessary for the purpose of providing for a liability the nature of which is clearly defined and that is either likely to be incurred or certain to be incurred but uncertain as to amount or as to the date on which it will arise.

(5) For the purposes of subsection (2)(c) a company is in the same group as another company if it is a holding company or subsidiary of that company or a subsidiary of a holding company of that company.

Supplementary

[1.766]
683 Definitions for this Chapter

(1) In this Chapter—

"distributable profits", in relation to the giving of any financial assistance—

- (a) means those profits out of which the company could lawfully make a distribution equal in value to that assistance, and
- (b) includes, in a case where the financial assistance consists of or includes, or is treated as arising in consequence of, the sale, transfer or other disposition of a non-cash asset, any profit that, if the company were to make a distribution of that character would be available for that purpose (see section 846); and

"distribution" has the same meaning as in Part 23 (distributions) (see section 829).

(2) In this Chapter—

- (a) a reference to a person incurring a liability includes his changing his financial position by making an agreement or arrangement (whether enforceable or unenforceable, and whether made on his own account or with any other person) or by any other means, and
- (b) a reference to a company giving financial assistance for the purposes of reducing or discharging a liability incurred by a person for the purpose of the acquisition of shares includes its giving such assistance for the purpose of wholly or partly restoring his financial position to what it was before the acquisition took place.

CHAPTER 3 REDEEMABLE SHARES

[1.767]
684 Power of limited company to issue redeemable shares

(1) A limited company having a share capital may issue shares that are to be redeemed or are liable to be redeemed at the option of the company or the shareholder ("redeemable shares"), subject to the following provisions.

(2) The articles of a private limited company may exclude or restrict the issue of redeemable shares.

(3) A public limited company may only issue redeemable shares if it is authorised to do so by its articles.

(4) No redeemable shares may be issued at a time when there are no issued shares of the company that are not redeemable.

[1.768]

685 Terms and manner of redemption

(1) The directors of a limited company may determine the terms, conditions and manner of redemption of shares if they are authorised to do so—

(a) by the company's articles, or

(b) by a resolution of the company.

(2) A resolution under subsection (1)(b) may be an ordinary resolution, even though it amends the company's articles.

(3) Where the directors are authorised under subsection (1) to determine the terms, conditions and manner of redemption of shares—

(a) they must do so before the shares are allotted, and

(b) any obligation of the company to state in a statement of capital the rights attached to the shares extends to the terms, conditions and manner of redemption.

(4) Where the directors are not so authorised, the terms, conditions and manner of redemption of any redeemable shares must be stated in the company's articles.

[1.769]

686 Payment for redeemable shares

(1) Redeemable shares in a limited company may not be redeemed unless they are fully paid.

(2) The terms of redemption of shares in a limited company may provide that the amount payable on redemption may, by agreement between the company and the holder of the shares, be paid on a date later than the redemption date.

(3) Unless redeemed in accordance with a provision authorised by subsection (2), the shares must be paid for on redemption.

[1.770]

687 Financing of redemption

(1) A private limited company may redeem redeemable shares out of capital in accordance with Chapter 5.

(2) Subject to that, redeemable shares in a limited company may only be redeemed out of—

(a) distributable profits of the company, or

(b) the proceeds of a fresh issue of shares made for the purposes of the redemption.

(3) Any premium payable on redemption of shares in a limited company must be paid out of distributable profits of the company, subject to the following provision.

(4) If the redeemable shares were issued at a premium, any premium payable on their redemption may be paid out of the proceeds of a fresh issue of shares made for the purposes of the redemption, up to an amount equal to—

(a) the aggregate of the premiums received by the company on the issue of the shares redeemed, or

(b) the current amount of the company's share premium account (including any sum transferred to that account in respect of premiums on the new shares),

whichever is the less.

(5) The amount of the company's share premium account is reduced by a sum corresponding (or by sums in the aggregate corresponding) to the amount of any payment made under subsection (4).

(6) This section is subject to section 735(4) (terms of redemption enforceable in a winding up).

[1.771]

688 Redeemed shares treated as cancelled

Where shares in a limited company are redeemed—

(a) the shares are treated as cancelled, and

(b) the amount of the company's issued share capital is diminished accordingly by the nominal value of the shares redeemed.

[1.772]

689 Notice to registrar of redemption

(1) If a limited company redeems any redeemable shares it must within one month after doing so give notice to the registrar, specifying the shares redeemed.

(2) The notice must be accompanied by a statement of capital.

(3) The statement of capital must state with respect to the company's share capital immediately following the redemption—

(a) the total number of shares of the company,

(b) the aggregate nominal value of those shares,

[(ba) the aggregate amount (if any) unpaid on those shares (whether on account of their nominal value or by way of premium), and]

(c) for each class of shares—

(i) prescribed particulars of the rights attached to the shares,

(ii) the total number of shares of that class, and

(iii) the aggregate nominal value of shares of that class, . . .

(d) . . .

(4) If default is made in complying with this section, an offence is committed by—

(a) the company, and

(b) every officer of the company who is in default.

(5) A person guilty of an offence under this section is liable on summary conviction to a fine not exceeding level 3 on the standard scale and, for continued contravention, a daily default fine not exceeding one-tenth of level 3 on the standard scale.

NOTES

Sub-s (3): para (ba) inserted, and para (d) and the preceding word repealed, by the Small Business, Enterprise and Employment Act 2015, s 97, Sch 6, paras 1, 13, as from 30 June 2016.

Orders: the Companies (Shares and Share Capital) Order 2009, SI 2009/388 at **[4.211]**. For a summary of all statutory instruments made under this Act, see Appendix 4 at **[A4]**.

CHAPTER 4 PURCHASE OF OWN SHARES

General provisions

[1.773]

690 Power of limited company to purchase own shares

(1) A limited company having a share capital may purchase its own shares (including any redeemable shares), subject to—

(a) the following provisions of this Chapter, and

(b) any restriction or prohibition in the company's articles.

(2) A limited company may not purchase its own shares if as a result of the purchase there would no longer be any issued shares of the company other than redeemable shares or shares held as treasury shares.

[1.774]

691 Payment for purchase of own shares

(1) A limited company may not purchase its own shares unless they are fully paid.

(2) Where a limited company purchases its own shares, the shares must be paid for on purchase.

[(3) But subsection (2) does not apply in a case where a private limited company is purchasing shares for the purposes of or pursuant to an employees' share scheme.]

NOTES

Sub-s (3): added by the Companies Act 2006 (Amendment of Part 18) Regulations 2013, SI 2013/999, reg 3, as from 30 April 2013.

[1.775]

692 Financing of purchase of own shares

[(1) A private limited company may purchase its own shares out of capital in accordance with Chapter 5.

(1ZA) If authorised to do so by its articles, a private limited company may purchase its own shares out of capital otherwise than in accordance with Chapter 5, up to an aggregate purchase price in a financial year of the lower of—

(a) £15,000, or

(b) the nominal value of 5% of its fully paid share capital as at the beginning of the financial year.]

(1A) If the share capital of the company is not denominated in sterling, the value in sterling of the share capital shall be calculated for the purposes of subsection [(1ZA)(b)] at an appropriate spot rate of exchange.

(1B) The rate must be a rate prevailing on a day specified in the resolution authorising the purchase of the shares.]

(2) [Subject to subsections (1) and (1ZA)]—

(a) a limited company may only purchase its own shares out of—

(i) distributable profits of the company, or

(ii) the proceeds of a fresh issue of shares made for the purpose of financing the purchase, and

(b) any premium payable on the purchase by a limited company of its own shares must be paid out of distributable profits of the company, subject to subsection (3).

(3) If the shares to be purchased were issued at a premium, any premium payable on their purchase by the company may be paid out of the proceeds of a fresh issue of shares made for the purpose of financing the purchase, up to an amount equal to—

(a) the aggregate of the premiums received by the company on the issue of the shares purchased, or

(b) the current amount of the company's share premium account (including any sum transferred to that account in respect of premiums on the new shares),

whichever is the less.

(4) The amount of the company's share premium account is reduced by a sum corresponding (or by sums in the aggregate corresponding) to the amount of any payment made under subsection (3).

(5) This section has effect subject to section 735(4) (terms of purchase enforceable in a winding up).

NOTES

Sub-ss (1)–(1B) were substituted (for the original sub-s (1)), and the words in the first (outer) pair of square brackets in sub-s (2) were substituted, by the Companies Act 2006 (Amendment of Part 18) Regulations 2013, SI 2013/999, reg 4, as from 30 April 2013.

Sub-s (1) was further substituted, the figure in square brackets in sub-s (1A) was substituted, and the words in the second (inner) pair of square brackets in sub-s (2) were substituted, by the Companies Act 2006 (Amendment of Part 18) Regulations 2015, SI 2015/532, regs 2, 3, as from 6 April 2015.

Authority for purchase of own shares

[1.776]

693 Authority for purchase of own shares

(1) A limited company may only purchase its own shares—

(a) by an off-market purchase, [authorised in accordance with section 693A or] in pursuance of a contract approved in advance in accordance with section 694;

(b) by a market purchase, authorised in accordance with section 701.

(2) A purchase is "off-market" if the shares either—

(a) are purchased otherwise than on a recognised investment exchange, or

(b) are purchased on a recognised investment exchange but are not subject to a marketing arrangement on the exchange.

(3) For this purpose a company's shares are subject to a marketing arrangement on a recognised investment exchange if—

- (a) they are listed under Part 6 of the Financial Services and Markets Act 2000 (c 8), or
- (b) the company has been afforded facilities for dealings in the shares to take place on the exchange—
  - (i) without prior permission for individual transactions from the authority governing that investment exchange, and
  - (ii) without limit as to the time during which those facilities are to be available.

(4) A purchase is a "market purchase" if it is made on a recognised investment exchange and is not an off-market purchase by virtue of subsection (2)(b).

(5) In this section "recognised investment exchange" means a recognised investment exchange (within the meaning of Part 18 of the Financial Services and Markets Act 2000) other than an overseas exchange (within the meaning of that Part).

NOTES

Sub-s (1): words in square brackets inserted by the Companies Act 2006 (Amendment of Part 18) Regulations 2013, SI 2013/999, reg 6, as from 30 April 2013.

[1.777]

[693A Authority for off-market purchase for the purposes of or pursuant to an employees' share scheme

(1) A company may make an off-market purchase of its own shares for the purposes of or pursuant to an employees' share scheme if the purchase has first been authorised by a resolution of the company under this section.

(2) That authority—

- (a) may be general or limited to the purchase of shares of a particular class or description, and
- (b) may be unconditional or subject to conditions.

(3) The authority must—

- (a) specify the maximum number of shares authorised to be acquired, and
- (b) determine both the maximum and minimum prices that may be paid for the shares.

(4) The authority may be varied, revoked or from time to time renewed by a resolution of the company.

(5) A resolution conferring, varying or renewing authority must specify a date on which it is to expire, which must not be later than five years after the date on which the resolution is passed.

(6) A company may make a purchase of its own shares after the expiry of the time limit specified if—

- (a) the contract of purchase was concluded before the authority expired, and
- (b) the terms of the authority permitted the company to make a contract of purchase that would or might be executed wholly or partly after its expiration.

(7) A resolution to confer or vary authority under this section may determine the maximum or minimum price for purchase by—

- (a) specifying a particular sum, or
- (b) providing a basis or formula for calculating the amount of the price (but without reference to any person's discretion or opinion).

(8) Chapter 3 of Part 3 (resolutions affecting a company's constitution) applies to a resolution under this section.]

NOTES

Inserted by the Companies Act 2006 (Amendment of Part 18) Regulations 2013, SI 2013/999, reg 7, as from 30 April 2013.

Authority for off-market purchase

[1.778]

694 Authority for off-market purchase

(1) [Subject to section 693A,] a company may only make an off-market purchase of its own shares in pursuance of a contract approved prior to the purchase in accordance with this section.

(2) Either—

- (a) the terms of the contract must be authorised by a . . . resolution of the company before the contract is entered into, or
- (b) the contract must provide that no shares may be purchased in pursuance of the contract until its terms have been authorised by a . . . resolution of the company.

(3) The contract may be a contract, entered into by the company and relating to shares in the company, that does not amount to a contract to purchase the shares but under which the company may (subject to any conditions) become entitled or obliged to purchase the shares.

(4) The authority conferred by a resolution under this section may be varied, revoked or from time to time renewed by a . . . resolution of the company.

(5) In the case of a public company a resolution conferring, varying or renewing authority must specify a date on which the authority is to expire, which must not be later than [five years] after the date on which the resolution is passed.

(6) A resolution conferring, varying, revoking or renewing authority under this section is subject to—

section 695 (exercise of voting rights), and
section 696 (disclosure of details of contract).

NOTES

Sub-s (1): words in square brackets inserted by the Companies Act 2006 (Amendment of Part 18) Regulations 2013, SI 2013/999, reg 8, as from 30 April 2013.

Sub-ss (2), (4): words omitted repealed by SI 2013/999, reg 5(a), as from 30 April 2013.

Sub-s (5): words in square brackets substituted by the Companies (Share Capital and Acquisition by Company of its Own Shares) Regulations 2009, SI 2009/2022, reg 4(1), as from 1 October 2009.

[1.779]

695 Resolution authorising off-market purchase: exercise of voting rights

(1) This section applies to a resolution to confer, vary, revoke or renew authority for the purposes of section 694 (authority for off-market purchase of own shares).

(2) Where the resolution is proposed as a written resolution, a member who holds shares to which the resolution relates is not an eligible member.

(3) Where the resolution is proposed at a meeting of the company, it is not effective if—

(a) any member of the company holding shares to which the resolution relates exercises the voting rights carried by any of those shares in voting on the resolution, and

(b) the resolution would not have been passed if he had not done so.

(4) For this purpose—

(a) a member who holds shares to which the resolution relates is regarded as exercising the voting rights carried by those shares not only if he votes in respect of them on a poll on the question whether the resolution shall be passed, but also if he votes on the resolution otherwise than on a poll;

(b) any member of the company may demand a poll on that question;

(c) a vote and a demand for a poll by a person as proxy for a member are the same respectively as a vote and a demand by the member.

[1.780]

696 Resolution authorising off-market purchase: disclosure of details of contract

(1) This section applies in relation to a resolution to confer, vary, revoke or renew authority for the purposes of section 694 (authority for off-market purchase of own shares).

(2) A copy of the contract (if it is in writing) or a memorandum setting out its terms (if it is not) must be made available to members—

(a) in the case of a written resolution, by being sent or submitted to every eligible member at or before the time at which the proposed resolution is sent or submitted to him;

(b) in the case of a resolution at a meeting, by being made available for inspection by members of the company both—

(i) at the company's registered office for not less than 15 days ending with the date of the meeting, and

(ii) at the meeting itself.

(3) A memorandum of contract terms so made available must include the names of the members holding shares to which the contract relates.

(4) A copy of the contract so made available must have annexed to it a written memorandum specifying such of those names as do not appear in the contract itself.

(5) The resolution is not validly passed if the requirements of this section are not complied with.

[1.781]

697 Variation of contract for off-market purchase

(1) A company may only agree to a variation of a contract authorised under section 694 (authority for off-market purchase) if the variation is approved in advance in accordance with this section.

(2) The terms of the variation must be authorised by a . . . resolution of the company before it is agreed to.

(3) That authority may be varied, revoked or from time to time renewed by a . . . resolution of the company.

(4) In the case of a public company a resolution conferring, varying or renewing authority must specify a date on which the authority is to expire, which must not be later than [five years] after the date on which the resolution is passed.

(5) A resolution conferring, varying, revoking or renewing authority under this section is subject to—

section 698 (exercise of voting rights), and

section 699 (disclosure of details of variation).

NOTES

Sub-ss (2), (3): words omitted repealed by the Companies Act 2006 (Amendment of Part 18) Regulations 2013, SI 2013/999, reg 5(b), as from 30 April 2013.

Sub-s (4): words in square brackets substituted by the Companies (Share Capital and Acquisition by Company of its Own Shares) Regulations 2009, SI 2009/2022, reg 4(1), as from 1 October 2009.

[1.782]

698 Resolution authorising variation: exercise of voting rights

(1) This section applies to a resolution to confer, vary, revoke or renew authority for the purposes of section 697 (variation of contract for off-market purchase of own shares).

(2) Where the resolution is proposed as a written resolution, a member who holds shares to which the resolution relates is not an eligible member.

(3) Where the resolution is proposed at a meeting of the company, it is not effective if—

(a) any member of the company holding shares to which the resolution relates exercises the voting rights carried by any of those shares in voting on the resolution, and

(b) the resolution would not have been passed if he had not done so.

(4) For this purpose—

(a) a member who holds shares to which the resolution relates is regarded as exercising the voting rights carried by those shares not only if he votes in respect of them on a poll on the question whether the resolution shall be passed, but also if he votes on the resolution otherwise than on a poll;

(b) any member of the company may demand a poll on that question;

(c) a vote and a demand for a poll by a person as proxy for a member are the same respectively as a vote and a demand by the member.

[1.783]

699 Resolution authorising variation: disclosure of details of variation

(1) This section applies in relation to a resolution under section 697 (variation of contract for off-market purchase of own shares).

(2) A copy of the proposed variation (if it is in writing) or a written memorandum giving details of the proposed variation (if it is not) must be made available to members—

- (a) in the case of a written resolution, by being sent or submitted to every eligible member at or before the time at which the proposed resolution is sent or submitted to him;
- (b) in the case of a resolution at a meeting, by being made available for inspection by members of the company both—
  - (i) at the company's registered office for not less than 15 days ending with the date of the meeting, and
  - (ii) at the meeting itself.

(3) There must also be made available as mentioned in subsection (2) a copy of the original contract or, as the case may be, a memorandum of its terms, together with any variations previously made.

(4) A memorandum of the proposed variation so made available must include the names of the members holding shares to which the variation relates.

(5) A copy of the proposed variation so made available must have annexed to it a written memorandum specifying such of those names as do not appear in the variation itself.

(6) The resolution is not validly passed if the requirements of this section are not complied with.

[1.784]

700 Release of company's rights under contract for off-market purchase

(1) An agreement by a company to release its rights under a contract approved under section 694 (authorisation of off-market purchase) is void unless the terms of the release agreement are approved in advance in accordance with this section.

(2) The terms of the proposed agreement must be authorised by a . . . resolution of the company before the agreement is entered into.

(3) That authority may be varied, revoked or from time to time renewed by a . . . resolution of the company.

(4) In the case of a public company a resolution conferring, varying or renewing authority must specify a date on which the authority is to expire, which must not be later than [five years] after the date on which the resolution is passed.

(5) The provisions of—

section 698 (exercise of voting rights), and

section 699 (disclosure of details of variation),

apply to a resolution authorising a proposed release agreement as they apply to a resolution authorising a proposed variation.

NOTES

Sub-ss (2), (3): words omitted repealed by the Companies Act 2006 (Amendment of Part 18) Regulations 2013, SI 2013/999, reg 5(c), as from 30 April 2013.

Sub-s (4): words in square brackets substituted by the Companies (Share Capital and Acquisition by Company of its Own Shares) Regulations 2009, SI 2009/2022, reg 4(1), as from 1 October 2009.

Authority for market purchase

[1.785]

701 Authority for market purchase

(1) A company may only make a market purchase of its own shares if the purchase has first been authorised by a resolution of the company.

(2) That authority—

- (a) may be general or limited to the purchase of shares of a particular class or description, and
- (b) may be unconditional or subject to conditions.

(3) The authority must—

- (a) specify the maximum number of shares authorised to be acquired, and
- (b) determine both the maximum and minimum prices that may be paid for the shares.

(4) The authority may be varied, revoked or from time to time renewed by a resolution of the company.

(5) A resolution conferring, varying or renewing authority must specify a date on which it is to expire, which must not be later than [five years] after the date on which the resolution is passed.

(6) A company may make a purchase of its own shares after the expiry of the time limit specified if—

- (a) the contract of purchase was concluded before the authority expired, and
- (b) the terms of the authority permitted the company to make a contract of purchase that would or might be executed wholly or partly after its expiration.

(7) A resolution to confer or vary authority under this section may determine either or both the maximum and minimum price for purchase by—

- (a) specifying a particular sum, or
- (b) providing a basis or formula for calculating the amount of the price (but without reference to any person's discretion or opinion).

(8) Chapter 3 of Part 3 (resolutions affecting a company's constitution) applies to a resolution under this section.

NOTES

Sub-s (5): words in square brackets substituted by the Companies (Share Capital and Acquisition by Company of its Own Shares) Regulations 2009, SI 2009/2022, reg 4(2), as from 1 October 2009.

[1.786]

702 Copy of contract or memorandum to be available for inspection

(1) This section applies where a company has entered into—

(a) a contract approved under section 694 (authorisation of contract for off-market purchase), or

(b) a contract for a purchase authorised under section 701 (authorisation of market purchase).

(2) The company must keep available for inspection—

(a) a copy of the contract, or

(b) if the contract is not in writing, a written memorandum setting out its terms.

(3) The copy or memorandum must be kept available for inspection from the conclusion of the contract until the end of the period of ten years beginning with—

(a) the date on which the purchase of all the shares in pursuance of the contract is completed, or

(b) the date on which the contract otherwise determines.

(4) The copy or memorandum must be kept available for inspection—

(a) at the company's registered office, or

(b) at a place specified in regulations under section 1136.

(5) The company must give notice to the registrar—

(a) of the place at which the copy or memorandum is kept available for inspection, and

(b) of any change in that place,

unless it has at all times been kept at the company's registered office.

(6) Every copy or memorandum required to be kept under this section must be kept open to inspection without charge—

(a) by any member of the company, and

(b) in the case of a public company, by any other person.

(7) The provisions of this section apply to a variation of a contract as they apply to the original contract.

[1.787]

703 Enforcement of right to inspect copy or memorandum

(1) If default is made in complying with section 702(2), (3) or (4) or default is made for 14 days in complying with section 702(5), or an inspection required under section 702(6) is refused, an offence is committed by—

(a) the company, and

(b) every officer of the company who is in default.

(2) A person guilty of an offence under this section is liable on summary conviction to a fine not exceeding level 3 on the standard scale and, for continued contravention, a daily default fine not exceeding one-tenth of level 3 on the standard scale.

(3) In the case of refusal of an inspection required under section 702(6) the court may by order compel an immediate inspection.

[1.788]

704 No assignment of company's right to purchase own shares

The rights of a company under a contract authorised under—

[(za) section 693A (authority for off-market purchase for the purposes of or pursuant to an employees' share scheme),]

(a) section 694 (authority for off-market purchase), or

(b) section 701 (authority for market purchase)

are not capable of being assigned.

NOTES

Para (za) inserted by the Companies Act 2006 (Amendment of Part 18) Regulations 2013, SI 2013/999, reg 9, as from 30 April 2013.

[1.789]

705 Payments apart from purchase price to be made out of distributable profits

(1) A payment made by a company in consideration of—

(a) acquiring any right with respect to the purchase of its own shares in pursuance of a contingent purchase contract approved under section 694 (authorisation of off-market purchase),

(b) the variation of any contract approved under that section, or

(c) the release of any of the company's obligations with respect to the purchase of any of its own shares under a contract—

(i) approved under section 694, or

(ii) authorised under section 701 (authorisation of market purchase),

must be made out of the company's distributable profits.

(2) If this requirement is not met in relation to a contract, then—

(a) in a case within subsection (1)(a), no purchase by the company of its own shares in pursuance of that contract may be made under this Chapter;

(b) in a case within subsection (1)(b), no such purchase following the variation may be made under this Chapter;

(c) in a case within subsection (1)(c), the purported release is void.

[1.790]

706 Treatment of shares purchased

Where a limited company makes a purchase of its own shares in accordance with this Chapter, then—

(a) if section 724 (treasury shares) applies, the shares may be held and dealt with in accordance with Chapter 6;

(b) if that section does not apply—

(i) the shares are treated as cancelled, and

(ii) the amount of the company's issued share capital is diminished accordingly by the nominal value of the shares cancelled.

[1.791]

707 Return to registrar of purchase of own shares

(1) Where a company purchases shares under this Chapter, it must deliver a return to the registrar within the period of 28 days beginning with the date on which the shares are delivered to it.

(2) The return must distinguish—

(a) shares in relation to which section 724 (treasury shares) applies and shares in relation to which that section does not apply, and

(b) shares in relation to which that section applies—

(i) that are cancelled forthwith (under section 729 (cancellation of treasury shares)), and

(ii) that are not so cancelled.

(3) The return must state, with respect to shares of each class purchased—

(a) the number and nominal value of the shares, and

(b) the date on which they were delivered to the company.

(4) In the case of a public company the return must also state—

(a) the aggregate amount paid by the company for the shares, and

(b) the maximum and minimum prices paid in respect of shares of each class purchased.

(5) Particulars of shares delivered to the company on different dates and under different contracts may be included in a single return.

In such a case the amount required to be stated under subsection (4)(a) is the aggregate amount paid by the company for all the shares to which the return relates.

(6) If default is made in complying with this section an offence is committed by every officer of the company who is in default.

(7) A person guilty of an offence under this section is liable—

(a) on conviction on indictment, to a fine;

(b) on summary conviction to a fine not exceeding the statutory maximum and, for continued contravention, a daily default fine not exceeding [one-tenth of the greater of £5,000 or the amount corresponding to level 4 on the standard scale for summary offences].

NOTES

Sub-s (7): words in square brackets substituted (for the original words "one-tenth of the statutory maximum") by the Legal Aid, Sentencing and Punishment of Offenders Act 2012 (Fines on Summary Conviction) Regulations 2015, SI 2015/664, regs 3, 5, Sch 3, Pt 1, para 9(1), (17), as from 12 March 2015, in relation to England and Wales only (except in relation to (a) fines for offences committed before 12 March 2015, (b) the operation of restrictions on fines that may be imposed on a person aged under 18, or (c) fines that may be imposed on a person convicted by a magistrates' court who is to be sentenced as if convicted on indictment).

[1.792]

708 Notice to registrar of cancellation of shares

(1) If on the purchase by a company of any of its own shares in accordance with this Part—

(a) section 724 (treasury shares) does not apply (so that the shares are treated as cancelled), or

(b) that section applies but the shares are cancelled forthwith (under section 729 (cancellation of treasury shares)),

the company must give notice of cancellation to the registrar, within the period of 28 days beginning with the date on which the shares are delivered to it, specifying the shares cancelled.

(2) The notice must be accompanied by a statement of capital[, except where the statement of capital would be the same as a statement of capital that is required to be delivered to the registrar under section 720B(1)].

(3) The statement of capital must state with respect to the company's share capital immediately following the cancellation—

(a) the total number of shares of the company,

(b) the aggregate nominal value of those shares,

[(ba) the aggregate amount (if any) unpaid on those shares (whether on account of their nominal value or by way of premium), and]

(c) for each class of shares—

(i) prescribed particulars of the rights attached to the shares,

(ii) the total number of shares of that class, and

(iii) the aggregate nominal value of shares of that class, . . .

(d) . . .

(4) If default is made in complying with this section, an offence is committed by—

(a) the company, and

(b) every officer of the company who is in default.

(5) A person guilty of an offence under this section is liable on summary conviction to a fine not exceeding level 3 on the standard scale and, for continued contravention, a daily default fine not exceeding one-tenth of level 3 on the standard scale.

NOTES

Sub-s (2): words in square brackets inserted by the Companies Act 2006 (Amendment of Part 18) Regulations 2015, SI 2015/532, regs 2, 4, as from 6 April 2015.

Sub-s (3): para (ba) inserted, and para (d) and the preceding word repealed, by the Small Business, Enterprise and Employment Act 2015, s 97, Sch 6, paras 1, 14, as from 30 June 2016.

Orders: the Companies (Shares and Share Capital) Order 2009, SI 2009/388 at **[4.211]**. For a summary of all statutory instruments made under this Act, see Appendix 4 at **[A4]**.

CHAPTER 5 REDEMPTION OR PURCHASE BY PRIVATE COMPANY OUT OF CAPITAL

Introductory

[1.793]

709 Power of private limited company to redeem or purchase own shares out of capital

(1) A private limited company may in accordance with this Chapter, but subject to any restriction or prohibition in the company's articles, make a payment in respect of the redemption or purchase of its own shares otherwise than out of distributable profits or the proceeds of a fresh issue of shares.

(2) References below in this Chapter to payment out of capital are to any payment so made, whether or not it would be regarded apart from this section as a payment out of capital.

[(3) This Chapter is subject to section 692(1ZA) (purchase of own shares up to annual limit).]

NOTES

Sub-s (3): added by the Companies Act 2006 (Amendment of Part 18) Regulations 2015, SI 2015/532, regs 2, 5, as from 6 April 2015.

The permissible capital payment

[1.794]

710 The permissible capital payment

(1) The payment that may, in accordance with this Chapter, be made by a company out of capital in respect of the redemption or purchase of its own shares is such amount as, after applying for that purpose—

(a) any available profits of the company, and

(b) the proceeds of any fresh issue of shares made for the purposes of the redemption or purchase,

is required to meet the price of redemption or purchase.

(2) That is referred to below in this Chapter as "the permissible capital payment" for the shares.

[1.795]

711 Available profits

(1) For the purposes of this Chapter the available profits of the company, in relation to the redemption or purchase of any shares, are the profits of the company that are available for distribution (within the meaning of Part 23).

(2) But the question whether a company has any profits so available, and the amount of any such profits, shall be determined in accordance with section 712 instead of in accordance with sections 836 to 842 in that Part.

[1.796]

712 Determination of available profits

(1) The available profits of the company are determined as follows.

(2) First, determine the profits of the company by reference to the following items as stated in the relevant accounts—

(a) profits, losses, assets and liabilities,

(b) provisions of the following kinds—

(i) where the relevant accounts are Companies Act accounts, provisions of a kind specified for the purposes of this subsection by regulations under section 396;

(ii) where the relevant accounts are IAS accounts, provisions of any kind;

(c) share capital and reserves (including undistributable reserves).

(3) Second, reduce the amount so determined by the amount of—

(a) any distribution lawfully made by the company, and

(b) any other relevant payment lawfully made by the company out of distributable profits,

after the date of the relevant accounts and before the end of the relevant period.

(4) For this purpose "other relevant payment lawfully made" includes—

(a) financial assistance lawfully given out of distributable profits in accordance with Chapter 2,

(b) payments lawfully made out of distributable profits in respect of the purchase by the company of any shares in the company, and

(c) payments of any description specified in section 705 (payments other than purchase price to be made out of distributable profits) lawfully made by the company.

(5) The resulting figure is the amount of available profits.

(6) For the purposes of this section "the relevant accounts" are any accounts that—

(a) are prepared as at a date within the relevant period, and

(b) are such as to enable a reasonable judgment to be made as to the amounts of the items mentioned in subsection (2).

(7) In this section "the relevant period" means the period of three months ending with the date on which [the solvency statement is made in accordance with section 720A or] the directors' statement is made in accordance with section 714.

NOTES

Sub-s (7): words in square brackets inserted by the Companies Act 2006 (Amendment of Part 18) Regulations 2013, SI 2013/999, reg 10, as from 30 April 2013.

Regulations under section 396: see the notes to that section at **[1.451]**. See also the Small Companies and Groups (Accounts and Directors' Report) Regulations 2008, SI 2008/409, reg 12 (at **[4.49]**), and the Large and Medium-sized Companies and Groups (Accounts and Reports) Regulations 2008, SI 2008/410, reg 12 (at **[4.71]**) which provide that Sch 7 to SI 2008/409 (at **[4.57]**, **[4.58]**) and Sch 9 to SI 2008/410 (at **[4.112]**, **[4.113]**) define "provisions" for the purpose of those Regulations and for the purposes of sub-s (2)(b)(i) above.

[1.797]

713 Requirements for payment out of capital

(1) A payment out of capital by a private company for the redemption or purchase of its own shares is not lawful unless the requirements of the following sections are met—

section 714 (directors' statement and auditor's report);
section 716 (approval by special resolution);
section 719 (public notice of proposed payment);
section 720 (directors' statement and auditor's report to be available for inspection).

(2) This is subject [to section 720A and] to any order of the court under section 721 (power of court to extend period for compliance on application by persons objecting to payment).

NOTES

Sub-s (2): words in square brackets inserted by the Companies Act 2006 (Amendment of Part 18) Regulations 2013, SI 2013/999, reg 11, as from 30 April 2013.

[1.798]

714 Directors' statement and auditor's report

(1) The company's directors must make a statement in accordance with this section.
(2) The statement must specify the amount of the permissible capital payment for the shares in question.
(3) It must state that, having made full inquiry into the affairs and prospects of the company, the directors have formed the opinion—

- (a) as regards its initial situation immediately following the date on which the payment out of capital is proposed to be made, that there will be no grounds on which the company could then be found unable to pay its debts, and
- (b) as regards its prospects for the year immediately following that date, that having regard to—
  - (i) their intentions with respect to the management of the company's business during that year, and
  - (ii) the amount and character of the financial resources that will in their view be available to the company during that year,

  the company will be able to continue to carry on business as a going concern (and will accordingly be able to pay its debts as they fall due) throughout that year.

(4) In forming their opinion for the purposes of subsection (3)(a), the directors must take into account all of the company's liabilities (including any contingent or prospective liabilities).
(5) The directors' statement must be in the prescribed form and must contain such information with respect to the nature of the company's business as may be prescribed.
(6) It must in addition have annexed to it a report addressed to the directors by the company's auditor stating that—

- (a) he has inquired into the company's state of affairs,
- (b) the amount specified in the statement as the permissible capital payment for the shares in question is in his view properly determined in accordance with sections 710 to 712, and
- (c) he is not aware of anything to indicate that the opinion expressed by the directors in their statement as to any of the matters mentioned in subsection (3) above is unreasonable in all the circumstances.

NOTES

Orders: the Companies (Shares and Share Capital) Order 2009, SI 2009/388 at **[4.211]**. For a summary of all statutory instruments made under this Act, see Appendix 4 at **[A4]**.

[1.799]

715 Directors' statement: offence if no reasonable grounds for opinion

(1) If the directors make a statement under section 714 without having reasonable grounds for the opinion expressed in it, an offence is committed by every director who is in default.
(2) A person guilty of an offence under this section is liable—

- (a) on conviction on indictment, to imprisonment for a term not exceeding two years or a fine (or both);
- (b) on summary conviction—
  - (i) in England and Wales, to imprisonment for a term not exceeding twelve months or a fine not exceeding the statutory maximum (or both);
  - (ii) in Scotland or Northern Ireland, to imprisonment for a term not exceeding six months or a fine not exceeding the statutory maximum (or both).

NOTES

Offences under this section: see further s 1131 at **[1.1301]**.

[1.800]

716 Payment to be approved by special resolution

(1) The payment out of capital must be approved by a special resolution of the company.
(2) The resolution must be passed on, or within the week immediately following, the date on which the directors make the statement required by section 714.
(3) A resolution under this section is subject to—

section 717 (exercise of voting rights), and
section 718 (disclosure of directors' statement and auditors' report).

[1.801]

717 Resolution authorising payment: exercise of voting rights

(1) This section applies to a resolution under section 716 (authority for payment out of capital for redemption or purchase of own shares).

(2) Where the resolution is proposed as a written resolution, a member who holds shares to which the resolution relates is not an eligible member.

(3) Where the resolution is proposed at a meeting of the company, it is not effective if—

(a) any member of the company holding shares to which the resolution relates exercises the voting rights carried by any of those shares in voting on the resolution, and

(b) the resolution would not have been passed if he had not done so.

(4) For this purpose—

(a) a member who holds shares to which the resolution relates is regarded as exercising the voting rights carried by those shares not only if he votes in respect of them on a poll on the question whether the resolution shall be passed, but also if he votes on the resolution otherwise than on a poll;

(b) any member of the company may demand a poll on that question;

(c) a vote and a demand for a poll by a person as proxy for a member are the same respectively as a vote and a demand by the member.

[1.802]

718 Resolution authorising payment: disclosure of directors' statement and auditor's report

(1) This section applies to a resolution under section 716 (resolution authorising payment out of capital for redemption or purchase of own shares).

(2) A copy of the directors' statement and auditor's report under section 714 must be made available to members—

(a) in the case of a written resolution, by being sent or submitted to every eligible member at or before the time at which the proposed resolution is sent or submitted to him;

(b) in the case of a resolution at a meeting, by being made available for inspection by members of the company at the meeting.

(3) The resolution is ineffective if this requirement is not complied with.

[1.803]

719 Public notice of proposed payment

(1) Within the week immediately following the date of the resolution under section 716 the company must cause to be published in the Gazette a notice—

(a) stating that the company has approved a payment out of capital for the purpose of acquiring its own shares by redemption or purchase or both (as the case may be),

(b) specifying—

(i) the amount of the permissible capital payment for the shares in question, and

(ii) the date of the resolution,

(c) stating where the directors' statement and auditor's report required by section 714 are available for inspection, and

(d) stating that any creditor of the company may at any time within the five weeks immediately following the date of the resolution apply to the court under section 721 for an order preventing the payment.

(2) Within the week immediately following the date of the resolution the company must also either—

(a) cause a notice to the same effect as that required by subsection (1) to be published in an appropriate national newspaper, or

(b) give notice in writing to that effect to each of its creditors.

(3) "An appropriate national newspaper" means a newspaper circulating throughout the part of the United Kingdom in which the company is registered.

(4) Not later than the day on which the company—

(a) first publishes the notice required by subsection (1), or

(b) if earlier, first publishes or gives the notice required by subsection (2),

the company must deliver to the registrar a copy of the directors' statement and auditor's report required by section 714.

[1.804]

720 Directors' statement and auditor's report to be available for inspection

(1) The directors' statement and auditor's report must be kept available for inspection throughout the period—

(a) beginning with the day on which the company—

(i) first publishes the notice required by section 719(1), or

(ii) if earlier, first publishes or gives the notice required by section 719(2), and

(b) ending five weeks after the date of the resolution for payment out of capital.

(2) They must be kept available for inspection—

(a) at the company's registered office, or

(b) at a place specified in regulations under section 1136.

(3) The company must give notice to the registrar—

(a) of the place at which the statement and report are kept available for inspection, and

(b) of any change in that place,

unless they have at all times been kept at the company's registered office.

(4) They must be open to the inspection of any member or creditor of the company without charge.

(5) If default is made for 14 days in complying with subsection (3), or an inspection under subsection (4) is refused, an offence is committed by—

(a) the company, and

(b) every officer of the company who is in default.

(6) A person guilty of an offence under this section is liable on summary conviction to a fine not exceeding level 3 on the standard scale and, for continued contravention, a daily default fine not exceeding one-tenth of level 3 on the standard scale.

(7) In the case of a refusal of an inspection required by subsection (4), the court may by order compel an immediate inspection.

[Requirements for payment out of capital: employees' share schemes

[1.805]

720A Reduced requirements for payment out of capital for purchase of own shares for the purposes of or pursuant to an employees' share scheme

(1) Section 713(1) does not apply to the purchase out of capital by a private company of its own shares for the purposes of or pursuant to an employees' share scheme when approved by special resolution supported by a solvency statement.

(2) For the purposes of this section a resolution is supported by a solvency statement if—

(a) the directors of the company make a solvency statement (see section 643) not more than 15 days before the date on which the resolution is passed, and

(b) the resolution and solvency statement are registered in accordance with section 720B.

(3) Where the resolution is proposed as a written resolution, a copy of the solvency statement must be sent or submitted to every eligible member at or before the time at which the proposed resolution is sent or submitted to the member.

(4) Where the resolution is proposed at a general meeting, a copy of the solvency statement must be made available for inspection by members of the company throughout that meeting.

(5) The validity of a resolution is not affected by a failure to comply with subsection (3) or (4).

(6) Section 717 (resolution authorising payment: exercise of voting rights) applies to a resolution under this section as it applies to a resolution under section 716.]

NOTES

Inserted, together with the preceding heading and s 720B, by the Companies Act 2006 (Amendment of Part 18) Regulations 2013, SI 2013/999, reg 12, as from 30 April 2013.

[1.806]

[720B Registration of resolution and supporting documents for purchase of own shares for the purposes of or pursuant to an employees' share scheme

(1) Within 15 days after the passing of the resolution for a payment out of capital by a private company for the purchase of its own shares for the purposes of or pursuant to an employees' share scheme the company must deliver to the registrar—

(a) a copy of the solvency statement,

(b) a copy of the resolution, and

(c) a statement of capital.

(2) The statement of capital must state with respect to the company's share capital as reduced by the resolution—

(a) the total number of shares of the company,

(b) the aggregate nominal value of those shares,

[(ba) the aggregate amount (if any) unpaid on those shares (whether on account of their nominal value or by way of premium), and]

(c) for each class of shares—

(i) prescribed particulars of the rights attached to the shares,

(ii) the total number of shares of that class, and

(iii) the aggregate nominal value of shares of that class, . . .

(d) . . .

(3) The registrar must register the documents delivered to him under subsection (1) on receipt.

(4) The resolution does not take effect until those documents are registered.

(5) The company must also deliver to the registrar, within 15 days after the resolution is passed, a statement by the directors confirming that the solvency statement was—

(a) made not more than 15 days before the date on which the resolution was passed, and

(b) provided to members in accordance with section 720A(3) or (4).

(6) The validity of a resolution is not affected by—

(a) a failure to deliver the documents required to be delivered to the registrar under subsection (1) within the time specified in that subsection, or

(b) a failure to comply with subsection (5).

(7) If the company delivers to the registrar a solvency statement that was not provided to members in accordance with section 720A(3) or (4), an offence is committed by every officer of the company who is in default.

(8) If default is made in complying with this section, an offence is committed by—

(a) the company, and

(b) every officer of the company who is in default.

(9) A person guilty of an offence under subsection (7) or (8) is liable—

(a) on conviction on indictment, to a fine;

(b) on summary conviction, to a fine not exceeding the statutory maximum.]

NOTES

Inserted as noted to s 720A at **[1.805]**.

Sub-s (2): para (ba) inserted, and para (d) and the preceding word repealed, by the Small Business, Enterprise and Employment Act 2015, s 97, Sch 6, paras 1, 15, as from 30 June 2016.

Objection to payment by members or creditors

[1.807]

721 Application to court to cancel resolution

(1) Where a private company passes a special resolution approving a payment out of capital for the redemption or purchase of any of its shares—

(a) any member of the company (other than one who consented to or voted in favour of the resolution), and

(b) any creditor of the company,

may apply to the court for the cancellation of the resolution.

(2) The application—

(a) must be made within five weeks after the passing of the resolution, and

(b) may be made on behalf of the persons entitled to make it by such one or more of their number as they may appoint in writing for the purpose.

(3) On an application under this section the court may if it thinks fit—

(a) adjourn the proceedings in order that an arrangement may be made to the satisfaction of the court—

(i) for the purchase of the interests of dissentient members, or

(ii) for the protection of dissentient creditors, and

(b) give such directions and make such orders as it thinks expedient for facilitating or carrying into effect any such arrangement.

(4) Subject to that, the court must make an order either cancelling or confirming the resolution, and may do so on such terms and conditions as it thinks fit.

(5) If the court confirms the resolution, it may by order alter or extend any date or period of time specified—

(a) in the resolution, or

(b) in any provision of this Chapter applying to the redemption or purchase to which the resolution relates.

(6) The court's order may, if the court thinks fit—

(a) provide for the purchase by the company of the shares of any of its members and for the reduction accordingly of the company's capital, and

(b) make any alteration in the company's articles that may be required in consequence of that provision.

(7) The court's order may, if the court thinks fit, require the company not to make any, or any specified, amendments of its articles without the leave of the court.

[1.808]

722 Notice to registrar of court application or order

(1) On making an application under section 721 (application to court to cancel resolution) the applicants, or the person making the application on their behalf, must immediately give notice to the registrar.

This is without prejudice to any provision of rules of court as to service of notice of the application.

(2) On being served with notice of any such application, the company must immediately give notice to the registrar.

(3) Within 15 days of the making of the court's order on the application, or such longer period as the court may at any time direct, the company must deliver to the registrar a copy of the order.

(4) If a company fails to comply with subsection (2) or (3) an offence is committed by—

(a) the company, and

(b) every officer of the company who is in default.

(5) A person guilty of an offence under this section is liable on summary conviction to a fine not exceeding level 3 on the standard scale and, for continued contravention, a daily default fine not exceeding one-tenth of level 3 on the standard scale.

Supplementary provisions

[1.809]

723 [Time when payment out of capital to be made or shares to be surrendered]

(1) The payment out of capital[, if made in accordance with a resolution under section 716] must be made—

(a) no earlier than five weeks after the date on which the resolution under section 716 is passed, and

(b) no more than seven weeks after that date.

[(1A) Shares to be purchased in accordance with a resolution under section 720A must be surrendered—

(a) no earlier than five weeks after the date on which the resolution under section 720A is passed, and

(b) no later than seven weeks after that date.]

(2) This is subject to any exercise of the court's powers under section 721(5) (power to alter or extend time where resolution confirmed after objection).

NOTES

The section heading was substituted by the Companies Act 2006 (Amendment of Part 18) Regulations 2015, SI 2015/532, regs 2, 6(a), as from 6 April 2015.

Words in square brackets in sub-s (1) inserted, and sub-s (1A) originally inserted, by the Companies Act 2006 (Amendment of Part 18) Regulations 2013, SI 2013/999, reg 13, as from 30 April 2013.

Sub-s (1A) was subsequently substituted by SI 2015/532, regs 2, 6(b), as from 6 April 2015.

CHAPTER 6 TREASURY SHARES

[1.810]

724 Treasury shares

[(1) This section applies where—

(a) a limited company makes a purchase of its own shares in accordance with Chapter 4, and

[(b) the purchase is made out of distributable profits].

(2) . . .

(3) Where this section applies the company may—

(a) hold the shares (or any of them), or

(b) deal with any of them, at any time, in accordance with section 727 or 729.

(4) Where shares are held by the company, the company must be entered in its register of members [(or, as the case may be, the company's name must be delivered to the registrar under Chapter 2A of Part 8)] as the member holding the shares.

(5) In the Companies Acts references to a company holding shares as treasury shares are to the company holding shares that—

(a) were (or are treated as having been) purchased by it in circumstances in which this section applies, and

(b) have been held by the company continuously since they were so purchased (or treated as purchased).

NOTES

Sub-s (1) substituted, and sub-s (2) repealed, by the Companies Act 2006 (Amendment of Part 18) Regulations 2013, SI 2013/999, reg 14, as from 30 April 2013.

Sub-s (1)(b) was further substituted by the Companies Act 2006 (Amendment of Part 18) Regulations 2015, SI 2015/532, regs 2, 7, as from 6 April 2015.

The words in square brackets in sub-s (4) were inserted by the Small Business, Enterprise and Employment Act 2015, s 94, Sch 5, Pt 2, paras 11, 25, as from 30 June 2016.

725 *(S 725 (Treasury shares: maximum holdings) was repealed by the Companies (Share Capital and Acquisition by Company of its Own Shares) Regulations 2009, SI 2009/2022, reg 5(1), as from 1 October 2009, subject to transitional provisions in paras (2), (3) of that regulation. Those transitional provisions are now regarded as spent.)*

[1.811]

726 Treasury shares: exercise of rights

(1) This section applies where shares are held by a company as treasury shares.

(2) The company must not exercise any right in respect of the treasury shares, and any purported exercise of such a right is void.

This applies, in particular, to any right to attend or vote at meetings.

(3) No dividend may be paid, and no other distribution (whether in cash or otherwise) of the company's assets (including any distribution of assets to members on a winding up) may be made to the company, in respect of the treasury shares.

(4) Nothing in this section prevents—

(a) an allotment of shares as fully paid bonus shares in respect of the treasury shares, or

(b) the payment of any amount payable on the redemption of the treasury shares (if they are redeemable shares).

(5) Shares allotted as fully paid bonus shares in respect of the treasury shares are treated as if purchased by the company, at the time they were allotted, in circumstances in which section 724(1) (treasury shares) applied.

[1.812]

727 Treasury shares: disposal

(1) Where shares are held as treasury shares, the company may at any time—

(a) sell the shares (or any of them) for a cash consideration, or

(b) transfer the shares (or any of them) for the purposes of or pursuant to an employees' share scheme.

(2) In subsection (1)(a) "cash consideration" means—

(a) cash received by the company, or

(b) a cheque received by the company in good faith that the directors have no reason for suspecting will not be paid, or

(c) a release of a liability of the company for a liquidated sum, or

(d) an undertaking to pay cash to the company on or before a date not more than 90 days after the date on which the company agrees to sell the shares, or

(e) payment by any other means giving rise to a present or future entitlement (of the company or a person acting on the company's behalf) to a payment, or credit equivalent to payment, in cash.

For this purpose "cash" includes foreign currency.

(3) The Secretary of State may by order provide that particular means of payment specified in the order are to be regarded as falling within subsection (2)(e).

(4) If the company receives a notice under section 979 (takeover offers: right of offeror to buy out minority shareholders) that a person desires to acquire shares held by the company as treasury shares, the company must not sell or transfer the shares to which the notice relates except to that person.

(5) An order under this section is subject to negative resolution procedure.

NOTES

Orders: the Companies (Shares and Share Capital) Order 2009, SI 2009/388 at **[4.211]**. For a summary of all statutory instruments made under this Act, see Appendix 4 at **[A4]**.

[1.813]

728 Treasury shares: notice of disposal

(1) Where shares held by a company as treasury shares—

(a) are sold, or

(b) are transferred for the purposes of an employees' share scheme,

the company must deliver a return to the registrar not later than 28 days after the shares are disposed of.

(2) The return must state with respect to shares of each class disposed of—

(a) the number and nominal value of the shares, and

(b) the date on which they were disposed of.

(3) Particulars of shares disposed of on different dates may be included in a single return.

(4) If default is made in complying with this section an offence is committed by every officer of the company who is in default.

(5) A person guilty of an offence under this section is liable—

(a) on conviction on indictment, to a fine;

(b) on summary conviction, to a fine not exceeding the statutory maximum and, for continued contravention, a daily default fine not exceeding [one-tenth of the greater of £5,000 or the amount corresponding to level 4 on the standard scale for summary offences].

NOTES

Sub-s (5): words in square brackets substituted (for the original words "one-tenth of the statutory maximum") by the Legal Aid, Sentencing and Punishment of Offenders Act 2012 (Fines on Summary Conviction) Regulations 2015, SI 2015/664, regs 3, 5, Sch 3, Pt 1, para 9(1), (18), as from 12 March 2015, in relation to England and Wales only (except in relation to (a) fines for offences committed before 12 March 2015, (b) the operation of restrictions on fines that may be imposed on a person aged under 18, or (c) fines that may be imposed on a person convicted by a magistrates' court who is to be sentenced as if convicted on indictment).

[1.814]

729 Treasury shares: cancellation

(1) Where shares are held as treasury shares, the company may at any time cancel the shares (or any of them).

(2), (3) . . .

(4) If company cancels shares held as treasury shares, the amount of the company's share capital is reduced accordingly by the nominal amount of the shares cancelled.

(5) The directors may take any steps required to enable the company to cancel its shares under this section without complying with the provisions of Chapter 10 of Part 17 (reduction of share capital).

NOTES

Sub-ss (2), (3): repealed by the Companies Act 2006 (Amendment of Part 18) Regulations 2013, SI 2013/999, reg 15, as from 30 April 2013.

[1.815]

730 Treasury shares: notice of cancellation

(1) Where shares held by a company as treasury shares are cancelled, the company must deliver a return to the registrar not later than 28 days after the shares are cancelled.

This does not apply to shares that are cancelled forthwith on their acquisition by the company (see section 708).

(2) The return must state with respect to shares of each class cancelled—

(a) the number and nominal value of the shares, and

(b) the date on which they were cancelled.

(3) Particulars of shares cancelled on different dates may be included in a single return.

(4) The notice must be accompanied by a statement of capital.

(5) The statement of capital must state with respect to the company's share capital immediately following the cancellation—

(a) the total number of shares of the company,

(b) the aggregate nominal value of those shares,

[(ba) the aggregate amount (if any) unpaid on those shares (whether on account of their nominal value or by way of premium), and]

(c) for each class of shares—

(i) prescribed particulars of the rights attached to the shares,

(ii) the total number of shares of that class, and

(iii) the aggregate nominal value of shares of that class, . . .

(d) . . .

(6) If default is made in complying with this section, an offence is committed by—

(a) the company, and

(b) every officer of the company who is in default.

(7) A person guilty of an offence under this section is liable on summary conviction to a fine not exceeding level 3 on the standard scale and, for continued contravention, a daily default fine not exceeding one-tenth of level 3 on the standard scale.

NOTES

Sub-s (5): para (ba) inserted, and para (d) and the preceding word repealed, by the Small Business, Enterprise and Employment Act 2015, s 97, Sch 6, paras 1, 16, as from 30 June 2016.

Orders: the Companies (Shares and Share Capital) Order 2009, SI 2009/388 at **[4.211]**. For a summary of all statutory instruments made under this Act, see Appendix 4 at **[A4]**.

[1.816]

731 Treasury shares: treatment of proceeds of sale

(1) Where shares held as treasury shares are sold, the proceeds of sale must be dealt with in accordance with this section.

(2) If the proceeds of sale are equal to or less than the purchase price paid by the company for the shares, the proceeds are treated for the purposes of Part 23 (distributions) as a realised profit of the company.

(3) If the proceeds of sale exceed the purchase price paid by the company—

(a) an amount equal to the purchase price paid is treated as a realised profit of the company for the purposes of that Part, and

(b) the excess must be transferred to the company's share premium account.

(4) For the purposes of this section—

(a) the purchase price paid by the company must be determined by the application of a weighted average price method, and

(b) if the shares were allotted to the company as fully paid bonus shares, the purchase price paid for them is treated as nil.

[1.817]

732 Treasury shares: offences

(1) If a company contravenes any of the provisions of this Chapter (except section 730 (notice of cancellation)), an offence is committed by—

(a) the company, and

(b) every officer of the company who is in default.

(2) A person guilty of an offence under this section is liable—

(a) on conviction on indictment, to a fine;

(b) on summary conviction to a fine not exceeding the statutory maximum.

CHAPTER 7 SUPPLEMENTARY PROVISIONS

[1.818]

733 The capital redemption reserve

(1) In the following circumstances a company must transfer amounts to a reserve, called the "capital redemption reserve".

(2) Where under this Part shares of a limited company are redeemed or purchased wholly out of the company's profits, the amount by which the company's issued share capital is diminished in accordance with—

(a) section 688(b) (on the cancellation of shares redeemed), or

(b) section 706(b)(ii) (on the cancellation of shares purchased),

must be transferred to the capital redemption reserve.

(3) If—

(a) the shares are redeemed or purchased wholly or partly out of the proceeds of a fresh issue, and

(b) the aggregate amount of the proceeds is less than the aggregate nominal value of the shares redeemed or purchased,

the amount of the difference must be transferred to the capital redemption reserve.

This does not apply in the case of a private company if, in addition to the proceeds of the fresh issue, the company applies a payment out of capital under Chapter 5 [or under section 692(1ZA)] in making the redemption or purchase.

(4) The amount by which a company's share capital is diminished in accordance with section 729(4) (on the cancellation of shares held as treasury shares) must be transferred to the capital redemption reserve.

(5) The company may use the capital redemption reserve to pay up new shares to be allotted to members as fully paid bonus shares.

(6) Subject to that, the provisions of the Companies Acts relating to the reduction of a company's share capital apply as if the capital redemption reserve were part of its paid up share capital.

NOTES

Sub-s (3): words in square brackets inserted by the Companies Act 2006 (Amendment of Part 18) Regulations 2015, SI 2015/532, regs 2, 8, as from 6 April 2015.

[1.819]

734 Accounting consequences of payment out of capital

(1) This section applies where a payment out of capital is made in accordance with Chapter 5 [or section 692(1ZA)] (redemption or purchase of own shares by private company out of capital).

[(1A) In relation to a payment under section 692(1ZA) references to the permissible capital payment are to the purchase price of the shares or (if less) the part of it met out of the payment under section 692(1ZA) and any proceeds of a fresh issue used to make the purchase.]

(2) If the permissible capital payment is less than the nominal amount of the shares redeemed or purchased, the amount of the difference must be transferred to the company's capital redemption reserve.

(3) If the permissible capital payment is greater than the nominal amount of the shares redeemed or purchased—

(a) the amount of any capital redemption reserve, share premium account or fully paid share capital of the company, and

(b) any amount representing unrealised profits of the company for the time being standing to the credit of any revaluation reserve maintained by the company,

may be reduced by a sum not exceeding (or by sums not in total exceeding) the amount by which the permissible capital payment exceeds the nominal amount of the shares.

(4) Where the proceeds of a fresh issue are applied by the company in making a redemption or purchase of its own shares in addition to a payment out of capital under [Chapter 5], the references in subsections (2) and (3) to the permissible capital payment are to be read as referring to the aggregate of that payment and those proceeds.

NOTES

The words in square brackets in sub-s (1) were inserted, sub-s (1A) was inserted, and the words in square brackets in sub-s (4) were substituted, by the Companies Act 2006 (Amendment of Part 18) Regulations 2015, SI 2015/532, regs 2, 9, as from 6 April 2015.

[1.820]

735 Effect of company's failure to redeem or purchase

(1) This section applies where a company—

(a) issues shares on terms that they are or are liable to be redeemed, or

(b) agrees to purchase any of its shares.

(2) The company is not liable in damages in respect of any failure on its part to redeem or purchase any of the shares.

This is without prejudice to any right of the holder of the shares other than his right to sue the company for damages in respect of its failure.

(3) The court shall not grant an order for specific performance of the terms of redemption or purchase if the company shows that it is unable to meet the costs of redeeming or purchasing the shares in question out of distributable profits.

(4) If the company is wound up and at the commencement of the winding up any of the shares have not been redeemed or purchased, the terms of redemption or purchase may be enforced against the company.

When shares are redeemed or purchased under this subsection, they are treated as cancelled.

(5) Subsection (4) does not apply if—

(a) the terms provided for the redemption or purchase to take place at a date later than that of the commencement of the winding up, or

(b) during the period—

(i) beginning with the date on which the redemption or purchase was to have taken place, and

(ii) ending with the commencement of the winding up,

the company could not at any time have lawfully made a distribution equal in value to the price at which the shares were to have been redeemed or purchased.

(6) There shall be paid in priority to any amount that the company is liable under subsection (4) to pay in respect of any shares—

(a) all other debts and liabilities of the company (other than any due to members in their character as such), and

(b) if other shares carry rights (whether as to capital or as to income) that are preferred to the rights as to capital attaching to the first-mentioned shares, any amount due in satisfaction of those preferred rights.

Subject to that, any such amount shall be paid in priority to any amounts due to members in satisfaction of their rights (whether as to capital or income) as members.

[1.821]

736 Meaning of "distributable profits"

In this Part (except in Chapter 2 (financial assistance): see section 683) "distributable profits", in relation to the making of any payment by a company, means profits out of which the company could lawfully make a distribution (within the meaning given by section 830) equal in value to the payment.

[1.822]

737 General power to make further provision by regulations

(1) The Secretary of State may by regulations modify the provisions of this Part.

(2) The regulations may—

(a) amend or repeal any of the provisions of this Part, or

(b) make such other provision as appears to the Secretary of State appropriate in place of any of the provisions of this Part.

(3) Regulations under this section may make consequential amendments or repeals in other provisions of this Act, or in other enactments.

(4) Regulations under this section are subject to affirmative resolution procedure.

NOTES

Regulations: the Companies (Share Capital and Acquisition by Company of its Own Shares) Regulations 2009, SI 2009/2022 at **[4.369]**; the Companies Act 2006 (Amendment of Part 18) Regulations 2013, SI 2013/999; the Companies Act 2006 (Amendment of Part 18) Regulations 2015, SI 2015/532. For a summary of all statutory instruments made under this Act, see Appendix 4 at **[A4]**.

PART 19 DEBENTURES

General provisions

[1.823]

738 Meaning of "debenture"

In the Companies Acts "debenture" includes debenture stock, bonds and any other securities of a company, whether or not constituting a charge on the assets of the company.

[1.824]

739 Perpetual debentures

(1) A condition contained in debentures, or in a deed for securing debentures, is not invalid by reason only that the debentures are made—

(a) irredeemable, or

(b) redeemable only—

(i) on the happening of a contingency (however remote), or

(ii) on the expiration of a period (however long),

any rule of equity to the contrary notwithstanding.

(2) Subsection (1) applies to debentures whenever issued and to deeds whenever executed.

[1.825]

740 Enforcement of contract to subscribe for debentures

A contract with a company to take up and pay for debentures of the company may be enforced by an order for specific performance.

[1.826]

741 Registration of allotment of debentures

(1) A company must register an allotment of debentures as soon as practicable and in any event within two months after the date of the allotment.

(2) If a company fails to comply with this section, an offence is committed by—

(a) the company, and

(b) every officer of the company who is in default.

(3) A person guilty of an offence under this section is liable on summary conviction to a fine not exceeding level 3 on the standard scale and, for continued contravention, a daily default fine not exceeding one-tenth of level 3 on the standard scale.

(4) For the duties of the company as to the issue of the debentures, or certificates of debenture stock, see Part 21 (certification and transfer of securities)

[1.827]

742 Debentures to bearer (Scotland)

Notwithstanding anything in the statute of the Scots Parliament of 1696, chapter 25, debentures to bearer issued in Scotland are valid and binding according to their terms.

[1.828]

743 Register of debenture holders

(1) Any register of debenture holders of a company that is kept by the company must be kept available for inspection—

(a) at the company's registered office, or

(b) at a place specified in regulations under section 1136.

(2) A company must give notice to the registrar of the place where any such register is kept available for inspection and of any change in that place.

(3) No such notice is required if the register has, at all times since it came into existence, been kept available for inspection at the company's registered office.

(4) If a company makes default for 14 days in complying with subsection (2), an offence is committed by—

(a) the company, and

(b) every officer of the company who is in default.

(5) A person guilty of an offence under this section is liable on summary conviction to a fine not exceeding level 3 on the standard scale and, for continued contravention, a daily default fine not exceeding one-tenth of level 3 on the standard scale.

(6) References in this section to a register of debenture holders include a duplicate—

(a) of a register of debenture holders that is kept outside the United Kingdom, or

(b) of any part of such a register.

[1.829]

744 Register of debenture holders: right to inspect and require copy

(1) Every register of debenture holders of a company must, except when duly closed, be open to the inspection—

(a) of the registered holder of any such debentures, or any holder of shares in the company, without charge, and

(b) of any other person on payment of such fee as may be prescribed.

(2) Any person may require a copy of the register, or any part of it, on payment of such fee as may be prescribed.

(3) A person seeking to exercise either of the rights conferred by this section must make a request to the company to that effect.

(4) The request must contain the following information—

(a) in the case of an individual, his name and address;

(b) in the case of an organisation, the name and address of an individual responsible for making the request on behalf of the organisation;

(c) the purpose for which the information is to be used; and

(d) whether the information will be disclosed to any other person, and if so—

(i) where that person is an individual, his name and address,

(ii) where that person is an organisation, the name and address of an individual responsible for receiving the information on its behalf, and

(iii) the purpose for which the information is to be used by that person.

(5) For the purposes of this section a register is "duly closed" if it is closed in accordance with provision contained—

(a) in the articles or in the debentures,

(b) in the case of debenture stock in the stock certificates, or

(c) in the trust deed or other document securing the debentures or debenture stock.

The total period for which a register is closed in any year must not exceed 30 days.

(6) References in this section to a register of debenture holders include a duplicate—

(a) of a register of debenture holders that is kept outside the United Kingdom, or

(b) of any part of such a register.

NOTES

Regulations: the Companies (Fees for Inspection and Copying of Company Records) (No 2) Regulations 2007, SI 2007/3535 at **[4.16]**. For a summary of all statutory instruments made under this Act, see Appendix 4 at **[A4]**.

[1.830]

745 Register of debenture holders: response to request for inspection or copy

(1) Where a company receives a request under section 744 (register of debenture holders: right to inspect and require copy), it must within five working days either—

(a) comply with the request, or

(b) apply to the court.

(2) If it applies to the court it must notify the person making the request.

(3) If on an application under this section the court is satisfied that the inspection or copy is not sought for a proper purpose—

(a) it shall direct the company not to comply with the request, and

(b) it may further order that the company's costs (in Scotland, expenses) on the application be paid in whole or in part by the person who made the request, even if he is not a party to the application.

(4) If the court makes such a direction and it appears to the court that the company is or may be subject to other requests made for a similar purpose (whether made by the same person or different persons), it may direct that the company is not to comply with any such request.

The order must contain such provision as appears to the court appropriate to identify the requests to which it applies.

(5) If on an application under this section the court does not direct the company not to comply with the request, the company must comply with the request immediately upon the court giving its decision or, as the case may be, the proceedings being discontinued.

[1.831]

746 Register of debenture holders: refusal of inspection or default in providing copy

(1) If an inspection required under section 744 (register of debenture holders: right to inspect and require copy) is refused or default is made in providing a copy required under that section, otherwise than in accordance with an order of the court, an offence is committed by—

(a) the company, and

(b) every officer of the company who is in default.

(2) A person guilty of an offence under this section is liable on summary conviction to a fine not exceeding level 3 on the standard scale and, for continued contravention, a daily default fine not exceeding one-tenth of level 3 on the standard scale.

(3) In the case of any such refusal or default the court may by order compel an immediate inspection or, as the case may be, direct that the copy required be sent to the person requesting it.

[1.832]

747 Register of debenture holders: offences in connection with request for or disclosure of information

(1) It is an offence for a person knowingly or recklessly to make in a request under section 744 (register of debenture holders: right to inspect and require copy) a statement that is misleading, false or deceptive in a material particular.

(2) It is an offence for a person in possession of information obtained by exercise of either of the rights conferred by that section—

(a) to do anything that results in the information being disclosed to another person, or

(b) to fail to do anything with the result that the information is disclosed to another person,

knowing, or having reason to suspect, that person may use the information for a purpose that is not a proper purpose.

(3) A person guilty of an offence under this section is liable—

(a) on conviction on indictment, to imprisonment for a term not exceeding two years or a fine (or both);

(b) on summary conviction—

(i) in England and Wales, to imprisonment for a term not exceeding twelve months or to a fine not exceeding the statutory maximum (or both);

(ii) in Scotland or Northern Ireland, to imprisonment for a term not exceeding six months, or to a fine not exceeding the statutory maximum (or both).

NOTES

Offences under this section: see further s 1131 at **[1.1301]**.

[1.833]

748 Time limit for claims arising from entry in register

(1) Liability incurred by a company—

(a) from the making or deletion of an entry in the register of debenture holders, or

(b) from a failure to make or delete any such entry,

is not enforceable more than ten years after the date on which the entry was made or deleted or, as the case may be, the failure first occurred.

(2) This is without prejudice to any lesser period of limitation (and, in Scotland, to any rule that the obligation giving rise to the liability prescribes before the expiry of that period).

Supplementary provisions

[1.834]

749 Right of debenture holder to copy of deed

(1) Any holder of debentures of a company is entitled, on request and on payment of such fee as may be prescribed, to be provided with a copy of any trust deed for securing the debentures.

(2) If default is made in complying with this section, an offence is committed by every officer of the company who is in default.

(3) A person guilty of an offence under this section is liable on summary conviction to a fine not exceeding level 3 on the standard scale and, for continued contravention, a daily default fine not exceeding one-tenth of level 3 on the standard scale.

(4) In the case of any such default the court may direct that the copy required be sent to the person requiring it.

NOTES

Regulations: the Companies (Fees for Inspection and Copying of Company Records) (No 2) Regulations 2007, SI 2007/3535 at **[4.16]**. For a summary of all statutory instruments made under this Act, see Appendix 4 at **[A4]**.

[1.835]

750 Liability of trustees of debentures

(1) Any provision contained in—

(a) a trust deed for securing an issue of debentures, or

(b) any contract with the holders of debentures secured by a trust deed,

is void in so far as it would have the effect of exempting a trustee of the deed from, or indemnifying him against, liability for breach of trust where he fails to show the degree of care and diligence required of him as trustee, having regard to the provisions of the trust deed conferring on him any powers, authorities or discretions.

(2) Subsection (1) does not invalidate—

(a) a release otherwise validly given in respect of anything done or omitted to be done by a trustee before the giving of the release;

(b) any provision enabling such a release to be given—

(i) on being agreed to by a majority of not less than 75% in value of the debenture holders present and voting in person or, where proxies are permitted, by proxy at a meeting summoned for the purpose, and

(ii) either with respect to specific acts or omissions or on the trustee dying or ceasing to act.

(3) This section is subject to section 751 (saving for certain older provisions).

[1.836]
751 Liability of trustees of debentures: saving for certain older provisions
(1) Section 750 (liability of trustees of debentures) does not operate—
- (a) to invalidate any provision in force on the relevant date so long as any person—
  - (i) then entitled to the benefit of the provision, or
  - (ii) afterwards given the benefit of the provision under subsection (3) below,

  remains a trustee of the deed in question, or
- (b) to deprive any person of any exemption or right to be indemnified in respect of anything done or omitted to be done by him while any such provision was in force.

(2) The relevant date for this purpose is—
- (a) 1st July 1948 in a case where section 192 of the Companies Act 1985 (c 6) applied immediately before the commencement of this section;
- (b) 1st July 1961 in a case where Article 201 of the Companies (Northern Ireland) Order 1986 (SI 1986/1032 (NI 6)) then applied.

(3) While any trustee of a trust deed remains entitled to the benefit of a provision saved by subsection (1) above the benefit of that provision may be given either—
- (a) to all trustees of the deed, present and future, or
- (b) to any named trustees or proposed trustees of it,

by a resolution passed by a majority of not less than 75% in value of the debenture holders present in person or, where proxies are permitted, by proxy at a meeting summoned for the purpose.
(4) A meeting for that purpose must be summoned in accordance with the provisions of the deed or, if the deed makes no provision for summoning meetings, in a manner approved by the court.

[1.837]
752 Power to re-issue redeemed debentures
(1) Where a company has redeemed debentures previously issued, then unless—
- (a) provision to the contrary (express or implied) is contained in the company's articles or in any contract made by the company, or
- (b) the company has, by passing a resolution to that effect or by some other act, manifested its intention that the debentures shall be cancelled,

the company may re-issue the debentures, either by re-issuing the same debentures or by issuing new debentures in their place.
This subsection is deemed always to have had effect.
(2) On a re-issue of redeemed debentures the person entitled to the debentures has (and is deemed always to have had) the same priorities as if the debentures had never been redeemed.
(3) The re-issue of a debenture or the issue of another debenture in its place under this section is treated as the issue of a new debenture for the purposes of stamp duty.
It is not so treated for the purposes of any provision limiting the amount or number of debentures to be issued.
(4) A person lending money on the security of a debenture re-issued under this section which appears to be duly stamped may give the debenture in evidence in any proceedings for enforcing his security without payment of the stamp duty or any penalty in respect of it, unless he had notice (or, but for his negligence, might have discovered) that the debenture was not duly stamped. In that case the company is liable to pay the proper stamp duty and penalty.

[1.838]
753 Deposit of debentures to secure advances
Where a company has deposited any of its debentures to secure advances from time to time on current account or otherwise, the debentures are not treated as redeemed by reason only of the company's account having ceased to be in debit while the debentures remained so deposited.

[1.839]
754 Priorities where debentures secured by floating charge
(1) This section applies where debentures of a company registered in England and Wales or Northern Ireland are secured by a charge that, as created, was a floating charge.
(2) If possession is taken, by or on behalf of the holders of the debentures, of any property comprised in or subject to the charge, and the company is not at that time in the course of being wound up, the company's preferential debts shall be paid out of assets coming to the hands of the persons taking possession in priority to any claims for principal or interest in respect of the debentures.
(3) "Preferential debts" means the categories of debts listed in Schedule 6 to the Insolvency Act 1986 (c 45) or Schedule 4 to the Insolvency (Northern Ireland) Order 1989 (SI 1989/2405 (NI 19)).
For the purposes of those Schedules "the relevant date" is the date of possession being taken as mentioned in subsection (2).
(4) Payments under this section shall be recouped, as far as may be, out of the assets of the company available for payment of general creditors.

PART 20 PRIVATE AND PUBLIC COMPANIES

CHAPTER 1 PROHIBITION OF PUBLIC OFFERS BY PRIVATE COMPANIES

[1.840]
755 Prohibition of public offers by private company
(1) A private company limited by shares or limited by guarantee and having a share capital must not—
- (a) offer to the public any securities of the company, or
- (b) allot or agree to allot any securities of the company with a view to their being offered to the public.

(2) Unless the contrary is proved, an allotment or agreement to allot securities is presumed to be made with a view to their being offered to the public if an offer of the securities (or any of them) to the public is made—

(a) within six months after the allotment or agreement to allot, or

(b) before the receipt by the company of the whole of the consideration to be received by it in respect of the securities.

(3) A company does not contravene this section if—

(a) it acts in good faith in pursuance of arrangements under which it is to re-register as a public company before the securities are allotted, or

(b) as part of the terms of the offer it undertakes to re-register as a public company within a specified period, and that undertaking is complied with.

(4) The specified period for the purposes of subsection (3)(b) must be a period ending not later than six months after the day on which the offer is made (or, in the case of an offer made on different days, first made).

(5) In this Chapter "securities" means shares or debentures.

[1.841]

756 Meaning of "offer to the public"

(1) This section explains what is meant in this Chapter by an offer of securities to the public.

(2) An offer to the public includes an offer to any section of the public, however selected.

(3) An offer is not regarded as an offer to the public if it can properly be regarded, in all the circumstances, as—

(a) not being calculated to result, directly or indirectly, in securities of the company becoming available to persons other than those receiving the offer, or

(b) otherwise being a private concern of the person receiving it and the person making it.

(4) An offer is to be regarded (unless the contrary is proved) as being a private concern of the person receiving it and the person making it if—

(a) it is made to a person already connected with the company and, where it is made on terms allowing that person to renounce his rights, the rights may only be renounced in favour of another person already connected with the company; or

(b) it is an offer to subscribe for securities to be held under an employees' share scheme and, where it is made on terms allowing that person to renounce his rights, the rights may only be renounced in favour of—

(i) another person entitled to hold securities under the scheme, or

(ii) a person already connected with the company.

(5) For the purposes of this section "person already connected with the company" means—

(a) an existing member or employee of the company,

(b) a member of the family of a person who is or was a member or employee of the company,

(c) the widow or widower, or surviving civil partner, of a person who was a member or employee of the company,

(d) an existing debenture holder of the company, or

(e) a trustee (acting in his capacity as such) of a trust of which the principal beneficiary is a person within any of paragraphs (a) to (d).

(6) For the purposes of subsection (5)(b) the members of a person's family are the person's spouse or civil partner and children (including step-children) and their descendants.

[1.842]

757 Enforcement of prohibition: order restraining proposed contravention

(1) If it appears to the court—

(a) on an application under this section, or

(b) in proceedings under Part 30 (protection of members against unfair prejudice),

that a company is proposing to act in contravention of section 755 (prohibition of public offers by private companies), the court shall make an order under this section.

(2) An order under this section is an order restraining the company from contravening that section.

(3) An application for an order under this section may be made by—

(a) a member or creditor of the company, or

(b) the Secretary of State.

NOTES

With regard to proceedings under this section, see further the Companies (Authorised Minimum) Regulations 2008, SI 2008/729, reg 6 at **[4.134]** (Determination of exchange rates by the court in certain proceedings), and the Companies (Authorised Minimum) Regulations 2009, SI 2009/2425, reg 6 at **[4.386]** (Determination of exchange rates by the court in certain proceedings).

[1.843]

758 Enforcement of prohibition: orders available to the court after contravention

(1) This section applies if it appears to the court—

(a) on an application under this section, or

(b) in proceedings under Part 30 (protection of members against unfair prejudice),

that a company has acted in contravention of section 755 (prohibition of public offers by private companies).

(2) The court must make an order requiring the company to re-register as a public company unless it appears to the court—

(a) that the company does not meet the requirements for re-registration as a public company, and

(b) that it is impractical or undesirable to require it to take steps to do so.

(3) If it does not make an order for re-registration, the court may make either or both of the following—

(a) a remedial order (see section 759), or

(b) an order for the compulsory winding up of the company.

(4) An application under this section may be made by—

(a) a member of the company who—

(i) was a member at the time the offer was made (or, if the offer was made over a period, at any time during that period), or
(ii) became a member as a result of the offer,
(b) a creditor of the company who was a creditor at the time the offer was made (or, if the offer was made over a period, at any time during that period), or
(c) the Secretary of State.

NOTES

With regard to proceedings under this section, see further the Companies (Authorised Minimum) Regulations 2008, SI 2008/729, reg 6 at **[4.134]** (Determination of exchange rates by the court in certain proceedings), and the Companies (Authorised Minimum) Regulations 2009, SI 2009/2425, reg 6 at **[4.386]** (Determination of exchange rates by the court in certain proceedings).

[1.844]
759 Enforcement of prohibition: remedial order

(1) A "remedial order" is an order for the purpose of putting a person affected by anything done in contravention of section 755 (prohibition of public offers by private company) in the position he would have been in if it had not been done.
(2) The following provisions are without prejudice to the generality of the power to make such an order.
(3) Where a private company has—
(a) allotted securities pursuant to an offer to the public, or
(b) allotted or agreed to allot securities with a view to their being offered to the public,
a remedial order may require any person knowingly concerned in the contravention of section 755 to offer to purchase any of those securities at such price and on such other terms as the court thinks fit.
(4) A remedial order may be made—
(a) against any person knowingly concerned in the contravention, whether or not an officer of the company;
(b) notwithstanding anything in the company's constitution (which includes, for this purpose, the terms on which any securities of the company are allotted or held);
(c) whether or not the holder of the securities subject to the order is the person to whom the company allotted or agreed to allot them.
(5) Where a remedial order is made against the company itself, the court may provide for the reduction of the company's capital accordingly.

[1.845]
760 Validity of allotment etc not affected

Nothing in this Chapter affects the validity of any allotment or sale of securities or of any agreement to allot or sell securities.

CHAPTER 2 MINIMUM SHARE CAPITAL REQUIREMENT FOR PUBLIC COMPANIES

[1.846]
761 Public company: requirement as to minimum share capital

(1) A company that is a public company (otherwise than by virtue of re-registration as a public company) must not do business or exercise any borrowing powers unless the registrar has issued it with a certificate under this section (a "trading certificate").
(2) The registrar shall issue a trading certificate if, on an application made in accordance with section 762, he is satisfied that the nominal value of the company's allotted share capital is not less than the authorised minimum.
(3) For this purpose a share allotted in pursuance of an employees' share scheme shall not be taken into account unless paid up as to—
(a) at least one-quarter of the nominal value of the share, and
(b) the whole of any premium on the share.
(4) A trading certificate has effect from the date on which it is issued and is conclusive evidence that the company is entitled to do business and exercise any borrowing powers.

[1.847]
762 Procedure for obtaining certificate

(1) An application for a certificate under section 761 must—
(a) state that the nominal value of the company's allotted share capital is not less than the authorised minimum,
(b) specify the amount, or estimated amount, of the company's preliminary expenses,
(c) specify any amount or benefit paid or given, or intended to be paid or given, to any promoter of the company, and the consideration for the payment or benefit, . . .
(d) be accompanied by a statement of compliance[, and
(e) be accompanied by a statement of the aggregate amount paid up on the shares of the company on account of their nominal value].
(2) The statement of compliance is a statement that the company meets the requirements for the issue of a certificate under section 761.
(3) The registrar may accept the statement of compliance as sufficient evidence of the matters stated in it.

NOTES

Sub-s (1): word omitted from para (c) repealed, and para (e) (and the preceding word) inserted, by the Small Business, Enterprise and Employment Act 2015, s 98(1), (3), as from 30 June 2016.

[1.848]
763 The authorised minimum

(1) "The authorised minimum", in relation to the nominal value of a public company's allotted share capital is—
(a) £50,000, or

(b) the prescribed euro equivalent.

(2) The Secretary of State may by order prescribe the amount in euros that is for the time being to be treated as equivalent to the sterling amount of the authorised minimum.

(3) This power may be exercised from time to time as appears to the Secretary of State to be appropriate.

(4) The amount prescribed shall be determined by applying an appropriate spot rate of exchange to the sterling amount and rounding to the nearest 100 euros.

(5) An order under this section is subject to negative resolution procedure.

(6) This section has effect subject to any exercise of the power conferred by section 764 (power to alter authorised minimum).

NOTES

Regulations: the Companies (Authorised Minimum) Regulations 2008, SI 2008/729 at **[4.130]**; the Companies (Authorised Minimum) Regulations 2009, SI 2009/2425 at **[4.381]** (reg 2 of which prescribes €57,100 as the equivalent amount for the purposes of sub-s (1) (subject to transitional provisions in reg 9 of those Regulations)). For a summary of all statutory instruments made under this Act, see Appendix 4 at **[A4]**.

[1.849]

764 Power to alter authorised minimum

(1) The Secretary of State may by order—

- (a) alter the sterling amount of the authorised minimum, and
- (b) make a corresponding alteration of the prescribed euro equivalent.

(2) The amount of the prescribed euro equivalent shall be determined by applying an appropriate spot rate of exchange to the sterling amount and rounding to the nearest 100 euros.

(3) An order under this section that increases the authorised minimum may—

- (a) require a public company having an allotted share capital of which the nominal value is less than the amount specified in the order to—
  - (i) increase that value to not less than that amount, or
  - (ii) re-register as a private company;
- (b) make provision in connection with any such requirement for any of the matters for which provision is made by this Act relating to—
  - (i) a company's registration, re-registration or change of name,
  - (ii) payment for shares comprised in a company's share capital, and
  - (iii) offers to the public of shares in or debentures of a company,

  including provision as to the consequences (in criminal law or otherwise) of a failure to comply with any requirement of the order;
- (c) provide for any provision of the order to come into force on different days for different purposes.

(4) An order under this section is subject to affirmative resolution procedure.

NOTES

Orders: no Orders have been made under this section.

[1.850]

765 Authorised minimum: application of initial requirement

(1) The initial requirement for a public company to have allotted share capital of a nominal value not less than the authorised minimum, that is—

- (a) the requirement in section 761(2) for the issue of a trading certificate, or
- (b) the requirement in section 91(1)(a) for re-registration as a public company,

must be met either by reference to allotted share capital denominated in sterling or by reference to allotted share capital denominated in euros (but not partly in one and partly in the other).

(2) Whether the requirement is met is determined in the first case by reference to the sterling amount and in the second case by reference to the prescribed euro equivalent.

(3) No account is to be taken of any allotted share capital of the company denominated in a currency other than sterling or, as the case may be, euros.

(4) If the company could meet the requirement either by reference to share capital denominated in sterling or by reference to share capital denominated in euros, it must elect in its application for a trading certificate or, as the case may be, for re-registration as a public company which is to be the currency by reference to which the matter is determined.

[1.851]

766 Authorised minimum: application where shares denominated in different currencies etc

(1) The Secretary of State may make provision by regulations as to the application of the authorised minimum in relation to a public company that—

- [(a) has shares denominated—
  - (i) in more than one currency, or
  - (ii) in a currency other than sterling or euros,]
- (b) redenominates the whole or part of its allotted share capital, or
- (c) allots new shares.

(2) The regulations may make provision as to the currencies, exchange rates and dates by reference to which it is to be determined whether the nominal value of the company's allotted share capital is less than the authorised minimum.

(3) The regulations may provide that where—

- (a) a company has redenominated the whole or part of its allotted share capital, and
- (b) the effect of the redenomination is that the nominal value of the company's allotted share capital is less than the authorised minimum,

the company must re-register as a private company.

(4) Regulations under subsection (3) may make provision corresponding to any provision made by sections 664 to 667 (re-registration as private company in consequence of cancellation of shares).

(5) Any regulations under this section have effect subject to section 765 (authorised minimum: application of initial requirement).

(6) Regulations under this section are subject to negative resolution procedure.

NOTES

Sub-s (1): para (a) substituted by the Companies Act 2006 (Consequential Amendments and Transitional Provisions) Order 2011, SI 2011/1265, art 28(1), (2), as from 12 May 2011.

Regulations: the Companies (Authorised Minimum) Regulations 2008, SI 2008/729 at **[4.130]**; the Companies (Authorised Minimum) Regulations 2009, SI 2009/2425 at **[4.381]**. For a summary of all statutory instruments made under this Act, see Appendix 4 at **[A4]**.

[1.852]

767 Consequences of doing business etc without a trading certificate

(1) If a company does business or exercises any borrowing powers in contravention of section 761, an offence is committed by—

- (a) the company, and
- (b) every officer of the company who is in default.

(2) A person guilty of an offence under subsection (1) is liable—

- (a) on conviction on indictment, to a fine;
- (b) on summary conviction, to a fine not exceeding the statutory maximum.

(3) A contravention of section 761 does not affect the validity of a transaction entered into by the company, but if a company—

- (a) enters into a transaction in contravention of that section, and
- (b) fails to comply with its obligations in connection with the transaction within 21 days from being called on to do so,

the directors of the company are jointly and severally liable to indemnify any other party to the transaction in respect of any loss or damage suffered by him by reason of the company's failure to comply with its obligations.

(4) The directors who are so liable are those who were directors at the time the company entered into the transaction.

PART 21 CERTIFICATION AND TRANSFER OF SECURITIES

CHAPTER 1 CERTIFICATION AND TRANSFER OF SECURITIES: GENERAL

Share certificates

[1.853]

768 Share certificate to be evidence of title

(1) In the case of a company registered in England and Wales or Northern Ireland, a certificate under the common seal of the company specifying any shares held by a member is prima facie evidence of his title to the shares.

(2) In the case of a company registered in Scotland—

- (a) a certificate under the common seal of the company specifying any shares held by a member, or
- (b) a certificate specifying any shares held by a member and subscribed by the company in accordance with the Requirements of Writing (Scotland) Act 1995 (c 7),

is sufficient evidence, unless the contrary is shown, of his title to the shares.

Issue of certificates etc on allotment

[1.854]

769 Duty of company as to issue of certificates etc on allotment

(1) A company must, within two months after the allotment of any of its shares, debentures or debenture stock, complete and have ready for delivery—

- (a) the certificates of the shares allotted,
- (b) the debentures allotted, or
- (c) the certificates of the debenture stock allotted.

(2) Subsection (1) does not apply—

- (a) if the conditions of issue of the shares, debentures or debenture stock provide otherwise,
- (b) in the case of allotment to a financial institution (see section 778), or
- (c) in the case of an allotment of shares if, following the allotment, the company has issued a share warrant in respect of the shares (see section 779).

(3) If default is made in complying with subsection (1) an offence is committed by every officer of the company who is in default.

(4) A person guilty of an offence under subsection (3) is liable on summary conviction to a fine not exceeding level 3 on the standard scale and, for continued contravention, a daily default fine not exceeding one-tenth of level 3 on the standard scale.

Transfer of securities

[1.855]

770 Registration of transfer

(1) A company may not register a transfer of shares in or debentures of the company unless—

- (a) a proper instrument of transfer has been delivered to it, or
- (b) the transfer—
  - (i) is an exempt transfer within the Stock Transfer Act 1982 (c 41), or
  - (ii) is in accordance with regulations under Chapter 2 of this Part.

(2) Subsection (1) does not affect any power of the company to register as shareholder or debenture holder a person to whom the right to any shares in or debentures of the company has been transmitted by operation of law.

[(3) If an election under Chapter 2A of Part 8 is in force in respect of the company, references in this section to registering a transfer (or a person) are to be read as references to delivering particulars of that transfer (or person) to the registrar under that Chapter.]

NOTES

Sub-s (3): added by the Small Business, Enterprise and Employment Act 2015, s 94, Sch 5, Pt 2, paras 11, 26, as from 30 June 2016.

[1.856]

771 Procedure on transfer being lodged

(1) When a transfer of shares in or debentures of a company has been lodged with the company, the company must either—

(a) register the transfer, or

(b) give the transferee notice of refusal to register the transfer, together with its reasons for the refusal,

as soon as practicable and in any event within two months after the date on which the transfer is lodged with it.

(2) If the company refuses to register the transfer, it must provide the transferee with such further information about the reasons for the refusal as the transferee may reasonably request.

This does not include copies of minutes of meetings of directors.

[(2A) If an election is in force under Chapter 2A of Part 8 in respect of the company, references in this section to registering the transfer are to be read as references to delivering particulars of the transfer to the registrar in accordance with that Chapter.]

(3) If a company fails to comply with this section, an offence is committed by—

(a) the company, and

(b) every officer of the company who is in default.

(4) A person guilty of an offence under this section is liable on summary conviction to a fine not exceeding level 3 on the standard scale and, for continued contravention, a daily default fine not exceeding one-tenth of level 3 on the standard scale.

(5) This section does not apply—

(a) in relation to a transfer of shares if the company has issued a share warrant in respect of the shares (see section 779);

(b) in relation to the transmission of shares or debentures by operation of law.

NOTES

Sub-s (2A): inserted by the Small Business, Enterprise and Employment Act 2015, s 94, Sch 5, Pt 2, paras 11, 27, as from 30 June 2016.

[1.857]

772 Transfer of shares on application of transferor

On the application of the transferor of any share or interest in a company, the company shall enter in its register of members the name of the transferee [(or, as the case may be, deliver the name of the transferee to the registrar under Chapter 2A of Part 8)] in the same manner and subject to the same conditions as if the application for the entry [(or delivery)] were made by the transferee.

NOTES

Words in square brackets inserted by the Small Business, Enterprise and Employment Act 2015, s 94, Sch 5, Pt 2, paras 11, 28, as from 30 June 2016.

[1.858]

773 Execution of share transfer by personal representative

An instrument of transfer of the share or other interest of a deceased member of a company—

(a) may be made by his personal representative although the personal representative is not himself a member of the company, and

(b) is as effective as if the personal representative had been such a member at the time of the execution of the instrument.

[1.859]

774 Evidence of grant of probate etc

The production to a company of any document that is by law sufficient evidence of the grant of—

(a) probate of the will of a deceased person,

(b) letters of administration of the estate of a deceased person, or

(c) confirmation as executor of a deceased person,

shall be accepted by the company as sufficient evidence of the grant.

[1.860]

775 Certification of instrument of transfer

(1) The certification by a company of an instrument of transfer of any shares in, or debentures of, the company is to be taken as a representation by the company to any person acting on the faith of the certification that there have been produced to the company such documents as on their face show a prima facie title to the shares or debentures in the transferor named in the instrument.

(2) The certification is not to be taken as a representation that the transferor has any title to the shares or debentures.

(3) Where a person acts on the faith of a false certification by a company made negligently, the company is under the same liability to him as if the certification had been made fraudulently.

(4) For the purposes of this section—

(a) an instrument of transfer is certificated if it bears the words "certificate lodged" (or words to the like effect);

(b) the certification of an instrument of transfer is made by a company if—

(i) the person issuing the instrument is a person authorised to issue certificated instruments of transfer on the company's behalf, and

(ii) the certification is signed by a person authorised to certificate transfers on the company's behalf or by an officer or employee either of the company or of a body corporate so authorised;

(c) a certification is treated as signed by a person if—

(i) it purports to be authenticated by his signature or initials (whether handwritten or not), and

(ii) it is not shown that the signature or initials was or were placed there neither by himself nor by a person authorised to use the signature or initials for the purpose of certificating transfers on the company's behalf.

Issue of certificates etc on transfer

[1.861]

776 Duty of company as to issue of certificates etc on transfer

(1) A company must, within two months after the date on which a transfer of any of its shares, debentures or debenture stock is lodged with the company, complete and have ready for delivery—

(a) the certificates of the shares transferred,

(b) the debentures transferred, or

(c) the certificates of the debenture stock transferred.

(2) For this purpose a "transfer" means—

(a) a transfer duly stamped and otherwise valid, or

(b) an exempt transfer within the Stock Transfer Act 1982 (c 41),

but does not include a transfer that the company is for any reason entitled to refuse to register and does not register.

(3) Subsection (1) does not apply—

(a) if the conditions of issue of the shares, debentures or debenture stock provide otherwise,

(b) in the case of a transfer to a financial institution (see section 778), or

(c) in the case of a transfer of shares if, following the transfer, the company has issued a share warrant in respect of the shares (see section 779).

(4) Subsection (1) has effect subject to section 777 (cases where the Stock Transfer Act 1982 applies).

(5) If default is made in complying with subsection (1) an offence is committed by every officer of the company who is in default.

(6) A person guilty of an offence under this section is liable on summary conviction to a fine not exceeding level 3 on the standard scale and, for continued contravention, a daily default fine not exceeding one-tenth of level 3 on the standard scale.

[1.862]

777 Issue of certificates etc: cases within the Stock Transfer Act 1982

(1) Section 776(1) (duty of company as to issue of certificates etc on transfer) does not apply in the case of a transfer to a person where, by virtue of regulations under section 3 of the Stock Transfer Act 1982, he is not entitled to a certificate or other document of or evidencing title in respect of the securities transferred.

(2) But if in such a case the transferee—

(a) subsequently becomes entitled to such a certificate or other document by virtue of any provision of those regulations, and

(b) gives notice in writing of that fact to the company,

section 776 (duty to company as to issue of certificates etc) has effect as if the reference in subsection (1) of that section to the date of the lodging of the transfer were a reference to the date of the notice.

Issue of certificates etc on allotment or transfer to financial institution

[1.863]

778 Issue of certificates etc: allotment or transfer to financial institution

(1) A company—

(a) of which shares or debentures are allotted to a financial institution,

(b) of which debenture stock is allotted to a financial institution, or

(c) with which a transfer for transferring shares, debentures or debenture stock to a financial institution is lodged,

is not required in consequence of that allotment or transfer to comply with section 769(1) or 776(1) (duty of company as to issue of certificates etc).

(2) A "financial institution" means—

(a) a recognised clearing house [or a recognised CSD] acting in relation to a recognised investment exchange, or

(b) a nominee of—

(i) a recognised clearing house [or a recognised CSD] acting in that way, or

(ii) a recognised investment exchange,

designated for the purposes of this section in the rules of the recognised investment exchange in question.

(3) Expressions used in subsection (2) have the same meaning as in Part 18 of the Financial Services and Markets Act 2000 (c 8).

NOTES

Sub-s (2): words in square brackets inserted by the Central Securities Depositories Regulations 2017, SI 2017/1064, reg 10, Schedule, para 11(1), (2), as from 28 November 2017.

Share warrants

[1.864]

779 [Prohibition on issue of new share warrants and effect of existing share warrants]

(1) A company limited by shares may, if so authorised by its articles, issue with respect to any fully paid shares a warrant (a "share warrant") stating that the bearer of the warrant is entitled to the shares specified in it.

(2) A share warrant issued under the company's common seal or (in the case of a company registered in Scotland) subscribed in accordance with the Requirements of Writing (Scotland) Act 1995 (c 7) entitles the bearer to the shares specified in it and the shares may be transferred by delivery of the warrant.

(3) A company that issues a share warrant may, if so authorised by its articles, provide (by coupons or otherwise) for the payment of the future dividends on the shares included in the warrant.

[(4) No share warrant may be issued by a company (irrespective of whether its articles purport to authorise it to do so) on or after the day on which section 84 of the Small Business, Enterprise and Employment Act 2015 comes into force.]

NOTES

Section heading substituted, and sub-s (4) added, by the Small Business, Enterprise and Employment Act 2015, s 84(1), (2), as from 26 May 2015. See further ss 85, 86 of the 2015 Act at **[9.520]**, **[9.521]**.

780 (*Repealed by the Small Business, Enterprise and Employment Act 2015, s 84, Sch 4, Pt 2, paras 22, 26, as from 26 May 2015, except in relation to a share warrant surrendered for cancellation before that date.*)

[1.865]

781 Offences in connection with share warrants (Scotland)

(1) If in Scotland a person—

(a) with intent to defraud, forges or alters, or offers, utters, disposes of, or puts off, knowing the same to be forged or altered, any share warrant or coupon, or any document purporting to be a share warrant or coupon issued in pursuance of this Act, or

(b) by means of any such forged or altered share warrant, coupon or document—

(i) demands or endeavours to obtain or receive any share or interest in a company under this Act, or

(ii) demands or endeavours to receive any dividend or money payment in respect of any such share or interest,

knowing the warrant, coupon or document to be forged or altered,

he commits an offence.

(2) If in Scotland a person without lawful authority or excuse (of which proof lies on him)—

(a) engraves or makes on any plate, wood, stone, or other material, any share warrant or coupon purporting to be—

(i) a share warrant or coupon issued or made by any particular company in pursuance of this Act, or

(ii) a blank share warrant or coupon so issued or made, or

(iii) a part of such a share warrant or coupon, or

(b) uses any such plate, wood, stone, or other material, for the making or printing of any such share warrant or coupon, or of any such blank share warrant or coupon or of any part of such a share warrant or coupon, or

(c) knowingly has in his custody or possession any such plate, wood, stone, or other material,

he commits an offence.

(3) A person guilty of an offence under subsection (1) is liable on summary conviction to imprisonment for a term not exceeding six months or to a fine not exceeding level 5 on the standard scale (or both).

(4) A person guilty of an offence under subsection (2) is liable—

(a) on conviction on indictment, to imprisonment for a term not exceeding seven years or a fine (or both);

(b) on summary conviction, to imprisonment for a term not exceeding six months or a fine not exceeding the statutory maximum (or both).

Supplementary provisions

[1.866]

782 Issue of certificates etc: court order to make good default

(1) If a company on which a notice has been served requiring it to make good any default in complying with—

(a) section 769(1) (duty of company as to issue of certificates etc on allotment),

(b) section 776(1) (duty of company as to issue of certificates etc on transfer), or

(c) section 780(1) (duty of company as to issue of certificates etc on surrender of share warrant),

fails to make good the default within ten days after service of the notice, the person entitled to have the certificates or the debentures delivered to him may apply to the court.

(2) The court may on such an application make an order directing the company and any officer of it to make good the default within such time as may be specified in the order.

(3) The order may provide that all costs (in Scotland, expenses) of and incidental to the application are to be borne by the company or by an officer of it responsible for the default.

CHAPTER 2 EVIDENCING AND TRANSFER OF TITLE TO SECURITIES WITHOUT WRITTEN INSTRUMENT

Introductory

[1.867]

783 Scope of this Chapter

In this Chapter—

(a) "securities" means shares, debentures, debenture stock, loan stock, bonds, units of a collective investment scheme within the meaning of the Financial Services and Markets Act 2000 (c 8) and other securities of any description;

(b) references to title to securities include any legal or equitable interest in securities;

(c) references to a transfer of title include a transfer by way of security;

(d) references to transfer without a written instrument include, in relation to bearer securities, transfer without delivery.

[1.868]

784 Power to make regulations

(1) The power to make regulations under this Chapter is exercisable by the Treasury and the Secretary of State, either jointly or concurrently.

(2) References in this Chapter to the authority having power to make regulations shall accordingly be read as references to both or either of them, as the case may require.

(3) Regulations under this Chapter are subject to affirmative resolution procedure.

Powers exercisable

[1.869]

785 Provision enabling procedures for evidencing and transferring title

(1) Provision may be made by regulations for enabling title to securities to be evidenced and transferred without a written instrument.

(2) The regulations may make provision—

(a) for procedures for recording and transferring title to securities, and

(b) for the regulation of those procedures and the persons responsible for or involved in their operation.

(3) The regulations must contain such safeguards as appear to the authority making the regulations appropriate for the protection of investors and for ensuring that competition is not restricted, distorted or prevented.

(4) The regulations may, for the purpose of enabling or facilitating the operation of the procedures provided for by the regulations, make provision with respect to the rights and obligations of persons in relation to securities dealt with under the procedures.

(5) The regulations may include provision for the purpose of giving effect to—

(a) the transmission of title to securities by operation of law;

(b) any restriction on the transfer of title to securities arising by virtue of the provisions of any enactment or instrument, court order or agreement;

(c) any power conferred by any such provision on a person to deal with securities on behalf of the person entitled.

(6) The regulations may make provision with respect to the persons responsible for the operation of the procedures provided for by the regulations—

(a) as to the consequences of their insolvency or incapacity, or

(b) as to the transfer from them to other persons of their functions in relation to those procedures.

[(7) The regulations may confer functions on any person, including—

(a) the function of giving guidance or issuing a code of practice in relation to any provision made by the regulations, and

(b) the function of making rules for the purposes of any provision made by the regulations.

(8) The regulations may, in prescribed cases, confer immunity from liability in damages.]

NOTES

Sub-ss (7), (8): added by the Financial Services Act 2012, s 112, as from 24 January 2013.

Regulations: the Companies Act 2006 (Consequential Amendments) (Uncertificated Securities) Order 2009, SI 2009/1889; the Uncertificated Securities (Amendment) Regulations 2013, SI 2013/632; the Alternative Investment Fund Managers Regulations 2013, SI 2013/1773; the Uncertificated Securities (Amendment and EU Exit) Regulations 2019, SI 2019/679 at **[12.123]**. Also, by virtue of s 1297 of this Act (continuity of law) the Uncertificated Securities Regulations 2001, SI 2001/3755 (at **[6.40]**), the Uncertificated Securities (Amendment) (Eligible Debt Securities) Regulations 2003, SI 2003/1633, and the Uncertificated Securities (Amendment) Regulations 2007, SI 2007/124 (as amended by further SIs made under s 207 of the Companies Act 1989) have effect as if made under this section. Note also that the Local Authority (Stocks and Bonds) (Amendment) Regulations 1999, SI 1999/1409, and the Local Authority (Stocks and Bonds) (Amendment) Regulations 2000, SI 2000/1680 (originally made under the Companies Act 1989, s 207) also have effect as if made under this section. These Regulations amend the Local Authority (Stocks and Bonds) Regulations 1974, SI 1974/519 which provide for the manner in which stock or bonds shall be issued by a local authority, and are considered to be outside the scope of this work. For a summary of all statutory instruments made under this Act, see Appendix 4 at **[A4]**.

[1.870]

786 Provision enabling or requiring arrangements to be adopted

(1) Regulations under this Chapter may make provision—

(a) enabling the members of a company or of any designated class of companies to adopt, by ordinary resolution, arrangements under which title to securities is required to be evidenced or transferred (or both) without a written instrument; or

(b) requiring companies, or any designated class of companies, to adopt such arrangements.

(2) The regulations may make such provision—

(a) in respect of all securities issued by a company, or

(b) in respect of all securities of a specified description.

(3) The arrangements provided for by regulations making such provision as is mentioned in subsection (1)—

(a) must not be such that a person who but for the arrangements would be entitled to have his name entered in the company's register of members [(or, as the case may be, delivered to the registrar under Chapter 2A of Part 8)] ceases to be so entitled, and

(b) must be such that a person who but for the arrangements would be entitled to exercise any rights in respect of the securities continues to be able effectively to control the exercise of those rights.

(4) The regulations may—

(a) prohibit the issue of any certificate by the company in respect of the issue or transfer of securities,

(b) require the provision by the company to holders of securities of statements (at specified intervals or on specified occasions) of the securities held in their name, and

(c) make provision as to the matters of which any such certificate or statement is, or is not, evidence.

(5) In this section—

(a) references to a designated class of companies are to a class designated in the regulations or by order under section 787; and

(b) "specified" means specified in the regulations.

NOTES

Sub-s (3): words in square brackets inserted by the Small Business, Enterprise and Employment Act 2015, s 94, Sch 5, Pt 2, paras 11, 29, as from 30 June 2016.

[1.871]

787 Provision enabling or requiring arrangements to be adopted: order-making powers

(1) The authority having power to make regulations under this Chapter may by order—

(a) designate classes of companies for the purposes of section 786 (provision enabling or requiring arrangements to be adopted);

(b) provide that, in relation to securities of a specified description—

(i) in a designated class of companies, or

(ii) in a specified company or class of companies,

specified provisions of regulations made under this Chapter by virtue of that section either do not apply or apply subject to specified modifications.

(2) In subsection (1) "specified" means specified in the order.

(3) An order under this section is subject to negative resolution procedure.

NOTES

Orders: no Orders have been made under this section.

Supplementary

[1.872]

788 Provision that may be included in regulations

Regulations under this Chapter may—

(a) modify or exclude any provision of any enactment or instrument, or any rule of law;

(b) apply, with such modifications as may be appropriate, the provisions of any enactment or instrument (including provisions creating criminal offences);

(c) require the payment of fees, or enable persons to require the payment of fees, of such amounts as may be specified in the regulations or determined in accordance with them;

(d) empower the authority making the regulations to delegate to any person willing and able to discharge them any functions of the authority under the regulations.

[1.873]

789 Duty to consult

Before making—

(a) regulations under this Chapter, or

(b) any order under section 787,

the authority having power to make regulations under this Chapter must carry out such consultation as appears to it to be appropriate.

[1.874]

790 Resolutions to be forwarded to registrar

Chapter 3 of Part 3 (resolutions affecting a company's constitution) applies to a resolution passed by virtue of regulations under this Chapter.

[PART 21A INFORMATION ABOUT PEOPLE WITH SIGNIFICANT CONTROL

CHAPTER 1 INTRODUCTION

[1.875]

790A Overview

This Part is arranged as follows—

(a) the remaining provisions of this Chapter identify the companies to which this Part applies and explain some key terms, including what it means to have "significant control" over a company,

(b) Chapter 2 imposes duties on companies to gather information, and on others to supply information, to enable companies to keep the register required by Chapter 3,

(c) Chapter 3 requires companies to keep a register, referred to as a register of people with significant control over the company, and to make the register available to the public,

(d) Chapter 4 gives private companies the option of using an alternative method of record-keeping, and

(e) Chapter 5 makes provision for excluding certain material from the information available to the public.]

NOTES

Part 21A (originally ss 790A–790V, 790W–790ZG) was inserted by the Small Business, Enterprise and Employment Act 2015, s 81, Sch 3, Pt 1, para 1, as from 26 May 2015 (for the purposes of enabling the exercise of any power to make provision by regulations, rules or order made by statutory instrument or to prepare and issue guidance), as from 6 April 2016 (in so far as not in force, but subject as follows), and as from 30 June 2016 (in so far as relating to ss 790M(9)(c) and 790W–790ZE).

[1.876]

[790B Companies to which this Part applies

(1) This Part applies to companies other than—

[(a) companies with voting shares admitted to trading on a [UK regulated market or an EU regulated market], and]

(b) companies of any description specified by the Secretary of State by regulations.

(2) In deciding whether to specify a description of company, the Secretary of State is to have regard to the extent to which companies of that description are bound by disclosure and transparency rules (in the United Kingdom or elsewhere) [which are contained in international standards and are equivalent to those applicable to companies referred to in subsection (1)(a)].

(3) . . .

(4) Regulations under this section are subject to affirmative resolution procedure.

[(5) In this section—

"voting shares" means shares carrying voting rights;

"voting rights" means rights to vote at general meetings of the company in question, including rights that arise only in certain circumstances.]]

NOTES

Inserted as noted to s 790A at **[1.875]**.

Sub-s (1)(a) was substituted, the words in square brackets in sub-s (2) were substituted, sub-s (3) was repealed, and sub-s (5) was added, by the Information about People with Significant Control (Amendment) Regulations 2017, SI 2017/693, regs 4, 5, as from 26 June 2017 (for transitional arrangements, see Schedule, Pt 1 to the 2017 Regulations at **[10.1195]**).

Words in square brackets in sub-s (1)(a) substituted by the Companies, Limited Liability Partnerships and Partnerships (Amendment etc) (EU Exit) Regulations 2019, SI 2019/348, reg 6, Sch 1, paras 1, 10, as from IP completion day (as defined in the European Union (Withdrawal Agreement) Act 2020, s 39).

Regulations: the Register of People with Significant Control Regulations 2016, SI 2016/339 at **[4.559]**. For a summary of all statutory instruments made under this Act, see Appendix 4 at **[A4]**.

[1.877]

[790C Key terms

(1) This section explains some key terms used in this Part.

(2) References to a person with (or having) "significant control" over a company are to an individual who meets one or more of the specified conditions in relation to the company.

(3) The "specified conditions" are those specified in Part 1 of Schedule 1A.

(4) Individuals with significant control over a company are either "registrable" or "non-registrable" in relation to the company—

[(a) they are "non-registrable" if they do not hold any interest in the company except through one or more legal entities over each of which they have significant control and—

(i) as respects any shares or right in the company which they hold indirectly as described in paragraph 9(1)(b)(i) of Schedule 1A, the legal entity through which the shares or right are held is a relevant legal entity in relation to the company; and

(ii) as respects any shares or right in the company which they hold indirectly as described in paragraph 9(1)(b)(ii) of Schedule 1A, at least one of the legal entities in the chain is a relevant legal entity in relation to the company;]

(b) otherwise, they are "registrable",

and references to a "registrable person" in relation to a company are to an individual with significant control over the company who is registrable in relation to that company.

(5) A "legal entity" is a body corporate or a firm that is a legal person under the law by which it is governed.

(6) In relation to a company, a legal entity is a "relevant legal entity" if—

(a) it would have come within the definition of a person with significant control over the company if it had been an individual, and

(b) it is subject to its own disclosure requirements.

(7) A legal entity is "subject to its own disclosure requirements" if—

(a) this Part applies to it (whether by virtue of section 790B or another enactment that extends the application of this Part),

[(aa) it is an eligible Scottish partnership within the meaning of regulation 3(2) of the Scottish Partnerships (Register of People with Significant Control) Regulations 2017,]

[(b) it has voting shares admitted to trading on a [UK regulated market or an EU regulated market],]

(c) it is of a description specified in regulations under section 790B (or that section as extended), or

(d) it is of a description specified by the Secretary of State by regulations made under this paragraph.

(8) A relevant legal entity is either "registrable" or "non-registrable" in relation to a company—

[(a) it is "non-registrable" if it does not hold any interest in the company except through one or more other legal entities over each of which it has significant control and—

(i) as respects any shares or right in the company which it holds indirectly as described in paragraph 9(1)(b)(i) of Schedule 1A, the legal entity through which the shares or right are held is also a relevant legal entity in relation to the company; and

(ii) as respects any shares or right in the company which it holds indirectly as described in paragraph 9(1)(b)(ii) of Schedule 1A, at least one of the legal entities in the chain is also a relevant legal entity in relation to the company;]

(b) otherwise, it is "registrable",

and references to a "registrable relevant legal entity" in relation to a company are to a relevant legal entity which is registrable in relation to that company.

(9) For the purposes of subsections (4) and (8)—

(a) whether someone—

(i) holds an interest in a company, or

(ii) holds that interest through another legal entity,

is to be determined in accordance with Part 2 of Schedule 1A;

(b) whether someone has significant control over that other legal entity is to be determined in accordance with subsections (2) and (3) and Part 1 of Schedule 1A, reading references in those provisions to the company as references to that other entity.

(10) The register that a company is required to keep under section 790M (register of people with significant control over a company) is referred to as the company's "PSC register".

(11) In deciding whether to specify a description of legal entity under paragraph (d) of subsection (7), the Secretary of State is to have regard to the extent to which entities of that description are bound by disclosure and transparency rules (in the United Kingdom or elsewhere) [equivalent] to the ones applying to an entity falling within any other paragraph of that subsection.

(12) Subject to express provision in this Part and to any modification prescribed by regulations under this subsection, this Part is to be read and have effect as if each of the following were an individual, even if they are legal persons under the laws by which they are governed—

- (a) a corporation sole,
- (b) a government or government department of a country or territory or a part of a country or territory,
- (c) an international organisation whose members include two or more countries or territories (or their governments),
- (d) a local authority or local government body in the United Kingdom or elsewhere.

(13) Regulations under subsection (7)(d) are subject to affirmative resolution procedure.

(14) Subject to subsection (13), regulations under this section are subject to negative resolution procedure.

[(15) In this section "voting shares" has the same meaning as in section 790B.]]

NOTES

Inserted as noted to s 790A at **[1.875]**.

Sub-ss (4), (8): para (a) substituted by the Companies Act 2006 (Amendment of Part 21A) Regulations 2016, SI 2016/136, reg 2, as from 5 April 2016.

Sub-s (7): para (aa) inserted by the Scottish Partnerships (Register of People with Significant Control) Regulations 2017, SI 2017/694, reg 78, as from 26 June 2017, subject to transitional provisions in reg 80 of the 2017 Regulations at **[10.1276]**. Para (b) substituted by the Information about People with Significant Control (Amendment) Regulations 2017, SI 2017/693, regs 4, 6(1), (2), as from 26 June 2017 (for transitional arrangements, see Schedule, Pt 1 to the 2017 Regulations at **[10.1195]**). Words in square brackets in para (b) substituted by the Companies, Limited Liability Partnerships and Partnerships (Amendment etc) (EU Exit) Regulations 2019, SI 2019/348, reg 6, Sch 1, paras 1, 11, as from IP completion day (as defined in the European Union (Withdrawal Agreement) Act 2020, s 39).

Sub-s (11): word in square brackets substituted by SI 2017/693, regs 4, 6(1), (3), as from 26 June 2017 (for transitional arrangements, see Schedule, Pt 1 to the 2017 Regulations at **[10.1195]**).

Sub-s (15): added by SI 2017/693, regs 4, 6(1), (4), as from 26 June 2017 (for transitional arrangements, see Schedule, Pt 1 to the 2017 Regulations at **[10.1195]**).

Regulations: the Register of People with Significant Control Regulations 2016, SI 2016/339 at **[4.559]**. For a summary of all statutory instruments made under this Act, see Appendix 4 at **[A4]**.

[CHAPTER 2 INFORMATION-GATHERING

Duty on companies

[1.878]

790D Company's duty to investigate and obtain information

(1) A company to which this Part applies must take reasonable steps—

- (a) to find out if there is anyone who is a registrable person or a registrable relevant legal entity in relation to the company, and
- (b) if so, to identify them.

(2) Without limiting subsection (1), a company to which this Part applies must give notice to anyone whom it knows or has reasonable cause to believe to be a registrable person or a registrable relevant legal entity in relation to it.

(3) The notice, if addressed to an individual, must require the addressee—

- (a) to state whether or not he or she is a registrable person in relation to the company (within the meaning of this Part), and
- (b) if so, to confirm or correct any particulars of his or hers that are included in the notice, and supply any that are missing.

(4) The notice, if addressed to a legal entity, must require the addressee—

- (a) to state whether or not it is a registrable relevant legal entity in relation to the company (within the meaning of this Part), and
- (b) if so, to confirm or correct any of its particulars that are included in the notice, and supply any that are missing.

(5) A company to which this Part applies may also give notice to a person under this section if it knows or has reasonable cause to believe that the person—

- (a) knows the identity of someone who falls within subsection (6), or
- (b) knows the identity of someone likely to have that knowledge.

(6) The persons who fall within this subsection are—

- (a) any registrable person in relation to the company;
- (b) any relevant legal entity in relation to the company;
- (c) any entity which would be a relevant legal entity in relation to the company but for the fact that section 790C(6)(b) does not apply in respect of it.

(7) A notice under subsection (5) may require the addressee—

- (a) to state whether or not the addressee knows the identity of—
  - (i) any person who falls within subsection (6), or
  - (ii) any person likely to have that knowledge, and
- (b) if so, to supply any particulars of theirs that are within the addressee's knowledge, and state whether or not the particulars are being supplied with the knowledge of each of the persons concerned.

(8) A notice under this section must state that the addressee is to comply with the notice by no later than the end of the period of one month beginning with the date of the notice.

(9) The Secretary of State may by regulations make further provision about the giving of notices under this section, including the form and content of any such notices and the manner in which they must be given.

(10) Regulations under subsection (9) are subject to negative resolution procedure.

(11) A company is not required to take steps or give notice under this section with respect to a registrable person or registrable relevant legal entity if—

(a) the company has already been informed of the person's status as a registrable person or registrable relevant legal entity in relation to it, and been supplied with all the particulars, and

(b) in the case of a registrable person, the information and particulars were provided either by the person concerned or with his or her knowledge.

(12) A person to whom a notice under subsection (5) is given is not required by that notice to disclose any information in respect of which a claim to legal professional privilege (in Scotland, to confidentiality of communications) could be maintained in legal proceedings.

(13) In this section—

(a) a reference to knowing the identity of a person includes knowing information from which that person can be identified, and

(b) "particulars" means—

(i) in the case of a registrable person or a registrable relevant legal entity, the required particulars (see section 790K), and

(ii) in any other case, any particulars that will allow the person to be contacted by the company.]

NOTES

Inserted as noted to s 790A at **[1.875]**.

[1.879]

[790E Company's duty to keep information up-to-date

(1) This section applies if particulars of a registrable person or registrable relevant legal entity are stated in a company's PSC register.

(2) The company must give notice to the person or entity if the company knows or has reasonable cause to believe that a relevant change has occurred.

(3) In the case of a registrable person, a "relevant change" occurs if—

(a) the person ceases to be a registrable person in relation to the company, or

(b) any other change occurs as a result of which the particulars stated for the person in the PSC register are incorrect or incomplete.

(4) In the case of a registrable relevant legal entity, a "relevant change" occurs if—

(a) the entity ceases to be a registrable relevant legal entity in relation to the company, or

(b) any other change occurs as a result of which the particulars stated for the entity in the PSC register are incorrect or incomplete.

(5) The company must give the notice—

[(a)] as soon as reasonably practicable[, and

(b) in any event before the end of the period of 14 days beginning with the earlier of the day] after it learns of the change [and the day after it] first has reasonable cause to believe that the change has occurred.

(6) The notice must require the addressee—

(a) to confirm whether or not the change has occurred, and

(b) if so—

(i) to state the date of the change, and

(ii) to confirm or correct the particulars included in the notice, and supply any that are missing from the notice.

(7) Subsections (8) to (10) of section 790D apply to notices under this section as to notices under that section.

(8) A company is not required to give notice under this section if—

(a) the company has already been informed of the relevant change, and

(b) in the case of a registrable person, that information was provided either by the person concerned or with his or her knowledge.]

NOTES

Inserted as noted to s 790A at **[1.875]**.

Sub-s (5): words in square brackets inserted or substituted by the Information about People with Significant Control (Amendment) Regulations 2017, SI 2017/693, regs 4, 7, as from 26 June 2017 (for transitional arrangements, see Schedule, Pt 1 to the 2017 Regulations at **[10.1195]**).

[1.880]

[790F Failure by company to comply with information duties

(1) If a company fails to comply with a duty under section 790D or 790E to take steps or give notice, an offence is committed by—

(a) the company, and

(b) every officer of the company who is in default.

(2) A person guilty of an offence under this section is liable—

(a) on conviction on indictment, to imprisonment for a term not exceeding two years or a fine (or both);

(b) on summary conviction—

(i) in England and Wales, to imprisonment for a term not exceeding twelve months or a fine (or both);

(ii) in Scotland, to imprisonment for a term not exceeding twelve months or to a fine not exceeding the statutory maximum (or both);

(iii) in Northern Ireland, to imprisonment for a term not exceeding six months or to a fine not exceeding the statutory maximum (or both).]

NOTES

Inserted as noted to s 790A at **[1.875]**.

[Duty on others

[1.881]

790G Duty to supply information

(1) This section applies to a person if—

(a) the person is a registrable person or a registrable relevant legal entity in relation to a company,

(b) the person knows that to be the case or ought reasonably to do so,

(c) the required particulars of the person are not stated in the company's PSC register,

(d) the person has not received notice from the company under section 790D(2), and

(e) the circumstances described in paragraphs (a) to (d) have continued for a period of at least one month.

(2) The person must—

(a) notify the company of the person's status (as a registrable person or registrable relevant legal entity) in relation to the company,

(b) state the date, to the best of the person's knowledge, on which the person acquired that status, and

(c) give the company the required particulars (see section 790K).

(3) The duty under subsection (2) must be complied with by the end of the period of one month beginning with the day on which all the conditions in subsection (1)(a) to (e) were first met with respect to the person.]

NOTES

Inserted as noted to s 790A at **[1.875]**.

[1.882]

[790H Duty to update information

(1) This section applies to a person if—

(a) the required particulars of the person (whether a registrable person or a registrable relevant legal entity) are stated in a company's PSC register,

(b) a relevant change occurs,

(c) the person knows of the change or ought reasonably to do so,

(d) the company's PSC register has not been altered to reflect the change, and

(e) the person has not received notice from the company under section 790E by the end of the period of one month beginning with the day on which the change occurred.

(2) The person must—

(a) notify the company of the change,

(b) state the date on which it occurred, and

(c) give the company any information needed to update the PSC register.

(3) The duty under subsection (2) must be complied with by the later of—

(a) the end of the period of 2 months beginning with the day on which the change occurred, and

(b) the end of the period of one month beginning with the day on which the person discovered the change.

(4) "Relevant change" has the same meaning as in section 790E.]

NOTES

Inserted as noted to s 790A at **[1.875]**.

[Compliance

[1.883]

790I Enforcement of disclosure requirements

Schedule 1B contains provisions for when a person (whether an individual or a legal entity) fails to comply with a notice under section 790D or 790E or a duty under section 790G or 790H.]

NOTES

Inserted as noted to s 790A at **[1.875]**.

[Exemption from information and registration requirements

[1.884]

790J Power to make exemptions

(1) The Secretary of State may exempt a person (whether an individual or a legal entity) under this section.

(2) The effect of an exemption is—

(a) the person is not required to comply with any notice under section 790D(2) or 790E (but if a notice is received, the person must bring the existence of the exemption to the attention of the company that sent it),

(b) companies are not obliged to take steps or give notice under those sections to or with respect to that person,

(c) notices under section 790D(5) do not require anyone else to give any information about that person,

(d) the duties imposed by sections 790G and 790H do not apply to that person, and

(e) the person does not count for the purposes of section 790M as a registrable person or, as the case may be, a registrable relevant legal entity in relation to any company.

(3) The Secretary of State must not grant an exemption under this section unless the Secretary of State is satisfied that, having regard to any undertaking given by the person to be exempted, there are special reasons why that person should be exempted.]

NOTES

Inserted as noted to s 790A at **[1.875]**.

[Required particulars

[1.885]
790K Required particulars
(1) The "required particulars" of an individual who is a registrable person are—
(a) name,
(b) a service address,
(c) the country or state (or part of the United Kingdom) in which the individual is usually resident,
(d) nationality,
(e) date of birth,
(f) usual residential address,
(g) the date on which the individual became a registrable person in relation to the company in question,
(h) the nature of his or her control over that company (see Schedule 1A), and
(i) if, in relation to that company, restrictions on using or disclosing any of the individual's PSC particulars are in force under regulations under section 790ZG, that fact.
(2) In the case of a person in relation to which this Part has effect by virtue of section 790C(12) as if the person were an individual, the "required particulars" are—
(a) name,
(b) principal office,
(c) the legal form of the person and the law by which it is governed,
(d) the date on which it became a registrable person in relation to the company in question, and
(e) the nature of its control over the company (see Schedule 1A).
(3) The "required particulars" of a registrable relevant legal entity are—
(a) corporate or firm name,
(b) registered or principal office,
(c) the legal form of the entity and the law by which it is governed,
(d) if applicable, the register of companies in which it is entered (including details of the state) and its registration number in that register,
(e) the date on which it became a registrable relevant legal entity in relation to the company in question, and
(f) the nature of its control over that company (see Schedule 1A).
(4) Section 163(2) (particulars of directors to be registered: individuals) applies for the purposes of subsection (1).
(5) The Secretary of State may by regulations make further provision about the particulars required by subsections (1)(h), (2)(e) and (3)(f).
(6) Regulations under subsection (5) are subject to negative resolution procedure.]

NOTES
Inserted as noted to s 790A at **[1.875]**.
Transitional provision: see the Register of People with Significant Control Regulations 2016, SI 2016/339, reg 47 (at **[4.606]**) which provides that where an individual or a relevant legal entity is registrable in relation to a company on 6 April 2016, the date on which the individual or entity became a registrable person or a registrable relevant legal entity, as the case may be, in relation to the company in question is deemed to be 6 April 2016 for the purposes of sub-ss (1)(g), (2)(d) and (3)(e) above.
Regulations: the Register of People with Significant Control Regulations 2016, SI 2016/339 at **[4.559]**. For a summary of all statutory instruments made under this Act, see Appendix 4 at **[A4]**.

[1.886]
[790L Required particulars: power to amend
(1) The Secretary of State may by regulations amend section 790K so as to add to or remove from any of the lists of required particulars.
(2) Regulations under this section are subject to affirmative resolution procedure.]

NOTES
Inserted as noted to s 790A at **[1.875]**.

[CHAPTER 3 REGISTER OF PEOPLE WITH SIGNIFICANT CONTROL

[1.887]
790M Duty to keep register
(1) A company to which this Part applies must keep a register of people with significant control over the company.
(2) The required particulars of any individual with significant control over the company who is "registrable" in relation to the company must be entered in the register [before the end of the period of 14 days beginning with the day after all the required particulars of that individual are first confirmed].
(3) The company must not enter any of the individual's particulars in the register until they have all been confirmed.
(4) Particulars of any individual with significant control over the company who is "non-registrable" in relation to the company must not be entered in the register.
[(5) The required particulars of any entity that is a registrable relevant legal entity in relation to the company must be entered in the register before the end of the period of 14 days beginning with the day after the company first has all the required particulars of that entity.]
(6) If the company becomes aware of a relevant change (within the meaning of section 790E) with respect to a registrable person . . . whose particulars are stated in the register[, the company must enter in the register—
(a) the changes to the required particulars resulting from the relevant change, and
(b) the date on which the relevant change occurred,
before the end of the period of 14 days beginning with the day after all of those changes and that date are first confirmed].
[(6A) If the company becomes aware of a relevant change (within the meaning of section 790E) with respect to a registrable relevant legal entity whose particulars are stated in the register, the company must enter in the register—
(a) the changes to the required particulars resulting from the relevant change, and

(b) the date on which the relevant change occurred,

before the end of the period of 14 days beginning with the day after the company first has details of all of those changes and that date.]

(7) The Secretary of State may by regulations require additional matters to be noted in a company's PSC register.

[(7A) If a company is required by regulations made under subsection (7) to note an additional matter in its PSC register, the company must note the additional matter before the end of the period of 14 days beginning with the day after the requirement arises.]

(8) Regulations under subsection (7) are subject to affirmative resolution procedure.

(9) A person's required particulars, [a change to such particulars and the date of any relevant change with respect to a person], are considered for the purposes of this section to have been "confirmed" if—

(a) the person supplied or confirmed them to the company (whether voluntarily, pursuant to a duty imposed by this Part or otherwise),

(b) another person did so but with that person's knowledge, or

(c) they were included in a statement of initial significant control delivered to the registrar under section 9 by subscribers wishing to form the company.

(10) In the case of someone who was a registrable person or a registrable relevant legal entity in relation to the company on its incorporation—

(a) the date to be entered in the register as the date on which the individual became a registrable person, or the entity became a registrable relevant legal entity, is to be the date of incorporation, and

(b) in the case of a registrable person, that particular is deemed to have been "confirmed".

(11) For the purposes of this section—

(a) if a person's usual residential address is the same as his or her service address, the entry for him or her in the register may state that fact instead of repeating the address (but this does not apply in a case where the service address is stated to be "The company's registered office");

(b) nothing in section 126 (trusts not to be entered on register) affects what may be entered in a company's PSC register or is receivable by the registrar in relation to people with significant control over a company (even if they are members of the company);

(c) see section 790J (exemptions) for cases where a person does not count as a registrable person or a registrable relevant legal entity.

(12) If a company makes default in complying with this section, an offence is committed by—

(a) the company, and

(b) every officer of the company who is in default.

(13) A person guilty of an offence under this section is liable on summary conviction to a fine not exceeding level 3 on the standard scale and, for continued contravention, a daily default fine not exceeding one-tenth of level 3 on the standard scale.

(14) A company to which this Part applies is not by virtue of anything done for the purposes of this section affected with notice of, or put upon inquiry as to, the rights of any person in relation to any shares or rights in or with respect to the company.]

NOTES

Inserted as noted to s 790A at **[1.875]**.

Words in square brackets in sub-ss (2), (9) substituted, sub-s (5) substituted, words omitted from sub-s (6) repealed, words in square brackets in that subsection substituted, and sub-s (6A), (7A) inserted, by the Information about People with Significant Control (Amendment) Regulations 2017, SI 2017/693, regs 4, 8, as from 26 June 2017 (for transitional arrangements, see Schedule, Pt 1 to the 2017 Regulations at **[10.1195]**).

Temporary modification: the Companies etc (Filing Requirements) (Temporary Modifications) Regulations 2020, SI 2020/645, reg 13 provided for the following temporary modification of this section. By virtue of the Corporate Insolvency and Governance Act 2020, s 39(8), the modification applied from 27 June 2020 to the end of the day on 5 April 2021 (subject to the saving provision in s 39(9) which provides that the expiry of s 39 on 5 April 2021 does not affect the continued operation of any Regulations made under that section for the purpose of determining the length of any period that begins before the expiry):

(1) The modifications in paragraph (2) apply to a company in respect of which an election under section 790X is in force.

(2) Section 790M (duty to keep register) is to have effect as if for each reference to "14 days" there were substituted a reference to "42 days".

Regulations: the Register of People with Significant Control Regulations 2016, SI 2016/339 at **[4.559]**. For a summary of all statutory instruments made under this Act, see Appendix 4 at **[A4]**.

[1.888]

[790N Register to be kept available for inspection

(1) A company's PSC register must be kept available for inspection—

(a) at its registered office, or

(b) at a place specified in regulations under section 1136.

(2) A company must give notice to the registrar of the place where its PSC register is kept available for inspection and of any change in that place.

(3) No such notice is required if the register has, at all times since it came into existence, been kept available for inspection at the company's registered office.

(4) If a company makes default for 14 days in complying with subsection (2), an offence is committed by—

(a) the company, and

(b) every officer of the company who is in default.

(5) A person guilty of an offence under this section is liable on summary conviction to a fine not exceeding level 3 on the standard scale and, for continued contravention, a daily default fine not exceeding one-tenth of level 3 on the standard scale.]

NOTES

Inserted as noted to s 790A at **[1.875]**.

Temporary modification: this section was modified by the Companies etc (Filing Requirements) (Temporary Modifications) Regulations 2020, SI 2020/645, reg 14. By virtue of the Corporate Insolvency and Governance Act 2020, s 39(8), the modification applied from 27 June 2020 to the end of the day on 5 April 2021 (subject to the saving provision in s 39(9) which provides that the expiry of s 39 on 5 April 2021 does not affect the continued operation of any Regulations made under that section for the purpose of determining the length of any period that began before the expiry). As modified, sub-s (4) above had effect as if for the reference to "14 days" there were substituted a reference to "42 days".

[1.889]

[790O Rights to inspect and require copies

(1) A company's PSC register must be open to the inspection of any person without charge.

(2) Any person may require a copy of a company's PSC register, or any part of it, on payment of such fee as may be prescribed.

(3) A person seeking to exercise either of the rights conferred by this section must make a request to the company to that effect.

(4) The request must contain the following information—

(a) in the case of an individual, his or her name and address,

(b) in the case of an organisation, the name and address of an individual responsible for making the request on behalf of the organisation, and

(c) the purpose for which the information is to be used.]

NOTES

Inserted as noted to s 790A at **[1.875]**.

Regulations: the Register of People with Significant Control Regulations 2016, SI 2016/339 at **[4.559]**. For a summary of all statutory instruments made under this Act, see Appendix 4 at **[A4]**.

[1.890]

[790P PSC register: response to request for inspection or copy

(1) Where a company receives a request under section 790O, it must within 5 working days either—

(a) comply with the request, or

(b) apply to the court.

(2) If it applies to the court, it must notify the person making the request.

(3) If on an application under this section the court is satisfied that the inspection or copy is not sought for a proper purpose—

(a) it must direct the company not to comply with the request, and

(b) it may further order that the company's costs (in Scotland, expenses) on the application be paid in whole or in part by the person who made the request, even if that person is not a party to the application.

(4) If the court makes such a direction and it appears to the court that the company is or may be subject to other requests made for a similar purpose (whether made by the same person or different persons), it may direct that the company is not to comply with any such request.

The order must contain such provision as appears to the court appropriate to identify the requests to which it applies.

(5) If on an application under this section the court does not direct the company not to comply with the request, the company must comply with the request immediately upon the court giving its decision or, as the case may be, the proceedings being discontinued.]

NOTES

Inserted as noted to s 790A at **[1.875]**.

[1.891]

[790Q PSC register: refusal of inspection or default in providing copy

(1) If an inspection required under section 790O is refused or default is made in providing a copy required under that section, otherwise than in accordance with an order of the court, an offence is committed by—

(a) the company, and

(b) every officer of the company who is in default.

(2) A person guilty of an offence under this section is liable on summary conviction to a fine not exceeding level 3 on the standard scale and, for continued contravention, a daily default fine not exceeding one-tenth of level 3 on the standard scale.

(3) In the case of any such refusal or default the court may by order compel an immediate inspection or, as the case may be, direct that the copy required be sent to the person requesting it.]

NOTES

Inserted as noted to s 790A at **[1.875]**.

[1.892]

[790R PSC register: offences in connection with request for or disclosure of information

(1) It is an offence for a person knowingly or recklessly to make in a request under section 790O a statement that is misleading, false or deceptive in a material particular.

(2) It is an offence for a person in possession of information obtained by exercise of either of the rights conferred by that section—

(a) to do anything that results in the information being disclosed to another person, or

(b) to fail to do anything with the result that the information is disclosed to another person,

knowing, or having reason to suspect, that person may use the information for a purpose that is not a proper purpose.

(3) A person guilty of an offence under this section is liable—

(a) on conviction on indictment, to imprisonment for a term not exceeding two years or a fine (or both);

(b) on summary conviction—

(i) in England and Wales, to imprisonment for a term not exceeding twelve months or to a fine (or both);

(ii) in Scotland, to imprisonment for a term not exceeding twelve months or to a fine not exceeding the statutory maximum (or both);

(iii) in Northern Ireland, to imprisonment for a term not exceeding six months or to a fine not exceeding the statutory maximum (or both).]

NOTES

Inserted as noted to s 790A at **[1.875]**.

[1.893]

[790S Information as to state of register

(1) Where a person inspects the PSC register, or the company provides a person with a copy of the register or any part of it, the company must inform the person of the most recent date (if any) on which alterations were made to the register and whether there are further alterations to be made.

(2) If a company fails to provide the information required under subsection (1), an offence is committed by—

(a) the company, and

(b) every officer of the company who is in default.

(3) A person guilty of an offence under this section is liable on summary conviction to a fine not exceeding level 3 on the standard scale.]

NOTES

Inserted as noted to s 790A at **[1.875]**.

[1.894]

790T Protected information

(1) Section 790N and subsections (1) and (2) of section 790O are subject to—

(a) section 790ZF (protection of information as to usual residential address), and

(b) any provision of regulations made under section 790ZG (protection of material).

(2) Subsection (1) is not to be taken to affect the generality of the power conferred by virtue of section 790ZG(3)(f).

NOTES

Inserted as noted to s 790A at **[1.875]**.

[1.895]

[790U Removal of entries from the register

(1) An entry relating to an individual who used to be a registrable person may be removed from the company's PSC register after the expiration of 10 years from the date on which the individual ceased to be a registrable person in relation to the company.

(2) An entry relating to an entity that used to be a registrable relevant legal entity may be removed from the company's PSC register after the expiration of 10 years from the date on which the entity ceased to be a registrable relevant legal entity in relation to the company.]

NOTES

Inserted as noted to s 790A at **[1.875]**.

[1.896]

[790V Power of court to rectify register

(1) If—

(a) the name of any person is, without sufficient cause, entered in or omitted from a company's PSC register as a registrable person or registrable relevant legal entity, or

(b) default is made or unnecessary delay takes place in entering on the PSC register the fact that a person has ceased to be a registrable person or registrable relevant legal entity,

the person aggrieved or any other interested party may apply to the court for rectification of the register.

(2) The court may either refuse the application or may order rectification of the register and payment by the company of any damages sustained by any party aggrieved.

(3) On such an application, the court may—

(a) decide any question as to whether the name of any person who is a party to the application should or should not be entered in or omitted from the register, and

(b) more generally, decide any question necessary or expedient to be decided for rectification of the register.

(4) In the case of a company required by this Act to send information stated in its PSC register to the registrar of companies, the court, when making an order for rectification of the register, must by its order direct notice of the rectification to be given to the registrar.

(5) The reference in this section to "any other interested party" is to—

(a) any member of the company, and

(b) any other person who is a registrable person or a registrable relevant legal entity in relation to the company.]

NOTES

Inserted as noted to s 790A at **[1.875]**.

[1.897]

[790VA Notification of changes to the registrar

(1) Subsection (2) applies where a company—

(a) enters required particulars in its PSC register,

(b) alters required particulars in its PSC register, or

(c) notes in its PSC register an additional matter that is required to be noted by regulations under section 790M(7).

(2) The company must give notice to the registrar of the change made to its PSC register, and the date on which the change was made, before the end of the period of 14 days beginning with the day after it makes the change.

(3) If default is made in complying with this section, an offence is committed by—

(a) the company, and

(b) every officer of the company who is in default.

(4) For the purpose of subsection (3) a shadow director is treated as an officer of the company.

(5) A person guilty of an offence under this section is liable on summary conviction to a fine not exceeding level 3 on the standard scale and, for continued contravention, a daily default fine not exceeding one-tenth of level 3 on the standard scale.]

NOTES

Inserted by the Information about People with Significant Control (Amendment) Regulations 2017, SI 2017/693, regs 4, 9, as from 26 June 2017 (for transitional arrangements, see Schedule, Pt 1 to the 2017 Regulations at **[10.1195]**).

Temporary modification: this section was modified by the Companies etc (Filing Requirements) (Temporary Modifications) Regulations 2020, SI 2020/645, reg 15. By virtue of the Corporate Insolvency and Governance Act 2020, s 39(8), the modification applied from 27 June 2020 to the end of the day on 5 April 2021 (subject to the saving provision in s 39(9) which provides that the expiry of s 39 on 5 April 2021 does not affect the continued operation of any Regulations made under that section for the purpose of determining the length of any period that began before the expiry). As modified, sub-s (2) above had effect as if for the reference to "14 days" there were substituted a reference to "42 days".

[CHAPTER 4 ALTERNATIVE METHOD OF RECORD-KEEPING

[1.898]

790W Introductory

(1) This Chapter sets out rules allowing private companies to keep information on the register kept by the registrar instead of entering it in their PSC register.

(2) The register kept by the registrar (see section 1080) is referred to in this Chapter as "the central register".

(3) Chapter 3 must be read with this Chapter.

(4) Nothing in this Chapter affects the duties imposed by Chapter 2.

(5) Where an election under section 790X is in force in respect of a company, references in Chapter 2 to the company's PSC register are to be read as references to the central register.]

NOTES

Inserted as noted to s 790A at **[1.875]**.

[1.899]

[790X Right to make an election

(1) An election may be made under this section—

(a) by the subscribers wishing to form a private company under this Act, or

(b) by the private company itself once it is formed and registered.

(2) The election is of no effect unless—

(a) notice of the intention to make the election was given to each eligible person at least 14 days before the day on which the election was made, and

(b) no objection was received by the subscribers or, as the case may be, the company from any eligible person within that notice period.

(3) A person is an "eligible person" if—

(a) in a case of an election by the subscribers wishing to form a private company, the person's particulars would, but for the election, be required to be entered in the company's PSC register on its incorporation, and

(b) in the case of an election by the company itself—

(i) the person is a registrable person or a registrable relevant legal entity in relation to the company, and

(ii) the person's particulars are stated in the company's PSC register.

(4) An election under this section is made by giving notice of election to the registrar.

(5) If the notice is given by subscribers wishing to form a private company—

(a) it must be given when the documents required to be delivered under section 9 are delivered to the registrar, and

(b) it must be accompanied by a statement confirming that no objection was received as mentioned in subsection (2).

(6) If the notice is given by the company, it must be accompanied by—

(a) a statement confirming that no objection was received as mentioned in subsection (2), and

(b) a statement containing all the information that is required to be contained in the company's PSC register as at the date of the notice in respect of matters that are current as at that date.

(7) The company must where necessary update the statement sent under subsection (6)(b) to ensure that the final version delivered to the registrar contains all the information that is required to be contained in the company's PSC register as at the time immediately before the election takes effect (see section 790Y) in respect of matters that are current as at that time.

(8) The obligation in subsection (7) to update the statement includes an obligation to rectify it (where necessary) in consequence of the company's PSC register being rectified (whether before or after the election takes effect).

(9) If default is made in complying with subsection (7), an offence is committed by—

(a) the company, and

(b) every officer of the company who is in default.

For this purpose a shadow director is treated as an officer of the company.

(10) A person guilty of an offence under this section is liable on summary conviction to a fine not exceeding level 3 on the standard scale and, for continued contravention, a daily default fine not exceeding one-tenth of level 3 on the standard scale.

(11) A reference in this Chapter to matters that are current as at a given date or time is a reference to—

(a) persons who are a registrable person or registrable relevant legal entity in relation to the company as at that date or time and whose particulars are required to be contained in the company's PSC register as at that date or time, and

(b) any other matters that are current as at that date or time.]

NOTES

Inserted as noted to s 790A at **[1.875]**.

[1.900]

[790Y Effective date of election

(1) An election made under section 790X takes effect when the notice of election is registered by the registrar.

(2) The election remains in force until either—

(a) the company ceases to be a private company, or

(b) a notice of withdrawal sent by the company under section 790ZD is registered by the registrar,

whichever occurs first.]

NOTES

Inserted as noted to s 790A at **[1.875]**.

[1.901]

[790Z Effect of election on obligations under Chapter 3

(1) The effect of an election under section 790X on a company's obligations under Chapter 3 is as follows.

(2) The company's obligation to maintain a PSC register does not apply with respect to the period when the election is in force.

(3) This means that, during that period—

(a) the company must continue to keep a PSC register in accordance with Chapter 3 (a "historic" register) containing all the information that was required to be stated in that register as at the time immediately before the election took effect, but

(b) the company does not have to update that register to reflect any changes that occur after that time.

(4) The provisions of Chapter 3 (including the rights to inspect or require copies of the PSC register) continue to apply to the historic register during the period when the election is in force.

(5) The company must place a note in its historic register—

(a) stating that an election under section 790X is in force,

(b) recording when that election took effect, and

(c) indicating that up-to-date information about people with significant control over the company is available for public inspection on the central register.

(6) Subsections (12) and (13) of section 790M apply if a company makes default in complying with subsection (5) as they apply if a company makes default in complying with that section.

(7) The obligations under this section with respect to a historic register do not apply in a case where the election was made by subscribers wishing to form a private company.]

NOTES

Inserted as noted to s 790A at **[1.875]**.

[1.902]

[790ZA Duty to notify registrar of changes

(1) The duty under subsection (2) applies during the period when an election under section 790X is in force.

(2) The company must deliver to the registrar any information that the company would during that period have been obliged under Chapter 3 to enter in its PSC register, had the election not been in force.

(3) The information must be delivered as soon as reasonably practicable after the company becomes aware of it and, in any event, no later than the time by which the company would have been required to enter the information in its PSC register.

(4) If default is made in complying with this section, an offence is committed by—

(a) the company, and

(b) every officer of the company who is in default.

For this purpose a shadow director is treated as an officer of the company.

(5) A person guilty of an offence under this section is liable on summary conviction to a fine not exceeding level 3 on the standard scale and, for continued contravention, a daily default fine not exceeding one-tenth of level 3 on the standard scale.]

NOTES

Inserted as noted to s 790A at **[1.875]**.

[1.903]

[790ZB Information as to state of central register

(1) When a person inspects or requests a copy of material on the central register relating to a company in respect of which an election under section 790X is in force, the person may ask the company to confirm that all information that the company is required to deliver to the registrar under this Chapter has been delivered.

(2) If a company fails to respond to a request under subsection (1), an offence is committed by—

(a) the company, and

(b) every officer of the company who is in default.

(3) A person guilty of an offence under this section is liable on summary conviction to a fine not exceeding level 3 on the standard scale.]

NOTES

Inserted as noted to s 790A at **[1.875]**.

[1.904]

[790ZC Power of court to order company to remedy default or delay

(1) This section applies if—

(a) the name of a person is without sufficient cause included in, or omitted from, information that a company delivers to the registrar under this Chapter concerning persons who are a registrable person or a registrable relevant legal entity in relation to the company, or

(b) default is made or unnecessary delay takes place in informing the registrar under this Chapter that a person—

(i) has become a registrable person or a registrable relevant legal entity in relation to the company, or

(ii) has ceased to be a registrable person or a registrable relevant legal entity in relation to it.

(2) The person aggrieved, or any other interested party, may apply to the court for an order requiring the company to deliver to the registrar the information (or statements) necessary to rectify the position.

(3) The court may either refuse the application or may make the order and order the company to pay any damages sustained by any party aggrieved.

(4) On such an application the court may decide—

(a) any question as to whether the name of any person who is a party to the application should or should not be included in or omitted from information delivered to the registrar under this Chapter about persons who are a registrable person or a registrable relevant legal entity in relation to the company, and

(b) any question necessary or expedient to be decided for rectifying the position.

(5) Nothing in this section affects a person's rights under section 1095 or 1096 (rectification of register on application to registrar or under court order).

(6) The reference in this section to "any other interested party" is to—

(a) any member of the company, and

(b) any other person who is a registrable person or a registrable relevant legal entity in relation to the company.]

NOTES

Inserted as noted to s 790A at **[1.875]**.

[1.905]

[790ZD Withdrawing the election

(1) A company may withdraw an election made by or in respect of it under section 790X.

(2) Withdrawal is achieved by giving notice of withdrawal to the registrar.

(3) The withdrawal takes effect when the notice is registered by the registrar.

(4) The effect of withdrawal is that the company's obligation under Chapter 3 to maintain a PSC register applies from then on with respect to the period going forward.

(5) This means that, when the withdrawal takes effect—

(a) the company must enter in its PSC register all the information that is required to be contained in that register in respect of matters that are current as at that time,

(b) the company must also retain in its register all the information that it was required under section 790Z(3)(a) to keep in a historic register while the election was in force, but

(c) the company is not required to enter in its register information relating to the period when the election was in force that is no longer current.

(6) The company must place a note in its PSC register—

(a) stating that the election under section 790X has been withdrawn,

(b) recording when that withdrawal took effect, and

(c) indicating that information about people with significant control over the company relating to the period when the election was in force that is no longer current is available for public inspection on the central register.

(7) Subsections (12) and (13) of section 790M apply if a company makes default in complying with subsection (6) as they apply if a company makes default in complying with that section.]

NOTES

Inserted as noted to s 790A at **[1.875]**.

[1.906]

[790ZE Power to extend option to public companies

(1) The Secretary of State may by regulations amend this Act—

(a) to extend this Chapter (with or without modification) to public companies or public companies of a class specified in the regulations, and

(b) to make such other amendments as the Secretary of State thinks fit in consequence of that extension.

(2) Regulations under this section are subject to affirmative resolution procedure.]

NOTES

Inserted as noted to s 790A at **[1.875]**.

[CHAPTER 5 PROTECTION FROM DISCLOSURE

[1.907]

790ZF Protection of information as to usual residential address

(1) The provisions of sections 240 to 244 (directors' residential addresses: protection from disclosure) apply to information within subsection (2) as to protected information within the meaning of those sections.

(2) The information within this subsection is—

(a) information as to the usual residential address of a person with significant control over a company, and
(b) the information that such a person's service address is his or her usual residential address.
(3) Subsection (1) does not apply to information relating to a person if an application under regulations made under section 790ZG has been granted with respect to that information and not been revoked.]

NOTES

Inserted as noted to s 790A at **[1.875]**.

Regulations: the Register of People with Significant Control Regulations 2016, SI 2016/339 at **[4.559]**; the Registrar of Companies (Fees) (Amendment) Regulations 2016, SI 2016/621. For a summary of all statutory instruments made under this Act, see Appendix 4 at **[A4]**.

[1.908]
[790ZG Power to make regulations protecting material

(1) The Secretary of State may by regulations make provision requiring the registrar and the company to refrain from using or disclosing PSC particulars of a prescribed kind (or to refrain from doing so except in prescribed circumstances) where an application is made to the registrar requesting them to refrain from so doing.
(2) "PSC particulars" are particulars of a person with significant control over the company—
(a) including a person who used to be such a person, but
(b) excluding any person in relation to which this Part has effect by virtue of section 790C(12) as if the person were an individual.
(3) Regulations under this section may make provision as to—
(a) who may make an application,
(b) the grounds on which an application may be made,
(c) the information to be included in and documents to accompany an application,
(d) how an application is to be determined,
(e) the duration of and procedures for revoking the restrictions on use and disclosure,
(f) the operation of sections 790N to 790S in cases where an application is made, and
(g) the charging of fees by the registrar for disclosing PSC particulars where the regulations permit disclosure, by way of exception, in prescribed circumstances.
(4) Provision under subsection (3)(d) and (e) may in particular—
(a) confer a discretion on the registrar;
(b) provide for a question to be referred to a person other than the registrar for the purposes of determining the application or revoking the restrictions.
(5) Regulations under this section are subject to affirmative resolution procedure.
(6) Nothing in this section or in regulations made under it affects the use or disclosure of particulars of a person in any other capacity (for example, the use or disclosure of particulars of a person in that person's capacity as a member or director of the company).]

NOTES

Inserted as noted to s 790A at **[1.875]**.

Regulations: the Register of People with Significant Control Regulations 2016, SI 2016/339 at **[4.559]**. For a summary of all statutory instruments made under this Act, see Appendix 4 at **[A4]**.

PART 22 INFORMATION ABOUT INTERESTS IN A COMPANY'S SHARES

Introductory

[1.909]
791 Companies to which this Part applies

This Part applies only to public companies.

[1.910]
792 Shares to which this Part applies

(1) References in this Part to a company's shares are to the company's issued shares of a class carrying rights to vote in all circumstances at general meetings of the company (including any shares held as treasury shares).
(2) The temporary suspension of voting rights in respect of any shares does not affect the application of this Part in relation to interests in those or any other shares.

Notice requiring information about interests in shares

[1.911]
793 Notice by company requiring information about interests in its shares

(1) A public company may give notice under this section to any person whom the company knows or has reasonable cause to believe—
(a) to be interested in the company's shares, or
(b) to have been so interested at any time during the three years immediately preceding the date on which the notice is issued.
(2) The notice may require the person—
(a) to confirm that fact or (as the case may be) to state whether or not it is the case, and
(b) if he holds, or has during that time held, any such interest, to give such further information as may be required in accordance with the following provisions of this section.
(3) The notice may require the person to whom it is addressed to give particulars of his own present or past interest in the company's shares (held by him at any time during the three year period mentioned in subsection (1)(b)).
(4) The notice may require the person to whom it is addressed, where—
(a) his interest is a present interest and another interest in the shares subsists, or
(b) another interest in the shares subsisted during that three year period at a time when his interest subsisted,
to give, so far as lies within his knowledge, such particulars with respect to that other interest as may be required by the notice.

(5) The particulars referred to in subsections (3) and (4) include—
  (a) the identity of persons interested in the shares in question, and
  (b) whether persons interested in the same shares are or were parties to—
    (i) an agreement to which section 824 applies (certain share acquisition agreements), or
    (ii) an agreement or arrangement relating to the exercise of any rights conferred by the holding of the shares.

(6) The notice may require the person to whom it is addressed, where his interest is a past interest, to give (so far as lies within his knowledge) particulars of the identity of the person who held that interest immediately upon his ceasing to hold it.

(7) The information required by the notice must be given within such reasonable time as may be specified in the notice.

[1.912]
794 Notice requiring information: order imposing restrictions on shares

(1) Where—
  (a) a notice under section 793 (notice requiring information about interests in company's shares) is served by a company on a person who is or was interested in shares in the company, and
  (b) that person fails to give the company the information required by the notice within the time specified in it,

the company may apply to the court for an order directing that the shares in question be subject to restrictions.

For the effect of such an order see section 797.

(2) If the court is satisfied that such an order may unfairly affect the rights of third parties in respect of the shares, the court may, for the purpose of protecting those rights and subject to such terms as it thinks fit, direct that such acts by such persons or descriptions of persons and for such purposes as may be set out in the order shall not constitute a breach of the restrictions.

(3) On an application under this section the court may make an interim order. Any such order may be made unconditionally or on such terms as the court thinks fit.

(4) Sections 798 to 802 make further provision about orders under this section.

[1.913]
795 Notice requiring information: offences

(1) A person who—
  (a) fails to comply with a notice under section 793 (notice requiring information about interests in company's shares), or
  (b) in purported compliance with such a notice—
    (i) makes a statement that he knows to be false in a material particular, or
    (ii) recklessly makes a statement that is false in a material particular,

commits an offence.

(2) A person does not commit an offence under subsection (1)(a) if he proves that the requirement to give information was frivolous or vexatious.

(3) A person guilty of an offence under this section is liable—
  (a) on conviction on indictment, to imprisonment for a term not exceeding two years or a fine (or both);
  (b) on summary conviction—
    (i) in England and Wales, to imprisonment for a term not exceeding twelve months or to a fine not exceeding the statutory maximum (or both);
    (ii) in Scotland or Northern Ireland, to imprisonment for a term not exceeding six months, or to a fine not exceeding the statutory maximum (or both).

NOTES

Offences under this section: see further s 1131 at **[1.1301]**.

[1.914]
796 Notice requiring information: persons exempted from obligation to comply

(1) A person is not obliged to comply with a notice under section 793 (notice requiring information about interests in company's shares) if he is for the time being exempted by the Secretary of State from the operation of that section.

(2) The Secretary of State must not grant any such exemption unless—
  (a) he has consulted the Governor of the Bank of England, and
  (b) he (the Secretary of State) is satisfied that, having regard to any undertaking given by the person in question with respect to any interest held or to be held by him in any shares, there are special reasons why that person should not be subject to the obligations imposed by that section.

Orders imposing restrictions on shares

[1.915]
797 Consequences of order imposing restrictions

(1) The effect of an order under section 794 that shares are subject to restrictions is as follows—
  (a) any transfer of the shares is void;
  (b) no voting rights are exercisable in respect of the shares;
  (c) no further shares may be issued in right of the shares or in pursuance of an offer made to their holder;
  (d) except in a liquidation, no payment may be made of sums due from the company on the shares, whether in respect of capital or otherwise.

(2) Where shares are subject to the restriction in subsection (1)(a), an agreement to transfer the shares is void.

This does not apply to an agreement to transfer the shares on the making of an order under section 800 made by virtue of subsection (3)(b) (removal of restrictions in case of court-approved transfer).

(3) Where shares are subject to the restriction in subsection (1)(c) or (d), an agreement to transfer any right to be issued with other shares in right of those shares, or to receive any payment on them (otherwise than in a liquidation), is void.

This does not apply to an agreement to transfer any such right on the making of an order under section 800 made by virtue of subsection (3)(b) (removal of restrictions in case of court-approved transfer).

(4) The provisions of this section are subject—

(a) to any directions under section 794(2) or section 799(3) (directions for protection of third parties), and

(b) in the case of an interim order under section 794(3), to the terms of the order.

[1.916]

798 Penalty for attempted evasion of restrictions

(1) This section applies where shares are subject to restrictions by virtue of an order under section 794.

(2) A person commits an offence if he—

(a) exercises or purports to exercise any right—

(i) to dispose of shares that to his knowledge, are for the time being subject to restrictions, or

(ii) to dispose of any right to be issued with any such shares, or

(b) votes in respect of any such shares (whether as holder or proxy), or appoints a proxy to vote in respect of them, or

(c) being the holder of any such shares, fails to notify of their being subject to those restrictions a person whom he does not know to be aware of that fact but does know to be entitled (apart from the restrictions) to vote in respect of those shares whether as holder or as proxy, or

(d) being the holder of any such shares, or being entitled to a right to be issued with other shares in right of them, or to receive any payment on them (otherwise than in a liquidation), enters into an agreement which is void under section 797(2) or (3).

(3) If shares in a company are issued in contravention of the restrictions, an offence is committed by—

(a) the company, and

(b) every officer of the company who is in default.

(4) A person guilty of an offence under this section is liable—

(a) on conviction on indictment, to a fine;

(b) on summary conviction, to a fine not exceeding the statutory maximum.

(5) The provisions of this section are subject—

(a) to any directions under—

section 794(2) (directions for protection of third parties), or

section 799 or 800 (relaxation or removal of restrictions), and

(b) in the case of an interim order under section 794(3), to the terms of the order.

[1.917]

799 Relaxation of restrictions

(1) An application may be made to the court on the ground that an order directing that shares shall be subject to restrictions unfairly affects the rights of third parties in respect of the shares.

(2) An application for an order under this section may be made by the company or by any person aggrieved.

(3) If the court is satisfied that the application is well-founded, it may, for the purpose of protecting the rights of third parties in respect of the shares, and subject to such terms as it thinks fit, direct that such acts by such persons or descriptions of persons and for such purposes as may be set out in the order do not constitute a breach of the restrictions.

[1.918]

800 Removal of restrictions

(1) An application may be made to the court for an order directing that the shares shall cease to be subject to restrictions.

(2) An application for an order under this section may be made by the company or by any person aggrieved.

(3) The court must not make an order under this section unless—

(a) it is satisfied that the relevant facts about the shares have been disclosed to the company and no unfair advantage has accrued to any person as a result of the earlier failure to make that disclosure, or

(b) the shares are to be transferred for valuable consideration and the court approves the transfer.

(4) An order under this section made by virtue of subsection (3)(b) may continue, in whole or in part, the restrictions mentioned in section 797(1)(c) and (d) (restrictions on issue of further shares or making of payments) so far as they relate to a right acquired or offer made before the transfer.

(5) Where any restrictions continue in force under subsection (4)—

(a) an application may be made under this section for an order directing that the shares shall cease to be subject to those restrictions, and

(b) subsection (3) does not apply in relation to the making of such an order.

[1.919]

801 Order for sale of shares

(1) The court may order that the shares subject to restrictions be sold, subject to the court's approval as to the sale.

(2) An application for an order under subsection (1) may only be made by the company.

(3) Where the court has made an order under this section, it may make such further order relating to the sale or transfer of the shares as it thinks fit.

(4) An application for an order under subsection (3) may be made—

(a) by the company,

(b) by the person appointed by or in pursuance of the order to effect the sale, or

(c) by any person interested in the shares.

(5) On making an order under subsection (1) or (3) the court may order that the applicant's costs (in Scotland, expenses) be paid out of the proceeds of sale.

[1.920]

802 Application of proceeds of sale under court order

(1) Where shares are sold in pursuance of an order of the court under section 801, the proceeds of the sale, less the costs of the sale, must be paid into court for the benefit of the persons who are beneficially interested in the shares.

(2) A person who is beneficially interested in the shares may apply to the court for the whole or part of those proceeds to be paid to him.

(3) On such an application the court shall order the payment to the applicant of—

(a) the whole of the proceeds of sale together with any interest on them, or

(b) if another person had a beneficial interest in the shares at the time of their sale, such proportion of the proceeds and interest as the value of the applicant's interest in the shares bears to the total value of the shares.

This is subject to the following qualification.

(4) If the court has ordered under section 801(5) that the costs (in Scotland, expenses) of an applicant under that section are to be paid out of the proceeds of sale, the applicant is entitled to payment of his costs (or expenses) out of those proceeds before any person interested in the shares receives any part of those proceeds.

Power of members to require company to act

[1.921]

803 Power of members to require company to act

(1) The members of a company may require it to exercise its powers under section 793 (notice requiring information about interests in shares).

(2) A company is required to do so once it has received requests (to the same effect) from members of the company holding at least 10% of such of the paid-up capital of the company as carries a right to vote at general meetings of the company (excluding any voting rights attached to any shares in the company held as treasury shares).

(3) A request—

(a) may be in hard copy form or in electronic form,

(b) must—

(i) state that the company is requested to exercise its powers under section 793,

(ii) specify the manner in which the company is requested to act, and

(iii) give reasonable grounds for requiring the company to exercise those powers in the manner specified, and

(c) must be authenticated by the person or persons making it.

[1.922]

804 Duty of company to comply with requirement

(1) A company that is required under section 803 to exercise its powers under section 793 (notice requiring information about interests in company's shares) must exercise those powers in the manner specified in the requests.

(2) If default is made in complying with subsection (1) an offence is committed by every officer of the company who is in default.

(3) A person guilty of an offence under this section is liable—

(a) on conviction on indictment, to a fine;

(b) on summary conviction, to a fine not exceeding the statutory maximum.

[1.923]

805 Report to members on outcome of investigation

(1) On the conclusion of an investigation carried out by a company in pursuance of a requirement under section 803 the company must cause a report of the information received in pursuance of the investigation to be prepared.

The report must be made available for inspection within a reasonable period (not more than 15 days) after the conclusion of the investigation.

(2) Where—

(a) a company undertakes an investigation in pursuance of a requirement under section 803, and

(b) the investigation is not concluded within three months after the date on which the company became subject to the requirement,

the company must cause to be prepared in respect of that period, and in respect of each succeeding period of three months ending before the conclusion of the investigation, an interim report of the information received during that period in pursuance of the investigation.

(3) Each such report must be made available for inspection within a reasonable period (not more than 15 days) after the end of the period to which it relates.

(4) The reports must be retained by the company for at least six years from the date on which they are first made available for inspection and must be kept available for inspection during that time—

(a) at the company's registered office, or

(b) at a place specified in regulations under section 1136.

(5) The company must give notice to the registrar—

(a) of the place at which the reports are kept available for inspection, and

(b) of any change in that place,

unless they have at all times been kept at the company's registered office.

(6) The company must within three days of making any report prepared under this section available for inspection, notify the members who made the requests under section 803 where the report is so available.

(7) For the purposes of this section an investigation carried out by a company in pursuance of a requirement under section 803 is concluded when—

(a) the company has made all such inquiries as are necessary or expedient for the purposes of the requirement, and

(b) in the case of each such inquiry—

(i) a response has been received by the company, or

(ii) the time allowed for a response has elapsed.

[1.924]

806 Report to members: offences

(1) If default is made for 14 days in complying with section 805(5) (notice to registrar of place at which reports made available for inspection) an offence is committed by—

(a) the company, and

(b) every officer of the company who is in default.

(2) A person guilty of an offence under subsection (1) is liable on summary conviction to a fine not exceeding level 3 on the standard scale and, for continued contravention, a daily default fine not exceeding one-tenth of level 3 on the standard scale.

(3) If default is made in complying with any other provision of section 805 (report to members on outcome of investigation), an offence is committed by every officer of the company who is in default.

(4) A person guilty of an offence under subsection (3) is liable—

(a) on conviction on indictment, to a fine;

(b) on summary conviction, to a fine not exceeding the statutory maximum.

[1.925]

807 Right to inspect and request copy of reports

(1) Any report prepared under section 805 must be open to inspection by any person without charge.

(2) Any person is entitled, on request and on payment of such fee as may be prescribed, to be provided with a copy of any such report or any part of it. The copy must be provided within ten days after the request is received by the company.

(3) If an inspection required under subsection (1) is refused, or default is made in complying with subsection (2), an offence is committed by—

(a) the company, and

(b) every officer of the company who is in default.

(4) A person guilty of an offence under this section is liable on summary conviction to a fine not exceeding level 3 on the standard scale and, for continued contravention, a daily default fine not exceeding one-tenth of level 3 on the standard scale.

(5) In the case of any such refusal or default the court may by order compel an immediate inspection or, as the case may be, direct that the copy required be sent to the person requiring it.

NOTES

Regulations: the Companies (Fees for Inspection and Copying of Company Records) Regulations 2007, SI 2007/2612 at **[4.11]**. For a summary of all statutory instruments made under this Act, see Appendix 4 at **[A4]**.

Register of interests disclosed

[1.926]

808 Register of interests disclosed

(1) The company must keep a register of information received by it in pursuance of a requirement imposed under section 793 (notice requiring information about interests in company's shares).

(2) A company which receives any such information must, within three days of the receipt, enter in the register—

(a) the fact that the requirement was imposed and the date on which it was imposed, and

(b) the information received in pursuance of the requirement.

(3) The information must be entered against the name of the present holder of the shares in question or, if there is no present holder or the present holder is not known, against the name of the person holding the interest.

(4) The register must be made up so that the entries against the names entered in it appear in chronological order.

(5) If default is made in complying with this section an offence is committed by—

(a) the company, and

(b) every officer of the company who is in default.

(6) A person guilty of an offence under this section is liable on summary conviction to a fine not exceeding level 3 on the standard scale and, for continued contravention, a daily default fine not exceeding one-tenth of level 3 on the standard scale.

(7) The company is not by virtue of anything done for the purposes of this section affected with notice of, or put upon inquiry as to, the rights of any person in relation to any shares.

[1.927]

809 Register to be kept available for inspection

(1) The register kept under section 808 (register of interests disclosed) must be kept available for inspection—

(a) at the company's registered office, or

(b) at a place specified in regulations under section 1136.

(2) A company must give notice to the registrar of companies of the place where the register is kept available for inspection and of any change in that place.

(3) No such notice is required if the register has at all times been kept available for inspection at the company's registered office.

(4) If default is made in complying with subsection (1), or a company makes default for 14 days in complying with subsection (2), an offence is committed by—

(a) the company, and

(b) every officer of the company who is in default.

(5) A person guilty of an offence under this section is liable on summary conviction to a fine not exceeding level 3 on the standard scale and, for continued contravention, a daily default fine not exceeding one-tenth of level 3 on the standard scale.

[1.928]

810 Associated index

(1) Unless the register kept under section 808 (register of interests disclosed) is kept in such a form as itself to constitute an index, the company must keep an index of the names entered in it.

(2) The company must make any necessary entry or alteration in the index within ten days after the date on which any entry or alteration is made in the register.

(3) The index must contain, in respect of each name, a sufficient indication to enable the information entered against it to be readily found.

(4) The index must be at all times kept available for inspection at the same place as the register.

(5) If default is made in complying with this section, an offence is committed by—

(a) the company, and

(b) every officer of the company who is in default.

(6) A person guilty of an offence under this section is liable on summary conviction to a fine not exceeding level 3 on the standard scale and, for continued contravention, a daily default fine not exceeding one-tenth of level 3 on the standard scale.

[1.929]

811 Rights to inspect and require copy of entries

(1) The register required to be kept under section 808 (register of interests disclosed), and any associated index, must be open to inspection by any person without charge.

(2) Any person is entitled, on request and on payment of such fee as may be prescribed, to be provided with a copy of any entry in the register.

(3) A person seeking to exercise either of the rights conferred by this section must make a request to the company to that effect.

(4) The request must contain the following information—

(a) in the case of an individual, his name and address;

(b) in the case of an organisation, the name and address of an individual responsible for making the request on behalf of the organisation;

(c) the purpose for which the information is to be used; and

(d) whether the information will be disclosed to any other person, and if so—

(i) where that person is an individual, his name and address,

(ii) where that person is an organisation, the name and address of an individual responsible for receiving the information on its behalf, and

(iii) the purpose for which the information is to be used by that person.

NOTES

Regulations: the Companies (Fees for Inspection and Copying of Company Records) Regulations 2007, SI 2007/2612 at **[4.11]**. For a summary of all statutory instruments made under this Act, see Appendix 4 at **[A4]**.

[1.930]

812 Court supervision of purpose for which rights may be exercised

(1) Where a company receives a request under section 811 (register of interests disclosed: right to inspect and require copy), it must—

(a) comply with the request if it is satisfied that it is made for a proper purpose, and

(b) refuse the request if it is not so satisfied.

(2) If the company refuses the request, it must inform the person making the request, stating the reason why it is not satisfied.

(3) A person whose request is refused may apply to the court.

(4) If an application is made to the court—

(a) the person who made the request must notify the company, and

(b) the company must use its best endeavours to notify any persons whose details would be disclosed if the company were required to comply with the request.

(5) If the court is not satisfied that the inspection or copy is sought for a proper purpose, it shall direct the company not to comply with the request.

(6) If the court makes such a direction and it appears to the court that the company is or may be subject to other requests made for a similar purpose (whether made by the same person or different persons), it may direct that the company is not to comply with any such request.

The order must contain such provision as appears to the court appropriate to identify the requests to which it applies.

(7) If the court does not direct the company not to comply with the request, the company must comply with the request immediately upon the court giving its decision or, as the case may be, the proceedings being discontinued.

[1.931]

813 Register of interests disclosed: refusal of inspection or default in providing copy

(1) If an inspection required under section 811 (register of interests disclosed: right to inspect and require copy) is refused or default is made in providing a copy required under that section, otherwise than in accordance with [section 812], an offence is committed by—

(a) the company, and

(b) every officer of the company who is in default.

(2) A person guilty of an offence under this section is liable on summary conviction to a fine not exceeding level 3 on the standard scale and, for continued contravention, a daily default fine not exceeding one-tenth of level 3 on the standard scale.

(3) In the case of any such refusal or default the court may by order compel an immediate inspection or, as the case may be, direct that the copy required be sent to the person requesting it.

NOTES

Sub-s (1): words in square brackets substituted by the Small Business, Enterprise and Employment Act 2015, s 83, as from 26 May 2015.

[1.932]

814 Register of interests disclosed: offences in connection with request for or disclosure of information

(1) It is an offence for a person knowingly or recklessly to make in a request under section 811 (register of interests disclosed: right to inspect or require copy) a statement that is misleading, false or deceptive in a material particular.

(2) It is an offence for a person in possession of information obtained by exercise of either of the rights conferred by that section—

(a) to do anything that results in the information being disclosed to another person, or

(b) to fail to do anything with the result that the information is disclosed to another person,

knowing, or having reason to suspect, that person may use the information for a purpose that is not a proper purpose.

(3) A person guilty of an offence under this section is liable—

(a) on conviction on indictment, to imprisonment for a term not exceeding two years or a fine (or both);

(b) on summary conviction—

(i) in England and Wales, to imprisonment for a term not exceeding twelve months or to a fine not exceeding the statutory maximum (or both);

(ii) in Scotland or Northern Ireland, to imprisonment for a term not exceeding six months, or to a fine not exceeding the statutory maximum (or both).

NOTES

Offences under this section: see further s 1131 at **[1.1301]**.

[1.933]

815 Entries not to be removed from register

(1) Entries in the register kept under section 808 (register of interests disclosed) must not be deleted except in accordance with—

section 816 (old entries), or

section 817 (incorrect entry relating to third party).

(2) If an entry is deleted in contravention of subsection (1), the company must restore it as soon as reasonably practicable.

(3) If default is made in complying with subsection (1) or (2), an offence is committed by—

(a) the company, and

(b) every officer of the company who is in default.

(4) A person guilty of an offence under this section is liable on summary conviction to a fine not exceeding level 3 on the standard scale and, for continued contravention of subsection (2), a daily default fine not exceeding one-tenth of level 3 on the standard scale.

[1.934]

816 Removal of entries from register: old entries

A company may remove an entry from the register kept under section 808 (register of interests disclosed) if more than six years have elapsed since the entry was made.

[1.935]

817 Removal of entries from register: incorrect entry relating to third party

(1) This section applies where in pursuance of an obligation imposed by a notice under section 793 (notice requiring information about interests in company's shares) a person gives to a company the name and address of another person as being interested in shares in the company.

(2) That other person may apply to the company for the removal of the entry from the register.

(3) If the company is satisfied that the information in pursuance of which the entry was made is incorrect, it shall remove the entry.

(4) If an application under subsection (3) is refused, the applicant may apply to the court for an order directing the company to remove the entry in question from the register.

The court may make such an order if it thinks fit.

[1.936]

818 Adjustment of entry relating to share acquisition agreement

(1) If a person who is identified in the register kept by a company under section 808 (register of interests disclosed) as being a party to an agreement to which section 824 applies (certain share acquisition agreements) ceases to be a party to the agreement, he may apply to the company for the inclusion of that information in the register.

(2) If the company is satisfied that he has ceased to be a party to the agreement, it shall record that information (if not already recorded) in every place where his name appears in the register as a party to the agreement.

(3) If an application under this section is refused (otherwise than on the ground that the information has already been recorded), the applicant may apply to the court for an order directing the company to include the information in question in the register.

The court may make such an order if it thinks fit.

[1.937]

819 Duty of company ceasing to be public company

(1) If a company ceases to be a public company, it must continue to keep any register kept under section 808 (register of interests disclosed), and any associated index, until the end of the period of six years after it ceased to be such a company.

(2) If default is made in complying with this section, an offence is committed by—

(a) the company, and

(b) every officer of the company who is in default.

(3) A person guilty of an offence under this section is liable on summary conviction to a fine not exceeding level 3 on the standard scale and, for continued contravention, a daily default fine not exceeding one-tenth of level 3 on the standard scale.

Meaning of interest in shares

[1.938]

820 Interest in shares: general

(1) This section applies to determine for the purposes of this Part whether a person has an interest in shares.

(2) In this Part—

(a) a reference to an interest in shares includes an interest of any kind whatsoever in the shares, and

(b) any restraints or restrictions to which the exercise of any right attached to the interest is or may be subject shall be disregarded.

(3) Where an interest in shares is comprised in property held on trust, every beneficiary of the trust is treated as having an interest in the shares.

(4) A person is treated as having an interest in shares if—

(a) he enters into a contract to acquire them, or

(b) not being the registered holder, he is entitled—

(i) to exercise any right conferred by the holding of the shares, or

(ii) to control the exercise of any such right.

(5) For the purposes of subsection (4)(b) a person is entitled to exercise or control the exercise of a right conferred by the holding of shares if he—

(a) has a right (whether subject to conditions or not) the exercise of which would make him so entitled, or

(b) is under an obligation (whether subject to conditions or not) the fulfilment of which would make him so entitled.

(6) A person is treated as having an interest in shares if—

(a) he has a right to call for delivery of the shares to himself or to his order, or

(b) he has a right to acquire an interest in shares or is under an obligation to take an interest in shares.

This applies whether the right or obligation is conditional or absolute.

(7) Persons having a joint interest are treated as each having that interest.

(8) It is immaterial that shares in which a person has an interest are unidentifiable.

[1.939]

821 Interest in shares: right to subscribe for shares

(1) Section 793 (notice by company requiring information about interests in its shares) applies in relation to a person who has, or previously had, or is or was entitled to acquire, a right to subscribe for shares in the company as it applies in relation to a person who is or was interested in shares in that company.

(2) References in that section to an interest in shares shall be read accordingly.

[1.940]

822 Interest in shares: family interests

(1) For the purposes of this Part a person is taken to be interested in shares in which—

(a) his spouse or civil partner, or

(b) any infant child or step-child of his,

is interested.

(2) In relation to Scotland "infant" means a person under the age of 18 years.

[1.941]

823 Interest in shares: corporate interests

(1) For the purposes of this Part a person is taken to be interested in shares if a body corporate is interested in them and—

(a) the body or its directors are accustomed to act in accordance with his directions or instructions, or

(b) he is entitled to exercise or control the exercise of one-third or more of the voting power at general meetings of the body.

(2) For the purposes of this section a person is treated as entitled to exercise or control the exercise of voting power if—

(a) another body corporate is entitled to exercise or control the exercise of that voting power, and

(b) he is entitled to exercise or control the exercise of one-third or more of the voting power at general meetings of that body corporate.

(3) For the purposes of this section a person is treated as entitled to exercise or control the exercise of voting power if—

(a) he has a right (whether or not subject to conditions) the exercise of which would make him so entitled, or

(b) he is under an obligation (whether or not subject to conditions) the fulfilment of which would make him so entitled.

[1.942]

824 Interest in shares: agreement to acquire interests in a particular company

(1) For the purposes of this Part an interest in shares may arise from an agreement between two or more persons that includes provision for the acquisition by any one or more of them of interests in shares of a particular public company (the "target company" for that agreement).

(2) This section applies to such an agreement if—

(a) the agreement includes provision imposing obligations or restrictions on any one or more of the parties to it with respect to their use, retention or disposal of their interests in the shares of the target company acquired in pursuance of the agreement (whether or not together with any other interests of theirs in the company's shares to which the agreement relates), and

(b) an interest in the target company's shares is in fact acquired by any of the parties in pursuance of the agreement.

(3) The reference in subsection (2) to the use of interests in shares in the target company is to the exercise of any rights or of any control or influence arising from those interests (including the right to enter into an agreement for the exercise, or for control of the exercise, of any of those rights by another person).

(4) Once an interest in shares in the target company has been acquired in pursuance of the agreement, this section continues to apply to the agreement so long as the agreement continues to include provisions of any description mentioned in subsection (2).

This applies irrespective of—

(a) whether or not any further acquisitions of interests in the company's shares take place in pursuance of the agreement;

(b) any change in the persons who are for the time being parties to it;

(c) any variation of the agreement.

References in this subsection to the agreement include any agreement having effect (whether directly or indirectly) in substitution for the original agreement.

(5) In this section—

(a) "agreement" includes any agreement or arrangement, and

(b) references to provisions of an agreement include—

(i) undertakings, expectations or understandings operative under an arrangement, and

(ii) any provision whether express or implied and whether absolute or not.

References elsewhere in this Part to an agreement to which this section applies have a corresponding meaning.

(6) This section does not apply—

(a) to an agreement that is not legally binding unless it involves mutuality in the undertakings, expectations or understandings of the parties to it; or

(b) to an agreement to underwrite or sub-underwrite an offer of shares in a company, provided the agreement is confined to that purpose and any matters incidental to it.

[1.943]

825 Extent of obligation in case of share acquisition agreement

(1) For the purposes of this Part each party to an agreement to which section 824 applies is treated as interested in all shares in the target company in which any other party to the agreement is interested apart from the agreement (whether or not the interest of the other party was acquired, or includes any interest that was acquired, in pursuance of the agreement).

(2) For those purposes an interest of a party to such an agreement in shares in the target company is an interest apart from the agreement if he is interested in those shares otherwise than by virtue of the application of section 824 (and this section) in relation to the agreement.

(3) Accordingly, any such interest of the person (apart from the agreement) includes for those purposes any interest treated as his under section 822 or 823 (family or corporate interests) or by the application of section 824 (and this section) in relation to any other agreement with respect to shares in the target company to which he is a party.

(4) A notification with respect to his interest in shares in the target company made to the company under this Part by a person who is for the time being a party to an agreement to which section 824 applies must—

(a) state that the person making the notification is a party to such an agreement,

(b) include the names and (so far as known to him) the addresses of the other parties to the agreement, identifying them as such, and

(c) state whether or not any of the shares to which the notification relates are shares in which he is interested by virtue of section 824 (and this section) and, if so, the number of those shares.

Other supplementary provisions

[1.944]

826 Information protected from wider disclosure

(1) Information in respect of which a company is for the time being entitled to any exemption conferred by regulations under section 409(3) (information about related undertakings to be given in notes to accounts: exemption where disclosure harmful to company's business)—

(a) must not be included in a report under section 805 (report to members on outcome of investigation), and

(b) must not be made available under section 811 (right to inspect and request copy of entries).

(2) Where any such information is omitted from a report under section 805, that fact must be stated in the report.

[1.945]

827 Reckoning of periods for fulfilling obligations

Where the period allowed by any provision of this Part for fulfilling an obligation is expressed as a number of days, any day that is not a working day shall be disregarded in reckoning that period.

[1.946]

828 Power to make further provision by regulations

(1) The Secretary of State may by regulations amend—

(a) the definition of shares to which this Part applies (section 792),

(b) the provisions as to notice by a company requiring information about interests in its shares (section 793), and

(c) the provisions as to what is taken to be an interest in shares (sections 820 and 821).

(2) The regulations may amend, repeal or replace those provisions and make such other consequential amendments or repeals of provisions of this Part as appear to the Secretary of State to be appropriate.

(3) Regulations under this section are subject to affirmative resolution procedure.

NOTES

Regulations: no Regulations have been made under this section.

PART 23 DISTRIBUTIONS

CHAPTER 1 RESTRICTIONS ON WHEN DISTRIBUTIONS MAY BE MADE

Introductory

[1.947]

829 Meaning of "distribution"

(1) In this Part "distribution" means every description of distribution of a company's assets to its members, whether in cash or otherwise, subject to the following exceptions.

(2) The following are not distributions for the purposes of this Part—

(a) an issue of shares as fully or partly paid bonus shares;

(b) the reduction of share capital—

(i) by extinguishing or reducing the liability of any of the members on any of the company's shares in respect of share capital not paid up, or

(ii) by repaying paid-up share capital;

(c) the redemption or purchase of any of the company's own shares out of capital (including the proceeds of any fresh issue of shares) or out of unrealised profits in accordance with Chapter 3, 4 or 5 of Part 18;

(d) a distribution of assets to members of the company on its winding up.

General rules

[1.948]

830 Distributions to be made only out of profits available for the purpose

(1) A company may only make a distribution out of profits available for the purpose.

(2) A company's profits available for distribution are its accumulated, realised profits, so far as not previously utilised by distribution or capitalisation, less its accumulated, realised losses, so far as not previously written off in a reduction or reorganisation of capital duly made.

(3) Subsection (2) has effect subject to sections 832[, 833A] and 835 (investment companies [and Solvency 2 insurance companies]).

NOTES

Sub-s (3): number in first pair of square brackets inserted, and words in second pair of square brackets substituted, by the Companies Act 2006 (Distributions of Insurance Companies) Regulations 2016, SI 2016/1194, reg 2(1), (2), as from 30 December 2016 (in relation to distributions made on or after that date by reference to relevant accounts (within the meaning of s 836) prepared for any period ending on or after 1 January 2016).

[1.949]

831 Net asset restriction on distributions by public companies

(1) A public company may only make a distribution—

(a) if the amount of its net assets is not less than the aggregate of its called-up share capital and undistributable reserves, and

(b) if, and to the extent that, the distribution does not reduce the amount of those assets to less than that aggregate.

(2) For this purpose a company's "net assets" means the aggregate of the company's assets less the aggregate of its liabilities.

(3) "Liabilities" here includes—

(a) where the relevant accounts are Companies Act accounts, provisions of a kind specified for the purposes of this subsection by regulations under section 396;

(b) where the relevant accounts are IAS accounts, provisions of any kind.

(4) A company's undistributable reserves are—

(a) its share premium account;

(b) its capital redemption reserve;

(c) the amount by which its accumulated, unrealised profits (so far as not previously utilised by capitalisation) exceed its accumulated, unrealised losses (so far as not previously written off in a reduction or reorganisation of capital duly made);

(d) any other reserve that the company is prohibited from distributing—

(i) by any enactment (other than one contained in this Part), or

(ii) by its articles.

The reference in paragraph (c) to capitalisation does not include a transfer of profits of the company to its capital redemption reserve.

(5) A public company must not include any uncalled share capital as an asset in any accounts relevant for purposes of this section.

(6) Subsection (1) has effect subject to sections 832 and 835 (investment companies etc: distributions out of accumulated revenue profits).

NOTES

Regulations under section 396: see the notes to that section at **[1.451]**. See also the Large and Medium-sized Companies and Groups (Accounts and Reports) Regulations 2008, SI 2008/410, reg 12 (at **[4.71]**) which provides that Sch 9 to those Regulations (at **[4.112]**, **[4.113]**) defines "provisions" for the purpose of those Regulations and for the purposes of sub-s (3)(a) above.

Distributions by investment companies [or Solvency 2 insurance companies]

NOTES

Words in square brackets in the preceding heading inserted by the Companies Act 2006 (Distributions of Insurance Companies) Regulations 2016, SI 2016/1194, reg 2(1), (3), as from 30 December 2016 (in relation to distributions made on or after that date by reference to relevant accounts (within the meaning of s 836) prepared for any period ending on or after 1 January 2016).

[1.950]

832 Distributions by investment companies out of accumulated revenue profits

(1) An investment company may make a distribution out of its accumulated, realised revenue profits if the following conditions are met.

(2) It may make such a distribution only if, and to the extent that, its accumulated, realised revenue profits, so far as not previously utilised by a distribution or capitalisation, exceed its accumulated revenue losses (whether realised or unrealised), so far as not previously written off in a reduction or reorganisation of capital duly made.

(3) It may make such a distribution only—

(a) if the amount of its assets is at least equal to one and a half times the aggregate of its liabilities to creditors, and

(b) if, and to the extent that, the distribution does not reduce that amount to less than one and a half times that aggregate.

(4) For this purpose a company's liabilities to creditors include—

(a) in the case of Companies Act accounts, provisions of a kind specified for the purposes of this subsection by regulations under section 396;

(b) in the case of IAS accounts, provisions for liabilities to creditors.

(5) The following conditions must also be met—

[(a) the company's shares must be shares admitted to trading on a [UK regulated market];]

(b) during the relevant period it must not have—

(i) . . .

(ii) applied any unrealised profits . . . in paying up debentures or amounts unpaid on its issued shares;

(c) it must have given notice to the registrar under section 833(1) (notice of intention to carry on business as an investment company)—

(i) before the beginning of the relevant period, or

(ii) as soon as reasonably practicable after the date of its incorporation.

(6) For the purposes of this section—

(a) . . .

(b) the "relevant period" is the period beginning with—

(i) the first day of the accounting reference period immediately preceding that in which the proposed distribution is to be made, or

(ii) where the distribution is to be made in the company's first accounting reference period, the first day of that period,

and ending with the date of the distribution.

(7) The company must not include any uncalled share capital as an asset in any accounts relevant for purposes of this section.

NOTES

Paragraph (a) of sub-s (5) was substituted, and the words omitted from that subsection and from sub-s (6) were repealed, by the Companies Act 2006 (Amendment of Part 23) (Investment Companies) Regulations 2012, SI 2012/952, reg 2(1)–(3), as from 6 April 2012.

Words in square brackets in sub-s (5)(a) substituted by the Companies, Limited Liability Partnerships and Partnerships (Amendment etc) (EU Exit) Regulations 2019, SI 2019/348, reg 6, Sch 1, paras 1, 12, as from IP completion day (as defined in the European Union (Withdrawal Agreement) Act 2020, s 39) (for transitional provisions see Sch 4, para 3 to the 2019 Regulations at **[12.105]**).

Regulations under section 396: see the notes to that section at **[1.451]**. See also the Large and Medium-sized Companies and Groups (Accounts and Reports) Regulations 2008, SI 2008/410, reg 12 (at **[4.71]**) which provides that Sch 9 to those Regulations (at **[4.112]**, **[4.113]**) defines "provisions" for the purpose of those Regulations and for the purposes of sub-s (4)(a) above.

[1.951]

833 Meaning of "investment company"

(1) In this Part an "investment company" means a public company that—

(a) has given notice (which has not been revoked) to the registrar of its intention to carry on business as an investment company, and

(b) since the date of that notice has complied with the following [requirement].

(2) [The requirement is]—

(a) that the business of the company consists of investing its funds [in shares, land or other assets], with the aim of spreading investment risk and giving members of the company the benefit of the results of the management of its funds;

(b)–(d) . . .

(3) . . .

(4) Notice to the registrar under this section may be revoked at any time by the company on giving notice to the registrar that it no longer wishes to be an investment company within the meaning of this section.

(5) On giving such a notice, the company ceases to be such a company.

NOTES

The words in square brackets in sub-ss (1), (2) were substituted, and sub-s (2)(b)–(d) and sub-s (3) were repealed, by the Companies Act 2006 (Amendment of Part 23) (Investment Companies) Regulations 2012, SI 2012/952, reg 2(1), (4)–(6), as from 6 April 2012, in relation to accounting reference periods of an existing investment company beginning on or after 6 April 2012.

[1.952]

[833A Distributions by insurance companies authorised under the Solvency 2 Directive

(1) This section applies in relation to any authorised insurance company carrying on long-term business that is authorised in accordance with Article 14 of the Solvency 2 Directive.

(2) For the purposes of section 830(2), the realised profit or loss of the company for the period in respect of which its relevant accounts (within the meaning of section 836) are prepared is taken to be the amount given by the formula in subsection (4) (with a positive figure taken to be a realised profit and a negative figure taken to be a realised loss).

(3) But the company's profits available for distribution are limited to an amount that does not exceed its accumulated profits (whether realised or not), so far as not previously utilised by distribution or capitalisation, less its accumulated losses (whether realised or not), so far as not previously written off in a reduction or reorganisation of capital duly made.

(4) The formula is A – L – D,

where—

"A" is the total value of the company's assets;

"L" is the total value of the company's liabilities; and

"D" is the total value of the items within subsection (5) relating to the company;

and, in each case, the value is to be determined as at the date of the company's balance sheet that forms part of the accounts mentioned in subsection (2).

(5) The items within this subsection are—

(a) if the value of shares held by the company in a qualifying investment subsidiary exceeds the value of the consideration given by it for their acquisition, the amount of that excess;

(b) any asset of the company representing a surplus in a defined benefit pension scheme;

(c) if the value of the assets held by the company in a ring-fenced fund exceeds the value of the liabilities incurred by the company in respect of that fund, the amount of that excess;

(d) the amount of any liability of the company in respect of deferred tax shown in the company's balance sheet that relates to any asset within paragraph (a), (b) or (c);

(e) if—

(i) the company has permission under regulation 42 of the Solvency 2 Regulations 2015 to apply a matching adjustment to a relevant risk-free interest rate term structure to calculate the best estimate of a portfolio of the company's life insurance or reinsurance obligations, and

(ii) the value of the portfolio of the company's assets assigned by the company to cover the best estimate exceeds the value of the portfolio of the company's life insurance or reinsurance obligations,

the amount of that excess; and

(f) the following capital items of the company—

(i) paid-in ordinary share capital together with any related share premium account;

(ii) paid-in preference shares which are not liabilities of the company together with any related share premium account;

(iii) capital redemption reserve; and

(iv) any other reserve that the company is prohibited from distributing (ignoring this Part for this purpose).

(6) So far as anything falls within more than one of the above paragraphs of subsection (5), its value is to be taken into account only once.

(7) The company's assets and liabilities must be valued in accordance with—

(a) rules made by the Prudential Regulation Authority under Part 9A of the Financial Services and Markets Act 2000 implementing Articles 75 to 85, and 308b to 308e, of the Solvency 2 Directive; and

(b) Articles 7 to 61 of Commission Delegated Regulation (EU) 2015/35 supplementing that directive.

(8) If the company carries on both long-term business and other insurance business—

(a) this section is to be applied on the assumption that the company carries on only the long-term business; and

(b) the remainder of this Part is to be applied on the assumption that the company carries on only that other insurance business;

and, in applying paragraph (a) or (b), such apportionments of amounts referable to the long-term business or other insurance business are to be made as are just and reasonable.

(9) In this section—

"best estimate", "paid-in ordinary share capital", "paid-in preference shares", "relevant risk-free interest rate term structure" and "ring-fenced fund" have the same meaning as in the Solvency 2 Directive and any directly applicable regulations made under it;

"defined benefit pension scheme" means a pension scheme (as defined by section 1(5) of the Pension Schemes Act 1993) which is a defined benefits scheme within the meaning given by section 2 of the Pension Schemes Act 2015;

"long-term business" means business that consists of effecting or carrying out contracts of long-term insurance (and this definition must be read with section 22 of the Financial Services and Markets Act 2000, any relevant order under that section and Schedule 2 to that Act);

"qualifying investment subsidiary" means an undertaking in which the company holds a participation within the meaning given by Article 13(20) of the Solvency 2 Directive and which is not held by the company as part of its portfolio of investments;

"Solvency 2 Directive" means Directive 2009/138/EC of the European Parliament and of the Council on the taking-up and pursuit of the business of Insurance and Reinsurance (Solvency II).]

NOTES

Inserted by the Companies Act 2006 (Distributions of Insurance Companies) Regulations 2016, SI 2016/1194, reg 2(1), (4), as from 30 December 2016 (in relation to distributions made on or after that date by reference to relevant accounts (within the meaning of s 836) prepared for any period ending on or after 1 January 2016).

834, 835 (*Repealed by the Companies Act 2006 (Amendment of Part 23) (Investment Companies) Regulations 2012, SI 2012/952, reg 2(1), (7), as from 6 April 2012.*)

CHAPTER 2 JUSTIFICATION OF DISTRIBUTION BY REFERENCE TO ACCOUNTS

Justification of distribution by reference to accounts

[1.953]

836 Justification of distribution by reference to relevant accounts

(1) Whether a distribution may be made by a company without contravening this Part is determined by reference to the following items as stated in the relevant accounts—

(a) profits, losses, assets and liabilities;

(b) provisions of the following kinds—

(i) where the relevant accounts are Companies Act accounts, provisions of a kind specified for the purposes of this subsection by regulations under section 396;

(ii) where the relevant accounts are IAS accounts, provisions of any kind;

(c) share capital and reserves (including undistributable reserves).

(2) The relevant accounts are the company's last annual accounts, except that—

(a) where the distribution would be found to contravene this Part by reference to the company's last annual accounts, it may be justified by reference to interim accounts, and

(b) where the distribution is proposed to be declared during the company's first accounting reference period, or before any accounts have been circulated in respect of that period, it may be justified by reference to initial accounts.

(3) The requirements of—

section 837 (as regards the company's last annual accounts),

section 838 (as regards interim accounts), and

section 839 (as regards initial accounts),

must be complied with, as and where applicable.

(4) If any applicable requirement of those sections is not complied with, the accounts may not be relied on for the purposes of this Part and the distribution is accordingly treated as contravening this Part.

NOTES

Regulations under section 396: see the notes to that section at **[1.451]**. See also the Small Companies and Groups (Accounts and Directors' Report) Regulations 2008, SI 2008/409, reg 12 (at **[4.49]**), and the Large and Medium-sized Companies and Groups (Accounts and Reports) Regulations 2008, SI 2008/410, reg 12 (at **[4.71]**) which provide that Sch 7 to SI 2008/409 (at **[4.57]**, **[4.58]**) and Sch 9 to SI 2008/410 (at **[4.112]**, **[4.113]**) define "provisions" for the purpose of those Regulations and for the purposes of sub-s (1)(b)(i) above.

Requirements applicable in relation to relevant accounts

[1.954]

837 Requirements where last annual accounts used

(1) The company's last annual accounts means the company's individual accounts—

(a) that were last circulated to members in accordance with section 423 (duty to circulate copies of annual accounts and reports), . . .

(b) . . .

(2) The accounts must have been properly prepared in accordance with this Act, or have been so prepared subject only to matters that are not material for determining (by reference to the items mentioned in section 836(1)) whether the distribution would contravene this Part.

(3) Unless the company is exempt from audit and the directors take advantage of that exemption, the auditor must have made his report on the accounts.

(4) If that report was qualified—

(a) the auditor must have stated in writing (either at the time of his report or subsequently) whether in his opinion the matters in respect of which his report is qualified are material for determining whether a distribution would contravene this Part, and

(b) a copy of that statement must—

(i) in the case of a private company, have been circulated to members in accordance with section 423, or

(ii) in the case of a public company, have been laid before the company in general meeting.

(5) An auditor's statement is sufficient for the purposes of a distribution if it relates to distributions of a description that includes the distribution in question, even if at the time of the statement it had not been proposed.

NOTES

Sub-s (1): para (b) (and the preceding word) repealed by the Companies Act 2006 (Strategic Report and Directors' Report) Regulations 2013, SI 2013/1970, reg 14, Schedule, paras 1, 23, in respect of financial years ending on or after 30 September 2013.

[1.955]

838 Requirements where interim accounts used

(1) Interim accounts must be accounts that enable a reasonable judgment to be made as to the amounts of the items mentioned in section 836(1).

(2) Where interim accounts are prepared for a proposed distribution by a public company, the following requirements apply.

(3) The accounts must have been properly prepared, or have been so prepared subject to matters that are not material for determining (by reference to the items mentioned in section 836(1)) whether the distribution would contravene this Part.

(4) "Properly prepared" means prepared in accordance with sections 395 to 397 (requirements for company individual accounts), applying those requirements with such modifications as are necessary because the accounts are prepared otherwise than in respect of an accounting reference period.

(5) The balance sheet comprised in the accounts must have been signed in accordance with section 414.

(6) A copy of the accounts must have been delivered to the registrar.

Any requirement of Part 35 of this Act as to the delivery of a certified translation into English of any document forming part of the accounts must also have been met.

[1.956]

839 Requirements where initial accounts used

(1) Initial accounts must be accounts that enable a reasonable judgment to be made as to the amounts of the items mentioned in section 836(1).

(2) Where initial accounts are prepared for a proposed distribution by a public company, the following requirements apply.

(3) The accounts must have been properly prepared, or have been so prepared subject to matters that are not material for determining (by reference to the items mentioned in section 836(1)) whether the distribution would contravene this Part.

(4) "Properly prepared" means prepared in accordance with sections 395 to 397 (requirements for company individual accounts), applying those requirements with such modifications as are necessary because the accounts are prepared otherwise than in respect of an accounting reference period.

(5) The company's auditor must have made a report stating whether, in his opinion, the accounts have been properly prepared.

(6) If that report was qualified—

(a) the auditor must have stated in writing (either at the time of his report or subsequently) whether in his opinion the matters in respect of which his report is qualified are material for determining whether a distribution would contravene this Part, and

[(b) a copy of that statement must have been laid before the company in general meeting.]

(7) A copy of the accounts, of the auditor's report and of any auditor's statement must have been delivered to the registrar.

Any requirement of Part 35 of this Act as to the delivery of a certified translation into English of any of those documents must also have been met.

NOTES

Sub-s (6): para (b) substituted by the Companies Act 2006 (Consequential Amendments, Transitional Provisions and Savings) Order 2009, SI 2009/1941, art 2(1), Sch 1, para 260(1), (4), as from 1 October 2009.

Application of provisions to successive distributions etc

[1.957]

840 Successive distributions etc by reference to the same accounts

(1) In determining whether a proposed distribution may be made by a company in a case where—

(a) one or more previous distributions have been made in pursuance of a determination made by reference to the same relevant accounts, or

(b) relevant financial assistance has been given, or other relevant payments have been made, since those accounts were prepared,

the provisions of this Part apply as if the amount of the proposed distribution was increased by the amount of the previous distributions, financial assistance and other payments.

(2) The financial assistance and other payments that are relevant for this purpose are—

(a) financial assistance lawfully given by the company out of its distributable profits;

(b) financial assistance given by the company in contravention of section 678 or 679 (prohibited financial assistance) in a case where the giving of that assistance reduces the company's net assets or increases its net liabilities;

(c) payments made by the company in respect of the purchase by it of shares in the company, except a payment lawfully made otherwise than out of distributable profits;

(d) payments of any description specified in section 705 (payments apart from purchase price of shares to be made out of distributable profits).

(3) In this section "financial assistance" has the same meaning as in Chapter 2 of Part 18 (see section 677).

(4) For the purpose of applying subsection (2)(b) in relation to any financial assistance—

(a) "net assets" means the amount by which the aggregate amount of the company's assets exceeds the aggregate amount of its liabilities, and

(b) "net liabilities" means the amount by which the aggregate amount of the company's liabilities exceeds the aggregate amount of its assets,

taking the amount of the assets and liabilities to be as stated in the company's accounting records immediately before the financial assistance is given.

(5) For this purpose a company's liabilities include any amount retained as reasonably necessary for the purposes of providing for any liability—

(a) the nature of which is clearly defined, and

(b) which is either likely to be incurred or certain to be incurred but uncertain as to amount or as to the date on which it will arise.

CHAPTER 3 SUPPLEMENTARY PROVISIONS

Accounting matters

[1.958]

841 Realised losses and profits and revaluation of fixed assets

(1) The following provisions have effect for the purposes of this Part.

(2) The following are treated as realised losses—

(a) in the case of Companies Act accounts, provisions of a kind specified for the purposes of this paragraph by regulations under section 396 (except revaluation provisions);

(b) in the case of IAS accounts, provisions of any kind (except revaluation provisions).

(3) A "revaluation provision" means a provision in respect of a diminution in value of a fixed asset appearing on a revaluation of all the fixed assets of the company, or of all of its fixed assets other than goodwill.

(4) For the purpose of subsections (2) and (3) any consideration by the directors of the value at a particular time of a fixed asset is treated as a revaluation provided—

(a) the directors are satisfied that the aggregate value at that time of the fixed assets of the company that have not actually been revalued is not less than the aggregate amount at which they are then stated in the company's accounts, and

(b) it is stated in a note to the accounts—

(i) that the directors have considered the value of some or all of the fixed assets of the company without actually revaluing them,

(ii) that they are satisfied that the aggregate value of those assets at the time of their consideration was not less than the aggregate amount at which they were then stated in the company's accounts, and

(iii) that accordingly, by virtue of this subsection, amounts are stated in the accounts on the basis that a revaluation of fixed assets of the company is treated as having taken place at that time.

(5) Where—

(a) on the revaluation of a fixed asset, an unrealised profit is shown to have been made, and

(b) on or after the revaluation, a sum is written off or retained for depreciation of that asset over a period,

an amount equal to the amount by which that sum exceeds the sum which would have been so written off or retained for the depreciation of that asset over that period, if that profit had not been made, is treated as a realised profit made over that period.

NOTES

Regulations under section 396: see the notes to that section at **[1.451]**. See also the Small Companies and Groups (Accounts and Directors' Report) Regulations 2008, SI 2008/409, reg 12 (at **[4.49]**), and the Large and Medium-sized Companies and Groups (Accounts and Reports) Regulations 2008, SI 2008/410, reg 12 (at **[4.71]**) which provide that Sch 7 to SI 2008/409 (at **[4.57]**, **[4.58]**) and Sch 9 to SI 2008/410 (at **[4.112]**, **[4.113]**) define "provisions" for the purpose of those Regulations and for the purposes of sub-s (2)(a) above.

[1.959]

842 Determination of profit or loss in respect of asset where records incomplete

In determining for the purposes of this Part whether a company has made a profit or loss in respect of an asset where—

(a) there is no record of the original cost of the asset, or

(b) a record cannot be obtained without unreasonable expense or delay,

its cost is taken to be the value ascribed to it in the earliest available record of its value made on or after its acquisition by the company.

[1.960]

843 Realised profits and losses of long-term insurance business [of certain insurance companies]

[(1) The provisions of this section have effect for the purposes of this Part as it applies in relation to an authorised insurance company carrying on long-term business, other than—

(a) a person to whom section 833A applies; or

(b) an insurance special purpose vehicle.]

(2) An amount included in the relevant part of the company's balance sheet that—

(a) represents a surplus in the fund or funds maintained by it in respect of its long-term business, and

(b) has not been allocated to policy holders or, as the case may be, carried forward unappropriated in accordance with asset identification rules made under [Part 9A] of the Financial Services and Markets Act 2000 (c 8),

is treated as a realised profit.

(3) For the purposes of subsection (2)—

(a) the relevant part of the balance sheet is that part of the balance sheet that represents accumulated profit or loss;

(b) a surplus in the fund or funds maintained by the company in respect of its long-term business means an excess of the assets representing that fund or those funds over the liabilities of the company attributable to its long-term business, as shown by an actuarial investigation.

(4) A deficit in the fund or funds maintained by the company in respect of its long-term business is treated as a realised loss.

For this purpose a deficit in any such fund or funds means an excess of the liabilities of the company attributable to its long-term business over the assets representing that fund or those funds, as shown by an actuarial investigation.

(5) Subject to subsections (2) and (4), any profit or loss arising in the company's long-term business is to be left out of account.

(6) For the purposes of this section an "actuarial investigation" means an investigation made into the financial condition of an authorised insurance company in respect of its long-term business—

(a) carried out once in every period of twelve months in accordance with rules made under [Part 9A] of the Financial Services and Markets Act 2000, or

(b) carried out in accordance with a requirement imposed under section 166 of that Act,

by an actuary appointed as actuary to the company.

(7) In this section "long-term business" means business that consists of effecting or carrying out contracts of long-term insurance.

This definition must be read with section 22 of the Financial Services and Markets Act 2000, any relevant order under that section and Schedule 2 to that Act.

[(8) In this section "insurance special purpose vehicle" means a special purpose vehicle within the meaning of [Article 13(26) of Directive 2009/138/EC of the European Parliament and of the Council of 25 November 2009 on the taking-up and pursuit of the business of Insurance and Reinsurance (Solvency II)].]

NOTES

Sub-s (1): substituted by the Companies Act 2006 (Distributions of Insurance Companies) Regulations 2016, SI 2016/1194, reg 2(1), (5), as from 30 December 2016 (in relation to distributions made on or after that date by reference to relevant accounts (within the meaning of s 836) prepared for any period ending on or after 1 January 2016).

Sub-ss (2), (6): words in square brackets substituted by the Financial Services Act 2012, s 114(1), Sch 18, Pt 2, paras 110, 117, as from 1 April 2013.

Sub-s (8): added by SI 2007/3253, reg 2(3), Sch 3, para 2(1)(b), as from 10 December 2007. Words in square brackets substituted by the Solvency 2 Regulations 2015, SI 2015/575, reg 59, Sch 1, Pt 2, para 25, as from 1 January 2016.

[1.961]

844 Treatment of development costs

(1) Where development costs are shown or included as an asset in a company's accounts, any amount shown or included in respect of those costs is treated—

(a) for the purposes of section 830 (distributions to be made out of profits available for the purpose) as a realised loss, and

(b) for the purposes of section 832 (distributions by investment companies out of accumulated revenue profits) as a realised revenue loss.

This is subject to the following exceptions.

(2) Subsection (1) does not apply to any part of that amount representing an unrealised profit made on revaluation of those costs.

(3) Subsection (1) does not apply if—

(a) there are special circumstances in the company's case justifying the directors in deciding that the amount there mentioned is not to be treated as required by subsection (1),

(b) it is stated—

(i) in the case of Companies Act accounts, in the note required by regulations under section 396 as to the reasons for showing development costs as an asset, or

(ii) in the case of IAS accounts, in any note to the accounts,

that the amount is not to be so treated, and

(c) the note explains the circumstances relied upon to justify the decision of the directors to that effect.

Distributions in kind

[1.962]

845 Distributions in kind: determination of amount

(1) This section applies for determining the amount of a distribution consisting of or including, or treated as arising in consequence of, the sale, transfer or other disposition by a company of a non-cash asset where—

(a) at the time of the distribution the company has profits available for distribution, and

(b) if the amount of the distribution were to be determined in accordance with this section, the company could make the distribution without contravening this Part.

(2) The amount of the distribution (or the relevant part of it) is taken to be—

(a) in a case where the amount or value of the consideration for the disposition is not less than the book value of the asset, zero;

(b) in any other case, the amount by which the book value of the asset exceeds the amount or value of any consideration for the disposition.

(3) For the purposes of subsection (1)(a) the company's profits available for distribution are treated as increased by the amount (if any) by which the amount or value of any consideration for the disposition exceeds the book value of the asset.

(4) In this section "book value", in relation to an asset, means—

(a) the amount at which the asset is stated in the relevant accounts, or

(b) where the asset is not stated in those accounts at any amount, zero.

(5) The provisions of Chapter 2 (justification of distribution by reference to accounts) have effect subject to this section.

[1.963]

846 Distributions in kind: treatment of unrealised profits

(1) This section applies where—

(a) a company makes a distribution consisting of or including, or treated as arising in consequence of, the sale, transfer or other disposition by the company of a non-cash asset, and

(b) any part of the amount at which that asset is stated in the relevant accounts represents an unrealised profit.

(2) That profit is treated as a realised profit—

(a) for the purpose of determining the lawfulness of the distribution in accordance with this Part (whether before or after the distribution takes place), and

(b) for the purpose of the application, in relation to anything done with a view to or in connection with the making of the distribution, of any provision of regulations under section 396 under which only realised profits are to be included in or transferred to the profit and loss account.

Consequences of unlawful distribution

[1.964]

847 Consequences of unlawful distribution

(1) This section applies where a distribution, or part of one, made by a company to one of its members is made in contravention of this Part.

(2) If at the time of the distribution the member knows or has reasonable grounds for believing that it is so made, he is liable—

(a) to repay it (or that part of it, as the case may be) to the company, or

(b) in the case of a distribution made otherwise than in cash, to pay the company a sum equal to the value of the distribution (or part) at that time.

(3) This is without prejudice to any obligation imposed apart from this section on a member of a company to repay a distribution unlawfully made to him.

(4) This section does not apply in relation to—

(a) financial assistance given by a company in contravention of section 678 or 679, or

(b) any payment made by a company in respect of the redemption or purchase by the company of shares in itself.

Other matters

[1.965]

848 Saving for certain older provisions in articles

(1) Where immediately before the relevant date a company was authorised by a provision of its articles to apply its unrealised profits in paying up in full or in part unissued shares to be allotted to members of the company as fully or partly paid bonus shares, that provision continues (subject to any alteration of the articles) as authority for those profits to be so applied after that date.

(2) For this purpose the relevant date is—

(a) for companies registered in Great Britain, 22nd December 1980;

(b) for companies registered in Northern Ireland, 1st July 1983.

[1.966]

849 Restriction on application of unrealised profits

A company must not apply an unrealised profit in paying up debentures or any amounts unpaid on its issued shares.

[1.967]

850 Treatment of certain older profits or losses

(1) Where the directors of a company are, after making all reasonable enquiries, unable to determine whether a particular profit made before the relevant date is realised or unrealised, they may treat the profit as realised.

(2) Where the directors of a company, after making all reasonable enquiries, are unable to determine whether a particular loss made before the relevant date is realised or unrealised, they may treat the loss as unrealised.

(3) For the purposes of this section the relevant date is—

(a) for companies registered in Great Britain, 22nd December 1980;

(b) for companies registered in Northern Ireland, 1st July 1983.

[1.968]

851 Application of rules of law restricting distributions

(1) Except as provided in this section, the provisions of this Part are without prejudice to any rule of law restricting the sums out of which, or the cases in which, a distribution may be made.

(2) For the purposes of any rule of law requiring distributions to be paid out of profits or restricting the return of capital to members—

(a) section 845 (distributions in kind: determination of amount) applies to determine the amount of any distribution or return of capital consisting of or including, or treated as arising in consequence of the sale, transfer or other disposition by a company of a non-cash asset; and

(b) section 846 (distributions in kind: treatment of unrealised profits) applies as it applies for the purposes of this Part.

(3) In this section references to distributions are to amounts regarded as distributions for the purposes of any such rule of law as is referred to in subsection (1).

[1.969]

852 Saving for other restrictions on distributions

The provisions of this Part are without prejudice to any enactment, or any provision of a company's articles, restricting the sums out of which, or the cases in which, a distribution may be made.

[1.970]

853 Minor definitions

(1) The following provisions apply for the purposes of this Part.

(2) References to profit or losses of any description—

(a) are to profits or losses of that description made at any time, and

(b) except where the context otherwise requires, are to profits or losses of a revenue or capital character.

(3) "Capitalisation", in relation to a company's profits, means any of the following operations (whenever carried out)—

(a) applying the profits in wholly or partly paying up unissued shares in the company to be allotted to members of the company as fully or partly paid bonus shares, or

(b) transferring the profits to capital redemption reserve.

(4) References to "realised profits" and "realised losses", in relation to a company's accounts, are to such profits or losses of the company as fall to be treated as realised in accordance with principles generally accepted at the time when the accounts are prepared, with respect to the determination for accounting purposes of realised profits or losses.

(5) Subsection (4) is without prejudice to—

(a) the construction of any other expression (where appropriate) by reference to accepted accounting principles or practice, or

(b) any specific provision for the treatment of profits or losses of any description as realised.

(6) "Fixed assets" means assets of a company which are intended for use on a continuing basis in the company's activities.

[PART 24 ANNUAL CONFIRMATION OF ACCURACY OF INFORMATION ON REGISTER

[1.971]

853A Duty to deliver confirmation statements

(1) Every company must, before the end of the period of 14 days after the end of each review period, deliver to the registrar—

(a) such information as is necessary to ensure that the company is able to make the statement referred to in paragraph (b), and

(b) a statement (a "confirmation statement") confirming that all information required to be delivered by the company to the registrar in relation to the confirmation period concerned under any duty mentioned in subsection (2) either—

(i) has been delivered, or

(ii) is being delivered at the same time as the confirmation statement.

(2) The duties are—

(a) any duty to notify a relevant event (see section 853B);

(b) any duty under sections 853C to [853H].

(3) In this Part "confirmation period"—

(a) in relation to a company's first confirmation statement, means the period beginning with the day of the company's incorporation and ending with the date specified in the statement ("the confirmation date");

(b) in relation to any other confirmation statement of a company, means the period beginning with the day after the confirmation date of the last such statement and ending with the confirmation date of the confirmation statement concerned.

(4) The confirmation date of a confirmation statement must be no later than the last day of the review period concerned.

(5) For the purposes of this Part, each of the following is a review period—

(a) the period of 12 months beginning with the day of the company's incorporation;

(b) each period of 12 months beginning with the day after the end of the previous review period.

(6) But where a company delivers a confirmation statement with a confirmation date which is earlier than the last day of the review period concerned, the next review period is the period of 12 months beginning with the day after the confirmation date.

(7) For the purpose of making a confirmation statement, a company is entitled to assume that any information has been properly delivered to the registrar if it has been delivered within the period of 5 days ending with the date on which the statement is delivered.

(8) But subsection (7) does not apply in a case where the company has received notice from the registrar that such information has not been properly delivered.]

NOTES

A new Part 24 (ss 853A–853L) was substituted for the original Part 24 (originally ss 854–859) by the Small Business, Enterprise and Employment Act 2015, s 92, as from 1 May 2016 (only for the purpose of enabling the registrar to impose the requirements referred to in s 853F(6)), and as from 30 June 2016 (otherwise), except in relation to annual returns to be made up to a return date before 30 June 2016.

Sub-s (2): figure in square brackets substituted by the Information about People with Significant Control (Amendment) Regulations 2017, SI 2017/693, reg 10(1), (2), as from 26 June 2017 (for transitional arrangements, see Schedule, Pt 1 to the 2017 Regulations at **[10.1195]**).

Temporary modification: this section was modified by the Companies etc (Filing Requirements) (Temporary Modifications) Regulations 2020, SI 2020/645, reg 16. By virtue of the Corporate Insolvency and Governance Act 2020, s 39(8), the modification applied from 27 June 2020 to the end of the day on 5 April 2021 (subject to the saving provision in s 39(9) which provides that the expiry of s 39 on 5 April 2021 does not affect the continued operation of any Regulations made under that section for the purpose of determining the length of any period that began before the expiry). As modified, sub-s (1) above had effect as if for the reference to "14 days" there were substituted a reference to "42 days".

[1.972]

[853B Duties to notify a relevant event

The following duties are duties to notify a relevant event—

(a) the duty to give notice of a change in the address of the company's registered office (see section 87);

(b) in the case of a company in respect of which an election is in force under section 128B (election to keep membership information on central register), the duty to deliver anything as mentioned in section 128E;

(c) the duty to give notice of a change as mentioned in section 167 (change in directors or in particulars required to be included in register of directors or register of directors' residential addresses);

(d) in the case of a company in respect of which an election is in force under section 167A (election to keep information in register of directors or register of directors' residential addresses on central register), the duty to deliver anything as mentioned in section 167D;

(e) in the case of a private company with a secretary or a public company, the duty to give notice of a change as mentioned in section 276 (change in secretary or joint secretaries or in particulars required to be included in register of secretaries);

(f) in the case of a private company with a secretary in respect of which an election is in force under section 279A (election to keep information in register of secretaries on central register), the duty to deliver anything as mentioned in section 279D;

[(fa) in the case of a company to which Part 21A (information about people with significant control) applies, and in respect of which an election is not in force under section 790X (election to keep information in PSC register on central register), the duty to give notice of a change as mentioned in section 790VA (notification to the registrar of changes to the company's PSC register);]

(g) in the case of a company in respect of which an election is in force under section 790X (election to keep information in PSC register on central register), the duty to deliver anything as mentioned in section 790ZA;

(h) in the case of a company which, in accordance with regulations under section 1136, keeps any company records at a place other than its registered office, any duty under the regulations to give notice of a change in the address of that place.]

NOTES

Substituted as noted to s 853A at **[1.971]**.

Para (fa) inserted by the Information about People with Significant Control (Amendment) Regulations 2017, SI 2017/693, reg 10(1), (3), as from 26 June 2017 (for transitional arrangements, see Schedule, Pt 1 to the 2017 Regulations at **[10.1195]**).

[1.973]

[853C Duty to notify a change in company's principal business activities

(1) This section applies where—

(a) a company makes a confirmation statement, and

(b) there has been a change in the company's principal business activities during the confirmation period concerned.

(2) The company must give notice to the registrar of the change at the same time as it delivers the confirmation statement.

(3) The information as to the company's new principal business activities may be given by reference to one or more categories of any prescribed system of classifying business activities.]

NOTES

Substituted as noted to s 853A at **[1.971]**.

The Standard Industrial Classification 2007 is prescribed for the purposes of sub-s (3) above, see the note to s 9 at **[1.9]** *ante*.

Regulations: the Companies and Limited Liability Partnerships (Filing Requirements) Regulations 2016, SI 2016/599 at **[4.640]**.

[1.974]

[853D Duty to deliver statement of capital

(1) This section applies where a company having a share capital makes a confirmation statement.

(2) The company must deliver a statement of capital to the registrar at the same time as it delivers the confirmation statement.

(3) Subsection (2) does not apply if there has been no change in any of the matters required to be dealt with by the statement of capital since the last such statement was delivered to the registrar.

(4) The statement of capital must state with respect to the company's share capital at the confirmation date—

(a) the total number of shares of the company,

(b) the aggregate nominal value of those shares,

(c) the aggregate amount (if any) unpaid on those shares (whether on account of their nominal value or by way of premium), and

(d) for each class of shares—

(i) prescribed particulars of the rights attached to the shares,

(ii) the total number of shares of that class, and

(iii) the aggregate nominal value of shares of that class.]

NOTES

Substituted as noted to s 853A at **[1.971]**.

[1.975]

[853E Duty to notify trading status of shares

(1) This section applies where a company having a share capital makes a confirmation statement.

(2) The company must deliver to the registrar a statement dealing with the matters mentioned in subsection (4) at the same time as it delivers the confirmation statement.

(3) Subsection (2) does not apply if and to the extent that the last statement delivered to the registrar under this section applies equally to the confirmation period concerned.

(4) The matters are—

(a) whether any of the company's shares were, at any time during the confirmation period concerned, shares admitted to trading on a relevant market or on any other market which is outside the United Kingdom, and

(b) if so, whether both of the conditions mentioned in subsection (5) were satisfied throughout the confirmation period concerned.

(5) The conditions are that—

(a) there were shares of the company which were shares admitted to trading on a relevant market;

(b) the company was a DTR5 issuer.

(6) In this Part—

"DTR5 issuer" means an issuer to which Chapter 5 of the Disclosure Rules and Transparency Rules sourcebook made by the Financial Conduct Authority (as amended or replaced from time to time) applies;

["relevant market" means—

(a) a recognised investment exchange, as defined in section 285(1)(a) (exemption for recognised exemption exchanges and clearance houses) of the Financial Services and Markets Act 2000 ("the Act"); and

(b) any other market which is a [UK regulated market or an EU regulated market], but not an overseas investment exchange, as defined by section 313 (interpretation of Part 18) of the Act].]

NOTES

Substituted as noted to s 853A at **[1.971]**.

Sub-s (6): definition "relevant market" substituted by the Financial Services and Markets Act 2000 (Markets in Financial Instruments) Regulations 2017, SI 2017/701, reg 50(3), Sch 4, para 9(1), (6), as from 3 January 2018. Words in square brackets in para (b) of the definition "relevant market" substituted by the Companies, Limited Liability Partnerships and Partnerships (Amendment etc) (EU Exit) Regulations 2019, SI 2019/348, reg 6, Sch 1, paras 1, 13, as from IP completion day (as defined in the European Union (Withdrawal Agreement) Act 2020, s 39).

[1.976]

[853F Duty to deliver shareholder information: non-traded companies

(1) This section applies where—

(a) a non-traded company makes a confirmation statement, and

(b) there is no election in force under section 128B in respect of the company.

(2) A "non-traded company" is a company none of whose shares were, at any time during the confirmation period concerned, shares admitted to trading on a relevant market or on any other market which is outside the United Kingdom.

(3) The company must deliver the information falling within subsection (5) to the registrar at the same time as it delivers the confirmation statement.

(4) Subsection (3) does not apply if and to the extent that the information most recently delivered to the registrar under this section applies equally to the confirmation period concerned.

(5) The information is—

(a) the name (as it appears in the company's register of members) of every person who was at any time during the confirmation period a member of the company,

(b) the number of shares of each class held at the end of the confirmation date concerned by each person who was a member of the company at that time,

(c) the number of shares of each class transferred during the confirmation period concerned by or to each person who was a member of the company at any time during that period, and

(d) the dates of registration of those transfers.

(6) The registrar may impose requirements about the form in which information of the kind mentioned in subsection (5)(a) is delivered for the purpose of enabling the entries on the register relating to any given person to be easily found.]

NOTES

Substituted as noted to s 853A at **[1.971]**.

[1.977]

[853G Duty to deliver shareholder information: certain traded companies

(1) This section applies where a traded company makes a confirmation statement.

(2) A "traded company" is a company any of whose shares were, at any time during the confirmation period concerned, shares admitted to trading on a relevant market or on any other market which is outside the United Kingdom.

(3) But a company is not a traded company if throughout the confirmation period concerned—

(a) there were shares of the company which were shares admitted to trading on a relevant market, and

(b) the company was a DTR5 issuer.

(4) The company must deliver the information falling within subsection (6) to the registrar at the same time as it delivers the confirmation statement.

(5) Subsection (4) does not apply if and to the extent the information most recently delivered to the registrar under this section applies equally to the confirmation period concerned.

(6) The information is—

(a) the name and address (as they appear in the company's register of members) of each person who, at the end of the confirmation date concerned, held at least 5% of the issued shares of any class of the company, and

(b) the number of shares of each class held by each such person at that time.]

NOTES

Substituted as noted to s 853A at **[1.971]**.

[1.978]

[853H Duty to deliver information about exemption from Part 21A

(1) This section applies where a company . . . to which Part 21A does not apply (information about people with significant control, see section 790B), makes a confirmation statement.

(2) The company must deliver to the registrar a statement of the fact that it is a company to which Part 21A does not apply at the same time as it delivers the confirmation statement.

(3) Subsection (2) does not apply if the last statement delivered to the registrar under this section applies equally to the confirmation period concerned.]

NOTES

Substituted as noted to s 853A at **[1.971]**.

Sub-s (1): words omitted repealed by the Information about People with Significant Control (Amendment) Regulations 2017, SI 2017/693, reg 10(1), (4), as from 26 June 2017 (for transitional arrangements, see Schedule, Pt 1 to the 2017 Regulations at **[10.1195]**).

853I (*Substituted as noted to s 853A ante. Repealed by the Information about People with Significant Control (Amendment) Regulations 2017, SI 2017/693, reg 10(1), (5), as from 26 June 2017 (for transitional arrangements, see Schedule, Pt 1 to the 2017 Regulations at* **[10.1195]**).)

[1.979]
[853J Power to amend duties to deliver certain information
(1) The Secretary of State may by regulations make provision about the duties on a company in relation to the delivery of information falling within section 853E(4), 853F(5), 853G(6) [or 853H(2)] (referred to in this section as "relevant information").
(2) The regulations may, in particular, make provision requiring relevant information to be delivered—
(a) on such occasions as may be prescribed;
(b) at such intervals as may be prescribed.
(3) The regulations may amend or repeal the provisions of sections 853A, 853B and 853E to [853H].
(4) The regulations may provide—
(a) that where a company fails to comply with any duty to deliver relevant information an offence is committed by—
(i) the company,
(ii) every director of the company,
(iii) in the case of a private company with a secretary or a public company, every secretary of the company, and
(iv) every other officer of the company who is in default;
(b) that a person guilty of such an offence is liable on summary conviction—
(i) in England and Wales, to a fine and, for continued contravention, a daily default fine not exceeding the greater of £500 and one-tenth of level 4 on the standard scale;
(ii) in Scotland or Northern Ireland, to a fine not exceeding level 5 on the standard scale and, for continued contravention, a daily default fine not exceeding one-tenth of level 5 on the standard scale;
(c) that, in the case of continued contravention, an offence is also committed by every officer of the company who did not commit an offence under provision made under paragraph (a) in relation to the initial contravention but who is in default in relation to the continued contravention;
(d) that a person guilty of such an offence is liable on summary conviction—
(i) in England and Wales, to a fine not exceeding the greater of £500 and one-tenth of level 4 on the standard scale for each day on which the contravention continues and the person is in default;
(ii) in Scotland or Northern Ireland, to a fine not exceeding one-tenth of level 5 on the standard scale for each day on which the contravention continues and the person is in default.
(5) The regulations may provide that, for the purposes of any provision made under subsection (4), a shadow director is to be treated as a director.
(6) Regulations under this section are subject to affirmative resolution procedure.]

NOTES
Substituted as noted to s 853A at **[1.971]**.
Sub-ss (1), (3): word and figures in square brackets substituted by the Information about People with Significant Control (Amendment) Regulations 2017, SI 2017/693, reg 10(1), (6), as from 26 June 2017 (for transitional arrangements, see Schedule, Pt 1 to the 2017 Regulations at **[10.1195]**).

[1.980]
[853K Confirmation statements: power to make further provision by regulations
(1) The Secretary of State may by regulations make further provision as to the duties to deliver information to the registrar to which a confirmation statement is to relate.
(2) The regulations may—
(a) amend or repeal the provisions of sections 853A to [853H], and
(b) provide for exceptions from the requirements of those sections as they have effect from time to time.
(3) Regulations under this section which provide that a confirmation statement must relate to a duty to deliver information not for the time being mentioned in section 853A(2) are subject to affirmative resolution procedure.
(4) Any other regulations under this section are subject to negative resolution procedure.]

NOTES
Substituted as noted to s 853A at **[1.971]**.
Sub-s (2): figure in square brackets substituted by the Information about People with Significant Control (Amendment) Regulations 2017, SI 2017/693, reg 10(1), (7), as from 26 June 2017 (for transitional arrangements, see Schedule, Pt 1 to the 2017 Regulations at **[10.1195]**).

[1.981]
[853L Failure to deliver confirmation statement
(1) If a company fails to deliver a confirmation statement before the end of the period of 14 days after the end of a review period an offence is committed by—
(a) the company,
(b) every director of the company,
(c) in the case of a private company with a secretary or a public company, every secretary of the company, and
(d) every other officer of the company who is in default.
For this purpose a shadow director is treated as a director.
(2) A person guilty of an offence under subsection (1) is liable on summary conviction—
(a) in England and Wales to a fine, and, for continued contravention, a daily default fine not exceeding the greater of £500 and one-tenth of level 4 on the standard scale;
(b) in Scotland or Northern Ireland, to a fine not exceeding level 5 on the standard scale and, for continued contravention, a daily default fine not exceeding one-tenth of level 5 on the standard scale.
(3) The contravention continues until such time as a confirmation statement specifying a confirmation date no later than the last day of the review period concerned is delivered by the company to the registrar.
(4) It is a defence for a director or secretary charged with an offence under subsection (1)(b) or (c) to prove that the person took all reasonable steps to avoid the commission or continuation of the offence.

(5) In the case of continued contravention, an offence is also committed by every officer of the company who did not commit an offence under subsection (1) in relation to the initial contravention but who is in default in relation to the continued contravention.

(6) A person guilty of an offence under subsection (5) is liable on summary conviction—

(a) in England and Wales, to a fine not exceeding the greater of £500 and one-tenth of level 4 on the standard scale for each day on which the contravention continues and the person is in default;

(b) in Scotland or Northern Ireland, to a fine not exceeding one-tenth of level 5 on the standard scale for each day on which the contravention continues and the person is in default.]

NOTES

Substituted as noted to s 853A at **[1.971]**.

Temporary modification: this section was modified by the Companies etc (Filing Requirements) (Temporary Modifications) Regulations 2020, SI 2020/645, reg 17. By virtue of the Corporate Insolvency and Governance Act 2020, s 39(8), the modification applied from 27 June 2020 to the end of the day on 5 April 2021 (subject to the saving provision in s 39(9) which provides that the expiry of s 39 on 5 April 2021 does not affect the continued operation of any Regulations made under that section for the purpose of determining the length of any period that began before the expiry). As modified, sub-s (1) above had effect as if for the reference to "14 days" there were substituted a reference to "42 days".

PART 25 COMPANY CHARGES

NOTES

See further the Banking Act 2009, s 252 which provides as follows—

"252 Registration of charges

(1) Part 25 of the Companies Act 2006 (registration of charges) does not apply to a charge if the person interested in it is—

(a) the Bank of England,

(b) the central bank of a country or territory outside the United Kingdom, or

(c) the European Central Bank.

(2) The reference in subsection (1) to Part 25 of the Companies Act 2006 includes a reference to—

(a) Part 12 of the Companies Act 1985 (which has effect until the commencement of Part 25 of the 2006 Act),

(b) Part 13 of the Companies (Northern Ireland) Order 1986 (which has effect until the commencement of Part 25 of the 2006 Act), and

(c) any provision about registration of charges made under section 1052 of the Companies Act 2006 (overseas companies).".

[CHAPTER A1 REGISTRATION OF COMPANY CHARGES

Company charges

[1.982]

859A Charges created by a company

(1) Subject to subsection (6), this section applies where a company creates a charge.

(2) The registrar must register the charge if, before the end of the period allowed for delivery, the company or any person interested in the charge delivers to the registrar for registration a section 859D statement of particulars.

(3) Where the charge is created or evidenced by an instrument, the registrar is required to register it only if a certified copy of the instrument is delivered to the registrar with the statement of particulars.

(4) "The period allowed for delivery" is 21 days beginning with the day after the date of creation of the charge (see section 859E), unless an order allowing an extended period is made under section 859F(3).

(5) Where an order is made under section 859F(3) a copy of the order must be delivered to the registrar with the statement of particulars.

(6) This section does not apply to—

(a) a charge in favour of a landlord on a cash deposit given as a security in connection with the lease of land;

(b) a charge created by a member of Lloyd's (within the meaning of the Lloyd's Act 1982) to secure its obligations in connection with its underwriting business at Lloyd's;

(c) a charge excluded from the application of this section by or under any other Act.

(7) In this Part—

"cash" includes foreign currency,

"charge" includes—

(a) a mortgage;

(b) a standard security, assignation in security, and any other right in security constituted under the law of Scotland, including any heritable security, but not including a pledge, and

"company" means a UK-registered company.]

NOTES

Chapter 1A (ss 859A–859Q) was inserted by the Companies Act 2006 (Amendment of Part 25) Regulations 2013, SI 2013/600, reg 2, Sch 1, as from 6 April 2013, subject to transitional provisions as detailed in the final note below.

Temporary modification: the Companies etc (Filing Requirements) (Temporary Modifications) Regulations 2020, SI 2020/645, reg 18 provided for the following temporary modification of this section. By virtue of the Corporate Insolvency and Governance Act 2020, s 39(8), the modification applied from 27 June 2020 to the end of the day on 5 April 2021 (subject to the saving provision in s 39(9) which provides that the expiry of s 39 on 5 April 2021 does not affect the continued operation of any Regulations made under that section for the purpose of determining the length of any period that begins before the expiry):

(1) Section 859A(4) (charges created by a company) is to have effect as if for the reference to "21 days" there were substituted a reference to "31 days".

(2) Paragraph (1) does not apply in respect of a period allowed for delivery under section 859A which has been extended by the court under section 859F.

Transitional provisions (charges created before 6 April 2013): the Companies Act 2006 (Amendment of Part 25)

Regulations 2013, SI 2013/600, reg 6 provides as follows—

"6 Application and transitional provisions

(1) Subject to paragraph (3) the provisions amending the Companies Act 2006 set out in Schedule 1 and the consequential amendments set out in Schedule 2 apply to charges created on or after 6th April 2013.

(2) Subject to paragraph (3), the provisions of Part 25 of the Companies Act 2006 as they stood immediately before 6th April 2013 continue to apply to charges created before 6th April 2013.

(3) Sections 859K, 859L and 859O of the Companies Act 2006 also apply to charges created before 6th April 2013.".

[1.983]

[859B Charge in series of debentures

(1) This section applies where—

(a) a company creates a series of debentures containing a charge, or giving a charge by reference to another instrument, and

(b) debenture holders of that series are entitled to the benefit of the charge pari passu.

(2) The registrar must register the charge if, before the end of the period allowed for delivery, the company or any person interested in the charge delivers to the registrar for registration, a section 859D statement of particulars which also contains the following—

(a) either—

(i) the name of each of the trustees for the debenture holders, or

(ii) where there are more than four such persons, the names of any four persons listed in the charge instrument as trustees for the debenture holders, and a statement that there are other such persons;

(b) the dates of the resolutions authorising the issue of the series;

(c) the date of the covering instrument (if any) by which the series is created or defined.

(3) Where the charge is created or evidenced by an instrument, the registrar is required to register it only if a certified copy of the instrument is delivered to the registrar with the statement of particulars.

(4) Where the charge is not created or evidenced by an instrument, the registrar is required to register it only if a certified copy of one of the debentures in the series is delivered to the registrar with the statement of particulars.

(5) For the purposes of this section a statement of particulars is taken to be a section 859D statement of particulars even if it does not contain the names of the debenture holders.

(6) "The period allowed for delivery" is—

(a) if there is a deed containing the charge, 21 days beginning with the day after the date on which the deed is executed;

(b) if there is no deed containing the charge, 21 days beginning with the day after the date on which the first debenture of the series is executed.

(7) Where an order is made under section 859F(3) a copy of the order must be delivered to the registrar with the statement of particulars.

(8) In this section "deed" means—

(a) a deed governed by the law of England and Wales or Northern Ireland, or

(b) an instrument governed by a law other than the law of England and Wales or Northern Ireland which requires delivery under that law in order to take effect.]

NOTES

Inserted as noted to s 859A at **[1.982]**.

Temporary modification: the Companies etc (Filing Requirements) (Temporary Modifications) Regulations 2020, SI 2020/645, reg 19 provided for the following temporary modification of this section. By virtue of the Corporate Insolvency and Governance Act 2020, s 39(8), the modification applied from 27 June 2020 to the end of the day on 5 April 2021 (subject to the saving provision in s 39(9) which provides that the expiry of s 39 on 5 April 2021 does not affect the continued operation of any Regulations made under that section for the purpose of determining the length of any period that begins before the expiry):

(1) Section 859B(6) (charge in series of debentures) is to have effect as if for each reference to "21 days" there were substituted in each place where it occurs a reference to "31 days".

(2) Paragraph (1) does not apply in respect of a period allowed for delivery under section 859B which has been extended by the court under section 859F.

[1.984]

[859C Charges existing on property or undertaking acquired

(1) This section applies where a company acquires property or undertaking which is subject to a charge of a kind which would, if it had been created by the company after the acquisition of the property or undertaking, have been capable of being registered under section 859A.

(2) The registrar must register the charge if the company or any person interested in the charge delivers to the registrar for registration a section 859D statement of particulars.

(3) Where the charge is created or evidenced by an instrument, the registrar is required to register it only if a certified copy of the instrument is delivered to the registrar with the statement of particulars.]

NOTES

Inserted as noted to s 859A at **[1.982]**.

[1.985]

[859D Particulars to be delivered to registrar

(1) A statement of particulars relating to a charge created by a company is a "section 859D statement of particulars" if it contains the following particulars—

(a) the registered name and number of the company;

(b) the date of creation of the charge and (if the charge is one to which section 859C applies) the date of acquisition of the property or undertaking concerned;

(c) where the charge is created or evidenced by an instrument, the particulars listed in subsection (2);

(d) where the charge is not created or evidenced by an instrument, the particulars listed in subsection (3).

(2) The particulars referred to in subsection (1)(c) are—

(a) any of the following—

(i) the name of each of the persons in whose favour the charge has been created or of the security agents or trustees holding the charge for the benefit of one or more persons; or,

(ii) where there are more than four such persons, security agents or trustees, the names of any four such persons, security agents or trustees listed in the charge instrument, and a statement that there are other such persons, security agents or trustees;

(b) whether the instrument is expressed to contain a floating charge and, if so, whether it is expressed to cover all the property and undertaking of the company;

(c) whether any of the terms of the charge prohibit or restrict the company from creating further security that will rank equally with or ahead of the charge;

(d) whether (and if so, a short description of) any land, ship, aircraft or intellectual property that is registered or required to be registered in the United Kingdom, is subject to a charge (which is not a floating charge) or fixed security included in the instrument;

(e) whether the instrument includes a charge (which is not a floating charge) or fixed security over—

(i) any tangible or corporeal property, or

(ii) any intangible or incorporeal property,

not described in paragraph (d).

(3) The particulars referred to in subsection (1)(d) are—

(a) a statement that there is no instrument creating or evidencing the charge;

(b) the names of each of the persons in whose favour the charge has been created or the names of any security agents or trustees holding the charge for the benefit of one or more persons;

(c) the nature of the charge;

(d) a short description of the property or undertaking charged;

(e) the obligations secured by the charge.

(4) In this section "fixed security" has the meaning given in section 486(1) of the Companies Act 1985.

(5) In this section "intellectual property" includes—

(a) any patent, trade mark, registered design, copyright or design right;

(b) any licence under or in respect of any such right.]

NOTES

Inserted as noted to s 859A at **[1.982]**.

[1.986]

[859E Date of creation of charge

(1) For the purposes of this Part, a charge of the type described in column 1 of the Table below is taken to be created on the date given in relation to it in column 2 of that Table.

1 Type of charge	***2 When charge created***
Standard security	The date of its recording in the Register of Sasines or its registration in the Land Register of Scotland
Charge other than a standard security, where created or evidenced by an instrument	Where the instrument is a deed that has been executed and has immediate effect on execution and delivery, the date of delivery
	Where the instrument is a deed that has been executed and held in escrow, the date of delivery into escrow
	Where the instrument is a deed that has been executed and held as undelivered, the date of delivery
	Where the instrument is not a deed and has immediate effect on execution, the date of execution
	Where the instrument is not a deed and does not have immediate effect on execution, the date on which the instrument takes effect
Charge other than a standard security, where not created or evidenced by an instrument	The date on which the charge comes into effect.

(2) Where a charge is created or evidenced by an instrument made between two or more parties, references in the Table in subsection (1) to execution are to execution by all the parties to the instrument whose execution is essential for the instrument to take effect as a charge.

(3) This section applies for the purposes of this Chapter even if further forms, notices, registrations or other actions or proceedings are necessary to make the charge valid or effectual for any other purposes.

(4) For the purposes of this Chapter, the registrar is entitled without further enquiry to accept a charge as created on the date given as the date of creation of the charge in a section 859D statement of particulars.

(5) In this section "deed" means—

(a) a deed governed by the law of England and Wales or Northern Ireland, or

(b) an instrument governed by a law other than the law of England and Wales or Northern Ireland which requires delivery under that law in order to take effect.

(6) References in this section to delivery, in relation to a deed, include delivery as a deed where required.]

NOTES

Inserted as noted to s 859A at **[1.982]**.

[1.987]

[859F Extension of period allowed for delivery

(1) Subsection (3) applies if the court is satisfied that—

(a) neither the company nor any other person interested in the charge has delivered to the registrar the documents required under section 859A or (as the case may be) 859B before the end of the period allowed for delivery under the section concerned, and

(b) the requirement in subsection (2) is met.

(2) The requirement is—

(a) that the failure to deliver those documents—

(i) was accidental or due to inadvertence or to some other sufficient cause, or

(ii) is not of a nature to prejudice the position of creditors or shareholders of the company, or

(b) that on other grounds it is just and equitable to grant relief.

(3) The court may, on the application of the company or a person interested, and on such terms and conditions as seem to the court just and expedient, order that the period allowed for delivery be extended.]

NOTES

Inserted as noted to s 859A at **[1.982]**.

[1.988]

[859G Personal information etc in certified copies

(1) The following are not required to be included in a certified copy of an instrument or debenture delivered to the registrar for the purposes of any provision of this Chapter—

(a) personal information relating to an individual (other than the name of an individual);

(b) the number or other identifier of a bank or securities account of a company or individual;

(c) a signature.

(2) The registrar is entitled without further enquiry, to accept the certified copy of an instrument whether or not any of the information in subsection (1) is contained within the instrument.]

NOTES

Inserted as noted to s 859A at **[1.982]**.

[Consequence of non-delivery

[1.989]

859H Consequence of failure to deliver charges

(1) This section applies if—

(a) a company creates a charge to which section 859A or 859B applies, and

(b) the documents required by section 859A or (as the case may be) 859B are not delivered to the registrar by the company or another person interested in the charge before the end of the relevant period allowed for delivery.

(2) "The relevant period allowed for delivery" is—

(a) the period allowed for delivery under the section in question, or

(b) if an order under section 859F(3) has been made, the period allowed by the order.

(3) Where this section applies, the charge is void (so far as any security on the company's property or undertaking is conferred by it) against—

(a) a liquidator of the company,

(b) an administrator of the company, and

(c) a creditor of the company.

(4) Subsection (3) is without prejudice to any contract or obligation for repayment of the money secured by the charge; and when a charge becomes void under this section, the money secured by it immediately becomes payable.]

NOTES

Inserted as noted to s 859A at **[1.982]**.

[The register

[1.990]

859I Entries on the register

(1) This section applies where a charge is registered in accordance with a provision of this Chapter.

(2) The registrar must—

(a) allocate to the charge a unique reference code and place a note in the register recording that reference code; and

(b) include in the register any documents delivered under section 859A(3) or (5), 859B(3), (4) or (7), or 859C(3).

(3) The registrar must give a certificate of the registration of the charge to the person who delivered to the registrar a section 859D statement of particulars relating to the charge.

(4) The certificate must state—

(a) the registered name and number of the company in respect of which the charge was registered; and

(b) the unique reference code allocated to the charge.

(5) The certificate must be signed by the registrar or authenticated by the registrar's official seal.

(6) In the case of registration under section 859A or 859B, the certificate is conclusive evidence that the documents required by the section concerned were delivered to the registrar before the end of the relevant period allowed for delivery.

(7) "The relevant period allowed for delivery" is—

(a) the period allowed for delivery under the section in question, or

(b) if an order under section 859F(3) has been made, the period allowed by the order.]

NOTES

Inserted as noted to s 859A at **[1.982]**.

[1.991]

[859J Company holding property or undertaking as trustee

(1) Where a company is acting as trustee of property or undertaking which is the subject of a charge delivered for registration under this Chapter, the company or any person interested in the charge may deliver to the registrar a statement to that effect.

(2) A statement delivered after the delivery for registration of the charge must include—

(a) the registered name and number of the company; and

(b) the unique reference code allocated to the charge.]

NOTES

Inserted as noted to s 859A at **[1.982]**.

[1.992]

[859K Registration of enforcement of security

(1) Subsection (2) applies where a person—

(a) obtains an order for the appointment of a receiver or manager of a company's property or undertaking, or

(b) appoints such a receiver or manager under powers contained in an instrument.

(2) The person must, within 7 days of the order or of the appointment under those powers—

(a) give notice to the registrar of that fact, and

(b) if the order was obtained, or the appointment made, by virtue of a registered charge held by the person give the registrar a notice containing—

(i) in the case of a charge created before 6th April 2013, the information specified in subsection (4);

(ii) in the case of a charge created on or after 6th April 2013, the unique reference code allocated to the charge.

(3) Where a person appointed receiver or manager of a company's property or undertaking under powers contained in an instrument ceases to act as such a receiver or manager, the person must, on so ceasing—

(a) give notice to the registrar of that fact, and

(b) give the registrar a notice containing—

(i) in the case of a charge created before 6th April 2013, the information specified in subsection (4), or

(ii) in the case of a charge created on or after 6th April 2013, the unique reference code allocated to the charge.

(4) The information referred to in subsections (2)(b)(i) and (3)(b)(i) is—

(a) the date of the creation of the charge;

(b) a description of the instrument (if any) creating or evidencing the charge;

(c) short particulars of the property or undertaking charged.

(5) The registrar must include in the register—

(a) a fact of which notice is given under subsection (2)(a), and

(b) a fact of which notice is given under subsection (3)(a).

(6) A person who makes default in complying with the requirements of subsections (2) or (3) of this section commits an offence.

(7) A person guilty of an offence under this section is liable on summary conviction to a fine not exceeding level 3 on the standard scale and, for continued contravention, a daily default fine not exceeding one-tenth of level 3 on the standard scale.

(8) This section applies only to a receiver or manager appointed—

(a) by a court in England and Wales or Northern Ireland, or

(b) under an instrument governed by the law of England and Wales or Northern Ireland.

(9) This section does not apply to a receiver appointed under Chapter 2 of Part 3 of the Insolvency Act 1986 (receivers (Scotland)).]

NOTES

Inserted as noted to s 859A at **[1.982]**.

[1.993]

[859L Entries of satisfaction and release

(1) Subsection (5) applies if the statement set out in subsection (2) and the particulars set out in subsection (4) are delivered to the registrar with respect to a registered charge.

(2) The statement referred to in subsection (1) is a statement to the effect that—

(a) the debt for which the charge was given has been paid or satisfied in whole or in part, or

(b) all or part of the property or undertaking charged—

(i) has been released from the charge, or

(ii) has ceased to form part of the company's property or undertaking.

(3) Where a statement within subsection (2)(b) relates to part only of the property or undertaking charged, the statement must include a short description of that part.

(4) The particulars referred to in subsection (1) are—

(a) the name and address of the person delivering the statement and an indication of their interest in the charge;

(b) the registered name and number of the company that—

(i) created the charge (in a case within section 859A or 859B), or

(ii) acquired the property or undertaking subject to the charge (in a case within section 859C);

(c) in respect of a charge created before 6th April 2013—

(i) the date of creation of the charge;

(ii) a description of the instrument (if any) by which the charge is created or evidenced;

(iii) short particulars of the property or undertaking charged;

(d) in respect of a charge created on or after 6th April 2013, the unique reference code allocated to the charge.

(5) The registrar must include in the register—

(a) a statement of satisfaction in whole or in part, or
(b) a statement of the fact that all or part of the property or undertaking has been released from the charge or has ceased to form part of the company's property or undertaking (as the case may be).]

NOTES

Inserted as noted to s 859A at **[1.982]**.

[1.994]

[859M Rectification of register

(1) Subsection (3) applies if the court is satisfied that—
(a) there has been an omission or mis-statement in any statement or notice delivered to the registrar in accordance with this Chapter, and
(b) the requirement in subsection (2) is met.

(2) The requirement is that the court is satisfied—
(a) that the omission or mis-statement—
(i) was accidental or due to inadvertence or to some other sufficient cause, or
(ii) is not of a nature to prejudice the position of creditors or shareholders of the company, or
(b) that on other grounds it is just and equitable to grant relief.

(3) The court may, on the application of the company or a person interested, and on such terms and conditions as seem to the court just and expedient, order that the omission or mis-statement be rectified.

(4) A copy of the court's order must be sent by the applicant to the registrar for registration.]

NOTES

Inserted as noted to s 859A at **[1.982]**.

[1.995]

[859N Replacement of instrument or debenture

(1) Subsection (2) applies if the court is satisfied that—
(a) a copy of an instrument or debenture delivered to the registrar under this Chapter contains material which could have been omitted under section 859G;
(b) the wrong instrument or debenture was delivered to the registrar; or
(c) the copy was defective.

(2) The court may, on the application of the company or a person interested, and on such terms and conditions as seem to the court just and expedient, order that the copy of the instrument or debenture be removed from the register and replaced.]

(3) A copy of the court's order must be sent by the applicant to the registrar for registration.

NOTES

Inserted as noted to s 859A at **[1.982]**.

[1.996]

[859O Notification of addition to or amendment of charge

(1) This section applies where, after the creation of a charge, the charge is amended by adding or amending a term that—
(a) prohibits or restricts the creation of any fixed security or any other charge having priority over, or ranking pari passu with, the charge; or
(b) varies, or otherwise regulates the order of, the ranking of the charge in relation to any fixed security or any other charge.

(2) Either the company that created the charge or the person taking the benefit of the charge (or another charge referred to in subsection (1)(b)) may deliver to the registrar for registration—
(a) a certified copy of the instrument effecting the amendment, variation or regulation, and
(b) a statement of the particulars set out in subsection (3).

(3) The particulars to be included in the statement are—
(a) the registered name and number of the company;
(b) in the case of a charge created before 6th April 2013—
(i) the date of creation of the charge;
(ii) a description of the instrument (if any) by which the charge was created or evidenced;
(iii) short particulars of the property or undertaking charged as set out when the charge was registered;
(c) in the case of a charge created on or after 6th April 2013, (where allocated) the unique reference code allocated to the charge.

(4) Subsections (1) to (3) do not affect the continued application of section 466 of the Companies Act 1985.

(5) In this section "fixed security" has the meaning given in section 486(1) of the Companies Act 1985.]

NOTES

Inserted as noted to s 859A at **[1.982]**.

[Companies' records and registers

[1.997]

859P Companies to keep copies of instruments creating and amending charges

(1) A company must keep available for inspection a copy of every—
(a) instrument creating a charge capable of registration under this Chapter, and
(b) instrument effecting any variation or amendment of such a charge.

(2) In the case of a charge contained in a series of uniform debentures, a copy of one of the debentures of the series is sufficient for the purposes of subsection (1)(a).

(3) If the particulars referred to in section 859D(1) or the particulars of the property or undertaking charged are not contained in the instrument creating the charge, but are instead contained in other documents which are referred to in or otherwise incorporated into the instrument, then the company must also keep available for inspection a copy of those other documents.
(4) It is sufficient for the purposes of subsection (1)(a) if the company keeps a copy of the instrument in the form delivered to the registrar under section 859A(3), 859B(3) or (4) or 859C(3).
(5) Where a translation has been delivered to the registrar in accordance with section 1105, the company must keep available for inspection a copy of the translation.]

NOTES

Inserted as noted to s 859A at **[1.982]**.

[1.998]
[859Q Instruments creating charges to be available for inspection

(1) This section applies to documents required to be kept available for inspection under section 859P (copies of instruments creating and amending charges).
(2) The documents must be kept available for inspection—
(a) at the company's registered office, or
(b) at a place specified in regulations under section 1136.
(3) The company must give notice to the registrar—
(a) of the place at which the documents are kept available for inspection, and
(b) of any change in that place,
unless they have at all times been kept at the company's registered office.
(4) The documents must be open to the inspection—
(a) of any creditor or member of the company, without charge, and
(b) of any other person, on payment of such fee as may be prescribed.
(5) If default is made for 14 days in complying with subsection (3) or an inspection required under subsection (4) is refused, an offence is committed by—
(a) the company, and
(b) every officer of the company who is in default.
(6) A person guilty of an offence under this section is liable on summary conviction to a fine not exceeding level 3 on the standard scale and, for continued contravention, a daily default fine not exceeding one-tenth of level 3 on the standard scale.
(7) If an inspection required under subsection (4) is refused the court may by order compel an immediate inspection.
(8) Where the company and a person wishing to carry out an inspection under subsection (4) agree, the inspection may be carried out by electronic means.]

NOTES

Inserted as noted to s 859A at **[1.982]**.

Temporary modification: this section was modified by the Companies etc (Filing Requirements) (Temporary Modifications) Regulations 2020, SI 2020/645, reg 20. By virtue of the Corporate Insolvency and Governance Act 2020, s 39(8), the modification applied from 27 June 2020 to the end of the day on 5 April 2021 (subject to the saving provision in s 39(9) which provides that the expiry of s 39 on 5 April 2021 does not affect the continued operation of any Regulations made under that section for the purpose of determining the length of any period that began before the expiry). As modified, sub-s (5) above had effect as if for the reference to "14 days" there were substituted a reference to "42 days".

CHAPTER 1 COMPANIES REGISTERED IN ENGLAND AND WALES OR IN NORTHERN IRELAND

Requirement to register company charges

[1.999]
860 Charges created by a company

(1) A company that creates a charge to which this section applies must deliver the prescribed particulars of the charge, together with the instrument (if any) by which the charge is created or evidenced, to the registrar for registration before the end of the period allowed for registration.
(2) Registration of a charge to which this section applies may instead be effected on the application of a person interested in it.
(3) Where registration is effected on the application of some person other than the company, that person is entitled to recover from the company the amount of any fees properly paid by him to the registrar on registration.
(4) If a company fails to comply with subsection (1), an offence is committed by—
(a) the company, and
(b) every officer of it who is in default.
(5) A person guilty of an offence under this section is liable—
(a) on conviction on indictment, to a fine;
(b) on summary conviction, to a fine not exceeding the statutory maximum.
(6) Subsection (4) does not apply if registration of the charge has been effected on the application of some other person.
(7) This section applies to the following charges—
(a) a charge on land or any interest in land, other than a charge for any rent or other periodical sum issuing out of land,
(b) a charge created or evidenced by an instrument which, if executed by an individual, would require registration as a bill of sale,
(c) a charge for the purposes of securing any issue of debentures,
(d) a charge on uncalled share capital of the company,
(e) a charge on calls made but not paid,
(f) a charge on book debts of the company,

(g) *a floating charge on the company's property or undertaking,*
(h) *a charge on a ship or aircraft, or any share in a ship,*
(i) *a charge on goodwill or on any intellectual property.*

NOTES

Chapters 1 and 2 of Part 25 (ss 860–892) were repealed by the Companies Act 2006 (Amendment of Part 25) Regulations 2013, SI 2013/600, reg 3, as from 6 April 2013, except in relation to charges created before that date (see the transitional provisions note at **[1.982]**).

[1.1000]

861 Charges which have to be registered: supplementary

(1) The holding of debentures entitling the holder to a charge on land is not, for the purposes of section 860(7)(a), an interest in the land.

(2) It is immaterial for the purposes of this Chapter where land subject to a charge is situated.

(3) The deposit by way of security of a negotiable instrument given to secure the payment of book debts is not, for the purposes of section 860(7)(f), a charge on those book debts.

(4) For the purposes of section 860(7)(i), "intellectual property" means—

(a) *any patent, trade mark, registered design, copyright or design right;*
(b) *any licence under or in respect of any such right.*

(5) In this Chapter—

"charge" includes mortgage, and

"company" means a company registered in England and Wales or in Northern Ireland.

NOTES

Repealed (except in relation to charges created before 6 April 2013); see s 860 at **[1.999]**.

[1.1001]

862 Charges existing on property acquired

(1) This section applies where a company acquires property which is subject to a charge of a kind which would, if it had been created by the company after the acquisition of the property, have been required to be registered under this Chapter.

(2) The company must deliver the prescribed particulars of the charge, together with a certified copy of the instrument (if any) by which the charge is created or evidenced, to the registrar for registration.

(3) Subsection (2) must be complied with before the end of the period allowed for registration.

(4) If default is made in complying with this section, an offence is committed by—

(a) *the company, and*
(b) *every officer of it who is in default.*

(5) A person guilty of an offence under this section is liable—

(a) *on conviction on indictment, to a fine;*
(b) *on summary conviction, to a fine not exceeding the statutory maximum.*

NOTES

Repealed (except in relation to charges created before 6 April 2013); see s 860 at **[1.999]**.

Special rules about debentures

[1.1002]

863 Charge in series of debentures

(1) Where a series of debentures containing, or giving by reference to another instrument, any charge to the benefit of which debenture holders of that series are entitled pari passu is created by a company, it is for the purposes of section 860(1) sufficient if the required particulars, together with the deed containing the charge (or, if there is no such deed, one of the debentures of the series), are delivered to the registrar before the end of the period allowed for registration.

(2) The following are the required particulars—

(a) *the total amount secured by the whole series, and*
(b) *the dates of the resolutions authorising the issue of the series and the date of the covering deed (if any) by which the series is created or defined, and*
(c) *a general description of the property charged, and*
(d) *the names of the trustees (if any) for the debenture holders.*

(3) Particulars of the date and amount of each issue of debentures of a series of the kind mentioned in subsection (1) must be sent to the registrar for entry in the register of charges.

(4) Failure to comply with subsection (3) does not affect the validity of the debentures issued.

(5) Subsections (2) to (6) of section 860 apply for the purposes of this section as they apply for the purposes of that section, but as if references to the registration of a charge were references to the registration of a series of debentures.

NOTES

Repealed (except in relation to charges created before 6 April 2013); see s 860 at **[1.999]**.

[1.1003]

864 Additional registration requirement for commission etc in relation to debentures

(1) Where any commission, allowance or discount has been paid or made either directly or indirectly by a company to a person in consideration of his—

(a) *subscribing or agreeing to subscribe, whether absolutely or conditionally, for debentures in a company, or*
(b) *procuring or agreeing to procure subscriptions, whether absolute or conditional, for such debentures,*

the particulars required to be sent for registration under section 860 shall include particulars as to the amount or rate per cent. of the commission, discount or allowance so paid or made.

(2) The deposit of debentures as security for a debt of the company is not, for the purposes of this section, treated as the issue of debentures at a discount.

(3) Failure to comply with this section does not affect the validity of the debentures issued.

NOTES

Repealed (except in relation to charges created before 6 April 2013); see s 860 at **[1.999]**.

[1.1004]

865 Endorsement of certificate on debentures

(1) The company shall cause a copy of every certificate of registration given under section 869 to be endorsed on every debenture or certificate of debenture stock which is issued by the company, and the payment of which is secured by the charge so registered.

(2) But this does not require a company to cause a certificate of registration of any charge so given to be endorsed on any debenture or certificate of debenture stock issued by the company before the charge was created.

(3) If a person knowingly and wilfully authorises or permits the delivery of a debenture or certificate of debenture stock which under this section is required to have endorsed on it a copy of a certificate of registration, without the copy being so endorsed upon it, he commits an offence.

(4) A person guilty of an offence under this section is liable on summary conviction to a fine not exceeding level 3 on the standard scale.

NOTES

Repealed (except in relation to charges created before 6 April 2013); see s 860 at **[1.999]**.

Charges in other jurisdictions

[1.1005]

866 Charges created in, or over property in, jurisdictions outside the United Kingdom

(1) Where a charge is created outside the United Kingdom comprising property situated outside the United Kingdom, the delivery to the registrar of a verified copy of the instrument by which the charge is created or evidenced has the same effect for the purposes of this Chapter as the delivery of the instrument itself.

(2) Where a charge is created in the United Kingdom but comprises property outside the United Kingdom, the instrument creating or purporting to create the charge may be sent for registration under section 860 even if further proceedings may be necessary to make the charge valid or effectual according to the law of the country in which the property is situated.

NOTES

Repealed (except in relation to charges created before 6 April 2013); see s 860 at **[1.999]**.

[1.1006]

867 Charges created in, or over property in, another United Kingdom jurisdiction

(1) Subsection (2) applies where—

(a) a charge comprises property situated in a part of the United Kingdom other than the part in which the company is registered, and

(b) registration in that other part is necessary to make the charge valid or effectual under the law of that part of the United Kingdom.

(2) The delivery to the registrar of a verified copy of the instrument by which the charge is created or evidenced, together with a certificate stating that the charge was presented for registration in that other part of the United Kingdom on the date on which it was so presented has, for the purposes of this Chapter, the same effect as the delivery of the instrument itself.

NOTES

Repealed (except in relation to charges created before 6 April 2013); see s 860 at **[1.999]**.

Orders charging land: Northern Ireland

[1.1007]

868 Northern Ireland: registration of certain charges etc affecting land

(1) Where a charge imposed by an order under Article 46 of the 1981 Order or notice of such a charge is registered in the Land Registry against registered land or any estate in registered land of a company, the Registrar of Titles shall as soon as may be cause two copies of the order made under Article 46 of that Order or of any notice under Article 48 of that Order to be delivered to the registrar.

(2) Where a charge imposed by an order under Article 46 of the 1981 Order is registered in the Registry of Deeds against any unregistered land or estate in land of a company, the Registrar of Deeds shall as soon as may be cause two copies of the order to be delivered to the registrar.

(3) On delivery of copies under this section, the registrar shall—

(a) register one of them in accordance with section 869, and

(b) not later than 7 days from that date of delivery, cause the other copy together with a certificate of registration under section 869(5) to be sent to the company against which judgment was given.

(4) Where a charge to which subsection (1) or (2) applies is vacated, the Registrar of Titles or, as the case may be, the Registrar of Deeds shall cause a certified copy of the certificate of satisfaction lodged under Article 132(1) of the 1981 Order to be delivered to the registrar for entry of a memorandum of satisfaction in accordance with section 872.

(5) In this section—

"the 1981 Order" means the Judgments Enforcement (Northern Ireland) Order 1981 (SI 1981/226 (NI 6));

"the Registrar of Deeds" means the registrar appointed under the Registration of Deeds Act (Northern Ireland) 1970 (c 25);

"Registry of Deeds" has the same meaning as in the Registration of Deeds Acts;

"Registration of Deeds Acts" means the Registration of Deeds Act (Northern Ireland) 1970 and every statutory provision for the time being in force amending that Act or otherwise relating to the registry of deeds, or the registration of deeds, orders or other instruments or documents in such registry;

"the Land Registry" and "the Registrar of Titles" are to be construed in accordance with section 1 of the Land Registration Act (Northern Ireland) 1970 (c 18);

"registered land" and "unregistered land" have the same meaning as in Part 3 of the Land Registration Act (Northern Ireland) 1970.

NOTES

Repealed (except in relation to charges created before 6 April 2013); see s 860 at **[1.999]**.

The register of charges

[1.1008]

869 Register of charges to be kept by registrar

(1) The registrar shall keep, with respect to each company, a register of all the charges requiring registration under this Chapter.

(2) In the case of a charge to the benefit of which holders of a series of debentures are entitled, the registrar shall enter in the register the required particulars specified in section 863(2).

(3) In the case of a charge imposed by the Enforcement of Judgments Office under Article 46 of the Judgments Enforcement (Northern Ireland) Order 1981, the registrar shall enter in the register the date on which the charge became effective.

(4) In the case of any other charge, the registrar shall enter in the register the following particulars—

(a) if it is a charge created by a company, the date of its creation and, if it is a charge which was existing on property acquired by the company, the date of the acquisition,

(b) the amount secured by the charge,

(c) short particulars of the property charged, and

(d) the persons entitled to the charge.

(5) The registrar shall give a certificate of the registration of any charge registered in pursuance of this Chapter, stating the amount secured by the charge.

(6) The certificate—

(a) shall be signed by the registrar or authenticated by the registrar's official seal, and

(b) is conclusive evidence that the requirements of this Chapter as to registration have been satisfied.

(7) The register kept in pursuance of this section shall be open to inspection by any person.

NOTES

Repealed (except in relation to charges created before 6 April 2013); see s 860 at **[1.999]**.

[1.1009]

870 The period allowed for registration

(1) The period allowed for registration of a charge created by a company is—

(a) 21 days beginning with the day after the day on which the charge is created, or

(b) if the charge is created outside the United Kingdom, 21 days beginning with the day after the day on which the instrument by which the charge is created or evidenced (or a copy of it) could, in due course of post (and if despatched with due diligence) have been received in the United Kingdom.

(2) The period allowed for registration of a charge to which property acquired by a company is subject is—

(a) 21 days beginning with the day after the day on which the acquisition is completed, or

(b) if the property is situated and the charge was created outside the United Kingdom, 21 days beginning with the day after the day on which the instrument by which the charge is created or evidenced (or a copy of it) could, in due course of post (and if despatched with due diligence) have been received in the United Kingdom.

(3) The period allowed for registration of particulars of a series of debentures as a result of section 863 is—

(a) if there is a deed containing the charge mentioned in section 863(1), 21 days beginning with the day after the day on which that deed is executed, or

(b) if there is no such deed, 21 days beginning with the day after the day on which the first debenture of the series is executed.

NOTES

Repealed (except in relation to charges created before 6 April 2013); see s 860 at **[1.999]**.

[1.1010]

871 Registration of enforcement of security

(1) If a person obtains an order for the appointment of a receiver or manager of a company's property, or appoints such a receiver or manager under powers contained in an instrument, he shall within 7 days of the order or of the appointment under those powers, give notice of the fact to the registrar.

(2) Where a person appointed receiver or manager of a company's property under powers contained in an instrument ceases to act as such receiver or manager, he shall, on so ceasing, give the registrar notice to that effect.

(3) The registrar must enter a fact of which he is given notice under this section in the register of charges.

(4) A person who makes default in complying with the requirements of this section commits an offence.

(5) A person guilty of an offence under this section is liable on summary conviction to a fine not exceeding level 3 on the standard scale and, for continued contravention, a daily default fine not exceeding one-tenth of level 3 on the standard scale.

NOTES

Repealed (except in relation to charges created before 6 April 2013); see s 860 at **[1.999]**.

[1.1011]

872 Entries of satisfaction and release

(1) Subsection (2) applies if a statement is delivered to the registrar verifying with respect to a registered charge—

- *(a) that the debt for which the charge was given has been paid or satisfied in whole or in part, or*
- *(b) that part of the property or undertaking charged has been released from the charge or has ceased to form part of the company's property or undertaking.*

(2) The registrar may enter on the register a memorandum of satisfaction in whole or in part, or of the fact part of the property or undertaking has been released from the charge or has ceased to form part of the company's property or undertaking (as the case may be).

(3) Where the registrar enters a memorandum of satisfaction in whole, the registrar shall if required send the company a copy of it.

NOTES

Repealed (except in relation to charges created before 6 April 2013); see s 860 at **[1.999]**.

[1.1012]

873 Rectification of register of charges

(1) Subsection (2) applies if the court is satisfied—

- *(a) that the failure to register a charge before the end of the period allowed for registration, or the omission or mis-statement of any particular with respect to any such charge or in a memorandum of satisfaction—*
  - *(i) was accidental or due to inadvertence or to some other sufficient cause, or*
  - *(ii) is not of a nature to prejudice the position of creditors or shareholders of the company, or*
- *(b) that on other grounds it is just and equitable to grant relief.*

(2) The court may, on the application of the company or a person interested, and on such terms and conditions as seem to the court just and expedient, order that the period allowed for registration shall be extended or, as the case may be, that the omission or mis-statement shall be rectified.

NOTES

Repealed (except in relation to charges created before 6 April 2013); see s 860 at **[1.999]**.

Avoidance of certain charges

[1.1013]

874 Consequence of failure to register charges created by a company

(1) If a company creates a charge to which section 860 applies, the charge is void (so far as any security on the company's property or undertaking is conferred by it) against—

- *(a) a liquidator of the company,*
- *(b) an administrator of the company, and*
- *(c) a creditor of the company,*

unless that section is complied with.

(2) Subsection (1) is subject to the provisions of this Chapter.

(3) Subsection (1) is without prejudice to any contract or obligation for repayment of the money secured by the charge; and when a charge becomes void under this section, the money secured by it immediately becomes payable.

NOTES

Repealed (except in relation to charges created before 6 April 2013); see s 860 at **[1.999]**.

Companies' records and registers

[1.1014]

875 Companies to keep copies of instruments creating charges

(1) A company must keep available for inspection a copy of every instrument creating a charge requiring registration under this Chapter, including any document delivered to the company under section 868(3)(b) (Northern Ireland: orders imposing charges affecting land).

(2) In the case of a series of uniform debentures, a copy of one of the debentures of the series is sufficient.

NOTES

Repealed (except in relation to charges created before 6 April 2013); see s 860 at **[1.999]**.

[1.1015]

876 Company's register of charges

(1) Every limited company shall keep available for inspection a register of charges and enter in it—

- *(a) all charges specifically affecting property of the company, and*
- *(b) all floating charges on the whole or part of the company's property or undertaking.*

(2) The entry shall in each case give a short description of the property charged, the amount of the charge and, except in the cases of securities to bearer, the names of the persons entitled to it.

(3) If an officer of the company knowingly and wilfully authorises or permits the omission of an entry required to be made in pursuance of this section, he commits an offence.

(4) A person guilty of an offence under this section is liable—

- *(a) on conviction on indictment, to a fine;*
- *(b) on summary conviction, to a fine not exceeding the statutory maximum.*

NOTES

Repealed (except in relation to charges created before 6 April 2013); see s 860 at **[1.999]**.

[1.1016]

877 Instruments creating charges and register of charges to be available for inspection

(1) This section applies to—

(a) documents required to be kept available for inspection under section 875 (copies of instruments creating charges), and

(b) a company's register of charges kept in pursuance of section 876.

(2) The documents and register must be kept available for inspection—

(a) at the company's registered office, or

(b) at a place specified in regulations under section 1136.

(3) The company must give notice to the registrar—

(a) of the place at which the documents and register are kept available for inspection, and

(b) of any change in that place,

unless they have at all times been kept at the company's registered office.

(4) The documents and register shall be open to the inspection—

(a) of any creditor or member of the company without charge, and

(b) of any other person on payment of such fee as may be prescribed.

(5) If default is made for 14 days in complying with subsection (3) or an inspection required under subsection (4) is refused, an offence is committed by—

(a) the company, and

(b) every officer of the company who is in default.

(6) A person guilty of an offence under this section is liable on summary conviction to a fine not exceeding level 3 on the standard scale and, for continued contravention, a daily default fine not exceeding one-tenth of level 3 on the standard scale.

(7) If an inspection required under subsection (4) is refused the court may by order compel an immediate inspection.

NOTES

Repealed (except in relation to charges created before 6 April 2013); see s 860 at **[1.999]**.

Regulations: the Companies (Fees for Inspection of Company Records) Regulations 2008, SI 2008/3007 at **[4.177]**. For a summary of all statutory instruments made under this Act, see Appendix 4 at **[A4]**.

CHAPTER 2 COMPANIES REGISTERED IN SCOTLAND

Charges requiring registration

[1.1017]

878 Charges created by a company

(1) A company that creates a charge to which this section applies must deliver the prescribed particulars of the charge, together with a copy certified as a correct copy of the instrument (if any) by which the charge is created or evidenced, to the registrar for registration before the end of the period allowed for registration.

(2) Registration of a charge to which this section applies may instead be effected on the application of a person interested in it.

(3) Where registration is effected on the application of some person other than the company, that person is entitled to recover from the company the amount of any fees properly paid by him to the registrar on the registration.

(4) If a company fails to comply with subsection (1), an offence is committed by—

(a) the company, and

(b) every officer of the company who is in default.

(5) A person guilty of an offence under this section is liable—

(a) on conviction on indictment, to a fine;

(b) on summary conviction, to a fine not exceeding the statutory maximum.

(6) Subsection (4) does not apply if registration of the charge has been effected on the application of some other person.

(7) This section applies to the following charges—

(a) a charge on land or any interest in such land, other than a charge for any rent or other periodical sum payable in respect of the land,

(b) a security over incorporeal moveable property of any of the following categories—

(i) goodwill,

(ii) a patent or a licence under a patent,

(iii) a trademark,

(iv) a copyright or a licence under a copyright,

(v) a registered design or a licence in respect of such a design,

(vi) a design right or a licence under a design right,

(vii) the book debts (whether book debts of the company or assigned to it), and

(viii) uncalled share capital of the company or calls made but not paid,

(c) a security over a ship or aircraft or any share in a ship,

(d) a floating charge.

NOTES

Repealed (except in relation to charges created before 6 April 2013); see s 860 at **[1.999]**.

[1.1018]

879 Charges which have to be registered: supplementary

(1) A charge on land, for the purposes of section 878(7)(a), includes a charge created by a heritable security within the meaning of section 9(8) of the Conveyancing and Feudal Reform (Scotland) Act 1970 (c 35).

(2) The holding of debentures entitling the holder to a charge on land is not, for the purposes of section 878(7)(a), deemed to be an interest in land.

(3) It is immaterial for the purposes of this Chapter where land subject to a charge is situated.

(4) The deposit by way of security of a negotiable instrument given to secure the payment of book debts is not, for the purposes of section 878(7)(b)(vii), to be treated as a charge on those book debts.

(5) References in this Chapter to the date of the creation of a charge are—

(a) in the case of a floating charge, the date on which the instrument creating the floating charge was executed by the company creating the charge, and

(b) in any other case, the date on which the right of the person entitled to the benefit of the charge was constituted as a real right.

(6) In this Chapter "company" means an incorporated company registered in Scotland.

NOTES

Repealed (except in relation to charges created before 6 April 2013); see s 860 at **[1.999]**.

[1.1019]

880 Duty to register charges existing on property acquired

(1) Subsection (2) applies where a company acquires any property which is subject to a charge of any kind as would, if it had been created by the company after the acquisition of the property, have been required to be registered under this Chapter.

(2) The company must deliver the prescribed particulars of the charge, together with a copy (certified to be a correct copy) of the instrument (if any) by which the charge was created or is evidenced, to the registrar for registration before the end of the period allowed for registration.

(3) If default is made in complying with this section, an offence is committed by—

(a) the company, and

(b) every officer of it who is in default.

(4) A person guilty of an offence under this section is liable—

(a) on conviction on indictment, to a fine;

(b) on summary conviction, to a fine not exceeding the statutory maximum.

NOTES

Repealed (except in relation to charges created before 6 April 2013); see s 860 at **[1.999]**.

[1.1020]

881 Charge by way of ex facie absolute disposition, etc

(1) For the avoidance of doubt, it is hereby declared that, in the case of a charge created by way of an ex facie absolute disposition or assignation qualified by a back letter or other agreement, or by a standard security qualified by an agreement, compliance with section 878(1) does not of itself render the charge unavailable as security for indebtedness incurred after the date of compliance.

(2) Where the amount secured by a charge so created is purported to be increased by a further back letter or agreement, a further charge is held to have been created by the ex facie absolute disposition or assignation or (as the case may be) by the standard security, as qualified by the further back letter or agreement.

(3) In that case, the provisions of this Chapter apply to the further charge as if—

(a) references in this Chapter (other than in this section) to a charge were references to the further charge, and

(b) references to the date of the creation of a charge were references to the date on which the further back letter or agreement was executed.

NOTES

Repealed (except in relation to charges created before 6 April 2013); see s 860 at **[1.999]**.

Special rules about debentures

[1.1021]

882 Charge in series of debentures

(1) Where a series of debentures containing, or giving by reference to any other instrument, any charge to the benefit of which the debenture-holders of that series are entitled pari passu, is created by a company, it is sufficient for purposes of section 878 if the required particulars, together with a copy of the deed containing the charge (or, if there is no such deed, of one of the debentures of the series) are delivered to the registrar before the end of the period allowed for registration.

(2) The following are the required particulars—

(a) the total amount secured by the whole series,

(b) the dates of the resolutions authorising the issue of the series and the date of the covering deed (if any) by which the security is created or defined,

(c) a general description of the property charged,

(d) the names of the trustees (if any) for the debenture-holders, and

(e) in the case of a floating charge, a statement of any provisions of the charge and of any instrument relating to it which prohibit or restrict or regulate the power of the company to grant further securities ranking in priority to, or pari passu with, the floating charge, or which vary or otherwise regulate the order of ranking of the floating charge in relation to subsisting securities.

(3) Where more than one issue is made of debentures in the series, particulars of the date and amount of each issue of debentures of the series must be sent to the registrar for entry in the register of charges.

(4) Failure to comply with subsection (3) does not affect the validity of any of those debentures.

(5) Subsections (2) to (6) of section 878 apply for the purposes of this section as they apply for the purposes of that section but as if for the reference to the registration of the charge there was substituted a reference to the registration of the series of debentures.

NOTES

Repealed (except in relation to charges created before 6 April 2013); see s 860 at **[1.999]**.

[1.1022]

883 Additional registration requirement for commission etc in relation to debentures

(1) Where any commission, allowance or discount has been paid or made either directly or indirectly by a company to a person in consideration of his—

(a) subscribing or agreeing to subscribe, whether absolutely or conditionally, for debentures in a company, or

(b) procuring or agreeing to procure subscriptions, whether absolute or conditional, for such debentures,

the particulars required to be sent for registration under section 878 shall include particulars as to the amount or rate per cent. of the commission, discount or allowance so paid or made.

(2) The deposit of debentures as security for a debt of the company is not, for the purposes of this section, treated as the issue of debentures at a discount.

(3) Failure to comply with this section does not affect the validity of the debentures issued.

NOTES

Repealed (except in relation to charges created before 6 April 2013); see s 860 at **[1.999]**.

Charges on property outside the United Kingdom

[1.1023]

884 Charges on property outside United Kingdom

Where a charge is created in the United Kingdom but comprises property outside the United Kingdom, the copy of the instrument creating or purporting to create the charge may be sent for registration under section 878 even if further proceedings may be necessary to make the charge valid or effectual according to the law of the country in which the property is situated.

NOTES

Repealed (except in relation to charges created before 6 April 2013); see s 860 at **[1.999]**.

The register of charges

[1.1024]

885 Register of charges to be kept by registrar

(1) The registrar shall keep, with respect to each company, a register of all the charges requiring registration under this Chapter.

(2) In the case of a charge to the benefit of which holders of a series of debentures are entitled, the registrar shall enter in the register the required particulars specified in section 882(2).

(3) In the case of any other charge, the registrar shall enter in the register the following particulars—

(a) if it is a charge created by a company, the date of its creation and, if it is a charge which was existing on property acquired by the company, the date of the acquisition,

(b) the amount secured by the charge,

(c) short particulars of the property charged,

(d) the persons entitled to the charge, and

(e) in the case of a floating charge, a statement of any of the provisions of the charge and of any instrument relating to it which prohibit or restrict or regulate the company's power to grant further securities ranking in priority to, or pari passu with, the floating charge, or which vary or otherwise regulate the order of ranking of the floating charge in relation to subsisting securities.

(4) The registrar shall give a certificate of the registration of any charge registered in pursuance of this Chapter, stating—

(a) the name of the company and the person first-named in the charge among those entitled to the benefit of the charge (or, in the case of a series of debentures, the name of the holder of the first such debenture issued), and

(b) the amount secured by the charge.

(5) The certificate—

(a) shall be signed by the registrar or authenticated by the registrar's official seal, and

(b) is conclusive evidence that the requirements of this Chapter as to registration have been satisfied.

(6) The register kept in pursuance of this section shall be open to inspection by any person.

NOTES

Repealed (except in relation to charges created before 6 April 2013); see s 860 at **[1.999]**.

[1.1025]

886 The period allowed for registration

(1) The period allowed for registration of a charge created by a company is—

(a) 21 days beginning with the day after the day on which the charge is created, or

(b) if the charge is created outside the United Kingdom, 21 days beginning with the day after the day on which a copy of the instrument by which the charge is created or evidenced could, in due course of post (and if despatched with due diligence) have been received in the United Kingdom.

(2) The period allowed for registration of a charge to which property acquired by a company is subject is—

(a) 21 days beginning with the day after the day on which the transaction is settled, or

(b) if the property is situated and the charge was created outside the United Kingdom, 21 days beginning with the day after the day on which a copy of the instrument by which the charge is created or evidenced could, in due course of post (and if despatched with due diligence) have been received in the United Kingdom.

(3) The period allowed for registration of particulars of a series of debentures as a result of section 882 is—

(a) if there is a deed containing the charge mentioned in section 882(1), 21 days beginning with the day after the day on which that deed is executed, or

(b) if there is no such deed, 21 days beginning with the day after the day on which the first debenture of the series is executed.

NOTES

Repealed (except in relation to charges created before 6 April 2013); see s 860 at **[1.999]**.

[1.1026]

887 Entries of satisfaction and relief

(1) Subsection (2) applies if a statement is delivered to the registrar verifying with respect to any registered charge—

(a) that the debt for which the charge was given has been paid or satisfied in whole or in part, or

(b) that part of the property charged has been released from the charge or has ceased to form part of the company's property.

(2) If the charge is a floating charge, the statement must be accompanied by either—

(a) a statement by the creditor entitled to the benefit of the charge, or a person authorised by him for the purpose, verifying that the statement mentioned in subsection (1) is correct, or

(b) a direction obtained from the court, on the ground that the statement by the creditor mentioned in paragraph (a) could not be readily obtained, dispensing with the need for that statement.

(3) The registrar may enter on the register a memorandum of satisfaction (in whole or in part) regarding the fact contained in the statement mentioned in subsection (1).

(4) Where the registrar enters a memorandum of satisfaction in whole, he shall, if required, furnish the company with a copy of the memorandum.

(5) Nothing in this section requires the company to submit particulars with respect to the entry in the register of a memorandum of satisfaction where the company, having created a floating charge over all or any part of its property, disposes of part of the property subject to the floating charge.

NOTES

Repealed (except in relation to charges created before 6 April 2013); see s 860 at **[1.999]**.

[1.1027]

888 Rectification of register of charges

(1) Subsection (2) applies if the court is satisfied—

(a) that the failure to register a charge before the end of the period allowed for registration, or the omission or mis-statement of any particular with respect to any such charge or in a memorandum of satisfaction—

(i) was accidental or due to inadvertence or to some other sufficient cause, or

(ii) is not of a nature to prejudice the position of creditors or shareholders of the company, or

(b) that on other grounds it is just and equitable to grant relief.

(2) The court may, on the application of the company or a person interested, and on such terms and conditions as seem to the court just and expedient, order that the period allowed for registration shall be extended or, as the case may be, that the omission or mis-statement shall be rectified.

NOTES

Repealed (except in relation to charges created before 6 April 2013); see s 860 at **[1.999]**.

Avoidance of certain charges

[1.1028]

889 Charges void unless registered

(1) If a company creates a charge to which section 878 applies, the charge is void (so far as any security on the company's property or any part of it is conferred by the charge) against—

(a) the liquidator of the company,

(b) an administrator of the company, and

(c) any creditor of the company

unless that section is complied with.

(2) Subsection (1) is without prejudice to any contract or obligation for repayment of the money secured by the charge; and when a charge becomes void under this section the money secured by it immediately becomes payable.

NOTES

Repealed (except in relation to charges created before 6 April 2013); see s 860 at **[1.999]**.

Companies' records and registers

[1.1029]

890 Copies of instruments creating charges to be kept by company

(1) Every company shall cause a copy of every instrument creating a charge requiring registration under this Chapter to be kept available for inspection.

(2) In the case of a series of uniform debentures, a copy of one debenture of the series is sufficient.

NOTES

Repealed (except in relation to charges created before 6 April 2013); see s 860 at **[1.999]**.

[1.1030]

891 Company's register of charges

(1) Every company shall keep available for inspection a register of charges and enter in it all charges specifically affecting property of the company, and all floating charges on any property of the company.

(2) There shall be given in each case a short description of the property charged, the amount of the charge and, except in the case of securities to bearer, the names of the persons entitled to it.

(3) If an officer of the company knowingly and wilfully authorises or permits the omission of an entry required to be made in pursuance of this section, he commits an offence.

(4) A person guilty of an offence under this section is liable—

(a) on conviction on indictment, to a fine;

(b) on summary conviction, to a fine not exceeding the statutory maximum.

NOTES

Repealed (except in relation to charges created before 6 April 2013); see s 860 at **[1.999]**.

[1.1031]

892 Instruments creating charges and register of charges to be available for inspection

(1) This section applies to—

(a) documents required to be kept available for inspection under section 890 (copies of instruments creating charges), and

(b) a company's register of charges kept in pursuance of section 891.

(2) The documents and register must be kept available for inspection—

(a) at the company's registered office, or

(b) at a place specified in regulations under section 1136.

(3) The company must give notice to the registrar—

(a) of the place at which the documents and register are kept available for inspection, and

(b) of any change in that place,

unless they have at all times been kept at the company's registered office.

(4) The documents and register shall be open to the inspection—

(a) of any creditor or member of the company without charge, and

(b) of any other person on payment of such fee as may be prescribed.

(5) If default is made for 14 days in complying with subsection (3) or an inspection required under subsection (4) is refused, an offence is committed by—

(a) the company, and

(b) every officer of the company who is in default.

(6) A person guilty of an offence under this section is liable on summary conviction to a fine not exceeding level 3 on the standard scale and, for continued contravention, a daily default fine not exceeding one-tenth of level 3 on the standard scale.

(7) If an inspection required under subsection (4) is refused the court may by order compel an immediate inspection.

NOTES

Repealed (except in relation to charges created before 6 April 2013); see s 860 at **[1.999]**.

Regulations: the Companies (Fees for Inspection of Company Records) Regulations 2008, SI 2008/3007 at **[4.177]**. For a summary of all statutory instruments made under this Act, see Appendix 4 at **[A4]**.

CHAPTER 3 POWERS OF THE SECRETARY OF STATE

[1.1032]

893 Power to make provision for effect of registration in special register

(1) In this section a "special register" means a register, other than [the register], in which a charge to which [Chapter A1] applies is required or authorised to be registered.

(2) The Secretary of State may by order make provision for facilitating the making of information-sharing arrangements between the person responsible for maintaining a special register ("the responsible person") and the registrar that meet the requirement in subsection (4).

"Information-sharing arrangements" are arrangements to share and make use of information held by the registrar or by the responsible person.

(3) If the Secretary of State is satisfied that appropriate information-sharing arrangements have been made, he may by order provide that—

(a) the registrar is authorised not to register a charge of a specified description under [Chapter A1],

(b) a charge of a specified description that is registered in the special register within a specified period is to be treated as if it had been registered (and certified by the registrar as registered) in accordance with the requirements of [Chapter A1], and

(c) the other provisions of [Chapter A1] apply to a charge so treated with specified modifications.

(4) The information-sharing arrangements must ensure that persons inspecting the [register]—

(a) are made aware, in a manner appropriate to the inspection, of the existence of charges in the special register which are treated in accordance with provision so made, and

(b) are able to obtain information from the special register about any such charge.

(5) An order under this section may—

(a) modify any enactment or rule of law which would otherwise restrict or prevent the responsible person from entering into or giving effect to information-sharing arrangements,

(b) authorise the responsible person to require information to be provided to him for the purposes of the arrangements,

(c) make provision about—

(i) the charging by the responsible person of fees in connection with the arrangements and the destination of such fees (including provision modifying any enactment which would otherwise apply in relation to fees payable to the responsible person), and

(ii) the making of payments under the arrangements by the registrar to the responsible person,

(d) require the registrar to make copies of the arrangements available to the public (in hard copy or electronic form).

(6) In this section "specified" means specified in an order under this section.

(7) A description of charge may be specified, in particular, by reference to one or more of the following—

(a) the type of company by which it is created,

(b) the form of charge which it is,

(c) the description of assets over which it is granted,

(d) the length of the period between the date of its registration in the special register and the date of its creation.

(8) Provision may be made under this section relating to registers maintained under the law of a country or territory outside the United Kingdom.

(9) An order under this section is subject to negative resolution procedure.

NOTES

Sub-s (1): words in first pair of square brackets substituted (for the original words "the register of charges kept under this Part"), and words in second pair of square brackets substituted (for the original words "Chapter 1 or Chapter 2"), by the Companies Act 2006 (Amendment of Part 25) Regulations 2013, SI 2013/600, reg 5, Sch 2, para 3(1), (2)(a), (b), as from 6 April 2013, in relation to charges created on or after that date (see further the transitional provisions note at **[1.982]**).

Sub-s (3): words in first pair of square brackets substituted (for the original words "Chapter 1 or Chapter 2"), and words in second and third pairs of square brackets substituted (for the original words "Chapter 1 or, as the case may be, Chapter 2"), by SI 2013/600, reg 5, Sch 2, para 3(1), (2)(c)–(e), as from 6 April 2013, in relation to charges created on or after that date (see further the transitional provisions note at **[1.982]**).

Sub-s (4): word in square brackets substituted (for the original words "register of charges") by the Companies Act 2006 (Amendment of Part 25) Regulations 2013, SI 2013/600, reg 5, Sch 2, para 3(1), (2)(f), as from 6 April 2013, in relation to charges created on or after that date (see further the transitional provisions note at **[1.982]**).

Orders: no Orders have been made under this section.

[1.1033]

894 General power to make amendments to this Part

(1) The Secretary of State may by regulations under this section—

(a) amend this Part by altering, adding or repealing provisions,

(b) make consequential amendments or repeals in this Act or any other enactment (whether passed or made before or after this Act).

(2) Regulations under this section are subject to affirmative resolution procedure.

NOTES

Regulations: the Companies Act 2006 (Amendment of Part 25) Regulations 2013, SI 2013/600. For a summary of all statutory instruments made under this Act, see Appendix 4 at **[A4]**.

PART 26 ARRANGEMENTS AND RECONSTRUCTIONS[: GENERAL]

NOTES

Word in square brackets in the preceding heading added by the Corporate Insolvency and Governance Act 2020, s 7, Sch 9, Pt 2, paras 30, 35(1), (2), as from 26 June 2020.

Application of this Part

[1.1034]

895 Application of this Part

(1) The provisions of this Part apply where a compromise or arrangement is proposed between a company and—

(a) its creditors, or any class of them, or

(b) its members, or any class of them.

(2) In this Part—

"arrangement" includes a reorganisation of the company's share capital by the consolidation of shares of different classes or by the division of shares into shares of different classes, or by both of those methods; and

"company"—

(a) in section 900 (powers of court to facilitate reconstruction or amalgamation) means a company within the meaning of this Act, and

(b) elsewhere in this Part means any company liable to be wound up under the Insolvency Act 1986 (c 45) or the Insolvency (Northern Ireland) Order 1989 (SI 1989/2405 (NI 19)).

(3) The provisions of this Part have effect subject to Part 27 (mergers and divisions of public companies) where that Part applies (see sections 902 and 903).

Meeting of creditors or members

[1.1035]

896 Court order for holding of meeting

(1) The court may, on an application under this section, order a meeting of the creditors or class of creditors, or of the members of the company or class of members (as the case may be), to be summoned in such manner as the court directs.

(2) An application under this section may be made by—

(a) the company,

(b) any creditor or member of the company,

[(c) if the company is being wound up, the liquidator, or

(d) if the company is in administration, the administrator.]

[(3) Section 323 (representation of corporations at meetings) applies to a meeting of creditors under this section as to a meeting of the company (references to a member of the company being read as references to a creditor).]

[(4) This section is subject to section 899A (moratorium debts, etc).]

NOTES

Sub-s (2): paras (c), (d) substituted (for the original para (c) and the word "or" preceding it) by the Companies Act 2006 (Consequential Amendments etc) Order 2008, SI 2008/948, art 3(1), Sch 1, Pt 2, para 249(1), (2), as from 6 April 2008.

Sub-s (3): added by SI 2008/948, art 3(1), Sch 1, Pt 2, para 249(1), (3), as from 6 April 2008.

Sub-s (4): added by the Corporate Insolvency and Governance Act 2020, s 7, Sch 9, Pt 2, paras 30, 35(1), (3), as from 26 June 2020.

Temporary restriction on initiating certain insolvency arrangements (rent debts): see the Commercial Rent (Coronavirus) Act 2022, s 25 (at **[9.701]**), which provides as follows—

"(1) This section applies where the matter of relief from payment of a protected rent debt has been referred to arbitration.

(2) During the relevant period—

(a) no proposal for a company voluntary arrangement under section 1 of the Insolvency Act 1986 which relates to the whole or part of the debt may be made,

(b) no proposal for an individual voluntary arrangement under section 256A of that Act, or an application for an interim order under section 253 of that Act, which relates to the whole or part of the debt may be made, and

(c) no application for a compromise or arrangement under section 896 or 901C of the Companies Act 2006 (court orders for holding of meetings) which relates to the whole or part of the debt may be made.

(3) In this section "the relevant period" means the period beginning with the day on which an arbitrator is appointed and ending with—

(a) where the arbitrator makes an award in accordance with section 14, the day which is 12 months after the day on which that award is made,

(b) where the arbitrator makes an award dismissing a reference under section 13(2) or (3), the day on which that award is made,

(c) where an award made in accordance with section 14 is set aside on appeal, the day on which that decision is made, or

(d) where the arbitration proceedings are abandoned or withdrawn by the parties, the day of that abandonment or withdrawal.

(4) This section, so far as relating to a company voluntary arrangement and a compromise or arrangement under section 899 or 901F of the Companies Act 2006, applies to limited liability partnerships (as well as to companies).".

[1.1036]

897 Statement to be circulated or made available

(1) Where a meeting is summoned under section 896—

(a) every notice summoning the meeting that is sent to a creditor or member must be accompanied by a statement complying with this section, and

(b) every notice summoning the meeting that is given by advertisement must either—

(i) include such a statement, or

(ii) state where and how creditors or members entitled to attend the meeting may obtain copies of such a statement.

(2) The statement must—

(a) explain the effect of the compromise or arrangement, and

(b) in particular, state—

(i) any material interests of the directors of the company (whether as directors or as members or as creditors of the company or otherwise), and

(ii) the effect on those interests of the compromise or arrangement, in so far as it is different from the effect on the like interests of other persons.

(3) Where the compromise or arrangement affects the rights of debenture holders of the company, the statement must give the like explanation as respects the trustees of any deed for securing the issue of the debentures as it is required to give as respects the company's directors.

(4) Where a notice given by advertisement states that copies of an explanatory statement can be obtained by creditors or members entitled to attend the meeting, every such creditor or member is entitled, on making application in the manner indicated by the notice, to be provided by the company with a copy of the statement free of charge.

(5) If a company makes default in complying with any requirement of this section, an offence is committed by—

(a) the company, and

(b) every officer of the company who is in default.

This is subject to subsection (7) below.

(6) For this purpose the following are treated as officers of the company—

(a) a liquidator or administrator of the company, and

(b) a trustee of a deed for securing the issue of debentures of the company.

(7) A person is not guilty of an offence under this section if he shows that the default was due to the refusal of a director or trustee for debenture holders to supply the necessary particulars of his interests.

(8) A person guilty of an offence under this section is liable—

(a) on conviction on indictment, to a fine;

(b) on summary conviction, to a fine not exceeding the statutory maximum.

[1.1037]

898 Duty of directors and trustees to provide information

(1) It is the duty of—

(a) any director of the company, and

(b) any trustee for its debenture holders,

to give notice to the company of such matters relating to himself as may be necessary for the purposes of section 897 (explanatory statement to be circulated or made available).

(2) Any person who makes default in complying with this section commits an offence.

(3) A person guilty of an offence under this section is liable on summary conviction to a fine not exceeding level 3 on the standard scale.

Court sanction for compromise or arrangement

[1.1038]

899 Court sanction for compromise or arrangement

(1) If a majority in number representing 75% in value of the creditors or class of creditors or members or class of members (as the case may be), present and voting either in person or by proxy at the meeting summoned under section 896, agree a compromise or arrangement, the court may, on an application under this section, sanction the compromise or arrangement.

[(1A) Subsection (1) is subject to section 899A (moratorium debts, etc).]

(2) An application under this section may be made by—

(a) the company,
(b) any creditor or member of the company,
[(c) if the company is being wound up, the liquidator, or
(d) if the company is in administration, the administrator.]

(3) A compromise or [arrangement] sanctioned by the court is binding on—
(a) all creditors or the class of creditors or on the members or class of members (as the case may be), and
(b) the company or, in the case of a company in the course of being wound up, the liquidator and contributories of the company.

(4) The court's order has no effect until a copy of it has been delivered to the registrar.

[(5) . . .]

NOTES

Sub-s (1A): inserted by the Corporate Insolvency and Governance Act 2020, s 7, Sch 9, Pt 2, paras 30, 35(1), (4)(a), as from 26 June 2020.

Sub-s (2): paras (c), (d) substituted (for the original para (c) and the word "or" preceding it) by the Companies Act 2006 (Consequential Amendments etc) Order 2008, SI 2008/948, art 3(1), Sch 1, Pt 2, para 250(1), (2), as from 6 April 2008.

Sub-s (3): word in square brackets substituted by the Companies Act 2006 (Consequential Amendments and Transitional Provisions) Order 2011, SI 2011/1265, art 28(1), (3), as from 12 May 2011.

Sub-s (5): originally added by SI 2008/948, art 3(1), Sch 1, Pt 2, para 250(1), (3), as from 6 April 2008. Subsequently repealed by the Corporate Insolvency and Governance Act 2020, s 7, Sch 9, Pt 2, paras 30, 35(1), (4)(b), as from 26 June 2020.

[Special cases

[1.1039]

899A Moratorium debts, etc

(1) This section applies where—
(a) an application under section 896 in respect of a compromise or arrangement is made before the end of the period of 12 weeks beginning with the day after the end of any moratorium for the company under Part A1 of the Insolvency Act 1986 or Part 1A of the Insolvency (Northern Ireland) Order 1989 (SI 1989/2405 (NI 19)), and
(b) the creditors with whom the compromise or arrangement is proposed include any relevant creditors (see subsection (2)).

(2) In this section "relevant creditor" means—
(a) a creditor in respect of a moratorium debt, or
(b) a creditor in respect of a priority pre-moratorium debt.

(3) The relevant creditors may not participate in the meeting summoned under section 896.

(4) For the purposes of section 897 (statement to be circulated or made available)—
(a) the requirement in section 897(1)(a) is to be read as including a requirement to send each relevant creditor a statement complying with section 897;
(b) any reference to creditors entitled to attend the meeting summoned under section 896 includes a reference to relevant creditors.

(5) The court may not sanction the compromise or arrangement under section 899 if it includes provision in respect of any relevant creditor who has not agreed to it.

(6) In this section—

"moratorium debt"—
(a) in the case of a moratorium under Part A1 of the Insolvency Act 1986, has the same meaning as in section 174A of that Act;
(b) in the case of a moratorium under Part 1A of the Insolvency (Northern Ireland) Order 1989, has the same meaning as in Article 148A of that Order;

"priority pre-moratorium debt"—
(a) in the case of a moratorium under Part A1 of the Insolvency Act 1986, has the same meaning as in section 174A of that Act;
(b) in the case of a moratorium under Part 1A of the Insolvency (Northern Ireland) Order 1989, has the same meaning as in Article 148A of that Order.]

NOTES

Commencement: 26 June 2020.

Inserted, together with the preceding heading, by the Corporate Insolvency and Governance Act 2020, s 7, Sch 9, Pt 2, paras 30, 35(1), (5), as from 26 June 2020.

Reconstructions and amalgamations

[1.1040]

900 Powers of court to facilitate reconstruction or amalgamation

(1) This section applies where application is made to the court under section 899 to sanction a compromise or arrangement and it is shown that—
(a) the compromise or arrangement is proposed for the purposes of, or in connection with, a scheme for the reconstruction of any company or companies, or the amalgamation of any two or more companies, and
(b) under the scheme the whole or any part of the undertaking or the property of any company concerned in the scheme ("a transferor company") is to be transferred to another company ("the transferee company").

(2) The court may, either by the order sanctioning the compromise or arrangement or by a subsequent order, make provision for all or any of the following matters—
(a) the transfer to the transferee company of the whole or any part of the undertaking and of the property or liabilities of any transferor company;
(b) the allotting or appropriation by the transferee company of any shares, debentures, policies or other like interests in that company which under the compromise or arrangement are to be allotted or appropriated by that company to or for any person;

(c) the continuation by or against the transferee company of any legal proceedings pending by or against any transferor company;
(d) the dissolution, without winding up, of any transferor company;
(e) the provision to be made for any persons who, within such time and in such manner as the court directs, dissent from the compromise or arrangement;
(f) such incidental, consequential and supplemental matters as are necessary to secure that the reconstruction or amalgamation is fully and effectively carried out.

(3) If an order under this section provides for the transfer of property or liabilities—
(a) the property is by virtue of the order transferred to, and vests in, the transferee company, and
(b) the liabilities are, by virtue of the order, transferred to and become liabilities of that company.

(4) The property (if the order so directs) vests freed from any charge that is by virtue of the compromise or arrangement to cease to have effect.

(5) In this section—
"property" includes property, rights and powers of every description; and
"liabilities" includes duties.

(6) Every company in relation to which an order is made under this section must cause a copy of the order to be delivered to the registrar within seven days after its making.

(7) If default is made in complying with subsection (6) an offence is committed by—
(a) the company, and
(b) every officer of the company who is in default.

(8) A person guilty of an offence under subsection (7) is liable on summary conviction to a fine not exceeding level 3 on the standard scale and, for continued contravention, a daily default fine not exceeding one-tenth of level 3 on the standard scale.

Obligations of company with respect to articles etc

[1.1041]

901 Obligations of company with respect to articles etc

(1) This section applies—
(a) to any order under section 899 (order sanctioning compromise or arrangement), and
(b) to any order under section 900 (order facilitating reconstruction or amalgamation) that alters the company's constitution.

(2) If the order amends—
(a) the company's articles, or
(b) any resolution or agreement to which Chapter 3 of Part 3 applies (resolution or agreement affecting a company's constitution),

the copy of the order delivered to the registrar by the company under section 899(4) or section 900(6) must be accompanied by a copy of the company's articles, or the resolution or agreement in question, as amended.

(3) Every copy of the company's articles issued by the company after the order is made must be accompanied by a copy of the order, unless the effect of the order has been incorporated into the articles by amendment.

(4) In this section—
(a) references to the effect of the order include the effect of the compromise or arrangement to which the order relates; and
(b) in the case of a company not having articles, references to its articles shall be read as references to the instrument constituting the company or defining its constitution.

(5) If a company makes default in complying with this section an offence is committed by—
(a) the company, and
(b) every officer of the company who is in default.

(6) A person guilty of an offence under this section is liable on summary conviction to a fine not exceeding level 3 on the standard scale.

[PART 26A ARRANGEMENTS AND RECONSTRUCTIONS: COMPANIES IN FINANCIAL DIFFICULTY

Application of this Part

[1.1042]

901A Application of this Part

(1) The provisions of this Part apply where conditions A and B are met in relation to a company.

(2) Condition A is that the company has encountered, or is likely to encounter, financial difficulties that are affecting, or will or may affect, its ability to carry on business as a going concern.

(3) Condition B is that—
(a) a compromise or arrangement is proposed between the company and—
(i) its creditors, or any class of them, or
(ii) its members, or any class of them, and
(b) the purpose of the compromise or arrangement is to eliminate, reduce or prevent, or mitigate the effect of, any of the financial difficulties mentioned in subsection (2).

(4) In this Part—
"arrangement" includes a reorganisation of the company's share capital by the consolidation of shares of different classes or by the division of shares into shares of different classes, or by both of those methods;
"company"—
(a) in section 901J (powers of court to facilitate reconstruction or amalgamation) means a company within the meaning of this Act, and
(b) elsewhere in this Part means any company liable to be wound up under the Insolvency Act 1986 or the Insolvency (Northern Ireland) Order 1989 (SI 1989/2405 (NI 19)).

(5) The provisions of this Part have effect subject to Part 27 (mergers and divisions of public companies) where that Part applies (see sections 902 and 903).]

NOTES

Commencement: 26 June 2020.

Part 26A was inserted by the Corporate Insolvency and Governance Act 2020, s 7, Sch 9, Pt 1, para 1, as from 26 June 2020.

[1.1043]

[901B Power to exclude companies providing financial services, etc

(1) The Secretary of State may by regulations provide that this Part does not apply—

(a) where the company in respect of which a compromise or arrangement is proposed is an authorised person, or an authorised person of a specified description;

(b) where—

(i) a compromise or arrangement is proposed between a company, or a company of a specified description, and any creditors of the company, and

(ii) those creditors consist of or include creditors of a specified description.

(2) In this section—

"authorised person" has the same meaning as in the Financial Services and Markets Act 2000 (see section 31 of that Act);

"specified" means specified in the regulations.

(3) Regulations under this section are subject to affirmative resolution procedure.]

NOTES

Commencement: 26 June 2020.

Inserted as noted to s 901A at **[1.1042]**.

[Meeting of creditors or members

[1.1044]

901C Court order for holding of meeting

(1) The court may, on an application under this subsection, order a meeting of the creditors or class of creditors, or of the members of the company or class of members (as the case may be), to be summoned in such manner as the court directs.

(2) An application under subsection (1) may be made by—

(a) the company,

(b) any creditor or member of the company,

(c) if the company is being wound up, the liquidator, or

(d) if the company is in administration, the administrator.

(3) Every creditor or member of the company whose rights are affected by the compromise or arrangement must be permitted to participate in a meeting ordered to be summoned under subsection (1).

(4) But subsection (3) does not apply in relation to a class of creditors or members of the company if, on an application under this subsection, the court is satisfied that none of the members of that class has a genuine economic interest in the company.

(5) An application under subsection (4) is to be made by the person who made the application under subsection (1) in respect of the compromise or arrangement.

(6) Section 323 (representation of corporations at meetings) applies to a meeting of creditors under this section as to a meeting of the company (references to a member of the company being read as references to a creditor).

(7) This section is subject to section 901H (moratorium debts, etc).]

NOTES

Commencement: 26 June 2020.

Inserted as noted to s 901A at **[1.1042]**.

Temporary restriction on initiating certain insolvency arrangements (rent debts): see the note at s 896 at **[1.1035]** *ante*.

[1.1045]

[901D Statement to be circulated or made available

(1) Where a meeting is summoned under section 901C—

(a) every notice summoning the meeting that is sent to a creditor or member must be accompanied by a statement complying with this section, and

(b) every notice summoning the meeting that is given by advertisement must either—

(i) include such a statement, or

(ii) state where and how creditors or members entitled to attend the meeting may obtain copies of such a statement.

(2) The statement must—

(a) explain the effect of the compromise or arrangement, and

(b) in particular, state—

(i) any material interests of the directors of the company (whether as directors or as members or as creditors of the company or otherwise), and

(ii) the effect on those interests of the compromise or arrangement, in so far as it is different from the effect on the like interests of other persons.

(3) Where the compromise or arrangement affects the rights of debenture holders of the company, the statement must give the like explanation as respects the trustees of any deed for securing the issue of the debentures as it is required to give as respects the company's directors.

(4) Where a notice given by advertisement states that copies of an explanatory statement can be obtained by creditors or members entitled to attend the meeting, every such creditor or member is entitled, on making application in the manner indicated by the notice, to be provided by the company with a copy of the statement free of charge.

(5) If a company makes default in complying with any requirement of this section, an offence is committed by—
(a) the company, and
(b) every officer of the company who is in default.
This is subject to subsection (7).
(6) For this purpose the following are treated as officers of the company—
(a) a liquidator or administrator of the company, and
(b) a trustee of a deed for securing the issue of debentures of the company.
(7) A person is not guilty of an offence under this section if the person shows that the default was due to the refusal of a director or trustee for debenture holders to supply the necessary particulars of the director's or (as the case may be) the trustee's interests.
(8) A person guilty of an offence under this section is liable—
(a) on conviction on indictment, to a fine;
(b) on summary conviction in England and Wales, to a fine;
(c) on summary conviction in Scotland or Northern Ireland, to a fine not exceeding the statutory maximum.]

NOTES

Commencement: 26 June 2020.
Inserted as noted to s 901A at **[1.1042]**.

[1.1046]
901E Duty of directors and trustees to provide information

(1) It is the duty of—
(a) any director of the company, and
(b) any trustee for its debenture holders,
to give notice to the company of such matters relating to that director or trustee as may be necessary for the purposes of section 901D (explanatory statement to be circulated or made available).
(2) Any person who makes default in complying with this section commits an offence.
(3) A person guilty of an offence under this section is liable on summary conviction to a fine not exceeding level 3 on the standard scale.]

NOTES

Commencement: 26 June 2020.
Inserted as noted to s 901A at **[1.1042]**.

[Court sanction for compromise or arrangement

[1.1047]
901F Court sanction for compromise or arrangement

(1) If a number representing 75% in value of the creditors or class of creditors or members or class of members (as the case may be), present and voting either in person or by proxy at the meeting summoned under section 901C, agree a compromise or arrangement, the court may, on an application under this section, sanction the compromise or arrangement.
(2) Subsection (1) is subject to—
(a) section 901G (sanction for compromise or arrangement where one or more classes dissent), and
(b) section 901H (moratorium debts, etc).
(3) An application under this section may be made by—
(a) the company,
(b) any creditor or member of the company,
(c) if the company is being wound up, the liquidator, or
(d) if the company is in administration, the administrator.
(4) Where the court makes an order under this section in relation to a company that is in administration or is being wound up, the court may by the order—
(a) provide for the appointment of the administrator or liquidator to cease to have effect;
(b) stay or sist all proceedings in the administration or the winding up;
(c) impose any requirements with respect to the conduct of the administration or the winding up which the court thinks appropriate for facilitating the compromise or arrangement.
(5) A compromise or arrangement sanctioned by the court is binding—
(a) on all creditors or the class of creditors or on the members or class of members (as the case may be), and
(b) on the company or, in the case of a company in the course of being wound up, the liquidator and contributories of the company.
(6) The court's order has no effect until a copy of it has been—
(a) in the case of an overseas company that is not required to register particulars under section 1046, published in the Gazette, or
(b) in any other case, delivered to the registrar.]

NOTES

Commencement: 26 June 2020.
Inserted as noted to s 901A at **[1.1042]**.

[1.1048]
[901G Sanction for compromise or arrangement where one or more classes dissent

(1) This section applies if the compromise or arrangement is not agreed by a number representing at least 75% in value of a class of creditors or (as the case may be) of members of the company ("the dissenting class"), present and voting either in person or by proxy at the meeting summoned under section 901C.
(2) If conditions A and B are met, the fact that the dissenting class has not agreed the compromise or arrangement does not prevent the court from sanctioning it under section 901F.

(3) Condition A is that the court is satisfied that, if the compromise or arrangement were to be sanctioned under section 901F, none of the members of the dissenting class would be any worse off than they would be in the event of the relevant alternative (see subsection (4)).

(4) For the purposes of this section "the relevant alternative" is whatever the court considers would be most likely to occur in relation to the company if the compromise or arrangement were not sanctioned under section 901F.

(5) Condition B is that the compromise or arrangement has been agreed by a number representing 75% in value of a class of creditors or (as the case may be) of members, present and voting either in person or by proxy at the meeting summoned under section 901C, who would receive a payment, or have a genuine economic interest in the company, in the event of the relevant alternative.

(6) The Secretary of State may by regulations amend this section for the purpose of—

(a) adding to the conditions that must be met for the purposes of this section;

(b) removing or varying any of those conditions.

(7) Regulations under subsection (6) are subject to affirmative resolution procedure.]

NOTES

Commencement: 26 June 2020.

Inserted as noted to s 901A at **[1.1042]**.

[Special cases

[1.1049]

901H Moratorium debts, etc

(1) This section applies where—

(a) an application under section 901C(1) in respect of a compromise or arrangement is made before the end of the period of 12 weeks beginning with the day after the end of any moratorium for the company under Part A1 of the Insolvency Act 1986 or Part 1A of the Insolvency (Northern Ireland) Order 1989 (SI 1989/2405 (NI 19)), and

(b) the creditors with whom the compromise or arrangement is proposed include any relevant creditors (see subsection (2)).

(2) In this section "relevant creditor" means—

(a) a creditor in respect of a moratorium debt, or

(b) a creditor in respect of a priority pre-moratorium debt.

(3) The relevant creditors may not participate in the meeting summoned under section 901C.

(4) For the purposes of section 901D (statement to be circulated or made available)—

(a) the requirement in section 901D(1)(a) is to be read as including a requirement to send each relevant creditor a statement complying with section 901D;

(b) any reference to creditors entitled to attend the meeting summoned under section 901C includes a reference to relevant creditors.

(5) The court may not sanction the compromise or arrangement under section 901F if it includes provision in respect of any relevant creditor who has not agreed to it.

(6) In this section—

"moratorium debt"—

(a) in the case of a moratorium under Part A1 of the Insolvency Act 1986, has the same meaning as in section 174A of that Act;

(b) in the case of a moratorium under Part 1A of the Insolvency (Northern Ireland) Order 1989, has the same meaning as in Article 148A of that Order;

"priority pre-moratorium debt"—

(a) in the case of a moratorium under Part A1 of the Insolvency Act 1986, has the same meaning as in section 174A of that Act;

(b) in the case of a moratorium under Part 1A of the Insolvency (Northern Ireland) Order 1989, has the same meaning as in Article 148A of that Order.]

NOTES

Commencement: 26 June 2020.

Inserted as noted to s 901A at **[1.1042]**.

[1.1050]

[901I Pension schemes

(1) In a case where the company in respect of which a compromise or arrangement is proposed is or has been an employer in respect of an occupational pension scheme that is not a money purchase scheme, any notice or other document required to be sent to a creditor of the company must also be sent to the Pensions Regulator.

(2) In a case where the company in respect of which a compromise or arrangement is proposed is an employer in respect of an eligible scheme, any notice or other document required to be sent to a creditor of the company must also be sent to the Board of the Pension Protection Fund ("the Board").

(3) The Secretary of State may by regulations provide that, in a case where—

(a) the company in respect of which a compromise or arrangement is proposed is an employer in respect of an eligible scheme, and

(b) the trustees or managers of the scheme are a creditor of the company,

the Board may exercise any rights, or any rights of a specified description, that are exercisable under this Part by the trustees or managers as a creditor of the company.

(4) Regulations under this section may provide that the Board may exercise any such rights—

(a) to the exclusion of the trustees or managers of the scheme, or

(b) in addition to the exercise of those rights by the trustees or managers of the scheme.

(5) Regulations under this section—

(a) may specify conditions that must be met before the Board may exercise any such rights;

(b) may provide for any such rights to be exercisable by the Board for a specified period;

(c) may make provision in connection with any such rights ceasing to be so exercisable at the end of such a period.

(6) Regulations under this section are subject to affirmative resolution procedure (but see subsection (7)).

(7) During the period of six months beginning with the day on which this section comes into force, regulations under this section are subject to approval after being made (and subsection (6) does not apply).

(8) For the purposes of subsection (7), section 1291 has effect as if any reference in that section to a period of 28 days were to a period of 40 days.

(9) In this section—

"eligible scheme" means any pension scheme that is an eligible scheme for the purposes of section 126 of the Pensions Act 2004 or Article 110 of the Pensions (Northern Ireland) Order 2005 (SI 2005/255 (NI 1));

"employer"—

(a) in subsection (1), means an employer within the meaning of section 318(1) of the Pensions Act 2004 or Article 2(2) of the Pensions (Northern Ireland) Order 2005;

(b) in subsections (2) and (3)—

(i) in the case of a pension scheme that is an eligible scheme for the purposes of section 126 of the Pensions Act 2004, has the same meaning as it has for the purposes of Part 2 of that Act (see section 318(1) and (4) of that Act);

(ii) in the case of a pension scheme that is an eligible scheme for the purposes of Article 110 of the Pensions (Northern Ireland) Order 2005, has the same meaning as it has for the purposes of Part 3 of that Order (see Article 2(2) and (5) of that Order);

"money purchase scheme" means a pension scheme that is a money purchase scheme for the purposes of the Pension Schemes Act 1993 (see section 181(1) of that Act) or the Pension Schemes (Northern Ireland) Act 1993 (see section 176(1) of that Act);

"occupational pension scheme" and "pension scheme" have the meaning given by section 1 of the Pension Schemes Act 1993;

"specified" means specified in regulations under this section.]

NOTES

Commencement: 26 June 2020.

Inserted as noted to s 901A at **[1.1042]**.

Regulations: the Pension Protection Fund (Moratorium and Arrangements and Reconstructions for Companies in Financial Difficulty) Regulations 2020, SI 2020/693; the Pension Protection Fund (Moratorium and Arrangements and Reconstructions for Companies in Financial Difficulty) (Amendment and Revocation) Regulations 2020, SI 2020/990. For a summary of all statutory instruments made under this Act, see Appendix 4 at **[A4]**

[Reconstructions and amalgamations

[1.1051]

901J Powers of court to facilitate reconstruction or amalgamation

(1) This section applies where application is made to the court under section 901F to sanction a compromise or arrangement and it is shown that—

(a) the compromise or arrangement is proposed in connection with a scheme for the reconstruction of any company or companies, or the amalgamation of any two or more companies, and

(b) under the scheme the whole or any part of the undertaking or the property of any company concerned in the scheme (a "transferor company") is to be transferred to another company ("the transferee company").

(2) The court may, either by the order sanctioning the compromise or arrangement or by a subsequent order, make provision for all or any of the following matters—

(a) the transfer to the transferee company of the whole or any part of the undertaking and of the property or liabilities of any transferor company;

(b) the allotting or appropriation by the transferee company of any shares, debentures, policies or other like interests in that company which under the compromise or arrangement are to be allotted or appropriated by that company to or for any person;

(c) the continuation by or against the transferee company of any legal proceedings pending by or against any transferor company;

(d) the dissolution, without winding up, of any transferor company;

(e) the provision to be made for any persons who, within such time and in such manner as the court directs, dissent from the compromise or arrangement;

(f) such incidental, consequential and supplemental matters as are necessary to secure that the reconstruction or amalgamation is fully and effectively carried out.

(3) If an order under this section provides for the transfer of property or liabilities—

(a) the property is by virtue of the order transferred to, and vests in, the transferee company, and

(b) the liabilities are, by virtue of the order, transferred to and become liabilities of that company.

(4) The property (if the order so directs) vests freed from any charge that is by virtue of the compromise or arrangement to cease to have effect.

(5) In this section—

"property" includes property, rights and powers of every description; and

"liabilities" includes duties.

(6) Every company in relation to which an order is made under this section must cause a copy of the order to be delivered to the registrar within seven days after its making.

(7) If default is made in complying with subsection (6) an offence is committed by—

(a) the company, and

(b) every officer of the company who is in default.

(8) A person guilty of an offence under subsection (7) is liable on summary conviction to a fine not exceeding level 3 on the standard scale and, for continued contravention, a daily default fine not exceeding one-tenth of level 3 on the standard scale.]

NOTES

Commencement: 26 June 2020.

Inserted as noted to s 901A at **[1.1042]**.

[Obligations of company with respect to articles etc

[1.1052]

901K Obligations of company with respect to articles etc

(1) This section applies—

(a) to any order under section 901F (order sanctioning compromise or arrangement), and

(b) to any order under section 901J (order facilitating reconstruction or amalgamation) that alters the company's constitution.

(2) If—

(a) the order amends—

(i) the company's articles, or

(ii) any resolution or agreement to which Chapter 3 of Part 3 applies (resolution or agreement affecting a company's constitution), and

(b) a copy of the order is required to be delivered to the registrar by the company under section 901F(6)(b) or section 901J(6),

the copy of the order delivered to the registrar must be accompanied by a copy of the company's articles, or the resolution or agreement in question, as amended.

(3) Every copy of the company's articles issued by the company after the order is made must be accompanied by a copy of the order, unless the effect of the order has been incorporated into the articles by amendment.

(4) In this section—

(a) references to the effect of the order include the effect of the compromise or arrangement to which the order relates, and

(b) in the case of a company not having articles, references to its articles are to be read as references to the instrument constituting the company or defining its constitution.

(5) If a company makes default in complying with this section an offence is committed by—

(a) the company, and

(b) every officer of the company who is in default.

(6) A person guilty of an offence under this section is liable on summary conviction to a fine not exceeding level 3 on the standard scale.]

NOTES

Commencement: 26 June 2020.

Inserted as noted to s 901A at **[1.1042]**.

[Power to amend Act

[1.1053]

901L Power to amend Act

(1) The Secretary of State may by regulations make any amendment of this Act which the Secretary of State considers necessary or expedient for the purposes of, in consequence of, or for giving full effect to this Part.

(2) Regulations under this section are subject to affirmative resolution procedure.]

NOTES

Commencement: 26 June 2020.

Inserted as noted to s 901A at **[1.1042]**.

PART 27 MERGERS AND DIVISIONS OF PUBLIC COMPANIES

CHAPTER 1 INTRODUCTORY

[1.1054]

902 Application of this Part

(1) This Part applies where—

(a) a compromise or arrangement is proposed between a public company and—

(i) its creditors or any class of them, or

(ii) its members or any class of them,

for the purposes of, or in connection with, a scheme for the reconstruction of any company or companies or the amalgamation of any two or more companies,

(b) the scheme involves—

(i) a merger (as defined in section 904), or

(ii) a division (as defined in section 919), and

(c) the consideration for the transfer (or each of the transfers) envisaged is to be shares in the transferee company (or one or more of the transferee companies) receivable by members of the transferor company (or transferor companies), with or without any cash payment to members.

(2) In this Part—

(a) a "new company" means a company formed for the purposes of, or in connection with, the scheme, and

(b) an "existing company" means a company other than one formed for the purposes of, or in connection with, the scheme.

(3) This Part does not apply where the company in respect of which the compromise or arrangement is proposed is being wound up.

[1.1055]

903 Relationship of this Part to [Parts 26 and 26A]

(1) The court must not sanction the compromise or arrangement under [Part 26 (arrangements and reconstructions: general) or Part 26A (arrangements and reconstructions: companies in financial difficulty)] unless the relevant requirements of this Part have been complied with.

(2) The requirements applicable to a merger are specified in sections 905 to 914. Certain of those requirements, and certain general requirements of [Parts 26 and 26A], are modified or excluded by the provisions of sections 915 to [918A].

(3) The requirements applicable to a division are specified in sections 920 to 930. Certain of those requirements, and certain general requirements of [Parts 26 and 26A], are modified or excluded by the provisions of sections 931 to 934.

NOTES

The figure in square brackets in sub-s (2) was substituted by the Companies (Reporting Requirements in Mergers and Divisions) Regulations 2011, SI 2011/1606, regs 3, 4, as from 1 August 2011 (except in relation to any merger or division the draft terms of which were adopted before that date).

All other words in square brackets in this section were substituted by the Corporate Insolvency and Governance Act 2020, s 7, Sch 9, Pt 2, paras 30, 36(1), (2), as from 26 June 2020.

CHAPTER 2 MERGER

Introductory

[1.1056]

904 Mergers and merging companies

(1) The scheme involves a merger where under the scheme—

(a) the undertaking, property and liabilities of one or more public companies, including the company in respect of which the compromise or arrangement is proposed, are to be transferred to another existing public company (a "merger by absorption"), or

(b) the undertaking, property and liabilities of two or more public companies, including the company in respect of which the compromise or arrangement is proposed, are to be transferred to a new company, whether or not a public company, (a "merger by formation of a new company").

(2) References in this Part to "the merging companies" are—

(a) in relation to a merger by absorption, to the transferor and transferee companies;

(b) in relation to a merger by formation of a new company, to the transferor companies.

Requirements applicable to merger

[1.1057]

905 Draft terms of scheme (merger)

(1) A draft of the proposed terms of the scheme must be drawn up and adopted by the directors of the merging companies.

(2) The draft terms must give particulars of at least the following matters—

(a) in respect of each transferor company and the transferee company—

(i) its name,

(ii) the address of its registered office, and

(iii) whether it is a company limited by shares or a company limited by guarantee and having a share capital;

(b) the number of shares in the transferee company to be allotted to members of a transferor company for a given number of their shares (the "share exchange ratio") and the amount of any cash payment;

(c) the terms relating to the allotment of shares in the transferee company;

(d) the date from which the holding of shares in the transferee company will entitle the holders to participate in profits, and any special conditions affecting that entitlement;

(e) the date from which the transactions of a transferor company are to be treated for accounting purposes as being those of the transferee company;

(f) any rights or restrictions attaching to shares or other securities in the transferee company to be allotted under the scheme to the holders of shares or other securities in a transferor company to which any special rights or restrictions attach, or the measures proposed concerning them;

(g) any amount of benefit paid or given or intended to be paid or given—

(i) to any of the experts referred to in section 909 (expert's report), or

(ii) to any director of a merging company,

and the consideration for the payment of benefit.

(3) The requirements in subsection (2)(b), (c) and (d) are subject to section 915 (circumstances in which certain particulars not required).

[1.1058]

906 Publication of draft terms [by registrar] (merger)

(1) The directors of each of the merging companies must deliver a copy of the draft terms to the registrar.

(2) The registrar must publish in the Gazette notice of receipt by him from that company of a copy of the draft terms.

(3) That notice must be published at least one month before the date of any meeting of that company summoned for the purpose of approving the scheme.

[(4) The requirements in this section are subject to section 906A (publication of draft terms on company website).]

NOTES

The words in square brackets in the section heading were inserted, and sub-s (4) was added, by the Companies (Reporting Requirements in Mergers and Divisions) Regulations 2011, SI 2011/1606, regs 3, 5, as from 1 August 2011 (except in relation to any merger the draft terms of which were adopted before that date).

[1.1059]
[906A Publication of draft terms on company website (merger)
(1) Section 906 does not apply in respect of a company if the conditions in subsections (2) to (6) are met.
(2) The first condition is that the draft terms are made available on a website which—
(a) is maintained by or on behalf of the company, and
(b) identifies the company.
(3) The second condition is that neither access to the draft terms on the website nor the supply of a hard copy of them from the website is conditional on payment of a fee or otherwise restricted.
(4) The third condition is that the directors of the company deliver to the registrar a notice giving details of the website.
(5) The fourth condition is that the registrar publishes the notice in the Gazette at least one month before the date of any meeting of the company summoned for the purpose of approving the scheme.
(6) The fifth condition is that the draft terms remain available on the website throughout the period beginning one month before, and ending on, the date of any such meeting.]

NOTES
Inserted by the Companies (Reporting Requirements in Mergers and Divisions) Regulations 2011, SI 2011/1606, regs 3, 6, as from 1 August 2011 (except in relation to any merger the draft terms of which were adopted before that date).

[1.1060]
907 Approval of members of merging companies
(1) The scheme must be approved by a majority in number, representing 75% in value, of each class of members of each of the merging companies, present and voting either in person or by proxy at a meeting.
(2) This requirement is subject to sections 916, 917[, 917A] and 918 (circumstances in which meetings of members not required).

NOTES
Sub-s (2): figure in square brackets inserted by the Corporate Insolvency and Governance Act 2020, s 7, Sch 9, Pt 2, paras 30, 36(1), (3), as from 26 June 2020.

[1.1061]
908 Directors' explanatory report (merger)
(1) The directors of each of the merging companies must draw up and adopt a report.
(2) The report must consist of—
[(a) the required statement explaining the effect of the compromise or arrangement,] and
(b) insofar as that statement does not deal with the following matters, a further statement—
(i) setting out the legal and economic grounds for the draft terms, and in particular for the share exchange ratio, and
(ii) specifying any special valuation difficulties.
[(2A) In subsection (2) "the required statement explaining the effect of the compromise or arrangement" means—
(a) in a case where a meeting is summoned under section 896 in relation to the compromise or arrangement, the statement required by section 897;
(b) in a case where a meeting is summoned under section 901C in relation to the compromise or arrangement, the statement required by section 901D.]
(3) The requirement in this section is subject to section 915 (circumstances in which reports not required)[, section 915A (other circumstances in which reports and inspection not required) and section 918A (agreement to dispense with reports etc)].

NOTES
Sub-s (2): para (a) substituted by the Corporate Insolvency and Governance Act 2020, s 7, Sch 9, Pt 2, paras 30, 36(1), (4)(a), as from 26 June 2020.
Sub-s (2A): inserted by the Corporate Insolvency and Governance Act 2020, s 7, Sch 9, Pt 2, paras 30, 36(1), (4)(b), as from 26 June 2020.
Sub-s (3): words in square brackets added by the Companies (Reporting Requirements in Mergers and Divisions) Regulations 2011, SI 2011/1606, regs 3, 7, as from 1 August 2011 (except in relation to any merger the draft terms of which were adopted before that date).

[1.1062]
909 Expert's report (merger)
(1) An expert's report must be drawn up on behalf of each of the merging companies.
(2) The report required is a written report on the draft terms to the members of the company.
(3) The court may on the joint application of all the merging companies approve the appointment of a joint expert to draw up a single report on behalf of all those companies.

If no such appointment is made, there must be a separate expert's report to the members of each merging company drawn up by a separate expert appointed on behalf of that company.
(4) The expert must be a person who—
(a) is eligible for appointment as a statutory auditor (see section 1212), and
(b) meets the independence requirement in section 936.
(5) The expert's report must—
(a) indicate the method or methods used to arrive at the share exchange ratio;
(b) give an opinion as to whether the method or methods used are reasonable in all the circumstances of the case, indicate the values arrived at using each such method and (if there is more than one method) give an opinion on the relative importance attributed to such methods in arriving at the value decided on;
(c) describe any special valuation difficulties that have arisen;
(d) state whether in the expert's opinion the share exchange ratio is reasonable; and

(e) in the case of a valuation made by a person other than himself (see section 935), state that it appeared to him reasonable to arrange for it to be so made or to accept a valuation so made.

(6) The expert (or each of them) has—

(a) the right of access to all such documents of all the merging companies, and

(b) the right to require from the companies' officers all such information,

as he thinks necessary for the purposes of making his report.

(7) The requirement in this section is subject to section 915 (circumstances in which reports not required)[, section 915A (other circumstances in which reports and inspection not required)] [and section 918A (agreement to dispense with expert's report)].

NOTES

Sub-s (7): words in first pair of square brackets inserted by the Companies (Reporting Requirements in Mergers and Divisions) Regulations 2011, SI 2011/1606, regs 3, 8, as from 1 August 2011 (except in relation to any merger the draft terms of which were adopted before that date). Words in second pair of square brackets inserted by the Companies (Mergers and Divisions of Public Companies) (Amendment) Regulations 2008, SI 2008/690, reg 2(1), as from 6 April 2008.

[1.1063]

910 Supplementary accounting statement (merger)

[(1) This section applies if the last annual accounts of any of the merging companies relate to a financial year ending before—

(a) the date seven months before the first meeting of the company summoned for the purposes of approving the scheme, or

(b) if no meeting of the company is required (by virtue of any of sections 916 to 918), the date six months before the directors of the company adopt the draft terms of the scheme.

(1A) If the company has not made public a half-yearly financial report relating to a period ending on or after the date mentioned in subsection (1), the directors of the company must prepare a supplementary accounting statement.]

(2) That statement must consist of—

(a) a balance sheet dealing with the state of affairs of the company as at a date not more than three months before the draft terms were adopted by the directors, and

(b) where the company would be required under section 399 to prepare group accounts if that date were the last day of a financial year, a consolidated balance sheet dealing with the state of affairs of the company and the undertakings that would be included in such a consolidation.

(3) The requirements of this Act . . . as to the balance sheet forming part of a company's annual accounts, and the matters to be included in notes to it, apply to the balance sheet required for an accounting statement under this section, with such modifications as are necessary by reason of its being prepared otherwise than as at the last day of a financial year.

(4) The provisions of section 414 as to the approval and signing of accounts apply to the balance sheet required for an accounting statement under this section.

[(5) In this section "half-yearly financial report" means a report of that description required to be made public by rules under section 89A of the Financial Services and Markets Act 2000 (transparency rules).

(6) The requirement in this section is subject to section 915A (other circumstances in which reports and inspection not required) and section 918A (agreement to dispense with reports etc).]

NOTES

Sub-ss (1), (1A) were substituted (for the original sub-s (1)), and sub-ss (5), (6) were added, by the Companies (Reporting Requirements in Mergers and Divisions) Regulations 2011, SI 2011/1606, regs 3, 9, as from 1 August 2011 (except in relation to any merger the draft terms of which were adopted before that date).

Sub-s (3): words omitted repealed by the International Accounting Standards and European Public Limited-Liability Company (Amendment etc) (EU Exit) Regulations 2019, SI 2019/685, reg 19, Sch 1, Pt 1, paras 1, 24, in relation to accounts for financial years beginning on or after IP completion day (as defined in the European Union (Withdrawal Agreement) Act 2020, s 39) (note also that in relation to accounts for financial years which begin before but end on or after IP completion day, the enactments amended by Parts 1–3 of Sch 1 to the 2019 Regulations have effect as if the UK were a member State until the end of the financial year in question).

[1.1064]

911 Inspection of documents (merger)

(1) The members of each of the merging companies must be able, during the period specified below—

(a) to inspect at the registered office of that company copies of the documents listed below relating to that company and every other merging company, and

(b) to obtain copies of those documents or any part of them on request free of charge.

(2) The period referred to above is the period—

(a) beginning one month before, and

(b) ending on the date of,

the first meeting of the members, or any class of members, of the company for the purposes of approving the scheme.

(3) The documents referred to above are—

(a) the draft terms;

(b) the directors' explanatory report;

(c) the expert's report;

(d) the company's annual accounts and reports for the last three financial years ending on or before the first meeting of the members, or any class of members, of the company summoned for the purposes of approving the scheme; . . .

(e) any supplementary accounting statement required by section 910[; and

(f) if no statement is required by section 910 because the company has made public a recent half-yearly financial report (see subsection (1A) of that section), that report].

[(3A) The requirement in subsection (1)(a) is subject to section 911A(1) (publication of documents on company website).]

(4) The requirements of subsection (3)(b) and (c) are subject to section 915 (circumstances in which reports not required) [and section 918A (agreement to dispense with reports etc)].

[(5) Section 1145 (right to hard copy) does not apply to a document sent or supplied in accordance with subsection (1)(b) to a member who has consented to information being sent or supplied by the company by electronic means and has not revoked that consent.

(6) Part 4 of Schedule 5 (communications by means of a website) does not apply for the purposes of subsection (1)(b) (but see section 911A(5)).

(7) The requirements in this section are subject to section 915A (other circumstances in which reports and inspection not required).]

NOTES

The word omitted from sub-s (3)(d) was repealed, sub-s (3)(f) and the preceding word were added, the words in square brackets in sub-s (4) were added, and sub-ss (3A), (5)–(7) were inserted and added respectively, by the Companies (Reporting Requirements in Mergers and Divisions) Regulations 2011, SI 2011/1606, regs 3, 10, as from 1 August 2011 (except in relation to any merger the draft terms of which were adopted before that date).

[1.1065]

[911A Publication of documents on company website (merger)

(1) Section 911(1)(a) does not apply to a document if the conditions in subsections (2) to (4) are met in relation to that document.

This is subject to subsection (6).

(2) The first condition is that the document is made available on a website which—

- (a) is maintained by or on behalf of the company, and
- (b) identifies the company.

(3) The second condition is that access to the document on the website is not conditional on payment of a fee or otherwise restricted.

(4) The third condition is that the document remains available on the website throughout the period beginning one month before, and ending on, the date of any meeting of the company summoned for the purpose of approving the scheme.

(5) A person is able to obtain a copy of a document as required by section 911(1)(b) if—

- (a) the conditions in subsections (2) and (3) are met in relation to that document, and
- (b) the person is able, throughout the period specified in subsection (4)—
  - (i) to retain a copy of the document as made available on the website, and
  - (ii) to produce a hard copy of it.

(6) Where members of a company are able to obtain copies of a document only as mentioned in subsection (5), section 911(1)(a) applies to that document even if the conditions in subsections (2) to (4) are met.]

NOTES

Inserted by the Companies (Reporting Requirements in Mergers and Divisions) Regulations 2011, SI 2011/1606, regs 3, 11, as from 1 August 2011 (except in relation to any merger the draft terms of which were adopted before that date).

[1.1066]

[911B Report on material changes of assets of merging companies

(1) The directors of each of the merging companies must report—

- (a) to every meeting of the members, or any class of members, of that company summoned for the purpose of agreeing to the scheme, and
- (b) to the directors of every other merging company,

any material changes in the property and liabilities of that company between the date when the draft terms were adopted and the date of the meeting in question.

(2) The directors of each of the other merging companies must in turn—

- (a) report those matters to every meeting of the members, or any class of members, of that company summoned for the purpose of agreeing to the scheme, or
- (b) send a report of those matters to every member entitled to receive notice of such a meeting.

(3) The requirement in this section is subject to section 915A (other circumstances in which reports and inspection not required) and section 918A (agreement to dispense with reports etc).]

NOTES

Inserted by the Companies (Reporting Requirements in Mergers and Divisions) Regulations 2011, SI 2011/1606, regs 3, 12, as from 1 August 2011 (except in relation to any merger the draft terms of which were adopted before that date).

[1.1067]

912 Approval of articles of new transferee company (merger)

[(1)] In the case of a merger by formation of a new company, the articles of the transferee company, or a draft of them, must be approved by ordinary resolution of . . . each of the transferor companies. [This is subject to subsection (2).]

[(2) In the case of a compromise or arrangement to be sanctioned under Part 26A, it is not necessary for the articles of the transferee company (or a draft of them) to be approved by ordinary resolution of the company in respect of which the compromise or arrangement is proposed.]

NOTES

Sub-s (1) was numbered as such, the words in square brackets in that subsection were inserted, and sub-s (2) was added, by the Corporate Insolvency and Governance Act 2020, s 7, Sch 9, Pt 2, paras 30, 36(1), (5), as from 26 June 2020.

The words omitted from sub-s (1) were repealed by the Companies (Reporting Requirements in Mergers and Divisions) Regulations 2011, SI 2011/1606, regs 3, 13, as from 1 August 2011 (except in relation to any merger the draft terms of which were adopted before that date).

[1.1068]

913 Protection of holders of securities to which special rights attached (merger)

(1) The scheme must provide that where any securities of a transferor company (other than shares) to which special rights are attached are held by a person otherwise than as a member or creditor of the company, that person is to receive rights in the transferee company of equivalent value.

(2) Subsection (1) does not apply if—

(a) the holder has agreed otherwise, or

(b) the holder is, or under the scheme is to be, entitled to have the securities purchased by the transferee company on terms that the court considers reasonable.

[1.1069]

[914 No allotment of shares to transferor company or transferee company (merger)

The scheme must not provide for any shares in the transferee company to be allotted to—

(a) a transferor company (or its nominee) in respect of shares in the transferor company held by the transferor company itself (or its nominee); or

(b) the transferee company (or its nominee) in respect of shares in a transferor company held by the transferee company (or its nominee).]

NOTES

Substituted by the Companies (Mergers and Divisions of Public Companies) (Amendment) Regulations 2008, SI 2008/690, reg 3, as from 6 April 2008. Note that the original s 914 was due to come into force on 6 April 2008 and was, therefore, substituted without ever coming into effect.

Exceptions where shares of transferor company held by transferee company

[1.1070]

915 Circumstances in which certain particulars and reports not required (merger)

(1) This section applies in the case of a merger by absorption where all of the relevant securities of the transferor company (or, if there is more than one transferor company, of each of them) are held by or on behalf of the transferee company.

(2) The draft terms of the scheme need not give the particulars mentioned in section 905(2)(b), (c) or (d) (particulars relating to allotment of shares to members of transferor company).

(3) [In a case where a meeting has been summoned under section 896 in relation to the compromise or arrangement, section 897] (explanatory statement to be circulated or made available) does not apply.

[(3A) In a case where a meeting has been summoned under section 901C in relation to the compromise or arrangement, section 901D (explanatory statement to be circulated or made available) does not apply.]

(4) The requirements of the following sections do not apply—

section 908 (directors' explanatory report),

section 909 (expert's report).

(5) The requirements of section 911 (inspection of documents) so far as relating to any document required to be drawn up under the provisions mentioned in [subsection (4)] above do not apply.

(6) In this section "relevant securities", in relation to a company, means shares or other securities carrying the right to vote at general meetings of the company.

NOTES

Sub-s (3): words in square brackets substituted by the Corporate Insolvency and Governance Act 2020, s 7, Sch 9, Pt 2, paras 30, 36(1), (6)(a), as from 26 June 2020.

Sub-s (3A): inserted by the Corporate Insolvency and Governance Act 2020, s 7, Sch 9, Pt 2, paras 30, 36(1), (6)(b), as from 26 June 2020.

Sub-s (5): words in square brackets substituted by the Companies Act 2006 (Consequential Amendments and Transitional Provisions) Order 2011, SI 2011/1265 art 28(1), (4), as from 12 May 2011.

[1.1071]

[915A Other circumstances in which reports and inspection not required (merger)

(1) This section applies in the case of a merger by absorption where 90% or more (but not all) of the relevant securities of the transferor company (or, if there is more than one transferor company, of each of them) are held by or on behalf of the transferee company.

(2) If the conditions in subsections (3) and (4) are met, the requirements of the following sections do not apply—

(a) section 908 (directors' explanatory report),

(b) section 909 (expert's report),

(c) section 910 (supplementary accounting statement),

(d) section 911 (inspection of documents), and

(e) section 911B (report on material changes of assets of merging company).

(3) The first condition is that the scheme provides that every other holder of relevant securities has the right to require the transferee company to acquire those securities.

(4) The second condition is that, if a holder of securities exercises that right, the consideration to be given for those securities is fair and reasonable.

(5) The powers of the court under section 900(2) [or, as the case may be, section 901J(2)] (power to facilitate reconstruction or amalgamation) include the power to determine, or make provision for the determination of, the consideration to be given for securities acquired under this section.

(6) In this section—

"other holder" means a person who holds securities of the transferor company otherwise than on behalf of the transferee company (and does not include the transferee company itself);

"relevant securities", in relation to a company, means shares or other securities carrying the right to vote at general meetings of the company.]

NOTES

Inserted by the Companies (Reporting Requirements in Mergers and Divisions) Regulations 2011, SI 2011/1606, regs 3, 14, as from 1 August 2011 (except in relation to any merger the draft terms of which were adopted before that date).

Sub-s (5): words in square brackets inserted by the Corporate Insolvency and Governance Act 2020, s 7, Sch 9, Pt 2, paras 30, 36(1), (7), as from 26 June 2020.

[1.1072]

916 Circumstances in which meeting of members of transferee company not required (merger)

(1) This section applies in the case of a merger by absorption where 90% or more (but not all) of the relevant securities of the transferor company (or, if there is more than one transferor company, of each of them) are held by or on behalf of the transferee company.

(2) It is not necessary for the scheme to be approved at a meeting of the members, or any class of members, of the transferee company if the court is satisfied that the following conditions have been complied with.

[(3) The first condition is that either subsection (3A) or subsection (3B) is satisfied.

(3A) This subsection is satisfied if publication of notice of receipt of the draft terms by the registrar took place in respect of the transferee company at least one month before the date of the first meeting of members, or any class of members, of the transferor company summoned for the purpose of agreeing to the scheme.

(3B) This subsection is satisfied if—

(a) the conditions in section 906A(2) to (4) are met in respect of the transferee company,

(b) the registrar published the notice mentioned in subsection (4) of that section in the Gazette at least one month before the date of the first meeting of members, or any class of members, of the transferor company summoned for the purpose of agreeing to the scheme, and

(c) the draft terms remained available on the website throughout the period beginning one month before, and ending on, that date.]

[(4) The second condition is that subsection (4A) or (4B) is satisfied for each of the documents listed in the applicable paragraphs of section 911(3)(a) to (f) relating to the transferee company and the transferor company (or, if there is more than one transferor company, each of them).

(4A) This subsection is satisfied for a document if the members of the transferee company were able during the period beginning one month before, and ending on, the date mentioned in subsection (3A) to inspect that document at the registered office of that company.

(4B) This subsection is satisfied for a document if—

(a) the document is made available on a website which is maintained by or on behalf of the transferee company and identifies the company,

(b) access to the document on the website is not conditional on the payment of a fee or otherwise restricted, and

(c) the document remains available on the website throughout the period beginning one month before, and ending on, the date mentioned in subsection (3A).

(4C) The third condition is that the members of the transferee company were able to obtain copies of the documents mentioned in subsection (4), or any part of those documents, on request and free of charge, throughout the period beginning one month before, and ending on, the date mentioned in subsection (3A).

(4D) For the purposes of subsection (4C)—

(a) section 911A(5) applies as it applies for the purposes of section 911(1)(b), and

(b) Part 4 of Schedule 5 (communications by means of a website) does not apply.]

(5) The [fourth] condition is that—

(a) one or more members of the transferee company, who together held not less than 5% of the paid-up capital of the company which carried the right to vote at general meetings of the company (excluding any shares in the company held as treasury shares) would have been able, during that period, to require a meeting of each class of members to be called for the purpose of deciding whether or not to agree to the scheme, and

(b) no such requirement was made.

(6) In this section "relevant securities", in relation to a company, means shares or other securities carrying the right to vote at general meetings of the company.

NOTES

Sub-ss (3)–(3B) were substituted (for the original sub-s (3)), sub-ss (4)–(4D) were substituted (for the original sub-s (4)), and the word in square brackets in sub-s (5) was substituted, by the Companies (Reporting Requirements in Mergers and Divisions) Regulations 2011, SI 2011/1606, regs 3, 15, as from 1 August 2011 (except in relation to any merger the draft terms of which were adopted before that date).

[1.1073]

917 Circumstances in which no meetings required (merger)

(1) This section applies in the case of a merger by absorption where all of the relevant securities of the transferor company (or, if there is more than one transferor company, of each of them) are held by or on behalf of the transferee company.

(2) It is not necessary for the scheme to be approved at a meeting of the members, or any class of members, of any of the merging companies if the court is satisfied that the following conditions have been complied with.

[(3) The first condition is that either subsection (3A) or subsection (3B) is satisfied.

(3A) This subsection is satisfied if publication of notice of receipt of the draft terms by the registrar took place in respect of all the merging companies at least one month before the date of the court's order.

(3B) This subsection is satisfied if—

(a) the conditions in section 906A(2) to (4) are met in respect of each of the merging companies,

(b) in each case, the registrar published the notice mentioned in subsection (4) of that section in the Gazette at least one month before the date of the court's order, and

(c) the draft terms remained available on the website throughout the period beginning one month before, and ending on, that date.]

[(4) The second condition is that subsection (4A) or (4B) is satisfied for each of the documents listed in the applicable paragraphs of section 911(3)(a) to (f) relating to the transferee company and the transferor company (or, if there is more than one transferor company, each of them).

(4A) This subsection is satisfied for a document if the members of the transferee company were able during the period beginning one month before, and ending on, the date mentioned in subsection (3A) to inspect that document at the registered office of that company.

(4B) This subsection is satisfied for a document if—

(a) the document is made available on a website which is maintained by or on behalf of the transferee company and identifies the company,

(b) access to the document on the website is not conditional on the payment of a fee or otherwise restricted, and

(c) the document remains available on the website throughout the period beginning one month before, and ending on, the date mentioned in subsection (3A).

(4C) The third condition is that the members of the transferee company were able to obtain copies of the documents mentioned in subsection (4), or any part of those documents, on request and free of charge, throughout the period beginning one month before, and ending on, the date mentioned in subsection (3A).

(4D) For the purposes of subsection (4C)—

(a) section 911A(5) applies as it applies for the purposes of section 911(1)(b), and

(b) Part 4 of Schedule 5 (communications by means of a website) does not apply.]

(5) The [fourth] condition is that—

(a) one or more members of the transferee company, who together held not less than 5% of the paid-up capital of the company which carried the right to vote at general meetings of the company (excluding any shares in the company held as treasury shares) would have been able, during that period, to require a meeting of each class of members to be called for the purpose of deciding whether or not to agree to the scheme, and

(b) no such requirement was made.

(6) In this section "relevant securities", in relation to a company, means shares or other securities carrying the right to vote at general meetings of the company.

NOTES

Sub-ss (3)–(3B) were substituted (for the original sub-s (3)), sub-ss (4)–(4D) were substituted (for the original sub-s (4)), and the word in square brackets in sub-s (5) was substituted, by the Companies (Reporting Requirements in Mergers and Divisions) Regulations 2011, SI 2011/1606, regs 3, 16, as from 1 August 2011 (except in relation to any merger the draft terms of which were adopted before that date).

Other exceptions

[1.1074]

[917A Other circumstances in which meeting of members of transferor company not required (merger)

In the case of a compromise or arrangement to be sanctioned under Part 26A, it is not necessary for the scheme to be approved by the members of the company in respect of which the compromise or arrangement is proposed.]

NOTES

Commencement: 26 June 2020.

Inserted by the Corporate Insolvency and Governance Act 2020, s 7, Sch 9, Pt 2, paras 30, 36(1), (8), as from 26 June 2020.

[1.1075]

918 Other circumstances in which meeting of members of transferee company not required (merger)

(1) In the case of any merger by absorption, it is not necessary for the scheme to be approved by the members of the transferee company if the court is satisfied that the following conditions have been complied with.

[(2) The first condition is that either subsection (2A) or subsection (2B) is satisfied.

(2A) This subsection is satisfied if publication of notice of receipt of the draft terms by the registrar took place in respect of the transferee company at least one month before the date of the first meeting of members, or any class of members, of the transferor company (or, if there is more than one transferor company, any of them) summoned for the purposes of agreeing to the scheme.

(2B) This subsection is satisfied if—

(a) the conditions in section 906A(2) to (4) are met in respect of the transferee company,

(b) the registrar published the notice mentioned in subsection (4) of that section in the Gazette at least one month before the date of the first meeting of members, or any class of members, of the transferor company (or, if there is more than one transferor company, any of them) summoned for the purposes of agreeing to the scheme, and

(c) the draft terms remained available on the website throughout the period beginning one month before, and ending on, that date.]

[(3) The second condition is that subsection (3A) or (3B) is satisfied for each of the documents listed in the applicable paragraphs of section 911(3) relating to the transferee company and the transferor company (or, if there is more than one transferor company, each of them).

(3A) This subsection is satisfied for a document if the members of the transferee company were able during the period beginning one month before, and ending on, the date of any such meeting as is mentioned in subsection (2A) to inspect that document at the registered office of that company.

(3B) This subsection is satisfied for a document if—

(a) the document is made available on a website which is maintained by or on behalf of the transferee company and identifies the company,

(b) access to the document on the website is not conditional on the payment of a fee or otherwise restricted, and

(c) the document remains available on the website throughout the period beginning one month before, and ending on, the date of any such meeting as is mentioned in subsection (2A).

(3C) The third condition is that the members of the transferee company were able to obtain copies of the documents mentioned in subsection (3), or any part of those documents, on request and free of charge, throughout the period beginning one month before, and ending on, the date of any such meeting as is mentioned in subsection (2A).

(3D) For the purposes of subsection (3C)—

(a) section 911A(5) applies as it applies for the purposes of section 911(1)(b), and

(b) Part 4 of Schedule 5 (communications by means of a website) does not apply.]

(4) The [fourth] condition is that—

(a) one or more members of that company, who together held not less than 5% of the paid-up capital of the company which carried the right to vote at general meetings of the company (excluding any shares in the company held as treasury shares) would have been able, during that period, to require a meeting of each class of members to be called for the purpose of deciding whether or not to agree to the scheme, and

(b) no such requirement was made.

NOTES

Sub-ss (2)–(2B) were substituted (for the original sub-s (2)), sub-ss (3)–(3D) were substituted (for the original sub-s (3)), and the word in square brackets in sub-s (4) was substituted, by the Companies (Reporting Requirements in Mergers and Divisions) Regulations 2011, SI 2011/1606, regs 3, 17, as from 1 August 2011 (except in relation to any merger the draft terms of which were adopted before that date).

[1.1076]

[918A Agreement to dispense with [reports etc] (merger)

(1) If all members holding shares in, and all persons holding other securities of, the [the merging companies], being shares or securities that carry a right to vote in general meetings of the company in question, so agree, [the following requirements do not apply].

[(1A) The requirements that may be dispensed with under this section are—

(a) the requirements of—

(i) section 908 (directors' explanatory report),

(ii) section 909 (expert's report),

(iii) section 910 (supplementary accounting statement), and

(iv) section 911B (report on material changes of assets of merging company); and

(b) the requirements of section 911 (inspection of documents) so far as relating to any document required to be drawn up under sections 908, 909 or 910.]

(2) For the purposes of this section—

(a) the members, or holders of other securities, of a company, and

(b) whether shares or other securities carry a right to vote in general meetings of the company,

are determined as at the date of [the relevant application].

[(3) In subsection (2) "the relevant application" means—

(a) in the case of a compromise or arrangement to be sanctioned under Part 26, the application to the court under section 896;

(b) in the case of a compromise or arrangement to be sanctioned under Part 26A, the application to the court under section 901C(1).]]

NOTES

Inserted by the Companies (Mergers and Divisions of Public Companies) (Amendment) Regulations 2008, SI 2008/690, reg 2(2), as from 6 April 2008.

The words in square brackets in the section heading and in sub-s (1) were substituted, and sub-s (1A) was inserted, by the Companies (Reporting Requirements in Mergers and Divisions) Regulations 2011, SI 2011/1606, regs 3, 18, as from 1 August 2011 (except in relation to any merger the draft terms of which were adopted before that date).

The words in square brackets in sub-s (2) were substituted, and sub-s (3) was added, by the Corporate Insolvency and Governance Act 2020, s 7, Sch 9, Pt 2, paras 30, 36(1), (9), as from 26 June 2020.

CHAPTER 3 DIVISION

Introductory

[1.1077]

919 Divisions and companies involved in a division

(1) The scheme involves a division where under the scheme the undertaking, property and liabilities of the company in respect of which the compromise or arrangement is proposed are to be divided among and transferred to two or more companies each of which is either—

(a) an existing public company, or

(b) a new company (whether or not a public company).

(2) References in this Part to the companies involved in the division are to the transferor company and any existing transferee companies.

Requirements to be complied with in case of division

[1.1078]

920 Draft terms of scheme (division)

(1) A draft of the proposed terms of the scheme must be drawn up and adopted by the directors of each of the companies involved in the division.

(2) The draft terms must give particulars of at least the following matters—

(a) in respect of the transferor company and each transferee company—

(i) its name,

(ii) the address of its registered office, and

(iii) whether it is a company limited by shares or a company limited by guarantee and having a share capital;

(b) the number of shares in a transferee company to be allotted to members of the transferor company for a given number of their shares (the "share exchange ratio") and the amount of any cash payment;

(c) the terms relating to the allotment of shares in a transferee company;

(d) the date from which the holding of shares in a transferee company will entitle the holders to participate in profits, and any special conditions affecting that entitlement;

(e) the date from which the transactions of the transferor company are to be treated for accounting purposes as being those of a transferee company;

(f) any rights or restrictions attaching to shares or other securities in a transferee company to be allotted under the scheme to the holders of shares or other securities in the transferor company to which any special rights or restrictions attach, or the measures proposed concerning them;

(g) any amount of benefit paid or given or intended to be paid or given—

(i) to any of the experts referred to in section 924 (expert's report), or

(ii) to any director of a company involved in the division,

and the consideration for the payment of benefit.

(3) The draft terms must also—

(a) give particulars of the property and liabilities to be transferred (to the extent that these are known to the transferor company) and their allocation among the transferee companies;

(b) make provision for the allocation among and transfer to the transferee companies of any other property and liabilities that the transferor company has acquired or may subsequently acquire; and

(c) specify the allocation to members of the transferor company of shares in the transferee companies and the criteria upon which that allocation is based.

[1.1079]

921 Publication of draft terms [by registrar] (division)

(1) The directors of each company involved in the division must deliver a copy of the draft terms to the registrar.

(2) The registrar must publish in the Gazette notice of receipt by him from that company of a copy of the draft terms.

(3) That notice must be published at least one month before the date of any meeting of that company summoned for the purposes of approving the scheme.

(4) The requirements in this section are subject to [section 921A (publication of draft terms on company website) and] section 934 (power of court to exclude certain requirements).

NOTES

Section heading, sub-s (4): words in square brackets inserted by the Companies (Reporting Requirements in Mergers and Divisions) Regulations 2011, SI 2011/1606, regs 3, 19, as from 1 August 2011 (except in relation to any division the draft terms of which were adopted before that date).

[1.1080]

[921A Publication of draft terms on company website (division)

(1) Section 921 does not apply in respect of a company if the conditions in subsections (2) to (6) are met.

(2) The first condition is that the draft terms are made available on a website which—

(a) is maintained by or on behalf of the company, and

(b) identifies the company.

(3) The second condition is that neither access to the draft terms on the website nor the supply of a hard copy of them from the website is conditional on payment of a fee or otherwise restricted.

(4) The third condition is that the directors of the company deliver to the registrar a notice giving details of the website.

(5) The fourth condition is that the registrar publishes the notice in the Gazette at least one month before the date of any meeting of the company summoned for the purpose of approving the scheme.

(6) The fifth condition is that the draft terms remain available on the website throughout the period beginning one month before, and ending on, the date of any such meeting.]

NOTES

Inserted by the Companies (Reporting Requirements in Mergers and Divisions) Regulations 2011, SI 2011/1606, regs 3, 20, as from 1 August 2011 (except in relation to any division the draft terms of which were adopted before that date).

[1.1081]

922 Approval of members of companies involved in the division

(1) The [scheme] must be approved by a majority in number, representing 75% in value, of each class of members of each of the companies involved in the division, present and voting either in person or by proxy at a meeting.

(2) This requirement is subject to sections 931[, 931A] and 932 (circumstances in which meeting of members not required).

NOTES

Word and number in square brackets substituted by the Corporate Insolvency and Governance Act 2020, s 7, Sch 9, Pt 2, paras 30, 36(1), (10), as from 26 June 2020.

[1.1082]

923 Directors' explanatory report (division)

(1) The directors of the transferor and each existing transferee company must draw up and adopt a report.

(2) The report must consist of—

[(a) the required statement explaining the effect of the compromise or arrangement,] and

(b) insofar as that statement does not deal with the following matters, a further statement—

(i) setting out the legal and economic grounds for the draft terms, and in particular for the share exchange ratio and for the criteria on which the allocation to the members of the transferor company of shares in the transferee companies was based, and

(ii) specifying any special valuation difficulties.

[(2A) In subsection (2) "the required statement explaining the effect of the compromise or arrangement" means—

(a) in a case where a meeting is summoned under section 896 in relation to the compromise or arrangement, the statement required by section 897;

(b) in a case where a meeting is summoned under section 901C in relation to the compromise or arrangement, the statement required by section 901D.]

(3) The report must also state—

(a) whether a report has been made to any transferee company under section 593 (valuation of non-cash consideration for shares), and

(b) if so, whether that report has been delivered to the registrar of companies.

(4) The requirement in this section is subject to section 933 (agreement to dispense with reports etc) [and section 933A (certain requirements excluded where shareholders given proportional rights)].

NOTES

Sub-s (2): para (a) substituted by the Corporate Insolvency and Governance Act 2020, s 7, Sch 9, Pt 2, paras 30, 36(1), (11)(a), as from 26 June 2020.

Sub-s (2A): inserted by the Corporate Insolvency and Governance Act 2020, s 7, Sch 9, Pt 2, paras 30, 36(1), (11)(b), as from 26 June 2020.

Sub-s (4): words in square brackets inserted by the Companies (Reporting Requirements in Mergers and Divisions) Regulations 2011, SI 2011/1606, regs 3, 21, as from 1 August 2011 (except in relation to any division the draft terms of which were adopted before that date).

[1.1083]

924 Expert's report (division)

(1) An expert's report must be drawn up on behalf of each company involved in the division.

(2) The report required is a written report on the draft terms to the members of the company.

(3) The court may on the joint application of the companies involved in the division approve the appointment of a joint expert to draw up a single report on behalf of all those companies.

If no such appointment is made, there must be a separate expert's report to the members of each company involved in the division drawn up by a separate expert appointed on behalf of that company.

(4) The expert must be a person who—

(a) is eligible for appointment as a statutory auditor (see section 1212), and

(b) meets the independence requirement in section 936.

(5) The expert's report must—

(a) indicate the method or methods used to arrive at the share exchange ratio;

(b) give an opinion as to whether the method or methods used are reasonable in all the circumstances of the case, indicate the values arrived at using each such method and (if there is more than one method) give an opinion on the relative importance attributed to such methods in arriving at the value decided on;

(c) describe any special valuation difficulties that have arisen;

(d) state whether in the expert's opinion the share exchange ratio is reasonable; and

(e) in the case of a valuation made by a person other than himself (see section 935), state that it appeared to him reasonable to arrange for it to be so made or to accept a valuation so made.

(6) The expert (or each of them) has—

(a) the right of access to all such documents of the companies involved in the division, and

(b) the right to require from the companies' officers all such information,

as he thinks necessary for the purposes of making his report.

(7) The requirement in this section is subject to section 933 (agreement to dispense with reports etc) [and section 933A (certain requirements excluded where shareholders given proportional rights)].

NOTES

Sub-s (7): words in square brackets inserted by the Companies (Reporting Requirements in Mergers and Divisions) Regulations 2011, SI 2011/1606, regs 3, 22, as from 1 August 2011 (except in relation to any division the draft terms of which were adopted before that date).

[1.1084]

925 Supplementary accounting statement (division)

[(1) This section applies if the last annual accounts of a company involved in the division relate to a financial year ending before—

(a) the date seven months before the first meeting of the company summoned for the purposes of approving the scheme, or

(b) if no meeting of the company is required (by virtue of section 931[, 931A] or 932), the date six months before the directors of the company adopt the draft terms of the scheme.

(1A) If the company has not made public a half-yearly financial report relating to a period ending on or after the date mentioned in subsection (1), the directors of the company must prepare a supplementary accounting statement.]

(2) That statement must consist of—

(a) a balance sheet dealing with the state of affairs of the company as at a date not more than three months before the draft terms were adopted by the directors, and

(b) where the company would be required under section 399 to prepare group accounts if that date were the last day of a financial year, a consolidated balance sheet dealing with the state of affairs of the company and the undertakings that would be included in such a consolidation.

(3) The requirements of this Act . . . as to the balance sheet forming part of a company's annual accounts, and the matters to be included in notes to it, apply to the balance sheet required for an accounting statement under this section, with such modifications as are necessary by reason of its being prepared otherwise than as at the last day of a financial year.

(4) The provisions of section 414 as to the approval and signing of accounts apply to the balance sheet required for an accounting statement under this section.

[(4A) In this section "half-yearly financial report" means a report of that description required to be made public by rules under section 89A of the Financial Services and Markets Act 2000 (transparency rules).]

(5) The requirement in this section is subject to section 933 (agreement to dispense with reports etc) [and section 933A (certain requirements excluded where shareholders given proportional rights)].

NOTES

Sub-ss (1), (1A) were substituted (for the original sub-s (1)), sub-s (4A) was inserted, and the words in square brackets in sub-s (5) were added, by the Companies (Reporting Requirements in Mergers and Divisions) Regulations 2011, SI 2011/1606, regs 3, 23, as from 1 August 2011 (except in relation to any division the draft terms of which were adopted before that date).

The figure in square brackets in sub-s (1)(b) was inserted by the Corporate Insolvency and Governance Act 2020, s 7, Sch 9, Pt 2, paras 30, 36(1), (12), as from 26 June 2020.

Sub-s (3): words omitted repealed by the International Accounting Standards and European Public Limited-Liability Company (Amendment etc) (EU Exit) Regulations 2019, SI 2019/685, reg 19, Sch 1, Pt 1, paras 1, 25, in relation to accounts for financial years beginning on or after IP completion day (as defined in the European Union (Withdrawal Agreement) Act 2020, s 39) (note also that in relation to accounts for financial years which begin before but end on or after IP completion day, the enactments amended by Parts 1–3 of Sch 1 to the 2019 Regulations have effect as if the UK were a member State until the end of the financial year in question).

[1.1085]

926 Inspection of documents (division)

(1) The members of each company involved in the division must be able, during the period specified below—

(a) to inspect at the registered office of that company copies of the documents listed below relating to that company and every other company involved in the division, and
(b) to obtain copies of those documents or any part of them on request free of charge.

(2) The period referred to above is the period—

(a) beginning one month before, and
(b) ending on the date of,

the first meeting of the members, or any class of members, of the company for the purposes of approving the scheme.

(3) The documents referred to above are—

(a) the draft terms;
(b) the directors' explanatory report;
(c) the expert's report;
(d) the company's annual accounts and reports for the last three financial years ending on or before the first meeting of the members, or any class of members, of the company summoned for the purposes of approving the scheme; . . .
(e) any supplementary accounting statement required by section 925[; and
(f) if no statement is required by section 925 because the company has made public a recent half-yearly financial report (see subsection (1A) of that section), that report].

[(3A) The requirement in subsection (1)(a) is subject to section 926A(1) (publication of documents on company website).]

(4) The requirements in subsection (3)(b), (c) and (e) are subject to section 933 (agreement to dispense with reports etc)[, section 933A (certain requirements excluded where shareholders given proportional rights)] and section 934 (power of court to exclude certain requirements).

[(5) Section 1145 (right to hard copy) does not apply to a document sent or supplied in accordance with subsection (1)(b) to a member who has consented to information being sent or supplied by the company by electronic means and has not revoked that consent.

(6) Part 4 of Schedule 5 (communications by means of a website) does not apply for the purposes of subsection (1)(b) (but see section 926A(5)).]

NOTES

The word omitted from sub-s (3)(d) was repealed, sub-s (3)(f) and the preceding word were added, the words in square brackets in sub-s (4) were inserted, and sub-ss (3A), (5), (6) were inserted and added respectively, by the Companies (Reporting Requirements in Mergers and Divisions) Regulations 2011, SI 2011/1606, regs 3, 24, as from 1 August 2011 (except in relation to any division the draft terms of which were adopted before that date).

[1.1086]

[926A Publication of documents on company website (division)

(1) Section 926(1)(a) does not apply to a document if the conditions in subsections (2) to (4) are met in relation to that document.

This is subject to subsection (6).

(2) The first condition is that the document is made available on a website which—

(a) is maintained by or on behalf of the company, and
(b) identifies the company.

(3) The second condition is that access to the document on the website is not conditional on payment of a fee or otherwise restricted.

(4) The third condition is that the document remains available on the website throughout the period beginning one month before, and ending on, the date of any meeting of the company summoned for the purpose of approving the scheme.

(5) A person is able to obtain a copy of a document as required by section 926(1)(b) if—

(a) the conditions in subsections (2) and (3) are met in relation to that document, and
(b) the person is able, throughout the period specified in subsection (4)—
(i) to retain a copy of the document as made available on the website, and
(ii) to produce a hard copy of it.

(6) Where members of a company are able to obtain copies of a document only as mentioned in subsection (5), section 926(1)(a) applies to that document even if the conditions in subsections (2) to (4) are met.]

NOTES

Inserted by the Companies (Reporting Requirements in Mergers and Divisions) Regulations 2011, SI 2011/1606, regs 3, 25, as from 1 August 2011 (except in relation to any division the draft terms of which were adopted before that date).

[1.1087]

927 Report on material changes of assets of transferor company (division)

(1) The directors of the transferor company must report—
(a) to every meeting of the members, or any class of members, of that company summoned for the purpose of agreeing to the scheme, and
(b) to the directors of each existing transferee company,

any material changes in the property and liabilities of the transferor company between the date when the draft terms were adopted and the date of the meeting in question.

(2) The directors of each existing transferee company must in turn—
(a) report those matters to every meeting of the members, or any class of members, of that company summoned for the purpose of agreeing to the scheme, or
(b) send a report of those matters to every member entitled to receive notice of such a meeting.

(3) The requirement in this section is subject to section 933 (agreement to dispense with reports etc) [and section 933A (certain requirements excluded where shareholders given proportional rights)].

NOTES

Sub-s (3): words in square brackets added by the Companies (Reporting Requirements in Mergers and Divisions) Regulations 2011, SI 2011/1606, regs 3, 26, as from 1 August 2011 (except in relation to any division the draft terms of which were adopted before that date).

[1.1088]

928 Approval of articles of new transferee company (division)

[(1)] The articles of every new transferee company, or a draft of them, must be approved by ordinary resolution of the transferor company.

[(2) Subsection (1) does not apply in the case of a compromise or arrangement to be sanctioned under Part 26A.]

NOTES

Sub-s (1) numbered as such, and sub-s (2) added, by the Corporate Insolvency and Governance Act 2020, s 7, Sch 9, Pt 2, paras 30, 36(1), (13), as from 26 June 2020.

[1.1089]

929 Protection of holders of securities to which special rights attached (division)

(1) The scheme must provide that where any securities of the transferor company (other than shares) to which special rights are attached are held by a person otherwise than as a member or creditor of the company, that person is to receive rights in a transferee company of equivalent value.

(2) Subsection (1) does not apply if—
(a) the holder has agreed otherwise, or
(b) the holder is, or under the scheme is to be, entitled to have the securities purchased by a transferee company on terms that the court considers reasonable.

[1.1090]

[930 No allotment of shares to transferor company or to transferee company (division)

The scheme must not provide for any shares in a transferee company to be allotted to—
(a) the transferor company (or its nominee) in respect of shares in the transferor company held by the transferor company itself (or its nominee); or
(b) a transferee company (or its nominee) in respect of shares in the transferor company held by the transferee company (or its nominee).]

NOTES

Substituted by the Companies (Mergers and Divisions of Public Companies) (Amendment) Regulations 2008, SI 2008/690, reg 4, as from 6 April 2008. Note that the original s 930 was due to come into force on 6 April 2008 and was, therefore, substituted without ever coming into effect.

Exceptions where shares of transferor company held by transferee company

[1.1091]

931 Circumstances in which meeting of members of transferor company not required (division)

(1) This section applies in the case of a division where all of the shares or other securities of the transferor company carrying the right to vote at general meetings of the company are held by or on behalf of one or more existing transferee companies.

(2) It is not necessary for the scheme to be approved by a meeting of the members, or any class of members, of the transferor company if the court is satisfied that the following conditions have been complied with.

[(3) The first condition is that either subsection (3A) or subsection (3B) is satisfied.

(3A) This subsection is satisfied if publication of notice of receipt of the draft terms by the registrar took place in respect of all the companies involved in the division at least one month before the date of the court's order.

(3B) This subsection is satisfied if—

(a) the conditions in section 921A(2) to (4) are met in respect of each of the companies involved in the division,
(b) in each case, the registrar published the notice mentioned in subsection (4) of that section in the Gazette at least one month before the date of the court's order, and
(c) the draft terms remained available on the website throughout the period beginning one month before, and ending on, that date.]

[(4) The second condition is that subsection (4A) or (4B) is satisfied for each of the documents listed in the applicable paragraphs of section 926(3) relating to every company involved in the division.

(4A) This subsection is satisfied for a document if the members of every company involved in the division were able during the period beginning one month before, and ending on, the date of the court's order to inspect that document at the registered office of their company.

(4B) This subsection is satisfied for a document if—
(a) the document is made available on a website which is maintained by or on behalf of the company to which it relates and identifies the company,
(b) access to the document on the website is not conditional on payment of a fee or otherwise restricted, and
(c) the document remains available on the website throughout the period beginning one month before, and ending on, the date of the court's order.

(4C) The third condition is that the members of every company involved in the division were able to obtain copies of the documents mentioned in subsection (4), or any part of those documents, on request and free of charge, throughout the period beginning one month before, and ending on, the date of the court's order.

(4D) For the purposes of subsection (4C)—
(a) section 926A(5) applies as it applies for the purposes of section 926(1)(b), and
(b) Part 4 of Schedule 5 (communications by means of a website) does not apply.]

(5) . . .

(6) The fourth condition is that the directors of the transferor company have sent—
(a) to every member who would have been entitled to receive notice of a meeting to agree to the scheme (had any such meeting been called), and
(b) to the directors of every existing transferee company,

a report of any material change in the property and liabilities of the transferor company between the date when the terms were adopted by the directors and the date one month before the date of the court's order.

NOTES

Sub-ss (3)–(3B) were substituted (for the original sub-s (3)), sub-ss (4)–(4D) were substituted (for the original sub-s (4)), and sub-s (5) was repealed, by the Companies (Reporting Requirements in Mergers and Divisions) Regulations 2011, SI 2011/1606, regs 3, 27, as from 1 August 2011 (except in relation to any division the draft terms of which were adopted before that date).

Other exceptions

[1.1092]

[931A Other circumstances in which meeting of members of transferor company not required (division)

[In the case of a compromise or arrangement to be sanctioned under Part 26A, it is not necessary for the scheme to be approved by the members of the transferor company.]

NOTES

Commencement: 26 June 2020.

Inserted by the Corporate Insolvency and Governance Act 2020, s 7, Sch 9, Pt 2, paras 30, 36(1), (14), as from 26 June 2020.

[1.1093]

932 Circumstances in which meeting of members of transferee company not required (division)

(1) In the case of a division, it is not necessary for the scheme to be approved by the members of a transferee company if the court is satisfied that the following conditions have been complied with in relation to that company.

[(2) The first condition is that either subsection (2A) or subsection (2B) is satisfied.

(2A) This subsection is satisfied if publication of notice of receipt of the draft terms by the registrar took place in respect of the transferee company at least one month before the date of the first meeting of members of the transferor company summoned for the purposes of agreeing to the scheme.

(2B) This subsection is satisfied if—
(a) the conditions in section 921A(2) to (4) are met in respect of the transferee company,
(b) the registrar published the notice mentioned in subsection (4) of that section in the Gazette at least one month before the date of the first meeting of members of the transferor company summoned for the purposes of agreeing to the scheme, and
(c) the draft terms remained available on the website throughout the period beginning one month before, and ending on, that date.]

[(3) The second condition is that subsection (3A) or (3B) is satisfied for each of the documents listed in the applicable paragraphs of section 926(3) relating to the transferee company and every other company involved in the division.

(3A) This subsection is satisfied for a document if the members of the transferee company were able during the period beginning one month before, and ending on, the date mentioned in subsection (2A) to inspect that document at the registered office of that company.

(3B) This subsection is satisfied for a document if—
(a) the document is made available on a website which is maintained by or on behalf of the transferee company and identifies the company,
(b) access to the document on the website is not conditional on payment of a fee or otherwise restricted, and
(c) the document remains available on the website throughout the period beginning one month before, and ending on, the date mentioned in subsection (2A).

(3C) The third condition is that the members of the transferee company were able to obtain copies of the documents mentioned in subsection (3), or any part of those documents, on request and free of charge, throughout the period beginning one month before, and ending on, the date mentioned in subsection (2A).

(3D) For the purposes of subsection (3C)—

(a) section 926A(5) applies as it applies for the purposes of section 926(1)(b), and

(b) Part 4 of Schedule 5 (communications by means of a website) does not apply.]

(4) The [fourth] condition is that—

(a) one or more members of that company, who together held not less than 5% of the paid-up capital of the company which carried the right to vote at general meetings of the company (excluding any shares in the company held as treasury shares) would have been able, during that period, to require a meeting of each class of members to be called for the purpose of deciding whether or not to agree to the scheme, and

(b) no such requirement was made.

(5) The [first, second and third] conditions above are subject to section 934 (power of court to exclude certain requirements).

NOTES

Sub-ss (2)–(2B) were substituted (for the original sub-s (2)), sub-ss (3)–(3D) were substituted (for the original sub-s (3)), and the words in square brackets in sub-ss (4), (5) were substituted, by the Companies (Reporting Requirements in Mergers and Divisions) Regulations 2011, SI 2011/1606, regs 3, 28, as from 1 August 2011 (except in relation to any division the draft terms of which were adopted before that date).

[1.1094]

933 Agreement to dispense with reports etc (division)

(1) If all members holding shares in, and all persons holding other securities of, the companies involved in the division, being shares or securities that carry a right to vote in general meetings of the company in question, so agree, the following requirements do not apply.

(2) The requirements that may be dispensed with under this section are—

(a) the requirements of—

(i) section 923 (directors' explanatory report),

(ii) section 924 (expert's report),

(iii) section 925 (supplementary accounting statement), and

(iv) section 927 (report on material changes in assets of transferor company); and

(b) the requirements of section 926 (inspection of documents) so far as relating to any document required to be drawn up under the provisions mentioned in paragraph (a)(i), (ii) or (iii) above.

(3) For the purposes of this section—

(a) the members, or holders of other securities, of a company, and

(b) whether shares or other securities carry a right to vote in general meetings of the company,

are determined as at the date of [the relevant application].

[(4) In subsection (3) "the relevant application" means—

(a) in the case of a compromise or arrangement to be sanctioned under Part 26, the application to the court under section 896;

(b) in the case of a compromise or arrangement to be sanctioned under Part 26A, the application to the court under section 901C(1).]

NOTES

Words in square brackets in sub-s (3) substituted, and sub-s (4) added, by the Corporate Insolvency and Governance Act 2020, s 7, Sch 9, Pt 2, paras 30, 36(1), (15), as from 26 June 2020.

[1.1095]

[933A Certain requirements excluded where shareholders given proportional rights (division)

(1) This section applies in the case of a division where each of the transferee companies is a new company.

(2) If all the shares in each of the transferee companies are to be allotted to the members of the transferor company in proportion to their rights in the allotted share capital of the transferor company, the following requirements do not apply.

(3) The requirements which do not apply are—

(a) the requirements of—

(i) section 923 (directors' explanatory report),

(ii) section 924 (expert's report),

(iii) section 925 (supplementary accounting statement), and

(iv) section 927 (report on material changes in assets of transferor company); and

(b) the requirements of section 926 (inspection of documents) so far as relating to any document required to be drawn up under the provisions mentioned in paragraph (a)(i), (ii) or (iii) above.]

NOTES

Inserted by the Companies (Reporting Requirements in Mergers and Divisions) Regulations 2011, SI 2011/1606, regs 3, 29, as from 1 August 2011 (except in relation to any division the draft terms of which were adopted before that date).

[1.1096]

934 Power of court to exclude certain requirements (division)

(1) In the case of a division, the court may by order direct that—

(a) in relation to any company involved in the division, the requirements of—

(i) section 921 (publication of draft terms), and

(ii) section 926 (inspection of documents),

do not apply, and

(b) in relation to an existing transferee company, section 932 (circumstances in which meeting of members of transferee company not required) has effect with the omission of the [first, second and third] conditions specified in that section,

if the court is satisfied that the following conditions will be fulfilled in relation to that company.

(2) The first condition is that the members of that company will have received, or will have been able to obtain free of charge, copies of the documents listed in section 926—

(a) in time to examine them before the date of the first meeting of the members, or any class of members, of that company summoned for the purposes of agreeing to the scheme, or

(b) in the case of an existing transferee company where in the circumstances described in section 932 no meeting is held, in time to require a meeting as mentioned in subsection (4) of that section.

(3) The second condition is that the creditors of that company will have received or will have been able to obtain free of charge copies of the draft terms in time to examine them—

(a) before the date of the first meeting of the members, or any class of members, of the company summoned for the purposes of agreeing to the scheme, or

(b) in the circumstances mentioned in subsection (2)(b) above, at the same time as the members of the company.

(4) The third condition is that no prejudice would be caused to the members or creditors of the transferor company or any transferee company by making the order in question.

NOTES

Sub-s (1): words in square brackets substituted by the Companies (Reporting Requirements in Mergers and Divisions) Regulations 2011, SI 2011/1606, regs 3, 30, as from 1 August 2011 (except in relation to any division the draft terms of which were adopted before that date).

CHAPTER 4 SUPPLEMENTARY PROVISIONS

Expert's report and related matters

[1.1097]

935 Expert's report: valuation by another person

(1) Where it appears to an expert—

(a) that a valuation is reasonably necessary to enable him to draw up his report, and

(b) that it is reasonable for that valuation, or part of it, to be made by (or for him to accept a valuation made by) another person who—

(i) appears to him to have the requisite knowledge and experience to make the valuation or that part of it, and

(ii) meets the independence requirement in section 936,

he may arrange for or accept such a valuation, together with a report which will enable him to make his own report under section 909 or 924.

(2) Where any valuation is made by a person other than the expert himself, the latter's report must state that fact and must also—

(a) state the former's name and what knowledge and experience he has to carry out the valuation, and

(b) describe so much of the undertaking, property and liabilities as was valued by the other person, and the method used to value them, and specify the date of the valuation.

[1.1098]

936 Experts and valuers: independence requirement

(1) A person meets the independence requirement for the purposes of section 909 or 924 (expert's report) or section 935 (valuation by another person) only if—

(a) he is not—

(i) an officer or employee of any of the companies concerned in the scheme, or

(ii) a partner or employee of such a person, or a partnership of which such a person is a partner;

(b) he is not—

(i) an officer or employee of an associated undertaking of any of the companies concerned in the scheme, or

(ii) a partner or employee of such a person, or a partnership of which such a person is a partner; and

(c) there does not exist between—

(i) the person or an associate of his, and

(ii) any of the companies concerned in the scheme or an associated undertaking of such a company,

a connection of any such description as may be specified by regulations made by the Secretary of State.

(2) An auditor of a company is not regarded as an officer or employee of the company for this purpose.

(3) For the purposes of this section—

(a) the "companies concerned in the scheme" means every transferor and existing transferee company;

(b) "associated undertaking", in relation to a company, means—

(i) a parent undertaking or subsidiary undertaking of the company, or

(ii) a subsidiary undertaking of a parent undertaking of the company; and

(c) "associate" has the meaning given by section 937.

(4) Regulations under this section are subject to negative resolution procedure.

NOTES

Regulations: no Regulations have been made under this section.

[1.1099]

937 Experts and valuers: meaning of "associate"

(1) This section defines "associate" for the purposes of section 936 (experts and valuers: independence requirement).

(2) In relation to an individual, "associate" means—

(a) that individual's spouse or civil partner or minor child or step-child,

(b) any body corporate of which that individual is a director, and
(c) any employee or partner of that individual.

(3) In relation to a body corporate, "associate" means—
(a) any body corporate of which that body is a director,
(b) any body corporate in the same group as that body, and
(c) any employee or partner of that body or of any body corporate in the same group.

(4) In relation to a partnership that is a legal person under the law by which it is governed, "associate" means—
(a) any body corporate of which that partnership is a director,
(b) any employee of or partner in that partnership, and
(c) any person who is an associate of a partner in that partnership.

(5) In relation to a partnership that is not a legal person under the law by which it is governed, "associate" means any person who is an associate of any of the partners.

(6) In this section, in relation to a limited liability partnership, for "director" read "member".

Powers of the court

[1.1100]
938 Power of court to summon meeting of members or creditors of existing transferee company

(1) The court may order a meeting of—
(a) the members of an existing transferee company, or any class of them, or
(b) the creditors of an existing transferee company, or any class of them, to be summoned in such manner as the court directs.

(2) An application for such an order may be made by—
(a) the company concerned,
(b) a member or creditor of the company, or
[(c) if the company is being wound up, the liquidator, or
(d) if the company is in administration, the administrator.]

[(3) Section 323 (representation of corporations at meetings) applies to a meeting of creditors under this section as to a meeting of the company (references to a member being read as references to a creditor).]

NOTES

Sub-s (2): paras (c), (d) substituted (for the original para (c)) by the Companies Act 2006 (Consequential Amendments, Transitional Provisions and Savings) Order 2009, SI 2009/1941, art 2(1), Sch 1, para 260(1), (5), as from 1 October 2009.

Sub-s (3): added by the Companies Act 2006 (Consequential Amendments etc) Order 2008, SI 2008/948, art 3(1), Sch 1, Pt 2, para 251, as from 6 April 2008.

[1.1101]
939 Court to fix date for transfer of undertaking etc of transferor company

(1) Where the court sanctions the compromise or arrangement, it must—
(a) in the order sanctioning the compromise or arrangement, or
(b) in a subsequent order under section 900 [or, as the case may be, section 901J] (powers of court to facilitate reconstruction or amalgamation),

fix a date on which the transfer (or transfers) to the transferee company (or transferee companies) of the undertaking, property and liabilities of the transferor company is (or are) to take place.

(2) Any such order that provides for the dissolution of the transferor company must fix the same date for the dissolution.

(3) If it is necessary for the transferor company to take steps to ensure that the undertaking, property and liabilities are fully transferred, the court must fix a date, not later than six months after the date fixed under subsection (1), by which such steps must be taken.

(4) In that case, the court may postpone the dissolution of the transferor company until that date.

(5) The court may postpone or further postpone the date fixed under subsection (3) if it is satisfied that the steps mentioned cannot be completed by the date (or latest date) fixed under that subsection.

NOTES

Sub-s (1): words in square brackets in para (b) inserted by the Corporate Insolvency and Governance Act 2020, s 7, Sch 9, Pt 2, paras 30, 36(1), (16), as from 26 June 2020.

Liability of transferee companies

[1.1102]
940 Liability of transferee companies for each other's defaults

(1) In the case of a division, each transferee company is jointly and severally liable for any liability transferred to any other transferee company under the scheme to the extent that the other company has made default in satisfying that liability.

This is subject to the following provisions.

(2) If[, in the case of a compromise or arrangement to be sanctioned under Part 26,] a majority in number representing 75% in value of the creditors or any class of creditors of the transferor company, present and voting either in person or by proxy at a meeting summoned for the purposes of agreeing to the scheme, so agree, subsection (1) does not apply in relation to the liabilities owed to the creditors or that class of creditors.

[(2A) If, in the case of a compromise or arrangement to be sanctioned under Part 26A, a number representing 75% in value of the creditors or any class of creditors of the transferor company, present and voting either in person or by proxy at a meeting summoned for the purposes of agreeing to the scheme, so agree, subsection (1) does not apply in relation to the liabilities owed to the creditors or that class of creditors.]

(3) A transferee company is not liable under this section for an amount greater than the net value transferred to it under the scheme.

The "net value transferred" is the value at the time of the transfer of the property transferred to it under the scheme less the amount at that date of the liabilities so transferred.

NOTES

Words in square brackets in sub-s (2) inserted, and sub-s (2A) inserted, by the Corporate Insolvency and Governance Act 2020, s 7, Sch 9, Pt 2, paras 30, 36(1), (17), as from 26 June 2020.

[Disruption of websites

[1.1103]

940A Disregard of website failures beyond control of company

(1) A failure to make information or a document available on the website throughout a period specified in any of the provisions mentioned in subsection (2) is to be disregarded if—

(a) it is made available on the website for part of that period, and

(b) the failure to make it available throughout that period is wholly attributable to circumstances that it would not be reasonable to have expected the company to prevent or avoid.

(2) The provisions referred to above are—

(a) section 906A(6),

(b) section 911A(4),

(c) section 916(3B) and (4B),

(d) section 917(3B) and (4B),

(e) section 918(2B) and (3B),

(f) section 921A(6),

(g) section 926A(4),

(h) section 931(3B) and (4B), and

(i) section 932(2B) and (3B).]

NOTES

Inserted, together with the preceding heading, by the Companies (Reporting Requirements in Mergers and Divisions) Regulations 2011, SI 2011/1606, regs 3, 31, as from 1 August 2011 (except in relation to any merger or division the draft terms of which were adopted before that date).

Interpretation

[1.1104]

941 Meaning of "liabilities" and "property"

In this Part—

"liabilities" includes duties;

"property" includes property, rights and powers of every description.

PART 28 TAKEOVERS ETC

NOTES

The Directive of the European Parliament and of the Council (2004/25/EC) on takeover bids had to be implemented by 20 May 2006 and, as this Act had not completed Parliamentary passage by that date, this was achieved by means of the Takeovers Directive (Interim Implementation) Regulations 2006, SI 2006/1183. The 2006 Regulations were revoked by the Companies Act 2006 (Commencement No 2, Consequential Amendments, Transitional Provisions and Savings) Order 2007, SI 2007/1093, art 7, Sch 5, as from 6 April 2007 (the same date as this Part came into force). The revocation of SI 2006/1183 was subject to certain savings contained in Sch 6, paras 2, 3 to the 2007 Order.

As to the application of this Part to the Isle of Man, see the note to s 965 at **[1.1127]**.

CHAPTER 1 THE TAKEOVER PANEL

The Panel and its rules

[1.1105]

942 The Panel

(1) The body known as the Panel on Takeovers and Mergers ("the Panel") is to have the functions conferred on it by or under this Chapter.

(2) The Panel may do anything that it considers necessary or expedient for the purposes of, or in connection with, its functions.

(3) The Panel may make arrangements for any of its functions to be discharged by—

(a) a committee or sub-committee of the Panel, or

(b) an officer or member of staff of the Panel, or a person acting as such.

This is subject to section 943(4) and (5).

[1.1106]

943 Rules

[(1) The Panel must make rules—

(a) giving effect to the general principles in Part 1 of Schedule 1C, and

(b) in accordance with Part 2 of that Schedule.]

[(1A) Rules must specify the percentage of voting rights that gives a person control of a company for the purposes of this Chapter and how it is to be calculated.]

(2) Rules made by the Panel may also make other provision—

(a) for or in connection with the regulation of—

(i) takeover bids,

(ii) merger transactions, and

(iii) transactions (not falling within sub-paragraph (i) or (ii)) that have or may have, directly or indirectly, an effect on the ownership or control of companies;

(b) for or in connection with the regulation of things done in consequence of, or otherwise in relation to, any such bid or transaction;

(c) about cases where—

(i) any such bid or transaction is, or has been, contemplated or apprehended, or
(ii) an announcement is made denying that any such bid or transaction is intended.

(3) The provision that may be made under subsection (2) includes, in particular, provision for a matter that is, or is similar to, a matter provided for by the Panel in the City Code on Takeovers and Mergers as it had effect immediately before the passing of this Act.

(4) In relation to rules made by virtue of section 957 (fees and charges), functions under this section may be discharged either by the Panel itself or by a committee of the Panel (but not otherwise).

(5) In relation to rules of any other description, the Panel must discharge its functions under this section by a committee of the Panel.

(6) Section 1 (meaning of "company") does not apply for the purposes of this section.

(7) In this section "takeover bid" includes a takeover bid within the meaning [given by paragraph 20(1) of Schedule 1C].

(8) . . .

(9) A reference to rules in the following provisions of this Chapter is to rules under this section.

NOTES

All amendments to this section were made by the Takeovers (Amendment) (EU Exit) Regulations 2019, SI 2019/217, regs 2, 3, as from IP completion day (as defined in the European Union (Withdrawal Agreement) Act 2020, s 39).

As to Rules made by the Takeover Panel under this section, see: www.thetakeoverpanel.org.uk.

[1.1107]

944 Further provisions about rules

(1) Rules may—
(a) make different provision for different purposes;
(b) make provision subject to exceptions or exemptions;
(c) contain incidental, supplemental, consequential or transitional provision;
(d) authorise the Panel to dispense with or modify the application of rules in particular cases and by reference to any circumstances.

Rules made by virtue of paragraph (d) must require the Panel to give reasons for acting as mentioned in that paragraph.

(2) Rules must be made by an instrument in writing.

(3) Immediately after an instrument containing rules is made, the text must be made available to the public, with or without payment, in whatever way the Panel thinks appropriate.

(4) A person is not to be taken to have contravened a rule if he shows that at the time of the alleged contravention the text of the rule had not been made available as required by subsection (3).

(5) The production of a printed copy of an instrument purporting to be made by the Panel on which is endorsed a certificate signed by an officer of the Panel authorised by it for that purpose and stating—
(a) that the instrument was made by the Panel,
(b) that the copy is a true copy of the instrument, and
(c) that on a specified date the text of the instrument was made available to the public as required by subsection (3),

is evidence (or in Scotland sufficient evidence) of the facts stated in the certificate.

(6) A certificate purporting to be signed as mentioned in subsection (5) is to be treated as having been properly signed unless the contrary is shown.

(7) A person who wishes in any legal proceedings to rely on an instrument by which rules are made may require the Panel to endorse a copy of the instrument with a certificate of the kind mentioned in subsection (5).

[1.1108]

945 Rulings

(1) The Panel may give rulings on the interpretation, application or effect of rules.

(2) To the extent and in the circumstances specified in rules, and subject to any review or appeal, a ruling has binding effect.

[1.1109]

946 Directions

Rules may contain provision conferring power on the Panel to give any direction that appears to the Panel to be necessary in order—
(a) to restrain a person from acting (or continuing to act) in breach of rules;
(b) to restrain a person from doing (or continuing to do) a particular thing, pending determination of whether that or any other conduct of his is or would be a breach of rules;
(c) otherwise to secure compliance with rules.

Information

[1.1110]

947 Power to require documents and information

(1) The Panel may by notice in writing require a person—
(a) to produce any documents that are specified or described in the notice;
(b) to provide, in the form and manner specified in the notice, such information as may be specified or described in the notice.

(2) A requirement under subsection (1) must be complied with—
(a) at a place specified in the notice, and
(b) before the end of such reasonable period as may be so specified.

(3) This section applies only to documents and information reasonably required in connection with the exercise by the Panel of its functions.

(4) The Panel may require—

(a) any document produced to be authenticated, or

(b) any information provided (whether in a document or otherwise) to be verified,

in such manner as it may reasonably require.

(5) The Panel may authorise a person to exercise any of its powers under this section.

(6) A person exercising a power by virtue of subsection (5) must, if required to do so, produce evidence of his authority to exercise the power.

(7) The production of a document in pursuance of this section does not affect any lien that a person has on the document.

(8) The Panel may take copies of or extracts from a document produced in pursuance of this section.

(9) A reference in this section to the production of a document includes a reference to the production of—

(a) a hard copy of information recorded otherwise than in hard copy form, or

(b) information in a form from which a hard copy can be readily obtained.

(10) A person is not required by this section to disclose documents or information in respect of which a claim to legal professional privilege (in Scotland, to confidentiality of communications) could be maintained in legal proceedings.

[1.1111]

948 Restrictions on disclosure

(1) This section applies to information (in whatever form)—

(a) relating to the private affairs of an individual, or

(b) relating to any particular business,

that is provided to the Panel in connection with the exercise of its functions.

(2) No such information may, during the lifetime of the individual or so long as the business continues to be carried on, be disclosed without the consent of that individual or (as the case may be) the person for the time being carrying on that business.

(3) Subsection (2) does not apply to any disclosure of information that—

(a) is made for the purpose of facilitating the carrying out by the Panel of any of its functions,

(b) is made to a person specified in Part 1 of Schedule 2,

(c) is of a description specified in Part 2 of that Schedule, or

(d) is made in accordance with Part 3 of that Schedule.

(4) The Secretary of State may amend Schedule 2 by order subject to negative resolution procedure.

(5) An order under subsection (4) must not—

(a) amend Part 1 of Schedule 2 by specifying a person unless the person exercises functions of a public nature (whether or not he exercises any other function);

(b) amend Part 2 of Schedule 2 by adding or modifying a description of disclosure unless the purpose for which the disclosure is permitted is likely to facilitate the exercise of a function of a public nature;

(c) amend Part 3 of Schedule 2 so as to have the effect of permitting disclosures to be made to a body other than one that exercises functions of a public nature in a country or territory outside the United Kingdom.

(6) Subsection (2) does not apply to—

(a) the disclosure by an authority within subsection (7) of information disclosed to it by the Panel in reliance on subsection (3);

(b) the disclosure of such information by anyone who has obtained it directly or indirectly from an authority within subsection (7).

(7) The authorities within this subsection are—

[(a) the Financial Conduct Authority;

(aa) the Prudential Regulation Authority;

(ab) the Bank of England;]

(b), (c) . . .

(8) This section does not prohibit the disclosure of information if the information is or has been available to the public from any other source.

(9) Nothing in this section authorises the making of a disclosure in contravention of [the data protection legislation].

NOTES

Sub-s (7): paras (a), (aa), (ab) substituted (for the original para (a)) by the Financial Services Act 2012, s 114(1), Sch 18, Pt 2, paras 110, 118, as from 1 April 2013. Paras (b) and (c) repealed by the Takeovers (Amendment) (EU Exit) Regulations 2019, SI 2019/217, regs 2, 4, as from IP completion day (as defined in the European Union (Withdrawal Agreement) Act 2020, s 39).

Sub-s (9): words in square brackets substituted by the Data Protection Act 2018, s 211, Sch 19, Pt 1, paras 120, 124, as from 25 May 2018 (for transitional provisions and savings relating to the repeal of the Data Protection Act 1998, see Sch 20 to the 2018 Act).

Orders: the Companies Act 2006 (Amendment of Schedule 2) (No 2) Order 2009, SI 2009/1208. For a summary of all statutory instruments made under this Act, see Appendix 4 at **[A4]**.

[1.1112]

949 Offence of disclosure in contravention of section 948

(1) A person who discloses information in contravention of section 948 is guilty of an offence, unless—

(a) he did not know, and had no reason to suspect, that the information had been provided as mentioned in section 948(1), or

(b) he took all reasonable steps and exercised all due diligence to avoid the commission of the offence.

(2) A person guilty of an offence under this section is liable—

(a) on conviction on indictment, to imprisonment for a term not exceeding two years or a fine (or both);

(b) on summary conviction—

(i) in England and Wales, to imprisonment for a term not exceeding twelve months or to a fine not exceeding the statutory maximum (or both);

(ii) in Scotland or Northern Ireland, to imprisonment for a term not exceeding six months, or to a fine not exceeding the statutory maximum (or both).

(3) Where a company or other body corporate commits an offence under this section, an offence is also committed by every officer of the company or other body corporate who is in default.

NOTES

Offences under this section: see further s 1131 at **[1.1301]**.

Co-operation

[1.1113]

950 Panel's duty of co-operation

(1) The Panel must take such steps as it considers appropriate to co-operate with—

[(a) the Financial Conduct Authority;

(aa) the Prudential Regulation Authority;

(ab) the Bank of England;]

(b) . . .

(c) any other person or body that exercises functions of a public nature, under legislation in any country or territory outside the United Kingdom, that appear to the Panel to be similar to its own functions or those of the [Financial Conduct Authority or the Prudential Regulation Authority or similar to the regulatory functions of the Bank of England].

(2) Co-operation may include the sharing of information that the Panel is not prevented from disclosing.

NOTES

Sub-s (1): paras (a), (aa), (ab) substituted (for the original para (a)), and words in square brackets in para (c) substituted, by the Financial Services Act 2012, s 114(1), Sch 18, Pt 2, paras 110, 119, as from 1 April 2013. Para (b) repealed by the Takeovers (Amendment) (EU Exit) Regulations 2019, SI 2019/217, regs 2, 5, as from IP completion day (as defined in the European Union (Withdrawal Agreement) Act 2020, s 39).

Hearings and appeals

[1.1114]

951 Hearings and appeals

(1) Rules must provide for a decision of the Panel to be subject to review by a committee of the Panel (the "Hearings Committee") at the instance of such persons affected by the decision as are specified in the rules.

(2) Rules may also confer other functions on the Hearings Committee.

(3) Rules must provide for there to be a right of appeal against a decision of the Hearings Committee to an independent tribunal (the "Takeover Appeal Board") in such circumstances and subject to such conditions as are specified in the rules.

(4) Rules may contain—

(a) provision as to matters of procedure in relation to proceedings before the Hearings Committee (including provision imposing time limits);

(b) provision about evidence in such proceedings;

(c) provision as to the powers of the Hearings Committee dealing with a matter referred to it;

(d) provision about enforcement of decisions of the Hearings Committee and the Takeover Appeal Board.

(5) Rules must contain provision—

(a) requiring the Panel, when acting in relation to any proceedings before the Hearings Committee or the Takeover Appeal Board, to do so by an officer or member of staff of the Panel (or a person acting as such);

(b) preventing a person who is or has been a member of the committee mentioned in section 943(5) from being a member of the Hearings Committee or the Takeover Appeal Board;

(c) preventing a person who is a member of the committee mentioned in section 943(5), of the Hearings Committee or of the Takeover Appeal Board from acting as mentioned in paragraph (a).

Contravention of rules etc

[1.1115]

952 Sanctions

(1) Rules may contain provision conferring power on the Panel to impose sanctions on a person who has—

(a) acted in breach of rules, or

(b) failed to comply with a direction given by virtue of section 946.

(2) Subsection (3) applies where rules made by virtue of subsection (1) confer power on the Panel to impose a sanction of a kind not provided for by the City Code on Takeovers and Mergers as it had effect immediately before the passing of this Act.

(3) The Panel must prepare a statement (a "policy statement") of its policy with respect to—

(a) the imposition of the sanction in question, and

(b) where the sanction is in the nature of a financial penalty, the amount of the penalty that may be imposed.

An element of the policy must be that, in making a decision about any such matter, the Panel has regard to the factors mentioned in subsection (4).

(4) The factors are—

(a) the seriousness of the breach or failure in question in relation to the nature of the rule or direction contravened;

(b) the extent to which the breach or failure was deliberate or reckless;

(c) whether the person on whom the sanction is to be imposed is an individual.

(5) The Panel may at any time revise a policy statement.

(6) The Panel must prepare a draft of any proposed policy statement (or revised policy statement) and consult such persons about the draft as the Panel considers appropriate.

(7) The Panel must publish, in whatever way it considers appropriate, any policy statement (or revised policy statement) that it prepares.

(8) In exercising, or deciding whether to exercise, its power to impose a sanction within subsection (2) in the case of any particular breach or failure, the Panel must have regard to any relevant policy statement published and in force at the time when the breach or failure occurred.

[1.1116]
953 Failure to comply with rules about bid documentation

(1) This section applies where a takeover bid is made for a company that has securities carrying voting rights admitted to trading on a regulated market in the United Kingdom.
(2) Where an offer document published in respect of the bid does not comply with offer document rules, an offence is committed by—
(a) the person making the bid, and
(b) where the person making the bid is a body of persons, any director, officer or member of that body who caused the document to be published.
(3) A person commits an offence under subsection (2) only if—
(a) he knew that the offer document did not comply, or was reckless as to whether it complied, and
(b) he failed to take all reasonable steps to secure that it did comply.
(4) Where a response document published in respect of the bid does not comply with response document rules, an offence is committed by any director or other officer of the company referred to in subsection (1) who—
(a) knew that the response document did not comply, or was reckless as to whether it complied, and
(b) failed to take all reasonable steps to secure that it did comply.
(5) Where an offence is committed under subsection (2)(b) or (4) by a company or other body corporate ("the relevant body")—
(a) subsection (2)(b) has effect as if the reference to a director, officer or member of the person making the bid included a reference to a director, officer or member of the relevant body;
(b) subsection (4) has effect as if the reference to a director or other officer of the company referred to in subsection (1) included a reference to a director, officer or member of the relevant body.
(6) A person guilty of an offence under this section is liable—
(a) on conviction on indictment, to a fine;
(b) on summary conviction, to a fine not exceeding the statutory maximum.
(7) Nothing in this section affects any power of the Panel in relation to the enforcement of its rules.
(8) Section 1 (meaning of "company") does not apply for the purposes of this section.
(9) In this section—
"designated" means designated in rules;
"offer document" means a document required to be published by rules [made in accordance with paragraph 12(1) to (3) of Schedule 1C];
["offer document rules" means rules under section 943(1) designated as rules made in accordance with paragraph 12(4) of Schedule 1C;]
"response document" means a document required to be published by rules [made in accordance with paragraph 18 of Schedule 1C];
["response document rules" means rules under section 943(1) designated as rules made in accordance with paragraph 18(1) of Schedule 1C;]
"securities" means shares or debentures;
"takeover bid" has the [meaning given by paragraph 20(1) of Schedule 1C];
"voting rights" means rights to vote at general meetings of the company in question, including rights that arise only in certain circumstances.

NOTES

Sub-s (9): the words in square brackets in the definitions "offer document", "response document", and "takeover bid" were substituted, and the definitions "offer document rules" and "response document rules" were substituted, by the Takeovers (Amendment) (EU Exit) Regulations 2019, SI 2019/217, regs 2, 6, as from IP completion day (as defined in the European Union (Withdrawal Agreement) Act 2020, s 39).

[1.1117]
954 Compensation

(1) Rules may confer power on the Panel to order a person to pay such compensation as it thinks just and reasonable if he is in breach of a rule the effect of which is to require the payment of money.
(2) Rules made by virtue of this section may include provision for the payment of interest (including compound interest).

[1.1118]
955 Enforcement by the court

(1) If, on the application of the Panel, the court is satisfied—
(a) that there is a reasonable likelihood that a person will contravene a rule-based requirement, or
(b) that a person has contravened a rule-based requirement or a disclosure requirement,
the court may make any order it thinks fit to secure compliance with the requirement.
(2) In subsection (1) "the court" means the High Court or, in Scotland, the Court of Session.
(3) Except as provided by subsection (1), no person—
(a) has a right to seek an injunction, or
(b) in Scotland, has title or interest to seek an interdict or an order for specific performance,
to prevent a person from contravening (or continuing to contravene) a rule-based requirement or a disclosure requirement.
(4) In this section—
"contravene" includes fail to comply;
"disclosure requirement" means a requirement imposed under section 947;
"rule-based requirement" means a requirement imposed by or under rules.

[1.1119]

956 No action for breach of statutory duty etc

(1) Contravention of a rule-based requirement or a disclosure requirement does not give rise to any right of action for breach of statutory duty.

(2) Contravention of a rule-based requirement does not make any transaction void or unenforceable or (subject to any provision made by rules) affect the validity of any other thing.

(3) In this section—

(a) "contravention" includes failure to comply;

(b) "disclosure requirement" and "rule-based requirement" have the same meaning as in section 955.

Funding

[1.1120]

957 Fees and charges

(1) Rules may provide for fees or charges to be payable to the Panel for the purpose of meeting any part of its expenses.

(2) A reference in this section or section 958 to expenses of the Panel is to any expenses that have been or are to be incurred by the Panel in, or in connection with, the discharge of its functions, including in particular—

(a) payments in respect of the expenses of the Takeover Appeal Board;

(b) the cost of repaying the principal of, and of paying any interest on, any money borrowed by the Panel;

(c) the cost of maintaining adequate reserves.

[1.1121]

958 Levy

(1) For the purpose of meeting any part of the expenses of the Panel, the Secretary of State may by regulations provide for a levy to be payable to the Panel—

(a) by specified persons or bodies, or persons or bodies of a specified description, or

(b) on transactions, of a specified description, in securities on specified markets.

In this subsection "specified" means specified in the regulations.

(2) The power to specify (or to specify descriptions of) persons or bodies must be exercised in such a way that the levy is payable only by persons or bodies that appear to the Secretary of State—

(a) to be capable of being directly affected by the exercise of any of the functions of the Panel, or

(b) otherwise to have a substantial interest in the exercise of any of those functions.

(3) Regulations under this section may in particular—

(a) specify the rate of the levy and the period in respect of which it is payable at that rate;

(b) make provision as to the times when, and the manner in which, payments are to be made in respect of the levy.

(4) In determining the rate of the levy payable in respect of a particular period, the Secretary of State—

(a) must take into account any other income received or expected by the Panel in respect of that period;

(b) may take into account estimated as well as actual expenses of the Panel in respect of that period.

(5) The Panel must—

(a) keep proper accounts in respect of any amounts of levy received by virtue of this section;

(b) prepare, in relation to each period in respect of which any such amounts are received, a statement of account relating to those amounts in such form and manner as is specified in the regulations.

Those accounts must be audited, and the statement certified, by persons appointed by the Secretary of State.

(6) Regulations under this section—

(a) are subject to affirmative resolution procedure if subsection (7) applies to them;

(b) otherwise, are subject to negative resolution procedure.

(7) This subsection applies to—

(a) the first regulations under this section;

(b) any other regulations under this section that would result in a change in the persons or bodies by whom, or the transactions on which, the levy is payable.

(8) If a draft of an instrument containing regulations under this section would, apart from this subsection, be treated for the purposes of the Standing Orders of either House of Parliament as a hybrid instrument, it is to proceed in that House as if it were not such an instrument.

NOTES

Regulations: no Regulations have been made under this section.

[1.1122]

959 Recovery of fees, charges or levy

An amount payable by any person or body by virtue of section 957 or 958 is a debt due from that person or body to the Panel, and is recoverable accordingly.

Miscellaneous and supplementary

[1.1123]

960 Panel as party to proceedings

The Panel is capable (despite being an unincorporated body) of—

(a) bringing proceedings under this Chapter in its own name;

(b) bringing or defending any other proceedings in its own name.

[1.1124]

961 Exemption from liability in damages

(1) Neither the Panel, nor any person within subsection (2), is to be liable in damages for anything done (or omitted to be done) in, or in connection with, the discharge or purported discharge of the Panel's functions.

(2) A person is within this subsection if—

(a) he is (or is acting as) a member, officer or member of staff of the Panel, or

(b) he is a person authorised under section 947(5).

(3) Subsection (1) does not apply—

(a) if the act or omission is shown to have been in bad faith, or

(b) so as to prevent an award of damages in respect of the act or omission on the ground that it was unlawful as a result of section 6(1) of the Human Rights Act 1998 (c 42) (acts of public authorities incompatible with Convention rights).

[1.1125]

962 Privilege against self-incrimination

(1) A statement made by a person in response to—

(a) a requirement under section 947(1), or

(b) an order made by the court under section 955 to secure compliance with such a requirement,

may not be used against him in criminal proceedings in which he is charged with an offence to which this subsection applies.

(2) Subsection (1) applies to any offence other than an offence under one of the following provisions (which concern false statements made otherwise than on oath)—

(a) section 5 of the Perjury Act 1911 (c 6);

(b) section 44(2) of the Criminal Law (Consolidation) (Scotland) Act 1995 (c 39);

(c) Article 10 of the Perjury (Northern Ireland) Order 1979 (SI 1979/1714 (NI 19)).

[1.1126]

963 Annual reports

(1) After the end of each financial year the Panel must publish a report.

(2) The report must—

(a) set out how the Panel's functions were discharged in the year in question;

(b) include the Panel's accounts for that year;

(c) mention any matters the Panel considers to be of relevance to the discharge of its functions.

964 (*Amends FSMA 2000, ss 144, 349, 354, 417, and repeals s 143 (power to make rules endorsing the City Code on Takeovers and Mergers etc). Repealed in part by the Financial Services Act 2012, s 114(2), Sch 19, as from 1 April 2013.*)

[1.1127]

965 Power to extend to Isle of Man and Channel Islands

Her Majesty may by Order in Council direct that any of the provisions of this Chapter extend, with such modifications as may be specified in the Order, to the Isle of Man or any of the Channel Islands.

NOTES

Orders: the Companies Act 2006 (Extension of Takeover Panel Provisions) (Isle of Man) Order 2019, SI 2019/567 at **[4.675]**. This Order (which came into force on IP completion day (as defined in the European Union (Withdrawal Agreement) Act 2020, s 39)) provides that this Chapter (including Sch 2 post) shall extend to the Isle of Man with the modifications set out in the Schedule to the Order. It also revokes the Companies Act 2006 (Extension of Takeover Panel Provisions) (Isle of Man) Order 2008, SI 2008/3122, and the Companies Act 2006 (Extension of Takeover Panel Provisions) (Isle of Man) Order 2009, SI 2009/1378 (as from IP completion day), partly to reflect changes in responsibility for company registration on the Isle of Man, and partly to deal with the UK's withdrawal from the EU. For a summary of all statutory instruments made under this Act, see Appendix 4 at **[A4]**.

CHAPTER 2 IMPEDIMENTS TO TAKEOVERS

Opting in and opting out

[1.1128]

966 Opting in and opting out

(1) A company may by special resolution (an "opting-in resolution") opt in for the purposes of this Chapter if the following [five] conditions are met in relation to the company.

(2) The first condition is that the company has voting shares admitted to trading on a [UK] regulated market.

[(3) The second condition is that the company's articles of association do not contain any restrictions on the transfer of shares or, if they do contain any such restrictions, provide that they are not to apply to—

(a) transfers to the offeror, or at the offeror's direction to another person, during the offer period, or

(b) transfers to any person at a time during the offer period when the offeror holds shares amounting to not less than 75% in value of all the voting shares in the company.

(3A) The third condition is that the company's articles of association—

(a) do not contain any restrictions on rights to vote at a general meeting of the company, or

(b) if they do contain any such restrictions, provide that they are not to have effect on rights to vote at a general meeting of the company that—

(i) decides whether to take any action which might result in the frustration of the takeover bid, or

(ii) is held at a time when the offeror holds shares amounting to not less than 75% in value of all the voting shares in the company,

unless the restrictions are compensated for by specific pecuniary advantages.

(3B) The fourth condition is that the company's articles of association do not contain any other provision which would be incompatible with the requirements of subsection (3C).

(3C) Those requirements are—

(a) multiple-vote shares are to carry only one vote each at a general meeting of the company that decides whether to take any action which might result in the frustration of the takeover bid,

(b) multiple-vote shares are to carry only one vote each at a general meeting of the company which—

(i) is the first such meeting to be held after the end of the offer period,

(ii) is held at a time when the offeror holds shares amounting to not less than 75% in value of all the voting shares in the company, and

(iii) is called at the offeror's request under section 969 in order to amend the company's articles of association or to appoint or remove members of the board of directors, and

(c) at a time during the offer period when the offeror holds shares amounting to not less than 75% in value of all the voting shares in the company, shareholders are not to have any extraordinary rights to appoint or remove members of the board of directors.

(3D) The references in subsections (3A)(b) and (3C)(a) to voting at a general meeting of the company that decides whether to take any action which might result in the frustration of the takeover bid includes a reference to voting on a written resolution concerned with that question.

(3E) For the purposes of subsections (3A)(b)(i) and (3C)(a), action which might result in the frustration of the takeover bid is any action of that kind specified in rules under section 943(1) made in accordance with paragraphs 17 or 18 of Schedule 1C.

(3F) The references in subsections (3), (3A) and (3C) to voting shares in the company do not include—

(a) debentures, or

(b) shares that, under the company's articles of association, do not normally carry rights to vote at its general meetings (for example, shares carrying rights to vote that, under those articles, arise only where specified pecuniary advantages are not provided).

(3G) In subsection (3C), "multiple-vote shares" means shares included in a distinct and separate class and carrying more than one vote each.]

(4) The [fifth] condition is that—

(a) no shares conferring special rights in the company are held by—

(i) a minister,

(ii) a nominee of, or any other person acting on behalf of, a minister, or

(iii) a company directly or indirectly controlled by a minister,

and

(b) no such rights are exercisable by or on behalf of a minister under any enactment.

(5) A company may revoke an opting-in resolution by a further special resolution (an "opting-out resolution").

(6) . . .

(7) In subsection (4) "minister" means—

(a) the holder of an office in Her Majesty's Government in the United Kingdom;

(b) the Scottish Ministers;

(c) a Minister within the meaning given by section 7(3) of the Northern Ireland Act 1998 (c 47);

[(d) the Welsh Ministers;]

and for the purposes of that subsection "minister" also includes the Treasury, the Board of Trade [and] the Defence Council . . .

(8) The Secretary of State may by order subject to negative resolution procedure provide that subsection (4) applies in relation to a specified person or body that exercises functions of a public nature as it applies in relation to a minister. "Specified" means specified in the order.

NOTES

In sub-s (7), para (d) and the word "and" in square brackets were inserted, and the words omitted were repealed, by the Government of Wales Act 2006 (Consequential Modifications and Transitional Provisions) Order 2007, SI 2007/1388, art 3, Sch 1, para 142, as from 25 May 2007.

All other amendments to this section were made by the Takeovers (Amendment) (EU Exit) Regulations 2019, SI 2019/217, regs 2, 7, as from IP completion day (as defined in the European Union (Withdrawal Agreement) Act 2020, s 39).

Orders: no Orders have been made under this section.

[1.1129]

967 Further provision about opting-in and opting-out resolutions

(1) An opting-in resolution or an opting-out resolution must specify the date from which it is to have effect (the "effective date").

(2) The effective date of an opting-in resolution may not be earlier than the date on which the resolution is passed.

(3) The [second, third, fourth and fifth] conditions in section 966 must be met at the time when an opting-in resolution is passed, but the first one does not need to be met until the effective date.

(4) An opting-in resolution passed before the time when voting shares of the company are admitted to trading on a [UK] regulated market complies with the requirement in subsection (1) if, instead of specifying a particular date, it provides for the resolution to have effect from that time.

(5) An opting-in resolution passed before the commencement of this section complies with the requirement in subsection (1) if, instead of specifying a particular date, it provides for the resolution to have effect from that commencement.

(6) The effective date of an opting-out resolution may not be earlier than the first anniversary of the date on which a copy of the opting-in resolution was forwarded to the registrar.

(7) Where a company has passed an opting-in resolution, any alteration of its articles of association that would prevent the [second, third or fourth condition] in section 966 from being met is of no effect until the effective date of an opting-out resolution passed by the company.

NOTES

All amendments to this section were made by the Takeovers (Amendment) (EU Exit) Regulations 2019, SI 2019/217, regs 2, 8, as from IP completion day (as defined in the European Union (Withdrawal Agreement) Act 2020, s 39).

Consequences of opting in

[1.1130]

968 Effect on contractual restrictions

(1) The following provisions have effect where a takeover bid is made for an opted-in company.

(2) An agreement to which this section applies is invalid in so far as it places any restriction—

(a) on the transfer to the offeror, or at his direction to another person, of shares in the company during the offer period;

(b) on the transfer to any person of shares in the company at a time during the offer period when the offeror holds shares amounting to not less than 75% in value of all the voting shares in the company;

(c) on rights to vote at a general meeting of the company that decides whether to take any action which might result in the frustration of the bid;

(d) on rights to vote at a general meeting of the company that—

(i) is the first such meeting to be held after the end of the offer period, and

(ii) is held at a time when the offeror holds shares amounting to not less than 75% in value of all the voting shares in the company.

(3) This section applies to an agreement—

(a) entered into between a person holding shares in the company and another such person on or after 21st April 2004, or

(b) entered into at any time between such a person and the company,

and it applies to such an agreement even if the law applicable to the agreement (apart from this section) is not the law of a part of the United Kingdom.

(4) The reference in subsection (2)(c) to rights to vote at a general meeting of the company that decides whether to take any action which might result in the frustration of the bid includes a reference to rights to vote on a written resolution concerned with that question.

(5) For the purposes of subsection (2)(c), action which might result in the frustration of a bid is any action of that kind specified in rules under section 943(1) [made in accordance with paragraph 17 or 18 of Schedule 1C].

(6) If a person suffers loss as a result of any act or omission that would (but for this section) be a breach of an agreement to which this section applies, he is entitled to compensation, of such amount as the court considers just and equitable, from any person who would (but for this section) be liable to him for committing or inducing the breach.

(7) In subsection (6) "the court" means the High Court or, in Scotland, the Court of Session.

(8) A reference in this section to voting shares in the company does not include—

(a) debentures, or

(b) shares that, under the company's articles of association, do not normally carry rights to vote at its general meetings (for example, shares carrying rights to vote that, under those articles, arise only where specified pecuniary advantages are not provided).

NOTES

Sub-s (5): words in square brackets substituted by the Takeovers (Amendment) (EU Exit) Regulations 2019, SI 2019/217, regs 2, 9, as from IP completion day (as defined in the European Union (Withdrawal Agreement) Act 2020, s 39).

[1.1131]

969 Power of offeror to require general meeting to be called

(1) Where a takeover bid is made for an opted-in company, the offeror may by making a request to the directors of the company require them to call a general meeting of the company if, at the date at which the request is made, he holds shares amounting to not less than 75% in value of all the voting shares in the company.

(2) The reference in subsection (1) to voting shares in the company does not include—

(a) debentures, or

(b) shares that, under the company's articles of association, do not normally carry rights to vote at its general meetings (for example, shares carrying rights to vote that, under those articles, arise only where specified pecuniary advantages are not provided).

(3) Sections 303 to 305 (members' power to require general meetings to be called) apply as they would do if subsection (1) above were substituted for subsections (1) to (3) of section 303, and with any other necessary modifications.

Supplementary

[1.1132]

970 Communication of decisions

(1) A company that has passed an opting-in resolution or an opting-out resolution must notify—

(a) the Panel, . . .

(b) . . .

(2) Notification must be given within 15 days after the resolution is passed . . .

(3) If a company fails to comply with this section, an offence is committed by—

(a) the company, and

(b) every officer of it who is in default.

(4) A person guilty of an offence under this section is liable on summary conviction to a fine not exceeding level 3 on the standard scale and, for continued contravention, a daily default fine not exceeding one-tenth of level 3 on the standard scale.

NOTES

Sub-ss (1), (2): words omitted repealed by the Takeovers (Amendment) (EU Exit) Regulations 2019, SI 2019/217, regs 2, 10, as from IP completion day (as defined in the European Union (Withdrawal Agreement) Act 2020, s 39).

[1.1133]
971 Interpretation of this Chapter
(1) In this Chapter—

. . .

["offeror", in relation to a takeover bid, means the person making the bid]

"offer period", in relation to a takeover bid, means the time allowed for acceptance of the bid by rules under section 943(1) [made in accordance with paragraph 13 of Schedule 1C];

"opted-in company" means a company in relation to which—

(a) an opting-in resolution has effect, and

(b) the conditions in section 966(2) and (4) continue to be met;

"opting-in resolution" has the meaning given by section 966(1);

"opting-out resolution" has the meaning given by section 966(5);

["takeover bid" has the meaning given by paragraph 20(1) of Schedule 1C;]

. . .

"voting rights" means rights to vote at general meetings of the company in question, including rights that arise only in certain circumstances;

"voting shares" means shares carrying voting rights.

(2) For the purposes of this Chapter—

(a) securities of a company are treated as shares in the company if they are convertible into or entitle the holder to subscribe for such shares;

(b) debentures issued by a company are treated as shares in the company if they carry voting rights.

NOTES

Sub-s (1): all amendments to this subsection were made by the Takeovers (Amendment) (EU Exit) Regulations 2019, SI 2019/217, regs 2, 11, as from IP completion day (as defined in the European Union (Withdrawal Agreement) Act 2020, s 39).

[1.1134]
972 Transitory provision
(1) Where a takeover bid is made for an opted-in company, section 368 of the Companies Act 1985 (c 6) (extraordinary general meeting on members' requisition) and section 378 of that Act (extraordinary and special resolutions) have effect as follows until their repeal by this Act.

(2) Section 368 has effect as if a members' requisition included a requisition of a person who—

(a) is the offeror in relation to the takeover bid, and

(b) holds at the date of the deposit of the requisition shares amounting to not less than 75% in value of all the voting shares in the company.

(3) In relation to a general meeting of the company that—

(a) is the first such meeting to be held after the end of the offer period, and

(b) is held at a time when the offeror holds shares amounting to not less than 75% in value of all the voting shares in the company,

section 378(2) (meaning of "special resolution") has effect as if "14 days' notice" were substituted for "21 days' notice".

(4) A reference in this section to voting shares in the company does not include—

(a) debentures, or

(b) shares that, under the company's articles of association, do not normally carry rights to vote at its general meetings (for example, shares carrying rights to vote that, under those articles, arise only where specified pecuniary advantages are not provided).

[1.1135]
973 Power to extend to Isle of Man and Channel Islands
Her Majesty may by Order in Council direct that any of the provisions of this Chapter extend, with such modifications as may be specified in the Order, to the Isle of Man or any of the Channel Islands.

CHAPTER 3 "SQUEEZE-OUT" AND "SELL-OUT"

Takeover offers

[1.1136]
974 Meaning of "takeover offer"
(1) For the purposes of this Chapter an offer to acquire shares in a company is a "takeover offer" if the following two conditions are satisfied in relation to the offer.

(2) The first condition is that it is an offer to acquire—

(a) all the shares in a company, or

(b) where there is more than one class of shares in a company, all the shares of one or more classes,

other than shares that at the date of the offer are already held by the offeror. Section 975 contains provision supplementing this subsection.

(3) The second condition is that the terms of the offer are the same—

(a) in relation to all the shares to which the offer relates, or

(b) where the shares to which the offer relates include shares of different classes, in relation to all the shares of each class.

Section 976 contains provision treating this condition as satisfied in certain circumstances.

(4) In subsections (1) to (3) "shares" means shares, other than relevant treasury shares, that have been allotted on the date of the offer (but see subsection (5)).

(5) A takeover offer may include among the shares to which it relates—

(a) all or any shares that are allotted after the date of the offer but before a specified date;

(b) all or any relevant treasury shares that cease to be held as treasury shares before a specified date;

(c) all or any other relevant treasury shares.

(6) In this section—

"relevant treasury shares" means shares that—

(a) are held by the company as treasury shares on the date of the offer, or

(b) become held by the company as treasury shares after that date but before a specified date;

"specified date" means a date specified in or determined in accordance with the terms of the offer.

(7) Where the terms of an offer make provision for their revision and for acceptances on the previous terms to be treated as acceptances on the revised terms, then, if the terms of the offer are revised in accordance with that provision—

(a) the revision is not to be regarded for the purposes of this Chapter as the making of a fresh offer, and

(b) references in this Chapter to the date of the offer are accordingly to be read as references to the date of the original offer.

[1.1137]

975 Shares already held by the offeror etc

(1) The reference in section 974(2) to shares already held by the offeror includes a reference to shares that he has contracted to acquire, whether unconditionally or subject to conditions being met.

This is subject to subsection (2).

(2) The reference in section 974(2) to shares already held by the offeror does not include a reference to shares that are the subject of a contract—

(a) intended to secure that the holder of the shares will accept the offer when it is made, and

(b) entered into—

(i) by deed and for no consideration,

(ii) for consideration of negligible value, or

(iii) for consideration consisting of a promise by the offeror to make the offer.

(3) In relation to Scotland, this section applies as if the words "by deed and" in subsection (2)(b)(i) were omitted.

(4) The condition in section 974(2) is treated as satisfied where—

(a) the offer does not extend to shares that associates of the offeror hold or have contracted to acquire (whether unconditionally or subject to conditions being met), and

(b) the condition would be satisfied if the offer did extend to those shares.

(For further provision about such shares, see section 977(2)).

[1.1138]

976 Cases where offer treated as being on same terms

(1) The condition in section 974(3) (terms of offer to be the same for all shares or all shares of particular classes) is treated as satisfied where subsection (2) or (3) below applies.

(2) This subsection applies where—

(a) shares carry an entitlement to a particular dividend which other shares of the same class, by reason of being allotted later, do not carry,

(b) there is a difference in the value of consideration offered for the shares allotted earlier as against that offered for those allotted later,

(c) that difference merely reflects the difference in entitlement to the dividend, and

(d) the condition in section 974(3) would be satisfied but for that difference.

(3) This subsection applies where—

(a) the law of a country or territory outside the United Kingdom—

(i) precludes an offer of consideration in the form, or any of the forms, specified in the terms of the offer ("the specified form"), or

(ii) precludes it except after compliance by the offeror with conditions with which he is unable to comply or which he regards as unduly onerous,

(b) the persons to whom an offer of consideration in the specified form is precluded are able to receive consideration in another form that is of substantially equivalent value, and

(c) the condition in section 974(3) would be satisfied but for the fact that an offer of consideration in the specified form to those persons is precluded.

[1.1139]

977 Shares to which an offer relates

(1) Where a takeover offer is made and, during the period beginning with the date of the offer and ending when the offer can no longer be accepted, the offeror—

(a) acquires or unconditionally contracts to acquire any of the shares to which the offer relates, but

(b) does not do so by virtue of acceptances of the offer,

those shares are treated for the purposes of this Chapter as excluded from those to which the offer relates.

(2) For the purposes of this Chapter shares that an associate of the offeror holds or has contracted to acquire, whether at the date of the offer or subsequently, are not treated as shares to which the offer relates, even if the offer extends to such shares.

In this subsection "contracted" means contracted unconditionally or subject to conditions being met.

(3) This section is subject to section 979(8) and (9).

[1.1140]

978 Effect of impossibility etc of communicating or accepting offer

(1) Where there are holders of shares in a company to whom an offer to acquire shares in the company is not communicated, that does not prevent the offer from being a takeover offer for the purposes of this Chapter if—

(a) those shareholders have no registered address in the United Kingdom,

(b) the offer was not communicated to those shareholders in order not to contravene the law of a country or territory outside the United Kingdom, and

(c) either—

(i) the offer is published in the Gazette, or

(ii) the offer can be inspected, or a copy of it obtained, at a place in [the United Kingdom] or on a website, and a notice is published in the Gazette specifying the address of that place or website.

(2) Where an offer is made to acquire shares in a company and there are persons for whom, by reason of the law of a country or territory outside the United Kingdom, it is impossible to accept the offer, or more difficult to do so, that does not prevent the offer from being a takeover offer for the purposes of this Chapter.

(3) It is not to be inferred—

(a) that an offer which is not communicated to every holder of shares in the company cannot be a takeover offer for the purposes of this Chapter unless the requirements of paragraphs (a) to (c) of subsection (1) are met, or

(b) that an offer which is impossible, or more difficult, for certain persons to accept cannot be a takeover offer for those purposes unless the reason for the impossibility or difficulty is the one mentioned in subsection (2).

NOTES

Sub-s (1): words in square brackets in sub-para (c)(ii) substituted by the Takeovers (Amendment) (EU Exit) Regulations 2019, SI 2019/217, regs 2, 12, as from IP completion day (as defined in the European Union (Withdrawal Agreement) Act 2020, s 39).

"Squeeze-out"

[1.1141]

979 Right of offeror to buy out minority shareholder

(1) Subsection (2) applies in a case where a takeover offer does not relate to shares of different classes.

(2) If the offeror has, by virtue of acceptances of the offer, acquired or unconditionally contracted to acquire—

(a) not less than 90% in value of the shares to which the offer relates, and

(b) in a case where the shares to which the offer relates are voting shares, not less than 90% of the voting rights carried by those shares,

he may give notice to the holder of any shares to which the offer relates which the offeror has not acquired or unconditionally contracted to acquire that he desires to acquire those shares.

(3) Subsection (4) applies in a case where a takeover offer relates to shares of different classes.

(4) If the offeror has, by virtue of acceptances of the offer, acquired or unconditionally contracted to acquire—

(a) not less than 90% in value of the shares of any class to which the offer relates, and

(b) in a case where the shares of that class are voting shares, not less than 90% of the voting rights carried by those shares,

he may give notice to the holder of any shares of that class to which the offer relates which the offeror has not acquired or unconditionally contracted to acquire that he desires to acquire those shares.

(5) In the case of a takeover offer which includes among the shares to which it relates—

(a) shares that are allotted after the date of the offer, or

(b) relevant treasury shares (within the meaning of section 974) that cease to be held as treasury shares after the date of the offer,

the offeror's entitlement to give a notice under subsection (2) or (4) on any particular date shall be determined as if the shares to which the offer relates did not include any allotted, or ceasing to be held as treasury shares, on or after that date.

(6) Subsection (7) applies where—

(a) the requirements for the giving of a notice under subsection (2) or (4) are satisfied, and

(b) there are shares in the company which the offeror, or an associate of his, has contracted to acquire subject to conditions being met, and in relation to which the contract has not become unconditional.

(7) The offeror's entitlement to give a notice under subsection (2) or (4) shall be determined as if—

(a) the shares to which the offer relates included shares falling within paragraph (b) of subsection (6), and

(b) in relation to shares falling within that paragraph, the words "by virtue of acceptances of the offer" in subsection (2) or (4) were omitted.

(8) Where—

(a) a takeover offer is made,

(b) during the period beginning with the date of the offer and ending when the offer can no longer be accepted, the offeror—

(i) acquires or unconditionally contracts to acquire any of the shares to which the offer relates, but

(ii) does not do so by virtue of acceptances of the offer, and

(c) subsection (10) applies,

then for the purposes of this section those shares are not excluded by section 977(1) from those to which the offer relates, and the offeror is treated as having acquired or contracted to acquire them by virtue of acceptances of the offer.

(9) Where—

(a) a takeover offer is made,

(b) during the period beginning with the date of the offer and ending when the offer can no longer be accepted, an associate of the offeror acquires or unconditionally contracts to acquire any of the shares to which the offer relates, and

(c) subsection (10) applies,

then for the purposes of this section those shares are not excluded by section 977(2) from those to which the offer relates.

(10) This subsection applies if—

(a) at the time the shares are acquired or contracted to be acquired as mentioned in subsection (8) or (9) (as the case may be), the value of the consideration for which they are acquired or contracted to be acquired ("the acquisition consideration") does not exceed the value of the consideration specified in the terms of the offer, or

(b) those terms are subsequently revised so that when the revision is announced the value of the acquisition consideration, at the time mentioned in paragraph (a), no longer exceeds the value of the consideration specified in those terms.

[1.1142]

980 Further provision about notices given under section 979

(1) A notice under section 979 must be given in the prescribed manner.

(2) No notice may be given under section 979(2) or (4) after the end of—

- (a) the period of three months beginning with the day after the last day on which the offer can be accepted, or
- (b) the period of six months beginning with the date of the offer, where that period ends earlier and the offer is one to which subsection (3) below applies.

(3) This subsection applies to an offer if the time allowed for acceptance of the offer is not governed by rules under section 943(1) [made in accordance with paragraph 13 or 14 of Schedule 1C].

(4) At the time when the offeror first gives a notice under section 979 in relation to an offer, he must send to the company—

- (a) a copy of the notice, and
- (b) a statutory declaration by him in the prescribed form, stating that the conditions for the giving of the notice are satisfied.

(5) Where the offeror is a company (whether or not a company within the meaning of this Act) the statutory declaration must be signed by a director.

(6) A person commits an offence if—

- (a) he fails to send a copy of a notice or a statutory declaration as required by subsection (4), or
- (b) he makes such a declaration for the purposes of that subsection knowing it to be false or without having reasonable grounds for believing it to be true.

(7) It is a defence for a person charged with an offence for failing to send a copy of a notice as required by subsection (4) to prove that he took reasonable steps for securing compliance with that subsection.

(8) A person guilty of an offence under this section is liable—

- (a) on conviction on indictment, to imprisonment for a term not exceeding two years or a fine (or both);
- (b) on summary conviction—
  - (i) in England and Wales, to imprisonment for a term not exceeding twelve months or to a fine not exceeding the statutory maximum (or both) and, for continued contravention, a daily default fine not exceeding [one-fiftieth of the greater of £5,000 or the amount corresponding to level 4 on the standard scale for summary offences];
  - (ii) in Scotland or Northern Ireland, to imprisonment for a term not exceeding six months, or to a fine not exceeding the statutory maximum (or both) and, for continued contravention, a daily default fine not exceeding one-fiftieth of the statutory maximum.

NOTES

Sub-s (3): words in square brackets substituted by the Takeovers (Amendment) (EU Exit) Regulations 2019, SI 2019/217, regs 2, 13, as from IP completion day (as defined in the European Union (Withdrawal Agreement) Act 2020, s 39).

Sub-s (8): words in square brackets substituted (for the original words "one-fiftieth of the statutory maximum") by the Legal Aid, Sentencing and Punishment of Offenders Act 2012 (Fines on Summary Conviction) Regulations 2015, SI 2015/664, regs 3, 5, Sch 3, Pt 1, para 9(1), (20), as from 12 March 2015, (except in relation to (a) fines for offences committed before 12 March 2015, (b) the operation of restrictions on fines that may be imposed on a person aged under 18, or (c) fines that may be imposed on a person convicted by a magistrates' court who is to be sentenced as if convicted on indictment).

Offences under this section: see further s 1131 at **[1.1301]**.

Orders and Regulations: no Orders or Regulations have been made under this section, but by virtue of s 1297 *post*, the Companies (Forms) Regulations 1985, SI 1985/854, Forms 980(1), 980dec, as prescribed by the Companies (Forms) (Amendment) Regulations 1987, SI 1987/752, have effect as if made hereunder. For a summary of all statutory instruments made under this Act, see Appendix 4 at **[A4]**.

[1.1143]

981 Effect of notice under section 979

(1) Subject to section 986 (applications to the court), this section applies where the offeror gives a shareholder a notice under section 979.

(2) The offeror is entitled and bound to acquire the shares to which the notice relates on the terms of the offer.

(3) Where the terms of an offer are such as to give the shareholder a choice of consideration, the notice must give particulars of the choice and state—

- (a) that the shareholder may, within six weeks from the date of the notice, indicate his choice by a written communication sent to the offeror at an address specified in the notice, and
- (b) which consideration specified in the offer will apply if he does not indicate a choice.

The reference in subsection (2) to the terms of the offer is to be read accordingly.

(4) Subsection (3) applies whether or not any time-limit or other conditions applicable to the choice under the terms of the offer can still be complied with.

(5) If the consideration offered to or (as the case may be) chosen by the shareholder—

- (a) is not cash and the offeror is no longer able to provide it, or
- (b) was to have been provided by a third party who is no longer bound or able to provide it,

the consideration is to be taken to consist of an amount of cash, payable by the offeror, which at the date of the notice is equivalent to the consideration offered or (as the case may be) chosen.

(6) At the end of six weeks from the date of the notice the offeror must immediately—

- (a) send a copy of the notice to the company, and
- (b) pay or transfer to the company the consideration for the shares to which the notice relates.

Where the consideration consists of shares or securities to be allotted by the offeror, the reference in paragraph (b) to the transfer of the consideration is to be read as a reference to the allotment of the shares or securities to the company.

(7) If the shares to which the notice relates are registered, the copy of the notice sent to the company under subsection (6)(a) must be accompanied by an instrument of transfer executed on behalf of the holder of the shares by a person appointed by the offeror.

On receipt of that instrument the company must register the offeror as the holder of those shares.

(8) If the shares to which the notice relates are transferable by the delivery of warrants or other instruments, the copy of the notice sent to the company under subsection (6)(a) must be accompanied by a statement to that effect. On receipt of that statement the company must issue the offeror with warrants or other instruments in respect of the shares, and those already in issue in respect of the shares become void.

(9) The company must hold any money or other consideration received by it under subsection (6)(b) on trust for the person who, before the offeror acquired them, was entitled to the shares in respect of which the money or other consideration was received.

Section 982 contains further provision about how the company should deal with such money or other consideration.

[1.1144]

982 Further provision about consideration held on trust under section 981(9)

(1) This section applies where an offeror pays or transfers consideration to the company under section 981(6).

(2) The company must pay into a separate bank account that complies with subsection (3)—

(a) any money it receives under paragraph (b) of section 981(6), and

(b) any dividend or other sum accruing from any other consideration it receives under that paragraph.

(3) A bank account complies with this subsection if the balance on the account—

(a) bears interest at an appropriate rate, and

(b) can be withdrawn by such notice (if any) as is appropriate.

(4) If—

(a) the person entitled to the consideration held on trust by virtue of section 981(9) cannot be found, and

(b) subsection (5) applies,

the consideration (together with any interest, dividend or other benefit that has accrued from it) must be paid into court.

(5) This subsection applies where—

(a) reasonable enquiries have been made at reasonable intervals to find the person, and

(b) twelve years have elapsed since the consideration was received, or the company is wound up.

(6) In relation to a company registered in Scotland, subsections (7) and (8) apply instead of subsection (4).

(7) If the person entitled to the consideration held on trust by virtue of section 981(9) cannot be found and subsection (5) applies—

(a) the trust terminates,

(b) the company or (if the company is wound up) the liquidator must sell any consideration other than cash and any benefit other than cash that has accrued from the consideration, and

(c) a sum representing—

(i) the consideration so far as it is cash,

(ii) the proceeds of any sale under paragraph (b), and

(iii) any interest, dividend or other benefit that has accrued from the consideration,

must be deposited in the name of the Accountant of Court in a separate bank account complying with subsection (3) and the receipt for the deposit must be transmitted to the Accountant of Court.

(8) Section [150 of the Bankruptcy (Scotland) Act 2016]) (so far as consistent with this Act) applies (with any necessary modifications) to sums deposited under subsection (7) as it applies to sums deposited under section [148(3)] of that Act.

(9) The expenses of any such enquiries as are mentioned in subsection (5) may be paid out of the money or other property held on trust for the person to whom the enquiry relates.

NOTES

Sub-s (8): words and figure in square brackets substituted by the Bankruptcy (Scotland) Act 2016 (Consequential Provisions and Modifications) Order 2016, SI 2016/1034, art 7(1), (3), Sch 1, para 29(1), (6), as from 30 November 2016 (except in relation to (i) a sequestration as regards which the petition is presented, or the debtor application is made before that date; or (ii) a trust deed executed before that date).

"Sell-out"

[1.1145]

983 Right of minority shareholder to be bought out by offeror

(1) Subsections (2) and (3) apply in a case where a takeover offer relates to all the shares in a company.

For this purpose a takeover offer relates to all the shares in a company if it is an offer to acquire all the shares in the company within the meaning of section 974.

(2) The holder of any voting shares to which the offer relates who has not accepted the offer may require the offeror to acquire those shares if, at any time before the end of the period within which the offer can be accepted—

(a) the offeror has by virtue of acceptances of the offer acquired or unconditionally contracted to acquire some (but not all) of the shares to which the offer relates, and

(b) those shares, with or without any other shares in the company which he has acquired or contracted to acquire (whether unconditionally or subject to conditions being met)—

(i) amount to not less than 90% in value of all the voting shares in the company (or would do so but for section 990(1)), and

(ii) carry not less than 90% of the voting rights in the company (or would do so but for section 990(1)).

(3) The holder of any non-voting shares to which the offer relates who has not accepted the offer may require the offeror to acquire those shares if, at any time before the end of the period within which the offer can be accepted—

(a) the offeror has by virtue of acceptances of the offer acquired or unconditionally contracted to acquire some (but not all) of the shares to which the offer relates, and

(b) those shares, with or without any other shares in the company which he has acquired or contracted to acquire (whether unconditionally or subject to conditions being met), amount to not less than 90% in value of all the shares in the company (or would do so but for section 990(1)).

(4) If a takeover offer relates to shares of one or more classes and at any time before the end of the period within which the offer can be accepted—

(a) the offeror has by virtue of acceptances of the offer acquired or unconditionally contracted to acquire some (but not all) of the shares of any class to which the offer relates, and

(b) those shares, with or without any other shares of that class which he has acquired or contracted to acquire (whether unconditionally or subject to conditions being met)—

(i) amount to not less than 90% in value of all the shares of that class, and

(ii) in a case where the shares of that class are voting shares, carry not less than 90% of the voting rights carried by the shares of that class,

the holder of any shares of that class to which the offer relates who has not accepted the offer may require the offeror to acquire those shares.

(5) For the purposes of subsections (2) to (4), in calculating 90% of the value of any shares, shares held by the company as treasury shares are to be treated as having been acquired by the offeror.

(6) Subsection (7) applies where—

(a) a shareholder exercises rights conferred on him by subsection (2), (3) or (4),

(b) at the time when he does so, there are shares in the company which the offeror has contracted to acquire subject to conditions being met, and in relation to which the contract has not become unconditional, and

(c) the requirement imposed by subsection (2)(b), (3)(b) or (4)(b) (as the case may be) would not be satisfied if those shares were not taken into account.

(7) The shareholder is treated for the purposes of section 985 as not having exercised his rights under this section unless the requirement imposed by paragraph (b) of subsection (2), (3) or (4) (as the case may be) would be satisfied if—

(a) the reference in that paragraph to other shares in the company which the offeror has contracted to acquire unconditionally or subject to conditions being met were a reference to such shares which he has unconditionally contracted to acquire, and

(b) the reference in that subsection to the period within which the offer can be accepted were a reference to the period referred to in section 984(2).

(8) A reference in subsection (2)(b), (3)(b), (4)(b), (6) or (7) to shares which the offeror has acquired or contracted to acquire includes a reference to shares which an associate of his has acquired or contracted to acquire.

[1.1146]

984 Further provision about rights conferred by section 983

(1) Rights conferred on a shareholder by subsection (2), (3) or (4) of section 983 are exercisable by a written communication addressed to the offeror.

(2) Rights conferred on a shareholder by subsection (2), (3) or (4) of that section are not exercisable after the end of the period of three months from—

(a) the end of the period within which the offer can be accepted, or

(b) if later, the date of the notice that must be given under subsection (3) below.

(3) Within one month of the time specified in subsection (2), (3) or (4) (as the case may be) of that section, the offeror must give any shareholder who has not accepted the offer notice in the prescribed manner of—

(a) the rights that are exercisable by the shareholder under that subsection, and

(b) the period within which the rights are exercisable.

If the notice is given before the end of the period within which the offer can be accepted, it must state that the offer is still open for acceptance.

(4) Subsection (3) does not apply if the offeror has given the shareholder a notice in respect of the shares in question under section 979.

(5) An offeror who fails to comply with subsection (3) commits an offence.

If the offeror is a company, every officer of that company who is in default or to whose neglect the failure is attributable also commits an offence.

(6) If an offeror other than a company is charged with an offence for failing to comply with subsection (3), it is a defence for him to prove that he took all reasonable steps for securing compliance with that subsection.

(7) A person guilty of an offence under this section is liable—

(a) on conviction on indictment, to a fine;

(b) on summary conviction, to a fine not exceeding the statutory maximum and, for continued contravention, a daily default fine not exceeding [one-fiftieth of the greater of £5,000 or the amount corresponding to level 4 on the standard scale for summary offences].

NOTES

Sub-s (7): words in square brackets substituted (for the original words "one-fiftieth of the statutory maximum") by the Legal Aid, Sentencing and Punishment of Offenders Act 2012 (Fines on Summary Conviction) Regulations 2015, SI 2015/664, regs 3, 5, Sch 3, Pt 1, para 9(1), (21), as from 12 March 2015, in relation to England and Wales only (except in relation to (a) fines for offences committed before 12 March 2015, (b) the operation of restrictions on fines that may be imposed on a person aged under 18, or (c) fines that may be imposed on a person convicted by a magistrates' court who is to be sentenced as if convicted on indictment).

Orders and Regulations: no Orders or Regulations have been made under this section.

[1.1147]

985 Effect of requirement under section 983

(1) Subject to section 986, this section applies where a shareholder exercises his rights under section 983 in respect of any shares held by him.

(2) The offeror is entitled and bound to acquire those shares on the terms of the offer or on such other terms as may be agreed.

(3) Where the terms of an offer are such as to give the shareholder a choice of consideration—

(a) the shareholder may indicate his choice when requiring the offeror to acquire the shares, and

(b) the notice given to the shareholder under section 984(3)—
(i) must give particulars of the choice and of the rights conferred by this subsection, and
(ii) may state which consideration specified in the offer will apply if he does not indicate a choice.

The reference in subsection (2) to the terms of the offer is to be read accordingly.

(4) Subsection (3) applies whether or not any time-limit or other conditions applicable to the choice under the terms of the offer can still be complied with.

(5) If the consideration offered to or (as the case may be) chosen by the shareholder—
(a) is not cash and the offeror is no longer able to provide it, or
(b) was to have been provided by a third party who is no longer bound or able to provide it,

the consideration is to be taken to consist of an amount of cash, payable by the offeror, which at the date when the shareholder requires the offeror to acquire the shares is equivalent to the consideration offered or (as the case may be) chosen.

Supplementary

[1.1148]
986 Applications to the court

(1) Where a notice is given under section 979 to a shareholder the court may, on an application made by him, order—
(a) that the offeror is not entitled and bound to acquire the shares to which the notice relates, or
(b) that the terms on which the offeror is entitled and bound to acquire the shares shall be such as the court thinks fit.

(2) An application under subsection (1) must be made within six weeks from the date on which the notice referred to in that subsection was given.

If an application to the court under subsection (1) is pending at the end of that period, section 981(6) does not have effect until the application has been disposed of.

(3) Where a shareholder exercises his rights under section 983 in respect of any shares held by him, the court may, on an application made by him or the offeror, order that the terms on which the offeror is entitled and bound to acquire the shares shall be such as the court thinks fit.

(4) On an application under subsection (1) or (3)—
(a) the court may not require consideration of a higher value than that specified in the terms of the offer ("the offer value") to be given for the shares to which the application relates unless the holder of the shares shows that the offer value would be unfair;
(b) the court may not require consideration of a lower value than the offer value to be given for the shares.

(5) No order for costs or expenses may be made against a shareholder making an application under subsection (1) or (3) unless the court considers that—
(a) the application was unnecessary, improper or vexatious,
(b) there has been unreasonable delay in making the application, or
(c) there has been unreasonable conduct on the shareholder's part in conducting the proceedings on the application.

(6) A shareholder who has made an application under subsection (1) or (3) must give notice of the application to the offeror.

(7) An offeror who is given notice of an application under subsection (1) or (3) must give a copy of the notice to—
(a) any person (other than the applicant) to whom a notice has been given under section 979;
(b) any person who has exercised his rights under section 983.

(8) An offeror who makes an application under subsection (3) must give notice of the application to—
(a) any person to whom a notice has been given under section 979;
(b) any person who has exercised his rights under section 983.

(9) Where a takeover offer has not been accepted to the extent necessary for entitling the offeror to give notices under subsection (2) or (4) of section 979 the court may, on an application made by him, make an order authorising him to give notices under that subsection if it is satisfied that—
(a) the offeror has after reasonable enquiry been unable to trace one or more of the persons holding shares to which the offer relates,
(b) the requirements of that subsection would have been met if the person, or all the persons, mentioned in paragraph (a) above had accepted the offer, and
(c) the consideration offered is fair and reasonable.

This is subject to subsection (10).

(10) The court may not make an order under subsection (9) unless it considers that it is just and equitable to do so having regard, in particular, to the number of shareholders who have been traced but who have not accepted the offer.

[1.1149]
987 Joint offers

(1) In the case of a takeover offer made by two or more persons jointly, this Chapter has effect as follows.

(2) The conditions for the exercise of the rights conferred by section 979 are satisfied—
(a) in the case of acquisitions by virtue of acceptances of the offer, by the joint offerors acquiring or unconditionally contracting to acquire the necessary shares jointly;
(b) in other cases, by the joint offerors acquiring or unconditionally contracting to acquire the necessary shares either jointly or separately.

(3) The conditions for the exercise of the rights conferred by section 983 are satisfied—
(a) in the case of acquisitions by virtue of acceptances of the offer, by the joint offerors acquiring or unconditionally contracting to acquire the necessary shares jointly;
(b) in other cases, by the joint offerors acquiring or contracting (whether unconditionally or subject to conditions being met) to acquire the necessary shares either jointly or separately.

(4) Subject to the following provisions, the rights and obligations of the offeror under sections 979 to 985 are respectively joint rights and joint and several obligations of the joint offerors.

(5) A provision of sections 979 to 986 that requires or authorises a notice or other document to be given or sent by or to the joint offerors is complied with if the notice or document is given or sent by or to any of them (but see subsection (6)).

(6) The statutory declaration required by section 980(4) must be made by all of the joint offerors and, where one or more of them is a company, signed by a director of that company.

(7) In sections 974 to 977, 979(9), 981(6), 983(8) and 988 references to the offeror are to be read as references to the joint offerors or any of them.

(8) In section 981(7) and (8) references to the offeror are to be read as references to the joint offerors or such of them as they may determine.

(9) In sections 981(5)(a) and 985(5)(a) references to the offeror being no longer able to provide the relevant consideration are to be read as references to none of the joint offerors being able to do so.

(10) In section 986 references to the offeror are to be read as references to the joint offerors, except that—

- (a) an application under subsection (3) or (9) may be made by any of them, and
- (b) the reference in subsection (9)(a) to the offeror having been unable to trace one or more of the persons holding shares is to be read as a reference to none of the offerors having been able to do so.

Interpretation

[1.1150]

988 Associates

(1) In this Chapter "associate", in relation to an offeror, means—

- (a) a nominee of the offeror,
- (b) a holding company, subsidiary or fellow subsidiary of the offeror or a nominee of such a holding company, subsidiary or fellow subsidiary,
- (c) a body corporate in which the offeror is substantially interested,
- (d) a person who is, or is a nominee of, a party to a share acquisition agreement with the offeror, or
- (e) (where the offeror is an individual) his spouse or civil partner and any minor child or step-child of his.

(2) For the purposes of subsection (1)(b) a company is a fellow subsidiary of another body corporate if both are subsidiaries of the same body corporate but neither is a subsidiary of the other.

(3) For the purposes of subsection (1)(c) an offeror has a substantial interest in a body corporate if—

- (a) the body or its directors are accustomed to act in accordance with his directions or instructions, or
- (b) he is entitled to exercise or control the exercise of one-third or more of the voting power at general meetings of the body.

Subsections (2) and (3) of section 823 (which contain provision about when a person is treated as entitled to exercise or control the exercise of voting power) apply for the purposes of this subsection as they apply for the purposes of that section.

(4) For the purposes of subsection (1)(d) an agreement is a share acquisition agreement if—

- (a) it is an agreement for the acquisition of, or of an interest in, shares to which the offer relates,
- (b) it includes provisions imposing obligations or restrictions on any one or more of the parties to it with respect to their use, retention or disposal of such shares, or their interests in such shares, acquired in pursuance of the agreement (whether or not together with any other shares to which the offer relates or any other interests of theirs in such shares), and
- (c) it is not an excluded agreement (see subsection (5)).

(5) An agreement is an "excluded agreement"—

- (a) if it is not legally binding, unless it involves mutuality in the undertakings, expectations or understandings of the parties to it, or
- (b) if it is an agreement to underwrite or sub-underwrite an offer of shares in a company, provided the agreement is confined to that purpose and any matters incidental to it.

(6) The reference in subsection (4)(b) to the use of interests in shares is to the exercise of any rights or of any control or influence arising from those interests (including the right to enter into an agreement for the exercise, or for control of the exercise, of any of those rights by another person).

(7) In this section—

- (a) "agreement" includes any agreement or arrangement;
- (b) references to provisions of an agreement include—
  - (i) undertakings, expectations or understandings operative under an arrangement, and
  - (ii) any provision whether express or implied and whether absolute or not.

[1.1151]

989 Convertible securities

(1) For the purposes of this Chapter securities of a company are treated as shares in the company if they are convertible into or entitle the holder to subscribe for such shares.

References to the holder of shares or a shareholder are to be read accordingly.

(2) Subsection (1) is not to be read as requiring any securities to be treated—

- (a) as shares of the same class as those into which they are convertible or for which the holder is entitled to subscribe, or
- (b) as shares of the same class as other securities by reason only that the shares into which they are convertible or for which the holder is entitled to subscribe are of the same class.

[1.1152]

990 Debentures carrying voting rights

(1) For the purposes of this Chapter debentures issued by a company to which subsection (2) applies are treated as shares in the company if they carry voting rights.

(2) This subsection applies to a company that has voting shares, or debentures carrying voting rights, which are admitted to trading on a regulated market.

(3) In this Chapter, in relation to debentures treated as shares by virtue of subsection (1)—

(a) references to the holder of shares or a shareholder are to be read accordingly;
(b) references to shares being allotted are to be read as references to debentures being issued.

[1.1153]
991 Interpretation

(1) In this Chapter—

"the company" means the company whose shares are the subject of a takeover offer;

"date of the offer" means—

(a) where the offer is published, the date of publication;
(b) where the offer is not published, or where any notices of the offer are given before the date of publication, the date when notices of the offer (or the first such notices) are given;

and references to the date of the offer are to be read in accordance with section 974(7) (revision of offer terms) where that applies;

"non-voting shares" means shares that are not voting shares;

"offeror" means (subject to section 987) the person making a takeover offer;

"voting rights" means rights to vote at general meetings of the company, including rights that arise only in certain circumstances;

"voting shares" means shares carrying voting rights.

(2) For the purposes of this Chapter a person contracts unconditionally to acquire shares if his entitlement under the contract to acquire them is not (or is no longer) subject to conditions or if all conditions to which it was subject have been met.

A reference to a contract becoming unconditional is to be read accordingly.

CHAPTER 4 AMENDMENTS TO PART 7 OF THE COMPANIES ACT 1985

[1.1154]
992 Matters to be dealt with in directors' report

(1)–(5) *(Amended CA 1985, ss 234ZZA, 251 and added Sch 7, Pt 7 to that Act (all of which were repealed with savings by this Act).)*

(6) The amendments made by this section apply in relation to directors' reports for financial years beginning on or after 20th May 2006.

PART 29 FRAUDULENT TRADING

[1.1155]
993 Offence of fraudulent trading

(1) If any business of a company is carried on with intent to defraud creditors of the company or creditors of any other person, or for any fraudulent purpose, every person who is knowingly a party to the carrying on of the business in that manner commits an offence.

(2) This applies whether or not the company has been, or is in the course of being, wound up.

(3) A person guilty of an offence under this section is liable—

(a) on conviction on indictment, to imprisonment for a term not exceeding ten years or a fine (or both);
(b) on summary conviction—
   (i) in England and Wales, to imprisonment for a term not exceeding twelve months or a fine not exceeding the statutory maximum (or both);
   (ii) in Scotland or Northern Ireland, to imprisonment for a term not exceeding six months or a fine not exceeding the statutory maximum (or both).

NOTES

Offences under this section: see further s 1131 at **[1.1301]**.

Deferred Prosecution Agreements: as to the application of Deferred Prosecution Agreements to an offence under this section (ie, an agreement between a designated prosecutor and a person accused of a crime (P) whereby proceedings against P in respect of the alleged offence are automatically suspended as soon as they are instituted if P agrees to comply with certain requirements), see s 45 of, and Sch 17, Pt 1 and Sch 17, Pt 2, para 24 to, the Crime and Courts Act 2013.

PART 30 PROTECTION OF MEMBERS AGAINST UNFAIR PREJUDICE

NOTES

With regard to proceedings under this Part, see further the Companies (Authorised Minimum) Regulations 2008, SI 2008/729, reg 6 at **[4.134]** (Determination of exchange rates by the court in certain proceedings), and the Companies (Authorised Minimum) Regulations 2009, SI 2009/2425, reg 6 at **[4.386]** (Determination of exchange rates by the court in certain proceedings).

Main provisions

[1.1156]
994 Petition by company member

(1) A member of a company may apply to the court by petition for an order under this Part on the ground—

(a) that the company's affairs are being or have been conducted in a manner that is unfairly prejudicial to the interests of members generally or of some part of its members (including at least himself), or
(b) that an actual or proposed act or omission of the company (including an act or omission on its behalf) is or would be so prejudicial.

[(1A) For the purposes of subsection (1)(a), a removal of the company's auditor from office—

(a) on grounds of divergence of opinions on accounting treatments or audit procedures, or
(b) on any other improper grounds,

shall be treated as being unfairly prejudicial to the interests of some part of the company's members.]

(2) The provisions of this Part apply to a person who is not a member of a company but to whom shares in the company have been transferred or transmitted by operation of law as they apply to a member of a company.

(3) In this section, and so far as applicable for the purposes of this section in the other provisions of this Part, "company" means—

(a) a company within the meaning of this Act, or

(b) a company that is not such a company but is a statutory water company within the meaning of the Statutory Water Companies Act 1991 (c 58).

NOTES

Sub-s (1A): inserted by the Statutory Auditors and Third Country Auditors Regulations 2007, SI 2007/3494, reg 42, as from 6 April 2008, except in relation to auditors appointed for financial years beginning before that date.

[1.1157]

995 Petition by Secretary of State

(1) This section applies to a company in respect of which—

(a) the Secretary of State has received a report under section 437 of the Companies Act 1985 (c 6) (inspector's report);

(b) the Secretary of State has exercised his powers under section 447 or 448 of that Act (powers to require documents and information or to enter and search premises);

(c) the Secretary of State[, the Financial Conduct Authority, the Prudential Regulation Authority or the Bank of England] has exercised his or its powers under Part 11 of the Financial Services and Markets Act 2000 (c 8) (information gathering and investigations); or

(d) the Secretary of State has received a report from an investigator appointed by him[, the Financial Conduct Authority, the Prudential Regulation Authority or the Bank of England] under that Part.

(2) If it appears to the Secretary of State that in the case of such a company—

(a) the company's affairs are being or have been conducted in a manner that is unfairly prejudicial to the interests of members generally or of some part of its members, or

(b) an actual or proposed act or omission of the company (including an act or omission on its behalf) is or would be so prejudicial,

he may apply to the court by petition for an order under this Part.

(3) The Secretary of State may do this in addition to, or instead of, presenting a petition for the winding up of the company.

(4) In this section, and so far as applicable for the purposes of this section in the other provisions of this Part, "company" means any body corporate that is liable to be wound up under the Insolvency Act 1986 (c 45) or the Insolvency (Northern Ireland) Order 1989 (SI 1989/2405 (NI 19)).

NOTES

Sub-s (1): words in square brackets in paras (c), (d) substituted by the Financial Services Act 2012, s 114(1), Sch 18, Pt 2, paras 110, 120, as from 1 April 2013.

[1.1158]

996 Powers of the court under this Part

(1) If the court is satisfied that a petition under this Part is well founded, it may make such order as it thinks fit for giving relief in respect of the matters complained of.

(2) Without prejudice to the generality of subsection (1), the court's order may—

(a) regulate the conduct of the company's affairs in the future;

(b) require the company—

 (i) to refrain from doing or continuing an act complained of, or

 (ii) to do an act that the petitioner has complained it has omitted to do;

(c) authorise civil proceedings to be brought in the name and on behalf of the company by such person or persons and on such terms as the court may direct;

(d) require the company not to make any, or any specified, alterations in its articles without the leave of the court;

(e) provide for the purchase of the shares of any members of the company by other members or by the company itself and, in the case of a purchase by the company itself, the reduction of the company's capital accordingly.

Supplementary provisions

[1.1159]

997 Application of general rule-making powers

The power to make rules under section 411 of the Insolvency Act 1986 (c 45) or Article 359 of the Insolvency (Northern Ireland) Order 1989 (SI 1989/2405 (NI 19)), so far as relating to a winding-up petition, applies for the purposes of a petition under this Part.

[1.1160]

998 Copy of order affecting company's constitution to be delivered to registrar

(1) Where an order of the court under this Part—

(a) alters the company's constitution, or

(b) gives leave for the company to make any, or any specified, alterations to its constitution,

the company must deliver a copy of the order to the registrar.

(2) It must do so within 14 days from the making of the order or such longer period as the court may allow.

(3) If a company makes default in complying with this section, an offence is committed by—

(a) the company, and

(b) every officer of the company who is in default.

(4) A person guilty of an offence under this section is liable on summary conviction to a fine not exceeding level 3 on the standard scale and, for continued contravention, a daily default fine not exceeding one-tenth of level 3 on the standard scale.

[1.1161]

999 Supplementary provisions where company's constitution altered

(1) This section applies where an order under this Part alters a company's constitution.

(2) If the order amends—

(a) a company's articles, or

(b) any resolution or agreement to which Chapter 3 of Part 3 applies (resolution or agreement affecting a company's constitution),

the copy of the order delivered to the registrar by the company under section 998 must be accompanied by a copy of the company's articles, or the resolution or agreement in question, as amended.

(3) Every copy of a company's articles issued by the company after the order is made must be accompanied by a copy of the order, unless the effect of the order has been incorporated into the articles by amendment.

(4) If a company makes default in complying with this section an offence is committed by—

(a) the company, and

(b) every officer of the company who is in default.

(5) A person guilty of an offence under this section is liable on summary conviction to a fine not exceeding level 3 on the standard scale.

PART 31 DISSOLUTION AND RESTORATION TO THE REGISTER

CHAPTER 1 STRIKING OFF

Registrar's power to strike off defunct company

[1.1162]

1000 Power to strike off company not carrying on business or in operation

(1) If the registrar has reasonable cause to believe that a company is not carrying on business or in operation, the registrar may send to the company [a communication] inquiring whether the company is carrying on business or in operation.

(2) If the registrar does not within [14 days of sending] [the communication] receive any answer to it, the registrar must within 14 days after the expiration of [that period] send to the company [a second communication referring to the first communication], and stating—

(a) that no answer to it has been received, and

(b) that if an answer is not received to the second [communication] within [14 days] from its date, a notice will be published in the Gazette with a view to striking the company's name off the register..

(3) If the registrar—

(a) receives an answer to the effect that the company is not carrying on business or in operation, or

(b) does not within [14 days] after sending the second [communication] receive any answer,

the registrar may publish in the Gazette, and send to the company . . . . , a notice that at the expiration of [2 months] from the date of the notice the name of the company mentioned in it will, unless cause is shown to the contrary, be struck off the register and the company will be dissolved.

(4) At the expiration of the time mentioned in the notice the registrar may, unless cause to the contrary is previously shown by the company, strike its name off the register.

(5) The registrar must publish notice in the Gazette of the company's name having been struck off the register.

(6) On the publication of the notice in the Gazette the company is dissolved.

(7) However—

(a) the liability (if any) of every director, managing officer and member of the company continues and may be enforced as if the company had not been dissolved, and

(b) nothing in this section affects the power of the court to wind up a company the name of which has been struck off the register.

NOTES

Sub-s (1): words "a communication" in square brackets substituted by the Companies (Striking Off) (Electronic Communications) Order 2014, SI 2014/1602, art 2(1), (2)(a), as from 11 July 2014.

Sub-s (2) is amended as follows:

Words "14 days of sending" in square brackets substituted by the Small Business, Enterprise and Employment Act 2015, s 103(1), (2)(a)(i), (5), as from 10 October 2015.

Words "the communication" in square brackets substituted by virtue of SI 2014/1602, art 2(1), (2)(b), as from 11 July 2014.

Words "that period" in square brackets substituted by the Small Business, Enterprise and Employment Act 2015, s 103(1), (2)(a)(ii), (5), as from 10 October 2015.

Words "a second communication referring to the first communication" in square brackets substituted by SI 2014/1602, art 2(1), (2)(b), as from 11 July 2014.

Word "communication" in square brackets in para (b) substituted by SI 2014/1602, art 2(1), (2)(c), as from 11 July 2014.

Words "14 days" in square brackets in para (b) substituted by the Small Business, Enterprise and Employment Act 2015, s 103(1), (2)(a)(iii), (5), as from 10 October 2015.

Sub-s (3) is amended as follows:

Words "14 days" in square brackets in para (b) substituted by the Small Business, Enterprise and Employment Act 2015, s 103(1), (2)(b)(i), (5), as from 10 October 2015.

Word "communication" in square brackets in para (b) substituted by SI 2014/1602, art 2(1), (2)(d), as from 11 July 2014.

Words omitted repealed by SI 2014/1602, art 2(1), (2)(e), as from 11 July 2014.

Words "2 months" in square brackets substituted by the Small Business, Enterprise and Employment Act 2015, s 103(1), (2)(b)(ii), (5), as from 10 October 2015.

[1.1163]

1001 Duty to act in case of company being wound up

(1) If, in a case where a company is being wound up—

(a) the registrar has reasonable cause to believe—

(i) that no liquidator is acting, or

(ii) that the affairs of the company are fully wound up, and

(b) the returns required to be made by the liquidator have not been made for a period of six consecutive months,

the registrar must publish in the Gazette and send to the company or the liquidator (if any) a notice that at the expiration of [2 months] from the date of the notice the name of the company mentioned in it will, unless cause is shown to the contrary, be struck off the register and the company will be dissolved.

(2) At the expiration of the time mentioned in the notice the registrar may, unless cause to the contrary is previously shown by the company, strike its name off the register.

(3) The registrar must publish notice in the Gazette of the company's name having been struck off the register.

(4) On the publication of the notice in the Gazette the company is dissolved.

(5) However—

- (a) the liability (if any) of every director, managing officer and member of the company continues and may be enforced as if the company had not been dissolved, and
- (b) nothing in this section affects the power of the court to wind up a company the name of which has been struck off the register.

NOTES

Sub-s (1): words in square brackets substituted by the Small Business, Enterprise and Employment Act 2015, s 103(1), (3), (6), as from 10 October 2015.

[1.1164]

1002 Supplementary provisions as to service of [communication] or notice

[(1) If the registrar is not able to send a communication or notice under section 1000 or 1001 to a company in accordance with Schedule 4, the communication may be sent to an officer of the company at an address for that officer that has been notified to the registrar by the company.]

(2) If there is no officer of the company whose name and address are known to the registrar, the [communication] or notice may be sent to each of the persons who subscribed the memorandum (if their addresses are known to the registrar).

[(3) A notice to be sent to a liquidator under section 1001 may be sent to the address of the liquidator's last known place of business or to an address specified by the liquidator to the registrar for the purpose of receiving notices, or notices of that kind.]

[(4) In this section "address" has the same meaning as in section 1148(1).]

NOTES

The words in square brackets in the section heading and in sub-s (2) were substituted, sub-ss (1) and (3) were substituted, and sub-s (4) was added, by the Companies (Striking Off) (Electronic Communications) Order 2014, SI 2014/1602, art 2(1), (3), as from 11 July 2014.

Voluntary striking off

[1.1165]

1003 Striking off on application by company

(1) On application by a company, the registrar of companies may strike the company's name off the register.

(2) The application—

- (a) must be made on the company's behalf by its directors or by a majority of them, and
- (b) must contain the prescribed information.

(3) The registrar may not strike a company off under this section until after the expiration of [2 months] from the publication by the registrar in the Gazette of a notice—

- (a) stating that the registrar may exercise the power under this section in relation to the company, and
- (b) inviting any person to show cause why that should not be done.

(4) The registrar must publish notice in the Gazette of the company's name having been struck off.

(5) On the publication of the notice in the Gazette the company is dissolved.

(6) However—

- (a) the liability (if any) of every director, managing officer and member of the company continues and may be enforced as if the company had not been dissolved, and
- (b) nothing in this section affects the power of the court to wind up a company the name of which has been struck off the register.

NOTES

Sub-s (3): words in square brackets substituted by the Small Business, Enterprise and Employment Act 2015, s 103(1), (4), (7), as from 10 October 2015.

Regulations: the Registrar of Companies and Applications for Striking Off Regulations 2009, SI 2009/1803 at **[4.317]**. For a summary of all statutory instruments made under this Act, see Appendix 4 at **[A4]**.

[1.1166]

1004 Circumstances in which application not to be made: activities of company

(1) An application under section 1003 (application for voluntary striking off) on behalf of a company must not be made if, at any time in the previous three months, the company has—

- (a) changed its name,
- (b) traded or otherwise carried on business,
- (c) made a disposal for value of property or rights that, immediately before ceasing to trade or otherwise carry on business, it held for the purpose of disposal for gain in the normal course of trading or otherwise carrying on business, or
- (d) engaged in any other activity, except one which is—
  - (i) necessary or expedient for the purpose of making an application under that section, or deciding whether to do so,
  - (ii) necessary or expedient for the purpose of concluding the affairs of the company,
  - (iii) necessary or expedient for the purpose of complying with any statutory requirement, or

(iv) specified by the Secretary of State by order for the purposes of this sub-paragraph.

(2) For the purposes of this section, a company is not to be treated as trading or otherwise carrying on business by virtue only of the fact that it makes a payment in respect of a liability incurred in the course of trading or otherwise carrying on business.

(3) The Secretary of State may by order amend subsection (1) for the purpose of altering the period in relation to which the doing of the things mentioned in paragraphs (a) to (d) of that subsection is relevant.

(4) An order under this section is subject to negative resolution procedure.

(5) It is an offence for a person to make an application in contravention of this section.

(6) In proceedings for such an offence it is a defence for the accused to prove that he did not know, and could not reasonably have known, of the existence of the facts that led to the contravention.

(7) A person guilty of an offence under this section is liable—

(a) on conviction on indictment, to a fine;

(b) on summary conviction, to a fine not exceeding the statutory maximum.

NOTES

Orders: no Orders have been made under this section.

[1.1167]

1005 Circumstances in which application not to be made: other proceedings not concluded

(1) An application under section 1003 (application for voluntary striking off) on behalf of a company must not be made at a time when—

(a) an application to the court under Part 26 [or 26A] has been made on behalf of the company for the sanctioning of a compromise or arrangement and the matter has not been finally concluded;

(b) a voluntary arrangement in relation to the company has been proposed under Part 1 of the Insolvency Act 1986 (c 45) or Part 2 of the Insolvency (Northern Ireland) Order 1989 (SI 1989/2405 (NI 19)) and the matter has not been finally concluded;

(c) the company is in administration under Part 2 of that Act or Part 3 of that Order;

(d) paragraph 44 of Schedule B1 to that Act or paragraph 45 of Schedule B1 to that Order applies (interim moratorium on proceedings where application to the court for an administration order has been made or notice of intention to appoint administrator has been filed);

(e) the company is being wound up under Part 4 of that Act or Part 5 of that Order, whether voluntarily or by the court, or a petition under that Part for winding up of the company by the court has been presented and not finally dealt with or withdrawn;

(f) there is a receiver or manager of the company's property;

(g) the company's estate is being administered by a judicial factor.

(2) For the purposes of subsection (1)(a), the matter is finally concluded if—

(a) the application has been withdrawn,

(b) the application has been finally dealt with without a compromise or arrangement being sanctioned by the court, or

(c) a compromise or arrangement has been sanctioned by the court and has, together with anything required to be done under any provision made in relation to the matter by order of the court, been fully carried out.

(3) For the purposes of subsection (1)(b), the matter is finally concluded if—

(a) no meetings are to be summoned under section 3 of the Insolvency Act 1986 (c 45) or Article 16 of the Insolvency (Northern Ireland) Order 1989,

(b) meetings summoned under that section or Article fail to approve the arrangement with no, or the same, modifications,

(c) an arrangement approved by meetings summoned under that section, or in consequence of a direction under section 6(4)(b) of that Act or Article 19(4)(b) of that Order, has been fully implemented, or

(d) the court makes an order under section 6(5) of that Act or Article 19(5) of that Order revoking approval given at previous meetings and, if the court gives any directions under section 6(6) of that Act or Article 19(6) of that Order, the company has done whatever it is required to do under those directions.

(4) It is an offence for a person to make an application in contravention of this section.

(5) In proceedings for such an offence it is a defence for the accused to prove that he did not know, and could not reasonably have known, of the existence of the facts that led to the contravention.

(6) A person guilty of an offence under this section is liable—

(a) on conviction on indictment, to a fine;

(b) on summary conviction, to a fine not exceeding the statutory maximum.

NOTES

Sub-s (1): words in square brackets inserted by the Corporate Insolvency and Governance Act 2020, s 7, Sch 9, Pt 2, paras 30, 37(1), (2), as from 26 June 2020.

[1.1168]

1006 Copy of application to be given to members, employees, etc

(1) A person who makes an application under section 1003 (application for voluntary striking off) on behalf of a company must secure that, within seven days from the day on which the application is made, a copy of it is given to every person who at any time on that day is—

(a) a member of the company,

(b) an employee of the company,

(c) a creditor of the company,

(d) a director of the company,

(e) a manager or trustee of any pension fund established for the benefit of employees of the company, or

(f) a person of a description specified for the purposes of this paragraph by regulations made by the Secretary of State.

Regulations under paragraph (f) are subject to negative resolution procedure.

(2) Subsection (1) does not require a copy of the application to be given to a director who is a party to the application.

(3) The duty imposed by this section ceases to apply if the application is withdrawn before the end of the period for giving the copy application.

(4) A person who fails to perform the duty imposed on him by this section commits an offence.

If he does so with the intention of concealing the making of the application from the person concerned, he commits an aggravated offence.

(5) In proceedings for an offence under this section it is a defence for the accused to prove that he took all reasonable steps to perform the duty.

(6) A person guilty of an offence under this section (other than an aggravated offence) is liable—

- (a) on conviction on indictment, to a fine;
- (b) on summary conviction, to a fine not exceeding the statutory maximum.

(7) A person guilty of an aggravated offence under this section is liable—

- (a) on conviction on indictment, to imprisonment for a term not exceeding seven years or a fine (or both);
- (b) on summary conviction—
  - (i) in England and Wales, to imprisonment for a term not exceeding twelve months or to a fine not exceeding the statutory maximum (or both);
  - (ii) in Scotland or Northern Ireland, to imprisonment for a term not exceeding six months, or to a fine not exceeding the statutory maximum (or both).

NOTES

Offences under this section: see further s 1131 at **[1.1301]**.

Regulations: no Regulations have been made under this section.

[1.1169]

1007 Copy of application to be given to new members, employees, etc

(1) This section applies in relation to any time after the day on which a company makes an application under section 1003 (application for voluntary striking off) and before the day on which the application is finally dealt with or withdrawn.

(2) A person who is a director of the company at the end of a day on which a person (other than himself) becomes—

- (a) a member of the company,
- (b) an employee of the company,
- (c) a creditor of the company,
- (d) a director of the company,
- (e) a manager or trustee of any pension fund established for the benefit of employees of the company, or
- (f) a person of a description specified for the purposes of this paragraph by regulations made by the Secretary of State,

must secure that a copy of the application is given to that person within seven days from that day.

Regulations under paragraph (f) are subject to negative resolution procedure.

(3) The duty imposed by this section ceases to apply if the application is finally dealt with or withdrawn before the end of the period for giving the copy application.

(4) A person who fails to perform the duty imposed on him by this section commits an offence.

If he does so with the intention of concealing the making of the application from the person concerned, he commits an aggravated offence.

(5) In proceedings for an offence under this section it is a defence for the accused to prove—

- (a) that at the time of the failure he was not aware of the fact that the company had made an application under section 1003, or
- (b) that he took all reasonable steps to perform the duty.

(6) A person guilty of an offence under this section (other than an aggravated offence) is liable—

- (a) on conviction on indictment, to a fine;
- (b) on summary conviction, to a fine not exceeding the statutory maximum.

(7) A person guilty of an aggravated offence under this section is liable—

- (a) on conviction on indictment, to imprisonment for a term not exceeding seven years or a fine (or both);
- (b) on summary conviction—
  - (i) in England and Wales, to imprisonment for a term not exceeding twelve months or to a fine not exceeding the statutory maximum (or both);
  - (ii) in Scotland or Northern Ireland, to imprisonment for a term not exceeding six months, or to a fine not exceeding the statutory maximum (or both).

NOTES

Offences under this section: see further s 1131 at **[1.1301]**.

Regulations: no Regulations have been made under this section.

[1.1170]

1008 Copy of application: provisions as to service of documents

(1) The following provisions have effect for the purposes of—

section 1006 (copy of application to be given to members, employees, etc), and
section 1007 (copy of application to be given to new members, employees, etc).

(2) A document is treated as given to a person if it is—

- (a) delivered to him, or
- (b) left at his proper address, or
- (c) sent by post to him at that address.

(3) For the purposes of subsection (2) and section 7 of the Interpretation Act 1978 (c 30) (service of documents by post) as it applies in relation to that subsection, the proper address of a person is—

(a) in the case of a firm incorporated or formed in the United Kingdom, its registered or principal office;

(b) in the case of a firm incorporated or formed outside the United Kingdom—

(i) if it has a place of business in the United Kingdom, its principal office in the United Kingdom, or

(ii) if it does not have a place of business in the United Kingdom, its registered or principal office;

(c) in the case of an individual, his last known address.

(4) In the case of a creditor of the company a document is treated as given to him if it is left or sent by post to him—

(a) at the place of business of his with which the company has had dealings by virtue of which he is a creditor of the company, or

(b) if there is more than one such place of business, at each of them.

[1.1171]

1009 Circumstances in which application to be withdrawn

(1) This section applies where, at any time on or after the day on which a company makes an application under section 1003 (application for voluntary striking off) and before the day on which the application is finally dealt with or withdrawn—

(a) the company—

(i) changes its name,

(ii) trades or otherwise carries on business,

(iii) makes a disposal for value of any property or rights other than those which it was necessary or expedient for it to hold for the purpose of making, or proceeding with, an application under that section, or

(iv) engages in any activity, except one to which subsection (4) applies;

(b) an application is made to the court under Part 26 [or 26A] on behalf of the company for the sanctioning of a compromise or arrangement;

(c) a voluntary arrangement in relation to the company is proposed under Part 1 of the Insolvency Act 1986 (c 45) or Part 2 of the Insolvency (Northern Ireland) Order 1989 (SI 1989/2405 (NI 19));

(d) an application to the court for an administration order in respect of the company is made under paragraph 12 of Schedule B1 to that Act or paragraph 13 of Schedule B1 to that Order;

(e) an administrator is appointed in respect of the company under paragraph 14 or 22 of Schedule B1 to that Act or paragraph 15 or 23 of Schedule B1 to that Order, or a copy of notice of intention to appoint an administrator of the company under any of those provisions is filed with the court;

(f) there arise any of the circumstances in which, under section 84(1) of that Act or Article 70 of that Order, the company may be voluntarily wound up;

(g) a petition is presented for the winding up of the company by the court under Part 4 of that Act or Part 5 of that Order;

(h) a receiver or manager of the company's property is appointed; or

(i) a judicial factor is appointed to administer the company's estate.

(2) A person who, at the end of a day on which any of the events mentioned in subsection (1) occurs, is a director of the company must secure that the company's application is withdrawn forthwith.

(3) For the purposes of subsection (1)(a), a company is not treated as trading or otherwise carrying on business by virtue only of the fact that it makes a payment in respect of a liability incurred in the course of trading or otherwise carrying on business.

(4) The excepted activities referred to in subsection (1)(a)(iv) are—

(a) any activity necessary or expedient for the purposes of—

(i) making, or proceeding with, an application under section 1003 (application for voluntary striking off),

(ii) concluding affairs of the company that are outstanding because of what has been necessary or expedient for the purpose of making, or proceeding with, such an application, or

(iii) complying with any statutory requirement;

(b) any activity specified by the Secretary of State by order for the purposes of this subsection.

An order under paragraph (b) is subject to negative resolution procedure.

(5) A person who fails to perform the duty imposed on him by this section commits an offence.

(6) In proceedings for an offence under this section it is a defence for the accused to prove—

(a) that at the time of the failure he was not aware of the fact that the company had made an application under section 1003, or

(b) that he took all reasonable steps to perform the duty.

(7) A person guilty of an offence under this section is liable—

(a) on conviction on indictment, to a fine;

(b) on summary conviction, to a fine not exceeding the statutory maximum.

NOTES

Sub-s (1): words in square brackets inserted by the Corporate Insolvency and Governance Act 2020, s 7, Sch 9, Pt 2, paras 30, 37(1), (3), as from 26 June 2020.

Orders: no Orders have been made under this section.

[1.1172]

1010 Withdrawal of application

An application under section 1003 is withdrawn by notice to the registrar.

[1.1173]

1011 Meaning of "creditor"

In this Chapter "creditor" includes a contingent or prospective creditor.

CHAPTER 2 PROPERTY OF DISSOLVED COMPANY

Property vesting as bona vacantia

[1.1174]

1012 Property of dissolved company to be bona vacantia

(1) When a company is dissolved, all property and rights whatsoever vested in or held on trust for the company immediately before its dissolution (including leasehold property, but not including property held by the company on trust for another person) are deemed to be *bona vacantia* and—

(a) accordingly belong to the Crown, or to the Duchy of Lancaster or to the Duke of Cornwall for the time being (as the case may be), and

(b) vest and may be dealt with in the same manner as other *bona vacantia* accruing to the Crown, to the Duchy of Lancaster or to the Duke of Cornwall.

(2) Subsection (1) has effect subject to the possible restoration of the company to the register under Chapter 3 (see section 1034).

[1.1175]

1013 Crown disclaimer of property vesting as bona vacantia

(1) Where property vests in the Crown under section 1012, the Crown's title to it under that section may be disclaimed by a notice signed by the Crown representative, that is to say the Treasury Solicitor, or, in relation to property in Scotland, the Queen's and Lord Treasurer's Remembrancer.

(2) The right to execute a notice of disclaimer under this section may be waived by or on behalf of the Crown either expressly or by taking possession.

(3) A notice of disclaimer must be executed within three years after—

(a) the date on which the fact that the property may have vested in the Crown under section 1012 first comes to the notice of the Crown representative, or

(b) if ownership of the property is not established at that date, the end of the period reasonably necessary for the Crown representative to establish the ownership of the property.

(4) If an application in writing is made to the Crown representative by a person interested in the property requiring him to decide whether he will or will not disclaim, any notice of disclaimer must be executed within twelve months after the making of the application or such further period as may be allowed by the court.

(5) A notice of disclaimer under this section is of no effect if it is shown to have been executed after the end of the period specified by subsection (3) or (4).

(6) A notice of disclaimer under this section must be delivered to the registrar and retained and registered by him.

(7) Copies of it must be published in the Gazette and sent to any persons who have given the Crown representative notice that they claim to be interested in the property.

(8) This section applies to property vested in the Duchy of Lancaster or the Duke of Cornwall under section 1012 as if for references to the Crown and the Crown representative there were respectively substituted references to the Duchy of Lancaster and to the Solicitor to that Duchy, or to the Duke of Cornwall and to the Solicitor to the Duchy of Cornwall, as the case may be.

[1.1176]

1014 Effect of Crown disclaimer

(1) Where notice of disclaimer is executed under section 1013 as respects any property, that property is deemed not to have vested in the Crown under section 1012.

(2) The following sections contain provisions as to the effect of the Crown disclaimer—

sections 1015 to 1019 apply in relation to property in England and Wales or Northern Ireland;
sections 1020 to 1022 apply in relation to property in Scotland.

Effect of Crown disclaimer: England and Wales and Northern Ireland

[1.1177]

1015 General effect of disclaimer

(1) The Crown's disclaimer operates so as to terminate, as from the date of the disclaimer, the rights, interests and liabilities of the company in or in respect of the property disclaimed.

(2) It does not, except so far as is necessary for the purpose of releasing the company from any liability, affect the rights or liabilities of any other person.

[1.1178]

1016 Disclaimer of leaseholds

(1) The disclaimer of any property of a leasehold character does not take effect unless a copy of the disclaimer has been served (so far as the Crown representative is aware of their addresses) on every person claiming under the company as underlessee or mortgagee, and either—

(a) no application under section 1017 (power of court to make vesting order) is made with respect to that property before the end of the period of 14 days beginning with the day on which the last notice under this paragraph was served, or

(b) where such an application has been made, the court directs that the disclaimer shall take effect.

(2) Where the court gives a direction under subsection (1)(b) it may also, instead of or in addition to any order it makes under section 1017, make such order as it thinks fit with respect to fixtures, tenant's improvements and other matters arising out of the lease.

(3) In this section the "Crown representative" means—

(a) in relation to property vested in the Duchy of Lancaster, the Solicitor to that Duchy;

(b) in relation to property vested in the Duke of Cornwall, the Solicitor to the Duchy of Cornwall;

(c) in relation to property in Scotland, the Queen's and Lord Treasurer's Remembrancer;

(d) in relation to other property, the Treasury Solicitor.

[1.1179]

1017 Power of court to make vesting order

(1) The court may on application by a person who—

(a) claims an interest in the disclaimed property, or

(b) is under a liability in respect of the disclaimed property that is not discharged by the disclaimer,

make an order under this section in respect of the property.

(2) An order under this section is an order for the vesting of the disclaimed property in, or its delivery to—

(a) a person entitled to it (or a trustee for such a person), or

(b) a person subject to such a liability as is mentioned in subsection (1)(b) (or a trustee for such a person).

(3) An order under subsection (2)(b) may only be made where it appears to the court that it would be just to do so for the purpose of compensating the person subject to the liability in respect of the disclaimer.

(4) An order under this section may be made on such terms as the court thinks fit.

(5) On a vesting order being made under this section, the property comprised in it vests in the person named in that behalf in the order without conveyance, assignment or transfer.

[1.1180]

1018 Protection of persons holding under a lease

(1) The court must not make an order under section 1017 vesting property of a leasehold nature in a person claiming under the company as underlessee or mortgagee except on terms making that person—

(a) subject to the same liabilities and obligations as those to which the company was subject under the lease, or

(b) if the court thinks fit, subject to the same liabilities and obligations as if the lease had been assigned to him.

(2) Where the order relates to only part of the property comprised in the lease, subsection (1) applies as if the lease had comprised only the property comprised in the vesting order.

(3) A person claiming under the company as underlessee or mortgagee who declines to accept a vesting order on such terms is excluded from all interest in the property.

(4) If there is no person claiming under the company who is willing to accept an order on such terms, the court has power to vest the company's estate and interest in the property in any person who is liable (whether personally or in a representative character, and whether alone or jointly with the company) to perform the lessee's covenants in the lease.

(5) The court may vest that estate and interest in such a person freed and discharged from all estates, incumbrances and interests created by the company.

[1.1181]

1019 Land subject to rentcharge

Where in consequence of the disclaimer land that is subject to a rentcharge vests in any person, neither he nor his successors in title are subject to any personal liability in respect of sums becoming due under the rentcharge, except sums becoming due after he, or some person claiming under or through him, has taken possession or control of the land or has entered into occupation of it.

Effect of Crown disclaimer: Scotland

[1.1182]

1020 General effect of disclaimer

(1) The Crown's disclaimer operates to determine, as from the date of the disclaimer, the rights, interests and liabilities of the company, and the property of the company, in or in respect of the property disclaimed.

(2) It does not (except so far as is necessary for the purpose of releasing the company and its property from liability) affect the rights or liabilities of any other person.

[1.1183]

1021 Power of court to make vesting order

(1) The court may—

(a) on application by a person who either claims an interest in disclaimed property or is under a liability not discharged by this Act in respect of disclaimed property, and

(b) on hearing such persons as it thinks fit,

make an order for the vesting of the property in or its delivery to any persons entitled to it, or to whom it may seem just that the property should be delivered by way of compensation for such liability, or a trustee for him.

(2) The order may be made on such terms as the court thinks fit.

(3) On a vesting order being made under this section, the property comprised in it vests accordingly in the person named in that behalf in the order, without conveyance or assignation for that purpose.

[1.1184]

1022 Protection of persons holding under a lease

(1) Where the property disclaimed is held under a lease the court must not make a vesting order in favour of a person claiming under the company, whether—

(a) as sub-lessee, or

(b) as creditor in a duly registered or (as the case may be) recorded heritable security over a lease,

except on the following terms.

(2) The person must by the order be made subject—

(a) to the same liabilities and obligations as those to which the company was subject under the lease in respect of the property, or

(b) if the court thinks fit, only to the same liabilities and obligations as if the lease had been assigned to him.

In either event (if the case so requires) the liabilities and obligations must be as if the lease had comprised only the property comprised in the vesting order.

(3) A sub-lessee or creditor declining to accept a vesting order on such terms is excluded from all interest in and security over the property.

(4) If there is no person claiming under the company who is willing to accept an order on such terms, the court has power to vest the company's estate and interest in the property in any person liable (either personally or in a representative character, and either alone or jointly with the company) to perform the lessee's obligations under the lease.

(5) The court may vest that estate and interest in such a person freed and discharged from all interests, rights and obligations created by the company in the lease or in relation to the lease.

(6) For the purposes of this section a heritable security—

(a) is duly recorded if it is recorded in the Register of Sasines, and

(b) is duly registered if registered in accordance with the [Land Registration etc (Scotland) Act 2012 (asp 5)].

NOTES

Sub-s (6): words in square brackets substituted by the Land Registration etc (Scotland) Act 2012, s 119, Sch 5, para 50(1), (4), as from 8 December 2014.

Supplementary provisions

[1.1185]

1023 Liability for rentcharge on company's land after dissolution

(1) This section applies where on the dissolution of a company land in England and Wales or Northern Ireland that is subject to a rentcharge vests by operation of law in the Crown or any other person ("the proprietor").

(2) Neither the proprietor nor his successors in title are subject to any personal liability in respect of sums becoming due under the rentcharge, except sums becoming due after the proprietor, or some person claiming under or through him, has taken possession or control of the land or has entered into occupation of it.

(3) In this section "company" includes any body corporate.

CHAPTER 3 RESTORATION TO THE REGISTER

Administrative restoration to the register

[1.1186]

1024 Application for administrative restoration to the register

(1) An application may be made to the registrar to restore to the register a company that has been struck off the register under section 1000 or 1001 (power of registrar to strike off defunct company).

(2) An application under this section may be made whether or not the company has in consequence been dissolved.

(3) An application under this section may only be made by a former director or former member of the company.

(4) An application under this section may not be made after the end of the period of six years from the date of the dissolution of the company.

For this purpose an application is made when it is received by the registrar.

[1.1187]

1025 Requirements for administrative restoration

(1) On an application under section 1024 the registrar shall restore the company to the register if, and only if, the following conditions are met.

(2) The first condition is that the company was carrying on business or in operation at the time of its striking off.

(3) The second condition is that, if any property or right previously vested in or held on trust for the company has vested as *bona vacantia*, the Crown representative has signified to the registrar in writing consent to the company's restoration to the register.

(4) It is the applicant's responsibility to obtain that consent and to pay any costs (in Scotland, expenses) of the Crown representative—

(a) in dealing with the property during the period of dissolution, or

(b) in connection with the proceedings on the application,

that may be demanded as a condition of giving consent.

(5) The third condition is that the applicant has—

(a) delivered to the registrar such documents relating to the company as are necessary to bring up to date the records kept by the registrar, and

(b) paid any penalties under section 453 or corresponding earlier provisions (civil penalty for failure to deliver accounts) that were outstanding at the date of dissolution or striking off.

(6) In this section the "Crown representative" means—

(a) in relation to property vested in the Duchy of Lancaster, the Solicitor to that Duchy;

(b) in relation to property vested in the Duke of Cornwall, the Solicitor to the Duchy of Cornwall;

(c) in relation to property in Scotland, the Queen's and Lord Treasurer's Remembrancer;

(d) in relation to other property, the Treasury Solicitor.

[1.1188]

1026 Application to be accompanied by statement of compliance

(1) An application under section 1024 (application for administrative restoration to the register) must be accompanied by a statement of compliance.

(2) The statement of compliance required is a statement—

(a) that the person making the application has standing to apply (see subsection (3) of that section), and

(b) that the requirements for administrative restoration (see section 1025) are met.

(3) The registrar may accept the statement of compliance as sufficient evidence of those matters.

[1.1189]

1027 Registrar's decision on application for administrative restoration

(1) The registrar must give notice to the applicant of the decision on an application under section 1024 (application for administrative restoration to the register).

(2) If the decision is that the company should be restored to the register, the restoration takes effect as from the date that notice is sent.

(3) In the case of such a decision, the registrar must—

(a) enter on the register a note of the date as from which the company's restoration to the register takes effect, and

(b) cause notice of the restoration to be published in the Gazette.

(4) The notice under subsection (3)(b) must state—

(a) the name of the company or, if the company is restored to the register under a different name (see section 1033), that name and its former name,

(b) the company's registered number, and

(c) the date as from which the restoration of the company to the register takes effect.

[1.1190]

1028 Effect of administrative restoration

(1) The general effect of administrative restoration to the register is that the company is deemed to have continued in existence as if it had not been dissolved or struck off the register.

(2) The company is not liable to a penalty under section 453 or any corresponding earlier provision (civil penalty for failure to deliver accounts) for a financial year in relation to which the period for filing accounts and reports ended—

(a) after the date of dissolution or striking off, and

(b) before the restoration of the company to the register.

(3) The court may give such directions and make such provision as seems just for placing the company and all other persons in the same position (as nearly as may be) as if the company had not been dissolved or struck off the register.

(4) An application to the court for such directions or provision may be made any time within three years after the date of restoration of the company to the register.

[1.1191]

[1028A Administrative restoration of company with share warrants

(1) This section applies in relation to a company which has been struck off the register under section 1000 or 1001 and which, at the time it was struck off, had any share warrant in issue.

(2) If the registrar restores the company to the register under section 1025, the share warrant and the shares specified in it are cancelled with effect from the date the restoration takes effect.

(3) If as a result of subsection (2) the company has no issued share capital, the company must, before the end of the period of one month beginning with the date the restoration takes effect, allot at least one share in the company; and section 549(1) does not apply to such an allotment.

(4) The company must, before the end of the period of 15 days beginning with the date the restoration takes effect, deliver a statement of capital to the registrar.

(5) Subsection (4) does not apply in a case where the company is required under subsection (3) to make an allotment (because in such a case section 555 will apply).

(6) The statement of capital must state with respect to the company's share capital as reduced by the cancellation of the share warrant and the shares specified in it—

(a) the total number of shares of the company,

(b) the aggregate nominal value of those shares,

(c) the aggregate amount (if any) unpaid on those shares (whether on account of their nominal value or by way of premium), and

(d) for each class of shares—

(i) prescribed particulars of the rights attached to the shares,

(ii) the total number of shares of that class, and

(iii) the aggregate nominal value of shares of that class.

(7) Where a share warrant is cancelled in accordance with subsection (2), the company must, as soon as reasonably practicable—

(a) enter the date the cancellation takes effect in its register of members, or

(b) where an election is in force under section 128B of the Companies Act 2006 (option to keep membership information on central register) in respect of the company, deliver that information to the registrar as if it were information required to be delivered under section 128E of that Act.

(8) Subsection (9) applies where—

(a) any property or right previously vested in or held on trust for the company in respect of any share specified in a share warrant has vested as *bona vacantia* (see section 1012), and

(b) the warrant and the share are cancelled on the restoration of the company in accordance with this section.

(9) On restoration of the company, that property or right—

(a) may not be returned to the company, and

(b) accordingly, remains vested as *bona vacantia*.

(10) If default is made in complying with subsection (3) or (4), an offence is committed by—

(a) the company, and

(b) every officer of the company who is in default.

For this purpose a shadow director is treated as an officer of the company.

(11) A person guilty of an offence under this section is liable—

(a) on conviction on indictment, to a fine;

(b) on summary conviction—

(i) in England and Wales, to a fine;

(ii) in Scotland or Northern Ireland, to a fine not exceeding the statutory maximum.]

NOTES

Inserted by the Small Business, Enterprise and Employment Act 2015, s 84, Sch 4, Pt 2, paras 22, 27(1), as from 26 May 2015.

[1.1192]

1029 Application to court for restoration to the register

(1) An application may be made to the court to restore to the register a company—

(a) that has been dissolved under Chapter 9 of Part 4 of the Insolvency Act 1986 (c 45) or Chapter 9 of Part 5 of the Insolvency (Northern Ireland) Order 1989 (SI 1989/2405 (NI 19)) (dissolution of company after winding up),

(b) that is deemed to have been dissolved under paragraph 84(6) of Schedule B1 to that Act or paragraph 85(6) of Schedule B1 to that Order (dissolution of company following administration), or

(c) that has been struck off the register—

(i) under section 1000 or 1001 (power of registrar to strike off defunct company), or

(ii) under section 1003 (voluntary striking off),

whether or not the company has in consequence been dissolved.

(2) An application under this section may be made by—

(a) the Secretary of State,

(b) any former director of the company,

(c) any person having an interest in land in which the company had a superior or derivative interest,

(d) any person having an interest in land or other property—

(i) that was subject to rights vested in the company, or

(ii) that was benefited by obligations owed by the company,

(e) any person who but for the company's dissolution would have been in a contractual relationship with it,

(f) any person with a potential legal claim against the company,

(g) any manager or trustee of a pension fund established for the benefit of employees of the company,

(h) any former member of the company (or the personal representatives of such a person),

(i) any person who was a creditor of the company at the time of its striking off or dissolution,

(j) any former liquidator of the company,

(k) where the company was struck off the register under section 1003 (voluntary striking off), any person of a description specified by regulations under section 1006(1)(f) or 1007(2)(f) (persons entitled to notice of application for voluntary striking off),

or by any other person appearing to the court to have an interest in the matter.

[1.1193]

1030 When application to the court may be made

(1) An application to the court for restoration of a company to the register may be made at any time for the [purpose of—

(a) bringing] proceedings against the company for damages for personal [injury;

(b) an insurer (within the meaning of the Third Parties (Rights Against Insurers) Act 2010) bringing proceedings against a third party in the name of that company in respect of that company's liability for damages for personal injury.]

(2) No order shall be made on such an application if it appears to the court that the proceedings would fail by virtue of any enactment as to the time within which proceedings must be brought.

(3) In making that decision the court must have regard to its power under section 1032(3) (power to give consequential directions etc) to direct that the period between the dissolution (or striking off) of the company and the making of the order is not to count for the purposes of any such enactment.

(4) In any other case an application to the court for restoration of a company to the register may not be made after the end of the period of six years from the date of the dissolution of the company, subject as follows.

(5) In a case where—

(a) the company has been struck off the register under section 1000 or 1001 (power of registrar to strike off defunct company),

(b) an application to the registrar has been made under section 1024 (application for administrative restoration to the register) within the time allowed for making such an application, and

(c) the registrar has refused the application,

an application to the court under this section may be made within 28 days of notice of the registrar's decision being issued by the registrar, even if the period of six years mentioned in subsection (4) above has expired.

(6) For the purposes of this section—

(a) "personal injury" includes any disease and any impairment of a person's physical or mental condition; and

(b) references to damages for personal injury include—

(i) any sum claimed by virtue of section 1(2)(c) of the Law Reform (Miscellaneous Provisions) Act 1934 (c 41) or section 14(2)(c) of the Law Reform (Miscellaneous Provisions) Act (Northern Ireland) 1937 (1937 c 9 (NI)) (funeral expenses)), and

(ii) damages under the Fatal Accidents Act 1976 (c 30), the [Damages (Scotland) Act 2011 (asp 7)] or the Fatal Accidents (Northern Ireland) Order 1977 (SI 1977/1251 (NI 18)).

NOTES

Sub-s (1): words in square brackets substituted by the Third Parties (Rights Against Insurers) Act 2010 (Consequential Amendment of Companies Act 2006) Regulations 2018, SI 2018/1162, reg 2, as from 23 November 2018.

Sub-s (6): words in square brackets substituted by the Damages (Scotland) Act 2011, s 15, Sch 1, para 9, as from 7 July 2011.

[1.1194]

1031 Decision on application for restoration by the court

(1) On an application under section 1029 the court may order the restoration of the company to the register—

(a) if the company was struck off the register under section 1000 or 1001 (power of registrar to strike off defunct companies) and the company was, at the time of the striking off, carrying on business or in operation;

(b) if the company was struck off the register under section 1003 (voluntary striking off) and any of the requirements of sections 1004 to 1009 was not complied with;

(c) if in any other case the court considers it just to do so.

(2) If the court orders restoration of the company to the register, the restoration takes effect on a copy of the court's order being delivered to the registrar.

(3) The registrar must cause to be published in the Gazette notice of the restoration of the company to the register.

(4) The notice must state—

(a) the name of the company or, if the company is restored to the register under a different name (see section 1033), that name and its former name,

(b) the company's registered number, and

(c) the date on which the restoration took effect.

[1.1195]

1032 Effect of court order for restoration to the register

(1) The general effect of an order by the court for restoration to the register is that the company is deemed to have continued in existence as if it had not been dissolved or struck off the register.

(2) The company is not liable to a penalty under section 453 or any corresponding earlier provision (civil penalty for failure to deliver accounts) for a financial year in relation to which the period for filing accounts and reports ended—

(a) after the date of dissolution or striking off, and

(b) before the restoration of the company to the register.

(3) The court may give such directions and make such provision as seems just for placing the company and all other persons in the same position (as nearly as may be) as if the company had not been dissolved or struck off the register.

(4) The court may also give directions as to—

(a) the delivery to the registrar of such documents relating to the company as are necessary to bring up to date the records kept by the registrar,

(b) the payment of the costs (in Scotland, expenses) of the registrar in connection with the proceedings for the restoration of the company to the register,

(c) where any property or right previously vested in or held on trust for the company has vested as *bona vacantia*, the payment of the costs (in Scotland, expenses) of the Crown representative—

(i) in dealing with the property during the period of dissolution, or

(ii) in connection with the proceedings on the application.

(5) In this section the "Crown representative" means—

(a) in relation to property vested in the Duchy of Lancaster, the Solicitor to that Duchy;

(b) in relation to property vested in the Duke of Cornwall, the Solicitor to the Duchy of Cornwall;

(c) in relation to property in Scotland, the Queen's and Lord Treasurer's Remembrancer;

(d) in relation to other property, the Treasury Solicitor.

[1.1196]

[1032A Restoration by court of company with share warrants

(1) This section applies in relation to a company falling within section 1029(1) if, at the time it was dissolved, deemed to be dissolved or (as the case may be) struck off, it had any share warrant in issue.

(2) If the court orders the restoration of the company to the register, the order must also cancel the share warrant and the shares specified in it with effect from the date the restoration takes effect.

(3) If as a result of subsection (2) the company has no issued share capital, the company must, before the end of the period of one month beginning with the date the restoration takes effect, allot at least one share in the company; and section 549(1) does not apply to such an allotment.

(4) Subsection (6) applies in a case where—

(a) the application under section 1029 was made by a person mentioned in subsection (2)(b) or (h) of that section, or

(b) the court order specifies that it applies.

(5) But subsection (6) does not apply in any case where the company is required under subsection (3) to make an allotment (because in such a case section 555 will apply).

(6) In a case where this subsection applies, the company must, before the end of the period of 15 days beginning with the date the restoration takes effect, deliver a statement of capital to the registrar.

(7) The statement of capital must state with respect to the company's share capital as reduced by the cancellation of the share warrant and the shares specified in it—

(a) the total number of shares of the company,

(b) the aggregate nominal value of those shares,

(c) the aggregate amount (if any) unpaid on those shares (whether on account of their nominal value or by way of premium), and

(d) for each class of shares—

(i) prescribed particulars of the rights attached to the shares,

(ii) the total number of shares of that class, and

(iii) the aggregate nominal value of shares of that class.

(8) Where a share warrant is cancelled by an order as mentioned in subsection (2), the company must, as soon as reasonably practicable—

(a) enter the date the cancellation takes effect in its register of members, or

(b) where an election is in force under section 128B of the Companies Act 2006 (option to keep membership information on central register) in respect of the company, deliver that information to the registrar as if it were information required to be delivered under section 128E of that Act.

(9) Subsection (10) applies where—

(a) any property or right previously vested in or held on trust for the company in respect of any share specified in a share warrant has vested as *bona vacantia* (see section 1012), and

(b) the warrant and the share are cancelled on the restoration of the company in accordance with this section.

(10) On restoration of the company, that property or right—

(a) may not be returned to the company, and

(b) accordingly, remains vested as *bona vacantia*.

(11) If default is made in complying with subsection (3) or (6), an offence is committed by—

(a) the company, and

(b) every officer of the company who is in default.

For this purpose a shadow director is treated as an officer of the company.

(12) A person guilty of an offence under this section is liable—

(a) on conviction on indictment, to a fine;

(b) on summary conviction—

(i) in England and Wales, to a fine;

(ii) in Scotland or Northern Ireland, to a fine not exceeding the statutory maximum.]

NOTES

Inserted by the Small Business, Enterprise and Employment Act 2015, s 84, Sch 4, Pt 2, paras 22, 28(1), as from 26 May 2015.

Supplementary provisions

[1.1197]

1033 Company's name on restoration

(1) A company is restored to the register with the name it had before it was dissolved or struck off the register, subject to the following provisions.

(2) If at the date of restoration the company could not be registered under its former name without contravening section 66 (name not to be the same as another in the registrar's index of company names), it must be restored to the register—

(a) under another name specified—

(i) in the case of administrative restoration, in the application to the registrar, or

(ii) in the case of restoration under a court order, in the court's order, or

(b) as if its registered number was also its name.

References to a company's being registered in a name, and to registration in that context, shall be read as including the company's being restored to the register.

(3) If a company is restored to the register under a name specified in the application to the registrar, the provisions of—

section 80 (change of name: registration and issue of new certificate of incorporation), and
section 81 (change of name: effect),

apply as if the application to the registrar were notice of a change of name.

(4) If a company is restored to the register under a name specified in the court's order, the provisions of—

section 80 (change of name: registration and issue of new certificate of incorporation), and
section 81 (change of name: effect),

apply as if the copy of the court order delivered to the registrar were notice of a change a name.

(5) If the company is restored to the register as if its registered number was also its name—

(a) the company must change its name within 14 days after the date of the restoration,

(b) the change may be made by resolution of the directors (without prejudice to any other method of changing the company's name),

(c) the company must give notice to the registrar of the change, and

(d) sections 80 and 81 apply as regards the registration and effect of the change.

(6) If the company fails to comply with subsection (5)(a) or (c) an offence is committed by—

(a) the company, and

(b) every officer of the company who is in default.

(7) A person guilty of an offence under subsection (6) is liable on summary conviction to a fine not exceeding level 5 on the standard scale and, for continued contravention, a daily default fine not exceeding [one-tenth of the greater of £5,000 or level 4 on the standard scale].

NOTES

Sub-s (7): words in square brackets substituted (for the original words "one-tenth of level 5 on the standard scale") by the Legal Aid, Sentencing and Punishment of Offenders Act 2012 (Fines on Summary Conviction) Regulations 2015, SI 2015/664, regs 3, 5, Sch 3, Pt 1, para 9(1), (22), as from 12 March 2015, in relation to England and Wales only (except in relation to (a) fines for offences committed before 12 March 2015, (b) the operation of restrictions on fines that may be imposed on a person aged under 18, or (c) fines that may be imposed on a person convicted by a magistrates' court who is to be sentenced as if convicted on indictment).

[1.1198]

1034 Effect of restoration to the register where property has vested as bona vacantia

(1) The person in whom any property or right is vested by section 1012 (property of dissolved company to be *bona vacantia*) may dispose of, or of an interest in, that property or right despite the fact that the company may be restored to the register under this Chapter.

(2) If the company is restored to the register—

(a) the restoration does not affect the disposition (but without prejudice to its effect in relation to any other property or right previously vested in or held on trust for the company), and

(b) the Crown or, as the case may be, the Duke of Cornwall shall pay to the company an amount equal to—

(i) the amount of any consideration received for the property or right or, as the case may be, the interest in it, or

(ii) the value of any such consideration at the time of the disposition,

or, if no consideration was received an amount equal to the value of the property, right or interest disposed of, as at the date of the disposition.

(3) There may be deducted from the amount payable under subsection (2)(b) the reasonable costs of the Crown representative in connection with the disposition (to the extent that they have not been paid as a condition of administrative restoration or pursuant to a court order for restoration).

(4) Where a liability accrues under subsection (2) in respect of any property or right which before the restoration of the company to the register had accrued as *bona vacantia* to the Duchy of Lancaster, the Attorney General of that Duchy shall represent Her Majesty in any proceedings arising in connection with that liability.

(5) Where a liability accrues under subsection (2) in respect of any property or right which before the restoration of the company to the register had accrued as *bona vacantia* to the Duchy of Cornwall, such persons as the Duke of Cornwall (or other possessor for the time being of the Duchy) may appoint shall represent the Duke (or other possessor) in any proceedings arising out of that liability.

(6) In this section the "Crown representative" means—

- (a) in relation to property vested in the Duchy of Lancaster, the Solicitor to that Duchy;
- (b) in relation to property vested in the Duke of Cornwall, the Solicitor to the Duchy of Cornwall;
- (c) in relation to property in Scotland, the Queen's and Lord Treasurer's Remembrancer;
- (d) in relation to other property, the Treasury Solicitor.

PART 32 COMPANY INVESTIGATIONS: AMENDMENTS

[1.1199]

1035 Powers of Secretary of State to give directions to inspectors

(This section inserts CA 1985, ss 446A, 446B at **[5.28]**, **[5.29]** *and amends ss 431, 432, 437 and 442 at* **[5.17]**, **[5.18]**, **[5.21]** *and* **[5.24]**.*)*

[1.1200]

1036 Resignation, removal and replacement of inspectors

(This section inserts CA 1985, ss 446C, 446D at **[5.30]**, **[5.31]**.*)*

[1.1201]

1037 Power to obtain information from former inspectors etc

(This section inserts CA 1985, s 446E at **[5.32]** *and amends ss 451A and 452 at* **[5.40]** *and* **[5.41]**.*)*

[1.1202]

1038 Power to require production of documents

(This section substitutes CA 1985, ss 434(6) and 447(9) at **[5.19]**, **[5.33]**.*)*

1039 (*This section amended the Company Directors Disqualification Act 1986, s 8, and was repealed by the Small Business, Enterprise and Employment Act 2015, s 111, Sch 7, Pt 2, para 5, as from 26 May 2015.*)

PART 33 UK COMPANIES NOT FORMED UNDER COMPANIES LEGISLATION

CHAPTER 1 COMPANIES NOT FORMED UNDER COMPANIES LEGISLATION BUT AUTHORISED TO REGISTER

[1.1203]

1040 Companies authorised to register under this Act

(1) This section applies to—

- (a) any company that was in existence on 2nd November 1862 (including any company registered under the Joint Stock Companies Acts), and
- (b) any company formed after that date (whether before or after the commencement of this Act)—
  - (i) in pursuance of an Act of Parliament other than this Act or any of the former Companies Acts,
  - (ii) in pursuance of letters patent, or
  - (iii) that is otherwise duly constituted according to law,

  [other than a company registered under Part 4 of the Risk Transformation Regulations 2017].

(2) Any such company may on making application register under this Act.

(3) Subject to the following provisions, it may register as an unlimited company, as a company limited by shares or as a company limited by guarantee.

(4) A company having the liability of its members limited by Act of Parliament or letters patent—

- (a) may not register under this section unless it is a joint stock company, and
- (b) may not register under this section as an unlimited company or a company limited by guarantee.

(5) A company that is not a joint stock company may not register under this section as a company limited by shares.

(6) The registration of a company under this section is not invalid by reason that it has taken place with a view to the company's being wound up.

NOTES

Sub-s (1): words in square brackets in para (b) added by the Risk Transformation Regulations 2017, SI 2017/1212, reg 190, Sch 4, para 4(a), as from 8 December 2017.

Note: as to the registration of a company on an application under this section, see the Companies (Companies Authorised to Register) Regulations 2009, SI 2009/2437 at **[4.400]**.

[1.1204]

1041 Definition of "joint stock company"

(1) For the purposes of section 1040 (companies authorised to register under this Act) "joint stock company" means a company—

- (a) having a permanent paid-up or nominal share capital of fixed amount divided into shares, also of fixed amount, or held and transferable as stock, or divided and held partly in one way and partly in the other, and
- (b) formed on the principle of having for its members the holders of those shares or that stock, and no other persons.

(2) Such a company when registered with limited liability under this Act is deemed a company limited by shares.

[1.1205]

1042 Power to make provision by regulations

(1) The Secretary of State may make provision by regulations—

(a) for and in connection with registration under section 1040 (companies authorised to register under this Act), and

(b) as to the application to companies so registered of the provisions of the Companies Acts.

(2) Without prejudice to the generality of that power, regulations under this section may make provision corresponding to any provision formerly made by Chapter 2 of Part 22 of the Companies Act 1985 (c 6).

(3) Regulations under this section are subject to negative resolution procedure.

NOTES

Regulations: the Companies (Companies Authorised to Register) Regulations 2009, SI 2009/2437 at **[4.400]**; the Companies and Limited Liability Partnerships (Filing Requirements) Regulations 2015, SI 2015/1695; the Companies and Limited Liability Partnerships (Filing Requirements) Regulations 2016, SI 2016/599 at **[4.640]**. For a summary of all statutory instruments made under this Act, see Appendix 4 at **[A4]**.

CHAPTER 2 UNREGISTERED COMPANIES

[1.1206]

1043 Unregistered companies

(1) This section applies to bodies corporate incorporated in and having a principal place of business in the United Kingdom, other than—

(a) bodies incorporated by, or registered under, a public general Act of Parliament;

(b) bodies not formed for the purpose of carrying on a business that has for its object the acquisition of gain by the body or its individual members;

(c) bodies for the time being exempted from this section by direction of the Secretary of State;

(d) open-ended investment companies;

[(e) protected cell companies registered under Part 4 of the Risk Transformation Regulations 2017].

(2) The Secretary of State may make provision by regulations applying specified provisions of the Companies Acts to all, or any specified description of, the bodies to which this section applies.

(3) The regulations may provide that the specified provisions of the Companies Acts apply subject to any specified limitations and to such adaptations and modifications (if any) as may be specified.

(4) This section does not—

(a) repeal or revoke in whole or in part any enactment, royal charter or other instrument constituting or regulating any body in relation to which provisions of the Companies Acts are applied by regulations under this section, or

(b) restrict the power of Her Majesty to grant a charter in lieu or supplementary to any such charter.

But in relation to any such body the operation of any such enactment, charter or instrument is suspended in so far as it is inconsistent with any of those provisions as they apply for the time being to that body.

(5) In this section "specified" means specified in the regulations.

(6) Regulations under this section are subject to negative resolution procedure.

NOTES

Sub-s (1): para (e) added by the Risk Transformation Regulations 2017, SI 2017/1212, reg 190, Sch 4, para 4(b), as from 8 December 2017.

Regulations: the Unregistered Companies Regulations 2009, SI 2009/2436 at **[4.389]**; the Companies and Limited Liability Partnerships (Accounts and Audit Exemptions and Change of Accounting Framework) Regulations 2012, SI 2012/2301; the Unregistered Companies (Amendment) Regulations 2013, SI 2013/1972; the Companies and Limited Liability Partnerships (Filing Requirements) Regulations 2015, SI 2015/1695; the Companies and Limited Liability Partnerships (Filing Requirements) Regulations 2016, SI 2016/599 at **[4.640]**. For a summary of all statutory instruments made under this Act, see Appendix 4 at **[A4]**.

PART 34 OVERSEAS COMPANIES

Introductory

[1.1207]

1044 Overseas companies

In the Companies Acts an "overseas company" means a company incorporated outside the United Kingdom.

[1.1208]

1045 Company contracts and execution of documents by companies

(1) The Secretary of State may make provision by regulations applying sections 43 to 52 (formalities of doing business and other matters) to overseas companies, subject to such exceptions, adaptations or modifications as may be specified in the regulations.

(2) Regulations under this section are subject to negative resolution procedure.

NOTES

Regulations: the Overseas Companies (Execution of Documents and Registration of Charges) Regulations 2009, SI 2009/1917 at **[4.326]**. For a summary of all statutory instruments made under this Act, see Appendix 4 at **[A4]**.

Registration of particulars

[1.1209]

1046 Duty to register particulars

(1) The Secretary of State may make provision by regulations requiring an overseas company—

(a) to deliver to the registrar for registration a return containing specified particulars, and

(b) to deliver to the registrar with the return specified documents.

(2) The regulations—

(a) must, in the case of a company other than a Gibraltar company, require the company to register particulars if the company opens a branch in the United Kingdom, and

(b) may, in the case of a Gibraltar company, require the company to register particulars if the company opens a branch in the United Kingdom, and

(c) may, in any case, require the registration of particulars in such other circumstances as may be specified.

(3) In subsection (2)—

"branch" means a branch within the meaning of the Eleventh Company Law Directive (89/666/EEC);

"Gibraltar company" means a company incorporated in Gibraltar.

(4) The regulations may provide that where a company has registered particulars under this section and any alteration is made—

(a) in the specified particulars, or

(b) in any document delivered with the return,

the company must deliver to the registrar for registration a return containing specified particulars of the alteration.

(5) The regulations may make provision—

(a) requiring the return under this section to be delivered for registration to the registrar for a specified part of the United Kingdom, and

(b) requiring it to be so delivered before the end of a specified period.

(6) The regulations may make different provision according to—

(a) the place where the company is incorporated, and

(b) the activities carried on (or proposed to be carried on) by it.

This is without prejudice to the general power to make different provision for different cases.

(7) In this section "specified" means specified in the regulations.

(8) Regulations under this section are subject to affirmative resolution procedure.

NOTES

Regulations: the Overseas Companies Regulations 2009, SI 2009/1801 at **[4.216]**. For a summary of all statutory instruments made under this Act, see Appendix 4 at **[A4]**.

[1.1210]

1047 Registered name of overseas company

(1) Regulations under section 1046 (duty to register particulars) must require an overseas company that is required to register particulars to register its name.

(2) This may be—

(a) the company's corporate name (that is, its name under the law of the country or territory in which it is incorporated) or

(b) an alternative name specified in accordance with section 1048.

(3) . . .

(4) . . . the following provisions of Part 5 (a company's name) apply in relation to the registration of the name of an overseas company—

(a) section 53 (prohibited names);

(b) sections 54 to 56 (sensitive words and expressions);

[(ba) section 57 (permitted characters etc);]

(c) section 65 (inappropriate use of indications of company type or legal form);

(d) sections 66 to 74 (similarity to other names);

(e) section 75 (provision of misleading information etc);

(f) section 76 (misleading indication of activities).

(5) . . .

(6) Any reference in the provisions mentioned in subsection (4) . . . to a change of name shall be read as a reference to registration of a different name under section 1048.

NOTES

Sub-ss (3) and (5) were repealed, sub-s (4)(ba) was inserted, and the words omitted from sub-ss (4) and (6) were repealed, by the Companies, Limited Liability Partnerships and Partnerships (Amendment etc) (EU Exit) Regulations 2019, SI 2019/348, reg 6, Sch 1, paras 1, 14, as from IP completion day (as defined in the European Union (Withdrawal Agreement) Act 2020, s 39).

Regulations: the Overseas Companies Regulations 2009, SI 2009/1801 at **[4.216]**. For a summary of all statutory instruments made under this Act, see Appendix 4 at **[A4]**.

[1.1211]

1048 Registration under alternative name

(1) An overseas company that is required to register particulars under section 1046 may at any time deliver to the registrar for registration a statement specifying a name, other than its corporate name, under which it proposes to carry on business in the United Kingdom.

(2) An overseas company that has registered an alternative name may at any time deliver to the registrar of companies for registration a statement specifying a different name under which it proposes to carry on business in the United Kingdom (which may be its corporate name or a further alternative) in substitution for the name previously registered.

(3) The alternative name for the time being registered under this section is treated for all purposes of the law applying in the United Kingdom as the company's corporate name.

(4) This does not—

(a) affect the references in this section or section 1047 to the company's corporate name,

(b) affect any rights or obligation of the company, or

(c) render defective any legal proceedings by or against the company.

(5) Any legal proceedings that might have been continued or commenced against the company by its corporate name, or any name previously registered under this section, may be continued or commenced against it by its name for the time being so registered.

Other requirements

[1.1212]

1049 Accounts and reports: general

(1) The Secretary of State may make provision by regulations requiring an overseas company that is required to register particulars under section 1046—

(a) to prepare the like accounts [and strategic report] and directors' report, and

(b) to cause to be prepared such an auditor's report,

as would be required if the company were formed and registered under this Act.

(2) The regulations may for this purpose apply, with or without modifications, all or any of the provisions of—

Part 15 (accounts and reports), and

Part 16 (audit).

(3) The Secretary of State may make provision by regulations requiring an overseas company to deliver to the registrar copies of—

(a) the accounts and reports prepared in accordance with the regulations, or

(b) the accounts and reports that it is required to prepare and have audited under the law of the country in which it is incorporated.

(4) Regulations under this section are subject to negative resolution procedure.

NOTES

Sub-s (1): words in square brackets in para (a) inserted by the Companies Act 2006 (Strategic Report and Directors' Report) Regulations 2013, SI 2013/1970, reg 14, Schedule, paras 1, 24, in respect of financial years ending on or after 30 September 2013.

Regulations: the Overseas Companies Regulations 2009, SI 2009/1801 at **[4.216]**; the Companies etc (Filing Requirements) (Temporary Modifications) Regulations 2020, SI 2020/645 at **[4.681]**). For a summary of all statutory instruments made under this Act, see Appendix 4 at **[A4]**.

[1.1213]

1050 Accounts and reports: credit or financial institutions

(1) This section applies to a credit or financial institution—

(a) that is incorporated or otherwise formed outside the United Kingdom and Gibraltar,

(b) whose head office is outside the United Kingdom and Gibraltar, and

(c) that has a branch in the United Kingdom.

(2) In subsection (1) "branch" means a place of business that forms a legally dependent part of the institution and conducts directly all or some of the operations inherent in its business.

(3) The Secretary of State may make provision by regulations requiring an institution to which this section applies—

(a) to prepare the like accounts [and strategic report] and directors' report, and

(b) to cause to be prepared such an auditor's report,

as would be required if the institution were a company formed and registered under this Act.

(4) The regulations may for this purpose apply, with or without modifications, all or any of the provisions of—

Part 15 (accounts and reports), and

Part 16 (audit).

(5) The Secretary of State may make provision by regulations requiring an institution to which this section applies to deliver to the registrar copies of—

(a) accounts and reports prepared in accordance with the regulations, or

(b) accounts and reports that it is required to prepare and have audited under the law of the country in which the institution has its head office.

(6) Regulations under this section are subject to negative resolution procedure.

NOTES

Sub-s (3): words in square brackets in para (a) inserted by the Companies Act 2006 (Strategic Report and Directors' Report) Regulations 2013, SI 2013/1970, reg 14, Schedule, paras 1, 25, in respect of financial years ending on or after 30 September 2013.

Regulations: the Overseas Companies Regulations 2009, SI 2009/1801 at **[4.216]**; the Companies etc (Filing Requirements) (Temporary Modifications) Regulations 2020, SI 2020/645 at **[4.681]**. For a summary of all statutory instruments made under this Act, see Appendix 4 at **[A4]**.

[1.1214]

1051 Trading disclosures

(1) The Secretary of State may by regulations make provision requiring overseas companies carrying on business in the United Kingdom—

(a) to display specified information in specified locations,

(b) to state specified information in specified descriptions of document or communication, and

(c) to provide specified information on request to those they deal with in the course of their business.

(2) The regulations—

(a) shall in every case require a company that has registered particulars under section 1046 to disclose the name registered by it under section 1047, and

(b) may make provision as to the manner in which any specified information is to be displayed, stated or provided.

(3) The regulations may make provision corresponding to that made by—

section 83 (civil consequences of failure to make required disclosure), and

section 84 (criminal consequences of failure to make required disclosure).

(4) In this section "specified" means specified in the regulations.

(5) Regulations under this section are subject to affirmative resolution procedure.

NOTES

Regulations: the Overseas Companies Regulations 2009, SI 2009/1801 at **[4.216]**. For a summary of all statutory instruments made under this Act, see Appendix 4 at **[A4]**.

[1.1215]

1052 Company charges

(1) The Secretary of State may by regulations make provision about the registration of specified charges over property in the United Kingdom of a registered overseas company.

(2) The power in subsection (1) includes power to make provision about—

(a) a registered overseas company that—

(i) has particulars registered in more than one part of the United Kingdom;

(ii) has property in more than one part of the United Kingdom;

(b) the circumstances in which property is to be regarded, for the purposes of the regulations, as being, or not being, in the United Kingdom or in a particular part of the United Kingdom;

(c) the keeping by a registered overseas company of records and registers about specified charges and their inspection;

(d) the consequences of a failure to register a charge in accordance with the regulations;

(e) the circumstances in which a registered overseas company ceases to be subject to the regulations.

(3) The regulations may for this purpose apply, with or without modifications, any of the provisions of Part 25 (company charges).

(4) The regulations may modify any reference in an enactment to Part 25, or to a particular provision of that Part, so as to include a reference to the regulations or to a specified provision of the regulations.

(5) Regulations under this section are subject to negative resolution procedure.

(6) In this section—

"registered overseas company" means an overseas company that has registered particulars under section 1046(1), and

"specified" means specified in the regulations.

NOTES

Regulations: the Overseas Companies (Execution of Documents and Registration of Charges) Regulations 2009, SI 2009/1917 at **[4.326]**; the Overseas Companies (Execution of Documents and Registration of Charges) (Amendment) Regulations 2011, SI 2011/2194. For a summary of all statutory instruments made under this Act, see Appendix 4 at **[A4]**.

[1.1216]

1053 Other returns etc

(1) This section applies to overseas companies that are required to register particulars under section 1046.

(2) The Secretary of State may make provision by regulations requiring the delivery to the registrar of returns—

(a) by a company to which this section applies that—

(i) is being wound up, or

(ii) becomes or ceases to be subject to insolvency proceedings, or an arrangement or composition or any analogous proceedings;

(b) by the liquidator of a company to which this section applies.

(3) The regulations may specify—

(a) the circumstances in which a return is to be made,

(b) the particulars to be given in it, and

(c) the period within which it is to be made.

(4) The Secretary of State may make provision by regulations requiring notice to be given to the registrar of the appointment in relation to a company to which this section applies of a judicial factor (in Scotland).

(5) The regulations may include provision corresponding to any provision made by section 1154 of this Act (duty to notify registrar of certain appointments).

(6) Regulations under this section are subject to affirmative resolution procedure.

NOTES

Regulations: the Overseas Companies Regulations 2009, SI 2009/1801 at **[4.216]**. For a summary of all statutory instruments made under this Act, see Appendix 4 at **[A4]**.

Supplementary

[1.1217]

1054 Offences

(1) Regulations under this Part may specify the person or persons responsible for complying with any specified requirement of the regulations.

(2) Regulations under this Part may make provision for offences, including provision as to—

(a) the person or persons liable in the case of any specified contravention of the regulations, and

(b) circumstances that are, or are not, to be a defence on a charge of such an offence.

(3) The regulations must not provide—

(a) for imprisonment, or

(b) for the imposition on summary conviction of a fine exceeding level 5 on the standard scale and, for continued contravention, a daily default fine not exceeding [one-tenth of the greater of £5,000 or level 4 on the standard scale].

(4) In this section "specified" means specified in the regulations.

NOTES

Sub-s (5): words in square brackets substituted (for the original words "one-tenth of level 5 on the standard scale") by the Legal Aid, Sentencing and Punishment of Offenders Act 2012 (Fines on Summary Conviction) Regulations 2015, SI 2015/664, regs 3, 5, Sch 3, Pt 1, para 9(1), (13), as from 12 March 2015, in relation to England and Wales only (except in relation to (a) fines for offences committed before 12 March 2015, (b) the operation of restrictions on fines that may be imposed on a person aged under 18, or (c) fines that may be imposed on a person convicted by a magistrates' court who is to be sentenced as if convicted on indictment). Note also that this amendment does not authorise the alteration of a fine or maximum fine that applies in respect of an offence that is, immediately before 12 March 2015, contained in an instrument made under the legislation amended (whether or not the instrument is in force).

Regulations: the Overseas Companies Regulations 2009, SI 2009/1801 at **[4.216]**. For a summary of all statutory instruments made under this Act, see Appendix 4 at **[A4]**.

[1.1218]

1055 Disclosure of individual's residential address: protection from disclosure

Where regulations under section 1046 (overseas companies: duty to register particulars) require an overseas company to register particulars of an individual's usual residential address, they must contain provision corresponding to that made by Chapter 8 of Part 10 (directors' residential addresses: protection from disclosure).

NOTES

Regulations under s 1046: see that section at **[1.1209]**.

[1.1219]

1056 Requirement to identify persons authorised to accept service of documents

Regulations under section 1046 (overseas companies: duty to register particulars) must require an overseas company to register—

(a) particulars identifying every person resident in the United Kingdom authorised to accept service of documents on behalf of the company, or
(b) a statement that there is no such person.

NOTES

Regulations under s 1046: see that section at **[1.1209]**.

[1.1220]

1057 Registrar to whom returns, notices etc to be delivered

(1) This section applies to an overseas company that is required to register or has registered particulars under section 1046 in more than one part of the United Kingdom.

(2) The Secretary of State may provide by regulations that, in the case of such a company, anything authorised or required to be delivered to the registrar under this Part is to be delivered—

(a) to the registrar for each part of the United Kingdom in which the company is required to register or has registered particulars, or
(b) to the registrar for such part or parts of the United Kingdom as may be specified in or determined in accordance with the regulations.

(3) Regulations under this section are subject to negative resolution procedure.

NOTES

Regulations: no Regulations have been made under this section.

[1.1221]

1058 Duty to give notice of ceasing to have registrable presence

(1) The Secretary of State may make provision by regulations requiring an overseas company—

(a) if it has registered particulars following the opening of a branch, in accordance with regulations under section 1046(2)(a) or (b), to give notice to the registrar if it closes that branch;
(b) if it has registered particulars in other circumstances, in accordance with regulations under section 1046(2)(c), to give notice to the registrar if the circumstances that gave rise to the obligation to register particulars cease to obtain.

(2) The regulations must provide for the notice to be given to the registrar for the part of the United Kingdom to which the original return of particulars was delivered.

(3) The regulations may specify the period within which notice must be given.

(4) Regulations under this section are subject to negative resolution procedure.

NOTES

Regulations: the Overseas Companies Regulations 2009, SI 2009/1801 at **[4.216]**. For a summary of all statutory instruments made under this Act, see Appendix 4 at **[A4]**.

[1.1222]

1059 Application of provisions in case of relocation of branch

For the purposes of this Part—

(a) the relocation of a branch from one part of the United Kingdom to another counts as the closing of one branch and the opening of another;
(b) the relocation of a branch within the same part of the United Kingdom does not.

PART 35 THE REGISTRAR OF COMPANIES

[Scheme of this Part

[1.1223]

1059A Scheme of this Part

(1) The scheme of this Part is as follows.

(2) The following provisions apply generally (to the registrar, to any functions of the registrar, or to documents delivered to or issued by the registrar under any enactment, as the case may be)—

sections 1060(1) and (2) and 1061 to 1063 (the registrar),
sections 1068 to 1071 (delivery of documents to the registrar),
sections 1072 to 1076 (requirements for proper delivery),
sections 1080(1), (4) and (5) and 1092 (keeping and production of records),
section 1083 (preservation of original documents),
[section 1084A (recording optional information on register)]
sections 1108 to 1110 (language requirements: transliteration),
sections 1111 and 1114 to 1119 (supplementary provisions).

(3) The following provisions apply in relation to companies (to companies or for the purposes of the Companies Acts, as the case may be)—

section 1060(3) and (4) (references to the registrar in the Companies Acts),
sections 1064 and 1065 (certificates of incorporation),
section 1066 (companies' registered numbers),
sections 1077 to [1079A (public notice of certain information)],
sections 1080(2) and (3), 1081, 1082 and 1084 (the register),
sections 1085 to 1091 (inspection of the register),
sections 1093 to 1098 (correction or removal of material on the register),
section 1106 (voluntary filing of translations),
sections 1112 and 1113 (supplementary provisions).

(4) The following provisions apply as indicated in the provisions concerned—

section 1067 (registered numbers of UK establishments of overseas companies),
sections 1099 to 1101 (the registrar's index of company names),
sections 1102 to 1105 and 1107 (language requirements: translation).

(5) Unless the context otherwise requires, the provisions of this Part apply to an overseas company as they apply to a company as defined in section 1.]

NOTES

Inserted, together with the preceding heading, by the Companies Act 2006 (Part 35) (Consequential Amendments, Transitional Provisions and Savings) Order 2009, SI 2009/1802, arts 2, 3, as from 1 October 2009.

Sub-s (1): words in square brackets inserted by the Small Business, Enterprise and Employment Act 2015, s 95(2), as from 26 May 2015.

Sub-s (3): words in square brackets substituted by the Companies Act 2006 (Interconnection of Registers) Order 2014, SI 2014/1557, arts 2, 3, as from 7 July 2014.

The registrar

[1.1224]

1060 The registrar

(1) There shall continue to be—

(a) a registrar of companies for England and Wales,
(b) a registrar of companies for Scotland, and
(c) a registrar of companies for Northern Ireland.

(2) The registrars shall be appointed by the Secretary of State.

(3) In the Companies Acts "the registrar of companies" and "the registrar" mean the registrar of companies for England and Wales, Scotland or Northern Ireland, as the case may require.

(4) References in the Companies Acts to registration in a particular part of the United Kingdom are to registration by the registrar for that part of the United Kingdom.

[1.1225]

1061 The registrar's functions

(1) The registrar shall continue—

[(a) to perform the functions conferred on the registrar by or under the Companies Acts or any other enactment, and]
(b) to perform such functions on behalf of the Secretary of State, in relation to the registration of companies or other matters, as the Secretary of State may from time to time direct.

(2) . . .

(3) References in this Act to the functions of the registrar are to functions within subsection (1)(a) or (b).

NOTES

Sub-s (1): para (a) substituted by the Companies Act 2006 (Part 35) (Consequential Amendments, Transitional Provisions and Savings) Order 2009, SI 2009/1802, arts 2, 4(a), as from 1 October 2009.

Sub-s (2): repealed by SI 2009/1802, arts 2, 4(b), as from 1 October 2009.

[1.1226]

1062 The registrar's official seal

The registrar shall have an official seal for the authentication of documents in connection with the performance of the registrar's functions.

[1.1227]

1063 Fees payable to registrar

(1) The Secretary of State may make provision by regulations requiring the payment to the registrar of fees in respect of—

(a) the performance of any of the registrar's functions, or

(b) the provision by the registrar of services or facilities for purposes incidental to, or otherwise connected with, the performance of any of the registrar's functions.

(2) The matters for which fees may be charged include—

(a) the performance of a duty imposed on the registrar or the Secretary of State,

(b) the receipt of documents delivered to the registrar, and

(c) the inspection, or provision of copies, of documents kept by the registrar.

(3) The regulations may—

(a) provide for the amount of the fees to be fixed by or determined under the regulations;

(b) provide for different fees to be payable in respect of the same matter in different circumstances;

(c) specify the person by whom any fee payable under the regulations is to be paid;

(d) specify when and how fees are to be paid.

(4) Regulations under this section are subject to negative resolution procedure.

(5) In respect of the performance of functions or the provision of services or facilities—

(a) for which fees are not provided for by regulations, or

(b) in circumstances other than those for which fees are provided for by regulations,

the registrar may determine from time to time what fees (if any) are chargeable.

(6) Fees received by the registrar are to be paid into the Consolidated Fund.

(7) *(Amends the Limited Partnerships Act 1907, ss 16, 17 at* **[9.72]**, **[9.73]**.)

NOTES

Regulations: the Registrar of Companies (Fees) (Limited Partnerships and Newspaper Proprietors) Regulations 2009, SI 2009/2392 at **[4.370]**; the Registrar of Companies (Fees) (Limited Partnerships) (Amendment) Regulations 2011, SI 2011/319; the Registrar of Companies (Fees) (Companies, Overseas Companies and Limited Liability Partnerships) Regulations 2012, SI 2012/1907 at **[4.452]**; the Registrar of Companies (Fees) (European Economic Interest Grouping and European Public Limited-Liability Company) Regulations 2012, SI 2012/1908 at **[4.470]**; the Registrar of Companies (Fees) (Amendment) Regulations 2016, SI 2016/621. Note also that the Companies Act 2006 (Commencement No 8, Transitional Provisions and Savings) Order 2008, SI 2008/2860, Sch 2, para 94 (fees payable to registrar) provides that any Regulations under s 708 of the 1985 Act (fees payable to registrar) that are in force immediately before 1 October 2009 have effect on or after that date as if made under this section (see the Open-Ended Investment Companies (Investment Companies with Variable Capital) (Fees) Regulations 1998, SI 1998/3087, and the Companies (Fees) Regulations 2004, SI 2004/2621). Note also that the Limited Liability Partnerships (Application of Companies Act 2006) Regulations 2009, SI 2009/1804, Sch 1, Pt 9, para 36 at **[10.417]** provides that any Regulations made s 708 of the 1985 Act (as it applies to LLPs) that are in force immediately before that date also have effect, on or after that date, as if made under this section (see the Limited Liability Partnerships (Fees) Regulations 2004, SI 2004/2620). For a summary of all statutory instruments made under this Act, see Appendix 4 at **[A4]**.

Certificates of incorporation

[1.1228]

1064 Public notice of issue of certificate of incorporation

(1) The registrar must cause to be published—

(a) in the Gazette, or

(b) in accordance with section 1116 (alternative means of giving public notice),

notice of the issue by the registrar of any certificate of incorporation of a company.

(2) The notice must state the name and registered number of the company and the date of issue of the certificate.

(3) This section applies to a certificate of incorporation issued under—

(a) section 80 (change of name),

(b) section 88 (Welsh companies), or

(c) any provision of Part 7 (re-registration),

as well as to the certificate issued on a company's formation.

[1.1229]

1065 Right to certificate of incorporation

Any person may require the registrar to provide him with a copy of any certificate of incorporation of a company, signed by the registrar or authenticated by the registrar's seal.

Registered numbers

[1.1230]

1066 Company's registered numbers

(1) The registrar shall allocate to every company a number, which shall be known as the company's registered number.

(2) Companies' registered numbers shall be in such form, consisting of one or more sequences of figures or letters, as the registrar may determine.

(3) The registrar may on adopting a new form of registered number make such changes of existing registered numbers as appear necessary.

(4) A change of a company's registered number has effect from the date on which the company is notified by the registrar of the change.

(5) For a period of three years beginning with that date any requirement to disclose the company's registered number imposed by regulations under section 82 or section 1051 (trading disclosures) is satisfied by the use of either the old number or the new.

(6) In this section "company" includes an overseas company whose particulars have been registered under section 1046, other than a company that appears to the registrar not to be required to register particulars under that section.

[1.1231]

1067 Registered numbers of [UK establishments] of overseas company

(1) The registrar shall allocate to every [UK establishment] of an overseas company whose particulars are registered under section 1046 a number, which shall be known as [the UK establishment's registered number].

(2) [The registered numbers of UK establishments of overseas companies] shall be in such form, consisting of one or more sequences of figures or letters, as the registrar may determine.

(3) The registrar may on adopting a new form of registered number make such changes of existing registered numbers as appear necessary.

(4) A change of [the registered number of a UK establishment] has effect from the date on which the company is notified by the registrar of the change.

(5) For a period of three years beginning with that date any requirement to disclose [the UK establishment's registered number] imposed by regulations under section 1051 (trading disclosures) is satisfied by the use of either the old number or the new.

[(6) In this Part "establishment", in relation to an overseas company, means—

(a) a branch within the meaning of the Eleventh Company Law Directive (89/666/EEC), or

(b) a place of business that is not such a branch,

and "UK establishment" means an establishment in the United Kingdom.]

NOTES

All amendments to this section were made by the Companies Act 2006 (Part 35) (Consequential Amendments, Transitional Provisions and Savings) Order 2009, SI 2009/1802, arts 2, 5, as from 1 October 2009.

Delivery of documents to the registrar

[1.1232]

1068 Registrar's requirements as to form, authentication and manner of delivery

(1) The registrar may impose requirements as to the form, authentication and manner of delivery of documents required or authorised to be delivered to the registrar under any enactment.

(2) As regards the form of the document, the registrar may—

(a) require the contents of the document to be in a standard form;

(b) impose requirements for the purpose of enabling the document to be scanned or copied.

(3) As regards authentication, the registrar may—

(a) require the document to be authenticated by a particular person or a person of a particular description;

(b) specify the means of authentication;

[(c) require the document to contain or be accompanied by the name or registered number (or both) of the company (or other body) to which it relates.]

(4) As regards the manner of delivery, the registrar may specify requirements as to—

(a) the physical form of the document (for example, hard copy or electronic form);

(b) the means to be used for delivering the document (for example, by post or electronic means);

(c) the address to which the document is to be sent;

(d) in the case of a document to be delivered by electronic means, the hardware and software to be used, and technical specifications (for example, matters relating to protocol, security, anti-virus protection or encryption).

(5) The registrar must secure that [an enhanced disclosure document] (see section 1078) may be delivered to the registrar by electronic means.

(6) The power conferred by this section does not authorise the registrar to require documents to be delivered by electronic means (see section 1069).

[(6A) But the power conferred by this section does authorise the registrar to require any document permitted or required to be delivered to the registrar under Chapter 2A of Part 8 (option to keep membership information on central register) [or Chapter 4 of Part 21A (option to keep PSC information on central register)] to be delivered by electronic means.]

(7) Requirements imposed under this section must not be inconsistent with requirements imposed by any enactment with respect to the form, authentication or manner of delivery of the document concerned.

NOTES

Sub-s (3): para (c) substituted by the Companies Act 2006 (Part 35) (Consequential Amendments, Transitional Provisions and Savings) Order 2009, SI 2009/1802, arts 2, 6, as from 1 October 2009.

Sub-s (5): words in square brackets substituted by the Companies, Limited Liability Partnerships and Partnerships (Amendment etc) (EU Exit) Regulations 2019, SI 2019/348, reg 6, Sch 1, paras 1, 15, as from IP completion day (as defined in the European Union (Withdrawal Agreement) Act 2020, s 39).

Sub-s (6A): inserted by the Small Business, Enterprise and Employment Act 2015, s 94, Sch 5, Pt 2, paras 11, 30, as from 30 June 2016. Words in square brackets inserted by s 81 of, and Sch 3, Pt 2, paras 3, 7 to, the 2015 Act, as from the same date.

[1.1233]

1069 Power to require delivery by electronic means

(1) The Secretary of State may make regulations requiring documents that are authorised or required to be delivered to the registrar to be delivered by electronic means.

(2) Any such requirement to deliver documents by electronic means is effective only if registrar's rules have been published with respect to the detailed requirements for such delivery.

(3) Regulations under this section are subject to affirmative resolution procedure.

NOTES

Regulations: the Reports on Payments to Governments Regulations 2014, SI 2014/3209; the Register of Overseas Entities (Delivery, Protection and Trust Services) Regulations 2022, SI 2022/870 at **[10.1376]**. For a summary of all statutory instruments made under this Act, see Appendix 4 at **[A4]**.

[1.1234]

1070 Agreement for delivery by electronic means

(1) The registrar may agree with a company [(or other body)] that documents relating to the company [(or other body)] that are required or authorised to be delivered to the registrar—

(a) will be delivered by electronic means, except as provided for in the agreement, and

(b) will conform to such requirements as may be specified in the agreement or specified by the registrar in accordance with the agreement.

(2) An agreement under this section may relate to all or any description of documents to be delivered to the registrar.

(3) Documents in relation to which an agreement is in force under this section must be delivered in accordance with the agreement.

NOTES

Sub-s (1): words in square brackets inserted by the Companies Act 2006 (Part 35) (Consequential Amendments, Transitional Provisions and Savings) Order 2009, SI 2009/1802, arts 2, 7, as from 1 October 2009.

[1.1235]

1071 Document not delivered until received

(1) A document is not delivered to the registrar until it is received by the registrar.

(2) Provision may be made by registrar's rules as to when a document is to be regarded as received.

Requirements for proper delivery

[1.1236]

1072 Requirements for proper delivery

(1) A document delivered to the registrar is not properly delivered unless all the following requirements are met—

(a) the requirements of the provision under which the document is to be delivered to the registrar as regards—

(i) the contents of the document, and

(ii) form, authentication and manner of delivery;

(b) any applicable requirements under—

section 1068 (registrar's requirements as to form, authentication and manner of delivery),

section 1069 (power to require delivery by electronic means), or

section 1070 (agreement for delivery by electronic means);

(c) any requirements of this Part as to the language in which the document is drawn up and delivered or as to its being accompanied on delivery by a certified translation into English;

(d) in so far as it consists of or includes names and addresses, any requirements of this Part as to permitted characters, letters or symbols or as to its being accompanied on delivery by a certificate as to the transliteration of any element;

(e) any applicable requirements under section 1111 (registrar's requirements as to certification or verification);

(f) any requirement of regulations under section 1082 (use of unique identifiers);

(g) any requirements as regards payment of a fee in respect of its receipt by the registrar.

(2) A document that is not properly delivered is treated for the purposes of the provision requiring or authorising it to be delivered as not having been delivered, subject to the provisions of section 1073 (power to accept documents not meeting requirements for proper delivery).

[1.1237]

1073 Power to accept documents not meeting requirements for proper delivery

(1) The registrar may accept (and register) a document that does not comply with the requirements for proper delivery.

(2) A document accepted by the registrar under this section is treated as received by the registrar for the purposes of section 1077 (public notice of receipt of certain documents).

(3) No objection may be taken to the legal consequences of a document's being accepted (or registered) by the registrar under this section on the ground that the requirements for proper delivery were not met.

(4) The acceptance of a document by the registrar under this section does not affect—

(a) the continuing obligation to comply with the requirements for proper delivery, or

(b) subject as follows, any liability for failure to comply with those requirements.

(5) For the purposes of—

(a) section 453 (civil penalty for failure to file accounts and reports), and

(b) any enactment imposing a daily default fine for failure to deliver the document,

the period after the document is accepted does not count as a period during which there is default in complying with the requirements for proper delivery.

(6) But if, subsequently—

(a) the registrar issues a notice under section 1094(4) in respect of the document (notice of administrative removal from the register), and

(b) the requirements for proper delivery are not complied with before the end of the period of 14 days after the issue of that notice,

any subsequent period of default does count for the purposes of those provisions.

[1.1238]

1074 Documents containing unnecessary material

(1) This section applies where a document delivered to the registrar contains unnecessary material.

(2) "Unnecessary material" means material that—

(a) is not necessary in order to comply with an obligation under any enactment, and

(b) is not specifically authorised to be delivered to the registrar.

(3) For this purpose an obligation to deliver a document of a particular description, or conforming to certain requirements, is regarded as not extending to anything that is not needed for a document of that description or, as the case may be, conforming to those requirements.

(4) If the unnecessary material cannot readily be separated from the rest of the document, the document is treated as not meeting the requirements for proper delivery.

(5) If the unnecessary material can readily be separated from the rest of the document, the registrar may register the document either—

(a) with the omission of the unnecessary material, or

(b) as delivered.

[1.1239]

1075 Informal correction of document

(1) A document delivered to the registrar may be corrected by the registrar if it appears to the registrar to be incomplete or internally inconsistent.

(2) This power is exercisable only—

(a) on instructions, and

(b) if [the company (or other body) to which the document relates] has given (and has not withdrawn) its consent to instructions being given under this section.

(3) The following requirements must be met as regards the instructions—

(a) the instructions must be given in response to an enquiry by the registrar;

(b) the registrar must be satisfied that the person giving the instructions is authorised to do so—

(i) by the person by whom the document was delivered, or

(ii) by the company [(or other body)] to which the document relates;

(c) the instructions must meet any requirements of registrar's rules as to—

(i) the form and manner in which they are given, and

(ii) authentication.

(4) [The consent of the company (or other body)] to instructions being given under this section (and any withdrawal of such consent)—

(a) may be in hard copy or electronic form, and

(b) must be notified to the registrar.

(5) This section applies in relation to documents delivered under Part 25 (company charges) by a person other than the company [(or other body)] as if the references to the company [(or other body)] were to the company [(or other body)] or the person by whom the document was delivered.

(6) A document that is corrected under this section is treated, for the purposes of any enactment relating to its delivery, as having been delivered when the correction is made.

(7) The power conferred by this section is not exercisable if the document has been registered under section 1073 (power to accept documents not meeting requirements for proper delivery).

NOTES

All words in square brackets in this section were substituted or inserted by the Companies Act 2006 (Part 35) (Consequential Amendments, Transitional Provisions and Savings) Order 2009, SI 2009/1802, arts 2, 8, as from 1 October 2009.

[1.1240]

1076 Replacement of document not meeting requirements for proper delivery

(1) The registrar may accept a replacement for a document previously delivered that—

(a) did not comply with the requirements for proper delivery, or

(b) contained unnecessary material (within the meaning of section 1074).

(2) A replacement document must not be accepted unless the registrar is satisfied that it is delivered by—

(a) the person by whom the original document was delivered, or

(b) the company [(or other body)] to which the original document relates, and that it complies with the requirements for proper delivery.

(3) The power of the registrar to impose requirements as to the form and manner of delivery includes power to impose requirements as to the identification of the original document and the delivery of the replacement in a form and manner enabling it to be associated with the original.

(4) This section does not apply where the original document was delivered under Part 25 (company charges) (but see [section 859M (rectification of register)]).

NOTES

Sub-s (2): words in square brackets inserted by the Companies Act 2006 (Part 35) (Consequential Amendments, Transitional Provisions and Savings) Order 2009, SI 2009/1802, arts 2, 9, as from 1 October 2009.

Sub-s (4): words in square brackets substituted (for the original words "sections 873 and 888 (rectification of register of charges)") by the Companies Act 2006 (Amendment of Part 25) Regulations 2013, SI 2013/600, reg 5, Sch 2, para 3(1), (3), as from 6 April 2013, in relation to charges created on or after that date (see further the transitional provisions note at **[1.982]**).

Public notice of receipt of certain documents

[1.1241]

1077 Public notice of receipt of certain documents

(1) The registrar must cause to be published—

(a) in the Gazette, or

(b) in accordance with section 1116 (alternative means of giving public notice),

notice of the receipt by the registrar of any document that, on receipt, is [an enhanced disclosure document] (see section 1078).

(2) The notice must state the name and registered number of the company, the description of document and the date of receipt.

(3) The registrar is not required to cause notice of the receipt of a document to be published before the date of incorporation of the company to which the document relates.

NOTES

Sub-s (1): words in square brackets substituted by the Companies, Limited Liability Partnerships and Partnerships (Amendment etc) (EU Exit) Regulations 2019, SI 2019/348, reg 6, Sch 1, paras 1, 16, as from IP completion day (as defined in the European Union (Withdrawal Agreement) Act 2020, s 39).

[1.1242]

1078 [Enhanced disclosure documents]

(1) [The enhanced disclosure documents are as follows]

. . .

(2) In the case of every company—

Constitutional documents

1. The company's memorandum and articles.
2. Any amendment of the company's articles (including every resolution or agreement required to be embodied in or annexed to copies of the company's articles issued by the company).
3. After any amendment of the company's articles, the text of the articles as amended.
4. Any notice of a change of the company's name.

Directors

1. The statement of proposed officers required on formation of the company.
2. Notification of any change among the company's directors.
3. Notification of any change in the particulars of directors required to be delivered to the registrar.

[Accounts and reports etc]

1. All documents required to be delivered to the registrar under section 441 (annual accounts and reports).

[1A. All documents delivered to the registrar under sections 394A(2)(e), 448A(2)(e) and 479A(2)(e) (qualifying subsidiary companies: conditions for exemption from the audit, preparation and filing of individual accounts).]

2. [Any confirmation statement delivered by the company under section 853A].

Registered office

Notification of any change of the company's registered office.

Winding up

1. Copy of any winding-up order in respect of the company.
2. Notice of the appointment of liquidators.
3. Order for the dissolution of a company on a winding up.
4. Return by a liquidator of the final meeting of a company on a winding up.

(3) In the case of a public company—

Share capital

1. Any statement of capital and initial shareholdings.
2. Any return of allotment and the statement of capital accompanying it.
3. Copy of any resolution under section 570 or 571 (disapplication of pre-emption rights).
4. Copy of any report under section 593 or 599 as to the value of a non-cash asset.
5. Statement of capital accompanying notice given under section 625 (notice by company of redenomination of shares).
6. Statement of capital accompanying notice given under section 627 (notice by company of reduction of capital in connection with redenomination of shares).
7. Notice delivered under section 636 (notice of new name of class of shares) or 637 (notice of variation of rights attached to shares).
8. Statement of capital accompanying order delivered under section 649 (order of court confirming reduction of capital).
9. Notification (under section 689) of the redemption of shares and the statement of capital accompanying it.
10. Statement of capital accompanying return delivered under section 708 (notice of cancellation of shares on purchase of own shares) or 730 (notice of cancellation of shares held as treasury shares).
11. Any statement of compliance delivered under section 762 (statement that company meets conditions for issue of trading certificate).

[12. Any statement delivered under section 762(1)(e) (statement of the aggregate amount paid up on shares on account of their nominal value).]

Mergers and divisions

1. Copy of any draft of the terms of a scheme required to be delivered to the registrar under section 906 or 921.
2. Copy of any order under [section 899, 900, 901F or 901J] in respect of a compromise or arrangement to which Part 27 (mergers and divisions of public companies) applies.

[(3A) In the case of a private company which applies to re-register as a public company, the statement delivered under section 94(2)(e) (statement of the aggregate amount paid up on shares on account of their nominal value).]

(4) Where a private company re-registers as a public company (see section 96)—

(a) the last statement of capital relating to the company received by the registrar under any provision of the Companies Acts becomes [an enhanced disclosure document], and

(b) section 1077 (public notice of receipt of certain documents) applies as if the statement had been received by the registrar when the re-registration takes effect.

[(4A) Where a company is required by regulation 14 of the Reports on Payments to Governments Regulations 2014 to deliver to the registrar a report or consolidated report on payments to governments, that report or consolidated report.

(4B) Where a company is required by regulation 15 of the Reports on Payments to Governments Regulations 2014 to deliver to the registrar information on payments to governments which is contained in a report or consolidated report prepared in accordance with equivalent reporting requirements (within the meaning of those Regulations), that information.]

(5) In the case of an overseas company, such particulars, returns and other documents required to be delivered under Part 34 as may be specified by the Secretary of State by regulations.

(6) Regulations under subsection (5) are subject to negative resolution procedure.

NOTES

Section heading: words in square brackets substituted by the Companies, Limited Liability Partnerships and Partnerships (Amendment etc) (EU Exit) Regulations 2019, SI 2019/348, reg 6, Sch 1, paras 1, 17(a), as from IP completion day (as defined in the European Union (Withdrawal Agreement) Act 2020, s 39).

Sub-s (1): words in square brackets substituted, and words omitted repealed, by SI 2019/348, reg 6, Sch 1, paras 1, 17(b), as from IP completion day (as defined in the European Union (Withdrawal Agreement) Act 2020, s 39).

Sub-s (2): para 1A under the heading "Accounts reports and returns" was inserted by the Companies and Limited Liability Partnerships (Accounts and Audit Exemptions and Change of Accounting Framework) Regulations 2012, SI 2012/2301, regs 2, 19, as from 1 October 2012 (in relation to accounts for financial years ending on or after that date). Other words in square brackets substituted by the Small Business, Enterprise and Employment Act 2015, s 93(1), (5), as from 30 June 2016.

Sub-s (3): para 12 added by the Small Business, Enterprise and Employment Act 2015, s 98(1), (4)(a), as from 30 June 2016. Words "section 899, 900, 901F or 901J" in square brackets substituted by the Corporate Insolvency and Governance Act 2020, s 7, Sch 9, Pt 2, paras 30, 38, as from 26 June 2020.

Sub-s (3A): inserted by the Small Business, Enterprise and Employment Act 2015, s 98(1), (4)(b), as from 30 June 2016.

Sub-s (4): words in square brackets substituted by SI 2019/348, reg 6, Sch 1, paras 1, 17(c), as from IP completion day (as defined in the European Union (Withdrawal Agreement) Act 2020, s 39).

Sub-ss (4A), (4B): inserted by the Reports on Payments to Governments Regulations 2014, SI 2014/3209, reg 20(1), as from 1 December 2014, in relation to a financial year of an undertaking beginning on or after 1 January 2015 (note that this amendment does not apply in relation to a financial year beginning before 1 January 2016 of an undertaking that is a subsidiary undertaking and whose parent undertaking is required to prepare consolidated group accounts in a member State other than the UK).

Regulations: the Overseas Companies Regulations 2009, SI 2009/1801 at **[4.216]**. For a summary of all statutory instruments made under this Act, see Appendix 4 at **[A4]**.

[1.1243]

1079 Effect of failure to give public notice

(1) A company is not entitled to rely against other persons on the happening of any event to which this section applies unless—

(a) the event has been officially notified at the material time, or

(b) the company shows that the person concerned knew of the event at the material time.

(2) The events to which this section applies are—

(a) an amendment of the company's articles,

(b) a change among the company's directors,

(c) (as regards service of any document on the company) a change of the company's registered office,

(d) the making of a winding-up order in respect of the company, or

(e) the appointment of a liquidator in a voluntary winding up of the company.

(3) If the material time falls—

(a) on or before the 15th day after the date of official notification, or

(b) where the 15th day was not a working day, on or before the next day that was,

the company is not entitled to rely on the happening of the event as against a person who shows that he was unavoidably prevented from knowing of the event at that time.

(4) "Official notification" means—

(a) in relation to an amendment of the company's articles, notification in accordance with section 1077 (public notice of receipt by registrar of certain documents) of the amendment and the amended text of the articles;

(b) in relation to anything else stated in [an enhanced disclosure document], notification of that document in accordance with that section;

(c) in relation to the appointment of a liquidator in a voluntary winding up, notification of that event in accordance with section 109 of the Insolvency Act 1986 (c 45) or Article 95 of the Insolvency (Northern Ireland) Order 1989 (SI 1989/2405 (NI 19)).

NOTES

Sub-s (4): words in square brackets substituted by the Companies, Limited Liability Partnerships and Partnerships (Amendment etc) (EU Exit) Regulations 2019, SI 2019/348, reg 6, Sch 1, paras 1, 18, as from IP completion day (as defined in the European Union (Withdrawal Agreement) Act 2020, s 39).

1079A *(S 1079A (Provision of information for publication on European e-Justice portal) originally inserted by the Companies Act 2006 (Interconnection of Registers) Order 2014, SI 2014/1557, arts 2, 5, as from 7 July 2014. Subsequently repealed by the Companies, Limited Liability Partnerships and Partnerships (Amendment etc) (EU Exit) Regulations 2019, SI 2019/348, reg 6, Sch 1, paras 1, 19, as from IP completion day (as defined in the European Union (Withdrawal Agreement) Act 2020, s 39).)*

[Notice of receipt of documents about new directors

[1.1244]

1079B Duty to notify directors

(1) This section applies whenever the registrar registers either of the following documents—

(a) the statement of proposed officers required on formation of a company, or

(b) notice under section 167 or 167D of a person having become a director of a company.

(2) As soon as reasonably practicable after registering the document, the registrar must notify—

(a) in the case of a statement of proposed officers, the person or each person named in the statement as a director of the company, or

(b) in the case of a notice under section 167 or 167D, the person named in the document as having become a director of the company.

(3) The notice must—

(a) state that the person is named in the document as a director of the company, and

(b) include such information relating to the office and duties of a director (or such details of where information of that sort can be found) as the Secretary of State may from time to time direct the registrar to include.

(4) The notice may be sent in hard copy or electronic form to any address for the person that the registrar has received from either the subscribers or the company.]

NOTES

Inserted, together with the preceding heading, by the Small Business, Enterprise and Employment Act 2015, s 101, as from 10 October 2015.

The register

[1.1245]

1080 The register

(1) The registrar shall continue to keep records of—

(a) the information contained in documents delivered to the registrar under any enactment, [and

(b) certificates issued by the registrar under any enactment].

(2) The records relating to companies are referred to collectively in the Companies Acts as "the register".

(3) Information deriving from [an enhanced disclosure document (see section 1078) delivered to the registrar,] must be kept by the registrar in electronic form.

(4) Subject to that, information contained in documents delivered to the registrar may be recorded and kept in any form the registrar thinks fit, provided it is possible to inspect it and produce a copy of it.

This is sufficient compliance with any duty of the registrar to keep, file or register the document or to record the information contained in it.

(5) The records kept by the registrar must be such that information relating to a company [or other registered body] is associated with [that body], in such manner as the registrar may determine, so as to enable all the information relating to [the body] to be retrieved.

NOTES

Sub-s (1): para (b) and the word immediately preceding it were substituted (for the original paras (b), (c)) by the Companies Act 2006 (Part 35) (Consequential Amendments, Transitional Provisions and Savings) Order 2009, SI 2009/1802, arts 2, 10(1), (2), as from 1 October 2009.

Sub-s (3): words in square brackets substituted by the Companies, Limited Liability Partnerships and Partnerships (Amendment etc) (EU Exit) Regulations 2019, SI 2019/348, reg 6, Sch 1, paras 1, 20, as from IP completion day (as defined in the European Union (Withdrawal Agreement) Act 2020, s 39).

Sub-s (5): words in first pair of square brackets inserted, and other words in square brackets substituted, by SI 2009/1802, arts 2, 10(1), (3), as from 1 October 2009.

[1.1246]

1081 Annotation of the register

(1) The registrar must place a note in the register recording—

(a) the date on which a document is delivered to the registrar;

(b) if a document is corrected under section 1075, the nature and date of the correction;

(c) if a document is replaced (whether or not material derived from it is removed), the fact that it has been replaced and the date of delivery of the replacement;

(d) if material is removed—

(i) what was removed (giving a general description of its contents),

(ii) under what power, and

(iii) the date on which that was done;

[(e) if a document is rectified under section 859M, the nature and date of rectification;

(f) if a document is replaced under section 859N, the fact that it has been replaced and the date of delivery of the replacement.]

[(1A) If the registrar registers a document delivered by a company under section 128E that, by virtue of subsection (3)(a), (b) or (c) of that section, does not specify the relevant date, the registrar must place a note in the register recording as that date the date on which the document was registered by the registrar.]

(2) The Secretary of State may make provision by regulations—

(a) authorising or requiring the registrar to annotate the register in such other circumstances as may be specified in the regulations, and

(b) as to the contents of any such annotation.

(3) No annotation is required in the case of a document that by virtue of section 1072(2) (documents not meeting requirements for proper delivery) is treated as not having been delivered.

(4) A note may be removed if it no longer serves any useful purpose.

(5) Any duty or power of the registrar with respect to annotation of the register is subject to the court's power under section 1097 (powers of court on ordering removal of material from the register) to direct—

(a) that a note be removed from the register, or

(b) that no note shall be made of the removal of material that is the subject of the court's order.

(6) Notes placed in the register in accordance with subsection (1) [or (1A)], or in pursuance of regulations under subsection (2), are part of the register for all purposes of the Companies Acts.

(7) Regulations under this section are subject to negative resolution procedure.

NOTES

Sub-s (1): paras (e), (f) inserted by the Companies Act 2006 (Amendment of Part 25) Regulations 2013, SI 2013/600, reg 5, Sch 2, para 3(1), (4), as from 6 April 2013, in relation to charges created on or after that date (see further the transitional provisions note at **[1.982]**).

Sub-s (1A): inserted by the Small Business, Enterprise and Employment Act 2015, s 94, Sch 5, Pt 2, paras 11, 31(1), (2), as from 30 June 2016.

Sub-s (6): words in square brackets substituted by the Small Business, Enterprise and Employment Act 2015, s 94, Sch 5, Pt 2, paras 11, 31(1), (3), as from 30 June 2016.

Regulations: the Registrar of Companies and Applications for Striking Off Regulations 2009, SI 2009/1803 at **[4.317]**. For a summary of all statutory instruments made under this Act, see Appendix 4 at **[A4]**.

[1.1247]

1082 Allocation of unique identifiers

(1) The Secretary of State may make provision for the use, in connection with the register, of reference numbers ("unique identifiers") to identify each person who—

(a) is a director of a company,

(b) is secretary (or a joint secretary) of a company, or

(c) in the case of an overseas company whose particulars are registered under section 1046, holds any such position as may be specified for the purposes of this section by regulations under that section.

(2) The regulations may—

(a) provide that a unique identifier may be in such form, consisting of one or more sequences of letters or numbers, as the registrar may from time to time determine;

(b) make provision for the allocation of unique identifiers by the registrar;

(c) require there to be included, in any specified description of documents delivered to the registrar, as well as a statement of the person's name—

(i) a statement of the person's unique identifier, or

(ii) a statement that the person has not been allocated a unique identifier;

(d) enable the registrar to take steps where a person appears to have more than one unique identifier to discontinue the use of all but one of them.

(3) The regulations may contain provision for the application of the scheme in relation to persons appointed, and documents registered, before the commencement of this Act.

(4) The regulations may make different provision for different descriptions of person and different descriptions of document.

(5) Regulations under this section are subject to affirmative resolution procedure.

NOTES

Regulations: no Regulations have been made under this section.

[1.1248]

1083 Preservation of original documents

(1) The originals of documents delivered to the registrar in hard copy form must be kept for three years after they are received by the registrar, after which they may be destroyed provided the information contained in them has been [recorded].

This is subject to section 1087(3) (extent of obligation to retain material not available for public inspection).

(2) The registrar is under no obligation to keep the originals of documents delivered in electronic form, provided the information contained in them has been [recorded].

(3) This section applies to documents held by the registrar when this section comes into force as well as to documents subsequently received.

NOTES

Sub-ss (1), (2): words in square brackets substituted by the Companies Act 2006 (Part 35) (Consequential Amendments, Transitional Provisions and Savings) Order 2009, SI 2009/1802, arts 2, 11, as from 1 October 2009.

[1.1249]

1084 Records relating to companies that have been dissolved etc

(1) This section applies where—

(a) a company is dissolved,

(b) an overseas company ceases to have any connection with the United Kingdom by virtue of which it is required to register particulars under section 1046, or

(c) a credit or financial institution ceases to be within section 1050 (overseas institutions required to file accounts with the registrar).

(2) At any time after two years from the date on which it appears to the registrar that—

(a) the company has been dissolved,

(b) the overseas company has ceased to have any connection with the United Kingdom by virtue of which it is required to register particulars under section 1046, or

(c) the credit or financial institution has ceased to be within section 1050 (overseas institutions required to file accounts with the registrar),

the registrar may direct that records relating to the company or institution may be removed to the Public Record Office or, as the case may be, the Public Record Office of Northern Ireland.

(3) Records in respect of which such a direction is given shall be disposed of under the enactments relating to that Office and the rules made under them.

(4) In subsection (1)(a) "company" includes a company provisionally or completely registered under the Joint Stock Companies Act 1844 (c 110).

[(4A) This section has effect subject to section 1087ZA (required particulars available for public inspection for limited period).]

(5) This section does not extend to Scotland.

NOTES

Sub-s (4A): inserted by the Money Laundering and Terrorist Financing (Amendment) Regulations 2019, SI 2019/1511, reg 16(1), (3), as from 10 January 2020.

[1.1250]

[1084A Recording of optional information on register

(1) The Secretary of State may make provision by regulations authorising a company or other body to deliver optional information of a prescribed description to the registrar.

(2) In this section "optional information", in relation to a company or other body, means information about the company or body which, but for the regulations, the company or body would not be obliged or authorised under any enactment to deliver to the registrar.

(3) The regulations may, in particular, include provision—

- (a) imposing requirements on a company or other body in relation to keeping any of its optional information recorded on the register up to date;
- (b) about the consequences of a company or other body failing to do so.

(4) Regulations under this section are subject to affirmative resolution procedure.]

NOTES

Inserted by the Small Business, Enterprise and Employment Act 2015, s 95(1), as from 26 May 2015.

Inspection etc of the register

[1.1251]

1085 Inspection of the register

(1) Any person may inspect the register.

(2) The right of inspection extends to the originals of documents delivered to the registrar in hard copy form if, and only if, the record kept by the registrar of the contents of the document is illegible or unavailable.

The period for which such originals are to be kept is limited by section 1083(1).

(3) This section has effect subject to section 1087 (material not available for public inspection) [and section 1087ZA (required particulars available for public inspection for limited period)].

NOTES

Sub-s (3): words in square brackets inserted by the Money Laundering and Terrorist Financing (Amendment) Regulations 2019, SI 2019/1511, reg 16(1), (4), as from 10 January 2020.

[1.1252]

1086 Right to copy of material on the register

(1) Any person may require a copy of any material on the register.

(2) The fee for any such copy of material derived from [an enhanced disclosure document] (see section 1078), whether in hard copy or electronic form, must not exceed the administrative cost of providing it.

(3) This section has effect subject to section 1087 (material not available for public inspection) [and section 1087ZA (required particulars available for public inspection for limited period)].

NOTES

Sub-s (2): words in square brackets substituted by the Companies, Limited Liability Partnerships and Partnerships (Amendment etc) (EU Exit) Regulations 2019, SI 2019/348, reg 6, Sch 1, paras 1, 21, as from IP completion day (as defined in the European Union (Withdrawal Agreement) Act 2020, s 39).

Sub-s (3): words in square brackets inserted by the Money Laundering and Terrorist Financing (Amendment) Regulations 2019, SI 2019/1511, reg 16(1), (5), as from 10 January 2020.

[1.1253]

1087 Material not available for public inspection

(1) The following material must not be made available by the registrar for public inspection—

- (a) the contents of any document sent to the registrar containing views expressed pursuant to section 56 (comments on proposal by company to use certain words or expressions in company name);
- (b) protected information within section 242(1) (directors' residential addresses: restriction on disclosure by registrar) or any corresponding provision of regulations under section 1046 (overseas companies);
- [(ba) representations received by the registrar in response to a notice under—
  - (i) section 245(2) (notice of proposal to put director's usual residential address on the public record), or
  - (ii) any corresponding provision of regulations under section 1046 (overseas companies);]
- [(bb) information to which sections 240 to 244 are applied by section 790ZF(1) (residential addresses of people with significant control over the company) or any corresponding provision of regulations under section 1046 (overseas companies);
- (bc) information that, by virtue of regulations under section 790ZG or any corresponding provision of regulations under section 1046, the registrar must omit from the material on the register that is available for inspection;]
- (c) any application to the registrar under section 1024 (application for administrative restoration to the register) that has not yet been determined or was not successful;
- (d) any document received by the registrar in connection with the giving or withdrawal of consent under section 1075 (informal correction of documents);

[(da) information falling within section 1087A(1) (information about a person's date of birth);]

(e) any application or other document delivered to the registrar under section 1088 (application to make address unavailable for public inspection) and any address in respect of which such an application is successful;

(f) any application or other document delivered to the registrar under section 1095 (application for rectification of register);

(g) any court order under section 1096 (rectification of the register under court order) that the court has directed under section 1097 (powers of court on ordering removal of material from the register) is not to be made available for public inspection;

[(ga) any application or other document delivered to the registrar under section 1097A (rectification of company registered office) other than an order or direction of the court;]

[(h) the contents of—

(i) any instrument creating or evidencing a charge, or

(ii) any certified or verified copy of an instrument creating or evidencing a charge,

delivered to the registrar under Part 25 (company charges) or regulations under section 1052 (overseas companies);]

(i) any e-mail address, identification code or password deriving from a document delivered for the purpose of authorising or facilitating electronic filing procedures or providing information by telephone;

[(j) the contents of any documents held by the registrar pending a decision of the Regulator of Community Interest Companies under—

(i) section 36A of the Companies (Audit, Investigations and Community Enterprise) Act 2004 (eligibility for registration as community interest company),

(ii) section 38 of that Act (eligibility for conversion to community interest company), or

(iii) section 55 of that Act (eligibility for conversion from community interest company to charity),

and that the registrar is not later required to record;]

(k) any other material excluded from public inspection by or under any other enactment.

(2) A restriction applying by reference to material deriving from a particular description of document does not affect the availability for public inspection of the same information contained in material derived from another description of document in relation to which no such restriction applies.

(3) Material to which this section applies need not be retained by the registrar for longer than appears to the registrar reasonably necessary for the purposes for which the material was delivered to the registrar.

NOTES

Sub-s (1) is amended as follows:

Para (ba) inserted, and para (h) substituted, by the Companies Act 2006 (Part 35) (Consequential Amendments, Transitional Provisions and Savings) Order 2009, SI 2009/1802, arts 2, 12, as from 1 October 2009.

Paras (bb), (bc) inserted by the Small Business, Enterprise and Employment Act 2015, s 81, Sch 3, Pt 2, paras 3, 8, as from 6 April 2016.

Para (da) inserted by s 96(1), (2) of the 2015 Act, as from 10 October 2015. Para (ga) inserted by s 99(2) of the 2015 Act, as from 26 May 2015.

Para (h) subsequently repealed by the Companies Act 2006 (Amendment of Part 25) Regulations 2013, SI 2013/600, reg 5, Sch 2, para 3(1), (5), as from 6 April 2013, in relation to charges created on or after that date (see further the transitional provisions note at **[1.982]**).

Para (j) substituted by the Companies Act 2006 (Consequential Amendments, Transitional Provisions and Savings) Order 2009, SI 2009/1941, art 2(1), Sch 1, para 260(1), (6), as from 1 October 2009.

[1.1254]

[1087ZA Required particulars available for public inspection for limited period

(1) This section applies where—

(a) a notice is given to the registrar by a company under section 790VA (notification of changes to the registrar), or

(a) a document is delivered to the registrar by a company under section 790ZA (duty to notify registrar of changes).

(2) The notice or document, and any record of the information contained in the notice or document, must not be made available by the registrar for public inspection after the expiration of ten years beginning with the date on which the company is dissolved.

(3) The power in section 1084(2) (power of registrar to direct that records of a company that has been dissolved may be removed to the Public Record Office etc) may not be exercised in relation to the notice or document, or any record of the information contained in the notice or document, before the expiration of ten years beginning with the date on which the company is dissolved.

(4) Subsection (2) does not affect the availability for public inspection of the same information contained in material derived from another description of document in relation to which no such restriction applies.]

NOTES

Commencement: 10 January 2020.

Inserted by the Money Laundering and Terrorist Financing (Amendment) Regulations 2019, SI 2019/1511, reg 16(1), (6), as from 10 January 2020.

[1.1255]

[1087A Information about a person's date of birth

(1) Information falls within this subsection at any time ("the relevant time") if—

(a) it is DOB information,

(b) it is contained in a document delivered to the registrar that is protected at the relevant time as regards that information,

(c) the document is one in which such information is required to be stated, and

(d) if the document has more than one part, the part in which the information is contained is a part in which such information is required to be stated.

(2) "DOB information" is information as to the day of the month (but not the month or year) on which a relevant person was born.

(3) A "relevant person" is an individual—

(a) who is a director of a company, or

(b) whose particulars are stated in a company's PSC register as a registrable person in relation to that company (see Part 21A).

(4) A document delivered to the registrar is "protected" at any time unless—

(a) it is an election period document,

(b) subsection (7) applies to it at the time, or

(c) it was registered before this section comes into force.

(5) As regards DOB information about a relevant person in his or her capacity as a director of the company, each of the following is an "election period document"—

(a) a statement of the company's proposed officers delivered under section 9 in circumstances where the subscribers gave notice of election under section 167A (election to keep information on central register) in respect of the company's register of directors when the statement was delivered;

(b) a document delivered by the company under section 167D (duty to notify registrar of changes while election in force).

(6) As regards DOB information about a relevant person in his or her capacity as someone whose particulars are stated in the company's PSC register, each of the following is an "election period document"—

(a) a statement of initial significant control delivered under section 9 in circumstances where the subscribers gave notice of election under section 790X in respect of the company when the statement was delivered;

(b) a document containing a statement or updated statement delivered by the company under section 790X(6)(b) or (7) (statement accompanying notice of election made after incorporation);

(c) a document delivered by the company under section 790ZA (duty to notify registrar of changes while election in force).

(7) This subsection applies to a document if—

(a) the DOB information relates to the relevant person in his or her capacity as a director of the company,

(b) an election under section 167A is or has previously been in force in respect of the company's register of directors,

(c) the document was delivered to the registrar at some point before that election took effect,

(d) the relevant person was a director of the company when that election took effect, and

(e) the document was either—

(i) a statement of proposed officers delivered under section 9 naming the relevant person as someone who was to be a director of the company, or

(ii) notice given under section 167 of the relevant person having become a director of the company.

(8) Information about a person does not cease to fall within subsection (1) when he or she ceases to be a relevant person and, to that extent, references in this section to a relevant person include someone who used to be a relevant person.

(9) Nothing in subsection (1) obliges the registrar to check other documents or (as the case may be) other parts of the document to ensure the absence of DOB information.]

NOTES

Inserted, together with s 1087B, by the Small Business, Enterprise and Employment Act 2015, s 96(1), (3), as from 10 October 2015 (sub-ss (1), (2) (3)(a), (4)(c), (8), (9)), and as from 30 June 2016 (sub-ss (3)(b), (4)(a), (b), (5)–(7)).

[1.1256]

[1087B Disclosure of DOB information

(1) The registrar must not disclose restricted DOB information unless—

(a) the same information about the relevant person (whether in the same or a different capacity) is made available by the registrar for public inspection as a result of being contained in another description of document in relation to which no restriction under section 1087 applies (see subsection (2) of that section), or

(b) disclosure of the information by the registrar is permitted by subsection (2) or another provision of this Act.

(2) The registrar may disclose restricted DOB information—

(a) to a public authority specified for the purposes of this subsection by regulations made by the Secretary of State, or

(b) to a credit reference agency.

(3) Subsections (3) to (8) of section 243 (permitted use or disclosure of directors' residential addresses etc by the registrar) apply for the purposes of subsection (2) as for the purposes of that section (reading references there to protected information as references to restricted DOB information).

(4) This section does not apply to restricted DOB information about a relevant person in his or her capacity as someone whose particulars are stated in the company's PSC register if an application under regulations made under section 790ZG (regulations for protecting PSC particulars) has been granted with respect to that information and not been revoked.

(5) "Restricted DOB information" means information falling within section 1087A(1).]

NOTES

Inserted, together with s 1087A, by the Small Business, Enterprise and Employment Act 2015, s 96(1), (3), as from 26 May 2015 (for the purposes of enabling the exercise of any power to make provision by regulations), as from 10 October 2015 (except for sub-s (4)), and as from 30 June 2016 (sub-s (4)).

Regulations: the Companies (Disclosure of Date of Birth Information) Regulations 2015, SI 2015/1694 at **[4.552]**; the Companies and Limited Liability Partnerships (Filing Requirements) Regulations 2016, SI 2016/599 at **[4.640]**; the

Registrar of Companies (Fees) (Amendment) Regulations 2016, SI 2016/621. For a summary of all statutory instruments made under this Act, see Appendix 4 at **[A4]**.

[1.1257]

1088 Application to registrar to make address unavailable for public inspection

(1) The Secretary of State may make provision by regulations requiring the registrar, on application, to make an address on the register unavailable for public inspection.

(2) The regulations may make provision as to—

(a) who may make an application,

(b) the grounds on which an application may be made,

(c) the information to be included in and documents to accompany an application,

(d) the notice to be given of an application and of its outcome, and

(e) how an application is to be determined.

(3) Provision under subsection (2)(e) may in particular—

(a) confer a discretion on the registrar;

(b) provide for a question to be referred to a person other than the registrar for the purposes of determining the application.

(4) An application must specify the address to be removed from the register and indicate where on the register it is.

(5) The regulations may provide—

(a) that an address is not to be made unavailable for public inspection under this section unless replaced by a service address, and

(b) that in such a case the application must specify a service address.

(6) Regulations under this section are subject to affirmative resolution procedure.

NOTES

Confidentiality orders under the Companies Act 1985: a director or secretary in relation to whom a confidentiality order under CA 1985, s 723B was in force immediately before 1 October 2009 is treated on and after that date as if (a) they had made an application under this section in respect of any address that immediately before that date was contained in "confidential records" as defined in s 723D(3) of the 1985 Act, and (b) that application had been determined by the registrar in their favour. For general transitional provisions in connection with the continuation of protection afforded by confidentiality orders under the 1985 Act, see the Companies Act 2006 (Commencement No 8, Transitional Provisions and Savings) Order 2008, SI 2008/2860, Sch 2, paras 36–39.

Regulations and Orders: the Companies (Disclosure of Address) Regulations 2009, SI 2009/214 at **[4.191]**; the Companies Act 2006 (Consequential Amendments, Transitional Provisions and Savings) Order 2009, SI 2009/1941 at **[4.355]**; the Register of People with Significant Control Regulations 2016, SI 2016/339 at **[4.559]**; the Companies (Disclosure of Address) (Amendment) Regulations 2018, SI 2018/528. For a summary of all statutory instruments made under this Act, see Appendix 4 at **[A4]**.

[1.1258]

1089 Form of application for inspection or copy

(1) The registrar may specify the form and manner in which application is to be made for—

(a) inspection under section 1085, or

(b) a copy under section 1086.

(2) [Applications in respect of an enhanced disclosure document] may be submitted to the registrar in hard copy or electronic form, as the applicant chooses.

This does not affect the registrar's power under subsection (1) above to impose requirements in respect of other matters.

NOTES

Sub-s (2): words in square brackets substituted by the Companies, Limited Liability Partnerships and Partnerships (Amendment etc) (EU Exit) Regulations 2019, SI 2019/348, reg 6, Sch 1, paras 1, 22, as from IP completion day (as defined in the European Union (Withdrawal Agreement) Act 2020, s 39).

[1.1259]

1090 Form and manner in which copies to be provided

(1) The following provisions apply as regards the form and manner in which copies are to be provided under section 1086.

(2) [Copies of an enhanced disclosure document] must be provided in hard copy or electronic form, as the applicant chooses.

This is subject to the following proviso.

(3) The registrar is not obliged by subsection (2) to provide copies in electronic form of a document that was delivered to the registrar in hard copy form if—

(a) the document was delivered to the registrar on or before 31st December 1996, or

(b) the document was delivered to the registrar on or before 31st December 2006 and ten years or more elapsed between the date of delivery and the date of receipt of the first application for a copy on or after 1st January 2007.

(4) Subject to the preceding provisions of this section, the registrar may determine the form and manner in which copies are to be provided.

NOTES

Sub-s (2): words in square brackets substituted by the Companies, Limited Liability Partnerships and Partnerships (Amendment etc) (EU Exit) Regulations 2019, SI 2019/348, reg 6, Sch 1, paras 1, 23, as from IP completion day (as defined in the European Union (Withdrawal Agreement) Act 2020, s 39).

[1.1260]

1091 Certification of copies as accurate

(1) Copies provided under section 1086 in hard copy form must be certified as true copies unless the applicant dispenses with such certification.

(2) Copies so provided in electronic form must not be certified as true copies unless the applicant expressly requests such certification.

(3) A copy provided under section 1086, certified by the registrar (whose official position it is unnecessary to prove) to be an accurate record of the contents of the original document, is in all legal proceedings admissible in evidence—

(a) as of equal validity with the original document, and

(b) as evidence (in Scotland, sufficient evidence) of any fact stated in the original document of which direct oral evidence would be admissible.

(4) The Secretary of State may make provision by regulations as to the manner in which such a certificate is to be provided in a case where the copy is provided in electronic form.

(5) Except in the case of [an enhanced disclosure document] (see section 1078), copies provided by the registrar may, instead of being certified in writing to be an accurate record, be sealed with the registrar's official seal.

NOTES

Sub-s (5): words in square brackets substituted by the Companies, Limited Liability Partnerships and Partnerships (Amendment etc) (EU Exit) Regulations 2019, SI 2019/348, reg 6, Sch 1, paras 1, 24, as from IP completion day (as defined in the European Union (Withdrawal Agreement) Act 2020, s 39).

Regulations: the Companies (Registrar, Languages and Trading Disclosures) Regulations 2006, SI 2006/3429 at **[4.1]**. For a summary of all statutory instruments made under this Act, see Appendix 4 at **[A4]**.

[1.1261]

1092 Issue of process for production of records kept by the registrar

(1) No process for compelling the production of a record kept by the registrar shall issue from any court except with the permission of the court.

(2) Any such process shall bear on it a statement that it is issued with the permission of the court.

Correction or removal of material on the register

[1.1262]

1093 Registrar's notice to resolve inconsistency on the register

(1) Where it appears to the registrar that the information contained in a document delivered to the registrar is inconsistent with other information on the register, the registrar may give notice to the company to which the document relates—

(a) stating in what respects the information contained in it appears to be inconsistent with other information on the register, and

(b) requiring the company to take steps to resolve the inconsistency.

(2) The notice must—

(a) state the date on which it is issued, and

(b) require the delivery to the registrar, within 14 days after that date, of such replacement or additional documents as may be required to resolve the inconsistency.

(3) If the necessary documents are not delivered within the period specified, an offence is committed by—

(a) the company, and

(b) every officer of the company who is in default.

(4) A person guilty of an offence under subsection (3) is liable on summary conviction to a fine not exceeding level 5 on the standard scale and, for continued contravention, a daily default fine not exceeding [one-tenth of the greater of £5,000 or level 4 on the standard scale].

NOTES

Sub-s (4): words in square brackets substituted (for the original words "one-tenth of level 5 on the standard scale") by the Legal Aid, Sentencing and Punishment of Offenders Act 2012 (Fines on Summary Conviction) Regulations 2015, SI 2015/664, regs 3, 5, Sch 3, Pt 1, para 9(1), (23), as from 12 March 2015, in relation to England and Wales only (except in relation to (a) fines for offences committed before 12 March 2015, (b) the operation of restrictions on fines that may be imposed on a person aged under 18, or (c) fines that may be imposed on a person convicted by a magistrates' court who is to be sentenced as if convicted on indictment).

[1.1263]

1094 Administrative removal of material from the register

(1) The registrar may remove from the register anything that there was power, but no duty, to include.

(2) This power is exercisable, in particular, so as to remove—

(a) unnecessary material within the meaning of section 1074, and

(b) material derived from a document that has been replaced under—

section 1076 (replacement of document not meeting requirements for proper delivery), or

section 1093 (notice to remedy inconsistency on the register).

(3) This section does not authorise the removal from the register of—

(a) anything whose registration has had legal consequences in relation to the company as regards—

(i) its formation,

(ii) a change of name,

(iii) its re-registration,

(iv) its becoming or ceasing to be a community interest company,

(v) a reduction of capital,

(vi) a change of registered office,

(vii) the registration of a charge, . . .

(viii) its dissolution[, or]

[(ix) a change in its membership particulars of which were delivered to the registrar under section 128E (duty to notify registrar of changes while election to keep information on central register is in force);]

(b) an address that is a person's registered address for the purposes of section 1140 (service of documents on directors, secretaries and others).

(4) On or before removing any material under this section (otherwise than at the request of the company) the registrar must give notice—

(a) to the person by whom the material was delivered (if the identity, and name and address of that person are known), or

(b) to the company to which the material relates (if notice cannot be given under paragraph (a) and the identity of that company is known).

(5) The notice must—

(a) state what material the registrar proposes to remove, or has removed, and on what grounds, and

(b) state the date on which it is issued.

NOTES

Sub-s (3): word omitted from sub-para (a)(vii) repealed, word in square brackets in sub-para (a)(viii) inserted, and sub-para (a)(ix) added, by the Small Business, Enterprise and Employment Act 2015, s 94, Sch 5, Pt 2, paras 11, 32, as from 30 June 2016.

[1.1264]

1095 Rectification of register on application to registrar

(1) The Secretary of State may make provision by regulations requiring the registrar, on application, to remove from the register material of a description specified in the regulations that—

(a) derives from anything invalid or ineffective or that was done without the authority of the company, or

(b) is factually inaccurate, or is derived from something that is factually inaccurate or forged.

(2) The regulations may make provision as to—

(a) who may make an application,

(b) the information to be included in and documents to accompany an application,

(c) the notice to be given of an application and of its outcome,

(d) a period in which objections to an application may be made, and

(e) how an application is to be determined.

(3) An application must—

(a) specify what is to be removed from the register and indicate where on the register it is, and

(b) be accompanied by a statement that the material specified in the application complies with this section and the regulations.

(4) If no objections are made to the application, the registrar may accept the statement as sufficient evidence that the material specified in the application should be removed from the register.

[(4A) Subsections (4B) and (4C) apply, in place of subsection (4), in a case where—

(a) the material specified in the application is material naming a person—

(i) in a statement of a company's proposed officers as a person who is to be a director of the company, or

(ii) in a notice given by a company under section 167 or 167D as a person who has become a director of the company, and

(b) the application is made by or on behalf of the person named and is accompanied by a statement that the person did not consent to act as director of the company.

(4B) If the company provides the registrar with the necessary evidence within the time required by the regulations, the registrar must not remove the material from the register.

(4C) If the company does not provide the registrar with the necessary evidence within that time—

(a) the material is conclusively presumed for the purposes of this section to be derived from something that is factually inaccurate, and

(b) the registrar must accept the applicant's statement as sufficient evidence that the material should be removed from the register.

(4D) "The necessary evidence" is—

(a) evidence sufficient to satisfy the registrar that the person did consent to act as director of the company, plus

(b) a statement by the company that the evidence provided by it is true and is not misleading or deceptive in any material particular.]

(5) Where anything is removed from the register under this section the registration of which had legal consequences as mentioned in section 1094(3), any person appearing to the court to have a sufficient interest may apply to the court for such consequential orders as appear just with respect to the legal effect (if any) to be accorded to the material by virtue of its having appeared on the register.

(6) Regulations under this section are subject to affirmative resolution procedure.

NOTES

Sub-ss (4A)–(4D): inserted by the Small Business, Enterprise and Employment Act 2015, s 102, as from 6 April 2016.

Regulations: the Registrar of Companies and Applications for Striking Off Regulations 2009, SI 2009/1803 at **[4.317]**; the Registrar of Companies and Applications for Striking Off (Amendment) Regulations 2016, SI 2016/441. For a summary of all statutory instruments made under this Act, see Appendix 4 at **[A4]**.

[1.1265]

[1095A Rectification of register to resolve a discrepancy

(1) This section applies where—

(a) *a discrepancy* in information relating to a company is reported to the registrar under regulation 30A(2) [or (2B)] of the Money Laundering, Terrorist Financing and Transfer of Funds (Information on the Payer) Regulations 2017 (requirement to report discrepancies in information about beneficial ownership), and

(b) the registrar determines, having investigated *the discrepancy* under regulation 30A(5) of those Regulations, that there is *a discrepancy*.

(2) The registrar may remove material from the register if doing so is necessary to resolve the discrepancy.]

NOTES

Commencement: 10 January 2020.

Inserted by the Money Laundering and Terrorist Financing (Amendment) Regulations 2019, SI 2019/1511, reg 16(1), (7), as from 10 January 2020.

Sub-s (1): for the words in italics there are substituted the words "a material discrepancy", and the words "or (2B)" in square brackets are inserted, by the Money Laundering and Terrorist Financing (Amendment) (No 2) Regulations 2022 SI 2022/860, reg 16(a), as from 1 April 2023.

Sub-s (2): the first words in italics are repealed, and for the second words in italics there are substituted the words "a material discrepancy, by SI 2022/860, reg 16(b), as from 1 April 2023.

[1.1266]

1096 Rectification of the register under court order

(1) The registrar shall remove from the register any material—

(a) that derives from anything that the court has declared to be invalid or ineffective, or to have been done without the authority of the company, or

(b) that a court declares to be factually inaccurate, or to be derived from something that is factually inaccurate, or forged,

and that the court directs should be removed from the register.

(2) The court order must specify what is to be removed from the register and indicate where on the register it is.

(3) The court must not make an order for the removal from the register of anything the registration of which had legal consequences as mentioned in section 1094(3) unless satisfied—

(a) that the presence of the material on the register has caused, or may cause, damage to the company, and

(b) that the company's interest in removing the material outweighs any interest of other persons in the material continuing to appear on the register.

(4) Where in such a case the court does make an order for removal, it may make such consequential orders as appear just with respect to the legal effect (if any) to be accorded to the material by virtue of its having appeared on the register.

(5) A copy of the court's order must be sent to the registrar for registration.

(6) This section does not apply where the court has other, specific, powers to deal with the matter, for example under—

(a) the provisions of Part 15 relating to the revision of defective accounts and reports, or

(b) section [859M (rectification of register)].

NOTES

Sub-s (6): words in square brackets substituted (for the original words "873 and 888 (rectification of the register of charges)") by the Companies Act 2006 (Amendment of Part 25) Regulations 2013, SI 2013/600, reg 5, Sch 2, para 3(1), (6), as from 6 April 2013, in relation to charges created on or after that date (see further the transitional provisions note at **[1.982]**).

[1.1267]

1097 Powers of court on ordering removal of material from the register

(1) Where the court makes an order for the removal of anything from the register under section 1096 (rectification of the register), it may give directions under this section.

(2) It may direct that any note on the register that is related to the material that is the subject of the court's order shall be removed from the register.

(3) It may direct that its order shall not be available for public inspection as part of the register.

(4) It may direct—

(a) that no note shall be made on the register as a result of its order, or

(b) that any such note shall be restricted to such matters as may be specified by the court.

(5) The court shall not give any direction under this section unless it is satisfied—

(a) that—

(i) the presence on the register of the note or, as the case may be, of an unrestricted note, or

(ii) the availability for public inspection of the court's order,

may cause damage to the company, and

(b) that the company's interest in non-disclosure outweighs any interest of other persons in disclosure.

[1.1268]

[1097A Rectification of register relating to company registered office

(1) The Secretary of State may make provision by regulations requiring the registrar, on application, to change the address of a company's registered office if the registrar is satisfied that the company is not authorised to use the address.

(2) The applicant and the company must provide such information as the registrar may require for the purposes of determining such an application.

(3) The regulations may make provision as to—

(a) who may make an application,

(b) the information to be included in and documents to accompany an application,

(c) the notice to be given of an application and of its outcome,

(d) the period in which objections to an application may be made,

(e) how an application is to be determined, including in particular the evidence, or descriptions of evidence, which the registrar may without further enquiry rely on to be satisfied that the company is authorised to use the address,

(f) the referral of the application, or any question relating to the application, by the registrar for determination by the court,

(g) the registrar requiring a company to provide an address to be the company's registered office,

(h) the nomination by the registrar of an address (a "default address") to be the company's registered office,

(i) the effect of the registration of any change.

(4) Subject to further provision which may be made by virtue of subsection (3)(i), the change takes effect upon it being registered by the registrar, but until the end of the period of 14 days beginning with the date on which it is registered a person may validly serve any document on the company at the address previously registered.

(5) Provision made by virtue of subsection (3)(i) may in particular include provision, in relation to the registration of a default address—

(a) for the suspension, for up to 28 days beginning with the date on which it is registered, of duties of the company under this Act relating to the inspection of company records or to the provision, disclosure or display of information,

(b) that the default address may not be used for the purpose of keeping the company's registers, indexes or other documents,

(c) for there to be no requirement that documents delivered to the default address for the company must be opened,

(d) for the collection of such documents by the company, or the forwarding of such documents to the company,

(e) for the circumstances in which, and the period of time after which, such documents may be destroyed,

(f) about evidence, or descriptions of evidence, that the registrar may require a company to provide if giving notice to the registrar to change the address of its registered office from a default address.

(6) The applicant or the company may appeal the outcome of an application under this section to the court.

(7) On an appeal, the court must direct the registrar to register such address as the registered office of the company as the court considers appropriate in all the circumstances of the case.

(8) The regulations may make further provision about an appeal and in particular—

(a) provision about the time within which an appeal must be brought and the grounds on which an appeal may be brought,

(b) provision for the suspension, pending the outcome of an appeal, of duties of the company under this Act relating to the inspection of company records or to the provision, disclosure or display of information,

(c) further provision about directions by virtue of subsection (7).

(9) The regulations may include such provision applying (including applying with modifications), amending or repealing an enactment contained in this Act as the Secretary of State considers necessary or expedient in consequence of any provision made by the regulations.

(10) Regulations under this section are subject to affirmative resolution procedure.]

NOTES

Inserted by the Small Business, Enterprise and Employment Act 2015, s 99(1), as from 26 May 2015.

Regulations: the Companies (Address of Registered Office) Regulations 2016, SI 2016/423 at **[4.621]**. For a summary of all statutory instruments made under this Act, see Appendix 4 at **[A4]**.

[1.1269]

1098 Public notice of removal of certain material from the register

(1) The registrar must cause to be published—

(a) in the Gazette, or

(b) in accordance with section 1116 (alternative means of giving public notice),

notice of the removal from the register of [an enhanced disclosure document] (see section 1078) or of any material derived from such a document.

(2) The notice must state the name and registered number of the company, the description of document and the date of receipt.

NOTES

Sub-s (1): words in square brackets in para (b) substituted by the Companies, Limited Liability Partnerships and Partnerships (Amendment etc) (EU Exit) Regulations 2019, SI 2019/348, reg 6, Sch 1, paras 1, 25, as from IP completion day (as defined in the European Union (Withdrawal Agreement) Act 2020, s 39).

The registrar's index of company names

[1.1270]

1099 The registrar's index of company names

(1) The registrar of companies must keep an index of the names of the companies and other bodies to which this section applies.

This is "the registrar's index of company names".

(2) This section applies to—

(a) UK-registered companies;

(b) any body to which any provision of the Companies Acts applies by virtue of regulations under section 1043 (unregistered companies); and

(c) overseas companies that have registered particulars with the registrar under section 1046, other than companies that appear to the registrar not to be required to do so.

(3) This section also applies to—

(a) limited partnerships registered in the United Kingdom;

(b) limited liability partnerships incorporated in the United Kingdom;

[(c) UK Economic Interest Groupings;

(ca) EEIG establishments, within the meaning of regulation 2(1) of the European Economic Interest Grouping Regulations 1989;]

(d) open-ended investment companies authorised in the United Kingdom;

(e) societies registered under [the Co-operative and Community Benefit Societies Act 2014] or the Industrial and Provident Societies Act (Northern Ireland) 1969 (c 24 (NI));
[(f) protected cell companies registered under Part 4 of the Risk Transformation Regulations 2017];
[(f) charitable incorporated organisations within the meaning of Part 11 of the Charities Act 2011;
(g) Scottish charitable incorporated organisations within the meaning of Chapter 7, Part 1 of the Charities and Trustee Investment (Scotland) Act 2005 (asp 10)];

(4) The Secretary of State may by order amend subsection (3)—
(a) by the addition of any description of body;
(b) by the deletion of any description of body.

(5) Any such order is subject to negative resolution procedure.

NOTES

Sub-s (3) is amended as follows:

Paras (c), (ca) substituted (for the original paras (c)) by the European Economic Interest Grouping (Amendment) (EU Exit) Regulations 2018, SI 2018/1299, reg 62(1), (2), as from IP completion day (as defined in the European Union (Withdrawal Agreement) Act 2020, s 39).

Words in square brackets in para (e) substituted by the Co-operative and Community Benefit Societies Act 2014, s 151, Sch 4, Pt 2, paras 99, 101, as from 1 August 2014.

First para (f) added by the Risk Transformation Regulations 2017, SI 2017/1212, reg 190, Sch 4, para 4(c), as from 8 December 2017.

Second para (f), and para (g), added by the Company Names (Listed Bodies) Order 2017, SI 2017/1233, art 2, as from 1 January 2018.

Orders: the Company Names (Listed Bodies) Order 2017, SI 2017/1233 (which amends this section as noted above). For a summary of all statutory instruments made under this Act, see Appendix 4 at **[A4]**.

[1.1271]

1100 Right to inspect index

Any person may inspect the registrar's index of company names.

[1.1272]

1101 Power to amend enactments relating to bodies other than companies

(1) The Secretary of State may by regulations amend the enactments relating to any description of body for the time being within section 1099(3) (bodies other than companies whose names are to be entered in the registrar's index), so as to—
(a) require the registrar to be provided with information as to the names of bodies registered, incorporated, authorised or otherwise regulated under those enactments, and
(b) make provision in relation to such bodies corresponding to that made by—
section 66 (company name not to be the same as another in the index), and
sections 67 and 68 (power to direct change of company name in case of similarity to existing name).

(2) Regulations under this section are subject to affirmative resolution procedure.

NOTES

Regulations: the Limited Liability Partnerships (Application of Companies Act 2006) Regulations 2009, SI 2009/1804 at **[10.319]**. For a summary of all statutory instruments made under this Act, see Appendix 4 at **[A4]**.

Language requirements: translation

[1.1273]

1102 Application of language requirements

(1) The provisions listed below apply to all documents required to be delivered to the registrar under any provision of—
(a) the Companies Acts, or
(b) the Insolvency Act 1986 (c 45) or the Insolvency (Northern Ireland) Order 1989 (SI 1989/2405 (NI 19)).

(2) The Secretary of State may make provision by regulations applying all or any of the listed provisions, with or without modifications, in relation to documents delivered to the registrar under any other enactment.

(3) The provisions are—
section 1103 (documents to be drawn up and delivered in English),
section 1104 (documents relating to Welsh companies),
section 1105 (documents that may be drawn up and delivered in other languages),
section 1107 (certified translations).

(4) Regulations under this section are subject to negative resolution procedure.

NOTES

Regulations: the European Public Limited-Liability Company (Amendment) Regulations 2009, SI 2009/2400; the Reports on Payments to Governments (Amendment) Regulations 2015, SI 2015/1928. For a summary of all statutory instruments made under this Act, see Appendix 4 at **[A4]**.

[1.1274]

1103 Documents to be drawn up and delivered in English

(1) The general rule is that all documents required to be delivered to the registrar must be drawn up and delivered in English.

(2) This is subject to—
section 1104 (documents relating to Welsh companies) and
section 1105 (documents that may be drawn up and delivered in other languages).

[1.1275]

1104 Documents relating to Welsh companies

(1) Documents relating to a Welsh company may be drawn up and delivered to the registrar in Welsh.

(2) On delivery to the registrar any such document must be accompanied by a certified translation into English, unless it is—

(a) of a description excepted from that requirement by regulations made by the Secretary of State, or

(b) in a form prescribed in Welsh (or partly in Welsh and partly in English) by virtue of section 26 of the Welsh Language Act 1993 (c 38).

(3) Where a document is properly delivered to the registrar in Welsh without a certified translation into English, the registrar must obtain such a translation if the document is to be available for public inspection.

The translation is treated as if delivered to the registrar in accordance with the same provision as the original.

(4) A Welsh company may deliver to the registrar a certified translation into Welsh of any document in English that relates to the company and is or has been delivered to the registrar.

(5) Section 1105 (which requires certified translations into English of documents delivered to the registrar in another language) does not apply to a document relating to a Welsh company that is drawn up and delivered in Welsh.

NOTES

Regulations: the Registrar of Companies and Applications for Striking Off Regulations 2009, SI 2009/1803 at **[4.317]**; the Companies and Limited Liability Partnerships (Accounts and Audit Exemptions and Change of Accounting Framework) Regulations 2012, SI 2012/2301. For a summary of all statutory instruments made under this Act, see Appendix 4 at **[A4]**.

[1.1276]

1105 Documents that may be drawn up and delivered in other languages

(1) Documents to which this section applies may be drawn up and delivered to the registrar in a language other than English, but when delivered to the registrar they must be accompanied by a certified translation into English.

(2) This section applies to—

(a) agreements required to be forwarded to the registrar under Chapter 3 of Part 3 (agreements affecting the company's constitution);

(b) documents required to be delivered under section 400(2)(e) or section 401(2)(f) (company included in accounts of larger group: required to deliver copy of group accounts);

(c) [certified copies] delivered under Part 25 (company charges);

(d) documents of any other description specified in regulations made by the Secretary of State.

(3) Regulations under this section are subject to negative resolution procedure.

NOTES

Sub-s (2): words in square brackets substituted (for the original words "instruments or copy instruments required to be") by the Companies Act 2006 (Amendment of Part 25) Regulations 2013, SI 2013/600, reg 5, Sch 2, para 3(1), (7), as from 6 April 2013, in relation to charges created on or after that date (see further the transitional provisions note at **[1.982]**).

Regulations: the Companies (Registrar, Languages and Trading Disclosures) Regulations 2006, SI 2006/3429 at **[4.1]**; the Overseas Companies Regulations 2009, SI 2009/1801 at **[4.216]**; the Registrar of Companies and Applications for Striking Off Regulations 2009, SI 2009/1803 at **[4.317]**; the Overseas Companies (Execution of Documents and Registration of Charges) Regulations 2009, SI 2009/1917 at **[4.326]**; the Companies and Limited Liability Partnerships (Accounts and Audit Exemptions and Change of Accounting Framework) Regulations 2012, SI 2012/2301; the Reports on Payments to Governments Regulations 2014, SI 2014/3209. For a summary of all statutory instruments made under this Act, see Appendix 4 at **[A4]**.

[1.1277]

1106 Voluntary filing of translations

(1) A company may deliver to the registrar one or more certified translations of any document relating to the company that is or has been delivered to the registrar.

(2) The Secretary of State may by regulations specify—

(a) the languages, and

(b) the descriptions of document,

in relation to which this facility is available.

(3) The regulations must provide that it is available as from 1st January 2007—

(a) in relation to all the official languages of the European Union, and

(b) in relation to all documents subject to the Directive disclosure requirements (see section 1078).

(4) The power of the registrar to impose requirements as to the form and manner of delivery includes power to impose requirements as to the identification of the original document and the delivery of the translation in a form and manner enabling it to be associated with the original.

(5) Regulations under this section are subject to negative resolution procedure.

(6) This section does not apply where the original document was delivered to the registrar before this section came into force.

NOTES

Regulations: the Companies (Registrar, Languages and Trading Disclosures) Regulations 2006, SI 2006/3429 at **[4.1]**. For a summary of all statutory instruments made under this Act, see Appendix 4 at **[A4]**.

[1.1278]

1107 Certified translations

(1) In this Part a "certified translation" means a translation certified to be a correct translation.

(2) In the case of any discrepancy between the original language version of a document and a certified translation—

(a) the company may not rely on the translation as against a third party, but

(b) a third party may rely on the translation unless the company shows that the third party had knowledge of the original.

(3) A "third party" means a person other than the company or the registrar.

Language requirements: transliteration

[1.1279]
1108 Transliteration of names and addresses: permitted characters

(1) Names and addresses in a document delivered to the registrar must contain only letters, characters and symbols (including accents and other diacritical marks) that are permitted.

(2) The Secretary of State may make provision by regulations—

- (a) as to the letters, characters and symbols (including accents and other diacritical marks) that are permitted, and
- (b) permitting or requiring the delivery of documents in which names and addresses have not been transliterated into a permitted form.

(3) Regulations under this section are subject to negative resolution procedure.

NOTES

Regulations: the Registrar of Companies and Applications for Striking Off Regulations 2009, SI 2009/1803 at **[4.317]**; the European Economic Interest Grouping (Amendment) Regulations 2009, SI 2009/2399; the European Public Limited-Liability Company (Amendment) Regulations 2009, SI 2009/2400; the Companies and Limited Liability Partnerships (Accounts and Audit Exemptions and Change of Accounting Framework) Regulations 2012, SI 2012/2301. For a summary of all statutory instruments made under this Act, see Appendix 4 at **[A4]**.

[1.1280]
1109 Transliteration of names and addresses: voluntary transliteration into Roman characters

(1) Where a name or address is or has been delivered to the registrar in a permitted form using other than Roman characters, [the company (or other body) to which the document relates] may deliver to the registrar a transliteration into Roman characters.

(2) The power of the registrar to impose requirements as to the form and manner of delivery includes power to impose requirements as to the identification of the original document and the delivery of the transliteration in a form and manner enabling it to be associated with the original.

NOTES

Sub-s (1): words in square brackets substituted by the Companies Act 2006 (Part 35) (Consequential Amendments, Transitional Provisions and Savings) Order 2009, SI 2009/1802, arts 2, 13, as from 1 October 2009.

[1.1281]
1110 Transliteration of names and addresses: certification

(1) The Secretary of State may make provision by regulations requiring the certification of transliterations and prescribing the form of certification.

(2) Different provision may be made for compulsory and voluntary transliterations.

(3) Regulations under this section are subject to negative resolution procedure.

NOTES

Regulations: no Regulations have been made under this section.

Supplementary provisions

[1.1282]
1111 Registrar's requirements as to certification or verification

(1) Where a document required or authorised to be delivered to the registrar under any enactment is required—

- (a) to be certified as an accurate translation or transliteration, or
- (b) to be certified as a correct copy or verified,

the registrar may impose requirements as to the person, or description of person, by whom the certificate or verification is to be given.

(2) The power conferred by section 1068 (registrar's requirements as to form, authentication and manner of delivery) is exercisable in relation to the certificate or verification as if it were a separate document.

(3) Requirements imposed under this section must not be inconsistent with requirements imposed by any enactment with respect to the certification or verification of the document concerned.

[1.1283]
1112 General false statement offence

(1) It is an offence for a person knowingly or recklessly—

- (a) to deliver or cause to be delivered to the registrar, for any purpose of the Companies Acts, a document, or
- (b) to make to the registrar, for any such purpose, a statement,

that is misleading, false or deceptive in a material particular.

(2) A person guilty of an offence under this section is liable—

- (a) on conviction on indictment, to imprisonment for a term not exceeding two years or a fine (or both);
- (b) on summary conviction—
  - (i) in England and Wales, to imprisonment for a term not exceeding twelve months or to a fine not exceeding the statutory maximum (or both);
  - (ii) in Scotland or Northern Ireland, to imprisonment for a term not exceeding six months, or to a fine not exceeding the statutory maximum (or both).

NOTES

Offences under this section: see further s 1131 at **[1.1301]**.

[1.1284]
1113 Enforcement of company's filing obligations

(1) This section applies where a company has made default in complying with any obligation under the Companies Acts—

- (a) to deliver a document to the registrar, or

(b) to give notice to the registrar of any matter.

(2) The registrar, or any member or creditor of the company, may give notice to the company requiring it to comply with the obligation.

(3) If the company fails to make good the default within 14 days after service of the notice, the registrar, or any member or creditor of the company, may apply to the court for an order directing the company, and any specified officer of it, to make good the default within a specified time.

(4) The court's order may provide that all costs (in Scotland, expenses) of or incidental to the application are to be borne by the company or by any officers of it responsible for the default.

(5) This section does not affect the operation of any enactment making it an offence, or imposing a civil penalty, for the default.

[1.1285]
1114 Application of provisions about documents and delivery

(1) In this Part—

(a) "document" means information recorded in any form, and

(b) references to delivering a document include forwarding, lodging, registering, sending, producing or submitting it or (in the case of a notice) giving it.

(2) Except as otherwise provided, this Part applies in relation to the supply to the registrar of information otherwise than in documentary form as it applies in relation to the delivery of a document.

[1.1286]
1115 Supplementary provisions relating to electronic communications

(1) Registrar's rules may require a company [(or other body)] to give any necessary consents to the use of electronic means for communications by the registrar to the company [(or other body)] as a condition of making use of any facility to deliver material to the registrar by electronic means.

(2) A document that is required to be signed by the registrar or authenticated by the registrar's seal shall, if sent by electronic means, be authenticated in such manner as may be specified by registrar's rules.

NOTES

Sub-s (1): words in square brackets inserted by the Companies Act 2006 (Part 35) (Consequential Amendments, Transitional Provisions and Savings) Order 2009, SI 2009/1802, arts 2, 14, as from 1 October 2009.

[1.1287]
1116 Alternative to publication in the Gazette

(1) Notices that would otherwise need to be published by the registrar in the Gazette may instead be published by such means as may from time to time be approved by the registrar in accordance with regulations made by the Secretary of State.

(2) The Secretary of State may make provision by regulations as to what alternative means may be approved.

(3) The regulations may, in particular—

(a) require the use of electronic means;

(b) require the same means to be used—

(i) for all notices or for all notices of specified descriptions, and

(ii) whether [the company (or other body) to which the notice relates] is registered in England and Wales, Scotland or Northern Ireland;

(c) impose conditions as to the manner in which access to the notices is to be made available.

(4) Regulations under this section are subject to negative resolution procedure.

(5) Before starting to publish notices by means approved under this section the registrar must publish at least one notice to that effect in the Gazette.

(6) Nothing in this section prevents the registrar from giving public notice both in the Gazette and by means approved under this section.

In that case, the requirement of public notice is met when notice is first given by either means.

NOTES

Sub-s (3): words in square brackets substituted by the Companies Act 2006 (Part 35) (Consequential Amendments, Transitional Provisions and Savings) Order 2009, SI 2009/1802, arts 2, 15, as from 1 October 2009.

Regulations: no Regulations have been made under this section.

[1.1288]
1117 Registrar's rules

(1) Where any provision of this Part enables the registrar to make provision, or impose requirements, as to any matter, the registrar may make such provision or impose such requirements by means of rules under this section.

This is without prejudice to the making of such provision or the imposing of such requirements by other means.

(2) Registrar's rules—

(a) may make different provision for different cases, and

(b) may allow the registrar to disapply or modify any of the rules.

(3) The registrar must—

(a) publicise the rules in a manner appropriate to bring them to the notice of persons affected by them, and

(b) make copies of the rules available to the public (in hard copy or electronic form).

[1.1289]
1118 Payments into the Consolidated Fund

Nothing in the Companies Acts or any other enactment as to the payment of receipts into the Consolidated Fund shall be read as affecting the operation in relation to the registrar of section 3(1) of the Government Trading Funds Act 1973 (c 63).

[1.1290]

1119 Contracting out of registrar's functions

(1) Where by virtue of an order made under section 69 of the Deregulation and Contracting Out Act 1994 (c 40) a person is authorised by the registrar to accept delivery of any class of documents that are under any enactment to be delivered to the registrar, the registrar may direct that documents of that class shall be delivered to a specified address of the authorised person.

Any such direction must be printed and made available to the public (with or without payment).

(2) A document of that class that is delivered to an address other than the specified address is treated as not having been delivered.

(3) Registrar's rules are not subordinate legislation for the purposes of section 71 of the Deregulation and Contracting Out Act 1994 (functions excluded from contracting out).

1120 (*Repealed by the Companies Act 2006 (Part 35) (Consequential Amendments, Transitional Provisions and Savings) Order 2009, SI 2009/1802, arts 2, 16, as from 1 October 2009.*)

PART 36 OFFENCES UNDER THE COMPANIES ACTS

Liability of officer in default

[1.1291]

1121 Liability of officer in default

(1) This section has effect for the purposes of any provision of the Companies Acts to the effect that, in the event of contravention of an enactment in relation to a company, an offence is committed by every officer of the company who is in default.

(2) For this purpose "officer" includes—

(a) any director, manager or secretary, and

(b) any person who is to be treated as an officer of the company for the purposes of the provision in question.

(3) An officer is "in default" for the purposes of the provision if he authorises or permits, participates in, or fails to take all reasonable steps to prevent, the contravention.

[1.1292]

1122 Liability of company as officer in default

(1) Where a company is an officer of another company, it does not commit an offence as an officer in default unless one of its officers is in default.

(2) Where any such offence is committed by a company the officer in question also commits the offence and is liable to be proceeded against and punished accordingly.

(3) In this section "officer" and "in default" have the meanings given by section 1121.

[1.1293]

1123 Application to bodies other than companies

(1) Section 1121 (liability of officers in default) applies to a body other than a company as it applies to a company.

(2) As it applies in relation to a body corporate other than a company—

(a) the reference to a director of the company shall be read as referring—

(i) where the body's affairs are managed by its members, to a member of the body,

(ii) in any other case, to any corresponding officer of the body, and

(b) the reference to a manager or secretary of the company shall be read as referring to any manager, secretary or similar officer of the body.

(3) As it applies in relation to a partnership—

(a) the reference to a director of the company shall be read as referring to a member of the partnership, and

(b) the reference to a manager or secretary of the company shall be read as referring to any manager, secretary or similar officer of the partnership.

(4) As it applies in relation to an unincorporated body other than a partnership—

(a) the reference to a director of the company shall be read as referring—

(i) where the body's affairs are managed by its members, to a member of the body,

(ii) in any other case, to a member of the governing body, and

(b) the reference to a manager or secretary of the company shall be read as referring to any manager, secretary or similar officer of the body.

Offences under the Companies Act 1985

[1.1294]

1124 Amendments of the Companies Act 1985

Schedule 3 contains amendments of the Companies Act 1985 (c 6) relating to offences.

General provisions

[1.1295]

1125 Meaning of "daily default fine"

(1) This section defines what is meant in the Companies Acts where it is provided that a person guilty of an offence is liable on summary conviction to a fine not exceeding a specified amount "and, for continued contravention, a daily default fine" not exceeding a specified amount.

(2) This means that the person is liable on a second or subsequent summary conviction of the offence to a fine not exceeding the latter amount for each day on which the contravention is continued (instead of being liable to a fine not exceeding the former amount).

[1.1296]

1126 Consents required for certain prosecutions

(1) This section applies to proceedings for an offence under any of the following provisions—

section 458, 460 or 949 of this Act (offences of unauthorised disclosure of information);

section 953 of this Act (failure to comply with rules about takeover bid documents);
section 448, 449, 450, 451 or 453A of the Companies Act 1985 (c 6) (offences in connection with company investigations);
section 798 of this Act or section 455 of the Companies Act 1985 (offence of attempting to evade restrictions on shares);
[section 1112 of this Act (general false statement offence);
paragraph 5 or 6 of Schedule 1B to this Act (breach of certain restrictions imposed under that Schedule)].

(2) No such proceedings are to be brought in England and Wales except by or with the consent of—
(a) in the case of an offence under—
(i) section 458, 460 or 949 of this Act,
(ii) section 953 of this Act, . . .
(iii) section 448, 449, 450, 451 or 453A of the Companies Act 1985, [or
(iv) section 1112 of this Act,]
the Secretary of State or the Director of Public Prosecutions;
(b) in the case of an offence under section 798 of[, or paragraph 5 or 6 of Schedule 1B to,] this Act or section 455 of the Companies Act 1985, the Secretary of State.

(3) No such proceedings are to be brought in Northern Ireland except by or with the consent of—
(a) in the case of an offence under—
(i) section 458, 460 or 949 of this Act,
(ii) section 953 of this Act, . . .
(iii) section 448, 449, 450, 451 or 453A of the Companies Act 1985, [or
(iv) section 1112 of this Act,]
the Secretary of State or the Director of Public Prosecutions for Northern Ireland;
(b) in the case of an offence under section 798 of[, or paragraph 5 or 6 of Schedule 1B to,] this Act or section 455 of the Companies Act 1985, the Secretary of State.

NOTES

Words omitted repealed, and words in square brackets inserted, by the Small Business, Enterprise and Employment Act 2015, s 81, Sch 3, Pt 2, paras 3, 9, as from 6 April 2016.

[1.1297]
1127 Summary proceedings: venue

(1) Summary proceedings for any offence under the Companies Acts may be taken—
(a) against a body corporate, at any place at which the body has a place of business, and
(b) against any other person, at any place at which he is for the time being.

(2) This is without prejudice to any jurisdiction exercisable apart from this section.

[1.1298]
1128 Summary proceedings: time limit for proceedings

(1) An information relating to an offence under the Companies Acts that is triable by a magistrates' court in England and Wales may be so tried if it is laid—
(a) at any time within three years after the commission of the offence, and
(b) within twelve months after the date on which evidence sufficient in the opinion of the Director of Public Prosecutions or the Secretary of State (as the case may be) to justify the proceedings comes to his knowledge.

(2) Summary proceedings in Scotland for an offence under the Companies Acts—
(a) must not be commenced after the expiration of three years from the commission of the offence;
(b) subject to that, may be commenced at any time—
(i) within twelve months after the date on which evidence sufficient in the Lord Advocate's opinion to justify the proceedings came to his knowledge, or
(ii) where such evidence was reported to him by the Secretary of State, within twelve months after the date on which it came to the knowledge of the latter.

Section 136(3) of the Criminal Procedure (Scotland) Act 1995 (c 46) (date when proceedings deemed to be commenced) applies for the purposes of this subsection as for the purposes of that section.

(3) A magistrates' court in Northern Ireland has jurisdiction to hear and determine a complaint charging the commission of a summary offence under the Companies Acts provided that the complaint is made—
(a) within three years from the time when the offence was committed, and
(b) within twelve months from the date on which evidence sufficient in the opinion of the Director of Public Prosecutions for Northern Ireland or the Secretary of State (as the case may be) to justify the proceedings comes to his knowledge.

(4) For the purposes of this section a certificate of the Director of Public Prosecutions, the Lord Advocate, the Director of Public Prosecutions for Northern Ireland or the Secretary of State (as the case may be) as to the date on which such evidence as is referred to above came to his notice is conclusive evidence.

[1.1299]
1129 Legal professional privilege

In proceedings against a person for an offence under the Companies Acts, nothing in those Acts is to be taken to require any person to disclose any information that he is entitled to refuse to disclose on grounds of legal professional privilege (in Scotland, confidentiality of communications).

[1.1300]
1130 Proceedings against unincorporated bodies

(1) Proceedings for an offence under the Companies Acts alleged to have been committed by an unincorporated body must be brought in the name of the body (and not in that of any of its members).

(2) For the purposes of such proceedings—
(a) any rules of court relating to the service of documents have effect as if the body were a body corporate, and

(b) the following provisions apply as they apply in relation to a body corporate—
   (i) in England and Wales, section 33 of the Criminal Justice Act 1925 (c 86) and Schedule 3 to the Magistrates' Courts Act 1980 (c 43),
   (ii) in Scotland, sections 70 and 143 of the Criminal Procedure (Scotland) Act 1995 (c 46),
   (iii) in Northern Ireland, section 18 of the Criminal Justice Act (Northern Ireland) 1945 (c 15 (NI)) and Article 166 of and Schedule 4 to the Magistrates' Courts (Northern Ireland) Order 1981 (SI 1981/1675 (NI 26)).

(3) A fine imposed on an unincorporated body on its conviction of an offence under the Companies Acts must be paid out of the funds of the body.

[1.1301]
1131 Imprisonment on summary conviction in England and Wales: transitory provision
(1) This section applies to any provision of the Companies Acts that provides that a person guilty of an offence is liable on summary conviction in England and Wales to imprisonment for a term not exceeding twelve months.
(2) In relation to an offence committed before [2 May 2022], for "twelve months" substitute "six months".

NOTES
Sub-s (2): words in square brackets substituted by the Criminal Justice Act 2003 (Commencement No 33) and Sentencing Act 2020 (Commencement No 2) Regulations 2022, SI 2022/500, reg 5, Schedule, Pt 1, as from 28 April 2022.

Production and inspection of documents

[1.1302]
1132 Production and inspection of documents where offence suspected
(1) An application under this section may be made—
   (a) in England and Wales, to a judge of the High Court by the Director of Public Prosecutions, the Secretary of State or a chief officer of police;
   (b) in Scotland, to one of the Lords Commissioners of Justiciary by the Lord Advocate;
   (c) in Northern Ireland, to the High Court by the Director of Public Prosecutions for Northern Ireland, the Department of Enterprise, Trade and Investment or a chief superintendent of the Police Service of Northern Ireland.

(2) If on an application under this section there is shown to be reasonable cause to believe—
   (a) that any person has, while an officer of a company, committed an offence in connection with the management of the company's affairs, and
   (b) that evidence of the commission of the offence is to be found in any documents in the possession or control of the company,

an order under this section may be made.
(3) The order may—
   (a) authorise any person named in it to inspect the documents in question, or any of them, for the purpose of investigating and obtaining evidence of the offence, or
   (b) require the secretary of the company, or such other officer of it as may be named in the order, to produce the documents (or any of them) to a person named in the order at a place so named.

(4) This section applies also in relation to documents in the possession or control of a person carrying on the business of banking, so far as they relate to the company's affairs, as it applies to documents in the possession or control of the company, except that no such order as is referred to in subsection (3)(b) may be made by virtue of this subsection.
(5) The decision under this section of a judge of the High Court, any of the Lords Commissioners of Justiciary or the High Court is not appealable.
(6) In this section "document" includes information recorded in any form.

Supplementary

[1.1303]
1133 Transitional provision
The provisions of this Part except section 1132 do not apply to offences committed before the commencement of the relevant provision.

PART 37 COMPANIES: SUPPLEMENTARY PROVISIONS

Company records

[1.1304]
1134 Meaning of "company records"
In this Part "company records" means—
   (a) any register, index, accounting records, agreement, memorandum, minutes or other document required by the Companies Acts to be kept by a company, and
   (b) any register kept by a company of its debenture holders.

[1.1305]
1135 Form of company records
(1) Company records—
   (a) may be kept in hard copy or electronic form, and
   (b) may be arranged in such manner as the directors of the company think fit,

provided the information in question is adequately recorded for future reference.
(2) Where the records are kept in electronic form, they must be capable of being reproduced in hard copy form.
(3) If a company fails to comply with this section, an offence is committed by every officer of the company who is in default.
(4) A person guilty of an offence under this section is liable on summary conviction to a fine not exceeding level 3 on the standard scale and, for continued contravention, a daily default fine not exceeding one-tenth of level 3 on the standard scale.

(5) Any provision of an instrument made by a company before 12th February 1979 that requires a register of holders of the company's debentures to be kept in hard copy form is to be read as requiring it to be kept in hard copy or electronic form.

[1.1306]

1136 Regulations about where certain company records to be kept available for inspection

(1) The Secretary of State may make provision by regulations specifying places other than a company's registered office at which company records required to be kept available for inspection under a relevant provision may be so kept in compliance with that provision.

(2) The "relevant provisions" are—

section 114 (register of members);
[section 128D (historic register of members);]
section 162 (register of directors);
section 228 (directors' service contracts);
section 237 (directors' indemnities);
section 275 (register of secretaries);
section 358 (records of resolutions etc);
section 702 (contracts relating to purchase of own shares);
section 720 (documents relating to redemption or purchase of own shares out of capital by private company);
section 743 (register of debenture holders);
[section 790M (register of people with significant control over a company);
section 790Z (historic PSC register);]
section 805 (report to members of outcome of investigation by public company into interests in its shares);
section 809 (register of interests in shares disclosed to public company);
[section 859Q (instruments creating charges)].

(3) The regulations may specify a place by reference to the company's principal place of business, the part of the United Kingdom in which the company is registered, the place at which the company keeps any other records available for inspection or in any other way.

(4) The regulations may provide that a company does not comply with a relevant provision by keeping company records available for inspection at a place specified in the regulations unless conditions specified in the regulations are met.

(5) The regulations—

(a) need not specify a place in relation to each relevant provision;
(b) may specify more than one place in relation to a relevant provision.

(6) A requirement under a relevant provision to keep company records available for inspection is not complied with by keeping them available for inspection at a place specified in the regulations unless all the company's records subject to the requirement are kept there.

(7) Regulations under this section are subject to negative resolution procedure.

NOTES

Sub-s (2) is amended as follows:

Words in first pair of square brackets inserted by the Small Business, Enterprise and Employment Act 2015, s 94, Sch 5, Pt 2, paras 11, 33, as from 30 June 2016.

Words in second pair of square brackets inserted by s 81 of, and Sch 3, Pt 2, paras 3, 10 to, the 2015 Act, as from 26 May 2015.

Words in third pair of square brackets substituted (for the original words "section 877 (instruments creating charges and register of charges: England and Wales); section 892 (instruments creating charges and register of charges: Scotland)") by the Companies Act 2006 (Amendment of Part 25) Regulations 2013, SI 2013/600, reg 5, Sch 2, para 3(1), (8), as from 6 April 2013, in relation to charges created on or after that date (see further the transitional provisions note at **[1.982]**).

Regulations: the Companies (Company Records) Regulations 2008, SI 2008/3006 at **[4.168]**. For a summary of all statutory instruments made under this Act, see Appendix 4 at **[A4]**.

[1.1307]

1137 Regulations about inspection of records and provision of copies

(1) The Secretary of State may make provision by regulations as to the obligations of a company that is required by any provision of the Companies Acts—

(a) to keep available for inspection any company records, or
(b) to provide copies of any company records.

(2) A company that fails to comply with the regulations is treated as having refused inspection or, as the case may be, having failed to provide a copy.

(3) The regulations may—

(a) make provision as to the time, duration and manner of inspection, including the circumstances in which and extent to which the copying of information is permitted in the course of inspection, and
(b) define what may be required of the company as regards the nature, extent and manner of extracting or presenting any information for the purposes of inspection or the provision of copies.

(4) Where there is power to charge a fee, the regulations may make provision as to the amount of the fee and the basis of its calculation.

(5) Nothing in any provision of this Act or in the regulations shall be read as preventing a company—

(a) from affording more extensive facilities than are required by the regulations, or
(b) where a fee may be charged, from charging a lesser fee than that prescribed or none at all.

(6) Regulations under this section are subject to negative resolution procedure.

NOTES

Regulations: the Companies (Fees for Inspection and Copying of Company Records) Regulations 2007, SI 2007/2612 at **[4.11]**; the Companies (Fees for Inspection and Copying of Company Records) (No 2) Regulations 2007, SI 2007/3535 at

[4.16]; the Companies (Company Records) Regulations 2008, SI 2008/3006 at **[4.168]**; the Companies (Fees for Inspection of Company Records) Regulations 2008, SI 2008/3007 at **[4.177]**. For a summary of all statutory instruments made under this Act, see Appendix 4 at **[A4]**.

[1.1308]

1138 Duty to take precautions against falsification

(1) Where company records are kept otherwise than in bound books, adequate precautions must be taken—

(a) to guard against falsification, and

(b) to facilitate the discovery of falsification.

(2) If a company fails to comply with this section, an offence is committed by every officer of the company who is in default.

(3) A person guilty of an offence under this section is liable on summary conviction to a fine not exceeding level 3 on the standard scale and, for continued contravention, a daily default fine not exceeding one-tenth of level 3 on the standard scale.

(4) This section does not apply to the documents required to be kept under—

(a) section 228 (copy of director's service contract or memorandum of its terms); or

(b) section 237 (qualifying indemnity provision).

Service addresses

[1.1309]

1139 Service of documents on company

(1) A document may be served on a company registered under this Act by leaving it at, or sending it by post to, the company's registered office.

(2) A document may be served on an overseas company whose particulars are registered under section 1046—

(a) by leaving it at, or sending it by post to, the registered address of any person resident in the United Kingdom who is authorised to accept service of documents on the company's behalf, or

(b) if there is no such person, or if any such person refuses service or service cannot for any other reason be effected, by leaving it at or sending by post to any place of business of the company in the United Kingdom.

(3) For the purposes of this section a person's "registered address" means any address for the time being shown as a current address in relation to that person in the part of the register available for public inspection.

(4) Where a company registered in Scotland or Northern Ireland carries on business in England and Wales, the process of any court in England and Wales may be served on the company by leaving it at, or sending it by post to, the company's principal place of business in England and Wales, addressed to the manager or other head officer in England and Wales of the company.

Where process is served on a company under this subsection, the person issuing out the process must send a copy of it by post to the company's registered office.

(5) Further provision as to service and other matters is made in the company communications provisions (see section 1143).

[1.1310]

1140 Service of documents on directors, secretaries and others

(1) A document may be served on a person to whom this section applies by leaving it at, or sending it by post to, the person's registered address.

(2) This section applies to—

(a) a director or secretary of a company;

(b) in the case of an overseas company whose particulars are registered under section 1046, a person holding any such position as may be specified for the purposes of this section by regulations under that section;

(c) a person appointed in relation to a company as—

(i) a judicial factor (in Scotland),

(ii) [an interim manager] appointed under [section 76 of the Charities Act 2011] [or section 33 of Charities Act (Northern Ireland) 2008], or

(iii) a manager appointed under section 47 of the Companies (Audit, Investigations and Community Enterprise) Act 2004 (c 27).

(3) This section applies whatever the purpose of the document in question.

It is not restricted to service for purposes arising out of or in connection with the appointment or position mentioned in subsection (2) or in connection with the company concerned.

(4) For the purposes of this section a person's "registered address" means any address for the time being shown as a current address in relation to that person in the part of the register available for public inspection.

(5) If notice of a change of that address is given to the registrar, a person may validly serve a document at the address previously registered until the end of the period of 14 days beginning with the date on which notice of the change is registered.

(6) Service may not be effected by virtue of this section at an address—

(a) if notice has been registered of the termination of the appointment in relation to which the address was registered and the address is not a registered address of the person concerned in relation to any other appointment;

(b) in the case of a person holding any such position as is mentioned in subsection (2)(b), if the overseas company has ceased to have any connection with the United Kingdom by virtue of which it is required to register particulars under section 1046.

(7) Further provision as to service and other matters is made in the company communications provisions (see section 1143).

(8) Nothing in this section shall be read as affecting any enactment or rule of law under which permission is required for service out of the jurisdiction.

NOTES

Sub-s (2): words in first pair of square brackets in sub-para (c)(ii) substituted by the Companies Act 2006 (Consequential Amendments, Transitional Provisions and Savings) Order 2009, SI 2009/1941, art 2(1), Sch 1, para 260(1), (7)(a), as from 1 October 2009. Words in second pair of square brackets in sub-para (c)(ii) substituted by the Charities Act 2011, s 354, Sch 7, Pt 2, para 115(a), as from 14 March 2012. Words in third pair of square brackets in sub-para (c)(ii) inserted by the Charities Act (Northern Ireland) 2008, s 183, Sch 8, para 13(3), as from 24 June 2013.

Regulations: the Overseas Companies Regulations 2009, SI 2009/1801 at **[4.216]**. For a summary of all statutory instruments made under this Act, see Appendix 4 at **[A4]**.

[1.1311]
1141 Service addresses

(1) In the Companies Acts a "service address", in relation to a person, means an address at which documents may be effectively served on that person.
(2) The Secretary of State may by regulations specify conditions with which a service address must comply.
(3) Regulations under this section are subject to negative resolution procedure.

NOTES

Regulations: the Companies Act 2006 (Annual Return and Service Addresses) Regulations 2008, SI 2008/3000 (see the note at **[4.167]**). For a summary of all statutory instruments made under this Act, see Appendix 4 at **[A4]**.

[1.1312]
1142 Requirement to give service address

Any obligation under the Companies Acts to give a person's address is, unless otherwise expressly provided, to give a service address for that person.

Sending or supplying documents or information

[1.1313]
1143 The company communications provisions

(1) The provisions of sections 1144 to 1148 and Schedules 4 and 5 ("the company communications provisions") have effect for the purposes of any provision of the Companies Acts that authorises or requires documents or information to be sent or supplied by or to a company.
(2) The company communications provisions have effect subject to any requirements imposed, or contrary provision made, by or under any enactment.
(3) In particular, in their application in relation to documents or information to be sent or supplied to the registrar, they have effect subject to the provisions of Part 35.
(4) For the purposes of subsection (2), provision is not to be regarded as contrary to the company communications provisions by reason only of the fact that it expressly authorises a document or information to be sent or supplied in hard copy form, in electronic form or by means of a website.

[1.1314]
1144 Sending or supplying documents or information

(1) Documents or information to be sent or supplied to a company must be sent or supplied in accordance with the provisions of Schedule 4.
(2) Documents or information to be sent or supplied by a company must be sent or supplied in accordance with the provisions of Schedule 5.
(3) The provisions referred to in subsection (2) apply (and those referred to in subsection (1) do not apply) in relation to documents or information that are to be sent or supplied by one company to another.

[1.1315]
1145 Right to hard copy version

(1) Where a member of a company or a holder of a company's debentures has received a document or information from the company otherwise than in hard copy form, he is entitled to require the company to send him a version of the document or information in hard copy form.
(2) The company must send the document or information in hard copy form within 21 days of receipt of the request from the member or debenture holder.
(3) The company may not make a charge for providing the document or information in that form.
(4) If a company fails to comply with this section, an offence is committed by the company and every officer of it who is in default.
(5) A person guilty of an offence under this section is liable on summary conviction to a fine not exceeding level 3 on the standard scale and, for continued contravention, a daily default fine not exceeding one-tenth of level 3 on the standard scale.

[1.1316]
1146 Requirement of authentication

(1) This section applies in relation to the authentication of a document or information sent or supplied by a person to a company.
(2) A document or information sent or supplied in hard copy form is sufficiently authenticated if it is signed by the person sending or supplying it.
(3) A document or information sent or supplied in electronic form is sufficiently authenticated—
  (a) if the identity of the sender is confirmed in a manner specified by the company, or
  (b) where no such manner has been specified by the company, if the communication contains or is accompanied by a statement of the identity of the sender and the company has no reason to doubt the truth of that statement.
(4) Where a document or information is sent or supplied by one person on behalf of another, nothing in this section affects any provision of the company's articles under which the company may require reasonable evidence of the authority of the former to act on behalf of the latter.

[1.1317]

1147 Deemed delivery of documents and information

(1) This section applies in relation to documents and information sent or supplied by a company.

(2) Where—

(a) the document or information is sent by post (whether in hard copy or electronic form) to an address in the United Kingdom, and

(b) the company is able to show that it was properly addressed, prepaid and posted,

it is deemed to have been received by the intended recipient 48 hours after it was posted.

(3) Where—

(a) the document or information is sent or supplied by electronic means, and

(b) the company is able to show that it was properly addressed,

it is deemed to have been received by the intended recipient 48 hours after it was sent.

(4) Where the document or information is sent or supplied by means of a website, it is deemed to have been received by the intended recipient—

(a) when the material was first made available on the website, or

(b) if later, when the recipient received (or is deemed to have received) notice of the fact that the material was available on the website.

(5) In calculating a period of hours for the purposes of this section, no account shall be taken of any part of a day that is not a working day.

(6) This section has effect subject to—

(a) in its application to documents or information sent or supplied by a company to its members, any contrary provision of the company's articles;

(b) in its application to documents or information sent or supplied by a company to its debentures holders, any contrary provision in the instrument constituting the debentures;

(c) in its application to documents or information sent or supplied by a company to a person otherwise than in his capacity as a member or debenture holder, any contrary provision in an agreement between the company and that person.

[1.1318]

1148 Interpretation of company communications provisions

(1) In the company communications provisions—

"address" includes a number or address used for the purposes of sending or receiving documents or information by electronic means;

"company" includes any body corporate;

"document" includes summons, notice, order or other legal process and registers.

(2) References in the company communications provisions to provisions of the Companies Acts authorising or requiring a document or information to be sent or supplied include all such provisions, whatever expression is used, and references to documents or information being sent or supplied shall be construed accordingly.

(3) References in the company communications provisions to documents or information being sent or supplied by or to a company include references to documents or information being sent or supplied by or to the directors of a company acting on behalf of the company.

Requirements as to independent valuation

[1.1319]

1149 Application of valuation requirements

The provisions of sections 1150 to 1153 apply to the valuation and report required by—

section 93 (re-registration as public company: recent allotment of shares for non-cash consideration);

section 593 (allotment of shares of public company in consideration of non-cash asset);

section 599 (transfer of non-cash asset to public company).

[1.1320]

1150 Valuation by qualified independent person

(1) The valuation and report must be made by a person ("the valuer") who—

(a) is eligible for appointment as a statutory auditor (see section 1212), and

(b) meets the independence requirement in section 1151.

(2) However, where it appears to the valuer to be reasonable for the valuation of the consideration, or part of it, to be made by (or for him to accept a valuation made by) another person who—

(a) appears to him to have the requisite knowledge and experience to value the consideration or that part of it, and

(b) is not an officer or employee of—

(i) the company, or

(ii) any other body corporate that is that company's subsidiary or holding company or a subsidiary of that company's holding company,

or a partner of or employed by any such officer or employee,

he may arrange for or accept such a valuation, together with a report which will enable him to make his own report under this section.

(3) The references in subsection (2)(b) to an officer or employee do not include an auditor.

(4) Where the consideration or part of it is valued by a person other than the valuer himself, the latter's report must state that fact and shall also—

(a) state the former's name and what knowledge and experience he has to carry out the valuation, and

(b) describe so much of the consideration as was valued by the other person, and the method used to value it, and specify the date of that valuation.

[1.1321]

1151 The independence requirement

(1) A person meets the independence requirement for the purposes of section 1150 only if—

(a) he is not—
  (i) an officer or employee of the company, or
  (ii) a partner or employee of such a person, or a partnership of which such a person is a partner;
(b) he is not—
  (i) an officer or employee of an associated undertaking of the company, or
  (ii) a partner or employee of such a person, or a partnership of which such a person is a partner; and
(c) there does not exist between—
  (i) the person or an associate of his, and
  (ii) the company or an associated undertaking of the company,

a connection of any such description as may be specified by regulations made by the Secretary of State.

(2) An auditor of the company is not regarded as an officer or employee of the company for this purpose.

(3) In this section—

"associated undertaking" means—
  (a) a parent undertaking or subsidiary undertaking of the company, or
  (b) a subsidiary undertaking of a parent undertaking of the company; and

"associate" has the meaning given by section 1152.

(4) Regulations under this section are subject to negative resolution procedure.

NOTES

Regulations: no Regulations have been made under this section.

[1.1322]

1152 Meaning of "associate"

(1) This section defines "associate" for the purposes of section 1151 (valuation: independence requirement).

(2) In relation to an individual, "associate" means—
(a) that individual's spouse or civil partner or minor child or step-child,
(b) any body corporate of which that individual is a director, and
(c) any employee or partner of that individual.

(3) In relation to a body corporate, "associate" means—
(a) any body corporate of which that body is a director,
(b) any body corporate in the same group as that body, and
(c) any employee or partner of that body or of any body corporate in the same group.

(4) In relation to a partnership that is a legal person under the law by which it is governed, "associate" means—
(a) any body corporate of which that partnership is a director,
(b) any employee of or partner in that partnership, and
(c) any person who is an associate of a partner in that partnership.

(5) In relation to a partnership that is not a legal person under the law by which it is governed, "associate" means any person who is an associate of any of the partners.

(6) In this section, in relation to a limited liability partnership, for "director" read "member".

[1.1323]

1153 Valuer entitled to full disclosure

(1) A person carrying out a valuation or making a report with respect to any consideration proposed to be accepted or given by a company, is entitled to require from the officers of the company such information and explanation as he thinks necessary to enable him to—
(a) carry out the valuation or make the report, and
(b) provide any note required by section 596(3) or 600(3) (note required where valuation carried out by another person).

(2) A person who knowingly or recklessly makes a statement to which this subsection applies that is misleading, false or deceptive in a material particular commits an offence.

(3) Subsection (2) applies to a statement—
(a) made (whether orally or in writing) to a person carrying out a valuation or making a report, and
(b) conveying or purporting to convey any information or explanation which that person requires, or is entitled to require, under subsection (1).

(4) A person guilty of an offence under subsection (2) is liable—
(a) on conviction on indictment, to imprisonment for a term not exceeding two years or a fine (or both);
(b) on summary conviction—
  (i) in England and Wales, to imprisonment for a term not exceeding twelve months or to a fine not exceeding the statutory maximum (or both);
  (ii) in Scotland or Northern Ireland, to imprisonment for a term not exceeding six months, or to a fine not exceeding the statutory maximum (or both).

NOTES

Offences under this section: see further s 1131 at **[1.1301]**.

Notice of appointment of certain officers

[1.1324]

1154 Duty to notify registrar of certain appointments etc

(1) Notice must be given to the registrar of the appointment in relation to a company of—
(a) a judicial factor (in Scotland),
(b) [an interim manager] appointed under [section 76 of the Charities Act 2011] [or section 33 of the Charities Act (Northern Ireland) 2008], or
(c) a manager appointed under section 47 of the Companies (Audit, Investigations and Community Enterprise) Act 2004 (c 27).

(2) The notice must be given—

(a) in the case of appointment of a judicial factor, by the judicial factor;

(b) in the case of appointment of [an interim manager] under [section 76 of the Charities Act 2011], by the Charity Commission;

[(bb) in the case of appointment of a receiver or manager under section 33 of the Charities Act (Northern Ireland) 2008, by the Charity Commission for Northern Ireland;]

(c) in the case of appointment of a manager under section 47 of the Companies (Audit, Investigations and Community Enterprise) Act 2004, by the Regulator of Community Interest Companies.

(3) The notice must specify an address at which service of documents (including legal process) may be effected on the person appointed.

Notice of a change in the address for service may be given to the registrar by the person appointed.

(4) Where notice has been given under this section of the appointment of a person, notice must also be given to the registrar of the termination of the appointment. This notice must be given by the person specified in subsection (2).

NOTES

Sub-ss (1), (2): words "an interim manager" in square brackets substituted by the Companies Act 2006 (Consequential Amendments, Transitional Provisions and Savings) Order 2009, SI 2009/1941, art 2(1), Sch 1, para 260(1), (7)(b), as from 1 October 2009. Words "section 76 of the Charities Act 2011" in square brackets substituted by the Charities Act 2011, s 354, Sch 7, Pt 2, para 115(b), as from 14 March 2012. Words "or section 33 of the Charities Act (Northern Ireland) 2008" in square brackets in sub-s (1)(b) inserted, and sub-s (2)(bb) inserted, by the Charities Act (Northern Ireland) 2008, s 183, Sch 8, para 13(4), (5), as from 24 June 2013.

[1.1325]

1155 Offence of failure to give notice

(1) If a judicial factor fails to give notice of his appointment in accordance with section 1154 within the period of 14 days after the appointment he commits an offence.

(2) A person guilty of an offence under this section is liable on summary conviction to a fine not exceeding level 5 on the standard scale and, for continued contravention, a daily default fine not exceeding one-tenth of level 5 on the standard scale.

Courts and legal proceedings

[1.1326]

1156 Meaning of "the court"

(1) Except as otherwise provided, in the Companies Acts "the court" means—

(a) in England and Wales, the High Court or [the] county court;

(b) in Scotland, the Court of Session or the sheriff court;

(c) in Northern Ireland, the High Court.

(2) The provisions of the Companies Acts conferring jurisdiction on "the court" as defined above have effect subject to any enactment or rule of law relating to the allocation of jurisdiction or distribution of business between courts in any part of the United Kingdom.

(3), (4) . . .

NOTES

Word in square brackets in sub-s (1)(a) substituted, and sub-ss (3), (4) repealed, by the Crime and Courts Act 2013, s 17, Sch 9, Pt 2, para 43, as from 22 April 2014.

[1.1327]

1157 Power of court to grant relief in certain cases

(1) If in proceedings for negligence, default, breach of duty or breach of trust against—

(a) an officer of a company, or

(b) a person employed by a company as auditor (whether he is or is not an officer of the company),

it appears to the court hearing the case that the officer or person is or may be liable but that he acted honestly and reasonably, and that having regard to all the circumstances of the case (including those connected with his appointment) he ought fairly to be excused, the court may relieve him, either wholly or in part, from his liability on such terms as it thinks fit.

(2) If any such officer or person has reason to apprehend that a claim will or might be made against him in respect of negligence, default, breach of duty or breach of trust—

(a) he may apply to the court for relief, and

(b) the court has the same power to relieve him as it would have had if it had been a court before which proceedings against him for negligence, default, breach of duty or breach of trust had been brought.

(3) Where a case to which subsection (1) applies is being tried by a judge with a jury, the judge, after hearing the evidence, may, if he is satisfied that the defendant (in Scotland, the defender) ought in pursuance of that subsection to be relieved either in whole or in part from the liability sought to be enforced against him, withdraw the case from the jury and forthwith direct judgment to be entered for the defendant (in Scotland, grant decree of absolvitor) on such terms as to costs (in Scotland, expenses) or otherwise as the judge may think proper.

PART 38 COMPANIES: INTERPRETATION

Meaning of "UK-registered company"

[1.1328]

1158 Meaning of "UK-registered company"

In the Companies Acts "UK-registered company" means a company registered under this Act.

The expression does not include an overseas company that has registered particulars under section 1046.

Meaning of "subsidiary" and related expressions

[1.1329]

1159 Meaning of "subsidiary" etc

(1) A company is a "subsidiary" of another company, its "holding company", if that other company—

(a) holds a majority of the voting rights in it, or
(b) is a member of it and has the right to appoint or remove a majority of its board of directors, or
(c) is a member of it and controls alone, pursuant to an agreement with other members, a majority of the voting rights in it,

or if it is a subsidiary of a company that is itself a subsidiary of that other company.

(2) A company is a "wholly-owned subsidiary" of another company if it has no members except that other and that other's wholly-owned subsidiaries or persons acting on behalf of that other or its wholly-owned subsidiaries.

(3) Schedule 6 contains provisions explaining expressions used in this section and otherwise supplementing this section.

(4) In this section and that Schedule "company" includes any body corporate.

[1.1330]

1160 Meaning of "subsidiary" etc: power to amend

(1) The Secretary of State may by regulations amend the provisions of section 1159 (meaning of "subsidiary" etc) and Schedule 6 (meaning of "subsidiary" etc: supplementary provisions) so as to alter the meaning of the expressions "subsidiary", "holding company" or "wholly-owned subsidiary".

(2) Regulations under this section are subject to negative resolution procedure.

(3) Any amendment made by regulations under this section does not apply for the purposes of enactments outside the Companies Acts unless the regulations so provide.

(4) So much of section 23(3) of the Interpretation Act 1978 (c 30) as applies section 17(2)(a) of that Act (effect of repeal and re-enactment) to deeds, instruments and documents other than enactments does not apply in relation to any repeal and re-enactment effected by regulations under this section.

NOTES

Regulations: no Regulations have been made under this section.

Meaning of "undertaking" and related expressions

[1.1331]

1161 Meaning of "undertaking" and related expressions

(1) In the Companies Acts "undertaking" means—
(a) a body corporate or partnership, or
(b) an unincorporated association carrying on a trade or business, with or without a view to profit.

(2) In the Companies Acts references to shares—
(a) in relation to an undertaking with capital but no share capital, are to rights to share in the capital of the undertaking; and
(b) in relation to an undertaking without capital, are to interests—
 (i) conferring any right to share in the profits or liability to contribute to the losses of the undertaking, or
 (ii) giving rise to an obligation to contribute to the debts or expenses of the undertaking in the event of a winding up.

(3) Other expressions appropriate to companies shall be construed, in relation to an undertaking which is not a company, as references to the corresponding persons, officers, documents or organs, as the case may be, appropriate to undertakings of that description.

This is subject to provision in any specific context providing for the translation of such expressions.

(4) References in the Companies Acts to "fellow subsidiary undertakings" are to undertakings which are subsidiary undertakings of the same parent undertaking but are not parent undertakings or subsidiary undertakings of each other.

(5) In the Companies Acts "group undertaking", in relation to an undertaking, means an undertaking which is—
(a) a parent undertaking or subsidiary undertaking of that undertaking, or
(b) a subsidiary undertaking of any parent undertaking of that undertaking.

[1.1332]

1162 Parent and subsidiary undertakings

(1) This section (together with Schedule 7) defines "parent undertaking" and "subsidiary undertaking" for the purposes of the Companies Acts.

(2) An undertaking is a parent undertaking in relation to another undertaking, a subsidiary undertaking, if—
(a) it holds a majority of the voting rights in the undertaking, or
(b) it is a member of the undertaking and has the right to appoint or remove a majority of its board of directors, or
(c) it has the right to exercise a dominant influence over the undertaking—
 (i) by virtue of provisions contained in the undertaking's articles, or
 (ii) by virtue of a control contract, or
(d) it is a member of the undertaking and controls alone, pursuant to an agreement with other shareholders or members, a majority of the voting rights in the undertaking.

(3) For the purposes of subsection (2) an undertaking shall be treated as a member of another undertaking—
(a) if any of its subsidiary undertakings is a member of that undertaking, or
(b) if any shares in that other undertaking are held by a person acting on behalf of the undertaking or any of its subsidiary undertakings.

(4) An undertaking is also a parent undertaking in relation to another undertaking, a subsidiary undertaking, if—
(a) it has the power to exercise, or actually exercises, dominant influence or control over it, or
(b) it and the subsidiary undertaking are managed on a unified basis.

(5) A parent undertaking shall be treated as the parent undertaking of undertakings in relation to which any of its subsidiary undertakings are, or are to be treated as, parent undertakings; and references to its subsidiary undertakings shall be construed accordingly.

(6) Schedule 7 contains provisions explaining expressions used in this section and otherwise supplementing this section.

(7) In this section and that Schedule references to shares, in relation to an undertaking, are to allotted shares.

Other definitions

[1.1333]

1163 "Non-cash asset"

(1) In the Companies Acts "non-cash asset" means any property or interest in property, other than cash.

For this purpose "cash" includes foreign currency.

(2) A reference to the transfer or acquisition of a non-cash asset includes—

(a) the creation or extinction of an estate or interest in, or a right over, any property, and

(b) the discharge of a liability of any person, other than a liability for a liquidated sum.

[1.1334]

1164 Meaning of "banking company" and "banking group"

(1) This section defines "banking company" and "banking group" for the purposes of the Companies Acts.

(2) "Banking company" means a person who has permission under [Part 4A] of the Financial Services and Markets Act 2000 (c 8) to accept deposits, other than—

(a) a person who is not a company, and

(b) a person who has such permission only for the purpose of carrying on another regulated activity in accordance with permission under that Part.

(3) The definition in subsection (2) must be read with section 22 of that Act, any relevant order under that section and Schedule 2 to that Act.

(4) References to a banking group are to a group where the parent company is a banking company or where—

(a) the parent company's principal subsidiary undertakings are wholly or mainly credit institutions, and

(b) the parent company does not itself carry on any material business apart from the acquisition, management and disposal of interests in subsidiary undertakings.

"Group" here means a parent undertaking and its subsidiary undertakings.

(5) For the purposes of subsection (4)—

(a) a parent company's principal subsidiary undertakings are the subsidiary undertakings of the company whose results or financial position would principally affect the figures shown in the group accounts, and

(b) the management of interests in subsidiary undertakings includes the provision of services to such undertakings.

NOTES

Sub-s (2): words in square brackets substituted by the Financial Services Act 2012, s 114(1), Sch 18, Pt 2, paras 110, 121, as from 1 April 2013.

[1.1335]

1165 Meaning of "insurance company" and related expressions

(1) This section defines "insurance company", "authorised insurance company", "insurance group" and "insurance market activity" for the purposes of the Companies Acts.

(2) An "authorised insurance company" means a person (whether incorporated or not) who has permission under [Part 4A] of the Financial Services and Markets Act 2000 (c 8) to effect or carry out contracts of insurance.

(3) An "insurance company" means—

(a) an authorised insurance company, or

(b) any other person (whether incorporated or not) who—

(i) carries on insurance market activity, or

(ii) may effect or carry out contracts of insurance under which the benefits provided by that person are exclusively or primarily benefits in kind in the event of accident to or breakdown of a vehicle.

(4) Neither expression includes a friendly society within the meaning of the Friendly Societies Act 1992 (c 40).

(5) References to an insurance group are to a group where the parent company is an insurance company or where—

(a) the parent company's principal subsidiary undertakings are wholly or mainly insurance companies, and

(b) the parent company does not itself carry on any material business apart from the acquisition, management and disposal of interests in subsidiary undertakings.

"Group" here means a parent undertaking and its subsidiary undertakings.

(6) For the purposes of subsection (5)—

(a) a parent company's principal subsidiary undertakings are the subsidiary undertakings of the company whose results or financial position would principally affect the figures shown in the group accounts, and

(b) the management of interests in subsidiary undertakings includes the provision of services to such undertakings.

(7) "Insurance market activity" has the meaning given in section 316(3) of the Financial Services and Markets Act 2000.

(8) References in this section to contracts of insurance and to the effecting or carrying out of such contracts must be read with section 22 of that Act, any relevant order under that section and Schedule 2 to that Act.

NOTES

Sub-s (2): words in square brackets substituted by the Financial Services Act 2012, s 114(1), Sch 18, Pt 2, paras 110, 122, as from 1 April 2013.

[1.1336]

1166 "Employees' share scheme"

For the purposes of the Companies Acts an employees' share scheme is a scheme for encouraging or facilitating the holding of shares in or debentures of a company by or for the benefit of—

(a) the bona fide employees or former employees of—

(i) the company,
(ii) any subsidiary of the company, or
(iii) the company's holding company or any subsidiary of the company's holding company, or
(b) the spouses, civil partners, surviving spouses, surviving civil partners, or minor children or step-children of such employees or former employees.

[1.1337]
1167 Meaning of "prescribed"
In the Companies Acts "prescribed" means prescribed (by order or by regulations) by the Secretary of State.

[1.1338]
1168 Hard copy and electronic form and related expressions
(1) The following provisions apply for the purposes of the Companies Acts.
(2) A document or information is sent or supplied in hard copy form if it is sent or supplied in a paper copy or similar form capable of being read.
References to hard copy have a corresponding meaning.
(3) A document or information is sent or supplied in electronic form if it is sent or supplied—
(a) by electronic means (for example, by e-mail or fax), or
(b) by any other means while in an electronic form (for example, sending a disk by post).
References to electronic copy have a corresponding meaning.
(4) A document or information is sent or supplied by electronic means if it is—
(a) sent initially and received at its destination by means of electronic equipment for the processing (which expression includes digital compression) or storage of data, and
(b) entirely transmitted, conveyed and received by wire, by radio, by optical means or by other electromagnetic means.
References to electronic means have a corresponding meaning.
(5) A document or information authorised or required to be sent or supplied in electronic form must be sent or supplied in a form, and by a means, that the sender or supplier reasonably considers will enable the recipient—
(a) to read it, and
(b) to retain a copy of it.
(6) For the purposes of this section, a document or information can be read only if—
(a) it can be read with the naked eye, or
(b) to the extent that it consists of images (for example photographs, pictures, maps, plans or drawings), it can be seen with the naked eye.
(7) The provisions of this section apply whether the provision of the Companies Acts in question uses the words "sent" or "supplied" or uses other words (such as "deliver", "provide", "produce" or, in the case of a notice, "give") to refer to the sending or supplying of a document or information.

[1.1339]
1169 Dormant companies
(1) For the purposes of the Companies Acts a company is "dormant" during any period in which it has no significant accounting transaction.
(2) A "significant accounting transaction" means a transaction that is required by section 386 to be entered in the company's accounting records.
(3) In determining whether or when a company is dormant, there shall be disregarded—
(a) any transaction arising from the taking of shares in the company by a subscriber to the memorandum as a result of an undertaking of his in connection with the formation of the company;
(b) any transaction consisting of the payment of—
(i) a fee to the registrar on a change of the company's name,
(ii) a fee to the registrar on the re-registration of the company,
(iii) a penalty under section 453 (penalty for failure to file accounts), or
(iv) a fee to the registrar for the registration of [a confirmation statement].
(4) Any reference in the Companies Acts to a body corporate other than a company being dormant has a corresponding meaning.

NOTES
Sub-s (3): words in square brackets substituted by the Small Business, Enterprise and Employment Act 2015, s 93(1), (6), as from 30 June 2016.

[1.1340]
1170 Meaning of "EEA State" and related expressions
In the Companies Acts—
["EEA State" has the meaning given by Schedule 1 to the Interpretation Act 1978;]
"EEA company" and "EEA undertaking" mean a company or undertaking governed by the law of an EEA State.

NOTES
Definition "EEA State" substituted by the Companies (EEA State) Regulations 2007, SI 2007/732, reg 3, as from 9 March 2007.

[1.1341]
[1170A Receiver or manager and certain related references
(1) Any reference in the Companies Acts to a receiver or manager of the property of a company, or to a receiver of it, includes a receiver or manager or (as the case may be) a receiver of part only of that property and a receiver of the income arising from the property or from part of it.

(2) Any reference in the Companies Acts to the appointment of a receiver or manager under powers contained in an instrument includes an appointment made under powers that by virtue of an enactment are implied in and have effect as if contained in an instrument.]

NOTES

Inserted, together with s 1170B, by the Companies Act 2006 (Consequential Amendments, Transitional Provisions and Savings) Order 2009, SI 2009/1941, art 2(1), Sch 1, para 260(1), (8), as from 1 October 2009.

[1.1342]
[1170B Meaning of "contributory"

(1) In the Companies Acts "contributory" means every person liable to contribute to the assets of a company in the event of its being wound up.

(2) For the purposes of all proceedings for determining, and all proceedings prior to the final determination of, the persons who are to be deemed contributories, the expression includes any person alleged to be a contributory.

(3) The reference in subsection (1) to persons liable to contribute to the assets does not include a person so liable by virtue of a declaration by the court under—

(a) section 213 of the Insolvency Act 1986 or Article 177 of the Insolvency (Northern Ireland) Order 1989 (fraudulent trading), or

(b) section 214 of that Act or Article 178 of that Order (wrongful trading).]

NOTES

Inserted as noted to s 1170A at **[1.1341]**.

[1.1343]
1171 The former Companies Acts

In the Companies Acts—

"the former Companies Acts" means—

(a) the Joint Stock Companies Acts, the Companies Act 1862 (c 89), the Companies (Consolidation) Act 1908 (c 69), the Companies Act 1929 (c 23), the Companies Act (Northern Ireland) 1932 (c 7 (NI)), the Companies Acts 1948 to 1983, the Companies Act (Northern Ireland) 1960 (c 22 (NI)), the Companies (Northern Ireland) Order 1986 (SI 1986/1032 (NI 6)) and the Companies Consolidation (Consequential Provisions) (Northern Ireland) Order 1986 (SI 1986/1035 (NI 9)), and

(b) the provisions of the Companies Act 1985 (c 6) and the Companies Consolidation (Consequential Provisions) Act 1985 (c 9) that are no longer in force;

"the Joint Stock Companies Acts" means the Joint Stock Companies Act 1856 (c 47), the Joint Stock Companies Acts 1856, 1857 (20 & 21 Vict c 14), the Joint Stock Banking Companies Act 1857 (c 49), and the Act to enable Joint Stock Banking Companies to be formed on the principle of limited liability (1858 c 91), but does not include the Joint Stock Companies Act 1844 (c 110).

General

[1.1344]
1172 References to requirements of this Act

References in the company law provisions of this Act to the requirements of this Act include the requirements of regulations and orders made under it.

[1.1345]
1173 Minor definitions: general

(1) In the Companies Acts—

["the Audit Regulation" means Regulation 537/2014 of the European Parliament and of the Council on specific requirements regarding statutory audit of public interest entities;]

"body corporate" and "corporation" include a body incorporated outside the United Kingdom, but do not include—

(a) a corporation sole, or

(b) a partnership that, whether or not a legal person, is not regarded as a body corporate under the law by which it is governed;

["the competent authority" means the Financial Reporting Council Limited;]

["credit institution" means a credit institution as defined in Article 4(1)(1) of Regulation (EU) No 575/2013 of the European Parliament and of the Council;]

["the data protection legislation" has the same meaning as in the Data Protection Act 2018 (see section 3 of that Act);]

["EU regulated market" has the meaning given in Article 2.1.13B of Regulation (EU) No 600/2014 of the European Parliament and of the Council of 15 May 2014 and amending Regulation (EU) No 648/2012;]

"financial institution" means a financial institution within the meaning of Article 1.1 of the Council Directive on the obligations of branches established in a Member State of credit and financial institutions having their head offices outside that Member State regarding the publication of annual accounting documents (the Bank Branches Directive, 89/ 117/EEC);

"firm" means any entity, whether or not a legal person, that is not an individual and includes a body corporate, a corporation sole and a partnership or other unincorporated association;

"the Gazette" means—

(a) as respects companies registered in England and Wales, the London Gazette,

(b) as respects companies registered in Scotland, the Edinburgh Gazette, and

(c) as respects companies registered in Northern Ireland, the Belfast Gazette;

"hire-purchase agreement" has the same meaning as in the Consumer Credit Act 1974 (c 39);

"officer", in relation to a body corporate, includes a director, manager or secretary;

"parent company" means a company that is a parent undertaking (see section 1162 and Schedule 7);

"regulated activity" has the meaning given in section 22 of the Financial Services and Markets Act 2000 (c 8);

["regulated market" has the meaning given in Article 2.1.13 of Regulation (EU) No 600/2014 of the European Parliament and of the Council of 15 May 2014 and amending Regulation (EU) No 648/2012;]

["transferable securities" has the meaning given by Article 2.1.24 of Regulation (EU) No 600/2014 of the European Parliament and of the Council of 15 May 2014 and amending Regulation (EU) No 648/2012;]

["UK regulated market" has the meaning given in Article 2.1.13A of Regulation (EU) No 600/2014 of the European Parliament and of the Council of 15 May 2014 and amending Regulation (EU) No 648/2012;]

"working day", in relation to a company, means a day that is not a Saturday or Sunday, Christmas Day, Good Friday or any day that is a bank holiday under the Banking and Financial Dealings Act 1971 (c 80) in the part of the United Kingdom where the company is registered.

(2) . . .

NOTES

Sub-s (1) is amended as follows:

Definitions "the Audit Regulation" and "the competent authority" inserted by the Statutory Auditors and Third Country Auditors Regulations 2016, SI 2016/649, reg 15, Sch 3, Pt 4, para 27, as from 17 June 2016.

Definition "credit institution" substituted by the Capital Requirements Regulations 2013, SI 2013/3115, reg 46(1), Sch 2, Pt 2, para 42(1), (2), as from 1 January 2014.

Definition "the data protection legislation" inserted by the Data Protection Act 2018, s 211, Sch 19, Pt 1, paras 120, 124, as from 25 May 2018 (for transitional provisions and savings relating to the repeal of the Data Protection Act 1998, see Sch 20 to the 2018 Act).

Definitions "EU regulated market" and "UK regulated market" inserted, and definition "regulated market" substituted, by the Accounts and Reports (Amendment) (EU Exit) Regulations 2019, SI 2019/145, reg 5, Sch 2, Pt 1, paras 1, 18(a), as from IP completion day (as defined in the European Union (Withdrawal Agreement) Act 2020, s 39) (in so far as the new definitions do not apply to enactments which operate by reference to financial years), and in relation to financial years beginning on or after IP completion day (otherwise) (for effect and transitional provisions see regs 2(a)(ii) and 7 of the 2019 Regulations at **[12.77]** and **[12.79]**).

Definition "transferable securities" originally inserted by the Companies, Partnerships and Groups (Accounts and Reports) Regulations 2015, SI 2015/980, reg 12, in relation to (a) financial years beginning on or after 1 January 2016, and (b) a financial year of a company beginning on or after 1 January 2015, but before 1 January 2016, if the directors of the company so decide. Subsequently substituted by the Companies, Limited Liability Partnerships and Partnerships (Amendment etc) (EU Exit) Regulations 2019, SI 2019/348, reg 6, Sch 1, paras 1, 26, as from IP completion day (as defined in the European Union (Withdrawal Agreement) Act 2020, s 39).

Sub-s (2): repealed by SI 2019/145, reg 5, Sch 2, Pt 1, paras 1, 18(b), as from IP completion day (as defined in the European Union (Withdrawal Agreement) Act 2020, s 39).

[1.1346]

1174 Index of defined expressions

Schedule 8 contains an index of provisions defining or otherwise explaining expressions used in the Companies Acts.

PART 39 COMPANIES: MINOR AMENDMENTS

1175 (*This section introduced the amendments made by Sch 9 and was repealed by the Deregulation Act 2015, s 107, Sch 23, Pt 1, para 1, as from 26 May 2015.*)

[1.1347]

1176 Power of Secretary of State to bring civil proceedings on company's behalf

(1)–(3) *(Repeal CA 1985, s 438, and amend ss 439, 453 of that Act at* **[5.22]**, **[5.42]**.*)*

(4) Nothing in this section affects proceedings brought under section 438 before the commencement of this section.

[1.1348]

1177 Repeal of certain provisions about company directors

The following provisions of Part 10 of the Companies Act 1985 shall cease to have effect—

section 311 (prohibition on tax-free payments to directors);
sections 323 and 327 (prohibition on directors dealing in share options);
sections 324 to 326 and 328 to 329, and Parts 2 to 4 of Schedule 13 (register of directors' interests);
sections 343 and 344 (special procedure for disclosure by banks).

[1.1349]

1178 Repeal of requirement that certain companies publish periodical statement

The following provisions shall cease to have effect—

section 720 of the Companies Act 1985 (c 6) (certain companies to publish periodical statement), and
Schedule 23 to that Act (form of statement under section 720).

[1.1350]

1179 Repeal of requirement that Secretary of State prepare annual report

Section 729 of the Companies Act 1985 (annual report to Parliament by Secretary of State on matters within the Companies Acts) shall cease to have effect.

[1.1351]

1180 Repeal of certain provisions about company charges

Part 4 of the Companies Act 1989 (c 40) (registration of company charges), which has not been brought into force, is repealed.

[1.1352]

1181 Access to constitutional documents of RTE and RTM companies

(1) The Secretary of State may by order—

(a) amend Chapter 1 of Part 1 of the Leasehold Reform, Housing and Urban Development Act 1993 (c 28) for the purpose of facilitating access to the provisions of the articles or any other constitutional document of RTE companies;

(b) amend Chapter 1 of Part 2 of the Commonhold and Leasehold Reform Act 2002 (c 15) (leasehold reform) for the purpose of facilitating access to the provisions of the articles or any other constitutional document of RTM companies.

(2) References in subsection (1) to provisions of a company's articles or any other constitutional document include any provisions included in those documents by virtue of any enactment.

(3) An order under this section is subject to negative resolution procedure.

(4) In this section—

"RTE companies" has the same meaning as in Chapter 1 of Part 1 of the Leasehold Reform, Housing and Urban Development Act 1993;

"RTM companies" has the same meaning as in Chapter 1 of Part 2 of the Commonhold and Leasehold Reform Act 2002.

NOTES

Orders: no Orders have been made under this section.

PART 40 COMPANY DIRECTORS: FOREIGN DISQUALIFICATION ETC

Introductory

[1.1353]

1182 Persons subject to foreign restrictions

(1) This section defines what is meant by references in this Part to a person being subject to foreign restrictions.

(2) A person is subject to foreign restrictions if under the law of a country or territory outside the United Kingdom—

(a) he is, by reason of misconduct or unfitness, disqualified to any extent from acting in connection with the affairs of a company,

(b) he is, by reason of misconduct or unfitness, required—

(i) to obtain permission from a court or other authority, or

(ii) to meet any other condition,

before acting in connection with the affairs of a company, or

(c) he has, by reason of misconduct or unfitness, given undertakings to a court or other authority of a country or territory outside the United Kingdom—

(i) not to act in connection with the affairs of a company, or

(ii) restricting the extent to which, or the way in which, he may do so.

(3) The references in subsection (2) to acting in connection with the affairs of a company are to doing any of the following—

(a) being a director of a company,

(b) acting as receiver of a company's property, or

(c) being concerned or taking part in the promotion, formation or management of a company.

(4) In this section—

(a) "company" means a company incorporated or formed under the law of the country or territory in question, and

(b) in relation to such a company—

"director" means the holder of an office corresponding to that of director of a UK company; and

"receiver" includes any corresponding officer under the law of that country or territory.

[1.1354]

1183 Meaning of "the court" and "UK company"

In this Part—

"the court" means—

(a) in England and Wales, the High Court or [the county court];

(b) in Scotland, the Court of Session or the sheriff court;

(c) in Northern Ireland, the High Court;

"UK company" means a company registered under this Act.

NOTES

Words in square brackets substituted by the Crime and Courts Act 2013, s 17, Sch 9, Pt 3, para 52, as from 22 April 2014.

Power to disqualify

[1.1355]

1184 Disqualification of persons subject to foreign restrictions

(1) The Secretary of State may make provision by regulations disqualifying a person subject to foreign restrictions from—

(a) being a director of a UK company,

(b) acting as receiver of a UK company's property, or

(c) in any way, whether directly or indirectly, being concerned or taking part in the promotion, formation or management of a UK company.

(2) The regulations may provide that a person subject to foreign restrictions—

(a) is disqualified automatically by virtue of the regulations, or

(b) may be disqualified by order of the court on the application of the Secretary of State.

(3) The regulations may provide that the Secretary of State may accept an undertaking (a "disqualification undertaking") from a person subject to foreign restrictions that he will not do anything which would be in breach of a disqualification under subsection (1).

(4) In this Part—

(a) a "person disqualified under this Part" is a person—

(i) disqualified as mentioned in subsection (2)(a) or (b), or

(ii) who has given and is subject to a disqualification undertaking;

(b) references to a breach of a disqualification include a breach of a disqualification undertaking.

(5) The regulations may provide for applications to the court by persons disqualified under this Part for permission to act in a way which would otherwise be in breach of the disqualification.

(6) The regulations must provide that a person ceases to be disqualified under this Part on his ceasing to be subject to foreign restrictions.

(7) Regulations under this section are subject to affirmative resolution procedure.

NOTES

Regulations: no Regulations have been made under this section.

[1.1356]

1185 Disqualification regulations: supplementary

(1) Regulations under section 1184 may make different provision for different cases and may in particular distinguish between cases by reference to—

(a) the conduct on the basis of which the person became subject to foreign restrictions;

(b) the nature of the foreign restrictions;

(c) the country or territory under whose law the foreign restrictions were imposed.

(2) Regulations under section 1184(2)(b) or (5) (provision for applications to the court)—

(a) must specify the grounds on which an application may be made;

(b) may specify factors to which the court shall have regard in determining an application.

(3) The regulations may, in particular, require the court to have regard to the following factors—

(a) whether the conduct on the basis of which the person became subject to foreign restrictions would, if done in relation to a UK company, have led a court to make a disqualification order on an application under the Company Directors Disqualification Act 1986 (c 46) or the Company Directors Disqualification (Northern Ireland) Order 2002 (SI 2002/3150 (NI 4));

(b) in a case in which the conduct on the basis of which the person became subject to foreign restrictions would not be unlawful if done in relation to a UK company, the fact that the person acted unlawfully under foreign law;

(c) whether the person's activities in relation to UK companies began after he became subject to foreign restrictions;

(d) whether the person's activities (or proposed activities) in relation to UK companies are undertaken (or are proposed to be undertaken) outside the United Kingdom.

(4) Regulations under section 1184(3) (provision as to undertakings given to the Secretary of State) may include provision allowing the Secretary of State, in determining whether to accept an undertaking, to take into account matters other than criminal convictions notwithstanding that the person may be criminally liable in respect of those matters.

(5) Regulations under section 1184(5) (provision for application to court for permission to act) may include provision—

(a) entitling the Secretary of State to be represented at the hearing of the application, and

(b) as to the giving of evidence or the calling of witnesses by the Secretary of State at the hearing of the application.

[1.1357]

1186 Offence of breach of disqualification

(1) Regulations under section 1184 may provide that a person disqualified under this Part who acts in breach of the disqualification commits an offence.

(2) The regulations may provide that a person guilty of such an offence is liable—

(a) on conviction on indictment, to imprisonment for a term not exceeding two years or a fine (or both);

(b) on summary conviction—

(i) in England and Wales, to imprisonment for a term not exceeding twelve months or to a fine not exceeding the statutory maximum (or both);

(ii) in Scotland or Northern Ireland, to imprisonment for a term not exceeding six months, or to a fine not exceeding the statutory maximum (or both).

(3) In relation to an offence committed before [2 May 2022], for "twelve months" in subsection (2)(b)(i) substitute "six months".

NOTES

Sub-s (3): words in square brackets substituted by the Criminal Justice Act 2003 (Commencement No 33) and Sentencing Act 2020 (Commencement No 2) Regulations 2022, SI 2022/500, reg 5, Schedule, Pt 1, as from 28 April 2022.

Power to make persons liable for company's debts

[1.1358]

1187 Personal liability for debts of company

(1) The Secretary of State may provide by regulations that a person who, at a time when he is subject to foreign restrictions—

(a) is a director of a UK company, or

(b) is involved in the management of a UK company,

is personally responsible for all debts and other liabilities of the company incurred during that time.

(2) A person who is personally responsible by virtue of this section for debts and other liabilities of a company is jointly and severally liable in respect of those debts and liabilities with—

(a) the company, and

(b) any other person who (whether by virtue of this section or otherwise) is so liable.

(3) For the purposes of this section a person is involved in the management of a company if he is concerned, whether directly or indirectly, or takes part, in the management of the company.

(4) The regulations may make different provision for different cases and may in particular distinguish between cases by reference to—

(a) the conduct on the basis of which the person became subject to foreign restrictions;
(b) the nature of the foreign restrictions;
(c) the country or territory under whose law the foreign restrictions were imposed.

(5) Regulations under this section are subject to affirmative resolution procedure.

NOTES

Regulations: no Regulations have been made under this section.

Power to require statements to be sent to the registrar of companies

[1.1359]
1188 Statements from persons subject to foreign restrictions

(1) The Secretary of State may make provision by regulations requiring a person who—

(a) is subject to foreign restrictions, and
(b) is not disqualified under this Part,

to send a statement to the registrar if he does anything that, if done by a person disqualified under this Part, would be in breach of the disqualification.

(2) The statement must include such information as may be specified in the regulations relating to—

(a) the person's activities in relation to UK companies, and
(b) the foreign restrictions to which the person is subject.

(3) The statement must be sent to the registrar within such period as may be specified in the regulations.

(4) The regulations may make different provision for different cases and may in particular distinguish between cases by reference to—

(a) the conduct on the basis of which the person became subject to foreign restrictions;
(b) the nature of the foreign restrictions;
(c) the country or territory under whose law the foreign restrictions were imposed.

(5) Regulations under this section are subject to affirmative resolution procedure.

NOTES

Regulations: no Regulations have been made under this section.

[1.1360]
1189 Statements from persons disqualified

(1) The Secretary of State may make provision by regulations requiring a statement or notice sent to the registrar of companies under any of the provisions listed below that relates (wholly or partly) to a person who—

(a) is a person disqualified under this Part, or
(b) is subject to a disqualification order or disqualification undertaking under the Company Directors Disqualification Act 1986 (c 46) or the Company Directors Disqualification (Northern Ireland) Order 2002 (SI 2002/3150 (NI 4)),

to be accompanied by an additional statement.

(2) The provisions referred to above are—

(a) section 12 (statement of a company's proposed officers),
(b) section 167(2) (notice of person having become director), and
(c) section 276 (notice of a person having become secretary or one of joint secretaries).

(3) The additional statement is a statement that the person has obtained permission from a court, on an application under section 1184(5) or (as the case may be) for the purposes of section 1(1)(a) of the Company Directors Disqualification Act 1986 (c 46) or Article 3(1) of the Company Directors Disqualification (Northern Ireland) Order 2002 (SI 2002/3150 (NI 4)), to act in the capacity in question.

(4) Regulations under this section are subject to affirmative resolution procedure.

NOTES

Regulations: no Regulations have been made under this section.

[1.1361]
1190 Statements: whether to be made public

(1) Regulations under section 1188 or 1189 (statements required to be sent to registrar) may provide that a statement sent to the registrar of companies under the regulations is to be treated as a record relating to a company for the purposes of section 1080 (the companies register).

(2) The regulations may make provision as to the circumstances in which such a statement is to be, or may be—

(a) withheld from public inspection, or
(b) removed from the register.

(3) The regulations may, in particular, provide that a statement is not to be withheld from public inspection or removed from the register unless the person to whom it relates provides such information, and satisfies such other conditions, as may be specified.

(4) The regulations may provide that section 1081 (note of removal of material from the register) does not apply, or applies with such modifications as may be specified, in the case of material removed from the register under the regulations.

(5) In this section "specified" means specified in the regulations.

[1.1362]
1191 Offences

(1) Regulations under section 1188 or 1189 may provide that it is an offence for a person—

(a) to fail to comply with a requirement under the regulations to send a statement to the registrar;

(b) knowingly or recklessly to send a statement under the regulations to the registrar that is misleading, false or deceptive in a material particular.

(2) The regulations may provide that a person guilty of such an offence is liable—

(a) on conviction on indictment, to imprisonment for a term not exceeding two years or a fine (or both);

(b) on summary conviction—

(i) in England and Wales, to imprisonment for a term not exceeding twelve months or to a fine not exceeding the statutory maximum (or both);

(ii) in Scotland or Northern Ireland, to imprisonment for a term not exceeding six months, or to a fine not exceeding the statutory maximum (or both).

(3) In relation to an offence committed before [2 May 2022], for "twelve months" in subsection (2)(b)(i) substitute "six months".

NOTES

Sub-s (3): words in square brackets substituted by the Criminal Justice Act 2003 (Commencement No 33) and Sentencing Act 2020 (Commencement No 2) Regulations 2022, SI 2022/500, reg 5, Schedule, Pt 1, as from 28 April 2022.

PART 41 BUSINESS NAMES

CHAPTER 1 RESTRICTED OR PROHIBITED NAMES

Introductory

[1.1363]

1192 Application of this Chapter

(1) This Chapter applies to any person carrying on business in the United Kingdom.

(2) The provisions of this Chapter do not prevent—

(a) an individual carrying on business under a name consisting of his surname without any addition other than a permitted addition, or

(b) individuals carrying on business in partnership under a name consisting of the surnames of all the partners without any addition other than a permitted addition.

(3) The following are the permitted additions—

(a) in the case of an individual, his forename or initial;

(b) in the case of a partnership—

(i) the forenames of individual partners or the initials of those forenames, or

(ii) where two or more individual partners have the same surname, the addition of "s" at the end of that surname;

(c) in either case, an addition merely indicating that the business is carried on in succession to a former owner of the business.

Sensitive words or expressions

[1.1364]

1193 Name suggesting connection with government or public authority

(1) A person must not, without the approval of the Secretary of State, carry on business in the United Kingdom under a name that would be likely to give the impression that the business is connected with—

(a) Her Majesty's Government, any part of the Scottish administration[, the Welsh Assembly Government] or Her Majesty's Government in Northern Ireland,

(b) any local authority, or

(c) any public authority specified for the purposes of this section by regulations made by the Secretary of State.

(2) For the purposes of this section—

"local authority" means—

(a) a local authority within the meaning of the Local Government Act 1972 (c 70), the Common Council of the City of London or the Council of the Isles of Scilly,

(b) a council constituted under section 2 of the Local Government etc (Scotland) Act 1994 (c 39), or

(c) a district council in Northern Ireland;

"public authority" includes any person or body having functions of a public nature.

(3) Regulations under this section are subject to affirmative resolution procedure.

(4) A person who contravenes this section commits an offence.

(5) Where an offence under this section is committed by a body corporate, an offence is also committed by every officer of the body who is in default.

(6) A person guilty of an offence under this section is liable on summary conviction to a fine not exceeding level 3 on the standard scale and, for continued contravention, a daily default fine not exceeding one-tenth of level 3 on the standard scale.

NOTES

Sub-s (1): words in square brackets inserted by the Government of Wales Act 2006 (Consequential Modifications, Transitional Provisions and Saving) Order 2009, SI 2009/2958, arts 8, 11, as from 6 November 2009.

National Assembly for Wales: see the note to s 54 at **[1.55]** in relation to the renaming of the National Assembly for Wales.

Regulations: the Company, Limited Liability Partnership and Business (Names and Trading Disclosures) Regulations 2015, SI 2015/17 at **[4.514]**. For a summary of all statutory instruments made under this Act, see Appendix 4 at **[A4]**.

[1.1365]

1194 Other sensitive words or expressions

(1) A person must not, without the approval of the Secretary of State, carry on business in the United Kingdom under a name that includes a word or expression for the time being specified in regulations made by the Secretary of State under this section.

(2) Regulations under this section are subject to approval after being made.

(3) A person who contravenes this section commits an offence.
(4) Where an offence under this section is committed by a body corporate, an offence is also committed by every officer of the body who is in default.
(5) A person guilty of an offence under this section is liable on summary conviction to a fine not exceeding level 3 on the standard scale and, for continued contravention, a daily default fine not exceeding one-tenth of level 3 on the standard scale.

NOTES

Chamber of commerce: by the Company and Business Names (Chamber of Commerce, etc) Act 1999, s 1 (as amended), the Secretary of State is required to include the title "chamber of commerce" (and its Welsh equivalent "siambr fasnach") in the list of controlled titles maintained in accordance with regulations made under this section.

Regulations: the Company, Limited Liability Partnership and Business Names (Sensitive Words and Expressions) Regulations 2014, SI 2014/3140 at **[4.503]**. For a summary of all statutory instruments made under this Act, see Appendix 4 at **[A4]**.

[1.1366]
1195 Requirement to seek comments of government department or other relevant body
(1) The Secretary of State may by regulations under—
- (a) section 1193 (name suggesting connection with government or public authority), or
- (b) section 1194 (other sensitive words or expressions),

require that, in connection with an application for the approval of the Secretary of State under that section, the applicant must seek the view of a specified Government department or other body.
(2) Where such a requirement applies, the applicant must request the specified department or other body (in writing) to indicate whether (and if so why) it has any objections to the proposed name.
(3) He must submit to the Secretary of State a statement that such a request has been made and a copy of any response received from the specified body.
(4) If these requirements are not complied with, the Secretary of State may refuse to consider the application for approval.
(5) In this section "specified" means specified in the regulations.

NOTES

Regulations: the Company, Limited Liability Partnership and Business Names (Sensitive Words and Expressions) Regulations 2014, SI 2014/3140 at **[4.503]**; the Company, Limited Liability Partnership and Business (Names and Trading Disclosures) Regulations 2015, SI 2015/17 at **[4.514]**. For a summary of all statutory instruments made under this Act, see Appendix 4 at **[A4]**.

[1.1367]
1196 Withdrawal of Secretary of State's approval
(1) This section applies to approval given for the purposes of—
section 1193 (name suggesting connection with government or public authority), or
section 1194 (other sensitive words or expressions).
(2) If it appears to the Secretary of State that there are overriding considerations of public policy that require such approval to be withdrawn, the approval may be withdrawn by notice in writing given to the person concerned.
(3) The notice must state the date as from which approval is withdrawn.

Misleading names

[1.1368]
1197 Name containing inappropriate indication of company type or legal form
(1) The Secretary of State may make provision by regulations prohibiting a person from carrying on business in the United Kingdom under a name consisting of or containing specified words, expressions or other indications—
- (a) that are associated with a particular type of company or form of organisation, or
- (b) that are similar to words, expressions or other indications associated with a particular type of company or form of organisation.

(2) The regulations may prohibit the use of words, expressions or other indications—
- (a) in a specified part, or otherwise than in a specified part, of a name;
- (b) in conjunction with, or otherwise than in conjunction with, such other words, expressions or indications as may be specified.

(3) In this section "specified" means specified in the regulations.
(4) Regulations under this section are subject to negative resolution procedure.
(5) A person who uses a name in contravention of regulations under this section commits an offence.
(6) Where an offence under this section is committed by a body corporate, an offence is also committed by every officer of the body who is in default.
(7) A person guilty of an offence under this section is liable on summary conviction to a fine not exceeding level 3 on the standard scale and, for continued contravention, a daily default fine not exceeding one-tenth of level 3 on the standard scale.

NOTES

Regulations: the Company, Limited Liability Partnership and Business (Names and Trading Disclosures) Regulations 2015, SI 2015/17 at **[4.514]**. For a summary of all statutory instruments made under this Act, see Appendix 4 at **[A4]**.

[1.1369]
1198 Name giving misleading indication of activities
(1) A person must not carry on business in the United Kingdom under a name that gives so misleading an indication of the nature of the activities of the business as to be likely to cause harm to the public.
(2) A person who uses a name in contravention of this section commits an offence.

(3) Where an offence under this section is committed by a body corporate, an offence is also committed by every officer of the body who is in default.

(4) A person guilty of an offence under this section is liable on summary conviction to a fine not exceeding level 3 on the standard scale and, for continued contravention, a daily default fine not exceeding one-tenth of level 3 on the standard scale.

Supplementary

[1.1370]

1199 Savings for existing lawful business names

(1) This section has effect in relation to—

sections 1192 to 1196 (sensitive words or expressions), and

section 1197 (inappropriate indication of company type or legal form).

(2) Those sections do not apply to the carrying on of a business by a person who—

(a) carried on the business immediately before the date on which this Chapter came into force, and

(b) continues to carry it on under the name that immediately before that date was its lawful business name.

(3) Where—

(a) a business is transferred to a person on or after the date on which this Chapter came into force, and

(b) that person carries on the business under the name that was its lawful business name immediately before the transfer,

those sections do not apply in relation to the carrying on of the business under that name during the period of twelve months beginning with the date of the transfer.

(4) In this section "lawful business name", in relation to a business, means a name under which the business was carried on without contravening—

(a) section 2(1) of the Business Names Act 1985 (c 7) or Article 4(1) of the Business Names (Northern Ireland) Order 1986 (SI 1986/1033 NI 7)), or

(b) after this Chapter has come into force, the provisions of this Chapter.

CHAPTER 2 DISCLOSURE REQUIRED IN CASE OF INDIVIDUAL OR PARTNERSHIP

Introductory

[1.1371]

1200 Application of this Chapter

(1) This Chapter applies to an individual or partnership carrying on business in the United Kingdom under a business name.

References in this Chapter to "a person to whom this Chapter applies" are to such an individual or partnership.

(2) For the purposes of this Chapter a "business name" means a name other than—

(a) in the case of an individual, his surname without any addition other than a permitted addition;

(b) in the case of a partnership—

(i) the surnames of all partners who are individuals, and

(ii) the corporate names of all partners who are bodies corporate,

without any addition other than a permitted addition.

(3) The following are the permitted additions—

(a) in the case of an individual, his forename or initial;

(b) in the case of a partnership—

(i) the forenames of individual partners or the initials of those forenames, or

(ii) where two or more individual partners have the same surname, the addition of "s" at the end of that surname;

(c) in either case, an addition merely indicating that the business is carried on in succession to a former owner of the business.

[1.1372]

[1201 Information required to be disclosed

(1) The "information required by this Chapter" is—

(a) in the case of an individual, the individual's name;

(b) in the case of a partnership, the name of each member of the partnership;

and, in relation to each person so named, an address at which service of any document relating in any way to the business will be effective.

(2) If the individual or partnership has a place of business in the United Kingdom, the address must be in the United Kingdom.

(3) If the individual or partnership does not have a place of business in the United Kingdom, the address must be an address at which service of documents can be effected by physical delivery and the delivery of documents is capable of being recorded by the obtaining of an acknowledgement of delivery.]

NOTES

Substituted by the Companies Act 2006 (Substitution of Section 1201) Regulations 2009, SI 2009/3182, reg 2, as from 28 December 2009.

Disclosure requirements

[1.1373]

1202 Disclosure required: business documents etc

(1) A person to whom this Chapter applies must state the information required by this Chapter, in legible characters, on all—

(a) business letters,

(b) written orders for goods or services to be supplied to the business,

(c) invoices and receipts issued in the course of the business, and

(d) written demands for payment of debts arising in the course of the business.

This subsection has effect subject to section 1203 (exemption for large partnerships if certain conditions met).
(2) A person to whom this Chapter applies must secure that the information required by this Chapter is immediately given, by written notice, to any person with whom anything is done or discussed in the course of the business and who asks for that information.
(3) The Secretary of State may by regulations require that such notices be given in a specified form.
(4) Regulations under this section are subject to negative resolution procedure.

NOTES

Regulations: no Regulations have been made under this section.

[1.1374]

1203 Exemption for large partnerships if certain conditions met

(1) Section 1202(1) (disclosure required in business documents) does not apply in relation to a document issued by a partnership of more than 20 persons if the following conditions are met.
(2) The conditions are that—

- (a) the partnership maintains at its principal place of business a list of the names of all the partners,
- (b) no partner's name appears in the document, except in the text or as a signatory, and
- (c) the document states in legible characters the address of the partnership's principal place of business and that the list of the partners' names is open to inspection there.

(3) Where a partnership maintains a list of the partners' names for the purposes of this section, any person may inspect the list during office hours.
(4) Where an inspection required by a person in accordance with this section is refused, an offence is committed by any member of the partnership concerned who without reasonable excuse refused the inspection or permitted it to be refused.
(5) A person guilty of an offence under subsection (4) is liable on summary conviction to a fine not exceeding level 3 on the standard scale and, for continued contravention, a daily default fine not exceeding one-tenth of level 3 on the standard scale.

[1.1375]

1204 Disclosure required: business premises

(1) A person to whom this Chapter applies must, in any premises—

- (a) where the business is carried on, and
- (b) to which customers of the business or suppliers of goods or services to the business have access,

display in a prominent position, so that it may easily be read by such customers or suppliers, a notice containing the information required by this Chapter.
(2) The Secretary of State may by regulations require that such notices be displayed in a specified form.
(3) Regulations under this section are subject to negative resolution procedure.

NOTES

Regulations: no Regulations have been made under this section.

Consequences of failure to make required disclosure

[1.1376]

1205 Criminal consequences of failure to make required disclosure

(1) A person who without reasonable excuse fails to comply with the requirements of—
section 1202 (disclosure required: business documents etc), or
section 1204 (disclosure required: business premises),
commits an offence.
(2) Where an offence under this section is committed by a body corporate, an offence is also committed by every officer of the body who is in default.
(3) A person guilty of an offence under this section is liable on summary conviction to a fine not exceeding level 3 on the standard scale and, for continued contravention, a daily default fine not exceeding one-tenth of level 3 on the standard scale.
(4) References in this section to the requirements of section 1202 or 1204 include the requirements of regulations under that section.

[1.1377]

1206 Civil consequences of failure to make required disclosure

(1) This section applies to any legal proceedings brought by a person to whom this Chapter applies to enforce a right arising out of a contract made in the course of a business in respect of which he was, at the time the contract was made, in breach of section 1202(1) or (2) (disclosure in business documents etc) or section 1204(1) (disclosure at business premises).
(2) The proceedings shall be dismissed if the defendant (in Scotland, the defender) to the proceedings shows—

- (a) that he has a claim against the claimant (pursuer) arising out of the contract that he has been unable to pursue by reason of the latter's breach of the requirements of this Chapter, or
- (b) that he has suffered some financial loss in connection with the contract by reason of the claimant's (pursuer's) breach of those requirements,

unless the court before which the proceedings are brought is satisfied that it is just and equitable to permit the proceedings to continue.
(3) References in this section to the requirements of this Chapter include the requirements of regulations under this Chapter.
(4) This section does not affect the right of any person to enforce such rights as he may have against another person in any proceedings brought by that person.

CHAPTER 3 SUPPLEMENTARY

[1.1378]

1207 Application of general provisions about offences

The provisions of sections 1121 to 1123 (liability of officer in default) and 1125 to 1131 (general provisions about offences) apply in relation to offences under this Part as in relation to offences under the Companies Acts.

[1.1379]

1208 Interpretation

In this Part—

"business" includes a profession;

"initial" includes any recognised abbreviation of a name;

"partnership" means—

(a) a partnership within the Partnership Act 1890 (c 39), or

(b) a limited partnership registered under the Limited Partnerships Act 1907 (c 24),

or a firm or entity of a similar character formed under the law of a country or territory outside the United Kingdom;

"surname", in relation to a peer or person usually known by a British title different from his surname, means the title by which he is known.

PART 42 STATUTORY AUDITORS

NOTES

Transfer of functions: Part 3 of the Statutory Auditors (Amendment of Companies Act 2006 and Delegation of Functions etc) Order 2012, SI 2012/1741 transfers the functions of the Secretary of State under Part 42 of this Act to the Financial Reporting Council Limited (subject to a number of specified exceptions and reservations). It revokes the Statutory Auditors (Delegation of Functions etc) Order 2008, SI 2008/496 (as from 2 July 2012) whereby functions under Part 42 were transferred to the Professional Oversight Board. See **[4.430]** et seq. See also the Local Audit (Delegation of Functions) and Statutory Audit (Delegation of Functions) Order 2014, SI 2014/2009 which transfers the functions of the Secretary of State under this Part, as applied with modifications to local audits by the Local Audit and Accountability Act 2014, Sch 5.

CHAPTER 1 INTRODUCTORY

[1.1380]

1209 Main purposes of Part

The main purposes of this Part are—

(a) to secure that only persons who are properly supervised and appropriately qualified are appointed as statutory auditors, and

(b) to secure that audits by persons so appointed are carried out properly, with integrity and with a proper degree of independence.

[1.1381]

1210 Meaning of "statutory auditor" etc

(1) In this Part "statutory auditor" means—

(a) a person appointed as auditor under Part 16 of this Act,

(b) a person appointed as auditor under section 77 of or Schedule 11 to the Building Societies Act 1986 (c 53),

[(c) a person appointed as auditor of a friendly society under section 72 of or Schedule 14 to the Friendly Societies Act 1992, where that society is—

(i) an insurer, or

(ii) an issuer whose transferable securities are admitted to trading on a [UK regulated market];]

(d) . . .

[(e) a person appointed as auditor for the purposes of regulation 5 of the Insurance Accounts Directive (Lloyd's Syndicate and Aggregate Accounts) Regulations 2008 or appointed to report on the "aggregate accounts" within the meaning of those Regulations,]

[(f) a person appointed as auditor of an insurance undertaking for the purposes of the Insurance Accounts Directive (Miscellaneous Insurance Undertakings) Regulations 2008,]

[(g) . . .]

(h) a person appointed as auditor of a prescribed person under a prescribed enactment authorising or requiring the appointment;

and the expressions "statutory audit" and "statutory audit work" are to be construed accordingly.

(2) In this Part "audited person" means the person in respect of whom a statutory audit is conducted.

(3) In subsection (1)—

. . .

"friendly society" means a friendly society within the meaning of the Friendly Societies Act 1992 (c 40);

. . .

["insurer" means a person who would be an insurance undertaking, as defined in Article 2(1) of Council Directive 91/674/EEC of 19 December 1991 of the European Parliament and of the Council on the annual accounts and consolidated accounts of insurance undertakings as that Article had effect immediately before IP completion day, were the United Kingdom a member State;]

["issuer" has the same meaning as in Part 6 of the Financial Services and Markets Act 2000 (see section 102A(6));]

"prescribed" means prescribed, or of a description prescribed, by order made by the Secretary of State for the purposes of subsection (1)(h);

[. . .]

(4) An order under this section is subject to negative resolution procedure.

NOTES

Sub-s (1) is amended as follows:

Para (c) substituted by the Statutory Auditors and Third Country Auditors Regulations 2017, SI 2017/516, reg 13(1), (2)(a), in relation to financial years of friendly societies beginning on or after 17 June 2016. Words in square brackets in sub-para (c)(ii) substituted by the Statutory Auditors and Third Country Auditors (Amendment) (EU Exit) Regulations 2019, SI 2019/177, regs 10, 11(a), as from IP completion day (as defined in the European Union (Withdrawal Agreement) Act 2020, s 39).

Para (d) repealed, and para (f) substituted, by the Insurance Accounts Directive (Miscellaneous Insurance Undertakings) Regulations 2008, SI 2008/565, reg 15, as from 6 April 2008, in relation to insurance undertakings' financial years beginning on or after that date, and auditors appointed in respect of those financial years.

Para (e) substituted by the Insurance Accounts Directive (Lloyd's Syndicate and Aggregate Accounts) Regulations 2008, SI 2008/1950, reg 31, in relation to financial years beginning on or after 1 January 2009.

Para (g) substituted by the Bank Accounts Directive (Miscellaneous Banks) Regulations 2008, SI 2008/567, reg 14, as from 6 April 2008, in relation to qualifying banks' financial years beginning on or after that date, and auditors appointed in respect of those financial years. Subsequently repealed by the Statutory Auditors Regulations 2017, SI 2017/1164, reg 19, Sch 4, as from 1 January 2018, in relation to financial years of qualifying banks beginning on or after 30 November 2018 (see**[4.671]** et seq).

Sub-s (3) is amended as follows:

Definition "bank" (omitted) repealed by SI 2019/177, regs 10, 11(b)(i), as from IP completion day (as defined in the European Union (Withdrawal Agreement) Act 2020, s 39).

Definition "industrial and provident society" (omitted) repealed by SI 2008/565, reg 15, as from 6 April 2008, in relation to insurance undertakings' financial years beginning on or after that date, and auditors appointed in respect of those financial years.

Definition "insurer" substituted by SI 2019/177, regs 10, 11(b)(ii), as from IP completion day (as defined in the European Union (Withdrawal Agreement) Act 2020, s 39). Note that reg 11(b)(ii) of the 2019 Regulations was amended by the Companies and Statutory Auditors etc (Consequential Amendments) (EU Exit) Regulations 2020, SI 2020/523, reg 14(d), with effect from immediately before IP completion day (and that the effect of the amendment has been incorporated in the text set out above).

Definition "issuer" inserted by SI 2017/516, reg 13(1), (2)(b), in relation to financial years of friendly societies beginning on or after 17 June 2016.

Definition "regulated market" (omitted) originally inserted by SI 2017/516, reg 13(1), (2)(b), in relation to financial years of friendly societies beginning on or after 17 June 2016. Subsequently repealed by SI 2019/177, regs 10, 11(b)(iii), as from IP completion day (as defined in the European Union (Withdrawal Agreement) Act 2020, s 39).

Regulations: the Partnerships (Accounts) Regulations 2008, SI 2008/569 at **[10.202]** (reg 14 of which provides that for the purposes of sub-s (1)(h) a qualifying partnership is a prescribed person, and reg 4(1)(b) is a prescribed enactment); the Limited Liability Partnerships (Accounts and Audit) (Application of Companies Act 2006) Regulations 2008, SI 2008/1911 at **[10.223]** (reg 48 of which provides that for the purposes of sub-s (1)(h) an LLP is a prescribed person, and Pt 16 of this Act (as applied to LLPs) is a prescribed enactment); the Unregistered Companies Regulations 2009, SI 2009/2436 at **[4.389]** (reg 6 of which provides that for the purposes of sub-s (1)(h) an unregistered company is a prescribed person, and Pt 16 of this Act (as applied to unregistered companies) is a prescribed enactment). For a summary of all statutory instruments made under this Act, see Appendix 4 at **[A4]**.

[1.1382]

1211 Eligibility for appointment as a statutory auditor: overview

A person is eligible for appointment as a statutory auditor only if the person is so eligible—

(a) by virtue of Chapter 2 (individuals and firms), or

(b) by virtue of Chapter 3 (Comptroller and Auditor General, etc).

CHAPTER 2 INDIVIDUALS AND FIRMS

Eligibility for appointment

[1.1383]

1212 Individuals and firms: eligibility for appointment as a statutory auditor

(1) An individual or firm is eligible for appointment as a statutory auditor if the individual or firm—

(a) is a member of a recognised supervisory body, and

(b) is eligible for appointment under the rules of that body.

(2) In the cases to which section 1222 applies (individuals retaining only 1967 Act authorisation) a person's eligibility for appointment as a statutory auditor is restricted as mentioned in that section.

[1.1384]

1213 Effect of ineligibility

(1) No person may act as statutory auditor of an audited person if he is ineligible for appointment as a statutory auditor.

(2) If at any time during his term of office a statutory auditor becomes ineligible for appointment as a statutory auditor, he must immediately—

(a) resign his office (with immediate effect), and

(b) give notice in writing to the audited person that he has resigned by reason of his becoming ineligible for appointment.

(3) A person is guilty of an offence if—

(a) he acts as a statutory auditor in contravention of subsection (1), or

(b) he fails to give the notice mentioned in paragraph (b) of subsection (2) in accordance with that subsection.

(4) A person guilty of an offence under subsection (3) is liable—

(a) on conviction on indictment, to a fine;

(b) on summary conviction, to a fine not exceeding the statutory maximum.

(5) A person is guilty of an offence if—

(a) he has been convicted of an offence under subsection (3)(a) or this subsection, and

(b) he continues to act as a statutory auditor in contravention of subsection (1) after the conviction.

(6) A person is guilty of an offence if—

(a) he has been convicted of an offence under subsection (3)(b) or this subsection, and

(b) he continues, after the conviction, to fail to give the notice mentioned in subsection (2)(b).

(7) A person guilty of an offence under subsection (5) or (6) is liable—

(a) on conviction on indictment, to a fine;

(b) on summary conviction, to a fine not exceeding [one-tenth of the greater of £5,000 or the amount corresponding to level 4 on the standard scale for summary offences] for each day on which the act or the failure continues.

(8) In proceedings against a person for an offence under this section it is a defence for him to show that he did not know and had no reason to believe that he was, or had become, ineligible for appointment as a statutory auditor.

NOTES

Sub-s (7): words in square brackets substituted (for the original words "one-tenth of the statutory maximum") by the Legal Aid, Sentencing and Punishment of Offenders Act 2012 (Fines on Summary Conviction) Regulations 2015, SI 2015/664, regs 3, 5, Sch 3, Pt 1, para 9(1), (24), as from 12 March 2015, in relation to England and Wales only (except in relation to (a) fines for offences committed before 12 March 2015, (b) the operation of restrictions on fines that may be imposed on a person aged under 18, or (c) fines that may be imposed on a person convicted by a magistrates' court who is to be sentenced as if convicted on indictment).

Independence requirement

[1.1385]

1214 Independence requirement

(1) A person may not act as statutory auditor of an audited person if one or more of subsections (2), (3) and (4) apply to him.

(2) This subsection applies if the person is—

(a) an officer or employee of the audited person, or

(b) a partner or employee of such a person, or a partnership of which such a person is a partner.

(3) This subsection applies if the person is—

(a) an officer or employee of an associated undertaking of the audited person, or

(b) a partner or employee of such a person, or a partnership of which such a person is a partner.

(4) This subsection applies if there exists, between—

(a) the person or an associate of his, and

(b) the audited person or an associated undertaking of the audited person,

a connection of any such description as may be specified by regulations made by the Secretary of State.

(5) An auditor of an audited person is not to be regarded as an officer or employee of the person for the purposes of subsections (2) and (3).

(6) In this section "associated undertaking", in relation to an audited person, means—

(a) a parent undertaking or subsidiary undertaking of the audited person, or

(b) a subsidiary undertaking of a parent undertaking of the audited person.

(7) Regulations under subsection (4) are subject to negative resolution procedure.

NOTES

Regulations: no Regulations have been made under this section.

[1.1386]

1215 Effect of lack of independence

(1) If at any time during his term of office a statutory auditor becomes prohibited from acting by section 1214(1), he must immediately—

(a) resign his office (with immediate effect), and

(b) give notice in writing to the audited person that he has resigned by reason of his lack of independence.

(2) A person is guilty of an offence if—

(a) he acts as a statutory auditor in contravention of section 1214(1), or

(b) he fails to give the notice mentioned in paragraph (b) of subsection (1) in accordance with that subsection.

(3) A person guilty of an offence under subsection (2) is liable—

(a) on conviction on indictment, to a fine;

(b) on summary conviction, to a fine not exceeding the statutory maximum.

(4) A person is guilty of an offence if—

(a) he has been convicted of an offence under subsection (2)(a) or this subsection, and

(b) he continues to act as a statutory auditor in contravention of section 1214(1) after the conviction.

(5) A person is guilty of an offence if—

(a) he has been convicted of an offence under subsection (2)(b) or this subsection, and

(b) after the conviction, he continues to fail to give the notice mentioned in subsection (1)(b).

(6) A person guilty of an offence under subsection (4) or (5) is liable—

(a) on conviction on indictment, to a fine;

(b) on summary conviction, to a fine not exceeding [one-tenth of the greater of £5,000 or the amount corresponding to level 4 on the standard scale for summary offences] for each day on which the act or the failure continues.

(7) In proceedings against a person for an offence under this section it is a defence for him to show that he did not know and had no reason to believe that he was, or had become, prohibited from acting as statutory auditor of the audited person by section 1214(1).

NOTES

Sub-s (6): words in square brackets substituted (for the original words "one-tenth of the statutory maximum") by the Legal Aid, Sentencing and Punishment of Offenders Act 2012 (Fines on Summary Conviction) Regulations 2015, SI 2015/664, regs 3, 5, Sch 3, Pt 1, para 9(1), (25), as from 12 March 2015, in relation to England and Wales only (except in relation to (a) fines for offences committed before 12 March 2015, (b) the operation of restrictions on fines that may be imposed on a person aged under 18, or (c) fines that may be imposed on a person convicted by a magistrates' court who is to be sentenced as if convicted on indictment).

Effect of appointment of a partnership

[1.1387]

1216 Effect of appointment of a partnership

(1) This section applies where a partnership constituted under the law of—

(a) England and Wales,

(b) Northern Ireland, or

(c) any other country or territory in which a partnership is not a legal person,

is by virtue of this Chapter appointed as statutory auditor of an audited person.

(2) Unless a contrary intention appears, the appointment is an appointment of the partnership as such and not of the partners.

(3) Where the partnership ceases, the appointment is to be treated as extending to—

(a) any appropriate partnership which succeeds to the practice of that partnership, or

(b) any other appropriate person who succeeds to that practice having previously carried it on in partnership.

(4) For the purposes of subsection (3)—

(a) a partnership is to be regarded as succeeding to the practice of another partnership only if the members of the successor partnership are substantially the same as those of the former partnership, and

(b) a partnership or other person is to be regarded as succeeding to the practice of a partnership only if it or he succeeds to the whole or substantially the whole of the business of the former partnership.

(5) Where the partnership ceases and the appointment is not treated under subsection (3) as extending to any partnership or other person, the appointment may with the consent of the audited person be treated as extending to an appropriate partnership, or other appropriate person, who succeeds to—

(a) the business of the former partnership, or

(b) such part of it as is agreed by the audited person is to be treated as comprising the appointment.

(6) For the purposes of this section, a partnership or other person is "appropriate" if it or he—

(a) is eligible for appointment as a statutory auditor by virtue of this Chapter, and

(b) is not prohibited by section 1214(1) from acting as statutory auditor of the audited person.

NOTES

See the Companies Act 2006 (Consequential Amendments etc) Order 2008, SI 2008/948, art 5 (at **[4.140]**) which provides that this section applies (subject to specified modifications) in relation to any statutory appointment where eligibility for the appointment depends on eligibility for appointment as a statutory auditor under this Part. For these purposes, a "statutory appointment" means an appointment in pursuance of an enactment authorising or requiring the making of the appointment, but only where that enactment was passed or made before 6 April 2008.

Supervisory bodies

[1.1388]

1217 Supervisory bodies

(1) In this Part a "supervisory body" means a body established in the United Kingdom (whether a body corporate or an unincorporated association) which maintains and enforces rules as to—

(a) the eligibility of persons for appointment as a statutory auditor, and

(b) the conduct of statutory audit work,

which are binding on persons seeking appointment or acting as a statutory auditor . . . because they are members of that body . . .

[(1A) The rules referred to in [paragraphs 9(1A) and 10C(3) (bar on appointment as director or other [officer),] paragraph 9(3)(b) (confidentiality of information)] [and paragraph 12(3)(b)(v) (temporary prohibition from exercising functions in a firm)] of Schedule 10 must also be binding on persons who—

(a) have sought appointment or acted as a statutory auditor, and

(b) have been members of the body at any time after the commencement of this Part.]

(2) In this Part references to the members of a supervisory body are to the persons who, whether or not members of the body, are subject to its rules in seeking appointment or acting as a statutory auditor.

(3) In this Part references to the rules of a supervisory body are to the rules (whether or not laid down by the body itself) which the body [or the competent authority] has power to enforce and which are relevant for the purposes of this Part.

This includes rules relating to the admission or expulsion of members of the body, so far as relevant for the purposes of this Part.

(4) Schedule 10 has effect with respect to the recognition of supervisory bodies for the purposes of this Part.

NOTES

Sub-s (1): words omitted repealed by the Statutory Auditors and Third Country Auditors Regulations 2007, SI 2007/3494, reg 4(1), (2), as from 6 April 2008.

Sub-s (1A): inserted by SI 2007/3494, reg 4(1), (3), as from 6 April 2008. Words in first (outer) pair of square brackets substituted by the Statutory Auditors and Third Country Auditors Regulations 2016, SI 2016/649, reg 15, Sch 3, Pt 5, para 29(1), (2), as from 17 June 2016. Word in second (inner) pair of square brackets substituted, and words in third pair of square brackets inserted, by the Statutory Auditors and Third Country Auditors Regulations 2017, SI 2017/516, reg 13(1), (3), as from 1 May 2017.

Sub-s (3): words in square brackets inserted by SI 2016/649, reg 15, Sch 3, Pt 5, para 29(1), (3), as from 17 June 2016.

[1.1389]

1218 Exemption from liability for damages

(1) No person within subsection (2) is to be liable in damages for anything done or omitted in the discharge or purported discharge of functions to which this subsection applies.

(2) The persons within this subsection are—

(a) any recognised supervisory body,

(b) any officer or employee of a recognised supervisory body, and

(c) any member of the governing body of a recognised supervisory body.

(3) Subsection (1) applies to the functions of a recognised supervisory body so far as relating to, or to matters arising out of, any of the following—

- (a) rules, practices, powers and arrangements of the body to which the requirements of Part 2 of Schedule 10 apply;
- (b) the obligations with which paragraph 20 of that Schedule requires the body to comply;
- (c) any guidance issued by the body;
- (d) the obligations imposed on the body by or by virtue of this Part [or by or by virtue of the Statutory Auditors and Third Country Auditors Regulations 2016;]
- [(e) the obligations imposed on the body by or by virtue of the Audit Regulation].

(4) The reference in subsection (3)(c) to guidance issued by a recognised supervisory body is a reference to any guidance or recommendation which is—

- (a) issued or made by it to all or any class of its members or persons seeking to become members, and
- (b) relevant for the purposes of this Part[, the Statutory Auditors and Third Country Auditors Regulations 2016 or the Audit Regulation],

including any guidance or recommendation relating to the admission or expulsion of members of the body, so far as relevant for the purposes of this Part[, the Statutory Auditors and Third Country Auditors Regulations 2016 or the Audit Regulation].

(5) Subsection (1) does not apply—

- (a) if the act or omission is shown to have been in bad faith, or
- (b) so as to prevent an award of damages in respect of the act or omission on the ground that it was unlawful as a result of section 6(1) of the Human Rights Act 1998 (c 42) (acts of public authorities incompatible with Convention rights).

NOTES

Sub-ss (3), (4): words in square brackets inserted by the Statutory Auditors and Third Country Auditors Regulations 2016, SI 2016/649, reg 15, Sch 3, Pt 5, para 30, as from 17 June 2016.

Professional qualifications

[1.1390]

1219 Appropriate qualifications

(1) A person holds an appropriate qualification for the purposes of this Chapter if and only if—

- (a) he holds a recognised professional qualification obtained in the United Kingdom,
- (b) immediately before the commencement of this Chapter, he—
  - (i) held an appropriate qualification for the purposes of Part 2 of the Companies Act 1989 (c 40) (eligibility for appointment as company auditor) by virtue of section 31(1)(a) or (c) of that Act, or
  - (ii) was treated as holding an appropriate qualification for those purposes by virtue of section 31(2), (3) or (4) of that Act,
- (c) immediately before the commencement of this Chapter, he—
  - (i) held an appropriate qualification for the purposes of Part III of the Companies (Northern Ireland) Order 1990 (SI 1990/593 (NI 5)) by virtue of Article 34(1)(a) or (c) of that Order, or
  - (ii) was treated as holding an appropriate qualification for those purposes by virtue of Article 34(2), (3) or (4) of that Order,
- (d) he is within subsection (2), [or]
- (e) . . .
- (f) subject to any direction under section 1221(5), he is regarded for the purposes of this Chapter as holding an approved [third country] qualification.

(2) A person is within this subsection if—

- (a) before 1st January 1990, he began a course of study or practical training leading to a professional qualification in accountancy offered by a body established in the United Kingdom,
- (b) he obtained that qualification on or after 1st January 1990 and before 1st January 1996, and
- (c) the Secretary of State [approved his qualification before 1st October 2018] as an appropriate qualification for the purposes of this Chapter.

(3) . . .

NOTES

Sub-s (1): word in square brackets in para (d) inserted, para (e) repealed, and words in square brackets in para (f) substituted, by the Statutory Auditors and Third Country Auditors Regulations 2007, SI 2007/3494, reg 5, as from 6 April 2008.

Sub-s (2): words in square brackets in para (c) substituted by the Statutory Auditors and Third Country Auditors Regulations 2017, SI 2017/516, reg 13(1), (4)(a), as from 1 May 2017.

Sub-s (3): repealed by SI 2017/516, reg 13(1), (4)(b), as from 1 October 2018.

[1.1391]

1220 Qualifying bodies and recognised professional qualifications

(1) In this Part a "qualifying body" means a body established in the United Kingdom (whether a body corporate or an unincorporated association) which offers a professional qualification in accountancy.

(2) In this Part references to the rules of a qualifying body are to the rules (whether or not laid down by the body itself) which the body has power to enforce and which are relevant for the purposes of this Part.

This includes, so far as so relevant, rules relating to—

- (a) admission to or expulsion from a course of study leading to a qualification,
- (b) the award or deprivation of a qualification, or
- (c) the approval of a person for the purposes of giving practical training or the withdrawal of such approval.

(3) Schedule 11 has effect with respect to the recognition for the purposes of this Part of a professional qualification offered by a qualifying body.

[1.1392]

1221 Approval of [third country] qualifications

(1) The Secretary of State may declare that the following are to be regarded for the purposes of this Chapter as holding an approved [third country] qualification—

(a) persons who are qualified to audit accounts under the law of a specified [third country], or

(b) persons who hold a specified professional qualification in accountancy obtained in a specified [third country].

[(1A) A declaration under subsection (1)(a) or (b) must contain provision to the effect that a person is not to be regarded as holding an approved third country qualification for the purposes of this Chapter unless the person—

(a) already holds a professional qualification which covers all the subjects which are covered by a recognised professional qualification and which are subjects of which knowledge is essential for the pursuit of the profession of statutory auditor, or

(b) holds a professional qualification which does not cover all those subjects and has met whichever of the requirements of subsection (1B) is specified in the declaration.

(1B) The declaration must specify that the condition in subsection (1A)(b) is satisfied in one of the following ways—

(a) only by passing an aptitude test in accordance with subsection (7A),

(b) only by completing an adaptation period in accordance with subsections (7C) and (7D), or

(c) either by passing an aptitude test in accordance with subsection (7A) or by completing an adaptation period in accordance with subsections (7C) and (7D), according to the choice of the person.]

(2) A declaration under subsection (1)(b) may be expressed to be subject to the satisfaction of any specified requirement or requirements.

(3) The Secretary of State may make a declaration under subsection (1) only if he is satisfied that—

(a) in the case of a declaration under subsection (1)(a), the fact that the persons in question are qualified to audit accounts under the law of the specified [third country], [taken with any requirement or requirements to be specified under subsection (1A)] or

(b) in the case of a declaration under subsection (1)(b), the specified professional qualification taken with any requirement or requirements to be specified under [subsections (1A) or (2)],

affords an assurance of professional competence equivalent to that afforded by a recognised professional qualification.

(4) The Secretary of State may make a declaration under subsection (1) only if he is satisfied that the treatment that the persons who are the subject of the declaration will receive as a result of it is comparable to the treatment which is, or is likely to be, afforded in the specified [third country] or a part of it to—

(a) in the case of a declaration under subsection (1)(a), some or all persons who are eligible to be appointed as a statutory auditor, and

(b) in the case of a declaration under subsection (1)(b), some or all persons who hold a corresponding recognised professional qualification.

(5) The Secretary of State may direct that persons holding an approved [third country] qualification are not to be treated as holding an appropriate qualification for the purposes of this Chapter unless they hold such additional educational qualifications as the Secretary of State may specify for the purpose of ensuring that such persons have an adequate knowledge of the law and practice in the United Kingdom relevant to the audit of accounts.

(6) The Secretary of State may give different directions in relation to different approved [third country] qualifications.

(7) The Secretary of State may, if he thinks fit, having regard to the considerations mentioned in subsections (3) and (4), withdraw a declaration under subsection (1) in relation to—

(a) persons becoming qualified to audit accounts under the law of the specified [third country] after such date as he may specify, or

(b) persons obtaining the specified professional qualification after such date as he may specify.

[(7A) An aptitude test required for the purposes of subsection [(1B)]—

(a) must test the person's knowledge of subjects—

(i) that are covered by a recognised professional qualification,

(ii) that are not covered by the professional qualification already held by the person, and

(iii) the knowledge of which is essential for the pursuit of the profession of statutory auditor;

(b) may test the person's knowledge of rules of professional conduct;

(c) must not test the person's knowledge of any other matters.

(7B) . . .]

[(7C) An adaptation period is a period, not exceeding three years, in which the person ("the applicant") pursues the profession of statutory auditor under the supervision of another person who holds an appropriate qualification, subject to an assessment ("the ability assessment") of the applicant's ability to pursue the profession of statutory auditor in the United Kingdom.

(7D) The adaptation period must be completed, and the ability assessment must be carried out, in accordance with the rules and practices of a recognised supervisory body (see paragraph 7A of Schedule 10).]

(8) The Secretary of State may, if he thinks fit, having regard to the considerations mentioned in subsections (3) and (4), vary or revoke a requirement specified under subsection (2) from such date as he may specify.

(9) . . .

NOTES

Section heading, sub-ss (1), (4)–(7): words in square brackets substituted by the Statutory Auditors and Third Country Auditors Regulations 2007, SI 2007/3494, reg 6(1)–(3), as from 6 April 2008.

Sub-ss (1A), (1B): substituted (for sub-s (1A)) by the Statutory Auditors Regulations 2017, SI 2017/1164, reg 3, Sch 1, paras 7, 21(a), as from 1 April 2018 (see **[4.671]** et seq). Sub-s (1A) was originally inserted by SI 2007/3494, reg 6(1), (4), as from 6 April 2008.

Sub-s (3): words in first pair of square brackets substituted by SI 2007/3494, reg 6(1), (2), as from 6 April 2008. Words in second pair of square brackets inserted, and words in final pair of square brackets substituted, by SI 2017/1164, reg 3, Sch 1, paras 7, 21(b), as from 1 April 2018 (see **[4.671]** et seq).

Sub-ss (7A), (7B): inserted by SI 2007/3494, reg 6(1), (4), (5), as from 6 April 2008. Figure in square brackets in sub-s (7A) substituted, and sub-s (7B) repealed, by SI 2017/1164, reg 3, Sch 1, paras 7, 21(c), (d), as from 1 April 2018 (see **[4.671]** et seq).

Sub-ss (7C), (7D): inserted by SI 2017/1164, reg 3, Sch 1, paras 7, 21(e), as from 1 April 2018 (see **[4.671]** et seq).

Sub-s (9): repealed by SI 2007/3494, reg 6(1), (6), as from 6 April 2008.

[1.1393]

1222 Eligibility of individuals retaining only 1967 Act authorisation

(1) A person whose only appropriate qualification is based on his retention of an authorisation originally granted by the Board of Trade or the Secretary of State under section 13(1) of the Companies Act 1967 (c 81) is eligible only for appointment as auditor of an unquoted company.

(2) A company is "unquoted" if, at the time of the person's appointment, neither the company, nor any parent undertaking of which it is a subsidiary undertaking, is a quoted company within the meaning of section 385(2).

(3) References to a person eligible for appointment as a statutory auditor by virtue of this Part in enactments relating to eligibility for appointment as auditor of a person other than a company do not include a person to whom this section applies.

Information

[1.1394]

1223 Matters to be notified to the Secretary of State

(1) The Secretary of State may require a recognised supervisory body or a recognised qualifying body—

- (a) to notify him immediately of the occurrence of such events as he may specify in writing and to give him such information in respect of those events as is so specified;
- (b) to give him, at such times or in respect of such periods as he may specify in writing, such information as is so specified.

(2) The notices and information required to be given must be such as the Secretary of State may reasonably require for the exercise of his functions under this Part.

(3) The Secretary of State may require information given under this section to be given in a specified form or verified in a specified manner.

(4) Any notice or information required to be given under this section must be given in writing unless the Secretary of State specifies or approves some other manner.

[1.1395]

[1223ZA Matters to be notified to the competent authority

(1) The competent authority may require a recognised supervisory body—

- (a) to notify the competent authority immediately of the occurrence of such events as the competent authority may specify in writing and to give the competent authority such information in respect of those events as is so specified;
- (b) to give the competent authority, at such times or in respect of such periods as the competent authority may specify in writing, such information as is so specified.

(2) The notices and information required to be given must be such as the competent authority may reasonably require for the exercise of its functions under this Part, the Statutory Auditors and Third Country Auditors Regulations 2016 or the Audit Regulation.

(3) The competent authority may require information given under this section to be given in a specified form or verified in a specified manner.

(4) Any notice or information required to be given under this section must be given in writing unless the competent authority specifies or approves some other manner.]

NOTES

Inserted by the Statutory Auditors and Third Country Auditors Regulations 2016, SI 2016/649, reg 15, Sch 3, Pt 5, para 31, as from 17 June 2016.

[1.1396]

[1223A Notification of matters relevant to [approved third country competent authorities]

[(1) A recognised supervisory body must notify the Secretary of State—

- (a) if a notifiable person becomes eligible for appointment as a statutory auditor, unless the notifiable person is an individual;
- (b) if a notifiable person's eligibility for appointment as a statutory auditor is withdrawn;
- (c) of the reasons for any such withdrawal.]

(2) A recognised supervisory body must also notify the Secretary of State of any reasonable grounds it has for suspecting that—

- (a) a person has contravened the law of the United Kingdom, or [an equivalent third country or transitional third country], and
- (b) the act or omission constituting that contravention took place on the territory of an [equivalent third country or transitional third country].

(3) In this section "notifiable person" means a member of the recognised supervisory body in question—

- (a) who is also [a third country auditor that has been approved by an approved third country competent authority]; and
- (b) in respect of whom the [approved third country] competent authority is not the recognised supervisory body itself.]

NOTES

Inserted by the Statutory Auditors and Third Country Auditors Regulations 2007, SI 2007/3494, reg 7, as from 6 April 2008.

Section heading: words in square brackets substituted by the Statutory Auditors and Third Country Auditors (Amendment) (EU Exit) Regulations 2019, SI 2019/177, regs 10, 12(a), as from IP completion day (as defined in the European Union (Withdrawal Agreement) Act 2020, s 39).

Sub-s (1): substituted by the Statutory Auditors and Third Country Auditors Regulations 2016, SI 2016/649, reg 15, Sch 3, Pt 5, para 32, as from 17 June 2016.

Sub-ss (2), (3): words in square brackets substituted by SI 2019/177, regs 10, 12(b), (c), as from IP completion day (as defined in the European Union (Withdrawal Agreement) Act 2020, s 39).

[1.1397]

1224 The Secretary of State's power to call for information

(1) The Secretary of State may by notice in writing require a person within subsection (2) to give him such information as he may reasonably require for the exercise of his functions under this Part.

(2) The persons within this subsection are—

(a) any recognised supervisory body,

(b) any recognised qualifying body, and

(c) any person eligible for appointment as a statutory auditor by virtue of this Chapter.

(3) The Secretary of State may require that any information which he requires under this section is to be given within such reasonable time and verified in such manner as he may specify.

[1.1398]

[1224ZA The competent authority's power to call for information

(1) The competent authority may by notice in writing require any recognised supervisory body to give the competent authority such information as it may reasonably require for the exercise of its functions under this Part, the Statutory Auditors and Third Country Auditors Regulations 2016 or the Audit Regulation.

(2) The competent authority may require that any information which it requires under this section is to be given within such reasonable time and verified in such manner as it may specify.]

NOTES

Inserted by the Statutory Auditors and Third Country Auditors Regulations 2016, SI 2016/649, reg 15, Sch 3, Pt 5, para 33, as from 17 June 2016.

[1.1399]

[1224A Restrictions on disclosure

(1) This section applies to information (in whatever form)—

(a) relating to the private affairs of an individual, or

(b) relating to any particular business,

that is provided to a body to which this section applies in connection with the exercise of its functions under this Part, [sections 522 to 524 (notification to appropriate audit authority of resignation or removal of auditor), the Statutory Auditors and Third Country Auditors Regulations 2016 or the Audit Regulation].

(2) This section applies to—

(a) a recognised supervisory body,

(b) a recognised qualifying body,

[(c) the competent authority,]

(d) the Independent Supervisor,

(e) the Secretary of State, and

(f) a body designated by the Secretary of State under section 1252 (delegation of the Secretary of State's functions).

(3) No such information may, during the lifetime of the individual or so long as the business continues to be carried on, be disclosed without the consent of that individual or (as the case may be) the person for the time being carrying on that business.

(4) Subsection (3) does not apply to any disclosure of information that—

(a) is made for the purpose of facilitating the carrying out by the body of any of its functions,

(b) is made to a person specified in Part 1 of Schedule 11A,

(c) is of a description specified in Part 2 of that Schedule, or

(d) is made in accordance with Part 3 of that Schedule.

(5) . . .

(6) This section does not prohibit the disclosure of information if the information is or has been available to the public from any other source.

(7) Nothing in this section authorises the making of a disclosure in contravention of [the data protection legislation].]

NOTES

Inserted by the Statutory Auditors and Third Country Auditors Regulations 2007, SI 2007/3494, reg 8(1), (3), as from 6 April 2008.

Sub-ss (1), (2): words in square brackets substituted by the Statutory Auditors and Third Country Auditors Regulations 2016, SI 2016/649, reg 15, Sch 3, Pt 5, para 34, as from 17 June 2016.

Sub-s (5): repealed by the Statutory Auditors and Third Country Auditors (Amendment) (EU Exit) Regulations 2019, SI 2019/177, regs 10, 13, as from IP completion day (as defined in the European Union (Withdrawal Agreement) Act 2020, s 39).

Sub-s (7): words in square brackets substituted by the Data Protection Act 2018, s 211, Sch 19, Pt 1, paras 120, 125, as from 25 May 2018 (for transitional provisions and savings relating to the repeal of the Data Protection Act 1998, see Sch 20 to the 2018 Act).

[1.1400]

[1224B Offence of disclosure in contravention of section 1224A

(1) A person who discloses information in contravention of section 1224A (restrictions on disclosure) is guilty of an offence, unless—

(a) he did not know, and had no reason to suspect, that the information had been provided as mentioned in section 1224A(1), or

(b) he took all reasonable steps and exercised all due diligence to avoid the commission of the offence.

(2) A person guilty of an offence under this section is liable—
 (a) on conviction on indictment, to imprisonment for a term not exceeding two years or a fine (or both);
 (b) on summary conviction—
  (i) in Scotland, to imprisonment for a term not exceeding 12 months or to a fine not exceeding the statutory maximum, or to both;
  (ii) in England and Wales or Northern Ireland, to imprisonment for a term not exceeding three months or to a fine not exceeding the statutory maximum, or to both.]

NOTES

Inserted by the Statutory Auditors and Third Country Auditors Regulations 2007, SI 2007/3494, reg 8(1), as from 6 April 2008.

Enforcement

[1.1401]

[1225 Enforcement: general

(1) This section applies if at any time it appears to the Secretary of State—
 (a) in the case of a recognised supervisory body, that any requirement of Part 2 or 3 of Schedule 10 is not satisfied,
 (b) in the case of a recognised professional qualification offered by a recognised qualifying body, that any requirement of Part 2 of Schedule 11 is not satisfied, . . .
 (c) that a recognised supervisory body or a recognised qualifying body has not complied with an obligation imposed on it by or by virtue of this Part (other than an obligation to pay a financial penalty under section 1225D), [or]
 [(d) that a recognised supervisory body has not complied with an obligation imposed on it by or by virtue of the Statutory Auditors and Third Country Auditors Regulations 2016].

(2) The Secretary of State may do any one or more of the following—
 (a) give a direction to the body under section 1225A;
 (b) make an application to the court in respect of the body under section 1225C;
 (c) impose a financial penalty on the body under section 1225D.

(3) Subsection (2) is without prejudice to the powers of the Secretary of State under paragraph 3 of Schedule 10 and paragraph 3 of Schedule 11 (revocation of recognition orders) [or the powers of the competent authority under regulation 3 of the Statutory Auditors and Third Country Auditors Regulations 2016].]

NOTES

This section and ss 1225A–1225G were substituted (for the original s 1225) by the Statutory Auditors (Amendment of Companies Act 2006 and Delegation of Functions etc) Order 2012, SI 2012/1741, art 4, as from 2 July 2012.

Sub-s (1): word omitted from para (b) repealed, and para (d) (and the preceding word) inserted, by the Statutory Auditors and Third Country Auditors Regulations 2016, SI 2016/649, reg 15, Sch 3, Pt 5, para 35(1), (2), as from 17 June 2016.

Sub-s (3): words in square brackets inserted by SI 2016/649, reg 15, Sch 3, Pt 5, para 35(1), (3), as from 17 June 2016.

[1.1402]

[1225A Directions: general

(1) A direction under this section is one directing a body to take such steps as the Secretary of State considers will—
 (a) secure that the requirement in question is satisfied or the obligation in question is complied with, or
 (b) mitigate the effect, or prevent the recurrence, of the failure to satisfy the requirement or comply with the obligation.

(2) A direction under this section—
 (a) may only require a body to take steps which it has power to take;
 (b) may require a body to refrain from taking a particular course of action.

(3) The power to give a direction under this section is subject to any provision made by or under any other enactment.

(4) The Secretary of State may take such steps as the Secretary of State considers appropriate to monitor the extent to which a direction under this section is being, or has been, complied with.]

NOTES

Substituted as noted to s 1225 at **[1.1401]**.

[1.1403]

[1225B Directions: supplementary

(1) Before giving a direction to a body under section 1225A, the Secretary of State must give the body a notice (a "notice of proposed direction") accompanied by a copy of the proposed direction.

(2) A notice of proposed direction must—
 (a) state that the Secretary of State proposes to give the body a direction in the form of the accompanying draft,
 (b) identify the requirement or obligation in question and state why it appears to the Secretary of State that the requirement is not satisfied or the obligation has not been complied with,
 (c) specify a period within which the body may make written representations with respect to the proposal.

(3) The period specified under subsection (2)(c)—
 (a) must begin with the date on which the notice of proposed direction is given to the body, and
 (b) must not be less than 14 days.

(4) Written representations made by the body within the period specified under subsection (2)(c) must be considered by the Secretary of State.

(5) After considering any such representations or, in their absence, on the expiry of the period specified under subsection (2)(c), the Secretary of State must decide whether to give the body the proposed direction.

(6) The Secretary of State must give notice of the decision (a "direction decision notice") to the body.

(7) Where the Secretary of State decides to give the proposed direction, the direction decision notice must—

(a) contain the direction,
(b) state the time at which the direction is to take effect, and
(c) specify the Secretary of State's reasons for the decision to give the direction.

(8) Where the Secretary of State decides to give the proposed direction, the Secretary of State must publish the direction decision notice in such manner as the Secretary of State considers appropriate for bringing the direction to the attention of persons likely to be affected.

(9) The Secretary of State may revoke a direction given to a body under section 1225A and, where doing so, must—
(a) give the body notice of the revocation, and
(b) publish the notice in the same manner as the direction decision notice was published.]

NOTES

Substituted as noted to s 1225 at **[1.1401]**.

[1.1404]

[1225C Compliance orders

(1) If on an application under this section in respect of a body, the court decides that a requirement is not satisfied or an obligation has not been complied with, the court may, subject to subsection (2), order the body to take such steps as it considers will secure that the requirement is satisfied or the obligation is complied with.

(2) Where the obligation is an obligation to comply with a direction under section 1225A, the court may not order compliance with the direction unless it also decides that—
(a) the requirement in respect of which the direction was given is not satisfied, or
(b) the obligation in respect of which the direction was given has not been complied with.

(3) In this section, "the court" means the High Court or, in Scotland, the Court of Session.]

NOTES

Substituted as noted to s 1225 at **[1.1401]**.

[1.1405]

[1225D Financial penalties: general

(1) A financial penalty imposed on a body under this section is a financial penalty of such amount as the Secretary of State considers appropriate, subject to subsection (2).

(2) In deciding what amount is appropriate the Secretary of State—
(a) must have regard to the nature of the requirement which is not satisfied or the obligation which has not been complied with; and
(b) must not take into account the Secretary of State's costs in discharging functions under this Part.

(3) A financial penalty under this section is payable to the Secretary of State.

(4) In sections 1225E to 1225G, references to a penalty are to a financial penalty under this section.]

NOTES

Substituted as noted to s 1225 at **[1.1401]**.

[1.1406]

[1225E Financial penalties: supplementary

(1) Before imposing a penalty on a body, the Secretary of State must give the body a notice (a "notice of proposed penalty")—
(a) stating that the Secretary of State proposes to impose a penalty and the amount of the penalty proposed,
(b) identifying the requirement or obligation in question and stating why it appears to the Secretary of State that the requirement is not satisfied or the obligation has not been complied with, and
(c) specifying a period within which the body may make written representations with respect to the proposed penalty.

(2) The period specified under subsection (1)(c)—
(a) must begin with the date on which the notice of proposed penalty is given to the body, and
(b) must not be less than 21 days.

(3) Written representations made by the body before the end of the period specified under subsection (1)(c) must be considered by the Secretary of State.

(4) After considering any such representations or, in their absence, on the expiry of the period specified under subsection (1)(c), the Secretary of State must decide—
(a) whether to impose a penalty, and
(b) where the Secretary of State decides to do so, whether to reduce the proposed amount of the penalty.

(5) The Secretary of State must give notice of the decision (a "penalty decision notice") to the body.

(6) Where the Secretary of State decides to impose a penalty, the penalty decision notice must—
(a) state that the Secretary of State has imposed a penalty on the body and its amount,
(b) identify the requirement or obligation in question and state—
  (i) why it appears to the Secretary of State that the requirement is not satisfied or the obligation has not been complied with, or
  (ii) where, by that time, the requirement is satisfied or the obligation has been complied with, why it appeared to the Secretary of State when giving the notice of proposed penalty that the requirement was not satisfied or the obligation had not been complied with, and
(c) specify a time by which the penalty is required to be paid.

(7) The time specified under subsection (6)(c) must be at least 3 months after the date on which the penalty decision notice is given to the body.

(8) Where the Secretary of State decides to impose a penalty, the Secretary of State must publish the penalty decision notice and must do so in such manner as the Secretary of State considers appropriate for bringing the penalty to the attention of persons likely to be affected.

(9) The Secretary of State may rescind a penalty imposed on a body under section 1225D and, where doing so, must—

(a) give the body notice of the rescission, and

(b) publish the notice in the same manner as the penalty decision notice was published.]

NOTES

Substituted as noted to s 1225 at **[1.1401]**.

[1.1407]

[1225F Appeals against financial penalties

(1) A body on which a penalty is imposed may appeal to the court on one or more of the appeal grounds.

(2) The appeal grounds are—

(a) that, before the giving of the notice under section 1225E(1), the requirement in respect of which the penalty was imposed was satisfied or the obligation in respect of which the penalty was imposed had been complied with;

(b) that, where the penalty was imposed in respect of a failure to comply with a direction under section 1225A, before the giving of the notice under section 1225B(6), the requirement in respect of which the direction was given was satisfied or the obligation in respect of which the direction was given had been complied with;

(c) that any of the requirements of section 1225E have not been complied with in relation to the imposition of the penalty and the interests of the body have been substantially prejudiced by the non-compliance;

(d) that the amount of the penalty is unreasonable;

(e) that it was unreasonable of the Secretary of State to require the penalty imposed to be paid by the time specified in the notice under section 1225E(5).

(3) An appeal under subsection (1) must be made within the period of 3 months beginning with the day on which the notice under section 1225E(5) is given to the body in respect of the penalty.

(4) On any such appeal, where the court considers it appropriate to do so in all the circumstances of the case and is satisfied of one or more of the appeal grounds, the court may—

(a) quash the penalty,

(b) substitute a penalty of such lesser amount as the court considers appropriate, or

(c) in the case of the appeal ground in subsection (2)(e), substitute a later time for the time specified in the notice under section 1225E(5).

(5) Where the court substitutes a penalty of a lesser amount, it may require the payment of interest on the substituted penalty, accruing from the time specified in the notice under section 1225E(5) or such later time as the court considers just and equitable.

(6) Where the court substitutes a later time for the time specified in the notice under section 1225E(5), it may require the payment of interest on the penalty, accruing from the substituted time or such later time as the court considers just and equitable.

(7) Where the court dismisses the appeal, it may require the payment of interest on the penalty, accruing from the time specified in the notice under section 1225E(5).

(8) Where the court requires the payment of interest under this section, the interest is payable at such rate as the court considers just and equitable.

(9) Except as provided by this section, the validity of a penalty is not to be questioned by any legal proceedings whatever.

(10) In this section "the court" means the High Court or, in Scotland, the Court of Session.]

NOTES

Substituted as noted to s 1225 at **[1.1401]**.

[1.1408]

[1225G Recovery of financial penalties

(1) If the whole or any part of a penalty is not paid by the time by which it is required to be paid, the unpaid balance from time to time carries interest at the rate for the time being specified in section 17 of the Judgments Act 1838 (c 110) (unless a different rate is specified by the court under section 1225F(8)).

(2) If an appeal is made under section 1225F in relation to a penalty, the penalty is not required to be paid until the appeal has been determined or withdrawn.

(3) Subsection (2) does not prevent the court from specifying that interest is to accrue from an earlier date under section 1225F.

(4) Where a penalty, or any portion of it, has not been paid by the time when it is required to be paid and—

(a) no appeal relating to the penalty has been made under section 1225F during the period within which such an appeal can be made, or

(b) an appeal has been made under that section and has been determined or withdrawn,

the Secretary of State may recover from the body, as a debt due to the Secretary of State, any of the penalty and any interest which has not been paid.]

NOTES

Substituted as noted to s 1225 at **[1.1401]**.

CHAPTER 3 AUDITORS GENERAL

Eligibility for appointment

[1.1409]

1226 Auditors General: eligibility for appointment as a statutory auditor

(1) In this Part "Auditor General" means—

(a) the Comptroller and Auditor General,

(b) the Auditor General for Scotland,

(c) the Auditor General for Wales, or
(d) the Comptroller and Auditor General for Northern Ireland.

(2) An Auditor General is eligible for appointment as a statutory auditor.

(3) Subsection (2) is subject to any suspension notice having effect under section 1234 (notices suspending eligibility for appointment as a statutory auditor).

Conduct of audits

[1.1410]

1227 Individuals responsible for audit work on behalf of Auditors General

An Auditor General must secure that each individual responsible for statutory audit work on behalf of that Auditor General is eligible for appointment as a statutory auditor by virtue of Chapter 2.

The Independent Supervisor

[1.1411]

1228 Appointment of the Independent Supervisor

(1) The Secretary of State must appoint a body ("the Independent Supervisor") to discharge the function mentioned in section 1229(1) ("the supervision function").

(2) An appointment under this section must be made by order.

(3) The order has the effect of making the body appointed under subsection (1) designated under section 5 of the Freedom of Information Act 2000 (c 36) (further powers to designate public authorities).

(4) A body may be appointed under this section only if it is a body corporate or an unincorporated association which appears to the Secretary of State—

(a) to be willing and able to discharge the supervision function, and
(b) to have arrangements in place relating to the discharge of that function which are such as to be likely to ensure that the conditions in subsection (5) are met.

(5) The conditions are—

(a) that the supervision function will be exercised effectively, and
(b) where the order is to contain any requirements or other provisions specified under subsection (6), that that function will be exercised in accordance with any such requirements or provisions.

(6) An order under this section may contain such requirements or other provisions relating to the exercise of the supervision function by the Independent Supervisor as appear to the Secretary of State to be appropriate.

(7) An order under this section is subject to negative resolution procedure.

NOTES

Orders: the Statutory Auditors (Amendment of Companies Act 2006 and Delegation of Functions etc) Order 2012, SI 2012/1741 at **[4.430]**. See Part 4 of the Order (arts 17–21) which concerns the appointment of the Financial Reporting Council Limited as "Independent Supervisor" of the Auditors General. Article 17 revokes the Independent Supervisor Appointment Order 2007, SI 2007/3534 (as from 2 July 2012) whereby the Professional Oversight Body performed this supervisory function. Article 18 appoints the Financial Reporting Council Limited. Article 19 makes provision for the content of reports prepared by the Independent Supervisor. Article 20 imposes certain consultation and record-keeping requirements. Article 21 makes transitional provisions. For a summary of all statutory instruments made under this Act, see Appendix 4 at **[A4]**.

Supervision of Auditors General

[1.1412]

1229 Supervision of Auditors General by the Independent Supervisor

(1) The Independent Supervisor must supervise the performance by each Auditor General of his functions as a statutory auditor.

[(2) The Independent Supervisor must discharge that duty by—

(a) establishing supervision arrangements itself, or
(b) entering into supervision arrangements with one or more [recognised supervisory bodies].

(2A) If the Independent Supervisor enters into supervision arrangements with one or more bodies, it must oversee the effective operation of those supervision arrangements.]

(3) For this purpose "supervision arrangements" are arrangements [established by the Independent Supervisor or] entered into by the Independent Supervisor with a body, for the purposes of this section, in accordance with which [the Independent Supervisor or] the body does . . . the following—

(a) determines standards relating to professional integrity and independence which must be applied by an Auditor General in statutory audit work;
(b) determines technical standards which must be applied by an Auditor General in statutory audit work and the manner in which those standards are to be applied in practice;
(c) monitors the performance of statutory audits carried out by an Auditor General;
(d) investigates any matter arising from the performance by an Auditor General of a statutory audit;
(e) holds disciplinary hearings in respect of an Auditor General which appear to be desirable following the conclusion of such investigations;
(f) decides whether (and, if so, what) disciplinary action should be taken against an Auditor General to whom such a hearing related.

[(3A) The requirements of [paragraphs 9 to 10C and 12 to 16] of Schedule 10 (requirements for recognition of a supervisory body) apply in relation to supervision arrangements as they apply in relation to the rules, practices and arrangements of supervisory bodies.]

(4) The Independent Supervisor may enter into supervision arrangements with a body despite any relationship that may exist between the Independent Supervisor and that body.

(5) The Independent Supervisor must notify each Auditor General in writing of any supervision arrangements that it [establishes or] enters into under this section.

[(5A) The Independent Supervisor must, at least once in every calendar year, deliver to the Secretary of State a summary of the results of any inspections conducted for the purposes of subsection (3)(c).]

(6) Supervision arrangements within subsection (3)(f) may, in particular, provide for the payment by an Auditor General of a fine to any person [or, in the case of the Auditor General for Wales, for payment by the Wales Audit Office of such a fine.

(7) Any fine received by the Independent Supervisor under supervision arrangements is to be paid into the Consolidated Fund.

NOTES

Sub-ss (2), (2A): substituted, for the original sub-s (2), by the Statutory Auditors and Third Country Auditors Regulations 2007, SI 2007/3494, reg 9(1), (2), as from 6 April 2008. Words in square brackets in sub-s (2) substituted by the Statutory Auditors and Third Country Auditors Regulations 2016, SI 2016/649, reg 15, Sch 3, Pt 5, para 36(1), (2), as from 17 June 2016.

Sub-s (3): words in square brackets inserted, and words omitted repealed, by SI 2007/3494, reg 9(1), (3), as from 6 April 2008.

Sub-s (3A): inserted by SI 2007/3494, reg 9(1), (4), as from 6 April 2008. Words in square brackets substituted by SI 2016/649, reg 15, Sch 3, Pt 5, para 36(1), (3), as from 17 June 2016.

Sub-s (5): words in square brackets inserted by SI 2007/3494, reg 9(1), (5), as from 6 April 2008.

Sub-s (5A): inserted by SI 2007/3494, reg 9(1), (6), as from 6 April 2008.

Sub-s (6): words in square brackets inserted by the Public Audit (Wales) Act 2013, s 34, Sch 4, paras 80, 81, as from 1 April 2014.

As to the duty of the Independent Supervisor to consult with the Auditors General (and such other persons as seem to it to be appropriate) before amending, revoking, establishing or entering into a supervision arrangement for the purposes of this section, see the Statutory Auditors (Amendment of Companies Act 2006 and Delegation of Functions etc) Order 2012, SI 2012/1741, art 20 at **[4.447]**.

[1.1413]

1230 Duties of Auditors General in relation to supervision arrangements

(1) Each Auditor General must—

- (a) comply with any standards of the kind mentioned in subsection (3)(a) or (b) of section 1229 determined under the supervision arrangements,
- (b) take such steps as may be reasonably required of that Auditor General to enable his performance of statutory audits to be monitored by means of inspections carried out under the supervision arrangements, and
- (c) comply with any decision of the kind mentioned in subsection (3)(f) of that section made under the supervision arrangements.

[(2) Each Auditor General must—

- (a) if the Independent Supervisor has established supervision arrangements, pay to the Independent Supervisor;
- (b) if the Independent Supervisor has entered into supervision arrangements with a body, pay to that body,

such proportion of the costs incurred by the Independent Supervisor or body for the purposes of the arrangements as the Independent Supervisor may notify to him in writing.]

(3) Expenditure under subsection (2) is—

- (a) . . .
- (b) in the case of expenditure of the Comptroller and Auditor General for Northern Ireland, to be regarded as expenditure of the Northern Ireland Audit Office for the purposes of Article 6(1) of the Audit (Northern Ireland) Order 1987 (SI 1987/460 (NI 5)),
- [(c) in the case of expenditure of the Auditor General for Wales, to be regarded as expenditure of the Wales Audit Office for the purposes of section 20 of the Public Audit (Wales) Act 2013].

(4) In this section "the supervision arrangements" means the arrangements [established or] entered into under section 1229.

NOTES

Sub-s (2): substituted by the Statutory Auditors and Third Country Auditors Regulations 2007, SI 2007/3494, reg 10(1), (2), as from 6 April 2008.

Sub-s (3): para (a) repealed by the Budget Responsibility and National Audit Act 2011, s 26, Sch 5, Pt 2, paras 29, 30, as from 1 April 2012. Para (c) inserted by the Public Audit (Wales) Act 2013, s 34, Sch 4, paras 80, 82, as from 1 April 2014.

Sub-s (4): words in square brackets inserted by SI 2007/3494, reg 10(1), (3), as from 6 April 2008.

Reporting requirement

[1.1414]

1231 Reports by the Independent Supervisor

(1) The Independent Supervisor must, at least once in each calendar year, prepare a report on the discharge of its functions.

(2) The Independent Supervisor must give a copy of each report prepared under subsection (1) to—

- (a) the Secretary of State;
- (b) the First Minister in Scotland;
- (c) the First Minister and the deputy First Minister in Northern Ireland;
- [(d) The First Minister for Wales].

(3) The Secretary of State must lay before each House of Parliament a copy of each report received by him under subsection (2)(a).

[(3A) The First Minister for Wales must lay before the National Assembly for Wales a copy of each report received by him under subsection (2)(d).]

(4) In relation to a calendar year during which an appointment of a body as the Independent Supervisor is made or revoked by an order under section 1228, this section applies with such modifications as may be specified in the order.

NOTES

Sub-s (2): para (d) substituted by the Government of Wales Act 2006 (Consequential Modifications, Transitional Provisions and Saving) Order 2009, SI 2009/2958, arts 8, 12(1), (2), as from 6 November 2009.

Sub-s (3A): inserted by SI 2009/2958, arts 8, 12(1), (3), (4), as from 6 November 2009.

National Assembly for Wales: see the note to s 54 at **[1.55]** in relation to the renaming of the National Assembly for Wales.

Orders: the Statutory Auditors (Amendment of Companies Act 2006 and Delegation of Functions etc) Order 2012, SI 2012/1741 at **[4.430]**. For a summary of all statutory instruments made under this Act, see Appendix 4 at **[A4]**.

Information

[1.1415]

1232 Matters to be notified to the Independent Supervisor

(1) The Independent Supervisor may require an Auditor General—

(a) to notify the Independent Supervisor immediately of the occurrence of such events as it may specify in writing and to give it such information in respect of those events as is so specified;

(b) to give the Independent Supervisor, at such times or in respect of such periods as it may specify in writing, such information as is so specified.

(2) The notices and information required to be given must be such as the Independent Supervisor may reasonably require for the exercise of the functions conferred on it by or by virtue of this Part.

(3) The Independent Supervisor may require information given under this section to be given in a specified form or verified in a specified manner.

(4) Any notice or information required to be given under this section must be given in writing unless the Independent Supervisor specifies or approves some other manner.

[1.1416]

1233 The Independent Supervisor's power to call for information

(1) The Independent Supervisor may by notice in writing require an Auditor General to give it such information as it may reasonably require for the exercise of the functions conferred on it by or by virtue of this Part.

(2) The Independent Supervisor may require that any information which it requires under this section is to be given within such reasonable time and verified in such manner as it may specify.

Enforcement

[1.1417]

1234 Suspension notices

(1) The Independent Supervisor may issue—

(a) a notice (a "suspension notice") suspending an Auditor General's eligibility for appointment as a statutory auditor in relation to all persons, or any specified person or persons, indefinitely or until a date specified in the notice;

(b) a notice amending or revoking a suspension notice previously issued to an Auditor General.

(2) In determining whether it is appropriate to issue a notice under subsection (1), the Independent Supervisor must have regard to—

(a) the Auditor General's performance of the obligations imposed on him by or by virtue of this Part, and

(b) the Auditor General's performance of his functions as a statutory auditor.

(3) A notice under subsection (1) must—

(a) be in writing, and

(b) state the date on which it takes effect (which must be after the period of three months beginning with the date on which it is issued).

(4) Before issuing a notice under subsection (1), the Independent Supervisor must—

(a) give written notice of its intention to do so to the Auditor General, and

(b) publish the notice mentioned in paragraph (a) in such manner as it thinks appropriate for bringing it to the attention of any other persons who are likely to be affected.

(5) A notice under subsection (4) must—

(a) state the reasons for which the Independent Supervisor proposes to act, and

(b) give particulars of the rights conferred by subsection (6).

(6) A person within subsection (7) may, within the period of three months beginning with the date of service or publication of the notice under subsection (4) or such longer period as the Independent Supervisor may allow, make written representations to the Independent Supervisor and, if desired, oral representations to a person appointed for that purpose by the Independent Supervisor.

(7) The persons within this subsection are—

(a) the Auditor General, and

(b) any other person who appears to the Independent Supervisor to be affected.

(8) The Independent Supervisor must have regard to any representations made in accordance with subsection (6) in determining—

(a) whether to issue a notice under subsection (1), and

(b) the terms of any such notice.

(9) If in any case the Independent Supervisor considers it appropriate to do so in the public interest it may issue a notice under subsection (1), without regard to the restriction in subsection (3)(b), even if—

(a) no notice has been given or published under subsection (4), or

(b) the period of time for making representations in pursuance of such a notice has not expired.

(10) On issuing a notice under subsection (1), the Independent Supervisor must—

(a) give a copy of the notice to the Auditor General, and

(b) publish the notice in such manner as it thinks appropriate for bringing it to the attention of persons likely to be affected.

(11) In this section "specified" means specified in, or of a description specified in, the suspension notice in question.

[1.1418]

1235 Effect of suspension notices

(1) An Auditor General must not act as a statutory auditor at any time when a suspension notice issued to him in respect of the audited person has effect.

(2) If at any time during an Auditor General's term of office as a statutory auditor a suspension notice issued to him in respect of the audited person takes effect, he must immediately—

(a) resign his office (with immediate effect), and

(b) give notice in writing to the audited person that he has resigned by reason of his becoming ineligible for appointment.

(3) A suspension notice does not make an Auditor General ineligible for appointment as a statutory auditor for the purposes of section 1213 (effect of ineligibility: criminal offences).

[1.1419]
1236 Compliance orders

(1) If at any time it appears to the Independent Supervisor that an Auditor General has failed to comply with an obligation imposed on him by or by virtue of this Part, the Independent Supervisor may make an application to the court under this section.

(2) If on an application under this section the court decides that the Auditor General has failed to comply with the obligation in question, it may order the Auditor General to take such steps as the court directs for securing that the obligation is complied with.

(3) In this section "the court" means the High Court or, in Scotland, the Court of Session.

Proceedings

[1.1420]
1237 Proceedings involving the Independent Supervisor

(1) If the Independent Supervisor is an unincorporated association, any relevant proceedings may be brought by or against it in the name of any body corporate whose constitution provides for the establishment of the body.

(2) For this purpose "relevant proceedings" means proceedings brought in or in connection with the exercise of any function by the body as the Independent Supervisor.

(3) Where an appointment under section 1228 is revoked, the revoking order may make such provision as the Secretary of State thinks fit with respect to pending proceedings.

Grants

[1.1421]
1238 Grants to the Independent Supervisor

(*Inserts the Companies (Audit, Investigations and Community Enterprise) Act 2004, s 16(2)(ka) at* **[5.216]**.)

CHAPTER 4 THE REGISTER OF AUDITORS ETC

[1.1422]
1239 The register of auditors

(1) The Secretary of State must make regulations requiring the keeping of a register of—

(a) the persons eligible for appointment as a statutory auditor, and

(b) third country auditors (see Chapter 5) who apply to be registered in the specified manner and in relation to whom specified requirements are met.

(2) The regulations must require each person's entry in the register to contain—

(a) his name and address,

(b) in the case of an individual eligible for appointment as a statutory auditor, the specified information relating to any firm on whose behalf he is responsible for statutory audit work,

(c) in the case of a firm eligible for appointment as a statutory auditor, the specified information relating to the individuals responsible for statutory audit work on its behalf,

(d) in the case of an individual or firm eligible for appointment as a statutory auditor by virtue of Chapter 2, the name of the relevant supervisory body, . . .

(e) in the case of a firm eligible for appointment as a statutory auditor by virtue of Chapter 2 . . . , the information mentioned in subsection (3), [and

(f) in the case of a third country auditor which is a firm, the name and address of each person who is—

(i) an owner or shareholder of the firm, or

(ii) a member of the firm's administrative or management body],

and may require each person's entry to contain other specified information.

(3) The information referred to in subsection (2)(e) is—

(a) in relation to a body corporate, except where paragraph (b) applies, the name and address of each person who is a director of the body or holds any shares in it;

(b) in relation to a limited liability partnership, the name and address of each member of the partnership;

(c) in relation to a corporation sole, the name and address of the individual for the time being holding the office by the name of which he is the corporation sole;

(d) in relation to a partnership, the name and address of each partner.

(4) The regulations may provide that different parts of the register are to be kept by different persons.

(5) The regulations may impose such obligations as the Secretary of State thinks fit on—

(a) recognised supervisory bodies,

(b) any body designated by order under section 1252 (delegation of Secretary of State's functions),

(c) persons eligible for appointment as a statutory auditor,

(d) third country auditors,

(e) . . .

(f) the Independent Supervisor appointed under section 1228,

[(g) the competent authority].

(6) The regulations may include—

(a) provision requiring that specified entries in the register be open to inspection at times and places specified or determined in accordance with the regulations;

(b) provision enabling a person to require a certified copy of specified entries in the register;

(c) provision authorising the charging of fees for inspection, or the provision of copies, of such reasonable amount as may be specified or determined in accordance with the regulations.

(7) The Secretary of State may direct in writing that the requirements imposed by the regulations . . . , or such of those requirements as are specified in the direction, are not to apply, in whole or in part, in relation to a particular registered third country auditor or class of registered third country auditors.

(8) The obligations imposed by regulations under this section on such persons as are mentioned in subsection (5)(b) or (e) are enforceable on the application of the Secretary of State by injunction or, in Scotland, by an order under section 45 of the Court of Session Act 1988 (c 36).

(9) In this section "specified" means specified by regulations under this section.

(10) Regulations under this section are subject to negative resolution procedure.

NOTES

Sub-s (2): words omitted from paras (d) and (e) repealed, and para (f) (and the word immediately preceding it) inserted, by the Statutory Auditors and Third Country Auditors Regulations 2007, SI 2007/3494, reg 30(1)–(4), as from 6 April 2008.

Sub-s (5): para (e) repealed, and para (g) inserted, by the Statutory Auditors and Third Country Auditors Regulations 2016, SI 2016/649, reg 15, Sch 3, Pt 5, para 37, as from 17 June 2016.

Sub-s (7): words omitted repealed by SI 2007/3494, reg 30(1), (5), as from 6 April 2008.

Regulations and Orders: the Statutory Auditors and Third Country Auditors Regulations 2007, SI 2007/3494; the Statutory Auditors and Third Country Auditors (Amendment) Regulations 2011, SI 2011/1856; the Statutory Auditors (Amendment of Companies Act 2006 and Delegation of Functions etc) Order 2012, SI 2012/1741 at **[4.430]**; the Statutory Auditors and Third Country Auditors Regulations 2013, SI 2013/1672 at **[4.482]**; the Statutory Auditors and Third Country Auditors (Amendment) (EU Exit) Regulations 2019, SI 2019/177 at **[12.83]**. For a summary of all statutory instruments made under this Act, see Appendix 4 at **[A4]**.

[1.1423]

1240 Information to be made available to public

(1) The Secretary of State may make regulations requiring a person eligible for appointment as a statutory auditor, or a member of a specified class of such persons, to keep and make available to the public specified information, including information regarding—

(a) the person's ownership and governance,

(b) the person's internal controls with respect to the quality and independence of its audit work,

(c) the person's turnover, and

(d) the audited persons of whom the person has acted as statutory auditor.

(2) Regulations under this section may—

(a) impose such obligations as the Secretary of State thinks fit on persons eligible for appointment as a statutory auditor;

(b) require the information to be made available to the public in a specified manner.

(3) In this section "specified" means specified by regulations under this section.

(4) Regulations under this section are subject to negative resolution procedure.

NOTES

Regulations: no Regulations have been made under this section.

[CHAPTER 4A EQUIVALENT THIRD COUNTRIES AND TRANSITIONAL THIRD COUNTRIES

[1.1424]

1240A Power to approve third countries as equivalent or transitional third countries

(1) The Secretary of State may by regulations grant to a third country, or make provision for the grant to a third country of—

(a) approval as an equivalent third country,

(b) provisional approval, for a period of up to seven years, as an equivalent third country, or

(c) transitional approval, for a period of up to seven years, as a transitional third country,

in relation to the comparability of the third country's audit regulatory regime to the audit regulatory regime of the United Kingdom.

(2) Regulations under subsection (1) may (among other things)—

(a) specify the procedure for assessing the audit regulatory regime of a third country;

(b) set out the considerations which must be taken into account, or may be taken into account, by the Secretary of State when determining—

(i) whether the third country has an audit regulatory regime comparable to that of the United Kingdom,

(ii) whether to grant approval, provisional approval or transitional approval, and

(iii) the period for which provisional approval or transitional approval should be granted;

(c) specify the procedure for the granting of approval, provisional approval or transitional approval;

(d) set out a list of third countries that have been granted approval, provisional approval or transitional approval;

(e) make provision for the amendment, suspension or withdrawal of approval, provisional approval or transitional approval.

(3) In this section, "audit regulatory regime" in relation to a country or territory, means the system of public oversight, quality assurance, investigations and sanctions for auditors in that country or territory.

(4) Regulations under this section are subject to negative resolution procedure.]

NOTES

Commencement: 13 November 2019.

Chapters 4A, 4B (ss 1240A, 1240B) inserted by the Statutory Auditors and Third Country Auditors (Amendment) (EU Exit) Regulations 2019, SI 2019/177, regs 10, 14, as from 13 November 2019.

Regulations: the Statutory Auditors and Third Country Auditors (Amendment) (EU Exit) Regulations 2020, SI 2020/108 at **[12.171]**; the Statutory Auditors and Third Country Auditors (Amendment) (EU Exit) (No 2) Regulations 2020, SI 2020/1247;

the Statutory Auditors and Third Country Auditors (Amendment) Regulations 2022, SI 2022/762. For a summary of all statutory instruments made under this Act, see Appendix 4 at **[A4]**.

[CHAPTER 4B APPROVED THIRD COUNTRY COMPETENT AUTHORITIES

[1.1425]

1240B Power to approve third country competent authorities

(1) The Secretary of State may by regulations grant to a third country competent authority, or make provision for the grant to a third country competent authority of—

(a) approval as an approved third country competent authority, or

(b) provisional approval, for a period of up to seven years, as an approved third country competent authority,

in relation to the exchange of audit working papers and investigation reports.

(2) Regulations under subsection (1) may (among other things)—

(a) specify the procedure for assessing the adequacy of the third country competent authority, in relation to the authority's ability to co-operate with the competent authority on the exchange of audit working papers and investigation reports;

(b) set out the considerations which must be taken into account, or may be taken into account, by the Secretary of State when determining—

(i) whether to grant approval or provisional approval, and

(ii) in relation to the granting of provisional approval, the period of the approval;

(c) specify the procedure for the granting of an approval or a provisional approval;

(d) set out a list of third country competent authorities that have been granted an approval or a provisional approval;

(e) make provision for the amendment, suspension or withdrawal of an approval or a provisional approval.

(3) Regulations under this section are subject to negative resolution procedure.]

NOTES

Commencement: 13 November 2019.

Chapters 4A, 4B (ss 1240A, 1240B) inserted by the Statutory Auditors and Third Country Auditors (Amendment) (EU Exit) Regulations 2019, SI 2019/177, regs 10, 14, as from 13 November 2019.

Regulations: the Statutory Auditors and Third Country Auditors (Amendment) (EU Exit) Regulations 2020, SI 2020/108 at **[12.171]**; the Statutory Auditors and Third Country Auditors (Amendment) (EU Exit) (No 2) Regulations 2020, SI 2020/1247; the Statutory Auditors and Third Country Auditors (Amendment) Regulations 2022, SI 2022/762. For a summary of all statutory instruments made under this Act, see Appendix 4 at **[A4]**.

CHAPTER 5 REGISTERED THIRD COUNTRY AUDITORS

Introductory

[1.1426]

1241 [Meaning of "registered third country auditor" and ["UK-traded third country company"]]

(1) In this Part—

. . .

"registered third country auditor" means a third country auditor who is entered in the register kept in accordance with regulations under section 1239(1).

(2) [In this Part "[UK-traded third country company]" means a body corporate—]

(a) which is incorporated or formed under the law of [a third country],

(b) whose transferable securities are admitted to trading on a [UK regulated market] . . . , and

(c) which has not been excluded, or is not of a description of bodies corporate which has been excluded, from this definition by an order made by the Secretary of State.

(3) . . .

(4) An order under this section is subject to negative resolution procedure.

NOTES

Section heading: substituted by the Statutory Auditors and Third Country Auditors Regulations 2007, SI 2007/3494, reg 31(1), (2), as from 6 April 2008. Words in square brackets substituted by the Statutory Auditors and Third Country Auditors (Amendment) (EU Exit) Regulations 2019, SI 2019/177, regs 10, 15(a), as from IP completion day (as defined in the European Union (Withdrawal Agreement) Act 2020, s 39).

Sub-s (1): definition "third country auditor" (omitted) repealed by SI 2007/3494, reg 31(1), (3), as from 6 April 2008.

Sub-s (2): words in first (outer) pair of square brackets and words in square brackets in para (a) substituted by SI 2007/3494, reg 31(1), (4), as from 6 April 2008. Words in second (inner) pair of square brackets and words in square brackets in para (b) substituted, and words omitted from that paragraph repealed, by SI 2019/177, regs 10, 15(b), as from IP completion day (as defined in the European Union (Withdrawal Agreement) Act 2020, s 39)

Sub-s (3): repealed by SI 2019/177, regs 10, 15(b), as from IP completion day (as defined in the European Union (Withdrawal Agreement) Act 2020, s 39).

UK-traded third country company: see further the Statutory Auditors and Third Country Auditors Regulations 2016, SI 2016/649, reg 21(1)–(3) which provide as follows. Note that the regulation set out below is reproduced as amended by the Statutory Auditors and Third Country Auditors (Amendment) (EU Exit) Regulations 2019, SI 2019/177, regs 65, 72, as from IP completion day (as defined in the European Union (Withdrawal Agreement) Act 2020, s 39)—

"21 Exclusion of large debt securities issuer from definition of "[UK-traded third country company]"

(1) A large debt securities issuer is excluded from the definition of "[UK-traded third country company]" for the purposes of Part 42 of the Act.

(2) In paragraph (1) "large debt securities issuer" means a body corporate whose only issued transferable securities admitted to trading on a [UK regulated market] are debt securities, the denomination per unit of which is not less than—

(a) 50,000 euros or an equivalent amount, in the case of securities admitted to trading on a [UK regulated market] before 31st December 2010,

(b) 100,000 euros or an equivalent amount, in the case of securities admitted to trading on a [UK regulated market] on or after 31st December 2010.

(3) In paragraph (2)—

"an equivalent amount" means an amount of a currency other than euros which at the date the security was issued was equivalent to the relevant amount of euros; and

"debt securities" has the same meaning as in Article 2(1)(b) of Directive 2004/109/EC of the European Parliament and of the Council on the harmonisation of transparency requirements in relation to information about issuers whose securities are admitted to trading on a regulated market and amending Directive 2001/43/EC.".

Regulations: the Statutory Auditors and Third Country Auditors Regulations 2007, SI 2007/3494; the Statutory Auditors and Third Country Auditors Regulations 2016, SI 2016/649 at **[4.650]**; the Statutory Auditors and Third Country Auditors (Amendment) (EU Exit) Regulations 2019, SI 2019/177 at **[12.83]**. For a summary of all statutory instruments made under this Act, see Appendix 4 at **[A4]**.

Duties

[1.1427]

1242 Duties of registered third country auditors

(1) A registered third country auditor [who audits the accounts of a [UK-traded third country company]] must participate in—

(a) arrangements within paragraph 1 of Schedule 12 (arrangements for independent monitoring of audits . . .), and

(b) arrangements within paragraph 2 of that Schedule (arrangements for independent investigation for disciplinary purposes . . .).

(2) A registered third country auditor must—

(a) take such steps as may be reasonably required of it to enable its performance of [audits of accounts of [UK-traded third country companies]] to be monitored by means of inspections carried out under the arrangements mentioned in subsection (1)(a), and

(b) comply with any decision as to disciplinary action to be taken against it made under the arrangements mentioned in subsection (1)(b).

(3) Schedule 12 makes further provision with respect to the arrangements in which registered third country auditors are required to participate.

(4) The Secretary of State may direct in writing that subsections (1) to (3) are not to apply, in whole or in part, in relation to—

[(a)] a particular registered third country auditor or class of registered third country auditors;

[(b) audits of the accounts of a particular [UK-traded third country company] or class of [UK-traded third country companies];

(c) audits by a particular registered third country auditor or class of registered third country auditors of the accounts of a particular [UK-traded third country company] or class of [UK-traded third country companies]].

NOTES

Sub-s (1): words in first (outer) pair of square brackets inserted, and first words omitted repealed, by the Statutory Auditors and Third Country Auditors Regulations 2007, SI 2007/3494, reg 32(1), (2), as from 29 June 2008. Words in second (inner) pair of square brackets substituted by the Statutory Auditors and Third Country Auditors (Amendment) (EU Exit) Regulations 2019, SI 2019/177, regs 10, 16(a), as from IP completion day (as defined in the European Union (Withdrawal Agreement) Act 2020, s 39. Second words omitted repealed by the Statutory Auditors and Third Country Auditors Regulations 2013, SI 2013/1672, reg 14, as from 1 October 2013.

Sub-s (2): words in first (outer) pair of square brackets in para (a) substituted by SI 2007/3494, reg 32(1), (3), as from 29 June 2008. Words in second (inner) pair of square brackets substituted by SI 2019/177, regs 10, 16(b), as from IP completion day (as defined in the European Union (Withdrawal Agreement) Act 2020, s 39).

Sub-s (4): para (a) designated as such, and paras (b)–(d) added by the Statutory Auditors and Third Country Auditors (Amendment) Regulations 2011, SI 2011/1856, reg 4, as from 1 September 2011 (note that reg 1(5) of the 2011 Regulations provides that a direction given under sub-s (4) above by virtue of the amendments made by reg 4 does not apply in respect of the audit of accounts for a period beginning before 2 July 2010). All the other words in square brackets in this subsection were substituted by SI 2019/177, regs 10, 16(c), (d), as from IP completion day (as defined in the European Union (Withdrawal Agreement) Act 2020, s 39). Note that reg 16(c), (d) of the 2019 Regulations were inserted by the Statutory Auditors, Third Country Auditors and International Accounting Standards (Amendment) (EU Exit) Regulations 2019, SI 2019/1392, regs 2, 5, with effect from immediately before IP completion day.

Information

[1.1428]

1243 Matters to be notified to the Secretary of State

(1) The Secretary of State may require a registered third country auditor—

(a) to notify him immediately of the occurrence of such events as he may specify in writing and to give him such information in respect of those events as is so specified;

(b) to give him, at such times or in respect of such periods as he may specify in writing, such information as is so specified.

(2) The notices and information required to be given must be such as the Secretary of State may reasonably require for the exercise of his functions under this Part.

(3) The Secretary of State may require information given under this section to be given in a specified form or verified in a specified manner.

(4) Any notice or information required to be given under this section must be given in writing unless the Secretary of State specifies or approves some other manner.

[1.1429]

1244 The Secretary of State's power to call for information

(1) The Secretary of State may by notice in writing require a registered third country auditor to give him such information as he may reasonably require for the exercise of his functions under this Part.

(2) The Secretary of State may require that any information which he requires under this section is to be given within such reasonable time and verified in such manner as he may specify.

Enforcement

[1.1430]

1245 Compliance orders

(1) If at any time it appears to the Secretary of State that a registered third country auditor has failed to comply with an obligation imposed on him by or by virtue of this Part, the Secretary of State may make an application to the court under this section.

(2) If on an application under this section the court decides that the auditor has failed to comply with the obligation in question, it may order the auditor to take such steps as the court directs for securing that the obligation is complied with.

(3) In this section "the court" means the High Court or, in Scotland, the Court of Session.

[1.1431]

1246 Removal of third country auditors from the register of auditors

(1) The Secretary of State may, by regulations, confer on the person keeping the register in accordance with regulations under section 1239(1) power to remove a third country auditor from the register.

(2) Regulations under this section must require the person keeping the register, in determining whether to remove a third country auditor from the register, to have regard to the auditor's compliance with obligations imposed on him by or by virtue of this Part.

(3) Where provision is made under section 1239(4) (different parts of the register to be kept by different persons), references in this section to the person keeping the register are to the person keeping that part of the register which relates to third country auditors.

(4) Regulations under this section are subject to negative resolution procedure.

NOTES

Regulations: the Statutory Auditors and Third Country Auditors Regulations 2007, SI 2007/3494; the Statutory Auditors and Third Country Auditors (Amendment) Regulations 2011, SI 2011/1856; the Statutory Auditors and Third Country Auditors Regulations 2013, SI 2013/1672 at **[4.482]**; the Statutory Auditors and Third Country Auditors (Amendment) (EU Exit) Regulations 2019, SI 2019/177 at **[12.83]**. For a summary of all statutory instruments made under this Act, see Appendix 4 at **[A4]**.

[1.1432]

1247 Grants to bodies concerned with arrangements under Schedule 12

(*Inserts the Companies (Audit, Investigations and Community Enterprise) Act 2004, s 16(2)(kb) at* **[5.216]**.)

CHAPTER 6 SUPPLEMENTARY AND GENERAL

Power to require second company audit

[1.1433]

1248 Secretary of State's power to require second audit of a company

(1) This section applies where a person appointed as statutory auditor of a company was not an appropriate person for any part of the period during which the audit was conducted.

(2) The Secretary of State may direct the company concerned to retain an appropriate person—

- (a) to conduct a second audit of the relevant accounts, or
- (b) to review the first audit and to report (giving his reasons) whether a second audit is needed.

(3) For the purposes of subsections (1) and (2) a person is "appropriate" if he—

- (a) is eligible for appointment as a statutory auditor or, if the person is an Auditor General, for appointment as statutory auditor of the company, and
- (b) is not prohibited by section 1214(1) (independence requirement) from acting as statutory auditor of the company.

(4) The Secretary of State must send a copy of a direction under subsection (2) to the registrar of companies.

(5) The company is guilty of an offence if—

- (a) it fails to comply with a direction under subsection (2) within the period of 21 days beginning with the date on which it is given, or
- (b) it has been convicted of a previous offence under this subsection and the failure to comply with the direction which led to the conviction continues after the conviction.

(6) The company must—

- (a) send a copy of a report under subsection (2)(b) to the registrar of companies, and
- (b) if the report states that a second audit is needed, take such steps as are necessary for the carrying out of that audit.

(7) The company is guilty of an offence if—

- (a) it fails to send a copy of a report under subsection (2)(b) to the registrar within the period of 21 days beginning with the date on which it receives it,
- (b) in a case within subsection (6)(b), it fails to take the steps mentioned immediately it receives the report, or
- (c) it has been convicted of a previous offence under this subsection and the failure to send a copy of the report, or take the steps, which led to the conviction continues after the conviction.

(8) A company guilty of an offence under this section is liable on summary conviction—

- (a) in a case within subsection (5)(a) or (7)(a) or (b), to a fine not exceeding level 5 on the standard scale, and
- (b) in a case within subsection (5)(b) or (7)(c), to a fine not exceeding [one-tenth of the greater of £5,000 or level 4 on the standard scale] for each day on which the failure continues.

(9) In this section "registrar of companies" has the meaning given by section 1060.

NOTES

Sub-s (8): words in square brackets substituted (for the original words "one-tenth of level 5 on the standard scale") by the Legal Aid, Sentencing and Punishment of Offenders Act 2012 (Fines on Summary Conviction) Regulations 2015, SI 2015/664, regs 3, 5, Sch 3, Pt 1, para 9(1), (26), as from 12 March 2015, in relation to England and Wales only (except in relation to (a) fines for offences committed before 12 March 2015, (b) the operation of restrictions on fines that may be imposed on a person aged under 18, or (c) fines that may be imposed on a person convicted by a magistrates' court who is to be sentenced as if convicted on indictment).

[1.1434]

1249 Supplementary provision about second audits

(1) If a person accepts an appointment, or continues to act, as statutory auditor of a company at a time when he knows he is not an appropriate person, the company may recover from him any costs incurred by it in complying with the requirements of section 1248.

For this purpose "appropriate" is to be construed in accordance with subsection (3) of that section.

(2) Where a second audit is carried out under section 1248, any statutory or other provision applying in relation to the first audit applies also, in so far as practicable, in relation to the second audit.

(3) A direction under section 1248(2) is, on the application of the Secretary of State, enforceable by injunction or, in Scotland, by an order under section 45 of the Court of Session Act 1988 (c 36).

False and misleading statements

[1.1435]

1250 Misleading, false and deceptive statements

(1) A person is guilty of an offence if—

(a) for the purposes of or in connection with any application under this Part, or

(b) in purported compliance with any requirement imposed on him by or by virtue of this Part,

he knowingly or recklessly furnishes information which is misleading, false or deceptive in a material particular.

(2) It is an offence for a person whose name does not appear on the register of auditors kept under regulations under section 1239 in an entry made under subsection (1)(a) of that section to describe himself as a registered auditor or so to hold himself out as to indicate, or be reasonably understood to indicate, that he is a registered auditor.

(3) It is an offence for a person whose name does not appear on the register of auditors kept under regulations under that section in an entry made under subsection (1)(b) of that section to describe himself as a registered third country auditor or so to hold himself out as to indicate, or be reasonably understood to indicate, that he is a registered third country auditor.

(4) It is an offence for a body which is not a recognised supervisory body or a recognised qualifying body to describe itself as so recognised or so to describe itself or hold itself out as to indicate, or be reasonably understood to indicate, that it is so recognised.

(5) A person guilty of an offence under subsection (1) is liable—

(a) on conviction on indictment, to imprisonment for a term not exceeding two years or to a fine (or both);

(b) on summary conviction—

(i) in England and Wales, to imprisonment for a term not exceeding twelve months or to a fine not exceeding the statutory maximum (or both),

(ii) in Scotland or Northern Ireland, to imprisonment for a term not exceeding six months or to a fine not exceeding the statutory maximum (or both).

In relation to an offence committed before [2 May 2022], for "twelve months" in paragraph (b)(i) substitute "six months".

(6) Subject to subsection (7), a person guilty of an offence under subsection (2), (3) or (4) is liable on summary conviction—

(a) in England and Wales, to imprisonment for a term not exceeding 51 weeks or to a fine not exceeding level 5 on the standard scale (or both),

(b) in Scotland or Northern Ireland, to imprisonment for a term not exceeding six months or to a fine not exceeding level 5 on the standard scale (or both).

In relation to an offence committed before the commencement of section 281(5) of the Criminal Justice Act 2003, for "51 weeks" in paragraph (a) substitute "six months".

(7) Where a contravention of subsection (2), (3) or (4) involves a public display of the offending description, the maximum fine that may be imposed is an amount equal to level 5 on the standard scale multiplied by the number of days for which the display has continued.

(8) It is a defence for a person charged with an offence under subsection (2), (3) or (4) to show that he took all reasonable precautions and exercised all due diligence to avoid the commission of the offence.

NOTES

Sub-s (5): words in square brackets substituted by the Criminal Justice Act 2003 (Commencement No 33) and Sentencing Act 2020 (Commencement No 2) Regulations 2022, SI 2022/500, reg 5, Schedule, Pt 1, as from 28 April 2022.

Fees

[1.1436]

1251 Fees

(1) An applicant for a recognition order under this Part must pay such fee in respect of his application as the Secretary of State may by regulations prescribe; and no application is to be regarded as duly made unless this subsection is complied with.

(2) The Secretary of State may by regulations prescribe periodical fees to be paid by—

(a) every recognised supervisory body,

(b) every recognised qualifying body,

(c) every Auditor General, and

(d) every registered third country auditor.

(3) Fees received by the Secretary of State by virtue of this Part are to be paid into the Consolidated Fund.
(4) Regulations under this section are subject to negative resolution procedure.

NOTES

Regulations: no Regulations have been made under this section.

[Duty of Secretary of State to Report on Inspections

[1.1437]

1251A Duty of the Secretary of State to report on inspections

The Secretary of State must, at least once in every calendar year, publish a report containing a summary of the results of inspections that are delivered to him—

(a) by the Independent Supervisor under section 1229(5A);
(b) by a recognised supervisory body under [paragraph 13(12)] of Schedule 10.]

NOTES

Inserted, together with the preceding heading, by the Statutory Auditors and Third Country Auditors Regulations 2007, SI 2007/3494, reg 11, as from 6 April 2008.

Words in square brackets substituted by the Statutory Auditors and Third Country Auditors Regulations 2016, SI 2016/649, reg 15, Sch 3, Pt 5, para 38, as from 17 June 2016.

Delegation of Secretary of State's functions

[1.1438]

1252 Delegation of the Secretary of State's functions

(1) The Secretary of State may make an order under this section (a "delegation order") for the purpose of enabling functions of the Secretary of State under this Part to be exercised by a body designated by the order.
(2) The body designated by a delegation order may be either—

(a) a body corporate which is established by the order, or
(b) subject to section 1253, a body [(including the competent authority, and whether] a body corporate or an unincorporated association) which is already in existence ("an existing body").

(3) A delegation order has the effect of making the body designated by the order designated under section 5 of the Freedom of Information Act 2000 (c 36) (further powers to designate public authorities).
(4) A delegation order has the effect of transferring to the body designated by it all functions of the Secretary of State under this Part—

(a) subject to such exceptions and reservations as may be specified in the order, and
(b) except—
  (i) his functions in relation to the body itself, and
  (ii) his functions under section 1228 (appointment of Independent Supervisor).

(5) A delegation order may confer on the body designated by it such other functions supplementary or incidental to those transferred as appear to the Secretary of State to be appropriate.
(6) Any transfer of functions under the following provisions must be subject to the reservation that the functions remain exercisable concurrently by the Secretary of State—

(a) section 1224 (power to call for information from recognised bodies etc);
(b) section 1244 (power to call for information from registered third country auditors);
(c) section 1254 (directions to comply with international obligations).

(7) Any transfer of—

(a) the function of refusing to make a declaration under section 1221(1) (approval of [third country] qualifications) on the grounds referred to in section 1221(4) (lack of comparable treatment), or
(b) the function of withdrawing such a declaration under section 1221(7) on those grounds,

must be subject to the reservation that the function is exercisable only with the consent of the Secretary of State.
(8) A delegation order may be amended or, if it appears to the Secretary of State that it is no longer in the public interest that the order should remain in force, revoked by a further order under this section.
(9) Where functions are transferred or resumed, the Secretary of State may by order confer or, as the case may be, take away such other functions supplementary or incidental to those transferred or resumed as appear to him to be appropriate.
(10) Where a delegation order is made, Schedule 13 has effect with respect to—

(a) the status of the body designated by the order in exercising functions of the Secretary of State under this Part,
(b) the constitution and proceedings of the body where it is established by the order,
(c) the exercise by the body of certain functions transferred to it, and
(d) other supplementary matters.

(11) An order under this section which has the effect of transferring or resuming any functions is subject to affirmative resolution procedure.
(12) Any other order under this section is subject to negative resolution procedure.

NOTES

Sub-s (2): words in square brackets substituted by the Statutory Auditors and Third Country Auditors Regulations 2016, SI 2016/649, reg 15, Sch 3, Pt 5, para 39, as from 17 June 2016.

Sub-s (7): words in square brackets substituted by the Statutory Auditors and Third Country Auditors Regulations 2007, SI 2007/3494, reg 12, as from 6 April 2008.

Orders and Regulations: the Statutory Auditors (Amendment of Companies Act 2006 and Delegation of Functions etc) Order 2012, SI 2012/1741 at **[4.430]**; the Local Audit (Delegation of Functions) and Statutory Audit (Delegation of Functions) Order 2014, SI 2014/2009; the Statutory Auditors and Third Country Auditors Regulations 2016, SI 2016/649 at **[4.650]**; the Statutory Auditors and Third Country Auditors (Amendment) (EU Exit) Regulations 2019, SI 2019/177 at **[12.83]**. For a summary of all statutory instruments made under this Act, see Appendix 4 at **[A4]**.

[1.1439]

1253 Delegation of functions to an existing body

(1) The Secretary of State's power to make a delegation order under section 1252 which designates an existing body is exercisable in accordance with this section.

(2) The Secretary of State may make such a delegation order if it appears to him that—

(a) the body is able and willing to exercise the functions that would be transferred by the order, and

(b) the body has arrangements in place relating to the exercise of those functions which are such as to be likely to ensure that the conditions in subsection (3) are met.

(3) The conditions are—

(a) that the functions in question will be exercised effectively, and

(b) where the delegation order is to contain any requirements or other provisions specified under subsection (4), that those functions will be exercised in accordance with any such requirements or provisions.

(4) The delegation order may contain such requirements or other provision relating to the exercise of the functions by the designated body as appear to the Secretary of State to be appropriate.

(5) An existing body—

(a) may be designated by a delegation order under section 1252, and

(b) may accordingly exercise functions of the Secretary of State in pursuance of the order,

despite any involvement of the body in the exercise of any functions under arrangements within . . . paragraph 1 or 2 of Schedule 12.

NOTES

Sub-s (5): words omitted repealed by the Statutory Auditors and Third Country Auditors Regulations 2016, SI 2016/649, reg 15, Sch 3, Pt 5, para 40, as from 17 June 2016.

Orders: the Statutory Auditors (Amendment of Companies Act 2006 and Delegation of Functions etc) Order 2012, SI 2012/1741 (see the note preceding s 1209 at **[1.1380]**); the Local Audit (Delegation of Functions) and Statutory Audit (Delegation of Functions) Order 2014, SI 2014/2009. For a summary of all statutory instruments made under this Act, see Appendix 4 at **[A4]**.

[Cooperation with Foreign Competent Authorities

[1.1440]

1253A Requests to foreign competent authorities

The Secretary of State may request from . . . a third country competent authority such assistance, information or investigation as he may reasonably require in connection with the exercise of his functions under this Part.]

NOTES

Inserted, together with the preceding heading and ss 1253B, 1253C, by the Statutory Auditors and Third Country Auditors Regulations 2007, SI 2007/3494, reg 14(1), as from 6 April 2008.

Words omitted repealed by the Statutory Auditors and Third Country Auditors (Amendment) (EU Exit) Regulations 2019, SI 2019/177, regs 10, 17, as from IP completion day (as defined in the European Union (Withdrawal Agreement) Act 2020, s 39).

[1.1441]

[1253B Requests from [approved third country competent authorities]

[(1) The Secretary of State must take all necessary steps to—

(a) ensure that an investigation is carried out, or

(b) provide any other assistance or information,

if requested to do so by an [approved third country competent authority] . . .]

[(1A) Where the request includes a request for the transfer of audit working papers and investigation reports, the Secretary of State must act in accordance with section 1253D.]

(2) Within 28 days following the date on which he receives the request, the Secretary of State must—

(a) provide the assistance or information required by [the requesting authority] under subsection (1)(b), or

(b) notify [the requesting authority] of the reasons why he has not done so.

(3) But the Secretary of State need not take steps to comply with a request under subsection (1) if—

(a) he considers that complying with the request may prejudice the sovereignty, security or public order of the United Kingdom;

(b) legal proceedings have been brought in the United Kingdom (whether continuing or not) in relation to the persons and matters to which the request relates; or

(c) disciplinary action has been taken by a recognised supervisory body in relation to the persons and matters to which the request relates.

[(4) . . .]]

NOTES

Inserted as noted to s 1253A at **[1.1440]**. By virtue of reg 14(2) of the 2007 Regulations, this section applies only to investigations, assistance or information relating to auditors appointed for financial years beginning on or after 6 April 2008.

Section heading: words in square brackets substituted by the Statutory Auditors and Third Country Auditors (Amendment) (EU Exit) Regulations 2019, SI 2019/177, regs 10, 18(a), as from IP completion day (as defined in the European Union (Withdrawal Agreement) Act 2020, s 39).

Sub-s (1): substituted by the Statutory Auditors and Third Country Auditors Regulations 2016, SI 2016/649, reg 15, Sch 3, Pt 5, para 41(1), (2), as from 17 June 2016. Words in square brackets substituted, and words omitted repealed, by SI 2019/177, regs 10, 18(b), as from IP completion day (as defined in the European Union (Withdrawal Agreement) Act 2020, s 39).

Sub-s (1A): inserted by SI 2019/177, regs 10, 18(c), as from IP completion day (as defined in the European Union (Withdrawal Agreement) Act 2020, s 39).

Sub-s (2): words in square brackets substituted by SI 2016/649, reg 15, Sch 3, Pt 5, para 41(1), (3), as from 17 June 2016.

Sub-s (4): originally added by SI 2016/649, reg 15, Sch 3, Pt 5, para 41(1), (4), as from 17 June 2016. Subsequently repealed by SI 2019/177, regs 10, 18(d), as from IP completion day (as defined in the European Union (Withdrawal Agreement) Act 2020, s 39).

[1.1442]

[1253C Notification to [approved third country] competent authorities . . .

[(1) If the Secretary of State receives notice from a recognised supervisory body under section 1223A(1) (notification of matters relevant to [approved third country competent authorities]) that—

(a) a person has become eligible for appointment as a statutory auditor, or

(b) a person's eligibility for appointment as a statutory auditor has been withdrawn,

the Secretary of State must notify the relevant [approved third country competent authority].]

(2) In subsection (1) "the [approved third country competent authority]" means the [approved third country competent authority] which has approved the person concerned . . . to carry out audits of annual accounts or consolidated accounts . . .

(3) The notification under subsection (1) must include the name of the person concerned and[, in a case where a person's eligibility for appointment as a statutory auditor has been withdrawn, the reasons for the withdrawal].

(4) The Secretary of State must notify the relevant [approved third country competent authority] if he has reasonable grounds for suspecting that—

(a) a person has contravened the law of the United Kingdom, or any [equivalent third country or transitional third country, relating to audit], and

(b) the act or omission constituting that contravention took place on the territory of [an equivalent third country or transitional third country].

(5) In subsection (4) "the relevant [approved third country competent country or territory]" means the [approved third country competent country or territory] for the [country or territory] in which the suspected contravention took place.

(6) The notification under subsection (4) must include the name of the person concerned and the grounds for the Secretary of State's suspicion.]

NOTES

Inserted as noted to s 1253A at **[1.1440]**.

Section heading: the words in square brackets were inserted, and the words omitted were repealed, by the Statutory Auditors and Third Country Auditors (Amendment) (EU Exit) Regulations 2019, SI 2019/177, regs 10, 19(a), as from IP completion day (as defined in the European Union (Withdrawal Agreement) Act 2020, s 39).

Sub-s (1): substituted by the Statutory Auditors and Third Country Auditors Regulations 2016, SI 2016/649, reg 15, Sch 3, Pt 5, para 42(1), (2), as from 17 June 2016. Words in square brackets substituted by SI 2019/177, regs 10, 19(b), as from IP completion day (as defined in the European Union (Withdrawal Agreement) Act 2020, s 39).

Sub-s (2): words in square brackets substituted, and words omitted repealed, by SI 2019/177, regs 10, 19(c), as from IP completion day (as defined in the European Union (Withdrawal Agreement) Act 2020, s 39).

Sub-s (3): words in square brackets substituted by SI 2016/649, reg 15, Sch 3, Pt 5, para 42(1), (3), as from 17 June 2016.

Sub-ss (4), (5): words in square brackets substituted by SI 2019/177, regs 10, 19(d), (e), as from IP completion day (as defined in the European Union (Withdrawal Agreement) Act 2020, s 39).

[Transfer of Papers to Third Countries

[1.1443]

[1253D Restriction on transfer of audit working papers to third countries

(1) [Audit working papers and investigation reports] must not be transferred to a third country competent authority [unless the third country competent authority is an approved third country competent authority and the transfers are made] in accordance with—

(a) section 1253DA (transfer by Secretary of State),

(b) section 1253DB (transfer by statutory auditor with approval of Secretary of State), or

(c) section 1253DC (transfer by statutory auditor for purposes of investigation of auditor).

(2) . . .

(3) Nothing in the sections referred to in subsection (1) authorises the making of a disclosure in contravention of [the data protection legislation].]

NOTES

Sections 1253D, 1253DA–1253DE were substituted for the original s 1253D (as inserted by the Statutory Auditors and Third Country Auditors Regulations 2007, SI 2007/3494, reg 15(1), as from 6 April 2008) by the Companies Act 2006 (Transfer of Audit Working Papers to Third Countries) Regulations 2010, SI 2010/2537, reg 2, as from 15 November 2010.

Sub-s (1): words in first pair of square brackets substituted by the Statutory Auditors and Third Country Auditors Regulations 2016, SI 2016/649, reg 15, Sch 3, Pt 3, para 43, as from 17 June 2016, in relation to financial years beginning on or after that date. Words in second pair of square brackets substituted by the Statutory Auditors and Third Country Auditors (Amendment) (EU Exit) Regulations 2019, SI 2019/177, regs 10, 20(a), as from IP completion day (as defined in the European Union (Withdrawal Agreement) Act 2020, s 39).

Sub-s (2): repealed by SI 2019/177, regs 10, 20(b), as from IP completion day (as defined in the European Union (Withdrawal Agreement) Act 2020, s 39).

Sub-s (3): words in square brackets substituted by the Data Protection Act 2018, s 211, Sch 19, Pt 1, paras 120, 126, as from 25 May 2018 (for transitional provisions and savings relating to the repeal of the Data Protection Act 1998, see Sch 20 to the 2018 Act).

[1.1444]

[1253DA Transfer by Secretary of State

(1) The Secretary of State may transfer [audit working papers and investigation reports] to an approved third country competent authority if the following conditions are met (but see also section 1253DD).

(2) The first condition is that the authority has made a request to the Secretary of State for the transfer of the [audit working papers and investigation reports].

(3) The second condition is that the [audit working papers and investigation reports] relate to audits of companies that—

(a) have issued securities in the third country in which the authority is established, or

(b) form part of a group issuing statutory consolidated accounts in that third country.

(4) The third condition is that the authority has entered into arrangements with the Secretary of State in accordance with section 1253E.]

NOTES

Substituted as noted to s 1253D at **[1.1443]**.

Words in square brackets substituted by the Statutory Auditors and Third Country Auditors Regulations 2016, SI 2016/649, reg 15, Sch 3, Pt 3, para 44, as from 17 June 2016, in relation to financial years beginning on or after that date.

[1.1445]

[1253DB Transfer by statutory auditor with approval of Secretary of State

(1) A statutory auditor may transfer [audit working papers and investigation reports] to an approved third country competent authority if the transfer is made—

(a) with the prior approval of the Secretary of State, and

(b) in accordance with rules of a recognised supervisory body meeting the requirements of paragraph 16AA of Schedule 10.

(2) The Secretary of State must not approve a transfer of [audit working papers and investigation reports] to an approved third country competent authority for the purposes of this section unless the following conditions are met (see also section 1253DD).

(3) The first condition is that the authority has made a request to the Secretary of State for the transfer of the [audit working papers and investigation reports].

(4) The second condition is that the [audit working papers and investigation reports] relate to audits of companies that—

(a) have issued securities in the third country in which the authority is established, or

(b) form part of a group issuing statutory consolidated accounts in that third country.

(5) The third condition is that the authority has entered into arrangements with the Secretary of State in accordance with section 1253E.]

NOTES

Substituted as noted to s 1253D at **[1.1443]**.

Words in square brackets substituted by the Statutory Auditors and Third Country Auditors Regulations 2016, SI 2016/649, reg 15, Sch 3, Pt 3, para 45, as from 17 June 2016, in relation to financial years beginning on or after that date.

[1.1446]

[1253DC Transfer by statutory auditor for purposes of investigation of auditor

A statutory auditor may transfer [audit working papers and investigation reports] to a third country competent authority if the transfer is made—

(a) for the purposes of an investigation of an auditor or audit firm, and

(b) in accordance with rules of a recognised supervisory body meeting the requirements of paragraph 16AB of Schedule 10.]

NOTES

Substituted as noted to s 1253D at **[1.1443]**.

Words in square brackets substituted by the Statutory Auditors and Third Country Auditors Regulations 2016, SI 2016/649, reg 15, Sch 3, Pt 3, para 46, as from 17 June 2016, in relation to financial years beginning on or after that date.

[1.1447]

[1253DD Agreement of [third country competent authority]

(1) This section applies where—

(a) an approved third country competent authority makes a request to the Secretary of State for the transfer of [audit working papers and investigation reports] which relate to the audit of the consolidated accounts of a group, and

(b) the [audit working papers and investigation reports] that are the subject of the request—

(i) have been created by the auditor of a subsidiary that is located in [an equivalent third country or transitional third country] in relation to the audit of that subsidiary, and

(ii) are in the possession of a statutory auditor.

(2) In the case of a transfer by the Secretary of State under section 1253DA, the transfer must not take place unless the [third country competent authority] responsible for the auditor of the subsidiary has given its express agreement to the transfer.

(3) In the case of a transfer by a statutory auditor under section 1253DB, the Secretary of State must not approve the transfer unless the [third country competent authority] responsible for the auditor of the subsidiary has given its express agreement to the transfer.]

NOTES

Substituted as noted to s 1253D at **[1.1443]**.

The words "audit working papers and investigation reports" in square brackets in sub-s (1)(a), (b) were substituted by the Statutory Auditors and Third Country Auditors Regulations 2016, SI 2016/649, reg 15, Sch 3, Pt 3, para 47, as from 17 June 2016, in relation to financial years beginning on or after that date.

All other words in square brackets in this section were substituted by the Statutory Auditors and Third Country Auditors (Amendment) (EU Exit) Regulations 2019, SI 2019/177, regs 10, 21, as from IP completion day (as defined in the European Union (Withdrawal Agreement) Act 2020, s 39).

[1.1448]

[1253DE Transfer by means of inspection

(1) This section applies in the case of a transfer of [audit working papers and investigation reports] if—

(a) it is a transfer to an approved third country competent authority . . . ,

(b) it is a transfer under section 1253DA or 1253DB, and

(c) it is to take place by means of an inspection in the United Kingdom by the authority.

(2) The Secretary of State must participate in the inspection.

(3) The inspection must be under the leadership of the Secretary of State unless the Secretary of State otherwise permits.]

NOTES

Substituted as noted to s 1253D at **[1.1443]**.

Sub-s (1): words in square brackets substituted by the Statutory Auditors and Third Country Auditors Regulations 2016, SI 2016/649, reg 15, Sch 3, Pt 3, para 48, as from 17 June 2016, in relation to financial years beginning on or after that date. Words omitted repealed by the Statutory Auditors and Third Country Auditors (Amendment) (EU Exit) Regulations 2019, SI 2019/177, regs 10, 22, as from IP completion day (as defined in the European Union (Withdrawal Agreement) Act 2020, s 39).

[1.1449]
[1253E Working arrangements for transfer of papers

(1) The Secretary of State may enter into arrangements with a third country competent authority relating to the transfer of [audit working papers and investigation reports]—

(a) from the third country competent authority or a third country auditor regulated by that authority to the Secretary of State, and

(b) from the Secretary of State or a statutory auditor to the third country competent authority.

(2) The arrangements must provide that a request by the Secretary of State or the third country competent authority for a transfer mentioned in subsection (1) must be accompanied by a statement explaining the reasons for the request.

(3) The arrangements must—

(a) provide that the Secretary of State may not use [audit working papers and investigation reports] obtained from the third country competent authority or a third country auditor regulated by that authority except in connection with one or more of the functions mentioned in subsection (4), and

(b) include comparable provision in relation to [audit working papers and investigation reports] obtained by the third country competent authority from the Secretary of State or a statutory auditor.

(4) Those functions are—

(a) quality assurance functions which meet requirements equivalent to those of [regulation 9 of the Statutory Auditors and Third Country Auditors Regulations 2016];

(b) investigation or disciplinary functions which meet requirements equivalent to those of [regulations 5 to 8 and 10 of the Statutory Auditors and Third Country Auditors Regulations 2016];

(c) public oversight functions which meet requirements equivalent to those of [regulation 3 of the Statutory Auditors and Third Country Auditors Regulations 2016].

(5) The arrangements must—

(a) provide that the Secretary of State, a person exercising the functions of the Secretary of State and persons employed or formerly employed in discharging those functions must be subject to obligations of confidentiality as to personal data, professional secrets and sensitive commercial information contained in [audit working papers and investigation reports] transferred to the Secretary of State, . . .

(b) provide that the third country competent authority and persons involved in exercising its functions are subject to comparable obligations in relation to [audit working papers and investigation reports] transferred to the authority, [and]

[(c) ensure that the protection of the commercial interests of any audited person, including its industrial and intellectual property, is not undermined].

(6) The arrangements must—

(a) provide that the Secretary of State may refuse, or direct a statutory auditor to refuse, a request from the third country competent authority for a transfer of [audit working papers and investigation reports] in a case mentioned in subsection (7)(a) or (b), and

(b) provide that the third country competent authority has comparable rights in relation to a request from the Secretary of State.

(7) Those cases are—

(a) where the transfer of the papers would adversely affect the sovereignty, security or public order . . . of the United Kingdom;

(b) where legal proceedings have been brought in the United Kingdom (whether continuing or not) in relation to the persons and matters to which the request relates.

[(7A) The arrangements must—

(a) provide that the Secretary of State may only disclose confidential information received from the third country competent authority—

(i) with the agreement of that authority or for purposes for which that authority has given its agreement,

(ii) where disclosure is required by law, or

(iii) where disclosure is necessary in connection with legal proceedings, and

(b) provide that the third country competent authority may only disclose confidential information received from the Secretary of State—

(i) with the Secretary of State's agreement or for purposes for which the Secretary of State has given agreement,

(ii) where disclosure is required by law, or

(iii) where disclosure is necessary in connection with legal proceedings.]

(8), (9) . . .]

NOTES

Originally inserted by the Statutory Auditors and Third Country Auditors Regulations 2007, SI 2007/3494, reg 15(1), as from 6 April 2008.

Subsequently substituted by the Companies Act 2006 (Transfer of Audit Working Papers to Third Countries) Regulations 2010, SI 2010/2537, reg 3, as from 15 November 2010.

The words "audit working papers and investigation reports" in square brackets (in each place they occur) were substituted, the word omitted from sub-s (5)(a) was repealed, sub-s (5)(c) and the preceding word were inserted, and sub-s (7A) was inserted, by the Statutory Auditors and Third Country Auditors Regulations 2016, SI 2016/649, reg 15, Sch 3, Pt 3, para 49, as from 17 June 2016, in relation to financial years beginning on or after that date.

The words in square brackets in sub-s (4) were substituted, the words omitted from sub-s (7) were repealed, and sub-ss (8) and (9) were repealed, by the Statutory Auditors and Third Country Auditors (Amendment) (EU Exit) Regulations 2019, SI 2019/177, regs 10, 23, as from IP completion day (as defined in the European Union (Withdrawal Agreement) Act 2020, s 39).

[1.1450]

[1253F Publication of working arrangements

If the Secretary of State enters into working arrangements in accordance with section 1253E, he must publish on a website without undue delay—

(a) the name of the third country competent authority with which he has entered into such arrangements, and

(b) the country or territory in which it is established.]

NOTES

Inserted as noted to s 1253D at **[1.1443]**.

International obligations

[1.1451]

1254 Directions to comply with international obligations

(1) If it appears to the Secretary of State—

[(a) that any action proposed to be taken by—

(i) a recognised supervisory body,

(ii) a recognised qualifying body,

(iii) a person keeping a register of auditors, or part of such a register, in accordance with regulations under section 1239(1),

(iv) a body exercising functions under arrangements within Schedule 12,

(v) the Independent Supervisor,

(vi) the competent authority, or

(vii) a body designated by order under section 1252,

would be incompatible with [retained EU obligations] or any other international obligations of the United Kingdom, or]

(b) that any action which that body has power to take is required for the purpose of implementing any such obligations,

he may direct the body not to take or, as the case may be, to take the action in question.

(2) A direction may include such supplementary or incidental requirements as the Secretary of State thinks necessary or expedient.

(3) A direction under this section given to [the Independent Supervisor[, the competent authority] or] a body designated by order under section 1252 is enforceable on the application of the Secretary of State by injunction or, in Scotland, by an order under section 45 of the Court of Session Act 1988 (c 36).

NOTES

Sub-s (1): para (a) substituted by the Statutory Auditors and Third Country Auditors Regulations 2017, SI 2017/516, reg 13(1), (7), as from 1 May 2017. The words "retained EU obligations" in square brackets were substituted by the Statutory Auditors and Third Country Auditors (Amendment) (EU Exit) Regulations 2019, SI 2019/177, regs 10, 24, as from IP completion day (as defined in the European Union (Withdrawal Agreement) Act 2020, s 39).

Sub-s (3): words in first (outer) pair of square brackets inserted by SI 2007/3494, reg 16(1), (3), as from 6 April 2008. Words in second (inner) pair of square brackets inserted by SI 2016/649, reg 15, Sch 3, Pt 5, para 50(1), (3), as from 17 June 2016.

General provision relating to offences

[1.1452]

1255 Offences by bodies corporate, partnerships and unincorporated associations

(1) Where an offence under this Part committed by a body corporate is proved to have been committed with the consent or connivance of, or to be attributable to any neglect on the part of, an officer of the body, or a person purporting to act in any such capacity, he as well as the body corporate is guilty of the offence and liable to be proceeded against and punished accordingly.

(2) Where an offence under this Part committed by a partnership is proved to have been committed with the consent or connivance of, or to be attributable to any neglect on the part of, a partner, he as well as the partnership is guilty of the offence and liable to be proceeded against and punished accordingly.

(3) Where an offence under this Part committed by an unincorporated association (other than a partnership) is proved to have been committed with the consent or connivance of, or to be attributable to any neglect on the part of, any officer of the association or any member of its governing body, he as well as the association is guilty of the offence and liable to be proceeded against and punished accordingly.

[1.1453]

1256 Time limits for prosecution of offences

(1) An information relating to an offence under this Part which is triable by a magistrates' court in England and Wales may be so tried if it is laid at any time within the period of twelve months beginning with the date on which evidence sufficient in the opinion of the Director of Public Prosecutions or the Secretary of State to justify the proceedings comes to his knowledge.

(2) Proceedings in Scotland for an offence under this Part may be commenced at any time within the period of twelve months beginning with the date on which evidence sufficient in the Lord Advocate's opinion to justify proceedings came to his knowledge or, where such evidence was reported to him by the Secretary of State, within the period of twelve months beginning with the date on which it came to the knowledge of the Secretary of State.

(3) For the purposes of subsection (2) proceedings are to be deemed to be commenced on the date on which a warrant to apprehend or cite the accused is granted, if the warrant is executed without undue delay.

(4) A complaint charging an offence under this Part which is triable by a magistrates' court in Northern Ireland may be so tried if it is made at any time within the period of twelve months beginning with the date on which evidence sufficient in the opinion of the Director of Public Prosecutions for Northern Ireland or the Secretary of State to justify the proceedings comes to his knowledge.

(5) This section does not authorise—

(a) in the case of proceedings in England and Wales, the trial of an information laid,

(b) in the case of proceedings in Scotland, the commencement of proceedings, or

(c) in the case of proceedings in Northern Ireland, the trial of a complaint made,

more than three years after the commission of the offence.

(6) For the purposes of this section a certificate of the Director of Public Prosecutions, the Lord Advocate, the Director of Public Prosecutions for Northern Ireland or the Secretary of State as to the date on which such evidence as is referred to above came to his knowledge is conclusive evidence.

(7) Nothing in this section affects proceedings within the time limits prescribed by section 127(1) of the Magistrates' Courts Act 1980 (c 43), section 331 of the Criminal Procedure (Scotland) Act 1975 or Article 19 of the Magistrates' Courts (Northern Ireland) Order 1981 (SI 1981/1675 (NI 26)) (the usual time limits for criminal proceedings).

NOTES

Note: following the transfer of most of the Secretary of State's functions under this Part (see further the introductory notes to this Part *ante*) the references in sub-ss (1), (2), (4) and (6) above to the Secretary of State have effect as references to the Secretary of State or the Financial Reporting Council Limited; see the Statutory Auditors (Amendment of Companies Act 2006 and Delegation of Functions etc) Order 2012, SI 2012/1741, art 14.

[1.1454]

1257 Jurisdiction and procedure in respect of offences

(1) Summary proceedings for an offence under this Part may, without prejudice to any jurisdiction exercisable apart from this section, be taken—

(a) against a body corporate or unincorporated association at any place at which it has a place of business, and

(b) against an individual at any place where he is for the time being.

(2) Proceedings for an offence alleged to have been committed under this Part by an unincorporated association must be brought in the name of the association (and not in that of any of its members), and for the purposes of any such proceedings any rules of court relating to the service of documents apply as in relation to a body corporate.

(3) Section 33 of the Criminal Justice Act 1925 (c 86) and Schedule 3 to the Magistrates' Courts Act 1980 (c 43) (procedure on charge of offence against a corporation) apply in a case in which an unincorporated association is charged in England and Wales with an offence under this Part as they apply in the case of a corporation.

(4) Section 18 of the Criminal Justice Act (Northern Ireland) 1945 (c 15 (NI)) and Article 166 and Schedule 4 to the Magistrates' Courts (Northern Ireland) Order 1981 (SI 1981/1675 (NI 26)) (procedure on charge of offence against a corporation) apply in a case in which an unincorporated association is charged in Northern Ireland with an offence under this Part as they apply in the case of a corporation.

(5) In relation to proceedings on indictment in Scotland for an offence alleged to have been committed under this Part by an unincorporated association, section 70 of the Criminal Procedure (Scotland) Act 1995 (proceedings on indictment against bodies corporate) applies as if the association were a body corporate.

(6) A fine imposed on an unincorporated association on its conviction of such an offence must be paid out of the funds of the association.

Notices etc

[1.1455]

1258 Service of notices

(1) This section has effect in relation to any notice, direction or other document required or authorised by or by virtue of this Part to be given to or served on any person other than the Secretary of State.

(2) Any such document may be given to or served on the person in question—

(a) by delivering it to him,

(b) by leaving it at his proper address, or

(c) by sending it by post to him at that address.

(3) Any such document may—

(a) in the case of a body corporate, be given to or served on an officer of that body;

(b) in the case of a partnership, be given to or served on any partner;

(c) in the case of an unincorporated association other than a partnership, be given to or served on any member of the governing body of that association.

(4) For the purposes of this section and section 7 of the Interpretation Act 1978 (c 30) (service of documents by post) in its application to this section, the proper address of any person is his last known address (whether of his residence or of a place where he carries on business or is employed) and also—

(a) in the case of a person who is eligible under the rules of a recognised supervisory body for appointment as a statutory auditor and who does not have a place of business in the United Kingdom, the address of that body;

(b) in the case of a body corporate or an officer of that body, the address of the registered or principal office of that body in the United Kingdom;

(c) in the case of an unincorporated association other than a partnership or a member of its governing body, its principal office in the United Kingdom.

[1.1456]

1259 Documents in electronic form

(1) This section applies where—

(a) section 1258 authorises the giving or sending of a notice, direction or other document by its delivery to a particular person ("the recipient"), and
(b) the notice, direction or other document is transmitted to the recipient—
  (i) by means of an electronic communications network, or
  (ii) by other means but in a form that requires the use of apparatus by the recipient to render it intelligible.

(2) The transmission has effect for the purposes of this Part as a delivery of the notice, direction or other document to the recipient, but only if the recipient has indicated to the person making the transmission his willingness to receive the notice, direction or other document in the form and manner used.

(3) An indication to a person for the purposes of subsection (2)—
(a) must be given to the person in such manner as he may require,
(b) may be a general indication or an indication that is limited to notices, directions or other documents of a particular description,
(c) must state the address to be used,
(d) must be accompanied by such other information as the person requires for the making of the transmission, and
(e) may be modified or withdrawn at any time by a notice given to the person in such manner as he may require.

(4) In this section "electronic communications network" has the same meaning as in the Communications Act 2003 (c 21).

Interpretation

[1.1457]
1260 Meaning of "associate"

(1) In this Part "associate", in relation to a person, is to be construed as follows.
(2) In relation to an individual, "associate" means—
(a) that individual's spouse, civil partner or minor child or step-child,
(b) any body corporate of which that individual is a director, and
(c) any employee or partner of that individual.
(3) In relation to a body corporate, "associate" means—
(a) any body corporate of which that body is a director,
(b) any body corporate in the same group as that body, and
(c) any employee or partner of that body or of any body corporate in the same group.
(4) In relation to a partnership constituted under the law of Scotland, or any other country or territory in which a partnership is a legal person, "associate" means—
(a) any body corporate of which that partnership is a director,
(b) any employee of or partner in that partnership, and
(c) any person who is an associate of a partner in that partnership.
(5) In relation to a partnership constituted under the law of England and Wales or Northern Ireland, or the law of any other country or territory in which a partnership is not a legal person, "associate" means any person who is an associate of any of the partners.
(6) In subsections (2)(b), (3)(a) and (4)(a), in the case of a body corporate which is a limited liability partnership, "director" is to be read as "member".

[1.1458]
1261 Minor definitions

(1) In this Part, unless a contrary intention appears—
"address" means—
  (a) in relation to an individual, his usual residential or business address;
  (b) in relation to a firm, its registered or principal office in the United Kingdom;

[. . .]
["the Audit Regulation" means Regulation 537/2014 of the European Parliament and of the Council on specific requirements regarding statutory audit of public interest entities;]
[. . .]
["audit working papers and investigation reports" means—
  (a) any documents which are or have been held by a statutory auditor . . . or a third country auditor and which are related to the conduct of an audit conducted by that auditor;
  (b) any report of an inspection of the conduct of an audit by a statutory auditor . . . or a third country auditor, or
  (c) any report of an investigation into the conduct of a statutory auditor . . . or a third country auditor,]

"company" means any company or other body the accounts of which must be audited in accordance with Part 16;
["the competent authority" means the Financial Reporting Council Limited,]
["the data protection legislation" has the same meaning as in the Data Protection Act 2018 (see section 3 of that Act);]
"director", in relation to a body corporate, includes any person occupying in relation to it the position of a director (by whatever name called) and any person in accordance with whose directions or instructions (not being advice given in a professional capacity) the directors of the body are accustomed to act;
[. . .]
[. . .]
"firm" means any entity, whether or not a legal person, which is not an individual and includes a body corporate, a corporation sole and a partnership or other unincorporated association;
"group", in relation to a body corporate, means the body corporate, any other body corporate which is its holding company or subsidiary and any other body corporate which is a subsidiary of that holding company;
"holding company" and "subsidiary" are to be read in accordance with section 1159 and Schedule 6;

"officer", in relation to a body corporate, includes a director, a manager, a secretary or, where the affairs of the body are managed by its members, a member;

"parent undertaking" and "subsidiary undertaking" are to be read in accordance with section 1162 and Schedule 7;

["regulated market" has the meaning given in Article 2(1)(13) of Regulation (EU) No 600/2014 of the European Parliament and of the Council of 15 May 2014 and amending Regulation (EU) No 648/2012;]

["third country" means a country or territory [other than the United Kingdom];]

["third country auditor" means a person, other than [. . .] a person eligible for appointment as a statutory auditor, who is eligible to conduct audits of the accounts of bodies corporate incorporated or formed under the law of a third country in accordance with the law of that country;]

["third country competent authority" means a body established in a third country exercising functions related to the regulation or oversight of auditors];

["transfer", in relation to audit working papers [and investigation reports], includes physical and electronic transfer and allowing access to such papers];

["transferable securities" has the meaning given in Article 2(1)(24) of Regulation (EU) No 600/2014 of the European Parliament and of the Council of 15 May 2014 and amending Regulation (EU) No 648/2012;

"UK regulated market" has the meaning given in Article 2(1)(13A) of Regulation (EU) No 600/2014 of the European Parliament and of the Council of 15 May 2014 and amending Regulation (EU) No 648/2012;]

(2) For the purposes of this Part a body is to be regarded as "established in the United Kingdom" if and only if—

(a) it is incorporated or formed under the law of the United Kingdom or a part of the United Kingdom, or

(b) its central management and control are exercised in the United Kingdom;

and any reference to a qualification "obtained in the United Kingdom" is to a qualification obtained from such a body.

[(2A) . . .]

(3) The Secretary of State may by regulations make such modifications of this Part as appear to him to be necessary or appropriate for the purposes of its application in relation to any firm, or description of firm, which is not a body corporate or a partnership.

(4) Regulations under subsection (3) are subject to negative resolution procedure.

NOTES

Sub-s (1) is amended as follows:

Definition "the Audit Directive" (omitted) originally inserted by the Statutory Auditors and Third Country Auditors Regulations 2007, SI 2007/3494, reg 2(1), (2), as from 6 April 2008. Subsequently repealed by the Statutory Auditors and Third Country Auditors (Amendment) (EU Exit) Regulations 2019, SI 2019/177, regs 10, 25(a)(i), as from IP completion day (as defined in the European Union (Withdrawal Agreement) Act 2020, s 39.

Definition "the Audit Regulation" inserted by SI 2016/649, reg 15, Sch 3, Pts 1, 5, paras 1, 51(1), (2)(a), as from 17 June 2016.

Definition "audit working papers" (omitted) originally inserted by SI 2007/3494, reg 2(1), (2), as from 6 April 2008. Subsequently repealed by SI 2016/649, reg 15, Sch 3, Pt 3, para 1(1), (2)(c), as from 17 June 2016, in relation to financial years beginning on or after that date.

Definition "audit working papers and investigation reports" inserted by SI 2016/649, reg 15, Sch 3, Pts 1, 5, paras 1, 51(1), (2)(a), as from 17 June 2016 in relation to financial years beginning on or after that date. The words omitted were repealed by SI 2019/177, regs 10, 25(a)(ii), as from IP completion day (as defined in the European Union (Withdrawal Agreement) Act 2020, s 39).

Definition "the competent authority" inserted by SI 2016/649, reg 15, Sch 3, Pts 1, 5, paras 1, 51(1), (2)(a), as from 17 June 2016.

Definition "the data protection legislation" inserted by the Data Protection Act 2018, s 211, Sch 19, Pt 1, paras 120, 127, as from 25 May 2018 (for transitional provisions and savings relating to the repeal of the Data Protection Act 1998, see Sch 20 to the 2018 Act).

Definition "EEA auditor" (omitted) originally inserted by SI 2007/3494, reg 2(1), (2)), as from 6 April 2008. This definition was repealed by SI 2019/177, regs 10, 25(a)(iii), as from IP completion day (as defined in the European Union (Withdrawal Agreement) Act 2020, s 39).

Definition "EEA competent authority" (omitted) originally inserted by SI 2007/3494, reg 2(1), (2), as from 6 April 2008. Subsequently repealed by SI 2019/177, regs 10, 25(a)(iii), as from IP completion day (as defined in the European Union (Withdrawal Agreement) Act 2020, s 39).

Definition "regulated market" inserted by SI 2019/177, regs 10, 25(a)(iv), as from IP completion day (as defined in the European Union (Withdrawal Agreement) Act 2020, s 39).

Definition "third country" inserted by SI 2007/3494, reg 2(1), (2), as from 6 April 2008. Words in square brackets substituted by SI 2019/177, regs 10, 25(a)(v), as from IP completion day (as defined in the European Union (Withdrawal Agreement) Act 2020, s 39).

Definition "third country auditor" inserted by SI 2007/3494, reg 2(1), (2), as from 6 April 2008. The words omitted were originally inserted by SI 2016/649, reg 15, Sch 3, Pt 3, para 51(1), (2)(d), as from 17 June 2016; and were subsequently repealed by SI 2019/177, regs 10, 25(a)(vi), as from IP completion day (as defined in the European Union (Withdrawal Agreement) Act 2020, s 39).

Definition "third country competent authority" inserted by SI 2007/3494, reg 2(1), (2), as from 6 April 2008.

Definition "transfer" inserted by SI 2010/2537, reg 6(1), (4), as from 15 November 2010. Words in square brackets inserted by SI 2016/649, reg 15, Sch 3, Pt 3, para 51(1), (2)(e), as from 17 June 2016, in relation to financial years beginning on or after that date.

Definition "transferable securities" inserted by SI 2019/177, regs 10, 25(a)(vi), as from IP completion day (as defined in the European Union (Withdrawal Agreement) Act 2020, s 39).

Definition "UK regulated market" inserted by SI 2019/177, regs 10, 25(a)(vi), as from IP completion day (as defined in the European Union (Withdrawal Agreement) Act 2020, s 39).

Sub-s (2A): originally inserted by SI 2007/3494, reg 1(1), (3), as from 6 April 2008. Subsequently repealed by SI 2019/177, regs 10, 25(b), as from IP completion day (as defined in the European Union (Withdrawal Agreement) Act 2020, s 39).

Regulations: no Regulations have been made under this section.

[1.1459]

1262 Index of defined expressions

The following Table shows provisions defining or otherwise explaining expressions used in this Part (other than provisions defining or explaining an expression used only in the same section)—

Expression	*Provision*
address	section 1261(1)
appropriate qualification	section 1219
[approved third country competent authority	[section 1240B(1)]]
[approved third country qualification	section 1221(1)]
associate	section 1260
[Audit Directive	[paragraph 20A of Schedule 10]]
audited person	section 1210(2)
Auditor General	section 1226(1)
[Audit Regulation	section 1261(1)]
[audit regulatory regime	section 1240A(3)]
[. . .	. . .]
[audit working papers and investigation reports	section 1261(1)]
company	section 1261(1)
[competent authority	section 1261(1)]
[the data protection legislation	section 1261(1)]
delegation order	section 1252(1)
director (of a body corporate)	section 1261(1)
[EEA auditor	[paragraph 20A of Schedule 10]]
[EEA competent authority	[paragraph 20A of Schedule 10]]
enactment	section 1293
[equivalent third country	section 1240A(1)]
established in the United Kingdom	section 1261(2)
firm	section 1261(1)
group (in relation to a body corporate)	section 1261(1)
holding company	section 1261(1)
main purposes of this Part	section 1209
member (of a supervisory body)	section 1217(2)
obtained in the United Kingdom	section 1261(2)
officer	section 1261(1)
parent undertaking	section 1261(1)
qualifying body	section 1220(1)
recognised, in relation to a professional qualification	section 1220(3) and Schedule 11
recognised, in relation to a qualifying body	paragraph 1(2) of Schedule 11
recognised, in relation to a supervisory body	section 1217(4) and Schedule 10
registered third country auditor	section 1241(1)
[regulated market	section 1261(1)]
rules of a qualifying body	section 1220(2)
rules of a supervisory body	section 1217(3)
statutory auditor, statutory audit and statutory audit work	section 1210(1)
subsidiary	section 1261(1)
supervisory body	section 1217(1)
subsidiary undertaking	section 1261(1)
[third country	section 1261(1)]
third country auditor . . .	[section 1261(1)]
[third country competent authority	section 1261(1)]
[transferable securities	section 1261(1)]
[transfer (in relation to audit working papers)	Section 1261(1)]
[transitional third country	section 1240A(1)]
[UK regulated market	section 1261(1)]
[[UK-traded third country company]	section 1241(2)]

NOTES

Entries "approved third country competent authority" and "transfer (in relation to audit working papers)" inserted by the Companies Act 2006 (Transfer of Audit Working Papers to Third Countries) Regulations 2010, SI 2010/2537, reg 6(5), as from 15 November 2010.

Entries "approved third country qualification", "audit regulatory regime", "equivalent third country", "regulated market", "transferable securities", "transitional third country", and "UK regulated market" inserted by the Statutory Auditors and Third Country Auditors (Amendment) (EU Exit) Regulations 2019, SI 2019/177, regs 10, 26(a), as from IP completion day (as defined in the European Union (Withdrawal Agreement) Act 2020, s 39).

Words in square brackets in the entries "approved third country competent authority", "Audit Directive", "EEA auditor", "EEA competent authority", and "UK-traded third country company" substituted by SI 2019/177, regs 10, 26(b)–(f), as from IP completion day (as defined in the European Union (Withdrawal Agreement) Act 2020, s 39).

Entries "Audit Regulation", "audit working papers and investigation reports" and "competent authority" inserted, and entry "audit working papers" (omitted) repealed, by the Statutory Auditors and Third Country Auditors Regulations 2016, SI 2016/649, reg 15, Sch 3, Pt 3, para 52, as from 17 June 2016 (note that the insertion of the definition "audit working papers and investigation reports" and the repeal of the definition "audit working papers" applies in relation to financial years beginning on or after that date).

Entry "the data protection legislation" inserted by the Data Protection Act 2018, s 211, Sch 19, Pt 1, paras 120, 128, as from 25 May 2018 (for transitional provisions and savings relating to the repeal of the Data Protection Act 1998, see Sch 20 to the 2018 Act).

Words omitted from the entry relating to "third country auditor" repealed, and words in square bracket substituted, by SI 2007/3494, reg 3(1), (3), as from 6 April 2008.

Other entries in square brackets inserted by the Statutory Auditors and Third Country Auditors Regulations 2007, SI 2007/3494, reg 3(1), (2), as from 6 April 2008.

Miscellaneous and general

[1.1460]

1263 Power to make provision in consequence of changes affecting accountancy bodies

(1) The Secretary of State may by regulations make such amendments of enactments as appear to him to be necessary or expedient in consequence of any change of name, merger or transfer of engagements affecting—

(a) a recognised supervisory body or recognised qualifying body, or

(b) a body of accountants referred to in, or approved, authorised or otherwise recognised for the purposes of, any other enactment.

(2) Regulations under this section are subject to negative resolution procedure.

NOTES

Regulations: no Regulations have been made under this section.

[1.1461]

1264 Consequential amendments

Schedule 14 contains consequential amendments relating to this Part.

PART 43 TRANSPARENCY OBLIGATIONS AND RELATED MATTERS

Introductory

[1.1462]

1265 The transparency obligations directive

(Amends FSMA 2000, s 103 at **[7.234]**.)

Transparency obligations

[1.1463]

1266 Transparency rules

(1) *(Inserts FSMA 2000, ss 89A–89G at* **[7.197]** *et seq.)*

(2) The effectiveness for the purposes of section 155 of the Financial Services and Markets Act 2000 (c 8) (consultation on proposed rules) of things done by the Financial Services Authority before this section comes into force with a view to making transparency rules (as defined in the provisions to be inserted in that Act by subsection (1) above) is not affected by the fact that those provisions were not then in force.

[1.1464]

1267 Competent authority's power to call for information

(Inserts FSMA 2000, ss 89H–89J at **[7.203]** et seq.)

[1.1465]

1268 Powers exercisable in case of infringement of transparency obligation

(Inserts FSMA 2000, ss 89K–89N at **[7.206]** et seq.)

Other matters

[1.1466]

1269 Corporate governance rules

(Inserts FSMA 2000, s 89O at **[7.211]**.)

[1.1467]

1270 Liability for false or misleading statements in certain publications

(Inserts FSMA 2000, ss 90A, 90B at **[7.222]** et seq.)

[1.1468]

1271 Exercise of powers where UK is host member State

(Inserted FSMA 2000, s 100A (now repealed).)

[1.1469]

1272 Transparency obligations and related matters: minor and consequential amendments

(1) Schedule 15 to this Act makes minor and consequential amendments in connection with the provision made by this Part.

(2) In that Schedule—

Part 1 contains amendments of the Financial Services and Markets Act 2000 (c 8);

Part 2 contains amendments of the Companies (Audit, Investigations and Community Enterprise) Act 2004 (c 27).

1273 *(S 1273 (Corporate governance regulations) was repealed by the Official Listing of Securities, Prospectus and Transparency (Amendment etc) (EU Exit) Regulations 2019, SI 2019/707, reg 39, as from IP completion day (as defined in the European Union (Withdrawal Agreement) Act 2020, s 39).)*

PART 44 MISCELLANEOUS PROVISIONS

Regulation of actuaries etc

[1.1470]

1274 Grants to bodies concerned with actuarial standards etc

(Substitutes the Companies (Audit, Investigations and Community Enterprise) Act 2004, s 16(2)(l)–(t) (for the original para (l)) and amends sub-s (5) at **[5.216]**.)

[1.1471]

1275 Levy to pay expenses of bodies concerned with actuarial standards etc

(1)–(5) *(Amend the Companies (Audit, Investigations and Community Enterprise) Act 2004, s 17 at* **[5.217]***)*

(6) The above amendments have effect in relation to any exercise of the power to make regulations under section 17 of the Companies (Audit, Investigations and Community Enterprise) Act 2004 after this section comes into force, regardless of when the expenses to be met by the levy in respect of which the regulations are made were incurred.

(7) *(Amends the Pensions Act 2004, Sch 3 (outside the scope of this work).)*

[1.1472]

1276 Application of provisions to Scotland and Northern Ireland

(Amends the Companies (Audit, Investigations and Community Enterprise) Act 2004, ss 16, 66 at **[5.216]**, **[5.269]**.)

Information as to exercise of voting rights by institutional investors

[1.1473]

1277 Power to require information about exercise of voting rights

(1) The Treasury or the Secretary of State may make provision by regulations requiring institutions to which this section applies to provide information about the exercise of voting rights attached to shares to which this section applies.

(2) This power is exercisable in accordance with—

section 1278 (institutions to which information provisions apply),

section 1279 (shares to which information provisions apply), and

section 1280 (obligations with respect to provision of information).

(3) In this section and the sections mentioned above—

(a) references to a person acting on behalf of an institution include—

(i) any person to whom authority has been delegated by the institution to take decisions as to any matter relevant to the subject matter of the regulations, and

(ii) such other persons as may be specified; and

(b) "specified" means specified in the regulations.

(4) The obligation imposed by regulations under this section is enforceable by civil proceedings brought by—

(a) any person to whom the information should have been provided, or

(b) a specified regulatory authority.

(5) Regulations under this section may make different provision for different descriptions of institution, different descriptions of shares and for other different circumstances.

(6) Regulations under this section are subject to affirmative resolution procedure.

NOTES

Regulations: no Regulations have been made under this section.

[1.1474]

1278 Institutions to which information provisions apply

(1) The institutions to which section 1277 applies are—

(a) unit trust schemes within the meaning of the Financial Services and Markets Act 2000 (c 8) in respect of which an order is in force under section 243 of that Act;

(b) open-ended investment companies incorporated by virtue of regulations under section 262 of that Act;

(c) companies approved for the purposes of [Chapter 4 of Part 24 of the Corporation Tax Act 2010] (investment trusts);

(d) pension schemes as defined in section 1(5) of the Pension Schemes Act 1993 (c 48) or the Pension Schemes (Northern Ireland) Act 1993 (c 49);

(e) undertakings authorised under the Financial Services and Markets Act 2000 to carry on long-term insurance business (that is, the activity of effecting or carrying out contracts of long-term insurance within the meaning of the Financial Services and Markets (Regulated Activities) Order 2001 (SI 2001/544);

(f) . . .

(2) Regulations under that section may—

(a) provide that the section applies to other descriptions of institution;

(b) provide that the section does not apply to a specified description of institution.

(3) The regulations must specify by whom, in the case of any description of institution, the duty imposed by the regulations is to be fulfilled.

NOTES

Sub-s (1): words in square brackets in para (c) substituted by the Corporation Tax Act 2010, s 1177, Sch 1, Pt 2, paras 487, 490 (note that the 2010 Act comes into force on 1 April 2010 and has effect, for corporation tax purposes for accounting periods ending on or after that day, and for income tax and capital gains tax purposes for the tax year 2010–11 and subsequent tax years; see s 1184(1) of the 2010 Act). Para (f) repealed by the Alternative Investment Fund Managers Regulations 2013, SI 2013/1773, reg 80, Sch 1, Part 2, para 42, as from 22 July 2013.

Regulations under s 1277: see that section *ante*.

[1.1475]

1279 Shares to which information provisions apply

(1) The shares to which section 1277 applies are shares—

(a) of a description traded on a specified market, and

(b) in which the institution has, or is taken to have, an interest.

Regulations under that section may provide that the section does not apply to shares of a specified description.

(2) For this purpose an institution has an interest in shares if the shares, or a depositary certificate in respect of them, are held by it, or on its behalf.

A "depositary certificate" means an instrument conferring rights (other than options)—

(a) in respect of shares held by another person, and

(b) the transfer of which may be effected without the consent of that person.

(3) Where an institution has an interest—

(a) in a specified description of collective investment scheme (within the meaning of the Financial Services and Markets Act 2000 (c 8)), or

(b) in any other specified description of scheme or collective investment vehicle,

it is taken to have an interest in any shares in which that scheme or vehicle has or is taken to have an interest.

(4) For this purpose a scheme or vehicle is taken to have an interest in shares if it would be regarded as having such an interest in accordance with subsection (2) if it was an institution to which section 1277 applied.

NOTES

Regulations under s 1277: see that section *ante*.

[1.1476]

1280 Obligations with respect to provision of information

(1) Regulations under section 1277 may require the provision of specified information about—

(a) the exercise or non-exercise of voting rights by the institution or any person acting on its behalf,

(b) any instructions given by the institution or any person acting on its behalf as to the exercise or non-exercise of voting rights, and

(c) any delegation by the institution or any person acting on its behalf of any functions in relation to the exercise or non-exercise of voting rights or the giving of such instructions.

(2) The regulations may require information to be provided in respect of specified occasions or specified periods.

(3) Where instructions are given to act on the recommendations or advice of another person, the regulations may require the provision of information about what recommendations or advice were given.

(4) The regulations may require information to be provided—

(a) in such manner as may be specified, and

(b) to such persons as may be specified, or to the public, or both.

(5) The regulations may provide—

(a) that an institution may discharge its obligations under the regulations by referring to information disclosed by a person acting on its behalf, and

(b) that in such a case it is sufficient, where that other person acts on behalf of more than one institution, that the reference is to information given in aggregated form, that is—

(i) relating to the exercise or non-exercise by that person of voting rights on behalf of more than one institution, or

(ii) relating to the instructions given by that person in respect of the exercise or non-exercise of voting rights on behalf of more than one institution, or

(iii) relating to the delegation by that person of functions in relation to the exercise or non-exercise of voting rights, or the giving of instructions in respect of the exercise or non-exercise of voting rights, on behalf of more than one institution.

(6) References in this section to instructions are to instructions of any description, whether general or specific, whether binding or not and whether or not acted upon.

NOTES

Regulations under s 1277: see that section *ante*.

Disclosure of information under the Enterprise Act 2002

[1.1477]

1281 Disclosure of information under the Enterprise Act 2002

(Inserts the Enterprise Act 2002, s 241A (outside the scope of this work).)

Expenses of winding up

[1.1478]

1282 Payment of expenses of winding up

(Sub-s (1) inserts the Insolvency Act 1986, s 176ZA at **[9.306]***; sub-s (2) makes a corresponding amendment to the Insolvency (Northern Ireland) Order 1989.)*

Commonhold associations

[1.1479]

1283 Amendment of memorandum or articles of commonhold association

(Amends the Commonhold and Leasehold Reform Act 2002, Sch 3 (outside the scope of this work).)

PART 45 NORTHERN IRELAND

[1.1480]

1284 Extension of Companies Acts to Northern Ireland

(1) The Companies Acts as defined by this Act (see section 2) extend to Northern Ireland.

(2) The Companies (Northern Ireland) Order 1986 (SI 1986/1032 (NI 6)), the Companies Consolidation (Consequential Provisions) (Northern Ireland) Order 1986 (SI 1986/1035 (NI 9)) and Part 3 of the Companies (Audit, Investigations and Community Enterprise) Order 2005 (SI 2005/1967 (NI 17)) shall cease to have effect accordingly.

[1.1481]

1285 Extension of GB enactments relating to [UK Societas]

(1) The enactments in force in Great Britain relating to [UK Societas] extend to Northern Ireland.

(2) The following enactments shall cease to have effect accordingly—

(a) the European Public Limited-Liability Company Regulations (Northern Ireland) 2004 (SR 2004/417), and

(b) the European Public Limited-Liability Company (Fees) Regulations (Northern Ireland) 2004 (SR 2004/418).

[(3) In this section "UK Societas" means a United Kingdom Societas within the meaning of Council Regulation 2157/2001/EC of 8 October 2001 on the Statute for a European Company.]

NOTES

Words in square brackets in the section heading and in sub-s (1) substituted, and sub-s (3) substituted, by the International Accounting Standards and European Public Limited-Liability Company (Amendment etc) (EU Exit) Regulations 2019, SI 2019/685, reg 21, Sch 3, Pt 3, para 20, as from IP completion day (as defined in the European Union (Withdrawal Agreement) Act 2020, s 39).

[1.1482]

1286 Extension of GB enactments relating to certain other forms of business organisation

(1) The enactments in force in Great Britain relating to—

(a) limited liability partnerships,

(b) limited partnerships,

(c) open-ended investment companies, . . .

(d) European Economic Interest Groupings, [and]

[(e) UK Economic Interest Groupings,]

extend to Northern Ireland.

(2) The following enactments shall cease to have effect accordingly—

(a) the Limited Liability Partnerships Act (Northern Ireland) 2002 (c 12 (NI));

(b) the Limited Partnerships Act 1907 (c 24) as it formerly had effect in Northern Ireland;

(c) the Open-Ended Investment Companies Act (Northern Ireland) 2002 (c 13 (NI));

(d) the European Economic Interest Groupings Regulations (Northern Ireland) 1989 (SR 1989/216).

NOTES

Sub-s (1): the word omitted from para (c) was repealed, and para (e) and the preceding word were inserted, by the European Economic Interest Grouping (Amendment) (EU Exit) Regulations 2018, SI 2018/1299, reg 62(1), (3), as from IP completion day (as defined in the European Union (Withdrawal Agreement) Act 2020, s 39).

[1.1483]

1287 Extension of enactments relating to business names

(1) The provisions of Part 41 of this Act (business names) extend to Northern Ireland.

(2) The Business Names (Northern Ireland) Order 1986 (SI 1986/1033 (NI 7)) shall cease to have effect accordingly.

PART 46 GENERAL SUPPLEMENTARY PROVISIONS

Regulations and orders

[1.1484]

1288 Regulations and orders: statutory instrument

Except as otherwise provided, regulations and orders under this Act shall be made by statutory instrument.

[1.1485]

1289 Regulations and orders: negative resolution procedure

Where regulations or orders under this Act are subject to "negative resolution procedure" the statutory instrument containing the regulations or order shall be subject to annulment in pursuance of a resolution of either House of Parliament.

[1.1486]

1290 Regulations and orders: affirmative resolution procedure

Where regulations or orders under this Act are subject to "affirmative resolution procedure" the regulations or order must not be made unless a draft of the statutory instrument containing them has been laid before Parliament and approved by a resolution of each House of Parliament.

[1.1487]

1291 Regulations and orders: approval after being made

(1) Regulations or orders under this Act that are subject to "approval after being made"—

(a) must be laid before Parliament after being made, and

(b) cease to have effect at the end of 28 days beginning with the day on which they were made unless during that period they are approved by resolution of each House.

(2) In reckoning the period of 28 days no account shall be taken of any time during which Parliament is dissolved or prorogued or during which both Houses are adjourned for more than four days.

(3) The regulations or order ceasing to have effect does not affect—

(a) anything previously done under them or it, or

(b) the making of new regulations or a new order.

[1.1488]

1292 Regulations and orders: supplementary

(1) Regulations or orders under this Act may—

(a) make different provision for different cases or circumstances,

(b) include supplementary, incidental and consequential provision, and

(c) make transitional provision and savings.

(2) Any provision that may be made by regulations under this Act may be made by order; and any provision that may be made by order under this Act may be made by regulations.

(3) Any provision that may be made by regulations or order under this Act for which no Parliamentary procedure is prescribed may be made by regulations or order subject to negative or affirmative resolution procedure.

(4) Any provision that may be made by regulations or order under this Act subject to negative resolution procedure may be made by regulations or order subject to affirmative resolution procedure.

[“Bank of England”

[1.1489]

1292A “Bank of England”

In this Act, except in section 796, references to the Bank of England do not include the Bank acting in its capacity as the Prudential Regulation Authority.]

NOTES

Inserted by the Bank of England and Financial Services (Consequential Amendments) Regulations 2017, SI 2017/80, reg 2, Schedule, Pt 1, para 18, as from 1 March 2017.

Meaning of “enactment”

[1.1490]

1293 Meaning of “enactment”

In this Act, unless the context otherwise requires, “enactment” includes—

(a) an enactment contained in subordinate legislation within the meaning of the Interpretation Act 1978 (c 30),

[(aa) an enactment contained in, or in an instrument made under, a Measure or Act of the National Assembly for Wales,]

(b) an enactment contained in, or in an instrument made under, an Act of the Scottish Parliament, and

(c) an enactment contained in, or in an instrument made under, Northern Ireland legislation within the meaning of the Interpretation Act 1978.

NOTES

Para (aa) inserted by the Small Business, Enterprise and Employment Act 2015, s 90(4), as from 26 May 2015.

National Assembly for Wales: see the note to s 54 at **[1.55]** in relation to the renaming of the National Assembly for Wales.

Consequential and transitional provisions

[1.1491]

1294 Power to make consequential amendments etc

(1) The Secretary of State or the Treasury may by order make such provision amending, repealing or revoking any enactment to which this section applies as they consider necessary or expedient in consequence of any provision made by or under this Act.

(2) This section applies to—

(a) any enactment passed or made before the passing of this Act,

(b) any enactment contained in this Act or in subordinate legislation made under it, and

(c) any enactment passed or made before the end of the session after that in which this Act is passed.

(3) Without prejudice to the generality of the power conferred by subsection (1), orders under this section may—

(a) make provision extending to other forms of organisation any provision made by or under this Act in relation to companies, or

(b) make provision corresponding to that made by or under this Act in relation to companies,

in either case with such adaptations or other modifications as appear to the Secretary of State or the Treasury to be necessary or expedient.

(4) The references in subsection (3) to provision made by this Act include provision conferring power to make provision by regulations, orders or other subordinate legislation.

(5) Amendments and repeals made under this section are additional, and without prejudice, to those made by or under any other provision of this Act.

(6) Orders under this section are subject to affirmative resolution procedure.

NOTES

Orders and Regulations: the Companies Act 2006 (Commencement No 2, Consequential Amendments, Transitional Provisions and Savings) Order 2007, SI 2007/1093; the Companies Act 2006 (Commencement No 3, Consequential Amendments, Transitional Provisions and Savings) Order 2007, SI 2007/2194; the Companies Act 2006 (Consequential Amendments etc) Order 2008, SI 2008/948 at **[4.136]**; the Companies Act 2006 (Consequential Amendments) (Taxes and National Insurance) Order 2008, SI 2008/954; the Overseas Companies Regulations 2009, SI 2009/1801 at **[4.216]**; the Companies Act 2006 (Part 35) (Consequential Amendments, Transitional Provisions and Savings) Order 2009, SI 2009/1802; the Limited Liability Partnerships (Application of Companies Act 2006) Regulations 2009, SI 2009/1804 at

[10.319]; the Companies Act 2006 (Consequential Amendments) (Uncertificated Securities) Order 2009, SI 2009/1889; the Companies Act 2006 (Consequential Amendments) (Taxes and National Insurance) Order 2009, SI 2009/1890; the Companies Act 2006 (Consequential Amendments, Transitional Provisions and Savings) Order 2009, SI 2009/1941 at **[4.355]**; the Companies Act 2006 (Consequential Amendments and Transitional Provisions) Order 2011, SI 2011/1265 at **[4.425]**; the Company, Limited Liability Partnership and Business (Names and Trading Disclosures) Regulations 2015, SI 2015/17 at **[4.514]**. For a summary of all statutory instruments made under this Act, see Appendix 4 at **[A4]**.

[1.1492]

1295 Repeals

The enactments specified in Schedule 16, which include enactments that are no longer of practical utility, are repealed to the extent specified.

[1.1493]

1296 Power to make transitional provision and savings

(1) The Secretary of State or the Treasury may by order make such transitional provision and savings as they consider necessary or expedient in connection with the commencement of any provision made by or under this Act.

(2) An order may, in particular, make such adaptations of provisions brought into force as appear to be necessary or expedient in consequence of other provisions of this Act not yet having come into force.

(3) Transitional provision and savings made under this section are additional, and without prejudice, to those made by or under any other provision of this Act.

(4) Orders under this section are subject to negative resolution procedure.

NOTES

Orders: the Companies Act 2006 (Commencement No 1, Transitional Provisions and Savings) Order 2006, SI 2006/3428; the Companies Act 2006 (Commencement No 2, Consequential Amendments, Transitional Provisions and Savings) Order 2007, SI 2007/1093; the Companies Act 2006 (Commencement No 3, Consequential Amendments, Transitional Provisions and Savings) Order 2007, SI 2007/2194; the Companies Act 2006 (Commencement No 4 and Commencement No 3 (Amendment)) Order 2007, SI 2007/2607; the Companies Act 2006 (Commencement No 5, Transitional Provisions and Savings) Order 2007, SI 2007/3495; the Companies Act 2006 (Commencement No 6, Saving and Commencement Nos 3 and 5 (Amendment)) Order 2008, SI 2008/674; the Companies Act 2006 (Consequential Amendments etc) Order 2008, SI 2008/948 at **[4.136]**; the Companies Act 2006 (Consequential Amendments) (Taxes and National Insurance) Order 2008, SI 2008/954; the Companies Act 2006 (Commencement No 7, Transitional Provisions and Savings) Order 2008, SI 2008/1886; the Companies Act 2006 (Commencement No 8, Transitional Provisions and Savings) Order 2008, SI 2008/2860; the Companies Act 2006 (Part 35) (Consequential Amendments, Transitional Provisions and Savings) Order 2009, SI 2009/1802; the Limited Liability Partnerships (Application of Companies Act 2006) Regulations 2009, SI 2009/1804 at **[10.319]**; the Companies Act 2006 (Consequential Amendments, Transitional Provisions and Savings) Order 2009, SI 2009/1941 at **[4.355]**; the Registrar of Companies (Fees) (Limited Partnerships and Newspaper Proprietors) Regulations 2009, SI 2009/2392 at **[4.370]**; the Companies Act 2006 and Limited Liability Partnerships (Transitional Provisions and Savings) (Amendment) Regulations 2009, SI 2009/2476 at **[4.424]**; the Companies Act 2006 (Consequential Amendments and Transitional Provisions) Order 2011, SI 2011/1265 at **[4.425]**; the Companies and Limited Liability Partnerships (Forms, etc) Amendment Regulations 2013, SI 2013/1947; the Company, Limited Liability Partnership and Business (Names and Trading Disclosures) Regulations 2015, SI 2015/17 at **[4.514]**. For a summary of all statutory instruments made under this Act, see Appendix 4 at **[A4]**.

[1.1494]

1297 Continuity of the law

(1) This section applies where any provision of this Act re-enacts (with or without modification) an enactment repealed by this Act.

(2) The repeal and re-enactment does not affect the continuity of the law.

(3) Anything done (including subordinate legislation made), or having effect as if done, under or for the purposes of the repealed provision that could have been done under or for the purposes of the corresponding provision of this Act, if in force or effective immediately before the commencement of that corresponding provision, has effect thereafter as if done under or for the purposes of that corresponding provision.

(4) Any reference (express or implied) in this Act or any other enactment, instrument or document to a provision of this Act shall be construed (so far as the context permits) as including, as respects times, circumstances or purposes in relation to which the corresponding repealed provision had effect, a reference to that corresponding provision.

(5) Any reference (express or implied) in any enactment, instrument or document to a repealed provision shall be construed (so far as the context permits), as respects times, circumstances and purposes in relation to which the corresponding provision of this Act has effect, as being or (according to the context) including a reference to the corresponding provision of this Act.

(6) This section has effect subject to any specific transitional provision or saving contained in this Act.

(7) References in this section to this Act include subordinate legislation made under this Act.

(8) In this section "subordinate legislation" has the same meaning as in the Interpretation Act 1978 (c 30).

NOTES

General saving for existing companies etc: see the Companies Act 2006 (Commencement No 8, Transitional Provisions and Savings) Order 2008, SI 2008/2860, Sch 2, para 1(2), (3).

References to companies registered or re-registered under earlier legislation: see the Companies Act 2006 (Consequential Amendments, Transitional Provisions and Savings) Order 2009, SI 2009/1941, art 3 at **[4.357]**.

See also the Companies Act 2006 (Commencement No 3, Consequential Amendments, Transitional Provisions and Savings) Order 2007, SI 2007/2194, art 12(1), the Companies Act 2006 (Commencement No 5, Transitional Provisions and Savings) Order 2007, SI 2007/3495, art 12(2), the Companies Act 2006 (Commencement No 6, Saving and Commencement Nos 3 and 5 (Amendment)) Order 2008, SI 2008/674, art 6(2), the Companies Act 2006 (Consequential Amendments etc) Order 2008, SI 2008/948, art 12, and the Companies Act 2006 (Commencement No 8, Transitional Provisions and Savings) Order 2008, SI 2008/2860, art 8, which provide that the amendments and repeals made by those Orders do not affect the operation of this section.

PART 47 FINAL PROVISIONS

[1.1495]

1298 Short title

The short title of this Act is the Companies Act 2006.

[1.1496]

1299 Extent

Except as otherwise provided (or the context otherwise requires), the provisions of this Act extend to the whole of the United Kingdom.

[1.1497]

1300 Commencement

(1) The following provisions come into force on the day this Act is passed—

(a) Part 43 (transparency obligations and related matters), except the amendment in paragraph 11(2) of Schedule 15 of the definition of "regulated market" in Part 6 of the Financial Services and Markets Act 2000 (c 8),

(b) in Part 44 (miscellaneous provisions)—
section 1274 (grants to bodies concerned with actuarial standards etc), and
section 1276 (application of provisions to Scotland and Northern Ireland),

(c) Part 46 (general supplementary provisions), except section 1295 and Schedule 16 (repeals), and

(d) this Part.

(2) The other provisions of this Act come into force on such day as may be appointed by order of the Secretary of State or the Treasury.

NOTES

Orders: the Companies Act 2006 (Commencement No 1, Transitional Provisions and Savings) Order 2006, SI 2006/3428; the Companies Act 2006 (Commencement No 2, Consequential Amendments, Transitional Provisions and Savings) Order 2007, SI 2007/1093; the Companies Act 2006 (Commencement No 3, Consequential Amendments, Transitional Provisions and Savings) Order 2007, SI 2007/2194; the Companies Act 2006 (Commencement No 4 and Commencement No 3 (Amendment)) Order 2007, SI 2007/2607; the Companies Act 2006 (Commencement No 5, Transitional Provisions and Savings) Order 2007, SI 2007/3495; the Companies Act 2006 (Commencement No 6, Saving and Commencement Nos 3 and 5 (Amendment)) Order 2008, SI 2008/674; the Companies Act 2006 (Commencement No 7, Transitional Provisions and Savings) Order 2008, SI 2008/1886; the Companies Act 2006 (Commencement No 8, Transitional Provisions and Savings) Order 2008, SI 2008/2860; the Companies Act 2006 (Consequential Amendments, Transitional Provisions and Savings) Order 2009, SI 2009/1941; the Companies Act 2006 and Limited Liability Partnerships (Transitional Provisions and Savings) (Amendment) Regulations 2009, SI 2009/2476; the Companies and Limited Liability Partnerships (Forms, etc) Amendment Regulations 2013, SI 2013/1947. For a summary of all statutory instruments made under this Act, see Appendix 4 at **[A4]**.

SCHEDULES

SCHEDULE 1
CONNECTED PERSONS: REFERENCES TO AN INTEREST IN SHARES OR DEBENTURES

Sections 254 and 255

Introduction

[1.1498]

1. (1) The provisions of this Schedule have effect for the interpretation of references in sections 254 and 255 (directors connected with or controlling a body corporate) to an interest in shares or debentures.

(2) The provisions are expressed in relation to shares but apply to debentures as they apply to shares.

General provisions

2. (1) A reference to an interest in shares includes any interest of any kind whatsoever in shares.

(2) Any restraints or restrictions to which the exercise of any right attached to the interest is or may be subject shall be disregarded.

(3) It is immaterial that the shares in which a person has an interest are not identifiable.

(4) Persons having a joint interest in shares are deemed each of them to have that interest.

Rights to acquire shares

3. (1) A person is taken to have an interest in shares if he enters into a contract to acquire them.

(2) A person is taken to have an interest in shares if—

(a) he has a right to call for delivery of the shares to himself or to his order, or

(b) he has a right to acquire an interest in shares or is under an obligation to take an interest in shares,

whether the right or obligation is conditional or absolute.

(3) Rights or obligations to subscribe for shares are not to be taken for the purposes of sub-paragraph (2) to be rights to acquire or obligations to take an interest in shares.

(4) A person ceases to have an interest in shares by virtue of this paragraph—

(a) on the shares being delivered to another person at his order—

(i) in fulfilment of a contract for their acquisition by him, or

(ii) in satisfaction of a right of his to call for their delivery;

(b) on a failure to deliver the shares in accordance with the terms of such a contract or on which such a right falls to be satisfied;

(c) on the lapse of his right to call for the delivery of shares.

Right to exercise or control exercise of rights

4. (1) A person is taken to have an interest in shares if, not being the registered holder, he is entitled—

(a) to exercise any right conferred by the holding of the shares, or

(b) to control the exercise of any such right.

(2) For this purpose a person is taken to be entitled to exercise or control the exercise of a right conferred by the holding of shares if he—

(a) has a right (whether subject to conditions or not) the exercise of which would make him so entitled, or

(b) is under an obligation (whether or not so subject) the fulfilment of which would make him so entitled.

(3) A person is not by virtue of this paragraph taken to be interested in shares by reason only that—

(a) he has been appointed a proxy to exercise any of the rights attached to the shares, or

(b) he has been appointed by a body corporate to act as its representative at any meeting of a company or of any class of its members.

Bodies corporate

5. (1) A person is taken to be interested in shares if a body corporate is interested in them and—

(a) the body corporate or its directors are accustomed to act in accordance with his directions or instructions, or

(b) he is entitled to exercise or control the exercise of more than one-half of the voting power at general meetings of the body corporate.

(2) For the purposes of sub-paragraph (1)(b) where—

(a) a person is entitled to exercise or control the exercise of more than one-half of the voting power at general meetings of a body corporate, and

(b) that body corporate is entitled to exercise or control the exercise of any of the voting power at general meetings of another body corporate,

the voting power mentioned in paragraph (b) above is taken to be exercisable by that person.

Trusts

6. (1) Where an interest in shares is comprised in property held on trust, every beneficiary of the trust is taken to have an interest in shares, subject as follows.

(2) So long as a person is entitled to receive, during the lifetime of himself or another, income from trust property comprising shares, an interest in the shares in reversion or remainder or (as regards Scotland) in fee shall be disregarded.

(3) A person is treated as not interested in shares if and so long as he holds them—

(a) under the law in force in any part of the United Kingdom, as a bare trustee or as a custodian trustee, or

(b) under the law in force in Scotland, as a simple trustee.

(4) There shall be disregarded any interest of a person subsisting by virtue of—

(a) an authorised unit trust scheme (within the meaning of section 237 of the Financial Services and Markets Act 2000 (c 8));

(b) a scheme made under section 22 or 22A of the Charities Act 1960 (c 58), section 25 of the Charities Act (Northern Ireland) 1964 (c 33 (NI))[, section 24 or 25 of the Charities Act 1993[, section 44 or 45 of the Charities Act (Northern Ireland) 2008] or section 96 or 100 of the Charities Act 2011,], section 11 of the Trustee Investments Act 1961 (c 62) or section 42 of the Administration of Justice Act 1982 (c 53); or

(c) the scheme set out in the Schedule to the Church Funds Investment Measure 1958 (1958 No 1).

(5) There shall be disregarded any interest—

(a) of the Church of Scotland General Trustees or of the Church of Scotland Trust in shares held by them;

(b) of any other person in shares held by those Trustees or that Trust otherwise than as simple trustees.

"The Church of Scotland General Trustees" are the body incorporated by the order confirmed by the Church of Scotland (General Trustees) Order Confirmation Act 1921 (1921 c xxv), and "the Church of Scotland Trust" is the body incorporated by the order confirmed by the Church of Scotland Trust Order Confirmation Act 1932 (1932 c xxi).

NOTES

Para 6: words in first (outer) pair of square brackets in sub-para (4)(b) substituted by the Charities Act 2011, s 354, Sch 7, Pt 2, para 116, as from 14 March 2012. Words in second (inner) pair of square brackets in that sub-paragraph inserted by the Charities Act (Northern Ireland) 2008, s 183, Sch 8, para 13(6), as from a day to be appointed.

Charities Act 1960; Charities Act 1993: repealed (see now the Charities Act 2011).

[SCHEDULE 1A
REFERENCES TO PEOPLE WITH SIGNIFICANT CONTROL OVER A COMPANY

Section 790C

PART 1 THE SPECIFIED CONDITIONS

Introduction

[1.1499]

1. This Part of this Schedule specifies the conditions at least one of which must be met by an individual ("X") in relation to a company ("company Y") in order for the individual to be a person with "significant control" over the company.

Ownership of shares

2. The first condition is that X holds, directly or indirectly, more than 25% of the shares in company Y.

Ownership of voting rights

3. The second condition is that X holds, directly or indirectly, more than 25% of the voting rights in company Y.

Ownership of right to appoint or remove directors

4. The third condition is that X holds the right, directly or indirectly, to appoint or remove a majority of the board of directors of company Y.

Significant influence or control

5. The fourth condition is that X has the right to exercise, or actually exercises, significant influence or control over company Y.

Trusts, partnerships etc

6. The fifth condition is that—

(a) the trustees of a trust or the members of a firm that, under the law by which it is governed, is not a legal person meet any of the other specified conditions (in their capacity as such) in relation to company Y, or would do so if they were individuals, and

(b) X has the right to exercise, or actually exercises, significant influence or control over the activities of that trust or firm.]

NOTES

Inserted by the Small Business, Enterprise and Employment Act 2015, s 81, Sch 3, Pt 1, para 2, as from 6 April 2016.

[PART 2 HOLDING AN INTEREST IN A COMPANY ETC

Introduction

[1.1500]

7. This Part of this Schedule specifies the circumstances in which, for the purposes of section 790C(4) or (8)—

(a) a person ("V") is to be regarded as holding an interest in a company ("company W");

(b) an interest held by V in company W is to be regarded as held through a legal entity.

Holding an interest

8. (1) V holds an interest in company W if—

(a) V holds shares in company W, directly or indirectly,

(b) V holds, directly or indirectly, voting rights in company W,

(c) V holds, directly or indirectly, the right to appoint or remove any member of the board of directors of company W,

(d) V has the right to exercise, or actually exercises, significant influence or control over company W, or

(e) sub-paragraph (2) is satisfied.

(2) This sub-paragraph is satisfied where—

(a) the trustees of a trust or the members of a firm that, under the law by which it is governed, is not a legal person hold an interest in company W in a way mentioned in sub-paragraph (1)(a) to (d), and

(b) V has the right to exercise, or actually exercises, significant influence or control over the activities of that trust or firm.

Interests held through a legal entity

9. (1) This paragraph applies where V—

(a) holds an interest in company W by virtue of indirectly holding shares or a right, and

(b) does so by virtue of having a majority stake (see paragraph 18) in—

(i) a legal entity ("L") which holds the shares or right directly, or

(ii) a legal entity that is part of a chain of legal entities such as is described in paragraph 18(1)(b) or (2)(b) that includes L.

(2) Where this paragraph applies, V holds the interest in company W—

(a) through L, and

(b) through each other legal entity in the chain mentioned in sub-paragraph (1)(b)(ii).]

NOTES

Inserted by the Small Business, Enterprise and Employment Act 2015, s 81, Sch 3, Pt 1, para 2, as from 6 April 2016.

[PART 3 SUPPLEMENTARY PROVISION

Introduction

[1.1501]

10. This Part sets out rules for the interpretation of this Schedule.

Joint interests

11. If two or more persons each hold a share or right jointly, each of them is treated for the purposes of this Schedule as holding that share or right.

Joint arrangements

12. (1) If shares or rights held by a person and shares or rights held by another person are the subject of a joint arrangement between those persons, each of them is treated for the purposes of this Schedule as holding the combined shares or rights of both of them.

(2) A "joint arrangement" is an arrangement between the holders of shares (or rights) that they will exercise all or substantially all the rights conferred by their respective shares (or rights) jointly in a way that is pre-determined by the arrangement.

(3) "Arrangement" has the meaning given by paragraph 21.

Calculating shareholdings

13. (1) In relation to a legal entity that has a share capital, a reference to holding "more than 25% of the shares" in that entity is to holding shares comprised in the issued share capital of that entity of a nominal value exceeding (in aggregate) 25% of that share capital.

(2) In relation to a legal entity that does not have a share capital—

(a) a reference to holding shares in that entity is to holding a right to share in the capital or, as the case may be, profits of that entity;

(b) a reference to holding "more than 25% of the shares" in that entity is to holding a right or rights to share in more than 25% of the capital or, as the case may be, profits of that entity.

Voting rights

14. (1) A reference to the voting rights in a legal entity is to the rights conferred on shareholders in respect of their shares (or, in the case of an entity not having a share capital, on members) to vote at general meetings of the entity on all or substantially all matters.

(2) In relation to a legal entity that does not have general meetings at which matters are decided by the exercise of voting rights—

(a) a reference to exercising voting rights in the entity is to be read as a reference to exercising rights in relation to the entity that are equivalent to those of a person entitled to exercise voting rights in a company;

(b) a reference to exercising more than 25% of the voting rights in the entity is to be read as a reference to exercising the right under the constitution of the entity to block changes to the overall policy of the entity or to the terms of its constitution.

15. In applying this Schedule, the voting rights in a legal entity are to be reduced by any rights held by the entity itself.

Rights to appoint or remove members of the board

16. A reference to the right to appoint or remove a majority of the board of directors of a legal entity is to the right to appoint or remove directors holding a majority of the voting rights at meetings of the board on all or substantially all matters.

17. References to a board of directors, in the case of an entity that does not have such a board, are to be read as references to the equivalent management body of that entity.

Shares or rights held "indirectly"

18. (1) A person holds a share "indirectly" if the person has a majority stake in a legal entity and that entity—

(a) holds the share in question, or

(b) is part of a chain of legal entities—

(i) each of which (other than the last) has a majority stake in the entity immediately below it in the chain, and

(ii) the last of which holds the share.

(2) A person holds a right "indirectly" if the person has a majority stake in a legal entity and that entity—

(a) holds that right, or

(b) is part of a chain of legal entities—

(i) each of which (other than the last) has a majority stake in the entity immediately below it in the chain, and

(ii) the last of which holds that right.

(3) For these purposes, A has a "majority stake" in B if—

(a) A holds a majority of the voting rights in B,

(b) A is a member of B and has the right to appoint or remove a majority of the board of directors of B,

(c) A is a member of B and controls alone, pursuant to an agreement with other shareholders or members, a majority of the voting rights in B, or

(d) A has the right to exercise, or actually exercises, dominant influence or control over B.

(4) In the application of this paragraph to the right to appoint or remove a majority of the board of directors, a legal entity is to be treated as having the right to appoint a director if—

(a) a person's appointment as director follows necessarily from that person's appointment as director of the legal entity, or

(b) the directorship is held by the legal entity itself.

Shares held by nominees

19. A share held by a person as nominee for another is to be treated for the purposes of this Schedule as held by the other (and not by the nominee).

Rights treated as held by person who controls their exercise

20. (1) Where a person controls a right, the right is to be treated for the purposes of this Schedule as held by that person (and not by the person who in fact holds the right, unless that person also controls it).

(2) A person "controls" a right if, by virtue of any arrangement between that person and others, the right is exercisable only—

(a) by that person,

(b) in accordance with that person's directions or instructions, or

(c) with that person's consent or concurrence.

21. (1) "Arrangement" includes—

(a) any scheme, agreement or understanding, whether or not it is legally enforceable, and

(b) any convention, custom or practice of any kind.

(2) But something does not count as an arrangement unless there is at least some degree of stability about it (whether by its nature or terms, the time it has been in existence or otherwise).

Rights exercisable only in certain circumstances etc

22. (1) Rights that are exercisable only in certain circumstances are to be taken into account only—
- (a) when the circumstances have arisen, and for so long as they continue to obtain, or
- (b) when the circumstances are within the control of the person having the rights.

(2) But rights that are exercisable by an administrator or by creditors while a legal entity is in relevant insolvency proceedings are not to be taken into account even while the entity is in those proceedings.

(3) "Relevant insolvency proceedings" means—
- (a) administration within the meaning of the Insolvency Act 1986,
- (b) administration within the meaning of the Insolvency (Northern Ireland) Order 1989 (SI 1989/2405 (NI 19)), or
- (c) proceedings under the insolvency law of another country or territory during which an entity's assets and affairs are subject to the control or supervision of a third party or creditor.

(4) Rights that are normally exercisable but are temporarily incapable of exercise are to continue to be taken into account.

Rights attached to shares held by way of security

23. Rights attached to shares held by way of security provided by a person are to be treated for the purposes of this Schedule as held by that person—
- (a) where apart from the right to exercise them for the purpose of preserving the value of the security, or of realising it, the rights are exercisable only in accordance with that person's instructions, and
- (b) where the shares are held in connection with the granting of loans as part of normal business activities and apart from the right to exercise them for the purpose of preserving the value of the security, or of realising it, the rights are exercisable only in that person's interests.

Significant influence or control

24. (1) The Secretary of State must issue guidance about the meaning of "significant influence or control" for the purposes of this Schedule.

(2) Regard must be had to that guidance in interpreting references in this Schedule to "significant influence or control".

(3) Before issuing guidance under this paragraph the Secretary of State must lay a draft of it before Parliament.

(4) If, within the 40-day period, either House of Parliament resolves not to approve the draft guidance, the Secretary of State must take no further steps in relation to it.

(5) If no such resolution is made within that period, the Secretary of State must issue and publish the guidance in the form of the draft.

(6) Sub-paragraph (4) does not prevent a new draft of proposed guidance from being laid before Parliament.

(7) In this section "the 40-day period", in relation to draft guidance, means the period of 40 days beginning with the day on which the draft is laid before Parliament (or, if it is not laid before each House on the same day, the later of the days on which it is laid).

(8) In calculating the 40-day period, no account is to be taken of any period during which—
- (a) Parliament is dissolved or prorogued, or
- (b) both Houses are adjourned for more than 4 days.

(9) The Secretary of State may revise guidance issued under this paragraph, and a reference in this paragraph to guidance includes a reference to revised guidance.

Limited partnerships

25. (1) An individual does not meet the specified condition in paragraph 2, 3 or 4 in relation to a company by virtue only of being a limited partner.

(2) An individual does not meet the specified condition in paragraph 2, 3 or 4 in relation to a company by virtue only of, directly or indirectly—
- (a) holding shares, or
- (b) holding a right,

in or in relation to a limited partner which (in its capacity as such) would meet the condition if it were an individual.

(3) Sub-paragraphs (1) and (2) do not apply for the purposes of determining whether the requirement set out in paragraph (a) of the specified condition in paragraph 6 is met.

(4) In this paragraph "limited partner" means—
- (a) a limited partner in a limited partnership registered under the Limited Partnerships Act 1907 (other than one who takes part in the management of the partnership business), or
- (b) a foreign limited partner.

(5) In this paragraph "foreign limited partner" means an individual who—
- (a) participates in arrangements established under the law of a country or territory outside the United Kingdom, and
- (b) has the characteristics prescribed by regulations made by the Secretary of State.

(6) Regulations under this paragraph may, in particular, prescribe characteristics by reference to—
- (a) the nature of arrangements;
- (b) the nature of an individual's participation in the arrangements.

(7) Regulations under this paragraph are subject to affirmative resolution procedure.]

NOTES

Inserted by the Small Business, Enterprise and Employment Act 2015, s 81, Sch 3, Pt 1, para 2, as from 26 May 2015 (for the purposes of enabling the exercise of any power to make provision by regulations, rules or order made by statutory instrument or to prepare and issue guidance), and as from 6 April 2016 (otherwise).

Regulations: the Register of People with Significant Control Regulations 2016, SI 2016/339 at **[4.559]**. For a summary of all statutory instruments made under this Act, see Appendix 4 at **[A4]**.

[PART 4 POWER TO AMEND THRESHOLDS ETC

[1.1502]

26. (1) The Secretary of State may by regulations amend this Schedule for a permitted purpose.

(2) The permitted purposes are—

(a) to replace any or all references in this Schedule to a percentage figure with references to some other (larger or smaller) percentage figure;

(b) to change or supplement the specified conditions in Part 1 of this Schedule so as to include circumstances (for example, circumstances involving more complex structures) that give individuals a level of control over company Y broadly similar to the level of control given by the other specified conditions;

(c) in consequence of any provision made by virtue of paragraph (b), to change or supplement Part 2 of this Schedule so that circumstances specified in that Part in which a person is to be regarded as holding an interest in a company correspond to any of the specified conditions, or would do so but for the extent of the interest.

(3) Regulations under this paragraph are subject to affirmative resolution procedure.]

NOTES

Inserted by the Small Business, Enterprise and Employment Act 2015, s 81, Sch 3, Pt 1, para 2, as from 26 May 2015.

[SCHEDULE 1B
ENFORCEMENT OF DISCLOSURE REQUIREMENTS

Section 790I

Right to issue restrictions notice

[1.1503]

1. (1) This paragraph applies if—

(a) a notice under section 790D or 790E is served by a company on a person who has a relevant interest in the company, and

(b) the person fails to comply with that notice within the time specified in it.

(2) The company may give the person a notice under this paragraph (a "warning notice") informing the person that it is proposing to issue the person with a notice (a "restrictions notice") with respect to the relevant interest.

(3) The company may issue the restrictions notice if, by the end of the period of one month beginning with the date on which the warning notice was given—

(a) the person has not complied with the notice served under section 790D or 790E, and

(b) the company has not been provided with a valid reason sufficient to justify the person's failure to comply with the notice served under that section.

(4) A restrictions notice is issued on a person by sending the notice to the person.

(5) The effect of a restrictions notice is set out in paragraph 3.

(6) In deciding whether to issue a restrictions notice, the company must have regard to the effect of the notice on the rights of third parties in respect of the relevant interest.

Relevant interests

2. (1) For the purposes of this Schedule, a person has a relevant interest in a company if the person—

(a) holds any shares in the company,

(b) holds any voting rights in the company, or

(c) holds the right to appoint or remove any member of the board of directors of the company.

(2) References to "the relevant interest" are to the shares or right in question.

(3) Part 3 of Schedule 1A applies for the interpretation of sub-paragraph (1) save that, where the relevant interest is by virtue of paragraph 19 or 20 of that Schedule treated for the purposes of that Schedule as held by a person other than the person who in fact holds the interest, both the holder and the other person are to be regarded for the purposes of this Schedule as having the relevant interest.

Effect of restrictions notice

3. (1) The effect of a restrictions notice issued under paragraph 1 with respect to a relevant interest is as follows—

(a) any transfer of the interest is void,

(b) no rights are exercisable in respect of the interest,

(c) no shares may be issued in right of the interest or in pursuance of an offer made to the interest-holder,

(d) except in a liquidation, no payment may be made of sums due from the company in respect of the interest, whether in respect of capital or otherwise.

(2) An agreement to transfer an interest that is subject to the restriction in sub-paragraph (1)(a) is void.

(3) Sub-paragraph (2) does not apply to an agreement to transfer the interest on the making of an order under paragraph 8 made by virtue of sub-paragraph (3)(b) of that paragraph (removal of restrictions in case of court-approved transfer).

(4) An agreement to transfer any associated right (otherwise than in a liquidation) is void.

(5) Sub-paragraph (4) does not apply to an agreement to transfer any such right on the making of an order under paragraph 8 made by virtue of sub-paragraph (3)(b) of that paragraph (removal of restrictions in case of court-approved transfer).

(6) An "associated right", in relation to a relevant interest, is—

(a) a right to be issued with any shares issued in right of the relevant interest, or

(b) a right to receive payment of any sums due from the company in respect of the relevant interest.

(7) The provisions of this section are subject to any directions given under paragraph 4.

Protection of third party rights

4. (1) The court may give a direction under this paragraph if, on application by any person aggrieved, the court is satisfied that a restrictions notice issued by the company under paragraph 1 unfairly affects the rights of third parties in respect of the relevant interest.

(2) The direction is given for the purpose of protecting those third party rights.

(3) The direction is a direction that certain acts will not constitute a breach of the restrictions placed on the relevant interest by the restrictions notice.

(4) An order containing a direction under this paragraph—

(a) must specify the acts that will not constitute a breach of the restrictions, and

(b) may confine the direction to cases where those acts are done by persons, or for purposes, described in the order.

(5) The direction may be given subject to such terms as the court thinks fit.

Breach of restrictions

5. (1) A person commits an offence if the person does anything listed in sub-paragraph (2) knowing that the interest is subject to restrictions.

(2) The things are—

(a) exercising or purporting to exercise any right to dispose of a relevant interest,

(b) exercising or purporting to exercise any right to dispose of any right to be issued with a relevant interest, or

(c) voting in respect of a relevant interest (whether as holder of the interest or as proxy) or appointing a proxy to vote in respect of a relevant interest.

(3) A person who has a relevant interest that the person knows to be subject to restrictions commits an offence if the person—

(a) knows a person to be entitled (apart from the restrictions) to vote in respect of the interest, whether as holder or as proxy,

(b) does not know the person to be aware of the fact that the interest is subject to restrictions, and

(c) fails to notify the person of that fact.

(4) A person commits an offence if the person—

(a) either has a relevant interest that the person knows to be subject to restrictions or is entitled to an associated right, and

(b) enters in that capacity into an agreement that is void by virtue of paragraph 3(2) or (4).

(5) References in this Schedule to an interest being "subject to restrictions" are to an interest being subject to restrictions by virtue of a restrictions notice under paragraph 1.

6. If shares in a company are issued in contravention of a restriction imposed by virtue of a restrictions notice under paragraph 1, an offence is committed by—

(a) the company, and

(b) every officer of the company who is in default.

7. (1) A person guilty of an offence under paragraph 5 or 6 is liable—

(a) on conviction on indictment, to a fine;

(b) on summary conviction—

(i) in England and Wales, to a fine,

(ii) in Scotland or Northern Ireland, to a fine not exceeding the statutory maximum.

(2) The provisions of those paragraphs are subject to any direction given under paragraph 4 or 8.

Relaxation of restrictions

8. (1) An application may be made to the court for an order directing that the relevant interest cease to be subject to restrictions.

(2) An application for an order under this paragraph may be made by the company in question or by any person aggrieved.

(3) The court must not make an order under this paragraph unless—

(a) it is satisfied that the information required by the notice served under section 790D or 790E has been disclosed to the company and no unfair advantage has accrued to any person as a result of the earlier failure to make that disclosure, or

(b) the relevant interest is to be transferred for valuable consideration and the court approves the transfer.

(4) An order under this paragraph made by virtue of sub-paragraph (3)(b) may continue, in whole or in part, the restrictions mentioned in paragraph 3(1)(c) and (d) so far as they relate to a right acquired or offer made before the transfer.

(5) Where any restrictions continue in force under sub-paragraph (4)—

(a) an application may be made under this paragraph for an order directing that the relevant interest cease to be subject to those restrictions, and

(b) sub-paragraph (3) does not apply in relation to the making of such an order.

Orders for sale

9. (1) The court may order that the relevant interest subject to restrictions be sold subject to the court's approval as to the sale.

(2) An application for an order under sub-paragraph (1) may only be made by the company in question.

(3) If the court makes an order under this paragraph, it may make such further order relating to the sale or transfer of the interest as it thinks fit.

(4) An application for an order under sub-paragraph (3) may be made—
- (a) by the company in question,
- (b) by the person appointed by or in pursuance of the order to effect the sale, or
- (c) by any person with an interest in the relevant interest.

(5) On making an order under sub-paragraph (1) or (3), the court may order that the applicant's costs (in Scotland, expenses) be paid out of the proceeds of sale.

10. (1) If a relevant interest is sold in pursuance of an order under paragraph 9, the proceeds of the sale, less the costs of the sale, must be paid into court for the benefit of those who are beneficially interested in the relevant interest.

(2) A person who is beneficially interested in the relevant interest may apply to the court for the whole or part of those proceeds to be paid to that person.

(3) On such an application, the court must order the payment to the applicant of—
- (a) the whole of the proceeds of sale together with any interest on the proceeds, or
- (b) if another person was also beneficially interested in the relevant interest at the time of the sale, such proportion of the proceeds (and any interest) as the value of the applicant's interest bears to the total value of the relevant interest.

(4) If the court has ordered under paragraph 9 that the costs (in Scotland, expenses) of an applicant under that paragraph are to be paid out of the proceeds of sale, the applicant is entitled to payment of those costs (or expenses) out of the proceeds before any person receives any part of the proceeds under this paragraph.

Company's power to withdraw restrictions notice

11. A company that issues a person with a restrictions notice under paragraph 1 must by notice withdraw the restrictions notice if—
- (a) it is satisfied that there is a valid reason sufficient to justify the person's failure to comply with the notice served under section 790D or 790E,
- (b) the notice served under section 790D or 790E is complied with, or
- (c) it discovers that the rights of a third party in respect of the relevant interest are being unfairly affected by the restrictions notice.

Supplementary provision

12. (1) The Secretary of State may by regulations make provision about the procedure to be followed by companies in issuing and withdrawing restrictions notices.

(2) The regulations may in particular make provision about—
- (a) the form and content of warning notices and restrictions notices, and the manner in which they must be given,
- (b) the factors to be taken into account in deciding what counts as a "valid reason" sufficient to justify a person's failure to comply with a notice under section 790D or 790E, and
- (c) the effect of withdrawing a restrictions notice on matters that are pending with respect to the relevant interest when the notice is withdrawn.

(3) Regulations under this paragraph are subject to negative resolution procedure.

Offences for failing to comply with notices

13. (1) A person to whom a notice under section 790D or 790E is addressed commits an offence if the person—
- (a) fails to comply with the notice, or
- (b) in purported compliance with the notice—
  - (i) makes a statement that the person knows to be false in a material particular, or
  - (ii) recklessly makes a statement that is false in a material particular.

(2) Where the person is a legal entity, an offence is also committed by every officer of the entity who is in default.

(3) A person does not commit an offence under sub-paragraph (1)(a) (or sub-paragraph (2) as it applies in relation to that sub-paragraph) if the person proves that the requirement to give information was frivolous or vexatious.

(4) A person guilty of an offence under this paragraph is liable—
- (a) on conviction on indictment, to imprisonment for a term not exceeding two years or a fine (or both);
- (b) on summary conviction—
  - (i) in England and Wales, to imprisonment for a term not exceeding twelve months or to a fine (or both);
  - (ii) in Scotland, to imprisonment for a term not exceeding twelve months or to a fine not exceeding the statutory maximum (or both);
  - (iii) in Northern Ireland, to imprisonment for a term not exceeding six months or to a fine not exceeding the statutory maximum (or both).

Offences for failing to provide information

14. (1) A person commits an offence if the person—
- (a) fails to comply with a duty under section 790G or 790H, or
- (b) in purported compliance with such a duty—
  - (i) makes a statement that the person knows to be false in a material particular, or
  - (ii) recklessly makes a statement that is false in a material particular.

(2) Where the person is a legal entity, an offence is also committed by every officer of the entity who is in default.

(3) A person guilty of an offence under this paragraph is liable—

(a) on conviction on indictment, to imprisonment for a term not exceeding two years or a fine (or both);

(b) on summary conviction—

(i) in England and Wales, to imprisonment for a term not exceeding twelve months or to a fine (or both);

(ii) in Scotland, to imprisonment for a term not exceeding twelve months or to a fine not exceeding the statutory maximum (or both);

(iii) in Northern Ireland, to imprisonment for a term not exceeding six months or to a fine not exceeding the statutory maximum (or both).]

NOTES

Inserted by the Small Business, Enterprise and Employment Act 2015, s 81, Sch 3, Pt 1, para 2, as from 26 May 2015 (for the purposes of enabling the exercise of any power to make provision by regulations, rules or order made by statutory instrument or to prepare and issue guidance), and as from 6 April 2016 (otherwise).

Regulations: the Register of People with Significant Control Regulations 2016, SI 2016/339 at **[4.559]**. For a summary of all statutory instruments made under this Act, see Appendix 4 at **[A4]**.

[SCHEDULE 1C
RULES OF THE TAKEOVER PANEL: GENERAL PRINCIPLES AND OTHER PROVISION

Section 943

PART 1 GENERAL PRINCIPLES

[1.1504]

1. (1) All holders of the securities of an offeree company of the same class must be afforded equivalent treatment.

(2) If a person acquires control of a company, the other holders of securities must be protected.

2. (1) The holders of the securities of an offeree company must have sufficient time and information to enable them to reach a properly informed decision on the takeover bid.

(2) Where it advises the holders of securities, the board of directors of the offeree company must give its views on the effects of implementation of the takeover bid on—

(a) employment,

(b) conditions of employment, and

(c) the locations of the company's places of business.

3. The board of directors of an offeree company must act in the interests of the company as a whole and must not deny the holders of securities the opportunity to decide on the merits of the takeover bid.

4. False markets must not be created in the securities of—

(a) the offeree company,

(b) if the offeror is a company, that company, or

(c) any other company concerned by the takeover bid,

in such a way that the rise or fall of the prices of the securities becomes artificial and the normal functioning of the markets is distorted.

5. An offeror must announce a takeover bid only after—

(a) ensuring that the offeror can fulfil in full any cash consideration, if such is offered, and

(b) taking all reasonable measures to secure the implementation of any other type of consideration.

6. An offeree company must not be hindered in the conduct of its affairs for longer than is reasonable by a takeover bid for its securities.

NOTES

Commencement: IP completion day (as defined in the European Union (Withdrawal Agreement) Act 2020, s 39).

Inserted by the Takeovers (Amendment) (EU Exit) Regulations 2019, SI 2019/217, regs 2, 14, Schedule, as from IP completion day (as defined in the European Union (Withdrawal Agreement) Act 2020, s 39).

PART 2 OTHER PROVISION

Protection of minority shareholders, the mandatory takeover bid and the equitable price

[1.1505]

7. (1) Rules must ensure that a person ("P") is required to make a takeover bid ("a mandatory takeover bid") where—

(a) P, or any person acting in concert with P, has acquired securities in a company, and

(b) the acquired securities, when added to any existing securities held by P or by persons acting in concert with P, directly or indirectly give P control of that company.

(2) Rules must ensure that the mandatory takeover bid must be addressed at the earliest opportunity to all of the holders of those securities for all their holdings at the equitable price.

(3) Rules must ensure that where control has been acquired following a voluntary takeover bid to all the holders of securities for all their holdings, the obligation referred to in sub-paragraph (1) to make a mandatory takeover bid no longer applies.

8. (1) For the purposes of paragraph 7, "the equitable price" is the highest price paid for the same securities by the offeror, or by persons acting in concert with the offeror, over a period, determined by rules, of not less than 6 and not more than 12 months before the mandatory takeover bid is announced.

(2) Rules must ensure that if, after the mandatory takeover bid has been made public and before the offer closes for acceptance, the offeror or any person acting in concert with the offeror purchases securities at a price higher than the offer price, the offeror must increase the offer consideration so that it is not less than the highest price paid for the securities so acquired.

(3) Rules may confer power on the Panel to adjust the equitable price in circumstances and in accordance with criteria that are clearly determined.

(4) Rules must ensure that any decision by the Panel to adjust the equitable price must be substantiated and made public.

9. (1) Rules must ensure that the offeror may offer by way of consideration for the securities which are the subject of the mandatory takeover bid—

(a) securities,
(b) cash, or
(c) a combination of both.

(2) Rules must ensure that cash must be offered—

(a) as an alternative where the consideration offered does not consist of liquid securities admitted to trading on a UK regulated market, and
(b) at least as an alternative where the securities purchased for cash over a relevant period by the offeror or by persons acting in concert with the offeror, taken together, carry 5% or more of the voting rights in the offeree company.

(3) "A relevant period" is a period—

(a) beginning at the same time as the period determined in accordance with paragraph 8(1), and
(b) ending when the offer closes for acceptance.

(4) Rules may require that cash must be offered, at least as an alternative, in all cases.

10. Any rules that make provision to protect the interests of the holders of securities that goes beyond the provision referred to in paragraphs 7 to 9 must not hinder the normal course of a takeover bid.

Information concerning takeover bids

11. (1) Rules must ensure that a decision to make a takeover bid must be made public without delay and the Panel must be informed of the bid.

(2) Rules may require that the Panel is informed before such a decision is made public.

(3) Rules must ensure that, as soon as the takeover bid has been made public, the boards of directors of the offeree company and of the offeror must inform—

(a) the representatives of their respective employees, or
(b) where there are no such representatives, the employees themselves.

12. (1) Rules must ensure that an offeror must draw up and make public in good time an offer document containing the information necessary to enable the holders of the offeree company's securities to reach a properly informed decision on the takeover bid.

(2) Rules must ensure that, before the offer document is made public, the offeror must provide a copy to the Panel.

(3) Rules must ensure that, when the offer document is made public, the boards of directors of the offeree company and of the offeror must communicate it—

(a) to the representatives of their respective employees, or
(b) where there are no such representatives, to the employees themselves.

(4) Rules must ensure that the offer document must state at least—

(a) the terms of the takeover bid,
(b) the identity of the offeror and, where the offeror is a company, the company's type, name and registered office,
(c) the securities or, where appropriate, the class or classes of securities for which the takeover bid is made,
(d) the consideration offered for each security or class of securities and, in the case of a mandatory takeover bid, the method employed in determining it, with particulars of the way in which that consideration is to be paid,
(e) the compensation offered for the rights which might be removed as a result of a company's opting-in resolution under Chapter 2, with particulars of the way in which that compensation is to be paid and the method employed in determining it,
(f) the maximum and minimum percentages or quantities of securities which the offeror undertakes to acquire,
(g) details of any existing holdings of the offeror, and of any person acting in concert with the offeror, in the offeree company,
(h) all the conditions to which the takeover bid is subject,
(i) the offeror's intentions with regard to the future business of the offeree company,
(j) the offeror's intentions with regard to the safeguarding of the jobs of the employees and management of the offeree company, including any material change in the conditions of employment,
(k) the offeror's strategic plans for the offeree company, and their likely repercussions on employment and the locations of the company's places of business,
(l) if the offeror is a company and in so far as it is affected by the takeover bid—
    (i) the offeror's intentions with regard to its future business,
    (ii) the offeror's intentions with regard to the safeguarding of the jobs of its employees and management, including any material change in the conditions of employment, and
    (iii) the offeror's strategic plans for itself, and their likely repercussions on employment and the locations of its places of business,
(m) the time allowed for acceptance of the takeover bid,
(n) where the consideration offered includes securities of any kind, information concerning those securities,
(o) information concerning the financing for the takeover bid,
(p) the identity of persons acting in concert with the offeror or with the offeree company and, in the case of companies, the types, names, registered offices and relationships with the offeror and, where possible, with the offeree company, and
(q) the national law which will govern contracts concluded between the offeror and the holders of the offeree company's securities as a result of the takeover bid and the competent courts.

Time allowed for acceptance

13. (1) Rules must ensure that, subject to any provision made in accordance with paragraph 14, the time allowed for the acceptance of a takeover bid must not be less than the period of two weeks nor more than the period of 10 weeks beginning with the day after the date of publication of the offer document.

(2) Rules may provide that the maximum period allowed for acceptance of a takeover bid may be extended on the condition that the offeror gives at least two weeks' notice of the offeror's intention to close the takeover bid.

14. (1) Rules may contain provision changing the time allowed for the acceptance of a takeover bid in specific cases.

(2) Rules may confer power on the Panel to grant a derogation from the time allowed for the acceptance of a takeover bid in order to allow the offeree company to call a general meeting of the company to consider the takeover bid.

Disclosure

15. Rules must ensure that a takeover bid must be made public in such a way as to ensure market transparency and integrity for the securities of—

(a) the offeree company,
(b) if the offeror is a company, that company, or
(c) any other company affected by the takeover bid,

in particular in order to prevent the publication or dissemination of false or misleading information.

16. Rules must ensure that all information and documents required by provision made in accordance with paragraphs 11 and 12 must be disclosed in such a manner as to ensure that they are both readily and promptly available—

(a) to the holders of securities admitted to trading on a UK regulated market who are located in the United Kingdom, and
(b) to the representatives of the employees of the offeree company and of the offeror, or where there are no such representatives, to the employees themselves.

Obligations of the board of directors of the offeree company

17. (1) Rules must ensure that, during the relevant period, the board of directors of the offeree company must obtain the prior authorisation of a general meeting of the company given for this purpose—

(a) before taking any action, other than seeking alternative takeover bids, which may result in the frustration of the bid, and
(b) in particular, before issuing any shares which may result in a lasting impediment to the offeror's acquiring control of the offeree company.

(2) "The relevant period"—

(a) begins when the board of directors of the offeree company receives the information that a decision to make a takeover bid has been made public, or at such earlier stage as rules may determine, and
(b) ends when the result of the bid is made public or the bid lapses.

(3) Rules must ensure that, with regard to decisions taken before the beginning of the relevant period and not yet partly or fully implemented, a general meeting of the company must approve or confirm any decision—

(a) which does not form part of the normal course of the company's business, and
(b) the implementation of which may result in the frustration of the takeover bid.

(4) For the purposes of this paragraph, where a company has a two-tier board structure, "board of directors" means both the management board and the supervisory board.

18. (1) Rules must ensure that the board of directors of the offeree company must draw up and make public a document setting out its opinion of the takeover bid and the reasons for the opinion, including its views on—

(a) the effects of implementation of the takeover bid on all the company's interests and specifically employment, and
(b) the offeror's strategic plans for the offeree company and their likely repercussions on employment and the locations of the company's places of business as set out in the offer document in accordance with paragraph 12(4)(k).

(2) Rules must ensure that the board of directors of the offeree company must at the same time communicate that opinion—

(a) to the representatives of its employees, or
(b) where there are no such representatives, to the employees themselves.

(3) Rules must ensure that, where the board of directors of the offeree company receives in good time a separate opinion from the representatives of its employees on the effects of the takeover bid on employment, that opinion must be appended to the document.

Other rules applicable to the conduct of takeover bids

19. Rules must make provision governing the conduct of takeover bids which must address at least—

(a) the lapsing of takeover bids,
(b) the revision of takeover bids,
(c) competing takeover bids,
(d) the disclosure of the results of takeover bids, and
(e) the irrevocability of takeover bids and the conditions permitted.

Interpretation

20. (1) In this Schedule—

"offer document" means a document required to be published by rules made in accordance with paragraph 12;
"offeree company" means a company, the securities of which are the subject of a takeover bid;
"offeror", in relation to a takeover bid, means the person making the bid;

"rules" means rules made by the Panel under section 943(1);

"securities" means transferable securities carrying voting rights in a company;

"takeover bid" means a public offer made to the holders of the securities of a company to acquire some or all of those securities, whether mandatory or voluntary, which follows or has as its objective the acquisition of control of that company, but does not include cases where the offer is made by the company itself;

"voting rights" means rights to vote at general meetings of the company in question.

(2) For the purposes of this Schedule, securities are of one class if the rights attached to them are in all respects uniform; and for that purpose the rights attached to securities are not regarded as different from those attached to other securities by reason only that they do not carry the same rights to dividends in the twelve months immediately following their allotment.

(3) In this Schedule, "persons acting in concert" means persons who co-operate with the offeror or the offeree company on the basis of an agreement or understanding aimed at—

(a) acquiring control of the offeree company, or

(b) frustrating the successful outcome of a takeover bid.

(4) For the purposes of this Schedule, where a person ("A") is a subsidiary undertaking of another person ("B") within the meaning of section 420 of the Financial Services and Markets Act 2000 (but disregarding subsections (2)(b) and (3) of that section, and subsections (2)(c) and (4)(b) of section 1162 of the Companies Act 2006)—

(a) A is deemed to be acting in concert with B and with any other subsidiary undertakings of B, and

(b) B and those subsidiary undertakings are deemed to be acting in concert with A.

21. (1) In this Schedule, other than in the listed provisions, "company" means a company that has securities admitted to trading on a UK regulated market.

(2) The listed provisions are—

paragraph 4(b) and (c);

paragraph 12(4)(b), (l) and (p);

paragraph 15(b) and (c).

(3) Section 1 (meaning of "company") does not apply for the purposes of the listed provisions."

NOTES

Commencement: IP completion day (as defined in the European Union (Withdrawal Agreement) Act 2020, s 39).

Inserted by the Takeovers (Amendment) (EU Exit) Regulations 2019, SI 2019/217, regs 2, 14, Schedule, as from IP completion day (as defined in the European Union (Withdrawal Agreement) Act 2020, s 39).

SCHEDULE 2
SPECIFIED PERSONS, DESCRIPTIONS OF DISCLOSURES ETC FOR THE PURPOSES OF SECTION 948

Section 948

[PART 1 SPECIFIED PERSONS

(A) UNITED KINGDOM

[1.1506]

1. The Secretary of State.

2. The Department of Enterprise, Trade and Investment for Northern Ireland.

3. The Treasury.

4. The Bank of England.

[**5.** The Financial Conduct Authority.

5A. The Prudential Regulation Authority.]

6. The Commissioners for Her Majesty's Revenue and Customs.

7. The Lord Advocate.

8. The Director of Public Prosecutions.

9. The Director of Public Prosecutions for Northern Ireland.

10. A constable.

11. A procurator fiscal.

12. The Scottish Ministers.

(B) JERSEY

1. The Minister for Economic Development.

2. The Minister for Treasury and Resources.

3. The Jersey Financial Services Commission.

4. The Comptroller of Income Tax.

5. The Agent of the Impôts.

6. Her Majesty's Attorney General for Jersey.

7. The Viscount.

8. A police officer (within the meaning of the Interpretation (Jersey) Law 1954: see Part 1 of the Schedule to that Law).

(C) GUERNSEY

1. The Commerce and Employment Department.

2. The Treasury and Resources Department.

3. The Guernsey Financial Services Commission.

4. The Director of Income Tax.

5. The Chief Officer of Customs and Excise.

6. Her Majesty's Procureur.

7. A police officer (within the meaning of the Companies (Guernsey) Law 2008: see section 532 of that Law).

(D) ISLE OF MAN

1. (1) The members and officers of each of the Departments constituted by section 1(1) of the Government Departments Act 1987 (an Act of Tynwald: c 13).

(2) In sub-paragraph (1) "member" has the same meaning as it has by virtue of section 7(1) of that Act.

2. The Treasury of the Isle of Man.

3. The Financial Supervision Commission of the Isle of Man.

4. Her Majesty's Attorney General of the Isle of Man.

5. A constable (within the meaning of the Interpretation Act 1976 (an Act of Tynwald: c 11): see section 3 of that Act).]

NOTES

Substituted by the Companies Act 2006 (Amendment of Schedule 2) (No 2) Order 2009, SI 2009/1208, art 2, Schedule, as from 1 July 2009.

Part (A), paras 5, 5A: substituted (for the original para 5) by the Financial Services Act 2012, s 114(1), Sch 18, Pt 2, paras 110, 123(1), (2), as from 1 April 2013.

Application to the Isle of Man: see notes to s 965 at **[1.1127]**.

[PART 2 SPECIFIED DESCRIPTIONS OF DISCLOSURES

(A) UNITED KINGDOM

[1.1507]

1. A disclosure for the purpose of enabling or assisting a person authorised under section 457 of this Act (revision of defective accounts: persons authorised to apply to court) to exercise their functions.

2. A disclosure for the purpose of enabling or assisting an inspector appointed under Part 14 of the Companies Act 1985 (c 6) (investigation of companies and their affairs, etc) to exercise their functions.

3. A disclosure for the purpose of enabling or assisting a person authorised under section 447 of the Companies Act 1985 (power to require production of documents) or section 84 of the Companies Act 1989 (c 40) (exercise of powers by officer etc) to exercise their functions.

4. A disclosure for the purpose of enabling or assisting a person appointed under section 167 of the Financial Services and Markets Act 2000 (c 8) (general investigations) to conduct an investigation to exercise their functions.

5. A disclosure for the purpose of enabling or assisting a person appointed under section 168 of the Financial Services and Markets Act 2000 (investigations in particular cases) to conduct an investigation to exercise their functions.

6. A disclosure for the purpose of enabling or assisting a person appointed under section 169(1)(b) of the Financial Services and Markets Act 2000 (investigation in support of overseas regulator) to conduct an investigation to exercise their functions.

7. A disclosure for the purpose of enabling or assisting the body corporate responsible for administering the scheme referred to in section 225 of the Financial Services and Markets Act 2000 (the ombudsman scheme) to exercise its functions.

8. A disclosure for the purpose of enabling or assisting a person appointed under paragraph 4 or 5 of Schedule 17 to the Financial Services and Markets Act 2000 (the panel of ombudsmen or the Chief Ombudsman) to exercise their functions.

9. A disclosure for the purpose of enabling or assisting a person appointed under regulations made under section 262(1) and (2)(k) of the Financial Services and Markets Act 2000 (investigations into open-ended investment companies) to conduct an investigation to exercise their functions.

10. A disclosure for the purpose of enabling or assisting a person appointed under section 284 of the Financial Services and Markets Act 2000 (investigations into affairs of certain collective investment schemes) to conduct an investigation to exercise their functions.

11. A disclosure for the purpose of enabling or assisting the investigator appointed under [section 84 of the Financial Services Act 2012] (arrangements for investigation of complaints) to exercise their functions.

12. A disclosure for the purpose of enabling or assisting a person appointed by the Treasury to hold an inquiry into matters relating to financial services (including an inquiry under [section 69 of the Financial Services Act 2012]) to exercise their functions.

13. A disclosure for the purpose of enabling or assisting the Secretary of State or the Treasury to exercise any of their functions under any of the following—

(a) the Companies Acts;
(b) the Insolvency Act 1986 (c 45);

(c) the Company Directors Disqualification Act 1986 (c 46);
(d) Part 3 (investigations and powers to obtain information) or 7 (financial markets and insolvency) of the Companies Act 1989 (c 40);
(e) Part 5 of the Criminal Justice Act 1993 (c 36) (insider dealing);
(f) the Financial Services and Markets Act 2000;
(g) Part 42 of this Act (statutory auditors).

14. A disclosure for the purpose of enabling or assisting the Scottish Ministers to exercise their functions under the enactments relating to insolvency.

15. A disclosure for the purpose of enabling or assisting the Department of Enterprise, Trade and Investment for Northern Ireland to exercise any powers conferred on it by the enactments relating to companies or insolvency.

16. A disclosure for the purpose of enabling or assisting a person appointed or authorised by the Department of Enterprise, Trade and Investment for Northern Ireland under the enactments relating to companies or insolvency to exercise their functions.

17. A disclosure for the purpose of enabling or assisting an official receiver (including the Accountant in Bankruptcy in Scotland and the Official Assignee in Northern Ireland) to exercise their functions under the enactments relating to insolvency.

18. . . .

19. A disclosure for the purpose of enabling or assisting a body that is for the time being a recognised professional body for the purposes of section 391 of the Insolvency Act 1986 (recognised professional bodies) to exercise its functions as such.

20. A disclosure for the purpose of enabling or assisting the Pensions Regulator to exercise the functions conferred on it by or by virtue of any of the following—
(a) the Pension Schemes Act 1993 (c 48);
(b) the Pensions Act 1995 (c 26);
(c) the Welfare Reform and Pensions Act 1999 (c 30);
(d) the Pensions Act 2004 (c 35);
(e) any enactment in force in Northern Ireland corresponding to any of those enactments.

21. A disclosure for the purpose of enabling or assisting the Board of the Pension Protection Fund to exercise the functions conferred on it by or by virtue of Part 2 of the Pensions Act 2004 or any enactment in force in Northern Ireland corresponding to that Part.

22. A disclosure for the purpose of enabling or assisting the Bank of England to exercise its functions.

23. A disclosure for the purpose of enabling or assisting the Commissioners for Her Majesty's Revenue and Customs to exercise their functions.

24. A disclosure for the purpose of enabling or assisting organs of the Society of Lloyd's (being organs constituted by or under the Lloyd's Act 1982 (c. xiv)) to exercise their functions under or by virtue of the Lloyd's Acts 1871 to 1982.

25. A disclosure for the purpose of enabling or assisting the [Competition and Markets Authority] to exercise its functions under any of the following—
(a) the Fair Trading Act 1973 (c 41);
(b), (c) . . .
(d) the Competition Act 1980 (c 21);
(e) the Competition Act 1998 (c 41);
(f) the Financial Services and Markets Act 2000 (c 8);
(g) the Enterprise Act 2002 (c 40);
(h) . . .
(i) the Business Protection from Misleading Marketing Regulations 2008 (SI 2008/1276);
(j) the Consumer Protection from Unfair Trading Regulations 2008 (SI 2008/1277);
[(k) Parts 3 and 4 of the Enterprise and Regulatory Reform Act 2013];
[(l) Schedule 3 to the Consumer Rights Act 2015].

26. . . .

27. A disclosure with a view to the institution of, or otherwise for the purposes of, proceedings before the Competition Appeal Tribunal.

28. A disclosure for the purpose of enabling or assisting an enforcer under Part 8 of the Enterprise Act 2002 (enforcement of consumer legislation) to exercise their functions under that Part.

29. A disclosure for the purpose of enabling or assisting the Charity Commission to exercise its functions.

30. A disclosure for the purpose of enabling or assisting the Attorney General to exercise their functions in connection with charities.

31. A disclosure for the purpose of enabling or assisting the [Gambling Commission] to exercise its functions under sections 5 to 10 and 15 of the National Lottery etc Act 1993 (c 39) (licensing and power of Secretary of State to require information).

32. A disclosure by the [Gambling Commission] to [the Comptroller and Auditor General] for the purpose of enabling or assisting the Comptroller and Auditor General to carry out an examination under Part 2 of the National Audit Act 1983 (c 44) into the economy, effectiveness and efficiency with which the [Gambling Commission] has used its resources in discharging its functions under sections 5 to 10 of the National Lottery etc Act 1993.

[33. A disclosure for the purposes of enabling or assisting a regulator under Schedule 3 to the Consumer Rights Act 2015 other than the Competition and Markets Authority to exercise its functions under that Schedule.]

34. A disclosure for the purpose of enabling or assisting an enforcement authority under [the Consumer Contracts (Information, Cancellation and Additional Charges) Regulations 2013] to exercise its functions under those Regulations.

35. A disclosure for the purpose of enabling or assisting an enforcement authority under the Financial Services (Distance Marketing) Regulations 2004 (SI 2004/2095) to exercise its functions under those Regulations.

36. A disclosure for the purpose of enabling or assisting a local weights and measures authority in England and Wales to exercise its functions under section 230(2) of the Enterprise Act 2002 (c 40) (notice of intention to prosecute, etc).

[36A. A disclosure for the purpose of enabling or assisting the lead enforcement authority (as defined in section 33(1) of the Estate Agents Act 1979) to exercise its functions under the Estate Agents Act 1979.]

37. A disclosure for the purpose of enabling or assisting the [Financial Conduct Authority or the Prudential Regulation Authority] to exercise its functions under any of the following—

(a) the legislation relating to friendly societies . . . ;
[(aa) the Consumer Credit Act 1974;]
[(ab) the Credit Unions Act 1979;]
(b) the Building Societies Act 1986 (c 53);
(c) Part 7 of the Companies Act 1989 (c 40) (financial markets and insolvency);
(d) the Financial Services and Markets Act 2000 (c 8);
[(e) the Co-operative and Community Benefit Societies Act 2014].

38. . . .

39. A disclosure for the purpose of enabling or assisting a body corporate established in accordance with section 212(1) of the Financial Services and Markets Act 2000 (compensation scheme manager) to exercise its functions.

40. (1) A disclosure for the purpose of enabling or assisting a recognised investment exchange[, a recognised clearing house or a recognised CSD] to exercise its functions as such.

(2) In sub-paragraph (1) "recognised investment exchange"[, "recognised clearing house" and "recognised CSD"] have the same meaning as in section 285 of the Financial Services and Markets Act 2000.

41. A disclosure for the purpose of enabling or assisting a person [who is an operator of a relevant system for the purposes of the Uncertificated Securities Regulations 2001 (SI 2001/3755)] to exercise their functions.

42. A disclosure for the purpose of enabling or assisting a body designated under section 326(1) of the Financial Services and Markets Act 2000 (designated professional bodies) to exercise its functions in its capacity as a body designated under that section.

43. A disclosure with a view to the institution of, or otherwise for the purposes of, civil proceedings arising under or by virtue of the Financial Services and Markets Act 2000.

44. A disclosure for the purpose of enabling or assisting a body designated by order under section 1252 of this Act (delegation of functions of Secretary of State) to exercise its functions under Part 42 of this Act (statutory auditors).

45. A disclosure for the purpose of enabling or assisting a recognised supervisory or qualifying body, within the meaning of Part 42 of this Act, to exercise its functions as such.

46. A disclosure for the purpose of enabling or assisting the Regulator of Community Interest Companies to exercise functions under the Companies (Audit, Investigations and Community Enterprise) Act 2004 (c 27).

47. A disclosure for the purpose of enabling or assisting a person authorised by the Secretary of State under Part 2, 3 or 4 of the Proceeds of Crime Act 2002 (c 29) to exercise their functions.

48. A disclosure with a view to the institution of, or otherwise for the purposes of, proceedings on an application under section 6, 7 or 8 of the Company Directors Disqualification Act 1986 (c 46) (disqualification for unfitness).

[49. A disclosure with a view to the institution of, or otherwise for the purposes of, proceedings before the Upper Tribunal in respect of—

[(a) a decision of the Financial Conduct Authority;
(aa) a decision of the Prudential Regulation Authority;]
(b) a decision of the Bank of England; or
(c) a decision of a person relating to the assessment of any compensation or consideration under the Banking (Special Provisions) Act 2008 or the Banking Act 2009.]

50. A disclosure for the purposes of proceedings before [a tribunal in relation to a decision of the Pensions Regulator].

51. A disclosure for the purpose of enabling or assisting a body appointed under section 14 of the Companies (Audit, Investigations and Community Enterprise) Act 2004 (supervision of periodic accounts and reports of issuers of listed securities) to exercise functions mentioned in subsection (2) of that section.

52. (1) A disclosure with a view to the institution of, or otherwise for the purposes of, disciplinary proceedings relating to the performance by a lawyer, auditor, accountant, valuer or actuary of their professional duties.

(2) In sub-paragraph (1) "lawyer" means—

(a) a person who for the purposes of the Legal Services Act 2007 (c 29) is an authorised person in relation to an activity that constitutes a reserved legal activity (within the meaning of that Act),
(b) a solicitor or barrister in Northern Ireland,
(c) a solicitor or advocate in Scotland, or
(d) a person who is a member, and entitled to practise as such, of a legal profession regulated in a jurisdiction outside the United Kingdom.

(3) Until the coming into force of section 18 of the Legal Services Act 2007, the following is substituted for paragraph (a) of sub-paragraph (2) above—

"(a) a solicitor or barrister in England and Wales,".

53. (1) A disclosure with a view to the institution of, or otherwise for the purposes of, disciplinary proceedings relating to the performance by a public servant of their duties.

(2) In sub-paragraph (1) "public servant" means—

(a) an officer or employee of the Crown, or

(b) an officer or employee of any public or other authority for the time being designated for the purposes of this paragraph by the Secretary of State by order subject to negative resolution procedure.

(B) JERSEY

1. A disclosure for the purpose of enabling or assisting an inspector appointed under Part 19 of the Companies (Jersey) Law 1991 to exercise their functions.

2. A disclosure for the purpose of enabling or assisting a person appointed under Article 33 of the Financial Services (Jersey) Law 1998 to exercise their functions.

3. A disclosure for the purpose of enabling or assisting an inspector appointed under Article 22 of the Collective Investment Funds (Jersey) Law 1988 to exercise their functions.

4. A disclosure for the purpose of enabling or assisting the Minister for Economic Development to exercise functions under any of the following—

(a) the Bankruptcy Désastre (Jersey) Law 1990;

(b) the Companies (Jersey) Law 1991;

(c) the Financial Services (Jersey) Law 1998.

5. A disclosure for the purpose of enabling or assisting the Comptroller of Income Tax to exercise their functions.

6. A disclosure for the purpose of enabling or assisting the Agent of the Impôts to exercise their functions.

7. A disclosure for the purpose of enabling or assisting the Jersey Competition Regulatory Authority to exercise its functions.

8. A disclosure for the purpose of enabling or assisting Her Majesty's Attorney General for Jersey to exercise their functions in connection with charities.

9. A disclosure for the purpose of enabling or assisting Her Majesty's Attorney General for Jersey to exercise their functions under the Distance Selling (Jersey) Law 2007.

10. A disclosure for the purpose of enabling or assisting the Viscount to exercise their functions in relation to désastre or in relation to Part 2 of the Proceeds of Crime (Jersey) Law 1999.

11. A disclosure with a view to the institution of, or otherwise for the purposes of, proceedings on an application under Article 78 of the Companies (Jersey) Law 1991 (disqualification orders).

12. (1) A disclosure with a view to the institution of, or otherwise for the purposes of, disciplinary proceedings relating to the performance by a solicitor, advocate, foreign lawyer, auditor, accountant, valuer or actuary of their professional duties.

(2) In sub-paragraph (1)—

(a) "solicitor" means a person who has been admitted as a solicitor under the Advocates and Solicitors (Jersey) Law 1997;

(b) "advocate" means a person who has been admitted to the Bar under that Law; and

(c) "foreign lawyer" means a person who has not been admitted as mentioned in paragraph (a) or (b) but is a member, and entitled to practise as such, of a legal profession regulated within a jurisdiction outside Jersey.

13. (1) A disclosure with a view to the institution of, or otherwise for the purposes of, disciplinary proceedings relating to the performance by a public servant of their duties.

(2) In sub-paragraph (1) "public servant" means—

(a) an individual who holds office under, or is employed by, the Crown,

(b) a member, officer or employee of the States of Jersey or an officer or employee in an administration of the States of Jersey,

(c) a member, officer or employee of the Jersey Financial Services Commission, or

(d) any person exercising public functions who is declared by Order of the Minister for Economic Development to be a public servant for the purposes of paragraph 25 of the Schedule to the Companies (Takeovers and Mergers Panel) (Jersey) Law 2009.

(C) GUERNSEY

1. A disclosure for the purpose of enabling or assisting the Registrar of Companies appointed under the Companies (Guernsey) Law 2008 to exercise their functions under that Law.

2. A disclosure for the purpose of enabling or assisting a person appointed under—

(a) section 27E or 41I of the Protection of Investors (Bailiwick of Guernsey) Law 1987,

(b) section 27 of the Banking Supervision (Bailiwick of Guernsey) Law 1994,

(c) section 10 of the Company Securities (Insider Dealing) (Bailiwick of Guernsey) Law 1996,

(d) section 24 of the Regulation of Fiduciaries, Administration Businesses and Company Directors (Bailiwick of Guernsey) Law 2000,

(e) section 69 of the Insurance Business (Bailiwick of Guernsey) Law 2002,

(f) section 46 of the Insurance Managers and Insurance Intermediaries (Bailiwick of Guernsey) Law 2002,

(g) section 19 of the Registration of Non-Regulated Financial Services Business (Bailiwick of Guernsey) Law 2008, to exercise their functions.

3. A disclosure for the purpose of enabling or assisting Her Majesty's Procureur to exercise their functions in connection with charities.

4. A disclosure for the purpose of enabling or assisting the Guernsey Banking Deposit Compensation Scheme, established under section 46 of the Banking Supervision (Bailiwick of Guernsey) Law 1987 by the Banking Deposit Compensation Scheme (Bailiwick of Guernsey) Ordinance 2008, to exercise its functions.

5. A disclosure for the purpose of enabling or assisting any supervisory body or professional oversight body to exercise its functions under Part XVIA of the Companies (Guernsey) Law 2008 (regulation of auditors).

6. A disclosure with a view to the institution of, or otherwise for the purposes of, proceedings on an application under Part XXV of the Companies (Guernsey) Law 2008 (disqualification orders).

7. (1) A disclosure with a view to the institution of, or otherwise for the purposes of, disciplinary proceedings relating to the performance by an Advocate of the Royal Court, foreign lawyer, auditor, accountant, valuer or actuary of their professional duties.

(2) In sub-paragraph (1) "foreign lawyer" means a person who has not been admitted as an Advocate of the Royal Court, but is a member, and entitled to practise as such, of a legal profession regulated within a jurisdiction outside Guernsey.

8. (1) A disclosure with a view to the institution of, or otherwise for the purposes of, disciplinary proceedings relating to the performance by a public servant of their duties.

(2) In sub-paragraph (1) "public servant" means—

(a) an officer or employee of the Crown,

(b) a member, officer or employee of the States of Guernsey,

(c) a member, officer or employee of the Guernsey Financial Services Commission, or

(d) any person exercising public functions who is declared by regulations of the Commerce and Employment Department to be a public servant for the purposes of paragraph 17 of Schedule 6 to the Companies (Guernsey) Law 2008.

(D) ISLE OF MAN

1. A disclosure for the purpose of enabling or assisting an inspector appointed by the High Court of the Isle of Man under the enactments of the Isle of Man relating to companies to discharge their functions.

2. A disclosure for the purpose of enabling or assisting a person conducting an investigation under—

(a) section 16 of the Collective Investment Schemes Act 2008 (an Act of Tynwald: c 7);

(b) Schedule 2 to the Financial Services Act 2008 (an Act of Tynwald: c 8); or

(c) Schedule 5 to the Insurance Act 2008 (an Act of Tynwald: c 16),

to exercise their functions.

3. A disclosure for the purpose of enabling or assisting the Financial Supervision Commission of the Isle of Man to exercise any of its functions.

4. A disclosure for the purpose of enabling or assisting an auditor of a permitted person (within the meaning of the Financial Services Act 2008 (an Act of Tynwald)) to exercise their functions.

5. A disclosure for the purpose of enabling or assisting the Office of Fair Trading of the Isle of Man to exercise its functions under Schedule 4 to the Financial Services Act 2008 (an Act of Tynwald) in relation to a financial services dispute within the meaning of paragraph 1(1) of that Schedule.

6. A disclosure for the purpose of enabling or assisting an adjudicator appointed under paragraph 4 of Schedule 4 to the Financial Services Act 2008 (an Act of Tynwald) to exercise their functions.

7. A disclosure for the purpose of enabling or assisting the body administering a scheme under section 25 of the Financial Services Act 2008 (an Act of Tynwald) (compensation schemes) to exercise its functions under the scheme.

8. A disclosure with a view to the institution of, or otherwise for the purposes of, civil proceedings arising under or by virtue of the Financial Services Act 2008 (an Act of Tynwald).

9. A disclosure for the purpose of enabling or assisting—

(a) the Insurance and Pensions Authority of the Isle of Man; or

(b) the Retirement Benefits Schemes Supervisor of the Isle of Man,

to exercise its functions under the Retirement Benefits Schemes Act 2000 (an Act of Tynwald: c 14).

10. A disclosure for the purpose of enabling or assisting the Assessor of Income Tax to exercise their functions under enactments of the Isle of Man relating to income tax.

11. A disclosure for the purpose of enabling or assisting the Office of Fair Trading of the Isle of Man to exercise its functions under any of the following—

(a) the Unsolicited Goods and Services (Isle of Man) Act 1974 (an Act of Tynwald: c 5);

(b) the Moneylenders Act 1991 (an Act of Tynwald: c 6);

(c) the Consumer Protection Act 1991 (an Act of Tynwald: c 11);

(d) the Fair Trading Act 1996 (an Act of Tynwald: c 15).

12. A disclosure for the purpose of enabling or assisting the Department of Local Government and the Environment of the Isle of Man to exercise its functions under the Estate Agents Act 1975 (an Act of Tynwald: c 6) or the Estate Agents Act 1999 (an Act of Tynwald: c 7).

13. A disclosure for the purpose of enabling or assisting Her Majesty's Attorney General of the Isle of Man to exercise their functions in connection with charities.

14. A disclosure for the purpose of enabling or assisting the Treasury of the Isle of Man to exercise its functions under the enactments of the Isle of Man relating to companies, insurance companies or insolvency.

15. A disclosure for the purpose of enabling or assisting an official receiver appointed in the Isle of Man to exercise their functions under the enactments of the Isle of Man relating to insolvency.

16. (1) A disclosure with a view to the institution of, or otherwise for the purposes of, disciplinary proceedings relating to the performance by an advocate, registered legal practitioner, auditor, accountant, valuer or actuary of their professional duties.

(2) In sub-paragraph (1)—

"advocate" means a person who is qualified to act as an advocate in any court in the Island in accordance with section 7 of the Advocates Act 1976 (an Act of Tynwald: c 27);

"registered legal practitioner" means a legal practitioner within the meaning of section 10 of the Legal Practitioners Registration Act 1986 (an Act of Tynwald: c 15) who is registered within the meaning of that Act.

17. (1) A disclosure with a view to the institution of, or otherwise for the purposes of, disciplinary proceedings relating to the performance by a public servant of their duties.

(2) In sub-paragraph (1) "public servant" means—

(a) an officer or employee of the Crown, or

(b) an officer or employee of any public or other authority for the time being designated for the purposes of this paragraph by order made by the Council of Ministers of the Isle of Man.

(E) GENERAL

1. A disclosure for the purpose of enabling or assisting—

(a) the European Central Bank, or

(b) the central bank of any country or territory outside the British Islands,

to exercise its functions.

2. (1) A disclosure for the purpose of enabling or assisting an overseas regulatory authority to exercise its regulatory functions.

(2) In sub-paragraph (1) "overseas regulatory authority" and "regulatory functions" have the same meaning as in section 82 of the Companies Act 1989 (assistance for overseas regulatory authorities).

3. A disclosure with a view to the institution of, or otherwise for the purposes of, criminal proceedings in the British Islands or elsewhere.

4. A disclosure for the purpose of the provision of a summary or collection of information framed in such a way as not to enable the identity of any person to whom the information relates to be ascertained.

5. . . .]

NOTES

Substituted by the Companies Act 2006 (Amendment of Schedule 2) (No 2) Order 2009, SI 2009/1208, art 2, Schedule, as from 1 July 2009.

Part A, paras 11, 12: words in square brackets substituted by the Financial Services Act 2012, s 114(1), Sch 18, Pt 2, paras 110, 123(1), (3), as from 1 April 2013.

Part A, para 18: repealed by the Deregulation Act 2015, s 19, Sch 6, Pt 6, para 22(15)(a), as from 1 October 2015.

Part A, para 25: words in first pair of square brackets substituted, and sub-para (k) added, by the Enterprise and Regulatory Reform Act 2013 (Competition) (Consequential, Transitional and Saving Provisions) Order 2014, SI 2014/892, art 2, Sch 1, Pt 2, paras 167, 168(a), as from 1 April 2014. Sub-para (b) repealed by the Financial Services and Markets Act 2000 (Regulated Activities) (Amendment) (No 2) Order 2013, SI 2013/1881, art 28, Schedule, Pt 1, para 11(a), as from 1 April 2014. Sub-para (c) repealed by the Public Bodies (Abolition of the National Consumer Council and Transfer of the Office of Fair Trading's Functions in relation to Estate Agents etc) Order 2014, SI 2014/631, art 5(3), Sch 2, para 5(1), (2)(a), as from 31 March 2014. Sub-para (h) repealed, and sub-para (l) added, by the Consumer Rights Act 2015, s 75, Sch 4, paras 36, 37(1), (2), as from 1 October 2015 (for transitional provisions in relation to the continued application of the Unfair Terms in Consumer Contracts Regulations 1999, see the Consumer Rights Act 2015 (Commencement No 3, Transitional Provisions, Savings and Consequential Amendments) Order 2015, SI 2015/1630, art 6).

Part A, para 26: repealed by SI 2014/892, art 2, Sch 1, Pt 2, paras 167, 168(b), as from 1 April 2014.

Part A, para 31: words in square brackets substituted by the Public Bodies (Merger of the Gambling Commission and the National Lottery Commission) Order 2013, SI 2013/2329, art 4, Schedule, para 29(a)(i), as from 1 October 2013.

Part A, para 32: words in first and third pairs of square brackets substituted by SI 2013/2329, art 4, Schedule, para 29(a)(ii), as from 1 October 2013. Words in second pair of square brackets substituted by the Budget Responsibility and National Audit Act 2011, s 26, Sch 5, Pt 2, paras 29, 31, as from 1 April 2012.

Part A, para 33: substituted by the Consumer Rights Act 2015, s 75, Sch 4, paras 36, 37(1), (3), as from 1 October 2015 (for transitional provisions, see the first note relating to the 2015 Act above).

Part A, para 34: words in square brackets substituted by the Consumer Contracts (Information, Cancellation and Additional Charges) Regulations 2013, SI 2013/3134, reg 47, Sch 4, para 6(a), as from 13 June 2014, in relation to contracts entered into on or after that date.

Part A, para 36A: inserted SI 2014/631, art 5(3), Sch 2, para 5(1), (2)(b), as from 31 March 2014.

Part A, para 37: words first pair of square brackets substituted by the Financial Services Act 2012, s 114(1), Sch 18, Pt 2, paras 110, 123(1), (3)(c), as from 1 April 2013. Sub-para (aa) inserted by the Financial Services Act 2012 (Consumer Credit) Order 2013, SI 2013/1882, art 10(4)(a), as from 1 April 2014. Words omitted from sub-para (a) repealed, and sub-paras (ab), (e) inserted, by the Co-operative and Community Benefit Societies Act 2014, s 151, Sch 4, Pt 2, paras 99, 102, as from 1 August 2014.

Part A, para 38: repealed by the Financial Services Act 2012, s 114(2), Sch 19, as from 1 April 2013.

Part A, para 40: words in square brackets substituted by the Central Securities Depositories Regulations 2017, SI 2017/1064, reg 10, Schedule, para 11(1), (3), as from 28 November 2017.

Part A, para 41: words in square brackets substituted by the Uncertificated Securities (Amendment and EU Exit) Regulations 2019, SI 2019/679, reg 2(1), (2), as from 27 March 2019, for transitional provisions and savings see regs 11, 12 of the 2019 Regulations at **[12.125]** et seq).

Part A, para 49: substituted by the Transfer of Tribunal Functions Order 2010, SI 2010/22, art 5(1), Sch 2, paras 141, 142(a), as from 6 April 2010. Sub-paras (a), (aa) substituted (for the original sub-para (a)) by the Financial Services Act 2012, s 114(1), Sch 18, Pt 2, paras 110, 123(1), (3)(d), as from 1 April 2013.

Part A, para 50: words in square brackets substituted by SI 2010/22, art 5(1), Sch 2, paras 141, 142(b).

Part E, para 5: repealed by the Takeovers (Amendment) (EU Exit) Regulations 2019, SI 2019/217, regs 2, 15, as from IP completion day (as defined in the European Union (Withdrawal Agreement) Act 2020, s 39).

Application to the Isle of Man: see notes to s 965 at **[1.1127]**.

[PART 3 OVERSEAS REGULATORY BODIES

[1.1508]

1. (1) A disclosure is made in accordance with this Part of this Schedule if—

(a) it is made to a person or body exercising relevant functions under legislation in a country or territory outside the British Islands, and

(b) it is made for the purpose of enabling or assisting that person or body to exercise those functions.

(2) "Relevant functions" for this purpose are functions of a public nature that appear to the Panel to be similar to its own functions or those of the [Financial Conduct Authority or the Prudential Regulation Authority or similar to the regulatory functions of the Bank of England].

2. In determining whether to disclose information to a person or body in accordance with this Part of this Schedule, the Panel must have regard to the following considerations—

(a) whether the use that the person or body is likely to make of the information is sufficiently important to justify making the disclosure;

(b) whether the person or body has adequate arrangements to prevent the information from being used or further disclosed, otherwise than—

(i) for the purposes of carrying out the functions mentioned in paragraph 1(1)(a), or

(ii) for other purposes substantially similar to those for which information disclosed to the Panel could be used or further disclosed.]

NOTES

Substituted by the Companies Act 2006 (Amendment of Schedule 2) (No 2) Order 2009, SI 2009/1208, art 2, Schedule, as from 1 July 2009.

Para 1: words in square brackets substituted by the Financial Services Act 2012, s 114(1), Sch 18, Pt 2, paras 110, 123(1), (4), as from 1 April 2013.

Application to the Isle of Man: see notes to s 965 at **[1.1127]**.

SCHEDULE 3
AMENDMENTS OF REMAINING PROVISIONS OF THE COMPANIES ACT 1985 RELATING TO OFFENCES

Section 1124

[1.1509]

(This Schedule amends CA 1985, ss 444, 448, 449, 450, 451, 453A and 455 at **[5.26]** et seq.)

SCHEDULE 4
DOCUMENTS AND INFORMATION SENT OR SUPPLIED TO A COMPANY

Section 1144(1)

PART 1 INTRODUCTION

Application of Schedule

[1.1510]

1. (1) This Schedule applies to documents or information sent or supplied to a company.

(2) It does not apply to documents or information sent or supplied by another company (see section 1144(3) and Schedule 5).

PART 2 COMMUNICATIONS IN HARD COPY FORM

Introduction

[1.1511]

2. A document or information is validly sent or supplied to a company if it is sent or supplied in hard copy form in accordance with this Part of this Schedule.

Method of communication in hard copy form

3. (1) A document or information in hard copy form may be sent or supplied by hand or by post to an address (in accordance with paragraph 4).

(2) For the purposes of this Schedule, a person sends a document or information by post if he posts a prepaid envelope containing the document or information.

Address for communications in hard copy form

4. A document or information in hard copy form may be sent or supplied—

(a) to an address specified by the company for the purpose;

(b) to the company's registered office;

(c) to an address to which any provision of the Companies Acts authorises the document or information to be sent or supplied.

PART 3 COMMUNICATIONS IN ELECTRONIC FORM

Introduction

[1.1512]

5. A document or information is validly sent or supplied to a company if it is sent or supplied in electronic form in accordance with this Part of this Schedule.

Conditions for use of communications in electronic form

6. A document or information may only be sent or supplied to a company in electronic form if—

(a) the company has agreed (generally or specifically) that the document or information may be sent or supplied in that form (and has not revoked that agreement), or

(b) the company is deemed to have so agreed by a provision in the Companies Acts.

Address for communications in electronic form

7. (1) Where the document or information is sent or supplied by electronic means, it may only be sent or supplied to an address—

(a) specified for the purpose by the company (generally or specifically), or

(b) deemed by a provision in the Companies Acts to have been so specified.

(2) Where the document or information is sent or supplied in electronic form by hand or by post, it must be sent or supplied to an address to which it could be validly sent if it were in hard copy form.

PART 4 OTHER AGREED FORMS OF COMMUNICATION

[1.1513]

8. A document or information that is sent or supplied to a company otherwise than in hard copy form or electronic form is validly sent or supplied if it is sent or supplied in a form or manner that has been agreed by the company.

SCHEDULE 5
COMMUNICATIONS BY A COMPANY

Section 1144(2)

PART 1 INTRODUCTION

Application of this Schedule

[1.1514]

1. This Schedule applies to documents or information sent or supplied by a company.

PART 2 COMMUNICATIONS IN HARD COPY FORM

Introduction

[1.1515]

2. A document or information is validly sent or supplied by a company if it is sent or supplied in hard copy form in accordance with this Part of this Schedule.

Method of communication in hard copy form

3. (1) A document or information in hard copy form must be—

(a) handed to the intended recipient, or

(b) sent or supplied by hand or by post to an address (in accordance with paragraph 4).

(2) For the purposes of this Schedule, a person sends a document or information by post if he posts a prepaid envelope containing the document or information.

Address for communications in hard copy form

4. (1) A document or information in hard copy form may be sent or supplied by the company—

(a) to an address specified for the purpose by the intended recipient;

(b) to a company at its registered office;

(c) to a person in his capacity as a member of the company at his address as shown in the company's register of members;

(d) to a person in his capacity as a director of the company at his address as shown in the company's register of directors;

(e) to an address to which any provision of the Companies Acts authorises the document or information to be sent or supplied.

[(1A) Sub-paragraph (1) has effect—

(a) where an election under section 128B is in force, as if the reference in paragraph (c) to the company's register of members were a reference to the register kept by the registrar under section 1080, and

(b) where an election under section 167A is in force in respect of the company's register of directors, as if the reference in paragraph (d) to the company's register of directors were a reference to the register kept by the registrar under section 1080.]

(2) Where the company is unable to obtain an address falling within sub-paragraph (1), the document or information may be sent or supplied to the intended recipient's last address known to the company.

NOTES

Para 4: sub-para (1A) inserted by the Small Business, Enterprise and Employment Act 2015, s 94, Sch 5, Pt 2, paras 11, 34(a), as from 30 June 2016.

PART 3 COMMUNICATIONS IN ELECTRONIC FORM

Introduction

[1.1516]

5. A document or information is validly sent or supplied by a company if it is sent in electronic form in accordance with this Part of this Schedule.

Agreement to communications in electronic form

6. A document or information may only be sent or supplied by a company in electronic form—

(a) to a person who has agreed (generally or specifically) that the document or information may be sent or supplied in that form (and has not revoked that agreement), or

(b) to a company that is deemed to have so agreed by a provision in the Companies Acts.

Address for communications in electronic form

7. (1) Where the document or information is sent or supplied by electronic means, it may only be sent or supplied to an address—

(a) specified for the purpose by the intended recipient (generally or specifically), or

(b) where the intended recipient is a company, deemed by a provision of the Companies Acts to have been so specified.

(2) Where the document or information is sent or supplied in electronic form by hand or by post, it must be—

(a) handed to the intended recipient, or

(b) sent or supplied to an address to which it could be validly sent if it were in hard copy form.

PART 4 COMMUNICATIONS BY MEANS OF A WEBSITE

Use of website

[1.1517]

8. A document or information is validly sent or supplied by a company if it is made available on a website in accordance with this Part of this Schedule.

Agreement to use of website

9. A document or information may only be sent or supplied by the company to a person by being made available on a website if the person—

(a) has agreed (generally or specifically) that the document or information may be sent or supplied to him in that manner, or

(b) is taken to have so agreed under—

(i) paragraph 10 (members of the company etc), or

(ii) paragraph 11 (debenture holders),

and has not revoked that agreement.

Deemed agreement of members of company etc to use of website

10. (1) This paragraph applies to a document or information to be sent or supplied to a person—

(a) as a member of the company, or

(b) as a person nominated by a member in accordance with the company's articles to enjoy or exercise all or any specified rights of the member in relation to the company, or

(c) as a person nominated by a member under section 146 to enjoy information rights.

(2) To the extent that—

(a) the members of the company have resolved that the company may send or supply documents or information to members by making them available on a website, or

(b) the company's articles contain provision to that effect,

a person in relation to whom the following conditions are met is taken to have agreed that the company may send or supply documents or information to him in that manner.

(3) The conditions are that—

(a) the person has been asked individually by the company to agree that the company may send or supply documents or information generally, or the documents or information in question, to him by means of a website, and

(b) the company has not received a response within the period of 28 days beginning with the date on which the company's request was sent.

(4) A person is not taken to have so agreed if the company's request—

(a) did not state clearly what the effect of a failure to respond would be, or

(b) was sent less than twelve months after a previous request made to him for the purposes of this paragraph in respect of the same or a similar class of documents or information.

(5) Chapter 3 of Part 3 (resolutions affecting a company's constitution) applies to a resolution under this paragraph.

Deemed agreement of debenture holders to use of website

11. (1) This paragraph applies to a document or information to be sent or supplied to a person as holder of a company's debentures.

(2) To the extent that—

(a) the relevant debenture holders have duly resolved that the company may send or supply documents or information to them by making them available on a website, or

(b) the instrument creating the debenture in question contains provision to that effect,

a debenture holder in relation to whom the following conditions are met is taken to have agreed that the company may send or supply documents or information to him in that manner.

(3) The conditions are that—

(a) the debenture holder has been asked individually by the company to agree that the company may send or supply documents or information generally, or the documents or information in question, to him by means of a website, and

(b) the company has not received a response within the period of 28 days beginning with the date on which the company's request was sent.

(4) A person is not taken to have so agreed if the company's request—

(a) did not state clearly what the effect of a failure to respond would be, or

(b) was sent less than twelve months after a previous request made to him for the purposes of this paragraph in respect of the same or a similar class of documents or information.

(5) For the purposes of this paragraph—

(a) the relevant debenture holders are the holders of debentures of the company ranking *pari passu* for all purposes with the intended recipient, and

(b) a resolution of the relevant debenture holders is duly passed if they agree in accordance with the provisions of the instruments creating the debentures.

Availability of document or information

12. (1) A document or information authorised or required to be sent or supplied by means of a website must be made available in a form, and by a means, that the company reasonably considers will enable the recipient—

(a) to read it, and

(b) to retain a copy of it.

(2) For this purpose a document or information can be read only if—

(a) it can be read with the naked eye, or

(b) to the extent that it consists of images (for example photographs, pictures, maps, plans or drawings), it can be seen with the naked eye.

Notification of availability

13. (1) The company must notify the intended recipient of—

(a) the presence of the document or information on the website,

(b) the address of the website,

(c) the place on the website where it may be accessed, and

(d) how to access the document or information.

(2) The document or information is taken to be sent—

(a) on the date on which the notification required by this paragraph is sent, or

(b) if later, the date on which the document or information first appears on the website after that notification is sent.

Period of availability on website

14. (1) The company must make the document or information available on the website throughout—

(a) the period specified by any applicable provision of the Companies Acts, or

(b) if no such period is specified, the period of 28 days beginning with the date on which the notification required under paragraph 13 is sent to the person in question.

(2) For the purposes of this paragraph, a failure to make a document or information available on a website throughout the period mentioned in sub-paragraph (1) shall be disregarded if—

(a) it is made available on the website for part of that period, and

(b) the failure to make it available throughout that period is wholly attributable to circumstances that it would not be reasonable to have expected the company to prevent or avoid.

PART 5 OTHER AGREED FORMS OF COMMUNICATION

[1.1518]

15. A document or information that is sent or supplied otherwise than in hard copy or electronic form or by means of a website is validly sent or supplied if it is sent or supplied in a form or manner that has been agreed by the intended recipient.

PART 6 SUPPLEMENTARY PROVISIONS

Joint holders of shares or debentures

[1.1519]

16. (1) This paragraph applies in relation to documents or information to be sent or supplied to joint holders of shares or debentures of a company.

(2) Anything to be agreed or specified by the holder must be agreed or specified by all the joint holders.

(3) Anything authorised or required to be sent or supplied to the holder may be sent or supplied either—

(a) to each of the joint holders, or

(b) to the holder whose name appears first in the register of members or the relevant register of debenture holders.

[(3A) Where an election under section 128B is in force, the reference in sub-paragraph (3)(b) to the register of members is to be read as a reference to the register kept by the registrar under section 1080."]

(4) This paragraph has effect subject to anything in the company's articles.

Death or bankruptcy of holder of shares

17. (1) This paragraph has effect in the case of the death or bankruptcy of a holder of a company's shares.

(2) Documents or information required or authorised to be sent or supplied to the member may be sent or supplied to the persons claiming to be entitled to the shares in consequence of the death or bankruptcy—

(a) by name, or

(b) by the title of representatives of the deceased, or trustee of the bankrupt, or by any like description, at the address in the United Kingdom supplied for the purpose by those so claiming.

(3) Until such an address has been so supplied, a document or information may be sent or supplied in any manner in which it might have been sent or supplied if the death or bankruptcy had not occurred.

(4) This paragraph has effect subject to anything in the company's articles.

(5) References in this paragraph to the bankruptcy of a person include—

(a) the sequestration of the estate of a person;

(b) a person's estate being the subject of a protected trust deed (within the meaning of the Bankruptcy (Scotland) Act [2016]).

In such a case the reference in sub-paragraph (2)(b) to the trustee of the bankrupt is to be read as the [trustee or interim trustee (under that Act)] on the sequestrated estate or, as the case may be, the trustee under the protected deed.

NOTES

Para 16: sub-para (3A) inserted by the Small Business, Enterprise and Employment Act 2015, s 94, Sch 5, Pt 2, paras 11, 34(b), as from 30 June 2016.

Para 17: year "2016" in square brackets and words in square brackets substituted by the Bankruptcy (Scotland) Act 2016 (Consequential Provisions and Modifications) Order 2016, SI 2016/1034, art 7(1), (3), Sch 1, para 29(1), (7), as from 30 November 2016 (except in relation to (i) a sequestration as regards which the petition is presented, or the debtor application is made before that date; or (ii) a trust deed executed before that date).

SCHEDULE 6
MEANING OF "SUBSIDIARY" ETC: SUPPLEMENTARY PROVISIONS

Section 1159

Introduction

[1.1520]

1. The provisions of this Part of this Schedule explain expressions used in section 1159 (meaning of "subsidiary" etc) and otherwise supplement that section.

Voting rights in a company

2. In section 1159(1)(a) and (c) the references to the voting rights in a company are to the rights conferred on shareholders in respect of their shares or, in the case of a company not having a share capital, on members, to vote at general meetings of the company on all, or substantially all, matters.

Right to appoint or remove a majority of the directors

3. (1) In section 1159(1)(b) the reference to the right to appoint or remove a majority of the board of directors is to the right to appoint or remove directors holding a majority of the voting rights at meetings of the board on all, or substantially all, matters.

(2) A company shall be treated as having the right to appoint to a directorship if—

(a) a person's appointment to it follows necessarily from his appointment as director of the company, or

(b) the directorship is held by the company itself.

(3) A right to appoint or remove which is exercisable only with the consent or concurrence of another person shall be left out of account unless no other person has a right to appoint or, as the case may be, remove in relation to that directorship.

Rights exercisable only in certain circumstances or temporarily incapable of exercise

4. (1) Rights which are exercisable only in certain circumstances shall be taken into account only—

(a) when the circumstances have arisen, and for so long as they continue to obtain, or

(b) when the circumstances are within the control of the person having the rights.

(2) Rights which are normally exercisable but are temporarily incapable of exercise shall continue to be taken into account.

Rights held by one person on behalf of another

5. Rights held by a person in a fiduciary capacity shall be treated as not held by him.

6. (1) Rights held by a person as nominee for another shall be treated as held by the other.

(2) Rights shall be regarded as held as nominee for another if they are exercisable only on his instructions or with his consent or concurrence.

Rights attached to shares held by way of security

7. Rights attached to shares held by way of security shall be treated as held by the person providing the security—

(a) where apart from the right to exercise them for the purpose of preserving the value of the security, or of realising it, the rights are exercisable only in accordance with his instructions, and

(b) where the shares are held in connection with the granting of loans as part of normal business activities and apart from the right to exercise them for the purpose of preserving the value of the security, or of realising it, the rights are exercisable only in his interests.

Rights attributed to holding company

8. (1) Rights shall be treated as held by a holding company if they are held by any of its subsidiary companies.

(2) Nothing in paragraph 6 or 7 shall be construed as requiring rights held by a holding company to be treated as held by any of its subsidiaries.

(3) For the purposes of paragraph 7 rights shall be treated as being exercisable in accordance with the instructions or in the interests of a company if they are exercisable in accordance with the instructions of or, as the case may be, in the interests of—

(a) any subsidiary or holding company of that company, or

(b) any subsidiary of a holding company of that company.

Disregard of certain rights

9. The voting rights in a company shall be reduced by any rights held by the company itself.

Supplementary

10. References in any provision of paragraphs 5 to 9 to rights held by a person include rights falling to be treated as held by him by virtue of any other provision of those paragraphs but not rights which by virtue of any such provision are to be treated as not held by him.

SCHEDULE 7
PARENT AND SUBSIDIARY UNDERTAKINGS: SUPPLEMENTARY PROVISIONS

Section 1162

Introduction

[1.1521]

1. The provisions of this Schedule explain expressions used in section 1162 (parent and subsidiary undertakings) and otherwise supplement that section.

Voting rights in an undertaking

2. (1) In section 1162(2)(a) and (d) the references to the voting rights in an undertaking are to the rights conferred on shareholders in respect of their shares or, in the case of an undertaking not having a share capital, on members, to vote at general meetings of the undertaking on all, or substantially all, matters.

(2) In relation to an undertaking which does not have general meetings at which matters are decided by the exercise of voting rights the references to holding a majority of the voting rights in the undertaking shall be construed as references to having the right under the constitution of the undertaking to direct the overall policy of the undertaking or to alter the terms of its constitution.

Right to appoint or remove a majority of the directors

3. (1) In section 1162(2)(b) the reference to the right to appoint or remove a majority of the board of directors is to the right to appoint or remove directors holding a majority of the voting rights at meetings of the board on all, or substantially all, matters.

(2) An undertaking shall be treated as having the right to appoint to a directorship if—

(a) a person's appointment to it follows necessarily from his appointment as director of the undertaking, or
(b) the directorship is held by the undertaking itself.

(3) A right to appoint or remove which is exercisable only with the consent or concurrence of another person shall be left out of account unless no other person has a right to appoint or, as the case may be, remove in relation to that directorship.

Right to exercise dominant influence

4. (1) For the purposes of section 1162(2)(c) an undertaking shall not be regarded as having the right to exercise a dominant influence over another undertaking unless it has a right to give directions with respect to the operating and financial policies of that other undertaking which its directors are obliged to comply with whether or not they are for the benefit of that other undertaking.

(2) A "control contract" means a contract in writing conferring such a right which—

(a) is of a kind authorised by the articles of the undertaking in relation to which the right is exercisable, and
(b) is permitted by the law under which that undertaking is established.

(3) This paragraph shall not be read as affecting the construction of section 1162(4)(a).

Rights exercisable only in certain circumstances or temporarily incapable of exercise

5. (1) Rights which are exercisable only in certain circumstances shall be taken into account only—

(a) when the circumstances have arisen, and for so long as they continue to obtain, or
(b) when the circumstances are within the control of the person having the rights.

(2) Rights which are normally exercisable but are temporarily incapable of exercise shall continue to be taken into account.

Rights held by one person on behalf of another

6. Rights held by a person in a fiduciary capacity shall be treated as not held by him.

7. (1) Rights held by a person as nominee for another shall be treated as held by the other.

(2) Rights shall be regarded as held as nominee for another if they are exercisable only on his instructions or with his consent or concurrence.

Rights attached to shares held by way of security

8. Rights attached to shares held by way of security shall be treated as held by the person providing the security—

(a) where apart from the right to exercise them for the purpose of preserving the value of the security, or of realising it, the rights are exercisable only in accordance with his instructions, and
(b) where the shares are held in connection with the granting of loans as part of normal business activities and apart from the right to exercise them for the purpose of preserving the value of the security, or of realising it, the rights are exercisable only in his interests.

Rights attributed to parent undertaking

9. (1) Rights shall be treated as held by a parent undertaking if they are held by any of its subsidiary undertakings.

(2) Nothing in paragraph 7 or 8 shall be construed as requiring rights held by a parent undertaking to be treated as held by any of its subsidiary undertakings.

(3) For the purposes of paragraph 8 rights shall be treated as being exercisable in accordance with the instructions or in the interests of an undertaking if they are exercisable in accordance with the instructions of or, as the case may be, in the interests of any group undertaking.

Disregard of certain rights

10. The voting rights in an undertaking shall be reduced by any rights held by the undertaking itself.

Supplementary

11. References in any provision of paragraphs 6 to 10 to rights held by a person include rights falling to be treated as held by him by virtue of any other provision of those paragraphs but not rights which by virtue of any such provision are to be treated as not held by him.

SCHEDULE 8
INDEX OF DEFINED EXPRESSIONS

Section 1174

[1.1522]

. . .	. . .
accounting reference date and accounting reference period	section 391
accounting standards (in Part 15)	section 464
accounts meeting	section 437(3)
acquisition, in relation to a non-cash asset	section 1163(2)
address	
— generally in the Companies Acts	section 1142
— in the company communications provisions	section 1148(1)
affirmative resolution procedure, in relation to regulations and orders	section 1290
allotment (time of)	section 558
allotment of equity securities (in Chapter 3 of Part 17)	[section 560(2) and (3)]
allotted share capital and allotted shares	section 546(1)(b) and (2)
annual accounts (in Part 15)	section 471
annual accounts and reports (in Part 15)	section 471
annual general meeting	section 336
. . .	. . .
appropriate audit authority (in sections 522, 523 and 524)	section 525(1)
appropriate rate of interest	
— in Chapter 5 of Part 17	section 592
— in Chapter 6 of Part 17	section 609
approval after being made, in relation to regulations and orders	section 1291
arrangement	
— in Chapter 7 of Part 17	section 616(1)
— in Part 26	section 895(2)
[— in Part 26A	section 901A(4)]
articles	section 18
associate (in Chapter 3 of Part 28)	section 988
associated bodies corporate and associated company (in Part 10)	section 256
[the Audit Regulation	section 1173(1)]
authenticated, in relation to a document or information sent or supplied to a company	section 1146
authorised group, of members of a company (in Part 14)	section 370(3)
authorised insurance company	section 1165(2)
authorised minimum (in relation to share capital of public company)	section 763
available profits (in Chapter 5 of Part 18)	sections 711 and 712
banking company and banking group	section 1164
body corporate	section 1173(1)
called-up share capital	section 547
capital redemption reserve	section 733
capitalisation in relation to a company's profits (in Part 23)	section 853(3)
cash (in relation to paying up or allotting shares)	section 583

cause of action, in relation to derivative proceedings (in Chapter 2 of Part 11)	section 265(7)
[the central register	
— in Chapter 2A of Part 8	section 128A(2)
— in Chapter 4 of Part 21A	section 790W(2)]
certified translation (in Part 35)	section 1107
charge (in [Chapter A1] of Part 25)	[section 859A(7)]
circulation date, in relation to a written resolution (in Part 13)	section 290
class of shares	section 629
the Companies Acts	section 2
Companies Act accounts	sections 395(1)(a) and 403(2)(a)
Companies Act group accounts	section 403(2)(a)
Companies Act individual accounts	section 395(1)(a)
companies involved in the division (in Part 27)	section 919(2)
company	
— generally in the Companies Acts	section 1
— in Chapter 7 of Part 17	section 616(1)
— in [Chapter A1] of Part 25	[section 859A(7)]
— in Chapter 2 of Part 25	*section 879(6)*
— in Part 26	section 895(2)
[— in Part 26A	section 901A(4)]
[— in Schedule 1C (see Chapter 1 of Part 28)	paragraph 21 of Schedule 1C]
— in Chapter 3 of Part 28	section 991(1)
— in the company communications provisions	section 1148(1)
the company communications provisions	section 1143
the company law provisions of this Act	section 2(2)
company records (in Part 37)	section 1134
[the competent authority	section 1173(1)]
[confirmation date (in Part 24)	section 853A(3)]
[confirmation period (in Part 24)	section 853A(3)]
[confirmation statement	section 853A(1)]
connected with, in relation to a director (in Part 10)	sections 252 to 254
constitution, of a company	
— generally in the Companies Acts	section 17
— in Part 10	section 257
[contributory	section 1170B]
controlling, of a body corporate by a director (in Part 10)	section 255
[corporate governance statement and separate corporate governance statement	
— in Part 15	section 472A
— in Part 16	section 538A]
corporation	section 1173(1)
the court	section 1156
credit institution	section 1173(1)
credit transaction (in Chapter 4 of Part 10)	section 202
creditor (in Chapter 1 of Part 31)	section 1011
daily default fine	section 1125
[the data protection legislation	section 1173(1)]
date of the offer (in Chapter 3 of Part 28)	section 991(1)
debenture	section 738
derivative claim (in Chapter 1 of Part 11)	section 260
derivative proceedings (in Chapter 2 of Part 11)	section 265
. . .	
director	
— generally in the Companies Acts	section 250
— in Chapter 8 of Part 10	section 240(3)

— in Chapter 1 of Part 11	section 260(5)
— in Chapter 2 of Part 11	section 265(7)
— in Part 14	section 379(1)
[directors' remuneration policy (in Chapter 4A of Part 10)	section 226A(1)]
directors' remuneration report	section 420
directors' report	section 415
distributable profits	
— in Chapter 2 of Part 18	section 683(1)
— elsewhere in Part 18	section 736
distribution	
— in Chapter 2 of Part 18	section 683(1)
— in Part 23	section 829
division (in Part 27)	section 919
document	
— in Part 35	section 1114(1)
— in the company communications provisions	section 1148(1)
dormant, in relation to a company or other body corporate	section 1169
[DTR5 issuer (in Part 24)	section 853E(6)]
EEA State and related expressions	section 1170
electronic form, electronic copy, electronic means	
— generally in the Companies Acts	section 1168(3) and (4)
— in relation to communications to a company	Part 3 of Schedule 4
— in relation to communications by a company	Part 3 of Schedule 5
eligible members, in relation to a written resolution	section 289
e-money issuer	
— in Part 15	section 474(1)
— in Part 16	section 539
employees' share scheme	section 1166
employer and employee (in Chapter 1 of Part 18)	section 676
enactment	section 1293
[enhanced disclosure documents	section 1078]
equity securities (in Chapter 3 of Part 17)	section 560(1)
equity share capital	section 548
equity shares (in Chapter 7 of Part 17)	section 616(1)
[establishment of an overseas company (in Part 35)	section 1067(6)]
[EU regulated market	section 1173(1)]
[exempt reasons, in relation to an auditor of a company ceasing to hold office (in Chapter 4 of Part 16)	section 519A]
existing company (in Part 27)	section 902(2)
fellow subsidiary undertakings	section 1161(4)
financial assistance (in Chapter 2 of Part 18)	section 677
financial institution	section 1173(1)
financial year, of a company	section 390
firm	section 1173(1)
fixed assets (in Part 23)	section 853
the former Companies Acts	section 1171
the Gazette	section 1173(1)
group (in Part 15)	section 474(1)
group undertaking	section 1161(5)
hard copy form and hard copy	
— generally in the Companies Acts	section 1168(2)
— in relation to communications to a company	Part 2 of Schedule 4
— in relation to communications by a company	Part 2 of Schedule 5
hire-purchase agreement	section 1173(1)
holder of shares (in Chapter 3 of Part 17)	section 574
holding company	section 1159 (and see section 1160 and

	Schedule 6)
IAS accounts	sections 395(1)(b) and 403(1) and (2)(b)
IAS group accounts	section 403(1) and (2)(b)
IAS individual accounts	section 395(1)(b)
. . .	. . .
included in the consolidation, in relation to group accounts (in Part 15)	section 474(1)
individual accounts	section 394
information rights (in Part 9)	section 146(3)
insurance company	section 1165(3)
insurance group	section 1165(5)
insurance market activity	section 1165(7)
interest in shares (for the purposes of Part 22)	sections 820 to 825
international accounting standards (in Part 15)	section 474(1)
investment company (in Part 23)	section 833
. . .	. . .
issued share capital and issued shares	section 546(1)(a) and (2)
the issuing company (in Chapter 7 of Part 17)	section 610(6)
the Joint Stock Companies Acts	section 1171
[legal entity (in Part 21A)	section 790C(5)]
liabilities (in Part 27)	section 941
liability, references to incurring, reducing or discharging (in Chapter 2 of Part 18)	section 683(2)
limited by guarantee	section 3(3)
limited by shares	section 3(2)
limited company	section 3
the main register (of members) (in Chapter 3 of Part 8)	section 131(1)
. . .	. . .
market purchase, by a company of its own shares (in Chapter 4 of Part 18)	section 693(4)
member, of a company	
— generally in the Companies Acts	section 112
— in Chapter 1 of Part 11	section 260(5)
— in Chapter 2 of Part 11	section 265(7)
memorandum of association	section 8
merger (in Part 27)	section 904
merging companies (in Part 27)	section 904(2)
merger by absorption (in Part 27)	section 904(1)(a)
merger by formation of a new company (in Part 27)	section 904(1)(b)
[MiFID investment firm	
— in Part 15	section 474(1)
— in Part 16	section 539]
negative resolution procedure, in relation to regulations and orders	section 1289
net assets (in Part 7)	section 92
new company (in Part 27)	section 902(2)
non-cash asset	section 1163
[non-public interest company (in Chapter 4 of Part 16)	section 519A]
[. . .	. . .]
non-voting shares (in Chapter 3 of Part 28)	section 991(1)
number, in relation to shares	section 540(4)(b)
off-market purchase, by a company of its own shares (in Chapter 4 of Part 18)	section 693(2)
offer period (in Chapter 2 of Part 28)	section 971(1)
offer to the public (in Chapter 1 of Part 20)	section 756
offeror	
[— in Schedule 1C (see Chapter 1 of Part 28)	paragraph 20(1) of Schedule 1C]

— in Chapter 2 of Part 28	section 971(1)
— in Chapter 3 of Part 28	section 991(1)
officer, in relation to a body corporate	section 1173(1)
officer in default	section 1121
official seal, of registrar	section 1062
opted-in company (in Chapter 2 of Part 28)	section 971(1)
opting-in resolution (in Chapter 2 of Part 28)	section 966(1)
opting-out resolution (in Chapter 2 of Part 28)	section 966(5)
ordinary resolution	section 282
ordinary shares (in Chapter 3 of Part 17)	section 560(1)
organisation (in Part 14)	section 379(1)
other relevant transactions or arrangements (in Chapter 4 of Part 10)	section 210
overseas company	section 1044
overseas branch register	section 129(1)
paid up	section 583
the Panel (in Part 28)	section 942
parent company	section 1173(1)
parent undertaking	section 1162 (and see Schedule 7)
payment for loss of office (in Chapter 4 of Part 10)	section 215
[payment for loss of office (in Chapter 4A of Part 10)	section 226A(1)]
pension scheme (in Chapter 1 of Part 18)	section 675
period for appointing auditors, in relation to a private company	section 485(2)
period for filing, in relation to accounts and reports for a financial year	section 442
permissible capital payment (in Chapter 5 of Part 18)	section 710
political donation (in Part 14)	section 364
political expenditure (in Part 14)	section 365
political organisation (in Part 14)	section 363(2)
prescribed	section 1167
private company	section 4
profit and loss account (in Part 15)	section 474(1) and (2)
profits and losses (in Part 23)	section 853(2)
profits available for distribution (for the purposes of Part 23)	section 830(2)
property (in Part 27)	section 941
protected information (in Chapter 8 of Part 10)	section 240
provision for entrenchment, in relation to a company's articles	section 22
[PSC register	section 790C(5)]
public company	section 4
[public interest company (in Chapter 4 of Part 16)	section 519A]
publication, in relation to accounts and reports (in sections 433 to 435)	section 436
[qualified, in relation to an auditor's report etc	
— in Part 15	section 474(1)
— in Part 16	section 539]
qualifying shares (in Chapter 6 of Part 18)	section 724(2)
qualifying third party indemnity provision (in Chapter 7 of Part 10)	section 234
qualifying pension scheme indemnity provision (in Chapter 7 of Part 10)	section 235
quasi-loan (in Chapter 4 of Part 10)	section 199
quoted company	
[— in Chapter 4A of Part 10	section 226A(1)]
— in Part 13	section 361
— in Part 15	section 385
— in Chapter 5 of Part 16	section 531 (and section 385)

realised profits and losses (in Part 23)	section 853(4)
[receiver or manager (and certain related references)	section 1170A]
redeemable shares	section 684(1)
redenominate	section 622(1)
redenomination reserve	section 628
the register	section 1080
[registered number, of a company (or an overseas company)	section 1066 (and section 1059A(5))]
[registered number, of a UK establishment of an overseas company	section 1067]
register of charges, kept by registrar	
— in England and Wales and Northern Ireland	*section 869*
— in Scotland	*section 885*
register of directors	section 162
register of directors' residential addresses	section 165
register of members	section 113
register of secretaries	section 275
. . .	. . .
. . .	. . .
registered office, of a company	section 86
[registrable person (in Part 21A)	section 790C(4)]
[registrable relevant legal entity (in Part 21A)	section 790C(8)]
registrar and registrar of companies	section 1060
registrar's index of company names	section 1099
registrar's rules	section 1117
registration in a particular part of the United Kingdom	section 1060(4)
regulated activity	
— generally in the Companies Acts	section 1173(1)
— in Part 15	section 474(1)
regulated market	section 1173(1)
relevant accounts (in Part 23)	section 836(2)
[relevant legal entity (in Part 21A)	section 790C(6)]
[relevant market (in Part 24)	section 853E(6)]
[remuneration payment (in Chapter 4A of Part 10)	section 226A(1)]
requirements for proper delivery (in Part 35)	section 1072 (and see section 1073)
requirements of this Act	section 1172
[. . .	. . .]
[review period (in Part 24)	section 853A(5) and (6)]
[section 172(1) statement	section 414CZA(1)]
securities (and related expressions)	
— in Chapter 1 of Part 20	section 755(5)
— in Chapter 2 of Part 21	section 783
senior statutory auditor	section 504
sent or supplied, in relation to documents or information (in the company communications provisions)	section 1148(2) and (3)
service address	section 1141
service contract, of a director (in Part 10)	section 227
shadow director	section 251
share	
— generally in the Companies Acts	section 540 (and see section 1161(2))
— in Part 22	section 792
— in section 1162 and Schedule 7	section 1162(7)
share capital, company having a	section 545
share exchange ratio	
— in Chapter 2 of Part 27	section 905(2)
— in Chapter 3 of Part 27	section 920(2)
share premium account	section 610(1)

share warrant	section 779(1)
[significant control (in Part 21A)	section 790C(2)]
[small companies exemption (in relation to directors' report)	section 415A]
small companies regime, [(for accounts)]	section 381
solvency statement (in sections 641 to 644)	section 643
special notice, in relation to a resolution	section 312
special resolution	section 283
statutory accounts	section 434(3)
subsidiary	section 1159 (and see section 1160 and Schedule 6)
subsidiary undertaking	section 1162 (and see Schedule 7)
. . .	. . .
[takeover bid	
— in section 943	section 943(7)
— in Schedule 1C	paragraph 20(1) of Schedule 1C
— in section 953	section 953(9)
— in Chapter 2 of Part 28	section 971(1)]
takeover offer (in Chapter 3 of Part 28)	section 974
. . .	
[traded company	
— in Part 13	section 360C
— in Part 15	section 474(1)]
[. . .	. . .]
trading certificate	section 761(1)
transfer, in relation to a non-cash asset	section 1163(2)
[transferable securities	section 1173(1)]
treasury shares	section 724(5)
turnover	
— in Part 15	section 474(1)
— in Part 16	section 539
UCITS management company	
— in Part 15	section 474(1)
— in Part 16	section 539
[UK-adopted international accounting standards (in Part 15)	section 474(1)]
[UK establishment of an overseas company (in Part 35)	section 1067(6)]
UK-registered company	section 1158
[UK regulated market	section 1173(1)]
uncalled share capital	section 547
unconditional, in relation to a contract to acquire shares (in Chapter 3 of Part 28)	section 991(2)
undistributable reserves	section 831(4)
undertaking	section 1161(1)
unique identifier	section 1082
unlimited company	section 3
unquoted company (in Part 15)	section 385
[unquoted traded company (in Chapter 4A of Part 10)	section 226A(1)]
voting rights	
[— in Schedule 1C (see Chapter 1 of Part 28)	paragraph 20(1) of Schedule 1C]
— in Chapter 2 of Part 28	section 971(1)
— in Chapter 3 of Part 28	section 991(1)
— in section 1159 and Schedule 6	paragraph 2 of Schedule 6
— in section 1162 and Schedule 7	paragraph 2 of Schedule 7
voting shares	
— in Chapter 2 of Part 28	section 971(1)
— in Chapter 3 of Part 28	section 991(1)
website, communication by a company by means of	Part 4 of Schedule 5

Welsh company	section 88
wholly-owned subsidiary	section 1159(2) (and see section 1160 and Schedule 6)
working day, in relation to a company	section 1173(1)
written resolution	section 288

NOTES

Entry "abbreviated accounts" (omitted) repealed by the Companies, Partnerships and Groups (Accounts and Reports) Regulations 2015, SI 2015/980, reg 13(1), (2), in relation to (a) financial years beginning on or after 1 January 2016, and (b) a financial year of a company beginning on or after 1 January 2015, but before 1 January 2016, if the directors of the company so decide (subject to transitional provisions, etc, in regs 2, 3 of the 2015 Regulations as noted to s 380 at **[1.430]**).

Words in square brackets in entry "allotment of equity securities (in Chapter 3 of Part 17)" substituted by the Companies Act 2006 (Allotment of Shares and Right of Pre-emption) (Amendment) Regulations 2009, SI 2009/2561, reg 2(6), as from 1 October 2009.

Entry "annual return" (omitted) repealed, and entries "confirmation date (in Part 24)", "confirmation period (in Part 24)", "confirmation statement", "DTR5 issuer (in Part 24)", "relevant market (in Part 24)", and "review period (in Part 24)" inserted, by the Small Business, Enterprise and Employment Act 2015, s 93(7), as from 30 June 2016.

In the entry "arrangement", words in square brackets inserted by the Corporate Insolvency and Governance Act 2020, s 7, Sch 9, Pt 2, paras 30, 39(1), (2), as from 26 June 2020.

Entries "the Audit Regulation" and "the competent authority" inserted by the Statutory Auditors and Third Country Auditors Regulations 2016, SI 2016/649, reg 15, Sch 3, Pt 4, para 28, as from 17 June 2016.

Entry "the central register" inserted by the Small Business, Enterprise and Employment Act 2015, s 94, Sch 5, Pt 2, paras 11, 35, as from 30 June 2016.

In the entry "charge (in Chapter A1 of Part 25)" the words "Chapter A1" in square brackets were substituted (for the original words "Chapter 1") and the words in square brackets in the second column were substituted (for the original words "section 861(5)") by the Companies Act 2006 (Amendment of Part 25) Regulations 2013, SI 2013/600, reg 5, Sch 2, para 3(1), (9)(a), as from 6 April 2013, in relation to charges created on or after that date (see further the transitional provisions note at **[1.982]**).

In the entry "company" the words "Chapter A1" in square brackets were substituted (for the original words "Chapter 1"), and the words "section 859A(7)" in square brackets in the second column were substituted (for the original words "section 861(5)"), by SI 2013/600, reg 5, Sch 2, para 3(1), (9)(b), as from 6 April 2013, in relation to charges created on or after that date (see further the transitional provisions note at **[1.982]**).

In the entry "company", the entry relating to "Chapter 2 of Part 25" was repealed by SI 2013/600, reg 5, Sch 2, para 3(1), (9)(b), as from 6 April 2013, in relation to charges created on or after that date (see further the transitional provisions note at **[1.982]**).

In the entry "company", the entry relating to "Part 26A" was inserted by the Corporate Insolvency and Governance Act 2020, s 7, Sch 9, Pt 2, paras 30, 39(1), (3), as from 26 June 2020.

In the entry "company", the entry relating to "Schedule 1C" was inserted by the Takeovers (Amendment) (EU Exit) Regulations 2019, SI 2019/217, regs 2, 16(a), as from IP completion day (as defined in the European Union (Withdrawal Agreement) Act 2020, s 39).

Entries "contributory" and "receiver or manager (and certain related references)" inserted by the Companies Act 2006 (Consequential Amendments, Transitional Provisions and Savings) Order 2009, SI 2009/1941, art 2(1), Sch 1, para 260(1), (9), as from 1 October 2009.

Entry "corporate governance statement and separate corporate governance statement" inserted by the Companies Act 2006 (Accounts, Reports and Audit) Regulations 2009, SI 2009/1581, reg 9, in relation to financial years beginning on or after 29 June 2008 which have not ended before 27 June 2009.

Entry "the data protection legislation" inserted by the Data Protection Act 2018, s 211, Sch 19, Pt 1, paras 120, 129, as from 25 May 2018 (for transitional provisions and savings relating to the repeal of the Data Protection Act 1998, see Sch 20 to the 2018 Act).

Entry "Directive disclosure requirements" (omitted) repealed, and entry "enhanced disclosure documents" inserted, by the Companies, Limited Liability Partnerships and Partnerships (Amendment etc) (EU Exit) Regulations 2019, SI 2019/348, reg 6, Sch 1, paras 1, 27, as from IP completion day (as defined in the European Union (Withdrawal Agreement) Act 2020, s 39).

Entries "directors' remuneration policy (in Chapter 4A of Part 10)", "payment for loss of office (in Chapter 4A of Part 10)" and "remuneration payment (in Chapter 4A of Part 10)" inserted, and words in square brackets in the entry "quoted company" inserted, by the Enterprise and Regulatory Reform Act 2013, s 81(1), (5), (11), (12), as from 1 October 2013.

Entries "establishment of an overseas company (in Part 35)", "registered number, of a company (or an overseas company)", "registered number, of a UK establishment of an overseas company" and "UK establishment of an overseas company (in Part 35)" inserted, and entries "registered number, of a branch of an overseas company" and "registered number, of a company" (omitted) repealed, by the Companies Act 2006 (Part 35) (Consequential Amendments, Transitional Provisions and Savings) Order 2009, SI 2009/1802, arts 2, 17, as from 1 October 2009.

Entries "EU regulated market" and "UK regulated market" inserted by the Accounts and Reports (Amendment) (EU Exit) Regulations 2019, SI 2019/145, reg 5, Sch 2, Pt 1, paras 1, 19, in relation to financial years beginning on or after IP completion day (as defined in the European Union (Withdrawal Agreement) Act 2020, s 39) (for transitional provisions see reg 7 of the 2019 Regulations at **[12.79]**).

Entry "IAS Regulation (in Part 15)" (omitted) repealed by the International Accounting Standards and European Public Limited-Liability Company (Amendment etc) (EU Exit) Regulations 2019, SI 2019/685, reg 19, Sch 1, Pt 1, paras 1, 26(a), in relation to accounts for financial years beginning on or after IP completion day (as defined in the European Union (Withdrawal Agreement) Act 2020, s 39) (note also that in relation to accounts for financial years which begin before but end on or after IP completion day, the enactments amended by Parts 1–3 of Sch 1 to the 2019 Regulations have effect as if the UK were a member State until the end of the financial year in question).

Entry "ISD investment firm" (omitted) repealed, and entry "MiFID investment firm" inserted, by the Markets in Financial Instruments Directive (Consequential Amendments) Regulations 2007, SI 2007/2932, reg 3(8), as from 1 November 2007.

Entries "legal entity", "PSC register", "registrable person (in Part 21A)", "registrable relevant legal entity (in Part 21A)", "relevant legal entity (in Part 21A)", and "significant control (in Part 21A)" inserted, by the Small Business, Enterprise and Employment Act 2015, s 81, Sch 3, Pt 2, paras 3, 11, as from 6 April 2016.

Entry "major audit" (omitted) repealed, and entries "exempt reasons, in relation to an auditor of a company ceasing to hold office (in Chapter 4 of Part 16)", "non-public interest company (in Chapter 4 of Part 16)", and "public interest company (in Chapter 4 of Part 16)" inserted, by the Deregulation Act 2015, s 18(5), Sch 5, Pt 1, paras 1, 12, as from 1 October 2015, in relation to financial years beginning on or after that date.

The entries "non-traded company (in Part 24)", "return period (in Part 24)", and "traded company (in Part 24)" (all now omitted) were originally inserted by the Companies Act 2006 (Annual Return and Service Addresses) Regulations 2008, SI 2008/3000, reg 9, as from 1 October 2009 (in relation to annual returns made up to that date or a later date). Entries "non-traded company (in Part 24)" and "traded company (in Part 24)" subsequently repealed by the Companies Act 2006 (Annual Returns) Regulations 2011, SI 2011/1487, reg 5, as from 1 October 2011 (in relation to annual returns made up to that date or a later date). Note that the definitions "non-traded company (in Part 24)" and "return period (in Part 24)" were also repealed by the Small Business, Enterprise and Employment Act 2015, s 93(7), as from 30 June 2016.

In the entry "offeror", the words in square brackets were inserted by SI 2019/217, regs 2, 16(b), as from IP completion day (as defined in the European Union (Withdrawal Agreement) Act 2020, s 39).

Entry "qualified, in relation to an auditor's report etc" substituted by SI 2015/980, reg 13(1), (3), as from the same dates and for the same purposes as specified in the first note relating to the 2015 Regulations above.

Entry "register of charges, kept by registrar" in italics repealed by SI 2013/600, reg 5, Sch 2, para 3(1), (9)(c), as from 6 April 2013, in relation to charges created on or after that date (see further the transitional provisions note at **[1.982]**).

Entry "section 172(1) statement" inserted by the Companies (Miscellaneous Reporting) Regulations 2018, SI 2018/860, regs 2, 6, in relation to the financial years of companies beginning on or after 1 January 2019.

Entry "small companies exemption (in relation to directors' report)" inserted by the Companies Act 2006 (Amendment) (Accounts and Reports) Regulations 2008, SI 2008/393, reg 6(11), as from 6 April 2008, in relation to financial years beginning on or after that date.

Words in square brackets in the entry "small companies regime" substituted by SI 2008/393, reg 6(12), as from 6 April 2008, in relation to financial years beginning on or after that date.

Entry "summary financial statement" (omitted) repealed by the Companies Act 2006 (Strategic Report and Directors' Report) Regulations 2013, SI 2013/1970, reg 14, Schedule, paras 1, 26, in respect of financial years ending on or after 30 September 2013.

Entry "takeover bid" substituted by SI 2019/217, regs 2, 16(c), as from IP completion day (as defined in the European Union (Withdrawal Agreement) Act 2020, s 39).

Entry "the Takeovers Directive" (omitted) repealed by SI 2019/217, regs 2, 16(d), as from IP completion day (as defined in the European Union (Withdrawal Agreement) Act 2020, s 39).

Entry "traded company" originally inserted by the Companies (Shareholders' Rights) Regulations 2009, SI 2009/1632, reg 21(2), as from 3 August 2009, in relation to meetings of which notice is given, or first given, on or after that date; and subsequently substituted by SI 2015/980, reg 13(1), (4), as from the same dates and for the same purposes as specified in the first note relating to the 2015 Regulations above.

Entry "transferable securities" inserted by SI 2015/980, reg 13(1), (5), as from the same dates and for the same purposes as specified in the first note relating to the 2015 Regulations above.

Entry "UK-adopted international accounting standards (in Part 15)" inserted by SI 2019/685, reg 19, Sch 1, Pt 1, paras 1, 26(b), in relation to accounts for financial years beginning on or after IP completion day (as defined in the European Union (Withdrawal Agreement) Act 2020, s 39) (note also that in relation to accounts for financial years which begin before but end on or after IP completion day, the enactments amended by Parts 1–3 of Sch 1 to the 2019 Regulations have effect as if the UK were a member State until the end of the financial year in question).

Entry "unquoted traded company (in Chapter 4A of Part 10)" inserted by the Companies (Directors' Remuneration Policy and Directors' Remuneration Report) Regulations 2019, SI 2019/970, regs 3, 27, as from 10 June 2019 (for transitional provisions, etc, see reg 2 of the 2019 Regulations at **[4.680]**).

In the entry "voting rights", the words in square brackets were inserted by SI 2019/217, regs 2, 16(e), as from IP completion day (as defined in the European Union (Withdrawal Agreement) Act 2020, s 39).

SCHEDULE 9
REMOVAL OF SPECIAL PROVISIONS ABOUT ACCOUNTS AND AUDIT OF CHARITABLE COMPANIES

(*Part 1 amended CA 1985, and Part 2 contained amendments to the Companies (Northern Ireland) Order 1986. Both Parts were repealed by the Deregulation Act 2015, s 107, Sch 23, Pt 1, para 1, as from 26 May 2015. Note that Part 2 was repealed without ever coming into force.*)

SCHEDULE 10
RECOGNISED SUPERVISORY BODIES

Section 1217

PART 1 GRANT AND REVOCATION OF RECOGNITION OF A SUPERVISORY BODY

Application for recognition of supervisory body

[1.1523]

1. (1) A supervisory body may apply to the Secretary of State for an order declaring it to be a recognised supervisory body for the purposes of this Part of this Act ("a recognition order").

(2) Any such application must be—

(a) made in such manner as the Secretary of State may direct, and

(b) accompanied by such information as the Secretary of State may reasonably require for the purpose of determining the application.

(3) At any time after receiving an application and before determining it the Secretary of State may require the applicant to furnish additional information.

(4) The directions and requirements given or imposed under sub-paragraphs (2) and (3) may differ as between different applications.

(5) The Secretary of State may require any information to be furnished under this paragraph to be in such form or verified in such manner as he may specify.

(6) Every application must be accompanied by—

(a) a copy of the applicant's rules, and

(b) a copy of any guidance issued by the applicant in writing.

(7) The reference in sub-paragraph (6)(b) to guidance issued by the applicant is a reference to any guidance or recommendation—

(a) issued or made by it to all or any class of its members or persons seeking to become members,

(b) relevant for the purposes of this Part, and

(c) intended to have continuing effect,

including any guidance or recommendation relating to the admission or expulsion of members of the body, so far as relevant for the purposes of this Part.

Grant and refusal of recognition

2. (1) The Secretary of State may, on an application duly made in accordance with paragraph 1 and after being furnished with all such information as he may require under that paragraph, make or refuse to make a recognition order in respect of the applicant.

[(2) The Secretary of State may make a recognition order only if it appears to him, from the information furnished by the body and having regard to other information in his possession, that—

(a) the requirements of Part 2 of this Schedule are satisfied in the case of that body,

(b) the body is able to perform all of the tasks which can be delegated by the competent authority under regulation 3 of the Statutory Auditors and Third Country Auditors Regulations 2016, and

(c) the body is organised in such a way that conflicts of interest are avoided.]

(3) The Secretary of State may refuse to make a recognition order in respect of a body if he considers that its recognition is unnecessary having regard to the existence of one or more other bodies which—

(a) maintain and enforce rules as to the appointment and conduct of statutory auditors, and

(b) have been or are likely to be recognised.

(4) Where the Secretary of State refuses an application for a recognition order he must give the applicant a written notice to that effect—

(a) specifying which requirements, in the opinion of the Secretary of State, are not satisfied, or

(b) stating that the application is refused on the ground mentioned in sub-paragraph (3).

(5) A recognition order must state the date on which it takes effect.

Revocation of recognition

3. [(1) A recognition order in respect of a body may be revoked by a further order made by the Secretary of State if at any time it appears to him—

(a) that any requirement of Part 2 or 3 of this Schedule, other than a requirement relating to a task delegated to the body under regulation 3 of the Statutory Auditors and Third Country Auditors Regulations 2016, is not satisfied in the case of the body,

(b) that the body has failed to comply with any obligation imposed on it by or by virtue of this Part of this Act, other than an obligation relating to a task delegated to the body under regulation 3 of the Statutory Auditors and Third Country Auditors Regulations 2016, or

(c) that the continued recognition of the body is undesirable having regard to the existence of one or more other bodies which have been or are to be recognised.]

[(1A) A recognition order in respect of a body may be revoked by a further order made by the Secretary of State if at any time—

(a) one or more tasks delegated to the body under regulation 3 of the Statutory Auditors and Third Country Auditors Regulations 2016 has been reclaimed by the competent authority, and

(b) it appears to the Secretary of State that the continued recognition of the body is undesirable having regard to the circumstances in which the task or tasks were reclaimed.]

(2) An order revoking a recognition order must state the date on which it takes effect, which must be after the period of three months beginning with the date on which the revocation order is made.

(3) Before revoking a recognition order the Secretary of State must—

(a) give written notice of his intention to do so to the recognised body,

(b) take such steps as he considers reasonably practicable for bringing the notice to the attention of the members of the body, and

(c) publish the notice in such manner as he thinks appropriate for bringing it to the attention of any other persons who are in his opinion likely to be affected.

(4) A notice under sub-paragraph (3) must—

(a) state the reasons for which the Secretary of State proposes to act, and

(b) give particulars of the rights conferred by sub-paragraph (5).

(5) A person within sub-paragraph (6) may, within the period of three months beginning with the date of service or publication of the notice under sub-paragraph (3) or such longer period as the Secretary of State may allow, make written representations to the Secretary of State and, if desired, oral representations to a person appointed for that purpose by the Secretary of State.

(6) The persons within this sub-paragraph are—

(a) the recognised body on which a notice is served under sub-paragraph (3),

(b) any member of the body, and

(c) any other person who appears to the Secretary of State to be affected.

(7) The Secretary of State must have regard to any representations made in accordance with sub-paragraph (5) in determining whether to revoke the recognition order.

(8) If in any case the Secretary of State considers it essential to do so in the public interest he may revoke a recognition order without regard to the restriction imposed by sub-paragraph (2), even if—

(a) no notice has been given or published under sub-paragraph (3), or

(b) the period of time for making representations in pursuance of such a notice has not expired.

(9) An order revoking a recognition order may contain such transitional provision as the Secretary of State thinks necessary or expedient.

(10) A recognition order may be revoked at the request or with the consent of the recognised body and any such revocation is not subject to—

(a) the restrictions imposed by sub-paragraphs (1)[, (1A)] and (2), or

(b) the requirements of sub-paragraphs (3) to (5) and (7).

(11) On making an order revoking a recognition order in respect of a body the Secretary of State must—

(a) give written notice of the making of the order to the body,

(b) take such steps as he considers reasonably practicable for bringing the making of the order to the attention of the members of the body, and

(c) publish a notice of the making of the order in such manner as he thinks appropriate for bringing it to the attention of any other persons who are in his opinion likely to be affected.

Transitional provision

4. A recognition order made and not revoked under—

(a) paragraph 2(1) of Schedule 11 to the Companies Act 1989 (c 40), or

(b) paragraph 2(1) of Schedule 11 to the Companies (Northern Ireland) Order 1990 (SI 1990/593 (NI 5)),

before the commencement of this Chapter of this Part of this Act is to have effect after the commencement of this Chapter as a recognition order made under paragraph 2(1) of this Schedule.

Orders not statutory instruments

5. Orders under this Part of this Schedule shall not be made by statutory instrument.

NOTES

Para 2: sub-para (2) substituted by the Statutory Auditors and Third Country Auditors Regulations 2016, SI 2016/649, reg 15, Sch 3, Pt 5, paras 53, 54, as from 17 June 2016.

Para 3: sub-para (1) substituted, sub-para (1A) inserted, and figure in square brackets in sub-para (10)(a) inserted, by SI 2016/649, reg 15, Sch 3, Pt 5, paras 53, 55, as from 17 June 2016.

Transfer of functions: as to the transfer of the functions of the Secretary of State under Part 42 of this Act (which includes this Schedule) see the note preceding s 1209 at **[1.1380]**.

PART 2 REQUIREMENTS FOR RECOGNITION OF A SUPERVISORY BODY

[Delegation etc of tasks by competent authority

[1.1524]

5A. The body ("B") must have rules providing that—

(a) in circumstances where and to the extent that a task delegated to the body is reclaimed by the competent authority under regulation 3 of the Statutory Auditors and Third Country Auditors Regulations 2016, the competent authority may apply rules (and may vary the rules it applies) made by B in accordance with the requirements of this Part of this Schedule,

(b) in circumstances where and to the extent that a task delegated to B is reclaimed by the competent authority under regulation 3 of the Statutory Auditors and Third Country Auditors Regulations 2016 and is delegated to another recognised supervisory body, the other recognised supervisory body may apply rules (and may vary the rules it applies) made by B in accordance with the requirements of this Part of the Schedule, and

(c) in circumstances where and to the extent that a task is not delegated to B by the competent authority under regulation 3 of the Statutory Auditors and Third Country Auditors Regulations 2016, the competent authority may apply rules (and may vary the rules it applies) made by B in accordance with the requirements of paragraphs 12 to 16 of this Schedule.

Consultation

5B. The body must consult with the competent authority and with other recognised supervisory bodies in making or varying rules in accordance with the requirements of this Schedule.]

Holding of appropriate qualification

6. (1) The body must have rules to the effect that a person is not eligible for appointment as a statutory auditor unless—

(a) in the case of an individual [other than [a third country auditor]], he holds an appropriate qualification,

[(aa) in the case of an individual who is [a third country auditor]—

(i) he holds an appropriate qualification,

(ii) he has been authorised on or before 5 April 2008 to practise the profession of company auditor pursuant to the European Communities (Recognition of Professional Qualifications) (First General System) Regulations 2005 (SI 2005/18) and has fulfilled any requirements imposed pursuant to regulation 6 of those Regulations, or

[(iii) he meets the requirements of sub-paragraph (1A)].]

(b) in the case of a firm . . . —

(i) each individual responsible for statutory audit work on behalf of the firm is eligible for appointment as a statutory auditor, and

(ii) the firm is controlled by qualified persons (see paragraph 7 below),

[(c) . . .]

[(1A) The requirements of this sub-paragraph are that—

(a) the individual holds a professional qualification which covers all the subjects that are covered by a recognised professional qualification and that are subjects of which knowledge is essential for the pursuit of the profession of statutory auditor, or

(b) the individual is an EEA auditor who—

(i) on or before IP completion day, holds a professional qualification which does not cover all those subjects,

(ii) on or before IP completion day, has been approved by the body or is in the process of seeking approval from the body, and

(iii) has met whichever of the requirements of sub-paragraph (1B) is specified in the body's rules.

(1B) For the purposes of sub-paragraph (1A)(b)(iii), the body's rules must specify one of the following requirements—

(a) a requirement to pass an aptitude test in accordance with sub-paragraph (2),

(b) a requirement to complete an adaptation period in accordance with sub-paragraphs (2B) and (2C), or

(c) a requirement either to pass an aptitude test in accordance with sub-paragraph (2) or to complete an adaptation period in accordance with sub-paragraphs (2B) and (2C), according to the choice of the individual.]

[(2) The aptitude test—

(a) must test the person's knowledge of subjects—

(i) that are covered by a recognised professional qualification,

(ii) that are not covered by the professional qualification already held by the person, and

(iii) the knowledge of which is essential for the pursuit of the profession of statutory auditor;

(b) may test the person's knowledge of rules of professional conduct;

(c) must not test the person's knowledge of any other matters.

(2A) . . .]

[(2B) An adaptation period is a period, not exceeding three years, in which the individual ("the applicant") pursues the profession of statutory auditor under the supervision of an individual who holds an appropriate qualification, subject to an assessment ("the ability assessment") of the applicant's ability to pursue the profession of statutory auditor in the United Kingdom.

(2C) Where the body's rules specify [a requirement that may or must be met by completing an adaptation period]—

(a) the body must have rules governing the adaptation period and the ability assessment, having regard to the circumstances of each applicant and, in particular, to the fact that each applicant is a qualified professional in [an EEA State],

(b) the applicant may be required to undergo further training during the adaptation period,

(c) the applicant's performance during the adaptation period must be assessed by the body, and

(d) the body must determine the applicant's professional status during the adaptation period.]

(3) A firm which has ceased to comply with the conditions mentioned in sub-paragraph (1)(b) may be permitted to remain eligible for appointment as a statutory auditor for a period of not more than three months.

7. (1) This paragraph explains what is meant in paragraph 6(1)(b) by a firm being "controlled by qualified persons".

(2) In this paragraph references to a person being qualified are—

[(a) in relation to an individual, to that individual's—

(i) holding an appropriate qualification, or

(ii) being a third country auditor and meeting the requirements of paragraph 6(1)(aa)(ii) or 6(1A);]

(b) in relation to a firm, to its—

(i) being eligible for appointment as a statutory auditor, . . .

(ii) . . .

(3) A firm is to be treated as controlled by qualified persons if, and only if—

(a) a majority of the members of the firm are qualified persons, and

(b) where the firm's affairs are managed by a board of directors, committee or other management body, a majority of that body are qualified persons or, if the body consists of two persons only, at least one of them is a qualified person.

(4) A majority of the members of a firm means—

(a) where under the firm's constitution matters are decided upon by the exercise of voting rights, members holding a majority of the rights to vote on all, or substantially all, matters;

(b) in any other case, members having such rights under the constitution of the firm as enable them to direct its overall policy or alter its constitution.

(5) A majority of the members of the management body of a firm means—

(a) where matters are decided at meetings of the management body by the exercise of voting rights, members holding a majority of the rights to vote on all, or substantially all, matters at such meetings;

(b) in any other case, members having such rights under the constitution of the firm as enable them to direct its overall policy or alter its constitution.

(6) Paragraphs 5 to 11 of Schedule 7 to this Act (rights to be taken into account and attribution of rights) apply for the purposes of this paragraph.

[**7A.** (1) The body must have rules and practices governing the adaptation period and the ability assessment referred to in section 1221 (approval of third country qualifications), and the following provisions of this paragraph apply in any case within that section.

(2) The body must have regard to the circumstances of each applicant in relation to the adaptation period, and the ability assessment, to be required of the applicant.

(3) The applicant may be required to undergo further training during the adaptation period.

(4) The applicant's performance during the adaptation period must be assessed by the body.

(5) The body must determine the applicant's professional status during the adaptation period.]

Auditors to be fit and proper persons

8. (1) The body must have adequate rules and practices designed to ensure that the persons eligible under its rules for appointment as a statutory auditor are fit and proper persons to be so appointed.

(2) The matters which the body may take into account for this purpose in relation to a person must include—

(a) any matter relating to any person who is or will be employed by or associated with him for the purposes of or in connection with statutory audit work;

(b) in the case of a body corporate, any matter relating to—

(i) any director or controller of the body,

(ii) any other body corporate in the same group, or

(iii) any director or controller of any such other body; and

(c) in the case of a partnership, any matter relating to—

(i) any of the partners,

(ii) any director or controller of any of the partners,

(iii) any body corporate in the same group as any of the partners, or

(iv) any director or controller of any such other body.

(3) Where the person is a limited liability partnership, in sub-paragraph (2)(b) "director" is to be read as "member".

(4) In sub-paragraph (2)(b) and (c) "controller", in relation to a body corporate, means a person who either alone or with an associate or associates is entitled to exercise or control the exercise of 15% or more of the rights to vote on all, or substantially all, matters at general meetings of the body or another body corporate of which it is a subsidiary.

Professional integrity and independence

9. (1) The body must have adequate rules and practices designed to ensure that—

(a) statutory audit work is conducted properly and with integrity, . . .

(b) persons are not appointed as statutory auditors in circumstances in which they have an interest likely to conflict with the proper conduct of the audit,

[(c) persons appointed as statutory auditors take steps to safeguard their independence [in accordance with the standards mentioned in sub-paragraph (3A)],

(d) persons appointed as statutory auditors record [the matters required to be recorded in accordance with those standards.]

(e) . . .

[(1A) The body must have adequate rules and practices designed to ensure that, except where the audited person is a public interest entity—

(a) an individual who has been appointed as statutory auditor may not be appointed as a director or other officer of the audited person or be concerned in the management of the audited person during a period of not less than one year determined in standards set by the competent authority and commencing on the date on which the individual's appointment as a statutory auditor ended;

(b) a key audit partner of a firm which has been appointed as statutory auditor may not be appointed as a director or other officer of the audited person or be concerned in the management of the audited person during a period of not less than one year to be determined in standards set by the competent authority and commencing on the date on which the firm's appointment as a statutory auditor ended.]

(2) . . .

[(3) The body must also have adequate rules and practices designed to ensure that—

(a) . . .

(b) any rule of law relating to the confidentiality of information received in the course of statutory audit work by persons appointed as statutory auditors is complied with; . . .

(c) . . .]

[(3A) The rules and practices mentioned in sub-paragraphs (1) and (3) must include provision requiring compliance with standards for the time being determined by the competent authority under the Statutory Auditors and Third Country Auditors Regulations 2016.]

[(4) The rules referred to in [sub-paragraphs (1A) and (3)(b)] must apply to persons who are no longer members of the body as they apply to members and any fine imposed in the enforcement of those rules shall be recoverable by the body as a debt due to it from the person obliged to pay it.]

[(5) An auditor is not to be regarded as an officer of the audited person for the purposes of sub-paragraph (1A) (a) and (b).]

Technical standards

10. (1) The body must have rules and practices as to—

(a) the technical standards to be applied in statutory audit work, and

(b) the manner in which those standards are to be applied in practice.

[(2) The rules and practices mentioned in sub-paragraph (1) must include provision requiring compliance with any standards for the time being determined by the competent authority under the Statutory Auditors and Third Country Auditors Regulations 2016.]

[Technical standards for group audits

10A. (1) The body must have rules and practices as to technical standards ensuring that group auditors—

(a) review for the purposes of a group audit the audit work conducted by other persons, and

(b) record that review.

[(2) The rules and practices mentioned in sub-paragraph (1) must include provision requiring compliance with any standards for the time being determined by the competent authority under the Statutory Auditors and Third Country Auditors Regulations 2016.]

[(3) The body must have rules and practices ensuring that group auditors retain copies of any documents necessary for the purposes of any review in accordance with those standards.]

(4)–(6) . . .

(7) In this paragraph—

"group auditor" means a person appointed as statutory auditor to conduct an audit of group accounts;
"group" has the same meaning as in Part 15 of this Act (see section 474).]

[. . .

10B. . . .

Public interest entity independence requirements

10C. (1), (2) . . .

[(3) The body must have adequate rules and practices designed to ensure that—

(a) an individual who has been appointed as statutory auditor of a public interest entity may not be appointed as a director or other officer of the entity or be concerned in the management of the entity during a period of not less than two years to be determined in standards set by the competent authority and commencing on the date on which the individual's appointment as statutory auditor ended;

(b) a key audit partner of a firm which has been appointed as statutory auditor of a public interest entity may not be appointed as a director or other officer or be concerned in the management of the entity during a period of not less than two years to be determined in standards set by the competent authority and commencing on the date on which the firm's appointment as statutory auditor ended.]

(4) The rules referred to in sub-paragraph (3) must apply to persons who are no longer members of the body as they apply to members and any fine imposed in the enforcement of those rules shall be recoverable by the body as a debt due to it from the person obliged to pay it.

(5) An auditor of a public interest entity is not to be regarded as an officer of the entity for the purposes of sub-paragraph (3)(a) and (b).

(6) . . .]

Procedures for maintaining competence

[11. The body must have rules and practices designed to ensure that persons eligible for appointment as statutory auditors take part in appropriate programmes of continuing education in order to maintain their theoretical knowledge, professional skills and values at a sufficiently high level.]

Monitoring and enforcement

12. [(1) The body must—

(a) have adequate resources for the effective monitoring and enforcement of compliance with its rules, and
(b) ensure that those resources may not be influenced improperly by the persons monitored.

(1A) The body must—

(a) have adequate arrangements for the effective monitoring and enforcement of compliance with its rules, and
(b) ensure that those arrangements operate independently of the persons monitored.]

[(2) The arrangements for monitoring must make provision for that function to be performed by the competent authority or any body to whom that authority has delegated tasks in accordance with regulation 3 of the Statutory Auditors and Third Country Auditors Regulations 2016.]

[(3) The arrangements for enforcement must—

(a) make provision for that function to be performed by the competent authority or any body to whom that authority has delegated tasks in accordance with regulation 3 of the Statutory Auditors and Third Country Auditors Regulations 2016;
(b) include provision for sanctions which include—
  (i) the withdrawal of eligibility for appointment as a statutory auditor;
  (ii) a notice requiring the person responsible for any breach to cease the conduct amounting to a breach and to abstain from repeating such conduct;
  (iii) a public statement identifying the person responsible for any breach and the nature of the breach (which may take the form of a reprimand or a severe reprimand);
  (iv) a temporary prohibition preventing a person responsible for any breach from carrying out statutory audits or signing audit reports;
  (v) a temporary prohibition of up to three years preventing a person responsible for any breach from exercising specified functions in a firm that is eligible for appointment as a statutory auditor or in a public interest entity;
  (vi) a declaration that the audit report does not satisfy the audit reporting requirements and, where appropriate, a declaration as to the proportion of the audit fee that is not payable as a result;
  (vii) an appropriate financial penalty;
  (viii) a requirement to take action to mitigate the effect or prevent the recurrence of the contravention;
  (ix) exclusion from membership of the body; and
(c) include provision for the body to make available to the public information relating to the steps it has taken to ensure the effective enforcement of its rules.]

[(4) The sanctions referred to in sub-paragraph (3)(b)(v) must apply to persons who are no longer members of the body as they apply to members.

(5) The information to be made available to the public under sub-paragraph (3)(c) must include the following information (which the body must continue to make available in accordance with sub-paragraph (7)) in relation to sanctions the body imposes—

(a) information concerning the type of contravention and its nature;
(b) the identity of the person sanctioned, unless any of the circumstances mentioned in sub-paragraph (6) applies; and
(c) where a sanction is subject to appeal, information concerning the status and outcome of any appeal.

(6) The circumstances in which the identity of the person sanctioned must not be made available to the public are—

(a) where that person is an individual and the body considers the publication of personal data would be disproportionate;
(b) where publication would jeopardise the stability of financial markets;
(c) where publication would jeopardise an ongoing criminal investigation; and
(d) where publication would cause disproportionate damage to any institution or individual involved.

(7) Information in relation to sanctions mentioned in sub-paragraph (3) must continue to be made available for a proportionate period and must be published on the body's website for at least five years after the relevant date.

(8) In sub-paragraph (7), "the relevant date" means—
(a) where the body imposes a sanction and that decision is appealed, the date on which the appeal is determined;
(b) where the body imposes a sanction and that decision is not appealed, the date by which any appeal was required to be lodged.]

[Monitoring of audits

13. (1) The body must—
(a) have adequate arrangements for enabling the performance by its members of statutory audit functions to be monitored by means of inspections, where functions relating to the monitoring of the audits are the subject of a delegation of tasks to the body under regulation 3 of the Statutory Auditors and Third Country Auditors Regulations 2016;
(b) in the case of members of the body who perform any statutory audit functions in respect of audits where functions relating to the monitoring of the audits are not the subject of such a delegation—
(i) have arrangements for the monitoring of those audits by the competent authority in accordance with those Regulations and, in respect of public interest entities, Article 26 of the EU Audit Regulation; and
(ii) have rules and practices designed to ensure that a sanction imposed by the competent authority in accordance with those Regulations is to be treated as if it were a sanction which the body had determined under arrangements for enforcement within paragraph 12;
(c) in the case of members of the body who perform any third country audit functions—
(i) have arrangements for the monitoring of those audits by the competent authority in accordance with the Statutory Auditors and Third Country Auditors Regulations 2016; and
(ii) have rules and practices designed to ensure that a sanction imposed by the competent authority in accordance with those Regulations is to be treated as if it were a sanction which the body had determined under arrangements for enforcement within paragraph 12; and
(d) have rules designed to ensure that members of the body take such steps as may reasonably be required of them to enable their performance of any statutory audit functions or third country audit functions to be monitored by means of inspections.

(2) Any monitoring of members of the body under the Statutory Auditors and Third Country Auditors Regulations 2016 or Article 26 of the EU Audit Regulation is to be regarded (so far as their performance of statutory audit functions, or of third country audit functions, is concerned) as monitoring of compliance with the body's rules for the purposes of paragraph 12(1) and (1A).

(3) The arrangements referred to in sub-paragraph (1)(a) must—
(a) make provision for inspections to be conducted by the competent authority or any recognised supervisory body to whom that authority has delegated tasks in accordance with regulation 3 of the Statutory Auditors and Third Country Auditors Regulations 2016; and
(b) include an inspection which is conducted in relation to each person eligible for appointment as a statutory auditor—
(i) at such frequency as the body considers appropriate given the risks arising from the statutory audit work undertaken by the person eligible for appointment as a statutory auditor; and
(ii) at least once every six years in the case of a person who, during any of the previous five years, has carried out a statutory audit of an entity not subject to the small companies regime (see section 381).

(4) The arrangements must provide that the determination by the body of the frequency of inspections under sub-paragraph (3)(b)(i) is subject to any direction by the competent authority.

(5) The inspection must be conducted by persons who—
(a) have an appropriate professional education;
(b) have experience of—
(i) statutory audit work, . . .
[(ii) equivalent work, for the purposes of an appointment of a person to conduct inspections made prior to IP completion day, on the audit of accounts under the law of an EEA State, or part of an EEA State, or
(iii) equivalent work, for the purpose of an appointment of a person to conduct inspections, on the audit of accounts under the law of—
(aa) an equivalent third country or part of an equivalent third country, or
(bb) a transitional third country or part of a transitional third country;]
(c) have received adequate training in the conduct of inspections;
(d) have declared that they do not have any interests likely to conflict with the proper conduct of the inspection;
(e) have not been an employee or partner or member of the management body of the person subject to inspection and have not been otherwise associated with that person for at least three years before the inspection.

(6) The inspection must review one or more statutory audits in which the person to whom the inspection relates has participated.

(7) The inspection must include an assessment of—
(a) the person's compliance with the standards set by the competent authority under the Statutory Auditors and Third Country Auditors Regulations 2016;

(b) the resources allocated by the person to statutory audit work;
(c) in the case of an inspection in relation to a firm, its internal quality control system;
(d) the remuneration received by the person in respect of statutory audit work.

(8) The inspection must be appropriate and proportionate in view of the scale and complexity of the statutory audit work of the person subject to inspection.

(9) Where undertaking inspections of statutory audits of undertakings that qualify as small (see sections 382 and 383) or medium sized (see sections 465 and 466) the body must take account of the fact that the standards determined by the competent authority under the Statutory Auditors and Third Country Auditors Regulations 2016 are designed to be applied in a manner that is proportionate to the scale and complexity of the business of the audited person.

(10) An inspection conducted in relation to a firm may be treated as an inspection of all individuals responsible for statutory audit work on behalf of that firm, if the firm has a common quality assurance policy with which each such individual is required to comply.

(11) The main conclusions of the inspection must be recorded in a report which is made available to—
(a) the person to whom the inspection relates, and
(b) the body.

(12) The body must, at least once in every calendar year, deliver to the Secretary of State a summary of the results of inspections conducted under this paragraph.

Membership, eligibility and discipline

14. The rules and practices of the body relating to—
(a) the admission and expulsion of members,
(b) the grant and withdrawal of eligibility for appointment as a statutory auditor by the body, where this task has been delegated to the body by the competent authority under regulation 3 of the Statutory Auditors and Third Country Auditors Regulations 2016, and
(c) the enforcement action the body takes in respect of its members, where tasks related to the competent authority's responsibility for imposing and enforcing sanctions have been delegated to the body under that regulation,

must be fair and reasonable and include adequate provision for appeals.]

Investigation of complaints

15. (1) The body must have effective arrangements for the investigation of complaints against—
(a) persons who are eligible under its rules for appointment as a statutory auditor, and
(b) the body in respect of matters arising out of its functions as a supervisory body.

[(2) The arrangements mentioned in sub-paragraph (1) must make provision for the whole or part of the function of investigating those complaints to be performed by the competent authority under the Statutory Auditors and Third Country Auditors Regulations 2016.]

[Independent investigation for enforcement purposes

16. (1) The body must have rules and practices designed to ensure that, where the competent authority has decided that any particular enforcement action should be taken against a member of the body following the conclusion of an investigation under the Statutory Auditors and Third Country Auditors Regulations 2016, that decision is to be treated as if it were a decision made by the body in enforcement proceedings against the member.

(2) The body must have adequate arrangements as part of its rules and practices—
(a) to facilitate the conduct of investigations into non-delegated cases by the competent authority in connection with the performance of statutory audit functions or third country audit functions by members of the body;
(b) for the holding by the competent authority of hearings relating to members of the body in accordance with the Statutory Auditors and Third Country Auditors Regulations 2016, where necessary following those investigations; and
(c) for making decisions by the competent authority following those investigations as to whether (and, if so, what) enforcement action should be taken against members of the body.

(3) "Non-delegated cases" means matters relating to tasks which have not been delegated to the body by the competent authority under regulation 3 of the Statutory Auditors and Third Country Auditors Regulations 2016.]

[Transfer of papers to third countries

16A. (1) The body must have adequate rules and practices designed to ensure that a person eligible under its rules for appointment as a statutory auditor transfers [audit working papers and investigation reports] to a third country competent authority only in accordance with the requirements of—
(a) paragraph 16AA (transfer to approved third country competent authority), or
(b) paragraph 16AB (transfer for purposes of investigation).

(2) The body must also have adequate rules and practices designed to ensure that a person eligible under its rules for appointment as a statutory auditor must refuse to transfer [audit working papers and investigation reports] to a third country competent authority if the Secretary of State directs under section 1253E(6) that such a transfer should not take place.

Transfer to approved third country competent authority

16AA. The requirements of this paragraph are that—
(a) the transfer is to an approved third country competent authority, and
(b) . . . the Secretary of State has approved the transfer.

Transfer for purposes of investigation of auditor

16AB. (1) The requirements of this paragraph are that—
(a) the transfer to the third country competent authority is made for the purposes of an investigation of an auditor or audit firm, and

(b) the following conditions are met.

(2) The first condition is that the authority has requested the [audit working papers and investigation reports] for the purposes of an investigation which has been initiated by itself or another third country competent authority established in the same third country.

(3) The second condition is that the [audit working papers and investigation reports] relate to audits of companies that—

(a) have issued securities in that third country, or

(b) form part of a group issuing statutory consolidated accounts in that third country.

(4) The third condition is that, where the authority has made the request for the [audit working papers and investigation reports] directly to the statutory auditor, the authority has given the Secretary of State advance notice of the request, indicating the reasons for it.

(5) The fourth condition is that the authority has entered into arrangements with the Secretary of State in accordance with section 1253E.]

Meeting of claims arising out of audit work

17. (1) The body must have adequate rules or arrangements designed to ensure that persons eligible under its rules for appointment as a statutory auditor take such steps as may reasonably be expected of them to secure that they are able to meet claims against them arising out of statutory audit work.

(2) This may be achieved by professional indemnity insurance or other appropriate arrangements.

Register of auditors and other information to be made available

18. The body must have rules requiring persons eligible under its rules for appointment as a statutory auditor to comply with any obligations imposed on them by—

(a) requirements under section 1224 (Secretary of State's power to call for information);

(b) regulations under section 1239 (the register of auditors);

(c) regulations under section 1240 (information to be made available to the public).

Taking account of costs of compliance

19. The body must have satisfactory arrangements for taking account, in framing its rules, of the cost to those to whom the rules would apply of complying with those rules and any other controls to which they are subject.

Promotion and maintenance of standards

20. The body must be able and willing—

(a) to promote and maintain high standards of integrity in the conduct of statutory audit work, and

(b) to co-operate, by the sharing of information and otherwise, with the Secretary of State and any other authority, body or person having responsibility in the United Kingdom for the qualification, supervision or regulation of auditors.

[Supplementary: funding of arrangements

20ZA (1) This paragraph applies where, under regulation 3 of the Statutory Auditors and Third Country Auditors Regulations 2016, the competent authority has delegated the task of approving persons as eligible for appointment as statutory auditors to a body ("B").

(2) B must pay the costs incurred by—

(a) the competent authority in carrying out activities mentioned in paragraphs 9 to 10C, 12, 13 and 16, or

(b) another recognised supervisory body, in carrying out those activities as a result of the competent authority delegating a task to the other body,

in relation to any statutory auditor bound by B's rules.]

[Interpretation

20A. [(1)] In this Part of this Schedule—

["the Audit Directive" means Directive 2006/43/EC of the European Parliament and of the Council on statutory audits of annual accounts and consolidated accounts, amending Council Directives 78/660/EEC and 83/349/EEC and repealing Council Directive 84/253/EEC;]

"audit reporting requirements" has the meaning given by regulation 2 of the Statutory Auditors and Third Country Auditors Regulations 2016 as amended from time to time;

["EEA auditor" means an individual or firm approved in accordance with the Audit Directive by an EEA competent authority to carry out audits of annual accounts or consolidated accounts required by European Union law;

"EEA competent authority" means a competent authority within the meaning of Article 2(10) of the Audit Directive of an EEA State;]

"issuer" has the same meaning as in Part 6 of the Financial Services and Markets Act 2000 (see section 102A(6));

["key audit partner" means—

(a) an individual who is eligible for appointment as a statutory auditor and who is designated by an audit firm for a particular audit engagement as being primarily responsible for carrying out the statutory audit on behalf of the audit firm;

(b) in the case of a group audit, any of the following—

(i) an individual who is eligible for appointment as a statutory auditor and who is designated by an audit firm as being primarily responsible for carrying out the statutory audit of the consolidated accounts of the group on behalf of the audit firm;

(ii) an individual who is eligible to conduct the audit of the accounts of any material subsidiary undertaking and who is designated as being primarily responsible for that audit; or

(c) an individual who is eligible for appointment as a statutory auditor and who signs the audit report.]

"public interest entity" means—

(a) an issuer whose transferable securities are admitted to trading on a [UK regulated market];

(b) a credit institution within the meaning given by Article 4(1)(1) of Regulation (EU) No 575/2013 of the European Parliament and of the Council, [which is a CRR firm within the meaning of Article 4(1)(2A) of that Regulation];

[(c) a person who would be an insurance undertaking as defined in Article 2(1) of Council Directive 91/674/EEC of 19 December 1991 of the European Parliament and of the Council on the annual accounts and consolidated accounts of insurance undertakings as that Article had effect immediately before IP completion day, were the United Kingdom a member State;]

. . .

"statutory audit function" means any function performed as a statutory auditor;

"third country audit function" means any function related to the audit of a [UK-traded third country company] or of [a body corporate] whose transferable securities are admitted to trading on a regulated market situated or operating in [an equivalent third country or transitional third country]; and

[. . .]

[(2) For the purposes of this Schedule, Gibraltar is to be treated as if it were an EEA State and subject to the Audit Directive.]

NOTES

Paras 5A, 5B: inserted by the Statutory Auditors and Third Country Auditors Regulations 2016, SI 2016/649, reg 15, Sch 3, Pt 5, paras 53, 56, as from 17 June 2016.

Para 6 is amended as follows:

The words in the first (outer) pair of square brackets in sub-para (1)(a) were inserted by the Statutory Auditors and Third Country Auditors Regulations 2007, SI 2007/3494, reg 17(1), (2), as from 6 April 2008.

Sub-para (1)(aa) was inserted by SI 2007/3494, reg 17(1), (3), as from 6 April 2008.

The words "a third country auditor" in square brackets in sub-paras (1)(a) and (aa) were substituted, and the words omitted from sub-para (1)(b) were repealed, by the Statutory Auditors and Third Country Auditors (Amendment) (EU Exit) Regulations 2019, SI 2019/177, regs 27, 28(za)–(zc), as from IP completion day (as defined in the European Union (Withdrawal Agreement) Act 2020, s 39). Note that SI 2019/177, reg 28(za)–(zc) were inserted by the Companies and Statutory Auditors etc (Consequential Amendments) (EU Exit) Regulations 2020, SI 2020/523, reg 14(e)(i), with effect from immediately before IP completion day.

Sub-para (1)(aa)(iii) was substituted by SI 2016/649, reg 15, Sch 3, Pt 5, paras 53, 57(1), (2), as from 17 June 2016.

Sub-para (1)(c) was originally inserted by SI 2016/649, reg 15, Sch 3, Pt 5, paras 53, 57(1), (4), as from 17 June 2016. Subsequently repealed by SI 2019/177, regs 27, 28(a), as from IP completion day (as defined in the European Union (Withdrawal Agreement) Act 2020, s 39). Note that the 2019 Regulations originally provided for the substitution of this sub-paragraph, but they were amended by SI 2020/523, reg 14(e)(ii), with effect from immediately before IP completion day. That amendment provided for the repeal of the sub-paragraph instead.

Sub-paras (1A), (1B) originally inserted by SI 2016/649, reg 15, Sch 3, Pt 5, paras 53, 57(1), (5), as from 17 June 2016. Subsequently substituted by SI 2019/177, regs 27, 28(b), (c), as from IP completion day (as defined in the European Union (Withdrawal Agreement) Act 2020, s 39). Note that reg 28(b) of the 2019 Regulations was amended by the Statutory Auditors, Third Country Auditors and International Accounting Standards (Amendment) (EU Exit) Regulations 2019, SI 2019/1392, reg 6, with effect from immediately before IP completion day (and that SI 2019/1392, reg 6 was itself amended by the Companies and Statutory Auditors etc (Consequential Amendments) (EU Exit) Regulations 2020, SI 2020/523, reg 27, with effect from immediately before IP completion day). Note also that reg 28(c) of the 2019 Regulations was amended by the International Accounting Standards, Statutory Auditors and Third Country Auditors (Amendment) (EU Exit) Regulations 2020, SI 2020/335, regs 6, 7, as from immediately before IP completion day. All amendments have been incorporated in the text set out above.

Sub-paras (2), (2A) substituted (for the original sub-para (2)) by SI 2007/3494, reg 17(1), (4), as from 6 April 2008. Sub-para (2A) subsequently repealed by SI 2016/649, reg 15, Sch 3, Pt 5, paras 53, 57(1), (6), as from 17 June 2016.

Sub-paras (2B), (2C) inserted by SI 2016/649, reg 15, Sch 3, Pt 5, paras 53, 57(1), (7), as from 17 June 2016. Words in square brackets in sub-para (2C) substituted by SI 2019/177, regs 27, 28(d), (da), as from IP completion day (as defined in the European Union (Withdrawal Agreement) Act 2020, s 39). Note that reg 28(da) of the 2019 Regulations was inserted by SI 2020/523, reg 14(e)(iii), with effect from immediately before IP completion day.

Para 7: sub-para (2)(a) was substituted, and sub-para (b)(ii) and the preceding word were repealed, by SI 2019/177, regs 27, 29, as from IP completion day (as defined in the European Union (Withdrawal Agreement) Act 2020, s 39). Note that reg 29 of the 2019 Regulations was substituted by SI 2020/523, reg 14(f), with effect from immediately before IP completion day.

Para 7A: inserted by the Statutory Auditors Regulations 2017, SI 2017/1164, reg 3, Sch 1, paras 7, 22, as from 1 April 2018 (see **[4.671]** et seq).

Para 9: word omitted from sub-para (1)(a) repealed, sub-paras (1)(c)–(e) inserted, and sub-paras (3), (4) substituted, by SI 2007/3494, reg 19, as from 6 April 2008. Words in square brackets in sub-paras (1)(c), (d) and (4) substituted, sub-paras (1)(e), (2) repealed, sub-paras (1A), (3A) inserted, words omitted from sub-para (3) repealed, and sub-para (5) added, by SI 2016/649, reg 15, Sch 3, Pt 5, paras 53, 58, as from 17 June 2016.

Para 10: sub-para (2) substituted by SI 2016/649, reg 15, Sch 3, Pt 5, paras 53, 59, as from 17 June 2016.

Para 10A: inserted by SI 2007/3494, reg 20, as from 6 April 2008. Sub-paras (2), (3) substituted, and sub-paras (4)–(6) repealed, by SI 2016/649, reg 15, Sch 3, Pt 5, paras 53, 60, as from 17 June 2016.

Para 10B: inserted, together with para 10C, by SI 2007/3494, reg 21, as from 6 April 2008. Subsequently repealed by SI 2016/649, reg 15, Sch 3, Pt 5, paras 53, 61, as from 17 June 2016.

Para 10C: inserted as noted above. Sub-paras (1), (2), (6) repealed, and sub-para (3) substituted, by SI 2016/649, reg 15, Sch 3, Pt 5, paras 53, 62, as from 17 June 2016.

Para 11: substituted by SI 2016/649, reg 15, Sch 3, Pt 5, paras 53, 63, as from 17 June 2016.

Para 12: sub-paras (1), (1A) substituted (for the original sub-para (1)), and sub-para (3) added, by SI 2007/3494, reg 22, as from 6 April 2008. Sub-paras (2), (3) substituted, and sub-paras (4)–(8) added, by SI 2016/649, reg 15, Sch 3, Pt 5, paras 53, 64, as from 17 June 2016.

Para 13: was substituted by SI 2007/3494, reg 23, as from 6 April 2008. It was further substituted (together with para 14) by SI 2016/649, reg 15, Sch 3, Pt 5, paras 53, 65, as from 17 June 2016 (note that reg 1(9) of the 2016 Regulations (at **[4.650]**) provides that the substitution of para 13 does not apply to enforcement action which is taken following an inspection under arrangements mentioned in that paragraph and which began before 17 June 2016). The word omitted from sub-para (5)(b)(i) was repealed, and sub-paras (5)(b)(ii), (iii) were substituted (for the original sub-para (5)(b)(ii)), by SI 2019/177, regs 27, 30, as from

IP completion day (as defined in the European Union (Withdrawal Agreement) Act 2020, s 39). Note that reg 30 of the 2019 Regulations was amended by SI 2020/523, reg 14(g), with effect from immediately before IP completion day (and that the effect of the amendment has been incorporated in the text set out above).

Para 14: substituted by SI 2016/649, reg 15, Sch 3, Pt 5, paras 53, 65, as from 17 June 2016.

Para 15: sub-para (2) substituted by SI 2016/649, reg 15, Sch 3, Pt 5, paras 53, 66, as from 17 June 2016.

Para 16: substituted by SI 2016/649, reg 15, Sch 3, Pt 5, paras 53, 67, as from 17 June 2016. Note that reg 1(8) of the 2016 Regulations (at **[4.650]**) provides that the substitution of para 16 does not apply to investigations under arrangements mentioned in that paragraph which occur as a result of a complaint or referral made before 17 June 2016.

Paras 16A, 16AA, 16AB: substituted for the original para 16A (as inserted by SI 2007/3494, regs 20, 24, as from 6 April 2008) by the Companies Act 2006 (Transfer of Audit Working Papers to Third Countries) Regulations 2010, SI 2010/2537, reg 5, as from 15 November 2010 (note that reg 8 of the 2010 Regulations provides that notwithstanding Sch 4, para 38 to the Companies Act 2006 (Commencement No 5, Transitional Provisions and Savings) Order 2007 (which limits the application of certain provisions of the Companies Act 2006, including this Schedule), paras 16A, 16AA, 16AB (as inserted by the 2010 Regulations) apply in relation to the supervision of auditors appointed for any financial year). The words in square brackets in paras 16A and 16AB were substituted by SI 2016/649, reg 15, Sch 3, Pt 5, paras 53, 68, 69, as from 17 June 2016, in relation to financial years beginning on or after that date. The words omitted from para 16AA were repealed by SI 2019/177, regs 27, 31, as from IP completion day (as defined in the European Union (Withdrawal Agreement) Act 2020, s 39).

Para 20ZA: inserted by SI 2016/649, reg 15, Sch 3, Pt 5, paras 53, 70, as from 17 June 2016.

Para 20A was originally inserted by SI 2007/3494, reg 25, as from 6 April 2008; and subsequently substituted by SI 2016/649, reg 15, Sch 3, Pt 5, paras 53, 68, 71, as from 17 June 2016. It has subsequently been amended as follows:

Para (1) numbered as such by SI 2019/177, regs 27, 32(a), as from IP completion day (as defined in the European Union (Withdrawal Agreement) Act 2020, s 39).

Definitions "the Audit Directive", "EEA auditor", and "EEA competent authority" inserted by SI 2019/177, regs 27, 32(b), (c), as from IP completion day (as defined in the European Union (Withdrawal Agreement) Act 2020, s 39).

Definition "key audit partner" substituted by the Statutory Auditors and Third Country Auditors (Amendment) (EU Exit) Regulations 2020, SI 2020/108, reg 15(1), (3), as from 22 February 2020.

The words in square brackets in para (a) of the definition "public interest entity" were substituted by SI 2019/177, regs 27, 32(d)(i), as from IP completion day (as defined in the European Union (Withdrawal Agreement) Act 2020, s 39) (for transitional provisions in relation to audits of accounts for financial years that begin before IP completion day, see Sch 4 to the 2019 Regulations at **[12.88]**).

The words in square brackets in para (b) of the definition "public interest entity" were substituted, and para (c) of the definition was substituted, by SI 2019/177, regs 27, 32(d)(ii), (iii), as from IP completion day (as defined in the European Union (Withdrawal Agreement) Act 2020, s 39). Note that reg 32(d)(iii) of the 2019 Regulations was amended by SI 2020/523, reg 14(h), with effect from immediately before IP completion day (and that the effect of the amendment has been incorporated in the text set out above).

Definition "regulated market" (omitted) repealed by SI 2019/177, regs 27, 32(e), as from IP completion day (as defined in the European Union (Withdrawal Agreement) Act 2020, s 39).

Words in square brackets in the definition "third country audit function" substituted by SI 2019/177, regs 27, 32(f), as from IP completion day (as defined in the European Union (Withdrawal Agreement) Act 2020, s 39).

Definition "transferable securities" (omitted) repealed by SI 2019/177, regs 27, 32(g), as from IP completion day (as defined in the European Union (Withdrawal Agreement) Act 2020, s 39).

Sub-para (2) was added by SI 2019/177, regs 27, 32(h), as from IP completion day (as defined in the European Union (Withdrawal Agreement) Act 2020, s 39).

Transfer of functions: as to the transfer of the functions of the Secretary of State under Part 42 of this Act (which includes this Schedule) see the note preceding s 1209 at **[1.1380]**.

PART 3

(This Part was repealed by the Statutory Auditors and Third Country Auditors Regulations 2016, SI 2016/649, reg 15, Sch 3, Pt 5, paras 53, 72, as from 17 June 2016, subject to the following transitional provisions in reg 1 of those Regulations: (i) in so far as relating to paras 21 to 22B of this Part, this repeal does not apply in relation to financial years beginning before 17 June 2016; (ii) in so far as relating to para 24, this repeal does not apply to investigations under arrangements mentioned in that paragraph which occur as a result of a complaint or referral made before 17 June 2016; (iii) in so far as relating to paras 23, 23A, this repeal does not apply to enforcement action which is taken following an inspection under arrangements mentioned in those paragraphs and which begins before 17 June 2016.)

SCHEDULE 11
RECOGNISED PROFESSIONAL QUALIFICATIONS

Section 1220

PART 1 GRANT AND REVOCATION OF RECOGNITION OF A PROFESSIONAL QUALIFICATION

Application for recognition of professional qualification

[1.1525]

1. (1) A qualifying body may apply to the Secretary of State for an order declaring a qualification offered by it to be a recognised professional qualification for the purposes of this Part of this Act ("a recognition order").

(2) In this Part of this Act "a recognised qualifying body" means a qualifying body offering a recognised professional qualification.

(3) Any application must be—

(a) made in such manner as the Secretary of State may direct, and

(b) accompanied by such information as the Secretary of State may reasonably require for the purpose of determining the application.

(4) At any time after receiving an application and before determining it the Secretary of State may require the applicant to furnish additional information.

(5) The directions and requirements given or imposed under sub-paragraphs (3) and (4) may differ as between different applications.

(6) The Secretary of State may require any information to be furnished under this paragraph to be in such form or verified in such manner as he may specify.

(7) In the case of examination standards, the verification required may include independent moderation of the examinations over such a period as the Secretary of State considers necessary.

(8) Every application must be accompanied by—

(a) a copy of the applicant's rules, and

(b) a copy of any guidance issued by the applicant in writing.

(9) The reference in sub-paragraph (8)(b) to guidance issued by the applicant is a reference to any guidance or recommendation—

(a) issued or made by it to all or any class of persons holding or seeking to hold a qualification, or approved or seeking to be approved by the body for the purposes of giving practical training,

(b) relevant for the purposes of this Part of this Act, and

(c) intended to have continuing effect,

including any guidance or recommendation relating to a matter within sub-paragraph (10).

(10) The matters within this sub-paragraph are—

(a) admission to or expulsion from a course of study leading to a qualification,

(b) the award or deprivation of a qualification, and

(c) the approval of a person for the purposes of giving practical training or the withdrawal of such an approval,

so far as relevant for the purposes of this Part of this Act.

Grant and refusal of recognition

2. (1) The Secretary of State may, on an application duly made in accordance with paragraph 1 and after being furnished with all such information as he may require under that paragraph, make or refuse to make a recognition order in respect of the qualification in relation to which the application was made.

(2) The Secretary of State may make a recognition order only if it appears to him, from the information furnished by the applicant and having regard to any other information in his possession, that the requirements of Part 2 of this Schedule are satisfied in relation to the qualification.

(3) Where the Secretary of State refuses an application for a recognition order he must give the applicant a written notice to that effect specifying which requirements, in his opinion, are not satisfied.

(4) A recognition order must state the date on which it takes effect.

Revocation of recognition

3. (1) A recognition order may be revoked by a further order made by the Secretary of State if at any time it appears to him—

(a) that any requirement of Part 2 of this Schedule is not satisfied in relation to the qualification to which the recognition order relates, or

(b) that the qualifying body has failed to comply with any obligation imposed on it by or by virtue of this Part of this Act.

(2) An order revoking a recognition order must state the date on which it takes effect, which must be after the period of three months beginning with the date on which the revocation order is made.

(3) Before revoking a recognition order the Secretary of State must—

(a) give written notice of his intention to do so to the qualifying body,

(b) take such steps as he considers reasonably practicable for bringing the notice to the attention of persons holding the qualification or in the course of studying for it, and

(c) publish the notice in such manner as he thinks appropriate for bringing it to the attention of any other persons who are in his opinion likely to be affected.

(4) A notice under sub-paragraph (3) must—

(a) state the reasons for which the Secretary of State proposes to act, and

(b) give particulars of the rights conferred by sub-paragraph (5).

(5) A person within sub-paragraph (6) may, within the period of three months beginning with the date of service or publication or such longer period as the Secretary of State may allow, make written representations to the Secretary of State and, if desired, oral representations to a person appointed for that purpose by the Secretary of State.

(6) The persons within this sub-paragraph are—

(a) the qualifying body on which a notice is served under sub-paragraph (3),

(b) any person holding the qualification or in the course of studying for it, and

(c) any other person who appears to the Secretary of State to be affected.

(7) The Secretary of State must have regard to any representations made in accordance with sub-paragraph (5) in determining whether to revoke the recognition order.

(8) If in any case the Secretary of State considers it essential to do so in the public interest he may revoke a recognition order without regard to the restriction imposed by sub-paragraph (2), even if—

(a) no notice has been given or published under sub-paragraph (3), or

(b) the period of time for making representations in pursuance of such a notice has not expired.

(9) An order revoking a recognition order may contain such transitional provision as the Secretary of State thinks necessary or expedient.

(10) A recognition order may be revoked at the request or with the consent of the qualifying body and any such revocation is not subject to—

(a) the restrictions imposed by sub-paragraphs (1) and (2), or

(b) the requirements of sub-paragraphs (3) to (5) and (7).

(11) On making an order revoking a recognition order the Secretary of State must—

(a) give written notice of the making of the order to the qualifying body,

(b) take such steps as he considers reasonably practicable for bringing the making of the order to the attention of persons holding the qualification or in the course of studying for it, and

(c) publish a notice of the making of the order in such manner as he thinks appropriate for bringing it to the attention of any other persons who are in his opinion likely to be affected.

Transitional provision

4. A recognition order made and not revoked under—

(a) paragraph 2(1) of Schedule 12 to the Companies Act 1989 (c 40), or

(b) paragraph 2(1) of Schedule 12 to the Companies (Northern Ireland) Order 1990 (SI 1990/593 (NI 5)),

before the commencement of this Chapter of this Part of this Act is to have effect after the commencement of this Chapter as a recognition order made under paragraph 2(1) of this Schedule.

Orders not statutory instruments

5. Orders under this Part of this Schedule shall not be made by statutory instrument.

NOTES

Transfer of functions: as to the transfer of the functions of the Secretary of State under Part 42 of this Act (which includes this Schedule) see the note preceding s 1209 at **[1.1380]**.

PART 2 REQUIREMENTS FOR RECOGNITION OF A PROFESSIONAL QUALIFICATION

Entry requirements

[1.1526]

6. (1) The qualification must only be open to persons who—

(a) have attained university entrance level, or

(b) have a sufficient period of professional experience.

(2) In relation to a person who has not been admitted to a university or other similar establishment in the United Kingdom, "attaining university entrance level" means—

(a) being educated to such a standard as would entitle him to be considered for such admission on the basis of—

(i) academic or professional qualifications obtained in the United Kingdom and recognised by the Secretary of State to be of an appropriate standard, or

(ii) academic or professional qualifications obtained outside the United Kingdom which the Secretary of State considers to be of an equivalent standard, or

(b) being assessed, on the basis of written tests of a kind appearing to the Secretary of State to be adequate for the purpose (with or without oral examination), as of such a standard of ability as would entitle him to be considered for such admission.

(3) The assessment, tests and oral examination referred to in sub-paragraph (2)(b) may be conducted by—

(a) the qualifying body, or

(b) some other body approved by the Secretary of State.

(4) The reference in sub-paragraph (1)(b) to "a sufficient period of professional experience" is to not less than seven years' experience in a professional capacity in the fields of finance, law and accountancy.

Requirement for theoretical instruction or professional experience

7. (1) The qualification must be restricted to persons who—

(a) have completed a course of theoretical instruction in the subjects prescribed for the purposes of paragraph 8, or

(b) have a sufficient period of professional experience.

(2) The reference in sub-paragraph (1)(b) to "a sufficient period of professional experience" is to not less than seven years' experience in a professional capacity in the fields of finance, law and accountancy.

Examination

8. (1) The qualification must be restricted to persons who have passed an examination (at least part of which is in writing) testing—

(a) theoretical knowledge of the subjects prescribed for the purposes of this paragraph by regulations made by the Secretary of State, and

(b) ability to apply that knowledge in practice,

and requiring a standard of attainment at least equivalent to that required to obtain a degree from a university or similar establishment in the United Kingdom.

(2) The qualification may be awarded to a person without his theoretical knowledge of a subject being tested by examination if he has passed a university or other examination of equivalent standard in that subject or holds a university degree or equivalent qualification in it.

(3) The qualification may be awarded to a person without his ability to apply his theoretical knowledge of a subject in practice being tested by examination if he has received practical training in that subject which is attested by an examination or diploma recognised by the Secretary of State for the purposes of this paragraph.

(4) Regulations under this paragraph are subject to negative resolution procedure.

Practical training

9. (1) The qualification must be restricted to persons who have completed at least three years' practical training of which—

(a) part was spent being trained in statutory audit work, and

(b) a substantial part was spent being trained in statutory audit work or other audit work of a description approved by the Secretary of State as being similar to statutory audit work.

(2) For the purpose of sub-paragraph (1) "statutory audit work" includes the work of a person appointed as the auditor of a person under the law of a country or territory outside the United Kingdom where it appears to the Secretary of State that the law and practice with respect to the audit of accounts is similar to that in the United Kingdom.

(3) The training must be given by persons approved by the body offering the qualification as persons whom the body is satisfied, in the light of undertakings given by them and the supervision to which they are subject (whether by the body itself or some other body or organisation), will provide adequate training.

(4) At least two-thirds of the training must be given by a person—

(a) eligible for appointment as a statutory auditor, or

(b) eligible for a corresponding appointment as an auditor under the law of [an EEA State], or part of [an EEA State] . . .

[(5) For the purpose of sub-paragraph (4), Gibraltar is to be treated as if it were an EEA State.]

Supplementary provision with respect to a sufficient period of professional experience

10. (1) Periods of theoretical instruction in the fields of finance, law and accountancy may be deducted from the required period of professional experience, provided the instruction—

(a) lasted at least one year, and

(b) is attested by an examination recognised by the Secretary of State for the purposes of this paragraph;

but the period of professional experience may not be so reduced by more than four years.

(2) The period of professional experience together with the practical training required in the case of persons satisfying the requirement in paragraph 7 by virtue of having a sufficient period of professional experience must not be shorter than the course of theoretical instruction referred to in that paragraph and the practical training required in the case of persons satisfying the requirement of that paragraph by virtue of having completed such a course.

The body offering the qualification

11. (1) The body offering the qualification must have—

(a) rules and arrangements adequate to ensure compliance with the requirements of paragraphs 6 to 10, and

(b) adequate arrangements for the effective monitoring of its continued compliance with those requirements.

(2) The arrangements must include arrangements for monitoring—

(a) the standard of the body's examinations, and

(b) the adequacy of the practical training given by the persons approved by it for that purpose.

NOTES

Para 9: words in square brackets in sub-para (4)(b) substituted by the Statutory Auditors and Third Country Auditors Regulations 2007, SI 2007/3494, reg 44, as from 6 April 2008. The words omitted from sub-para (4)(b) were repealed, and sub-para (5) was added, by the Statutory Auditors and Third Country Auditors (Amendment) (EU Exit) Regulations 2019, SI 2019/177, regs 33, 34, as from IP completion day (as defined in the European Union (Withdrawal Agreement) Act 2020, s 39).

Transfer of functions: as to the transfer of the functions of the Secretary of State under Part 42 of this Act (which includes this Schedule) see the note preceding s 1209 at **[1.1380]**.

Regulations: the Statutory Auditors and Third Country Auditors Regulations 2007, SI 2007/3494. For a summary of all statutory instruments made under this Act, see Appendix 4 at **[A4]**.

[SCHEDULE 11A
SPECIFIED PERSONS, DESCRIPTIONS, DISCLOSURES ETC FOR THE PURPOSES OF SECTION 1224A

PART 1 SPECIFIED PERSONS

[1.1527]

1. The Secretary of State.

2. The Department of Enterprise, Trade and Investment for Northern Ireland.

3. The Treasury.

4. The Bank of England.

[**5.** The Financial Conduct Authority.

5A. The Prudential Regulation Authority.]

6. The Commissioners for Her Majesty's Revenue and Customs.

7. The Lord Advocate.

8. The Director of Public Prosecutions.

9. The Director of Public Prosecutions for Northern Ireland.

10. A constable.

11. A procurator fiscal.

12. The Scottish Ministers.

13. A body designated by the Secretary of State under section 1252 (delegation of the Secretary of State's functions).

14. A recognised supervisory body.

15. A recognised qualifying body.

[**16.** The competent authority.]

17. The Independent Supervisor.

[17A. A recognised supervisory body as defined in section 1217(4) and Schedule 10 as they have effect by virtue of Schedule 5 to the Local Audit and Accountability Act 2014.

17B. A recognised qualifying body as defined in section 1219(13) as it has effect by virtue of that Schedule.

17C. A body designated by the Secretary of State under section 1252 (delegation of the Secretary of State's functions) as it has effect by virtue of that Schedule.

17D. A body with which a recognised supervisory body within the meaning of that Act is participating in arrangements for the purposes of paragraph 23 (independent monitoring of certain audits) or 24 (independent investigation of public interest cases) of Schedule 10 as it has effect by virtue of that Schedule.]]

NOTES

Inserted by the Statutory Auditors and Third Country Auditors Regulations 2007, SI 2007/3494, reg 10(2), Schedule, as from 6 April 2008.

Paras 5, 5A: substituted (for the original para 5) by the Financial Services Act 2012, s 114(1), Sch 18, Pt 2, paras 110, 124(1), (2), as from 1 April 2013.

Para 16: substituted by the Statutory Auditors and Third Country Auditors Regulations 2016, SI 2016/649, reg 15, Sch 3, Pt 5, paras 53, 73(1), (2), as from 17 June 2016.

Paras 17A–17D: added by the Local Audit and Accountability Act 2014, s 45, Sch 12, para 78, as from 1 April 2015.

Transfer of functions: as to the transfer of the functions of the Secretary of State under Part 42 of this Act (which includes this Schedule) see the note preceding s 1209 at **[1.1380]**.

[PART 2 SPECIFIED DESCRIPTIONS OF DISCLOSURES

[1.1528]

18. A disclosure for the purpose of enabling or assisting a person authorised under section 457 of this Act (persons authorised to apply to court) to exercise his functions.

19. A disclosure for the purpose of enabling or assisting an inspector appointed under Part 14 of the Companies Act 1985 (investigation of companies and their affairs, etc) to exercise his functions.

20. A disclosure for the purpose of enabling or assisting a person authorised under section 447 of the Companies Act 1985 (power to require production of documents) or section 84 of the Companies Act 1989 (c 40) (exercise of powers by officer etc) to exercise his functions.

21. A disclosure for the purpose of enabling or assisting a person appointed under section 167 of the Financial Services and Markets Act 2000 (c 8) (general investigations) to conduct an investigation to exercise his functions.

22. A disclosure for the purpose of enabling or assisting a person appointed under section 168 of the Financial Services and Markets Act 2000 (investigations in particular cases) to conduct an investigation to exercise his functions.

23. A disclosure for the purpose of enabling or assisting a person appointed under section 169(1)(b) of the Financial Services and Markets Act 2000 (investigation in support of overseas regulator) to conduct an investigation to exercise his functions.

24. A disclosure for the purpose of enabling or assisting the body corporate responsible for administering the scheme referred to in section 225 of the Financial Services and Markets Act 2000 (the ombudsman scheme) to exercise its functions.

25. A disclosure for the purpose of enabling or assisting a person appointed under paragraph 4 (the panel of ombudsmen) or 5 (the Chief Ombudsman) of Schedule 17 to the Financial Services and Markets Act 2000 to exercise his functions.

26. A disclosure for the purpose of enabling or assisting a person appointed under regulations made under section 262(1) and (2)(k) of the Financial Services and Markets Act 2000 (investigations into open-ended investment companies) to conduct an investigation to exercise his functions.

27. A disclosure for the purpose of enabling or assisting a person appointed under section 284 of the Financial Services and Markets Act 2000 (investigations into affairs of certain collective investment schemes) to conduct an investigation to exercise his functions.

28. A disclosure for the purpose of enabling or assisting the investigator appointed under [section 84 of the Financial Services Act 2012] (arrangements for investigation of complaints) to exercise his functions.

29. A disclosure for the purpose of enabling or assisting a person appointed by the Treasury to hold an inquiry into matters relating to financial services (including an inquiry under [section 69 of the Financial Services Act 2012]) to exercise his functions.

30. A disclosure for the purpose of enabling or assisting the Secretary of State or the Treasury to exercise any of their functions under any of the following—

(a) the Companies Acts;
(b) Part 5 of the Criminal Justice Act 1993 (c 36) (insider dealing);
(c) the Insolvency Act 1986 (c 45);
(d) the Company Directors Disqualification Act 1986 (c 46);
(e) Part 42 of this Act (statutory auditors)
(f) Part 3 (investigations and powers to obtain information) or 7 (financial markets and insolvency) of the Companies Act 1989 (c 40);
(g) the Financial Services and Markets Act 2000.

31. A disclosure for the purpose of enabling or assisting the Scottish Ministers to exercise their functions under the enactments relating to insolvency.

32. A disclosure for the purpose of enabling or assisting the Department of Enterprise, Trade and Investment for Northern Ireland to exercise any powers conferred on it by the enactments relating to companies or insolvency.

33. A disclosure for the purpose of enabling or assisting a person appointed or authorised by the Department of Enterprise, Trade and Investment for Northern Ireland under the enactments relating to companies or insolvency to exercise his functions.

34. A disclosure for the purpose of enabling or assisting the Pensions Regulator to exercise the functions conferred on it by or by virtue of any of the following—

(a) the Pension Schemes Act 1993 (c 48);
(b) the Pensions Act 1995 (c 26);
(c) the Welfare Reform and Pensions Act 1999 (c 30);
(d) the Pensions Act 2004 (c 35);
(e) any enactment in force in Northern Ireland corresponding to any of those enactments.

35. A disclosure for the purpose of enabling or assisting the Board of the Pension Protection Fund to exercise the functions conferred on it by or by virtue of Part 2 of the Pensions Act 2004 or any enactment in force in Northern Ireland corresponding to that Part.

36. A disclosure for the purpose of enabling or assisting—

(a) the Bank of England,
(b) the European Central Bank, or
(c) the central bank of any country or territory outside the United Kingdom, to exercise its functions.

37. A disclosure for the purpose of enabling or assisting the Commissioners for Her Majesty's Revenue and Customs to exercise their functions.

38. A disclosure for the purpose of enabling or assisting organs of the Society of Lloyd's (being organs constituted by or under the Lloyd's Act 1982 (c xiv)) to exercise their functions under or by virtue of the Lloyd's Acts 1871 to 1982.

39. A disclosure for the purpose of enabling or assisting the [Competition and Markets Authority] to exercise its functions under any of the following—

(a) the Fair Trading Act 1973 (c 41);
(b), (c) . . .
(d) the Competition Act 1980 (c 21);
(e) the Competition Act 1998 (c 41);
(f) the Financial Services and Markets Act 2000 (c 8);
(g) the Enterprise Act 2002 (c 40);
(h) the Control of Misleading Advertisements Regulations 1988 (SI 1988/915);
[(i) Schedule 3 to the Consumer Rights Act 2015;]
[(j) Parts 3 and 4 of the Enterprise and Regulatory Reform Act 2013].

40. . . .

41. A disclosure with a view to the institution of, or otherwise for the purposes of, proceedings before the Competition Appeal Tribunal.

42. A disclosure for the purpose of enabling or assisting an enforcer under Part 8 of the Enterprise Act 2002 (enforcement of consumer legislation) to exercise its functions under that Part.

43. A disclosure for the purpose of enabling or assisting the Takeover Panel to perform any of its functions under Part 28 of this Act (takeovers etc).

44. A disclosure for the purpose of enabling or assisting the Charity Commission to exercise its functions.

45. A disclosure for the purpose of enabling or assisting the Attorney General to exercise his functions in connection with charities.

46. A disclosure for the purpose of enabling or assisting the [Gambling Commission] to exercise its functions under sections 5 to 10 (licensing) and 15 (power of Secretary of State to require information) of the National Lottery etc Act 1993 (c 39).

47. A disclosure by the [Gambling Commission] to [the Comptroller and Auditor General] for the purpose of enabling or assisting the Comptroller and Auditor General to carry out an examination under Part 2 of the National Audit Act 1983 (c 44) into the economy, effectiveness and efficiency with which the [Gambling Commission] has used its resources in discharging its functions under sections 5 to 10 of the National Lottery etc Act 1993.

[48. A disclosure for the purposes of enabling or assisting a regulator under Schedule 3 to the Consumer Rights Act 2015 other than the Competition and Markets Authority to exercise its functions under that Schedule.]

49. A disclosure for the purpose of enabling or assisting an enforcement authority under [the Consumer Contracts (Information, Cancellation and Additional Charges) Regulations 2013] to exercise its functions under those Regulations.

50. A disclosure for the purpose of enabling or assisting an enforcement authority under the Financial Services (Distance Marketing) Regulations 2004 (SI 2004/2095) to exercise its functions under those Regulations.

51. A disclosure for the purpose of enabling or assisting a local weights and measures authority in England and Wales to exercise its functions under section 230(2) of the Enterprise Act 2002 (c 40) (notice of intention to prosecute, etc).

[51A. A disclosure for the purpose of enabling or assisting the lead enforcement authority (as defined in section 33(1) of the Estate Agents Act 1979) to exercise its functions under the Estate Agents Act 1979.]

52. A disclosure for the purpose of enabling or assisting the [Financial Conduct Authority or the Prudential Regulation Authority] to exercise its functions under any of the following—

(a) the legislation relating to friendly societies . . . ;
[(aa) the Consumer Credit Act 1974;]

[(ab) the Credit Unions Act 1979;]
(b) the Building Societies Act 1986 (c 53);
(c) Part 7 of the Companies Act 1989 (c 40) (financial markets and insolvency);
(d) the Financial Services and Markets Act 2000 (c 8);
[(e) the Co-operative and Community Benefit Societies Act 2014].

53. . . .

54. A disclosure for the purpose of enabling or assisting a body corporate established in accordance with section 212(1) of the Financial Services and Markets Act 2000 (compensation scheme manager) to exercise its functions.

55. A disclosure for the purpose of enabling or assisting a recognised investment exchange[, a recognised clearing house or a recognised CSD] to exercise its functions as such.

"Recognised investment exchange"[, "recognised clearing house" and "recognised CSD"] have the same meaning as in section 285 of the Financial Services and Markets Act 2000.

56. A disclosure for the purpose of enabling or assisting a person [who is an operator of a relevant system for the purposes of the Uncertificated Securities Regulations 2001 (SI 2001/3755)] to exercise his functions.

57. A disclosure for the purpose of enabling or assisting a body designated under section 326(1) of the Financial Services and Markets Act 2000 (designated professional bodies) to exercise its functions in its capacity as a body designated under that section.

58. A disclosure with a view to the institution of, or otherwise for the purposes of, civil proceedings arising under or by virtue of the Financial Services and Markets Act 2000.

59. A disclosure for the purpose of enabling or assisting a body designated by order under section 1252 of this Act (delegation of functions of Secretary of State) to exercise its functions under Part 42 of this Act (statutory auditors).

60. A disclosure for the purpose of enabling or assisting a recognised supervisory or qualifying body, within the meaning of Part 42 of this Act, to exercise its functions as such.

61. A disclosure for the purpose of making available to an audited person information relating to a statutory audit of that person's accounts.

[62. A disclosure for the purpose of making available to the public information relating to inspections carried out under regulation 9 (monitoring of audits by the competent authority) of the Statutory Auditors and Third Country Auditors Regulations 2016 (SI 2016/649), provided such information does not identify any audited person.]

63. A disclosure for the purpose of enabling or assisting an official receiver (including the Accountant in Bankruptcy in Scotland and the Official Assignee in Northern Ireland) to exercise his functions under the enactments relating to insolvency.

64. . . .

65. A disclosure for the purpose of enabling or assisting a body that is for the time being a recognised professional body for the purposes of section 391 of the Insolvency Act 1986 (recognised professional bodies) to exercise its functions as such.

66. A disclosure for the purpose of enabling or assisting an overseas regulatory authority to exercise its regulatory functions.

"Overseas regulatory authority" and "regulatory functions" have the same meaning as in section 82 of the Companies Act 1989.

67. A disclosure for the purpose of enabling or assisting the Regulator of Community Interest Companies to exercise functions under the Companies (Audit, Investigations and Community Enterprise) Act 2004 (c 27).

68. A disclosure with a view to the institution of, or otherwise for the purposes of, criminal proceedings.

69. A disclosure for the purpose of enabling or assisting a person authorised by the Secretary of State under Part 2, 3 or 4 of the Proceeds of Crime Act 2002 (c 29) to exercise his functions.

70. A disclosure with a view to the institution of, or otherwise for the purposes of, proceedings on an application under section 6, 7 or 8 of the Company Directors Disqualification Act 1986 (c 46) (disqualification for unfitness).

[71. A disclosure with a view to the institution of, or otherwise for the purposes of, proceedings before the Upper Tribunal in respect of—
[(a) a decision of the Financial Conduct Authority;
(aa) a decision of the Prudential Regulation Authority;]
(b) a decision of the Bank of England; or
(c) a decision of a person relating to the assessment of any compensation or consideration under the Banking (Special Provisions) Act 2008 or the Banking Act 2009.]

72. A disclosure for the purposes of proceedings before the Financial Services Tribunal by virtue of the Financial Services and Markets Act 2000 (Transitional Provisions) (Partly Completed Procedures) Order 2001 (SI 2001/3592).

73. A disclosure for the purposes of proceedings before [a tribunal in relation to a decision of the Pensions Regulator].

74. A disclosure for the purpose of enabling or assisting a body appointed under section 14 of the Companies (Audit, Investigations and Community Enterprise) Act 2004 (supervision of periodic accounts and reports of issuers of listed securities) to exercise functions mentioned in subsection (2) of that section.

75. A disclosure with a view to the institution of, or otherwise for the purposes of, disciplinary proceedings relating to the performance by a relevant lawyer, foreign lawyer, auditor, accountant, valuer or actuary of his professional duties.

In this paragraph—

"foreign lawyer" means a person (other than a relevant lawyer) who is a foreign lawyer within the meaning of section 89(9) of the Courts and Legal Services Act 1990;

"relevant lawyer" means—

(a) a person who, for the purposes of the Legal Services Act 2007, is an authorised person in relation to an activity which constitutes a reserved legal activity (within the meaning of that Act),

(b) a solicitor or barrister in Northern Ireland, or

(c) a solicitor or advocate in Scotland.

76. A disclosure with a view to the institution of, or otherwise for the purposes of, disciplinary proceedings relating to the performance by a public servant of his duties.

"Public servant" means an officer or employee of the Crown.

77. A disclosure for the purpose of the provision of a summary or collection of information framed in such a way as not to enable the identity of any person to whom the information relates to be ascertained.

78. A disclosure in pursuance of any [retained EU obligation].]

NOTES

Inserted by the Statutory Auditors and Third Country Auditors Regulations 2007, SI 2007/3494, reg 10(2), Schedule, as from 6 April 2008.

Paras 28, 29: words in square brackets substituted by the Financial Services Act 2012, s 114(1), Sch 18, Pt 2, paras 110, 124(1), (3), as from 1 April 2013.

Para 39: words in first pair of square brackets substituted, and sub-para (j) added, by the Enterprise and Regulatory Reform Act 2013 (Competition) (Consequential, Transitional and Saving Provisions) Order 2014, SI 2014/892, art 2, Sch 1, Pt 2, paras 167, 169(a), as from 1 April 2014. Sub-para (b) repealed by the Financial Services and Markets Act 2000 (Regulated Activities) (Amendment) (No 2) Order 2013, SI 2013/1881, art 28, Schedule, Pt 1, para 11(b), as from 1 April 2014. Sub-para (c) repealed by the Public Bodies (Abolition of the National Consumer Council and Transfer of the Office of Fair Trading's Functions in relation to Estate Agents etc) Order 2014, SI 2014/631, art 5(3), Sch 2, para 5(1), (3)(a), as from 31 March 2014. Sub-para (i) substituted by the Consumer Rights Act 2015, s 75, Sch 4, paras 36, 38(1), (2), as from 1 October 2015 (for transitional provisions in relation to the continued application of the Unfair Terms in Consumer Contracts Regulations 1999, see the Consumer Rights Act 2015 (Commencement No 3, Transitional Provisions, Savings and Consequential Amendments) Order 2015, SI 2015/1630, art 6).

Para 40: repealed by SI 2014/892, art 2, Sch 1, Pt 2, paras 167, 169(b), as from 1 April 2014.

Para 46: words in square brackets substituted by the Public Bodies (Merger of the Gambling Commission and the National Lottery Commission) Order 2013, SI 2013/2329, art 4, Schedule, para 29(b)(i), as from 1 October 2013.

Para 47: words in first and third pairs of square brackets substituted by SI 2013/2329, art 4, Schedule, para 29(b)(ii), as from 1 October 2013. Words in second pair of square brackets substituted by the Budget Responsibility and National Audit Act 2011, s 26, Sch 5, Pt 2, paras 29, 31, as from 1 April 2012.

Para 48: substituted by the Consumer Rights Act 2015, s 75, Sch 4, paras 36, 38(1), (3), as from 1 October 2015 (for transitional provisions, see the first note relating to the 2015 Act above).

Para 49: words in square brackets substituted by the Consumer Contracts (Information, Cancellation and Additional Charges) Regulations 2013, SI 2013/3134, reg 47, Sch 4, para 6(b), as from 13 June 2014, in relation to contracts entered into on or after that date.

Para 51A: inserted by SI 2014/631, art 5(3), Sch 2, para 5(1), (3)(b), as from 31 March 2014.

Para 52: words in first pair of square brackets substituted by the Financial Services Act 2012, s 114(1), Sch 18, Pt 2, paras 110, 124(1), (3)(c), as from 1 April 2013. Sub-para (aa) inserted by the Financial Services Act 2012 (Consumer Credit) Order 2013, SI 2013/1882, art 10(4)(b), as from 1 April 2014. Words omitted from sub-para (a) repealed, and sub-paras (ab), (e) inserted, by the Co-operative and Community Benefit Societies Act 2014, s 151, Sch 4, Pt 2, paras 99, 103, as from 1 August 2014.

Para 53: repealed by the Financial Services Act 2012, s 114(2), Sch 19, as from 1 April 2013.

Para 55: words in square brackets substituted by the Central Securities Depositories Regulations 2017, SI 2017/1064, reg 10, Schedule, para 11(1), (4), as from 28 November 2017.

Para 56: words in square brackets substituted by the Uncertificated Securities (Amendment and EU Exit) Regulations 2019, SI 2019/679, reg 2(1), (3), as from 27 March 2019, for transitional provisions and savings see regs 11, 12 of the 2019 Regulations at **[12.125]** et seq).

Para 62: substituted by the Statutory Auditors and Third Country Auditors Regulations 2017, SI 2017/516, reg 13(1), (9), as from 1 May 2017.

Para 64: repealed by the Deregulation Act 2015, s 19, Sch 6, Pt 7, para 22(15)(b), as from 1 October 2015.

Para 71: substituted by the Transfer of Tribunal Functions Order 2010, SI 2010/22, art 5(1), Sch 2, paras 141, 143(a), as from 6 April 2010. Sub-paras (a), (aa) substituted (for the original sub-para (a)) by the Financial Services Act 2012, s 114(1), Sch 18, Pt 2, paras 110, 124(1), (3)(d), as from 1 April 2013.

Para 73: words in square brackets substituted by SI 2010/22, art 5(1), Sch 2, paras 141, 143(b), as from 6 April 2010.

Para 78: words in square brackets substituted by the Statutory Auditors and Third Country Auditors (Amendment) (EU Exit) Regulations 2019, SI 2019/177, regs 33, 35(a), as from IP completion day (as defined in the European Union (Withdrawal Agreement) Act 2020, s 39).

Transfer of functions: as to the transfer of the functions of the Secretary of State under Part 42 of this Act (which includes this Schedule) see the note preceding s 1209 at **[1.1380]**.

[PART 3 OVERSEAS REGULATORY BODIES

[1.1529]

79. A disclosure is made in accordance with this Part of this Schedule if it is made to an [approved third country competent authority] in accordance with section 1253B (requests from [approved third country competent authorities]).

80. A disclosure is made in accordance with this Part of this Schedule if it is—

(a) a transfer of [audit working papers and investigation reports] to a third country competent authority in accordance with rules imposed under paragraph 16A of Schedule 10 (transfer of papers to third countries), or

(b) a disclosure other than a transfer of [audit working papers and investigation reports] made to a third country competent authority for the purpose of enabling or assisting the authority to exercise its functions.]

NOTES

Inserted by the Statutory Auditors and Third Country Auditors Regulations 2007, SI 2007/3494, reg 10(2), Schedule, as from 6 April 2008.

Para 79: words in square brackets substituted by the Statutory Auditors and Third Country Auditors (Amendment) (EU Exit) Regulations 2019, SI 2019/177, regs 33, 35(b), as from IP completion day (as defined in the European Union (Withdrawal Agreement) Act 2020, s 39).

Para 80: words in square brackets substituted by the Statutory Auditors and Third Country Auditors Regulations 2016, SI 2016/649, reg 15, Sch 3, Pt 3, para 73(1), (3), as from 17 June 2016, in relation to financial years beginning on or after that date.

Transfer of functions: as to the transfer of the functions of the Secretary of State under Part 42 of this Act (which includes this Schedule) see the note preceding s 1209 at **[1.1380]**.

SCHEDULE 12
ARRANGEMENTS IN WHICH REGISTERED THIRD COUNTRY AUDITORS ARE REQUIRED TO PARTICIPATE

Section 1242

Arrangements for independent monitoring of audits of [UK-traded third country companies]

[1.1530]

1. (1) The arrangements referred to in section 1242(1)(a) are appropriate arrangements—

(a) for enabling the performance by the registered third country auditor of [functions related to the audit of [UK-traded third country companies]] to be monitored by means of inspections carried out under the arrangements, and

(b) for ensuring that the carrying out of such monitoring and inspections is done independently of the registered third country auditor.

(2) . . .

Arrangements for independent investigations for disciplinary purposes

2. [(1) The arrangements referred to in section 1242(1)(b) are appropriate arrangements—

(a) for the carrying out of investigations into matters arising in connection with the performance of functions related to the audit of [UK-traded third country companies] by the registered third country auditor,

(b) where it appears to be desirable following the conclusion of such investigations—

(i) for the holding, subject to sub-paragraph (1A), of disciplinary hearings relating to the registered third country auditor,

(ii) unless the interests of justice otherwise require, for any such hearings to be held in public, and

(iii) for decisions to be made as to whether (and, if so, what) disciplinary action should be taken against the registered third country auditor, and

(c) for ensuring that the carrying out of those investigations, the holding of those hearings and the making of those decisions are done independently of the registered third country auditor.

(1A) The arrangements may provide that decisions to take disciplinary action, and decisions as to what that action should be, may be made in respect of a registered third country auditor without the holding of a disciplinary hearing relating to that registered third country auditor where the registered third country auditor agrees in writing that such a hearing need not be held.]

(2) In this paragraph—

"disciplinary action" includes the imposition of a fine; and

. . .

Supplementary: arrangements to operate independently of third country auditor

3. (1) This paragraph applies for the purposes of—

(a) paragraph 1(1)(b), or

(b) [paragraph 2(1)(c)].

(2) Arrangements are not to be regarded as appropriate for the purpose of ensuring that a thing is done independently of the registered third country auditor unless they are designed to ensure that the registered third country auditor—

(a) will have no involvement in the appointment or selection of any of the persons who are to be responsible for doing that thing, and

(b) will not otherwise be involved in the doing of that thing.

(3) Sub-paragraph (2) imposes a minimum requirement and does not preclude the possibility that additional criteria may need to be satisfied in order for the arrangements to be regarded as appropriate for the purpose in question.

Supplementary: funding of arrangements

4. (1) The registered third country auditor must pay any of the costs of maintaining any relevant arrangements which the arrangements provide are to be paid by it.

(2) For this purpose "relevant arrangements" are arrangements within paragraph 1 or 2 in which the registered third country auditor is obliged to participate.

Supplementary: scope of arrangements

5. Arrangements may qualify as arrangements within either of paragraphs 1 and 2 even though the matters for which they provide are more extensive in any respect than those mentioned in the applicable paragraph.

Specification of particular arrangements by the Secretary of State

6. (1) If there exist two or more sets of arrangements within paragraph 1 or within paragraph 2, the obligation of a registered third country auditor under section 1242(1)(a) or (b), as the case may be, is to participate in such set of arrangements as the Secretary of State may by order specify.

(2) An order under sub-paragraph (1) is subject to negative resolution procedure.

NOTES

Para 1: words "UK-traded third country companies" in the heading preceding this paragraph, and in sub-para (1)(a), substituted by the Statutory Auditors and Third Country Auditors (Amendment) (EU Exit) Regulations 2019, SI 2019/177, regs 33, 36(a), (b), as from IP completion day (as defined in the European Union (Withdrawal Agreement) Act 2020, s 39). Words in first (outer) pair of square brackets in sub-para (1)(a) substituted, and sub-para (2) repealed, by the Statutory Auditors and Third Country Auditors Regulations 2007, SI 2007/3494, reg 33(1)–(3), as from 29 June 2008.

Para 2: sub-paras (1), (1A) substituted (for the original sub-para (1)) by the Statutory Auditors and Third Country Auditors Regulations 2013, SI 2013/1672, reg 17(1), (2), as from 1 October 2013. Words in square brackets in sub-para (1)(a) substituted by SI 2019/177, regs 33, 36(c), as from IP completion day (as defined in the European Union (Withdrawal Agreement) Act 2020, s 39). Definition omitted from sub-para (2) repealed by SI 2007/3494, reg 33(1), (4), as from 29 June 2008.

Para 3: words in square brackets substituted by SI 2013/1672, reg 17(1), (3), as from 1 October 2013.

Transfer of functions: as to the transfer of the functions of the Secretary of State under Part 42 of this Act (which includes this Schedule) see the note preceding s 1209 at **[1.1380]**.

SCHEDULE 13
SUPPLEMENTARY PROVISIONS WITH RESPECT TO DELEGATION ORDER

Section 1252

Operation of this Schedule

[1.1531]

1. (1) This Schedule has effect in relation to a body designated by a delegation order under section 1252 as follows—

(a) paragraphs 2 to 12 have effect in relation to the body where it is established by the order;

(b) paragraphs 2 and 6 to 11 have effect in relation to the body where it is an existing body;

(c) paragraph 13 has effect in relation to the body where it is an existing body that is an unincorporated association.

(2) In their operation in accordance with sub-paragraph (1)(b), paragraphs 2 and 6 apply only in relation to—

(a) things done by or in relation to the body in or in connection with the exercise of functions transferred to it by the delegation order, and

(b) functions of the body which are functions so transferred.

(3) Any power conferred by this Schedule to make provision by order is a power to make provision by an order under section 1252.

Status

2. The body is not to be regarded as acting on behalf of the Crown and its members, officers and employees are not to be regarded as Crown servants.

Name, members and chairman

3. (1) The body is to be known by such name as may be specified in the delegation order.

(2) The body is to consist of such persons (not being less than eight) as the Secretary of State may appoint after such consultation as he thinks appropriate.

(3) The chairman of the body is to be such person as the Secretary of State may appoint from among its members.

(4) The Secretary of State may make provision by order as to—

(a) the terms on which the members of the body are to hold and vacate office;

(b) the terms on which a person appointed as chairman is to hold and vacate the office of chairman.

Financial provisions

4. (1) The body must pay to its chairman and members such remuneration, and such allowances in respect of expenses properly incurred by them in the performance of their duties, as the Secretary of State may determine.

(2) As regards any chairman or member in whose case the Secretary of State so determines, the body must pay or make provision for the payment of—

(a) such pension, allowance or gratuity to or in respect of that person on his retirement or death, or

(b) such contributions or other payment towards the provision of such a pension, allowance or gratuity,

as the Secretary of State may determine.

(3) Where—

(a) a person ceases to be a member of the body otherwise than on the expiry of his term of office, and

(b) it appears to the Secretary of State that there are special circumstances which make it right for that person to receive compensation,

the body must make a payment to him by way of compensation of such amount as the Secretary of State may determine.

Proceedings

5. (1) The delegation order may contain such provision as the Secretary of State considers appropriate with respect to the proceedings of the body.

(2) The delegation order may, in particular—

(a) authorise the body to discharge any functions by means of committees consisting wholly or partly of members of the body;

(b) provide that the validity of proceedings of the body, or of any such committee, is not affected by any vacancy among the members or any defect in the appointment of any member.

Fees

6. (1) The body may retain fees payable to it.

(2) The fees must be applied for—

(a) meeting the expenses of the body in discharging its functions, and

(b) any purposes incidental to those functions.

(3) Those expenses include any expenses incurred by the body on such staff, accommodation, services and other facilities as appear to it to be necessary or expedient for the proper performance of its functions.

(4) In prescribing the amount of fees in the exercise of the functions transferred to it the body must prescribe such fees as appear to it sufficient to defray those expenses, taking one year with another.

(5) Any exercise by the body of the power to prescribe fees requires the approval of the Secretary of State.

(6) The Secretary of State may, after consultation with the body, by order vary or revoke any regulations prescribing fees made by the body.

Legislative functions

7. (1) Regulations or an order made by the body in the exercise of the functions transferred to it must be made by instrument in writing, but not by statutory instrument.

(2) The instrument must specify the provision of this Part of this Act under which it is made.

(3) The Secretary of State may by order impose such requirements as he thinks necessary or expedient as to the circumstances and manner in which the body must consult on any regulations or order it proposes to make.

(4) Nothing in this Part applies to make regulations or an order made by the body subject to negative resolution procedure or affirmative resolution procedure.

8. (1) Immediately after an instrument is made it must be printed and made available to the public with or without payment.

(2) A person is not to be taken to have contravened any regulation or order if he shows that at the time of the alleged contravention the instrument containing the regulation or order had not been made available as required by this paragraph.

9. (1) The production of a printed copy of an instrument purporting to be made by the body on which is endorsed a certificate signed by an officer of the body authorised by it for the purpose and stating—

(a) that the instrument was made by the body,

(b) that the copy is a true copy of the instrument, and

(c) that on a specified date the instrument was made available to the public as required by paragraph 8,

is evidence (or, in Scotland, sufficient evidence) of the facts stated in the certificate.

(2) A certificate purporting to be signed as mentioned in sub-paragraph (1) is to be deemed to have been duly signed unless the contrary is shown.

(3) Any person wishing in any legal proceedings to cite an instrument made by the body may require the body to cause a copy of it to be endorsed with such a certificate as is mentioned in this paragraph.

Report and accounts

10. (1) The body must, at least once in each calendar year for which the delegation order is in force, make a report to the Secretary of State on—

(a) the discharge of the functions transferred to it, and

(b) such other matters as the Secretary of State may by order require.

(2) The delegation order may modify sub-paragraph (1) as it has effect in relation to the calendar year in which the order comes into force or is revoked.

(3) The Secretary of State must lay before Parliament copies of each report received by him under this paragraph.

(4) The following provisions of this paragraph apply as follows—

(a) sub-paragraphs (5) and (6) apply only where the body is established by the order, and

(b) sub-paragraphs (7) and (8) apply only where the body is an existing body.

(5) The Secretary of State may, with the consent of the Treasury, give directions to the body with respect to its accounts and the audit of its accounts.

(6) A person may only be appointed as auditor of the body if he is eligible for appointment as a statutory auditor.

(7) Unless the body is a company to which section 394 (duty to prepare individual company accounts) applies, the Secretary of State may, with the consent of the Treasury, give directions to the body with respect to its accounts and the audit of its accounts.

(8) Whether or not the body is a company to which section 394 applies, the Secretary of State may direct that any provisions of this Act specified in the directions are to apply to the body, with or without any modifications so specified.

Other supplementary provisions

11. (1) The transfer of a function to a body designated by a delegation order does not affect anything previously done in the exercise of the function transferred; and the resumption of a function so transferred does not affect anything previously done in exercise of the function resumed.

(2) The Secretary of State may by order make such transitional and other supplementary provision as he thinks necessary or expedient in relation to the transfer or resumption of a function.

(3) The provision that may be made in connection with the transfer of a function includes, in particular, provision—

(a) for modifying or excluding any provision of this Part of this Act in its application to the function transferred;

(b) for applying to the body designated by the delegation order, in connection with the function transferred, any provision applying to the Secretary of State which is contained in or made under any other enactment;

(c) for the transfer of any property, rights or liabilities from the Secretary of State to that body;

(d) for the carrying on and completion by that body of anything in the process of being done by the Secretary of State when the order takes effect;

(e) for the substitution of that body for the Secretary of State in any instrument, contract or legal proceedings.

(4) The provision that may be made in connection with the resumption of a function includes, in particular, provision—

(a) for the transfer of any property, rights or liabilities from that body to the Secretary of State;

(b) for the carrying on and completion by the Secretary of State of anything in the process of being done by that body when the order takes effect;

(c) for the substitution of the Secretary of State for that body in any instrument, contract or legal proceedings.

12. Where a delegation order is revoked, the Secretary of State may by order make provision—

(a) for the payment of compensation to persons ceasing to be employed by the body established by the delegation order;

(b) as to the winding up and dissolution of the body.

13. (1) This paragraph applies where the body is an unincorporated association.

(2) Any relevant proceedings may be brought by or against the body in the name of any body corporate whose constitution provides for the establishment of the body.

(3) In sub-paragraph (2) "relevant proceedings" means proceedings brought in or in connection with the exercise of any transferred function.

(4) In relation to proceedings brought as mentioned in sub-paragraph (2), any reference in paragraph 11(3)(e) or (4)(c) to the body replacing or being replaced by the Secretary of State in any legal proceedings is to be read with the appropriate modifications.

NOTES

Orders and Regulations: the Statutory Auditors (Amendment of Companies Act 2006 and Delegation of Functions etc) Order 2012, SI 2012/1741 at **[4.430]** (see further the note preceding s 1209 at **[1.1380]**); the Local Audit (Delegation of Functions) and Statutory Audit (Delegation of Functions) Order 2014, SI 2014/2009; the Statutory Auditors and Third Country Auditors Regulations 2016, SI 2016/649 at **[4.650]**. For a summary of all statutory instruments made under this Act, see Appendix 4 at **[A4]**.

SCHEDULE 14
STATUTORY AUDITORS: CONSEQUENTIAL AMENDMENTS

Section 1264

[1.1532]

(Amends the Companies (Audit, Investigations and Community Enterprise) Act 2004, s 16 at **[5.216]**.)

SCHEDULE 15
TRANSPARENCY OBLIGATIONS AND RELATED MATTERS: MINOR AND CONSEQUENTIAL AMENDMENTS

Section 1272

PART 1 AMENDMENTS OF THE FINANCIAL SERVICES AND MARKETS ACT 2000

[1.1533]

(Amends FSMA 2000, ss 73, 73A, 90 (and the preceding heading), 91, 96B, 97, 99, 102A, 103, 429 (see **[7.1]** *et seq.)*

NOTES

Paras 2, 9 (which amended ss73 and 99 of the 2000 Act) were repealed by the Financial Services Act 2012, s 114(2), Sch 19, as from 1 April 2013.

PART 2 AMENDMENTS OF THE COMPANIES (AUDIT, INVESTIGATIONS AND COMMUNITY ENTERPRISE) ACT 2004

[1.1534]

(Amends the Companies (Audit, Investigations and Community Enterprise) Act 2004, ss 14, 15 at **[5.209]**, **[5.210]**.)

SCHEDULE 16
REPEALS

Section 1295

COMPANY LAW REPEALS (GREAT BRITAIN)

[1.1535]

Short title and chapter	*Extent of repeal*
Companies Act 1985 (c 6)	Sections 1 to 430F. In section 437— (a) in subsection (1), the second sentence, and (b) subsections (1B) and (1C). Section 438. In section 439— (a) in subsection (2), ", or is ordered to pay the whole or any part of the costs of proceedings brought under section 438",

Short title and chapter	Extent of repeal
	(b) subsections (3) and (7), and
	(c) in subsection (8), "; and any such liability imposed by subsection (2) is (subject as mentioned above) a liability also to indemnify all persons against liability under subsection (3)".
	Section 442(2).
	Section 446.
	In section 448(7), the words "and liable to a fine." to the end.
	Section 449(7).
	Section 450(4).
	Section 451(3).
	In section 453(1A)—
	(a) paragraph (b), and
	(b) paragraph (d) and the word "and" preceding it.
	Section 453A(6).
	Sections 458 to 461.
	Sections 651 to 746.
	Schedules 1 to 15B.
	Schedules 20 to 25.
Insolvency Act 1985 (c 65)	Schedule 6.
Insolvency Act 1986 (c 45)	In Schedule 13, in Part 1, the entries relating to the following provisions of the Companies Act 1985—
	(a) section 13(4),
	(b) section 44(7),
	(c) section 103(7),
	(d) section 131(7),
	(e) section 140(2),
	(f) section 156(3),
	(g) section 173(4),
	(h) section 196,
	(i) section 380(4),
	(j) section 461(6),
	(k) section 462(5),
	(l) section 463(2),
	(m) section 463(3),
	(n) section 464(6),
	(o) section 657(2),
	(p) section 658(1), and
	(q) section 711(2).
Building Societies Act 1986 (c 53)	Section 102C(5).
Finance Act 1988 (c 39)	In section 117(3), from the beginning to "that section";".
	In section 117(4), the words "and (3)".
Water Act 1989 (c 15)	In Schedule 25, paragraph 71(3).
Companies Act 1989 (c 40)	Sections 1 to 22.
	Section 56(5).
	Sections 57 and 58.
	Section 64(2).
	Section 66(3).
	Section 71.
	Sections 92 to 110.
	Sections 113 to 138.
	Section 139(1) to (3).
	Sections 141 to 143.
	Section 144(1) to (3) and (6).
	Section 207.
	Schedules 1 to 9.

Short title and chapter	*Extent of repeal*
	In Schedule 10, paragraphs 1 to 24.
	Schedules 15 to 17.
	In Schedule 18, paragraphs 32 to 38.
	In Schedule 19, paragraphs 1 to 9 and 11 to 21.
Age of Legal Capacity (Scotland) Act 1991 (c 50)	In Schedule 1, paragraph 39.
Water Consolidation (Consequential Provisions) Act 1991 (c 60)	In Schedule 1, paragraph 40(2).
Charities Act 1992 (c 41)	In Schedule 6, paragraph 11.
Charities Act 1993 (c 10)	In Schedule 6, paragraph 20.
Criminal Justice Act 1993 (c 36)	In Schedule 5, paragraph 4.
Welsh Language Act 1993 (c 38)	Section 30.
Pension Schemes Act 1993 (c 48)	In Schedule 8, paragraph 16.
Trade Marks Act 1994 (c 26)	In Schedule 4, in paragraph 1(2), the reference to the Companies Act 1985.
Deregulation and Contracting Out Act 1994 (c 40)	Section 13(1).
	Schedule 5.
	In Schedule 16, paragraphs 8 to 10.
Requirements of Writing (Scotland) Act 1995 (c 7)	In Schedule 4, paragraphs 51 to 56.
Criminal Procedure (Consequential Provisions) (Scotland) Act 1995 (c 40)	In Schedule 4, paragraph 56(3) and (4).
Disability Discrimination Act 1995 (c 50)	In Schedule 6, paragraph 4.
Financial Services and Markets Act 2000 (c 8)	Section 143.
	Section 263.
Limited Liability Partnerships Act 2000 (c 12)	In the Schedule, paragraph 1.
Political Parties, Elections and Referendums Act 2000 (c 41)	Sections 139 and 140.
	Schedule 19.
	In Schedule 23, paragraphs 12 and 13.
Criminal Justice and Police Act 2001 (c 16)	Section 45.
	In Schedule 2, paragraph 17.
Enterprise Act 2002 (c 40)	In Schedule 17, paragraphs 3 to 8.
Companies (Audit, Investigations and Community Enterprise) Act 2004 (c 27)	Sections 7 to 10.
	Section 11(1).
	Sections 12 and 13.
	Sections 19 and 20.
	Schedule 1.
	In Schedule 2, paragraphs 5 to 10, 22 to 24 and 26.
	In Schedule 6, paragraphs 1 to 9.
Civil Partnership Act 2004 (c 33)	In Schedule 27, paragraphs 99 to 105.
Constitutional Reform Act 2005 (c 4)	In Schedule 11, in paragraph 4(3), the reference to the Companies Act 1985.

REPEALS AND REVOCATIONS RELATING TO NORTHERN IRELAND

Short title and chapter	*Extent of repeal or revocation*
Companies (Northern Ireland) Order 1986 (SI 1986/1032 (NI 6))	The whole Order.
Companies Consolidation (Consequential Provisions) (Northern Ireland) Order 1986 (SI 1986/1035 (NI 9))	The whole Order.
Business Names (Northern Ireland) Order 1986 (SI 1986/1033 (NI 7))	The whole Order.
Industrial Relations (Northern Ireland) Order 1987 (SI 1987/936 NI 9))	Article 3.

Short title and chapter	Extent of repeal or revocation
Finance Act 1988 (c 39)	In section 117(3), the words from "and for" to the end.
Companies (Northern Ireland) Order 1989 (SI 1989/2404 (NI 18))	The whole Order.
Insolvency (Northern Ireland) Order 1989 (SI 1989/2405 (NI 19))	In Schedule 7, in the entry relating to Article 166(4), the word "office". In Schedule 9, Part I.
European Economic Interest Groupings Regulations (Northern Ireland) 1989 (SR 1989/216)	The whole Regulations.
Companies (Northern Ireland) Order 1990 (SI 1990/593 (NI 5))	The whole Order.
Companies (No 2) (Northern Ireland) Order 1990 (SI 1990/1504 (NI 10))	Parts II to IV.
	Part VI.
	Schedules 1 to 6.
Criminal Justice Act 1993 (c 36)	In Schedule 5, Part 2.
	Schedule 6.
Financial Provisions (Northern Ireland) Order 1993 (SI 1993/1252 (NI 5))	Article 15.
Deregulation and Contracting Out Act 1994 (c 40)	Section 13(2).
	Schedule 6.
Pensions (Northern Ireland) Order 1995 (SI 1995/3213 (NI 22))	In Schedule 3, paragraph 7.
Deregulation and Contracting Out (Northern Ireland) Order 1996 (SI 1996/1632 (NI 11))	Article 11.
	Schedule 2.
	In Schedule 5, paragraph 4.
Youth Justice and Criminal Evidence Act 1999 (c 23)	In Schedule 4, paragraph 18.
Limited Liability Partnerships Act (Northern Ireland) 2002 (c 12 (NI))	The whole Act.
Open-Ended Investment Companies Act (Northern Ireland) 2002 (c 13)	The whole Act.
Company Directors Disqualification (Northern Ireland) Order 2002 (SI 2002/3150 (NI 4))	In Schedule 3, paragraphs 3 to 5.
Companies (Audit, Investigations and Community Enterprise) Act 2004 (c 27)	Section 11(2). In Schedule 2, paragraphs 11 to 15.
Law Reform (Miscellaneous Provisions) (Northern Ireland) Order 2005 (SI 2005/1452 (NI 7))	Article 4(2).
Companies (Audit, Investigations and Community Enterprise) (Northern Ireland) Order 2005 (SI 2005/1967 (NI 17))	The whole Order.

OTHER REPEALS

Short title and chapter	Extent of repeal or revocation
Limited Partnerships Act 1907 (c 24)	In section 16(1)—
	(a) the words ", and there shall be paid for such inspection such fees as may be appointed by the Board of Trade, not exceeding 5p for each inspection", and
	(b) the words from "and there shall be paid for such certificate" to the end.
	In section 17—
	(a) the words "(but as to fees with the concurrence of the Treasury)", and
	(b) paragraph (a).
Business Names Act 1985 (c 7)	The whole Act.
Companies Act 1989 (c 40)	Sections 24 to 54.
	Schedules 11 to 13.
Criminal Procedure (Consequential	In Schedule 4, paragraph 74(2).

Short title and chapter	*Extent of repeal or revocation*
Provisions) (Scotland) Act 1995 (c 40)	
Companies (Audit, Investigations and Community Enterprise) Act 2004 (c 27)	Sections 1 to 6.
	In Schedule 2, Part 1.
Civil Partnership Act 2004 (c 33)	In Schedule 27, paragraph 128.

PART 2
COMPANIES ACT 2006 – COMMENCEMENT

TABLE OF COMMENCEMENTS FOR THE COMPANIES ACT 2006

[2.1]

NOTES

The commencement of the Companies Act 2006 is provided for by s 1300 (at **[1.1497]**). See also the Orders made under that section, ie: the Companies Act 2006 (Commencement No 1, Transitional Provisions and Savings) Order 2006, SI 2006/3428, the Companies Act 2006 (Commencement No 2, Consequential Amendments, Transitional Provisions and Savings) Order 2007, SI 2007/1093, the Companies Act 2006 (Commencement No 3, Consequential Amendments, Transitional Provisions and Savings) Order 2007, SI 2007/2194, the Companies Act 2006 (Commencement No 4 and Commencement No 3 (Amendment)) Order 2007, SI 2007/2607, the Companies Act 2006 (Commencement No 5, Transitional Provisions and Savings) Order 2007, SI 2007/3495, the Companies Act 2006 (Commencement No 6, Saving and Commencement Nos 3 and 5 (Amendment)) Order 2008, SI 2008/674, the Companies Act 2006 (Commencement No 7, Transitional Provisions and Savings) Order 2008, SI 2008/1886, and the Companies Act 2006 (Commencement No 8, Transitional Provisions and Savings) Order 2008, SI 2008/2860.

Note that the Commencement Orders which were previously included in full in this Part of the Handbook have been moved to an online only Appendix (Appendix 10) in order to free up space for more recent legislation.

This table lists the commencement dates for each section of, and Schedule to, the 2006 Act (including those sections and Schedules subsequently added to the Act). The substitution of a whole section or Schedule is also noted and, in such cases, the commencement date is deemed to be the date on which the substitution took effect. Where a section or Schedule has been repealed, the entry is reproduced in italics. Where a section or Schedule name has been amended (or where a Part or Chapter heading has been amended) the amendment has been incorporated in the table below, but no details of the amending provision are given. The table does not give details of amendments to the text of an individual section or Schedule.

Where a date has been appointed for a section or Schedule the number of the relevant commencement order is given in the same column – or the abbreviation 'RA' (Royal Assent) is used, as appropriate. Details of commencements for limited purposes, transitional adaptations, transitional provisions and savings, etc, are given in the footnotes to this table. Where transitional adaptations, transitional provisions and savings are subsequently amended or revoked, details are not given in the footnotes below but are noted on both the provision of the commencement order concerned and in the notes to the affected provision of the 2006 Act. See in particular the Companies Act 2006 (Commencement No 8, Transitional Provisions and Savings) Order 2008, SI 2008/2860, art 6 (Revocation of spent transitional adaptations), which revokes many of the transitional adaptations in earlier Orders as from 1 October 2009.

Other abbreviations used in this table are as follows:

— CO No 1: the Companies Act 2006 (Commencement No 1, Transitional Provisions and Savings) Order 2006, SI 2006/3428.
— CO No 2: the Companies Act 2006 (Commencement No 2, Consequential Amendments, Transitional Provisions and Savings) Order 2007, SI 2007/1093.
— CO No 3: the Companies Act 2006 (Commencement No 3, Consequential Amendments, Transitional Provisions and Savings) Order 2007, SI 2007/2194.
— CO No 4: the Companies Act 2006 (Commencement No 4 and Commencement No 3 (Amendment)) Order 2007, SI 2007/2607.
— CO No 5: the Companies Act 2006 (Commencement No 5, Transitional Provisions and Savings) Order 2007, SI 2007/3495.
— CO No 6: the Companies Act 2006 (Commencement No 6, Saving and Commencement Nos 3 and 5 (Amendment)) Order 2008, SI 2008/674.
— CO No 7: the Companies Act 2006 (Commencement No 7, Transitional Provisions and Savings) Order 2008, SI 2008/1886.
— CO No 8: the Companies Act 2006 (Commencement No 8, Transitional Provisions and Savings) Order 2008, SI 2008/2860.
— GB: Great Britain.
— NI: Northern Ireland.

Provision of CA 2006	Commencement
Part 1: General Introductory Provisions	
1 Companies	1 Oct 2009 (CO No 8)
2 The Companies Acts	1 Jan 2007 (certain purposes) (CO No 1)[1] 20 Jan 2007 (certain purposes) (CO No 1)[1] 6 Apr 2007 (otherwise) (CO No 2)[2]
3 Limited and unlimited companies	1 Oct 2009 (CO No 8)
4 Private and public companies	1 Oct 2009 (CO No 8)
5 Companies limited by guarantee and having share capital	1 Oct 2009 (CO No 8)
6 Community interest companies	1 Oct 2009 (CO No 8)
Part 2: Company Formation	
7 Method of forming company	1 Oct 2009 (CO No 8)[129]
8 Memorandum of association	20 Jan 2007 (certain purposes) (CO No 1)[3] 1 Oct 2009 (otherwise) (CO No 8)[129]
9 Registration documents	1 Oct 2009 (CO No 8)[129]
10 Statement of capital and initial shareholdings	20 Jan 2007 (certain purposes) (CO No 1)[3] 1 Oct 2009 (otherwise) (CO No 8)[129]

Provision of CA 2006	Commencement
11 Statement of guarantee	20 Jan 2007 (certain purposes) (CO No 1)[3] 1 Oct 2009 (otherwise) (CO No 8)[129]
12 Statement of proposed officers	1 Oct 2009 (CO No 8)[129]
12A Statement of initial significant control[231]	30 Jun 2016
13 Statement of compliance	1 Oct 2009 (CO No 8)[129]
14 Registration	1 Oct 2009 (CO No 8)[129]
15 Issue of certificate of incorporation	1 Oct 2009 (CO No 8)[129]
16 Effect of registration	1 Oct 2009 (CO No 8)[129]
Part 3: A Company's Constitution	
Chapter 1: Introductory	
17 A company's constitution	1 Oct 2007 (certain purposes) (CO No 3)[4] 6 Apr 2008 (certain purposes) (CO No 5)[107] 1 Oct 2009 (otherwise) (CO No 8)
Chapter 2: Articles of Association	
18 Articles of association	1 Oct 2009 (CO No 8)[130]
19 Power of Secretary of State to prescribe model articles	20 Jan 2007 (certain purposes) (CO No 1)[3] 1 Oct 2009 (otherwise) (CO No 8)[130]
20 Default application of model articles	1 Oct 2009 (CO No 8)[130]
21 Amendment of articles	1 Oct 2009 (CO No 8)[131]
22 Entrenched provisions of the articles	1 Oct 2009 (sub-ss (1), (3) (4)); *not in force* (sub-s (2)) (CO No 8)[202]
23 Notice to registrar of existence of restriction on amendment of articles	1 Oct 2009 (CO No 8)[132]
24 Statement of compliance where amendment of articles restricted	1 Oct 2009 (CO No 8)
25 Effect of alteration of articles on company's members	1 Oct 2009 (CO No 8)
26 Registrar to be sent copy of amended articles	1 Oct 2009 (CO No 8)[133]
27 Registrar's notice to comply in case of failure with respect to amended articles	1 Oct 2009 (CO No 8)
28 Existing companies: provisions of memorandum treated as provisions of articles	1 Oct 2009 (CO No 8)[134]
Chapter 3: Resolutions and Agreements Affecting a Company's Constitution	
29 Resolutions and agreements affecting a company's constitution	1 Oct 2007 (CO No 3)[5]
30 Copies of resolutions or agreements to be forwarded to registrar	1 Oct 2007 (CO No 3)[5]
Chapter 4: Miscellaneous and Supplementary Provisions	
31 Statement of company's objects	1 Oct 2009 (CO No 8)
32 Constitutional documents to be provided to members	20 Jan 2007 (certain purposes) (CO No 1)[3] 1 Oct 2009 (otherwise) (CO No 8)[135]
33 Effect of company's constitution	1 Oct 2009 (CO No 8)
34 Notice to registrar where company's constitution altered by enactment	1 Oct 2009 (CO No 8)[136]
35 Notice to registrar where company's constitution altered by order	1 Oct 2009 (CO No 8)[137]
36 Documents to be incorporated in or accompany copies of articles issued by company	1 Oct 2009 (CO No 8)[138]
37 Right to participate in profits otherwise than as member void	1 Oct 2009 (CO No 8)
38 Application to single member companies of enactments and rules of law	1 Oct 2009 (CO No 8)
Part 4: A Company's Capacity and Related Matters	
39 A company's capacity	1 Oct 2009 (CO No 8)[139]
40 Power of directors to bind the company	1 Oct 2009 (CO No 8)
41 Constitutional limitations: transactions involving directors or their associates	1 Oct 2009 (CO No 8)
42 Constitutional limitations: companies that are charities	1 Oct 2009 (CO No 8)

Provision of CA 2006	Commencement
43 Company contracts	1 Oct 2009 (CO No 8)
44 Execution of documents	6 Apr 2008 (CO No 5)[71]
45 Common seal	1 Oct 2009 (CO No 8)
46 Execution of deeds	1 Oct 2009 (CO No 8)
47 Execution of deeds or other documents by attorney	1 Oct 2009 (CO No 8)[140]
48 Execution of documents by companies	1 Oct 2009 (CO No 8)
49 Official seal for use abroad	1 Oct 2009 (CO No 8)
50 Official seal for share certificates etc	1 Oct 2009 (CO No 8)
51 Pre-incorporation contracts, deeds and obligations	1 Oct 2009 (CO No 8)
52 Bills of exchange and promissory notes	1 Oct 2009 (CO No 8)
Part 5: A Company's Name	
Chapter 1: General Requirements	
53 Prohibited names	1 Oct 2009 (CO No 8)
54 Names suggesting connection with government or public authority	20 Jan 2007 (certain purposes) (CO No 1)[3] 1 Oct 2009 (otherwise) (CO No 8)[141]
55 Other sensitive words or expressions	20 Jan 2007 (certain purposes) (CO No 1)[3] 1 Oct 2009 (otherwise) (CO No 8)[141]
56 Duty to seek comments of government department or other specified body	20 Jan 2007 (certain purposes) (CO No 1)[3] 1 Oct 2009 (otherwise) (CO No 8)[141]
57 Permitted characters etc	20 Jan 2007 (certain purposes) (CO No 1)[3] 1 Oct 2009 (otherwise) (CO No 8)[141]
Chapter 2: Indications of Company Type or Legal Form	
58 Public limited companies	1 Oct 2009 (CO No 8)
59 Private limited companies	1 Oct 2009 (CO No 8)
60 Exemption from requirement as to use of "limited"	20 Jan 2007 (certain purposes) (CO No 1)[3] 1 Oct 2009 (otherwise) (CO No 8)
61 Continuation of existing exemption: companies limited by shares	1 Oct 2009 (CO No 8)
62 Continuation of existing exemption: companies limited by guarantee	1 Oct 2009 (CO No 8)
63 Exempt company: restriction on amendment of articles	1 Oct 2009 (CO No 8)
64 Power to direct change of name in case of company ceasing to be entitled to exemption	1 Oct 2009 (CO No 8)
65 Inappropriate use of indications of company type or legal form	20 Jan 2007 (certain purposes) (CO No 1)[3] 1 Oct 2009 (otherwise) (CO No 8)[141]
Chapter 3: Similarity to Other Names	
66 Name not to be the same as another in the index	20 Jan 2007 (certain purposes) (CO No 1)[3] 1 Oct 2009 (otherwise) (CO No 8)[141]
67 Power to direct change of name in case of similarity to existing name	20 Jan 2007 (certain purposes) (CO No 1)[3] 1 Oct 2009 (otherwise) (CO No 8)
68 Direction to change name: supplementary provisions	1 Oct 2009 (CO No 8)
69 Objection to company's registered name	1 Oct 2008 (CO No 5)
70 Company names adjudicators	1 Oct 2008 (CO No 5)
71 Procedural rules	1 Oct 2008 (CO No 5)
72 Decision of adjudicator to be made available to public	1 Oct 2008 (CO No 5)
73 Order requiring name to be changed	1 Oct 2008 (CO No 5)[111]
74 Appeal from adjudicator's decision	1 Oct 2008 (CO No 5)
Chapter 4: Other Powers of the Secretary of State	
75 Provision of misleading information etc	1 Oct 2009 (CO No 8)
76 Misleading indication of activities	1 Oct 2009 (CO No 8)
77 Change of name	1 Oct 2009 (CO No 8)[142]
78 Change of name by special resolution	1 Oct 2009 (CO No 8)[142]
79 Change of name by means provided for in company's articles	1 Oct 2009 (CO No 8)
80 Change of name: registration and issue of new certificate of incorporation	1 Oct 2009 (CO No 8)[142]
81 Change of name: effect	1 Oct 2009 (CO No 8)[142]

Provision of CA 2006	Commencement
Chapter 6: Trading Disclosures	
82 Requirement to disclose company name etc	20 Jan 2007 (certain purposes) (CO No 1)[3] 1 Oct 2008 (otherwise) (CO No 5)
83 Civil consequences of failure to make required disclosure	1 Oct 2008 (CO No 5)
84 Criminal consequences of failure to make required disclosures	20 Jan 2007 (certain purposes) (CO No 1)[3] 1 Oct 2008 (otherwise) (CO No 5)
85 Minor variations in form of name to be left out of account	1 Oct 2008 (CO No 5)[112]
Part 6: A Company's Registered Office	
86 A company's registered office	1 Oct 2009 (CO No 8)
87 Change of address of registered office	1 Oct 2009 (CO No 8)
88 Welsh companies	1 Oct 2009 (CO No 8)
Part 7: Re-Registration as a Means of Altering a Company's Status	
89 Alteration of status by re-registration	1 Oct 2009 (CO No 8)[143]
90 Re-registration of private company as public	1 Oct 2009 (CO No 8)[143]
91 Requirements as to share capital	1 Oct 2009 (CO No 8)[143]
92 Requirements as to net assets	1 Oct 2009 (CO No 8)[143]
93 Recent allotment of shares for non-cash consideration	1 Oct 2009 (CO No 8)[143]
94 Application and accompanying documents	1 Oct 2009 (CO No 8)[143]
95 Statement of proposed secretary	1 Oct 2009 (CO No 8)[143]
96 Issue of certificate of incorporation on re-registration	1 Oct 2009 (CO No 8)[143]
97 Re-registration of public company as private limited company	1 Oct 2009 (CO No 8)[143]
98 Application to court to cancel resolution	1 Oct 2009 (CO No 8)[143]
99 Notice to registrar of court application or order	1 Oct 2009 (CO No 8)[143]
100 Application and accompanying documents	1 Oct 2009 (CO No 8)[143]
101 Issue of certificate of incorporation on re-registration	1 Oct 2009 (CO No 8)[143]
102 Re-registration of private limited company as unlimited	1 Oct 2009 (CO No 8)[143]
103 Application and accompanying documents	20 Jan 2007 (certain purposes) (CO No 1)[3] 1 Oct 2009 (otherwise) (CO No 8)[143]
104 Issue of certificate of incorporation on re-registration	1 Oct 2009 (CO No 8)[143]
105 Re-registration of unlimited company as limited	1 Oct 2009 (CO No 8)[143]
106 Application and accompanying documents	1 Oct 2009 (CO No 8)[143]
107 Issue of certificate of incorporation on re-registration	1 Oct 2009 (CO No 8)[143]
108 Statement of capital required where company already has share capital	20 Jan 2007 (certain purposes) (CO No 1)[3] 1 Oct 2009 (otherwise) (CO No 8)[143]
109 Re-registration of public company as private and unlimited	1 Oct 2009 (CO No 8)
110 Application and accompanying documents	20 Jan 2007 (certain purposes) (CO No 1)[3] 1 Oct 2009 (otherwise) (CO No 8)
111 Issue of certificate of incorporation on re-registration	1 Oct 2009 (CO No 8)
Part 8: A Company's Members	
Chapter 1: The Members of a Company	
112 The members of a company	1 Oct 2009 (CO No 8)
Chapter 2: Register of Members	
112A Alternative method of record-keeping[231]	30 Jun 2016
113 Register of members	1 Oct 2009 (CO No 8)
114 Register to be kept available for inspection	1 Oct 2009 (CO No 8)
115 Index of members	1 Oct 2009 (CO No 8)
116 Rights to inspect and require copies	20 Jan 2007 (certain purposes) (CO No 1)[3]

Provision of CA 2006	Commencement
	1 Oct 2007 (otherwise) (CO No 3)[6]
117 Register of members: response to request for inspection or copy	1 Oct 2007 (CO No 3)[6]
118 Register of members: refusal of inspection or default in providing copy	1 Oct 2007 (CO No 3)[6]
119 Register of members: offences in connection with request for or disclosure of information	1 Oct 2007 (CO No 3)[6]
120 Information as to state of register and index	1 Oct 2009 (CO No 8)[144]
121 Removal of entries relating to former members	6 Apr 2008 (CO No 5)[72]
122 Share warrants	1 Oct 2009 (CO No 8)
123 Single member companies	1 Oct 2009 (CO No 8)
124 Company holding its own shares as treasury shares	1 Oct 2009 (CO No 8)
125 Power of court to rectify register	1 Oct 2009 (CO No 8)
126 Trusts not to be entered on register	1 Oct 2009 (CO No 8)
127 Register to be evidence	1 Oct 2009 (CO No 8)
128 Time limit for claims arising from entry in register	6 Apr 2008 (CO No 5)[73]
Chapter 2A: Option to keep information on central register[231]	
128A Introduction	30 Jun 2016
128B Right to make an election	30 Jun 2016
128C Effective date of election	30 Jun 2016
128D Effect of election on obligations under Chapter 2	30 Jun 2016
128E Duty to notify registrar of changes	30 Jun 2016
128F Information as to state of central register	30 Jun 2016
128G Power of court to order company to remedy default or delay	30 Jun 2016
128H Central register to be evidence	30 Jun 2016
128I Time limits for claims arising from delivery to registrar	30 Jun 2016
128J Withdrawing the election	30 Jun 2016
128K Power to extend option to public companies	30 Jun 2016
Chapter 3: Overseas Branch Registers	
129 Overseas branch registers	20 Jan 2007 (certain purposes) (CO No 1)[3] 1 Oct 2009 (otherwise) (CO No 8)
130 Notice of opening of overseas branch register	1 Oct 2009 (CO No 8)
131 Keeping of overseas branch register	20 Jan 2007 (certain purposes) (CO No 1)[3] 1 Oct 2009 (otherwise) (CO No 8)
132 Register or duplicate to be kept available for inspection in UK	1 Oct 2009 (CO No 8)
133 Transactions in shares registered in overseas branch register	1 Oct 2009 (CO No 8)
134 Jurisdiction of local courts	1 Oct 2009 (CO No 8)
135 Discontinuance of overseas branch register	1 Oct 2009 (CO No 8)
Chapter 4: Prohibition on Subsidiary being Member of its Holding Company	
136 Prohibition on subsidiary being a member of its holding company	1 Oct 2009 (CO No 8)
137 Shares acquired before prohibition became applicable	1 Oct 2009 (CO No 8)
138 Subsidiary acting as personal representative or trustee	1 Oct 2009 (CO No 8)
139 Interests to be disregarded: residual interest under pension scheme or employees' share scheme	1 Oct 2009 (CO No 8)
140 Interests to be disregarded: employer's rights of recovery under pension scheme or employees' share scheme	1 Oct 2009 (CO No 8)
141 Subsidiary acting as authorised dealer in securities	1 Oct 2009 (CO No 8)
142 Protection of third parties in other cases where subsidiary acting as dealer in securities	1 Oct 2009 (CO No 8)
143 Application of provisions to companies not limited by shares	1 Oct 2009 (CO No 8)

Provision of CA 2006	Commencement
144 Application of provisions to nominees	1 Oct 2009 (CO No 8)
Part 9: Exercise of Members' Rights	
145 Effect of provisions of articles as to enjoyment or exercise of members' rights	1 Oct 2007 (CO No 3)[7]
146 Traded companies: nomination of persons to enjoy information rights	1 Oct 2007 (CO No 3)[7]
147 Information rights: form in which copies to be provided	1 Oct 2007 (CO No 3)[7]
148 Termination or suspension of nomination	1 Oct 2007 (CO No 3)[7]
149 Information as to possible rights in relation to voting	1 Oct 2007 (CO No 3)[7]
150 Information rights: status of rights	1 Oct 2007 (CO No 3)[7]
151 Information rights: power to amend	20 Jan 2007 (certain purposes) (CO No 1)[3] 1 Oct 2007 (otherwise) (CO No 3)
152 Exercise of rights where shares held on behalf of others: exercise in different ways	1 Oct 2007 (CO No 3)[7]
153 Exercise of rights where shares held on behalf of others: members' requests	1 Oct 2007 (CO No 3)[7]
Part 10: A Company's Directors	
Chapter 1: Appointment and Removal of Directors	
154 Companies required to have directors	1 Oct 2007 (CO No 3)
155 Companies required to have at least one director who is a natural person[251]	1 Oct 2008 (CO No 5)[113]
156 Direction requiring company to make appointment	1 Oct 2008 (CO No 5)[114]
156A Each director to be a natural person[231]	*Not in force*
156B Power to provide for exceptions from requirement that each director be a natural person[231]	*Not in force*
156C Existing director who is not a natural person[231]	*Not in force*
157 Minimum age for appointment as director	1 Oct 2008 (CO No 5)
158 Power to provide for exceptions from minimum age requirement	20 Jan 2007 (certain purposes) (CO No 1)[3] 1 Oct 2008 (otherwise) (CO No 5)
159 Existing under-age directors	1 Oct 2008 (CO No 5)
160 Appointment of directors of public company to be voted on individually	1 Oct 2007 (CO No 3)
161 Validity of acts of directors	1 Oct 2007 (CO No 3)[8]
161A Alternative method of record-keeping[231]	30 Jun 2016
162 Register of directors	20 Jan 2007 (certain purposes) (CO No 1)[3] 1 Oct 2009 (otherwise) (CO No 8)[145]
163 Particulars of directors to be registered: individuals	1 Oct 2009 (CO No 8)[145]
164 Particulars of directors to be registered: corporate directors and firms	1 Oct 2009 (CO No 8)[145]
165 Register of directors' residential addresses	1 Oct 2009 (CO No 8)[145]
166 Particulars of directors to be registered: power to make regulations	20 Jan 2007 (certain purposes) (CO No 1)[3] 1 Oct 2009 (otherwise) (CO No 8)[145]
167 Duty to notify registrar of changes	1 Oct 2009 (CO No 8)[145]
167A Right to make an election[231]	30 Jun 2016
167B Effective date of election[231]	30 Jun 2016
167C Effect of election on obligations under sections 162 to 167[231]	30 Jun 2016
167D Duty to notify registrar of changes[231]	30 Jun 2016
167E Withdrawing the election[231]	30 Jun 2016
167F Power to extend option to public companies[231]	30 Jun 2016
168 Resolution to remove director	1 Oct 2007 (CO No 3)
169 Director's right to protest against removal	1 Oct 2007 (CO No 3)[9]
Chapter 2: General Duties of Directors	
170 Scope and nature of general duties	1 Oct 2007 (CO No 3)[10]
171 Duty to act within powers	1 Oct 2007 (CO No 3)
172 Duty to promote the success of the	1 Oct 2007 (CO No 3)

Provision of CA 2006	Commencement
company	
173 Duty to exercise independent judgment	1 Oct 2007 (CO No 3)
174 Duty to exercise reasonable care, skill and diligence	1 Oct 2007 (CO No 3)
175 Duty to avoid conflicts of interest	1 Oct 2008 (CO No 5)[115]
176 Duty not to accept benefits from third parties	1 Oct 2008 (CO No 5)
177 Duty to declare interest in proposed transaction or arrangement	1 Oct 2008 (CO No 5)[116]
178 Civil consequences of breach of general duties	1 Oct 2007 (CO No 3)[10]
179 Cases within more than one of the general duties	1 Oct 2007 (CO No 3)
180 Consent, approval or authorisation by members	1 Oct 2007 (CO No 3)[10a]
181 Modification of provisions in relation to charitable companies	1 Oct 2007 (CO No 3)[10]
Chapter 3: Declaration of Interest in Existing Transaction or Arrangement	
182 Declaration of interest in existing transaction or arrangement	1 Oct 2008 (CO No 5)[117]
183 Offence of failure to declare interest	1 Oct 2008 (CO No 5)[117]
184 Declaration made by notice in writing	1 Oct 2008 (CO No 5)[117]
185 General notice treated as sufficient declaration	1 Oct 2008 (CO No 5)[117]
186 Declaration of interest in case of company with sole director	1 Oct 2008 (CO No 5)[117]
187 Declaration of interest in existing transaction by shadow director	1 Oct 2008 (CO No 5)[117]
Chapter 4: Transactions with Directors Requiring Approval of Members	
188 Directors' long-term service contracts: requirement of members' approval	1 Oct 2007 (CO No 3)[11]
189 Directors' long-term service contracts: civil consequences of contravention	1 Oct 2007 (CO No 3)[11]
190 Substantial property transactions: requirement of members' approval	1 Oct 2007 (CO No 3)[12]
191 Meaning of "substantial"	1 Oct 2007 (CO No 3)[12]
192 Exception for transactions with members or other group companies	1 Oct 2007 (CO No 3)[12]
193 Exception in case of company in winding up or administration	1 Oct 2007 (CO No 3)[12]
194 Exception for transactions on recognised investment exchange	1 Oct 2007 (CO No 3)[12]
195 Property transactions: civil consequences of contravention	1 Oct 2007 (CO No 3)[12]
196 Property transactions: effect of subsequent affirmation	1 Oct 2007 (CO No 3)[12]
197 Loans to directors: requirement of members' approval	1 Oct 2007 (CO No 3)[13]
198 Quasi-loans to directors: requirement of members' approval	1 Oct 2007 (CO No 3)[13]
199 Meaning of "quasi-loan" and related expressions	1 Oct 2007 (CO No 3)[13]
200 Loans or quasi-loans to persons connected with directors: requirement of members' approval	1 Oct 2007 (CO No 3)[13]
201 Credit transactions: requirement of members' approval	1 Oct 2007 (CO No 3)[13]
202 Meaning of "credit transaction"	1 Oct 2007 (CO No 3)[13]
203 Related arrangements: requirement of members' approval	1 Oct 2007 (CO No 3)[13]
204 Exception for expenditure on company business	1 Oct 2007 (CO No 3)[13]
205 Exception for expenditure on defending proceedings etc	1 Oct 2007 (CO No 3)[13]
206 Exception for expenditure in connection with regulatory action or investigation	1 Oct 2007 (CO No 3)[13]
207 Exceptions for minor and business	1 Oct 2007 (CO No 3)[13]

Provision of CA 2006	Commencement
transactions	
208 Exceptions for intra-group transactions	1 Oct 2007 (CO No 3)[13]
209 Exceptions for money-lending companies	1 Oct 2007 (CO No 3)[13]
210 Other relevant transactions or arrangements	1 Oct 2007 (CO No 3)[13]
211 The value of transactions and arrangements	1 Oct 2007 (CO No 3)[13]
212 The person for whom a transaction or arrangement is entered into	1 Oct 2007 (CO No 3)[13]
213 Loans etc: civil consequences of contravention	1 Oct 2007 (CO No 3)[13]
214 Loans etc: effect of subsequent affirmation	1 Oct 2007 (CO No 3)[13]
215 Payments for loss of office	1 Oct 2007 (CO No 3)[14]
216 Amounts taken to be payments for loss of office	1 Oct 2007 (CO No 3)[14]
217 Payment by company: requirement of members' approval	1 Oct 2007 (CO No 3)[14]
218 Payment in connection with transfer of undertaking etc: requirement of members' approval	1 Oct 2007 (CO No 3)[14]
219 Payment in connection with share transfer: requirement of members' approval	1 Oct 2007 (CO No 3)[14]
220 Exception for payments in discharge of legal obligations etc	1 Oct 2007 (CO No 3)[14]
221 Exception for small payments	1 Oct 2007 (CO No 3)[14]
222 Payments made without approval: civil consequences	1 Oct 2007 (CO No 3)[14]
223 Transactions requiring members' approval: application of provisions to shadow directors	1 Oct 2007 (CO No 3)
224 Approval by written resolution: accidental failure to send memorandum	1 Oct 2007 (CO No 3)
225 Cases where approval is required under more than one provision	1 Oct 2007 (CO No 3)
226 Requirement of consent of Charity Commission: companies that are charities[216]	*1 Oct 2007 (CO No 3)*
Chapter 4A: Directors of Quoted Companies and Traded Companies: Special Provision[222]	
226A Key definitions	1 Oct 2013
226B Remuneration payments	1 Oct 2013
226C Loss of office payments	1 Oct 2013
226D Sections 226B and 226C: supplementary	1 Oct 2013
226E Payments made without approval: civil consequences	1 Oct 2013
226F Relationship with requirements under Chapter 4	1 Oct 2013
Chapter 5: Directors' Service Contracts	
227 Directors' service contracts	1 Oct 2007 (CO No 3)
228 Copy of contract or memorandum of terms to be available for inspection	1 Oct 2007 (CO No 3)[15]
229 Right of member to inspect and request copy	20 Jan 2007 (certain purposes) (CO No 1)[3] 1 Oct 2007 (otherwise) (CO No 3)[15]
230 Directors' service contracts: application of provisions to shadow directors	1 Oct 2007 (CO No 3)[15]
Chapter 6: Contracts with Sole Members who are Directors	
231 Contract with sole member who is also a director	1 Oct 2007 (CO No 3)[16]
Chapter 7: Directors' Liabilities	
232 Provisions protecting directors from liability	1 Oct 2007 (CO No 3)[17]
233 Provision of insurance	1 Oct 2007 (CO No 3)[17]
234 Qualifying third party indemnity provision	1 Oct 2007 (CO No 3)[17]
235 Qualifying pension scheme indemnity provision	1 Oct 2007 (CO No 3)[17]
236 Qualifying indemnity provision to be disclosed in directors' report	1 Oct 2007 (CO No 3)[17]
237 Copy of qualifying indemnity provision to be available for inspection	1 Oct 2007 (CO No 3)[18]
238 Right of member to inspect and request copy	20 Jan 2007 (certain purposes) (CO No 1)[3] 1 Oct 2007 (otherwise) (CO No 3)[18]

Provision of CA 2006	Commencement
239 Ratification of acts of directors	1 Oct 2007 (CO No 3)[19]
Chapter 8: Directors' Residential Addresses: Protection From Disclosure	
240 Protected information	1 Oct 2009 (CO No 8)[145]
241 Protected information: restriction on use or disclosure by company	1 Oct 2009 (CO No 8)[145]
242 Protected information: restriction on use or disclosure by registrar	1 Oct 2009 (CO No 8)[145]
243 Permitted use or disclosure by the registrar	20 Jan 2007 (certain purposes) (CO No 1)[3] 1 Oct 2009 (otherwise) (CO No 8)[145]
244 Disclosure under court order	1 Oct 2009 (CO No 8)[145]
245 Circumstances in which registrar may put address on the public record	1 Oct 2009 (CO No 8)[145]
246 Putting the address on the public record	1 Oct 2009 (CO No 8)[145]
Chapter 9: Supplementary Provisions	
247 Power to make provision for employees on cessation or transfer of business	1 Oct 2009 (CO No 8)[20]
248 Minutes of directors' meetings	1 Oct 2007 (CO No 3)[21]
249 Minutes as evidence	1 Oct 2007 (CO No 3)[21]
250 "Director"	1 Oct 2007 (CO No 3)
251 "Shadow director"	1 Oct 2007 (CO No 3)
252 Persons connected with a director	1 Oct 2007 (CO No 3)
253 Members of a director's family	1 Oct 2007 (CO No 3)
254 Director "connected with" a body corporate	1 Oct 2007 (CO No 3)
255 Director "controlling" a body corporate	1 Oct 2007 (CO No 3)
256 Associated bodies corporate	1 Oct 2007 (CO No 3)
257 References to company's constitution	1 Oct 2007 (CO No 3)
258 Power to increase financial limits	20 Jan 2007 (certain purposes) (CO No 1)[3] 1 Oct 2007 (otherwise) (CO No 3)
259 Transactions under foreign law	1 Oct 2007 (CO No 3)
Part 11: Derivative Claims and Proceedings by Members	
Chapter 1: Derivative Claims in England and Wales or Northern Ireland	
260 Derivative claims	1 Oct 2007 (CO No 3)[22]
261 Application for permission to continue derivative claim	1 Oct 2007 (CO No 3)[22]
262 Application for permission to continue claim as a derivative claim	1 Oct 2007 (CO No 3)[22]
263 Whether permission to be given	20 Jan 2007 (certain purposes) (CO No 1)[3] 1 Oct 2007 (otherwise) (CO No 3)[22]
264 Application for permission to continue derivative claim brought by another member	1 Oct 2007 (CO No 3)[22]
Chapter 2: Derivative Proceedings in Scotland	
265 Derivative proceedings	1 Oct 2007 (CO No 3)
266 Requirement for leave and notice	1 Oct 2007 (CO No 3)[22]
267 Application to continue proceedings as derivative proceedings	1 Oct 2007 (CO No 3)[22]
268 Granting of leave	20 Jan 2007 (certain purposes) (CO No 1)[3] 1 Oct 2007 (otherwise) (CO No 3)
269 Application by member to be substituted for member pursuing derivative proceedings	1 Oct 2007 (CO No 3)
Part 12: Company Secretaries	
270 Private company not required to have secretary	6 Apr 2008 (CO No 5)[74]
271 Public company required to have secretary	6 Apr 2008 (CO No 5)
272 Direction requiring public company to appoint secretary	6 Apr 2008 (CO No 5)[75]
273 Qualifications of secretaries of public companies	6 Apr 2008 (CO No 5)[76]
274 Discharge of functions where office vacant or secretary unable to act	6 Apr 2008 (CO No 5)[75]
274A Alternative method of record-keeping[231]	30 Jun 2016
275 Duty to keep register of secretaries	20 Jan 2007 (certain purposes) (CO No 1)[3]

Provision of CA 2006	Commencement
	1 Oct 2009 (otherwise) (CO No 8)[145]
276 Duty to notify registrar of changes	1 Oct 2009 (CO No 8)[145]
277 Particulars of secretaries to be registered: individuals	1 Oct 2009 (CO No 8)[145]
278 Particulars of secretaries to be registered: corporate secretaries and firms	1 Oct 2009 (CO No 8)[145]
279 Particulars of secretaries to be registered: power to make regulations	20 Jan 2007 (certain purposes) (CO No 1)[3] 1 Oct 2009 (otherwise) (CO No 8)[145]
279A Right to make an election[231]	30 Jun 2016
279B Effective date of election[231]	30 Jun 2016
279C Effect of election on obligations under sections 275 and 276[231]	30 Jun 2016
279D Duty to notify registrar of changes[231]	30 Jun 2016
279E Withdrawing the election[231]	30 Jun 2016
279F Power to extend option to public companies[231]	30 Jun 2016
280 Acts done by person in dual capacity	6 Apr 2008 (CO No 5)
Part 13: Resolutions and Meetings	
Chapter 1: General Provisions About Resolutions	
281 Resolutions	1 Oct 2007 (CO No 3)[23]
282 Ordinary resolutions	1 Oct 2007 (CO No 3)[23]
283 Special resolutions	1 Oct 2007 (CO No 3)[23]
284 Votes: general rules	1 Oct 2007 (CO No 3)[23]
285 Voting by proxy[204]	3 Aug 2009
285A Voting rights on poll or written resolution[204]	3 Aug 2009
286 Votes of joint holders of shares	1 Oct 2007 (CO No 3)[23]
287 Saving for provisions of articles as to determination of entitlement to vote	1 Oct 2007 (CO No 3)[23]
Chapter 2: Written Resolutions	
288 Written resolutions of private companies	1 Oct 2007 (CO No 3)[24]
289 Eligible members	1 Oct 2007 (CO No 3)[24]
290 Circulation date	1 Oct 2007 (CO No 3)[24]
291 Circulation of written resolutions proposed by directors	1 Oct 2007 (CO No 3)[24]
292 Members' power to require circulation of written resolution	1 Oct 2007 (CO No 3)[24]
293 Circulation of written resolution proposed by members	1 Oct 2007 (CO No 3)[24]
294 Expenses of circulation	1 Oct 2007 (CO No 3)[24]
295 Application not to circulate members' statement	1 Oct 2007 (CO No 3)[24]
296 Procedure for signifying agreement to written resolution	1 Oct 2007 (CO No 3)[24]
297 Period for agreeing to written resolution	1 Oct 2007 (CO No 3)[24]
298 Sending documents relating to written resolutions by electronic means	1 Oct 2007 (CO No 3)[24]
299 Publication of written resolution on website	1 Oct 2007 (CO No 3)[24]
300 Relationship between this Chapter and provisions of company's articles	1 Oct 2007 (CO No 3)[24]
Chapter 3: Resolutions at Meetings	
301 Resolutions at general meetings	1 Oct 2007 (CO No 3)
302 Directors' power to call general meetings	1 Oct 2007 (CO No 3)
303 Members' power to require directors to call general meeting	1 Oct 2007 (CO No 3)[25]
304 Directors' duty to call meetings required by members	1 Oct 2007 (CO No 3)[25]
305 Power of members to call meeting at company's expense	1 Oct 2007 (CO No 3)[25]
306 Power of court to order meeting	1 Oct 2007 (CO No 3)[26]
307 Notice required of general meeting	1 Oct 2007 (CO No 3)[27]

Provision of CA 2006	Commencement
307A Notice required of general meeting: certain meetings of traded companies[205]	3 Aug 2009
308 Manner in which notice to be given	20 Jan 2007 (CO No 1)
309 Publication of notice of meeting on website	20 Jan 2007 (CO No 1)
310 Persons entitled to receive notice of meetings	1 Oct 2007 (CO No 3)[27]
311 Contents of notices of meetings	1 Oct 2007 (CO No 3)[27]
311A Traded companies: publication of information in advance of general meeting[205]	3 Aug 2009
312 Resolution requiring special notice	1 Oct 2007 (CO No 3)[28]
313 Accidental failure to give notice of resolution or meeting	1 Oct 2007 (CO No 3)[29]
314 Members' power to require circulation of statements	1 Oct 2007 (CO No 3)[30]
315 Company's duty to circulate members' statement	1 Oct 2007 (CO No 3)[30]
316 Expenses of circulating members' statement	1 Oct 2007 (CO No 3)[30]
317 Application not to circulate members' statement	1 Oct 2007 (CO No 3)[30]
318 Quorum at meetings	1 Oct 2007 (CO No 3)[31]
319 Chairman of meeting	1 Oct 2007 (CO No 3)[31]
319A Traded companies: questions at meetings[205]	3 Aug 2009
320 Declaration by chairman on a show of hands	1 Oct 2007 (CO No 3)[31]
321 Right to demand a poll	1 Oct 2007 (CO No 3)[31]
322 Voting on a poll	1 Oct 2007 (CO No 3)[31]
322A Voting on a poll: votes cast in advance[205]	1 Aug 2009
323 Representation of corporations at meetings	1 Oct 2007 (CO No 3)[31]
324 Rights to appoint proxies	1 Oct 2007 (CO No 3)[31]
324A Obligation of proxy to vote in accordance with instructions[205]	1 Aug 2009
325 Notice of meeting to contain statement of rights	1 Oct 2007 (CO No 3)[31]
326 Company-sponsored invitations to appoint proxies	1 Oct 2007 (CO No 3)[31]
327 Notice required of appointment of proxy etc	1 Oct 2007 (except sub-s (2)(c)) (CO No 3)[31] *Never in force* (sub-s (2)(c))[200]
328 Chairing meetings	1 Oct 2007 (CO No 3)[31]
329 Right of proxy to demand a poll	1 Oct 2007 (CO No 3)[31]
330 Notice required of termination of proxy's authority	1 Oct 2007 (except sub-s (6)(c)) (CO No 3)[31] *Never in force* (sub-s (6)(c))[200]
331 Saving for more extensive rights conferred by articles	1 Oct 2007 (CO No 3)[31]
332 Resolution passed at adjourned meeting	1 Oct 2007 (CO No 3)
333 Sending documents relating to meetings etc in electronic form	20 Jan 2007 (CO No 1)
333A Traded company: duty to provide electronic address for receipt of proxies etc[205]	1 Aug 2009
334 Application to class meetings	1 Oct 2007 (CO No 3)[32]
335 Application to class meetings: companies without a share capital	1 Oct 2007 (CO No 3)[32]
Chapter 4: Public Companies and Traded Companies: Additional Requirements for AGMs	
336 Public companies and traded companies: annual general meeting	1 Oct 2007 (CO No 3)[33]
337 Public companies and traded companies: notice of AGM	1 Oct 2007 (CO No 3)[33]
338 Public companies: members' power to require circulation of resolutions for AGMs	1 Oct 2007 (CO No 3)[33]
338A Traded companies: members' power to include other matters in business dealt with at AGM[205]	1 Aug 2009
339 Public companies: company's duty to circulate members' resolutions for AGMs	1 Oct 2007 (CO No 3)[33]
340 Public companies: expenses of circulating members' resolutions for AGM	1 Oct 2007 (CO No 3)[33]
340A Traded companies: duty to circulate members'	1 Aug 2009

Provision of CA 2006	Commencement
matters for AGM[205]	
340B Traded companies: expenses of circulating members' matters to be dealt with at AGM[205]	1 Aug 2009
Chapter 5: Additional Requirements for Quoted Companies and Traded Companies	
341 Results of poll to be made available on website	1 Oct 2007 (CO No 3)
342 Members' power to require independent report on poll	1 Oct 2007 (CO No 3)[34]
343 Appointment of independent assessor	1 Oct 2007 (CO No 3)[34]
344 Independence requirement	20 Jan 2007 (certain purposes) (CO No 1)[3] 1 Oct 2007 (otherwise) (CO No 3)[34]
345 Meaning of "associate"	1 Oct 2007 (CO No 3)[34]
346 Effect of appointment of a partnership	1 Oct 2007 (CO No 3)[34]
347 The independent assessor's report	1 Oct 2007 (CO No 3)[34]
348 Rights of independent assessor: right to attend meeting etc	1 Oct 2007 (CO No 3)[34]
349 Rights of independent assessor: right to information	1 Oct 2007 (CO No 3)[34]
350 Offences relating to provision of information	1 Oct 2007 (CO No 3)[34]
351 Information to be made available on website	1 Oct 2007 (CO No 3)[34]
352 Application of provisions to class meetings	1 Oct 2007 (CO No 3)[34]
353 Requirements as to website availability	1 Oct 2007 (CO No 3)[34]
354 Power to limit or extend the types of company to which provisions of this Chapter apply	20 Jan 2007 (certain purposes) (CO No 1)[3] 1 Oct 2007 (otherwise) (CO No 3)[34]
Chapter 6: Records of Resolutions and Meetings	
355 Records of resolutions and meetings etc	1 Oct 2007 (CO No 3)[35]
356 Records as evidence of resolutions etc	1 Oct 2007 (CO No 3)[35]
357 Records of decisions by sole member	1 Oct 2007 (CO No 3)[35]
358 Inspection of records of resolutions and meetings	20 Jan 2007 (certain purposes) (CO No 1)[3] 1 Oct 2007 (otherwise) (CO No 3)[35]
359 Records of resolutions and meetings of class of members	1 Oct 2007 (CO No 3)[35]
Chapter 7: Supplementary Provisions	
360 Computation of periods of notice etc: clear day rule	1 Oct 2007 (CO No 3)
360A Electronic meetings and voting[205]	3 Aug 2009
360AA Traded companies: confirmation of receipt of electronic voting[255]	3 Sep 2020
360B Traded companies: requirements for participating in and voting at general meetings[205]	3 Aug 2009
360BA Traded companies: right to confirmation of vote after a general meeting[255]	3 Sep 2020
360C Meaning of "traded company"[205]	3 Aug 2009
361 Meaning of "quoted company"	1 Oct 2007 (CO No 3)
Part 14: Control of Political Donations and Expenditure	
362 Introductory	1 Oct 2007 (GB subject to an exception) (CO No 3) 1 Nov 2007 (NI subject to an exception) (CO No 3) 1 Oct 2008 (exception noted above) (CO No 3)[36]
363 Political parties, organisations etc to which this Part applies	1 Oct 2007 (GB subject to an exception) (CO No 3) 1 Nov 2007 (NI subject to an exception) (CO No 3) 1 Oct 2008 (exception noted above) (CO No 3)[36]
364 Meaning of "political donation"	1 Oct 2007 (GB subject to an exception) (CO No 3) 1 Nov 2007 (NI subject to an exception) (CO No 3) 1 Oct 2008 (exception noted above) (CO No 3)[36]
365 Meaning of "political expenditure"	1 Oct 2007 (GB subject to an exception) (CO No 3) 1 Nov 2007 (NI subject to an exception) (CO No 3) 1 Oct 2008 (exception noted above) (CO No 3)[36]
366 Authorisation required for donations or expenditure	1 Oct 2007 (GB subject to an exception) (CO No 3) 1 Nov 2007 (NI subject to an exception) (CO No 3) 1 Oct 2008 (exception noted above) (CO No 3)[36]
367 Form of authorising resolution	1 Oct 2007 (GB subject to an exception) (CO No 3) 1 Nov 2007 (NI subject to an exception) (CO No 3)

Provision of CA 2006	Commencement
	1 Oct 2008 (exception noted above) (CO No 3)[36]
368 Period for which resolution has effect	1 Oct 2007 (GB) (CO No 3) 1 Nov 2007 (NI) (CO No 3)[36]
369 Liability of directors in case of unauthorised donation or expenditure	20 Jan 2007 (certain purposes) (CO No 1)[3] 1 Oct 2007 (otherwise, GB) (CO No 3) 1 Nov 2007 (otherwise, NI) (CO No 3)[36]
370 Enforcement of directors' liabilities by shareholder action	1 Oct 2007 (GB) (CO No 3) 1 Nov 2007 (NI) (CO No 3)[36]
371 Enforcement of directors' liabilities by shareholder action: supplementary	1 Oct 2007 (GB) (CO No 3) 1 Nov 2007 (NI) (CO No 3)[36]
372 Costs of shareholder action	1 Oct 2007 (GB) (CO No 3) 1 Nov 2007 (NI) (CO No 3)[36]
373 Information for purposes of shareholder action	1 Oct 2007 (GB) (CO No 3) 1 Nov 2007 (NI) (CO No 3)[36]
374 Trade unions	1 Oct 2007 (GB) (CO No 3) 1 Nov 2007 (NI) (CO No 3)[36]
375 Subscription for membership of trade association	1 Oct 2007 (GB) (CO No 3) 1 Nov 2007 (NI) (CO No 3)[36]
376 All-party parliamentary groups	1 Oct 2007 (GB) (CO No 3) 1 Nov 2007 (NI) (CO No 3)[36]
377 Political expenditure exempted by order	20 Jan 2007 (certain purposes) (CO No 1)[3] 1 Oct 2007 (otherwise, GB) (CO No 3) 1 Nov 2007 (otherwise, NI) (CO No 3)[36]
378 Donations not amounting to more than £5,000 in any twelve month period	1 Oct 2007 (GB subject to an exception) (CO No 3) 1 Nov 2007 (NI subject to an exception) (CO No 3) 1 Oct 2008 (exception noted above) (CO No 3)[36]
379 Minor definitions	1 Oct 2007 (GB) (CO No 3) 1 Nov 2007 (NI) (CO No 3)[36]
Part 15: Accounts and Reports	
Chapter 1: Introduction	
380 Scheme of this Part	6 Apr 2008 (CO No 5)[77]
381 Companies subject to the small companies regime	6 Apr 2008 (CO No 5)[77]
382 Companies qualifying as small: general	6 Apr 2008 (CO No 5)[77]
383 Companies qualifying as small: parent companies	6 Apr 2008 (CO No 5)[77]
384 Companies excluded from the small companies regime	6 Apr 2008 (CO No 5)[77]
384A Companies qualifying as micro-entities	1 Dec 2013[226]
384B Companies excluded from being treated as micro-entities	1 Dec 2013[226]
385 Quoted and unquoted companies	20 Jan 2007 (certain purposes) (CO No 1)[3] 1 Oct 2007 (certain purposes) (CO No 3)[4] 6 Apr 2008 (otherwise) (CO No 5)[77]
Chapter 2: Accounting Records	
386 Duty to keep accounting records	6 Apr 2008 (CO No 5)[77]
387 Duty to keep accounting records: offence	6 Apr 2008 (CO No 5)[77]
388 Where and for how long records to be kept	6 Apr 2008 (CO No 5)[77]
389 Where and for how long records to be kept: offences	6 Apr 2008 (CO No 5)[77]
Chapter 3: A Company's Financial Year	
390 A company's financial year	6 Apr 2008 (CO No 5)
391 Accounting reference periods and accounting reference date	6 Apr 2008 (CO No 5)
392 Alteration of accounting reference date	6 Apr 2008 (CO No 5)[77]
Chapter 4: Annual Accounts	
393 Accounts to give true and fair view	6 Apr 2008 (CO No 5)[77]
394 Duty to prepare individual accounts	6 Apr 2008 (CO No 5)[77]
394A Individual accounts: exemption for dormant subsidiaries[219]	1 Oct 2012
394B Companies excluded from the dormant subsidiaries exemption[219]	1 Oct 2012
394C Dormant subsidiaries exemption: parent undertak-	1 Oct 2012

Provision of CA 2006	Commencement
ing declaration of guarantee[219]	
395 Individual accounts: applicable accounting framework	6 Apr 2008 (CO No 5)[77]
396 Companies Act individual accounts	20 Jan 2007 (certain purposes) (CO No 1)[3] 6 Apr 2008 (otherwise) (CO No 5)[77]
397 IAS individual accounts	6 Apr 2015[236]
398 Option to prepare group accounts[244]	*6 Apr 2008 (CO No 5)*[77]
399 Duty to prepare group accounts	6 Apr 2008 (CO No 5)[77]
400 Exemption for company included in UK group accounts of larger group	6 Apr 2008 (CO No 5)[77]
401 Exemption for company included in non-UK group accounts of larger group	6 Apr 2008 (CO No 5)[77]
402 Exemption if no subsidiary undertakings need be included in the consolidation	6 Apr 2008 (CO No 5)[77]
403 Group accounts: applicable accounting framework	6 Apr 2008 (CO No 5)[77]
404 Companies Act group accounts	20 Jan 2007 (certain purposes) (CO No 1)[3] 6 Apr 2008 (otherwise) (CO No 5)[77]
405 Companies Act group accounts: subsidiary undertakings included in the consolidation	6 Apr 2008 (CO No 5)[77]
406 IAS group accounts	6 Apr 2015[236]
407 Consistency of financial reporting within group	6 Apr 2008 (CO No 5)[77]
408 Individual profit and loss account where group accounts prepared	6 Apr 2008 (CO No 5)[77]
409 Information about related undertakings	20 Jan 2007 (certain purposes) (CO No 1)[3] 6 Apr 2008 (otherwise) (CO No 5)[77]
410 Information about related undertakings: alternative compliance[233]	*6 Apr 2008 (CO No 5)*[77]
410A Information about off-balance sheet arrangements[122]	6 Apr 2008
411 Information about employee numbers and costs	6 Apr 2008 (CO No 5)[77]
412 Information about directors' benefits: remuneration	20 Jan 2007 (certain purposes) (CO No 1)[3] 6 Apr 2008 (otherwise) (CO No 5)[77]
413 Information about directors' benefits: advances, credit and guarantees	6 Apr 2008 (CO No 5)[77]
414 Approval and signing of accounts	6 Apr 2008 (CO No 5)[77]
Chapter 4A: Strategic Report[225]	
414A Duty to prepare strategic report	1 Oct 2013
414B Strategic report: small companies exemption	1 Oct 2013
414C Contents of strategic report	1 Oct 2013
414CZA Section 172(1) statement	1 Jan 2019[170]
414CA Non-financial and sustainability information statement	26 Dec 2016[242]
414CB Contents of non-financial and sustainability information statement	26 Dec 2016[242]
414D Approval and signing of strategic report	1 Oct 2013
Chapter 5: Directors' Report	
415 Duty to prepare directors' report	6 Apr 2008 (CO No 5)[77]
415A Directors' report: small companies exemption[122]	6 Apr 2008
416 Contents of directors' report: general	20 Jan 2007 (certain purposes) (CO No 1)[3] 6 Apr 2008 (otherwise) (CO No 5)[77]
417 Contents of directors' report: business review[228]	*1 Oct 2007 (CO No 3)*[37]
418 Contents of directors' report: statement as to disclosure to auditors	6 Apr 2008 (CO No 5)[77]
419 Approval and signing of directors' report	6 Apr 2008 (CO No 5)[77]
419A Approval and signing of separate corporate governance statement[199]	27 Jun 2009
Chapter 6: Quoted Companies and Traded Companies: Directors' Remuneration Report	
420 Duty to prepare directors' remuneration report	6 Apr 2008 (CO No 5)[77]
421 Contents of directors' remuneration report	20 Jan 2007 (certain purposes) (CO No 1)[3] 6 Apr 2008 (otherwise) (CO No 5)[77]

Provision of CA 2006	Commencement
422 Approval and signing of directors' remuneration report	6 Apr 2008 (CO No 5)[77]
422A Revisions to directors' remuneration policy[223]	25 Apr 2013 (for the purposes of enabling the exercise of any power to make provision by regulations) 1 Oct 2013 (otherwise)
Chapter 7: Publication of Accounts and Reports	
423 Duty to circulate copies of annual accounts and reports	6 Apr 2008 (CO No 5)[77]
424 Time allowed for sending out copies of accounts and reports	6 Apr 2008 (CO No 5)[77]
425 Default in sending out copies of accounts and reports: offences	6 Apr 2008 (CO No 5)[77]
426 Option to provide strategic report with supplementary material	20 Jan 2007 (certain purposes) (CO No 1)[3] 6 Apr 2008 (otherwise) (CO No 5)[77]
426A Supplementary material	1 Oct 2013[225]
426B Section 172(1) statement to be made available on website	1 Jan 2019[170]
427 Form and contents of summary financial statement: unquoted companies[228]	*20 Jan 2007 (certain purposes) (CO No 1)*[3] *6 Apr 2008 (otherwise) (CO No 5)*[77]
428 Form and contents of summary financial statement: quoted companies[228]	*20 Jan 2007 (certain purposes) (CO No 1)*[3] *6 Apr 2008 (otherwise) (CO No 5)*[77]
429 Summary financial statements: offences[228]	*6 Apr 2008 (CO No 5)*[77]
430 Quoted companies and traded companies: annual accounts and reports to be made available on website	6 Apr 2008 (CO No 5)[77]
431 Right of member or debenture holder to copies of accounts and reports: unquoted companies	6 Apr 2008 (CO No 5)[77]
432 Right of member or debenture holder to copies of accounts and reports: quoted companies	6 Apr 2008 (CO No 5)[77]
433 Name of signatory to be stated in published copies of accounts and reports	6 Apr 2008 (CO No 5)[77]
434 Requirements in connection with publication of statutory accounts	6 Apr 2008 (CO No 5)[77]
435 Requirements in connection with publication of non-statutory accounts	6 Apr 2008 (CO No 5)[77]
436 Meaning of "publication" in relation to accounts and reports	6 Apr 2008 (CO No 5)[77]
Chapter 8: Public Companies: Laying of Accounts and Reports Before General Meeting	
437 Public companies: laying of accounts and reports before general meeting	6 Apr 2008 (CO No 5)[77]
438 Public companies: offence of failure to lay accounts and reports	6 Apr 2008 (CO No 5)[77]
Chapter 9: Quoted Companies and Traded Companies: Members' Approval of Directors' Remuneration Report	
439 Quoted companies and traded companies: members' approval of directors' remuneration report	6 Apr 2008 (CO No 5)[77]
439A Quoted companies and traded companies: members' approval of directors' remuneration policy[223]	1 Oct 2013
440 Quoted companies and traded companies: offences in connection with procedure for approval	6 Apr 2008 (CO No 5)[77]
Chapter 10: Filing of Accounts and Reports	
441 Duty to file accounts and reports with the registrar	6 Apr 2008 (CO No 5)[77]
442 Period allowed for filing accounts	6 Apr 2008 (CO No 5)[77]
443 Calculation of period allowed	6 Apr 2008 (CO No 5)[77]
444 Filing obligations of companies subject to small companies regime	20 Jan 2007 (certain purposes) (CO No 1)[3] 6 Apr 2008 (otherwise) (CO No 5)[77]
444A Filing obligations of companies entitled to small companies exemption in relation to directors' report[122]	6 Apr 2008
445 Filing obligations of medium-sized companies	20 Jan 2007 (certain purposes) (CO No 1)[3] 6 Apr 2008 (otherwise) (CO No 5)[77]
446 Filing obligations of unquoted companies	6 Apr 2008 (CO No 5)[77]
447 Filing obligations of quoted companies	6 Apr 2008 (CO No 5)[77]

Provision of CA 2006	Commencement
448 Unlimited companies exempt from obligation to file accounts	6 Apr 2008 (CO No 5)[77]
448A Dormant subsidiaries exempt from obligation to file accounts[219]	1 Oct 2012
448B Companies excluded from the dormant subsidiaries exemption[219]	1 Oct 2012
448C Dormant subsidiaries filing exemption: parent undertaking declaration of guarantee[219]	1 Oct 2012
449 Special auditor's report where abbreviated accounts delivered[233]	*6 Apr 2008 (CO No 5)*[77]
450 Approval and signing of abbreviated accounts[233]	*6 Apr 2008 (CO No 5)*[77]
451 Default in filing accounts and reports: offences	6 Apr 2008 (CO No 5)[77]
452 Default in filing accounts and reports: court order	6 Apr 2008 (CO No 5)[77]
453 Civil penalty for failure to file accounts and reports	20 Jan 2007 (certain purposes) (CO No 1)[3] 6 Apr 2008 (otherwise) (CO No 5)[77]
Chapter 11: Revision of Defective Accounts and Reports	
454 Voluntary revision of accounts etc	20 Jan 2007 (certain purposes) (CO No 1)[3] 6 Apr 2008 (otherwise) (CO No 5)[77]
455 Secretary of State's notice in respect of accounts or reports	6 Apr 2008 (CO No 5)[77]
456 Application to court in respect of defective accounts or reports	6 Apr 2008 (CO No 5)[77]
457 Other persons authorised to apply to the court	20 Jan 2007 (certain purposes) (CO No 1)[3] 6 Apr 2008 (otherwise) (CO No 5)[77]
458 Disclosure of information by tax authorities	6 Apr 2008 (CO No 5)[77]
459 Power of authorised person to require documents, information and explanations	6 Apr 2008 (CO No 5)[77]
460 Restrictions on disclosure of information obtained under compulsory powers	6 Apr 2008 (CO No 5)[77]
461 Permitted disclosure of information obtained under compulsory powers	6 Apr 2008 (CO No 5)[77]
462 Power to amend categories of permitted disclosure	20 Jan 2007 (certain purposes) (CO No 1)[3] 6 Apr 2008 (otherwise) (CO No 5)[77]
Chapter 12: Supplementary Provisions	
463 Liability for false or misleading statements in reports and statements	20 Jan 2007 (CO No 1)[38]
464 Accounting standards	20 Jan 2007 (certain purposes) (CO No 1)[3] 6 Apr 2008 (otherwise) (CO No 5)[77]
465 Companies qualifying as medium-sized: general	6 Apr 2008 (CO No 5)[77]
466 Companies qualifying as medium-sized: parent companies	6 Apr 2008 (CO No 5)[77]
467 Companies excluded from being treated as medium-sized	6 Apr 2008 (CO No 5)[77]
468 General power to make further provision about accounts and reports	20 Jan 2007 (certain purposes) (CO No 1)[3] 6 Apr 2008 (otherwise) (CO No 5)[77]
469 Preparation and filing of accounts in euros	6 Apr 2008 (CO No 5)[77]
470 Power to apply provisions to banking partnerships	20 Jan 2007 (certain purposes) (CO No 1)[3] 6 Apr 2008 (otherwise) (CO No 5)[77]
471 Meaning of "annual accounts" and related expressions	6 Apr 2008 (CO No 5)[77]
472 Notes to the accounts	6 Apr 2008 (CO No 5)[77]
472A Meaning of "corporate governance statement" etc[199]	27 Jun 2009
473 Parliamentary procedure for certain regulations under this Part	20 Jan 2007 (certain purposes) (CO No 1)[3] 6 Apr 2008 (otherwise) (CO No 5)[77]
474 Minor definitions	6 Apr 2008 (CO No 5)[77]
Part 16: Audit	
Chapter 1: Requirement for Audited Accounts	
475 Requirement for audited accounts	6 Apr 2008 (CO No 5)[78]
476 Right of members to require audit	6 Apr 2008 (CO No 5)[78]

Provision of CA 2006	Commencement
477 Small companies: conditions for exemption from audit	6 Apr 2008 (CO No 5)[78]
478 Companies excluded from small companies exemption	6 Apr 2008 (CO No 5)[78]
479 Availability of small companies exemption in case of group company	6 Apr 2008 (CO No 5)[78]
479A Subsidiary companies: conditions for exemption from audit[219]	1 Oct 2012
479B Companies excluded from the subsidiary companies audit exemption[219]	1 Oct 2012
479C Subsidiary companies audit exemption: parent undertaking declaration of guarantee[219]	1 Oct 2012
480 Dormant companies: conditions for exemption from audit	6 Apr 2008 (CO No 5)[78]
481 Companies excluded from dormant companies exemption	6 Apr 2008 (CO No 5)[78]
482 Non-profit-making companies subject to public sector audit	6 Apr 2008 (CO No 5)[78]
483 Scottish public sector companies: audit by Auditor General for Scotland	20 Jan 2007 (certain purposes) (CO No 1)[3] 6 Apr 2008 (otherwise) (CO No 5)[78]
484 General power of amendment by regulations	20 Jan 2007 (certain purposes) (CO No 1)[3] 6 Apr 2008 (otherwise) (CO No 5)[78]
Chapter 2: Appointment of Auditors	
485 Appointment of auditors of private company: general	1 Oct 2007 (CO No 3)[39]
485A Appointment of auditors of private company: additional requirements for public interest entities with audit committees	17 Jun 2016[237]
485B Appointment of auditors of private company: additional requirements for public interest entities without audit committees	17 Jun 2016[237]
485C Restriction on appointment of auditor of private company which is a public interest entity	17 Jun 2016[245]
486 Appointment of auditors of private company: default power of Secretary of State	1 Oct 2007 (CO No 3)[39]
486A Defective appointments: default power of Secretary of State	1 Jan 2018[198]
487 Term of office of auditors of private company	1 Oct 2007 (CO No 3)[39]
487A Maximum engagement period: transitional arrangements[237]	*17 Jun 2016*[246]
488 Prevention by members of deemed re-appointment of auditor	1 Oct 2007 (CO No 3)[39]
489 Appointment of auditors of public company: general	6 Apr 2008 (CO No 5)[79]
489A Appointment of auditors of public company: additional requirements for public interest entities with audit committees	17 Jun 2016[237]
489B Appointment of auditors of public company: additional requirements for public interest entities without audit committees	17 Jun 2016[237]
489C Restriction on appointment of auditor of public company which is a public interest entity	17 Jun 2016[245]
490 Appointment of auditors of public company: default power of Secretary of State	6 Apr 2008 (CO No 5)[79]
490A Defective appointments: default power of Secretary of State	1 Jan 2018[198]
491 Term of office of auditors of public company	6 Apr 2008 (CO No 5)[79]
491A Maximum engagement period: transitional arrangements[246]	*17 Jun 2016*[237]
492 Fixing of auditor's remuneration	6 Apr 2008 (CO No 5)[79]
493 Disclosure of terms of audit appointment	20 Jan 2007 (certain purposes) (CO No 1)[3] 6 Apr 2008 (otherwise) (CO No 5)[79]

Provision of CA 2006	Commencement
494 Disclosure of services provided by auditor or associates and related remuneration	20 Jan 2007 (certain purposes) (CO No 1)[3] 6 Apr 2008 (otherwise) (CO No 5)[79]
494ZA The maximum engagement period	17 Jun 2016[245]
494A Interpretation	17 Jun 2016[237]
Chapter 3: Functions of Auditor	
495 Auditor's report on company's annual accounts	6 Apr 2008 (CO No 5)[80]
496 Auditor's report on strategic report and directors' report	6 Apr 2015[236]
497 Auditor's report on auditable part of directors' remuneration report	6 Apr 2008 (CO No 5)[80]
497A Auditor's report on separate corporate governance statement[199]	6 Apr 2015[236]
498 Duties of auditor	6 Apr 2008 (CO No 5)[80]
498A Auditor's duties in relation to separate corporate governance statement[199]	27 Jun 2009
499 Auditor's general right to information	6 Apr 2008 (CO No 5)[80]
500 Auditor's right to information from overseas subsidiaries	6 Apr 2008 (CO No 5)[80]
501 Auditor's rights to information: offences	6 Apr 2008 (CO No 5)[80]
502 Auditor's rights in relation to resolutions and meetings	6 Apr 2008 (CO No 5)[80]
503 Signature of auditor's report	6 Apr 2008 (CO No 5)[80]
504 Senior statutory auditor	20 Jan 2007 (certain purposes) (CO No 1)[3] 6 Apr 2008 (otherwise) (CO No 5)[80]
505 Names to be stated in published copies of auditor's report	6 Apr 2008 (CO No 5)[80]
506 Circumstances in which names may be omitted	6 Apr 2008 (CO No 5)[80]
507 Offences in connection with auditor's report	6 Apr 2008 (CO No 5)[80]
508 Guidance for regulatory and prosecuting authorities: England, Wales and Northern Ireland	6 Apr 2008 (CO No 5)[80]
509 Guidance for regulatory authorities: Scotland	6 Apr 2008 (CO No 5)[80]
Chapter 4: Removal, Resignation, etc of Auditors	
510 Resolution removing auditor from office	6 Apr 2008 (CO No 5)[81]
511 Special notice required for resolution removing auditor from office	6 Apr 2008 (CO No 5)[81]
511A Public interest companies: application to court to remove auditor from office	17 Jun 2016[237]
512 Notice to registrar of resolution removing auditor from office[239]	*6 Apr 2008 (CO No 5)*[81]
513 Rights of auditor who has been removed from office	6 Apr 2008 (CO No 5)[81]
514 Failure to re-appoint auditor: special procedure required for written resolution	6 Apr 2008 (CO No 5)[81]
515 Failure to re-appoint auditor: special notice required for resolution at general meeting	6 Apr 2008 (CO No 5)[81]
516 Resignation of auditor	6 Apr 2008 (CO No 5)[81]
517 Notice to registrar of resignation of auditor[239]	*6 Apr 2008 (CO No 5)*[81]
518 Rights of resigning auditor	6 Apr 2008 (CO No 5)[81]
519 Statement by auditor to be sent to company	6 Apr 2008 (CO No 5)[81]
519A Meaning of "public interest company", "non-public interest company" and "exempt reasons"[234]	1 Oct 2015
520 Company's duties in relation to statement	6 Apr 2008 (CO No 5)[81]
521 Copy of statement to be sent to registrar	6 Apr 2008 (CO No 5)[81]
522 Duty of auditor to send statement to appropriate audit authority	6 Apr 2008 (CO No 5)[81]
523 Duty of company to notify appropriate audit authority	6 Apr 2008 (CO No 5)[81]
524 Provision of information to accounting authorities	6 Apr 2008 (CO No 5)[81]
525 Meaning of "appropriate audit authority"	6 Apr 2008 (CO No 5)[81]

Provision of CA 2006	Commencement
526 Effect of casual vacancies	6 Apr 2008 (CO No 5)[81]
Chapter 5: Quoted Companies: Right of Members to Raise Audit Concerns at Accounts Meeting	
527 Members' power to require website publication of audit concerns	6 Apr 2008 (CO No 5)[82]
528 Requirements as to website availability	6 Apr 2008 (CO No 5)
529 Website publication: company's supplementary duties	6 Apr 2008 (CO No 5)
530 Website publication: offences	6 Apr 2008 (CO No 5)
531 Meaning of "quoted company"	6 Apr 2008 (CO No 5)
Chapter 6: Auditors' Liability	
532 Voidness of provisions protecting auditors from liability	6 Apr 2008 (CO No 5)
533 Indemnity for costs of successfully defending proceedings	6 Apr 2008 (CO No 5)[124]
534 Liability limitation agreements	6 Apr 2008 (CO No 5)
535 Terms of liability limitation agreement	20 Jan 2007 (certain purposes) (CO No 1)[3] 6 Apr 2008 (otherwise) (CO No 5)
536 Authorisation of agreement by members of the company	6 Apr 2008 (CO No 5)[83]
537 Effect of liability limitation agreement	6 Apr 2008 (CO No 5)
538 Disclosure of agreement by company	20 Jan 2007 (certain purposes) (CO No 1)[3] 6 Apr 2008 (otherwise) (CO No 5)
Chapter 7: Supplementary Provisions	
538A Meaning of "corporate governance statement" etc[199]	27 Jun 2009
539 Minor definitions	6 Apr 2008 (CO No 5)
Part 17: A Company's Share Capital	
Chapter 1: Shares and Share Capital of a Company	
540 Shares	1 Oct 2007 (sub-ss (1), (4) certain purposes) (CO No 3)[40] 6 Apr 2008 (sub-ss (1), (4) certain purposes) (CO No 5)[107] 1 Oct 2009 (otherwise) (CO No 8)[146]
541 Nature of shares	1 Oct 2009 (CO No 8)
542 Nominal value of shares	1 Oct 2009 (CO No 8)
543 Numbering of shares	1 Oct 2009 (CO No 8)
544 Transferability of shares	6 Apr 2008 (CO No 5)
545 Companies having a share capital	1 Oct 2007 (certain purposes) (CO No 3)[4] 6 Apr 2008 (certain purposes) (CO No 5)[107] 1 Oct 2009 (otherwise) (CO No 8)
546 Issued and allotted share capital	6 Apr 2007 (certain purposes) (CO No 2)[41] 1 Oct 2007 (certain purposes) (CO No 3)[4] 1 Nov 2007 (certain purposes) (CO No 3)[42] 6 Apr 2008 (certain purposes) (CO No 5)[107] 1 Oct 2009 (otherwise) (CO No 8)
547 Called-up share capital	1 Oct 2009 (CO No 8)
548 Equity share capital	1 Oct 2007 (certain purposes) (CO No 3)[4] 6 Apr 2008 (certain purposes) (CO No 5)[107] 1 Oct 2009 (otherwise) (CO No 8)
Chapter 2: Allotment of Shares: General Provisions	
549 Exercise by directors of power to allot shares etc	1 Oct 2009 (CO No 8)
550 Power of directors to allot shares etc: private company with only one class of shares	1 Oct 2009 (CO No 8)[147]
551 Power of directors to allot shares etc: authorisation by company	1 Oct 2009 (CO No 8)[148]
552 General prohibition of commissions, discounts and allowances	1 Oct 2009 (CO No 8)
553 Permitted commission	1 Oct 2009 (CO No 8)
554 Registration of allotment	1 Oct 2009 (CO No 8)[149]
555 Return of allotment by limited company	20 Jan 2007 (certain purposes) (CO No 1)[3]

Provision of CA 2006	Commencement
	1 Oct 2009 (otherwise) (CO No 8)
556 Return of allotment by unlimited company allotting new class of shares	20 Jan 2007 (certain purposes) (CO No 1)[3] 1 Oct 2009 (otherwise) (CO No 8)
557 Offence of failure to make return	1 Oct 2009 (CO No 8)
558 When shares are allotted	6 Apr 2007 (certain purposes) (CO No 2)[41] 1 Oct 2009 (otherwise) (CO No 8)
559 Provisions about allotment not applicable to shares taken on formation	1 Oct 2009 (CO No 8)
Chapter 3: Allotment of Equity Securities: Existing Shareholders': Right of Pre-emption	
560 Meaning of "equity securities" and related expressions	1 Oct 2009 (CO No 8)
561 Existing shareholders' right of pre-emption	1 Oct 2009 (CO No 8)[150]
562 Communication of pre-emption offers to shareholders	20 Jan 2007 (certain purposes) (CO No 1)[3] 1 Oct 2009 (otherwise) (CO No 8)[150]
563 Liability of company and officers in case of contravention	1 Oct 2009 (CO No 8)[150]
564 Exception to pre-emption right: bonus shares	1 Oct 2009 (CO No 8)[150]
565 Exception to pre-emption right: issue for non-cash consideration	1 Oct 2009 (CO No 8)[150]
566 Exceptions to pre-emption right: employees' share schemes[201]	1 Oct 2009
566A Exception to pre-emption right: companies in financial difficulty[254]	26 Jun 2020
567 Exclusion of requirements by private companies	1 Oct 2009 (CO No 8)[150]
568 Exclusion of pre-emption right: articles conferring corresponding right	1 Oct 2009 (CO No 8)[150]
569 Disapplication of pre-emption rights: private company with only one class of shares	1 Oct 2009 (CO No 8)[150]
570 Disapplication of pre-emption rights: directors acting under general authorisation	1 Oct 2009 (CO No 8)[150]
571 Disapplication of pre-emption rights by special resolution	1 Oct 2009 (CO No 8)[150]
572 Liability for false statement in directors' statement	1 Oct 2009 (CO No 8)[150]
573 Disapplication of pre-emption rights: sale of treasury shares	1 Oct 2009 (CO No 8)[150]
574 References to holder of shares in relation to offer	1 Oct 2009 (CO No 8)[150]
575 Saving for other restrictions on offer or allotment	1 Oct 2009 (CO No 8)[150]
576 Saving for certain older pre-emption requirements	1 Oct 2009 (CO No 8)[150]
577 Provisions about pre-emption not applicable to shares taken on formation	1 Oct 2009 (CO No 8)[150]
Chapter 4: Public Companies: Allotment Where Issue Not Fully Subscribed	
578 Public companies: allotment where issue not fully subscribed	1 Oct 2009 (CO No 8)[151]
579 Public companies: effect of irregular allotment where issue not fully subscribed	1 Oct 2009 (CO No 8)[151]
Chapter 5: Payment for Shares	
580 Shares not to be allotted at a discount	1 Oct 2009 (CO No 8)
581 Provision for different amounts to be paid on shares	1 Oct 2009 (CO No 8)
582 General rule as to means of payment	1 Oct 2009 (CO No 8)
583 Meaning of payment in cash	20 Jan 2007 (certain purposes) (CO No 1)[3] 1 Oct 2009 (otherwise) (CO No 8)[152]
584 Public companies: shares taken by subscribers of memorandum	1 Oct 2009 (CO No 8)
585 Public companies: must not accept undertaking to do work or perform services	1 Oct 2009 (CO No 8)
586 Public companies: shares must be at least one-quarter paid up	1 Oct 2009 (CO No 8)
587 Public companies: payment by long-term undertaking	1 Oct 2009 (CO No 8)

Provision of CA 2006	Commencement
588 Liability of subsequent holders of shares	1 Oct 2009 (CO No 8)
589 Power of court to grant relief	1 Oct 2009 (CO No 8)[153]
590 Penalty for contravention of this Chapter	1 Oct 2009 (CO No 8)
591 Enforceability of undertakings to do work etc	1 Oct 2009 (CO No 8)
592 The appropriate rate of interest	20 Jan 2007 (certain purposes) (CO No 1)[3] 1 Oct 2009 (otherwise) (CO No 8)
Chapter 6: Public Companies: Independent Valuation of Non-Cash Consideration	
593 Public company: valuation of non-cash consideration for shares	1 Oct 2009 (CO No 8)
594 Exception to valuation requirement: arrangement with another company	1 Oct 2009 (CO No 8)
595 Exception to valuation requirement: merger or division	1 Oct 2009 (CO No 8)
596 Non-cash consideration for shares: requirements as to valuation and report	1 Oct 2009 (CO No 8)
597 Copy of report to be delivered to registrar	1 Oct 2009 (CO No 8)
598 Public company: agreement for transfer of non-cash asset in initial period	1 Oct 2009 (CO No 8)
599 Agreement for transfer of non-cash asset: requirement of independent valuation	1 Oct 2009 (CO No 8)
600 Agreement for transfer of non-cash asset: requirements as to valuation and report	1 Oct 2009 (CO No 8)
601 Agreement for transfer of non-cash asset: requirement of approval by members	1 Oct 2009 (CO No 8)
602 Copy of resolution to be delivered to registrar	1 Oct 2009 (CO No 8)
603 Adaptation of provisions in relation to company re-registering as public	1 Oct 2009 (CO No 8)
604 Agreement for transfer of non-cash asset: effect of contravention	1 Oct 2009 (CO No 8)
605 Liability of subsequent holders of shares	1 Oct 2009 (CO No 8)
606 Power of court to grant relief	1 Oct 2009 (CO No 8)[153]
607 Penalty for contravention of this Chapter	1 Oct 2009 (CO No 8)[152]
608 Enforceability of undertakings to do work etc	1 Oct 2009 (CO No 8)
609 The appropriate rate of interest	20 Jan 2007 (certain purposes) (CO No 1)[3] 1 Oct 2009 (otherwise) (CO No 8)
Chapter 7: Share Premiums	
610 Application of share premiums	1 Oct 2008 (certain purposes) (CO No 7)[127] 1 Oct 2009 (otherwise) (CO No 8)
611 Group reconstruction relief	1 Oct 2009 (CO No 8)
612 Merger relief	1 Oct 2009 (CO No 8)
613 Merger relief: meaning of 90% equity holding	1 Oct 2009 (CO No 8)
614 Power to make further provision by regulations	20 Jan 2007 (certain purposes) (CO No 1)[3] 1 Oct 2009 (otherwise) (CO No 8)
615 Relief may be reflected in company's balance sheet	1 Oct 2009 (CO No 8)
616 Interpretation of this Chapter	1 Oct 2009 (CO No 8)
Chapter 8: Alteration of Share Capital	
617 Alteration of share capital of limited company	1 Oct 2009 (CO No 8)
618 Sub-division or consolidation of shares	1 Oct 2009 (CO No 8)
619 Notice to registrar of sub-division or consolidation	20 Jan 2007 (certain purposes) (CO No 1)[3] 1 Oct 2009 (otherwise) (CO No 8)
620 Reconversion of stock into shares	1 Oct 2009 (CO No 8)
621 Notice to registrar of reconversion of stock into shares	20 Jan 2007 (certain purposes) (CO No 1)[3] 1 Oct 2009 (otherwise) (CO No 8)
622 Redenomination of share capital	1 Oct 2009 (CO No 8)
623 Calculation of new nominal values	1 Oct 2009 (CO No 8)
624 Effect of redenomination	1 Oct 2009 (CO No 8)
625 Notice to registrar of redenomination	20 Jan 2007 (certain purposes) (CO No 1)[3] 1 Oct 2009 (otherwise) (CO No 8)

Provision of CA 2006	Commencement
626 Reduction of capital in connection with redenomination	1 Oct 2009 (CO No 8)
627 Notice to registrar of reduction of capital in connection with redenomination	20 Jan 2007 (certain purposes) (CO No 1)[3] 1 Oct 2009 (otherwise) (CO No 8)
628 Redenomination reserve	1 Oct 2009 (CO No 8)
Chapter 9: Classes of Share and Class Rights	
629 Classes of shares	1 Oct 2007 (certain purposes) (CO No 3)[4] 6 Apr 2008 (certain purposes) (CO No 5)[107] 1 Oct 2009 (otherwise) (CO No 8)
630 Variation of class rights: companies having a share capital	1 Oct 2009 (CO No 8)
631 Variation of class rights: companies without a share capital	1 Oct 2009 (CO No 8)[154]
632 Variation of class rights: saving for court's powers under other provisions	1 Oct 2009 (CO No 8)
633 Right to object to variation: companies having a share capital	1 Oct 2009 (CO No 8)
634 Right to object to variation: companies without a share capital	1 Oct 2009 (CO No 8)[154]
635 Copy of court order to be forwarded to the registrar	1 Oct 2009 (CO No 8)
636 Notice of name or other designation of class of shares	1 Oct 2009 (CO No 8)[155]
637 Notice of particulars of variation of rights attached to shares	1 Oct 2009 (CO No 8)[156]
638 Notice of new class of members	1 Oct 2009 (CO No 8)[157]
639 Notice of name or other designation of class of members	1 Oct 2009 (CO No 8)[158]
640 Notice of particulars of variation of class rights	1 Oct 2009 (CO No 8)[159]
Chapter 10: Reduction of Share Capital	
641 Circumstances in which a company may reduce its share capital	1 Oct 2008 (sub-ss (1)(a), (2)–(6)) (CO No 7)[125] 1 Oct 2009 (otherwise) (CO No 8)
642 Reduction of capital supported by solvency statement	1 Oct 2008 (CO No 7)
643 Solvency statement	20 Jan 2007 (certain purposes) (CO No 1)[3] 1 Oct 2008 (otherwise) (CO No 7)
644 Registration of resolution and supporting documents	20 Jan 2007 (certain purposes) (CO No 1)[3] 1 Oct 2008 (otherwise) (CO No 7)[125]
645 Application to court for order of confirmation	1 Oct 2009 (CO No 8)[160]
646 Creditors entitled to object to reduction	1 Oct 2009 (CO No 8)[160]
647 Offences in connection with list of creditors	1 Oct 2009 (CO No 8)[160]
648 Court order confirming reduction	1 Oct 2009 (CO No 8)[160]
649 Registration of order and statement of capital	20 Jan 2007 (certain purposes) (CO No 1)[3] 1 Oct 2009 (otherwise) (CO No 8)[160]
650 Public company reducing capital below authorised minimum	1 Oct 2009 (CO No 8)[160]
651 Expedited procedure for re-registration as a private company	1 Oct 2009 (CO No 8)[160]
652 Liability of members following reduction of capital	1 Oct 2008 (certain purposes) (CO No 7)[127] 1 Oct 2009 (otherwise) (CO No 8)[161]
653 Liability to creditor in case of omission from list of creditors	1 Oct 2009 (CO No 8)[161]
Chapter 11: Miscellaneous and Supplementary Provisions	
654 Treatment of reserve arising from reduction of capital	20 Jan 2007 (certain purposes) (CO No 1)[3] 1 Oct 2008 (otherwise) (CO No 7)[126]
655 Shares no bar to damages against company	1 Oct 2009 (CO No 8)
656 Public companies: duty of directors to call meeting on serious loss of capital	1 Oct 2009 (CO No 8)
657 General power to make further provision by regulations	20 Jan 2007 (certain purposes) (CO No 1)[3] 1 Oct 2009 (otherwise) (CO No 8)

Provision of CA 2006	Commencement
Part 18: Acquisition by Limited Company of its Own Shares	
Chapter 1: General Provisions	
658 General rule against limited company acquiring its own shares	1 Oct 2009 (CO No 8)
659 Exceptions to general rule	1 Oct 2009 (CO No 8)
660 Treatment of shares held by nominee	1 Oct 2009 (CO No 8)
661 Liability of others where nominee fails to make payment in respect of shares	1 Oct 2009 (CO No 8)
662 Duty to cancel shares in public company held by or for the company	1 Oct 2009 (CO No 8)[162]
663 Notice of cancellation of shares	20 Jan 2007 (certain purposes) (CO No 1)[3] 1 Oct 2009 (otherwise) (CO No 8)[162]
664 Re-registration as private company in consequence of cancellation	1 Oct 2009 (CO No 8)[162]
665 Issue of certificate of incorporation on re-registration	1 Oct 2009 (CO No 8)[162]
666 Effect of failure to re-register	1 Oct 2009 (CO No 8)[162]
667 Offence in case of failure to cancel shares or re-register	1 Oct 2009 (CO No 8)[162]
668 Application of provisions to company re-registering as public company	1 Oct 2009 (CO No 8)[162]
669 Transfer to reserve on acquisition of shares by public company or nominee	1 Oct 2009 (CO No 8)
670 Public companies: general rule against lien or charge on own shares	1 Oct 2009 (CO No 8)
671 Interests to be disregarded in determining whether company has beneficial interest	1 Oct 2009 (CO No 8)
672 Residual interest under pension scheme or employees' share scheme	1 Oct 2009 (CO No 8)
673 Employer's charges and other rights of recovery	1 Oct 2009 (CO No 8)
674 Rights as personal representative or trustee	1 Oct 2009 (CO No 8)
675 Meaning of "pension scheme"	1 Oct 2009 (CO No 8)
676 Application of provisions to directors	1 Oct 2009 (CO No 8)
Chapter 2: Financial Assistance for Purchase of Own Shares	
677 Meaning of "financial assistance"	1 Oct 2009 (CO No 8)
678 Assistance for acquisition of shares in public company	1 Oct 2009 (CO No 8)
679 Assistance by public company for acquisition of shares in its private holding company	1 Oct 2009 (CO No 8)
680 Prohibited financial assistance an offence	1 Oct 2009 (CO No 8)
681 Unconditional exceptions	1 Oct 2009 (CO No 8)
682 Conditional exceptions	1 Oct 2009 (CO No 8)
683 Definitions for this Chapter	1 Oct 2009 (CO No 8)
Chapter 3: Redeemable Shares	
684 Power of limited company to issue redeemable shares	1 Oct 2009 (CO No 8)
685 Terms and manner of redemption	1 Oct 2009 (CO No 8)
686 Payment for redeemable shares	1 Oct 2009 (CO No 8)[163]
687 Financing of redemption	1 Oct 2009 (CO No 8)
688 Redeemed shares treated as cancelled	1 Oct 2009 (CO No 8)
689 Notice to registrar of redemption	20 Jan 2007 (certain purposes) (CO No 1)[3] 1 Oct 2009 (otherwise) (CO No 8)[164]
Chapter 4: Purchase of Own Shares	
690 Power of limited company to purchase own shares	1 Oct 2009 (CO No 8)
691 Payment for purchase of own shares	1 Oct 2009 (CO No 8)
692 Financing of purchase of own shares	1 Oct 2009 (CO No 8)
693 Authority for purchase of own shares	1 Oct 2009 (CO No 8)[165]
693A Authority for off-market purchase for the purposes of or pursuant to an employees' share scheme[224]	30 Apr 2013

Part 2 CA 2006 commencement

Provision of CA 2006	Commencement
694 Authority for off-market purchase	1 Oct 2009 (CO No 8)[165]
695 Resolution authorising off-market purchase: exercise of voting rights	1 Oct 2009 (CO No 8)[165]
696 Resolution authorising off-market purchase: disclosure of details of contract	1 Oct 2009 (CO No 8)[165]
697 Variation of contract for off-market purchase	1 Oct 2009 (CO No 8)[165]
698 Resolution authorising variation: exercise of voting rights	1 Oct 2009 (CO No 8)[165]
699 Resolution authorising variation: disclosure of details of variation	1 Oct 2009 (CO No 8)[165]
700 Release of company's rights under contract for off-market purchase	1 Oct 2009 (CO No 8)[165]
701 Authority for market purchase	1 Oct 2009 (CO No 8)[165]
702 Copy of contract or memorandum to be available for inspection	1 Oct 2009 (CO No 8)
703 Enforcement of right to inspect copy or memorandum	1 Oct 2009 (CO No 8)
704 No assignment of company's right to purchase own shares	1 Oct 2009 (CO No 8)
705 Payments apart from purchase price to be made out of distributable profits	1 Oct 2009 (CO No 8)
706 Treatment of shares purchased	1 Oct 2009 (CO No 8)
707 Return to registrar of purchase of own shares	1 Oct 2009 (CO No 8)[166]
708 Notice to registrar of cancellation of shares	20 Jan 2007 (certain purposes) (CO No 1)[3] 1 Oct 2009 (otherwise) (CO No 8)[166]
Chapter 5: Redemption or Purchase by Private Company Out of Capital	
709 Power of private limited company to redeem or purchase own shares out of capital	1 Oct 2009 (CO No 8)[167]
710 The permissible capital payment	1 Oct 2009 (CO No 8)[167]
711 Available profits	1 Oct 2009 (CO No 8)[167]
712 Determination of available profits	1 Oct 2009 (CO No 8)[167]
713 Requirements for payment out of capital	1 Oct 2009 (CO No 8)[167]
714 Directors' statement and auditor's report	20 Jan 2007 (certain purposes) (CO No 1)[3] 1 Oct 2009 (otherwise) (CO No 8)[167]
715 Directors' statement: offence if no reasonable grounds for opinion	1 Oct 2009 (CO No 8)[167]
716 Payment to be approved by special resolution	1 Oct 2009 (CO No 8)[167]
717 Resolution authorising payment: exercise of voting rights	1 Oct 2009 (CO No 8)[167]
718 Resolution authorising payment: disclosure of directors' statement and auditor's report	1 Oct 2009 (CO No 8)[167]
719 Public notice of proposed payment	1 Oct 2009 (CO No 8)[167]
720 Directors' statement and auditor's report to be available for inspection	1 Oct 2009 (CO No 8)[167]
720A Reduced requirements for payment out of capital for purchase of own shares for the purposes of or pursuant to an employees' share scheme[224]	30 Apr 2013
720B Registration of resolution and supporting documents for purchase of own shares for the purposes of or pursuant to an employees' share scheme[224]	30 Apr 2013
721 Application to court to cancel resolution	1 Oct 2009 (CO No 8)[167]
722 Notice to registrar of court application or order	1 Oct 2009 (CO No 8)[167]
723 Time when payment out of capital to be made or shares to be surrendered	1 Oct 2009 (CO No 8)[167]
Chapter 6: Treasury Shares	
724 Treasury shares	1 Oct 2009 (CO No 8)
725 Treasury shares: maximum holdings[208]	*1 Oct 2009 (CO No 8)*
726 Treasury shares: exercise of rights	1 Oct 2009 (CO No 8)
727 Treasury shares: disposal	20 Jan 2007 (certain purposes) (CO No 1)[3] 1 Oct 2009 (otherwise) (CO No 8)[168]
728 Treasury shares: notice of disposal	1 Oct 2009 (CO No 8)

Provision of CA 2006	Commencement
729 Treasury shares: cancellation	1 Oct 2009 (CO No 8)
730 Treasury shares: notice of cancellation	20 Jan 2007 (certain purposes) (CO No 1)[3] 1 Oct 2009 (otherwise) (CO No 8)[169]
731 Treasury shares: treatment of proceeds of sale	1 Oct 2009 (CO No 8)
732 Treasury shares: offences	1 Oct 2009 (CO No 8)
Chapter 7: Supplementary Provisions	
733 The capital redemption reserve	1 Oct 2008 (certain purposes) (CO No 7)[127] 1 Oct 2009 (otherwise) (CO No 8)
734 Accounting consequences of payment out of capital	1 Oct 2009 (CO No 8)
735 Effect of company's failure to redeem or purchase	1 Oct 2009 (CO No 8)
736 Meaning of "distributable profits"	1 Oct 2009 (CO No 8)
737 General power to make further provision by regulations	20 Jan 2007 (certain purposes) (CO No 1)[3] 1 Oct 2009 (otherwise) (CO No 8)
Part 19: Debentures	
738 Meaning of "debenture"	6 Apr 2008 (CO No 5)
739 Perpetual debentures	6 Apr 2008 (CO No 5)
740 Enforcement of contract to subscribe for debentures	6 Apr 2008 (CO No 5)
741 Registration of allotment of debentures	6 Apr 2008 (CO No 5)[84]
742 Debentures to bearer (Scotland)	6 Apr 2008 (CO No 5)
743 Register of debenture holders	6 Apr 2008 (CO No 5)[85]
744 Register of debenture holders: right to inspect and require copy	20 Jan 2007 (certain purposes) (CO No 1)[3] 6 Apr 2008 (otherwise) (CO No 5)[86]
745 Register of debenture holders: response to request for inspection or copy	6 Apr 2008 (CO No 5)[86]
746 Register of debenture holders: refusal of inspection or default in providing copy	6 Apr 2008 (CO No 5)[86]
747 Register of debenture holders: offences in connection with request for or disclosure of information	6 Apr 2008 (CO No 5)[86]
748 Time limit for claims arising from entry in register	6 Apr 2008 (CO No 5)[87]
749 Right of debenture holder to copy of deed	20 Jan 2007 (certain purposes) (CO No 1)[3] 6 Apr 2008 (otherwise) (CO No 5)[86]
750 Liability of trustees of debentures	6 Apr 2008 (CO No 5)
751 Liability of trustees of debentures: saving for certain older provisions	6 Apr 2008 (CO No 5)
752 Power to re-issue redeemed debentures	6 Apr 2008 (CO No 5)
753 Deposit of debentures to secure advances	6 Apr 2008 (CO No 5)
754 Priorities where debentures secured by floating charge	6 Apr 2008 (CO No 5)
Part 20: Private and Public Companies	
Chapter 1: Prohibition of Public Offers by Private Companies	
755 Prohibition of public offers by private company	6 Apr 2008 (CO No 5)[88]
756 Meaning of "offer to the public"	6 Apr 2008 (CO No 5)[88]
757 Enforcement of prohibition: order restraining proposed contravention	6 Apr 2008 (CO No 5)
758 Enforcement of prohibition: orders available to the court after contravention	6 Apr 2008 (CO No 5)[89]
759 Enforcement of prohibition: remedial order	6 Apr 2008 (CO No 5)[89]
760 Validity of allotment etc not affected	6 Apr 2008 (CO No 5)
Chapter 2: Minimum Share Capital Requirement for Public Companies	
761 Public company: requirement as to minimum share capital	6 Apr 2008 (CO No 5)[90]
762 Procedure for obtaining certificate	6 Apr 2008 (CO No 5)[91]
763 The authorised minimum	20 Jan 2007 (certain purposes) (CO No 1)[3] 6 Apr 2008 (otherwise) (CO No 5)
764 Power to alter authorised minimum	20 Jan 2007 (certain purposes) (CO No 1)[3] 6 Apr 2008 (otherwise) (CO No 5)
765 Authorised minimum: application of initial requirement	6 Apr 2008 (CO No 5)[92]

Part 2 CA 2006 commencement

Provision of CA 2006	Commencement
766 Authorised minimum: application where shares denominated in different currencies etc	20 Jan 2007 (certain purposes) (CO No 1)[3] 6 Apr 2008 (otherwise) (CO No 5)[92]
767 Consequences of doing business etc without a trading certificate	6 Apr 2008 (CO No 5)[93]
Part 21: Certification and Transfer of Securities	
Chapter 1: Certification and Transfer of Securities: General	
768 Share certificate to be evidence of title	6 Apr 2008 (CO No 5)
769 Duty of company as to issue of certificates etc on allotment	6 Apr 2008 (CO No 5)
770 Registration of transfer	6 Apr 2008 (CO No 5)
771 Procedure on transfer being lodged	6 Apr 2008 (CO No 5)[94]
772 Transfer of shares on application of transferor	6 Apr 2008 (CO No 5)
773 Execution of share transfer by personal representative	6 Apr 2008 (CO No 5)
774 Evidence of grant of probate etc	6 Apr 2008 (CO No 5)
775 Certification of instrument of transfer	6 Apr 2008 (CO No 5)
776 Duty of company as to issue of certificates etc on transfer	6 Apr 2008 (CO No 5)
777 Issue of certificates etc: cases within the Stock Transfer Act 1982	6 Apr 2008 (CO No 5)
778 Issue of certificates etc: allotment or transfer to financial institution	6 Apr 2008 (CO No 5)
779 Prohibition on issue of new share warrants and effect of existing share warrants	6 Apr 2008 (CO No 5)
780 Duty of company as to issue of certificates on surrender of share warrant[229]	*6 Apr 2008 (CO No 5)*[95]
781 Offences in connection with share warrants (Scotland)	6 Apr 2008 (CO No 5)
782 Issue of certificates etc: court order to make good default	6 Apr 2008 (CO No 5)
Chapter 2: Evidencing and Transfer of Title to Securities Without Written Instrument	
783 Scope of this Chapter	6 Apr 2008 (CO No 5)
784 Power to make regulations	20 Jan 2007 (certain purposes) (CO No 1)[3] 6 Apr 2008 (otherwise) (CO No 5)
785 Provision enabling procedures for evidencing and transferring title	20 Jan 2007 (certain purposes) (CO No 1)[3] 6 Apr 2008 (otherwise) (CO No 5)
786 Provision enabling or requiring arrangements to be adopted	20 Jan 2007 (certain purposes) (CO No 1)[3] 6 Apr 2008 (otherwise) (CO No 5)
787 Provision enabling or requiring arrangements to be adopted: order-making powers	20 Jan 2007 (certain purposes) (CO No 1)[3] 6 Apr 2008 (otherwise) (CO No 5)
788 Provision that may be included in regulations	20 Jan 2007 (certain purposes) (CO No 1)[3] 6 Apr 2008 (otherwise) (CO No 5)
789 Duty to consult	20 Jan 2007 (certain purposes) (CO No 1)[3] 6 Apr 2008 (otherwise) (CO No 5)
790 Resolutions to be forwarded to registrar	6 Apr 2008 (CO No 5)
Part 21A: Information about people with significant control[231]	
Chapter 1: Introduction	
790A Overview	26 May 2015 (for the purposes of making regulations, rules or orders, and to prepare and issue guidance); 6 Apr 2016 (otherwise)
790B Companies to which this Part applies	26 May 2015 (for the purposes of making regulations, rules or orders, and to prepare and issue guidance); 6 Apr 2016 (otherwise)
790C Key terms	26 May 2015 (for the purposes of making regulations, rules or orders, and to prepare and issue guidance); 6 Apr 2016 (otherwise)
Chapter 2: Information-gathering	
790D Company's duty to investigate and obtain information	26 May 2015 (for the purposes of making regulations, rules or orders, and to prepare and issue guidance); 6 Apr 2016 (otherwise)
790E Company's duty to keep information up-to-date	26 May 2015 (for the purposes of making regulations, rules or orders, and to prepare and issue guidance);

Provision of CA 2006	Commencement
	6 Apr 2016 (otherwise)
790F Failure by company to comply with information duties	26 May 2015 (for the purposes of making regulations, rules or orders, and to prepare and issue guidance); 6 Apr 2016 (otherwise)
790G Duty to supply information	26 May 2015 (for the purposes of making regulations, rules or orders, and to prepare and issue guidance); 6 Apr 2016 (otherwise)
790H Duty to update information	26 May 2015 (for the purposes of making regulations, rules or orders, and to prepare and issue guidance); 6 Apr 2016 (otherwise)
790I Enforcement of disclosure requirements	26 May 2015 (for the purposes of making regulations, rules or orders, and to prepare and issue guidance); 6 Apr 2016 (otherwise)
790J Power to make exemptions	26 May 2015 (for the purposes of making regulations, rules or orders, and to prepare and issue guidance); 6 Apr 2016 (otherwise)
790K Required particulars	26 May 2015 (for the purposes of making regulations, rules or orders, and to prepare and issue guidance); 6 Apr 2016 (otherwise)
790L Required particulars: power to amend	26 May 2015 (for the purposes of making regulations, rules or orders, and to prepare and issue guidance); 6 Apr 2016 (otherwise)
Chapter 3: Register of people with significant control	
790M Duty to keep register	26 May 2015 (for the purposes of making regulations, rules or orders, and to prepare and issue guidance); 6 Apr 2016 (otherwise)
790N Register to be kept available for inspection	26 May 2015 (for the purposes of making regulations, rules or orders, and to prepare and issue guidance); 6 Apr 2016 (otherwise)
790O Rights to inspect and require copies	26 May 2015 (for the purposes of making regulations, rules or orders, and to prepare and issue guidance); 6 Apr 2016 (otherwise)
790P PSC register: response to request for inspection or copy	26 May 2015 (for the purposes of making regulations, rules or orders, and to prepare and issue guidance); 6 Apr 2016 (otherwise)
790Q PSC register: refusal of inspection or default in providing copy	26 May 2015 (for the purposes of making regulations, rules or orders, and to prepare and issue guidance); 6 Apr 2016 (otherwise)
790R PSC register: offences in connection with request for or disclosure of information	26 May 2015 (for the purposes of making regulations, rules or orders, and to prepare and issue guidance); 6 Apr 2016 (otherwise)
790S Information as to state of register	26 May 2015 (for the purposes of making regulations, rules or orders, and to prepare and issue guidance); 6 Apr 2016 (otherwise)
790T Protected information	26 May 2015 (for the purposes of making regulations, rules or orders, and to prepare and issue guidance); 6 Apr 2016 (otherwise)
790U Removal of entries from the register	26 May 2015 (for the purposes of making regulations, rules or orders, and to prepare and issue guidance); 6 Apr 2016 (otherwise)
790V Power of court to rectify register	26 May 2015 (for the purposes of making regulations, rules or orders, and to prepare and issue guidance); 6 Apr 2016 (otherwise)
790VA Notification of changes to the registrar	26 Jun 2017[247]
Chapter 4: Alternative method of record-keeping	
790W Introductory	26 May 2015 (for the purposes of making regulations, rules or orders, and to prepare and issue guidance); 6 Apr 2016 (otherwise)
790X Right to make an election	26 May 2015 (for the purposes of making regulations, rules or orders, and to prepare and issue guidance); 6 Apr 2016 (otherwise)
790Y Effective date of election	26 May 2015 (for the purposes of making regulations, rules or orders, and to prepare and issue guidance); 6 Apr 2016 (otherwise)
790Z Effect of election on obligations under Chapter 3	26 May 2015 (for the purposes of making regulations, rules or orders, and to prepare and issue guidance);

Provision of CA 2006	Commencement
	6 Apr 2016 (otherwise)
790ZA Duty to notify registrar of changes	26 May 2015 (for the purposes of making regulations, rules or orders, and to prepare and issue guidance); 6 Apr 2016 (otherwise)
790ZB Information as to state of central register	26 May 2015 (for the purposes of making regulations, rules or orders, and to prepare and issue guidance); 6 Apr 2016 (otherwise)
790ZC Power of court to order company to remedy default or delay	26 May 2015 (for the purposes of making regulations, rules or orders, and to prepare and issue guidance); 6 Apr 2016 (otherwise)
790ZD Withdrawing the election	26 May 2015 (for the purposes of making regulations, rules or orders, and to prepare and issue guidance); 6 Apr 2016 (otherwise)
790ZE Power to extend option to public companies	26 May 2015 (for the purposes of making regulations, rules or orders, and to prepare and issue guidance); 6 Apr 2016 (otherwise)
Chapter 5: Protection from disclosure	
790ZF Protection of information as to usual residential address	26 May 2015 (for the purposes of making regulations, rules or orders, and to prepare and issue guidance); 6 Apr 2016 (otherwise)
790ZG Power to make regulations protecting material	26 May 2015 (for the purposes of making regulations, rules or orders, and to prepare and issue guidance); 6 Apr 2016 (otherwise)
Part 22: Information About Interests in a Company's Shares	
791 Companies to which this Part applies	20 Jan 2007 (CO No 1)
792 Shares to which this Part applies	20 Jan 2007 (CO No 1)
793 Notice by company requiring information about interests in its shares	20 Jan 2007 (CO No 1)
794 Notice requiring information: order imposing restrictions on shares	20 Jan 2007 (CO No 1)
795 Notice requiring information: offences	20 Jan 2007 (CO No 1)
796 Notice requiring information: persons exempted from obligation to comply	20 Jan 2007 (CO No 1)
797 Consequences of order imposing restrictions	20 Jan 2007 (CO No 1)
798 Penalty for attempted evasion of restrictions	20 Jan 2007 (CO No 1)
799 Relaxation of restrictions	20 Jan 2007 (CO No 1)
800 Removal of restrictions	20 Jan 2007 (CO No 1)
801 Order for sale of shares	20 Jan 2007 (CO No 1)
802 Application of proceeds of sale under court order	20 Jan 2007 (CO No 1)
803 Power of members to require company to act	20 Jan 2007 (CO No 1)
804 Duty of company to comply with requirement	20 Jan 2007 (CO No 1)
805 Report to members on outcome of investigation	20 Jan 2007 (CO No 1)
806 Report to members: offences	20 Jan 2007 (CO No 1)
807 Right to inspect and request copy of reports	20 Jan 2007 (CO No 1)
808 Register of interests disclosed	20 Jan 2007 (CO No 1)[70]
809 Register to be kept available for inspection	20 Jan 2007 (CO No 1)[70]
810 Associated index	20 Jan 2007 (CO No 1)
811 Rights to inspect and require copy of entries	20 Jan 2007 (sub-ss (1)–(3)) (CO No 1) 6 Apr 2008 (otherwise) (CO No 5)[96]
812 Court supervision of purpose for which rights may be exercised	6 Apr 2008 (CO No 5)[96]
813 Register of interests disclosed: refusal of inspection or default in providing copy	20 Jan 2007 (CO No 1)[43]
814 Register of interests disclosed: offences in connection with request for or disclosure of information	6 Apr 2008 (CO No 5)[96]
815 Entries not to be removed from register	20 Jan 2007 (CO No 1)
816 Removal of entries from register: old entries	20 Jan 2007 (CO No 1)
817 Removal of entries from register: incorrect entry relating to third party	20 Jan 2007 (CO No 1)
818 Adjustment of entry relating to share acquisition agreement	20 Jan 2007 (CO No 1)

Provision of CA 2006	Commencement
819 Duty of company ceasing to be public company	20 Jan 2007 (CO No 1)
820 Interest in shares: general	20 Jan 2007 (CO No 1)
821 Interest in shares: right to subscribe for shares	20 Jan 2007 (CO No 1)
822 Interest in shares: family interests	20 Jan 2007 (CO No 1)
823 Interest in shares: corporate interests	20 Jan 2007 (CO No 1)
824 Interest in shares: agreement to acquire interests in a particular company	20 Jan 2007 (CO No 1)
825 Extent of obligation in case of share acquisition agreement	20 Jan 2007 (CO No 1)
826 Information protected from wider disclosure	20 Jan 2007 (CO No 1)[43]
827 Reckoning of periods for fulfilling obligations	20 Jan 2007 (CO No 1)
828 Power to make further provision by regulations	20 Jan 2007 (CO No 1)
Part 23: Distributions	
Chapter 1: Restrictions on When Distributions may be Made	
829 Meaning of "distribution"	6 Apr 2008 (CO No 5)[97]
830 Distributions to be made only out of profits available for the purpose	6 Apr 2008 (CO No 5)[97]
831 Net asset restriction on distributions by public companies	6 Apr 2008 (CO No 5)[97]
832 Distributions by investment companies out of accumulated revenue profits	6 Apr 2008 (CO No 5)[97]
833 Meaning of "investment company"	6 Apr 2008 (CO No 5)[97]
833A Distributions by insurance companies authorised under the Solvency 2 Directive	30 Dec 2016[241]
834 Investment company: condition as to holdings in other companies[217]	*6 Apr 2008 (CO No 5)*[97]
835 Power to extend provisions relating to investment companies[217]	*20 Jan 2007 (certain purposes) (CO No 1)*[3] *6 Apr 2008 (otherwise) (CO No 5)*[97]
Chapter 2: Justification of Distribution by Reference to Accounts	
836 Justification of distribution by reference to relevant accounts	6 Apr 2008 (CO No 5)[97]
837 Requirements where last annual accounts used	6 Apr 2008 (CO No 5)[97]
838 Requirements where interim accounts used	6 Apr 2008 (CO No 5)[97]
839 Requirements where initial accounts used	6 Apr 2008 (CO No 5)[97]
840 Successive distributions etc by reference to the same accounts	6 Apr 2008 (CO No 5)[97]
Chapter 3: Supplementary Provisions	
841 Realised losses and profits and revaluation of fixed assets	6 Apr 2008 (CO No 5)[97]
842 Determination of profit or loss in respect of asset where records incomplete	6 Apr 2008 (CO No 5)[97]
843 Realised profits and losses of long-term insurance business of certain insurance companies	6 Apr 2008 (CO No 5)[97]
844 Treatment of development costs	6 Apr 2008 (CO No 5)[97]
845 Distributions in kind: determination of amount	6 Apr 2008 (CO No 5)[97]
846 Distributions in kind: treatment of unrealised profits	6 Apr 2008 (CO No 5)[97]
847 Consequences of unlawful distribution	6 Apr 2008 (CO No 5)[97]
848 Saving for certain older provisions in articles	6 Apr 2008 (CO No 5)[97]
849 Restriction on application of unrealised profits	6 Apr 2008 (CO No 5)[97]
850 Treatment of certain older profits or losses	6 Apr 2008 (CO No 5)[97]
851 Application of rules of law restricting distributions	6 Apr 2008 (CO No 5)[97]
852 Saving for other restrictions on distributions	6 Apr 2008 (CO No 5)[97]
853 Minor definitions	6 Apr 2008 (CO No 5)[97]
Part 24: Annual confirmation of accuracy of information on register[232]	
853A Duty to deliver confirmation statements	30 Jun 2016
853B Duties to notify a relevant event	30 Jun 2016
853C Duty to notify a change in company's principal business activities	30 Jun 2016

Provision of CA 2006	Commencement
853D Duty to deliver statement of capital	30 Jun 2016
853E Duty to notify trading status of shares	30 Jun 2016
853F Duty to deliver shareholder information: non-traded companies	1 May 2016 (for the purpose of enabling the registrar to impose the requirements referred to in sub-s (6) of this section); 30 Jun 2016 (otherwise)
853G Duty to deliver shareholder information: certain traded companies	30 Jun 2016
853H Duty to deliver information about exemption from Part 21A	30 Jun 2016
853I Duty to deliver information about people with significant control	*30 Jun 2016*[203]
853J Power to amend duties to deliver certain information	30 Jun 2016
853K Confirmation statements: power to make further provision by regulations	30 Jun 2016
853L Failure to deliver confirmation statement	30 Jun 2016
Part 25: Company Charges	
Chapter A1: Registration of Company Charges[220]	
859A Charges created by a company	6 Apr 2013
859B Charge in series of debentures	6 Apr 2013
859C Charges existing on property or undertaking acquired	6 Apr 2013
859D Particulars to be delivered to registrar	6 Apr 2013
859E Date of creation of charge	6 Apr 2013
859F Extension of period allowed for delivery	6 Apr 2013
859G Personal information etc in certified copies	6 Apr 2013
859H Consequence of failure to deliver charges	6 Apr 2013
859I Entries on the register	6 Apr 2013
859J Company holding property or undertaking as trustee	6 Apr 2013
859K Registration of enforcement of security	6 Apr 2013
859L Entries of satisfaction and release	6 Apr 2013
859M Rectification of register	6 Apr 2013
859N Replacement of instrument or debenture	6 Apr 2013
859O Notification of addition to or amendment of charge	6 Apr 2013
859P Companies to keep copies of instruments creating and amending charges	6 Apr 2013
859Q Instruments creating charges to be available for inspection	6 Apr 2013
Chapter 1: Companies Registered in England and Wales or in Northern Ireland[221]	
860 Charges created by a company	*20 Jan 2007 (certain purposes) (CO No 1)*[3] *1 Oct 2009 (otherwise) (CO No 8)*[171]
861 Charges which have to be registered: supplementary	*1 Oct 2009 (CO No 8)*
862 Charges existing on property acquired	*20 Jan 2007 (certain purposes) (CO No 1)*[3] *1 Oct 2009 (otherwise) (CO No 8)*[172]
863 Charge in series of debentures	*1 Oct 2009 (CO No 8)*[173]
864 Additional registration requirement for commission etc in relation to debentures	*1 Oct 2009 (CO No 8)*
865 Endorsement of certificate on debentures	*1 Oct 2009 (CO No 8)*
866 Charges created in, or over property in, jurisdictions outside the United Kingdom	*1 Oct 2009 (CO No 8)*
867 Charges created in, or over property in, another United Kingdom jurisdiction	*1 Oct 2009 (CO No 8)*
868 Northern Ireland: registration of certain charges etc affecting land	*1 Oct 2009 (CO No 8)*[174]
869 Register of charges to be kept by registrar	*1 Oct 2009 (CO No 8)*
870 The period allowed for registration	*1 Oct 2009 (CO No 8)*
871 Registration of enforcement of security	*1 Oct 2009 (CO No 8)*[175]

Provision of CA 2006	Commencement
872 Entries of satisfaction and release	*1 Oct 2009 (CO No 8)*[176]
873 Rectification of register of charges	*1 Oct 2009 (CO No 8)*
874 Consequence of failure to register charges created by a company	*1 Oct 2009 (CO No 8)*
875 Companies to keep copies of instruments creating charges	*1 Oct 2009 (CO No 8)*
876 Company's register of charges	*1 Oct 2009 (CO No 8)*
877 Instruments creating charges and register of charges to be available for inspection	*20 Jan 2007 (certain purposes) (CO No 1)*[3] 1 Oct 2009 (otherwise) (CO No 8)
Chapter 2: Companies Registered in Scotland[221]	
878 Charges created by a company	*20 Jan 2007 (certain purposes) (CO No 1)*[3] *1 Oct 2009 (otherwise) (CO No 8)*[171]
879 Charges which have to be registered: supplementary	*1 Oct 2009 (CO No 8)*
880 Duty to register charges existing on property acquired	*20 Jan 2007 (certain purposes) (CO No 1)*[3] *1 Oct 2009 (otherwise) (CO No 8)*[172]
881 Charge by way of ex facie absolute disposition, etc	*1 Oct 2009 (CO No 8)*
882 Charge in series of debentures	*1 Oct 2009 (CO No 8)*[173]
883 Additional registration requirement for commission etc in relation to debentures	*1 Oct 2009 (CO No 8)*
884 Charges on property outside United Kingdom	*1 Oct 2009 (CO No 8)*
885 Register of charges to be kept by registrar	*1 Oct 2009 (CO No 8)*
886 The period allowed for registration	*1 Oct 2009 (CO No 8)*
887 Entries of satisfaction and relief	*1 Oct 2009 (CO No 8)*[176]
888 Rectification of register of charges	*1 Oct 2009 (CO No 8)*
889 Charges void unless registered	*1 Oct 2009 (CO No 8)*
890 Copies of instruments creating charges to be kept by company	*1 Oct 2009 (CO No 8)*
891 Company's register of charges	*1 Oct 2009 (CO No 8)*
892 Instruments creating charges and register of charges to be available for inspection	*20 Jan 2007 (certain purposes) (CO No 1)*[3] *1 Oct 2009 (otherwise) (CO No 8)*
Chapter 3: Powers of the Secretary of State	
893 Power to make provision for effect of registration in special register	20 Jan 2007 (certain purposes) (CO No 1)[3] 1 Oct 2009 (otherwise) (CO No 8)
894 General power to make amendments to this Part	20 Jan 2007 (certain purposes) (CO No 1)[3] 1 Oct 2009 (otherwise) (CO No 8)
Part 26: Arrangements and Reconstructions: General	
895 Application of this Part	6 Apr 2008 (CO No 5)
896 Court order for holding of meeting	6 Apr 2008 (CO No 5)
897 Statement to be circulated or made available	6 Apr 2008 (CO No 5)
898 Duty of directors and trustees to provide information	6 Apr 2008 (CO No 5)
899 Court sanction for compromise or arrangement	6 Apr 2008 (CO No 5)
899A Moratorium debts, etc[254]	26 Jun 2020
900 Powers of court to facilitate reconstruction or amalgamation	6 Apr 2008 (CO No 5)
901 Obligations of company with respect to articles etc	6 Apr 2008 (CO No 5)[98]
Part 26A: Arrangements and Reconstructions: Companies in Financial Difficulty[254]	
901A Application of this Part	26 Jun 2020
901B Power to exclude companies providing financial services, etc	26 Jun 2020
901C Court order for holding of meeting	26 Jun 2020
901D Statement to be circulated or made available	26 Jun 2020
901E Duty of directors and trustees to provide information	26 Jun 2020
901F Court sanction for compromise or arrangement	26 Jun 2020
901G Sanction for compromise or arrangement where one or more classes dissent	26 Jun 2020

Provision of CA 2006	Commencement
901H Moratorium debts, etc	26 Jun 2020
901I Pension schemes	26 Jun 2020
901J Powers of court to facilitate reconstruction or amalgamation	26 Jun 2020
901K Obligations of company with respect to articles etc	26 Jun 2020
901L Power to amend Act	26 Jun 2020
Part 27: Mergers and Divisions of Public Companies	
Chapter 1: Introductory	
902 Application of this Part	6 Apr 2008 (CO No 5)
903 Relationship of this Part to Parts 26 and 26A	6 Apr 2008 (CO No 5)
Chapter 2: Merger	
904 Mergers and merging companies	6 Apr 2008 (CO No 5)
905 Draft terms of scheme (merger)	6 Apr 2008 (CO No 5)
906 Publication of draft terms by registrar (merger)	6 Apr 2008 (CO No 5)
906A Publication of draft terms on company website (merger)[215]	1 Aug 2011
907 Approval of members of merging companies	6 Apr 2008 (CO No 5)
908 Directors' explanatory report (merger)	6 Apr 2008 (CO No 5)
909 Expert's report (merger)	6 Apr 2008 (CO No 5)
910 Supplementary accounting statement (merger)	6 Apr 2008 (CO No 5)
911 Inspection of documents (merger)	6 Apr 2008 (CO No 5)
911A Publication of documents on company website (merger)[215]	1 Aug 2011
911B Report on material changes of assets of merging companies[215]	1 Aug 2011
912 Approval of articles of new transferee company (merger)	6 Apr 2008 (CO No 5)
913 Protection of holders of securities to which special rights attached (merger)	6 Apr 2008 (CO No 5)
914 No allotment of shares to transferor company or transferee company (merger)[210]	6 Apr 2008
915 Circumstances in which certain particulars and reports not required (merger)	6 Apr 2008 (CO No 5)
915A Other circumstances in which reports and inspection not required (merger)[215]	1 Aug 2011
916 Circumstances in which meeting of members of transferee company not required (merger)	6 Apr 2008 (CO No 5)
917 Circumstances in which no meetings required (merger)	6 Apr 2008 (CO No 5)
917A Other circumstances in which meeting of members of transferor company not required (merger)[254]	26 Jun 2020
918 Other circumstances in which meeting of members of transferee company not required (merger)	6 Apr 2008 (CO No 5)
918A Agreement to dispense with reports etc (merger)[123]	6 Apr 2008
Chapter 3: Division	
919 Divisions and companies involved in a division	6 Apr 2008 (CO No 5)
920 Draft terms of scheme (division)	6 Apr 2008 (CO No 5)
921 Publication of draft terms by registrar (division)	6 Apr 2008 (CO No 5)
921A Publication of draft terms on company website (division)[215]	1 Aug 2011
922 Approval of members of companies involved in the division	6 Apr 2008 (CO No 5)
923 Directors' explanatory report (division)	6 Apr 2008 (CO No 5)[99]
924 Expert's report (division)	6 Apr 2008 (CO No 5)
925 Supplementary accounting statement (division)	6 Apr 2008 (CO No 5)
926 Inspection of documents (division)	6 Apr 2008 (CO No 5)
926A Publication of documents on company website	1 Aug 2011

Provision of CA 2006	Commencement
(division)[215]	
927 Report on material changes of assets of transferor company (division)	6 Apr 2008 (CO No 5)
928 Approval of articles of new transferee company (division)	6 Apr 2008 (CO No 5)
929 Protection of holders of securities to which special rights attached (division)	6 Apr 2008 (CO No 5)
930 No allotment of shares to transferor company or to transferee company (division)[210]	6 Apr 2008
931 Circumstances in which meeting of members of transferor company not required (division)	6 Apr 2008 (CO No 5)
931A Other circumstances in which meeting of members of transferor company not required (division)[254]	26 Jun 2020
932 Circumstances in which meeting of members of transferee company not required (division)	6 Apr 2008 (CO No 5)
933 Agreement to dispense with reports etc (division)	6 Apr 2008 (CO No 5)
933A Certain requirements excluded where shareholders given proportional rights (division)[215]	1 Aug 2011
934 Power of court to exclude certain requirements (division)	6 Apr 2008 (CO No 5)
Chapter 4: Supplementary Provisions	
935 Expert's report: valuation by another person	6 Apr 2008 (CO No 5)
936 Experts and valuers: independence requirement	20 Jan 2007 (certain purposes) (CO No 1)[3] 6 Apr 2008 (otherwise) (CO No 5)
937 Experts and valuers: meaning of "associate"	6 Apr 2008 (CO No 5)
938 Power of court to summon meeting of members or creditors of existing transferee company	6 Apr 2008 (CO No 5)
939 Court to fix date for transfer of undertaking etc of transferor company	6 Apr 2008 (CO No 5)
940 Liability of transferee companies for each other's defaults	6 Apr 2008 (CO No 5)
940A Disregard of website failures beyond control of company[215]	1 Aug 2011
941 Meaning of "liabilities" and "property"	6 Apr 2008 (CO No 5)
Part 28: Takeovers etc	
Chapter 1: The Takeover Panel	
942 The Panel	6 Apr 2007 (CO No 2)
943 Rules	6 Apr 2007 (CO No 2)[44]
944 Further provisions about rules	6 Apr 2007 (CO No 2)
945 Rulings	6 Apr 2007 (CO No 2)
946 Directions	6 Apr 2007 (CO No 2)
947 Power to require documents and information	6 Apr 2007 (CO No 2)
948 Restrictions on disclosure	20 Jan 2007 (certain purposes) (CO No 1)[3] 6 Apr 2007 (otherwise) (CO No 2)
949 Offence of disclosure in contravention of section 948	6 Apr 2007 (CO No 2)
950 Panel's duty of co-operation	6 Apr 2007 (CO No 2)
951 Hearings and appeals	6 Apr 2007 (CO No 2)
952 Sanctions	6 Apr 2007 (CO No 2)
953 Failure to comply with rules about bid documentation	6 Apr 2007 (CO No 2)[44]
954 Compensation	6 Apr 2007 (CO No 2)
955 Enforcement by the court	6 Apr 2007 (CO No 2)
956 No action for breach of statutory duty etc	6 Apr 2007 (CO No 2)
957 Fees and charges	6 Apr 2007 (CO No 2)
958 Levy	20 Jan 2007 (certain purposes) (CO No 1)[3] 6 Apr 2007 (otherwise) (CO No 2)
959 Recovery of fees, charges or levy	6 Apr 2007 (CO No 2)
960 Panel as party to proceedings	6 Apr 2007 (CO No 2)

Provision of CA 2006	Commencement
961 Exemption from liability in damages	6 Apr 2007 (CO No 2)
962 Privilege against self-incrimination	6 Apr 2007 (CO No 2)
963 Annual reports	6 Apr 2007 (CO No 2)
964 Amendments to Financial Services and Markets Act 2000	6 Apr 2007 (CO No 2)
965 Power to extend to Isle of Man and Channel Islands	20 Jan 2007 (certain purposes) (CO No 1)[3] 6 Apr 2007 (otherwise) (CO No 2)
Chapter 2: Impediments to Takeovers	
966 Opting in and opting out	20 Jan 2007 (certain purposes) (CO No 1)[3] 6 Apr 2007 (otherwise) (CO No 2)
967 Further provision about opting-in and opting-out resolutions	6 Apr 2007 (CO No 2)
968 Effect on contractual restrictions	6 Apr 2007 (CO No 2)[45]
969 Power of offeror to require general meeting to be called	6 Apr 2007 (CO No 2)
970 Communication of decisions	6 Apr 2007 (CO No 2)
971 Interpretation of this Chapter	6 Apr 2007 (CO No 2)
972 Transitory provision	6 Apr 2007 (CO No 2)
973 Power to extend to Isle of Man and Channel Islands	20 Jan 2007 (certain purposes) (CO No 1)[3] 6 Apr 2007 (otherwise) (CO No 2)
Chapter 3: "Squeeze-Out" and "Sell-Out"	
974 Meaning of "takeover offer"	6 Apr 2007 (CO No 2)
975 Shares already held by the offeror etc	6 Apr 2007 (CO No 2)
976 Cases where offer treated as being on same terms	6 Apr 2007 (CO No 2)
977 Shares to which an offer relates	6 Apr 2007 (CO No 2)
978 Effect of impossibility etc of communicating or accepting offer	6 Apr 2007 (CO No 2)
979 Right of offeror to buy out minority shareholder	6 Apr 2007 (CO No 2)
980 Further provision about notices given under section 979	20 Jan 2007 (certain purposes) (CO No 1)[3] 6 Apr 2007 (otherwise) (CO No 2)
981 Effect of notice under section 979	6 Apr 2007 (CO No 2)
982 Further provision about consideration held on trust under section 981(9)	6 Apr 2007 (CO No 2)
983 Right of minority shareholder to be bought out by offeror	6 Apr 2007 (CO No 2)
984 Further provision about rights conferred by section 983	20 Jan 2007 (certain purposes) (CO No 1)[3] 6 Apr 2007 (otherwise) (CO No 2)
985 Effect of requirement under section 983	6 Apr 2007 (CO No 2)
986 Applications to the court	6 Apr 2007 (CO No 2)
987 Joint offers	6 Apr 2007 (CO No 2)
988 Associates	6 Apr 2007 (CO No 2)
989 Convertible securities	6 Apr 2007 (CO No 2)
990 Debentures carrying voting rights	6 Apr 2007 (CO No 2)
991 Interpretation	6 Apr 2007 (CO No 2)
Chapter 4: Amendments to Part 7 of the Companies Act 1985	
992 Matters to be dealt with in directors' report	6 Apr 2007 (CO No 2)
Part 29: Fraudulent Trading	
993 Offence of fraudulent trading	1 Oct 2007 (CO No 3)[46]
Part 30: Protection of Members Against Unfair Prejudice	
994 Petition by company member	1 Oct 2007 (CO No 3)[47]
995 Petition by Secretary of State	1 Oct 2007 (CO No 3)
996 Powers of the court under this Part	1 Oct 2007 (CO No 3)
997 Application of general rule-making powers	1 Oct 2007 (CO No 3)
998 Copy of order affecting company's constitution to be delivered to registrar	1 Oct 2007 (CO No 3)
999 Supplementary provisions where company's constitution altered	1 Oct 2007 (CO No 3)[48]

Provision of CA 2006	Commencement
Part 31: Dissolution and Restoration to the Register	
Chapter 1: Striking Off	
1000 Power to strike off company not carrying on business or in operation	1 Oct 2009 (CO No 8)
1001 Duty to act in case of company being wound up	1 Oct 2009 (CO No 8)
1002 Supplementary provisions as to service of communication or notice	1 Oct 2009 (CO No 8)
1003 Striking off on application by company	20 Jan 2007 (certain purposes) (CO No 1)[3] 1 Oct 2009 (otherwise) (CO No 8)
1004 Circumstances in which application not to be made: activities of company	20 Jan 2007 (certain purposes) (CO No 1)[3] 1 Oct 2009 (otherwise) (CO No 8)
1005 Circumstances in which application not to be made: other proceedings not concluded	1 Oct 2009 (CO No 8)
1006 Copy of application to be given to members, employees, etc	20 Jan 2007 (certain purposes) (CO No 1)[3] 1 Oct 2009 (otherwise) (CO No 8)
1007 Copy of application to be given to new members, employees, etc	20 Jan 2007 (certain purposes) (CO No 1)[3] 1 Oct 2009 (otherwise) (CO No 8)
1008 Copy of application: provisions as to service of documents	1 Oct 2009 (CO No 8)
1009 Circumstances in which application to be withdrawn	20 Jan 2007 (certain purposes) (CO No 1)[3] 1 Oct 2009 (otherwise) (CO No 8)
1010 Withdrawal of application	1 Oct 2009 (CO No 8)
1011 Meaning of "creditor"	1 Oct 2009 (CO No 8)
Chapter 2: Property of Dissolved Company	
1012 Property of dissolved company to be bona vacantia	1 Oct 2009 (CO No 8)[177]
1013 Crown disclaimer of property vesting as bona vacantia	1 Oct 2009 (CO No 8)[177]
1014 Effect of Crown disclaimer	1 Oct 2009 (CO No 8)[177]
1015 General effect of disclaimer	1 Oct 2009 (CO No 8)[177]
1016 Disclaimer of leaseholds	1 Oct 2009 (CO No 8)[177]
1017 Power of court to make vesting order	1 Oct 2009 (CO No 8)[177]
1018 Protection of persons holding under a lease	1 Oct 2009 (CO No 8)[177]
1019 Land subject to rentcharge	1 Oct 2009 (CO No 8)[177]
1020 General effect of disclaimer	1 Oct 2009 (CO No 8)[177]
1021 Power of court to make vesting order	1 Oct 2009 (CO No 8)[177]
1022 Protection of persons holding under a lease	1 Oct 2009 (CO No 8)[177]
1023 Liability for rentcharge on company's land after dissolution	1 Oct 2009 (CO No 8)[177]
Chapter 3: Restoration to the Register	
1024 Application for administrative restoration to the register	1 Oct 2009 (CO No 8)
1025 Requirements for administrative restoration	1 Oct 2009 (CO No 8)
1026 Application to be accompanied by statement of compliance	1 Oct 2009 (CO No 8)
1027 Registrar's decision on application for administrative restoration	1 Oct 2009 (CO No 8)
1028 Effect of administrative restoration	1 Oct 2009 (CO No 8)
1028A Administrative restoration of company with share warrants[231]	26 May 2015
1029 Application to court for restoration to the register	1 Oct 2009 (CO No 8)[178]
1030 When application to the court may be made	1 Oct 2009 (CO No 8)[178]
1031 Decision on application for restoration by the court	1 Oct 2009 (CO No 8)[178]
1032 Effect of court order for restoration to the register	1 Oct 2009 (CO No 8)[178]
1032A Restoration by court of company with share warrants[231]	26 May 2015
1033 Company's name on restoration	1 Oct 2009 (CO No 8)
1034 Effect of restoration to the register where property has vested as bona vacantia	1 Oct 2009 (CO No 8)[179]

Provision of CA 2006	Commencement
Part 32: Company Investigations: Amendments	
1035 Powers of Secretary of State to give directions to inspectors	1 Oct 2007 (CO No 3)[49]
1036 Resignation, removal and replacement of inspectors	1 Oct 2007 (CO No 3)[49]
1037 Power to obtain information from former inspectors etc	1 Oct 2007 (CO No 3)[49]
1038 Power to require production of documents	1 Oct 2007 (CO No 3)[49]
1039 Disqualification orders: consequential amendments[230]	*1 Oct 2007 (CO No 3)*[49]
Part 33: UK Companies Not Formed Under Companies Legislation	
Chapter 1: Companies Not Formed Under Companies Legislation but Authorised to Register	
1040 Companies authorised to register under this Act	1 Oct 2009 (CO No 8)[180]
1041 Definition of "joint stock company"	1 Oct 2009 (CO No 8)[180]
1042 Power to make provision by regulations	20 Jan 2007 (certain purposes) (CO No 1)[3] 1 Oct 2009 (otherwise) (CO No 8)[180]
Chapter 2: Unregistered Companies	
1043 Unregistered companies	20 Jan 2007 (certain purposes) (CO No 1)[3] 6 Apr 2007 (otherwise) (CO No 2)
Part 34: Overseas Companies	
1044 Overseas companies	1 Oct 2009 (CO No 8)
1045 Company contracts and execution of documents by companies	20 Jan 2007 (certain purposes) (CO No 1)[3] 1 Oct 2009 (otherwise) (CO No 8)
1046 Duty to register particulars	20 Jan 2007 (certain purposes) (CO No 1)[3] 1 Oct 2009 (otherwise) (CO No 8)
1047 Registered name of overseas company	1 Oct 2009 (CO No 8)
1048 Registration under alternative name	1 Oct 2009 (CO No 8)
1049 Accounts and reports: general	20 Jan 2007 (certain purposes) (CO No 1)[3] 1 Oct 2009 (otherwise) (CO No 8)
1050 Accounts and reports: credit or financial institutions	20 Jan 2007 (certain purposes) (CO No 1)[3] 1 Oct 2009 (otherwise) (CO No 8)
1051 Trading disclosures	20 Jan 2007 (certain purposes) (CO No 1)[3] 1 Oct 2009 (otherwise) (CO No 8)
1052 Company charges	20 Jan 2007 (certain purposes) (CO No 1)[3] 1 Oct 2009 (otherwise) (CO No 8)
1053 Other returns etc	20 Jan 2007 (certain purposes) (CO No 1)[3] 1 Oct 2009 (otherwise) (CO No 8)
1054 Offences	20 Jan 2007 (certain purposes) (CO No 1)[3] 1 Oct 2009 (otherwise) (CO No 8)
1055 Disclosure of individual's residential address: protection from disclosure	20 Jan 2007 (certain purposes) (CO No 1)[3] 1 Oct 2009 (otherwise) (CO No 8)
1056 Requirement to identify persons authorised to accept service of documents	20 Jan 2007 (certain purposes) (CO No 1)[3] 1 Oct 2009 (otherwise) (CO No 8)
1057 Registrar to whom returns, notices etc to be delivered	20 Jan 2007 (certain purposes) (CO No 1)[3] 1 Oct 2009 (otherwise) (CO No 8)
1058 Duty to give notice of ceasing to have registrable presence	20 Jan 2007 (certain purposes) (CO No 1)[3] 1 Oct 2009 (otherwise) (CO No 8)
1059 Application of provisions in case of relocation of branch	1 Oct 2009 (CO No 8)
Part 35: The Registrar of Companies	
1059A Scheme of this Part[206]	1 Oct 2009
1060 The registrar	6 Apr 2007 (certain purposes) (CO No 1)[50] 1 Oct 2009 (otherwise) (CO No 8)
1061 The registrar's functions	6 Apr 2007 (certain purposes) (CO No 1)[50] 1 Oct 2009 (otherwise) (CO No 8)
1062 The registrar's official seal	1 Oct 2009 (CO No 8)
1063 Fees payable to registrar	20 Jan 2007 (certain purposes) (CO No 1)[3] 6 Apr 2007 (GB otherwise) (CO No 1)[51] 1 Oct 2009 (NI otherwise) (CO No 8)[181]
1064 Public notice of issue of certificate of	1 Oct 2009 (CO No 8)[182]

Provision of CA 2006	Commencement
incorporation	
1065 Right to certificate of incorporation	1 Oct 2009 (CO No 8)[183]
1066 Company's registered numbers	1 Oct 2009 (CO No 8)
1067 Registered numbers of UK establishments of overseas company	1 Oct 2009 (CO No 8)
1068 Registrar's requirements as to form, authentication and manner of delivery	1 Jan 2007 (sub-s (5), and sub-ss (1)–(4), (6), (7)for certain purposes) (CO No 1)[52] 15 Dec 2007 (sub-ss (1)–(4), (6), (7)for certain purposes) (CO No 3)[53] 1 Oct 2009 (otherwise) (CO No 8)[184]
1069 Power to require delivery by electronic means	20 Jan 2007 (certain purposes) (CO No 1)[3] 1 Oct 2009 (otherwise) (CO No 8)[184]
1070 Agreement for delivery by electronic means	1 Oct 2009 (CO No 8)[185]
1071 Document not delivered until received	1 Oct 2009 (CO No 8)[186]
1072 Requirements for proper delivery	1 Oct 2009 (CO No 8)[187]
1073 Power to accept documents not meeting requirements for proper delivery	1 Oct 2009 (CO No 8)[187]
1074 Documents containing unnecessary material	1 Oct 2009 (CO No 8)[187]
1075 Informal correction of document	1 Oct 2009 (CO No 8)[188]
1076 Replacement of document not meeting requirements for proper delivery	1 Oct 2009 (CO No 8)[189]
1077 Public notice of receipt of certain documents	1 Jan 2007 (CO No 1)[54]
1078 Enhanced disclosure documents	1 Jan 2007 (CO No 1)[190]
1079 Effect of failure to give public notice	1 Jan 2007 (CO No 1)[190]
1079A Provision of information for publication on European e-Justice portal[227]	*7 Jul 2014*[252]
1079B Duty to notify directors[231]	10 Oct 2015
1080 The register	1 Jan 2007 (CO No 1)[54]
1081 Annotation of the register	20 Jan 2007 (certain purposes) (CO No 1)[3] 1 Oct 2009 (otherwise) (CO No 8)[191]
1082 Allocation of unique identifiers	20 Jan 2007 (certain purposes) (CO No 1)[3] 1 Oct 2009 (otherwise) (CO No 8)
1083 Preservation of original documents	1 Oct 2009 (CO No 8)
1084 Records relating to companies that have been dissolved etc	1 Oct 2009 (CO No 8)
1084A Recording of optional information on register[231]	26 May 2015
1085 Inspection of the register	1 Jan 2007 (CO No 1)[54]
1086 Right to copy of material on the register	1 Jan 2007 (CO No 1)
1087 Material not available for public inspection	1 Jan 2007 (CO No 1)[54]
1087ZA Required particulars available for public inspection for limited period[250]	10 Jan 2020
1087A Information about a person's date of birth[231]	10 Oct 2015 (sub-ss (1), (2) (3)(a), (4)(c), (8), (9)); 30 Jun 2016 (otherwise)
1087B Disclosure of DOB information[231]	26 May 2015 (in so far as relating to the power to make Regulations); 10 Oct 2015 (except for sub-s (4)); 30 Jun 2016 (sub-s (4))
1088 Application to registrar to make address unavailable for public inspection	1 Jan 2007 (CO No 1)
1089 Form of application for inspection or copy	1 Jan 2007 (CO No 1)
1090 Form and manner in which copies to be provided	1 Jan 2007 (CO No 1)
1091 Certification of copies as accurate	1 Jan 2007 (CO No 1)
1092 Issue of process for production of records kept by the registrar	1 Jan 2007 (CO No 1)
1093 Registrar's notice to resolve inconsistency on the register	1 Oct 2009 (CO No 8)[192]
1094 Administrative removal of material from the register	1 Oct 2009 (CO No 8)[193]
1095 Rectification of register on application to registrar	20 Jan 2007 (certain purposes) (CO No 1)[3] 1 Oct 2009 (otherwise) (CO No 8)[193]
1095A Rectification of register to resolve a discrepancy[250]	10 Jan 2020

Provision of CA 2006	Commencement
1096 Rectification of the register under court order	1 Oct 2009 (CO No 8)[193]
1097 Powers of court on ordering removal of material from the register	1 Oct 2009 (CO No 8)[193]
1097A Rectification of register relating to company registered office[231]	26 May 2015
1098 Public notice of removal of certain material from the register	1 Oct 2009 (CO No 8)[193]
1099 The registrar's index of company names	20 Jan 2007 (certain purposes) (CO No 1)[3] 1 Oct 2009 (otherwise) (CO No 8)
1100 Right to inspect index	1 Oct 2009 (CO No 8)
1101 Power to amend enactments relating to bodies other than companies	20 Jan 2007 (certain purposes) (CO No 1)[3] 1 Oct 2009 (otherwise) (CO No 8)
1102 Application of language requirements	1 Jan 2007 (CO No 1)
1103 Documents to be drawn up and delivered in English	1 Jan 2007 (CO No 1)[54]
1104 Documents relating to Welsh companies	1 Jan 2007 (CO No 1)[54a]
1105 Documents that may be drawn up and delivered in other languages	1 Jan 2007 (CO No 1)[55]
1106 Voluntary filing of translations	1 Jan 2007 (CO No 1)
1107 Certified translations	1 Jan 2007 (CO No 1)
1108 Transliteration of names and addresses: permitted characters	20 Jan 2007 (certain purposes) (CO No 1)[3] 1 Oct 2009 (otherwise) (CO No 8)[194]
1109 Transliteration of names and addresses: voluntary transliteration into Roman characters	1 Oct 2009 (CO No 8)[194]
1110 Transliteration of names and addresses: certification	20 Jan 2007 (certain purposes) (CO No 1)[3] 1 Oct 2009 (otherwise) (CO No 8)[194]
1111 Registrar's requirements as to certification or verification	1 Jan 2007 (CO No 1)[54b]
1112 General false statement offence	1 Oct 2009 (CO No 8)[195]
1113 Enforcement of company's filing obligations	1 Oct 2009 (CO No 8)
1114 Application of provisions about documents and delivery	1 Jan 2007 (certain purposes) (CO No 1)[56] 1 Oct 2009 (otherwise) (CO No 8)
1115 Supplementary provisions relating to electronic communications	1 Oct 2009 (CO No 8)
1116 Alternative to publication in the Gazette	20 Jan 2007 (certain purposes) (CO No 1)[3] 1 Oct 2009 (otherwise) (CO No 8)
1117 Registrar's rules	1 Jan 2007 (certain purposes) (CO No 1)[56] 6 Apr 2008 (certain purposes) (CO No 5)[106] 1 Oct 2009 (otherwise) (CO No 8)
1118 Payments into the Consolidated Fund	1 Oct 2009 (CO No 8)
1119 Contracting out of registrar's functions	1 Oct 2009 (CO No 8)
1120 Application of this Part to overseas companies[207]	*1 Jan 2007 (certain purposes) (CO No 1)*[56] *1 Oct 2009 (otherwise) (CO No 8)*
Part 36: Offences Under the Companies Acts	
1121 Liability of officer in default	20 Jan 2007 (certain purposes) (CO No 1)[57] 6 Apr 2007 (certain purposes) (CO No 2)[41] 1 Oct 2007 (certain purposes) (CO No 3)[58] 6 Apr 2008 (certain purposes) (CO No 5)[108] 1 Oct 2008 (certain purposes) (CO No 5)[108] 1 Oct 2009 (otherwise) (CO No 8)[196]
1122 Liability of company as officer in default	20 Jan 2007 (certain purposes) (CO No 1)[57] 6 Apr 2007 (certain purposes) (CO No 2)[41] 1 Oct 2007 (certain purposes) (CO No 3)[58] 6 Apr 2008 (certain purposes) (CO No 5)[108] 1 Oct 2008 (certain purposes) (CO No 5)[108] 1 Oct 2009 (otherwise) (CO No 8)[196]
1123 Application to bodies other than companies	6 Apr 2007 (certain purposes) (CO No 2)[41] 1 Oct 2007 (certain purposes) (CO No 3)[58] 6 Apr 2008 (certain purposes) (CO No 5)[108] 1 Oct 2008 (certain purposes) (CO No 5)[108] 1 Oct 2009 (otherwise) (CO No 8)[196]
1124 Amendments of the Companies Act 1985	1 Oct 2007 (CO No 3)
1125 Meaning of "daily default fine"	20 Jan 2007 (certain purposes) (CO No 1)[57]

Provision of CA 2006	Commencement
	6 Apr 2007 (certain purposes) (CO No 2)[41] 1 Oct 2007 (certain purposes) (CO No 3)[58] 6 Apr 2008 (certain purposes) (CO No 5)[108] 1 Oct 2008 (certain purposes) (CO No 5)[108] 1 Oct 2009 (otherwise) (CO No 8)[196]
1126 Consents required for certain prosecutions	20 Jan 2007 (certain purposes) (CO No 1)[57] 6 Apr 2007 (certain purposes) (CO No 2)[41] 1 Oct 2007 (certain purposes) (CO No 3)[58] 6 Apr 2008 (otherwise) (CO No 5)
1127 Summary proceedings: venue	20 Jan 2007 (certain purposes) (CO No 1)[57] 6 Apr 2007 (certain purposes) (CO No 2)[41] 1 Oct 2007 (certain purposes) (CO No 3)[58] 6 Apr 2008 (certain purposes) (CO No 5)[108] 1 Oct 2008 (certain purposes) (CO No 5)[108] 1 Oct 2009 (otherwise) (CO No 8)[196]
1128 Summary proceedings: time limit for proceedings	20 Jan 2007 (certain purposes) (CO No 1)[57] 6 Apr 2007 (certain purposes) (CO No 2)[41] 1 Oct 2007 (certain purposes) (CO No 3)[58] 6 Apr 2008 (certain purposes) (CO No 5)[108] 1 Oct 2008 (certain purposes) (CO No 5)[108] 1 Oct 2009 (otherwise) (CO No 8)[196]
1129 Legal professional privilege	20 Jan 2007 (certain purposes) (CO No 1)[57] 6 Apr 2007 (certain purposes) (CO No 2)[41] 1 Oct 2007 (certain purposes) (CO No 3)[58] 6 Apr 2008 (certain purposes) (CO No 5)[108] 1 Oct 2008 (certain purposes) (CO No 5)[108] 1 Oct 2009 (otherwise) (CO No 8)[196]
1130 Proceedings against unincorporated bodies	20 Jan 2007 (certain purposes) (CO No 1)[57] 6 Apr 2007 (certain purposes) (CO No 2)[41] 1 Oct 2007 (certain purposes) (CO No 3)[58] 6 Apr 2008 (certain purposes) (CO No 5)[108] 1 Oct 2008 (certain purposes) (CO No 5)[108] 1 Oct 2009 (otherwise) (CO No 8)[196]
1131 Imprisonment on summary conviction in England and Wales: transitory provision	20 Jan 2007 (certain purposes) (CO No 1)[57] 6 Apr 2007 (certain purposes) (CO No 2)[41] 1 Oct 2007 (certain purposes) (CO No 3)[58] 6 Apr 2008 (certain purposes) (CO No 5)[108] 1 Oct 2008 (certain purposes) (CO No 5)[108] 1 Oct 2009 (otherwise) (CO No 8)[196]
1132 Production and inspection of documents where offence suspected	6 Apr 2007 (certain purposes) (CO No 2)[41] 1 Oct 2007 (certain purposes) (CO No 3)[58] 6 Apr 2008 (certain purposes) (CO No 5)[108] 1 Oct 2008 (certain purposes) (CO No 5)[108] 1 Oct 2009 (otherwise) (CO No 8)[196]
1133 Transitional provision	20 Jan 2007 (certain purposes) (CO No 1)[57] 6 Apr 2007 (certain purposes) (CO No 2)[41] 1 Oct 2007 (certain purposes) (CO No 3)[58] 6 Apr 2008 (certain purposes) (CO No 5)[108] 1 Oct 2008 (certain purposes) (CO No 5)[108] 1 Oct 2009 (otherwise) (CO No 8)[196]
Part 37: Companies: Supplementary Provisions	
1134 Meaning of "company records"	6 Apr 2007 (certain purposes) (CO No 2)[41] 1 Oct 2009 (otherwise) (CO No 8)
1135 Form of company records	6 Apr 2007 (certain purposes) (CO No 2)[41] 1 Oct 2009 (otherwise) (CO No 8)
1136 Regulations about where certain company records to be kept available for inspection	20 Jan 2007 (certain purposes) (CO No 1)[3] 1 Oct 2009 (otherwise) (CO No 8)
1137 Regulations about inspection of records and provision of copies	20 Jan 2007 (certain purposes) (CO No 1)[3] 30 Sep 2007 (sub-ss (1), (4), (5)(b), (6)) (CO No 4) 1 Oct 2009 (otherwise) (CO No 8)
1138 Duty to take precautions against falsification	6 Apr 2007 (certain purposes) (CO No 2)[41] 1 Oct 2009 (otherwise) (CO No 8)
1139 Service of documents on company	6 Apr 2007 (certain purposes) (CO No 2)[41] 6 Apr 2008 (certain purposes) (CO No 5)[107] 1 Oct 2009 (otherwise) (CO No 8)
1140 Service of documents on directors, secretaries and others	6 Apr 2007 (certain purposes) (CO No 2)[41] 6 Apr 2008 (certain purposes) (CO No 5)[107] 1 Oct 2009 (otherwise) (CO No 8)

Provision of CA 2006	Commencement
1141 Service addresses	20 Jan 2007 (certain purposes) (CO No 1)[3] 1 Oct 2009 (otherwise) (CO No 8)
1142 Requirement to give service address	1 Oct 2009 (CO No 8)
1143 The company communications provisions	20 Jan 2007 (CO No 1)[43]
1144 Sending or supplying documents or information	20 Jan 2007 (CO No 1)
1145 Right to hard copy version	20 Jan 2007 (CO No 1)
1146 Requirement of authentication	20 Jan 2007 (CO No 1)
1147 Deemed delivery of documents and information	20 Jan 2007 (CO No 1)
1148 Interpretation of company communications provisions	20 Jan 2007 (CO No 1)
1149 Application of valuation requirements	1 Oct 2009 (CO No 8)
1150 Valuation by qualified independent person	1 Oct 2009 (CO No 8)
1151 The independence requirement	20 Jan 2007 (certain purposes) (CO No 1)[3] 1 Oct 2009 (otherwise) (CO No 8)
1152 Meaning of "associate"	1 Oct 2009 (CO No 8)
1153 Valuer entitled to full disclosure	1 Oct 2009 (CO No 8)
1154 Duty to notify registrar of certain appointments etc	1 Oct 2009 (CO No 8)[197]
1155 Offence of failure to give notice	1 Oct 2009 (CO No 8)[197]
1156 Meaning of "the court"	20 Jan 2007 (certain purposes) (CO No 1)[3] 1 Oct 2009 (otherwise) (CO No 8)
1157 Power of court to grant relief in certain cases	1 Oct 2008 (CO No 5)
Part 38: Companies: Interpretation	
1158 Meaning of "UK-registered company"	1 Oct 2007 (certain purposes) (CO No 3)[4] 1 Nov 2007 (certain purposes) (CO No 3)[42] 1 Oct 2009 (otherwise) (CO No 8)
1159 Meaning of "subsidiary" etc	6 Apr 2008 (certain purposes) (CO No 5)[109] 1 Oct 2009 (otherwise) (CO No 8)
1160 Meaning of "subsidiary" etc: power to amend	20 Jan 2007 (certain purposes) (CO No 1)[3] 6 Apr 2008 (certain purposes) (CO No 5)[109] 1 Oct 2009 (otherwise) (CO No 8)
1161 Meaning of "undertaking" and related expressions	6 Apr 2008 (CO No 5)
1162 Parent and subsidiary undertakings	6 Apr 2008 (CO No 5)
1163 "Non-cash asset"	1 Oct 2009 (CO No 8)
1164 Meaning of "banking company" and "banking group"	6 Apr 2008 (CO No 5)
1165 Meaning of "insurance company" and related expressions	6 Apr 2008 (CO No 5)
1166 "Employees' share scheme"	1 Oct 2009 (CO No 8)
1167 Meaning of "prescribed"	20 Jan 2007 (certain purposes) (CO No 1)[3] 30 Sep 2007 (otherwise) (CO No 4)
1168 Hard copy and electronic form and related expressions	1 Jan 2007 (certain purposes) (CO No 1)[59] 20 Jan 2007 (certain purposes) (CO No 1)[59] 6 Apr 2007 (certain purposes) (CO No 2)[41] 1 Oct 2007 (certain purposes) (CO No 3)[4] 15 Dec 2007 (certain purposes) (CO No 3)[60] 6 Apr 2008 (certain purposes) (CO No 5)[108] 1 Oct 2008 (certain purposes) (CO No 5)[108] 1 Oct 2009 (otherwise) (CO No 8)
1169 Dormant companies	6 Apr 2008 (CO No 5)
1170 Meaning of "EEA State" and related expressions	6 Apr 2007 (CO No 2)
1170A Receiver or manager and certain related references[209]	1 Oct 2009
1170B Meaning of "contributory"[209]	1 Oct 2009
1171 The former Companies Acts	1 Oct 2009 (CO No 8)
1172 References to requirements of this Act	6 Apr 2008 (CO No 5)
1173 Minor definitions: general	1 Jan 2007 (certain purposes) (CO No 1)[61] 20 Jan 2007 (certain purposes) (CO No 1)[61] 6 Apr 2007 (certain purposes) (CO No 2)[62] 1 Oct 2007 (certain purposes) (CO No 3)[63] 1 Nov 2007 (certain purposes) (CO No 3)[64]

Provision of CA 2006	Commencement
	6 Apr 2008 (certain purposes) (CO No 5)[100] 1 Oct 2008 (certain purposes) (CO No 3)[100] 1 Oct 2009 (otherwise) (CO No 8)
1174 Index of defined expressions	1 Oct 2009 (CO No 8)
Part 39: Companies: Minor Amendments	
1175 Removal of special provisions about accounts and audit of charitable companies[235]	*1 Apr 2008 (certain purposes) (CO No 6)*[120] *Never in force for other purposes*[200]
1176 Power of Secretary of State to bring civil proceedings on company's behalf	6 Apr 2007 (CO No 1)
1177 Repeal of certain provisions about company directors	6 Apr 2007 (CO No 1)
1178 Repeal of requirement that certain companies publish periodical statement	6 Apr 2007 (CO No 1)
1179 Repeal of requirement that Secretary of State prepare annual report	6 Apr 2007 (CO No 1)
1180 Repeal of certain provisions about company charges	1 Oct 2009 (CO No 8)
1181 Access to constitutional documents of RTE and RTM companies	20 Jan 2007 (certain purposes) (CO No 1)[3] 1 Oct 2009 (otherwise) (CO No 8)
Part 40: Company Directors: Foreign Disqualification etc	
1182 Persons subject to foreign restrictions	1 Oct 2009 (CO No 8)
1183 Meaning of "the court" and "UK company"	1 Oct 2009 (CO No 8)
1184 Disqualification of persons subject to foreign restrictions	20 Jan 2007 (certain purposes) (CO No 1)[3] 1 Oct 2009 (otherwise) (CO No 8)
1185 Disqualification regulations: supplementary	20 Jan 2007 (certain purposes) (CO No 1)[3] 1 Oct 2009 (otherwise) (CO No 8)
1186 Offence of breach of disqualification	20 Jan 2007 (certain purposes) (CO No 1)[3] 1 Oct 2009 (otherwise) (CO No 8)
1187 Personal liability for debts of company	20 Jan 2007 (certain purposes) (CO No 1)[3] 1 Oct 2009 (otherwise) (CO No 8)
1188 Statements from persons subject to foreign restrictions	20 Jan 2007 (certain purposes) (CO No 1)[3] 1 Oct 2009 (otherwise) (CO No 8)
1189 Statements from persons disqualified	20 Jan 2007 (certain purposes) (CO No 1)[3] 1 Oct 2009 (otherwise) (CO No 8)
1190 Statements: whether to be made public	1 Oct 2009 (CO No 8)
1191 Offences	20 Jan 2007 (certain purposes) (CO No 1)[3] 1 Oct 2009 (otherwise) (CO No 8)
Part 41: Business Names	
Chapter 1: Restricted or Prohibited Names	
1192 Application of this Chapter	1 Oct 2009 (CO No 8)
1193 Name suggesting connection with government or public authority	20 Jan 2007 (certain purposes) (CO No 1)[3] 1 Oct 2009 (otherwise) (CO No 8)
1194 Other sensitive words or expressions	20 Jan 2007 (certain purposes) (CO No 1)[3] 1 Oct 2009 (otherwise) (CO No 8)
1195 Requirement to seek comments of government department or other relevant body	20 Jan 2007 (certain purposes) (CO No 1)[3] 1 Oct 2009 (otherwise) (CO No 8)
1196 Withdrawal of Secretary of State's approval	1 Oct 2009 (CO No 8)
1197 Name containing inappropriate indication of company type or legal form	20 Jan 2007 (certain purposes) (CO No 1)[3] 1 Oct 2009 (otherwise) (CO No 8)
1198 Name giving misleading indication of activities	1 Oct 2009 (CO No 8)
1199 Savings for existing lawful business names	1 Oct 2009 (CO No 8)
Chapter 2: Disclosure Required in Case of Individual or Partnership	
1200 Application of this Chapter	1 Oct 2009 (CO No 8)
1201 Information required to be disclosed[211]	28 Dec 2009
1202 Disclosure required: business documents etc	20 Jan 2007 (certain purposes) (CO No 1)[3] 1 Oct 2009 (otherwise) (CO No 8)
1203 Exemption for large partnerships if certain conditions met	1 Oct 2009 (CO No 8)
1204 Disclosure required: business premises	20 Jan 2007 (certain purposes) (CO No 1)[3] 1 Oct 2009 (otherwise) (CO No 8)
1205 Criminal consequences of failure to make re-	1 Oct 2009 (CO No 8)

Provision of CA 2006	Commencement
quired disclosure	
1206 Civil consequences of failure to make required disclosure	1 Oct 2009 (CO No 8)
Chapter 3: Supplementary	
1207 Application of general provisions about offences	1 Oct 2009 (CO No 8)
1208 Interpretation	1 Oct 2009 (CO No 8)
Part 42: Statutory Auditors	
Chapter 1: Introductory	
1209 Main purposes of Part	6 Apr 2008 (CO No 5)
1210 Meaning of "statutory auditor" etc	20 Jan 2007 (certain purposes) (CO No 1)[3] 6 Apr 2008 (otherwise) (CO No 5)
1211 Eligibility for appointment as a statutory auditor: overview	6 Apr 2008 (CO No 5)
Chapter 2: Individuals and Firms	
1212 Individuals and firms: eligibility for appointment as a statutory auditor	6 Apr 2008 (CO No 5)[101]
1213 Effect of ineligibility	6 Apr 2008 (CO No 5)[101]
1214 Independence requirement	20 Jan 2007 (certain purposes) (CO No 1)[3] 6 Apr 2008 (otherwise) (CO No 5)[101]
1215 Effect of lack of independence	6 Apr 2008 (CO No 5)[101]
1216 Effect of appointment of a partnership	6 Apr 2008 (CO No 5)[101]
1217 Supervisory bodies	6 Apr 2008 (CO No 5)[102]
1218 Exemption from liability for damages	6 Apr 2008 (CO No 5)[102]
1219 Appropriate qualifications	6 Apr 2008 (CO No 5)[102]
1220 Qualifying bodies and recognised professional qualifications	6 Apr 2008 (CO No 5)[102]
1221 Approval of third country qualifications	6 Apr 2008 (CO No 5)[102]
1222 Eligibility of individuals retaining only 1967 Act authorisation	6 Apr 2008 (CO No 5)[102]
1223 Matters to be notified to the Secretary of State	6 Apr 2008 (CO No 5)
1223ZA Matters to be notified to the competent authority[238]	17 Jun 2016
1223A Notification of matters relevant to approved third country competent authorities[119]	6 Apr 2008
1224 The Secretary of State's power to call for information	6 Apr 2008 (CO No 5)
1224ZA The competent authority's power to call for information	17 Jun 2016[238]
1224A Restrictions on disclosure[119]	6 Apr 2008
1224B Offence of disclosure in contravention of section 1224A[119]	6 Apr 2008
1225 Enforcement: general[218]	2 Jul 2012
1225A Directions: general[218]	2 Jul 2012
1225B Directions: supplementary[218]	2 Jul 2012
1225C Compliance orders[218]	2 Jul 2012
1225D Financial penalties: general[218]	2 Jul 2012
1225E Financial penalties: supplementary[218]	2 Jul 2012
1225F Appeals against financial penalties[218]	2 Jul 2012
1225G Recovery of financial penalties[218]	2 Jul 2012
Chapter 3: Auditors General	
1226 Auditors General: eligibility for appointment as a statutory auditor	6 Apr 2008 (CO No 5)[103]
1227 Individuals responsible for audit work on behalf of Auditors General	6 Apr 2008 (CO No 5)
1228 Appointment of the Independent Supervisor	20 Jan 2007 (certain purposes) (CO No 1)[3] 6 Apr 2008 (otherwise) (CO No 5)
1229 Supervision of Auditors General by the Independent Supervisor	6 Apr 2008 (CO No 5)[103]
1230 Duties of Auditors General in relation to supervi-	6 Apr 2008 (CO No 5)[103]

Provision of CA 2006	Commencement
sion arrangements	
1231 Reports by the Independent Supervisor	20 Jan 2007 (certain purposes) (CO No 1)[3] 6 Apr 2008 (otherwise) (CO No 5)
1232 Matters to be notified to the Independent Supervisor	6 Apr 2008 (CO No 5)
1233 The Independent Supervisor's power to call for information	6 Apr 2008 (CO No 5)
1234 Suspension notices	6 Apr 2008 (CO No 5)
1235 Effect of suspension notices	6 Apr 2008 (CO No 5)
1236 Compliance orders	6 Apr 2008 (CO No 5)
1237 Proceedings involving the Independent Supervisor	20 Jan 2007 (certain purposes) (CO No 1)[3] 6 Apr 2008 (otherwise) (CO No 5)
1238 Grants to the Independent Supervisor	6 Apr 2008 (CO No 5)
Chapter 4: The Register of Auditors etc	
1239 The register of auditors	20 Jan 2007 (certain purposes) (CO No 1)[3] 6 Apr 2008 (otherwise) (CO No 5)
1240 Information to be made available to public	20 Jan 2007 (certain purposes) (CO No 1)[3] 6 Apr 2008 (otherwise) (CO No 5)
Chapter 4A: Equivalent Third Countries and Transitional Third Countries[248]	
1240A Power to approve third countries as equivalent or transitional third countries	IP completion day (as defined in the European Union (Withdrawal Agreement) Act 2020, s 39)
Chapter 4B: Approved Third Country Competent Authorities[248]	
1240B Power to approve third country competent authorities	IP completion day (as defined in the European Union (Withdrawal Agreement) Act 2020, s 39))
Chapter 5: Registered Third Country Auditors	
1241 Meaning of "registered third country auditor" and "UK-traded third country company"	20 Jan 2007 (certain purposes) (CO No 1)[3] 6 Apr 2008 (otherwise) (CO No 5)
1242 Duties of registered third country auditors	29 Jun 2008 (CO No 5)[110]
1243 Matters to be notified to the Secretary of State	29 Jun 2008 (CO No 5)[110]
1244 The Secretary of State's power to call for information	29 Jun 2008 (CO No 5)[110]
1245 Compliance orders	6 Apr 2008 (CO No 5)
1246 Removal of third country auditors from the register of auditors	20 Jan 2007 (certain purposes) (CO No 1)[3] 6 Apr 2008 (otherwise) (CO No 5)
1247 Grants to bodies concerned with arrangements under Schedule 12	6 Apr 2008 (CO No 5)
Chapter 6: Supplementary and General	
1248 Secretary of State's power to require second audit of a company	6 Apr 2008 (CO No 5)[104]
1249 Supplementary provision about second audits	6 Apr 2008 (CO No 5)[104]
1250 Misleading, false and deceptive statements	6 Apr 2008 (CO No 5)[104]
1251 Fees	20 Jan 2007 (certain purposes) (CO No 1)[3] 6 Apr 2008 (otherwise) (CO No 5)[104]
1251A Duty of the Secretary of State to report on inspections[119]	6 Apr 2008
1252 Delegation of the Secretary of State's functions	20 Jan 2007 (certain purposes) (CO No 1)[3] 6 Apr 2008 (otherwise) (CO No 5)
1253 Delegation of functions to an existing body	20 Jan 2007 (certain purposes) (CO No 1)[3] 6 Apr 2008 (otherwise) (CO No 5)
1253A Requests to foreign competent authorities[119]	6 Apr 2008
1253B Requests from approved third country competent authorities[119]	6 Apr 2008
1253C Notification to approved third country competent authorities[119]	6 Apr 2008
1253D Restriction on transfer of audit working papers to third countries[213]	6 Apr 2008
1253DA Transfer by Secretary of State[213]	15 Nov 2010
1253DB Transfer by statutory auditor with approval of Secretary of State[213]	15 Nov 2010
1253DC Transfer by statutory auditor for purposes of investigation of auditor[213]	15 Nov 2010

Part 2 CA 2006 commencement

Provision of CA 2006	Commencement
1253DD Agreement of third country competent authority[213]	15 Nov 2010
1253DE Transfer by means of inspection[213]	15 Nov 2010
1253E Working arrangements for transfer of papers[214]	6 Apr 2008
1253F Publication of working arrangements[119]	6 Apr 2008
1254 Directions to comply with international obligations	6 Apr 2008 (CO No 5)[104]
1255 Offences by bodies corporate, partnerships and unincorporated associations	6 Apr 2008 (CO No 5)[104]
1256 Time limits for prosecution of offences	6 Apr 2008 (CO No 5)[104]
1257 Jurisdiction and procedure in respect of offences	6 Apr 2008 (CO No 5)[104]
1258 Service of notices	6 Apr 2008 (CO No 5)[104]
1259 Documents in electronic form	6 Apr 2008 (CO No 5)[104]
1260 Meaning of "associate"	6 Apr 2008 (CO No 5)
1261 Minor definitions	20 Jan 2007 (certain purposes) (CO No 1)[3] 6 Apr 2008 (otherwise) (CO No 5)
1262 Index of defined expressions	6 Apr 2008 (CO No 5)
1263 Power to make provision in consequence of changes affecting accountancy bodies	20 Jan 2007 (certain purposes) (CO No 1)[3] 6 Apr 2008 (otherwise) (CO No 5)
1264 Consequential amendments	6 Apr 2008 (CO No 5)
Part 43: Transparency Obligations and Related Matters	
1265 The transparency obligations directive	8 Nov 2006 (RA)
1266 Transparency rules	8 Nov 2006 (RA)
1267 Competent authority's power to call for information	8 Nov 2006 (RA)
1268 Powers exercisable in case of infringement of transparency obligation	8 Nov 2006 (RA)
1269 Corporate governance rules	8 Nov 2006 (RA)
1270 Liability for false or misleading statements in certain publications	8 Nov 2006 (RA)
1271 Exercise of powers where UK is host member State	8 Nov 2006 (RA)
1272 Transparency obligations and related matters: minor and consequential amendments	8 Nov 2006 (certain purposes) (RA) 1 Oct 2008 (otherwise)[65]
1273 *Corporate governance regulations*[253]	*8 Nov 2006 (RA)*
Part 44: Miscellaneous Provisions	
1274 Grants to bodies concerned with actuarial standards etc	8 Nov 2006 (RA)
1275 Levy to pay expenses of bodies concerned with actuarial standards etc	1 Oct 2009 (CO No 8)
1276 Application of provisions to Scotland and Northern Ireland	8 Nov 2006 (RA)
1277 Power to require information about exercise of voting rights	20 Jan 2007 (certain purposes) (CO No 1)[3] 1 Oct 2008 (otherwise) (CO No 5)
1278 Institutions to which information provisions apply	20 Jan 2007 (certain purposes) (CO No 1)[3] 1 Oct 2008 (otherwise) (CO No 5)
1279 Shares to which information provisions apply	20 Jan 2007 (certain purposes) (CO No 1)[3] 1 Oct 2008 (otherwise) (CO No 5)
1280 Obligations with respect to provision of information	20 Jan 2007 (certain purposes) (CO No 1)[3] 1 Oct 2008 (otherwise) (CO No 5)
1281 Disclosure of information under the Enterprise Act 2002	6 Apr 2007 (CO No 1)
1282 Payment of expenses of winding up	6 Apr 2008 (CO No 5)[105]
1283 Amendment of memorandum or articles of commonhold association	1 Oct 2009 (CO No 8)
Part 45: Northern Ireland	
1284 Extension of Companies Acts to Northern Ireland	1 Jan 2007 (certain purposes) (CO No 1) 20 Jan 2007 (certain purposes) (CO No 1) 6 Apr 2007 (certain purposes) (CO No 1 & CO No 2) 30 Sep 2007 (certain purposes) (CO No 4)

Provision of CA 2006	Commencement
	1 Oct 2007 (certain purposes) (CO No 3) 1 Nov 2007 (certain purposes) (CO No 3) 15 Dec 2007 (certain purposes) (CO No 3) 6 Apr 2008 (certain purposes) (CO No 5) 1 Oct 2008 (certain purposes) (CO No 3 & CO No 5 & CO No 7) 1 Oct 2009 (otherwise) (CO No 8)[66]
1285 Extension of GB enactments relating to UK Societas	1 Oct 2009 (CO No 8)
1286 Extension of GB enactments relating to certain other forms of business organisation	1 Oct 2008 (certain purposes) (CO No 7)[128] 1 Oct 2009 (otherwise) (CO No 8)
1287 Extension of enactments relating to business names	1 Oct 2009 (CO No 8)
Part 46: General Supplementary Provisions	
1288 Regulations and orders: statutory instrument	8 Nov 2006 (RA)
1289 Regulations and orders: negative resolution procedure	8 Nov 2006 (RA)
1290 Regulations and orders: affirmative resolution procedure	8 Nov 2006 (RA)
1291 Regulations and orders: approval after being made	8 Nov 2006 (RA)
1292 Regulations and orders: supplementary	8 Nov 2006 (RA)
1292A "Bank of England"	1 Mar 2017[243]
1293 Meaning of "enactment"	8 Nov 2006 (RA)
1294 Power to make consequential amendments etc	8 Nov 2006 (RA)
1295 Repeals	See Sch 16 below
1296 Power to make transitional provision and savings	8 Nov 2006 (RA)
1297 Continuity of the law	8 Nov 2006 (RA)
Part 47: Final Provisions	
1298 Short title	8 Nov 2006 (RA)
1299 Extent	8 Nov 2006 (RA)
1300 Commencement	8 Nov 2006 (RA)
Schedules	
Schedule 1—Connected Persons: References to an Interest in Shares or Debentures	1 Oct 2007 (CO No 3)[118]
Schedule 1A—References to People with Significant Control Over a Company[231]	
Part 1—The specified conditions	6 Apr 2016
Part 2—Holding an interest in a company etc	6 Apr 2016
Part 3—Supplementary Provision	26 May 2015 (for the purposes of enabling the exercise of any power to make provision by regulations made by statutory instrument or to prepare and issue guidance); 6 Apr 2016 (otherwise)
Part 4—Power to amend thresholds etc	26 May 2015
Schedule 1B—Enforcement of Disclosure Requirements[231]	26 May 2015 (for the purposes of enabling the exercise of any power to make provision by regulations made by statutory instrument); 6 Apr 2016 (otherwise)
Schedule 1C—Rules of the Takeover Panel: General Principles and other Provision[249]	
Part 1—General Principles	IP completion day (as defined in the European Union (Withdrawal Agreement) Act 2020, s 39)
Part 2—Other Provision	IP completion day (as defined in the European Union (Withdrawal Agreement) Act 2020, s 39)
Schedule 2—Specified Persons, Descriptions of Disclosures etc for the Purposes of Section 948[212]	
Part 1—Specified Persons	1 Jul 2009
Part 2—Specified Descriptions of Disclosures	1 Jul 2009
Part 3—Overseas Regulatory Bodies	1 Jul 2009
Schedule 3—Amendments of Remaining Provisions of the Companies Act 1985 Relating to Offences	1 Oct 2007 (CO No 3)[67]

Provision of CA 2006	Commencement
Schedule 4—Documents and Information Sent or Supplied to a Company	
Part 1—Introduction	20 Jan 2007 (CO No 1)
Part 2—Communications in Hard Copy Form	20 Jan 2007 (CO No 1)
Part 3—Communications in Electronic Form	20 Jan 2007 (CO No 1)
Part 4—Other Agreed Forms of Communication	20 Jan 2007 (CO No 1)
Schedule 5—Communications by a Company	
Part 1—Introduction	20 Jan 2007 (CO No 1)
Part 2—Communications in Hard Copy Form	20 Jan 2007 (CO No 1)
Part 3—Communications in Electronic Form	20 Jan 2007 (CO No 1)[68]
Part 4—Communications by Means of a Website	20 Jan 2007 (CO No 1)[68]
Part 5—Other Agreed Forms of Communication	20 Jan 2007 (CO No 1)
Part 6—Supplementary Provisions	20 Jan 2007 (CO No 1)
Schedule 6—Meaning of "Subsidiary" etc: Supplementary Provisions	6 Apr 2008 (certain purposes) (CO No 5)[109] 1 Oct 2009 (otherwise) (CO No 8)
Schedule 7—Parent and Subsidiary Undertakings: Supplementary Provisions	6 Apr 2008 (CO No 5)
Schedule 8—Index of Defined Expressions	1 Oct 2009 (CO No 8)
Schedule 9—Removal of Special Provisions About Accounts and Audit of Charitable Companies[235]	
Part 1—The Companies Act 1985 (c 6)	*1 Apr 2008 (CO No 6)*[121]
Part 2—The Companies (Northern Ireland) Order 1986 (SI 1986/1032 (NI 6)	*Never in force*[200]
Schedule 10—Recognised Supervisory Bodies	
Part 1—Grant and Revocation of Recognition of a Supervisory Body	6 Apr 2008 (CO No 5)[102]
Part 2—Requirements for Recognition of a Supervisory Body	6 Apr 2008 (CO No 5)[102]
Part 3—Arrangements in which Recognised Supervisory Bodies are Required to Participate[240]	*6 Apr 2008 (CO No 5)*[102]
Schedule 11—Recognised Professional Qualifications	
Part 1—Grant and Revocation of Recognition of a Professional Qualification	6 Apr 2008 (CO No 5)[102]
Part 2—Requirements for Recognition of a Professional Qualification	20 Jan 2007 (certain purposes) (CO No 1)[3] 6 Apr 2008 (otherwise) (CO No 5)[102]
Schedule 11A—Specified Persons, Descriptions, Disclosures etc for the Purposes of Section 1224A[119]	
Part 1—Specified Persons	6 Apr 2008
Part 2—Specified Descriptions of Disclosures	6 Apr 2008
Part 3—Overseas Regulatory Bodies	6 Apr 2008
Schedule 12—Arrangements in which Registered Third Country Auditors are Required to Participate	20 Jan 2007 (certain purposes) (CO No 1)[3] 29 Jun 2008 (otherwise) (CO No 5)[110]
Schedule 13—Supplementary Provisions with Respect to Delegation Order	20 Jan 2007 (certain purposes) (CO No 1)[3] 6 Apr 2008 (otherwise) (CO No 5)
Schedule 14—Statutory Auditors: Consequential Amendments	6 Apr 2008 (CO No 5)
Schedule 15—Transparency Obligations and Related Matters: Minor and Consequential Amendments	
Part 1—Amendments of the Financial Services and Markets Act 2000	8 Nov 2006 (certain purposes) (RA) 1 Oct 2008 (otherwise)[65]
Part 2—Amendments of the Companies (Audit, Investigations and Community Enterprise) Act 2004	8 Nov 2006 (RA)
Schedule 16—Repeals	1 Jan 2007 (in part) (CO No 1) 20 Jan 2007 (in part) (CO No 1) 6 Apr 2007 (in part) (CO No 1 & CO No 2) 1 Oct 2007 (in part) (CO No 3) 1 Apr 2008 (in part) (CO No 5 & CO No 6) 1 Oct 2008 (in part) (CO No 5 & CO No 7)

Provision of CA 2006	Commencement
	1 Oct 2009 (in part) (CO No 8) Not in force (otherwise)[69]

NOTES

1 CO No 1, arts 2(2), 3(2) provide that this section shall come into force on 1 Jan 2007 and 20 Jan 2007 respectively so far as is necessary for the purposes of the provisions of this Act brought into force on those dates by that Order. For transitional adaptations of s 2, see CO No 1, Sch 1, para 1.

2 For transitional adaptations of s 2, see CO No 2, Sch 1, para 1.

3 CO No 1, art 3(3) provides that the provisions CA 2006, in so far as not brought into force by s 1300(1) of that Act, or arts 2, 3(1), (2) of that Order, come into force on 20 Jan 2007 for the purpose of enabling the exercise of powers to make Orders or Regulations by statutory instrument.

4 CO No 3, art 2(3) provides that this section shall come into force on 1 Oct 2007 so far as is necessary for the purposes of the provisions of this Act brought into force on that date by art 2(1), (2) of that Order. For transitional adaptations of ss 17, 1158, see CO No 3, Sch 1, paras 1, 21.

5 For transitional provisions, see CO No 3, Sch 3, para 1.

6 For transitional provisions, see CO No 3, Sch 3, para 2. For transitional adaptations of s 116, see CO No 3, Sch 1, para 2.

7 For transitional provisions, see CO No 3, Sch 3, para 3. For transitional adaptations of ss 145, 146, 153, see CO No 3, Sch 1, paras 3–5.

8 For transitional provisions, see CO No 3, Sch 3, para 4.

9 For transitional provisions, see CO No 3, Sch 3, para 5.

10 For transitional adaptations of ss 170, 178, 181, see CO No 3, Sch 1, paras 6–9.

10a For transitional adaptations of s 180, see CO No 3, Sch 1, para 8. For transitional provisions, see CO No 5, Sch 4, Pt 3, para 49.

11 For transitional provisions, see CO No 3, Sch 3, para 6.

12 For transitional provisions, see CO No 3, Sch 3, para 7. For transitional adaptations of s 191, see CO No 3, Sch 1, para 10.

13 For transitional provisions, see CO No 3, Sch 3, paras 8–11. For transitional adaptations of s 205, see CO No 3, Sch 1, para 11 and CO No 5, Sch 1, Pt 1, para 1.

14 For transitional provisions, see CO No 3, Sch 3, para 12.

15 For transitional provisions, see CO No 3, Sch 3, para 13.

16 For transitional provisions, see CO No 3, Sch 3, para 14.

17 For transitional provisions, see CO No 3, Sch 3, para 15. For transitional adaptations of s 234, see CO No 3, Sch 1, para 12 and CO No 5, Sch 1, Pt 1, para 2.

18 For transitional provisions, see CO No 3, Sch 3, para 16.

19 For transitional provisions, see CO No 3, Sch 3, para 17.

20 CO No 3, art 2(1)(d) originally provided that s 247 would come into force on 1 Oct 2007 (subject to transitional provisions in Sch 3, para 18 to that Order). Article 2(1)(d) was amended by CO No 4, art 4(1) (with effect from 30 Sep 2007) so that the commencement of this section on 1 Oct 2007 was reversed. The transitional provisions in Sch 3, para 18 were revoked at the same time. This section was commenced by CO No 8 (for transitional provisions see Sch 2, para 40 to that Order).

21 For transitional provisions, see CO No 3, Sch 3, para 19.

22 For transitional provisions, see CO No 3, Sch 3, paras 20, 21.

23 For transitional provisions, see CO No 3, Sch 3, paras 22, 23.

24 For transitional provisions, see CO No 3, Sch 3, para 24. For transitional adaptations of s 288 and the transitional insertion of ss 300A–300D, see CO No 3, Sch 1, para 13.

25 For transitional provisions, see CO No 3, Sch 3, para 25.

26 For transitional adaptations of s 306, see CO No 3, Sch 1, para 14.

27 For transitional provisions, see CO No 3, Sch 3, para 26.

28 For transitional provisions, see CO No 3, Sch 3, para 27.

29 For transitional provisions, see CO No 3, Sch 3, para 28.

30 For transitional provisions, see CO No 3, Sch 3, para 29.

31 For transitional provisions, see CO No 3, Sch 3, para 30.

32 For transitional provisions, see CO No 3, Sch 3, para 31.

33 For transitional provisions, see CO No 3, Sch 3, paras 32–38. For transitional adaptations of s 336, see CO No 3, Sch 1, para 15.

34 For transitional provisions, see CO No 3, Sch 3, para 39.

35 For transitional provisions, see CO No 3, Sch 3, para 40.

36 CO No 3, arts 2(2), 3(1) provide that Part 14 shall come into force on 1 Oct 2007 (in relation to Great Britain) and 1 Nov 2007 (in relation to Northern Ireland) except in so far as it relates to independent election candidates. Article 5 of that Order specifies certain words in ss 362–367, 378 which, accordingly, do not come into force until 1 Oct 2008. For transitional provisions in connection with the commencement of all of Part 14, see CO No 3, Sch 3, paras 41, 42.

37 For transitional provisions, see CO No 3, Sch 3, para 43. For transitional adaptations of s 417, see CO No 3, Sch 1, para 16.

38 For transitional provisions, see CO No 1, Sch 5, Pt 2, para 3.

39 For transitional provisions, see CO No 3, Sch 3, paras 44, 45. For transitional adaptations of ss 485, 487, see CO No 3, Sch 1, paras 17, 18.

40 CO No 3, art 2(3) provides that sub-ss (1), (4) shall come into force on 1 Oct 2007 so far as is necessary for the purposes of the provisions of this Act brought into force on that date by art 2(1), (2) of that Order.

41 CO No 2, art 2(2) provides that this section shall come into force on 6 Apr 2007 so far as is necessary for the purposes of the provisions of this Act brought into force on that date by that Order. For transitional adaptations of s 1139, see CO No 2, Sch 1, para 5.

42 CO No 3, art 3(2) provides that this section shall come into force on 1 Nov 2007 so far as is necessary for the purposes of the provisions of this Act brought into force on that date by art 3(1) of that Order. For transitional adaptations of s 1158, see CO No 3, Sch 1, para 21.

43 For transitional adaptations of ss 813, 826, 1143, see CO No 1, Sch 1, paras 2, 3 14.

44 For transitional adaptations of ss 943, 953, see CO No 2, Sch 1, paras 2, 3.

45 For transitional adaptations of s 968, see CO No 2, Sch 1, para 4.

46 For transitional provisions, see CO No 3, Sch 3, para 46.

47 For transitional adaptations of s 994, see CO No 3, Sch 1, para 19.

48 For transitional provisions, see CO No 3, Sch 3, para 47.

49 For transitional provisions, see CO No 3, Sch 3, para 48.

50 CO No 1, art 4(3) provides that this section shall come into force on 6 Apr 2007 so far as is necessary for the purposes of the provisions of this Act brought into force on that date by that Order.

51 For transitional provisions, see CO No 1, Sch 5, Pt 3, para 6. Note also that the commencement of this section on 6 Apr 2007 by CO No 1 does not extend to Northern Ireland (see art 4(4) of that Order).

52 CO No 1, art 2(2) provides that sub-ss (1)–(4), (6), (7) shall come into force on 1 Jan 2007 so far as is necessary for the purposes of the provisions of this Act brought into force on that date by that Order.

53 CO No 3, art 4(1) (as amended by SI 2007/2974) provides that sub-ss (1)–(4), (6), (7) shall come into force on 15 Dec 2007 so far as necessary for the purposes of the Companies (Cross-Border Mergers) Regulations 2007.

54 For transitional adaptations of ss 1077, 1080, 1085, 1087, 1103, see CO No 1, Sch 1, paras 4, 7–10.

54a For transitional adaptations of s 1104, see CO No 1, Sch 1, para 11. For savings in relation to the Companies (Welsh Language Forms and Documents) Regulations 1994, see CO No 1, Sch 5, para 1.

54b For savings in relation to the Companies (Welsh Language Forms and Documents) Regulations 1994, see CO No 1, Sch 5, para 1.

55 For transitional adaptations of s 1105, see CO No 1, Sch 1, para 12.

56 CO No 1, art 2(2) provides that this section shall come into force on 1 Jan 2007 so far as is necessary for the purposes of the provisions of this Act brought into force on that date by that Order. For transitional adaptations of s 1120, see CO No 1, Sch 1, para 13.

57 CO No 1, art 3(2) provides that this section shall come into force on 20 Jan 2007 so far as is necessary for the purposes of the provisions of this Act brought into force on that date by that Order.

58 CO No 3, art 2(1)(l) provides that ss 1121–1123, 1125–1133 shall come into force on 1 Oct 2007 in so far as applying to offences under CA 1985, Pts XIV, XV. Article 2(3)(h) of that Order further provides that ss 1121, 1122, 1125, 1127–1133 shall come into force on the same date so far as is necessary for the purposes of the provisions of this Act brought into force on that date by art 2(1), (2) of that Order.

59 CO No 1, arts 2(2), 3(2) provide that this section shall come into force on 1 Jan 2007 and 20 Jan 2007 respectively so far as is necessary for the purposes of the provisions of this Act brought into force on those dates by that Order.

60 CO No 3, art 4(2) provides that this section shall come into force on 15 Dec 2007 so far as is necessary for the purposes of the provisions of this Act brought into force on that date by art 4(1) of that Order.

61 CO No 1, arts 2(2), 3(2) provide that specified definitions in this section shall come into force on 1 Jan 2007 and 20 Jan 2007 respectively so far as is necessary for the purposes of the provisions of this Act brought into force on those dates by that Order.

62 CO No 2, art 2(2) provides that specified definitions in this section shall come into force on 6 Apr 2007 so far as is necessary for the purposes of the provisions of this Act brought into force on that date by that Order.

63 CO No 3, art 2(3) provides that specified definitions in this section shall come into force on 1 Oct 2007 so far as is necessary for the purposes of the provisions of this Act brought into force on that date by art 2(1), (2) of that Order.

64 CO No 3, art 3(2) provides that specified definitions in this section shall come into force on 1 Nov 2007 so far as is necessary for the purposes of the provisions of this Act brought into force on that date by art 3(1) of that Order.

65 Part 43 (ss 1265–1273, Sch 15) came into force on Royal Assent except in so far as relating to the amendment in Sch 15, Pt 1, para 11(2) to this Act to the definition of "regulated market" in FSMA 2000, s 103; see s 1300 of this Act (at **[1.1497]**). Sch 15, Pt 1, para 11(2) (and s 1272 in so far as it introduces Sch 15) was brought into force on 1 Oct 2008 by CO No 7.

66 CO No 1, arts 2(2), 3(2), 4(3) provide that this section shall come into force on 1 Jan 2007, 20 Jan 2007 and 6 Apr 2007 respectively so far as is necessary for the purposes of the provisions of this Act brought into force on those dates by that Order. For transitional adaptations of s 1284, see CO No 1, Sch 1, para 15. CO No 2, art 2(1)(e) also provides that s 1284(1) comes into force on 6 Apr 2007 so far as relating to the provisions commenced by art 2(1)(a)–(c) of that Order and in so far as it relates to Part 2 of the Companies (Audit, Investigations and Community Enterprise) Act 2004. CO No 2, art 5 further provides that s 1284(2) comes into force on 6 Apr 2007 in so far as relating to the repeals specified in Sch 2 to that Order. CO No 3, arts 2(4), 3(2), 4(2) and 5(2) provide that this section shall come into force on 1 Oct 2007, 1 Nov 2007, 15 Dec 2007 and 1 Oct 2008 so far as is necessary for the purposes of the provisions of this Act brought into force on those dates by arts 2(1)(a)–(j), 3(1), 4(1) and 5(1) of that Order respectively. CO No 3, art 8 further provides that s 1284(2) comes into force on 1 Oct 2007 in so far as relating to the repeals specified in Sch 2 to that Order. CO No 5, arts 3(5), 5(4) provide that this section shall come into force on 6 Apr 2008 and 1 Oct 2008 respectively so far as is necessary for the purposes of the provisions of this Act brought into force on those dates by arts 3(1)(a)–(t), (2), (3), 5(1)–(3) of that Order. CO No 7, art 2(d) provides that sub-s (1) shall come into force on 1 Oct 2008 so far as is necessary for the purposes of the provisions of this Act brought into force on that date by art 2(a)–(c) of that Order. CO No 8, art 3 brings this section into force in 1 Oct 2009 for all remaining purposes; for transitional provisions, see Sch 2, para 114 to that Order.

67 For transitional adaptations of Sch 3, see CO No 3, Sch 1, para 20.

68 For transitional provisions, see CO No 1, Sch 5, Pt 2, paras 4, 5. For transitional adaptations of Sch 5, Pt 4, see CO No 1, Sch 1, para 16.

69 Not yet in force, repeals *of or in*: (i) the Companies Act 1985, ss 726(2), 746 (and provisions of the 1985 Act which have already been repealed by other enactments); (ii) the Insolvency Act 1986, Sch 13, Pt 1 (entries relating to ss 156(3), 462(5), 463(2), 463(3), 464(6)); (iii) the Companies Act 1989, ss 56(5), 57, 64(2), 66(3), 71, 116(3), 125(2), 130(6), 135, 144(2), (6); (iv) the Water Consolidation (Consequential Provisions) Act 1991; (v) the Charities Act 1992; (vi) the Criminal Procedure (Consequential Provisions) (Scotland) Act 1995, Sch 4, para 56(3) (it is thought that the intention of CO No 8 was to repeal this paragraph rather than para 56(4) as stated); (vii) the Financial Services and Markets Act

2000, ss 143, 263 (note that s143 no longer exists following the substitution of Part 9A (ss 137A–137T, 138A–138O, 139A, 139B, 140A–140H, 141A) for the original Part X (ss 138–164); note also that s 263 is spent following the repeal of CA 1985, s 716 (which it amended)); (viii) the Companies (Audit, Investigations and Community Enterprise) Act 2004, Sch 2, paras 6, 26 (both of which are spent following the repeal of the CA 1985 provision that they amended); (ix) the Civil Partnership Act 2004, Sch 27, para 103 (it is thought that the intention of SI 2008/2860 was to repeal this paragraph rather than para 104 as stated); (x) the Constitutional Reform Act 2005. Note: repeals of Northern Ireland legislation by Sch 16 that are yet to be commenced are not noted.

70 For transitional provisions, see CO No 1, Sch 5, Pt 2, para 2(3), (4).

71 For transitional provisions, see CO No 5, Sch 4, Pt 1, para 1.

72 For transitional provisions, see CO No 5, Sch 4, Pt 1, para 2.

73 For transitional provisions, see CO No 5, Sch 4, Pt 1, para 3.

74 For transitional provisions, see CO No 5, Sch 4, Pt 1, para 4. For transitional adaptations, see CO No 5, Sch 1, Pt 1, para 3.

75 For transitional adaptations, see CO No 5, Sch 1, Pt 1, paras 4, 5.

76 For transitional provisions, see CO No 5, Sch 4, Pt 1, para 5.

77 For transitional provisions, see CO No 5, Sch 4, Pt 1, paras 6–8. For transitional adaptations of ss 444–447, 449, see CO No 5, Sch 1, Pt 1, paras 6–10.

78 For transitional provisions, see CO No 5, Sch 4, Pt 1, para 9.

79 For transitional provisions, see CO No 5, Sch 4, Pt 1, paras 10, 11.

80 For transitional provisions, see CO No 5, Sch 4, Pt 1, para 12.

81 For transitional provisions, see CO No 5, Sch 4, Pt 1, paras 13–17.

82 For transitional provisions, see CO No 5, Sch 4, Pt 1, para 18.

83 For transitional provisions, see CO No 5, Sch 4, Pt 1, para 19.

84 For transitional provisions, see CO No 5, Sch 4, Pt 1, para 20.

85 For transitional provisions, see CO No 5, Sch 4, Pt 1, para 21.

86 For transitional provisions, see CO No 5, Sch 4, Pt 1, para 22.

87 For transitional provisions, see CO No 5, Sch 4, Pt 1, para 23.

88 For transitional provisions, see CO No 5, Sch 4, Pt 1, para 24.

89 For transitional provisions, see CO No 5, Sch 4, Pt 1, para 25.

90 For transitional provisions, see CO No 5, Sch 4, Pt 1, para 26.

91 For transitional provisions, see CO No 5, Sch 4, Pt 1, paras 27, 28.

92 For transitional adaptations, see CO No 5, Sch 1, Pt 1, paras 12, 13.

93 For transitional provisions, see CO No 5, Sch 4, Pt 1, para 29.

94 For transitional provisions, see CO No 5, Sch 4, Pt 1, para 30.

95 For transitional provisions, see CO No 5, Sch 4, Pt 1, para 31.

96 For transitional provisions, see CO No 5, Sch 4, Pt 1, para 32.

97 For transitional provisions, see CO No 5, Sch 4, Pt 1, paras 33–35. For transitional adaptations of ss 829, 832, 833, 838–840, 847, see CO No 5, Sch 1, Pt 1, paras 14–20.

98 For transitional provisions, see CO No 5, Sch 4, Pt 1, para 36.

99 For transitional adaptations, see CO No 5, Sch 1, Pt 1, para 21.

100 Certain specified definitions come into force on 6 Apr 2008 (see CO No 5, art 3(1)(t) at. Also, arts 3(3)(j) and 5(3)(c) of that Order provide that specified definitions in this section shall come into force on 6 Apr 2008 and 1 Oct 2008 respectively so far as is necessary for the purposes of the provisions of this Act brought into force on those dates by arts 3(1)(a)–(t), (2), 5(1)(a)–(f) of that Order.

101 For transitional provisions, see CO No 5, Sch 4, Pt 1, para 37.

102 For transitional provisions, see CO No 5, Sch 4, Pt 1, para 38.

103 For transitional provisions, see CO No 5, Sch 4, Pt 1, para 40.

104 For transitional provisions, see CO No 5, Sch 4, Pt 1, para 41.

105 For transitional provisions, see CO No 5, Sch 4, Pt 1, para 43.

106 CO No 5, art 3(2) provides that sub-ss (1), (2) come into force on 6 Apr 2008 so far as may be necessary for the purpose of enabling rules to be made under this section before the date on which the section is brought generally into force, and sub-s (3) has effect accordingly.

107 CO No 5, art 3(3)(a)–(f), (h) provides that this section shall come into force on 6 Apr 2008 so far as is necessary for the purposes of the provisions of this Act brought into force on that date by art 3(1)(a)–(t), (2) of that Order.

108 CO No 5, arts 3(3)(g), (i), 5(3)(a), (b) provide that this section shall come into force on 6 Apr 2008 and 1 Oct 2008 respectively so far as is necessary for the purposes of the provisions of this Act brought into force on those dates by arts 3(1)(a)–(t), (2), 5(1)(a)–(f) of that Order.

109 CO No 5, art 3(4) provides that ss 1159, 1160 and Sch 6 shall come into force on 6 Apr 2008 so far as is necessary for the purposes of the provisions of this Act brought into force on that date by art 3(1)(u) of that Order.

110 For transitional provisions, see CO No 5, Sch 4, Pt 2, para 45.

111 For transitional adaptations, see CO No 5, Sch 1, Pt 2, para 22.

112 For transitional adaptations, see CO No 5, Sch 1, Pt 2, para 23.

113 For transitional provisions, see CO No 5, Sch 4, Pt 3, para 46.

114 For transitional adaptations, see CO No 5, Sch 1, Pt 2, para 24.

115 For transitional provisions, see CO No 5, Sch 4, Pt 3, para 47.

116 For transitional provisions, see CO No 5, Sch 4, Pt 3, para 48.

117 For transitional provisions, see CO No 5, Sch 4, Pt 3, paras 47(4), 50.

118 CO No 3, art 2(1)(d) brings into force ss 254, 255 of this Act (the enabling sections for this Schedule) on 1 Oct 2007. Although not specifically mentioned in that commencement order, it is believed that the intention was also to bring Sch 1 into force on the same date.

119 Inserted by SI 2007/3494 (subject, in certain cases, to transitional provisions contained in those Regulations).

120 CO No 6, art 3(1)(a) provides that this section shall come into force on 1 Apr 2008 in so far as it relates to CA 1985,

Pt VII. For transitional provisions see art 3(2), (3) of that Order.

121 For transitional provisions see CO No 6, art 3(2), (3).

122 Inserted by SI 2008/393, in relation to financial years beginning on or after 6 Apr 2008.

123 Inserted by SI 2008/690.

124 For transitional adaptations, see CO No 5, Sch 1, Pt 1, para 11.

125 For transitional adaptations, see CO No 7, arts 3, 4.

126 For transitional provisions see CO No 7, art 7(2).

127 CO No 7, art 2(c) provides that ss 610(2)–(4), 652(1), (3), 733(5), (6) shall come into force on 1 Oct 2008 in so far as relating to a reduction of capital under ss 641(1)(a), (2)–(6) and 642–644. For transitional adaptations of s 652, see art 5 of that Order.

128 CO No 7, art 2(e) provides s 1286(1)(a), (2)(a) shall come into force on 1 Oct 2008 in so far as relating to the application to LLPs of the subject matter of Pt 15 (accounts and reports), Pt 16 (audit) and Pt 42 (statutory auditors). This applies in relation to accounts and the audit of accounts for financial years beginning on or after that date (see art 7(3)).

129 For transitional provisions, see CO No 8, Sch 2, para 2.

130 For transitional provisions, see CO No 8, Sch 2, para 3.

131 For transitional provisions, see CO No 8, Sch 2, para 4.

132 For transitional provisions, see CO No 8, Sch 2, para 5.

133 For transitional provisions, see CO No 8, Sch 2, para 6.

134 For transitional provisions, see CO No 8, Sch 2, paras 7–10.

135 For transitional provisions, see CO No 8, Sch 2, para 11.

136 For transitional provisions, see CO No 8, Sch 2, para 12.

137 For transitional provisions, see CO No 8, Sch 2, para 13.

138 For transitional provisions, see CO No 8, Sch 2, para 14.

139 For transitional provisions, see CO No 8, Sch 2, para 15.

140 For transitional provisions, see CO No 8, Sch 2, para 16.

141 For transitional provisions, see CO No 8, Sch 2, paras 17, 18.

142 For transitional provisions, see CO No 8, Sch 2, para 19.

143 For transitional provisions, see CO No 8, Sch 2, para 22.

144 For transitional provisions, see CO No 8, Sch 2, para 23.

145 For transitional provisions, see CO No 8, Sch 2, paras 25–39.

146 For transitional provisions, see CO No 8, Sch 2, para 41.

147 For transitional provisions, see CO No 8, Sch 2, paras 43, 44.

148 For transitional provisions, see CO No 8, Sch 2, para 45.

149 For transitional provisions, see CO No 8, Sch 2, para 46.

150 For transitional provisions, see CO No 8, Sch 2, paras 49–55.

151 For transitional provisions, see CO No 8, Sch 2, para 56.

152 For transitional provisions, see CO No 8, Sch 2, para 57.

153 For transitional provisions, see CO No 8, Sch 2, para 58.

154 For transitional provisions, see CO No 8, Sch 2, para 61.

155 For transitional provisions, see CO No 8, Sch 2, para 62.

156 For transitional provisions, see CO No 8, Sch 2, para 63.

157 For transitional provisions, see CO No 8, Sch 2, para 64.

158 For transitional provisions, see CO No 8, Sch 2, para 65.

159 For transitional provisions, see CO No 8, Sch 2, para 66.

160 For transitional provisions, see CO No 8, Sch 2, para 68.

161 For transitional provisions, see CO No 8, Sch 2, para 69.

162 For transitional provisions, see CO No 8, Sch 2, paras 70–72.

163 For transitional provisions, see CO No 8, Sch 2, para 73.

164 For transitional provisions, see CO No 8, Sch 2, para 74.

165 For transitional provisions, see CO No 8, Sch 2, paras 75, 76.

166 For transitional provisions, see CO No 8, Sch 2, para 77.

167 For transitional provisions, see CO No 8, Sch 2, para 78.

168 For transitional provisions, see CO No 8, Sch 2, para 79.

169 For transitional provisions, see CO No 8, Sch 2, para 80.

170 Inserted by SI 2018/860, in relation to the financial years of companies beginning on or after 1 Jan 2019.

171 For transitional provisions, see CO No 8, Sch 2, para 82.

172 For transitional provisions, see CO No 8, Sch 2, para 83.

173 For transitional provisions, see CO No 8, Sch 2, para 84.

174 For transitional provisions, see CO No 8, Sch 2, para 85.

175 For transitional provisions, see CO No 8, Sch 2, para 86.

176 For transitional provisions, see CO No 8, Sch 2, para 87.

177 For transitional provisions, see CO No 8, Sch 2, para 88.

178 For transitional provisions, see CO No 8, Sch 2, paras 90, 91.

179 For transitional provisions, see CO No 8, Sch 2, para 92.

180 For transitional provisions, see CO No 8, Sch 2, para 93.

181 For transitional provisions, see CO No 8, Sch 2, para 94.

182 For transitional provisions, see CO No 8, Sch 2, para 95.

183 For transitional provisions, see CO No 8, Sch 2, para 96.

184 For transitional provisions, see CO No 8, Sch 2, para 97.

185 For transitional provisions, see CO No 8, Sch 2, para 98.

186 For transitional provisions, see CO No 8, Sch 2, para 99.
187 For transitional provisions, see CO No 8, Sch 2, para 100.
188 For transitional provisions, see CO No 8, Sch 2, para 101.
189 For transitional provisions, see CO No 8, Sch 2, para 102.
190 For transitional adaptations of ss 1078, 1079, see CO No 1, Sch 1, paras 5, 6. For savings in relation to those transitional adaptations, see CO No 8, Sch 2, paras 103, 104.
191 For transitional provisions, see CO No 8, Sch 2, para 105.
192 For transitional provisions, see CO No 8, Sch 2, para 106.
193 For transitional provisions, see CO No 8, Sch 2, para 107.
194 For transitional provisions, see CO No 8, Sch 2, para 108.
195 For transitional provisions, see CO No 8, Sch 2, para 109.
196 For transitional provisions, see CO No 8, art 7, and Sch 2, para 116.
197 For transitional provisions, see CO No 8, Sch 2, para 112.
198 Inserted by SI 2017/1164, as from 1 Jan 2018, in relation to financial years of companies beginning on or after 17 Jun 2016 (as to the application of the 2017 Regulations, see **[4.671]** et seq).
199 Inserted by SI 2009/1581, in relation to financial years beginning on or after 29 Jun 2008 which have not ended before the date of coming into force of the 2009 Regulations.
200 The government announced that they do not intend to commence ss 327(2)(c), 330(6)(c), 1175 (in so far as relating to Northern Ireland) or Sch 9, Pt 2; see the written ministerial statements for 6 Nov 2008. Those provisions were subsequently repealed by the Deregulation Act 2015 as from 26 May 2015 meaning that, in effect, ss 327 and 330 are fully in force.
201 Substituted by SI 2009/2561.
202 For transitional provisions, see CO No 8, Sch 2, para 4. Note also that sub-s (2) was originally scheduled to come into force on 1 Oct 2009. CO No 8 was amended by SI 2009/2476 (as from 30 Sep 2009) to stop this happening. See the note for those Regulations at **[4.424]**.
203 Repealed by SI 2017/693, as from 26 Jun 2017, subject to transitional arrangements.
204 Sections 285, 285A were substituted (for the original s 285) by SI 2009/1632, in relation to meetings of which notice is given, or first given, on or after 3 Aug 2009.
205 Inserted by SI 2009/1632, in relation to meetings of which notice is given, or first given, on or after 3 Aug 2009.
206 Inserted by SI 2009/1802.
207 Repealed by SI 2009/1802, as from 1 Oct 2009.
208 Repealed by SI 2009/2022, as from 1 Oct 2009.
209 Inserted by SI 2009/1941.
210 Substituted by SI 2008/690.
211 Substituted by SI 2009/3182.
212 Substituted by SI 2009/1208.
213 Sections 1253D, 1253DA–1253DE were substituted (for the original s 1253D) by SI 2010/2537. Section 1253D was originally inserted by SI 2007/3494.
214 Section 1253E was substituted by SI 2010/2537. It was originally inserted by SI 2007/3494.
215 Inserted by SI 2011/1606, except in relation to any merger or division the draft terms of which were adopted before 1 Aug 2011.
216 Repealed by the Charities Act 2011, as from 14 Mar 2012.
217 Repealed by SI 2012/952, as from 6 Apr 2012.
218 Sections 1225, 1225A–1225G were substituted for the original s 1225 by SI 2012/1741.
219 Inserted by SI 2012/2301, in relation to accounts for financial years ending on or after 1 Oct 2012.
220 Inserted by SI 2013/600, in relation to charges created on or after 6 Apr 2013 (with the exception of ss 859K, 859L, 859O which also apply to charges created before that date).
221 Repealed by SI 2013/600, as from 6 Apr 2013, except in relation to charges created before that date. See also the footnote above.
222 Inserted by the Enterprise and Regulatory Reform Act 2013, except in relation to remuneration payments or payments for loss of office that are required to be made under an agreement entered into before 27 Jun 2012 or in consequence of any other obligation arising before that date.
223 Inserted by the Enterprise and Regulatory Reform Act 2013.
224 Inserted by SI 2013/999.
225 Inserted by SI 2013/1970, as from 1 Oct 2013 (in respect of financial years ending on or after 30 Sep 2013).
226 Inserted by SI 2013/3008, as from 1 Dec 2013 (in relation to (a) financial years ending on or after 30 Sep 2013, and (b) companies, which deliver the accounts required by s 444 of this Act to the registrar on or after 1 Dec 2013).
227 Inserted by SI 2014/1557.
228 Repealed by SI 2013/1970, in respect of financial years ending on or after 30 Sep 2013.
229 Repealed by the Small Business, Enterprise and Employment Act 2015, as from 26 May 2015, except in relation to a share warrant surrendered for cancellation before that date.
230 Repealed by the Small Business, Enterprise and Employment Act 2015, as from 26 May 2015.
231 Inserted by the Small Business, Enterprise and Employment Act 2015.
232 The original Part 24 (ss 854–859) was substituted by a new Part 24 (ss 853A–853L) by the Small Business, Enterprise and Employment Act 2015, as from 1 May 2016 (for the purpose of enabling the registrar to impose the requirements referred to in s 853F(6) of the 2006 Act), and as from 30 Jun 2016 (otherwise) except in relation to annual returns to be made up to a return date before 30 Jun 2016.
233 Repealed by SI 2015/980, as from 6 Apr 2015, in relation to (a) financial years beginning on or after 1 Jan 2016, and (b) a financial year of a company beginning on or after 1 Jan 2015, but before 1 Jan 2016, if the directors of the company so decide (subject to transitional provisions, etc, in regs 2, 3 of the 2015 Regulations).
234 Inserted by the Deregulation Act 2015, as from 1 Oct 2015, in relation to financial years beginning on or after that date (and subject to transitional provisions).

235 Repealed by the Deregulation Act 2015, as from 26 May 2015.

236 Substituted by SI 2015/980, as from 6 Apr 2015, in relation to (a) financial years beginning on or after 1 Jan 2016, and (b) a financial year of a company beginning on or after 1 Jan 2015, but before 1 Jan 2016, if the directors of the company so decide (subject to transitional provisions, etc, in regs 2, 3 of the 2015 Regulations).

237 Inserted by SI 2016/649, as from 17 Jun 2016, in relation to financial years beginning on or after that date.

238 Inserted by SI 2016/649.

239 Repealed by the Deregulation Act 2015, as from 1 Oct 2015, in relation to financial years beginning on or after that date (and subject to transitional provisions).

240 Repealed by SI 2016/649, as from 17 Jun 2016 (subject to transitional provisions).

241 Inserted by SI 2016/1194, as from 30 Dec 2016 (in relation to distributions made on or after that date by reference to relevant accounts (within the meaning of s 836) prepared for any period ending on or after 1 Jan 2016).

242 Inserted by SI 2016/1245, as from 26 Dec 2016, in relation to the financial years of companies and qualifying partnerships beginning on or after 1 Jan 2017 (and only in relation to companies (as defined by s 1 of the 2006 Act) and qualifying partnerships (as defined in the Partnerships (Accounts) Regulations 2008, reg 3)).

243 Inserted by SI 2017/80.

244 Repealed by SI 2016/1245, regs 2, 3(2)(b), as from 26 Dec 2016 (a) in relation to the financial years of companies and qualifying partnerships beginning on or after 1 January 2017; and (b) only in relation to companies, and qualifying partnerships.

245 Inserted by SI 2017/516, as from 1 May 2017, in relation to financial years of companies beginning on or after 17 Jun 2016.

246 Repealed by SI 2017/516, as from 1 May 2017, in relation to financial years of companies beginning on or after 17 Jun 2016.

247 Inserted by SI 2017/693 (subject to transitional arrangements in the Schedule to the Regulations).

248 Inserted by SI 2019/177.

249 Inserted by SI 2019/217.

250 Inserted by SI 2019/1511.

251 Repealed by the Small Business, Enterprise and Employment Act 2015, as from a day to be appointed.

252 Repealed by SI 2019/348, as from IP completion day (as defined in the European Union (Withdrawal Agreement) Act 2020, s 39).

253 Repealed by SI 2019/707, as from IP completion day (as defined in the European Union (Withdrawal Agreement) Act 2020, s 39).

254 Inserted by the Corporate Insolvency and Governance Act 2020.

255 S 360AA inserted by SI 2020/717, as from 3 Sep 2020, in relation to votes cast on or after that date. S 360BA inserted by SI 2020/717, as from 3 Sep 2020, in relation to votes cast at a general meeting which takes place on or after that date.

PART 3
COMPANIES ACT 2006: SUPPORTING MATERIALS, ETC

FINANCIAL REPORTING COUNCIL: THE UK CORPORATE GOVERNANCE CODE (JULY 2018)

[3.1]

NOTES

See the Financial Reporting Council website at: www.frc.org.uk/.

CONTENTS

INTRODUCTION

[3.2]

The first version of the UK Corporate Governance Code (the Code) was published in 1992 by the Cadbury Committee. It defined corporate governance as 'the system by which companies are directed and controlled. Boards of directors are responsible for the governance of their companies. The shareholders' role in governance is to appoint the directors and the auditors and to satisfy themselves that an appropriate governance structure is in place.' This remains true today, but the environment in which companies, their shareholders and wider stakeholders operate continues to develop rapidly.

Companies do not exist in isolation. Successful and sustainable businesses underpin our economy and society by providing employment and creating prosperity. To succeed in the long-term, directors and the companies they lead need to build and maintain successful relationships with a wide range of stakeholders. These relationships will be successful and enduring if they are based on respect, trust and mutual benefit. Accordingly, a company's culture should promote integrity and openness, value diversity and be responsive to the views of shareholders and wider stakeholders.

Over the years the Code has been revised and expanded to take account of the increasing demands on the UK's corporate governance framework. The principle of collective responsibility within a unitary board has been a success and – alongside the stewardship activities of investors – played a vital role in delivering high standards of governance and encouraging long-term investment. Nevertheless, the debate about the nature and extent of the framework has intensified as a result of financial crises and high-profile examples of inadequate governance and misconduct, which have led to poor outcomes for a wide range of stakeholders.

At the heart of this Code is an updated set of Principles that emphasise the value of good corporate governance to long-term sustainable success. By applying the Principles, following the more detailed Provisions and using the associated guidance, companies can demonstrate throughout their reporting how the governance of the company contributes to its long-term sustainable success and achieves wider objectives.

Achieving this depends crucially on the way boards and companies apply the spirit of the Principles. The Code does not set out a rigid set of rules; instead it offers flexibility through the application of Principles and through 'comply or explain' Provisions and supporting guidance. It is the responsibility of boards to use this flexibility wisely and of investors and their advisors to assess differing company approaches thoughtfully.

REPORTING ON THE CODE

The 2018 Code focuses on the application of the Principles. The Listing Rules require companies to make a statement of how they have applied the Principles, in a manner that would enable shareholders to evaluate how the Principles have been applied. The ability of investors to evaluate the approach to governance is important. Reporting should cover the application of the Principles in the context of the particular circumstances of the company and how the board has set the company's purpose and strategy, met objectives and achieved outcomes through the decisions it has taken.

It is important to report meaningfully when discussing the application of the Principles and to avoid boilerplate reporting. The focus should be on how these have been applied, articulating what action has been taken and the resulting outcomes. High-quality reporting will include signposting and cross-referencing to those parts of the annual report that describe how the Principles have been applied. This will help investors with their evaluation of company practices.

The effective application of the Principles should be supported by high-quality reporting on the Provisions. These operate on a 'comply or explain' basis and companies should avoid a 'tick-box approach'. An alternative to complying with a Provision may be justified in particular circumstances based on a range of factors, including the size, complexity, history and ownership structure of a company. Explanations should set out the background, provide a clear rationale for the action the company is taking, and explain the impact that the action has had. Where a departure from a Provision is intended to be limited in time, the explanation should indicate when the company expects to conform to the Provision. Explanations are a positive opportunity to communicate, not an onerous obligation.

In line with their responsibilities under the UK Stewardship Code, investors should engage constructively and discuss with the company any departures from recommended practice. In their consideration of explanations, investors and their advisors should pay due regard to a company's individual circumstances. While they have every right to challenge explanations if they are unconvincing, these must not be evaluated in a mechanistic way. Investors and their advisors should also give companies sufficient time to respond to enquiries about corporate governance.

Corporate governance reporting should also relate coherently to other parts of the annual report – particularly the Strategic Report and other complementary information – so that shareholders can effectively assess the quality of the company's governance arrangements, and the board's activities and contributions. This should include providing information that enables shareholders to assess how the directors have performed their duty under section 172 of the Companies Act 2006 (the Act) to promote the success of the company. Nothing in this Code overrides or is intended as an interpretation of the statutory statement of directors' duties in the Act.

The Code is also supported by the *Guidance on Board Effectiveness* (the Guidance). We encourage boards and companies to use this to support their activities. The Guidance does not set out the 'right way' to apply the Code. It is intended to stimulate thinking on how boards can carry out their role most effectively. The Guidance is designed to help boards with their actions and decisions when reporting on the application of the Code's Principles. The board should also take into account the Financial Reporting Council's *Guidance on Audit Committees* and *Guidance on Risk Management, Internal Control and Related Financial and Business Reporting*.

APPLICATION

The Code is applicable to all companies with a premium listing, whether incorporated in the UK or elsewhere. The new Code applies to accounting periods beginning on or after 1 January 2019.

For parent companies with a premium listing, the board should ensure that there is adequate co-operation within the group to enable it to discharge its governance responsibilities under the Code effectively. This includes the communication of the parent company's purpose, values and strategy.

Externally managed investment companies (which typically have a different board and company structure that may affect the relevance of particular Principles) may wish to use the Association of Investment Companies' Corporate Governance Code to meet their obligations under the Code. In addition, the Association of Financial Mutuals produces an annotated version of the Code for mutual insurers to use.

1. BOARD LEADERSHIP AND COMPANY PURPOSE

[3.3]

Principles

A. A successful company is led by an effective and entrepreneurial board, whose role is to promote the long-term sustainable success of the company, generating value for shareholders and contributing to wider society.

B. The board should establish the company's purpose, values and strategy, and satisfy itself that these and its culture are aligned. All directors must act with integrity, lead by example and promote the desired culture.

C. The board should ensure that the necessary resources are in place for the company to meet its objectives and measure performance against them. The board should also establish a framework of prudent and effective controls, which enable risk to be assessed and managed.

D. In order for the company to meet its responsibilities to shareholders and stakeholders, the board should ensure effective engagement with, and encourage participation from, these parties.

E. The board should ensure that workforce policies and practices are consistent with the company's values and support its long-term sustainable success. The workforce should be able to raise any matters of concern.

PROVISIONS

1. The board should assess the basis on which the company generates and preserves value over the long-term. It should describe in the annual report how opportunities and risks to the future success of the business have been considered and addressed, the sustainability of the company's business model and how its governance contributes to the delivery of its strategy.

2. The board should assess and monitor culture. Where it is not satisfied that policy, practices or behaviour throughout the business are aligned with the company's purpose, values and strategy, it should seek assurance that management has taken corrective action. The annual report should explain the board's activities and any action taken. In addition, it should include an explanation of the company's approach to investing in and rewarding its workforce.

3. In addition to formal general meetings, the chair should seek regular engagement with major shareholders in order to understand their views on governance and performance against the strategy. Committee chairs should seek engagement with shareholders on significant matters related to their areas of responsibility. The chair should ensure that the board as a whole has a clear understanding of the views of shareholders.

4. When 20 per cent or more of votes have been cast against the board recommendation for a resolution, the company should explain, when announcing voting results, what actions it intends to take to consult shareholders in order to understand the reasons behind the result. An update on the views received from shareholders and actions taken should be published no later than six months after the shareholder meeting. The board should then provide a final summary in the annual report and, if applicable, in the explanatory notes to resolutions at the next shareholder meeting, on what impact the feedback has had on the decisions the board has taken and any actions or resolutions now proposed.[1]

5. The board should understand the views of the company's other key stakeholders and describe in the annual report how their interests and the matters set out in section 172 of the Companies Act 2006 have been considered in board discussions and decision-making.[2] The board should keep engagement mechanisms under review so that they remain effective.

For engagement with the workforce,[3] one or a combination of the following methods should be used:
- a director appointed from the workforce;
- a formal workforce advisory panel;
- a designated non-executive director.

If the board has not chosen one or more of these methods, it should explain what alternative arrangements are in place and why it considers that they are effective.

6. There should be a means for the workforce to raise concerns in confidence and – if they wish – anonymously. The board should routinely review this and the reports arising from its operation. It should ensure that arrangements are in place for the proportionate and independent investigation of such matters and for follow-up action.

7. The board should take action to identify and manage conflicts of interest, including those resulting from significant shareholdings, and ensure that the influence of third parties does not compromise or override independent judgement.

8. Where directors have concerns about the operation of the board or the management of the company that cannot be resolved, their concerns should be recorded in the board minutes. On resignation, a non-executive director should provide a written statement to the chair, for circulation to the board, if they have any such concerns.

NOTES

1 Details of significant votes against and related company updates are available on the Public Register maintained by The Investment Association – www.theinvestmentassociation.org/publicregister.html

2 The Companies (Miscellaneous Reporting) Regulations 2018 require directors to explain how they have had regard to various matters in performing their duty to promote the success of the company in section 172 of the Companies Act 2006. The Financial Reporting Council's Guidance on the Strategic Report supports reporting on the legislative requirement.

3 See the Guidance on Board Effectiveness Section 1 for a description of 'workforce' in this context.

2. DIVISION OF RESPONSIBILITIES

[3.4]

Principles

F. The chair leads the board and is responsible for its overall effectiveness in directing the company. They should demonstrate objective judgement throughout their tenure and promote a culture of openness and debate. In addition, the chair facilitates constructive board relations and the effective contribution of all non-executive directors, and ensures that directors receive accurate, timely and clear information.

G. The board should include an appropriate combination of executive and non-executive (and, in particular, independent non-executive) directors, such that no one individual or small group of individuals dominates the board's decision-making. There should be a clear division of responsibilities between the leadership of the board and the executive leadership of the company's business.

H. Non-executive directors should have sufficient time to meet their board responsibilities. They should provide constructive challenge, strategic guidance, offer specialist advice and hold management to account.

I. The board, supported by the company secretary, should ensure that it has the policies, processes, information, time and resources it needs in order to function effectively and efficiently.

PROVISIONS

9. The chair should be independent on appointment when assessed against the circumstances set out in Provision 10. The roles of chair and chief executive should not be exercised by the same individual. A chief executive should not become chair of the same company. If, exceptionally, this is proposed by the board, major shareholders should be consulted ahead of appointment. The board should set out its reasons to all shareholders at the time of the appointment and also publish these on the company website.

10. The board should identify in the annual report each non-executive director it considers to be independent. Circumstances which are likely to impair, or could appear to impair, a non-executive director's independence include, but are not limited to, whether a director:
- is or has been an employee of the company or group within the last five years;
- has, or has had within the last three years, a material business relationship with the company, either directly or as a partner, shareholder, director or senior employee of a body that has such a relationship with the company;

- has received or receives additional remuneration from the company apart from a director's fee, participates in the company's share option or a performance-related pay scheme, or is a member of the company's pension scheme;
- has close family ties with any of the company's advisers, directors or senior employees;
- holds cross-directorships or has significant links with other directors through involvement in other companies or bodies;
- represents a significant shareholder; or
- has served on the board for more than nine years from the date of their first appointment.

Where any of these or other relevant circumstances apply, and the board nonetheless considers that the non-executive director is independent, a clear explanation should be provided.

11. At least half the board, excluding the chair, should be non-executive directors whom the board considers to be independent.

12. The board should appoint one of the independent non-executive directors to be the senior independent director to provide a sounding board for the chair and serve as an intermediary for the other directors and shareholders. Led by the senior independent director, the non-executive directors should meet without the chair present at least annually to appraise the chair's performance, and on other occasions as necessary.

13. Non-executive directors have a prime role in appointing and removing executive directors. Non-executive directors should scrutinise and hold to account the performance of management and individual executive directors against agreed performance objectives. The chair should hold meetings with the non-executive directors without the executive directors present.

14. The responsibilities of the chair, chief executive, senior independent director, board and committees should be clear, set out in writing, agreed by the board and made publicly available. The annual report should set out the number of meetings of the board and its committees, and the individual attendance by directors.

15. When making new appointments, the board should take into account other demands on directors' time. Prior to appointment, significant commitments should be disclosed with an indication of the time involved. Additional external appointments should not be undertaken without prior approval of the board, with the reasons for permitting significant appointments explained in the annual report. Full-time executive directors should not take on more than one non-executive directorship in a FTSE 100 company or other significant appointment.

16. All directors should have access to the advice of the company secretary, who is responsible for advising the board on all governance matters. Both the appointment and removal of the company secretary should be a matter for the whole board.

3. COMPOSITION, SUCCESSION AND EVALUATION

[3.5]

Principles

J. Appointments to the board should be subject to a formal, rigorous and transparent procedure, and an effective succession plan should be maintained for board and senior management.[4] Both appointments and succession plans should be based on merit and objective criteria[5] and, within this context, should promote diversity of gender, social and ethnic backgrounds, cognitive and personal strengths.

K. The board and its committees should have a combination of skills, experience and knowledge. Consideration should be given to the length of service of the board as a whole and membership regularly refreshed.

L. Annual evaluation of the board should consider its composition, diversity and how effectively members work together to achieve objectives. Individual evaluation should demonstrate whether each director continues to contribute effectively.

PROVISIONS

17. The board should establish a nomination committee to lead the process for appointments, ensure plans are in place for orderly succession to both the board and senior management positions, and oversee the development of a diverse pipeline for succession. A majority of members of the committee should be independent non-executive directors. The chair of the board should not chair the committee when it is dealing with the appointment of their successor.

18. All directors should be subject to annual re-election. The board should set out in the papers accompanying the resolutions to elect each director the specific reasons why their contribution is, and continues to be, important to the company's long-term sustainable success.

19. The chair should not remain in post beyond nine years from the date of their first appointment to the board. To facilitate effective succession planning and the development of a diverse board, this period can be extended for a limited time, particularly in those cases where the chair was an existing non-executive director on appointment. A clear explanation should be provided.

20. Open advertising and/or an external search consultancy should generally be used for the appointment of the chair and non-executive directors. If an external search consultancy is engaged it should be identified in the annual report alongside a statement about any other connection it has with the company or individual directors.

21. There should be a formal and rigorous annual evaluation of the performance of the board, its committees, the chair and individual directors. The chair should consider having a regular externally facilitated board evaluation. In FTSE 350 companies this should happen at least every three years. The external evaluator should be identified in the annual report and a statement made about any other connection it has with the company or individual directors.

22. The chair should act on the results of the evaluation by recognising the strengths and addressing any weaknesses of the board. Each director should engage with the process and take appropriate action when development needs have been identified.

23. The annual report should describe the work of the nomination committee, including:

- the process used in relation to appointments, its approach to succession planning and how both support developing a diverse pipeline;
- how the board evaluation has been conducted, the nature and extent of an external evaluator's contact with the board and individual directors, the outcomes and actions taken, and how it has or will influence board composition;
- the policy on diversity and inclusion, its objectives and linkage to company strategy, how it has been implemented and progress on achieving the objectives; and
- the gender balance of those in the senior management[6] and their direct reports.

NOTES

[4] The definition of 'senior management' for this purpose should be the executive committee or the first layer of management below board level, including the company secretary.

[5] Which protect against discrimination for those with protected characteristics within the meaning of the Equalities Act 2010.

[6] See footnote 4.

4. AUDIT, RISK AND INTERNAL CONTROL

[3.6]

Principles

M. The board should establish formal and transparent policies and procedures to ensure the independence and effectiveness of internal and external audit functions and satisfy itself on the integrity of financial and narrative statements.[7]

N. The board should present a fair, balanced and understandable assessment of the company's position and prospects.

O. The board should establish procedures to manage risk, oversee the internal control framework, and determine the nature and extent of the principal risks the company is willing to take in order to achieve its long-term strategic objectives.

PROVISIONS

24. The board should establish an audit committee of independent non-executive directors, with a minimum membership of three, or in the case of smaller companies, two.[8] The chair of the board should not be a member. The board should satisfy itself that at least one member has recent and relevant financial experience. The committee as a whole shall have competence relevant to the sector in which the company operates.

25. The main roles and responsibilities of the audit committee should include:

- monitoring the integrity of the financial statements of the company and any formal announcements relating to the company's financial performance, and reviewing significant financial reporting judgements contained in them;
- providing advice (where requested by the board) on whether the annual report and accounts, taken as a whole, is fair, balanced and understandable, and provides the information necessary for shareholders to assess the company's position and performance, business model and strategy;
- reviewing the company's internal financial controls and internal control and risk management systems, unless expressly addressed by a separate board risk committee composed of independent non-executive directors, or by the board itself;
- monitoring and reviewing the effectiveness of the company's internal audit function or, where there is not one, considering annually whether there is a need for one and making a recommendation to the board;
- conducting the tender process and making recommendations to the board, about the appointment, reappointment and removal of the external auditor, and approving the remuneration and terms of engagement of the external auditor;
- reviewing and monitoring the external auditor's independence and objectivity;
- reviewing the effectiveness of the external audit process, taking into consideration relevant UK professional and regulatory requirements;
- developing and implementing policy on the engagement of the external auditor to supply non-audit services, ensuring there is prior approval of non-audit services, considering the impact this may have on independence, taking into account the relevant regulations and ethical guidance in this regard, and reporting to the board on any improvement or action required; and
- reporting to the board on how it has discharged its responsibilities.

26. The annual report should describe the work of the audit committee, including:

- the significant issues that the audit committee considered relating to the financial statements, and how these issues were addressed;

- an explanation of how it has assessed the independence and effectiveness of the external audit process and the approach taken to the appointment or reappointment of the external auditor, information on the length of tenure of the current audit firm, when a tender was last conducted and advance notice of any retendering plans;
- in the case of a board not accepting the audit committee's recommendation on the external auditor appointment, reappointment or removal, a statement from the audit committee explaining its recommendation and the reasons why the board has taken a different position (this should also be supplied in any papers recommending appointment or reappointment);
- where there is no internal audit function, an explanation for the absence, how internal assurance is achieved, and how this affects the work of external audit; and
- an explanation of how auditor independence and objectivity are safeguarded, if the external auditor provides non-audit services.

27. The directors should explain in the annual report their responsibility for preparing the annual report and accounts, and state that they consider the annual report and accounts, taken as a whole, is fair, balanced and understandable, and provides the information necessary for shareholders to assess the company's position, performance, business model and strategy.

28. The board should carry out a robust assessment of the company's emerging and principal risks.[9] The board should confirm in the annual report that it has completed this assessment, including a description of its principal risks, what procedures are in place to identify emerging risks, and an explanation of how these are being managed or mitigated.

29. The board should monitor the company's risk management and internal control systems and, at least annually, carry out a review of their effectiveness and report on that review in the annual report. The monitoring and review should cover all material controls, including financial, operational and compliance controls.

30. In annual and half-yearly financial statements, the board should state whether it considers it appropriate to adopt the going concern basis of accounting in preparing them, and identify any material uncertainties to the company's ability to continue to do so over a period of at least twelve months from the date of approval of the financial statements.

31. Taking account of the company's current position and principal risks, the board should explain in the annual report how it has assessed the prospects of the company, over what period it has done so and why it considers that period to be appropriate. The board should state whether it has a reasonable expectation that the company will be able to continue in operation and meet its liabilities as they fall due over the period of their assessment, drawing attention to any qualifications or assumptions as necessary.

NOTES

[7] The board's responsibility to present a fair, balanced and understandable assessment extends to interim and other price-sensitive public records and reports to regulators, as well as to information required to be presented by statutory instruments.

[8] A smaller company is one that is below the FTSE 350 throughout the year immediately prior to the reporting year.

[9] Principal risks should include, but are not necessarily limited to, those that could result in events or circumstances that might threaten the company's business model, future performance, solvency or liquidity and reputation. In deciding which risks are principal risks companies should consider the potential impact and probability of the related events or circumstances, and the timescale over which they may occur.

5. REMUNERATION

[3.7]

Principles

P. Remuneration policies and practices should be designed to support strategy and promote long-term sustainable success. Executive remuneration should be aligned to company purpose and values, and be clearly linked to the successful delivery of the company's long-term strategy.

Q. A formal and transparent procedure for developing policy on executive remuneration and determining director and senior management[10] remuneration should be established. No director should be involved in deciding their own remuneration outcome.

R. Directors should exercise independent judgement and discretion when authorising remuneration outcomes, taking account of company and individual performance, and wider circumstances.

PROVISIONS

32. The board should establish a remuneration committee of independent non-executive directors, with a minimum membership of three, or in the case of smaller companies, two.[11] In addition, the chair of the board can only be a member if they were independent on appointment and cannot chair the committee. Before appointment as chair of the remuneration committee, the appointee should have served on a remuneration committee for at least 12 months.

33. The remuneration committee should have delegated responsibility for determining the policy for executive director remuneration and setting remuneration for the chair, executive directors and senior management.[12] It should review workforce[13] remuneration and related policies and the alignment of incentives and rewards with culture, taking these into account when setting the policy for executive director remuneration.

34. The remuneration of non-executive directors should be determined in accordance with the Articles of Association or, alternatively, by the board. Levels of remuneration for the chair and all non-executive directors should reflect the time commitment and responsibilities of the role. Remuneration for all non-executive directors should not include share options or other performance-related elements.

35. Where a remuneration consultant is appointed, this should be the responsibility of the remuneration committee. The consultant should be identified in the annual report alongside a statement about any other connection it has with the company or individual directors. Independent judgement should be exercised when evaluating the advice of external third parties and when receiving views from executive directors and senior management.[14]

36. Remuneration schemes should promote long-term shareholdings by executive directors that support alignment with long-term shareholder interests. Share awards granted for this purpose should be released for sale on a phased basis and be subject to a total vesting and holding period of five years or more. The remuneration committee should develop a formal policy for post-employment shareholding requirements encompassing both unvested and vested shares.

37. Remuneration schemes and policies should enable the use of discretion to override formulaic outcomes. They should also include provisions that would enable the company to recover and/or withhold sums or share awards and specify the circumstances in which it would be appropriate to do so.

38. Only basic salary should be pensionable. The pension contribution rates for executive directors, or payments in lieu, should be aligned with those available to the workforce. The pension consequences and associated costs of basic salary increases and any other changes in pensionable remuneration, or contribution rates, particularly for directors close to retirement, should be carefully considered when compared with workforce arrangements.

39. Notice or contract periods should be one year or less. If it is necessary to offer longer periods to new directors recruited from outside the company, such periods should reduce to one year or less after the initial period. The remuneration committee should ensure compensation commitments in directors' terms of appointment do not reward poor performance. They should be robust in reducing compensation to reflect departing directors' obligations to mitigate loss.

40. When determining executive director remuneration policy and practices, the remuneration committee should address the following:

- **clarity** – remuneration arrangements should be transparent and promote effective engagement with shareholders and the workforce;
- **simplicity** – remuneration structures should avoid complexity and their rationale and operation should be easy to understand;
- **risk** – remuneration arrangements should ensure reputational and other risks from excessive rewards, and behavioural risks that can arise from target-based incentive plans, are identified and mitigated;
- **predictability** – the range of possible values of rewards to individual directors and any other limits or discretions should be identified and explained at the time of approving the policy;
- **proportionality** – the link between individual awards, the delivery of strategy and the long-term performance of the company should be clear. Outcomes should not reward poor performance; and
- **alignment to culture** – incentive schemes should drive behaviours consistent with company purpose, values and strategy.

41. There should be a description of the work of the remuneration committee in the annual report, including:

- an explanation of the strategic rationale for executive directors' remuneration policies, structures and any performance metrics;
- reasons why the remuneration is appropriate using internal and external measures, including pay ratios and pay gaps;
- a description, with examples, of how the remuneration committee has addressed the factors in Provision 40;
- whether the remuneration policy operated as intended in terms of company performance and quantum, and, if not, what changes are necessary;
- what engagement has taken place with shareholders and the impact this has had on remuneration policy and outcomes;
- what engagement with the workforce has taken place to explain how executive remuneration aligns with wider company pay policy; and
- to what extent discretion has been applied to remuneration outcomes and the reasons why.

NOTES

[10] See footnote 4.

[11] See footnote 8.

[12] See footnote 4.

[13] See the Guidance on Board Effectiveness Section 5 for a description of 'workforce' in this context.

[14] See footnote 4.

See footnote 4.

See footnote 8.

See footnote 4.

See footnote 4.

TABLE OF ORIGINS FOR THE COMPANIES ACT 2006

[3.8]

NOTES

(1) This table shows the origin of the company law provisions of the Companies Act 2006 by reference to the enactments in force on the date that Act received Royal assent (subject to the note to the origins for Part 28). The Act received Royal Assent on 8 November 2006. Where an enactment had been amended before that date, the reference is to the text at that date; the table does not show the source of such amendments. [Editorial note: the "company law provisions of the Companies Act 2006" is defined by s 2 of the 2006 Act at **[1.2]**, ie, "(a) the provisions of Parts 1 to 39 of this Act, and (b) the provisions of Parts 45 to 47 of this Act so far as they apply for the purposes of those Parts"].

(2) The origin of a provision of the Companies Act 2006 in the Companies (Northern Ireland) Order 1986 is acknowledged where it makes significantly different provision in relation to Northern Ireland than in relation to England and Wales or, as the case may be, Great Britain.

(3) In the table—
"1985" means the Companies Act 1985 (c 6);
"IA 1986" means the Insolvency Act 1986 (c 45);
"1986" means the Companies (Northern Ireland) Order 1986, SI 1096/1032 (NI 6);
"ICTA" means the Income and Corporation Taxes Act 1988 (c 1);
"1989" means the Companies Act 1989 (c 40).

(4) The entry "drafting" indicates a new provision of a mechanical or editorial nature – for example, a provision defining an expression to avoid repetition or indicating where other relevant provisions are to be found.

(5) A reference followed by "(changed)" means that the provision referred to has been re-enacted with one or more changes. In general, a change is noted only in the primary context affected and not in every provision where a consequential change results The table does not show changes in the maximum penalties for offences.

(6) The entry "new" indicates a provision which has no predecessor in the repealed legislation or which is fundamentally different from its predecessor.

(7) The entries in the table are intended only as a general indication of what has changed and what is new. They should not be read as expressing any view as to the application or otherwise of any provision relating to enactments repealed and re-enacted.

CA 2006	*Origin*
PART 1 GENERAL INTRODUCTORY PROVISIONS	
1(1)	1985, s 735(1)(a), (b)
(2), (3)	drafting
2(1), (2)	1985, s 744 (changed)
3(1)–(4)	1985, s 1(2)
4(1), (2)	1985, s 1(3)
(3)	1985, s 1(3), 1986 art 12(3)
(4)	drafting
5(1)	1985, s 1(4)
(2)	1985, s 1(4), 1986 art 12(4)
(3)	1985, s 15(2)
6(1), (2)	drafting
PART 2 COMPANY FORMATION	
7(1), (2)	1985, s 1(1) (changed)
8(1)	new
(2)	1985, s 3(1)
9(1)	1985, s 10(1) (changed)
(2)	1985, s 2(1)(a), (b), (2), (3) (changed)
(3)	1985, s 10(4)
(4)	new
(5)	1985, s 10(1), (6)
(6)	1985, s 10(1)
10(1)–(5)	new
11(1)	drafting
(2)	new
(3)	1985, s 2(4) (changed)
12(1)	1985, s 10(2) (changed)
(2)	new
(3), first sentence	1985, s 10(3)
(3), second sentence	new
13(1), (2)	1985, s 12(3), (3A) (changed)
14	1985, s 12(1), (2)

CA 2006	*Origin*
15(1)	1985, s 13(1)
(2)	new
(3)	1985, s 13(2)
(4)	1985, s 13(7)(a)
16(1)	drafting
(2)	1985, s 13(3) (changed)
(3)	1985, s 13(4)
(4)	new
(5)	new
(6)	1985, s 13(5)
PART 3 A COMPANY'S CONSTITUTION	
Chapter 1 Introductory	
17	new
Chapter 2 Articles of association	
18(1)	new
(2)	1985, s 7(1) (changed)
(3)	1985, s 7(3) (changed)
(4)	1985, s 744
19(1)–(3)	1985, s 8(1), (4) (changed)
(4)	1985, s 8(3)
(5)	1985, s 8(5)
20(1), (2)	1985, s 8(2) (changed)
21(1)	1985, s 9(1)
(2), (3)	drafting
22(1)–(3)	new
23(1), (2)	new
24(1)–(4)	new
25(1)	1985, s 16(1)
(2)	1985, s 16(2)
26(1)	1985, s 18(2) (changed)
(2)	new
(3), (4)	1985, s 18(3) and Sch 24

Part 3 CA 2006 Supporting Materials

CA 2006	Origin
27(1)–(5)	new
28(1)–(3)	new
Chapter 3 Resolutions and agreements affecting a company's constitution	
29(1)	1985, s 380(4) (changed)
(2)	1985, s 380(4A)
30(1)	1985, s 380(1)
(2), (3)	1985, s 380(5) and Sch 24
(4)	1985, s 380(7)
Chapter 4 Miscellaneous and supplementary provisions	
31(1)–(5)	new
32(1)	1985, s 19(1) (changed)
(2)	new
(3), (4)	1985, s 19(2) (changed) and Sch 24
33(1)	1985, s 14(1) (changed)
(2)	1985, s 14(2) (changed)
34(1)	drafting
(2)	1985, s 18(1) (changed)
(3)	1985, s 18(2) (changed)
(4)	new
(5), (6)	1985, s 18(3) and Sch 24
35(1)–(5)	new
36(1), (2)	1985, s 380(2) (changed)
(3), (4)	1985, s 380(6) (changed) and Sch 24
(5)	1985, s 380(7)
37	1985, s 15(1)
38	Companies (Single Member Private Limited Companies) Regulations 1992 (SI 1992/1699) (changed)
PART 4 A COMPANY'S CAPACITY AND RELATED MATTERS	
39(1)	1985, s 35(1) (changed)
(2)	1985, s 35(4)
40(1)	1985, s 35A(1)
(2)	1985, s 35A(2) and 35B
(3)	1985, s 35A(3)
(4)	1985, s 35A(4)
(5)	1985, s 35A(5)
(6)	1985, s 35A(6)
41(1)	1985, s 322A(1), (4)
(2)	1985, s 322A(1), (2)
(3)	1985, s 322A(3)
(4)	1985, s 322A(5)
(5)	1985, s 322A(6)
(6)	1985, s 322A(7)
(7)	1985, s 322A(8)
42(1)	Charities Act 1993, s 65(1)
(2)	Charities Act 1993, s 65(2)
(3)	Charities Act 1993, s 65(3)
(4)	Charities Act 1993, s 65(4)
(5)	drafting
43(1), (2)	1985, s 36
44(1)	1985, s 36A(1)–(3)
(2)(a), (3), (4)	1985, s 36A(4)
(2)(b)	new
(5)	1985, s 36A(6) (changed)
(6)	1985, s 36A(4A)
(7)	1985, s 36A(8)
(8)	1985, s 36A(7)
45(1)	1985, s 36A(3)
(2)	1985, s 350(1)
(3)	1985, s 350(1) (changed)
(4), (5)	1985, s 350(2) and Sch 24
(6)	drafting
46(1)	1985, s 36AA(1)
(2)	1985, s 36AA(2)
47(1)	1985, s 38(1) (changed), (3)
(2)	1985, s 38(2) (changed)
48(1)	Requirements of Writing (Scotland) Act 1995 (c 7), s 15(3)
(2)	1985, s 36B(1)
(3)	1985, s 36B(2)
49(1)	1985, s 39(1) (changed)
(2)	1985, s 39(1)
(3)	1985, s 39(2), (2A)
(4)	1985, s 39(3)
(5)	1985, s 39(4)
(6)	1985, s 39(5)
50(1), (2)	1985, s 40(1)
51(1)	1985, s 36C(1)
(2)	1985, s 36C(2)
52	1985, s 37
PART 5 A COMPANY'S NAME	
Chapter 1 General requirements	
53	1985, s 26(1)(d), (e)
54(1)–(3)	1985, s 26(2)(a) and second sentence (changed)
55(1)	1985, s 26(2)(b) and 29(1)(a)
(2)	1985, s 29(6)
56(1)	1985, s 29(1)(b) (changed)
(2)	1985, s 29(2)
(3), (4)	1985, s 29(3) (changed)
(5)	drafting
57(1)–(5)	new
Chapter 2 Indications of company type or legal form	
58(1)	1985, s 25(1) and 27(4)(b)
(2)	1985, s 25(1) and 27(4)(d)
(3)	drafting
59(1)	1985, s 25(2) (opening words) and 27(4)(a)
(2)	1985, s 25(2)(b) and 27(4)(c)
(3)	1985, s 25(2)(a)
(4)	drafting
60(1)(a), (b)	new
(1)(c)	drafting
(2)	1985, s 30(5B)
(3)	1985, s 30(4)
(4)	new
61(1)	1985, s 30(2), 1986 art 40(2)
(2)–(4)	1985, s 30(2), (3) (changed)
62(1)–(3)	1985, s 30(2), (3) (changed)

CA 2006	*Origin*
63(1)	1985, s 31(1)
(2), (3)	1985, s 31(5) and Sch 24
(4), (5)	new
64(1)–(3)	1985, s 31(2) first sentence
(4)	1985, s 31(2) second sentence (changed)
(5), (6)	1985, s 31(6) and Sch 24
(7)	1985, s 31(3)
65(1)–(5)	1985, s 26(1)(a), (b), (bb), (bbb) (changed)
Chapter 3 Similarity to other names	
66(1)	1985, s 26(1)(c)
(2), (3)	1985, s 26(3) (changed)
(4)–(6)	new
67(1)	1985, s 28(2)
(2)–(6)	new
68(1)	drafting
(2)	1985, s 28(2) full out
(3)	1985, s 28(4)
(4)	1985, s 28(2) full out and (4)
(5), (6)	1985, s 28(5) and Sch 24
69(1)–(7)	new
70(1)–(6)	new
71(1)–(4)	new
72(1), (2)	new
73(1)–(6)	new
74(1)–(5)	new
Chapter 4 Other powers of the Secretary of State	
75(1), (2)	1985, s 28(3)
(3)	1985, s 28(4)
(4)	1985, s 28(3)
(5), (6)	1985, s 28(5) and Sch 24
76(1)	1985, s 32(1)
(2)	new
(3)	1985, s 32(2)
(4), (5)	1985, s 32(3)
(6), (7)	1985, s 32(4) (changed) and Sch 24
Chapter 5 Change of name	
77(1)(a)	1985, s 28(1)
(1)(b)	new
(2)	drafting
78(1)–(3)	new
79(1), (2)	new
80(1), (2)	1985, s 28(6) and 32(5) (changed)
(3)	1985, s 28(6) and 32(5)
81(1)	1985, s 28(6) and 32(5)
(2), (3)	1985, s 28(7) and 32(6)
Chapter 6 Trading disclosures	
82(1), (2)	1985, ss 348(1), 349(1), 351(1), (2), Business Names Act 1985, s 4(1) (changed)
(3)–(5)	new
83(1), (2)	Business Names Act 1985, s 5(1)
(3)	Business Names Act 1985, s 5(2)

CA 2006	*Origin*
84(1), (2)	1985, ss 348(2), 349(2), (3), 351(5), Business Names Act 1985, s 7 (changed)
(3)	new
85(1), (2)	new
PART 6 A COMPANY'S REGISTERED OFFICE	
86	1985, s 287(1)
87(1)	1985, s 287(3)
(2)	1985, s 287(4)
(3)	1985, s 287(5)
(4)	1985, s 287(6)
88(1)	drafting
(2)	1985, s 2(2)
(3), (4)	new
PART 7 RE-REGISTRATION AS A MEANS OF ALTERING A COMPANY'S STATUS	
89	drafting
90(1)	1985, s 43(1) (changed)
(2)	1985, s 43(1); drafting
(3)	1985, s 43(2)
(4)	1985, s 48(1), (2)
91(1)	1985, s 45(1)–(4)
(2)	1985, s 45(5), 1986 art 55(5)
(3)	1985, s 45(6)
(4)	1985, s 45(7)
(5)	1985, s 47(3) (changed)
92(1)	1985, s 43(3)(b), (c), (4)
(2)	1985, s 43(e)(ii)
(3), (4)	1985, s 46(2), (3)
(5), (6)	1985, s 46(4)
93(1)	1985, s 44(1)
(2)	1985, s 44(2), drafting
(3)–(5)	1985, s 44(4), (5)
(6)	1985, s 44(6), (7)(b)
(7)	1985, s 44(2), (7)(a)
94(1)	new
(2)	1985, s 43(3)(a)–(d)
(3)	1985, s 43(e)(i)
(4)	1985, s 47(2)
95(1)–(3)	new
96(1), (2)	1985, s 47(1)
(3)	new
(4), (5)	1985, s 47(4), (5)
97(1)	1985, s 53(1) (changed)
(2)	new
(3)	1985, s 53(2)
98(1)	1985, s 54(1), (2)
(2)	1985, s 54(3)
(3), (4)	1985, s 54(5)
(5)	1985, s 54(6)
(6)	1985, s 54(8)
99(1), (2)	1985, s 54(4) (changed)
(3)	1985, s 54(7)
(4), (5)	1985, s 54(10), Sch 24
100(1)	new
(2)	1985, s 53(1)(b) (changed)

CA 2006	*Origin*
(3), (4)	new
101(1), (2)	1985, s 55(1)
(3)	new
(4), (5)	1985, s 55(2), (3)
102(1)	1985, s 49(1), (4), (8)(a) (changed)
(2)	1985, s 49(2)
(3)	1985, s 49(5)–(7) (changed)
(4)	1985, s 49(9)
(5)	new
103(1)	new
(2)	1985, s 49(8)(a), (c), (d)
(3), (4)	1985, s 49(8)(b), (8A) (changed)
(5)	new
104(1), (2)	1985, s 50(1)(b)
(3)	new
(4), (5)	1985, s 50(2), (3)
105(1)	1985, s 51(1) (changed)
(2)	1985, s 51(2)
(3), (4)	1985, s 51(3)
106(1)	new
(2)	1985, s 51(5) (changed)
(3)–(5)	new
107(1), (2)	1985, s 52(1)
(3)	new
(4), (5)	1985, s 52(2), (3)
108(1)–(5)	new
109(1)–(5)	new
110(1)–(5)	new
111(1)–(5)	new
PART 8 A COMPANY'S MEMBERS	
Chapter 1 The members of a company	
112(1)	1985, s 22(1) (changed)
(2)	1985, s 22(2)
Chapter 2 Register of members	
113(1), (2)	1985, s 352(1), (2)
(3), (4)	1985, s 352(3)
(5)	new
(6)	1985, s 352(4)
(7), (8)	1985, s 352(5), Sch 24
114(1)	1985, s 353(1) (changed)
(2)	1985, s 353(2)
(3)	1985, s 353(3)
(4)	1985, s 353(3), 1986 art 361(3)
(5), (6)	1985, s 353(4), Sch 24
115(1), (2)	1985, s 354(1)
(3)	1985, s 354(2)
(4)	1985, s 354(3) (changed)
(5), (6)	1985, s 354(4), Sch 24
116(1)	1985, s 356(1) (changed)
(2)	1985, s 356(3) first branch
(3), (4)	new
117(1)–(5)	new
118(1), (2)	1985, s 356(5), Sch 24 (changed)
(3)	1985, s 356(6)

CA 2006	*Origin*
119(1)–(3)	new
120(1)–(4)	new
121	1985, s 352(6) (changed)
122(1)	1985, s 355(1) (changed)
(2)	1985, s 355(4)
(3)	1985, s 355(5)
(4), (5)	1985, s 355(2), (3)
(6)	1985, s 355(4)
123(1)	new
(2), (3)	1985, s 352A(1), (2) (changed)
(4), (5)	1985, s 352A(3), Sch 24
124(1), (2)	1985, s 352(3A)
125(1)–(4)	1985, s 359(1)–(4)
126	1985, s 360
127	1985, s 361
128(1), (2)	1985, s 352(7)
Chapter 3 Overseas branch registers	
129(1)	1985, s 362(1), (2) opening words
(2)	1985, Sch 14, Pt 1
(3), (4)	new
(5)	1985, s 362(2)(b), (c)
130(1)	1985, s 362(3), Sch 14, Pt 2, para 1(1), (2)
(2), (3)	1985, s 362(3), Sch 14, Pt 2, para 1(3), Sch 24
131(1)	1985, s 362(3), Sch 14, Pt 2, para 2(1)
(2), (3)	new
(4)	1985, s 362(3), Sch 14, Pt 2, para 7
132(1), (2)	1985, s 362(3), Sch 14, Pt 2, para 4(1) (changed)
(3), (4)	1985, s 362(3), Sch 14, Pt 2, para 4(2), Sch 24
133(1), (2)	1985, s 362(3), Sch 14, Pt 2, para 5
(3)	1985, s 362(3), Sch 14, Pt 2, para 8
134(1), (2)	1985, s 362(3), Sch 14, Pt 2, para 3(1) (changed)
(3)	1985, s 362(3), Sch 14, Pt 2, para 3(2)
135(1), (2)	1985, s 362(3), Sch 14, Pt 2, para 6
(3)	1985, s 362(3), Sch 14, Pt 2, para 1(1), (2)
(4), (5)	1985, s 362(3), Sch 14, Pt 2, para 1(3), Sch 24
Chapter 4 Prohibition on subsidiary being member of its holding company	
136(1)	1985, s 23(1)
(2)	drafting
137(1)	1985, s 23(4), (5)
(2)	1985, s 23(4), 1986 art 33(4)
(3), (4)	1985, s 23(6)
138(1), (2)	1985, s 23(2), Sch 2, para 4(1), (2); drafting
139(1)–(4)	1985, Sch 2, para 1(1)–(4)
(5)	1985, Sch 2, para 5(2)

CA 2006	Origin
(6)	1985, Sch 2, para 5(2), (3)
140(1), (2)	1985, Sch 2, para 3(1), (2)
(3), (4)	1985, Sch 2, para 5(2), (3)
141(1), (2)	1985, s 23(3)
141(3), (4)	1985, s 23(3A), (3B)
(5)	1985, s 23(3BA)
142(1), (2)	1985, s 23(3C)
143	1985, s 23(8)
144	1985, s 23(7)
PART 9 EXERCISE OF MEMBERS' RIGHTS	
145(1)–(4)	new
146(1)–(5)	new
147(1)–(6)	new
148(1)–(8)	new
149(1)–(3)	new
150(1)–(7)	new
151(1)–(3)	new
152(1)–(4)	new
153(1), (2)	new
PART 10 A COMPANY'S DIRECTORS	
Chapter 1 Appointment and removal of directors	
154(1)	1985, s 282(3)
(2)	1985, s 282(1) (changed)
155(1), (2)	new
156(1)–(7)	new
157(1)–(6)	new
158(1)–(5)	new
159(1)–(4)	new
160(1)–(4)	1985, s 292(1)–(4)
161(1), (2)	1985, s 285 (changed)
162(1)–(3)	1985, s 288(1) (changed)
(4)	new
(5)	1985, s 288(3)
(6)	1985, s 288(4), (6)
(7)	1985, s 288(4), Sch 24
(8)	1985, s 288(5)
163(1)	1985, s 289(1)(a) (changed)
(2)	1985, s 289(2)(a)
(3)	new
(4)	1985, s 289(2)(b) (changed)
(5)	new
164	1985, s 289(1)(b) (changed)
165(1)–(6)	new
166(1), (2)	new
167(1), (2)	1985, s 288(2) (changed)
(3)	new
(4)	1985, s 288(4), (6)
(5)	1985, s 288(4), Sch 24
168(1)	1985, s 303(1) (changed)
(2)–(5)	1985, s 303(2)–(5)
169(1), (2)	1985, s 304(1)
(3), (4)	1985, s 304(2), (3)
(5)	1985, s 304(4) (changed)
(6)	1985, s 304(5)
Chapter 2 General duties of directors	
170(1)–(5)	new
171	new
172(1)	1985, s 309(1) (changed)
(2), (3)	new
173(1), (2)	new
174(1), (2)	new
175(1)–(7)	new
176(1)–(5)	new
177(1)–(6)	new
178(1), (2)	new
179	new
180(1)–(5)	new
181(1)–(5)	new
Chapter 3 Declaration of interest in existing transaction or arrangement	
182(1)	1985, s 317(1), (5) (changed)
(2)	1985, s 317(2) (changed)
(3)–(6)	new
183(1)	1985, s 317(7)
(2)	1985, s 317(7), Sch 24
184(1)–(5)	new
185(1), (2)	1985, s 317(3) (changed)
(3)	new
(4)	1985, s 317(4)
186(1), (2)	new
187(1)–(4)	1985, s 317(8) (changed)
Chapter 4 Transactions with directors requiring approval of members	
188(1)	1985, s 319(1) (changed)
(2)	1985, s 319(3) (changed)
(3)	1985, s 319(1) (changed)
(4)	1985, s 319(2) (changed)
(5)	1985, s 319(5), para 7 of Sch 15A (changed)
(6)	1985, s 319(4)
(7)	1985, s 319(7)(a)
189	1985, s 319(6)
190(1), (2)	1985, s 320(1) (changed)
(3)	new
(4)	1985, s 321(1)
(5), (6)	new
191(1)–(5)	1985, s 320(2) (changed)
192	1985, s 321(2)(a), (3) (changed)
193(1), (2)	1985, s 321(2)(b) (changed)
194(1), (2)	1985, s 321(4)
195(1)	1985, s 322(1), (3)
(2)	1985, s 322(1), (2)(a), (b)
(3)	1985, s 322(3), (4)
(4)	1985, s 322(3)
(5)	1985, s 322(4)
(6)	1985, s 322(5)
(7)	1985, s 322(6)
(8)	1985, s 322(4)
196	1985, s 322(2)(c)
197(1)	1985, s 330(2) (changed)
(2)–(5)	new
198(1)	1985, s 330(3), s 331(6)

CA 2006	Origin
(2)	1985, s 330(3)(a), (c) (changed)
(3)–(6)	new
199(1)	1985, s 331(3)
(2), (3)	1985, s 331(4)
200(1)	1985, s 330(3), s 331(6)
(2)	1985, s 330(3)(b), (c) (changed)
(3)–(6)	new
201(1)	1985, s 330(4), s 331(6)
(2)	1985, s 330(4) (changed)
(3)–(6)	new
202(1)	1985, s 331(7)
(2)	1985, s 331(9)(b)
(3)	1985, s 331(8), (10)
203(1)	1985, s 330(6), (7) (changed)
(2)–(5)	new
(6)	1985, s 330(6)
204(1)	1985, s 337(1), (2) (changed)
(2)	1985, s 337(3), s 339(1), (2) (changed)
205(1)	1985, s 337A(1), (3) (changed)
(2)	1985, s 337A(4)
(3)	1985, s 337A(5)
(4)	1985, s 337A(6)
(5)	1985, s 337A(2)
206	new
207(1)	1985, s 334, s 339(1), (2) (changed)
(2)	1985, s 335(1), s 339(1), (2) (changed)
(3)	1985, s 335(2)
208(1)	1985, s 333, s 336(a) (changed)
(2)	1985, s 336(b) (changed)
209(1)	1985, s 338(1), (3)
(2)	1985, s 338(2)
(3), (4)	1985, s 338(6) (changed)
210(1)	1985, s 339(1)
(2)	1985, s 339(2)
(3)	1985, s 339(2), (3)
(4)	1985, s 339(2), (3)
(5)	1985, s 339(5)
211(1)	1985, s 339(6) and, s 340(1)
(2)	1985, s 340(2)
(3)	1985, s 340(3)
(4)	1985, s 340(6)
(5)	1985, s 340(4)
(6)	1985, s 340(5)
(7)	1985, s 340(7) (changed)
212	1985, s 331(9)(a)–(d)
213(1), (2)	1985, s 341(1)
(3), (4)	1985, s 341(2)
(5)	1985, s 341(3)
(6)	1985, s 341(4)
(7)	1985, s 341(5)
(8)	1985, s 341(3)
214	new
215(1)	1985, s 312, s 313(1), s 314(1) (changed)

CA 2006	Origin
(2)–(4)	new
216(1), (2)	1985, s 316(2) (changed)
217(1)	1985, s 312
(2)	new
(3)	1985, s 312 (changed)
(4)	new
218(1)	1985, s 313(1)
(2)	new
(3)	1985, s 313(1) (changed)
(4)	new
(5)	1985, s 316(1)
219(1)	1985, s 314(1), s 315(1)(b) (changed)
(2)	1985, s 315(1)(b)
(3), (4)	new
(5)	1985, s 315(3)
(6)	new
(7)	1985, s 316(1)
220(1)	1985, s 316(3) (changed)
(2)–(5)	new
221(1)–(4)	new
222(1)	new
(2)	1985, s 313(2)
(3)	1985, s 315(1)
(4), (5)	new
223(1)	1985, s 319(6), 320(3), 330(5)
(2)	new
224(1) and (2)	new
225(1)–(3)	new
226	new
Chapter 5 Directors' service contracts	
227	new
228(1)	1985, s 318(1)
(2)	1985, s 318(2), (3) (changed)
(3)	new
(4)	1985, s 318(4)
(5)	1985, s 318(8) (changed)
(6)	1985, s 318(8), Sch 24
(7)	1985, s 318(10)
229(1)	1985, s 318(7)
(2)	new
(3)	1985, s 318(8) (changed)
(4)	1985, s 318(8), Sch 24
(5)	1985, s 318(9) (changed)
230	1985, s 318(6)
Chapter 6 Contracts with sole members who are directors	
231(1)	1985, s 322B(1), (2) (changed)
(2)	1985, s 322B(1)
(3)	1985, s 322B(4) (changed)
(4)	1985, s 322B(4), Sch 24
(5)	1985, s 322B(3)
(6)	1985, s 322B(6)
(7)	1985, s 322B(5)
Chapter 7 Directors' liabilities	
232(1)	1985, s 309A(1), (2)

CA 2006	Origin
(2)	1985, s 309A(1), (3) (changed)
(3)	1985, s 309A(6)
(4)	new
233	1985, s 309A(5)
234(1)	1985, s 309A(4)
(2)	1985, s 309B(1), (2)
(3)	1985, s 309B(3), (4)
(4)	1985, s 309B(5)
(5)	1985, s 309B(6), (7)
(6)	1985, s 309B(4)(c)
235(1)–(6)	new
236(1)	1985, s 309C(1) (changed)
(2), (3)	1985, s 309C(2)
(4), (5)	1985, s 309C(3)
237(1)	1985, s 309C(4), (5)
(2)	1985, s 309C(5), s 318(1)
(3)	1985, s 309C(5), s 318(2), (3) (changed)
(4)	new
(5)	1985, s 309C(5), s 318(4)
(6)	1985, s 309C(5), s 318(8) (changed).
(7)	1985, s 309C(5), s 318(8), Sch 24
(8)	1985, s 309C(5), s 318(10)
(9)	new
238(1)	1985, s 309C(5), s 318(7)
(2)	new
(3)	1985, s 309C(5), s 318(8) (changed)
(4)	1985, s 309C(5), 1985, s 318(8), Sch 24
(5)	1985, s 309C(5), s 318(9) (changed)
239(1)–(7)	new
Chapter 8 Directors' residential addresses: protection from disclosure	
240(1)–(3)	new
241(1), (2)	new
242(1)–(3)	new
243(1)–(8)	new
244(1)–(4)	new
245(1)–(6)	new
246(1)–(7)	new
Chapter 9 Supplementary provisions	
247(1)	1985, s 719(1)
(2)	1985, s 719(2) (changed)
(3)	new
(4)	1985, s 719(3)
(5)	1985, s 719(3) (changed)
(6)	1985, s 719(3)
(7)	1985, s 719(4) (changed)
248(1)	1985, s 382(1)
(2)	new
(3)	1985, s 382(5) (changed)
(4)	1985, s 382(5), Sch 24
249(1)	1985, s 382(2)
(2)	1985, s 382(4)

CA 2006	Origin
250	1985, s 741(1)
251(1), (2)	1985, s 741(2)
(3)	1985, s 741(3)
252(1)	1985, s 346(1)
(2)	1985, s 346(2), (3) (changed)
(3)	1985, s 346(2)
253(1)	drafting
(2)	1985, s 346(2), (3) (changed)
(3)	new
254(1)	1985, s 346(1)
(2)	1985, s 346(4)
(3)	1985, s 346(7)
(4)	1985, s 346(8)
(5)	1985, s 346(4)
(6)	1985, s 346(6)
255(1)	1985, s 346(1)
(2)	1985, s 346(5)
(3)	1985, s 346(7)
(4)	1985, s 346(8)
(5)	1985, s 346(5)
(6)	1985, s 346(6)
256	new
257(1), (2)	new
258(1)	1985, s 345(1)
(2)	1985, s 345(2)
(3)	1985, s 345(3)
259	1985, s 347
PART 11 DERIVATIVE CLAIMS AND PROCEEDINGS BY MEMBERS	
Chapter 1 Derivative claims in England and Wales or Northern Ireland	
260(1)–(5)	new
261(1)–(4)	new
262(1)–(5)	new
263(1)–(7)	new
264(1)–(5)	new
Chapter 2 Derivative proceedings in Scotland	
265(1)–(7)	new
266(1)–(5)	new
267(1)–(5)	new
268(1)–(6)	new
269(1)–(5)	new
PART 12 COMPANY SECRETARIES	
270(1), (2)	new
(3)	1985, s 283(3) (changed)
271	1985, s 283(1) (changed)
272(1)–(7)	new
273(1), (2)	1985, s 286(1) (changed)
(3)	1985, s 286(2)
274	1985, s 283(3) (changed)
275(1)–(3)	1985, s 288(1) (changed)
(4)	new
(5)	1985, s 288(3)
(6)	1985, s 288(4), (6)
(7)	1985, s 288(4), Sch 24
(8)	1985, s 288(5)

Part 3 CA 2006 Supporting Materials

CA 2006	*Origin*
276(1), (2)	1985, s 288(2)
(3)	1985, s 288(4), (6) (changed)
(4)	1985, s 288(4), Sch 24
277(1)	1985, s 290(1)(a) (changed)
(2)	1985, s 289(2)(a), s 290(3)
(3)	new
(4)	1985, s 289(2)(b), s 290(3) (changed)
(5)	new
278(1)	1985, s 290(1)(b) (changed)
(2)	1985, s 290(2)
279(1), (2)	new
280	1985, s 284
PART 13 RESOLUTIONS AND MEETINGS	
Chapter 1 General provisions about resolutions	
281(1)–(4)	new
282(1)–(5)	new
283(1)	1985, s 378(1), (2) (changed)
(2), (3)	new
(4)	1985, s 378(1), (2) (changed)
(5)	1985, s 378(1), (2), (5) (changed)
(6)	1985, s 378(2) (changed)
284(1)	1985, s 370(6)
(2)	Table A, para 54 (changed)
(3)	1985, s 370(6), Table A, para 54 (changed)
(4)	1985, s 370(1), Table A, para 54
285(1)–(3)	new
286(1)–(3)	Table A, para 55
287	new
Chapter 2 Written resolutions	
288(1)	new
(2)	1985, s 381A(7), Sch 15A, para 1
(3)	new
(4)	1985, s 381A(1) (changed)
(5)	1985, s 381A(4)
289(1)	1985, s 381A(1) (changed)
(2)	new
290	new
291(1)–(7)	new
292(1)–(6)	new
293(1)–(7)	new
294(1), (2)	new
295(1), (2)	new
296(1)	1985, s 381A(2) (changed)
(2)–(4)	new
297(1), (2)	new
298(1), (2)	new
299(1), (2)	new
300	1985, s 381C(1)
Chapter 3 Resolutions at meetings	
301	1985, s 378(6) (changed)
302	Table A, para 37
303(1)	1985, s 368(1)
(2)	1985, s 368(1), (2), (2A)
(3)	1985, s 368(2) (changed)
(4)	1985, s 368(3) (changed)
(5)	new
(6)	1985, s 368(3) (changed)
304(1)	1985, s 368(4), (8)
(2), (3)	new
(4)	1985, s 368(7)
305(1)	1985, s 368(4)
(2)	new
(3)	1985, s 368(4)
(4)	1985, s 368(5)
(5)	new
(6), (7)	1985, s 368(6)
306(1), (2)	1985, s 371(1)
(3), (4)	1985, s 371(2)
(5)	1985, s 371(3)
307(1)	new
(2)	1985, s 369(1), (2) (changed)
(3)	1985, s 369(1), (2)
(4)	1985, s 369(3) (changed)
(5), (6)	1985, s 369(4) (changed)
(7)	drafting
308	1985, s 369(4A), (4B) (changed)
309(1)	1985, s 369(4B)
(2)	1985, s 369(4C) (changed)
(3)	1985, s 369(4B)(d)
310(1)	1985, s 370(2), Table A, para 38 (changed)
(2)	Table A, para 38 (changed)
(3)	new
(4)	1985, s 370(1), Table A, para 38
311(1), (2)	Table A, para 38
312(1)	1985, s 379(1)
(2)	1985, s 379(2)
(3)	1985, s 379(2) (changed)
(4)	1985, s 379(3)
313(1), (2)	1985 Table A, para 39 (changed)
314(1)	1985, s 376(1)(b)
(2), (3)	1985, s 376(2) (changed)
(4)	1985, s 376(1), s 377(1)(a) (changed)
315(1)	1985, s 376(3), (5)
(2)	1985, s 376(1)
(3)	1985, s 376(7)
(4)	1985, s 376(7), Sch 24
316(1)	new
(2)	1985, s 376(1), s 377(1)(b) (changed)
317(1)	1985, s 377(3) (changed)
(2)	1985, s 377(3)
318(1)	1985, s 370A
(2)	1985, s 370(1), (4) (changed)
(3)	1985, s 370A (changed)
319(1)	1985, s 370(5)
(2)	1985, s 370(1)
320(1)	1985, s 378(4), Table A, para 47

CA 2006	*Origin*
(2)	Table A, para 47
(3)	1985, s 378(4), Table A, paras 47 and 48 (changed)
321(1)	1985, s 373(1)(a)
(2)	1985, s 373(1)(b) (changed)
322	1985, s 374
323(1)	1985, s 375(1)(a)
(2), (3)	1985, s 375(2) (changed)
(4)	new
324(1)	1985, s 372(1) (changed)
(2)	1985, s 372(2)(b) (changed)
325(1)	1985, s 372(3) (changed)
(2)	new
(3)	1985, s 372(4)
(4)	1985, s 372(4), Sch 24
326(1), (2)	1985, s 372(6)
(3)	1985, s 372(6) (changed)
(4)	1985, s 372(6), Sch 24
327(1)	1985, s 372(5)
(2)	1985, s 372(5) (changed)
(3)	new
328(1), (2)	new
329(1)	1985, s 373(2)
(2)	1985, s 373(2) (changed)
330(1)–(7)	Table A, para 63 (changed)
331	new
332	1985, s 381
333(1)–(4)	new
334(1)–(3)	1985, s 125(6) (changed)
(4)	1985, s 125(6)(a)
(5)	new
(6)	1985, s 125(6)(b)
(7)	1985, s 125(7), (8)
335(1)–(6)	new
Chapter 4 Public companies: additional requirements for AGMs	
336(1)	1985, s 366(1) (changed)
(2)	new
(3)	1985, s 366(4) (changed)
(4)	1985, s 366(4), Sch 24
337(1)	1985, s 366(1)
(2)	1985, s 369(3)(a)
338(1)	1985, s 376(1)(b)
(2)	new
(3)	1985, s 376(2) (changed)
(4)	1985, s 376(1), s 377(1)(a), (2) (changed)
339(1)	1985, s 376(3), (5)
(2)	1985, s 376(1)
(3)	1985, s 376(6)
(4)	1985, s 376(7)
(5)	1985, s 376(7), Sch 24
340(1)	new
(2)	1985, s 376(1), s 377(1)(b) (changed)
Chapter 5 Additional requirements for quoted companies	

CA 2006	*Origin*
341(1)–(6)	new
342(1)–(4)	new
343(1)–(6)	new
344(1)–(4)	new
345(1)–(6)	new
346(1)–(5)	new
347(1)–(4)	new
348(1)–(4)	new
349(1)–(5)	new
350(1)–(5)	new
351(1)–(5)	new
352(1), (2)	new
353(1)–(5)	new
354(1)–(4)	new
Chapter 6 Records of resolutions and meetings	
355(1)	1985, s 382(1), s 382A(1) (changed)
(2)	new
(3)	1985, s 382(5) (changed)
(4)	1985, s 382(5), Sch 24
356(1)	drafting
(2), (3)	1985, s 382A(2)
(4)	1985, s 382(2)
(5)	1985, s 382(4)
357(1), (2)	1985, s 382B(1)
(3)	1985, s 382B(2)
(4)	1985, s 382B(2), Sch 24
(5)	1985, s 382B(3)
358(1)	1985, s 383(1) (changed)
(2)	new
(3)	1985, s 383(1)
(4)	1985, s 383(3) (changed)
(5)	1985, s 383(4) (changed)
(6)	1985, s 383(4), Sch 24
(7)	1985, s 383(5)
359	new
Chapter 7 Supplementary provisions	
360(1), (2)	new
361	new
PART 14 CONTROL OF POLITICAL DONATIONS AND EXPENDITURE	
362	1985, s 347A(1) (changed)
363(1)	1985, s 347A(6), (7)(a), (9)
(2)	1985, s 347A(6)(b), (7)(b), (c) (changed)
(3)	new
(4)	drafting
364(1)	drafting
(2)	1985, s 347A(4)
(3)	new
(4)	new
365(1)	1985, s 347A(5) (changed)
(2)	new
366(1)	1985, s 347C(1) (changed)
(2)	1985, s 347C(1), 347D(1), (2), (3) (changed)

CA 2006	Origin
(3)	1985, s 347D(3) (changed)
(4)	new
(5)	1985, s 347A(10), s 347C(1), s 347D(2), (3)
(6)	1985, s 347C(6), s 347D(9)
367(1), (2)	new
(3)	1985, s 347C(2), s 347D(4) (changed)
(4)	new
(5)	1985, s 347C(4), s 347D(6)
(6)	1985, s 347C(2), s 347D(4) (changed)
(7)	new
368(1)	1985, s 347C(3)(b), s 347D(5)
(2)	1985, s 347C(3), s 347D(5)
369(1)	1985, s 347F(1)
(2)	1985, s 347F(2), (3), (4)
(3)	1985, s 347F(2), (6) (changed)
(4)	new
(5)	1985, s 347F(3)
(6)	1985, s 347F(5)
370(1)	1985, s 347I(1) (changed)
(2)	1985, s 347I(1)
(3)	1985, s 54(2), s 347I(2) (changed)
(4)	1985, s 347I(3)
(5)	new
371(1)	1985, s 347I(3)
(2)	1985, s 347I(4), (5)
(3)	1985, s 347I(6)
(4)	1985, s 347I(7)
(5)	1985, s 347I(8)
372(1)	1985, s 347J(1)
(2)	1985, s 347J(2)
(3)	1985, s 347J(3)
(4)	1985, s 347J(4), (5)
(5)	1985, s 347J(6)
373(1)	1985, s 347K(1)
(2)	1985, s 347K(2)
374(1)–(3)	new
375(1)	1985, s 347B(1)
(2)	1985, s 347B(2) (changed)
376(1), (2)	1985, s 347B(3)
377(1)	1985, s 347B(8)
(2)	1985, s 347B(10)
(3)	1985, s 347B(9)
(4)	1985, s 347B(11)
378(1)	1985, ss 347B(4), (6), (7) (changed)
(2)	new
(3)	1985, s 347B(5)
379(1)	1985, s 347A(3), (8)
(2)	1985, s 347A(10)
PART 15 ACCOUNTS AND REPORTS	
Chapter 1 Introduction	
380(1)–(4)	drafting
381	drafting
382(1)	1985, s 247(1)(a)
(2)	1985, s 247(1)(b), (2)
(3), (4)	1985, s 247(3), (4)
(5)	1985, s 247(5) (changed)
(6)	1985, s 247(6), Sch 4, para 56(2), (3)
(7)	drafting
383(1)	1985, s 247A(3)
(2)	1985, s 249(1)(a)
(3)	1985, s 249(1)(b), (2)
(4)	1985, s 249(3)
(5), (6)	1985, s 249(4)
(7)	1985, s 249(5), (6)
384(1)	1985, s 247A(1)–(1B)
(2)	1985, s 247A(2) (changed)
(3)	1985, s 247A(2A)
385(1)	new
(2)	1985, s 262(1) "quoted company"
(3)	drafting
(4)–(6)	new
Chapter 2 Accounting records	
386(1), (2)	1985, s 221(1)
(3)–(5)	1985, s 221(2)–(4)
387(1), (2)	1985, s 221(5)
(3)	1985, s 221(6), Sch 24
388(1)–(3)	1985, s 222(1)–(3)
(4), (5)	1985, s 222(5)
389(1), (2)	1985, s 222(4)
(3)	1985, s 222(6)
(4)	1985, s 222(4), (6), Sch 24
Chapter 3 A company's financial year	
390(1)–(5)	1985, s 223(1)–(5)
391(1)	1985, s 224(1)
(2)	1985, s 224(2), (3)
(3)	1986 art 232(2), (3)
(4)	1985, s 224(3A), 1986 art 232(3A)
(5)–(7)	1985, s 224(4)–(6)
392(1)	1985, s 225(1)
(2)–(6)	1985, s 225(3)–(7)
Chapter 4 Annual accounts	
393(1), (2)	new
394	1985, s 226(1)
395(1)–(5)	1985, s 226(2)–(6)
396(1), (2)	1985, s 226A(1), (2)
(3)	1985, s 226A(3) (changed)
(4)	1985, s 226A(4)
(5)	1985, s 226A(5), (6)
397	1985, s 226B
398	1985, ss 227(8), 248(1) (changed)
399(1), (2)	1985, ss 227(1), (8), 248(1), (2) (changed)
(3)	1985, s 227(8)
(4)	new
400(1), (2)	1985, s 228(1), (2)

CA 2006	Origin
(3)	1985, s 228(5)
(4)	1985, s 228(3)
(5)	1985, s 228(4)
(6)	1985, s 228(6)
401(1), (2)	1985, s 228A(1), (2)
(3)	1985, s 228A(5)
(4)	1985, s 228A(3)
(5)	1985, s 228A(4)
(6)	1985, s 228A(6)
402	1985, s 229(5)
403(1)–(6)	1985, s 227(2)–(7)
404(1), (2)	1985, s 227A(1), (2)
(3)	1985, s 227A(3) (changed)
(4)	1985, s 227A(4)
(5)	1985, s 227A(5), (6)
405(1), (2)	1985, s 229(1), (2)
(3), (4)	1985, s 229(3)
406	1985, s 227B
407(1)–(5)	1985, s 227C(1)–(5)
408(1)	1985, s 230(1) (changed)
(2)	1985, s 230(2) (changed)
(3), (4)	1985, s 230(3), (4)
409(1), (2)	1985, s 231(1), (2) (changed)
(3), (4)	1985, s 231(3) (changed)
(5)	1985, s 231(4)
410(1), (2)	1985, s 231(5)
(3)	1985, s 231(6)
(4), (5)	1985, s 231(7), Sch 24
411(1)	1985, ss 231A(1), 246(3)(b)(ai)
(2)	1985, s 231A(5)
(3)–(5)	1985, s 231A(2)–(4)
(6)	1985, s 231A(7), Sch 4, para 94(1), (2)
(7)	1985, s 231A(6)
412(1)–(4)	new
(5)	1985, s 232(3)
(6)	1985, s 232(4), Sch 24
413(1)–(8)	new
414(1), (2)	1985, s 233(1), (2)
(3)	1985, s 246(8)
(4), (5)	1985, s 233(5) (changed), Sch 24
Chapter 5 Directors' report	
415(1)	1985, s 234(1)
(2), (3)	1985, s 234(2), (3)
(4), (5)	1985, s 234(5), Sch 24
416(1)	1985, s 234ZZA(1)(a), (b)
(2)	1985, s 234ZZA(2)
(3)	1985, ss 234ZZA(1)(c), 246(4)(a)
(4)	1985, s 234ZZA(3), (4) (changed)
417(1)	1985, ss 234(1)(a), 246(4)(a)
(2)	new
(3), (4)	1985, s 234ZZB(1), (2)
(5)	new
(6)	1985, s 234ZZB(3), (5)
(7)	1985, s 246A(2A)
(8)	1985, s 234ZZB(4)
(9)	1985, s 234ZZB(6)
(10), (11)	new
418(1)	1985, s 234ZA(1)
(2)	1985, ss 234(1)(b), 234ZA(2)
(3), (4)	1985, s 234ZA(3), (4)
(5), (6)	1985, s 234ZA(6), Sch 24
419(1)	1985, s 234A(1)
(2)	1985, s 246(8)(b)
(3), (4)	1985, ss 234(5), 234A(4) (changed), Sch 24
Chapter 6 Quoted companies: directors' remuneration report	
420(1)	1985, s 421(1)
(2)	1985, s 234B(3), (4) (changed)
(3)	1985, s 234B(3), Sch 24
421(1), (2)	1985, s 234B(1), (2) (changed)
(3)	1985, s 234B(5), (6)
(4)	1985, s 234B(6), Sch 24
422(1)	1985, s 234C(1)
(2), (3)	1985, s 234C(4) (changed), Sch 24
Chapter 7 Publication of accounts and reports	
423(1)	1985, s 238(1), (1A)
(2), (3)	new
(4)	1985, s 238(3)
(5)	1985, s 238(6)
(6)	drafting
424(1)–(3)	1985, s 238(1) (changed)
(4)	1985, s 238(4) (changed)
(5)	new
(6)	drafting
425(1), (2)	1985, s 238(5), Sch 24
426(1)	1985, s 251(1)
(2), (3)	1985, s 251(2)
(4)	drafting
(5)	new
(6)	1985, s 251(5)
427(1)	1985, s 251(1) "summary financial statement"
(2)	1985, s 251(3)
(3)	1985, s 251(3A)
(4)	1985, s 251(4)
(5)	new
(6)	1985, s 251(5)
428(1)	1985, s 251(1) "summary financial statement"
(2)	1985, s 251(3)
(3)	1985, s 251(3A)
(4)	1985, s 251(4)
(5)	new
(6)	1985, s 251(5)
429(1), (2)	1985, s 251(6), Sch 24
430(1)–(7)	new
431(1), (2)	1985, s 239(1), (2)
(3), (4)	1985, s 239(3), Sch 24

CA 2006	Origin
432(1), (2)	1985, s 239(1), (2)
(3), (4)	1985, s 239(3), Sch 24
433(1)–(3)	1985, ss 233(3), 234A(2) and 234C(2)
(4), (5)	1985, ss 233(6)(a), 234A(4)(a) and 234C(4)(a), Sch 24
434(1)	1985, s 240(1) (changed)
(2)	1985, s 240(2) (changed)
(3)	1985, s 240(5)
(4), (5)	1985, s 240(6), Sch 24
(6)	1985, s 251(7)
435(1), (2)	1985, s 240(3) (changed)
(3)	1985, s 240(5) (changed)
(4)	new
(5), (6)	1985, s 240(6), Sch 24
(7)	1985, s 251(7)
436(1), (2)	1985, ss 233(3), 234A(2), 234C(2), 240(4) (changed)
Chapter 8 Public companies: laying of accounts and reports before general meeting	
437(1)	1985, s 241(1) (changed)
(2)	1985, s 241(2)
(3)	drafting
438(1)–(3)	1985, s 241(2)–(4)
(4)	1985, s 241(2), Sch 24
Chapter 9 Quoted companies: members' approval of directors' remuneration report	
439(1)	1985, s 241A(1), (3)
(2)	1985, s 241A(4)
(3)	1985, s 241A(5), (7)
(4)	1985, s 241A(6)
(5)	1985, s 241A(8)
(6)	1985, s 241A(2), (12)
440(1)	1985, s 241A(9)
(2), (3)	1985, s 241A(10), (11)
(4)	1985, s 241A(9), (10), Sch 24
(5)	1985, s 241A(2), (12)
Chapter 10 Filing of accounts and reports	
441(1)	1985, s 242(1)
(2)	drafting
442(1)	drafting
(2), (3)	1985, s 244(1), (2) (changed)
(4), (5)	1985, s 244(4), (5)
(6)	new
(7)	1985, s 244(6)
443(1)–(5)	new
444(1)	1985, ss 242(1)(a), (b), 246(5)
(2)	1985, ss 242(1)(d), 249E(1)(b) (changed)
(3)	1985, s 246(5), (6) (changed)
(4)	1985, s 247B(2)
(5)	1985, s 246(8)
(6)	1985, ss 233(4), 234A(3), 246(7)
(7)	1985, s 236(3)
445(1)	1985, ss 242(1)(a), (b), 246A(1)
(2)	1985, ss 242(1)(d), 249E(1)(b) (changed)
(3)	1985, s 246A(2), (3) (changed)

CA 2006	Origin
(4)	1985, s 247B(2)
(5)	1985, ss 233(4), 234A(3) (changed)
(6)	new
(7)	drafting
446(1)	1985, s 242(1)(a), (b)
(2)	1985, ss 242(1)(d), 249E(1)(b)
(3)	1985, ss 233(4), 234A(3) (changed)
(4)	new
(5)	drafting
447(1)	1985, s 242(1)(a), (b), (c)
(2)	1985, ss 242(1)(d)
(3)	1985, ss 233(4), 234A(3), 234C(3) (changed)
(4)	new
448(1)–(3)	1985, s 254(1)–(3)
(4)	1985, s 254(4)
(5)	1985, s 244(6)
449(1)–(5)	1985, s 247B(1)–(5)
450(1), (2)	1985, ss 233(1), (2), 246(7)
(3)	1985, s 246(8), 246A(4)
(4), (5)	1985, s 233(5), Sch 24
451(1)	1985, s 242(2)
(2), (3)	1985, s 242(4), (5)
(4)	1985, s 242(2), Sch 24
452(1), (2)	1985, s 242(3)
453(1)	1985, s 242A(1)
(2)	1985, s 242A(2) (changed)
(3), (4)	1985, s 242A(3), (4)
(5)	new
Chapter 11 Revision of defective accounts and reports	
454(1)–(3)	1985, s 245(1)–(3)
(4)	1985, s 245(4) (changed)
(5)	1985, s 245(5)
455(1), (2)	1985, s 245A(1)
(3)–(5)	1985, s 245A(2)–(4)
456(1)–(3)	1985, s 245B(1)–(3)
(4)	1985, s 245B(3A)
(5)–(8)	1985, s 245B(4)–(7)
457(1)	1985, s 245C(1)
(2), (3)	1985, s 245C(2), (3)
(4)	1985, s 245C(4B)
(5)	1985, s 245C(1A), (4A)
(6)	1985, s 245C(5)
(7)	1985, s 245C(4)
458(1)	1985, s 245D(1), (3)
(2)	1985, s 245D(2)
(3)	1985, s 245E(1), (2)
(4)	1985, s 245E(3), (4) (changed)
(5)	1985, s 245E(3), Sch 24
459(1)–(8)	1985, s 245F(1)–(8)
460(1), (2)	1985, s 245G(1), (2)
(3)	drafting; 1985, s 245G(3), (10)
(4)	1985, s 245G(7)(a), (8)
(5)	1985, s 245G(7)(b), Sch 24

CA 2006	*Origin*
461(1)	1985, s 245G(3)
(2)	1985, s 245G(3)(a)
(3)	1985, s 245G(3)(b), Sch 7B, Pt 1
(4)	1985, s 245G(3)(c), Sch 7B, Pt 2
(5), (6)	1985, s 245G(3)(d), Sch 7B, Pt 3
(7)	1985, s 245G(11)
462(1)–(3)	1985, s 245G(4)–(6)
Chapter 12 Supplementary provisions	
463(1)–(6)	new
464(1), (2)	1985, s 256(1), (2)
(3)	1985, s 256(4)
465(1)	1985, s 247(1)(a)
(2)	1985, s 247(1)(b), (2)
(3), (4)	1985, s 247(3), (4)
(5)	1985, s 247(5) (changed)
(6)	1985, s 247(6), Sch 4, para 56(2), (3)
(7)	drafting
466(1)	1985, s 247A(3)
(2)	1985, s 249(1)(a)
(3)	1985, s 249(1)(b), (2)
(4)	1985, s 249(3)
(5), (6)	1985, s 249(4)
(7)	1985, s 249(5), (6)
467(1)	1985, s 247A(1)–(1B)
(2)	1985, s 247A(2)
(3)	1985, s 247A(2A)
468(1)–(5)	new
469(1)–(4)	1985, s 242B(1)–(4) (changed)
470(1)	1985, s 255D(1)
(2)	1985, s 255D(2), (2A)
(3)	1985, s 255D(5)
(4)	1985, s 255D(4)
471(1)	1985, s 262(1) "annual accounts"
(2), (3)	1985, s 238(1A); drafting
472(1), (2)	1985, s 261(1), (2)
473(1)–(4)	1985, s 257(2), (3) (changed)
474(1)	1985, ss 262(1), 744 "regulated activity"
(2)	1985, s 262(2)
PART 16 AUDIT	
Chapter 1 Requirement for audited accounts	
475(1)	1985, s 235(1) (changed)
(2), (3)	1985, s 249B(4)
(4)	1985, s 249B(5)
476(1)–(3)	1985, s 249B(2)
477(1)	1985, s 249A(1)
(2)	1985, s 249A(3)
(3)	1985, s 249A(6)
(4)	1985, s 249A(3)(a), (7)
(5)	drafting
478	1985, s 249B(1)(a)–(e)
479(1)–(3)	1985, s 249B(1)(f), (1A)–(1C)
(4)	drafting

CA 2006	*Origin*
(5), (6)	1985, s 249B(1)(C)
480(1), (2)	1985, s 249AA(1), (2)
(3)	drafting
481	1985, s 249AA(3)
482(1)–(4)	new
483(1)–(5)	new
484(1)	1985, s 257(1)
484(2)	1985, s 257(4)(c)
484(3)	1985, s 257 (2)(b), (d)
484(4)	1985, s 257 (3)
Chapter 2 Appointment of auditors	
485(1)	1985, s 384(1)
(2)–(5)	new
486(1), (2)	1985, s 387(1), (2)
(3), (4)	1985, s 387(2), Sch 24
487(1)–(4)	new
488(1)–(3)	new
489(1)	1985, s 384(1) (changed)
(2)	1985, ss 384(2), 385(2)
(3)	1985, ss 385(3), 388(1) (changed)
(4)	1985, s 385(2), (4) (changed)
(5)	drafting
490(1), (2)	1985, s 387(1), (2)
(3), (4)	1985, s 387(2), Sch 24
491(1)	1985, s 385(2) (changed)
(2)	drafting
492(1)	1985, s 390A(1)
(2), (3)	1985, s 390A(2)
(4), (5)	1985, s 390A(4), (5)
493(1)–(4)	new
494(1)	1985, s 390B(1), (8)
(2)–(4)	1985, s 390B(2)–(4)
(5)	1985, s 390B(5)(a)
(6)	1985, s 390B(9)
Chapter 3 Functions of auditor	
495(1)	1985, s 235(1); drafting
(2)	1985, s 235(1A)
(3)	1985, s 235(1B), (2)
(4)	1985, s 235(2A)
496	1985, s 235(3)
497(1), (2)	1985, s 235(4), (5)
498(1)–(4)	1985, s 237(1)–(4)
(5)	1985, s 237(4A)
499(1), (2)	1985, s 389A(1), (2)
(3)	1985, s 389A(6)
(4)	1985, s 389A(7)
500(1)–(3)	1985, s 389A(3)–(5)
(4)	1985, s 389A(6)
(5)	1985, s 389A(7)
501(1)	1985, s 389B(1)
(2)	1985, s 389B(1), Sch 24
(3)	1985, s 389B(2), (3) (changed)
(4)	1985, s 389B(4)
(5)	1985, s 389B(4), Sch 24

CA 2006	Origin
(6)	1985, s 389B(5)
502(1)	1985, s 390(2)
(2)	1985, s 390(1)
(3)	1985, s 390(3)
503(1), (2)	1985, s 236(1)
(3)	new
504(1)–(4)	new
505(1), (2)	1985, s 236(2) (changed)
(3), (4)	1985, s 236(4), Sch 24
506(1), (2)	new
507(1)–(4)	new
508(1)–(4)	new
509(1)–(4)	new
Chapter 4 Removal, resignation, etc of auditors	
510(1), (2)	1985, s 391(1); drafting
(3)	1985, s 391(3)
(4)	drafting
511(1)	1985, s 391A(1)(a)
(2)–(6)	1985, s 391A(2)–(6)
512(1)	1985, s 391(2)
(2), (3)	1985, s 391(2), Sch 24
513(1), (2)	1985, s 391(4)
514(1)–(8)	new
515(1)	1985, s 391A(1)(b)
(2)	1985, s 391A(1) opening words (changed)
(3)–(7)	1985, s 391A(2)–(6)
516(1), (2)	1985, s 392(1)
(3)	1985, s 392(2)
517(1)	1985, s 392(3)
(2), (3)	1985, s 392(3), Sch 24
518(1)–(4)	1985, s 392A(1)–(4)
(5)	1985, s 392A(5)
(6), (7)	1985, s 392(5), Sch 24
(8)–(10)	1985, s 392A(6)–(8)
519(1)–(3)	1985, s 394(1) (changed)
(4)	1985, s 394(2) (changed)
(5), (6)	1985, s 394A(1), (2)
(7)	1985, s 394(1), Sch 24
520(1)	drafting
(2), (3)	1985, s 394(3), (4)
(4)	1985, s 394(6)
(5)	1985, s 394(7) (changed)
(6)	1985, s 394A(4)
(7)	new
(8)	1985, s 394A(4), Sch 24 (changed)
521(1)	1985, s 394(5)
(2)	1985, s 394(7)
(3), (4)	1985, s 394A(1), (2)
(5)	1985, s 394A(1), Sch 24
522(1)–(8)	new
523(1)–(6)	new
524(1)–(4)	new
525(1)–(3)	new
526	1985, s 388(2)

CA 2006	Origin
Chapter 5 Quoted companies: right of members to raise audit concerns at accounts meeting	
527(1)–(6)	new
528(1)–(5)	new
529(1)–(4)	new
530(1), (2)	new
531(1), (2)	new
Chapter 6 Auditors' liability	
532(1)	1985, s 310(1) (changed)
(2)	1985, s 310(2), drafting
(3)	1985, s 310(1)
(4)	new
533	1985, s 310(3)(b)
534(1)–(3)	new
535(1)–(5)	new
536(1)–(5)	new
537(1)–(3)	new
538(1)–(3)	new
Chapter 7 Supplementary provisions	
539	1985, ss 262(1)
PART 17 A COMPANY'S SHARE CAPITAL	
Chapter 1 Shares and share capital of a company	
540(1)	1985, s 744 ("share")
(2), (3)	new
(4)	1985, s 744 ("share"), drafting
541	1985, s 182(1)(a)
542(1)–(5)	new
543(1), (2)	1985, s 182(2)
544(1), (2)	1985, s 182(1)(b)
(3)	drafting
545	new
546(1), (2)	new
547	1985, s 737(1), (2)
548	1985, s 744 ("equity share capital")
Chapter 2 Allotment of shares: general provisions	
549(1)	1985, s 80(1), (2) (changed)
(2), (3)	1985, s 80(2)
(4)	1985, s 80(9)
(5)	1985, s 80(9), Sch 24
(6)	1985, s 80(10) (changed)
550	new
551(1)	1985, s 80(1), (2)
(2)	1985, s 80(3)
(3)	1985, s 80(4)
(4)	1985, s 80(4), (5)
(5)	1985, s 80(5)
(6)	1985, s 80(6)
(7)	1985, s 80(7)
(8)	1985, s 80(8)
(9)	drafting
552(1)	1985, s 98(1)
(2)	1985, s 98(2)
(3)	1985, s 98(3)
553(1)	1985, s 97(1)

CA 2006	Origin
(2)	1985, s 97(2)(a)
(3)	1985, s 98(4)
554(1)–(5)	new
555(1)	1985, s 88(1)
(2)	1985, s 88(2) (changed)
(3), (4)	new
556(1)	1985, s 128(1), (2) (changed)
(2), (3)	1985, s 128(1)
(4)	1985, s 128(2)
557(1)	1985, s 88(5), s 128(5) (changed)
(2)	1985, s 88(5), s 128(5), Sch 24
(3)	1985, s 88(6) (changed)
558	1985, s 738(1)
559	1985, s 80(2)(a)
Chapter 3 Allotment of equity securities: existing shareholders' right of pre-emption	
560(1)	1985, s 94(2), (5)
(2)	1985, s 94(3), (3A)
561(1)	1985, s 89(1)
(2)	1985, s 89(4)
(3)	1985, s 94(3)
(4)	1985, s 89(6)
(5)	drafting
562(1)	1985, s 90(1)
(2)	new
(3)	1985, s 90(5) (changed)
(4)	1985, s 90(6)
(5)	1985, s 90(6) (changed)
(6), (7)	new
563(1), (2)	1985, s 92(1)
(3)	1985, s 92(2)
564	1985, s 94(2)
565	1985, s 89(4)
566	1985, s 89(5)
567(1), (2)	1985, s 91(1)
(3), (4)	1985, s 91(2)
568(1)	1985, s 89(2), (3)
(2)	1985, s 89(3)
(3)	1985, s 90(1)
(4)	1985, s 92(1)
(5)	1985, s 92(2)
569(1), (2)	new
570(1), (2)	1985, s 95(1)
(3)	1985, s 95(3)
(4)	1985, s 95(4)
571(1), (2)	1985, s 95(2)
(3)	1985, s 95(3)
(4)	1985, s 95(4)
(5), (6)	1985, s 95(5)
(7)	1985, s 95(5), Sch 15A, para 3(1), (2)
572(1), (2)	1985, s 95(6)
(3)	1985, s 95(6), Sch 24
573(1)	1985, s 95(2A)
(2)	1985, s 95(1), (2A)
(3)	1985, s 95(1), (2A), (4)

CA 2006	Origin
(4)	1985, s 95(2), (2A)
(5)	1985, s 95(1), (2A), (4), (5), Sch 15A, para 3(1), (2)
574(1), (2)	1985, s 94(7)
575(1)	1985, s 93(1)
(2)	1985, s 93(2)
576(1)	1985, s 96(1), (2)
(2)	1985, s 96(3)
(3)	1985, s 96(4)
577	1985, s 94(2)
Chapter 4 Public companies: allotment where issue not fully subscribed	
578(1)	1985, s 84(1)
(2)	1985, s 84(2)
(3)	1985, s 84(3) (changed)
(4)	1985, s 84(4)
(5)	1985, s 84(4), (5)
(6)	1985, s 84(6)
579(1), (2)	1985, s 85(1)
(3)	1985, s 85(2)
(4)	1985, s 85(3)
Chapter 5 Payment for shares	
580(1)	1985, s 100(1)
(2)	1985, s 100(2)
581	1985, s 119
582(1)	1985, s 99(1)
(2)	1985, s 99(4)
(3)	1985, s 99(1)
583(1)	drafting
(2)–(3)(d)	1985, s 738(2)
(3)(e), (4)	new
(4)	new
(5)	1985, s 738(3)
(6)	1985, s 738(4)
(7)	new
584	1985, s 106
585(1)	1985, s 99(2)
(2)	1985, s 99(3)
(3)	1985, s 99(5)
586(1)	1985, s 101(1)
(2)	1985, s 101(2)
(3)	1985, s 101(3), (4)
(4)	1985, s 101(5)
587(1)	1985, s 102(1)
(2)	1985, s 102(2)
(3)	1985, s 102(3), (4)
(4)	1985, s 102(5), (6)
(5)	1985, s 102(7)
588(1)	1985, s 112(1), (5)(a)
(2)	1985, s 112(3)
(3)	1985, s 112(4)
(4)	1985, s 112(5)(b)
589(1), (2)	1985, s 113(1)
(3)	1985, s 113(2), (3) (changed)
(4)	1985, s 113(4)
(5)	1985, s 113(5)

CA 2006	Origin
(6)	1985, s 113(6), (7)
590(1)	1985, s 114
(2)	1985, s 114., Sch 24
591(1), (2)	1985, s 115(1)
592(1), (2)	1985, s 107
Chapter 6 Public companies: independent valuation of non-cash consideration	
593(1)	1985, s 103(1)
(2)	1985, s 103(2)
(3)	1985, s 103(6)
(4)	drafting
594(1)–(3)	1985, s 103(3)
(4), (5)	1985, s 103(4)
(6)	1985, s 103(7)
595(1), (2)	1985, s 103(5)
(3)	1985, s 103(7)(b)
596(1)	drafting
(2)	1985, s 108(4)
(3)	1985, s 108(6)
(4), (5)	1985, s 108(7)
597(1), (2)	1985, s 111(1)
(3), (4)	1985, s 111(3), Sch 24
(5), (6)	1985, ss 88(6), 111(3)
598(1)	1985, s 104(1)
(2)	1985, s 104(2)
(3)	drafting
(4)	1985, s 104(6)(a)
(5)	1985, s 104(6)(b)
599(1)	1985, s 104(4)(a), (b), (d)
(2)	1985, s 104(5)(a)
(3)	1985, s 104(4)(d)
(4)	1985, s 104(5)(b)
600(1)	drafting
(2)	1985, s 109(2)(a), (b)
(3)	1985, s 108(6)(a), (b), (c), 109(2)(c), (d)
(4), (5)	1985, s 109(3)
601(1), (2)	1985, s 104(4)(c), (d)
(3)	1985, s 104(4)(c) (changed)
602(1)	1985, s 111(2)
(2), (3)	1985, s 111(4), Sch 24
603	1985, s 104(3)
604(1)	1985, s 105(1)
(2)	1985, s 105(2)
(3)	1985, s 105(3)
605(1)	1985, s 112(1)
(2)	1985, s 112(2)
(3)	1985, s 112(3)
(4)	1985, s 112(4)
606(1)	1985, s 113(1)
(2)	1985, s 113(2), (3) (changed)
(3)	1985, s 113(4)
(4)	1985, s 113(5)
(5)	1986, s 113(6), (7)
(6)	1986, s 113(8)
607(1)	drafting

CA 2006	Origin
(2)	1985, s 114
(3)	1985, s 114, Sch 24
608(1), (2)	1985, s 115(1)
609(1), (2)	1985, s 107
Chapter 7 Share premiums	
610(1)	1985, s 130(1)
(2), (3)	1985, s 130(2) (changed)
(4)	1985, s 130(3)
(5), (6)	1985, s 130(4)
611(1)	1985, s 132(1)
(2)	1985, s 132(2)
(3)	1985, s 132(3)
(4)	1985, s 132(4)
(5)	1985, s 132(5)
612(1)	1985, s 131(1)
(2)	1985, s 131(2)
(3)	1985, s 131(3)
(4)	1985, s 131(1), 132(8)
613(1)	drafting
(2), (3)	1985, s 131(4)
(4)	1985, s 131(5)
(5)	1985, s 131(6)
614(1)	1985, s 134(1)
(2)	1985, s 134(3)
615	1985, s 133(1)
616(1)	1985, s 131(7), 133(4)
(2)	1985, s 133(2)
(3)	1985, s 133(3)
Chapter 8 Alteration of share capital	
617(1)	1985, s 121(1) (changed)
(2)	1985, s 121(2)(a) (changed)
(3)	1985, s 121(2)(b), (c), (d) (changed)
(4), (5)	new
618(1)	1985, s 121(2)(b), (d)
(2)	1985, s 121(3) (changed)
(3)	1985, s 121(4) (changed)
(4), (5)	new
619(1)	1985, s 122(1)(a), (d)
(2), (3)	1985, s 122(1) (changed)
(4)	1985, s 122(2)
(5)	1985, s 122(2), Sch 24
620(1)	1985, s 121(2)(c) (changed)
(2)	1985, s 121(4) (changed)
(3)	new
621(1)	1985, s 122(1)(c)
(2), (3)	new
(4)	1985, s 122(2)
(5)	1985, s 122(2), Sch 24
622(1)–(8)	new
623	new
624(1)–(3)	new
625(1)–(5)	new
626(1)–(6)	new
627(1)–(8)	new

CA 2006	*Origin*
628(1)–(3)	new
Chapter 9 Classes of share and class rights	
629(1)	new
(2)	1985, s 128(2)
630(1)	1985, s 125(1)
(2)–(4)	1985, s 125(2) (changed)
(5)	1985, s 125(7)
(6)	1985, s 125(8)
631(1)–(6)	new
632	1985, s 126 (changed)
633(1)	1985, s 127(1)(b)
(2)	1985, s 127(2), (2A)
(3)	1985, s 127(2)
(4)	1985, s 127(3)
(5)	1985, s 127(4)
(6)	1985, s 127(6)
634(1)–(6)	new
635(1)–(3)	1985, s 127(5)
636(1)	1985, s 128(4) (changed)
(2)	1985, s 128(5)
(3)	1985, s 128(5), Sch 24
637(1)	1985, s 128(3) (changed)
(2)	1985, s 128(5)
(3)	1985, s 128(5), Sch 24
638(1)	1985, s 129(1) (changed)
(2)	1985, s 129(4)
(3)	1985, s 129(4), Sch 24
639(1)	1985, s 129(3) (changed)
(2)	1985, s 129(4)
(3)	1985, s 129(4), Sch 24
640(1)	1985, s 129(2) (changed)
(2)	1985, s 129(4)
(3)	1985, s 129(4), Sch 24
Chapter 10 Reduction of share capital	
641(1)–(3)	1985, s 135(1) (changed)
(4)	1985, s 135(2)
(5), (6)	new
642(1)–(4)	new
643(1)–(5)	new
644(1)–(9)	new
645(1)	1985, s 136(1)
(2)	1985, s 136(2), (6)
(3)	1985, s 136(6)
(4)	1985, s 136(2)
646(1)	1985, s 136(3)
(2), (3)	1985, s 136(4)
(4), (5)	1985, s 136(5)
647(1)	1985, s 141 (changed)
(2)	1985, s 141, Sch 24
648(1), (2)	1985, s 137(1)
(3)	1985, s 137(2)(b)
(4)	1985, s 137(2)(a), (3)
649(1)	1985, s 138(1) (changed)
(2)	new
(3)	1985, s 138(2) (changed)
(4)	1985, s 138(3) (changed)

CA 2006	*Origin*
(5)	1985, s 138(4) (changed)
(6)	1985, s 138(4)
650(1)	1985, s 139(1)
(2)	1985, s 139(2)
(3)	drafting
651(1), (2)	1985, s 139(3)
(3)	1985, s 139(4) (changed)
(4)	1985, s 139(5)
(5)	new
(6)	1985, s 139(5)(a)
(7)	1985, s 139(5)(b)
652(1)	1985, s 140(1) (changed)
(2)	drafting
(3)	1985, s 140(5)
653(1)	1985, s 140(2)
(2)	1985, s 140(3)
(3)	1985, s 140(4)
(4)	drafting
Chapter 11 Miscellaneous and supplementary provisions	
654(1)–(3)	new
655	1985, s 111A
656(1)–(3)	1985, s 142(1)
(4)	1985, s 142(2) (changed)
(5)	1985, s 142(2), Sch 24
(6)	1985, s 142(3)
657(1)–(4)	new
PART 18 ACQUISITION BY LIMITED COMPANY OF ITS OWN SHARES	
Chapter 1 General provisions	
658(1)	1985, s 143(1)
(2)	1985, s 143(2)
(3)	1985, s 143(2), Sch 24
659(1), (2)	1985, s 143(3)
660(1), (2)	1985, s 144(1) (changed)
(3)	1985, s 145(1), (2)(a)
661(1), (2)	1985, s 144(2) (changed)
(3)	1985, s 144(3)
(4)	1985, s 144(4)
(5)	1985, s 145(2)(a)
662(1)	1985, s 146(1)
(2)	1985, s 146(2)
(3)	1985, s 146(2), (3)
(4)	1985, s 147(1)
(5), (6)	1985, s 146(4)
663(1)	1985, s 122(1)(f)
(2), (3)	new
(4)	1985, s 122(2)
(5)	1985, s 122(2), Sch 24
664(1), (2)	1985, s 147(2) (changed)
(3)	new
(4)	1985, s 147(3) (changed)
(5), (6)	new
665(1), (2)	1985, s 147(4)
(3)	new
(4)	1985, s 147(4)(a) (changed)

CA 2006	Origin
(5)	1985, s 147(4)(b)
666(1), (2)	1985, s 149(1)
667(1), (2)	1985, s 149(2)
(3)	1985, s 149(2), Sch 24
668(1), (2)	1985, s 148(1)
(3)	1985, s 148(2)
669(1), (2)	1985, s 148(4)
670(1)	1985, s 150(1)
(2)	1985, s 150(2)
(3)	1985, s 150(3)
(4)	1985, s 150(4)
671	1985, s 145(3), s 146(1), s 148(3)
672(1)	1985, Sch 2, para 1(1)
(2)	1985, Sch 2, para 1(2)
(3)	1985, Sch 2, para 1(3)
(4)	1985, Sch 2, para 1(4)
(5)	1985, Sch 2, para 2(3)
(6)	1985, Sch 2, para 2(4)
673(1)	1985, Sch 2, para 3(1)(a), (2)
(2)	1985, Sch 2, para 3(1)(b), (2)(a)
674	1985, Sch 2, para 4(1), (3)
675(1), (2)	1985, Sch 2, para 5(1), (2)
676	1985, Sch 2, para 5(1), (3)
Chapter 2 Financial assistance for purchase of own shares	
677(1)	1985, s 152(1)(a)
(2), (3)	1985, s 152(2)
678(1)	1985, s 151(1) (changed)
(2)	1985, s 153(1)
(3)	1985, s 151(2) (changed)
(4)	1985, s 153(2)
(5)	drafting
679(1)	1985, s 151(1) (changed)
(2)	1985, s 153(1) (changed)
(3)	1985, s 151(2) (changed)
(4)	1985, s 153(2) (changed)
(5)	drafting
680(1)	1985, s 151(3)
(2)	1985, s 151(3), Sch 24
681(1), (2)	1985, s 153(3)
682(1)	1985, s 153(4), s 154(1)
(2)	1985, s 153(4)
(3), (4)	1985, s 154(2)
(5)	1985, s 153(5)
683(1)	1985, s 152(1)(b), (c)
(2)	1985, s 152(3)
Chapter 3 Redeemable shares	
684(1)	1985, s 159(1) (changed)
(2)	new
(3)	1985, s 159(1) (changed)
(4)	1985, s 159(2)
685(1)–(4)	new
686(1)–(3)	1985, s 159(3) (changed)
687(1)–(3)	1985, s 160(1)
(4), (5)	1985, s 160(2)

CA 2006	Origin
(6)	1985, s 160(1)
688	1985, s 160(4) (changed)
689(1)	1985, s 122(1)(e)
(2), (3)	new
(4)	1985, s 122(2)
(5)	1985, s 122(2), Sch 24
Chapter 4 Purchase of own shares	
690(1)	1985, s 162(1) (changed)
(2)	1985, s 162(3)
691(1), (2)	1985, s 159(3), s 162(2)
692(1), (2)	1985, s 160(1), s 162(2)
(3), (4)	1985, s 160(2), s 162(2)
(5)	1985, s 160(1), s 162(2)
693(1)	1985, s 164(1), s 166(1)
(2)	1985, s 163(1)
(3)	1985, s 163(2)
(4)	1985, s 163(3)
(5)	1985, s 163(4), (5)
694(1)	1985, s 164(1)
(2)	1985, s 164(2), s 165(2) (changed)
(3)	1985, s 165(1)
(4)	1985, s 164(3), 165(2)
(5)	1985, s 164(4), 165(2)
(6)	drafting
695(1)	1985, s 164(5), 165(2)
(2)	1985, Sch 15A, para 5(1), (2)
(3), (4)	1985, s 164(5), s 165(2)
696(1)	1985, s 164(6), s 165(2)
(2)	1985, s 164(6), s 165(2), Sch 15A, para 5(3), (4)
(3)–(5)	1985, s 164(6), s 165(2)
697(1), (2)	1985, s 164(7)
(3)	1985, s 164(3), (7)
(4)	1985, s 164(4), (7)
(5)	drafting
698(1)	1985, s 164(5), (7)
(2)	1985, Sch 15A, para 5(1), (2)
(3), (4)	1985, s 164(5), (7)
699(1)	1985, s 164(6), (7)
(2)	1985, s 164(6), (7), Sch 15A, para 5(3)
(3)–(6)	1985, s 164(6), (7)
700(1), (2)	1985, s 167(2)
(3)	1985, s 164(3), (7), s 167(2)
(4)	1985, s 164(4), (7), s 167(2)
(5)	1985, s 164(5), (6), (7), s 167(2)
701(1)	1985, s 166(1)
(2)	1985, s 166(2)
(3)	1985, s 166(3)(a), (b)
(4)	1985, s 166(4)
(5)	1985, s 166(3)(c), (4)
(6)	1985, s 166(5)
(7)	1985, s 166(6)
(8)	1985, s 166(7)
702(1)–(4)	1985, s 169(4) (changed)

CA 2006	Origin
(5)	new
(6)	1985, s 169(5)
(7)	1985, s 169(9)
703(1)	1985, s 169(7) (changed)
(2)	1985, s 169(7), Sch 24
(3)	1985, s 169(8)
704	1985, s 167(1)
705(1)	1985, s 168(1)
(2)	1985, s 168(2)
706	1985, s 160(4), s 162(2), (2B)
707(1)–(3)	1985, s 169(1), (1A), (1B) (changed)
(4)	1985, s 169(2)
(5)	1985, s 169(3)
(6)	1985, s 169(6)
(7)	1985, s 169(6), Sch 24
708(1)	1985, s 169(1), (1A), (1B) (changed)
(2), (3)	new
(4)	1985, s 169(6)
(5)	1985, s 169(6), Sch 24
Chapter 5 Redemption or purchase by private company out of capital	
709(1)	1985, s 171(1) (changed)
(2)	1985, s 171(2)
710(1), (2)	1985, s 171(3)
711(1), (2)	1985, s 172(1)
712(1)	drafting
(2)	1985, s 172(2)
(3)	1985, s 172(4)
(4)	1985, s 172(5)
(5)	drafting
(6)	1985, s 172(3)
(7)	1985, s 172(6)
713(1), (2)	1985, s 173(1)
714(1)–(3)	1985, s 173(3) (changed)
(4)	1985, s 173(4) (changed)
(5), (6)	1985, s 173(5) (changed)
715(1)	1985, s 173(6)
(2)	1985, s 173(6), Sch 24
716(1)	1985, s 173(2)
(2)	1985, s 174(1)
(3)	drafting
717(1)	drafting
(2)	1985, Sch 15A, para 6(1), (2)
(3)	1985, s 174(2)
(4)	1985, s 174(3), (5)
718(1)	drafting
(2)	1985, s 174(4), Sch 15A, para 6(1), (3)
(3)	1985, s 174(4)
719(1)	1985, s 175(1)
(2)	1985, s 175(2)
(3)	1985, s 175(3)
(4)	1985, s 175(4), (5)
720(1)	1985, s 175(4), (6)(a)
(2)	1985, s 175(6)(a) (changed)
(3)	new
(4)	1985, s 175(6)(b)
(5)	1985, s 175(7) (changed)
(6)	1985, s 175(7), Sch 24
(7)	1985, s 175(8)
721(1)	1985, s 176(1)
(2)	1985, s 176(1), (2)
(3)	1985, s 177(1)
(4), (5)	1985, s 177(2)
(6)	1985, s 177(3)
(7)	1985, s 177(4)
722(1)	new
(2)	1985, s 176(3)(a)
(3)	1985, s 176(3)(b)
(4)	1985, s 176(4)
(5)	1985, s 176(4), Sch 24
723(1)	1985, s 174(1)
(2)	drafting
Chapter 6 Treasury shares	
724(1)	1985, s 162(2B)
(2)	1985, s 162(4)
(3)	1985, s 162A(1)
(4)	1985, s 162A(2)
(5)	1985, s 162A(3)
725(1)	1985, s 162B(1)
(2)	1985, s 162B(2)
(3)	1985, s 162B(3)
(4)	1985, s 143(2A)
726(1)	1985, s 162C(1)
(2)	1985, s 162C(2), (3)
(3)	1985, s 162C(4)
(4)	1985, s 162C(5)
(5)	1985, s 162C(6)
727(1)	1985, s 162D(1)(a), (b)
(2)	1985, s 162D(2) (changed)
(3)	1985, s 162D(3)
(4), (5)	new
728(1)	1985, s 169A(1)(b)(ii), (2)
(2)	1985, s 169A(2)
(3)	1985, s 169A(3)
(4)	1985, s 169A(4)
(5)	1985, s 169A(4), Sch 24
729(1)	1985, s 162D(1)(c)
(2)	1985, s 162E(1)
(3)	1985, s 162E(2)
(4)	1985, s 162D(4)
(5)	1985, s 162D(5)
730(1)	1985, s 169A(1)(b)(i), (2)
(2)	1985, s 169A(2)
(3)	1985, s 169A(3)
(4), (5)	new
(6)	1985, s 169A(4)
(7)	1985, s 169A(4), Sch 24
731(1)	1985, s 162F(1)
(2)	1985, s 162F(2)

CA 2006	Origin
(3)	1985, s 162F(3)
(4)	1985, s 162F(4), (5)
732(1)	1985, s 162G (changed)
(2)	1985, s 162G
Chapter 7 Supplementary provisions	
733(1), (2)	1985, s 170(1)
(3)	1985, s 170(2), (3)
(4)	1985, s 170(1)
(5), (6)	1985, s 170(4)
734(1)	drafting
(2)	1985, s 171(4)
(3)	1985, s 171(5)
(4)	1985, s 171(6)
735(1)	1985, s 178(1)
(2)	1985, s 178(2), (3)
(3)	1985, s 178(3)
(4)	1985, s 178(4)
(5)	1985, s 178(5)
(6)	1985, s 178(6)
736	1985, s 181(a)
737(1)–(4)	new
PART 19 DEBENTURES	
738	1985, s 744 ("debenture")
739(1), (2)	1985, s 193
740	1985, s 195
741(1)–(4)	new
742	1985, s 197
743(1)	new
(2)	1985, s 190(5) (changed)
(3)	1985, s 190(6)
(4), (5)	new
(6)	1985, s 190(1), (5)
744(1)	1985, s 191(1)
(2)	1985, s 191(2)
(3), (4)	new
(5)	1985, s 191(6)
(6)	new
745(1)–(5)	new
746(1)	1985, s 191(4) (changed)
(2)	1985, s 191(4), Sch 24
(3)	1985, s 191(5)
747(1)–(3)	new
748(1)	1985, s 191(7) (changed)
(2)	1985, s 191(7)
749(1)	1985, s 191(3)
(2)	1985, s 191(4)
(3)	1985, s 191(4), Sch 24
(4)	1985, s 191(5)
750(1)	1985, s 192(1)
(2)	1985, s 192(2)
(3)	1985, s 192(1)
751(1)	1985, s 192(3)
(2)	1985, s 192(3), 1986 art 201(3)
(3), (4)	1985, s 192(4)
752(1)	1985, s 194(1)
(2)	1985, s 194(2)
(3)	1985, s 194(4)
(4)	1985, s 194(5)
753	1985, s 194(3)
754(1)	1985, s 196(1)
(2)	1985, s 196(2)
(3)	1985, s 196(3)
(4)	1985, s 196(4)
PART 20 PUBLIC AND PRIVATE COMPANIES	
Chapter 1 Prohibition of public offers by private companies	
755(1)	1985, s 81(1) (changed)
(2)	1985, s 58(3)
(3), (4)	new
(5)	drafting
756(1), (2)	1985, s 742A(1)
(3)	1985, s 742A(2)
(4)	1985, s 742A(3), (4), and (5)
(5)	1985, s 742A(3)(a), (6)(b) (changed)
(6)	1985, s 742A(6)(a)
757(1)–(3)	new
758(1)–(4)	new
759(1)–(5)	new
760	1985, s 81(3)
Chapter 2 Minimum share capital requirement for public companies	
761(1)	1985, s 117(1)
(2)	1985, s 117(2) (changed)
(3)	1985, s 117(4)
(4)	1985, s 117(6) (changed)
762(1)	1985, s 117(3) (changed)
(2)	new
(3)	1985, s 117(5)
763(1)	1985, s 118(1) (changed)
(2)–(6)	new
764(1)	1985, s 118(1) (changed)
(2)	new
(3)	1985, s 118(2)
(4)	1985, s 118(3)
765(1)–(4)	new
766(1)–(6)	new
767(1)	1985, s 117(7)
(2)	1985, s 117(7), Sch 24
(3)	1985, s 117(8)
(4)	new
PART 21 CERTIFICATION AND TRANSFER OF SECURITIES	
Chapter 1 Certification and transfer of securities: general	
768(1)	1985, s 186(1)(a)
(2)	1985, s 186(1)(b), (2)
769(1)	1985, s 185(1)(a)
(2)	1985, s 185(1), (4)(a), (b)
(3)	1985, s 185(5)
(4)	1985, s 185(5), Sch 24
770(1)	1985, s 183(1)
(2)	1985, s 183(2)

CA 2006	Origin
771(1)–(6)	new
772	1985, s 183(4)
773	1985, s 183(3)
774	1985, s 187
775(1), (2)	1985, s 184(1)
(3)	1985, s 184(2)
(4)	1985, s 184(3)
776(1)	1985, s 185(1)(b)
(2)	1985, s 185(2)
(3)	1985, s 185(1), (4)(c)
(4)	drafting
(5)	1985, s 185(5)
(6)	1985, s 185(5), Sch 24
777(1), (2)	1985, s 185(3)
778(1)	1985, s 185(4), (4A)
(2)	1985, s 185(4B), (4C)
(3)	1985, s 185(4D)
779(1)	1985, s 188(1)
(2)	1985, s 188(2)
(3)	1985, s 188(3)
780(1)–(4)	new
781(1)	1985, s 189(1)
(2)	1985, s 189(2)
(3)	1985, s 189(1), Sch 24
(4)	1985, s 189(2), Sch 24
782(1)	1985, s 185(6)
(2), (3)	1985, s 185(7)
Chapter 2 Evidencing and transfer of title to securities without written instrument	
783	1989, s 207(1), (10)
784(1), (2)	new
(3)	1989, s 207(9)
785(1)	1989, s 207(1)
(2)	1989, s 207(2)
(3)	1989, s 207(3)
(4)	1989, s 207(4)
(5)	1989, s 207(5)
(6)	1989, s 207(6)
786(1)–(5)	new
787(1)–(3)	new
788	1989, s 207(7)
789	new
790	new
PART 22 INFORMATION ABOUT INTERESTS IN A COMPANY'S SHARES	
791	new
792(1)	1985, s 198(2) (changed)
(2)	1985, s 198(2)(b)
793(1), (2)	1985, s 212(1) (changed)
(3)	1985, s 212(2)(a)
(4)	1985, s 212(2)(b)
(5)	1985, s 212(3)
(6)	1985, s 212(2)(c)
(7)	1985, s 212(4)
794(1)	1985, s 216(1)
(2)	1985, s 216(1B)

CA 2006	Origin
(3)	1985, s 216(1A)
(4)	drafting
795(1)	1985, s 216(3)
(2)	1985, s 216(4)
(3)	1985, s 216(3), Sch 24
796(1), (2)	1985, s 216(5)
797(1)	1985, s 454(1)
(2)	1985, s 454(2)
(3)	1985, s 454(3)
(4)	1985, s 454(2), (3)
798(1), (2)	1985, s 455(1)
(3)	1985, s 455(2)
(4)	1985, s 455(2), Sch 24
(5)	1985, s 455(1), (2)
799(1)	1985, s 456(1A)
(2)	1985, s 456(2)
(3)	1985, s 456(1A)
800(1)	1985, s 456(1)
(2)	1985, s 456(2)
(3)	1985, s 456(3)
(4)	1985, s 456(6)
(5)	1985, s 456(7)
801(1), (2)	1985, s 456(4)
(3), (4)	1985, s 456(5)
(5)	1985, s 457(3)
802(1), (2)	1985, s 457(1)
(3)	1985, s 457(2)
(4)	1985, s 457(3)
803(1), (2)	1985, s 214(1) (changed)
(3)	1985, s 214(2) (changed)
804(1)	1985, s 214(4)
(2)	1985, s 214(5) (changed)
(3)	1985, s 214(5), Sch 24
805(1)	1985, s 215(1), (3)
(2)	1985, s 215(2)
(3)	1985, s 215(2), (3)
(4)	1985, s 215(7) (changed)
(5)	new
(6)	1985, s 215(5)
(7)	1985, s 215(6)
806(1), (2)	new
(3)	1985, s 215(8) (changed)
(4)	1985, s 215(8), Sch 24
807(1)	1985, s 215(7)(b), s 219(1)
(2)	1985, s 215(7)(b), s 219(2)
(3)	1985, s 215(7)(b), s 219(3)
(4)	1985, s 215(7)(b), s 219(3), Sch 24
(5)	1985, s 215(7)(b), s 219(4)
808(1)	1985, s 213(1)
(2)	1985, s 211(3), s 213(1), (3)
(3)	1985, s 213(1) (changed)
(4)	1985, s 211(5), s 213(3)
(5)	1985, s 211(10), s 213(3)
(6)	1985, s 211(10), s 213(3), Sch 24

CA 2006	Origin
(7)	1985, s 211(4), s 213(3)
809(1)	1985, s 211(8), s 213(3) (changed)
(2), (3)	1985, s 211(8), s 213(3), s 325(5), Sch 13, para 27
(4), (5)	new
810(1)–(3)	1985, s 211(6), s 213(3)
(4)	1985, s 211(8), s 213(3)
(5), (6)	new
811(1)	1985, s 211(8)(b), s 213(3), s 219(1)
(2)	1985, s 211(8)(b), s 213(3), s 219(2) (changed)
(3)	new
(4)	new
812(1)–(7)	new
813(1)	1985, s 211(8)(b), s 213(3), s 219(3) (changed)
(2)	1985, s 211(8)(b), s 213(3), s 219(3), Sch 24
(3)	1985, s 211(8)(b), s 213(3), s 219(4)
814(1)–(3)	new
815(1)	1985, s 218(1)
(2)	1985, s 218(2)
(3)	1985, s 218(3)
(4)	1985, s 218(3), Sch 24
816	1985, s 217(1) (changed)
817(1)	1985, s 217(2) (changed)
(2), (3)	1985, s 217(3)
(4)	1985, s 217(5)
818(1), (2)	1985, s 217(4)
(3)	1985, s 217(5)
819(1)	1985, s 211(7), s 213(3)
(2)	1985, s 211(10), s 213(3)
(3)	1985, s 211(10), s 213(3), Sch 24
820(1)	1985, s 208(1), s 212(5)
(2)	1985, s 208(2), s 212(5)
(3)	1985, s 208(3), s 212(5)
(4)	1985, s 208(4), s 212(5)
(5)	1985, s 208(6), s 212(5)
(6)	1985, s 208(5), s 212(5)
(7)	1985, s 208(7), s 212(5)
(8)	1985, s 208(8), s 212(5)
821(1), (2)	1985, s 212(6)
822(1), (2)	1985, s 203(1), s 212(5)
823(1)	1985, s 203(2), s 212(5)
(2)	1985, s 203(3), s 212(5)
(3)	1985, s 203(4), s 212(5)
824(1)	1985, s 204(1), (2), s 212(5)
(2)	1985, s 204(2), s 212(5)
(3)	1985, s 204(3), s 212(5)
(4)	1985, s 204(4), s 212(5)
(5)	1985, s 204(5), s 212(5)
(6)	1985, s 204(6), s 212(5)
825(1)	1985, s 205(1), s 212(5)
(2)	1985, s 205(2), s 212(5)

CA 2006	Origin
(3)	1985, s 205(3), s 212(5)
(4)	1985, s 205(4), s 212(5)
826(1)	1985, s 211(9), s 213(3), s 215(4)
(2)	1985, s 215(4)
827	1985, s 220(2) (changed)
828(1), (2)	1985, s 210A(1)
(3)	1985, s 210A(5)

PART 23 DISTRIBUTIONS

Chapter 1 Restrictions on when distributions may be made

CA 2006	Origin
829(1), (2)	1985, s 263(2)
830(1)	1985, s 263(1)
(2), (3)	1985, s 263(3)
831(1)	1985, s 264(1)
(2), (3)	1985, s 264(2)
(4)	1985, s 264(3)
(5)	1985, s 264(4)
(6)	1985, s 264(1)
832(1)–(3)	1985, s 265(1)
(4)	1985, s 265(2)
(5)	1985, s 265(4), (6)
(6)	1985, s 265(4A), (5)
(7)	1985, s 265(3)
833(1)	1985, s 266(1)
(2)	1985, s 266(2)
(3)	1985, s 266(2A)
(4), (5)	1985, s 266(3)
834(1)	1985, s 266(2)(b)
(2)	1985, s 266(4), ICTA, s 842(1A)
(3)	1985, s 266(4), ICTA, s 842(2)
(4)	1985, s 266(4), ICTA, s 842(3)
(5)	1985, s 266(4), ICTA, s 838, s 842(1A), (4)
835(1)	1985, s 267(1)
(2)	1985, s 267(2)(b)

Chapter 2 Justification of distribution by reference to accounts

CA 2006	Origin
836(1)	1985, s 270(1), (2)
(2)	1985, s 270(3), (4)
(3), (4)	1985, s 270(5)
837(1)	1985, s 270(3)
(2)	1985, s 271(2)
(3)	1985, s 271(3)
(4)	1985, s 271(3), (4)
(5)	1985, s 271(5)
838(1)	1985, s 270(4)
(2)	1985, s 272(1)
(3)	1985, s 272(2)
(4), (5)	1985, s 272(3)
(6)	1985, s 272(4), (5)
839(1)	1985, s 270(4)
(2)	1985, s 273(1)
(3)	1985, s 273(2)
(4)	1985, s 272(3), s 273(3)
(5)	1985, s 273(4)

CA 2006	Origin
(6)	1985, s 273(4), (5)
(7)	1985, s 273(6), (7)
840(1)	1985, s 274(1), (2)
(2)	1985, s 274(2)
(3)	1985, s 274(3) ("financial assistance")
(4)	1985, s 154(2)(a), s 274(3) ("net assets" and "net liabilities")
(5)	1985, s 154(2)(b), s 274(3) ("net liabilities")
Chapter 3 Supplementary provisions	
841(1), (2)	1985, s 275(1)
(3)	1985, s 275(1A)
(4)	1985, s 275(4), (5), (6)
(5)	1985, s 275(2)
842	1985, s 275(3)
843(1)	1985, s 268(1)
(2)	1985, s 268(1)(a)
(3)	1985, s 268(2)(aa), (a)
(4)	1985, s 268(1)(b), (2)(b)
(5)	1985, s 268(1)
(6)	1985, s 268(3)(a)
(7)	1985, s 268(3)(b), (4)
844(1)	1985, s 269(1)
(2), (3)	1985, s 269(2)
845(1)–(5)	new
846(1), (2)	1985, s 276 (changed)
847(1), (2)	1985, s 277(1)
(3), (4)	1985, s 277(2)
848(1)	1985, s 278
(2)	1985, s 278, 1986 art 286
849	1985, s 263(4)
850(1), (2)	1985, s 263(5)
(3)	1985, s 263(5), 1986 art 271(5)
851(1)	1985, s 281 (changed)
(2), (3)	new
852	1985, s 281
853(1)	1985, s 280(1)
(2)	1985, s 280(3)
(3)	1985, s 280(2)
(4), (5)	1985, s 262(3), s 742(2)
(6)	1985, s 262(1), s 742(1)
PART 24 A COMPANY'S ANNUAL RETURN	
854(1), (2)	1985, s 363(1)
(3)	1985, s 363(2) (changed)
855(1)	1985, s 364(1) (changed)
(2)	1985, s 364(2)
(3)	1985, s 364(3)
856(1)	1985, s 364A(1)
(2)	1985, s 364A(2), (3) (changed)
(3)	1985, s 364A(4) (changed)
(4)	1985, s 364A(5)
(5)	1985, s 364A(6)
(6)	1985, s 364A(8)
857(1), (2)	1985, s 365(1)
(3)	1985, s 365(2)
858(1)	1985, s 363(3), (4) (changed)

CA 2006	Origin
(2)	1985, s 363(3), (4), Sch 24
(3)	1985, s 363(3)
(4)	1985, s 363(4)
(5)	new
859	1985, s 365(3)
PART 25 COMPANY CHARGES	
Chapter 1 Companies registered in England and Wales or in Northern Ireland	
860(1)	1985, ss 395(1), 399(1)
(2)	1985, s 399(1)
(3)	1985, s 399(2)
(4)–(6)	1985, s 399(3), Sch 24 (changed)
(7)	1985, s 396(1)
861(1)	1985, s 396(3)
(2)	1985, s 396(1)(d)
(3)	1985, s 396(2)
(4)	1985, s 396(3A)
(5)	1985, ss 395(1) ("company"), 396(4) ("charge"), 400(1) ("company")
862(1)	1985, s 400(1)
(2), (3)	1985, s 400(2)
(4), (5)	1985, s 400(4), Sch 24 (changed)
863(1)–(4)	1985, s 397(1)
(5)	1985, s 399(1)–(3)
864(1)	1985, s 397(2)
(2)	1985, s 397(3)
(3)	1985, s 397(2)
865(1)	1985, s 402(1)
(2)	1985, s 402(2)
(3), (4)	1985, s 402(3), Sch 24
866(1)	1985, s 398(1)
(2)	1985, s 398(3)
867(1), (2)	1985, s 398(4)
868(1), (2)	1986 art 408(1)
(3)	1986 art 408(2)
(4)	1986 art 408(3)
(5)	Drafting
869(1)	1985, s 401(1) (opening words)
(2)	1985, s 401(1)(a)
(3)	1986 art 409(2)(b)
(4)	1985, s 401(1)(b)
(5), (6)	1985, s 401(2)
(7)	1985, s 401(3)
870(1)	1985, ss 395(1), 398(2)
(2)	1985, s 400(2), (3)
(3)	1985, s 397(1)
871(1)	1985, s 405(1)
(2)	1985, s 405(2)
(3)	1985, s 405(1), (2)
(4), (5)	1985, s 405(4), Sch 24
872(1), (2)	1985, s 403(1) (changed)
(3)	1985, s 403(2)
873(1)	1985, s 404(1)
(2)	1985, s 404(2)

CA 2006	Origin
874(1), (2)	1985, s 395(1)
(3)	1985, s 395(2)
875(1)	1985, s 406(1), 1986 art 414(1)
(2)	1985, s 406(2)
876(1)	1985, s 407(1)
(2)	1985, s 407(2)
(3), (4)	1985, s 407(3), Sch 24
877(1)	1985, s 408(1)
(2)	1985, ss 406(1), 407(1), 408(1) (changed)
(3)	new
(4)	1985, s 408(1), (2) (changed)
(5), (6)	1985, s 408(3), Sch 24 (changed)
(7)	1985, s 408(4)
Chapter 2 Companies registered in Scotland	
878(1)	1985, ss 410(2), 415(1)
(2)	1985, s 415(1)
(3)	1985, s 415(2)
(4)–(6)	1985, s 415(3), Sch 24 (changed)
(7)	1985, s 410(4)
879(1)	1985, s 410(4)(a)
(2)	1985, s 413(1)
(3)	1985, s 410(4)(a)
(4)	1985, s 412
(5)	1985, s 410(5)
(6)	1985, s 410(5) ("company")
880(1), (2)	1985, s 416(1)
(3), (4)	1985, s 416(3), Sch 24 (changed)
881(1)	1985, s 414(1)
(2), (3)	1985, s 414(2)
882(1)–(4)	1985, s 413(2)
(5)	1985, s 415(1)–(3)
883(1)–(3)	1985, s 413(3)
884	1985, s 411(2)
885(1)	1985, s 417(1)
(2)	1985, s 417(2)
(3)	1985, s 417(3)
(4)	1985, s 418(1), (2)(b)
(5)	1985, s 418(2)(a), (c)
(6)	1985, s 417(4)
886(1)	1985, ss 410(2), 411(1)
(2)	1985, s 416(1), (2)
(3)	1985, s 413(2)
887(1)	1985, s 419(1) (changed)
(2)	1985, s 419(1B)(a), (c), (3) (changed)
(3)	1985, s 419(1)
(4)	1985, s 419(2)
(5)	1985, s 419(4)
888(1), (2)	1985, s 420
889(1)	1985, s 410(2)
(2)	1985, s 410(3)
890(1)	1985, s 421(1)
(2)	1985, s 421(2)

CA 2006	Origin
891(1)	1985, s 422(1)
(2)	1985, s 422(2)
(3), (4)	1985, s 422(3), Sch 24
892(1)	1985, s 423(1)
(2)	1985, ss 421(1), 422(1), 423(1) (changed)
(3)	new
(4)	1985, s 423(1), (2) (changed)
(5), (6)	1985, s 423(3), Sch 24 (changed)
(7)	1985, s 423(4)
Chapter 3 Powers of the Secretary of State	
893(1)–(9)	new
894(1), (2)	new
PART 26 ARRANGEMENTS AND RECONSTRUCTIONS	
895(1)	1985, s 425(1)
(2)	1985, ss 425(6), 427(6)
(3)	drafting
896(1), (2)	1985, s 425(1)
897(1)	1985, s 426(1), (2), (3)
(2)	1985, s 426(2)
(3)	1985, s 426(4)
(4)	1985, s 426(5)
(5)–(8)	1985, s 426(6), Sch 24
898(1)–(3)	1985, s 426(7), Sch 24
899(1)	1985, s 425(2)
(2)	new
(3)	1985, s 425(2)
(4)	1985, s 425(3)
900(1)	1985, s 427(1), (2)
(2)	1985, s 427(2), (3)
(3), (4)	1985, s 427(4)
(5)	1985, s 427(6)
(6)–(8)	1985, s 427(5), Sch 24
901(1), (2)	new
(3), (4)	1985, s 425(3) (changed)
(5), (6)	1985, s 425(4), Sch 24
PART 27 MERGERS AND DIVISIONS OF PUBLIC COMPANIES	
Chapter 1 Introductory	
902(1)	1985, s 427A(1)
(2)	drafting
(3)	1985, s 427A(4)
903(1)	1985, s 427A(1)
(2), (3)	drafting
Chapter 2 Merger	
904(1)	1985, s 427A(2) Cases 1 and 2
(2)	drafting
905(1)	1985, Sch 15B, para 2(1)(a)
(2), (3)	1985, Sch 15B, para 2(2)
906(1), (2)	1985, Sch 15B, para 2(1)(b)
(3)	1985, Sch 15B, para 2(1)(c)
907(1)	1985, s 425(2), Sch 15B, para 1
(2)	1985, s 427A(1) closing words, Sch 15B, para 1 opening words
908(1)	1985, Sch 15B, para 3(a)

CA 2006	*Origin*
(2)	1985, Sch 15B, para 4(1)
(3)	1985, Sch 15B, para 3 opening words
909(1)	1985, Sch 15B, para 3(d)
(2)	1985, Sch 15B, para 5(1)
(3)	1985, Sch 15B, para 5(1), (2)
(4)	1985, Sch 15B, para 5(3)
(5)	1985, Sch 15B, para 5(7)
(6)	1985, Sch 15B, para 5(8)
(7)	1985, Sch 15B, para 3 opening words
910(1)	1985, Sch 15B, para 6(1)(e)
(2)	1985, Sch 15B, para 6(2)
(3)	1985, Sch 15B, para 6(3) (changed)
(4)	1985, Sch 15B, para 6(4)
911(1), (2)	1985, Sch 15B, para 3(e)
(3)	1985, Sch 15B, para 6(1)
(4)	1985, Sch 15B, para 3 opening words
912	1985, Sch 15B, para 3(f)
913(1)	1985, Sch 15B, para 8(1)
(2)	1985, Sch 15B, para 8(2)
914	1985, Sch 15B, para 7
915(1)	1985, Sch 15B, para 12(1)
(2)	1985, Sch 15B, para 12(2)
(3)–(5)	1985, Sch 15B, para 12(3)
(6)	1985, Sch 15B, para 12(1)(a), (b)
916(1)	1985, Sch 15B, para 14(1)
(2)	1985, Sch 15B, para 14(2)
(3)–(5)	1985, Sch 15B paras 10(2), 14(3)
(6)	1985, Sch 15B para14(1)(a), (b)
917(1)	1985, Sch 15B, para 12(1)
(2)	1985, Sch 15B, para 12(4)
(3)–(5)	1985, Sch 15B, para 12(5)
(6)	1985, Sch 15B, para 12(1)(a), (b)
918(1)	1985, Sch 15B, para 10(1)
(2)–(4)	1985, Sch 15B, para 10(2)
Chapter 3 Division	
919(1)	1985, s 427A(2) Case 3
(2)	drafting
920(1)	1985, Sch 15B, para 2(1)(a)
(2)	1985, Sch 15B, para 2(2)
(3)	1985, Sch 15B, para 2(3)
921(1), (2)	1985, Sch 15B, para 2(1)(b)
(3)	1985, Sch 15B, para 2(1)(c)
(4)	1985, Sch 15B, para 2(1)(b), (c) opening words
922(1)	1985, s 425(2), Sch 15B, para 1
(2)	1985, s 427A(1) closing words, Sch 15B, para 1 opening words
923(1)	1985, Sch 15B, para 3(a)
(2)	1985, Sch 15B, para 4(1)
(3)	1985, Sch 15B, para 4(2)
(4)	1985, Sch 15B, para 3 opening words
924(1)	1985, Sch 15B, para 3(d)
(2)	1985, Sch 15B, para 5(1)
(3)	1985, Sch 15B, para 5(1), (2)
(4)	1985, Sch 15B, para 5(3)
(5)	1985, Sch 15B, para 5(7)
(6)	1985, Sch 15B, para 5(8)
(7)	1985, Sch 15B, para 3 opening words
925(1)	1985, Sch 15B, para 6(1)(e)
(2)	1985, Sch 15B, para 6(2)
(3)	1985, Sch 15B, para 6(3) (changed)
(4)	1985, Sch 15B, para 6(4)
(5)	1985, Sch 15B, para 3 opening words
926(1), (2)	1985, Sch 15B, para 3(e)
(3)	1985, Sch 15B, para 6(1)
(4)	1985, Sch 15B, para 3 opening words
927(1)	1985, Sch 15B, para 3(b)
(2)	1985, Sch 15B, para 3(c)
(3)	1985, Sch 15B, para 3 opening words
928	1985, Sch 15B, para 3(f)
929(1)	1985, Sch 15B, para 8(1)
(2)	1985, Sch 15B, para 8(2)
930	1985, Sch 15B, para 7
931(1)	1985, Sch 15B, para 13(1)
(2)	1985, Sch 15B, para 13(2)
(3)	1985, Sch 15B paras 12(5)(a), 13(3)(a)
(4)	1985, Sch 15B, para 13(3)(b)
(5)	1985, Sch 15B paras 12(5)(c), 13(3)(a)
(6)	1985, Sch 15B, para 13(3)(c)
932(1)	1985, Sch 15B, para 10(1)
(2)–(4)	1985, Sch 15B, para 10(2)
(5)	1985, Sch 15B, para 10(2) opening words
933(1)–(3)	1985, Sch 15B, para 11(1), (2)
934(1)	1985, Sch 15B, para 11(1), (3)
(2)	1985, Sch 15B, para 11(4)(a), (b)
(3)	1985, Sch 15B, para 11(4)(c)
(4)	1985, Sch 15B, para 11(4)(d)
Chapter 4 Supplementary provisions	
935(1)	1985, Sch 15B, para 5(4) (changed)
(2)	1985, Sch 15B, para 5(6)
936(1)–(4)	new
937(1)–(6)	new
938(1), (2)	1985, s 427A(3)
939(1)	1985, Sch 15B, para 9(1), (2)
(2)	1985, Sch 15B, para 9(2)
(3), (4)	1985, Sch 15B, para 9(3)
(5)	1985, Sch 15B, para 9(4)
940(1)	1985, Sch 15B, para 15(1)
(2)	1985, Sch 15B, para 15(2)
(3)	1985, Sch 15B, para 15(1)

CA 2006	Origin
941	1985, ss 427(6), 427A(8)
PART 28 TAKEOVERS ETC	
[Note: The Takeovers Directive (Interim Implementation) Regulations 2006, SI 2006/1183 are based on the provisions of this Part. So although the regulations came into force on 20 May 2006 and so before the date of Royal assent to the Companies Act 2006, they are not cited as origins for those provisions].	
Chapter 1 The Takeover Panel	
942(1)–(3)	new
943(1)–(9)	new
944(1)–(7)	new
945(1), (2)	new
946	new
947(1)–(10)	new
948(1)–(9)	new
949(1)–(3)	new
950(1), (2)	new
951(1)–(5)	new
952(1)–(8)	new
953(1)–(9)	new
954(1), (2)	new
955(1)–(4)	new
956(1)–(3)	new
957(1), (2)	new
958(1)–(8)	new
959	new
960	new
961(1)–(3)	new
962(1), (2)	new
963(1), (2)	new
964(1)–(6)	new
965	new
Chapter 2 Impediments to takeovers	
966(1)–(8)	new
967(1)–(7)	new
968(1)–(8)	new
969(1)–(3)	new
970(1)–(4)	new
971(1), (2)	new
972(1)–(4)	new
973	new
Chapter 3 "Squeeze-out" and "sell-out"	
974(1)–(3)	1985, s 428(1), drafting
(4), (5)	1985, s 428(2)
(6)	1985, s 428(2A)
(7)	1985, s 428(7)
975(1), (2)	1985, s 428(5) (changed)
(3)	1985, s 428(6) (changed)
(4)	1985, s 430E(1)
976(1)	1985, s 428(3)
(2)	new
(3)	1985, s 428(4)
977(1)	1985, s 429(8) (changed)
(2)	1985, s 430E(1) (changed)
(3)	drafting
978(1)–(3)	new

CA 2006	Origin
979(1), (2)	1985, s 429(1) (changed)
(3), (4)	1985, s 429(2) (changed)
(5)–(7)	new
(8)	1985, s 429(8) (changed)
(9)	1985, ss 429(8), 430E(2) (changed)
(10)	1985, s 429(8) (changed)
980(1)	1985, s 429(4)
(2)	1985, s 429(3) (changed)
(3)	new
(4)	1985, s 429(4)
(5)	1985, s 429(5)
(6)	1985, s 429(6)
(7)	1985, s 429(7)
(8)	1985, s 429(6), Sch 24
981(1)	1985, s 430(1)
(2)	1985, s 430(2)
(3)	1985, s 430(3)
(4)	1985, s 430(4)
(5)	1985, s 430(4) (changed)
(6)	1985, s 430(5), (8)
(7)	1985, s 430(6)
(8)	1985, s 430(7)
(9)	1985, s 430(9), drafting
982(1)	drafting
(2), (3)	1985, s 430(10)
(4), (5)	1985, s 430(11)
(6)	1985, s 430(12)
(7)	1985, s 430(13)
(8)	1985, s 430(14)
(9)	1985, s 430(15)
983(1)	1985, s 430A(1), (1A)
(2), (3)	1985, s 430A(1) (changed)
(4)	1985, s 430A(2) (changed)
(5)	1985, s 430A(2A)
(6), (7)	new
(8)	1985, s 430E(3)
984(1)	1985, s 430A(1)
(2)	1985, s 430A(4) (changed)
(3)	1985, s 430A(3)
(4)	1985, s 430A(5)
(5)	1985, s 430A(6)
(6)	1985, s 430A(7)
(7)	1985, s 430A(6), Sch 24
985(1)	1985, s 430B(1)
(2)	1985, s 430B(2)
(3)	1985, s 430B(3)
(4)	1985, s 430B(4)
(5)	1985, s 430B(4) (changed)
986(1)	1985, s 430C(1)
(2)	1985, s 430C(1), (2)
(3)	1985, s 430C(3)
(4)	new
(5)	1985, s 430C(4)
(6)–(8)	new

CA 2006	*Origin*
(9), (10)	1985, s 430C(5)
987(1)	1985, s 430D(1)
(2), (3)	1985, s 430D(2) (changed)
(4)	1985, s 430D(4) (changed)
(5), (6)	1985, s 430D(3)
(7)	1985, s 430D(4)
(8)	1985, s 430D(5)
(9)	1985, s 430D(6)
(10)	1985, s 430D(7)
988(1)	1985, s 430E(4), (8)
(2)	1985, s 430E(5)
(3)	1985, s 430E(6), (7)
(4)	1985, ss 204(2)(a), 430E(4)(d)
(5)	1985, ss 204(6), 430E(7)
(6)	1985, s 204(3)
(7)	1985, ss 204(5), 430E(7)
989(1)	1985, s 430F(1)
(2)	1985, s 430F(2)
990(1)–(3)	new
991(1)	1985, s 428(8) ("the company" and "the offeror"), new ("date of the offer", "non-voting shares", "voting rights" and "voting shares")
(2)	new
Chapter 4 Amendments to Part 7 of the Companies Act 1985	
992(1)–(6)	new (amends 1985 Pt 7)
PART 29 FRAUDULENT TRADING	
993(1)–(3)	1985, s 458, Sch 24
PART 30 PROTECTION OF MEMBERS AGAINST UNFAIR PREJUDICE	
994(1)	1985, s 459(1)
(2)	1985, s 459(2)
(3)	1985, s 459(3)
995(1)	1985, s 460(1A)
(2), (3)	1985, s 460(1)
(4)	1985, s 460(2)
996(1)	1985, s 461(1)
(2)	1985, s 461(2), (3)
997	1985, s 461(6)
998(1)–(4)	1985, s 461(5)
999(1)–(5)	new
PART 31 DISSOLUTION AND RESTORATION TO THE REGISTER	
Chapter 1 Striking off	
1000(1)	1985, s 652(1)
(2)	1985, s 652(2)
(3)	1985, s 652(3)
(4)–(6)	1985, s 652(5)
(7)	1985, s 652(6)
1001(1)	1985, s 652(4)
(2)–(4)	1985, s 652(5)
(5)	1985, s 652(6)
1002(1)–(3)	1985, s 652(7)
1003(1)	1985, s 652A(1) (changed)
(2)	1985, s 652A(2) (changed)

CA 2006	*Origin*
(3)	1985, s 652A(3)
(4)	1985, s 652A(4)
(5)	1985, s 652A(5)
(6)	1985, s 652A(6), (7)
1004(1)	1985, s 652B(1)
(2)	1985, s 652B(2)
(3)	1985, s 652B(9)
(4)	1985, s 652D(5)(c)
(5)	1985, s 652E(1)
(6)	1985, s 652E(3)
(7)	1985, s 652E(1), Sch 24
1005(1)	1985, s 652B(3)
(2)	1985, s 652B(4)
(3)	1985, s 652B(5)
(4)	1985, s 652E(1)
(5)	1985, s 652E(3)
(6)	1985, s 652E(1), Sch 24
1006(1)	1985, ss 652B(6), 652D(5)(c)
(2)	1985, s 652B(7)
(3)	1985, s 652B(8)
(4)	1985, s 652E(1), (2)
(5)	1985, s 652E(4)
(6)	1985, s 652E(1), Sch 24
(7)	1985, s 652E(2), Sch 24
1007(1)	1985, s 652C(1)
(2)	1985, ss 652C(2), 652D(5)(c)
(3)	1985, s 652C(3)
(4)	1985, s 652E(1), (2)
(5)	1985, s 652E(5)
(6)	1985, s 652E(1), Sch 24
(7)	1985, s 652E(2), Sch 24
1008(1), (2)	1985, s 652D(1)
(3)	1985, s 652D(2), (3)
(4)	1985, s 652D(4)
1009(1)	1985, s 652C(4)
(2)	1985, s 652C(5)
(3)	1985, s 652C(7)
(4)	1985, ss 652C(6), 652D(5)(c)
(5)	1985, s 652E(1)
(6)	1985, s 652E(5)
(7)	1985, s 652E(1), Sch 24
1010	1985, s 652D(6)
1011	1985, s 652D(8)
Chapter 2 Property of dissolved company	
1012(1)	1985, s 654(1)
(2)	1985, s 654(2)
1013(1)	1985, s 656(1)
(2)	1985, s 656(2) (changed)
(3)–(5)	1985, s 656(3) (changed)
(6), (7)	1985, s 656(5)
(8)	1985, s 656(6)
1014(1)	1985, s 657(1)
(2)	drafting
1015(1), (2)	1985, s 657(2), IA 1986, s 178(4)

CA 2006	Origin
1016(1)	1985, s 657(2), IA 1986, s 179(1)
(2)	1985, s 657(2), IA 1986, s 179(2)
(3)	drafting
1017(1)	1985, s 657(2), IA 1986, s 181(2), (3)
(2)	1985, s 657(2), IA 1986, s 181(3)
(3)	1985, s 657(2), IA 1986, s 181(4)
(4)	1985, s 657(2), IA 1986, s 181(3)
(5)	1985, s 657(2), IA 1986, s 181(6)
1018(1)	1985, s 657(2), IA 1986, s 182(1)
(2)	1985, s 657(2), IA 1986, s 182(2)
(3)	1985, s 657(2), IA 1986, s 182(4)
(4), (5)	1985, s 657(2), IA 1986, s 182(3)
1019	1985, s 657(2), IA 1986, s 180(1), (2)
1020(1), (2)	1985, s 657(4)
1021(1), (2)	1985, s 657(5)
(3)	1985, s 657(6)
1022(1)	1985, Sch 20, para 5
(2)	1985, Sch 20, para 6
(3)	1985, Sch 20, para 7
(4), (5)	1985, Sch 20, para 8
(6)	1985, Sch 20, para 9
1023(1)	1985, s 658(1), IA, s 180(1)
(2)	1985, s 658(1), IA, s 180(2)
(3)	1985, s 658(2)
Chapter 3 Restoration to the register	
1024(1)–(4)	new
1025(1)–(6)	new
1026(1)–(3)	new
1027(1)–(4)	new
1028(1)–(4)	new
1029(1), (2)	new
1030(1)–(6)	new
1031(1)–(4)	new
1032(1)–(5)	new
1033(1)–(7)	new
1034(1)	1985, s 655(1)
(2)	1985, s 655(2)
(3)	new
(4)	1985, s 655(3)
(5)	1985, s 655(4)
(6)	drafting
PART 32 COMPANY INVESTIGATIONS: AMENDMENTS	
1035(1)–(5)	new (inserts 1985, ss 446A and 446B; amends 1985 s, s 431, 432, 437 and 442)
1036	new (inserts 1985, ss 446C and 446D)
1037(1)–(3)	new (inserts 1985, s 446E; amends 1985, ss 451A and 452)
1038(1), (2)	new (amends 1985, ss 434 and 447)
1039	new (amends Company Directors Disqualification Act 1986, s 8)
PART 33 UK COMPANIES NOT FORMED UNDER THE COMPANIES LEGISLATION	
Chapter 1 Companies not formed under companies legislation but authorised to register	
1040(1)	1985, s 680(1)(a), (b), (1A), (2)
(2), (3)	1985, s 680(1) (closing words)
(4)	1985, s 680(3), (4)
(5)	1985, s 680(5)
(6)	1985, s 680(1) (closing words)
1041(1)	1985, s 683(1)
(2)	1985, s 683(2)
1042(1)–(3)	new
Chapter 2 Unregistered companies	
1043(1)	1985, s 718(1), (2)
(2)	1985, s 718(3) (changed)
(3)	1985, s 718(1) (changed)
(4)	1985, s 718(5)
(5)	1985, s 718(1), (3)
(6)	1985, s 718(6)
PART 34 OVERSEAS COMPANIES	
1044	1985, s 744 ("overseas company") (changed)
1045(1), (2)	1989, s 130(6)
1046(1)–(8)	new
1047(1)–(6)	new
1048(1), (2)	1985, s 694(4) (changed)
(3)–(5)	1985, s 694(5)
1049(1)–(4)	new
1050(1)–(6)	new
1051(1)–(5)	new
1052(1)–(6)	new
1053(1)–(6)	new
1054(1)–(4)	new
1055	new
1056	new
1057(1)–(3)	new
1058(1)–(4)	new
1059	1985, s 695A(4)
PART 35 THE REGISTRAR OF COMPANIES	
1060(1), (2)	1985, s 704(2)
(3)	1985, s 744 ("the registrar of companies" and "the registrar")
(4)	drafting
1061(1)–(3)	drafting
1062	1985, s 704(4) (changed)
1063(1)–(3)	1985, s 708(1) (changed)
(4)	1985, s 708(2), (3) (changed)
(5)	1985, s 708(5) (changed)
(6)	1985, s 708(4)

CA 2006	*Origin*
(7)	new
1064(1)–(3)	1985, s 711(1)(a) (changed)
1065	1985, s 710
1066(1)–(3)	1985, s 705(1)–(3)
(4), (5)	1985, s 705(4)
(6)	1985, s 705(5)(za)
1067(1)	1985, s 705A(1), (2) (changed)
(2)	1985, s 705A(3)
(3)	1985, s 705A(4)
(4), (5)	1985, s 705A(5)
1068(1)–(7)	new
1069(1)–(3)	new
1070(1)–(3)	new
1071(1), (2)	new
1072(1), (2)	new
1073(1)–(6)	new
1074(1)–(5)	new
1075(1)–(7)	new
1076(1)–(4)	new
1077(1)	1985, s 711(1) opening words
(2), (3)	new
1078(1)	drafting
(2), (3)	1985, s 711(1) (changed)
(4)	new
(5), (6)	new
1079(1)–(3)	1985, s 42(1)
(4)	1985, s 711(2) (changed)
1080(1), (2)	drafting
(3)	new
(4)	1985, s 707A(1)
(5)	new
1081(1)–(7)	new
1082(1)–(5)	new
1083(1)	1985, s 707A(2) (changed)
(2), (3)	new
1084(1)–(3)	1985, s 707A(3) (changed)
(4)	1985, s 707A(4)
(5)	1985, s 707A(3)
1085(1)	1985, s 709(1) opening words
(2)	1985, s 709(2) (changed)
(3)	drafting
1086(1)	1985, s 709(1)(a), (b)
(2)	new
(3)	drafting
1087(1)–(3)	new
1088(1)–(6)	new
1089(1), (2)	new
1090(1)–(4)	new
1091(1), (2)	new
(3)	1985, s 709(3)
(4)	new
(5)	1985, s 709(4)
1092(1), (2)	1985, s 709(5)
1093(1)–(4)	new
1094(1)–(5)	new
1095(1)–(6)	new

CA 2006	*Origin*
1096(1)–(6)	new
1097(1)–(5)	new
1098(1), (2)	new
1099(1)–(3)	1985, s 714(1) (changed)
(4), (5)	1985, s 714(2)
1100	1985, s 709(1) opening words
1101(1), (2)	new
1102(1)–(4)	new
1103(1), (2)	new
1104(1), (2)	1985, s 710B(1)–(3)
(3)	1985, s 710B(4)
(4)	1985, s 710B(5)
(5)	drafting
1105(1)–(3)	new
1106(1)–(6)	new
1107(1)	drafting
1107(2), (3)	new
1108(1)–(3)	new
1109(1), (2)	new
1110(1)–(3)	new
1111(1)–(3)	new
1112(1), (2)	new
1113(1)–(3)	1985, s 713(1)
(4), (5)	1985, s 713(2), (3)
1114(1)	1985, s 715A(1) "document", (2)
(2)	new
1115(1)	new
(2)	1985, s 710A(2)
1116(1)–(6)	new
1117(1)–(3)	new
1118	drafting
1119(1), (2)	1985, s 704(7), (8)
(3)	new
1120	new
PART 36 OFFENCES UNDER THE COMPANIES ACTS	
1121(1)	1985, s 730(5)
(2)	1985, s 744 "officer"
(3)	1985, s 730(5) (changed)
1122(1)–(3)	new
1123(1)–(4)	new
1124 and Sch 3	new (amend 1985 Act)
1125(1)	drafting
(2)	1985, s 730(4)
1126(1)	1985, s 732(1)
(2)	1985, s 732(2) (changed)
(3)	1986 art 680(2) (changed)
1127(1), (2)	1985, s 731(1)
1128(1)	1985, s 731(2)
(2)	1985, s 731(3)
(3)	1986 art 679(2)
(4)	1985, s 731(4), 1986 art 679(3)
1129	1985, s 732(3) (changed)
1130(1)	1985, s 734(1) (changed)
(2)	1985, s 734(1), (3), (4)
(3)	1985, s 734(2)

CA 2006	Origin
1131(1), (2)	new
1132(1), (2)	1985, s 721(1)
(3)–(5)	1985, s 721(2)–(4)
(6)	drafting
1133	new
PART 37 COMPANIES: SUPPLEMENTARY PROVISIONS	
1134	1985, s 722(1) (changed)
1135(1)	1985, ss 722(1), 723(1) (changed)
(2)	new
(3), (4)	new
(5)	1985, s 723(2)
1136(1)–(7)	new
1137(1), (2)	1985, s 723A(1)
(3)	1985, s 723A(2), (3)
(4)	1985, s 723A(4)
(5), (6)	1985, s 723A(6), (7)
1138(1)	1985, s 722(2)
(2), (3)	1985, s 722(3), Sch 24
(4)	new
1139(1)	1985, s 725(1)
(2)	1985, s 695(1), (2) (changed)
(3)	new
(4)	1985, s 725(2), (3)
(5)	drafting
1140(1)–(8)	new
1141(1)	drafting
(2), (3)	new
1142	new
1143(1)–(4), Schs 4 and 5	new
1144(1)–(3)	new
1145(1)–(5)	new
1146(1)–(4)	new
1147(1)–(6)	new
1148(1)–(3)	new
1149	drafting
1150(1)	1985, s 108(1) (changed)
(2), (3)	1985, s 108(2), (3)
(4)	1985, s 108(5)
1151(1)–(4)	new
1152(1)–(6)	new
1153(1)	1985, s 110(1)
(2), (3)	1985, s 110(2), (3)
(4)	1985, s 110(2), Sch 24
1154(1)–(4)	new
1155(1), (2)	new
1156(1)–(3)	1985, s 744 "the court", IA 1986, s 117 (changed)
1157(1)–(3)	1985, s 727(1)–(3)
PART 38 COMPANIES: INTERPRETATION	
1158	drafting
1159(1), (2)	1985, s 736(1), (2)
(3) and Sch 6	1985, s 736A(1)–(11)
(4)	1985, ss 736(3), 736A(12)
1160(1)	1985, s 736B(1)

CA 2006	Origin
(2)–(4)	1985, s 736B(3)–(5)
1161(1)–(5)	1985, s 259(1)–(5)
1162(1)–(5)	1985, s 258(1)–(5)
(6) and Sch 7	1985, s 258(6) and Sch 10A
1163(1), (2)	1985, s 739(1), (2)
1164(1)–(3)	1985, s 742B(1)–(3)
(4)	1985, s 255A(4)
(5)	1985, s 255A(5A)
1165(1)	drafting
(2)–(4)	1985, s 742C(1)–(4)
(5)	1985, s 255A(5)
(6)	1985, s 255A(5A)
(7)	1985, s 744 "insurance market activity"
(8)	1985, s 742C(5)
1166	1985, s 743
1167	1985, s 744 "prescribed"
1168(1)–(7)	new
1169(1)	1985, s 249AA(4)
(2), (3)	1985, s 249AA(5)–(7)
(4)	drafting
1170	1985, s 744 "EEA State", drafting
1171 "the former Companies Acts"	1985, s 735(1)(c) (changed)
"the Joint Stock Companies Acts"	1985, s 735(3)
1172	drafting
1173(1) "body corporate" and "corporation"	new
"credit institution"	1985, s 262 "credit institution" (changed)
"financial institution"	1985, s 699A(3) "financial institution"
"firm"	new
"the Gazette"	1985, s 744 "the Gazette"
"hire-purchase agreement"	1985, s 744 "hire purchase agreement"
"officer"	1985, s 744 "officer"
"parent company"	1985, ss 258(1) and 742(1)
"regulated activity"	1985, s 744 "regulated activity"
"regulated market"	1985 passim (changed)
"working day"	drafting
(2)	drafting
1174 and Sch 8	drafting
PART 39 COMPANIES: MINOR AMENDMENTS	
1175(1), (2), Sch 9	new (amend 1985, Pt 7 and 1986, Pt 8)
1176(1)–(3)	new (repeals 1985, s 438, amends 1985, ss 439 and 453)
1177	new (repeals 1985, ss 311, 323 and 327, 324–326, 328, 329, Pts 2–4 of Sch 13 and ss 343 and 344)
1178	new (repeals 1985, s 720 and Sch 23)
1179	new (repeals 1985, s 729)
1180	new (repeals 1985, Pt 4)
1181(1)–(4)	new (power to amend)

TABLES OF DESTINATIONS (COMPANIES ACTS 1985 AND 1989)

[3.9]

NOTES

(1) The table identifies the provisions of the Companies Act 1985 (c 6) that are repealed and re-enacted (with or without changes) by the Companies Act 2006 and identifies the corresponding provisions in that Act.

(2) The table is based on the table of origins. So it only shows a provision of the Companies Act 2006 as a destination of a provision of the Companies Act 1985 if the latter is cited in that table as an origin for the new provision.

(3) A repealed provision of the Companies Act 1985 may not be listed in this table because the provision is spent or it is otherwise unnecessary to re-enact it, because the new provision is fundamentally different from the existing provision or because as a matter of policy it has been decided to repeal the existing provision without replacing it.

(4) There is no entry for Schedule 24 to the Companies Act 1985 (punishment of offences) in the table. This is cited in the table of origins as the origin for a large number of provisions in the Companies Act 2006.

(5) A section at the end of the table identifies the substantive provisions of the Companies Act 1989 (c 40) that are repealed and re-enacted by the Companies Act 2006.

COMPANIES ACT 1985

CA 1985	*CA 2006*
1 Mode of forming incorporated company	
(1)	s 7(1), (2) (changed)
(2)	s 3(1)–(4)
(3)	s 4(1)–(3)
(4)	s 5(1), (2)
2 Requirements with respect to memorandum	
(1)	s 9(2)
(2)	ss 9(2), 88(2)
(3)	s 9(2) (changed)
(4)	s 11(3) (changed)
3 Forms of memorandum	
(1)	s 8(2)
7 Articles prescribing regulations for companies	
(1)	s 18(2) (changed)
(3)	s 18(3) (changed)
8 Tables A, C, D and E	
(1)	s 19(1)–(3) (changed)
(2)	s 20(1), (2) (changed)
(3)	s 19(4)
(4)	s 19(1)–(3) (changed)
(5)	s 19(5)
9 Alteration of articles by special resolution	
(1), (2)	s 21(1)
10 Documents to be sent to registrar	
(1)	s 9(1), (5), (6) (changed)
(2)	s 12(1) (changed)
(3)	s 12(3)
(4)	s 9(3)
(6)	s 9(5)
12 Duty of registrar	
(1), (2)	s 14
(3), (3A)	s 13(1), (2) (changed)
13 Effect of registration	
(1)	s 15(1)
(2)	s 15(3)
(3)	s 16(2) (changed)
(4)	s 16(3)
(5)	s 16(6)
(7)	s 15(4)
14 Effect of memorandum and articles	
(1)	s 33(1) (changed)
(2)	s 33(2) (changed)
15 Memorandum and articles of company limited by guarantee	
(1)	s 37
(2)	s 5(3)
16 Effect of alteration on company's members	
(1)	s 25(1)
(2)	s 25(2)
18 Amendments of memorandum or articles to be registered	
(1)	s 34(2) (changed)
(2)	ss 26(1), 34(3) (changed)
(3)	ss 26(3), (4), 34(5), (6)
19 Copies of memorandum and articles to be given to members	
(1)	s 32(1) (changed)
(2)	s 32(3), (4) (changed)
22 Definition of "member"	
(1)	s 112(1) (changed)
(2)	s 112(2)
23 Membership of holding company	
(1)	s 136(1)
(2)	s 138(1), (2)
(3)	s 141(1), (2)
(3A)	s 141(3)
(3B)	s 141(4)
(3BA)	s 141(5)
(3C)	s 142(1), (2)
(4), (5)	s 137(1), (2)
(6)	s 137(3), (4)
(7)	s 144
(8)	s 143
25 Name as stated in memorandum	
(1)	s 58(1), (2)
(2)	s 59(1), (2), (3)
26 Prohibition on registration of certain names	
(1)	ss 53, 65(1)–(5), 66(1) (changed)
(2)	ss 54(1)–(3) and 55(1) (changed)
(3)	s 66(2), (3) (changed)
27 Alternatives of statutory designations	
(4)	ss 58(1), (2), 59(1), (2)

Part 3 CA 2006 Supporting Materials

CA 1985	CA 2006
28 Change of name	
(1)	s 77(1)
(2)	ss 67(1), 68(2), (3)
(3)	s 75(1), (2), (4)
(4)	ss 68(3), 75(3)
(5)	ss 68(5), (6), 75(5), (6)
(6)	ss 80(1)–(3), 81(1)
(7)	s 81(2), (3)
29 Regulations about names	
(1)	ss 55(1), 56(1)
(2)	s 56(2)
(3)	s 56(3), (4) (changed)
(6)	s 55(2)
30 Exemption from requirement of "limited" as part of the name	
(2), (3)	ss 61(1)–(4), 62(1)–(3) (changed)
(4)	s 60(3)
(5B)	s 60(2)
31 Provisions applying to company exempt under s 30	
(1)	s 63(1)
(2)	s 64(1)–(4) (changed)
(3)	s 64(7)
(5)	s 63(2), (3)
(6)	s 64(5), (6)
32 Power to require company to abandon misleading name	
(1)	s 76(1)
(2)	s 76(3)
(3)	s 76(4), (5)
(4)	s 76(6), (7) (changed)
(5)	ss 80(1)–(3), 81(1)
(6)	s 81(2), (3)
35 A company's capacity not limited by its memorandum	
(1)	s 39(1) (changed)
(4)	s 39(2)
35A Power of directors to bind the company	
(1)	s 40(1)
(2)	s 40(2)
(3)	s 40(3)
(4)	s 40(4)
(5)	s 40(5)
(6)	s 40(6)
35B No duty to enquire as to capacity of company or authority of directors	
	s 40(2)
36 Company contracts: England and Wales	
(1), (2)	s 43(1), (2)
36A Execution of documents: England and Wales	
(2)	ss 44(1)
(3)	s 45(1)
(4)	s 44(2), (3), (4)
(4A)	s 44(6)
(6)	s 44(5)
(7)	s 44(8)
(8)	s 44(7)
36AA Execution of deeds: England and Wales	
(1)	s 46(1)
(2)	s 46(2)
36B Execution of documents by companies	
(1)	s 48(2)
(2)	s 48(3)
36C Pre-incorporation contracts, deeds and obligations	
(1)	s 51(1)
(2)	s 51(2)
37 Bills of exchange and promissory notes	
	s 52
38 Execution of deeds abroad	
(1)	s 47(1) (changed)
(2)	s 47(2)
(3)	s 47(1)
39 Power of company to have official seal for use abroad	
(1)	s 49(1), (2) (changed)
(2), (2A)	s 49(3)
(3)	s 49(4)
(4)	s 49(5)
(5)	s 49(6)
40 Official seal for share certificates, etc	
(1)	s 50(1), (2)
42 Events affecting a company's status	
(1)	s 1079(1)–(3)
43 Re-registration of private company as public	
(1)	s 90(1), (2) (changed)
(2)	s 90(3)
(3)	ss 92(1), (2), 94(2), (3)
(4)	s 92(1)
44 Consideration for shares recently allotted to be valued	
(1)	s 93(1)
(2)	s 93(2), (7)
(4), (5)	s 93(3)–(5)
(6)	s 93(6)
(7)	s 93(6), (7)
45 Additional requirements relating to share capital	
(1)–(4)	s 91(1)
46 Meaning of "unqualified report" in s 43(3)	
(2)	s 92(3)
(3)	s 92(4)
(4)	s 92(5), (6)
47 Certificate of re-registration under s 43	
(1)	s 96(1), (2)
(2)	s 94(4)
(3)	s 91(5) (changed)
(4)	s 96(4)
(5)	s 96(5)
48 Modification for unlimited company re-registering	
(1), (2)	s 90(4)
(5)	s 91(2)
(6)	s 91(3)
(7)	s 91(4)

CA 1985	*CA 2006*
49 Re-registration of limited company as unlimited	
(1)	s 102(1)
(2)	s 102(2)
(4)	s 102(1)
(5)–(7)	s 102(3)
(8)	ss 102(1), 103(2)–(4) (changed)
(8A)	s 103(3), (4) (changed)
(9)	s 102(4)
50 Certificate of re-registration under s 49	
(1)	s 104(1), (2)
(2)	s 104(4)
(3)	s 104(5)
51 Re-registration of unlimited company as limited	
(1)	s 105(1) (changed)
(2)	s 105(2)
(3)	s 105(3), (4)
(5)	s 106(2)
52 Certificate of re-registration under s 51	
(1)	s 107(1), (2)
(2)	s 107(4)
(3)	s 107(5)
53 Re-registration of public company as private	
(1)	ss 97(1), 100(2) (changed)
(2)	s 97(3)
54 Litigated objection to resolution under s 53	
(1)	s 98(1)
(2)	ss 98(1), 370(3) (changed)
(3)	s 98(2)
(4)	s 99(1), (2) (changed)
(5)	s 98(3), (4)
(6)	s 98(5), (6)
(7)	s 99(3)
(8)	s 98(6)
(10)	s 99(4), (5)
55 Certificate of re-registration under s 53	
(1)	s 101(1), (2)
(2)	s 101(4)
(3)	s 101(5)
58 Document offering shares etc for sale deemed a prospectus	
(3)	s 755(2)
80 Authority of company required for certain allotments	
(1)	s 549(1),s 551(1) (changed)
(2)	ss 549(1)–(3), 551(1), 559
(3)	s 551(2)
(4)	s 551(3), (4)
(5)	s 551(5)
(6)	s 551(6)
(7)	s 551(7)
(8)	s 551(8)
(9)	s 549(4), (5)
(10)	s 549(6) (changed)
81 Restriction on public offers by private company	
(1)	s 755(1)
(3)	s 760

CA 1985	*CA 2006*
84 Allotment where issue not fully subscribed	
(1)	s 578(1)
(2)	s 578(2)
(3)	s 578(3) (changed)
(4)	s 578(4), (5)
(5)	s 578(5)
(6)	s 578(6)
85 Effect of irregular allotment	
(1)	s 579(1), (2)
(2)	s 579(3)
(3)	s 579(4)
88 Return as to allotments, etc	
(1)	s 555(1)
(2)	s 555(2) (changed)
(5)	s 557(1), (2)
(6)	ss 557(3), 597(5), (6)
89 Offers to shareholders to be on pre-emptive basis	
(1)	s 561(1)
(2)	s 568(1)
(3)	s 568(1), (2)
(4)	ss 561(2), 565
(5)	s 566
(6)	s 561(4)
90 Communication of pre-emption offers to shareholders	
(1)	s 562(1)
(2)	s 568(3)
(5)	s 562(3) (changed)
(6)	s 562(4), (5) (changed)
91 Exclusion of ss 89, 90 by private company	
(1)	s 567(1), (2)
(2)	s 567(3), (4)
92 Consequences of contravening ss 89, 90	
(1)	ss 563(1), (2), 568(4)
(2)	ss 563(3), 568(5)
93 Saving for other restrictions as to offers	
(1)	s 575(1)
(2)	s 575(2)
94 Definitions for ss 89–96	
(2)	ss 560(1), 564, 577
(3)	ss 560(2), 561(3)
(3A)	s 560(2)
(5)	s 560(1)
(7)	s 574(1), (2)
95 Disapplication of pre-emption rights	
(1)	ss 570(1), (2), 573(2), (3), (5)
(2)	ss 571(1), (2), 573(4)
(2A)	s 573(1)–(5l)
(3)	ss 570(3), 571(3)
(4)	ss 570(4), 571(4), 573(3), (5)
(5)	ss 571(5)–(7), 573(5) (changed)
(6)	s 572(1)–(3)
96 Saving for company's pre-emption procedure operative before 1982	
(1), (2)	s 576(1)
(3)	s 576(2)

CA 1985	*CA 2006*
(4)	s 576(3)
97 Power of company to pay commissions	
(1)	s 553(1)
(2)	s 553(2)
98 Apart from s 97, commissions and discounts barred	
(1)	s 552(1)
(2)	s 552(2)
(3)	s 552(3)
(4)	s 553(3)
99 General rules as to payment for shares on allotment	
(1)	s 582(1), (3)
(2)	s 585(1)
(3)	s 585(2)
(4)	s 582(2)
(5)	s 585(3)
100 Prohibition on allotment of shares at a discount	
(1)	s 580(1)
(2)	s 580(2)
101 Shares to be allotted as at least one-quarter paid-up	
(1)	s 586(1)
(2)	s 586(2)
(3), (4)	s 586(3)
(5)	s 586(4)
102 Restriction on payment by long-term undertaking	
(1)	s 587(1)
(2)	s 587(2)
(3), (4)	s 587(3)
(5), (6)	s 587(4)
(7)	s 587(5)
103 Non-cash consideration to be valued before allotment	
(1)	s 593(1)
(2)	s 593(2)
(3)	s 594(1)–(3)
(4)	s 594(4), (5)
(5)	s 595(1), (2)
(6)	s 593(3)
(7)	ss 594(6), 595(3)
104 Transfer to public company of non-cash asset in initial period	
(1)	s 598(1)
(2)	s 598(2)
(3)	s 603
(4)	ss 599(1), (3), 601(1)–(3) (changed)
(5)	s 599(2), (4)
(6)	s 598(4), (5)
105 Agreements contravening s 104	
(1)	s 604(1)
(2)	s 604(2)
(3)	s 604(3)
106 Shares issued to subscribers of memorandum	
	s 584
107 Meaning of "the appropriate rate"	
	ss 592(1), (2), 609(1), (2)
108 Valuation and report (s 103)	

CA 1985	*CA 2006*
(1)	s 1150(1) (changed)
(2)	s 1150(2)
(3)	s 1150(3)
(4)	s 596(2)
(5)	s 1150(4)
(6)	ss 596(3), 600(3)
(7)	s 596(4), (5)
109 Valuation and report (s 104)	
(2)	s 600(2), (3)
(3)	s 600(4), (5)
110 Entitlement of valuer to full disclosure	
(1)	s 1153(1)
(2)	s 1153(2), (4)
(3)	s 1153(3)
111 Matters to be communicated to registrar	
(1)	s 597(1), (2)
(2)	s 602(1)
(3)	s 597(3)–(6)
(4)	s 602(2), (3)
111A Right to damages, &c not affected	
	s 655
112 Liability of subsequent holders of shares allotted	
(1)	ss 588(1), 605(1)
(2)	s 605(2)
(3)	ss 588(2), 605(3)
(4)	ss 588(3), 605(4)
(5)	s 588(1), (4)
113 Relief in respect of certain liabilities under ss 99 ff	
(1)	ss 589(1), (2), 606(1)
(2)	ss 589(3), 606(2) (changed)
(3)	ss 589(3), 606(2)
(4)	ss 589(4), 606(3)
(5)	ss 589(5), 606(4)
(6), (7)	ss 589(6), 606(5)
(8)	s 606(6)
114 Penalty for contravention	
	ss 590(1), (2), 607(2), (3)
115 Undertakings to do work, etc	
(1)	ss 591(1), (2), 608(1), (2)
117 Public company share capital requirements	
(1)	s 761(1)
(2)	s 761(2) (changed)
(3)	s 762(1) (changed)
(4)	s 761(3)
(5)	s 762(3)
(6)	s 761(4) (changed)
(7)	s 767(1), (2)
(8)	s 767(3)
118 The authorised minimum	
(1)	ss 763(1), 764(1) (changed)
(2)	s 764(3)
(3)	s 764(4)
119 Provision for different amounts to be paid on shares	
	s 581

CA 1985	CA 2006
121 Alteration of share capital (limited companies)	
(1)	s 617(1) (changed)
(2)	ss 617(2), (3), 618(1), 620(1) (changed)
(3)	s 618(2)
(4)	ss 618(3), 620(2) (changed)
122 Notice to registrar of alteration	
(1)	ss 619(1)–(3), 621(1), 663(1), 689(1) (changed)
(2)	ss 619(4), (5), 621(4), (5), 663(4), (5), 689(4), (5)
125 Variation of class rights	
(1)	s 630(1)
(2)	s 630(2)–(4) (changed)
(6)	ss 334(1)–(4), (6) (changed)
(7)	ss 334(7), 630(5)
(8)	s 630(6)
126 Saving for court's powers under other provisions	
	s 632
127 Shareholders' right to object to variation	
(1)	s 633(1)
(2)	s 633(2), (3)
(2A)	s 633(2)
(3)	s 633(4)
(4)	s 633(5)
(5)	s 635(1)–(3)
(6)	s 633(6)
128 Registration of particulars of special rights	
(1)	s 556(1)–(3) (changed)
(2)	ss 556(1), (4), 629(2)
(3)	s 637(1) (changed)
(4)	s 636(1) (changed)
(5)	ss 557(1), (2), 636(2), (3), 637(2), (3) (changed)
129 Registration of newly created class rights	
(1)	s 638(1) (changed)
(2)	s 640(1) (changed)
(3)	s 639(1) (changed)
(4)	ss 638(2), (3), 639(2), (3), 640(2), (3)
130 Application of share premiums	
(1)	s 610(1)
(2)	s 610(2), (2) (changed)
(3)	s 610(4)
(4)	s 610(5), (6)
131 Merger relief	
(1)	s 612(1), (4)
(2)	s 612(2)
(3)	s 612(3)
(4)	s 613(2), (3)
(5)	s 613(4)
(6)	s 613(5)
(7)	s 616(1)
132 Relief in respect of group reconstructions	
(1)	s 611(1)
(2)	s 611(2)
(3)	s 611(3)
(4)	s 611(4)
(5)	s 611(5)
(8)	s 612(4)
133 Provisions supplementing ss 131, 132	
(1)	s 615
(2)	s 616(2)
(3)	s 616(3)
(4)	s 616(1)
134 Provision for extending or restricting relief from s 130	
(1)	s 614(1)
(3)	s 614(2)
135 Special resolution for reduction of share capital	
(1)	s 641(1)–(3) (changed)
(2)	s 641(4)
136 Application to court for order of confirmation	
(1)	s 645(1)
(2)	ss 645(2), (4), 646(4)
(3)	s 646(1)
(4)	s 646(2), (3)
(5)	s 646(4), (5)
(6)	s 645(2), (3)
137 Court order confirming reduction	
(1)	s 648(1), (2)
(2)	s 648(3), (4)
(3)	s 648(4)
138 Registration of order and minute of reduction	
(1)	s 649(1) (changed)
(2)	s 649(3) (changed)
(3)	s 649(4) (changed)
(4)	s 649(5), (6) (changed)
139 Public company reducing capital below authorised minimum	
(1)	s 650(1)
(2)	s 650(2)
(3)	s 651(1), (2)
(4)	s 651(3) (changed)
(5)	s 651(4), (6), (7)
140 Liability of members on reduced shares	
(1)	s 652(1) (changed)
(2)	s 653(1)
(3)	s 653(2)
(4)	s 653(3)
(5)	s 653(3)
141 Penalty for concealing name of creditor, etc	
	s 647(1), (2) (changed)
142 Duty of directors on serious loss of capital	
(1)	s 656(1)–(3)
(2)	s 656(4), (5) (changed)
(3)	s 656(6)
143 General rule against company acquiring own shares	
(1)	s 658(1)
(2)	s 658(2), (3)
(2A)	s 725(4)
(3)	s 659(1), (2)

Part 3 CA 2006 Supporting Materials

CA 1985	*CA 2006*
144 Acquisition of shares by company's nominee	
(1)	s 660(1), (2) (changed)
(2)	s 661(1), (2) (changed)
(3)	s 661(3)
(4)	s 661(4)
145 Exceptions from s 144	
(1)	s 660(3)
(2)	ss 660(3), 661(5)
(3)	s 671
146 Treatment of shares held by or for public company	
(1)	ss 662(1), 671
(2)	s 662(2), (3)
(3)	s 662(3)
(4)	s 662(5), (6)
147 Matters arising out of compliance with s 146(2)	
(2)	s 664(1), (2)
(3)	s 664(4) (changed)
(4)	s 665(1), (2), (4), (5) (changed)
148 Further provisions supplementing ss 146, 147	
(1)	s 668(1), (2)
(2)	s 668(3)
(3)	s 671
(4)	s 669(1), (2)
149 Sanctions for non-compliance	
(1)	s 666(1), (2)
(2)	s 667(1)–(3)
150 Charges of public companies on own shares	
(1)	s 670(1)
(2)	s 670(2)
(3)	s 670(3)
(4)	s 670(4)
151 Financial assistance generally prohibited	
(1)	ss 678(1), 679(1) (changed)
(2)	ss 678(3), 679(3) (changed)
(3)	s 680(1), (2)
152 Definitions for this Chapter	
(1)	ss 677(1), 683(1)
(2)	s 677(2), (3)
(3)	s 683(2)
153 Transactions not prohibited by s 151	
(1)	ss 678(2), 679(2) (changed)
(2)	ss 678(4), 679(4)
(3)	s 681(1), (2)
(4)	s 682(1), (2)
(5)	s 682(5)
154 Special restriction for public companies	
(1)	s 682(1)
(2)	ss 682(3), (4), 840(4), (5)
159 Power to issue redeemable shares	
(1)	s 684(1), (3) (changed)
(2)	s 684(4)
(3)	ss 686(1)–(3) (changed), 691(1), (2)
160 Financing etc of redemption	
(1)	ss 687(1)–(3), (6), 692(1), (2), (5)

CA 1985	*CA 2006*
(2)	ss 687(4), (5), 692(3), (4)
(4)	ss 688, 706 (changed)
162 Power of company to purchase own shares	
(1)	s 690(1) (changed)
(2)	ss 691(1), (2), 692(1)–(5)
(2A)	s 706
(2B)	ss 706, 724(1)
(3)	s 690(2)
(4)	s 724(2)
162A Treasury shares	
(1)	s 724(3)
(2)	s 724(4)
(3)	s 724(5)
162B Treasury shares: maximum holdings	
(1)	s 725(1)
(2)	s 725(2)
(3)	s 725(4)
162C Treasury shares: voting and other rights	
(1)	s 726(1)
(2), (3)	s 726(2)
(4)	s 726(3)
(5)	s 726(4)
(6)	s 726(5)
162D Treasury shares: disposal and cancellation	
(1)	ss 727(1), 729(1)
(2)	s 727(2) (changed)
(3)	s 727(3)
(4)	s 729(4)
(5)	s 729(5)
162E Treasury shares: mandatory cancellation	
(1)	s 729(2)
(2)	s 729(3)
162F Treasury shares: proceeds of sale	
(1)	s 731(1)
(2)	s 731(2)
(3)	s 731(3)
(4), (5)	s 731(4)
162G Treasury shares: penalty for contravention	
	s 732(1), (2) (changed)
163 Definitions of "off-market" and "market" purchase	
(1)	s 693(2)
(2)	s 693(3)
(3)	s 693(4)
(4), (5)	s 693(5)
164 Authority for off-market purchase	
(1)	ss 693(1), 694(1)
(2)	s 694(2) (changed)
(3)	ss 694(4), 697(3), 700(3)
(4)	ss 694(5), 697(4), 700(4)
(5)	ss 694(1), (3), (4), 698(1), (3), (4), 700(5)
(6)	ss 696(1)–(5), 699(1)–(6), 700(5) (changed)
(7)	ss 697(1)–(4), 698(1), (3), (4), 699(1)–(6), 700(3)–(5)

CA 1985	CA 2006
165 Authority for contingent purchase contract	
(1)	s 694(3)
(2)	ss 694(2), (4), (5), 695(1), (3), (5), 696(1)–(5)
166 Authority for market purchase	
(1)	ss 693(1), 701(1)
(2)	s 701(2)
(3)	s 701(3), (5)
(4)	s 701(4), (5)
(5)	s 701(6)
(6)	s 701(7)
(7)	s 701(8)
167 Assignment or release of company's right to purchase own shares	
(1)	s 704
(2)	s 700(1)–(5)
168 Payments apart from purchase price to be made out of distributable profits	
(1)	s 705(1)
(2)	s 705(2)
169 Disclosure by company of purchase of own shares	
(1)	ss 707(1)–(3), 708(1) (changed)
(1A)	ss 707(1)–(3), 708(1) (changed)
(1B)	ss 707(1)–(3), 708(1) (changed)
(2)	s 707(4)
(3)	s 707(5)
(4)	s 702(1)–(4) (changed)
(5)	s 702(6)
(6)	ss 707(6), (7), 708(4), (5)
(7)	s 703(1), (2) (changed)
(8)	s 703(3)
(9)	s 702(7)
169A Disclosure by company of cancellation or disposal of treasury shares	
(1)	ss 728(1), 730(1)
(2)	ss 728(2), 730(2)
(3)	ss 728(3), 730(3)
(4)	ss 728(4), (5), 730(6), (7)
170 The capital redemption reserve	
(1)	s 733(1), (2), (4)
(2), (3)	s 733(3)
(4)	s 733(5), (6)
171 Power of private companies to redeem or purchase own shares out of capital	
(1)	s 709(1) (changed)
(2)	s 709(2)
(3)	s 710(1), (2)
(4)	s 734(2)
(5)	s 734(3)
(6)	s 734(4)
172 Availability of profits for purposes of s 171	
(1)	s 711(1), (2)
(2)	s 712(2)
(3)	s 712(6)
(4)	s 712(3)
(5)	s 712(4)
(6)	s 712(7)
173 Conditions for payment out of capital	
(1)	s 713(1), (2)
(2)	s 716(1)
(3)	s 714(1)–(3)
(4)	s 714(4) (changed)
(5)	s 714(5), (6) (changed)
(6)	s 715(1), (2)
174 Procedure for special resolution under s 173	
(1)	ss 716(2), 723(1)
(2)	s 717(3)
(3)	s 717(4)
(4)	s 718(2), (3) (changed)
(5)	s 717(5)
175 Publicity for proposed payment out of capital	
(1)	s 719(1)
(2)	s 719(2)
(3)	s 719(3)
(4)	ss 719(4), 720(1)
(5)	s 719(4)
(6)	s 720(1), (2), (4) (changed)
(7)	s 720(5), (6)
(8)	s 720(7)
176 Objections by company's members or creditors	
(1)	s 721(1), (2)
(2)	s 721(2)
(3)	s 722(2), (3)
(4)	s 722(4), (5)
177 Powers of court on application under s 176	
(1)	s 721(3)
(2)	s 721(4), (5)
(3)	s 721(6)
(4)	s 721(7)
178 Effect of company's failure to redeem or purchase	
(1)	s 735(1)
(2)	s 735(2)
(3)	s 735(2), (3)
(4)	s 735(4)
(5)	s 735(5)
(6)	s 735(6)
181 Definitions for Chapter VII	
	s 736
182 Nature, transfer and numbering of shares	
(1)	ss 541, 544(1), (2)
(2)	s 543(1), (2)
183 Transfer and registration	
(1)	s 770(1)
(2)	s 770(2)
(3)	s 773
(4)	s 772
184 Certification of transfers	
(1)	s 775(1), (2)
(2)	s 775(3)
(3)	s 775(4)
185 Duty of company as to issue of certificates	
(1)	ss 769(1), (2), 776(1), (3)

CA 1985	CA 2006
(2)	s 776(2)
(3)	s 777(1), (2)
(4)	ss 769(2), 776(3), 778(1)
(4A)	s 778(1)
(4B), (4C)	s 778(2)
(4D)	s 778(3)
(5)	ss 769(3), (4), 776(5), (6)
(6)	s 782(1)
(7)	s 782(2), (3)
186 Certificate to be evidence of title	
(1)	s 768(1), (2)
(2)	s 768(2)
187 Evidence of grant of probate or confirmation as executor	
	s 774
188 Issue and effect of share warrant to bearer	
(1)	s 779(1)
(2)	s 779(2)
(3)	s 779(3)
189 Offences in connections with share warrants (Scotland)	
(1)	s 781(1), (3)
(2)	s 781(2), (4)
190 Register of debenture holders	
(1)	s 743(6)
(5)	s 743(2), (6) (changed)
(6)	s 743(3)
191 Right to inspect register	
(1)	s 744(1)
(2)	s 744(2)
(3)	s 749(1)
(4)	ss 746(1), (2), 749(2), (3)
(5)	ss 746(3), 749(4)
(6)	s 744(5)
(7)	s 748(1), (2) (changed)
192 Liability of trustees of debentures	
(1)	s 750(1), (3)
(2)	s 750(2)
(3)	s 751(1), (2)
(4)	s 751(3), (4)
193 Perpetual debentures	
	s 739(1), (2)
194 Power to re-issue redeemed debentures	
(1)	s 752(1)
(2)	s 752(2)
(3)	s 753
(4)	s 752(3)
(5)	s 752(4)
195 Contract to subscribe for debentures	
	s 740
196 Payment of debts out of assets subject to floating charge (England and Wales)	
(1)	s 754(1)
(2)	s 754(2)
(3)	s 754(3)
(4)	s 754(4)
197 Debentures to bearer (Scotland)	

CA 1985	CA 2006
	s 742
198 Obligation of disclosure: the cases in which it may arise and "the relevant time"	
(2)	s 792(1), (2) (changed)
203 Notification of family and corporate interests	
(1)	s 822(1), (2)
(2)	s 823(1)
(3)	s 832(2)
(4)	s 823(3)
204 Agreement to acquire interests in a particular company	
(1)	s 824(1)
(2)	ss 824(1), (2), 988(4)
(3)	ss 824(3), 988(6)
(4)	s 824(4)
(5)	ss 824(5), 988(7)
(6)	ss 824(6), 988(5)
205 Obligation of disclosure arising under s 204	
(1)	s 825(1)
(2)	s 825(2)
(3)	s 825(3)
(4)	s 825(4)
207 Interests in shares by attribution	
(1)	ss 783, 785(1)
(2)	s 785(2)
(3)	s 785(3)
(4)	s 785(4)
(5)	s 785(5)
(6)	s 785(6)
(7)	s 788
(9)	s 784(3)
(10)	s 783
208 Interests in shares which are to be notified	
(1)	s 820(1)
(2)	s 820(2)
(3)	s 820(3)
(4)	s 820(4)
(5)	s 820(6)
(6)	s 820(5)
(7)	s 820(7)
(8)	s 820(8)
210A Power to make further provision by regulations	
(1)	s 828(1), (2)
(5)	s 828(3)
211 Register of interests in shares	
(3)	s 808(2)
(4)	s 808(7)
(5)	s 808(4)
(6)	s 810(1)–(3)
(7)	s 819(1)
(8)	ss 809(1), 810(4), 811(1), (2), 813(1)–(3) (changed)
(9)	s 826(1)
(10)	ss 808(5), (6), 819(2), (3)
212 Company investigations	
(1)	s 793(1), (2) (changed)
(2)	s 793(3), (4), (6)

CA 1985	CA 2006
(3)	s 793(5)
(4)	s 793(7)
(5)	ss 820(1)–(8), 822(1), (2), 823(1)–(3), 824(1)–(6), 825(1)–(4)
(6)	s 821(1), (2)
213 Registration of interests disclosed under s 212	
(1)	s 808(1)–(3) (changed)
(3)	ss 808(2), (4)–(7), 809(1), 810(1)–(4), 811(1), (2), 813(1)–(3), 819(1)–(3), 826(1)
214 Company investigation on requisition by members	
(1)	s 803(1), (2) (changed)
(2)	s 803(3) (changed)
(4)	s 804(1)
(5)	s 804(2), (3) (changed)
215 Company report to members	
(1)	s 805(1)
(2)	s 805(2), (3)
(3)	s 805(1), (3)
(4)	s 826(1), (2)
(5)	s 805(6)
(6)	s 805(7)
(7)	ss 805(4), 807(1)–(5)
(8)	s 806(3), (4)
216 Penalty for failure to provide information	
(1)	s 794(1)
(1A)	s 794(3)
(1B)	s 794(2)
(3)	s 795(1), (3)
(4)	s 795(2)
(5)	s 796(1), (2)
217 Removal of entries from register	
(1)	s 816 (changed)
(2)	s 817(1) (changed)
(3)	s 817(2), (3)
(4)	s 818(1), (2)
(5)	ss 817(4), 818(3)
218 Otherwise, entries not to be removed	
(1)	s 815(1)
(2)	s 815(2)
(3)	s 815(3), (4)
219 Inspection of register and reports	
(1)	s 807(1), 811(1)
(2)	s 807(2), 811(2)
(3)	ss 807(3), (4), 813(1), (2) (changed)
(4)	ss 807(5), 813(3)
220 Definitions for Part VI	
(2)	s 827
221 Duty to keep accounting records	
(1)	s 386(1), (2)
(2)–(4)	s 386(3)–(5)
(5)	s 387(1), (2)
(6)	s 387(3)
222 Where and for how long records to be kept	
(1)–(3)	s 388(1)–(3)
(4)	s 389(1), (2), (4)
(5)	s 388(4), (5)
(6)	s 389(3), (4)
223 A company's financial year	
(1)–(5)	s 390(1)–(5)
224 Accounting reference periods and accounting reference date	
(1)	s 391(1)
(2), (3)	s 391(2)
(3A)	s 391(4)
(4)–(6)	s 391(5)–(7)
225 Alteration of accounting reference date	
(1)	s 392(1)
(3)–(7)	s 392(2)–(6)
226 Duty to prepare individual accounts	
(1)	s 394
(2)–(6)	s 395(1)–(5)
226A Companies Act individual accounts	
(1), (2)	s 396(1), (2)
(3)	s 396(3) (changed)
(4)	s 396(4)
(5), (6)	s 396(5)
226B IAS individual accounts	
	s 397
227 Duty to prepare group accounts	
(1)	s 399(2)
(2)–(7)	s 403(1)–(6)
(8)	s 399(2), (3)
227A Companies Act group accounts	
(1), (2)	s 404(1), (2)
(3)	s 404(3) (changed)
(4)	s 404(4)
(5), (6)	s 404(5)
227B IAS group accounts	
	s 406
227C Consistency of accounts	
(1)–(5)	s 407(1)–(5)
228 Exemption for parent companies included in accounts of larger group	
(1), (2)	s 400(1), (2)
(3)	s 400(4)
(4)	s 400(5)
(5)	s 400(3)
(6)	s 400(6)
228A Exemption for parent companies included in non-EEA group accounts	
(1), (2)	s 401(1), (2)
(3)	s 401(4)
(4)	s 401(5)
(5)	s 401(3)
(6)	s 401(6)
229 Subsidiary undertakings included in the consolidation	
(1), (2)	s 405(1), (2)
(3)	s 405(3), (4)

CA 1985	CA 2006
(5)	s 402
230 Treatment of individual profit and loss account where group accounts prepared	
(1)	s 408(1) (changed)
(2)	s 408(2) (changed)
(3), (40	s 408(3), (4)
231 Disclosure required in notes to accounts: related undertakings	
(1), (2)	s 409(1), (2) (changed)
(3)	s 409(3), (4) (changed)
(4)	s 409(5)
(5)	s 410(1), (2)
(6)	s 410(3)
(7)	s 410(4), (5)
231A Disclosure required in notes to annual accounts: particulars of staff	
(1)	s 411(1)
(2)–(4)	s 411(3)–(5)
(5)	s 411(2)
(6)	s 411(7)
(7)	s 411(6)
232 Disclosure required in notes to accounts: emoluments and other benefits of directors and others	
(3)	s 412(5)
(4)	s 412(6)
233 Approval and signing of accounts	
(1), (2)	ss 414(1), (2), 450(1), (2)
(3)	ss 433(1)–(3), 436(1), (2),
(4)	ss 444(6), 445(5), 446(3), 447(3) (changed)
(5)	s 414(4), (5) (changed)
(6)(a)	s 433(4), (5),
234 Duty to prepare directors' report	
(1)	ss 415(1), 417(1), 418(2)
(2), (3)	s 415(2), (3)
(5)	ss 415(4), (5), 419(3), (4)
234ZZA Directors' report: general requirements	
(1)	s 416(1), (3)
(2)	s 416(2)
(3), (4)	s 416(4) (changed)
234ZZB Directors' report: business review	
(1), (2)	s 417(3), (4)
(3)	s 417(6)
(4)	s 417(8)
(5)	s 417(6)
(6)	s 417(9)
234ZA Statement as to disclosure of information to auditors	
(1)–(4)	s 418(1)–(4)
(6)	s 418(5), (6)
234A Approval and signing of directors' report	
(1)	s 419(1)
(2)	ss 433(1)–(3), 436(1), (2)
(3)	ss 444(6), 445(5), 446(3), 447(3)
(4)	ss 419(3), (4), 433(4), (5)
234B Duty to prepare directors' remuneration report	
(1)	ss 420(1), 421(1), (2)

CA 1985	CA 2006
(2)	s 421(1), (2)
(3), (4)	s 420(2), (3)
(5), (6)	s 421(3), (4)
234C Approval and signing of directors' remuneration report	
(1)	s 422(1)
(2)	ss 433(1)–(3), 436(1), (2)
(3)	s 447(3)
(4)	s 422(2), (3)
235 Auditors' report	
(1)	ss 475(1), 495(1)
(1A)	s 495(2)
(1B), (2)	s 495(3)
(2A)	s 495(4)
(3)	s 496
(4), (5)	s 497(1), (2)
236 Signature of auditors' report	
(1)	s 503(1), (2)
(2)	s 505(1), (2) (changed)
(3)	s 444(7) (changed)
(4)	s 505(3), (4)
237 Duties of auditors	
(1)–(4)	s 498(1)–(4)
(4A)	s 498(5)
238 Persons entitled to receive copies of accounts and reports	
(1), (1A)	ss 423(1), 424(1)–(3) (changed)
(3)	s 423(4)
(4)	s 424(4) (changed)
(5)	s 425(1), (2)
(6)	s 423(5)
239 Right to demand copies of accounts and reports	
(1), (2)	ss 431(1), (2), 432(1), (2)
(3)	ss 431(3), (4), 432(3), (4)
240 Requirements in connection with publication of accounts	
(1)	s 434(1) (changed)
(2)	s 434(2) (changed)
(3)	s 435(1), (2) (changed)
(4)	s 436(1), (2) (changed)
(5)	ss 434(3), 435(3) (changed)
(6)	s 435(5), (6)
241 Accounts and reports to be laid before company in general meeting	
(1)	s 437(1) (changed)
(2)	ss 437(2), 438(1), (4)
(3), (4)	s 438(2), (3)
241A Members' approval of directors' remuneration report	
(1), (3)	s 439(1)
(4)	s 439(2)
(5)	s 439(3)
(6)	s 439(4)
(7)	s 439(3)
(8)	s 439(5)
(9)	s 440(1), (4)
(10)	s 440(2)–(4)

CA 1985	CA 2006
(11)	s 440(2), (3)
(12)	s 439(6)
242 Accounts and reports to be delivered to the registrar	
(1)	ss 441(1), 444(1), (2), 445(1), (2), 446(1), (2), 447(1), (2) (changed)
(2)	s 451(1)
(3)	s 452(1), (2)
(4), (5)	s 451(2), (3)
242A Civil penalty for failure to deliver accounts	
(1)	s 453(1)
(2)	s 453(2) (changed)
(3), (4)	s 453(3), (4)
242B Delivery and publication of accounts in ECUs	
(1)–(4)	s 469(1)–(4)
244 Period allowed for laying and delivering accounts and reports	
(1), (2)	s 442(2), (3) (changed)
(4), (5)	s 442(4), (5)
(6)	s 442(7)
245 Voluntary revision of annual accounts or directors' report	
(1)–(3)	s 454(1)–(3)
(4)	s 454(4) (changed)
(5)	s 454(5)
245A Secretary of State's notice in respect of annual accounts	
(1)	s 455(1), (2)
(2)–(4)	s 455(3)–(5)
245B Application to court in respect of defective accounts	
(1)–(3)	s 456(1)–(3)
(3A)	s 456(4)
(4)–(7)	s 456(5)–(8)
245C Other persons authorised to apply to court	
(1)	s 457(1)
(1A)	s 457(5)
(2), (3)	s 457(2), (3)
(4)	s 457(7)
(4A)	s 457(5)
(4B)	s 457(4)
(5)	s 457(6)
245D Disclosure of information held by Inland Revenue to persons authorised to apply to court	
(1)	s 458(1)
(2)	s 458(2)
(3)	s 458(1)
245E Restrictions on use and further disclosure of information disclosed under section 245D	
(1), (2)	s 458(3)
(3)	s 458(4), (5)
(4)	s 458(4) (changed)
(5)	ss 1126, 1130
245F Power of authorised persons to require documents, information and explanations	
(1)–(8)	s 459(1)–(8)
245G Restrictions on further disclosure of information	

CA 1985	CA 2006
obtained under section 245F	
(1), (2)	s 460(1), (2)
(3)	ss 460(3), 461(1)–(6)
(4)–(6)	s 462(1)–(3)
(7)	s 460(4), (5)
(8)	s 460(4)
(9)	ss 1126, 1130
(10)	s 460(3)
(11)	s 461(7)
246 Special provisions for small companies	
(3)	s 411(1)
(4)	ss 416(3), 417(1)
(5)	s 444(1), (3) (changed)
(6)	s 444(3) (changed)
(7)	ss 444(6), 450(1), (2)
(8)	ss 414(3), 419(2), 444(5), 450(3)
246A Special provisions for medium-sized companies	
(1)	s 445(1)
(2)	s 445(3) (changed)
(2A)	s 417(7)
(3)	s 445(3) (changed)
(4)	s 450(3)
247 Qualification of company as small or medium-sized	
(1)(a)	ss 382(1), 465(1)
(1)(b), (2)	ss 382(2), 465(2)
(3), (4)	ss 382(3), (4), 465(3), (4)
(5)	ss 382(5), 465(5) (changed)
(6)	ss 382(6), 465(6)
247A Cases in which special provisions do not apply	
(1)–(1B)	ss 384(1), 467(1)
(2)	ss 384(2), 467(2) (changed)
(2A)	ss 384(3), 467(3)
(3)	ss 383(1), 466(1)
247B Special auditors' report	
(1)	s 449(1)
(2)	ss 444(4), 445(4), 449(2)
(3)–(5)	s 449(3)–(5)
248 Exemption for small and medium-sized groups	
(1), (2)	ss 398, 399(1), (2) (changed)
249 Qualification of group as small or medium-sized	
(1)(a)	s 466(2)
(1)(b), (2)	s 466(3)
(3)	s 466(4)
(4)	s 466(5), (6)
(5), (6)	s 466(7)
249A Exemptions from audit	
(1)	s 477(1)
(3)	s 477(2), (4)
(6)	s 477(3)
(7)	s 477(4)
249AA Dormant companies	
(1), (2)	s 480(1), (2)
(3)	s 481
(4)	s 1169(1)
(5)–(7)	s 1169(2), (3)

CA 1985	*CA 2006*
249B Cases where exemptions not available	
(1)	ss 478, 479(1)–(3)
(1A)	s 479(3)
(1B)	s 479(1)–(3)
(1C)	s 479(2), (5), (6)
(2), (3)	s 476(1)–(3)
(4)	s 475(2), (3)
(5)	s 475(4)
249E Effect of exemptions	
(1)(b)	ss 444(2), 445(2), 446(2) (changed)
251 Provision of summary financial statement to shareholders	
(1)	ss 426(1), 427(1)
(2)	s 426(2), (3)
(3)	ss 427(2), 428(2)
(3A)	ss 427(3), 428(3)
(4)	ss 427(4), 428(4)
(5)	ss 427(6), 428(6)
(6)	s 429(1), (2)
(7)	ss 434(6), 435(7)
254 Exemption from requirement to deliver accounts and reports	
(1)–(3)	s 448(1)–(3)
(4)	s 448(4)
255A Special provisions for banking and insurance groups	
(4)	s 1164(5)
(5)	s 1165(5)
(5A)	ss 1164(5), 1165(6)
255D Power to apply provisions to banking partnerships	
(1)	s 470(1)
(2), (2A)	s 470(2)
(4)	s 470(4)
(5)	s 470(3)
256 Accounting standards	
(1), (2)	s 464(1), (2)
(4)	s 464(3)
257 Power of Secretary of State to alter accounting requirements	
(1)	s 484(1)
(2)	ss 473(1)–(4) (changed), 484(3)
(3)	s 484(4)
(4)(c)	s 484(2)
258 Parent and subsidiary undertakings	
(1)–(6)	s 1162(1)–(6)
259 Meaning of "undertaking" and related expressions	
(1)	ss 1161(1), 1173 "parent company"
(2)–(5)	s 1161(2)–(5)
261 Notes to the accounts	
(1), (2)	s 472(1), (2)
262 Minor definitions	
(1)	ss 474(1), 539, 835(6), 1173 "credit institution" (changed)
(2)	s 474(2)
(3)	s 853(4), (5)

CA 1985	*CA 2006*
263 Certain distributions prohibited	
(1)	s 830(1)
(2)	s 829(1), (2)
(3)	s 830(2), (3)
(4)	s 849
(5)	s 850(1)–(3)
264 Restriction on distribution of assets	
(1)	s 831(1), (6)
(2)	s 831(2), (3)
(3)	s 831(4)
(4)	s 831(5)
265 Other distributions by investment companies	
(1)	s 832(1)–(3)
(2)	s 832(4)
(3)	s 832(7)
(4)	s 832(5)
(4A)	s 832(6)
(5)	s 832(6)
(6)	s 832(5)
266 Meaning of "investment company"	
(1)	s 833(1)
(2)	ss 833(2), 834(1)
(2A)	s 833(3)
(3)	s 833(4), (5)
(4)	s 834(2)–(5)
267 Extension of ss 265, 266 to other companies	
(1)	s 835(1)
(2)	s 835(2)
268 Realised profits of insurance company with long term business	
(1)	s 843(1), (2), (4), (5)
(2)	s 843(3), (4)
(3)	s 843(6), (7)
(4)	s 843(7)
269 Treatment of development costs	
(1)	s 844(1)
(2)	s 844(2), (3)
270 Distribution to be justified by reference to company's accounts	
(1), (2)	s 836(1)
(3)	ss 836(2), 837(1)
(4)	ss 836(2), 838(1), 839(1)
(5)	s 836(3), (4)
271 Requirements for last annual accounts	
(2)	s 837(2)
(3)	s 837(3), (4)
(4)	s 837(4)
(5)	s 837(5)
272 Requirements for interim accounts	
(1)	s 838(2)
(2)	s 838(3)
(3)	ss 838(4), (5), 839(4)
(4), (5)	s 838(6)
273 Requirements for initial accounts	
(1)	s 839(2)
(2)	s 839(3)

CA 1985	CA 2006
(3)	s 839(4)
(4)	s 839(5), (6)
(5)	s 839(6)
(6), (7)	s 839(7)
274 Method of applying s 270 to successive distributions	
(1)	s 840(1)
(2)	s 840(1), (2)
(3)	s 840(3)–(5)
275 Treatment of assets in the relevant accounts	
(1)	s 841(1), (2)
(1A)	s 841(3)
(2)	s 841(5)
(3)	s 842
(4)–(6)	s 841(4)
276 Distributions in kind	
	s 846(1), (2) (changed)
277 Consequences of unlawful distribution	
(1)	s 847(1), (2)
(2)	s 847(3), (4)
278 Saving for provision in articles operative before Act of 1980	
	s 848(1), (2)
280 Definitions for Part VIII	
(1)	s 853(1)
(2)	s 853(2)
(3)	s 853(3)
281 Saving for other restraints on distribution	
	ss 851, 852 (changed)
282 Directors	
(1)	s 154(2) (changed)
(3)	s 154(1)
283 Secretary	
(1)	s 271 (changed)
(3)	ss 270(3), 274 (changed)
284 Acts done by person in dual capacity	
	s 280
285 Validity of acts of directors	
	s 161(1), (2) (changed)
286 Qualifications of company secretaries	
(1)	s 273(1), (2) (changed)
(2)	s 273(3)
287 Registered office	
(1)	s 86
(3)	s 87(1)
(4)	s 87(2)
(5)	s 87(3)
(6)	s 87(4)
288 Register of directors and secretaries	
(1)	ss 162(1)–(3), 275(1)–(3) (changed)
(2)	ss 167(1), (2), 276(1), (2)
(3)	ss 162(5), 275(5)
(4)	ss 162(6), (7), 167(4), (5), 275(6), (7), 276(3), (4)
(5)	ss 162(8), 275(8)
(6)	ss 162(6), 167(4), 275(6), 276(3)

CA 1985	CA 2006
289 Particulars of directors to be registered under s 288	
(1)	ss 163(1), 164 (changed)
(2)	ss 163(2), (4), 277(2), (4) (changed)
290 Particulars of secretaries to be registered under s 288	
(1)	ss 277(1), 278(1) (changed)
(2)	s 278(2)
(3)	s 277(2), (4)
292 Appointment of directors to be voted on individually	
(1)	s 160(1)
(2)	s 160(2)
(3)	s 160(3)
(4)	s 160(4)
303 Resolution to remove director	
(1)	s 168(1) (changed)
(2)	s 168(2)
(3)	s 168(3)
(4)	s 168(4)
(5)	s 168(5)
304 Director's right to protest removal	
(1)	s 169(1), (2)
(2)	s 169(3)
(3)	s 169(4)
(4)	s 169(5)
(5)	s 169(6)
309 Directors to have regard to interests of employees	
(1)	s 172(1)
309A Provisions protecting directors from liability	
(1)	s 232(1), (2)
(2)	s 232(1)
(3)	s 232(2)
(4)	s 234(1)
(5)	s 233
(6)	s 232(3)
309B Qualifying third party indemnity provisions	
(1), (2)	s 234(2)
(3)	s 234(3)
(4)	s 234(3), (6)
(5)	s 234(4)
(6), (7)	s 234(5)
309C Disclosure of qualifying third party indemnity provisions	
(1)	s 236(1) (changed)
(2)	s 236(2), (3)
(3)	s 236(4), (5) (changed)
(4)	s 237(1)
(5)	ss 237(1)–(3), (5)–(8), 238(1), (3)–(5)
310 Provisions protecting auditors from liability	
(1)	s 532(1), (3) (changed)
(2)	s 532(2)
(3)	s 533
312 Payment to director for loss of office, etc	
	ss 215(1), 217(1), (3) (changed)

CA 1985	*CA 2006*
313 Company approval for property transfer	
(1)	ss 215(1), 218(1), (3) (changed)
(2)	s 222(2)
314 Director's duty of disclosure on takeover, etc	
(1)	ss 215(1), 219(1) (changed)
315 Consequences of non-compliance with s 314	
(1)	ss 219(1), (2), 222(3) (changed)
(3)	s 219(5)
316 Provisions supplementing ss 312 to 315	
(1)	ss 218(5), 219(7)
(2)	s 216(1), (2) (changed)
(3)	s 220(1)
317 Directors to disclose interest in contracts	
(1)	s 182(1) (changed)
(2)	s 182(2) (changed)
(3)	s 185(1), (2) (changed)
(4)	s 185(4)
(5)	s 185(1) (changed)
(7)	s 183(1), (2)
(8)	s 187(1)–(4)
318 Director's service contracts to be open to inspection	
(1)	ss 228(1), 237(2)
(2), (3)	ss 228(2), 237(3) (changed)
(4)	ss 228(4), 237(5)
(6)	s 230
(7)	ss 229(1), 238(1)
(8)	ss 228(5), (6), 229(3), (4), 237(6), (7), 238(3), (4) (changed)
(9)	ss 229(5), 238(5) (changed)
(10)	ss 228(7), 237(8)
319 Director's contract of employment for more than 5 years	
(1)	s 188(1), (3) (changed)
(2)	s 188(4) (changed)
(3)	s 188(2) (changed)
(4)	s 188(6)
(5)	s 188(5)
(6)	s 189
(7)	ss 188(7), 223(1)
320 Substantial property transactions involving directors, etc	
(1)	s 190(1), (2) (changed)
(2)	s 191(1)–(5) (changed)
(3)	s 223(1)
321 Exceptions from s 320	
(1)	s 190(4)
(2)	ss 192, 193(1), (2) (changed)
(3)	s 192
(4)	s 194(1), (2)
322 Liabilities arising from contravention of s 320	
(1)	s 195(1), (2)
(2)	ss 195(2) and 196
(3)	s 195(1), (3), (4)
(4)	s 195(3), (5), (8)
(5)	s 195(6)
(6)	s 195(7)
322A Invalidity of certain transactions involving directors, etc	
(1)	s 41(1), (2)
(2)	s 41(2)
(3)	s 41(3)
(4)	s 41(1)
(5)	s 41(4)
(6)	s 41(5)
(7)	s 41(6)
(8)	s 41(7)
322B Contracts with sole members who are directors	
(1)	s 231(1), (2) (changed)
(2)	s 231(1)
(3)	s 231(5)
(4)	s 231(3), (4) (changed)
(5)	s 231(7)
(6)	s 231(6)
325 Register of directors' interests notified under s 324	
(5)	s 809(2), (3)
330 General restriction on loans etc to directors and persons connected with them	
(2)	s 197(1) (changed)
(3)	ss 198(1), (2) (changed), 200(1), (2)
(4)	s 201(1), (2) (changed)
(5)	s 223(1)
(6)	s 203(1), (6) (changed)
(7)	s 203(1) (changed)
331 Definitions for ss 330 ff	
(3)	s 199(1)
(4)	s 199(2), (3)
(6)	ss 198(1), 200(1), 201(1)
(7)	s 202(1)
(8)	s 202(3)
(9)	ss 202(2), 212
(10)	s 202(3)
333 Inter-company loans in same group	
	s 208(1) (changed)
334 Loans of small amounts	
	s 207(1) (changed)
335 Minor and business transactions	
(1)	s 207(2) (changed)
(2)	s 207(3)
336 Transactions at behest of holding company	
	208(1), (2) (changed)
337 Funding of director's expenditure on duty to company	
(1), (2)	s 204(1) (changed)
(3)	s 204(2) (changed)
337A Funding of director's expenditure on defending proceedings	
(1)	s 205(1) (changed)
(2)	s 205(5)
(3)	s 205(1) (changed)
(4)	s 205(2)
(5)	s 205(3)

CA 1985	*CA 2006*
(6)	s 205(4)
338 Loan or quasi-loan by money-lending company	
(1)	s 209(1)
(2)	s 209(2)
(3)	s 209(1)
(6)	s 209(3), (4)
339 "Relevant amounts" for purposes of ss 334 ff	
(1)	ss 204(2), 207(1), (2), 210(1)
(2)	ss 204(2), 207(1), (2), 210(2)–(4)
(3)	s 210(3), (4)
(5)	s 210(5)
(6)	s 211(1)
340 "Value" of transactions and arrangements	
(2)	s 211(2)
(3)	s 211(3)
(4)	s 211(5)
(5)	s 211(6)
(6)	s 211(4)
(7)	s 211(7) (changed)
341 Civil remedies for breach of s 330	
(1)	s 213(1), (2)
(2)	s 213(3), (4)
(3)	s 213(5), (8)
(4)	s 213(6)
(5)	s 213(7)
345 Power to increase financial limits	
(1)	s 258(1)
(2)	s 258(2)
(3)	s 258(3)
346 "Connected persons", etc	
(1)	ss 252(1), 254(1), 255(1)
(2), (3)	ss 252(2), (3), 253(2) (changed)
(4)	s 254(2), (5)
(5)	s 255(2), (5)
(6)	ss 254(6), 255(6)
(7)	ss 254(3), 255(3)
(8)	ss 254(4), 255(4)
347 Transactions under foreign law	
	s 259
347A Introductory provisions	
(1)	s 362 (changed)
(3)	s 379(1)
(4)	s 364(2)
(5)	s 365(1) (changed)
(6)	s 363(1), (2)
(7)	s 363(1), (2) (changed)
(8)	s 379(1)
(9)	s 363(1)
(10)	ss 366(5), 379(2)
347B Exemptions	
(1)	s 375(1)
(2)	s 375(2) (changed)
(3)	s 376(1), (2)
(4)	s 378(1) (changed)
(5)	s 378(3)
(6), (7)	s 378(1) (changed)
(8)	s 377(1)
(9)	s 377(3)
(10)	s 377(2)
(11)	s 377(4)
347C Prohibition on donations and political expenditure by companies	
(1)	s 366(1), (2), (5) (changed)
(2)	s 367(3), (6) (changed)
(3)	s 368(1), (2)
(4)	s 367(5)
(6)	s 366(6)
347D Special rules for subsidiaries	
(1)	s 366(2)
(2)	s 366(2), (5) (changed)
(3)	s 366(2), (3), (5) (changed)
(4)	s 367(3), (6) (changed)
(5)	s 368(1), (2)
(6)	s 367(5)
(9)	s 366(6)
347F Remedies for breach of prohibitions on company donations etc	
(1)	s 369(1)
(2)	s 369(2), (3) (changed)
(3)	s 369(2), (5)
(4)	s 369(2)
(5)	s 369(6)
(6)	s 369(3) (changed)
347I Enforcement of directors' liabilities by shareholder action	
(1)	s 370(1), (2) (changed)
(2)	s 370(3)
(3)	ss 370(4), 371(1)
(4), (5)	s 371(2)
(6)	s 371(3)
(7)	s 371(4)
(8)	s 371(5)
347J Costs of shareholder action	
(1)	s 372(1)
(2)	s 372(2)
(3)	s 372(3)
(4), (5)	s 372(4)
(6)	s 372(5)
347K Information for purposes of shareholder action	
(1)	s 373(1)
(2)	s 373(2)
348 Company name to appear outside place of business	
(1)	s 82(1), (2)
(2)	s 84(1), (2)
349 Company's name to appear in its correspondence, etc	
(1)	s 82(1), (2)
(2), (3)	s 84(1), (2)
350 Company seal	
(1)	s 45(2), (3) (changed)
(2)	s 45(4), (5)

CA 1985	*CA 2006*
351 Particulars in correspondence etc	
(1), (2)	s 82(1), (2)
(5)	s 84(1), (2)
352 Obligation to keep and enter up register	
(1)	s 113(1)
(2)	s 113(2)
(3)	s 113(3), (4)
(4)	s 113(6)
(5)	s 113(7), (8)
(6)	s 121 (changed)
(7)	s 128(1), (2)
352A Statement that company has only one member	
(1)	s 123(2) (changed)
(2)	s 123(3) (changed)
(3)	s 123(4), (5)
(3A)	s 124(1), (2)
353 Location of register	
(1)	s 114(1) (changed)
(2)	s 114(2)
(3)	s 114(3), (4)
(4)	s 114(5), (6)
354 Index of members	
(1)	s 115(1), (2)
(2)	s 115(3)
(3)	s 115(4) (changed)
(4)	s 115(5), (6)
355 Entries in register in relation to share warrants	
(1)	s 122(1) (changed)
(2)	s 122(4)
(3)	s 122(5)
(4)	s 122(2), (6)
(5)	s 122(3)
356 Inspection of register and index	
(1)	s 116(1) (changed)
(3)	s 116(2)
(5)	s 118(1), (2) (changed)
(6)	s 118(3)
359 Power of court to rectify register	
(1)	s 125(1)
(2)	s 125(2)
(3)	s 125(3)
(4)	s 125(4)
360 Trusts not to be entered on register in England and Wales	
	s 126
361 Register to be evidence	
	s 127
362 Overseas branch registers	
(1)	s 129(1)
(2)	s 129(1), (5)
(3)	ss 130(1)–(3), 131(1), (4), 132(1)–(4), 133(1)–(3), 134(1)–(3), 135(1)–(5)
363 Duty to deliver annual returns	
(1)	s 854(1), (2)
(2)	s 854(3) (changed)
(3)	s 858(1)–(3)

CA 1985	*CA 2006*
(4)	s 858(1), (2), (4) (changed)
364 Contents of annual return: general	
(1)	s 855(1) (changed)
(2)	s 855(2)
(3)	s 855(3)
364A Contents of annual return: particulars of share capital and shareholders	
(1)	s 856(1)
(2)	s 856(2)
(3)	s 856(2) (changed)
(4)	s 856(3)
(5)	s 856(4)
(6)	s 856(5)
(8)	s 856(6)
365 Supplementary provisions: regulations and interpretation	
(1)	s 857(1), (2)
(2)	s 857(3)
(3)	s 859
366 Annual general meeting	
(1)	ss 336(1), 337(1)
(4)	s 336(3), (4)
368 Extraordinary general meeting on members' requisition	
(1)	s 303(1), (2)
(2)	s 303(2), (3) (changed)
(2A)	s 303(2)
(3)	s 303(4), (6) (changed)
(4)	ss 304(1), 305(1), (3)
(5)	s 305(4)
(6)	s 305(6), (7)
(7)	s 304(4)
(8)	s 304(1)
369 Length of notice for calling meetings	
(1), (2)	s 307(2), (3) (changed)
(3)	ss 307(4), 337(2) (changed)
(4)	s 307(5), (6) (changed)
(4A)	s 308 (changed)
(4B)	ss 308, 309(1), (3) (changed)
(4C)	s 309(2)
370 General provisions as to meetings and votes	
(1)	ss 284(4), 310(4), 318(2), 319(2)
(2)	s 310(1)
(4)	s 318(2) (changed)
(5)	s 319(1)
(6)	s 284(1), (3)
370A Quorum at meetings of the sole member	
	s 318(1), (3) (changed)
371 Power of court to order meeting	
(1)	s 306(1), (2)
(2)	s 306(3), (4)
(3)	s 306(5)
372 Proxies	
(1)	s 324(1)
(2)	s 324(2) (changed)
(3)	s 325(1) (changed)
(4)	s 325(3), (4)

CA 1985	CA 2006
(5)	s 327(1), (2) (changed)
(6)	s 326(1)–(4) (changed)
373 Right to demand a poll	
(1)	s 321(1), (2) (changed)
(2)	s 329(1), (2) (changed)
374 Voting on a poll	
	s 322
375 Representation of corporations at meetings	
(1)	s 323(1)
(2)	s 323(2), (3) (changed)
376 Circulation of members' resolutions	
(1)	ss 314(1), (4), 315(2), 316(2), 338(1), (4), 339(2), 340(2)
(2)	ss 314(2), (3), 338(3)
(3)	ss 315(1), 339(1)
(5)	ss 315(1), 339(1)
(6)	s 339(3)
(7)	ss 315(3), (4), 339(4), (5)
377 In certain cases, compliance with s 376 not required	
(1)	ss 314(4), 316(2), 338(4), 340(2) (changed)
(3)	s 317(1), (2) (changed)
378 Extraordinary and special resolutions	
(1)	s 283(1), (4), (5) (changed)
(2)	s 283(1), (4)–(6) (changed)
(4)	s 320(1), (3)
(5)	s 283(5) (changed)
(6)	s 301 (changed)
379 Resolution requiring special notice	
(1)	s 312(1)
(2)	s 312(2), (3) (changed)
(3)	s 312(4)
380 Registration, etc of resolutions and agreements	
(1)	s 30(1)
(2)	s 36(1), (2) (changed)
(4)	s 29(1) (changed)
(4A)	s 29(2)
(5)	s 30(2), (3)
(6)	s 36(3), (4) (changed)
(7)	ss 30(4), 36(5)
381 Resolution passed at adjourned meeting	
	s 332
381A Written resolutions of private companies	
(1)	ss 288(1), 289(1) (changed)
(2)	s 296(1) (changed)
(4)	s 288(5)
(7)	s 288(2)
381C Written resolutions: supplementary provisions	
(1)	s 300
382 Minutes of meetings	
(1)	ss 248(1), 355(1)
(2)	ss 249(1), 356(4)
(4)	ss 249(2), 356(5)
(5)	ss 248(3), (4), 355(3), (4) (changed)
382A Recording of written resolutions	

CA 1985	CA 2006
(1)	s 355(1) (changed)
(2)	s 356(2), (3)
382B Recording of decisions by the sole member	
(1)	s 357(1), (2)
(2)	s 357(3), (4)
(3)	s 357(5)
383 Inspection of minute books	
(1)	s 358(1), (3) (changed)
(3)	s 358(4) (changed)
(4)	s 358(5), (6) (changed)
(5)	s 358(7)
384 Duty to appoint auditors	
(1)	ss 485(1), 489(1) (changed)
(2)	s 489(2)
385 Appointment at general meeting at which accounts laid	
(2)	ss 489(2), (4), 491(1) (changed)
(3)	s 489(3) (changed)
(4)	s 489(4) (changed)
387 Appointment by Secretary of State in default of appointment by company	
(1)	ss 486(1), 490(1)
(2)	ss 486(2)–(4), 490(2)–(4)
388 Filling of casual vacancies	
(1)	ss 489(3), 526
389A Rights to information	
(1)	s 499(1)
(2)	s 499(2)
(3)	s 500(1)
(4)	s 500(2)
(5)	s 500(3)
(6)	ss 499(3), 500(4)
(7)	ss 499(4) 500(5)
389B Offences relating to the provision of information to auditors	
(1)	s 501(1), (2)
(2)	s 501(3)
(3)	s 501(3) (changed)
(4)	s 501(4), (5)
(5)	s 501(6)
390 Right to attend company meetings, &c	
(1)	s 502(2)
(2)	s 502(1)
(3)	s 502(2)
390A Remuneration of auditors	
(1)	s 492(1)
(2)	s 492(2), (3)
(4)	s 492(4)
(5)	s 492(5)
390B Disclosure of services provided by auditors or associates and related remuneration	
(1)	ss 494(1), 501(1), (2)
(2)	s 494(2)
(3)	s 494(3)
(4)	s 494(4)
(5)	s 494(5)
(8)	s 494(1)

Part 3 CA 2006 Supporting Materials

CA 1985	CA 2006
(9)	s 494(6)
391 Removal of auditors	
(1)	s 510(1), (2)
(2)	s 512(1)–(3)
(3)	s 510(3)
(4)	s 513(1), (2)
391A Rights of auditors who are removed or not re-appointed	
(1)	ss 511(1), 515(1), (2) (changed)
(2)	ss 511(2), 515(3)
(3)	ss 511(3), 515(4)
(4)	ss 511(4), 515(5)
(5)	ss 511(5), 515(6)
(6)	ss 511(6), 515(7)
392 Resignation of auditors	
(1)	s 516(1), (2)
(2)	s 516(3)
(3)	s 517(1)–(3)
392A Rights of resigning auditors	
(1)	s 518(1)
(2)	s 518(2)
(3)	s 518(3)
(4)	s 518(4)
(5)	s 518(5)–(7)
(6)	s 518(8)
(7)	s 518(9)
(8)	s 518(10)
394 Statement by person ceasing to hold office as auditor	
(1)	s 519(1)–(3), (7) (changed)
(2)	s 519(4) (changed)
(3)	s 520(2)
(4)	s 520(3)
(5)	s 521(1)
(6)	s 520(4)
(7)	ss 520(5), 521(2) (changed)
394A Offences of failing to comply with s 394	
(1)	ss 519(5), 521(3)–(5)
(2)	ss 519(6), 521(4)
(4)	s 520(6), (8) (changed)
395 Certain charges void if not registered	
(1)	ss 860(1), 861(5), 870(1), 874(1), (2)
(2)	s 874(3)
396 Charges which have to be registered	
(1)	ss 860(7), 861(2)
(2)	s 861(3)
(3)	s 861(1)
(3A)	s 861(4)
(4)	s 861(5)
397 Formalities of registration (debentures)	
(1)	ss 863(1)–(4), 870(3)
(2)	s 864(1), (3)
(3)	s 864(2)
398 Verification of charge on property outside United Kingdom	
(1)	s 866(1)
(2)	s 870(1)
(3)	s 866(2)
(4)	s 867(1), (2)
399 Company's duty to register charges it creates	
(1)	ss 860(1), (2), 863(5)
(2)	ss 860(3), 863(5)
(3)	ss 860(4)–(6), 863(5)
400 Charges existing on property acquired	
(1)	ss 861(5), 862(1)
(2)	ss 862(2), (3), 870(2)
(3)	s 870(2)
(4)	s 862(4), (5) (changed)
401 Register of charges to be kept by registrar of companies	
(1)	s 869(1), (2), (4)
(2)	s 869(5), (6)
(3)	s 869(7)
402 Endorsement of certificate on debentures	
(1)	s 865(1)
(2)	s 865(2)
(3)	s 865(3), (4)
403 Entries of satisfaction and release	
(1)	s 872(1), (2) (changed)
(2)	s 872(3)
404 Rectification of register of charges	
(1)	s 873(1)
(2)	s 873(2)
405 Registration of enforcement of security	
(1)	s 871(1), (3)
(2)	s 871(2), (3)
(4)	s 871(4), (5)
406 Companies to keep copies of instrument creating charges	
(1)	ss 875(1), 877(2) (changed)
(2)	s 875(2)
407 Company's register of charges	
(1)	ss 876(1), 877(2) (changed)
(2)	s 876(2)
(3)	s 876(3), (4)
408 Right to inspect instruments which create charges, etc	
(1)	s 877(1), (2), (4) (changed)
(2)	s 877(2) (changed)
(3)	s 877(5), (6)
(4)	s 877(7)
410 Charges void unless registered	
(1)	s 878(1)
(2)	ss 886(1), 889(1)
(3)	s 889(2)
(4)	ss 878(7), 879(1), (3)
(5)	s 879(5), (6)
411 Charges on property outside United Kingdom	
(1)	s 886(1)
(2)	s 884

CA 1985	*CA 2006*
412 Negotiable instrument to secure book debts	
	s 879(4)
413 Charges associated with debentures	
(1)	s 879(2)
(2)	ss 882(1)–(4), 886(3)
(3)	s 883(1)–(3)
414 Charge by way of ex facie absolute disposition, etc	
(1)	s 881(1)
(2)	s 881(2), (3)
415 Company's duty to register charges created by it	
(1)	ss 878(1), (2), 882(5)
(2)	s 878(3), 882(5)
(3)	s 878(4)–(6), 882(5)
416 Duty to register charges existing on property acquired	
(1)	ss 880(1), (2), 886(2)
(2)	s 886(2)
(3)	s 880(3), (4) (changed)
417 Register of charges to be kept by registrar of companies	
(1)	s 885(1)
(2)	s 885(2)
(3)	s 885(3)
(4)	s 886(6)
418 Certificate of registration to be issued	
(1)	s 885(4)
(2)	s 885(4), (5)
419 Entries of satisfaction and release	
(1)	s 887(1), (3) (changed)
(1B)	s 887(2)
(2)	s 887(4)
(3)	s 887(2) (changed)
(4)	s 887(5)
420 Rectification of register	
	s 888(1), (2)
421 Copies of instruments creating charges to be kept by company	
(1)	ss 890(1), 892(2) (changed)
(2)	s 890(2)
422 Company's register of charges	
(1)	ss 891(1), 892(2) (changed)
(2)	s 891(2)
(3)	s 891(3), (4)
423 Right to inspect copies of instruments, and company's register	
(1)	s 892(1), (2), (4) (changed)
(2)	s 892(4) (changed)
(3)	s 892(5), (6)
(4)	s 892(7)
425 Power of company to compromise with creditors and members	
(1)	ss 895(1), 896(1), (2)
(2)	ss 899(1), (3), 907(1), 922(1)
(3)	s 899(4), 901(3), (4) (changed)
(4)	s 901(5) and (6)
(6)	s 895(2)

CA 1985	*CA 2006*
426 Information as to compromise to be circulated	
(1)	s 897(1)
(2)	s 897(1), (2)
(3)	s 897(1)
(4)	s 897(3)
(5)	s 897(4)
(6)	ss 895(1), 897(5)–(8)
(7)	s 898(1)–(3)
427 Provisions for facilitating company reconstruction or amalgamation	
(1)	s 900(1)
(2)	s 900(1), (2)
(3)	s 900(2)
(4)	s 900(3), (4)
(5)	s 900(6)–(8)
(6)	ss 900(5), 941
427A Application of ss 425–427 to mergers and divisions of public companies	
(1)	ss 902(1), 903(1), 907(2), 922(2)
(2)	ss 904(1), 919(1)
(3)	s 938(1), (2)
(4)	s 902(3)
(8)	s 941
428 Takeover offers	
(1)	s 974(1)–(3)
(2)	s 974(4), (5)
(2A)	s 974(6)
(3)	s 976(1)
(4)	s 976(3)
(5)	s 975(1), (2) (changed)
(6)	s 975(3) (changed)
(7)	s 974(7)
(8)	s 991(1)
429 Right of offeror to buy out minority shareholders	
(1)	s 979(1), (2) (changed)
(2)	s 979(3), (4) (changed)
(3)	s 980(2) (changed)
(4)	s 980(1), (4)
(5)	s 980(5)
(6)	s 980(6), (8)
(7)	s 980(7)
(8)	ss 977(1), 979(8)–(10) (changed)
430 Effect of notice under s 429	
(1)	s 981(1)
(2)	s 981(2)
(3)	s 981(3)
(4)	s 981(4), (5) (changed)
(5)	s 981(6)
(6)	s 981(7)
(7)	s 981(8)
(8)	s 981(6)
(9)	s 981(9)
(10)	s 982(2), (3)
(11)	s 982(4), (5)
(12)	s 982(6)

Part 3 CA 2006 Supporting Materials

CA 1985	CA 2006
(13)	s 982(7)
(14)	s 982(8)
(15)	s 982(9)
430A Right of minority shareholder to be bought out by offeror	
(1)	ss 983(1)–(3), 984(1)
(1A)	s 983(1)
(2)	s 983(4)
(2A)	s 983(5)
(3)	s 984(3)
(4)	s 984(2)
(5)	s 984(4)
(6)	s 984(5), (7)
(7)	s 984(6)
430B Effect of requirement under s 430A	
(1)	s 985(1)
(2)	s 985(2)
(3)	s 985(3)
(4)	s 985(4), (5) (changed)
430C Applications to the court	
(1)	s 986(1), (2)
(2)	s 986(2)
(3)	s 986(3)
(4)	s 986(5)
(5)	s 986(9), (10)
430D Joint offers	
(1)	s 987(1)
(2)	s 987(2), (3) (changed)
(3)	s 987(5), (6)
(4)	s 987(4), (7)
(5)	s 987(8)
(6)	s 987(9)
(7)	s 987(10)
430E Associates	
(1)	ss 975(4), 977(2) (changed)
(2)	s 979(9)
(3)	s 983(8)
(4)	s 988(1), (4)
(5)	s 988(2)
(6)	s 988(3)
(7)	s 988(3), (5), (7)
(8)	s 988(1)
430F Convertible securities	
(1)	s 989(1)
(2)	s 989(2)
458 Punishment for fraudulent trading	
	s 993(1)–(3)
459 Order on application of company member	
(1)	s 994(1)
(2)	s 994(2)
(3)	s 994(3)
460 Order on application of Secretary of State	
(1)	s 995(2), (3)
(1A)	s 995(1)
(2)	s 995(4)
461 Provisions as to petitions and orders under this Part	
(1)	s 996(1)
(2)	s 996(2)
(3)	s 996(2)
(5)	s 998(1)–(4)
(6)	s 997
652 Registrar may strike defunct company off register	
(1)	s 1000(1)
(2)	s 1000(2)
(3)	s 1000(3)
(4)	s 1001(1)
(5)	ss 1000(4)–(6), 1001(2)–(4)
(6)	ss 1000(7), 1001(5)
(7)	s 1002(1)–(3)
652A Registrar may strike private company off register on application	
(1)	s 1003(1) (changed)
(2)	s 1003(2) (changed)
(3)	s 1003(3)
(4)	s 1003(4)
(5)	s 1003(5)
(6)	s 1003(6)
(7)	s 1003(6)
652B Duties in connection with making application under section 652A	
(1)	s 1004(1)
(2)	s 1004(2)
(3)	s 1005(1)
(4)	s 1005(2)
(5)	s 1005(3)
(6)	s 1006(1)
(7)	s 1006(2)
(8)	s 1006(3)
(9)	s 1004(3)
652C Directors' duties following application under section 652A	
(1)	s 1007(1)
(2)	s 1007(2)
(3)	s 1007(3)
(4)	s 1009(1)
(5)	s 1009(2)
(6)	s 1009(4)
(7)	s 1009(3)
652D Sections 652B and 652C: supplementary provisions	
(1)	s 1008(1), (2)
(2)	s 1008(3)
(3)	s 1008(3)
(4)	s 1008(4)
(5)(c)	ss 1004(4), 1006(1), 1007(2), 1009(4)
(6)	s 1010
(8)	s 1011
652E Sections 652B and 652C: enforcement	
(1)	ss 1004(5), (7), 1005(4), (6), 1006(4), (6), 1007(4), (6), 1009(5), (7)

CA 1985	CA 2006
(2)	ss 1006(4), (7), 1007(4), (7)
(3)	ss 1004(6), 1005(5)
(4)	s 1006(5)
(5)	ss 1007(5), 1009(6)
654 Property of dissolved company to be bona vacantia	
(1)	s 1012(1)
(2)	s 1012(2)
655 Effect on s 654 of company's revival after dissolution	
(1)	s 1034(1)
(2)	s 1034(2)
(3)	s 1034(4)
(4)	s 1034(5)
656 Crown disclaimer of property vesting as bona vacantia	
(1)	s 1013(1)
(2)	s 1013(2) (changed)
(3)	s 1013(3)–(5) (changed)
(5)	s 1013(6), (7)
(6)	s 1013(8)
657 Effect of Crown disclaimer under s 656	
(1)	s 1014(1)
(2)	ss 1015(1), (2), 1016(1), (2), 1017(1)–(5), 1018(1)–(5), 1019
(4)	s 1020(1), (2)
(5)	s 1021(1), (2)
(6)	s 1021(3)
658 Liability for rentcharge on company's land after dissolution	
(1)	s 1023(1), (2)
(2)	s 1023(3)
680 Companies capable of being registered under this Chapter	
(1)(a), (b)	s 1040(1)
(1) (closing words)	s 1040(2), (3), (6)
(1A)	s 1040(1)
(2)	s 1040(1)
(3)	s 1040(4)
(4)	s 1040(4)
(5)	s 1040(5)
683 Definition of "joint stock company"	
(1)	s 1041(1)
(2)	s 1041(2)
694 Regulation of oversea companies in respect of their names	
(4)	s 1048(1), (2) (changed)
(5)	s 1048(3)–(5)
695 Service of documents on oversea company	
(1), (2)	s 1139(2) (changed)
695A Registrar to whom documents to be delivered: companies to which section 690A applies	
(4)	s 1059
699A Credit and financial institutions to which the Bank Branches Directive (89/117/EEC) applies	
(3) ("financial institution")	s 1173(1)
704 Registration offices	
(2)	s 1060(1), (2)
(4)	s 1062 (changed)

CA 1985	CA 2006
(7), (8)	s 1119(1), (2)
705 Companies' registered numbers	
(1)–(3)	s 1066(1)–(3)
(4)	s 1066(4), (5)
(5)(za)	s 1066(6)
705A Registration of branches of oversea companies	
(1)	s 1067(1) (changed)
(2)	s 1067(1)
(3)	s 1067(2)
(4)	s 1067(3)
(5)	s 1067(4), (5)
707A The keeping of company records by the registrar	
(1)	s 1080(4)
(2)	s 1083(1) (changed)
(3)	s 1084(1)–(3) (changed), (5)
(4)	s 1084(4)
708 Fees payable to registrar	
(1)	s 1063(1)–(3) (changed)
(2), (3)	s 1063(4) (changed)
(4)	s 1063(6)
(5)	s 1063(5) (changed)
709 Inspection, &c. of records kept by the registrar	
(1) opening words	s 1085(1) and s 1100
(1)(a), (b)	s 1086(1)
(2)	s 1085(2) (changed)
(3)	s 1091(3)
(4)	s 1091(5)
(5)	s 1092(1), (2)
710 Certificate of incorporation	
	s 1065
710A Provision and authentication by registrar of documents in non-legible form	
(2)	s 1115(2)
710B Documents relating to Welsh companies	
(1)–(3)	s 1104(1), (2)
(4)	s 1104(3)
(5)	s 1104(4)
711 Public notice by registrar of receipt and issue of certain documents	
(1)	ss 1064(1)–(3), 1077(1)–(3), 1078(2), (3) (changed)
(2)	s 1079(4) (changed)
713 Enforcement of company's duty to make returns	
(1)	s 1113(1)–(3)
(2), (3)	s 1113(4), (5)
714 Registrar's index of company and corporate names	
(1)	s 1099(1)–(3) (changed)
(2)	s 1099(4), (5)
715A Interpretation	
(1) ("document"), (2)	s 1114(1)
718 Unregistered companies	
(1)	s 1043(1), (3), (5) (changed)
(2)	s 1043(1)
(3)	s 1043(2), (5) (changed)
(5)	s 1043(4)
(6)	s 1043(6)

Part 3 CA 2006 Supporting Materials

CA 1985	CA 2006
719 Power of company to provide for employees on cessation or transfer of business	
(1)	s 247(1)
(2)	s 247(2) (changed)
(3)	s 247(4)–(6) (changed)
(4)	s 247(7) (changed)
721 Production and inspection of books where offence suspected	
(1)	s 1132(1), (2)
(2)–(4)	s 1132(3)–(5)
722 Form of company registers, etc	
(1)	ss 1134 and 1135(1) (changed)
(2)	s 1138(1)
(3)	s 1138(2), (3)
723 Use of computers for company records	
(1)	s 1135(1) (changed)
(2)	s 1135(5)
723A Obligations of company as to inspections of registers, &c.	
(1)	s 1137(1), (2)
(2)	s 1137(3)
(3)	s 1137(3)
(4)	s 1137(4)
(6), (7)	s 1137(5), (6)
725 Service of documents	
(1)	s 1139(1)
(2)	s 1139(4)
(3)	s 1139(4)
727 Power of court to grant relief in certain cases	
(1)–(3)	s 1157(1)–(3)
730 Punishment of offences	
(4)	s 1125(2)
(5)	s 1121(1), (3) (changed)
731 Summary proceedings	
(1)	s 1127(1), (2)
(2)	s 1128(1)
(3)	s 1128(2)
(4)	s 1128(4)
732 Prosecution by public authorities	
(1)	s 1126(1)
(2)	s 1126(2) (changed)
(3)	s 1129 (changed)
734 Criminal proceedings against unincorporated bodies	
(1)	s 1130(1), (2) (changed)
(2)	s 1130(3)
(3)	s 1130(2)
(4)	s 1130(2)
735 "Company", etc	
(1)(a), (b)	s 1(1)
(1)(c)	s 1171 (changed)
(3)	s 1171
736 "Subsidiary"; "holding company" and "wholly-owned subsidiary"	
(1), (2)	s 1159(1), (2)
(3)	s 1159(4)
736A Provisions supplementing s 736	

CA 1985	CA 2006
(1)–(11)	s 1159(3), Sch 6
736B Power to amend ss 736 and 736A	
(1)	s 1160(1)
(3)–(5)	s 1160(2)–(4)
737 "Called-up share capital"	
(1), (2)	s 547
738 "Allotment" and "paid up"	
(1)	s 558
(2)	s 583(2)–(3)(d)
(3)	s 583(5)
(4)	s 583(6)
739 "Non-cash asset"	
(1), (2)	s 1163(1), (2)
741 "Director" and "shadow director"	
(1)	s 250
(2)	s 251(1), (2)
(3)	s 251(3)
742 Expressions used in connection with accounts	
(1) ("fixed assets")	s 853(6)
(1) ("parent company")	s 1173(1)
(2)	s 853(4), (5)
742A Meaning of "offer to the public"	
(1)	s 756(1), (2)
(2)	s 756(3)
(3)	s 756(4), (5)(a)–(d) (changed)
(4)	s 756(4)
(5)	s 756(4)
(6)	s 756(5)(e), (6)
742B Meaning of "banking company"	
(1)–(3)	s 1164(1)–(3)
742C Meaning of "insurance company" and "authorised insurance company"	
(1)–(4)	s 1165(2)–(4)
(5)	s 1165(8)
743 "Employees' share scheme"	
	s 1166
744 Expressions used generally in this Act	
"articles"	s 18(4)
"the Companies Acts"	s 2(1), (2) (changed)
"the court"	s 1156(1)–(3) (changed)
"debenture"	s 738
"EEA State"	s 1170
"equity share capital"	s 548
"the Gazette"	s 1173(1)
"hire-purchase agreement"	s 1173(1)
"insurance market activity"	s 1165(7)
"officer"	ss 1121(2), 1173(1)
"oversea company"	s 1044 (changed)
"prescribed"	s 1167
"the registrar of companies" and "the registrar"	s 1060(3)
"regulated activity"	s 1173(1)
"share"	s 540(1), (4)
744A Index of defined expressions	

CA 1985	CA 2006
	Sch 8
Sch 2 Interpretation of references to "beneficial interest"	
Part 1 References in sections 23, 145, 146 and 148	
para 1(1)	ss 139(1), 672(1)
para 1(2)	ss 139(2), 672(2)
para 1(3)	ss 139(3), 672(3)
para 1(4)	ss 139(4), 672(4)
para 2(3)	s 672(5)
para 2(4)	s 672(6)
para 3(1), (2)	ss 140(1), (2), 673(1), (2)
para 4(1)	ss 138(1), (2), 674
para 4(2)	s 138(1)
para 4(3)	s 674
para 5(1)	ss 675(1), (2), 676
para 5(2)	ss 139(5), (6), 140(3), 675(1), (2)
para 5(3)	ss 139(6), 140(4), 676
Sch 4 Form and content of company accounts	
Part 3 Notes to the accounts	
para 56(2), (3)	ss 382(6), 465(6)
Part 7 Interpretation of Schedule	
para 94(1), (2)	s 411(6)
Sch 7B Specified persons, descriptions of disclosures etc for the purposes of section 245G	
Part 1 Specified persons	
	s 461(1)
Part 2 Specified descriptions of disclosures	
	s 461(4)
Part 3 Overseas regulatory bodies	
	s 461(5), (6)
Sch 10A Parent and subsidiary undertakings: supplementary provisions	
para 1	Sch 7, para 1
para 2(1)	Sch 7, para 2(1)
para 2(2)	Sch 7, para 2(2)
para 3(1)	Sch 7, para 3(1)
para 3(2)	Sch 7, para 3(2)
para 3(2)	Sch 7, para 3(3)
para 4(1)	Sch 7, para 4(1)
para 4(2)	Sch 7, para 4(2)
para 4(3)	Sch 7, para 4(3)
para 5(1)	Sch 7, para 5(1)
para 5(2)	Sch 7, para 5(2)
para 6	Sch 7, para 6
para 7(1)	Sch 7, para 7(1)
para 7(2)	Sch 7, para 7(2)
para 8	Sch 7, para 8
para 9(1)	Sch 7, para 9(1)
para 9(2)	Sch 7, para 9(2)
para 9(3)	Sch 7, para 9(3)
para 10	Sch 7, para 10
para 11	Sch 7, para 11
Sch 13 Provisions supplementing and interpreting sections 324 to 328	
Part 4 Provisions with respect to register of directors' interests to be kept under section 325	
para 27	s 809(2), (3)

CA 1985	CA 2006
Sch 14 Overseas branch registers	
Part 1 Countries and territories in which overseas branch register may be kept	
	s 129(2)
Part 2 General provisions with respect to overseas branch registers	
para 1(1), (2)	ss 130(1), 135(3)
para 1(3)	ss 130(2), (3), 135(4), (5)
para 2(1)	s 131(1)
para 3(1)	s 134(1), (2) (changed)
para 3(2)	s 134(3)
para 4(1)	s 132(1), (2) (changed)
para 4(2)	s 132(3), (4)
para 5	s 133(1), (2)
para 6	s 135(1), (2)
para 7	s 131(4)
Sch 15A Written resolutions of private companies	
Part 1 Exceptions	
para 1	s 288(2)
Part 2 Adaptation of procedural requirements	
para 3(1), (2)	ss 571(7), 573(5)
para 5(1), (2)	ss 695(2), 698(2)
para 5(3), (4)	ss 696(2), 699(2)
para 6(1)	ss 717(2), 718(2)
para 6(2)	s 717(2)
para 6(3)	s 718(2)
para 7	s 188(5)
Sch 15B Provisions subject to which ss 425–427 have effect in their application to mergers and divisions of public companies	
para 1	ss 907(1), (2), 922(1), (2)
para 2(1)	ss 905(1), 906(1)–(3), 920(1), 921(1)–(4)
para 2(2)	ss 905(2), (3), 920(2)
para 2(3)	s 920(3)
para 3	ss 908(1), (3), 909(1), (7), 911(1), (2), (4), 912, 923(1), (4), 924(1), (7), 925(5), 926(1), (2), (4), 927(1)–(3), 928
para 4(1)	ss 908(2), 923(2)
para 4(2)	s 923(3)
para 5(1)	ss 909(2), (3), 924(2), (3)
para 5(2)	ss 909(3), 924(3)
para 5(3)	ss 909(4), 924(4)
para 5(4)	s 935(1) (changed)
para 5(6)	s 935(2)
para 5(7)	ss 909(5), 924(5)
para 5(8)	ss 909(6), 924(6)
para 6(1)	ss 910(1), 911(3), 925(1), 926(3)
para 6(2)	ss 910(2), 925(2)
para 6(3)	ss 910(3), 925(3) (changed)
para 6(4)	ss 910(4), 925(4),
para 7	ss 914, 930
para 8(1)	ss 913(1), 929(1)
para 8(2)	ss 913(2), 929(2)
para 9(1)	s 939(1)
para 9(2)	s 939(1), (2)

CA 1985	CA 2006
para 9(3)	s 939(3), (4)
para 9(4)	s 939(5)
para 10(1)	ss 918(1), 932(1)
para 10(2)	ss 916(3)–(5), 918(2)–(4), 932(2)–(5)
para 11(1)	s 933(1)–(3), 934(1)
para 11(2)	s 933(1)–(3)
para 11(3)	s 934(1)
para 11(4)	s 934(2)–(4)
para 12(1)	ss 915(1), (6), 917(1), (6)
para 12(2)	s 915(2)
para 12(3)	s 915(3)–(5)
para 12(4)	s 917(2)
para 12(5)	ss 917(3)–(5), 931(3), (5)
para 13(1)	s 931(1)
para 13(2)	s 931(2)
para 13(3)	s 931(3), (4), (6)

CA 1985	CA 2006
para 14(1)	s 916(1)
para 14(2)	s 916(2)
para 14(3)	s 916(3)–(5)
para 15(1)	s 940(1)
para 15(2)	s 940(2)
para 15(3)	s 940(3)
Sch 20 Vesting of disclaimed property; protection of third parties	
Part 2 Crown disclaimer under section 656 (Scotland only)	
para 5	s 1022(1)
para 6	s 1022(2)
para 7	s 1022(3)
para 8	s 1022(4), (5)
para 9	s 1022(6)

COMPANIES ACT 1989

(1) Section 130(6) of the Companies Act 1989 (power by regulations to apply provisions relating to company contracts and execution of documents by companies to overseas companies) is re-enacted in section 1045 of the Companies Act 2006.

(2) Section 207 of the Companies Act 1989 (transfer of securities) is re-enacted in sections 783, 784(3), 785 and 788 of the Companies Act 2006.

MINISTERIAL STATEMENTS ON DUTIES OF DIRECTORS

COMPANIES ACT 2006
DUTIES OF COMPANY DIRECTORS
MINISTERIAL STATEMENTS
DTI
JUNE 2007

Introduction

Rt Hon Margaret Hodge MP MBE (Minister of State for Industry and the Regions)

[3.10]
I know that the new statutory duties of directors set out in Part 10 of the Companies Act 2006 were keenly debated while the Bill was going through Parliament, and I am sure they will continue to be seen as one of the most significant parts of the Act.

During those debates, I and the other Ministers were questioned about the meaning of the provisions. Some of our responses and statements may be helpful to people interested in what the provisions mean, and I am pleased to be publishing this structured collection of what we believe are the most useful of them.

There are two ways of looking at the statutory statement of directors' duties: on the one the hand it simply codifies the existing common law obligations of company directors; on the other – especially in section 172: the duty to act in the interests of the company – it marks a radical departure in articulating the connection between what is good for a company and what is good for society at large.

Continuity

The statutory expression of the duties is essentially the same as the existing duties established by case law, the only major exception being the new procedures for dealing with conflicts of interest.

The simple high-level guidance for directors in the box on the following page illustrates the way in which the codification maintains continuity with the existing law: this advice on how a director has to live up to his position of trust is applicable to the pre-existing common law as well as to the new codification. For most directors, who are working hard and put the interests of their company before their own, there will be no need to change their behaviour.

Guidance for company directors—

(1) Act in the company's best interests, taking everything you think relevant into account.
(2) Obey the company's constitution and decisions taken under it.
(3) Be honest, and remember that the company's property belongs to it and not to you or to its shareholders.
(4) Be diligent, careful and well informed about the company's affairs. If you have any special skills or experience, use them.
(5) Make sure the company keeps records of your decisions.
(6) Remember that you remain responsible for the work you give to others.
(7) Avoid situations where your interests conflict with those of the company. When in doubt disclose potential conflicts quickly.
(8) Seek external advice where necessary, particularly if the company is in financial difficulty.

Change

But compared with most text-book definitions of the common law duties of directors, the new statutory statement captures a cultural change in the way in which companies conduct their business. There was a time when business success in the interests of shareholders was thought to be in conflict with society's aspirations for people who work in the company or in supply chain companies, for the long-term well-being of the community and for the protection of the environment. The law is now based on a new approach. Pursuing the interests of shareholders and embracing wider responsibilities are complementary purposes, not contradictory ones.

I strongly believe that businesses perform better, and are more sustainable in the long term, when they have regard to a wider group of issues in pursuing success. That is a common-sense approach that reflects a modern view of the way in which businesses operate in their community: they interact with customers and suppliers; they make sure that employees are motivated and properly rewarded; and they think about their impact on communities and the environment. They do so at least partly because it makes good business sense.

The new expression of the duties is part of the wider recognition and encouragement of change in the Act. The enhanced business review, which for quoted companies must now include information on environmental, employee, social and community issues, is another key example that builds on the growing consensus that it is good business sense for companies to embrace wider social responsibilities.

I am sure that directors' duties will continue to evolve as times change and as societal norms are transformed. Corporate social responsibility has developed and evolved over time. The relationship between business interests and the wider world is changing all the time. The best way of achieving lasting cultural change is to go with the tide and the broad consensus of opinion.

Margaret Hodge

Notes on the ministerial statements

The quotations should be read in conjunction with the Act itself (available in hard copy at www.tsoshop.co.uk or online at www.opsi.gov.uk) and should not be regarded as a substitute for reading that Act or seeking legal advice. Full explanatory notes on the provisions of the Act are also available at www.tsoshop.co.uk and at www.opsi.gov.uk together with tables of origins and destinations for the Act's provisions.

It should be noted that on occasion the Parliamentary quotes have been edited in order to make it easier to read them. References to Hansard have been given so the full discussion can be seen if so desired.

Companies Act 2006 – Duties of directors

Collated Hansard extracts from debates on Companies Bill (originally Company Law Reform Bill)

Background

"The law commissions and the Company Law Review concluded that a statutory statement of duties would be helpful . . . it is important that . . . flexibility and ability to note changing circumstances are not lost".

Lord Goldsmith, Lords Grand Committee, 6 February 2006, column 242

"First . . . .the origins of the general duties [is] . . . that they are based in certain common law rules and equitable principles . . . the statutory statement replaces the common rule equitable principle . . . once the Act is passed, one will go to the statutory statement of duties to identify the duties to identify the duty the director owed".

Lord Goldsmith, Lords Grand Committee, 6 February 2006, column 243

" . . . the main purpose in codifying the general duties of directors is to make what is expected of directors clearer and to make the law more accessible to them and to others".

Lord Goldsmith, Lords Grand Committee, 6 February 2006, column 254

"We should remind ourselves that being a company director is a wonderful thing for the person who is a company director. But it is a position of great responsibility which involves running the affairs of a company for the benefit of other people. It is a heavy responsibility we should not water down".

Lord Goldsmith, Lords Grand Committee, 6 February 2006, column 291

Interpretation by the courts

"The courts should be left to interpret the words Parliament passes".

Lord Goldsmith, Lords Grand Committee, 6 February 2006, column 243

"Although the duties in relation to directors have developed in a distinctive way, they are often manifestations of more general principles . . . [it] is intended to enable the courts to continue to have regard to development in the common law rules and equitable principles applying to these other types of fiduciary relationships. The advantage of that is it will enable the statutory duties to develop in line with relevant developments in the law as it applies elsewhere."

Lord Goldsmith, Lords Grand Committee, 6 February 2006, column 244

Effect of codification

"One proposition [is] that the result of this codification will be increased litigation. That is not how we see it . . . as in existing law, the general duties are owed by the director to the company. It follows that, as now, only the company can enforce them. Directors are liable to the company for loss to the company, and not more widely. It is quite rare for companies to sue their directors for breach of duty. That may well continue to be the position."

Lord Goldsmith, Lords Grand Committee, 6 February 2006, column 242

Effect of the provision of new duties

"[On] the provision of new duties, we do not see why that should lead to increased litigation either. For example . . . the need to have regard to the interests of employees as part of the main duty to promote the success of the company . . . was part of case law before becoming statute. It is an important principle, and plays a crucial part in business decisions . . . however . . . there is not evidence of which we are aware that it has led to legalistic decision making by companies, or people turning away from bringing their talent to the world of enterprise. We have no reason to expect that there will be a greater degree of litigation on those duties than there is now".

Lord Goldsmith, Lords Grand Committee, 6 February 2006, column 243

Statement of general duties

"The statement of general duties . . . is not intended to be an exhaustive list of all the duties owed by a director to his company. The directors may owe a wide range of duties to their companies in addition to the general duties listed. Those are general, basic duties which it is seen as right and important to set out in this way. The statement that these are the general duties does not allow a director to escape any other obligation he has, including obligations under the Insolvency Act 1986."

Lord Goldsmith, Lords Grand Committee, 6 February 2006, column 249

Enlightened shareholder value

"The Company Law Review considered and consulted on two main options. The first was "enlightened shareholder value", under which a director must first act in the way that he or she considers, in good faith, would be most likely to promote the success of the company for its members . . . The Government agrees this is the right approach. It resolves any confusion in the mind of directors as to what that the interests of the company are, and prevents any inclination to identify those interests with their own. It also prevents confusion between the interests of those who depend on the company and those of the members".

Lord Goldsmith, Lords Grand Committee, 6 February 2006, column 255

"For the first time, the Bill includes a statutory statement of directors' general duties. It provides a code of conduct that sets out how directors are expected to behave. That enshrines in statue what the law review called "enlightened shareholder value". It recognises that directors will be more likely to achieve long term sustainable success for the benefit of their shareholders if their companies pay attention to a wider range of matters . . . Directors will be required to promote the success of the company in the collective best interest of the shareholders, but in doing so they will have to have regard to a wider range of factors, including the interests of employees and the environment".

Alistair Darling, Commons Second Reading, 6 June 2006, column 125

Duty to promote the success of the company

"What is success? The starting point is that it is essentially for the members of the company to define the objective they wish to achieve. Success means what the members collectively want the company to achieve. For a commercial company, success will usually mean long-term increase in value. For certain companies, such as charities and community interest companies, it will mean the attainment of the objectives for which the company has been established".

Lord Goldsmith, Lords Grand Committee, 6 February 2006, column 255

" . . . for a commercial company, success will normally mean long-term increase in value, but the company's constitution and decisions made under it may also lay down the appropriate success model for the company. . . . it is essentially for the members of a company to define the objectives they wish to achieve. The normal way for that to be done—the traditional way—is that the members do it at the time the company is established. In the old style, it would have been set down in the company's memorandum. That is changing . . . but the principle does not change that those who establish the company will start off by setting out what they hope to achieve. For most people who invest in companies, there is never any doubt about it—money. That is what they want. They want a long-term increase in the company. It is not a snap poll to be taken at any point in time."

Lord Goldsmith, Lords Grand Committee, 6 February 2006, column 258

" . . . it is for the directors, by reference to those things we are talking about – the objective of the company – to judge and form a good faith judgment about what is to be regarded as success for the members as a whole . . . .they will need to look at the company's constitution, shareholder decisions and anything else that they consider relevant in helping them to reach that judgement . . . the duty is to promote the success for the benefit of the members as a whole – that is, for the members as a collective body – not only to benefit the majority shareholders, or any particular shareholder or section of shareholders, still less the interests of directors who might happen to be shareholders themselves. That is an important statement of the way in which directors need to look at this judgement they have to make".

Lord Goldsmith, Lords Grand Committee, 6 February 2006, column 256

" . . . we have included the words "amongst other matters". We want to be clear that the list of factors [for a director to have regard to] is not exhaustive".

Lord Goldsmith, Lords Grand Committee, 9 May 2006, column 846

"The clause does not impose a requirement on directors to keep records, as some people have suggested, in any circumstances in which they would not have to do so now."

Margaret Hodge, Commons Committee, 11 July 2006, column 592

"The Government believe that our enlightened shareholder value approach will be mutually beneficial to business and society. We do not, however, claim that the interests of the company and of its employees will always be identical; regrettably, it will sometimes be necessary, for example, to lay off staff. The drafting . . . must therefore clearly point directors towards their overarching objective. We have made it clear that [the clause] will make a difference, and a very important difference. The words "have regard to" mean "think about"; they are absolutely not about just ticking boxes. If "thinking about" leads to the conclusion, as we believe it will in many cases, that the proper course is to act positively to achieve the objectives in the clause, that will be what the director's duty is. In other words "have regard to" means "give proper consideration to" . . . Consideration of the factors will be an integral part of the duty to promote the success of the company for the benefit of its members as a whole. The clause makes it clear that a director is to have regard to the factors in fulfilling that duty. The decisions taken by a director and the weight given to the factors will continue to be a matter for his good faith judgment.".

Margaret Hodge, Commons Report, 17 October 2006, column 789

Duty to exercise independent judgement

" . . . the clause does not mean that a director has to form his judgement totally independently from anyone or anything. It does not actually mean that the director has to be independent himself. He can have an interest in the matter . . . It is the exercise of the judgement of a director that must be independent in the sense of it being his own judgement . . . The duty does not prevent a director from relying on the advice or work of others, but the final judgement must be his responsibility. He clearly cannot be expected to do everything himself. Indeed, in certain circumstances directors may be in breach of duty if they fail to take appropriate advice – for example, legal advice. As with all advice, slavish reliance is not acceptable, and the obtaining of outside advice does not absolve directors from exercising their judgement on the basis of such advice".

Lord Goldsmith, Lords Grand Committee, 6 February 2006, column 282

Standard of care owed by a director

" . . . the standard of care which a director owes is enormously important . . . it is now accepted that the duty of care . . . is accurately stated in Section 214(4) of the Insolvency Act 1986 . . . . Under the clause you take account both of the general knowledge, skills and experience that may be reasonably expected of a person carrying out those functions and the general knowledge, skills and experience that that director has. It is a cumulative requirement . . . I want to emphasise the point that it is not making a change from what is already the common law".

Lord Goldsmith, Lords Grand Committee, 6 February 2006, column 284

Duty to avoid conflicts of interest

" . . . the law already recognises that potential conflicts in certain circumstances are to be avoided . . . there is currently no absolute rule prohibiting directors from holding multiple directorships or even from engaging in business that competes with the company of which they are a director, but obviously a tension results from that degree of tolerance and the fiduciary duties which the director owes. The solution to it is . . . there is no prohibition of a conflict or potential conflict as long as it is has been authorised by the directors in accordance with the requirements set out in [the Act]".

Lord Goldsmith, Lords Grand Committee, 6 February 2006, column 288

" . . . we do not say that this should happen just because in the mind of a director it is all right; there should be a process for the company, through its members or directors, to make that decision, and that is what these new regulations permit".

Lord Goldsmith, Lords Grand Committee, 6 February 2006, column 289

"Following consultation, the Government have already adjusted the provision . . . to use instead the expression "if the situation cannot reasonably be regarded as likely to give rise to a conflict of interest". This introduces the concept of reasonableness which makes the situation easier from the point of view of a director and avoids a very harsh test, although it is still a heavy duty and intended to be so."

Lord Goldsmith, Lords Grand Committee, 6 February 2006, column 293

"So far as private companies are concerned, the default position is that the directors may authorise the matter unless there is a provision in the company's constitution saying otherwise. In the case of a public company . . . [d]irectors may authorise the matter only if the company's constitution includes provisions saying they can do so. It must follow that if the constitution does not do so, steps will have to be taken to amend it to that effect and the members of the company will be able to take a view about whether they think that is a good move".

Lord Goldsmith, Lords Grand Committee, 6 February 2006, column 294

" . . . the authorisation has to be given without relying on the votes of directors seeking the authorisation or any other director with an interest in it . . . . Those directors cannot count towards the quorum either . . . .[and] any requirements under the common law for what is necessary for a valid authorisation remain in force . . . Finally, in general terms, the directors who are giving the authorisation will need to comply with the general duties imposed on them. Those will include, specifically, the general duty . . . to act in such a way that in good faith they consider that authorisation is the course of action most likely to promote the success of the company".

Lord Goldsmith, Lords Grand Committee, 9 February 2006, column 327

" . . . the duty does not apply if the situation cannot reasonably be regarded as being likely to give rise to a conflict of interest. If the matter falls outside the ambit of the company's business, a real conflict of interest is unlikely".

Lord Goldsmith, Lords Grand Committee, 9 May 2006, column 864

" . . . the company's articles may contain provisions for dealing with conflicts of interests, and directors will not be in breach of duty if they act in accordance with those provisions. Examples might include arrangements whereby the directors withdraw from any board meeting at which the matters relating to conflicts of interest are discussed . . . our amendments will allow all the normal, perfectly acceptable, lawful ways in which companies and their directors deal with conflicts of interest to continue."

Lord Sainsbury of Turville, Lords Report, 23 May 2006, column 722

Duty not to accept benefits from third parties

" . . . the purpose of the clause . . . is to impose on a director a duty not to accept benefits from third parties. It applies only to benefits conferred because the director is a director of the company or because of something that the director does or doesn't do as director. The word "benefit" . . . includes benefits of any description, including non-financial benefits. The clause codifies . . . [the] long-standing rule, prohibiting the exploitation of the position of director for personal benefit. It does not apply to benefits that the director receives from the company, or from any associated company, or from any person acting on behalf of any of those companies . . . . I . . . draw attention to the fact that benefits are prohibited by the duty only if their acceptance is likely to give rise to a conflict of interest".

Lord Goldsmith, Lords Grand Committee, 9 February 2006, column 330

Duty to declare interest in proposed transaction or arrangement

"[This] clause . . . is deliberately intended to apply only to proposed transactions . . . if a company is told that a director has an interest in a proposed transaction, it can decide whether to enter into the transaction, on what terms and with what safeguards. [As for] "a director is treated as being aware of matters he ought reasonably to be aware" . . . I believe that the test is objective – that is, one judges objectively whether this is a matter of which the director ought to be aware reasonably".

Lord Goldsmith, Lords Grand Committee, 9 February 2006, column 334

Civil consequences of breach of general duties

" . . . we take the view that the "duty to exercise reasonable care, skill and diligence" is not a fiduciary duty. It may be owed by someone who is a fiduciary. But that is not the same thing . . . It is important to keep to the principle that these are enforceable in the same way as any other fiduciary duty owed to the company by its directors."

Lord Goldsmith, Lords Grand Committee, 9 February 2006, column 336

Consent, approval or authorisation by members

"[The Bill] permitted director authorisation of what would otherwise be impermissible conflicts of interests [and] . . . required declarations of interest in proposed company transactions. In both those cases, the general duty no longer requires the consent of the members. The common law rules or principles that refer to the failure to have had a conflict of interest approved by the member of a company under certain circumstances need to be set aside . . . . However . . . the company's constitution can reverse the change and can insist on certain steps being taken requiring the consent of the members in certain circumstances".

Lord Goldsmith, Lords Grand Committee, 9 February 2006, column 337

Indemnifying directors

" . . . the starting point for our reform package was a principle . . . that companies should be prohibited from exempting directors from, or indemnifying them against, liability for negligence, default, breach of duty or breach of trust in relation to the company. However the reform package also recognised that companies should be permitted to indemnify directors in respect of third-party claims in most circumstances . . . There are four main possible exceptions to indemnification: criminal penalties; penalties imposed by regulatory bodies: costs incurred by the director in defending criminal proceedings in which he is convicted; and costs incurred by the director in defending civil proceedings brought by the company in which final judgement is given against him".

Lord Goldsmith, Lords Grand Committee, 9 February 2006, column 364

"[The Companies (Audit, Investigations and Community Enterprise) Act 2004] . . . closed an important loophole concerning the indemnification of directors by third parties. It used to be the practice in some groups that one group company would indemnify the director of another group company . . . in effect to circumvent the rule that the company could not indemnify its own directors. We take the view that . . . continu[ing] to make directors properly accountable for what they do in relation to the company . . . should stand".

Lord Goldsmith, Lords Grand Committee, 9 February 2006, column 366

"It is also important to remember that at the same time as the loophole was closed, important reforms were introduced that permit all companies to indemnify directors against third-party claims, subject to . . . [certain] requirements. Although we agree that indemnification by a parent company of the directors is less likely to result in attempts at circumvention of the prohibition than indemnification by a wholly owned subsidiary company of the director of a holding company, we still believe there is scope for mischief. We cannot . . . accept [any] amendment".

Lord Sainsbury of Turville, Lords Report, 23 May 2006, column 724

Shadow directors

"The law is still developing. It would not be right for the general duties not to apply at all to a shadow directors, but the law may develop in such a way that some do and some don't. It is right to leave those areas, as now, to the courts . . . "

Lord Goldsmith, Lords Grand Committee, 9 May 2006, column 828

NOTES

Note that the OPSI website (www.opsi.gov.uk) is now www.legislation.gov.uk.

PART 4
COMPANIES ACT 2006 STATUTORY INSTRUMENTS

COMPANIES (REGISTRAR, LANGUAGES AND TRADING DISCLOSURES) REGULATIONS 2006

(SI 2006/3429)

NOTES

Made: 20 December 2006.

Authority: European Communities Act 1972, s 2(2); Limited Liability Partnerships Act 2000, ss 15, 17; Companies Act 2006, ss 1091(4), 1105(2)(d), 1106(2).

Commencement: 1 January 2007.

These Regulations are reproduced as amended by: the Companies (Trading Disclosures) Regulations 2008, SI 2008/495.

For a summary of all Orders and Regulations made under the Companies Act 2006, see Appendix 4 at **[A4]**.

General note: statutory Instruments made under the European Communities Act 1972: the 1972 Act was repealed by the European Union (Withdrawal) Act 2018, s 1, as from exit day (as defined in s 20 of that Act (ie, 11pm on 31 January 2020)). However, provision was made for the continuation in force of any subordinate legislation made under the authority of s 2(2) of the 1972 Act by s 1B(1)–(5) of the 2018 Act at **[12.3]**. Note that sub-ss (1)–(5) of s 1B of the 2018 Act were repealed by s 1B(6) of the 2018 Act as from IP completion day (as defined in the European Union (Withdrawal Agreement) Act 2020, s 39) (ie, 11pm on 31 December 2020)). For the status of "EU-derived domestic legislation" after IP completion day, see s 2 of the 2018 Act at **[12.4]**. That section provides that (subject to ss 5, 5A of, and Sch 1 to, the 2018 Act) EU-derived domestic legislation, as it had effect in domestic law immediately before IP completion day, continues to have effect in domestic law on and after IP completion day.

[4.1]

1 Citation, commencement and interpretation

(1) These Regulations may be cited as the Companies (Registrar, Languages and Trading Disclosures) Regulations 2006 and shall come into force on 1st January 2007.

(2) In these Regulations—

"the 1985 Act" means the Companies Act 1985,

"the 1986 Order" means the Companies (Northern Ireland) Order 1986, and

"the 2006 Act" means the Companies Act 2006.

[4.2]

2 Certification of electronic copies by registrar

(1) Where—

(a) a person requires a copy of material on the register under section 1086 of the 2006 Act,

(b) that person expressly requests that the copy be certified as a true copy, and

(c) the registrar provides the copy in electronic form,

the registrar's certificate that the copy is an accurate record of the contents of the original document must be provided in accordance with the following provisions.

(2) The certificate must be authenticated by means of an electronic signature that—

(a) is uniquely linked to the registrar,

(b) indicates that the registrar has caused it to be applied,

(c) is created using means that the registrar can maintain under his sole control, and

(d) is linked—

(i) to the certificate, and

(ii) to the copy provided under section 1086 of the 2006 Act

in such a manner that any subsequent change of the data comprised in either is detectable.

(3) For the purposes of this regulation, an "electronic signature" means data in electronic form which are attached to or logically associated with other electronic data and which serve as a method of authentication.

[4.3]

3 Provisions requiring office copies to be delivered to the registrar

(1) In the following provisions (which require an office copy of certain orders to be delivered to the registrar) for "an office copy" substitute "a copy"—

(a) section 54(7) of the 1985 Act and article 64(7) of the 1986 Order (order on litigated objection to resolution that public company be re-registered as private),

(b) section 425(3) of the 1985 Act and article 418(3) of the 1986 Order (order sanctioning compromise or arrangement),

(c) section 427(5) of the 1985 Act and article 420(5) of the 1986 Order (order sanctioning compromise or arrangement),

(d) section 201(4) of the Insolvency Act 1986 and article 166(4) of the Insolvency (Northern Ireland) Order 1989 (order deferring date at which dissolution of company after winding up is to take effect).

(2) In—

(a) Form 139, in Schedule 3 to the Companies (Forms) Regulations 1985 and

(b) Form 149, in Schedule 3 to the Companies (Forms) Regulations (Northern Ireland) 1986,

for "Office copy" substitute "Copy".

(3) For the purposes of their application to limited liability partnerships by the Limited Liability Partnerships Regulations 2001 or the Limited Liability Partnerships Regulations (Northern Ireland) 2004, the provisions specified in paragraph (1)(b), (c) and (d) have effect as if not amended by this regulation.

[4.4]

4 Language requirements: contracts relating to allotments of shares

Section 1105 of the 2006 Act (documents that may be drawn up and delivered in languages other than English) applies to contracts required to be delivered to the registrar under section 88(2)(b)(i) of the 1985 Act or article 98(2)(b)(i) of the 1986 Order.

[4.5]

5 Voluntary filing of translations

The facility described in section 1106 of the 2006 Act (voluntary filing of translations) is available in relation to—

(a) all the official languages of the European Union, and

(b) all documents subject to the Directive disclosure requirements.

6, 7 *(Reg 6 introduced Schs 1 and 2 to these Regulations (amendments to the Companies Act 1985 and the Companies (Northern Ireland) Order 1986), and was revoked by the Companies (Trading Disclosures) Regulations 2008, SI 2008/495, reg 11, as from 1 October 2008. Reg 7 amends the Insolvency Act 1986, s 188 at* **[9.320]**, *and the Insolvency (Northern Ireland) Order 1989.)*

SCHEDULES 1 AND 2

(Sch 1 amended the Companies Act 1985, ss 349, 351, 705, Sch 24, and was revoked by the Companies (Trading Disclosures) Regulations 2008, SI 2008/495, reg 11, as from 1 October 2008. Sch 2 amended the Companies (Northern Ireland) Order 1986, and was also revoked by SI 2008/495, reg 11, as from 1 October 2008.)

COMPANIES (POLITICAL EXPENDITURE EXEMPTION) ORDER 2007

(SI 2007/2081)

NOTES

Made: 18 July 2007.

Authority: Companies Act 2006, ss 377, 1292(1)(c).

Commencement: 1 October 2007 (in relation to Great Britain); 1 November 2007 (in relation to Northern Ireland).

For a summary of all Orders and Regulations made under the Companies Act 2006, see Appendix 4 at **[A4]**.

This Order is reproduced as amended by: the Companies, Limited Liability Partnerships and Partnerships (Amendment etc) (EU Exit) Regulations 2019, SI 2019/348.

[4.6]

1 Citation, commencement and interpretation

(1) This Order may be cited as the Companies (Political Expenditure Exemption) Order 2007 and shall come into force—

(a) for the purposes of its application to Great Britain, on 1st October 2007;

(b) for the purposes of its application to Northern Ireland, on 1st November 2007.

(2) In this Order, "news material" means material relating to—

(a) news,

(b) public and political affairs,

(c) public and political events, or

(d) views, opinion or comment on such news, affairs or events.

[4.7]

2 Exemption from authorisation

Political expenditure is exempt from the need for authorisation under Part 14 of the Companies Act 2006 if it is—

(a) political expenditure to which article 3 applies, and

(b) incurred by a company to which article 4 applies.

[4.8]

3 Description of political expenditure

(1) This article applies to political expenditure incurred in respect of the preparation, publication or dissemination of news material, where that material contains matter which would render that preparation, publication or dissemination on the part of the company an activity on the part of the company that is capable of being reasonably regarded as intended—

(a) to affect public support for a political party or other political organisation, or an independent election candidate, or

(b) to influence voters in relation to any national or regional referendum held under the law of [the United Kingdom].

(2) Until 1st October 2008, paragraph (1)(a) has effect as if the words "or an independent election candidate" were omitted.

NOTES

Para (1): words in square brackets substituted by the Companies, Limited Liability Partnerships and Partnerships (Amendment etc) (EU Exit) Regulations 2019, SI 2019/348, reg 7, Sch 2, paras 1, 2, as from IP completion day (as defined in the European Union (Withdrawal Agreement) Act 2020, s 39).

[4.9]

4 Description of company

(1) This article applies to any company whose ordinary course of business includes, or is proposed to include, the publication or dissemination to the public, or any part of the public, of news material, or the preparation of such material for publication or dissemination to the public, or any part of the public.

(2) For the purposes of paragraph (1), it is to be irrelevant—

(a) by which means or modes the news material is to be prepared, published or disseminated; or

(b) where the public, or any part of the public, to which such material is published or disseminated is located or the identity or description of the public or any part of it.

COMPANIES (INTEREST RATE FOR UNAUTHORISED POLITICAL DONATION OR EXPENDITURE) REGULATIONS 2007 (NOTE)

(SI 2007/2242)

[4.10]

NOTES

These Regulations were made on 25 July 2007 under the Companies Act 2006, ss 369(5)(b) and 1167 and came into force on 1 October 2007 (for the purpose of their application to Great Britain) and on 1 November 2007 (for the purpose of their application to Northern Ireland). Under the Companies Act 2006, s 369, where a company has made a political donation or incurred political expenditure without the authorisation required by CA 2006 the directors are liable to make good to the company the amount of the unauthorised donation or expenditure with interest. These Regulations set the rate of interest to be applied at 8% per annum.

COMPANIES (FEES FOR INSPECTION AND COPYING OF COMPANY RECORDS) REGULATIONS 2007

(SI 2007/2612)

NOTES

Made: 6 September 2007.

Authority: Companies Act 2006, ss 116(1)(b), (2), 229(2), 238(2), 358(4), 807(2), 811(2), 1137(1), (4), 1167, 1292(1)(a), (c).

Commencement: 1 October 2007.

For a summary of all Orders and Regulations made under the Companies Act 2006, see Appendix 4 at **[A4]**.

[4.11]

1 Citation, commencement and interpretation

(1) These Regulations may be cited as the Companies (Fees for Inspection and Copying of Company Records) Regulations 2007 and shall come into force on 1st October 2007.

(2) In these Regulations—

"the Act" means the Companies Act 2006; and

"the Commencement Order" means the Companies Act 2006 (Commencement No 3, Consequential Amendments, Transitional Provisions and Savings) Order 2007.

[4.12]

2 Fee for inspection of registers

For the purpose of section 116(1)(b) of the Act (inspection of register and index of members' names) the fee prescribed is £3.50 for each hour or part thereof during which the right of inspection is exercised.

[4.13]

3 Fee for copy of registers

(1) For the purposes of the following sections of the Act—

(a) section 116(2) (copy of company's register of members); and

(b) section 811(2) (copy of entries in register of interests in shares disclosed),

the fee prescribed is—

(i) the amount per number of entries copied by the company as set out in paragraph (2); and

(ii) the reasonable costs incurred by the company in delivering the copy of the entries to the person entitled to be provided with that copy.

(2) The amounts per number of entries copied are—

(a) £1 for each of the first 5 entries;

(b) £30 for the next 95 entries or part thereof;

(c) £30 for the next 900 entries or part thereof;

(d) £30 for the next 99,000 entries or part thereof; and

(e) £30 for the remainder of the entries in the register or part thereof.

[4.14]

4 Fee for copy of company records

For the purposes of the following sections of the Act—

(a) section 229(2) (copy of director's service contract or memorandum setting out the terms of that contract);

(b) section 238(2) (copy of director's qualifying indemnity provision);

(c) section 358(4) (copy of records of resolutions and meetings); and

(d) section 807(2) (copy of report under section 805 of the Act),

the fee prescribed is—

(i) 10 pence per 500 words or part thereof copied; and

(ii) the reasonable costs incurred by the company in delivering the copy of the company record to the person entitled to be provided with that copy.

[4.15]

5 Revocation and savings: Great Britain

(1) (*Revokes the Companies (Inspection and Copying of Registers, Indices and Documents) Regulations 1991, SI 1991/1998, Sch 2, paras 1(d), 2(b), (d), 3(b), subject to the savings in paras (2), (3) below.*)

(2) The fees prescribed in the following paragraphs of Schedule 2 to the 1991 Regulations—

(a) paragraph 1(d) (fee for inspection of register of members and index); and

(b) paragraph 2(d) (fee for copies of entries in the register of members),

shall continue to apply in respect of requests relating to the register of members or the index of members' names of a company which are subject to section 356 of the Companies Act 1985 by virtue of paragraph 2(2) of Schedule 3 to the Commencement Order.

(3) The fee prescribed in paragraph 3(b) of Schedule 2 to the 1991 Regulations shall continue to apply in respect of requests relating to minutes of general meetings which are subject to section 383 of the Companies Act 1985 by virtue of paragraph 40(2) of Schedule 3 to the Commencement Order.

6 *((Revocation and savings: Northern Ireland) outside the scope of this work.)*

COMPANIES (FEES FOR INSPECTION AND COPYING OF COMPANY RECORDS) (NO 2) REGULATIONS 2007

(SI 2007/3535)

NOTES

Made: 17 December 2007.

Authority: Companies Act 2006, ss 744(1)(b), (2), 749(1), 1137(1), (4), 1167, 1292(1)(a), (c).

Commencement: 6 April 2008.

For a summary of all Orders and Regulations made under the Companies Act 2006, see Appendix 4 at **[A4]**.

[4.16]

1 Citation, commencement and interpretation

(1) These Regulations may be cited as the Companies (Fees for Inspection and Copying of Company Records) (No 2) Regulations 2007 and come into force on 6th April 2008.

(2) In these Regulations—

(a) "the Act" means the Companies Act 2006; and

(b) "the Commencement Order" means the Companies Act 2006 (Commencement No 5, Transitional Provisions and Savings) Order 2007.

[4.17]

2 Fee for inspection of register of debenture holders

For the purpose of section 744(1)(b) of the Act (inspection of register of debenture holders) the fee prescribed is £3.50 for each hour or part thereof during which the right of inspection is exercised.

[4.18]

3 Fee for copy of register of debenture holders

(1) The fee prescribed for the purpose of section 744(2) of the Act (copy of entries in register of debenture holders) is—

(a) the amount per number of entries copied by the company as set out in paragraph (2); and

(b) the reasonable costs incurred by the company in delivering the copy of the entries to the person entitled to be provided with that copy.

(2) The amounts per number of entries copied are—

(a) £1 for each of the first 5 entries;

(b) £30 for the next 95 entries or part thereof;

(c) £30 for the next 900 entries or part thereof;

(d) £30 for the next 99,000 entries or part thereof; and

(e) £30 for the remainder of the entries in the register or part thereof.

[4.19]

4 Fee for copy of debenture trust deed

The fee prescribed for the purpose of section 749(1) of the Act (right of debenture holder to copy of debenture trust deed) is—

(a) 10 pence per 500 words or part thereof copied; and

(b) the reasonable costs incurred by the company in delivering the copy of the debenture trust deed or part thereof to the person entitled to be provided with it.

[4.20]

5 Revocation and savings: Great Britain

(1) (*Revokes the Companies (Inspection and Copying of Registers, Indices and Documents) Regulations 1991, SI 1991/1998, Sch 2, paras 1(a), 2(a), 3(a), subject to the savings in para (2) below.*)

(2) The fees prescribed in paragraphs 1(a), 2(a) and 3(a) of Schedule 2 to the 1991 Regulations shall continue to apply in respect of requests relating to the register of debenture holders or a debenture trust deed of a company which are subject to section 191(1) to (6) of the Companies Act 1985 by virtue of paragraph 22(2) of Schedule 4 to the Commencement Order.

6 (*(Revocation and savings: Northern Ireland) outside the scope of this work.*)

COMPANIES (REVISION OF DEFECTIVE ACCOUNTS AND REPORTS) REGULATIONS 2008

(SI 2008/373)

NOTES

Made: 19 February 2008.

Authority: Companies Act 2006, ss 454(3), (4), 1292(1)(a), (c).

Commencement: 6 April 2008.

For a summary of all Orders and Regulations made under the Companies Act 2006, see Appendix 4 at **[A4]**.

These Regulations are reproduced as amended by: the Companies (Revision of Defective Accounts and Reports) (Amendment) (No 2) Regulations 2013, SI 2013/2224 (which revoked and replaced the Companies (Revision of Defective Accounts and Reports) (Amendment) Regulations 2013, SI 2013/1971 because of a number of defects in the original Regulations); the Companies, Partnerships and Groups (Accounts and Reports) Regulations 2015, SI 2015/980; the Statutory Auditors Regulations 2017, SI 2017/1164; the International Accounting Standards and European Public Limited-Liability Company (Amendment etc) (EU Exit) Regulations 2019, SI 2019/685.

ARRANGEMENT OF REGULATIONS

PART 1
INTRODUCTION

PART 2
REVISED ACCOUNTS AND REPORTS

PART 3
AUDITOR'S REPORTS

PART 4
EFFECT OF REVISION

PART 5
PUBLICATION, LAYING AND DELIVERY OF REVISED ACCOUNTS ETC

PART 7
COMPANIES EXEMPT FROM AUDIT

PART 8
FINAL PROVISIONS

PART 1 INTRODUCTION

[4.21]

1 Citation, commencement and application

(1) These Regulations may be cited as the Companies (Revision of Defective Accounts and Reports) Regulations 2008.

(2) These Regulations come into force on 6th April 2008 and apply in relation to companies' financial years beginning on or after that date.

[4.22]

2 Interpretation

(1) In these Regulations—

"the 2006 Act" means the Companies Act 2006;

"date of the original annual accounts" means the date on which the original annual accounts were approved by the board of directors under section 414 of the 2006 Act (approval and signing of accounts);

"date of the original directors' remuneration report" means the date on which the original directors' remuneration report was approved by the board of directors under section 422 of the 2006 Act (approval and signing of directors' remuneration report);

["date of the original revised directors' remuneration policy" means the date on which the original revised directors' remuneration policy prepared in accordance with section 422A of the 2006 Act(d) was approved by the board of directors under section 422A of the 2006 Act (approval and signing of revised directors' remuneration policy);]

"date of the original directors' report" means the date on which the original directors' report was approved by the board of directors under section 419 of the 2006 Act (approval and signing of directors' report);

["date of the original strategic report" means the date on which the original strategic report was approved by the board of directors under section 414D of the 2006 Act(a) (approval and signing of strategic report);]

"date of revision" means the date on which revised accounts are approved by the board of directors under regulation 4 or (as the case may be) a revised [report or] [policy] is approved by them under regulation [4A,] [5, 6 or 6A];

["original", in relation to annual accounts, or a strategic report or directors' report or directors' remuneration report or revised directors' remuneration policy, means the annual accounts or (as the case may be) strategic report or directors' report or directors' remuneration report or revised directors' remuneration policy which are the subject of revision by, respectively, revised accounts or a revised report or policy . . . ;]

"revised accounts" mean revised annual accounts of a company prepared by the directors under section 454 of the 2006 Act (voluntary revision of accounts etc), either through revision by replacement or revision by supplementary note; in the latter case the revised accounts comprise the original annual accounts together with the supplementary note;

["revised directors' remuneration policy" means a revised directors' remuneration policy within the meaning of section 422A of the 2006 Act;]

["revised policy" means a revised revised directors' remuneration policy prepared by the directors under section 454 of the 2006 Act, either through revision by replacement or revision by supplementary note; in the latter case the revised policy comprises the original directors' remuneration policy together with the supplementary note;

"revised report" means a revised strategic report, revised directors' report or revised directors' remuneration report prepared by the directors under section 454 of the 2006 Act, either through revision by replacement or revision by supplementary note; in the latter case the revised report comprises the original strategic report, directors' report or directors' remuneration report together with the supplementary note;]

["revised report or policy" means a revised report or a revised policy;]

"revision by replacement" means revision by the preparation of a replacement set of accounts, [strategic report or] directors' report or directors' remuneration report, [revised directors' remuneration policy], in substitution for the original annual accounts, [strategic report or] directors' report or directors' remuneration report, [revised directors' remuneration policy]; and

"revision by supplementary note" means revision by the preparation of a note indicating corrections to be made to the original annual accounts, [strategic report,] directors' report or directors' remuneration report [or revised directors' remuneration policy].

(2) References in these Regulations to a member or members of a company include a reference to a person nominated to enjoy information rights under section 146 of the 2006 Act (traded companies: nomination of persons to enjoy information rights).

(3) References in these Regulations to provisions or requirements of the 2006 Act as to matters to be included in annual accounts and reports include relevant provisions of the Small Companies and Groups (Accounts and Directors' Report) Regulations 2008 and the Large and Medium-sized Companies and Groups (Accounts and Reports) Regulations 2008.

NOTES

Para (1) is amended as follows:

Definitions "date of the original revised directors' remuneration policy", "date of the original strategic report", and "revised directors' remuneration policy", inserted by the Companies (Revision of Defective Accounts and Reports) (Amendment) (No 2) Regulations 2013, SI 2013/2224, regs 3, 4(a), (b), (e), as from 1 October 2013, in respect of financial years ending on or after 30 September 2013.

The words in the first pair of square brackets in the definition "date of revision" were substituted, and the figure in the third pair of square brackets was inserted, by the Statutory Auditors Regulations 2017, SI 2017/1164, regs 6, 7(a), as from 1 January 2018 (as to the application of the 2017 Regulations, see **[4.671]** et seq). The word in the second pair of square brackets in the definition "date of revision" were inserted by virtue of, and the words in the final pair of square brackets were substituted, by SI 2013/2224, regs 3, 4(c), as from 1 October 2013, in respect of financial years ending on or after 30 September 2013.

Definition "original" substituted by SI 2013/2224, regs 3, 4(d), as from 1 October 2013, in respect of financial years ending on or after 30 September 2013. Words omitted revoked by the Companies, Partnerships and Groups (Accounts and Reports) Regulations 2015, SI 2015/980, reg 43(1), (2), as from 6 April 2015, in relation to (a) financial years beginning on or after 1 January 2016, and (b) a financial year of a company beginning on or after 1 January 2015, but before 1 January 2016, if the directors of the company so decide (see **[4.549]** *post*).

Definitions "revised policy" and "revised report" inserted, and definition "revised report or policy" substituted, by SI 2017/1164, regs 6, 7(b), (c), as from 1 January 2018 (as to the application of the 2017 Regulations, see **[4.671]** et seq).

Words in square brackets in the definitions "revision by replacement" and "revision by supplementary note" inserted by SI 2013/2224, regs 3, 4(g), (h), as from 1 October 2013, in respect of financial years ending on or after 30 September 2013.

PART 2 REVISED ACCOUNTS AND REPORTS

[4.23]

3 Content of revised accounts or revised report

(1) Subject to regulation 19(1), the provisions of the 2006 Act . . . as to the matters to be included in the annual accounts of a company apply to revised accounts as if the revised accounts were prepared and approved by the directors as at the date of the original annual accounts.

(2) In particular—

(a) in the case of Companies Act accounts—

(i) section 393 of the 2006 Act (accounts to give true and fair view),

(ii) section 396(2) of that Act (Companies Act individual accounts: true and fair view), and

(iii) section 404(2) of that Act (Companies Act group accounts: true and fair view), and

(b) in the case of IAS accounts, section 393 of the 2006 Act and [UK-adopted international accounting standards],

apply so as to require a true and fair view to be shown in the revised accounts of the matters referred to in those accounts, viewed as at the date of the original annual accounts.

(3) In the case of Companies Act accounts, paragraph 13(b) of Schedule 1 to the Small Companies and Groups (Accounts and Directors' Report) Regulations 2008 or (where applicable) paragraph 13(b) of Schedule 1 to the Large and Medium-sized Companies and Groups (Accounts and Reports) Regulations 2008 apply to revised accounts as if the reference in those paragraphs to the date on which the accounts were signed was to the date of the original annual accounts.

[(4) The provisions of the 2006 Act as to the matters to be included in a strategic report, directors' report, directors' remuneration report or revised directors' remuneration policy apply to a revised report or policy as if the revised report or policy were prepared and approved by the directors of the company as at the date of the original strategic report, directors' report, directors' remuneration report or revised directors' remuneration policy.]

NOTES

Para (1): words omitted revoked by the International Accounting Standards and European Public Limited-Liability Company (Amendment etc) (EU Exit) Regulations 2019, SI 2019/685, reg 19, Sch 1, Pt 2, para 55(1), (2)(a), in relation to accounts for financial years beginning on or after IP completion day (as defined in the European Union (Withdrawal Agreement) Act 2020, s 39) (note also that in relation to accounts for financial years which begin before but end on or after IP completion day, the enactments amended by Parts 1–3 of Sch 1 to the 2019 Regulations have effect as if the UK were a member State until the end of the financial year in question).

Para (2): words in square brackets in sub-para (b) substituted by SI 2019/685, reg 19, Sch 1, Pt 2, para 55(1), (2)(b) (as to the application of this amendment, see the first note relating to SI 2019/685 above).

Para (4): substituted by the Companies (Revision of Defective Accounts and Reports) (Amendment) (No 2) Regulations 2013, SI 2013/2224, regs 3, 5, as from 1 October 2013, in respect of financial years ending on or after 30 September 2013.

[4.24]

4 Approval and signature of revised accounts

(1) Section 414 of the 2006 Act applies to revised accounts, save that in the case of revision by supplementary note, it applies as if it required a signature on the supplementary note instead of on the company's balance sheet.

(2) Where copies of the original annual accounts have been sent out to members under section 423(1) of the 2006 Act (duty to circulate copies of annual accounts and reports), laid before the company in general meeting under section 437(1) of that Act (public companies: laying of accounts and reports before general meeting) in the case of a public company, or delivered to the registrar under section 441(1) of that Act (duty to file accounts and reports with the registrar), the directors must before approving the revised accounts under section 414, cause statements as to the following matters to be made in a prominent position in the revised accounts (in the case of a revision by supplementary note, in that note)—

(a) in the case of a revision by replacement—

(i) that the revised accounts replace the original annual accounts for the financial year (specifying it),

(ii) that they are now the statutory accounts of the company for that financial year,

(iii) that they have been prepared as at the date of the original annual accounts and not as at the date of revision and accordingly do not deal with events between those dates,

(iv) the respects in which the original annual accounts did not comply with the requirements of the 2006 Act, and

(v) any significant amendments made consequential upon the remedying of those defects,

(b) in the case of a revision by supplementary note—

(i) that the note revises in certain respects the original annual accounts of the company and is to be treated as forming part of those accounts, and

(ii) that the annual accounts have been revised as at the date of the original annual accounts and not as at the date of revision and accordingly do not deal with events between those dates,

and must, when approving the revised accounts, cause the date on which the approval is given to be stated in them (in the case of revision by supplementary note, in that note); section 414(4) and (5) apply with respect to a failure to comply with this paragraph as if the requirements of this paragraph were requirements of Part 15 of that Act.

[4.25]

[4A Approval and signature of revised strategic report

(1) Section 414D(1) and (2) of the 2006 Act applies to a revised strategic report, save that in the case of revision by supplementary note, they shall apply as if they required the signature to be on the supplementary note.

(2) Where the original strategic report has been sent out to members under section 423(1) of the 2006 Act, laid before the company in general meeting under section 437(1) of that Act in the case of a public company, or delivered to the registrar under section 441(1), the directors shall, before approving the revised report under section 414E, cause statements as to the following matters to be made in a prominent position in the revised report (in the case of a revision by supplementary note, in that note)—

(a) in the case of a revision by replacement—

(i) that the revised report replaces the original report for the financial year (specifying it),

(ii) that it has been prepared as at the date of the original strategic report and not as at the date of revision and accordingly does not deal with any events between those dates,

(iii) the respects in which the original strategic report did not comply with the requirements of the 2006 Act, and

(iv) any significant amendments made consequential upon the remedying of those defects,

(b) in the case of revision by a supplementary note—

(i) that the note revises in certain respects the original strategic report of the company and is to be treated as forming part of that report, and

(ii) that the strategic report has been revised as at the date of the original strategic report and not as at the date of the revision and accordingly does not deal with events between those dates,

and shall, when approving the revised report, cause the date on which the approval is given to be stated in it (in the case of a revision by supplementary note, in that note); section 414A(5) of the 2006 Act shall apply with respect to a failure to comply with this paragraph as if the requirements of this paragraph were requirements of Part 15 of that Act.]

NOTES

Inserted by the Companies (Revision of Defective Accounts and Reports) (Amendment) (No 2) Regulations 2013, SI 2013/2224, regs 3, 6, as from 1 October 2013, in respect of financial years ending on or after 30 September 2013.

[4.26]

5 Approval and signature of revised directors' report

(1) Section 419 of the 2006 Act applies to a revised directors' report, save that in the case of revision by supplementary note, it applies as if it required the signature to be on the supplementary note.

(2) Where copies of the original directors' report have been sent out to members under section 423(1) of the 2006 Act, laid before the company in general meeting under section 437(1) of that Act in the case of a public company, or delivered to the registrar under section 441(1), the directors must, before approving the revised report under section 419, cause statements as to the following matters to be made in a prominent position in the revised report (in the case of a revision by supplementary note, in that note)—

(a) in the case of a revision by replacement—

(i) that the revised report replaces the original report for the financial year (specifying it),

(ii) that it has been prepared as at the date of the original directors' report and not as at the date of revision and accordingly does not deal with any events between those dates,

(iii) the respects in which the original directors' report did not comply with the requirements of the 2006 Act, and

(iv) any significant amendments made consequential upon the remedying of those defects,

(b) in the case of a revision by supplementary note—

(i) that the note revises in certain respects the original directors' report of the company and is to be treated as forming part of that report, and

(ii) that the directors' report has been revised as at the date of the original directors' report and not as at the date of the revision and accordingly does not deal with events between those dates,

and must, when approving the revised report, cause the date on which the approval is given to be stated in [it] (in the case of a revision by supplementary note, in that note); section 419(3) and (4) of the 2006 Act apply with respect to a failure to comply with this paragraph as if the requirements of this paragraph were requirements of Part 15 of that Act.

NOTES

Para (2): word in square brackets substituted by the Statutory Auditors Regulations 2017, SI 2017/1164, regs 6, 8, as from 1 January 2018.

[4.27]

6 Approval and signature of revised directors' remuneration report

(1) Section 422 of the 2006 Act applies to a revised directors' remuneration report, save that in the case of revision by supplementary note, it applies as if it required the signature to be on the supplementary note.

(2) Where copies of the original directors' remuneration report have been sent out to members under section 423(1) of the 2006 Act, laid before the company in general meeting under section 437(1) of that Act in the case of a public company, or delivered to the registrar under section 441(1) of that Act, the directors must, before approving the revised report under section 422, cause statements as to the following matters to be made in a prominent position in the revised report (in the case of a revision by supplementary note, in that note)—

(a) in the case of a revision by replacement—

(i) that the revised report replaces the original report for the financial year (specifying it),

(ii) that it has been prepared as at the date of the original directors' remuneration report and not as at the date of revision and accordingly does not deal with any events between those dates,

(iii) the respects in which the original directors' remuneration report did not comply with the requirements of the 2006 Act, and

(iv) any significant amendments made consequential upon the remedying of those defects,

(b) in the case of a revision by supplementary note—

(i) that the note revises in certain respects the original directors' remuneration report of the company and is to be treated as forming part of that report, and

(ii) that the directors' remuneration report has been revised as at the date of the original directors' remuneration report and not as at the date of the revision and accordingly does not deal with events between those dates,

and must, when approving the revised report, cause the date on which the approval is given to be stated in it (in the case of a revision by supplementary note, in that note); section 422(2) and (3) of the 2006 Act apply with respect to a failure to comply with this paragraph as if the requirements of this paragraph were requirements of Part 15 of that Act.

[4.28]

[6A Approval and signature of revised revised directors' remuneration policy

Section 422A of the 2006 Act applies to a revised revised directors' remuneration policy, save that in the case of revision by supplementary note, it applies as if it required the signature to be on the supplementary note.]

NOTES

Inserted by the Companies (Revision of Defective Accounts and Reports) (Amendment) (No 2) Regulations 2013, SI 2013/2224, regs 3, 7, as from 1 October 2013, in respect of financial years ending on or after 30 September 2013.

PART 3 AUDITOR'S REPORTS

[4.29]

7 Auditor's report on revised accounts and revised report

[(1) Subject to paragraph (2), where a company has revised its accounts and its strategic report, directors' report or directors' remuneration report under section 454 of the 2006 Act, a company's current auditor or auditors shall make a report or (as the case may be) further report under section 495 of the 2006 Act (auditor's report on company's annual accounts), to the company's members on those revised accounts and revised reports, and—

(za) subject to the modifications in paragraph (1A), the requirements of sections 495 to 497 of the 2006 Act apply, as appropriate, to the report on the revised accounts or the revised report as they applied to the, or would have applied to a, report on the original annual accounts, strategic report, directors' report or directors' remuneration report,]

(a) section 498 of that Act (duties of auditor) applies with any necessary modifications, and

(b) section 495(1) does not apply with respect to the revised accounts.

[(1A) The modifications are that—

(a) for the references to the report on the company's annual accounts in sections 495(1), 496(1) and 497(1) there were substituted a reference to the report under this regulation,

(b) the—

(i) requirements of the 2006 Act . . . in accordance with which the revised accounts must have been prepared, referred to in section 495(3)(c),

(ii) the applicable legal requirements in accordance with which the revised strategic report and revised directors' report must have been prepared, referred to in section 496(1)(a)(ii), and

(iii) the requirements of the 2006 Act in accordance with which the revised directors' remuneration report must have been properly prepared, referred to in section 497(1)(b),

are construed in accordance with regulation 3]

(2) Where the auditor's report on the original annual accounts was not made by the company's current auditor, the directors of the company may resolve that the report required by paragraph (1) is to be made by the person or persons who made that report, provided that that person or those persons agree to do so and would be qualified for appointment as auditor of the company.

(3) . . .

The [auditor's] report must also state whether in the auditor's opinion the original annual accounts failed to comply with the requirements of the 2006 Act *and, where applicable, Article 4 of the IAS Regulation* in the respects identified by the directors (in the case of a revision by replacement) in the statement required by regulation 4(2)(a)(iv) . . .

(4) . . .

(5) Sections 503 to 506 of the 2006 Act (signature of auditor's report) apply to an auditor's report under this regulation as they apply to an auditor's report under section 495(1) of that Act, with any necessary modifications.

(6) An auditor's report under this regulation shall, upon being signed under section 503 of the 2006 Act as so applied, be, as from the date of signature, the auditor's report on the annual accounts of the company in place of the report on the original annual accounts.

NOTES

The words in square brackets in para (1) were substituted, para (1A) was inserted, the first and final words omitted from para (3) were revoked, the word in square brackets in that paragraph was inserted, and para (4) was revoked, by the Statutory Auditors Regulations 2017, SI 2017/1164, regs 6, 9, as from 1 January 2018 (as to the application of the 2017 Regulations, see **[4.671]** et seq).

The words omitted from para (1A), and the second words omitted from para (3), were revoked by the International Accounting Standards and European Public Limited-Liability Company (Amendment etc) (EU Exit) Regulations 2019, SI 2019/685, reg 19, Sch 1, Pt 2, para 55(1), (3), in relation to accounts for financial years beginning on or after IP completion day (as defined in the European Union (Withdrawal Agreement) Act 2020, s 39) (note also that in relation to accounts for financial years which begin before but end on or after IP completion day, the enactments amended by Parts 1–3 of Sch 1 to the 2019 Regulations have effect as if the UK were a member State until the end of the financial year in question).

[4.30]

8 Auditor's report where company ceases to be exempt from audit

(1) Where as a result of the revisions to the accounts, the company is no longer entitled to exemption from audit under Chapter 1 of Part 16 of the 2006 Act, the company shall cause an auditor's report on the revised accounts to be prepared.

(2) The auditor's report must be delivered to the registrar within 28 days after the date of revision of the accounts.

(3) Sections 451 (default in filing accounts and reports: offences) and 452 (default in filing accounts: court order) of the 2006 Act apply with respect to a failure to comply with the requirements of this regulation as they apply with respect to a failure to comply with the requirements of section 441 of that Act but as if—

(a) the references in section 451(1) and in section 452(1)(a) to "the period for filing those accounts and reports" were references to the period of 28 days referred to in paragraph (2); the reference in section 451(1) and (2) to "that period" are to be construed accordingly, and

(b) the references in section 451(3) to "the documents in question" and "this Part" were, respectively, a reference to the auditor's report referred to in paragraph (2) and the provisions of Part 16 of the 2006 Act as applied by these Regulations.

[4.31]

9 Auditor's report on revised report alone

[(1) Subject to paragraph (2), where a company has revised its strategic report, directors' report or directors' remuneration report under section 454 of the 2006 Act but has not revised its annual accounts, a company's current auditor shall make a report or (as the case may be) further report to the company's members on any revised report prepared under section 454 of that Act if the relevant annual accounts have not been revised at the same time, and—

(a) subject to the modifications in paragraph (1A), the requirements of section s496 and 497 of the 2006 Act apply, as appropriate, to the report on the revised report as they applied to the, or would have applied to a, report on the original strategic report, directors' report or directors' remuneration report,

(b) section 498 of that Act (duties of auditor) applies with any necessary modifications, and

(c) section 495(1) does not apply with respect to the revised reports.

(1A) The modifications are that—

(a) for the references to the report on the company's annual accounts in sections 496(1) and 497(1) there were substituted a reference to the report under this regulation,

(b) the—

(i) applicable legal requirements in accordance with which the revised strategic report and revised directors' report must have been prepared, referred to in section 496(1)(a)(ii), and

(ii) requirements of the 2006 Act in accordance with which the revised directors' remuneration report must have been properly prepared, referred to in section 497(1)(b),

are construed in accordance with regulation 3.]

(2) Where the auditor's report on the annual accounts for the financial year covered by the revised report was not made by the company's current auditor, the directors of the company may resolve that the report required by paragraph (1) is to be made by the person or persons who made that report, provided that that person or those persons agree to do so and would be qualified for appointment as auditor of the company.

(3), (4) . . .

(5) Sections 503 to 506 of the 2006 Act apply to an auditor's report under this regulation as they apply to an auditor's report under section 495 of that Act, with any necessary modifications.

NOTES

Paras (1), (1A) were substituted (for the original para (1)), and paras (3), (4) were revoked, by the Statutory Auditors Regulations 2017, SI 2017/1164, regs 6, 10, as from 1 January 2018 (as to the application of the 2017 Regulations, see **[4.671]** et seq).

PART 4 EFFECT OF REVISION

[4.32]

10 Effect of revision of accounts

(1) Upon the directors approving revised accounts under regulation 4, the provisions of the 2006 Act have effect as if the revised accounts were, as from the date of their approval, the annual accounts of the company in place of the original annual accounts.

(2) In particular, the revised accounts shall as from that date be the company's annual accounts for the relevant financial year for the purposes of the following provisions of the 2006 Act—

(a) section 431 (right of member or debenture holder to copies of accounts and reports: unquoted companies),

(b) section 432 (right of member or debenture holder to copies of accounts and reports: quoted companies),

(c) section 434(3) (requirements in connection with publication of statutory accounts), and

(d) sections 423 (duty to circulate copies of annual accounts and reports), 437 (public companies; laying of accounts and reports before general meeting) and 441 (duty to file accounts and reports with the registrar), if the requirements of those sections have not been complied with prior to the date of revision.

[4.33]

11 Effect of revision of report

[(1) Subject to the following provisions of these Regulations upon the directors approving a revised report or policy under regulations [4A,] 5, 6 or 6A the provisions of the 2006 Act have effect as if the revised report or policy was, as from the date of its approval, the strategic report, directors' report, directors' remuneration report or revised directors' remuneration policy (as the case may be) in place of the original strategic report, directors' report, directors' remuneration report or revised directors' remuneration policy (as the case may be).]

(2) In particular, the revised report [or policy] shall as from that date be [the strategic report or] the directors' report or the directors' remuneration report [or revised directors' remuneration policy] for the relevant financial year for the purposes of—

(a) sections 431 and 432 of the 2006 Act, and

(b) sections 423, 437 and 441 of that Act if the requirements of those sections have not been complied with prior to the date of revision.

NOTES

Para (1): substituted by the Companies (Revision of Defective Accounts and Reports) (Amendment) (No 2) Regulations 2013, SI 2013/2224, regs 3, 10(a), as from 1 October 2013, in respect of financial years ending on or after 30 September 2013. Figure in square brackets inserted by the Statutory Auditors Regulations 2017, SI 2017/1164, regs 6, 11, as from 1 January 2018 (as to the application of the 2017 Regulations, see **[4.671]** et seq).

Para (2): words in square brackets inserted by SI 2013/2224, regs 3, 10(b), as from 1 October 2013, in respect of financial years ending on or after 30 September 2013.

PART 5 PUBLICATION, LAYING AND DELIVERY OF REVISED ACCOUNTS ETC

[4.34]

12 Publication of revised accounts and reports

(1) This regulation has effect where the directors have prepared revised accounts or a revised report under section 454 of the 2006 Act and copies of the original annual accounts or report have been sent to any person under section 423 or 146 of that Act.

(2) The directors must send to any such person—

(a) in the case of a revision by replacement, a copy of the revised accounts, or (as the case may be) the revised report, together with a copy of the auditor's report on those accounts, or (as the case may be) on that report, or

(b) in the case of a revision by supplementary note, a copy of that note together with a copy of the auditor's report on the revised accounts, or (as the case may be) on the revised report,

not more than 28 days after the date of revision.

(3) The directors must also, not more than 28 days after the revision, send a copy of the revised accounts or (as the case may be) revised report, together with a copy of the auditor's report on those accounts or (as the case may be) on that report, to any person who is not a person entitled to receive a copy under paragraph (2) but who is, as at the date of revision—

(a) a member of the company,

(b) a holder of the company's debentures, or

(c) a person who is entitled to receive notice of general meetings,

unless the company would be entitled at that date to send to that person a [copy of strategic report and supplementary material] under section 426 of the 2006 Act (option to provide [copy of strategic report and supplementary material]). Section 423(2) to (4) of that Act apply to this paragraph as they apply to section 423(1).

(4) Section 425 of the 2006 Act (default in sending out copies of accounts and reports: offences) applies to a default in complying with this regulation as if the provisions of this regulation were provisions of section 423 and as if the references in that section to "the company" and "every officer of the company who is in default" were a reference to each of the directors who approved the revised accounts under regulation 4 or revised report under regulation 5 or 6.

(5) Where, prior to the date of revision of the original annual accounts, the company had completed sending out copies of those accounts under section 423 of the 2006 Act, references in that Act to the day on which accounts are sent out under section 423 are to be construed as referring to the day on which the original accounts were sent out (applying section 423(5) as necessary) notwithstanding that those accounts have been revised; where the company had not completed, prior to the date of revision, the sending out of copies of those accounts under that section, such references are to the day, or the last day, on which the revised accounts are sent out.

NOTES

Para (3): words in square brackets substituted by the Companies (Revision of Defective Accounts and Reports) (Amendment) (No 2) Regulations 2013, SI 2013/2224, regs 3, 11, as from 1 October 2013, in respect of financial years ending on or after 30 September 2013.

[4.35]

13 Laying of revised accounts or a revised report

(1) This regulation has effect where the directors of a public company have prepared revised accounts or a revised report under section 454 of the 2006 Act and copies of the original annual accounts or report have been laid before a general meeting under section 437 of that Act.

(2) A copy of the revised accounts or (as the case may be) the revised report, together with a copy of the auditor's report on those accounts, or (as the case may be) on that report, must be laid before the next general meeting of the company held after the date of revision at which any annual accounts for a financial year are laid, unless the revised accounts, or (as the case may be) the revised report, have already been laid before an earlier general meeting.

(3) Section 438 of the 2006 Act (public companies: offence of failure to lay accounts and reports) applies with respect to a failure to comply with the requirements of this regulation as it has effect with respect to a failure to comply with the requirements of section 437 of that Act but as if—

(a) the reference in section 438(1) to "the period allowed" was a reference to the period between the date of revision of the revised accounts or (as the case may be) the revised report and the date of the next general meeting of the company held after the date of revision at which any annual accounts for a financial year are laid; references in section 438(1) and (2) to "that period" are to be construed accordingly; and

(b) the references in section 438(3) to "the documents in question" and "this Part" were, respectively, a reference to the documents referred to in paragraph (2) and the provisions of Part 15 of the 2006 Act as applied by these Regulations.

[4.36]

14 Delivery of revised accounts or a revised report

(1) This regulation has effect where the directors have prepared revised accounts or a revised report under section 454 of the 2006 Act and a copy of the original annual accounts or report has been delivered to the registrar under section 441(1) of that Act.

(2) The directors of the company must, within 28 days of the date of revision, deliver to the registrar—

- (a) in the case of a revision by replacement, a copy of the revised accounts or (as the case may be) the revised report, together with a copy of the auditor's report on those accounts or (as the case may be) on that report, or
- (b) in the case of a revision by supplementary note, a copy of that note, together with a copy of the auditor's report on the revised accounts or (as the case may be) on the revised report.

(3) Sections 451 (default in filing accounts and reports: offences) and 452 (default in filing accounts: court order) of the 2006 Act apply with respect to a failure to comply with the requirements of this regulation as they apply with respect to a failure to comply with the requirements of section 441 of that Act but as if—

- (a) the references in section 451(1) and in section 452(1)(a) to "the period for filing those accounts and reports" were references to the period of 28 days referred to in paragraph (2); the references in section 451(1) and (2) to "that period" are to be construed accordingly, and
- (b) the references in section 451(3) to "the documents in question" and "this Part" were, respectively, a reference to the documents referred to in paragraph (2) and the provisions of Part 15 of the 2006 Act as applied by these Regulations.

15–17 *(Regs 15, 16 revoked by the Companies, Partnerships and Groups (Accounts and Reports) Regulations 2015, SI 2015/980, reg 43(1), (3), as from 6 April 2015, in relation to (a) financial years beginning on or after 1 January 2016, and (b) a financial year of a company beginning on or after 1 January 2015, but before 1 January 2016, if the directors of the company so decide (see* **[4.549]** *post). Reg 17 revoked by the Companies (Revision of Defective Accounts and Reports) (Amendment) (No 2) Regulations 2013, SI 2013/2224, regs 3, 12, as from 1 October 2013 in respect of financial years ending on or after 30 September 2013.)*

PART 7 COMPANIES EXEMPT FROM AUDIT

[4.37]

18 Companies exempt from audit under section 477[, 479A] or 480

Where, in respect of any financial year, a company is exempt under section 477 (small companies: conditions for exemption from audit)[, 479A (subsidiary companies: conditions for exemption from audit)] or 480 (dormant companies: conditions for exemption from audit) of the 2006 Act from the requirements of that Act relating to the audit of accounts, these Regulations apply as if they omitted any reference to an auditor's report, or to the making of such a report.

NOTES

Words in square brackets inserted by the Statutory Auditors Regulations 2017, SI 2017/1164, regs 6, 12, as from 1 January 2018 (as to the application of the 2017 Regulations, see **[4.671]** et seq).

PART 8 FINAL PROVISIONS

[4.38]

19 Modifications of the 2006 Act

(1) Where the provisions of the 2006 Act as to the matters to be included in the annual accounts of a company or (as the case may be) in a [strategic report or a] directors' report or directors' remuneration report have been amended after the date of the original annual accounts or (as the case may be) [strategic report,] directors' report or directors' remuneration report but prior to the date of revision, references in regulations 3 and 7(3) to the provisions of that Act are to be construed as references to the provisions of that Act as in force at the date of the original annual accounts or (as the case may be) [strategic report,] directors' report or directors' remuneration report.

(2), (3) . . .

NOTES

The words "strategic report," in para (1) were inserted, and para (2) was revoked, by the Statutory Auditors Regulations 2017, SI 2017/1164, regs 6, 13, as from 1 January 2018 (as to the application of the 2017 Regulations, see **[4.671]** et seq).

The other words in square brackets in para (1) were inserted, and para (3) was revoked, by the Companies (Revision of Defective Accounts and Reports) (Amendment) (No 2) Regulations 2013, SI 2013/2224, regs 3, 13, as from 1 October 2013, in respect of financial years ending on or after 30 September 2013. Note that para (3) continues to apply to financial years ending before 30 September 2013 (see reg 14 of the 2013 Regulations).

[4.39]

20 Revocations etc

(1) The Companies (Revision of Defective Accounts and Report) Regulations 1990 and the Companies (Revision of Defective Accounts and Report) Regulations (Northern Ireland) 1991 are revoked.

(2) Notwithstanding the revocation of the regulations specified in paragraph (1), the provisions of those regulations continue to apply in relation to financial years of a company beginning before 6th April 2008.

[4.40]

[21 Review

(1) The Secretary of State must from time to time—

- (a) carry out a review of the regulatory provision in these Regulations to which amendments have been made by Part 3 of the Statutory Auditor Regulations 2017, and
- (b) publish a report setting out the conclusions of the review.

(2) The first report must be published before 1st January 2023.

(3) Subsequent reports must be published at intervals not exceeding 5 years.

(4) Section 30(3) of the Small Business, Enterprise and Employment Act 2015 requires that a review carried out under this regulation must, so far as is reasonable, have regard to how Article 28 of Directive 2006/43/EC of the European Parliament and of the Council on statutory audits of annual accounts and consolidated accounts, amending Council Directives 78/660/EEC and 83/349/EEC and repealing Council Directive 84/253/EEC is implemented in other member States.

(5) Section 30(4) of the Small Business, Enterprise and Employment Act 2015 requires that a report published under this regulation must, in particular—

- (a) set out the objectives intended to be achieved by the regulatory provision referred to in paragraph (1)(a),
- (b) assess the extent to which those objectives are achieved,
- (c) assess whether those objectives remain appropriate, and
- (d) if those objectives remain appropriate, assess the extent to which they could be achieved in another way which involves less onerous regulatory provision.

(6) In this regulation, "regulatory provision" has the same meaning as in sections 28 to 32 of the Small Business, Enterprise and Employment Act 2015 (see section 32 of that Act).]

NOTES

Added by the Statutory Auditors Regulations 2017, SI 2017/1164, regs 6, 14, as from 1 January 2018 (as to the application of the 2017 Regulations, see **[4.671]** et seq).

SMALL COMPANIES AND GROUPS (ACCOUNTS AND DIRECTORS' REPORT) REGULATIONS 2008

(SI 2008/409)

NOTES

Made: 19 February 2008.

Authority: Companies Act 2006, ss 396(3), 404(3), 409(1), (3), 412(1), (3), 416(4), 444(3)(a), (b), 677(3)(a), 712(2)(b)(i), 836(1)(b)(i), 1292(1)(a), (c).

Commencement: 6 April 2008.

For a summary of all Orders and Regulations made under the Companies Act 2006, see Appendix 4 at **[A4]**.

These Regulations are reproduced as amended by: the Partnerships (Accounts) Regulations 2008, SI 2008/569; the Companies Act 2006 (Accounts, Reports and Audit) Regulations 2009, SI 2009/1581; the Companies Act 2006 (Strategic Report and Directors' Report) Regulations 2013, SI 2013/1970; the Companies and Partnerships (Accounts and Audit) Regulations 2013, SI 2013/2005; the Small Companies (Micro-Entities' Accounts) Regulations 2013, SI 2013/3008; the Companies, Partnerships and Groups (Accounts and Reports) Regulations 2015, SI 2015/980; the Companies, Partnerships and Groups (Accounts and Reports) (No 2) Regulations 2015, SI 2015/1672; the Accounts and Reports (Amendment) (EU Exit) Regulations 2019, SI 2019/145; the International Accounting Standards and European Public Limited-Liability Company (Amendment etc) (EU Exit) Regulations 2019, SI 2019/685.

Application: these Regulations are applied (i) to limited liability partnerships, see the Small Limited Liability Partnerships (Accounts) Regulations 2008, SI 2008/1912 at **[10.288]**; (ii) to partnerships, see the Partnerships (Accounts) Regulations 2008, SI 2008/569 at **[10.202]**.

ARRANGEMENT OF REGULATIONS

PART 1
INTRODUCTION

PART 2
FORM AND CONTENT OF INDIVIDUAL ACCOUNTS

PART 3
DIRECTORS' REPORT

PART 4
FORM AND CONTENT OF GROUP ACCOUNTS

PART 5
INTERPRETATION

SCHEDULES

PART 1 INTRODUCTION

[4.41]

1 Citation and interpretation

(1) These Regulations may be cited as the Small Companies and Groups (Accounts and Directors' Report) Regulations 2008.

(2) In these Regulations "the 2006 Act" means the Companies Act 2006.

[4.42]

2 Commencement and application

(1) These Regulations come into force on 6th April 2008.

(2) They apply in relation to financial years beginning on or after 6th April 2008.

(3) They apply to companies which are subject to the small companies regime under Part 15 of the 2006 Act (see section 381 of that Act).

PART 2 FORM AND CONTENT OF INDIVIDUAL ACCOUNTS

[4.43]

3 Companies Act individual accounts

(1) [Subject to the following provisions of this regulation and regulation 5A,] Companies Act individual accounts under section 396 of the 2006 Act (Companies Act: individual accounts) must comply with the provisions of Schedule 1 to these Regulations as to the form and content of the balance sheet and profit and loss account, and additional information to be provided by way of notes to the accounts.

[(1A) Sections C (alternative accounting rules) and D (fair value accounting) in Part 2 of Schedule 1 to these Regulations do not apply to a company which qualifies as a micro-entity in relation to a financial year (see sections 384A and 384B of the 2006 Act) and whose accounts for that year are prepared in accordance with the exemption permitted by—

(a) regulation 5A, or

(b) paragraph 1(1A) of Section A in Part 1 of Schedule 1 to these Regulations.]

(2) . . .

(3) Accounts are treated as having complied with any provision of Schedule 1 to these Regulations if they comply instead with the corresponding provision of Schedule 1 to the Large and Medium-Sized Companies and Groups (Accounts and Reports) Regulations 2008.

NOTES

Words in square brackets in para (1) inserted, and para (1A) inserted, by the Small Companies (Micro-Entities' Accounts) Regulations 2013, SI 2013/3008, reg 9(1), (2), as from 1 December 2013, in relation to (a) financial years ending on or after 30 September 2013, and (b) companies which deliver the accounts required by s 444 of this Act to the registrar on or after 1 December 2013.

Para (2) revoked by the Companies, Partnerships and Groups (Accounts and Reports) Regulations 2015, SI 2015/980, reg 14(1), (2), as from 6 April 2015, in relation to (a) financial years beginning on or after 1 January 2016, and (b) a financial year of a company beginning on or after 1 January 2015, but before 1 January 2016, if the directors of the company so decide (see **[4.549]** *post*).

4, 5 *(Revoked by the Companies, Partnerships and Groups (Accounts and Reports) Regulations 2015, SI 2015/980, reg 14(1), (3), (4), as from 6 April 2015, in relation to (a) financial years beginning on or after 1 January 2016, and (b) a financial year of a company beginning on or after 1 January 2015, but before 1 January 2016, if the directors of the company so decide (see* **[4.549]** *post).)*

[4.44]

[5A Companies Act individual accounts: micro-entities—notes to the accounts

Nothing in Schedule 1, 2 or 3 to these Regulations requires the Companies Act individual accounts of a company for a financial year in which the company qualifies as a micro-entity (see sections 384A and 384B of the 2006 Act) to contain any information by way of notes to the accounts, except that the company is required to disclose by way of notes to the accounts the information required by paragraph 57 in Part 3 of Schedule 1.]

NOTES

Inserted by the Small Companies (Micro-Entities' Accounts) Regulations 2013, SI 2013/3008, reg 9(1), (5), as from 1 December 2013, in relation to (a) financial years ending on or after 30 September 2013, and (b) companies which deliver the accounts required by s 444 of this Act to the registrar on or after 1 December 2013.

6 *(Revoked by the Companies, Partnerships and Groups (Accounts and Reports) Regulations 2015, SI 2015/980, reg 14(1), (5), as from 6 April 2015, in relation to (a) financial years beginning on or after 1 January 2016, and (b) a financial year of a company beginning on or after 1 January 2015, but before 1 January 2016, if the directors of the company so decide (see* **[4.549]** *post).)*

PART 3 DIRECTORS' REPORT

[4.45]

7 Directors' report

The report which the directors of a company are required to prepare under section 415 of the 2006 Act (duty to prepare directors' report) must disclose the matters specified in Schedule 5 to these Regulations.

PART 4 FORM AND CONTENT OF GROUP ACCOUNTS

[4.46]

8 Companies Act group accounts

(1) Where the directors of a parent company which—

(a) is subject to the small companies regime, and

(b) has prepared Companies Act individual accounts in accordance with regulation 3,

prepare Companies Act group accounts under section 398 of the 2006 Act (option to prepare group accounts), those accounts must comply with the provisions of . . . Schedule 6 to these Regulations as to the form and content of the consolidated balance sheet and consolidated profit and loss account, and additional information to be provided by way of notes to the accounts.

(2) Accounts are treated as having complied with any provision of Part 1 of Schedule 6 if they comply instead with the corresponding provision of Schedule 6 to the Large and Medium-Sized Companies and Groups (Accounts and Reports) Regulations 2008.

NOTES

Para (1): words omitted revoked by the Companies, Partnerships and Groups (Accounts and Reports) Regulations 2015, SI 2015/980, reg 15(1), (2), as from 6 April 2015, in relation to (a) financial years beginning on or after 1 January 2016, and (b) a financial year of a company beginning on or after 1 January 2015, but before 1 January 2016, if the directors of the company so decide (see **[4.549]** *post*).

9 *(Revoked by the Companies, Partnerships and Groups (Accounts and Reports) Regulations 2015, SI 2015/980, reg 15(1), (3), as from 6 April 2015, in relation to (a) financial years beginning on or after 1 January 2016, and (b) a financial year of a company beginning on or after 1 January 2015, but before 1 January 2016, if the directors of the company so decide (see* **[4.549]** *post).)*

[4.47]

10 Information about related undertakings (Companies Act or IAS group accounts)

(1) Companies Act or IAS group accounts must comply with the provisions of Part 2 of Schedule 6 to these Regulations as to information about related undertakings to be given in notes to the company's accounts.

(2) Information otherwise required to be given by Part 2 of Schedule 6 need not be disclosed with respect to an undertaking that—

(a) is established under the law of a country outside the United Kingdom, or

(b) carries on business outside the United Kingdom,

if the conditions specified in section 409(4) of the 2006 Act are met (see section 409(5) of the 2006 Act for disclosure required where advantage taken of this exemption).

This paragraph does not apply in relation to the information required by paragraphs 26 and 35 of Schedule 6 to these Regulations.

[4.48]

11 Accounts for delivery to registrar of companies (Companies Act group accounts)

Companies Act group accounts delivered to the registrar of companies under section 444 of the 2006 Act need not give the information required by—

(a) . . .

(b) paragraph 25 of Schedule 6 to these Regulations (shares of company held by subsidiary undertakings).

NOTES

Para (a) revoked by the Companies, Partnerships and Groups (Accounts and Reports) Regulations 2015, SI 2015/980, reg 15(1), (4), as from 6 April 2015, in relation to (a) financial years beginning on or after 1 January 2016, and (b) a financial year of a company beginning on or after 1 January 2015, but before 1 January 2016, if the directors of the company so decide (see **[4.549]** *post*).

PART 5 INTERPRETATION

[4.49]

12 Definition of "provisions"

Schedule 7 to these Regulations defines "provisions" for the purpose of these Regulations and for the purposes of—

(a) section 677(3)(a) (Companies Act accounts: relevant provisions for purposes of financial assistance) in Part 18 of the 2006 Act,

(b) section 712(2)(b)(i) (Companies Act accounts: relevant provisions to determine available profits for redemption or purchase by private company out of capital) in that Part, . . .
(c) section 836(1)(b)(i) (Companies Act accounts: relevant provisions for distribution purposes) in Part 23 of that Act[, and
(d) section 841(2)(a) (Companies Act accounts: provisions to be treated as realised losses) in that Part].

NOTES

The word omitted from para (b) was revoked, and para (d) (and the word immediately preceding it) was added, by the Companies Act 2006 (Accounts, Reports and Audit) Regulations 2009, SI 2009/1581, reg 11(1), (2), as from 27 June 2009, in relation to financial years beginning on or after 6 April 2008 which have not ended before 27 June 2009.

[4.50]

13 General interpretation

Schedule 8 to these Regulations contains general definitions for the purposes of these Regulations.

SCHEDULES

SCHEDULE 1
COMPANIES ACT INDIVIDUAL ACCOUNTS

Regulation 3(1)

PART 1 GENERAL RULES AND FORMATS
SECTION A GENERAL RULES

[4.51]

1. (1) Subject to the following provisions of this Schedule—
(a) every balance sheet of a company must show the items listed in either of the balance sheet formats in Section B of this Part, and
(b) every profit and loss account must show the items listed in [either] of the profit and loss account formats in Section B.

[(1A) But, subject to the following provisions of this Schedule, in relation to a company which qualifies as a micro-entity in relation to a financial year (see sections 384A and 384B of the 2006 Act)—
(a) the only items which must be shown on the company's balance sheet for that year are those listed in either of the balance sheet formats in Section C of this Part, and
(b) the only items which must be shown on the company's profit and loss account for that year are those listed in the profit and loss account format in Section C.]

(2) References in this Schedule to the items listed in any of the formats in Section B [and Section C] are to those items read together with any of the notes following the formats which apply to those items.

(3) [Subject to paragraph 1A] the items must be shown in the order and under the headings and sub-headings given in the particular format used, but—
(a) the notes to the formats may permit alternative positions for any particular items, and
(b) the heading or sub-heading for any item does not have to be distinguished by any letter or number assigned to that item in the format used.

[1A. (1) Where appropriate to the circumstances of a company's business, the company's directors may, with reference to one of the formats in Section B, draw up an abridged balance sheet showing only those items in that format preceded by letters and roman numerals, provided that—
(a) in the case of format 1, note (5) of the notes to the formats is complied with,
(b) in the case of format 2, notes (5) and (10) of those notes are complied with, and
(c) all of the members of the company have consented to the drawing up of the abridged balance sheet.

(2) Where appropriate to the circumstances of a company's business, the company's directors may, with reference to one of the formats in Section B, draw up an abridged profit and loss account, combining under one item called "Gross profit or loss"—
(a) items 1, 2, 3 and 6 in the case of format 1, and
(b) items 1 to 5 in the case of format 2

provided that, in either case, all of the members of the company have consented to the drawing up of the abridged profit and loss account.

(3) Such consent as is referred to in sub-paragraphs (1) and (2) may only be given as regards the preparation of, as appropriate, the balance sheet or profit and loss account in respect of the preceding financial year.

(4) Sub-paragraphs (1) and (2) do not apply in relation to the preparation of, as appropriate, a company's balance sheet or profit and loss account for a particular financial year if the company was a charity at any time within that year.

1B. (1) The company's directors may adapt one of the balance sheet formats in Section B so to distinguish between current and non-current items in a different way, provided that—
(a) the information given is at least equivalent to that which would have been required by the use of such format had it not been thus adapted, and
(b) the presentation of those items is in accordance with generally accepted accounting principles or practice.

(2) The company's directors may, otherwise than pursuant to paragraph 1A(2), adapt one of the profit and loss account formats in Section B, provided that—
(a) the information given is at least equivalent to that which would have been required by the use of such format had it not been thus adapted, and
(b) the presentation is in accordance with generally accepted accounting principles or practice.

1C So far as is practicable, the following provisions of Section A of this Part of this Schedule apply to the balance sheet or profit or loss account of a company notwithstanding any such abridgment or adaptation pursuant to paragraph 1A or 1B.]

2. (1) Where in accordance with [paragraph 1(1)] a company's balance sheet or profit and loss account for any financial year has been prepared by reference to one of the formats in Section B, the company's directors must use the same format in preparing Companies Act individual accounts for subsequent financial years, unless in their opinion there are special reasons for a change.

(2) Particulars of any such change must be given in a note to the accounts in which the new format is first used, and the reasons for the change must be explained.

[2A. Where in accordance with paragraph 1(1A) a company's balance sheet or profit and loss account for any financial year has been prepared by reference to one of the formats in Section C, the company's directors must use the same format in preparing Companies Act individual accounts for subsequent financial years, unless in their opinion there are special reasons for a change.]

3. (1) Any item required to be shown in a company's balance sheet or profit and loss account may be shown in greater detail than required by the particular format used.

(2) The balance sheet or profit and loss account may include an item representing or covering the amount of any asset or liability, income or expenditure not otherwise covered by any of the items listed in the format used, save that none of the following may be treated as assets in any balance sheet—

- (a) preliminary expenses,
- (b) expenses of, and commission on, any issue of shares or debentures,
- (c) costs of research.

4. (1) Where the special nature of the company's business requires it, the company's directors must adapt the arrangement, headings and sub-headings otherwise required in respect of items given an Arabic number in the balance sheet or profit and loss account format used.

(2) The directors may combine items to which Arabic numbers are given in any of the formats set out in Section B if—

- (a) their individual amounts are not material to assessing the state of affairs or profit or loss of the company for the financial year in question, or
- (b) the combination facilitates that assessment.

(3) Where sub-paragraph (2)(b) applies, the individual amounts of any items which have been combined must be disclosed in a note to the accounts.

5. (1) Subject to sub-paragraph (2), the directors must not include a heading or sub-heading corresponding to an item in the balance sheet or profit and loss account format used if there is no amount to be shown for that item for the financial year to which the balance sheet or profit and loss account relates.

(2) Where an amount can be shown for the item in question for the immediately preceding financial year that amount must be shown under the heading or sub-heading required by the format for that item.

6. Every profit and loss account [other than one prepared by reference to the format in Section C] must show the amount of a company's profit or loss . . . before taxation.

7. (1) For every item shown in the balance sheet or profit and loss account the corresponding amount for the immediately preceding financial year must also be shown.

(2) Where that corresponding amount is not comparable with the amount to be shown for the item in question in respect of the financial year to which the balance sheet or profit and loss account relates, the former amount may be adjusted, and particulars of the non-comparability and of any adjustment must be disclosed in a note to the accounts.

8. Amounts in respect of items representing assets or income may not be set off against amounts in respect of items representing liabilities or expenditure (as the case may be), or vice versa.

9. The company's directors must, in determining how amounts are presented within items in the profit and loss account and balance sheet, have regard to the substance of the reported transaction or arrangement, in accordance with generally accepted accounting principles or practice.

[9A. Where an asset or liability relates to more than one item in the balance sheet, the relationship of such asset or liability to the relevant items must be disclosed either under those items or in the notes to the accounts.]

SECTION B [THE REQUIRED FORMATS FOR THE ACCOUNTS OF COMPANIES OTHER THAN MICRO-ENTITIES]

Balance sheet formats

Format 1

A Called up share capital not paid [(1)]

B Fixed assets

- I Intangible assets
  - 1 Goodwill [(2)]
  - 2 Other intangible assets [(3)]
- II Tangible assets
  - 1 Land and buildings
  - 2 Plant and machinery etc
- III Investments
  - 1 Shares in group undertakings and participating interests
  - 2 Loans to group undertakings and undertakings in which the company has a participating interest

Part 4 CA 2006 SIs

3 Other investments other than loans
4 Other investments [4]

C Current assets
I Stocks
1 Stocks
2 Payments on account
II Debtors [5]
1 Trade debtors
2 Amounts owed by group undertakings and undertakings in which the company has a participating interest
3 Other debtors [1]
III Investments
1 Shares in group undertakings
2 Other investments [4]
IV Cash at bank and in hand

D Prepayments and accrued income [6]

E Creditors: amounts falling due within one year
1 Bank loans and overdrafts
2 Trade creditors
3 Amounts owed to group undertakings and undertakings in which the company has a participating interest
4 Other creditors [7]

F Net current assets (liabilities) [8]

G Total assets less current liabilities

H Creditors: amounts falling due after more than one year
1 Bank loans and overdrafts
2 Trade creditors
3 Amounts owed to group undertakings and undertakings in which the company has a participating interest
4 Other creditors [7]

I Provisions for liabilities

J Accruals and deferred income [7]

K Capital and reserves
I Called up share capital [9]
II Share premium account
III Revaluation reserve
IV Other reserves
V Profit and loss account

Balance sheet formats

Format 2

ASSETS

A Called up share capital not paid [1]

B Fixed assets
I Intangible assets
1 Goodwill [2]
2 Other intangible assets [3]
II Tangible assets
1 Land and buildings
2 Plant and machinery etc
III Investments
1 Shares in group undertakings and participating interests
2 Loans to group undertakings and undertakings in which the company has a participating interest
3 Other investments other than loans
4 Other investments [4]

C Current assets
I Stocks
1 Stocks
2 Payments on account
II Debtors [5]
1 Trade debtors
2 Amounts owed by group undertakings and undertakings in which the company has a participating interest
3 Other debtors [1]
III Investments
1 Shares in group undertakings
2 Other investments [4]
IV Cash at bank and in hand

D Prepayments and accrued income [6]

[CAPITAL, RESERVES AND LIABILITIES]

A Capital and reserves
- I Called up share capital [(9)]
- II Share premium account
- III Revaluation reserve
- IV Other reserves
- V Profit and loss account

B Provisions for liabilities

C Creditors [(10)]
- 1 Bank loans and overdrafts
- 2 Trade creditors
- 3 Amounts owed to group undertakings and undertakings in which the company has a participating interest
- 4 Other creditors [(7)]

D Accruals and deferred income [(7)]

Notes on the balance sheet formats

(1) Called up share capital not paid

(Formats 1 and 2, items A and C II 3)

This item may either be shown at item A or included under item C II 3 in Format 1 or 2.

(2) Goodwill

(Formats 1 and 2, item B I 1)

Amounts representing goodwill must only be included to the extent that the goodwill was acquired for valuable consideration.

(3) Other intangible assets

(Formats 1 and 2, item B I 2)

Amounts in respect of concessions, patents, licences, trade marks and similar rights and assets must only be included in a company's balance sheet under this item if either—

(a) the assets were acquired for valuable consideration and are not required to be shown under goodwill, or

(b) the assets in question were created by the company itself.

(4) Others: Other investments

(Formats 1 and 2, items B III 4 and C III 2)

Where amounts in respect of own shares held are included under either of these items, the nominal value of such shares must be shown separately.

(5) Debtors

(Formats 1 and 2, items C II 1 to 3)

The amount falling due after more than one year must be shown separately for each item included under debtors [and, in the case of format 2, the aggregate amount falling due after more than one year must also be shown].

(6) Prepayments and accrued income

(Formats 1 and 2, item D.)

This item may alternatively be included under item C II 3 in Format 1 or 2.

(7) Other creditors

(Format 1, items E 4, H 4 and J and Format 2, items C 4 and D.)

There must be shown separately—

(a) the amount of any convertible loans, and

(b) the amount for creditors in respect of taxation and social security.

Payments received on account of orders must be included in so far as they are not shown as deductions from stocks.

In Format 1, accruals and deferred income may be shown under item J or included under item E 4 or H 4, or both (as the case may require). In Format 2, accruals and deferred income may be shown under item D or within item C 4 under Liabilities.

(8) Net current assets (liabilities)

(Format 1, item F)

In determining the amount to be shown under this item any prepayments and accrued income must be taken into account wherever shown.

(9) Called up share capital

(Format 1, item K I and Format 2, Liabilities item A I)

The amount of allotted share capital and the amount of called up share capital which has been paid up must be shown separately.

(10) Creditors

(Format 2, Liabilities items C 1 to 4)

Amounts falling due within one year and after one year must be shown separately for each of these items and for the aggregate of all of these items . . .

Profit and loss account formats

Format 1
(see note (14) below)

1 Turnover
2 Cost of sales[11]
3 Gross profit or loss
4 Distribution costs[11]
5 Administrative expenses[11]
6 Other operating income
7 Income from shares in group undertakings
8 Income from participating interests
9 Income from other fixed asset investments[12]
10 Other interest receivable and similar income[12]
11 Amounts written off investments
12 Interest payable and similar [expenses][13]
13 Tax on profit or loss . . .
14 Profit or loss . . . after taxation
15–18 Extraordinary income
19 Other taxes not shown under the above items
20 Profit or loss for the financial year

Profit and loss account formats

Format 2

1 Turnover
2 Change in stocks of finished goods and in work in progress
3 Own work capitalised
4 Other operating income
5
 (a) Raw materials and consumables
 (b) Other external charges
6 Staff costs
 (a) wages and salaries
 (b) social security costs
 (c) other pension costs
7
 (a) Depreciation and other amounts written off tangible and intangible fixed assets
 [(b) Amounts written off current assets, to the extent that they exceed write-offs which are normal in the undertaking concerned]
8 Other operating [expenses]
9 Income from shares in group undertakings
10 Income from participating interests
11 Income from other fixed asset investments[12]
12 Other interest receivable and similar income[12]
13 Amounts written off investments
14 Interest payable and similar [expenses][13]
15 Tax on profit or loss . . .
16 Profit or loss . . . after taxation
17–20 Extraordinary income
21 Other taxes not shown under the above items
22 Profit or loss for the financial year

Profit and loss account formats

Formats 3, 4

. . .

Notes on the profit and loss account formats

(11) Cost of sales: distribution costs: administrative expenses

(Format 1, items 2, 4 and 5 . . .)

These items must be stated after taking into account any necessary provisions for depreciation or diminution in value of assets.

(12) Income from other fixed asset investments: other interest receivable and similar income

(Format 1, items 9 and 10; Format 2, items 11 and 12; . . .)

Income and interest derived from group undertakings must be shown separately from income and interest derived from other sources.

(13) Interest payable and similar [expenses]

(Format 1, item 12; Format 2, item 14; . . .)

The amount payable to group undertakings must be shown separately.

(14) . . .

[SECTION C THE REQUIRED FORMATS FOR THE ACCOUNTS OF MICRO-ENTITIES

Format 1

A Called up share capital not paid

B Fixed assets

C Current assets

D Prepayments and accrued income

E Creditors: amounts falling due within one year

F Net current assets (liabilities)

G Total assets less current liabilities

H Creditors: amounts falling due after more than one year

I Provisions for liabilities

J Accruals and deferred income

K Capital and reserves

Format 2

ASSETS

A Called up share capital not paid

B Fixed assets

C Current Assets

D Prepayments and accrued income

[CAPITAL, RESERVES AND LIABILITIES]

A Capital and reserves

B Provisions for liabilities

C Creditors[(1)]

D Accruals and deferred income

Notes on the balance sheet formats

(1) Creditors

(Format 2, item C under Liabilities)

Aggregate amounts falling due within one year and after one year must be shown separately.

Profit and loss account format

A Turnover

B Other income

C Cost of raw materials and consumables

D Staff costs

E Depreciation and other amounts written off assets

F Other charges

G Tax

H Profit or loss.]

NOTES

Section A

Word in square brackets in para 1(1)(b) substituted, words in square brackets in para 1(3) inserted, paras 1A–1C, 9A inserted, and words omitted from para 6 revoked, by the Companies, Partnerships and Groups (Accounts and Reports) Regulations 2015, SI 2015/980, reg 16(1), (2), as from 6 April 2015, in relation to (a) financial years beginning on or after 1 January 2016, and (b) a financial year of a company beginning on or after 1 January 2015, but before 1 January 2016, if the directors of the company so decide (see **[4.549]** *post*).

Para 1(1A) was inserted, the words in square brackets in para 1(2) were inserted, the words in square brackets in para 2(1) were substituted, para 2A was inserted, and the words in square brackets in para 6 were inserted, by the Small Companies (Micro-Entities' Accounts) Regulations 2013, SI 2013/3008, reg 10(1), (2), as from 1 December 2013, in relation to (a) financial years ending on or after 30 September 2013, and (b) companies which deliver the accounts required by s 444 of this Act to the registrar on or after 1 December 2013.

Section B

The heading was substituted by SI 2013/3008, reg 10(1), (3), as from 1 December 2013, in relation to (a) financial years ending on or after 30 September 2013, and (b) companies which deliver the accounts required by s 444 of this Act to the registrar on or after 1 December 2013.

Words "CAPITAL, RESERVES AND LIABILITIES" in square brackets substituted by SI 2015/980, reg 16(1), (3)(a) (as to the application of this amendment see the first note relating to the 2015 Regulations above).

Words in square brackets in note (5) of the Notes on the balance sheet formats substituted by SI 2015/980, reg 16(1), (3)(b) (as to the application of this amendment see the first note relating to the 2015 Regulations above).

Words omitted from note (10) of the Notes on the balance sheet formats revoked by SI 2015/980, reg 16(1), (3)(c) (as to the application of this amendment see the first note relating to the 2015 Regulations above).

In profit and loss account format 1, word in square brackets in item 12 substituted, words omitted from items 13, 14 revoked, and items 15–18 revoked, by SI 2015/980, reg 16(1), (3)(d) (as to the application of this amendment see the first note relating to the 2015 Regulations above).

In profit and loss account format 2, para (b) of item 7 substituted, words in square brackets in items 8 and 14 substituted, words omitted from items 15, 16 revoked, and items 17–20 revoked, by SI 2015/980, reg 16(1), (3)(e) (as to the application of this amendment see the first note relating to the 2015 Regulations above).

Profit and loss account formats 3 and 4 revoked by SI 2015/980, reg 16(1), (3)(f), (g) (as to the application of this amendment see the first note relating to the 2015 Regulations above).

Words omitted from notes (11), (12) of the Notes on the profit and loss account formats revoked, word "expenses" in square brackets in note (13) substituted, words omitted from note (13) revoked, and note (14) revoked, by SI 2015/980, reg 16(1), (3)(h)–(k) (as to the application of this amendment see the first note relating to the 2015 Regulations above).

Section C

Added by SI 2013/3008, reg 10(1), (4), as from 1 December 2013, in relation to (a) financial years ending on or after 30 September 2013, and (b) companies which deliver the accounts required by s 444 of this Act to the registrar on or after 1 December 2013.

Words "CAPITAL, RESERVES AND LIABILITIES" in square brackets substituted by SI 2015/980, reg 16(1), (4) (as to the application of this amendment see the first note relating to the 2015 Regulations above).

PART 2 ACCOUNTING PRINCIPLES AND RULES

SECTION A ACCOUNTING PRINCIPLES

Preliminary

[4.52]

10. (1) The amounts to be included in respect of all items shown in a company's accounts must be determined in accordance with the principles set out in this Section.

(2) But if it appears to the company's directors that there are special reasons for departing from any of those principles in preparing the company's accounts in respect of any financial year they may do so, in which case particulars of the departure, the reasons for it and its effect must be given in a note to the accounts.

Accounting principles

11. The company is presumed to be carrying on business as a going concern.

12. Accounting policies [and measurement bases] must be applied consistently within the same accounts and from one financial year to the next.

13. The amount of any item must be determined on a prudent basis, and in particular—

(a) only profits realised at the balance sheet date must be included in the profit and loss account, . . .

(b) all liabilities which have arisen in respect of the financial year to which the accounts relate or a previous financial year must be taken into account, including those which only become apparent between the balance sheet date and the date on which it is signed on behalf of the board of directors in accordance with section 414 of the 2006 Act (approval and signing of accounts) [and]

[(c) all provisions for diminution of value must be recognised, whether the result of the financial year is a profit or a loss].

14. All income and charges relating to the financial year to which the accounts relate must be taken into account, without regard to the date of receipt or payment.

15. In determining the aggregate amount of any item, the amount of each individual asset or liability that falls to be taken into account must be determined separately.

[**15A.** The opening balance sheet for each financial year shall correspond to the closing balance sheet for the preceding financial year.]

SECTION B HISTORICAL COST ACCOUNTING RULES

Preliminary

16. Subject to Sections C and D of this Part of this Schedule, the amounts to be included in respect of all items shown in a company's accounts must be determined in accordance with the rules set out in this Section.

Fixed Assets

General rules

17. (1) The amount to be included in respect of any fixed asset must be its purchase price or production cost.

(2) This is subject to any provision for depreciation or diminution in value made in accordance with paragraphs 18 to 20.

Rules for depreciation and diminution in value

18. In the case of any fixed asset which has a limited useful economic life, the amount of—

(a) its purchase price or production cost, or

(b) where it is estimated that any such asset will have a residual value at the end of the period of its useful economic life, its purchase price or production cost less that estimated residual value,

must be reduced by provisions for depreciation calculated to write off that amount systematically over the period of the asset's useful economic life.

19. (1) Where a fixed asset investment of a description falling to be included under item B.III of either of the balance sheet formats set out in [Section B of] Part 1 of this Schedule has diminished in value, provisions for diminution in value may be made in respect of it and the amount to be included in respect of it may be reduced accordingly.

(2) Provisions for diminution in value must be made in respect of any fixed asset which has diminished in value if the reduction in its value is expected to be permanent (whether its useful economic life is limited or not), and the amount to be included in respect of it must be reduced accordingly.

[(3) Provisions made under sub-paragraph (1) or (2) must be charged to the profit and loss account and disclosed separately in a note to the accounts if not shown separately in the profit and loss account.]

20. (1) Where the reasons for which any provision was made in accordance with paragraph 19 have ceased to apply to any extent, that provision must be written back to the extent that it is no longer necessary.

[(1A) But provision made in accordance with paragraph 19(2) in respect of goodwill must not be written back to any extent.]

[(2) Any amounts written back under sub-paragraph (1) must be recognised in the profit and loss account and disclosed separately in a note to the accounts if not shown separately in the profit and loss account.]

[Intangible Assets

21. (1) Where this is in accordance with generally accepted accounting principles or practice, development costs may be included in "other intangible assets" under "fixed assets" in the balance sheet formats set out in Section B of Part 1 of this Schedule.

(2) If any amount is included in a company's balance sheet in respect of development costs, the note on accounting policies (see paragraph 44 of this Schedule) must include the following information—

(a) the period over which the amount of those costs originally capitalised is being or is to be written off, and

(b) the reasons for capitalising the development costs in question.

22. (1) Intangible assets must be written off over the useful economic life of the intangible asset.

(2) Where in exceptional cases the useful life of intangible assets cannot be reliably estimated, such assets must be written off over a period chosen by the directors of the company.

(3) The period referred to in sub-paragraph (2) must not exceed ten years.

(4) There must be disclosed in a note to the accounts the period referred to in sub-paragraph (2) and the reasons for choosing that period.]

Current assets

23. Subject to paragraph 24, the amount to be included in respect of any current asset must be its purchase price or production cost.

24. (1) If the net realisable value of any current asset is lower than its purchase price or production cost, the amount to be included in respect of that asset must be the net realisable value.

(2) Where the reasons for which any provision for diminution in value was made in accordance with sub-paragraph (1) have ceased to apply to any extent, that provision must be written back to the extent that it is no longer necessary.

Miscellaneous and Supplementary Provisions

Excess of money owed over value received as an asset item

25. (1) Where the amount repayable on any debt owed by a company is greater than the value of the consideration received in the transaction giving rise to the debt, the amount of the difference may be treated as an asset.

(2) Where any such amount is so treated—

(a) it must be written off by reasonable amounts each year and must be completely written off before repayment of the debt, and

(b) if the current amount is not shown as a separate item in the company's balance sheet, it must be disclosed in a note to the accounts.

Assets included at a fixed amount

26. [(1) Subject to sub-paragraph (2), the following may be included at a fixed quantity and value in the balance sheet formats set out in Section B of Part 1 of this Schedule—

(a) assets which fall to be included amongst the fixed assets of a company under the item "intangible assets", and

(b) raw materials and consumables within the item "stocks".]

(2) Sub-paragraph (1) applies to assets of a kind which are constantly being replaced where—

(a) their overall value is not material to assessing the company's state of affairs, and

(b) their quantity, value and composition are not subject to material variation.

Determination of purchase price or production cost

27. (1) The purchase price of an asset is to be determined by adding to the actual price paid any expenses incidental to its acquisition [and then subtracting any incidental reductions in the cost of acquisition].

(2) The production cost of an asset is to be determined by adding to the purchase price of the raw materials and consumables used the amount of the costs incurred by the company which are directly attributable to the production of that asset.

(3) In addition, there may be included in the production cost of an asset—

(a) a reasonable proportion of the costs incurred by the company which are only indirectly attributable to the production of that asset, but only to the extent that they relate to the period of production, and

(b) interest on capital borrowed to finance the production of that asset, to the extent that it accrues in respect of the period of production,

provided, however, in a case within paragraph (b), that the inclusion of the interest in determining the cost of that asset and the amount of the interest so included is disclosed in a note to the accounts.

(4) In the case of current assets distribution costs may not be included in production costs.

28. (1) The purchase price or production cost of—

(a) any assets which[, by virtue of regulation 3(1) and Section B of Part 1 of this Schedule,] fall to be included under any item shown in a company's balance sheet under the general item "stocks", and

(b) any assets which are fungible assets (including investments),

may be determined by the application of any of the methods mentioned in sub-paragraph (2) in relation to any such assets of the same class, provided that the method chosen is one which appears to the directors to be appropriate in the circumstances of the company.

(2) Those methods are—

(a) the method known as "first in, first out" (FIFO),

(b) the method known as "last in, first out" (LIFO),

(c) a weighted average price, and

(d) any other method [reflecting generally accepted best practice].

(3) For the purposes of this paragraph, assets of any description must be regarded as fungible if assets of that description are substantially indistinguishable one from another.

Substitution of original stated amount where price or cost unknown

29. (1) This paragraph applies where—

(a) there is no record of the purchase price or production cost of any asset of a company or of any price, expenses or costs relevant for determining its purchase price or production cost in accordance with paragraph 27, or

(b) any such record cannot be obtained without unreasonable expense or delay.

(2) In such a case, the purchase price or production cost of the asset must be taken, for the purposes of paragraphs 17 to 24, to be the value ascribed to it in the earliest available record of its value made on or after its acquisition or production by the company.

[29A. Equity method in respect of participating interests

(1) Participating interests may be accounted for using the equity method.

(2) If participating interests are accounted for using the equity method—

(a) the proportion of profit or loss attributable to a participating interest and recognised in the profit and loss account may be that proportion which corresponds to the amount of any dividends, and

(b) where the profit attributable to a participating interest and recognised in the profit and loss account exceeds the amount of any dividends, the difference must be placed in a reserve which cannot be distributed to shareholders.

(3) The reference to "dividends" in sub-paragraph (2) includes dividends already paid and those whose payment can be claimed.]

SECTION C ALTERNATIVE ACCOUNTING RULES

Preliminary

30. (1) The rules set out in Section B are referred to below in this Schedule as the historical cost accounting rules.

(2) Those rules, with the omission of paragraphs 16, 22 and 26 to 29, are referred to below in this Part of this Schedule as the depreciation rules; and references below in this Schedule to the historical cost accounting rules do not include the depreciation rules as they apply by virtue of paragraph 33.

31. Subject to paragraphs 33 to 35, the amounts to be included in respect of assets of any description mentioned in paragraph 32 may be determined on any basis so mentioned.

Alternative accounting rules

32. (1) Intangible fixed assets, other than goodwill, may be included at their current cost.

(2) Tangible fixed assets may be included at a market value determined as at the date of their last valuation or at their current cost.

(3) Investments of any description falling to be included under item B III of either of the balance sheet formats set out Part 1 of this Schedule may be included either—

(a) at a market value determined as at the date of their last valuation, or

(b) at a value determined on any basis which appears to the directors to be appropriate in the circumstances of the company.

But in the latter case particulars of the method of valuation adopted and of the reasons for adopting it must be disclosed in a note to the accounts.

(4), (5) . . .

Application of the depreciation rules

33. (1) Where the value of any asset of a company is determined on any basis mentioned in paragraph 32, that value must be, or (as the case may require) be the starting point for determining, the amount to be included in respect of that asset in the company's accounts, instead of its purchase price or production cost or any value previously so determined for that asset.

The depreciation rules apply accordingly in relation to any such asset with the substitution for any reference to its purchase price or production cost of a reference to the value most recently determined for that asset on any basis mentioned in paragraph 32.

(2) The amount of any provision for depreciation required in the case of any fixed asset by paragraphs 18 to 20 as they apply by virtue of sub-paragraph (1) is referred to below in this paragraph as the adjusted amount, and the amount of any provision which would be required by any of those paragraphs in the case of that asset according to the historical cost accounting rules is referred to as the historical cost amount.

(3) Where sub-paragraph (1) applies in the case of any fixed asset the amount of any provision for depreciation in respect of that asset—

(a) included in any item shown in the profit and loss account in respect of amounts written off assets of the description in question, or

(b) taken into account in stating any item so shown which is required by note *(11)* of the notes on the profit and loss account formats set out in Part 1 of this Schedule to be stated after taking into account any necessary provision for depreciation or diminution in value of assets included under it,

may be the historical cost amount instead of the adjusted amount, provided that the amount of any difference between the two is shown separately in the profit and loss account or in a note to the accounts.

Additional information to be provided in case of departure from historical cost accounting rules

34. (1) This paragraph applies where the amounts to be included in respect of assets covered by any items shown in a company's accounts have been determined on any basis mentioned in paragraph 32.

(2) The items affected and the basis of valuation adopted in determining the amounts of the assets in question in the case of each such item must be disclosed in [the note on accounting policies (see paragraph 44 of this Schedule)].

[(3) In the case of each balance sheet item affected, the comparable amounts determined according to the historical cost accounting rules must be shown in a note to the accounts.]

(4) In sub-paragraph (3), references in relation to any item to the comparable amounts determined as there mentioned are references to—

(a) the aggregate amount which would be required to be shown in respect of that item if the amounts to be included in respect of all the assets covered by that item were determined according to the historical cost accounting rules, and

(b) the aggregate amount of the cumulative provisions for depreciation or diminution in value which would be permitted or required in determining those amounts according to those rules.

Revaluation reserve

35. (1) With respect to any determination of the value of an asset of a company on any basis mentioned in paragraph 32, the amount of any profit or loss arising from that determination (after allowing, where appropriate, for any provisions for depreciation or diminution in value made otherwise than by reference to the value so determined and any adjustments of any such provisions made in the light of that determination) must be credited or (as the case may be) debited to a separate reserve ("the revaluation reserve").

(2) The amount of the revaluation reserve must be shown in the company's balance sheet under a separate sub-heading in the position given for the item "revaluation reserve" in [under "Capital and reserves"] Format 1 or 2 of the balance sheet formats set out in Part 1 of this Schedule . . .

(3) An amount may be transferred—

(a) from the revaluation reserve—

(i) to the profit and loss account, if the amount was previously charged to that account or represents realised profit, or

(ii) on capitalisation,

(b) to or from the revaluation reserve in respect of the taxation relating to any profit or loss credited or debited to the reserve.

The revaluation reserve must be reduced to the extent that the amounts transferred to it are no longer necessary for the purposes of the valuation method used.

(4) In sub-paragraph (3)(a)(ii) "capitalisation", in relation to an amount standing to the credit of the revaluation reserve, means applying it in wholly or partly paying up unissued shares in the company to be allotted to members of the company as fully or partly paid shares.

(5) The revaluation reserve must not be reduced except as mentioned in this paragraph.

(6) The treatment for taxation purposes of amounts credited or debited to the revaluation reserve must be disclosed in a note to the accounts.

SECTION D FAIR VALUE ACCOUNTING

Inclusion of financial instruments at fair value

36. (1) Subject to sub-paragraphs (2) to (5), financial instruments (including derivatives) may be included at fair value.

(2) Sub-paragraph (1) does not apply to financial instruments that constitute liabilities unless—

(a) they are held as part of a trading portfolio,

(b) they are derivatives, or

(c) they are financial instruments falling within sub-paragraph (4).

(3) Unless they are financial instruments falling within sub-paragraph (4), sub-paragraph (1) does not apply to—

(a) financial instruments (other than derivatives) held to maturity,

(b) loans and receivables originated by the company and not held for trading purposes,

(c) interests in subsidiary undertakings, associated undertakings and joint ventures,

(d) equity instruments issued by the company,

(e) contracts for contingent consideration in a business combination, or

(f) other financial instruments with such special characteristics that the instruments, according to generally accepted accounting principles or practice, should be accounted for differently from other financial instruments.

[(4) Financial instruments which under [UK-adopted international accounting standards] may be included in accounts at fair value, may be so included, provided that the disclosures required by such accounting standards are made.]

(5) If the fair value of a financial instrument cannot be determined reliably in accordance with paragraph 37, sub-paragraph (1) does not apply to that financial instrument.

(6) In this paragraph—

"associated undertaking" has the meaning given by paragraph 19 of Schedule 6 to these Regulations;

"joint venture" has the meaning given by paragraph 18 of that Schedule.

Determination of fair value

37. (1) The fair value of a financial instrument is its value determined in accordance with this paragraph.

(2) If a reliable market can readily be identified for the financial instrument, its fair value is to be determined by reference to its market value.

(3) If a reliable market cannot readily be identified for the financial instrument but can be identified for its components or for a similar instrument, its fair value is determined by reference to the market value of its components or of the similar instrument.

(4) If neither sub-paragraph (2) nor (3) applies, the fair value of the financial instrument is a value resulting from generally accepted valuation models and techniques.

(5) Any valuation models and techniques used for the purposes of sub-paragraph (4) must ensure a reasonable approximation of the market value.

Hedged items

38. A company may include any assets and liabilities, or identified portions of such assets or liabilities, that qualify as hedged items under a fair value hedge accounting system at the amount required under that system.

[Other assets that may be included at fair value

39. (1) This paragraph applies to—

(a) stocks

(b) investment property, and

(c) living animals and plants.

(2) Such stocks, investment property, and living animals and plants may be included at fair value, provided that, as the case maybe, all such stocks, investment property, and living animals and plants are so included where their fair value can reliably be determined.

(3) In this paragraph, "fair value" means fair value determined in accordance with generally accepted accounting principles or practice.]

Accounting for changes in value

40. (1) This paragraph applies where a financial instrument is valued in accordance with paragraph 36 or 38 or an asset is valued in accordance with paragraph 39.

(2) Notwithstanding paragraph 13 in this Part of this Schedule, and subject to sub-paragraphs (3) and (4), a change in the value of the financial instrument or of the investment property or living animal or plant must be included in the profit and loss account.

(3) Where—

(a) the financial instrument accounted for is a hedging instrument under a hedge accounting system that allows some or all of the change in value not to be shown in the profit and loss account, or

(b) the change in value relates to an exchange difference arising on a monetary item that forms part of a company's net investment in a foreign entity,

the amount of the change in value must be credited to or (as the case may be) debited from a separate reserve ("the fair value reserve").

(4) Where the instrument accounted for—

(a) is an available for sale financial asset, and

(b) is not a derivative,

the change in value may be credited to or (as the case may be) debited from the fair value reserve.

The fair value reserve

41. (1) The fair value reserve must be adjusted to the extent that the amounts shown in it are no longer necessary for the purposes of paragraph 40(3) or (4).

(2) . . .

NOTES

Section A

Words in square brackets in para 12 inserted, word omitted from para 13(a) revoked, para 13(c) and the preceding word inserted, and para 15A inserted, by the Companies, Partnerships and Groups (Accounts and Reports) Regulations 2015,

SI 2015/980, reg 17(1), (2), as from 6 April 2015, in relation to (a) financial years beginning on or after 1 January 2016, and (b) a financial year of a company beginning on or after 1 January 2015, but before 1 January 2016, if the directors of the company so decide (see **[4.549]** *post*).

Section B

The words in square brackets in paras 19(1) and 28(1)(a) were inserted, and para 26(1) was substituted, by the Small Companies (Micro-Entities' Accounts) Regulations 2013, SI 2013/3008, reg 11, as from 1 December 2013, in relation to (a) financial years ending on or after 30 September 2013, and (b) companies which deliver the accounts required by s 444 of this Act to the registrar on or after 1 December 2013.

Para 19(3) substituted by SI 2015/980, reg 17(1), (3)(a) (as to the application of this amendment see the first note relating to the 2015 Regulations above).

Para 20(1A) inserted by the Companies, Partnerships and Groups (Accounts and Reports) (No 2) Regulations 2015, SI 2015/1672, reg 3, as from 1 October 2015, in relation to (a) financial years beginning on or after 1 January 2016, and (b) a financial year of a company beginning on or after 1 January 2015 but before 1 January 2016, if the directors of the company have decided, pursuant to reg 2(2)(b) of the Companies, Partnerships and Groups (Accounts and Reports) Regulations 2015, that the amendments made by those Regulations have effect in relation to that financial year.

Para 20(2) substituted by SI 2015/980, reg 17(1), (3)(b) (as to the application of this amendment see the first note relating to the 2015 Regulations above).

Paras 21, 22 substituted by SI 2015/980, reg 17(1), (3)(c) (as to the application of this amendment see the first note relating to the 2015 Regulations above).

Words in square brackets in para 27(1) inserted, words in square brackets in para 28(2)(d) substituted, and para 29A inserted, by SI 2015/980, reg 17(1), (3)(d)–(f) (as to the application of this amendment see the first note relating to the 2015 Regulations above).

Section C

Paras 32(4), (5) revoked, words in square brackets in para 34(2) substituted, para 34(3) substituted, words in square brackets in para 35(2) inserted, and words omitted from that paragraph revoked, by SI 2015/980, reg 17(1), (4) (as to the application of this amendment see the first note relating to the 2015 Regulations above).

Section D

Para 36(4) substituted by SI 2015/980, reg 17(1), (5)(a) (as to the application of this amendment see the first note relating to the 2015 Regulations above). The words in square brackets were substituted by the International Accounting Standards and European Public Limited-Liability Company (Amendment etc) (EU Exit) Regulations 2019, SI 2019/685, reg 19, Sch 1, Pt 2, para 56(a), in relation to accounts for financial years beginning on or after IP completion day (as defined in the European Union (Withdrawal Agreement) Act 2020, s 39) (note also that in relation to accounts for financial years which begin before but end on or after IP completion day, the enactments amended by Parts 1–3 of Sch 1 to the 2019 Regulations have effect as if the UK were a member State until the end of the financial year in question).

Para 39 substituted by SI 2015/980, reg 17(1), (5)(b) (as to the application of this amendment see the first note relating to the 2015 Regulations above).

Para 41(2) revoked by SI 2015/980, reg 17(1), (5)(c) (as to the application of this amendment see the first note relating to the 2015 Regulations above).

PART 3 NOTES TO THE ACCOUNTS

[Preliminary

[4.53]

42. (1) Any information required in the case of a company by the following provisions of this Part of this Schedule must be given by way of a note to the accounts.

(2) These notes must be presented in the order in which, where relevant, the items to which they relate are presented in the balance sheet and in the profit and loss account.]

. . .

43. . . .

Disclosure of accounting policies

44. The accounting policies adopted by the company in determining the amounts to be included in respect of items shown in the balance sheet and in determining the profit or loss of the company must be stated (including such policies with respect to the depreciation and diminution in value of assets).

Information Supplementing the Balance Sheet

45. Paragraphs [46 to 58] require information which either supplements the information given with respect to any particular items shown in the balance sheet or is otherwise relevant to assessing the company's state of affairs in the light of the information so given.

. . .

46, 47. . . .

Fixed assets

48. (1) In respect of each item which is or would but for paragraph 4(2)(b) be shown under the general item "fixed assets" in the company's balance sheet the following information must be given—

(a) the appropriate amounts in respect of that item as at the date of the beginning of the financial year and as at the balance sheet date respectively,

(b) the effect on any amount shown in the balance sheet in respect of that item of—

- (i) any revision of the amount in respect of any assets included under that item made during that year on any basis mentioned in paragraph 32,
- (ii) acquisitions during that year of any assets,
- (iii) disposals during that year of any assets, and
- (iv) any transfers of assets of the company to and from that item during that year.

(2) The reference in sub-paragraph (1)(a) to the appropriate amounts in respect of any item as at any date there mentioned is a reference to amounts representing the aggregate amounts determined, as at that date, in respect of assets falling to be included under that item on either of the following bases, that is to say—

(a) on the basis of purchase price or production cost (determined in accordance with paragraphs 27 and 28), or

(b) on any basis mentioned in paragraph 32,

(leaving out of account in either case any provisions for depreciation or diminution in value).

(3) In respect of each item within sub-paragraph (1) there must also be stated—

(a) the cumulative amount of provisions for depreciation or diminution in value of assets included under that item as at each date mentioned in sub-paragraph (1)(a),

(b) the amount of any such provisions made in respect of the financial year,

(c) the amount of any adjustments made in respect of any such provisions during that year in consequence of the disposal of any assets, and

(d) the amount of any other adjustments made in respect of any such provisions during that year.

49. Where any fixed assets of the company (other than listed investments) are included under any item shown in the company's balance sheet at an amount determined on any basis mentioned in paragraph 32, the following information must be given—

(a) the years (so far as they are known to the directors) in which the assets were severally valued and the several values, and

(b) in the case of assets that have been valued during the financial year, the names of the persons who valued them or particulars of their qualifications for doing so and (whichever is stated) the bases of valuation used by them.

. . .

50. . . .

[Information about fair value of assets and liabilities

51. (1) This paragraph applies where financial instruments or other assets have been valued in accordance with, as appropriate, paragraph 36, 38 or 39.

(2) There must be stated—

(a) the significant assumptions underlying the valuation models and techniques used to determine the fair values,

(b) for each category of financial instrument or other asset, the fair value of the assets in that category and the changes in value—

(i) included directly in the profit and loss account, or

(ii) credited to or (as the case may be) debited from the fair value reserve,

in respect of those assets, and

(c) for each class of derivatives, the extent and nature of the instruments, including significant terms and conditions that may affect the amount, timing and certainty of future cash flows.

(3) Where any amount is transferred to or from the fair value reserve during the financial year, there must be stated in tabular form—

(a) the amount of the reserve as at the date of the beginning of the financial year and as at the balance sheet date respectively, and

(b) the amount transferred to or from the reserve during that year.]

52. . . .

. . .

53. . . .

[Information about revalued fixed assets

54. (1) This paragraph applies where fixed assets are measured at revalued amounts.

(2) Where this paragraph applies, the following information must be given in tabular form—

(a) movements in the revaluation reserve in the financial year, with an explanation of the tax treatment of items therein, and

(b) the carrying amount in the balance sheet that would have been recognised had the fixed assets not been revalued.]

Details of indebtedness

55. (1) For the aggregate of all items shown under "creditors" in the company's balance sheet there must be stated the aggregate of the following amounts—

(a) the amount of any debts included under "creditors" which are payable or repayable otherwise than by instalments and fall due for payment or repayment after the end of the period of five years beginning with the day next following the end of the financial year, and

(b) in the case of any debts so included which are payable or repayable by instalments, the amount of any instalments which fall due for payment after the end of that period.

(2) In respect of each item shown under "creditors" in the company's balance sheet there must be stated the aggregate amount of any debts included under that item in respect of which any security has been given by the company [with an indication of the nature and form of any such security].

(3) References above in this paragraph to an item shown under "creditors" in the company's balance sheet include references, where amounts falling due to creditors within one year and after more than one year are distinguished in the balance sheet—

(a) in a case within sub-paragraph (1), to an item shown under the latter of those categories,

(b) in a case within sub-paragraph (2), to an item shown under either of those categories.

References to items shown under "creditors" include references to items which would but for paragraph 4(2)(b) be shown under that heading.

56. . . .

[Guarantees and other financial commitments

57. (1) The total amount of any financial commitments, guarantees and contingencies that are not included in the balance sheet must be stated.

(2) An indication of the nature and form of any valuable security given by the company in respect of commitments, guarantees and contingencies within sub-paragraph (1) must be given.

(3) The total amount of any commitments within sub-paragraph (1) concerning pensions must be separately disclosed.

(4) The total amount of any commitments within sub-paragraph (1) which are undertaken on behalf of or for the benefit of—

(a) any parent undertaking, fellow subsidiary undertaking or any subsidiary undertaking of the company, or
(b) any undertaking in which the company has a participating interest

must be separately stated and those within paragraph (a) must also be stated separately from those within paragraph (b).]

. . .

58–60. . . .

Miscellaneous matters

61. (1) Where any amount relating to any preceding financial year is included in any item in the profit and loss account, the effect must be stated.

[(2) The amount and nature of any individual items of income or expenditure of exceptional size or incidence must be stated.]

. . .

62–63. . . .

[Post balance sheet events

64. The nature and financial effect of material events arising after the balance sheet date which are not reflected in the profit and loss account or balance sheet must be stated.

Parent undertaking information

65 Where the company is a subsidiary undertaking, the following information must be given in respect of the parent undertaking of the smallest group of undertakings for which group accounts are drawn up of which the company is a member—

(a) the name of the parent undertaking which draws up the group accounts,
(b) the address of the undertaking's registered office (whether in or outside the United Kingdom), or
(c) if it is unincorporated, the address of its principal place of business.

Related party transactions

66 (1) Particulars may be given of transactions which the company has entered into with related parties, and must be given if such transactions are material and have not been concluded under normal market conditions with—

(a) owners holding a participating interest in the company;
(b) companies in which the company itself has a participating interest; and
(c) the company's directors.

(2) Particulars of the transactions required to be disclosed under sub-paragraph (1) must include—

(a) the amount of such transactions,
(b) the nature of the related party relationship, and
(c) other information about the transactions necessary for an understanding of the financial position of the company.

(3) Information about individual transactions may be aggregated according to their nature, except where separate information is necessary of an understanding of the effects of the related party transactions on the financial position of the company.

(4) Particulars need not be given of transactions entered into between two or more members of a group, provided that any subsidiary undertaking which is a party to the transaction is wholly-owned by such a member.

(5) In this paragraph, "related party" has the same meaning as in [UK-adopted international accounting standards].]

NOTES

Para 42: substituted by the Companies, Partnerships and Groups (Accounts and Reports) Regulations 2015, SI 2015/980, reg 18(1), (2), as from 6 April 2015, in relation to (a) financial years beginning on or after 1 January 2016, and (b) a financial year of a company beginning on or after 1 January 2015, but before 1 January 2016, if the directors of the company so decide (see **[4.549]** *post*).

Paras 43, 46, 47, 50, 52, 53, 56, 58–60, 62, 63 revoked by SI 2015/980, reg 18(1), (3), (5)–(7), (8), (9), (15)–(17), (19), (20) (as to the application of this amendment see the first note relating to the 2015 Regulations above).

Para 45: words in square brackets substituted by SI 2015/980, reg 18(1), (4) (as to the application of this amendment see the first note relating to the 2015 Regulations above).

Paras 51, 54, 57: substituted by SI 2015/980, reg 18(1), (8), (11), (14) (as to the application of this amendment see the first note relating to the 2015 Regulations above).

Para 55: words in square brackets in sub-para (2) inserted by SI 2015/980, reg 18(1), (12) (as to the application of this amendment see the first note relating to the 2015 Regulations above).

Para 61: sub-para (2) substituted (for the original sub-paras (2), (3)) by SI 2015/980, reg 18(1), (18) (as to the application of this amendment see the first note relating to the 2015 Regulations above).

Paras 64–66: added by SI 2015/980, reg 18(1), (21) (as to the application of this amendment see the first note relating to the 2015 Regulations above). The words in square brackets in para 66(5) were substituted by the International

Accounting Standards and European Public Limited-Liability Company (Amendment etc) (EU Exit) Regulations 2019, SI 2019/685, reg 19, Sch 1, Pt 2, para 56(b), in relation to accounts for financial years beginning on or after IP completion day (as defined in the European Union (Withdrawal Agreement) Act 2020, s 39) (note also that in relation to accounts for financial years which begin before but end on or after IP completion day, the enactments amended by Parts 1–3 of Sch 1 to the 2019 Regulations have effect as if the UK were a member State until the end of the financial year in question).

SCHEDULES 2–4 *(Schedules 2–4 revoked by the Companies, Partnerships and Groups (Accounts and Reports) Regulations 2015, SI 2015/980, regs 19–21, as from 6 April 2015, in relation to (a) financial years beginning on or after 1 January 2016, and (b) a financial year of a company beginning on or after 1 January 2015, but before 1 January 2016, if the directors of the company so decide (see* **[4.549]** *post).)*

SCHEDULE 5
MATTERS TO BE DEALT WITH IN DIRECTORS' REPORT

Regulation 7

Introduction

[4.54]

1. In addition to the information required by section 416 of the 2006 Act, the directors' report must contain the following information.

Political donations and expenditure

2. (1) If—

(a) the company (not being the wholly-owned subsidiary of a company incorporated in the United Kingdom) has in the financial year—

(i) made any political donation to any political party or other political organisation,

(ii) made any political donation to any independent election candidate, or

(iii) incurred any political expenditure, and

(b) the amount of the donation or expenditure, or (as the case may be) the aggregate amount of all donations and expenditure falling within paragraph (a), exceeded £2000,

the directors' report for the year must contain the following particulars.

(2) Those particulars are—

(a) as respects donations falling within sub-paragraph (1)(a)(i) or (ii)—

(i) the name of each political party, other political organisation or independent election candidate to whom any such donation has been made, and

(ii) the total amount given to that party, organisation or candidate by way of such donations in the financial year; and

(b) as respects expenditure falling within sub-paragraph (1)(a)(iii), the total amount incurred by way of such expenditure in the financial year.

(3) If—

(a) at the end of the financial year the company has subsidiaries which have, in that year, made any donations or incurred any such expenditure as is mentioned in sub-paragraph (1)(a), and

(b) it is not itself the wholly-owned subsidiary of a company incorporated in the United Kingdom,

the directors' report for the year is not, by virtue of sub-paragraph (1), required to contain the particulars specified in sub-paragraph (2).

But, if the total amount of any such donations or expenditure (or both) made or incurred in that year by the company and the subsidiaries between them exceeds £2000, the directors' report for the year must contain those particulars in relation to each body by whom any such donation or expenditure has been made or incurred.

(4) Any expression used in this paragraph which is also used in Part 14 of the 2006 Act (control of political donations and expenditure) has the same meaning as in that Part.

3. (1) If the company (not being the wholly-owned subsidiary of a company incorporated in the United Kingdom) has in the financial year made any contribution to a [non-UK] political party, the directors' report for the year must contain—

(a) a statement of the amount of the contribution, or

(b) (if it has made two or more such contributions in the year) a statement of the total amount of the contributions.

(2) If—

(a) at the end of the financial year the company has subsidiaries which have, in that year, made any such contributions as are mentioned in sub-paragraph (1), and

(b) it is not itself the wholly-owned subsidiary of a company incorporated in the United Kingdom,

the directors' report for the year is not, by virtue of sub-paragraph (1), required to contain any such statement as is there mentioned, but it must instead contain a statement of the total amount of the contributions made in the year by the company and the subsidiaries between them.

(3) In this paragraph, "contribution", in relation to an organisation, means—

(a) any gift of money to the organisation (whether made directly or indirectly);

(b) any subscription or other fee paid for affiliation to, or membership of, the organisation; or

(c) any money spent (otherwise than by the organisation or a person acting on its behalf) in paying any expenses incurred directly or indirectly by the organisation.

(4) In this paragraph, "[non-UK] political party" means any political party which carries on, or proposes to carry on, its activities wholly outside the [United Kingdom].

. . .

4. . . .

Disclosure concerning employment etc of disabled persons

5. (1) This paragraph applies to the directors' report where the average number of persons employed by the company in each week during the financial year exceeded 250.

(2) That average number is the quotient derived by dividing, by the number of weeks in the financial year, the number derived by ascertaining, in relation to each of those weeks, the number of persons who, under contracts of service, were employed in the week (whether throughout it or not) by the company, and adding up the numbers ascertained.

(3) The directors' report must in that case contain a statement describing such policy as the company has applied during the financial year—

(a) for giving full and fair consideration to applications for employment by the company made by disabled persons, having regard to their particular aptitudes and abilities,

(b) for continuing the employment of, and for arranging appropriate training for, employees of the company who have become disabled persons during the period when they were employed by the company, and

(c) otherwise for the training, career development and promotion of disabled persons employed by the company.

(4) In this paragraph—

(a) "employment" means employment other than employment to work wholly or mainly outside the United Kingdom, and "employed" and "employee" are to be construed accordingly; and

(b) "disabled person" means the same as in the Disability Discrimination Act 1995.

. . .

6. . . .

NOTES

Para 3: words in square brackets substituted by the Accounts and Reports (Amendment) (EU Exit) Regulations 2019, SI 2019/145, reg 6, Sch 3, para 1, in relation to financial years beginning on or after IP completion day (as defined in the European Union (Withdrawal Agreement) Act 2020, s 39) (for transitional provisions see reg 7 of the 2019 Regulations at **[12.79]**).

Paras 4, 6: revoked by the Companies Act 2006 (Strategic Report and Directors' Report) Regulations 2013, SI 2013/1970, reg 8, as from 1 October 2013 (in respect of financial years ending on or after 30 September 2013).

SCHEDULE 6
GROUP ACCOUNTS

Regulations 8(1) and 10

PART 1 FORM AND CONTENT OF COMPANIES ACT GROUP ACCOUNTS

General rules

[4.55]

1. (1) Subject to [the following provisions of this Schedule], group accounts must comply so far as practicable with the provisions of Schedule 1 to these Regulations (Companies Act individual accounts) as if the undertakings included in the consolidation ("the group") were a single company.

[(1A) Paragraph 1A of Schedule 1 to these Regulations does not apply to group accounts.]

(2) For item B III in each balance sheet format set out in [Section B of Part 1 of] that Schedule substitute—

"B III Investments
1 Shares in group undertakings
2 Interests in associated undertakings
3 Other participating interests
4 Loans to group undertakings and undertakings in which a participating interest is held
5 Other investments other than loans
6 Others".

(3) In the profit and loss account formats [in Section B of Part 1 of that Schedule] replace the items headed "Income from participating interests", that is—

(a) in Format 1, item 8, [and]

(b) in Format 2, item 10,

(c), (d) . . .

by two items: "Income from interests in associated undertakings" and "Income from other participating interests".

2. (1) The consolidated balance sheet and profit and loss account must incorporate in full the information contained in the individual accounts of the undertakings included in the consolidation, subject to the adjustments authorised or required by the following provisions of this Schedule and to such other adjustments (if any) as may be appropriate in accordance with generally accepted accounting principles or practice.

[(1A) Group accounts must be drawn up as at the same date as the accounts of the parent company.]

(2) If the financial year of a subsidiary undertaking included in the consolidation does not end with that of the parent company, the group accounts must be made up—

(a) from the accounts of the subsidiary undertaking for its financial year last ending before the end of the parent company's financial year, provided that year ended no more than three months before that of the parent company, or

(b) from interim accounts prepared by the subsidiary undertaking as at the end of the parent company's financial year.

3. (1) Where assets and liabilities to be included in the group accounts have been valued or otherwise determined by undertakings according to accounting rules differing from those used for the group accounts, the values or amounts must be adjusted so as to accord with the rules used for the group accounts.

(2) If it appears to the directors of the parent company that there are special reasons for departing from sub-paragraph (1) they may do so, but particulars of any such departure, the reasons for it and its effect must be given in a note to the accounts.

(3) The adjustments referred to in this paragraph need not be made if they are not material for the purpose of giving a true and fair view.

4. Any differences of accounting rules as between a parent company's individual accounts for a financial year and its group accounts must be disclosed in a note to the latter accounts and the reasons for the difference given.

5. Amounts that in the particular context of any provision of this Schedule are not material may be disregarded for the purposes of that provision.

Elimination of group transactions

6. (1) Debts and claims between undertakings included in the consolidation, and income and expenditure relating to transactions between such undertakings, must be eliminated in preparing the group accounts.

(2) Where profits and losses resulting from transactions between undertakings included in the consolidation are included in the book value of assets, they must be eliminated in preparing the group accounts.

(3) The elimination required by sub-paragraph (2) may be effected in proportion to the group's interest in the shares of the undertakings.

(4) Sub-paragraphs (1) and (2) need not be complied with if the amounts concerned are not material for the purpose of giving a true and fair view.

Acquisition and merger accounting

7. (1) The following provisions apply where an undertaking becomes a subsidiary undertaking of the parent company.

(2) That event is referred to in those provisions as an "acquisition", and references to the "undertaking acquired" are to be construed accordingly.

8. An acquisition must be accounted for by the acquisition method of accounting unless the conditions for accounting for it as a merger are met and the merger method of accounting is adopted.

9. (1) The acquisition method of accounting is as follows.

(2) The identifiable assets and liabilities of the undertaking acquired must be included in the consolidated balance sheet at their fair values as at the date of acquisition.

(3) The income and expenditure of the undertaking acquired must be brought into the group accounts only as from the date of the acquisition.

(4) There must be set off against the acquisition cost of the interest in the shares of the undertaking held by the parent company and its subsidiary undertakings the interest of the parent company and its subsidiary undertakings in the adjusted capital and reserves of the undertaking acquired.

(5) The resulting amount if positive must be treated as goodwill, and if negative as a negative consolidation difference.

[(6) Negative goodwill may be transferred to the consolidated profit and loss account where such a treatment is in accordance with the principles and rules of Part 2 of Schedule 1 to these Regulations.]

[10. The conditions for accounting for an acquisition as a merger are—

(a) that the undertaking whose shares are acquired is ultimately controlled by the same party both before and after the acquisition,

(b) that the control referred to in paragraph (a) is not transitory, and

(c) that adoption of the merger method accords with generally accepted accounting principles or practice.]

11. (1) The merger method of accounting is as follows.

(2) The assets and liabilities of the undertaking acquired must be brought into the group accounts at the figures at which they stand in the undertaking's accounts, subject to any adjustment authorised or required by this Schedule.

(3) The income and expenditure of the undertaking acquired must be included in the group accounts for the entire financial year, including the period before the acquisition.

(4) The group accounts must show corresponding amounts relating to the previous financial year as if the undertaking acquired had been included in the consolidation throughout that year.

(5) There must be set off against the aggregate of—

(a) the appropriate amount in respect of qualifying shares issued by the parent company or its subsidiary undertakings in consideration for the acquisition of shares in the undertaking acquired, and

(b) the fair value of any other consideration for the acquisition of shares in the undertaking acquired, determined as at the date when those shares were acquired,

the nominal value of the issued share capital of the undertaking acquired held by the parent company and its subsidiary undertakings.

(6) The resulting amount must be shown as an adjustment to the consolidated reserves.

(7) In sub-paragraph (5)(a) "qualifying shares" means—

(a) shares in relation to which any of the following provisions applies (merger relief), and in respect of which the appropriate amount is the nominal value—

(i) section 131 of the Companies Act 1985,

(ii) Article 141 of the Companies (Northern Ireland) Order 1986, or

(iii) section 612 of the 2006 Act, or

(b) shares in relation to which any of the following provisions applies (group reconstruction relief), and in respect of which the appropriate amount is the nominal value together with any minimum premium value within the meaning of that section—

(i) section 132 of the Companies Act 1985,
(ii) Article 142 of the Companies (Northern Ireland) Order 1986, or
(iii) section 611 of the 2006 Act.

12. (1) Where a group is acquired, paragraphs 9 to 11 apply with the following adaptations.

(2) References to shares of the undertaking acquired are to be construed as references to shares of the parent undertaking of the group.

(3) Other references to the undertaking acquired are to be construed as references to the group; and references to the assets and liabilities, income and expenditure and capital and reserves of the undertaking acquired must be construed as references to the assets and liabilities, income and expenditure and capital and reserves of the group after making the set-offs and other adjustments required by this Schedule in the case of group accounts.

13. (1) The following information with respect to acquisitions taking place in the financial year must be given in a note to the accounts.

(2) There must be stated—

(a) the name of the undertaking acquired or, where a group was acquired, the name of the parent undertaking of that group, and
(b) whether the acquisition has been accounted for by the acquisition or the merger method of accounting;

and in relation to an acquisition which significantly affects the figures shown in the group accounts, the following further information must be given.

(3) The composition and fair value of the consideration for the acquisition given by the parent company and its subsidiary undertakings must be stated.

(4) Where the acquisition method of accounting has been adopted, the book values immediately prior to the acquisition, and the fair values at the date of acquisition, of each class of assets and liabilities of the undertaking or group acquired must be stated in tabular form, including a statement of the amount of any goodwill or negative consolidation difference arising on the acquisition, together with an explanation of any significant adjustments made.

(5) In ascertaining for the purposes of sub-paragraph (4) the profit or loss of a group, the book values and fair values of assets and liabilities of a group or the amount of the assets and liabilities of a group, the set-offs and other adjustments required by this Schedule in the case of group accounts must be made.

14. (1) There must also be stated in a note to the accounts the cumulative amount of goodwill resulting from acquisitions in that and earlier financial years which has been written off otherwise than in the consolidated profit and loss account for that or any earlier financial year.

(2) That figure must be shown net of any goodwill attributable to subsidiary undertakings or businesses disposed of prior to the balance sheet date.

15. Where during the financial year there has been a disposal of an undertaking or group which significantly affects the figure shown in the group accounts, there must be stated in a note to the accounts—

(a) the name of that undertaking or, as the case may be, of the parent undertaking of that group, and
(b) the extent to which the profit or loss shown in the group accounts is attributable to profit or loss of that undertaking or group.

16. The information required by paragraph 13, 14 or 15 need not be disclosed with respect to an undertaking which—

(a) is established under the law of a country outside the United Kingdom, or
(b) carries on business outside the United Kingdom,

if in the opinion of the directors of the parent company the disclosure would be seriously prejudicial to the business of that undertaking or to the business of the parent company or any of its subsidiary undertakings and the Secretary of State agrees that the information should not be disclosed.

[16A. Where an acquisition has taken place in the financial year and the merger method of accounting has been adopted, the notes to the accounts must also disclose—

(a) the address of the registered office of the undertaking acquired (whether in or outside the United Kingdom),
(b) the name of the party referred to in paragraph 10(a),
(c) the address of the registered office of that party (whether in or outside the United Kingdom), and
(d) the information referred to in paragraph 11(6).]

[Non-controlling interests

17. (1) The formats set out in Section B of Part 1 of Schedule 1 to these Regulations have effect in relation to group accounts with the following additions.

(2) In the Balance Sheet Formats there must be shown, as a separate item and under the heading "non-controlling interests", the amount of capital and reserves attributable to shares in subsidiary undertakings included in the consolidation held by or on behalf of persons other than the parent company and its subsidiary undertakings.

(3) In the Profit and Loss Account Formats there must be shown, as a separate item and under the heading "non-controlling interests", the amount of any profit or loss attributable to shares in subsidiary undertakings included in the consolidation held by or on behalf of persons other than the parent company and its subsidiary undertakings.

(4) For the purposes of paragraph (4) of Schedule 1 (power to adapt or combine items)—

(a) the additional item required by sub-paragraph (2) above is treated as one to which a letter is assigned, and
(b) the additional item required by sub-paragraph (3) above is treated as one to which an Arabic number is assigned.]

Joint ventures

18. (1) Where an undertaking included in the consolidation manages another undertaking jointly with one or more undertakings not included in the consolidation, that other undertaking ("the joint venture") may, if it is not—

(a) a body corporate, or

(b) a subsidiary undertaking of the parent company,

be dealt with in the group accounts by the method of proportional consolidation.

(2) The provisions of this Schedule relating to the preparation of consolidated accounts [and sections 402 and 405 of the 2006 Act] apply, with any necessary modifications, to proportional consolidation under this paragraph.

[(3) In addition to the disclosure of the average number of employees employed during the financial year (see section 411(7) of the 2006 Act), there must be a separate disclosure in the notes to the accounts of the average number of employees employed by undertakings that are proportionately consolidated.]

Associated undertakings

19. (1) An "associated undertaking" means an undertaking in which an undertaking included in the consolidation has a participating interest and over whose operating and financial policy it exercises a significant influence, and which is not—

(a) a subsidiary undertaking of the parent company, or

(b) a joint venture dealt with in accordance with paragraph 18.

(2) Where an undertaking holds 20% or more of the voting rights in another undertaking, it is presumed to exercise such an influence over it unless the contrary is shown.

(3) The voting rights in an undertaking means the rights conferred on shareholders in respect of their shares or, in the case of an undertaking not having a share capital, on members, to vote at general meetings of the undertaking on all, or substantially all, matters.

(4) The provisions of paragraphs 5 to 11 of Schedule 7 to the 2006 Act (parent and subsidiary undertakings: rights to be taken into account and attribution of rights) apply in determining for the purposes of this paragraph whether an undertaking holds 20% or more of the voting rights in another undertaking.

20. (1) The interest of an undertaking in an associated undertaking, and the amount of profit or loss attributable to such an interest, must be shown by the equity method of accounting (including dealing with any goodwill arising in accordance with paragraphs 17 to 20 and 22 of Schedule 1 to these Regulations).

(2) Where the associated undertaking is itself a parent undertaking, the net assets and profits or losses to be taken into account are those of the parent and its subsidiary undertakings (after making any consolidation adjustments).

(3) The equity method of accounting need not be applied if the amounts in question are not material for the purpose of giving a true and fair view.

[Deferred tax balances

20A. Deferred tax balances must be recognised on consolidation where it is probable that a charge to tax will arise within the foreseeable future for one of the undertakings included in the consolidation.

Related Party Transactions

20B Paragraph 66 of Schedule 1 to these Regulations applies to transactions which the parent company, or other undertakings included in the consolidation, have entered into with related parties, unless they are intra-group transactions.]

NOTES

The words "Section B of Part 1 of" in square brackets in para 1(2), and the words "in Section B of Part 1 of that Schedule" in square brackets in para 1(3), were inserted by the Small Companies (Micro-Entities' Accounts) Regulations 2013, SI 2013/3008, reg 12(a), as from 1 December 2013, in relation to (a) financial years ending on or after 30 September 2013, and (b) companies which deliver the accounts required by s 444 of this Act to the registrar on or after 1 December 2013.

All other amendment to this Part were made by the Companies, Partnerships and Groups (Accounts and Reports) Regulations 2015, SI 2015/980, reg 22, as from 6 April 2015, in relation to (a) financial years beginning on or after 1 January 2016, and (b) a financial year of a company beginning on or after 1 January 2015, but before 1 January 2016, if the directors of the company so decide (see **[4.549]** *post*).

PART 2 INFORMATION ABOUT RELATED UNDERTAKINGS WHERE COMPANY PREPARING GROUP ACCOUNTS (COMPANIES ACT OR IAS GROUP ACCOUNTS)

Introduction and interpretation

[4.56]

21. In this Part of this Schedule "the group" means the group consisting of the parent company and its subsidiary undertakings.

Subsidiary undertakings

22. (1) The following information must be given with respect to the undertakings that are subsidiary undertakings of the parent company at the end of the financial year.

(2) The name of each undertaking must be stated.

(3) There must be stated—

[(a) the address of the undertaking's registered office (whether in or outside the United Kingdom),]

(b) if it is unincorporated, the address of its principal place of business.

(4) It must also be stated whether the subsidiary undertaking is included in the consolidation and, if it is not, the reasons for excluding it from consolidation must be given.

(5) It must be stated with respect to each subsidiary undertaking by virtue of which of the conditions specified in section 1162(2) or (4) of the 2006 Act it is a subsidiary undertaking of its immediate parent undertaking.

That information need not be given if the relevant condition is that specified in subsection (2)(a) of that section (holding of a majority of the voting rights) and the immediate parent undertaking holds the same proportion of the shares in the undertaking as it holds voting rights.

Holdings in subsidiary undertakings

23. (1) The following information must be given with respect to the shares of a subsidiary undertaking held—

(a) by the parent company, and

(b) by the group,

and the information under paragraphs (a) and (b) must (if different) be shown separately.

(2) There must be stated—

(a) the identity of each class of shares held, and

(b) the proportion of the nominal value of the shares of that class represented by those shares.

Financial information about subsidiary undertakings not included in the consolidation

24. (1) There must be shown with respect to each subsidiary undertaking not included in the consolidation—

(a) the aggregate amount of its capital and reserves as at the end of its relevant financial year, and

(b) its profit or loss for that year.

(2) That information need not be given if the group's investment in the undertaking is included in the accounts by way of the equity method of valuation or if—

(a) the undertaking is not required by any provision of the 2006 Act to deliver a copy of its balance sheet for its relevant financial year and does not otherwise publish that balance sheet in the United Kingdom or elsewhere, and

(b) the holding of the group is less than 50% of the nominal value of the shares in the undertaking.

(3) Information otherwise required by this paragraph need not be given if it is not material.

(4) For the purposes of this paragraph the "relevant financial year" of a subsidiary undertaking is—

(a) if its financial year ends with that of the company, that year, and

(b) if not, its financial year ending last before the end of the company's financial year.

Shares of company held by subsidiary undertakings

25. (1) The number, description and amount of the shares in the company held by or on behalf of its subsidiary undertakings must be disclosed.

(2) Sub-paragraph (1) does not apply in relation to shares in the case of which the subsidiary undertaking is concerned as personal representative or, subject as follows, as trustee.

(3) The exception for shares in relation to which the subsidiary undertaking is concerned as trustee does not apply if the company or any of its subsidiary undertakings is beneficially interested under the trust, otherwise than by way of security only for the purposes of a transaction entered into by it in the ordinary course of a business which includes the lending of money.

(4) Part 2 of Schedule 2 to these Regulations has effect for the interpretation of the reference in sub-paragraph (3) to a beneficial interest under a trust.

Joint ventures

26. (1) The following information must be given where an undertaking is dealt with in the consolidated accounts by the method of proportional consolidation in accordance with paragraph 18 of this Schedule (joint ventures)—

(a) the name of the undertaking,

[(b) the address of the undertaking's registered office (whether in or outside the United Kingdom),]

(c) the factors on which joint management of the undertaking is based, and

(d) the proportion of the capital of the undertaking held by [or on behalf of] undertakings included in the consolidation.

(2) Where the financial year of the undertaking did not end with that of the company, there must be stated the date on which a financial year of the undertaking last ended before that date.

Associated undertakings

27. (1) The following information must be given where an undertaking included in the consolidation has an interest in an associated undertaking.

(2) The name of the associated undertaking must be stated.

(3) There must be stated—

[(a) the address of the undertaking's registered office (whether in or outside the United Kingdom),]

(b) if it is unincorporated, the address of its principal place of business.

(4) The following information must be given with respect to the shares of the undertaking held—

(a) by the parent company, and

(b) by the group,

and the information under paragraphs (a) and (b) must be shown separately.

(5) There must be stated—

(a) the identity of each class of shares held, and

(b) the proportion of the nominal value of the shares of that class represented by those shares.

(6) In this paragraph "associated undertaking" has the meaning given by paragraph 19 of this Schedule; and the information required by this paragraph must be given notwithstanding that paragraph 20(3) of this Schedule (materiality) applies in relation to the accounts themselves.

Other significant holdings of parent company or group

28. (1) The information required by paragraphs 29 and 30 must be given where at the end of the financial year the parent company has a significant holding in an undertaking which is not one of its subsidiary undertakings and does not fall within paragraph 26 (joint ventures) or paragraph 27 (associated undertakings).

(2) A holding is significant for this purpose if—

(a) it amounts to 20% or more of the nominal value of any class of shares in the undertaking, or

(b) the amount of the holding (as stated or included in the company's individual accounts) exceeds 20% of the amount of its assets (as so stated).

29. (1) The name of the undertaking must be stated.

(2) There must be stated—

[(a) the address of the undertaking's registered office (whether in or outside the United Kingdom),]

(b) if it is unincorporated, the address of its principal place of business.

(3) The following information must be given with respect to the shares of the undertaking held by the parent company.

(4) There must be stated—

(a) the identity of each class of shares held, and

(b) the proportion of the nominal value of the shares of that class represented by those shares.

30. (1) There must also be stated—

(a) the aggregate amount of the capital and reserves of the undertaking as at the end of its relevant financial year, and

(b) its profit or loss for that year.

(2) That information need not be given in respect of an undertaking if—

(a) the undertaking is not required by any provision of the 2006 Act to deliver a copy of its balance sheet for its relevant financial year and does not otherwise publish that balance sheet in the United Kingdom or elsewhere, and

(b) the company's holding is less than 50% of the nominal value of the shares in the undertaking.

(3) Information otherwise required by this paragraph need not be given if it is not material.

(4) For the purposes of this paragraph the "relevant financial year" of an undertaking is—

(a) if its financial year ends with that of the company, that year, and

(b) if not, its financial year ending last before the end of the company's financial year.

31. (1) The information required by paragraphs 32 and 33 must be given where at the end of the financial year the group has a significant holding in an undertaking which is not a subsidiary undertaking of the parent company and does not fall within paragraph 26 (joint ventures) or paragraph 27 (associated undertakings).

(2) A holding is significant for this purpose if—

(a) it amounts to 20% or more of the nominal value of any class of shares in the undertaking, or

(b) the amount of the holding (as stated or included in the group accounts) exceeds 20% of the amount of the group's assets (as so stated).

32. (1) The name of the undertaking must be stated.

(2) There must be stated—

[(a) the address of the undertaking's registered office (whether in or outside the United Kingdom),]

(b) if it is unincorporated, the address of its principal place of business.

(3) The following information must be given with respect to the shares of the undertaking held by the group.

(4) There must be stated—

(a) the identity of each class of shares held, and

(b) the proportion of the nominal value of the shares of that class represented by those shares.

33. (1) There must also be stated—

(a) the aggregate amount of the capital and reserves of the undertaking as at the end of its relevant financial year, and

(b) its profit or loss for that year.

(2) That information need not be given if—

(a) the undertaking is not required by any provision of the 2006 Act to deliver a copy of its balance sheet for its relevant financial year and does not otherwise publish that balance sheet in the United Kingdom or elsewhere, and

(b) the holding of the group is less than 50% of the nominal value of the shares in the undertaking.

(3) Information otherwise required by this paragraph need not be given if it is not material.

(4) For the purposes of this paragraph the "relevant financial year" of an outside undertaking is—

(a) if its financial year ends with that of the parent company, that year, and

(b) if not, its financial year ending last before the end of the parent company's financial year.

Parent company's or group's membership of certain undertakings

34. (1) The information required by this paragraph must be given where at the end of the financial year the parent company or group is a member of a qualifying undertaking.

(2) There must be stated—

(a) the name and legal form of the undertaking, and

(b) the address of the undertaking's registered office (whether in or outside the United Kingdom) or, if it does not have such an office, its head office (whether in or outside the United Kingdom).

(3) Where the undertaking is a qualifying partnership there must also be stated either—

(a) that a copy of the latest accounts of the undertaking has been or is to be appended to the copy of the company's accounts sent to the registrar under section 444 of the 2006 Act, or

(b) the name of at least one body corporate (which may be the company) in whose group accounts the undertaking has been or is to be dealt with on a consolidated basis.

(4) Information otherwise required by sub-paragraph (2) need not be given if it is not material.

(5) Information otherwise required by sub-paragraph (3)(b) need not be given if the notes to the company's accounts disclose that advantage has been taken of the exemption conferred by regulation 7 of the [Partnerships (Accounts) Regulations 2008].

[(6) In sub-paragraph (1) "member", in relation to a qualifying undertaking which is a qualifying partnership, has the same meaning as in the Partnerships (Accounts) Regulations 2008.

(7) In this paragraph—

"dealt with on a consolidated basis" and "qualifying partnership" have the same meanings as in the Partnerships (Accounts) Regulations 2008;

"qualifying undertaking" means—

(a) a qualifying partnership, or

(b) an unlimited company each of whose members is—

(i) a limited company,

(ii) another unlimited company each of whose members is a limited company,

(iii) a Scottish partnership which is not a limited partnership, each of whose members is a limited company, or

(iv) a Scottish partnership which is a limited partnership, each of whose general partners is a limited company.

(8) In sub-paragraph (7) the references to a limited company, another unlimited company, a Scottish partnership which is not a limited partnership or a Scottish partnership which is a limited partnership include a comparable undertaking incorporated in or formed under the law of a country or territory outside the United Kingdom.

(9) In sub-paragraph (7) "general partner" means—

(a) in relation to a Scottish partnership which is a limited partnership, a person who is a general partner within the meaning of the Limited Partnerships Act 1907, and

(b) in relation to an undertaking incorporated in or formed under the law of any country or territory outside the United Kingdom and which is comparable to a Scottish partnership which is a limited partnership, a person comparable to such a general partner.

(10) In sub-paragraphs (7), (8) and (9) "limited partnership" means a partnership registered under the Limited Partnerships Act 1907.]

Parent undertaking drawing up accounts for larger group

35. (1) Where the parent company is itself a subsidiary undertaking, the following information must be given with respect to that parent undertaking of the company which heads—

(a) the largest group of undertakings for which group accounts are drawn up and of which that company is a member, and

(b) the smallest such group of undertakings.

(2) The name of the parent undertaking must be stated.

(3) There must be stated—

(a) if the undertaking is incorporated outside the United Kingdom, the country in which it is incorporated,

(b) if it is unincorporated, the address of its principal place of business.

(4) If copies of the group accounts referred to in sub-paragraph (1) are available to the public, there must also be stated the addresses from which copies of the accounts can be obtained.

Identification of ultimate parent company

36. (1) Where the parent company is itself a subsidiary undertaking, the following information must be given with respect to the company (if any) regarded by the directors as being that company's ultimate parent company.

(2) The name of that company must be stated.

(3) If that company is incorporated outside the United Kingdom, the country in which it is incorporated must be stated (if known to the directors).

(4) In this paragraph "company" includes any body corporate.

Construction of references to shares held by parent company or group

37. (1) References in this Part of this Schedule to shares held by the parent company or the group are to be construed as follows.

(2) For the purposes of paragraphs 23, 27(4) and (5) and 28 to 30 (information about holdings in subsidiary and other undertakings)—

(a) there must be attributed to the parent company shares held on its behalf by any person; but

(b) there must be treated as not held by the parent company shares held on behalf of a person other than the company.

(3) References to shares held by the group are to any shares held by or on behalf of the parent company or any of its subsidiary undertakings; but any shares held on behalf of a person other than the parent company or any of its subsidiary undertakings are not to be treated as held by the group.

(4) Shares held by way of security must be treated as held by the person providing the security—

(a) where apart from the right to exercise them for the purpose of preserving the value of the security, or of realising it, the rights attached to the shares are exercisable only in accordance with his instructions, and

(b) where the shares are held in connection with the granting of loans as part of normal business activities and apart from the right to exercise them for the purpose of preserving the value of the security, or of realising it, the rights attached to the shares are exercisable only in his interests.

NOTES

Para 22: sub-para (3)(a) substituted by the Companies, Partnerships and Groups (Accounts and Reports) Regulations 2015, SI 2015/980, reg 23(1), (2), as from 6 April 2015, in relation to (a) financial years beginning on or after 1 January 2016, and

(b) a financial year of a company beginning on or after 1 January 2015, but before 1 January 2016, if the directors of the company so decide (see **[4.549]** *post*).

Para 26: words in square brackets in sub-para (1)(d) inserted, and sub-para (1)(b) substituted, by SI 2015/980, reg 23(1), (3), (4) (as to the application of this amendment see the first note relating to the 2015 Regulations above).

Para 27: sub-para (3)(a) substituted by SI 2015/980, reg 23(1), (5) (as to the application of this amendment see the first note relating to the 2015 Regulations above).

Para 29: sub-para (2)(a) substituted by SI 2015/980, reg 23(1), (6) (as to the application of this amendment see the first note relating to the 2015 Regulations above).

Para 32: sub-para (2)(a) substituted by SI 2015/980, reg 23(1), (7) (as to the application of this amendment see the first note relating to the 2015 Regulations above).

Para 34 is amended as follows:

Words in square brackets in sub-para (5) substituted by the Partnerships (Accounts) Regulations 2008, SI 2008/569, reg 17(1)(b), as from 6 April 2008, in relation to qualifying partnerships' financial years beginning on or after that date, and auditors appointed in respect of those financial years.

Sub-paras (6)–(10) substituted (for the original sub-para (6)) by the Companies and Partnerships (Accounts and Audit) Regulations 2013, SI 2013/2005, reg 5, in relation to a financial year of a company beginning on or after 1 October 2013.

SCHEDULE 7
INTERPRETATION OF TERM "PROVISIONS"

Regulation 12

PART 1 MEANING FOR PURPOSES OF THESE REGULATIONS

Definition of "Provisions"

[4.57]

1. (1) In these Regulations, references to provisions for depreciation or diminution in value of assets are to any amount written off by way of providing for depreciation or diminution in value of assets.

(2) Any reference in the profit and loss account formats set out in Part 1 of Schedule 1 to these Regulations to the depreciation of, or amounts written off, assets of any description is to any provision for depreciation or diminution in value of assets of that description.

2. References in these Regulations to provisions for liabilities are to any amount retained as reasonably necessary for the purpose of providing for any liability the nature of which is clearly defined and which is either likely to be incurred, or certain to be incurred but uncertain as to amount or as to the date on which it will arise.

[2A. At the balance sheet date, a provision must represent the best estimate of the expenses likely to be incurred or, in the case of a liability, of the amount required to meet that liability.

2B. Provisions must not be used to adjust the values of assets.]

NOTES

Paras 2A, 2B: inserted by the Companies, Partnerships and Groups (Accounts and Reports) Regulations 2015, SI 2015/980, reg 24, as from 6 April 2015, in relation to (a) financial years beginning on or after 1 January 2016, and (b) a financial year of a company beginning on or after 1 January 2015, but before 1 January 2016, if the directors of the company so decide (see **[4.549]** *post*).

PART 2 MEANING FOR PURPOSES OF PARTS 18 AND 23 OF THE 2006 ACT

Financial assistance for purchase of own shares

[4.58]

3. The specified provisions for the purposes of section 677(3)(a) of the 2006 Act (Companies Act accounts: relevant provisions for purposes of financial assistance) are provisions for liabilities within paragraph 2 of this Schedule.

Redemption or purchase by private company out of capital

4. The specified provisions for the purposes of section 712(2)(b)(i) of the 2006 Act (Companies Act accounts: relevant provisions to determine available profits for redemption or purchase out of capital) are provisions of any of the kinds mentioned in paragraphs 1 and 2 of this Schedule.

Justification of distribution by references to accounts

5. The specified provisions for the purposes of section 836(1)(b)(i) of the 2006 Act (Companies Act accounts: relevant provisions for distribution purposes) are provisions of any of the kinds mentioned in paragraphs 1 and 2 of this Schedule.

[Realised losses

6. The specified provisions for the purposes of section 841(2)(a) of the 2006 Act (Companies Act accounts: treatment of provisions as realised losses) are provisions of any of the kinds mentioned in paragraphs 1 and 2 of this Schedule.]

NOTES

Para 6: added by the Companies Act 2006 (Accounts, Reports and Audit) Regulations 2009, SI 2009/1581, reg 11(1), (3), as from 27 June 2009, in relation to financial years beginning on or after 6 April 2008 which have not ended before 27 June 2009.

SCHEDULE 8
GENERAL INTERPRETATION

Regulation 13

Financial instruments

[4.59]

1. References to "derivatives" include commodity-based contracts that give either contracting party the right to settle in cash or in some other financial instrument, except where such contracts—

(a) were entered into for the purpose of, and continue to meet, the company's expected purchase, sale or usage requirements,
(b) were designated for such purpose at their inception, and
(c) are expected to be settled by delivery of the commodity.

2. [(1) The expressions listed in sub-paragraph (2) have the same meaning as they have in Directive 2013/34/EU of the European Parliament and of the Council of 26 June 2013 on the annual financial statements etc of certain types of undertakings.]

(2) Those expressions are "available for sale financial asset", "business combination", "commodity-based contracts", "derivative", "equity instrument", "exchange difference", "fair value hedge accounting system", "financial fixed asset", "financial instrument", "foreign entity", "hedge accounting", "hedge accounting system", "hedged items", "hedging instrument", "held for trading purposes", "held to maturity", "monetary item", "receivables", "reliable market" and "trading portfolio".

Fixed and current assets

3. "Fixed assets" means assets of a company which are intended for use on a continuing basis in the company's activities, and "current assets" means assets not intended for such use.

Historical cost accounting rules

4. References to the historical cost accounting rules are to be read in accordance with paragraph 30 of Schedule 1 to these Regulations.

Listed investments

5. (1) "Listed investment" means an investment as respects which there has been granted a listing on—
(a) a recognised investment exchange other than an overseas investment exchange, or
(b) a stock exchange of repute outside the United Kingdom.

(2) "Recognised investment exchange" and "overseas investment exchange" have the meaning given in Part 18 of the Financial Services and Markets Act 2000.

Loans

6. A loan is treated as falling due for repayment, and an instalment of a loan is treated as falling due for payment, on the earliest date on which the lender could require repayment or (as the case may be) payment, if he exercised all options and rights available to him.

Materiality

7. Amounts which in the particular context of any provision of Schedule 1 to these Regulations are not material may be disregarded for the purposes of that provision.

Participating interests

8. (1) A "participating interest" means an interest held by an undertaking in the shares of another undertaking which it holds on a long-term basis for the purpose of securing a contribution to its activities by the exercise of control or influence arising from or related to that interest.

(2) A holding of 20% or more of the shares of the undertaking is to be presumed to be a participating interest unless the contrary is shown.

(3) The reference in sub-paragraph (1) to an interest in shares includes—
(a) an interest which is convertible into an interest in shares, and
(b) an option to acquire shares or any such interest,

and an interest or option falls within paragraph (a) or (b) notwithstanding that the shares to which it relates are, until the conversion or the exercise of the option, unissued.

(4) For the purposes of this paragraph an interest held on behalf of an undertaking is to be treated as held by it.

(5) In the balance sheet and profit and loss formats set out in [Section B of] Part 1 of Schedule 1 . . . to these Regulations, "participating interest" does not include an interest in a group undertaking.

(6) For the purpose of this paragraph as it applies in relation to the expression "participating interest"—
(a) in those formats as they apply in relation to group accounts, and
(b) in paragraph 19 of Schedule 6 (group accounts: undertakings to be accounted for as associated undertakings),

the references in sub-paragraphs (1) to (4) to the interest held by, and the purposes and activities of, the undertaking concerned are to be construed as references to the interest held by, and the purposes and activities of, the group (within the meaning of paragraph 1 of that Schedule).

Purchase price

9. "Purchase price", in relation to an asset of a company or any raw materials or consumables used in the production of such an asset, includes any consideration (whether in cash or otherwise) given by the company in respect of that asset or those materials or consumables, as the case may be.

Realised profits and losses

10. "Realised profits" and "realised losses" have the same meaning as in section 853(4) and (5) of the 2006 Act.

Staff costs

11. (1) "Social security costs" means any contributions by the company to any state social security or pension scheme, fund or arrangement.

(2) "Pension costs" includes—
(a) any costs incurred by the company in respect of any pension scheme established for the purpose of providing pensions for persons currently or formerly employed by the company,
(b) any sums set aside for the future payment of pensions directly by the company to current or former employees, and

(c) any pensions paid directly to such persons without having first been set aside.

(3) Any amount stated in respect of the item "social security costs" or in respect of the item "wages and salaries" in [the profit and loss account [Format 2] in Section B of Part 1 of Schedule 1] must be determined by reference to payments made or costs incurred in respect of all persons employed by the company during the financial year under contracts of service.

NOTES

Para 2: sub-para (1) substituted by the Companies, Partnerships and Groups (Accounts and Reports) Regulations 2015, SI 2015/980, reg 25(1), (2), as from 6 April 2015, in relation to (a) financial years beginning on or after 1 January 2016, and (b) a financial year of a company beginning on or after 1 January 2015, but before 1 January 2016, if the directors of the company so decide (see **[4.549]** *post*).

Para 8: words in square brackets in sub-para (5) inserted by the Small Companies (Micro-Entities' Accounts) Regulations 2013, SI 2013/3008, reg 13(1), (2), as from 1 December 2013, in relation to (a) financial years ending on or after 30 September 2013, and (b) companies which deliver the accounts required by s 444 of this Act to the registrar on or after 1 December 2013. Words omitted from sub-para (5) revoked by SI 2015/980, reg 25(1), (3) (as to the application of this amendment see the first note relating to the 2015 Regulations above).

Para 11: words in first (outer) pair of square brackets in sub-para (3) substituted by SI 2013/3008, reg 13(1), (3), as from 1 December 2013, in relation to (a) financial years ending on or after 30 September 2013, and (b) companies which deliver the accounts required by s 444 of this Act to the registrar on or after 1 December 2013. Words in second (inner) pair of square brackets in sub-para (3) substituted by SI 2015/980, reg 25(1), (4) (as to the application of this amendment see the first note relating to the 2015 Regulations above).

LARGE AND MEDIUM-SIZED COMPANIES AND GROUPS (ACCOUNTS AND REPORTS) REGULATIONS 2008

(SI 2008/410)

NOTES

Made: 19 February 2008.

Authority: Companies Act 2006, ss 396(3), 404(3), 409(1)–(3), 412(1)–(3), 416(4), 421(1), (2), 445(3)(a), (b), 677(3)(a), 712(2)(b)(i), 831(3)(a), 832(4)(a), 836(1)(b)(i), 1292(1)(a), (c).

Commencement: 6 April 2008.

For a summary of all Orders and Regulations made under the Companies Act 2006, see Appendix 4 at **[A4]**.

These Regulations are reproduced as amended by: the Partnerships (Accounts) Regulations 2008, SI 2008/569; the Companies Act 2006 (Accounts, Reports and Audit) Regulations 2009, SI 2009/1581; the Financial Services Act 2012 (Consequential Amendments and Transitional Provisions) Order 2013, SI 2013/472; the Companies Act 2006 (Strategic Report and Directors' Report) Regulations 2013, SI 2013/1970; the Large and Medium-sized Companies and Groups (Accounts and Reports) (Amendment) Regulations 2013, SI 2013/1981; the Companies and Partnerships (Accounts and Audit) Regulations 2013, SI 2013/2005; the Solvency 2 Regulations 2015, SI 2015/575; the Companies, Partnerships and Groups (Accounts and Reports) Regulations 2015, SI 2015/980; the Companies, Partnerships and Groups (Accounts and Reports) (No 2) Regulations 2015, SI 2015/1672; the Limited Liability Partnerships, Partnerships and Groups (Accounts and Audit) Regulations 2016, SI 2016/575; the Companies (Miscellaneous Reporting) Regulations 2018, SI 2018/860; the Companies (Directors' Report) and Limited Liability Partnerships (Energy and Carbon Report) Regulations 2018, SI 2018/1155; the Accounts and Reports (Amendment) (EU Exit) Regulations 2019, SI 2019/145; the Takeovers (Amendment) (EU Exit) Regulations 2019, SI 2019/217; the International Accounting Standards and European Public Limited-Liability Company (Amendment etc) (EU Exit) Regulations 2019, SI 2019/685; the Companies (Directors' Remuneration Policy and Directors' Remuneration Report) Regulations 2019, SI 2019/970.

Application: these Regulations are applied (i) to limited liability partnerships, see the Large and Medium-sized Limited Liability Partnerships (Accounts) Regulations 2008, SI 2008/1913 at **[10.302]**; (ii) to partnerships, see the Partnerships (Accounts) Regulations 2008, SI 2008/569 at **[10.202]**; (iii) to insurance undertakings, see the Insurance Accounts Directive (Miscellaneous Insurance Undertakings) Regulations 2008, SI 2008/565.

ARRANGEMENT OF REGULATIONS

PART 4
DIRECTORS' REMUNERATION REPORT

PART 5
INTERPRETATION

PART 6
REVIEW

SCHEDULES

PART 1 INTRODUCTION

[4.60]

1 Citation and interpretation

(1) These Regulations may be cited as the Large and Medium-sized Companies and Groups (Accounts and Reports) Regulations 2008.

(2) In these Regulations "the 2006 Act" means the Companies Act 2006.

[4.61]

2 Commencement and application

(1) These Regulations come into force on 6th April 2008.

(2) Subject to paragraph (3), they apply in relation to financial years beginning on or after 6th April 2008.

(3) The requirement for disclosure in paragraph 4 of Schedule 8 to these Regulations (directors' remuneration report: disclosure relating to consideration of conditions in company and group) applies in relation to financial years beginning on or after 6th April 2009.

(4) These Regulations apply to companies other than those which are subject to the small companies regime under Part 15 of the 2006 Act.

PART 2 FORM AND CONTENT OF ACCOUNTS

[4.62]

3 Companies Act individual accounts (companies other than banking and insurance companies)

(1) Subject to regulation 4, the directors of a company—

(a) for which they are preparing Companies Act individual accounts under section 396 of the 2006 Act (Companies Act: individual accounts), and

(b) which is not a banking company or an insurance company,

must comply with the provisions of Schedule 1 to these Regulations as to the form and content of the balance sheet and profit and loss account, and additional information to be provided by way of notes to the accounts.

(2) The profit and loss account of a company that falls within section 408 of the 2006 Act (individual profit and loss account where group accounts prepared) need not contain the information specified in paragraphs 65 to 69 of Schedule 1 to these Regulations (information supplementing the profit and loss account).

[4.63]

4 Medium-sized companies: exemptions for Companies Act individual accounts

(1) This regulation applies to a company—

(a) which qualifies as medium-sized in relation to a financial year under section 465 of the 2006 Act, and

(b) the directors of which are preparing Companies Act individual accounts under section 396 of that Act for that year.

[(2A) The individual accounts for the year need not comply with paragraph 45 (disclosure with respect to compliance with accounting standards) of Schedule 1 to these Regulations.

(2B) Paragraph 72 (related party transactions) applies with the modification that only particulars of transactions which have not been concluded under normal market conditions with the following must be disclosed—

(a) owners holding a participating interest in the company;

(b) companies in which the company itself has a participating interest; and

(c) the company's directors.]

(3) . . .

NOTES

Paras (2A), (2B) substituted (for the original para (2)), and para (3), revoked, by the Companies, Partnerships and Groups (Accounts and Reports) Regulations 2015, SI 2015/980, reg 26, as from 6 April 2015, in relation to (a) financial years beginning on or after 1 January 2016, and (b) a financial year of a company beginning on or after 1 January 2015, but before 1 January 2016, if the directors of the company so decide (see **[4.549]** *post*).

[4.64]

5 Companies Act individual accounts: banking companies

(1) The directors of a company—

(a) for which they are preparing Companies Act individual accounts under section 396 of the 2006 Act, and

(b) which is a banking company,

must comply with the provisions of Schedule 2 to these Regulations as to the form and content of the balance sheet and profit and loss account, and additional information to be provided by way of notes to the accounts.

(2) The profit and loss account of a banking company that falls within section 408 of the 2006 Act (individual profit and loss account where group accounts prepared) need not contain the information specified in paragraphs 85 to 91 of Schedule 2 to these Regulations (information supplementing the profit and loss account).

(3) Accounts prepared in accordance with this regulation must contain a statement that they are prepared in accordance with the provisions of these Regulations relating to banking companies.

[4.65]

6 Companies Act individual accounts: insurance companies

(1) The directors of a company—

(a) for which they are preparing Companies Act individual accounts under section 396 of the 2006 Act, and

(b) which is an insurance company,

must comply with the provisions of Schedule 3 to these Regulations as to the form and content of the balance sheet and profit and loss account, and additional information to be provided by way of notes to the accounts.

(2) The profit and loss account of a company that falls within section 408 of the 2006 Act (individual profit and loss account where group accounts prepared) need not contain the information specified in paragraphs 83 to 89 of Schedule 3 to these Regulations (information supplementing the profit and loss account).

(3) Accounts prepared in accordance with this regulation must contain a statement that they are prepared in accordance with the provisions of these Regulations relating to insurance companies.

[4.66]

7 Information about related undertakings (Companies Act or IAS individual or group accounts)

(1) Companies Act or IAS individual or group accounts must comply with the provisions of Schedule 4 to these Regulations as to information about related undertakings to be given in notes to the company's accounts.

(2) In Schedule 4—

Part 1 contains provisions applying to all companies
Part 2 contains provisions applying only to companies not required to prepare group accounts
Part 3 contains provisions applying only to companies required to prepare group accounts
Part 4 contains additional disclosures for banking companies and groups
Part 5 contains interpretative provisions.

(3) Information otherwise required to be given by Schedule 4 need not be disclosed with respect to an undertaking that—

(a) is established under the law of a country outside the United Kingdom, or
(b) carries on business outside the United Kingdom,

if the conditions specified in section 409(4) of the 2006 Act are met (see section 409(5) of the 2006 Act for disclosure required where advantage taken of this exemption).

This paragraph does not apply in relation to the information otherwise required by paragraph 3, 7 or 21 of Schedule 4.

[4.67]

8 Information about directors' benefits: remuneration (Companies Act or IAS individual or group accounts: quoted and unquoted companies)

(1) Companies Act or IAS individual or group accounts must comply with the provisions of Schedule 5 to these Regulations as to information about directors' remuneration to be given in notes to the company's accounts.

(2) In Schedule 5—

Part 1 contains provisions applying to quoted and unquoted companies,
Part 2 contains provisions applying only to unquoted companies, and
Part 3 contains supplementary provisions.

[4.68]

9 Companies Act group accounts

(1) Subject to paragraphs (2) and (3), where the directors of a parent company prepare Companies Act group accounts under section 403 of the 2006 Act (group accounts: applicable accounting framework), those accounts must comply with the provisions of Part 1 of Schedule 6 to these Regulations as to the form and content of the consolidated balance sheet and consolidated profit and loss account, and additional information to be provided by way of notes to the accounts.

(2) The directors of the parent company of a banking group preparing Companies Act group accounts must do so in accordance with the provisions of Part 1 of Schedule 6 as modified by Part 2 of that Schedule.

(3) The directors of the parent company of an insurance group preparing Companies Act group accounts must do so in accordance with the provisions of Part 1 of Schedule 6 as modified by Part 3 of that Schedule.

(4) Accounts prepared in accordance with paragraph (2) or (3) must contain a statement that they are prepared in accordance with the provisions of these Regulations relating to banking groups or to insurance groups, as the case may be.

PART 3 DIRECTORS' REPORT

[4.69]

10 Directors' report

(1) The report which the directors of a company are required to prepare under section 415 of the 2006 Act (duty to prepare directors' report) must disclose the matters specified in Schedule 7 to these Regulations.

[(2) In Schedule 7—

Part 1 relates to matters of a general nature including political donations and expenditure,
Part 2 relates to the acquisition by a company of its own shares or a charge on them,
Part 3 relates to the employment, training and advancement of disabled persons,
[Part 4 relates to the engagement by the company with employees, suppliers, customers and others]
Part 6 relates to certain disclosures required by publicly traded companies, . . .
Part 7 relates to disclosures in relation to greenhouse gas [emissions, energy consumption and energy efficiency action by quoted companies,]
[Part 7A relates to disclosures in relation to greenhouse gas emissions, energy consumption and energy efficiency action by unquoted companies, and]
[Part 8 relates to the statement of corporate governance arrangements].]

NOTES

Para (2): was substituted by the Companies Act 2006 (Strategic Report and Directors' Report) Regulations 2013, SI 2013/1970, reg 7(1), (2), as from 1 October 2013 (in respect of financial years ending on or after 30 September 2013), and is amended as follows:

Part 4 CA 2006 SIs

The entry relating to Part 4 was substituted, the word omitted from the entry relating to Part 6 was revoked, and the entry relating to "Part 8" was added, by the Companies (Miscellaneous Reporting) Regulations 2018, SI 2018/860, regs 7, 8, in relation to the financial years of companies beginning on or after 1 January 2019.

Words in square brackets in the entry relating to Part 7 substituted, and the entry relating to Part 7A inserted, by the Companies (Directors' Report) and Limited Liability Partnerships (Energy and Carbon Report) Regulations 2018, SI 2018/1155, regs 3, 4, as from 1 April 2019, in respect of financial years beginning on or after that date.

PART 4 DIRECTORS' REMUNERATION REPORT

[4.70]

11 Directors' remuneration report (quoted companies [and traded companies])

(1) The remuneration report which the directors of a quoted company [or unquoted traded company] are required to prepare under section 420 of the 2006 Act (duty to prepare directors' remuneration report) must contain the information specified in Schedule 8 to these Regulations, and must comply with any requirement of that Schedule as to how information is to be set out in the report.

[(1A) The document setting out a revised directors' remuneration policy in accordance with section 422A of the 2006 Act must contain the information specified in Schedule 8 to these Regulations, and must comply with any requirements in that Schedule as to how that information is to be set out.]

(2) . . .

(3) For the purposes of section 497 in Part 16 of the 2006 Act (auditor's report on auditable part of directors' remuneration report), "the auditable part" of a directors' remuneration report is [the information set out in the report as identified in Part 5] of Schedule 8 to these Regulations.

NOTES

The words in square brackets in the regulation heading and in para (1) were inserted by the Companies (Directors' Remuneration Policy and Directors' Remuneration Report) Regulations 2019, SI 2019/970, regs 28, 29, as from 10 June 2019 (for transitional provisions, etc, see reg 2 of the 2019 Regulations at **[4.680]**).

Para (1A) was inserted, para (2) was revoked, and the words in square brackets in para (3) were substituted, by the Large and Medium-sized Companies and Groups (Accounts and Reports) (Amendment) Regulations 2013, SI 2013/1981, reg 2, as from 1 October 2013, except in respect of a company's financial year ending before 30 September 2013.

PART 5 INTERPRETATION

[4.71]

12 Definition of "provisions"

Schedule 9 to these Regulations defines "provisions" for the purposes of these Regulations and for the purposes of—

- (a) section 677(3)(a) (Companies Act accounts: relevant provisions for purposes of financial assistance) in Part 18 of the 2006 Act,
- (b) section 712(2)(b)(i) (Companies Act accounts: relevant provisions to determine available profits for redemption or purchase by private company out of capital) in that Part, . . .
- (c) sections 831(3)(a) (Companies Act accounts: net asset restriction on public company distributions), 832(4)(a) (Companies Act accounts: investment companies distributions) and 836(1)(b)(i) (Companies Act accounts: relevant provisions for distribution purposes) in Part 23 of that Act[, and
- (d) section 841(2)(a) (Companies Act accounts: provisions to be treated as realised losses) in that Part].

NOTES

The word omitted from para (b) was revoked, and para (d) (and the word immediately preceding it) was added, by the Companies Act 2006 (Accounts, Reports and Audit) Regulations 2009, SI 2009/1581, reg 12(1), (2), as from 27 June 2009, in relation to financial years beginning on or after 6 April 2008 which have not ended before 27 June 2009.

[4.72]

13 General interpretation

Schedule 10 to these Regulations contains general definitions for the purposes of these Regulations.

[PART 6 REVIEW

[4.73]

14 Review

(1) The Secretary of State must from time to time—

- [(a) carry out a review, respectively, of the provisions of these Regulations to which amendments have been made by—
  - (i) Part 6 of the Limited Liability Partnerships, Partnerships and Groups (Accounts and Audit) Regulations 2016 ("the 2016 Regulations"), . . .
  - (ii) Part 3 of the Companies (Miscellaneous Reporting) Regulations 2018, and]
  - [(iii) Part 2 of the Companies (Directors' Report) and Limited Liability Partnerships (Energy and Carbon Report) Regulations 2018, and]
- (b) set out the conclusions of [each review] in a [separate] report, and
- (c) publish the report.

(2) The report must, in particular—

- (a) set out the objectives intended to be achieved by those provisions,
- (b) assess the extent to which those objectives are achieved,
- (c) assess whether those objectives remain appropriate, and
- (d) if those objectives remain appropriate, assess the extent to which they could be achieved in another way which involves less onerous regulatory provision.

(3) . . .

(4) The first report under [paragraph (1)(a)(i)] must be published before the end of the period of 5 years beginning with the date on which the 2016 Regulations come into force.

[(4A) The first report under paragraph (1)(a)(ii) must be published before the end of the period of 5 years beginning with the date on which Part 3 of the Companies (Miscellaneous Reporting) Regulations 2018 comes into force.]

[(4B) The first report under paragraph (1)(a)(iii) must be published before the end of the period of 5 years beginning with the date on which the Companies (Directors' Report) and Limited Liability Partnerships (Energy and Carbon Report) Regulations 2018 come into force.]

(5) Subsequent reports under [[paragraphs (1)(a)(i) to (iii)] respectively] must be published at intervals not exceeding 5 years.

(6) In this regulation, "regulatory provision" has the meaning given by section 32(4) of the Small Business, Enterprise and Employment Act 2015.]

NOTES

Inserted, together with the preceding Part heading, by the Limited Liability Partnerships, Partnerships and Groups (Accounts and Audit) Regulations 2016, SI 2016/575, regs 65, 67, as from 17 May 2016.

Para (1) is amended as follows:

Sub-para (a) was substituted by the Companies (Miscellaneous Reporting) Regulations 2018, SI 2018/860, regs 7, 9(1), (2), in relation to the financial years of companies beginning on or after 1 January 2019.

The word omitted from sub-para (a)(i) was revoked, and sub-para (a)(iii) was inserted, by the Companies (Directors' Report) and Limited Liability Partnerships (Energy and Carbon Report) Regulations 2018, SI 2018/1155, regs 3, 5(1), (2), as from 1 April 2019, in respect of financial years beginning on or after that date.

Words in first pair of square brackets in sub-para (b) substituted, and word in second pair of square brackets inserted, by SI 2018/860, regs 7, 9(1), (3), in relation to the financial years of companies beginning on or after 1 January 2019.

Para (3): revoked by the Accounts and Reports (Amendment) (EU Exit) Regulations 2019, SI 2019/145, reg 6, Sch 3, paras 2, 3, as from IP completion day (as defined in the European Union (Withdrawal Agreement) Act 2020, s 39).

Para (4): words in square brackets substituted by SI 2018/860, regs 7, 9(1), (5), in relation to the financial years of companies beginning on or after 1 January 2019.

Para (4A): inserted by SI 2018/860, regs 7, 9(1), (6), in relation to the financial years of companies beginning on or after 1 January 2019.

Para (4B): inserted by SI 2018/1155, regs 3, 5(1), (3), as from 1 April 2019, in respect of financial years beginning on or after that date.

Para (5): words in first (outer) pair of square brackets (ie, now only the word "respectively") substituted by SI 2018/860, regs 7, 9(1), (7), in relation to the financial years of companies beginning on or after 1 January 2019. Words in second (inner) pair of square brackets (ie, the words "paragraphs (1)(a)(i) to (iii)") substituted by SI 2018/1155, regs 3, 5(1), (4), as from 1 April 2019, in respect of financial years beginning on or after that date.

SCHEDULES

SCHEDULE 1
COMPANIES ACT INDIVIDUAL ACCOUNTS: COMPANIES WHICH ARE NOT BANKING OR INSURANCE COMPANIES

Regulation 3(1)

PART 1 GENERAL RULES AND FORMATS

SECTION A GENERAL RULES

[4.74]

1. (1) Subject to the following provisions of this Schedule—

(a) every balance sheet of a company must show the items listed in either of the balance sheet formats in Section B of this Part, and

(b) every profit and loss account must show the items listed in [either] of the profit and loss account formats in Section B.

(2) References in this Schedule to the items listed in any of the formats in Section B are to those items read together with any of the notes following the formats which apply to those items.

(3) [Subject to paragraph 1A,] the items must be shown in the order and under the headings and sub-headings given in the particular format used, but—

(a) the notes to the formats may permit alternative positions for any particular items, and

(b) the heading or sub-heading for any item does not have to be distinguished by any letter or number assigned to that item in the format used.

[1A. (1) The company's directors may adapt one of the balance sheet formats in Section B so to distinguish between current and non-current items in a different way, provided that—

(a) the information given is at least equivalent to that which would have been required by the use of such format had it not been thus adapted, and

(b) the presentation of those items is in accordance with generally accepted accounting principles or practice.

(2) The company's directors may adapt one of the profit and loss account formats in Section B, provided that—

(a) the information given is at least equivalent to that which would have been required by the use of such format had it not been thus adapted, and

(b) the presentation is in accordance with generally accepted accounting principles or practice.

(3) So far as is practicable, the following provisions of Section A of this Part of this Schedule apply to the balance sheet or profit or loss account of a company notwithstanding any such adaptation pursuant to this paragraph.]

2. (1) Where in accordance with paragraph 1 a company's balance sheet or profit and loss account for any financial year has been prepared by reference to one of the formats in Section B, the company's directors must use the same format in preparing Companies Act individual accounts for subsequent financial years, unless in their opinion there are special reasons for a change.

(2) Particulars of any such change must be given in a note to the accounts in which the new format is first used, and the reasons for the change must be explained.

3. (1) Any item required to be shown in a company's balance sheet or profit and loss account may be shown in greater detail than required by the particular format used.

(2) The balance sheet or profit and loss account may include an item representing or covering the amount of any asset or liability, income or expenditure not otherwise covered by any of the items listed in the format used, save that none of the following may be treated as assets in any balance sheet—

(a) preliminary expenses,

(b) expenses of, and commission on, any issue of shares or debentures, and

(c) costs of research.

4. (1) Where the special nature of the company's business requires it, the company's directors must adapt the arrangement, headings and sub-headings otherwise required in respect of items given an Arabic number in the balance sheet or profit and loss account format used.

(2) The directors may combine items to which Arabic numbers are given in any of the formats in Section B if—

(a) their individual amounts are not material to assessing the state of affairs or profit or loss of the company for the financial year in question, or

(b) the combination facilitates that assessment.

(3) Where sub-paragraph (2)(b) applies, the individual amounts of any items which have been combined must be disclosed in a note to the accounts.

5. (1) Subject to sub-paragraph (2), the directors must not include a heading or sub-heading corresponding to an item in the balance sheet or profit and loss account format used if there is no amount to be shown for that item for the financial year to which the balance sheet or profit and loss account relates.

(2) Where an amount can be shown for the item in question for the immediately preceding financial year that amount must be shown under the heading or sub-heading required by the format for that item.

6. Every profit and loss account must show the amount of a company's profit or loss . . . before taxation.

7. (1) For every item shown in the balance sheet or profit and loss account the corresponding amount for the immediately preceding financial year must also be shown.

(2) Where that corresponding amount is not comparable with the amount to be shown for the item in question in respect of the financial year to which the balance sheet or profit and loss account relates, the former amount may be adjusted, and particulars of the non-comparability and of any adjustment must be disclosed in a note to the accounts.

8. Amounts in respect of items representing assets or income may not be set off against amounts in respect of items representing liabilities or expenditure (as the case may be), or vice versa.

9. The company's directors must, in determining how amounts are presented within items in the profit and loss account and balance sheet, have regard to the substance of the reported transaction or arrangement, in accordance with generally accepted accounting principles or practice.

[9A. Where an asset or liability relates to more than one item in the balance sheet, the relationship of such asset or liability to the relevant items must be disclosed either under those items or in the notes to the accounts.]

SECTION B THE REQUIRED FORMATS FOR ACCOUNTS

Balance sheet formats

Format 1

A Called up share capital not paid [(1)]

B Fixed assets

I Intangible assets

1 Development costs

2 Concessions, patents, licences, trade marks and similar rights and assets [(2)]

3 Goodwill [(3)]

4 Payments on account

II Tangible assets

1 Land and buildings

2 Plant and machinery

3 Fixtures, fittings, tools and equipment

4 Payments on account and assets in course of construction

III Investments

1 Shares in group undertakings

2 Loans to group undertakings

3 Participating interests

4 Loans to undertakings in which the company has a participating interest

5 Other investments other than loans

6 Other loans

7 Own shares [(4)]

C Current assets

I Stocks
  1 Raw materials and consumables
  2 Work in progress
  3 Finished goods and goods for resale
  4 Payments on account
II Debtors [5]
  1 Trade debtors
  2 Amounts owed by group undertakings
  3 Amounts owed by undertakings in which the company has a participating interest
  4 Other debtors
  5 Called up share capital not paid [1]
  6 repayments and accrued income [6]
III Investments
  1 Shares in group undertakings
  2 Own shares [4]
  3 Other investments
IV Cash at bank and in hand

D Prepayments and accrued income [6]

E Creditors: amounts falling due within one year
  1 Debenture loans [7]
  2 Bank loans and overdrafts
  3 Payments received on account [8]
  4 Trade creditors
  5 Bills of exchange payable
  6 Amounts owed to group undertakings
  7 Amounts owed to undertakings in which the company has a participating interest
  8 Other creditors including taxation and social security [9]
  9 Accruals and deferred income [10]

F Net current assets (liabilities) [11]

G Total assets less current liabilities

H Creditors: amounts falling due after more than one year
  1 Debenture loans [7]
  2 Bank loans and overdrafts
  3 Payments received on account [8]
  4 Trade creditors
  5 Bills of exchange payable
  6 Amounts owed to group undertakings
  7 Amounts owed to undertakings in which the company has a participating interest
  8 Other creditors including taxation and social security [9]
  9 Accruals and deferred income [10]

I Provisions for liabilities
  1 Pensions and similar obligations
  2 Taxation, including deferred taxation
  3 Other provisions

J Accruals and deferred income [10]

K Capital and reserves
  I Called up share capital [12]
  II Share premium account
  III Revaluation reserve
  IV Other reserves
    1 Capital redemption reserve
    2 Reserve for own shares
    3 Reserves provided for by the articles of association
    [4 Other reserves, including the fair value reserve]
  V Profit and loss account

Balance sheet formats

Format 2

ASSETS

A Called up share capital not paid [1]

B Fixed assets
  I Intangible assets
    1 Development costs
    2 Concessions, patents, licences, trade marks and similar rights and assets [2]
    3 Goodwill [3]
    4 Payments on account
  II Tangible assets
    1 Land and buildings

2 Plant and machinery
3 Fixtures, fittings, tools and equipment
4 Payments on account and assets in course of construction

III Investments
1 Shares in group undertakings
2 Loans to group undertakings
3 participating interests
4 Loans to undertakings in which the company has a participating interest
5 Other investments other than loans
6 Other loans
7 Own shares [(4)]

C Current assets

I Stocks
1 Raw materials and consumables
2 Work in progress
3 Finished goods and goods for resale
4 Payments on account

II Debtors [(5)]
1 Trade debtors
2 Amounts owed by group undertakings
3 Amounts owed by undertakings in which the company has a participating interest
4 Other debtors
5 Called up share capital not paid [(1)]
6 Prepayments and accrued income [(6)]

III Investments
1 Shares in group undertakings
2 Own shares [(4)]
3 Other investments

IV Cash at bank and in hand

D Prepayments and accrued income [(6)]

[CAPITAL, RESERVES AND LIABILITIES]

A Capital and reserves

I Called up share capital [(12)]
II Share premium account
III Revaluation reserve
IV Other reserves
1 Capital redemption reserve
2 Reserve for own shares
3 Reserves provided for by the articles of association
[4 Other reserves, including the fair value reserve]
V Profit and loss account

B Provisions for liabilities
1 Pensions and similar obligations
2 Taxation, including deferred taxation
3 Other provisions

C Creditors [(13)]
1 Debenture loans [(7)]
2 Bank loans and overdrafts
3 Payments received on account [(8)]
4 Trade creditors
5 Bills of exchange payable
6 Amounts owed to group undertakings
7 Amounts owed to undertakings in which the company has a participating interest
8 Other creditors including taxation and social security [(9)]
9 Accruals and deferred income [(10)]

D Accruals and deferred income [(10)]

Notes on the balance sheet formats

(1) Called up share capital not paid

(Formats 1 and 2, items A and CII.5.)

This item may be shown in either of the two positions given in formats 1 and 2.

(2) Concessions, patents, licences, trade marks and similar rights and assets

(Formats 1 and 2, item B.I.2.)

Amounts in respect of assets are only to be included in a company's balance sheet under this item if either—

(a) the assets were acquired for valuable consideration and are not required to be shown under goodwill, or
(b) the assets in question were created by the company itself.

(3) Goodwill

(Formats 1 and 2, item B.I.3.)

Amounts representing goodwill are only to be included to the extent that the goodwill was acquired for valuable consideration.

(4) Own shares

(Formats 1 and 2, items B.III.7 and CIII.2.)

The nominal value of the shares held must be shown separately.

(5) Debtors

(Formats 1 and 2, items CII.1 to 6.)

The amount falling due after more than one year must be shown separately for each item included under debtors.

(6) Prepayments and accrued income

(Formats 1 and 2, items CII.6 and D.)

This item may be shown in either of the two positions given in formats 1 and 2.

(7) Debenture loans

(Format 1, items E.1 and H.1 and format 2, item C1.)

The amount of any convertible loans must be shown separately.

(8) Payments received on account

(Format 1, items E.3 and H.3 and format 2, item C3.)

Payments received on account of orders must be shown for each of these items in so far as they are not shown as deductions from stocks.

(9) Other creditors including taxation and social security

(Format 1, items E.8 and H.8 and format 2, item C8.)

The amount for creditors in respect of taxation and social security must be shown separately from the amount for other creditors.

(10) Accruals and deferred income

(Format 1, items E.9, H.9 and J and format 2, items C9 and D.)

The two positions given for this item in format 1 at E.9 and H.9 are an alternative to the position at J, but if the item is not shown in a position corresponding to that at J it may be shown in either or both of the other two positions (as the case may require).

The two positions given for this item in format 2 are alternatives.

(11) Net current assets (liabilities)

(Format 1, item F.)

In determining the amount to be shown for this item any amounts shown under "prepayments and accrued income" must be taken into account wherever shown.

(12) Called up share capital

(Format 1, item K.I and format 2, item A.I.)

The amount of allotted share capital and the amount of called up share capital which has been paid up must be shown separately.

(13) Creditors

(Format 2, items C1 to 9.)

Amounts falling due within one year and after one year must be shown separately for each of these items and for the aggregate of all of these items.

Profit and loss account formats

Format 1
(see note [14] below)

1 Turnover

2 Cost of sales [14]

3 Gross profit or loss

4 Distribution costs [14]

5 Administrative expenses [14]

6 Other operating income

7 Income from shares in group undertakings

8 Income from participating interests

9 Income from other fixed asset investments [15]

10 Other interest receivable and similar income [15]

11 Amounts written off investments

12 Interest payable and similar [expenses] [16]

13 Tax on profit or loss . . .

14 Profit or loss . . . after taxation

15–18 . . .

19 Other taxes not shown under the above items

20 Profit or loss for the financial year

Profit and loss account formats

Format 2

1 Turnover

2 Change in stocks of finished goods and in work in progress

3 Own work capitalised

4 Other operating income

5

(a) Raw materials and consumables
(b) Other external [expenses]

6 Staff costs
(a) wages and salaries
(b) social security costs
(c) other pension costs

7

(a) Depreciation and other amounts written off tangible and intangible fixed assets
[(b) Amounts written off current assets, to the extent that they exceed write-offs which are normal in the undertaking concerned]

8 Other operating [expenses]

9 Income from shares in group undertakings

10 Income from participating interests

11 Income from other fixed asset investments (15)

12 Other interest receivable and similar income (15)

13 Amounts written off investments

14 Interest payable and similar [expenses] (16)

15 Tax on profit or loss . . .

16 Profit or loss . . . after taxation

17–20 Extraordinary income

21 Other taxes not shown under the above items

22 Profit or loss for the financial year

Profit and loss account formats

Formats 3, 4

. . .

Notes on the profit and loss account formats

(14) Cost of sales: distribution costs: administrative expenses

(Format 1, items 2, 4 and 5 . . .)

These items must be stated after taking into account any necessary provisions for depreciation or diminution in value of assets.

(15) Income from other fixed asset investments: other interest receivable and similar income

(Format 1, items 9 and 10; format 2, items 11 and 12; . . .).)

Income and interest derived from group undertakings must be shown separately from income and interest derived from other sources.

(16) Interest payable and similar [expenses]

(Format 1, item 12; format 2, item 14; . . .).)

The amount payable to group undertakings must be shown separately.

(17) [Format 1]

The amount of any provisions for depreciation and diminution in value of tangible and intangible fixed assets falling to be shown under [item 7(a) in format 2] respectively in formats 2 and 4 must be disclosed in a note to the accounts in any case where the profit and loss account is prepared using format 1 . . .).

NOTES

All amendments to this Part were made by the Companies, Partnerships and Groups (Accounts and Reports) Regulations 2015, SI 2015/980, reg 27, as from 6 April 2015, in relation to (a) financial years beginning on or after 1 January 2016, and (b) a financial year of a company beginning on or after 1 January 2015, but before 1 January 2016, if the directors of the company so decide (see **[4.549]** *post*).

PART 2 ACCOUNTING PRINCIPLES AND RULES

SECTION A ACCOUNTING PRINCIPLES

Preliminary

[4.75]

10. (1) The amounts to be included in respect of all items shown in a company's accounts must be determined in accordance with the principles set out in this Section.

(2) But if it appears to the company's directors that there are special reasons for departing from any of those principles in preparing the company's accounts in respect of any financial year they may do so, in which case particulars of the departure, the reasons for it and its effect must be given in a note to the accounts.

Accounting principles

11. The company is presumed to be carrying on business as a going concern.

12. Accounting policies [and measurement bases] must be applied consistently within the same accounts and from one financial year to the next.

13. The amount of any item must be determined on a prudent basis, and in particular—

(a) only profits realised at the balance sheet date are to be included in the profit and loss account, . . .

(b) all liabilities which have arisen in respect of the financial year to which the accounts relate or a previous financial year must be taken into account, including those which only become apparent between the balance sheet date and the date on which it is signed on behalf of the board of directors in accordance with section 414 of the 2006 Act (approval and signing of accounts), [and]

[(c) all provisions for diminution of value must be recognised, whether the result of the financial year is a profit or a loss].

14. All income and charges relating to the financial year to which the accounts relate must be taken into account, without regard to the date of receipt or payment.

15. In determining the aggregate amount of any item, the amount of each individual asset or liability that falls to be taken into account must be determined separately.

[**15A.** The opening balance sheet for each financial year shall correspond to the closing balance sheet for the preceding financial year.]

SECTION B HISTORICAL COST ACCOUNTING RULES

Preliminary

16. Subject to Sections C and D of this Part of this Schedule, the amounts to be included in respect of all items shown in a company's accounts must be determined in accordance with the rules set out in this Section.

Fixed assets

General rules

17. (1) The amount to be included in respect of any fixed asset must be its purchase price or production cost.

(2) This is subject to any provision for depreciation or diminution in value made in accordance with paragraphs 18 to 20.

Rules for depreciation and diminution in value

18. In the case of any fixed asset which has a limited useful economic life, the amount of—

(a) its purchase price or production cost, or

(b) where it is estimated that any such asset will have a residual value at the end of the period of its useful economic life, its purchase price or production cost less that estimated residual value,

must be reduced by provisions for depreciation calculated to write off that amount systematically over the period of the asset's useful economic life.

19. (1) Where a fixed asset investment falling to be included under item B.III of either of the balance sheet formats set out in Part 1 of this Schedule has diminished in value, provisions for diminution in value may be made in respect of it and the amount to be included in respect of it may be reduced accordingly.

(2) Provisions for diminution in value must be made in respect of any fixed asset which has diminished in value if the reduction in its value is expected to be permanent (whether its useful economic life is limited or not), and the amount to be included in respect of it must be reduced accordingly.

[(3) Provisions made under sub-paragraph (1) or (2) must be charged to the profit and loss account and disclosed separately in a note to the accounts if not shown separately in the profit and loss account.]

20. (1) Where the reasons for which any provision was made in accordance with paragraph 19 have ceased to apply to any extent, that provision must be written back to the extent that it is no longer necessary.

[(1A) But provision made in accordance with paragraph 19(2) in respect of goodwill must not be written back to any extent.]

[(2) Any amounts written back under sub-paragraph (1) must be recognised in the profit and loss account and disclosed separately in a note to the accounts if not shown separately in the profit and loss account.]

[Intangible Assets

21. (1) Where this is in accordance with generally accepted accounting principles or practice, development costs may be included in "other intangible assets" under "fixed assets" in the balance sheet formats set out in Section B of Part 1 of this Schedule.

(2) If any amount is included in a company's balance sheet in respect of development costs, the note on accounting policies (see paragraph 44 of this Schedule) must include the following information—

(a) the period over which the amount of those costs originally capitalised is being or is to be written off, and
(b) the reasons for capitalising the development costs in question.

22. (1) Intangible assets must be written off over the useful economic life of the intangible asset.

(2) Where in exceptional cases the useful life of intangible assets cannot be reliably estimated, such assets must be written off over a period chosen by the directors of the company.

(3) The period referred to in sub-paragraph (2) must not exceed ten years.

(4) There must be disclosed in a note to the accounts the period referred to in sub-paragraph (2) and the reasons for choosing that period.]

Current assets

23. Subject to paragraph 24, the amount to be included in respect of any current asset must be its purchase price or production cost.

24. (1) If the net realisable value of any current asset is lower than its purchase price or production cost, the amount to be included in respect of that asset must be the net realisable value.

(2) Where the reasons for which any provision for diminution in value was made in accordance with sub-paragraph (1) have ceased to apply to any extent, that provision must be written back to the extent that it is no longer necessary.

Miscellaneous and supplementary provisions

Excess of money owed over value received as an asset item

25. (1) Where the amount repayable on any debt owed by a company is greater than the value of the consideration received in the transaction giving rise to the debt, the amount of the difference may be treated as an asset.

(2) Where any such amount is so treated—
(a) it must be written off by reasonable amounts each year and must be completely written off before repayment of the debt, and
(b) if the current amount is not shown as a separate item in the company's balance sheet, it must be disclosed in a note to the accounts.

Assets included at a fixed amount

26. (1) Subject to sub-paragraph (2), assets which fall to be included—
(a) amongst the fixed assets of a company under the item "tangible assets", or
(b) amongst the current assets of a company under the item "raw materials and consumables",
may be included at a fixed quantity and value.

(2) Sub-paragraph (1) applies to assets of a kind which are constantly being replaced where—
(a) their overall value is not material to assessing the company's state of affairs, and
(b) their quantity, value and composition are not subject to material variation.

Determination of purchase price or production cost

27. (1) The purchase price of an asset is to be determined by adding to the actual price paid any expenses incidental to its acquisition [and then subtracting any incidental reductions in the cost of acquisition].

(2) The production cost of an asset is to be determined by adding to the purchase price of the raw materials and consumables used the amount of the costs incurred by the company which are directly attributable to the production of that asset.

(3) In addition, there may be included in the production cost of an asset—
(a) a reasonable proportion of the costs incurred by the company which are only indirectly attributable to the production of that asset, but only to the extent that they relate to the period of production, and
(b) interest on capital borrowed to finance the production of that asset, to the extent that it accrues in respect of the period of production,
provided, however, in a case within paragraph (b), that the inclusion of the interest in determining the cost of that asset and the amount of the interest so included is disclosed in a note to the accounts.

(4) In the case of current assets distribution costs may not be included in production costs.

28. (1) The purchase price or production cost of—
(a) any assets which fall to be included under any item shown in a company's balance sheet under the general item "stocks", and
(b) any assets which are fungible assets (including investments),
may be determined by the application of any of the methods mentioned in sub-paragraph (2) in relation to any such assets of the same class, provided that the method chosen is one which appears to the directors to be appropriate in the circumstances of the company.

(2) Those methods are—
(a) the method known as "first in, first out" (FIFO),
(b) the method known as "last in, first out" (LIFO),
(c) a weighted average price, and
(d) any other method [reflecting generally accepted best practice].

(3) Where in the case of any company—
(a) the purchase price or production cost of assets falling to be included under any item shown in the company's balance sheet has been determined by the application of any method permitted by this paragraph, and
(b) the amount shown in respect of that item differs materially from the relevant alternative amount given below in this paragraph,
the amount of that difference must be disclosed in a note to the accounts.

(4) Subject to sub-paragraph (5), for the purposes of sub-paragraph (3)(b), the relevant alternative amount, in relation to any item shown in a company's balance sheet, is the amount which would have been shown in respect of that item if assets of any class included under that item at an amount determined by any method permitted by this paragraph had instead been included at their replacement cost as at the balance sheet date.

(5) The relevant alternative amount may be determined by reference to the most recent actual purchase price or production cost before the balance sheet date of assets of any class included under the item in question instead of by reference to their replacement cost as at that date, but only if the former appears to the directors of the company to constitute the more appropriate standard of comparison in the case of assets of that class.

Substitution of original stated amount where price or cost unknown

29. (1) This paragraph applies where—

(a) there is no record of the purchase price or production cost of any asset of a company or of any price, expenses or costs relevant for determining its purchase price or production cost in accordance with paragraph 27, or

(b) any such record cannot be obtained without unreasonable expense or delay.

(2) In such a case, the purchase price or production cost of the asset must be taken, for the purposes of paragraphs 17 to 24, to be the value ascribed to it in the earliest available record of its value made on or after its acquisition or production by the company.

[Equity method in respect of participating interests

29A. (1) Participating interests may be accounted for using the equity method.

(2) If participating interests are accounted for using the equity method—

(a) the proportion of profit or loss attributable to a participating interest and recognised in the profit and loss account may be that proportion which corresponds to the amount of any dividends, and

(b) where the profit attributable to a participating interest and recognised in the profit and loss account exceeds the amount of any dividends, the difference must be placed in a reserve which cannot be distributed to shareholders.

(3) The reference to "dividends" in sub-paragraph (2) includes dividends already paid and those whose payment can be claimed.]

SECTION C ALTERNATIVE ACCOUNTING RULES

Preliminary

30. (1) The rules set out in Section B are referred to below in this Schedule as the historical cost accounting rules.

(2) Those rules, with the omission of paragraphs 16, 22 and 26 to 29, are referred to below in this Part of this Schedule as the depreciation rules; and references below in this Schedule to the historical cost accounting rules do not include the depreciation rules as they apply by virtue of paragraph 33.

31. Subject to paragraphs 33 to 35, the amounts to be included in respect of assets of any description mentioned in paragraph 32 may be determined on any basis so mentioned.

Alternative accounting rules

32. (1) Intangible fixed assets, other than goodwill, may be included at their current cost.

(2) Tangible fixed assets may be included at a market value determined as at the date of their last valuation or at their current cost.

(3) Investments of any description falling to be included under item B III of either of the balance sheet formats set out in Part 1 of this Schedule may be included either—

(a) at a market value determined as at the date of their last valuation, or

(b) at a value determined on any basis which appears to the directors to be appropriate in the circumstances of the company.

But in the latter case particulars of the method of valuation adopted and of the reasons for adopting it must be disclosed in a note to the accounts.

(4), (5) . . .

Application of the depreciation rules

33. (1) Where the value of any asset of a company is determined on any basis mentioned in paragraph 32, that value must be, or (as the case may require) be the starting point for determining, the amount to be included in respect of that asset in the company's accounts, instead of its purchase price or production cost or any value previously so determined for that asset.

The depreciation rules apply accordingly in relation to any such asset with the substitution for any reference to its purchase price or production cost of a reference to the value most recently determined for that asset on any basis mentioned in paragraph 32.

(2) The amount of any provision for depreciation required in the case of any fixed asset by paragraphs 18 to 20 as they apply by virtue of sub-paragraph (1) is referred to below in this paragraph as the adjusted amount, and the amount of any provision which would be required by any of those paragraphs in the case of that asset according to the historical cost accounting rules is referred to as the historical cost amount.

(3) Where sub-paragraph (1) applies in the case of any fixed asset the amount of any provision for depreciation in respect of that asset—

(a) included in any item shown in the profit and loss account in respect of amounts written off assets of the description in question, or

(b) taken into account in stating any item so shown which is required by note (14) of the notes on the profit and loss account formats set out in Part 1 of this Schedule to be stated after taking into account any necessary provision for depreciation or diminution in value of assets included under it,

may be the historical cost amount instead of the adjusted amount, provided that the amount of any difference between the two is shown separately in the profit and loss account or in a note to the accounts.

Additional information to be provided in case of departure from historical cost accounting rules

34. (1) This paragraph applies where the amounts to be included in respect of assets covered by any items shown in a company's accounts have been determined on any basis mentioned in paragraph 32.

(2) The items affected and the basis of valuation adopted in determining the amounts of the assets in question in the case of each such item must be disclosed in [the note on accounting policies (see paragraph 44 of this Schedule].

[(3) In the case of each balance sheet item affected, the comparable amounts determined according to the historical cost accounting rules must be shown in a note to the accounts.]

(4) In sub-paragraph (3), references in relation to any item to the comparable amounts determined as there mentioned are references to—

(a) the aggregate amount which would be required to be shown in respect of that item if the amounts to be included in respect of all the assets covered by that item were determined according to the historical cost accounting rules, and

(b) the aggregate amount of the cumulative provisions for depreciation or diminution in value which would be permitted or required in determining those amounts according to those rules.

Revaluation reserve

35. (1) With respect to any determination of the value of an asset of a company on any basis mentioned in paragraph 32, the amount of any profit or loss arising from that determination (after allowing, where appropriate, for any provisions for depreciation or diminution in value made otherwise than by reference to the value so determined and any adjustments of any such provisions made in the light of that determination) must be credited or (as the case may be) debited to a separate reserve ("the revaluation reserve").

(2) The amount of the revaluation reserve must be shown in the company's balance sheet under a separate sub-heading in the position given for the item "revaluation reserve" [under "Capital and reserves"] in format 1 or 2 of the balance sheet formats set out in Part 1 of this Schedule, . . .

(3) An amount may be transferred—

(a) from the revaluation reserve—

(i) to the profit and loss account, if the amount was previously charged to that account or represents realised profit, or

(ii) on capitalisation,

(b) to or from the revaluation reserve in respect of the taxation relating to any profit or loss credited or debited to the reserve.

The revaluation reserve must be reduced to the extent that the amounts transferred to it are no longer necessary for the purposes of the valuation method used.

(4) In sub-paragraph (3)(a)(ii) "capitalisation", in relation to an amount standing to the credit of the revaluation reserve, means applying it in wholly or partly paying up unissued shares in the company to be allotted to members of the company as fully or partly paid shares.

(5) The revaluation reserve must not be reduced except as mentioned in this paragraph.

(6) The treatment for taxation purposes of amounts credited or debited to the revaluation reserve must be disclosed in a note to the accounts.

SECTION D FAIR VALUE ACCOUNTING

Inclusion of financial instruments at fair value

36. (1) Subject to sub-paragraphs (2) to (5), financial instruments (including derivatives) may be included at fair value.

(2) Sub-paragraph (1) does not apply to financial instruments that constitute liabilities unless—

(a) they are held as part of a trading portfolio,

(b) they are derivatives, or

(c) they are financial instruments falling within sub-paragraph (4).

(3) Unless they are financial instruments falling within sub-paragraph (4), sub-paragraph (1) does not apply to—

(a) financial instruments (other than derivatives) held to maturity,

(b) loans and receivables originated by the company and not held for trading purposes,

(c) interests in subsidiary undertakings, associated undertakings and joint ventures,

(d) equity instruments issued by the company,

(e) contracts for contingent consideration in a business combination, or

(f) other financial instruments with such special characteristics that the instruments, according to generally accepted accounting principles or practice, should be accounted for differently from other financial instruments.

[(4) Financial instruments which under [UK-adopted international accounting standards] may be included in accounts at fair value, may be so included, provided that the disclosures required by such accounting standards are made.]

(5) If the fair value of a financial instrument cannot be determined reliably in accordance with paragraph 37, sub-paragraph (1) does not apply to that financial instrument.

(6) In this paragraph—

"associated undertaking" has the meaning given by paragraph 19 of Schedule 6 to these Regulations;

"joint venture" has the meaning given by paragraph 18 of that Schedule.

Determination of fair value

37. (1) The fair value of a financial instrument is its value determined in accordance with this paragraph.

(2) If a reliable market can readily be identified for the financial instrument, its fair value is determined by reference to its market value.

(3) If a reliable market cannot readily be identified for the financial instrument but can be identified for its components or for a similar instrument, its fair value is determined by reference to the market value of its components or of the similar instrument.

(4) If neither sub-paragraph (2) nor (3) applies, the fair value of the financial instrument is a value resulting from generally accepted valuation models and techniques.

(5) Any valuation models and techniques used for the purposes of sub-paragraph (4) must ensure a reasonable approximation of the market value.

Hedged items

38. A company may include any assets and liabilities, or identified portions of such assets or liabilities, that qualify as hedged items under a fair value hedge accounting system at the amount required under that system.

[Other assets that may be included at fair value

39. (1) This paragraph applies to—

(a) stocks,
(b) investment property, and
(c) living animals and plants.

(2) Such stocks, investment property, and living animals and plants may be included at fair value, provided that, as the case may be, all such stocks, investment property, and living animals and plants are so included where their fair value can reliably be determined.

(3) In this paragraph, "fair value" means fair value determined in accordance with generally accepted accounting principles or practice.]

Accounting for changes in value

40. (1) This paragraph applies where a financial instrument is valued in accordance with paragraph 36 or 38 or an asset is valued in accordance with paragraph 39.

(2) Notwithstanding paragraph 13 in this Part of this Schedule, and subject to sub-paragraphs (3) and (4), a change in the value of the financial instrument or of the investment property or living animal or plant must be included in the profit and loss account.

(3) Where—

(a) the financial instrument accounted for is a hedging instrument under a hedge accounting system that allows some or all of the change in value not to be shown in the profit and loss account, or
(b) the change in value relates to an exchange difference arising on a monetary item that forms part of a company's net investment in a foreign entity,

the amount of the change in value must be credited to or (as the case may be) debited from a separate reserve ("the fair value reserve").

(4) Where the instrument accounted for—

(a) is an available for sale financial asset, and
(b) is not a derivative,

the change in value may be credited to or (as the case may be) debited from the fair value reserve.

The fair value reserve

41. (1) The fair value reserve must be adjusted to the extent that the amounts shown in it are no longer necessary for the purposes of paragraph 40(3) or (4).

(2) The treatment for taxation purposes of amounts credited or debited to the fair value reserve must be disclosed in a note to the accounts.

NOTES

Section A

Para 12: words in square brackets inserted by the Companies, Partnerships and Groups (Accounts and Reports) Regulations 2015, SI 2015/980, reg 28(1), (2)(a), as from 6 April 2015, in relation to (a) financial years beginning on or after 1 January 2016, and (b) a financial year of a company beginning on or after 1 January 2015, but before 1 January 2016, if the directors of the company so decide (see **[4.549]** *post*).

Para 13: word omitted from sub-para (a) revoked, word in square brackets in sub-para (b) inserted, and sub-para (c) added, by SI 2015/980, reg 28(1), (2)(b) (as to the application of this amendment see the first note above).

Para 15A: inserted by SI 2015/980, reg 28(1), (2)(c) (as to the application of this amendment see the first note above).

Section B

Para 19: sub-para (3) substituted by SI 2015/980, reg 28(1), (3)(a) (as to the application of this amendment see the first note above).

Para 20 is amended as follows:

Sub-para (1A) inserted by the Companies, Partnerships and Groups (Accounts and Reports) (No 2) Regulations 2015, SI 2015/1672, reg 4(1), (2), as from 1 October 2015, in relation to (a) financial years beginning on or after 1 January 2016, and (b) a financial year of a company beginning on or after 1 January 2015 but before 1 January 2016, if the directors of the company have decided, pursuant to reg 2(2)(b) of the Companies, Partnerships and Groups (Accounts and Reports) Regulations 2015, that the amendments made by those Regulations have effect in relation to that financial year.

Sub-para (2) substituted by SI 2015/980, reg 28(1), (3)(b) (as to the application of this amendment see the first note above).

Paras 21, 22: substituted by SI 2015/980, reg 28(1), (3)(c) (as to the application of this amendment see the first note above).

Para 27: words in square brackets in sub-para (1) inserted by SI 2015/980, reg 28(1), (3)(d) (as to the application of this amendment see the first note above).

Para 28: words in square brackets in sub-para (2)(d) substituted by SI 2015/980, reg 28(1), (3)(e) (as to the application of this amendment see the first note above).

Para 29A: inserted by SI 2015/980, reg 28(1), (3)(f) (as to the application of this amendment see the first note above).

Section C

Para 32: sub-paras (4), (5) revoked by SI 2015/980, reg 28(1), (4)(a) (as to the application of this amendment see the first note above).

Para 34: words in square brackets in sub-para (2) substituted, and sub-para (3) substituted, by SI 2015/980, reg 28(1), (4)(b), (c) (as to the application of this amendment see the first note above).

Para 35: words in square brackets in sub-para (2) inserted, and words omitted from that sub-paragraph revoked, by SI 2015/980, reg 28(1), (4)(d) (as to the application of this amendment see the first note above).

Section D

Para 36: sub-para (4) substituted by SI 2015/980, reg 28(1), (5)(a) (as to the application of this amendment see the first note above). Words in square brackets in sub-para (4) substituted by the International Accounting Standards and European Public Limited-Liability Company (Amendment etc) (EU Exit) Regulations 2019, SI 2019/685, reg 19, Sch 1, Pt 2, para 57(1), (2)(a), in relation to accounts for financial years beginning on or after IP completion day (as defined in the European Union (Withdrawal Agreement) Act 2020, s 39) (note also that in relation to accounts for financial years which begin before but end on or after IP completion day, the enactments amended by Parts 1–3 of Sch 1 to the 2019 Regulations have effect as if the UK were a member State until the end of the financial year in question).

Para 39: substituted by SI 2015/980, reg 28(1), (5)(b) (as to the application of this amendment see the first note above).

PART 3 NOTES TO THE ACCOUNTS

[Preliminary

[4.76]

42. (1) Any information required in the case of a company by the following provisions of this Part of this Schedule must be given by way of a note to the accounts.

(2) These notes must be presented in the order in which, where relevant, the items to which they relate are presented in the balance sheet and in the profit and loss account.]

General

Reserves and dividends

43. There must be stated—

(a) any amount set aside or proposed to be set aside to, or withdrawn or proposed to be withdrawn from, reserves,

(b) the aggregate amount of dividends paid in the financial year (other than those for which a liability existed at the immediately preceding balance sheet date),

(c) the aggregate amount of dividends that the company is liable to pay at the balance sheet date, and

(d) the aggregate amount of dividends that are proposed before the date of approval of the accounts, and not otherwise disclosed under sub-paragraph (b) or (c).

Disclosure of accounting policies

44. The accounting policies adopted by the company in determining the amounts to be included in respect of items shown in the balance sheet and in determining the profit or loss of the company must be stated (including such policies with respect to the depreciation and diminution in value of assets).

45. It must be stated whether the accounts have been prepared in accordance with applicable accounting standards and particulars of any material departure from those standards and the reasons for it must be given (see regulation 4(2) for exemption for medium-sized companies).

Information supplementing the balance sheet

46. Paragraphs 47 to 64 require information which either supplements the information given with respect to any particular items shown in the balance sheet or is otherwise relevant to assessing the company's state of affairs in the light of the information so given.

Share capital and debentures

47. (1) The following information must be given with respect to the company's share capital—

(a) where shares of more than one class have been allotted, the number and aggregate nominal value of shares of each class allotted, and

(b) where shares are held as treasury shares, the number and aggregate nominal value of the treasury shares and, where shares of more than one class have been allotted, the number and aggregate nominal value of the shares of each class held as treasury shares.

(2) In the case of any part of the allotted share capital that consists of redeemable shares, the following information must be given—

(a) the earliest and latest dates on which the company has power to redeem those shares,

(b) whether those shares must be redeemed in any event or are liable to be redeemed at the option of the company or of the shareholder, and

(c) whether any (and, if so, what) premium is payable on redemption.

48. If the company has allotted any shares during the financial year, the following information must be given—

(a) the classes of shares allotted, and

(b) as respects each class of shares, the number allotted, their aggregate nominal value, and the consideration received by the company for the allotment.

49. (1) With respect to any contingent right to the allotment of shares in the company the following particulars must be given—

(a) the number, description and amount of the shares in relation to which the right is exercisable,

(b) the period during which it is exercisable, and

(c) the price to be paid for the shares allotted.

(2) In sub-paragraph (1) "contingent right to the allotment of shares" means any option to subscribe for shares and any other right to require the allotment of shares to any person whether arising on the conversion into shares of securities of any other description or otherwise.

50. (1) If the company has issued any debentures during the financial year to which the accounts relate, the following information must be given—

(a) the classes of debentures issued, and

(b) as respects each class of debentures, the amount issued and the consideration received by the company for the issue.

(2) Where any of the company's debentures are held by a nominee of or trustee for the company, the nominal amount of the debentures and the amount at which they are stated in the accounting records kept by the company in accordance with section 386 of the 2006 Act (duty to keep accounting records) must be stated.

Fixed assets

51. (1) In respect of each item which is or would but for paragraph 4(2)(b) be shown under the general item "fixed assets" in the company's balance sheet the following information must be given—

(a) the appropriate amounts in respect of that item as at the date of the beginning of the financial year and as at the balance sheet date respectively,

(b) the effect on any amount shown in the balance sheet in respect of that item of—

(i) any revision of the amount in respect of any assets included under that item made during that year on any basis mentioned in paragraph 32,

(ii) acquisitions during that year of any assets,

(iii) disposals during that year of any assets, and

(iv) any transfers of assets of the company to and from that item during that year.

(2) The reference in sub-paragraph (1)(a) to the appropriate amounts in respect of any item as at any date there mentioned is a reference to amounts representing the aggregate amounts determined, as at that date, in respect of assets falling to be included under that item on either of the following bases, that is to say—

(a) on the basis of purchase price or production cost (determined in accordance with paragraphs 27 and 28), or

(b) on any basis mentioned in paragraph 32,

(leaving out of account in either case any provisions for depreciation or diminution in value).

(3) In respect of each item within sub-paragraph (1) there must also be stated—

(a) the cumulative amount of provisions for depreciation or diminution in value of assets included under that item as at each date mentioned in sub-paragraph (1)(a),

(b) the amount of any such provisions made in respect of the financial year,

(c) the amount of any adjustments made in respect of any such provisions during that year in consequence of the disposal of any assets, and

(d) the amount of any other adjustments made in respect of any such provisions during that year.

52. Where any fixed assets of the company (other than listed investments) are included under any item shown in the company's balance sheet at an amount determined on any basis mentioned in paragraph 32, the following information must be given—

(a) the years (so far as they are known to the directors) in which the assets were severally valued and the several values, and

(b) in the case of assets that have been valued during the financial year, the names of the persons who valued them or particulars of their qualifications for doing so and (whichever is stated) the bases of valuation used by them.

53. In relation to any amount which is or would but for paragraph 4(2)(b) be shown in respect of the item "land and buildings" in the company's balance sheet there must be stated—

(a) how much of that amount is ascribable to land of freehold tenure and how much to land of leasehold tenure, and

(b) how much of the amount ascribable to land of leasehold tenure is ascribable to land held on long lease and how much to land held on short lease.

Investments

54. (1) In respect of the amount of each item which is or would but for paragraph 4(2)(b) be shown in the company's balance sheet under the general item "investments" (whether as fixed assets or as current assets) there must be stated how much of that amount is ascribable to listed investments.

(2) Where the amount of any listed investments is stated for any item in accordance with sub-paragraph (1), the following amounts must also be stated—

(a) the aggregate market value of those investments where it differs from the amount so stated, and

(b) both the market value and the stock exchange value of any investments of which the former value is, for the purposes of the accounts, taken as being higher than the latter.

[Information about fair value of assets and liabilities

55. (1) This paragraph applies where financial instruments or other assets have been valued in accordance with, as appropriate, paragraph 36, 38 or 39.

(2) There must be stated—

(a) the significant assumptions underlying the valuation models and techniques used to determine the fair value of the instruments or other assets,

(b) for each category of financial instrument or other asset, the fair value of the assets in that category and the changes in value—

(i) included directly in the profit and loss account, or

(ii) credited to or (as the case may be) debited from the fair value reserve,

in respect of those assets, and

(c) for each class of derivatives, the extent and nature of the instruments, including significant terms and conditions that may affect the amount, timing and certainty of future cash flows.

(3) Where any amount is transferred to or from the fair value reserve during the financial year, there must be stated in tabular form—

(a) the amount of the reserve as at the date of the beginning of the financial year and as at the balance sheet date respectively,

(b) the amount transferred to or from the reserve during the year, and

(c) the source and application respectively of the amounts so transferred.]

56. Where the company has derivatives that it has not included at fair value, there must be stated for each class of such derivatives—

(a) the fair value of the derivatives in that class, if such a value can be determined in accordance with paragraph 37, and

(b) the extent and nature of the derivatives.

57. (1) This paragraph applies if—

(a) the company has financial fixed assets that could be included at fair value by virtue of paragraph 36,

(b) the amount at which those items are included under any item in the company's accounts is in excess of their fair value, and

(c) the company has not made provision for diminution in value of those assets in accordance with paragraph 19(1) of this Schedule.

(2) There must be stated—

(a) the amount at which either the individual assets or appropriate groupings of those individual assets are included in the company's accounts,

(b) the fair value of those assets or groupings, and

(c) the reasons for not making a provision for diminution in value of those assets, including the nature of the evidence that provides the basis for the belief that the amount at which they are stated in the accounts will be recovered.

Information where investment property and living animals and plants included at fair value

58. (1) This paragraph applies where the amounts to be included in a company's accounts in respect of [stocks,] investment property or living animals and plants have been determined in accordance with paragraph 39.

(2) The balance sheet items affected and the basis of valuation adopted in determining the amounts of the assets in question in the case of each such item must be disclosed in a note to the accounts.

(3) In the case of investment property, for each balance sheet item affected there must be shown, either separately in the balance sheet or in a note to the accounts—

(a) the comparable amounts determined according to the historical cost accounting rules, or

(b) the differences between those amounts and the corresponding amounts actually shown in the balance sheet in respect of that item.

(4) In sub-paragraph (3), references in relation to any item to the comparable amounts determined in accordance with that sub-paragraph are to—

(a) the aggregate amount which would be required to be shown in respect of that item if the amounts to be included in respect of all the assets covered by that item were determined according to the historical cost accounting rules, and

(b) the aggregate amount of the cumulative provisions for depreciation or diminution in value which would be permitted or required in determining those amounts according to those rules.

Reserves and provisions

59. (1) This paragraph applies where any amount is transferred—

(a) to or from any reserves, or

(b) to any provision for liabilities, or

(c) from any provision for liabilities otherwise than for the purpose for which the provision was established,

and the reserves or provisions are or would but for paragraph 4(2)(b) be shown as separate items in the company's balance sheet.

(2) The following information must be given in respect of the aggregate of reserves or provisions included in the same item [in tabular form]—

(a) the amount of the reserves or provisions as at the date of the beginning of the financial year and as at the balance sheet date respectively,

(b) any amounts transferred to or from the reserves or provisions during that year, and

(c) the source and application respectively of any amounts so transferred.

(3) Particulars must be given of each provision included in the item "other provisions" in the company's balance sheet in any case where the amount of that provision is material.

Provision for taxation

60. The amount of any provision for deferred taxation must be stated separately from the amount of any provision for other taxation.

Details of indebtedness

61. (1) For the aggregate of all items shown under "creditors" in the company's balance sheet there must be stated the aggregate of the following amounts—

(a) the amount of any debts included under "creditors" which are payable or repayable otherwise than by instalments and fall due for payment or repayment after the end of the period of five years beginning with the day next following the end of the financial year, and

(b) in the case of any debts so included which are payable or repayable by instalments, the amount of any instalments which fall due for payment after the end of that period.

(2) Subject to sub-paragraph (3), in relation to each debt falling to be taken into account under sub-paragraph (1), the terms of payment or repayment and the rate of any interest payable on the debt must be stated.

(3) If the number of debts is such that, in the opinion of the directors, compliance with sub-paragraph (2) would result in a statement of excessive length, it is sufficient to give a general indication of the terms of payment or repayment and the rates of any interest payable on the debts.

(4) In respect of each item shown under "creditors" in the company's balance sheet there must be stated—

(a) the aggregate amount of any debts included under that item in respect of which any security has been given by the company, and

(b) an indication of the nature [and form] of the securities so given.

(5) References above in this paragraph to an item shown under "creditors" in the company's balance sheet include references, where amounts falling due to creditors within one year and after more than one year are distinguished in the balance sheet—

(a) in a case within sub-paragraph (1), to an item shown under the latter of those categories, and

(b) in a case within sub-paragraph (4), to an item shown under either of those categories.

References to items shown under "creditors" include references to items which would but for paragraph 4(2)(b) be shown under that heading.

62. If any fixed cumulative dividends on the company's shares are in arrear, there must be stated—

(a) the amount of the arrears, and

(b) the period for which the dividends or, if there is more than one class, each class of them are in arrear.

[Guarantees and other financial commitments

63. (1) Particulars must be given of any charge on the assets of the company to secure the liabilities of any other person including the amount secured.

(2) Particulars and the total amount of any financial commitments, guarantees and contingencies that are not included in the balance sheet must be disclosed.

(3) An indication of the nature and form of any valuable security given by the company in respect of commitments, guarantees and contingencies within sub-paragraph (2) must be given.

(4) The total amount of any commitments within sub-paragraph (2) concerning pensions must be separately disclosed.

(5) Particulars must be given of pension commitments which are included in the balance sheet.

(6) Where any commitment within sub-paragraph (4) or (5) relates wholly or partly to pensions payable to past directors of the company separate particulars must be given of that commitment.

(7) The total amount of any commitments, guarantees and contingencies within sub-paragraph (2) which are undertaken on behalf of or for the benefit of—

(a) any parent undertaking or fellow subsidiary undertaking of the company,

(b) any subsidiary undertaking of the company, or

(c) any undertaking in which the company has a participating interest

must be separately stated and those within each of paragraphs (a), (b) and (c) must also be stated separately from those within any other of those paragraphs.]

Miscellaneous matters

64. (1) Particulars must be given of any case where the purchase price or production cost of any asset is for the first time determined under paragraph 29.

(2) Where any outstanding loans made under the authority of section 682(2)(b), (c) or (d) of the 2006 Act (various cases of financial assistance by a company for purchase of its own shares) are included under any item shown in the company's balance sheet, the aggregate amount of those loans must be disclosed for each item in question.

Information supplementing the profit and loss account

65. Paragraphs 66 to 69 require information which either supplements the information given with respect to any particular items shown in the profit and loss account or otherwise provides particulars of income or expenditure of the company or of circumstances affecting the items shown in the profit and loss account (see regulation 3(2) for exemption for companies falling within section 408 of the 2006 Act (individual profit and loss account where group accounts prepared)).

Separate statement of certain items of income and expenditure

66. (1) Subject to sub-paragraph (2), there must be stated the amount of the interest on or any similar charges in respect of bank loans and overdrafts, and loans of any other kind made to the company.

(2) Sub-paragraph (1) does not apply to interest or charges on loans to the company from group undertakings, but, with that exception, it applies to interest or charges on all loans, whether made on the security of debentures or not.

Particulars of tax

67. (1) Particulars must be given of any special circumstances which affect liability in respect of taxation of profits, income or capital gains for the financial year or liability in respect of taxation of profits, income or capital gains for succeeding financial years.

(2) The following amounts must be stated—

(a) the amount of the charge for United Kingdom corporation tax,

(b) if that amount would have been greater but for relief from double taxation, the amount which it would have been but for such relief,

(c) the amount of the charge for United Kingdom income tax, and

(d) the amount of the charge for taxation imposed outside the United Kingdom of profits, income and (so far as charged to revenue) capital gains.

[These amounts must be stated separately in respect of each of the amounts which is or would but for paragraph 4(2)(b) be shown under the item "tax on profit or loss" in the profit and loss account].

Particulars of turnover

68. (1) If in the course of the financial year the company has carried on business of two or more classes that, in the opinion of the directors, differ substantially from each other, the amount of the turnover attributable to each class must be stated and the class described (see regulation 4(3)(b) for exemption for medium-sized companies in accounts delivered to registrar).

(2) If in the course of the financial year the company has supplied markets that, in the opinion of the directors, differ substantially from each other, the amount of the turnover attributable to each such market must also be stated.

In this paragraph "market" means a market delimited by geographical bounds.

(3) In analysing for the purposes of this paragraph the source (in terms of business or in terms of market) of turnover, the directors of the company must have regard to the manner in which the company's activities are organised.

(4) For the purposes of this paragraph—

(a) classes of business which, in the opinion of the directors, do not differ substantially from each other must be treated as one class, and

(b) markets which, in the opinion of the directors, do not differ substantially from each other must be treated as one market,

and any amounts properly attributable to one class of business or (as the case may be) to one market which are not material may be included in the amount stated in respect of another.

(5) Where in the opinion of the directors the disclosure of any information required by this paragraph would be seriously prejudicial to the interests of the company, that information need not be disclosed, but the fact that any such information has not been disclosed must be stated.

Miscellaneous matters

69. (1) Where any amount relating to any preceding financial year is included in any item in the profit and loss account, the effect must be stated.

[(2) The amount, nature and effect of any individual items of income or expenditure which are of exceptional size or incidence must be stated.]

Sums denominated in foreign currencies

70. Where any sums originally denominated in foreign currencies have been brought into account under any items shown in the balance sheet format or profit and loss account formats, the basis on which those sums have been translated into sterling (or the currency in which the accounts are drawn up) must be stated.

Dormant companies acting as agents

71. Where the directors of a company take advantage of the exemption conferred by section 480 of the 2006 Act (dormant companies: exemption from audit), and the company has during the financial year in question acted as an agent for any person, the fact that it has so acted must be stated.

Related party transactions

72. (1) Particulars may be given of transactions which the company has entered into with related parties, and must be given if such transactions are material and have not been concluded under normal market conditions (see [regulation 4(2B) for a modification] for medium-sized companies).

(2) The particulars of transactions required to be disclosed by sub-paragraph (1) must include—

(a) the amount of such transactions,

(b) the nature of the related party relationship, and

(c) other information about the transactions necessary for an understanding of the financial position of the company.

(3) Information about individual transactions may be aggregated according to their nature, except where separate information is necessary for an understanding of the effects of related party transactions on the financial position of the company.

(4) Particulars need not be given of transactions entered into between two or more members of a group, provided that any subsidiary undertaking which is a party to the transaction is wholly-owned by such a member.

(5) In this paragraph, "related party" has the same meaning as in [UK-adopted international accounting standards].

[Post balance sheet events

72A. The nature and financial effect of material events arising after the balance sheet date which are not reflected in the profit and loss account or balance sheet must be stated.

Appropriations

72B. Particulars must be given of the proposed appropriation of profit or treatment of loss or, where applicable, particulars of the actual appropriation of the profits or treatment of the losses.]

NOTES

Paras 42, 55, 63: substituted by the Companies, Partnerships and Groups (Accounts and Reports) Regulations 2015, SI 2015/980, reg 29(1)–(3), (7), as from 6 April 2015, in relation to (a) financial years beginning on or after 1 January 2016, and (b) a financial year of a company beginning on or after 1 January 2015, but before 1 January 2016, if the directors of the company so decide (see **[4.549]** *post*).

Paras 58, 59, 61: words in square brackets inserted by SI 2015/980, reg 29(1), (4)–(6) (as to the application of this amendment see the first note relating to the 2015 Regulations above).

Para 67: words in square brackets in sub-para (2) substituted by SI 2015/980, reg 29(1), (8) (as to the application of this amendment see the first note relating to the 2015 Regulations above).

Para 69: sub-para (2) substituted (for the original sub-paras (2), (3)) by SI 2015/980, reg 29(1), (9) (as to the application of this amendment see the first note relating to the 2015 Regulations above).

Para 72: words in square brackets in sub-para (1) substituted by SI 2015/980, reg 29(1), (10) (as to the application of this amendment see the first note relating to the 2015 Regulations above). Words in square brackets in sub-para (5) substituted by the International Accounting Standards and European Public Limited-Liability Company (Amendment etc) (EU Exit) Regulations 2019, SI 2019/685, reg 19, Sch 1, Pt 2, para 57(1), (2)(b), in relation to accounts for financial years beginning on or after IP completion day (as defined in the European Union (Withdrawal Agreement) Act 2020, s 39) (note also that in relation to accounts for financial years which begin before but end on or after IP completion day, the enactments amended by Parts 1–3 of Sch 1 to the 2019 Regulations have effect as if the UK were a member State until the end of the financial year in question).

Paras 72A, 72B: inserted by SI 2015/980, reg 29(1), (11) (as to the application of this amendment see the first note relating to the 2015 Regulations above).

PART 4

(Revoked by the Companies, Partnerships and Groups (Accounts and Reports) Regulations 2015, SI 2015/980, reg 30, as from 6 April 2015, in relation to (a) financial years beginning on or after 1 January 2016, and (b) a financial year of a company beginning on or after 1 January 2015, but before 1 January 2016, if the directors of the company so decide (see ***[4.549]*** *post).*

PART 5 SPECIAL PROVISIONS WHERE THE COMPANY IS AN INVESTMENT COMPANY

[4.77]

74. (1) Paragraph 35 does not apply to the amount of any profit or loss arising from a determination of the value of any investments of an investment company on any basis mentioned in paragraph 32(3).

(2) Any provisions made by virtue of paragraph 19(1) or (2) in the case of an investment company in respect of any fixed asset investments need not be charged to the company's profit and loss account provided they are either—

- (a) charged against any reserve account to which any amount excluded by sub-paragraph (1) from the requirements of paragraph 35 has been credited, or
- (b) shown as a separate item in the company's balance sheet under the sub-heading "other reserves".

(3) For the purposes of this paragraph, as it applies in relation to any company, "fixed asset investment" means any asset falling to be included under any item shown in the company's balance sheet under the subdivision "investments" under the general item "fixed assets".

75. (1) Any distribution made by an investment company which reduces the amount of its net assets to less than the aggregate of its called-up share capital and undistributable reserves shall be disclosed in a note to the company's accounts.

(2) For purposes of this paragraph, a company's net assets are the aggregate of its assets less the aggregate of its liabilities (including any provision for liabilities within paragraph 2 of Schedule 9 to these Regulations that is made in Companies Act accounts and any provision that is made in IAS accounts); and "undistributable reserves" has the meaning given by section 831(4) of the 2006 Act.

(3) A company shall be treated as an investment company for the purposes of this Part of this Schedule in relation to any financial year of the company if—

- (a) during the whole of that year it was an investment company as defined by section 833 of the 2006 Act, and
- (b) it was not at any time during that year prohibited from making a distribution by virtue of section 832 of the 2006 Act due to either or both of the conditions specified in section 832(5)(a) or (b) (no distribution where capital profits have been distributed etc) not being met.

SCHEDULE 2
BANKING COMPANIES: COMPANIES ACT INDIVIDUAL ACCOUNTS

Regulation 5(1)

PART 1 GENERAL RULES AND FORMATS

SECTION A GENERAL RULES

[4.78]

1. Subject to the following provisions of this Part of this Schedule—

- (a) every balance sheet of a company must show the items listed in the balance sheet format set out in Section B of this Part, and
- (b) every profit and loss account must show the items listed in either of the profit and loss account formats in Section B.

2. (1) References in this Part of this Schedule to the items listed in any of the formats set out in Section B, are to those items read together with any of the notes following the formats which apply to those items.

(2) The items must be shown in the order and under the headings and sub-headings given in the particular format used, but—

- (a) the notes to the formats may permit alternative positions for any particular items,
- (b) the heading or sub-heading for any item does not have to be distinguished by any letter or number assigned to that item in the format used, and
- (c) where the heading of an item in the format used contains any wording in square brackets, that wording may be omitted if not applicable to the company.

3. (1) Where in accordance with paragraph 1 a company's profit and loss account for any financial year has been prepared by reference to one of the formats in Section B, the company's directors must use the same format in preparing the profit and loss account for subsequent financial years, unless in their opinion there are special reasons for a change.

(2) Particulars of any change must be given in a note to the accounts in which the new format is first used, and the reasons for the change must be explained.

4. (1) Any item required to be shown in a company's balance sheet or profit and loss account may be shown in greater detail than required by the particular format used.

(2) The balance sheet or profit and loss account may include an item representing or covering the amount of any asset or liability, income or expenditure not specifically covered by any of the items listed in the format used, save that none of the following may be treated as assets in any balance sheet—

(a) preliminary expenses,

(b) expenses of, and commission on, any issue of shares or debentures, and

(c) costs of research.

5. (1) Items to which lower case letters are assigned in any of the formats in Section B may be combined in a company's accounts for any financial year if—

(a) their individual amounts are not material for the purpose of giving a true and fair view, or

(b) the combination facilitates the assessment of the state of affairs or profit or loss of the company for that year.

(2) Where sub-paragraph (1)(b) applies, the individual amounts of any items so combined must be disclosed in a note to the accounts and any notes required by this Schedule to the items so combined must, notwithstanding the combination, be given.

6. (1) Subject to sub-paragraph (2), the directors must not include a heading or sub-heading corresponding to an item in the balance sheet or profit and loss account format used if there is no amount to be shown for that item for the financial year to which the balance sheet or profit and loss account relates.

(2) Where an amount can be shown for the item in question for the immediately preceding financial year, that amount must be shown under the heading or sub-heading required by the format for that item.

7. (1) For every item shown in the balance sheet or profit and loss account the corresponding amount for the immediately preceding financial year must also be shown.

(2) Where that corresponding amount is not comparable with the amount to be shown for the item in question in respect of the financial year to which the balance sheet or profit and loss account relates, the former amount may be adjusted, and particulars of the non-comparability and of any adjustment must be disclosed in a note to the accounts.

8. (1) Subject to the following provisions of this paragraph and without prejudice to note (6) to the balance sheet format, amounts in respect of items representing assets or income may not be set off against amounts in respect of items representing liabilities or expenditure (as the case may be), or vice versa.

(2) Charges required to be included in profit and loss account format 1, items 11(a) and 11(b) or format 2, items A7(a) and A7(b) may be set off against income required to be included in format 1, items 12(a) and 12(b) or format 2, items B5(a) and B5(b) and the resulting figure shown as a single item (in format 2 at position A7 if negative and at position B5 if positive).

(3) Charges required to be included in profit and loss account format 1, item 13 or format 2, item A8 may also be set off against income required to be included in format 1, item 14 or format 2, item B6 and the resulting figure shown as a single item (in format 2 at position A8 if negative and at position B6 if positive).

9. (1) Assets must be shown under the relevant balance sheet headings even where the company has pledged them as security for its own liabilities or for those of third parties or has otherwise assigned them as security to third parties.

(2) A company may not include in its balance sheet assets pledged or otherwise assigned to it as security unless such assets are in the form of cash in the hands of the company.

(3) Assets acquired in the name of and on behalf of third parties must not be shown in the balance sheet.

10. The company's directors must, in determining how amounts are presented within items in the profit and loss account and balance sheet, have regard to the substance of the reported transaction or arrangement, in accordance with generally accepted accounting principles or practice.

[10A. Where an asset or liability relates to more than one item in the balance sheet, the relationship of such asset or liability to the relevant items must be disclosed either under those items or in the notes to the accounts.]

SECTION B THE REQUIRED FORMATS

Balance sheet format

ASSETS

1 Cash and balances at central [or post office] banks (1)

2 Treasury bills and other eligible bills (20)

(a) Treasury bills and similar securities (2)

(b) Other eligible bills (3)

3 Loans and advances to banks (4) (20)

(a) Repayable on demand

(b) Other loans and advances

4 Loans and advances to customers (5) (20)

5 Debt securities [and other fixed-income securities] (6) (20)

(a) Issued by public bodies

(b) Issued by other issuers

6 Equity shares [and other variable-yield securities]

7 Participating interests

8 Shares in group undertakings

9 Intangible fixed assets (7)

10 Tangible fixed assets (8)

11 Called up capital not paid (9)

12 Own shares [10]

13 Other assets

14 Called up capital not paid [9]

15 Prepayments and accrued income

Total assets

LIABILITIES

1 Deposits by banks [11] [20]

(a) Repayable on demand

(b) With agreed maturity dates or periods of notice

2 Customer accounts [12] [20]

(a) Repayable on demand

(b) With agreed maturity dates or periods of notice

3 Debt securities in issue [13] [20]

(a) Bonds and medium term notes

(b) Others

4 Other liabilities

5 Accruals and deferred income

6 Provisions for liabilities

(a) Provisions for pensions and similar obligations

(b) Provisions for tax

(c) Other provisions

7 Subordinated liabilities [14] [20]

8 Called up share capital [15]

9 Share premium account

10 Reserves

(a) Capital redemption reserve

(b) Reserve for own shares

(c) Reserves provided for by the articles of association

(d) Other reserves

11 Revaluation reserve

12 Profit and loss account

Total liabilities

MEMORANDUM ITEMS

1 Contingent liabilities [16]

(1) Acceptances and endorsements

(2) Guarantees and assets pledged as collateral security [17]

(3) Other contingent liabilities

2 Commitments [18]

(1) Commitments arising out of sale and option to resell transactions [19]

(2) Other commitments

Notes on the balance sheet format and memorandum items

(1) Cash and balances at central [or post office] banks

(Assets item 1.)

Cash is to comprise all currency including foreign notes and coins.

Only those balances which may be withdrawn without notice and which are deposited with central or post office banks of the country or countries in which the company is established may be included in this item. All other claims on central or post office banks must be shown under assets items 3 or 4.

(2) Treasury bills and other eligible bills: Treasury bills and similar securities

(Assets item 2.(a).)

Treasury bills and similar securities are to comprise treasury bills and similar debt instruments issued by public bodies which are eligible for refinancing with central banks of the country or countries in which the company is established. Any treasury bills or similar debt instruments not so eligible must be included under assets item 5(a).

(3) Treasury bills and other eligible bills: Other eligible bills

(Assets item 2.(b).)

Other eligible bills are to comprise all bills purchased to the extent that they are eligible, under national law, for refinancing with the central banks of the country or countries in which the company is established.

(4) Loans and advances to banks

(Assets item 3.)

Loans and advances to banks are to comprise all loans and advances to domestic or foreign credit institutions made by the company arising out of banking transactions. However loans and advances to credit institutions represented by debt securities or other fixed-income securities must be included under assets item 5 and not this item.

(5) Loans and advances to customers

(Assets item 4.)

Loans and advances to customers are to comprise all types of assets in the form of claims on domestic and foreign customers other than credit institutions. However loans and advances represented by debt securities or other fixed-income securities must be included under assets item 5 and not this item.

(6) Debt securities [and other fixed-income securities]

(Assets item 5.)

This item is to comprise transferable debt securities and any other transferable fixed-income securities issued by credit institutions, other undertakings or public bodies. Debt securities and other fixed-income securities issued by public bodies are, however, only to be included in this item if they may not be shown under assets item 2.

Where a company holds its own debt securities these must not be included under this item but must be deducted from liabilities item 3.(a) or (b), as appropriate.

Securities bearing interest rates that vary in accordance with specific factors, for example the interest rate on the inter-bank market or on the Euromarket, are also to be regarded as fixed- income securities to be included under this item.

(7) Intangible fixed assets

(Assets item 9.)

This item is to comprise—

(a) development costs,
(b) concessions, patents, licences, trade marks and similar rights and assets,
(c) goodwill, and
(d) payments on account.

Amounts are, however, to be included in respect of (b) only if the assets were acquired for valuable consideration or the assets in question were created by the company itself.

Amounts representing goodwill are only to be included to the extent that the goodwill was acquired for valuable consideration.

The amount of any goodwill included in this item must be disclosed in a note to the accounts.

(8) Tangible fixed assets

(Assets item 10.)

This item is to comprise—

(a) land and buildings,
(b) plant and machinery,
(c) fixtures and fittings, tools and equipment, and
(d) payments on account and assets in the course of construction.

The amount included in this item with respect to land and buildings occupied by the company for its own activities must be disclosed in a note to the accounts.

(9) Called up capital not paid

(Assets items 11 and 14.)

The two positions shown for this item are alternatives.

(10) Own shares

(Assets item 12.)

The nominal value of the shares held must be shown separately under this item.

(11) Deposits by banks

(Liabilities item 1.)

Deposits by banks are to comprise all amounts arising out of banking transactions owed to other domestic or foreign credit institutions by the company. However liabilities in the form of debt securities and any liabilities for which transferable certificates have been issued must be included under liabilities item 3 and not this item.

(12) Customer accounts

(Liabilities item 2.)

This item is to comprise all amounts owed to creditors that are not credit institutions. However liabilities in the form of debt securities and any liabilities for which transferable certificates have been issued must be shown under liabilities item 3 and not this item.

(13) Debt securities in issue

(Liabilities item 3.)

This item is to include both debt securities and debts for which transferable certificates have been issued, including liabilities arising out of own acceptances and promissory notes. (Only acceptances which a company has issued for its own refinancing and in respect of which it is the first party liable are to be treated as own acceptances.)

(14) Subordinated liabilities

(Liabilities item 7.)

This item is to comprise all liabilities in respect of which there is a contractual obligation that, in the event of winding up or bankruptcy, they are to be repaid only after the claims of other creditors have been met.

This item must include all subordinated liabilities, whether or not a ranking has been agreed between the subordinated creditors concerned.

(15) Called up share capital

(Liabilities item 8.)

The amount of allotted share capital and the amount of called up share capital which has been paid up must be shown separately.

(16) Contingent liabilities

(Memorandum item 1.)

This item is to include all transactions whereby the company has underwritten the obligations of a third party.

Liabilities arising out of the endorsement of rediscounted bills must be included in this item. Acceptances other than own acceptances must also be included.

(17) Contingent liabilities: Guarantees and assets pledged as collateral security

(Memorandum item 1(2).)

This item is to include all guarantee obligations incurred and assets pledged as collateral security on behalf of third parties, particularly in respect of sureties and irrevocable letters of credit.

(18) Commitments

(Memorandum item 2.)

This item is to include every irrevocable commitment which could give rise to a credit risk.

(19) Commitments: Commitments arising out of sale and option to resell transactions

(Memorandum item 2(1).)

This item is to comprise commitments entered into by the company in the context of sale and option to resell transactions.

(20) Claims on, and liabilities to, undertakings in which a participating interest is held or group undertakings

(Assets items 2 to 5, liabilities items 1 to 3 and 7.)

The following information must be given either by way of subdivision of the relevant items or by way of notes to the accounts.

The amount of the following must be shown for each of assets items 2 to 5—

(a) claims on group undertakings included therein, and

(b) claims on undertakings in which the company has a participating interest included therein.

The amount of the following must be shown for each of liabilities items 1, 2, 3 and 7—

(i) liabilities to group undertakings included therein, and

(ii) liabilities to undertakings in which the company has a participating interest included therein.

Special rules

11 Subordinated assets

(1) The amount of any assets that are subordinated must be shown either as a subdivision of any relevant asset item or in the notes to the accounts; in the latter case disclosure must be by reference to the relevant asset item or items in which the assets are included.

(2) In the case of assets items 2 to 5 in the balance sheet format, the amounts required to be shown by note (20) to the format as sub-items of those items must be further subdivided so as to show the amount of any claims included therein that are subordinated.

(3) For this purpose, assets are subordinated if there is a contractual obligation to the effect that, in the event of winding up or bankruptcy, they are to be repaid only after the claims of other creditors have been met, whether or not a ranking has been agreed between the subordinated creditors concerned.

12 Syndicated loans

(1) Where a company is a party to a syndicated loan transaction the company must include only that part of the total loan which it itself has funded.

(2) Where a company is a party to a syndicated loan transaction and has agreed to reimburse (in whole or in part) any other party to the syndicate any funds advanced by that party or any interest thereon upon the occurrence of any event, including the default of the borrower, any additional liability by reason of such a guarantee must be included as a contingent liability in Memorandum item 1(2).

13 Sale and repurchase transactions

(1) The following rules apply where a company is a party to a sale and repurchase transaction.

(2) Where the company is the transferor of the assets under the transaction—

(a) the assets transferred must, notwithstanding the transfer, be included in its balance sheet,

(b) the purchase price received by it must be included in its balance sheet as an amount owed to the transferee, and

(c) the value of the assets transferred must be disclosed in a note to its accounts.

(3) Where the company is the transferee of the assets under the transaction, it must not include the assets transferred in its balance sheet but the purchase price paid by it to the transferor must be so included as an amount owed by the transferor.

14 Sale and option to resell transactions

(1) The following rules apply where a company is a party to a sale and option to resell transaction.

(2) Where the company is the transferor of the assets under the transaction, it must not include in its balance sheet the assets transferred but it must enter under Memorandum item 2 an amount equal to the price agreed in the event of repurchase.

(3) Where the company is the transferee of the assets under the transaction it must include those assets in its balance sheet.

15 Managed funds

(1) For the purposes of this paragraph, "managed funds" are funds which the company administers in its own name but on behalf of others and to which it has legal title.

(2) The company must, in any case where claims and obligations arising in respect of managed funds fall to be treated as claims and obligations of the company, adopt the following accounting treatment.

(3) Claims and obligations representing managed funds are to be included in the company's balance sheet, with the notes to the accounts disclosing the total amount included with respect to such assets and liabilities in the balance sheet and showing the amount included under each relevant balance sheet item in respect of such assets or (as the case may be) liabilities.

Profit and loss account formats

Format 1

Vertical layout

1 Interest receivable (1)
   (1) Interest receivable and similar income arising from debt securities [and other fixed-income securities]
   (2) Other interest receivable and similar income

2 Interest payable (2)

3 Dividend income
   (a) Income from equity shares [and other variable-yield securities]
   (b) Income from participating interests
   (c) Income from shares in group undertakings

4 Fees and commissions receivable (3)

5 Fees and commissions payable (4)

6 Dealing [profits] [losses] (5)

7 Other operating income

8 Administrative expenses
   (a) Staff costs
      (i) Wages and salaries
      (ii) Social security costs
      (iii) Other pension costs
   (b) Other administrative expenses

9 Depreciation and amortisation (6)

10 Other operating charges

11 Provisions
   (a) Provisions for bad and doubtful debts (7)
   (b) Provisions for contingent liabilities and commitments (8)

12 Adjustments to provisions
   (a) Adjustments to provisions for bad and doubtful debts (9)
   (b) Adjustments to provisions for contingent liabilities and commitments (10)

13 Amounts written off fixed asset investments (11)

14 Adjustments to amounts written off fixed asset investments (12)

15 [Profit] [loss] on ordinary activities before tax

16 Tax on [profit] [loss] on ordinary activities

17 [Profit] [loss] on ordinary activities after tax

18 Extraordinary income

19 Extraordinary charges

20 Extraordinary [profit] [loss]

21 Tax on extraordinary [profit] [loss]

22 Extraordinary [profit] [loss] after tax

23 Other taxes not shown under the preceding items

24 [Profit] [loss] for the financial year

Profit and loss account formats

Format 2

Horizontal layout

A Charges
   1 Interest payable (2)
   2 Fees and commissions payable (4)
   3 Dealing losses (5)
   4 Administrative expenses
      (a) Staff costs
         (i) Wages and salaries
         (ii) Social security costs
         (iii) Other pension costs
      (b) Other administrative expenses
   5 Depreciation and amortisation (6)

6 Other operating charges
7 Provisions
(a) Provisions for bad and doubtful debts [7]
(b) Provisions for contingent liabilities and commitments [8]
8 Amounts written off fixed asset investments [11]
9 Profit on ordinary activities before tax
10 Tax on [profit] [loss] on ordinary activities
11 Profit on ordinary activities after tax
12 Extraordinary charges
13 Tax on extraordinary [profit] [loss]
14 Extraordinary loss after tax
15 Other taxes not shown under the preceding items
16 Profit for the financial year

B Income
1 Interest receivable [1]
(1) Interest receivable and similar income arising from debt securities [and other fixed-income securities]
(2) Other interest receivable and similar income
2 Dividend income
(a) Income from equity shares [and other variable-yield securities]
(b) Income from participating interests
(c) Income from shares in group undertakings
3 Fees and commissions receivable [3]
4 Dealing profits [5]
5 Adjustments to provisions
(a) Adjustments to provisions for bad and doubtful debts [9]
(b) Adjustments to provisions for contingent liabilities and commitments [10]
6 Adjustments to amounts written off fixed asset investments [12]
7 Other operating income
8 Loss on ordinary activities before tax
9 Loss on ordinary activities after tax
10 Extraordinary income
11 Extraordinary profit after tax
12 Loss for the financial year

Notes on the profit and loss account formats

(1) Interest receivable

(Format 1, item 1; format 2, item B1.)

This item is to include all income arising out of banking activities, including—

(a) income from assets included in assets items 1 to 5 in the balance sheet format, however calculated,
(b) income resulting from covered forward contracts spread over the actual duration of the contract and similar in nature to interest, and
(c) fees and commissions receivable similar in nature to interest and calculated on a time basis or by reference to the amount of the claim (but not other fees and commissions receivable).

(2) Interest payable

(Format 1, item 2; format 2, item A1.)

This item is to include all expenditure arising out of banking activities, including—

(a) charges arising out of liabilities included in liabilities items 1, 2, 3 and 7 in the balance sheet format, however calculated,
(b) charges resulting from covered forward contracts, spread over the actual duration of the contract and similar in nature to interest, and
(c) fees and commissions payable similar in nature to interest and calculated on a time basis or by reference to the amount of the liability (but not other fees and commissions payable).

(3) Fees and commissions receivable

(Format 1, item 4; format 2, item B3.)

Fees and commissions receivable are to comprise income in respect of all services supplied by the company to third parties, but not fees or commissions required to be included under interest receivable (format 1, item 1; format 2, item B1).

In particular the following fees and commissions receivable must be included (unless required to be included under interest receivable)—

(a) fees and commissions for guarantees, loan administration on behalf of other lenders and securities transactions,
(b) fees, commissions and other income in respect of payment transactions, account administration charges and commissions for the safe custody and administration of securities,
(c) fees and commissions for foreign currency transactions and for the sale and purchase of coin and precious metals, and
(d) fees and commissions charged for brokerage services in connection with savings and insurance contracts and loans.

(4) Fees and commissions payable

(Format 1, item 5; format 2, item A2.)

Fees and commissions payable are to comprise charges for all services rendered to the company by third parties but not fees or commissions required to be included under interest payable (format 1, item 2; format 2, item A1).

In particular the following fees and commissions payable must be included (unless required to be included under interest payable)—

(a) fees and commissions for guarantees, loan administration and securities transactions;
(b) fees, commissions and other charges in respect of payment transactions, account administration charges and commissions for the safe custody and administration of securities;
(c) fees and commissions for foreign currency transactions and for the sale and purchase of coin and precious metals; and
(d) fees and commissions for brokerage services in connection with savings and insurance contracts and loans.

(5) Dealing [profits] [losses]

(Format 1, item 6; format 2, items B4 and A3.)

This item is to comprise—

(a) the net profit or net loss on transactions in securities which are not held as financial fixed assets together with amounts written off or written back with respect to such securities, including amounts written off or written back as a result of the application of paragraph 33(1),
(b) the net profit or loss on exchange activities, save in so far as the profit or loss is included in interest receivable or interest payable (format 1, items 1 or 2; format 2, items B1 or A1), and
(c) the net profits and losses on other dealing operations involving financial instruments, including precious metals.

(6) Depreciation and amortisation

(Format 1, item 9; format 2, item A5.)

This item is to comprise depreciation and other amounts written off in respect of balance sheet assets items 9 and 10.

(7) Provisions: Provisions for bad and doubtful debts

(Format 1, item 11(a); format 2, item A7(a).)

Provisions for bad and doubtful debts are to comprise charges for amounts written off and for provisions made in respect of loans and advances shown under balance sheet assets items 3 and 4.

(8) Provisions: Provisions for contingent liabilities and commitments

(Format 1, item 11(b); format 2, item A7(b).)

This item is to comprise charges for provisions for contingent liabilities and commitments of a type which would, if not provided for, be shown under Memorandum items 1 and 2.

(9) Adjustments to provisions: Adjustments to provisions for bad and doubtful debts

(Format 1, item 12(a); format 2, item B5(a).)

This item is to include credits from the recovery of loans that have been written off, from other advances written back following earlier write offs and from the reduction of provisions previously made with respect to loans and advances.

(10) Adjustments to provisions: Adjustments to provisions for contingent liabilities and commitments

(Format 1, item 12(b); format 2, item B5(b).)

This item comprises credits from the reduction of provisions previously made with respect to contingent liabilities and commitments.

(11) Amounts written off fixed asset investments

(Format 1, item 13; format 2, item A8.)

Amounts written off fixed asset investments are to comprise amounts written off in respect of assets which are transferable securities held as financial fixed assets, participating interests and shares in group undertakings and which are included in assets items 5 to 8 in the balance sheet format.

(12) Adjustments to amounts written off fixed asset investments

(Format 1, item 14; format 2, item B6.)

Adjustments to amounts written off fixed asset investments are to include amounts written back following earlier write offs and provisions in respect of assets which are transferable securities held as financial fixed assets, participating interests and group undertakings and which are included in assets items 5 to 8 in the balance sheet format.

NOTES

Section A: para 10A inserted by the Companies, Partnerships and Groups (Accounts and Reports) Regulations 2015, SI 2015/980, reg 31, as from 6 April 2015, in relation to (a) financial years beginning on or after 1 January 2016, and (b) a financial year of a company beginning on or after 1 January 2015, but before 1 January 2016, if the directors of the company so decide (see **[4.549]** *post*).

PART 2 ACCOUNTING PRINCIPLES AND RULES

SECTION A ACCOUNTING PRINCIPLES

Preliminary

[4.79]

16. (1) The amounts to be included in respect of all items shown in a company's accounts must be determined in accordance with the principles set out in this Section.

(2) But if it appears to the company's directors that there are special reasons for departing from any of those principles in preparing the company's accounts in respect of any financial year they may do so, in which case particulars of the departure, the reasons for it and its effect must be given in a note to the accounts.

Accounting principles

17. The company is presumed to be carrying on business as a going concern.

18. Accounting policies [and measurement bases] must be applied consistently within the same accounts and from one financial year to the next.

19. The amount of any item must be determined on a prudent basis, and in particular—

(a) only profits realised at the balance sheet date are to be included in the profit and loss account, . . .

(b) all liabilities which have arisen in respect of the financial year to which the accounts relate or a previous financial year must be taken into account, including those which only become apparent between the balance sheet date and the date on which it is signed on behalf of the board of directors in accordance with section 414 of the 2006 Act (approval and signing of accounts), [and]

[(c) all provisions for diminution of value must be recognised, whether the result of the financial year is a profit or a loss].

20. All income and charges relating to the financial year to which the accounts relate must be taken into account, without regard to the date of receipt or payment.

21. In determining the aggregate amount of any item, the amount of each individual asset or liability that falls to be taken into account must be determined separately.

[21A The opening balance sheet for each financial year shall correspond to the closing balance sheet for the preceding financial year.]

SECTION B HISTORICAL COST ACCOUNTING RULES

Preliminary

22. Subject to Sections C and D of this Part of this Schedule, the amounts to be included in respect of all items shown in a company's accounts must be determined in accordance with the rules set out in this Section.

Fixed assets

General rules

23. (1) The amount to be included in respect of any fixed asset is its cost.

(2) This is subject to any provision for depreciation or diminution in value made in accordance with paragraphs 24 to 26.

Rules for depreciation and diminution in value

24. In the case of any fixed asset which has a limited useful economic life, the amount of—

(a) its cost, or

(b) where it is estimated that any such asset will have a residual value at the end of the period of its useful economic life, its cost less that estimated residual value,

must be reduced by provisions for depreciation calculated to write off that amount systematically over the period of the asset's useful economic life.

25. (1) Where a fixed asset investment to which sub-paragraph (2) applies has diminished in value, provisions for diminution in value may be made in respect of it and the amount to be included in respect of it may be reduced accordingly.

(2) This sub-paragraph applies to fixed asset investments of a description falling to be included under assets item 7 (participating interests) or 8 (shares in group undertakings) in the balance sheet format, or any other holding of securities held as a financial fixed asset.

(3) Provisions for diminution in value must be made in respect of any fixed asset which has diminished in value if the reduction in its value is expected to be permanent (whether its useful economic life is limited or not), and the amount to be included in respect of it must be reduced accordingly.

[(4) Provisions made under this paragraph must be charged to the profit and loss account and disclosed separately in a note to the accounts if they have not been shown separately in the profit and loss account.]

26. (1) Where the reasons for which any provision was made in accordance with paragraph 25 have ceased to apply to any extent, that provision must be written back to the extent that it is no longer necessary.

[(1A) But provision made in accordance with paragraph 25(3) in respect of goodwill must not be written back to any extent.]

[(2) Any amounts written back under sub-paragraph (1) must be recognised in the profit and loss account and disclosed separately in a note to the accounts if not shown separately in the profit and loss account.]

[Intangible assets

27. (1) Where this is in accordance with generally accepted accounting principles or practice, development costs may be included under assets item 9 in the balance sheet format.

(2) If any amount is included in a company's balance sheet in respect of development costs, the note on accounting policies (see paragraph 53 of this Schedule) must include the following information—

(a) the period over which the amount of those costs originally capitalised is being or is to be written off, and

(b) the reasons for capitalising the development costs in question.

28. (1) Intangible assets must be written off over the useful economic life of the intangible asset.

(2) Where in exceptional cases the useful life of intangible assets cannot be reliably estimated, such assets must be written off over a period chosen by the directors of the company.

(3) The period referred to in sub-paragraph (2) must not exceed ten years.

(4) There must be disclosed in a note to the accounts the period referred to in sub-paragraph (2) and the reasons for choosing that period.]

Treatment of fixed assets

29. (1) Assets included in assets items 9 (intangible fixed assets) and 10 (tangible fixed assets) in the balance sheet format must be valued as fixed assets.

(2) Other assets falling to be included in the balance sheet must be valued as fixed assets where they are intended for use on a continuing basis in the company's activities.

Financial fixed assets

30. (1) Debt securities, including fixed-income securities, held as financial fixed assets must be included in the balance sheet at an amount equal to their maturity value plus any premium, or less any discount, on their purchase, subject to the following provisions of this paragraph.

(2) The amount included in the balance sheet with respect to such securities purchased at a premium must be reduced each financial year on a systematic basis so as to write the premium off over the period to the maturity date of the security and the amounts so written off must be charged to the profit and loss account for the relevant financial years.

(3) The amount included in the balance sheet with respect to such securities purchased at a discount must be increased each financial year on a systematic basis so as to extinguish the discount over the period to the maturity date of the security and the amounts by which the amount is increased must be credited to the profit and loss account for the relevant years.

(4) The notes to the accounts must disclose the amount of any unamortized premium or discount not extinguished which is included in the balance sheet by virtue of sub-paragraph (1).

(5) For the purposes of this paragraph "premium" means any excess of the amount paid for a security over its maturity value and "discount" means any deficit of the amount paid for a security over its maturity value.

Current assets

31. The amount to be included in respect of loans and advances, debt or other fixed-income securities and equity shares or other variable yield securities not held as financial fixed assets must be their cost, subject to paragraphs 32 and 33.

32. (1) If the net realisable value of any asset referred to in paragraph 31 is lower than its cost, the amount to be included in respect of that asset is the net realisable value.

(2) Where the reasons for which any provision for diminution in value was made in accordance with sub-paragraph (1) have ceased to apply to any extent, that provision must be written back to the extent that it is no longer necessary.

33. (1) Subject to paragraph 32, the amount to be included in the balance sheet in respect of transferable securities not held as financial fixed assets may be the higher of their cost or their market value at the balance sheet date.

(2) The difference between the cost of any securities included in the balance sheet at a valuation under sub-paragraph (1) and their market value must be shown (in aggregate) in the notes to the accounts.

Miscellaneous and supplementary provisions

Excess of money owed over value received as an asset item

34. (1) Where the amount repayable on any debt owed by a company is greater than the value of the consideration received in the transaction giving rise to the debt, the amount of the difference may be treated as an asset.

(2) Where any such amount is so treated—

(a) it must be written off by reasonable amounts each year and must be completely written off before repayment of the debt, and

(b) if the current amount is not shown as a separate item in the company's balance sheet, it must be disclosed in a note to the accounts.

Determination of cost

35. (1) The cost of an asset that has been acquired by the company is to be determined by adding to the actual price paid any expenses incidental to its acquisition [and then subtracting any incidental reductions in the cost of acquisition].

(2) The cost of an asset constructed by the company is to be determined by adding to the purchase price of the raw materials and consumables used the amount of the costs incurred by the company which are directly attributable to the construction of that asset.

(3) In addition, there may be included in the cost of an asset constructed by the company—

(a) a reasonable proportion of the costs incurred by the company which are only indirectly attributable to the construction of that asset, but only to the extent that they relate to the period of construction, and

(b) interest on capital borrowed to finance the construction of that asset, to the extent that it accrues in respect of the period of construction,

provided, however, in a case within paragraph (b), that the inclusion of the interest in determining the cost of that asset and the amount of the interest so included is disclosed in a note to the accounts.

36. (1) The cost of any assets which are fungible assets (including investments), may be determined by the application of any of the methods mentioned in sub-paragraph (2) in relation to any such assets of the same class, provided that the method chosen is one which appears to the directors to be appropriate in the circumstances of the company.

(2) Those methods are—

(a) the method known as "first in, first out" (FIFO),

(b) the method known as "last in, first out" (LIFO),

(c) a weighted average price, and

(d) any other method [reflecting generally accepted best practice].

(3) Where in the case of any company—

(a) the cost of assets falling to be included under any item shown in the company's balance sheet has been determined by the application of any method permitted by this paragraph, and

(b) the amount shown in respect of that item differs materially from the relevant alternative amount given below in this paragraph,

the amount of that difference must be disclosed in a note to the accounts.

(4) Subject to sub-paragraph (5), for the purposes of sub-paragraph (3)(b), the relevant alternative amount, in relation to any item shown in a company's balance sheet, is the amount which would have been shown in respect of that item if assets of any class included under that item at an amount determined by any method permitted by this paragraph had instead been included at their replacement cost as at the balance sheet date.

(5) The relevant alternative amount may be determined by reference to the most recent actual purchase price before the balance sheet date of assets of any class included under the item in question instead of by reference to their replacement cost as at that date, but only if the former appears to the directors of the company to constitute the more appropriate standard of comparison in the case of assets of that class.

Substitution of original stated amount where price or cost unknown

37. (1) This paragraph applies where—

(a) there is no record of the purchase price of any asset acquired by a company or of any price, expenses or costs relevant for determining its cost in accordance with paragraph 35, or

(b) any such record cannot be obtained without unreasonable expense or delay.

(2) In such a case, its cost is to be taken, for the purposes of paragraphs 23 to 33, to be the value ascribed to it in the earliest available record of its value made on or after its acquisition by the company.

SECTION C ALTERNATIVE ACCOUNTING RULES

Preliminary

38. (1) The rules set out in Section B are referred to below in this Schedule as the historical cost accounting rules.

(2) Paragraphs 23 to 26 and 30 to 34 are referred to below in this Section as the depreciation rules; and references below in this Schedule to the historical cost accounting rules do not include the depreciation rules as they apply by virtue of paragraph 41.

39. Subject to paragraphs 41 to 43, the amounts to be included in respect of assets of any description mentioned in paragraph 40 may be determined on any basis so mentioned.

Alternative accounting rules

40. (1) Intangible fixed assets, other than goodwill, may be included at their current cost.

(2) Tangible fixed assets may be included at a market value determined as at the date of their last valuation or at their current cost.

(3) Investments of any description falling to be included under assets items 7 (participating interests) or 8 (shares in group undertakings) of the balance sheet format and any other securities held as financial fixed assets may be included either—

(a) at a market value determined as at the date of their last valuation, or

(b) at a value determined on any basis which appears to the directors to be appropriate in the circumstances of the company.

But in the latter case particulars of the method of valuation adopted and of the reasons for adopting it must be disclosed in a note to the accounts.

(4) . . .

Application of the depreciation rules

41. (1) Where the value of any asset of a company is determined in accordance with paragraph 40, that value must be, or (as the case may require) be the starting point for determining, the amount to be included in respect of that asset in the company's accounts, instead of its cost or any value previously so determined for that asset.

The depreciation rules apply accordingly in relation to any such asset with the substitution for any reference to its cost of a reference to the value most recently determined for that asset in accordance with paragraph 40.

(2) The amount of any provision for depreciation required in the case of any fixed asset by paragraphs 24 to 26 as they apply by virtue of sub-paragraph (1) is referred to below in this paragraph as the adjusted amount, and the amount of any provision which would be required by any of those paragraphs in the case of that asset according to the historical cost accounting rules is referred to as the historical cost amount.

(3) Where sub-paragraph (1) applies in the case of any fixed asset the amount of any provision for depreciation in respect of that asset included in any item shown in the profit and loss account in respect of amounts written off assets of the description in question may be the historical cost amount instead of the adjusted amount, provided that the amount of any difference between the two is shown separately in the profit and loss account or in a note to the accounts.

Additional information to be provided in case of departure from historical cost accounting rules

42. (1) This paragraph applies where the amounts to be included in respect of assets covered by any items shown in a company's accounts have been determined in accordance with paragraph 40.

(2) The items affected and the basis of valuation adopted in determining the amounts of the assets in question in the case of each such item must be disclosed in a note to the accounts.

[(3) In the case of each balance sheet item affected, the comparable amounts determined according to the historical cost accounting rules must be shown in a note to the accounts.]

(4) In sub-paragraph (3), references in relation to any item to the comparable amounts determined as there mentioned are references to—

(a) the aggregate amount which would be required to be shown in respect of that item if the amounts to be included in respect of all the assets covered by that item were determined according to the historical cost accounting rules, and

(b) the aggregate amount of the cumulative provisions for depreciation or diminution in value which would be permitted or required in determining those amounts according to those rules.

Revaluation reserve

43. (1) With respect to any determination of the value of an asset of a company in accordance with paragraph 40, the amount of any profit or loss arising from that determination (after allowing, where appropriate, for any provisions for depreciation or diminution in value made otherwise than by reference to the value so determined and any adjustments of any such provisions made in the light of that determination) must be credited or (as the case may be) debited to a separate reserve ("the revaluation reserve").

(2) The amount of the revaluation reserve must be shown in the company's balance sheet under liabilities item 11 in the balance sheet format, . . .

(3) An amount may be transferred—

(a) from the revaluation reserve—

(i) to the profit and loss account, if the amount was previously charged to that account or represents realised profit, or

(ii) on capitalisation,

(b) to or from the revaluation reserve in respect of the taxation relating to any profit or loss credited or debited to the reserve.

The revaluation reserve must be reduced to the extent that the amounts transferred to it are no longer necessary for the purposes of the valuation method used.

(4) In sub-paragraph (3)(a)(ii) "capitalisation", in relation to an amount standing to the credit of the revaluation reserve, means applying it in wholly or partly paying up unissued shares in the company to be allotted to members of the company as fully or partly paid shares.

(5) The revaluation reserve must not be reduced except as mentioned in this paragraph.

(6) The treatment for taxation purposes of amounts credited or debited to the revaluation reserve must be disclosed in a note to the accounts.

SECTION D FAIR VALUE ACCOUNTING

Inclusion of financial instruments at fair value

44. (1) Subject to sub-paragraphs (2) to (5), financial instruments (including derivatives) may be included at fair value.

(2) Sub-paragraph (1) does not apply to financial instruments that constitute liabilities unless—

(a) they are held as part of a trading portfolio,

(b) they are derivatives, or

(c) they are financial instruments falling within sub-paragraph (4).

(3) Unless they are financial instruments falling within sub-paragraph (4), sub-paragraph (1) does not apply to—

(a) financial instruments (other than derivatives) held to maturity,

(b) loans and receivables originated by the company and not held for trading purposes,

(c) interests in subsidiary undertakings, associated undertakings and joint ventures,

(d) equity instruments issued by the company,

(e) contracts for contingent consideration in a business combination, or

(f) other financial instruments with such special characteristics that the instruments, according to generally accepted accounting principles or practice, should be accounted for differently from other financial instruments.

[(4) Financial instruments which under [UK-adopted international accounting standards] may be included in accounts at fair value, may be so included, provided that the disclosures required by such accounting standards are made.]

(5) If the fair value of a financial instrument cannot be determined reliably in accordance with paragraph 45, sub-paragraph (1) does not apply to that financial instrument.

(6) In this paragraph—

"associated undertaking" has the meaning given by paragraph 19 of Schedule 6 to these Regulations;

"joint venture" has the meaning given by paragraph 18 of that Schedule.

Determination of fair value

45. (1) The fair value of a financial instrument is its value determined in accordance with this paragraph.

(2) If a reliable market can readily be identified for the financial instrument, its fair value is determined by reference to its market value.

(3) If a reliable market cannot readily be identified for the financial instrument but can be identified for its components or for a similar instrument, its fair value is determined by reference to the market value of its components or of the similar instrument.

(4) If neither sub-paragraph (2) nor (3) applies, the fair value of the financial instrument is a value resulting from generally accepted valuation models and techniques.

(5) Any valuation models and techniques used for the purposes of sub-paragraph (4) must ensure a reasonable approximation of the market value.

Hedged items

46. A company may include any assets and liabilities, or identified portions of such assets or liabilities, that qualify as hedged items under a fair value hedge accounting system at the amount required under that system.

[Other assets that may be included at fair value

47. (1) This paragraph applies to—

(a) investment property, and

(b) living animals and plants.

(2) Such investment property and living animals and plants may be included at fair value, provided that, as the case may be, all such investment property or living animals and plants are so included where their fair value can be reliably determined.

(3) In this paragraph, "fair value" means fair value determined in accordance with generally accepted accounting principles or practice.]

Accounting for changes in value

48. (1) This paragraph applies where a financial instrument is valued in accordance with paragraph 44 or 46 or an asset is valued in accordance with paragraph 47.

(2) Notwithstanding paragraph 19 in this Part of this Schedule, and subject to sub-paragraphs (3) and (4), a change in the value of the financial instrument or of the investment property or living animal or plant must be included in the profit and loss account.

(3) Where—

(a) the financial instrument accounted for is a hedging instrument under a hedge accounting system that allows some or all of the change in value not to be shown in the profit and loss account, or

(b) the change in value relates to an exchange difference arising on a monetary item that forms part of a company's net investment in a foreign entity,

the amount of the change in value must be credited to or (as the case may be) debited from a separate reserve ("the fair value reserve").

(4) Where the instrument accounted for—

(a) is an available for sale financial asset, and

(b) is not a derivative,

the change in value may be credited to or (as the case may be) debited from the fair value reserve.

The fair value reserve

49. (1) The fair value reserve must be adjusted to the extent that the amounts shown in it are no longer necessary for the purposes of paragraph 48(3) or (4).

(2) The treatment for taxation purposes of amounts credited or debited to the fair value reserve must be disclosed in a note to the accounts.

Assets and liabilities denominated in foreign currencies

50. (1) Subject to the following sub-paragraphs, amounts to be included in respect of assets and liabilities denominated in foreign currencies must be in sterling (or the currency in which the accounts are drawn up) after translation at an appropriate spot rate of exchange prevailing at the balance sheet date.

(2) An appropriate rate of exchange prevailing on the date of purchase may however be used for assets held as financial fixed assets and assets to be included under assets items 9 (intangible fixed assets) and 10 (tangible fixed assets) in the balance sheet format, if they are not covered or not specifically covered in either the spot or forward currency markets.

(3) An appropriate spot rate of exchange prevailing at the balance sheet date must be used for translating uncompleted spot exchange transactions.

(4) An appropriate forward rate of exchange prevailing at the balance sheet date must be used for translating uncompleted forward exchange transactions.

(5) This paragraph does not apply to any assets or liabilities held, or any transactions entered into, for hedging purposes or to any assets or liabilities which are themselves hedged.

51. (1) Subject to sub-paragraph (2), any difference between the amount to be included in respect of an asset or liability under paragraph 50 and the book value, after translation into sterling (or the currency in which the accounts are drawn up) at an appropriate rate, of that asset or liability must be credited or, as the case may be, debited to the profit and loss account.

(2) In the case, however, of assets held as financial fixed assets, of assets to be included under assets items 9 (intangible fixed assets) and 10 (tangible fixed assets) in the balance sheet format and of transactions undertaken to cover such assets, any such difference may be deducted from or credited to any non-distributable reserve available for the purpose.

NOTES

Section A

All amendments to Section A were made by the Companies, Partnerships and Groups (Accounts and Reports) Regulations 2015, SI 2015/980, reg 32(1), (2), as from 6 April 2015, in relation to (a) financial years beginning on or after 1 January 2016, and (b) a financial year of a company beginning on or after 1 January 2015, but before 1 January 2016, if the directors of the company so decide (see **[4.549]** *post*).

Section B

Para 26(1A) was inserted by the Companies, Partnerships and Groups (Accounts and Reports) (No 2) Regulations 2015, SI 2015/1672, reg 4(3), (4), as from 1 October 2015, in relation to (a) financial years beginning on or after 1 January 2016, and (b) a financial year of a company beginning on or after 1 January 2015 but before 1 January 2016, if the directors of the company have decided, pursuant to reg 2(2)(b) of the Companies, Partnerships and Groups (Accounts and Reports) Regulations 2015, that the amendments made by those Regulations have effect in relation to that financial year.

All other amendments to Section B were made by SI 2015/980, reg 32(1), (3) (as to the application of these amendments see the first note above).

Section C

All amendments to Section C were made by SI 2015/980, reg 32(1), (4) (as to the application of these amendments see the first note above).

Section D

Para 44: sub-para (4) substituted by SI 2015/980, reg 32(1), (5)(a) (as to the application of this amendment see the first note above). Words in square brackets in sub-para (4) substituted by the International Accounting Standards and European Public Limited-Liability Company (Amendment etc) (EU Exit) Regulations 2019, SI 2019/685, reg 19, Sch 1, Pt 2, para 57(1), (3)(a), in relation to accounts for financial years beginning on or after IP completion day (as defined in the European Union (Withdrawal Agreement) Act 2020, s 39) (note also that in relation to accounts for financial years which begin before but end on or after IP completion day, the enactments amended by Parts 1–3 of Sch 1 to the 2019 Regulations have effect as if the UK were a member State until the end of the financial year in question).

Para 47: substituted by SI 2015/980, reg 32(1), (5)(b) (as to the application of this amendment see the first note above).

PART 3 NOTES TO THE ACCOUNTS

[Preliminary

[4.80]

52. (1) Any information required in the case of a company by the following provisions of this Part of this Schedule must be given by way of a note to the accounts.

(2) These notes must be presented in the order in which, where relevant, the items to which they relate are presented in the balance sheet and in the profit and loss account.]

General

Disclosure of accounting policies

53. The accounting policies adopted by the company in determining the amounts to be included in respect of items shown in the balance sheet and in determining the profit or loss of the company must be stated (including such policies with respect to the depreciation and diminution in value of assets).

54. It must be stated whether the accounts have been prepared in accordance with applicable accounting standards and particulars of any material departure from those standards and the reasons for it must be given.

Sums denominated in foreign currencies

55. Where any sums originally denominated in foreign currencies have been brought into account under any items shown in the balance sheet format or profit and loss account formats, the basis on which those sums have been translated into sterling (or the currency in which the accounts are drawn up) must be stated.

Reserves and dividends

56. There must be stated—

(a) any amount set aside or proposed to be set aside to, or withdrawn or proposed to be withdrawn from, reserves,
(b) the aggregate amount of dividends paid in the financial year (other than those for which a liability existed at the immediately preceding balance sheet date),
(c) the aggregate amount of dividends that the company is liable to pay at the balance sheet date, and
(d) the aggregate amount of dividends that are proposed before the date of approval of the accounts, and not otherwise disclosed under sub-paragraph (b) or (c).

Information supplementing the balance sheet

57. Paragraphs 58 to 84 require information which either supplements the information given with respect to any particular items shown in the balance sheet or is otherwise relevant to assessing the company's state of affairs in the light of the information so given.

Share capital and debentures

58. (1) Where shares of more than one class have been allotted, the number and aggregate nominal value of shares of each class allotted must be given.

(2) In the case of any part of the allotted share capital that consists of redeemable shares, the following information must be given—

(a) the earliest and latest dates on which the company has power to redeem those shares,
(b) whether those shares must be redeemed in any event or are liable to be redeemed at the option of the company or of the shareholder, and
(c) whether any (and, if so, what) premium is payable on redemption.

59. If the company has allotted any shares during the financial year, the following information must be given—

(a) the classes of shares allotted, and
(b) as respects each class of shares, the number allotted, their aggregate nominal value and the consideration received by the company for the allotment.

60. (1) With respect to any contingent right to the allotment of shares in the company the following particulars must be given—

(a) the number, description and amount of the shares in relation to which the right is exercisable,
(b) the period during which it is exercisable, and
(c) the price to be paid for the shares allotted.

(2) In sub-paragraph (1) "contingent right to the allotment of shares" means any option to subscribe for shares and any other right to require the allotment of shares to any person whether arising on the conversion into shares of securities of any other description or otherwise.

61. (1) If the company has issued any debentures during the financial year to which the accounts relate, the following information must be given—

(a) the classes of debentures issued, and

(b) as respects each class of debentures, the amount issued and the consideration received by the company for the issue.

(2) Where any of the company's debentures are held by a nominee of or trustee for the company, the nominal amount of the debentures and the amount at which they are stated in the accounting records kept by the company in accordance with section 386 of the 2006 Act (duty to keep accounting records) must be stated.

Fixed assets

62. (1) In respect of any fixed assets of the company included in any assets item in the company's balance sheet the following information must be given by reference to each such item—

(a) the appropriate amounts in respect of those assets included in the item as at the date of the beginning of the financial year and as at the balance sheet date respectively,

(b) the effect on any amount shown included in the item in respect of those assets of—

(i) any determination during that year of the value to be ascribed to any of those assets in accordance with paragraph 40,

(ii) acquisitions during that year of any fixed assets,

(iii) disposals during that year of any fixed assets, and

(iv) any transfers of fixed assets of the company to and from that item during that year.

(2) The reference in sub-paragraph (1)(a) to the appropriate amounts in respect of any fixed assets (included in an assets item) as at any date there mentioned is a reference to amounts representing the aggregate amounts determined, as at that date, in respect of fixed assets falling to be included under the item on either of the following bases—

(a) on the basis of cost (determined in accordance with paragraphs 35 and 36), or

(b) on any basis permitted by paragraph 40,

(leaving out of account in either case any provisions for depreciation or diminution in value).

(3) In addition, in respect of any fixed assets of the company included in any assets item in the company's balance sheet, there must be stated (by reference to each such item)—

(a) the cumulative amount of provisions for depreciation or diminution in value of those assets included under that item as at each date mentioned in sub-paragraph (1)(a),

(b) the amount of any such provisions made in respect of the financial year,

(c) the amount of any adjustments made in respect of any such provisions during that year in consequence of the disposal of any of those assets, and

(d) the amount of any other adjustments made in respect of any such provisions during that year.

(4) The requirements of this paragraph need not be complied with to the extent that a company takes advantage of the option of setting off charges and income afforded by paragraph 8(3) in Part 1 of this Schedule.

63. Where any fixed assets of the company (other than listed investments) are included under any item shown in the company's balance sheet at an amount determined in accordance with paragraph 40, the following information must be given—

(a) the years (so far as they are known to the directors) in which the assets were severally valued and the several values, and

(b) in the case of assets that have been valued during the financial year, the names of the persons who valued them or particulars of their qualifications for doing so and (whichever is stated) the bases of valuation used by them.

64. In relation to any amount which is included under assets item 10 in the balance sheet format (tangible fixed assets) with respect to land and buildings there must be stated—

(a) how much of that amount is ascribable to land of freehold tenure and how much to land of leasehold tenure, and

(b) how much of the amount ascribable to land of leasehold tenure is ascribable to land held on long lease and how much to land held on short lease.

65. There must be disclosed separately the amount of—

(a) any participating interests, and

(b) any shares in group undertakings that are held in credit institutions.

[Information about fair value of assets and liabilities

66. (1) This paragraph applies where financial instruments or other assets have been valued in accordance with, as appropriate, paragraph 44, 46 or 47.

(2) There must be stated—

(a) the significant assumptions underlying the valuation models and techniques used to determine the fair value of the financial instruments or other assets,

(b) for each category of financial instrument or other asset, the fair value of the assets in that category and the changes in value—

(i) included directly in the profit and loss account, or

(ii) credited to or (as the case may be) debited from the fair value reserve,

in respect of those assets, and

(c) for each class of derivatives, the extent and nature of the instruments, including significant terms and conditions that may affect the amount, timing and certainty of future cash flows.

(3) Where any amount is transferred to or from the fair value reserve during the financial year, there must be stated in tabular form—

(a) the amount of the reserve as at the date of the beginning of the financial year and as at the balance sheet date respectively,

(b) the amount transferred to or from the reserve during the year, and

(c) the source and application respectively of the amounts so transferred.]

67. Where the company has derivatives that it has not included at fair value, there must be stated for each class of such derivatives—

(a) the fair value of the derivatives in that class, if such a value can be determined in accordance with paragraph 45, and

(b) the extent and nature of the derivatives.

68. (1) This paragraph applies if—

(a) the company has financial fixed assets that could be included at fair value by virtue of paragraph 44,

(b) the amount at which those items are included under any item in the company's accounts is in excess of their fair value, and

(c) the company has not made provision for diminution in value of those assets in accordance with paragraph 25(1) in Part 2 of this Schedule.

(2) There must be stated—

(a) the amount at which either the individual assets or appropriate groupings of those individual assets are included in the company's accounts,

(b) the fair value of those assets or groupings, and

(c) the reasons for not making a provision for diminution in value of those assets, including the nature of the evidence that provides the basis for the belief that the amount at which they are stated in the accounts will be recovered.

Information where investment property and living animals and plants included at fair value

69. (1) This paragraph applies where the amounts to be included in a company's accounts in respect of investment property or living animals and plants have been determined in accordance with paragraph 47.

(2) The balance sheet items affected and the basis of valuation adopted in determining the amounts of the assets in question in the case of each such item must be disclosed in a note to the accounts.

(3) In the case of investment property, for each balance sheet item affected there must be shown, either separately in the balance sheet or in a note to the accounts—

(a) the comparable amounts determined according to the historical cost accounting rules, or

(b) the differences between those amounts and the corresponding amounts actually shown in the balance sheet in respect of that item.

(4) In sub-paragraph (3), references in relation to any item to the comparable amounts determined in accordance with that sub-paragraph are to—

(a) the aggregate amount which would be required to be shown in respect of that item if the amounts to be included in respect of all the assets covered by that item were determined according to the historical cost accounting rules, and

(b) the aggregate amount of the cumulative provisions for depreciation or diminution in value which would be permitted or required in determining those amounts according to those rules.

Reserves and provisions

70. (1) This paragraph applies where any amount is transferred—

(a) to or from any reserves, or

(b) to any provision for liabilities, or

(c) from any provision for liabilities otherwise than for the purpose for which the provision was established,

and the reserves or provisions are or would but for paragraph 5(1) in Part 1 of this Schedule be shown as separate items in the company's balance sheet.

(2) The following information must be given in respect of the aggregate of reserves or provisions included in the same item [in tabular form]—

(a) the amount of the reserves or provisions as at the date of the beginning of the financial year and as at the balance sheet date respectively,

(b) any amounts transferred to or from the reserves or provisions during that year, and

(c) the source and application respectively of any amounts so transferred.

(3) Particulars must be given of each provision included in liabilities item 6.(c) (other provisions) in the company's balance sheet in any case where the amount of that provision is material.

Provision for taxation

71. The amount of any provision for deferred taxation must be stated separately from the amount of any provision for other taxation.

Maturity analysis

72. (1) A company must disclose separately for each of assets items 3.(b) and 4 and liabilities items 1.(b), 2.(b) and 3.(b) the aggregate amount of the loans and advances and liabilities included in those items broken down into the following categories—

(a) those repayable in not more than three months,

(b) those repayable in more than three months but not more than one year,

(c) those repayable in more than one year but not more than five years,

(d) those repayable in more than five years,

from the balance sheet date.

(2) A company must also disclose the aggregate amounts of all loans and advances falling within assets item 4 (loans and advances to customers) which are—

(a) repayable on demand, or

(b) are for an indeterminate period, being repayable upon short notice.

(3) For the purposes of sub-paragraph (1), where a loan or advance or liability is repayable by instalments, each such instalment is to be treated as a separate loan or advance or liability.

Debt and other fixed-income securities

73. A company must disclose the amount of debt and fixed-income securities included in assets item 5 (debt securities [and other fixed-income securities]) and the amount of such securities included in liabilities item 3.(a) (bonds and medium term notes) that (in each case) will become due within one year of the balance sheet date.

Subordinated liabilities

74. (1) The following information must be disclosed in relation to any borrowing included in liabilities item 7 (subordinated liabilities) that exceeds 10% of the total for that item—

(a) its amount,
(b) the currency in which it is denominated,
(c) the rate of interest and the maturity date (or the fact that it is perpetual),
(d) the circumstances in which early repayment may be demanded,
(e) the terms of the subordination, and
(f) the existence of any provisions whereby it may be converted into capital or some other form of liability and the terms of any such provisions.

(2) The general terms of any other borrowings included in liabilities item 7 must also be stated.

Fixed cumulative dividends

75. If any fixed cumulative dividends on the company's shares are in arrear, there must be stated—

(a) the amount of the arrears, and
(b) the period for which the dividends or, if there is more than one class, each class of them are in arrear.

Details of assets charged

76. (1) There must be disclosed, in relation to each liabilities and memorandum item of the balance sheet format—

(a) the aggregate amount of any assets of the company which have been charged to secure any liability or potential liability included under that item,
(b) the aggregate amount of the liabilities or potential liabilities so secured, and
(c) an indication of the nature of the security given.

(2) Particulars must also be given of any other charge on the assets of the company to secure the liabilities of any other person, including, where practicable, the amount secured.

[Guarantees and other financial commitments

77. (1) Particulars and the total amount of any financial commitments, guarantees and contingencies that are not included in the balance sheet must be disclosed.

(2) An indication of the nature and form of any valuable security given by the company in respect of commitments, guarantees and contingencies within sub-paragraph (1) must be given.

(3) The total amount of any commitments within sub-paragraph (1) concerning pensions must be separately disclosed.

(4) Particulars must be given of pension commitments which are included in the balance sheet.

(5) Where any commitment within sub-paragraph (3) or (4) relates wholly or partly to pensions payable to past directors of the company separate particulars must be given of that commitment.

(6) The total amount of any commitments, guarantees and contingencies within sub-paragraph (1) which are undertaken on behalf of or for the benefit of—

(a) any parent undertaking or fellow subsidiary undertaking of the company,
(b) any subsidiary undertaking of the company, or
(c) any undertaking in which the company has a participating interest

must be separately stated and those within each of paragraphs (a), (b) and (c) must also be stated separately from those within any other of those paragraphs.

(7) There must be disclosed the nature and amount of any contingent liabilities and commitments included in Memorandum items 1 and 2 which are material in relation to the company's activities.]

Memorandum items: Group undertakings

78. (1) With respect to contingent liabilities required to be included under Memorandum item 1 in the balance sheet format, there must be stated in a note to the accounts the amount of such contingent liabilities incurred on behalf of or for the benefit of—

(a) any parent undertaking or fellow subsidiary undertaking, or
(b) any subsidiary undertaking,

of the company; in addition the amount incurred in respect of the undertakings referred to in paragraph (a) must be stated separately from the amount incurred in respect in respect of the undertakings referred to in paragraph (b).

(2) With respect to commitments required to be included under Memorandum item 2 in the balance sheet format, there must be stated in a note to the accounts the amount of such commitments undertaken on behalf of or for the benefit of—

(a) any parent undertaking or fellow subsidiary undertaking, or
(b) any subsidiary undertaking,

of the company; in addition the amount incurred in respect of the undertakings referred to in paragraph (a) must be stated separately from the amount incurred in respect of the undertakings referred to in paragraph (b).

Transferable securities

79. (1) There must be disclosed for each of assets items 5 to 8 in the balance sheet format the amount of transferable securities included under those items that are listed and the amount of those that are unlisted.

(2) In the case of each amount shown in respect of listed securities under sub-paragraph (1), there must also be disclosed the aggregate market value of those securities, if different from the amount shown.

(3) There must also be disclosed for each of assets items 5 and 6 the amount of transferable securities included under those items that are held as financial fixed assets and the amount of those that are not so held, together with the criterion used by the directors to distinguish those held as financial fixed assets.

Leasing transactions

80. The aggregate amount of all property (other than land) leased by the company to other persons must be disclosed, broken down so as to show the aggregate amount included in each relevant balance sheet item.

Assets and liabilities denominated in a currency other than sterling (or the currency in which the accounts are drawn up)

81. (1) The aggregate amount, in sterling (or the currency in which the accounts are drawn up), of all assets denominated in a currency other than sterling (or the currency used) together with the aggregate amount, in sterling (or the currency used), of all liabilities so denominated, is to be disclosed.

(2) For the purposes of this paragraph an appropriate rate of exchange prevailing at the balance sheet date must be used to determine the amounts concerned.

Sundry assets and liabilities

82. Where any amount shown under either of the following items is material, particulars must be given of each type of asset or liability included in that item, including an explanation of the nature of the asset or liability and the amount included with respect to assets or liabilities of that type—

(a) assets item 13 (other assets),
(b) liabilities item 4 (other liabilities).

Unmatured forward transactions

83. (1) The following must be disclosed with respect to unmatured forward transactions outstanding at the balance sheet date—

(a) the categories of such transactions, by reference to an appropriate system of classification,
(b) whether, in the case of each such category, they have been made, to any material extent, for the purpose of hedging the effects of fluctuations in interest rates, exchange rates and market prices or whether they have been made, to any material extent, for dealing purposes.

(2) Transactions falling within sub-paragraph (1) must include all those in relation to which income or expenditure is to be included in—

(a) format 1, item 6 or format 2, items B4 or A3 (dealing [profits][losses]),
(b) format 1, items 1 or 2, or format 2, items B1 or A1, by virtue of notes (1)(b) and (2)(b) to the profit and loss account formats (forward contracts, spread over the actual duration of the contract and similar in nature to interest).

Miscellaneous matters

84. (1) Particulars must be given of any case where the cost of any asset is for the first time determined under paragraph 37 in Part 2 of this Schedule.

(2) Where any outstanding loans made under the authority of section 682(2)(b), (c) or (d) of the 2006 Act (various cases of financial assistance by a company for purchase of its own shares) are included under any item shown in the company's balance sheet, the aggregate amount of those loans must be disclosed for each item in question.

Information supplementing the profit and loss account

85. Paragraphs 86 to 91 require information which either supplements the information given with respect to any particular items shown in the profit and loss account or otherwise provides particulars of income or expenditure of the company or of circumstances affecting the items shown in the profit and loss account (see regulation 5(2) for exemption for companies falling within section 408 of the 2006 Act (individual profit and loss account where group accounts prepared)).

Particulars of tax

86. (1) Particulars must be given of any special circumstances which affect liability in respect of taxation of profits, income or capital gains for the financial year or liability in respect of taxation of profits, income or capital gains for succeeding financial years.

(2) The following amounts must be stated—

(a) the amount of the charge for United Kingdom corporation tax,
(b) if that amount would have been greater but for relief from double taxation, the amount which it would have been but for such relief,
(c) the amount of the charge for United Kingdom income tax, and
(d) the amount of the charge for taxation imposed outside the United Kingdom of profits, income and (so far as charged to revenue) capital gains.

These amounts must be stated separately in respect of each of the amounts which is shown under the following items in the profit and loss account, that is to say format 1 item 16, format 2 item A10 (tax on [profit][loss] on ordinary activities) and format 1 item 21, format 2 item A13 (tax on extraordinary [profit][loss]).

Particulars of income

87. (1) A company must disclose, with respect to income included in the following items in the profit and loss account formats, the amount of that income attributable to each of the geographical markets in which the company has operated during the financial year—

(a) format 1 item 1, format 2 item B1 (interest receivable),
(b) format 1 item 3, format 2 item B2 (dividend income),
(c) format 1 item 4, format 2 item B3 (fees and commissions receivable),
(d) format 1 item 6, format 2 item B4 (dealing profits), and

(e) format 1 item 7, format 2 item B7 (other operating income).

(2) In analysing for the purposes of this paragraph the source of any income, the directors must have regard to the manner in which the company's activities are organised.

(3) For the purposes of this paragraph, markets which do not differ substantially from each other shall be treated as one market.

(4) Where in the opinion of the directors the disclosure of any information required by this paragraph would be seriously prejudicial to the interests of the company, that information need not be disclosed, but the fact that any such information has not been disclosed must be stated.

Management and agency services

88. A company providing any management and agency services to customers must disclose that fact, if the scale of such services provided is material in the context of its business as a whole.

Subordinated liabilities

89. Any amounts charged to the profit and loss account representing charges incurred during the year with respect to subordinated liabilities must be disclosed.

Sundry income and charges

90. Where any amount to be included in any of the following items is material, particulars must be given of each individual component of the figure, including an explanation of their nature and amount—

(a) in format 1—

(i) items 7 and 10 (other operating income and charges),

(ii) items 18 and 19 (extraordinary income and charges);

(b) in format 2—

(i) items A6 and B7 (other operating charges and income),

(ii) items A12 and B10 (extraordinary charges and income).

Miscellaneous matters

91. (1) Where any amount relating to any preceding financial year is included in any item in the profit and loss account, the effect must be stated.

[(2) The amount, nature and effect of any individual items of income or expenditure which are of exceptional size or incidence must be stated.]

Related party transactions

92. (1) Particulars may be given of transactions which the company has entered into with related parties, and must be given if such transactions are material and have not been concluded under normal market conditions.

(2) The particulars of transactions required to be disclosed by sub-paragraph (1) must include—

(a) the amount of such transactions,

(b) the nature of the related party relationship, and

(c) other information about the transactions necessary for an understanding of the financial position of the company.

(3) Information about individual transactions may be aggregated according to their nature, except where separate information is necessary for an understanding of the effects of related party transactions on the financial position of the company.

(4) Particulars need not be given of transactions entered into between two or more members of a group, provided that any subsidiary undertaking which is a party to the transaction is wholly-owned by such a member.

(5) In this paragraph, "related party" has the same meaning as in [UK-adopted international accounting standards].

[Post balance sheet events

92A. The nature and financial effect of material events arising after the balance sheet date which are not reflected in the profit and loss account of balance sheet must be stated.

Appropriations

92B. Particulars must be given of the proposed appropriation of profit or treatment of loss or, where applicable, particulars of the actual appropriation of the profits or treatment of the losses.]

NOTES

Paras 52, 66, 77: substituted by the Companies, Partnerships and Groups (Accounts and Reports) Regulations 2015, SI 2015/980, reg 33(1)–(3), (5), as from 6 April 2015, in relation to (a) financial years beginning on or after 1 January 2016, and (b) a financial year of a company beginning on or after 1 January 2015, but before 1 January 2016, if the directors of the company so decide (see **[4.549]** *post*).

Para 72: words in square brackets in sub-para (2) inserted by SI 2015/980, reg 33(1), (4) (as to the application of this amendment see the first note relating to the 2015 Regulations above).

Para 91: sub-para (2) substituted by SI 2015/980, reg 33(1), (6) (as to the application of this amendment see the first note relating to the 2015 Regulations above).

Para 92: words in square brackets in sub-para (5) substituted by the International Accounting Standards and European Public Limited-Liability Company (Amendment etc) (EU Exit) Regulations 2019, SI 2019/685, reg 19, Sch 1, Pt 2, para 57(1), (3)(b), in relation to accounts for financial years beginning on or after IP completion day (as defined in the European Union (Withdrawal Agreement) Act 2020, s 39) (note also that in relation to accounts for financial years which begin before but end on or after IP completion day, the enactments amended by Parts 1–3 of Sch 1 to the 2019 Regulations have effect as if the UK were a member State until the end of the financial year in question).

Paras 92A, 92B: inserted by SI 2015/980, reg 33(1), (7) (as to the application of these amendments see the first note relating to the 2015 Regulations above).

PART 4 INTERPRETATION OF THIS SCHEDULE

Definitions for this Schedule

[4.81]
93. The following definitions apply for the purposes of this Schedule.

Financial fixed assets

94. "Financial fixed assets" means loans and advances and securities held as fixed assets; participating interests and shareholdings in group undertakings are to be regarded as financial fixed assets.

Financial instruments

95. For the purposes of this Schedule, references to "derivatives" include commodity-based contracts that give either contracting party the right to settle in cash or in some other financial instrument, except when such contracts—

(a) were entered into for the purpose of, and continue to meet, the company's expected purchase, sale or usage requirements,
(b) were designated for such purpose at their inception, and
(c) are expected to be settled by delivery of the commodity.

96. (1) The expressions listed in sub-paragraph (2) have the same meaning in paragraphs 44 to 49, 66 to 68 and 95 of this Schedule as they have in Council Directives [2013/34/EU on the annual financial statements etc of certain types of undertaking] and 86/635/EEC on the annual accounts and consolidated accounts of banks and other financial institutions.

(2) Those expressions are "available for sale financial asset", "business combination", "commodity-based contracts", "derivative", "equity instrument", "exchange difference", "fair value hedge accounting system", "financial fixed asset", "financial instrument", "foreign entity", "hedge accounting", "hedge accounting system", "hedged items", "hedging instrument", "held for trading purposes", "held to maturity", "monetary item", "receivables", "reliable market" and "trading portfolio".

Repayable on demand

97. "Repayable on demand", in connection with deposits, loans or advances, means that they can at any time be withdrawn or demanded without notice or that a maturity or period of notice of not more than 24 hours or one working day has been agreed for them.

Sale and repurchase transaction

98. (1) "Sale and repurchase transaction" means a transaction which involves the transfer by a credit institution or customer ("the transferor") to another credit institution or customer ("the transferee") of assets subject to an agreement that the same assets, or (in the case of fungible assets) equivalent assets, will subsequently be transferred back to the transferor at a specified price on a date specified or to be specified by the transferor.

(2) The following are not to be regarded as sale and repurchase transactions for the purposes of sub-paragraph (1)—

(a) forward exchange transactions,
(b) options,
(c) transactions involving the issue of debt securities with a commitment to repurchase all or part of the issue before maturity, or
(d) any similar transactions.

Sale and option to resell transaction

99. "Sale and option to resell transaction" means a transaction which involves the transfer by a credit institution or customer ("the transferor") to another credit institution or customer ("the transferee") of assets subject to an agreement that the transferee is entitled to require the subsequent transfer of the same assets, or (in the case of fungible assets) equivalent assets, back to the transferor at the purchase price or another price agreed in advance on a date specified or to be specified.

NOTES

Para 96: words in square brackets in sub-para (1) substituted by the Companies, Partnerships and Groups (Accounts and Reports) Regulations 2015, SI 2015/980, reg 33(8), as from 6 April 2015, in relation to (a) financial years beginning on or after 1 January 2016, and (b) a financial year of a company beginning on or after 1 January 2015, but before 1 January 2016, if the directors of the company so decide (see **[4.549]** *post*).

SCHEDULE 3
INSURANCE COMPANIES: COMPANIES ACT INDIVIDUAL ACCOUNTS

Regulation 6(1)

PART 1 GENERAL RULES AND FORMATS

SECTION A GENERAL RULES

[4.82]
1. (1) Subject to the following provisions of this Schedule—

(a) every balance sheet of a company must show the items listed in the balance sheet format in Section B of this Part, and
(b) every profit and loss account must show the items listed in the profit and loss account format in Section B.

(2) References in this Schedule to the items listed in any of the formats in Section B are to those items read together with any of the notes following the formats which apply to those items.

(3) The items must be shown in the order and under the headings and sub-headings given in the particular format, but—

(a) the notes to the formats may permit alternative positions for any particular items, and

(b) the heading or sub-heading for any item does not have to be distinguished by any letter or number assigned to that item in the format used.

2. (1) Any item required to be shown in a company's balance sheet or profit and loss account may be shown in greater detail than required by the particular format.

(2) The balance sheet or profit and loss account may include an item representing or covering the amount of any asset or liability, income or expenditure not specifically covered by any of the items listed in the formats set out in Section B, save that none of the following may be treated as assets in any balance sheet—

(a) preliminary expenses,
(b) expenses of, and commission on, any issue of shares or debentures, and
(c) costs of research.

3. (1) The directors may combine items to which Arabic numbers are given in the balance sheet format set out in Section B (except for items concerning technical provisions and the reinsurers' share of technical provisions), and items to which lower case letters in parentheses are given in the profit and loss account format so set out (except for items within items I.1 and 4 and II.1, 5 and 6) if—

(a) their individual amounts are not material for the purpose of giving a true and fair view, or
(b) the combination facilitates the assessment of the state of affairs or profit or loss of the company for the financial year in question.

(2) Where sub-paragraph (1)(b) applies—

(a) the individual amounts of any items which have been combined must be disclosed in a note to the accounts, and
(b) any notes required by this Schedule to the items so combined must, notwithstanding the combination, be given.

4. (1) Subject to sub-paragraph (2), the directors must not include a heading or sub-heading corresponding to an item in the balance sheet or profit and loss account format used if there is no amount to be shown for that item for the financial year to which the balance sheet or profit and loss account relates.

(2) Where an amount can be shown for the item in question for the immediately preceding financial year that amount must be shown under the heading or sub-heading required by the format for that item.

5. (1) For every item shown in the balance sheet or profit and loss account the corresponding amount for the immediately preceding financial year must also be shown.

(2) Where that corresponding amount is not comparable with the amount to be shown for the item in question in respect of the financial year to which the balance sheet or profit and loss account relates, the former amount may be adjusted, and particulars of the non-comparability and of any adjustment must be disclosed in a note to the accounts.

6. Subject to the provisions of this Schedule, amounts in respect of items representing assets or income may not be set off against amounts in respect of items representing liabilities or expenditure (as the case may be), or vice versa.

7. (1) The provisions of this Schedule which relate to long-term business apply, with necessary modifications, to business which consists of effecting or carrying out relevant contracts of general insurance which—

(a) is transacted exclusively or principally according to the technical principles of long-term business, and
(b) is a significant amount of the business of the company.

(2) For the purposes of paragraph (1), a contract of general insurance is a relevant contract if the risk insured against relates to—

(a) accident, or
(b) sickness.

(3) Sub-paragraph (2) must be read with—

(a) section 22 of the Financial Services and Markets Act 2000,
(b) the Financial Services and Markets Act 2000 (Regulated Activities) Order 2001, and
(c) Schedule 2 to that Act.

8. The company's directors must, in determining how amounts are presented within items in the profit and loss account and balance sheet, have regard to the substance of the reported transaction or arrangement, in accordance with generally accepted accounting principles or practice.

[8A. Where an asset or liability relates to more than one item in the balance sheet, the relationship of such asset or liability to the relevant items must be disclosed either under those items or in the notes to the accounts.]

SECTION B THE REQUIRED FORMATS

9. (1) Where in respect of any item to which an Arabic number is assigned in the balance sheet or profit and loss account format, the gross amount and reinsurance amount or reinsurers' share are required to be shown, a sub-total of those amounts must also be given.

(2) Where in respect of any item to which an Arabic number is assigned in the profit and loss account format, separate items are required to be shown, then a separate sub-total of those items must also be given in addition to any sub-total required by sub-paragraph (1).

10. (1) In the profit and loss account format set out below—

(a) the heading "Technical account—General business" is for business which consists of effecting or carrying out contracts of general business; and
(b) the heading "Technical account—Long-term business" is for business which consists of effecting or carrying out contracts of long-term insurance.

(2) In sub-paragraph (1), references to—

(a) contracts of general or long-term insurance, and
(b) the effecting or carrying out of such contracts,

must be read with section 22 of the Financial Services and Markets Act 2000, the Financial Services and Markets Act 2000 (Regulated Activities) Order 2001, and Schedule 2 to that Act.

Balance sheet format

ASSETS

A Called up share capital not paid (1)

B Intangible assets
- 1 Development costs
- 2 Concessions, patents, licences, trade marks and similar rights and assets (2)
- 3 Goodwill (3)
- 4 Payments on account

C Investments
- I Land and buildings (4)
- II Investments in group undertakings and participating interests
  - 1 Shares in group undertakings
  - 2 Debt securities issued by, and loans to, group undertakings
  - 3 Participating interests
  - 4 Debt securities issued by, and loans to, undertakings in which the company has a participating interest
- III Other financial investments
  - 1 Shares and other variable-yield securities and units in unit trusts
  - 2 Debt securities and other fixed-income securities (5)
  - 3 Participation in investment pools (6)
  - 4 Loans secured by mortgages (7)
  - 5 Other loans (7)
  - 6 Deposits with credit institutions (8)
  - 7 Other (9)
- IV Deposits with ceding undertakings (10)

D Assets held to cover linked liabilities (11)

Da Reinsurers' share of technical provisions (12)
- 1 Provision for unearned premiums
- 2 Long-term business provision
- 3 Claims outstanding
- 4 Provisions for bonuses and rebates
- 5 Other technical provisions
- 6 Technical provisions for unit-linked liabilities

E Debtors (13)
- I Debtors arising out of direct insurance operations
  - 1 Policyholders
  - 2 Intermediaries
- II Debtors arising out of reinsurance operations
- III Other debtors
- IV Called up share capital not paid (1)

F Other assets
- I Tangible assets
  - 1 Plant and machinery
  - 2 Fixtures, fittings, tools and equipment
  - 3 Payments on account (other than deposits paid on land and buildings) and assets (other than buildings) in course of construction
- II Stocks
  - 1 Raw materials and consumables
  - 2 Work in progress
  - 3 Finished goods and goods for resale
  - 4 Payments on account
- III Cash at bank and in hand
- IV Own shares (14)
- V Other (15)

G Prepayments and accrued income
- I Accrued interest and rent (16)
- II Deferred acquisition costs (17)
- III Other prepayments and accrued income

LIABILITIES

A Capital and reserves
- I Called up share capital or equivalent funds
- II Share premium account
- III Revaluation reserve
- IV Reserves
  - 1 Capital redemption reserve
  - 2 Reserve for own shares

3 Reserves provided for by the articles of association

4 Other reserves

V Profit and loss account

B Subordinated liabilities [18]

Ba Fund for future appropriations [19]

C Technical provisions

1 Provision for unearned premiums [20]

(a) gross amount

(b) reinsurance amount [12]

2 Long-term business provision [20] [21] [26]

(a) gross amount

(b) reinsurance amount [12]

3 Claims outstanding [22]

(a) gross amount

(b) reinsurance amount [12]

4 Provision for bonuses and rebates [23]

(a) gross amount

(b) reinsurance amount [12]

5 Equalisation provision [24]

6 Other technical provisions [25]

(a) gross amount

(b) reinsurance amount [12]

D Technical provisions for linked liabilities [26]

(a) gross amount

(b) reinsurance amount [12]

E Provisions for other risks

I Provisions for pensions and similar obligations

2 Provisions for taxation

3 Other provisions

F Deposits received from reinsurers [27]

G Creditors [28]

I Creditors arising out of direct insurance operations

II Creditors arising out of reinsurance operations

III Debenture loans [29]

IV Amounts owed to credit institutions

V Other creditors including taxation and social security

H Accruals and deferred income

Notes on the balance sheet format

(1) Called up share capital not paid

(Assets items A and E.IV.)

This item may be shown in either of the positions given in the format.

(2) Concessions, patents, licences, trade marks and similar rights and assets

(Assets item B.2.)

Amounts in respect of assets are only to be included in a company's balance sheet under this item if either—

(a) the assets were acquired for valuable consideration and are not required to be shown under goodwill, or

(b) the assets in question were created by the company itself.

(3) Goodwill

(Assets item B.3.)

Amounts representing goodwill are only to be included to the extent that the goodwill was acquired for valuable consideration.

(4) Land and buildings

(Assets item CI.)

The amount of any land and buildings occupied by the company for its own activities must be shown separately in the notes to the accounts.

(5) Debt securities and other fixed-income securities

(Assets item CIII.2.)

This item is to comprise transferable debt securities and any other transferable fixed-income securities issued by credit institutions, other undertakings or public bodies, in so far as they are not covered by assets item CII.2 or CII.4.

Securities bearing interest rates that vary in accordance with specific factors, for example the interest rate on the inter-bank market or on the Euromarket, are also to be regarded as debt securities and other fixed-income securities and so be included under this item.

(6) Participation in investment pools

(Assets item CIII.3.)

This item is to comprise shares held by the company in joint investments constituted by several undertakings or pension funds, the management of which has been entrusted to one of those undertakings or to one of those pension funds.

(7) Loans secured by mortgages and other loans

(Assets items CIII.4 and CIII.5.)

Loans to policyholders for which the policy is the main security are to be included under "Other loans" and their amount must be disclosed in the notes to the accounts. Loans secured by mortgage are to be shown as such even where they are also secured by insurance policies. Where the amount of "Other loans" not secured by policies is material, an appropriate breakdown must be given in the notes to the accounts.

(8) Deposits with credit institutions

(Assets item CIII.6.)

This item is to comprise sums the withdrawal of which is subject to a time restriction. Sums deposited with no such restriction must be shown under assets item F.III even if they bear interest.

(9) Other

(Assets item CIII.7.)

This item is to comprise those investments which are not covered by assets items CIII.1 to 6. Where the amount of such investments is significant, they must be disclosed in the notes to the accounts.

(10) Deposits with ceding undertakings

(Assets item CIV.)

Where the company accepts reinsurance this item is to comprise amounts, owed by the ceding undertakings and corresponding to guarantees, which are deposited with those ceding undertakings or with third parties or which are retained by those undertakings.

These amounts may not be combined with other amounts owed by the ceding insurer to the reinsurer or set off against amounts owed by the reinsurer to the ceding insurer.

Securities deposited with ceding undertakings or third parties which remain the property of the company must be entered in the company's accounts as an investment, under the appropriate item.

(11) Assets held to cover linked liabilities

(Assets item D)

In respect of long-term business, this item is to comprise investments made pursuant to long- term policies under which the benefits payable to the policyholder are wholly or partly to be determined by reference to the value of, or the income from, property of any description (whether or not specified in the contract) or by reference to fluctuations in, or in an index of, the value of property of any description (whether or not so specified).

This item is also to comprise investments which are held on behalf of the members of a tontine and are intended for distribution among them.

(12) Reinsurance amounts

(Assets item Da: liabilities items C1.(b), 2.(b), 3.(b), 4.(b) and 6.(b) and D.(b).)

The reinsurance amounts may be shown either under assets item Da or under liabilities items C1.(b), 2.(b), 3.(b), 4.(b) and 6.(b) and D.(b).

The reinsurance amounts are to comprise the actual or estimated amounts which, under contractual reinsurance arrangements, are deducted from the gross amounts of technical provisions.

As regards the provision for unearned premiums, the reinsurance amounts must be calculated according to the methods referred to in paragraph 50 below or in accordance with the terms of the reinsurance policy.

(13) Debtors

(Assets item E.)

Amounts owed by group undertakings and undertakings in which the company has a participating interest must be shown separately as sub-items of assets items E.I, II and III.

(14) Own shares

(Assets item F.IV.)

The nominal value of the shares must be shown separately under this item.

(15) Other

(Assets item F.V.)

This item is to comprise those assets which are not covered by assets items F.I to IV. Where such assets are material they must be disclosed in the notes to the accounts.

(16) Accrued interest and rent

(Assets item G.I.)

This item is to comprise those items that represent interest and rent that have been earned up to the balance-sheet date but have not yet become receivable.

(17) Deferred acquisition costs

(Assets item G.II.)

This item is to comprise the costs of acquiring insurance policies which are incurred during a financial year but relate to a subsequent financial year ("deferred acquisition costs"), except in so far as—

(a) allowance has been made in the computation of the long-term business provision made under paragraph 52 below and shown under liabilities item C2 or D in the balance sheet, for—
   (i) the explicit recognition of such costs, or
   (ii) the implicit recognition of such costs by virtue of the anticipation of future income from which such costs may prudently be expected to be recovered, or

(b) allowance has been made for such costs in respect of general business policies by a deduction from the provision for unearned premiums made under paragraph 50 below and shown under liabilities item CI in the balance sheet.

Deferred acquisition costs arising in general business must be distinguished from those arising in long-term business.

In the case of general business, the amount of any deferred acquisition costs must be established on a basis compatible with that used for unearned premiums.

There must be disclosed in the notes to the accounts—

(c) how the deferral of acquisition costs has been treated (unless otherwise expressly stated in the accounts), and

(d) where such costs are included as a deduction from the provisions at liabilities item CI, the amount of such deduction, or

(e) where the actuarial method used in the calculation of the provisions at liabilities item C2 or D has made allowance for the explicit recognition of such costs, the amount of the costs so recognised.

(18) Subordinated liabilities

(Liabilities item B.)

This item is to comprise all liabilities in respect of which there is a contractual obligation that, in the event of winding up or of bankruptcy, they are to be repaid only after the claims of all other creditors have been met (whether or not they are represented by certificates).

(19) Fund for future appropriations

(Liabilities item Ba.)

This item is to comprise all funds the allocation of which either to policyholders or to shareholders has not been determined by the end of the financial year.

Transfers to and from this item must be shown in item II.12a in the profit and loss account.

(20) Provision for unearned premiums

(Liabilities item C1.)

In the case of long-term business the provision for unearned premiums may be included in liabilities item C2 rather than in this item.

The provision for unearned premiums is to comprise the amount representing that part of gross premiums written which is estimated to be earned in the following financial year or to subsequent financial years.

(21) Long-term business provision

(Liabilities item C2.)

This item is to comprise the actuarially estimated value of the company's liabilities (excluding technical provisions included in liabilities item D), including bonuses already declared and after deducting the actuarial value of future premiums.

This item is also to comprise claims incurred but not reported, plus the estimated costs of settling such claims.

(22) Claims outstanding

(Liabilities item C3.)

This item is to comprise the total estimated ultimate cost to the company of settling all claims arising from events which have occurred up to the end of the financial year (including, in the case of general business, claims incurred but not reported) less amounts already paid in respect of such claims.

(23) Provision for bonuses and rebates

(Liabilities item C4.)

This item is to comprise amounts intended for policyholders or contract beneficiaries by way of bonuses and rebates as defined in Note *(5)* on the profit and loss account format to the extent that such amounts have not been credited to policyholders or contract beneficiaries or included in liabilities item Ba or in liabilities item C2.

(24) Equalisation provision

(Liabilities item C5.)

This item is to comprise the amount of any equalisation reserve maintained in respect of general business by the company, in accordance with the rules [made by the Financial Conduct Authority or the Prudential Regulation Authority] under Part 10 of the Financial Services and Markets Act 2000.

This item is also to comprise any amounts which, in accordance with Council Directive 87/343/EEC of 22nd June 1987, are required to be set aside by a company to equalise fluctuations in loss ratios in future years or to provide for special risks.

A company which otherwise constitutes reserves to equalise fluctuations in loss ratios in future years or to provide for special risks must disclose that fact in the notes to the accounts.

(25) Other technical provisions

(Liabilities item C6.)

This item is to comprise, inter alia, the provision for unexpired risks as defined in paragraph 91 below. Where the amount of the provision for unexpired risks is significant, it must be disclosed separately either in the balance sheet or in the notes to the accounts.

(26) Technical provisions for linked liabilities

(Liabilities item D.)

This item is to comprise technical provisions constituted to cover liabilities relating to investment in the context of long-term policies under which the benefits payable to policyholders are wholly or partly to be determined by reference to the value of, or the income from, property of any description (whether or not specified in the contract) or by reference to fluctuations in, or in an index of, the value of property of any description (whether or not so specified).

Any additional technical provisions constituted to cover death risks, operating expenses or other risks (such as benefits payable at the maturity date or guaranteed surrender values) must be included under liabilities item C2.

This item must also comprise technical provisions representing the obligations of a tontine's organiser in relation to its members.

(27) Deposits received from reinsurers

(Liabilities item F.)

Where the company cedes reinsurance, this item is to comprise amounts deposited by or withheld from other insurance undertakings under reinsurance contracts. These amounts may not be merged with other amounts owed to or by those other undertakings.

Where the company cedes reinsurance and has received as a deposit securities which have been transferred to its ownership, this item is to comprise the amount owed by the company by virtue of the deposit.

(28) Creditors

(Liabilities item G.)

Amounts owed to group undertakings and undertakings in which the company has a participating interest must be shown separately as sub-items.

(29) Debenture loans

(Liabilities item G.III.)

The amount of any convertible loans must be shown separately.

11 Additional items

(1) Every balance sheet of a company which carries on long-term business must show separately as an additional item the aggregate of any amounts included in liabilities item A (capital and reserves) which are required not to be treated as realised profits under section 843 of the 2006 Act.

(2) A company which carries on long-term business must show separately, in the balance sheet or in the notes to the accounts, the total amount of assets representing the long-term fund valued in accordance with the provisions of this Schedule.

12 Managed funds

(1) For the purposes of this paragraph "managed funds" are funds of a group pension fund—

(a) the management of which constitutes long-term insurance business, and

(b) which the company administers in its own name but on behalf of others, and

(c) to which it has legal title.

(2) The company must, in any case where assets and liabilities arising in respect of managed funds fall to be treated as assets and liabilities of the company, adopt the following accounting treatment: assets and liabilities representing managed funds are to be included in the company's balance sheet, with the notes to the accounts disclosing the total amount included with respect to such assets and liabilities in the balance sheet and showing the amount included under each relevant balance sheet item in respect of such assets or (as the case may be) liabilities.

13 Deferred acquisition costs

The costs of acquiring insurance policies which are incurred during a financial year but which relate to a subsequent financial year must be deferred in a manner specified in Note *(17)* on the balance sheet format.

Profit and loss account format

I Technical account—General business

1 Earned premiums, net of reinsurance

(a) gross premiums written (1)

(b) outward reinsurance premiums (2)

(c) change in the gross provision for unearned premiums

(d) change in the provision for unearned premiums, reinsurers' share

2 Allocated investment return transferred from the non-technical account (item III.6) (10)

2a Investment income (8) (10)

(a) income from participating interests, with a separate indication of that derived from group undertakings

(b) income from other investments, with a separate indication of that derived from group undertakings

(aa) income from land and buildings

(bb) income from other investments

(c) value re-adjustments on investments

(d) gains on the realisation of investments

3 Other technical income, net of reinsurance

4 Claims incurred, net of reinsurance (4)

(a) claims paid

(aa) gross amount

(bb) reinsurers' share

(b) change in the provision for claims

(aa) gross amount

(bb) reinsurers' share

5 Changes in other technical provisions, net of reinsurance, not shown under other headings

6 Bonuses and rebates, net of reinsurance (5)

7 Net operating expenses

(a) acquisition costs (6)

(b) change in deferred acquisition costs

(c) administrative expenses (7)

(d) reinsurance commissions and profit participation

8 Other technical charges, net of reinsurance

8a Investment expenses and charges (8)

(a) investment management expenses, including interest

(b) value adjustments on investments

(c) losses on the realisation of investments

9 Change in the equalisation provision
10 Sub-total (balance on the technical account for general business) (item III.1)

II Technical account—Long-term business
1 Earned premiums, net of reinsurance
(a) gross premiums written [(1)]
(b) outward reinsurance premiums [(2)]
(c) change in the provision for unearned premiums, net of reinsurance [(3)]
2 Investment income [(8) (10)]
(a) income from participating interests, with a separate indication of that derived from group undertakings
(b) income from other investments, with a separate indication of that derived from group undertakings
(aa) income from land and buildings
(bb) income from other investments
(c) value re-adjustments on investments
(d) gains on the realisation of investments
3 Unrealised gains on investments [(9)]
4 Other technical income, net of reinsurance
5 Claims incurred, net of reinsurance [(4)]
(a) claims paid
(aa) gross amount
(bb) reinsurers' share
(b) change in the provision for claims
(aa) gross amount
(bb) reinsurers' share
6 Change in other technical provisions, net of reinsurance, not shown under other headings
(a) Long-term business provision, net of reinsurance [(3)]
(aa) gross amount
(bb) reinsurers' share
(b) other technical provisions, net of reinsurance
7 Bonuses and rebates, net of reinsurance [(5)]
8 Net operating expenses
(a) acquisition costs [(6)]
(b) change in deferred acquisition costs
(c) administrative expenses [(7)]
(d) reinsurance commissions and profit participation
9 Investment expenses and charges [(8)]
(a) investment management expenses, including interest
(b) value adjustments on investments
(c) losses on the realisation of investments
10 Unrealised losses on investments [(9)]
11 Other technical charges, net of reinsurance
11a Tax attributable to the long-term business
12 Allocated investment return transferred to the non-technical account (item III.4)
12a Transfers to or from the fund for future appropriations
13 Sub-total (balance on the technical account—long-term business) (item III.2)

III Non-technical account
1 Balance on the general business technical account (item I.10)
2 Balance on the long-term business technical account (item II.13)
2a Tax credit attributable to balance on the long-term business technical account
3 Investment income [(8)]
(a) income from participating interests, with a separate indication of that derived from group undertakings
(b) income from other investments, with a separate indication of that derived from group undertakings
(aa) income from land and buildings
(bb) income from other investments
(c) value re-adjustments on investments
(d) gains on the realisation of investments
3a Unrealised gains on investments [(9)]
4 Allocated investment return transferred from the long-term business technical account (item II.12) [(10)]
5 Investment expenses and charges [(8)]
(a) investment management expenses, including interest
(b) value adjustments on investments
(c) losses on the realisation of investments
5a Unrealised losses on investments [(9)]
6 Allocated investment return transferred to the general business technical account (item I.2) [(10)]
7 Other income
8 Other charges, including value adjustments
8a Profit or loss on ordinary activities before tax
9 Tax on profit or loss on ordinary activities
10 Profit or loss on ordinary activities after tax
11 Extraordinary income

12 Extraordinary charges
13 Extraordinary profit or loss
14 Tax on extraordinary profit or loss
15 Other taxes not shown under the preceding items
16 Profit or loss for the financial year

Notes on the profit and loss account format

(1) Gross premiums written

(General business technical account: item I.1.(a).

Long-term business technical account: item II.1.(a).)

This item is to comprise all amounts due during the financial year in respect of insurance contracts entered into regardless of the fact that such amounts may relate in whole or in part to a later financial year, and must include inter alia—

(i) premiums yet to be determined, where the premium calculation can be done only at the end of the year;
(ii) single premiums, including annuity premiums, and, in long-term business, single premiums resulting from bonus and rebate provisions in so far as they must be considered as premiums under the terms of the contract;
(iii) additional premiums in the case of half-yearly, quarterly or monthly payments and additional payments from policyholders for expenses borne by the company;
(iv) in the case of co-insurance, the company's portion of total premiums;
(v) reinsurance premiums due from ceding and retroceding insurance undertakings, including portfolio entries,

after deduction of cancellations and portfolio withdrawals credited to ceding and retroceding insurance undertakings.

The above amounts must not include the amounts of taxes or duties levied with premiums.

(2) Outward reinsurance premiums

(General business technical account: item I.1.(b).

Long-term business technical account: item II.1.(b).)

This item is to comprise all premiums paid or payable in respect of outward reinsurance contracts entered into by the company. Portfolio entries payable on the conclusion or amendment of outward reinsurance contracts must be added; portfolio withdrawals receivable must be deducted.

(3) Change in the provision for unearned premiums, net of reinsurance

(Long-term business technical account: items II.1.(c) and II.6.(a).)

In the case of long-term business, the change in unearned premiums may be included either in item II.1.(c) or in item II.6.(a) of the long-term business technical account.

(4) Claims incurred, net of reinsurance

(General business technical account: item I.4.

Long-term business technical account: item II.5.)

This item is to comprise all payments made in respect of the financial year with the addition of the provision for claims (but after deducting the provision for claims for the preceding financial year).

These amounts must include annuities, surrenders, entries and withdrawals of loss provisions to and from ceding insurance undertakings and reinsurers and external and internal claims management costs and charges for claims incurred but not reported such as are referred to in paragraphs 53(2) and 55 below.

Sums recoverable on the basis of subrogation and salvage (within the meaning of paragraph 53 below) must be deducted.

Where the difference between—

(a) the loss provision made at the beginning of the year for outstanding claims incurred in previous years, and
(b) the payments made during the year on account of claims incurred in previous years and the loss provision shown at the end of the year for such outstanding claims,

is material, it must be shown in the notes to the accounts, broken down by category and amount.

(5) Bonuses and rebates, net of reinsurance

(General business technical account: item I.6.

Long-term business technical account: item II.7.)

Bonuses are to comprise all amounts chargeable for the financial year which are paid or payable to policyholders and other insured parties or provided for their benefit, including amounts used to increase technical provisions or applied to the reduction of future premiums, to the extent that such amounts represent an allocation of surplus or profit arising on business as a whole or a section of business, after deduction of amounts provided in previous years which are no longer required.

Rebates are to comprise such amounts to the extent that they represent a partial refund of premiums resulting from the experience of individual contracts.

Where material, the amount charged for bonuses and that charged for rebates must be disclosed separately in the notes to the accounts.

(6) Acquisition costs

(General business technical account: item I.7.(a).

Long-term business technical account: item II.8.(a).)

This item is to comprise the costs arising from the conclusion of insurance contracts. They must cover both direct costs, such as acquisition commissions or the cost of drawing up the insurance document or including the insurance contract in the portfolio, and indirect costs, such as advertising costs or the administrative expenses connected with the processing of proposals and the issuing of policies.

In the case of long-term business, policy renewal commissions must be included under item II.8.(c) in the long-term business technical account.

(7) Administrative expenses

(General business technical account: item I.7.(c).

Long-term business technical account: item II.8.(c).)

This item must include the costs arising from premium collection, portfolio administration, handling of bonuses and rebates, and inward and outward reinsurance. They must in particular include staff costs and depreciation provisions in respect of office furniture and equipment in so far as these need not be shown under acquisition costs, claims incurred or investment charges.

Item II.8.(c) must also include policy renewal commissions.

(8) Investment income, expenses and charges

(General business technical account: items I.2a and 8a.

Long-term business technical account: items II.2 and 9.

Non-technical account: items III.3 and 5.)

Investment income, expenses and charges must, to the extent that they arise in the long-term fund, be disclosed in the long-term business technical account. Other investment income, expenses and charges must either be disclosed in the non-technical account or attributed between the appropriate technical and non-technical accounts. Where the company makes such an attribution it must disclose the basis for it in the notes to the accounts.

(9) Unrealised gains and losses on investments

(Long-term business technical account: items II.3 and 10.

Non-technical account: items III.3a and 5a.)

In the case of investments attributed to the long-term fund, the difference between the valuation of the investments and their purchase price or, if they have previously been valued, their valuation as at the last balance sheet date, may be disclosed (in whole or in part) in item II.3 or II.10 (as the case may be) of the long-term business technical account, and in the case of investments shown as assets under assets item D (assets held to cover linked liabilities) must be so disclosed.

In the case of other investments, the difference between the valuation of the investments and their purchase price or, if they have previously been valued, their valuation as at the last balance sheet date, may be disclosed (in whole or in part) in item III.3a or III.5a (as the case may require) of the non-technical account.

(10) Allocated investment return

(General business technical account: item I.2.

Long-term business technical account: item II.2.

Non-technical account: items III.4 and 6.)

The allocated return may be transferred from one part of the profit and loss account to another.

Where part of the investment return is transferred to the general business technical account, the transfer from the non-technical account must be deducted from item III.6 and added to item I.2.

Where part of the investment return disclosed in the long-term business technical account is transferred to the non-technical account, the transfer to the non-technical account shall be deducted from item II.12 and added to item III.4.

The reasons for such transfers (which may consist of a reference to any relevant statutory requirement) and the bases on which they are made must be disclosed in the notes to the accounts.

NOTES

Para 8A: inserted by the Companies, Partnerships and Groups (Accounts and Reports) Regulations 2015, SI 2015/980, reg 34, as from 6 April 2015, in relation to (a) financial years beginning on or after 1 January 2016, and (b) a financial year of a company beginning on or after 1 January 2015, but before 1 January 2016, if the directors of the company so decide (see **[4.549]** *post*).

Para 10: words in square brackets in note 24 of the notes on balance sheet format substituted by the Financial Services Act 2012 (Consequential Amendments and Transitional Provisions) Order 2013, SI 2013/472, art 3, Sch 2, para 135(a), as from 1 April 2013.

PART 2 ACCOUNTING PRINCIPLES AND RULES

SECTION A ACCOUNTING PRINCIPLES

Preliminary

[4.83]

14. The amounts to be included in respect of all items shown in a company's accounts must be determined in accordance with the principles set out in this Section.

15. But if it appears to the company's directors that there are special reasons for departing from any of those principles in preparing the company's accounts in respect of any financial year they may do so, in which case particulars of the departure, the reasons for it and its effect must be given in a note to the accounts.

Accounting principles

16. The company is presumed to be carrying on business as a going concern.

17. Accounting policies [and measurement bases] must be applied consistently within the same accounts and from one financial year to the next.

18. The amount of any item must be determined on a prudent basis, and in particular—

(a) subject to note (9) on the profit and loss account format, only profits realised at the balance sheet date are to be included in the profit and loss account, . . .

(b) all liabilities which have arisen in respect of the financial year to which the accounts relate or a previous financial year must be taken into account, including those which only become apparent between the balance sheet date and the date on which it is signed on behalf of the board of directors in accordance with section 414 of the 2006 Act (approval and signing of accounts), [and]

[(c) all provisions for diminution of value must be recognised, whether the result of the financial year is a profit or a loss].

19. All income and charges relating to the financial year to which the accounts relate are to be taken into account, without regard to the date of receipt or payment.

20. In determining the aggregate amount of any item, the amount of each individual asset or liability that falls to be taken into account must be determined separately.

[20A. The opening balance sheet for each financial year shall correspond to the closing balance sheet for the preceding financial year.]

Valuation

21. (1) The amounts to be included in respect of assets of any description mentioned in paragraph 22 (valuation of assets: general) must be determined either—

(a) in accordance with that paragraph and paragraph 24 (but subject to paragraphs 27 to 29), or

(b) so far as applicable to an asset of that description, in accordance with Section C (valuation at fair value).

(2) The amounts to be included in respect of assets of any description mentioned in paragraph 24 (alternative valuation of fixed-income securities) may be determined—

(a) in accordance with that paragraph (but subject to paragraphs 27 to 29), or

(b) so far as applicable to an asset of that description, in accordance with Section C

(3) The amounts to be included in respect of assets which—

(a) are not assets of a description mentioned in paragraph 22 or 23, but

(b) are assets of a description to which Section C is applicable,

may be determined in accordance with that Section.

(4) Subject to sub-paragraphs (1) to (3), the amounts to be included in respect of all items shown in a company's accounts are determined in accordance with Section C

SECTION B CURRENT VALUE ACCOUNTING RULES

Valuation of assets: general

22. (1) Subject to paragraph 24, investments falling to be included under assets item C (investments) must be included at their current value calculated in accordance with paragraphs 25 and 26.

(2) Investments falling to be included under assets item D (assets held to cover linked liabilities) must be shown at their current value calculated in accordance with paragraphs 25 and 26.

23. (1) Intangible assets other than goodwill may be shown at their current cost.

(2) Assets falling to be included under assets items F.I (tangible assets) and F.IV (own shares) in the balance sheet format may be shown at their current value calculated in accordance with paragraphs 25 and 26 or at their current cost.

(3) Assets falling to be included under assets item F.II (stocks) may be shown at current cost.

Alternative valuation of fixed-income securities

24. (1) This paragraph applies to debt securities and other fixed-income securities shown as assets under assets items CII (investments in group undertakings and participating interests) and CIII (other financial investments).

(2) Securities to which this paragraph applies may either be valued in accordance with paragraph 22 or their amortised value may be shown in the balance sheet, in which case the provisions of this paragraph apply.

(3) Subject to sub-paragraph (4), where the purchase price of securities to which this paragraph applies exceeds the amount repayable at maturity, the amount of the difference—

(a) must be charged to the profit and loss account, and

(b) must be shown separately in the balance sheet or in the notes to the accounts.

(4) The amount of the difference referred to in sub-paragraph (3) may be written off in instalments so that it is completely written off when the securities are repaid, in which case there must be shown separately in the balance sheet or in the notes to the accounts the difference between the purchase price (less the aggregate amount written off) and the amount repayable at maturity.

(5) Where the purchase price of securities to which this paragraph applies is less than the amount repayable at maturity, the amount of the difference must be released to income in instalments over the period remaining until repayment, in which case there must be shown separately in the balance sheet or in the notes to the accounts the difference between the purchase price (plus the aggregate amount released to income) and the amount repayable at maturity.

(6) Both the purchase price and the current value of securities valued in accordance with this paragraph must be disclosed in the notes to the accounts.

(7) Where securities to which this paragraph applies which are not valued in accordance with paragraph 22 are sold before maturity, and the proceeds are used to purchase other securities to which this paragraph applies, the difference between the proceeds of sale and their book value may be spread uniformly over the period remaining until the maturity of the original investment.

Meaning of "current value"

25. (1) Subject to sub-paragraph (5), in the case of investments other than land and buildings, current value means market value determined in accordance with this paragraph.

(2) In the case of listed investments, market value means the value on the balance sheet date or, when the balance sheet date is not a stock exchange trading day, on the last stock exchange trading day before that date.

(3) Where a market exists for unlisted investments, market value means the average price at which such investments were traded on the balance sheet date or, when the balance sheet date is not a trading day, on the last trading day before that date.

(4) Where, on the date on which the accounts are drawn up, listed or unlisted investments have been sold or are to be sold within the short term, the market value must be reduced by the actual or estimated realisation costs.

(5) Except where the equity method of accounting is applied, all investments other than those referred to in sub-paragraphs (2) and (3) must be valued on a basis which has prudent regard to the likely realisable value.

26. (1) In the case of land and buildings, current value means the market value on the date of valuation, where relevant reduced as provided in sub-paragraphs (4) and (5).

(2) Market value means the price at which land and buildings could be sold under private contract between a willing seller and an arm's length buyer on the date of valuation, it being assumed that the property is publicly exposed to the market, that market conditions permit orderly disposal and that a normal period, having regard to the nature of the property, is available for the negotiation of the sale.

(3) The market value must be determined through the separate valuation of each land and buildings item, carried out at least every five years in accordance with generally recognised methods of valuation.

(4) Where the value of any land and buildings item has diminished since the preceding valuation under sub-paragraph (3), an appropriate value adjustment must be made.

(5) The lower value arrived at under sub-paragraph (4) must not be increased in subsequent balance sheets unless such increase results from a new determination of market value arrived at in accordance with sub-paragraphs (2) and (3).

(6) Where, on the date on which the accounts are drawn up, land and buildings have been sold or are to be sold within the short term, the value arrived at in accordance with sub-paragraphs (2) and (4) must be reduced by the actual or estimated realisation costs.

(7) Where it is impossible to determine the market value of a land and buildings item, the value arrived at on the basis of the principle of purchase price or production cost is deemed to be its current value.

Application of the depreciation rules

27. (1) Where—

(a) the value of any asset of a company is determined in accordance with paragraph 22 or 23, and

(b) in the case of a determination under paragraph 22, the asset falls to be included under assets item CI,

that value must be, or (as the case may require) must be the starting point for determining, the amount to be included in respect of that asset in the company's accounts, instead of its cost or any value previously so determined for that asset.

Paragraphs 36 to 41 and 43 apply accordingly in relation to any such asset with the substitution for any reference to its cost of a reference to the value most recently determined for that asset in accordance with paragraph 22 or 23 (as the case may be).

(2) The amount of any provision for depreciation required in the case of any asset by paragraph 37 or 38 as it applies by virtue of sub-paragraph (1) is referred to below in this paragraph as the adjusted amount, and the amount of any provision which would be required by that paragraph in the case of that asset according to the historical cost accounting rules is referred to as the historical cost amount.

(3) Where sub-paragraph (1) applies in the case of any asset the amount of any provision for depreciation in respect of that asset included in any item shown in the profit and loss account in respect of amounts written off assets of the description in question may be the historical cost amount instead of the adjusted amount, provided that the amount of any difference between the two is shown separately in the profit and loss account or in a note to the accounts.

Additional information to be provided

28. (1) This paragraph applies where the amounts to be included in respect of assets covered by any items shown in a company's accounts have been determined in accordance with paragraph 22 or 23.

(2) The items affected and the basis of valuation adopted in determining the amounts of the assets in question in the case of each such item must be disclosed in a note to the accounts.

(3) The purchase price of investments valued in accordance with paragraph 22 must be disclosed in the notes to the accounts.

(4) In the case of each balance sheet item valued in accordance with paragraph 23 either—

(a) the comparable amounts determined according to the historical cost accounting rules (without any provision for depreciation or diminution in value), or

(b) the differences between those amounts and the corresponding amounts actually shown in the balance sheet in respect of that item,

must be shown separately in the balance sheet or in a note to the accounts.

(5) In sub-paragraph (4), references in relation to any item to the comparable amounts determined as there mentioned are references to—

(a) the aggregate amount which would be required to be shown in respect of that item if the amounts to be included in respect of all the assets covered by that item were determined according to the historical cost accounting rules, and

(b) the aggregate amount of the cumulative provisions for depreciation or diminution in value which would be permitted or required in determining those amounts according to those rules.

Revaluation reserve

29. (1) Subject to sub-paragraph (7), with respect to any determination of the value of an asset of a company in accordance with paragraph 22 or 23, the amount of any profit or loss arising from that determination (after allowing, where appropriate, for any provisions for depreciation or diminution in value made otherwise than by reference to the value so determined and any adjustments of any such provisions made in the light of that determination) must be credited or (as the case may be) debited to a separate reserve ("the revaluation reserve").

(2) The amount of the revaluation reserve must be shown in the company's balance sheet under liabilities item A.III, but need not be shown under the name "revaluation reserve".

(3) An amount may be transferred—

(a) from the revaluation reserve—

(i) to the profit and loss account, if the amount was previously charged to that account or represents realised profit, or

(ii) on capitalisation,

(b) to or from the revaluation reserve in respect of the taxation relating to any profit or loss credited or debited to the reserve.

The revaluation reserve must be reduced to the extent that the amounts transferred to it are no longer necessary for the purposes of the valuation method used.

(4) In sub-paragraph (3)(a)(ii) "capitalisation", in relation to an amount standing to the credit of the revaluation reserve, means applying it in wholly or partly paying up unissued shares in the company to be allotted to members of the company as fully or partly paid shares.

(5) The revaluation reserve must not be reduced except as mentioned in this paragraph.

(6) The treatment for taxation purposes of amounts credited or debited to the revaluation reserve must be disclosed in a note to the accounts.

(7) This paragraph does not apply to the difference between the valuation of investments and their purchase price or previous valuation shown in the long-term business technical account or the non-technical account in accordance with note (9) on the profit and loss account format.

SECTION C VALUATION AT FAIR VALUE

Inclusion of financial instruments at fair value

30. (1) Subject to sub-paragraphs (2) to (5), financial instruments (including derivatives) may be included at fair value.

(2) Sub-paragraph (1) does not apply to financial instruments that constitute liabilities unless—

(a) they are held as part of a trading portfolio,

(b) they are derivatives, or

(c) they are financial instruments falling within paragraph (4).

(3) Except where they fall within paragraph (4), or fall to be included under assets item D (assets held to cover linked liabilities), sub-paragraph (1) does not apply to—

(a) financial instruments (other than derivatives) held to maturity,

(b) loans and receivables originated by the company and not held for trading purposes,

(c) interests in subsidiary undertakings, associated undertakings and joint ventures,

(d) equity instruments issued by the company,

(e) contracts for contingent consideration in a business combination, or

(f) other financial instruments with such special characteristics that the instruments, according to generally accepted accounting principles or practice, should be accounted for differently from other financial instruments.

[(4) Financial instruments which under [UK-adopted international accounting standards] may be included in accounts at fair value, may be so included, provided that the disclosures required by such accounting standards are made.]

(5) If the fair value of a financial instrument cannot be determined reliably in accordance with paragraph 31, sub-paragraph (1) does not apply to that financial instrument.

(6) In this paragraph—

"associated undertaking" has the meaning given by paragraph 19 of Schedule 6 to these Regulations; and

"joint venture" has the meaning given by paragraph 18 of that Schedule.

Determination of fair value

31. (1) The fair value of a financial instrument is its value determined in accordance with this paragraph.

(2) If a reliable market can readily be identified for the financial instrument, its fair value is determined by reference to its market value.

(3) If a reliable market cannot readily be identified for the financial instrument but can be identified for its components or for a similar instrument, its fair value is determined by reference to the market value of its components or of the similar instrument.

(4) If neither sub-paragraph (2) nor (3) applies, the fair value of the financial instrument is a value resulting from generally accepted valuation models and techniques.

(5) Any valuation models and techniques used for the purposes of sub-paragraph (4) must ensure a reasonable approximation of the market value.

Hedged items

32. A company may include any assets and liabilities, or identified portions of such assets or liabilities, that qualify as hedged items under a fair value hedge accounting system at the amount required under that system.

[Other assets that may be included at fair value

33. (1) This paragraph applies to—

(a) investment property, and

(b) living animals and plants.

(2) Such investment property and living animals and plants may be included at fair value provided that, as the case may be, all such investment property or living animals and plants are so included where their fair value can be reliably determined.

(3) In this paragraph, "fair value" means fair value determined in accordance with generally accepted accounting principles or practice.]

Accounting for changes in value

34. (1) This paragraph applies where a financial instrument is valued in accordance with paragraph 30 or 32 or an asset is valued in accordance with paragraph 33.

(2) Notwithstanding paragraph 18 in this Part of this Schedule, and subject to sub-paragraphs (3) and (4), a change in the value of the financial instrument or of the investment property or living animal or plant must be included in the profit and loss account.

(3) Where—

(a) the financial instrument accounted for is a hedging instrument under a hedge accounting system that allows some or all of the change in value not to be shown in the profit and loss account, or

(b) the change in value relates to an exchange difference arising on a monetary item that forms part of a company's net investment in a foreign entity,

the amount of the change in value must be credited to or (as the case may be) debited from a separate reserve ("the fair value reserve").

(4) Where the instrument accounted for—

(a) is an available for sale financial asset, and

(b) is not a derivative,

the change in value may be credited to or (as the case may be) debited from the fair value reserve.

The fair value reserve

35. (1) The fair value reserve must be adjusted to the extent that the amounts shown in it are no longer necessary for the purposes of paragraph 34(3) or (4).

(2) The treatment for taxation purposes of amounts credited or debited to the fair value reserve must be disclosed in a note to the accounts.

SECTION D HISTORICAL COST ACCOUNTING RULES

Valuation of assets

General rules

36. (1) The rules in this Section are "the historical cost accounting rules".

(2) Subject to any provision for depreciation or diminution in value made in accordance with paragraph 37 or 38, the amount to be included in respect of any asset in the balance sheet format is its cost.

37. In the case of any asset included under assets item B (intangible assets), CI (land and buildings), F.I (tangible assets) or F.II (stocks) which has a limited useful economic life, the amount of—

(a) its cost, or

(b) where it is estimated that any such asset will have a residual value at the end of the period of its useful economic life, its cost less that estimated residual value,

must be reduced by provisions for depreciation calculated to write off that amount systematically over the period of the asset's useful economic life.

38. (1) This paragraph applies to any asset included under assets item B (intangible assets), C (investments), F.I (tangible assets) or F.IV (own shares).

(2) Where an asset to which this paragraph applies has diminished in value, provisions for diminution in value may be made in respect of it and the amount to be included in respect of it may be reduced accordingly.

(3) Provisions for diminution in value must be made in respect of any asset to which this paragraph applies if the reduction in its value is expected to be permanent (whether its useful economic life is limited or not), and the amount to be included in respect of it must be reduced accordingly.

(4) Any provisions made under sub-paragraph (2) or (3) which are not shown in the profit and loss account must be disclosed (either separately or in aggregate) in a note to the accounts.

39. (1) Where the reasons for which any provision was made in accordance with paragraph 38 have ceased to apply to any extent, that provision must be written back to the extent that it is no longer necessary.

[(1A) But provision made in accordance with paragraph 38(2) or (3) in respect of goodwill must not be written back to any extent.]

(2) Any amounts written back in accordance with sub-paragraph (1) which are not shown in the profit and loss account must be disclosed (either separately or in aggregate) in a note to the accounts.

40. (1) This paragraph applies to assets included under assets items E.I, II and III (debtors) and F.III (cash at bank and in hand) in the balance sheet.

(2) If the net realisable value of an asset to which this paragraph applies is lower than its cost the amount to be included in respect of that asset is the net realisable value.

(3) Where the reasons for which any provision for diminution in value was made in accordance with sub-paragraph (2) have ceased to apply to any extent, that provision must be written back to the extent that it is no longer necessary.

[Intangible assets

41. (1) Where this is in accordance with generally accepted accounting principles or practice, development costs may be included under assets item B (intangible assets) in the balance sheet format.

(2) If any amount is included in a company's balance sheet in respect of development costs, the note on accounting policies (see paragraph 61 of this Schedule) must include the following information—

(a) the period over which the amount of those costs originally capitalised is being or is to be written off, and

(b) the reasons for capitalising the development costs in question.

42. (1) Intangible assets must be written off over the useful economic life of the intangible asset.

(2) Where in exceptional cases the useful life of intangible assets cannot be reliably estimated, such assets must be written off over a period chosen by the directors of the company.

(3) The period referred to in sub-paragraph (2) must not exceed ten years.

(4) There must be disclosed in a note to the accounts the period referred to in sub-paragraph (2) and the reasons for choosing that period.]

Miscellaneous and supplementary provisions

Excess of money owed over value received as an asset item

43. (1) Where the amount repayable on any debt owed by a company is greater than the value of the consideration received in the transaction giving rise to the debt, the amount of the difference may be treated as an asset.

(2) Where any such amount is so treated—

(a) it must be written off by reasonable amounts each year and must be completely written off before repayment of the debt, and

(b) if the current amount is not shown as a separate item in the company's balance sheet, it must be disclosed in a note to the accounts.

Assets included at a fixed amount

44. (1) Subject to sub-paragraph (2), assets which fall to be included under assets item F.I (tangible assets) in the balance sheet format may be included at a fixed quantity and value.

(2) Sub-paragraph (1) applies to assets of a kind which are constantly being replaced where—

(a) their overall value is not material to assessing the company's state of affairs, and

(b) their quantity, value and composition are not subject to material variation.

Determination of cost

45. (1) The cost of an asset that has been acquired by the company is to be determined by adding to the actual price paid any expenses incidental to its acquisition [and then subtracting any incidental reductions in the cost of acquisition].

(2) The cost of an asset constructed by the company is to be determined by adding to the purchase price of the raw materials and consumables used the amount of the costs incurred by the company which are directly attributable to the construction of that asset.

(3) In addition, there may be included in the cost of an asset constructed by the company—

(a) a reasonable proportion of the costs incurred by the company which are only indirectly attributable to the construction of that asset, but only to the extent that they relate to the period of construction, and

(b) interest on capital borrowed to finance the construction of that asset, to the extent that it accrues in respect of the period of construction,

provided, however, in a case within paragraph (b), that the inclusion of the interest in determining the cost of that asset and the amount of the interest so included is disclosed in a note to the accounts.

46. (1) The cost of any assets which are fungible assets may be determined by the application of any of the methods mentioned in sub-paragraph (2) in relation to any such assets of the same class, provided that the method chosen is one which appears to the directors to be appropriate in the circumstances of the company.

(2) Those methods are—

(a) the method known as "first in, first out" (FIFO),

(b) the method known as "last in, first out" (LIFO),

(c) a weighted average price, and

(d) any other method [reflecting generally accepted best practice].

(3) Where in the case of any company—

(a) the cost of assets falling to be included under any item shown in the company's balance sheet has been determined by the application of any method permitted by this paragraph, and

(b) the amount shown in respect of that item differs materially from the relevant alternative amount given below in this paragraph,

the amount of that difference must be disclosed in a note to the accounts.

(4) Subject to sub-paragraph (5), for the purposes of sub-paragraph (3)(b), the relevant alternative amount, in relation to any item shown in a company's balance sheet, is the amount which would have been shown in respect of that item if assets of any class included under that item at an amount determined by any method permitted by this paragraph had instead been included at their replacement cost as at the balance sheet date.

(5) The relevant alternative amount may be determined by reference to the most recent actual purchase price before the balance sheet date of assets of any class included under the item in question instead of by reference to their replacement cost as at that date, but only if the former appears to the directors of the company to constitute the more appropriate standard of comparison in the case of assets of that class.

Substitution of original amount where price or cost unknown

47. (1) This paragraph applies where—

(a) there is no record of the purchase price of any asset acquired by a company or of any price, expenses or costs relevant for determining its cost in accordance with paragraph 45, or

(b) any such record cannot be obtained without unreasonable expense or delay.

(2) In such a case, the cost of the asset must be taken, for the purposes of paragraphs 36 to 42, to be the value ascribed to it in the earliest available record of its value made on or after its acquisition by the company.

SECTION E RULES FOR DETERMINING PROVISIONS

Preliminary

48. Provisions which are to be shown in a company's accounts are to be determined in accordance with this Section.

Technical provisions

49. The amount of technical provisions must at all times be sufficient to cover any liabilities arising out of insurance contracts as far as can reasonably be foreseen.

Provision for unearned premiums

50. (1) The provision for unearned premiums must in principle be computed separately for each insurance contract, save that statistical methods (and in particular proportional and flat rate methods) may be used where they may be expected to give approximately the same results as individual calculations.

(2) Where the pattern of risk varies over the life of a contract, this must be taken into account in the calculation methods.

Provision for unexpired risks

51. The provision for unexpired risks (as defined in paragraph 91) must be computed on the basis of claims and administrative expenses likely to arise after the end of the financial year from contracts concluded before that date, in so far as their estimated value exceeds the provision for unearned premiums and any premiums receivable under those contracts.

Long-term business provision

52. (1) The long-term business provision must in principle be computed separately for each long-term contract, save that statistical or mathematical methods may be used where they may be expected to give approximately the same results as individual calculations.

(2) A summary of the principal assumptions in making the provision under sub-paragraph (1) must be given in the notes to the accounts.

(3) The computation must be made annually by a Fellow of the Institute or Faculty of Actuaries [with due regard to generally accepted actuarial principles and] on the basis of recognised actuarial methods . . .

Provisions for claims outstanding

General business

53. (1) A provision must in principle be computed separately for each claim on the basis of the costs still expected to arise, save that statistical methods may be used if they result in an adequate provision having regard to the nature of the risks.

(2) This provision must also allow for claims incurred but not reported by the balance sheet date, the amount of the allowance being determined having regard to past experience as to the number and magnitude of claims reported after previous balance sheet dates.

(3) All claims settlement costs (whether direct or indirect) must be included in the calculation of the provision.

(4) Recoverable amounts arising out of subrogation or salvage must be estimated on a prudent basis and either deducted from the provision for claims outstanding (in which case if the amounts are material they must be shown in the notes to the accounts) or shown as assets.

(5) In sub-paragraph (4), "subrogation" means the acquisition of the rights of policy holders with respect to third parties, and "salvage" means the acquisition of the legal ownership of insured property.

(6) Where benefits resulting from a claim must be paid in the form of annuity, the amounts to be set aside for that purpose must be calculated by recognised actuarial methods, and paragraph 54 does not apply to such calculations.

(7) Implicit discounting or deductions, whether resulting from the placing of a current value on a provision for an outstanding claim which is expected to be settled later at a higher figure or otherwise effected, is prohibited.

54. (1) Explicit discounting or deductions to take account of investment income is permitted, subject to the following conditions—

- (a) the expected average interval between the date for the settlement of claims being discounted and the accounting date must be at least four years;
- (b) the discounting or deductions must be effected on a recognised prudential basis;
- (c) when calculating the total cost of settling claims, the company must take account of all factors that could cause increases in that cost;
- (d) the company must have adequate data at its disposal to construct a reliable model of the rate of claims settlements;
- (e) the rate of interest used for the calculation of present values must not exceed a rate prudently estimated to be earned by assets of the company which are appropriate in magnitude and nature to cover the provisions for claims being discounted during the period necessary for the payment of such claims, and must not exceed either—
  - (i) a rate justified by the performance of such assets over the preceding five years, or
  - (ii) a rate justified by the performance of such assets during the year preceding the balance sheet date.

(2) When discounting or effecting deductions, the company must, in the notes to the accounts, disclose—

- (a) the total amount of provisions before discounting or deductions,
- (b) the categories of claims which are discounted or from which deductions have been made,
- (c) for each category of claims, the methods used, in particular the rates used for the estimates referred to in sub-paragraph (1)(d) and (e), and the criteria adopted for estimating the period that will elapse before the claims are settled.

Long-term business

55. The amount of the provision for claims must be equal to the sums due to beneficiaries, plus the costs of settling claims.

Equalisation reserves

56. The amount of any equalisation reserve maintained in respect of general business by the company, in accordance with the rules [made by the Financial Conduct Authority or the Prudential Regulation Authority] under Part 10 of the Financial Services and Markets Act 2000, must be determined in accordance with such rules.

Accounting on a non-annual basis

57. (1) Either of the methods described in paragraphs 58 and 59 may be applied where, because of the nature of the class or type of insurance in question, information about premiums receivable or claims payable (or both) for the underwriting years is insufficient when the accounts are drawn up for reliable estimates to be made.

(2) The use of either of the methods referred to in sub-paragraph (1) must be disclosed in the notes to the accounts together with the reasons for adopting it.

(3) Where one of the methods referred to in sub-paragraph (1) is adopted, it must be applied systematically in successive years unless circumstances justify a change.

(4) In the event of a change in the method applied, the effect on the assets, liabilities, financial position and profit or loss must be stated in the notes to the accounts.

(5) For the purposes of this paragraph and paragraph 58, "underwriting year" means the financial year in which the insurance contracts in the class or type of insurance in question commenced.

58. (1) The excess of the premiums written over the claims and expenses paid in respect of contracts commencing in the underwriting year shall form a technical provision included in the technical provision for claims outstanding shown in the balance sheet under liabilities item C3.

(2) The provision may also be computed on the basis of a given percentage of the premiums written where such a method is appropriate for the type of risk insured.

(3) If necessary, the amount of this technical provision must be increased to make it sufficient to meet present and future obligations.

(4) The technical provision constituted under this paragraph must be replaced by a provision for claims outstanding estimated in accordance with paragraph 53 as soon as sufficient information has been gathered and not later than the end of the third year following the underwriting year.

(5) The length of time that elapses before a provision for claims outstanding is constituted in accordance with sub-paragraph (4) must be disclosed in the notes to the accounts.

59. (1) The figures shown in the technical account or in certain items within it must relate to a year which wholly or partly precedes the financial year (but by no more than 12 months).

(2) The amounts of the technical provisions shown in the accounts must if necessary be increased to make them sufficient to meet present and future obligations.

(3) The length of time by which the earlier year to which the figures relate precedes the financial year and the magnitude of the transactions concerned must be disclosed in the notes to the accounts.

NOTES

Section A

Para 17: words in square brackets inserted by the Companies, Partnerships and Groups (Accounts and Reports) Regulations 2015, SI 2015/980, reg 35(1), (2)(a), as from 6 April 2015, in relation to (a) financial years beginning on or after 1 January 2016, and (b) a financial year of a company beginning on or after 1 January 2015, but before 1 January 2016, if the directors of the company so decide (see **[4.549]** *post*).

Para 18: word omitted from sub-para (a) revoked, word in square brackets in sub-para (b) inserted, and sub-para (c) added, by SI 2015/980, reg 35(1), (2)(b) (as to the application of this amendment see the first note above).

Para 20A: inserted by SI 2015/980, reg 35(1), (2)(c) (as to the application of this amendment see the first note above).

Section C

Para 30: sub-para (4) substituted by SI 2015/980, reg 35(1), (3)(a) (as to the application of this amendment see the first note above). Words in square brackets in sub-para (4) substituted by the International Accounting Standards and European Public Limited-Liability Company (Amendment etc) (EU Exit) Regulations 2019, SI 2019/685, reg 19, Sch 1, Pt 2, para 57(1), (4)(a), in relation to accounts for financial years beginning on or after IP completion day (as defined in the European Union (Withdrawal Agreement) Act 2020, s 39) (note also that in relation to accounts for financial years which begin before but end on or after IP completion day, the enactments amended by Parts 1–3 of Sch 1 to the 2019 Regulations have effect as if the UK were a member State until the end of the financial year in question).

Para 33: substituted by SI 2015/980, reg 35(1), (3)(b) (as to the application of this amendment see the first note above).

Section D

Para 39: sub-para (1A) inserted by the Companies, Partnerships and Groups (Accounts and Reports) (No 2) Regulations 2015, SI 2015/1672, reg 4(5), (6), as from 1 October 2015, in relation to (a) financial years beginning on or after 1 January 2016, and (b) a financial year of a company beginning on or after 1 January 2015 but before 1 January 2016, if the directors of the company have decided, pursuant to reg 2(2)(b) of the Companies, Partnerships and Groups (Accounts and Reports) Regulations 2015, that the amendments made by those Regulations have effect in relation to that financial year.

Paras 41, 42: substituted by SI 2015/980, reg 35(1), (4)(a) (as to the application of this amendment see the first note above).

Para 45: words in square brackets in sub-para (1) inserted by SI 2015/980, reg 35(1), (4)(b) (as to the application of this amendment see the first note above).

Para 46: words in square brackets in sub-para (2)(d) substituted by SI 2015/980, reg 35(1), (4)(c) (as to the application of this amendment see the first note above).

Section E

Para 52: the words in the square brackets in sub-para (3) were inserted, and the words omitted were revoked, by the Accounts and Reports (Amendment) (EU Exit) Regulations 2019, SI 2019/145, reg 6, Sch 3, paras 2, 4(a), in relation to financial years beginning on or after IP completion day (as defined in the European Union (Withdrawal Agreement) Act 2020, s 39) (for transitional provisions see reg 7 of the 2019 Regulations at **[12.79]**).

Para 56: words in square brackets substituted by the Financial Services Act 2012 (Consequential Amendments and Transitional Provisions) Order 2013, SI 2013/472, art 3, Sch 2, para 135(b), as from 1 April 2013.

PART 3 NOTES TO THE ACCOUNTS

[Preliminary

[4.84]

60. (1) Any information required in the case of a company by the following provisions of this Part of this Schedule must be given by way of a note to the accounts.

(2) These notes must be presented in the order in which, where relevant, the items to which they relate are presented in the balance sheet and in the profit and loss account.]

General

Disclosure of accounting policies

61. The accounting policies adopted by the company in determining the amounts to be included in respect of items shown in the balance sheet and in determining the profit or loss of the company must be stated (including such policies with respect to the depreciation and diminution in value of assets).

62. It must be stated whether the accounts have been prepared in accordance with applicable accounting standards and particulars of any material departure from those standards and the reasons for it must be given.

Sums denominated in foreign currencies

63. Where any sums originally denominated in foreign currencies have been brought into account under any items shown in the balance sheet or profit and loss account format, the basis on which those sums have been translated into sterling (or the currency in which the accounts are drawn up) must be stated.

Reserves and dividends

64. There must be stated—

(a) any amount set aside or proposed to be set aside to, or withdrawn or proposed to be withdrawn from, reserves,
(b) the aggregate amount of dividends paid in the financial year (other than those for which a liability existed at the immediately preceding balance sheet date),
(c) the aggregate amount of dividends that the company is liable to pay at the balance sheet date, and
(d) the aggregate amount of dividends that are proposed before the date of approval of the accounts, and not otherwise disclosed under sub-paragraph (b) or (c).

Information Supplementing the Balance Sheet

Share capital and debentures

65. (1) Where shares of more than one class have been allotted, the number and aggregate nominal value of shares of each class allotted must be given.

(2) In the case of any part of the allotted share capital that consists of redeemable shares, the following information must be given—

(a) the earliest and latest dates on which the company has power to redeem those shares,
(b) whether those shares must be redeemed in any event or are liable to be redeemed at the option of the company or of the shareholder, and
(c) whether any (and, if so, what) premium is payable on redemption.

66. If the company has allotted any shares during the financial year, the following information must be given—

(a) the classes of shares allotted, and
(b) as respects each class of shares, the number allotted, their aggregate nominal value and the consideration received by the company for the allotment.

67. (1) With respect to any contingent right to the allotment of shares in the company the following particulars must be given—

(a) the number, description and amount of the shares in relation to which the right is exercisable,
(b) the period during which it is exercisable, and
(c) the price to be paid for the shares allotted.

(2) In sub-paragraph (1) "contingent right to the allotment of shares" means any option to subscribe for shares and any other right to require the allotment of shares to any person whether arising on the conversion into shares of securities of any other description or otherwise.

68. (1) If the company has issued any debentures during the financial year to which the accounts relate, the following information must be given—

(a) the classes of debentures issued, and
(b) as respects each class of debentures, the amount issued and the consideration received by the company for the issue.

(2) Where any of the company's debentures are held by a nominee of or trustee for the company, the nominal amount of the debentures and the amount at which they are stated in the accounting records kept by the company in accordance with section 386 of the 2006 Act (duty to keep accounting records) must be stated.

Assets

69. (1) In respect of any assets of the company included in assets items B (intangible assets), CI (land and buildings) and CII (investments in group undertakings and participating interests) in the company's balance sheet the following information must be given by reference to each such item—

(a) the appropriate amounts in respect of those assets included in the item as at the date of the beginning of the financial year and as at the balance sheet date respectively,
(b) the effect on any amount included in assets item B in respect of those assets of—
    (i) any determination during that year of the value to be ascribed to any of those assets in accordance with paragraph 23,

(ii) acquisitions during that year of any assets,
(iii) disposals during that year of any assets, and
(iv) any transfers of assets of the company to and from the item during that year.

(2) The reference in sub-paragraph (1)(a) to the appropriate amounts in respect of any assets (included in an assets item) as at any date there mentioned is a reference to amounts representing the aggregate amounts determined, as at that date, in respect of assets falling to be included under the item on either of the following bases—
(a) on the basis of cost (determined in accordance with paragraphs 45 and 46), or
(b) on any basis permitted by paragraph 22 or 23,
(leaving out of account in either case any provisions for depreciation or diminution in value).

(3) In addition, in respect of any assets of the company included in any assets item in the company's balance sheet, there must be stated (by reference to each such item)—
(a) the cumulative amount of provisions for depreciation or diminution in value of those assets included under the item as at each date mentioned in sub-paragraph (1)(a),
(b) the amount of any such provisions made in respect of the financial year,
(c) the amount of any adjustments made in respect of any such provisions during that year in consequence of the disposal of any of those assets, and
(d) the amount of any other adjustments made in respect of any such provisions during that year.

70. Where any assets of the company (other than listed investments) are included under any item shown in the company's balance sheet at an amount determined on any basis mentioned in paragraph 22 or 23, the following information must be given—
(a) the years (so far as they are known to the directors) in which the assets were severally valued and the several values, and
(b) in the case of assets that have been valued during the financial year, the names of the persons who valued them or particulars of their qualifications for doing so and (whichever is stated) the bases of valuation used by them.

71. In relation to any amount which is included under assets item CI (land and buildings) there must be stated—
(a) how much of that amount is ascribable to land of freehold tenure and how much to land of leasehold tenure, and
(b) how much of the amount ascribable to land of leasehold tenure is ascribable to land held on long lease and how much to land held on short lease.

Investments

72. In respect of the amount of each item which is shown in the company's balance sheet under assets item C (investments) there must be stated how much of that amount is ascribable to listed investments.

[Information about fair value of assets and liabilities

73. (1) This paragraph applies where financial instruments or other assets have been valued in accordance with, as appropriate, paragraph 30, 32 or 33.

(2) There must be stated—
(a) the significant assumptions underlying the valuation models and techniques used to determine the fair value of the financial instruments or other assets,
(b) in the case of financial instruments, their purchase price, the items affected and the basis of valuation,
(c) for each category of financial instrument or other asset, the fair value of the assets in that category and the changes in value—
(i) included directly in the profit and loss account, or
(ii) credited to or (as the case may be) debited from the fair value reserve,
in respect of those assets, and
(c) for each class of derivatives, the extent and nature of the instruments, including significant terms and conditions that may affect the amount, timing and certainty of future cash flows.

(3) Where any amount is transferred to or from the fair value reserve during the financial year, there must be stated in tabular form—
(a) the amount of the reserve as at the date of the beginning of the financial year and as at the balance sheet date respectively,
(b) the amount transferred to or from the reserve during the year, and
(c) the source and application respectively of the amounts so transferred.]

74. Where the company has derivatives that it has not included at fair value, there must be stated for each class of such derivatives—
(a) the fair value of the derivatives in that class, if such a value can be determined in accordance with paragraph 31, and
(b) the extent and nature of the derivatives.

75. (1) This paragraph applies if—
(a) the company has financial fixed assets that could be included at fair value by virtue of paragraph 30,
(b) the amount at which those assets are included under any item in the company's accounts is in excess of their fair value, and
(c) the company has not made provision for diminution in value of those assets in accordance with paragraph 38(2) of this Schedule.

(2) There must be stated—
(a) the amount at which either the individual assets or appropriate groupings of those individual assets are included in the company's accounts,
(b) the fair value of those assets or groupings, and

(c) the reasons for not making a provision for diminution in value of those assets, including the nature of the evidence that provides the basis for the belief that the amount at which they are stated in the accounts will be recovered.

Information where investment property and living animals and plants included at fair value

76. (1) This paragraph applies where the amounts to be included in a company's accounts in respect of investment property or living animals and plants have been determined in accordance with paragraph 33.

(2) The balance sheet items affected and the basis of valuation adopted in determining the amounts of the assets in question in the case of each such item must be disclosed in a note to the accounts.

(3) In the case of investment property, for each balance sheet item affected there must be shown, either separately in the balance sheet or in a note to the accounts—

(a) the comparable amounts determined according to the historical cost accounting rules, or

(b) the differences between those amounts and the corresponding amounts actually shown in the balance sheet in respect of that item.

(4) In sub-paragraph (3), references in relation to any item to the comparable amounts determined in accordance with that sub-paragraph are to—

(a) the aggregate amount which would be required to be shown in respect of that item if the amounts to be included in respect of all the assets covered by that item were determined according to the historical cost accounting rules, and

(b) the aggregate amount of the cumulative provisions for depreciation or diminution in value which would be permitted or required in determining those amounts according to those rules.

Reserves and provisions

77. (1) This paragraph applies where any amount is transferred—

(a) to or from any reserves,

(b) to any provisions for other risks, or

(c) from any provisions for other risks otherwise than for the purpose for which the provision was established,

and the reserves or provisions are or would but for paragraph 3(1) be shown as separate items in the company's balance sheet.

(2) The following information must be given in respect of the aggregate of reserves or provisions included in the same item—

(a) the amount of the reserves or provisions as at the date of the beginning of the financial year and as at the balance sheet date respectively,

(b) any amounts transferred to or from the reserves or provisions during that year, and

(c) the source and application respectively of any amounts so transferred.

(3) Particulars must be given of each provision included in liabilities item E.3 (other provisions) in the company's balance sheet in any case where the amount of that provision is material.

Provision for taxation

78. The amount of any provision for deferred taxation must be stated separately from the amount of any provision for other taxation.

Details of indebtedness

79. (1) In respect of each item shown under "creditors" in the company's balance sheet there must be stated the aggregate of the following amounts—

(a) the amount of any debts included under that item which are payable or repayable otherwise than by instalments and fall due for payment or repayment after the end of the period of five years beginning with the day next following the end of the financial year, and

(b) in the case of any debts so included which are payable or repayable by instalments, the amount of any instalments which fall due for payment after the end of that period.

(2) Subject to sub-paragraph (3), in relation to each debt falling to be taken into account under sub-paragraph (1), the terms of payment or repayment and the rate of any interest payable on the debt must be stated.

(3) If the number of debts is such that, in the opinion of the directors, compliance with sub-paragraph (2) would result in a statement of excessive length, it is sufficient to give a general indication of the terms of payment or repayment and the rates of any interest payable on the debts.

(4) In respect of each item shown under "creditors" in the company's balance sheet there must be stated—

(a) the aggregate amount of any debts included under that item in respect of which any security has been given by the company, and

(b) an indication of the nature of the securities so given.

(5) References above in this paragraph to an item shown under "creditors" in the company's balance sheet include references, where amounts falling due to creditors within one year and after more than one year are distinguished in the balance sheet—

(a) in a case within sub-paragraph (1), to an item shown under the latter of those categories, and

(b) in a case within sub-paragraph (4), to an item shown under either of those categories.

References to items shown under "creditors" include references to items which would but for paragraph 3(1)(b) be shown under that heading.

80. If any fixed cumulative dividends on the company's shares are in arrear, there must be stated—

(a) the amount of the arrears, and

(b) the period for which the dividends or, if there is more than one class, each class of them are in arrear.

[Guarantees and other financial commitments

81. (1) Particulars must be given of any charge on the assets of the company to secure the liabilities of any other person including the amount secured.

(2) Particulars and the total amount of any financial commitments, guarantees and contingencies (excluding those which arise out of insurance contracts) that are not included in the balance sheet must be disclosed.

(3) An indication of the nature and form of any valuable security given by the company in respect of commitments, guarantees and contingencies within sub-paragraph (2) must be given.

(4) The total amount of any commitments within sub-paragraph (2) concerning pensions must be separately disclosed.

(5) Particulars must be given of pension commitments which are included in the balance sheet.

(6) Where any commitment within sub-paragraph (4) or (5) relates wholly or partly to pensions payable to past directors of the company separate particulars must be given of that commitment.

(7) The total amount of any commitments, guarantees and contingencies within sub-paragraph (2) which are undertaken on behalf of or for the benefit of—

(a) any parent undertaking or fellow subsidiary undertaking of the company,

(b) any subsidiary undertaking of the company, or

(c) any undertaking in which the company has a participating interest

must be separately stated and those within each of paragraphs (a), (b) and (c) must also be stated separately from those within any other of those paragraphs.]

Miscellaneous matters

82. (1) Particulars must be given of any case where the cost of any asset is for the first time determined under paragraph 47.

(2) Where any outstanding loans made under the authority of section 682(2)(b), (c) or (d) of the 2006 Act (various cases of financial assistance by a company for purchase of its own shares) are included under any item shown in the company's balance sheet, the aggregate amount of those loans must be disclosed for each item in question.

Information supplementing the profit and loss account

Separate statement of certain items of income and expenditure

83. (1) Subject to sub-paragraph (2), there must be stated the amount of the interest on or any similar charges in respect of—

(a) bank loans and overdrafts, and

(b) loans of any other kind made to the company.

(2) Sub-paragraph (1) does not apply to interest or charges on loans to the company from group undertakings, but, with that exception, it applies to interest or charges on all loans, whether made on the security of debentures or not.

Particulars of tax

84. (1) Particulars must be given of any special circumstances which affect liability in respect of taxation of profits, income or capital gains for the financial year or liability in respect of taxation of profits, income or capital gains for succeeding financial years.

(2) The following amounts must be stated—

(a) the amount of the charge for United Kingdom corporation tax,

(b) if that amount would have been greater but for relief from double taxation, the amount which it would have been but for such relief,

(c) the amount of the charge for United Kingdom income tax, and

(d) the amount of the charge for taxation imposed outside the United Kingdom of profits, income and (so far as charged to revenue) capital gains.

Those amounts must be stated separately in respect of each of the amounts which is shown under the following items in the profit and loss account, that is to say item III.9 (tax on profit or loss on ordinary activities) and item III.14 (tax on extraordinary profit or loss).

Particulars of business

85. (1) As regards general business a company must disclose—

(a) gross premiums written,

(b) gross premiums earned,

(c) gross claims incurred,

(d) gross operating expenses, and

(e) the reinsurance balance.

(2) The amounts required to be disclosed by sub-paragraph (1) must be broken down between direct insurance and reinsurance acceptances, if reinsurance acceptances amount to 10 per cent or more of gross premiums written.

(3) Subject to sub-paragraph (4), the amounts required to be disclosed by sub-paragraphs (1) and (2) with respect to direct insurance must be further broken down into the following groups of classes—

(a) accident and health,

(b) motor (third party liability),

(c) motor (other classes),

(d) marine, aviation and transport,

(e) fire and other damage to property,

(f) third-party liability,

(g) credit and suretyship,

(h) legal expenses,

(i) assistance, and

(j) miscellaneous,

where the amount of the gross premiums written in direct insurance for each such group exceeds 10 million Euros.

(4) The company must in any event disclose the amounts relating to the three largest groups of classes in its business.

86. (1) As regards long-term business, the company must disclose—

(a) gross premiums written, and

(b) the reinsurance balance.

(2) Subject to sub-paragraph (3)—

(a) gross premiums written must be broken down between those written by way of direct insurance and those written by way of reinsurance, and

(b) gross premiums written by way of direct insurance must be broken down—

(i) between individual premiums and premiums under group contracts,

(ii) between periodic premiums and single premiums, and

(iii) between premiums from non-participating contracts, premiums from participating contracts and premiums from contracts where the investment risk is borne by policyholders.

(3) Disclosure of any amount referred to in sub-paragraph (2)(a) or (2)(b)(i), (ii) or (iii) is not required if it does not exceed 10 per cent of the gross premiums written or (as the case may be) of the gross premiums written by way of direct insurance.

87. (1) Subject to sub-paragraph (2), there must be disclosed as regards both general and long- term business the total gross direct insurance premiums resulting from contracts concluded by the company—

[(a) in the country in which its head office is located, and]

(b) . . .

(c) in other countries.

(2) Disclosure of any amount referred to in sub-paragraph (1) is not required if it does not exceed 5 per cent of total gross premiums.

Commissions

88. There must be disclosed the total amount of commissions for direct insurance business accounted for in the financial year, including acquisition, renewal, collection and portfolio management commissions.

Miscellaneous matters

89. (1) Where any amount relating to any preceding financial year is included in any item in the profit and loss account, the effect must be stated.

[(2) The amount, nature and effect of any individual items of income or expenditure which are of exceptional size or incidence must be stated.]

Related party transactions

90. (1) Particulars may be given of transactions which the company has entered into with related parties, and must be given if such transactions are material and have not been concluded under normal market conditions.

(2) The particulars of transactions required to be disclosed by sub-paragraph (1) must include—

(a) the amount of such transactions,

(b) the nature of the related party relationship, and

(c) other information about the transactions necessary for an understanding of the financial position of the company.

(3) Information about individual transactions may be aggregated according to their nature, except where separate information is necessary for an understanding of the effects of related party transactions on the financial position of the company.

(4) Particulars need not be given of transactions entered into between two or more members of a group, provided that any subsidiary undertaking which is a party to the transaction is wholly-owned by such a member.

(5) In this paragraph, "related party" has the same meaning as in [UK-adopted international accounting standards].

[Post balance sheet events

90A. The nature and financial effect of material events arising after the balance sheet date which are not reflected in the profit and loss account of balance sheet must be stated.

Appropriations

90B. Particulars must be given of the proposed appropriation of profit or treatment of loss or, where applicable, particulars of the actual appropriation of the profits or treatment of the losses.]

NOTES

Paras 60, 73, 81: substituted by the Companies, Partnerships and Groups (Accounts and Reports) Regulations 2015, SI 2015/980, reg 36(1)–(4), as from 6 April 2015, in relation to (a) financial years beginning on or after 1 January 2016, and (b) a financial year of a company beginning on or after 1 January 2015, but before 1 January 2016, if the directors of the company so decide (see **[4.549]** *post*).

Para 87: sub-para (a) was substituted, and sub-para (b) was revoked, by the Accounts and Reports (Amendment) (EU Exit) Regulations 2019, SI 2019/145, reg 6, Sch 3, paras 2, 4(b), in relation to financial years beginning on or after IP completion day (as defined in the European Union (Withdrawal Agreement) Act 2020, s 39) (for transitional provisions see reg 7 of the 2019 Regulations at **[12.79]**).

Para 89: sub-para (2) substituted (for the original sub-paras (2), (3)) by SI 2015/980, reg 36(1), (5) (as to the application of this amendment see the first note above).

Para 90: words in square brackets in sub-para (5) substituted by the International Accounting Standards and European Public Limited-Liability Company (Amendment etc) (EU Exit) Regulations 2019, SI 2019/685, reg 19, Sch 1, Pt 2, para 57(1), (4)(b), in relation to accounts for financial years beginning on or after IP completion day (as defined in the European Union (Withdrawal Agreement) Act 2020, s 39) (note also that in relation to accounts for financial years which begin before but end on or after IP completion day, the enactments amended by Parts 1–3 of Sch 1 to the 2019 Regulations have effect as if the UK were a member State until the end of the financial year in question).

Paras 90A, 90B: inserted by SI 2015/980, reg 36(1), (6) (as to the application of this amendment see the first note above).

PART 4 INTERPRETATION OF THIS SCHEDULE

Definitions for this Schedule

[4.85]

91. The following definitions apply for the purposes of this Schedule and its interpretation—

"general business" means business which consists of effecting or carrying out contracts of general insurance;

"long-term business" means business which consists of effecting or carrying out contracts of long-term insurance;

"long-term fund" means the fund or funds maintained by a company in respect of its long-term business in accordance with [rules made by the Financial Conduct Authority or the Prudential Regulation Authority] under Part 10 of the Financial Services and Markets Act 2000;

"policyholder" has the meaning given by article 3 of the Financial Services and Markets Act 2000 (Meaning of "Policy" and "Policyholder") Order 2001;

"provision for unexpired risks" means the amount set aside in addition to unearned premiums in respect of risks to be borne by the company after the end of the financial year, in order to provide for all claims and expenses in connection with insurance contracts in force in excess of the related unearned premiums and any premiums receivable on those contracts.

NOTES

Para 91: words in square brackets in the definition "long-term fund" substituted by the Financial Services Act 2012 (Consequential Amendments and Transitional Provisions) Order 2013, SI 2013/472, art 3, Sch 2, para 135(c), as from 1 April 2013.

SCHEDULE 4
INFORMATION ON RELATED UNDERTAKINGS REQUIRED WHETHER PREPARING COMPANIES ACT OR IAS ACCOUNTS

Regulation 7

PART 1 PROVISIONS APPLYING TO ALL COMPANIES

Subsidiary undertakings

[4.86]

1. (1) The following information must be given where at the end of the financial year the company has subsidiary undertakings.

(2) The name of each subsidiary undertaking must be stated.

(3) There must be stated with respect to each subsidiary undertaking—

[(a) the address of the undertaking's registered office (whether in or outside the United Kingdom),]

(b) if it is unincorporated, the address of its principal place of business.

Financial information about subsidiary undertakings

2. (1) There must be disclosed with respect to each subsidiary undertaking not included in consolidated accounts by the company—

(a) the aggregate amount of its capital and reserves as at the end of its relevant financial year, and

(b) its profit or loss for that year.

(2) That information need not be given if the company is exempt by virtue of section 400 or 401 of the 2006 Act from the requirement to prepare group accounts (parent company included in accounts of larger group).

(3) That information need not be given if the company's investment in the subsidiary undertaking is included in the company's accounts by way of the equity method of valuation.

(4) That information need not be given if—

(a) the subsidiary undertaking is not required by any provision of the 2006 Act to deliver a copy of its balance sheet for its relevant financial year and does not otherwise publish that balance sheet in the United Kingdom or elsewhere, and

(b) the company's holding is less than 50% of the nominal value of the shares in the undertaking.

(5) Information otherwise required by this paragraph need not be given if it is not material.

(6) For the purposes of this paragraph the "relevant financial year" of a subsidiary undertaking is—

(a) if its financial year ends with that of the company, that year, and

(b) if not, its financial year ending last before the end of the company's financial year.

Shares and debentures of company held by subsidiary undertakings

3. (1) The number, description and amount of the shares in the company held by or on behalf of its subsidiary undertakings must be disclosed.

(2) Sub-paragraph (1) does not apply in relation to shares in the case of which the subsidiary undertaking is concerned as personal representative or, subject as follows, as trustee.

(3) The exception for shares in relation to which the subsidiary undertaking is concerned as trustee does not apply if the company, or any of its subsidiary undertakings, is beneficially interested under the trust, otherwise than by way of security only for the purposes of a transaction entered into by it in the ordinary course of a business which includes the lending of money.

(4) Part 5 of this Schedule has effect for the interpretation of the reference in sub-paragraph (3) to a beneficial interest under a trust.

Significant holdings in undertakings other than subsidiary undertakings

4. (1) The information required by paragraphs 5 and 6 must be given where at the end of the financial year the company has a significant holding in an undertaking which is not a subsidiary undertaking of the company, and which does not fall within paragraph 18 (joint ventures) or 19 (associated undertakings).

(2) A holding is significant for this purpose if—

(a) it amounts to 20% or more of the nominal value of any class of shares in the undertaking, or

(b) the amount of the holding (as stated or included in the company's individual accounts) exceeds one-fifth of the amount (as so stated) of the company's assets.

5. (1) The name of the undertaking must be stated.

(2) There must be stated—

[(a) the address of the undertaking's registered office (whether in or outside the United Kingdom),]

(b) if it is unincorporated, the address of its principal place of business.

(3) There must also be stated—

(a) the identity of each class of shares in the undertaking held by the company, and

(b) the proportion of the nominal value of the shares of that class represented by those shares.

6. (1) Subject to paragraph 14, there must also be stated—

(a) the aggregate amount of the capital and reserves of the undertaking as at the end of its relevant financial year, and

(b) its profit or loss for that year.

(2) That information need not be given in respect of an undertaking if—

(a) the undertaking is not required by any provision of the 2006 Act to deliver a copy of its balance sheet for its relevant financial year and does not otherwise publish that balance sheet in the United Kingdom or elsewhere, and

(b) the company's holding is less than 50% of the nominal value of the shares in the undertaking.

(3) Information otherwise required by this paragraph need not be given if it is not material.

(4) For the purposes of this paragraph the "relevant financial year" of an undertaking is—

(a) if its financial year ends with that of the company, that year, and

(b) if not, its financial year ending last before the end of the company's financial year.

Membership of certain undertakings

7. (1) The information required by this paragraph must be given where at the end of the financial year the company is a member of [an undertaking having unlimited liability].

(2) There must be stated—

(a) the name and legal form of the undertaking, and

(b) the address of the undertaking's registered office (whether in or outside the United Kingdom) or, if it does not have such an office, its head office (whether in or outside the United Kingdom).

(3) Where the undertaking is a qualifying partnership there must also be stated either—

(a) that a copy of the latest accounts of the undertaking has been or is to be appended to the copy of the company's accounts sent to the registrar under section 444 of the 2006 Act, or

(b) the name of at least one body corporate (which may be the company) in whose group accounts the undertaking has been or is to be dealt with on a consolidated basis.

(4) Information otherwise required by sub-paragraph (2) need not be given if it is not material.

(5) Information otherwise required by sub-paragraph (3)(b) need not be given if the notes to the company's accounts disclose that advantage has been taken of the exemption conferred by regulation 7 of the [Partnerships (Accounts) Regulations 2008].

[(6) . . .

(7) In this paragraph—

"dealt with on a consolidated basis" and "qualifying partnership" have the same meanings as in the Partnerships (Accounts) Regulations 2008;

. . .

(8)–(10) . . .

Parent undertaking drawing up accounts for larger group

8. (1) Where the company is a subsidiary undertaking, the following information must be given with respect to the parent undertaking of—

(a) the largest group of undertakings for which group accounts are drawn up and of which the company is a member, and

(b) the smallest such group of undertakings.

(2) The name of the parent undertaking must be stated.

(3) There must be stated—

[(a) the address of the undertaking's registered office (whether in or outside the United Kingdom),]

(b) if it is unincorporated, the address of its principal place of business.

(4) If copies of the group accounts referred to in sub-paragraph (1) are available to the public, there must also be stated the addresses from which copies of the accounts can be obtained.

Identification of ultimate parent company

9. (1) Where the company is a subsidiary undertaking, the following information must be given with respect to the company (if any) regarded by the directors as being the company's ultimate parent company.

(2) The name of that company must be stated.

(3) If that company is incorporated outside the United Kingdom, the country in which it is incorporated must be stated (if known to the directors).

(4) In this paragraph "company" includes any body corporate.

NOTES

Para 1: sub-para (3)(a) substituted by the Companies, Partnerships and Groups (Accounts and Reports) Regulations 2015, SI 2015/980, reg 37(1), (2), as from 6 April 2015, in relation to (a) financial years beginning on or after 1 January 2016, and (b) a financial year of a company beginning on or after 1 January 2015, but before 1 January 2016, if the directors of the company so decide (see **[4.549]** *post*).

Para 5: sub-para (2)(a) substituted by SI 2015/980, reg 37(1), (3) (as to the application of this amendment see the first note above).

Para 7 is amended as follows:

Words in square brackets in sub-para (1) substituted by SI 2015/980, reg 37(1), (4)(a) (as to the application of this amendment see the first note above).

Words in square brackets in sub-para (5) substituted by the Partnerships (Accounts) Regulations 2008, SI 2008/569, reg 17(2), as from 6 April 2008, in relation to qualifying partnerships' financial years beginning on or after that date, and auditors appointed in respect of those financial years.

Sub-paras (6)–(10) substituted (for the original sub-para (6)) by the Companies and Partnerships (Accounts and Audit) Regulations 2013, SI 2013/2005, reg 6, in relation to a financial year of a company beginning on or after 1 October 2013.

Sub-paras (6), (8)–(10) subsequently revoked by SI 2015/980, reg 37(1), (4)(b), (d)–(f) (as to the application of this amendment see the first note above).

Definition "qualifying undertaking" omitted from sub-para (7) revoked by SI 2015/980, reg 37(1), (4)(c) (as to the application of this amendment see the first note above).

Para 8: sub-para (3)(a) substituted by SI 2015/980, reg 37(1), (5) (as to the application of this amendment see the first note above).

PART 2 COMPANIES NOT REQUIRED TO PREPARE GROUP ACCOUNTS

Reason for not preparing group accounts

[4.87]

10. (1) The reason why the company is not required to prepare group accounts must be stated.

(2) If the reason is that all the subsidiary undertakings of the company fall within the exclusions provided for in section 405 of the 2006 Act (Companies Act group accounts: subsidiary undertakings included in the consolidation), it must be stated with respect to each subsidiary undertaking which of those exclusions applies.

Holdings in subsidiary undertakings

11. (1) There must be stated in relation to shares of each class held by the company in a subsidiary undertaking—

(a) the identity of the class, and

(b) the proportion of the nominal value of the shares of that class represented by those shares.

(2) The shares held by or on behalf of the company itself must be distinguished from those attributed to the company which are held by or on behalf of a subsidiary undertaking.

Financial years of subsidiary undertakings

12. Where—

(a) disclosure is made under paragraph 2(1) with respect to a subsidiary undertaking, and

(b) that undertaking's financial year does not end with that of the company,

there must be stated in relation to that undertaking the date on which its last financial year ended (last before the end of the company's financial year).

Exemption from giving information about significant holdings in non-subsidiary undertakings

13. (1) The information otherwise required by paragraph 6 (significant holdings in undertakings other than subsidiary undertaking) need not be given if—

(a) the company is exempt by virtue of section 400 or 401 of the 2006 Act from the requirement to prepare group accounts (parent company included in accounts of larger group), and

(b) the investment of the company in all undertakings in which it has such a holding as is mentioned in sub-paragraph (1) is shown, in aggregate, in the notes to the accounts by way of the equity method of valuation.

Construction of references to shares held by company

14. (1) References in Parts 1 and 2 of this Schedule to shares held by a company are to be construed as follows.

(2) For the purposes of paragraphs 2, 11 and 12 (information about subsidiary undertakings)—

(a) there must be attributed to the company any shares held by a subsidiary undertaking, or by a person acting on behalf of the company or a subsidiary undertaking; but

(b) there must be treated as not held by the company any shares held on behalf of a person other than the company or a subsidiary undertaking.

(3) For the purposes of paragraphs 4 to 6 (information about undertakings other than subsidiary undertakings)—

(a) there must be attributed to the company shares held on its behalf by any person; but

(b) there must be treated as not held by a company shares held on behalf of a person other than the company.

(4) For the purposes of any of those provisions, shares held by way of security must be treated as held by the person providing the security—

(a) where apart from the right to exercise them for the purpose of preserving the value of the security, or of realising it, the rights attached to the shares are exercisable only in accordance with that person's instructions, and

(b) where the shares are held in connection with the granting of loans as part of normal business activities and apart from the right to exercise them for the purpose of preserving the value of the security, or of realising it, the rights attached to the shares are exercisable only in that person's interests.

PART 3 COMPANIES REQUIRED TO PREPARE GROUP ACCOUNTS

Introductory

[4.88]

15. In this Part of this Schedule "the group" means the group consisting of the parent company and its subsidiary undertakings.

Subsidiary undertakings

16. (1) In addition to the information required by paragraph 2, the following information must also be given with respect to the undertakings which are subsidiary undertakings of the parent company at the end of the financial year.

(2) It must be stated whether the subsidiary undertaking is included in the consolidation and, if it is not, the reasons for excluding it from consolidation must be given.

(3) It must be stated with respect to each subsidiary undertaking by virtue of which of the conditions specified in section 1162(2) or (4) of the 2006 Act it is a subsidiary undertaking of its immediate parent undertaking.

That information need not be given if the relevant condition is that specified in subsection (2)(a) of that section (holding of a majority of the voting rights) and the immediate parent undertaking holds the same proportion of the shares in the undertaking as it holds voting rights.

Holdings in subsidiary undertakings

17. (1) The following information must be given with respect to the shares of a subsidiary undertaking held—

(a) by the parent company, and
(b) by the group,

and the information under paragraphs (a) and (b) must (if different) be shown separately.

(2) There must be stated—

(a) the identity of each class of shares held, and
(b) the proportion of the nominal value of the shares of that class represented by those shares.

Joint ventures

18. (1) The following information must be given where an undertaking is dealt with in the consolidated accounts by the method of proportional consolidation in accordance with paragraph 18 of Schedule 6 to these Regulations (joint ventures)—

[(a) the name of the undertaking,
(b) the address of the undertaking's registered office (whether in or outside the United Kingdom),]
(c) the factors on which joint management of the undertaking is based, and
(d) the proportion of the capital of the undertaking held by undertakings included in the consolidation.

(2) Where the financial year of the undertaking did not end with that of the company, there must be stated the date on which a financial year of the undertaking last ended before that date.

Associated undertakings

19. (1) The following information must be given where an undertaking included in the consolidation has an interest in an associated undertaking.

(2) The name of the associated undertaking must be stated.

(3) There must be stated—

(a) if the undertaking is incorporated outside the United Kingdom, the country in which it is incorporated,
[(b) the address of the undertaking's registered office (whether in or outside the United Kingdom),]

(4) The following information must be given with respect to the shares of the undertaking held—

(a) by the parent company, and
(b) by the group,

and the information under paragraphs (a) and (b) must be shown separately.

(5) There must be stated—

(a) the identity of each class of shares held, and
(b) the proportion of the nominal value of the shares of that class represented by those shares.

(6) In this paragraph "associated undertaking" has the meaning given by paragraph 19 of Schedule 6 to these Regulations; and the information required by this paragraph must be given notwithstanding that paragraph 21(3) of that Schedule (materiality) applies in relation to the accounts themselves.

Requirement to give information about other significant holdings of parent company or group

20. (1) The information required by paragraphs 5 and 6 must also be given where at the end of the financial year the group has a significant holding in an undertaking which is not a subsidiary undertaking of the parent company and does not fall within paragraph 18 (joint ventures) or 19 (associated undertakings), as though the references to the company in those paragraphs were a reference to the group.

(2) A holding is significant for this purpose if—

(a) it amounts to 20% or more of the nominal value of any class of shares in the undertaking, or
(b) the amount of the holding (as stated or included in the group accounts) exceeds one-fifth of the amount of the group's assets (as so stated).

(3) For the purposes of those paragraphs as applied to a group the "relevant financial year" of an outside undertaking is—

(a) if its financial year ends with that of the parent company, that year, and
(b) if not, its financial year ending last before the end of the parent company's financial year.

Group's membership of certain undertakings

21. The information required by paragraph 7 must also be given where at the end of the financial year the group is a member of [an undertaking having unlimited liability].

Construction of references to shares held by parent company or group

22. (1) References in Parts 1 and 3 of this Schedule to shares held by that parent company or group are to be construed as follows.

(2) For the purposes of paragraphs 4 to 6, 17, 19(4) and (5) and 12 (information about holdings in subsidiary and other undertakings)—

(a) there must be attributed to the parent company shares held on its behalf by any person; but

(b) there must be treated as not held by the parent company shares held on behalf of a person other than the company.

(3) References to shares held by the group are to any shares held by or on behalf of the parent company or any of its subsidiary undertakings; but any shares held on behalf of a person other than the parent company or any of its subsidiary undertakings are not to be treated as held by the group.

(4) Shares held by way of security must be treated as held by the person providing the security—

(a) where apart from the right to exercise them for the purpose of preserving the value of the security, or of realising it, the rights attached to the shares are exercisable only in accordance with his instructions, and

(b) where the shares are held in connection with the granting of loans as part of normal business activities and apart from the right to exercise them for the purpose of preserving the value of the security, or of realising it, the rights attached to the shares are exercisable only in his interests.

NOTES

Para 18 is amended as follows:

Sub-paras (1)(a), (b) substituted by the Limited Liability Partnerships, Partnerships and Groups (Accounts and Audit) Regulations 2016, SI 2016/575, regs 65, 66, in relation to (a) financial years beginning on or after 1 January 2016, and (b) a financial year of a company beginning on or after 1 January 2015, but before 1 January 2016, if (i) the directors of the company have decided, pursuant to regulation 2(2)(b) of the Companies, Partnerships and Groups (Accounts and Reports) Regulations 2015, that the amendments made by those Regulations have effect in relation to that financial year, and (ii) a copy of the company's accounts for that financial year has not been delivered to the registrar in accordance with ss 445, 446 or 447 of the Companies Act 2006 before 17 May 2016.

Para 19: sub-para (3)(b) substituted by SI 2015/980, reg 38(1), (3), as from 6 April 2015, in relation to (a) financial years beginning on or after 1 January 2016, and (b) a financial year of a company beginning on or after 1 January 2015, but before 1 January 2016, if the directors of the company so decide (see **[4.549]** *post*).

Para 21: words in square brackets substituted by SI 2015/980, reg 38(1), (4) (as to the application of this amendment see the note relating to the 2015 Regulations above).

PART 4 ADDITIONAL DISCLOSURES FOR BANKING COMPANIES AND GROUPS

[4.89]

23. (1) This paragraph applies where accounts are prepared in accordance with the special provisions of Schedules 2 and 6 relating to banking companies or groups.

(2) The information required by paragraph 5 of this Schedule, modified where applicable by paragraph 20 (information about significant holdings of the company or group in undertakings other than subsidiary undertakings) need only be given in respect of undertakings (otherwise falling within the class of undertakings in respect of which disclosure is required) in which the company or group has a significant holding amounting to 20 % or more of the nominal value of the shares in the undertaking.

In addition any information required by those paragraphs may be omitted if it is not material.

(3) Paragraphs 14(3) and (4) and 22(3) and (4) of this Schedule apply with necessary modifications for the purposes of this paragraph.

PART 5 INTERPRETATION OF REFERENCES TO "BENEFICIAL INTEREST"

Residual interests under pension and employees' share schemes

[4.90]

24. (1) Where shares in an undertaking are held on trust for the purposes of a pension scheme or an employees' share scheme, there must be disregarded any residual interest which has not vested in possession, being an interest of the undertaking or any of its subsidiary undertakings.

(2) In this paragraph a "residual interest" means a right of the undertaking in question (the "residual beneficiary") to receive any of the trust property in the event of—

(a) all the liabilities arising under the scheme having been satisfied or provided for, or

(b) the residual beneficiary ceasing to participate in the scheme, or

(c) the trust property at any time exceeding what is necessary for satisfying the liabilities arising or expected to arise under the scheme.

(3) In sub-paragraph (2) references to a right include a right dependent on the exercise of a discretion vested by the scheme in the trustee or any other person; and references to liabilities arising under a scheme include liabilities that have resulted or may result from the exercise of any such discretion.

(4) For the purposes of this paragraph a residual interest vests in possession—

(a) in a case within sub-paragraph (2)(a), on the occurrence of the event there mentioned, whether or not the amount of the property receivable pursuant to the right mentioned in that sub-paragraph is then ascertained,

(b) in a case within sub-paragraph (2)(b) or (c), when the residual beneficiary becomes entitled to require the trustee to transfer to that beneficiary any of the property receivable pursuant to that right.

Employer's charges and other rights of recovery

25. (1) Where shares in an undertaking are held on trust there must be disregarded—

(a) if the trust is for the purposes of a pension scheme, any such rights as are mentioned in sub-paragraph (2),

(b) if the trust is for the purposes of an employees' share scheme, any such rights as are mentioned in paragraph (a) of that sub-paragraph, being rights of the undertaking or any of its subsidiary undertakings.

(2) The rights referred to are—

(a) any charge or lien on, or set-off against, any benefit or other right or interest under the scheme for the purpose of enabling the employer or former employer of a member of the scheme to obtain the discharge of a monetary obligation due to him from the member, and

(b) any right to receive from the trustee of the scheme, or as trustee of the scheme to retain, an amount that can be recovered or retained under section 61 of the Pension Schemes Act 1993 or section 57 of the Pension Schemes (Northern Ireland) Act 1993 (deduction of contributions equivalent premium from refund of scheme contributions) or otherwise as reimbursement or partial reimbursement for any contributions equivalent premium paid in connection with the scheme under Chapter 3 of Part 3 of that Act.

Trustee's right to expenses, remuneration, indemnity etc

26. Where an undertaking is a trustee, there must be disregarded any rights which the undertaking has in its capacity as trustee including, in particular, any right to recover its expenses or be remunerated out of the trust property and any right to be indemnified out of that property for any liability incurred by reason of any act or omission of the undertaking in the performance of its duties as trustee.

Supplementary

27. (1) This Schedule applies in relation to debentures as it applies in relation to shares.

(2) "Pension scheme" means any scheme for the provision of benefits consisting of or including relevant benefits for or in respect of employees or former employees; and "relevant benefits" means any pension, lump sum, gratuity or other like benefit given or to be given on retirement or on death or in anticipation of retirement or, in connection with past service, after retirement or death.

(3) In sub-paragraph (2) of this paragraph and in paragraph 25(2) "employee" and "employer" are to be read as if a director of an undertaking were employed by it.

SCHEDULE 5
INFORMATION ABOUT BENEFITS OF DIRECTORS

Regulation 8

PART 1 PROVISIONS APPLYING TO QUOTED AND UNQUOTED COMPANIES

Total amount of directors' remuneration etc

[4.91]

1. (1) There must be shown—

(a) the aggregate amount of remuneration paid to or receivable by directors in respect of qualifying services;

(b) the aggregate of the amount of gains made by directors on the exercise of share options;

(c) the aggregate of the amount of money paid to or receivable by directors, and the net value of assets (other than money and share options) received or receivable by directors, under long term incentive schemes in respect of qualifying services; and

(d) the aggregate value of any company contributions—

(i) paid, or treated as paid, to a pension scheme in respect of directors' qualifying services, and

(ii) by reference to which the rate or amount of any money purchase benefits that may become payable will be calculated.

(2) There must be shown the number of directors (if any) to whom retirement benefits are accruing in respect of qualifying services—

(a) under money purchase schemes, and

(b) under defined benefit schemes.

(3) In the case of a company which is not a quoted company and whose equity share capital is not listed on the market known as AIM—

(a) sub-paragraph (1) has effect as if paragraph (b) were omitted and, in paragraph (c), "assets" did not include shares; and

(b) the number of each of the following (if any) must be shown, namely—

(i) the directors who exercised share options, and

(ii) the directors in respect of whose qualifying services shares were received or receivable under long term incentive schemes.

PART 2 PROVISIONS APPLYING ONLY TO UNQUOTED COMPANIES

Details of highest paid director's emoluments etc

[4.92]

2. (1) Where the aggregates shown under paragraph 1(1)(a), (b) and (c) total £200,000 or more, there must be shown—

(a) so much of the total of those aggregates as is attributable to the highest paid director, and

(b) so much of the aggregate mentioned in paragraph 1(1)(d) as is so attributable.

(2) Where sub-paragraph (1) applies and the highest paid director has performed qualifying services during the financial year by reference to which the rate or amount of any defined benefits that may become payable will be calculated, there must also be shown—

(a) the amount at the end of the year of his accrued pension, and

(b) where applicable, the amount at the end of the year of his accrued lump sum.

(3) Subject to sub-paragraph (4), where sub-paragraph (1) applies in the case of a company which is not a listed company, there must also be shown—

(a) whether the highest paid director exercised any share options, and

(b) whether any shares were received or receivable by that director in respect of qualifying services under a long term incentive scheme.

(4) Where the highest paid director has not been involved in any of the transactions specified in sub-paragraph (3), that fact need not be stated.

Excess retirement benefits of directors and past directors

3. (1) Subject to sub-paragraph (2), there must be shown the aggregate amount of—

(a) so much of retirement benefits paid to or receivable by directors under pension schemes, and

(b) so much of retirement benefits paid to or receivable by past directors under such schemes,

as (in each case) is in excess of the retirement benefits to which they were respectively entitled on the date on which the benefits first became payable or 31st March 1997, whichever is the later.

(2) Amounts paid or receivable under a pension scheme need not be included in the aggregate amount if—

(a) the funding of the scheme was such that the amounts were or, as the case may be, could have been paid without recourse to additional contributions, and

(b) amounts were paid to or receivable by all pensioner members of the scheme on the same basis.

(3) In sub-paragraph (2), "pensioner member", in relation to a pension scheme, means any person who is entitled to the present payment of retirement benefits under the scheme.

(4) In this paragraph—

(a) references to retirement benefits include benefits otherwise than in cash, and

(b) in relation to so much of retirement benefits as consists of a benefit otherwise than in cash, references to their amount are to the estimated money value of the benefit,

and the nature of any such benefit must also be disclosed.

Compensation to directors for loss of office

4. (1) There must be shown the aggregate amount of any compensation to directors or past directors in respect of loss of office.

(2) This includes compensation received or receivable by a director or past director—

(a) for loss of office as director of the company, or

(b) for loss, while director of the company or on or in connection with his ceasing to be a director of it, of—

(i) any other office in connection with the management of the company's affairs, or

(ii) any office as director or otherwise in connection with the management of the affairs of any subsidiary undertaking of the company.

(3) In this paragraph references to compensation for loss of office include—

(a) compensation in consideration for, or in connection with, a person's retirement from office, and

(b) where such a retirement is occasioned by a breach of the person's contract with the company or with a subsidiary undertaking of the company—

(i) payments made by way of damages for the breach, or

(ii) payments made by way of settlement or compromise of any claim in respect of the breach.

(4) In this paragraph—

(a) references to compensation include benefits otherwise than in cash, and

(b) in relation to such compensation references to its amount are to the estimated money value of the benefit.

The nature of any such compensation must be disclosed.

Sums paid to third parties in respect of directors' services

5. (1) There must be shown the aggregate amount of any consideration paid to or receivable by third parties for making available the services of any person—

(a) as a director of the company, or

(b) while director of the company—

(i) as director of any of its subsidiary undertakings, or

(ii) otherwise in connection with the management of the affairs of the company or any of its subsidiary undertakings.

(2) In sub-paragraph (1)—

(a) the reference to consideration includes benefits otherwise than in cash, and

(b) in relation to such consideration the reference to its amount is to the estimated money value of the benefit.

The nature of any such consideration must be disclosed.

(3) For the purposes of this paragraph a "third party" means a person other than—

(a) the director himself or a person connected with him or a body corporate controlled by him, or

(b) the company or any of its subsidiary undertakings.

PART 3 SUPPLEMENTARY PROVISIONS

General nature of obligations

[4.93]

6. (1) This Schedule requires information to be given only so far as it is contained in the company's books and papers or the company has the right to obtain it from the persons concerned.

(2) For the purposes of this Schedule any information is treated as shown if it is capable of being readily ascertained from other information which is shown.

Provisions as to amounts to be shown

7. (1) The following provisions apply with respect to the amounts to be shown under this Schedule.

(2) The amount in each case includes all relevant sums, whether paid by or receivable from the company, any of the company's subsidiary undertakings or any other person.

(3) References to amounts paid to or receivable by a person include amounts paid to or receivable by a person connected with him or a body corporate controlled by him (but not so as to require an amount to be counted twice).

(4) Except as otherwise provided, the amounts to be shown for any financial year are—

(a) the sums receivable in respect of that year (whenever paid), or

(b) in the case of sums not receivable in respect of a period, the sums paid during that year.

(5) Sums paid by way of expenses allowance that are charged to United Kingdom income tax after the end of the relevant financial year must be shown in a note to the first accounts in which it is practicable to show them and must be distinguished from the amounts to be shown apart from this provision.

(6) Where it is necessary to do so for the purpose of making any distinction required in complying with this Schedule, the directors may apportion payments between the matters in respect of which they have been paid or are receivable in such manner as they think appropriate.

Exclusion of sums liable to be accounted for to company etc

8. (1) The amounts to be shown under this Schedule do not include any sums that are to be accounted for—

(a) to the company or any of its subsidiary undertakings, or

(b) by virtue of sections 219 and 222(3) of the 2006 Act (payments in connection with share transfers: duty to account) to persons who sold their shares as a result of the offer made.

(2) Where—

(a) any such sums are not shown in a note to the accounts for the relevant financial year on the ground that the person receiving them is liable to account for them, and

(b) the liability is afterwards wholly or partly released or is not enforced within a period of two years,

those sums, to the extent to which the liability is released or not enforced, must be shown in a note to the first accounts in which it is practicable to show them and must be distinguished from the amounts to be shown apart from this provision.

Meaning of "remuneration"

9. (1) In this Schedule "remuneration" of a director includes—

(a) salary, fees and bonuses, sums paid by way of expenses allowance (so far as they are chargeable to United Kingdom income tax), and

(b) subject to sub-paragraph (2), the estimated money value of any other benefits received by the director otherwise than in cash.

(2) The expression does not include—

(a) the value of any share options granted to the director or the amount of any gains made on the exercise of any such options,

(b) any company contributions paid, or treated as paid, under any pension scheme or any benefits to which the director is entitled under any such scheme, or

(c) any money or other assets paid to or received or receivable by the director under any long term incentive scheme.

Meaning of "highest paid director"

10. In this Schedule, "the highest paid director" means the director to whom is attributable the greatest part of the total of the aggregates shown under paragraph 1(1)(a), (b) and (c).

Meaning of "long term incentive scheme"

11. (1) In this Schedule "long term incentive scheme" means an agreement or arrangement—

(a) under which money or other assets may become receivable by a director, and

(b) which includes one or more qualifying conditions with respect to service or performance which cannot be fulfilled within a single financial year.

(2) For this purpose the following must be disregarded—

(a) bonuses the amount of which falls to be determined by reference to service or performance within a single financial year;

(b) compensation for loss of office, payments for breach of contract and other termination payments; and

(c) retirement benefits.

Meaning of "shares" and "share option" and related expressions

12. In this Schedule—

(a) "shares" means shares (whether allotted or not) in the company, or any undertaking which is a group undertaking in relation to the company, and includes a share warrant as defined by section 779(1) of the 2006 Act; and

(b) "share option" means a right to acquire shares.

Meaning of "pension scheme" and related expressions

13. [(1) In this Schedule—

"pension scheme" means a retirement benefits scheme within the meaning given by section 150(1) of the Finance Act 2004 which is—

(a) one in which the company participates, or

(b) one to which the company paid a contribution during the financial year; and

"retirement benefits" means relevant benefits within the meaning given by section 393B of the Income Tax (Earnings and Pensions) Act 2003 read as if subsection (2) were omitted.]

(2) In this Schedule "accrued pension" and "accrued lump sum", in relation to any pension scheme and any director, mean respectively the amount of the annual pension, and the amount of the lump sum, which would be payable under the scheme on his attaining normal pension age if—

(a) he had left the company's service at the end of the financial year,

(b) there was no increase in the general level of prices in the United Kingdom during the period beginning with the end of that year and ending with his attaining that age,

(c) no question arose of any commutation of the pension or inverse commutation of the lump sum, and

(d) any amounts attributable to voluntary contributions paid by the director to the scheme, and any money purchase benefits which would be payable under the scheme, were disregarded.

(3) In this Schedule, "company contributions", in relation to a pension scheme and a director, means any payments (including insurance premiums) made, or treated as made, to the scheme in respect of the director by a person other than the director.

(4) In this Schedule, in relation to a director—

"defined benefits" means retirement benefits payable under a pension scheme that are not money purchase benefits;

"defined benefit scheme" means a pension scheme that is not a money purchase scheme;

"money purchase benefits" means retirement benefits payable under a pension scheme the rate or amount of which is calculated by reference to payments made, or treated as made, by the director or by any other person in respect of the director and which are not average salary benefits; and

"money purchase scheme" means a pension scheme under which all of the benefits that may become payable to or in respect of the director are money purchase benefits.

(5) In this Schedule, "normal pension age", in relation to any pension scheme and any director, means the age at which the director will first become entitled to receive a full pension on retirement of an amount determined without reduction to take account of its payment before a later age (but disregarding any entitlement to pension upon retirement in the event of illness, incapacity or redundancy).

(6) Where a pension scheme provides for any benefits that may become payable to or in respect of any director to be whichever are the greater of—

(a) money purchase benefits as determined by or under the scheme; and

(b) defined benefits as so determined,

the company may assume for the purposes of this paragraph that those benefits will be money purchase benefits, or defined benefits, according to whichever appears more likely at the end of the financial year.

(7) For the purpose of determining whether a pension scheme is a money purchase or defined benefit scheme, any death in service benefits provided for by the scheme are to be disregarded.

References to subsidiary undertakings

14. (1) Any reference in this Schedule to a subsidiary undertaking of the company, in relation to a person who is or was, while a director of the company, a director also, by virtue of the company's nomination (direct or indirect) of any other undertaking, includes that undertaking, whether or not it is or was in fact a subsidiary undertaking of the company.

(2) Any reference to a subsidiary undertaking of the company—

(a) for the purposes of paragraph 1 (remuneration etc) is to an undertaking which is a subsidiary undertaking at the time the services were rendered, and

(b) for the purposes of paragraph 4 (compensation for loss of office) is to a subsidiary undertaking immediately before the loss of office as director.

Other minor definitions

15. (1) In this Schedule—

"net value", in relation to any assets received or receivable by a director, means value after deducting any money paid or other value given by the director in respect of those assets;

"qualifying services", in relation to any person, means his services as a director of the company, and his services while director of the company—

(a) as director of any of its subsidiary undertakings; or

(b) otherwise in connection with the management of the affairs of the company or any of its subsidiary undertakings.

(2) References in this Schedule to a person being "connected" with a director, and to a director "controlling" a body corporate, are to be construed in accordance with sections 252 to 255 of the 2006 Act.

(3) For the purposes of this Schedule, remuneration paid or receivable or share options granted in respect of a person's accepting office as a director are treated as emoluments paid or receivable or share options granted in respect of his services as a director.

NOTES

Para 13: sub-para (1) substituted by the Companies (Miscellaneous Reporting) Regulations 2018, SI 2018/860, regs 7, 10, as from 7 August 2018.

SCHEDULE 6
COMPANIES ACT GROUP ACCOUNTS

Regulation 9

PART 1 GENERAL RULES

General rules

[4.94]

1. (1) Group accounts must comply so far as practicable with the provisions of Schedule 1 to these Regulations as if the undertakings included in the consolidation ("the group") were a single company (see Parts 2 and 3 of this Schedule for modifications for banking and insurance groups).

(2) Where the parent company is treated as an investment company for the purposes of Part 5 of Schedule 1 (special provisions for investment companies) the group must be similarly treated.

2. (1) The consolidated balance sheet and profit and loss account must incorporate in full the information contained in the individual accounts of the undertakings included in the consolidation, subject to the adjustments authorised or required by the following provisions of this Schedule and to such other adjustments (if any) as may be appropriate in accordance with generally accepted accounting principles or practice.

[(1A) Group accounts must be drawn up as at the same date as the accounts of the parent company.]

(2) If the financial year of a subsidiary undertaking included in the consolidation does not end with that of the parent company, the group accounts must be made up—

(a) from the accounts of the subsidiary undertaking for its financial year last ending before the end of the parent company's financial year, provided that year ended no more than three months before that of the parent company, or

(b) from interim accounts prepared by the subsidiary undertaking as at the end of the parent company's financial year.

3. (1) Where assets and liabilities to be included in the group accounts have been valued or otherwise determined by undertakings according to accounting rules differing from those used for the group accounts, the values or amounts must be adjusted so as to accord with the rules used for the group accounts.

(2) If it appears to the directors of the parent company that there are special reasons for departing from sub-paragraph (1) they may do so, but particulars of any such departure, the reasons for it and its effect must be given in a note to the accounts.

(3) The adjustments referred to in this paragraph need not be made if they are not material for the purpose of giving a true and fair view.

4. Any differences of accounting rules as between a parent company's individual accounts for a financial year and its group accounts must be disclosed in a note to the latter accounts and the reasons for the difference given.

5. Amounts that in the particular context of any provision of this Schedule are not material may be disregarded for the purposes of that provision.

Elimination of group transactions

6. (1) Debts and claims between undertakings included in the consolidation, and income and expenditure relating to transactions between such undertakings, must be eliminated in preparing the group accounts.

(2) Where profits and losses resulting from transactions between undertakings included in the consolidation are included in the book value of assets, they must be eliminated in preparing the group accounts.

(3) The elimination required by sub-paragraph (2) may be effected in proportion to the group's interest in the shares of the undertakings.

(4) Sub-paragraphs (1) and (2) need not be complied with if the amounts concerned are not material for the purpose of giving a true and fair view.

Acquisition and merger accounting

7. (1) The following provisions apply where an undertaking becomes a subsidiary undertaking of the parent company.

(2) That event is referred to in those provisions as an "acquisition", and references to the "undertaking acquired" are to be construed accordingly.

8. An acquisition must be accounted for by the acquisition method of accounting unless the conditions for accounting for it as a merger are met and the merger method of accounting is adopted.

9. (1) The acquisition method of accounting is as follows.

(2) The identifiable assets and liabilities of the undertaking acquired must be included in the consolidated balance sheet at their fair values as at the date of acquisition.

(3) The income and expenditure of the undertaking acquired must be brought into the group accounts only as from the date of the acquisition.

(4) There must be set off against the acquisition cost of the interest in the shares of the undertaking held by the parent company and its subsidiary undertakings the interest of the parent company and its subsidiary undertakings in the adjusted capital and reserves of the undertaking acquired.

(5) The resulting amount if positive must be treated as goodwill, and if negative as a negative consolidation difference.

[(6) Negative goodwill may be transferred to the consolidated profit and loss account where such a treatment is in accordance with the principles and rules of Part 2 of Schedule 1 to these Regulations.]

[10. The conditions for accounting for an acquisition as a merger are—

(a) that the undertaking whose shares are acquired is ultimately controlled by the same party both before and after the acquisition,

(b) that the control referred to in paragraph (a) is not transitory, and

(c) that adoption of the merger method accords with generally accepted accounting principles or practice.]

11. (1) The merger method of accounting is as follows.

(2) The assets and liabilities of the undertaking acquired must be brought into the group accounts at the figures at which they stand in the undertaking's accounts, subject to any adjustment authorised or required by this Schedule.

(3) The income and expenditure of the undertaking acquired must be included in the group accounts for the entire financial year, including the period before the acquisition.

(4) The group accounts must show corresponding amounts relating to the previous financial year as if the undertaking acquired had been included in the consolidation throughout that year.

(5) There must be set off against the aggregate of—

(a) the appropriate amount in respect of qualifying shares issued by the parent company or its subsidiary undertakings in consideration for the acquisition of shares in the undertaking acquired, and

(b) the fair value of any other consideration for the acquisition of shares in the undertaking acquired, determined as at the date when those shares were acquired,

the nominal value of the issued share capital of the undertaking acquired held by the parent company and its subsidiary undertakings.

(6) The resulting amount must be shown as an adjustment to the consolidated reserves.

(7) In sub-paragraph (5)(a) "qualifying shares" means—

(a) shares in relation to which any of the following provisions applies (merger relief), and in respect of which the appropriate amount is the nominal value—

(i) section 131 of the Companies Act 1985,

(ii) Article 141 of the Companies (Northern Ireland) Order 1986, or

(iii) section 612 of the 2006 Act, or

(b) shares in relation to which any of the following provisions applies (group reconstruction relief), and in respect of which the appropriate amount is the nominal value together with any minimum premium value within the meaning of that section—

(i) section 132 of the Companies Act 1985,

(ii) Article 142 of the Companies (Northern Ireland) Order 1986, or

(iii) section 611 of the 2006 Act.

12. (1) Where a group is acquired, paragraphs 9 to 11 apply with the following adaptations.

(2) References to shares of the undertaking acquired are to be construed as references to shares of the parent undertaking of the group.

(3) Other references to the undertaking acquired are to be construed as references to the group; and references to the assets and liabilities, income and expenditure and capital and reserves of the undertaking acquired must be construed as references to the assets and liabilities, income and expenditure and capital and reserves of the group after making the set-offs and other adjustments required by this Schedule in the case of group accounts.

13. (1) The following information with respect to acquisitions taking place in the financial year must be given in a note to the accounts.

(2) There must be stated—

(a) the name of the undertaking acquired or, where a group was acquired, the name of the parent undertaking of that group, and

(b) whether the acquisition has been accounted for by the acquisition or the merger method of accounting;

and in relation to an acquisition which significantly affects the figures shown in the group accounts, the following further information must be given.

(3) The composition and fair value of the consideration for the acquisition given by the parent company and its subsidiary undertakings must be stated.

(4) Where the acquisition method of accounting has been adopted, the book values immediately prior to the acquisition, and the fair values at the date of acquisition, of each class of assets and liabilities of the undertaking or group acquired must be stated in tabular form, including a statement of the amount of any goodwill or negative consolidation difference arising on the acquisition, together with an explanation of any significant adjustments made.

(5) In ascertaining for the purposes of sub-paragraph (4) the profit or loss of a group, the book values and fair values of assets and liabilities of a group or the amount of the assets and liabilities of a group, the set-offs and other adjustments required by this Schedule in the case of group accounts must be made.

14. (1) There must also be stated in a note to the accounts the cumulative amount of goodwill resulting from acquisitions in that and earlier financial years which has been written off otherwise than in the consolidated profit and loss account for that or any earlier financial year.

(2) That figure must be shown net of any goodwill attributable to subsidiary undertakings or businesses disposed of prior to the balance sheet date.

15. Where during the financial year there has been a disposal of an undertaking or group which significantly affects the figure shown in the group accounts, there must be stated in a note to the accounts—

(a) the name of that undertaking or, as the case may be, of the parent undertaking of that group, and

(b) the extent to which the profit or loss shown in the group accounts is attributable to profit or loss of that undertaking or group.

16. The information required by paragraph 13, 14 or 15 need not be disclosed with respect to an undertaking which—

(a) is established under the law of a country outside the United Kingdom, or

(b) carries on business outside the United Kingdom,

if in the opinion of the directors of the parent company the disclosure would be seriously prejudicial to the business of that undertaking or to the business of the parent company or any of its subsidiary undertakings and the Secretary of State agrees that the information should not be disclosed.

[16A. Where an acquisition has taken place in the financial year and the merger method of accounting has been adopted, the notes to the accounts must also disclose—

(a) the address of the registered office of the undertaking acquired (whether in or outside the United Kingdom),

(b) the name of the party referred to in paragraph 10(a),

(c) the address of the registered office of that party (whether in or outside the United Kingdom), and

(d) the information referred to in paragraph 11(6).]

[Non-controlling interests

17. (1) The formats set out in Schedule 1 to these Regulations have effect in relation to group accounts with the following additions.

(2) In the balance sheet formats there must be shown, as a separate item and under the heading "non-controlling interests", the amount of capital and reserves attributable to shares in subsidiary undertakings included in the consolidation held by or on behalf of persons other than the parent company and its subsidiary undertakings.

(3) In the profit and loss account formats there must be shown, as a separate item and under the heading "non-controlling interests", the amount of any profit or loss attributable to shares in subsidiary undertakings included in the consolidation held by or on behalf of persons other than the parent company and its subsidiary undertakings.

(4) For the purposes of paragraph 4(1) and (2) of Schedule 1 (power to adapt or combine items)—

(a) the additional item required by sub-paragraph (2) above is treated as one to which a letter is assigned, and

(b) the additional item required by sub-paragraph (3) above is treated as one to which an Arabic number is assigned.]

Joint ventures

18. (1) Where an undertaking included in the consolidation manages another undertaking jointly with one or more undertakings not included in the consolidation, that other undertaking ("the joint venture") may, if it is not—

(a) a body corporate, or

(b) a subsidiary undertaking of the parent company,

be dealt with in the group accounts by the method of proportional consolidation.

(2) The provisions of this Schedule relating to the preparation of consolidated accounts [and sections 402 and 405 of the 2006 Act] apply, with any necessary modifications, to proportional consolidation under this paragraph.

[(3) In addition to the disclosure of the average number of employees employed during the financial year (see section 411(7) of the 2006 Act), there must be a separate disclosure in the notes to the accounts of the average number of employees employed by undertakings that are proportionately consolidated.]

Associated undertakings

19. (1) An "associated undertaking" means an undertaking in which an undertaking included in the consolidation has a participating interest and over whose operating and financial policy it exercises a significant influence, and which is not—

(a) a subsidiary undertaking of the parent company, or

(b) a joint venture dealt with in accordance with paragraph 18.

(2) Where an undertaking holds 20% or more of the voting rights in another undertaking, it is presumed to exercise such an influence over it unless the contrary is shown.

(3) The voting rights in an undertaking means the rights conferred on shareholders in respect of their shares or, in the case of an undertaking not having a share capital, on members, to vote at general meetings of the undertaking on all, or substantially all, matters.

(4) The provisions of paragraphs 5 to 11 of Schedule 7 to the 2006 Act (parent and subsidiary undertakings: rights to be taken into account and attribution of rights) apply in determining for the purposes of this paragraph whether an undertaking holds 20% or more of the voting rights in another undertaking.

20. (1) The formats set out in Schedule 1 to these Regulations have effect in relation to group accounts with the following modifications.

(2) In the balance sheet formats replace the items headed "Participating interests", that is—

(a) in format 1, item B.III.3, and

(b) in format 2, item B.III.3 under the heading "ASSETS",

by two items: "Interests in associated undertakings" and "Other participating interests".

(3) In the profit and loss account formats replace the items headed "Income from participating interests", that is—

(a) in format 1, item 8, [and]

(b) in format 2, item 10,

(c), (d) . . .

by two items: "Income from interests in associated undertakings" and "Income from other participating interests".

21. (1) The interest of an undertaking in an associated undertaking, and the amount of profit or loss attributable to such an interest, must be shown by the equity method of accounting (including dealing with any goodwill arising in accordance with paragraphs 17 to 20 and 22 of Schedule 1 to these Regulations).

(2) Where the associated undertaking is itself a parent undertaking, the net assets and profits or losses to be taken into account are those of the parent and its subsidiary undertakings (after making any consolidation adjustments).

(3) The equity method of accounting need not be applied if the amounts in question are not material for the purpose of giving a true and fair view.

Related party transactions

22. Paragraph 72 of Schedule 1 to these Regulations applies to transactions which the parent company, or other undertakings included in the consolidation, have entered into with related parties, unless they are intra group transactions.

[Total amount of directors' remuneration etc

22A. Paragraph 1 of Schedule 5 to these Regulations applies to group accounts with the modification that only the amounts and values referred to in that paragraph received or receivable by the directors of the parent company from the parent company and any of its subsidiary undertakings must be disclosed in the notes to the accounts.

Deferred tax balances

22B. Deferred tax balances must be recognised on consolidation where it is probable that a charge to tax will arise within the foreseeable future for one of the undertakings included in the consolidation.]

NOTES

All amendment to this Part were made by the Companies, Partnerships and Groups (Accounts and Reports) Regulations 2015, SI 2015/980, reg 39(1)–(10), as from 6 April 2015, in relation to (a) financial years beginning on or after 1 January 2016, and (b) a financial year of a company beginning on or after 1 January 2015, but before 1 January 2016, if the directors of the company so decide (see **[4.549]** *post*).

PART 2 MODIFICATIONS FOR BANKING GROUPS

General application of provisions applicable to individual accounts

[4.95]

23. In its application to banking groups, Part 1 of this Schedule has effect with the following modifications.

24. In paragraph 1 of this Schedule—

(a) the reference in sub-paragraph (1) to the provisions of Schedule 1 to these Regulations is to be construed as a reference to the provisions of Schedule 2 to these Regulations, and

(b) sub-paragraph (2) is to be omitted.

[24A. In paragraph 9 of this Schedule, the reference in sub-paragraph (6) to Schedule 1 is to these Regulations is to be construed as a reference to Schedule 2.]

[Non-controlling interests and associated undertakings

25. (1) This paragraph adapts paragraphs 17 and 20 (which require items in respect of "non-controlling interests" and associated undertakings to be added to the formats set out in Schedule 1 to these Regulations) to the formats prescribed by Schedule 2 to these Regulations.

(2) In paragraph 17—

(a) in sub-paragraph (1), for the reference to Schedule 1 to these Regulations, substitute a reference to Schedule 2,

(b) sub-paragraph (3) is to apply as if the reference to "a separate item" were a reference to "separate items" and the reference to "the amount of any profit or loss" were a reference to the following—

  (i) the amount of any profit or loss on ordinary activities, and

  (ii) the amount of any profit or loss on extraordinary activities, and

(c) sub-paragraph (4) is not to apply, but for the purposes of paragraph 5(1) of Part 1 of Schedule 2 to these Regulations (power to combine items) the additional items required by the foregoing provisions of this paragraph are to be treated as items to which a letter is assigned.

(3) Paragraph 20(2) is to apply with respect to a balance sheet prepared under Schedule 2 to these Regulations as if it required assets item 7 (participating interests) in the balance sheet format to be replaced by the two replacement items referred to in that paragraph.

(4) Paragraph 20(3) is not to apply, but the following items in the profit and loss account formats—

(a) format 1 item 3(b) (income from participating interests),

(b) format 2 item B2(b) (income from participating interests),

are replaced by the following—

  (i) "Income from participating interests other than associated undertakings", to be shown at position 3(b) in format 1 and position B2(b) in format 2, and

  (ii) "Income from associated undertakings", to be shown at an appropriate position.]

26. In paragraph 21(1) of this Schedule, for the references to paragraphs 17 to 20 and 22 of Schedule 1 to these Regulations substitute references to paragraphs 23 to 26 and 28 of Schedule 2 to these Regulations.

Related party transactions

27. In paragraph 22 of this Schedule, for the reference to paragraph 72 of Schedule 1 to these Regulations substitute a reference to paragraph 92 of Schedule 2 to these Regulations.

Foreign currency translation

28. Any difference between—

(a) the amount included in the consolidated accounts for the previous financial year with respect to any undertaking included in the consolidation or the group's interest in any associated undertaking, together with the amount of any transactions undertaken to cover any such interest, and

(b) the opening amount for the financial year in respect of those undertakings and in respect of any such transactions,

arising as a result of the application of paragraph 50 of Schedule 2 to these Regulations may be credited to (where (a) is less than (b)), or deducted from (where (a) is greater than (b)), (as the case may be) consolidated reserves.

29. Any income and expenditure of undertakings included in the consolidation and associated undertakings in a foreign currency may be translated for the purposes of the consolidated accounts at the average rates of exchange prevailing during the financial year.

Information as to undertaking in which shares held as a result of financial assistance operation

30. (1) The following provisions apply where the parent company of a banking group has a subsidiary undertaking which—

(a) is a credit institution of which shares are held as a result of a financial assistance operation with a view to its reorganisation or rescue, and

(b) is excluded from consolidation under section 405(3)(c) of the 2006 Act (interest held with a view to resale).

(2) Information as to the nature and terms of the operations must be given in a note to the group accounts, and there must be appended to the copy of the group accounts delivered to the registrar in accordance with section 441 of the 2006 Act a copy of the undertaking's latest individual accounts and, if it is a parent undertaking, its latest group accounts.

If the accounts appended are required by law to be audited, a copy of the auditor's report must also be appended.

(3) Any requirement of Part 35 of the 2006 Act as to the delivery to the registrar of a certified translation into English must be met in relation to any document required to be appended by sub-paragraph (2).

(4) The above requirements are subject to the following qualifications—

(a) an undertaking is not required to prepare for the purposes of this paragraph accounts which would not otherwise be prepared, and if no accounts satisfying the above requirements are prepared none need be appended;

(b) the accounts of an undertaking need not be appended if they would not otherwise be required to be published, or made available for public inspection, anywhere in the world, but in that case the reason for not appending the accounts must be stated in a note to the consolidated accounts.

(5) Where a copy of an undertaking's accounts is required to be appended to the copy of the group accounts delivered to the registrar, that fact must be stated in a note to the group accounts.

NOTES

Para 24A: inserted by the Companies, Partnerships and Groups (Accounts and Reports) Regulations 2015, SI 2015/980, reg 39(1), (11), as from 6 April 2015, in relation to (a) financial years beginning on or after 1 January 2016, and (b) a financial year of a company beginning on or after 1 January 2015, but before 1 January 2016, if the directors of the company so decide (see **[4.549]** *post*).

Para 25: substituted by SI 2015/980, reg 39(1), (12) (as to the application of this amendment see the first note above).

PART 3 MODIFICATIONS FOR INSURANCE GROUPS

General application of provisions applicable to individual accounts

[4.96]

31. In its application to insurance groups, Part 1 of this Schedule has effect with the following modifications.

32. In paragraph 1 of this Schedule—

(a) the reference in sub-paragraph (1) to the provisions of Schedule 1 to these Regulations is to be construed as a reference to the provisions of Schedule 3 to these Regulations, and

(b) sub-paragraph (2) is to be omitted.

Financial years of subsidiary undertakings

33. In paragraph 2(2)(a), for "three months" substitute "six months".

Assets and liabilities to be included in group accounts

34. In paragraph 3, after sub-paragraph (1) insert—

"(1A) Sub-paragraph (1) is not to apply to those liabilities items the valuation of which by the undertakings included in a consolidation is based on the application of provisions applying only to insurance undertakings, nor to those assets items changes in the values of which also affect or establish policyholders' rights.

(1B) Where sub-paragraph (1A) applies, that fact must be disclosed in the notes to the consolidated accounts.".

Elimination of group transactions

35. For sub-paragraph (4) of paragraph 6 substitute—

"(4) Sub-paragraphs (1) and (2) need not be complied with—

(a) where a transaction has been concluded according to normal market conditions and a policyholder has rights in respect of the transaction, or

(b) if the amounts concerned are not material for the purpose of giving a true and fair view.

(5) Where advantage is taken of sub-paragraph (4)(a) that fact must be disclosed in the notes to the accounts, and where the transaction in question has a material effect on the assets, liabilities, financial position and profit or loss of all the undertakings included in the consolidation that fact must also be so disclosed.".

[35A. In paragraph 9 of this Schedule, the reference in sub-paragraph (6) to Schedule 1 to these Regulations is to be construed as a reference to Schedule 3 to these Regulations.]

[Non-controlling interests

36. In paragraph 17—

(a) in sub-paragraph (1), for the reference to Schedule 1 to these Regulations, substitute a reference to Schedule 3,

(b) sub-paragraph (3) is to apply as if the reference to "a separate item" were a reference to "separate items" and as if the reference to "the amount of any profit or loss" were a reference to the following—

(i) the amount of any profit or loss on ordinary activities, and

(ii) the amount of any profit or loss on extraordinary activities, and

(c) for sub-paragraph (4), substitute—

"(4) Paragraph 3(1) of Schedule 3 to these Regulations (power to combine items) does not apply in relation to the additional items required by the above provisions of this paragraph.".]

Associated undertakings

37. In paragraph 20—

(a) in sub-paragraph (1), for the reference to Schedule 1 to these Regulations substitute a reference to Schedule 3 to these Regulations, and

(b) for sub-paragraphs (2) and (3) substitute—

"(2) In the balance sheet format, replace asset item CII.3 (participating interests) with two items, "Interests in associated undertakings" and "Other participating interests".

(3) In the profit and loss account format, replace items II.2.(a) and III.3.(a) (income from participating interests, with a separate indication of that derived from group undertakings) with—

(a) "Income from participating interests other than associated undertakings, with a separate indication of that derived from group undertakings", to be shown as items II.2.(a) and III.3.(a), and

(b) "Income from associated undertakings", to be shown as items II.2.(aa) and III.3.(aa).".

38. In paragraph 21(1) of this Schedule, for the references to paragraphs 17 to 20 and 22 of Schedule 1 to these Regulations, substitute references to paragraphs 36 to 39 and 42 of Schedule 3 to these Regulations.

Related party transactions

39. In paragraph 22 of this Schedule, for the reference to paragraph 72 of Schedule 1 to these Regulations substitute a reference to paragraph 90 of Schedule 3 to these Regulations.

Modifications of Schedule 3 to these Regulations for purposes of paragraph 31

40. (1) For the purposes of paragraph 31 of this Schedule, Schedule 3 to these Regulations is to be modified as follows.

(2) The information required by paragraph 11 (additional items) need not be given.

(3) In the case of general business, investment income, expenses and charges may be disclosed in the non-technical account rather than in the technical account.

(4) In the case of subsidiary undertakings which are not authorised to carry on long-term business in the United Kingdom, notes (8) and (9) to the profit and loss account format have effect as if references to investment income, expenses and charges arising in the long-term fund or to investments attributed to the long-term fund were references to investment income, expenses and charges or (as the case may be) investments relating to long-term business.

(5) In the case of subsidiary undertakings which do not have a head office in the United Kingdom, the computation required by paragraph 52 must be made annually by an actuary or other specialist in the field on the basis of recognised actuarial methods.

(6) The information required by paragraphs 85 to 88 need not be shown.

NOTES

Para 35A: inserted by the Companies, Partnerships and Groups (Accounts and Reports) Regulations 2015, SI 2015/980, reg 39(1), (13), as from 6 April 2015, in relation to (a) financial years beginning on or after 1 January 2016, and (b) a financial year of a company beginning on or after 1 January 2015, but before 1 January 2016, if the directors of the company so decide (see **[4.549]** *post*).

Para 36: substituted by SI 2015/980, reg 39(1), (14) (as to the application of this amendment see the first note above).

SCHEDULE 7
MATTERS TO BE DEALT WITH IN DIRECTORS' REPORT

Regulation 10

PART 1 MATTERS OF A GENERAL NATURE

Introduction

[4.97]

1. In addition to the information required by section 416 of the 2006 Act, the directors' report must contain the following information.

[1A. Where a company has chosen in accordance with section 414C(11) to set out in the company's strategic report information required by this Schedule to be contained in the directors' report it shall state in the directors' report that it has done so and in respect of which information it has done so.]

. . .

2. . . .

Political donations and expenditure

3. (1) If—

(a) the company (not being the wholly-owned subsidiary of a company incorporated in the United Kingdom) has in the financial year—

(i) made any political donation to any political party or other political organisation,

(ii) made any political donation to any independent election candidate, or

(iii) incurred any political expenditure, and

(b) the amount of the donation or expenditure, or (as the case may be) the aggregate amount of all donations and expenditure falling within paragraph (a), exceeded £2000,

the directors' report for the year must contain the following particulars.

(2) Those particulars are—

(a) as respects donations falling within sub-paragraph (1)(a)(i) or (ii)—

(i) the name of each political party, other political organisation or independent election candidate to whom any such donation has been made, and

(ii) the total amount given to that party, organisation or candidate by way of such donations in the financial year; and

(b) as respects expenditure falling within sub-paragraph (1)(a)(iii), the total amount incurred by way of such expenditure in the financial year.

(3) If—

(a) at the end of the financial year the company has subsidiaries which have, in that year, made any donations or incurred any such expenditure as is mentioned in sub-paragraph (1)(a), and

(b) it is not itself the wholly-owned subsidiary of a company incorporated in the United Kingdom,

the directors' report for the year is not, by virtue of sub-paragraph (1), required to contain the particulars specified in sub-paragraph (2).

But, if the total amount of any such donations or expenditure (or both) made or incurred in that year by the company and the subsidiaries between them exceeds £2000, the directors' report for the year must contain those particulars in relation to each body by whom any such donation or expenditure has been made or incurred.

(4) Any expression used in this paragraph which is also used in Part 14 of the 2006 Act (control of political donations and expenditure) has the same meaning as in that Part.

4. (1) If the company (not being the wholly-owned subsidiary of a company incorporated in the United Kingdom) has in the financial year made any contribution to a [non-UK] political party, the directors' report for the year must contain—

(a) a statement of the amount of the contribution, or

(b) (if it has made two or more such contributions in the year) a statement of the total amount of the contributions.

(2) If—

(a) at the end of the financial year the company has subsidiaries which have, in that year, made any such contributions as are mentioned in sub-paragraph (1), and

(b) it is not itself the wholly-owned subsidiary of a company incorporated in the United Kingdom,

the directors' report for the year is not, by virtue of sub-paragraph (1), required to contain any such statement as is there mentioned, but it must instead contain a statement of the total amount of the contributions made in the year by the company and the subsidiaries between them.

(3) In this paragraph, "contribution", in relation to an organisation, means—

(a) any gift of money to the organisation (whether made directly or indirectly);

(b) any subscription or other fee paid for affiliation to, or membership of, the organisation; or

(c) any money spent (otherwise than by the organisation or a person acting on its behalf) in paying any expenses incurred directly or indirectly by the organisation.

(4) In this paragraph, "[non-UK] political party" means any political party which carries on, or proposes to carry on, its activities wholly outside the [United Kingdom].

5. . . .

Financial instruments

6. (1) In relation to the use of financial instruments by a company, the directors' report must contain an indication of—

(a) the financial risk management objectives and policies of the company, including the policy for hedging each major type of forecasted transaction for which hedge accounting is used, and

(b) the exposure of the company to price risk, credit risk, liquidity risk and cash flow risk,

unless such information is not material for the assessment of the assets, liabilities, financial position and profit or loss of the company.

(2) In relation to a group directors' report sub-paragraph (1) has effect as if the references to the company were references to the company and its subsidiary undertakings included in the consolidation.

(3) In sub-paragraph (1) the expressions "hedge accounting", "price risk", "credit risk", "liquidity risk" and "cash flow risk" have the same meaning as they have in [Directive 2013/34/EU of the European Parliament and of the Council on the annual financial statements, consolidated financial statements and related reports of certain types of undertakings].

Miscellaneous

7. (1) The directors' report must contain—

(a) particulars of any important events affecting the company which have occurred since the end of the financial year,

(b) an indication of likely future developments in the business of the company,

(c) an indication of the activities (if any) of the company in the field of research and development, and

(d) (unless the company is an unlimited company) an indication of the existence of branches (as defined in section 1046(3) of the 2006 Act) of the company outside the United Kingdom.

(2) In relation to a group directors' report paragraphs (a), (b) and (c) of sub-paragraph (1) have effect as if the references to the company were references to the company and its subsidiary undertakings included in the consolidation.

NOTES

Para 1A inserted, and paras 2, 5 revoked, by the Companies Act 2006 (Strategic Report and Directors' Report) Regulations 2013, SI 2013/1970, reg 7(1), (3)(a), (b), as from 1 October 2013 (in respect of financial years ending on or after 30 September 2013).

Para 4: words in square brackets substituted by the Accounts and Reports (Amendment) (EU Exit) Regulations 2019, SI 2019/145, reg 6, Sch 3, paras 2, 5(a), in relation to financial years beginning on or after IP completion day (as defined in the European Union (Withdrawal Agreement) Act 2020, s 39) (for transitional provisions see reg 7 of the 2019 Regulations at **[12.79]**).

Para 6: words in square brackets in sub-para (3) substituted by the Accounts and Reports (Amendment) (EU Exit) Regulations 2019, SI 2019/145, reg 4, Sch 1, para 2, as from 6 February 2019.

PART 2 DISCLOSURE REQUIRED BY COMPANY ACQUIRING ITS OWN SHARES ETC

[4.98]

8. This Part of this Schedule applies where shares in a [public] company—

(a) are purchased by the company or are acquired by it by forfeiture or surrender in lieu of forfeiture, or in pursuance of any of the following provisions (acquisition of own shares by company limited by shares)—
  (i) section 143(3) of the Companies Act 1985,
  (ii) Article 153(3) of the Companies (Northern Ireland) Order 1986, or
  (iii) section 659 of the 2006 Act, or

(b) are acquired by another person in circumstances where paragraph (c) or (d) of any of the following provisions applies (acquisition by company's nominee, or by another with company financial assistance, the company having a beneficial interest)—
  (i) section 146(1) of the Companies Act 1985,
  (ii) Article 156(1) of the Companies (Northern Ireland) Order 1986, or
  (iii) section 662(1) of the 2006 Act applies, or

(c) are made subject to a lien or other charge taken (whether expressly or otherwise) by the company and permitted by any of the following provisions (exceptions from general rule against a company having a lien or charge on its own shares)—
  (i) section 150(2) or (4) of the Companies Act 1985,
  (ii) Article 160(2) or (4) of the Companies (Northern Ireland) Order 1986, or
  (iii) section 670(2) or (4) of the 2006 Act.

9. The directors' report for a financial year must state—

(a) the number and nominal value of the shares so purchased, the aggregate amount of the consideration paid by the company for such shares and the reasons for their purchase;

(b) the number and nominal value of the shares so acquired by the company, acquired by another person in such circumstances and so charged respectively during the financial year;

(c) the maximum number and nominal value of shares which, having been so acquired by the company, acquired by another person in such circumstances or so charged (whether or not during that year) are held at any time by the company or that other person during that year;

(d) the number and nominal value of the shares so acquired by the company, acquired by another person in such circumstances or so charged (whether or not during that year) which are disposed of by the company or that other person or cancelled by the company during that year;

(e) where the number and nominal value of the shares of any particular description are stated in pursuance of any of the preceding sub-paragraphs, the percentage of the called-up share capital which shares of that description represent;

(f) where any of the shares have been so charged the amount of the charge in each case; and

(g) where any of the shares have been disposed of by the company or the person who acquired them in such circumstances for money or money's worth the amount or value of the consideration in each case.

NOTES

Para 8: word in square brackets inserted by the Companies Act 2006 (Strategic Report and Directors' Report) Regulations 2013, SI 2013/1970, reg 7(1), (3)(c), as from 1 October 2013 (in respect of financial years ending on or after 30 September 2013).

PART 3 DISCLOSURE CONCERNING EMPLOYMENT ETC OF DISABLED PERSONS

[4.99]

10. (1) This Part of this Schedule applies to the directors' report where the average number of persons employed by the company . . . during the financial year exceeded 250.

[(2) The average number of persons employed by the company in the year is determined as follows—

(a) find for each month in the financial year the number of persons employed under contracts of service by the company in that month (whether throughout the month or not),

(b) add together the monthly totals, and

(c) divide by the number of months in the financial year.]

(3) The directors' report must in that case contain a statement describing such policy as the company has applied during the financial year—

(a) for giving full and fair consideration to applications for employment by the company made by disabled persons, having regard to their particular aptitudes and abilities,

(b) for continuing the employment of, and for arranging appropriate training for, employees of the company who have become disabled persons during the period when they were employed by the company, and

(c) otherwise for the training, career development and promotion of disabled persons employed by the company.

(4) In this Part—

(a) "employment" means employment other than employment to work wholly or mainly outside the United Kingdom, and "employed" and "employee" are to be construed accordingly; and

(b) "disabled person" means the same as in the Disability Discrimination Act 1995.

NOTES

Para 10: the words omitted from sub-para (1) were revoked, and sub-para (2) was substituted, by the Companies (Miscellaneous Reporting) Regulations 2018, SI 2018/860, regs 11, 12, in relation to the financial years of companies beginning on or after 1 January 2019.

[PART 4 ENGAGEMENT WITH EMPLOYEES, SUPPLIERS, CUSTOMERS AND OTHERS

Engagement with employees

[4.100]

11. (1) Unless the company is exempted under paragraph 11A, the directors' report for a financial year must contain a statement—

(a) describing the action that has been taken during the financial year to introduce, maintain or develop arrangements aimed at—

(i) providing employees systematically with information on matters of concern to them as employees,

(ii) consulting employees or their representatives on a regular basis so that the views of employees can be taken into account in making decisions which are likely to affect their interests,

(iii) encouraging the involvement of employees in the company's performance through an employees' share scheme or by some other means, and

(iv) achieving a common awareness on the part of all employees of the financial and economic factors affecting the performance of the company, and

(b) summarising—

(i) how the directors have engaged with employees, and

(ii) how the directors have had regard to employee interests, and the effect of that regard, including on the principal decisions taken by the company during the financial year.

(2) Nothing in sub-paragraph (1)(b) requires the disclosure of information about impending developments or matters in the course of negotiation if the disclosure would, in the opinion of the directors, be seriously prejudicial to the interests of the company.

(3) In sub-paragraph (1) "employee" does not include a person employed to work wholly or mainly outside the United Kingdom.

11A. (1) A company is exempted under this paragraph—

(a) in relation to its first financial year if the qualifying condition is met in that year;

(b) in relation to a subsequent financial year—

(i) if the qualifying condition is met in that year and was also met in relation to the preceding financial year;

(ii) if—

(aa) the qualifying condition is met in that year, and

(bb) the company was exempted in relation to the preceding financial year, or

(iii) if—

(aa) the qualifying condition was met in the preceding financial year, and

(bb) the company was exempted in relation to the preceding financial year.

(2) The qualifying condition is met by a company in a year in which the average number of persons employed by the company during the financial year is not more than 250.

(3) The average number of persons employed by the company in the year is determined as follows—

(a) find for each month in the financial year the number of persons employed under contracts of service by the company in that month (whether throughout the month or not),

(b) add together the monthly totals, and

(c) divide by the number of months in the financial year.

(4) Where the company is a parent company the average number of persons employed by the company refers to the number within the group.

(5) In this paragraph no regard is to be had to a person employed to work wholly or mainly outside the United Kingdom.

Engagement with suppliers, customers and others in a business relationship with the company

11B. (1) Unless the company is exempted under paragraph 11C, the directors' report for the financial year must contain a statement summarising how the directors have had regard to the need to foster the company's business relationships with suppliers, customers and others, and the effect of that regard, including on the principal decisions taken by the company during the financial year.

(2) Nothing in sub-paragraph (1) requires the disclosure of information about impending developments or matters in the course of negotiation if the disclosure would, in the opinion of the directors, be seriously prejudicial to the interests of the company.

11C. (1) A company is exempted under this paragraph—

(a) in relation to its first financial year if the qualifying conditions are met in that year;

(b) in relation to a subsequent financial year—

(i) if the qualifying conditions are met in that year and were also met in relation to the preceding financial year;

(ii) if—

(aa) the qualifying conditions are met in that year, and

(bb) the company was exempted in relation to the preceding financial year, or

(iii) if—

(aa) the qualifying conditions were met in the preceding financial year, and

(bb) the company was exempted in relation to the preceding financial year.

(2) The qualifying conditions are met by a company in a year in which it satisfies two or more of the following requirements—

1. Turnover	not more than £36 million

2. Balance sheet total	not more than £18 million
3. Number of employees	not more than 250

(3) In sub-paragraph (2)—

(a) for a period that is a company's financial year but is not in fact a year the figure for turnover must be proportionately adjusted,

(b) the balance sheet total means the aggregate of the amounts shown as assets in the company's balance sheet,

(c) the number of employees means the average number of persons employed by the company in the year, determined as follows—

(i) find for each month in the financial year the number of persons employed under contracts of service by the company in that month (whether throughout the month or not),

(ii) add together the monthly totals, and

(iii) divide by the number of months in the financial year.]

NOTES

This Part was substituted by the Companies (Miscellaneous Reporting) Regulations 2018, SI 2018/860, regs 11, 13, in relation to the financial years of companies beginning on or after 1 January 2019.

PART 5 POLICY AND PRACTICE ON PAYMENT OF CREDITORS

. . .

NOTES

This Part was revoked by the Companies Act 2006 (Strategic Report and Directors' Report) Regulations 2013, SI 2013/1970, reg 7(1), (3)(d), as from 1 October 2013 (in respect of financial years ending on or after 30 September 2013).

PART 6 DISCLOSURE REQUIRED BY CERTAIN PUBLICLY-TRADED COMPANIES

[4.101]

13. (1) This Part of this Schedule applies to the directors' report for a financial year if the company had securities carrying voting rights admitted to trading on a [UK] regulated market at the end of that year.

(2) The report must contain detailed information, by reference to the end of that year, on the following matters—

(a) the structure of the company's capital, including in particular—

(i) the rights and obligations attaching to the shares or, as the case may be, to each class of shares in the company, and

(ii) where there are two or more such classes, the percentage of the total share capital represented by each class;

(b) any restrictions on the transfer of securities in the company, including in particular—

(i) limitations on the holding of securities, and

(ii) requirements to obtain the approval of the company, or of other holders of securities in the company, for a transfer of securities;

(c) in the case of each person with a significant direct or indirect holding of securities in the company, such details as are known to the company of—

(i) the identity of the person,

(ii) the size of the holding, and

(iii) the nature of the holding;

(d) in the case of each person who holds securities carrying special rights with regard to control of the company—

(i) the identity of the person, and

(ii) the nature of the rights;

(e) where—

(i) the company has an employees' share scheme, and

(ii) shares to which the scheme relates have rights with regard to control of the company that are not exercisable directly by the employees,

how those rights are exercisable;

(f) any restrictions on voting rights, including in particular—

(i) limitations on voting rights of holders of a given percentage or number of votes,

(ii) deadlines for exercising voting rights, and

(iii) arrangements by which, with the company's co-operation, financial rights carried by securities are held by a person other than the holder of the securities;

(g) any agreements between holders of securities that are known to the company and may result in restrictions on the transfer of securities or on voting rights;

(h) any rules that the company has about—

(i) appointment and replacement of directors, or

(ii) amendment of the company's articles of association;

(i) the powers of the company's directors, including in particular any powers in relation to the issuing or buying back by the company of its shares;

(j) any significant agreements to which the company is a party that take effect, alter or terminate upon a change of control of the company following a takeover bid, and the effects of any such agreements;

(k) any agreements between the company and its directors or employees providing for compensation for loss of office or employment (whether through resignation, purported redundancy or otherwise) that occurs because of a takeover bid.

(3) For the purposes of sub-paragraph (2)(a) a company's capital includes any securities in the company that are not admitted to trading on a regulated market.

(4) For the purposes of sub-paragraph (2)(c) a person has an indirect holding of securities if—

(a) they are held on his behalf, or

(b) he is able to secure that rights carried by the securities are exercised in accordance with his wishes.

(5) Sub-paragraph (2)(j) does not apply to an agreement if—

(a) disclosure of the agreement would be seriously prejudicial to the company, and

(b) the company is not under any other obligation to disclose it.

(6) In this paragraph—

"securities" means shares or debentures;

"takeover bid" has the same meaning as in [paragraph 20(1) of Schedule 1C to the Companies Act 2006];

. . .

"voting rights" means rights to vote at general meetings of the company in question, including rights that arise only in certain circumstances.

14. The directors' report must also contain any necessary explanatory material with regard to information that is required to be included in the report by this Part.

NOTES

Para 13: word in square brackets in sub-para (1) inserted by the Accounts and Reports (Amendment) (EU Exit) Regulations 2019, SI 2019/145, reg 6, Sch 3, paras 2, 5(b), in relation to financial years beginning on or after IP completion day (as defined in the European Union (Withdrawal Agreement) Act 2020, s 39) (for transitional provisions see reg 7 of the 2019 Regulations at **[12.79]**). The words in square brackets in the definition "takeover bid" in sub-para (6) were substituted, and the definition "the Takeovers Directive" (omitted) was revoked, by the Takeovers (Amendment) (EU Exit) Regulations 2019, SI 2019/217, regs 17, 18, as from IP completion day (as defined in the European Union (Withdrawal Agreement) Act 2020, s 39).

[PART 7 DISCLOSURES CONCERNING GREENHOUSE GAS EMISSIONS[, ENERGY CONSUMPTION AND ENERGY EFFICIENCY ACTION BY QUOTED COMPANIES]

[4.102]

15. (1) [Subject to sub-paragraph (1A),] this Part of this Schedule applies to the directors' report for a financial year if the company is a quoted company.

[(1A) This Part does not apply if—

(a) the company is a subsidiary undertaking at the end of the financial year;

(b) the company is included in the group report of a parent undertaking; and

(c) the group report is prepared for a financial year of the parent undertaking that ends at the same time as, or before the end of, the company's financial year; and—

(i) if the group report is a group directors' report—

(aa) of a quoted company, it complies with this Part of this Schedule other than in reliance on paragraph 15(5)(b); or

(bb) of an unquoted company, it complies with Part 7A of this Schedule other than in reliance on paragraph 20D(7)(b); or

(ii) if the group report is a group energy and carbon report, it complies with Part 7A of this Schedule as applied and modified by regulation 12B of the Limited Liability Partnerships (Accounts and Audit) (Application of Companies Act 2006) Regulations 2008 other than in reliance on paragraph 20D(7)(b).

(1B) For the purpose of sub-paragraph (1A), "group energy and carbon report" means a report prepared in accordance with section 415(2) of the 2006 Act as applied and modified by regulation 12B of the Limited Liability Partnerships (Accounts and Audit) (Application of Companies Act 2006) Regulations 2008;]

(2) The report must state the annual quantity of emissions in tonnes of carbon dioxide equivalent from activities for which that company is responsible including—

(a) the combustion of fuel; and

(b) the operation of any facility.

(3) The report must state the annual quantity of emissions in tonnes of carbon dioxide equivalent resulting from the purchase of electricity, heat, steam or cooling by the company for its own use.

[(3A) The report must state a figure, in kWh, which is the aggregate of—

(a) the annual quantity of energy consumed from activities for which the company is responsible, including—

(i) the combustion of fuel; and

(ii) the operation of any facility; and

(b) the annual quantity of energy consumed resulting from the purchase of electricity, heat, steam or cooling by the company for its own use.

(3B) The report must state what proportion of the figures reported in accordance with sub-paragraphs (2) and (3) relate to emissions in the United Kingdom and offshore area.

(3C) The report must state what proportion of the figure reported in accordance with sub-paragraph (3A) relates to energy consumed in the United Kingdom and offshore area.

(3D) If the company has in the financial year to which the report relates taken any measures for the purpose of increasing the company's energy efficiency, the report must contain a description of the principal measures taken for that purpose.]

(4) Sub-paragraphs [(2) to (3D) and paragraphs 16 and 17] apply only to the extent that it is practical for the company to obtain the information in question; but where it is not practical for the company to obtain some or all of that information, the report must state what information is not included and why.

[(5) Nothing in sub-paragraphs (2) to (3D) and paragraphs 16 and 17 requires the disclosure of information if—

(a) the company consumed 40,000 kWh of energy or less during the period in respect of which the directors' report is prepared and the report states that the information is not disclosed for that reason; or

(b) the disclosure would, in the opinion of the directors, be seriously prejudicial to the interests of the company, and the report states that the information is not disclosed for that reason.]

[15A. (1) If the report is a group directors' report, subject to sub-paragraph (2), paragraph 15(2) to (3A), (3D) and (5)(a) and paragraph 17 have effect as if references to the company were references to the company and its subsidiary undertakings included in the consolidation that are quoted companies, unquoted companies or limited liability partnerships.

(2) The company may exclude from the report any information which relates to—

(a) a subsidiary undertaking that is a quoted company and which that quoted company would not be required to include in its directors' report by this Part of this Schedule;

(b) a subsidiary undertaking that is an unquoted company and which that unquoted company would not be required to include in its directors' report by Part 7A of this Schedule;

(c) a subsidiary undertaking that is a limited liability partnership and which that limited liability partnership would not be required to include in its energy and carbon report by section 416(2) of the 2006 Act as applied and modified by regulation 12B of the Limited Liability Partnerships (Accounts and Audit) (Application of Companies Act 2006) Regulations 2008.

(3) For the purpose of this paragraph, "limited liability partnership" means a limited liability partnership registered under the Limited Liability Partnerships Act 2000.]

16. The directors' report must state the methodologies used to calculate the information disclosed under paragraph 15(2)[, (3) and (3A)].

17. The directors' report must state at least one ratio which expresses the . . . company's annual emissions in relation to a quantifiable factor associated with the company's activities.

18. With the exception of the first year for which the directors' report contains the information required by paragraphs 15(2) and (3) and 17, the report must state not only the information required by paragraphs 15(2) and (3) and 17, but also that information as disclosed in the report for the preceding financial year.

[18A. With the exception of the first year for which the directors' report contains the information required by paragraph 15(3A) to (3D), the report must state not only the information required by paragraph 15(3A) to (3D) but that information as disclosed in the report for the preceding financial year.]

19. The directors' report must state . . . the period for which it is reporting the information required by paragraph 15(2) [if it] is different to the period in respect of which the directors' report is prepared.

[19A The period for which the directors' report is reporting the information required by paragraph 15(3) and (3A) must be the same as the period for which it is reporting the information required by paragraph 15(2).]

20. The following definitions apply for the purposes of this Part of this Schedule—

"emissions" means emissions into the atmosphere of a greenhouse gas as defined in section 92 of the Climate Change Act 2008 which are attributable to human activity;

["energy" means all forms of energy products where "energy products" means combustible fuels, heat, renewable energy, electricity, or any other form of energy;

"energy efficiency" means the ratio of output of performance, service, goods or energy to input of energy;

"kWh" means kilowatt hours;

"offshore area" means the areas comprising—

(a) the sea adjacent to the United Kingdom from the low water mark to the landward baseline of the United Kingdom territorial sea;

(b) the United Kingdom territorial sea;

(c) the sea in any designated area within the meaning of section 1(7) of the Continental Shelf Act 1964; and

(d) the sea in any area for the time being designated under section 41(3) of the Marine and Coastal Access Act 2009,

and includes the places above those areas, and the bed and subsoil of the sea within those areas;]

"tonne of carbon dioxide equivalent" has the meaning given in section 93(2) of the Climate Change Act 2008.]

NOTES

Inserted by the Companies Act 2006 (Strategic Report and Directors' Report) Regulations 2013, SI 2013/1970, reg 7(1), (3)(e), as from 1 October 2013 (in respect of financial years ending on or after 30 September 2013).

Part heading: words in square brackets inserted by the Companies (Directors' Report) and Limited Liability Partnerships (Energy and Carbon Report) Regulations 2018, SI 2018/1155, regs 3, 6(1), (2), as from 1 April 2019, in respect of financial years beginning on or after that date.

Para 15 is amended as follows:

Words in square brackets in sub-para (1) inserted by SI 2018/1155, regs 3, 6(1), (3)(a), as from 1 April 2019, in respect of financial years beginning on or after that date.

Sub-paras (1A), (1B), (3A)–(3D) and (5) inserted and added respectively by SI 2018/1155, regs 3, 6(1), (3)(b), (c), (e), as from 1 April 2019, in respect of financial years beginning on or after that date.

Words in square brackets in sub-para (4) substituted by SI 2018/1155, regs 3, 6(1), (3)(d), as from 1 April 2019, in respect of financial years beginning on or after that date.

Paras 15A, 18A, 19A: inserted by SI 2018/1155, regs 3, 6(1), (4), (7), (9), as from 1 April 2019, in respect of financial years beginning on or after that date.

Para 16: words in square brackets substituted by SI 2018/1155, regs 3, 6(1), (5), as from 1 April 2019, in respect of financial years beginning on or after that date.

Para 17: word omitted revoked by SI 2018/1155, regs 3, 6(1), (6), as from 1 April 2019, in respect of financial years beginning on or after that date.

Para 19: word omitted revoked, and words in square brackets substituted, by SI 2018/1155, regs 3, 6(1), (8), as from 1 April 2019, in respect of financial years beginning on or after that date.

Para 20: definitions in square brackets inserted by SI 2018/1155, regs 3, 6(1), (10), as from 1 April 2019, in respect of financial years beginning on or after that date.

[PART 7A DISCLOSURES CONCERNING GREENHOUSE GAS EMISSIONS, ENERGY CONSUMPTION AND ENERGY EFFICIENCY ACTION BY UNQUOTED COMPANIES

[4.103]

20A. (1) Unless the company is exempted under paragraph 20B or 20C, and subject to sub-paragraph (2), this Part of this Schedule applies to the directors' report for a financial year if the company is an unquoted company.

(2) This Part does not apply if—

(a) the company is a subsidiary undertaking at the end of the financial year;

(b) the company is included in the group report of a parent undertaking; and

(c) the group report is prepared for a financial year of the parent undertaking that ends at the same time as, or before the end of, the company's financial year; and—

(i) if the group report is a group directors' report—

(aa) of a quoted company, it complies with Part 7 of this Schedule other than in reliance on paragraph 15(5)(b); or

(bb) of an unquoted company, it complies with this Part of this Schedule other than in reliance on paragraph 20D(7)(b); or

(ii) if the group report is a group energy and carbon report, it complies with this Part of this Schedule as applied and modified by regulation 12B of the Limited Liability Partnerships (Accounts and Audit) (Application of Companies Act 2006) Regulations 2008 other than in reliance on paragraph 20D(7)(b).

(3) For the purpose of sub-paragraph (2), "group energy and carbon report" means a report prepared in accordance with section 415(2) of the 2006 Act as applied and modified by regulation 12B of the Limited Liability Partnerships (Accounts and Audit) (Application of Companies Act 2006) Regulations 2008.

20B. (1) Unless the company is a parent company, the company is exempted under this paragraph—

(a) in relation to its first financial year if the qualifying conditions in sub-paragraph (2) are met in that year;

(b) in relation to a subsequent financial year—

(i) if the qualifying conditions are met in that year and were also met in relation to the preceding financial year;

(ii) if—

(aa) the qualifying conditions are met in that year, and

(bb) the company was exempted in relation to the preceding financial year; or

(iii) if—

(aa) the qualifying conditions were met in the preceding financial year, and

(bb) the company was exempted in relation to the preceding financial year.

(2) The qualifying conditions referred to in sub-paragraph (1) are met by a company in a year in which it satisfies two or more of the following requirements—

1. Turnover	not more than £36 million
2. Balance sheet total	not more than £18 million
3. Number of employees	not more than 250

(3) For the purposes of sub-paragraph (2)—

(a) for a period that is a company's financial year but is not in fact a year the figure for turnover must be proportionately adjusted;

(b) the balance sheet total means the aggregate of the amounts shown as assets in the company's balance sheet;

(c) the number of employees means the average number of persons employed by the company in the year, determined as follows—

(i) find for each month in the financial year the number of persons employed under contracts of service by the company in that month (whether throughout the month or not),

(ii) add together the monthly totals, and

(iii) divide by the number of months in the financial year.

20C. (1) A parent company is exempted under this paragraph—

(a) in relation to the parent company's first financial year if the qualifying conditions in sub-paragraph (2) are met in that year by the group headed by it;

(b) in relation to a subsequent financial year of the parent company—

(i) if the qualifying conditions are met in that year and the preceding financial year by the group headed by the parent company;

(ii) if—

(aa) the qualifying conditions are met in that year by the group, and

(bb) the parent company was exempted in relation to the preceding financial year; or

(iii) if—

(aa) the qualifying conditions were met in the preceding financial year by the group, and

(bb) the parent company was exempted in relation to the preceding financial year.

(2) The qualifying conditions referred to in sub-paragraph (1) are met by a group in a year in which it satisfies two or more of the following requirements—

1. Aggregate turnover	not more than £36 million net (or £43.2 million gross)
2. Aggregate balance sheet total	not more than £18 million net (or £21.6 million gross)

Part 4 CA 2006 SIs

3. Aggregate number of employees	not more than 250

(3) For the purposes of sub-paragraph (2), the aggregate figures are to be ascertained by aggregating the relevant figures determined in accordance with paragraph 20B for each member of the group.

(4) In relation to the aggregate figures for turnover and balance sheet total—

(a) "net" means after any set-offs and other adjustments made to eliminate group transactions—

(i) in the case of Companies Act accounts, in accordance with regulations under section 404 of the 2006 Act,

(ii) in the case of IAS accounts, in accordance with international accounting standards;

(b) "gross" means without those set-offs and other adjustments; and

(c) a company may satisfy any requirements in sub-paragraph (2) on the basis of either the net or the gross figure.

(5) For the purposes of sub-paragraph (2)—

(a) the figures for each subsidiary undertaking must be those included in its individual accounts for the relevant financial year, that is—

(i) if its financial year ends with that of the parent company, that financial year, and

(ii) if not, its financial year ending last before the end of the financial year of the parent company; or

(b) if those figures cannot be obtained without disproportionate expense or undue delay, the latest available figures may be taken.

20D. (1) The directors' report must state the annual quantity of emissions in tonnes of carbon dioxide equivalent resulting from activities for which the company is responsible involving—

(a) the combustion of gas; or

(b) the consumption of fuel for the purposes of transport.

(2) The report must state the annual quantity of emissions in tonnes of carbon dioxide equivalent resulting from the purchase of electricity by the company for its own use, including for the purposes of transport.

(3) The report must state a figure, in kWh, which is the aggregate of—

(a) the annual quantity of energy consumed from activities for which the company is responsible involving—

(i) the combustion of gas; or

(ii) the consumption of fuel for the purposes of transport; and

(b) the annual quantity of energy consumed resulting from the purchase of electricity by the company for its own use, including for the purposes of transport.

(4) If the company has in the financial year to which the report relates taken any measures for the purpose of increasing the company's energy efficiency, the report must contain a description of the principal measures taken for that purpose.

(5) The figures reported in accordance with sub-paragraphs (1) to (3)—

(a) if the company is an offshore undertaking, may exclude emissions and energy consumed outside of the United Kingdom and offshore area;

(b) in any other case, may exclude emissions and energy consumed outside of the United Kingdom.

(6) Sub-paragraphs (1) to (4) and paragraphs 20F and 20G apply only to the extent that it is practical for the company to obtain the information in question; but where it is not practical for the company to obtain some or all of that information, the report must state what information is not included and why.

(7) Nothing in sub-paragraphs (1) to (4) and paragraphs 20F and 20G requires the disclosure of information if—

(a) the company consumed 40,000 kWh of energy or less in the United Kingdom during the period in respect of which the directors' report is prepared, and the report states that the information is not disclosed for that reason; or

(b) the disclosure would, in the opinion of the directors, be seriously prejudicial to the interests of the company, and the report states that the information is not disclosed for that reason.

20E. (1) If the report is a group directors' report, subject to sub-paragraph (2) and (3), paragraph 20D(1) to (4) and (7)(a) and paragraph 20G have effect as if references to the company were references to the company and its subsidiary undertakings included in the consolidation that are quoted companies, unquoted companies or limited liability partnerships.

(2) If a subsidiary undertaking is a quoted company, paragraph 20D(1) to (4) have effect as if references to the disclosures required were references to the disclosures required for the purpose of paragraph 15(2) to (3D) of Part 7 of this Schedule.

(3) The company may exclude from the report any information which relates to—

(a) a subsidiary undertaking that is a quoted company and which that quoted company would not be required to include in its directors' report by Part 7 of this Schedule;

(b) a subsidiary undertaking that is an unquoted company and which that unquoted company would not be required to include in its directors' report by this Part of this Schedule;

(c) a subsidiary undertaking that is a limited liability partnership and which that limited liability partnership would not be required to include in its energy and carbon report by section 416(2) of the 2006 Act as applied and modified by regulation 12B of the Limited Liability Partnerships (Accounts and Audit) (Application of Companies Act 2006) Regulations 2008.

(4) For the purpose of this paragraph, "limited liability partnership" means a limited liability partnership registered under the Limited Liability Partnerships Act 2000.

20F. The directors' report must state the methodologies used to calculate the information disclosed under paragraph 20D(1), (2) and (3).

20G. The directors' report must state at least one ratio which expresses the company's annual emissions in relation to a quantifiable factor associated with the company's activities.

20H. With the exception of the first year for which the directors' report contains the information required by paragraphs 20D(1) to (4) and 20G, the report must state not only the information required by those paragraphs, but also that information as disclosed in the report for the preceding financial year.

20I. The directors' report must state the period for which it is reporting the information required by paragraph 20D(1) if it is different to the period in respect of which the directors' report is prepared.

20J. The period for which the directors' report is reporting the information required by paragraph 20D(2) and (3) must be the same as the period for which it is reporting the information required by paragraph 20D(1).

20K. The following definitions apply for the purposes of this Part of this Schedule—

"aircraft" means a self-propelled machine that can move through the air other than against the earth's surface;

"emissions", "energy" and "energy efficiency" have the same meaning as in Part 7 of this Schedule;

"for the purposes of transport" means, in relation to the consumption of fuel or the purchase of electricity, for consumption by an aircraft, road-going vehicle, train or a vessel during the course of any journey which—

(a) starts,

(b) ends, or

(c) both starts and ends

within the United Kingdom;

"gas" means, except in the definition of "offshore activity", any combustible substance which is gaseous at a temperature of 15 degrees Celsius and a pressure of 101.325 kPa (1013.25 mb) and which consists wholly or mainly of methane, ethane, propane, butane, hydrogen or carbon monoxide, or a combination of those, or a combustible mixture of those and air;

"kWh" means kilowatt hours;

"offshore activity" means activity which includes—

(a) the exploitation of mineral resources in or under the shore or bed of waters in the offshore area,

(b) the conversion of a place under the shore or bed of such waters for the purpose of storing gas,

(c) the storage of gas in, under or over such waters or the recovery of gas so stored,

(d) the unloading of gas at a place in, under or over such waters, or

(e) the provision of accommodation for persons who work on or from an offshore installation which is maintained for the production of petroleum or the storage or unloading of gas

where storing gas includes storing gas with a view to its permanent disposal and where "gas" for this purpose means gas within the meaning of section 2(4) of the Energy Act 2008 or carbon dioxide;

"offshore area" has the same meaning as in Part 7 of this Schedule;

"offshore installation" means an installation or structure used for carrying on a relevant offshore activity, and which is situated in the waters of, or in the seabed in, the offshore area, but excluding a ship or a floating structure which is not being maintained on station during the course of a relevant offshore activity; and for this purpose "relevant offshore activity" means an activity falling within paragraphs (a) to (d) of the definition of "offshore activity";

"offshore undertaking" means an undertaking whose activities consist wholly or mainly of offshore activities;

"road-going vehicle" means any vehicle—

(a) in respect of which a vehicle licence is required under the Vehicle Excise and Registration Act 1994; or

(b) which is an exempt vehicle under that Act;

"tonne of carbon dioxide equivalent" has the same meaning as in Part 7 of this Schedule;

"train" has the meaning given in section 83 of the Railways Act 1993;

"vessel" means any boat or ship which is self-propelled and operates in or under water.]

NOTES

Inserted by the Companies (Directors' Report) and Limited Liability Partnerships (Energy and Carbon Report) Regulations 2018, SI 2018/1155, regs 3, 7, as from 1 April 2019, in respect of financial years beginning on or after that date.

[PART 8 STATEMENT OF CORPORATE GOVERNANCE ARRANGEMENTS

[4.104]

21. This Part of this Schedule applies to the directors' report for a financial year unless the company is exempted under paragraph 22.

22. A company is exempted under this paragraph if—

(a) it is required to provide a corporate governance statement,

(b) it is a community interest company within the meaning of section 26 of the Companies (Audit, Investigations and Community Enterprise) Act 2004, or

(c) it is a charitable company within the meaning of section 193 of the Charities Act 2011.

23. (1) The directors' report for a company's first financial year must include a statement of its corporate governance arrangements in accordance with paragraph 26 if the qualifying conditions are met in that year.

(2) In relation to any subsequent financial year, the directors' report must include a statement of the company's corporate governance arrangements—

(a) if the qualifying conditions are met in that year and were also met in relation to the preceding financial year;

(b) if—

(i) the qualifying conditions are met in that year, and

(ii) the directors' report was required to provide a statement of the company's corporate governance arrangements in relation to the preceding financial year, or

(c) if—

(i) the qualifying conditions were met in the preceding financial year, and

(ii) the directors' report was required to provide a statement of the company's corporate governance arrangements in relation to the preceding financial year.

(3) The qualifying conditions are met by a company in a year in which it satisfies either or both of the following requirements—

(a) it has more than 2000 employees;

(b) it has—

(i) a turnover of more than £200 million, and

(ii) a balance sheet total of more than £2 billion.

24. In paragraph 23(3)—

(a) for a period that is a company's financial year but is not in fact a year, the figure for turnover must be proportionately adjusted,

(b) the balance sheet total means the aggregate of the amounts shown as assets in the company's balance sheet, and

(c) the number of employees means the average number of persons employed by the company in the year, determined as follows—

(i) find for each month in the financial year the number of persons employed under contracts of service by the company in that month (whether throughout the month or not),

(ii) add together the monthly totals, and

(iii) divide by the number of months in the financial year.

25. In this Part—

"corporate governance", in relation to a company, means—

(a) the nature, constitution or functions of the organs of the company,

(b) the manner in which organs of the company conduct themselves,

(c) the requirements imposed on organs of the company,

(d) the relationship between different organs of the company, and

(e) the relationship between the organs of the company and the members of the company, and

"corporate governance code" means a code of practice on corporate governance.

26. (1) The directors' report must include a statement (a "statement of corporate governance arrangements") which states—

(a) which corporate governance code, if any, the company applied in the financial year,

(b) how the company applied any corporate governance code reported under sub-paragraph (a), and

(c) if the company departed from any corporate governance code reported under sub-paragraph (a), the respects in which it did so, and its reasons for so departing.

(2) If the company has not applied any corporate governance code for the financial year, the statement of corporate governance arrangements must explain the reasons for that decision, and explain what arrangements for corporate governance were applied for that year.

27. (1) This paragraph applies if—

(a) a company is required by this Part to include a statement of corporate governance arrangements in its directors' report for a financial year, and

(b) the company is an unquoted company in relation to that financial year.

(2) The company must ensure that the statement of corporate governance arrangements—

(a) is made available on a website, and

(b) remains so available until—

(i) the statement of corporate governance arrangements for the company's next financial year is made available in accordance with this paragraph, or

(ii) if the obligation under this paragraph to make a statement of corporate governance arrangements available does not arise in relation to the company's next financial year, the end of the company's next financial year.

(3) Sub-paragraph (2) applies whether a company's statement of corporate governance arrangements is located in the directors' report, or in the strategic report as permitted by section 414C(11) of the 2006 Act.

(4) The statement of corporate governance arrangements must be made available on a website that—

(a) is maintained by or on behalf of the company, and

(b) identifies the company in question.

(5) Access to the statement of corporate governance arrangements made available on the website under sub-paragraph (2), and the ability to obtain a hard copy of the statement from the website, must not be—

(a) conditional on the payment of a fee, or

(b) otherwise restricted, except so far as necessary to comply with any enactment or regulatory requirement (in the United Kingdom or elsewhere).

(6) The statement of corporate governance arrangements—

(a) must be made available on a website as soon as reasonably practicable, and

(b) must be kept available throughout the period specified in sub-paragraph (2)(b)(i) or (as the case may be) (ii).

(7) A failure to make the statement of corporate governance arrangements available on a website throughout the period specified in sub-paragraph (2)(b)(i) or (as the case may be) (ii) is disregarded if—

(a) the statement is made available on the website for part of that period, and

(b) the failure is wholly attributable to circumstances that it would not be reasonable to have expected the company to prevent or avoid.

(8) In the event of default in complying with this paragraph, an offence is committed by every officer of the company who is in default.

(9) A person guilty of an offence under sub-paragraph (8) is liable on summary conviction to a fine not exceeding level 3 on the standard scale.]

NOTES

Inserted by the Companies (Miscellaneous Reporting) Regulations 2018, SI 2018/860, regs 11, 14, in relation to the financial years of companies beginning on or after 1 January 2019.

[SCHEDULE 8
QUOTED COMPANIES [AND TRADED COMPANIES]: DIRECTORS' REMUNERATION REPORT
PART 1 INTRODUCTORY

[4.105]

1. (1) In the directors' remuneration report for a financial year ("the relevant financial year") there must be shown, subject to sub-paragraph (2), the information specified in Parts 2, 3, and 4.

(2) The directors' remuneration policy as specified in Part 4, may, subject to subparagraph (3), be omitted from the directors' remuneration report for a financial year, if the company does not intend, at the accounts meeting at which the report is to be laid, to move a resolution to approve the directors' remuneration policy in accordance with section 439A of the 2006 Act.

(3) Where the directors' remuneration policy is omitted from the report in accordance with sub-paragraph (2), there must be set out in the report the following information—

(a) the date of the last general meeting of the company at which a resolution was moved by the company in respect of that directors' remuneration policy and at which that policy was approved; and

(b) where, on the company's website or at some other place, a copy of that directors' remuneration policy may be inspected by the members of the company.

2. (1) Information required to be shown in the report for or in respect of a particular person must be shown in the report in a manner that links the information to that person identified by name.

(2) Nothing in this Schedule prevents the directors setting out in the report any such additional information as they think fit, and any item required to be shown in the report may be shown in greater detail than required by the provisions of this Schedule.

[(2A) The directors' remuneration report must not include personal data of a director that falls within a special category of data listed in Article 9(1) of Regulation (EU) 2016/679 of the European Parliament and of the Council of 27 April 2016 on the protection of natural persons with regard to the processing of personal data and on the free movement of such data, or personal data which refers to the family situation of individual directors.]

(3) Where the requirements of this Schedule make reference to a "director" those requirements may be complied with in such manner as to distinguish between directors who perform executive functions and those who do not.

(4) Any requirement of this Schedule to provide information in respect of a director may, in respect of those directors who do not perform executive functions, be omitted or otherwise modified where that requirement is not applicable to such a director and in such a case, particulars of, and the reasons for, the omission or modification must be given in the report.

(5) Any requirement of this Schedule to provide information in respect of performance measures or targets does not require the disclosure of information which, in the opinion of the directors, is commercially sensitive in respect of the company.

(6) Where information that would otherwise be required to be in the report is not included in reliance on sub-paragraph (5), particulars of, and the reasons for, the omission must be given in the report and an indication given of when (if at all) the information is to be reported to the members of the company.

(7) Where any provision of this Schedule requires a sum or figure to be given in respect of any financial year preceding the relevant financial year, in the first directors' remuneration report prepared in accordance with this Schedule, that sum or figure may, where the sum or figure is not readily available from the reports and accounts of the company prepared for those years, be given as an estimate and a note of explanation provided in the report.

[(8) A person is to be treated as a director of a company for the purposes of this Schedule (other than in the references to directors in paragraphs 2(2), 2(5), 3, 5(2), 6(1)(b), 10(3), 22(1), 23(c), 24(4), and 48) if the person—

(a) is the company's chief executive officer (however described) or, where such a function exists in the company, the company's deputy chief executive officer (however described), but

(b) is not a director of the company.]]

NOTES

This Schedule was substituted by the Large and Medium-sized Companies and Groups (Accounts and Reports) (Amendment) Regulations 2013, SI 2013/1981, reg 4, Schedule, as from 1 October 2013, except in respect of a company's financial year ending before 30 September 2013 (note also that the provisions of Part 6 of Schedule 8 apply to a revised directors' remuneration policy set out in a document in accordance with the Companies Act 2006, s 422A(3) on or after 1 October 2013).

The words in square brackets in the Schedule heading were inserted, and sub-paras 2(2A) and (8) were inserted and added respectively, by the Companies (Directors' Remuneration Policy and Directors' Remuneration Report) Regulations 2019, SI 2019/970, regs 30, 31(1)–(3), in relation to a directors' remuneration report for a financial year of a company beginning on or after 10 June 2019 (see further reg 2 of the 2019 Regulations at **[4.680]**).

[PART 2 ANNUAL STATEMENT

[4.106]

3. The directors' remuneration report must contain a statement by the director who fulfils the role of chair of the remuneration committee (or, where there is no such person, by a director nominated by the directors to make the statement) summarising for the relevant financial year—

(a) the major decisions on directors' remuneration;

[(aa) any discretion which has been exercised in the award of directors' remuneration;]

(b) any substantial changes relating to directors' remuneration made during the year; and

(c) the context in which those changes occurred and decisions have been taken.]

NOTES

This Schedule was substituted as noted to Part 1 of this Schedule at **[4.105]**.

Para 3: sub-para (aa) inserted by the Companies (Miscellaneous Reporting) Regulations 2018, SI 2018/860, regs 15, 16, in relation to the financial years of companies beginning on or after 1 January 2019.

[PART 3 ANNUAL REPORT ON REMUNERATION

[4.107]

4. Single total figure of remuneration for each director

(1) The directors' remuneration report must, for the relevant financial year, for each person who has served as a director of the company at any time during that year, set out in a table in the form set out in paragraph 5 ("the single total figure table") the information prescribed by paragraphs 6 and 7 below.

(2) The report may set out in separate tables the information to be supplied in respect of directors who perform executive functions and those who do not.

(3) Unless otherwise indicated the sums set out in the table are those in respect of the relevant financial year and relate to the director's performance of, or agreement to perform, qualifying services.

5. (1) The form of the table required by paragraph 4 is—

[Single Total Figure Table

	a	b	c	d	e	Total	Total Fixed Remuneration	Total Variable Remuneration
Director 1	xxx	xxx	xxx	xxx	xxx	xxx	xxx	xxx
Director 2	xxx	xxx	xxx	xxx	xxx	xxx	xxx	xxx]

(2) The directors may choose to display the table using an alternative orientation, in which case references in this Schedule to columns are to be read as references to rows.

6. (1) In addition to the columns described in paragraph 7, columns—

(a) must be included to set out any other items in the nature of remuneration (other than items required to be disclosed under paragraph 15) which are not set out in the columns headed "(a)" to "(e)"; and

(b) may be included if there are any sub-totals or other items which the directors consider necessary in order to assist the understanding of the table.

(2) Any additional columns must be inserted before the column marked "Total".

7. (1) Subject to paragraph 9, in the single total figure table, the sums that are required to be set out in the columns are—

(a) in the column headed "a", the total amount of salary and fees;

(b) in the column headed "b", all taxable benefits;

(c) in the column headed "c", money or other assets received or receivable for the relevant financial year as a result of the achievement of performance measures and targets relating to a period ending in that financial year other than—

(i) those which result from awards made in a previous financial year and where final vesting is determined as a result of the achievement of performance measures or targets relating to a period ending in the relevant financial year; or

(ii) those receivable subject to the achievement of performance measures or targets in a future financial year;

(d) in the column headed "d", money or other assets received or receivable for periods of more than one financial year where final vesting—

(i) is determined as a result of the achievement of performance measures or targets relating to a period ending in the relevant financial year; and

(ii) is not subject to the achievement of performance measures or targets in a future financial year;

(e) in the column headed "e", all pension related benefits including—

(i) payments (whether in cash or otherwise) in lieu of retirement benefits;

(ii) all benefits in year from participating in pension schemes;

(f) in the column headed "Total", the total amount of the sums set out in the previous columns;

[(g) in the column headed "Total Fixed Remuneration", the total amount of the sums set out in columns headed "a", "b" and "e" and any additional columns relevant to this calculation;

(h) in the column headed "Total Variable Remuneration", the total amount of the sums set out in columns headed "c" and "d" and any additional columns relevant to this calculation.]

(2) Where it is necessary to assist the understanding of the table by the creation of subtotals the columns headed "a" to "e" may be set out in an order other than the one set out in paragraph 5.

8. (1) In respect of any items in paragraph 7(1)(c) or (d) where the performance measures or targets are substantially (but not fully) completed by the end of the relevant financial year—

(a) the sum given in the table may include sums which relate to the following financial year; but

(b) where such sums are included, those sums must not be included in the corresponding column of the single total figure table prepared for that following financial year; and

(c) a note to the table must explain the basis of the calculation.

(2) Where any money or other assets reported in the single total figure table in the directors' remuneration report prepared in respect of any previous financial year are the subject of a recovery of sums paid or the withholding of any sum for any reason in the relevant financial year—

(a) the recovery or withholding so attributable must be shown in a separate column in the table as a negative value and deducted from the column headed "Total"; and

(b) an explanation for the recovery or withholding and the basis of the calculation must be given in a note to the table.

(3) Where the calculations in accordance with paragraph 10 (other than in respect of a recovery or withholding) result in a negative value, the result must be expressed as zero in the relevant column in the table.

9. (1) Each column in the single total figure table must contain, in such manner as to permit comparison, two sums as follows—

(a) the sum set out in the corresponding column in the report prepared in respect of the financial year preceding the relevant financial year; and

(b) the sum for the relevant financial year.

(2) When, in the single total figure table, a sum is given in the column which relates to the preceding financial year and that sum, when set out in the report for that preceding year was given as an estimated sum, then in the relevant financial year—

(a) it must be given as an actual sum;

(b) the amount representing the difference between the estimate and the actual must not be included in the column relating to the relevant financial year; and

(c) details of the calculation of the revised sum must be given in a note to the table.

10. (1) The methods to be used to calculate the sums required to be set out in the single total figure table are—

(a) for the column headed "a", cash paid to or receivable by the person in respect of the relevant financial year;

(b) for the column headed "b", the gross value before payment of tax;

(c) for column "c", the total cash equivalent including any amount deferred, other than where the deferral is subject to the achievement of further performance measures or targets in a future financial year;

(d) for column "d"—

(i) the cash value of any monetary award;

(ii) the value of any shares or share options awarded, calculated by—

(aa) multiplying the original number of shares granted by the proportion that vest (or an estimate);

(bb) multiplying the total arrived at in (aa) by the market price of shares at the date on which the shares vest; and

(iii) the value of any additional cash or shares receivable in respect of dividends accrued (actually or notionally);

(e) for the column headed "e",—

(i) for the item in paragraph 7(1)(e)(i), the cash value;

(ii) for the item in paragraph 7(1)(e)(ii), what the aggregate pension input amount would be across all the pension schemes of the company or group in which the director accrues benefits, calculated using the method set out in section 229 of the Finance Act 2004 where—

(aa) references to "pension input period" are to be read as references to the company's financial year, or where a person becomes a director during the financial year, the period starting on the date the person became a director and ending at the end of the financial year;

(bb) all pension schemes of the company or group which provide relevant benefits to the director are deemed to be registered schemes;

(cc) all pension contributions paid by the director during the pension input period are deducted from the pension input amount;

(dd) in the application of section 234 of that Act, the figure 20 is substituted for the figure 16 each time it appears;

(ee) subsections 229(3) and (4) do not apply; and

(ff) section 277 of that Act is read as follows—

"277 Valuation assumptions

For the purposes of this Part the valuation assumptions in relation to a person, benefits and a date are—

(a) if the person has not left the employment to which the arrangement relates on or before the date, that the person left that employment on the date with a prospective right to benefits under the arrangement,

(b) if the person has not reached such age (if any) as must have been reached to avoid any reduction in the benefits on account of age, that on the date the person is entitled to receive the benefits without any reduction on account of age, and

(c) that the person's right to receive the benefits had not been occasioned by physical or mental impairment.".

(2) For the item in paragraph 7(1)(e)(ii) where there has not been a company contribution to the pension scheme in respect of the director, but if such a contribution had been made it would have been measured for pension input purposes under section 233(1)(b) of the Finance Act 2004, when calculating the pension input amount for the purposes of subparagraph (1)(e)(ii) it should be calculated as if the cash value of any contribution notionally allocated to the scheme in respect of the person by or on behalf of the company including any adjustment made for any notional investment return achieved during the relevant financial year were a contribution paid by the employer in respect of the individual for the purposes of section 233(1)(b) of the Finance Act 2004.

(3) For the purposes of the calculation in sub-paragraph (1)(d)(ii)—

(a) where the market price of shares at the date on which the shares vest is not ascertainable by the date on which the remuneration report is approved by the directors, an estimate of the market price of the shares shall be calculated on the basis of an average market value over the last quarter of the relevant financial year; and

(b) where the award was an award of shares or share options, the cash amount the individual was or will be required to pay to acquire the share must be deducted from the total.

11. Definitions applicable to the single total figure table

(1) In paragraph 7(1)(b) "taxable benefits" includes—

(a) sums paid by way of expenses allowance that are—

(i) chargeable to United Kingdom income tax (or would be if the person were an individual, or would be if the person were resident in the United Kingdom for tax purposes), and

(ii) paid to or receivable by the person in respect of qualifying services; and

(b) any benefits received by the person, other than salary, (whether or not in cash) that—

(i) are emoluments of the person, and

(ii) are received by the person in respect of qualifying services.

(2) A payment or other benefit received in advance of a director commencing qualifying services, but in anticipation of performing qualifying services, is to be treated as if received on the first day of performance of the qualifying services.

12. Additional requirements in respect of the single total figure table

(1) In respect of the sum required to be set out by paragraph 7(1)(b), there must be set out after the table a summary identifying—

(a) the types of benefits the value of which is included in the sum set out in the column headed "b"; and

(b) the value (where significant).

(2) For every component the value of which is included in the sums required to be set out in the columns headed "c" and "d" of the table by paragraphs 7(1)(c) and (d), there must be set out after the table the relevant details.

(3) In sub-paragraph (2) "the relevant details" means—

(a) details of any performance measures and the relative weighting of each;

(b) within each performance measure, the performance targets set at the beginning of the performance period and corresponding value of the award achievable;

(c) for each performance measure, details of actual performance relative to the targets set and measured over the relevant reporting period, and the resulting level of award; and

[(ca) the amount of the award or, where this is not ascertainable, an estimate of the amount of the award, that is attributable to share price appreciation;]

(d) where any discretion has been exercised in respect of the award, particulars must be given of how the discretion was exercised[, how the resulting level of award was determined and whether the discretion has been exercised as a result of share price appreciation or depreciation].

(4) For each component the value of which is included in the sum set out in the column headed "c" of the table, the report must state if any amount was deferred, the percentage deferred, whether it was deferred in cash or shares, if relevant, and whether the deferral was subject to any conditions other than performance measures.

(5) Where additional columns are included in accordance with paragraph 6(1)(a), there must be set out in a note to the table the basis on which the sums in the column were calculated, and other such details as are necessary for an understanding of the sums set out in the column, including any performance measures relating to that component of remuneration or if there are none, an explanation of why not.

13. Total pension entitlements

(1) The directors' remuneration report must, for each person who has served as a director of the company at any time during the relevant financial year, and who has a prospective entitlement to defined benefits or cash balance benefits (or to benefits under a hybrid arrangement which includes such benefits) in respect of qualifying services, contain the following information in respect of pensions—

(a) details of those rights as at the end of that year, including the person's normal retirement date;

(b) a description of any additional benefit that will become receivable by a director in the event that that director retires early; and

(c) where a person has rights under more than one type of pension benefit identified in column headed "e" of the single total figure table, separate details relating to each type of pension benefit.

(2) For the purposes of this paragraph, "defined benefits", "cash balance benefits" and "hybrid arrangement" have the same meaning as in section 152 of the Finance Act 2004.

(3) "Normal retirement date" means an age specified in the pension scheme rules (or otherwise determined) as the earliest age at which, while the individual continues to accrue benefits under the pension scheme, entitlement to a benefit arises—

(a) without consent (whether of an employer, the trustees or managers of the scheme or otherwise), and

(b) without an actuarial reduction,

but disregarding any special provision as to early repayment on grounds of ill health, redundancy or dismissal.

14. Scheme interests awarded during the financial year

(1) The directors' remuneration report must for each person who has served as a director of the company at any time during the relevant financial year contain a table setting out—

(a) details of the scheme interests awarded to the person during the relevant financial year; and

(b) for each scheme interest—

(i) a description of the type of interest awarded;

(ii) a description of the basis on which the award is made;

(iii) the face value of the award;

(iv) the percentage of scheme interests that would be receivable if the minimum performance was achieved;

(v) for a scheme interest that is a share option, an explanation of any difference between the exercise price per share and the price specified under paragraph 14(3); [and any change in the exercise price or date;]

(vi) the end of the period over which the performance measures and targets for that interest have to be achieved (or if there are different periods for different measures and targets, the end of whichever of those periods ends last); and

(vii) a summary of the performance measures and targets if not set out elsewhere in the report.

(2) In respect of a scheme interest relating to shares or share options, "face value" means the maximum number of shares that would vest if all performance measures and targets are met multiplied by either—

(a) the share price at date of grant or

(b) the average share price used to determine the number of shares awarded.

(3) Where the report sets out the face value of an award in respect of a scheme interest relating to shares or share options, the report must specify—

(a) whether the face value has been calculated using the share price at date of grant or the average share price;

(b) where the share price at date of grant is used, the amount of that share price and the date of grant;

(c) where the average share price is used, what that price was and the period used for calculating the average.

15. Payments to past directors

The directors' remuneration report must, for the relevant financial year, contain details of any payments of money or other assets to any person who was not a director of the company at the time the payment was made, but who had been a director of the company before that time, excluding—

(a) any payments falling within paragraph 16;

(b) any payments which are shown in the single total figure table;

(c) any payments which have been disclosed in a previous directors' remuneration report of the company;

(d) any payments which are below a *de minimis* threshold set by the company and stated in the report;

(e) payments by way of regular pension benefits commenced in a previous year or dividend payments in respect of scheme interests retained after leaving office; and

(f) payments in respect of employment with or any other contractual service performed for the company other than as a director.

16. Payments for loss of office

The directors' remuneration report must for the relevant financial year set out, for each person who has served as a director of the company at any time during that year, or any previous year, excluding payments which are below a *de minimis* threshold set by the company and stated in the report—

(a) the total amount of any payment for loss of office paid to or receivable by the person in respect of that financial year, broken down into each component comprised in that payment and the value of each component;

(b) an explanation of how each component was calculated;

(c) any other payments paid to or receivable by the person in connection with the termination of qualifying services, whether by way of compensation for loss of office or otherwise, including the treatment of outstanding incentive awards that vest on or following termination; and

(d) where any discretion was exercised in respect of the payment, an explanation of how it was exercised.

17. Statement of directors' shareholding and share interests

The directors' remuneration report for the relevant financial year must contain, for each person who has served as a director of the company at any time during that year—

(a) a statement of any requirements or guidelines for the director to own shares in the company and state whether or not those requirements or guidelines have been met;

(b) in tabular form or forms—

(i) the total number of interests in shares in the company of the director including interests of connected persons (as defined for the purposes of section 96B(2) of the Financial Services and Markets Act 2000);

(ii) total number of scheme interests differentiating between—

(aa) shares and share options; and

(bb) those with or without performance measures;

(iii) details of those scheme interests (which may exclude any details included elsewhere in the report); and

(iv) details of share options which are—

(aa) vested but unexercised; and

(bb) exercised in the relevant financial year.

18. Performance graph and table

(1) The directors' remuneration report must—

(a) contain a line graph that shows for each of—

(i) a holding of shares of that class of the company's equity share capital whose listing, or admission to dealing, has resulted in the company falling within the definition of "quoted company" [or "unquoted traded company"], and

(ii) a hypothetical holding of shares made up of shares of the same kinds and number as those by reference to which a broad equity market index is calculated,

a line drawn by joining up points plotted to represent, for each of the financial years in the relevant period, the total shareholder return on that holding; and

(b) state the name of the index selected for the purposes of the graph and set out the reasons for selecting that index.

(2) The report must also set out in tabular form the following information for each of the financial years in the relevant period in respect of the director undertaking the role of chief executive officer—

(a) total remuneration as set out in the single total figure table;

(b) the sum set out in the table in column headed "c" in the single total figure table expressed as a percentage of the maximum that could have been paid in respect of that component in the financial year; and

(c) the sum set out in column headed "d" in the single total figure table restated as a percentage of the number of shares vesting against the maximum number of shares that could have been received, or, where paid in money and other assets, as a percentage of the maximum that could have been paid in respect of that component in the financial year.

(3) For the purposes of sub-paragraphs (1), (2) and (6), "relevant period" means the specified period of financial years of which the last is the relevant financial year.

(4) Where the relevant financial year—

(a) is the company's first financial year for which the performance graph is prepared in accordance with this paragraph, "specified" in sub-paragraph (3) means "five";

(b) is the company's "second", "third", "fourth", "fifth" financial year in which the report is prepared in accordance with this Schedule, "specified" in sub-paragraph (3) means "six", "seven", "eight", "nine" as the case may be; and

(c) is any financial year after the fifth financial year in which the report is prepared in accordance with this Schedule, "specified" means "ten".

(5) Sub-paragraph (2) may be complied with by use of either—

(a) a sum based on the information supplied in the directors' remuneration reports for those previous years, or,

(b) where no such report has been compiled, a suitable corresponding sum.

(6) For the purposes of sub-paragraph (1), the "total shareholder return" for a relevant period on a holding of shares must be calculated using a fair method that—

(a) takes as its starting point the percentage change over the period in the market price of the holding;

(b) involves making—

(i) the assumptions specified in sub-paragraph (7) as to reinvestment of income, and

(ii) the assumption specified in sub-paragraph (9) as to the funding of liabilities; and

(c) makes provision for any replacement of shares in the holding by shares of a different description;

and the same method must be used for each of the holdings mentioned in sub-paragraph (1).

(7) The assumptions as to reinvestment of income are—

(a) that any benefit in the form of shares of the same kind as those in the holding is added to the holding at the time the benefit becomes receivable; and

(b) that any benefit in cash, and an amount equal to the value of any benefit not in cash and not falling within paragraph (a), is applied at the time the benefit becomes receivable in the purchase at their market price of shares of the same kind as those in the holding and that the shares purchased are added to the holding at that time.

(8) In sub-paragraph (7) "benefit" means any benefit (including, in particular, any dividend) receivable in respect of any shares in the holding by the holder from the company of whose share capital the shares form part.

(9) The assumption as to the funding of liabilities is that, where the holder has a liability to the company of whose capital the shares in the holding form part, shares are sold from the holding—

(a) immediately before the time by which the liability is due to be satisfied, and

(b) in such numbers that, at the time of the sale, the market price of the shares sold equals the amount of the liability in respect of the shares in the holding that are not being sold.

(10) In sub-paragraph (9) "liability" means a liability arising in respect of any shares in the holding or from the exercise of a right attached to any of those shares.

19. [Annual percentage change in remuneration of directors and employees]

(1) The directors' remuneration report must set out (in a manner which permits comparison) in relation to each of the kinds of remuneration required to be set out in each of the columns headed "a", "b" and "c" of the single total figure table the following information—

[(a) the annual percentage change over the five financial years preceding the relevant financial year in respect of each director; and

(b) the average percentage change, from financial year to subsequent financial year, over the five financial years preceding the relevant financial year in respect of the employees of the company on a full time equivalent basis.]

(2), (3) . . .

[(4) For the purposes of sub-paragraphs (1)(a) and (1)(b) the "five financial years" referred to must include financial years beginning on or after 10th June 2019 and where five financial years have not passed since that date the annual percentage change must be calculated for all financial years since that date preceding the relevant financial year.

(5) "Employee" for purposes of this paragraph means any employee other than a director.]

[19A. Pay ratio information in relation to the total remuneration of the director undertaking the role of chief executive officer

(1) If paragraph 19B applies to the company for the relevant financial year the directors' remuneration report must contain pay ratio information specified in paragraphs 19C to 19G.

(2) Where the company is a parent company, the pay ratio information must relate to the group and not the company, and references in paragraphs 19C, 19D and 19G to the company's UK employees should be read as references to the UK employees of all the companies within the group.

19B. Requirement to provide pay ratio information

(1) This paragraph applies to a company—

(a) in relation to its first financial year if the qualifying condition is met in that year;

(b) in relation to a subsequent financial year—

(i) if the qualifying condition is met in that year and was also met in relation to the preceding financial year,

(ii) if—

(aa) the qualifying condition is met in that year, and

(bb) the paragraph applied to the company in the preceding financial year, or

(iii) if—

(aa) the qualifying condition was met in the preceding financial year, and

(bb) the paragraph applied to the company in the preceding financial year.

(2) The qualifying condition is met by a company in a year in which the average number of UK employees of the company is more than 250.

(3) The average number of UK employees of the company is determined as follows—

(a) find for each month in the financial year the number of UK employees in that month (whether employed throughout the month or not),

(b) add together the monthly totals, and

(c) divide by the number of months in the financial year.

(4) Where the company is a parent company the average number of UK employees refers to the number of UK employees within the group.

19C. Pay ratios table

(1) The directors' remuneration report must set out in the form of the table in sub-paragraph (2) ("pay ratios table") the following information for the relevant financial year—

(a) in the first column, the year in which that financial year ends,

(b) in the second column, the method set out in paragraph 19D used by the company to determine Y25, Y50 and Y75, and

(c) in subsequent columns, the specified ratios ("pay ratios").

(2) The form of the pay ratios table is—

Pay ratios table

Year	*Method*	*25th percentile pay ratio*	*Median pay ratio*	*75th percentile pay ratio*
[year]	[Option A, B or C]	(X/Y25):1	(X/Y50):1	(X/Y75):1

Where—

X is the remuneration of the director undertaking the role of chief executive officer ("CEO"), using the total for the CEO in the single total figure table. Where more than one person has undertaken the role of CEO in the relevant financial year, X means the total remuneration in the single total figure table paid to persons in relation to the period those persons were undertaking the role of CEO in the relevant financial year;

Y25 is the pay and benefits figure relating to P25;

Y50 is the pay and benefits figure relating to P50;

Y75 is the pay and benefits figure relating to P75.

(3) In this paragraph and paragraphs 19D to 19G—

"P25" is a UK employee whose pay and benefits are on the 25th percentile of pay and benefits of the company's UK employees for the relevant financial year;

"P50" is a UK employee whose pay and benefits are on the 50th percentile of pay and benefits of the company's UK employees for the relevant financial year;

"P75" is a UK employee whose pay and benefits are on the 75th percentile of pay and benefits of the company's UK employees for the relevant financial year;

"pay and benefits" of a UK employee means the employee's full-time equivalent pay and benefits, calculating the applicable components in paragraph 7(1)(a) to (e) by reference to paragraph 10, save that in paragraph 7(1)(a) "salary" means "wages and salary".

(4) If the relevant financial year is not the first financial year in which the requirement in sub-paragraph (1) applied to the company, the pay ratios table must also show, in separate rows, information for earlier financial years in accordance with sub-paragraphs (5) and (6).

(5) The earlier financial years for which information must be shown under sub-paragraph (4) are—

(a) the first financial year in which the requirement in sub-paragraph (1) applied to the company and every subsequent financial year before the relevant financial year, or

(b) if the application of paragraph (a) would require the company to show information in respect of more than nine earlier financial years, the nine financial years immediately preceding the relevant financial year.

(6) The information required to be shown by sub-paragraph (4) is—

(a) for a financial year in which the requirement in sub-paragraph (1) applied to the company, the information that was required by that sub-paragraph to be included in the pay ratios table in respect of that financial year;

(b) for a financial year in which that requirement did not apply, the year of that financial year and the statement "The company was exempt from reporting pay ratios for this financial year".

19D. Pay ratios methods

(1) The company must choose one of the methods set out in sub-paragraph (2) to determine the Y25, Y50 and Y75 figures to use in the pay ratios for the relevant financial year, but for a subsequent financial year may choose to use a different one of those methods.

(2) The methods for determining Y25, Y50 and Y75 are—

(a) "Option A" set out in sub-paragraph (3),
(b) "Option B" set out in sub-paragraph (4), or
(c) "Option C" set out in sub-paragraph (5).

(3) Under Option A the company must calculate the pay and benefits of all its UK employees for the relevant financial year in order to identify P25, P50 and P75, and use the pay and benefits figures for those UK employees as Y25, Y50 and Y75.

(4) Under Option B the company must determine Y25, Y50 and Y75 as follows—
(a) as a starting point, use the most recent hourly rate gender pay gap information for all UK employees of the company to identify three UK employees as the best equivalents of P25, P50 and P75,
(b) use available data for the relevant financial year for the best equivalents to calculate the pay and benefits figures for each for the relevant financial year, and
(c) make any necessary adjustment to the pay and benefit figures to ensure that the best equivalents are reasonably representative of P25, P50 and P75 for the relevant financial year.

(5) Under Option C the company may determine Y25, Y50 and Y75 as follows—
(a) as a starting point, use data other than, or in addition to, gender pay gap information to identify three UK employees as the best equivalents of P25, P50 and P75, and in so doing—
(i) the company must not use data that relates to any year prior to the preceding financial year, and
(ii) if the company has gender pay gap information available, it must not use data that is less up to date than the gender pay gap information,
(b) use available data for the relevant financial year for the best equivalents to calculate the pay and benefits for each in relation to the relevant financial year, and
(c) make any necessary adjustment to the pay and benefit figures to ensure that the best equivalents are reasonably representative of P25, P50 and P75 for the relevant financial year.

(6) When using any of the options, the company may—
(a) determine Y25, Y50 and Y75 with reference to a day no earlier than three months before the last day of the relevant financial year, using a projected calculation of the salary component of pay and benefits;
(b) omit any component other than salary from pay and benefits to determine Y25, Y50 and Y75, provided the company includes in its report a statement required by paragraph 19E(f);
(c) calculate any component of pay and benefits, other than salary, using a different methodology than that set out in paragraph 10 to determine Y25, Y50 and Y75, provided the company includes in its report a statement required by paragraph 19E(g).

(7) When using Option B or C, if the company does not have the data available for any component of pay and benefits corresponding to paragraph 7(1)(b) to (e), the company may use a reasonable estimate of that component to determine Y25, Y50 and Y75.

(8) In this paragraph gender pay gap information means the most recent data collected in accordance with the Equality Act 2010 (Gender Pay Gap Information) Regulations 2017.

19E. Additional requirements in respect of the pay ratios table

The directors' remuneration report must set out the following information after the pay ratios table—
(a) an explanation of why the company chose Option A, B or C as the preferred method for calculating the pay ratio for the relevant financial year,
(b) if the company was required to report pay ratio information in the preceding financial year, and the company then used a different option to determine Y25, Y50 and Y75, an explanation for the change,
(c) the day by reference to which the company determined Y25, Y50 and Y75,
(d) where the company has used Option B—
(i) a brief explanation of how the best equivalents are reasonably representative of P25, P50 and P75, and
(ii) whether, and if so how, it has relied on the use of estimates or adjustments,
(e) where the company has used Option C—
(i) the methodology used for estimating the best equivalents, describing any estimates, adjustments, or material assumptions, and
(ii) a brief explanation of how the best equivalents are reasonably representative of P25, P50 and P75,
(f) where the company has omitted any component from pay and benefits in reliance on paragraph 19D(6)(b), the component omitted and the reason for the omission, and if the company omitted any component in the previous financial year, whether the company has continued to omit that component,
(g) where the company has used a different methodology from that set out in paragraph 10 to calculate a component of pay and benefits, a description of the different methodology and why the methodology in paragraph 10 was not used,
(h) a brief explanation of any assumptions or statistical modelling used to determine full-time equivalent remuneration.

19F. The directors' remuneration report must set out the following figures for each of Y25, Y50, and Y75 after the information required by paragraph 19E—
(a) total pay and benefits, and
(b) the salary component of total pay and benefits.

19G. The directors' remuneration report must set out a summary for the relevant financial year after the information required by paragraph 19F, explaining—
(a) any reduction or increase in the relevant financial year's pay ratios compared to the pay ratios of the preceding financial year (if the company recorded pay ratio information for that financial year),
(b) whether a reduction or an increase in a pay ratio is attributable to a change in—
(i) the remuneration of the CEO, or the pay and benefits of the company's UK employees taken as a whole;

(ii) the company's employment models (including any increase in the proportion of the company's employees employed to work wholly or mainly outside the UK, and any increase in the proportion of the company's workforce that is not employed by the company under contracts of service);

(iii) the use of a different option to calculate Y25, Y50 and Y75,

(c) any trend in the median pay ratio over the period of financial years covered by the pay ratios table, and

(d) whether, and if so why, the company believes the median pay ratio for the relevant financial year is consistent with the pay, reward and progression policies for the company's UK employees taken as a whole.]

20. Relative importance of spend on pay

(1) The directors' remuneration report must set out in a graphical or tabular form that shows in respect of the relevant financial year and the immediately preceding financial year the actual expenditure of the company, and the difference in spend between those years, on—

(a) remuneration paid to or receivable by all employees of the group;

(b) distributions to shareholders by way of dividend and share buyback; and

(c) any other significant distributions and payments or other uses of profit or cashflow deemed by the directors to assist in understanding the relative importance of spend on pay.

(2) There must be set out in a note to the report an explanation in respect of subparagraph (1)(c) why the particular matters were chosen by the directors and how the amounts were calculated.

(3) Where the matters chosen for the report in respect of sub-paragraph (1)(c) in the relevant financial year are not the same as the other items set out in the report for previous years, an explanation for that change must be given.

21. Statement of implementation of remuneration policy in the following financial year

(1) The directors' remuneration report must contain a statement describing how the company intends to implement the approved directors' remuneration policy in the financial year following the relevant financial year.

(2) The statement must include, where applicable, the—

(a) performance measures and relative weightings for each; and

(b) performance targets determined for the performance measures and how awards will be calculated.

(3) Where this is not the first year of the approved remuneration policy, the statement should detail any significant changes in the way that the remuneration policy will be implemented in the next financial year compared to how it was implemented in the relevant financial year [and any deviations from the procedure for the implementation of the remuneration policy set out in the policy].

(4) This statement need not include information that is elsewhere in the report, including any disclosed in the directors' remuneration policy.

22. Consideration by the directors of matters relating to directors' remuneration

(1) If a committee of the company's directors has considered matters relating to the directors' remuneration for the relevant financial year, the directors' remuneration report must—

(a) name each director who was a member of the committee at any time when the committee was considering any such matter;

(b) state whether any person provided to the committee advice, or services, that materially assisted the committee in their consideration of any such matter and name any person that has done so;

(c) in the case of any person named under paragraph (b), who is not a director of the company (other than a person who provided legal advice on compliance with any relevant legislation), state—

(i) the nature of any other services that that person has provided to the company during the relevant financial year;

(ii) by whom that person was appointed, whether or not by the committee and how they were selected;

(iii) whether and how the remuneration committee has satisfied itself that the advice received was objective and independent; and

(iv) the amount of fee or other charge paid by the company to that person for the provision of the advice or services referred to in paragraph (b) and the basis on which it was charged.

(2) In sub-paragraph (1)(b) "person" includes (in particular) any director of the company who does not fall within sub-paragraph (1)(a).

(3) Sub-paragraph (1)(c) does not apply where the person was, at the time of the provision of the advice or service, an employee of the company.

(4) This paragraph also applies to a committee which considers remuneration issues during the consideration of an individual's nomination as a director.

23. Statement of voting at general meeting

The directors' remuneration report must contain a statement setting out in respect of the last general meeting at which a resolution of the following kind was moved by the company—

(a) in respect of a resolution to approve the directors' remuneration report, the percentage of votes cast for and against and the number of votes withheld;

(b) in respect of a resolution to approve the directors' remuneration policy, the percentage of votes cast for and against and the number of votes withheld; and,

(c) where there was a significant percentage of votes against either such resolution, a summary of the reasons for those votes, as far as known to the directors, and any actions taken by the directors in response to those concerns.]

NOTES

This Schedule was substituted as noted to Part 1 of this Schedule at **[4.105]**.

Para 5: the table was substituted by the Companies (Directors' Remuneration Policy and Directors' Remuneration Report) Regulations 2019, SI 2019/970, regs 30, 31(4), in relation to a directors' remuneration report for a financial year of a company beginning on or after 10 June 2019 (see further reg 2 of the 2019 Regulations at **[4.680]**).

Para 7: sub-paras (1)(g) and (h) added by SI 2019/970, regs 30, 31(5), in relation to a directors' remuneration report for a financial year of a company beginning on or after 10 June 2019 (see further reg 2 of the 2019 Regulations at **[4.680]**).

Para 12: sub-para (3)(ca) was inserted, and the words in square brackets in sub-para (3)(d) were substituted, by the Companies (Miscellaneous Reporting) Regulations 2018, SI 2018/860, regs 15, 17(a), in relation to the financial years of companies beginning on or after 1 January 2019.

Para 14: words in square brackets in sub-para (1)(b)(v) inserted by SI 2019/970, regs 30, 31(6), in relation to a directors' remuneration report for a financial year of a company beginning on or after 10 June 2019 (see further reg 2 of the 2019 Regulations at **[4.680]**).

Para 18: words in square brackets in sub-para (1)(a)(i) inserted by SI 2019/970, regs 30, 31(7), in relation to a directors' remuneration report for a financial year of a company beginning on or after 10 June 2019 (see further reg 2 of the 2019 Regulations at **[4.680]**).

Para 19: the heading was substituted, sub-paras (1)(a) and (b) were substituted, sub-paras (2) and (3) were revoked, and sub-paras (4) and (5) were added, by SI 2019/970, regs 30, 31(8), in relation to a directors' remuneration report for a financial year of a company beginning on or after 10 June 2019 (see further reg 2 of the 2019 Regulations at **[4.680]**).

Paras 19A–19G: inserted by SI 2018/860, regs 15, 17(b), in relation to the financial years of companies beginning on or after 1 January 2019.

Para 21: words in square brackets in sub-para (3) inserted by SI 2019/970, regs 30, 31(9), in relation to a directors' remuneration report for a financial year of a company beginning on or after 10 June 2019 (see further reg 2 of the 2019 Regulations at **[4.680]**).

[PART 4 DIRECTORS' REMUNERATION POLICY

[4.108]

24. Introductory

(1) The information required to be included in the directors' remuneration report by the provisions of this Part must be set out in a separate part of the report and constitutes the directors' remuneration policy of the company.

[(1A) The directors' remuneration policy must explain the decision-making process followed for its determination, review and implementation, including measures to avoid or manage conflicts of interest and, where applicable, the role of the remuneration committee or other committees concerned except that this explanation need not include information that is elsewhere in the directors' remuneration report.]

(2) Where a company intends to move a resolution at a meeting of the company to approve a directors' remuneration policy and it is intended that some or all of the provisions of the last approved directors' remuneration policy are to continue to apply after the resolution is approved, this fact must be stated in the policy which is the subject of the resolution and it must be made clear which provisions of the last approved policy are to continue to apply and for what period of time it is intended that they shall apply.

(3) Notwithstanding the requirements of this Part, the directors' remuneration policy part of the report must set out all those matters for which the company requires approval for the purposes of Chapter 4A of Part 10 of the 2006 Act.

(4) Where any provision of the directors' remuneration policy provides for the exercise by the directors of a discretion on any aspect of the policy, the policy must clearly set out the extent of that discretion in respect of any such variation, change or amendment.

(5) The directors' remuneration policy (or revised directors' remuneration policy) of a company in respect of which a company moves a resolution for approval in accordance with section 439A of the 2006 Act must, on the first occasion that such a resolution is moved after 1st October 2013 set out the date from which it is intended by the company that that policy is to take effect.

25. Future policy table

(1) The directors' remuneration report must contain in tabular form a description of each of the components of the remuneration package for the directors of the company which are comprised in the directors' remuneration policy of the company.

(2) Where the report complies with sub-paragraph (1) by reference to provisions which apply generally to all directors, the table must also include any particular arrangements which are specific to any director individually.

(3) References in this Part to "component parts of the remuneration package" include, but are not limited to, all those items which are relevant for the purposes of the single total figure table.

26. In respect of each of the components described in the table there must be set out the following information—

- (a) how that component supports the short and long-term strategic objectives of the company (or, where the company is a parent company, the group);
- (b) an explanation of how that component of the remuneration package operates [and information on any deferral periods];
- [(ba) where the company awards share-based remuneration, information on any vesting periods and any holding periods;]
- (c) the maximum that may be paid in respect of that component (which may be expressed in monetary terms, or otherwise);
- (d) where applicable, a description of the framework used to assess performance including—
  - (i) a description of any performance measures which apply and, where more than one performance measure applies, an indication of the weighting of the performance measure or group of performance measures;
  - (ii) details of any performance period; and
  - (iii) the amount (which may be expressed in monetary terms or otherwise) that may be paid in respect of —
    - (aa) the minimum level of performance that results in any payment under the policy, and
    - (bb) any further levels of performance set in accordance with the policy;
- (e) an explanation as to whether there are any provisions for the recovery of sums paid or the withholding of the payment of any sum.

27. There must accompany the table notes which set out—

(a) in respect of any component falling within paragraph 26(d)(i)–(iii), an explanation of why any performance measures were chosen and how any performance targets are set;

(b) in respect of any component (other than salary, fees, benefits or pension) which is not subject to performance measures, an explanation of why there are no such measures;

(c) if any component did not form part of the remuneration package in the last approved directors' remuneration policy, why that component is now contained in the remuneration package;

(d) in respect of any component which did form a part of such a package, what changes have been made to it and why; and

(e) an explanation of the differences (if any) in the company's policy on the remuneration of directors from the policy on the remuneration of employees generally (within the company, or where the company is a parent company, the group).

28. The information required by paragraph 25 may, in respect of directors not performing an executive function, be set out in a separate table and there must be set out in that table the approach of the company to the determination of—

(a) the fee payable to such directors;

(b) any additional fees payable for any other duties to the company;

(c) such other items as are to be considered in the nature of remuneration.

29. Approach to recruitment remuneration

(1) The directors' remuneration policy must contain a statement of the principles which would be applied by the company when agreeing the components of a remuneration package for the appointment of directors.

(2) The statement must set out the various components which would be considered for inclusion in that package and the approach to be adopted by the company in respect of each component.

(3) The statement must, subject to sub-paragraph (4), set out the maximum level of variable remuneration which may be granted (which can be expressed in monetary terms or otherwise).

(4) Remuneration which constitutes compensation for the forfeit of any award under variable remuneration arrangements entered into with a previous employer is not included within sub-paragraph (3) of this paragraph, but is subject to the requirements of subparagraphs (1) and (2).

30. Service contracts

The directors' remuneration policy must contain a description of any obligation on the company which—

(a) is contained in all directors' service contracts;

(b) is contained in the service contracts of any one or more existing directors (not being covered by paragraph (a)); or

(c) it is proposed would be contained in directors' service contracts to be entered into by the company

and which could give rise to, or impact on, remuneration payments or payments for loss of office but which is not disclosed elsewhere in this report.

[30A. The directors' remuneration policy must contain an indication of the duration of directors' service contracts or arrangements with the directors.]

31. Where the directors' service contracts are not kept available for inspection at the company's registered office, the report must give details of where the contracts are kept, and if the contracts are available on a website, a link to that website.

32. The provisions of paragraphs 30 and 31 relating to directors' service contracts apply in like manner to the terms of letters of appointment of directors.

33. Illustrations of application of remuneration policy

The directors' remuneration report must, in respect of each person who is a director (other than a director who is not performing an executive function), set out in the form of a bar chart an indication of the level of remuneration that would be received by the director in accordance with the directors' remuneration policy in the first year to which the policy applies.

34. (1) The bar chart must contain separate bars representing—

(a) minimum remuneration receivable, that is to say, including, but not limited to, salary, fees, benefits and pension;

(b) the remuneration receivable if the director was, in respect of any performance measures or targets, performing in line with the company's expectation;

(c) maximum remuneration receivable (not allowing for any share price appreciation).

(2) Each bar of the chart must contain separate parts which represent—

(a) salary, fees, benefits, pension and any other item falling within sub-paragraph 34(1)(a);

(b) remuneration where performance measures or targets relate to one financial year;

(c) remuneration where performance measures or targets relate to more than one financial year.

(3) Each bar must show—

(a) percentage of the total comprised by each of the parts; and

(b) total value of remuneration expected for each bar.

35. (1) A narrative description of the basis of calculation and assumptions used to compile the bar chart must be set out to enable an understanding of the charts presented.

(2) In complying with sub-paragraph (1) it is not necessary for any matter to be included in the narrative description which has been set out in the future policy table required by paragraph 25.

[35A. The directors' remuneration report must, in respect of each person who is a director (other than a director who is not performing an executive function)—

(a) set out for performance targets or measures relating to more than one financial year, an indication of the maximum remuneration receivable assuming company share price appreciation of 50% during the relevant performance period, and
(b) provide a short description of the basis of the calculation reported under sub-paragraph (a).]

36. Policy on payment for loss of office

The directors' remuneration policy must set out the company's policy on the setting of notice periods under directors' service contracts.

37. The directors' remuneration policy must also set out the principles on which the determination of payments for loss of office will be approached including—
(a) an indication of how each component of the payment will be calculated;
(b) whether, and if so how, the circumstances of the director's loss of office and performance during the period of qualifying service are relevant to any exercise of discretion; and
(c) any contractual provision agreed prior to 27th June 2012 that could impact on the quantum of the payment.

38. Statement of consideration of employment conditions elsewhere in company

The directors' remuneration policy must contain a statement of how pay and employment conditions of employees (other than directors) of the company and, where the company is a parent company, of the group of other undertakings within the same group as the company, were taken into account when setting the policy for directors' remuneration.

39. The statement must also set out—
(a) whether, and if so, how, the company consulted with employees when drawing up the directors' remuneration policy set out in this part of the report;
(b) whether any remuneration comparison measurements were used and if so, what they were, and how that information was taken into account.

40. Statement of consideration of shareholder views

The directors' remuneration policy must contain a statement of whether, and if so how, any views in respect of directors' remuneration expressed to the company by shareholders (whether at a general meeting or otherwise) have been taken into account in the formulation of the directors' remuneration policy.]

NOTES

This Schedule was substituted as noted to Part 1 of this Schedule at **[4.105]**.

Para 24: sub-para (1A) inserted by the Companies (Directors' Remuneration Policy and Directors' Remuneration Report) Regulations 2019, SI 2019/970, regs 30, 32(1), in relation to a relevant directors' remuneration policy that was approved under the Companies Act 2006, s 439A on or after 10 June 2019 (see further reg 2 of the 2019 Regulations at **[4.680]**).

Para 26: words in square brackets in sub-para (b) inserted, and sub-para (ba) inserted, by SI 2019/970, regs 30, 32(2), in relation to a relevant directors' remuneration policy that was approved under the Companies Act 2006, s 439A on or after 10 June 2019 (see further reg 2 of the 2019 Regulations at **[4.680]**).

Para 30A: inserted by SI 2019/970, regs 30, 32(3), in relation to a relevant directors' remuneration policy that was approved under the Companies Act 2006, s 439A on or after 10 June 2019 (see further reg 2 of the 2019 Regulations at **[4.680]**).

Para 35A: inserted by the Companies (Miscellaneous Reporting) Regulations 2018, SI 2018/860, regs 15, 18, in relation to the financial years of companies beginning on or after 1 January 2019.

[PART 5 PROVISIONS OF THE DIRECTORS' REMUNERATION REPORT WHICH ARE SUBJECT TO AUDIT

[4.109]

41. The information contained in the directors' remuneration report which is subject to audit is the information required by paragraphs 4 to 17 (inclusive) of Part 3 of this Schedule.]

NOTES

This Schedule was substituted as noted to Part 1 of this Schedule at **[4.105]**.

[PART 6 REVISED DIRECTORS' REMUNERATION POLICY

[4.110]

42. A revised directors' remuneration policy prepared in accordance with section 422A of the 2006 Act must contain all those matters required by Part 4 of this Schedule to be in the directors' remuneration policy[, and a description and explanation of all significant revisions].

43. A revised directors' remuneration policy must be set out in the same manner as required by Part 4 of this Schedule in respect of that part of the directors' remuneration report.]

NOTES

This Schedule was substituted as noted to Part 1 of this Schedule at **[4.105]**.

Para 42: words in square brackets inserted by the Companies (Directors' Remuneration Policy and Directors' Remuneration Report) Regulations 2019, SI 2019/970, regs 30, 32(4), in relation to a relevant directors' remuneration policy that was approved under the Companies Act 2006, s 439A on or after 10 June 2019 (see further reg 2 of the 2019 Regulations at **[4.680]**).

[PART 7 INTERPRETATION AND SUPPLEMENTARY

[4.111]

44. (1) In this Schedule—

"amount", in relation to a gain made on the exercise of a share option, means the difference between—
(a) the market price of the shares on the day on which the option was exercised; and
(b) the price actually paid for the shares;

"company contributions", in relation to a pension scheme and a person, means any payments (including insurance premiums) made, or treated as made, to the scheme in respect of the person by anyone other than the person;

"emoluments" of a person—

(a) include salary, fees and bonuses, sums paid by way of expenses allowance (so far as they are chargeable to United Kingdom income tax or would be if the person were an individual or would be if the person were resident in the United Kingdom for tax purposes), but

(b) do not include any of the following, namely—

(i) the value of any share options granted to him or the amount of any gains made on the exercise of any such options;

(ii) any company contributions paid, or treated as paid, in respect of him under any pension scheme or any benefits to which he is entitled under any such scheme; or

(iii) any money or other assets paid to or received or receivable by him under any scheme;

"pension scheme" means a retirement benefits scheme within the meaning given by section 150(1) of the Finance Act 2004 which is—

(a) one in which the company participates or

(b) one to which the company paid a contribution during the financial year;

"performance measure" is the measure by which performance is to be assessed, but does not include any condition relating to service:

"performance target" is the specific level of performance to be attained in respect of that performance measure;

"qualifying services", in relation to any person, means his services as a director of the company, and his services at any time while he is a director of the company—

(a) as a director of an undertaking that is a subsidiary undertaking of the company at that time;

(b) as a director of any other undertaking of which he is a director by virtue of the company's nomination (direct or indirect); or

(c) otherwise in connection with the management of the affairs of the company or any such subsidiary undertaking or any such other undertaking;

"remuneration committee" means a committee of directors of the company having responsibility for considering matters related to the remuneration of directors;

"retirement benefits" means relevant benefits within the meaning given by section 393B of the Income Tax (Earnings and Pensions) Act 2003 read as if subsection (2) were omitted;

"scheme" (other than a pension scheme) means any agreement or arrangement under which money or other assets may become receivable by a person and which includes one or more qualifying conditions with respect to service or performance that cannot be fulfilled within a single financial year, and for this purpose the following must be disregarded, namely—

(a) any payment the amount of which falls to be determined by reference to service or performance within a single financial year;

(b) compensation in respect of loss of office, payments for breach of contract and other termination payments; and

(c) retirement benefits;

"scheme interest" means an interest under a scheme;

"shares" means shares (whether allotted or not) in the company, or any undertaking which is a group undertaking in relation to the company, and includes a share warrant as defined by section 779(1) of the 2006 Act;

"share option" means a right to acquire shares;

["UK employee" means a person employed under a contract of service by the company, other than a person employed to work wholly or mainly outside the United Kingdom;]

["unquoted traded company" means a traded company (as defined in section 360C of the Companies Act 2006) that is not a quoted company (as defined in section 385 of the Companies Act 2006);]

"value" in relation to shares received or receivable on any day by a person who is or has been a director of a company, means the market price of the shares on that day.

(2) In this Schedule "compensation in respect of loss of office" includes compensation received or receivable by a person for—

(a) loss of office as director of the company, or

(b) loss, while director of the company or on or in connection with his ceasing to be a director of it, of—

(i) any other office in connection with the management of the company' affairs; or

(ii) any office as director or otherwise in connection with the management of the affairs of any undertaking that, immediately before the loss, is a subsidiary undertaking of the company or an undertaking of which he is a director by virtue of the company's nomination (direct or indirect);

(c) compensation in consideration for, or in connection with, a person's retirement from office; and

(d) where such a retirement is occasioned by a breach of the person's contract with the company or with an undertaking that, immediately before the breach, is a subsidiary undertaking of the company or an undertaking of which he is a director by virtue of the company's nomination (direct or indirect)—

(i) payments made by way of damages for the breach; or

(ii) payments made by way of settlement or compromise of any claim in respect of the breach.

(3) References in this Schedule to compensation include benefits otherwise than in cash; and in relation to such compensation references in this Schedule to its amounts are to the estimated money value of the benefit.

(4) References in this Schedule to a person being "connected" with a director, and to a director "controlling" a body corporate, are to be construed in accordance with sections 252 to 255 of the 2006 Act.

45. For the purposes of this Schedule emoluments paid or receivable or share options granted in respect of a person's accepting office as a director are to be treated as emoluments paid or receivable or share options granted in respect of his services as a director.

46. (1) The following applies with respect to the amounts to be shown under this Schedule.

(2) The amount in each case includes all relevant sums paid by or receivable from—

(a) the company; and

(b) the company's subsidiary undertakings; and

(c) any other person,

except sums to be accounted for to the company or any of its subsidiary undertakings or any other undertaking of which any person has been a director while director of the company, by virtue of section 219 of the 2006 Act (payment in connection with share transfer: requirement of members' approval), to past or present members of the company or any of its subsidiaries or any class of those members.

(3) Reference to amounts paid to or receivable by a person include amounts paid to or receivable by a person connected with the person or a body corporate controlled by the person (but not so as to require an amount to be counted twice).

47. (1) The amounts to be shown for any financial year under Part 3 of this Schedule are the sums receivable in respect of that year (whenever paid) or, in the case of sums not receivable in respect of a period, the sums paid during that year.

(2) But where—

(a) any sums are not shown in the directors' remuneration report for the relevant financial year on the ground that the person receiving them is liable to account for them as mentioned in paragraph 46(2), but the liability is thereafter wholly or partly released or is not enforced within a period of 2 years; or

(b) any sums paid by way of expenses allowance are charged to United Kingdom income tax after the end of the relevant financial year or, in the case of any such sums paid otherwise than to an individual, it does not become clear until the end of the relevant financial year that those sums would be charged to such tax were the person an individual,

those sums must, to the extent to which the liability is released or not enforced or they are charged as mentioned above (as the case may be), be shown in the first directors' remuneration report in which it is practicable to show them and must be distinguished from the amounts to be shown apart from this provision.

48. Where it is necessary to do so for the purpose of making any distinction required by the preceding paragraphs in an amount to be shown in compliance with this Schedule, the directors may apportion any payments between the matters in respect of which these have been paid or are receivable in such manner as they think appropriate.

49. The Schedule requires information to be given only so far as it is contained in the company's books and papers, available to members of the public or the company has the right to obtain it.]

NOTES

This Schedule was substituted as noted to Part 1 of this Schedule at **[4.105]**.

Para 44: definition "UK employee" in sub-para (1) inserted by the Companies (Miscellaneous Reporting) Regulations 2018, SI 2018/860, regs 15, 19, in relation to the financial years of companies beginning on or after 1 January 2019. Definition "unquoted traded company" in sub-para (1) inserted by the Companies (Directors' Remuneration Policy and Directors' Remuneration Report) Regulations 2019, SI 2019/970, regs 30, 33, as from 10 June 2019 (for transitional provisions, etc, see reg 2 of the 2019 Regulations at **[4.680]**).

SCHEDULE 9
INTERPRETATION OF TERM "PROVISIONS"

Regulation 12

PART 1 MEANING FOR PURPOSES OF THESE REGULATIONS

Definition of "Provisions"

[4.112]

1. (1) In these Regulations, references to provisions for depreciation or diminution in value of assets are to any amount written off by way of providing for depreciation or diminution in value of assets.

(2) Any reference in the profit and loss account formats or the notes to them set out in Schedule 1, 2 or 3 to these Regulations to the depreciation of, or amounts written off, assets of any description is to any provision for depreciation or diminution in value of assets of that description.

2. References in these Regulations to provisions for liabilities or, in the case of insurance companies, to provisions for other risks are to any amount retained as reasonably necessary for the purpose of providing for any liability the nature of which is clearly defined and which is either likely to be incurred, or certain to be incurred but uncertain as to amount or as to the date on which it will arise.

[2A. At the balance sheet date, a provision must represent the best estimate of the expenses likely to be incurred or, in the case of a liability, of the amount required to meet that liability.

2B. Provisions must not be used to adjust the value of assets.]

NOTES

Paras 2A, 2B: inserted by the Companies, Partnerships and Groups (Accounts and Reports) Regulations 2015, SI 2015/980, reg 40, as from 6 April 2015, in relation to (a) financial years beginning on or after 1 January 2016, and (b) a financial year of a company beginning on or after 1 January 2015, but before 1 January 2016, if the directors of the company so decide (see **[4.549]** *post*).

PART 2 MEANING FOR PURPOSES OF PARTS 18 AND 23 OF THE 2006 ACT

Financial assistance for purchase of own shares

[4.113]

3. The specified provisions for the purposes of section 677(3)(a) of the 2006 Act (Companies Act accounts: relevant provisions for purposes of financial assistance) are provisions within paragraph 2 of this Schedule.

Redemption or purchase by private company out of capital

4. The specified provisions for the purposes of section 712(2)(b)(i) of the 2006 Act (Companies Act accounts: relevant provisions to determine available profits for redemption or purchase out of capital) are provisions of any of the kinds mentioned in paragraphs 1 and 2 of this Schedule.

Net asset restriction on public companies distributions

5. The specified provisions for the purposes of section 831(3)(a) of the 2006 Act (Companies Act accounts: net asset restriction on public company distributions) are—

(a) provisions within paragraph 2 of this Schedule, and

(b) in the case of an insurance company, any amount included under liabilities items Ba (fund for future appropriations), C (technical provisions) and D (technical provisions for linked liabilities) in a balance sheet drawn up in accordance with Schedule 3 to these Regulations.

Distributions by investment companies

6. The specified provisions for the purposes of section 832(4)(a) of the 2006 Act (Companies Act accounts: investment companies distributions) are provisions within paragraph 2 of this Schedule.

Justification of distribution by references to accounts

7. The specified provisions for the purposes of section 836(1)(b)(i) of the 2006 Act (Companies Act accounts: relevant provisions for distribution purposes)—

(a) are provisions of any of the kinds mentioned in paragraphs 1 and 2 of this Schedule, and

(b) in the case of an insurance company, any amount included under liabilities items Ba (fund for future appropriations), C (technical provisions) and D (technical provisions for linked liabilities) in a balance sheet drawn up in accordance with Schedule 3 to these Regulations.

[Realised losses

8 The specified provisions for the purposes of section 841(2)(a) of the 2006 Act (Companies Act accounts: treatment of provisions as realised losses) are provisions of any of the kinds mentioned in paragraphs 1 and 2 of this Schedule.]

NOTES

Para 8: added by the Companies Act 2006 (Accounts, Reports and Audit) Regulations 2009, SI 2009/1581, reg 12(1), (4), as from 27 June 2009, in relation to financial years beginning on or after 6 April 2008 which have not ended before 27 June 2009.

SCHEDULE 10
GENERAL INTERPRETATION

Regulation 13

Capitalisation

[4.114]

1. "Capitalisation", in relation to work or costs, means treating that work or those costs as a fixed asset.

Financial instruments

2. Save in Schedule 2 to these Regulations, references to "derivatives" include commodity-based contracts that give either contracting party the right to settle in cash or in some other financial instrument, except where such contracts—

(a) were entered into for the purpose of, and continue to meet, the company's expected purchase, sale or usage requirements,

(b) were designated for such purpose at their inception, and

(c) are expected to be settled by delivery of the commodity (for banking companies, see the definition in paragraph 94 of Schedule 2 to these Regulations).

3. [(1) Save in Schedule 2 to these Regulations, the expressions listed in sub-paragraph (2) have the same meaning as they have in Directive 2013/34/EC of the European Parliament and of the Council of 26 June 2013 on the annual financial statements etc of certain types of undertakings and Council Directive 91/674/EEC of 19 December 1991 on the annual accounts and consolidated accounts of insurance undertakings (for banking companies, see the definition in paragraph 96 of Schedule 2 to these Regulations).]

(2) Those expressions are "available for sale financial asset", "business combination", "commodity-based contracts", "derivative", "equity instrument", "exchange difference", "fair value hedge accounting system", "financial fixed asset", "financial instrument", "foreign entity", "hedge accounting", "hedge accounting system", "hedged items", "hedging instrument", "held for trading purposes", "held to maturity", "monetary item", "receivables", "reliable market" and "trading portfolio".

Fixed and current assets

4. "Fixed assets" means assets of a company which are intended for use on a continuing basis in the company's activities, and "current assets" means assets not intended for such use.

Fungible assets

5. "Fungible assets" means assets of any description which are substantially indistinguishable one from another.

Historical cost accounting rules

6. References to the historical cost accounting rules are to be read in accordance with paragraph 30 of Schedule 1, paragraph 38 of Schedule 2 and paragraph 36(1) of Schedule 3 to these Regulations.

Leases

7. (1) "Long lease" means a lease in the case of which the portion of the term for which it was granted remaining unexpired at the end of the financial year is not less than 50 years.

(2) "Short lease" means a lease which is not a long lease.

(3) "Lease" includes an agreement for a lease.

Listed investments

8. (1) "Listed investment" means an investment as respects which there has been granted a listing on—

(a) a recognised investment exchange other than an overseas investment exchange, or

(b) a stock exchange of repute outside the United Kingdom.

(2) "Recognised investment exchange" and "overseas investment exchange" have the meaning given in Part 18 of the Financial Services and Markets Act 2000.

Loans

9. A loan or advance (including a liability comprising a loan or advance) is treated as falling due for repayment, and an instalment of a loan or advance is treated as falling due for payment, on the earliest date on which the lender could require repayment or (as the case may be) payment, if he exercised all options and rights available to him.

Materiality

10. Amounts which in the particular context of any provision of Schedules 1, 2 or 3 to these Regulations are not material may be disregarded for the purposes of that provision.

Participating interests

11. (1) A "participating interest" means an interest held by an undertaking in the shares of another undertaking which it holds on a long-term basis for the purpose of securing a contribution to its activities by the exercise of control or influence arising from or related to that interest.

(2) A holding of 20% or more of the shares of the undertaking is to be presumed to be a participating interest unless the contrary is shown.

(3) The reference in sub-paragraph (1) to an interest in shares includes—

(a) an interest which is convertible into an interest in shares, and

(b) an option to acquire shares or any such interest,

and an interest or option falls within paragraph (a) or (b) notwithstanding that the shares to which it relates are, until the conversion or the exercise of the option, unissued.

(4) For the purposes of this regulation an interest held on behalf of an undertaking is to be treated as held by it.

(5) In the balance sheet and profit and loss formats set out in Schedules 1, 2 and 3 to these Regulations, "participating interest" does not include an interest in a group undertaking.

(6) For the purpose of this regulation as it applies in relation to the expression "participating interest"—

(a) in those formats as they apply in relation to group accounts, and

(b) in paragraph 19 of Schedule 6 (group accounts: undertakings to be accounted for as associated undertakings),

the references in sub-paragraphs (1) to (4) to the interest held by, and the purposes and activities of, the undertaking concerned are to be construed as references to the interest held by, and the purposes and activities of, the group (within the meaning of paragraph 1 of that Schedule).

Purchase price

12. "Purchase price", in relation to an asset of a company or any raw materials or consumables used in the production of such an asset, includes any consideration (whether in cash or otherwise) given by the company in respect of that asset or those materials or consumables, as the case may be.

Realised profits and realised losses

13. "Realised profits" and "realised losses" have the same meaning as in section 853(4) and (5) of the 2006 Act.

Staff costs

14. (1) "Social security costs" means any contributions by the company to any state social security or pension scheme, fund or arrangement.

(2) "Pension costs" includes—

(a) any costs incurred by the company in respect of any pension scheme established for the purpose of providing pensions for persons currently or formerly employed by the company,

(b) any sums set aside for the future payment of pensions directly by the company to current or former employees, and

(c) any pensions paid directly to such persons without having first been set aside.

(3) Any amount stated in respect of the item "social security costs" or in respect of the item "wages and salaries" in the company's profit and loss account must be determined by reference to payments made or costs incurred in respect of all persons employed by the company during the financial year under contracts of service.

Scots land tenure

15. In the application of these Regulations to Scotland, "land of freehold tenure" means land in respect of which the company is the owner; "land of leasehold tenure" means land of which the company is the tenant under a lease.

NOTES

Para 3: sub-para (1) substituted by the Companies, Partnerships and Groups (Accounts and Reports) Regulations 2015, SI 2015/980, reg 41, as from 6 April 2015, in relation to (a) financial years beginning on or after 1 January 2016, and (b) a financial year of a company beginning on or after 1 January 2015, but before 1 January 2016, if the directors of the company so decide (see **[4.549]** *post*).

COMPANIES (DISCLOSURE OF AUDITOR REMUNERATION AND LIABILITY LIMITATION AGREEMENTS) REGULATIONS 2008

(SI 2008/489)

NOTES

Made: 23 February 2008.

Authority: Companies Act 2006, ss 494, 538, 1292(1)(a); European Communities Act 1972, s 2(2) (see also the note "Statutory Instruments made under the European Communities Act 1972" preceding paragraph **[4.1]** *ante*).

Commencement: 6 April 2008.

For a summary of all Orders and Regulations made under the Companies Act 2006, see Appendix 4 at **[A4]**.

These Regulations are reproduced as amended by: the Companies (Disclosure of Auditor Remuneration and Liability Limitation Agreements) (Amendment) Regulations 2011, SI 2011/2198; the Statutory Auditors and Third Country Auditors Regulations 2016, SI 2016/649.

Application: these Regulations are applied (i) to partnerships, see the Partnerships (Accounts) Regulations 2008, SI 2008/569 at **[10.202]**; (ii) to insurance undertakings, see the Insurance Accounts Directive (Miscellaneous Insurance Undertakings) Regulations 2008, SI 2008/565.

ARRANGEMENT OF REGULATIONS

PART 1
INTRODUCTORY

PART 2
DISCLOSURE OF REMUNERATION

PART 3
LIABILITY LIMITATION AGREEMENTS

SCHEDULES

PART 1 INTRODUCTORY

[4.115]

1 Citation and commencement

These Regulations may be cited as the Companies (Disclosure of Auditor Remuneration and Liability Limitation Agreements) Regulations 2008 and come into force on 6th April 2008.

[4.116]

2 Application and revocation

(1) Regulations 3 to 7 do not apply to the accounts of a company for any financial year beginning before 6th April 2008.

(2) The Companies (Disclosure of Auditor Remuneration) Regulations 2005 continue to apply to the accounts of a company for any financial year beginning before 6th April 2008.

(3) Subject to paragraph (2), the Companies (Disclosure of Auditor Remuneration) Regulations 2005 are revoked.

[4.117]

3 Interpretation

(1) In these Regulations—

"the Act" means the Companies Act 2006;

"associated pension scheme" means, in relation to a company, a scheme for the provision of benefits for or in respect of directors or employees (or former directors or employees) of the company or any subsidiary of the company where—

(a) the benefits consist of or include any pension, lump sum, gratuity or other like benefit given or to be given on retirement or on death or in anticipation of retirement or, in connection with past service, after retirement or death; and

(b) either—

(i) a majority of the trustees are appointed by, or by a person acting on behalf of, the company or a subsidiary of the company; or

(ii) the company, or a subsidiary of the company, exercises a dominant influence over the appointment of the auditor (if any) of the scheme;

Part 4 CA 2006 SIs

"parent" means a parent undertaking (as defined in section 1162 of the Act) which is a body corporate, and "parent company" is a parent which is a company;

"principal terms" has the meaning in section 536(4) of the Act;

"remuneration" includes payments in respect of expenses and benefits in kind;

"subsidiary" means a subsidiary undertaking (as defined in section 1162 of the Act) which is a body corporate, and "subsidiary company" is a subsidiary which is a company.

(2) For the purposes of these Regulations—

(a) a company is small in relation to a financial year if the small companies regime as defined in section 381 of the Act applies to it for that year;

(b) a company is medium-sized in relation to a financial year if—

(i) it qualifies as medium-sized in relation to that year under section 465 of the Act; and

(ii) it is not excluded from being medium-sized under section 467(1) of the Act;

(c) references to an associate of a company are references to—

(i) any subsidiary of that company, other than a subsidiary in respect of which severe long-term restrictions substantially hinder the exercise of the rights of the company over the assets or management of that subsidiary; and

(ii) any scheme which is an associated pension scheme in relation to that company; and

(d) a person is an associate, or a distant associate, of a company's auditor if that person is specified as such by Schedule 1 to these Regulations.

PART 2 DISCLOSURE OF REMUNERATION

[4.118]

4 Disclosure of remuneration: small and medium-sized companies

(1) A note to the annual accounts of a . . . medium-sized company must disclose the amount of any remuneration receivable by the company's auditor for the auditing of those accounts.

(2) Where the remuneration includes benefits in kind, the nature and estimated money-value of those benefits must also be disclosed in a note.

(3) Where more than one person has been appointed as a company's auditor in respect of the period to which the accounts relate, separate disclosure is required in respect of the remuneration of each such person.

(4) . . .

NOTES

Para (1): words omitted revoked by the Statutory Auditors and Third Country Auditors Regulations 2016, SI 2016/649, reg 18(1), (2)(a), as from 17 June 2016, in relation to financial years beginning on or after 1 January 2016 (see reg 1(4) of the 2016 Regulations).

Para (4): revoked by SI 2016/649, reg 18(1), (2)(b), as from 17 June 2016.

[4.119]

5 Disclosure of remuneration: other companies

(1) A note to the annual accounts of a company which is not a small or medium-sized company must disclose the amount of—

(a) any remuneration receivable by the company's auditor[, or an associate of the company's auditor,] for the auditing of those accounts; and

(b) subject to paragraph (6) and regulation 6(2), any remuneration receivable in respect of the period to which the accounts relate by—

(i) the company's auditor; or

(ii) any person who was, at any time during the period to which the accounts relate, an associate of the company's auditor,

for the supply of other services to the company or any associate of the company.

(2) Where the remuneration includes benefits in kind, the nature and estimated money-value of those benefits must also be disclosed in a note.

(3) Separate disclosure is required in respect of the auditing of the accounts in question and of each type of service specified in [Schedule 2A], but not in respect of each service falling within a type of service.

(4) Separate disclosure is required in respect of services supplied to the company and its subsidiaries on the one hand and to associated pension schemes on the other.

(5) Where more than one person has been appointed as a company's auditor in respect of the period to which the accounts relate, separate disclosure is required in respect of the remuneration of each such person and his associates.

(6) Disclosure is not required of remuneration receivable for the supply of services falling within [paragraph 8 of Schedule 2A] supplied by a distant associate of the company's auditor where the total remuneration receivable for all of those services supplied by that associate does not exceed either—

(a) £10,000, or

(b) 1% of the total audit remuneration received by the company's auditor in the most recent financial year of the auditor which ended no later than the end of the financial year of the company to which the accounts relate.

(7) In paragraph (6)(b)—

(a) "financial year of the auditor" means—

(i) the period of not more than 18 months in respect of which the auditor's profit and loss account is required to be made up (whether by law or by or in accordance with the auditor's constitution (if any)), or

(ii) failing any such requirement, the period of 12 months beginning with 1st April;

(b) "total audit remuneration received" means the total remuneration received for the auditing pursuant to legislation (including that of countries and territories outside the United Kingdom) of any accounts of any person.

NOTES

Words in square brackets in para (1) inserted, and words in square brackets in paras (3), (6) substituted, by the Companies (Disclosure of Auditor Remuneration and Liability Limitation Agreements) (Amendment) Regulations 2011, SI 2011/2198, regs 2–4, as from 1 October 2011, in relation to the accounts of a company for any financial year beginning on or after that date.

[4.120]

6 Group Accounts

(1) Group accounts must comply with regulation 5(1)(b) as if the undertakings included in the consolidation were a single company except where the group—

(a) qualifies as small or medium-sized under section 383 or 466 of the Act; and
(b) is not an ineligible group under section 384(2) or 467(2) of the Act.

(2) A note to the individual accounts of—

(a) a parent company which is required to prepare and does prepare group accounts in accordance with the Act; and
[(b) a subsidiary company where—
(i) its parent is required to prepare and does prepare group accounts in accordance with the Act,
(ii) the company is included in the consolidation, and
(iii) the statutory auditor is the same for both the company and its parent;]

does not have to disclose the information required by regulation 5(1)(b) if the conditions in paragraph (3) are satisfied.

(3) Those conditions are that—

(a) the group accounts are required to comply with paragraph (1); and
(b) the individual accounts state that the group accounts are so required.

NOTES

Para (2): sub-para (b) substituted by the Statutory Auditors and Third Country Auditors Regulations 2016, SI 2016/649, reg 18(1), (3), as from 17 June 2016, in relation to financial years beginning on or after that date (see reg 1(4) of the 2016 Regulations).

[4.121]

7 Duty of auditor to supply information

The auditor of a company must supply the directors of the company with such information as is necessary to enable the disclosure required by regulation 5(1)(b) or 6(1) to be made.

PART 3 LIABILITY LIMITATION AGREEMENTS

[4.122]

8 Disclosure of liability limitation agreements

(1) A company which has entered into a liability limitation agreement must disclose—

(a) its principal terms; and
(b) the date of the resolution approving the agreement or the agreement's principal terms or, in the case of a private company, the date of the resolution waiving the need for such approval,

in a note to the company's annual accounts.

(2) The annual accounts in which the disclosure required by paragraph (1) must be made shall be those for the financial year to which the agreement relates unless the agreement was entered into too late for it to be reasonably practicable for the disclosure to be made in those accounts.

(3) If the agreement was entered into too late for it to be reasonably practicable for the disclosure required by paragraph (1) to be made in the accounts for the financial year to which the agreement relates, the disclosure shall be made in a note to the company's next following annual accounts.

SCHEDULES

SCHEDULE 1
ASSOCIATES OF A COMPANY'S AUDITOR

Regulation 3(2)(d)

[4.123]

1. Each of the following shall be regarded as an associate of a company's auditor—

(a) any person controlled by the company's auditor or by any associate of the company's auditor (whether alone or through two or more persons acting together to secure or exercise control), but only if that control does not arise solely by virtue of the company's auditor or any associate of the company's auditor acting—
(i) as an insolvency practitioner in relation to any person;
(ii) in the capacity of a receiver, or a receiver or manager, of the property of a company or other body corporate; or
(iii) as a judicial factor on the estate of any person;
(b) any person who, or group of persons acting together which, has control of the company's auditor;
(c) any person using a trading name which is the same as or similar to a trading name used by the company's auditor, but only if the company's auditor uses that trading name with the intention of creating the impression of a connection between the auditor and that other person;
(d) any person who is a party to an arrangement with the company's auditor, with or without any other person, under which costs, profits, quality control, business strategy or significant professional resources are shared.

2. Where a company's auditor is a partnership, each of the following shall also be regarded as an associate of the auditor—

(a) any other partnership which has a partner in common with the company's auditor;

(b) any partner in the company's auditor;

(c) any body corporate which is in the same group as a body corporate which is a partner in the company's auditor;

(d) any body corporate which is in the same group as a body corporate which is a partner in a partnership which has a partner in common with the company's auditor;

(e) any body corporate of which a partner in the company's auditor is a director.

3. Where a company's auditor is a body corporate (other than one which is also a partnership as defined in paragraph 5(c)), each of the following shall also be regarded as an associate of the auditor—

(a) any other body corporate which has a director in common with the company's auditor;

(b) any director of the company's auditor;

(c) any body corporate which is in the same group as a body corporate which is a director of the company's auditor;

(d) any body corporate which is in the same group as a body corporate which has a director in common with the company's auditor;

(e) any partnership in which a director of the company's auditor is a partner;

(f) any body corporate which is in the same group as the company's auditor;

(g) any partnership in which any body corporate which is in the same group as the company's auditor is a partner.

4. A distant associate of a company's auditor is a person who is an associate of that auditor by reason only that that person is an associate within one or more of—

(a) paragraph 1(a) where the person in question is controlled by a distant associate of the company's auditor but not by the auditor or by an associate who is not a distant associate;

(b) paragraph 2(a), (d) or (e);

(c) paragraph 3(a), (d) or (e).

5. In this Schedule—

(a) "acting as an insolvency practitioner" shall be construed in accordance with section 388 of the Insolvency Act 1986 or Article 3 of the Insolvency (Northern Ireland) Order 1989;

(b) "partner" includes a member of a limited liability partnership;

(c) "partnership" includes a limited liability partnership and a partnership constituted under the law of a country or a territory outside the United Kingdom;

(d) a reference to "a receiver, or a receiver or manager, of the property of a company or other body corporate" includes a receiver, or (as the case may be) a receiver or manager, of part only of that property;

(e) a person able, directly or indirectly to control or materially to influence the operating and financial policy of another person shall be treated as having control of that other person; and

(f) a body corporate is in the same group as another body corporate if it is a parent or subsidiary of that body corporate, or a subsidiary of a parent of that body corporate.

[SCHEDULE 2A
TYPE OF SERVICE IN RESPECT OF WHICH DISCLOSURE IS TO BE MADE

Regulation 5(3)

[4.124]

1. The auditing of accounts of any associate of the company.

2. Audit-related assurance services.

3. Taxation compliance services.

4. All taxation advisory services not falling within paragraph 3.

5. Internal audit services.

6. All assurance services not falling within paragraphs 1 to 5.

7. All services relating to corporate finance transactions entered into, or proposed to be entered into, by or on behalf of the company or any of its associates not falling within paragraphs 1 to 6.

8. All non-audit services not falling within paragraphs 2 to 7.]

NOTES

Schedule 2A was substituted (for the original Sch 2) by the Companies (Disclosure of Auditor Remuneration and Liability Limitation Agreements) (Amendment) Regulations 2011, SI 2011/2198, reg 5, Schedule, as from 1 October 2011, in relation to the accounts of a company for any financial year beginning on or after that date.

COMPANIES (LATE FILING PENALTIES) AND LIMITED LIABILITY PARTNERSHIPS (FILING PERIODS AND LATE FILING PENALTIES) REGULATIONS 2008

(SI 2008/497)

NOTES

Made: 23 February 2008.

Authority: Companies Act 1985, s 247(1), (4)(a), (d); Limited Liability Partnerships Act 2000, s 15(a); Companies Act 2006, ss 453, 1292(1)(a), (c). Note that s 247 of the 1985 Act was repealed by CA 2006, as from 6 April 2008, subject to savings in relation to financial years beginning before that date.

Commencement: 6 April 2008.

For a summary of all Orders and Regulations made under the Companies Act 2006, see Appendix 4 at **[A4]**.

These Regulations are reproduced as amended by: the Limited Liability Partnerships (Accounts and Audit) (Application of Companies Act 2006) Regulations 2008, SI 2008/1911.

[4.125]

1 Citation, coming into force and interpretation

(1) These Regulations may be cited as the Companies (Late Filing Penalties) and Limited Liability Partnerships (Filing Periods and Late Filing Penalties) Regulations 2008.

(2) These Regulations come into force on 6th April 2008.

(3) References in these Regulations to late filing, or to a failure to comply with filing requirements, are to a failure to comply with the requirements of section 441 of the Companies Act 2006 (which apply in relation to financial years beginning on or after 6th April 2008) in relation to a company's accounts and reports before the end of the period for filing those accounts and reports.

(4) For the purposes of regulations 2 and 4, whether a company is a public company or a private company depends upon its status at the end of the financial year in question.

[4.126]

2 Late filing penalties under the Companies Act 2006 as from 6th April 2008

(1) This regulation applies where the requirements of section 441 of the Companies Act 2006 are complied with before 1st February 2009.

(2) The amount of the civil penalty to which a company is liable under section 453 of the Companies Act 2006 in a case of late filing is that shown in the following table:

Length of period	Public company	Private company
Not more than 3 months	£500	£100
More than 3 months but not more than 6 months	£1,000	£250
More than 6 months	£2,000	£500

(3) The first column of the table ("length of period") refers to the length of the period between the end of the period for filing the accounts and reports in question and the day on which the requirements of section 441 are complied with.

3 *(This regulation inserted the Companies Act 1985, s 242A(2A), and applied where the requirements of s 242(1) of that Act were complied with on or after 6 April 2008. Note that s 242 of the 1985 Act was repealed by CA 2006, as from 6 April 2008, subject to savings in relation to financial years beginning before that date.)*

[4.127]

4 Late filing penalties under the Companies Act 2006 as from 1st February 2009

(1) This regulation applies where the requirements of section 441 of the Companies Act 2006 are complied with on or after 1st February 2009.

(2) The amount of the civil penalty to which a company is liable under section 453 of the Companies Act 2006 in a case of late filing is that shown in the following table or, if there was a failure to comply with filing requirements in relation to the previous financial year of the company and that previous financial year had begun on or after 6th April 2008, double that shown in the table:

Length of period	Public company	Private company
Not more than 1 month	£750	£150
More than 1 month but not more than 3 months	£1,500	£375
More than 3 months but not more than 6 months	£3,000	£750
More than 6 months	£7,500	£1,500

(3) The first column of the table ("length of period") refers to the length of the period between the end of the period for filing the accounts and reports in question and the day on which the requirements of section 441 are complied with.

5 *(This regulation substituted the table in sub-s (2) of the Companies Act 1985, s 242A, and applied where the requirements of s 242(1) of that Act (which continued to apply in relation to financial years beginning before 6 April 2008 and, in the case of LLPs, in relation to financial years beginning on or after that date) were complied with on or after 1 February 2009. Note that s 242A of the 1985 Act was repealed by CA 2006, as from 6 April 2008, subject to savings in relation to financial years beginning before that date.)*

[4.128]

6 Limited liability partnerships: filing periods and late filing penalties

(1) Section 443 of the Companies Act 2006 (calculation of period allowed for filing accounts and reports) applies to limited liability partnerships with the modification in Part 1 of the Schedule to these Regulations.

(2) Schedule 1 to the Limited Liability Partnership Regulations 2001 is amended as provided in Part 2 of the Schedule to these Regulations.

(3) This regulation applies to accounts and auditors' reports for financial years beginning on or after 6th April 2008[, but paragraph (1) does not apply to accounts or reports for financial years beginning on or after 1st October 2008].

NOTES

Para (3): words in square brackets added by the Limited Liability Partnerships (Accounts and Audit) (Application of Companies Act 2006) Regulations 2008, SI 2008/1911, reg 22(2), as from 1 October 2008.

SCHEDULE

Regulation 6

PART 1 MODIFICATION OF SECTION 443 OF THE COMPANIES ACT 2006 IN ITS APPLICATION TO LIMITED LIABILITY PARTNERSHIPS

[4.129]

In subsection (1), for the words "the period for filing a company's reports and accounts" substitute "the period allowed for delivering the accounts and the auditor's report".

(Part 2 of the Schedule amended the Limited Liability Partnerships Regulations 2001, SI 2001/1090, Sch 1 (which was revoked by the Limited Liability Partnerships (Accounts and Audit) (Application of Companies Act 2006) Regulations 2008, SI 2008/1911, reg 58(1)(a), as from 1 October 2008, except in relation to accounts for, and otherwise as regards, financial years beginning before that date).)

COMPANIES (AUTHORISED MINIMUM) REGULATIONS 2008

(SI 2008/729)

NOTES

Made: 12 March 2008.

Authority: Companies Act 2006, ss 763(2), 766(1)(a), (2), 1292(1)(a), (b).

Commencement: 6 April 2008.

For a summary of all Orders and Regulations made under the Companies Act 2006, see Appendix 4 at **[A4]**.

These Regulations are reproduced as amended by: the Companies (Authorised Minimum) Regulations 2009, SI 2009/2425; the EEA Passport Rights (Amendment, etc, and Transitional Provisions) (EU Exit) Regulations 2018, SI 2018/1149.

Note: to a large extent these Regulations have been replaced by the Companies (Authorised Minimum) Regulations 2009, SI 2009/2425 at **[4.381]**. However, the 2009 Regulations only revoked reg 2 of these Regulations. These Regulations provide for the application of the authorised minimum requirement for the purposes of relevant provisions of the Companies Act 1985 (and the Companies (Northern Ireland) Order 1986), which require a public company to re-register as a private company where certain events cause the nominal value of its allotted its share capital to fall below the authorised minimum, in the case where the company has or will have shares denominated in more than one currency.

ARRANGEMENT OF REGULATIONS

[4.130]

1 Citation, commencement and interpretation

(1) These Regulations may be cited as the Companies (Authorised Minimum) Regulations 2008 and shall come into force on 6th April 2008.

(2) In these Regulations—

"the 1985 Act" means the Companies Act 1985;

"the 1986 Order" means the Companies (Northern Ireland) Order 1986;

"the 2006 Act" means the Companies Act 2006;

"the appropriate spot rate of exchange" is to be interpreted in accordance with regulation 4(1);

"the certified spot rate" has the meaning given in regulation 4(3);

"published spot rate" has the meaning given in regulation 4(2);

"reference date" is to be interpreted in accordance with regulation 4(7) and (8);

"relevant day" is to be interpreted in accordance with regulation 4(5) and (6); and

"working day" means a day which is not a Saturday or Sunday, Christmas Day, Good Friday or any day that is a bank holiday under the Banking and Financial Dealings Act 1971 in England and Wales.

2 *(Revoked by the Companies (Authorised Minimum) Regulations 2009, SI 2009/2425, reg 8, as from 1 October 2009. Note that prior to its revocation, this regulation provided that for the purposes of the definition of "the authorised* *minimum" in s 763(1) of the 2006 Act, the amount in euros that is to be treated as equivalent to the sterling amount is €65,600. For transitional provisions in relation to the revocation of this regulation, see reg 9 of the 2009 Regulations at* **[4.388]***.)*

[4.131]

3 Application of the authorised minimum where a public company has shares denominated in more than one currency

(1) This regulation applies for either of the purposes in paragraphs (2) and (3).

(2) The first purpose is to determine whether, for the purposes of section 139 of the 1985 Act or Article 149 of the 1986 Order, a court order under section 137 of the 1985 Act or Article 147 of the 1986 Order has the effect of bringing the nominal value of a public company's allotted share capital below the authorised minimum.

(3) The second purpose is to determine whether, for the purposes of section 146(2)(b) of the 1985 Act or Article 156(2)(b) of the 1986 Order, the cancellation of a public company's shares under that section or that Article will have the effect of bringing the nominal value of the company's allotted share capital below the authorised minimum.

(4) This regulation applies only where the company has or will have allotted share capital denominated in more than one currency, taking account (where the purpose is that in paragraph (2)) of the effect of the court order or (where the purpose is that in paragraph (3)) of the cancellation of the shares.

(5) The nominal value of a public company's allotted share capital is to be treated as being below the authorised minimum if—

(a) the sterling value is less than £50,000; and

(b) the euro value is less than €65,600.

(6) The "sterling value" is the sum in sterling of—

(a) the nominal value of the company's allotted share capital denominated in sterling;

(b) the nominal value of the company's allotted share capital denominated in euros if it were to be converted into sterling at the appropriate spot rate of exchange; and

(c) the nominal value of the company's allotted share capital denominated in a currency other than sterling or euros if it were to be converted into sterling at the appropriate spot rate of exchange.

(7) The "euro value" is the sum in euros of—

(a) the nominal value of the company's allotted share capital denominated in euros;

(b) the nominal value of the company's allotted share capital denominated in sterling if it were to be converted into euros at the appropriate spot rate of exchange; and

(c) the nominal value of the company's allotted share capital denominated in a currency other than sterling or euros if it were to be converted into euros at the appropriate spot rate of exchange.

(8) Regulation 4 applies to determine the appropriate spot rate of exchange.

NOTES

Companies Act 1985, ss 137, 139, 146: repealed by the Companies Act 2006, as from 1 October 2009.

[4.132]

4 The appropriate spot rate of exchange

(1) The appropriate spot rate of exchange for a currency conversion referred to in regulation 3(6) and (7) is the published spot rate relevant to the currency conversion in question or, where the circumstances in paragraph (4) exist, the certified spot rate relevant to that currency conversion.

(2) The published spot rate is the middle spot exchange rate prevailing on the foreign exchange market at 4pm on the relevant day as published in respect of that day by the Financial Times.

(3) The certified spot rate is the middle spot exchange rate prevailing on the foreign exchange market at 4pm on the relevant day and stated in a certificate obtained by the company from—

(a) a person, nominated by the company, who under Part 4 of the Financial Services and Markets Act 2000 has permission to accept deposits; . . .

(b) . . .

(4) The circumstances in this paragraph exist where—

(a) the Financial Times has not, on or before the reference date, published an exchange rate referred to in paragraph (2) relevant to the currency conversion in question; or

(b) the Financial Times has, on or before the reference date, published what appears to be an exchange rate referred to in paragraph (2) relevant to the currency conversion in question but the company can show that there was a publication error; or

(c) there is no evidence of what (if any) was the rate referred to in paragraph (2) relevant to the currency conversion in question as published on or before the reference date by the Financial Times.

(5) Where the currency conversion is relevant to the calculation of the sterling value or the euro value for the purpose in regulation 3(2), the "relevant day" is the working day which immediately preceded the working day immediately preceding the date of the court order under section 137 of the 1985 Act or Article 147 of the 1986 Order.

(6) Where the currency conversion is relevant to the calculation of the sterling value or the euro value for the purpose in regulation 3(3), the "relevant day" is—

(a) in a case within section 146(1)(a) or (aa) of the 1985 Act or Article 156(1)(a) or (aa) of the 1986 Order, the working day immediately preceding the date of the forfeiture or surrender; and

(b) in a case within section 146(1)(b), (c) or (d) of the 1985 Act or Article 156(1)(b), (c) or (d) of the 1986 Order, the working day immediately preceding the date of the acquisition.

(7) Where the currency calculation is relevant to the calculation of the sterling value or the euro value for the purpose in regulation 3(2), the "reference date" is the date of the court order under section 137 of the 1985 Act or Article 147 of the 1986 Order.

(8) Where the currency conversion is relevant to the calculation of the sterling value or the euro value for the purpose in regulation 3(3), the "reference date" is—

(a) in the case within section 146(1)(a) or (aa) of the 1985 Act or Article 156(1)(a) or (aa) of the 1986 Order, the fifth working day following the date of the forfeiture or surrender; and

(b) in the case within section 146(1)(b), (c) or (d) of the 1985 Act or Article 156(1)(b), (c) or (d) of the 1986 Order, the fifth working day following the date of the acquisition.

NOTES

Para (3): sub-para (b) and the preceding word revoked by the EEA Passport Rights (Amendment, etc, and Transitional Provisions) (EU Exit) Regulations 2018, SI 2018/1149, reg 3, Schedule, Pt 3, para 54, as from IP completion day (as defined in the European Union (Withdrawal Agreement) Act 2020, s 39).

Companies Act 1985, ss 137, 146: repealed by the Companies Act 2006, as from 1 October 2009.

[4.133]

5 Registration of a court order confirming a capital reduction and applications by public companies for re-registration: assumptions which may be made by the registrar

(1) This regulation applies where—

(a) a public company delivers to the registrar under section 138 of the 1985 Act or Article 148 of the 1986 Order a copy of an order of the court confirming a reduction of its share capital and the court has not directed the order to be registered; or

(b) an application is made to the registrar under section 147(3) of the 1985 Act or Article 157(3) of the 1986 Order for re-registration of a public company as a private company.

(2) Where the circumstances in paragraph (3), (4) or (5) exist, the registrar may make (in a case within paragraph (1)(a)) the assumption in paragraph (6) or (in a case within paragraph (1)(b)) the assumption in paragraph (7).

(3) The circumstances in this paragraph are that—

(a) the company has or will have (taking account, where the case is within paragraph (1)(a), of the effect of the court order or, where the case is within paragraph (1)(b), of the effect of the cancellation of shares under section 146(2)(a) of the 1985 Act or Article 156(2)(a) of the 1986 Order) allotted share capital denominated in more than one currency;

(b) either the Financial Times did not publish, on or before the reference date, an exchange rate referred to in regulation 4(2) relevant to converting into sterling a currency in which the company's allotted share capital is denominated or it did not publish, on or before that date, such a rate relevant to converting such a currency into euros; and

(c) the company has not delivered to the registrar, in respect of every such currency for which the Financial Times did not publish such an exchange rate on or before the reference date, a copy of a certificate referred to in regulation 4(3).

(4) The circumstances in this paragraph are that—

(a) the company has or will have (taking account, where the case is within paragraph (1)(a), of the effect of the court order or, where the case is within paragraph (1)(b), of the effect of the cancellation of shares under section 146(2)(a) of the 1985 Act or Article 156(2)(a) of the 1986 Order) allotted share capital denominated in more than one currency;

(b) the Financial Times published, on or before the reference date, what appears to be an exchange rate referred to in regulation 4(2) relevant to converting into sterling or euros a currency in which the company's allotted share capital is denominated but the company can show that there was a publication error; and

(c) the company has not delivered to the registrar, for every currency in respect of which the company can show such a publication error, a copy of a certificate referred to in regulation 4(3).

(5) The circumstances in this paragraph are that—

(a) the company has or will have (taking account, where the case is within paragraph (1)(a), of the effect of the court order or, where the case is within paragraph (1)(b), of the effect of the cancellation of shares under section 146(2)(a) of the 1985 Act or Article 156(2)(a) of the 1986 Order) allotted share capital denominated in more than one currency;

(b) in respect of one or more of the exchange rates referred to in regulation 4(2) relevant to converting into sterling or euros the currencies in which the company's allotted share capital is denominated there is no evidence of what (if any) was the rate published on or before the reference date by the Financial Times; and

(c) the company has not delivered to the registrar, for every such currency in respect of which there is no such evidence, a copy of a certificate referred to in regulation 4(3).

(6) The registrar may (but is not required to) assume for the purposes of sections 138(1) and 139(2) of the 1985 Act or Articles 148(1) and 149(2) of the 1986 Order that the court order has the effect of bringing the nominal value of the company's allotted share capital below the authorised minimum.

(7) The registrar may (but is not required to) assume for the purposes of section 147(4) of the 1985 Act or Article 157(4) of the 1986 Order that the effect of the cancellation of shares under section 146(2)(a) of the 1985 Act or Article 156(2)(a) of the 1986 Order is or will be that the nominal value of the company's allotted share capital is brought below the authorised minimum.

NOTES

Companies Act 1985, ss 138, 139, 146, 147: repealed by the Companies Act 2006, as from 1 October 2009.

[4.134]

6 Determination of exchange rates by the court in certain proceedings

(1) This regulation applies to—

(a) proceedings against a public company or any officer of a public company for an offence under section 149(2) of the 1985 Act or Article 159(2) of the 1986 Order; and

(b) proceedings under section 757 or 758 or Part 30 of the 2006 Act.

(2) Where the circumstances in paragraph (3) exist, the court may make a determination referred to in paragraph (4) in the proceedings.

(3) The circumstances are that—

(a) in proceedings referred to in paragraph (1)(a) it is alleged that, or in proceedings referred to in paragraph (1)(b) the question arises whether, the effect of a cancellation of the company's shares under section 146(2)(a) of the 1985 Act or Article 156(2)(a) of the 1986 Order was or will be that the nominal value of the company's allotted share capital was or is brought below the authorised minimum; and

(b) as a result of that cancellation the company had (or continued to have) allotted share capital denominated in more than one currency.

(4) The court may make such determination as it thinks fit as to the exchange rate to be applied to a currency conversion referred to in regulation 3(6) and (7) where—

(a) the Financial Times did not publish, on or before the reference date, an exchange rate referred to in regulation 4(2) relevant to that currency conversion; or

(b) the Financial Times published, on or before the reference date, what appears to be an exchange rate referred to in regulation 4(2) relevant to that currency conversion but the company or officer of the company (as the case may be) can show that there was a publication error; or

(c) there is no evidence of what (if any) was the exchange rate referred to in regulation 4(2) as published on or before the reference date by the Financial Times relevant to that currency conversion,

and there has not been produced to the court in the proceedings a copy of a certificate referred to in regulation 4(3) in respect of that currency conversion.

(5) In this regulation, "the court" in relation to proceedings referred to in paragraph (1)(a) means the court of criminal jurisdiction in which the proceedings are brought.

NOTES

Companies Act 1985, ss 146, 149: repealed by the Companies Act 2006, as from 1 October 2009.

[4.135]

7 Exclusion of liability in respect of publication of spot rate

No person shall be liable to any other person as a result of—

(a) that or any other person having placed reliance for the purposes of these Regulations upon a rate published by the Financial Times; or

(b) any error in a rate published by the Financial Times which is relied upon for the purposes of these Regulations; or

(c) any act or omission as a result of which the Financial Times did not publish a rate capable of being relied upon for the purposes of these Regulations.

COMPANIES ACT 2006 (CONSEQUENTIAL AMENDMENTS ETC) ORDER 2008

(SI 2008/948)

NOTES

Made: 1 April 2008.

Authority: Companies Act 2006, ss 1292, 1294, 1296.

Commencement: 6 April 2008 (certain purposes); 1 October 2008 (otherwise); see art 2 at **[4.137]**.

For a summary of all Orders and Regulations made under the Companies Act 2006, see Appendix 4 at **[A4]**.

ARRANGEMENT OF ARTICLES

[4.136]

1 Citation

This Order may be cited as the Companies Act 2006 (Consequential Amendments etc) Order 2008.

[4.137]
2 Coming into force

(1) The provisions of this Order come into force as follows.

(2) Articles 1 to 3 and 5 to 12 and Schedules 1 and 2 come into force on 6th April 2008.

(3) Article 4 and Schedules 3 and 4 come into force on 1st October 2008.

[4.138]
3 Consequential amendments, repeals and revocations: 6th April 2008

(1) Schedule 1 to this Order contains amendments coming into force on 6th April 2008—

- (a) Part 1 contains amendments about eligibility for appointment as auditor and related matters;
- (b) Part 2 contains other amendments.

(2) Schedule 2 to this Order contains repeals and revocations coming into force on that date.

[4.139]
4 Consequential amendments, repeals and revocations: 1st October 2008

(1) Schedule 3 to this Order contains amendments coming into force on 1st October 2008.

(2) Schedule 4 to this Order contains repeals and revocations coming into force on that date.

[4.140]
5 Eligibility for appointment as statutory auditor: effect of appointing partnership

(1) Section 1216 of the Companies Act 2006 (effect of appointing partnership) applies in relation to any statutory appointment where eligibility for the appointment depends on eligibility for appointment as a statutory auditor under Part 42 of that Act.

(2) In subsection (6)(b) of that section as it applies by virtue of this article, the reference to being prohibited by virtue of section 1214(1) of that Act from acting as statutory auditor shall be read as including a reference to being prohibited or disqualified from acting, or ineligible or disqualified for appointment, on the ground of lack of independence (of any description) by virtue of any other enactment applying in relation to the appointment.

(3) For the purposes of this article a "statutory appointment" means an appointment in pursuance of an enactment authorising or requiring the making of the appointment.

(4) This article applies only where that enactment was passed or made before 6th April 2008.

[4.141]
6 Provisions referred to in amendments

(1) The following provisions have effect in relation to any amendment made by this Order.

(2) Any reference to the Companies Act 2006, the provisions of that Act or any particular provision of that Act includes any provision made under that Act or, as the case may be, the provision referred to.

(3) Any provision of the Companies Act 2006 referred to in the amendment has effect for the purposes of the amendment although not yet brought into force generally.

(4) Where by virtue of any transitional provision a provision of the Companies Act 2006 has effect only—

- (a) on or after a specified date, or
- (b) in relation to matters occurring or arising on or after a specified date,

any amendment substituting or inserting a reference to that provision has effect correspondingly.

(5) Without prejudice to the generality of paragraph (4), the provisions of paragraph 35 of Schedule 4 to the Companies Act 2006 (Commencement No 5, Transitional Provisions and Savings) Order 2007 apply in any case where the effect of an amendment made by this Order is that the lawfulness of a distribution depends on Part 23 of the Companies Act 2006, or any provision of that Part, applying in relation to accounts for financial years beginning before 6th April 2008.

[4.142]
7 Savings for provisions relating to execution of documents

(1) The repeal of provisions of section 36A of the Companies Act 1985 (execution of documents) does not affect the operation of that section as applied by the Foreign Companies (Execution of Documents) Regulations 1994.

(2) That section as so applied does not apply to companies registered in Northern Ireland to which section 44 of the Companies Act 2006 applies.

[4.143]
8

(1) The repeal of provisions of Article 46A of the Companies (Northern Ireland) Order 1986 (execution of documents) does not affect the operation of that Article—

- (a) in relation to a liquidator of a company, or
- (b) as applied by the Foreign Companies (Execution of Documents) Regulations (Northern Ireland) 2003.

(2) That Article as so applied does not apply to companies registered in Great Britain to which section 44 of the Companies Act 2006 applies.

[4.144]
9 Saving for accounting definitions

(1) The repeal of paragraphs 88 and 89 of Schedule 4 to the Companies Act 1985 (accounting definitions) does not affect the operation of those provisions for the purposes of section 152(2) or 172(2)(b)(i) of that Act.

(2) The repeal of paragraphs 87 and 88 of Schedule 4 to the Companies (Northern Ireland) Order 1986 (accounting definitions) does not affect the operation of those provisions for the purposes of Article 162(2) or 182(2)(b)(i) of that Order.

[4.145]

10 Saving for earlier consequential amendments

The repeal of section 50 of the Companies Act 1989 or Article 52 of the Companies (Northern Ireland) Order 1990 (appointment etc of auditors: power to make consequential amendments) does not affect any amendments made by regulations under that section or Article that are in force immediately before 6th April 2008.

[4.146]

11 Saving for limited liability partnerships

Nothing in this Order affects any provision of the Companies Act 1985 or the Companies (Northern Ireland) Order 1986 as applied by the Limited Liability Partnerships Regulations 2001 or the Limited Liability Partnerships Regulations (Northern Ireland) 2004 to limited liability partnerships.

[4.147]

12 General saving

The amendments, revocations and repeals made by this Order do not affect the operation of section 1297 of the Companies Act 2006 (continuity of the law).

SCHEDULES 1–4

(Sch 1 (Amendments Coming Into Force on 6th April 2008), Sch 2 (Repeals and Revocations Coming into Force on 6th April 2008), Sch 3 (Amendments Coming into Force on 1st October 2008), and Sch 4 (Repeals and Revocations Coming into Force on 1st October 2008) contain various amendments, repeals and revocations which, where relevant, have been incorporated at the appropriate place.)

COMPANY NAMES ADJUDICATOR RULES 2008

(SI 2008/1738)

NOTES

Made: 1 July 2008.

Authority: Companies Act 2006, s 71.

Commencement: 1 October 2008.

For a summary of all Orders and Regulations made under the Companies Act 2006, see Appendix 4 at **[A4]**.

These Rules are reproduced as amended by: the Public Bodies (Abolition of Administrative Justice and Tribunals Council) Order 2013, SI 2013/2042.

ARRANGEMENT OF RULES

Introductory

[4.148]

1 Citation, commencement and interpretation

(1) These Rules may be cited as the Company Names Adjudicator Rules 2008 and come into force on 1st October 2008.

(2) In these Rules—

"the Act" means the Companies Act 2006 and references to a "section" are to a section of the Act;

"the appropriate form" means the form determined by the Chief Adjudicator in relation to a particular matter; and

"the Office" means the office of the company names adjudicator at the Intellectual Property Office, Concept House, Cardiff Road, Newport, South Wales, NP10 8QQ.

(3) In these Rules references to the filing of any application or other document are to be construed as references to its being delivered to the adjudicator at the Office.

[4.149]

2 Forms and fees

(1) The Chief Adjudicator shall have the power to determine the form and content of any form required to be used by these Rules.

(2) Where a form is required to be used by these Rules that form shall be accompanied by the fee, if any, specified in the Schedule in respect of that matter.

Proceedings before the adjudicator

[4.150]

3 Procedure for objecting to a company's registered name

(1) An application under section 69(2) shall—

(a) be made on the appropriate form;

(b) include a concise statement of the grounds on which the application is made;

(c) include an address for service in the United Kingdom; and

(d) be filed at the Office.

(2) The adjudicator shall send a copy of the appropriate form to the primary respondent.

(3) The adjudicator shall specify a period within which the primary respondent must file its defence.

(4) The primary respondent, before the end of that period, shall file a counter-statement on the appropriate form, otherwise the adjudicator may treat it as not opposing the application and may make an order under section 73(1).

(5) In its counter-statement the primary respondent shall—

(a) include an address for service in the United Kingdom;

(b) include a concise statement of the grounds on which it relies;

(c) state which of the allegations in the statement of grounds of the applicant it admits and which it denies; and

(d) state which of the allegations it is unable to admit or deny, but which it requires the applicant to prove.

(6) Any member or director of the primary respondent who is joined as a respondent to the application must be joined before the end of a period specified by the adjudicator.

(7) The adjudicator shall send a copy of the appropriate form referred to in paragraph (4) to the applicant.

[4.151]

4 Evidence rounds

(1) When the period specified under rule 3(3) has expired, the adjudicator shall specify the periods within which evidence may be filed by the parties.

(2) All evidence must be—

(a) accompanied by the appropriate form, and

(b) copied to all other parties in the proceedings.

[4.152]

5 Decision of adjudicator and hearings

(1) Where the applicant files no evidence in support of its application the adjudicator may treat it as having withdrawn its application.

(2) The adjudicator may strike out the application or any defence in whole or in part if it is vexatious, has no reasonable prospect of success or is otherwise misconceived.

(3) Any party may, by filing the appropriate form, request to be heard in person before a decision is made by the adjudicator under the Act or these Rules.

(4) Following a request under rule 5(3) the adjudicator shall decide whether a decision can be made without an oral hearing in circumstances where—

(a) the primary respondent files no evidence; or

(b) the applicant files no evidence in reply to the respondent's evidence; or

(c) the decision will not terminate the proceedings.

(5) Where the adjudicator decides that a decision can be made without an oral hearing the adjudicator will specify a period for the parties to submit written submissions before making a decision.

(6) Where the adjudicator decides that a hearing is necessary he shall require the parties or their legal representatives to attend a hearing and shall give the parties at least 14 days' notice of the hearing.

(7) When the adjudicator has made a decision on the application under section 69(2) he shall send to the parties written notice of it, stating the reasons for his decision.

(8) The date on which the decision was sent to the parties shall be taken to be the date of the decision for the purposes of any appeal.

[4.153]

6 General powers of adjudicator in relation to proceedings before him

(1) At any stage of proceedings before him, the adjudicator may direct that the parties to the proceedings attend a case management conference or pre-hearing review.

(2) The adjudicator may give such directions as to the management of the proceedings as he thinks fit, and in particular he may—

- (a) direct a document to be filed or to be copied to a party to proceedings within a specified period;
- (b) allow for the electronic filing and sending of documents;
- (c) direct how documents filed or sent electronically are to be authenticated;
- (d) direct that a document shall not be available for public inspection;
- (e) require a translation of any document;
- (f) direct that a witness be cross-examined;
- (g) consolidate proceedings;
- (h) direct that proceedings are to be heard by more than one adjudicator;
- (i) direct that part of any proceedings be dealt with as separate proceedings; or
- (j) suspend or stay proceedings.

(3) The adjudicator may control the evidence by giving directions as to—

- (a) the issues on which he requires evidence;
- (b) the nature of the evidence which he requires to decide those issues; and
- (c) the way in which the evidence is to be placed before him,

and the adjudicator may use his power under this paragraph to exclude evidence which would otherwise be admissible.

[4.154]

7 Requests for extensions of time

(1) The adjudicator may extend (or further extend) any period which has been specified under any provision of these Rules even if the period has expired.

(2) Any party can request an extension of any time period specified under any provision of these Rules.

(3) Any request for a retrospective extension must be filed before the end of the period of 2 months beginning with the date the time period in question expired.

(4) Any request made under paragraph (2) shall be made on the appropriate form and shall include reasons why the extra time is required. A request for a retrospective extension shall also include reasons why the request is being made out of time.

[4.155]

8 Public proceedings

(1) Subject to paragraphs (3) and (4), any hearing before the adjudicator of proceedings relating to an application under section 69(2) shall be held in public.

(2) Any party to the proceedings may apply to the adjudicator for the hearing to be held in private.

(3) The adjudicator shall only grant an application under paragraph (2) where—

- (a) it is in the interests of justice for the hearing to be in held in private; and
- (b) all the parties to the proceedings have had an opportunity to be heard on the matter,

and where the application is granted the hearing shall be held in private.

(4) Any hearing of an application under paragraph (2) shall be held in private.

(5) In this rule a reference to a hearing includes any part of a hearing.

(6) . . .

(7) All documents connected to proceedings shall be available for public inspection unless the adjudicator directs otherwise.

NOTES

Para (6): revoked by the Public Bodies (Abolition of Administrative Justice and Tribunals Council) Order 2013, SI 2013/2042, art 2(2), Schedule, para 70, as from 19 August 2013.

[4.156]

9 Evidence in proceedings before the adjudicator

(1) Subject to rule 6(3), evidence filed under these Rules may be given—

- (a) by witness statement, affidavit or statutory declaration; or
- (b) in any other form which would be admissible as evidence in proceedings before the court,

and a witness statement may only be given in evidence if it includes a statement of truth.

(2) For the purposes of these Rules, a statement of truth—

- (a) means a statement that the person making the statement believes that the facts stated in a particular document are true; and
- (b) shall be dated and signed by the maker of the statement.

(3) In these Rules, a witness statement is a written statement signed by a person that contains the evidence which that person would be allowed to give orally.

[4.157]
10 Correction of irregularities of procedure

(1) Any irregularity in procedure may be rectified on such terms as the adjudicator may direct.

(2) Where rectification includes the amendment of a document by the adjudicator the parties will be given notice of this amendment.

Costs or expenses

[4.158]
11 Costs or expenses of proceedings

The adjudicator may, at any stage in any proceedings before him under the Act, award to any party by order such costs (in Scotland, expenses) as he considers reasonable, and direct how and by what parties they are to be paid.

[4.159]
12 Security for costs or expenses

An application for security for costs (in Scotland, caution for expenses) shall be made on the appropriate form. The adjudicator may require a person to give security for costs (in Scotland, caution for expenses) if he is satisfied, having regard to all the circumstances of the case, that it is just to require such security or caution.

Address for service

[4.160]
13 Address for service

(1) Where a person has provided an address for service in the United Kingdom under rule 3 he may substitute a new address for service in the United Kingdom by notifying the adjudicator on the appropriate form.

(2) Where the primary respondent has a registered office in the United Kingdom the adjudicator may treat this as the address for service in the United Kingdom unless and until an alternative address is provided.

Miscellaneous

[4.161]
14 Hours of business

(1) For the transaction of relevant business by the public under the Act the Office shall be open—
  (a) on Monday to Friday between 9.00 am and midnight; and
  (b) on Saturday between 9.00 am and 1.00 pm,
unless the day is an excluded day (see rule 15).

(2) For the transaction of all other business by the public under the Act the Office shall be open on Monday to Friday between 9.00 am and 5.00 pm unless the day is an excluded day (see rule 15).

(3) In this rule and in rule 15 "relevant business" means the filing of any application or other document.

[4.162]
15 Excluded days

(1) The following shall be excluded days for the transaction of any business by the public under the Act—
  (a) a Sunday;
  (b) Good Friday;
  (c) Christmas Day;
  (d) a day which is specified or proclaimed to be a bank holiday by or under section 1 of the Banking and Financial Dealings Act 1971; or
  (e) a Saturday where the previous Friday and the following Monday are both excluded days.

(2) Any application or document received on an excluded day shall be treated as having been filed on the next day on which the Office is open for relevant business.

(3) Where any period for filing any document ends on an excluded day that period shall be extended to the next day on which the Office is open for relevant business.

SCHEDULE
FEES

[4.163]

Form	Fee (£)
Form required by rule 3(1)	400
Form required by rule 3(4)	150
Form required by rule 4(2)	150
Form required by rule 5(3)	100
Form required by rule 7(4)	100
Form required by rule 12	150

COMPANIES (REDUCTION OF SHARE CAPITAL) ORDER 2008

(SI 2008/1915)

NOTES

Made: 17 July 2008.
Authority: Companies Act 2006, ss 643(3), 654, 1167.

Commencement: 1 October 2008.

For a summary of all Orders and Regulations made under the Companies Act 2006, see Appendix 4 at **[A4]**.

[4.164]

1

(1) This Order may be cited as the Companies (Reduction of Share Capital) Order 2008 and comes into force on 1st October 2008.

(2) In this Order, "the Act" means the Companies Act 2006.

[4.165]

2

A solvency statement under section 643 of the Act must—

(a) be in writing,

(b) indicate that it is a solvency statement for the purposes of section 642 of the Act, and

(c) be signed by each of the directors.

[4.166]

3

(1) If an unlimited company reduces its share capital—

(a) the prohibition in section 654(1) of the Act does not apply, and

(b) a reserve arising from the reduction is to be treated for the purposes of Part 23 of the Act as a realised profit.

(2) If a private company limited by shares reduces its share capital and the reduction is supported by a solvency statement but has not been the subject of an application to the court for an order confirming it—

(a) the prohibition in section 654(1) of the Act does not apply, and

(b) a reserve arising from the reduction is to be treated for the purposes of Part 23 of the Act as a realised profit.

(3) If a limited company having a share capital reduces its share capital and the reduction is confirmed by order of the court—

(a) the prohibition in section 654(1) of the Act does not apply, and

(b) a reserve arising from the reduction is to be treated for the purposes of Part 23 of the Act as a realised profit unless the court orders otherwise under section 648(1) of the Act.

(4) This article is without prejudice to any contrary provision of—

(a) an order of, or undertaking given to, the court,

(b) the resolution for, or any other resolution relevant to, the reduction of share capital, or

(c) the company's memorandum or articles of association.

COMPANIES ACT 2006 (ANNUAL RETURN AND SERVICE ADDRESSES) REGULATIONS 2008 (NOTE)

(SI 2008/3000)

[4.167]

NOTES

Made: 18 November 2008.

Authority: Companies Act 2006, ss 857, 1141, 1167, 1292(1). As to s 857 of the 2006 Act, see the notes below.

Commencement: 1 October 2009.

Reg 1 provides for citation and commencement.

Regs 2–4 amended the Companies Act 2006, s 855(1), and inserted s 855A of that Act. Note that the original Part 24 of the 2006 Act (ss 854–859) was substituted (by the Small Business, Enterprise and Employment Act 2015, s 92) by a new Part 24 (ss 853A–853L), except in relation to annual returns to be made up to a return date before 30 June 2016. Regs 2–4 are, therefore, effectively spent.

Reg 5 (Classification scheme for company type) and Sch 1 prescribed the classification scheme for the purposes of section 855(2) of the Companies Act 2006 as originally enacted. As noted above, Part 24 of the 2006 Act was subsequently substituted and, accordingly, this regulation and Sch 1 are effectively spent.

Reg 6 (Classification system for company's principal business activities) (as amended) provided that the Standard Industrial Classification 2007 was prescribed for the purposes of section 855(3) of the Companies Act 2006, with the addition of the codes and designations in Sch 2 to these Regulations. As noted above, Part 24 of the 2006 Act was subsequently substituted and, accordingly, this regulation and Sch 2 are effectively spent.

Regs 7 and 8 contained various amendments to the original Part 24 of the Companies Act 2006. As noted above, Part 24 of the 2006 Act was subsequently substituted and, accordingly, regs 7 and 8 are effectively spent.

Reg 9 contained a consequential amendment to Sch 8 to the 2006 Act. This regulation is now also effectively spent.

Reg 10 provides that for the purposes of section 1141 of the Companies Act 2006 (conditions with which a service address must comply) the conditions are that the service address must be a place where—

(a) the service of documents can be effected by physical delivery; and

(b) the delivery of documents is capable of being recorded by the obtaining of an acknowledgement of delivery.

Note: as to the classification scheme for company type, etc, see now the Companies and Limited Liability Partnerships (Filing Requirements) Regulations 2016, SI 2016/599 at **[4.640]**.

For a summary of all Orders and Regulations made under the Companies Act 2006, see Appendix 4 at **[A4]**.

COMPANIES (COMPANY RECORDS) REGULATIONS 2008

(SI 2008/3006)

NOTES

Made: 19 November 2008.
Authority: Companies Act 2006, ss 1136, 1137, 1292(1).
Commencement: 1 October 2009.
For a summary of all Orders and Regulations made under the Companies Act 2006, see Appendix 4 at **[A4]**.

ARRANGEMENT OF REGULATIONS

PART 1 INTRODUCTORY

[4.168]

1 Citation, commencement, application and interpretation

(1) These Regulations may be cited as the Companies (Company Records) Regulations 2008 and come into force on 1st October 2009.

(2) Part 4 applies to any request made on or after 1st October 2009 to be provided with a copy of a company record.

(3) In these Regulations "the Act" means the Companies Act 2006.

[4.169]

2 Revocations and saving

(1) The following Regulations are revoked subject to paragraph (2)—

(a) the Companies (Inspection and Copying of Registers, Indices and Documents) Regulations 1991 ("the 1991 Regulations"); and

(b) the Companies (Inspection and Copying of Registers, Indices and Documents) Regulations (Northern Ireland) 1993 ("the 1993 Regulations").

(2) The 1991 Regulations and the 1993 Regulations continue to apply to any request made before 1st October 2009 to be provided with a copy of a company record.

PART 2 ALTERNATIVE INSPECTION LOCATION

[4.170]

3 Single alternative inspection location

The specified place in respect of the relevant provisions listed in section 1136(2) of the Act—

(a) is a place that is situated in the part of the United Kingdom in which the company is registered;

(b) must be the same place for all the relevant provisions; and

(c) must have been notified to the registrar as being the company's alternative inspection location.

PART 3 INSPECTION OF COMPANY RECORDS

[4.171]

4 Inspection: private company

(1) A private company shall make its company records available for inspection by a person on a day which has been specified by that person ("the specified day") provided that—

(a) the specified day is a working day; and

(b) that person gives the company the required notice of the specified day.

(2) The required notice is at least 2 working days' notice of the specified day if the notice is given—

(a) during the period of notice for a general meeting or a class meeting; or

(b) where the company circulates a written resolution, during the period provided for in section 297(1) of the Act, provided that the notice given both begins and ends during the period referred to in sub-paragraph (a) or (b) (as the case may be).

(3) In all other cases the required notice is at least 10 working days' notice of the specified day.

(4) When the person gives notice of the specified day he shall also give notice of the time on that day at which he wishes to start the inspection (which shall be any time between 9 am and 3 pm) and the company shall make its company records available for inspection by that person for a period of at least 2 hours beginning with that time.

[4.172]
5 Inspection: public company

A public company shall make its company records available for inspection for at least 2 hours between 9 am and 5 pm on each working day.

[4.173]
6 Inspection: general

(1) A company is not required for the purposes of inspection of a company record to present information in that record in a different order, structure or form from that set out in that record.

(2) A company shall permit a person to make a copy of the whole or any part of a company record in the course of inspection at—

(a) the location at which the record is made available for inspection; and

(b) any time during which the record is made available for inspection,

but a company is not required to assist that person in making his copy of that record.

PART 4 PROVISION OF COPIES OF COMPANY RECORDS

[4.174]
7 Right to hard copy

Where a company is requested to provide a copy of a company record in hard copy form, the company shall provide that copy in hard copy form.

[4.175]
8 Copy in electronic form

(1) Where a person requests a company to provide a copy of a company record in electronic form, the company shall provide that copy in such electronic form as the company shall decide.

(2) But where a company keeps a company record in hard copy form only, it is not required to provide a copy of that record in electronic form.

(3) Where a company provides a copy of a company record in electronic form to a member of the company or to a holder of the company's debentures, the company is not required to provide a hard copy of that record in accordance with section 1145 of the Act.

[4.176]
9 Re-ordering of information in copy of record

A company is not required to present information in a copy of a company record that it provides in a different order, structure or form from that set out in the record.

COMPANIES (FEES FOR INSPECTION OF COMPANY RECORDS) REGULATIONS 2008

(SI 2008/3007)

NOTES

Made: 19 November 2008.

Authority: Companies Act 2006, ss 162(5)(b), 275(5)(b), 877(4)(b), 892(4)(b), 1137(4), 1167, 1292(1)(c). As to ss 877 and 892, see the note to reg 2 *post*.

Commencement: 1 October 2009.

For a summary of all Orders and Regulations made under the Companies Act 2006, see Appendix 4 at **[A4]**.

[4.177]
1 Citation, commencement and application

(1) These Regulations may be cited as the Companies (Fees for Inspection of Company Records) Regulations 2008 and come into force on 1st October 2009.

(2) These Regulations apply where a person inspects a register or instrument referred to in regulation 2 on or after 1st October 2009 regardless of the date on which the request to inspect that register or instrument was made.

[4.178]
2 Fee for inspection of company records

For the purposes of the following provisions of the Companies Act 2006—

(a) section 162(5)(b) (register of directors);

(b) section 275(5)(b) (register of secretaries);

(c) section 877(4)(b) (instruments creating charges and register of charges: England and Wales and Northern Ireland); and

(d) section 892(4)(b) (instruments creating charges and register of charges: Scotland),

the fee prescribed is £3.50 for each hour or part thereof during which the right of inspection is exercised.

NOTES

Note that Chapters 1 and 2 of Part 25 of the Companies Act 2006 (ss 860–892) were repealed by the Companies Act 2006 (Amendment of Part 25) Regulations 2013, SI 2013/600, as from 6 April 2013, except in relation to charges created before that date.

COMPANIES (REGISTRATION) REGULATIONS 2008

(SI 2008/3014)

NOTES

Made: 20 November 2008.
Authority: Companies Act 2006, ss 8(2), 10(3), 11(2), 103(2)(a), 110(2)(a), 1167, 1292(1)(a).
Commencement: 1 October 2009.
For a summary of all Orders and Regulations made under the Companies Act 2006, see Appendix 4 at **[A4]**.

ARRANGEMENT OF REGULATIONS

SCHEDULES

[4.179]
1 Citation, commencement and interpretation

(1) These Regulations may be cited as the Companies (Registration) Regulations 2008 and come into force on 1st October 2009.

(2) In these Regulations "the Act" means the Companies Act 2006.

[4.180]
2 Memorandum of association

For the purposes of section 8 of the Act—

(a) the memorandum of association of a company having a share capital shall be in the form set out in Schedule 1; and
(b) the memorandum of association of a company not having a share capital shall be in the form set out in Schedule 2.

[4.181]
3 Statement of capital and initial shareholdings

For the purposes of section 10(3) of the Act, the statement of capital and initial shareholdings shall contain the name and address of each subscriber to the memorandum of association.

[4.182]
4 Statement of guarantee

For the purposes of section 11(2) of the Act, the statement of guarantee shall contain the name and address of each subscriber to the memorandum of association.

[4.183]
5 Form of assent for re-registration of private limited company as unlimited

The form set out in Schedule 3 is the form prescribed for the purposes of section 103(2)(a) of the Act.

[4.184]
6 Form of assent for re-registration of public company as private and unlimited

The form set out in Schedule 4 is the form prescribed for the purposes of section 110(2)(a) of the Act.

SCHEDULES

SCHEDULE 1
COMPANY HAVING A SHARE CAPITAL

Regulation 2(a)

[4.185]

Memorandum of association of [*insert name of company*]

Each subscriber to this memorandum of association wishes to form a company under the Companies Act 2006 and agrees to become a member of the company and to take at least one share.

Memorandum of association of [*insert name of company*]	
Name of each subscriber	*Authentication by each subscriber*
Dated	

SCHEDULE 2
COMPANY NOT HAVING A SHARE CAPITAL

Regulation 2(b)

[4.186]

Memorandum of association of [*insert name of company*]	
Each subscriber to this memorandum of association wishes to form a company under the Companies Act 2006 and agrees to become a member of the company.	
Name of each subscriber	*Authentication by each subscriber*
Dated	

SCHEDULES 3 AND 4

(Sch 3 (as introduced by reg 5) sets out the form of assent for re-registration of private limited company as unlimited; Sch 4 (as introduced by reg 6) sets out the form of assent for re-registration of public company as private and unlimited; neither form is reproduced in this work but both are available at: www.legislation.gov.uk.*)*

COMPANIES (MODEL ARTICLES) REGULATIONS 2008

(SI 2008/3229)

NOTES

Made: 16 December 2008.

Authority: Companies Act 2006, s 19.

Commencement: 1 October 2009.

For a summary of all Orders and Regulations made under the Companies Act 2006, see Appendix 4 at **[A4]**.

Note (Model Articles): Sch 1 (Model Articles for Private Companies Limited by Shares), Sch 2 (Model Articles for Private Companies Limited by Guarantee), and Sch 3 (Model Articles for Public Companies) are not reproduced below, but are reproduced in Appendix 1 at **[A1.1]**, **[A1.2]**, and **[A1.3]** respectively. The provisions of these Regulations reproduced here have not been amended; as to amendments to the Model Articles, see Appendix 1.

[4.187]

1 Citation and Commencement

These Regulations may be cited as the Companies (Model Articles) Regulations 2008 and come into force on 1st October 2009.

[4.188]

2 Model articles for private companies limited by shares

Schedule 1 to these Regulations prescribes the model articles of association for private companies limited by shares.

[4.189]

3 Model articles for private companies limited by guarantee

Schedule 2 to these Regulations prescribes the model articles of association for private companies limited by guarantee.

[4.190]

4 Model articles for public companies

Schedule 3 to these Regulations prescribes the model articles of association for public companies.

SCHEDULES

SCHEDULES 1–3

(Sch 1 (Model Articles for Private Companies Limited by Shares), Sch 2 (Model Articles for Private Companies Limited by Guarantee), and Sch 3 (Model Articles for Public Companies) are reproduced in Appendix 1 at **[A1.1]**, **[A1.2]**, *and* **[A1.3]** *respectively.)*

COMPANIES (DISCLOSURE OF ADDRESS) REGULATIONS 2009

(SI 2009/214)

NOTES

Made: 1 February 2009.

Authority: Companies Act 2006, ss 243(2)–(6), 1088(1)–(3), (5), 1292(1), (4).

Commencement: 1 October 2009.

For a summary of all Orders and Regulations made under the Companies Act 2006, see Appendix 4 at **[A4]**.

These Regulations are reproduced as amended by: the Companies Act 2006 (Consequential Amendments, Transitional Provisions and Savings) Order 2009, SI 2009/1941; the European Public Limited-Liability Company (Amendment) Regulations 2009, SI 2009/2400; the Companies (Disclosure of Address) (Amendment) Regulations 2010, SI 2010/2156; the Postal Services Act 2011 (Consequential Modifications and Amendments) Order 2011, SI 2011/2085; the Housing (Scotland) Act 2010 (Consequential Provisions and Modifications) Order 2012, SI 2012/700; the Crime and Courts Act 2013; the Financial Services Act 2012 (Consequential Amendments and Transitional Provisions) Order 2013, SI 2013/472; the Energy Act 2013 (Office for Nuclear Regulation) (Consequential Amendments, Transitional Provisions and Savings) Order 2014, SI 2014/469; the Enterprise and Regulatory Reform Act 2013 (Competition) (Consequential, Transitional and Saving Provisions) (No 2) Order 2014, SI 2014/549; the Public Bodies (Abolition of the National Consumer Council and Transfer of the Office of Fair Trading's Functions in relation to Estate Agents etc) Order 2014, SI 2014/631; the Companies (Disclosure of Address) (Amendment) Regulations 2015, SI 2015/842; the Register of People with Significant Control Regulations 2016, SI 2016/339; the Limited Liability Partnerships (Register of People with Significant Control) Regulations 2016, SI 2016/340; the Immigration Act 2016 (Consequential Amendments) Regulations 2016, SI 2016/655; the Bank of England and Financial Services (Consequential Amendments) Regulations 2017, SI 2017/80; the Money Laundering, Terrorist Financing and Transfer of Funds (Information on the Payer) Regulations 2017, SI 2017/692; the Companies (Disclosure of Address) (Amendment) Regulations 2018, SI 2018/528; the Data Protection Act 2018; the Companies, Limited Liability Partnerships and Partnerships (Amendment etc) (EU Exit) Regulations 2019, SI 2019/348; the International Accounting Standards and European Public Limited-Liability Company (Amendment etc) (EU Exit) Regulations 2019, SI 2019/685.

Application: these Regulations are applied to Limited liability partnerships, see the Limited Liability Partnerships (Application of Companies Act 2006) Regulations 2009, SI 2009/1804 at **[10.319]**.

ARRANGEMENT OF REGULATIONS

PART 1

[4.191]

1 Citation, commencement and interpretation

(1) These Regulations may be cited as the Companies (Disclosure of Address) Regulations 2009 and come into force on 1st October 2009.

(2) In these Regulations—

"the Act" means the Companies Act 2006 and, unless the context otherwise requires, any reference to a numbered section is to a section so numbered in that Act;

"the 1985 Act" means the Companies Act 1985;

"the 1986 Order" means the Companies (Northern Ireland) Order 1986;

["the 2016 Regulations" means the Register of People with Significant Control Regulations 2016;]

"confidentiality order" means an order under section 723B of the 1985 Act (confidentiality orders);

"former name" means a name by which an individual was formerly known and which has been notified to the registrar under section 10 (documents to be sent to the registrar) or section 288 (register of directors and secretaries) of the 1985 Act, or Article 21 or 296 of the 1986 Order, [or regulation 80C of the SEs Regulations, or regulation 79 of the old SEs Regulations, or regulation 77 of the Northern Ireland SEs Regulations,] or section 12 (statement of proposed officers) or section 167 (duty to notify registrar of changes) of the Act;

"limited liability partnership" means a limited liability partnership incorporated under the Limited Liability Partnerships Act 2000 or Limited Liability Partnerships Act (Northern Ireland) 2002;

"name" means a person's Christian name (or other forename) and surname, except that in the case of—

(a) a peer; or

(b) an individual usually known by a title,

the title may be stated instead of his Christian name (or other forename) and surname or in addition to either or both of them;

["the Northern Ireland SEs Regulations" means the European Public Limited-Liability Company Regulations (Northern Ireland) 2004 [as they had effect at the time the address was filed];]

["the old SEs Regulations" means the SEs Regulations, disregarding the amendments made by the European Public Limited-Liability Company (Amendment) Regulations 2009;]

"permanent representative" means an individual who was a permanent representative for the purposes of sections 723B and 723C (effect of confidentiality orders) of the 1985 Act;

["police force" means—

(a) a police force within the meaning of section 101(1) of the Police Act 1996 (interpretation),

(b) the Police Service of Scotland within the meaning of section 6 of the Police and Fire Reform (Scotland) Act 2012 (the Police Service of Scotland),

(c) the Police Service of Northern Ireland and the Police Service of Northern Ireland Reserve within the meaning of section 1 of the Police (Northern Ireland) Act 2000 (name of the police in Northern Ireland),

and includes a police force constituted under, or referred to in, any corresponding earlier enactments;]

["registrable person" means a registrable person under Part 21A of the Act;]

"relevant body" means any police force and any other person whom the registrar considers may be able to assist in answering a question referred to that person by the registrar under these Regulations;

"relevant organisation" means the Government Communications Headquarters, the Secret Intelligence Service [or] the Security Service . . . ;

["the SEs Regulations" means the European Public Limited-Liability Company Regulations 2004 [as they had effect at the time the address was filed];]

"section 243 applicant" means an individual by whom or in respect of whom a section 243 application has been made but in respect of which application the registrar either has not made a determination, or has made a determination, not being a section 243 decision, and any appeal to the court in respect of that application under regulation 14 has not been determined by the court;

"section 243 application" means an application under section 243(4) (permitted use or disclosure by the registrar) for the purpose of requiring the registrar to refrain from disclosing protected information relating to a director to a credit reference agency;

"section 243 beneficiary" means—

(a) an individual who has made a section 243 application in respect of which a section 243 decision has been made; or

(b) an individual on whose behalf a company or a subscriber to a memorandum of association has made a section 243 application in respect of which a section 243 decision has been made; or

(c) an individual in relation to whom a confidentiality order was in force immediately before 1st October 2009 and who, by paragraph 37 of Schedule 2 to the Companies Act 2006 (Commencement No 8, Transitional Provisions and Savings) Order 2008 is treated as having made a section 243 application in respect of which a section 243 decision has been made;

"section 243 decision" means a determination by the registrar on a section 243 application in favour of the applicant;

"section 1088 application" means an application under section 1088 (application to registrar to make address unavailable for public inspection) for the purpose of requiring the registrar to make an address on the register unavailable for public inspection;

"section 1088 beneficiary" means a person who has made a section 1088 application in respect of which a section 1088 decision has been made;

"section 1088 decision" means a determination by the registrar on a section 1088 application [under regulation 10(1) or 11(1)] in favour of the applicant;

"specified public authority" means any public authority specified in Schedule 1 to these Regulations; and "working day" means a day that is not a Saturday or Sunday, Christmas Day, Good Friday or any day that is a bank holiday under the Banking and Financial Dealings Act 1971 in England and Wales.

NOTES

Para (2) is amended as follows

Definitions "the 2016 Regulations" and "registrable person" inserted by the Register of People with Significant Control Regulations 2016, SI 2016/339, reg 48, Sch 5, paras 1, 2, as from 6 April 2016.

Words in square brackets in definition "former name" inserted, and definition "the old SEs Regulations" inserted, by the European Public Limited-Liability Company (Amendment) Regulations 2009, SI 2009/2400, reg 42(1), (2), as from 1 October 2009.

Definitions "the Northern Ireland SEs Regulations" and "the SEs Regulations" inserted by SI 2009/2400, reg 42(1), (2), as from 1 October 2009. Words in square brackets in those definitions inserted by the International Accounting Standards and European Public Limited-Liability Company (Amendment etc) (EU Exit) Regulations 2019, SI 2019/685, reg 21, Sch 3, Pt 3, para 21(a), as from IP completion day (as defined in the European Union (Withdrawal Agreement) Act 2020, s 39).

Definition "police force" substituted, word in square brackets in the definition "relevant organisation" substituted, words omitted from that definition revoked, and words in square brackets in the definition "section 1088 decision" inserted, by the Companies (Disclosure of Address) (Amendment) Regulations 2018, SI 2018/528, reg 2, as from 26 April 2018.

PART 2 DISCLOSURE OF PROTECTED INFORMATION

[4.192]

2 Permitted disclosure by the registrar to specified public authorities

(1) The registrar may disclose protected information to a specified public authority where the conditions specified in paragraphs 2 and 3 of Schedule 2 are satisfied.

(2) A specified public authority shall deliver to the registrar such information or evidence as he may direct for the purpose of enabling him to determine in accordance with these Regulations whether to disclose protected information.

(3) The registrar may require such information or evidence to be verified in such manner as he may direct.

(4) The specified public authority must inform the registrar immediately of any change in respect of any statement delivered to the registrar pursuant to Schedule 2 or information or evidence provided for the purpose of enabling the registrar to determine whether to disclose protected information.

(5) The public authorities specified for the purposes of section 243(2) are set out in Schedule 1 to these Regulations.

[4.193]

3 Permitted disclosure by the registrar to credit reference agencies

(1) Subject to regulation 4, the registrar may disclose protected information to a credit reference agency where the conditions specified in paragraphs 6 to 10 of Schedule 2 are satisfied.

(2) The registrar may rely on a statement delivered to him by a credit reference agency under paragraph 10 of Schedule 2 as sufficient evidence of the matters stated in it.

(3) Notwithstanding paragraph (2), a credit reference agency shall deliver to the registrar such information or evidence in addition to the statement required by paragraph 10 of Schedule 2 as he may direct for the purpose of enabling him to determine in accordance with these Regulations whether to disclose protected information.

(4) The registrar may require such information or evidence to be verified in such manner as he may direct.

(5) The credit reference agency must inform the registrar immediately of any change in respect of any statement delivered to the registrar pursuant to Schedule 2 or information or evidence provided for the purpose of enabling the registrar to determine whether to disclose protected information.

[4.194]

4 Registrar to refrain from disclosure of protected information

The registrar shall refrain from disclosing protected information to a credit reference agency if such information relates to a section 243 beneficiary or a section 243 applicant.

[4.195]

5 Application under section 243 by an individual

(1) A section 243 application may be made to the registrar by an individual who is, or proposes to become, a director.

(2) The grounds on which an application under paragraph (1) may be made are that the individual making the application—

- (a) [reasonably believes] that there is a serious risk that he, or a person who lives with him, will be subjected to violence or intimidation as a result of the activities of at least one of—
  - (i) the companies of which he is, or proposes to become, a director;
  - (ii) the companies of which he was a director;
  - [(iia) the companies of which that individual is, or proposes to become, a registrable person;
  - (iib) the companies of which that individual used to be a registrable person;]
  - (iii) the overseas companies of which he is or has been a director, secretary or permanent representative; or,
  - (iv) the limited liability partnerships of which he is or has been a member; . . .
  - [(v) the limited liability partnerships of which that individual proposes to become a member;
  - (vi) the limited liability partnerships of which that individual is, or proposes to become, a registrable person under Part 21A of the Act as applied to LLPs by the Limited Liability Partnerships (Register of People with Significant Control) Regulations 2016; or
  - (vii) the limited liability partnerships of which that individual used to be a registrable person under Part 21A of the Act as applied to LLPs by the Limited Liability Partnerships (Register of People with Significant Control) Regulations 2016.]

(b) is or has been employed by a relevant [organisation [or a police force, or is or has been a constable in a police force]; or

(c) is the subject of an application made under regulation 25, 26 or 27 of the 2016 Regulations which has been determined by the registrar in favour of the applicant and that determination has not ceased to have effect under regulation 31 of those Regulations].

(3) The application shall—

(a) contain—

(i) a statement of the grounds on which the application is made;

(ii) the name and any former name of the applicant;

(iii) the date of birth of the applicant;

(iv) the usual residential address of the applicant;

[(iva) the e-mail address of the applicant, if any;]

(v) where the registrar has allocated a unique identifier to the applicant, that unique identifier;

(vi) the name and registered number of each company of which the applicant is, or proposes to become, a director;

[(via) the name and registered number of each company of which the applicant is, or proposes to become, a registrable person;]

(vii) where the grounds of the application are those described in paragraph [(2)(a)(ii), (iia), (iib), (iii) or (iv)], the name and registered number of the company, overseas company or limited liability partnership; . . .

[(viii) where the grounds of the application are those described in paragraph (2)(c), the name and registered number of the company in relation to which the determination was made, unless the determination relates to a proposed company which was never incorporated; and]

[(b) where the grounds of the application are those described in paragraph (2)(a) or (2)(b), be accompanied by evidence which supports the applicant's statement of the grounds on which the application is made].

(4) The registrar may refer to a relevant body any question relating to an assessment of—

(a) where the grounds of the application are those described in paragraph (2)(a), the nature and extent of any risk of violence or intimidation considered by the applicant to arise in relation to himself, or to a person who lives with him; or

(b) where the grounds of the application are those described in paragraph (2)(b), whether the applicant is or has been employed by a relevant organisation [or a police force, or is or has been a constable in a police force].

[(5) The registrar must determine the application and, within 7 days beginning with the date that the determination is made, send to the applicant notice of the determination.

(6) Where the application is unsuccessful, the notice under paragraph (5) must inform the applicant of the applicant's right to apply for permission to appeal against the determination within 28 days beginning with the date of the notice.]

NOTES

In para (2), sub-paras (a)(v)–(vii) were inserted by the Limited Liability Partnerships (Register of People with Significant Control) Regulations 2016, SI 2016/340, reg 5, Sch 3, para 8, as from 6 April 2016.

The words "or a police force, or is or has been a constable in a police force" in square brackets in sub-paras (2)(b) and (4)(b) were inserted by the Companies (Disclosure of Address) (Amendment) Regulations 2018, SI 2018/528, reg 3(1), (2), as from 26 April 2018.

All other amendments to this regulation were made by the Register of People with Significant Control Regulations 2016, SI 2016/339, reg 48, Sch 5, paras 1, 3, as from 6 April 2016.

[4.196]

[6 Application under section 243 by a company

(1) A company ("the applicant") may make a section 243 application to the registrar relating to an individual ("D") who is, or proposes to become, a director of the company.

(2) A company may only make an application under paragraph (1) where D has given consent for the company to make the application on D's behalf.

(3) The grounds on which an application under paragraph (1) may be made are that—

(a) the applicant reasonably believes that there is a serious risk that D, or a person who lives with D, will be subjected to violence or intimidation as a result of the applicant's activities; or

(b) D is the subject of an application made under regulation 25, 26 or 27 of the 2016 Regulations which has been determined by the registrar in favour of the applicant and that determination has not ceased to have effect under regulation 31 of those Regulations.

(4) Where the grounds of the application are those described in paragraph (3)(b), the application must only relate to one individual who is, or proposes to become, a director of the company.

(5) The application must contain—

(a) a statement of the grounds on which the application is made;

(b) confirmation that D consents to the making of the application;

(c) the name and registered number of the applicant;

(d) the address of the registered office of the applicant;

(e) the e-mail address of the applicant, if any;

(f) the name and any former name of D;

(g) the date of birth of D;

(h) the usual residential address of D;

(i) the e-mail address of D, if any;

(j) where the registrar has allocated a unique identifier to D, that unique identifier;

(k) where D is a director of another company, the name and registered number of that company; and

(l) where the grounds of the application are those described in paragraph (3)(b), the name and registered number of the company in relation to which the determination was made, unless the determination relates to a proposed company which was never incorporated.

(6) Where the grounds of the application are those described in paragraph (3)(a), the application must be accompanied by evidence which supports the applicant's statement of the grounds on which the application is made.

(7) The registrar may refer to a relevant body any question relating to an assessment of the nature or extent of any risk of violence or intimidation.

(8) The registrar must determine the application and, within 7 days beginning with the date that the determination is made, send to the applicant and to D notice of the determination.

(9) Where the application is unsuccessful, the notice under paragraph (8) must inform the applicant of the applicant's right to apply for permission to appeal against the determination within 28 days beginning with the date of the notice.]

NOTES

Substituted by the Register of People with Significant Control Regulations 2016, SI 2016/339, reg 48, Sch 5, paras 1, 4, as from 6 April 2016.

[4.197]

[7 Application under section 243 by a subscriber to a memorandum of association

(1) A subscriber to a memorandum of association ("the applicant") may make a section 243 application to the registrar relating to an individual ("D") who proposes to become, on or after the formation of the company to which the memorandum relates, a director of the company.

(2) A subscriber to a memorandum of association may only make an application under paragraph (1) where D has given consent for the subscriber to make the application on D's behalf.

(3) The grounds on which an application under paragraph (1) may be made are that—

(a) the applicant reasonably believes that there is a serious risk that D, or a person who lives D, will be subjected to violence or intimidation as a result of the proposed activities of the proposed company to which the memorandum relates; or

(b) D is the subject of an application made under regulation 25, 26 or 27 of the 2016 Regulations which has been determined by the registrar in favour of the applicant and that determination has not ceased to have effect under regulation 31 of those Regulations.

(4) Where the grounds of the application are those described in paragraph (3)(b), the application must only relate to one individual who proposes to become a director in relation to the proposed company.

(5) The application must contain—

(a) a statement of the grounds on which the application is made;
(b) confirmation that D consents to the making of the application;
(c) the name and any former name of the applicant;
(d) the usual residential address of the applicant;
(e) the e-mail address of the applicant, if any;
(f) the name of the proposed company to which the memorandum relates;
(g) the name and any former name of D;
(h) the date of birth of D;
(i) the usual residential address of D;
(j) the e-mail address of D, if any;
(k) where the registrar has allocated a unique identifier to D, that unique identifier;
(l) where D is a director of another company, the name and registered number of that company; and
(m) where the grounds of the application are those described in paragraph (3)(b), the name and registered number of the company in relation to which the determination was made, unless the determination relates to a proposed company which was never incorporated.

(6) Where the grounds of the application are those described in paragraph (3)(a), the application must be accompanied by evidence which supports the applicant's statement of the grounds on which the application is made.

(7) The registrar may refer to a relevant body any question relating to an assessment of the nature or extent of any risk of violence or intimidation.

(8) The registrar must determine the application and, within 7 days beginning with the date that the determination is made, send to the applicant and to D notice of the determination.

(9) Where the application is unsuccessful, the notice under paragraph (8) must inform the applicant of the applicant's right to apply for permission to appeal against the determination within 28 days beginning with the date of the notice.]

NOTES

Substituted by the Register of People with Significant Control Regulations 2016, SI 2016/339, reg 48, Sch 5, paras 1, 4, as from 6 April 2016.

[4.198]

8 Matters relating to a section 243 application

(1) For the purpose of regulations 5, 6 and 7 the registrar may direct that additional information or evidence should be delivered to him, what such information or evidence should be and how it should be verified.

(2) The registrar shall not make available for public inspection—

(a) any section 243 application; or
(b) any documents provided in support of that application.

(3) For the purpose of determining any section 243 application the registrar may accept any answer to a question referred in accordance with regulation 5(4), [6(7) or 7(7)] as providing sufficient evidence of—

(a) the nature and extent of any risk relevant to—

(i) where the grounds of the application are those described in regulation 5(2)(a), the applicant;

(ii) where the grounds of the application are those described in regulation [6(3)(a)], the directors on behalf of whom the application is made;

(iii) where the grounds of the application are those described in regulation [7(3)(a)], the proposed directors on behalf of whom the application is made,

or to persons who live with any of the above individuals, or

(b) whether an applicant is or has been employed by a relevant organisation [or a police force, or is or has been a constable in a police force].

NOTES

Para (3): words and figures in first, second and third pairs of square brackets substituted by the Register of People with Significant Control Regulations 2016, SI 2016/339, reg 48, Sch 5, paras 1, 5, as from 6 April 2016. Words in square brackets in sub-para (b) inserted by the Companies (Disclosure of Address) (Amendment) Regulations 2018, SI 2018/528, reg 3(1), (3), as from 26 April 2018.

PART 3 APPLICATION TO MAKE AN ADDRESS UNAVAILABLE FOR PUBLIC INSPECTION UNDER SECTION 1088

[4.199]

[9 Application under section 1088 to make an address unavailable for public inspection by an individual

(1) Where an individual's usual residential address is on the register, that individual may make a section 1088 application in respect of that address, where that address was placed on the register in the individual's capacity as—

(a) a proposed director or director or manager under—

(i) section 10 (documents to be sent to registrar), 288 (register of directors and secretaries), 363 (duty to deliver annual returns), 686 (other requirements for registration), 691 (documents to be delivered to registrar) or 692 (registration of altered particulars) of, or paragraph 2 of Schedule 21A (branch registration under the eleventh company law directive (89/666/EEC)) to, the 1985 Act,

(ii) article 21 (documents to be sent to registrar), 296 (register of directors and secretaries), 371 (duty to deliver annual returns), 635 (other requirements for registration), 641 (documents to be delivered to registrar) or 642 (registration of altered particulars) of, or paragraph 2 of Schedule 20A (branch registration under the eleventh company law directive (89/666/EEC)) to, the 1986 Order,

(iii) section 855 (contents of annual return: general),

(iv) section 12 (statement of proposed officers), 167 (duty to notify registrar of changes) or 167D (duty to notify registrar of changes), or regulations made under sections 1040 (companies authorised to register under this Act) or 1046 (duty to register particulars),

(v) regulation 83 (registration of a public company by the conversion of an SE) of the Northern Ireland SEs Regulations,

(vi) regulation 85 (registration of a public company by the conversion of an SE) of the SEs Regulations;

(b) a permanent representative under Schedule 21A to the 1985 Act, Schedule 20A to the 1986 Order or regulations made under section 1046;

(c) a proposed secretary or secretary under—

(i) section 10, 288, 363, 691 or 692 of, or paragraph 2 of Schedule 21A to, the 1985 Act,

(ii) article 21, 296, 371, 641 or 642 of, or paragraph 2 of Schedule 20A to, the 1986 Order,

(iii) section 855,

(iv) section 12, 95 (statement of proposed secretary), 276 (duty to notify registrar of changes), 279A (right to make an election) or 279D (duty to notify registrar of changes), or regulations made under sections 1040 or 1046,

(v) regulation 83 of the Northern Ireland SEs Regulations,

(vi) regulation 85 of the SEs Regulations;

(d) a proposed member or member of a Societas Europaea [or a member of a United Kingdom Societas] under—

(i) regulation 79 (register of members of supervisory organ) of the old SEs Regulations,

(ii) regulations 5 to 10 (registration of an SE) or 77 (register of members of supervisory organ) of the Northern Ireland SEs Regulations,

(iii) regulations 5 to 10 (registration of an SE) or 80C (duty to notify registrar of changes) of the SEs Regulations;

(e) a registrable person under—

(i) regulations 5 to 10 or 85 of the SEs Regulations,

(ii) section 9 (registration documents), 853I (duty to deliver information about people with significant control) or any obligation in Part 21A (information about people with significant control);

(f) a subscriber under—

(i) section 10 of the 1985 Act,

(ii) article 21 of the 1986 Order,

(iii) section 9 or regulations made under section 1040,

or any other obligation to file a memorandum of association;

(g) as a member or former member under—

(i) section 88 (return as to allotments, etc), 684 (requirements for registration by joint stock companies) or 363 of the 1985 Act,

(ii) article 98 (return as to allotments, etc), 633 (requirements for registration by joint stock companies) or 371 of the 1986 Order,

(iii) section 854 (duty to deliver annual returns) or regulations made under section 1040,

(iv) 128B (right to make an election), 128E (duty to notify registrar of changes) or 853G (duty to deliver shareholder information: certain traded companies),

or any other obligation to file with the registrar an annual return or a return of allotment of shares;

(2) The application must contain—

(a) the name and any former name of the applicant;

(b) the usual residential address of the applicant that is to be made unavailable for public inspection;

(c) an address for correspondence in respect of the application;

(d) the name and registered number of each company in respect of which the applicant has indicated in the application that the applicant's usual residential address was placed on the register;

(e) in respect of each company falling within sub-paragraph (d)—

(i) the name of the document in which that usual residential address appears on the register,

(ii) where that document is a form, the number and title of the form, and

(iii) the registration date of that document;

(f) where the application includes a company which is required to maintain a current address for the applicant on the register, the service address which is to replace the usual residential address;

(g) the date of birth of the applicant; and

(h) where the registrar has allotted a unique identifier to the applicant, that unique identifier.]

NOTES

Substituted by the Companies (Disclosure of Address) (Amendment) Regulations 2018, SI 2018/528, reg 4(1), (2), as from 26 April 2018; for transitional provisions see the note below.

Para (1): words in square brackets in sub-para (d) inserted by the International Accounting Standards and European Public Limited-Liability Company (Amendment etc) (EU Exit) Regulations 2019, SI 2019/685, reg 21, Sch 3, Pt 3, para 21(b), as from IP completion day (as defined in the European Union (Withdrawal Agreement) Act 2020, s 39).

Transitional provisions: note that reg 8 of the 2018 Regulations provides that if a s 1088 application was received by the registrar before 26 April 2018, the application must be dealt with by the registrar in accordance with these Regulations as they applied before that date.

[4.200]

10 Application under section 1088 to make an address unavailable for public inspection by a company

(1) A section 1088 application may be made to the registrar by a company in respect of the addresses of—

(a) all of its members and former members whose addresses were contained in—

(i) an annual return; or

(ii) a return of allotment of shares,

. . . ; or

(b) the subscribers to its memorandum of association . . . [, statement of capital and initial shareholdings or statement of guarantee,]

(2) The grounds on which an application under paragraph (1) may be made are that the company making the application considers that, as a result of its activities, the availability to members of the public of the addresses described in paragraph (1) creates a serious risk that its members or former members or subscribers, or persons who live at those addresses, will be subjected to violence or intimidation.

(3) The application shall—

(a) contain—

(i) the name of the applicant and its registered number; and

(ii) a statement of the grounds on which the application is made; and

(b) be accompanied by evidence—

(i) which supports the applicant's assertion that its application falls within the grounds stated in its application; or

(ii) where the court has made an order under section 117(3) (register of members: response to request for inspection or copy) directing the applicant not to comply with a request under section 116 (rights to inspect and require copies), a copy of that order.

(4) The registrar may refer to a relevant body any question relating to the assessment of the nature and extent of any risk of violence or intimidation considered by the applicant to arise in relation to any of its members or former members or subscribers, or persons who live at the addresses described in paragraph (1), as a result of its activities by virtue of the availability to members of the public of particulars of the addresses of such members or former members or subscribers.

(5) The registrar shall determine the application and send the applicant to its registered office notice of his determination on the section 1088 application within five working days of that determination being made.

NOTES

Para (1): words omitted revoked, and words in square brackets inserted, by the Companies (Disclosure of Address) (Amendment) Regulations 2018, SI 2018/528, reg 4(1), (3), as from 26 April 2018 (for transitional provisions see the note to reg 9 at **[4.199]**)).

[4.201]

11 Application under section 1088 to make an address unavailable for public inspection by a person who registers a charge

(1) A section 1088 application may be made to the registrar by a person who—

(a)

(i) . . . registered a charge under Part 12 of the 1985 Act (registration of charges) or Part 13 of the 1986 Order; or

(ii) has registered a charge under Part 25 of the Act (company charges) [or under regulations made under section 1052]; and

(b) is not the company which created the charge or acquired the property subject to a charge,

in respect of his address delivered to the registrar for the purposes of that registration.

(2) The grounds on which an application under paragraph (1) may be made are that the person making the application considers that there is a serious risk that he, or if applicable his employees, or persons who live with him or his employees, will be subjected to violence or intimidation as a result of the activities of the company which is, or was, subject to the charge.

(3) The application shall—

(a) contain—

(i) a statement of the grounds on which the application is made;

(ii) the name of the applicant, and where the applicant is a company, its registered number;

(iii) the address of the applicant that is to be made unavailable for public inspection;

(iv) the name and registered number of the company which is or was subject to the charge;

(v) an address for correspondence with the registrar in respect of the application;

(vi) where the applicant is the chargee, the service address which is to replace the address of the applicant on the register; and

(b) be accompanied by evidence which supports the applicant's assertion that there is a serious risk that he or, if applicable, his employees, or persons who live with him or his employees, will be subjected to violence or intimidation as a result of the activities of the company which is or was subject to the charge.

(4) The registrar may refer to a relevant body any question relating to the assessment of the nature and extent of any risk of violence or intimidation considered by the applicant to arise in relation to himself or, if applicable, his employees, or persons who live with him or his employees, as a result of the activities of the company which is or was subject to the charge.

(5) The registrar shall determine the application and send the applicant to the address stated in the application in accordance with paragraph (3)(a)(v) notice of his determination on the section 1088 application within five working days of that determination being made.

NOTES

Para (1): words omitted from sub-para (a)(i) revoked by the Companies (Disclosure of Address) (Amendment) Regulations 2018, SI 2018/528, reg 4(1), (4), as from 26 April 2018 (for transitional provisions see the note to reg 9 at **[4.199]**)). Words in square brackets in sub-para (a)(ii) inserted by the Companies Act 2006 (Consequential Amendments, Transitional Provisions and Savings) Order 2009, SI 2009/1941, art 2(1), Sch 1, para 270(1), (3), as from 1 October 2009.

[4.202]

12 Matters relevant to section 1088 applications

(1) For the purpose of regulations . . . 10 and 11 the registrar may direct that additional information or evidence should be delivered to him, what such information or evidence should be and how it should be verified.

(2) For the purpose of determining any section 1088 application the registrar may accept any answer to a question referred in accordance with regulation . . . 10(4) or 11(4) as providing sufficient evidence of—

(a) the nature and extent of any risk relevant to—

(i) . . .

(ii) where the grounds of the application are those described in regulation 10(2), the subscribers or members or former members of an applicant; or

(iii) where the grounds of the application are those described in regulation 11(2), where the applicant is an individual, the applicant, or any employees of an applicant,

or to persons who live with any of the above individuals or, in the case of members, former members or subscribers, to persons who live at their addresses, . . .

(b) . . .

NOTES

Words omitted revoked by the Companies (Disclosure of Address) (Amendment) Regulations 2018, SI 2018/528, reg 4(1), (5), as from 26 April 2018 (for transitional provisions see the note to reg 9 at **[4.199]**).

[4.203]

[13 Effect of a section 1088 application

(1) Paragraphs (2) to (4) apply in relation to a section 1088 application made under regulation 9.

(2) The registrar must make the specified address unavailable for public inspection in the places on the register where the applicant has indicated, in the application, that it appears.

(3) Where the application relates to an entry concerning a company which is required to maintain a current address for the applicant on the register, the registrar must make the specified address unavailable for public inspection by replacing it with the service address provided by the applicant.

(4) In any other case the registrar must make the specified address unavailable for public inspection by removing all elements of that address, except—

(a) for a United Kingdom address—

(i) the outward code from the postcode, or

(ii) where the address on the register does not include the outward code from the postcode, any information in that address that denotes a geographical area which is equivalent to or larger than the area represented by the outward code of the postcode which applies to that address; and

(b) for an address other than a United Kingdom address, the country or territory and the name of the next principal unit of geographical subdivision for that country or territory (eg the state, region, province, county, district, municipality or equivalent) if there is one included in that address as it appears on the register.

(5) Where a section 1088 application has been made under regulation 10(1) and has been determined in favour of the applicant, the registrar must make all of the members', former members' or subscribers' addresses unavailable for public inspection by removing the whole of those addresses.

(6) Where a section 1088 application has been made under regulation 11(1) and has been determined in favour of the applicant, the registrar must make the specified address unavailable for public inspection by removing the whole address and, where the applicant is the chargee, replacing it with the service address provided by the applicant.

(7) In this regulation—

"specified address" means the address specified in the application as being the one to be made unavailable for public inspection; and

"outward code" means the part of a postcode before the internal space but not the number and letters which come after that space.]

NOTES

Substituted by the Companies (Disclosure of Address) (Amendment) Regulations 2018, SI 2018/528, reg 4(1), (6), as from 26 April 2018 (for transitional provisions see the note to reg 9 at **[4.199]**).

PART 4 MATTERS RELATING TO APPLICATIONS UNDER SECTION 243 AND UNDER SECTION 1088

[4.204]

14 Appeals

(1) An applicant who has received notice under regulation 5(5), [6(8), 7(8)], . . . 10(5) or 11(5) that his application has been unsuccessful may appeal to the High Court or, in Scotland, the Court of Session on the grounds that the decision—

(a) is unlawful;

(b) is irrational or unreasonable;

(c) has been made on the basis of a procedural impropriety or otherwise contravenes the rules of natural justice.

(2) No appeal under this regulation may be brought unless the [permission] of the court has been obtained.

[(3) No application for such permission may be made after 28 days beginning with the date of the notice under regulation 5(5), 6(8), 7(8), . . . 10(5) or 11(5) unless the court is satisfied that there was good reason for the failure of the applicant to seek permission before the end of that period.

(3A) An applicant who seeks permission to appeal must serve written notice of the application on the registrar within 7 days beginning with the date on which the application for permission was issued.]

(4) The court determining an appeal may—

(a) dismiss the appeal; or

(b) quash the decision,

and where the court quashes a decision it may refer the matter to the registrar with a direction to reconsider it and make a determination in accordance with the findings of the court.

NOTES

Figures in square brackets in para (1) substituted, word in square brackets in para (2) substituted, and paras (3), (3A) substituted (for the original para (3)), by the Register of People with Significant Control Regulations 2016, SI 2016/339, reg 48, Sch 5, paras 1, 7, as from 6 April 2016.

Figures omitted from paras (1), (3) revoked by the Companies (Disclosure of Address) (Amendment) Regulations 2018, SI 2018/528, reg 5, as from 26 April 2018 (for transitional provisions see the note to reg 9 at **[4.199]**).

[4.205]

15 Duration of a section 243 decision or a section 1088 decision

(1) A section 243 decision shall continue to have effect until—

(a) either—

(i) the section 243 beneficiary, or

(ii) his personal representative,

has notified the registrar in writing that he wishes the section 243 decision to cease to apply; or

(b) the registrar has made a revocation decision in relation to that beneficiary,

whichever first occurs.

(2) A section 1088 decision shall continue to have effect until the registrar has made a revocation decision in relation to the section 1088 beneficiary.

(3) In this regulation—

"personal representative" means the executor, original or by representation, or administrator for the time being of a deceased person; and

"revocation decision" in relation to a section 243 decision or a section 1088 decision means a determination by the registrar to revoke that decision in accordance with regulation 16.

[4.206]

16 Revocation of a section 243 decision or a section 1088 decision

(1) The registrar may revoke a section 243 decision or a section 1088 decision at any time if he is satisfied that the section 243 beneficiary or section 1088 beneficiary, as the case may be, or any other person, in purported compliance with any provision of these Regulations, is found guilty of an offence under section 1112 (general false statement offence) ("a revocation decision").

(2) If the registrar proposes to make a revocation decision he shall send the beneficiary notice of his intention.

(3) The notice must—

(a) inform the beneficiary that he may, within the period of 28 days beginning with the date of the notice, deliver representations in writing to the registrar; and

(b) state that if representations are not received by the registrar within that period, the revocation decision will be made at the expiry of that period.

(4) If within the period specified in paragraph (3) the beneficiary delivers representations as to why the revocation decision should not be made, the registrar shall have regard to the representations in determining whether to make the revocation decision, and shall, within five working days of making his decision, send notice of it to the beneficiary.

(5) Any communication by the registrar in respect of a revocation decision or proposed revocation decision shall be sent to the beneficiary—

(a) in the case of an individual, to his usual residential address;
(b) in the case of a company, to its registered office; or
(c) in the case of a partnership, to the address specified in its section 1088 application.

(6) In this regulation—

"partnership" includes a limited liability partnership;

"section 243 beneficiary" includes where the section 243 decision was made following an application under regulation 6 or 7, the applicant.

SCHEDULES

SCHEDULE 1
SPECIFIED PUBLIC AUTHORITIES

Regulation 2

[4.207]

The Secretary of State;

[the Minister for the Cabinet Office;]

any Northern Ireland Department;

the Scottish Ministers;

the Welsh Ministers;

the Treasury;

[the Treasury Solicitor;]

the Commissioners for Her Majesty's Revenue and Customs;

the Bank of England [(including the Bank in its capacity as the Prudential Regulation Authority)];

the Director of Public Prosecutions;

the Director of Public Prosecutions for Northern Ireland;

the Serious Fraud Office;

the Secret Intelligence Service;

the Security Service;

the Government Communications Headquarters;

[the Financial Conduct Authority;

. . .]

[the Competition and Markets Authority];

the Pensions Regulator;

the Panel on Takeovers and Mergers;

the Regulator of Community Interest Companies;

the Registrar of Credit Unions for Northern Ireland;

. . .

the Office of the Information Commissioner;

the Charity Commission;

the Charity Commission for Northern Ireland;

the Office of the Scottish Charity Regulator;

[the Office of Communications];

the Gas and Electricity Markets Authority;

the Northern Ireland Authority for Utility Regulation;

the Gambling Commission;

[the National Crime Agency];

the Health and Safety Executive;

[the Office for Nuclear Regulation;]

the Health and Safety Executive for Northern Ireland;

the Food Standards Agency;

[the Gangmasters Labour and Abuse Authority;]

the Security Industry Authority;

a local authority within the meaning of section 54(2) of the Act;

an official receiver appointed under section 399 of the Insolvency Act 1986 (appointment, etc, of official receivers);

the Official Receiver for Northern Ireland;

the Crown Office and Procurator Fiscal Services;

[the Marine Management Organisation;]

a person acting as an insolvency practitioner within the meaning of section 388 of the Insolvency Act 1986 (meaning of "act as an insolvency practitioner") or Article 3 of the Insolvency (Northern Ireland) Order 1989 ("act as an insolvency practitioner");

an inspector appointed under Part 14 of the 1985 Act (investigation of companies and their affairs: requisition of documents) or Part 15 of the 1986 Order or a person appointed under regulation 30 of the Open-Ended Investment Companies Regulations 2001 (power to investigate) or regulation 22 of the Open-Ended Investment Companies Regulations (Northern Ireland) 2004;

any person authorised to exercise powers under section 447 of the 1985 Act (power to require documents and information), or section 84 of the Companies Act 1989 (exercise of powers by officers, etc) or Article 440 of the 1986 Order;

any person exercising functions conferred by Part 6 of the Financial Services and Markets Act 2000 (official listing) . . . ;

a person appointed to make a report under section 166 [or 166A] (reports by skilled persons) of the Financial Services and Markets Act 2000;

a person appointed to conduct an investigation under section 167 (appointment of persons to carry out general investigations) or 168(3) or (5) (appointment of persons to carry out investigations in particular cases) of the Financial Services and Markets Act 2000;

an inspector appointed under section 284 (power to investigate) of the Financial Services and Markets Act 2000;

. . .

a police force;

[the Scottish Housing Regulator];

[the lead enforcement authority (as defined in section 33(1) of the Estate Agents Act 1979) exercising functions under the Estate Agents Act 1979].

NOTES

Entry "the Minister for the Cabinet Office" inserted by the Companies (Disclosure of Address) (Amendment) Regulations 2015, SI 2015/842, reg 2, as from 30 June 2015.

Entry "the Treasury Solicitor" inserted, and entry "an overseas regulatory authority within the meaning of section 82 of the Companies Act 1989 (request for assistance by overseas regulatory authority)" (omitted) revoked, by the Register of People with Significant Control Regulations 2016, SI 2016/339, reg 48, Sch 5, paras 1, 8, as from 6 April 2016.

Words in square brackets in the entry "Bank of England" inserted by the Bank of England and Financial Services (Consequential Amendments) Regulations 2017, SI 2017/80, reg 2, Schedule, Pt 2, para 34(a), as from 1 March 2017.

Entries "the Financial Conduct Authority" and "the Prudential Regulation Authority" substituted (for the original entry "the Financial Services Authority"), words omitted from the entry beginning "any person exercising functions conferred by Part 6 of the Financial Services and Markets Act 2000 (official listing)" revoked, and words in square brackets in the entry beginning "a person appointed to make a report under section 166" inserted, by the Financial Services Act 2012 (Consequential Amendments and Transitional Provisions) Order 2013, SI 2013/472, art 3, Sch 2, para 157(a), as from 1 April 2013. Entry "the Prudential Regulation Authority" (omitted) subsequently revoked by SI 2017/80, reg 2, Schedule, Pt 2, para 34(b), as from 1 March 2017.

Entry "the Competition and Markets Authority" substituted (for the original entry "the Competition Commission"), and entry "the Office of Fair Trading" (omitted) revoked, by the Enterprise and Regulatory Reform Act 2013 (Competition) (Consequential, Transitional and Saving Provisions) (No 2) Order 2014, SI 2014/549, art 2, Schedule, Pt 2, para 37, as from 1 April 2014.

Entry "the Office of Communications" substituted (for the original entry "the Postal Services Commission") by the Postal Services Act 2011 (Consequential Modifications and Amendments) Order 2011, SI 2011/2085, art 5(1), Sch 1, para 79, as from 1 October 2011.

Entry "the National Crime Agency" substituted (for the original entry "the Serious Organised Crime Agency") by virtue of the Crime and Courts Act 2013, s 15(3), Sch 8, Pt 4, para 190, as from 7 October 2013.

Entry "the Office for Nuclear Regulation" inserted by the Energy Act 2013 (Office for Nuclear Regulation) (Consequential Amendments, Transitional Provisions and Savings) Order 2014, SI 2014/469, art 6(2), Sch 3, Pt 5, para 195, as from 1 April 2014.

Entry "the Gangmasters Labour and Abuse Authority" substituted (for the original entry "the Gangmasters Licensing Authority") by the Immigration Act 2016 (Consequential Amendments) Regulations 2016, SI 2016/655, reg 2, Schedule, Pt 2, para 4, as from 12 July 2016.

Entry "the Marine Management Organisation" inserted by the Companies (Disclosure of Address) (Amendment) Regulations 2010, SI 2010/2156, reg 2, as from 1 October 2010.

Entry "the Scottish Housing Regulator" inserted by the Housing (Scotland) Act 2010 (Consequential Provisions and Modifications) Order 2012, SI 2012/700, art 4, Schedule, Pt 2, para 20, as from 1 April 2012.

Entry beginning "the lead enforcement authority (as defined in section 33(1) of the Estate Agents Act 1979)" inserted by the Public Bodies (Abolition of the National Consumer Council and Transfer of the Office of Fair Trading's Functions in relation to Estate Agents etc) Order 2014, SI 2014/631, art 5(3), Sch 2, para 11, as from 31 March 2014.

SCHEDULE 2
CONDITIONS FOR PERMITTED DISCLOSURE

Regulations 2 and 3

PART 1 DISCLOSURE TO SPECIFIED PUBLIC AUTHORITIES

[4.208]

1. Paragraphs 2 and 3 set out the conditions specified for the disclosure of protected information by the registrar to a specified public authority.

2. The specified public authority has delivered to the registrar a statement that it intends to use the protected information only for the purpose of facilitating the carrying out by that specified public authority of a public function ("the permitted purpose").

3. Subject to paragraph 4, the specified public authority ("the authority") has delivered to the registrar a statement that it will, where it supplies a copy of the protected information to a processor for the purpose of processing the information for use in respect of the permitted purpose—

(a) ensure that the processor is one who carries on business in the European Economic Area [or in the United Kingdom];

(b) require that the information is not transmitted outside the [area comprising the United Kingdom and the European Economic Area] by the processor; and

(c) require that the processor does not disclose the information except to the authority or an employee of the authority.

4. Paragraph 3 does not apply where the specified public authority is the [National Crime Agency,] Secret Intelligence Service, Security Service or Government Communications Headquarters.

NOTES

Para 3: words in square brackets in sub-para (a) inserted, and words in square brackets in sub-para (b) substituted, by the Companies, Limited Liability Partnerships and Partnerships (Amendment etc) (EU Exit) Regulations 2019, SI 2019/348, reg 7, Sch 2, paras 9, 10(a), as from IP completion day (as defined in the European Union (Withdrawal Agreement) Act 2020, s 39) (for transitional provisions see Sch 4, para 5 to the 2019 Regulations at **[12.106]**).

Para 4: words in square brackets inserted by the Register of People with Significant Control Regulations 2016, SI 2016/339, reg 48, Sch 5, paras 1, 9, as from 6 April 2016.

PART 2 DISCLOSURE TO A CREDIT REFERENCE AGENCY

[4.209]

5. Paragraphs 6 to 10 set out the conditions specified for the disclosure of protected information by the registrar to a credit reference agency.

6. [(1)] The credit reference agency—

(a) is carrying on in the United Kingdom . . . a business comprising the furnishing of information relevant to the financial standing of individuals, being information collected by the agency for that purpose;

(b) maintains appropriate procedures—

  (i) to ensure that an independent person can investigate and audit the measures maintained by the agency for the purposes of ensuring the security of any protected information disclosed to that agency; and

  [(ii) for the purposes of ensuring that it complies with its [obligations under the data protection legislation (as defined in section 3 of the Data Protection Act 2018)];]

(c) has not been found guilty of an offence under—

  (i) section 1112 (general false statement offence) of the Act or section 2 of the Fraud Act 2006 (fraud by false representation); . . .

  (ii) section 47 (failure to comply with enforcement notice) of the Data Protection Act 1998 in circumstances where it has used the protected information for purposes other than those described in sub-paragraphs (a) to (e) of paragraph 7 below[; or

  (iii) section 144 of the Data Protection Act 2018 (false statements made in response to an information notice) or section 148 of that Act (destroying or falsifying information and documents etc)];

[(d) has not been given a penalty notice under section 155 of the Data Protection Act 2018 in circumstances described in paragraph (c)(ii), other than a penalty notice that has been cancelled].

[(2) . . .]

7. The credit reference agency has delivered to the registrar a statement that it intends to use the protected information only for the purposes of—

(a) providing an assessment of the financial standing of a person;

(b) meeting any obligations contained in [the Money Laundering, Terrorist Financing and Transfer of Funds (Information on the Payer) Regulations 2017] or any [rules made pursuant to section 137A of the Financial Services and Markets Act 2000 which relate to the prevention and detection of money laundering in connection with the carrying on of regulated activities by authorised persons] . . .

(c) conducting conflict of interest checks required or made necessary by any enactment;

(d) the provision of protected information to—

  (i) a public authority specified in Schedule 1 which has satisfied the requirements of paragraphs 2 and 3 of this Schedule; or

  (ii) a credit reference agency which has satisfied the requirements of this Part of this Schedule; or

(e) conducting checks for the prevention and detection of crime and fraud.

8. The credit reference agency has delivered to the registrar a statement that it intends to take delivery of and to use the protected information only in the United Kingdom . . .

9. The credit reference agency has delivered to the registrar a statement that it will, where it supplies a copy of the protected information to a processor for the purpose of processing the information for use in respect of the purposes referred to in paragraph 7—

(a) ensure that the processor is one who carries on business in the [United Kingdom];
(b) require that the information is not transmitted outside the [United Kingdom] by the processor; and
(c) require that the processor does not disclose the information except to the credit reference agency or an employee of the credit reference agency.

10. The credit reference agency has delivered to the registrar a statement that it meets the conditions in paragraph 6 above.

NOTES

Para 6: the words omitted from sub-para (1)(a) were revoked, the words in square brackets in sub-para (1)(b)(ii) were substituted, and sub-para (2) was revoked, by the Companies, Limited Liability Partnerships and Partnerships (Amendment etc) (EU Exit) Regulations 2019, SI 2019/348, reg 7, Sch 2, paras 9, 10(b), as from IP completion day (as defined in the European Union (Withdrawal Agreement) Act 2020, s 39) (for transitional provisions see Sch 4, para 5 to the 2019 Regulations at **[12.106]**). All other amendments to this paragraph were made by the Data Protection Act 2018, s 211, Sch 19, Pt 2, para 339, as from 25 May 2018 (for transitional provisions and savings relating to the repeal of the Data Protection Act 1998, see Sch 20 to the 2018 Act).

Para 7: words in first pair of square brackets in sub-para (b) substituted by the Money Laundering, Terrorist Financing and Transfer of Funds (Information on the Payer) Regulations 2017, SI 2017/692, reg 109, Sch 7, Pt 2, para 25, as from 26 June 2017. Words in second pair of square brackets in sub-para (b) substituted by the Financial Services Act 2012 (Consequential Amendments and Transitional Provisions) Order 2013, SI 2013/472, art 3, Sch 2, para 157(b), as from 1 April 2013. Words omitted from sub-para (b) revoked by SI 2019/348, reg 7, Sch 2, paras 9, 10(c), as from IP completion day (as defined in the European Union (Withdrawal Agreement) Act 2020, s 39) (for transitional provisions see Sch 4, para 5 to the 2019 Regulations at **[12.106]**).

Para 8: words omitted revoked by SI 2019/348, reg 7, Sch 2, paras 9, 10(d), as from IP completion day (as defined in the European Union (Withdrawal Agreement) Act 2020, s 39) (for transitional provisions see Sch 4, para 5 to the 2019 Regulations at **[12.106]**).

Para 9: words in square brackets substituted by SI 2019/348, reg 7, Sch 2, paras 9, 10(e), as from IP completion day (as defined in the European Union (Withdrawal Agreement) Act 2020, s 39) (for transitional provisions see Sch 4, para 5 to the 2019 Regulations at **[12.106]**).

PART 3 INTERPRETATION OF THIS SCHEDULE

[4.210]

11. (1) In this Schedule—

"processor" means any person who provides a service which consists of putting information into data form or processing information in data form and any reference to a processor includes a reference to his employees; and

"public function" includes—

(a) any function conferred by or in accordance with any provision contained in any enactment;
(b) . . .
(c) any similar function conferred on persons by or under provisions having effect as part of the law of a country or territory outside the United Kingdom; and
(d) any function exercisable in relation to the investigation of any criminal offence or for the purpose of any criminal proceedings.

(2) In this Schedule any reference to—

(a) an employee of any person who has access to protected information shall be deemed to include any person working or providing services for the purposes of that person or employed by or on behalf of, or working for, any person who is so working or who is supplying such a service; and
(b) the disclosure for the purpose of facilitating the carrying out of a public function includes disclosure in relation to, and for the purpose of, any proceedings whether civil, criminal or disciplinary in which the specified public authority engages while carrying out its public functions.

NOTES

Para 11: para (b) of the definition "public function" was revoked by the Companies, Limited Liability Partnerships and Partnerships (Amendment etc) (EU Exit) Regulations 2019, SI 2019/348, reg 7, Sch 2, paras 9, 10(f), as from IP completion day (as defined in the European Union (Withdrawal Agreement) Act 2020, s 39) (for transitional provisions see Sch 4, para 5 to the 2019 Regulations at **[12.106]**).

COMPANIES (SHARES AND SHARE CAPITAL) ORDER 2009

(SI 2009/388)

NOTES

Made: 26 February 2009.

Authority: Companies Act 2006, ss 10(2)(c)(i), 32(2)(c)(i), 108(3)(c)(i), 555(3)(a), (4)(c)(i), 556(3), 583(4), 619(3)(c)(i), 621(3)(c)(i), 625(3)(c)(i), 627(3)(c)(i), 644(2)(c)(i), 649(2)(c)(i), 663(3)(c)(i), 689(3)(c)(i), 708(3)(c)(i), 714(5), 727(3), 730(5)(c)(i), 1167.

Commencement: 1 October 2009.

For a summary of all Orders and Regulations made under the Companies Act 2006, see Appendix 4 at **[A4]**.

This Order is reproduced as amended by: the Companies and Limited Liability Partnerships (Filing Requirements) Regulations 2016, SI 2016/599.

[4.211]

1 Citation, commencement and interpretation

(1) This Order may be cited as the Companies (Shares and Share Capital) Order 2009 and shall come into force on 1st October 2009.

(2) In this Order, a reference to a section is a reference to a section of the Companies Act 2006.

[4.212]

2 Statements of capital, and returns of allotment by unlimited companies: prescribed particulars of the rights attached to shares

(1) The particulars in paragraph (3) are prescribed for the purposes of the provisions in paragraph (2).

(2) The provisions are—

(a) section 10(2)(c)(i);
(b) section 32(2)(c)(i);
(c) section 108(3)(c)(i);
(d) section 555(4)(c)(i);
(e) section 556(3);
(f) section 619(3)(c)(i);
(g) section 621(3)(c)(i);
(h) section 625(3)(c)(i);
(i) section 627(3)(c)(i);
(j) section 644(2)(c)(i);
(k) section 649(2)(c)(i);
(l) section 663(3)(c)(i);
(m) section 689(3)(c)(i);
(n) section 708(3)(c)(i); . . .
[(o) section 730(5)(c)(i); and
[(p) section 853D(4)(d)(i)].

(3) The particulars are—

(a) particulars of any voting rights attached to the shares, including rights that arise only in certain circumstances;
(b) particulars of any rights attached to the shares, as respects dividends, to participate in a distribution;
(c) particulars of any rights attached to the shares, as respects capital, to participate in a distribution (including on winding up); and
(d) whether the shares are to be redeemed or are liable to be redeemed at the option of the company or the shareholder.

NOTES

Para (2): word omitted from sub-para (n) revoked, and sub-paras (o), (p) substituted (for the original sub-para (o)), by the Companies and Limited Liability Partnerships (Filing Requirements) Regulations 2016, SI 2016/599, reg 5, Sch 3, para 11, as from 30 June 2016.

[4.213]

3 Prescribed information for a return of an allotment by a limited company

(1) The information in paragraph (2) is prescribed for the purposes of section 555(3)(a) (information to be contained in a return of an allotment by a limited company).

(2) The information is—

(a) the number of shares allotted;
(b) the amount paid up and the amount (if any) unpaid on each allotted share (whether on account of the nominal value of the share or by way of premium); and
(c) where the shares are allotted as fully or partly paid up (as to their nominal value or any premium on them) otherwise than in cash, the consideration for the allotment.

[4.214]

4 Shares deemed paid up in or allotted for cash, and sale of treasury shares for a cash consideration: meaning of cash consideration

(1) The creation of an obligation on the part of a settlement bank to make a relevant payment in respect of the allotment of a share to a system-member by means of a relevant system is to be regarded as a means of payment falling within section 583(3)(e).

(2) The creation of an obligation on the part of a settlement bank to make a relevant payment in respect of the payment up of a share by a system-member by means of a relevant system is to be regarded as a means of payment falling within section 583(3)(e).

(3) The creation of an obligation on the part of a settlement bank to make a relevant payment in respect of the transfer by a company to a system-member, by means of a relevant system, of a share held by the company as a treasury share is to be regarded as a means of payment falling within section 727(2)(e).

(4) In this article—

(a) the expressions "Operator", "relevant system", "rules", "settlement bank", "system-member" and "uncertificated" have the meanings given in the Uncertificated Securities Regulations 2001; and
(b) "relevant payment" means a payment in accordance with the rules and practices of an Operator of a relevant system.

[4.215]

5 Redemption or purchase of own shares out of capital by a private company: prescribed form of, and information with respect to the nature of the company's business to be contained in, a directors' statement

(1) The directors' statement required by section 714 (directors' statement to be made where a private company makes a payment out of capital for the redemption or purchase of its own shares) must—

(a) be in writing;
(b) indicate that it is a directors' statement made under that section; and
(c) be signed by each of the company's directors.

(2) The statement must state—

(a) whether the company's business includes that of a banking company; and
(b) whether its business includes that of an insurance company.

OVERSEAS COMPANIES REGULATIONS 2009

(SI 2009/1801)

NOTES

Made: 8 July 2009.

Authority: Companies Act 2006, ss 1046(1), (2), (4)–(6), 1047(1), 1049(1)–(3), 1050(3)–(5), 1051(1)–(3), 1053(2)–(5), 1054(1), (2), 1055, 1056, 1058(1)–(3), 1078(5), 1105(1), (2), 1140(2), 1292(1), (4), 1294.

Commencement: 1 October 2009.

For a summary of all Orders and Regulations made under the Companies Act 2006, see Appendix 4 at **[A4]**.

These Regulations are reproduced as amended by: the Postal Services Act 2011 (Consequential Modifications and Amendments) Order 2011, SI 2011/2085; the Housing (Scotland) Act 2010 (Consequential Provisions and Modifications) Order 2012, SI 2012/700; the Crime and Courts Act 2013; the Financial Services Act 2012 (Consequential Amendments and Transitional Provisions) Order 2013, SI 2013/472; the Energy Act 2013 (Office for Nuclear Regulation) (Consequential Amendments, Transitional Provisions and Savings) Order 2014, SI 2014/469; the Enterprise and Regulatory Reform Act 2013 (Competition) (Consequential, Transitional and Saving Provisions) (No 2) Order 2014, SI 2014/549; the Public Bodies (Abolition of the National Consumer Council and Transfer of the Office of Fair Trading's Functions in relation to Estate Agents etc) Order 2014, SI 2014/631; the Legal Aid, Sentencing and Punishment of Offenders Act 2012 (Fines on Summary Conviction) Regulations 2015, SI 2015/664; the Immigration Act 2016 (Consequential Amendments) Regulations 2016, SI 2016/655; the Bank of England and Financial Services (Consequential Amendments) Regulations 2017, SI 2017/80; the Money Laundering, Terrorist Financing and Transfer of Funds (Information on the Payer) Regulations 2017, SI 2017/692; the Financial Services Act 2012 (Mutual Societies) Order 2013, SI 2018/323; the Data Protection Act 2018; the Occupational Pension Schemes (Master Trusts) Regulations 2018, SI 2018/1030; the Accounts and Reports (Amendment) (EU Exit) Regulations 2019, SI 2019/145; the Companies, Limited Liability Partnerships and Partnerships (Amendment etc) (EU Exit) Regulations 2019, SI 2019/348.

Application to European Public Limited-Liability Companies (SEs): see the International Accounting Standards and European Public Limited-Liability Company (Amendment etc) (EU Exit) Regulations 2019, SI 2019/685, reg 19, Sch 3, Pt 1 at **[12.152]**.

ARRANGEMENT OF REGULATIONS

PART 1
INTRODUCTION

PART 2
INITIAL REGISTRATION OF PARTICULARS

PART 3
ALTERATION IN REGISTERED PARTICULARS

PART 4
USUAL RESIDENTIAL ADDRESSES: PROTECTION FROM DISCLOSURE

PART 1 INTRODUCTION

[4.216]

1 Citation and commencement

(1) These Regulations may be cited as the Overseas Companies Regulations 2009.

(2) These Regulations come into force on 1st October 2009.

[4.217]

2 Interpretation

In these Regulations—

"accounting documents"—

(a) in relation to an overseas company to which Chapter 2 of Part 5 applies (companies required to prepare and disclose accounts under parent law), has the meaning given by regulation 31(2), and

(b) in relation to a credit or financial institution to which Chapter 2 of Part 6 applies (institutions required to prepare accounts under parent law), has the meaning given by regulation 44(2);

"certified copy" means a copy certified as a correct copy;

"constitution", in relation to an overseas company, means the charter, statutes, memorandum and articles of association or other instrument constituting or defining the company's constitution;

"credit or financial institution" means a credit or financial institution to which section 1050 of the Companies Act 2006 applies;

"disclosure", in relation to a credit or financial institution to which Chapter 2 of Part 6 applies, has the meaning given by regulation 44(2);

"establishment" means—

(a) a branch within the meaning of the Eleventh Company Law Directive (89/666/EEC), or

(b) a place of business that is not such a branch,

and "UK establishment" means an establishment in the United Kingdom;

"financial period"—

(a) in relation to an overseas company to which Chapter 2 of Part 5 applies (companies required to prepare and disclose accounts under parent law), has the meaning given by regulation 31(2), and

(b) in relation to a credit or financial institution to which Chapter 2 of Part 6 applies (institutions required to prepare accounts under parent law), has the meaning given by regulation 44(2);

. . .

"former name", in the case of an individual, means a name by which the individual was formerly known for business purposes;

"name", in the case of an individual, means the person's Christian name (or other forename) and surname, except that in the case of—

(a) a peer, or

(b) an individual usually known by a title,

the title may be stated instead of the individual's Christian name (or other forename) and surname or in addition to either or both of them; and

"parent law"—

(a) in relation to an overseas company to which Chapter 2 of Part 5 applies (companies required to prepare and disclose accounts under parent law), has the meaning given by regulation 31(2), and

(b) in relation to a credit or financial institution to which Chapter 2 of Part 6 applies (institutions required to prepare accounts under parent law), has the meaning given by regulation 44(2).

NOTES

Definition "First Company Law Directive" (omitted) revoked by the Companies, Limited Liability Partnerships and Partnerships (Amendment etc) (EU Exit) Regulations 2019, SI 2019/348, reg 7, Sch 2, paras 3, 4, as from IP completion day (as defined in the European Union (Withdrawal Agreement) Act 2020, s 39).

PART 2 INITIAL REGISTRATION OF PARTICULARS

NOTES

Transitional provisions: see the Companies, Limited Liability Partnerships and Partnerships (Amendment etc) (EU Exit) Regulations 2019, SI 2019/348, Sch 4, para 4(1)–(3) at **[12.106]** which (as amended) provides as follows—

"(1) This paragraph applies to an overseas company that has a UK establishment immediately before [IP completion day].

(2) If there are additional registrable particulars in respect of that establishment, the company must, within the period of three months beginning on [IP completion day], deliver to the registrar a return containing those particulars.

(3) The requirement in sub-paragraph (2) is to be treated, for the purposes of Part 2 of the Overseas Companies Regulations 2009, as a requirement of that Part.".

[4.218]

3 Application and interpretation of Part

(1) This Part applies to an overseas company that opens a UK establishment.

(2) In this Part—

"director" includes shadow director; and

"secretary" includes any person occupying the position of secretary by whatever name called.

[4.219]

4 Duty to deliver return and documents

(1) The company must within one month of having opened a UK establishment—

(a) deliver to the registrar a return complying with the requirements of this Part, and

(b) deliver with the return the documents required by this Part.

(2) These requirements apply each time a company opens an establishment in the United Kingdom.

[4.220]

5 Particulars to be included in return

(1) The return must contain—

(a) the particulars specified in regulation 6 (particulars of the company), and

(b) the particulars specified in regulation 7 (particulars of the establishment).

(2) If at the time the return is delivered the company—

(a) has another UK establishment,

(b) has delivered a return in respect of that establishment containing the particulars specified in regulation 6, and

(c) has no outstanding obligation under Part 3 in respect of an alteration to those particulars,

the company may instead state in the return that those particulars are included in the particulars delivered in respect of another UK establishment (giving the registered number of that establishment).

[4.221]

6 Particulars of the company

(1) The particulars of the company to be included in the return are—

(a) the company's name,

(b) the company's legal form,
(c) if it is registered in the country of its incorporation, the identity of the register in which it is registered and the number with which it is so registered,
(d) a list of its directors and secretary, containing—
    (i) with respect to each director, the particulars specified in paragraph (3), and
    (ii) with respect to the secretary (or where there are joint secretaries, with respect to each of them) the particulars specified in paragraph (4),
(e) the extent of the powers of the directors or secretary to represent the company in dealings with third parties and in legal proceedings, together with a statement as to whether they may act alone or must act jointly and, if jointly, the name of any other person concerned, . . .
(f) whether the company is a credit or financial institution,
[(g) the law under which the company is incorporated,
(h) in the case of a company to which Chapter 2 of Part 5 or Chapter 2 of Part 6 applies (requirements to prepare and disclose accounts under parent law), the period for which the company is required by its parent law to prepare accounts, together with the period allowed for the preparation and public disclosure (if any) of accounts for such a period, and
(i) unless disclosed by the company's constitution (see regulation 8)—
    (i) the address of its principal place of business in its country of incorporation or, if applicable, its registered office,
    (ii) its objects, and
    (iii) the amount of its issued share capital].

(2) . . .

(3) The particulars referred to in paragraph (1)(d)(i) (directors) are—
(a) in the case of an individual—
    (i) name,
    (ii) any former name,
    (iii) a service address,
    (iv) usual residential address,
    (v) the country or state in which the individual is usually resident,
    (vi) nationality,
    (vii) business occupation (if any), and
    (viii) date of birth;
(b) in the case of a body corporate, or a firm that is a legal person under the law by which it is governed—
    (i) corporate or firm name,
    (ii) registered or principal office,
    (iii) . . .
    (iv) . . . particulars of—
        (aa) the legal form of the company or firm and the law by which it is governed, and
        (bb) if applicable, the register in which it is entered (including details of the state) and its registration number in that register.

(4) The particulars referred to in paragraph (1)(d)(ii) (secretary) are—
(a) in the case of an individual—
    (i) name,
    (ii) any former name, and
    (iii) a service address;
(b) in the case of a body corporate, or a firm that is a legal person under the law by which it is governed—
    (i) corporate or firm name,
    (ii) registered or principal office,
    (iii) . . .
    (iv) . . . particulars of—
        (aa) the legal form of the company or firm and the law by which it is governed, and
        (bb) if applicable, the register in which it is entered (including details of the state) and its registration number in that register.

But if all the partners in a firm are joint secretaries of the company it is sufficient to state the particulars that would be required if the firm were a legal person and the firm had been appointed secretary.

(5) For the purposes of paragraphs (3)(a)(ii) and (4)(a)(ii), where a person is or was formerly known by more than one former name, each of them must be stated.

(6) It is not necessary to include in the return particulars of a former name in the following cases—
(a) in the case of a peer or an individual normally known by a title, where the name is one by which the person was known previous to the adoption of or succession to the title,
(b) in the case of any person, where the former name—
    (i) was changed or disused before the person attained the age of 16 years, or
    (ii) has been changed or disused for 20 years or more.

(7) For the purposes of paragraph (3)(a)(iv) if the person's usual residential address is the same as the person's service address the return need only contain a statement to that effect.

NOTES

In para (1) sub-paras (g)–(i) were inserted, and all omitted words were revoked, by the Companies, Limited Liability Partnerships and Partnerships (Amendment etc) (EU Exit) Regulations 2019, SI 2019/348, reg 7, Sch 2, paras 3, 5, as from IP completion day (as defined in the European Union (Withdrawal Agreement) Act 2020, s 39). See also the transitional provisions note at the beginning of this Part.

[4.222]
7 Particulars of the establishment

(1) The particulars of the establishment to be included in the return are—

(a) address of the establishment,

(b) date on which it was opened,

(c) business carried on at it,

(d) name of the establishment if different from the name of the company,

(e) name and service address of every person resident in the United Kingdom authorised to accept service of documents on behalf of the company in respect of the establishment, or a statement that there is no such person,

(f) a list of every person authorised to represent the company as a permanent representative of the company in respect of the establishment, containing the following particulars with respect to each such person—

(i) name,

(ii) any former name,

(iii) service address, and

(iv) usual residential address,

(g) extent of the authority of any person falling within sub-paragraph (f), including whether that person is authorised to act alone or jointly, and

(h) if a person falling within sub-paragraph (f) is not authorised to act alone, the name of any person with whom they are authorised to act.

(2) For the purpose of paragraph (1)(f)(iv) if the person's usual residential address is the same as the person's service address the return need only contain a statement to that effect.

[4.223]
8 Documents to be delivered with the return: copy of company's constitution

(1) A certified copy of the company's constitution must be delivered to the registrar with the return.

(2) If at the time the return is delivered the company—

(a) has another UK establishment,

(b) has delivered a certified copy of the company's constitution with a return relating to that establishment, and

(c) has no outstanding obligation under Part 3 in respect of an alteration to its constitution,

the company may instead state in the return that a certified copy of the company's constitution has been delivered in respect of another UK establishment (giving the registered number of that establishment).

[4.224]
9 Documents to be delivered with the return: copies of accounting documents

(1) If the company is one to which Chapter 2 of Part 5 applies (companies required to prepare and disclose accounts under parent law), copies of the company's latest accounting documents must be delivered to the registrar with the return.

(2) The company's latest accounting documents means the accounting documents, prepared for a financial period of the company, last disclosed in accordance with its parent law before the end of the period allowed for delivery of the return or, if earlier, the date on which the company delivers the return.

(3) If at the time the return is delivered the company—

(a) has another UK establishment, and

(b) has delivered the documents required by paragraph (1) in connection with a return relating to that establishment,

the company may instead state in the return that the documents are included in the material delivered in respect of another UK establishment (giving the registered number of that establishment).

[4.225]
10 Statement as to future manner of compliance with accounting requirements

(1) If the company is one to which Part 5 applies (delivery of accounting documents: general), the return must state—

(a) in the case of a company to which Chapter 2 of that Part applies (companies required to file copies of accounting documents disclosed under parent law), whether it is intended to file copies of accounting documents in accordance with the provisions of that Chapter in respect of the establishment to which the return relates or in respect of another UK establishment;

(b) in the case of a company to which Chapter 3 of that Part applies (companies required to file accounts under UK law), whether it is intended to file accounts in accordance with the provisions of that Chapter in respect of the establishment to which the return relates or in respect of another UK establishment.

(2) If the return states that it is intended to file copies of accounting documents, or accounts, in respect of another UK establishment, it must give the registered number of that establishment.

[4.226]
11 Penalty for non-compliance

(1) If a company fails to comply with any of the requirements of this Part, an offence is committed by—

(a) the company, and

(b) every officer or agent of the company who knowingly and wilfully authorises or permits the default.

(2) A person guilty of an offence under paragraph (1) is liable on summary conviction to—

(a) a fine not exceeding level 3 on the standard scale, and

(b) for continued contravention, a daily default fine not exceeding one-tenth of level 3 on the standard scale.

PART 3 ALTERATION IN REGISTERED PARTICULARS

[4.227]

12 Application of Part

This Part applies to an overseas company that—

(a) has complied with Part 2 (initial registration of particulars) in respect of one or more UK establishments, and

(b) has not subsequently given notice under regulation 77 (notice of closure of UK establishment) in respect of all those establishments.

[4.228]

13 Return of alteration in registered particulars

(1) If an alteration is made in any of the particulars delivered under—

(a) regulation 6 (particulars of the company), or

(b) regulation 7 (particulars of the establishment),

the company must deliver to the registrar a return containing details of the alteration.

(2) Where a company has more than one UK establishment a return is required in respect of each UK establishment to which the alteration relates; but a return giving the registered numbers of more than one UK establishment is treated as a return in respect of each of them.

(3) An alteration in any of the particulars specified in regulation 6 (particulars of the company) is treated as relating to every UK establishment of the company.

(4) The details required of the alteration are—

(a) the particular that has been altered,

(b) details of the particular as altered, and

(c) the date on which the alteration was made.

(5) The return must also state—

(a) the company's name,

(b) the company's registered number, and

(c) the name (if different from the company's name) and registered number of each UK establishment to which the return relates.

(6) The period allowed for delivery of the return is—

(a) in the case of an alteration of any of the particulars specified in regulation 6 (particulars of the company), 21 days after the date on which notice of the alteration in question could have been received in the United Kingdom in due course of post (if despatched with due diligence);

(b) in the case of an alteration of any of the particulars specified in regulation 7 (particulars of the establishment), 21 days after the alteration is made.

[4.229]

14 Return of alteration in company's constitution

(1) If any alteration is made in the company's constitution the company must deliver to the registrar a return stating—

(a) that an alteration has been made to the company's constitution, and

(b) the date on which the alteration was made.

(2) The return must be accompanied by a certified copy of the constitution as altered.

(3) Where a company has more than one UK establishment a return is required in respect of each UK establishment to which the alteration relates; but a return giving the registered numbers of more than one UK establishment is treated as a return in respect of each of them.

(4) An alteration in the company's constitution is treated as relating to a UK establishment only if a copy of the constitution is included in the material registered in respect of that establishment.

(5) The return must also state—

(a) the company's name,

(b) the company's registered number, and

(c) the name (if different from the company's name) and registered number of each UK establishment to which the return relates.

(6) The period allowed for delivery of the return is 21 days after the date on which notice of the alteration in question could have been received in the United Kingdom in due course of post (if despatched with due diligence).

[4.230]

15 Return of alteration as regards filing of certified copy of constitution

(1) This regulation applies where—

(a) the company's return under Part 2 in respect of an establishment states that a certified copy of the company's constitution has been delivered in respect of another UK establishment, and

(b) that statement ceases to be true.

(2) The company must deliver to the registrar a further return in respect of the first-mentioned establishment—

(a) stating that the previous statement has ceased to be true, and

(b) either—

(i) accompanied by a certified copy of the company's constitution, or

(ii) stating that a copy of the company's constitution is included in the material delivered in respect of another UK establishment (giving the registered number of that establishment).

(3) Where the company has more than one UK establishment a return giving the registered numbers of more than one UK establishment is treated as a return in respect of each of them.

(4) The return must also state—

(a) the company's name,
(b) the company's registered number, and
(c) the name (if different from the company's name) and registered number of each UK establishment to which the return relates.

(5) The period allowed for delivery of the return is 21 days after the date on which notice of the fact that the statement in the earlier return has ceased to be true could have been received in the United Kingdom in due course of post (if despatched with due diligence).

(6) Where, after a company has made a return under this regulation, the statement mentioned in paragraph (2)(b)(ii) ceases to be true, paragraphs (2) to (5) (and this paragraph) apply again.

[4.231]
16 Return of alteration of manner of compliance with accounting requirements

(1) This regulation applies where—
(a) the company's return under Part 2 in respect of a UK establishment states an intention as to whether accounting documents, or accounts, are to be filed in accordance with the provisions of that Part in respect of that establishment or in respect of another UK establishment, and
(b) that intention changes.

(2) The company must deliver to the registrar a further return in respect of the first-mentioned establishment stating—
(a) that the intention has changed, and
(b) either—
(i) that it is intended to file accounting documents, or accounts, in respect of the establishment to which the return relates, or
(ii) that it is intended to file accounting documents, or accounts, in respect of another UK establishment (giving the registered number of that establishment).

(3) Where the company has more than one UK establishment a return giving the registered numbers of more than one UK establishment is treated as a return in respect of each of them.

(4) The return must also state—
(a) the company's name,
(b) the company's registered number, and
(c) the name (if different from the company's name) and registered number of each UK establishment to which the return relates.

(5) The period allowed for delivery of the return is 21 days after the date on which notice of the fact that the intention stated in the earlier return has changed could have been received in the United Kingdom in due course of post (if despatched with due diligence).

(6) Where, after a company has made a return under this regulation, the intention stated in accordance with paragraph (2)(b)(i) or (ii) changes again, paragraphs (2) to (5) (and this paragraph) apply again.

[4.232]
17 Penalty for non-compliance

(1) If a company fails to comply with any of the requirements of this Part within the period allowed, an offence is committed by—
(a) the company, and
(b) every officer or agent of the company who knowingly and wilfully authorises or permits the default.

(2) A person guilty of an offence under paragraph (1) is liable on summary conviction to—
(a) a fine not exceeding level 3 on the standard scale, and
(b) for continued contravention, a daily default fine not exceeding one-tenth of level 3 on the standard scale.

PART 4 USUAL RESIDENTIAL ADDRESSES: PROTECTION FROM DISCLOSURE

[4.233]
18 Application and interpretation of Part

(1) This Part applies to an overseas company that has one or more UK establishments in respect of which it has registered particulars under Part 2.

(2) In this Part—
"credit reference agency" means a person carrying on a business comprising the furnishing of information relevant to the financial standing of individuals, being information collected by the agency for that purpose;
"director" means a director of a company who is an individual and whose particulars have been delivered to the registrar under regulation 6(1)(d)(i);
"limited liability partnership" means a limited liability partnership incorporated under the Limited Liability Partnerships Act 2000 or Limited Liability Partnerships Act (Northern Ireland) 2002;
"permanent representative" means a permanent representative of a company whose particulars have been delivered to the registrar under regulation 7(1)(f);
"police force" means a police force within the meaning of section 101(1) of the Police Act 1996 (interpretation), section 50 of the Police (Scotland) Act 1967 (meaning of police area, etc) or section 1 of the Police (Northern Ireland) Act 2000 (name of the police in Northern Ireland); and
"specified public authority" means a public authority specified in Schedule 1.

[4.234]
19 Protected information

(1) This Part makes provision for protecting, in the case of a director or permanent representative of a company to which this Part applies—

(a) information as to their usual residential address;
(b) the information that their service address is their usual residential address.

(2) That information is referred to in this Part as "protected information".

(3) Information does not cease to be protected information on the person ceasing to be a director or permanent representative and references in this Part to a director or permanent representative include, to that extent, a person who was formerly a director or permanent representative.

[4.235]
20 Protected information: restriction on use or disclosure by company

(1) A company to which this Part applies must not use or disclose protected information about a director or permanent representative, except—
(a) for communicating with the individual concerned,
(b) in order to comply with any requirement in these Regulations as to particulars to be sent to the registrar, or
(c) in accordance with regulation 26 (disclosure under court order).

(2) Paragraph (1) does not prohibit the use or disclosure of protected information with the consent of the director or permanent representative.

[4.236]
21 Protected information: restriction on use or disclosure by registrar

(1) The registrar must omit protected information from the material on the register that is available for inspection where—
(a) it is contained in a document delivered to the registrar in which such information is required to be stated, and
(b) in the case of a document having more than one part, it is contained in a part of the document in which such information is required to be stated.

(2) The registrar is not obliged—
(a) to check other documents or (as the case may be) other parts of the document to ensure the absence of protected information, or
(b) to omit from the material that is available for public inspection anything registered before 1st October 2009.

(3) The registrar must not use or disclose protected information except—
(a) as permitted by regulations 22 to 24 (permitted use or disclosure by registrar), or
(b) in accordance with regulation 26 (disclosure under court order).

[4.237]
22 Permitted use of protected information by the registrar: communication

The registrar may use protected information for communicating with the director or permanent representative.

[4.238]
23 Permitted disclosure by the registrar: disclosure to specified public authority

(1) The registrar may disclose protected information to a specified public authority where the conditions set out in Part 1 of Schedule 2 are satisfied.

(2) A specified public authority must deliver to the registrar such information or evidence as the registrar may direct for the purpose of enabling the registrar to determine in accordance with these Regulations whether to disclose protected information.

(3) The registrar may require such information or evidence to be verified in such manner as the registrar may direct.

(4) The specified public authority must inform the registrar immediately of any change in respect of any statement delivered to the registrar pursuant to Schedule 2 or information or evidence provided for the purpose of enabling the registrar to determine whether to disclose protected information.

[4.239]
24 Permitted disclosure by the registrar: disclosure to credit reference agency

(1) Subject to regulation 25, the registrar may disclose protected information to a credit reference agency where the conditions set out in Part 2 of Schedule 2 are satisfied.

(2) The registrar may rely on a statement delivered by a credit reference agency under paragraph 10 of Schedule 2 as sufficient evidence of the matters stated in it.

(3) Notwithstanding paragraph (2), a credit reference agency shall deliver to the registrar such information or evidence in addition to the statement required by paragraph 10 of Schedule 2 as the registrar may direct for the purpose of enabling the registrar to determine in accordance with these Regulations whether to disclose protected information.

(4) The registrar may require such information or evidence to be verified in such manner as the registrar may direct.

(5) The credit reference agency must inform the registrar immediately of any change in respect of any statement delivered to the registrar pursuant to Schedule 2 or information or evidence provided for the purpose of enabling the registrar to determine whether to disclose protected information.

[4.240]
25 Application to prevent disclosure to credit reference agency

(1) An application may be made to the registrar to prevent the disclosure to a credit reference agency of protected information relating to a director or permanent representative (an "application for higher protection").

(2) An application for higher protection shall be made and determined in accordance with the provisions of Schedule 3.

(3) The registrar shall refrain from disclosing to a credit reference agency protected information relating to—
(a) an individual in respect of whom a successful application for higher protection has been made, or

(b) an individual in respect of whom an application for higher protection has been made where—
  (i) the registrar has not made a determination, or
  (ii) the registrar has made a determination rejecting the application and an appeal against that determination has been brought but has not been determined;

(c) an individual in relation to whom an order was in force under section 723B of the Companies Act 1985 (confidentiality orders) immediately before 1st October 2009 and who, by virtue of paragraph 21 of Schedule 8 (transitional provisions and savings: individuals with a confidentiality order) is to be treated as having made a successful application for higher protection.

[4.241]

26 Disclosure under court order

(1) The court may make an order for the disclosure of protected information by the company or by the registrar if—
  (a) there is evidence that service of documents at a service address other than the director or permanent representative's usual residential address is not effective to bring them to the notice of that individual, or
  (b) it is necessary or expedient for the information to be provided in connection with the enforcement of an order or decree of the court,

and the court is otherwise satisfied that it is appropriate to make the order.

(2) An order for disclosure by the registrar is to be made only if the company—
  (a) does not have the director or permanent representative's usual residential address,
  (b) no longer has a UK establishment and has given notice of that fact under regulation 77, or
  (c) has been dissolved.

(3) The order may be made on the application of a liquidator, creditor or member of the company, or any other person appearing to the court to have a sufficient interest.

(4) The order must specify the persons to whom, and purposes for which, disclosure is authorised.

[4.242]

27 Circumstances in which registrar may put address on the public record

(1) The registrar may put a director's or permanent representative's usual residential address on the public record if—
  (a) communications sent by the registrar to that individual and requiring a response within a specified period of time remain unanswered, or
  (b) there is evidence that service of documents at a service address provided in place of their usual residential address is not effective to bring them to the notice of the director or permanent representative.

(2) The registrar must give notice of the proposal—
  (a) to the director or permanent representative, and
  (b) to the company.

(3) The notice must—
  (a) state the grounds on which it is proposed to put the director's or permanent representative's usual residential address on the public record, and
  (b) specify a period within which representations may be made before that is done.

(4) The notice must be sent to the director or permanent representative at their usual residential address, unless it appears to the registrar that service at that address may be ineffective to bring it to their notice, in which case it may be sent to any service address provided in place of that address.

(5) The registrar must take account of any representations received within the specified period.

(6) What is meant by putting the address on the public record is explained in regulation 28.

[4.243]

28 Putting the address on the public record

(1) The registrar, on deciding in accordance with regulation 27 that a director's or permanent representative's usual residential address is to be put on the public record, shall proceed as if a return containing altered particulars had been given under Part 3—
  (a) stating that address as the director's or permanent representative's service address, and
  (b) stating that their usual residential address is the same as their service address.

(2) The registrar must give notice of having done so—
  (a) to the director or permanent representative, and
  (b) to the company.

(3) If the company has been notified by the director or permanent representative of a more recent address as their usual residential address, it must notify the registrar in accordance with regulation 13 (return of alteration in registered particulars).

(4) A director or permanent representative whose usual residential address has been put on the public record by the registrar under this regulation may not register a service address other than their usual residential address for a period of five years from the date of the registrar's decision.

[4.244]

29 Penalty for non-compliance

(1) If a company fails to comply with regulation 28(3) an offence is committed by—
  (a) the company, and
  (b) every officer of the company who is in default.

(2) A person guilty of an offence under paragraph (1) is liable on summary conviction to—
  (a) a fine not exceeding level 5 on the standard scale, and
  (b) for continued contravention, a daily default fine not exceeding [one-tenth of the greater of £5,000 or level 4 on the standard scale].

NOTES

Para (2): words in square brackets substituted (for the original words "one-tenth of level 5 on the standard scale") by the Legal Aid, Sentencing and Punishment of Offenders Act 2012 (Fines on Summary Conviction) Regulations 2015, SI 2015/664, regs 3, 5, Sch 3, Pt 1, para 13(1), (2), as from 12 March 2015, in relation to England and Wales only (except in relation to (a) fines for offences committed before 12 March 2015, (b) the operation of restrictions on fines that may be imposed on a person aged under 18, or (c) fines that may be imposed on a person convicted by a magistrates' court who is to be sentenced as if convicted on indictment).

PART 5 DELIVERY OF ACCOUNTING DOCUMENTS: GENERAL

CHAPTER 1 INTRODUCTORY PROVISIONS

[4.245]

30 Application of Part

This Part applies to every overseas company that has an establishment in the United Kingdom and is not—

(a) a credit or financial institution (as to which, see Part 6), or

(b) a company whose constitution does not limit the liability of its members.

CHAPTER 2 COMPANIES REQUIRED TO PREPARE AND DISCLOSE ACCOUNTS UNDER PARENT LAW

[4.246]

31 Application and interpretation of Chapter

(1) This Chapter applies to an overseas company to which this Part applies that—

(a) is required by its parent law to prepare, have audited and disclose accounts, . . .

(b) . . .

(2) In relation to a company to which this Chapter applies—

"accounting documents", in relation to a financial period of the company, means—

(a) the accounts of the company for the period, including if it has one or more subsidiaries, any consolidated accounts of the group,

(b) any annual report of the directors for the period,

(c) any report of the auditors on the accounts mentioned in sub-paragraph (a), and

(d) any report of the auditors on the report mentioned in sub-paragraph (b),

and for this purpose "subsidiaries" and "consolidated group accounts" have the meaning given to them by the company's parent law;

"financial period" means a period for which the company is required or permitted by its parent law to prepare accounts;

"parent law", in relation to a company, means the law of the country in which the company is incorporated; and references to disclose or disclosure are to public disclosure.

NOTES

Para (1): sub-para (b) and the preceding word were revoked by the Accounts and Reports (Amendment) (EU Exit) Regulations 2019, SI 2019/145, reg 6, Sch 3, paras 23, 24, as from IP completion day (as defined in the European Union (Withdrawal Agreement) Act 2020, s 39).

[4.247]

32 Duty to file copies of accounting documents disclosed under parent law

(1) The directors of a company to which this Chapter applies must deliver to the registrar a copy of all the accounting documents prepared in relation to a financial period of the company that are disclosed in accordance with its parent law.

(2) Where the company's parent law permits it to discharge its obligation with respect to the disclosure of accounting documents by disclosing documents in a modified form, the directors may discharge their obligation under paragraph (1) by delivering a copy of documents modified as permitted by that law.

(3) . . .

(4) This regulation does not apply in relation to copies of accounting documents disclosed under the company's parent law before—

(a) the date on which the company first delivered a return under Part 2 (initial registration of particulars) in respect of a UK establishment, or

(b) if earlier, the last day of the period allowed for delivery of a return under that Part in respect of its first UK establishment.

(5) The directors required by this regulation to deliver copies of accounting documents must deliver them in respect of each UK establishment that the company has at the end of the financial period to which the documents relate, subject as follows.

(6) Paragraph (5) does not require the delivery of copies of accounting documents in respect of an establishment if—

(a) a return in respect of that establishment has stated the intention to file copies of accounting documents in respect of another UK establishment (giving the registered number of that establishment), and

(b) copies of the accounting documents are delivered in respect of that establishment before the end of the period allowed for doing so.

NOTES

Para (3): revoked by the Accounts and Reports (Amendment) (EU Exit) Regulations 2019, SI 2019/145, reg 6, Sch 3, paras 23, 25, as from IP completion day (as defined in the European Union (Withdrawal Agreement) Act 2020, s 39).

[4.248]

33 Statement of details of parent law and other information

(1) The accounting documents delivered to the registrar under regulation 32 must be accompanied by a statement containing the following information.

(2) The information required is—

(a) the legislation under which the accounts have been prepared and . . . audited,

(b) whether those accounts have been prepared in accordance with a set of generally accepted accounting principles and, if so, the name of the organisation or other body which issued those principles, [and]

(c) . . .

[(d) whether those accounts have been audited in accordance with a set of generally accepted auditing standards and, if so, the name of the organisation or other body which issued those standards].

(e) . . .

NOTES

Para (2): the words omitted from sub-para (a) were revoked, the word in square brackets in sub-para (b) was inserted, sub-paras (c) and (e) were revoked, and sub-para (d) was substituted, by the Accounts and Reports (Amendment) (EU Exit) Regulations 2019, SI 2019/145, reg 6, Sch 3, paras 23, 26, as from IP completion day (as defined in the European Union (Withdrawal Agreement) Act 2020, s 39).

[4.249]

34 Period allowed for filing copies of accounting documents

The period allowed for delivery, in relation to a copy of a document required to be delivered under regulation 32, is three months from the date on which the document is required to be disclosed in accordance with the company's parent law.

NOTES

Temporary modification: the Companies etc (Filing Requirements) (Temporary Modifications) Regulations 2020, SI 2020/645, reg 41 provided for the following temporary modification of this regulation (as from 27 June 2020):

(1) The Overseas Companies Regulations 2009 are to have effect subject to the following modifications.

(2) Regulation 34 (period allowed for filing copies of accounting documents) is to have effect as if for the reference to "three months" there were substituted a reference to "six months".

(3) (Modifies reg 46 post.)

(4) This regulation expires at the end of the day on 5th April 2021.

(5) Paragraph (4) does not affect the continued operation of this regulation for the purpose of determining the length of any period that begins before the expiry.

[4.250]

35 Penalty for non-compliance

(1) If any of the requirements of this Chapter (other than that in regulation 33) are not complied with in relation to a company's accounting documents before the end of the period allowed for delivering copies of those documents, every person who immediately before the end of that period was a director of the company commits an offence.

(2) It is a defence for a person charged with such an offence to prove that they took all reasonable steps for securing that those requirements would be complied with before the end of that period.

(3) A person guilty of an offence under paragraph (1) is liable on summary conviction to a fine not exceeding level 5 on the standard scale and, for continued contravention, a daily default fine not exceeding [one-tenth of the greater of £5,000 or level 4 on the standard scale].

NOTES

Para (3): words in square brackets substituted (for the original words "one-tenth of level 5 on the standard scale") by the Legal Aid, Sentencing and Punishment of Offenders Act 2012 (Fines on Summary Conviction) Regulations 2015, SI 2015/664, regs 3, 5, Sch 3, Pt 1, para 13(1), (3), as from 12 March 2015, in relation to England and Wales only (except in relation to (a) fines for offences committed before 12 March 2015, (b) the operation of restrictions on fines that may be imposed on a person aged under 18, or (c) fines that may be imposed on a person convicted by a magistrates' court who is to be sentenced as if convicted on indictment).

CHAPTER 3 COMPANIES NOT REQUIRED TO PREPARE AND DISCLOSE ACCOUNTS UNDER PARENT LAW

[4.251]

36 Application of Chapter

This Chapter applies to an overseas company to which this Part applies that is not a company to which Chapter 2 of this Part applies.

[4.252]

37 A company's financial year

Sections 390 to 392 of the Companies Act 2006 apply in relation to a company to which this Chapter applies, modified so that they read as follows—

"390 A company's financial year

(1) A company's financial year is determined as follows.

(2) Its first financial year—

(a) begins with the first day of its first accounting reference period, and

(b) ends with the last day of that period or such other date, not more than seven days before or after the end of that period, as the directors may determine.

(3) Subsequent financial years—

(a) begin with the day immediately following the end of the company's previous financial year, and
(b) end with the last day of its next accounting reference period or such other date, not more than seven days before or after the end of that period, as the directors may determine.

391 Accounting reference periods and accounting reference date

(1) A company's accounting reference periods are determined according to its accounting reference date in each calendar year.

(2) The accounting reference date of a company is the last day of the month in which the anniversary of its becoming a relevant overseas company falls.

(3) A company's first accounting reference period is the period of more than six months, but not more than eighteen months, beginning with the date of its becoming a relevant overseas company and ending with its accounting reference date.

(4) Its subsequent accounting reference periods are successive periods of twelve months beginning immediately after the end of the previous accounting reference period and ending with its accounting reference date.

(5) This section has effect subject to the provisions of section 392.

392 Alteration of accounting reference date

(1) A company may by notice given to the registrar specify a new accounting reference date having effect in relation to—

(a) the company's current accounting reference period and subsequent periods, or
(b) the company's previous accounting reference period and subsequent periods.

A company's "previous accounting reference period" means the one immediately preceding its current accounting reference period.

(2) The notice must state whether the current or previous accounting reference period—

(a) is to be shortened, so as to come to an end on the first occasion on which the new accounting reference date falls or fell after the beginning of the period, or
(b) is to be extended, so as to come to an end on the second occasion on which that date falls or fell after the beginning of the period.

(3) A notice under this section may not be given in respect of a previous accounting reference period if the period for filing accounts for the financial year determined by reference to that accounting reference period has already expired.

(4) An accounting reference period may not be extended so as to exceed eighteen months and a notice under this section is ineffective if the current or previous accounting reference period as extended in accordance with the notice would exceed that limit.

This does not apply where the company is in administration under Part 2 of the Insolvency Act 1986 (c 45) or Part 3 of the Insolvency (Northern Ireland) Order 1989 (SI 1989/2405 (NI 19)).".

[4.253]

38 Duty to prepare accounts

Sections 394 to 397, 399, and 402 to 406 of the Companies Act 2006 apply in relation to a company to which this Chapter applies, modified so that they read as follows [(save that the modification of section 396 does not apply in relation to a company which is a scheme funder of a Master Trust scheme within the meanings given by section 39(1) of the Pension Schemes Act 2017 (interpretation of Part 1))]—

"394 Duty to prepare individual accounts

Subject to section 399 (duty to prepare group accounts), the directors of a company must prepare accounts for the company for each of its financial years.

Those accounts are referred to as the company's "individual accounts".

395 Individual accounts: applicable accounting framework

(1) A company's annual accounts may be prepared in accordance with—

(a) its parent law ("parent law individual accounts"),
(b) international accounting standards ("IAS individual accounts"), or
(c) section 396 ("overseas companies individual accounts").

(2) A company may only prepare parent law individual accounts if the content of such accounts includes that required by section 396.

396 Overseas companies individual accounts

(1) Overseas companies individual accounts must comprise—

(a) a balance sheet as at the last day of the financial year, and
(b) a profit and loss account.

(2) The accounts must comply with the provisions in Schedule 4 to the Overseas Companies Regulations as to—

(a) the content of the balance sheet and the profit and loss account, and
(b) additional information to be provided by way of notes to the accounts.

397 IAS individual accounts, parent law individual accounts and overseas company individual accounts

(1) Where the directors of a company prepare IAS individual accounts they must state in the notes—

(a) that the accounts have been prepared in accordance with international accounting standards,
(b) whether the accounts have been audited, and
(c) if they have been audited—
  (i) whether they have been audited in accordance with a set of generally accepted auditing standards, and
  (ii) if so, the name of the organisation or other body which issued those standards.

(2) Where the directors of a company prepare parent law individual accounts they must state in the notes—

(a) that the accounts have been prepared in accordance with the company's parent law,
(b) the legislation under which the accounts have been prepared,
(c) whether the accounts have been prepared in accordance with a set of generally accepted accounting principles, and if so, the name of the organisation or other body which issued those principles,
(d) whether the accounts have been audited, and
(e) if they have been audited—
  (i) whether they have been audited in accordance with a set of generally accepted auditing standards, and
  (ii) if so, the name of the organisation or other body which issued those standards.

(3) Where the directors of a company prepare overseas company individual accounts they must state in the notes—
(a) that the accounts have been prepared in accordance with section 396,
(b) whether the accounts have been prepared in accordance with a set of generally accepted accounting principles, and if so, the name of the organisation or other body which issued those principles,
(c) whether the accounts have been audited, and
(d) if they have been audited—
  (i) whether they have been audited in accordance with a set of generally accepted auditing standards, and
  (ii) if so, the name of the organisation or other body which issued those standards.

399 Duty to prepare group accounts

If at the end of a financial year a company is a parent company the directors must, instead of preparing individual accounts for the year, prepare group accounts for the year.

402 Exemption from duty to prepare group accounts

A parent company is exempt from the requirement to prepare group accounts where—
(a) it has prepared accounts under section 395(1)(a) and its parent law does not require consolidated accounts;
(b) it has prepared accounts under section 395(1)(b) and in accordance with the international accounting standards it is not required to prepare consolidated accounts;
(c) it has prepared accounts under section 395(1)(c) and if under section 405 all of the company's subsidiary undertakings could be excluded from the consolidation.

402A Holding company accounts to be regarded as group accounts

Where a company, being a parent company, is required by section 399 to prepare group accounts, and that company is itself the subsidiary of another company ("the holding company"), the group accounts of the holding company are deemed to satisfy the requirements of section 399 to prepare group accounts.

403 Group accounts: applicable accounting framework

(1) The group accounts of an overseas company may be prepared in accordance with—
(a) its parent law ("parent law group accounts"),
(b) international accounting standards ("IAS group accounts"), or
(c) section 404 ("overseas companies group accounts").

(2) A company may only prepare parent law group accounts if the content of such accounts includes that required by section 404.

404 Overseas companies group accounts

(1) Overseas companies group accounts must comprise—
(a) a consolidated balance sheet dealing with the state of affairs of the parent company and its subsidiary undertakings, and
(b) a consolidated profit and loss account dealing with the profit or loss of the parent company and its subsidiary undertakings.

(2) The accounts must comply with the provisions of Schedule 5 to the Overseas Companies Regulations as to—
(a) the content of the consolidated balance sheet and consolidated profit and loss account, and
(b) additional information to be provided by way of notes to the accounts.

405 Overseas companies group accounts: subsidiary undertakings included in the consolidation

(1) Where a parent company prepares overseas companies group accounts, all the subsidiary undertakings of the company must be included in the consolidation, subject to the following exceptions.

(2) A subsidiary undertaking may be excluded from the consolidation if its inclusion is not material (but two or more undertakings may be excluded only if they are not material taken together).

(3) A subsidiary undertaking may be excluded from consolidation where—
(a) severe long-term restrictions substantially hinder the exercise of the rights of the parent company over the assets or management of that undertaking, or
(b) the information necessary for the preparation of group accounts cannot be obtained without disproportionate expense or undue delay, or
(c) the interest of the parent company is held exclusively with a view to subsequent resale.

(4) The reference in subsection (3)(a) to the rights of the parent company and the reference in subsection (3)(c) to the interest of the parent company are, respectively, to rights and interests held by or attributed to the company for the purposes of the definition of "parent undertaking" (see section 1162) in the absence of which it would not be the parent company.

406 IAS group accounts, parent law group accounts and overseas company group accounts

(1) Where the directors of a company prepare IAS group accounts they must state in the notes—

(a) that the accounts have been prepared in accordance with international accounting standards,

(b) whether the accounts have been audited, and

(c) if they have been audited—

(i) whether they have been audited in accordance with a set of generally accepted auditing standards, and

(ii) if so, the name of the organisation or other body which issued those standards.

(2) Where the directors of a company prepare parent law group accounts they must state in the notes—

(a) that the accounts have been prepared in accordance with the company's parent law,

(b) the legislation under which the accounts have been prepared,

(c) whether the accounts have been prepared in accordance with a set of generally accepted accounting principles, and if so, the name of the organisation or other body which issued those principles,

(d) whether the accounts have been audited, and

(e) if they have been audited—

(i) whether they have been audited in accordance with a set of generally accepted auditing standards, and

(ii) if so, the name of the organisation or other body which issued those standards.

(3) Where the directors of a company prepare overseas company group accounts they must state in the notes—

(a) that the accounts have been prepared in accordance with section 404,

(b) whether the accounts have been prepared in accordance with a set of generally accepted accounting principles, and if so, the name of the organisation or other body which issued those principles,

(c) whether the accounts have been audited, and

(d) if they have been audited—

(i) whether they have been audited in accordance with a set of generally accepted auditing standards, and

(ii) if so, the name of the organisation or other body which issued those standards.".

NOTES

Words in square brackets inserted by the Occupational Pension Schemes (Master Trusts) Regulations 2018, SI 2018/1030, reg 32, as from 1 October 2018.

[4.254]

39 Approval and signing of accounts

Section 414 of the Companies Act 2006 applies in relation to a company to which this Chapter applies, modified so that it reads as follows—

"414 Approval and signing of accounts

(1) A company's annual accounts must be approved by the board of directors and signed on behalf of the board by a director of the company.

(2) The signature must be on the company's balance sheet.

(3) If annual accounts are approved that do not comply with the requirements of Part 15 as applied (with modifications) by Part 5 of the Overseas Companies Regulations, every director of the company who—

(a) knew that they did not comply, or was reckless as to whether they complied, and

(b) failed to take reasonable steps to secure compliance with those requirements or, as the case may be, to prevent the accounts from being approved,

commits an offence.

(4) A person guilty of an offence under this section is liable—

(a) on conviction on indictment, to a fine;

(b) on summary conviction, to a fine not exceeding the statutory maximum.".

[4.255]

40 Duty to file accounts

Sections 441 and 442 of the Companies Act 2006 apply in relation to a company to which this Chapter applies, modified so that they read as follows—

"441 Duty to file accounts with the registrar

(1) The directors of a company must deliver to the registrar for each financial year a copy of the company's annual accounts and such other reports as are required to be prepared.

(2) The copy of the balance sheet delivered to the registrar under this section must state the name of the person who signed it on behalf of the board.

(3) The directors required by this section to deliver accounts must deliver them in respect of each UK establishment that it has at the end of that year, subject as follows.

(4) Subsection (3) does not require the delivery of accounts in respect of an establishment if—

(a) a return under the Overseas Companies Regulations in respect of that establishment has stated the intention to file accounts in respect of another UK establishment (giving the registered number of that establishment), and

(b) the accounts are delivered in respect of that establishment before the end of the period allowed for doing so.

442 Period allowed for filing accounts

(1) This section specifies the period allowed for directors of a company to comply with their obligation under section 441 to deliver accounts for a financial year to the registrar.

This is referred to in sections 392 and 451 as the "period for filing" those accounts.

(2) The period is thirteen months after the end of the relevant accounting reference period.

This is subject to the following provisions of this section.

(3) If the relevant accounting reference period is the company's first and is a period of more than twelve months, the period allowed is thirteen months from the first anniversary of the company becoming a relevant overseas company.

(4) If the relevant accounting reference period is treated as shortened by virtue of a notice given under section 392, the period is—

(a) that applicable in accordance with the above provisions, or

(b) three months from the date of the notice under that section,

whichever last expires.

(5) If for any special reason the Secretary of State thinks fit he may, on an application made before the expiry of the period otherwise allowed, by notice in writing to a company extend that period by such further period as may be specified in the notice.

(6) In this section "the relevant accounting reference period" means the accounting reference period by reference to which the financial year for the accounts in question was determined.".

[4.256]

41 Penalty for non-compliance

Section 451 of the Companies Act 2006 applies in relation to a company to which this Chapter applies, modified so that it reads as follows—

"451 Default in filing accounts: offences

(1) If the requirements of section 441 (duty to file accounts) are not complied with in relation to a company's accounts for a financial year before the end of the period for filing those accounts, every person who immediately before the end of that period was a director of the company commits an offence.

(2) It is a defence for a person charged with such an offence to prove that he took all reasonable steps for securing that those requirements would be complied with before the end of that period.

(3) It is not a defence to prove that the documents in question were not in fact prepared as required by this Part.

(4) A person guilty of an offence under this section is liable on summary conviction to a fine not exceeding level 5 on the standard scale and, for continued contravention, a daily default fine not exceeding one-tenth of level 5 on the standard scale.".

[4.257]

42 Supplementary provisions

Sections 471, 472 and 474 of the Companies Act 2006 apply in relation to a company to which this Chapter applies, modified so that they read as follows—

"471 Meaning of "annual accounts"

In this Part a company's "annual accounts", in relation to a financial year, means the company's individual accounts for that year (see section 394) or, if applicable, the company's group accounts for that year (see section 399).

472 Notes to the accounts

(1) Information required by this Part to be given in notes to a company's annual accounts may be contained in the accounts or in a separate document annexed to the accounts.

(2) References in this Part to a company's annual accounts, or to a balance sheet or profit and loss account, include notes to the accounts.

474 Minor definitions

In this Part—

"balance sheet" includes a statement of financial position or other equivalent financial statement;

"group" means a parent undertaking and its subsidiary undertakings;

"IAS Regulation" means EC Regulation No 1606/2002 of the European Parliament and of the Council of 19th July 2002 on the application of international accounting standards;

"international accounting standards" means the international accounting standards, within the meaning of Article 2 of the IAS Regulation;

"Overseas Companies Regulations" means the Overseas Companies Regulations 2009 (SI 2009/1801);

"profit and loss account" includes an income statement or other equivalent financial statement;

"relevant overseas company" means a company to which Chapter 3 of Part 5 of the Overseas Companies Regulations applies,

and references to "this Part" are to be read as references to those sections of Part 15 of the Companies Act 2006 as applied (with modification) by the Overseas Companies Regulations and include Schedules 4 and 5 to those Regulations.".

PART 6 DELIVERY OF ACCOUNTING DOCUMENTS: CREDIT OR FINANCIAL INSTITUTIONS

CHAPTER 1 INTRODUCTORY PROVISIONS

[4.258]

43 Application and interpretation of Part

(1) This Part applies to every credit or financial institution that has a branch in the United Kingdom.

(2) In this Part "branch" means a place of business that forms a legally dependent part of the institution and conducts directly all or some of the operations inherent in its business.

CHAPTER 2 INSTITUTIONS REQUIRED TO PREPARE ACCOUNTS UNDER PARENT LAW

[4.259]

44 Application and interpretation of Chapter

(1) This Chapter applies to a credit or financial institution to which this Part applies that—

(a) is required by its parent law to prepare and have audited accounts; . . .

(b) . . .

(2) In relation to an institution to which this Chapter applies—

"accounting documents" in relation to a financial period of the institution, means—

(a) the accounts of the institution for the period, including, if it has one or more subsidiaries, any consolidated accounts of its group,

(b) any annual report of the directors for the period,

(c) any report of the auditors on the accounts mentioned in sub-paragraph (a),

(d) any report of the auditors on the report mentioned in sub-paragraph (b),

and for this purpose "subsidiaries" and "consolidated group accounts" have the meaning given to them by the institution's parent law;

"director", in the case of an institution which does not have directors, means persons occupying equivalent offices;

"disclosure" means public disclosure, except where an institution is not required under its parent law, any enactment having effect for the United Kingdom or its constitution to publicly disclose its accounts, in which case it means disclosure of the accounts to the persons for whose information they have been prepared;

"financial period" means a period for which the institution is required or permitted by its parent law to prepare accounts;

"parent law" means the law of the country in which the institution has its head office; and in the case of an institution which does not have directors, references to "directors" shall include the persons occupying equivalent offices.

NOTES

Para (1): sub-para (b) and the preceding word were revoked by the Accounts and Reports (Amendment) (EU Exit) Regulations 2019, SI 2019/145, reg 6, Sch 3, paras 23, 27, as from IP completion day (as defined in the European Union (Withdrawal Agreement) Act 2020, s 39).

[4.260]

45 Initial filing of copies of accounting documents

A credit or financial institution must within one month of becoming an institution to which this Chapter applies deliver to the registrar copies of the latest accounting documents of the institution prepared in accordance with its parent law to have been disclosed before the end of the period allowed for compliance with this regulation, or, if earlier, the date of compliance with it.

[4.261]

46 Filing of copies of subsequent accounting documents

(1) A credit or financial institution to which this Chapter applies must deliver to the registrar copies of all the accounting documents of the institution prepared in accordance with its parent law that are disclosed on or after the end of the period allowed for compliance with regulation 45, or, if earlier, the date on which it complies with that paragraph.

(2) The period allowed for delivery, in relation to a copy of a document required to be delivered under paragraph (1), is three months from the date on which the document is required to be disclosed in accordance with the institution's parent law.

NOTES

Temporary modification: the Companies etc (Filing Requirements) (Temporary Modifications) Regulations 2020, SI 2020/645, reg 41 provided for the following temporary modification of this regulation (as from 27 June 2020):

(1) The Overseas Companies Regulations 2009 are to have effect subject to the following modifications.

(2) (Modifies reg 34 ante.)

(3) Regulation 46(2) (filing of copies of subsequent accounting documents) is to have effect as if for the reference to "three months" there were substituted a reference to "six months".

(4) This regulation expires at the end of the day on 5th April 2021.

(5) Paragraph (4) does not affect the continued operation of this regulation for the purpose of determining the length of any period that begins before the expiry.

[4.262]

47 Statement of details of parent law and other information

(1) The copies of accounting documents delivered to the registrar under regulation 45 or 46 must be accompanied by a statement containing the following information.

(2) The information required is—

(a) the legislation under which the accounts have been prepared and . . . audited,

(b) whether those accounts have been prepared in accordance with a set of generally accepted accounting principles, and if so, the name of the organisation or other body which issued those principles, [and]

(c) . . .

[(d) whether those accounts have been audited in accordance with a set of generally accepted auditing standards, and if so, the name of the organisation or other body which issued those standards].

(e) . . .

NOTES

Para (2): the words omitted from sub-para (a) were revoked, the word in square brackets in sub-para (b) was inserted, sub-paras (c) and (e) were revoked, and sub-para (d) was substituted, by the Accounts and Reports (Amendment) (EU Exit) Regulations 2019, SI 2019/145, reg 6, Sch 3, paras 23, 28, as from IP completion day (as defined in the European Union (Withdrawal Agreement) Act 2020, s 39).

[4.263]

48 Supplementary provisions as to obligation to file copies of accounting documents

(1) The following provisions apply in relation to the obligations imposed by regulation 45 or 46.

(2) . . .

(3) Where the institution's parent law permits it to discharge an obligation with respect to the disclosure of accounting documents by disclosing documents in a modified form, it may discharge its obligation under regulations 45 and 46 by delivering copies of documents modified as permitted by that law.

NOTES

Para (2): revoked by the Accounts and Reports (Amendment) (EU Exit) Regulations 2019, SI 2019/145, reg 6, Sch 3, paras 23, 29, as from IP completion day (as defined in the European Union (Withdrawal Agreement) Act 2020, s 39).

[4.264]

49 Exception where documents available for inspection

(1) Neither regulation 45 nor regulation 46 requires an institution to deliver copies of accounting documents if at the end of the period allowed for compliance with those regulations—

(a) it is not required by its parent law to register them,

(b) they are made available for inspection at each branch of the institution in the United Kingdom, and

(c) copies of them are available on request at a cost not exceeding the cost of supplying them.

(2) Where—

(a) by virtue of paragraph (1) an institution is not required to deliver documents under regulation 45 or 46, and

(b) any of the conditions specified in paragraph (1) ceases to be met,

the institution must deliver the documents to the registrar for registration within seven days of the condition ceasing to be met.

[4.265]

50 Penalty for non-compliance

(1) If any of the requirements of this Chapter are not complied with before the end of the period allowed for delivery of copies of accounting documents, an offence is committed by every person who immediately before the end of that period was a director of the institution.

(2) It is a defence for a person charged with such an offence to prove that they took all reasonable steps for securing that those requirements would be complied with before the end of that period.

(3) A person guilty of an offence under paragraph (1) is liable on summary conviction to a fine not exceeding level 5 on the standard scale and, for continued contravention, a daily default fine not exceeding [one-tenth of the greater of £5,000 or level 4 on the standard scale].

NOTES

Para (3): words in square brackets substituted (for the original words "one-tenth of level 5 on the standard scale") by the Legal Aid, Sentencing and Punishment of Offenders Act 2012 (Fines on Summary Conviction) Regulations 2015, SI 2015/664, regs 3, 5, Sch 3, Pt 1, para 13(1), (4), as from 12 March 2015, in relation to England and Wales only (except in relation to (a) fines for offences committed before 12 March 2015, (b) the operation of restrictions on fines that may be imposed on a person aged under 18, or (c) fines that may be imposed on a person convicted by a magistrates' court who is to be sentenced as if convicted on indictment).

CHAPTER 3 INSTITUTIONS NOT REQUIRED TO PREPARE ACCOUNTS UNDER PARENT LAW

[4.266]

51 Application of Chapter

This Chapter applies to a credit or financial institution to which this Part applies that is not one to which Chapter 2 of this Part applies.

[4.267]

52 An institution's financial year

Sections 390 to 392 of the Companies Act 2006 apply in relation to an institution to which this Chapter applies, modified so that they read as follows—

"390 An institution's financial year

(1) An institution's financial year is determined as follows.

(2) Its first financial year—

(a) begins with the first day of its first accounting reference period, and

(b) ends with the last day of that period or such other date, not more than seven days before or after the end of that period, as the directors may determine.

(3) Subsequent financial years—

(a) begin with the day immediately following the end of the institution's previous financial year, and

(b) end with the last day of its next accounting reference period or such other date, not more than seven days before or after the end of that period, as the directors may determine.

391 Accounting reference periods and accounting reference date

(1) An institution's accounting reference periods are determined according to its accounting reference date in each calendar year.

(2) The accounting reference date of an institution is the last day of the month in which the anniversary of its becoming a relevant overseas institution falls.

(3) An institution's first accounting reference period is the period of more than six months, but not more than eighteen months, beginning with the date of its becoming a relevant overseas institution and ending with its accounting reference date.

(4) Its subsequent accounting reference periods are successive periods of twelve months beginning immediately after the end of the previous accounting reference period and ending with its accounting reference date.

(5) This section has effect subject to the provisions of section 392.

392 Alteration of accounting reference date

(1) An institution may by notice given to the registrar specify a new accounting reference date having effect in relation to—

- (a) the institution's current accounting reference period and subsequent periods, or
- (b) the institution's previous accounting reference period and subsequent periods.

An institution's "previous accounting reference period" means the one immediately preceding its current accounting reference period.

(2) The notice must state whether the current or previous accounting reference period—

- (a) is to be shortened, so as to come to an end on the first occasion on which the new accounting reference date falls or fell after the beginning of the period, or
- (b) is to be extended, so as to come to an end on the second occasion on which that date falls or fell after the beginning of the period.

(3) A notice under this section may not be given in respect of a previous accounting reference period if the period for filing accounts for the financial year determined by reference to that accounting reference period has already expired.

(4) An accounting reference period may not be extended so as to exceed eighteen months and a notice under this section is ineffective if the current or previous accounting reference period as extended in accordance with the notice would exceed that limit.

This does not apply where the institution is in administration under Part 2 of the Insolvency Act 1986 (c 45) or Part 3 of the Insolvency (Northern Ireland) Order 1989 (SI 1989/2405 (NI 19)).".

[4.268]

53 Duty to prepare accounts

Sections 394 to 397, 399, and 402 to 406 of the Companies Act 2006 apply in relation to an institution to which this Chapter applies, modified so that they read as follows—

"394 Duty to prepare individual accounts

Subject to section 399 (duty to prepare group accounts) the directors of an institution must prepare accounts for the institution for each of its financial years.

Those accounts are referred to as the institution's "individual accounts".

395 Individual accounts: applicable accounting framework

(1) An institution's annual accounts may be prepared in accordance with—

- (a) its parent law ("parent law individual accounts"),
- (b) international accounting standards ("IAS individual accounts"), or
- (c) section 396 ("overseas institutions individual accounts").

(2) An institution may only prepare parent law individual accounts if the content of such accounts includes that required by section 396.

396 Overseas institutions individual accounts

(1) Overseas institutions individual accounts must comprise—

- (a) a balance sheet as at the last day of the financial year, and
- (b) a profit and loss account.

(2) The accounts must comply with the provisions in Schedule 6 to the Overseas Companies Regulations as to—

- (a) the content of the balance sheet and the profit and loss account, and
- (b) additional information to be provided by way of notes to the accounts.

397 IAS individual accounts, parent law individual accounts and overseas institutions individual accounts

(1) Where the directors of an institution prepare IAS individual accounts they must state in the notes—

- (a) that the accounts have been prepared in accordance with international accounting standards,
- (b) whether the accounts have been audited, and
- (c) if they have been audited—
  - (i) whether they have been audited in accordance with a set of generally accepted auditing standards, and
  - (ii) if so, the name of the organisation or other body which issued those standards.

(2) Where the directors of an institution prepare parent law individual accounts they must state in the notes—

- (a) that the accounts have been prepared in accordance with the institution's parent law,
- (b) the legislation under which the accounts have been prepared,

(c) whether the accounts have been prepared in accordance with a set of generally accepted accounting principles, and if so, the name of the organisation or other body which issued those principles,

(d) whether the accounts have been audited, and

(e) if they have been audited—

(i) whether they have been audited in accordance with a set of generally accepted auditing standards, and

(ii) if so, the name of the organisation or other body which issued those standards.

(3) Where the directors of an institution prepare overseas institutions individual accounts they must state in the notes—

(a) that the accounts have been prepared in accordance with section 396,

(b) whether the accounts have been prepared in accordance with a set of generally accepted accounting principles, and if so, the name of the organisation or other body which issued those principles,

(c) whether the accounts have been audited, and

(d) if they have been audited—

(i) whether they have been audited in accordance with a set of generally accepted auditing standards, and

(ii) if so, the name of the organisation or other body which issued those standards.

399 Duty to prepare group accounts

If at the end of a financial year an institution is a parent institution the directors must, instead of preparing individual accounts for the year, prepare group accounts for the year.

402 Exemption from duty to prepare group accounts

A parent institution is exempt from the requirement to prepare group accounts where—

(a) it has prepared accounts under section 395(1)(a) and its parent law does not require consolidated accounts;

(b) it has prepared accounts under section 395(1)(b) and in accordance with the international accounting standards it is not required to prepare consolidated accounts;

(c) it has prepared accounts under section 395(1)(c) and if under section 405 all of the institution's subsidiary undertakings could be excluded from consolidation.

402A Holding institution accounts to be regarded as group accounts

Where an institution, being a parent institution, is required by section 399 to prepare group accounts, and that institution is itself the subsidiary of another institution ("the holding institution"), the group accounts of the holding institution may be deemed to satisfy the requirements of section 399 to prepare group accounts.

403 Group accounts: applicable accounting framework

(1) The group accounts of an institution may be prepared in accordance with—

(a) its parent law ("parent law group accounts"),

(b) international accounting standards ("IAS group accounts"), or

(c) section 404 ("overseas institutions group accounts").

(2) An institution may only prepare parent law group accounts if the content of such accounts includes that required by section 404.

404 Overseas institutions group accounts

(1) Overseas institutions group accounts must comprise—

(a) a consolidated balance sheet dealing with the state of affairs of the parent institution and its subsidiary undertakings, and

(b) a consolidated profit and loss account dealing with the profit or loss of the parent institution and its subsidiary undertakings.

(2) The accounts must comply with the provisions of Schedule 7 to the Overseas Companies Regulations as to—

(a) the content of the consolidated balance sheet and consolidated profit and loss account, and

(b) additional information to be provided by way of notes to the accounts.

405 Overseas institutions group accounts: subsidiary undertakings included in the consolidation

(1) Where a parent institution prepares overseas institutions group accounts, all the subsidiary undertakings of the institution must be included in the consolidation, subject to the following exceptions.

(2) A subsidiary undertaking may be excluded from the consolidation if its inclusion is not material (but two or more undertakings may be excluded only if they are not material taken together).

(3) A subsidiary undertaking may be excluded from consolidation where—

(a) severe long-term restrictions substantially hinder the exercise of the rights of the parent institution over the assets or management of that undertaking, or

(b) the information necessary for the preparation of group accounts cannot be obtained without disproportionate expense or undue delay, or

(c) the interest of the parent institution is held exclusively with a view to subsequent resale.

(4) The reference in subsection (3)(a) to the rights of the parent institution and the reference in subsection (3)(c) to the interest of the parent institution are, respectively, to rights and interests held by or attributed to the institution for the purposes of the definition of "parent undertaking" (see section 1162) in the absence of which it would not be the parent institution.

406 IAS group accounts, parent law group accounts and overseas institutions group accounts

(1) Where the directors of an institution prepare IAS group accounts they must state in the notes—

(a) that the accounts have been prepared in accordance with international accounting standards,

(b) whether the accounts have been audited, and
(c) if they have been audited—
(i) whether they have been audited in accordance with a set of generally accepted auditing standards, and
(ii) if so, the name of the organisation or other body which issued those standards.

(2) Where the directors of an institution prepare parent law group accounts they must state in the notes—
(a) that the accounts have been prepared in accordance with the institution's parent law,
(b) the legislation under which the accounts have been prepared,
(c) whether the accounts have been prepared in accordance with a set of generally accepted accounting principles, and if so, the name of the organisation or other body which issued those principles,
(d) whether the accounts have been audited, and
(e) if they have been audited—
(i) whether they have been audited in accordance with a set of generally accepted auditing standards, and
(ii) if so, the name of the organisation or other body which issued those standards.

(3) Where the directors of an institution prepare overseas institutions group accounts they must state in the notes—
(a) that the accounts have been prepared in accordance with section 404,
(b) whether the accounts have been prepared in accordance with a set of generally accepted accounting principles, and if so, the name of the organisation or other body which issued those principles,
(c) whether the accounts have been audited, and
(d) if they have been audited—
(i) whether they have been audited in accordance with a set of generally accepted auditing standards, and
(ii) if so, the name of the organisation or other body which issued those standards.".

[4.269]
54 Approval and signing of accounts

Section 414 of the Companies Act 2006 applies in relation to an institution to which this Chapter applies, modified so that it reads as follows—

"414 Approval and signing of accounts

(1) An institution's annual accounts must be approved by the board of directors and signed on behalf of the board by a director of the institution.
(2) The signature must be on the institution's balance sheet.
(3) If annual accounts are approved that do not comply with the requirements of Part 15 as applied (with modifications) by Part 6 of the Overseas Companies Regulations, every director of the institution who—
(a) knew that they did not comply, or was reckless as to whether they complied, and
(b) failed to take reasonable steps to secure compliance with those requirements or, as the case may be, to prevent the accounts from being approved,

commits an offence.
(4) A person guilty of an offence under this section is liable—
(a) on conviction on indictment, to a fine;
(b) on summary conviction, to a fine not exceeding the statutory maximum.".

[4.270]
55 Duty to file accounts

Sections 441 and 442 of the Companies Act 2006 apply in relation to an institution to which this Chapter applies, modified so that they read as follows—

"441 Duty to file accounts with the registrar

(1) The directors of an institution must deliver to the registrar for each financial year a copy of the institution's annual accounts and such other reports as are required to be prepared.
(2) The copy of the balance sheet delivered to the registrar under this section must state the name of the person who signed it on behalf of the board.

442 Period allowed for filing accounts

(1) This section specifies the period allowed for directors of an institution to comply with their obligation under section 441 to deliver accounts for a financial year to the registrar.
This is referred to in sections 392 and 451 as the "period for filing" those accounts.
(2) The period is thirteen months after the end of the relevant accounting reference period.
This is subject to the following provisions of this section.
(3) If the relevant accounting reference period is the institution's first and is a period of more than twelve months, the period allowed is thirteen months from the first anniversary of the institution becoming a relevant overseas institution.
(4) If the relevant accounting reference period is treated as shortened by virtue of a notice given under section 392, the period is—
(a) that applicable in accordance with the above provisions, or
(b) three months from the date of the notice under that section,

whichever last expires.

(5) If for any special reason the Secretary of State thinks fit he may, on an application made before the expiry of the period otherwise allowed, by notice in writing to an institution extend that period by such further period as may be specified in the notice.

(6) In this section "the relevant accounting reference period" means the accounting reference period by reference to which the financial year for the accounts in question was determined.".

[4.271]

56 Penalty for non-compliance

Section 451 of the Companies Act 2006 applies in relation to an institution to which this Chapter applies, modified so that it reads as follows—

"451 Default in filing accounts: offences

(1) If the requirements of section 441 (duty to file accounts) are not complied with in relation to an institution's accounts for a financial year before the end of the period for filing those accounts, every person who immediately before the end of that period was a director of the institution commits an offence.

(2) It is a defence for a person charged with such an offence to prove that he took all reasonable steps for securing that those requirements would be complied with before the end of that period.

(3) It is not a defence to prove that the documents in question were not in fact prepared as required by this Part.

(4) A person guilty of an offence under this section is liable on summary conviction to a fine not exceeding level 5 on the standard scale and, for continued contravention, a daily default fine not exceeding one-tenth of level 5 on the standard scale.".

[4.272]

57 Supplementary provisions

Sections 471, 472 and 474 of the Companies Act 2006 apply in relation to an institution to which this Chapter applies, modified so that they read as follows—

"471 Meaning of "annual accounts"

In this Part an institution's "annual accounts", in relation to a financial year, means the institution's individual accounts for that year (see section 394) or, if applicable, the institution's group accounts for that year (see section 399).

472 Notes to the accounts

(1) Information required by this Part to be given in notes to an institution's annual accounts may be contained in the accounts or in a separate document annexed to the accounts.

(2) References in this Part to an institution's annual accounts, or to a balance sheet or profit and loss account, include notes to the accounts.

474 Minor definitions

In this Part—

"balance sheet" includes a statement of financial position or other equivalent financial statement;

"directors", in the case of an institution which does not have directors, means persons occupying equivalent offices;

"group" means a parent institution and its subsidiary undertakings;

"IAS Regulation" means EC Regulation No 1606/2002 of the European Parliament and of the Council of 19th July 2002 on the application of international accounting standards;

"international accounting standards" means the international accounting standards, within the meaning of Article 2 of the IAS Regulation;

"Overseas Companies Regulations" means the Overseas Companies Regulations 2009 (SI 2009/1801);

"parent institution" means an institution that is a parent undertaking (see section 1162 of and Schedule 7 to the Companies Act 2006);

"profit and loss account" includes an income statement or other equivalent financial statement;

"relevant overseas institution" means an institution to which Chapter 3 of Part 6 of the Overseas Companies Regulations applies;

and references to "this Part" are references to those sections of Part 15 of the Companies Act 2006 as applied (with or without modification) by the Overseas Companies Regulations and include Schedules 6 and 7 to those Regulations.".

PART 7 TRADING DISCLOSURES

[4.273]

58 Application and interpretation of Part

(1) This Part applies to an overseas company that carries on business in the United Kingdom.

(2) In this Part—

(a) a reference to any type of document is a reference to a document of that type in hard copy, electronic or any other form;

(b) in relation to a company, a reference to "its websites" includes a reference to any part of a website relating to that company which that company has caused or authorised to appear.

[4.274]

59 Legibility of displays and disclosures

Any display or disclosure of information required by this Part must be in characters that can be read with the naked eye.

[4.275]
60 Requirement to display name etc at business location

(1) A company to which this Part applies must display the company's name and country of incorporation—
(a) at every location in the United Kingdom at which it carries on business, and
(b) at the service address of every person resident in the United Kingdom authorised to accept service of documents on behalf of the company.

(2) Paragraph (1)(a) does not apply to a location—
(a) that is primarily used for living accommodation;
(b) at which business is carried on by a company of which every director or permanent representative who is an individual is entitled to higher protection from disclosure of their residential address; or
(c) at which business is carried on by a company in respect of which a liquidator, administrator or administrative receiver has been appointed if the location is also a place of business of the liquidator, administrator or administrative receiver.

(3) The reference in paragraph (2)(b) to an individual who is entitled to higher protection from disclosure of their residential address is to an individual in respect of whom the registrar is prohibited from disclosing protected information to a credit reference agency.

[4.276]
61 Manner of display of name etc

(1) The following requirements apply where a company is required by regulation 60 to display its name and country of incorporation at a location in the United Kingdom.

(2) A company must display its name and country of incorporation in such a way so that they may be easily seen by any visitor to the location.

(3) The company's name and country of incorporation must be displayed continuously.

But, if the place of business is shared by six or more companies, this requirement is treated as met if the company's name and country of incorporation are displayed for at least fifteen continuous seconds at least once in every three minutes.

[4.277]
62 Company's name to appear on communications

A company to which this Part applies must state the company's name on all—
(a) its business letters, notices and other official publications;
(b) its bills of exchange, promissory notes, endorsements and order forms;
(c) cheques purporting to be signed by or on behalf of the company;
(d) orders for money, goods or services purporting to be signed by or on behalf of the company;
(e) its bills of parcels, invoices and other demands for payments, receipts, and letters of credit;
(f) its applications for licences to carry on a trade or activity;
(g) other forms of its business correspondence and documentation; and
(h) its websites,

that are used in carrying on the activities of its business in the United Kingdom.

[4.278]
63 Particulars to appear in business letters, order forms and websites

(1) An overseas company that has a UK establishment in respect of which it has registered particulars under Part 2 must state the particulars required by [paragraph (4)] on all—
(a) its business letters,
(b) its order forms, and
(c) its websites,

that are used in carrying on the activities of a UK establishment of the company.

(4) The particulars are—
(a) the company's country of incorporation,
(b) the identity of the registry, if any, in which the company is registered in its country of incorporation,
(c) if applicable, the number with which the company is registered in that registry,
(d) the location of its head office,
(e) the legal form of the company,
(f) if the liability of the members of the company is limited, the fact that it is a limited company, and
(g) if applicable, the fact that the company is being wound up, or is subject to other insolvency proceedings or an arrangement or composition or any analogous proceedings.

(5) If, in the case of an overseas company . . . having a share capital, there is reference to the amount of share capital on—
(a) its business letters,
(b) its order forms, or
(c) its websites,

the reference must be to paid up share capital.

(6) Paragraph (4)(g) does not apply to a company required to make disclosures under—
(a) section 39(1) or 188(a) of, or paragraph 16(1) of Schedule A1 or paragraph 45 of Schedule B1 to, the Insolvency Act 1986, or
(b) Article 49(1) or 159(1) of, or paragraph 27(1) of Schedule A1 or paragraph 46 of Schedule B1 to, the Insolvency (Northern Ireland) Order 1989.

NOTES

The words in square brackets in para (1) were substituted, and paras (2), (3) and the words omitted from para (5) were revoked, by the Companies, Limited Liability Partnerships and Partnerships (Amendment etc) (EU Exit) Regulations 2019,

SI 2019/348, reg 7, Sch 2, paras 3, 6, as from IP completion day (as defined in the European Union (Withdrawal Agreement) Act 2020, s 39) (for transitional provisions see Sch 4, para 4 to the 2019 Regulations at **[12.106]**).

[4.279]

64 Disclosure of names of directors

(1) Where a business letter of a company to which this Part applies includes the name of any director of the company, other than in the text or as a signatory, the letter must disclose the name of every director of the company.

(2) In the case of a body corporate, or a firm that is a legal person under the law by which it is governed, its corporate or firm name must be given.

[4.280]

65 Disclosures relating to address for service

(1) A company shall disclose the address of any person resident in the United Kingdom authorised to accept service of documents on behalf of the company to any person it deals with in the course of business who makes a written request to the company for that information.

(2) The company shall send a written response to that person within five working days of the receipt of that request.

[4.281]

66 Civil consequences of failure to make a required disclosure

(1) This regulation applies to any legal proceedings brought by a company to which this Part applies to enforce a right arising out of a contract made in the course of a business in respect of which, at the time the contract was made, there was a failure to comply with the requirements of this Part.

(2) The proceedings must be dismissed if it is shown that the defendant (in Scotland, the defender)—

(a) has a claim against the claimant (pursuer) arising out of the contract and has been unable to pursue that claim by reason of the latter's failure to comply with the requirements of this Part, or

(b) has suffered some financial loss in connection with the contract by reason of the claimant's (pursuer's) failure to comply with those requirements,

unless the court before which the proceedings are brought is satisfied that it is just and equitable to permit the proceedings to continue.

(3) This regulation does not affect the right of any person to enforce such rights as the person may have against another in any proceedings brought by the other.

[4.282]

67 Penalty for non-compliance

(1) Where a company fails, without reasonable excuse, to comply with any requirement of this Part, an offence is committed by—

(a) the company, and

(b) every officer of the company who is in default.

(2) A person guilty of an offence under paragraph (1) is liable on summary conviction to—

(a) a fine not exceeding level 3 on the standard scale, and

(b) for continued contravention, a daily default fine not exceeding one-tenth of level 3 on the standard scale.

(3) For the purposes of this regulation a shadow director is to be treated as an officer of the company.

PART 8 RETURNS IN CASE OF WINDING UP ETC

[4.283]

68 Application of Part

This Part applies to an overseas company that has one or more UK establishments.

[4.284]

69 Return in case of winding up

(1) Where a company to which this Part applies is being wound up, it must deliver to the registrar a return containing the following particulars—

(a) the company's name;

(b) whether the company is being wound up by an order of a court and if so, the name and address of the court and the date of the order;

(c) if the company is not being so wound up, as a result of what action the winding up has commenced;

(d) whether the winding up has been instigated by—

(i) the company's members,

(ii) the company's creditors, or

(iii) some other person (stating the person's identity); and

(e) the date on which the winding up became or will become effective.

(2) The return must be delivered not later than—

(a) if the winding up began before the company had a UK establishment, one month after the company first opens a UK establishment;

(b) if the winding up begins when the company has a UK establishment, 14 days after the date on which the winding up begins.

(3) Where the company has more than one UK establishment the obligation to deliver a return under this regulation applies in respect of each of them, but a return giving the registered numbers of more than one UK establishment is regarded as a return in respect of each establishment whose number is given.

(4) No return is required under this regulation in respect of winding up under the Insolvency Act 1986 or the Insolvency (Northern Ireland) Order 1989.

[4.285]

70 Returns to be made by liquidator

(1) A person appointed to be the liquidator of a company to which this Part applies must deliver to the registrar a return containing the following particulars—

(a) their name and address,

(b) date of the appointment, and

(c) a description of such of the person's powers, if any, as are derived otherwise than from the general law or the company's constitution.

(2) The period allowed for delivery of the return required by paragraph (1) is—

(a) if the liquidator was appointed before the company had a UK establishment (and continues in office at the date of the opening), one month after the company first opens a UK establishment;

(b) if the liquidator is appointed when the company has a UK establishment, 14 days after the date of the appointment.

(3) The liquidator of a company to which this Part applies must—

(a) on the termination of the winding up of the company, deliver a return to the registrar stating the name of the company and the date on which the winding up terminated;

(b) on the company ceasing to be registered in circumstances where ceasing to be registered is an event of legal significance, deliver a return to the registrar stating the name of the company and the date on which it ceased to be registered.

(4) The period allowed for delivery of the return required by paragraph (3)(a) or (b) is 14 days from the date of the event.

(5) Where the company has more than one UK establishment the obligation to deliver a return under this regulation applies in respect of each of them, but a return giving the registered numbers of more than one UK establishment is regarded as a return in respect of each establishment whose number is given.

(6) No return is required under this regulation in respect of a liquidator appointed under the Insolvency Act 1986 or the Insolvency (Northern Ireland) Order 1989.

[4.286]

71 Return in case of insolvency proceedings etc (other than winding up)

(1) Where a company to which this Part applies becomes subject to insolvency proceedings or an arrangement or composition or any analogous proceedings (other than proceedings for winding up of the company), it must deliver to the registrar a return containing the following particulars—

(a) the company's name;

(b) whether the proceedings are by an order of a court and if so, the name and address of the court and the date of the order;

(c) if the proceedings are not by an order of a court, as a result of what action the proceedings have been commenced;

(d) whether the proceedings have been commenced by—

(i) the company's members,

(ii) the company's creditors, or

(iii) some other person (giving the person's identity);

(e) the date on which the proceedings became or will become effective.

(2) The period allowed for delivery of the return required by paragraph (1) is—

(a) if the company became subject to the proceedings before it had a UK establishment, one month after the company first opens a UK establishment;

(b) if the company becomes subject to the proceedings when it has a UK establishment, 14 days from the date on which it becomes subject to the proceedings.

(3) Where a company to which this Part applies ceases to be subject to any of the proceedings referred to in paragraph (1) it must deliver to the registrar a return stating—

(a) the company's name, and

(b) the date on which it ceased to be subject to the proceedings.

(4) The period allowed for delivery of the return required by paragraph (3) is 14 days from the date on which it ceases to be subject to the proceedings.

(5) Where the company has more than one UK establishment the obligation to deliver a return under this regulation applies in respect of each of them, but a return giving the registered numbers of more than one UK establishment is regarded as a return in respect of each establishment whose number is given.

(6) No return is required under this regulation in respect of—

(a) a company's becoming or ceasing to be subject to a voluntary arrangement under Part 1 of the Insolvency Act 1986 or Part 2 of the Insolvency (Northern Ireland) Order 1989, or

(b) a company's entering administration under Part 2 and Schedule B1 of that Act or becoming or ceasing to be subject to an administration order under Part 3 of that Order.

[4.287]

72 Penalties for non-compliance

(1) If a company fails to comply with regulation 69(1) or 71(1) or (3) within the period allowed for compliance, an offence is committed by—

(a) the company, and

(b) every person who immediately before the end of that period was a director of the company.

(2) A liquidator who fails to comply with regulation 70(1) or (3)(a) or (b) within the period allowed for compliance commits an offence.

(3) A person who takes all reasonable steps to secure compliance with the requirements concerned does not commit an offence under this regulation.

(4) A person guilty of an offence under this regulation is liable—

(a) on conviction on indictment, to a fine;

(b) on summary conviction to a fine not exceeding the statutory maximum and, for continued contravention, a daily default fine not exceeding [one-fiftieth of the greater of £5,000 or the amount corresponding to level 4 on the standard scale for summary offences].

NOTES

Para (4): words in square brackets substituted (for the original words "one-fiftieth of the statutory maximum") by the Legal Aid, Sentencing and Punishment of Offenders Act 2012 (Fines on Summary Conviction) Regulations 2015, SI 2015/664, regs 3, 5, Sch 3, Pt 1, para 13(1), (5), as from 12 March 2015, in relation to England and Wales only (except in relation to (a) fines for offences committed before 12 March 2015, (b) the operation of restrictions on fines that may be imposed on a person aged under 18, or (c) fines that may be imposed on a person convicted by a magistrates' court who is to be sentenced as if convicted on indictment).

[4.288]

73 Notice of appointment of judicial factor

(1) Notice must be given to the registrar of the appointment in relation to a company to which this Part applies of a judicial factor (in Scotland).

(2) The notice must be given by the judicial factor.

(3) The notice must specify an address at which service of documents (including legal process) may be effected on the judicial factor.

(4) Notice of a change in the address for service may be given to the registrar by the judicial factor.

(5) A judicial factor who has notified the registrar of the appointment must also notify the registrar of the termination of the appointment.

[4.289]

74 Offence of failure to give notice

(1) A judicial factor who fails to give notice of the appointment in accordance with regulation 73 within the period of 14 days after the appointment commits an offence.

(2) A person guilty of an offence under this regulation is liable on summary conviction to—

(a) a fine not exceeding level 5 on the standard scale, and

(b) for continued contravention, a daily default fine not exceeding [one-tenth of the greater of £5,000 or level 4 on the standard scale].

NOTES

Para (2): words in square brackets substituted (for the original words "one-tenth of level 5 on the standard scale") by the Legal Aid, Sentencing and Punishment of Offenders Act 2012 (Fines on Summary Conviction) Regulations 2015, SI 2015/664, regs 3, 5, Sch 3, Pt 1, para 13(1), (6), as from 12 March 2015, in relation to England and Wales only (except in relation to (a) fines for offences committed before 12 March 2015, (b) the operation of restrictions on fines that may be imposed on a person aged under 18, or (c) fines that may be imposed on a person convicted by a magistrates' court who is to be sentenced as if convicted on indictment).

PART 9 MISCELLANEOUS PROVISIONS

[4.290]

75 Service of documents on director, secretary or permanent representative

The positions specified for the purposes of section 1140(2)(b) of the Companies Act 2006 (overseas companies that have registered particulars: persons on whom document may be served at registered address) are—

(a) director,

(b) secretary, and

(c) permanent representative.

[4.291]

76 [Enhanced disclosure documents]

The particulars, returns and other documents specified for the purposes of section 1078(5) of the Companies Act 2006 (overseas companies: [enhanced disclosure documents]) are—

(a) any return or document delivered under Part 2 (initial registration of particulars);

(b) any return or document delivered under Part 3 (alterations in registered particulars);

(c) any document delivered under Part 5 (delivery of accounting documents: general);

(d) any document delivered under Part 6 (delivery of accounting documents: credit or financial institutions);

(e) any return delivered under regulation 69 (return in case of winding up) or 70 (returns to be made by liquidator);

(f) any notice under regulation 77 (duty to give notice of closure of UK establishment).

NOTES

Words in square brackets substituted by the Companies, Limited Liability Partnerships and Partnerships (Amendment etc) (EU Exit) Regulations 2019, SI 2019/348, reg 7, Sch 2, paras 3, 7, as from IP completion day (as defined in the European Union (Withdrawal Agreement) Act 2020, s 39).

[4.292]

77 Duty to give notice of closure of UK establishment

(1) If an overseas company closes a UK establishment in respect of which it has registered particulars under Part 2, it must forthwith give notice of that fact to the registrar.

(2) From the date on which notice is given under paragraph (1) the company is no longer obliged to deliver documents to the registrar in respect of that establishment.

(3) If a company fails to comply with paragraph (1) an offence is committed by—
- (a) the company, and
- (b) every officer or agent of the company who knowingly and willingly authorises or permits the default.

(4) A person guilty of an offence under this regulation is liable on summary conviction to—
- (a) a fine not exceeding level 3 on the standard scale, and
- (b) for continued contravention, a daily default fine not exceeding one-tenth of level 3 on the standard scale.

PART 10 SUPPLEMENTARY PROVISIONS

[4.293]
78 Documents that may be drawn up and delivered in a language other than English

(1) The following documents are specified for the purposes of section 1105(2)(d) of the Companies Act 2006 as documents that may be drawn up and delivered to the registrar in a language other than English, but which must, when delivered to the registrar, be accompanied by a certified translation into English.

(2) The documents are—
- (a) a certified copy of the constitution required to be delivered under regulation 8, 14 or 15 of these Regulations;
- (b) copies of accounting documents required to be delivered under regulation 9, 32, 45 or 46;
- (c) copies of accounts required to be delivered under section 441 as modified by regulations 40 and 55.

[4.294]
79 Revocations

The following Regulations are revoked—
- (a) the Oversea Companies and Credit and Financial Institutions (Branch Disclosure) Regulations 1992,
- (b) the Part XXIII Companies and Credit and Financial Institutions (Branch Disclosure) Regulations (Northern Ireland) 1993.

[4.295]
80 Transitional provisions and savings

Schedule 8 contains transitional provisions and savings.

SCHEDULES
SCHEDULE 1
SPECIFIED PUBLIC AUTHORITIES

Regulation 18

[4.296]
The Secretary of State;

any Northern Ireland Department;

the Scottish Ministers;

the Welsh Ministers;

the Treasury;

the Commissioners for Her Majesty's Revenue and Customs;

the Bank of England [(including the Bank in its capacity as the Prudential Regulation Authority)];

the Director of Public Prosecutions;

the Director of Public Prosecutions for Northern Ireland;

the Serious Fraud Office;

the Secret Intelligence Service;

the Security Service;

the Government Communications Headquarters;

[the Financial Conduct Authority;

. . .]

. . .

the Pensions Regulator;

the Panel on Takeovers and Mergers;

the Regulator of Community Interest Companies;

. . .

[the Competition and Markets Authority;]

the Office of the Information Commissioner;

the Charity Commission;

the Charity Commission for Northern Ireland;

the Office of the Scottish Charity Regulator;

[the Office of Communications];

the Gas and Electricity Markets Authority;

the Northern Ireland Authority for Utility Regulation;

the Gambling Commission;

the Serious Organised Crime Agency;

the Health and Safety Executive;

the Health and Safety Executive for Northern Ireland;

the Food Standards Agency;

[the Gangmasters Labour and Abuse Authority;]

the Security Industry Authority;

a local authority within the meaning of section 54(2) of the Companies Act 2006;

an official receiver appointed under section 399 of the Insolvency Act 1986 (appointment, etc, of official receivers);

the Official Receiver for Northern Ireland;

the Crown Office and Procurator Fiscal Services;

a person acting as an insolvency practitioner within the meaning of section 388 of the Insolvency Act 1986 (meaning of "act as an insolvency practitioner") or Article 3 of the Insolvency (Northern Ireland) Order 1989 ("act as an insolvency practitioner");

an inspector appointed under Part 14 of the Companies Act 1985 (investigation of companies and their affairs: requisition of documents) or Part 15 of the Companies (Northern Ireland) Order 1986 or a person appointed under regulation 30 of the Open-Ended Investment Companies Regulations 2001 (power to investigate) or regulation 22 of the Open-Ended Investment Companies Regulations (Northern Ireland) 2004;

any person authorised to exercise powers under section 447 of the Companies Act 1985 (power to require documents and information), or section 84 of the Companies Act 1989 (exercise of powers by officers, etc) or Article 440 of the Companies (Northern Ireland) Order;

[any person exercising functions conferred by Part 6 of the Financial Services and Markets Act 2000 (official listing);]

a person appointed to make a report under section 166 [or section 166A] (reports by skilled persons) of the Financial Services and Markets Act 2000;

a person appointed to conduct an investigation under section 167 (appointment of persons to carry out general investigations) or 168(3) or (5) (appointment of persons to carry out investigations in particular cases) of the Financial Services and Markets Act 2000;

an inspector appointed under section 284 (power to investigate) of the Financial Services and Markets Act 2000;

an overseas regulatory authority within the meaning of section 82 of the Companies Act 1989 (request for assistance by overseas regulatory authority);

a police force;

[the Scottish Housing Regulator];

[the Office for Nuclear Regulation];

[the lead enforcement authority (as defined in section 33(1) of the Estate Agents Act 1979) exercising functions under the Estate Agents Act 1979].

NOTES

Words in square brackets in the entry "Bank of England" inserted, and entry "the Prudential Regulation Authority" (omitted) revoked, by the Bank of England and Financial Services (Consequential Amendments) Regulations 2017, SI 2017/80, reg 2, Schedule, Pt 2, para 35, as from 1 March 2017.

Entry "the Registrar of Credit Unions for Northern Ireland" (omitted) revoked by the Financial Services Act 2012 (Mutual Societies) Order 2013, SI 2018/323, art 2(c), Sch 4, Pt 2, para 10, as from 6 April 2018.

Entry "the Competition and Markets Authority" substituted (for the original entry "the Office of Fair Trading"), and entry "the Competition Commission" (omitted) revoked, by the Enterprise and Regulatory Reform Act 2013 (Competition) (Consequential, Transitional and Saving Provisions) (No 2) Order 2014, SI 2014/549, art 2, Schedule, Pt 2, para 39, as from 1 April 2014.

Entry "the Gangmasters Labour and Abuse Authority" substituted (for the original entry "the Gangmasters Licensing Authority") by the Immigration Act 2016 (Consequential Amendments) Regulations 2016, SI 2016/655, reg 2, Schedule, Pt 2, para 5, as from 12 July 2016.

Entry "the Office of Communications" substituted (for the original entry "the Postal Services Commission") by the Postal Services Act 2011 (Consequential Modifications and Amendments) Order 2011, SI 2011/2085, art 5(1), Sch 1, para 82, as from 1 October 2011.

Entry "the National Crime Agency" substituted (for the original entry "the Serious Organised Crime Agency") by virtue of the Crime and Courts Act 2013, s 15(3), Sch 8, Pt 4, para 190, as from 7 October 2013.

Entry "the Scottish Housing Regulator" inserted by the Housing (Scotland) Act 2010 (Consequential Provisions and Modifications) Order 2012, SI 2012/700, art 4, Schedule, Pt 2, para 21, as from 1 April 2012.

Entry "the Office for Nuclear Regulation" inserted by the Energy Act 2013 (Office for Nuclear Regulation) (Consequential Amendments, Transitional Provisions and Savings) Order 2014, SI 2014/469, art 6(2), Sch 3, Pt 5, para 196, as from 1 April 2014.

Entry beginning with the words "the lead enforcement authority (as defined in section 33(1) of the Estate Agents Act 1979)" inserted by the Public Bodies (Abolition of the National Consumer Council and Transfer of the Office of Fair Trading's Functions in relation to Estate Agents etc) Order 2014, SI 2014/631, art 5(3), Sch 2, para 12, as from 31 March 2014.

All other words in square brackets in this Schedule were substituted by the Financial Services Act 2012 (Consequential Amendments and Transitional Provisions) Order 2013, SI 2013/472, art 3, Sch 2, para 173(a), as from 1 April 2013.

SCHEDULE 2
CONDITIONS FOR PERMITTED DISCLOSURE

Regulations 23 and 24

PART 1 DISCLOSURE TO SPECIFIED PUBLIC AUTHORITY

[4.297]

1. Paragraphs 2 and 3 set out the conditions specified for the disclosure of protected information by the registrar to a specified public authority.

2. The specified public authority has delivered to the registrar a statement that it intends to use the protected information only for the purpose of facilitating the carrying out by that specified public authority of a public function ("the permitted purpose").

3. Subject to paragraph 4, the specified public authority ("the authority") has delivered to the registrar a statement that it will, where it supplies a copy of the protected information to a processor for the purpose of processing the information for use in respect of the permitted purpose—

(a) ensure that the processor is one who carries on business [in the United Kingdom or] in the European Economic Area;

(b) require that the information is not transmitted outside the [area comprising the United Kingdom and the European Economic Area] by the processor; and

(c) require that the processor does not disclose the information except to the authority or an employee of the authority.

4. Paragraph 3 does not apply where the specified public authority is the Secret Intelligence Service, Security Service or Government Communications Headquarters.

NOTES

Para 3: the words in square brackets in sub-para (a) were inserted, and the words in square brackets in sub-para (b) were substituted, by the Companies, Limited Liability Partnerships and Partnerships (Amendment etc) (EU Exit) Regulations 2019, SI 2019/348, reg 7, Sch 2, paras 3, 8(a), as from IP completion day (as defined in the European Union (Withdrawal Agreement) Act 2020, s 39) (for transitional provisions see Sch 4, para 5 to the 2019 Regulations at **[12.106]**).

PART 2 DISCLOSURE TO CREDIT REFERENCE AGENCY

[4.298]

5. Paragraphs 6 to 10 set out the conditions specified for the disclosure of protected information by the registrar to a credit reference agency.

6. [(1)] The credit reference agency—

(a) is carrying on in the United Kingdom . . . a business comprising the furnishing of information relevant to the financial standing of individuals, being information collected by the agency for that purpose;

(b) maintains appropriate procedures—

(i) to ensure that an independent person can investigate and audit the measures maintained by the agency for the purposes of ensuring the security of any protected information disclosed to that agency; and

[(ii) for the purposes of ensuring that it complies with its [obligations under the data protection legislation (as defined in section 3 of the Data Protection Act 2018)];]

(c) has not been found guilty of an offence under—

(i) section 1112 (general false statement offence) of the Companies Act 2006 or section 2 of the Fraud Act 2006 (fraud by false representation); . . .

(ii) section 47 (failure to comply with enforcement notice) of the Data Protection Act 1998 in circumstances where it has used the protected information for purposes other than those described in sub-paragraphs (a) to (e) of paragraph 7 below[; or

(iii) section 144 of the Data Protection Act 2018 (false statements made in response to an information notice) or section 148 of that Act (destroying or falsifying information and documents etc);]

[(d) has not been given a penalty notice under section 155 of the Data Protection Act 2018 in circumstances described in paragraph (c)(ii), other than a penalty notice that has been cancelled.]

[(2) . . .]

7. The credit reference agency has delivered to the registrar a statement that it intends to use that protected information only for the purposes of—

(a) providing an assessment of the financial standing of a person;

(b) meeting any obligations contained in [the Money Laundering, Terrorist Financing and Transfer of Funds (Information on the Payer) Regulations 2017] or any [rules made pursuant to section 137A of the Financial Services and Markets Act 2000 which relate to the prevention and detection of money laundering in connection with the carrying on of regulated activities by authorised persons], . . .

(c) conducting conflict of interest checks required or made necessary by any enactment;

(d) the provision of protected information to—

(i) a public authority specified in Schedule 1 which has satisfied the requirements of paragraphs 2 and 3 of this Schedule; or

(ii) a credit reference agency which has satisfied the requirements of this Part of this Schedule; or

(e) conducting checks for the prevention and detection of crime and fraud.

8. The credit reference agency has delivered to the registrar a statement that it intends to take delivery of and to use the protected information only in the United Kingdom . . .

9. The credit reference agency has delivered to the registrar a statement that it will, where it supplies a copy of the protected information to a processor for the purpose of processing the information for use in respect of the purposes referred to in paragraph 7—

(a) ensure that the processor is one who carries on business in the [United Kingdom];
(b) require that the information is not transmitted outside the [United Kingdom] by the processor; and
(c) require that the processor does not disclose the information except to the credit reference agency or an employee of the credit reference agency.

10. The credit reference agency has delivered to the registrar a statement that it meets the conditions in paragraph 6 above.

NOTES

Para 6: the words omitted from sub-para (1)(a) were revoked, the words in square brackets in sub-para (1)(b)(ii) were substituted, and sub-para (2) was revoked, by the Companies, Limited Liability Partnerships and Partnerships (Amendment etc) (EU Exit) Regulations 2019, SI 2019/348, reg 7, Sch 2, paras 3, 8(b), as from IP completion day (as defined in the European Union (Withdrawal Agreement) Act 2020, s 39) (for transitional provisions see Sch 4, para 5 to the 2019 Regulations at **[12.106]**). All other amendments to this paragraph were made by the Data Protection Act 2018, s 211, Sch 19, Pt 2, para 340, as from 25 May 2018 (for transitional provisions and savings relating to the repeal of the Data Protection Act 1998, see Sch 20 to the 2018 Act).

Para 7: words in first pair of square brackets in sub-para (b) substituted by the Money Laundering, Terrorist Financing and Transfer of Funds (Information on the Payer) Regulations 2017, SI 2017/692, reg 109, Sch 7, Pt 2, para 26, as from 26 June 2017. Words in second pair of square brackets in sub-para (b) substituted by the Financial Services Act 2012 (Consequential Amendments and Transitional Provisions) Order 2013, SI 2013/472, art 3, Sch 2, para 173(b), as from 1 April 2013. Words omitted from sub-para (b) revoked by SI 2019/348, reg 7, Sch 2, paras 3, 8(c), as from IP completion day (as defined in the European Union (Withdrawal Agreement) Act 2020, s 39) (for transitional provisions see Sch 4, para 5 to the 2019 Regulations at **[12.106]**).

Para 8: words omitted revoked by SI 2019/348, reg 7, Sch 2, paras 3, 8(d), as from IP completion day (as defined in the European Union (Withdrawal Agreement) Act 2020, s 39) (for transitional provisions see Sch 4, para 5 to the 2019 Regulations at **[12.106]**).

Para 9: words in square brackets substituted by SI 2019/348, reg 7, Sch 2, paras 3, 8(e), as from IP completion day (as defined in the European Union (Withdrawal Agreement) Act 2020, s 39) (for transitional provisions see Sch 4, para 5 to the 2019 Regulations at **[12.106]**).

PART 3 INTERPRETATION OF THIS SCHEDULE

[4.299]

11. (1) In this Schedule—

"processor" means any person who provides a service which consists of putting information into data form or processing information in data form, and any reference to a processor includes a reference to the processor's employees; and

"public function" includes—

(a) any function conferred by or in accordance with any provision contained in any enactment;
(b) . . .
(c) any similar function conferred on persons by or under provisions having effect as part of the law of a country or territory outside the United Kingdom; and
(d) any function exercisable in relation to the investigation of any criminal offence or for the purpose of any criminal proceedings.

(2) In this Schedule any reference to—

(a) an employee of any person who has access to protected information shall be deemed to include any person working or providing services for the purposes of that person or employed by or on behalf of, or working for, any person who is so working or who is supplying such a service; and
(b) the disclosure for the purpose of facilitating the carrying out of a public function includes disclosure in relation to, and for the purpose of, any proceedings whether civil, criminal or disciplinary in which the specified public authority engages while carrying out its public functions.

NOTES

Para 11: para (b) of the definition "public function" was revoked by the Companies, Limited Liability Partnerships and Partnerships (Amendment etc) (EU Exit) Regulations 2019, SI 2019/348, reg 7, Sch 2, paras 3, 8(e), as from IP completion day (as defined in the European Union (Withdrawal Agreement) Act 2020, s 39) (for transitional provisions see Sch 4, para 5 to the 2019 Regulations at **[12.106]**).

SCHEDULE 3
APPLICATION TO PREVENT DISCLOSURE OF ADDRESS TO CREDIT REFERENCE AGENCY

Regulation 25

[4.300]

1 Introductory

In this Schedule "application for higher protection" has the meaning given by regulation 25(1).

2 Application by the individual concerned

(1) An application for higher protection may be made to the registrar by an individual who is, or proposes to become, a director or permanent representative of a company to which Part 4 applies.

(2) The grounds on which an application may be made under this paragraph are that the applicant considers that there is a serious risk that the applicant, or a person who lives with the applicant, will be subjected to violence or intimidation as a result of the activities of at least one of—

(a) the overseas companies of which the applicant is, or proposes to become, a director or permanent representative;
(b) the overseas companies of which the applicant was a director or permanent representative or secretary;
(c) the companies of which the applicant is or has been a director; or
(d) the limited liability partnerships of which the applicant is or has been a member.

(3) The application must contain—

(a) a statement of the grounds on which the application is made;

(b) the name and any former name of the applicant;

(c) the date of birth of the applicant;

(d) the usual residential address of the applicant;

(e) where the registrar has allocated a unique identifier to the applicant, that unique identifier;

(f) the name and registered number of each overseas company of which the applicant is, or proposes to become, a director or permanent representative; and

(g) where the grounds of the application are those described in sub-paragraph (2)(b), (c) or (d), the name and registered number of the overseas company, company or limited liability partnership.

(4) The application must be accompanied by evidence which supports the applicant's statement of the grounds of the application.

(5) The registrar may refer to—

(a) a police force, or

(b) any other person whom the registrar considers may be able to assist in answering the question,

any question relating to an assessment of the nature and extent of any risk of violence or intimidation.

(6) The registrar shall—

(a) determine the application, and

(b) send notice of the determination to the applicant (to the applicant's usual residential address as stated in the application) within five working days of the determination's being made.

3 Application by company

(1) An application for higher protection may be made to the registrar by a company to which Part 4 applies on behalf of any of its directors or permanent representatives.

(2) The grounds on which an application under sub-paragraph (1) may be made are that the company considers that there is a serious risk that the director or permanent representative on behalf of whom the application is made, or a person who lives with that director or permanent representative, will be subjected to violence or intimidation as a result of the company's activities.

(3) The application must contain—

(a) a statement of the grounds on which the application is made;

(b) the name and registered number of the applicant;

(c) the name and any former name of each director or permanent representative on behalf of whom the application is made;

(d) the date of birth of each such director or permanent representative;

(e) the usual residential address of each such director or permanent representative;

(f) where the registrar has allocated a unique identifier to any such director or permanent representative, that unique identifier;

(g) the name and registered number of each UK-registered company or overseas company to which Part 4 applies of which each such director or permanent representative is a director or permanent representative.

(4) The application must be accompanied by evidence which supports the applicant's statement of the grounds of the application.

(5) The registrar may refer to—

(a) a police force, or

(b) any other person whom the registrar considers may be able to assist in answering the question,

any question relating to an assessment of the nature and extent of any risk of violence or intimidation.

(6) The registrar shall—

(a) determine the application, and

(b) send notice of the determination within five working days of its being made—

(i) to the applicant (to its registered office or, if it is not registered, to the address of its principal place of business in its country of incorporation), and

(ii) to each director or permanent representative on behalf of whom the application was made (to the usual residential address of the director or permanent representative as stated in the application).

4 Supplementary provisions relating to applications

(1) For the purpose of paragraphs 2(4) and 3(4) the registrar may direct that additional information or evidence should be delivered to him, what such information or evidence should be and how it should be verified.

(2) The registrar shall not make available for public inspection—

(a) any application for higher protection; or

(b) any documents provided in support of that application; or

(c) any representations received in connection with the revocation of a decision under paragraph 7.

(3) For the purpose of determining an application for higher protection the registrar may accept any answer to a question referred in accordance with paragraph 2(5) or 3(5) as providing sufficient evidence of the nature and extent of any risk of violence or intimidation.

(4) In paragraphs 2 and 3 "former name" means a name that has been notified to the registrar under regulation 6(3)(a)(ii) or 7(1)(f)(ii) and the definition in regulation 2 shall not apply.

5 Appeals

(1) An applicant who has received notice under paragraph 2 or 3 that the application has been unsuccessful may appeal to the High Court or, in Scotland, the Court of Session on the grounds that the decision—

(a) is unlawful;

(b) is irrational or unreasonable;

(c) has been made on the basis of a procedural impropriety or otherwise contravenes the rules of natural justice.

(2) No appeal under this paragraph may be brought unless the leave of the court has been obtained.

(3) An applicant must bring an appeal within 35 days of the date of the notice or, with the court's permission, after the end of such period, but only if the court is satisfied—

(a) where permission is sought before the end of that period, that there is good reason for the applicant being unable to bring the appeal in time; or

(b) where permission is sought after that time, that there was a good reason for the applicant's failure to bring the appeal in time and for any delay in applying for permission.

(4) The court determining an appeal may—

(a) dismiss the appeal, or

(b) quash the decision,

and where the court quashes a decision it may refer the matter to the registrar with a direction to reconsider it and make a determination in accordance with the findings of the court.

6 Duration of favourable decision on application

A decision of the registrar in favour of the applicant on an application for higher protection continues to have effect until—

(a) the registrar is notified by the individual in respect of whom the application was made (or their personal representative) of the wish that the decision should cease to apply, or

(b) the registrar revokes the decision in accordance with paragraph 7.

7 Revocation of favourable decision on application

(1) The registrar may revoke a decision in favour of the applicant on an application for higher protection if the individual in respect of whom the application was made, or any other person, is found guilty of an offence under section 1112 of the Companies Act 2006 (general false statement offence) committed in purporting to comply with any provision of this Schedule.

(2) The registrar must send to the individual notice of any proposal to revoke a decision under this paragraph.

(3) The notice must—

(a) inform the individual that they may, within the period of 28 days beginning with the date of the notice, deliver representations to the registrar, and

(b) state that if representations are not received by the registrar within that period, the decision will be revoked at the expiry of that period.

(4) If within the period specified in sub-paragraph (3) the individual delivers representations as to why the decision should not be revoked, the registrar must—

(a) have regard to the representations in determining whether to revoke the decision, and

(b) send notice of the determination to the individual within five working days of its being made.

(5) Any communication by the registrar under this paragraph in respect of a proposal or determination must be sent to the individual's usual residential address.

SCHEDULE 4
OVERSEAS COMPANIES INDIVIDUAL ACCOUNTS

Regulation 38

PART 1 GENERAL RULES

[4.301]

1. Subject to the following provisions of this Schedule—

(a) every balance sheet must show each of the line items required to be included in a balance sheet in accordance with international accounting standards;

(b) every profit and loss account must show each of the line items required to be included in a profit and loss account in accordance with international accounting standards;

(c) every balance sheet and profit and loss account must clearly indicate in what currency it is prepared.

2. (1) The company's directors must use the same line items in preparing overseas companies individual accounts for each financial year, unless in their opinion there are special reasons for a change.

(2) Particulars of any such change must be given in a note to the accounts in which the new line item is first used, and the reasons for the change must be explained.

3. Where the company's directors consider it appropriate, the balance sheet or the profit and loss account may show a combination of line items where they are of a similar nature.

4. (1) Items that are not of a similar nature or function shall be presented separately unless they are not material.

(2) For the purpose of this paragraph an item is "material" if it either supplements the information given with respect to any particular item shown in the balance sheet and profit and loss account or is otherwise relevant to assessing the company's state of affairs.

(3) Amounts which in the particular context of any provision of this Schedule are not material may be disregarded for the purposes of that provision.

5. (1) Where the nature of the company's business requires it, the company's directors must adapt the line items in the balance sheet or profit and loss account.

(2) The directors may combine items if—

(a) their individual amounts are not material to assessing the state of affairs or profit and loss of the company for the financial year in question, or

(b) the combination facilitates that assessment.

(3) Where sub-paragraph (2)(b) applies, the individual amounts of any items which have been combined must be disclosed in a note to the accounts.

6. (1) Subject to sub-paragraph (2), the directors may exclude an item in the balance sheet or profit and loss account if there is no amount to be shown for that item for the financial year to which the balance sheet or the profit and loss account relates.

(2) Where an amount can be shown for the item in question for the immediately preceding financial year that amount must be shown under the line item for that item.

7. (1) For every item shown in the balance sheet or profit and loss account the corresponding amount for the immediately preceding financial year must also be shown.

(2) Where that corresponding amount is not comparable with the amount to be shown for the item in question in respect of the financial year to which the balance sheet or profit and loss account relates, the former amount may be adjusted and particulars of the non-comparability and of any adjustment must be disclosed in a note to the accounts.

8. Amounts in respect of items representing assets or income may not be set off against amounts in respect of items representing liabilities or expenditure (as the case may be), or vice versa.

9. The company's directors must, in determining how amounts are presented within items in the profit and loss account and balance sheet, have regard to the substance of the reported transaction or arrangement, in accordance with generally accepted accounting principles or practice.

PART 2 ACCOUNTING PRINCIPLES AND RULES

Preliminary

[4.302]

10. (1) The amounts to be included in respect of all items shown in a company's accounts must be determined in accordance with the principles set out in this Part.

(2) But if it appears to the company's directors that there are special reasons for departing from any of those principles in preparing the company's accounts in respect of any financial year they may do so, in which case particulars of the departure, the reasons for it and its effect must be given in a note to the accounts.

Accounting principles

11. (1) The company is presumed to be carrying on business as a going concern.

(2) If the accounts are not prepared on a going concern basis, that fact shall be disclosed, together with the basis on which the accounts are prepared and the reason why the company is not a going concern.

12. Accounting policies must be applied consistently within the same accounts and from one financial year to the next.

13. All income and charges relating to the financial year to which the accounts relate must be taken into account, without regard to the date of receipt or payment.

14. In determining the aggregate amount of any item, the amount of each individual asset or liability that falls to be taken into account must be determined separately.

PART 3 NOTES TO THE ACCOUNTS

[4.303]

15. Any information required in the case of any company by the following provisions of this Part of this Schedule must (if not given in the company's accounts) be given by way of a note to the accounts.

16. The accounting policies adopted by the company in determining the amounts to be included in respect of items shown in the balance sheet and in determining the profit or loss of the company must be stated (including such policies with respect to the depreciation and diminution in value of assets).

17. It must be stated whether the accounts have been prepared in accordance with the applied accounting standards and particulars of any material departure from those standards and the reasons for it must be given.

18. The company must include in the statement of accounting policies—

(a) the measurement basis (or bases) used in preparing the accounts; and
(b) any other accounting policies used that are relevant to an understanding of the accounts.

19. (1) The company must provide information which is relevant to assessing the company's state of affairs.

(2) As a minimum that information must relate, where applicable, to—

(a) property, plant and equipment;
(b) investment property;
(c) intangible assets;
(d) financial assets;
(e) biological assets;
(f) inventories;
(g) trade and other receivables (and the amount falling due after more than one year must be shown separately for each item included under receivables);
(h) trade and other payables (and the amount falling due after more than one year must be shown separately for each item included under payables);
(i) provisions;
(j) financial liabilities;
(k) issued capital and reserves;
(l) finance costs;
(m) finance income;
(n) expenses and interest paid to group undertakings (this must be shown separately from expenses and interest paid to other entities);

(o) income and interest derived from group undertakings (this must be shown separately from income and interest derived from other sources);
(p) transactions with related parties;
(q) dividends;
(r) items described as other, sundry, miscellaneous or equivalent;
(s) guarantees;
(t) contingent liabilities;
(u) commitments;
(v) other off-balance sheet arrangements;
(w) financial instruments.

20. In this Schedule the expression "line item" has the same meaning as in international accounting standard 1 on the presentation of financial statements and includes "items", "layout items" and other equivalent terms.

SCHEDULE 5
OVERSEAS COMPANIES GROUP ACCOUNTS

Regulation 38

General rules

[4.304]

1. (1) Overseas companies group accounts must comply so far as practicable with the provisions of Schedule 4 as if the undertakings included in the consolidation ("the group") were a single company.

(2) In the case of overseas companies group accounts the minimum information listed in paragraph 19(2) of Schedule 4 must also relate to—
(a) investments accounted for using the equity method;
(b) minority interests, presented within equity.

2. The consolidated balance sheet and profit and loss account must incorporate in full the information contained in the individual accounts of the undertakings included in the consolidation, subject to the adjustments authorised or required by the following provisions of this Schedule and to such other adjustments (if any) as may be appropriate in accordance with generally accepted accounting principles or practice.

3. (1) Where assets and liabilities to be included in the group accounts have been valued or otherwise determined by undertakings according to accounting rules differing from those used for the group accounts, the values or amounts must be adjusted so as to accord with the rules used for the group accounts.

(2) If it appears to the directors of the parent company that there are special reasons for departing from sub-paragraph (1) they may do so, but particulars of any such departure, the reasons for it and its effect must be given in a note to the accounts.

(3) The adjustments referred to in this paragraph need not be made if they are not material.

4. Amounts that in the particular context of any provision of this Schedule are not material may be disregarded for the purposes of that provision.

Elimination of group transactions

5. (1) Debts and claims between undertakings included in the consolidation, and income and expenditure relating to transactions between such undertakings, must be eliminated in preparing the group accounts.

(2) Where profits and losses resulting from transactions between undertakings included in the consolidation are included in the book value of assets, they must be eliminated in preparing the group accounts.

(3) The elimination required by sub-paragraph (2) may be effected in proportion to the group's interest in the shares of the undertakings.

(4) Sub-paragraphs (1) and (2) need not be complied with if the amounts concerned are not material.

6. (1) The following provisions apply where an undertaking becomes a subsidiary undertaking of the parent company.

(2) That event is referred to in those provisions as an "acquisition", and references to the "undertaking acquired" are to be construed accordingly.

7. (1) An acquisition must be accounted for—
(a) by the acquisition method of accounting, or
(b) if the generally accepted accounting principles under which the accounts have been prepared allow it to be accounted for by another method, by that method.

(2) If an acquisition is accounted for in accordance with sub-paragraph (1)(b), the method used must be disclosed in the notes to the accounts.

Minority interests

8. (1) In the balance sheet there must be shown, as a separate item and under an appropriate line item, the amount of capital and reserves attributable to shares in subsidiary undertakings included in the consolidation held by or on behalf of persons other than the parent company and its subsidiary undertakings.

(2) In the profit and loss account formats there must be shown, as a separate item and under an appropriate line item—
(a) the amount of any profit or loss on ordinary activities, and
(b) the amount of any profit or loss on extraordinary activities,

attributable to shares in subsidiary undertakings included in the consolidation held by or on behalf of persons other than the parent company and its subsidiary undertakings.

Joint ventures

9. (1) Where an undertaking included in the consolidation manages another undertaking jointly with one or more undertakings not included in the consolidation, that other undertaking ("the joint venture") may, if it is not—

(a) a body corporate, or

(b) a subsidiary undertaking of the parent company,

be dealt with in the group accounts by the method of proportional consolidation.

(2) The provisions of this Schedule relating to the preparation of consolidated accounts apply, with any necessary modifications, to proportional consolidation under this paragraph.

Associated undertakings

10. An "associated undertaking" means an undertaking in which an undertaking included in the consolidation has a participating interest and over whose operating and financial policy it exercises a significant influence, and which is not—

(a) a subsidiary undertaking of the parent company, or

(b) a joint venture dealt with in accordance with paragraph 9.

11. (1) The interest of an undertaking in an associated undertaking, and the amount of profit or loss attributable to such an interest, shall be shown—

(a) by the equity method of accounting, or

(b) if the generally accepted accounting principles under which the accounts have been prepared allow it to be accounted for by another method, by that method.

(2) If an interest is accounted for in accordance with sub-paragraph (1)(b), the method used must be disclosed in the notes to the accounts.

(3) Where the associated undertaking is itself a parent undertaking, the net assets and profits or losses to be taken into account are those of the parent and its subsidiary undertakings (after making any consolidation adjustments).

SCHEDULE 6
CREDIT AND FINANCIAL INSTITUTIONS INDIVIDUAL ACCOUNTS

Regulation 53

PART 1 GENERAL RULES

[4.305]

1. Subject to the following provisions of this Schedule—

(a) every balance sheet must show each of the line items required to be included in a balance sheet in accordance with international accounting standards;

(b) every profit and loss account must show each of the line items required to be included in a profit and loss account in accordance with international accounting standards;

(c) every balance sheet and profit and loss account must clearly indicate in what currency it is prepared.

2. (1) The institution's directors must use the same line items in preparing overseas institutions individual accounts for each financial year, unless in their opinion there are special reasons for a change.

(2) Particulars of any such change must be given in a note to the accounts in which the new line item is first used, and the reasons for the change must be explained.

3. Where the institution's directors consider it appropriate, the balance sheet or the profit and loss account may show a combination of line items where they are of a similar nature.

4. (1) Items that are not of a similar nature or function shall be presented separately unless they are not material.

(2) For the purpose of this paragraph an item is "material" if it either supplements the information given with respect to any particular item shown in the balance sheet and profit and loss account or is otherwise relevant to assessing the institution's state of affairs.

(3) Amounts which in the particular context of any provision of this Schedule are not material may be disregarded for the purposes of that provision.

5. (1) Where the nature of the institution's business requires it, the directors must adapt the line items in the balance sheet or profit and loss account.

(2) The directors may combine items if—

(a) their individual amounts are not material to assessing the state of affairs or profit or loss of the institution for the financial year in question, or

(b) the combination facilitates that assessment.

(3) Where sub-paragraph (2)(b) applies, the individual amounts of any items which have been combined must be disclosed in a note to the accounts.

6. (1) Subject to sub-paragraph (2), the directors may exclude an item in the balance sheet or profit and loss account if there is no amount to be shown for that item for the financial year to which the balance sheet or the profit and loss account relates.

(2) Where an amount can be shown for the item in question for the immediately preceding financial year that amount must be shown under the line item for that item.

7. (1) For every item shown in the balance sheet or profit and loss account the corresponding amount for the immediately preceding financial year must also be shown.

(2) Where that corresponding amount is not comparable with the amount to be shown for the item in question in respect of the financial year to which the balance sheet or profit and loss account relates, the former amount may be adjusted and particulars of the non-comparability and of any adjustment must be disclosed in a note to the accounts.

8. Amounts in respect of items representing assets or income may not be set off against amounts in respect of items representing liabilities or expenditure (as the case may be), or vice versa.

9. The institution's directors must, in determining how amounts are presented within items in the profit and loss account and balance sheet, have regard to the substance of the reported transaction or arrangement, in accordance with generally accepted accounting principles or practice.

PART 2 ACCOUNTING PRINCIPLES AND RULES

[4.306]

10. (1) The amounts to be included in respect of all items shown in an institution's accounts must be determined in accordance with the principles set out in this Part.

(2) But if it appears to the directors that there are special reasons for departing from any of those principles in preparing the accounts in respect of any financial year they may do so, in which case particulars of the departure, the reasons for it and its effect must be given in a note to the accounts.

11. (1) The institution is presumed to be carrying on business as a going concern.

(2) If the accounts are not prepared on a going concern basis, that fact shall be disclosed, together with the basis on which the accounts are prepared and the reason why the institution is not a going concern.

12. Accounting policies must be applied consistently within the same accounts and from one financial year to the next.

13. All income and charges relating to the financial year to which the accounts relate must be taken into account, without regard to the date of receipt or payment.

14. In determining the aggregate amount of any item, the amount of each individual asset or liability that falls to be taken into account must be determined separately.

PART 3 NOTES TO THE ACCOUNTS

[4.307]

15. Any information required in the case of any institution by the following provisions of this Part of this Schedule must (if not given in the accounts) be given by way of a note to the accounts.

16. The accounting policies adopted by the institution in determining the amounts to be included in respect of items shown in the balance sheet and in determining the profit or loss of the institution must be stated (including such policies with respect to the depreciation and diminution in value of assets).

17. It must be stated whether the accounts have been prepared in accordance with the applied accounting standards and particulars of any material departure from those standards and the reasons for it must be given.

18. The institution must include in the statement of accounting policies—

(a) the measurement basis (or bases) used in preparing the accounts; and
(b) any other accounting policies used that are relevant to an understanding of the accounts.

19. (1) The institution must provide information which is relevant to assessing the institution's state of affairs.

(2) As a minimum that information must relate, where applicable, to—

(a) property, plant and equipment;
(b) investment property;
(c) intangible assets;
(d) financial assets;
(e) biological assets;
(f) inventories;
(g) trade and other receivables (and the amount falling due after more than one year must be shown separately for each item included under receivables);
(h) trade and other payables (and the amount falling due after more than one year must be shown separately for each item included under payables);
(i) provisions;
(j) financial liabilities;
(k) issued capital and reserves;
(l) finance costs;
(m) finance income;
(n) expenses and interest paid to group undertakings (this must be shown separately from expenses and interest paid to other entities);
(o) income and interest derived from group undertakings (this must be shown separately from income and interest derived from other sources);
(p) transactions with related parties;
(q) dividends;
(r) items described as other, sundry, miscellaneous or equivalent;
(s) guarantees;
(t) contingent liabilities;
(u) commitments;
(v) other off balance sheet arrangements;
(w) financial instruments.

20. In this Schedule the expression "line item" has the same meaning as in international accounting standard 1 on the presentation of financial statements and includes "items", "layout items" and other equivalent terms.

SCHEDULE 7
CREDIT AND FINANCIAL INSTITUTIONS GROUP ACCOUNTS

Regulation 53

General rules

[4.308]

1. (1) Overseas institutions group accounts must comply so far as practicable with the provisions of Schedule 6 as if the undertakings included in the consolidation ("the group") were a single institution.

(2) In the case of group accounts the minimum information listed in paragraph 19(2) of Schedule 6 must also relate to—

(a) investments accounted for using the equity method;
(b) minority interests, presented within equity.

2. The consolidated balance sheet and profit and loss account must incorporate in full the information contained in the individual accounts of the undertakings included in the consolidation, subject to the adjustments authorised or required by the following provisions of this Schedule and to such other adjustments (if any) as may be appropriate in accordance with generally accepted accounting principles or practice.

3. (1) Where assets and liabilities to be included in the group accounts have been valued or otherwise determined by undertakings according to accounting rules differing from those used for the group accounts, the values or amounts must be adjusted so as to accord with the rules used for the group accounts.

(2) If it appears to the directors of the parent institution that there are special reasons for departing from sub-paragraph (1) they may do so, but particulars of any such departure, the reasons for it and its effect must be given in a note to the accounts.

(3) The adjustments referred to in this paragraph need not be made if they are not material.

4. Amounts that in the particular context of any provision of this Schedule are not material may be disregarded for the purposes of that provision.

Elimination of group transactions

5. (1) Debts and claims between undertakings included in the consolidation, and income and expenditure relating to transactions between such undertakings, must be eliminated in preparing the group accounts.

(2) Where profits and losses resulting from transactions between undertakings included in the consolidation are included in the book value of assets, they must be eliminated in preparing the group accounts.

(3) The elimination required by sub-paragraph (2) may be effected in proportion to the group's interest in the shares of the undertakings.

(4) Sub-paragraphs (1) and (2) need not be complied with if the amounts concerned are not material.

6. (1) The following provisions apply where an undertaking becomes a subsidiary undertaking of the parent institution.

(2) That event is referred to in those provisions as an "acquisition", and references to the "undertaking acquired" are to be construed accordingly.

7. (1) An acquisition must be accounted for—

(a) by the acquisition method of accounting, or
(b) if the generally accepted accounting principles under which the accounts have been prepared allow it to be accounted for by another method, by that method.

(2) If an acquisition is accounted for in accordance with sub-paragraph (1)(b), the method used must be disclosed in the notes to the accounts.

Minority interests

8. (1) In the balance sheet there must be shown, as a separate item and under an appropriate line item, the amount of capital and reserves attributable to shares in subsidiary undertakings included in the consolidation held by or on behalf of persons other than the parent institution and its subsidiary undertakings.

(2) In the profit and loss account formats there must be shown, as a separate item and under an appropriate line item—

(a) the amount of any profit or loss on ordinary activities, and
(b) the amount of any profit or loss on extraordinary activities,

attributable to shares in subsidiary undertakings included in the consolidation held by or on behalf of persons other than the parent institution and its subsidiary undertakings.

Joint ventures

9. (1) Where an undertaking included in the consolidation manages another undertaking jointly with one or more undertakings not included in the consolidation, that other undertaking ("the joint venture") may, if it is not—

(a) a body corporate, or
(b) a subsidiary undertaking of the parent institution,

be dealt with in the group accounts by the method of proportional consolidation.

(2) The provisions of this Schedule relating to the preparation of consolidated accounts apply, with any necessary modifications, to proportional consolidation under this paragraph.

Associated undertakings

10. An "associated undertaking" means an undertaking in which an undertaking included in the consolidation has a participating interest and over whose operating and financial policy it exercises a significant influence, and which is not—

(a) a subsidiary undertaking of the parent institution, or

(b) a joint venture dealt with in accordance with paragraph 9.

11. (1) The interest of an undertaking in an associated undertaking, and the amount of profit or loss attributable to such an interest, shall be shown—

(a) by the equity method of accounting, or

(b) if the generally accepted accounting principles under which the accounts have been prepared allow it to be accounted for by another method, by that method.

(2) If an interest is accounted for in accordance with sub-paragraph (1)(b), the method used must be disclosed in the notes to the accounts.

(3) Where the associated undertaking is itself a parent undertaking, the net assets and profits or losses to be taken into account are those of the parent and its subsidiary undertakings (after making any consolidation adjustments).

SCHEDULE 8
TRANSITIONAL PROVISIONS AND SAVINGS

Regulation 80

PART 1 INTRODUCTION

Interpretation

[4.309]

1. In this Schedule—

"the 1985 Act" means the Companies Act 1985;

"the 1986 Order" means the Companies (Northern Ireland) Order 1986;

"the register" means the records kept by the registrar relating to overseas companies;

"the registrar" means the registrar of companies for England and Wales, Scotland or Northern Ireland.

Registration of returns and documents delivered before 1st October 2009

2. (1) The provisions of Chapter 1 of Part 23 of the 1985 Act or Chapter 1 of Part 23 of the 1986 Order (oversea companies: registration etc) continue to have effect on and after 1st October 2009 so far as necessary for the purposes of the registration of returns or other documents delivered to the registrar before that date.

(2) References in this Schedule to matters appearing on the register, or to documents held by the registrar, immediately before 1st October 2009 include any such return or other document that is subsequently registered.

PART 2 INITIAL REGISTRATION OF PARTICULARS

Company with existing registered branch

[4.310]

3. (1) An overseas company that immediately before 1st October 2009—

(a) had a branch in the United Kingdom, and

(b) had complied in respect of that branch with the requirements of paragraph 1(1) to (3) of Schedule 21A to the 1985 Act or paragraph 1(1) to (3) of Schedule 20A to the 1986 Order,

is treated as having complied in respect of that branch with the requirements of Part 2 of these Regulations (initial registration of particulars).

(2) Paragraphs 4 to 8 supplement sub-paragraph (1) and provide for particular things done under the 1985 Act or 1986 Order to be treated as if done under the corresponding provision of these Regulations.

4. (1) The following particulars about the company, as they appeared on the register immediately before 1st October 2009, are treated as if delivered and registered under regulation 6(1)—

(a) the company's name;

(b) the company's legal form;

(c) if it is registered in the country of its incorporation, the identity of the register in which it is registered and the number with which it is so registered;

(d) the list of its directors and secretaries, together with—

- (i) with respect to each director, the particulars specified in sub-paragraph (3), and
- (ii) with respect to each secretary, the particulars specified in sub-paragraph (4);

(e) the extent of the powers of the directors to represent the company in dealings with third parties and in legal proceedings, together with a statement as to whether they may act alone or must act jointly and, if jointly, the name of any other person concerned;

(f) whether the company is a credit or financial institution.

(2) In the case of a company that is not incorporated in an EEA State, the following particulars about the company, as they appeared on the register immediately before 1st October 2009, are treated as delivered and registered under regulation 6(2)—

(a) the law under which the company is incorporated;

(b) in the case of—

- (i) a company to which Chapter 2 of Part 5 of these Regulations applies (companies required to prepare and disclose accounts under parent law), or
- (ii) a company to which Chapter 2 of Part 6 of these Regulations applies (institutions required to prepare accounts under parent law),

the period for which the company is required by its parent law to prepare accounts, together with the period allowed for the preparation and public disclosure (if any) of accounts for such a period;

(c) unless disclosed by the company's constitution (see paragraph 6)—

- (i) the address of its principal place of business in its country of incorporation or, if applicable, its registered office,

(ii) its objects, and
(iii) the amount of its issued share capital.

(3) The particulars referred to in sub-paragraph (1)(d)(i) (directors) are—
(a) in the case of an individual—
(i) name,
(ii) any former name,
(iii) service address,
(iv) usual residential address,
(v) nationality,
(vi) business occupation (if any), and
(vii) date of birth;
(b) in the case of a body corporate, or a firm that is a legal person under the law by which it is governed—
(i) corporate or firm name, and
(ii) registered or principal office.

(4) The particulars referred to in sub-paragraph (1)(d)(ii)) (secretaries) are—
(a) in the case of an individual—
(i) name,
(ii) any former name, and
(iii) service address;
(b) in the case of a body corporate, or a firm that is a legal person under the law by which it is governed—
(i) corporate or firm name, and
(ii) registered or principal office.

(5) For the purposes of sub-paragraph (1)(f) the statement whether the company is an institution to which section 699A of the 1985 Act or Article 648A of the 1986 Order applies is treated as a statement whether the company is a credit or financial institution as defined for the purposes of these Regulations.

(6) For the purposes of sub-paragraphs (3)(a)(iii) and (4)(a)(iii) the individual's usual residential address as registered immediately before 1st October 2009 is treated as a service address.

5. (1) The following particulars about the branch, as they appeared on the register immediately before 1st October 2009, are treated as if delivered and registered under regulation 7—
(a) the address of the branch,
(b) the date on which it was opened,
(c) the business carried on at it,
(d) the name of the branch (if different from the company's name),
(e) the name and service address of every person resident in the United Kingdom authorised to accept service of documents on behalf of the company in respect of the branch, or a statement that there is no such person,
(f) the list of persons authorised to represent the company as a permanent representative of the company in respect of the branch, together with the following particulars of each such person—
(i) name,
(ii) any former name,
(iii) service address, and
(iv) usual residential address,
(g) the extent of the authority of any person falling within paragraph (f), including whether that person is authorised to act alone or jointly, and
(h) if a person falling within paragraph (f) is not authorised to act alone, the name of any person with whom they are authorised to act.

(2) For the purposes of sub-paragraph (1)(e) and (f)(iii), the individual's usual residential address as registered immediately before 1st October 2009 is treated as a service address.

6. (1) The certified copy of the company's constitution delivered under paragraph 5(a) of Schedule 21A to the 1985 Act or paragraph 5(a) of Schedule 20A to the 1986 Order, as held by the registrar immediately before 1st October 2009, is treated as if delivered and registered under regulation 8(1).

(2) Any certified translation delivered under paragraph 5(b) of Schedule 21A to that Act or paragraph 5(b) of Schedule 20A to that Order, as held by the registrar immediately before 1st October 2009, is treated as if delivered under regulation 8(1) in accordance with regulation 78 of these Regulations.

(3) The following, as they appeared on the register immediately before 1st October 2009, are treated as if delivered and registered under regulation 8(2)—
(a) any statement under paragraph 1(3)(b) of Schedule 21A to the 1985 Act or paragraph 1(3)(b) of Schedule 20A to the 1986 Order to the effect that a copy of the company's constitution is included in the material delivered in respect of another branch;
(b) the registered number of that other branch.

7. (1) Copies of accounting documents delivered under paragraph 6(1)(a) of Schedule 21A to the 1985 Act or paragraph 6(1)(a) of Schedule 20A to the 1986 Order, if not superseded by the delivery of copies of accounting documents for a subsequent financial period, are treated as if delivered and registered under regulation 9(1).

(2) A certified translation of any such document delivered under paragraph 6(1)(b) of Schedule 21A to that Act or paragraph 6(1)(b) of Schedule 20A to that Order is treated as if delivered under regulation 9(1) in accordance with regulation 78.

(3) The following, as they appeared on the register immediately before 1st October 2009, are treated as if delivered and registered under regulation 9(2)—
(a) any statement under paragraph 1(3)(b) of Schedule 21A to the 1985 Act or paragraph 1(3)(b) of Schedule 20A to the 1986 Order to the effect that copies of accounting documents are included in the material registered in respect of another branch;

(b) the registered number of that other branch.

8. (1) If the company is one to which Chapter 2 of Part 5 of these Regulations applies (companies required to prepare and disclose accounts under parent law), the following, as they appeared on the register immediately before 1st October 2009, are treated as if delivered and registered under regulation 10—

(a) the statement in the return in respect of a branch whether it is intended to file copies of accounting documents in respect of that branch or in respect of another branch;

(b) if the return states that it is intended to file copies of accounting documents in respect of another branch, the registered number of that branch.

(2) The statement of intention with respect to the registration of documents under paragraph 2(2) or 10(1) of Schedule 21D to the 1985 Act or paragraph 2(2) or 10(1) of Schedule 20D to the 1986 Order shall be read as a statement of intention with respect to the filing of copies of accounting documents under Chapter 2 of Part 5 of these Regulations.

Company with existing registered place of business

9. (1) An overseas company that immediately before 1st October 2009—

(a) had a place of business (other than a branch) in the United Kingdom, and

(b) had delivered to the registrar in respect of that place of business the documents required by section 691(1) of the 1985 Act of Article 641(1) of the 1986 Order,

is treated as having complied in respect of that place of business with the requirements of Part 2 of these Regulations (initial registration of particulars).

(2) Paragraphs 10 to 12 below supplement sub-paragraph (1) and provide for particular things done under the 1985 Act or 1986 Order to be treated as if done under the corresponding provision of these Regulations.

10. (1) The following particulars about the company, as they appeared on the register immediately before 1st October 2009, are treated as if delivered and registered under regulation 6(1)—

(a) the company's name;

(b) the list of the company's directors and secretaries together with—

(i) with respect to each director, the particulars specified in sub-paragraph (2), and

(ii) with respect to each secretary, the particulars specified in sub-paragraph (3).

(2) The particulars referred to in sub-paragraph (1)(b)(i) (directors) are—

(a) in the case of an individual—

(i) name,

(ii) any former name,

(iii) service address,

(iv) usual residential address,

(v) nationality,

(vi) business occupation (if any), and

(vii) date of birth;

(b) in the case of a body corporate or a firm that is a legal person under the law by which it is governed—

(i) its corporate or firm name, and

(ii) its registered or principal office.

(3) The particulars referred to in sub-paragraph (2)(b)(ii) (secretaries) are—

(a) in the case of an individual—

(i) name,

(ii) any former name, and

(iii) service address;

(b) in the case of a body corporate or a firm that is a legal person under the law by which it is governed—

(i) its corporate or firm name, and

(ii) its registered or principal office.

(4) For the purposes of sub-paragraph (1)(a) the company's name is treated as registered immediately before 1st October 2009 if it then appeared in the index maintained under section 714 of the 1985 Act or Article 663 of the 1986 Order (the registrar's index of company and corporate names).

(5) For the purposes of sub-paragraphs (2)(a)(iii) and (3)(a)(iii), the individual's usual residential address as registered immediately before 1st October 2009 is treated as a service address.

11. (1) The following particulars about the place of business, as they appeared on the register immediately before 1st October 2009, are treated as registered under regulation 7—

(a) the date on which the place of business was opened, and

(b) the name and service address of one or more persons resident in the United Kingdom authorised to accept service of documents on behalf of the company.

(2) For the purposes of sub-paragraph (1)(b) an individual's usual residential address as registered immediately before 1st October 2009 is treated as a service address.

12. (1) The certified copy of the company's constitution delivered under section 691(1)(a) of the 1985 Act or Article 641(1)(a) of the 1986 Order, as held by the registrar immediately before 1st October 2009, is treated as if delivered and registered under regulation 8(1).

(2) Any certified translation delivered under section 691(1)(a) of the 1985 Act or Article 641(1)(a) of the 1986 Order, as held by the registrar immediately before 1st October 2009, is treated as if delivered under regulation 8(1) in accordance with regulation 78.

Duty to deliver transitional return

13. (1) Where paragraph 3 or 9 applies in relation to an establishment, the company must deliver to the registrar not later than 31st March 2010 a transitional return in respect of the establishment.

(2) The return must contain such of the particulars specified in regulation 6 (particulars of the company) as are not treated as registered in respect of the establishment by virtue of paragraph 3 or 9.

Regulation 5(2) (reference to particulars included in those delivered in respect of another UK establishment) applies in relation to the return required by this paragraph as in relation to a return under Part 2 of these Regulations.

(3) The return must contain such of the particulars specified in regulation 7 (particulars of the establishment) as are not treated as registered by virtue of paragraph 5 or 11.

(4) If the company is one to which Part 5 of these Regulations applies (delivery of accounting documents: general), the return must—

(a) make any statement required by regulation 10 (statement as to future manner of compliance with accounting requirements) that is not treated as made by virtue of paragraph 8, and

(b) if the company states that it intends to file copies of accounting documents, or accounts, in respect of another UK establishment, give the registered number of that establishment.

(5) If the company is one to which Chapter 2 of Part 5 of these Regulations applies (companies required to prepare and disclose accounts under parent law), the return must, as regards any document specified in regulation 9(1) (copies of accounting documents) that is not treated as delivered by virtue of paragraph 7, either—

(a) be accompanied by the document, or

(b) make the statement specified in regulation 9(3) (statement that document included in those delivered in respect of another UK establishment).

(6) Sub-paragraph (5) does not apply if the company is required by its parent law to prepare and disclose accounts made up to a date before 1st October 2010.

Company with existing unregistered branch or place of business

14. (1) An overseas company that immediately before 1st October 2009—

(a) had a branch in the United Kingdom in respect of which it had not complied with paragraph 1(1) to (3) of Schedule 21A to the 1985 Act or paragraph 1(1) to (3) of Schedule 20A to the 1986 Order,

(b) had a place of business (other than a branch) in the United Kingdom in respect of which it had not complied with section 691 of the 1985 Act or Article 641 of the 1986 Order,

is treated for the purposes of these Regulations as if it had opened that establishment on 1st October 2009.

(2) This does not affect any liability under section 697(1) or (3) of the 1985 Act or Article 647(1) or (3) of the 1986 Order (penalties for non-compliance) in respect of failure to comply with the provisions mentioned in sub-paragraph (1)(a) or (b) before 1st October 2009.

PART 3 ALTERATIONS TO REGISTERED PARTICULARS

Alteration to registered particulars

[4.311]

15. (1) The provisions of the 1985 Act or 1986 Order relating to alterations of registered particulars continue to apply in relation to an alteration made before 1st October 2009.

(2) Those provisions are—

(a) in the case of a company subject to section 690A of the 1985 Act or Article 640A of the 1986 Order (branch registration under the 11th Company Law Directive), paragraph 7(1)(b) of Schedule 21A to that Act or paragraph 7(1)(b) of Schedule 20A to that Order;

(b) in the case of a company to which section 691 of the 1985 Act or Article 641 of the 1986 Order (registration of place of business other than branch) applies, section 692(1)(b) and (c) and (2) of that Act or Article 642(1)(b) and (c) and (2) of that Order.

(3) If a return giving the particulars of the alteration required by the 1985 Act or 1986 Order is duly delivered on or after 1st October 2009, Part 2 of this Schedule (initial registration of particulars) applies as if it had been delivered and registered immediately before that date.

(4) Regulation 13 (return of alteration in registered particulars) applies to alterations made on or after 1st October 2009.

Alteration in company's constitution

16. (1) The provisions of the 1985 Act or 1986 Order relating to alterations of the company's constitution continue to apply in relation to an alteration made before 1st October 2009.

(2) Those provisions are—

(a) in the case of a company subject to section 690A of the 1985 Act or Article 640A of the 1986 Order (branch registration under the 11th Company Law Directive), paragraph 7(1)(a) of Schedule 21A to that Act or paragraph 7(1)(a) of Schedule 20A to that Order;

(b) in the case of a company to which section 691 of the 1985 Act or Article 641 of the 1986 Order (registration of place of business other than branch) applies, section 692(1)(a) of that Act or Article 642(1)(a) of that Order.

(3) If the following are duly delivered on or after 1st October 2009—

(a) a return giving the particulars of the alteration required by the 1985 Act or 1986 Order,

(b) a certified copy of the company's constitution as altered, and

(c) any certified translation required by the 1985 Act or 1986 Order,

Part 2 of this Schedule (initial registration of particulars) applies as if they had been delivered and registered immediately before that date.

(4) Regulation 14 (return of alteration in company's constitution) applies to alterations made on or after 1st October 2009.

Alteration as regards filing of certified copy of constitution

17. (1) The provisions of paragraph 8 of Schedule 21A to the 1985 Act or paragraph 8 of Schedule 20A to the 1986 Order (statement that certified copy of company's constitution included in the material registered in respect of another UK branch ceasing to be true) continue to apply where that statement ceased to be true before 1st October 2009.

(2) If there is duly delivered on or after 1st October 2009—

(a) a certified copy of the company's constitution and any certified translation required by the 1985 Act or 1986 Order, or

(b) a return stating that those documents are included in the material registered in respect of another UK branch (giving the registered number of that other branch),

Part 2 of this Schedule (initial registration of particulars) applies as if they had been delivered and registered immediately before that date.

(3) Regulation 15 (return of alteration as regards filing of certified copy of constitution) applies where that statement ceases to be true on or after 1st October 2009.

PART 4 RESIDENTIAL ADDRESSES: PROTECTION FROM DISCLOSURE

Existing registered residential address treated as service address

[4.312]

18. (1) This paragraph applies where an address that immediately before 1st October 2009 appeared on the register as the usual residential address of a director, secretary or permanent representative of an overseas company is to be treated, on and after that date, as a service address.

(2) Any return of an alteration in any such residential address of a director, secretary or permanent representative of an overseas company occurring before 1st October 2009 that is received by the registrar on or after that date is treated as being or, as the case may be, including notification of a change of service address.

(3) The registrar may make such entries in the register as appear to be appropriate having regard to any provision to the effect mentioned in sub-paragraph (1) and to sub-paragraph (2).

(4) Where a residential address appears in the register as a service address by virtue of this paragraph, that address is not protected information for the purposes of Part 4 of these Regulations.

Residential addresses: protection from disclosure

19. (1) Regulation 21 (duty of registrar to omit protected information from material available for inspection) does not apply—

(a) to material delivered to the registrar before 1st October 2009, or

(b) to material delivered to the registrar on or after 1st October 2009 by virtue of paragraph 18 (return of alteration occurring before that date).

(2) In regulation 21(2)(b) (exclusion of material registered before commencement) the reference to things registered before 1st October 2009 is treated as including anything registered as a result of a return in accordance with paragraph 18(2) (return on or after 1st October 2009 of alteration occurring before that date).

(3) Sub-paragraphs (1) and (2) have effect subject to paragraph 21 below (which provides for the continued protection of information formerly protected by a confidentiality order).

20. In determining under regulation 27 whether to put a director or permanent representative's usual residential address on the public record, the registrar may take into account only—

(a) communications sent by the registrar on or after 1st October 2009, and

(b) evidence as to the effectiveness of service coming to the registrar's attention on or after that date.

Continuation of protection afforded by confidentiality orders under the 1985 Act

21. (1) A director or permanent representative of an overseas company in relation to whom a confidentiality order under section 723B of the 1985 Act was in force immediately before 1st October 2009 is treated on and after that date as if—

(a) they had made an application under regulation 25 (application to prevent disclosure of protected information by registrar to credit reference agency), and

(b) that application had been determined by the registrar in their favour.

(2) The provisions of Schedule 3 to these Regulations relating to decisions of the registrar in favour of an applicant (in particular, as to the duration and revocation of such a decision) apply accordingly.

(3) As those provisions apply in accordance with this paragraph any reference to an offence under section 1112 of the Companies Act 2006 (general false statement offence) shall be read as a reference to an offence under regulations under section 723E(1)(a) of the 1985 Act in relation to the application for the confidentiality order.

Effect of pending application for confidentiality order

22. (1) Section 723B(3) to (8) of the 1985 Act (application for confidentiality order) continue to apply in relation to an application for a confidentiality order made before 1st October 2009.

(2) Paragraph 21 (continuation of protection afforded by confidentiality orders) applies to an individual in respect of whom such an application has been made, and has not been determined or withdrawn, as to an individual in relation to whom a confidentiality order was in force immediately before that date.

(3) If the application is dismissed or withdrawn, that paragraph ceases to apply.

(4) If the application is successful that paragraph continues to apply as in the case of an individual in relation to whom a confidentiality order was in force immediately before 1st October 2009.

PART 5 DELIVERY OF ACCOUNTING DOCUMENTS: GENERAL

Companies required to prepare and disclose accounts under parent law

[4.313]

23. (1) This paragraph applies to companies to which Chapter 2 of Part 5 of these Regulations applies (companies required to prepare and disclose accounts under parent law).

(2) The provisions of that Chapter apply in relation to accounting documents first disclosed in accordance with the company's parent law on or after 1st October 2009.

(3) In the case of a company to which section 699AA of the 1985 Act or Article 648AA of the 1986 Order applied (company to which 11th Company Law Directive applies), the provisions of Part 1 of Schedule 21D to that Act or Part 1 of Schedule 20D to that Order continue to apply in relation to accounting documents first disclosed in accordance with the company's parent law before 1st October 2009.

(4) In the case of a company to which section 700 of the 1985 Act or Article 649 of the 1986 Order applied (company with place of business but not branch in UK), the relevant provisions of that Act or Order continue to apply in relation to the period between—

(a) the end of the last financial year of the company beginning before 1st October 2009, and

(b) the beginning of the first financial period of the company in respect of which accounting documents are first disclosed in accordance with the company's parent law on or after that date,

and that period shall be treated as a financial year of the company (if it would otherwise not be) for the purposes of those provisions.

(5) For the purposes of sub-paragraph (4)—

(a) the relevant provisions of the 1985 Act are sections 700 to 703 and the provisions applied by those sections;

(b) the relevant provisions of the 1986 Order are Articles 649 to 652 and the provisions applied by those Articles.

Companies not required to prepare and disclose accounts under parent law

24. (1) This paragraph applies to companies to which Chapter 3 of Part 5 of these Regulations applies (companies not required to prepare and disclose accounts under parent law).

(2) The provisions of that Chapter apply in relation to accounting documents for financial years of the company beginning on or after 1st October 2009.

(3) The provisions of—

(a) Part 2 of Schedule 21D to the 1985 Act or Part 2 of Schedule 20D to the 1986 Order (companies to which the 11th Company Law Directive applies), or

(b) sections 700 to 702 of that Act or Articles 649 to 652 of that Order (companies with place of business but not branch in the UK),

continue to apply in relation to accounting documents for financial years beginning before that date.

PART 6 DELIVERY OF ACCOUNTING DOCUMENTS: CREDIT OR FINANCIAL INSTITUTIONS

Institutions required to prepare accounts under parent law

[4.314]

25. (1) This paragraph applies to credit or financial institutions to which Chapter 2 of Part 6 of these Regulations applies (institutions required to prepare accounts under parent law).

(2) An institution that immediately before 1st October 2009—

(a) had a branch in the United Kingdom, and

(b) had complied with the requirements of paragraph 2 of Schedule 21C to the 1985 Act or paragraph 2 of Schedule 20C to the 1986 Order,

is treated as having complied with the requirements of regulation 45 (initial filing of copies of accounting documents).

(3) Regulation 46 (filing of copies of subsequent accounting documents) applies in relation to accounting documents first disclosed in accordance with the company's parent law on or after 1st October 2009.

(4) Paragraph 3 of Schedule 21C to the 1985 Act or paragraph 3 of Schedule 20D to the 1986 Order continues to apply in relation to accounting documents first disclosed in accordance with the company's parent law before 1st October 2009.

Institutions not require to prepare accounts under parent law

26. (1) This paragraph applies to credit or financial institutions to which Chapter 3 of Part 6 of these Regulations applies (institutions not required to prepare accounts under parent law).

(2) The provisions of that Chapter apply in relation to accounting documents for financial years of the institution beginning on or after 1st October 2009.

(3) The provisions of Part 2 of Schedule 21C to the 1985 Act or Part 2 of Schedule 20C to the 1986 Order continue to apply in relation to accounting documents for financial years beginning before that date.

PART 7 RETURNS IN CASE OF WINDING UP ETC

Return in case of winding up

[4.315]

27. (1) Regulation 69 (return in case of winding up) applies in relation to a winding up beginning on or after 1st October 2009.

(2) Section 703P(1) of the 1985 Act or Article 652P(1) of the 1986 Order (particulars to be delivered: winding up) continues to apply in relation to a winding up beginning before that date.

Returns to be made by liquidator

28. (1) Regulation 70(1) (return of appointment of liquidator) applies in relation to an appointment made on or after 1st October 2009.

(2) Section 703P(3) of the 1985 Act or Article 652P(3) of the 1986 Order continues to apply in relation to an appointment made before that date.

(3) Regulation 70(3) (return by liquidator where winding up terminates or company ceases to be registered) applies where the event concerned occurs on or after 1st October 2009.

(4) Section 703P(5) of the 1985 Act or Article 652P(5) of the 1986 Order continues to apply where the event occurred before that date.

Return in case of insolvency proceedings etc (other than winding up)

29. (1) Regulation 71 (return of insolvency proceedings etc) applies where the proceedings in question begin on or after 1st October 2009.

(2) Section 703Q of the 1985 Act or Article 652Q of the 1986 Order continues to apply where the proceedings began before that date.

Notice of appointment of judicial factor

30. Regulation 73 (notice of appointment of judicial factor) applies in relation to appointments made on or after 1st October 2009.

PART 8 SUPPLEMENTARY PROVISIONS

Saving for provisions as to form or manner in which documents to be delivered

[4.316]

31. (1) Any saving in this Schedule for the effect of a provision of the 1985 Act or 1986 Order requiring the use of a prescribed form extends to the form and the power under which it is prescribed.

(2) Any saving in this Schedule for the effect of a provision of the 1985 Act or 1986 Order requiring a document to be delivered to the registrar extends to section 707B of the 1985 Act or Article 656B of the 1986 Order (delivery to the registrar using electronic communications) so far as relating to the provision in question and the delivery of documents under it.

REGISTRAR OF COMPANIES AND APPLICATIONS FOR STRIKING OFF REGULATIONS 2009

(SI 2009/1803)

NOTES

Made: 8 July 2009.

Authority: Companies Act 2006, ss 1003(2)(b), 1081(2), 1095(1), (2), 1104(2)(a), 1105(2)(d), 1108(2), 1167, 1292(1), (3), (4).

Commencement: 1 October 2009.

For a summary of all Orders and Regulations made under the Companies Act 2006, see Appendix 4 at **[A4]**.

These Regulations are reproduced as amended by: the European Economic Interest Grouping (Amendment) Regulations 2009, SI 2009/2399; the European Public Limited-Liability Company (Amendment) Regulations 2009, SI 2009/2400; the Companies and Limited Liability Partnerships (Accounts and Audit Exemptions and Change of Accounting Framework) Regulations 2012, SI 2012/2301; the Companies Act 2006 (Amendment of Part 25) Regulations 2013, SI 2013/600; the European Economic Interest Grouping and European Public Limited-Liability Company (Amendment) Regulations 2014, SI 2014/2382; the Company, Limited Liability Partnership and Business (Names and Trading Disclosures) Regulations 2015, SI 2015/17; the Registrar of Companies and Applications for Striking Off (Amendment) Regulations 2016, SI 2016/441; the European Economic Interest Grouping (Amendment) (EU Exit) Regulations 2018, SI 2018/1299.

ARRANGEMENT OF REGULATIONS

SCHEDULES

[4.317]

1 Citation, commencement and interpretation

(1) These Regulations may be cited as the Registrar of Companies and Applications for Striking Off Regulations 2009 and come into force on 1st October 2009.

(2) In these Regulations—

(a) "relevant company form" has the meaning given in regulation 4(3);

(b) "relevant material" has the meaning given in regulation 4(2);

(c) "relevant overseas company form" has the meaning given in regulation 4(4); and

(d) "valid objection" has the meaning given in regulation 4(8).

[4.318]

2 Voluntary striking off: contents of an application

(1) An application under section 1003 of the Companies Act 2006 (application for voluntary striking off) must contain a declaration that neither section 1004 nor section 1005 of that Act prevents the application from being made.

(2) The declaration must be made by the directors who are making the application on behalf of the company.

[4.319]

3 Annotation of the register

Where it appears to the registrar that material on the register is misleading or confusing, the registrar may place a note in the register containing such information as appears to the registrar to be necessary to remedy, as far as possible, the misleading or confusing nature of the material.

[4.320]

4 Rectification of the register on application

(1) On application under this regulation . . . the registrar must remove from the register any relevant material that—

(a) derives from anything invalid or ineffective or that was done without the authority of the company or overseas company to which the material relates, or

(b) is factually inaccurate, or is derived from something that is factually inaccurate or forged.

[(1A) Paragraph (1) does not apply—

(a) in a case mentioned in section 1095(4A) of the Companies Act 2006 (application for removal from register of material about directors), if the registrar is required under section 1095(4B) of that Act not to remove the material from the register;

(b) in any other case, if there is a valid objection to the application.]

(2) "Relevant material" means material on the register that was included in, or is derived from material that was included in, a relevant company form or a relevant overseas company form delivered to the registrar by any person.

(3) A "relevant company form" is—

(a) a standard form required for giving notice under section 87 (change of address of registered office), [sections 167 or 167D] (changes relating to directors) or section 276 (changes relating to secretaries) of the Companies Act 2006; or

(b) so much of a standard form required for delivering an application under section 9 of that Act (application for registration of a company) as is required for the statement of a company's proposed officers referred to in section 9(4)(c).

(4) A "relevant overseas company form" is—

(a) so much of a standard form required for delivering a return under regulation 4 of the Overseas Companies Regulations 2009 as is required for—

(i) the list referred to in regulation 6(1)(d) of those Regulations (list of directors and secretary of an overseas company);

(ii) the names and service addresses referred to in regulation 7(1)(e) of those Regulations (names and service addresses of persons authorised to accept service of documents on behalf of an overseas company in respect of a UK establishment); or

(iii) the list referred to in regulation 7(1)(f) of those Regulations (list of permanent representatives of an overseas company in respect of a UK establishment); or

(b) so much of a standard form required for delivering a return under regulation 13 of those Regulations as is required for details of the alteration of particulars delivered under—

(i) regulation 6(1)(d) of those Regulations (directors and secretary);

(ii) regulation 7(1)(a) of those Regulations (address of UK establishment);

(iii) regulation 7(1)(e) of those Regulations (names and service addresses of persons authorised to accept service); or

(iv) regulation 7(1)(f) of those Regulations (list of permanent representatives).

(5) An application to the registrar for the removal from the register (on the grounds in paragraph (1)) of material that was included in a standard form required for giving notice under section 87 of the Companies Act 2006 (change of address of registered office), or of material that is derived from material that was included in such a form, may be made by (and only by) the company to which the material relates.

(6) An application to the registrar for the removal from the register (on the grounds in paragraph (1)) of material that was included in, or is derived from material that was included in, so much of a standard form required for delivering a return under regulation 13 of the Overseas Companies Regulations 2009 as is required for details of the alteration of particulars delivered under regulation 7(1)(a) of those Regulations (address of UK establishment) may be made by (and only by) the overseas company to which the material relates.

(7) An application to the registrar for the removal from the register on the grounds in paragraph (1) of relevant material other than material referred to in paragraph (5) or (6) may be made by (and only by)—

(a) the person by whom the relevant company form or relevant overseas company form (as the case may be) was delivered to the registrar;

(b) the company or overseas company to which the material relates; or

(c) any other person to whom the material relates.

[(7A) But an application specifying material of the kind mentioned in section 1095(4A)(a) of the Companies Act 2006 (material naming a person as a director), which is accompanied by a statement of the kind mentioned in section 1095(4A)(b) of that Act, may also be made on behalf of the person named in the material.]

(8) A "valid objection" is—

(a) an objection made in accordance with regulation 5(10) and (11) by a person to whom notice of the application was given under regulation 5(2), (3), (4) or (5), or

(b) an objection made in accordance with regulation 5(10) by any other person which is not an objection that the registrar is prevented from taking into account under regulation 5(12).

(9) In this regulation "required" means required by rules made by the registrar under section 1117 of the Companies Act 2006.

NOTES

The words omitted from para (1) were revoked, paras (1A), (7A) were inserted, and the words in square brackets in para (3) were substituted, by the Registrar of Companies and Applications for Striking Off (Amendment) Regulations 2016, SI 2016/441, reg 2(1), (2), as from 6 April 2016.

[4.321]

5 Applications to rectify: further requirements, objections and notices to be issued by the registrar

(1) An application to the registrar under regulation 4 must, in addition to satisfying the requirements of section 1095(3) of the Companies Act 2006—

(a) state the applicant's name and address;

(b) where the application is an application referred to in regulation 4(5) or (6), confirm that the applicant is the company or (as the case may be) the overseas company to which the relevant material which is the subject of the application relates;

[(ba) where the applicant is making the application in reliance on regulation 4(7A)—

(i) confirm that the person named in the relevant material which is the subject of the application has consented to the applicant making the application on that person's behalf; or

(ii) explain the basis on which the applicant is otherwise entitled to make the application on that person's behalf;]

(c) in any other case, state whether the applicant is a person mentioned in regulation 4(7)(a), a person mentioned in regulation 4(7)(b) or a person mentioned in regulation 4(7)(c); and

(d) state whether the relevant material which is the subject of the application—

(i) derives from anything invalid or ineffective;

(ii) derives from anything that was done without the authority of the company or overseas company to which the material relates;

(iii) is factually inaccurate or is derived from something that is factually inaccurate; or

(iv) is derived from something that is forged.

(2) Where the application is an application referred to in regulation 4(5), the registrar must give notice of the application to—

(a) the person who delivered the standard form mentioned in that regulation to the registrar (but only if the registrar knows the identity and name and address of that person);

(b) every person who (to the registrar's knowledge) was a director or secretary of the company at the time when the application was delivered to the registrar; and

(c) the company at the address of its registered office.

(3) Where the material which is the subject of the application relates to a company (rather than an overseas company), but the application is not an application referred to in regulation 4(5), the registrar must give notice of the application to—

(a) every person mentioned in regulation 4(7) whose identity and name and address the registrar knows (other than the applicant); and

(b) every person who (to the registrar's knowledge) was a director or secretary of the company at the time when the application was delivered to the registrar.

(4) Where the application is an application referred to in regulation 4(6), the registrar must give notice of the application to—

(a) the person who delivered the standard form mentioned in that regulation to the registrar (but only if the registrar knows the identity and name and address of that person);

(b) every person registered under regulation 4 or 13 of the Overseas Companies Regulations 2009, at the time when the application was delivered to the registrar, as a director or secretary of the overseas company;

(c) the persons mentioned in paragraph (6); and

(d) the overseas company.

(5) Where the material which is the subject of the application relates to an overseas company, but the application is not an application referred to in regulation 4(6), the registrar must give notice of the application to—

(a) every person mentioned in regulation 4(7) whose identity and name and address the registrar knows (other than the applicant);

(b) every person registered under regulation 4 or 13 of the Overseas Companies Regulations 2009, at the time when the application was delivered to the registrar, as a director or secretary of the overseas company; and

(c) the persons mentioned in paragraph (6).

(6) The persons are—

(a) every person registered under regulation 4 or 13 of the Overseas Companies Regulations 2009, at the time when the application was delivered to the registrar, as a person authorised to accept service of documents on behalf of the overseas company in respect of a UK establishment of the company; and

(b) every person registered under regulation 4 or 13 of those Regulations, at the time when the application was delivered to the registrar, as a permanent representative of the overseas company in respect of a UK establishment of the company.

(7) Where the material which is the subject of the application is material that was included in, or is derived from material that was included in, a relevant overseas company form described in regulation 4(4)(a)(ii) or (iii) or regulation 4(4)(b)(ii), (iii) or (iv), the notice which the registrar is required by paragraph (4) or (5) to give to the overseas company must be given to the company at the address which was, at the time when the application was delivered to the registrar, registered under regulation 4 or 13 of the Overseas Companies Regulations 2009 as the address of the company's UK establishment to which the material relates (and notice need not be given to the company at any other address).

(8) The notice given by the registrar under paragraph (2), (3), (4) or (5) must—

(a) where the material which is the subject of the application relates to a company (rather than an overseas company), state the name and registered number of the company to which the material relates;

(b) where the material which is the subject of the application relates to an overseas company, state the overseas company's name registered under regulation 4 or 13 of the Overseas Companies Regulations 2009 or section 1048 of the Companies Act 2006 and its registered number allocated under section 1066 of that Act;

(c) where the material which is the subject of the application is material that was included in, or is derived from material that was included in, a relevant overseas company form described in regulation 4(4)(a)(ii) or (iii) or regulation 4(4)(b)(ii), (iii) or (iv), state the registered number allocated under section 1067 of the Companies Act 2006 to the UK establishment to which the material relates;

(d) specify what is to be removed from the register and indicate where on the register it is;

(e) state the information provided to the registrar under paragraph (1)(d);

(f) state the date on which the notice is issued;

(g) give particulars of the recipient's right to object to the application and the requirements applying to that right under paragraphs (10) and (11);

(h) explain the effect of paragraph (13); and

(i) explain the effect of regulation 4(1) [and (1A)(b)] and of section 1095(4) of the Companies Act 2006.

(9) An objection to an application under regulation 4 may be made to the registrar by any person.

(10) An objection must be made by giving notice in writing to the registrar, and the notice must state the name and address of the person making the objection and identify the application to which the objection relates.

(11) A person to whom notice of an application was given under paragraph (2), (3), (4) or (5) and who wishes to object to the application must do so before the end of the period of 28 days beginning with the date on which that notice was issued (as stated in the notice).

(12) The registrar must not take account of an objection made by any other person after the end of the period of 28 days beginning with the date on which the notices under paragraph (2), (3), (4) or (5) were issued.

(13) If a valid objection is made to the application, the registrar must reject the application.

(14) When a valid objection is made, the registrar must also—

(a) send an acknowledgment of receipt to the person who made the objection;

(b) notify the applicant of the fact that an objection has been made; and

(c) notify every other person to whom the registrar gave notice under paragraph (2), (3), (4) or (5) (but not the person who made the objection or any other person who has made an objection).

(15) If no valid objection is made, the registrar must notify the applicant of that fact.

[(15A) Paragraphs (15B) to (15F) apply in a case mentioned in section 1095(4A) of the Companies Act 2006 (but not in any other case), in place of paragraphs (8)(g) to (i) and (9) to (15).

(15B) The notice of the application given by the registrar under paragraph (3) must—

(a) give particulars of—

   (i) the right of the company to which the application relates to provide the registrar with evidence that the person named in the material did consent to act as a director of the company; and

   (ii) the requirements applying to that right under paragraph (15C); and

(b) explain the effect of regulation 4(1) and (1A)(a), paragraph (15F) of this regulation and section 1095(4B) and (4C) of the Companies Act 2006.

(15C) If the company to which the application relates wishes to provide the registrar with evidence that the person named in the material did consent to act as a director of the company, it must, before the end of the period of 28 days beginning with the date on which the registrar's notice under paragraph (3) was issued (as stated in the notice)—

(a) provide the registrar with the evidence in writing (and identify the application to which the evidence relates); and

(b) provide the registrar with a statement by the company that the evidence provided by it is true and is not misleading or deceptive in any material particular.

(15D) If the registrar is provided by the company with evidence and a statement as mentioned in paragraph (15C), the registrar must send an acknowledgement of receipt to the company.

(15E) The registrar must notify the applicant and every person to whom a notice was given under paragraph (3) of the outcome of the application.

(15F) If the outcome of the application is that the registrar does not remove the material from the register, the notice to the applicant under paragraph (15E) must be accompanied by a copy of the evidence provided by the company to the registrar under paragraph (15C)(a).]

(16) In this regulation "UK establishment" has the meaning given in section 1067(6) of the Companies Act 2006.

NOTES

Sub-para (1)(ba) was inserted, the words in square brackets in sub-para (8)(i) were inserted, and paras (15A)–(15F) were inserted, by the Registrar of Companies and Applications for Striking Off (Amendment) Regulations 2016, SI 2016/441, reg 2(1), (3), as from 6 April 2016.

[4.322]

6 Documents relating to Welsh companies: exceptions to the requirement for a certified translation, and revocation of previous exceptions

(1) The documents in paragraph (2) are excepted from the requirement in section 1104(2) of the Companies Act 2006 that a document relating to a Welsh company must, on delivery to the registrar in Welsh, be accompanied by a certified translation into English.

(2) The documents are—

(a) a non-traded company's memorandum of association;

(b) a non-traded company's articles;

(c) a community interest company report prepared for a non-traded company under section 34 of the Companies (Audit, Investigations and Community Enterprise) Act 2004;

(d) a resolution or agreement which was agreed to by members of a non-traded company and to which Chapter 3 of Part 3 of the Companies Act 2006 applies, except for a resolution or agreement listed in paragraph (3);

(e) annual accounts and reports of a non-traded company required to be delivered to the registrar under Part 15 of the Companies Act 2006;

(f) a declaration referred to in regulation 11(1)(b) or regulation 12(1)(b) or (c) of the Community Interest Company Regulations 2005 which relates to a non-traded company;

(g) revised accounts and any revised report of a non-traded company, and any auditor's report on such revised accounts and reports, required to be delivered to the registrar by the Companies (Revision of Defective Accounts and Reports) Regulations 2008;

(h) a document required to be appended to the group accounts of a non-traded company by paragraph 30(2) of Schedule 6 to the Large and Medium-sized Companies and Groups (Accounts and Reports) Regulations 2008 (banking groups: information as to undertaking in which shares held as a result of financial assistance operation);

[(i) all documents to be delivered to the registrar by a non-traded company under sections 394A(2)(e), 448A(2)(e) and 479A(2)(e) of the Companies Act 2006 (qualifying subsidiaries: conditions for exemption from the audit, preparation and filing of individual accounts).]

(3) The following is the list of resolutions and agreements referred to in paragraph (2)(d)—

(a) a special resolution that—

(i) a private company should be re-registered as a public company;

(ii) a public company should be re-registered as a private limited company;

(iii) a private limited company should be re-registered as an unlimited company; or

(iv) an unlimited company should be re-registered as a limited company;

(b) a special resolution agreeing to the change of a company's name;

(c) a special resolution required by section 37 of the Companies (Audit, Investigations and Community Enterprise) Act 2004 (requirements for an existing company to become a community interest company);

(d) a resolution or agreement as altered by an enactment other than an enactment amending the general law, required to be delivered to the registrar under section 34 of the Companies Act 2006;

(e) a resolution or agreement as altered by an order of a court or other authority, required to be delivered to the registrar under section 35 or 999 of that Act;

(f) a special resolution under section 88(2) of that Act requiring the register to be amended so that it states that a company's registered office is to be situated in Wales;

(g) a special resolution under section 626 of that Act (reduction of capital in connection with redenomination);

(h) a special resolution under section 641(1)(a) of that Act (resolution for reducing the share capital of a private limited company supported by solvency statement);

(i) a resolution under section 664(1) of that Act that a public company should be re-registered as a private company to comply with section 662.

(4) For the purposes of paragraph (2)(g), "revised accounts" and "revised report" have the meanings given in regulation 2 of the Companies (Revision of Defective Accounts and Reports) Regulations 2008.

(5) *(Revokes the Companies (Welsh Language Forms and Documents) Regulations 1994, SI 1994/117, reg 4.)*

NOTES

Para (2): sub-para (i) added by the Companies and Limited Liability Partnerships (Accounts and Audit Exemptions and Change of Accounting Framework) Regulations 2012, SI 2012/2301, regs 2, 21(1), (2), as from 1 October 2012 (in relation to accounts for financial years ending on or after that date).

[4.323]

7 Documents that may be delivered under the Companies Acts in a language other than English

(1) The documents listed in paragraph (2) are specified for the purposes of section 1105(2)(d) of the Companies Act 2006 as documents which may be drawn up and delivered to the registrar under the Companies Acts in a language other than English but which must, when delivered to the registrar, be accompanied by a certified translation into English.

(2) The documents are—

(a) a memorandum of association;

(b) a company's articles;

(c) a valuation report required to be delivered to the registrar under section 94(2)(d) of the Companies Act 2006;

(d) any order made by a competent court in the United Kingdom or elsewhere;

[(e) copies of the consolidated accounts, the auditor's report and the consolidated annual report to be delivered to the registrar under sections 394A(2)(e), 448A(2)(e) or 479A(2)(e) of the Companies Act 2006 (qualifying subsidiaries: conditions for exemption from the audit, preparation and filing of individual accounts).]

NOTES

Para (2): sub-para (e) added by the Companies and Limited Liability Partnerships (Accounts and Audit Exemptions and Change of Accounting Framework) Regulations 2012, SI 2012/2301, regs 2, 21(1), (3), as from 1 October 2012 (in relation to accounts for financial years ending on or after that date).

[4.324]

8 Permitted characters and symbols for names and addresses in documents delivered to the registrar

(1) The characters and symbols specified in paragraph (3) are permitted for the purposes of section 1108(1) of the Companies Act 2006 (and names and addresses in documents delivered to the registrar must therefore contain only those characters and symbols).

(2) But the requirement in section 1108(1) does not apply to the following documents—

(a) a memorandum of association;
(b) a company's articles;
(c) an order made by a competent court in the United Kingdom or elsewhere;
(d) an agreement required to be forwarded to the registrar under Chapter 3 of Part 3 of the Companies Act 2006 (agreements affecting a company's constitution);
(e) a valuation report required to be delivered to the registrar under section 94(2)(d) of that Act;
(f) a document required to be delivered to the registrar under section 400(2)(e) or section 401(2)(f) of that Act (company included in accounts of larger group: required to deliver copy of group accounts);
(g) an instrument or copy instrument *required to be* delivered to the registrar under Part 25 of that Act (company charges);
(h) a certified copy of the constitution of an overseas company required to be delivered to the registrar under regulation 8, 14 or 15 of the Overseas Companies Regulations 2009;
(i) a copy of accounting documents of an overseas company required to be delivered to the registrar under regulation 9, 32, 45 or 46 of those Regulations;
(j) a copy of the annual accounts of an overseas company, or of a credit or financial institution to which Chapter 2 of Part 6 of the Overseas Companies Regulations 2009 applies, required to be delivered to the registrar under section 441 of the Companies Act 2006;
[(k) a contract for the formation of a [UK] Economic Interest Grouping;
(l) an amendment to such a contract;]
[(m) documents specified in respect of any of the Forms mentioned in regulations 5 to 11 of the European Public Limited-Liability Company Regulations 2004 (provisions relating to registration etc);
(n) copies of transfer proposals required to be delivered under regulation 68(1)(a) of those Regulations (publication of terms of transfer);
(o) copies of draft terms required to be delivered under regulation 68(2)(a) or (3)(a) of those Regulations (publication of terms for formation of holding SE or conversion of company into SE);
(p) copies of amendments to statutes required to be delivered under regulation 82(1)(a) of those Regulations (notification of amendments to statutes);
(q) documents required to be delivered . . . under regulation 85 of those Regulations (registration of a public company by conversion of SE);
(r) copies of draft terms required to be delivered under regulation 86 of those Regulations (publication of draft terms of conversion);]
[(s) copies of the consolidated accounts, the auditor's report and the consolidated annual report to be delivered to the registrar under sections 394A(2)(e), 448A(2)(e) or 479A(2)(e) of the Companies Act 2006 (qualifying subsidiaries: conditions for exemption from the audit, preparation and filing of individual accounts].

(3) The characters and symbols specified in this paragraph are—

(a) those in the Schedule;
(b) full stops, commas, colons, semi-colons and hyphens;
(c) the numerals 0, 1, 2, 3, 4, 5, 6, 7, 8 and 9.

(4) In this regulation the expressions "accounting documents", "certified copy" and "constitution" have the meanings given in the Overseas Companies Regulations 2009.

NOTES

Para (2) is amended as follows:

Words in italics in sub-para (g) revoked by the Companies Act 2006 (Amendment of Part 25) Regulations 2013, SI 2013/600, reg 5, Sch 2, para 5, as from 6 April 2013, in relation to charges created on or after that date (see further the transitional provisions note at **[1.982]**).

Sub-paras (k), (l) added by the European Economic Interest Grouping (Amendment) Regulations 2009, SI 2009/2399, reg 24, as from 1 October 2009.

The words in square brackets in sub-para (k) was substituted by the European Economic Interest Grouping (Amendment) (EU Exit) Regulations 2018, SI 2018/1299, reg 65, as from IP completion day (as defined in the European Union (Withdrawal Agreement) Act 2020, s 39).

Sub-paras (m)–(r) added by the European Public Limited-Liability Company (Amendment) Regulations 2009, SI 2009/2400, reg 43, as from 1 October 2009.

Words omitted from sub-para (q) revoked by the European Economic Interest Grouping and European Public Limited-Liability Company (Amendment) Regulations 2014, SI 2014/2382, reg 36, as from 1 October 2014.

Sub-para (s) added by the Companies and Limited Liability Partnerships (Accounts and Audit Exemptions and Change of Accounting Framework) Regulations 2012, SI 2012/2301, regs 2, 21(1), (3), as from 1 October 2012 (in relation to accounts for financial years ending on or after that date).

SCHEDULE
PERMITTED CHARACTERS AND SYMBOLS

Regulation 8(3)

[4.325]

[Characters and symbols referred to in regulation 8(3)(a)

A	À	Á	Â	Ã	Ä	Å	Ā	Ă	Ą
Ǻ	a	à	á	â	ã	ä	å	ā	ă
ą	ǻ	Æ	Ǽ	æ	ǽ	B	b	C	Ç
Ć	Ĉ	Ċ	Č	c	ç	ć	ĉ	ċ	č
D	Þ	Ď	Đ	d	þ	ď	đ	E	È
É	Ê	Ë	Ē	Ĕ	Ė	Ę	Ě	e	è
é	ê	ë	ē	ĕ	ė	ę	ě	F	f
G	Ĝ	Ğ	Ġ	Ģ	g	ĝ	ğ	ġ	ģ
H	Ĥ	Ħ	h	ĥ	ħ	I	Ì	Í	Î
Ï	Ĩ	Ī	Ĭ	Į	İ	i	ì	í	î
ï	ĩ	ī	ĭ	į	J	Ĵ	j	ĵ	K
Ķ	k	ķ	L	Ĺ	Ļ	Ľ	Ŀ	Ł	l
ĺ	ļ	ľ	ŀ	ł	M	m	N	Ñ	Ń
Ņ	Ň	Ŋ	n	ñ	ń	ņ	ň	ŋ	O
Ò	Ó	Ô	Õ	Ö	Ø	Ō	Ŏ	Ő	Ǿ
o	ò	ó	ô	õ	ö	ø	ō	ŏ	ő
ǿ	Œ	œ	P	p	Q	q	R	Ŕ	Ŗ
Ř	r	ŕ	ŗ	ř	S	Ś	Ŝ	Ş	Š
s	ś	ŝ	ş	š	T	Ţ	Ť	Ŧ	t
ţ	ť	ŧ	U	Ù	Ú	Û	Ü	Ũ	Ū
Ŭ	Ů	Ű	Ų	u	ù	ú	û	ü	ũ
ū	ŭ	ů	ű	ų	V	v	W	Ŵ	Ẁ
Ẃ	Ẅ	w	ŵ	ẁ	ẃ	ẅ	X	x	Y
Ỳ	Ý	Ŷ	Ÿ	y	ỳ	ý	ŷ	ÿ	Z
Ź	Ż	Ž	z	ź	ż	ž	&	@	£
$	€	¥	*	=	#	%	+	‘	’
'	(	)	[	]	{	}	<	>	!
«	»	?	“	”	″	\	/]		

NOTES

Table substituted by the Company, Limited Liability Partnership and Business (Names and Trading Disclosures) Regulations 2015, SI 2015/17, reg 30, Sch 6, para 5, as from 31 January 2015.

OVERSEAS COMPANIES (EXECUTION OF DOCUMENTS AND REGISTRATION OF CHARGES) REGULATIONS 2009

(SI 2009/1917)

NOTES

Made: 16 July 2009.

Authority: Companies Act 2006, ss 1045, 1052, 1105, 1292(1).

Commencement: 1 October 2009.

For a summary of all Orders and Regulations made under the Companies Act 2006, see Appendix 4 at **[A4]**.

These Regulations are reproduced as amended by: the Overseas Companies (Execution of Documents and Registration of Charges) (Amendment) Regulations 2011, SI 2011/2194.

Application to European Public Limited-Liability Companies (SEs): see the International Accounting Standards and European Public Limited-Liability Company (Amendment etc) (EU Exit) Regulations 2019, SI 2019/685, reg 19, Sch 3, Pt 1, at **[12.152]**.

ARRANGEMENT OF REGULATIONS

PART 1
INTRODUCTION

PART 2
EXECUTION OF DOCUMENTS ETC

PART 3
REGISTRATION OF CHARGES

Introduction

Charges requiring registration

Special rules for debentures

The register of charges

Companies' records and register

Supplementary provisions

SCHEDULES

PART 1 INTRODUCTION

[4.326]

1 Citation and commencement

(1) These Regulations may be cited as the Overseas Companies (Execution of Documents and Registration of Charges) Regulations 2009.

(2) These Regulations come into force on 1st October 2009.

[4.327]

2 Interpretation

In these Regulations—

"certified copy" means a copy certified as a correct copy;

"establishment" means—

(a) a branch within the meaning of the Eleventh Company Law Directive (89/666/EEC), or

(b) a place of business that is not such a branch, and

"UK establishment" means an establishment in the United Kingdom.

PART 2 EXECUTION OF DOCUMENTS ETC

[4.328]

3 Application of Part

This Part applies to all overseas companies.

[4.329]

4 Formalities of doing business under the law of England and Wales and Northern Ireland

Sections 43, 44 and 46 of the Companies Act 2006 apply to overseas companies, modified so that they read as follows—

"43 Company contracts

(1) Under the law of England and Wales or Northern Ireland a contract may be made—

(a) by an overseas company, by writing under its common seal or in any manner permitted by the laws of the territory in which the company is incorporated for the execution of documents by such a company, and

(b) on behalf of an overseas company, by any person who, in accordance with the laws of the territory in which the company is incorporated, is acting under the authority (express or implied) of that company.

(2) Any formalities required by law in the case of a contract made by an individual also apply, unless a contrary intention appears, to a contract made by or on behalf of an overseas company.

44 Execution of documents

(1) Under the law of England and Wales or Northern Ireland a document is executed by an overseas company—

(a) by the affixing of its common seal, or

(b) if it is executed in any manner permitted by the laws of the territory in which the company is incorporated for the execution of documents by such a company.

(2) A document which—

(a) is signed by a person who, in accordance with the laws of the territory in which an overseas company is incorporated, is acting under the authority (express or implied) of the company, and

(b) is expressed (in whatever form of words) to be executed by the company,

has the same effect in relation to that company as it would have in relation to a company incorporated in England and Wales or Northern Ireland if executed under the common seal of a company so incorporated.

(3) In favour of a purchaser a document is deemed to have been duly executed by an overseas company if it purports to be signed in accordance with subsection (2).

A "purchaser" means a purchaser in good faith for valuable consideration and includes a lessee, mortgagee or other person who for valuable consideration acquires an interest in property.

(4) Where a document is to be signed by a person on behalf of more than one overseas company, it is not duly signed by that person for the purposes of this section unless he signs it separately in each capacity.

(5) References in this section to a document being (or purporting to be) signed by a person who, in accordance with the laws of the territory in which an overseas company is incorporated, is acting under the authority (express or implied) of the company are to be read, in a case where that person is a firm, as references to its being (or purporting to be) signed by an individual authorised by the firm to sign on its behalf.

(6) This section applies to a document that is (or purports to be) executed by an overseas company in the name of or on behalf of another person whether or not that person is also an overseas company.

46 Execution of deeds

(1) A document is validly executed by an overseas company as a deed for the purposes of section 1(2)(b) of the Law of Property (Miscellaneous Provisions) Act 1989 (c 34) and for the purposes of the law of Northern Ireland if, and only if—

(a) it is duly executed by the company, and

(b) it is delivered as a deed.

(2) For the purposes of subsection (1)(b) a document is presumed to be delivered upon its being executed, unless a contrary intention is proved.".

[4.330]

5 Formalities of doing business under the law of Scotland

Section 48 of the Companies Act 2006 applies to overseas companies, modified so that it reads as follows—

"48 Execution of documents by overseas companies

(1) The following provision forms part of the law of Scotland only.

(2) For the purposes of any enactment—

(a) providing for a document to be executed by a company by affixing its common seal, or

(b) referring (in whatever terms) to a document so executed,

a document signed or subscribed by or on behalf of an overseas company in accordance with the provisions of the Requirements of Writing (Scotland) Act 1995 (c 7) has effect as if so executed.".

[4.331]

6 Other matters

Section 51 of the Companies Act 2006 applies to overseas companies, modified so that it reads as follows—

"51 Pre-incorporation contracts, deeds and obligations

(1) A contract that purports to be made by or on behalf of an overseas company at a time when the company has not been formed has effect, subject to any agreement to the contrary, as one made with the person purporting to act for the company or as agent for it, and he is personally liable on the contract accordingly.

(2) Subsection (1) applies—

(a) to the making of a deed under the law of England and Wales or Northern Ireland, and

(b) to the undertaking of an obligation under the law of Scotland,

as it applies to the making of a contract.".

7 *(Revokes the Foreign Companies (Execution of Documents) Regulations 1994, SI 1994/950, and the Foreign Companies (Execution of Documents) Regulations (Northern Ireland) 2003, SR 2003/5.)*

PART 3 REGISTRATION OF CHARGES

Introduction

[4.332]

8 Application and interpretation of Part

(1) This Part applies to an overseas company that is registered (as defined below).

(2) For the purposes of this Part—

(a) an overseas company becomes registered when it complies with Part 2 (initial registration of particulars) of the Overseas Companies Regulations 2009 in respect of one or more UK establishments and those particulars are registered, and

(b) an overseas company ceases to be registered when it gives notice under regulation 77 (notice of closure of UK establishment) of those regulations in respect of all its UK establishments and that notice is registered.

(3) For the purposes of this Part the particulars and notice referred to in paragraph (2) are not treated as registered unless and until they are on the register and accordingly available for public inspection.

(4) In this Part "charge"—

(a) in England and Wales and Northern Ireland, includes a mortgage;

(b) in Scotland, includes any right in security.

(5) In relation to a charge created under the law of Scotland, references in this Part to the date of creation of the charge are to—

(a) in the case of a floating charge, the date on which the instrument creating the floating charge was executed by the company creating the charge;

(b) in any other case, the date on which the right of the person entitled to the benefit of the charge was constituted as a real right.

NOTES

Para (5): revoked by the Overseas Companies (Execution of Documents and Registration of Charges) (Amendment) Regulations 2011, SI 2011/2194, reg 2(1), (2), as from 1 October 2011 (in relation to charges created by a company on or after that date).

Charges requiring registration

[4.333]

9 Charges requiring registration

(1) A charge requires registration under this Part if—

(a) it is created by a company to which this Part applies,

(b) the property subject to the charge is situated in the United Kingdom, and

(c) the charge is of a type requiring registration.

(2) Whether the conditions in paragraph (1)(a) and (b) are met is determined when the charge is created.

(3) The types of charge requiring registration are—

(a) a charge on land or any interest in land, other than a charge for rent or any other periodical sum issuing out of (in Scotland, payable in respect of) land;

(b) a charge created or evidenced by an instrument that, if executed by an individual, would require registration as a bill of sale;

(c) a charge for the purposes of securing any issue of debentures;

(d) a charge on uncalled share capital of the company;

(e) a charge on calls made but not paid;

(f) a charge on book debts of the company;

(g) a floating charge on the company's property or undertaking;

(h) a charge on a ship or aircraft, or any share in a ship;

(i) a charge on goodwill or on any intellectual property.

(4) For the purposes of paragraph (3)(a)—

(a) a charge on land includes a charge created by a heritable security within the meaning of section 9(8) of the Conveyancing and Feudal Reform (Scotland) Act 1970; and

(b) the holding of debentures entitling the holder to a charge on land is not an interest in the land.

(5) For the purposes of paragraph (3)(f) the deposit by way of security of a negotiable instrument given to secure the payment of book debts is not a charge on those book debts.

(6) For the purposes of paragraph (3)(i), "intellectual property" means—

(a) any patent, trade mark, registered design, copyright or design right; or

(b) any licence under or in respect of any such right.

NOTES

This regulation was revoked by the Overseas Companies (Execution of Documents and Registration of Charges) (Amendment) Regulations 2011, SI 2011/2194, reg 2(1), (3), as from 1 October 2011 (in relation to charges created by a company on or after that date).

[4.334]

10 Duty to deliver particulars of charge etc for registration

(1) A company to which this Part applies that creates a charge requiring registration must deliver the required particulars of the charge, together with a certified copy of the instrument (if any) by which the charge is created or evidenced, to the registrar before the end of the period allowed for registration.

(2) Registration of the charge may instead be effected on the application of a person interested in it.

(3) Where registration is effected on the application of some person other than the company, that person is entitled to recover from the company the amount of any fees properly paid by him to the registrar on registration.

(4) Paragraph (1) does not apply if the property subject to the charge is, at the end of the period allowed for registration, no longer situated in the United Kingdom.

NOTES

This regulation was revoked by the Overseas Companies (Execution of Documents and Registration of Charges) (Amendment) Regulations 2011, SI 2011/2194, reg 2(1), (3), as from 1 October 2011 (in relation to charges created by a company on or after that date).

[4.335]

11 The required particulars

(1) The required particulars are—

- *(a) the date of the creation of the charge,*
- *(b) a description of the instrument (if any) creating or evidencing the charge,*
- *(c) the amount secured by the charge,*
- *(d) the name and address of the person entitled to the charge, and*
- *(e) short particulars of the property charged.*

(2) In the case of a floating charge created under the law of Scotland, the required particulars include a statement as to any provisions of the charge and of any instrument relating to it—

- *(a) which prohibit or restrict or regulate the power of the company to grant further securities ranking in priority to, or pari passu with, the floating charge, or*
- *(b) which vary or otherwise regulate the order of ranking of the floating charge in relation to subsisting securities.*

NOTES

This regulation was revoked by the Overseas Companies (Execution of Documents and Registration of Charges) (Amendment) Regulations 2011, SI 2011/2194, reg 2(1), (3), as from 1 October 2011 (in relation to charges created by a company on or after that date).

[4.336]

12 The period allowed for registration

The period allowed for registration of the charge is—

- *(a) 21 days, beginning with the day after the day on which the charge is created, or*
- *(b) if the charge is created outside the United Kingdom, 21 days beginning with the day after the day on which the instrument by which the charge is created or evidenced (or a copy of it) could, in due course of post (and if despatched with due diligence) have been received in the United Kingdom.*

NOTES

This regulation was revoked by the Overseas Companies (Execution of Documents and Registration of Charges) (Amendment) Regulations 2011, SI 2011/2194, reg 2(1), (3), as from 1 October 2011 (in relation to charges created by a company on or after that date).

[4.337]

13 Charge by way of ex facie absolute disposition

(1) For the avoidance of doubt, it is hereby declared that, in the case of a charge created under the law of Scotland by way of an ex facie absolute disposition or assignation qualified by a back letter or other agreement, or by a standard security qualified by an agreement, compliance with regulation 10(1) does not of itself render the charge unavailable as security for indebtedness incurred after the date of compliance.

(2) Where the amount secured by a charge so created is purported to be increased by a further back letter or agreement, a further charge is held to have been created by the ex facie absolute disposition or assignation or (as the case may be) by the standard security, as qualified by the further back letter or agreement.

(3) In that case, the provisions of this Part apply to the further charge as if—

- *(a) references in this Part (other than in this regulation) to a charge were references to the further charge, and*
- *(b) references to the date of creation of a charge were references to the date on which the further back letter or agreement was executed.*

NOTES

This regulation was revoked by the Overseas Companies (Execution of Documents and Registration of Charges) (Amendment) Regulations 2011, SI 2011/2194, reg 2(1), (3), as from 1 October 2011 (in relation to charges created by a company on or after that date).

Special rules for debentures

[4.338]

14 Special rules about debentures: charge in series of debentures

(1) Where a series of debentures containing, or giving by reference to another instrument, any charge to the benefit of which debenture holders of that series are entitled pari passu is created by a company, it is for the purposes of regulation 10 sufficient if the following particulars, together with a certified copy of the instrument containing the charge (or, if there is no such instrument, a certified copy of one of the debentures of the series), are delivered to the registrar before the end of the period allowed for registration.

(2) The required particulars are—

- *(a) the total amount secured by the whole series,*
- *(b) the dates of the resolutions authorising the issue of the series and the date of the covering instrument (if any) by which the series is created or defined,*

(c) *a general description of the property charged, and*
(d) *the names of the trustees (if any) for the debenture holders.*

(3) In the case of a floating charge created under the law of Scotland, the required particulars include a statement as to any provisions of the charge and of any instrument relating to it—

(a) *which prohibit or restrict or regulate the power of the company to grant further securities ranking in priority to, or pari passu with, the floating charge, or*
(b) *which vary or otherwise regulate the order of ranking of the floating charge in relation to subsisting securities.*

(4) Where more than one issue is made of debentures in the series, particulars of the date and amount of each issue of debentures of the series must be sent to the registrar for entry in the register of charges.

NOTES

This regulation was revoked by the Overseas Companies (Execution of Documents and Registration of Charges) (Amendment) Regulations 2011, SI 2011/2194, reg 2(1), (3), as from 1 October 2011 (in relation to charges created by a company on or after that date).

[4.339]

15 Special rules about debentures: additional registration requirement for commission etc

(1) Where any commission, allowance or discount has been paid or made either directly or indirectly by a company to a person in consideration of their—

(a) *subscribing or agreeing to subscribe, whether absolutely or conditionally, for debentures in a company, or*
(b) *procuring or agreeing to procure subscriptions, whether absolute or conditional, for such debentures,*

the particulars required to be sent for registration under regulation 10 include particulars as to the amount or rate per cent. of the commission, discount or allowance so paid or made.

(2) The deposit of debentures as security for a debt of the company is not, for the purposes of this regulation, treated as the issue of debentures at a discount.

NOTES

This regulation was revoked by the Overseas Companies (Execution of Documents and Registration of Charges) (Amendment) Regulations 2011, SI 2011/2194, reg 2(1), (3), as from 1 October 2011 (in relation to charges created by a company on or after that date).

[4.340]

16 Special rules about debentures: period allowed for registration

The period allowed for registration of particulars of a series of debentures as a result of regulation 14 is—

(a) *if there is an instrument containing the charge mentioned in paragraph (1) of that regulation, 21 days beginning with the day after the date on which that instrument is executed;*
(b) *if there is no such instrument, 21 days beginning with the day after the day on which the first debenture of the series is executed.*

NOTES

This regulation was revoked by the Overseas Companies (Execution of Documents and Registration of Charges) (Amendment) Regulations 2011, SI 2011/2194, reg 2(1), (3), as from 1 October 2011 (in relation to charges created by a company on or after that date).

[4.341]

17 Special rules about debentures: endorsement of certificate on debentures

(1) The company shall cause a copy of every certificate of registration given under regulation 18(4) to be endorsed on every debenture or certificate of debenture stock which is issued by the company, and the payment of which is secured by the charge so registered.

(2) This does not require a company to cause a certificate of registration of any charge so given to be endorsed on any debenture or certificate of debenture stock issued by the company before the charge was created.

(3) A person commits an offence who knowingly and wilfully authorises or permits the delivery of a debenture or certificate of debenture stock which under this regulation is required to have endorsed on it a copy of a certificate of registration, without the copy being so endorsed upon it.

(4) A person guilty of an offence under this regulation is liable on summary conviction to a fine not exceeding level 3 on the standard scale.

NOTES

This regulation was revoked by the Overseas Companies (Execution of Documents and Registration of Charges) (Amendment) Regulations 2011, SI 2011/2194, reg 2(1), (3), as from 1 October 2011 (in relation to charges created by a company on or after that date).

The register of charges

[4.342]

18 The register of charges

(1) The registrar shall keep for each company to which this Part applies a register of all the charges requiring registration under this Part.

(2) The registrar shall enter in the register the particulars required to be delivered to the registrar under this Part.

(3) In the case of a charge imposed by the Enforcement of Judgments Office under Article 46 of the Judgments Enforcement (Northern Ireland) Order 1981, the registrar shall enter in the register the date on which the charge became effective.

(4) The registrar shall give a certificate of the registration of any charge registered in pursuance of this Part, stating the name of the company and the amount secured by the charge

(5) The certificate—

(a) shall be signed by the registrar or authenticated by the registrar's official seal, and

(b) is conclusive evidence that the requirements of this Part as to registration have been satisfied.

(6) The register kept in pursuance of this regulation shall be open to inspection by any person.

NOTES

This regulation was revoked by the Overseas Companies (Execution of Documents and Registration of Charges) (Amendment) Regulations 2011, SI 2011/2194, reg 2(1), (3), as from 1 October 2011 (in relation to charges created by a company on or after that date).

[4.343]

19 Consequences of failure to register

(1) If a company creates a charge requiring registration under this Part, the charge is void (so far as any security on the company's property or undertaking is conferred by it) against—

(a) a liquidator of the company,

(b) an administrator of the company, and

(c) a creditor of the company,

if regulation 10 (duty to deliver particulars of charge etc for registration) is not complied with.

(2) Failure to comply with—

(a) regulation 14(4) (special rules for debentures: duty to send particulars of each issue of debentures), or

(b) regulation 15 (special rules for debentures: additional registration requirement for commission etc),

does not affect the validity of the debentures issued.

(3) Paragraph (1) is without prejudice to any contract or obligation for repayment of the money secured by the charge; and when a charge becomes void under this regulation, the money secured by it immediately becomes payable.

NOTES

This regulation was revoked by the Overseas Companies (Execution of Documents and Registration of Charges) (Amendment) Regulations 2011, SI 2011/2194, reg 2(1), (3), as from 1 October 2011 (in relation to charges created by a company on or after that date).

[4.344]

20 Registration of enforcement of security

(1) A person who—

(a) obtains an order for the appointment of a receiver or manager of property of a company to which this Part applies, or

(b) appoints such a receiver or manager under powers contained in an instrument,

must give notice of the fact to the registrar within seven days of the order or of the appointment under those powers.

(2) A person appointed receiver or manager of a company's property under powers contained in an instrument who ceases to act as such receiver or manager must, on so ceasing, give the registrar notice to that effect.

(3) The registrar must enter a fact of which notice is given under this regulation in the register of charges.

(4) A person who makes default in complying with the requirements of paragraph (1) or (2) commits an offence.

(5) A person guilty of an offence under this regulation is liable on summary conviction to a fine not exceeding level 3 on the standard scale and, for continued contravention, a daily default fine not exceeding one-tenth of level 3 on the standard scale.

(6) This regulation does not apply in relation to the appointment of a receiver under section 51(1) or (2) of the Insolvency Act 1986 (appointment under law of Scotland by holder of floating charge or by court on application of holder), as respects which section 53(1) or 54(3) of that Act requires the delivery to the registrar of a copy of the instrument or interlocutor making the appointment.

NOTES

This regulation was revoked by the Overseas Companies (Execution of Documents and Registration of Charges) (Amendment) Regulations 2011, SI 2011/2194, reg 2(1), (3), as from 1 October 2011 (in relation to charges created by a company on or after that date).

[4.345]

21 Entries of satisfaction and release

(1) This regulation applies if a statement is delivered to the registrar verifying with respect to a registered charge—

(a) that the debt for which the charge was given has been paid or satisfied in whole or in part, or

(b) that part of the property or undertaking charged has been released from the charge or has ceased to form part of the company's property or undertaking.

(2) If the charge is a floating charge created under the law of Scotland, the statement must be accompanied by either—

(a) a statement by the creditor entitled to the benefit of the charge, or a person authorised by the creditor for that purpose, verifying that the statement mentioned in paragraph (1) is correct, or

(b) a direction obtained from the court, on the ground that the statement by the creditor mentioned in sub-paragraph (a) could not be readily obtained, dispensing with the need for that statement.

(3) The registrar may enter on the register a memorandum of satisfaction in whole or in part, or of the fact that part of the property or undertaking has been released from the charge or has ceased to form part of the company's property or undertaking (as the case may be).

(4) Where the registrar enters a memorandum of satisfaction in whole, the registrar must if required send the company a copy of it.

(5) Nothing in this regulation requires the company to submit particulars with respect to the entry in the register of a memorandum of satisfaction where the company, having created a floating charge under the law of Scotland over all or any part of its property, disposes of part of the property subject to the floating charge.

NOTES

This regulation was revoked by the Overseas Companies (Execution of Documents and Registration of Charges) (Amendment) Regulations 2011, SI 2011/2194, reg 2(1), (3), as from 1 October 2011 (in relation to charges created by a company on or after that date).

[4.346]
22 Rectification of register of charges

If the court is satisfied—

(a) that the failure to register a charge before the end of the period allowed for registration, or the omission or mis-statement of any particular with respect to any such charge or in a memorandum of satisfaction—
  (i) was accidental or due to inadvertence or to some other sufficient cause, or
  (ii) is not of a nature to prejudice the position of creditors or shareholders of the company, or

(b) that on other grounds it is just and equitable to grant relief,

the court may, on the application of the company or a person interested, and on such terms and conditions as seem to the court just and expedient, order that the period allowed for registration shall be extended or, as the case may be, that the omission or mis-statement shall be rectified.

NOTES

This regulation was revoked by the Overseas Companies (Execution of Documents and Registration of Charges) (Amendment) Regulations 2011, SI 2011/2194, reg 2(1), (3), as from 1 October 2011 (in relation to charges created by a company on or after that date).

Companies' records and register

[4.347]
23 Companies to keep available for inspection copies of instruments creating charges

(1) A company to which this Part applies must keep available for inspection a copy of every instrument creating a charge [referred to in regulation 24(1)].

(2) In the case of a series of uniform debentures, a copy of one of the debentures of the series is sufficient.

NOTES

Words in square brackets in para (1) substituted (for the original words "requiring registration under this Part"), and para (2) revoked, by the Overseas Companies (Execution of Documents and Registration of Charges) (Amendment) Regulations 2011, SI 2011/2194, reg 2(1), (4), as from 1 October 2011 (in relation to charges created by a company on or after that date).

[4.348]
24 Company's register of charges

[(1) Every company to which this Part applies must keep available for inspection a register of charges and must, as soon as practicable and in any event within 21 days of the creation of the charge, enter in it—

(a) any charge on land situated in the United Kingdom or any interest in such land;
(b) any charge on ships, aircraft or intellectual property registered in the United Kingdom; and
(c) any floating charge on the whole or part of the company's property or undertaking situated in the United Kingdom.]

(2) The entry must in each case give a short description of the property[, land or undertaking] charged, the amount of the charge and, except in the cases of securities to bearer, the names of the persons entitled to it.

[(2A) Paragraph (1)(c) does not apply to a floating charge which expressly excludes all property or undertaking of the company situated in the United Kingdom or which purports to be a fixed charge.

(2B) A charge on land, for the purposes of this regulation, includes a charge created by a heritable security within the meaning of section 9(8) of the Conveyancing and Feudal Reform (Scotland) Act 1970.

(2C) The holding of debentures entitling the holder to a charge on land is not, for the purposes of this regulation, an interest in land.]

(3) An officer of the company who knowingly and wilfully authorises or permits the omission of an entry required to be made in pursuance of this regulation commits an offence.

(4) A person guilty of an offence under this regulation is liable—

(a) on conviction on indictment, to a fine;
(b) on summary conviction, to a fine not exceeding the statutory maximum.

NOTES

Para (1) was substituted, the words in square brackets in para (2) were inserted, and paras (2A)–(2C) were inserted, by the Overseas Companies (Execution of Documents and Registration of Charges) (Amendment) Regulations 2011, SI 2011/2194, reg 2(1), (5), as from 1 October 2011 (in relation to charges created by a company on or after that date). The original para (1) read as follows—

"(1) Every company to which this Part applies must keep available for inspection a register of charges and must enter in it—

(a) all charges specifically affecting property of the company situated in the United Kingdom, and
(b) all floating charges on the whole or part of the company's property or undertaking situated in the United Kingdom.".

[4.349]

25 Copies of instruments and company's register of charges to be available for inspection

(1) This regulation applies to—

(a) documents required to be kept available for inspection under regulation 23 (copies of instruments creating charges), and

(b) a company's register of charges kept in pursuance of regulation 24.

(2) The documents and register must be kept available for inspection at a location in the United Kingdom at which the company carries on business notified to the registrar in accordance with paragraph (3).

(3) The company must give notice to the registrar—

(a) of the place at which the documents and register are kept available for inspection, within [21] days of the first [entry on the register] of a charge under [regulation 24(1)], and

(b) of any change in that place, within 14 days of any such change.

(4) The documents and register shall be open to the inspection—

(a) of any creditor or member of the company without charge, and

(b) of any other person on payment of £3.50 for each hour or part of an hour during which the right of inspection is exercised.

(5) If default is made in complying with paragraph (3) or an inspection required under paragraph (4) is refused, an offence is committed by—

(a) the company, and

(b) every officer of the company who is in default.

(6) A person guilty of an offence under this regulation is liable on summary conviction to a fine not exceeding level 3 on the standard scale and, for continued contravention, a daily default fine not exceeding one-tenth of level 3 on the standard scale.

(7) If an inspection required under paragraph (4) is refused the court may by order compel an immediate inspection.

NOTES

Para (3): words in square brackets substituted (for the original words "14", "registration", and "this Part" respectively) by the Overseas Companies (Execution of Documents and Registration of Charges) (Amendment) Regulations 2011, SI 2011/2194, reg 2(1), (6), as from 1 October 2011 (in relation to charges created by a company on or after that date). Note also that by virtue of reg 3 of the 2011 Regulations, these amendments do not apply where the company has given notice to the registrar of the place at which the documents and register are kept available for inspection in respect of a charge created before 1 October 2011).

[4.350]

26 Exercise of right of inspection

(1) A company to which this Part applies shall make the documents and register referred to in regulation 25 available for inspection by a person on a day which has been specified by that person ("the specified day") provided that—

(a) the specified day is a working day; and

(b) that person gives the company the required notice of the specified day.

(2) The required notice is at least 10 working days' notice of the specified day.

(3) When a person gives notice of the specified day he shall also give notice of the time on that day at which he wishes to start the inspection (which shall be any time between 9 am and 3 pm) and the company shall make its [documents and register] available for inspection by that person for a period of at least 2 hours beginning with that time.

(4) A company that fails to comply with this regulation is treated as having refused inspection.

NOTES

Para (3): words in square brackets substituted (for the original words "company records") by the Overseas Companies (Execution of Documents and Registration of Charges) (Amendment) Regulations 2011, SI 2011/2194, reg 2(1), (7), as from 1 October 2011 (in relation to charges created by a company on or after that date).

[4.351]

[26A Inspection by electronic means

Where the company and the person agree, the inspection referred to in regulation 26 may be carried out by electronic means.]

NOTES

Inserted by the Overseas Companies (Execution of Documents and Registration of Charges) (Amendment) Regulations 2011, SI 2011/2194, reg 2(1), (8), as from 1 October 2011 (in relation to charges created by a company on or after that date).

Supplementary provisions

[4.352]

27 Delivery of documents in language other than English

(1) The following documents are specified for the purposes of section 1105(2)(d) of the Companies Act 2006 as documents that may be drawn up and delivered to the registrar in a language other than English, but which must, when delivered to the registrar, be accompanied by a certified translation into English.

(2) The documents are a certified copy of a debenture or other instrument creating or evidencing a charge over the property of an overseas company to which this Part applies.

NOTES

This regulation was revoked by the Overseas Companies (Execution of Documents and Registration of Charges) (Amendment) Regulations 2011, SI 2011/2194, reg 2(1), (9), as from 1 October 2011 (in relation to charges created by a company on or after that date).

[4.353]

28 Transitional provisions and savings

The Schedule to these Regulations contains transitional provisions and savings.

SCHEDULE
REGISTRATION OF CHARGES: TRANSITIONAL PROVISIONS AND SAVINGS

Regulation 28

[4.354]

1 Introduction

In this Schedule—

"the 1985 Act" means the Companies Act 1985; and

"the 1986 Order" means the Companies (Northern Ireland) Order 1986.

2 Charge created by company

(1) The provisions of Part 12 of the 1985 Act relating to charges created by companies incorporated outside Great Britain continue to apply in relation to charges created before 1st October 2009.

(2) The provisions of Part 13 of the 1986 Order relating to charges created by companies incorporated outside Northern Ireland continue to apply in relation to charges created before 1st October 2009.

(3) The provisions of Part 3 of these Regulations apply to charges created on or after that date.

3 Charge in series of debentures

(1) The provisions of Part 12 of the 1985 Act relating to the registration of a series of debentures of a company incorporated outside Great Britain continue to apply where the first debenture of the series was executed before 1st October 2009.

(2) The provisions of Part 13 of the 1986 Order relating to the registration of a series of debentures of a company incorporated outside Northern Ireland continue to apply where the first debenture of the series was executed before 1st October 2009.

(3) The provisions of Part 3 of these Regulations apply where the first debenture of the series is executed on or after that date.

4 Charge on property acquired by company

(1) The provisions of Part 12 of the 1985 Act relating to charges existing on property acquired by a company incorporated outside Great Britain continue to apply to property acquired before 1st October 2009.

(2) The provisions of Part 13 of the 1986 Order relating to charges existing on property acquired by a company incorporated outside Northern Ireland continue to apply to property acquired before 1st October 2009.

5 Northern Ireland: registration of certain charges etc affecting land

Article 408 of the 1986 Order (Northern Ireland: registration of certain charges etc affecting land) continues to apply in relation to a charge against land, or an estate in land, of a company incorporated outside Northern Ireland imposed by an order under Article 46 of the Judgments Enforcement (Northern Ireland) Order 1981 made before 1st October 2009.

6 Registration of enforcement of security

(1) Section 405 of the 1985 Act or Article 413 of the 1986 Order (registration of enforcement of security) continues to apply where the order or appointment is made, or the receiver or manager ceases to act, before 1st October 2009.

(2) Regulation 20 applies where the order or appointment is made, or the receiver or manager ceases to act, on or after that date.

7 Entries of satisfaction and release

(1) Section 403 or 419 of the 1985 Act or Article 411 of the 1986 Order (entries of satisfaction and release) continues to apply where the relevant statutory declaration, statement or application and statutory declaration or statement is received by the registrar before 1st October 2009.

(2) Regulation 21 applies to statements delivered to the registrar on or after 1st October 2009.

COMPANIES ACT 2006 (CONSEQUENTIAL AMENDMENTS, TRANSITIONAL PROVISIONS AND SAVINGS) ORDER 2009

(SI 2009/1941)

NOTES

Made: 21 July 2008.

Authority: European Communities Act 1972, s 2(2); Companies Act 2006, ss 657, 1088, 1292, 1294, 1296(1), 1300(2); Charities Act 2006, s 75(4), (5) (see also the note "Statutory Instruments made under the European Communities Act 1972" preceding paragraph **[4.1]** *ante*).

Commencement: 1 October 2009.

For a summary of all Orders and Regulations made under the Companies Act 2006, see Appendix 4 at **[A4]**.

This Order is reproduced as amended by: the Companies Act 2006 (Consequential Amendments and Transitional Provisions) Order 2011, SI 2011/1265.

ARRANGEMENT OF ARTICLES

Introductory

Introductory

[4.355]

1 Citation and commencement

(1) This Order may be cited as the Companies Act 2006 (Consequential Amendments, Transitional Provisions and Savings) Order 2009.

(2) The provisions of this Order come into force on 1st October 2009.

Consequential amendments

[4.356]

2 Consequential amendments, repeals and revocations

(1) Schedule 1 to this Order contains consequential amendments.

(2) Schedule 2 to this Order contains other consequential repeals and revocations.

[4.357]

3 References to companies registered or re-registered under earlier legislation

A reference in any enactment to—

(a) a company formed and registered under the Companies Act 2006,
(b) a company registered but not formed under that Act, or
(c) a company re-registered under that Act,

includes a company treated as so formed and registered, registered or re-registered by virtue of section 1297(3) of that Act, including that provision as applied by paragraph 1(2) of Schedule 2 to the Companies Act 2006 (Commencement No 8, Transitional Provisions and Savings) Order 2008.

[4.358]

4 References to Northern Ireland directors disqualification orders

A reference in any enactment to a disqualification order under the Company Directors Disqualification (Northern Ireland) Order 2002 includes a disqualification order made under Part 2 of the Companies (Northern Ireland) Order 1989 that by virtue of section 29(3)(a) of the Interpretation Act (Northern Ireland) 1954 has effect as if made under the 2002 Order.

Transitional provisions

[4.359]

5 Change of name by existing or transitional company

(1) This article applies where, in the case of an existing or transitional company—

(a) the company's articles are deemed to contain a statement of its name by virtue of section 28 of the Companies Act 2006 (provisions of memorandum treated as provisions of articles), and
(b) the company changes its name (by any means) on or after 1st October 2009.

(2) The company is not required to amend its articles in order to effect the change of name.

(3) The deemed statement in the company's articles ceases to have effect when the change of name takes effect.

(4) The company is not required to send a copy of its articles to the registrar in accordance with section 26 of the Companies Act 2006.

(5) Where the company, in complying with any obligation to send a person a copy of its articles, relies on paragraph 9(1)(a) or (b) of Schedule 2 to the Companies Act 2006 (Commencement No 8, Transitional Provisions and Savings) Order 2008, it must—

(a) if it relies on paragraph 9(1)(a) (provisions of old-style memorandum appended to other provisions of articles), omit the provision stating the company's former name;

(b) if it relies on paragraph 9(1)(b) (copy of old-style memorandum with indication of provisions deemed to be provisions of the articles), indicate that the provision stating the company's former name is no longer effective.

(6) In this article—

"existing company" and "transitional company" have the same meaning as in the Companies Act 2006 (Commencement No 8, Transitional Provisions and Savings) Order 2008 (see article 2 of that Order); and

"old-style memorandum" has the same meaning as in paragraph 9(1) of Schedule 2 to that Order (see sub-paragraph (2) of that paragraph).

[4.360]

6 Companies that are charities: requirement of consent for affirmation of certain transactions

(1) Section 42(4) of the Companies Act 2006 (companies that are charities: requirement of consent for affirmation of certain transactions with directors or their associates) applies where the request for consent is received on or after 1st October 2009.

(2) Any request for consent under section 65(4) of the Charities Act 1993 or Article 9A(4) of the Charities (Northern Ireland) Order 1987 received but not determined before that date is treated as if made under section 42(4) of the Companies Act 2006.

(3) In relation to a decision under section 65(4) of the Charities Act 1993 made before 1st October 2009 the provisions of that Act as to appeals continue to have effect without the amendments made by this Order.

NOTES

Charities Act 1993, s 65: repealed by the Companies Act 2006 (Consequential Amendments, Transitional Provisions and Savings) Order 2009, SI 2009/1941,as from 1 October 2009.

[4.361]

7 Functions of registrar of companies for Northern Ireland: contracting out

(1) On the coming into force in relation to the registrar of companies for Northern Ireland of an order under Part 2 of the Deregulation and Contracting Out Act 1994, as amended by this Order, the provisions of the Deregulation and Contracting Out (Northern Ireland) Order 1996 relating to that registrar shall cease to have effect.

(2) Those provisions are—

(a) in Article 2(2), the definition of "registrar of companies";

(b) Article 11; and

(c) Part 1 of Schedule 2.

[4.362]

8 Amendments of insolvency legislation

(1) The amendments by this Order of the Insolvency Act 1986 ("the 1986 Act") and the Insolvency (Northern Ireland) Order 1989 ("the 1989 Order") apply as follows.

(2) They apply where, in a company voluntary arrangement, a moratorium comes into force in relation to a company on or after 1st October 2009.

(3) They apply where a company enters administration on or after 1st October 2009, except where—

(a) it enters administration by virtue of an administration order under paragraph 10 of Schedule B1 to the 1986 Act (or paragraph 11 of Schedule B1 to the 1989 Order) on an application made before 1st October 2009,

(b) the administration is immediately preceded by a voluntary liquidation in respect of which the resolution to wind up was passed before 1st October 2009, or

(c) the administration is immediately preceded by a liquidation on the making of a winding-up order on a petition which was presented before 1st October 2009.

(4) They apply where, in a receivership, a receiver or manager is appointed in respect of a company on or after 1st October 2009.

(5) They apply where a company goes into liquidation upon the passing on or after 1st October 2009 of a resolution to wind up.

(6) They apply where a company goes into voluntary liquidation under paragraph 83 of Schedule B1 to the 1986 Act (or paragraph 84 of Schedule B1 to the 1989 Order), except where the preceding administration—

(a) commenced before 1st October 2009, or

(b) is an administration which commenced by virtue of an administration order under paragraph 10 of Schedule B1 to the 1986 Act (or paragraph 11 of Schedule B1 to the 1989 Order) on an application which was made before 1st October 2009.

(7) They apply where a company goes into liquidation on the making of a winding-up order on a petition presented on or after 1st October 2009, except where the liquidation is immediately preceded by—

(a) an administration under paragraph 10 of Schedule B1 to the 1986 Act (or paragraph 11 of Schedule B1 to the 1989 Order) where the administration order was made on an application made before 1st October 2009,

(b) an administration in respect of which the appointment of an administrator under paragraph 14 or 22 of Schedule B1 to the 1986 Act (or paragraph 15 or 23 of Schedule B1 to the 1989 Order) took effect before 1st October 2009, or

(c) a voluntary liquidation in respect of which the resolution to wind up was passed before 1st October 2009.

Savings

[4.363]

9 Saving for unlimited liabilities of directors etc

The repeal of the provisions relating to unlimited liability of directors and others, that is—

(a) sections 306 and 307 of the Companies Act 1985 and section 75 of the Insolvency Act 1986, or

(b) Articles 314 and 315 of the Companies (Northern Ireland) Order 1986 and Article 62 of the Insolvency (Northern Ireland) Order 1989,

does not affect the operation of those provisions in relation to liabilities arising before 1st October 2009 or in connection with the holding of an office to which a person was appointed before that date on the understanding that their liability would be unlimited.

[4.364]

10 Saving for information obtained or report made under repealed NI provisions

(1) The operation of any provision about the disclosure of information—

(a) obtained under a repealed NI provision, or

(b) contained in a report made under a repealed NI provision,

is not affected by the repeal of that provision (or the repeal of the NI provision).

(2) So far as may be necessary for continuing the operation of any such provision—

(a) information obtained as mentioned in paragraph (1)(a) is to be treated in the same way as information obtained under the corresponding GB provision, and

(b) information contained in any such report as is mentioned in paragraph (1)(b) is to be treated in the same way as information contained in a report made under the corresponding GB provision.

(3) In this article—

"repealed NI provision" means a provision of Northern Ireland legislation that is repealed in consequence of the extension to Northern Ireland, by any provision of Part 45 of the Companies Act 2006, of provisions applying in Great Britain; and

"corresponding GB provision" means the corresponding provision so applied.

[4.365]

11 Saving for provisions relating to nature of liability of member or contributory

(1) The new provisions as to the nature of a member's or contributory's liability apply to liabilities arising on or after 1st October 2009 and the old provisions continue to apply to liabilities arising before that date.

(2) The new provisions are section 33(2) of the Companies Act 2006 and (in England and Wales) section 80 of the Insolvency Act 1986 as amended by this Order.

(3) The old provisions are—

(a) in England and Wales, section 14(2) of the Companies Act 1985 and section 80 of the Insolvency Act 1986 as it has effect before that amendment;

(b) in Northern Ireland, Articles 4(d)(ii) and 15(c) of the Limitation (Northern Ireland) Order 1989.

(4) For the purposes of this article a liability is treated as arising when the limitation period starts to run for the purposes of the Limitation Act 1980 or the Limitation (Northern Ireland) Order 1989.

[4.366]

12 Saving for earlier consequential amendments, transitional provisions and savings

(1) Schedule 3 to this Order contains provisions preserving the effect of the provisions of . . . the Companies Consolidation (Consequential Provisions) (Northern Ireland) Order 1986 relating to old public companies.

(2) The repeal of the other provisions of that . . . Order does not affect the operation of—

(a) any provision amending an enactment that remains in force;

(b) any transitional provision that remains capable of having effect in relation to the corresponding provision of the Companies Act 2006;

(c) any saving that remains capable of having effect in relation to the repeal of an enactment by that . . . Order.

NOTES

Words omitted revoked by the Companies Act 2006 (Consequential Amendments and Transitional Provisions) Order 2011, SI 2011/1265, art 4(1), (2), as from 12 May 2011.

[4.367]

13 Saving of power to order caution for expenses (in Scotland) or security for costs (in Northern Ireland)

(1) Schedule 1 to the Companies Act 2006 (Commencement No 8, Transitional Provisions and Savings) Order 2008 (repeals coming into force on 1st October 2009) is amended as follows—

(a) in Part 1 (Great Britain repeals), in the list of provisions of the Companies Act 1985, for "Sections 721 to 726" substitute "Sections 721 to 725 and 726(1)";

(b) in Part 2 (Northern Ireland repeals), in the list of provisions of the Companies (Northern Ireland) Order 1986, for "Articles 670 to 674" substitute "Articles 670 to 673".

(2) In Article 674 of the Companies (Northern Ireland) Order 1986 (power to order security for costs in Northern Ireland) the expression "limited company" has the same meaning as in the Companies Acts (see section 3 of the Companies Act 2006).

(3) That Article and section 726(2) of the Companies Act 1985 (power to order caution for expenses in Scotland) apply to a limited liability partnership registered under the Limited Liability Partnerships Act 2000 as they apply to a limited company.

SCHEDULES

SCHEDULES 1 AND 2

(Sch 1 contains consequential amendments which, in so far as relevant to this work, have been incorporated at the appropriate place; Sch 2 provides for other consequential repeals and revocations which, in so far as relevant to this work, have been incorporated at the appropriate place.)

SCHEDULE 3
PROVISIONS RELATING TO OLD PUBLIC COMPANIES

Article 12(1)

[4.368]

1 Meaning of "old public company"

[For the purposes of this Schedule an "old public company" is a company limited by shares, or a company limited by guarantee and having a share capital, in respect of which the following conditions are met—

(a) the company either existed on 1st July 1983 or was incorporated after that date pursuant to an application made before that date,

(b) on that date or, if later, on the day of the company's incorporation, the company was not or (as the case may be) would not have been a private company within the meaning of section 28 of the Companies Act (Northern Ireland) 1960, and

(c) the company has not since that date or the day of the company's incorporation (as the case may be) either been re-registered as a public company within the meaning of Article 12(3) of the Companies (Northern Ireland) Order or section 4(2) of the Companies Act 2006 or become a private company within the meaning of Article 12(3) of the Companies (Northern Ireland) Order or section 4(1) of the Companies Act 2006.]

2 Application of Companies Acts to old public companies

(1) References in the Companies Acts to—

(a) a public company, or

(b) a company other than a private company,

are to be read (unless the context otherwise requires) as including an old public company.

(2) References in the Companies Acts to a private company are to be read accordingly.

(3) Sub-paragraphs (1) and (2)—

(a) do not apply in relation to—

(i) Part 7 of the Companies Act 2006 (re-registration as a means of altering a company's status), and

(ii) sections 662 to 669 of that Act (treatment of shares held by or for public company) (see paragraph 7(1) and (2) below), and

(b) do not restrict the power to make provision by regulations under section 65 of that Act (inappropriate use of indications of company type or legal form).

3 Old public company re-registering as a public company

(1) Sections 90 to 96 of the Companies Act 2006 (re-registration as public company limited by shares) apply to an old public company.

(2) As they so apply—

(a) references to a private company shall be read as references to an old public company, and

(b) references to a special resolution of the company shall be read as references to a resolution of the directors.

(3) Chapter 3 of Part 3 of that Act (resolutions affecting a company's constitution) applies to any such resolution.

(4) References in this Schedule to re-registration as a public company, in relation to an old public company, are to re-registration by virtue of this paragraph.

4 Old public company becoming private: special resolution

(1) An old public company may pass a special resolution not to be re-registered as a public company.

(2) Sections 98 and 99 of the Companies Act 2006 (application to court to cancel resolution; notice to registrar of court application or order) apply to such a resolution as they would apply to a special resolution by a public company to be re-registered as private.

(3) If either—

(a) 28 days from the passing of the resolution elapse without an application being made under section 98 of the Companies Act 2006 (as applied), or

(b) such an application is made and proceedings are concluded on the application without the court making an order for the cancellation of the resolution,

the registrar of companies shall issue the company with a certificate stating that it is a private company.

(4) The company then becomes a private company by virtue of the issue of the certificate.

(5) For the purposes of sub-paragraph (3)(b), proceedings on the application are concluded—

(a) except in a case within the following paragraph, when the period mentioned in section 99(3) of the Companies Act 2006 (as applied) for delivering a copy of the court's order on the application to the registrar has expired, or

(b) when the company has been notified that the application has been withdrawn.

(6) A certificate issued to a company under sub-paragraph (3) is conclusive evidence that the requirements of this paragraph have been complied with and that the company is a private company.

5 Old public company becoming private: statutory declaration

(1) If an old public company delivers to the registrar a statutory declaration by a director or secretary of the company that the company does not at the time of the declaration satisfy the conditions for the company to be re-registered as public, the registrar shall issue the company with a certificate stating that it is a private company.

(2) The company then becomes a private company by virtue of the issue of the certificate.

(3) A certificate issued to a company under sub-paragraph (1) is conclusive evidence that the requirements of this paragraph have been complied with and that the company is a private company.

6 Failure by old public company to obtain new classification

(1) If at any time a company which is an old public company has not delivered to the registrar of companies a declaration under paragraph 5, the company and any officer of it who is in default is guilty of an offence unless at the time the company—

(a) has applied to be re-registered as a public company, and the application has not been refused or withdrawn, or

(b) has passed a special resolution not to be re-registered as a public company, and the resolution has not been revoked, and has not been cancelled under section 98 of the Companies Act 2006 as applied by paragraph 4.

(2) A person guilty of an offence under this paragraph is liable on summary conviction to a fine not exceeding level 3 on the standard scale and, for continued contravention, a daily default fine not exceeding one-tenth of level 3 on the standard scale.

7 Old public company holding, or having charge on, own shares

(1) In sections 662 to 669 of the Companies Act 2006 (treatment of shares held by or for public company) references to a public company do not include an old public company.

(2) Section 668 of that Act (application of sections 662 to 667 to private company re-registering as public company) applies to an old public company as to a private company.

(3) In the case of a company that—

(a) after [30th September 1984] remained an old public company, and

(b) did not before that date apply to be re-registered as a public company,

any charge on its own shares which was in existence on or immediately before that date is a permitted charge and not void under section 670 of the Companies Act 2006.

(4) . . .

8 Old public companies: trading under misleading name

(1) An old public company commits an offence if it carries on a trade, profession or business under a name that includes, as its last part, the words "public limited company" or "cwmni cyfyngedig cyhoeddus".

(2) Where an offence under this paragraph is committed by a company, an offence is also committed by every officer of the company who is in default.

(3) A person guilty of an offence under this paragraph is liable on summary conviction to a fine not exceeding level 3 on the standard scale and, for continued contravention, a daily default fine not exceeding one-tenth of level 3 on the standard scale.

9 Old public companies: payment for share capital

Sections 584 to 587 of the Companies Act 2006 (payment for shares: additional rules for public companies) apply to an old public company whose directors have passed and not revoked a resolution to be re-registered as a public company, as those sections apply to a public company.

NOTES

Para 1 substituted, words in square brackets in sub-para 7(3) substituted, and sub-para 7(4) revoked, by the Companies Act 2006 (Consequential Amendments and Transitional Provisions) Order 2011, SI 2011/1265, art 4(1), (3), as from 12 May 2011.

COMPANIES (SHARE CAPITAL AND ACQUISITION BY COMPANY OF ITS OWN SHARES) REGULATIONS 2009 (NOTE)

(SI 2009/2022)

[4.369]

NOTES

These Regulations were made on 21 July 2009 under the powers conferred by the Companies Act 2006, ss 562(6)(a), 657, 737, 1292(1)(c). They came into force on 1 October 2009.

Reg 1 of the Regulations provides for citation and commencement.

Reg 2 amends CA 2006, s 562 at **[1.644]** so that the minimum period for which rights issues must be kept open for acceptance is reduced from 21 days to 14 days.

Regulation 3 implements, in respect of CA 2006, the amendment made to Article 32(1) of Council Directive 77/91/EEC by Directive 2006/68/EC of the European Parliament and of the Council. That Directive was implemented in respect of CA 1985 by the Companies (Reduction of Capital) (Creditor Protection) Regulations 2008 (SI 2008/719)). The latter Directive amended the former as regards the formation of public companies and the maintenance and alteration of their capital. Regulation 3 also makes corresponding amendments to the law as it relates to private companies. Regulation 3 amends CA 2006, s 646 at **[1.729]**. Under s 645 of the 2006 Act a company may reduce its share capital by special resolution subject to confirmation by the court. Section 646 provides a procedure for identifying and producing a list of creditors entitled to object to a proposed capital reduction. Under s 648, before the court may confirm a reduction it must be satisfied that the consent of the listed creditors has been obtained or their claims have been discharged or have determined or have been secured by the company.

Regulation 3 amends s 646 to exclude from the list of creditors those who cannot show that there is a real likelihood that the proposed capital reduction would result in the company being unable to discharge their debts or claims when they fell due.

Regulation 4(1) amends ss 694(5), 697(4) and 700(4) of the 2006 Act at **[1.778]**, **[1.781]**, **[1.784]**. It increases from 18 months to five years the amount of time for which a public company may be authorised by special resolution of its members to make off-market purchases of its own shares, vary a contract for off-market purchase of its own shares or release its rights under a contract for off-market purchase of its own shares. Regulation 4(2) amends s 701(5) of the 2006 Act at **[1.785]**. It increases from 18 months to five years the amount of time for which a public or private company may be authorised by ordinary resolution of its members to make market purchases of its own shares.

Regulation 5 removes from companies the restriction that the maximum amount of their own shares which they may hold as treasury shares is limited to 10% of the nominal value of their issued share capital (or of the class of issued share capital in question). It repeals s 725 of the 2006 Act, subject to transitional provisions, as follows—

> "(2) Any outstanding obligation to dispose of or cancel excess shares arising under section 725(3) of that Act (duty to dispose of excess shares) shall cease to exist on 1st October 2009, whether or not the period mentioned in that provision has expired, but this is subject to paragraph (3).
> (3) This amendment does not affect any liability under section 732 of that Act (treasury shares: offences) in respect of a failure to comply with section 725(3) where the period mentioned in that provision expired before 1st October 2009.".

REGISTRAR OF COMPANIES (FEES) (LIMITED PARTNERSHIPS AND NEWSPAPER PROPRIETORS) REGULATIONS 2009

(SI 2009/2392)

NOTES

Made: 28 August 2009.

Authority: Companies Act 2006, ss 243(3), 1063(1)–(3), 1292(1).

Commencement: 1 October 2009.

For a summary of all Orders and Regulations made under the Companies Act 2006, see Appendix 4 at **[A4]**.

These Regulations are reproduced as amended by: the Registrar of Companies (Fees) (Limited Partnerships) (Amendment) Regulations 2011, SI 2011/319; the Deregulation Act 2015 (Consequential Amendments) Order 2015, SI 2015/971; the Registrar of Companies (Fees) (Amendment) Regulations 2016, SI 2016/621; the European Economic Interest Grouping (Amendment) (EU Exit) Regulations 2018, SI 2018/1299.

ARRANGEMENT OF REGULATIONS

SCHEDULES

[4.370]
1 Citation and commencement

These Regulations may be cited as the Registrar of Companies (Fees) (Limited Partnerships and Newspaper Proprietors) Regulations 2009 and come into force on 1st October 2009.

[4.371]
2 Interpretation

In these Regulations—

"Companies House Direct" and "CHD" mean the service by which information is accessed by the applicant in Hyper Text Markup Language using a website of the registrar by delivering a non-encrypted access code;

. . .

"limited liability partnership" means a body corporate incorporated under the Limited Liability Partnerships Act 2000;

"limited partnership" means a partnership registered under the Limited Partnerships Act 1907; and

. . .

NOTES

Definition "European Economic Interest Grouping" (omitted) revoked by the European Economic Interest Grouping (Amendment) (EU Exit) Regulations 2018, SI 2018/1299, reg 66(a), as from IP completion day (as defined in the European Union (Withdrawal Agreement) Act 2020, s 39).

Definition "the register of the proprietors of newspapers" (omitted) revoked by the Registrar of Companies (Fees) (Amendment) Regulations 2016, SI 2016/621, regs 14, 15, as from 30 June 2016.

[4.372]

3 Fees payable in respect of functions relating to the registration of documents by the registrar

Schedule 1 makes provision for the fees that are payable to the registrar in respect of the registration of documents relating to limited partnerships . . . by the registrar.

NOTES

Words omitted revoked by the Registrar of Companies (Fees) (Amendment) Regulations 2016, SI 2016/621, regs 14, 16, as from 30 June 2016.

[4.373]

4 Fees payable in respect of the inspection or provision of copies of documents kept by the registrar relating to limited partnerships

(1) Schedule 2 makes provision for the fees that are payable to the registrar in respect of the inspection, or provision of copies, of documents kept by the registrar relating to limited partnerships.

(2) The fees prescribed in relation to paragraph 4(a) of Schedule 2 are not payable in respect of any month for which the applicant pays a fee to the registrar for subscription to Companies House Direct under regulations providing for the payment of fees in respect of the functions of the registrar in relation to the inspection, or provision of copies, of documents kept by the registrar relating to companies, overseas companies, limited liability partnerships and [UK] Economic Interest Groupings.

NOTES

Para (2): word in square brackets substituted by the European Economic Interest Grouping (Amendment) (EU Exit) Regulations 2018, SI 2018/1299, reg 66(b), as from IP completion day (as defined in the European Union (Withdrawal Agreement) Act 2020, s 39).

[4.374]

5 Transitional provisions

Where any document is delivered to the registrar on or before 30th September 2009 to which any fee set under section 14 of the Newspaper Libel and Registration Act 1881 would have applied if registered on or before that date, and that document is registered on or after 1st October 2009, the fee prescribed in Schedule 1 in respect of that document shall not apply and any fee set under section 14 of the Newspaper Libel and Registrations Act 1881 shall apply.

[4.375]

6

Where any application is made to the registrar on or before 30th September 2009 in respect of the inspection of, or the provision of copies of, material kept by the registrar, the fee prescribed in Schedule 2 or determined by the registrar in the exercise of his powers under section 1063(5) of the Companies Act 2006 in respect of that application shall not apply and any fee payable under paragraph 6(2) of Schedule 5 to the Companies Act 2006 (Commencement No 1, Transitional Provisions and Savings) Order 2006 shall apply.

[4.376]

7 Revocation

Subject to Regulation 6, paragraph 6(2) of Schedule 5 to the Companies Act 2006 (Commencement No 1, Transitional Provisions and Savings) Order 2006 is revoked.

SCHEDULES

SCHEDULE 1
THE PERFORMANCE OF FUNCTIONS RELATING TO THE REGISTRATION OF DOCUMENTS BY THE REGISTRAR

Regulation 3

PART 1 INTERPRETATION

Meaning of . . . "the LP Act" and words and expressions used in those Acts

[4.377]

1. (1) In this Schedule—

. . .

"the LP Act" means the Limited Partnerships Act 1907.

[(2) Words and expressions used in the LP Act have the same meaning when used in this Schedule as they have in that Act.]

Meaning of "same day registration"

2. For the purposes of this Schedule a document is delivered for "same day registration" if—

(a) a request for same day registration and the document required to be delivered to the registrar in connection with that registration is received by the registrar by 3.00 pm on the day in question; and

(b) the registration is completed on that day.

General

3. Where, in relation to any matter in respect of which a fee is payable under this Schedule, the means of delivery to the registrar of the documents required to be delivered in relation to that matter, or the form of those documents, are not specified that fee is payable only in respect of documents that are delivered in hard copy form.

4. Where, in relation to any matter in respect of which a fee is payable under this Schedule, no provision is made for same day registration of the documents required to be delivered to the registrar in relation to that matter, that fee is only payable in respect of the delivery of documents other than for same day registration.

NOTES

Para 1: the words omitted from the preceding heading were revoked, in sub-para (1) the definition "the 1881 Act" (omitted) was revoked, and sub-para (2) was substituted, by the Registrar of Companies (Fees) (Amendment) Regulations 2016, SI 2016/621, regs 14, 17(1)–(4), as from 30 June 2016.

PART 2 FEES PAYABLE

Limited partnerships

[4.378]

5. In respect of the performance by the registrar of his functions in relation to the registration of documents delivered to him in respect of limited partnerships, the fee specified in relation to the matter below is payable on the registration of the documents so delivered relating to that matter—

Matter in relation to which the fee is payable	Amount of fee
(a) for the registration of a limited partnership under section 8 of the LP Act—	
(i) where the application is delivered for same day registration,	[£100.00]
(ii) where the application is delivered other than for same day registration.	£20.00

6. . . .

NOTES

Para 5: sum in square brackets substituted by the Registrar of Companies (Fees) (Limited Partnerships) (Amendment) Regulations 2011, SI 2011/319, reg 2, as from 6 April 2011.

Para 6: revoked by the Deregulation Act 2015 (Consequential Amendments) Order 2015, SI 2015/971, art 2, Sch 5, para 3, as from 26 May 2015. Note that para 6 was also revoked by the Registrar of Companies (Fees) (Amendment) Regulations 2016, SI 2016/621, regs 14, 17(1), (5), as from 30 June 2016.

SCHEDULE 2
THE PERFORMANCE OF FUNCTIONS RELATING TO THE INSPECTION OR PROVISION OF COPIES OF DOCUMENTS KEPT BY THE REGISTRAR IN RELATION TO LIMITED PARTNERSHIPS

Regulation 4

PART 1 INTERPRETATION

[4.379]

1 Means by which material kept by the registrar may be inspected and copies provided

In this Schedule—

"Companies House Contact Centre" and "CHCC" mean a contact centre maintained by or on behalf of the registrar through which a facility is provided for applying by telephone, fax or email for copies of material kept by the registrar;

"Companies House Information Centre" and "CHIC" mean an office of the registrar where facilities are made available for applicants to inspect and to obtain copies of material kept by the registrar.

2 Meaning of "same day delivery" and "same day collection"

For the purposes of this Schedule certificates and certified copies are provided for "same day delivery" or "same day collection" if—

(a) a request for same day delivery or same day collection is received by the registrar before 2.00pm on the day in question; and

(b) the appropriate certificate or certified copy is issued to the applicant on that day.

3 Meaning of "the LP Act" and words and expressions used in that Act

In this Schedule "the LP Act" means the Limited Partnerships Act 1907; and words and expressions used in that Act have the same meaning when used in this Schedule as they have in that Act.

PART 2 FEES PAYABLE

[4.380]

4 Companies House Direct

In respect of the performance of the registrar's functions in relation to the provision of certificates of registration in respect of limited partnerships, where an application for a certificate is made by means of CHD, the following fees are payable—

Matter in relation to which the fee is payable	Amount of fee
(a) for subscribing to CHD, for each calendar month payable in arrears at the end of that month;	[£4.00]
[(b) for a certificate of registration of a limited partnership, in hard copy form, under section 16 of the LP Act, applied for by means of CHD—	
(i) where that certificate is delivered by post other than by same day delivery and it is the first certificate relating to that limited partnership provided to an applicant on any one occasion,	[£15.00]
(ii) where that certificate is delivered by post by same delivery and it is the first certificate relating to that limited partnership provided to an applicant on any one occasion,	[£50.00]
(iii) where it is an additional certificate delivered by post (by same day delivery or not) relating to the same limited partnership provided to the same applicant on the same occasion;	£10.00]
[(c) for a certificate of registration of the type referred to in sub-paragraph (b) above applied for by means of CHD and made available for collection at a CHIC—	
(i) where that certificate is made available other than for same day collection and it is the first certificate relating to that limited partnership provided to an applicant on any one occasion,	[£15.00]
(ii) where that certificate is made available for same day collection and it is the first certificate relating to that limited partnership provided to an applicant on any one occasion,	[£50.00]
(iii) where it is an additional certificate made available for collection (for same day collection or not) relating to the same limited partnership provided to the same applicant on the same occasion.	£10.00]

5 Companies House Information Centre

In respect of the performance of the registrar's functions in relation to the inspection of material kept by the registrar and the provision of copies of material kept by the registrar in respect of limited partnerships, where an application for inspection or a copy is made at a CHIC, the following fees are payable—

Matter in relation to which the fee is payable	Amount of fee
(a) for the inspection, at a CHIC, of an original statement or application delivered to the registrar in hard copy form;	£6.00
(b) for the inspection and for a copy in hard copy form, of a statement or application of the type specified in sub-paragraph (a) above;	£9.00
(c) for a copy (without prior inspection), in hard copy form, of an original statement or application kept by the registrar in hard copy form applied for at a CHIC and delivered by post;	£3.00
(d) for a copy (without prior inspection), in hard copy form, of an original statement or application kept by the registrar in hard copy form applied for at a CHIC and made available for collection at a CHIC;	£3.00
(e) for a copy of or extract from, in hard copy form, a statement or application certified under section 16 of the LP Act, applied for at a CHIC and delivered to the applicant by post—	
(i) where the copy or extract consists of up to 10 pages (including the tenth page),	[£15.00]
(ii) for each subsequent page of the copy or extract,	£1.00
(iii) where any copy or extract is delivered by same day delivery;	[£50.00]
(f) for a copy of or extract from, in hard copy form, a statement or application certified under section 16 of the LP Act, applied for at a CHIC and made available for collection at a CHIC—	
(i) where the copy or extract consists of up to 10 pages (including the tenth page),	[£15.00]
(ii) for each subsequent page of the copy or extract,	£1.00
(iii) where any copy or extract is made available for same day collection;	[£50.00]
[(g) for a certificate of registration of a limited partnership, in hard copy form, under section 16 of the LP Act, applied for at a CHIC—	
(i) where that certificate is delivered by post other than by same day delivery and it is the first certificate relating to that limited partnership provided to an applicant on any one occasion,	[£15.00]
(ii) where that certificate is delivered by post by same day delivery and it is the first certificate relating to that limited partnership provided to an applicant on any one occasion,	[£50.00]
(iii) where it is an additional certificate delivered by post (by same day delivery or not) relating to the same limited partnership provided to the same applicant on the same occasion;	£10.00]
[(h) for a certificate of registration of the type referred to in sub-paragraph (g) above and	

Matter in relation to which the fee is payable	Amount of fee
applied for at a CHIC and made available for collection at a CHIC—	
(i) where that certificate is made available other than for same day collection and it is the first certificate relating to that limited partnership provided to an applicant on any one occasion,	[£15.00]
(ii) where that certificate is made available for same day collection and it is the first certificate relating to that limited partnership provided to an applicant on any one occasion,	[£50.00]
(iii) where it is an additional certificate made available for collection (for same day collection or not) relating to the same limited partnership provided to the same applicant on the same occasion.	£10.00]

Companies House Contact Centre

6 In respect of the performance of the registrar's functions in relation to the provision of copies of material kept by the registrar in respect of limited partnerships, where the application for a copy is made by means of a CHCC, the following fees are payable—

Matter in relation to which the fee is payable	Amount of fee
(a) for a copy, in hard copy form, provided on an application to a CHCC, of an original statement or application in relation to a limited partnership kept by the registrar in hard copy form and delivered by post;	£3.00
(b) for a copy, in hard copy form, provided on an application to a CHCC, of an original statement or application in relation to a limited partnership kept by the registrar in hard copy form and made available for collection at a CHIC;	£3.00
(c) for a copy of or extract from, in hard copy form, a statement or application certified under section 16 of the LP Act applied for at a CHCC—	
(i) where that copy or extract is delivered by post other than by same day delivery,	[£15.00]
(ii) where that copy or extract is delivered by post by same day delivery;	[£50.00]
(d) for a copy of or extract from, in hard copy form, a statement or application certified under section 16 of the LP Act, applied for at a CHCC and made available for collection at a CHIC—	
(i) where that copy or extract is made available for collection other than by same day collection,	[£15.00]
(ii) where that copy or extract is made available for same day collection;	[£50.00]
[(e) for a certificate of registration of a limited partnership, provided on application to a CHCC, in hard copy form, under section 16 of the LP Act—	
(i) where that certificate is delivered by post other than by same day delivery and it is the first certificate relating to that limited partnership provided to an applicant on any one occasion,	[£15.00]
(ii) where that certificate is delivered by post by same day delivery and it is the first certificate relating to that limited partnership provided to an applicant on any one occasion,	[£50.00]
(iii) where it is an additional certificate delivered by post (by same day delivery or not) relating to the same limited partnership provided to the same applicant on the same occasion;	£10.00]
[(f) for a certificate of registration of a limited partnership, provided on application to a CHCC, in hard copy form, under section 16 of the LP Act and made available for collection at a CHIC—	
(i) where that certificate is made available other than for same day collection and it is the first certificate relating to that limited partnership provided to an applicant on any one occasion,	[£15.00]
(ii) where that certificate is made available for same day collection and it is the first certificate relating to that limited partnership provided to an applicant on any one occasion,	[£50.00]
(iii) where it is an additional certificate made available for collection (for same day collection or not) relating to the same limited partnership provided to the same applicant on the same occasion.	£10.00]

NOTES

Para 4 is amended as follows:

The sum in square brackets in sub-para (a) was substituted by Registrar of Companies (Fees) (Limited Partnerships) (Amendment) Regulations 2011, SI 2011/319, reg 3(a), as from 6 April 2011.

Sub-paras (b), (c) were substituted by SI 2011/319, reg 3(b), (c), as from 6 April 2011.

All other sums in square brackets were substituted by the Registrar of Companies (Fees) (Amendment) Regulations 2016, SI 2016/621, regs 14, 18(1)–(5), as from 30 June 2016, except in respect of any application or request received by the registrar before that date.

Para 5 is amended as follows:

All sums in square brackets were substituted by SI 2016/621, regs 14, 18(1), (6)–(13), as from 30 June 2016, except in respect of any application or request received by the registrar before that date.

Sub-paras (g), (h) were substituted by SI 2011/319, reg 3(h), (i) respectively, as from 6 April 2011.

Para 6 is amended as follows:

All sums in square brackets were substituted by SI 2016/621, regs 14, 18(1), (14)–(21), as from 30 June 2016, except in respect of any application or request received by the registrar before that date.

Sub-paras (e), (f) were substituted by SI 2011/319, reg 3(n), (o) respectively, as from 6 April 2011.

COMPANIES (AUTHORISED MINIMUM) REGULATIONS 2009

(SI 2009/2425)

NOTES

Made: 4 September 2009.

Authority: Companies Act 2006, ss 763(2)–(4), 766(1)(a), (2), 1292(1), (2).

Commencement: 1 October 2009.

For a summary of all Orders and Regulations made under the Companies Act 2006, see Appendix 4 at **[A4]**.

These Regulations are reproduced as amended by: the EEA Passport Rights (Amendment, etc, and Transitional Provisions) (EU Exit) Regulations 2018, SI 2018/1149.

See also, the Companies (Authorised Minimum) Regulations 2008, SI 2008/729 at **[4.130]**.

ARRANGEMENT OF REGULATIONS

[4.381]

1 Citation, commencement and interpretation

(1) These Regulations may be cited as the Companies (Authorised Minimum) Regulations 2009 and come into force on 1st October 2009.

(2) In these Regulations—

"the appropriate spot rate of exchange" is to be interpreted in accordance with regulation 4(1);

"the certified spot rate" has the meaning given in regulation 4(3);

"published spot rate" has the meaning given in regulation 4(2);

"reference date" is to be interpreted in accordance with regulation 4(7) and (8);

"relevant day" is to be interpreted in accordance with regulation 4(5) and (6); and

"working day" means a day which is not a Saturday or Sunday, Christmas Day, Good Friday or any day that is a bank holiday under the Banking and Financial Dealings Act 1971 in England and Wales.

(3) In these Regulations a reference to any Part or section is, unless otherwise stated, a reference to a Part or section of the Companies Act 2006.

[4.382]

2 Authorised minimum in euros

For the purposes of the definition of "the authorised minimum" in section 763(1), but subject to regulation 9, the amount in euros that is to be treated as equivalent to the sterling amount is €57,100.

[4.383]

3 Application of the authorised minimum requirement for certain purposes

(1) This regulation applies for either of the purposes in paragraphs (2) and (3), and is subject to regulation 9.

(2) The first purpose is to determine, for the purposes of section 650, whether a reduction of a public company's share capital confirmed by a court order under section 648 has the effect of bringing the nominal value of the company's allotted share capital below the authorised minimum.

(3) The second purpose is to determine, for the purposes of section 662(2)(b), whether the cancellation of a public company's shares and the diminution of the amount of its share capital under section 662(2)(a) have the effect of bringing the nominal value of the company's allotted share capital below the authorised minimum.

(4) This regulation only applies where the company has allotted share capital denominated in more than one currency, taking account of the effect of the reduction of the company's share capital or (as the case may be) the effect of the cancellation of the company's shares and the diminution of the amount of its allotted share capital.

(5) The nominal value of a public company's allotted share capital is to be treated as being below the authorised minimum if—

(a) the sterling value is less than £50,000; and
(b) the euro value is less than €57,100.

(6) The "sterling value" is the sum in sterling of—

(a) the nominal value of the company's allotted share capital denominated in sterling;
(b) the nominal value of the company's allotted share capital denominated in euros if it were to be converted into sterling at the appropriate spot rate of exchange; and
(c) the nominal value of the company's allotted share capital denominated in a currency other than sterling or euros if it were to be converted into sterling at the appropriate spot rate of exchange.

(7) The "euro value" is the sum in euros of—
(a) the nominal value of the company's allotted share capital denominated in euros;
(b) the nominal value of the company's allotted share capital denominated in sterling if it were to be converted into euros at the appropriate spot rate of exchange; and
(c) the nominal value of the company's allotted share capital denominated in a currency other than sterling or euros if it were to be converted into euros at the appropriate spot rate of exchange.

[4.384]

4 The appropriate spot rate of exchange

(1) The appropriate spot rate of exchange for a currency conversion referred to in regulation 3(6) and (7) is the published spot rate relevant to the currency conversion in question or, where the circumstances in paragraph (4) exist, the certified spot rate relevant to that currency conversion.

(2) The published spot rate is the middle spot exchange rate prevailing on the foreign exchange market at 4pm on the relevant day as published in respect of that day by the Financial Times.

(3) The certified spot rate is the middle spot exchange rate prevailing on the foreign exchange market at 4pm on the relevant day and stated in a certificate obtained by the company from—
(a) a person, nominated by the company, who under Part 4 of the Financial Services and Markets Act 2000 has permission to accept deposits; . . .
(b) . . .

(4) The circumstances in this paragraph exist where—
(a) the Financial Times has not, on or before the reference date, published an exchange rate referred to in paragraph (2) relevant to the currency conversion in question; or
(b) the Financial Times has, on or before the reference date, published what appears to be an exchange rate referred to in paragraph (2) relevant to the currency conversion in question but the company can show that there was a publication error; or
(c) there is no evidence of what (if any) was the rate referred to in paragraph (2) relevant to the currency conversion in question as published on or before the reference date by the Financial Times.

(5) Where the currency conversion is relevant to the calculation of the sterling value or the euro value for the purpose in regulation 3(2), the "relevant day" is the working day which immediately preceded the working day immediately preceding the date of the court order.

(6) Where the currency conversion is relevant to the calculation of the sterling value or the euro value for the purpose in regulation 3(3), the "relevant day" is—
(a) in a case within section 662(1)(a) or (b), the working day immediately preceding the date of the forfeiture or surrender; and
(b) in a case within section 662(1)(c), (d) or (e), the working day immediately preceding the date of the acquisition.

(7) Where the currency calculation is relevant to the calculation of the sterling value or the euro value for the purpose in regulation 3(2), the "reference date" is the date of the court order.

(8) Where the currency conversion is relevant to the calculation of the sterling value or the euro value for the purpose in regulation 3(3), the "reference date" is—
(a) in a case within section 662(1)(a) or (b), the fifth working day following the date of the forfeiture or surrender; and
(b) in a case within section 662(1)(c), (d) or (e), the fifth working day following the date of the acquisition.

NOTES

Para (3): sub-para (b) and the preceding word were revoked by the EEA Passport Rights (Amendment, etc, and Transitional Provisions) (EU Exit) Regulations 2018, SI 2018/1149, reg 3, Schedule, Pt 3, para 56, as from IP completion day (as defined in the European Union (Withdrawal Agreement) Act 2020, s 39).

[4.385]

5 Registration of a court order confirming a capital reduction: assumptions which may be made by the registrar

(1) This regulation applies where a public company delivers to the registrar under section 649 a copy of an order of the court confirming a reduction of its share capital and the court has not directed the order to be registered.

(2) Where the circumstances in paragraph (3), (4) or (5) exist, the registrar may make the assumption in paragraph (6).

(3) The circumstances in this paragraph are that—
(a) taking account of the effect of the reduction of its capital, the company has allotted share capital denominated in more than one currency;
(b) either the Financial Times did not publish, on or before the reference date, an exchange rate referred to in regulation 4(2) relevant to converting into sterling a currency in which the company's allotted share capital is denominated or it did not publish, on or before that date, such a rate relevant to converting such a currency into euros; and
(c) the company has not delivered to the registrar, in respect of every such currency for which the Financial Times did not publish such an exchange rate on or before the reference date, a copy of a certificate referred to in regulation 4(3).

(4) The circumstances in this paragraph are that—

(a) taking account of the effect of the reduction of its share capital, the company has allotted share capital denominated in more than one currency;

(b) the Financial Times published, on or before the reference date, what appears to be an exchange rate referred to in regulation 4(2) relevant to converting into sterling or euros a currency in which the company's allotted share capital is denominated but the company can show that there was a publication error; and

(c) the company has not delivered to the registrar, for every currency in respect of which the company can show such a publication error, a copy of a certificate referred to in regulation 4(3).

(5) The circumstances in this paragraph are that—

(a) taking account of the effect of the reduction of its share capital, the company has allotted share capital denominated in more than one currency;

(b) in respect of one or more of the exchange rates referred to in regulation 4(2) relevant to converting into sterling or euros the currencies in which the company's allotted share capital is denominated there is no evidence of what (if any) was the rate published on or before the reference date by the Financial Times; and

(c) the company has not delivered to the registrar, for every such currency in respect of which there is no such evidence, a copy of a certificate referred to in regulation 4(3).

(6) The registrar may (but is not required to) assume for the purposes of sections 649(1) and 650(1) and (2) that the reduction of the company's share capital has the effect of bringing the nominal value of the company's allotted share capital below the authorised minimum.

[4.386]

6 Determination of exchange rates by the court in certain proceedings

(1) This regulation applies to—

(a) proceedings against a public company or any officer of a public company for an offence under section 667; and

(b) proceedings under section 757 or 758 or Part 30.

(2) Where the circumstances in paragraph (3) exist, the court may make a determination referred to in paragraph (4) in the proceedings.

(3) The circumstances are that—

(a) in proceedings under section 667 it is alleged that, or in proceedings referred to in paragraph (1)(b) the question arises whether, the effect of a cancellation of the company's shares and diminution of the amount of the company's share capital under section 662(2)(a) was that the nominal value of the company's allotted share capital was brought below the authorised minimum; and

(b) as a result of that cancellation and diminution the company had (or continued to have) allotted share capital denominated in more than one currency.

(4) The court may make such determination as it thinks fit as to the exchange rate to be applied to a currency conversion referred to in regulation 3(6) and (7) where—

(a) the Financial Times did not publish, on or before the reference date, an exchange rate referred to in regulation 4(2) relevant to that currency conversion; or

(b) the Financial Times published, on or before the reference date, what appears to be an exchange rate referred to in regulation 4(2) relevant to that currency conversion but the company or officer of the company (as the case may be) can show that there was a publication error; or

(c) there is no evidence of what (if any) was the exchange rate referred to in regulation 4(2) as published on or before the reference date by the Financial Times relevant to that currency conversion,

and there has not been produced to the court in the proceedings a copy of a certificate referred to in regulation 4(3) in respect of that currency conversion.

(5) In this regulation, "the court" in relation to proceedings referred to in paragraph (1)(a) means the court of criminal jurisdiction in which the proceedings are brought.

[4.387]

7 Exclusion of liability in respect of the publication or non-publication of a spot rate

No person shall be liable to any other person as a result of—

(a) that or any other person having placed reliance for the purposes of these Regulations upon a rate published by the Financial Times; or

(b) any error in a rate published by the Financial Times which is relied upon for the purposes of these Regulations; or

(c) any act or omission as a result of which the Financial Times did not publish a rate capable of being relied upon for the purposes of these Regulations.

8 *(Revokes the Companies (Authorised Minimum) Regulations 2008, SI 2008/729, reg 2.)*

[4.388]

9 Transitional provisions and savings

(1) The figure of €57,100 in regulation 2 is to be read as €65,600 where that regulation applies for any of the purposes in paragraph (2).

(2) The purposes are—

(a) to determine whether the nominal value of a public company's allotted share capital is less than the authorised minimum for the purposes of an application for a trading certificate under section 761 where the application was received by the registrar before 1st October 2009;

(b) to determine for the purposes of section 91(1)(a) whether the nominal value of a private company's allotted share capital is less than the authorised minimum in a case where the special resolution that the company should be re-registered as a public company was passed before 1st October 2009;

(c) to determine whether, for the purposes of section 139 of the Companies Act 1985 or Article 149 of the Companies (Northern Ireland) Order 1986, the effect of a reduction of share capital is to bring the nominal value of a company's allotted share capital below the authorised minimum;

(d) to determine for the purposes of section 650 whether the effect of a reduction of capital is to bring the nominal value of a company's allotted share capital below the authorised minimum in a case where the special resolution for reducing the company's share capital was passed before 1st October 2009;

(e) to determine for the purposes of section 662(2)(b) whether the effect of cancelling shares and diminishing a company's share capital under section 662(2)(a) is to bring the nominal value of the company's allotted share capital below the authorised minimum in a case where the period for complying with the obligations under section 662(2) began before 1st October 2009.

(3) The figure of €57,100 in regulation 3(5)(b) is to be read as €65,600 where that regulation applies for either of the purposes in paragraph (4).

(4) The purposes are—

(a) to determine for the purposes of section 650 whether the effect of a reduction of capital is to bring the nominal value of a company's allotted share capital below the authorised minimum in a case where the special resolution for reducing the company's share capital was passed before 1st October 2009;

(b) to determine for the purposes of section 662(2)(b) whether the effect of cancelling shares and diminishing a company's share capital under section 662(2)(a) is to bring the nominal value of the company's allotted share capital below the authorised minimum in a case where the period for complying with the obligations under section 662(2) began before 1st October 2009.

UNREGISTERED COMPANIES REGULATIONS 2009

(SI 2009/2436)

NOTES

Made: 4 September 2009.

Authority: Companies Act 2006, ss 1043, 1210(1)(h), 1292(2).

Commencement: 1 October 2009.

For a summary of all Orders and Regulations made under the Companies Act 2006, see Appendix 4 at **[A4]**.

These Regulations are reproduced as amended by: the Statutory Auditors (Amendment of Companies Act 2006 and Delegation of Functions etc) Order 2012, SI 2012/1741; the Companies and Limited Liability Partnerships (Accounts and Audit Exemptions and Change of Accounting Framework) Regulations 2012, SI 2012/2301; the Unregistered Companies (Amendment) Regulations 2013, SI 2013/1972; the Companies, Partnerships and Groups (Accounts and Reports) Regulations 2015, SI 2015/980; the Companies and Limited Liability Partnerships (Filing Requirements) Regulations 2015, SI 2015/1695; the Companies and Limited Liability Partnerships (Filing Requirements) Regulations 2016, SI 2016/599; the Information about People with Significant Control (Amendment) Regulations 2017, SI 2017/693; the Risk Transformation Regulations 2017, SI 2017/1212; the Takeovers (Amendment) (EU Exit) Regulations 2019, SI 2019/217; the Money Laundering and Terrorist Financing (Amendment) Regulations 2019, SI 2019/1511.

ARRANGEMENT OF REGULATIONS

SCHEDULES

[4.389]

1 Citation and commencement

(1) These Regulations may be cited as the Unregistered Companies Regulations 2009.

(2) These Regulations come into force on 1st October 2009.

[4.390]

2 Interpretation

In these Regulations—

(a) "unregistered company" means a body corporate incorporated in, and having a principal place of business in, the United Kingdom, other than—

(i) a body incorporated by, or registered under, a public general enactment,

(ii) a body not formed for the purpose of carrying on a business that has for its object the acquisition of gain by the body or its individual members,

(iii) a body for the time being exempted from section 1043 of the Companies Act 2006 by a direction of the Secretary of State under subsection (1)(c) of that section, . . .

(iv) an open-ended investment company, [or]

[(v) a protected cell company registered under Part 4 of the Risk Transformation Regulations 2017].

(b) "instrument constituting or regulating the company", in relation to an unregistered company, means any enactment, royal charter, letters patent, deed of settlement, contract of partnership, or other instrument constituting or regulating the company.

NOTES

In the definition "unregistered company", the word omitted from sub-para (iii) was revoked, the word in square brackets in sub-para (iv) was inserted, and sub-para (v) was added, by the Risk Transformation Regulations 2017, SI 2017/1212, reg 190, Sch 4, para 6, as from 8 December 2017.

[4.391]

3 Application of provisions of the Companies Acts

The provisions of the Companies Acts specified in Schedule 1 to these Regulations apply to an unregistered company as to a company within the meaning of section 1 of the Companies Act 2006, subject to any limitation, adaptation or modification specified in that Schedule.

[4.392]

4 References to registered office and registration

For the purposes of the application to an unregistered company of the provisions of the Companies Acts applying to it by virtue of these Regulations—

(a) any reference to the company's registered office shall be read as a reference to the company's principal office in the United Kingdom;

(b) any reference to the part of the United Kingdom in which the company is registered shall be read as a reference to the part of the United Kingdom in which the company's principal office is situated (and references to the registrar of companies shall be read accordingly);

(c) any reference to the company's registered number shall be read as a reference to the reference number allocated to the company by the registrar.

[4.393]

5 Other general adaptations

(1) In the application of any provision of the Companies Acts by virtue of these Regulations—

(a) any reference to a public company shall be read, in relation to an unregistered company, as referring to a company that has power under its constitution to offer its shares or debentures to the public;

(b) any reference to a private company shall be read, in relation to an unregistered company, as referring to a company that does not have power to offer its shares or debentures to the public;

(c) any reference to the company's constitution, or to its articles of association, shall be read, in relation to an unregistered company, as referring to any instrument constituting or regulating the company;

(d) any reference to the common seal of the company shall be read, in relation to an unregistered company, as referring to the common or authorised seal of the company.

(2) In the application of any provision of the Companies Acts to an unregistered company by virtue of these Regulations an expression defined, or otherwise having a particular meaning or effect, in relation to a company within the meaning of section 1 of the Companies Act 2006, has effect with any adaptations necessary to ensure a corresponding meaning or effect in relation to an unregistered company.

(3) Paragraphs (1) and (2) are subject to any specific adaptation or modification provided for in these Regulations.

[4.394]

6 Application of provisions relating to statutory auditors

For the purposes of section 1210(1)(h) of the Companies Act 2006 (meaning of "statutory auditor")—

(a) an unregistered company is a prescribed person, and

(b) Part 16 of that Act (audit) as applied to unregistered companies by these Regulations is a prescribed enactment.

(and accordingly a person appointed as auditor of an unregistered company under Part 16 of that Act as so applied is a statutory auditor).

[4.395]

7 Saving

Nothing in these Regulations affects the application of any provision to an unregistered company otherwise than by virtue of these Regulations.

[4.396]

8 Revocations

The following Regulations are revoked—

(a) the Companies (Unregistered Companies) Regulations 1985,

(b) the Companies (Unregistered Companies) Regulations (Northern Ireland) 1986, and

(c) the Companies Acts (Unregistered Companies) Regulations 2007.

[4.397]

9 Transitional provisions and savings

Schedule 2 contains transitional provisions and savings.

SCHEDULES

SCHEDULE 1
PROVISIONS OF THE COMPANIES ACTS APPLYING TO UNREGISTERED COMPANIES

Regulation 3

A company's constitution

[4.398]

1. Sections 26 and 27 of the Companies Act 2006 (filing obligations in connection with company's articles) apply to unregistered companies, modified so that they read as follows—

"26 Registrar to be sent copy of company's constitution

(1) A company must, not later than 15 days after the date of its incorporation, send to the registrar a copy of every instrument constituting or regulating the company.

(2) Where a company amends any instrument constituting or regulating the company, it must, not later than 15 days after the amendment takes effect, send to the registrar a copy of the instrument as amended.

(3) If a company fails to comply with subsection (1) or (2) an offence is committed by—

(a) the company, and

(b) every officer of the company who is in default.

(4) A person guilty of an offence under this section is liable on summary conviction to a fine not exceeding level 3 on the standard scale and, for continued contravention, a daily default fine not exceeding one-tenth of level 3 on the standard scale.

27 Registrar's notice to comply in case of failure with respect to company's constitution

(1) If it appears to the registrar that a company has failed to comply with—

(a) section 26(1) or (2) (registrar to be sent copy of company's constitution), or

(b) any enactment requiring the company to send to the registrar—

(i) a document making or evidencing an alteration in any instrument constituting or regulating the company, or

(ii) a copy of any such instrument as amended,

the registrar may give notice to the company requiring it to comply.

(2) The notice must—

(a) state the date on which it is issued, and

(b) require the company to comply within 28 days from that date.

(3) If the company complies with the notice within the specified time, no criminal proceedings may be brought in respect of the failure mentioned in subsection (1).

(4) If the company does not comply with the notice within the specified time, it is liable to a civil penalty of £200.

(5) This is in addition to any liability to criminal proceedings in respect of the failure mentioned in subsection (1).

(6) The penalty may be recovered by the registrar and is to be paid into the Consolidated Fund.".

2. Sections 34 and 35 of the Companies Act 2006 (notice to registrar where company's constitution altered) apply to unregistered companies, modified so that they read as follows—

"34 Notice to registrar where company's constitution altered by enactment

(1) This section applies where the constitution of a company is altered by an enactment, other than an enactment amending the general law.

(2) The company must give notice of the alteration to the registrar, specifying the enactment, not later than 15 days after the enactment comes into force.

(3) In the case of a special enactment the notice must be accompanied by a copy of the enactment.

(4) If the enactment amends any instrument constituting or regulating the company, the notice must be accompanied by a copy of the instrument in question, as amended.

(5) A "special enactment" means an enactment that is not a public general enactment, and includes—

(a) an Act for confirming a provisional order,

(b) any provision of a public general Act in relation to the passing of which any of the standing orders of the House of Lords or the House of Commons relating to Private Business applied, or

(c) any enactment to the extent that it is incorporated in or applied for the purposes of a special enactment.

(6) If a company fails to comply with this section an offence is committed by—

(a) the company, and

(b) every officer of the company who is in default.

(7) A person guilty of an offence under this section is liable on summary conviction to a fine not exceeding level 3 on the standard scale and, for continued contravention, a daily default fine not exceeding one-tenth of level 3 on the standard scale.

35 Notice to registrar where company's constitution altered by order

(1) Where the constitution of a company is altered by an order of a court or other authority, the company must give notice to the registrar of the alteration not later than 15 days after the alteration takes effect.

(2) The notice must be accompanied by—

(a) a copy of the order, and

(b) if the order amends any instrument constituting or regulating the company, a copy of the instrument in question, as amended.

(3) If a company fails to comply with this section an offence is committed by—

(a) the company, and

(b) every officer of the company who is in default.

(4) A person guilty of an offence under this section is liable on summary conviction to a fine not exceeding level 3 on the standard scale and, for continued contravention, a daily default fine not exceeding one-tenth of level 3 on the standard scale.

(5) This section does not apply where provision is made by another enactment for the delivery to the registrar of a copy of the order in question.".

A company's capacity and related matters

3. The following provisions of the Companies Act 2006 apply to unregistered companies—

(a) sections 39 and 40 (a company's capacity and power of directors to bind company);
(b) section 41 (constitutional limitations: transactions involving directors or their associates);
(c) section 42 (constitutional limitations: companies that are charities);
(d) sections 43, 44, 45(1) and 46 (formalities of doing business under the law of England and Wales or Northern Ireland);
(e) section 48 (execution of documents under the law of Scotland);
(f) section 50 (official seal for share certificates);
(g) section 51 (pre-incorporation contracts, deeds and obligations).

Trading disclosures

4. Sections 82 to 85 of the Companies Act 2006 (trading disclosures) apply to unregistered companies, modified so that they read as follows—

"82 Requirement to disclose company name and other particulars

(1) Every company must disclose its corporate name on—

(a) its business letters, notices and other official publications;
(b) its bills of exchange, promissory notes, endorsements and order forms;
(c) cheques purporting to be signed by or on behalf of the company;
(d) orders for money, goods or services purporting to be signed by or on behalf of the company;
(e) its bills of parcels, invoices and other demands for payment, receipts and letters of credit;
(f) its applications for licences to carry on a trade or activity;
(g) all other forms of its business correspondence and documentation; and
(h) its websites.

(2) Every company must disclose the further particulars set out in subsection (3) on—

(a) its business letters;
(b) its order forms; and
(c) its websites.

(3) The further particulars required are—

(a) the part of the United Kingdom in which the company's principal office is situated;
(b) the reference number allocated to the company by the registrar;
(c) the address of the company's principal office;
(d) the manner in which it was incorporated;
(e) if it is—
(i) a limited company, or
(ii) an investment company within the meaning of section 833,

that fact.

(4) If, in the case of a company having a share capital, there is a reference to the amount of share capital on—

(a) its business letters,
(b) its order forms, or
(c) its websites,

the reference must be to paid up share capital.

(5) In relation to a company, a reference to "its websites" includes a reference to any part of a website relating to that company which that company has caused or authorised to appear.

83 Civil consequences of failure to make required disclosure

(1) This section applies to any legal proceedings brought by a company to enforce a right arising out of a contract made in the course of a business in respect of which the company was, at the time the contract was made, in breach of section 82 (requirement to disclose company name and other particulars).

(2) The proceedings shall be dismissed if the defendant (in Scotland, the defender) to the proceedings shows—

(a) that he has a claim against the claimant (pursuer) arising out of the contract that he has been unable to pursue by reason of the latter's breach of section 82, or
(b) that he has suffered some financial loss in connection with the contract by reason of the claimant's (pursuer's) breach of section 82,

unless the court before which the proceedings are brought is satisfied that it is just and equitable to permit the proceedings to continue.

(3) This section does not affect the right of any person to enforce such rights as he may have against another person in any proceedings brought by that person.

84 Criminal consequences of failure to make required disclosure

(1) Where a company fails, without reasonable excuse, to comply with any requirement of section 82, an offence is committed by—

(a) the company; and
(b) every officer of the company who is in default.

(2) A person guilty of an offence under this section is liable on summary conviction to—

(a) a fine not exceeding level 3 on the standard scale; and

(b) for continued contravention, a daily default fine not exceeding one-tenth of level 3 on the standard scale.

(3) For the purposes of this section a shadow director is to be treated as an officer of the company.

85 Minor variations in form of name to be left out of account

For the purposes of this Chapter, in considering the name of a company no account is to be taken of—

(a) whether upper or lower case characters (or a combination of the two) are used, or

(b) whether diacritical marks or punctuation are present or absent,

provided there is no real likelihood of names differing only in those respects being taken to be different names.".

A company's principal office in the United Kingdom

5. Sections 86 and 87 of the Companies Act 2006 (a company's registered office) apply to unregistered companies, modified so that they read as follows—

"86 A company's principal office

(1) Communications and notices may at all times be addressed to a company at its principal office in the United Kingdom.

(2) A company must give notice to the registrar, not later than 15 days after the date of the incorporation of the company, of the address of its principal office in the United Kingdom.

(3) If a company fails to comply with subsection (2) an offence is committed by—

(a) the company, and

(b) every officer of the company who is in default.

(4) A person guilty of an offence under subsection (2) is liable on summary conviction to a fine not exceeding level 3 on the standard scale and, for continued contravention, a daily default fine not exceeding one-tenth of level 3 on the standard scale.

87 Change of principal office

(1) Where a company changes its principal office in the United Kingdom, it must send notice of the new address to the registrar not later than 15 days after the change takes effect.

(2) If a company fails to comply with subsection (1) an offence is committed by—

(a) the company, and

(b) every officer of the company who is in default.

(3) A person guilty of an offence under subsection (1) is liable on summary conviction to a fine not exceeding level 3 on the standard scale and, for continued contravention, a daily default fine not exceeding one-tenth of level 3 on the standard scale.

(4) Until the end of the period of 14 days beginning with the date on which the new address is registered a person may validly serve any document on the company at the address previously registered.

(5) For the purposes of any duty of a company—

(a) to keep available for inspection at its principal office in the United Kingdom any register or other document, or

(b) to mention the address of that office in any document,

a company that changes the address of its principal office in the United Kingdom may make the change as from such date as it may determine, but it is treated as failing to comply with that duty if it does not comply with subsection (1).

(6) Where a company unavoidably ceases to perform at its principal office in the United Kingdom any such duty as is mentioned in subsection (5)(a) but—

(a) resumes performance of that duty at other premises as soon as practicable, and

(b) gives notice to the registrar of a change in the address of its principal office in accordance with subsection (1),

it is not to be treated as having failed to comply with that duty.".

Directors and secretaries

6. (1) Sections 162 to 167 of the Companies Act 2006 (register of directors and register of directors' residential addresses) apply to unregistered companies.

(2) Section 162 (register of directors) applies with the following modifications—

(a) in subsection (3)(b) (places where register may be kept available for inspection), for "specified in regulations under section 1136" substitute "specified in Part 2 of the Companies (Company Records) Regulations 2008 (SI 2008/3006)";

(b) in subsection (5)(b) (inspection by non-member on payment), for "such fee as may be prescribed" substitute "the fee prescribed by regulation 2(a) of the Companies (Fees for Inspection of Company Records) Regulations 2008 (SI 2008/3007)".

7. (1) Sections 240 to 246 of the Companies Act 2006 (directors' residential addresses: protection from disclosure) apply to unregistered companies.

(2) Section 243 (permitted use or disclosure of protected information by the registrar) applies with the following modifications—

(a) in subsection (2)(a) for "by regulations made by the Secretary of State" substitute "in the Companies (Disclosure of Address) Regulations 2009 (SI 2009/214)";

(b) for subsection (3) substitute—

"(3) The provisions of the Companies (Disclosure of Address) Regulations 2009 (SI 2009/214) relating to disclosure of protected information under this section apply.

(3A) Those provisions are—

(a) Part 2 (disclosure of protected information),
(b) Part 4 (matters relating to applications), so far as relating to disclosure under this section, and
(c) any other provisions of the Regulations having effect for the purposes of those provisions.";

(c) omit subsections (4) to (6) and (8).

8. (1) Sections 275 to 279 of the Companies Act 2006 (register of secretaries) apply to unregistered companies.

(2) Section 275 applies with the following modifications—

(a) in subsection (3)(b) (places where register may be kept available for inspection), for "specified in regulations under section 1136" substitute "specified in Part 2 of the Companies (Company Records) Regulations 2008 (SI 2008/3006)";

(b) in subsection (5)(b) (inspection by non-member on payment), for "such fee as may be prescribed" substitute "the fee prescribed by regulation 2(a) of the Companies (Fees for Inspection of Company Records) Regulations 2008 (SI 2008/3007)".

Political donations and expenditure

9. (1) Sections 362 to 379 of the Companies Act 2006 (control of political donations and expenditure) apply to unregistered companies, with the following modifications.

(2) In section 369(5) (liability of directors to make good unauthorised donations or expenditure: interest), in paragraph (b) for "such rate as the Secretary of State may prescribe by regulations" substitute, "the rate specified in the Companies (Interest Rate for Unauthorised Political Donations or Expenditure) Regulations 2007 (SI 2007/2242)".

(3) In section 377 (exemption of certain political expenditure)—

(a) in subsection (1) for "an order of the Secretary of State under this section" substitute "articles 3 and 4 of the Companies (Political Expenditure Exemption) Order 2007 (SI 2007/2081)";
(b) omit subsection (2);
(c) in subsection (3) for "an order under this section" substitute "the articles mentioned in subsection (1)";
(d) omit subsection (4).

Accounts

10. [(1) Sections 380 to 414, 415 to 416, 418 to 419A, 423 to 425, 430 to 438, 441 to 469 and 471 to 474 of the Companies Act 2006 (accounts and reports) apply to unregistered companies, with the following modifications.]

(2) In section 383(6)(a) (small companies: determination of net amounts), for "regulations under section 404" substitute "Part 1 of Schedule 4 to the Small Companies and Groups (Accounts and Directors' Report) Regulations 2008 (SI 2008/409) or Schedule 3 to the Large and Medium-sized Companies and Groups (Accounts and Directors' Reports) Regulations 2008 (SI 2008/410)".

(3) In section 396 (Companies Act individual accounts)—

(a) for subsection (3) (requirements as to form and content of accounts etc) substitute—

"(3) The accounts must comply with the provisions of—
(a) regulation 3 of the Small Companies and Groups (Accounts and Directors' Report) Regulations 2008 (SI 2008/409), or
(b) regulations 3 and 4 of the Large and Medium-sized Companies and Groups (Accounts and Directors' Reports) Regulations 2008 (SI 2008/410),

as to the form and content of the balance sheet and profit and loss account, and additional information to be provided by way of notes to the accounts.";

(b) in subsection (4) (additional information) after "regulations" insert "specified in subsection (3)".

(4) In section 404 (Companies Act group accounts)—

(a) for subsection (3) (requirements as to form and content of accounts etc) substitute—

"(3) The accounts must comply with the provisions of—
(a) regulation 6 of the Small Companies and Groups (Accounts and Directors' Report) Regulations 2008 (SI 2008/409), or
(b) regulation 6 of the Large and Medium-sized Companies and Groups (Accounts and Directors' Reports) Regulations 2008 (SI 2008/410),

as to the form and content of the consolidated balance sheet and consolidated profit and loss account, and additional information to be provided by way of notes to the accounts.";

(b) in subsection (4) (additional information) after "regulations" insert "specified in subsection (3)".

(5) In section 409 (information about related undertakings), for subsections (1) to (3) substitute—

"(1) The notes to the company's annual accounts must contain the information about related undertakings required by—
(a) regulations 4 and 7 of the Small Companies and Groups (Accounts and Directors' Report) Regulations 2008 (SI 2008/409), or
(b) regulation 5 of the Large and Medium-sized Companies and Groups (Accounts and Directors' Reports) Regulations 2008 (SI 2008/410).

(2) That information need not be disclosed with respect to an undertaking that—
(a) is established under the law of a country outside the United Kingdom, or
(b) carries on business outside the United Kingdom,

if the following conditions are met.".

(6) In section 412 (information about directors' benefits: remuneration)—

(a) for subsections (1) to (3) substitute—

"(1) The information about directors' remuneration required by—

(a) the Small Companies and Groups (Accounts and Directors' Report) Regulations 2008 (SI 2008/409), or

(b) the Large and Medium-sized Companies and Groups (Accounts and Directors' Reports) Regulations 2008 (SI 2008/410),

must be given in notes to the company's annual accounts.";

(b) in subsection (4) for "and regulations made under it" substitute "and the regulations specified in subsection (1)";

(c) in subsection (5) for "regulations under this section" substitute "and the regulations specified in subsection (1)".

(7) In section 416 (contents of directors' report: general), for subsection (4) substitute—

"(4) The directors' report must comply with the provisions of—

(a) the Small Companies and Groups (Accounts and Directors' Report) Regulations 2008 (SI 2008/409), or

(b) the Large and Medium-sized Companies and Groups (Accounts and Directors' Reports) Regulations 2008 (SI 2008/410),

as to other matters to be included in the report.".

(8)–(11) . . .

(12) In section 444(3) (filing obligations of companies subject to small companies regime: copies of accounts and reports)—

(a) in paragraph (a) for "regulations made by the Secretary of State" substitute "regulation 5 of the Small Companies and Groups (Accounts and Directors' Report) Regulations 2008 (SI 2008/409)";

(b) in paragraph (b) for "the regulations" substitute "that regulation".

(13) In section 445(3) (filing obligations of medium-sized companies: copies of accounts and reports)—

(a) in paragraph (a) for "regulations made by the Secretary of State" substitute "regulation 4 of the Large and Medium-sized Companies and Groups (Accounts and Directors' Reports) Regulations 2008 (SI 2008/410)";

(b) in paragraph (b) for "the regulations" substitute "that regulation".

(14), (15) . . .

(16) In section 453 (civil penalty for failure to file accounts and reports)—

(a) in subsection (2) (determination of amount), for "regulations made by the Secretary of State" substitute "the relevant provisions of the Companies (Late Filing Penalties) and Limited Liability Partnerships (Filing Periods and Late Filing Penalties) Regulations 2008 (SI 2008/497)";

(b) omit subsection (5).

(17) In section 454 (voluntary revision of accounts), for subsections (3) to (5) substitute—

"(3) The provisions of the Companies (Revision of Defective Accounts) Regulations 2008 (SI 2008/373) apply.".

(18) In section 457 (other persons authorised to apply to the court)—

(a) for subsections (1) to (3) substitute—

"(1) The Companies (Defective Accounts and Directors' Reports) (Authorised Person) and Supervision of Accounts and Reports (Prescribed Body) Order 2008 (SI 2008/623) apply as regards—

(a) the persons authorised by the Secretary of State for the purposes of section 456 (application to court in respect of defective accounts or reports), and

(b) the requirements and other provisions applying to the exercise of functions as an authorised person.";

(b) omit subsections (5) to (7).

(19) In section 464 (accounting standards)—

[(a) in subsection (1) for "such body or bodies as may be prescribed by regulations" substitute "the Financial Reporting Council Limited";]

(b) omit subsection (3).

Audit

11. (1) Sections 475 to 481 and 484 to 539 of the Companies Act 2006 (audit) apply to unregistered companies, with the following modifications.

(2) Section 494 (disclosure of services provided by auditor or associates and related remuneration) is modified so that it reads as follows—

"494 Disclosure of services provided by auditor or associates and related remuneration

The Companies (Disclosure of Auditor Remuneration and Liability Limitation Agreements) Regulations 2008 (SI 2008/489) apply as regards the disclosure of—

(a) the nature of any services provided for a company by the company's auditor (whether in the capacity as auditor or otherwise) or by the auditor's associates;

(b) the amount of any remuneration received or receivable by the auditor, or the auditor's associates, in respect of any such services.".

(3) In section 504 (meaning of "senior statutory auditor"), in subsection (1)(b)(ii) for "by order of the Secretary of State" substitute "by the Statutory Auditors (Delegation of Functions etc) Order 2008 (SI 2008/496)".

(4) Section 538 (disclosure by company of liability limitation agreement) is modified so that it reads as follows—

"538 Disclosure of agreement by company
A company that has entered into a liability limitation agreement must make the disclosure in connection with the agreement required by the Companies (Disclosure of Auditor Remuneration and Liability Limitation Agreements) Regulations 2008 (SI 2008/489).".

Share certificates
12. (1) The following provisions of the Companies Act 2006 apply to unregistered companies—
(a) section 768 (share certificate to be evidence of title);
(b) section 778 (issue of certificates etc: allotment or transfer to financial institution).
(2) In section 778 as it applies to unregistered companies, for "section 769(1) or 776(1) (duty of company as to issue of certificates etc)" substitute "any provision of any instrument constituting or regulating the company".

[Information about people with significant control
12A. (1) Sections 790C to 790K of the Companies Act 2006 apply to unregistered companies, with the following modifications.
(2) In section 790C (key terms)—
(a) for subsection (7)(c) substitute—
"(c) it is a company with voting shares admitted to trading on a market listed in Schedule 1 to the Register of People with Significant Control Regulations 2016 (SI 2016/339)";
(b) for subsection (7)(d) substitute—
"(d) it is of a description specified in regulation 4 of and Schedule 1 to the Register of People with Significant Control Regulations 2016 (SI 2016/339) which apply, together with any other provisions of those Regulations having effect for the purposes of these provisions.";
(c) omit subsections (11), (13) and (14).
(3) In section 790D (company's duty to investigate and obtain information)—
(a) omit subsection (9);
(b) omit subsection (10).
(4) In section 790E (company's duty to keep information up-to-date) in subsection (7) for "subsections (8) to (10)" substitute "subsection (8)".
(5) In section 790K (required particulars)—
(a) for subsection (5) substitute—
"(5) Regulation 7 of and Schedule 2 to the Register of People with Significant Control Regulations 2016 (SI 2016/339) apply, with any other provisions of the Regulations having effect for the purposes of these provisions.";
(b) omit subsection (6).
12B. (1) Sections 790M to 790VA of the Companies Act 2006 apply to unregistered companies, with the following modifications.
(2) In section 790M (duty to keep register)—
(a) for subsection (7) substitute—
"(7) Part 4 of the Register of People with Significant Control Regulations 2016 (SI 2016/339) applies, with any other provisions of the Regulations having effect for the purposes of that Part.";
(b) omit subsection (8).
(3) In section 790O(2) for "on payment of such fee as may be prescribed" substitute "on payment of the fee prescribed in regulation 6 of the Register of People with Significant Control Regulations 2016 (SI 2016/339)".
(4) In section 790VA (notification of changes to the registrar) omit subsection (4).
12C. (1) Sections 790ZF and 790ZG apply to unregistered companies, with the following modifications.
(2) In section 790ZF—
(a) in subsection (1) for "sections 240 to 244" substitute "sections 240 to 242, 243(1), (2), and (7)";
(b) in subsection (3) for "regulations made under section 790ZG" substitute "Part 7 of the PSC Regulations";
(c) after subsection (3) insert—
"(4) Part 6 of the Register of People with Significant Control Regulations 2016 (SI 2016/339) applies, with any other provisions of the Regulations having effect for the purposes of that Part."
(3) For Section 790ZG as it applies to unregistered companies, substitute—
"790ZG Protection of secured information
(1) Part 7 of the Register of People with Significant Control Regulations 2016 (SI 2016/339) applies, with any other provisions of the Regulations having effect for the purposes of that Part.
(2) Nothing in the provisions referred to in subsection (1) affects the use or disclosure of particulars of a person in any other capacity (for example, the use or disclosure of particulars of a person in that person's capacity as a member or director of the company).
(3) In this section "secured information" means the required particulars (other than the particular required by section 790K(1)(i)) of a registrable person in relation to an unregistered company.""

[Confirmation statement
13. (1) Sections 853A to [853H] and sections 853K and 853L of the Companies Act 2006 apply to unregistered companies.

(2) Section 853B (duties to notify a relevant event) applies to unregistered companies with the following modifications—

(a) omit paragraphs (b), (d), (f) and (g); and

(b) for paragraph (h) substitute—

"(h) in the case of a company which keeps any company records at a place other than its registered office, the duty under sections 162(4) and 275(4) to give notice of a change in the address of that place.".

(3) Section 853C (duty to notify a change in company's principal business activities) applies with the modification that in subsection (3), for "any prescribed system of classifying business activities." substitute "the system of classifying business activities prescribed in regulation 7 of the Companies and Limited Liability Partnerships (Filing Requirements) Regulations 2016".]

Takeovers

14. [(A1) Schedule 1C to the Companies Act 2006 applies to unregistered companies.]

(1) Sections 966 to 973 of the Companies Act 2006 (impediments to takeovers) apply to unregistered companies.

(2) Sections 974 to 991 of that Act ("squeeze-out" and "sell-out") apply to unregistered companies, but so far as relating to the offeree company only if the unregistered company has voting shares admitted to trading on a regulated market.

Fraudulent trading

15. Section 993 of the Companies Act 2006 (fraudulent trading) applies to an unregistered company.

Company Investigations

16. Parts 14 and 15 of the Companies Act 1985 (company investigations etc) apply to unregistered companies.

The registrar of companies

17. (1) The application to unregistered companies by the following paragraphs of certain provisions of Part 35 of the Companies Act 2006 is without prejudice to the application in relation to unregistered companies of the provisions of that Part that are of general application.

(2) Those provisions are—

(a) sections 1060(1) and (2) and 1061 to 1063 (the registrar),

(b) sections 1068 to 1071 (delivery of documents to the registrar),

(c) sections 1072 to 1076 (requirements for proper delivery),

(d) sections 1080(1), (4) and (5) and 1092 (keeping and production of records),

(e) section 1083 (preservation of original documents),

(f) sections 1108 to 1110 (language requirements: transliteration),

(g) sections 1111 and 1114 to 1119 (supplementary provisions).

18. Section 1066 of the Companies Act 2006 (registered numbers) applies to unregistered companies, modified so that it reads as follows—

"1066 Companies' reference numbers

(1) The registrar shall allocate to every company a number, which shall be known as the company's reference number.

(2) Companies' reference numbers shall be in such form, consisting of one or more sequences of figures or letters, as the registrar may determine.

(3) The registrar may on adopting a new form of reference number make such changes of existing reference numbers as appear necessary.

(4) A change of a company's reference number has effect from the date on which the company is notified by the registrar of the change.

(5) For a period of three years beginning with that date any requirement to disclose the company's reference number imposed by section 82 (trading disclosures) is satisfied by the use of either the old number or the new.".

19. Sections 1077 to 1079 of the Companies Act 2006 (public notice of receipt of certain documents) apply to unregistered companies, modified so that they read as follows—

"1077 Public notice of receipt of certain documents

(1) The registrar must cause to be published—

(a) in the Gazette, or

(b) in accordance with section 1116 (alternative means of giving public notice),

notice of the receipt by the registrar of any document specified in section 1078.

(2) The notice must state the name and reference number of the company, the description of document and the date of receipt.

(3) The registrar is not required to cause notice of the receipt of a document to be published before the date of incorporation of the company to which the document relates.

1078 The section 1077 documents

The following documents are specified for the purposes of section 1077—

Constitutional documents

1 Any instrument constituting or regulating the company.

2 After any alteration of such an instrument, any copy of the instrument as amended.

3 Any notice of the change of the company's name.

[Accounts and reports etc]

1 All documents required to be delivered to the registrar under section 441 (annual accounts).

[1A All documents delivered to the registrar under sections 394A(2)(e), 448A(2)(e) and 479A(2)(e) (qualifying subsidiaries: conditions for exemption from the audit, preparation and filing of individual accounts).]

2 [Any confirmation statement delivered by the company].

Principal office

Notification of any change of the company's principal office in the United Kingdom.

Winding up

1 Copy of any winding-up order in respect of the company.
2 Notice of the appointment of liquidators.
3 Order for the dissolution of the company on a winding up.
4 Return by a liquidator of the final meeting of the company on a winding up.

1079 Effect of failure to give public notice

(1) A company is not entitled to rely against other persons on the happening of any event to which this section applies unless—

(a) the event has been officially notified at the material time, or
(b) the company shows that the person concerned knew of the event at the material time.

(2) The events to which this section applies are—

(a) (as regards service of any document on the company) a change of the company's principal office in the United Kingdom,
(b) the making of a winding-up order in respect of the company, or
(c) the appointment of a liquidator in a voluntary winding up of the company.

(3) If the material time falls—

(a) on or before the 15th day after the date of official notification, or
(b) where the 15th day was not a working day, on or before the next day that was,

the company is not entitled to rely on the happening of the event as against a person who shows that he was unavoidably prevented from knowing of the event at that time.

(4) "Official notification" means—

(a) in relation to anything stated in a document specified in section 1078, notification of that document in accordance with section 1077;
(b) in relation to the appointment of a liquidator in a voluntary winding up, notification of that event in accordance with section 109 of the Insolvency Act 1986 (c 45) or Article 95 of the Insolvency (Northern Ireland) Order 1989 (SI 1989/2405 (NI 19)).".

[19A. Section 1079B of the Companies Act 2006 (duty to notify directors) applies to unregistered companies in cases where the document registered by the registrar is a notice under section 167 of the Companies Act 2006 of a person having become a director of a company.]

20. (1) The following provisions of the Companies Act 2006 apply to unregistered companies—

(a) section 1080(2) and (4) (meaning of "register" and form in which documents to be recorded and kept);
(b) sections 1085 and 1086 (inspection of the register and right to take copies on the register);
(c) sections 1087 and 1088 (material not available for public inspection and application to registrar to make address unavailable for public inspection);
[(cza) section 1087ZA (required particulars available for public inspection for limited period);]
[(ca) sections 1087A and 1087B (DOB information);]
(d) sections 1089 and 1090 (form and manner of application for inspection or copy);
(e) section 1091 (certification of copies as accurate);
[(f) section 1095A (rectification of register to resolve a discrepancy)].

(2) In section 1087 (material not available for public inspection) as it applies to unregistered companies, in subsection (1)—

(a) omit paragraph (a);
(b) in paragraph (b) omit "or any corresponding provision of regulations under section 1046 (overseas companies)";
(c) in paragraph (ba), omit sub-paragraph (ii);
[(ca) for paragraph (bc) substitute—

"(bc) information which by virtue of Part 7 (secured information) of the Register of People with Significant Control Regulations 2016 (SI 2016/339) the registrar must omit from the material on the public register that is available for inspection;"]

[(d) omit paragraphs (c) and (d);
(e) omit paragraphs (e) to (g) and (j)].

[(2A) In section 1087B for sub-paragraph (3) substitute "The provisions of the Companies (Disclosure of Date of Birth Information) Regulations 2015 (SI 2015/1694) apply."]

(3) For section 1088 as it applies to unregistered companies substitute—

"1088 Application to registrar to make address unavailable for public inspection

(1) The relevant provisions of the Companies (Disclosure of Address) Regulations 2009 (SI 2009/214) apply with respect to applications to the registrar to make an address on the register unavailable for public inspection.

(2) Those provisions are—

(a) Part 3 (applications to make address unavailable for public inspection), and
(b) Part 4 (matters relating to application), so far as relating to such applications, and
(c) any other provisions of the Regulations having effect for the purposes of those provisions.".

(4) In section 1091 (certification of copies as accurate) as it applies to unregistered companies, for subsection (4) substitute—

"(4) Regulation 2 of the Companies (Registrar, Languages and Trading Disclosures) Regulations 2006 (SI 2006/3429) (certification of electronic copies by registrar) applies where the copy is provided in electronic form.".

[20A. (1) Schedule 1A (references to people with significant control over a company) to the Companies Act 2006 applies to unregistered companies, with the following modifications.

(2) In paragraph 25—

(a) in sub-paragraph (5)(b) for "by regulations made by the Secretary of State" substitute "in regulation 8 of the Register of People with Significant Control Regulations 2016 (SI 2016/339)", and

(b) omit sub-paragraphs (6) and (7).

(3) Omit paragraph 26.

20B. (1) Schedule 1B (enforcement of disclosure requirements) to the Companies Act 2006 applies to unregistered companies, with the following modifications.

(2) For paragraph 12 substitute—

12. Part 5 of the Register of People with Significant Control Regulations 2016 (SI 2016/339) applies, with any other provisions of the Regulations having effect for the purposes of that Part."]

Supplementary provisions

21. The provisions of the Companies Acts relating to offences, interpretation and other supplementary matters have effect in relation to unregistered companies so far as necessary for the purposes of the application and enforcement of the provisions applied to unregistered companies by these Regulations.

NOTES

Para 10 is amended as follows:

Sub-para (1) substituted, and sub-paras (8)–(11) revoked, by the Unregistered Companies (Amendment) Regulations 2013, SI 2013/1972, reg 2, as from 1 October 2013, in relation to accounts and reports for a financial year ending on or after 30 September 2013.

Sub-paras (14), (15) revoked by the Companies, Partnerships and Groups (Accounts and Reports) Regulations 2015, SI 2015/980, reg 44, as from 6 April 2015, in relation to (a) financial years beginning on or after 1 January 2016, and (b) a financial year of a company beginning on or after 1 January 2015, but before 1 January 2016, if the directors of the company so decide (see **[4.549]** *post*).

Words in square brackets in sub-para (19) substituted by the Statutory Auditors (Amendment of Companies Act 2006 and Delegation of Functions etc) Order 2012, SI 2012/1741, art 3, Schedule, Pt 2, para 10, as from 2 July 2012.

Paras 12A–12C: inserted by the Information about People with Significant Control (Amendment) Regulations 2017, SI 2017/693, regs 32, 33, as from 26 June 2017 (for transitional arrangements, see Schedule, Pt 3 to the 2017 Regulations at **[10.1197]**).

Para 13: substituted by the Companies and Limited Liability Partnerships (Filing Requirements) Regulations 2016, SI 2016/599, reg 4, Sch 2, paras 1, 2, as from 30 June 2016 (for transitional provisions see reg 4 of the 2016 Regulations at **[4.643]**). Figure in square brackets in sub-para (1) substituted by SI 2017/693, regs 32, 34, as from 26 June 2017 (for transitional arrangements, see Schedule, Pt 3 to the 2017 Regulations at **[10.1197]**).

Para 14: sub-para (A1) inserted by the Takeovers (Amendment) (EU Exit) Regulations 2019, SI 2019/217, regs 19, 20, as from IP completion day (as defined in the European Union (Withdrawal Agreement) Act 2020, s 39).

Para 19: in s 1078 as set out in this paragraph, the words "Accounts and returns" and "Any confirmation statement delivered by the company" in square brackets were substituted by SI 2016/599, reg 4, Sch 2, paras 1, 3, as from 30 June 2016. Other words in square brackets inserted by the Companies and Limited Liability Partnerships (Accounts and Audit Exemptions and Change of Accounting Framework) Regulations 2012, SI 2012/2301, regs 2, 23, as from 1 October 2012 (in relation to accounts for financial years ending on or after that date).

Para 19A: inserted by the Companies and Limited Liability Partnerships (Filing Requirements) Regulations 2015, SI 2015/1695, reg 9(1), (2), as from 10 October 2015. Note that this amendment does not apply in respect of a statement or notice received by the registrar before 10 October 2015.

Para 20: sub-para (1)(ca) inserted, and sub-paras (2)(d) and (e) substituted (for the original sub-para (2)(d)) by SI 2015/1695, reg 9(1), (3), as from 10 October 2015. Sub-para (1)(cza) inserted, and sub-para (1)(f) added, by the Money Laundering and Terrorist Financing (Amendment) Regulations 2019, SI 2019/1511, reg 18, as from 10 January 2020. Sub-paras (2)(ca) and (2A) inserted by SI 2017/693, regs 32, 35, as from 26 June 2017 (for transitional arrangements, see Schedule, Pt 3 to the 2017 Regulations at **[10.1197]**).

Paras 20A, 20B: inserted by SI 2017/693, regs 32, 36, as from 26 June 2017 (for transitional arrangements, see Schedule, Pt 3 to the 2017 Regulations at **[10.1197]**).

Temporary modification: this Schedule was modified by the Companies etc (Filing Requirements) (Temporary Modifications) Regulations 2020, SI 2020/645, reg 5. By virtue of the Corporate Insolvency and Governance Act 2020, s 39(8), the modification applied from 27 June 2020 to the end of the day on 5 April 2021 (subject to the saving provision in s 39(9) which provides that the expiry of s 39 on 5 April 2021 does not affect the continued operation of any Regulations made under that section for the purpose of determining the length of any period that began before the expiry). As modified, section 87, as it applies to unregistered companies by virtue of paragraph 5 above, had effect as if for the reference in subsection (1) to "15 days" there were substituted a reference to "42 days".

SCHEDULE 2
TRANSITIONAL PROVISIONS AND SAVINGS

Regulation 9

Introduction

[4.399]

1. (1) In this Schedule—

(a) "the 1985 Act" means the Companies Act 1985 and "the 1985 Regulations" means the Companies (Unregistered Companies) Regulations 1985;

(b) "the 1986 Order" means the Companies (Northern Ireland) Order 1986 and "the 1986 Regulations" means the Companies (Unregistered Companies) Regulations (Northern Ireland) 1986;

(c) "existing company" means an unregistered company that was incorporated before 1st October 2009.

(2) References in this Schedule to provisions of the 1985 Act or 1986 Order, or to provisions of the Companies Act 2006, are to those provisions as applied to unregistered companies.

A company's constitution

2. (1) Section 26(1) of the Companies Act 2006 (registrar to be sent copy of instruments constituting or regulating company) applies where the company is incorporated on or after 1st October 2009.

(2) Section 18 of the 1985 Act as modified by regulation 6(b)(ii) of the 1985 Regulations or Article 29 of the 1986 Order as modified by regulation 6(b)(ii) of the 1986 Regulations continues to apply where the company was incorporated before that date.

3. (1) Section 26(2) of the Companies Act 2006 (registrar to be sent copy of amended instrument constituting or regulating company) applies where the amendment takes effect on or after 1st October 2009.

(2) Section 18(2) and (3) of the 1985 Act or Article 29(2) and (3) of the 1986 Order continue to apply in relation to amendments taking effect before that date.

4. (1) Section 34 of the Companies Act 2006 (notice to registrar where company's constitution altered by enactment) applies where the enactment in question comes into force on or after 1st October 2009.

(2) Section 18(1) and (3) of the 1985 Act or Article 29(1) and (3) of the 1986 Order continue to apply in relation to alterations made by statutory provisions coming into force before that date.

5. Section 35 of the Companies Act 2006 (notice to registrar where company's constitution altered by order) applies in relation to orders made on or after 1st October 2009.

A company's capacity and related matters

6. (1) Section 39 of the Companies Act 2006 (a company's capacity) applies to acts of a company done on or after 1st October 2009.

(2) Section 35 of the 1985 Act or Article 45 of the 1986 Order continues to apply to acts of a company done before that date.

7. (1) Section 44 of the Companies Act 2006 (execution of documents) applies in relation to the execution of documents on or after 1st October 2009.

(2) Section 36A of the 1985 Act or Article 46A of the 1986 Order continues to apply in relation to documents executed before that date.

(3) For the purposes of this paragraph a document signed by one authorised signatory before 1st October 2009 and by another on or after that date is treated as executed on or after 1st October 2009.

A company's principal office in the United Kingdom

8. Section 86(2) of the Companies Act 2006 (registrar to be notified of address of company's principal office in the United Kingdom) applies where the company is incorporated on or after 1st October 2009.

Directors and secretaries

9. On and after 1st October 2009 the register of directors and secretaries kept by a company under section 288(1) of the 1985 Act or Article 296(1) of the 1986 Order shall be treated as two separate registers—

(a) a register of directors kept under and for the purposes of section 162 of the Companies Act 2006, and

(b) a register of secretaries kept under and for the purposes of section 275 of that Act.

10. (1) Subject to the following provisions, an existing company need not comply with any provision of the Companies Act 2006 requiring the company's register of directors or secretaries to contain particulars additional to those required by the 1985 Act or the 1986 Order until the earlier of—

(a) the date to which the company makes up its first annual return made up to a date on or after 1st October 2009, and

(b) the last date to which the company should have made up that return.

(2) Sub-paragraph (1) does not apply in relation to a director or secretary of whom particulars are first registered on or after 1st October 2009 (whether the director or secretary was appointed before, on or after that date).

(3) Sub-paragraph (1) ceases to apply in relation to a director or secretary whose registered particulars fall to be altered on or after 1st October 2009 because they have changed (whether the change occurred before, on or after that date).

(4) This paragraph does not affect the particulars required to be included in the company's annual return.

11. (1) In the case of an existing company—

(a) the relevant existing address of a director or secretary is deemed, on and after 1st October 2009, to be a service address, and

(b) any entry in the company's register of directors or secretaries stating that address is treated, on and after that date, as complying with the obligation in section 163(1)(b) or 277(1)(b) of the Companies Act 2006 to state a service address.

(2) The relevant existing address is—

(a) the address that immediately before 1st October 2009 appeared in the company's register of directors and secretaries as having been notified to the company under section 289(1A) or 290(1A) of the 1985 Act (service address notified by individual applying for confidentiality order in respect of usual residential address), or

(b) if no such address appeared, the address that immediately before that date appeared in the company's register of directors and secretaries as the director's or secretary's usual residential address.

(3) Any notification of a change of a relevant existing address occurring before 1st October 2009 that is received by the company on or after that date is treated as being or, as the case may be, including notification of a change of service address.

(4) The operation of this paragraph does not give rise to any duty to notify the registrar under section 167 or 276 of the Companies Act 2006 (duty to notify registrar of changes in particulars contained in register).

12. (1) An existing company must remove from its register of directors on 1st October 2009 any entry relating to a shadow director.

(2) Section 167 of the Companies Act 2006 (duty to notify registrar of changes) applies as if the shadow director had ceased to be a director on that date.

13. The removal by an existing company from its register of directors or secretaries on or after 1st October 2009 of particulars required by the 1985 Act or the 1986 Order but not required by the Companies Act 2006 does not give rise to any duty to notify the registrar under section 167 or 276 of the Companies Act 2006 (duty to notify registrar of changes in particulars contained in register).

14. (1) The duty of a company to keep a register of directors' residential addresses has effect on and after 1st October 2009.

(2) The entry on that register of information that immediately before that date was contained in the company's register of directors and secretaries does not give rise to any duty to notify the registrar under section 167 of the Companies Act 2006 (duty to notify registrar of changes in particulars contained in register).

15. (1) Sections 167 and 276 of the Companies Act 2006 (duty to notify registrar of changes) apply in relation to—

(a) a change among a company's directors or in its secretaries, or

(b) a change in the particulars contained in the register,

occurring on or after 1st October 2009.

(2) Sections 288(2), (4) and (6), 289 and 290 of the 1985 Act or Articles 296(2), (4) and (6), 297 and 298 of the 1986 Order (notification to registrar of changes) continue to apply in relation to a change occurring before that date.

16. (1) The registrar may make such entries in the register as appear to be appropriate having regard to paragraphs 10 to 14 and the information appearing on the register immediately before 1st October 2009 or notified to the registrar in accordance with paragraph 15(2).

(2) In particular, the registrar may record as a service address a relevant existing address (within the meaning of paragraph 11).

(3) Any notification of a change of a relevant existing address occurring before 1st October 2009 that is received by the registrar on or after that date is treated as being or, as the case may be, including notification of a change of service address.

17. Where a director's usual residential address appears as a service address—

(a) in the company's register of directors by virtue of paragraph 11, or

(b) in the register of companies by virtue of paragraph 16,

that address is not protected information for the purposes of Chapter 8 of Part 10 of the Companies Act 2006.

18. (1) Section 242(1) of the Companies Act 2006 (duty of registrar to omit protected information from material available for inspection) does not apply—

(a) to material delivered to the registrar before 1st October 2009, or

(b) to material delivered to the registrar on or after 1st October 2009 by virtue of paragraph 15(2) (notification of change occurring before that date).

(2) In section 242(2)(b) of the Companies Act 2006 (exclusion of material registered before commencement) the reference to things registered before Chapter 8 of Part 10 of that Act comes into force is treated as including anything registered as a result of a notification in accordance with paragraph 15(2) (notification on or after 1st October 2009 of change occurring before that date).

19. In determining under section 245(1) of the Companies Act 2006 whether to put a director's usual residential address on the public record, the registrar may take into account only—

(a) communications sent by the registrar on or after 1st October 2009, and

(b) evidence as to the effectiveness of service coming to the registrar's attention on or after that date.

Political donations and expenditure

20. (1) Sections 362 to 379 of the Companies Act 2006 (political donations and expenditure) apply to donations made or expenditure incurred on or after 1st October 2007.

(2) Section 379(2) of that Act applies as to the time when a donation is regarded as made or expenditure as incurred, including where it is made or incurred in pursuance of a contract entered into before that date.

(3) Part 10A of the 1985 Act continues to apply to donations or expenditure in relation to which the relevant time, as defined in section 347A(10) of that Act, is before that date.

(4) The repeal of that Part does not affect paragraph 3(4) of Schedule 7 to the 1985 Act (matters to be dealt with in directors' report: expressions to have same meaning as in Part 10A).

Accounts

21. (1) Sections 380 to 416, 418 to 469 and 471 to 474 of the Companies Act 2006 (accounts and reports) apply to accounts and reports for financial years beginning on or after 1st October 2009.

(2) The corresponding provisions of the 1985 Act or 1986 Order continue to apply to accounts and reports for financial years beginning before that date.

22. Any question whether—

(a) for the purposes of section 382, 383, 384(3) or 467(3) of the Companies Act 2006, a company or group qualified as small in a financial year beginning before 1st October 2009, or

(b) for the purposes of section 465 or 466 of that Act a company or group qualified as medium-sized in any such financial year,

is to be determined by reference to the corresponding provisions of the 1985 Act or 1986 Order.

Audit

23. (1) In Chapter 1 of Part 16 of the Companies Act 2006 (requirement for audited accounts)—

(a) sections 475 to 481 (general provisions) apply to accounts for financial years beginning on or after 1st October 2009; and

(b) section 484 (general power of amendment by regulations) applies accordingly.

(2) Sections 235(1), 249A(1), (3) and (6) to (7), 249AA and 249B of the 1985 Act or Articles 243(1), 257A(1), (3) and (6) to (7), 257AA and 257B of the 1986 Order continue to apply to accounts for financial years beginning before that date.

24. (1) Sections 485 to 488 of the Companies Act 2006 (appointment of auditors of private companies) apply in relation to appointments for financial years beginning on or after 1st October 2009.

(2) Sections 384 to 388A of the 1985 Act or Articles 392 to 396A of the 1986 Order continue to apply in relation to appointments for financial years beginning before that date.

(3) Where—

(a) a private company has elected under section 386 of the 1985 Act or Article 394 of the 1986 Order to dispense with the annual appointment of auditors, and

(b) the election is in force immediately before 1st October 2009.

section 487(2)(a) of the Companies Act 2006 (no deemed reappointment of auditors appointed by directors) does not prevent the deemed reappointment under that subsection of auditors first appointed before 1st October 2009.

25. (1) This paragraph applies where immediately before 1st October 2009 a resolution of a private company under section 390A of the 1985 Act or Article 398A of the 1986 Order (remuneration of auditors) was in force and was expressed (in whatever terms) to continue to have effect so long as a resolution under section 386 of that Act or Article 394 of that Order (election to dispense with annual appointment of auditors) continued in force.

(2) The repeal of section 386 of the 1985 Act or Article 394 of the 1986 Order does not affect the continued operation of the resolution, which shall continue to have effect until—

(a) it is revoked or superseded by a further resolution,

(b) the auditors to which it applies cease to hold office, or

(c) it otherwise ceases to have effect in accordance with its terms.

26. (1) In Chapter 2 of Part 16 of the Companies Act 2006 (appointment of auditors)—

(a) sections 489 and 490 (appointment of auditors by public companies) apply to appointments for financial years beginning on or after 1st October 2009;

(b) section 491 (term of office of auditors of public company) applies to auditors appointed for financial years beginning on or after that date.

(2) Sections 384, 385, 387 and 388(1), (3) and (4) of the 1985 Act or Articles 392, 393, 395 and 396(1), (3) and (4) of the 1986 Order continue to apply to appointments by public companies for financial years beginning before that date.

27. (1) The following provisions apply to auditors appointed for financial years beginning on or after 1st October 2009—

(a) section 492 (fixing of auditor's remuneration),

(b) section 493 (disclosure of terms of audit appointment), and

(c) section 494 (disclosure of services provided by auditor or associated and related remuneration).

(2) Sections 390A and 390B of the 1985 Act or Articles 398A and 398B of the 1986 Order continue to apply to auditors appointed for financial years beginning before that date.

(3) The repeal of section 390A of the 1985 Act and Article 398A of the 1986 Order (remuneration of auditors) does not affect the operation of any such resolution as is mentioned in paragraph 25 above.

28. (1) In Chapter 3 of Part 16 of the Companies Act 2006 (functions of auditor)—

(a) sections 495 to 498 (auditor's report and duties of auditor) apply to auditors' reports on accounts or reports for financial years beginning on or after 1st October 2009;

(b) sections 499 to 501 (rights of auditors) apply to auditors appointed for financial years beginning on or after that date;

(c) sections 503 to 509 (signature of auditor's report and offences in connection with auditor's report) apply to auditors' reports on accounts or reports for financial years beginning on or after that date.

(2) Sections 235 to 237, 389A and 389B of the 1985 Act or Articles 243 to 245, 397A and 397B of the 1986 Order continue to apply as regards financial years beginning before that date.

29. (1) Section 502 of the Companies Act 2006 (auditor's rights in relation to resolutions and meetings) applies to auditors appointed on or after 1st October 2009.

(2) Section 390 of the 1985 Act or Article 398 of the 1986 Order continues to apply to auditors appointed before that date.

30. (1) In Chapter 4 of Part 16 of that Act (removal, resignation, etc of auditors), sections 510 to 513 (removal of auditor) apply where notice of the intended resolution is given to the company on or after 1st October 2009.

(2) Sections 391 and 391A of the 1985 Act or Articles 399 and 399A of the 1986 Order continue to apply where notice of the intended resolution is given to the company before that date.

(3) In section 513 (rights of auditor removed from office) as it applies in relation to an auditor appointed before 1st October 2009, the reference to rights under section 502(2) shall be read as a reference to rights under section 390(1) of the 1985 Act or Article 398(1) of the 1986 Order.

31. (1) Sections 514 and 515 of the Companies Act 2006 (failure to re-appoint auditor) apply to appointments for financial years beginning on or after 1st October 2009.

(2) Section 391A of the 1985 Act or Article 399A of the 1986 Order continues to apply to appointments for financial years beginning before that date.

32. (1) Sections 516 to 518 of the Companies Act 2006 (resignation of auditor) apply to resignations occurring on or after 1st October 2009.

(2) Sections 392 and 392A of the 1985 Act or Articles 400 and 400A of the 1986 Order continue to apply to resignations occurring before that date.

(3) In section 518 (rights of resigning auditor) as it applies in relation to an auditor appointed before 1st October 2009, the reference to rights under section 502(2) shall be read as a reference to rights under section 390(1) of the 1985 Act or Article 398(1) of the 1986 Order.

33. (1) Sections 519 to 525 of the Companies Act 2006 (statement by auditor ceasing to hold office) apply where the auditor ceases to hold office on or after 1st October 2009.

(2) Sections 394 and 394A of the 1985 Act or Articles 401A and 401B of the 1986 Order continue to apply where the auditor ceases to hold office before that date.

34. (1) Section 526 of the Companies Act 2006 (effect of casual vacancies) applies where the vacancy occurs on or after 1st October 2009.

(2) Section 388(2) of the 1985 Act or Article 396(2) of the 1986 Order continues to apply where the vacancy occurred before that date.

35. In section 527 of the Companies Act 2006—

(a) subsection (1)(a) (matters relating to audit of company's accounts) applies to accounts for financial years beginning on or after 1st October 2009, and

(b) subsection (1)(b) (matters relating to circumstances connected with an auditor of the company) applies to auditors appointed for financial years beginning on or after that date.

36. A resolution passed before 1st October 2009 authorising a liability limitation agreement is effective for the purposes of section 536 of the Companies Act 2006 (authorisation of agreement by members of company) if it complies with the requirements of that section.

Annual return

37. (1) Sections 854 to 859 of the Companies Act 2006 (a company's annual return) apply to annual returns made up to a date on or after 1st October 2009.

(2) Sections 363 to 365 of the 1985 Act or Articles 371 to 373 of the 1986 Order continue to apply to annual returns made up to a date before 1st October 2009.

(3) Any reference in the Companies Act 2006 to a company's last return, or to a return delivered in accordance with Part 24 of that Act, shall be read as including (so far as necessary to ensure the continuity of the law) a return made up to a date before 1st October 2009 or delivered in accordance with the 1985 Act or the 1986 Order.

Fraudulent trading

38. (1) Section 458 of the 1985 Act or Article 451 of the 1986 Order (offences of fraudulent trading) continues to apply to offences completed before 1st October 2009.

(2) Where, in the case of an offence—

(a) a relevant event occurs before 1st October 2009, and

(b) another relevant event occurs on or after 1st October 2009,

the offence must be charged under section 993 of the Companies Act 2006 (and not under section 458 of the 1985 Act or Article 451 of the 1986 Order).

(3) If in the case of any such offence a relevant event occurred before 15th January 2007, section 993(3)(a) applies with the substitution of "seven years" for "ten years".

(4) "Relevant event" means an act, omission or other event (including any result of one or more acts or omissions) proof of which is required for conviction of the offence.

Company investigations

39. (1) The extension to Northern Ireland by section 1284 of the Companies Act 2006 of Parts 14 and 15 of the 1985 Act (company investigations) has effect to enable the exercise of the powers conferred by those Parts in relation to unregistered companies having their principal office in Northern Ireland, and otherwise in relation to Northern Ireland, on and after 1st October 2009.

(2) Parts 15 and 16 of the 1986 Order, and any other provision of that Order having effect for the purposes of Part 15, continue to apply (subject to sub-paragraph (3) below)—

(a) in relation to inspectors appointed under Part 15 before 1st October 2009 and matters arising in connection with or in consequence of any such appointment or any report of inspectors so appointed;

(b) in relation to any exercise before 1st October 2009 of any power of the Department of Enterprise, Trade and Investment in Northern Ireland not within paragraph (a), and matters arising in connection with or in consequence of any such exercise.

(3) A direction in force immediately before 1st October 2009 under Article 438(1A) or 449(1A) of the 1986 Order (direction limiting or relaxing restrictions on shares) shall continue in force and have effect on and after that date as if made under the corresponding provision of Part 14 of the 1985 Act, and the provisions of Part 15 of that Act shall apply accordingly.

Saving for provisions as to form or manner in which documents to be delivered

40. (1) Any saving in this Schedule for the effect of a provision of the 1985 Act or 1986 Order requiring use of a prescribed form extends to the form and the power under which it is prescribed.

(2) Any saving in this Schedule for the effect of a provision of the 1985 Act or 1986 Order requiring a document to be delivered to the registrar extends to section 707B of the 1985 Act or Article 656B of the 1986 Order (delivery to the registrar using electronic communications) so far as relating to the provision in question and the delivery of documents under it.

Savings for provisions relating to offences

41. (1) The repeal of any provision of the 1985 Act or 1986 Order creating an offence does not affect the continued operation of that provision in relation to an offence committed before 1st October 2009.

(2) Any saving in this Schedule for the effect of a provision of the 1985 Act or 1986 Order that creates an offence extends to the entry relating to that provision in Schedule 24 to that Act or Schedule 23 to that Order (punishment of offences).

(3) References in this paragraph to provisions of the 1985 Act or 1986 Order include provisions of regulations or orders made under that Act or Order.

COMPANIES (COMPANIES AUTHORISED TO REGISTER) REGULATIONS 2009

(SI 2009/2437)

NOTES

Made: 4 September 2009.

Authority: European Communities Act 1972, s 2(2); Companies Act 2006, ss 1042, 1292(1) (see also the note "Statutory Instruments made under the European Communities Act 1972" preceding paragraph **[4.1]** *ante*).

Commencement: 1 October 2009.

For a summary of all Orders and Regulations made under the Companies Act 2006, see Appendix 4 at **[A4]**.

These Regulations are reproduced as amended by: the Companies and Limited Liability Partnerships (Filing Requirements) Regulations 2015, SI 2015/1695; the Companies and Limited Liability Partnerships (Filing Requirements) Regulations 2016, SI 2016/599; the Companies, Limited Liability Partnerships and Partnerships (Amendment etc) (EU Exit) Regulations 2019, SI 2019/348.

ARRANGEMENT OF REGULATIONS

PART 1 INTRODUCTION

[4.400]

1 Citation and commencement

(1) These Regulations may be cited as the Companies (Companies Authorised to Register) Regulations 2009.

(2) These Regulations come into force on 1st October 2009.

PART 2 REGISTRATION REQUIREMENTS

Introduction

[4.401]

2 Application of this Part

(1) The provisions of this Part apply in relation to the registration of a company under the Companies Act 2006 in pursuance of section 1040 of that Act (companies not formed under companies legislation but authorised to register).

(2) In this Part—

- (a) references to a company are to a company authorised to register under that section (see subsections (1), (4) and (5) of that section); and
- (b) references to registration are to registration under that section.

Agreement of members to registration

[4.402]

3 Agreement of members to registration

(1) A company must not register without the assent of a majority of such of its members as are present in person or by proxy (in cases where proxies are allowed) at a general meeting summoned for the purpose.

(2) Where a company not having the liability of its members limited by an enactment or letters patent wishes to register as a limited company, the majority required to assent as required by paragraph (1) is not less than 75% of the members present in person or by proxy at the meeting.

(3) In computing any majority under this regulation when a poll is demanded, regard is to be had to the number of votes to which each member is entitled according to the company's regulations.

Requirements for registration

[4.403]

4 Registration documents

(1) An application for registration of the company must be delivered to the registrar together with the documents required by this regulation and a statement of compliance.

(2) The application for registration must state—

- (a) the name with which the company is proposed to be registered,
- (b) whether the company's registered office is to be situated in England and Wales (or in Wales), in Scotland or in Northern Ireland,
- (c) whether the liability of the members of the company is to be limited, and if so whether it is to be limited by shares or by guarantee, and
- (d) whether the company is to be a private or a public company.

(3) The application must contain—

- (a) in the case of a joint stock company, a statement of capital and initial shareholdings (see regulation 5);
- (b) in the case of a company that is to be limited by guarantee, a statement of guarantee (see regulation 6);
- (c) a statement of the company's proposed officers (see regulation 7).

(4) The application must contain—

- (a) a statement of the intended address of the company's registered office, and
- (b) a copy of any enactment, royal charter, letters patent, deed of settlement, contract of partnership or other instrument constituting or regulating the company.

(5) The application must be delivered—

- (a) to the registrar of companies for England and Wales, if the registered office of the company is to be situated in England and Wales (or in Wales);

(b) to the registrar of companies for Scotland, if the registered office of the company is to be situated in Scotland;

(c) to the registrar of companies for Northern Ireland, if the registered office of the company is to be situated in Northern Ireland.

[4.404]

5 Statement of capital and initial shareholdings

(1) The statement of capital and initial shareholdings required to be delivered in the case of a joint stock company must comply with this regulation.

(2) It must state—

(a) the total number of shares of the company that on a date specified in the statement ("the reference date") are held by members of the company,

(b) the aggregate nominal value of those shares,

[(ba) the aggregate amount (if any) unpaid on those shares (whether on account of their nominal value or by way of premium),]

(c) for each class of shares—

(i) the particulars specified in paragraph (4) below of the rights attached to the shares,

(ii) the total number of shares of that class, and

(iii) the aggregate nominal value of shares of that class, . . .

(d) . . .

(3) The reference date must be not more than 28 days before the date of the application for registration.

(4) The particulars referred to in paragraph (2)(c)(i) are—

(a) particulars of any voting rights attached to the shares, including rights that arise only in certain circumstances;

(b) particulars of any rights attached to the shares, as respects dividends, to participate in a distribution;

(c) particulars of any rights attached to the shares, as respects capital, to participate in a distribution (including on winding up); and

(d) whether the shares are to be redeemed or are liable to be redeemed at the option of the company or the shareholder.

(5) The statement of capital and initial shareholdings must also state—

(a) the names and service addresses of all persons who on the reference date were members of the company, and

(b) with respect to each member of the company—

(i) the number, nominal value (of each share) and class of shares held by that member on that date, and

(ii) the amount to be paid up and the amount (if any) to be unpaid on each share (whether on account of the nominal value of the share or by way of premium).

(6) For the purposes of paragraph (5)(a) a person's "name" means his Christian name (or other forename) and surname, except that in the case of—

(a) a peer, or

(b) an individual usually known by a title,

the title may be stated instead of his Christian name (or other forename) and surname or in addition to either or both of them.

(7) Where a member of the company holds shares of more than one class, the information required under paragraph (5)(b)(i) is required for each class.

NOTES

Para (2): sub-para (ba) inserted, and sub-para (d) and the preceding word revoked, by the Companies and Limited Liability Partnerships (Filing Requirements) Regulations 2016, SI 2016/599, reg 5, Sch 3, para 6, as from 30 June 2016.

[4.405]

6 Statement of guarantee

(1) Where the company proposes to register as a company limited by guarantee, the members' assent to its being registered (see regulation 3) must be accompanied by a resolution containing a statement of guarantee.

(2) The statement of guarantee required is a statement that each member undertakes that, if the company is wound up while he is a member, or within one year after he ceases to be a member, he will contribute to the assets of the company such amount as may be required for—

(a) payment of the debts and liabilities of the company contracted before he ceases to be a member,

(b) payment of the costs, charges and expenses of winding up, and

(c) adjustment of the rights of the contributories among themselves,

not exceeding a specified amount.

(3) The statement of guarantee required to be delivered to the registrar in the case of a company that is to be limited by guarantee is a copy of the resolution containing the statement of guarantee.

[4.406]

7 Statement of proposed officers

(1) The statement of the company's proposed officers required to be delivered to the registrar must contain the required particulars of—

(a) the person who is, or persons who are, to be a director or directors of the company on registration;

(b) in the case of a company that is to be a private company, any person who is (or any persons who are) to be the secretary (or joint secretaries) of the company on registration;

(c) in the case of a company that is to be a public company, the person who is (or the persons who are) to be the secretary (or joint secretaries) of the company on registration;

(d) . . .

(2) The required particulars are the particulars that will be required to be stated—

(a) in the case of a director, in the company's register of directors and register of residential addresses (see sections 162 to 165 of the Companies Act 2006);

(b) in the case of a secretary, in the company's register of secretaries (see sections 277 to 278 of that Act).

[(2A) The statement under paragraph (1) must be accompanied by a statement by the company that each person named as a director, as secretary or as one of joint secretaries has consented to act in the relevant capacity.]

(3) Regulation 7 of the Companies (Disclosure of Address) Regulations 2009 (disclosure of protected information: application under section 243 on behalf of proposed director) applies as if—

(a) references to a subscriber to the memorandum of association were to any member of the company, and

(b) references to the proposed company were to the company proposing to register.

NOTES

Sub-para (1)(d) revoked, and para (2A) inserted, by the Companies and Limited Liability Partnerships (Filing Requirements) Regulations 2015, SI 2015/1695, reg 10, as from 10 October 2015. Note that these amendments do not apply in respect of a statement or notice received by the registrar before 10 October 2015.

[4.407]
8 Statement of compliance

(1) The statement of compliance required to be delivered to the registrar is a statement that the requirements of this Part as to registration have been complied with.

(2) The registrar may accept the statement of compliance as sufficient evidence of compliance.

Registration as a public company

[4.408]
9 Registration as a public company

(1) A joint stock company may be registered as a public company limited by shares if—

(a) the following conditions are met, and

(b) the application for registration is accompanied by the documents specified in paragraph (4) below..

(2) The conditions are—

(a) that the requirements of section 91 of the Companies Act 2006 are met as regards its share capital;

(b) the requirements of section 92 of that Act are met as regards its net assets; and

(c) if section 93 of that Act applies (recent allotment of shares for non-cash consideration), that the requirements of that section are met.

(3) Sections 91 to 93 apply for this purpose as in the case of a private company applying to be re-registered under section 90 of the Companies Act 2006 (re-registration of private company as public), but as if any reference to the special resolution required by section 90 were to the joint stock company's resolution that it be a public company.

(4) The following documents must be delivered to the registrar together with the application for registration (as well as those required by regulation 4)—

(a) a copy of the resolution that the company be a public company;

(b) a copy of the balance sheet and other documents referred to in section 92(1); and

(c) if section 93 applies (recent allotment of shares for non-cash consideration), a copy of the valuation report (if any) under subsection (2)(a) of that section.

(5) The statement of compliance required to be delivered with the application is a statement that the requirements of this Part as to registration as a public company have been complied with.

(6) The registrar may accept the statement of compliance as sufficient evidence that the company is entitled to be registered as a public company.

Change of name on registration

[4.409]
10 Change of name on registration

(1) Where the name of a company seeking registration is a name by which it is precluded from being registered by any provision of the Companies Acts, either—

(a) because it is directly prohibited from being registered with that name, or

(b) because the Secretary of State would not approve the company being registered with that name,

the company may change its name with effect from the date on which it is registered.

(2) A change of name under this regulation requires the like assent of the company's members as is required by regulation 3 for registration.

Registration

[4.410]
11 Registration

If the registrar is satisfied that the requirements of this Part as to registration are complied with, the registrar shall register the documents delivered to him.

[4.411]
12 Issue of certificate of incorporation

(1) On the registration of a company, the registrar shall give a certificate that the company is incorporated.

(2) The certificate must state—

(a) the name and registered number of the company,

(b) the date of its incorporation,

(c) whether it is a limited or unlimited company, and if it is limited whether it is limited by shares or limited by guarantee,

(d) whether it is a private or a public company, and

(e) whether the company's registered office is situated in England and Wales (or in Wales), in Scotland or in Northern Ireland.

(3) The certificate must be signed by the registrar or authenticated by the registrar's official seal.

(4) The certificate is conclusive evidence that the requirements of this Part as to registration have been complied with and that the company is duly registered under the Companies Act 2006.

(5) Section 1064 of that Act (public notice of certificate of incorporation) applies to a certificate of incorporation issued under this regulation.

PART 3 EFFECT OF REGISTRATION

Introduction

[4.412]

13 Interpretation of this Part

In this Part—

"registration" means registration under the Companies Act 2006 in pursuance of section 1040 of that Act; and "instrument" includes a deed of settlement, a contract of partnership or letters patent.

Transfer of property, rights and liabilities

[4.413]

14 Transfer of property, rights and liabilities

(1) All property belonging to or vested in the company at the date of its registration passes to and vests in the company on registration for all the estate and interest of the company in the property.

(2) Registration does not affect the company's rights or liabilities in respect of any debt or obligation incurred, or contract entered into, by, to, with or on behalf of the company before registration.

[4.414]

15 Pending legal proceedings

(1) All actions and other legal proceedings which at the time of the company's registration are pending by or against the company, or the public officer or any member of it, may be continued in the same manner as if the registration had not taken place.

(2) Execution shall not issue against the effects of any individual member of the company on any judgment, decree or order obtained in such an action or proceeding; but in the event of the company's property and effects being insufficient to satisfy the judgment, decree or order, an order may be obtained for winding up the company.

The company's constitution

[4.415]

16 Constitutional provisions to have effect as if contained in articles of association

(1) All provisions contained in any enactment or other instrument constituting or regulating the company are deemed to be conditions and regulations of the company, in the same manner and with the same incidents as if so much of them as would, if the company had been formed and registered under the Companies Act 2006, be contained in registered articles of association.

(2) The provisions brought in by paragraph (1) include, in the case of a company registered as a company limited by guarantee, those of the resolution declaring the amount of the guarantee.

[4.416]

17 Power to substitute articles of association

A registered company may by special resolution alter the form of its constitution by substituting articles of association for any instrument constituting or regulating the company, other than an enactment, a royal charter or letters patent.

Application of the Companies Acts

[4.417]

18 General application of the Companies Acts

(1) Subject to the following regulations, the provisions of the Companies Acts apply to a registered company, and to its members and contributories, in the same manner as if it had been formed and registered under the Companies Act 2006.

(2) References in this and the following regulations to the Companies Acts—

(a) . . .

(b) do not include Part 2 of the Companies (Audit, Investigation and Community Enterprise) Act 2004 (community interest companies).

NOTES

Para (2): sub-para (a) revoked by the Companies, Limited Liability Partnerships and Partnerships (Amendment etc) (EU Exit) Regulations 2019, SI 2019/348, reg 8, Sch 3, paras 26, 27, as from IP completion day (as defined in the European Union (Withdrawal Agreement) Act 2020, s 39).

[4.418]

19 Exclusions

(1) The model articles of association prescribed by the Secretary of State under section 19 of the Companies Act 2006 do not apply unless adopted by special resolution.

(2) Provisions relating to the numbering of shares do not apply to a joint stock company whose shares are not numbered.

[4.419]

20 Restrictions on power to alter company's constitution

(1) Subject to the provisions of this Part, the company does not have power—

(a) to alter any provision contained in an enactment relating to the company,

(b) without the consent of the Secretary of State, to alter any provision contained in letters patent relating to the company.

(2) The company does not have power to alter any provision contained in a royal charter or letters patent with respect to the company's objects.

(3) Where by virtue of paragraph (1) or (2) a company does not have power to alter a provision, it does not have power to ratify acts of the directors in contravention of the provision.

[4.420]

21 Provisions as to capital structure

The provisions with respect to—

(a) the re-registration of an unlimited company as limited,

(b) the powers of an unlimited company on re-registration as a limited company to provide that a portion of its share capital shall not be capable of being called up except in the event of winding up, and

(c) the power of a limited company to determine that a portion of its share capital shall not be capable of being called up except in that event,

apply notwithstanding any provisions contained in any enactment, royal charter or other instrument constituting or regulating the company.

[4.421]

22 Saving for other powers to alter company's constitution

(1) Except as mentioned in paragraph (2), none of the provisions of this Part or of the Companies Acts affects any power of altering the company's constitution or regulations vested in the company by virtue of any enactment or other instrument constituting or regulating it.

(2) Paragraph (1) does not apply to the power of the court under section 996(2) of the Companies Act 2006 (protection of members against unfair prejudice: power of court to regulate the conduct of the company's affairs).

[4.422]

23 Status of banking company in Scotland

A banking company in Scotland that is incorporated by virtue of registration under these Regulations is deemed a bank incorporated, constituted or established by or under an Act of Parliament.

PART 4 TRANSITIONAL PROVISIONS AND SAVINGS

[4.423]

24 Transitional provisions and savings

(1) Part 2 of these Regulations has effect in accordance with paragraph 93 of Schedule 2 to the Companies Act 2006 (Commencement No 8, Transitional Provisions and Savings) Order 2008 (by virtue of which it applies to applications made on or after 1st October 2009).

(2) The transitional provisions and savings relating to the coming into force of the provisions of the Companies Acts in relation to companies as defined in section 1 of the Companies Act 2006 (companies formed and registered under that Act) also have effect in relation to those provisions as applied by Part 3 of these Regulations.

(3) In any such transitional provision or saving as applied by paragraph (2), a reference to a commencement date other than 1st October 2009 shall be read as a reference to 1st October 2009.

COMPANIES ACT 2006 AND LIMITED LIABILITY PARTNERSHIPS (TRANSITIONAL PROVISIONS AND SAVINGS) (AMENDMENT) REGULATIONS 2009 (NOTE)

(SI 2009/2476)

[4.424]

NOTES

These Regulations were made on 9 September 2009 under the powers conferred by the Companies Act 2006, ss 1292(2), 1296(1), 1300(2), and the Limited Liability Partnerships Act 2000, ss 15, 17.

Regulation 1 provides for citation and commencement. These Regulations come into force on 1 October 2009 (with the exception of the amendment to the Companies Act 2006 (Commencement No 8, Transitional Provisions and Savings) Order 2008, SI 2008/2860, art 3, which comes into force on 30 September 2009).

Regulation 2(1) and (2) amend art 3 of the 2008 Order so as to stop s 22(2) of CA 2006 coming into force on 1 October 2009.

Regulation 2(1) and (3) replace the transitional provisions and savings relating to ss 1012–1023 of the 2006 Act which come into force on 1 October 2009. Section 1012 provides for the property of a dissolved company to vest in the Crown as if it were bona vacantia. Sections 1013–1022 provide for the disclaimer by the Crown of title to such property and the effects of disclaimer. Sections 1012–1022 re-enact, with modifications, corresponding provisions of the Companies Act 1985 and the Companies (Northern Ireland) Order 1986 (SI 1986/1032). In particular, there are changes to the time periods within which the appropriate Crown representative must disclaim title to such property. Transitional provisions in para 88 of Schedule 2 to the 2008 Order provide for ss 1012–1022 of the 2006 Act to apply in relation to the property of a company dissolved on or after 1 October 2009, and for the provisions replaced by those sections to continue to apply in relation to the property of a company dissolved before that date.

Regulation 2(1) and (3) change the transitional provisions as they relate to the property of a company dissolved before 1 October 2009. The new law on disclaimer will apply in relation to such property if, at that date, the appropriate Crown representative has neither had notice that the property has vested in the Crown, nor received an application to consider disclaimer nor waived the right to disclaim. The old law will continue to apply in cases where the new law does not apply.

Sections 1012–1023 were applied to LLPs by regs 52–55 of the Limited Liability Partnerships (Application of Companies Act 2006) Regulations 2009 (SI 2009/1804). Paragraph 22 of Schedule 1 to those Regulations provides for transitional provisions corresponding to those for company property. Regulation 3 replaces those provisions with transitional provisions corresponding to those substituted, in relation to company property, by reg 2(1) and (3).

Regulation 2(1) and (4) add new savings to the 2008 Order. They relate to s 26(2)(a) of the Companies Act 1985 and s 2(1)(a) of the Business Names Act 1985, which have been repealed with effect from 1 October 2009. The effect is to save prohibitions on companies being registered by, or persons carrying on business under, a name which would be likely to give an impression of a connection with the Welsh Assembly Government. See now the amendments made to the Companies Act 2006, s 54 at **[1.55]**. See further, in relation to the renaming of the Welsh Assembly Government as the Welsh Government, the Wales Act 2014, s 4(4)(a). See also, in relation to the renaming of the National Assembly for Wales as the Senedd Cymru or the Welsh Parliament, the Senedd and Elections (Wales) Act 2020, s 2 (with effect from 6 May 2020).

COMPANIES ACT 2006 (CONSEQUENTIAL AMENDMENTS AND TRANSITIONAL PROVISIONS) ORDER 2011

(SI 2011/1265)

NOTES

Made: 11 May 2011.

Authority: Companies Act 2006, ss 1292, 1294, 1296.

Commencement: 12 May 2011.

For a summary of all Orders and Regulations made under the Companies Act 2006, see Appendix 4 at **[A4]**.

[4.425]

1 Citation and commencement

(1) This Order may be cited as the Companies Act 2006 (Consequential Amendments and Transitional Provisions) Order 2011.

(2) This Order comes into force on the day after the day on which it is made.

[4.426]

2 Repeal of the Companies Consolidation (Consequential Provisions) Act 1985 (c 9)

The Companies Consolidation (Consequential Provisions) Act 1985 is repealed.

3, 4 *(Arts 3, 4 contain amendments to the Companies Act 2006 (Commencement No 8, Transitional Provisions and Savings) Order 2008, SI 2008/2860 and the Companies Act 2006 (Consequential Amendments, Transitional Provisions and Savings) Order 2009, SI 2009/1941 (at* **[4.355]***) consequential on the repeal by art 2 of the Companies Consolidation (Consequential Provisions) Act 1985.)*

[4.427]

5

(1) Schedule 1 to this Order contains provisions preserving the effect of the provisions of the Companies Consolidation (Consequential Provisions) Act 1985 relating to old public companies.

(2) The repeal of the other provisions of that Act does not affect the operation of—

(a) any provision amending an enactment that remains in force;

(b) any transitional provision that remains capable of having effect in relation to the corresponding provision of the Companies Act 2006;

(c) any saving that remains capable of having effect in relation to the repeal of an enactment by that Act.

6–32 *(Arts 6–30 contain various consequential amendments which, in so far as relevant, have been incorporated at the appropriate place; art 31 introduces Sch 3 (transitional provisions and savings in connection with open-ended investment companies in Northern Ireland (outside the scope of this work)); art 32 revokes the Companies (Single Member Private Limited Companies) Regulations 1992, SI 1992/1699 and the Companies (Single Member Private Limited Companies) (Northern Ireland) Regulations 1992.)*

SCHEDULES

SCHEDULE 1
PROVISIONS RELATING TO OLD PUBLIC COMPANIES

Article 5(1)

[4.428]

1 Meaning of "old public company"

For the purposes of this Schedule an "old public company" is a company limited by shares, or a company limited by guarantee and having a share capital, in respect of which the following conditions are met—

(a) the company either existed on 22nd December 1980 or was incorporated after that date pursuant to an application made before that date,

(b) on that date or, if later, on the day of the company's incorporation, the company was not or (as the case may be) would not have been a private company within the meaning of section 28 of the Companies Act 1948, and

(c) the company has not since that date or the day of the company's incorporation (as the case may be) either been re-registered as a public company within the meaning of section 1(3) of the Companies Act 1985 or section 4(2) of the Companies Act 2006 or become a private company within the meaning of section 1(3) of the Companies Act 1985 or section 4(1) of the Companies Act 2006.

2 Application of Companies Acts to old public companies

(1) References in the Companies Acts to—

(a) a public company, or

(b) a company other than a private company,

are to be read (unless the context otherwise requires) as including an old public company.

(2) References in the Companies Acts to a private company are to be read accordingly.

(3) Sub-paragraphs (1) and (2)—

(a) do not apply in relation to—

(i) Part 7 of the Companies Act 2006 (re-registration as a means of altering a company's status), and

(ii) sections 662 to 669 of that Act (treatment of shares held by or for public company) (see paragraph 7(1) and (2) below), and

(b) do not restrict the power to make provision by regulations under section 65 of that Act (inappropriate use of indications of company type or legal form).

3 Old public company re-registering as a public company

(1) Sections 90 to 96 of the Companies Act 2006 (re-registration as public company limited by shares) apply to an old public company.

(2) As they so apply—

(a) references to a private company shall be read as references to an old public company, and

(b) references to a special resolution of the company shall be read as references to a resolution of the directors.

(3) Chapter 3 of Part 3 of that Act (resolutions affecting a company's constitution) applies to any such resolution.

(4) References in this Schedule to re-registration as a public company, in relation to an old public company, are to re-registration by virtue of this paragraph.

4 Old public company becoming private: special resolution

(1) An old public company may pass a special resolution not to be re-registered as a public company.

(2) Sections 98 and 99 of the Companies Act 2006 (application to court to cancel resolution; notice to registrar of court application or order) apply to such a resolution as they would apply to a special resolution by a public company to be re-registered as private.

(3) If either—

(a) 28 days from the passing of the resolution elapse without an application being made under section 98 of the Companies Act 2006 (as applied), or

(b) such an application is made and proceedings are concluded on the application without the court making an order for the cancellation of the resolution,

the registrar of companies shall issue the company with a certificate stating that it is a private company.

(4) The company then becomes a private company by virtue of the issue of the certificate.

(5) For the purposes of sub-paragraph (3)(b), proceedings on the application are concluded—

(a) except in a case within the following paragraph, when the period mentioned in section 99(3) of the Companies Act 2006 (as applied) for delivering a copy of the court's order on the application to the registrar has expired, or

(b) when the company has been notified that the application has been withdrawn.

(6) A certificate issued to a company under sub-paragraph (3) is conclusive evidence that the requirements of this paragraph have been complied with and that the company is a private company.

5 Old public company becoming private: statutory declaration

(1) If an old public company delivers to the registrar a statutory declaration by a director or secretary of the company that the company does not at the time of the declaration satisfy the conditions for the company to be re-registered as public, the registrar shall issue the company with a certificate stating that it is a private company.

(2) The company then becomes a private company by virtue of the issue of the certificate.

(3) A certificate issued to a company under sub-paragraph (1) is conclusive evidence that the requirements of this paragraph have been complied with and that the company is a private company.

6 Failure by old public company to obtain new classification

(1) If at any time a company which is an old public company has not delivered to the registrar of companies a declaration under paragraph 5, the company and any officer of it who is in default is guilty of an offence unless at the time the company—

(a) has applied to be re-registered as a public company, and the application has not been refused or withdrawn, or

(b) has passed a special resolution not to be re-registered as a public company, and the resolution has not been revoked, and has not been cancelled under section 98 of the Companies Act 2006, as applied by paragraph 4.

(2) A person guilty of an offence under this paragraph is liable on summary conviction to a fine not exceeding level 3 on the standard scale and, for continued contravention, a daily default fine not exceeding one-tenth of level 3 on the standard scale.

7 Old public company holding, or having charge on, own shares

(1) In sections 662 to 669 of the Companies Act 2006 (treatment of shares held by or for public company) references to a public company do not include an old public company.

(2) Section 668 of that Act (application of sections 662 to 667 to private company re-registering as public company) applies to an old public company as to a private company.

(3) In the case of a company that—

(a) after 22nd March 1982 remained an old public company, and

(b) did not before that date apply to be re-registered as a public company,

any charge on its own shares which was in existence on or immediately before that date is a permitted charge and not void under section 670 of the Companies Act 2006.

8 Old public companies: trading under misleading name

(1) An old public company commits an offence if it carries on a trade, profession or business under a name that includes, as its last part, the words "public limited company" or "cwmni cyfyngedig cyhoeddus".

(2) Where an offence under this paragraph is committed by a company, an offence is also committed by every officer of the company who is in default.

(3) A person guilty of an offence under this paragraph is liable on summary conviction to a fine not exceeding level 3 on the standard scale and, for continued contravention, a daily default fine not exceeding one-tenth of level 3 on the standard scale.

9 Old public companies: payment for share capital

Sections 584 to 587 of the Companies Act 2006 (payment for shares: additional rules for public companies) apply to an old public company whose directors have passed and not revoked a resolution to be re-registered as a public company, as those sections apply to a public company.

SCHEDULES 2 AND 3

(Sch 2 contains consequential amendments to the Open-ended Investment Companies Regulations 2001, SI 2001/1228; Sch 3 contains transitional provisions and savings in connection with open-ended investment companies in Northern Ireland (outside the scope of this work).)

SUPERVISION OF ACCOUNTS AND REPORTS (PRESCRIBED BODY) AND COMPANIES (DEFECTIVE ACCOUNTS AND DIRECTORS' REPORTS) (AUTHORISED PERSON) ORDER 2012 (NOTE)

(SI 2012/1439)

[4.429]

NOTES

This Order was made on 31 May 2012, under the powers conferred by the Companies Act 2006, ss 457(1), (2), (5), (6), 462, 1292(1)(b), (c), and the Companies (Audit, Investigations and Community Enterprise) Act 2004, ss 14(1), (5), (8), 15E. It came into force on 2 July 2012.

Articles 2–5 and 7, 8 were revoked by the Supervision of Accounts and Reports (Prescribed Body) and Companies (Defective Accounts and Reports) (Authorised Person) Order 2021, SI 2021/465, art 7, as from 6 May 2021 (see art 9 of the 2021 Order for transitional provisions in relation to the continuity of functions, etc at **[4.727]**).

The only provisions currently in force are art 1 (Citation, coming into force and interpretation); and art 6 (Amendments to categories of permitted disclosure) which amends the Companies (Audit, Investigation and Community Enterprise) Act 2004, s 15D at **[5.214]**, and CA 2006, s 461 at **[1.526]**.

For a summary of all Orders and Regulations made under the Companies Act 2006, see Appendix 4 at **[A4]**.

STATUTORY AUDITORS (AMENDMENT OF COMPANIES ACT 2006 AND DELEGATION OF FUNCTIONS ETC) ORDER 2012

(SI 2012/1741)

NOTES

Made: 2 July 2012.

Authority: European Communities Act 1972, s 2(2)(a), (b); Companies Act 2006, ss 464(1), (3), 504(1)(b)(ii), 525(1)(a)(ii), 1228(1), (2), (6), 1231(4), 1239, 1252(1), (2)(b), (4)(a), (5)–(8), 1253(4), 1292(1)(b), (c), (2), Sch 13, paras 7(3), 11(2), (3)(a) (see also the note "Statutory Instruments made under the European Communities Act 1972" preceding paragraph **[4.1]** *ante*).

Commencement: 2 July 2012.

For a summary of all Orders and Regulations made under the Companies Act 2006, see Appendix 4 at **[A4]**.

This Order is reproduced as amended by: the Local Audit (Delegation of Functions) and Statutory Audit (Delegation of Functions) Order 2014, SI 2014/2009; the Statutory Auditors and Third Country Auditors Regulations 2016, SI 2016/649; the Statutory Auditors Regulations 2017, SI 2017/1164; the Statutory Auditors and Third Country Auditors (Amendment) (EU Exit) Regulations 2019, SI 2019/177.

ARRANGEMENT OF ARTICLES

PART 1
INTRODUCTION

PART 1 INTRODUCTION

[4.430]
1 Citation and coming into force

(1) This Order may be cited as the Statutory Auditors (Amendment of Companies Act 2006 and Delegation of Functions etc) Order 2012.

(2) This Order comes into force on 2nd July 2012.

[4.431]
2 Interpretation

In this Order—

"the 2008 Regulations" means the Limited Liability Partnerships (Accounts and Audit) (Application of Companies Act 2006) Regulations 2008;
"the Act" means the Companies Act 2006;
"coming into force" means the coming into force of this Order;
"the designated body" means the Financial Reporting Council Limited; and
"LLPs" means limited liability partnerships.

[4.432]
3 Schedule

The Schedule (which makes minor and consequential amendments) has effect.

4, 5 *(Articles 4 and 5 (Part 2) provide as follows: art 4 substitutes the Companies Act 2006, ss 1225, 1225A–1225G (for the original s 1225) at* **[1.1401]** *et seq; art 5 amends Sch 10 to the 2006 Act at* **[1.1523]** *et seq.)*

PART 3 TRANSFER OF FUNCTIONS OF THE SECRETARY OF STATE

[4.433]
6 The Statutory Auditors (Delegation of Functions etc) Order 2008

The Statutory Auditors (Delegation of Functions etc) Order 2008 is revoked.

[4.434]
7 Transfer of functions

(1) The designated body is designated for the purpose of enabling it to exercise functions of the Secretary of State under Part 42 of the Act (statutory auditors).

(2) The functions of the Secretary of State under—

(a) section 1210(1)(h) of the Act (meaning of "statutory auditor" etc),
(b) section 1214(4) of the Act (power to specify connection between persons for purposes of independence requirement),
(c) section 1231(2)(a) (receipt of report by independent supervisor of auditors general),

(d) section 1231(3) of the Act (laying report by independent supervisor of auditors general before each House of Parliament),
(e) section 1237(3) of the Act (provision for pending proceedings in order revoking appointment of independent supervisor),
(f) section 1239(1)(b) of the Act (making regulations for register of third country auditors),
(g) section 1246 of the Act (regulations conferring power to remove third country auditors from the register of auditors),
(h) section 1261(3) of the Act (power to modify Part 42 of the Act (statutory auditors) for purposes of application to certain bodies), . . .
(i) section 1263 of the Act (power to amend enactments in consequence of changes affecting accountancy bodies),
[(j) section 1240A(1) of the Act (power to approve third countries as equivalent or transitional third countries), and
(k) section 1240B(1) of the Act (power to approve third country competent authorities),]

are not transferred by this Order.

(3) The transfer of the functions of the Secretary of State under—
(a) section 1224 of the Act (power to call for information from recognised bodies etc),
(b) section 1239(8) of the Act (obligations relating to register enforceable by injunction etc),
(c) section 1244 of the Act (power to call for information from registered third country auditors),
(d) section 1253A of the Act (requests to foreign competent authorities), and
(e) section 1254 of the Act (directions to comply with international obligations),

is subject to the reservation that these functions remain exercisable concurrently by the Secretary of State.

(4) The transfer of the functions of the Secretary of State of—
(a) refusing to make a declaration under section 1221(1) of the Act (approval of [third country qualification]) on the grounds referred to in section 1221(4) (lack of comparable treatment),
(b) withdrawing such a declaration under section 1221(7) of the Act on those grounds,
(c) refusing to comply with a request under section 1253B(1) of the Act (requests from [approved third country competent authorities]) on the grounds referred to in section 1253B(3)(a) (prejudice to sovereignty, security or public order), and
(d) refusing a request, or directing a statutory auditor to refuse a request, from a third country competent authority in a case referred to in section 1253E(7)(a) of the Act (prejudice to sovereignty, security or public order),

is subject to the reservation that these functions are exercisable only with the consent of the Secretary of State.

(5) The transfer of the function of the Secretary of State under section 1241(2)(c) of the Act (order to exclude bodies corporate from definition of "[UK-traded third country company]") is subject to the reservations that this function remains exercisable concurrently by the Secretary of State and is exercisable by the designated body only with the consent of the Secretary of State.

[(6) In this article—
(a) the reference in paragraph (1) to the functions of the Secretary of State under Part 42 of the Companies Act 2006 includes a reference to functions which have been amended by the Statutory Auditors and Third Country Auditors Regulations 2016[, the Statutory Auditors and Third Country Auditors Regulations 2017[, the Statutory Auditors Regulations 2017 and the Statutory Auditors and Third Country Auditors (Amendment) (EU Exit) Regulations 2019]]; and
(b) references to provisions of the Companies Act 2006 in paragraphs (2) to (5) include amendments made to those provisions by the Statutory Auditors and Third Country Auditors Regulations 2016[, the Statutory Auditors and Third Country Auditors Regulations 2017[, the Statutory Auditors Regulations 2017 and the Statutory Auditors and Third Country Auditors (Amendment) (EU Exit) Regulations 2019]].]

NOTES

Para (2): the word omitted from sub-para (h) was revoked, and sub-paras (j), (k) were inserted, by the Statutory Auditors and Third Country Auditors (Amendment) (EU Exit) Regulations 2019, SI 2019/177, regs 56, 57(a), as from IP completion day (as defined in the European Union (Withdrawal Agreement) Act 2020, s 39) (for transitional provisions, see Sch 4 to the 2019 Regulations at **[12.88]**).

Paras (4), (5): words in square brackets substituted by SI 2019/177, regs 56, 57(b)–(d), as from IP completion day (as defined in the European Union (Withdrawal Agreement) Act 2020, s 39) (for transitional provisions, see Sch 4 to the 2019 Regulations at **[12.88]**).

Para (6): added by the Statutory Auditors and Third Country Auditors Regulations 2016, SI 2016/649, reg 19, as from 17 June 2016. The words in the first and third (outer) pairs of square brackets were substituted by the Statutory Auditors Regulations 2017, SI 2017/1164, regs 17, 18, as from 6 April 2018 (as to the application of the 2017 Regulations, see **[4.671]** et seq). The words in the second and fourth (inner) pairs of square brackets were substituted by SI 2019/177, regs 56, 57(e), as from IP completion day (as defined in the European Union (Withdrawal Agreement) Act 2020, s 39) (for transitional provisions, see Sch 4 to the 2019 Regulations at **[12.88]**).

[4.435]

8 Appropriate audit authority

The functions of the designated body include the receipt of notices under sections 522 and 523 of the Act (notices of auditor ceasing to hold office) and, accordingly, the designated body is the appropriate audit authority under section 525(1)(a)(ii) of the Act.

[4.436]

9 Consultation requirement

(1) Before the designated body makes any order or regulations in exercise of the functions transferred to it by this Order, it must, unless paragraph (2) applies—
(a) publish the proposed order or regulations in such manner as appears to the body to be best calculated to bring the order or regulations to the attention of persons who may be affected by them;

(b) publish at the same time a statement that representations in respect of the proposals may be made to the body within a specified period which must not be less than [4 weeks] following the date of publication of the proposed order or regulations; and

(c) have regard to any representations duly made in accordance with the statement before making the order or regulations.

(2) Paragraph (1) does not apply in any case in which the body considers that the delay involved in complying with that paragraph would be prejudicial to the public interest.

NOTES

Para (1): words in square brackets substituted by the Local Audit (Delegation of Functions) and Statutory Audit (Delegation of Functions) Order 2014, SI 2014/2009, art 10, as from 19 August 2014.

[4.437]
10 Annual work programme

The designated body must publish a work programme at least once in every calendar year.

[4.438]
11 Requirements for recording decisions

The designated body must have satisfactory arrangements for—

(a) recording decisions made in the exercise of the functions transferred by this Order; and

(b) the safekeeping of the records of those decisions.

[4.439]
12 Matters notified to the designated body

(1) If under section 1223(1) or 1243(1) the designated body requires notification or the provision of information, it must notify the Secretary of State of the requirement without undue delay.

(2) If the Secretary of State so requests, the designated body must send the Secretary of State a copy of any notification or information received pursuant to the requirement.

[4.440]
13 Payment of amounts of financial penalties (less costs) by designated body to Secretary of State

(1) The designated body must, subject to subsection (2), pay the amount of a financial penalty under section 1225D to the Secretary of State as soon as reasonably practicable after it is paid to the body.

(2) The designated body may deduct and retain from the amount of any financial penalty a sum in respect of its reasonable costs incurred in relation to the imposition of that penalty up to the time of the giving of the relevant notice under section 1225E(5).

(3) The costs of the designated body referred to in subsection (2) are—

(a) its administrative costs (including any administrative costs incurred in determining that the requirement or obligation in respect of which the financial penalty was imposed had not been complied with);

(b) its costs of obtaining legal advice (including any legal advice in connection with determining that the requirement or obligation in respect of which the financial penalty was imposed had not been complied with);

(c) any other costs incurred in determining that the requirement or obligation in respect of which the financial penalty was imposed had not been complied with.

[4.441]
14 Time limits for prosecution of offences

Section 1256(1), (2), (4) and (6) of the Act (time limits for prosecution of offences) has effect as if the references to the Secretary of State were references to the Secretary of State or the designated body.

[4.442]
15 Appointment of body to issue guidance as to identifying senior statutory auditor

The designated body is appointed for the purposes of section 504(1)(b)(ii) of the Act (body to issue guidance on meaning of senior statutory auditor).

[4.443]
16 Transitional Provisions

(1) Anything which—

(a) relates to any function transferred by virtue of this Order; and

(b) is in the process of being done by or in relation to the body known as the Professional Oversight Board immediately before coming into force,

may be continued by or in relation to the designated body.

(2) Guidance issued by the body known as the Auditing Practices Board for the purposes mentioned in article 15 and which is in effect immediately before coming into force shall be treated as if it were issued by the designated body.

PART 4 APPOINTMENT OF THE INDEPENDENT SUPERVISOR

[4.444]
17 The Independent Supervisor Appointment Order 2007

The Independent Supervisor Appointment Order 2007 is revoked.

[4.445]
18 Appointment of Independent Supervisor

The designated body is appointed to discharge the function mentioned in section 1229(1) of the Act (supervision of Auditors General).

[4.446]

19 Requirements and provisions concerning the exercise of the supervision function

The report which is required under section 1231 of the Act (reports by the Independent Supervisor) must include—

(a) an account of how the Independent Supervisor has discharged the supervision function, including why it considers that this function has been discharged effectively;

(b) an account of the extent to which each Auditor General has complied with its duties under the Act;

(c) an account of any matters notified to the Independent Supervisor under section 1232 of the Act (matters to be notified to the Independent Supervisor);

(d) an account of the Independent Supervisor's enforcement activity, including the issue of any suspension notices and any applications for compliance orders; and

(e) an account of the activities carried out by the Independent Supervisor as a consequence of its status as a public authority for the purpose of the Freedom of Information Act 2000.

[4.447]

20

(1) Before amending, revoking, establishing or entering into a supervision arrangement for the purposes of section 1229 of the Act (supervision of Auditors General by the Independent Supervisor), the Independent Supervisor must consult with the Auditors General and such other persons as seem to it to be appropriate.

(2) The Independent Supervisor must have satisfactory arrangements for—

(a) recording decisions made in the exercise of the function mentioned in section 1229(1) of the Act; and

(b) the safekeeping of all material records.

[4.448]

21 Transitional Provisions

(1) Anything which—

(a) has been done by or in relation to the body known as the Professional Oversight Board for the purposes of or in connection with the function referred to in article 18; and

(b) is in effect immediately before coming into force,

is to be treated as if done by or in relation to the designated body.

(2) Anything which—

(a) relates to the function referred to in article 18; and

(b) is in the process of being done by or in relation to the body known as the Professional Oversight Board immediately before coming into force,

may be continued by or in relation to the designated body.

PART 5 PRESCRIPTION OF BODY TO ISSUE ACCOUNTING STANDARDS

[4.449]

22 The Accounting Standards (Prescribed Body) Regulations 2008

The Accounting Standards (Prescribed Body) Regulations 2008 are revoked.

[4.450]

23 Prescribed body

The designated body is prescribed for the purposes of section 464 of the Act.

[4.451]

24 Transitional Provisions

(1) Unless withdrawn, statements of standard accounting practice issued before coming into force for the purposes of section 464 of the Act are to be treated after coming into force as statements of standard accounting practice issued for those purposes by the designated body.

(2) The reference in paragraph (1) to statements of standard accounting practice issued before coming into force is to be taken to include statements issued for the purposes of either section 256 of the Companies Act 1985 or Article 264 of the Companies (Northern Ireland) Order 1986 where, by virtue of regulation 4 of the Accounting Standards (Prescribed Body) Regulations 2008, those statements fell to be treated as statements issued for the purposes of section 464 of the Act.

(3) Anything which—

(a) has been done by or in relation to the body known as the Accounting Standards Board for the purposes of or in connection with the issue of statements of standard accounting practice; and

(b) is in effect immediately before coming into force,

is to be treated as if done by or in relation to the designated body.

(4) Anything which—

(a) relates to the issue of statements of standard accounting practice; and

(b) is in the process of being done by or in relation to the body known as the Accounting Standards Board immediately before coming into force,

may be continued by or in relation to the designated body.

SCHEDULE

(The Schedule amends the Statutory Auditors and Third Country Auditors Regulations 2007, SI 2007/3494, reg 29 (revoked), the Limited Liability Partnerships (Accounts and Audit) (Application of Companies Act 2006) Regulations 2008, SI 2008/1911, regs 24, 46 (see the 2008 Regulations at **[10.223]** *et seq), the Unregistered Companies Regulations 2009, SI 2009/2436, Sch 1 at* **[4.398]**. *It also substitutes reg 25 of the 2008 Regulations and contains*

various amendments that are outside the scope of this work.)

REGISTRAR OF COMPANIES (FEES) (COMPANIES, OVERSEAS COMPANIES AND LIMITED LIABILITY PARTNERSHIPS) REGULATIONS 2012

(SI 2012/1907)

NOTES

Made: 18 July 2012.

Authority: Companies Act 2006, ss 243(3), 1063(1)–(3), 1292(1).

Commencement: 1 October 2012.

For a summary of all Orders and Regulations made under the Companies Act 2006, see Appendix 4 at **[A4]**.

These Regulations are reproduced as amended by: the Registrar of Companies (Fees) (Amendment) Regulations 2016, SI 2016/621.

ARRANGEMENT OF REGULATIONS

[4.452]

1 Citation and commencement

These Regulations may be cited as the Registrar of Companies (Fees) (Companies, Overseas Companies and Limited Liability Partnerships) Regulations 2012 and come into force on 1st October 2012.

[4.453]

2 Interpretation

In these Regulations—

"the 2006 Act" means the Companies Act 2006; and

"company" includes, where appropriate, a reference to a company to which section 1040 or 1043 of the 2006 Act applies.

[4.454]

3 Fees payable in respect of functions relating to the registration of documents by the registrar

Schedule 1 to these Regulations makes provision for the fees that are payable to the registrar in respect of the receipt of documents relating to companies, overseas companies and limited liability partnerships by the registrar and their registration.

[4.455]

4 Fees payable in respect of the inspection or provision of copies of documents kept by the registrar

Schedule 2 to these Regulations makes provision for the fees that are payable to the registrar in respect of the inspection, or provision of copies, of documents kept by the registrar relating to companies, overseas companies and limited liability partnerships.

[4.456]

5

The fees prescribed in relation to paragraphs 7(a), 8(a) and 10(a) of Schedule 2 to these Regulations are not payable in respect of any month for which the applicant pays a fee to the registrar for subscription to Companies House Direct, Extranet or XML (those terms are defined in paragraph 1 of Schedule 2) under regulations providing for the payment of fees in respect of the functions of the registrar in relation to the inspection, or provision of copies, of documents kept by the registrar relating to European Economic Interest Groupings and limited partnerships.

[4.457]

[6 Fees payable in respect of the disclosure of information not made available for public inspection

Schedule 3 to these Regulations makes provision for the fees that are payable to the registrar in respect of,

(a) the disclosure of protected information relating to a director of a company, a director and permanent representative of an overseas company and a member of a limited liability partnership,

(b) the disclosure of restricted DOB information relating to,

  (i) a director of a company,

  (ii) a director of an overseas company,

  (iii) a member of a limited liability partnership, and

  (iv) an individual whose particulars are stated in a company's or limited liability partnership's PSC register as a registrable person, and

(c) the disclosure of information within section 790ZF(2) of the 2006 Act or that section as applied to limited liability partnerships by regulation 31L of the Limited Liability Partnerships (Application of Companies Act 2006) Regulations 2009.]

NOTES

Substituted by the Registrar of Companies (Fees) (Amendment) Regulations 2016, SI 2016/621, regs 3, 4, as from 30 June 2016, except in respect of any application or request received by the registrar before that date.

[4.458]

7 Transitional provisions

(1) Where any document delivered to the registrar on or before 30th September 2012 is registered on or after 1st October 2012 the fee prescribed in Schedule 1 to the Regulations in respect of that document shall not apply and any fee payable in respect of that document by virtue of the Registrar of Companies (Fees) (Companies, Overseas Companies and Limited Liability Partnerships) Regulations 2009 shall apply.

(2) Where any application is made or subscription is payable to the registrar on or before 30th September 2012 in respect of the inspection of, or the provision of copies of, material kept by the registrar, the fee prescribed in Schedule 2 to these Regulations in respect of that application or subscription shall not apply and any fee payable under the Register of Companies (Fees) (Companies, Overseas Companies and Limited Liability Partnerships) Regulations 2009 shall apply.

(3) Where any application is made or subscription is payable to the registrar on or before 30th September 2012 in respect of the disclosure of protected information kept by the registrar, the fee prescribed in Schedule 3 to these Regulations in respect of that application or subscription shall not apply and any fee payable under the Registrar of Companies (Fees) (Companies, Overseas Companies and Limited Liability Partnerships) Regulations 2009 shall apply.

[4.459]

8 Revocation

The following regulations are revoked—

(a) the Registrar of Companies (Fees) (Companies, Overseas Companies and Limited Liability Partnerships) Regulations 2009;

(b) the Registrar of Companies (Fees) (Amendment) Regulations 2009; and

(c) the Registrar of Companies (Fees) (Companies, Overseas Companies and Limited Liability Partnerships) (Amendment) Regulations 2011.

SCHEDULES

SCHEDULE 1
THE PERFORMANCE OF FUNCTIONS RELATING TO THE RECEIPT OF DOCUMENTS BY THE REGISTRAR AND THEIR REGISTRATION

Regulation 3

PART 1 INTERPRETATION

[4.460]

1 Enactments and legal entities

(1) In this Schedule the following meanings are given to the enactments referred to and, where relevant, to the legal entities created under them—

the "2000 Act" means the Limited Liability Partnerships Act 2000 and "limited liability partnership" means a body corporate incorporated under that Act,

the "LLP Regulations" means the Limited Liability Partnerships (Application of Companies Act 2006) Regulations 2009,

the "OC Regulations" means the Overseas Companies Regulations 2009.

(2) In paragraph 11(d) in Part 2 of this Schedule, a reference to an "overseas company" includes a reference to any credit or financial institution to which section 1050 of the 2006 Act applies.

(3) Words and expressions used in the enactments set out in sub-paragraph (1) have the same meaning when used in this Schedule as they have in those enactments.

2 Means of electronic delivery to the registrar

In this Schedule—

"Web Incorporation Service" means a service by which the documents required to be delivered under section 9 of the 2006 Act are delivered to the registrar by electronic means using a website of the registrar;

"Software Incorporation Service" means a service by which the documents required to be delivered under section 9 of the 2006 Act are delivered to the registrar by electronic means other than using a website of the registrar.

3 Meaning of "relevant documents"

(1) For the purposes of paragraphs 8(f), 10(b) and 11(d) a "relevant document" is any document required or authorised to be delivered to the registrar in respect of a company, limited liability partnership or overseas company, as the case may be, by or under any provision of—

(a) the 2006 Act, or
(b) the 2000 Act, or
(c) the OC Regulations, or
(d) the LLP Regulations,

other than a document specified in sub-paragraph (2) below.

(2) A document is not a relevant document if—

(a) a fee is specified in this Schedule in relation to the registration of a document, or the performance by the registrar of a function, under any particular provision of the enactments listed in sub-paragraph (1) above; or
(b) that document is required or authorised to be delivered to the registrar by or under an excluded provision; and, for these purposes, an excluded provision is any provision of the enactments listed in sub-paragraph (1) above which is specified in Part 3 of this Schedule.

4 Meaning of "relevant period"

[(1) In this Schedule in relation to a company or a limited liability partnership a "relevant period" means one of the following periods—

(a) the period of 12 months beginning with the day of the company's or limited liability partnership's incorporation; or
(b) each period of 12 months beginning with the day after the end of the previous relevant period.]

(2) In this Schedule in relation to an overseas company a "relevant period" means one of the following periods—

(a) the period beginning with the registration of the documents required to be delivered to the registrar under Part 2 of the OC Regulations in respect of the opening of an establishment in the United Kingdom and ending immediately after the first delivery to the registrar of its accounting documents or, as the case may be, its annual accounts; or
(b) a period beginning immediately after a delivery of accounting documents or annual accounts to the registrar and ending immediately after delivery to the registrar of the next accounting documents or annual accounts.

5 Meaning of "same day registration"

For the purposes of this Schedule documents are delivered for "same day registration" if—

(a) a request for same day registration and all documents required to be delivered to the registrar in connection with that registration are received by the registrar before 3.00 pm on the day in question; and
(b) the registration is completed on that day.

6 General

Where, in relation to any matter in respect of which a fee is payable under this Schedule, the means of delivery to the registrar of the documents required to be delivered in relation to that matter, or the form of those documents are not specified, that fee is payable only in respect of documents that are delivered in hard copy form.

7 Where, in relation to any matter in respect of which a fee is payable under this Schedule, no provision is made for same day registration of the documents required to be delivered to the registrar in relation to that matter, that fee is only payable in respect of the delivery of documents other than for same day registration.

NOTES

Para 4: sub-para (1) substituted by the Registrar of Companies (Fees) (Amendment) Regulations 2016, SI 2016/621, regs 3, 5(1), (2), as from 30 June 2016 (subject to transitional provisions in respect of (inter alia) any registration where every document necessary for the registrar to effect such an act is delivered to the registrar before 30 June 2016; in relation to annual returns to be made up to a return date before 30 June 2016; and where any document delivered to the registrar on or before 29 June 2016 is registered on or after 30 June 2016 (etc); see regs 19–21 of the 2016 Regulations).

PART 2 FEES PAYABLE

[4.461]

8 Companies

Subject to paragraph 9, in respect of the performance by the registrar of his functions in relation to the registration of documents delivered to him in respect of companies, the fee specified in relation to each matter below is payable on the registration of the documents so delivered relating to that matter except as provided in sub-paragraphs (f) and (i)—

Matter in relation to which fee is payable	Amount of fee
(a) for the registration of a company under section 14 of the 2006 Act—	
(i) where the required documents are delivered by means of the Web Incorporation Service,	[£12.00]
(ii) where the required documents are delivered by means of the Software Incorpora-	£30.00

Matter in relation to which fee is payable	Amount of fee
tion Service for same day registration,	
(iii) where the required documents are delivered by means of the Software Incorporation Service other than for same day registration,	[£10.00]
(iv) where the required documents are delivered in hard copy form for same day registration,	£100.00
(v) where the required documents are delivered in hard copy form other than for same day registration except as provided in Paragraphs (vi) to (viii),	£40.00
(vi) . . .	. . .
(vii) where the required documents are delivered in respect of a community interest company within the meaning of section 26 of the Companies (Audit, Investigations and Community Enterprise) Act 2004 in hard copy form other than for same day registration,	£20.00
(viii) where the required documents are delivered in respect of an unlimited company in hard copy form other than for same day registration;	£20.00
(b) for the registration of a company under Chapter 1 of Part 33 of the 2006 Act;	£20.00
(c) for the re-registration of a company under Part 7 of the 2006 Act—	
(i) where the required documents are delivered for same day registration,	£50.00
(ii) where the required documents are delivered other than for same day registration;	£20.00
(d) for the re-registration of a company as a private company under section 651 of the 2006 Act—	
(i) where the required documents are delivered for same day registration,	£50.00
(ii) where the required documents are delivered other than for same day registration;	£20.00
(e) for the re-registration of a company as a private company under section 665 of the 2006 Act—	
(i) where the required documents are delivered for same day registration,	£50.00
(ii) where the required documents are delivered other than for same day registration;	£20.00
[(f) for the registration of all relevant documents in respect of a company delivered during a relevant period payable on the registration of a confirmation statement under section 853A of the 2006 Act with a confirmation date that falls within the relevant period, unless a confirmation statement with a confirmation date that falls within the same relevant period has been registered—	
(i) where the confirmation statement is delivered in hard copy form,	£40.00
(ii) where the confirmation statement is delivered by electronic means,	£13.00]
(g) for the registration of a change of name of a company under section 80 of the 2006 Act (other than a change made in response to a direction of the Secretary of State under section 64 or 67 of the 2006 Act, a determination by a company names adjudicator or a court under section 73(5) or 74(5) of that Act or on the restoration of the company to the register under section 1033(2)(a)(i) of that Act)—	
(i) where the required documents are delivered in hard copy form for same day registration,	£50.00
(ii) where the required documents are delivered in hard copy form other than for same day registration,	£10.00
(iii) where the required documents are delivered by electronic means for same day registration,	£30.00
(iv) where the required documents are delivered by electronic means other than for same day registration;	£8.00
[(h) for the registration of a charge under Part 25 of the 2006 Act—	
(i) where the required documents are delivered in hard copy form,	£23.00
(ii) where the required documents are delivered by electronic means;	£15.00]
(i) for the striking off the register of a company's name payable on an application under section 1003 of the 2006 Act;	£10.00
(j) for the registration of the reduction of share capital of a company under section 644 of the 2006 Act—	
(i) where the required documents are delivered for same day registration,	£50.00
(ii) where the required documents are delivered other than for same day registration;	£10.00
(k) for the registration of the reduction of share capital of a company under section 649 of the 2006 Act—	
(i) where the required documents are delivered for same day registration,	£50.00
(ii) where the required documents are delivered other than for same day registration.	£10.00

9 (1) The fee specified in paragraph 8(g) is not payable where the change of name relates solely to the indication of the particular type of company that the company whose name is changed becomes on its re-registration under Part 7 of the 2006 Act.

(2) Where a change of name is conditional on the occurrence of an event and that event occurs on or after 1st October 2012 the giving of notice of the event to the registrar, under section 78(3)(b) of the 2006 Act, is the required document for the registration of the change of name for the purposes of this Schedule.

10 Limited liability partnerships

In respect of the performance by the registrar of his functions in relation to the registration of documents delivered to him in respect of limited liability partnerships, the fee specified in relation to each matter set out below is payable on the registration of the documents so delivered relating to that matter except as provided in sub-paragraphs (b) and (e)—

Matter in relation to which fee is payable	Amount of fee
(a) for the registration of a limited liability partnership under section 3 of the 2000 Act—	
(i) where the required documents are delivered by electronic means for same day registration,	£30.00
(ii) where the required documents are delivered by electronic means other than for same day registration,	[£10.00]
(iii) where the required documents are delivered in hard copy form for same day registration,	£100.00
(iv) where the required documents are delivered in hard copy form other than for same day registration except as provided in Paragraph (v),	£40.00
(v) where the required documents are delivered in respect of a Welsh limited liability partnership in Welsh in hard copy form other than for same day registration;	£20.00
[(b) for the registration of all relevant documents in respect of a limited liability partnership delivered during a relevant period payable on the registration of a confirmation statement under section 853A of the 2006 Act as applied to limited liability partnerships by regulation 30 of the LLP Regulations with a confirmation date that falls within the relevant period, unless a confirmation statement with a confirmation date that falls within the same relevant period has been registered—	
(i) where the confirmation statement is delivered in hard copy form,	£40.00
(ii) where the confirmation statement is delivered by electronic means;	£13.00]
(c) for the registration of a change of name of a limited liability partnership under paragraph 5 of the Schedule to the 2000 Act (other than a change made in response to a direction of the Secretary of State under section 67 of the 2006 Act as applied by regulation 11 of the LLP Regulations, a determination by a company names adjudicator or a court under section 73(5) or 74(5) of the 2006 Act as applied by regulation 12 of the LLP Regulations or on the restoration of the limited liability partnership to the register under section 1033(2)(a)(i) of the 2006 Act as applied by regulation 58 of the LLP Regulations)—	
(i) where the required documents are delivered in hard copy form for same day registration,	£50.00
(ii) where the required documents are delivered in hard copy form other than for same day registration,	£10.00
(iii) where the required documents are delivered by electronic means for same day registration,	£30.00
(iv) where the required documents are delivered by electronic means other than for same day registration;	£8.00
[(d) for the registration of a charge under Part 25 of the 2006 Act as applied to limited liability partnerships by Part 9 of the LLP Regulations—	
(i) where the required documents are delivered in hard copy form,	£23.00
(ii) where the required documents are delivered by electronic means;	£15.00]
(e) for the striking off the register of a limited liability partnership's name payable on an application under section 1003 of the 2006 Act as applied to limited liability partnerships by regulation 51 of the LLP Regulations.	£10.00

11 Overseas companies

In respect of the performance by the registrar of his functions in relation to the registration of documents delivered to him in respect of overseas companies, the fee specified in relation to each matter set out below is payable on the registration of the documents so delivered relating to that matter except as provided in sub-paragraph (d)—

Matter in relation to which fee is payable	Amount of fee
(a) for the registration of documents required to be delivered to the registrar under Part 2 of the OC Regulations in respect of the opening of an establishment in the United Kingdom—	
(i) where the required documents are delivered for same day registration,	£100.00
(ii) where the required documents are delivered other than for same day registration;	£20.00

Matter in relation to which fee is payable	Amount of fee
(b) for the registration of an alteration to the registered particulars of an overseas company under Part 3 of the OC Regulations where the alteration is a change of the name of the overseas company—	
(i) where the required documents are delivered for same day registration,	£50.00
(ii) where the required documents are delivered other than for same day registration;	£10.00
(c) for the registration of an alternative name specified in accordance with section 1048 of the 2006 Act—	
(i) where the required documents are delivered for same day registration,	£50.00
(ii) where the required documents are delivered other than for same day registration;	£10.00
(d) for the registration of all relevant documents in respect of an overseas company delivered during a relevant period payable at the end of that period on registration of the accounting documents or, as the case may be, the annual accounts of the overseas company required to be delivered to the registrar under Parts 5 and 6 of the OC Regulations.	£20.00

NOTES

All amendments to this Part were made by the Registrar of Companies (Fees) (Amendment) Regulations 2016, SI 2016/621, regs 3, 5(1), (3)–(10), as from 30 June 2016 (for transitional provisions and savings see the note to Pt 1 of this Schedule at **[4.460]**).

PART 3 PROVISIONS REFERRED TO IN PARAGRAPH 3(2)(B)

[4.462]

12 Excluded provisions

For the purposes of paragraph 3(2)(b) of this Schedule, the excluded provisions are—

(a) in relation to a company, sections 1024 and 1088 of the 2006 Act;

(b) in relation to a limited liability partnership, sections 1024 and 1088 of the 2006 Act as applied by regulations 56 and 66 of the LLP Regulations; and

(c) in relation to an overseas company, section 1088 of the 2006 Act.

SCHEDULE 2
THE PERFORMANCE OF FUNCTIONS RELATING TO THE INSPECTION OR PROVISION OF COPIES OF DOCUMENTS KEPT BY THE REGISTRAR

Regulation 4

PART 1 INTERPRETATION

[4.463]

1 Means by which the register may be inspected and copies provided

In this Schedule—

"Companies House Contact Centre" and "CHCC" mean a contact centre maintained by or on behalf of the registrar through which a facility is provided for applying by telephone, fax and email for copies of material on the register;

"Companies House Direct" and "CHD" mean the service by which information is accessed by the applicant in Hyper Text Markup Language using a website of the registrar by delivering a non-encrypted access code;

"Companies House Information Centre" and "CHIC" mean an office of the registrar where facilities are made available for applicants to inspect the register and to obtain copies of material on the register and "searchroom terminal" [means a computer terminal through which information is accessed by an applicant by means of an access card at a CHIC;]

"Extranet" means the service by which information is accessed by means of the access codes of the applicant in Hyper Text Markup Language using a website of the registrar;

"WebCHeck" means the service by which information is accessed by the applicant in Hypertext Markup Language using a website of the registrar [at http://wck2.companieshouse.gov.uk] with no requirement for the applicant to deliver an access code;

"XML Gateway" and "XML" mean the service by which information is accessed by the applicant in Extensible Markup Language by means of a partially encrypted access code.

2 Company and limited liability partnership reports

In this Schedule—

"company report" means a report containing the information relating to a company set out in Part 3 of this Schedule in so far as recorded by the registrar in records kept by the registrar for the purposes of the 2006 Act;

"limited liability partnership report" means a report containing the information relating to a limited liability partnership set out in Part 4 of this Schedule in so far as recorded by the registrar in records kept by the registrar for the purposes of the 2006 Act as applied to limited liability partnerships by the LLP Regulations and the Limited Liability Partnerships (Accounts and Audit) (Application of Companies Act 2006) Regulations 2008.

3 Document packages

In this Schedule—

a "document package" means in relation to a company, one of the sets of copies of documents relating to a company (in so far as such documents are delivered to the registrar in respect of the company) as described in one of the paragraphs in Part 5 of this Schedule and with the maximum number of documents in each package being as specified in Part 2 of this Schedule, with the documents in the package being primarily determinable in reverse order of the dates of delivery to the registrar; and

a "document package" means in relation to a limited liability partnership, one of the sets of copies of documents relating to a limited liability partnership (in so far as such documents are delivered to the registrar in respect of the limited liability partnership) as described in one of the paragraphs in Part 6 of this Schedule and with the maximum number of documents in each package being as specified in Part 2 of this Schedule, with the documents in the package being primarily determinable in reverse order of the dates of delivery to the registrar.

4 Meaning of "same day delivery" and "same day collection"

For the purposes of this Schedule certificates and certified copies are provided for "same day delivery" or "same day collection" if—

(a) a request for same day delivery or same day collection is received by the registrar before 2.00 pm on the day in question; and

(b) the appropriate certificate or certified copy is issued to the applicant on that day.

5 Long list of members

Except where expressly provided to the contrary any references in this Schedule to a "document" or to "information" does not include a reference to a "long list of members" and, for the purposes of this Schedule, a "long list of members" has the meaning given to it in paragraph 12.

6 Enactments and legal entities

(1) Paragraph 1 of Schedule 1 to these Regulations applies to this Schedule as it does to that Schedule.

(2) References to a company in this Schedule include a reference to an overseas company except where express provision is made to the contrary.

NOTES

Para 1: words in square brackets in definition "Companies House Information Centre" substituted, and words in square brackets in definition "WebCHeck" inserted, by the Registrar of Companies (Fees) (Amendment) Regulations 2016, SI 2016/621, regs 3, 6(1)–(3), as from 30 June 2016, except in respect of any application or request received by the registrar before that date.

PART 2 FEES PAYABLE

[4.464]

7 Companies House Direct

In respect of the performance of the registrar's functions in relation to the inspection of the register and the provision of copies of material on the register, where an application for inspection or a copy is made by means of CHD, the following fees are payable—

Matter in relation to which fee is payable	Amount of fee
(a) for subscribing to CHD, for each calendar month payable in arrears at the end of that month;	£4.00
(b) for the inspection by means of CHD of particulars of—	
(i) directorships held by a named person,	£1.00
(ii) memberships of limited liability partnerships held by a named person;	£1.00
(c) for a copy provided by means of CHD of a company report or a limited liability partnership report;	£1.00
(d) for the inspection by means of CHD of a statement of particulars of a charge registered in respect of a company or a limited liability partnership;	£1.00
(e) for a copy provided by means of CHD (without prior inspection) of a document in respect of a company or a limited liability partnership;	£1.00
(f) for the inspection and provision of a copy of a document, by means of CHD, in respect of a company or a limited liability partnership;	£1.00
(g) for the delivery by post in hard copy form of a document specified in sub-paragraph (e) above applied for by means of CHD;	£3.00
(h) for the delivery by post in hard copy form of a document package of up to 50 documents applied for by means of CHD;	£20.00
(i) for the provision by means of CHD of a document package of up to 50 documents;	£4.00
(j) for a copy of a document or extract from a document in hard copy form, certified under section 1091 of the 2006 Act in relation to companies, and under that provision as applied to limited liability partnerships by regulation 66 of the LLP Regulations, applied for by means of CHD—	
(i) where that copy is delivered by post by same day delivery,	[£50.00]
(ii) where that copy is delivered by post other than by same day delivery,	[£15.00]
(iii) where that copy is made available for collection at a CHIC other than for same day collection,	[£15.00]
(iv) where that copy is made available for collection at a CHIC for same day collec-	[£50.00]

Matter in relation to which fee is payable	Amount of fee
tion;	
(k) for a copy certificate of incorporation in hard copy form under section 1065 of the 2006 Act, in relation to companies other than overseas companies, and under that provision as applied to limited liability partnerships by regulation 61 of the LLP Regulations, applied for by means of CHD—	
(i) where that certificate is delivered by post other than by same day delivery and it is the first certificate relating to that body corporate provided to an applicant on any one occasion,	[£15.00]
(ii) where that certificate is delivered by post by same day delivery and it is the first certificate relating to that body corporate provided to an applicant on any one occasion,	[£50.00]
(iii) where it is an additional certificate delivered by post (by same day delivery or not) relating to the same body corporate provided to the same applicant on the same occasion;	£10.00
(l) for a copy certificate of incorporation of the type referred to in sub-paragraph (k) applied for by means of CHD and made available for collection at a CHIC—	
(i) where that certificate is made available other than for same day collection and it is the first certificate relating to that body corporate provided to an applicant on any one occasion,	[£15.00]
(ii) where that certificate is made available for same day collection and it is the first certificate relating to that body corporate provided to an applicant on any one occasion,	[£50.00]
(iii) where it is an additional certificate made available for collection (for same day collection or not) relating to the same body corporate provided to the same applicant on the same occasion.	£10.00

8 Extranet

In respect of the performance of the registrar's functions in relation to the inspection of the register and the provision of copies of material on the register, where the application for inspection or a copy is made by means of Extranet, the following fees are payable—

Matter in relation to which fee is payable	Amount of fee
(a) for subscribing to Extranet, for each calendar month payable in arrears at the end of that month;	£4.70
(b) for the inspection by means of Extranet of particulars of—	
(i) directorships held by a named person,	£1.00
(ii) memberships of limited liability partnerships held by a named person;	£1.00
(c) for a copy provided by means of Extranet of a company report or a limited liability partnership report;	£1.00
(d) for the inspection by means of Extranet of a statement of particulars of a charge registered in respect of a company or a limited liability partnership;	£1.00
(e) for a copy provided by means of Extranet (without prior inspection) of a document in respect of a company or a limited liability partnership;	£1.00
(f) for the inspection and provision of a copy of a document by means of Extranet in respect of a company or a limited liability partnership;	£1.00
(g) for the provision by means of Extranet of a document package of up to 50 documents.	£4.00

9 WebCHeck

In respect of the performance of the registrar's functions in relation to the provision of copies of material on the register, where the application for a copy is made by means of WebCHeck, the following fees are payable—

Matter in relation to which fee is payable	Amount of fee
(a) for a copy provided by means of WebCHeck (without prior inspection) of a document in respect of a company or a limited liability partnership;	£1.00
(b) for a copy provided by means of WebCHeck of a company report or a limited liability partnership report.	£1.00

10 XML

In respect of the performance of the registrar's functions in relation to the inspection of the register and the provision of copies of material on the register, where the application for inspection or a copy is made by means of XML, the following fees are payable—

Matter in relation to which fee is payable	Amount of fee
(a) for subscribing to XML, for each calendar month payable in arrears at the end of that month;	£4.70
(b) for the inspection by means of XML of particulars of—	
(i) directorships held by a named person,	£1.00

Matter in relation to which fee is payable	Amount of fee
(ii) memberships of limited liability partnerships held by a named person;	£1.00
(c) for a copy provided by means of XML (without prior inspection) of a document in respect of a company or a limited liability partnership.	£1.00

11 Companies House Information Centre

In respect of the performance of the registrar's functions in relation to the inspection of the register and the provision of copies of material on the register, where the application for inspection or a copy is made at a CHIC, the following fees are payable—

Matter in relation to which fee is payable	Amount of fee
(a) for the inspection by means of a searchroom terminal of particulars of—	
(i) directorships held by a named person,	£1.00
(ii) memberships of a limited liability partnership held by a named person;	£1.00
(b) for the inspection by means of a searchroom terminal of a statement of particulars of a charge registered in respect of a company or a limited liability partnership;	£1.00
(c) for the inspection by means of a searchroom terminal of a company report or a limited liability partnership report;	£1.00
(d) for the provision of a document package of up to 25 documents applied for at a CHIC or by means of a searchroom terminal and made available for collection in hard copy form at a CHIC;	£7.00
(e) for the inspection of a document, by means of a searchroom terminal, in respect of a company or a limited liability partnership;	£1.00
(f) for a copy, in hard copy form, provided by means of a searchroom terminal, (without prior inspection) of a document in respect of a company or a limited liability partnership and made available for collection at a CHIC;	£1.00
(g) for a copy of any document specified in sub-paragraphs (a) to (c) and (e) above applied for at a CHIC and made available for collection at a CHIC;	£3.00
(h) for the inspection, at a CHIC, of an original document delivered to the registrar in hard copy form in respect of a company or a limited liability partnership when the record of the contents kept by the registrar is illegible or unavailable;	£6.00
(i) for the inspection and for a copy in hard copy form of a document of the type specified in sub-paragraph (h) above;	£9.00
(j) for a copy in hard copy form of a screen of information in respect of a company or a limited liability partnership displayed on a searchroom terminal [or any other computer] and made available for collection at a CHIC;	£0.10
(k) for a copy in hard copy form of a document or extract from a document certified under section 1091 of the 2006 Act in relation to companies, and under that provision as applied to limited liability partnerships by regulation 66 of the LLP Regulations, applied for at a CHIC and delivered to the applicant by post—	
(i) where the copy consists of up to 10 pages (including the tenth page),	[£15.00]
(ii) for each subsequent page of the copy,	£1.00
(iii) where any copy is delivered by same day delivery;	[£50.00]
(l) for a copy in hard copy form of a document or extract from a document certified under section 1091 of the 2006 Act in relation to companies, and under that provision as applied to limited liability partnerships by regulation 66 of the LLP Regulations, applied for at a CHIC and made available for collection at a CHIC—	
(i) where the copy consists of up to 10 pages (including the tenth page),	[£15.00]
(ii) for each subsequent page of the copy,	£1.00
(iii) where the copy is made available for same day collection;	[£50.00]
(m) for a copy certificate of incorporation in hard copy form under section 1065 of the 2006 Act, in relation to companies other than overseas companies, and under that provision as applied to limited liability partnerships by regulation 61 of the LLP Regulations, applied for at a CHIC—	
(i) where that certificate is delivered by post other than by same day delivery and it is the first certificate relating to that body corporate provided to an applicant on any one occasion,	[£15.00]
(ii) where that certificate is delivered by post by same day delivery and it is the first certificate relating to that body corporate provided to an applicant on any one occasion,	[£50.00]
(iii) where it is an additional certificate delivered by post (by same day delivery or not) relating to the same body corporate provided to the same applicant on the same occasion;	£10.00
(n) for a copy certificate of incorporation, in hard copy form, of the type referred to in sub-paragraph (m) above applied for at a CHIC and made available for collection at a CHIC—	

Matter in relation to which fee is payable	Amount of fee
(i) where that certificate is made available other than for same day collection and it is the first certificate relating to that body corporate provided to an applicant on any one occasion,	[£15.00]
(ii) where that certificate is made available for same day collection and it is the first certificate relating to that body corporate provided to an applicant on any one occasion,	[£50.00]
(iii) where it is an additional certificate made available for collection (for same day collection or not) relating to the same body corporate provided to the same applicant on the same occasion.	£10.00

12 Companies House Contact Centre

In respect of the performance of the registrar's functions in relation to provision of copies of material on the register, where the application for a copy is made by means of a CHCC, the following fees are payable—

Matter in relation to which fee is payable	Amount of fee
(a) for a copy, provided on an application to a CHCC, of a page of the registrar's index of company names kept under section 1099 of the 2006 Act delivered by post;	£2.00
(b) for a copy of the type specified in sub-paragraph (a) above, provided on an application to a CHCC, delivered by email;	£2.00
(c) for a copy, in hard copy form, provided on an application to a CHCC, of the particulars of the directors and secretary of a company or the members of a limited liability partnership delivered by post;	£3.00
(d) for a copy, provided on an application to a CHCC, of the particulars of the directors and secretary of a company or the members of a limited liability partnership delivered by email;	£3.00
(e) for a copy, provided on an application to a CHCC, of a statement of particulars of a charge registered in respect of a company or a limited liability partnership delivered by post;	£3.00
(f) for a copy, provided on an application to a CHCC, of a statement of particulars of a charge registered in respect of a company or a limited liability partnership delivered by email;	£3.00
(g) for a copy, in hard copy form, provided on an application to a CHCC, of a company report or a limited liability partnership report delivered by post;	£3.00
(h) for a copy, provided on an application to a CHCC, of a company report or a limited liability partnership report delivered by email;	£3.00
(i) for a copy, in hard copy form, provided on an application to a CHCC, of a document in respect of a company or a limited liability partnership delivered by post;	£3.00
(j) for a copy, provided on an application to a CHCC, of a document in respect of a company or a limited liability partnership delivered by email;	£3.00
(k) for a copy, provided on an application to a CHCC, of an original document delivered to the register before 1st January 1978 and kept by the registrar in hard copy form, in respect of a company and delivered by post;	£9.00
(l) for a copy, in hard copy form, of a long list of members of a company, other than an overseas company, provided on an application to a CHCC, delivered by post—	
(i) for the first 50 pages of the copy,	£12.50
(ii) for each additional page of the copy;	£0.20
(m) for a copy, in hard copy form, provided on an application to a CHCC, of a document or extract from a document, certified under section 1091 of the 2006 Act in relation to companies, and under that provision as applied to limited liability partnerships by regulation 66 of the LLP Regulations—	
(i) where that copy is delivered by post other than by same day delivery,	[£15.00]
(ii) where that copy is delivered by same day delivery;	[£50.00]
(n) for a copy, in hard copy form, provided on an application to a CHCC of a document or extract from a document of the type specified in sub-paragraph (m) above and made available for collection at a CHIC—	
(i) where that copy is made available for collection other than by same day collection,	[£15.00]
(ii) where that copy is made available for same day collection;	[£50.00]
(o) for a copy certificate of incorporation provided on an application to a CHCC, in hard copy form, under section 1065 of the 2006 Act, in relation to companies other than overseas companies, and under that provision as applied to limited liability partnerships by regulation 61 of the LLP Regulations—	
(i) where that certificate is delivered by post other than by same day delivery and it is the first certificate relating to that body corporate provided to an applicant on any one occasion,	[£15.00]
(ii) where that certificate is delivered by post by same day delivery and it is the first	[£50.00]

Matter in relation to which fee is payable	Amount of fee
certificate relating to that body corporate provided to an applicant on any one occasion,	
(iii) where it is an additional certificate delivered by post (by same day delivery or not) relating to the same body corporate provided to the same applicant on the same occasion;	£10.00
(p) for a copy certificate of incorporation of the type referred to in sub-paragraph (o) above, provided on an application to a CHCC, and made available for collection at a CHIC—	
(i) where that certificate is made available other than for same day collection and it is the first certificate relating to that body corporate provided to an applicant on any one occasion,	[£15.00]
(ii) where that certificate is made available for same day collection and it is the first certificate relating to that body corporate provided to an applicant on any one occasion,	[£50.00]
(iii) where it is an additional certificate made available for collection (for same day collection or not) relating to the same body corporate provided to the same applicant on the same occasion;	£10.00

and, for the purposes of this paragraph a "long list of members" means a list of members delivered to the registrar under section 856A or 856B of the 2006 Act in relation to companies which exceeds 49 pages and which is delivered in hard copy form.

NOTES

All sums and words in square brackets were substituted by the Registrar of Companies (Fees) (Amendment) Regulations 2016, SI 2016/621, regs 3, 6(1), (4)–(28), as from 30 June 2016, except in respect of any application or request received by the registrar before that date.

PART 3 CONTENTS OF COMPANY REPORT

[4.465]

13 Companies register information

Information relating to the company including its registered number, its date of incorporation, its name and the number of registered charges.

14 Any previous names of the company during the period of 20 years prior to the date to which the company report is made up.

15 A list of dates including those relating to latest annual accounts and annual returns and dates for the next such documents to be delivered to the registrar.

16 Charges and appointments

An applicant may elect to have either of the following sets of particulars—

(a) particulars of charges registered in respect of a company, or

(b) particulars of the directors and secretary of a company together with the particulars in sub-paragraph (a),

except an applicant using WebCHeck can only elect to have the sets of particulars in sub-paragraph (b).

17 Recent filing history

List of documents delivered to the registrar during the previous 18 months up to a maximum of 100 documents listed in the reverse order of the dates of delivery excluding returns of allotments unless requested by the applicant.

PART 4 CONTENTS OF LIMITED LIABILITY PARTNERSHIP REPORT

[4.466]

18 Limited liability partnership register information

Information relating to a limited liability partnership including its registered number, its date of incorporation, its name and the number of registered charges.

19 Any previous names of a limited liability partnership.

20 A list of dates including those relating to latest annual accounts and annual returns and dates for the next such documents to be delivered to the registrar.

21 Charges and appointments

An applicant may elect to have either of the following sets of particulars—

(a) particulars of charges registered in respect of a limited liability partnership, or

(b) particulars of the members of a limited liability partnership together with the particulars in sub-paragraph (a),

except an applicant using WebCHeck can only elect to have the sets of particulars in sub-paragraph (b).

22 Recent filing history

List of documents delivered to the registrar during the previous 18 months up to a maximum of 100 documents listed in the reverse order of the dates of delivery.

PART 5 DOCUMENT PACKAGES FOR COMPANIES

[4.467]

Listed below are the document packages and the documents included in each package:

23 General package

Incorporation documents and name change documents.

Resolutions and memorandum and articles of association.

Any documents relating to strike-off.

Latest annual accounts or, as the case may be, accounting documents and notices specifying accounting reference date or extending the period allowed for laying and delivering accounts and reports.

Latest annual return.

Notification of change among directors or in secretary or their particulars and changes in registered office in each case since the date to which the latest annual return was made up.

(at the option of the applicant) Returns of allotments of shares delivered to the registrar since the date to which the latest annual return giving full particulars of the members is made up.

(long list of members not available).

24 Current package

Latest annual accounts or, as the case may be, accounting documents and notices specifying accounting reference date or extending the period allowed for laying and delivering accounts and reports.

Latest annual return.

Notification of change among directors or in secretary or their particulars and changes in registered office in each case since the date to which the latest annual return was made up.

Any documents relating to strike-off.

(at the option of the applicant) Returns of allotments of shares delivered to the registrar since the date to which the latest annual return giving full particulars of the members is made up.

(long list of members not available).

25 Charges package

Charge related documents since incorporation.

The company report containing the particulars in paragraph 16(a) above.

26 Insolvency package

Company voluntary arrangements, administration, receivership, winding up, dissolution and strike-off related documents delivered to the registrar since April 1995.

27 Accounts package

Annual accounts, or as the case may be, accounting documents and notices specifying accounting reference date or extending the period allowed for laying and delivering accounts and reports delivered to the registrar over the previous 5 years.

28 Constitution package

The most recently delivered to the registrar of any of the documents specified below—

The certificate of incorporation where issued on incorporation, a change of name or re-registration.

The articles of association, or in the case of an existing company, the memorandum and articles of association.

Any resolutions and agreements affecting a company's constitution.

The statement of capital contained in the most recent annual return, or, where no annual return has been delivered, the statement of capital required by section 10 of the 2006 Act.

Any statement of capital delivered to the registrar under any of the following provisions of the 2006 Act—

Sections 108, 555, 619, 621, 625, 627, 644, 649, 663, 689, 708 and 730.

For the purposes of this paragraph an "existing company" is a company to which section 28 of the 2006 Act applies and a "statement of capital" is one delivered to the registrar under any of the provisions listed in respect of statements of capital above.

29 Package of documents delivered in a calendar year selected by the applicant

Documents delivered to the registrar by the company in a calendar year selected by the applicant (not available for years prior to 2003).

PART 6 DOCUMENT PACKAGES FOR LIMITED LIABILITY PARTNERSHIPS

[4.468]

Listed below are the document packages and the documents included in each package:

30 General package

Incorporation document and name change documents.

Any documents relating to strike-off.

Latest annual accounts and notices specifying accounting reference date or extending the period allowed for delivering the accounts and the auditor's report.

Latest annual return.

Notification of change among members or their particulars and changes in registered office in each case since the date to which the latest annual return was made up.

31 Current package

Latest annual accounts and notices specifying accounting reference date or extending the period allowed for delivering the accounts and the auditor's report.

Latest annual return.

Notification of change among members or their particulars and changes in registered office in each case since the date to which the latest annual return was made up.

Any documents relating to strike-off.

32 Charges package

Charge related documents since incorporation.

The limited liability partnership report containing the particulars in paragraph 21(a) above.

33 Insolvency package

Limited liability partnership voluntary arrangements, administration, receivership, winding up, dissolution and strike-off related documents delivered to the registrar since April 2001.

34 Accounts package

Annual accounts and notices specifying accounting reference date or extending the period allowed for delivering the accounts and the auditor's report delivered to the registrar over the previous 5 years.

35 Package of documents delivered in a calendar year selected by the applicant

Documents delivered to the registrar by the limited liability partnership in a calendar year selected by the applicant (not available for years prior to 2003).

[SCHEDULE 3
THE PERFORMANCE OF FUNCTIONS RELATING TO THE DISCLOSURE OF INFORMATION NOT MADE AVAILABLE FOR PUBLIC INSPECTION

Regulation 6

Interpretation

[4.469]

1. (1) In this Schedule—

"particulars of the usual residential address of a specified director" or "particulars of the usual residential address of a specified PSC" means the following information—

the house name or number,
the street,
the area,
the post town,
the region,
the country, and
the postcode, or

if appropriate a statement that the usual residential address is the same as a service address;

"the CDA Regulations" means the Companies (Disclosure of Address) Regulations 2009;

"the LLP Regulations" have the same meaning given to them in paragraph 1 of Schedule 1 to these Regulations;

"the LLP PSC Regulations" means the Limited Liability Partnerships (Register of People with Significant Control) Regulations 2016;

"the OC Regulations" have the same meaning given to them in paragraph 1 of Schedule 1 to these Regulations;

"PSC" means an individual whose particulars are stated in a company's or limited liability partnership's PSC register as a registrable person;

"the PSC Regulations" means the Register of People with Significant Control Regulations 2016.

2. In this Schedule—

(a) any reference to a director is also a reference to a member of a limited liability partnership; and

(b) any such reference in respect of an overseas company except in paragraph 4(b) is also a reference to a permanent representative of that company as that expression is used in the OC Regulations.

Protected information

3. Subject to paragraphs 6 and 7, in respect of the performance of the registrar's functions in relation to the inspection of the register and the provision of copies of material on the register, where that material is protected information to which section 242(1) of the 2006 Act or that section as applied to limited liability partnerships by regulation 19 of the LLP Regulations or regulation 21(1) of the OC Regulations apply, the following fees are payable—

Matters in relation to which a fee is payable	Amount of fee
(a) for an application by a specified public authority or a credit reference agency under regulations 2 and 3 of the CDA Regulations or those regulations as applied to limited liability partnerships by regulation 19 of the LLP Regulations or regulations 23 and 24 of the OC Regulations for the registrar to determine whether to disclose protected information to that authority or agency;	£54.00
(b) for the provision by means of an email of the particulars of the usual residential address of a specified director on the request of a specified public authority or a credit reference agency.	£5.00

Restricted DOB information

4. Subject to paragraphs 6 and 7, in respect of the performance of the registrar's functions in relation to the inspection of the register and the provision of copies of material on the register, where that material is restricted DOB information within section 1087A(1) of the 2006 Act or that section as applied to limited liability partnerships by regulation 66 of the LLP Regulations, the following fees are payable—

Matters in relation to which a fee is payable	Amount of fee
(a) for an application by a specified public authority or a credit reference agency under regulations 2 and 3 of the Companies (Disclosure of Date of Birth Information) Regulations 2015 or those regulations as applied to limited liability partnerships by regula-	£54.00

Matters in relation to which a fee is payable	Amount of fee
tion 66 of the LLP Regulations for the registrar to determine whether to disclose restricted DOB information to that authority or agency;	
(b) for the provision by means of an email of the day of the month on which a specified director was born on the request of a specified public authority or a credit reference agency.	£5.00
(c) for the provision by means of an email of the day of the month on which a specified PSC was born on the request of a specified public authority or a credit reference agency.	£5.00

Section 790ZF(2) information

5. Subject to paragraphs 6 and 7, in respect of the performance of the registrar's function in relation to the inspection of the register and the provision of copies of material on the register, where that material is information within section 790ZF(2) of the 2006 Act or that section as applied to limited liability partnerships by regulation 31L of the LLP Regulations, the following fees are payable—

Matters in relation to which a fee is payable	Amount of fee
(a) for an application by a specified public authority or a credit reference agency under regulations 22 and 23 of the PSC Regulations or those regulations as applied to limited liability partnerships by regulation 4 and Schedule 2 of the LLP PSC Regulations for the registrar to determine whether to disclose information within section 790ZF(2) of the 2006 Act to that authority or agency;	£54.00
(b) for the provision by means of an email of the particulars of the usual residential address of a specified PSC on the request of a specified public authority or a credit reference agency.	£5.00

Modifications to paragraphs 3(a), 4(a) and 5(a)

6. (1) Only one fee is payable under paragraph 3(a) where a specified public authority or a credit reference agency on the same occasion makes an application for the disclosure of protected information in respect of companies, limited liability partnerships and overseas companies (or any combination of them) to which the fee prescribed in paragraph 3(a) is payable.

(2) Only one fee is payable under paragraph 4(a) where a specified public authority or a credit reference agency on the same occasion makes an application for the disclosure of restricted DOB information in respect of companies, limited liability partnerships and overseas companies (or any combination of them) to which the fee prescribed in paragraph 4(a) is payable.

(3) Only one fee is payable under paragraph 5(a) where a specified public authority or a credit reference agency on the same occasion makes an application for the disclosure of information within section 790ZF(2) of the 2006 Act in respect of companies and limited liability partnerships to which the fee prescribed in paragraph 5(a) is payable.

(4) Only one fee is payable under paragraph 3(a), 4(a) or 5(a) where a specified public authority or a credit reference agency on the same occasion makes an application to which the fee prescribed in paragraphs 3(a), 4(a) and 5(a) (or any combination of them) is payable.

(5) The fee prescribed in paragraphs 3(a), 4(a) and 5(a) or any one or more of them is not payable where—

(a) a specified public authority or a credit reference agency makes an application to which the fee in paragraphs 3(a), 4(a) and 5(a) or any one or more of them is payable, and

(b) that authority or agency on an earlier occasion made an application to which the fee prescribed in paragraphs 3(a), 4(a) and 5(a) or any one or more of them was payable.

Modifications to paragraphs 3(b) and 4(b) and paragraphs 4(c) and 5(b)

7. (1) Only one fee is payable under paragraph 3(b) or 4(b) where—

(a) a specified public authority or a credit reference agency requests information to which the fee prescribed in paragraphs 3(b) and 4(b) is payable,

(b) those requests are made on the same occasion, and

(c) relate to the same specified director.

(2) Only one fee is payable under paragraph 4(c) or 5(b) where—

(a) a specified public authority or a credit reference agency requests information to which the fee prescribed in paragraphs 4(c) and 5(b) is payable,

(b) those requests are made on the same occasion, and

(c) relate to the same specified PSC.]

NOTES

Substituted by the Registrar of Companies (Fees) (Amendment) Regulations 2016, SI 2016/621, regs 3, 7, as from 30 June 2016, except in respect of any application or request received by the registrar before that date.

REGISTRAR OF COMPANIES (FEES) (EUROPEAN ECONOMIC INTEREST GROUPING AND EUROPEAN PUBLIC LIMITED-LIABILITY COMPANY) REGULATIONS 2012

(SI 2012/1908)

NOTES

Made: 18 July 2012.

Authority: Companies Act 2006, ss 1063(1)–(3), 1292(1).

Commencement: 1 October 2012.

For a summary of all Orders and Regulations made under the Companies Act 2006, see Appendix 4 at **[A4]**.

These Regulations are reproduced as amended by: the Registrar of Companies (Fees) (Amendment) Regulations 2016, SI 2016/621; the European Public Limited-Liability Company (Amendment etc) (EU Exit) Regulations 2018, SI 2018/1298; the European Economic Interest Grouping (Amendment) (EU Exit) Regulations 2018, SI 2018/1299.

ARRANGEMENT OF REGULATIONS

SCHEDULES

[4.470]

1 Citation and commencement

These Regulations may be cited as the Registrar of Companies (Fees) (European Economic Interest Grouping and European Public Limited-Liability Company) Regulations 2012 and come into force on 1st October 2012.

[4.471]

2 Interpretation

In these Regulations—

"the 2006 Act" means the Companies Act 2006;

"Companies House Direct" and "CHD" mean the service by which information is accessed by the applicant in Hyper Text Markup Language using a website of the registrar by delivering a non-encrypted access code;

["the EC Regulation" means Council Regulation 2157/2001/EC of 8 October 2001 on the Statute for a European Company;]

["EEIG establishment" has the meaning given in regulation 2(1) of the EEIG Regulations;]

["the "EEIG Regulations" means the European Economic Interest Grouping Regulations 1989;]

"Extranet" means the service by which information is accessed by means of the access codes of the applicant in Hyper Text Markup Language using a website of the registrar;

"limited liability partnership" means a body corporate incorporated under the Limited Liability Partnerships Act 2000;

"limited partnership" means a partnership registered under the Limited Partnerships Act 1907;

. . .

["UKEIG" has the meaning given in regulation 2(1) of the EEIG Regulations;]

"XML Gateway" and "XML" mean the service by which information is accessed by the applicant in Extensible Markup Language by means of a partially encrypted access code;

["UK Societas" means a European Public Limited-Liability Company, within the meaning of the EC Regulation, as it had effect immediately before [IP completion day], which was registered in the United Kingdom and which on [IP completion day] converted to a United Kingdom Societas within the meaning of the EC Regulation.]

NOTES

Definitions "the EC Regulation" and "UK Societas" inserted, and definition "SE" (omitted) revoked, by the European Public Limited-Liability Company (Amendment etc) (EU Exit) Regulations 2018, SI 2018/1298, regs 83, 84, as from IP completion day (as defined in the European Union (Withdrawal Agreement) Act 2020, s 39). Note with regard to the definition "UK Societas", that reg 84 of the 2018 Regulations was amended by the Companies and Statutory Auditors etc (Consequential

Amendments) (EU Exit) Regulations 2020, SI 2020/523, reg 3(k), with effect from immediately before IP completion day (and that the effect of this amendment has been incorporated into the text above).

Definition "EEIG establishment" substituted (for the original definition "EEIG"), and definition "UKEIG" inserted, by the European Economic Interest Grouping (Amendment) (EU Exit) Regulations 2018, SI 2018/1299, regs 23, 24, as from IP completion day (as defined in the European Union (Withdrawal Agreement) Act 2020, s 39).

Definition "the EEIG Regulations" inserted by the Registrar of Companies (Fees) (Amendment) Regulations 2016, SI 2016/621, regs 8, 9, as from 30 June 2016.

[4.472]

3 Fees payable in respect of functions relating to the registration of documents by the registrar

Schedule 1 makes provision for the fees that are payable to the registrar in respect of the registration of documents relating to [UKEIGs, EEIG establishments] and [UK Societates] by the registrar.

NOTES

Words in first pair of square brackets substituted by the European Economic Interest Grouping (Amendment) (EU Exit) Regulations 2018, SI 2018/1299, regs 23, 25, as from IP completion day (as defined in the European Union (Withdrawal Agreement) Act 2020, s 39).

Words in second pair of square brackets substituted by the European Public Limited-Liability Company (Amendment etc) (EU Exit) Regulations 2018, SI 2018/1298, regs 83, 85, as from IP completion day (as defined in the European Union (Withdrawal Agreement) Act 2020, s 39).

[4.473]

4 Fees payable in respect of the inspection or provision of copies of documents kept by the registrar relating to [UKEIGs and EEIG establishments]

(1) Schedule 2 makes provision for the fees that are payable to the registrar in respect of the inspection, or provision of copies, of documents kept by the registrar relating to [UKEIGs and EEIG establishments].

(2) The fees prescribed in relation to paragraphs 3(a), 4(a) and 6(a) of Schedule 2 are not payable in respect of any month for which the applicant pays a fee to the registrar for subscription to Companies House Direct, Extranet or XML under regulations providing for the payment of fees in respect of the functions of the registrar in relation to the inspection, or provision of copies, of documents kept by the registrar relating to companies, overseas companies, limited liability partnerships and limited partnerships

NOTES

Words in square brackets substituted by the European Economic Interest Grouping (Amendment) (EU Exit) Regulations 2018, SI 2018/1299, regs 23, 26, as from IP completion day (as defined in the European Union (Withdrawal Agreement) Act 2020, s 39).

[4.474]

[4A Fees payable in respect of the disclosure of restricted DOB information

Schedule 3 to these Regulations makes provision for the fees that are payable to the registrar in respect of the disclosure of restricted DOB information relating to a manager of [a UKEIG or an EEIG establishment]]

NOTES

Inserted by the Registrar of Companies (Fees) (Amendment) Regulations 2016, SI 2016/621, regs 8, 10, as from 30 June 2016, except in respect of any application or request received by the registrar before that date.

Words in square brackets substituted by the European Economic Interest Grouping (Amendment) (EU Exit) Regulations 2018, SI 2018/1299, regs 23, 27, as from IP completion day (as defined in the European Union (Withdrawal Agreement) Act 2020, s 39).

[4.475]

5 Transitional provisions

(1) Where any document delivered to the registrar on or before 30th September 2012 is registered on or after 1st October 2012 the fee prescribed in Schedule 1 to the Regulations in respect of that document shall not apply and any fee payable in respect of that document by virtue of the Registrar of Companies (Fees) (European Economic Interest Grouping and European Public Limited Liability Company) Regulations 2009 shall apply.

(2) Where any application is made or subscription is payable to the registrar on or before 30th September 2012 in respect of the inspection of, or the provision of copies of, material kept by the registrar, the fee prescribed in Schedule 2 to these Regulations in respect of that application or subscription shall not apply and any fee payable under the Registrar of Companies (Fees) (European Economic Interest Grouping and European Public Limited Liability Company) Regulations 2009 shall apply.

[4.476]

6 Revocation

The following regulations are revoked—

(a) the Registrar of Companies (Fees) (European Economic Interest Grouping and European Public Limited Liability Company) Regulations 2009; and

(b) the Registrar of Companies (Fees) (European Economic Interest Grouping) (Amendment) Regulations 2011.

SCHEDULES

SCHEDULE 1
THE PERFORMANCE OF FUNCTIONS RELATING TO THE REGISTRATION OF DOCUMENTS BY THE REGISTRAR

Regulation 3

PART 1 INTERPRETATION

[4.477]

1 [Words and expressions used in the EC Regulation]

(1) . . .

(2) Words and expressions used in the [EC Regulation] [and the EEIG Regulations] have the same meaning when used in this Schedule as they have in [that enactment].

2 Meaning of "same day registration"

For the purposes of this Schedule documents are delivered for "same day registration" if—

(a) a request for same day registration and all documents required to be delivered to the registrar in connection with that registration are received by the registrar by 3.00 pm on the day in question; and

(b) the registration is completed on that day.

3 General

Where, in relation to any matter in respect of which a fee is payable under this Schedule, the means of delivery to the registrar of the documents required to be delivered in relation to that matter, or the form of those documents are not specified, that fee is payable only in respect of documents that are delivered in hard copy form.

4 Where, in relation to any matter in respect of which a fee is payable under this Schedule, no provision is made for same day registration of the documents required to be delivered to the registrar in relation to that matter, that fee is only payable in respect of the delivery of documents other than for same day registration.

NOTES

Para 1: the words "and the EEIG Regulations" in square brackets in sub-para (2) were inserted by the Registrar of Companies (Fees) (Amendment) Regulations 2016, SI 2016/621, regs 8, 11(1)–(4), as from 30 June 2016 (for transitional provisions and savings see the note to **[4.460]**). All other amendments to para 1 were made by the European Public Limited-Liability Company (Amendment etc) (EU Exit) Regulations 2018, SI 2018/1298, regs 83, 86(a), (b), as from IP completion day (as defined in the European Union (Withdrawal Agreement) Act 2020, s 39).

PART 2 FEES PAYABLE

[4.478]

5 [UK Economic Interest Groupings and EEIG establishments]

In respect of the performance by the registrar of his functions in relation to the registration of documents delivered to him in respect of [UKEIGs and EEIG establishments], the fee specified in relation to each matter below is payable on the registration of the documents so delivered relating to that matter—

Matter in relation to which the fee is payable	Amount of fee
(a) . . .	. . .
(b) for the registration under regulation 12 of the EEIG Regulations of an EEIG [establishment];	£20.00
(c) for the registration of a change of name of [a UKEIG] under regulation 11 of the EEIG Regulations;	£10.00
(d) for the registration of a charge under paragraph 26 of Schedule 4 to the EEIG Regulations.	[£23.00]

6 [UK Societates]

In respect of the performance by the registrar of his functions in relation to the registration of documents delivered to him in respect of [UK Societates], the fee specified in relation to each matter below is payable on the registration of the documents so delivered relating to that matter—

Matter in relation to which the fee is payable	Amount of fee
(a) . . .	. . .
(b) for the registration of a public company by the conversion of [a UK Societas] in accordance with Article 66 of the EC Regulation;	£20.00
(c) . . .	. . .

NOTES

Para 5 is amended as follows:

The sum in square brackets in para (d) of the table was substituted by the Registrar of Companies (Fees) (Amendment) Regulations 2016, SI 2016/621, regs 8, 11(1)–(4), as from 30 June 2016 (for transitional provisions and savings see the note to **[4.460]**).

All other amendments to para 5 were made by the European Economic Interest Grouping (Amendment) (EU Exit) Regulations 2018, SI 2018/1299, regs 23, 28, as from IP completion day (as defined in the European Union (Withdrawal Agreement) Act 2020, s 39).

Para 6: all amendments were made by the European Public Limited-Liability Company (Amendment etc) (EU Exit) Regulations 2018, SI 2018/1298, regs 83, 86(c), as from IP completion day (as defined in the European Union (Withdrawal Agreement) Act 2020, s 39).

Note that fees in relation to EEIGs were prescribed by the European Economic Interest Grouping (Fees) Regulations 2004, SI 2004/2643. Those Regulations were revoked by the European Economic Interest Grouping and European Public Limited-Liability Company (Fees) Revocation Regulations 2009, SI 2009/2492, with the exception of Fee No 3 in Sch 2. That Fee is as follows (note that 'the principal Regulations' means the European Economic Interest Grouping Regulations 1989)—

Matter in respect of which fee is payable	Amount of fee
3. Registration of a charge under paragraph 4 of Schedule 4 to the principal Regulations	£13.00

SCHEDULE 2
THE PERFORMANCE OF FUNCTIONS RELATING TO THE INSPECTION OR PROVISION OF COPIES OF DOCUMENTS KEPT BY THE REGISTRAR IN RELATION TO [UKEIGS AND EEIG ESTABLISHMENTS]

Regulation 4

NOTES

Words in square brackets in the Schedule heading substituted by the European Economic Interest Grouping (Amendment) (EU Exit) Regulations 2018, SI 2018/1299, regs 23, 29(a), as from IP completion day (as defined in the European Union (Withdrawal Agreement) Act 2020, s 39).

PART 1 INTERPRETATION

[4.479]

1 Means by which the register may be inspected and copies provided

In this Schedule—

"Companies House Contact Centre" and "CHCC" mean a contact centre maintained by or on behalf of the registrar through which a facility is provided for applying by telephone, fax or e-mail for copies of material on the register;

"Companies House Information Centre" and "CHIC" mean an office of the registrar where facilities are made available for applicants to inspect the register and to obtain copies of material on the register and "searchroom terminal" [means a computer terminal through which information is accessed by an applicant by means of an access card at a CHIC;]

"WebCHeck" means the service by which information is accessed by the applicant in Hyper Text Markup Language using a website of the registrar [at http://wck2.companieshouse.gov.uk.] with no requirement for the applicant to deliver an access code.

2 Meaning of "same day delivery" and "same day collection"

For the purposes of this Schedule certified copies are provided for "same day delivery" or "same day collection" if—

(a) a request for same day delivery or same day collection is received by the registrar before 2.00pm on the day in question; and

(b) the appropriate certified copy is issued to the applicant on that day.

NOTES

Para 1: words in square brackets in definition "Companies House Information Centre" substituted, and words in square brackets in definition "WebCHeck" inserted, by the Registrar of Companies (Fees) (Amendment) Regulations 2016, SI 2016/621, regs 8, 12(1)–(3), as from 30 June 2016, except in respect of any application or request received by the registrar before that date.

PART 2 FEES PAYABLE

[4.480]

3 Companies House Direct

In respect of the performance of the registrar's function in relation to the inspection of material kept by the registrar and the provision of copies of material kept by the registrar in respect of [UKEIGs and EEIG establishments], where an application for inspection or a copy is made by means of CHD, the following fees are payable—

Matter in relation to which the fee is payable	Amount of fee
(a) for subscribing to CHD for each calendar month payable in arrears at the end of that month;	£4.00
(b) for the inspection by means of CHD of a statement of particulars of a charge registered in respect of [a UKEIG or an EEIG establishment];	£1.00
(c) for a copy provided by means of CHD (without prior inspection) of a document in respect of [a UKEIG or an EEIG establishment];	£1.00
(d) for the inspection and provision of a copy of a document, by means of CHD in respect of [a UKEIG or an EEIG establishment];	£1.00
(e) for the delivery by post in hard copy form of a document specified in sub-paragraph (c) above applied for by means of CHD;	£3.00
(f) for a copy of a document, or extract from a document, in hard copy form, certified under section 1091 of the 2006 Act in relation to [UKEIGs and EEIG establishments], applied for by means of CHD—	
—(i) where that copy or extract is delivered by post by same day delivery,	[£50.00]
—(ii) where that copy or extract is delivered by post other than by same day delivery,	[£15.00]
—(iii) where that copy or extract is made available for collection at a CHIC other than for same day collection,	[£15.00]

Matter in relation to which the fee is payable	Amount of fee
—(iv) where that copy or extract is made available for collection at a CHIC for same day collection.	[£50.00]

4 Extranet

In respect of the performance of the registrar's functions in relation to the inspection of material kept by the registrar and the provision of copies of material kept by the registrar in respect of [UKEIGs and EEIG establishments], where an application for inspection or a copy is made by means of Extranet, the following fees are payable—

Matter in relation to which the fee is payable	Amount of fee
(a) for subscribing to Extranet, for each calendar month payable in arrears at the end of that month;	£4.70
(b) for the inspection and provision of a copy of a document by means of Extranet in respect of [a UKEIG or an EEIG establishment];	£1.00
(c) for a copy provided by means of Extranet (without prior inspection) of a document in respect of [a UKEIG or an EEIG establishment].	£1.00

5 WebCHeck

In respect of the performance of the registrar's functions in relation to the provision of copies of material kept by the registrar in respect of [UKEIGs and EEIG establishments], where the application for a copy is made by means of WebCHeck, the following fee is payable—

Matter in relation to which the fee is payable	Amount of fee
(a) for a copy provided by means of WebCHeck (without prior inspection) of a document in respect of [a UKEIG or an EEIG establishment]	£1.00

6 XML

In respect of the performance of the registrar's functions in relation to the provision of copies of material kept by the registrar in respect of [UKEIGs and EEIG establishments], where the application for a copy is made by means of XML, the following fee is payable—

Matter in relation to which the fee is payable	Amount of fee
(a) for subscribing to XML, for each calendar month payable in arrears at the end of that month;	£4.70
(b) for a copy provided by means of XML (without prior inspection) of a document in respect of [a UKEIG or an EEIG establishment].	£1.00

7 Companies House Information Centre

In respect of the performance of the registrar's functions in relation to the inspection of material kept by the registrar and the provision of copies of material kept by the registrar in respect of [UKEIGs and EEIG establishments], where the application for inspection or a copy is made at a CHIC, the following fees are payable—

Matter in relation to which the fee is payable	Amount of fee
(a) for the inspection by means of a searchroom terminal of a statement of particulars of a charge registered in respect of [a UKEIG or an EEIG establishment];	£1.00
(b) for the inspection of a document by means of a searchroom terminal in respect of [a UKEIG or an EEIG establishment];	£1.00
(c) for a copy, in hard copy form, provided by means of a searchroom terminal (without prior inspection) of a document in respect of [a UKEIG or an EEIG establishment];	£1.00
(d) for a copy of any document specified in sub-paragraphs (a) and (b) above, applied for at a CHIC and made available at a CHIC;	£3.00
(e) for the inspection, at a CHIC, of an original document delivered to the registrar in hard copy form in respect of [a UKEIG or an EEIG establishment];	£6.00
(f) for the inspection and for a copy, in hard copy form of a document of the type specified in sub-paragraph (e) above;	£9.00
(g) for a copy in hard copy form of a screen of information in respect of [a UKEIG or an EEIG establishment] displayed on a searchroom terminal [or any other computer] and made available for collection at a CHIC;	£0.10
(h) for a copy, in hard copy form, of a document or extract from a document certified under section 1091 of the 2006 Act in relation to [a UKEIG or an EEIG establishment], applied for at a CHIC and delivered to the applicant by post—	
—(i) where the copy or extract consists of up to 10 pages (including the tenth page),	[£15.00]
—(ii) for each subsequent page of the copy or extract,	£1.00
—(iii) where any copy or extract is delivered by same day delivery;	[£50.00]
(i) for a copy, in hard copy form, of a document or an extract from a document certified under section 1091 of the 2006 Act in relation to [a UKEIG or an EEIG establishment], applied for at a CHIC and made available for collection at a CHIC—	

Matter in relation to which the fee is payable	Amount of fee
—(i) where the copy or extract consists of up to 10 pages (including the tenth page),	[£15.00]
—(ii) for each subsequent page of the copy or extract,	£1.00
—(iii) where the copy or extract is made available for same day collection.	[£50.00]

8 Companies House Contact Centre

In respect of the performance of the registrar's functions in relation to the provision of copies of material kept by the registrar in respect of [UKEIGs and EEIG establishments], where the application for a copy is made by means of a CHCC, the following fees are payable—

Matter in relation to which the fee is payable	Amount of fee
(a) for a copy, in hard copy form provided on application to a CHCC, of a statement of particulars of a charge registered in respect of [a UKEIG or an EEIG establishment] delivered by post;	£3.00
(b) for a copy provided on application to a CHCC, of a statement of particulars of a charge registered in respect of [a UKEIG or an EEIG establishment] delivered by e-mail;	£3.00
(c) for a copy, in hard copy form, provided on application to a CHCC of a document in respect of [a UKEIG or an EEIG establishment] delivered by post;	£3.00
(d) for a copy, provided on application to a CHCC of a document in respect of [a UKEIG or an EEIG establishment] delivered by e-mail;	£3.00
(e) for a copy, provided on application to a CHCC of an original document delivered to the registrar and kept by the registrar in hard copy form in respect of [a UKEIG or an EEIG establishment] and delivered by post;	£9.00
(f) for a copy, in hard copy form, provided on application to a CHCC, of a document or extract from a document, certified under section 1091 of the 2006 Act in relation to [a UKEIG or an EEIG establishment]—	
—(i) where that copy or extract is delivered by post other than by same day delivery,	[£15.00]
—(ii) where that copy or extract is delivered by post by same day delivery;	[£50.00]
(g) for a copy, in hard copy form, provided on application to a CHCC, of a document or extract from a document of the type specified in sub-paragraph (f) above and made available for collection at a CHIC—	
—(i) where that copy or extract is made available for collection other than for same day collection,	[£15.00]
—(ii) where that copy or extract is made available for same day collection.	[£50.00]

NOTES

The words "UKEIGs and EEIG establishments" and "a UKEIG or an EEIG establishment" (in each place that they occur) were substituted by the European Economic Interest Grouping (Amendment) (EU Exit) Regulations 2018, SI 2018/1299, regs 23, 29(b), as from IP completion day (as defined in the European Union (Withdrawal Agreement) Act 2020, s 39). Note that reg 29(b) of the 2018 Regulations provided, inter alia, for the substitution of the words "a UKEIG or an EEIG establishment" for the words "an EEIG" in para (f) of the table in para 3, and in the introductory wording of paras 5 and 6. Those provisions did not contain the word "an" before the abbreviation "EEIG" and, technically, this amendment could not be done. It is assumed that this was a drafting error and the words "UKEIGs and EEIG establishments" have been substituted for "EEIGs" in those provisions above.

All other amendments to this Part were made by the Registrar of Companies (Fees) (Amendment) Regulations 2016, SI 2016/621, regs 8, 12(1), (4)–(16), as from 30 June 2016, except in respect of any application or request received by the registrar before that date.

[SCHEDULE 3
THE PERFORMANCE OF FUNCTIONS RELATING TO THE DISCLOSURE OF RESTRICTED DOB INFORMATION

Regulation 4A

[4.481]

1. In respect of the performance of the registrar's function in relation to the inspection of material kept by the registrar and the provision of the copies of material kept by the registrar in respect of [UKEIGs and EEIG establishments], where that material is restricted DOB information to which section 1087A(1) of the 2006 Act as applied to [UKEIGs and EEIG establishments] by paragraph 32A of Schedule 4 to the EEIG Regulations applies, the following fees are payable—

Matters in relation to which a fee is payable	Amount of fee
(a) for an application by a specified public authority or a credit reference agency under regulations 2 and 3 of the Companies (Disclosure of Date of Birth Information) Regulations 2015 as applied to [UKEIGs and EEIG establishments] by paragraph 32A of Schedule 4 to the EEIG Regulations for the registrar to determine whether to disclose restricted DOB information to that authority or agency;	£54.00
(b) for the provision by means of an email of the day of the month on which a specified manager of [a UKEIG or an EEIG establishment] was	£5.00]

Matters in relation to which a fee is payable	Amount of fee
born on the request of a specified public authority or a credit reference agency.	

NOTES

Added by the Registrar of Companies (Fees) (Amendment) Regulations 2016, SI 2016/621, regs 8, 13, as from 30 June 2016, except in respect of any application or request received by the registrar before that date.

Words in square brackets substituted by the European Economic Interest Grouping (Amendment) (EU Exit) Regulations 2018, SI 2018/1299, regs 23, 30, as from IP completion day (as defined in the European Union (Withdrawal Agreement) Act 2020, s 39).

STATUTORY AUDITORS AND THIRD COUNTRY AUDITORS REGULATIONS 2013

(SI 2013/1672)

NOTES

Made: 4 July 2013.

Authority: Companies Act 2006, ss 1239(1)(b), (2)(a), (f), (5)(d), (6)(a), 1246(1), 1292(1); European Communities Act 1972, s 2(2) (see also the note "Statutory Instruments made under the European Communities Act 1972" preceding paragraph **[4.1]** *ante*).

Commencement: 30 July 2013 (regs 1–3, 13); 31 July 2013 (regs 4–12, Schedule); 1 October 2013 (regs 14–17).

For a summary of all Orders and Regulations made under the Companies Act 2006, see Appendix 4 at **[A4]**.

These Regulations are reproduced as amended by: the Statutory Auditors and Third Country Auditors Regulations 2016, SI 2016/649; the Statutory Auditors and Third Country Auditors (Amendment) (EU Exit) Regulations 2019, SI 2019/177.

ARRANGEMENT OF REGULATIONS

[4.482]
1 Citation

These Regulations may be cited as the Statutory Auditors and Third Country Auditors Regulations 2013.

[4.483]
2 Coming into force

These Regulations, except for regulations 1 to 3 and 13 to 17, come into force on 31st July 2013.

[4.484]
3

Regulations 1 to 3 and 13 come into force on 30th July 2013 and regulations 14 to 17 come into force on 1st October 2013.

[4.485]
4 Schedule

The regulations listed in the Schedule are revoked to the extent indicated in the Schedule.

[4.486]
5 Interpretation

In these Regulations—

"the Act" means the Companies Act 2006;

"the designated body" means the Financial Reporting Council Limited; and

"registered number" means the number allocated to a registered third country auditor by the designated body pursuant to regulation 10.

[4.487]
6 Register of third country auditors

(1) The designated body must keep the register of third country auditors referred to in section 1239(1)(b) of the Act.

(2) In relation to every registered third country auditor who is an individual, the register must contain the following information—

(a) the individual's name and address;
(b) the individual's registered number;
(c) an indication that the individual is a third country auditor;
(d) if responsible for audit work on behalf of a third country auditor which is a firm, the firm's name, address, registered number and, if it has a website, the website address;
(e) in the case of an individual who has registered with an EEA competent authority [under Article 45(1) of the Audit Directive]—
 (i) the name and address of that authority, and
 (ii) the registration number which that authority has allocated to the third country auditor; and
(f) the name and address of [each third country competent authority that] has authorised the individual to conduct audits in accordance with the law of a third country [and the registration number (if any) which each one has allocated to the individual].

(3) In relation to every registered third country auditor which is a firm, the register must contain the following information—
(a) the firm's name and address;
(b) the address of each of the firm's offices from which it carries out audits of [UK-traded third country companies];
(c) its registered number;
(d) an indication that it is a third country auditor;
(e) its contact information and, if it has a website, its website address;
(f) its legal form;
(g) the name and address of each person who is—
 (i) an owner or shareholder of the firm, or
 (ii) a member of the firm's administrative or management body;
(h) the name and address of every individual who performs audits of [UK-traded third country companies] on behalf of the firm and the registration number [(if any)] allocated to that individual by any [third country competent authority or other body] which has authorised the individual to conduct audits in accordance with the law of a third country;
(i) in the case of a firm which is a member of a network—
 (i) a list of the names and addresses of the other members of that network, or
 (ii) an indication of where that information is available to the public;
(j) in the case of a firm which has registered with an EEA competent authority [under Article 45(1) of the Audit Directive]—
 (i) the name and address of that authority, and
 (ii) the registration number which that authority has allocated to it; and
(k) the name and address of [each third country competent authority that] has authorised the firm to conduct audits in accordance with the law of a third country [and the registration number (if any) which each one has allocated to the firm].

(4) The register of third country auditors must be kept in electronic form.

(5) The information on the register must be kept available for inspection by any person by electronic means, unless it is excluded in accordance with paragraph (6).

(6) Information on the register relating to an individual may be excluded from being made available for inspection if making the information so available would create or be likely to create a serious risk that the individual, or any other person, would be subject to violence or intimidation.

[(7) In this regulation—

"Audit Directive" means Directive 2006/43/EC of the European Parliament and of the Council on statutory audits of annual accounts and consolidated accounts;

"EEA competent authority" means a competent authority within the meaning of Article 2(10) of the Audit Directive of an EEA State;

"network" means an association of persons other than a firm co-operating in audit work by way of—
 (a) profit sharing,
 (b) cost sharing,
 (c) common ownership, control or management,
 (d) common quality control policies and procedures,
 (e) common business strategy, or
 (f) use of a common brand name.

(8) For the purposes of this regulation, Gibraltar is to be treated as if it were an EEA State and subject to the Audit Directive.]

NOTES

All amendments to this regulation were made by the Statutory Auditors and Third Country Auditors (Amendment) (EU Exit) Regulations 2019, SI 2019/177, regs 58, 59, as from IP completion day (as defined in the European Union (Withdrawal Agreement) Act 2020, s 39) (for transitional provisions, see Sch 4 to the 2019 Regulations at **[12.88]**).

[4.488]

7 Application for registration of third country auditor

(1) A third country auditor may apply to the designated body for registration.

(2) An application for registration must be in writing.

(3) An application for registration must include—
(a) the information required for entry in the register (see regulation 6), other than the registered number;
(b) the statement required by regulation 8 (application statement);

(c) evidence demonstrating that the matters included in the statement required by regulation 8 (application statement) are correct;
(d) in respect of each [UK-traded third country company] for which the third country auditor provides an audit report—
    (i) the company's name and any number the company has by virtue of its incorporation,
    (ii) the third country or territory in which the company is incorporated or under the law of which it is formed,
    (iii) the accounting period to which the audit report relates, and
    (iv) a statement of the auditing standards and independence requirements applied to the audit; and
(e) a description of the third country auditor's internal quality control system,
(f) a statement of whether and, if so, when a quality assurance review has been carried out in respect of the third country auditor, and
(g) information required by the designated body about the outcome of a quality assurance review.

(4) For the purposes of paragraph (3)(c) a statement by the third country competent authority which oversees or regulates the third country auditor to the effect that the third country auditor is a fit and proper person to conduct audits in that third country may be treated as evidence demonstrating that the statement required by regulation 8(c) is correct.

(5) An application for registration must—
(a) in the case of a third country auditor who is an individual, be signed by the individual;
(b) in the case of a third country auditor which is a firm, be signed by a person authorised by the firm to sign on its behalf.

(6) An application may be delivered to the designated body by electronic means, if the designated body so agrees.

NOTES

Para (3): words in square brackets substituted by the Statutory Auditors and Third Country Auditors (Amendment) (EU Exit) Regulations 2019, SI 2019/177, regs 58, 60, as from IP completion day (as defined in the European Union (Withdrawal Agreement) Act 2020, s 39) (for transitional provisions, see Sch 4 to the 2019 Regulations at **[12.88]**).

[4.489]

8 Application statement

A third country auditor must make a statement for the purposes of an application under regulation 7 (application for registration of third country auditor) to the effect that—
(a) if an individual, the third country auditor holds a qualification which meets requirements equivalent to those which apply to an appropriate qualification for the purposes of section 1219 of the Act;
(b) if a firm—
    (i) a majority of the members of the firm's administrative or management body hold qualifications which meet requirements equivalent to those which apply to an appropriate qualification for the purposes of section 1219 of the Act, and
    (ii) each individual who conducts audits of [UK-traded third country companies] on behalf of the firm holds a qualification which meets requirements equivalent to those which apply to an appropriate qualification for the purposes of that section;
(c) the third country auditor is a fit and proper person to conduct audits of [];
[(d) the third country auditor conducts audits of [UK-traded third country companies] in accordance with—
    (i) the international auditing standards adopted by the European Commission in accordance with Article 26(3) of the Audit Directive [before IP completion day], or with standards which are equivalent,
    [(ia) the UK-adopted international standards adopted by the competent authority in accordance with regulation 4(3)(za) of the Statutory Auditors and Third Country Auditors Regulations 2016, or with standards, procedures or requirements which are equivalent,]
    (ii) any auditing standards, procedures or requirements imposed by the competent authority in accordance with [regulation 4(3)] of the Statutory Auditors and Third Country Auditors Regulations 2016, or with standards, procedures or requirements which are equivalent, and
    [(iii) any auditing standards, procedures or requirements imposed by the competent authority in accordance with the requirements set out in paragraphs 1 to 6 and 8 of Schedule 1 to the Statutory Auditors and Third Country Auditors Regulations 2016, or with any other equivalent standards, procedures or requirements];
(e) . . . and
(f) the third country auditor publishes on a website an annual transparency report equivalent to that required for auditors of public interest entities by [Article 13 of the Audit Regulation] (transparency report).

NOTES

Para (d) was substituted, para (e) was revoked, and words in square brackets in para (f) were substituted, by the Statutory Auditors and Third Country Auditors Regulations 2016, SI 2016/649, reg 20(1), (2), as from 17 June 2016.

All other amendments to this regulation were made by the Statutory Auditors and Third Country Auditors (Amendment) (EU Exit) Regulations 2019, SI 2019/177, regs 58, 61, as from IP completion day (as defined in the European Union (Withdrawal Agreement) Act 2020, s 39) (for transitional provisions, see Sch 4 to the 2019 Regulations at **[12.88]**). Note also that reg 61 of the 2019 Regulations was amended by the Companies and Statutory Auditors etc (Consequential Amendments) (EU Exit) Regulations 2020, SI 2020/523, reg 15(b), with effect from immediately before IP completion day; and that the effect of this amendment has been incorporated in the text above.

[4.490]

9 Acceptance and refusal of application for registration

(1) The designated body may register a third country auditor if the third country auditor has made an application in accordance with regulation 7 (application for registration of third country auditor).

(2) The designated body must refuse to register a third country auditor if it considers that the statement made pursuant to regulation 8 (application statement) is not correct.

(3) If the designated body refuses to register a third country auditor, it must give the third country auditor a written notice to that effect stating the reason for the refusal.

[4.491]
10 Allocation of registered number

The designated body must allocate a number to each third country auditor which it registers.

[4.492]
11 Duty to provide updated information

A registered third country auditor must take all reasonable steps to notify the designated body without undue delay of—

(a) any change or addition to the information specified in paragraphs (d) to (g) of regulation 7(3);
(b) any information or event which may lead the designated body to consider that the statement made pursuant to regulation 8 (application statement) is not correct;
(c) any information necessary to ensure that the information in the register relating to the registered third country auditor is correct.

[4.493]
12 Removal of registered third country auditor from the register

(1) If the designated body considers that the statement required by regulation 8 (application statement) made by a registered third country auditor is no longer correct, it must—

(a) notify the registered third country auditor of the steps that the registered third country auditor must take to ensure that the statement is correct, and
(b) if the registered third country auditor has not taken those steps on or before the date three months after the notification, remove the registered third country auditor from the register.

(2) The designated body may remove a registered third country auditor from the register if it considers that the registered third country auditor has failed to comply with any of the obligations of the registered third country auditor—

(a) regulation 11 (duty to provide updated information),
(b) section 1242 of the Act (duties of registered third country auditors),
(c) section 1243 of the Act (matters to be notified to the Secretary of State), or
(d) section 1244 of the Act (Secretary of State's power to call for information).

(3) The designated body may remove a registered third country auditor from the register if—

(a) it considers that the registered third country auditor—
    (i) has failed to apply the auditing standards and independence requirements set out in the statement referred to in paragraph (iv) of regulation 7(3)(d), or
    (ii) is not a fit and proper person to conduct audits of the accounts of [UK-traded third country companies], or
(b) it appears to the designated body that a competent authority which oversees or regulates the registered third country auditor considers that the registered third country auditor—
    (i) is not a fit and proper person to conduct audits in the country in which the authority is established, or
    (ii) is not eligible to conduct audits of the accounts of bodies corporate incorporated or formed under the law of that country.

NOTES

Para (3): words in square brackets in sub-para (a)(ii) substituted by the Statutory Auditors and Third Country Auditors (Amendment) (EU Exit) Regulations 2019, SI 2019/177, regs 58, 62, as from IP completion day (as defined in the European Union (Withdrawal Agreement) Act 2020, s 39) (for transitional provisions, see Sch 4 to the 2019 Regulations at **[12.88]**).

13–17 *(Reg 13 amended the commencement provisions of the Companies Act 2006 (Transfer of Audit Working Papers to Third Countries) Regulations 2010, SI 2010/2537 (the effect of this being to delay the coming into force of amendments to ss 1253D(2), 1253DE(1) and 1253E(8) of the Companies Act 2006) and was revoked by the Statutory Auditors and Third Country Auditors Regulations 2016, SI 2016/649, reg 20(1), (3), as from 17 June 2016; regs 14–17 amend ss 1242, 1253 of, and Schs, 10, 12 to, the 2006 Act.)*

SCHEDULE
REVOCATION OF REGULATIONS

(This Schedule revokes the Statutory Auditors and Third Country Auditors Regulations 2007, SI 2007/3494, regs 29, 34–40; the Statutory Auditors and Third Country Auditors (Amendment) Regulations 2008, SI 2008/499; the Statutory Auditors and Third Country Auditors (Amendment) (No 2) Regulations 2008, SI 2008/2639; the Statutory Auditors and Third Country Auditors (Amendment) Regulations 2009, SI 2009/2798; and the Statutory Auditors and Third Country Auditors (Amendment) Regulations 2011, SI 2011/1856, reg 4(1), (7).)

COMPANIES (RECEIPT OF ACCOUNTS AND REPORTS) REGULATIONS 2013

(SI 2013/1973)

NOTES

Made: 6 August 2013.

Authority: Companies Act 2006, s 426(1), (3).

Commencement: 1 October 2013.

For a summary of all Orders and Regulations made under the Companies Act 2006, see Appendix 4 at **[A4]**.

These Regulations are reproduced as amended by: the Accounts and Reports (Amendment) (EU Exit) Regulations 2019, SI 2019/145.

ARRANGEMENT OF REGULATIONS

[4.494]

1 Citation and commencement

(1) These Regulations may be cited as the Companies (Receipt of Accounts and Reports) Regulations 2013.

(2) These Regulations come into force on 1st October 2013 and apply in relation to annual accounts and reports prepared in respect of a company's financial year ending on or after 30th September 2013.

[4.495]

2 Interpretation

In these Regulations, unless otherwise stated—

"the 2006 Act" means the Companies Act 2006;

"full accounts and reports" means, in relation to a company, the annual accounts and reports, copies of which the company is required to send to the persons specified in section 423(1) of the 2006 Act.

[4.496]

3 Revocation and transitional provision

(1) The Companies (Summary Financial Statement) Regulations 2008 are revoked.

(2) A notification to the company under regulation 5(2) which is in force immediately before 1st October 2013 and the effect of a failure to respond before that date to an opportunity to elect to receive copies of the full accounts and reports under regulation 5(3) of the Companies (Summary Financial Statement) Regulations 2008 are treated on and after that date as if they were a notification or failure to respond under the provisions of regulation 6(2) and 6(3) of these Regulations.

[4.497]

4 Persons to whom a company may send strategic report with supplementary material

(1) Subject to these Regulations, a company may send a copy of its strategic report with supplementary material instead of a copy of its full accounts and reports to—

(a) a person specified in section 423(1) of the Companies Act 2006 (duty to circulate copies of annual accounts and reports); and

(b) a person nominated to enjoy information rights under section 146 of the Companies Act 2006 (traded companies: nomination of persons to enjoy information rights).

NOTES

This regulation is reproduced as it appears in the Queen's printer's copy; ie, there is no paragraph (2).

[4.498]

5 Cases in which sending of strategic report with supplementary material prohibited

(1) In the following cases a company may not send a copy of its strategic report with supplementary material to a person specified in regulation 4—

(a) in the case of any such person, where it is prohibited from doing so by any relevant provision of its constitution;

(b) in the case of any such person who is the holder of a debenture, where it is prohibited from doing so by a relevant provision in any instrument constituting or otherwise governing any of the company's debentures of which that person is a holder; or

(c) in the case of any such person (whether or not the holder of a debenture) where it is prohibited from sending a summary financial statement to any such person by any relevant provision of its constitution.

(2) In the following cases a company may not send a copy of its strategic report with supplementary material to a person specified in regulation 4 in relation to any financial year—

(a) where, in relation to that year, no auditor's report has been made in respect of the annual accounts of the company, or the strategic report, or the directors' report, or the auditable part of the directors' remuneration report, where relevant, under sections 495 (auditor's report on company's annual accounts), 496 (auditor's report on strategic report and directors' report) and 497 (auditor's report on auditable part of directors' remuneration report) of the 2006 Act respectively;

(b) where the period for filing accounts and reports for that year under section 442 of the 2006 Act (period for filing accounts) has expired;

(c) where the strategic report in respect of that financial year has not been approved by the board of directors and has not been signed on behalf of the board by a director of the company.

(3) For the purposes of paragraph (l) any provision (however expressed) which requires copies of the full accounts and reports to be sent to a person specified in regulation 4, or which forbids the sending of a copy of the strategic report with supplementary material under section 426 of the 2006 Act (option to provide strategic report with supplementary material), is a relevant provision.

[4.499]

6 Ascertainment of the wishes of a person specified in regulation 4

(1) A company may not send a copy of the strategic report with supplementary material to a person specified in regulation 4 unless the company has ascertained that the person does not wish to receive copies of its full accounts and reports, and paragraphs (2) and (3) apply for the ascertainment of whether or not such a person wishes to receive copies of the full accounts and reports for a financial year.

(2) Where a person specified in regulation 4 has expressly notified the company either that the person wishes to receive copies of the full accounts and reports or that the person wishes, instead of copies of those documents, to receive a copy of the strategic report with supplementary material, the company must send copies of the full accounts and reports or strategic report with supplementary material, as appropriate, to that person in respect of the financial years to which the notification applies.

(3) Where there has been no such express notification to the company by such a person, that person may be taken to have elected to receive a strategic report with supplementary material if the person fails to respond to an opportunity to elect to receive copies of the full accounts and reports given to the person either—

(a) by a consultation notice under regulation 7, or

(b) as part of a relevant consultation of that person's wishes by the company under regulation 8.

(4) For the purposes of paragraph (2) a notification has effect in relation to a financial year if it relates to that year (whether or not it has been given at the invitation of the company) and if it has been received by the company not later than 28 days before the first date on which copies of the full accounts and reports for that year are sent to the persons specified in regulation 4 in accordance with section 423 of the 2006 Act.

[4.500]

7 Consultation by notice

(1) A consultation notice under this regulation is notice given by a company to a person specified in regulation 4 which—

(a) states that for the future, so long as the person is a person so specified, the person will be sent a copy of the strategic report with supplementary material for each financial year instead of a copy of the company's full accounts and reports, unless the person notifies the company that the person wishes to receive full accounts and reports;

(b) states that the card or form accompanying the notice in accordance with regulation 9(3) must be returned by a date specified in the notice, being a date at least 21 days after service of the notice and not less than 28 days before the first date on which copies of the full accounts and reports for the next financial year for which that person is entitled to receive them are sent out to persons specified in regulation 4 in accordance with section 423 of the 2006 Act;

(c) includes a statement in a prominent position to the effect that the strategic report and supplementary material will not contain sufficient information to allow as full an understanding of the results and state of affairs of the company or group as would be provided by the full annual accounts and reports and that persons specified in regulation 4 requiring more detailed information have the right to obtain, free of charge, a copy of the company's last full accounts and reports.

NOTES

This regulation is reproduced as it appears in the Queen's printer's copy; ie, there is no paragraph (2).

[4.501]

8 Relevant consultation

(1) A company may conduct a relevant consultation to ascertain the wishes of a person specified in regulation 4.

(2) For the purposes of this regulation, a relevant consultation of the wishes of such a person is a notice given to that person which—

(a) states that for the future, so long as the person is a person specified in regulation 4, the person will be sent a strategic report with supplementary material instead of the full accounts and reports of the company, unless the person notifies the company that the person wishes to continue to receive full accounts and reports;

(b) accompanies a copy of the full accounts and reports; and

(c) accompanies a copy of a strategic report with supplementary material, with respect to the financial year covered by those full accounts and reports and which is identified in the notice as an example of the documents which that person will receive for the future, so long as the person is a person specified in regulation 4, unless the person notifies the company to the contrary.

[4.502]

9 Supplementary provisions

(1) The company communications provisions of the 2006 Act apply to any notice or other communication required or authorised to be sent to or by the company by any provision in these Regulations.

(2) This regulation and regulations 6, 7 and 8 apply to a person who is entitled, whether conditionally or unconditionally, to become a person specified in section 423(l) of the 2006 Act in relation to the company, but who has not yet become such a person, as they apply to a person specified in regulation 4.

(3) Subject to paragraph (4), a notice given under regulations 7 or 8 must be accompanied by a card or form—

(a) in respect of which, in the case of a card or form sent by post, any postage necessary for its return to the company has been, or will be, paid by the company, and

(b) which is so worded as to enable a person specified in regulation 4, by marking a box and returning the card or form, to notify the company that the person wishes to receive full accounts and reports for the next financial year for which the person is entitled to receive them as such a person and for all future financial years after that.

(4) The company need not pay the postage in respect of the return of the card or form in the following circumstances—

(a) if the address of a member to which notices are sent in accordance with the company's constitution is not within [the United Kingdom or] an EEA State,

(b) if the address of a debenture holder to which notices are sent in accordance with the terms of any instrument constituting or otherwise governing the debentures of which the person is a holder is not within [the United Kingdom or] an EEA State, or

(c) if the address of a person to whom paragraph (2) applies to which notices are sent, in accordance with the contractual provisions under which the person has a right (conditionally or unconditionally) to become a person specified in section 423(l) of the 2006 Act, is not within [the United Kingdom or] an EEA State.

NOTES

Para (4): words in square brackets inserted by the Accounts and Reports (Amendment) (EU Exit) Regulations 2019, SI 2019/145, reg 6, Sch 3, para 34, as from IP completion day (as defined in the European Union (Withdrawal Agreement) Act 2020, s 39).

COMPANY, LIMITED LIABILITY PARTNERSHIP AND BUSINESS NAMES (SENSITIVE WORDS AND EXPRESSIONS) REGULATIONS 2014

(SI 2014/3140)

NOTES

Made: 26 November 2014.

Authority: Companies Act 2006, ss 55(1), 56(1)(b), 1194(1), 1195(1)(b), 1292(1).

Commencement: 31 January 2015.

For a summary of all Orders and Regulations made under the Companies Act 2006, see Appendix 4 at **[A4]**.

These Regulations are reproduced as amended by: the Secretaries of State for Business, Energy and Industrial Strategy, for International Trade and for Exiting the European Union and the Transfer of Functions (Education and Skills) Order 2016, SI 2016/992; the Secretaries of State for Health and Social Care and for Housing, Communities and Local Government and Transfer of Functions (Commonhold Land) Order 2018, SI 2018/378.

ARRANGEMENT OF REGULATIONS

SCHEDULES

[4.503]

1 Citation and commencement

These Regulations may be cited as the Company, Limited Liability Partnership and Business Names (Sensitive Words and Expressions) Regulations 2014 and come into force on 31st January 2015.

[4.504]

2 Interpretation

(1) In these Regulations "the 2006 Act" means the Companies Act 2006.

(2) Any reference in these Regulations to section 55 or 88 of the 2006 Act includes a reference to that section as applied by regulation 8 or 17 of the Limited Liability Partnerships (Application of Companies Act 2006) Regulations 2009.

[4.505]

3 Specified words and expressions to which sections 55 and 1194 of the 2006 Act apply

The following words and expressions are specified for the purposes of sections 55(1) and 1194(1) of the 2006 Act—

(a) the words and expressions set out in Part 1 of Schedule 1;

(b) the plural and possessive forms of those words and expressions, and, where relevant, the feminine form; and

(c) in the case of the words and expressions set out in Part 1 of Schedule 1 which are marked with an asterisk, the grammatically mutated forms of those words and expressions.

[4.506]

4 Specified words and expressions to which section 55 of the 2006 Act applies

The following words and expressions are specified for the purposes of section 55(1) of the 2006 Act—

(a) the words and expressions set out in Part 2 of Schedule 1;

(b) the plural and possessive forms of those words and expressions, and, where relevant, the feminine form; and

(c) in the case of the words and expressions set out in Part 2 of Schedule 1 which are marked with an asterisk, the grammatically mutated forms of those words and expressions.

[4.507]

5 Applications where situation of registered office or principal place of business is irrelevant

In connection with an application for the approval of the Secretary of State under section 55 or 1194 of the 2006 Act in relation to a name that includes a word or expression specified in column (1) of Part 1 of Schedule 2, the applicant must seek the view of the Government department or other body set out opposite that word or expression in column (2) of Part 1 of Schedule 2.

[4.508]

6 Applications where situation of registered office or principal place of business is relevant

In connection with an application for the approval of the Secretary of State under section 55 or 1194 of the 2006 Act in relation to a name that includes a word or expression specified in column (1) of Part 2 of Schedule 2, the applicant must seek the view of a Government department or other body as follows—

(a) in the case of—

  (i) a company or limited liability partnership that has already been registered, whose registered office is situated in England and Wales;

  (ii) a proposed company or limited liability partnership that has not yet been registered under the 2006 Act, whose registered office is to be situated in England and Wales;

  (iii) a business, whose principal place of business is or is to be situated in England; and

  (iv) an overseas company (see section 1044 of the 2006 Act),

  the Government department or other body set out in column (2) of Part 2 of Schedule 2 opposite that word or expression;

(b) in the case of—

  (i) a company or limited liability partnership that has already been registered, that is a Welsh company or Welsh LLP (see section 88 of the 2006 Act);

  (ii) a proposed company or limited liability partnership that has not yet been registered, that is to be a Welsh company or Welsh LLP; and

  (iii) a business, whose principal place of business is or is to be situated in Wales,

  the Government department or other body set out in column (3) of Part 2 of Schedule 2 opposite that word or expression;

(c) in the case of—

  (i) a company or limited liability partnership that has already been registered, whose registered office is situated in Scotland;

  (ii) a proposed company or limited liability partnership that has not yet been registered, whose registered office is to be situated in Scotland; and

  (iii) a business, whose principal place of business is or is to be situated in Scotland,

  the Government department or other body set out in column (4) of Part 2 of Schedule 2 opposite that word or expression; and

(d) in the case of—

  (i) a company or limited liability partnership that has already been registered, whose registered office is situated in Northern Ireland;

  (ii) a proposed company or limited liability partnership that has not yet been registered, whose registered office is to be situated in Northern Ireland; and

  (iii) a business, whose principal place of business is or is to be situated in Northern Ireland,

  the Government department or other body set out in column (5) of Part 2 of Schedule 2 opposite that word or expression.

[4.509]

7 Revocation

The Company, Limited Liability Partnership and Business Names (Sensitive Words and Expressions) Regulations 2009 are revoked.

SCHEDULES

SCHEDULE 1
SPECIFIED WORDS AND EXPRESSIONS

Regulations 3 and 4

PART 1 WORDS AND EXPRESSIONS SPECIFIED FOR THE PURPOSES OF SECTIONS 55(1) AND 1194(1) OF THE 2006 ACT

[4.510]

Accredit
Accreditation
Accredited
Accrediting
Adjudicator
Association
Assurance
Assurer
Audit office
Auditor General
*Banc
Bank
Banking
Benevolent
*Breatannach
*Breatainn
*Brenhinol
*Brenin
*Brenhiniaeth
Britain
British
Chamber of commerce
Charitable
Charity
Charter
Chartered
Child maintenance
Child support
*Coimisean
*Comhairle
*Comisiwn
Commission
Co-operative
Council
*Cyngor
Dental
Dentistry
*Diùc
*Dug
Duke
Ei Fawrhydi
England
English
Federation
Friendly Society
Foundation
Fund
Government
*Gwasanaeth iechyd
Health centre
Health service
Health visitor
His Majesty
HPSS
HSC
Inspectorate
Institute
Institution
Insurance
Insurer
Judicial appointment
King
Licensing
*Llywodraeth
Medical centre
Midwife
Midwifery
*Mòrachd
Mutual
NHS
Northern Ireland
Northern Irish
Nurse
Nursing
Oifis sgrùdaidh
*Oilthigh
Ombudsman
*Ombwdsmon
*Parlamaid
Parliament
Parliamentarian
Parliamentary
Patent
Patentee
Police
Polytechnic
Post office
*Prifysgol
Prince

*Prionnsa
*Prydain
*Prydeinig
Queen
Reassurance
Reassurer
Registrar
Regulator
Reinsurance
Reinsurer
*Riaghaltas
*Rìgh
Rìoghachd Aonaichte
Rìoghail
Rìoghalachd
Royal
Royalty
Scotland
Scottish
Senedd
Sheffield
Siambr fasnach
Social service
Society
Special school
Standards
Stock exchange
Swyddfa archwilio
*Teyrnas Gyfunol
*Teyrnas Unedig
Trade union
Tribunal
Trust
*Tywysog
Underwrite
Underwriting
University
Wales
Welsh
Windsor

PART 2 WORDS AND EXPRESSIONS SPECIFIED FOR THE PURPOSES OF SECTION 55(1) OF THE 2006 ACT

[4.511]

Alba
Albannach
Na h-Alba
*Cymru
*Cymraeg
*Cymreig

SCHEDULE 2
LIST OF GOVERNMENT DEPARTMENTS AND OTHER BODIES WHOSE VIEWS MUST BE SOUGHT

Regulations 5 and 6

PART 1 APPLICATIONS WHERE SITUATION OF REGISTERED OFFICE OR PRINCIPAL PLACE OF BUSINESS IS IRRELEVANT

[4.512]

Column (1)	*Column (2)*
Word or expression specified under regulation 3	Specified Government department or other body whose view must be sought
Accredit	[Department for Business, Energy and Industrial Strategy]
Accreditation	[Department for Business, Energy and Industrial Strategy]
Accredited	[Department for Business, Energy and Industrial Strategy]
Accrediting	[Department for Business, Energy and Industrial Strategy]
Assurance	Financial Conduct Authority
Assurer	Financial Conduct Authority
Banc	Financial Conduct Authority
Bank	Financial Conduct Authority
Banking	Financial Conduct Authority
Brenhinol	The Welsh Assembly Government
Brenin	The Welsh Assembly Government
Brenhiniaeth	The Welsh Assembly Government
Child maintenance	Department for Work and Pensions
Child support	Department for Work and Pensions
Dental	General Dental Council
Dentistry	General Dental Council

Part 4 CA 2006 SIs

Diùc	The Scottish Government
Dug	The Welsh Assembly Government
Ei Fawrhydi	The Welsh Assembly Government
Friendly Society	Financial Conduct Authority
Fund	Financial Conduct Authority
Gwasanaeth iechyd	The Welsh Assembly Government
Health visitor	Nursing & Midwifery Council
HPSS	Department of Health, Social Services and Public Safety
HSC	Department of Health, Social Services and Public Safety
Insurance	Financial Conduct Authority
Insurer	Financial Conduct Authority
Judicial appointment	Ministry of Justice
Llywodraeth	The Welsh Assembly Government
Medical centre	Department of Health, Social Services and Public Safety
Midwife	Nursing & Midwifery Council
Midwifery	Nursing & Midwifery Council
Mòrachd	The Scottish Government
Mutual	Financial Conduct Authority
NHS	Department of Health [and Social Care]
Nurse	Nursing & Midwifery Council
Nursing	Nursing & Midwifery Council
Oifis sgrùdaidh	Audit Scotland
Oilthigh	The Scottish Government
Parlamaid	The Scottish Parliamentary Corporate Body
Parliament	The Corporate Officer of the House of Lords and The Corporate Officer of the House of Commons
Parliamentarian	The Corporate Officer of the House of Lords and The Corporate Officer of the House of Commons
Parliamentary	The Corporate Officer of the House of Lords and The Corporate Officer of the House of Commons
Patent	The Patent Office
Patentee	The Patent Office
Polytechnic	[Department for Education]
Prifysgol	The Welsh Assembly Government
Prionnsa	The Scottish Government
Reassurance	Financial Conduct Authority
Reassurer	Financial Conduct Authority
Reinsurance	Financial Conduct Authority
Reinsurer	Financial Conduct Authority
Riaghaltas	The Scottish Government
Rìgh	The Scottish Government
Rìoghail	The Scottish Government
Rìoghalachd	The Scottish Government
Senedd	The National Assembly for Wales
Sheffield	The Company of Cutlers in Hallamshire
Swyddfa archwilio	Auditor General for Wales
Tywysog	The Welsh Assembly Government
Underwrite	Financial Conduct Authority
Underwriting	Financial Conduct Authority

NOTES

Words in square brackets in the entry "NHS" inserted by the Secretaries of State for Health and Social Care and for Housing, Communities and Local Government and Transfer of Functions (Commonhold Land) Order 2018, SI 2018/378, art 15, Schedule, Pt 2, para 20(bb)(i), as from 11 April 2018.

All other words in square brackets were substituted by the Secretaries of State for Business, Energy and Industrial Strategy, for International Trade and for Exiting the European Union and the Transfer of Functions (Education and Skills) Order 2016, SI 2016/992, art 14, Schedule, Part 2, para 51(1), (2), as from 9 November 2016.

See further, in relation to the renaming of the Welsh Assembly Government as the Welsh Government, the Wales Act 2014, s 4(4)(a). See also, in relation to the renaming of the National Assembly for Wales as the Senedd Cymru or the Welsh

Parliament, the Senedd and Elections (Wales) Act 2020, s 2 (with effect from 6 May 2020).

PART 2 APPLICATIONS WHERE SITUATION OF REGISTERED OFFICE OR PRINCIPAL PLACE OF BUSINESS IS RELEVANT

[4.513]

Column (1)	*Column (2)*	*Column (3)*	*Column (4)*	*Column (5)*
Word or expression specified under regulation 3	*Specified Government department or other body whose view must be sought*			
	under regulation 6(a)	*under regulation 6(b)*	*under regulation 6(c)*	*under regulation 6(d)*
Audit office	Comptroller & Auditor General	Auditor General for Wales	Audit Scotland	Northern Ireland Audit Office
Charitable Charity	The Charity Commission	The Charity Commission	Office of the Scottish Charity Regulator	The Charity Commission
Duke His Majesty King Prince Queen Royal Royalty Windsor	Ministry of Justice	The Welsh Assembly Government	The Scottish Government	Ministry of Justice
Health centre Health service	Department of Health [and Social Care]	The Welsh Assembly Government	The Scottish Government	Department of Health, Social Services and Public Safety
Police	The Home Office	The Home Office	The Scottish Government	Department of Justice in Northern Ireland
Special school	Department for Education	The Welsh Assembly Government	The Scottish Government	Department of Education
University	[Department for Education]	The Welsh Assembly Government	The Scottish Government	Department for Employment and Learning

NOTES

Words in square brackets in the entries "Health centre" and "Health service" inserted by the Secretaries of State for Health and Social Care and for Housing, Communities and Local Government and Transfer of Functions (Commonhold Land) Order 2018, SI 2018/378, art 15, Schedule, Pt 2, para 20(bb)(ii), as from 11 April 2018.

Words in square brackets in the entry "University" substituted by the Secretaries of State for Business, Energy and Industrial Strategy, for International Trade and for Exiting the European Union and the Transfer of Functions (Education and Skills) Order 2016, SI 2016/992, art 14, Schedule, Part 2, para 51(1), (3), as from 9 November 2016.

See further, in relation to the renaming of the Welsh Assembly Government as the Welsh Government, the Wales Act 2014, s 4(4)(a). See also, in relation to the renaming of the National Assembly for Wales as the Senedd Cymru or the Welsh Parliament, the Senedd and Elections (Wales) Act 2020, s 2 (with effect from 6 May 2020).

COMPANY, LIMITED LIABILITY PARTNERSHIP AND BUSINESS (NAMES AND TRADING DISCLOSURES) REGULATIONS 2015

(SI 2015/17)

NOTES

Made: 7 January 2015.

Authority: Companies Act 2006, ss 54(1)(c), 56(1)(a), (5), 57(1)(a), (2), (5), 60(1)(b), 65(1), (2), (4), 66(2)–(4), (6), 82, 84, 1193(1)(c), 1195(1)(a), (5), 1197(1)–(3), 1292(1), (2), 1294, 1296.

Commencement: 31 January 2015.

For a summary of all Orders and Regulations made under the Companies Act 2006, see Appendix 4 at **[A4]**.

These Regulations are reproduced as amended by: the Bank of England and Financial Services (Consequential Amendments) Regulations 2017, SI 2017/80; the Risk Transformation Regulations 2017, SI 2017/1212; the European Economic Interest Grouping (Amendment) (EU Exit) Regulations 2018, SI 2018/1299; the Financial Guidance and Claims Act 2018 (Naming and Consequential Amendments) Regulations 2019, SI 2019/383.

ARRANGEMENT OF REGULATIONS

PART 1
INTRODUCTORY

PART 2
COMPANY NAMES

PART 3
LIMITED LIABILITY PARTNERSHIP NAMES

PART 4
OVERSEAS COMPANY NAMES

PART 5
BUSINESS NAMES

PART 6
TRADING DISCLOSURES

PART 7
MISCELLANEOUS

SCHEDULES

PART 1 INTRODUCTORY

[4.514]

1 Citation, commencement and interpretation

(1) These Regulations may be cited as the Company, Limited Liability Partnership and Business (Names and Trading Disclosures) Regulations 2015 and come into force on 31st January 2015.

(2) In these Regulations, "the Act" means the Companies Act 2006.

PART 2 COMPANY NAMES

[4.515]
2 Permitted characters

(1) This regulation sets out the characters, signs, symbols (including accents and other diacritical marks) and punctuation that may be used in the name of a company registered under the Act ("the permitted characters").

(2) The following permitted characters may be used in any part of the name—

- (a) any character, character with an accent or other diacritical mark, sign or symbol set out in table 1 in Schedule 1;
- (b) 0, 1, 2, 3, 4, 5, 6, 7, 8 or 9;
- (c) full stop, comma, colon, semi-colon or hyphen; and
- (d) any other punctuation referred to in column 1 of table 2 in Schedule 1 but only in one of the forms set out opposite that punctuation in column 2 of that table.

(3) The signs and symbols set out in table 3 in Schedule 1 are permitted characters that may be used but not as one of the first three permitted characters of the name.

(4) The name must not consist of more than 160 permitted characters.

(5) For the purposes of computing the number of permitted characters in paragraph (4) of this regulation (but not in paragraph (3) of this regulation), any blank space between one permitted character and another in the name shall be counted as though it was a permitted character.

[4.516]
3 Exemption from requirement as to use of "limited"

(1) A private company limited by guarantee is exempt from section 59 of the Act (requirement to have name ending with "limited" or permitted alternative) so long as it meets the following two conditions.

(2) The first condition is that the objects of that company are the promotion or regulation of commerce, art, science, education, religion, charity or any profession, and anything incidental or conducive to any of those objects.

(3) The second condition is that the company's articles—

- (a) require its income to be applied in promoting its objects;
- (b) prohibit the payment of dividends, or any return of capital, to its members; and
- (c) require all the assets that would otherwise be available to its members generally to be transferred on its winding up either—
  - (i) to another body with objects similar to its own; or
  - (ii) to another body the objects of which are the promotion of charity and anything incidental or conducive thereto,

(whether or not the body is a member of the company).

[4.517]
4 Inappropriate indication of company type or legal form: generally applicable provisions

(1) A company must not be registered under the Act by a name that includes, otherwise than at the end of the name, an expression or abbreviation specified in inverted commas in paragraph 3(a) to (f) of Schedule 2 (or any expression or abbreviation specified as similar).

(2) A company must not be registered under the Act by a name that includes in any part of the name an expression or abbreviation specified in inverted commas in paragraph 3(g) or (h) of Schedule 2 (or any expression or abbreviation specified as similar) unless that company is a RTE company within the meaning of section 4A of the Leasehold Reform, Housing and Urban Development Act 1993.

(3) A company must not be registered under the Act by a name that includes in any part of the name an expression or abbreviation specified in inverted commas in paragraph 3(i) or (j) of Schedule 2 (or any expression or abbreviation specified as similar) unless that company is a RTM company within the meaning of section 73 of the Commonhold and Leasehold Reform Act 2002.

(4) A company must not be registered under the Act by a name that includes in any part of the name an expression or abbreviation specified in inverted commas in paragraph 3(k) to (x) of Schedule 2 (or any expression or abbreviation specified as similar).

(5) A company must not be registered under the Act by a name that includes immediately before an expression or abbreviation specified in inverted commas in paragraph 3(a) to (j) of Schedule 2 an abbreviation specified in inverted commas in paragraph 3(y) of that Schedule (or any abbreviation specified as similar).

(6) Paragraph (1) is subject to regulations 5(b) and 6(b).

[4.518]
5 Inappropriate indication of company type or legal form: company exempt from requirement to have name ending in "limited"

A company which is exempt from section 59 of the Act (requirement to have name ending with "limited" or permitted alternative) under section 60 of the Act must not be registered under the Act by a name that concludes with—

- (a) a word specified in inverted commas in paragraph 1(c) or (d) of Schedule 2 (or any word specified as similar); or
- (b) an expression or abbreviation specified in inverted commas in paragraph 3(a) to (f) or (y) of Schedule 2 (or any expression or abbreviation specified as similar).

[4.519]
6 Inappropriate indication of company type or legal form: unlimited company

An unlimited company must not be registered under the Act by a name that concludes with—

- (a) a word or abbreviation specified in inverted commas in paragraph 1(a) or (b) of Schedule 2 (or any word or abbreviation specified as similar); or

(b) an expression or abbreviation specified in inverted commas in paragraph 3(a) to (f) or (y) of Schedule 2 (or any expression or abbreviation specified as similar).

[4.520]

7 Name not to be the same as another in the registrar's index of company names

For the purposes of section 66 of the Act (determining whether a name to be registered under the Act is the same as another name appearing in the registrar's index of company names) Schedule 3 has effect for setting out—

(a) the matters that are to be disregarded; and

(b) the words, expressions, signs and symbols that are to be regarded as the same.

[4.521]

8 Consent to registration of a name which is the same as another in the registrar's index of company names

(1) A company may be registered under the Act by a proposed same name if the conditions in paragraph (2) are met.

(2) The conditions are—

(a) the company or other body whose name already appears in the registrar's index of company names ("Body X") consents to the proposed same name being the name of a company ("Company Y");

(b) Company Y forms, or is to form, part of the same group as Body X; and

(c) Company Y provides to the registrar a copy of a statement made by Body X indicating—

(i) the consent of Body X as referred to in sub-paragraph (a); and

(ii) that Company Y forms, or is to form, part of the same group as Body X.

(3) If the proposed same name is to be taken by a company which has not yet been incorporated, the copy of such statement must be provided to the registrar instead by the person who delivers to the registrar the application for registration of the company (and the reference in paragraph (1) to the conditions in paragraph (2) shall be read accordingly).

(4) The registrar may accept the statement referred to in paragraph (2)(c) as sufficient evidence that the conditions referred to in paragraph (2)(a) and (b) have been met.

(5) If the consent referred to in paragraph (2)(a) is given by Body X, a subsequent withdrawal of that consent does not affect the registration of Company Y by that proposed same name.

(6) In this regulation—

(a) "group" has the meaning given in section 474(1) of the Act; and

(b) "proposed same name" means a name which is, due to the application of regulation 8 and Schedule 3, considered the same as a name appearing in the registrar's index of company names and differs from that name appearing in the index by any of the matters set out in inverted commas in paragraph 5 of Schedule 3.

[4.522]

9 Names with connection to Public Authorities

(1) Each of the persons and bodies set out in column (1) of Schedule 4 is specified for the purposes of section 54 of the Act.

(2) In connection with an application for the approval of the Secretary of State under section 54 of the Act in relation to a name that would be likely to give the impression of a connection with a public authority set out in column (1) of Schedule 4 the applicant must seek the view of the Government department or other body set out opposite that public authority in column (2) of Schedule 4.

[4.523]

10 Interpretation

In this Part—

(a) "expression or abbreviation specified as similar" has the meaning given in paragraph 4 of Schedule 2 and "abbreviation specified as similar" has the meaning that would be given to it in that paragraph if that paragraph made no reference to "expressions";

(b) "permitted characters" has the meaning given in regulation 2(1);

(c) "word or abbreviation specified as similar" has the meaning given in paragraph 2 of Schedule 2; and

(d) "word specified as similar" has the meaning given in paragraph 2 of Schedule 2.

PART 3 LIMITED LIABILITY PARTNERSHIP NAMES

[4.524]

11 Application to Limited Liability Partnerships

(1) In regulation 9 of these Regulations, any reference to section 54 of the Act includes a reference to that section as applied by regulation 8 of the Limited Liability Partnerships (Application of Companies Act 2006) Regulations 2009.

(2) The Limited Liability Partnerships (Application of Companies Act 2006) Regulations 2009 are amended by Schedule 5.

PART 4 OVERSEAS COMPANY NAMES

[4.525]

12 Interpretation and permitted characters

Regulations 2 and 10 apply to the name of an overseas company which is registered by that company under Part 34 of the Act (overseas companies) as they apply to the name of a company formed and registered under the Act.

[4.526]

13 Inappropriate indication of company type or legal form

(1) An overseas company must not be registered under the Act by a name that concludes with a word or abbreviation specified in inverted commas in paragraph 1(a) or (b) of Schedule 2 (or any word or abbreviation specified as similar) unless the liability of the members of the company is limited by its constitution.

(2) An overseas company must not be registered under the Act by a name that concludes with a word specified in inverted commas in paragraph 1(c) or (d) of Schedule 2 (or any word specified as similar) unless the liability of the members of the company is not limited by its constitution.

(3) An overseas company must not be registered under the Act by a name that includes in any part of the name an expression or abbreviation specified in inverted commas in paragraph 3 of Schedule 2 (or any expression or abbreviation specified as similar).

[4.527]
14 Name not to be the same as another in the registrar's index of company names

Regulation 7 applies to the name of an overseas company which is registered by that company under Part 34 of the Act as it applies to the name of a company formed and registered under the Act.

[4.528]
15 Consent to registration of a name which is the same as another in the registrar's index of company names

(1) Regulation 8 applies to the proposed same name of an overseas company as it applies to the proposed same name of a company formed and registered under the Act.

(2) In this regulation "proposed same name" has the same meaning as in regulation 8.

PART 5 BUSINESS NAMES

[4.529]
16 "Limited" and permitted alternatives

(1) A person must not carry on business in the United Kingdom under a name that concludes with any word or abbreviation set out in inverted commas in paragraph 1(a) or (b) of Schedule 2 unless that person is—

(a) a company or an overseas company registered in the United Kingdom by that name;
(b) an overseas company incorporated with that name;
(c) a society registered under the Co-operative and Community Benefit Societies Act 2014 or the Industrial and Provident Societies Act (Northern Ireland) 1969 by that name;
(d) an incorporated friendly society (as defined in section 116 of the Friendly Societies Act 1992) which has that name; . . .
(e) a company to which section 1040 of the Act (companies authorised to register under the Companies Act 2006) applies which has that name; [or]
[(f) a company registered under Part 4 of the Risk Transformation Regulations 2017 with that name].

(2) A person must not carry on business in the United Kingdom under a name that concludes with any word or abbreviation specified as similar to any word or abbreviation set out in inverted commas in paragraph 1(a) or (b) of Schedule 2.

NOTES

Para (1): the word omitted from sub-para (d) was revoked, the word in square brackets in sub-para (e) was inserted, and sub-para (f) was added, by the Risk Transformation Regulations 2017, SI 2017/1212, reg 190, Sch 4, para 7(a), as from 8 December 2017.

[4.530]
17 Other indications of legal form

(1) A person must not carry on business in the United Kingdom under a name that includes any expression or abbreviation set out in inverted commas in paragraph 3 of Schedule 2 unless that person is such a company, partnership, grouping or organisation as is indicated in that expression or abbreviation.

(2) A person must not carry on business in the United Kingdom under a name that includes any expression or abbreviation specified as similar to any expression or abbreviation set out in inverted commas in paragraph 3 of Schedule 2.

[4.531]
18 Names with connection to Public Authorities

(1) Each of the persons and bodies set out in column (1) of Schedule 4 is specified for the purposes of section 1193 of the Act.

(2) In connection with an application for the approval of the Secretary of State under section 1193 of the Act in relation to a name that would be likely to give the impression of a connection with a public authority set out in column (1) of Schedule 4 the applicant must seek the view of the Government department or other body set out opposite that public authority in column (2) of Schedule 4.

[4.532]
19 Savings and Transitional provisions

(1) Regulation 17 does not apply to the carrying on of a business under a name by a person who—

(a) carried on that business under that name immediately before these Regulations came into force; and
(b) continues to carry it on under that name,

if it was lawful for the business to be carried on under that name immediately before these Regulations came into force.

(2) Regulation 17 does not apply to the carrying on of a business under a name by a person to whom the business is transferred on or after the date on which these Regulations came into force—

(a) where that person continues to carry on the business under that name; and
(b) where it was lawful for the business to be carried on under that name immediately before the transfer,

during the period of 12 months beginning with the date of the transfer.

(3) Regulation 18 does not apply to the carrying on of a business by a person who—

(a) carried on the business immediately before the date on which these Regulations came into force, and

(b) continues to carry it on under the name that immediately before that date was its lawful business name.

(4) Regulation 18 does not apply in relation to the carrying on of the business under that name during the period of twelve months beginning with the date of the transfer where—

(a) a business is transferred to a person on or after the date on which these Regulations came into force, and

(b) that person carries on the business under the name that was its lawful business name immediately before the transfer,

(5) In this regulation "lawful business name", in relation to a business, means a name under which the business was carried on without contravening the provisions of Chapter 1 of Part 41 of the Act.

PART 6 TRADING DISCLOSURES

[4.533]

20 Legibility of displays and disclosures

Any display or disclosure of information required by this Part must be in characters that can be read with the naked eye.

[4.534]

21 Requirement to display registered name at registered office and inspection place

(1) A company shall display its registered name at—

(a) its registered office; and

(b) any inspection place.

(2) But paragraph (1) does not apply to any company which has at all times since its incorporation been dormant.

(3) Paragraph (1) shall also not apply to the registered office or an inspection place of a company where—

(a) in respect of that company, a liquidator, administrator or administrative receiver has been appointed; and

(b) the registered office or inspection place is also a place of business of that liquidator, administrator or administrative receiver.

[4.535]

22 Requirement to display registered name at other business locations

(1) This regulation applies to a location other than a company's registered office or any inspection place.

(2) A company shall display its registered name at any such location at which it carries on business.

(3) But paragraph (2) shall not apply to a location which is primarily used for living accommodation.

(4) Paragraph (2) shall also not apply to any location at which business is carried on by a company where—

(a) in respect of that company, a liquidator, administrator or administrative receiver has been appointed; and

(b) the location is also a place of business of that liquidator, administrator or administrative receiver.

(5) Paragraph (2) shall also not apply to any location at which business is carried on by a company of which every director who is an individual is a relevant director.

(6) In this regulation—

(a) "administrative receiver" has the meaning given—

(i) in England and Wales or Scotland, by section 251 of the Insolvency Act 1986, and

(ii) in Northern Ireland, by Article 5 of the Insolvency (Northern Ireland) Order 1989;

(b) "credit reference agency" has the meaning given in section 243(7) of the Act;

(c) "protected information" has the meaning given in section 240 of the Act; and

(d) "relevant director" means an individual in respect of whom the registrar is required by regulations made pursuant to section 243(4) of the Act to refrain from disclosing protected information to a credit reference agency.

[4.536]

23 Manner of display of registered name

(1) This regulation applies where a company is required to display its registered name at any office, place or location.

(2) Where that office, place or location is shared by no more than five companies, the registered name—

(a) shall be so positioned that it may be easily seen by any visitor to that office, place or location; and

(b) shall be displayed continuously.

(3) Where any such office, place or location is shared by six or more companies, each such company must ensure that either—

(a) its registered name is displayed for at least fifteen continuous seconds at least once every three minutes; or

(b) its registered name is available for inspection on a register by any visitor to that office, place or location.

[4.537]

24 Registered name to appear in communications

(1) Every company shall disclose its registered name on—

(a) its business letters, notices and other official publications;

(b) its bills of exchange, promissory notes, endorsements and order forms;

(c) cheques purporting to be signed by or on behalf of the company;

(d) orders for money, goods or services purporting to be signed by or on behalf of the company;

(e) its bills of parcels, invoices and other demands for payment, receipts and letters of credit;

(f) its applications for licences to carry on a trade or activity; and

(g) all other forms of its business correspondence and documentation.

(2) Every company shall disclose its registered name on its websites.

[4.538]

25 Further particulars to appear in business letters, order forms and websites

(1) Every company shall disclose the particulars set out in paragraph (2) on—

(a) its business letters;

(b) its order forms; and

(c) its websites.

(2) The particulars are—

(a) the part of the United Kingdom in which the company is registered;

(b) the company's registered number;

(c) the address of the company's registered office;

(d) in the case of a limited company exempt from the obligation to use the word "limited" as part of its registered name under section 60 of the Act, the fact that it is a limited company;

(e) in the case of a community interest company which is not a public company, the fact that it is a limited company; and

(f) in the case of an investment company within the meaning of section 833 of the Act, the fact that it is such a company.

(3) If, in the case of a company having a share capital, there is a disclosure as to the amount of share capital on—

(a) its business letters;

(b) its order forms; or

(c) its websites,

that disclosure must be as to paid up share capital.

[4.539]

26 Disclosure of names of directors

(1) Where a company's business letter includes the name of any director of that company, other than in the text or as a signatory, the letter must disclose the name of every director of that company.

(2) In paragraph (1), "name" has the following meanings—

(a) in the case of a director who is an individual, "name" has the meaning given in section 163(2) of the Act; and

(b) in the case of a director who is a body corporate or a firm that is a legal person under the law by which it is governed, "name" means corporate name or firm name.

[4.540]

27 Disclosures relating to registered office and inspection place

(1) A company shall disclose—

(a) the address of its registered office;

(b) any inspection place; and

(c) the type of company records which are kept at that office or place,

to any person it deals with in the course of business who makes a written request to the company for that information.

(2) The company shall send a written response to that person within five working days of the receipt of that request.

[4.541]

28 Offence

(1) Where a company fails, without reasonable excuse, to comply with any requirement in regulations 20 to 27, an offence is committed by—

(a) the company; and

(b) every officer of the company who is in default.

(2) A person guilty of an offence under paragraph (1) is liable on summary conviction to—

(a) a fine not exceeding level 3 on the standard scale; and

(b) for continued contravention, a daily default fine not exceeding one-tenth of level 3 on the standard scale.

(3) For the purposes of this regulation a shadow director is to be treated as an officer of the company.

[4.542]

29 Interpretation

In this Part—

(a) "company record" means—

(i) any register, index, accounting records, agreement, memorandum, minutes or other document required by the Companies Acts to be kept by a company; and

(ii) any register kept by a company of its debenture holders;

(b) "inspection place" means any location, other than a company's registered office, at which a company keeps available for inspection any company record which it is required under the Companies Acts to keep available for inspection;

(c) a reference to any type of document is a reference to a document of that type in hard copy, electronic or any other form; and

(d) in relation to a company, a reference to "its websites" includes a reference to any part of a website relating to that company which that company has caused or authorised to appear.

PART 7 MISCELLANEOUS

[4.543]

30 Revocations and Consequential Amendments

Schedule 6 (which contains revocations and consequential amendments) has effect.

SCHEDULES

SCHEDULE 1
CHARACTERS, SIGNS, SYMBOLS (INCLUDING ACCENTS AND OTHER DIACRITICAL MARKS) AND PUNCTUATION

Regulation 2

Table 1

[4.544]

Characters, signs and symbols				
A	À	Á	Â	Ã
Ä	Å	Ā	Ă	Ą
Ǻ	Æ	Ǽ	B	C
Ç	Ć	Ĉ	Ċ	Č
D	Þ	Ď	Đ	E
È	É	Ê	Ë	Ē
Ĕ	Ė	Ę	Ě	F
G	Ĝ	Ğ	Ġ	Ģ
H	Ĥ	Ħ	I	Ì
Í	Î	Ï	Ĩ	Ī
Ĭ	Į	İ	J	Ĵ
K	Ķ	L	Ĺ	Ļ
Ľ	Ŀ	Ł	M	N
Ñ	Ń	Ņ	Ň	Ŋ
O	Ò	Ó	Ô	Õ
Ö	Ø	Ō	Ŏ	Ő
Ǿ	Œ	P	Q	R
Ŕ	Ŗ	Ř	S	Ś
Ŝ	Ş	Š	T	Ţ
Ť	Ŧ	U	Ù	Ú
Û	Ü	Ũ	Ū	Ŭ
Ů	Ű	Ų	V	W
Ŵ	Ẁ	Ẃ	Ẅ	X
Y	Ỳ	Ý	Ŷ	Ÿ
Z	Ź	Ż	Ž	&
@	£	$	€	¥

Table 2	
Column 1 (type of punctuation)	*Column 2 (punctuation mark)*
Apostrophe	‘
	‘
	’
Bracket	(
	)
	[
	]
	{
	}
	<
	>
Exclamation mark	!
Guillemet	«
	»
Inverted comma	“
	”
	″
Question mark	?
Solidus	\
	/

Table 3: Signs and symbols
*
=
♯
%
+

SCHEDULE 2
SPECIFIED WORDS, EXPRESSIONS AND ABBREVIATIONS

Regulations 4 to 6, 10, 13, 16 and 17

[4.545]

1. The words and abbreviations specified are—

(a) "LIMITED" or (with or without full stops) the abbreviation "LTD";
(b) "CYFYNGEDIG" or (with or without full stops) the abbreviation "CYF";
(c) "UNLIMITED"; and
(d) "ANGHYFYNGEDIG".

2. The words and abbreviations specified as similar to the words and abbreviations set out in inverted commas in paragraph 1(a) and (b) and the words specified as similar to the words set out in inverted commas in paragraph 1(c) and (d) are any in which—

(a) one or more permitted characters has been omitted;
(b) one or more permitted characters has been added; or
(c) each of one or more permitted characters has been substituted by one or more other permitted characters,

in such a way as to be likely to mislead the public as to the legal form of a company or business if included in the registered name of the company or in a business name.

3. The expressions and abbreviations specified are—

(a) "PUBLIC LIMITED COMPANY" or (with or without full stops) the abbreviation "PLC";
(b) "CWMNI CYFYNGEDIG CYHOEDDUS" or (with or without full stops) the abbreviation "CCC";
(c) "COMMUNITY INTEREST COMPANY" or (with or without full stops) the abbreviation "CIC";
(d) "CWMNI BUDDIANT CYMUNEDOL" or (with or without full stops) the abbreviation "CBC";
(e) "COMMUNITY INTEREST PUBLIC LIMITED COMPANY" or (with or without full stops) the abbreviation "COMMUNITY INTEREST PLC";
(f) "CWMNI BUDDIANT CYMUNEDOL CYHOEDDUS CYFYNGEDIG" or (with or without full stops) the abbreviation "CWMNI BUDDIANT CYMUNEDOL CCC";
(g) "RIGHT TO ENFRANCHISEMENT" or (with or without full stops) the abbreviation "RTE";
(h) "HAWL I RYDDFREINIAD";
(i) "RIGHT TO MANAGE" or (with or without full stops) the abbreviation "RTM";
(j) "CWMNI RTM CYFYNGEDIG";
[(k) "UK ECONOMIC INTEREST GROUPING" or the abbreviation (with or without full stops) "UKEIG";]
(l) "INVESTMENT COMPANY WITH VARIABLE CAPITAL";
(m) "CWMNI BUDDSODDI Â CHYFALAF NEWIDIOL";
(n) "LIMITED PARTNERSHIP";
(o) "PARTNERIAETH CYFYNGEDIG";
(p) "LIMITED LIABILITY PARTNERSHIP";
(q) "PARTNERIAETH ATEBOLRWYDD CYFYNGEDIG";
(r) "OPEN-ENDED INVESTMENT COMPANY";
(s) "CWMNI BUDDSODDIAD PENAGORED";
(t) "CHARITABLE INCORPORATED ORGANISATION";
(u) "SEFYDLIAD ELUSENNOL CORFFOREDIG";
(v) "INDUSTRIAL AND PROVIDENT SOCIETY";
(w) "CO-OPERATIVE SOCIETY"
[(wa) "PROTECTED CELL COMPANY" or (with or without full stops) the abbreviations "PCC LIMITED" and "PCC LTD";
(wb) "CWMNI UNEDAU GWARCHODEDIG" or (with or without full stops) the abbreviations "CUG CYFYNGEDIG" and "CUG CYF";]
(x) "COMMUNITY BENEFIT SOCIETY"; and
(y) the following abbreviations (with or without full stops) of the expressions specified in sub-paragraphs (n), (o), (p), (q), (t) and (u) respectively, namely "LP", "PC", "LLP", "PAC", "CIO" and "SEC".

4. The expressions and abbreviations specified as similar to the expressions and abbreviations set out in inverted commas in paragraph 3 are any in which—

(a) one or more permitted characters has been omitted;
(b) one or more permitted characters has been added; or
(c) each of one or more permitted characters has been substituted by one or more other permitted characters,

in such a way as to be likely to mislead the public as to the legal form of a company or business if included in the registered name of the company or in a business name.

NOTES

Para 3 is amended as follows:

Sub-para (k) substituted by the European Economic Interest Grouping (Amendment) (EU Exit) Regulations 2018, SI 2018/1299, reg 67, as from IP completion day (as defined in the European Union (Withdrawal Agreement) Act 2020, s 39).

Sub-paras (wa), (wb) inserted by the Risk Transformation Regulations 2017, SI 2017/1212, reg 190, Sch 4, para 7(b), as from 8 December 2017. Note that this amendment does not apply in relation to a company which was registered under the Companies Act 2006 before that date (see reg 191 of the 2017 Regulations).

SCHEDULE 3
NAME SAME AS ANOTHER IN THE REGISTRAR'S INDEX OF COMPANY NAMES

Regulations 7 and 8

[4.546]

1. In determining whether a name is the same as another name appearing in the registrar's index of company names the provisions in this Schedule are to be applied in the order set out in the Schedule.

2. Regard each permitted character set out in column 1 of the table to this paragraph as the same as a corresponding permitted character, or combination of permitted characters, in column 2.

Column 1 (permitted characters)	*Column 2 (to be treated the same as)*
À Á Â Ã Ä Å Ā Ă Ą Ǻ	*A*
Æ Ǽ	*AE*
Ç Ć Ĉ Ċ Č	*C*
Þ Ď Đ	*D*
È É Ê Ë Ē Ĕ Ė Ę Ě	*E*
Ĝ Ğ Ġ Ģ	*G*
Ĥ Ħ	*H*
Ì Í Î Ï Ĩ Ī Ĭ Į İ	*I*
Ĵ	*J*
Ķ	*K*
Ĺ Ļ Ľ Ŀ Ł	*L*
Ñ Ń Ņ Ň Ŋ	*N*
Ò Ó Ô Õ Ö Ø Ō Ŏ Ő Ǿ	*O*
Œ	*OE CE*
Ŕ Ŗ Ř	*R*
Ś Ŝ Ş Š	*S*
Ţ Ť Ŧ	*T*
Ù Ú Û Ü Ũ Ū Ŭ Ů Ű Ų	*U*
Ŵ Ẁ Ẃ Ẅ	*W*
Ỳ Ý Ŷ Ÿ	*Y*
Ź Ż Ž	*Z*

3. Taking the name remaining after the application of paragraph 2, disregard any word, expression or abbreviation set out in inverted commas in Schedule 2 where it appears at the end of the name.

4. (1) Taking the name remaining after the application of paragraphs 2 and 3, regard each of the words, expressions, signs and symbols set out in inverted commas in any of the paragraphs of sub-paragraph (2) ("relevant matters") as the same as the other relevant matters set out in that paragraph where each relevant matter—

(a) is preceded by and followed by a blank space; or
(b) where the relevant matter is at the beginning of the name, where it is followed by a blank space.

(2) The words, expressions, signs and symbols are—

(a) "AND" and "&";
(b) "PLUS" and "+";
(c) "0", "ZERO" and "O";
(d) "1" and "ONE";
(e) "2", "TWO", "TO" and "TOO";
(f) "3" and "THREE";
(g) "4", "FOUR" and "FOR";
(h) "5" and "FIVE";
(i) "6" and "SIX";
(j) "7" and "SEVEN";
(k) "8" and "EIGHT";
(l) "9" and "NINE";
(m) "£" and "POUND";
(n) "€" and "EURO";
(o) "$" and "DOLLAR";
(p) "¥" and "YEN";
(q) "%", "PER CENT", "PERCENT", "PER CENTUM" and "PERCENTUM"; and
(r) "@" and "AT".

5. (1) Taking the name remaining after the application of paragraphs 2 to 4, disregard at the end of the name the matters set out in inverted commas in sub-paragraph (2) (or any combination of such matters) where the matter (or combination) is preceded by a blank space or by the following punctuation or symbol in inverted commas—

(a) a full stop; or
(b) "@".

(2) The matters are—

(a) "& CO";
(b) "& COMPANY";
(c) "AND CO";
(d) "AND COMPANY";
(e) "BIZ";
(f) "CO";
(g) "CO UK";
(h) "CO.UK";
(i) "COM";
(j) "COMPANY";
(k) "EU";
(l) "GB";
(m) "GREAT BRITAIN";
(n) "NET";
(o) "NI";
(p) "NORTHERN IRELAND";
(q) "ORG";
(r) "ORG UK";
(s) "ORG.UK";
(t) "UK";
(u) "UNITED KINGDOM";
(v) "WALES";
(w) "& CWMNI";
(x) "A'R CWMNI";
(y) "CWMNI";
(z) "CYM";
(aa) "CYMRU";
(bb) "DU";
(cc) "PF";
(dd) "PRYDAIN FAWR"; and
(ee) "Y DEYRNAS UNEDIG".

(3) The matters in sub-paragraph (2) include any matter in inverted commas that is preceded by and followed by brackets set out in column 2 of table 2 in Schedule 1.

6. Taking the name remaining after the application of paragraphs 2 to 5, disregard the following matters in any part of the name—

(a) any punctuation set out in regulation 2(2)(c) or in column 2 of table 2 in Schedule 1; and
(b) the following words and symbols set out in inverted commas—
  (i) "*";
  (ii) "="; and
  (iii) "#".

7. Taking the name remaining after the application of paragraphs 2 to 6, disregard the letter "S" at the end of the name.

8. (1) Taking the name remaining after the application of paragraphs 2 to 7, disregard any permitted character after the first 60 permitted characters of the name.

(2) For the purposes of computing the number of permitted characters in this paragraph, any blank space between one permitted character and another in the name shall be counted as though it was a permitted character.

9. Taking the name remaining after the application of paragraphs 2 to 8, disregard the following matters or any combination of the following matters set out in inverted commas where they appear at the beginning of the name—

(a) "@";
(b) "THE" (but only where followed by a blank space); and
(c) "WWW".

10. Taking the name remaining after the application of paragraphs 2 to 9, disregard blank spaces between permitted characters.

SCHEDULE 4
SPECIFIED "PUBLIC AUTHORITIES" AND LIST OF GOVERNMENT DEPARTMENTS AND OTHER BODIES WHOSE VIEWS MUST BE SOUGHT

Regulations 9 and 18

[4.547]

Column (1) **Public authority**	**Column (2)** **Government department or other body whose view must be sought**
Accounts Commission for Scotland	Accounts Commission for Scotland
Audit Commission for Local Authorities and the National Health Service in England	Audit Commission for Local Authorities and the National Health Service in England
Audit Scotland	Audit Scotland
Auditor General for Scotland	Auditor General For Scotland
Auditor General for Wales (known in Welsh as "Arch-	Auditor General for Wales (known in Welsh as "Arch-

Column (1) Public authority	Column (2) Government department or other body whose view must be sought
wilydd Cyffredinol Cymru")	wilydd Cyffredinol Cymru")
Comptroller and Auditor General	Comptroller and Auditor General
Comptroller and Auditor General for Northern Ireland	Comptroller and Auditor General for Northern Ireland
Financial Reporting Council	Financial Reporting Council
Financial Conduct Authority	Financial Conduct Authority
Health and Safety Executive	Health and Safety Executive
House of Commons	The Corporate Officer of the House of Commons
House of Lords	The Corporate Officer of the House of Lords
Law Commission	Ministry of Justice
[Money and Pensions Service	Department for Work and Pensions]
National Assembly for Wales (known in Welsh as "Cynulliad Cenedlaethol Cymru")	National Assembly for Wales Commission (known in Welsh as "Comisiwn Cynulliad Cenedlaethol Cymru")
National Assembly for Wales Commission (known in Welsh as "Comisiwn Cynulliad Cenedlaethol Cymru")	National Assembly for Wales Commission (known in Welsh as "Comisiwn Cynulliad Cenedlaethol Cymru")
Northern Ireland Assembly	Northern Ireland Assembly Commission
Northern Ireland Assembly Commission	Northern Ireland Assembly Commission
Northern Ireland Audit Office	Northern Ireland Audit Office
Office for Nuclear Regulation	Office for Nuclear Regulation
Prudential Regulation Authority	[the Governor and Company of the Bank of England]
Regional Agency for Public Health and Social Well-being.	Regional Agency for Public Health and Social Well-being.
Regional Health and Social Care Board	Regional Health and Social Care Board
Scottish Law Commission	Scottish Law Commission
The Governor and Company of the Bank of England	The Governor and Company of the Bank of England
The Pensions Advisory Service	Department for Work and Pensions
The Scottish Parliament	The Scottish Parliamentary Corporate Body
The Scottish Parliamentary Corporate Body	The Scottish Parliamentary Corporate Body
Wales Audit Office (known in Welsh as "Swyddfa Archwilio Cymru")	Wales Audit Office (known in Welsh as "Swyddfa Archwilio Cymru")

NOTES

Entry "Money and Pensions Service" inserted by the Financial Guidance and Claims Act 2018 (Naming and Consequential Amendments) Regulations 2019, SI 2019/383, reg 3, Schedule, Pt 2, para 25, as from 6 April 2019.

Words in square brackets in the entry "Prudential Regulation Authority" substituted by the Bank of England and Financial Services (Consequential Amendments) Regulations 2017, SI 2017/80, reg 2, Schedule, Pt 2, para 44, as from 1 March 2017.

National Assembly for Wales: see further, in relation to the renaming of the National Assembly for Wales as the Senedd Cymru or the Welsh Parliament, the Senedd and Elections (Wales) Act 2020, s 2 (with effect from 6 May 2020). See also ss 3–9 of the 2020 Act in relation to the renaming of Acts of the National Assembly for Wales, Members of the National Assembly for Wales, etc.

SCHEDULES 5 & 6

(Schedule 5 amends the Limited Liability Partnerships (Application of Companies Act 2006) Regulations 2009, SI 2009/1804 at **[10.319]** *et seq. Schedule 6 revokes the Company and Business Names (Miscellaneous Provisions) Regulations 2009, SI 2009/1085, the Company, Limited Liability Partnership and Business Names (Miscellaneous Provisions) (Amendment) Regulations 2009, SI 2009/2404, the Company, Limited Liability Partnership and Business Names (Public Authorities) Regulations 2009, SI 2009/2982, the Companies (Trading Disclosures) Regulations 2008, SI 2008/495, and the Companies (Trading Disclosures) (Amendment) Regulations 2009, SI 2009/218. It also amends the European Economic Interest Grouping Regulations 1989, SI 1989/638 at* **[10.13]** *et seq, the Registrar of Companies and Applications for Striking Off Regulations 2009, SI 2009/1803 at* **[4.317]** *et seq, and contains other amendments that are outside the scope of this work.)*

COMPANIES, PARTNERSHIPS AND GROUPS (ACCOUNTS AND REPORTS) REGULATIONS 2015

(SI 2015/980)

NOTES

Made: 26 March 2015.

Authority: European Communities Act 1972, s 2(2); Companies Act 2006, ss 396(3), 404(3), 409(1), (2), 412(1), (2), 468(1), (2), 473(2), 484, 1292(1) (see also the note "Statutory Instruments made under the European Communities Act 1972" preceding paragraph **[4.1]** *ante*).

Commencement: 6 April 2015.

For a summary of all Orders and Regulations made under the Companies Act 2006, see Appendix 4 at **[A4]**.

These Regulations are reproduced as amended by: the Companies, Partnerships and Groups (Accounts and Reports) (No 2) Regulations 2015, SI 2015/1672.

PART 1 INTRODUCTION

[4.548]

1 Citation and Interpretation

(1) These Regulations may be cited as the Companies, Partnerships and Groups (Accounts and Reports) Regulations 2015.

(2) In these Regulations—

"the Act" means the Companies Act 2006;

"the Small Companies Accounts Regulations" means the Small Companies and Groups (Accounts and Directors' Report) Regulations 2008; and

"the Large and Medium-sized Companies Accounts Regulations" means the Large and Medium-sized Companies and Groups (Accounts and Reports) Regulations 2008.

[4.549]

2 Commencement and Application

(1) These Regulations come into force on 6th April 2015.

(2) Subject to paragraph (3) and regulation 3, the amendments made by these Regulations have effect in relation to—

(a) financial years beginning on or after 1st January 2016, and

(b) a financial year of a company beginning on or after 1st January 2015, but before 1st January 2016, if the directors of the company so decide.

(3) Where—

(a) [by virtue of paragraph (2)(b) above and regulation 2(2)(b) of the Companies, Partnerships and Groups (Accounts and Reports) (No 2) Regulations 2015 ("the No 2 Regulations"), the amendments made by these Regulations and by regulations 3 and 4 of the No 2 Regulations] have effect in relation to a financial year beginning on or after 1st January 2015, but before 1st January 2016, and

(b) as a result the company qualifies as a small company in relation to that year,

the company is not exempt from the requirements of the Act relating to the audit of annual accounts for that year if the company would not have been so exempt had the amendments not had effect in relation to that year.

(4) In determining whether a company or group qualifies as small or medium-sized under section 382(2), 383(3), 465(2) or 466(3) of the Act (qualification in relation to subsequent financial year by reference to circumstances in preceding financial years) in relation to a financial year in relation to which the amendments made by these Regulations [and by regulations 3 and 4 of the No 2 Regulations] have effect, the company or group is to be treated as having qualified as small or medium-sized (as the case may be) in any previous year in which it would have so qualified if amendments to the same effect as the amendments made by these Regulations [and by regulations 3 and 4 of the No 2 Regulations] had had effect in relation to that previous year.

(5) Notwithstanding paragraph (2), the directors of a company cannot take advantage of subsection (2) of section 410 of the Act (information about related undertakings: alternative compliance) in relation to annual accounts of the company approved, pursuant to section 414 of the Act, on or after 1st July 2015.

NOTES

Words in square brackets in para (3) substituted, and words in square brackets in para (4) inserted, by the Companies, Partnerships and Groups (Accounts and Reports) (No 2) Regulations 2015, SI 2015/1672, reg 5(1), (2), as from 1 October 2015.

[4.550]

3 Disapplication of These Regulations to Limited Liability Partnerships

The amendments made by these Regulations to the Act, the Small Companies Accounts Regulations or the Large and Medium-sized Companies Accounts Regulations do not have effect in relation to the application of any provision of the Act or those regulations—

(a) to limited liability partnerships by the Limited Liability Partnerships (Accounts and Audit) (Application of Companies Act 2006) Regulations 2008, . . .

(b) to limited liability partnerships by the Small Limited Liability Partnerships (Accounts) Regulations 2008[, or

(c) to limited liability partnerships by the Large and Medium-sized Limited Liability Partnerships (Accounts) Regulations 2008].

NOTES

Word omitted from para (a) revoked, and para (c) (and the preceding word) added, by the Companies, Partnerships and Groups (Accounts and Reports) (No 2) Regulations 2015, SI 2015/1672, reg 5(1), (3), as from 1 October 2015.

4–44 (*Regs 4–13 (Part 2) amend the Companies Act 2006, Part 15 (Accounts and Reports) and Part 16 (Audit) at* **[1.430]** *et seq, and contain consequential amendments to Part 38 and Sch 8; regs 14–25 (Part 3) amend the Small Companies and Groups (Accounts and Directors' Report) Regulations 2008, SI 2008/409 at* **[4.41]**; *regs 26–41 amend the Large and Medium-sized Companies and Groups (Accounts and Reports) Regulations 2008, SI 2008/410 at* **[4.60]**; *reg 42 (Part 5) amends the Partnership (Accounts) Regulations 2008, SI 2008/569 at* **[10.202]**; *regs 43, 44 (Part 6) contain minor and consequential amendments.*)

ACCOUNTING STANDARDS (PRESCRIBED BODIES) (UNITED STATES OF AMERICA AND JAPAN) REGULATIONS 2015 (NOTE)

(SI 2015/1675)

[4.551]

NOTES

These Regulations were made on September 2015 under the Companies Act 2006, ss 464(1), (3), 1292(1). They cease to have effect on 30 September 2022, and have been omitted from this edition due to space considerations. For a summary of these Regulations, see Appendix 4 at **[A4]**.

COMPANIES (DISCLOSURE OF DATE OF BIRTH INFORMATION) REGULATIONS 2015

(SI 2015/1694)

NOTES

Made: 17 September 2015.

Authority: Companies Act 2006, ss 243(3), 1087B(2), (3), 1292(1).

Commencement: 10 October 2015.

For a summary of all Orders and Regulations made under the Companies Act 2006, see Appendix 4 at **[A4]**.

These Regulations are reproduced as amended by: the Companies and Limited Liability Partnerships (Filing Requirements) Regulations 2016, SI 2016/599; the Immigration Act 2016 (Consequential Amendments) Regulations 2016, SI 2016/655; the Bank of England and Financial Services (Consequential Amendments) Regulations 2017, SI 2017/80; the Money Laundering, Terrorist Financing and Transfer of Funds (Information on the Payer) Regulations 2017, SI 2017/692; the Financial Services Act 2012 (Mutual Societies) Order 2013, SI 2018/323; the Data Protection Act 2018; the Companies, Limited Liability Partnerships and Partnerships (Amendment etc) (EU Exit) Regulations 2019, SI 2019/348.

ARRANGEMENT OF REGULATIONS

SCHEDULES

[4.552]

1 Citation, commencement and interpretation

(1) These Regulations may be cited as the Companies (Disclosure of Date of Birth Information) Regulations 2015 and come into force on 10th October 2015.

(2) In these Regulations—

"the "Act" means the Companies Act 2006 and, unless the context otherwise requires, reference to a numbered section is a section so numbered in that Act;

"the 1985 Act" means the Companies Act 1985;

"the 1986 Order" means the Companies (Northern Ireland) Order 1986;

"specified public authority" means any public authority specified in Schedule 1 to these Regulations.

[4.553]

2 Permitted disclosure by the registrar to specified public authorities

(1) The registrar may disclose restricted DOB information to a specified public authority where the conditions specified in paragraphs 2 and 3 of Schedule 2 are satisfied.

(2) A specified public authority shall deliver to the registrar such information or evidence as the registrar may direct for the purpose of enabling the registrar to determine in accordance with these Regulations whether to disclose restricted DOB information to a specified public authority.

(3) The registrar may require such information or evidence to be verified in such manner as the registrar may direct.

(4) The specified public authority must inform the registrar immediately of any change in respect of any statement delivered to the registrar pursuant to Schedule 2 or information or evidence provided for the purpose of enabling the registrar to determine whether to disclose restricted DOB information.

(5) The public authorities specified for the purposes of section 1087B(2) are set out in Schedule 1 to these Regulations.

[4.554]

3 Permitted disclosure by the registrar to credit reference agencies

(1) The registrar may disclose restricted DOB information to a credit reference agency where the conditions specified in paragraphs 6 to 10 of Schedule 2 are satisfied.

(2) The registrar may rely on a statement delivered to the registrar by a credit reference agency under paragraph 10 of Schedule 2 as sufficient evidence of the matters stated in it.

(3) Notwithstanding paragraph (2), a credit reference agency shall deliver to the registrar such information or evidence in addition to the statement required by paragraph 10 of Schedule 2 as the registrar may direct for the purpose of enabling the registrar to determine in accordance with these Regulations whether to disclose restricted DOB information to a credit reference agency.

(4) The registrar may require such information or evidence to be verified in such manner as the registrar may direct.

(5) The credit reference agency must inform the registrar immediately of any change in respect of any statement delivered to the registrar pursuant to Schedule 2 or information or evidence provided for the purpose of enabling the registrar to determine whether to disclose restricted DOB information.

SCHEDULES

SCHEDULE 1
SPECIFIED PUBLIC AUTHORITIES

Regulation 2

[4.555]

The Secretary of State;

the Minister for the Cabinet Office;

any Northern Ireland Department;

the Scottish Ministers;

the Welsh Ministers;

the Treasury;

[the Treasury Solicitor;]

the Commissioners for Her Majesty's Revenue and Customs;

the Bank of England [(including the Bank in its capacity as the Prudential Regulation Authority)];

the Director of Public Prosecutions;

the Director of Public Prosecutions for Northern Ireland;

the Serious Fraud Office;

the Secret Intelligence Service;

the Security Service;

the Government Communications Headquarters;

the Financial Conduct Authority;

. . .

the Competition and Markets Authority;

the Pensions Regulator;

the Panel on Takeovers and Mergers;

the Regulator of Community Interest Companies;

. . .

the Office of the Information Commissioner;

the Charity Commission;

the Charity Commission for Northern Ireland;

the Office of the Scottish Charity Regulator;

the Office of Communications;

the Gas and Electricity Markets Authority;

the Northern Ireland Authority for Utility Regulation;

the Gambling Commission;

the National Crime Agency;

the Health and Safety Executive;

the Office for Nuclear Regulation;

the Health and Safety Executive for Northern Ireland;

the Food Standards Agency;

[the Gangmasters Labour and Abuse Authority];

the Security Industry Authority;

a local authority within the meaning of section 54(2) of the Act;

an official receiver appointed under section 399 of the Insolvency Act 1986 (appointment, etc, of official receivers);

the Official Receiver for Northern Ireland;

the Crown Office and Procurator Fiscal Services;

the Marine Management Organisation;

a person acting as an insolvency practitioner within the meaning of section 388 of the Insolvency Act 1986 (meaning of "act as an insolvency practitioner") or Article 3 of the Insolvency (Northern Ireland) Order 1989 ("act as an insolvency practitioner");

an inspector appointed under Part 14 of the 1985 Act (investigation of companies and their affairs: requisition of documents) or Part 15 of the 1986 Order or a person appointed under regulation 30 of the Open-Ended Investment Companies Regulations 2001 (power to investigate) or regulation 22 of the Open-Ended Investment Companies Regulations (Northern Ireland) 2004;

any person authorised to exercise powers under section 447 of the 1985 Act (power to require documents and information), or section 84 of the Companies Act 1989 (exercise of powers by officers, etc) or Article 440 of the 1986 Order;

any person exercising functions conferred by Part 6 of the Financial Services and Markets Act 2000 (official listing);

a person appointed to make a report under section 166 or 166A (reports by skilled persons) of the Financial Services and Markets Act 2000;

a person appointed to conduct an investigation under section 167 (appointment of persons to carry out general investigations) or 168(3) or (5) (appointment of persons to carry out investigations in particular cases) of the Financial Services and Markets Act 2000;

an inspector appointed under section 284 (power to investigate) of the Financial Services and Markets Act 2000;

. . .

a police force or police service within the meaning of section 101(1) of the Police Act 1996 (interpretation), section 6 of the Police and Fire Reform (Scotland) Act 2012 (the Police Service of Scotland) or section 1 of the Police (Northern Ireland) Act 2000 (name of the police in Northern Ireland);

the Scottish Housing Regulator;

the lead enforcement authority (as defined in section 33(1) of the Estate Agents Act 1979) exercising functions under the Estate Agents Act 1979.

NOTES

Entry relating to "the Treasury Solicitor" inserted, and entry "an overseas regulatory authority within the meaning of section 82 of the Companies Act 1989 (request for assistance by overseas regulatory authority)" (omitted) revoked, by the Companies and Limited Liability Partnerships (Filing Requirements) Regulations 2016, SI 2016/599, reg 5, Sch 3, paras 1, 2, as from 30 June 2016.

Words in square brackets in entry "Bank of England" inserted, and entry "the Prudential Regulation Authority" (omitted) revoked, by the Bank of England and Financial Services (Consequential Amendments) Regulations 2017, SI 2017/80, reg 2, Schedule, Pt 2, para 43, as from 1 March 2017.

Entry "the Registrar of Credit Unions for Northern Ireland" (omitted) revoked by the Financial Services Act 2012 (Mutual Societies) Order 2013, SI 2018/323, art 2(c), Sch 4, Pt 2, para 11, as from 6 April 2018.

Entry relating to "the Gangmasters Labour and Abuse Authority" substituted by the Immigration Act 2016 (Consequential Amendments) Regulations 2016, SI 2016/655, reg 2, Schedule, Pt 2, para 10, as from 12 July 2016.

SCHEDULE 2
CONDITIONS FOR PERMITTED DISCLOSURE

Regulations 2 and 3

PART 1 DISCLOSURE TO SPECIFIED PUBLIC AUTHORITIES

[4.556]

1. Paragraphs 2 and 3 set out the conditions specified for the disclosure of restricted DOB information by the registrar to a specified public authority.

2. The specified public authority has delivered to the registrar a statement that it intends to use the restricted DOB information only for the purpose of facilitating the carrying out by that specified public authority of a public function.

3. Subject to paragraph 4, the specified public authority ("the authority") has delivered to the registrar a statement that it will, where it supplies a copy of the restricted DOB information to a processor for the purpose of processing the information for use in respect of facilitating the carrying out of a public function by that authority—

(a) ensure that the processor is one who carries on business in the European Economic Area [or in the United Kingdom];

(b) require that the information is not transmitted outside the [area comprising the United Kingdom and the European Economic Area] by the processor; and

(c) require that the processor does not disclose the information except to the authority or an employee of the authority.

4. Paragraph 3 does not apply where the specified public authority is the [National Crime Agency,] Secret Intelligence Service, Security Service or Government Communications Headquarters.

NOTES

Para 3: the words in square brackets in sub-para (a) were inserted, and the words in square brackets in sub-para (b) were substituted, by the Companies, Limited Liability Partnerships and Partnerships (Amendment etc) (EU Exit) Regulations 2019, SI 2019/348, reg 7, Sch 2, paras 11, 12(a), as from IP completion day (as defined in the European Union (Withdrawal Agreement) Act 2020, s 39) (for transitional provisions see Sch 4, para 5 to the 2019 Regulations at **[12.106]**).

Para 4: words in square brackets inserted by the Companies and Limited Liability Partnerships (Filing Requirements) Regulations 2016, SI 2016/599, reg 5, Sch 3, paras 1, 3, as from 30 June 2016.

PART 2 DISCLOSURE TO A CREDIT REFERENCE AGENCY

[4.557]

5. Paragraphs 6 to 10 set out the conditions specified for the disclosure of restricted DOB information by the registrar to a credit reference agency.

6. [(1)] The credit reference agency—

(a) is carrying on in the United Kingdom . . . a business comprising the furnishing of information relevant to the financial standing of individuals, being information collected by the agency for that purpose;

(b) maintains appropriate procedures—

(i) to ensure that an independent person can investigate and audit the measures maintained by the agency for the purposes of ensuring the security of any restricted DOB information disclosed to that agency; and

[(ii) for the purposes of ensuring that it complies with its [obligations under the data protection legislation (as defined in section 3 of the Data Protection Act 2018)];]

(c) has not been found guilty of an offence under—

(i) section 1112 (general false statement offence) of the Act or section 2 of the Fraud Act 2006 (fraud by false representation); . . .

(ii) section 47 (failure to comply with enforcement notice) of the Data Protection Act 1998 in circumstances where it has used the restricted DOB information for purposes other than those described in sub-paragraphs (a) to (e) of paragraph 7 below[; or

(iii) section 144 of the Data Protection Act 2018 (false statements made in response to an information notice) or section 148 of that Act (destroying or falsifying information and documents etc);]

[(d) has not been given a penalty notice under section 155 of the Data Protection Act 2018 in circumstances described in paragraph (c)(ii), other than a penalty notice that has been cancelled.]

[(2) . . .]

7. The credit reference agency has delivered to the registrar a statement that it intends to use the restricted DOB information only for the purposes of—

(a) providing an assessment of the financial standing of a person;

(b) meeting any obligations contained in [the Money Laundering, Terrorist Financing and Transfer of Funds (Information on the Payer) Regulations 2017] or any rules made pursuant to section 137A of the Financial Services and Markets Act 2000 which relate to the prevention and detection of money laundering in connection with the carrying on of regulated activities by authorised persons . . .

(c) conducting conflict of interest checks required or made necessary by any enactment;

(d) the provision of restricted DOB information to—

(i) a specified public authority which has satisfied the requirements of paragraphs 2 and 3 of this Schedule; or

(ii) a credit reference agency which has satisfied the requirements of this Part of this Schedule; or

(e) conducting checks for the prevention and detection of crime and fraud.

8. The credit reference agency has delivered to the registrar a statement that it intends to take delivery of and to use the restricted DOB information only in the United Kingdom . . .

9. The credit reference agency has delivered to the registrar a statement that it will, where it supplies a copy of the restricted DOB information to a processor for the purpose of processing the information for use in respect of the purposes referred to in paragraph 7—

(a) ensure that the processor is one who carries on business in the [United Kingdom];

(b) require that the information is not transmitted outside the [United Kingdom] by the processor; and

(c) require that the processor does not disclose the information except to the credit reference agency or an employee of the credit reference agency.

10. The credit reference agency has delivered to the registrar a statement that it meets the conditions in paragraph 6 above.

NOTES

Para 6: the words omitted from sub-para (1)(a) were revoked, the words in square brackets in sub-para (1)(b)(ii) were substituted, and sub-para (2) was revoked, by the Companies, Limited Liability Partnerships and Partnerships (Amendment etc) (EU Exit) Regulations 2019, SI 2019/348, reg 7, Sch 2, paras 11, 12(b), as from IP completion day (as defined in the European Union (Withdrawal Agreement) Act 2020, s 39) (for transitional provisions see Sch 4, para 5 to the 2019 Regulations at **[12.106]**). All other amendments to this paragraph were made by the Data Protection Act 2018, s 211, Sch 19, Pt 2, para 384, as from 25 May 2018 (for transitional provisions and savings relating to the repeal of the Data Protection Act 1998, see Sch 20 to the 2018 Act).

Para 7: words in square brackets in sub-para (b) substituted by the Money Laundering, Terrorist Financing and Transfer of Funds (Information on the Payer) Regulations 2017, SI 2017/692, reg 109, Sch 7, Pt 2, para 32, as from 26 June 2017. Words omitted revoked by SI 2019/348, reg 7, Sch 2, paras 11, 12(c), as from IP completion day (as defined in the European Union (Withdrawal Agreement) Act 2020, s 39) (for transitional provisions see Sch 4, para 5 to the 2019 Regulations at **[12.106]**).

Para 8: words omitted revoked by SI 2019/348, reg 7, Sch 2, paras 11, 12(d), as from IP completion day (as defined in the European Union (Withdrawal Agreement) Act 2020, s 39) (for transitional provisions see Sch 4, para 5 to the 2019 Regulations at **[12.106]**).

Para 9: words in square brackets substituted by SI 2019/348, reg 7, Sch 2, paras 11, 12(e), as from IP completion day (as defined in the European Union (Withdrawal Agreement) Act 2020, s 39) (for transitional provisions see Sch 4, para 5 to the 2019 Regulations at **[12.106]**).

PART 3 INTERPRETATION OF THIS SCHEDULE

[4.558]

11. (1) In this Schedule—

"processor" means any person who provides a service which consists of putting information into data form or processing information in data form and any reference to a processor includes a reference to its employees; and

"public function" includes—

(a) any function conferred by or in accordance with any provision contained in any enactment;

(b) . . .

(c) any similar function conferred on persons by or under provisions having effect as part of the law of a country or territory outside the United Kingdom; and

(d) any function exercisable in relation to the investigation of any criminal offence or for the purpose of any criminal proceedings.

(2) In this Schedule any reference to—

(a) an employee of any person who has access to restricted DOB information shall be deemed to include any person working or providing services for the purposes of that person or employed by or on behalf of, or working for, any person who is so working or who is supplying such a service; and

(b) the disclosure for the purpose of facilitating the carrying out of a public function includes disclosure in relation to, and for the purpose of, any proceedings whether civil, criminal or disciplinary in which the specified public authority engages while carrying out its public functions.

NOTES

Para 11: para (b) of the definition "public function" was revoked by the Companies, Limited Liability Partnerships and Partnerships (Amendment etc) (EU Exit) Regulations 2019, SI 2019/348, reg 7, Sch 2, paras 11, 12(b), as from IP completion day (as defined in the European Union (Withdrawal Agreement) Act 2020, s 39) (for transitional provisions see Sch 4, para 5 to the 2019 Regulations at **[12.106]**).

REGISTER OF PEOPLE WITH SIGNIFICANT CONTROL REGULATIONS 2016

(SI 2016/339)

NOTES

Made: 15 March 2016

Authority: Companies Act 2006, ss 243, 790B(1)(b), 790C(7)(d), 790C(12), 790K(5), 790M(7), 790O(2), 790ZF, 790ZG, 1088, 1292, Sch 1A, para 25(5)(b), Sch 1B, paras 12(1), (2).

Commencement: 6 April 2016 (with the exception of Sch 5, para 6); 30 June 2016 (Sch 5, para 6).

For a summary of all Orders and Regulations made under the Companies Act 2006, see Appendix 4 at **[A4]**.

These Regulations are reproduced as amended by: the Immigration Act 2016 (Consequential Amendments) Regulations 2016, SI 2016/655; the Bank of England and Financial Services (Consequential Amendments) Regulations 2017, SI 2017/80; the Money Laundering, Terrorist Financing and Transfer of Funds (Information on the Payer) Regulations 2017, SI 2017/692; the Information about People with Significant Control (Amendment) Regulations 2017, SI 2017/693; the Data Protection Act 2018; the Companies, Limited Liability Partnerships and Partnerships (Amendment etc) (EU Exit) Regulations 2019, SI 2019/348.

Modifications: these Regulations are modified in their application to LLPs by the Limited Liability Partnerships (Register of People with Significant Control) Regulations 2016, SI 2016/340 at **[10.452]**.

These Regulations are modified in their application to European Public Limited-Liability Companies (SEs) by the European Public Limited-Liability Company (Register of People with Significant Control) Regulations 2016, SI 2016/375.

ARRANGEMENT OF REGULATIONS

PART 1 GENERAL INTRODUCTORY PROVISIONS

[4.559]

1 Citation and commencement

(1) These Regulations may be cited as the Register of People with Significant Control Regulations 2016.

(2) These Regulations come into force on 6th April 2016 other than paragraph 6 of Schedule 5, which comes into force on 30th June 2016.

[4.560]

2 Interpretation

In these Regulations—

"the Act" means the Companies Act 2006;

"the 2009 Regulations" means the Companies (Disclosure of Address) Regulations 2009;

"the 2016 Regulations" means the Limited Liability Partnerships (Register of People with Significant Control) Regulations 2016;

["credit institution" has the same meaning as in regulation 10(1) of the Money Laundering, Terrorist Financing and Transfer of Funds (Information on the Payer) Regulations 2017;]

["financial institution" has the same meaning as in regulation 10(2) of the Money Laundering, Terrorist Financing and Transfer of Funds (Information on the Payer) Regulations 2017;]

"former name" means a name by which an individual was formerly known for business purposes;

"limited liability partnership" means a limited liability partnership incorporated under the Limited Liability Partnerships Act 2000;

"name" means a person's forename and surname, except that in the case of—

(a) a peer; or
(b) an individual usually known by a title,

the title may be stated instead of that person's forename and surname or in addition to either or both of them;

"personal representative" means the executor or administrator for the time being of a deceased person;

"relevant body" means—

(a) a police force within the meaning of section 101(1) of the Police Act 1996;
(b) the Police Service of Northern Ireland; and
(c) the Police Service of Scotland;

"section 243 decision" means a determination under the 2009 Regulations which is a section 243 decision within the meaning of those Regulations;

"secured information" means the required particulars (other than the particular required by section 790K(1)(i) of the Act) of a registrable person in relation to a company;

"specified public authorities" has the meaning given in regulation 22(1);

"voting rights" means rights to vote at general meetings of the company or legal entity in question, including rights that arise only in certain circumstances, and in relation to a legal entity that does not have general meetings at which matters are decided by the exercise of voting rights, a reference to voting rights is to be read as a reference to rights in relation to the entity that are equivalent to those of a person entitled to exercise voting rights in a company;

"voting shares" means shares carrying voting rights; and

"withdrawal notice" has the meaning given in regulation 21.

NOTES

Definitions "credit institution" and "financial institution" inserted by the Information about People with Significant Control (Amendment) Regulations 2017, SI 2017/693, regs 11, 12, as from 26 June 2017 (for transitional arrangements, see Schedule, Pt 1 to the 2017 Regulations at **[10.1195]**).

PART 2 APPLICATION AND FEES

[4.561]

3 Companies to which Part 21A of the Act does not apply

A company is specified for the purpose of section 790B(1)(b) of the Act if it has voting shares admitted to trading—

(a) . . .
(b) on a market listed in Schedule 1.

NOTES

Para (a) revoked by the Information about People with Significant Control (Amendment) Regulations 2017, SI 2017/693, regs 11, 13, as from 26 June 2017 (for transitional arrangements, see Schedule, Pt 1 to the 2017 Regulations at **[10.1195]**).

[4.562]

4 Legal entities which are subject to their own disclosure requirements

A legal entity (other than one to which section 790C(7)(c) of the Act applies) is specified for the purpose of section 790C(7)(d) of the Act if it has voting shares admitted to trading—

(a) . . .

(b) on a market listed in Schedule 1.

NOTES

Para (a) revoked by the Information about People with Significant Control (Amendment) Regulations 2017, SI 2017/693, regs 11, 14, as from 26 June 2017 (for transitional arrangements, see Schedule, Pt 1 to the 2017 Regulations at **[10.1195]**).

[4.563]

5 Modification for persons covered by section 790C(12) of the Act

(1) The following modification is prescribed for the purpose of section 790C(12) of the Act.

(2) Sections 790M(2) to [(6A)] and (10) of the Act are not to be read and do not have effect as if a person within section 790C(12) of the Act were an individual.

NOTES

Para (2) figure in square brackets substituted by the Information about People with Significant Control (Amendment) Regulations 2017, SI 2017/693, regs 11, 15, as from 26 June 2017 (for transitional arrangements, see Schedule, Pt 1 to the 2017 Regulations at **[10.1195]**).

[4.564]

6 Fee for a copy of a company's PSC register

(1) The fee prescribed for the purpose of section 790O(2) of the Act is £12.

(2) That fee applies to any single request for a copy of a company's PSC register, or any part of it, regardless of how many parts are required to be copied.

PART 3 NATURE OF CONTROL AND FOREIGN LIMITED PARTNERS

[4.565]

7 Particulars required as to nature of control

(1) The particulars required by sections 790K(1)(h), 790K(2)(e) and 790K(3)(f) of the Act (particulars as to nature of control over the company) are—

(a) where the person meets the first specified condition, the statement listed in Part 1 of Schedule 2 which is applicable to that person;

(b) where the person meets the second specified condition, the statement listed in Part 2 of Schedule 2 which is applicable to that person;

(c) where the person meets the third specified condition, the statement listed in Part 3 of Schedule 2;

(d) where the person meets the fourth specified condition and does not meet the first, second or third specified condition, the statement listed in Part 4 of Schedule 2;

(e) where the person meets the fifth specified condition in connection with a trust, every statement listed in Part 5 of Schedule 2 which is applicable to that person;

(f) where the person meets the fifth specified condition in connection with a firm, every statement listed in Part 6 of Schedule 2 which is applicable to that person.

(2) Part 7 of Schedule 2 sets out a rule for the interpretation of Schedule 2.

[4.566]

8 Characteristics of a foreign limited partner

(1) The characteristics prescribed for the purposes of paragraph 25(5)(b) of Schedule 1A to the Act are that the individual—

(a) participates in a foreign limited partnership as a limited liability participant; or

(b) directly or indirectly, holds shares or a right in or in relation to a legal entity which participates in a foreign limited partnership as a limited liability participant.

(2) In this regulation—

(a) a "foreign limited partnership" is an arrangement which—

(i) is established under the law of a country or territory outside the United Kingdom;

(ii) consists of at least one person who has unlimited liability for the debts and obligations of the arrangement; and

(iii) consists of at least one person who has no, or limited, liability for the debts and obligations of the arrangement for so long as that person does not take part in the management of the arrangement's business; and

(b) a "limited liability participant" is a person who—

(i) has no, or limited, liability for the debts and obligations of the foreign limited partnership for so long as that person does not take part in the management of the foreign limited partnership's business; and

(ii) does not take part in the management of the foreign limited partnership's business.

PART 4 ADDITIONAL MATTERS

[4.567]

9 Additional matters to be noted in a PSC register

(1) The additional matters required to be noted in a company's PSC register under section 790M(7) of the Act are the matters required to be noted by regulations 10 to 17.

(2) Where any additional matter noted in a company's PSC register in accordance with regulation 10, 11, 12 or 13 ceases to be true, the company must note in its PSC register—

(a) that the additional matter has ceased to be true; and

(b) the date on which the additional matter ceased to be true.

[4.568]

10 Additional matters where there is no registrable person or registrable relevant legal entity

(1) This regulation applies where a company knows or has reasonable cause to believe that there is no registrable person or registrable relevant legal entity in relation to the company.

(2) The company must note in its PSC register that it knows or has reasonable cause to believe that there is no registrable person or registrable relevant legal entity in relation to the company.

[4.569]

11 Additional matters where there is an unidentified registrable person

(1) This regulation applies where a company—

(a) knows or has reasonable cause to believe that there is a registrable person in relation to the company; and

(b) has not been able to identify the registrable person.

(2) The company must—

(a) note in its PSC register that it knows or has reasonable cause to believe that there is a registrable person in relation to the company but it has not identified the registrable person; and

(b) make a separate note in its PSC register in respect of each registrable person which the company has been unable to identify.

[4.570]

12 Additional matters where an identified registrable person's particulars are not confirmed

(1) This regulation applies where—

(a) a company has identified a registrable person in relation to the company; and

(b) all the required particulars of that person have not been confirmed for the purposes of section 790M of the Act.

(2) The company must—

(a) note in its PSC register that it has identified a registrable person in relation to the company but all the required particulars of that person have not been confirmed; and

(b) make a separate note in its PSC register in respect of each registrable person which the company has been unable to identify.

[4.571]

13 Additional matters where a company's investigations are ongoing

(1) This regulation applies where a company—

(a) is not required to place a note in its PSC register by regulation 10, 11 or 12;

(b) has not entered, and is not required to enter, the required particulars of any registrable person or registrable relevant legal entity in its PSC register; and

(c) has not yet completed taking reasonable steps to find out if there is anyone who is a registrable person or a registrable relevant legal entity in relation to the company under section 790D of the Act.

(2) The company must note in its PSC register that it has not yet completed taking reasonable steps to find out if there is anyone who is a registrable person or a registrable relevant legal entity in relation to the company.

[4.572]

14 Additional matters where there is a failure to comply with a notice given under section 790D of the Act

(1) This regulation applies where—

(a) a company has given a notice under section 790D of the Act; and

(b) the addressee of the notice has failed to comply with the notice within the time specified in it.

(2) The company must—

(a) note in its PSC register that it has given a notice under section 790D of the Act which has not been complied with; and

(b) make a separate note in its PSC register in respect of each notice under section 790D which has not been complied with.

[4.573]

15 Additional matters where there is a failure to comply with a notice given under section 790E of the Act

(1) This regulation applies where—

(a) a company has given a notice under section 790E of the Act; and

(b) the addressee of the notice has failed to comply with the notice within the time specified in it.

(2) The company must note in the entry in its PSC register for the addressee that the addressee has failed to comply with a notice given by the company under section 790E of the Act.

[4.574]

16 Additional matters where a notice given under section 790D or section 790E of the Act is complied with after the time specified in the notice

(1) This regulation applies where—

(a) a note has been placed in a company's register under regulation 14 or 15; and

(b) the addressee of the notice to which the note relates has complied with the notice after the time specified in the notice.

(2) The company must note in its PSC register—

(a) that the notice has been complied with after the time specified in the notice; and

(b) the date on which the notice was complied with.

[4.575]

17 Additional matters where a company has issued a restrictions notice

(1) This regulation applies where a company has issued a restrictions notice under paragraph 1 of Schedule 1B to the Act.

(2) The company must—

(a) note in its PSC register that it has issued a restrictions notice under paragraph 1 of Schedule 1B to the Act; and

(b) make a separate note in its PSC register in respect of each registrable person which the company has been unable to identify.

(3) Where the company withdraws the restrictions notice under paragraph 11 of Schedule 1B to the Act, the company must note in its PSC register—

(a) that it has withdrawn the restrictions notice by giving a withdrawal notice; and

(b) the date specified in the withdrawal notice as the date on which the withdrawal notice was given.

(4) Where a court makes an order under paragraph 8 of Schedule 1B to the Act directing that a relevant interest in the company cease to be subject to restrictions, the company must note in its PSC register—

(a) that the court has made an order under paragraph 8 of Schedule 1B to the Act directing that a relevant interest in the company cease to be subject to restrictions; and

(b) the date on which that order takes effect.

PART 5 WARNING AND RESTRICTIONS NOTICES

[4.576]

18 Content of a warning notice

A warning notice given under paragraph 1 of Schedule 1B to the Act must—

(a) specify the date on which the warning notice is given;

(b) be accompanied by a copy of the notice given under section 790D or 790E of the Act to which the warning notice relates;

(c) identify the addressee's relevant interest in the company by reference to the shares or right in question;

(d) state that the company will consider reasons provided to it as to why the addressee failed to comply with the notice given under section 790D or 790E of the Act;

(e) explain the effect of a restrictions notice; and

(f) state that, by virtue of a restrictions notice, certain acts or failures to act may constitute an offence.

[4.577]

19 Content of a restrictions notice

A restrictions notice issued under paragraph 1 of Schedule 1B to the Act must—

(a) specify the date on which the restrictions notice is issued;

(b) be accompanied by a copy of the warning notice which preceded the restrictions notice;

(c) identify the addressee's relevant interest in the company by reference to the shares or right in question;

(d) explain the effect of the restrictions notice;

(e) state that, by virtue of the restrictions notice, certain acts or failures to act may constitute an offence; and

(f) state that an aggrieved person may apply to the court for an order directing that the relevant interest cease to be subject to restrictions.

[4.578]

20 Failure to comply with a section 790D or 790E notice: valid reason

A company must take into account any incapacity of the addressee of a notice given under section 790D or 790E of the Act in deciding what counts as a "valid reason" sufficient to justify the addressee's failure to comply with the notice.

[4.579]

21 Withdrawal of a restrictions notice

Where a company is required to withdraw a restrictions notice under paragraph 11 of Schedule 1B to the Act by notice (a "withdrawal notice"), the withdrawal notice must—

(a) be given before the end of the period of 14 days beginning with the day on which the company became required to withdraw the restrictions notice under that paragraph;

(b) specify the date on which the withdrawal notice is given;

(c) identify the addressee's relevant interest in the company by reference to the shares or right in question; and

(d) state that the relevant interest is no longer subject to restrictions.

PART 6 THE PROTECTION OF USUAL RESIDENTIAL ADDRESS INFORMATION

[4.580]

22 Permitted disclosure of usual residential address information by the registrar to specified public authorities

(1) The public authorities listed in Schedule 3 ("specified public authorities") are specified for the purposes of section 243 of the Act (as applied by section 790ZF of the Act).

(2) The conditions specified for the disclosure of information within section 790ZF(2) of the Act by the registrar to specified public authorities in accordance with section 243 of the Act (as applied by section 790ZF of the Act) are listed in Part 1 of Schedule 4.

[4.581]

23 Permitted disclosure of usual residential address information by the registrar to credit reference agencies

(1) The conditions specified for the disclosure of information within section 790ZF(2) of the Act by the registrar to a credit reference agency in accordance with section 243 of the Act (as applied by section 790ZF of the Act) are listed in Part 2 of Schedule 4.

(2) The registrar may rely on a statement delivered to the registrar by a credit reference agency under Part 2 of Schedule 4 as sufficient evidence of the matters stated in it.

[4.582]

24 Circumstances where the registrar must refrain from disclosure of usual residential address information

(1) The registrar must not disclose information within section 790ZF(2) of the Act to a credit reference agency if in relation to that information an application has been made under regulation 25, 26 or 27—

(a) which has not yet been determined by the registrar and has not been withdrawn under regulation 29;
(b) which has been determined by the registrar in favour of the applicant (but see paragraph (2));
(c) which was unsuccessful and the period for applying for permission to appeal in regulation 30(3) has not passed;
(d) which was unsuccessful and an appeal to the court in respect of that application under regulation 30 has not been determined by the court; or
(e) which was unsuccessful and the applicant has successfully appealed the determination.

(2) Paragraph (1)(b) does not apply where the determination has ceased to have effect under regulation 31.

(3) For the purposes of this regulation, an application is made when it has been registered by the registrar.

[4.583]

25 Application by an individual requiring the registrar to refrain from disclosing that individual's usual residential address information to a credit reference agency

(1) An individual who is, or proposes to become, a registrable person in relation to a company may make an application to the registrar requiring the registrar to refrain from disclosing to a credit reference agency information within section 790ZF(2) of the Act relating to that individual.

(2) The grounds on which an application may be made are that—

(a) the applicant reasonably believes that there is a serious risk that the applicant, or a person who lives with the applicant, will be subjected to violence or intimidation as a result of the activities of at least one of—
    (i) the companies in relation to which the applicant is, or proposes to become, a registrable person;
    (ii) the companies in relation to which the applicant used to be a registrable person;
    (iii) the limited liability partnerships in relation to which the applicant is, or proposes to become, a registrable person under the 2016 Regulations;
    (iv) the limited liability partnerships in relation to which the applicant used to be a registrable person under the 2016 Regulations;
    (v) the limited liability partnerships in relation to which the applicant is or proposes to become a member;
    (vi) the limited liability partnerships in relation to which the applicant used to be a member;
    (vii) the companies in relation to which the applicant is, or proposes to become, a director;
    (viii) the companies in relation to which the applicant used to be a director; or
    (ix) the overseas companies of which the applicant is or used to be a director, secretary or permanent representative; or
(b) a section 243 decision has been made in respect of the applicant which has not ceased to have effect under regulation 15 of the 2009 Regulations.

(3) The application must contain—

(a) a statement of the grounds on which the application is made;
(b) the name and any former name of the applicant;
(c) the date of birth of the applicant;
(d) the usual residential address of the applicant;
(e) the e-mail address of the applicant, if any;
(f) the name and registered number of each company in relation to which the applicant is, or proposes to become, a registrable person;
(g) where the grounds of the application are those described in paragraphs (2)(a)(ii) to (ix), the names and registered numbers of the companies, limited liability partnerships and overseas companies whose activities are relevant to the application; and
(h) where the grounds of the application are those described in paragraph (2)(b), the name and registered number of the company in relation to which the section 243 decision was made, unless the section 243 decision relates to a proposed company which was never incorporated.

(4) Where the grounds of the application are those described in paragraph (2)(a), the application must be accompanied by evidence which supports the applicant's statement of the grounds on which the application is made.

(5) The registrar must determine the application and, within 7 days beginning with the date that the determination is made, send to the applicant notice of the determination.

(6) Where the application is unsuccessful, the notice under paragraph (5) must inform the applicant of the applicant's right to apply for permission to appeal against the determination within 28 days beginning with the date of the notice.

[4.584]

26 Application by a company requiring the registrar to refrain from disclosing an individual's usual residential address information to a credit reference agency

(1) A company ("the applicant") may make an application to the registrar requiring the registrar to refrain from disclosing to a credit reference agency information within section 790ZF(2) of the Act relating to an individual ("R") who is, or proposes to become, a registrable person in relation to the company.

(2) A company may only make an application under paragraph (1) where R has given consent for the company to make the application on R's behalf.

(3) The grounds on which an application may be made are that—

(a) the applicant reasonably believes that there is a serious risk that R, or a person who lives with R, will be subjected to violence or intimidation as a result of the applicant's activities; or

(b) a section 243 decision has been made in respect of R which has not ceased to have effect under regulation 15 of the 2009 Regulations.

(4) Where the grounds of the application are those described in paragraph (3)(b), the application must only relate to one individual who is, or proposes to become, a registrable person in relation to the company.

(5) The application must contain—

(a) a statement of the grounds on which the application is made;

(b) confirmation that R consents to the making of the application;

(c) the name and registered number of the applicant;

(d) the address of the registered office of the applicant;

(e) the e-mail address of the applicant, if any;

(f) the name and any former name of R;

(g) the date of birth of R;

(h) the usual residential address of R;

(i) the e-mail address of R, if any;

(j) where R is a registrable person in relation to another company, the name and registered number of that company; and

(k) where the grounds of the application are those described in paragraph (3)(b), the name and registered number of the company in relation to which the section 243 decision was made, unless the section 243 decision relates to a proposed company which was never incorporated.

(6) Where the grounds of the application are those described in paragraph (3)(a), the application must be accompanied by evidence which supports the applicant's statement of the grounds on which the application is made.

(7) The registrar must determine the application and, within 7 days beginning with the date that the determination is made, send to the applicant and to R notice of the determination.

(8) Where the application is unsuccessful, the notice under paragraph (7) must inform the applicant of the applicant's right to apply for permission to appeal against the determination within 28 days beginning with the date of the notice.

[4.585]

27 Application by a subscriber to a memorandum of association requiring the registrar to refrain from disclosing an individual's usual residential address information to a credit reference agency

(1) A subscriber to a memorandum of association ("the applicant") may make an application to the registrar requiring the registrar to refrain from disclosing to a credit reference agency information within section 790ZF(2) relating to an individual ("R") who proposes to become, on or after the formation of the company to which the memorandum relates, a registrable person in relation to the company.

(2) A subscriber to a memorandum of association may only make an application under paragraph (1) where R has given consent for the subscriber to make the application on R's behalf.

(3) The grounds on which an application may be made are that—

(a) the applicant reasonably believes that there is a serious risk that R, or a person who lives with R, will be subjected to violence or intimidation as a result of the proposed activities of the company to which the memorandum relates; or

(b) a section 243 decision has been made in respect of R which has not ceased to have effect under regulation 15 of the 2009 Regulations.

(4) Where the grounds of the application are those described in paragraph (3)(b), the application must only relate to one individual who proposes to become a registrable person in relation to the proposed company.

(5) The application must contain—

(a) a statement of the grounds on which the application is made;

(b) confirmation that R consents to the making of the application;

(c) the name and any former name of the applicant;

(d) the usual residential address of the applicant;

(e) the e-mail address of the applicant, if any;

(f) the name of the proposed company to which the memorandum relates;

(g) the name and any former name of R;
(h) the date of birth of R;
(i) the usual residential address of R;
(j) the e-mail address of R, if any;
(k) where R is a registrable person in relation to another company, the name and registered number of that company; and
(l) where the grounds of the application are those described in paragraph (3)(b), the name and registered number of the company in relation to which the section 243 decision was made, unless the section 243 decision relates to a proposed company which was never incorporated.

(6) Where the grounds of the application are those described in paragraph (3)(a), the application must be accompanied by evidence which supports the applicant's statement of the grounds on which the application is made.

(7) The registrar must determine the application and, within 7 days beginning with the date that the determination is made, send to the applicant and to R notice of the determination.

(8) Where the application is unsuccessful, the notice under paragraph (7) must inform the applicant of the applicant's right to apply for permission to appeal against the determination within 28 days beginning with the date of the notice.

[4.586]
28 Matters relating to an application made under regulation 25, 26 or 27

(1) For the purpose of determining an application made under regulation 25, 26 or 27 the registrar may—
(a) direct that additional information or evidence should be delivered to the registrar;
(b) refer any question relating to an assessment of the nature or extent of any risk of violence or intimidation to a relevant body or to any other person the registrar considers may be able to assist in making the assessment; and
(c) accept any answer to a question referred under paragraph (1)(b) as providing sufficient evidence of the nature or extent of any risk.

(2) The registrar must not make available for public inspection—
(a) any application made under regulation 25, 26 or 27;
(b) any documents provided in support of that application;
(c) any notice provided under regulation 29 (notice of withdrawal of application);
(d) any notice provided under regulation 30(4) (notice of an appeal);
(e) any notice provided under regulation 31 (notice that determination no longer wanted); or
(f) any representations delivered under regulation 32 (representations as to why determination should not be revoked).

(3) A person who makes an application under regulation 25, 26 or 27 must inform the registrar in writing without delay upon becoming aware of any change to any information or evidence provided to the registrar in connection with the application.

[4.587]
29 Withdrawal of an application made under regulation 25, 26 or 27

If a person in relation to whom an application has been made under regulation 25, 26 or 27 that has not yet been determined notifies the registrar in writing that the person no longer wishes the registrar to determine the application, the registrar is not required to determine the application under regulation 25(5), 26(7) or 27(7) (as the case may be).

[4.588]
30 Appealing against a determination made under regulation 25, 26 or 27

(1) Subject to paragraph (2), an applicant who has received notice under regulation 25(5), 26(7) or 27(7) that the applicant's application has been unsuccessful may appeal to the High Court or, in Scotland, the Court of Session on the grounds that the determination—
(a) is unlawful;
(b) is irrational or unreasonable; or
(c) has been made on the basis of a procedural impropriety or otherwise contravenes the rules of natural justice.

(2) No appeal may be brought unless the permission of the court has been obtained.

(3) No application for such permission may be made after 28 days beginning with the date of the notice under regulation 25(5), 26(7) or 27(7) unless the court is satisfied that there was good reason for the failure of the applicant to seek permission before the end of that period.

(4) An applicant who seeks permission to appeal must serve written notice of the application on the registrar within 7 days beginning with the date on which the application for permission was issued.

(5) The court determining an appeal may—
(a) dismiss the appeal; or
(b) quash the determination.

(6) Where the court quashes a determination it may refer the matter to the registrar with a direction to reconsider it and make a determination in accordance with the findings of the court.

[4.589]
31 Duration of a determination made under regulation 25, 26 or 27

A determination made under regulation 25(5), 26(7) or 27(7) that an application is successful continues to have effect until—
(a) either—
(i) the person to whom the determination relates; or
(ii) that person's personal representative,

notifies the registrar in writing that he or she wishes the determination to cease to have effect; or

(b) the registrar revokes the determination under regulation 32.

[4.590]

32 Revocation of a determination made under regulation 25, 26 or 27

(1) The registrar may revoke a determination made under regulation 25(5), 26(7) or 27(7) that an application is successful if—

(a) the applicant in relation to the determination or (if different) any person to whom the application relates has been found guilty of an offence under section 1112 of the Act (general false statement offence) in respect of purported compliance with any provision of this Part;

(b) the registrar has sent a notice in accordance with paragraph (2) to the applicant in relation to the determination and (if different) the person to whom the determination relates; and

(c) the period of 28 days beginning with the date of that notice has expired.

(2) The notice mentioned in paragraph (1)(b) must inform the addressee—

(a) of the registrar's intention to revoke the determination;

(b) that the addressee may, within 28 days beginning with the date of the notice, deliver representations in writing to the registrar as to why the registrar should not revoke the determination; and

(c) that if the registrar receives such representations within that period, the registrar will have regard to the representations in deciding whether to revoke the determination.

(3) If within the period specified in paragraph (2)(b) the addressee of the notice delivers representations in writing to the registrar as to why the registrar should not revoke the determination, the registrar must have regard to the representations in deciding whether to revoke the determination.

(4) The registrar must send notice of the registrar's decision as to whether to revoke a determination to the applicant in relation to the determination and (if different) the person to whom the determination relates within 7 days beginning with the date of the decision.

PART 7 THE PROTECTION OF SECURED INFORMATION

[4.591]

33 Circumstances where the registrar must omit secured information from material on the register available for public inspection

(1) The registrar must omit secured information from the material on the register that is available for public inspection if—

(a) in relation to that information an application has been made under regulation 36, 37 or 38—

(i) which has not yet been determined by the registrar and has not been withdrawn under regulation 40;

(ii) which has been determined by the registrar in favour of the applicant (but see paragraph (4));

(iii) which was unsuccessful and a period of 42 days beginning with the date of the notice sent under regulation 36(5), 37(5) or 38(5) has not passed;

(iv) which was unsuccessful and an appeal to the court in respect of that application under regulation 41 has not been determined by the court; or

(v) which was unsuccessful and the applicant has successfully appealed the determination; and

(b) that information is contained in a document delivered to the registrar in which such information is required to be stated and, in the case of a document having more than one part, the information is contained in a part of the document in which such information is required to be stated.

(2) The registrar is not obliged to check documents, other than those described in paragraph (1)(b), to ensure the absence of secured information in relation to which an application under regulation 36, 37 or 38 has been made.

(3) If the secured information in relation to which an application under regulation 36, 37 or 38 is made is available for public inspection on the register at the time that the application is made, the registrar must comply with paragraph (1) as soon as reasonably practicable.

(4) Paragraph (1)(a)(ii) does not apply where the determination has ceased to have effect under regulation 43.

(5) For the purposes of this regulation an application under regulation 36, 37 or 38 is made when it has been registered by the registrar.

[4.592]

34 Circumstances where the registrar must not use or disclose secured information

(1) Subject to paragraph (3), the registrar must not use or disclose secured information if in relation to that information an application has been made under regulation 36, 37 or 38—

(a) which has not yet been determined by the registrar and has not been withdrawn under regulation 40;

(b) which has been determined by the registrar in favour of the applicant (but see paragraph (2));

(c) which was unsuccessful and a period of 42 days beginning with the date of the notice sent under regulation 36(5), 37(5) or 38(5) has not passed;

(d) which was unsuccessful and an appeal to the court in respect of that application under regulation 41 has not been determined by the court; or

(e) which was unsuccessful and the applicant has successfully appealed the determination.

(2) Paragraph (1)(b) does not apply where the determination has ceased to have effect under regulation 43.

(3) Where the prohibition in paragraph (1) applies in relation to secured information, the registrar may—

(a) use or disclose that secured information for communicating with the person to whom the application under regulation 36, 37 or 38 relates and, if different, the applicant; . . .

(b) disclose the secured information to a specified public authority where the conditions specified in Part 1 of Schedule 4 are satisfied[; and

(c) disclose such of the secured information as is specified in paragraph (3A) to a credit institution or a financial institution which satisfies the conditions specified in Part 2A of Schedule 4].

[(3A) The information specified for disclosure under paragraph (3)(c) is—

(a) name,
(b) a service address,
(c) the country or state (or part of the United Kingdom) in which the individual is usually resident,
(d) nationality,
(e) month and year of birth,
(f) the date on which the individual became a registrable person in relation to the company in question, and
(g) the nature of his or her control over that company (see Schedule 1A to the Act and regulation 7 of, and Schedule 2 to, these Regulations).

(3B) The registrar may rely on a statement delivered to the registrar by a credit institution or a financial institution under Part 2A of Schedule 4 as sufficient evidence of the matters stated in it.]

(4) For the purposes of this regulation an application under regulation 36, 37 or 38 is made when it has been registered by the registrar.

NOTES

The word omitted from sub-para (3)(a) was revoked, sub-para (3)(c) and the preceding word were added, and paras (3A), (3B) were inserted, by the Information about People with Significant Control (Amendment) Regulations 2017, SI 2017/693, regs 11,16, as from 26 June 2017 (for transitional arrangements, see Schedule, Pt 1 to the 2017 Regulations at **[10.1195]**).

[4.593]
35 Fee payable for the disclosure by the registrar of secured information

(1) On the disclosure of secured information under regulation 34(3)(b) the specified public authority to which the information is disclosed must pay a fee to the registrar for the disclosure of that information.

(2) The fee payable under paragraph (1) is—
(a) where the request for secured information by the specified public authority is made by reference to an individual, £5.00 per individual specified in the request; or
(b) where the request for secured information by the specified public authority is made by reference to a company, £5.00 per company specified in the request.

[4.594]
[35A Fee payable for the disclosure by the registrar of information to a credit institution or a financial institution

(1) On the disclosure of information under regulation 34(3)(c) the credit institution or the financial institution to which the information is disclosed must pay a fee to the registrar for the disclosure of the information.

(2) The fee payable under paragraph (1) is—
(a) where the request for information is made by reference to an individual, £5.00 per individual specified in the request; or
(b) where the request for information is made by reference to a company, £5.00 per company specified in the request.]

NOTES

Inserted by the Information about People with Significant Control (Amendment) Regulations 2017, SI 2017/693, regs 11, 17, as from 26 June 2017 (for transitional arrangements, see Schedule, Pt 1 to the 2017 Regulations at **[10.1195]**).

[4.595]
36 Application by an individual requiring the registrar to refrain from using or disclosing that individual's secured information

(1) An individual may make an application to the registrar requiring the registrar to refrain from using or disclosing secured information relating to that individual if that individual—
(a) is a registrable person in relation to a company;
(b) proposes to become a registrable person in relation to a company; or
(c) used to be a registrable person in relation to a company.

(2) The grounds on which an application may be made are that the applicant reasonably believes that if that secured information is disclosed by the registrar—
(a) the activities of that company; or
(b) one or more characteristics or personal attributes of the applicant when associated with that company,

will put the applicant or a person living with the applicant at serious risk of being subjected to violence or intimidation.

(3) The application must—
(a) contain—
(i) a statement of the grounds on which the application is made;
(ii) the name and any former name of the applicant;
(iii) the date of birth of the applicant;
(iv) the usual residential address of the applicant;
(v) the e-mail address of the applicant, if any;
(vi) the name and registered number of the company in relation to which the applicant is, proposes to become, or used to be a registrable person; and
(vii) if relevant, a statement that in relation to the applicant an application has also been made under regulation 25, 26 or 27 or a determination has been made in relation to an application under regulation 25(5), 26(7) or 27(7) in favour of the applicant; and
(b) be accompanied by evidence which supports the applicant's statement of the grounds on which the application is made.

(4) Where an individual who is or used to be a registrable person in relation to a company sends an application under paragraph (1) to the registrar in relation to that company, that individual must inform that company of that fact as soon as reasonably practicable.

(5) The registrar must determine the application and, within 7 days beginning with the date that the determination is made, send to the applicant notice of the determination.

(6) Where the application is unsuccessful, the notice under paragraph (5) must inform the applicant of the applicant's right to apply for permission to appeal against the determination within 28 days beginning with the date of the notice.

[4.596]

37 Application by a company requiring the registrar to refrain from using or disclosing an individual's secured information

(1) A company ("the applicant") may make an application to the registrar requiring the registrar to refrain from using or disclosing secured information relating to an individual ("S") who—

(a) is a registrable person;
(b) proposes to become a registrable person; or
(c) used to be a registrable person,

in relation to that company.

(2) A company may only make an application under paragraph (1) where S has given consent for the company to make the application on S's behalf.

(3) The grounds on which an application may be made are that the applicant reasonably believes that if the secured information is disclosed by the registrar—

(a) the activities of the applicant; or
(b) one or more characteristics or personal attributes of S when associated with the applicant,

will put S or a person living with S at serious risk of being subjected to violence or intimidation.

(4) The application must—

(a) contain—
   (i) a statement of the grounds on which the application is made;
   (ii) confirmation that S consents to the making of the application;
   (iii) the name and registered number of the applicant;
   (iv) the address of the registered office of the applicant;
   (v) the e-mail address of the applicant, if any;
   (vi) the name and any former name of S;
   (vii) the date of birth of S;
   (viii) the usual residential address of S; and
   (ix) the e-mail address of S, if any; and
(b) be accompanied by evidence which supports the applicant's statement of the grounds on which the application is made.

(5) The registrar must determine the application and, within 7 days beginning with the date that the determination is made, send to the applicant and to S notice of the determination.

(6) Where the application is unsuccessful, the notice under paragraph (5) must inform the applicant of the applicant's right to apply for permission to appeal against the determination within 28 days beginning with the date of the notice.

[4.597]

38 Application by a subscriber to a memorandum of association requiring the registrar to refrain from using or disclosing an individual's secured information

(1) A subscriber to a memorandum of association ("the applicant") may make an application to the registrar requiring the registrar to refrain from using or disclosing secured information relating to an individual ("S") who proposes to become, on or after the formation of the company to which the memorandum relates, a registrable person in relation to the company.

(2) A subscriber to a memorandum of association may only make an application under paragraph (1) where S has given consent for the subscriber to make the application on S's behalf.

(3) The grounds on which an application may be made are that the applicant reasonably believes that if the secured information is disclosed by the registrar—

(a) the proposed activities of the company to which the memorandum relates; or
(b) one or more characteristics or personal attributes of S when associated with the company to which the memorandum relates,

will put S or a person living with S at serious risk of being subjected to violence or intimidation.

(4) The application must—

(a) contain—
   (i) a statement of the grounds on which the application is made;
   (ii) confirmation that S consents to the making of the application;
   (iii) the name and any former name of the applicant;
   (iv) the usual residential address of the applicant;
   (v) the e-mail address of the applicant, if any;
   (vi) the name of the company to which the memorandum relates;
   (vii) the name and any former name of S;
   (viii) the date of birth of S;
   (ix) the usual residential address of S; and
   (x) the e-mail address of S, if any; and

(b) be accompanied by evidence which supports the applicant's statement of the grounds on which the application is made.

(5) The registrar must determine the application and, within 7 days beginning with the date that the determination is made, send to the applicant and to S notice of the determination.

(6) Where the application is unsuccessful, the notice under paragraph (5) must inform the applicant of the applicant's right to apply for permission to appeal against the determination within 28 days beginning with the date of the notice.

[4.598]

39 Matters relating to an application made under regulation 36, 37 or 38

(1) For the purpose of determining an application made under regulation 36, 37 or 38 the registrar may—

(a) direct that additional information or evidence should be delivered to the registrar;

(b) refer any question relating to an assessment of the nature or extent of any risk of violence or intimidation to a relevant body or to any other person the registrar considers may be able to assist in making that assessment; and

(c) accept any answer to a question referred under paragraph (1)(b) as providing sufficient evidence of the nature or extent of any risk.

(2) The registrar must not make available for public inspection—

(a) any application made under regulation 36, 37 or 38;

(b) any documents provided in support of that application;

(c) any notice provided under regulation 40 (notice of withdrawal of application);

(d) any notice provided under regulation 41 (notice of an appeal);

(e) any notice provided under regulation 43 (notice that determination no longer wanted);

(f) any notice provided under regulation 44 (representations as to why determination should not be revoked); or

(g) any notice provided under regulation 46 (notice that a person is no longer a registrable person).

(3) A person who makes an application under regulation 36, 37 or 38 must inform the registrar in writing without delay upon becoming aware of any change to any information or evidence provided to the registrar in connection with the application.

(4) For the purposes of this regulation an application under regulation 36, 37 or 38 is made when it has been registered by the registrar.

[4.599]

40 Withdrawal of an application made under regulation 36, 37 or 38

(1) If a person in relation to whom an application has been made under regulation 36, 37 or 38 that has not yet been determined notifies the registrar in writing that the person no longer wishes the registrar to determine the application, the registrar is not required to determine the application under regulation 36(5), 37(5) or 38(5) (as the case may be).

(2) Where a person in relation to whom an application under regulation 36 or 37 has been made sends a notice to the registrar under paragraph (1), that person must notify the company to which the application related of this fact as soon as reasonably practicable.

(3) Where a person in relation to whom an application under regulation 38 has been made sends a notice to the registrar under paragraph (1), that person must notify the subscriber to the memorandum of association who made the application and, if incorporated, the company to which the application related of this fact as soon as reasonably practicable.

(4) For the purposes of this regulation an application under regulation 36, 37 or 38 is made when it has been registered by the registrar.

[4.600]

41 Appealing against an unsuccessful application made under regulation 36, 37 or 38

(1) Subject to paragraph (2), an applicant who has received notice under regulation 36(5), 37(5) or 38(5) that the applicant's application has been unsuccessful may appeal to the High Court or, in Scotland, the Court of Session on the grounds that the determination—

(a) is unlawful;

(b) is irrational or unreasonable; or

(c) has been made on the basis of a procedural impropriety or otherwise contravenes the rules of natural justice.

(2) No appeal may be brought unless the permission of the court has been obtained.

(3) No application for such permission may be made after 28 days beginning with the date of the notice under regulation 36(5), 37(5) or 38(5) unless the court is satisfied that there was good reason for the failure of the applicant to seek permission before the end of that period.

(4) An applicant who seeks permission to appeal must serve written notice of the application on the registrar within 7 days beginning with the date on which the application for permission was issued.

(5) The court determining an appeal may—

(a) dismiss the appeal; or

(b) quash the determination.

(6) Where the court quashes a determination it may refer the matter to the registrar with a direction to reconsider it and make a determination in accordance with the findings of the court.

[4.601]

42 Unsuccessful determination made under regulation 36, 37 or 38

(1) This regulation applies where the registrar has made a determination in respect of an application made under regulation 36, 37 or 38 that is not in favour of the applicant.

(2) The registrar must make secured information on the register to which the application under regulation 36, 37 or 38 relates available for public inspection—

(a) where notice of an application for permission to appeal has not been served on the registrar in accordance with regulation 41(4), as soon as reasonably practicable after the end of the period of 42 days beginning with the date of the notice given under regulation 36(5), 37(5) or 38(5); or

(b) where notice of an application for permission to appeal has been served on the registrar in accordance with regulation 41(4), as soon as reasonably practicable after—

(i) the court has dismissed the application for permission to appeal or the appeal and there is no further appeal pending; or

(ii) the registrar becomes aware that the application for permission to appeal or the appeal has been subsequently withdrawn or abandoned.

(3) Where the registrar makes secured information available for public inspection on the register under this regulation, the registrar must notify the person to whom the secured information relates and the company to which the application under regulation 36, 37 or 38 related of that action as soon as reasonably practicable.

[4.602]

43 Duration of a determination under regulation 36, 37 or 38

(1) A determination under regulation 36(5), 37(5) or 38(5) that an application is successful continues to have effect until—

(a) either—

(i) the person to whom the determination relates; or

(ii) that person's personal representative,

notifies the registrar in writing that he or she wishes the determination to cease to have effect; or

(b) the registrar revokes the determination under regulation 44.

(2) Where a notice is given under paragraph (1)(a), the person giving the notice must also notify the company to which the application that was determined relates of the notice given to the registrar.

[4.603]

44 Revocation of a determination under regulation 36(5), 37(5) or 38(5)

(1) The registrar may revoke a determination made under regulation 36(5), 37(5) or 38(5) that an application is successful if—

(a) the applicant in relation to the determination or (if different) any person to whom the application relates has been found guilty of an offence under section 1112 of the Act (general false statement offence) in respect of purported compliance with any provision of this Part;

(b) the registrar has sent a notice in accordance with paragraph (2) to the applicant in relation to the determination and (if different) the person to whom the determination relates; and

(c) the period of 28 days beginning with the date of that notice has expired.

(2) The notice mentioned in paragraph (1)(b) must inform the addressee—

(a) of the registrar's intention to revoke the determination;

(b) that the addressee may, within 28 days beginning with the date of the notice, deliver representations in writing to the registrar as to why the registrar should not revoke the determination; and

(c) that if the registrar receives such representations within that period, the registrar will have regard to the representations in deciding whether to revoke the determination.

(3) If within the period specified in paragraph (2)(b) an addressee of the notice delivers representations in writing to the registrar as to why the registrar should not revoke the determination, the registrar must have regard to the representations in deciding whether to revoke the determination.

(4) The registrar must send notice of the registrar's decision as to whether to revoke a determination to the applicant in relation to the determination and (if different) the person to whom the determination relates within 7 days beginning with the date of the decision.

(5) Where the registrar has made a decision to revoke a determination, the registrar must make secured information on the register to which the determination relates available for public inspection as soon as reasonably practicable after sending the notice mentioned in paragraph (4).

(6) Where the registrar makes secured information available for public inspection on the register under this regulation, the registrar must notify the person to whom the secured information relates and the company to which the application under regulation 36, 37 or 38 related of that action as soon as reasonably practicable.

[4.604]

45 Protection by a company of secured information

(1) Subject to paragraph (2), a company must not use or disclose secured information relating to a person ("S") if—

(a) in relation to that information an application has been made under regulation 36, 37 or 38; and

(b) the company has not received notification under regulation 40(2), 40(3), 42(3), 43(2), 44(6) or 46(5)(b).

(2) The company may use or disclose secured information relating to S—

(a) for communicating with S;

(b) in order to comply with a requirement of the Act as to particulars to be sent to the registrar; . . .

(c) where S has given consent for the company to use or disclose secured information relating to S[; or

(d) to the extent necessary in order to comply with regulation 43 (corporate bodies: obligations) of the Money Laundering Terrorist Financing and Transfer of Funds (Information on the Payer) Regulations 2017].

(3) For the purposes of this regulation, an application has been made—

(a) under regulation 36(1)(a) or 36(1)(c) when the applicant has informed the company under regulation 36(4) that the applicant has made an application;

(b) under regulation 36(1)(b) when the company has received the particular required by section 790K(1)(i) of the Act in relation to that individual;
(c) under regulation 37 when the company sends the application to the registrar; or
(d) under regulation 38 when the subscriber to the memorandum sends an application to the registrar.

(4) Where a company is prohibited under paragraph (1) from using or disclosing any secured information, the company's PSC register is to be treated as not including that information for the purposes of sections 790N(1), 790O(1) and 790O(2) of the Act.

NOTES

Para (2): word omitted from sub-para (b) revoked, and sub-para (d) and the preceding word inserted, by the Information about People with Significant Control (Amendment) Regulations 2017, SI 2017/693, regs 11, 18, as from 26 June 2017 (for transitional arrangements, see Schedule, Pt 1 to the 2017 Regulations at **[10.1195]**).

PART 8 TRANSITIONAL PROVISIONS, AMENDMENTS TO THE 2009 REGULATIONS AND REVIEW

[4.605]

46 Transitional provision regarding the protection of secured information

(1) This regulation applies where—
(a) an individual is a registrable person on 6th April 2016 (a "protectable person");
(b) an application under regulation 36 or 37 is made in relation to the protectable person's secured information on or before 30th June 2016; and
(c) the registrar makes a determination that the application is unsuccessful.

(2) Subject to paragraph (4)—
(a) for the protected period, the registrar must not use or disclose that secured information and must omit that secured information from the material on the register that is available for public inspection; and
(b) where, before the expiry of the protected period, the protectable person ceases to be a registrable person in relation to the company to which the application relates and notifies the registrar in writing of that fact, after the expiry of the protected period the registrar must not use or disclose the secured information and must omit that secured information from the material on the register that is available for public inspection.

(3) A protectable person who sends a notice to the registrar under paragraph (2)(b) must—
(a) include in the notice the date on which that protectable person ceased to be a registrable person in relation to the company; and
(b) send a copy of the notice to the company.

(4) The registrar may use or disclose the secured information for communicating with the protectable person and, where the application was made under regulation 37, the company which made the application.

(5) Where the registrar has not received a notice under paragraph 2(b) before the expiry of the protected period, the registrar must, as soon as reasonably practicable after the expiry of that period—
(a) make the secured information on the register available for public inspection; and
(b) notify the protectable person and the company to which the application under regulation 36 or 37 related of that action.

(6) For the purposes of this regulation—
(a) an application under regulation 36 or 37 is made when it is registered by the registrar; and
(b) "protected period" means—
(i) where an appeal under regulation 41 has not been brought, 12 weeks beginning with the date of the notice sent under regulation 36(5) or 37(5);
(ii) where an appeal under regulation 41 has been brought and dismissed, 12 weeks beginning with the date the court dismissed the appeal in accordance with regulation 41(5); or
(iii) where an appeal under regulation 41 has been brought and subsequently withdrawn or abandoned, 12 weeks beginning with the date of the registrar becoming aware that such appeal has been withdrawn or abandoned.

[4.606]

47 Transitional provision for the purpose of section 790K

Where an individual or a relevant legal entity is registrable in relation to a company on 6th April 2016, the date on which the individual or entity became a registrable person or a registrable relevant legal entity, as the case may be, in relation to the company in question is deemed to be 6th April 2016 for the purposes of sections 790K(1)(g), 790K(2)(d) and 790K(3)(e) of the Act.

[4.607]

48 Amendments to the 2009 Regulations

Schedule 5 (which amends the 2009 Regulations) has effect.

49 (*Reg 49 requires the Secretary of State to review the operation and effect of these Regulations and publish a report within the period that the Secretary of State is obliged to review and report on Part 21A of the Companies Act 2006 by s 82 of the Small Business, Enterprise and Employment Act 2015. These Regulations must then be reviewed within every five years after that.*)

SCHEDULES

SCHEDULE 1
LIST OF MARKETS

Regulations 3 and 4

[4.608]

In Israel—

Tel Aviv Stock Exchange

In Japan—

Fukuoka Stock Exchange
Nagoya Stock Exchange
Osaka Securities Exchange
Sapporo Securities Exchange
Tokyo Stock Exchange

In Switzerland—

BX Berne Exchange
SIX Swiss Exchange

In the United States of America—

BATS Exchange, Inc
BATS Y-Exchange, Inc
BOX Options Exchange LLC
C2 Options Exchange, Incorporated
Chicago Board Options Exchange, Incorporated
Chicago Stock Exchange, Inc
EDGA Exchange, Inc
EDGX Exchange, Inc
International Securities Exchange, LLC
ISE Gemini LLC
Miami International Securities Exchange LLC
NASDAQ OMX BX, Inc
NASDAQ OMX PHLX LLC
The NASDAQ Stock Market LLC
National Stock Exchange, Inc
New York Stock Exchange LLC
NYSE Arca, Inc
NYSE MKT LLC

SCHEDULE 2
PARTICULARS REQUIRED AS TO NATURE OF CONTROL

Regulation 7

PART 1 FIRST CONDITION

[4.609]

1. A statement that the person holds, directly or indirectly, more than 25% but not more than 50% of the shares in the company.

2. A statement that the person holds, directly or indirectly, more than 50% but less than 75% of the shares in the company.

3. A statement that the person holds, directly or indirectly, 75% or more of the shares in the company.

PART 2 SECOND CONDITION

[4.610]

4. A statement that the person holds, directly or indirectly, more than 25% but not more than 50% of the voting rights in the company.

5. A statement that the person holds, directly or indirectly, more than 50% but less than 75% of the voting rights in the company.

6. A statement that the person holds, directly or indirectly, 75% or more of the voting rights in the company.

PART 3 THIRD CONDITION

[4.611]

7. A statement that the person holds the right, directly or indirectly, to appoint or remove a majority of the board of directors of the company.

PART 4 FOURTH CONDITION

[4.612]

8. A statement that the person has the right to exercise, or actually exercises, significant influence or control over the company.

PART 5 FIFTH CONDITION AND TRUSTS

[4.613]

9. A statement that—

(a) the person has the right to exercise, or actually exercises, significant influence or control over the activities of a trust; and

(b) the trustees of that trust (in their capacity as such) hold, directly or indirectly, more than 25% but not more than 50% of the shares in the company.

10. A statement that—

(a) the person has the right to exercise, or actually exercises, significant influence or control over the activities of a trust; and

(b) the trustees of that trust (in their capacity as such) hold, directly or indirectly, more than 50% but less than 75% of the shares in the company.

11. A statement that—

(a) the person has the right to exercise, or actually exercises, significant influence or control over the activities of a trust; and

(b) the trustees of that trust (in their capacity as such) hold, directly or indirectly, 75% or more of the shares in the company.

12. A statement that—

(a) the person has the right to exercise, or actually exercises, significant influence or control over the activities of a trust; and

(b) the trustees of that trust (in their capacity as such) hold, directly or indirectly, more than 25% but not more than 50% of the voting rights in the company.

13. A statement that—

(a) the person has the right to exercise, or actually exercises, significant influence or control over the activities of a trust; and

(b) the trustees of that trust (in their capacity as such) hold, directly or indirectly, more than 50% but less than 75% of the voting rights in the company.

14. A statement that—

(a) the person has the right to exercise, or actually exercises, significant influence or control over the activities of a trust; and

(b) the trustees of that trust (in their capacity as such) hold, directly or indirectly, 75% or more of the voting rights in the company.

15. A statement that—

(a) the person has the right to exercise, or actually exercises, significant influence or control over the activities of a trust; and

(b) the trustees of that trust (in their capacity as such) hold the right, directly or indirectly, to appoint or remove a majority of the board of directors of the company.

16. A statement that—

(a) the person has the right to exercise, or actually exercises, significant influence or control over the activities of a trust; and

(b) the trustees of that trust (in their capacity as such) have the right to exercise, or actually exercise, significant influence or control over the company.

PART 6 FIFTH CONDITION AND FIRMS

[4.614]

17. A statement that—

(a) the person has the right to exercise, or actually exercises, significant influence or control over the activities of a firm that, under the law by which it is governed, is not a legal person; and

(b) the members of that firm (in their capacity as such) hold, directly or indirectly, more than 25% but not more than 50% of the shares in the company.

18. A statement that—

(a) the person has the right to exercise, or actually exercises, significant influence or control over the activities of a firm that, under the law by which it is governed, is not a legal person; and

(b) the members of that firm (in their capacity as such) hold, directly or indirectly, more than 50% but less than 75% of the shares in the company.

19. A statement that—

(a) the person has the right to exercise, or actually exercises, significant influence or control over the activities of a firm that, under the law by which it is governed, is not a legal person; and

(b) the members of that firm (in their capacity as such) hold, directly or indirectly, 75% or more of the shares in the company.

20. A statement that—

(a) the person has the right to exercise, or actually exercises, significant influence or control over the activities of a firm that, under the law by which it is governed, is not a legal person; and

(b) the members of that firm (in their capacity as such) hold, directly or indirectly, more than 25% but not more than 50% of the voting rights in the company.

21. A statement that—

(a) the person has the right to exercise, or actually exercises, significant influence or control over the activities of a firm that, under the law by which it is governed, is not a legal person; and

(b) the members of that firm (in their capacity as such) hold, directly or indirectly, more than 50% but less than 75% of the voting rights in the company.

22. A statement that—

(a) the person has the right to exercise, or actually exercises, significant influence or control over the activities of a firm that, under the law by which it is governed, is not a legal person; and

(b) the members of that firm (in their capacity as such) hold, directly or indirectly, 75% or more of the voting rights in the company.

23. A statement that—

(a) the person has the right to exercise, or actually exercises, significant influence or control over the activities of a firm that, under the law by which it is governed, is not a legal person; and

(b) the members of that firm (in their capacity as such) hold the right, directly or indirectly, to appoint or remove a majority of the board of directors of the company.

24. A statement that—

(a) the person has the right to exercise, or actually exercises, significant influence or control over the activities of a firm that, under the law by which it is governed, is not a legal person; and

(b) the members of that firm (in their capacity as such) have the right to exercise, or actually exercise, significant influence or control over the company.

PART 7 INTERPRETATION OF SCHEDULE 2

[4.615]

25. In relation to a company that does not have a share capital, a reference to holding a particular percentage of shares in a company is to holding a right or rights to share in that percentage of capital or, as the case may be, profits of that company.

SCHEDULE 3
SPECIFIED PUBLIC AUTHORITIES

Regulation 22(1)

[4.616]

The Bank of England [(including the Bank in its capacity as the Prudential Regulation Authority)];

the Charity Commission;

the Charity Commission for Northern Ireland;

the Commissioners for Her Majesty's Revenue and Customs;

the Competition and Markets Authority;

the Crown Office and Procurator Fiscal Services;

the Director of Public Prosecutions;

the Director of Public Prosecutions for Northern Ireland;

the Financial Conduct Authority;

the Food Standards Agency;

the Gas and Electricity Markets Authority;

the Gambling Commission;

[the Gangmasters Labour and Abuse Authority;]

the Government Communications Headquarters;

the Health and Safety Executive;

the Health and Safety Executive for Northern Ireland;

the Marine Management Organisation;

the Minister for the Cabinet Office;

the National Crime Agency;

the Northern Ireland Authority for Utility Regulation;

any Northern Ireland Department;

the Office of Communications;

the Office of the Information Commissioner;

the Office for Nuclear Regulation;

the Office of the Scottish Charity Regulator;

the Official Receiver for Northern Ireland;

the Panel on Takeovers and Mergers;

the Pensions Regulator;

. . .

the Registry of Credit Unions and Industrial and Provident Societies for Northern Ireland;

the Regulator of Community Interest Companies;

the Scottish Housing Regulator;

the Scottish Ministers;

the Security Industry Authority;

the Secret Intelligence Service;

the Secretary of State;

the Security Service;

the Serious Fraud Office;

the Treasury;

the Treasury Solicitor;

the Welsh Ministers;

a local authority within the meaning of section 54(2) of the Act;

an official receiver appointed under section 399 of the Insolvency Act 1986 (appointment, etc, of official receivers);

a person acting as an insolvency practitioner within the meaning of section 388 of the Insolvency Act 1986 (meaning of "act as an insolvency practitioner") or article 3 of the Insolvency (Northern Ireland) Order 1989 ("act as an insolvency practitioner");

an inspector appointed under Part 14 of the Companies Act 1985 (investigation of companies and their affairs: requisition of documents) or a person appointed under regulation 30 of the Open-Ended Investment Companies Regulations 2001 (power to investigate) or regulation 30 of the Open-Ended Investment Companies Regulations (Northern Ireland) 2004;

any person authorised to exercise powers under section 447 of the Companies Act 1985 (power to require documents and information), or section 84 of the Companies Act 1989 (exercise of powers by officers, etc);

any person exercising functions conferred by Part 6 of the Financial Services and Markets Act 2000 (official listing);

a person appointed to make a report under section 166 or 166A (reports by skilled persons) of the Financial Services and Markets Act 2000;

a person appointed to conduct an investigation under section 167 (appointment of persons to carry out general investigations) or 168(3) or (5) (appointment of persons to carry out investigations in particular cases) of the Financial Services and Markets Act 2000;

a person appointed under section 284 (power to investigate) of the Financial Services and Markets Act 2000;

a police force within the meaning of section 101(1) of the Police Act 1996;

the Police Service of Northern Ireland;

the Police Service of Scotland;

the lead enforcement authority (as defined in section 33(1) of the Estate Agents Act 1979) exercising functions under the Estate Agents Act 1979.

NOTES

Words in square brackets in entry "Bank of England" inserted, and entry "the Prudential Regulation Authority" (omitted) revoked, by the Bank of England and Financial Services (Consequential Amendments) Regulations 2017, SI 2017/80, reg 2, Schedule, Pt 2, para 46, as from 1 March 2017.

Entry "the Gangmasters Labour and Abuse Authority" substituted by the Immigration Act 2016 (Consequential Amendments) Regulations 2016, SI 2016/655, reg 2, Schedule, Pt 2, para 12, as from 12 July 2016.

SCHEDULE 4
CONDITIONS FOR PERMITTED DISCLOSURE

Regulations 22(2), 23(1) and 34(3)

PART 1 DISCLOSURE TO SPECIFIED PUBLIC AUTHORITIES

[4.617]

1. The specified public authority has delivered to the registrar a statement that it intends to use the information only for the purpose of facilitating the carrying out by that specified public authority of a public function ("the permitted purpose").

2. Subject to paragraph 3, the specified public authority has delivered to the registrar a statement that, where it supplies a copy of the information to a processor for the purpose of processing the information for use in respect of the permitted purpose, the specified public authority will—

- (a) ensure that the processor is one who carries on business [in the United Kingdom or] in the European Economic Area;
- (b) require that the processor does not transmit the information outside the [area comprising the United Kingdom and the European Economic Area]; and
- (c) require that the processor does not disclose the information except to that specified public authority or an employee of that specified public authority.

3. Paragraph 2 does not apply where the specified public authority is the National Crime Agency, Secret Intelligence Service, Security Service or Government Communications Headquarters.

4. The specified public authority has delivered any information or evidence required by the registrar for the purpose of enabling the registrar to determine in accordance with these Regulations whether to disclose the information.

5. The specified public authority has complied with any requirement by the registrar to confirm the accuracy of the statements, information or evidence delivered to the registrar pursuant to this Part of this Schedule.

NOTES

Para 2: the words in square brackets in sub-para (a) were inserted, and the words in square brackets in sub-para (b) were substituted, by the Companies, Limited Liability Partnerships and Partnerships (Amendment etc) (EU Exit) Regulations 2019, SI 2019/348, reg 7, Sch 2, paras 13, 14(a), as from IP completion day (as defined in the European Union (Withdrawal Agreement) Act 2020, s 39) (for transitional provisions see Sch 4, para 5 to the 2019 Regulations at **[12.106]**).

PART 2 DISCLOSURE TO A CREDIT REFERENCE AGENCY

[4.618]

6. The credit reference agency—

(a) is carrying on in the United Kingdom . . . a business comprising the furnishing of information relevant to the financial standing of individuals, being information collected by the agency for that purpose;

(b) maintains appropriate procedures—

(i) to ensure that an independent person can investigate and audit the measures maintained by the agency for the purposes of ensuring the security of any information within section 790ZF(2) of the Act disclosed to that agency; and

[(ii) for the purposes of ensuring that it complies with its [obligations under the data protection legislation (as defined in section 3 of the Data Protection Act 2018)];]

(c) has not been found guilty of an offence under—

(i) section 1112 of the Act (general false statement offence);

(ii) section 2 of the Fraud Act 2006 (fraud by false representation); . . .

(iii) section 47 of the Data Protection Act 1998 (failure to comply with enforcement notice) in circumstances where it has used the information within section 790ZF(2) of the Act for purposes other than those described in sub-paragraphs (a) to (e) of paragraph 8;

[(iv) section 144 of the Data Protection Act 2018 (false statements made in response to an information notice); or

(v) section 148 of that Act (destroying or falsifying information and documents etc);]

[(d) has not been given a penalty notice under section 155 of the Data Protection Act 2018 in circumstances described in sub-paragraph (c)(iii), other than a penalty notice that has been cancelled.]

7. The credit reference agency has delivered to the registrar a statement that it meets the conditions in paragraph 6.

8. The credit reference agency has delivered to the registrar a statement that it intends to use the information within section 790ZF(2) of the Act only for the purposes of—

(a) providing an assessment of the financial standing of a person;

(b) meeting any obligations contained in—

(i) [the Money Laundering, Terrorist Financing and Transfer of Funds (Information on the Payer) Regulations 2017]; [or]

(ii) any rules made pursuant to section 137A of the Financial Services and Markets Act 2000 which relate to the prevention and detection of money laundering in connection with the carrying on of regulated activities by authorised persons; . . .

(iii) . . .

(c) conducting conflict of interest checks required or made necessary by any enactment;

(d) providing information within section 790ZF(2) of the Act to—

(i) a specified public authority which has satisfied the conditions of paragraphs 1 and 2 of Part 1 of this Schedule; or

(ii) a credit reference agency which has satisfied the requirements of this Part of this Schedule; or

(e) conducting checks for the prevention and detection of crime and fraud.

9. The credit reference agency has delivered to the registrar a statement that it intends to take delivery of and to use the information within section 790ZF(2) of the Act only in the United Kingdom . . .

10. The credit reference agency has delivered to the registrar a statement that it will, where it supplies a copy of the information within section 790ZF(2) of the Act to a processor for the purpose of processing the information for use in respect of the purposes referred to in paragraph 8—

(a) ensure that the processor is one who carries on business in the [United Kingdom];

(b) require that the processor does not transmit the information outside the [United Kingdom]; and

(c) require that the processor does not disclose the information except to the credit reference agency or an employee of the credit reference agency.

11. The credit reference agency has delivered any information or evidence required by the registrar for the purpose of enabling the registrar to determine in accordance with these Regulations whether to disclose the information within section 790ZF(2) of the Act.

12. The credit reference agency has complied with any requirement by the registrar to confirm the accuracy of the statements, information or evidence delivered to the registrar pursuant to this Part of this Schedule.

NOTES

Para 6: the words omitted from sub-para (a) were revoked, and the words in square brackets in sub-para (b)(ii) were substituted, by the Companies, Limited Liability Partnerships and Partnerships (Amendment etc) (EU Exit) Regulations 2019, SI 2019/348, reg 7, Sch 2, paras 13, 14(b), as from IP completion day (as defined in the European Union (Withdrawal Agreement) Act 2020, s 39) (for transitional provisions see Sch 4, para 5 to the 2019 Regulations at **[12.106]**). All other amendments to this paragraph were made by the Data Protection Act 2018, s 211, Sch 19, Pt 2, paras 399, 400, as from 25 May 2018 (for transitional provisions and savings relating to the repeal of the Data Protection Act 1998, see Sch 20 to the 2018 Act).

Para 8: the word "or" at the end of sub-para (b)(i) was inserted, and sub-para (b)(iii) and the preceding word were revoked, by SI 2019/348, reg 7, Sch 2, paras 13, 14(c), as from IP completion day (as defined in the European Union (Withdrawal Agreement) Act 2020, s 39) (for transitional provisions see Sch 4, para 5 to the 2019 Regulations at **[12.106]**). Words in first pair of square brackets in sub-para (b)(i) substituted by the Money Laundering, Terrorist Financing and Transfer of Funds (Information on the Payer) Regulations 2017, SI 2017/692, reg 109, Sch 7, Pt 2, para 34, as from 26 June 2017.

Para 9: words omitted revoked by SI 2019/348, reg 7, Sch 2, paras 13, 14(d), as from IP completion day (as defined in the European Union (Withdrawal Agreement) Act 2020, s 39) (for transitional provisions see Sch 4, para 5 to the 2019 Regulations at **[12.106]**).

Para 10: words in square brackets substituted by SI 2019/348, reg 7, Sch 2, paras 13, 14(e), as from IP completion day (as defined in the European Union (Withdrawal Agreement) Act 2020, s 39) (for transitional provisions see Sch 4, para 5 to the 2019 Regulations at **[12.106]**).

[PART 2A DISCLOSURE TO A CREDIT INSTITUTION OR A FINANCIAL INSTITUTION

[4.619]

12A. The credit institution or financial institution maintains appropriate procedures—

(a) to ensure that an independent person can investigate and audit the measures maintained by that institution for the purposes of ensuring the security of any information disclosed to it; and

[(b) for the purposes of ensuring that it complies with its [obligations under the data protection legislation (as defined in section 3 of the Data Protection Act 2018)].]

12B. The credit institution or financial institution has delivered to the registrar a statement confirming that it is a credit institution or, as the case may be, a financial institution, and that it meets the conditions in paragraph 12A.

12C. The credit institution or financial institution has delivered to the registrar a statement that it intends to use information only for the purpose of applying customer due diligence measures to the company in relation to which the information is secured, in accordance with the Money Laundering, Terrorist Financing and Transfer of Funds (Information on the Payer) Regulations 2017.

12D. The credit institution or financial institution has delivered to the registrar a statement that confirms the name and registered number of the company it is entering a transaction with which requires the institution to apply customer due diligence measures under those Regulations.

12E. The credit institution or financial institution has delivered to the registrar a statement that it intends to take delivery of and to use the information only in the United Kingdom.

12F. The credit institution or financial institution has delivered to the registrar a statement that it will, where it supplies a copy of the information to a processor for the purpose of processing the information for use in respect of the purpose referred to in paragraph 12C—

(a) ensure that the processor is one who carries on business in the [United Kingdom];

(b) require that the processor does not transmit the information outside the [United Kingdom]; and

(c) require that the processor does not disclose the information except to the credit institution or financial institution.

12G. The credit institution or financial institution has delivered any information or evidence required by the registrar for the purpose of enabling the registrar to determine in accordance with these Regulations whether to disclose the information.

12H. The credit institution or financial institution has complied with any requirement by the registrar to confirm the accuracy of the statements, information or evidence delivered to the registrar pursuant to this Part.]

NOTES

Inserted by the Information about People with Significant Control (Amendment) Regulations 2017, SI 2017/693, regs 11, 19, as from 26 June 2017 (for transitional arrangements, see Schedule, Pt 1 to the 2017 Regulations at **[10.1195]**).

Para 12A: sub-para (b) was substituted by the Data Protection Act 2018, s 211, Sch 19, Pt 2, paras 399, 401, as from 25 May 2018 (for transitional provisions and savings relating to the repeal of the Data Protection Act 1998, see Sch 20 to the 2018 Act). Words in square brackets in sub-para (b) substituted by the Companies, Limited Liability Partnerships and Partnerships (Amendment etc) (EU Exit) Regulations 2019, SI 2019/348, reg 7, Sch 2, paras 13, 14(f), as from IP completion day (as defined in the European Union (Withdrawal Agreement) Act 2020, s 39) (for transitional provisions see Sch 4, para 5 to the 2019 Regulations at **[12.106]**).

Para 12F: words in square brackets substituted by SI 2019/348, reg 7, Sch 2, paras 13, 14(g), as from IP completion day (as defined in the European Union (Withdrawal Agreement) Act 2020, s 39) (for transitional provisions see Sch 4, para 5 to the 2019 Regulations at **[12.106]**).

PART 3 INTERPRETATION OF THIS SCHEDULE

[4.620]

13. In this Schedule—

(a) "processor" means any person who provides a service which consists of putting information into data form or processing information in data form and any reference to a processor includes a reference to the processor's employees;

(b) "public function" includes—

(i) any function conferred by or in accordance with any provision contained in any enactment;

(ii) . . .

(iii) any similar function conferred on persons by or under provisions having effect as part of the law of a country or territory outside the United Kingdom; and

(iv) any function exercisable in relation to the investigation of any criminal offence or for the purpose of any criminal proceedings;

(c) any reference to an employee of any person who has access to information within section 790ZF(2) of the Act includes any person working or providing services for the purposes of that person or employed by or on behalf of, or working for, any person who is so working or who is supplying such a service; and

(d) any reference to the disclosure for the purpose of facilitating the carrying out of a public function includes disclosure in relation to, and for the purpose of, any proceedings whether civil, criminal or disciplinary in which the specified public authority engages while carrying out its public functions.

[14. . . .]

NOTES

Para 13: sub-para (b)(ii) revoked by the Companies, Limited Liability Partnerships and Partnerships (Amendment etc) (EU Exit) Regulations 2019, SI 2019/348, reg 7, Sch 2, paras 13, 14(h), as from IP completion day (as defined in the European Union (Withdrawal Agreement) Act 2020, s 39) (for transitional provisions see Sch 4, para 5 to the 2019 Regulations at **[12.106]**).

Para 14: originally added by the Data Protection Act 2018, s 211, Sch 19, Pt 2, paras 399, 402, as from 25 May 2018 (for transitional provisions and savings relating to the repeal of the Data Protection Act 1998, see Sch 20 to the 2018 Act). Subsequently revoked by SI 2019/348, reg 7, Sch 2, paras 13, 14(i), as from IP completion day (as defined in the European Union (Withdrawal Agreement) Act 2020, s 39) (for transitional provisions see Sch 4, para 5 to the 2019 Regulations at **[12.106]**).

SCHEDULE 5
AMENDMENTS TO THE 2009 REGULATIONS

(*Amends the Companies (Disclosure of Address) Regulations 2009, SI 2009/214 at* **[4.191]**.)

COMPANIES (ADDRESS OF REGISTERED OFFICE) REGULATIONS 2016

(SI 2016/423)

NOTES

Made: 23 March 2016.
Authority: Companies Act 2006, s 1097A; Limited Liability Partnerships Act 2000, s 15.
Commencement: 6 April 2016.
For a summary of all Orders and Regulations made under the Companies Act 2006, see Appendix 4 at **[A4]**.

ARRANGEMENT OF REGULATIONS

CITATION, COMMENCEMENT AND INTERPRETATION

[4.621]
1

(1) These Regulations may be cited as the Companies (Address of Registered Office) Regulations 2016 and come into force on 6th April 2016.

(2) In these Regulations—
- (a) "the 2015 Regulations" means the Company, Limited Liability Partnership and Business (Names and Trading Disclosures) Regulations 2015;
- (b) "the Act" means the Companies Act 2006;
- (c) "applicant" means the person who has made an application under regulation 2;
- (d) "default address" means an address nominated by the registrar by virtue of rules made under section 1117 of the Act;
- (e) "residential address" means the usual residential address of a director of a company stated in the company's register of directors' residential addresses and notified to the registrar under section 167 of the Act;
- (f) "service address" means—
  - (i) in the case of a director or secretary who is an individual, the address stated in the company's register of directors or register of secretaries respectively;
  - (ii) in the case of a director or secretary who is a body corporate or a firm that is a legal person under the law by which it is governed, the address of its registered or principal office stated in the company's register of directors or register of secretaries respectively;

  and notified to the registrar under section 167 or section 276 of the Act.

APPLICATION TO CHANGE A COMPANY REGISTERED OFFICE

[4.622]
2

An application to the registrar to change the address of a company's registered office may be made by any person.

[4.623]
3

An application to the registrar must—
(a) state the applicant's name and address;
(b) identify the company and the address of its registered office;
(c) include a statement explaining the grounds of the application; and
(d) provide any documents or information which supports the application.

[4.624]
4

(1) An application under these Regulations may be withdrawn by the applicant by written notice to the registrar.

(2) Where an application is withdrawn, the registrar must notify the company of the withdrawal.

[4.625]
5

Upon receiving an application, the registrar must either—
(a) dismiss the application if the registrar considers there is no reasonable chance of the application succeeding and notify the applicant of the decision under regulation 10; or
(b) give notice of the application to the company at—
(i) the address of its registered office;
(ii) the service address of every person who (to the registrar's knowledge) is a director or secretary of the company;
(iii) the residential address of every person who (to the registrar's knowledge) is a director of the company; and
(iv) an address specified by the company for communications in electronic form under paragraph 7 of Schedule 4 to the Act.

[4.626]
6

(1) The notice given under regulation 5(b) must—
(a) identify the name of the applicant;
(b) identify the grounds of the application;
(c) provide a copy of any documents or information which supported the application;
(d) state that the registrar will change the address of the company's registered office to a default address unless within a period specified in the notice by the registrar (the "specified period")—
(i) the company changes the address of its registered office in accordance with section 87 of the Act;
(ii) the company objects to the application and provides evidence to the satisfaction of the registrar that the company is authorised to use the address as its registered office; or
(iii) the applicant withdraws the application;
(e) provide an explanation of evidence that may satisfy the registrar that the company is authorised to use the address as its registered office.

(2) The specified period must be—
(a) at least 28 days beginning on the day after the day on which the notice was sent to the company; and
(b) may be extended at the discretion of the registrar at any time before the specified period ends.

DETERMINATION OF AN APPLICATION

[4.627]
7

The registrar, after the specified period, must change the address of a company's registered office to a default address if—
(a) the registrar is satisfied that the company is not authorised to use the address as its registered office; or
(b) the company does not respond to the registrar within the specified period.

[4.628]
8

The registrar must dismiss an application if—
(a) neither regulation 7(a) nor (b) applies; or
(b) the company delivers to the registrar a notice to change the address of the company's registered office under section 87 of the Act within the specified period.

[4.629]
9

For the purposes of determining the application, the registrar may—
(a) refer the application, or any question relating to the application, for determination by the court;
(b) without further enquiry rely on the evidence, or descriptions of evidence, listed in the Schedule, received in connection with an application under these Regulations, to be satisfied that the company is authorised to use the address; or
(c) consider information and documents received in connection with any previous application made under these Regulations that is materially the same as the current application.

NOTICE OF THE REGISTRAR'S DECISION

[4.630]
10

(1) Upon determining an application, the registrar must provide notice of the decision to—
- (a) the applicant; and
- (b) the company at each of the addresses listed in regulation 5.

(2) The notice must—
- (a) state the reasons for making the decision; and
- (b) provide a copy of any evidence upon which the registrar relied.

(3) Where the registrar changes the address of a company's registered office to a default address, the registrar must also provide details of the default address to the company.

EFFECT OF CHANGE OF ADDRESS

[4.631]
11

Where the registrar changes the address of a company's registered office under section 1097A(7) of the Act or these Regulations, the following duties of the company under the Act are suspended for a period of 28 days beginning on the day the address was changed—
- (a) the duty under the following sections of the Act to make company records available for inspection—
  - (i) section 114 (register of members);
  - (ii) section 162 (register of directors);
  - (iii) section 228 (directors' service contracts or memorandum of terms);
  - (iv) section 237 (directors' indemnities);
  - (v) section 275 (register of secretaries);
  - (vi) section 358 (records of resolutions etc);
  - (vii) sections 388 (accounting records);
  - (viii) section 702 (contracts relating to the purchase of own shares);
  - (ix) section 720 (documents relating to redemption or purchase of own shares out of capital by a private company);
  - (x) section 743 (register of debenture holders);
  - (xi) section 805 (report to members of outcome of investigation by public company into interests in its shares);
  - (xii) section 809 (register of interests in shares disclosed to public company); and
  - (xiii) section 859Q (instruments creating charges);
- (b) the duty to display a company's registered name at the company's registered office under regulation 21(1)(a) of the 2015 Regulations;
- (c) the duty to state information about the company's registered office in descriptions of document or communication specified under regulation 25(1) of the 2015 Regulations;
- (d) the duty to provide information about a company's registered office on request to those persons the company deals with in the course of business under regulation 27(1)(a) of the 2015 Regulations.

ADMINISTRATION OF THE DEFAULT ADDRESS

[4.632]
12

The default address may not be used for the purpose of keeping, or making available for inspection, the company's registers, indexes or other documents.

[4.633]
13

The registrar will not be required to open any documents delivered to the company at the default address.

[4.634]
14

(1) The registrar must provide for the collection by the company of any documents delivered to the company at the default address, unless the documents have been destroyed in accordance with paragraph (2).

(2) The registrar may destroy any document not collected by the company 12 months after receipt of the document.

[4.635]
15

Where the company has changed the address of its registered office from the default address to a new address under section 87 of the Act, the registrar may forward the documents to the new address.

APPEAL TO THE COURT

[4.636]
16

An appeal to the court under section 1097A(6) of the Act must be brought within a period of 28 days beginning on—
- (a) the day the address of a company's registered office is changed to a default address; or
- (b) where the registrar dismissed the application, the day a notice of the registrar's decision is sent under regulation 10.

[4.637]
17

Where an appeal is brought before the court by the company, the duty to display a company's registered name at the company's registered office under regulation 21(1)(a) of the 2015 Regulations is suspended until 28 days after the appeal is withdrawn or the court makes a decision.

CHANGE OF ADDRESS OF REGISTERED OFFICE UNDER SECTION 87 OF THE ACT

[4.638]
18

On receipt of a notice from a company under section 87 of the Act to change the address of the company's registered office from a default address, the registrar may require the company to provide—

(a) evidence, or descriptions of evidence, listed in the Schedule; or
(b) any other information or documents that show the company is authorised to use a proposed address as its registered office.

19–22 (*Regs 19–21 amend the Limited Liability Partnerships (Application of Companies Act 2006) Regulations 2009, SI 2009/1804 at* **[10.319]**. *Reg 22 requires the Secretary of State to review the operation and effect of these Regulations and publish a report within 5 years after they come into force and within every 5 years after that. Following a review it will fall to the Secretary of State to consider whether the Regulations should remain as they are, or be revoked or be amended. A further instrument would be needed to revoke the Regulations or to amend them.*)

SCHEDULE
EVIDENCE, OR DESCRIPTIONS OF EVIDENCE, THE REGISTRAR MAY RELY ON WITHOUT FURTHER ENQUIRY

Regulations 9(b) and 18(a)

[4.639]

1. Documentation evidencing proprietary rights of the company or a group undertaking, including leasehold or a freehold, in the address of the registered office, of the company.

2. A written agreement entitling the company or a group undertaking to use the address as the company's registered office.

3. A utility bill addressed to the company or a group undertaking at the address of the registered office and dated no more than 6 months before the date on which the registrar gives notice under regulation 5(b).

COMPANIES AND LIMITED LIABILITY PARTNERSHIPS (FILING REQUIREMENTS) REGULATIONS 2016

(SI 2016/599)

NOTES

Made: 6 June 2016.

Authority: Companies Act 2006, ss 9(5A), (5B), 243(3), 853C(3), 1042, 1043, 1087B(3), 1167, 1292; Limited Liability Partnerships Act 2000, ss 15(a), 17(1)–(3); Small Business, Enterprise and Employment Act 2015, s 159(1), (2).

Commencement: 30 June 2016.

For a summary of all Orders and Regulations made under the Companies Act 2006, see Appendix 4 at **[A4]**.

ARRANGEMENT OF REGULATIONS

SCHEDULES

[4.640]
1 Citation and commencement

These Regulations may be cited as the Companies and Limited Liability Partnerships (Filing Requirements) Regulations 2016 and come into force on 30th June 2016.

[4.641]

2 Interpretation

In these Regulations—

"the Act" means the Companies Act 2006;

"the 2009 Regulations" means the Limited Liability Partnerships (Application of the Companies Act 2006) Regulations 2009;

"annual return" means a return described in section 854 of the Act;

"LLP" means a limited liability partnership registered under the Limited Liability Partnerships Act 2000;

"registrar" has the meaning given in section 1060 of the Act; and

"return date" has the meaning given in section 854(2) of the Act.

[4.642]

3 Amendments to the 2009 Regulations

(1) Subject to paragraphs (2) to (4), Schedule 1 (which contains amendments to the 2009 Regulations) has effect.

(2) The substitution made by paragraph 5 of Schedule 1 does not have effect in relation to annual returns required by section 854 of the Act to be made up to a return date before 30th June 2016.

(3) In relation to an LLP that was incorporated on 30th June 2015, section 853A(5)(a) of the Act has effect as if it read—

"(a) the period of 12 months beginning with the day after the LLP's incorporation;"

(4) Any reference in section 853A of the Act, as applied to LLPs with modifications by paragraph 5 of Schedule 1, to a review period is to be read as including the period of 12 months beginning with the day after the LLP's last return date.

[4.643]

4 Amendments to the Unregistered Companies Regulations 2009

(1) Subject to paragraphs (2) to (5), Schedule 2 (which contains amendments to the Unregistered Companies Regulations 2009) has effect.

(2) The substitution made by paragraph 2 of Schedule 2 does not have effect in relation to an annual return of an unregistered company which is required by section 854 of the Act to be made up to a return date before 30th June 2016.

(3) Where an annual return of the kind described in paragraph (2) of this regulation is delivered to the registrar on or after 30th June 2016, section 856(2) of the Act (contents of annual return: information about shares and share capital) has effect as if it read—

"(2) The statement of capital must state with respect to the unregistered company's share capital at the return date—

(a) the total number of shares in the unregistered company,

(b) the aggregate nominal value of those shares,

(c) the aggregate amount (if any) unpaid on those shares (whether on account of their nominal value or by way of premium), and

(d) for each class of shares—

(i) the prescribed particulars of the rights attached to the shares,

(ii) the total number of shares of that class, and

(iii) the aggregate nominal value of shares of that class."

(4) In relation to an unregistered company that was incorporated on 30th June 2015, section 853A(5)(a) of the Act has effect as if it read—

"(a) the period of 12 months beginning with the day after the unregistered company's incorporation;"

(5) Any reference in section 853A of the Act, as applied to unregistered companies by paragraph 2 of Schedule 2, to a review period is to be read as including the period of 12 months beginning with the day after the unregistered company's last return date.

[4.644]

5 Consequential Amendments

Schedule 3 (which contains consequential amendments) has effect.

[4.645]

6 Classification scheme for company type

The classification scheme set out in the table in Schedule 4 is prescribed for the purposes of section 9(5A) (registration documents) of the Act.

[4.646]

7 Classification system for company's principal business activities

(1) The Standard Industrial Classification 2007 is prescribed for the purposes of section 9(5B) and section 853C(3) of the Act, with the addition of the codes and designations in the table in Schedule 5, where the code set out in column 1 of the table represents the designation opposite it in column 2 of the table.

(2) In paragraph (1), "Standard Industrial Classification 2007" means the UK Standard Industrial Classification of Economic Activities 2007, prepared by the Office for National Statistics and published by Palgrave MacMillan with the permission of the Office of Public Sector Information (OPSI) with ISBN number 978-0-230-21012-7.

[4.647]
8 Review

(1) The Secretary of the State must from time to time—
- (a) carry out a review of these Regulations;
- (b) set out the conclusions of the review in a report; and
- (c) publish the report.

(2) The report must in particular—
- (a) set out the objectives intended to be achieved by the regulatory system established by these Regulations;
- (b) assess the extent to which those objectives have been achieved; and
- (c) assess whether those objectives remain appropriate and, if so, the extent to which they could be achieved in another way that imposed less regulation.

(3) The first report under this regulation must be published before the end of the period of 5 years beginning with the day on which these Regulations come into force.

(4) Reports under this regulation are afterwards to be published at intervals not exceeding 5 years.

SCHEDULES

SCHEDULES 1–3

(Sch 1 amends the Limited Liability Partnerships (Application of the Companies Act 2006) Regulations 2009, SI 2009/1804 at **[10.319]** *et seq; Sch 2 amends the Unregistered Companies Regulations 2009, SI 2009/2436 at* **[4.389]** *et seq; Sch 3 contains various minor and consequential amendments which have been incorporated at the appropriate place.)*

SCHEDULE 4
CLASSIFICATION SCHEDULE FOR TYPE OF COMPANY

Regulation 6

[4.648]

Column 1 *Type of Company*	*Column 2* *Code*
Public limited company	T1
Private company limited by shares	T2
Private company limited by guarantee	T3
Private company limited by shares exempt under section 60 of the Act	T4
Private company limited by guarantee exempt under section 60 of the Act	T5
Private unlimited company with share capital	T6
Private unlimited company without share capital	T7

SCHEDULE 5
ADDITIONAL CODES AND DESIGNATIONS

Regulation 7

[4.649]

Column 1 *Codes*	*Column 2* *Designations*
74990	Non-trading company
98000	Residents' property management company
99999	Dormant company

STATUTORY AUDITORS AND THIRD COUNTRY AUDITORS REGULATIONS 2016

(SI 2016/649)

NOTES

Made: 15 June 2016.

Authority: Companies Act 2006, ss 494(1), (2)(b), (4)(a), 519A(5), 1241(2)(c), 1252(1), (8), 1292(1)(a), (2), (4), Sch 13, para 11(2); Companies (Audit, Investigations and Community Enterprise) Act 2004, s 18A(1), (3), (6); European Communities Act 1972, s 2(2) (see also the note "Statutory Instruments made under the European Communities Act 1972" preceding paragraph **[4.1]** *ante*).

Commencement: 17 June 2016.

For a summary of all Orders and Regulations made under the Companies Act 2006, see Appendix 4 at **[A4]**.

These Regulations are reproduced as amended by: the Statutory Auditors and Third Country Auditors Regulations 2017, SI 2017/516; the Statutory Auditors Regulations 2017, SI 2017/1164; the Statutory Auditors and Third Country Auditors (Amendment) (EU Exit) Regulations 2019, SI 2019/177; the Statutory Auditors and Third Country Auditors (Amendment) (EU Exit) Regulations 2020, SI 2020/108.

ARRANGEMENT OF REGULATIONS

PART 1
INTRODUCTION

PART 2
THE COMPETENT AUTHORITY

PART 3
RESTRICTIONS ON CHOICE OF AUDITOR

PART 4
MISCELLANEOUS

SCHEDULES

PART 1 INTRODUCTION

[4.650]

1 Citation, commencement and application

(1) These Regulations may be cited as the Statutory Auditors and Third Country Auditors Regulations 2016 and come into force—

- (a) on 17th June 2016, if the Regulations are made on or before 16th June 2016;
- (b) on the day after the day on which the Regulations are made, if they are made on or after 17th June 2016.

(2) The following provisions of Schedule 3 to these Regulations apply in relation to financial years beginning on or after 17th June 2016—

- (a) Part 3;
- (b) paragraphs 43 to 49;
- (c) in paragraph 51—
  - (i) sub-paragraph (2)(a), in so far as it relates to the insertion of the definition of "audit working papers and investigation reports";
  - (ii) sub-paragraphs (2)(c) and (e);
- (d) in paragraph 52—
  - (i) sub-paragraph (2), in so far as it relates to the insertion of the entry relating to "audit working papers and investigations reports";
  - (ii) sub-paragraph (3);
- (e) paragraphs 68 to 69;
- (f) paragraph 73(3).

(3) Paragraph 72 of Schedule 3, in so far as it relates to paragraphs 21 to 22B of Schedule 10 to the Act, does not apply in relation to financial years beginning before 17th June 2016.

(4) In regulation 18—

- (a) paragraph (2)(a) applies in relation to financial years beginning on or after 1st January 2016; and
- (b) paragraph (3) applies in relation to financial years beginning on or after the day on which these Regulations come into force.

(5) Standards set by the competent authority in accordance with Schedule 1 to these Regulations apply in relation to financial years beginning on or after 17th June 2016.

(6) Schedule 4 to these Regulations applies in relation to financial years beginning on or after 17th June 2016.

(7) Regulations 5 to 8 do not apply to decisions made by the competent authority following an investigation which commences before the day on which these Regulations come into force or occurs as a result of a complaint or referral made before that day.

(8) The amendments made by paragraphs 67 and 72 (in so far as it relates to paragraph 24 of Schedule 10) of Schedule 3 to these Regulations do not apply to investigations under arrangements mentioned in those paragraphs which occur as a result of a complaint or referral made before the day on which these Regulations come into force.

(9) The amendments made by paragraph 65 (in so far as it relates to paragraph 13 of Schedule 10) and by paragraph 72 (in so far as it relates to paragraphs 23 and 23A of that Schedule) of Schedule 3 do not apply to enforcement action which is taken following an inspection under arrangements mentioned in those paragraphs and which begins before the day on which these Regulations come into force.

(10) The amendment made by paragraph 3 of Schedule 3 to these Regulations does not apply where paragraph 23 of Schedule 10 to the Act continues to apply by virtue of paragraph (9) of this regulation.

(11) The amendment made by paragraph 1(2)(a) of Schedule 5 to these Regulations does not apply where paragraph 23 and 23A of Schedule 10 to the Act continue to apply by virtue of paragraph (9) of this regulation.

(12) The amendments made by these Regulations to Part 16 of the Companies Act 2006 do not have effect in relation to the application of any provision of that Part to limited liability partnerships by the Limited Liability Partnerships (Accounts and Audit) (Application of Companies Act 2006) Regulations 2008.

[4.651]

2 Interpretation

In these Regulations—

"the Act" means the Companies Act 2006;

"appropriate qualification", "audited person", ["equivalent third country",] . . . , . . . "firm", "group", "parent undertaking", ["regulated market",] "statutory audit", "statutory auditor", "statutory audit work", ["third country", "third country auditor", "transferable securities", "transitional third country" and "UK regulated market"] have the same meaning as in Part 42 of the Act;

"Audit Directive" means Directive 2006/43/EC of the European Parliament and of the Council on statutory audits of annual accounts and consolidated accounts, amending Council Directives 78/660/EEC and 83/349/EEC and repealing Council Directive 84/253/EEC;

"Audit Regulation" means Regulation (EU) 537/2014 of the European Parliament and of the Council of 16 April 2014 on specific requirements regarding statutory audit of public-interest entities and repealing Commission Decision 2005/909/EC;

"audit report" means the report required in accordance with the audit reporting requirements;

"audit reporting requirements" means the requirements of—

(a) sections 495 to 498A and 503 to 506 of the Act,

(b) sections 495, [496,] 498 and 503 to 506 of the Act as applied to an LLP by the Limited Liability Partnerships (Accounts and Audit) (Application of Companies Act 2006) Regulations 2008 (and "LLP" has the meaning given by regulation 3 of those Regulations),

(c) sections 495, 496 and 498 of the Act as applied to the auditor of a qualifying partnership, and sections 503 to 506 of that Act as applied in relation to the auditors' report for a qualifying partnership, by the Partnerships (Accounts) Regulations 2008 ("qualifying partnership" has the meaning given by regulation 3 of those Regulations),

(d) sections 495 to 498A [and 503 to 506] of the Act as applied to an unregistered company by the Unregistered Companies Regulations 2009 ("unregistered company" has the meaning given by regulation 2 of those Regulations),

(e) . . .

(f) sections 495[, 496] and 498 of the Act as applied to an auditor of an insurance undertaking and sections 503 to 506 of the Act as applied in relation to the auditor's report for an insurance undertaking, by the Insurance Accounts Directive (Miscellaneous Insurance Undertakings) Regulations 2008 ("insurance undertaking" has the meaning given by regulation 2 of those Regulations),

(g) sections 78 to 79 of the Building Societies Act 1986,

(h) sections 73 to 74C of the Friendly Societies Act 1992, in relation to the audit of a friendly society [which is subject to special requirements under that Act (see section 78A(3) of that Act)],

(i) regulations 3, 10 to 14 and 22 to 26 of the Insurance Accounts Directive (Lloyd's Syndicate and Aggregate Accounts) Regulations 2008,

(j) Articles 10 and 11 of the Audit Regulation;

"competent authority" means the Financial Reporting Council Limited;

"financial year" has the same meaning as in section 390 of the Act;

"group auditor" means the statutory auditor appointed to audit the consolidated accounts of a group and "group audit" shall be construed accordingly;

["international auditing standards" means International Standards on Auditing, International Standard on Quality Control and other related Standards issued from time to time by the International Federation of Accountants through the International Auditing and Assurance Standards Board, in so far as they are relevant to the statutory audit;]

"network" means an association of persons other than a firm co-operating in audit work by way of—

(a) profit-sharing,

(b) cost-sharing,

(c) common ownership, control or management,

(d) common quality control policies and procedures,

(e) common business strategy, or

(f) use of a common name;

"personal data" has the same meaning as in section 1(1) of the Data Protection Act 1998;

"public interest entity" means—

(a) an issuer whose transferable securities are admitted to trading on a [UK regulated market],

(b) a credit institution within the meaning given by Article 4(1)(1) of Regulation (EU) No 575/2013 of the European Parliament and of the Council, [which is a CRR firm within the meaning of Article 4(1)(2A) of that Regulation], or

[(c) a person who would be an insurance undertaking as defined in Article 2(1) of Council Directive 91/674/EEC of 19 December 1991 of the European Parliament and of the Council on the annual accounts of insurance undertakings as that Article had effect immediately before IP completion day, were the United Kingdom a member State;]

"issuer" . . . [has] the same meaning as in Part 6 of the Financial Services and Markets Act 2000;

"recognised supervisory body" means a supervisory body, within the meaning in section 1217(1) of the Act, recognised in accordance with Schedule 10 of that Act (and "member", in relation to a recognised supervisory body, has the meaning given by section 1217(2) of that Act);

"sanction" means any measure taken by the competent authority under regulation 5;

["third country competent authority" means a body established in a third country exercising functions related to the regulation or oversight of auditors;

"UK-adopted international standards" means the international auditing standards adopted by the competent authority in accordance with regulation 4(3)(za).]

. . .

NOTES

In the group of definitions beginning with the definition "appropriate qualification", all words in square brackets were inserted or substituted, and the definitions "EEA auditor" and "EEA competent authority" (omitted) were revoked, by the Statutory Auditors and Third Country Auditors (Amendment) (EU Exit) Regulations 2019, SI 2019/177, regs 65, 66(a), as from IP completion day (as defined in the European Union (Withdrawal Agreement) Act 2020, s 39) (for transitional provisions, see Sch 4 to the 2019 Regulations at **[12.88]**).

Figures and words in square brackets in paras (b), (d) and (f) of the definition "audit reporting requirements" inserted by the Statutory Auditors Regulations 2017, SI 2017/1164, regs 15, 16, as from 1 January 2018. Para (e) of that definition was revoked by reg 19 of, and Sch 4 to, the 2017 Regulations, as from 1 January 2018, in relation to financial years of qualifying banks beginning on or after 30 November 2018 (as to the application of the 2017 Regulations, see **[4.671]** et seq). Words in square brackets in sub-para (h) of that definition substituted by SI 2019/177, regs 65, 66(b), as from IP completion day (as defined in the European Union (Withdrawal Agreement) Act 2020, s 39) (for transitional provisions, see Sch 4 to the 2019 Regulations at **[12.88]**).

Definitions "international auditing standards", "third country competent authority", and "UK-adopted international standards" inserted by SI 2019/177, regs 65, 66(c), (g), as from IP completion day (as defined in the European Union (Withdrawal Agreement) Act 2020, s 39) (for transitional provisions, see Sch 4 to the 2019 Regulations at **[12.88]**).

Words in square brackets in the definition "public interest entity" substituted by SI 2019/177, regs 65, 66(d), as from IP completion day (as defined in the European Union (Withdrawal Agreement) Act 2020, s 39) (for transitional provisions, see Sch 4 to the 2019 Regulations at **[12.88]**). Note that reg 66(d) of the 2019 Regulations was amended by the Companies and Statutory Auditors etc (Consequential Amendments) (EU Exit) Regulations 2020, SI 2020/523, reg 15(c), with effect from immediately before IP completion day; and that the effect of the amendment has been incorporated in the text set out above.

In the definition "issuer", the words omitted were revoked, and the word in square brackets were substituted, by SI 2019/177, regs 65, 66(e), as from IP completion day (as defined in the European Union (Withdrawal Agreement) Act 2020, s 39) (for transitional provisions, see Sch 4 to the 2019 Regulations at **[12.88]**). Note that this was originally the definition ""issuer" and "regulated market"" and, therefore, the definition "regulated market" has effectively been revoked.

Definition "transferable securities" (omitted) revoked by SI 2019/177, regs 65, 66(f), as from IP completion day (as defined in the European Union (Withdrawal Agreement) Act 2020, s 39) (for transitional provisions, see Sch 4 to the 2019 Regulations at **[12.88]**).

Modification: unless the context otherwise requires, references to the Data Protection Act 1998 have effect as references to the Data Protection Act 2018 or, as the case may be, the data protection legislation. See the Data Protection Act 2018, Sch 19, Pt 3.

PART 2 THE COMPETENT AUTHORITY

[4.652]

3 The competent authority

(1) The competent authority is responsible for—

(a) the public oversight of statutory auditors under these Regulations;

(b) carrying out the tasks provided for in the Audit Regulation and for ensuring that the provisions of that Regulation are applied;

(c) the determination of technical standards (which must meet the requirements of [regulation 4(3) and] Schedule 1) and of other standards (which must meet the requirements of that Schedule) on professional ethics and internal quality control of statutory auditors and statutory audit work;

(d) the determination of the manner in which the standards determined under sub-paragraph (c) are to be applied in practice;

(e) the [imposition] of the standards determined under sub-paragraph (c) (including provision for securing compliance with those standards);

(f) the determination of criteria for the purpose of determining whether persons are eligible for appointment as statutory auditors;

(g) the application of the criteria determined under sub-paragraph (f) to determine whether persons are eligible for appointment as statutory auditors;

(h) registration of persons approved as eligible for appointment as statutory auditors under sub-paragraph (g);

(i) keeping the register and making it available for inspection;

(j) ensuring persons eligible for appointment as statutory auditors take part in appropriate programmes of continuing education in order to maintain their theoretical knowledge, professional skills and values at a sufficiently high level;
(k) monitoring (by means of inspections) of statutory auditors and audit work;
(l) investigations of statutory auditors and audit work; and
(m) imposing and enforcing sanctions.

(2) The competent authority—
(a) must consider whether and how tasks arising from its responsibility for the matters listed in sub-paragraphs (e) to (m) of paragraph (1) may be delegated to any recognised supervisory body; and
(b) subject to [paragraphs (5), (5A) and (5B)], may delegate such tasks to any recognised supervisory body.

(3) In exercising its duty under paragraph (2)(a), the competent authority—
(a) must consult the recognised supervisory bodies, and
(b) may consider the requirements of Schedule 10 to the Act (including the way in which recognised supervisory bodies discharge those requirements).

(4) The competent authority may delegate tasks to any recognised supervisory body in accordance with paragraphs (6) and (7).

(5) The competent authority may not delegate tasks related to any of the matters listed in Article 24(1)(a) to (c) of the Audit Regulation.

[(5A) Any delegation under paragraph (2) of the competent authority's responsibilities under sub-paragraphs (k), (l) or (m) of paragraph (1) must not prejudice the competent authority's ability to initiate and conduct an inspection or investigation of audit work by a statutory auditor itself, where necessary, and to take appropriate action.

(5B) In determining the delegation of tasks, the competent authority must ensure that conflicts of interest are avoided.]

(6) The competent authority must specify the tasks delegated (and may specify those tasks by reference to particular descriptions of activity for which the competent authority is responsible, particular descriptions of statutory auditor or particular descriptions of audited person) and any conditions under which those tasks are to be carried out (and may vary those conditions).

(7) The competent authority may specify (including by reference to particular descriptions of activity for which the competent authority is responsible, particular descriptions of statutory auditor or particular descriptions of audited person) exceptions to any delegation.

(8) The competent authority may reclaim tasks it has delegated, including those which relate to a particular description of activity for which the competent authority is responsible, particular description of statutory auditor or particular description of audited person.

(9) When the competent authority has reclaimed a task from a recognised supervisory body ('A') and delegated that task to another recognised supervisory body ('B'), section 1224ZA of the Act (as inserted by paragraph 33 of Schedule 3 to these Regulations) has effect so that the competent authority's power to call for information from A applies so that the competent authority may require A to provide such information as the competent authority considers that B reasonably requires for the performance of the task.

(10) The competent authority must make such arrangements as it considers necessary in relation to any of the matters for which it is responsible under this regulation, including arrangements for the performance by the competent authority of any task arising from its responsibility for those matters in the following circumstances—
(a) where the competent authority does not delegate a task to a recognised supervisory body;
(b) where the competent authority reclaims a task from a recognised supervisory body;
(c) where the recognition order in relation to a recognised supervisory body is revoked under paragraph 3 of Schedule 10 to the Act.

(11) An obligation which a statutory auditor has by virtue of any rules which a recognised supervisory body is required to have under Part 2 of Schedule 10 to the Act is an obligation which the statutory auditor owes to the competent authority including—
(a) where the competent authority reclaims a task from that recognised supervisory body, to the extent that the obligation arises from the competent authority having delegated that task to the body; or
(b) where the recognition order in relation to that recognised supervisory body is revoked under paragraph 3 of Schedule 10 to the Act, to any extent.

(12) The Secretary of State may give directions to the competent authority in connection with the delegation of tasks to the recognised supervisory bodies.

(13) Schedule 1 (which prescribes requirements for the standards the competent authority must determine in relation to the obligations of statutory auditors in relation to professional ethics, independence, objectivity and confidentiality) has effect.

[(14) The members of the management body of the competent authority must be individuals who—
(a) are knowledgeable in the areas relevant to statutory audit;
(b) are selected in accordance with an independent and transparent nomination procedure;
(c) during their period in office are non-practitioners, and in the three years preceding their appointment were non-practitioners.

(15) In paragraph (14), a "non-practitioner" is a person who is not—
(a) carrying out statutory audit work;
(b) a member of the ownership or management body of a firm that is eligible for appointment as a statutory auditor;
(c) employed by or otherwise associated with a firm that is eligible for appointment as a statutory auditor.]

NOTES

Para (1): words in square brackets in sub-para (c) inserted, and word in square brackets in sub-para (e) substituted, by the Statutory Auditors and Third Country Auditors (Amendment) (EU Exit) Regulations 2019, SI 2019/177, regs 65, 67, as from IP completion day (as defined in the European Union (Withdrawal Agreement) Act 2020, s 39) (for transitional provisions, see Sch 4 to the 2019 Regulations at **[12.88]**).

Para (2): words in square brackets in sub-para (b) substituted by SI 2019/177, regs 105, 106(a), as from 22 February 2019 (for transitional provisions, see Sch 4 to the 2019 Regulations at **[12.88]**).

Paras (5A). (5B): inserted by SI 2019/177, regs 105, 106(b), as from 22 February 2019 (for transitional provisions, see Sch 4 to the 2019 Regulations at **[12.88]**).

Paras (14). (15): added by SI 2019/177, regs 105, 106(c), as from 22 February 2019 (for transitional provisions, see Sch 4 to the 2019 Regulations at **[12.88]**).

[4.653]

4 General requirements of auditors

(1) A person appointed to conduct a statutory audit must conduct that audit in accordance with the relevant standards for the conduct of statutory audits.

(2) The relevant standards are—

(a) the standards of integrity, objectivity, professional competence, due care and professional scepticism as determined by the competent authority in accordance with Schedule 1;

(b) the international auditing standards adopted by the European Commission[, before IP completion day,] in accordance with Article 26(3) of the Audit Directive ("Commission-adopted international standards");

[(ba) any UK-adopted international standards adopted and imposed by the competent authority in accordance with paragraph (3)(za);]

(c) any auditing standards, procedures or requirements imposed by the competent authority in accordance with paragraph (3)(a);

(d) auditing procedures or requirements imposed by the competent authority in accordance with paragraph (3)(b); and

(e) the requirements of rules and practices of the recognised supervisory body of which the auditor is a member, provided that the rules and practices are rules and practices required by virtue of Part 2 of Schedule 10 to the Act.

(3) The competent authority may—

[(za) adopt and impose international auditing standards ("UK-adopted international standards") where those standards—

(i) have been developed with proper due process, public oversight and transparency;

(ii) are generally accepted internationally;

(iii) contribute a high level of credibility and quality to accounts of audited persons;

(iv) contribute to the public good; and

(v) are consistent with the relevant requirements listed in regulation 5(11);]

(a) impose auditing standards, procedures or requirements which do not cover the same subject-matter as [Commission-adopted or UK-adopted international standards]; or

(b) impose auditing procedures or requirements which cover the same subject-matter as [Commission-adopted or UK-adopted international standards] but are necessary—

(i) to give effect to any relevant requirement relating to the scope of statutory audit; or

(ii) to add to the credibility and quality of [].

[(3A) The Secretary of State may by regulations amend the requirements set out in Articles 7, 8 and 18 of the Audit Regulation and in paragraphs 1 to 15 of Schedule 1 to these Regulations, for the purpose of ensuring that, where the competent authority wishes to adopt international auditing standards under regulation 4(3)(za), those requirements are consistent with the standards that the competent authority wishes to adopt.

(3B) Regulations made under paragraph (3A) must not be made unless a draft of the statutory instrument containing them has been laid before Parliament and approved by a resolution of each House of Parliament.]

(4) In this regulation "relevant requirement" has the same meaning as in regulation 5.

NOTES

All amendments to this regulation were made by the Statutory Auditors and Third Country Auditors (Amendment) (EU Exit) Regulations 2019, SI 2019/177, regs 65, 68, as from IP completion day (as defined in the European Union (Withdrawal Agreement) Act 2020, s 39) (for transitional provisions, see Sch 4 to the 2019 Regulations at **[12.88]**). Note that reg 68 of the 2019 Regulations was amended by the Companies and Statutory Auditors etc (Consequential Amendments) (EU Exit) Regulations 2020, SI 2020/523, reg 15(d), with effect from immediately before IP completion day; and that the effect of the amendment has been incorporated in the text set out above.

[4.654]

5 The competent authority: sanctioning powers

(1) If the competent authority considers that a person ("A") has contravened a relevant requirement, it may—

(a) give a notice requiring A to cease the conduct giving rise to the contravention and to abstain from any repetition of that conduct,

(b) publish a statement (which may take the form of a reprimand or severe reprimand) to that effect,

(c) make an order prohibiting A permanently or for a specified period from carrying out statutory audits or signing audit reports,

(d) in a case where an audit report by A does not satisfy—

(i) the audit reporting requirements, or

(ii) the requirement in regulation 4(1),

make a declaration to that effect, and, where appropriate, order A to forego fees payable to A in connection with the carrying out of the statutory audit or to repay such fees,

(e) make an order prohibiting A for a specified period of up to three years from being a member of the management body of a firm that is eligible for appointment as a statutory auditor,

(f) make an order prohibiting A for a specified period of up to three years from acting as a director of or being otherwise concerned in the management of a public interest entity,

(g) impose on A a financial penalty of such amount as the competent authority considers appropriate,

(h) make an order requiring A to take such action as the competent authority considers will mitigate the effect or prevent the recurrence of the contravention,

(i) make an order excluding A from membership of one or more recognised supervisory bodies.

(2) The competent authority may only exercise the powers under paragraph (1) if A is eligible for appointment as a statutory auditor (or was so eligible at the time of the contravention).

(3) In determining the type and level of sanctions to be imposed under this regulation, the competent authority must take into account all relevant circumstances, including—

(a) the gravity and duration of the contravention;

(b) A's degree of responsibility;

(c) A's financial strength;

(d) the amount, so far as can be determined, of profits gained or losses avoided by A;

(e) the extent to which A has co-operated with the competent authority;

(f) any previous contravention by A of a relevant requirement.

(4) For the purpose of paragraph (3)(c), A's financial strength may be determined in such manner as the competent authority considers appropriate, including—

(a) where A is a firm by reference to A's total turnover; or

(b) where A is an individual by reference to A's annual income.

(5) The competent authority may make an order ("a costs order") requiring A to pay the costs reasonably incurred by the competent authority in determining whether A has contravened the requirement, including—

(a) its administrative costs;

(b) its costs of obtaining legal advice; and

(c) any costs incurred in considering any appeal by A.

(6) Where a recognised supervisory body has paid any part of the costs incurred by the competent authority, a costs order may include those costs and the competent authority must reimburse those costs to the recognised supervisory body.

(7) Any other sums received by the competent authority in payment of its costs or in payment of a financial penalty must be paid to the Secretary of State.

(8) Where the competent authority imposes a financial penalty on A or makes a costs order applying to A—

(a) it must specify a date by which the penalty is or the costs are required to be paid; and

(b) that date must be—

(i) in the case of a financial penalty, at least 28 days after the date on which the competent authority imposed the financial penalty, or

(ii) in the case of a costs order, at least 28 days after the date on which the competent authority made the costs order.

(9) The competent authority may not exercise the powers under this regulation if and to the extent that it has delegated a task under regulation 3 which arises from its responsibilities under regulation 3(1)(m).

(10) The competent authority must provide for an appeal against any decisions it makes under this regulation to be considered by an independent tribunal.

(11) In this regulation—

a "relevant requirement" means a requirement with which A must comply under—

(a) these Regulations (including the requirement under regulation 4(1)),

(b) the Audit Regulation,

(c) Parts 16 or 42 of the Act,

(d) Parts 10 to 12 of the Limited Liability Partnerships (Accounts and Audit) (Application of Companies Act 2006) Regulations 2008,

(e) Parts 2 and 3 of, or the Schedule to, the Partnerships (Accounts) Regulations 2008,

(f) Regulation 3 of, or Schedule 1 to, the Unregistered Companies Regulations 2009,

(g) . . .

(h) Parts 2 and 3 of, or Schedule 1 and 2 to, the Insurance Accounts Directive (Miscellaneous Insurance Undertakings) Regulations 2008,

(i) Part 8 of, or Schedule 11 to, the Building Societies Act 1986, or of any subordinate legislation made under that Part or that Schedule,

(j) Part 6 of, or Schedule 14 [or Schedule 14A] to, the Friendly Societies Act 1992, or of any subordinate legislation made under that Part of that Schedule, in so far as those provisions apply to [a friendly society that is subject to special requirements under that Act (see section 78A(3) of that Act)],

(k) Parts 2 and 3 of, or Schedules 1 and 3 to, the Insurance Accounts Directive (Lloyd's Syndicates and Aggregate Accounts) Regulations 2008, and

(l) a standard set under the arrangements required by Schedule 10 to the Act, where those paragraphs continue to apply by virtue of regulation 1 of these Regulations,

"subordinate legislation" means legislation made by way of statutory instrument, and

"turnover", in relation to a firm, means the amounts derived from the provision of goods and services within the United Kingdom, after deduction of—

(a) trade discounts,

(b) value added tax, and

(c) any other taxes based on the amounts so derived.

NOTES

Para (11): para (g) of the definition "relevant requirement" was revoked by the Statutory Auditors Regulations 2017, SI 2017/1164, reg 19, Sch 4, as from 1 January 2018, in relation to financial years of qualifying banks beginning on or after 30 November 2018 (as to the application of the 2017 Regulations, see **[4.671]** et seq). Words in first pair of square brackets in para (j) of that definition inserted by the Statutory Auditors and Third Country Auditors Regulations 2017, SI 2017/516, reg 14(1), (2), as from 1 May 2017. Words in second pair of square brackets in para (j) of that definition substituted by the Statutory Auditors and Third Country Auditors (Amendment) (EU Exit) Regulations 2019, SI 2019/177, regs 65, 69, as from IP completion day (as defined in the European Union (Withdrawal Agreement) Act 2020, s 39) (for transitional provisions, see Sch 4 to the 2019 Regulations at **[12.88]**).

[4.655]

6 Publication of sanctions and measures

(1) The competent authority shall publish, in accordance with paragraphs (2) to (5) details of the sanctions it imposes under regulation 5.

(2) The details published under paragraph (1) must include—

(a) information concerning the type of contravention and its nature;

(b) unless any of the circumstances mentioned in paragraph (3) applies, the identity of the person ("A") sanctioned under regulation 5; and

(c) where a sanction is subject to an appeal, information concerning the status and outcome of the appeal.

(3) The circumstances in which A's identity must not be published are—

(a) where A is an individual and the competent authority considers the publication of personal data would be disproportionate;

(b) where publication would jeopardise the stability of financial markets;

(c) where publication would jeopardise an ongoing criminal investigation; and

(d) where publication would cause disproportionate damage to any institution or individual involved.

(4) The competent authority shall ensure that—

(a) information published under this regulation remains published for a proportionate period, and

(b) is available on the competent authority's website for at least five years after the relevant date.

(5) In this regulation and in regulations 7 and 8, "the relevant date" means—

(a) where the competent authority imposes a sanction and that decision is appealed, the date on which the appeal is determined,

(b) where the competent authority imposes a sanction and that decision is not appealed, the date by which the appeal should have been lodged.

[4.656]

7 Enforcement of sanctions

(1) This regulation applies if—

(a) the competent authority has imposed a sanction under sub-paragraph (a), (c), (d) (insofar as it relates to an order to forego or repay fees), (e), (f), (g) or (h) of regulation 5(1) or made a costs order under regulation 5(5); and

(b) the person on whom the sanction or costs order was imposed—

(i) has not by the relevant date appealed against the decision, or

(ii) has appealed against the decision, but the appeal was unsuccessful or has been withdrawn.

(2) If on an application by the competent authority the court decides that a person has not complied with a sanction or costs order to which this regulation applies, the court may order that person to take such steps as the court considers will secure compliance with the sanction or costs order.

(3) In this regulation, "the court" means the High Court or, in Scotland, the Court of Session.

[4.657]

8 Recovery of financial penalties

(1) If the whole or any part of a financial penalty or costs order is not paid by the time by which it is required to be paid, the unpaid balance from time to time carries interest at the rate for the time being specified in section 17 of the Judgments Act 1838.

(2) Where a financial penalty or costs order, or any part of a financial penalty or costs order, has not been paid by the time when it is required to be paid and—

(a) no appeal has been made in respect of that penalty or costs order by the relevant date; or

(b) an appeal has been made in respect of that penalty or costs order, but has been determined or withdrawn,

the competent authority may recover from the person on whom the penalty or costs order was imposed, as a debt due to the competent authority, any of the penalty or costs order and any of the interest which has not been paid.

[4.658]

9 Monitoring of audits by the competent authority

(1) The competent authority must monitor the conduct of statutory audit work relating to public interest entities by means of a system of inspections that satisfies the requirements of Article 26 of the Audit Regulation.

(2) The competent authority must monitor the conduct of statutory audit work which does not relate to public interest entities in accordance with paragraphs (4) to (12).

(3) Paragraph (2) does not apply to the extent that the competent authority has delegated this task under regulation 3.

(4) The competent authority must have adequate arrangements for monitoring the conduct of statutory audit work and must ensure those arrangements operate independently of the persons monitored.

(5) The competent authority must have adequate resources for effectively monitoring the conduct of statutory audit work and ensure those resources may not be influenced improperly by the persons monitored.

(6) Monitoring the conduct of statutory audit work must be carried out by means of inspections which are conducted by persons who—

(a) have an appropriate professional education;
(b) have experience of—
  (i) statutory audit work, or
  [(ii) equivalent work, for the purposes of an appointment of a person to conduct inspections made prior to IP completion day, on the audit of accounts under the law of an EEA State, or part of an EEA State, or Gibraltar, or
  (iii) equivalent work, for the purposes of an appointment of a person to conduct inspections, on the audit of accounts under the law of—
    (aa) an equivalent third country, or part of an equivalent third country, or
    (bb) a transitional third country, or part of a transitional third country;]
(c) have received adequate training in the conduct of inspections;
(d) have declared that they do not have any interests likely to conflict with the proper conduct of the inspection;
(e) have not been an employee or partner or member of the management body of the person subject to inspection and have not been otherwise associated with that person for at least three years.

(7) An inspection must—

(a) review one or more statutory audits in which the person to whom the inspection relates has participated;
(b) in relation to the person to whom the inspection relates, include an assessment of—
  (i) that person's compliance with the standards [determined by] the competent authority under these Regulations;
  (ii) the resources allocated by that person to statutory audit work;
  (iii) if that person is a firm, its internal quality control system;
  (iv) the remuneration received by that person in respect of statutory audit work; and
(c) be appropriate and proportionate in view of the scale and complexity of the statutory audit work of the person subject to inspection.

(8) An inspection conducted in relation to a firm may be treated as an inspection of all individuals responsible for statutory audit work on behalf of that firm, if the firm has a common quality assurance policy with which each such individual is required to comply.

(9) The main conclusions of the inspection must be recorded in a report which is made available to—

(a) the person to whom the inspection relates; and
(b) the competent authority.

(10) An inspection must be carried out in relation to each person eligible for appointment as a statutory auditor—

(a) at such frequency as the competent authority considers appropriate given the risks arising from the statutory audit work undertaken by the person; and
(b) at least once every six years in the case of a person who, during any of the previous five years, has carried out a statutory audit of an audited person not subject to the small companies regime (within the meaning in section 381 of the Act).

(11) The competent authority must, at least once every calendar year, publish a report containing a summary of the results of inspections conducted under this regulation (and must publish this report at the same time that it publishes the information it is required to publish under Article 28(d) of the Audit Regulation).

(12) In relation to inspections of statutory audits of undertakings that qualify as small (by virtue of section 382 or 383 of the Act) or medium-sized (by virtue of section 465 or 466 of that Act), the competent authority must take account of the fact that the standards it has [determined] under these Regulations are designed to be applied in a manner that is proportionate to the scale and complexity of the business of the audited person.

NOTES

All amendments to this regulation were made by the Statutory Auditors and Third Country Auditors (Amendment) (EU Exit) Regulations 2019, SI 2019/177, regs 65, 70, as from IP completion day (as defined in the European Union (Withdrawal Agreement) Act 2020, s 39) (for transitional provisions, see Sch 4 to the 2019 Regulations at **[12.88]**). Note that reg 70 of the 2019 Regulations was amended by the Companies and Statutory Auditors etc (Consequential Amendments) (EU Exit) Regulations 2020, SI 2020/523, reg 15(e), with effect from immediately before IP completion day; and that the effect of the amendment has been incorporated in the text set out above.

[4.659]
10 Investigation powers

Schedule 2 (investigation powers) has effect.

[4.660]
11 Performance, monitoring and enforcement of third country audit functions

(1) Regulations 4 to 9 and Schedule 2 apply in relation to—

(a) the performance of third country audit functions by persons who are eligible for appointment as statutory auditors,
(b) the monitoring by the competent authority of the performance of third country audit functions by persons who are eligible for appointment as statutory auditors, and
(c) the imposition of sanctions by the competent authority in relation to the performance of third country audit functions by persons who are eligible for appointment as statutory auditors,

as they apply to the conduct of statutory audit work, the monitoring of that work and the imposition of sanctions in relation to that work, subject to the modifications set out in paragraphs (3) to (6).

(2) Paragraph (1) does not apply in respect of monitoring of the performance of third country audit functions—

[(a) for an audited entity which—
(i) is incorporated in an equivalent third country, or
(ii) is incorporated in a transitional third country; or]
(b) by a statutory auditor—
(i) who is also [eligible for appointment as an auditor of bodies corporate incorporated or formed under the law of an equivalent third country or a transitional third country], and
(ii) whose performance of third country audit functions is subject to the systems of public oversight, quality assurance and investigations and sanctions of the [third country competent authority in that equivalent third country or transitional third country].

(3) Regulations 4 to 9 and Schedule 2 apply but as if—
(a) for any cross-references to provisions within those regulations, there were substituted references to those provisions as they apply by virtue of this regulation; and
(b) for references to—
(i) "conduct of statutory audit work" or "conduct of a statutory audit" there were substituted references to "performance of third country audit functions", except in regulation 5(1)(c),
(ii) "statutory auditors", except in regulation 5(1)(e), or "persons appointed to conduct a statutory audit" there were substituted references to "a person who is eligible for appointment as a statutory auditor and who is appointed to perform third country audit functions",

and related expressions are to be construed accordingly.

(4) Regulation 4 applies but as if for paragraphs to (2) to (4) there were substituted—

"(2) The relevant standards are—
(a) the international auditing standards adopted by the European Commission in accordance with Article 26(3) of the Audit Directive [before IP completion day], or standards which are equivalent,
[(aa) the UK-adopted international standards adopted by the competent authority in accordance with regulation 4(3)(za), or standards which are equivalent,]
(b) any auditing standards, procedures or requirements imposed by the competent authority in relation to the conduct of statutory audit which do not cover the same subject-matter as the standards referred to in [paragraphs (a) or (aa),] or standards, procedures or requirements which are equivalent, and
[(c) any auditing standards, procedures or requirements imposed by the competent authority in accordance with the requirements set out in paragraphs 1 to 6 and 8 of Schedule 1, or with any other equivalent standards, procedures or requirements].

(3) The person who is eligible for appointment as a statutory auditor who is appointed to perform third country audit functions must, if not already required to do so by reason of carrying out statutory audits of public interest entities, publish on a website an annual transparency report equivalent to that required for auditors of public interest entities by Article 13 of the Audit Regulation (transparency report).".

(5) Regulation 5 applies but as if—
(a) paragraph (9) were omitted;
(b) for the definition of a "relevant requirement" in paragraph (11) were substituted—

"a "relevant requirement" means a requirement with which A must comply under—
(a) these Regulations (including the requirement under regulation 4(1)), or
(b) the Audit Regulation;"; and

(c) the definition of "subordinate legislation" in paragraph (11) were omitted.

(6) Regulation 9 applies but as if—
(a) for paragraph (1) were substituted—

"(1) The competent authority must monitor the performance of third country audit functions by persons eligible for appointment as statutory auditors, and may do so by means of a system of inspections.";

(b) in paragraph (2)—
(i) the words "which does not relate to public interest entities" were omitted, and
(ii) for "(4) to (12)" were substituted "(4) to (11)";
(c) paragraph (3) were omitted;
(d) in paragraph (6), sub-paragraph (b) were omitted;
(e) in paragraph (10)—
(i) after "statutory auditor" were inserted "in respect of their performance of third country audit functions"; and
(ii) sub-paragraph (b) were omitted;
(f) paragraph (12) were omitted.

(7) Schedule 2 applies but as if—
(a) in paragraph 1, sub-paragraphs (3) and (4) were omitted; and
(b) paragraph 4 were omitted.

(8) In this regulation, "third country audit function" means any function related to the audit of a [UK-traded third country company] or of [a body corporate] whose transferable securities are admitted to trading on a regulated market situated or operating in [an equivalent third country or a transitional third country].

NOTES

All amendments to this regulation were made by the Statutory Auditors and Third Country Auditors (Amendment) (EU Exit) Regulations 2019, SI 2019/177, regs 65, 71, as from IP completion day (as defined in the European Union (Withdrawal Agreement) Act 2020, s 39) (for transitional provisions, see Sch 4 to the 2019 Regulations at **[12.88]**). Note that reg 71 of the

2019 Regulations was amended by the Companies and Statutory Auditors etc (Consequential Amendments) (EU Exit) Regulations 2020, SI 2020/523, reg 15(f), with effect from immediately before IP completion day; and that the effect of the amendment has been incorporated in the text set out above.

PART 3 RESTRICTIONS ON CHOICE OF AUDITOR

[4.661]

[12 Contractual terms restricting choice of auditor

(1) This regulation applies to any term in a contract which, in relation to the conduct of a statutory audit of an audited person other than a person which is a public interest entity, provides for the restriction of the audited person's choice of statutory auditor to certain categories or lists of statutory auditors.

(2) A term to which this regulation applies has no effect.]

NOTES

Substituted by the Statutory Auditors and Third Country Auditors Regulations 2017, SI 2017/516, reg 14(1), (3), as from 1 May 2017.

PART 4 MISCELLANEOUS

[4.662]

13 Power to grant exemptions from the requirements of Article 4(2) of the Audit Regulation (limit on total fees charged for non-audit services)

(1) The competent authority may grant to a statutory auditor, in relation to the provision of services to an audited person, an exemption from the requirements of Article 4(2) of the Audit Regulation.

(2) The competent authority must be satisfied that exceptional circumstances exist before granting an exemption under this regulation.

(3) An exemption granted under this regulation may apply—

(a) for one financial year, or

(b) for two consecutive financial years.

[4.663]

[13A Provision of non-audit services

The competent authority may, within the standards on professional ethics that it determines in accordance with Schedule 1, allow the provision of the services referred to in points (a) (i), (a) (iv) to (a) (vii) and (f) of the second subparagraph of Article 5(1) of the Audit Regulation, provided that the following requirements are complied with—

(a) they have no direct or have immaterial effect, separately or in the aggregate on the audited accounts;

(b) the estimation of the effect on the audited accounts is comprehensively documented and explained in the additional report to the audit committee referred to in Article 11 of the Audit Regulation; and

(c) the principles of independence laid down in Part 42 of the Companies Act 2006 and these Regulations are complied with by the statutory auditor.]

NOTES

Inserted by the Statutory Auditors and Third Country Auditors (Amendment) (EU Exit) Regulations 2019, SI 2019/177, regs 105, 107, as from 22 February 2019 (for transitional provisions, see Sch 4 to the 2019 Regulations at **[12.88]**).

14 (*Amends the Partnerships (Accounts) Regulations 2008, SI 2008/569, reg 9.*)

[4.664]

15 Amendments to the Companies Act 2006

Schedule 3 has effect.

[4.665]

16 Amendments to the Building Societies Act 1986

Schedule 4 has effect.

[4.666]

17 Amendments to other enactments

Schedule 5 has effect.

18–20 (*Reg 18 amends the Companies (Disclosure of Auditor Remuneration and Liability Limitation Agreements) Regulations 2008, SI 2008/489; reg 19 amends the Statutory Auditors (Amendment of Companies Act 2006 and Delegation of Functions etc) Order 2012, SI 2012/1741; reg 20 amends the Statutory Auditors and Third Country Auditors Regulations 2013, SI 2013/1672.*)

[4.667]

21 Exclusion of large debt securities issuer from definition of ["UK-traded third country company"]

(1) A large debt securities issuer is excluded from the definition of ["UK-traded third country company"] for the purposes of Part 42 of the Act.

(2) In paragraph (1) "large debt securities issuer" means a body corporate whose only issued transferable securities admitted to trading on a [UK regulated market] are debt securities, the denomination per unit of which is not less than—

(a) 50,000 euros or an equivalent amount, in the case of securities admitted to trading on a [UK regulated market] before 31st December 2010,

(b) 100,000 euros or an equivalent amount, in the case of securities admitted to trading on a [UK regulated market] on or after 31st December 2010.

(3) In paragraph (2)—

"an equivalent amount" means an amount of a currency other than euros which at the date the security was issued was equivalent to the relevant amount of euros; and

"debt securities" has the same meaning as in Article 2(1)(b) of Directive 2004/109/EC of the European Parliament and of the Council on the harmonisation of transparency requirements in relation to information about issuers whose securities are admitted to trading on a regulated market and amending Directive 2001/43/EC.

(4) (*Revokes the Statutory Auditors and Third Country Auditors Regulations 2007, SI 2007/3434, reg 43.*)

NOTES

All words in square brackets were substituted by the Statutory Auditors and Third Country Auditors (Amendment) (EU Exit) Regulations 2019, SI 2019/177, regs 65, 72, as from IP completion day (as defined in the European Union (Withdrawal Agreement) Act 2020, s 39) (for transitional provisions, see Sch 4 to the 2019 Regulations at **[12.88]**).

22, 23 (*Reg 22 amends the Companies Act 2006 (Transfer of Audit Working Papers to Third Countries) Regulations 2010, SI 2010/2537; reg 23 amends the Companies (Bodies Concerned with Auditing Standards etc) (Exemption from Liability) Regulations 2016, SI 2016/571.*)

[4.668]

24 Review

(1) The Secretary of State must from time to time—

(a) carry out a review of the provisions of these Regulations,

(b) set out the conclusions of the review in a report, and

(c) publish the report.

(2) The report must, in particular—

(a) set out the objectives intended to be achieved by those provisions,

(b) assess the extent to which those objectives are achieved,

(c) assess whether those objectives remain appropriate, and

(d) if those objectives remain appropriate, assess the extent to which they could be achieved in another way which involves less onerous regulatory provision.

(3) . . .

(4) The first report under this regulation must be published before the end of the period of five years beginning with the date on which these Regulations come into force.

(5) Subsequent reports under this regulation must be published at intervals not exceeding five years.

(6) In this regulation, "regulatory provision" has the meaning given by section 32(4) of the Small Business, Enterprise and Employment Act 2015.

NOTES

Para (3): revoked by the Statutory Auditors and Third Country Auditors (Amendment) (EU Exit) Regulations 2019, SI 2019/177, regs 65, 73, as from IP completion day (as defined in the European Union (Withdrawal Agreement) Act 2020, s 39) (for transitional provisions, see Sch 4 to the 2019 Regulations at **[12.88]**).

SCHEDULES

SCHEDULE 1
REQUIREMENTS FOR PROFESSIONAL ETHICS, INDEPENDENCE, OBJECTIVITY, CONFIDENTIALITY, AUDITING STANDARDS AND AUDIT REPORTING

Regulation 3(13)

[4.669]

1. In this Schedule—

"A" means a person appointed as a statutory auditor,

["key audit partner" means—

(a) an individual who is eligible for appointment as a statutory auditor and who is designated by an audit firm for a particular audit engagement as being primarily responsible for carrying out the statutory audit on behalf of the audit firm;

(b) in the case of a group audit, any of the following—

(i) an individual who is eligible for appointment as a statutory auditor and who is designated by an audit firm as being primarily responsible for carrying out the statutory audit of the consolidated accounts of the group on behalf of the audit firm;

(ii) an individual who is eligible to conduct the audit of the accounts of any material subsidiary undertaking and who is designated as being primarily responsible for that audit; or

(c) an individual who is eligible for appointment as a statutory auditor and who signs the audit report,]

"relevant requirement" has the same meaning as in regulation 5.

2. (1) Standards must ensure that—

(a) A is subject to principles of professional ethics, covering at least A's public-interest function, A's integrity and objectivity and A's professional competence and due care;

(b) in carrying out statutory audit work, A—

(i) maintains professional scepticism throughout the audit;

(ii) maintains professional scepticism in particular when reviewing management estimates relating to fair values, the impairment of assets, provisions and future cash flow relevant to the audited person's ability to continue as a going concern;

(iii) recognises the possibility of a material misstatement due to facts or behaviour indicating irregularities, including fraud or error,

notwithstanding A's past experience of honesty and integrity on the part of the audited person's management and of the persons charged with the governance of the audited person.

(2) In this paragraph "professional scepticism" means an attitude that includes a questioning mind, being alert to conditions which may indicate possible misstatement due to error or fraud and a critical assessment of audit evidence.

(3) Standards must ensure that, during the relevant period A and any other individual in a position to influence the outcome of the statutory audit is independent of the audited person and not involved in the decision-taking of the audited person.

(4) In this paragraph "the relevant period" means—

(a) the [financial year of the account] to be audited; and

(b) the period during which the statutory audit is carried out.

3. (1) Standards must ensure that A takes all reasonable steps to ensure that, in carrying out statutory audit work, A's independence is not affected by—

(a) any existing or potential conflict of interest; or

(b) any business or other direct or indirect relationship with A or a person having a relevant connection with A.

(2) For the purposes of this paragraph a person has a relevant connection with A if that person—

(a) is a member of A's network;

(b) is a manager, auditor, employee or other individual whose services are placed at A's disposal or under A's control; or

(c) is directly or indirectly linked to A by control.

(3) Standards must ensure that A records in the audit working papers all significant threats to A's independence and the safeguards applied to mitigate those threats.

(4) In this paragraph "audit working papers" means any documents which are or have been held by A and are related to the conduct of the audit.

4. (1) Standards must ensure that A does not accept appointment as a statutory auditor (or, if already appointed, resigns from such an appointment) if there is any qualifying threat created by financial, personal business employment or other relationships between the audited person and-

(a) A,

(b) any member of A's network, or

(c) any individual in a position to influence the outcome of the statutory audit.

(2) In this paragraph "qualifying threat" means a threat of self-review, self-interest, advocacy, familiarity or intimidation which would cause an objective, reasonable and informed third party, taking into account any safeguards applied, to conclude that A's independence is compromised.

5. (1) Standards must ensure that—

(a) none of the persons mentioned in sub-paragraph (2), and

(b) no trust whose managerial responsibilities are discharged by, or which is directly or indirectly controlled by, or which is set up for the benefit of, or whose economic interests are substantially equivalent to those of any person mentioned in paragraphs (a), (b) or (c) of that sub-paragraph,

holds or has a material and direct beneficial interest in, or engages in any transaction in any financial instrument issued, guaranteed or otherwise supported by any audited person within (in the case of a person mentioned in sub-paragraph (2)(a)) the area of statutory audit work in which that person is directly involved or (in the case of a person mentioned in sub-paragraph (2)(b), (c) or (d)) the area of statutory audit work in which the person mentioned in sub-paragraph (a) to whom they have the connection described in sub-paragraph (2)(b), (c) or (d) as the case may be is involved.

(2) This sub-paragraph applies to—

(a) A, a key audit partner of A, an employee of A or any other individual—

(i) whose services are placed at A's disposal or under A's control, and

(ii) who is directly involved in statutory audit work;

(b) a person who is the spouse, civil partner or dependent child of any person mentioned in paragraph (a);

(c) any other relative of any person mentioned in paragraph (a) who (at any time in the period from the start of the financial year in respect of which the audit is being carried out to the date on which the audit report is signed) has lived in the same household as that person for at least one year;

(d) a firm whose managerial responsibilities are discharged by, or which is directly or indirectly controlled by, any person mentioned in paragraphs (a), (b) or (c) or in which any such person has a beneficial or other substantially equivalent economic interest.

(3) Sub-paragraph (1) does not prevent the owning of interests indirectly through diversified collective investment schemes, including managed funds, such as pensions or life insurance.

(4) Standards must ensure that none of the persons mentioned in sub-paragraph (2), who—

(a) owns financial instruments (except for interests of the kind mentioned in sub-paragraph (3)) of the audited person,

(b) owns financial instruments (except for interests of the kind mentioned in sub-paragraph (3)) of any person related to the audited person, in circumstances where owning those instruments may cause, or may be generally perceived as causing, a conflict of interest, or

(c) has a business or employment relationship with the audited person within the relevant period in circumstances that may cause, or may be generally perceived as causing, a conflict of interest,

participates in or otherwise influences the outcome of the statutory audit.

(5) In sub-paragraph (4), "the relevant period" has the same meaning as in paragraph 2(4).

(6) Standards must ensure A and any person mentioned in sub-paragraph (2) does not solicit or accept pecuniary or non-pecuniary gifts or favours from the audited person or from any person related to the audited person,

(7) In sub-paragraph (6) "pecuniary or non-pecuniary gifts" does not include gifts whose value an objective, reasonable and informed person would consider trivial or inconsequential.

6. Standards must ensure that if, during the [financial year of the account] to be audited, the audited person is acquired by, merges with or acquires another person, A shall—

(a) identify and evaluate any current or recent interests or relationships which could compromise A's independence and ability to continue carrying out the statutory audit after the effective date of the merger or acquisition, and

(b) as soon as possible, and in any event within three months—

  (i) take such steps as may be necessary to terminate any current interests or relationships which would compromise A's independence, and

  (ii) where possible, adopt safeguards that minimise any threats to A's independence arising from prior and current interests and relationships.

7. (1) Standards must ensure that—

(a) where A is an individual, A, and

(b) where A is a firm, A's key audit partner,

does not take up a relevant position with the audited person before the end of the cooling off period.

(2) Standards must also ensure that no person having a relevant connection with A takes up a relevant position with the audited person within one year of having been directly involved in the statutory audit of the audited person.

(3) In this paragraph—

"cooling off period" means—

  (a) in the case of a public interest entity, two years, and

  (b) in any other case, one year,

beginning with the day on which A ceased to be the audited person's statutory auditor or (if A is a firm), A's key audit partner ceased to be the key audit partner in connection with the statutory audit of the audited person;

"person having a relevant connection with A" means a person eligible for appointment as a statutory auditor, who is—

  (a) a partner (apart from a key audit partner) or employee of A, or

  (b) any individual whose services are placed at A's disposal or under A's control;

"relevant position" means—

  (a) any key management position,

  (b) membership of the audited person's audit committee,

  (c) membership of any body performing equivalent functions to an audit committee in relation to the audited person,

  (d) any other position as director of the audited person or, where the audited person's affairs are managed by a management body or other committee, membership of that management body or committee.

8. (1) Standards must ensure that, before accepting an appointment as a statutory auditor, A assesses and records—

(a) whether A is complying with the requirements of paragraphs 1 to 7 of this Schedule;

(b) whether there are any threats to A's independence and the safeguards applied to mitigate those threats;

(c) whether A has such competent employees, time and resources as are needed to carry out the statutory audit in an appropriate manner;

(d) where A is a firm, whether the key audit partner is approved [as eligible for appointment] as a statutory auditor . . .

(2) Standards ensuring the matters mentioned in this paragraph may apply simplified requirements in relation to the statutory audit of companies to which the small companies regime applies under section 381 of the Act.

9. (1) Standards must ensure adequate provision on confidentiality in relation to all information and documents to which A has access when carrying out a statutory audit, but such rules must not impede the enforcement of obligations under—

(a) these Regulations,

(b) the Audit Regulation, or

(c) Parts 16 and 42 of the Act.

(2) Standards ensuring the matters mentioned in sub-paragraph (1) must not prevent A from transferring relevant documents concerning the statutory audit to an auditor of the consolidated accounts of a parent undertaking in a third country where such documents are necessary for auditing the accounts of that undertaking.

(3) Standards must ensure that, where A ceases to hold office as statutory auditor, A provides A's successor as statutory auditor with access to all relevant information concerning the audited person, including information concerning the most recent audit.

(4) Standards ensuring the matters mentioned in sub-paragraph (1)—

(a) must apply to A in respect of an audit engagement after A has ceased that engagement, and

(b) must apply to A if he ceases to be eligible for appointment as a statutory auditor.

(5) Standards must ensure that any rule of law relating to the confidentiality of information received in the course of statutory audit work by persons appointed as statutory auditors is complied with.

(6) Standards must ensure that no firm is eligible for appointment as a statutory auditor unless the firm has arrangements to prevent any person from being able to exert any influence over the way in which a statutory audit is conducted in circumstances in which that influence would be likely to affect the independence or integrity of the audit.

10. (1) Standards must ensure that A—

(a) has appropriate policies and procedures to ensure that no partner, director, member or shareholder of A or partner, director, member or shareholder of any affiliate of A intervenes in the carrying out of statutory audit work in any way which jeopardises A's independence and objectivity in carrying out such work;
(b) has sound administrative and accounting procedures, internal quality control mechanisms (which are designed to secure compliance with decisions and procedures at all levels of A's working structure), effective procedures for risk assessment and effective control and safeguard arrangements for information processing systems;
(c) has appropriate policies and procedures to ensure that A's employees and any other individuals, whose services are placed at A's disposal or under A's control and who are directly involved in statutory audit activities, have appropriate knowledge and experience for the duties assigned;
(d) has appropriate policies and procedures to ensure that outsourcing of important audit functions is not undertaken in such a way as to impair the quality of A's internal quality control and the ability of the competent authority to supervise A's compliance with relevant requirements;
(e) has appropriate and effective organisational and administrative arrangements to prevent, identify, eliminate or manage and disclose any threats to their independence as referred to in paragraphs 2(3) and 3 to 8;
(f) has appropriate policies and procedures for carrying out statutory audits, coaching, supervising and reviewing the activities of A's employees and organising the structure of the audit file as referred to in paragraph 12(1)(f);
(g) establishes an internal quality control system to ensure the quality of a statutory audit, which—
  (i) covers at least the policies and procedures mentioned in paragraph (f); and
  (ii) in the case of a firm, ensures that responsibility for the system lies with an individual who . . . holds an appropriate qualification . . .
(h) uses appropriate systems, resources and procedures to ensure continuity and regularity in carrying out A's statutory audit work;
(i) has appropriate and effective organisational and administrative arrangements for dealing with and recording incidents which have, or may have, serious consequences, for integrity of A's statutory audit work;
(j) has in place adequate remuneration policies, including profit-sharing policies, providing sufficient performance incentives to secure audit quality (including provision that the amount of revenue that A derives from services other than statutory audit services must not form part of the performance evaluation and remuneration of any person involved in, or able to influence the carrying out of, the audit);
(k) monitors and evaluates the adequacy and effectiveness of A's systems, internal quality control mechanisms and arrangements established in accordance with these Regulations, the Audit Regulation or Parts 16 or 42 of the Act and takes appropriate measures to address any deficiencies;
(l) carries out an annual evaluation of the internal quality control system referred to in sub-paragraph (1)(g), keeps records of the findings of that evaluation and any proposed measure to modify the internal quality control system;
(m) documents and communicates to A's employees (and where A is a firm, communicates to A's partners or members) the policies and procedures referred to in this sub-paragraph;
(n) takes into consideration the scale and complexity of A's activities when complying with the requirements mentioned in this paragraph and is able to demonstrate to the competent authority that its policies and procedures are appropriate given the scale and complexity of those activities.

(2) The requirements of standards mentioned in sub-paragraph (1) may be simplified in relation to the statutory audit of companies which are exempt from the requirements of the Act relating to audit by virtue of section 477 of the Act.

(3) In this paragraph "affiliate", in relation to A, means any undertaking, regardless of its legal form, which is connected to A by means of common ownership, control or management.

11. (1) Standards must ensure that, when A is a firm, A—
(a) designates at least one key audit partner, and
(b) applies as its main criteria in selecting a key audit partner—
  (i) the need to secure the quality of the audit,
  (ii) the need to secure A's independence and competence in carrying out the audit,
(c) ensures the key audit partner is actively involved in carrying out the audit,
(d) provides any key audit partner with sufficient resources and with personnel that have the necessary competence and capabilities to carry out their duties appropriately.

(2) Standards must ensure that A devotes sufficient time to the engagement and assigns sufficient resources to enable A to carry out A's duties appropriately.

12. (1) Standards must ensure that A—
(a) keeps records of any breaches (other than breaches which A reasonably considers to be minor breaches) of any relevant requirement;
(b) keeps records of any consequences of any breach recorded in accordance with paragraph 12(1)(a), the measures taken to address such a breach and to modify A's internal quality control system;
(c) prepares an annual report containing an overview of any measures taken under paragraph (b) and communicates that report internally;
(d) documents any request for advice from an external expert, together with the advice received;
(e) maintains a client account record, which includes in respect of every statutory audit—
  (i) the audited person's name, address and place of business,
  (ii) when the statutory auditor is a firm, the name of the key audit partner or, where there is more than one key audit partner, the names of all the key audit partners,
  (iii) the fees charged for carrying out the statutory audit and for other services in any financial year;
(f) creates an audit file for each statutory audit, which meets the requirements of sub-paragraph (2).
(g) keeps records of any complaints made in writing about the performance of any statutory audit that A has carried out

(2) The requirements for an audit file are that—

- (a) it documents at least the matters recorded in accordance with paragraph 8;
- (b) in relation to a statutory audit of a public interest entity, it documents the matters recorded in accordance with Articles 6, 7 and 8 of the Audit Regulation;
- (c) it contains any other data and documents that are important in supporting the audit report;
- (d) in relation to a statutory audit of a public interest entity, it contains any other data and documents that are important in supporting the report to the audit committee required under Article 11 of the Audit Regulation;
- (e) it contains any other data and documents that are important for monitoring compliance with relevant requirements and other applicable legal requirements;
- (f) it is closed not more than sixty days after the date the audit report is signed in accordance with section 503 of the Act.

(3) The requirements of standards mentioned in sub-paragraph (1)(a) to (c) and (g) may be simplified in relation to the statutory audit of companies exempt from the requirements of the Act relating to audit by virtue of section 477 of the Act.

13. Standards must ensure that remuneration received or receivable by a statutory auditor in respect of statutory audit work—

- (a) is not influenced or determined by the statutory auditor providing other services to the audited person, or
- (b) cannot be based on any form of contingency.

14. Standards must ensure that the scope of statutory audit work does not include, save to the extent required by the audit reporting requirements, assurance on the future viability of the audited person or on the efficiency or effectiveness with which the directors or those concerned in the management of the audited person have conducted or will conduct its affairs.

15. (1) Standards must ensure that, in the case of a statutory audit of the consolidated accounts of a group of undertakings—

- (a) the group auditor bears full responsibility for the audit report,
- (b) where applicable, the group auditor bears full responsibility for ensuring the requirements of Articles 10 and 11 of the Audit Regulation are met,
- (c) the group auditor—
  - (i) evaluates and reviews the audit work carried out by any statutory auditors, . . . or third country auditors for the purpose of the group audit, and
  - (ii) documents the nature, timing and extent of the work so carried out, including, where applicable, the group auditor's review of the relevant parts of the audit documentation,
- (d) any documentation retained by the group auditor is such as to enable the competent authority (or, where appropriate, the recognised supervisory body of which the group auditor is a member) to review the work of the group auditor,
- (e) for the purposes of the group auditor's review mentioned in sub-paragraph (1)(c)(i), the group auditor—
  - (i) requests the agreement of the statutory auditor . . . or third country auditor to the transfer of relevant documentation during the conduct of the audit of consolidated [accounts] as a condition of the group auditor relying on the work of the statutory auditor . . . or third country auditor, and
  - (ii) if unable to request or secure the agreement mentioned in sub-paragraph (1)(e)(i), takes appropriate measures (including carrying out additional statutory audit work directly or outsourcing such work) and informs the competent authority (or where appropriate, the recognised supervisory body of which the group auditor is a member),

(2) Standards must ensure that a group auditor, who is subject to a quality assurance review or an investigation concerning the statutory audit of the consolidated [accounts] of a group of undertakings—

- (a) complies with any request by the competent authority for relevant documentation retained by the group auditor and concerning the audit work performed by the respective statutory auditors . . . or third country auditors for the purposes of the group audit (including any working papers relevant to the group audit);
- (b) in cases where the competent authority is unable to obtain documentation from the relevant competent authorities of a third country, complies with any request for additional documentation relating to audit work performed by third country auditors for the purposes of the group audit (including working papers relevant to the group audit);
- (c) in order to comply with any request under sub-paragraph (2)(b), the group auditor—
  - (i) retains copies of such documentation,
  - (ii) obtains the agreement of third country auditors to the group auditor having unrestricted access to such documentation on request,
  - (iii) retains documentation to show that the group auditor has undertaken the appropriate procedures in order to gain access to the audit documentation and evidence supporting the existence of any impediments to access, or
  - (iv) takes any other appropriate action.

16. (1) In relation to the audit of public interest entities, standards must ensure that A keeps key audit documents and information for at least five years following the creation of such documents and information.

(2) In this paragraph, "key audit documents and information" means—

[(a) the documents and information referred to, as appropriate, in—

- (i) articles 4(3), 6, 7, 8(4) to (7), 10, 11, 14 and 16(3) of the Audit Regulation,
- (ii) any rules made under section 340 of the Financial Services and Markets Act 2000,
- (iii) the Financial Services and Markets Act 2000 (Communications by Auditors) Regulations 2001,
- (iv) sections 485A to 485C, 489A to 489C and 494ZA of the Companies Act 2006,
- (v) paragraphs 3B to 3E of Schedule 11 to the Building Societies Act 1986,
- (vi) paragraphs 2 to 5 of Schedule 14A to the Friendly Societies Act 1992,
- (vii) sections 485A to 485C and 494ZA of the Companies Act, as applied to—

(aa) limited liability partnerships by the Limited Liability Partnerships (Accounts and Audit) (Application of Companies Act 2006) Regulations 2008 (see in particular regulation 36 and 38A), or

(bb) insurance undertakings by the Insurance Accounts Directive (Miscellaneous Insurance Undertakings) Regulations 2008 (see in particular regulation 6(1A)) ("insurance undertaking" has the meaning given by regulation 2 of those Regulations)].

(b) information recorded in accordance with the requirements of paragraphs 8, 10, 12 and 15 of this Schedule, and

(c) the audit report.

NOTES

The definition "key audit partner" in para 1 was substituted, and the words in square brackets in sub-para 2(4)(a), para 6, and sub-paras 15(1)(e)(i) and (2) were substituted, by the Statutory Auditors and Third Country Auditors (Amendment) (EU Exit) Regulations 2020, SI 2020/108, reg 17(1), (3), as from 22 February 2020.

The words in square brackets in sub-para 8(1)(d) were inserted, sub-para 16(2)(a) was substituted, and the words omitted from paras 8, 10, 15 were revoked, by the Statutory Auditors and Third Country Auditors (Amendment) (EU Exit) Regulations 2019, SI 2019/177, regs 65, 74, as from IP completion day (as defined in the European Union (Withdrawal Agreement) Act 2020, s 39) (for transitional provisions, see Sch 4 to the 2019 Regulations at **[12.88]**).

SCHEDULE 2
INVESTIGATION POWERS

Regulation 10

[4.670]

1. (1) The competent authority may for any purpose related to inspecting or investigating statutory audit work give notice to any statutory auditor ("A") requiring A to provide information specified in the notice.

(2) Information may be specified in a notice under sub-paragraph (1) only if it is information relating to the statutory audit of the annual accounts or the consolidated accounts of any audited person.

(3) The competent authority may give notice to any person mentioned in sub-paragraph (4) requiring that person to provide information relating to the statutory audit of the annual accounts or the consolidated accounts of any public interest entity.

(4) The persons to whom notice may be given under sub-paragraph (3) are—

(a) any person involved in the activities of a statutory auditor (including any person to whom a statutory auditor has outsourced such activities),

(b) any public interest entity,

(c) any subsidiary or parent of a public interest entity or any other subsidiary of a company of which a public interest entity is a subsidiary,

(d) any person otherwise having a connection to a statutory auditor carrying out the statutory audit of the annual accounts or consolidated accounts of a public interest entity.

(5) A notice under sub-paragraph (1) or (3) must be in writing and specify the purposes for which the information is required.

(6) A notice under sub-paragraph (1) or (3) may—

(a) specify the time within which and the manner in which the person to whom it is given must comply with it,

(b) require the creation of documents, or documents of a description, specified in the notice, and

(c) require the provision of those documents to the competent authority.

(7) A requirement to provide information or create a document is a requirement to do so in a legible form.

(8) A notice under sub-paragraph (1) or (3) does not require a person to provide any information or create any documents which the person would be entitled to refuse to provide or produce—

(a) in proceedings in the High Court on the grounds of legal professional privilege, or

(b) in proceedings in the Court of Session on the grounds of confidentiality of communications.

(9) In sub-paragraph (8) "communications" means—

(a) communications between a professional legal adviser and his client, or

(b) communications made in connection with or in contemplation of legal proceedings or for the purposes of those proceedings.

2. (1) If a person fails to comply with a notice under paragraph 1, the competent authority may make an application to the court.

(2) If it appears to the court that the person has failed to comply with the notice, it may make an order requiring the person to do anything that the court thinks it is reasonable for the person to do, for any of the purposes for which the notice was given, to ensure that the notice is complied with.

(3) Where the court makes an order under sub-paragraph (2)—

(a) it may require the person to meet the costs or expenses of the competent authority's application, or

(b) if the person is a company, partnership or unincorporated association, the court may require an officer who is responsible for the failure to meet those costs or expenses.

(4) In this paragraph—

"the court" means—

(a) the High Court,

(b) in relation to England and Wales, the county court,

(c) in relation to Northern Ireland, a county court,

(d) the Court of Session, or

(e) the sheriff;

"officer" means—

(a) in the case of a company, a director, manager, secretary or other similar officer,

(b) in the case of a limited liability partnership, a member,
(c) in the case of a partnership other than a limited liability partnership, a partner, and
(d) in the case of an unincorporated association, a person who is concerned in the management or control of its affairs.

3. (1) This paragraph applies if a person provides information (including information contained in a document created by the person) in response to a notice under paragraph 1.

(2) In any criminal proceedings against the person—
(a) no evidence relating to the information may be adduced by or on behalf of the prosecution, and
(b) no question relating to the information may be asked by or on behalf of the prosecution.

(3) Sub-paragraph (2) does not apply if, in the proceedings—
(a) evidence relating to the information is adduced by or on behalf of the person providing it, or
(b) a question relating to the information is asked by or on behalf of that person.

(4) Sub-paragraph (2) does not apply if the proceedings are for—
(a) an offence under paragraph 5 (obstruction),
(b) an offence under section 5 of the Perjury Act 1911 (false statutory declarations and other false statements without oath),
(c) an offence under section 44(2) of the Criminal Law (Consolidation)(Scotland) Act 1995 (false statements or declarations),
(d) an offence under Article 10 of the Perjury (Northern Ireland) Order 1979 (false statutory declarations and other false unsworn statements).

4. (1) An officer of the competent authority may, for the purposes of inspecting or investigating the statutory audit of a public interest entity, enter relevant premises at any reasonable time if—
(a) the requirements of sub-paragraph (3) are satisfied, or
(b) the occupier of the premises has waived those requirements.

(2) In this paragraph "relevant premises" means premises—
(a) in which a statutory auditor is carrying out a statutory audit, or
(b) where documents related to a statutory audit are kept,

and does not include premises used wholly or mainly as a dwelling.

(3) The requirements of this sub-paragraph are that—
(a) a notice in writing is given to the occupier of the premises by an officer of the competent authority,
(b) the notice sets out why entry is necessary and gives details of the statutory audit work subject to inspection (including the name of the audited person and the accounting years in question) and indicates the nature of the offence under paragraph 5, and
(c) there are at least two working days between the date the occupier of the premises receives the notice and the date of entry.

(4) An officer of the competent authority who enters premises under this paragraph must produce evidence of the officer's identity and authority to the occupier of the premises.

(5) An officer of the competent authority entering premises under this paragraph may—
(a) be accompanied by such persons and may take onto the premises such equipment as the officer thinks necessary,
(b) require a statutory auditor or any person acting on behalf of a statutory auditor to produce any documents relating to the statutory audit of the annual or consolidated accounts of a public interest entity to which the statutory auditor has access,
(c) require a statutory auditor or any person acting on behalf of a statutory auditor to give an explanation of any document produced under paragraph (b).

(6) Where a document required to be produced under sub-paragraph (5)(b) contains information recorded electronically, the power in that sub-paragraph includes power to require the production of a copy of the document in a form in which it can easily be taken away and in which it is visible and legible.

(7) This paragraph does not permit an officer of the competent authority to require a person to produce any document which the person would be entitled to refuse to produce—
(a) in proceedings in the High Court on the grounds of legal professional privilege, or
(b) in proceedings in the Court of Session on grounds of confidentiality of communications.

(8) In this paragraph—

"communications" means—
(a) communications between a professional legal adviser and the adviser's client, or
(b) communications made in connection with or in contemplation of legal proceedings or for the purposes of those proceedings.

"give", in relation to the giving of a notice to the occupier of premises, includes delivering it or leaving it at the premises or sending it there by post;

"working day" means a day other than—
(a) Saturday or Sunday,
(b) Christmas Day or Good Friday, or
(c) a day which is a bank holiday under the Banking and Financial Dealings Act 1971 in that part of the United Kingdom in which the premises are situated.

5. (1) A person commits an offence if the person—
(a) intentionally obstructs the competent authority or an officer of the competent authority in exercising or seeking to exercise a power under and in accordance with this Schedule,
(b) intentionally fails to comply with a requirement properly imposed by the competent authority or an officer of the competent authority under this Schedule,

(c) without reasonable excuse fails to give the competent authority or an officer of the competent authority any other assistance or information which the competent authority or officer may reasonably require for a purpose for which the competent authority or officer may exercise a power under this Schedule.

(2) A person commits an offence if, in giving information of a kind mentioned in sub-paragraph (1)(c), the person—

(a) makes a statement which the person knows is false or misleading in a material respect, or

(b) recklessly makes a statement which is false or misleading in a material respect.

(3) A person who is guilty of an offence under sub-paragraph (1) or (2) is liable on summary conviction to a fine not exceeding level 3 on the standard scale.

(4) Nothing in this paragraph requires a person to answer any question or give any information if to do so might incriminate that person.

SCHEDULES 3–5

(*Sch 3 amends the Companies Act 2006, Parts 15, 16, 38 and 42; Sch 4 amends the Building Societies Act 1986, Part 8; Sch 5 amends the Companies (Audit, Investigations and Community Enterprise) Act 2004, ss 15D, 16, and the Local Audit and Accountability Act 2014.*)

STATUTORY AUDITORS REGULATIONS 2017

(SI 2017/1164)

NOTES

Made: 28 November 2017.

Authority: European Communities Act 1972; Companies Act 2006, ss 454(3), (4), 1292(1)(a), (c); Liability Partnerships Act 2000, ss 15(a), 17 (see also the note "Statutory Instruments made under the European Communities Act 1972" preceding paragraph **[4.1]** *ante*).

Commencement: see reg 1 *post*.

For a summary of all Orders and Regulations made under the Companies Act 2006, see Appendix 4 at **[A4]**.

PART 1 INTRODUCTORY

[4.671]

1 Citation and commencement

(1) These Regulations may be cited as the Statutory Auditors Regulations 2017.

(2) Subject to paragraph (3), these Regulations come into force on 1 January 2018.

(3) The following provisions of these Regulations come into force on 6 April 2018—

(a) regulations 17 and 18;

(b) paragraphs 21 and 22 of Schedule 1;

(c) paragraphs 2(a), 4(b), 13(b) and 16(a) and (b) of Schedule 2.

[4.672]

2 Application and interpretation

(1) The amendments made by Part 1 of Schedule 1 have effect in relation to financial years of building societies beginning on or after 17th June 2016.

(2) The amendments made by Part 2 of Schedule 1 have effect in relation to financial years of friendly societies beginning on or after 17th June 2016.

(3) The amendments made by paragraphs 8 to 19 in Part 3 of Schedule 1 have effect in relation to financial years of companies beginning on or after 17th June 2016;

(4) The amendments made by Schedule 2 have effect in relation to financial years of insurance undertakings beginning on or after 17th June 2016.

(5) In Schedule 3—

(a) the amendments made by paragraphs 4 to 9 and 11 to 19 have effect in relation to financial years of limited liability partnerships beginning on or after 17 June 2016;

(b) the amendments made by paragraphs 2, 3 and 10 have effect in relation to financial years of limited liability partnerships beginning on or after 1 January 2017.

(6) Nothing in these Regulations makes any act or omission of any person occurring before 1st January 2018 an offence.

(7) These Regulations have no effect in relation to—

(a) copies of accounts and reports sent by the committee of management of a friendly society to the Financial Conduct Authority and, if appropriate, the Prudential Regulation Authority, under section 78(1) of the Friendly Societies Act 1992,

(b) copies of accounts and reports sent by the directors of a building society to the Financial Conduct Authority and, if appropriate, the Prudential Regulation Authority, under section 81(2) of the Building Societies Act 1986,

(c) copies of accounts and reports delivered by the directors of a company to the registrar under section 444, 444A, 445, 446 or 447 of the Companies Act 2006,

(d) an annual return, copy of a balance sheet or copy of an auditor's report sent by a registered society to the Financial Conduct Authority under section 89 of the Co-operative and Community Benefit Societies Act 2014 as modified by Schedule 1 to the Insurance Accounts Directive (Miscellaneous Insurance Undertakings) Regulations 2008,

(e) an annual return, copy of a balance sheet or copy of an auditor's report sent by a registered society to the registrar under section 48 of the Industrial and Provident Societies Act (Northern Ireland) 1969 as modified by Schedule 2 to the Insurance Accounts Directive (Miscellaneous Insurance Undertakings) Regulations 2008,

(f) the accounts and reports in respect of an insurance undertaking which is not a registered society which are prepared or caused to be prepared in accordance with regulation 3 of the Insurance Accounts Directive (Miscellaneous Insurance Undertakings) Regulations 2008, and

(g) copies of accounts and reports delivered by the designated members of an LLP to the registrar under section 444, 445 or 446 of the Companies Act 2006 as applied in respect of limited liability partnerships by the Limited Liability Partnerships (Accounts and Audit) (Application of Companies Act 2006) Regulations 2008,

before 1st January 2018.

(8) In this regulation—

"building society" means a building society within the meaning of the Building Societies Act 1986;

"company" means a company within the meaning of section 1(1) of the Companies Act 2006;

"financial year"—

(a) in relation to building societies, has the meaning given by sections 117 and 117A of the Building Societies Act 1986;

(b) in relation to companies, has the meaning given by section 390 of the Companies Act 2006;

(c) in relation to friendly societies, has the meaning given by section 118 of the Friendly Societies Act 1992;

(d) in relation to insurance undertakings, has the meaning given by regulation 2(6) of the Insurance Accounts Directive (Miscellaneous Insurance Undertakings) Regulations 2008;

(e) in relation to limited liability partnerships, has the meaning given by section 390 of the Companies Act 2006 as it has been applied in respect of limited liability partnerships by the Limited Liability Partnerships (Accounts and Audit) (Application of Companies Act 2006) Regulations 2008;

"friendly society" means a friendly society within the meaning of the Friendly Societies Act 1992;

"insurance undertaking" has the meaning given by regulation 2(2) to (4) of the Insurance Accounts Directive (Miscellaneous Insurance Undertakings) Regulations 2008;

"limited liability partnership" has the meaning given by section 1 of the Limited Liability Partnerships Act 2000;

"registered society" means—

(a) a registered society within the meaning given by section 1(1) of the Co-operative and Community Benefit Societies Act 2014; or

(b) a society registered or deemed to be registered under the Industrial and Provident Societies Act (Northern Ireland) 1969.

PARTS 2, 3

3–18 *(Reg 3 introduces Sch 1 to these Regulations (Amendments to primary legislation). Regs 4 and 5 introduce Schs 2 and 3 (Amendments to secondary legislation). Regs 6–14 amend the Companies (Revision of Defective Accounts and Reports) Regulations 2008, SI 2008/373 at* **[4.21]***. Regs 15, 16 amend the Statutory Auditors and Third Country Auditors Regulations 2016, SI 2016/649 at* **[4.650]***. Regs 17, 18 amend the Statutory Auditors (Amendment of Companies Act 2006 and Delegation of Functions etc) Order 2012, SI 2012/1741 at* **[4.430]***.)*

PART 4 REVOCATIONS, REPEALS AND SAVING

[4.673]

19 Revocations, repeals and saving

(1) The enactments listed in the table in Schedule 4 (revocations and repeals) are revoked or repealed to the extent specified.

(2) Other than in relation to entries 1 to 4 in the table, the revocations and repeals have effect in relation to financial years of qualifying banks beginning on or after 30th November 2018.

(3) In this regulation—

"financial year" has the meaning given by regulation 2(1) of the Bank Accounts Directive (Miscellaneous Banks) Regulations 2008;

"qualifying bank" has the meaning given by regulations 2(1) and 3 of those Regulations.

SCHEDULES

SCHEDULES 1–4

(Sch 1, Part 1 amends the Building Societies Act 1986. Sch 1, Part 2 amends the Friendly Societies Act 1992. Sch 1, Part 3 amends the Companies Act 2006 at **[1.1]***. Sch 2 amends the Insurance Accounts Directive (Miscellaneous Insurance Undertakings) Regulations 2008, SI 2008/565. Sch 3 amends the Limited Liability Partnerships (Accounts and Audit) (Application of Companies Act 2006) Regulations 2008, SI 2008/1911 at* **[10.223]***. Sch 4 revokes the Bank Accounts Directive (Miscellaneous Banks) Regulations 2008 (SI 2008/567) and contains minor and consequential repeals and revocations which, in so far as relevant to this Handbook, have been taken in at the appropriate place.)*

COMPANIES (MISCELLANEOUS REPORTING) REGULATIONS 2018 (NOTE)

(SI 2018/860)

[4.674]

NOTES

These Regulations were made on 17 July 2018 under powers conferred by the Companies Act 2006, ss 396(3), 404(3), 416(4), 421(1)–(2A), 468, 1292(1)(a), (c), and the Companies (Audit, Investigations and Community Enterprise) Act 2004, ss 34(3)(a) and 62(2).

The Regulations came into force as follows:

— Regs 1 and 10 came into force on 7 August 2018;

— Regs 20 to 23 came into force on 7 August 2018, and the amendments made by those regulations apply to community interest company reports for financial years ending on or after that date.

— All other regulations came into force on 1 January 2019, and the amendments made by regs 2 to 9 and 11 to 19 apply in relation to the financial years of companies beginning on or after that date.

These Regulations make changes to the reporting requirements in Part 15 of the Companies Act 2006 and in the Large and Medium-Sized Companies and Groups (Accounts and Reports) Regulations 2008 (SI 2008/410). These Regulations also amend the Community Interest Company Regulations 2005 (SI 2005/1788), to make it clear that small Community Interest Companies (CICs) must report on their directors' remuneration.

These Regulations extend to the whole of the UK.

Regulation 1 makes provision for differential commencement in relation to the provisions of these Regulations and for their application (see above).

Part 2 (regs 2 to 6) amends the Companies Act 2006, providing a new requirement to include a statement in the strategic report on how the directors have had regard to the matters set out in section 172 of that Act in the exercise of their duties. Those regulations provide as follows—

Regulation 2 introduces the amendments made by regs 3 to 6.

Regulation 3 amends CA 2006, s 414C (Contents of strategic report) at **[1.471]**.

Regulation 4 inserts CA 2006, s 414CZA (Section 172(1) statement) at **[1.472]**.

Regulation 5 inserts CA 2006, s 426B (Section 172(1) statement to be made available on website) at **[1.491]**.

Regulation 6 amends CA 2006, Sch 8 (Index of Defined Expressions) at **[1.1522]**.

Part 3 amends the Large and Medium-sized Companies and Groups (Accounts and Reports) Regulations 2008 (at **[4.60]**) to require companies to report additional information in the directors' report.

Regulation 7 introduces the amendments made by regs 8 to 19.

Regulation 8 makes a consequential amendment to reg 10 of the 2008 Regulations, and reg 9 amends the review clause in reg 14 of the 2008 Regulations to require a review of the amendments made by these Regulations.

Regulation 10 corrects definitions in Schedule 5 to the 2008 Regulations which refer to repealed legislation. This regulation will align the definitions in Schedule 5 with those in Schedule 8 to the 2008 Regulations (which were previously amended), as well as the definitions used in the new Schedule 4A to the Community Interest Company Regulations 2005 (inserted by reg 23 of, and the Schedule to, these Regulations).

Regulation 11 introduces the amendments made to Sch 7 to the 2018 Regulations by regs 12 to 14.

Regulation 12 aligns the formula provided in Schedule 7 to the 2008 Regulations for calculating the average number of employees with the formula used in the Companies Act 2006.

Regulation 13 amends Part 4 of Schedule 7 to the 2008 Regulations to require additional reporting on a company's engagement with its employees, and suppliers, customers and others in a business relationship, to provide further explanation on how the directors of the company have complied with the duty to have regard in section 172.

Regulation 14 inserts a new Part 8 into Schedule 7 to the 2008 Regulations requiring companies which in a financial year have more than 2000 employees, or a turnover of more than £200 million and a balance sheet total of more than £2 billion, to provide a statement of corporate governance arrangements in relation to that year.

Regulation 15 introduces the amendments made to Sch 8 to the 2018 Regulations by regs 16 to 19 to require additional information in the Directors' Remuneration Report.

Regulation 16 requires that the annual statement from the chair of the remuneration committee includes a summary of any discretion exercised by the remuneration committee in relation to the award of directors' remuneration.

Regulation 17 requires companies to report how much of a director's pay award is attributable to share price growth, and extends the requirement to report on the exercise of discretion in relation to the award to specifically address whether discretion has been exercised due to changes in share price. It also places new requirements on companies with more than 250 UK employees to report pay ratio information comparing the remuneration of the CEO with the 25th, 50th and 75th percentile of the full time equivalent remuneration of the company's UK employees. For a parent company within the meaning of the Companies Act 2006 the information must relate to the group.

Regulation 18 places a new requirement for companies to include in the remuneration policy an illustration, in relation to performance measures or targets, of the maximum remuneration of directors assuming share price growth of 50% during the performance period.

Regulation 19 inserts a new definition ("UK employee") into the interpretation provision for Schedule 8.

Part 4 (regs 20 to 23) amends the Community Interest Company Regulations 2005 at **[6.106]**.

These provisions remedy a gap created when Schedule 3 to the Small Companies and Groups (Accounts and Reports) Regulations 2008 was revoked by the Companies, Partnerships and Groups (Accounts and Reports) Regulations 2015. Section 34 of the Companies, Audit, Investigations and Enterprise Act 2004 requires regulations to make provision for community interest company reports to include information about the remuneration of directors. Regulation 23 amends the CIC Regulations by inserting Schedule 4A into the 2005 Regulations, the content of which is a reproduction of the revoked Schedule 3, with minor amendments to definitions to include cross-references to the appropriate legislation.

COMPANIES ACT 2006 (EXTENSION OF TAKEOVER PANEL PROVISIONS) (ISLE OF MAN) ORDER 2019

(SI 2019/567)

NOTES

Made: 13 March 2019.

Authority: Companies Act 2006, s 965.

Commencement: IP completion day (as defined in the European Union (Withdrawal Agreement) Act 2020, s 39).

For a summary of all Orders and Regulations made under the Companies Act 2006, see Appendix 4 at **[A4]**.

[4.675]

1 Citation and commencement

This Order may be cited as the Companies Act 2006 (Extension of Takeover Panel Provisions) (Isle of Man) Order 2019, and comes into operation on exit day (within the meaning of section 20 of the European Union (Withdrawal) Act 2018).

NOTES

Commencement: IP completion day (as defined in the European Union (Withdrawal Agreement) Act 2020, s 39).

As to the commencement of these Regulations, see the European Union (Withdrawal Agreement) Act 2020, Sch 5, para 1 (at **[12.53]**) which gives legal effect to the implementation period by 'non-textually amending' the coming into force dates of subordinate legislation which comes into force immediately before exit day, on exit day or at any time after exit day. This subordinate legislation will instead come into force immediately before the end of the implementation period (IP completion day), on IP completion day or (as the case maybe) at the time concerned after IP completion day.

[4.676]

2 Extension of Takeover Panel provisions to the Isle of Man

Chapter 1 of Part 28 of the Companies Act 2006 (takeovers etc: the Takeover Panel) shall extend to the Isle of Man with the modifications set out in the Schedule to this Order.

NOTES

Commencement: IP completion day (as defined in the European Union (Withdrawal Agreement) Act 2020, s 39).

[4.677]

3 Revocations

The Companies Act 2006 (Extension of Takeover Panel Provisions) (Isle of Man) Order 2008 and the Companies Act 2006 (Extension of Takeover Panel Provisions) (Isle of Man) Order 2009 are revoked.

NOTES

Commencement: IP completion day (as defined in the European Union (Withdrawal Agreement) Act 2020, s 39).

SCHEDULE
MODIFICATIONS SUBJECT TO WHICH CHAPTER 1 OF PART 28 OF THE COMPANIES ACT 2006 EXTENDS TO THE ISLE OF MAN

Article 2

[4.678]

1. (1) Section 943 (rules about takeovers) is modified as follows.

(2) For subsection (1) substitute—

> "(1) The Panel may make rules corresponding to the rules applying to takeover bids in the United Kingdom.".

(3) Omit subsection (1A).

2. In section 947(10) (power to require documents and information) omit "(in Scotland, to confidentiality of communications)".

3. In section 948—

(a) omit subsections (4) and (5);

(b) in subsection (7) after paragraph (ab) insert—

> "(ac) the Central Registry of the Isle of Man (established by the Central Registry Act 2018 (an Act of Tynwald: AT 13 of 2018));"; and

(c) in subsection (9) after "the data protection legislation" insert—

> "(within the meaning of regulation 5 of the GDPR and LED Implementing Regulations 2018 of the Isle of Man)".

4. In section 949 (offences) for subsection (2) substitute—

> "(2) A person guilty of an offence under this section is liable—
> (a) on conviction on information, to custody for a term not exceeding two years or a fine (or both);
> (b) on summary conviction to custody for a term not exceeding 12 months, or to a fine not exceeding level 5 on the standard scale (or both).
>
> The reference to the standard scale is to the scale set out in section 55 of the Interpretation Act 2015 (an Act of Tynwald: AT 11 of 2015).".

5. In section 950(1) (Panel's duty to co-operate) after paragraph (ab) insert—

"(ac) the Central Registry of the Isle of Man (established by the Central Registry Act 2018 (an Act of Tynwald: AT 13 of 2018));".

6. In section 953 (failure to comply with rules about bid documentation) for subsection (6) substitute—

"(6) A person guilty of an offence under this section is liable—
(a) on conviction on information, to custody for a term not exceeding two years or a fine (or both);
(b) on summary conviction to custody for a term not exceeding 12 months, or to a fine not exceeding level 5 on the standard scale (or both).
The reference to the standard scale is to the scale set out in section 55 of the Interpretation Act 2015 (an Act of Tynwald: AT 11 of 2015).".

7. In section 955 (enforcement by the court)—
(a) in subsection (2) for "or, in Scotland, the Court of Session" substitute "of the Isle of Man"; and
(b) omit subsection (3)(b).

8. In section 961(3) (extent of exemption from liability in damages) for "section 6(1) of the Human Rights Act 1998 (c 42)" substitute "section 6(1) of the Human Rights Act 2001 (an Act of Tynwald: AT 1 of 2001)".

9. In section 962 (privilege against self-incrimination) for subsection (2) substitute—

"(2) Subsection (1) applies to any offence other than one under section 5 of the Perjury Act 1952 (an Act of Tynwald: AT 8 of 1952) (which concerns false statutory declarations and other false statements without oath).".

10. Omit section 964 and 965 (amendments to the Financial Services and Markets Act 2000 and power to extend to the Isle of Man and the Channel Islands).

11. In Schedule 2 in section (D) (specified persons in the Isle of Man)—
(a) in paragraph 1—
(i) in sub-paragraph (1) for "members" substitute "Minister, members" and omit the words following "Departments";
(ii) for sub-paragraph (2) substitute—

"(2) Terms defined in section 7(1) of the Government Departments Act 1987 (an Act of Tynwald: AT 13 of 1987) have the same meaning in sub-paragraph (1) as they have in that Act.";

(b) for paragraph 3 substitute—

"**3.** The Central Registry of the Isle of Man (established by the Central Registry Act 2018 (an Act of Tynwald: AT 13 of 2018)).";

(c) for paragraph 5 substitute—

"**5.** A constable within the meaning of the Interpretation Act 2015 (an Act of Tynwald: AT 11 of 2015): see Schedule 1 to that Act.".

NOTES

Commencement: IP completion day (as defined in the European Union (Withdrawal Agreement) Act 2020, s 39).

COMPANIES (DIRECTORS' REMUNERATION POLICY AND DIRECTORS' REMUNERATION REPORT) REGULATIONS 2019

(SI 2019/970)

NOTES

Made: 22 May 2019.

Authority: European Communities Act 1972, s 2(2); Companies Act 2006, ss 421(1), 468(1), (2), 1292(1) (see also the note "Statutory Instruments made under the European Communities Act 1972" preceding paragraph **[4.1]** *ante*).

Commencement: 10 June 2019.

For a summary of all Orders and Regulations made under the Companies Act 2006, see Appendix 4 at **[A4]**.

PART 1 INTRODUCTORY

[4.679]

1 Citation and commencement

(1) These Regulations may be cited as the Companies (Directors' Remuneration Policy and Directors' Remuneration Report) Regulations 2019.

(2) These Regulations come into force on 10th June 2019.

[4.680]

2 Application, transitional provisions and interpretation

(1) The amendments made by—
(a) regulations 6 to 10 apply to a quoted company from the first date on or after 10th June 2019 on which a relevant directors' remuneration policy for the company approved under section 439A of the Companies Act 2006 takes effect;
(b) regulation 15 apply in relation to—
(i) a directors' remuneration report or directors' remuneration policy of a quoted company first required to be made available under section 430 of the Companies Act 2006 on or after 10th June 2019;

(ii) annual accounts and reports of an unquoted traded company for a financial year of the company beginning on or after 10th June 2019;

(c) regulation 31 apply in relation to a directors' remuneration report for a financial year of a company beginning on or after 10th June 2019;

(d) regulation 32 apply in relation to a relevant directors' remuneration policy that was approved under section 439A of the Companies Act 2006 on or after 10th June 2019.

(2) Where a company is an unquoted traded company immediately before the day on which these Regulations come into force and paragraph (4) does not apply—

(a) section 226D(6)of the Companies Act 2006 (as amended by regulation 9) applies as if—

(i) in the opening words "the earlier of" were omitted; and

(ii) paragraph (a) was omitted;

(b) section 439A(1)(a) of the Companies Act 2006 (as amended by regulation 20) applies to the company as if for "the day on which the company becomes a quoted company or (as the case may be) an unquoted traded company" there were substituted "1st January 2020 or at an earlier general meeting".

(3) Paragraph (4) applies if, immediately before the day on which these Regulations come into force, an unquoted traded company has a relevant directors' remuneration policy in effect which—

(a) was approved by a resolution passed by the members of the company at an accounts or other general meeting before 10th June 2019, and

(b) complied with the requirements of the Companies Act 2006 in relation to such policies.

(4) Where this paragraph applies—

(a) section 439A(1)(a) of the Companies Act 2006 does not apply to the company;

(b) the notice that was given of the intention to move a resolution to approve the policy is to be treated as having been given under section 439A(1) for the purpose of determining the period within which the next notice under that section must be given;

(c) regulation 2(1)(a) applies to the company as if it were a quoted company.

(5) In this regulation—

"directors' remuneration policy", "quoted company" and "unquoted traded company" have the same meanings as in section 226A(1) of the Companies Act 2006;

"directors' remuneration report" has the same meaning as in section 420 of the Companies Act 2006;

"relevant directors' remuneration policy" has the same meaning as in section 439A(7) of the Companies Act 2006.

PARTS 2, 3

3–33 *(Part 2 (regs 3–27) amends Parts 10, 15 and 16 of, and Sch 8 to, the Companies Act 2006 (at* **[1.1]** *et seq). Part 3 (regs 28–33) amends the Large and Medium-sized Companies and Groups (Accounts and Reports) Regulations 2008, SI 2008/410 (at* **[4.60]***).)*

COMPANIES ETC (FILING REQUIREMENTS) (TEMPORARY MODIFICATIONS) REGULATIONS 2020

(SI 2020/645)

NOTES

Made: 26 June 2020.

Authority: Companies Act 2006, ss 1049(3), 1050(5); Corporate Insolvency and Governance Act 2020, s 39(1), (4).

Commencement: 27 June 2020.

For a summary of all Orders and Regulations made under the Companies Act 2006, see Appendix 4 at **[A4]**.

PART 1 INTRODUCTORY

[4.681]

1 Citation and commencement

These Regulations may be cited as the Companies etc (Filing Requirements) (Temporary Modifications) Regulations 2020.

NOTES

Commencement: 27 June 2020.

[4.682]

2

These Regulations come into force on 27th June 2020.

NOTES

Commencement: 27 June 2020.

PART 2 MODIFICATIONS TO THE COMPANIES ACT 2006

[4.683]

3

(1) The Companies Act 2006 is modified in accordance with regulations 4 to 20.

(2) References to a section in this Part are to a section of that Act.

NOTES

Commencement: 27 June 2020.

[4.684]
4

Section 87(4)(b) (change of address of registered office) is to have effect as if for the reference to "14 days" there were substituted a reference to "42 days".

NOTES

Commencement: 27 June 2020.

[4.685]
5

Section 87, as it applies to unregistered companies by virtue of paragraph 5 of Schedule 1 to the Unregistered Companies Regulations 2009, is to have effect as if for the reference in subsection (1) to "15 days" there were substituted a reference to "42 days".

NOTES

Commencement: 27 June 2020.

[4.686]
6

Section 114(5) (register to be kept available for inspection) is to have effect as if for the reference to "14 days" there were substituted a reference to "42 days".

NOTES

Commencement: 27 June 2020.

[4.687]
7

Section 162(6) (register of directors) is to have effect as if for the reference to "14 days" there were substituted a reference to "42 days".

NOTES

Commencement: 27 June 2020.

[4.688]
8

Section 167(1) (duty to notify registrar of changes) is to have effect as if for the reference to "14 days" there were substituted a reference to "42 days".

NOTES

Commencement: 27 June 2020.

[4.689]
9

Section 275(6) (duty to keep register of secretaries) is to have effect as if for the reference to "14 days" there were substituted a reference to "42 days".

NOTES

Commencement: 27 June 2020.

[4.690]
10

Section 276(1) (duty to notify registrar of changes) is to have effect as if for the reference to "14 days" there were substituted a reference to "42 days".

NOTES

Commencement: 27 June 2020.

[4.691]
11

Section 442 (period allowed for filing accounts) is to have effect as if—

(a) in subsection (2)—
 (i) in paragraph (a) for the reference to "nine months" there were substituted a reference to "twelve months";
 (ii) in paragraph (b) for the reference to "six months" there were substituted a reference to "nine months";

(b) in subsection (3), in paragraph (a), for the reference to "nine months or six months" there were substituted a reference to "twelve months or nine months".

NOTES

Commencement: 27 June 2020.

[4.692]
12

Section 442, as it applies to limited liability partnerships, by virtue of regulation 17 of the Limited Liability Partnerships (Accounts and Audit) (Application of Companies Act 2006) Regulations 2008, is to have effect as if for each reference to "nine months" there were substituted a reference to "twelve months".

NOTES

Commencement: 27 June 2020.

[4.693]
13

(1) The modifications in paragraph (2) apply to a company in respect of which an election under section 790X is in force.

(2) Section 790M (duty to keep register) is to have effect as if for each reference to "14 days" there were substituted a reference to "42 days".

NOTES

Commencement: 27 June 2020.

[4.694]
14

Section 790N(4) (register to be kept available for inspection) is to have effect as if for the reference to "14 days" there were substituted a reference to "42 days".

NOTES

Commencement: 27 June 2020.

[4.695]
15

Section 790VA(2) (notification of changes to the registrar) is to have effect as if for the reference to "14 days" there were substituted a reference to "42 days".

NOTES

Commencement: 27 June 2020.

[4.696]
16

Section 853A(1) (duty to deliver confirmation statements) is to have effect as if for the reference to "14 days" there were substituted a reference to "42 days".

NOTES

Commencement: 27 June 2020.

[4.697]
17

Section 853L(1) (failure to deliver confirmation statement) is to have effect as if for the reference to "14 days" there were substituted a reference to "42 days".

NOTES

Commencement: 27 June 2020.

[4.698]
18

(1) Section 859A(4) (charges created by a company) is to have effect as if for the reference to "21 days" there were substituted a reference to "31 days".

(2) Paragraph (1) does not apply in respect of a period allowed for delivery under section 859A which has been extended by the court under section 859F.

NOTES

Commencement: 27 June 2020.

[4.699]
19

(1) Section 859B(6) (charge in series of debentures) is to have effect as if for each reference to "21 days" there were substituted in each place where it occurs a reference to "31 days".

(2) Paragraph (1) does not apply in respect of a period allowed for delivery under section 859B which has been extended by the court under section 859F.

NOTES

Commencement: 27 June 2020.

[4.700]
20

Section 859Q(5) (instruments creating charges to be available for inspection) is to have effect as if for the reference to "14 days" there were substituted a reference to "42 days".

NOTES

Commencement: 27 June 2020.

PART 3 MODIFICATIONS TO THE SCOTTISH PARTNERSHIPS (REGISTER OF PEOPLE WITH SIGNIFICANT CONTROL) REGULATIONS 2017

[4.701]
21

The Scottish Partnerships (Register of People with Significant Control) Regulations 2017 have effect subject to the modifications in regulations 22 to 36.

NOTES

Commencement: 27 June 2020.

[4.702]
22

Regulation 7 (notification of changes to the registration information) is to have effect as if for the reference to "14 days" there were substituted a reference to "42 days".

NOTES

Commencement: 27 June 2020.

[4.703]
23

Regulation 8(1) (effect of a partnership ceasing to be a Scottish qualifying partnership) is to have effect as if for the reference to "14 days" there were substituted a reference to "42 days".

NOTES

Commencement: 27 June 2020.

[4.704]
24

Regulation 19 (duty to deliver information to the registrar) is to have effect as if for each reference to "14 days" there were substituted in each place where it occurs a reference to "42 days".

NOTES

Commencement: 27 June 2020.

[4.705]
25

Regulation 20 (duty to deliver information about a relevant change) is to have effect as if for both references to "14 days" there were substituted a reference to "42 days".

NOTES

Commencement: 27 June 2020.

[4.706]
26

Regulation 23(2) (additional matters to be notified to the registrar where there is no registrable person or registrable relevant legal entity) is to have effect as if for the reference to "14 days" there were substituted a reference to "42 days".

NOTES

Commencement: 27 June 2020.

[4.707]
27

Regulation 24(2) (additional matters where there is an unidentified registrable person) is to have effect as if for the reference to "14 days" there were substituted a reference to "42 days".

NOTES

Commencement: 27 June 2020.

[4.708]
28

Regulation 25(2) (additional matters where an identified registrable person's particulars are not confirmed) is to have effect as if for the reference to "14 days" there were substituted a reference to "42 days".

NOTES

Commencement: 27 June 2020.

[4.709]
29

Regulation 26(2) (additional matters where investigations by an eligible Scottish partnership are ongoing) is to have effect as if for the reference to "14 days" there were substituted a reference to "42 days".

NOTES

Commencement: 27 June 2020.

[4.710]
30

Regulation 27(2) (additional matters where there is a failure to comply with a notice given under regulation 10) is to have effect as if for the reference to "14 days" there were substituted a reference to "42 days".

NOTES

Commencement: 27 June 2020.

[4.711]
31

Regulation 28(2) (additional matters where there is a failure to comply with a notice given under regulation 11) is to have effect as if for the reference to "14 days" there were substituted a reference to "42 days".

NOTES

Commencement: 27 June 2020.

[4.712]
32

Regulation 29(2) (additional matters where a notice given under regulation 10 or 11 is complied with after the time specified in the notice) is to have effect as if for the reference to "14 days" there were substituted a reference to "42 days".

NOTES

Commencement: 27 June 2020.

[4.713]
33

Regulation 30(2) (additional matters where an eligible Scottish partnership has issued a restrictions notice) is to have effect as if for the reference to "14 days" there were substituted a reference to "42 days".

NOTES

Commencement: 27 June 2020.

[4.714]
34

Regulation 31 (end-dating of additional matters) is to have effect as if for the reference to "14 days" there were substituted a reference to "42 days".

NOTES

Commencement: 27 June 2020.

[4.715]
35

Regulation 35(1) (duty to deliver a confirmation statement) is to have effect as if for the reference to "14 days" there were substituted a reference to "42 days".

NOTES

Commencement: 27 June 2020.

[4.716]
36

Regulation 38(1) (failure to deliver a confirmation statement) is to have effect as if for the reference to "14 days" there were substituted a reference to "42 days".

NOTES

Commencement: 27 June 2020.

PART 4 MODIFICATIONS TO OTHER LEGISLATION

[4.717]
37

Section 9(1) (registration of changes in partnerships) of the Limited Partnerships Act 1907 is to have effect as if for the reference to "seven days" there were substituted a reference to "42 days".

NOTES

Commencement: 27 June 2020.

[4.718]
38

(1) Section 466(4C)(a) of the Companies Act 1985 (alteration of floating charges) is to have effect as if for the reference to "21 days" there were substituted a reference to "31 days".

(2) Paragraph (1) does not apply in respect of a period allowed for delivery under section 466(4C) of the Companies Act 1985 which has been extended by the court under section 859F of the Companies Act 2006.

NOTES

Commencement: 27 June 2020.

[4.719]
39

Section 9(1) (registration of membership changes) of the Limited Liability Partnerships Act 2000 is to have effect as if—

(a) in paragraph (a), for the reference to "fourteen days" there were substituted a reference to "42 days", and
(b) in paragraph (b), for the reference to "14 days" there were substituted a reference to "42 days".

NOTES

Commencement: 27 June 2020.

[4.720]
40

Regulation 80C(1) (duty to notify registrar of changes) of the European Public Limited-Liability Company Regulations 2004 is to have effect as if for the reference to "14 days" there were substituted a reference to "42 days".

NOTES

Commencement: 27 June 2020.

[4.721]
41

(1) The Overseas Companies Regulations 2009 are to have effect subject to the following modifications.

(2) Regulation 34 (period allowed for filing copies of accounting documents) is to have effect as if for the reference to "three months" there were substituted a reference to "six months".

(3) Regulation 46(2) (filing of copies of subsequent accounting documents) is to have effect as if for the reference to "three months" there were substituted a reference to "six months".

(4) This regulation expires at the end of the day on 5th April 2021.

(5) Paragraph (4) does not affect the continued operation of this regulation for the purpose of determining the length of any period that begins before the expiry.

NOTES

Commencement: 27 June 2020.

SUPERVISION OF ACCOUNTS AND REPORTS (PRESCRIBED BODY) AND COMPANIES (DEFECTIVE ACCOUNTS AND REPORTS) (AUTHORISED PERSON) ORDER 2021

(SI 2021/465)

NOTES

Made: 13 April 2021.
Authority: Companies (Audit, Investigations and Community Enterprise) Act 2004, ss 14(1), (5), (8), (10), 18A(1), (3); Companies Act 2006, ss 457(1), (2), (5), (6), 1292(1)(b), (c).
Commencement: 6 May 2021.
For a summary of all Orders and Regulations made under the Companies Act 2006, see Appendix 4 at **[A4]**.

[4.722]
1 Citation, commencement and interpretation

(1) This Order may be cited as the Supervision of Accounts and Reports (Prescribed Body) and Companies (Defective Accounts and Reports) (Authorised Person) Order 2021.

(2) This Order comes into force on the 21st day after the day on which it is laid.

(3) In this Order—

"DGTR sourcebook" means the Disclosure Guidance and Transparency Rules sourcebook made by the Financial Conduct Authority under the Financial Services and Markets Act 2000, as it has effect on the day on which this Order is made;
"the 2004 Act" means the Companies (Audit, Investigations and Community Enterprise) Act 2004;
"the 2006 Act" means the Companies Act 2006;
"the FRC" means the Financial Reporting Council Limited;
"LLPs" means limited liability partnerships.

NOTES

Commencement: 6 May 2021.

[4.723]
2 Appointment in relation to issuers

(1) The FRC is appointed to exercise the functions mentioned in section 14(2) of the 2004 Act in respect of any issuer of transferable securities admitted to trading on a UK regulated market which is a body corporate.

(2) In paragraph (1), "issuer" does not include a person which is not required to comply with the reporting requirements of Section 1 of Chapter 4 (annual financial report) and Section 2 of Chapter 4 (half-yearly financial reports) of the DGTR sourcebook by virtue of—

(a) rule 4.4.1, rule 4.4.2 (exemptions) and TP 1.19 (exemption for certain large debt securities issuers) of the DGTR sourcebook, or

(b) applicable rules in the Listing Rules, Prospectus Regulation Rules and DGTR sourcebook of the Financial Conduct Authority Handbook made under the Financial Services and Markets Act 2000 (where the Listing Rules and the Prospectus Regulation Rules means those Rules as they had effect on the day on which this Order is made).

NOTES

Commencement: 6 May 2021.

[4.724]

3 Appointment in relation to accounts

The FRC is appointed to exercise the functions mentioned in section 14(2) of the 2004 Act under this Order only in respect of the periodic accounts and reports required to be produced under Section 1 of Chapter 4 (annual financial report) and Section 2 of Chapter 4 (half-yearly financial reports) of the DGTR sourcebook.

NOTES

Commencement: 6 May 2021.

[4.725]

4 Authorisation

The FRC is authorised for the purposes of section 456 of the 2006 Act (application to court in respect of defective accounts or reports).

NOTES

Commencement: 6 May 2021.

[4.726]

5 Requirements for recording decisions

The FRC must have satisfactory arrangements for—

(a) recording decisions made in connection with the functions it exercises by virtue of its appointment under articles 2 and 3 and its authorisation under article 4 of this Order; and

(b) the safekeeping of all material records.

NOTES

Commencement: 6 May 2021.

6–8 (*Reg 6 amends the Limited Liability Partnerships (Accounts and Audit) (Application of Companies Act 2006) Regulations 2008, SI 2008/1911 at* **[10.223]**. *Art 7 revokes the Supervision of Accounts and Reports (Prescribed Body) and Companies (Defective Accounts and Directors' Reports) (Authorised Person) Order 2012, 2012/1439 at* **[4.429]** *(with the exception of arts 1 and 6 (see the note ante)). Art 8 amends the Companies (Bodies Concerned with Auditing Standards etc) (Exemption from Liability) Regulations 2016, SI 2016/571.*)

[4.727]

9 Application and transitional provisions

(1) Articles 2 and 3 of this Order apply in respect of periodic accounts and reports relating to financial years beginning on or after 20th January 2007.

(2) Anything which—

(a) has been done by or in relation to the body known as the Conduct Committee of the FRC in connection with any of the functions referred to in this Order; and

(b) is in effect immediately before this Order comes into force,

is to be treated as if done by or in relation to the FRC.

(3) Anything which—

(a) relates to any of the functions referred to in this Order; and

(b) is in the process of being done by or in relation to the body known as the Conduct Committee of the FRC immediately before this Order comes into force,

may be continued by or in relation to the FRC.

NOTES

Commencement: 6 May 2021.

PART 5
OTHER COMPANIES PRIMARY LEGISLATION

COMPANIES ACT 1985

(1985 c 6)

NOTES

Repeal of this Act by the Companies Act 2006:

In so far as individual provisions of this Act had not already been repealed, the vast majority of this Act was repealed by the Companies Act 2006 (see s 1295 of, and Sch 16 to, the 2006 Act at **[1.1492]**, **[1.1535]** which repealed ss 1–430F, 438, 446, 458–461, 651–746 of, and Schs 1–15B, 20–25 to, this Act). The only provisions not repealed by the 2006 Act are: (a) Part XIV (Investigation of Companies and their Affairs; Requisition of Documents) (including Schs 15C, 15D but not including ss 438, 446 which were repealed); (b) Part XV (Orders Imposing Restrictions on Shares); (c) Part XVIII (Floating Charges and Receivers (Scotland)); and (d) section 747 (citation). For provision relating to the continuity of law, see s 1297 of the 2006 Act at **[1.1494]**.

Note also that Part XVIII (Floating Charges and Receivers (Scotland)) is repealed by the Bankruptcy and Diligence etc (Scotland) Act 2007, s 46(1), as from a day to be appointed. For savings see the introductory note to that Part (preceding **[5.53]**).

Abbreviations used in the notes in this Act are as follows:

— CO No 1: the Companies Act 2006 (Commencement No 1, Transitional Provisions and Savings) Order 2006, SI 2006/3428.
— CO No 2: the Companies Act 2006 (Commencement No 2, Consequential Amendments, Transitional Provisions and Savings) Order 2007, SI 2007/1093.
— CO No 3: the Companies Act 2006 (Commencement No 3, Consequential Amendments, Transitional Provisions and Savings) Order 2007, SI 2007/2194.
— CO No 4: the Companies Act 2006 (Commencement No 4 and Commencement No 3 (Amendment)) Order 2007, SI 2007/2607.
— CO No 5: the Companies Act 2006 (Commencement No 5, Transitional Provisions and Savings) Order 2007, SI 2007/3495.
— CO No 6: the Companies Act 2006 (Commencement No 6, Saving and Commencement Nos 3 and 5 (Amendment)) Order 2008, SI 2008/674.
— CO No 7: the Companies Act 2006 (Commencement No 7, Transitional Provisions and Savings) Order 2008, SI 2008/1886.
— CO No 8: the Companies Act 2006 (Commencement No 8, Transitional Provisions and Savings) Order 2008, SI 2008/2860.

Transitional adaptations: various commencement Orders made under the Companies Act 2006, s 1300 provided that certain sections of this Act shall have effect subject to specified transitional adaptations. In so far as these transitional adaptations had not been revoked (subject to certain savings) by earlier Orders, they were fully revoked by the Companies Act 2006 (Commencement No 8, Transitional Provisions and Savings) Order 2008, SI 2008/2860, art 6. Accordingly, they are not noted on the individual provisions below, but the commencement orders themselves are reproduced in full in the online only Appendix 10 of this Handbook.

Commencement: this Act came into force on 1 July 1985; see s 746 at **[5.70]**.

Offences under this Act: see CO No 8, Sch 2, para 116 (savings for provisions relating to offences). That paragraph provides that the repeal of any provision of this Act creating an offence does not affect the continued operation of that provision in relation to an offence committed before 1 October 2009. It also provides that such savings extend to Sch 24 to this Act (punishment of offences). Similar provision was made by CO No 5, Sch 4, Pt 1, para 44 which provided that the repeal of ss 732–734 of this Act does not affect the operation of those provisions in relation to offences committed before 6 April 2008.

See also the Companies Act 2006, ss 1131 at **[1.1301]** (imprisonment on summary conviction in England and Wales: transitory provision), and CO No 8, art 7 (prosecution of offences in transitional cases).

Limited liability partnerships: the provisions of this Act relating to companies were applied with modifications to limited liability partnerships by the Limited Liability Partnerships (Scotland) Regulations 2001, SSI 2001/128 at **[10.89]**, and the Limited Liability Partnerships Regulations 2001, SI 2001/1090 at **[10.99]**. Further provisions of this Act were applied to LLPs by the Limited Liability Partnership (No 2) Regulations 2002, SI 2002/913 (revoked as from 1 October 2009).

As the repeals of the provisions of this Act were commenced in stages by the various commencement orders made under the 2006 Act, savings provisions in those orders preserved the operation of the repealed provisions of this Act in so far as they applied to LLPs (see CO No 1, art 8(2), CO No 2, art 11(1), CO No 3, art 12(2), CO No 5, art 12(1), CO No 6, art 6(1), and SI 2008/948, art 11). Those articles provide that nothing in those Orders (which either (i) commence the repeals (or amendments) made to this Act by CA 2006, or (ii) amend this Act) affect the application of any provision of this Act (as applied by the Limited Liability Partnerships Regulations 2001) to LLPs. Art 11(2) of CO No 2 further provides that the repeal of s 723C(1)(a) by CA 2006 (brought into force by art 7(a) of CO No 1) does not apply to the application of the said s 723C(1)(a) to LLPs by the Limited Liability Partnerships (No 2) Regulations 2002. See also CO No 7, art 7(4) which provides that save as provided by art 2(e) of that Order (the commencement, on 1 October 2008, of s 1286(1)(a), (2)(a) of the 2006 Act in so far as relating to Parts 15, 16 and 42 of that Act) nothing in that Order affects any provision of this Act as applied by 2001 Regulations.

As to the revocation (subject to savings), as from 1 October 2008, of certain Parts of the LLP Regulations 2001 (most notably reg 3 and Sch 1 which applied Part VII of this Act to LLPs) see the Limited Liability Partnerships (Accounts and Audit) (Application of Companies Act 2006) Regulations 2008, SI 2008/1911, reg 58 at **[10.286]**. See also the Limited Liability Partnerships (Application of Companies Act 2006) Regulations 2009, SI 2009/1804 at **[10.319]** which applies various provisions of the Companies Act 2006 to LLPs, and revokes (as from 1 October 2009) most of Sch 2, Pt I to the 2001 Regulations (application of other provisions of this Act to LLPs) and also revokes SI 2002/913 and the Limited Liability Partnerships (Particulars of Usual Residential Address) (Confidentiality Orders) Regulations 2002, SI 2002/915. Schedule 1 to the 2009 Regulations (at **[10.409]** et seq) provides for detailed transitional provisions and savings in relation to the application of the 2006 Act to LLPs and the revocation of the 2001 Regulations in so far as they apply provisions of this Act to LLPs.

Currently, Part XIV (Investigation of Companies and their Affairs; Requisition of Documents) (including Schs 15C, 15D) still applies to LLPs by virtue of SI 2001/1090, Sch 2, Pt I. In addition, Part XVIII (Floating Charges and Receivers (Scotland)) still applies to LLPs by virtue of SI 2001/1090, Sch 2, Pt I and SSI 2001/128, Sch 1.

Application of this Act to other companies, etc: this Act, or particular parts of it, is applied to various other types of companies and bodies, *including* the following (note that the application of this Act to other bodies such as charities and building societies is not noted as it is considered outside the scope of this work).

UK Economic Interest Groupings (UKEIGs) and EEIG establishments: as to the application of Parts XIV, XVIII of this Act to UKEIGs and EEIG establishments, see the European Economic Interest Grouping Regulations 1989, SI 1989/638 at **[10.13]**. Note that the 1989 Regulations were amended by the European Economic Interest Grouping (Amendment) Regulations 2009, SI 2009/2399 which, inter alia, replaced references to provisions of this Act (other than Part XIV) with references to the equivalent provisions of the Companies Act 2006. Regulation 2 of the 2009 Regulations provides that in so far as relating to forms and other documents required to be delivered to the registrar, the amendments made by those Regulations do not have effect in any case where the obligation to deliver the form or other document arose before 1 October 2009 (ie, the date on which the amendments made by SI 2009/2399 took effect). The 1989 Regulations were also amended by the European Economic Interest Grouping (Amendment) (EU Exit) Regulations 2018, SI 2018/1299.

Unregistered companies: as to the application of Parts XIV, XV of this Act to unregistered companies, see the Unregistered Companies Regulations 2009, SI 2009/2436, Sch 1, para 16 at **[4.398]**. Note that the Companies (Unregistered Companies) Regulations 1985, SI 1985/680 applied certain provisions of this Act to unregistered companies before 1 October 2009. The 1985 Regulations were revoked by reg 8 of the 2009 Regulations subject to transitional provisions (in Sch 2 to the 2009 Regulations at **[4.399]**) in relation to the application of this Act to unregistered companies before that date.

Civil Procedure Rules: the Civil Procedure Rules 1998, SI 1998/3132, r 49, states that those Rules apply to proceedings under (a) the Companies Act 1985; (b) the Companies Act 2006; and (c) other legislation relating to companies and limited liability partnerships, subject to the provision of the relevant practice direction which applies to those proceedings.

Forms and Fees: as for forms for the purposes of the Companies Act 1985, see the Companies (Forms) Regulations 1985, SI 1985/854. A number of forms were revoked by the Companies and Limited Liability Partnerships (Forms, etc) Amendment Regulations 2013, SI 2013/1947, as from 1 October 2013 (see further the note for those Regulations in Appendix 4 at **[A4]**) but a few forms remain in use (see the Companies House website). As to fees, see the Companies (Inspectors' Reports) (Fees) Regulations 1981, SI 1981/1686, and the Companies (Fees) Regulations 2004, SI 2004/2621.

This Act is reproduced as amended by the following Acts:

1985	Insolvency Act 1985.
1986	FSA 1986; Insolvency Act 1986.
1989	Companies Act 1989.
1990	Law Reform (Miscellaneous Provisions) (Scotland) Act 1990.
1995	Requirements of Writing (Scotland) Act 1995.
1999	Youth Justice and Criminal Evidence Act 1999.
2004	Companies (Audit, Investigations and Community Enterprise) Act 2004; Pensions Act 2004.
2006	Charities Act 2006; Companies Act 2006.
2007	Bankruptcy and Diligence etc (Scotland) Act 2007; Legal Services Act 2007.
2012	Financial Services Act 2012.
2013	Financial Services (Banking Reform) Act 2013.
2015	Consumer Rights Act 2015; Deregulation Act 2015.
2018	Data Protection Act 2018.

This Act is reproduced as amended by the following SIs:

1991	Companies (Disclosure of Interests in Shares) (Orders imposing restrictions on shares) Regulations 1991, SI 1991/1646.
2001	Financial Services and Markets Act 2000 (Consequential Amendments and Repeals) Order 2001, SI 2001/3649.
2003	Companies (Acquisition of Own Shares) (Treasury Shares) Regulations 2003, SI 2003/1116.
2006	Companies (Disclosure of Information) (Designated Authorities) Order 2006, SI 2006/1644.
2007	Companies Act 2006 (Commencement No 3, Consequential Amendments, Transitional Provisions and Savings) Order 2007, SI 2007/2194.
2008	Companies Act 2006 (Consequential Amendments etc) Order 2008, SI 2008/948; Consumer Protection from Unfair Trading Regulations 2008, SI 2008/1277.
2009	Companies Act 2006 (Consequential Amendments, Transitional Provisions and Savings) Order 2009, SI 2009/1941.
2010	Transfer of Tribunal Functions Order 2010, SI 2010/22.
2011	Investment Bank Special Administration Regulations 2011, SI 2011/245; Treaty of Lisbon (Changes in Terminology) Order 2011, SI 2011/1043.
2013	Companies Act 2006 (Amendment of Part 25) Regulations 2013, SI 2013/600; Financial Services and Markets Act 2000 (Regulated Activities) (Amendment) (No 2) Order 2013, SI 2013/1881; Public Bodies (Merger of the Gambling Commission and the National Lottery Commission) Order 2013, SI 2013/2329; Consumer Contracts (Information, Cancellation and Additional Charges) Regulations 2013, SI 2013/3134.
2014	Enterprise and Regulatory Reform Act 2013 (Competition) (Consequential, Transitional and Saving Provisions) Order 2014, SI 2014/892; Public Bodies (Abolition of the National Consumer Council and Transfer of the Office of Fair Trading's Functions in relation to Estate Agents etc) Order 2014, SI 2014/631.
2015	Legal Aid, Sentencing and Punishment of Offenders Act 2012 (Fines on Summary Conviction) Regulations 2015, SI 2015/664.
2016	Companies (Disclosure of Information) (Specified Persons) Order 2016, SI 2016/741.
2017	Bank of England and Financial Services (Consequential Amendments) Regulations 2017, SI 2017/80; Cen-

	tral Securities Depositories Regulations 2017, SI 2017/1064.
2021	Payment and Electronic Money Institution Insolvency Regulations 2021, SI 2021/716.

ARRANGEMENT OF SECTIONS

PART XIV
INVESTIGATION OF COMPANIES AND THEIR AFFAIRS; REQUISITION OF DOCUMENTS

Appointment and functions of inspectors

Other powers of investigation available to the Secretary of State

Powers of Secretary of State to give directions to inspectors

Resignation, removal and replacement of inspectors

Power to obtain information from former inspectors etc

Requisition and seizure of books and papers

Supplementary

PART XV
ORDERS IMPOSING RESTRICTIONS ON SHARES (SECTION 445)

PART XVIII
FLOATING CHARGES AND RECEIVERS (SCOTLAND)

CHAPTER I FLOATING CHARGES

CHAPTER III GENERAL

PART XXV
MISCELLANEOUS AND SUPPLEMENTARY PROVISIONS

PART XXVII
FINAL PROVISIONS

SCHEDULES

An Act to consolidate the greater part of the Companies Acts

[11 March 1985]

PART I FORMATION AND REGISTRATION OF COMPANIES; JURIDICAL STATUS AND MEMBERSHIP

[5.1]
1–42

NOTES

This Part has been repealed as follows:

1 Mode of forming incorporated company	Repealed by CA 2006, as from 1 Oct 2009. Savings: CO No 8, Sch 2, para 2(1) provides that ss 7–16 of the Companies Act 2006 (company formation) apply to applications for registration received by the registrar on or after 1 Oct 2009. Sch 2, para 2(3) further provides that the corresponding provisions of this Act continue to apply to an application for registration if (a) it is received by the registrar, and (b) the requirements as to registration are met in relation to it, before that date. The corresponding provisions of this Act are as follows: ss 1(1), 2(1), (a), (b), (2)–(4), 3(1), 10(1), (2), (3), (4), (6), 12(1)–(3), (3A), 13(1)–(5), (7)(a) (see the table of origins at **[3.8]**).
2 Requirements with respect to memorandum	Repealed by CA 2006, as from 1 Oct 2009. For savings see the note to s 1.
3 Forms of memorandum	Repealed by CA 2006, as from 1 Oct 2009. For savings see the note to s 1.
3A Statement of company's objects: general commercial company	Repealed by CA 2006, as from 1 Oct 2009.
4 Resolution to alter objects	Repealed by CA 2006, as from 1 Oct 2009. Savings: CO No 8, Sch 2, para 110 provides that the repeal of ss 4–6 of this Act does not affect the application of those provisions in relation to a resolution agreed to before 1 Oct 2009.
5 Procedure for objecting to alteration	Repealed by CA 2006, as from 1 Oct 2009. For savings see the savings note to s 4.
6 Provisions supplementing ss 4, 5	Repealed by CA 2006, as from 1 Oct 2009. For savings see the savings note to s 4.
7 Articles prescribing regulations for companies	Repealed by CA 2006, as from 1 Oct 2009. Savings: CO No 8, Sch 2, para 3(1) provides that ss 7, 8 of this Act apply, and ss 18–20 of CA 2006 do not apply, to a company formed and registered under this Act on an application to which para 2(3) of that Schedule applies. Para 2(3) provides that the provisions of this Act corresponding to ss 7–16 of the 2006 Act continue to apply to an application for registration if (a) it is received by the registrar, and (b) the requirements as to registration are met in relation to it, before 1 Oct 2009.
8 Tables A, C, D and E	Repealed by CA 2006, as from 1 Oct 2009. For savings see the note to s 7.
8A Table G	Repealed by CA 2006, as from 1 Oct 2009.
9 Alteration of articles by special resolution	Repealed by CA 2006, as from 1 Oct 2009.
10 Documents to be sent to registrar	Repealed by CA 2006, as from 1 Oct 2009. For savings see the note to s 1.
11 Minimum authorised capital (public companies)	Repealed by CA 2006, as from 1 Oct 2009.
12 Duty of registrar	Repealed by CA 2006, as from 1 Oct 2009. For savings see the note to s 1.
13 Effect of registration	Repealed by CA 2006, as from 1 Oct 2009. For savings see the note to s 1.

14 Effect of memorandum and articles	Repealed by CA 2006, as from 1 Oct 2009: Saving for provisions relating to nature of liability of member or contributory: SI 2009/1941, art 11 (at **[4.365]**) provides that the new provisions as to the nature of a member's or contributory's liability (ie, CA 2006, s 33(2) and, in England and Wales, s 80 of the Insolvency Act 1986 as amended by that Order) apply to liabilities arising on or after 1 Oct 2009, and the old provisions (ie, CA 1985, s 14(2) and s 80 of the 1986 Act as it had effect prior to that amendment) continue to apply to liabilities arising before that date. Note also that for the purposes of art 11, a liability is treated as arising when the limitation period starts to run for the purposes of the Limitation Act 1980.
15 Memorandum and articles of company limited by guarantee	Repealed by CA 2006, as from 1 Oct 2009.
16 Effect of alteration on company's members	Repealed by CA 2006, as from 1 Oct 2009.
17 Conditions in memorandum which could have been in articles	Repealed by CA 2006, as from 1 Oct 2009.
18 Amendments of memorandum or articles to be registered	Repealed by CA 2006, as from 1 Oct 2009. Savings: CO No 8, Sch 2, para 6 provides that sub-ss (2), (3) continue to apply in relation to amendments taking effect before 1 Oct 2009. In addition, sub-ss (1), (3) continue to apply in relation to alterations made by statutory provisions coming into force before that date (see Sch 2, para 12 to that Order).
19 Copies of memorandum and articles to be given to members	Repealed by CA 2006, as from 1 Oct 2009. Savings: CO No 8, Sch 2, para 11 provides that this section continues to apply where the request was received by the company before 1 Oct 2009.
20 Issued copy of memorandum to embody alterations	Repealed by CA 2006, as from 1 Oct 2009.
21 Registered documentation of Welsh companies.	Repealed by the Welsh Language Act 1993, as from 1 Feb 1994.
22 Definition of "member"	Repealed by CA 2006, as from 1 Oct 2009.
23 Membership of holding company	Repealed by CA 2006, as from 1 Oct 2009.
24 Minimum membership for carrying on business	Repealed by CA 2006, as from 1 Oct 2009. Savings: CO No 8, Sch 2, para 24 provides that the repeal of this section does not affect any liability for debts of the company contracted before 1 Oct 2009.
25 Name as stated in memorandum	Repealed by CA 2006, as from 1 Oct 2009.
26 Prohibition on registration of certain names	Repealed by CA 2006, as from 1 Oct 2009. Savings: see CO No 8, Sch 2, para 114A which provides that the repeal of s 26(2)(a) does not affect the operation of that provision in relation to names suggesting a connection with the Welsh Assembly Government. See further, in relation to the renaming of the Welsh Assembly Government as the Welsh Government, the Wales Act 2014, s 4(4)(a). See also, in relation to the renaming of the National Assembly for Wales as the Senedd Cymru or the Welsh Parliament, the Senedd and Elections (Wales) Act 2020, s 2 (with effect from 6 May 2020).
27 Alternatives of statutory designations	Repealed by CA 2006, as from 1 Oct 2009.
28 Change of name	Repealed by CA 2006, as from 1 Oct 2009. Savings: CO No 8, Sch 2, para 19 provides that sub-ss (1), (6) and (7) above continue to apply to resolutions of which a copy is received by the registrar before 1 Oct 2009.
29 Regulations about names	Repealed by CA 2006, as from 1 Jan 2007 (in so far as relating to sub-s (4)), and as from 1 Oct 2009 (otherwise). Savings: CO No 8, Sch 2, para 18 provides that this section continues to apply in relation to applications received by the Secretary of State before 1 Oct 2009.
30 Exemption from requirement of "limited" as part of the name	Repealed by CA 2006, as from 1 Oct 2009.
31 Provisions applying to company exempt under s 30	Repealed by CA 2006, as from 1 Oct 2009. Savings: CO No 8, Sch 2, para 20 provides that sub-ss (2)–(4), (6) continue to apply where a direction under sub-s (2) was given before 1 October 2009.
32 Power to require company to abandon misleading name	Repealed by CA 2006, as from 1 Oct 2009. Savings: CO No 8, Sch 2, para 21 provides that this section continues to apply in relation to a direction given before 1 Oct 2009.
33 Prohibition on trading under misleading name	Repealed by CA 2006, as from 1 Oct 2009.
34 Penalty for improper use of "limited" or "cyfyngedig"	Repealed by CA 2006, as from 1 Oct 2009.
34A Penalty for improper use of "community interest company" etc	Repealed by CA 2006, as from 1 Oct 2009.

35 A company's capacity not limited by its memorandum	Repealed by CA 2006, as from 1 Oct 2009. Savings: CO No 8, Sch 2, para 15 provides that this section continues to apply to acts of a company carried out before 1 Oct 2009.
35A Power of directors to bind the company	Repealed by CA 2006, as from 1 Oct 2009.
35B No duty to enquire as to capacity of company or authority of directors	Repealed by CA 2006, as from 1 Oct 2009.
36 Company contracts: England and Wales	Repealed by CA 2006, as from 1 Oct 2009.
36A Execution of documents: England and Wales	Repealed by CA 2006, s 1295, Sch 16, as from 6 Apr 2008 (in part), and as from 1 Oct 2009 (otherwise). Savings: note that s 36A continues to apply in relation to documents executed before 6 Apr 2008; note also that a document signed by one authorised signatory before 6 Apr 2008 and by another on or after that date is treated as executed on or after 6 Apr 2008 (see CO No 5, Sch 4, Pt 1, para 1).
36AA Execution of deeds: England and Wales	Repealed by CA 2006, as from 1 Oct 2009.
36B Execution of documents by companies	Repealed by CA 2006, as from 1 Oct 2009.
36C Pre-incorporation documents, deeds and obligations	Repealed by CA 2006, as from 1 Oct 2009.
37 Bills of exchange and promissory notes	Repealed by CA 2006, as from 1 Oct 2009.
38 Execution of deeds abroad	Repealed by CA 2006, as from 1 Oct 2009. Savings: CO No 8, Sch 2, para 16 provides that this section continues to have effect where the power to act as a company's attorney was conferred before 1 Oct 2009 (including in relation to instruments executed by the attorney on behalf of the company on or after that date).
39 Power of company to have official seal for use abroad	Repealed by CA 2006, as from 1 Oct 2009.
40 Official seal for share certificates, etc	Repealed by CA 2006, as from 1 Oct 2009.
41 Authentication of documents	Repealed by CA 2006, as from 6 Apr 2007.
42 Events affecting a company's status	Repealed by CA 2006, as from 1 Jan 2007.

PART II RE-REGISTRATION AS A MEANS OF ALTERING A COMPANY'S STATUS

[5.2]
43–55

NOTES

This Part has been repealed as follows:

43 Re-registration of private company as public	Repealed by CA 2006, as from 1 Oct 2009. Savings: CO No 8, Sch 2, para 22 provides that ss 89–108 of CA 2006 (re-registration as a means of altering a company's status) apply to applications for re-registration received by the registrar on or after 1 Oct 2009; and that the corresponding provisions of this Act continue to apply to an application for re-registration if: (a) it is received by the registrar, and (b) the requirements for re-registration are met in relation to it, before that date.
44 Consideration for shares recently allotted to be valued	Repealed by CA 2006, as from 1 Oct 2009. For savings see the note to s 43.
45 Additional requirements relating to share capital	Repealed by CA 2006, as from 1 Oct 2009. For savings see the note to s 43.
46 Meaning of "unqualified report" in s 43(3)	Repealed by CA 2006, as from 1 Oct 2009. For savings see the note to s 43.
47 Certificate of re-registration under s 43	Repealed by CA 2006, as from 1 Oct 2009. For savings see the note to s 43.
48 Modification for unlimited company re-registering	Repealed by CA 2006, as from 1 Oct 2009. For savings see the note to s 43.
49 Re-registration of limited company as unlimited	Repealed by CA 2006, as from 1 Oct 2009. For savings see the note to s 43.
50 Certificate of re-registration under s 49	Repealed by CA 2006, as from 1 Oct 2009. For savings see the note to s 43.
51 Re-registration of unlimited company as limited	Repealed by CA 2006, as from 1 Oct 2009. For savings see the note to s 43.
52 Certificate of re-registration under	Repealed by CA 2006, as from 1 Oct 2009. For savings see the note to s 43.

s 51	
53 Re-registration of public company as private	Repealed by CA 2006, as from 1 Oct 2009. For savings see the note to s 43.
54 Litigated objection to resolution under s 53	Repealed by CA 2006, as from 1 Oct 2009. For savings see the note to s 43.
55 Certificate of re-registration under s 53	Repealed by CA 2006, as from 1 Oct 2009. For savings see the note to s 43.

PART III CAPITAL ISSUES

[5.3]
56–79

NOTES

This Part (ie, ss 56–79, Sch 3) (together with the other provisions mentioned in (i) and (ii) below) was repealed (subject to limited savings) in accordance with the notes set out below following the coming into force of the Public Offers of Securities Regulations 1995, SI 1995/1537 (now revoked).

Certain sections in this Part (ie, ss 58, 59, 60, 62 and Sch 3, para 2) were preserved by the Financial Services Act 1986 (Commencement) (No 13) Order 1995, SI 1995/1538 for the sole purpose of interpreting other provisions of this Act (ie, ss 81, 83, 246, 248 and 744).

Subject to the savings mentioned above, this Part was repealed by FSA 1986, s 212(3), Sch 17, Pt I as follows—

(i) to the extent to which they would apply in relation to any investment which is listed or the subject of an application for listing in accordance with FSA 1986, Pt IV—

(a) *as from 12 January 1987* for the purposes specified in art 5(a) of the Financial Services Act 1986 (Commencement) (No 3) Order 1986, SI 1986/2246, ie for all purposes relating to the admission of securities offered by or on behalf of a Minister of the Crown or a body corporate controlled by a Minister of the Crown or a subsidiary of such a body corporate to the Official List in respect of which an application is made after that date;

(b) *as from 16 February 1987* for the purposes specified in art 5(b) of SI 1986/2246, ie purposes relating to the admission of securities in respect of which an application is made after that date other than those referred to in art 5(a) of that Order (see (a) above) and otherwise for all purposes;

These repeals also affected ss 81–83, 86, 87, 709(2), (3), and specified words in ss 84, 85, 97, 693

(ii) *as from 29 April 1988* insofar as is necessary to have the effect that they cease to apply to a prospectus offering for subscription, or to any form of application for, units in a body corporate which is an open-ended investment company which is a recognised scheme (Financial Services Act 1986 (Commencement) (No 8) Order 1988, SI 1988/740, art 2, Schedule);

This repeal also affected ss 81–83, 86, 87, and specified words in ss 84, 85, 97, 449, 693, 744.

(iii) subject to NOTES below—

(a) *as from 31 December 1988* insofar as is necessary to have the effect that, to the extent that they do apply, they cease to apply to a prospectus offering for subscription, or to any application form for, units in an open-ended investment company which *does not* fulfil the conditions described in art 3(a)(i) or (a)(ii) of the Financial Services Act 1986 (Commencement) (No 10) Order 1988, SI 1988/1960. These conditions are—

(1) it is managed in and authorised under the law of a country or territory in respect of which an order under section 87 of the 1986 Act is in force on 31 December 1988 and which is of a class specified in that Order; or

(2) it is constituted in a member state in respect of which an order under para 10 of Sch 15 to the 1986 Act is in force on 31 December 1988 and which meets the requirements specified in that Order.

(b) *as from 1 March 1989* insofar as is necessary to have the effect that, to the extent that they do apply, they cease to apply to a prospectus offering for subscription, or to any application form for, units in an open-ended investment company which *does* fulfil the conditions described in art 3(a)(i) or (a)(ii) of SI 1988/1960 (set out above).

The dates above were appointed by SI 1988/1960, art 4, as amended by SI 1988/2285, art 6. The above repeals also affected s 693.

(iv)—

(a) *as from 1 May 1989* insofar as is necessary to have the effect that, to the extent that they do apply, they cease to apply to a prospectus offering for subscription, or to any application form for, units in an open-ended investment company falling within art 4(a) of SI 1988/2285, ie an open-ended investment company which fulfils the conditions described in art 2(a) of SI 1988/2285 (which are set out in NOTES to (iii) above), and which is a scheme of a class specified in the Schedule to the Financial Services (Designated Countries and Territories) (Overseas Collective Investment Schemes) (Bermuda) Order 1988, SI 1988/2284;

(b) *as from 28 February 1989* insofar as is necessary to have the effect that, to the extent that they do apply, they cease to apply to a prospectus offering for subscription, or to any application form for, units in an open-ended investment company falling within art 2(a) of SI 1988/2285 (which is set out in NOTES to (iii) above), but not within art 4(a) (which is set out in (iv)(a) above);

These dates were appointed by SI 1988/2285, art 5.

(v) *as from 19 June 1995* for all remaining purposes except for repeals of ss 58, 59, 60 (so far as necessary for the purposes of ss 81, 83, 246, 248, 744), Sch 3, para 2 (so far as necessary for the purposes of s 83(1)(a)) and s 62 (so far as necessary for the purposes of s 744) (SI 1995/1538, art 2(a)).

(vi) *as from 10 May 1999* so far as relates to repeals of or in (i) ss 82, 83, and the corresponding provisions of the Companies (Northern Ireland) Order 1986, SI 1986/1032, for all remaining purposes except for the purposes of prospectuses to which SI 1995/1537, reg 8 applies; and (ii) ss 86, 87, and the corresponding provisions of SI 1986/1032, for all remaining purposes (SI 1999/727).

NOTES: art 4, cited above, does not have effect in relation to a prospectus offering for subscription, or to any application form for, units in an open-ended investment company which fulfils the conditions described in art 2(a) of the Financial Services Act 1986 (Commencement) (No 11) Order 1988, SI 1988/2285, ie it is an open-ended investment company managed in and authorised under the law of Bermuda, units in which are, on 31 December 1988, included in the Official List of the International Stock Exchange of the United Kingdom and the Republic of Ireland Limited (SI 1988/2285, art 3).

In so far as this Part continued to have effect, it was completely repealed as follows—

(1) by the Financial Services and Markets Act 2000 (Consequential Amendments and Repeals) Order 2001, SI 2001/3649, art 5, as from 1 December 2001 (in the case of ss 59, 60);

(2) by CA 2006, as from 6 April 2008 (in the case of s 58);
(3) by CA 2006, as from 1 October 2009 (in the case of s 62 and Sch 3).

PART IV ALLOTMENT OF SHARES AND DEBENTURES

[5.4]
80–116

NOTES

This Part has been repealed as follows:

Repeal of certain provisions in this Part for certain purposes: ss 81–83, 86, 87 and specified words in ss 84(1), 85(1) and 97 were repealed by the Financial Services Act 1986, s 212(3), Sch 17, Pt I to the same extent and from the same sates as mentioned in paras (i) and (ii) of the note to Part III *ante*.

80 Authority of company required for certain allotments	Repealed by CA 2006, as from 1 Oct 2009. Transitional provisions: see CO No 8, Sch 2, para 45 which provides that an authorisation in force immediately before 1 Oct 2009 under ss 80, 80A has effect on and after that date as if given under CA 2006, s 551 (power of directors to allot shares etc: authorisation by company).
80A Election by private company as to duration of authority	Repealed by CA 2006, as from 1 Oct 2009. For savings see the note to s 80.
81 Restriction on public offers by private company	Repealed by CA 2006, as from 6 Apr 2008. Savings: see CO No 5, Sch 4, Pt 1, para 24 which provides that this section continues to apply to offers made before 6 Apr 2008. As to the previous repeal of this section by FSA 1986, see the note preceding this table.
82 Application for, and allotment of, shares and debentures	Repealed by CA 2006, as from 1 Oct 2009. As to the previous repeal of this section by FSA 1986, see the note preceding this table.
83 No allotment unless minimum subscription received	Repealed by CA 2006, as from 1 Oct 2009. As to the previous repeal of this section by FSA 1986, see the note preceding this table.
84 Allotment where issue not fully subscribed	Repealed by CA 2006, as from 1 Oct 2009. Savings: CO No 8, Sch 2, para 56 provides that this section and s 85 continue to apply where the offer was made, or a prospectus issued, before 1 Oct 2009.
85 Effect of irregular allotment	Repealed by CA 2006, as from 1 Oct 2009. For savings see the note to s 84.
86 Allotment of shares, etc to be dealt in on stock exchange	Repealed by CA 2006, as from 1 Oct 2009.
87 Operation of s 86 where prospectus offers shares for sale	Repealed by CA 2006, as from 1 Oct 2009.
88 Return as to allotments, etc	Repealed by CA 2006, as from 1 Oct 2009. Savings: CO No 8, Sch 2, para 47 provides that this section continues to apply to shares allotted before 1 Oct 2009.
89 Offers to shareholders to be on pre-emptive basis	Repealed by CA 2006, as from 1 Oct 2009. Savings and transitional provisions: for general savings and transitional provisions in connection with the commencement of the equivalent provisions of the 2006 Act (existing shareholders' right of pre-emption (ss 561–577)), see CO No 8, Sch 2, paras 49–55.
90 Communication of pre-emption offers to shareholders	Repealed by CA 2006, as from 1 Oct 2009. For savings and transitional provisions see the note to s 89.
91 Exclusion of ss 89, 90 by private company	Repealed by CA 2006, as from 1 Oct 2009. For savings and transitional provisions see the note to s 89.
92 Consequences of contravening ss 89, 90	Repealed by CA 2006, as from 1 Oct 2009. For savings and transitional provisions see the note to s 89.
93 Saving for other restrictions as to offers	Repealed by CA 2006, as from 1 Oct 2009. For savings and transitional provisions see the note to s 89.
94 Definitions for ss 89–96	Repealed by CA 2006, as from 1 Oct 2009. For savings and transitional provisions see the note to s 89.
95 Disapplication of pre-emption rights	Repealed by CA 2006, as from 1 Oct 2009. For savings and transitional provisions see the note to s 89.
96 Saving for company's pre-emption procedure operative before 1982	Repealed by CA 2006, as from 1 Oct 2009. For savings and transitional provisions see the note to s 89.
97 Power of company to pay commissions	Repealed by CA 2006, as from 1 Oct 2009. As to the previous repeal of this section by FSA 1986, see the note preceding this table.
98 Apart from s 97, commissions and discounts barred	Repealed by CA 2006, as from 1 Oct 2009.
99 General rules as to payment for shares on allotment	Repealed by CA 2006, as from 1 Oct 2009.
100 Prohibition on allotment of shares at a discount	Repealed by CA 2006, as from 1 Oct 2009.
101 Shares to be allotted as at least one-quarter paid-up	Repealed by CA 2006, as from 1 Oct 2009.
102 Restriction on payment by long-	Repealed by CA 2006, as from 1 Oct 2009.

term undertaking	
103 Non-cash consideration to be valued before allotment	Repealed by CA 2006, as from 1 Oct 2009.
104 Transfer to public company of non-cash asset in initial period	Repealed by CA 2006, as from 1 Oct 2009.
105 Agreements contravening s 104	Repealed by CA 2006, as from 1 Oct 2009.
106 Shares issued to subscribers of memorandum	Repealed by CA 2006, as from 1 Oct 2009.
107 Meaning of "the appropriate rate"	Repealed by CA 2006, as from 1 Oct 2009.
108 Valuation and report (s 103)	Repealed by CA 2006, as from 1 Oct 2009.
109 Valuation and report (s 104)	Repealed by CA 2006, as from 1 Oct 2009.
110 Entitlement of valuer to full disclosure	Repealed by CA 2006, as from 1 Oct 2009.
111 Matters to be communicated to registrar	Repealed by CA 2006, as from 1 Oct 2009.
111A Right to damages, &c not affected	Repealed by CA 2006, as from 1 Oct 2009.
112 Liability of subsequent holders of shares allotted	Repealed by CA 2006, as from 1 Oct 2009.
113 Relief in respect of certain liabilities under ss 99 ff	Repealed by CA 2006, as from 1 Oct 2009.
114 Penalty for contravention	Repealed by CA 2006, as from 1 Oct 2009. Savings: CO No 8, Sch 2, para 57 provides that this section continues to apply in relation to consideration received in pursuance of an obligation entered into before 1 Oct 2009.
115 Undertakings to do work, etc	Repealed by CA 2006, as from 1 Oct 2009.
116 Application of ss 99 ff to special cases	Repealed by CA 2006, as from 1 Oct 2009.

PART V SHARE CAPITAL, ITS INCREASE, MAINTENANCE AND REDUCTION

[5.5]
117–197

NOTES

This Part has been repealed as follows:

117 Public company share capital requirements	Repealed by CA 2006, as from 6 Apr 2008. Savings: CO No 5, Sch 4, Pt 1, paras 26, 27, 29 provide (i) that a certificate issued under this section has effect on and after 6 Apr 2008 as issued under CA 2006, s 761, (ii) s 762 of the 2006 Act applies to applications made on or after 6 Apr 2008 and sub-ss (1)–(5), (7A) of this section continue to apply to applications made before that date, and (iii) s 767 of the 2006 Act applies in relation to things done on or after 6 Apr 2008, and sub-ss (6)–(8) of this section continue to apply in relation to things done before that date.
118 The authorised minimum	Repealed by CA 2006, as from 6 Apr 2008.
119 Provision for different amounts to be paid on shares	Repealed by CA 2006, as from 1 Oct 2009.
120 Reserve liability of limited company	Repealed by CA 2006, as from 1 Oct 2009. Savings: CO No 8, Sch 2, para 67 provides that the repeal of this section does not affect the validity of any resolution that is in force immediately before 1 Oct 2009.
121 Alteration of share capital (limited companies)	Repealed by CA 2006, as from 1 Oct 2009. Savings: see CO No 8, Sch 2, para 42 (Saving for provisions as to amount of authorised share capital).
122 Notice to registrar of alteration	Repealed by CA 2006, as from 1 Oct 2009. Savings: see CO No 8, Sch 2, para 41.
123 Notice to registrar of increased share capital	Repealed by CA 2006, as from 1 Oct 2009.
124 Reserve capital of unlimited company	Repealed by CA 2006, as from 1 Oct 2009. Savings: CO No 8, Sch 2, para 67 provides that the repeal of this section does not affect the validity of any resolution that is in force immediately before 1 Oct 2009.

125 Variation of class rights	Repealed by CA 2006, as from 1 Oct 2007 (in so far as relating to sub-s (6)), and as from 1 Oct 2009 (otherwise). Savings: sub-s (6) (which applied (with the necessary modifications) ss 369, 370, 376 and 377 and the provisions of the articles relating to general meetings in relation to any meeting of shareholders in connection with the variation of the rights attached to a class of shares) continued to apply to meetings of which notice was given before 1 Oct 2007 (see CO No 3, Sch 3, para 31.
126 Saving for court's powers under other provisions	Repealed by CA 2006, as from 1 Oct 2009.
127 Shareholders' right to object to variation	Repealed by CA 2006, s 1295, Sch 16, as from 1 October 2009.
128 Registration of particulars of special rights	Repealed by CA 2006, as from 1 Oct 2009. Savings: see CO No 8, Sch 2, paras 48, 62, 63 which respectively provide as follows: (i) sub-ss (1), (2), (5) continue to apply to shares allotted before 1 Oct 2009; (ii) sub-ss (4), (5) continue to apply where the new name or other designation was assigned before that date; (iii) sub-ss (3), (5) continue to apply where the variation was made before that date.
129 Registration of newly created class rights	Repealed by CA 2006, as from 1 Oct 2009. Savings: see CO No 8, Sch 2, paras 64, 65, 66 which respectively provide as follows: (i) sub-ss (1), (4) continue to apply where a new class of members was created before 1 Oct 2009; (ii) sub-ss (3), (4) continue to apply where the name or other designation, or new name or other designation, was assigned before that date; (iii) sub-ss (2), (4) continue to apply where the variation was made before that date.
130 Application of share premiums	Repealed by CA 2006, as from 1 Oct 2009.
131 Merger relief	Repealed by CA 2006, as from 1 Oct 2009.
132 Relief in respect of group reconstructions	Repealed by CA 2006, as from 1 Oct 2009.
133 Provisions supplementing ss 131, 132	Repealed by CA 2006, as from 1 Oct 2009.
134 Provision for extending or restricting relief from s 130	Repealed by CA 2006, as from 1 Oct 2009.
135 Special resolution for reduction of share capital	Repealed by CA 2006, as from 1 Oct 2009.
136 Application to court for order of confirmation	Repealed by CA 2006, as from 1 Oct 2009. Savings: see CO No 8, Sch 2, paras 68, 69 (Reduction of capital confirmed by the court (ss 645 to 653)).
137 Court order confirming reduction	Repealed by CA 2006, as from 1 Oct 2009. For savings see the note to s 136.
138 Registration of order and minute of reduction	Repealed by CA 2006, as from 1 Oct 2009. For savings see the note to s 136.
139 Public company reducing capital below authorised minimum	Repealed by CA 2006, as from 1 Oct 2009. For savings see the note to s 136.
140 Liability of members on reduced shares	Repealed by CA 2006, as from 1 Oct 2009. For savings see the note to s 136.
141 Penalty for concealing name of creditor, etc	Repealed by CA 2006, as from 1 Oct 2009. For savings see the note to s 136.
142 Duty of directors on serious loss of capital	Repealed by CA 2006, as from 1 Oct 2009.
143 General rule against company acquiring own shares	Repealed by CA 2006, as from 1 Oct 2009.
144 Acquisition of shares by company's nominee	Repealed by CA 2006, as from 1 Oct 2009.
145 Exceptions from s 144	Repealed by CA 2006, as from 1 Oct 2009.
146 Treatment of shares held by or for public company	Repealed by CA 2006, as from 1 Oct 2009. Savings: see CO No 8, Sch 2, paras 70, 72 (Cancellation of shares in public company held by or for the company (ss 662 to 668)).
147 Matters arising out of compliance with s 146(2)	Repealed by CA 2006, as from 1 Oct 2009. For savings see the note to s 146.
148 Further provisions supplementing ss 146, 147	Repealed by CA 2006, as from 1 Oct 2009. For savings see the note to s 146.
149 Sanctions for non-compliance	Repealed by CA 2006, as from 1 Oct 2009. For savings see the note to s 146.
150 Charges of public companies on own shares	Repealed by CA 2006, as from 1 Oct 2009.

151 Financial assistance generally prohibited	Repealed by CA 2006, as from 1 Oct 2008 (in relation to the giving of financial assistance (on or after that date) by a private company for the purposes of the acquisition of shares in itself or another private company (see CO No 5, art 5(2)) and the savings note below), and as from 1 Oct 2009 (otherwise). Savings, etc: see CO No 5, Sch 4, Pt 3, paras 51, 52 (Repeal of prohibition on private companies giving financial assistance for acquisition of shares).
152 Definitions for this Chapter	Repealed by CA 2006, as from 1 Oct 2008 (in relation to the giving of financial assistance (on or after that date) by a private company for the purposes of the acquisition of shares in itself or another private company (see the notes to s 151), and as from 1 Oct 2009 (otherwise).
153 Transactions not prohibited by s 151	Repealed by CA 2006, as from 1 Oct 2008 (in relation to the giving of financial assistance (on or after that date) by a private company for the purposes of the acquisition of shares in itself or another private company (see the notes to s 151), and as from 1 Oct 2009 (otherwise).
154 Special restriction for public companies	Repealed by CA 2006, as from 1 Oct 2009.
155 Relaxation of s 151 for private companies	Repealed by CA 2006, as from 1 Oct 2008 (in relation to the giving of financial assistance (on or after that date) by a private company for the purposes of the acquisition of shares in itself or another private company (see the notes to s 151), and as from 1 Oct 2009 (otherwise).
156 Statutory declaration under s 155	Repealed by CA 2006, as from 1 Oct 2008 (in relation to the giving of financial assistance (on or after that date) by a private company for the purposes of the acquisition of shares in itself or another private company (see the notes to s 151), and as from 1 Oct 2009 (otherwise).
157 Special resolution under s 155	Repealed by CA 2006, as from 1 Oct 2008 (in relation to the giving of financial assistance (on or after that date) by a private company for the purposes of the acquisition of shares in itself or another private company (see the notes to s 151), and as from 1 Oct 2009 (otherwise).
158 Time for giving financial assistance under s 155	Repealed by CA 2006, as from 1 Oct 2008 (in relation to the giving of financial assistance (on or after that date) by a private company for the purposes of the acquisition of shares in itself or another private company (see the notes to s 151), and as from 1 Oct 2009 (otherwise).
159 Power to issue redeemable shares	Repealed by CA 2006, as from 1 Oct 2009. Savings: CO No 8, Sch 2, para 73 provides that CA 2006, s 686(2) (terms allowing for payment on date later than redemption date) applies (a) to shares issued on or after 1 Oct 2009, and (b) to shares issued before that date where the terms of redemption have been amended on or after that date to allow for payment on a date later than the redemption date. Furthermore, so much of sub-s (3) as requires payment on redemption continues to apply in any other case.
159A Terms and manner of redemption	Repealed by CA 2006, as from 1 Oct 2009.
160 Financing etc of redemption	Repealed by CA 2006, as from 1 Oct 2009.
161 Stamp duty on redemption of shares	Repealed by FA 1988, s 148, Sch 14, Pt XI, with effect from 22 Mar 1988.
162 Power of company to purchase own shares	Repealed by CA 2006, as from 1 Oct 2009.
162A Treasury shares	Repealed by CA 2006, as from 1 Oct 2009.
162B Treasury shares: maximum holdings	Repealed by CA 2006, as from 1 Oct 2009.
162C Treasury shares: voting and other rights	Repealed by CA 2006, as from 1 Oct 2009.
162D Treasury shares: disposal and cancellation	Repealed by CA 2006, as from 1 Oct 2009. Savings: CO No 8, Sch 2, para 79 provides that sub-s (1)(a) continues to apply where the contract for the sale of the shares was entered into before 1 Oct 2009.
162E Treasury shares: mandatory cancellation	Repealed by CA 2006, as from 1 Oct 2009.
162F Treasury shares: proceeds of sale	Repealed by CA 2006, as from 1 Oct 2009.
162G Treasury shares: penalty for contravention	Repealed by CA 2006, as from 1 Oct 2009.
163 Definitions of "off-market" and "market" purchase	Repealed by CA 2006, as from 1 Oct 2009.
164 Authority for off-market purchase	Repealed by CA 2006, as from 1 Oct 2009. Savings and transitional provisions: see CO No 8, Sch 2, paras 75–77 (Purchase of own shares (ss 690 to 708)).
165 Authority for contingent purchase contract	Repealed by CA 2006, as from 1 Oct 2009. For savings see the note to s 164.

166 Authority for market purchase	Repealed by CA 2006, as from 1 Oct 2009. Transitional provisions: CO No 8, Sch 2, para 75 provides that where immediately before 1 Oct 2009 a resolution is in force having been passed under ss 166 or 167(2), the resolution has effect on and after that date as if passed under the corresponding provision of CA 2006 and may be varied, revoked or renewed from time to time accordingly.
167 Assignment or release of company's right to purchase own shares	Repealed by CA 2006, as from 1 Oct 2009. For transitional provisions see the note to s 166.
168 Payments apart from purchase price to be made out of distributable profits	Repealed by CA 2006, as from 1 Oct 2009.
169 Disclosure by company of purchase of own shares	Repealed by CA 2006, as from 1 Oct 2009. For savings see the note to s 164.
169A Disclosure by company of cancellation or disposal of treasury shares	Repealed by CA 2006, as from 1 Oct 2009. Savings: CO No 8, Sch 2, para 80 provides that this section continues to apply to shares cancelled before 1 Oct 2009.
170 The capital redemption reserve	Repealed by CA 2006, as from 1 Oct 2009.
171 Power of private companies to redeem or purchase own shares out of capital	Repealed by CA 2006, as from 1 Oct 2009. Savings: CO No 8, Sch 2, para 78 provides that this section and ss 172–178 continue to apply where the statutory declaration required by s 173(3) was made before 1 Oct 2009.
172 Availability of profits for purposes of s 171	Repealed by CA 2006, as from 1 Oct 2009. For savings see the note to s 171.
173 Conditions for payment out of capital	Repealed by CA 2006, as from 1 Oct 2009. For savings see the note to s 171.
174 Procedure for special resolution under s 173	Repealed by CA 2006, as from 1 Oct 2009. For savings see the note to s 171.
175 Publicity for proposed payment out of capital	Repealed by CA 2006, as from 1 Oct 2009. For savings see the note to s 171.
176 Objections by company's members or creditors	Repealed by CA 2006, as from 1 Oct 2009. For savings see the note to s 171.
177 Powers of court on application under s 176	Repealed by CA 2006, as from 1 Oct 2009. For savings see the note to s 171.
178 Effect of company's failure to redeem or purchase	Repealed by CA 2006, as from 1 Oct 2009. For savings see the note to s 171.
179 Power for Secretary of State to modify this Chapter	Repealed by CA 2006, as from 1 Oct 2009.
180 Transitional cases arising under this Chapter; and savings	Repealed by CA 2006, as from 1 Oct 2009.
181 Definitions for Chapter VII	Repealed by CA 2006, as from 1 Oct 2009.
182 Nature, transfer and numbering of shares	Repealed by CA 2006, as from 1 Oct 2009.
183 Transfer and registration	Repealed by CA 2006, as from 6 Apr 2008.
184 Certification of transfers	Repealed by CA 2006, as from 6 Apr 2008.
185 Duty of company as to issue of certificates	Repealed by CA 2006, as from 6 Apr 2008.
186 Certificate to be evidence of title	Repealed by CA 2006, as from 6 Apr 2008.
187 Evidence of grant of probate or confirmation as executor	Repealed by CA 2006, as from 6 Apr 2008.
188 Issue and effect of share warrant to bearer	Repealed by CA 2006, as from 6 Apr 2008.
189 Offences in connection with share warrants (Scotland)	Repealed by CA 2006, as from 6 Apr 2008.
190 Register of debenture holders	Repealed by CA 2006, as from 6 Apr 2008.
191 Right to inspect register	Repealed by CA 2006, as from 6 Apr 2008. Savings: sub-ss (1)–(6) continue to apply to requests made before 6 Apr 2008; see CO No 5, Sch 4, Pt 1, para 22.
192 Liability of trustees of debentures	Repealed by CA 2006, as from 6 Apr 2008.
193 Perpetual debentures	Repealed by CA 2006, as from 6 Apr 2008.
194 Power to re-issue redeemed debentures	Repealed by CA 2006, as from 6 Apr 2008.
195 Contract to subscribe for debentures	Repealed by CA 2006, as from 6 Apr 2008.
196 Payment of debts out of assets subject to floating charge (England and Wales)	Repealed by CA 2006, as from 6 Apr 2008.

197 Debentures to bearer (Scotland)	Repealed by CA 2006, as from 6 Apr 2008.

PART VI DISCLOSURE OF INTERESTS IN SHARES

[5.6]
198–220

NOTES

This Part has been repealed as follows:

198 Obligation of disclosure: the cases in which it may arise and "the relevant time"	Repealed by the CA 2006, as from 20 Jan 2007. Savings: the repeal of ss 198–210 and 220 does not affect any obligation to which a person became subject under s 198 before 20 Jan 2007; see CO No 1, Sch 5, Pt 2, para 2(1).
199 Interests to be disclosed	Repealed by CA 2006, as from 20 Jan 2007. For savings see the note to s 198.
200 "Percentage level" in relation to notifiable interests	Repealed by CA 2006, as from 20 Jan 2007. For savings see the note to s 198.
201 The notifiable percentage	Repealed by CA 1989, s 212, Sch 24, as from 31 May 1990.
202 Particulars to be contained in notification	Repealed by CA 2006, as from 20 Jan 2007. For savings see the note to s 198.
203 Notification of family and corporate interests	Repealed by CA 2006, as from 20 Jan 2007. For savings see the note to s 198.
204 Agreement to acquire interests in a particular company	Repealed by CA 2006, as from 20 Jan 2007. For savings see the note to s 198.
205 Obligation of disclosure arising under s 204	Repealed by CA 2006, as from 20 Jan 2007. For savings see the note to s 198.
206 Obligation of persons acting together to keep each other informed	Repealed by CA 2006, as from 20 Jan 2007. For savings see the note to s 198.
207 Interests in shares by attribution	Repealed by CA 2006, as from 20 Jan 2007. For savings see the note to s 198.
208 Interests in shares which are to be notified	Repealed by CA 2006, as from 20 Jan 2007. For savings see the note to s 198.
209 Interests to be disregarded	Repealed by CA 2006, as from 20 Jan 2007. For savings see the note to s 198.
210 Other provisions about notification under this Part	Repealed by CA 2006, as from 20 Jan 2007. For savings see the note to s 198.
210A Power to make further provision by regulations	Repealed by CA 2006, as from 20 Jan 2007.
211 Register of interests in shares	Repealed by CA 2006, as from 20 Jan 2007.
212 Company investigations	Repealed by the CA 2006, as from 20 Jan 2007. Savings: the repeal of ss 212–220 does not affect the operation of those sections in relation to a notice issued by a company under s 212 before 20 Jan 2007; see CO No 1, Sch 5, Pt 2, para 2(2).
213 Registration of interests disclosed under s 212	Repealed by CA 2006, as from 20 Jan 2007. For savings see the note to s 212.
214 Company investigation on requisition by members	Repealed by CA 2006, as from 20 Jan 2007. For savings see the note to s 212.
215 Company report to members	Repealed by CA 2006, as from 20 Jan 2007. For savings see the note to s 212.
216 Penalty for failure to provide information	Repealed by CA 2006, as from 20 Jan 2007. For savings see the note to s 212.
217 Removal of entries from register	Repealed by CA 2006, as from 20 Jan 2007. For savings see the note to s 212.
218 Otherwise, entries not to be removed	Repealed by CA 2006, as from 20 Jan 2007. For savings see the note to s 212.
219 Inspection of register and reports	Repealed by CA 2006, as from 20 Jan 2007. For savings see the note to s 212.
220 Definitions for Part VI	Repealed by CA 2006, as from 20 Jan 2007. For savings see the notes to ss 198 and 212.

PART VII ACCOUNTS AND AUDIT

[5.7]
221–262A

NOTES

This Part has been repealed as follows:

221 Duty to keep accounting records	Repealed by CA 2006, as from 6 Apr 2008. Savings: this repeal does not apply in relation to accounts and reports for financial years beginning before 6 Apr 2008; see CO No 5, Sch 4, Pt 1, paras 6–9, 12(1), (2).
222 Where and for how long records to be kept	Repealed by CA 2006, as from 6 Apr 2008. For savings see the note to s 221.

223 A company's financial year	Repealed by CA 2006, as from 6 Apr 2008. For savings see the note to s 221.
224 Accounting reference periods and accounting reference date	Repealed by CA 2006, as from 6 Apr 2008. For savings see the note to s 221.
225 Alteration of accounting reference date	Repealed by CA 2006, as from 6 Apr 2008. For savings see the note to s 221.
226 Duty to prepare individual accounts	Repealed by CA 2006, as from 6 Apr 2008. For savings see the note to s 221.
226A Companies Act individual accounts	Repealed by CA 2006, as from 6 Apr 2008. For savings see the note to s 221.
226B IAS individual accounts	Repealed by CA 2006, as from 6 Apr 2008. For savings see the note to s 221.
227 Duty to prepare group accounts	Repealed by CA 2006, as from 6 Apr 2008. For savings see the note to s 221.
227A Companies Act group accounts	Repealed by CA 2006, as from 6 Apr 2008. For savings see the note to s 221.
227B IAS group accounts	Repealed by CA 2006, as from 6 Apr 2008. For savings see the note to s 221.
227C Consistency of accounts	Repealed by CA 2006, as from 6 Apr 2008. For savings see the note to s 221.
228 Exemption for parent companies included in accounts of larger group	Repealed by CA 2006, as from 6 Apr 2008. For savings see the note to s 221.
228A Exemption for parent companies included in non-EEA group accounts	Repealed by CA 2006, as from 6 Apr 2008. For savings see the note to s 221.
229 Subsidiary undertakings included in the consolidation	Repealed by CA 2006, as from 6 Apr 2008. For savings see the note to s 221.
230 Treatment of individual profit and loss account where group accounts prepared	Repealed by CA 2006, as from 6 Apr 2008. For savings see the note to s 221.
231 Disclosure required in notes to accounts: related undertakings	Repealed by CA 2006, as from 6 Apr 2008. For savings see the note to s 221.
231A Disclosure required in notes to annual accounts: particulars of staff	Repealed by CA 2006, as from 6 Apr 2008. For savings see the note to s 221.
232 Disclosure required in notes to accounts: emoluments and other benefits of directors and others	Repealed by CA 2006, as from 6 Apr 2008. For savings see the note to s 221.
233 Approval and signing of accounts	Repealed by CA 2006, as from 6 Apr 2008. For savings see the note to s 221.
234 Duty to prepare directors' report	Repealed by CA 2006, as from 6 Apr 2008. For savings see the note to s 221.
234ZZA Directors' report: general requirements	Repealed by CA 2006, as from 6 Apr 2008. For savings see the note to s 221.
234ZZB Directors' report: business review	Repealed by CA 2006, as from 1 Oct 2007. Savings: this repeal does not apply in relation to directors' reports for financial years beginning before 1 Oct 2007; see CO No 3, Sch 3, para 43.
234ZA Statement as to disclosure of information to auditors	Repealed by CA 2006, as from 6 Apr 2008. For savings see the note to s 221.
234A Approval and signing of directors' report	Repealed by CA 2006, as from 6 Apr 2008. For savings see the note to s 221.
234AA Duty to prepare operating and financial review	Repealed by SI 2005/3442, as from 12 Jan 2006.
234AB Approval and signing of operating and financial review	Repealed by SI 2005/3442, as from 12 Jan 2006.
234B Duty to prepare directors' remuneration report	Repealed by CA 2006, as from 6 Apr 2008. For savings see the note to s 221.
234C Approval and signing of directors' remuneration report	Repealed by CA 2006, as from 6 Apr 2008. For savings see the note to s 221.
235 Auditors' report	Repealed by CA 2006, as from 6 Apr 2008. For savings see the note to s 221.
236 Signature of auditors' report	Repealed by CA 2006, as from 6 Apr 2008. For savings see the note to s 221.
237 Duties of auditors	Repealed by CA 2006, as from 6 Apr 2008. For savings see the note to s 221.
238 Persons entitled to receive copies of accounts and reports	Repealed by CA 2006, as from 6 Apr 2008. For savings see the note to s 221.
238A Time allowed for sending out copies of accounts and reports	Repealed by CA 2006, as from 6 Apr 2008. For savings see the note to s 221.
239 Right to demand copies of accounts and reports	Repealed by CA 2006, as from 6 Apr 2008. For savings see the note to s 221.
240 Requirements in connection with publication of accounts	Repealed by CA 2006, as from 6 Apr 2008. For savings see the note to s 221.
241 Accounts and reports to be laid before company in general meeting	Repealed by CA 2006, as from 6 Apr 2008. For savings see the note to s 221.
241A Members' approval of directors' remuneration report	Repealed by CA 2006, as from 6 Apr 2008. For savings see the note to s 221.

242 Accounts and reports to be delivered to the registrar	Repealed by CA 2006, as from 6 Apr 2008. For savings see the note to s 221.
242A Civil penalty for failure to deliver accounts	Repealed by CA 2006, as from 6 Apr 2008. For savings see the note to s 221.
242B Delivery and publication of accounts in ECUs	Repealed by CA 2006, as from 6 Apr 2008. For savings see the note to s 221.
243 Penalty for non-compliance with s 241	Repealed by SI 2004/2947, as from 12 Nov 2004, in relation to companies' financial years which begin on or after 1 Jan 2005.
244 Period allowed for laying and delivering accounts and reports	Repealed by CA 2006, as from 6 Apr 2008. For savings see the note to s 221.
245 Voluntary revision of annual accounts or directors' report	Repealed by CA 2006, as from 6 Apr 2008. For savings see the note to s 221.
245A Secretary of State's notice in respect of annual accounts	Repealed by CA 2006, as from 6 Apr 2008. For savings see the note to s 221.
245B Application to court in respect of defective accounts	Repealed by CA 2006, as from 6 Apr 2008. For savings see the note to s 221.
245C Other persons authorised to apply to court	Repealed by CA 2006, as from 6 Apr 2008. For savings see the note to s 221.
245D Disclosure of information held by Inland Revenue to persons authorised to apply to court	Repealed by CA 2006, as from 6 Apr 2008. For savings see the note to s 221.
245E Restrictions on use and further disclosure of information disclosed under section 245D	Repealed by CA 2006, as from 6 Apr 2008. For savings see the note to s 221.
245F Power of authorised persons to require documents, information and explanations	Repealed by CA 2006, as from 6 Apr 2008. For savings see the note to s 221.
245G Restrictions on further disclosure of information obtained under section 245F	Repealed by CA 2006, as from 6 Apr 2008. For savings see the note to s 221.
246 Special provisions for small companies	Repealed by CA 2006, as from 6 Apr 2008. For savings see the note to s 221.
246A Special provisions for medium-sized companies	Repealed by CA 2006, as from 6 Apr 2008. For savings see the note to s 221.
247 Qualification of company as small or medium-sized	Repealed by CA 2006, as from 6 Apr 2008. For savings see the note to s 221.
247A Cases in which special provisions do not apply	Repealed by CA 2006, as from 6 Apr 2008. For savings see the note to s 221.
247B Special auditors' report	Repealed by CA 2006, as from 6 Apr 2008. For savings see the note to s 221.
248 Exemption for small and medium-sized groups	Repealed by CA 2006, as from 6 Apr 2008. For savings see the note to s 221.
248A Group accounts prepared by small company	Repealed by CA 2006, as from 6 Apr 2008. For savings see the note to s 221.
249 Qualification of group as small or medium-sized	Repealed by CA 2006, as from 6 Apr 2008. For savings see the note to s 221.
249A Exemptions from audit	Repealed by CA 2006, as from 6 Apr 2008. For savings see the note to s 221.
249AA Dormant companies	Repealed by CA 2006, as from 6 Apr 2008. For savings see the note to s 221.
249B Cases where exemptions not available	Repealed by CA 2006, as from 6 Apr 2008. For savings see the note to s 221.
249C The report required for the purposes of section 249A(2)	Repealed by CA 2006, as from 6 Apr 2008. For savings see the note to s 221.
249D The reporting accountant	Repealed by CA 2006, as from 6 Apr 2008. For savings see the note to s 221.
249E Effect of exemptions	Repealed by CA 2006, as from 6 Apr 2008. For savings see the note to s 221.
250 Power of Secretary of State to modify ss 247–250 and Sch 8	Repealed by SI 2000/1430, as from 26 May 2000, in relation to annual accounts and reports in respect of financial years ending two months or more after that date.
251 Provision of summary financial statement to shareholders	Repealed by CA 2006, as from 6 Apr 2008. For savings see the note to s 221.
252 Election to dispense with laying of accounts and reports before general meeting	Repealed by CA 2006, as from 1 Oct 2007. Savings: the repeal of ss 252, 253 have effect in relation to annual accounts and reports for financial years ending on or after 1 Oct 2007; see CO No 3, SI 2007/2194, Sch 3, para 49.
253 Right of shareholder to require laying of accounts	Repealed by CA 2006, as from 1 Oct 2007. For savings see the note to s 252.
254 Exemption from requirement to deliver accounts and reports	Repealed by CA 2006, as from 6 Apr 2008. For savings see the note to s 221.

255 Special provisions for banking and insurance companies	Repealed by CA 2006, as from 6 Apr 2008. For savings see the note to s 221.
255A Special provisions for banking and insurance groups	Repealed by CA 2006, as from 6 Apr 2008. For savings see the note to s 221.
255B Modification of disclosure requirements in relation to banking company or group	Repealed by CA 2006, as from 6 Apr 2008. For savings see the note to s 221.
255C Directors' report where accounts prepared in accordance with special provisions	Repealed by SI 1993/3246, as from 19 Dec 1993, subject to transitional provisions and exemptions in relation to certain companies.
255D Power to apply provisions to banking partnerships	Repealed by CA 2006, as from 6 Apr 2008. For savings see the note to s 221.
255E Delivery of accounting documents in Welsh only	Repealed by the Welsh Language Act 1993, as from 1 Feb 1994.
256 Accounting standards	Repealed by CA 2006, as from 6 Apr 2008. For savings see the note to s 221.
256A Reporting standards	Repealed by SI 2005/3442, as from 12 Jan 2006.
257 Power of Secretary of State to alter accounting requirements	Repealed by CA 2006, as from 6 Apr 2008. For savings see the note to s 221.
258 Parent and subsidiary undertakings	Repealed by CA 2006, as from 6 Apr 2008. For savings see the note to s 221.
259 Meaning of "undertaking" and related expressions	Repealed by CA 2006, as from 6 Apr 2008. For savings see the note to s 221.
260 Participating interests	Repealed by CA 2006, as from 6 Apr 2008. For savings see the note to s 221.
261 Notes to the accounts	Repealed by CA 2006, as from 6 Apr 2008. For savings see the note to s 221.
262 Minor definitions	Repealed by CA 2006, as from 6 Apr 2008. For savings see the note to s 221.
262A Index of defined expressions	Repealed by CA 2006, as from 6 Apr 2008. For savings see the note to s 221.

PART VIII DISTRIBUTION OF PROFITS AND ASSETS

[5.8]
263–281

NOTES

This Part has been repealed as follows:

263 Certain distributions prohibited	Repealed by CA2006, as from 6 Apr 2008. Savings: ss 263–281 continue to apply to distributions made before 6 Apr 2008; see CO No 5, Sch 4, Pt 1, para 33.
264 Restriction on distribution of assets	Repealed by CA 2006, as from 6 Apr 2008. For savings see the note to s 263.
265 Other distributions by investment companies	Repealed by CA 2006, as from 6 Apr 2008. For savings see the note to s 263.
266 Meaning of "investment company"	Repealed by CA 2006, as from 6 Apr 2008. For savings see the note to s 263.
267 Extension of ss 265, 266 to other companies	Repealed by CA 2006, as from 6 Apr 2008. For savings see the note to s 263.
268 Realised profits of insurance company with long term business	Repealed by CA 2006, as from 6 Apr 2008. For savings see the note to s 263.
269 Treatment of development costs	Repealed by CA 2006, as from 6 Apr 2008. For savings see the note to s 263.
270 Distribution to be justified by reference to company's accounts	Repealed by CA 2006, as from 6 Apr 2008. For savings see the note to s 263.
271 Requirements for last annual accounts	Repealed by CA 2006, as from 6 Apr 2008. For savings see the note to s 263.
272 Requirements for interim accounts	Repealed by CA 2006, as from 6 Apr 2008. For savings see the note to s 263.
273 Requirements for initial accounts	Repealed by CA 2006, as from 6 Apr 2008. For savings see the note to s 263.
274 Method of applying s 270 to successive distributions	Repealed by CA 2006, as from 6 Apr 2008. For savings see the note to s 263.
275 Treatment of assets in the relevant accounts	Repealed by CA 2006, as from 6 Apr 2008. For savings see the note to s 263.
276 Distributions in kind	Repealed by CA 2006, as from 6 Apr 2008. For savings see the note to s 263.
277 Consequences of unlawful distribution	Repealed by CA 2006, as from 6 Apr 2008. For savings see the note to s 263.
278 Saving for provision in articles operative before Act of 1980	Repealed by CA 2006, as from 6 Apr 2008. For savings see the note to s 263.
279 Distributions by banking or insurance companies	Repealed by CA 2006, as from 6 Apr 2008. For savings see the note to s 263.

280 Definitions for Part VIII	Repealed by CA 2006, as from 6 Apr 2008. For savings see the note to s 263.
281 Saving for other restraints on distribution	Repealed by CA 2006, as from 6 Apr 2008. For savings see the note to s 263.

PART IX A COMPANY'S MANAGEMENT; DIRECTORS AND SECRETARIES; THEIR QUALIFICATIONS, DUTIES AND RESPONSIBILITIES

[5.9]
282–310

NOTES

This Part has been repealed as follows:

282 Directors	Repealed by CA 2006, as from 1 Oct 2007.
283 Secretary	Repealed by CA 2006, as from 6 Apr 2008.
284 Acts done by person in dual capacity	Repealed by CA 2006, as from 6 Apr 2008.
285 Validity of acts of directors	Repealed by CA 2006, as from 1 Oct 2007. Savings: this repeal does not apply in relation to acts done before 1 Oct 2007; see CO No 3, Sch 3, para 4.
286 Qualifications of company secretaries	Repealed by CA 2006, as from 6 Apr 2008. Savings: this repeal does not apply in relation to company secretaries appointed before 6 Apr 2008; see CO No 5, Sch 4, Pt 1, para 5.
287 Registered office	Repealed by CA 2006, as from 1 Oct 2009.
288 Register of directors and secretaries	Repealed by CA 2006, as from 1 Oct 2009. Savings and transitional provisions: CO No 8, Sch 2, para 25 provides that on and after 1 Oct 2009 the register of directors and secretaries kept by a company under this section shall be treated as two separate registers: (a) a register of directors kept under and for the purposes of the CA 2006, s 162, and (b) a register of secretaries kept under and for the purposes of s 275 of that Act. See also Sch 2, para 31 to that Order which provides that sub-ss (2), (4) and (6) above continue to apply in relation to a change occurring before 1 Oct 2009.
288A	Repealed by CA 2006, as from 1 Oct 2009.
289 Particulars of directors to be registered under s 288	Repealed by CA 2006, as from 1 Oct 2009. Savings: CO No 8, Sch 2, para 31 provides that this section and s 290 continue to apply in relation to a change occurring before 1 Oct 2009.
290 Particulars of secretaries to be registered under s 288	Repealed by CA 2006, as from 1 Oct 2009. For savings see the note to s 289.
291 Share qualification of directors	Repealed by CA 2006, as from 1 Oct 2009.
292 Appointment of directors to be voted on individually	Repealed by CA 2006, as from 1 Oct 2007.
293 Age limit for directors	Repealed by CA 2006, as from 6 Apr 2007. Savings: CO No 1, Sch 5, para 7 provides that the repeal of sub-s (3) does not affect the validity of acts done by a person acting as director to whom that section applied.
294 Duty of director to disclose his age	Repealed by CA 2006, as from 6 Apr 2007.
295–302	Ss 295–299, 301, 302 repealed with savings by the Company Directors Disqualification Act 1986, as from 29 Dec 1986; s 300 repealed by the Insolvency Act 1985, as from 28 Apr 1986.
303 Resolution to remove director	Repealed by CA 2006, as from 1 Oct 2007.
304 Director's right to protest removal	Repealed by CA 2006, as from 1 Oct 2007. Savings: CO No 3, Sch 3, para 5 provides that sub-s (4) continues to apply where, in the case of an intended resolution to remove a director under s 303, the written representations made by the director concerned are received by the company before 1 Oct 2007.
305 Directors' names on company correspondence, etc	Repealed by CA 2006, as from 1 Oct 2008.
306 Limited company may have directors with unlimited liability	Repealed by CA 2006, as from 1 Oct 2009. Savings: SI 2009/1941, art 9 (at **[4.363]**) provides that the repeal of this section (and s 307) does not affect its operation in relation to liabilities arising before 1 Oct 2009 or in connection with the holding of an office to which a person was appointed before that date on the understanding that their liability would be unlimited.
307 Special resolution making liability of directors unlimited	Repealed by CA 2006, as from 1 Oct 2009. For savings see the note to s 306.
308 Assignment of office by directors	Repealed by CA 2006, as from 1 Oct 2009.
309 Directors to have regard to inter-	Repealed by CA 2006, as from 1 Oct 2007.

ests of employees	
309A Provisions protecting directors from liability	Repealed by CA 2006, as from 1 Oct 2007. Savings: ss 309A, 309B and 309C(1)–(3) and (6) continue to apply in relation to any provision to which they applied immediately before 1 Oct 2007; see CO No 3, Sch 3, paras 15–17.
309B Qualifying third party indemnity provisions	Repealed by CA 2006, as from 1 Oct 2007. For savings see the note to s 309A.
309C Disclosure of qualifying third party indemnity provisions	Repealed by CA 2006, as from 1 Oct 2007. For savings see the note to s 309A.
310 Provisions protecting auditors from liability	Repealed by CA 2006, as from 6 Apr 2008.

PART X ENFORCEMENT OF FAIR DEALING BY DIRECTORS

[5.10]
311–347

NOTES

This Part has been repealed as follows:

311 Prohibition on tax-free payments to directors	Repealed by CA 2006, as from 6 Apr 2007.
312 Payment to director for loss of office, etc	Repealed by CA 2006, as from 1 Oct 2007. Savings: this section and ss 313–316 continue to apply in relation to loss of office or retirement within the meaning of those provisions occurring before 1 Oct 2007; see CO No 3, Sch 3, para 12(3), (4).
313 Company approval for property transfer	Repealed by CA 2006, as from 1 Oct 2007. For savings see the note to s 311.
314 Director's duty of disclosure on takeover, etc	Repealed by CA 2006, as from 1 Oct 2007. For savings see the note to s 311.
315 Consequences of non-compliance with s 314	Repealed by CA 2006, as from 1 Oct 2007. For savings see the note to s 311.
316 Provisions supplementing ss 312–315	Repealed by CA 2006, as from 1 Oct 2007. For savings see the note to s 311.
317 Directors to disclose interest in contracts	Repealed by CA 2006, as from 1 Oct 2008. Savings: this section continues to apply in relation to a duty arising before 1 Oct 2008; see CO No 5, Sch 4, Pt 3, paras 48, 50.
318 Directors' service contracts to be open to inspection	Repealed by CA 2006, as from 1 Oct 2007. Savings: see CO No 3, Sch 3, para 13(4) which provides that this section continues to apply to: (a) any default before 1 Oct 2007 in complying with section 318(1) or (5); (b) any request for inspection under s 318(7) made before that date; (c) any duty to give notice under s 318(4) arising before that date.
319 Director's contract of employment for more than 5 years	Repealed by CA 2006, as from 1 Oct 2007. Savings: this section continues to apply to agreements made before 1 Oct 2007; see CO No 3, Sch 3, para 6.
320 Substantial property transactions involving directors, etc	Repealed by CA 2006, as from 1 Oct 2007. Savings: this section and ss 321, 322 continue to apply in relation to arrangements or transactions entered into before 1 Oct 2007 (see CO No 3, Sch 3, para 7).
321 Exceptions from s 320	Repealed by CA 2006, as from 1 Oct 2007. For savings see the note to s 320.
322 Liabilities arising from contravention of s 320	Repealed by CA 2006, as from 1 Oct 2007. For savings see the note to s 320.
322A Invalidity of certain transactions involving directors, etc	Repealed by CA 2006, as from 1 Oct 2009.
322B Contracts with sole members who are directors	Repealed by CA 2006, as from 1 Oct 2007. Savings: this section continues to apply to contracts entered into before 1 Oct 2007 (see CO No 3, Sch 3, para 14).
323 Prohibition on directors dealing in share options	Repealed by CA 2006, as from 6 Apr 2007.
324 Duty of director to disclose shareholdings in own company	Repealed by CA 2006, as from 6 Apr 2007.
325 Register of directors' interests notified under s 324	Repealed by CA 2006, as from 6 Apr 2007.
326 Sanctions for non-compliance	Repealed by CA 2006, as from 6 Apr 2007.
327 Extension of s 323 to spouses, civil partners and children	Repealed by CA 2006, as from 6 Apr 2007.
328 Extension of s 324 to spouses, civil partners and children	Repealed by CA 2006, as from 6 Apr 2007.

329 Duty to notify stock exchange of matters notified under preceding sections	Repealed by CA 2006, as from 6 Apr 2007.
330 General restriction on loans etc to directors and persons connected with them	Repealed by CA 2006, as from 1 Oct 2007. Savings: ss 330–342 continue to apply in relation to a contravention occurring before 1 Oct 2007; see CO No 3, Sch 3, paras 8–11.
331 Definitions for ss 330 ff	Repealed by CA 2006, as from 1 Oct 2007. For savings see the note to s 331.
332 Short-term quasi-loans	Repealed by CA 2006, as from 1 Oct 2007. For savings see the note to s 331.
333 Inter-company loans in same group	Repealed by CA 2006, as from 1 Oct 2007. For savings see the note to s 331.
334 Loans of small amounts	Repealed by CA 2006, as from 1 Oct 2007. For savings see the note to s 331.
335 Minor and business transactions	Repealed by CA 2006, as from 1 Oct 2007. For savings see the note to s 331.
336 Transactions at behest of holding company	Repealed by CA 2006, as from 1 Oct 2007. For savings see the note to s 331.
337 Funding of director's expenditure on duty to company	Repealed by CA 2006, as from 1 Oct 2007. For savings see the note to s 331.
337A Funding of director's expenditure on defending proceedings	Repealed by CA 2006, as from 1 Oct 2007. For savings see the note to s 331.
338 Loan or quasi-loan by money-lending company	Repealed by CA 2006, as from 1 Oct 2007. For savings see the note to s 331.
339 "Relevant amounts" for purposes of ss 334 ff	Repealed by CA 2006, as from 1 Oct 2007. For savings see the note to s 331.
340 "Value" of transactions and arrangements	Repealed by CA 2006, as from 1 Oct 2007. For savings see the note to s 331.
341 Civil remedies for breach of s 330	Repealed by CA 2006, as from 1 Oct 2007. For savings see the note to s 331.
342 Criminal penalties for breach of s 330	Repealed by CA 2006, as from 1 Oct 2007. For savings see the note to s 331.
343 Record of transactions not disclosed in company accounts	Repealed by CA 2006, as from 6 Apr 2007.
344 Exceptions from s 343	Repealed by CA 2006, as from 6 Apr 2007.
345 Power to increase financial limits	Repealed by CA 2006, as from 1 Oct 2007.
346 "Connected persons", etc	Repealed by CA 2006, as from 1 Oct 2007. Savings: see CO No 3, Sch 3, para 50 which provides that the repeal of this section (and Sch 13) does not affect: (a) s 317(3)(b) (directors to disclose interest in contracts); (b) ss 7E and 7F(3) of the Industrial and Provident Societies Act 1965 (transactions with committee members: whether person "connected with" committee member or "associated with" society); (c) s 96B(2)(a) of FSMA 2000 (disclosure rules: responsibility for compliance: meaning of person connected with person having managerial responsibilities within an issuer).
347 Transactions under foreign law	Repealed by CA 2006, as from 1 Oct 2007.

[PART XA CONTROL OF POLITICAL DONATIONS

[5.11]
347A–347K

NOTES

This Part has been repealed as follows:

347A Introductory provisions	Repealed by CA 2006, as from 1 Oct 2007. Savings: see CO No 3, Sch 3, para 41 which provides that this Part continues to apply to donations or expenditure in relation to which the relevant time, as defined in s 347A(10), is before 1 Oct 2007.
347B Exemptions	Repealed by CA 2006, as from 1 Oct 2007. For savings see the note to s 347A.
347C Prohibition on donations and political expenditure by companies	Repealed by CA 2006, as from 1 Oct 2007. For savings see the note to s 347A.
347D Special rules for subsidiaries	Repealed by CA 2006, as from 1 Oct 2007. For savings see the note to s 347A.
347E Special rule for parent company of non-GB subsidiary undertaking	Repealed by CA 2006, as from 1 Oct 2007. For savings see the note to s 347A.
347F Remedies for breach of prohibitions on company donations etc	Repealed by CA 2006, as from 1 Oct 2007. For savings see the note to s 347A.
347G Remedies for unauthorised donation or expenditure by non-GB subsidiary	Repealed by CA 2006, as from 1 Oct 2007. For savings see the note to s 347A.
347H Exemption of directors from liability in respect of unauthorised donation or expenditure	Repealed by CA 2006, as from 1 Oct 2007. For savings see the note to s 347A.

347I Enforcement of directors' liabilities by shareholder action	Repealed by CA 2006, as from 1 Oct 2007. For savings see the note to s 347A.
347J Costs of shareholder action	Repealed by CA 2006, as from 1 Oct 2007. For savings see the note to s 347A.
347K Information for purposes of shareholder action	Repealed by CA 2006, as from 1 Oct 2007. For savings see the note to s 347A.

PART XI COMPANY ADMINISTRATION AND PROCEDURE

[5.12]
348–394A

NOTES
This Part has been repealed as follows:

348 Company name to appear outside place of business	Repealed by CA 2006, as from 1 Oct 2008.
349 Company's name to appear in its correspondence, etc	Repealed by CA 2006, as from 1 Oct 2008.
350 Company seal	Repealed by CA 2006, as from 1 Oct 2009.
351 Particulars in correspondence etc	Repealed by CA 2006, as from 1 Oct 2008.
352 Obligation to keep and enter up register	Repealed by CA 2006, as from 6 Apr 2008 (in part), and as from 1 Oct 2009 (otherwise).
352A Statement that company has only one member	Repealed by CA 2006, as from 1 Oct 2009.
353 Location of register	Repealed by CA 2006, as from 1 Oct 2009.
354 Index of members	Repealed by CA 2006, as from 1 Oct 2009.
355 Entries in register in relation to share warrants	Repealed by CA 2006, as from 1 Oct 2009.
356 Inspection of register and index	Repealed by CA 2006, as from 1 Oct 2007. Savings: see CO No 3, Sch 3, para 2, which provides that this section and s 357 continue to apply to requests made before 1 Oct 2007 or after that date to a company that is so obliged.
357 Non-compliance with ss 353, 354, 356; agent's default	Repealed by CA 2006, as from 1 Oct 2007. For savings see the note to s 356.
358 Power to close register	Repealed by CA 2006, as from 1 Oct 2009.
359 Power of court to rectify register	Repealed by CA 2006, as from 1 Oct 2009.
360 Trusts not to be entered on register in England and Wales	Repealed by CA 2006, as from 1 Oct 2009.
361 Register to be evidence	Repealed by CA 2006, as from 1 Oct 2009.
362 Overseas branch registers	Repealed by CA 2006, as from 1 Oct 2009.
363 Duty to deliver annual returns	Repealed by CA 2006, as from 1 Oct 2009. Savings: CO No 8, Sch 2, para 81 provides that ss 363–365 continue to apply to annual returns made up to a date before 1 Oct 2009.
364 Contents of annual return: general	Repealed by CA 2006, as from 1 Oct 2009. For savings see the note to s 363.
364A Contents of annual return: particulars of share capital and shareholders	Repealed by CA 2006, as from 1 Oct 2009. For savings see the note to s 363.
364B Contents of annual return: information about shareholders: non-traded companies	Repealed by CA 2006, as from 1 Oct 2009. For savings see the note to s 363.
364C Contents of annual return: information about shareholders: traded companies	Repealed by CA 2006, as from 1 Oct 2009. For savings see the note to s 363.
364D Contents of annual return: information about shareholders: supplementary	Repealed by CA 2006, as from 1 Oct 2009. For savings see the note to s 363.
365 Supplementary provisions: regulations and interpretation	Repealed by CA 2006, as from 1 Oct 2009. For savings see the note to s 363.
366 Annual general meeting	Repealed by CA 2006, as from 1 Oct 2007. Savings: CO No 3, Sch 3, paras 22–40 make a variety of savings and transitional provisions in relation to the repeal of Chapter IV (ss 366–383) and the commencement of Part 13 of CA 2006 (Resolutions and Meetings). With regard to this section, see also CO No 3, Sch 3, para 10.
366A Election by private company to dispense with annual general meeting	Repealed by CA 2006, as from 20 Jan 2007 (in part), and as from 1 Oct 2007 (otherwise). For savings see the note to s 366.
367 Secretary of State's power to call meeting in default	Repealed by CA 2006, as from 1 Oct 2007. For savings see the note to s 366.

368 Extraordinary general meeting on members' requisition	Repealed by CA 2006, as from 1 Oct 2007. For savings see the note to s 366. See also CA 2006, s 972 at **[1.1134]**.
369 Length of notice for calling meetings	Repealed by CA 2006, as from 20 Jan 2007 (in part), and as from 1 Oct 2007 (otherwise). For savings see the note to s 366. See also CO No 1, Sch 5, Pt 2, paras 4, 5.
370 General provisions as to meetings and votes	Repealed by CA 2006, as from 1 Oct 2007. For savings see the note to s 366.
370A Quorum at meetings of the sole member	Repealed by CA 2006, as from 1 Oct 2007. For savings see the note to s 366.
371 Power of court to order meeting	Repealed by CA 2006, as from 1 Oct 2007. For savings see the note to s 366.
372 Proxies	Repealed by CA 2006, as from 20 Jan 2007 (in part), and as from 1 Oct 2007 (otherwise). For savings see the note to s 366.
373 Right to demand a poll	Repealed by CA 2006, as from 1 Oct 2007. For savings see the note to s 366.
374 Voting on a poll	Repealed by CA 2006, as from 1 Oct 2007. For savings see the note to s 366.
375 Representation of corporations at meetings	Repealed by CA 2006, as from 1 Oct 2007. For savings see the note to s 366.
376 Circulation of members' resolutions	Repealed by CA 2006, as from 1 Oct 2007. For savings see the note to s 366.
377 In certain cases, compliance with s 376 not required	Repealed by CA 2006, as from 1 Oct 2007. For savings see the note to s 366.
378 Extraordinary and special resolutions	Repealed by CA 2006, as from 1 Oct 2007. For savings see the note to s 366.
379 Resolution requiring special notice	Repealed by CA 2006, as from 1 Oct 2007. For savings see the note to s 366.
379A Elective resolution of private company	Repealed by CA 2006, as from 20 Jan 2007 (in part) and 1 Oct 2007 (in part), and as from 1 Oct 2009 (otherwise). For savings see the note to s 366.
380 Registration, etc of resolutions and agreements	Repealed by CA 2006, as from 1 Oct 2007 (in part) and 6 Apr 2008 (in part), and as from 1 Oct 2009 (otherwise). For savings see the note to s 366. Note also that CO No 8, Sch 2, para 14 provides that sub-ss (2), (6), (7) continue to apply to copies issued before 1 Oct 2009.
381 Resolution passed at adjourned meeting	Repealed by CA 2006, as from 1 Oct 2007. For savings see the note to s 366.
381A Written resolutions of private companies	Repealed by CA 2006, as from 1 Oct 2007. For savings see the note to s 366.
381B Duty to notify auditors of proposed written resolution	Repealed by CA 2006, as from 1 Oct 2007. For savings see the note to s 366.
381C Written resolutions: supplementary provisions	Repealed by CA 2006, as from 1 Oct 2007. For savings see the note to s 366.
382 Minutes of meetings	Repealed by CA 2006, as from 1 Oct 2007. For savings see the note to s 366. Note also CO No 3, Sch 3, para 19 which provides that this section continues to apply to meetings of directors held before 1 Oct 2007.
382A Recording of written resolutions	Repealed by CA 2006, as from 1 Oct 2007. For savings see the note to s 366.
382B Recording of decisions by the sole member	Repealed by CA 2006, as from 1 Oct 2007. For savings see the note to s 366.
383 Inspection of minute books	Repealed by CA 2006, as from 1 Oct 2007. For savings see the note to s 366.
384 Duty to appoint auditors	Repealed by CA 2006, as from 1 Oct 2007 (in so far as relating to private companies), and as from 6 Apr 2008 (otherwise). Savings: see CO No 3, Sch 3, para 44 which provides that ss 384–388A continue to apply in relation to the appointment of auditors of private companies for financial years beginning before 1 Oct 2007. See also CO No 5, Sch 4, Pt 1, para 10 which provides that ss 384, 385, 387, 388(1), (3), (4) continue to apply to appointments by public companies for financial years beginning before 6 Apr 2008.
385 Appointment at general meeting at which accounts laid	Repealed by CA 2006, as from 1 Oct 2007 (in so far as relating to private companies), and as from 6 Apr 2008 (otherwise). For savings see the note to s 384.
385A Appointment by private company which is not obliged to lay accounts	Repealed by CA 2006, as from 1 Oct 2007. For savings see the first part of the note to s 384.
386 Election by private company to dispense with annual appointment	Repealed by CA 2006, as from 1 Oct 2007. For savings see the first part of the note to s 384. See also CO No 3, Sch 3, para 45 which provides that the repeal of this section does not affect the continued operation of the resolution, which shall continue to have effect until (a) it is revoked or superseded by a further resolution, (b) the auditors to which it applies cease to hold office, or (c) it otherwise ceases to have effect in accordance with its terms.
387 Appointment by Secretary of State in default of appointment by	Repealed by CA 2006, as from 1 Oct 2007 (in so far as relating to private companies), and as from 6 Apr 2008 (otherwise). For savings see the note to

company	s 384.
388 Filling of casual vacancies	Repealed by CA 2006, as from 1 Oct 2007 (in so far as relating to private companies), and as from 6 Apr 2008 (otherwise). For savings see the note to s 384. See also CO No 5, Sch 4, Pt 1, para 17 which provides that sub-s (2) continues to apply where the vacancy occurred before 6 Apr 2008.
388A Certain companies exempt from obligation to appoint auditors	Repealed by CA 2006, as from 1 Oct 2007 (in so far as relating to private companies), and as from 6 Apr 2008 (otherwise). For savings see the first part of the note to s 384.
389 Qualification for appointment as auditor	Repealed by CA 1989, as from 1 Oct 1991.
389A Rights to information	Repealed by CA 2006, as from 6 Apr 2008. Savings: this section and s 389B continue to apply to financial years beginning before 6 Apr 2008 (see CO No 5, Sch 4, Pt 1, para 12(2)).
389B Offences relating to the provision of information to auditors	Repealed by CA 2006, as from 6 Apr 2008. For savings see the note to s 389A.
390 Right to attend company meetings, &c	Repealed by CA 2006, as from 6 Apr 2008. Savings: this section continues to apply to auditors appointed before 6 Apr 2008 (see CO No 5, Sch 4, Pt 1, para 12(4)).
390A Remuneration of auditors	Repealed by CA 2006, as from 6 Apr 2008. Savings: see CO No 5, Sch 4, Pt 1, para 11 which provides that this section and s 390B continue to apply to auditors appointed for financial years beginning before 6 Apr 2008, and that the repeal of this section does not affect the operation of any such resolution as is mentioned in Sch 3, para 45 to CO No 3.
390B Disclosure of services provided by auditors or associates and related remuneration	Repealed by CA 2006, as from 6 Apr 2008. For savings see the note to s 390A.
391 Removal of auditors	Repealed by CA 2006, as from 6 Apr 2008. Savings: see CO No 5, Sch 4, Pt 1, para 13 which provides that ss 391, 391A continue to apply where notice of the intended resolution is given to the company before 6 Apr 2008.
391A Rights of auditors who are removed or not re-appointed	Repealed by CA 2006, as from 6 Apr 2008. For savings see the note to s 391. Note also that this section continues to apply to appointments for financial years beginning before that date; see CO No 5, Sch 4, Pt 1, para 14.
392 Resignation of auditors	Repealed by CA 2006, as from 6 Apr 2008. Savings: see CO No 5, Sch 4, Pt 1, para 15 which provides that ss 392, 392A continue to apply to resignations occurring before 6 Apr 2008.
392A Rights of resigning auditors	Repealed by CA 2006, as from 6 Apr 2008. For savings see the note to s 392.
393 Termination of appointment of auditors not appointed annually	Repealed by CA 2006, as from 1 Oct 2007.
394 Statement by person ceasing to hold office as auditor	Repealed by CA 2006, as from 6 Apr 2008. Savings: see CO No 5, Sch 4, Pt 1, para 16 which provides that ss 394, 394A continue to apply where the auditor ceases to hold office before 6 Apr 2008.
394A Offences of failing to comply with s 394	Repealed by CA 2006, as from 6 Apr 2008. For savings see the note to s 394.

PART XII REGISTRATION OF CHARGES

[5.13]
395–424

NOTES

This Part has been repealed as follows:

395 Certain charges void if not registered	Repealed by CA 2006, as from 1 Oct 2009. Savings and transitional provisions: in connection with the repeal of this Part, see CO No 8, Sch 2, paras 82–87 (Company charges) and SI 2009/1917, Schedule (Registration of charges; transitional provisions and savings) at **[4.354]**.
396 Charges which have to be registered	Repealed by CA 2006, as from 1 Oct 2009. For savings see the note to s 395.
397 Formalities of registration (debentures)	Repealed by CA 2006, as from 1 Oct 2009. For savings see the note to s 395.
398 Verification of charge on property outside United Kingdom	Repealed by CA 2006, as from 1 Oct 2009. For savings see the note to s 395.
399 Company's duty to register charges it creates	Repealed by CA 2006, as from 1 Oct 2009. For savings see the note to s 395.
400 Charges existing on property acquired	Repealed by CA 2006, as from 1 Oct 2009. For savings see the note to s 395.
401 Register of charges to be kept by	Repealed by CA 2006, as from 1 Oct 2009. For savings see the note to s 395.

registrar of companies	
402 Endorsement of certificate on debentures	Repealed by CA 2006, as from 1 Oct 2009. For savings see the note to s 395.
403 Entries of satisfaction and release	Repealed by CA 2006, as from 1 Oct 2009. For savings see the note to s 395.
404 Rectification of register of charges	Repealed by CA 2006, as from 1 Oct 2009. For savings see the note to s 395.
405 Registration of enforcement of security	Repealed by CA 2006, as from 1 Oct 2009. For savings see the note to s 395.
406 Companies to keep copies of instruments creating charges	Repealed by CA 2006, as from 1 Oct 2009. For savings see the note to s 395.
407 Company's register of charges	Repealed by CA 2006, as from 1 Oct 2009. For savings see the note to s 395.
408 Right to inspect instruments which create charges, etc	Repealed by CA 2006, as from 1 Oct 2009. For savings see the note to s 395.
409 Charges on property in England and Wales created by overseas company	Repealed by CA 2006, as from 1 Oct 2009. For savings see the note to s 395.
410 Charges void unless registered	Repealed by CA 2006, as from 1 Oct 2009. For savings see the note to s 395.
411 Charges on property outside United Kingdom	Repealed by CA 2006, as from 1 Oct 2009. For savings see the note to s 395.
412 Negotiable instrument to secure book debts	Repealed by CA 2006, as from 1 Oct 2009. For savings see the note to s 395.
413 Charges associated with debentures	Repealed by CA 2006, as from 1 Oct 2009. For savings see the note to s 395.
414 Charge by way of ex facie absolute disposition, etc	Repealed by CA 2006, as from 1 Oct 2009. For savings see the note to s 395.
415 Company's duty to register charges created by it	Repealed by CA 2006, as from 1 Oct 2009. For savings see the note to s 395.
416 Duty to register charges existing on property acquired	Repealed by CA 2006, as from 1 Oct 2009. For savings see the note to s 395.
417 Register of charges to be kept by registrar of companies	Repealed by CA 2006, as from 1 Oct 2009. For savings see the note to s 395.
418 Certificate of registration to be issued	Repealed by CA 2006, as from 1 Oct 2009. For savings see the note to s 395.
419 Entries of satisfaction and relief	Repealed by CA 2006, as from 1 Oct 2009. For savings see the note to s 395.
420 Rectification of register	Repealed by CA 2006, as from 1 Oct 2009. For savings see the note to s 395.
421 Copies of instruments creating charges to be kept by company	Repealed by CA 2006, as from 1 Oct 2009. For savings see the note to s 395.
422 Company's register of charges	Repealed by CA 2006, as from 1 Oct 2009. For savings see the note to s 395.
423 Right to inspect copies of instruments, and company's register	Repealed by CA 2006, as from 1 Oct 2009. For savings see the note to s 395.
424 Extension of Chapter II	Repealed by CA 2006, as from 1 Oct 2009. For savings see the note to s 395.

PART XIII ARRANGEMENTS AND RECONSTRUCTIONS

[5.14]
425–427A

NOTES

This Part has been repealed as follows:

425 Power of company to compromise with creditors and members	Repealed by CA 2006, as from 6 Apr 2008. Savings and transitional provisions: see CO No 5, Sch 4, Pt 1, para 36 which provides that (i) s 425(3), (4) continue to apply to orders made before 6 Apr 2008; (ii) s 901 of CA 2006 (obligations of company with respect to articles etc) applies to orders of the court made on or after 6 Apr 2008, including orders made under s 425(2).
426 Information as to compromise to be circulated	Repealed by CA 2006, as from 6 Apr 2008.
427 Provisions for facilitating company reconstruction or amalgamation	Repealed by CA 2006, as from 6 Apr 2008.
427A Application of ss 425–427 to mergers and divisions of public companies	Repealed by CA 2006, as from 6 Apr 2008.

PART XIIIA TAKEOVER OFFERS

[5.15]
428–430F

NOTES

This Part has been repealed as follows:

428 Takeover offers	Repealed by CA 2006, as from 6 Apr 2007. Savings and transitional provisions: for savings regarding the operation of this Part in relation to a takeover offer where the date of the offer (within the meaning of s 428(1)) was before 6 Apr 2007, see CO No 2, Sch 6, para 1. Note also, that this Part was disapplied where a takeover offer (where the date of the offer was on or after 20 May 2006) was made for a company that had securities carrying voting rights admitted to trading on a regulated market; see SI 2006/1183, regs 29, 30. In such circumstances, Sch 2 to those Regulations applied. The 2006 Regulations were revoked, as from 6 Apr 2007, by SI 2007/1093, subject to certain savings in relation to (i) takeover offers (where the date of offer is before 6 Apr 2007) and (ii) offences committed before that date (see Sch 6, paras 2, 3 to the 2007 Order).
429 Right of offeror to buy out minority shareholders	Repealed by CA 2006, as from 6 Apr 2007. For savings see the note to s 428.
430 Effect of notice under s 429	Repealed by CA 2006, as from 6 Apr 2007. For savings see the note to s 428.
430A Right of minority shareholder to be bought out by offeror	Repealed by CA 2006, as from 6 Apr 2007. For savings see the note to s 428.
430B Effect of requirement under s 430A	Repealed by CA 2006, as from 6 Apr 2007. For savings see the note to s 428.
430C Applications to the court	Repealed by CA 2006, as from 6 Apr 2007. For savings see the note to s 428.
430D Joint offers	Repealed by CA 2006, as from 6 Apr 2007. For savings see the note to s 428.
430E Associates	Repealed by CA 2006, as from 6 Apr 2007. For savings see the note to s 428.
430F Convertible securities	Repealed by CA 2006, as from 6 Apr 2007. For savings see the note to s 428.

PART XIV INVESTIGATION OF COMPANIES AND THEIR AFFAIRS; REQUISITION OF DOCUMENTS

NOTES

Transitional provisions: for transitional provisions in relation to the extension of this Part (and Part XV) to Northern Ireland (by CA 2006, s 1284), see CO No 8, Sch 2, para 114.

Note also that the Companies (Audit, Investigations and Community Enterprise) Act 2004 (Commencement) and Companies Act 1989 (Commencement No 18) Order 2004, SI 2004/3322, arts 6–13 provided for various transitional provisions relating to company investigations in connection with the amendments made to this Part by the Companies (Audit, Investigations and Community Enterprise) Act 2004. The Act came into force for all purposes on 1 October 2005 and those transitional provisions are now regarded as spent.

Appointment and functions of inspectors

[5.16]
431 Investigation of a company on its own application or that of its members

(1) The Secretary of State may appoint one or more competent inspectors to investigate the affairs of a company and to [report the result of their investigations to him].

(2) The appointment may be made—

(a) in the case of a company having a share capital, on the application either of not less than 200 members or of members holding not less than one-tenth of the shares issued [(excluding any shares held as treasury shares)],

(b) in the case of a company not having a share capital, on the application of not less than one-fifth in number of the persons on the company's register of members, and

(c) in any case, on application of the company.

(3) The application shall be supported by such evidence as the Secretary of State may require for the purpose of showing that the applicant or applicants have good reason for requiring the investigation.

(4) The Secretary of State may, before appointing inspectors, require the applicant or applicants to give security, to an amount not exceeding £5,000, or such other sum as he may by order specify, for payment of the costs of the investigation.

An order under this subsection shall be made by statutory instrument subject to annulment in pursuance of a resolution of either House of Parliament.

NOTES

Sub-s (1): words in square brackets substituted by the Companies Act 2006, s 1035(2), as from 1 October 2007, with effect where an inspector is appointed under a provision of Pt XIV of this Act on or after that date.

Sub-s (2): words in square brackets in para (a) inserted by the Companies (Acquisition of Own Shares) (Treasury Shares) Regulations 2003, SI 2003/1116, reg 4, Schedule, para 28, as from 1 December 2003.

[5.17]
432 Other company investigations

(1) The Secretary of State shall appoint one or more competent inspectors to investigate the affairs of a company and [report the result of their investigations to him], if the court by order declares that its affairs ought to be so investigated.

(2) The Secretary of State may make such an appointment if it appears to him that there are circumstances suggesting—

(a) that the company's affairs are being or have been conducted with intent to defraud its creditors or the creditors of any other person, or otherwise for a fraudulent or unlawful purpose, or in a manner which is unfairly prejudicial to some part of its members, or

(b) that any actual or proposed act or omission of the company (including an act or omission on its behalf) is or would be so prejudicial, or that the company was formed for any fraudulent or unlawful purpose, or

(c) that persons concerned with the company's formation or the management of its affairs have in connection therewith been guilty of fraud, misfeasance or other misconduct towards it or towards its members, or

(d) that the company's members have not been given all the information with respect to its affairs which they might reasonably expect.

[(2A) Inspectors may be appointed under subsection (2) on terms that any report they may make is not for publication; and in such a case, the provisions of section 437(3) (availability and publication of inspectors' reports) do not apply.]

(3) Subsections (1) and (2) are without prejudice to the powers of the Secretary of State under section 431; and the power conferred by subsection (2) is exercisable with respect to a body corporate notwithstanding that it is in course of being voluntarily wound up.

(4) The reference in subsection (2)(a) to a company's members includes any person who is not a member but to whom shares in the company have been transferred or transmitted by operation of law.

NOTES

Sub-s (1): words in square brackets substituted by the Companies Act 2006, s 1035(3), as from 1 October 2007, with effect where an inspector is appointed under a provision of Pt XIV of this Act on or after that date.

Sub-s (2A): inserted by CA 1989, s 55, as from 21 February 1990.

[5.18]

433 Inspectors' powers during investigation

(1) If inspectors appointed under section 431 or 432 to investigate the affairs of a company think it necessary for the purposes of their investigation to investigate also the affairs of another body corporate which is or at any relevant time has been the company's subsidiary or holding company, or a subsidiary of its holding company or a holding company of its subsidiary, they have power to do so; and they shall report on the affairs of the other body corporate so far as they think that the results of their investigation of its affairs are relevant to the investigation of the affairs of the company first mentioned above.

(2) . . .

NOTES

Sub-s (2): repealed by FSA 1986, ss 182, 212(3), Sch 13, para 7, Sch 17, Pt I, as from 27 November 1986.

[5.19]

434 Production of documents and evidence to inspectors

(1) When inspectors are appointed under section 431 or 432, it is the duty of all officers and agents of the company, and of all officers and agents of any other body corporate whose affairs are investigated under section 433(1)—

(a) to produce to the inspectors all [documents] of or relating to the company or, as the case may be, the other body corporate which are in their custody or power,

(b) to attend before the inspectors when required to do so, and

(c) otherwise to give the inspectors all assistance in connection with the investigation which they are reasonably able to give.

[(2) If the inspectors consider that an officer or agent of the company or other body corporate, or any other person, is or may be in possession of information relating to a matter which they believe to be relevant to the investigation, they may require him—

(a) to produce to them any documents in his custody or power relating to that matter,

(b) to attend before them, and

(c) otherwise to give them all assistance in connection with the investigation which he is reasonably able to give;

and it is that person's duty to comply with the requirement.

(3) An inspector may for the purposes of the investigation examine any person on oath, and may administer an oath accordingly.]

(4) In this section a reference to officers or to agents includes past, as well as present, officers or agents (as the case may be); and "agents", in relation to a company or other body corporate, includes its bankers and solicitors and persons employed by it as auditors, whether these persons are or are not officers of the company or other body corporate.

(5) An answer given by a person to a question put to him in exercise of powers conferred by this section (whether as it has effect in relation to an investigation under any of sections 431 to 433, or as applied by any other section in this Part) may be used in evidence against him.

[(5A) However, in criminal proceedings in which that person is charged with an offence to which this subsection applies—

(a) no evidence relating to the answer may be adduced, and

(b) no question relating to it may be asked,

by or on behalf of the prosecution, unless evidence relating to it is adduced, or a question relating to it is asked, in the proceedings by or on behalf of that person.

(5B) Subsection (5A) applies to any offence other than—

(a) an offence under section 2 or 5 of the Perjury Act 1911 (false statements made on oath otherwise than in judicial proceedings or made otherwise than on oath); or

(b) an offence under section 44(1) or (2) of the Criminal Law (Consolidation) (Scotland) Act 1995 (false statements made on oath or otherwise than on oath)[; or

(c) an offence under Article 7 or 10 of the Perjury (Northern Ireland) Order 1979 (false statements made on oath otherwise than in judicial proceedings or made otherwise than on oath).]]

[(6) In this section "document" includes information recorded in any form.

(7) The power under this section to require production of a document includes power, in the case of a document not in hard copy form, to require the production of a copy of the document—

(a) in hard copy form, or

(b) in a form from which a hard copy can be readily obtained.

(8) An inspector may take copies of or extracts from a document produced in pursuance of this section.]

NOTES

Sub-s (1): word in square brackets substituted by CA 1989, s 56(1), (2), as from 21 February 1990.

Sub-ss (2), (3): substituted by CA 1989, s 56(1), (3), (4), as from 21 February 1990.

Sub-s (5A): inserted, together with sub-s (5B), by the Youth Justice and Criminal Evidence Act 1999, s 59, Sch 3, paras 4, 5, as from 14 April 2000 (in relation to England and Wales), and 1 January 2001 (in relation to Scotland).

Sub-s (5B): inserted as noted above. Para (c) (and the word immediately preceding it) inserted by the Companies Act 2006 (Consequential Amendments, Transitional Provisions and Savings) Order 2009, SI 2009/1941, art 2(1), Sch 1, para 57(1), (2), as from 1 October 2009.

Sub-ss (6)–(8): substituted (for the original sub-s (6) as added by CA 1989, s 56(1), (5), as from 21 February 1990) by the Companies Act 2006, s 1038(1), as from 1 October 2007, with effect where an inspector is appointed under a provision of Pt XIV of this Act on or after that date.

Solicitors: the reference to a solicitor in sub-s (4) includes a reference to a recognised body within the meaning of the Administration of Justice Act 1985, s 9; see the Solicitors' Recognised Bodies Order 1991, SI 1991/2684, arts 2–5, Sch 1.

435 (*Repealed by CA 1989, s 212, Sch 24, as from 21 February 1990.*)

[5.20]

436 Obstruction of inspectors treated as contempt of court

[(1) If any person—

(a) fails to comply with section 434(1)(a) or (c),

(b) refuses to comply with a requirement under section 434(1)(b) or (2), or

(c) refuses to answer any question put to him by the inspectors for the purposes of the investigation,

the inspectors may certify that fact in writing to the court.]

(3) The court may thereupon enquire into the case; and, after hearing any witnesses who may be produced against or on behalf of the alleged offender and after hearing any statement which may be offered in defence, the court may punish the offender in like manner as if he had been guilty of contempt of the court.

NOTES

Sub-s (1): substituted (for the original sub-ss (1), (2)) by CA 1989, s 56(6), as from 21 February 1990.

[5.21]

437 Inspectors' reports

(1) The inspectors may, and if so directed by the Secretary of State shall, make interim reports to the Secretary of State, and on the conclusion of their investigation shall make a final report to him.

. . .

[(1A) Any persons who have been appointed under section 431 or 432 may at any time and, if the Secretary of State directs them to do so, shall inform him of any matters coming to their knowledge as a result of their investigations.]

[(1B), (1C) . . .]

(2) If the inspectors were appointed under section 432 in pursuance of an order of the court, the Secretary of State shall furnish a copy of any report of theirs to the court.

[(2A) If the company is registered under the Companies Act 2006 in Northern Ireland, the Secretary of State must send a copy of any interim or final report by the inspectors to the Department of Enterprise, Trade and Investment in Northern Ireland.]

(3) In any case the Secretary of State may, if he thinks fit—

(a) forward a copy of any report made by the inspectors to the company's registered office,

(b) furnish a copy on request and on payment of the prescribed fee to—

(i) any member of the company or other body corporate which is the subject of the report,

(ii) any person whose conduct is referred to in the report,

(iii) the auditors of that company or body corporate,

(iv) the applicants for the investigation,

(v) any other person whose financial interests appear to the Secretary of State to be affected by the matters dealt with in the report, whether as a creditor of the company or body corporate, or otherwise, and

(c) cause any such report to be printed and published.

NOTES

Sub-s (1): words omitted repealed by the Companies Act 2006, ss 1035(4)(a) 1295, Sch 16, as from 1 October 2007, with effect where an inspector is appointed under a provision of Pt XIV of this Act on or after that date.

Sub-s (1A): inserted by FSA 1986, s 182, Sch 13, para 7, as from 15 November 1986 (for the purposes of anything done or which may be done under, or by virtue of, any provision brought into force by the Financial Services Act 1986 (Commencement No 1) Order 1986, SI 1986/1940), and as from 27 November 1986 (otherwise).

Sub-ss (1B), (1C): originally inserted by CA 1989, s 57, as from 21 February 1990. Subsequently repealed by the Companies Act 2006, ss 1035(4)(b) 1295, Sch 16, as from 1 October 2007, with effect where an inspector is appointed under a provision of Pt XIV of this Act on or after that date.

Sub-s (2A): inserted by the Companies Act 2006 (Consequential Amendments, Transitional Provisions and Savings) Order 2009, SI 2009/1941, art 2(1), Sch 1, para 57(1), (3), as from 1 October 2009.

Fees: see the Companies (Inspectors' Reports) (Fees) Regulations 1981, SI 1981/1686.

438 *(Repealed by the Companies Act 2006, ss 1176(1), (4), 1295, Sch 16, as from 6 April 2007, except in relation to proceedings brought under this section before that date.)*

[5.22]
439 Expenses of investigating a company's affairs

[(1) The expenses of an investigation under any of the powers conferred by this Part shall be defrayed in the first instance by the Secretary of State, but he may recover those expenses from the persons liable in accordance with this section.

There shall be treated as expenses of the investigation, in particular, such reasonable sums as the Secretary of State may determine in respect of general staff costs and overheads.]

(2) A person who is convicted on a prosecution instituted as a result of the investigation, . . . may in the same proceedings be ordered to pay those expenses to such extent as may be specified in the order.

(3) . . .

(4) A body corporate dealt with by [an inspectors' report], where the inspectors were appointed otherwise than of the Secretary of State's own motion, is liable except where it was the applicant for the investigation, and except so far as the Secretary of State otherwise directs.

[(5) Where inspectors were appointed—

(a) under section 431, or

(b) on an application under section 442(3),

the applicant or applicants for the investigation is or are liable to such extent (if any) as the Secretary of State may direct.]

(6) The report of inspectors appointed otherwise than of the Secretary of State's own motion may, if they think fit, and shall if the Secretary of State so directs, include a recommendation as to the directions (if any) which they think appropriate, in the light of their investigation, to be given under subsection (4) or (5) of this section.

(7) . . .

(8) Any liability to repay the Secretary of State imposed by [subsection (2)] above is (subject to satisfaction of his right to repayment) a liability also to indemnify all persons against liability under subsections (4) and (5); . . .

(9) A person liable under any one of those subsections is entitled to contribution from any other person liable under the same subsection, according to the amount of their respective liabilities under it.

(10) Expenses to be defrayed by the Secretary of State under this section shall, so far as not recovered under it, be paid out of money provided by Parliament.

NOTES

Sub-ss (1), (5): substituted by CA 1989, s 59(1), (2), (4), as from 21 February 1990.

Sub-s (2): words omitted repealed by the Companies Act 2006, ss 1176(2)(a), (4), 1295, Sch 16, as from 6 April 2007, except in relation to proceedings brought under s 438 before that date.

Sub-ss (3), (7): repealed by the Companies Act 2006, ss 1176(2)(b), (4), 1295, Sch 16, as from 6 April 2007, except in relation to proceedings brought under s 438 before that date.

Sub-s (4): words in square brackets substituted by CA 1989, s 59(1), (3), as from 21 February 1990.

Sub-s (8): words in square brackets substituted, and words omitted repealed, by the Companies Act 2006, ss 1176(2)(c), (4), 1295, Sch 16, as from 6 April 2007, except in relation to proceedings brought under s 438 before that date.

440 *(Repealed by CA 1989, ss 60(1), 212, Sch 24, as from 21 February 1990.)*

[5.23]
441 Inspectors' report to be evidence

(1) A copy of any report of inspectors appointed under [this Part], certified by the Secretary of State to be a true copy, is admissible in any legal proceedings as evidence of the opinion of the inspectors in relation to any matter contained in the report [and, in proceedings on an application under [section 8 of the Company Directors Disqualification Act 1986] [or Article 11 of the Company Directors Disqualification (Northern Ireland) Order 2002], as evidence of any fact stated therein].

(2) A document purporting to be such a certificate as is mentioned above shall be received in evidence and be deemed to be such a certificate, unless the contrary is proved.

NOTES

Sub-s (1): words in first pair of square brackets substituted by CA 1989, s 61, as from 21 February 1990. Words in second (outer) pair of square brackets added by the Insolvency Act 1985, s 109, Sch 6, para 3, as from 29 December 1986. Words in third (inner) pair of square brackets substituted by the Insolvency Act 1986, s 439(1), Sch 13, Pt I, as from 29 December 1986. Words in fourth (inner) pair of square brackets inserted by the Companies Act 2006 (Consequential Amendments, Transitional Provisions and Savings) Order 2009, SI 2009/1941, art 2(1), Sch 1, para 57(1), (4), as from 1 October 2009.

Other powers of investigation available to the Secretary of State

[5.24]
442 Power to investigate company ownership

(1) Where it appears to the Secretary of State that there is good reason to do so, he may appoint one or more competent inspectors to investigate and report on the membership of any company, and otherwise with respect to the company, for the purpose of determining the true persons who are or have been financially interested in the success or failure (real or apparent) of the company or able to control or materially to influence its policy.

(2) . . .

[(3) If an application for investigation under this section with respect to particular shares or debentures of a company is made to the Secretary of State by members of the company, and the number of applicants or the amount of shares held by them is not less than that required for an application for the appointment of inspectors under section 431(2)(a) or (b), then, subject to the following provisions, the Secretary of State shall appoint inspectors to conduct the investigation applied for.

(3A) The Secretary of State shall not appoint inspectors if he is satisfied that the application is vexatious; and where inspectors are appointed their terms of appointment shall exclude any matter in so far as the Secretary of State is satisfied that it is unreasonable for it to be investigated.

(3B) The Secretary of State may, before appointing inspectors, require the applicant or applicants to give security, to an amount not exceeding £5,000, or such other sum as he may by order specify, for payment of the costs of the investigation.

An order under this subsection shall be made by statutory instrument which shall be subject to annulment in pursuance of a resolution of either House of Parliament.

(3C) If on an application under subsection (3) it appears to the Secretary of State that the powers conferred by section 444 are sufficient for the purposes of investigating the matters which inspectors would be appointed to investigate, he may instead conduct the investigation under that section.]

(4) Subject to the terms of their appointment, the inspectors' powers extend to the investigation of any circumstances suggesting the existence of an arrangement or understanding which, though not legally binding, is or was observed or likely to be observed in practice and which is relevant to the purposes of the investigation.

NOTES

Sub-s (2): repealed by the Companies Act 2006, ss 1035(5), 1295, Sch 16, as from 1 October 2007, with effect where an inspector is appointed under a provision of Pt XIV of this Act on or after that date.

Sub-ss (3), (3A)–(3C): substituted (for the original sub-s (3)) by CA 1989, s 62, as from 21 February 1990.

[5.25]

443 Provisions applicable on investigation under s 442

(1) For purposes of an investigation under section 442, sections 433(1), 434, 436 and 437 apply with the necessary modifications of references to the affairs of the company or to those of any other body corporate, subject however to the following subsections.

(2) Those sections apply to—

(a) all persons who are or have been, or whom the inspector has reasonable cause to believe to be or have been, financially interested in the success or failure or the apparent success or failure of the company or any other body corporate whose membership is investigated with that of the company, or able to control or materially influence its policy (including persons concerned only on behalf of others), and

(b) any other person whom the inspector has reasonable cause to believe possesses information relevant to the investigation,

as they apply in relation to officers and agents of the company or the other body corporate (as the case may be).

(3) If the Secretary of State is of opinion that there is good reason for not divulging any part of a report made by virtue of section 442 and this section, he may under section 437 disclose the report with the omission of that part; and he may cause to be kept by the registrar of companies a copy of the report with that part omitted or, in the case of any other such report, a copy of the whole report.

(4) . . .

NOTES

Sub-s (4): repealed by CA 1989, s 212, Sch 24, as from 21 February 1990.

[5.26]

444 Power to obtain information as to those interested in shares, etc

(1) If it appears to the Secretary of State that there is good reason to investigate the ownership of any shares in or debentures of a company and that it is unnecessary to appoint inspectors for the purpose, he may require any person whom he has reasonable cause to believe to have or to be able to obtain any information as to the present and past interests in those shares or debentures and the names and addresses of the persons interested and of any persons who act or have acted on their behalf in relation to the shares or debentures to give any such information to the Secretary of State.

(2) For this purpose a person is deemed to have an interest in shares or debentures if he has any right to acquire or dispose of them or of any interest in them, or to vote in respect of them, or if his consent is necessary for the exercise of any of the rights of other persons interested in them, or if other persons interested in them can be required, or are accustomed, to exercise their rights in accordance with his instructions.

(3) A person who fails to give information required of him under this section, or who in giving such information makes any statement which he knows to be false in a material particular, or recklessly makes any statement which is false in a material particular, [commits an offence].

[(4) A person guilty of an offence under this section is liable—

(a) on conviction on indictment, to imprisonment for a term not exceeding two years or a fine (or both);

(b) on summary conviction—

(i) in England and Wales, to imprisonment for a term not exceeding twelve months or to a fine not exceeding the statutory maximum (or both) and, for continued contravention, a daily default fine not exceeding [one-fiftieth of the greater of £5,000 or the amount corresponding to level 4 on the standard scale for summary offences];

(ii) in Scotland or Northern Ireland, to imprisonment for a term not exceeding six months, or to a fine not exceeding the statutory maximum (or both) and, for continued contravention, a daily default fine not exceeding one-fiftieth of the statutory maximum.]

NOTES

Sub-s (3): words in square brackets substituted by the Companies Act 2006, s 1124, Sch 3, para 1(1), as from 1 October 2007 (except in relation to offences committed before that date (see s 1133 of the 2006 Act at **[1.1303]**)).

Sub-s (4): added by the Companies Act 2006, s 1124, Sch 3, para 1(2), as from 1 October 2007 (except in relation to offences committed before that date (see s 1133 of the 2006 Act at **[1.1303]**)). Words in square brackets substituted by the Legal Aid, Sentencing and Punishment of Offenders Act 2012 (Fines on Summary Conviction) Regulations 2015, SI 2015/664, reg 3, Sch 3, Pt 1, para 3, as from 12 March 2015 (except in relation to (a) fines for offences committed before 12 March 2015, (b) the operation of restrictions on fines that may be imposed on a person aged under 18, or (c) fines that may be imposed on a person convicted by a magistrates' court who is to be sentenced as if convicted on indictment).

[5.27]

445 Power to impose restrictions on shares and debentures

(1) If in connection with an investigation under either section 442 or 444 it appears to the Secretary of State that there is difficulty in finding out the relevant facts about any shares (whether issued or to be issued), he may by order direct that the shares shall until further order be subject to the restrictions of Part XV of this Act.

[(1A) If the Secretary of State is satisfied that an order under subsection (1) may unfairly affect the rights of third parties in respect of shares then the Secretary of State, for the purpose of protecting such rights and subject to such terms as he thinks fit, may direct that such acts by such persons or descriptions of persons and for such purposes as may be set out in the order, shall not constitute a breach of the restrictions of Part XV of this Act.]

(2) This section, and Part XV in its application to orders under it, apply in relation to debentures as in relation to shares [save that subsection (1A) shall not so apply].

NOTES

Sub-s (1A): inserted by the Companies (Disclosure of Interests in Shares) (Orders imposing restrictions on shares) Regulations 1991, SI 1991/1646, reg 5(a), as from 18 July 1991.

Sub-s (2): words in square brackets added by SI 1991/1646, reg 5(b), as from 18 July 1991.

446 (*Repealed by the Companies Act 2006, s 1295, Sch 16, as from 1 October 2007.*)

[Powers of Secretary of State to give directions to inspectors

[5.28]

446A General powers to give directions

(1) In exercising his functions an inspector shall comply with any direction given to him by the Secretary of State under this section.

(2) The Secretary of State may give an inspector appointed under section 431, 432(2) or 442(1) a direction—

- (a) as to the subject matter of his investigation (whether by reference to a specified area of a company's operation, a specified transaction, a period of time or otherwise), or
- (b) which requires the inspector to take or not to take a specified step in his investigation.

(3) The Secretary of State may give an inspector appointed under any provision of this Part a direction requiring him to secure that a specified report under section 437—

- (a) includes the inspector's views on a specified matter,
- (b) does not include any reference to a specified matter,
- (c) is made in a specified form or manner, or
- (d) is made by a specified date.

(4) A direction under this section—

- (a) may be given on an inspector's appointment,
- (b) may vary or revoke a direction previously given, and
- (c) may be given at the request of an inspector.

(5) In this section—

- (a) a reference to an inspector's investigation includes any investigation he undertakes, or could undertake, under section 433(1) (power to investigate affairs of holding company or subsidiary);
- (b) "specified" means specified in a direction under this section.]

NOTES

Inserted, together with the preceding heading and s 446B, by the Companies Act 2006, s 1035(1), as from 1 October 2007, with effect where an inspector is appointed under a provision of Pt XIV of this Act on or after that date.

[5.29]

[446B Direction to terminate investigation

(1) The Secretary of State may direct an inspector to take no further steps in his investigation.

(2) The Secretary of State may give a direction under this section to an inspector appointed under section 432(1) or 442(3) only on the grounds that it appears to him that—

- (a) matters have come to light in the course of the inspector's investigation which suggest that a criminal offence has been committed, and
- (b) those matters have been referred to the appropriate prosecuting authority.

(3) Where the Secretary of State gives a direction under this section, any direction already given to the inspector under section 437(1) to produce an interim report, and any direction given to him under section 446A(3) in relation to such a report, shall cease to have effect.

(4) Where the Secretary of State gives a direction under this section, the inspector shall not make a final report to the Secretary of State unless—

- (a) the direction was made on the grounds mentioned in subsection (2) and the Secretary of State directs the inspector to make a final report to him, or
- (b) the inspector was appointed under section 432(1) (appointment in pursuance of order of the court).

(5) An inspector shall comply with any direction given to him under this section.

(6) In this section, a reference to an inspector's investigation includes any investigation he undertakes, or could undertake, under section 433(1) (power to investigate affairs of holding company or subsidiary).]

NOTES

Inserted as noted to s 446A at **[5.28]**.

[Resignation, removal and replacement of inspectors

[5.30]

446C Resignation and revocation of appointment

(1) An inspector may resign by notice in writing to the Secretary of State.

(2) The Secretary of State may revoke the appointment of an inspector by notice in writing to the inspector.]

NOTES

Inserted, together with the preceding heading and s 446D, by the Companies Act 2006, s 1036, as from 1 October 2007, with effect where an inspector is appointed under a provision of Pt XIV of this Act on or after that date.

[5.31]

[446D Appointment of replacement inspectors

(1) Where—

(a) an inspector resigns,

(b) an inspector's appointment is revoked, or

(c) an inspector dies,

the Secretary of State may appoint one or more competent inspectors to continue the investigation.

(2) An appointment under subsection (1) shall be treated for the purposes of this Part (apart from this section) as an appointment under the provision of this Part under which the former inspector was appointed.

(3) The Secretary of State must exercise his power under subsection (1) so as to secure that at least one inspector continues the investigation.

(4) Subsection (3) does not apply if—

(a) the Secretary of State could give any replacement inspector a direction under section 446B (termination of investigation), and

(b) such a direction would (under subsection (4) of that section) result in a final report not being made.

(5) In this section, references to an investigation include any investigation the former inspector conducted under section 433(1) (power to investigate affairs of holding company or subsidiary).]

NOTES

Inserted as noted to s 446C at **[5.30]**.

[Power to obtain information from former inspectors etc

[5.32]

446E Obtaining information from former inspectors etc

(1) This section applies to a person who was appointed as an inspector under this Part—

(a) who has resigned, or

(b) whose appointment has been revoked.

(2) This section also applies to an inspector to whom the Secretary of State has given a direction under section 446B (termination of investigation).

(3) The Secretary of State may direct a person to whom this section applies to produce documents obtained or generated by that person during the course of his investigation to—

(a) the Secretary of State, or

(b) an inspector appointed under this Part.

(4) The power under subsection (3) to require production of a document includes power, in the case of a document not in hard copy form, to require the production of a copy of the document—

(a) in hard copy form, or

(b) in a form from which a hard copy can be readily obtained.

(5) The Secretary of State may take copies of or extracts from a document produced in pursuance of this section.

(6) The Secretary of State may direct a person to whom this section applies to inform him of any matters that came to that person's knowledge as a result of his investigation.

(7) A person shall comply with any direction given to him under this section.

(8) In this section—

(a) references to the investigation of a former inspector or inspector include any investigation he conducted under section 433(1) (power to investigate affairs of holding company or subsidiary), and

(b) "document" includes information recorded in any form.]

NOTES

Inserted, together with the preceding heading, by the Companies Act 2006, s 1037(1), as from 1 October 2007, with effect where an inspector is appointed under a provision of Pt XIV of this Act on or after that date.

Requisition and seizure of books and papers

[5.33]

[447 Power to require documents and information

(1) The Secretary of State may act under subsections (2) and (3) in relation to a company.

(2) The Secretary of State may give directions to the company requiring it—

(a) to produce such documents (or documents of such description) as may be specified in the directions;

(b) to provide such information (or information of such description) as may be so specified.

(3) The Secretary of State may authorise a person (an investigator) to require the company or any other person—

(a) to produce such documents (or documents of such description) as the investigator may specify;

(b) to provide such information (or information of such description) as the investigator may specify.

(4) A person on whom a requirement under subsection (3) is imposed may require the investigator to produce evidence of his authority.

(5) A requirement under subsection (2) or (3) must be complied with at such time and place as may be specified in the directions or by the investigator (as the case may be).

(6) The production of a document in pursuance of this section does not affect any lien which a person has on the document.

(7) The Secretary of State or the investigator (as the case may be) may take copies of or extracts from a document produced in pursuance of this section.

(8) A "document" includes information recorded in any form.

[(9) The power under this section to require production of a document includes power, in the case of a document not in hard copy form, to require the production of a copy of the document—

(a) in hard copy form, or

(b) in a form from which a hard copy can be readily obtained.]]

NOTES

Substituted by the Companies (Audit, Investigations and Community Enterprise) Act 2004, s 21, as from 6 April 2005.

Sub-s (3): para (c) (and the word immediately preceding it) inserted by the Companies Act 2006 (Consequential Amendments, Transitional Provisions and Savings) Order 2009, SI 2009/1941, art 2(1), Sch 1, para 57(1), (5), as from 1 October 2009.

Sub-s (9): substituted by the Companies Act 2006, s 1038(2), as from 1 October 2007.

[5.34]

[447A Information provided: evidence

(1) A statement made by a person in compliance with a requirement under section 447 may be used in evidence against him.

(2) But in criminal proceedings in which the person is charged with a relevant offence—

(a) no evidence relating to the statement may be adduced by or on behalf of the prosecution, and

(b) no question relating to it may be asked by or on behalf of the prosecution,

unless evidence relating to it is adduced or a question relating to it is asked in the proceedings by or on behalf of that person.

(3) A relevant offence is any offence other than the following—

(a) an offence under section 451,

(b) an offence under section 5 of the Perjury Act 1911 (false statement made otherwise than on oath), or

(c) an offence under section 44(2) of the Criminal Law (Consolidation) (Scotland) Act 1995 (false statement made otherwise than on oath)[; or

(d) an offence under Article 10 of the Perjury (Northern Ireland) Order 1979 (false statements made otherwise than on oath)].

NOTES

Inserted by the Companies (Audit, Investigations and Community Enterprise) Act 2004, s 25, Sch 2, Pt 3, paras 16, 17, as from 6 April 2005.

Sub-s (3): para (d) (and the preceding word) added by the Companies Act 2006 (Consequential Amendments, Transitional Provisions and Savings) Order 2009, SI 2009/1941, art 2(1), Sch 1, para 57(1), (5), as from 1 October 2009.

[5.35]

[448 Entry and search of premises

(1) A justice of the peace may issue a warrant under this section if satisfied on information on oath given by or on behalf of the Secretary of State, or by a person appointed or authorised to exercise powers under this Part, that there are reasonable grounds for believing that there are on any premises documents whose production has been required under this Part and which have not been produced in compliance with the requirement.

(2) A justice of the peace may also issue a warrant under this section if satisfied on information on oath given by or on behalf of the Secretary of State, or by a person appointed or authorised to exercise powers under this Part—

(a) that there are reasonable grounds for believing that an offence has been committed for which the penalty on conviction on indictment is imprisonment for a term of not less than two years and that there are on any premises documents relating to whether the offence has been committed,

(b) that the Secretary of State, or the person so appointed or authorised, has power to require the production of the documents under this Part, and

(c) that there are reasonable grounds for believing that if production was so required the documents would not be produced but would be removed from the premises, hidden, tampered with or destroyed.

(3) A warrant under this section shall authorise a constable, together with any other person named in it and any other constables—

(a) to enter the premises specified in the information, using such force as is reasonably necessary for the purpose;

(b) to search the premises and take possession of any documents appearing to be such documents as are mentioned in subsection (1) or (2), as the case may be, or to take, in relation to any such documents, any other steps which may appear to be necessary for preserving them or preventing interference with them;

(c) to take copies of any such documents; and

(d) to require any person named in the warrant to provide an explanation of them or to state where they may be found.

(4) If in the case of a warrant under subsection (2) the justice of the peace is satisfied on information on oath that there are reasonable grounds for believing that there are also on the premises other documents relevant to the investigation, the warrant shall also authorise the actions mentioned in subsection (3) to be taken in relation to such documents.

(5) A warrant under this section shall continue in force until the end of the period of one month beginning with the day on which it is issued.

(6) Any documents of which possession is taken under this section may be retained—

(a) for a period of three months; or

(b) if within that period proceedings to which the documents are relevant are commenced against any person for any criminal offence, until the conclusion of those proceedings.

(7) Any person who intentionally obstructs the exercise of any rights conferred by a warrant issued under this section or fails without reasonable excuse to comply with any requirement imposed in accordance with subsection (3)(d) is guilty of an offence . . .

[(7A) A person guilty of an offence under this section is liable—

(a) on conviction on indictment, to a fine;

(b) on summary conviction, to a fine not exceeding the statutory maximum.]

(8) For the purposes of sections 449 and 451A (provision for security of information) documents obtained under this section shall be treated as if they had been obtained under the provision of this Part under which their production was or, as the case may be, could have been required.

(9) In the application of this section to Scotland for the references to a justice of the peace substitute references to a justice of the peace or a sheriff, and for the references to information on oath substitute references to evidence on oath.

(10) In this section "document" includes information recorded in any form.]

NOTES

Substituted by CA 1989, s 64(1), as from 21 February 1990.

Sub-s (7): words omitted repealed by the Companies Act 2006, ss 1124, 1295, Sch 3, para 2(1), Sch 16, as from 1 October 2007 (except in relation to offences committed before that date (see s 1133 of the 2006 Act at **[1.1303]**)).

Sub-s (7A): inserted by the Companies Act 2006, s 1124, Sch 3, para 2(2), as from 1 October 2007 (except in relation to offences committed before that date (see s 1133 of the 2006 Act at **[1.1303]**)).

Take possession of, etc: the power of seizure conferred by sub-s (3) is a power to which Criminal Justice and Police Act 2001, s 50 applies (additional powers of seizure from premises); see s 50 of, and Sch 1, Pt 1, para 35 to, that Act.

[5.36]

[448A Protection in relation to certain disclosures: information provided to Secretary of State

(1) A person who makes a relevant disclosure is not liable by reason only of that disclosure in any proceedings relating to a breach of an obligation of confidence.

(2) A relevant disclosure is a disclosure which satisfies each of the following conditions—

(a) it is made to the Secretary of State otherwise than in compliance with a requirement under this Part;

(b) it is of a kind that the person making the disclosure could be required to make in pursuance of this Part;

(c) the person who makes the disclosure does so in good faith and in the reasonable belief that the disclosure is capable of assisting the Secretary of State for the purposes of the exercise of his functions under this Part;

(d) the information disclosed is not more than is reasonably necessary for the purpose of assisting the Secretary of State for the purposes of the exercise of those functions;

(e) the disclosure is not one falling within subsection (3) or (4).

(3) A disclosure falls within this subsection if the disclosure is prohibited by virtue of any enactment [whenever passed or made].

(4) A disclosure falls within this subsection if—

(a) it is made by a person carrying on the business of banking or by a lawyer, and

(b) it involves the disclosure of information in respect of which he owes an obligation of confidence in that capacity.

[(5) In this section "enactment" has the meaning given by section 1293 of the Companies Act 2006.]]

NOTES

Inserted by the Companies (Audit, Investigations and Community Enterprise) Act 2004, s 22, as from 6 April 2005.

Sub-s (3): words in square brackets inserted by the Companies Act 2006 (Consequential Amendments, Transitional Provisions and Savings) Order 2009, SI 2009/1941, art 2(1), Sch 1, para 57(1), (6)(a), as from 1 October 2009.

Sub-s (5): substituted by SI 2009/1941, art 2(1), Sch 1, para 57(1), (6)(b), as from 1 October 2009.

[5.37]

[449 Provision for security of information obtained

(1) This section applies to information (in whatever form) obtained—

(a) in pursuance of a requirement imposed under section 447;

(b) by means of a relevant disclosure within the meaning of section 448A(2);

(c) by an investigator in consequence of the exercise of his powers under section 453A.

(2) Such information must not be disclosed unless the disclosure—

(a) is made to a person specified in Schedule 15C, or

(b) is of a description specified in Schedule 15D.

(3) The Secretary of State may by order amend Schedules 15C and 15D.

(4) An order under subsection (3) must not—

(a) amend Schedule 15C by specifying a person unless the person exercises functions of a public nature (whether or not he exercises any other function);

(b) amend Schedule 15D by adding or modifying a description of disclosure unless the purpose for which the disclosure is permitted is likely to facilitate the exercise of a function of a public nature.

(5) An order under subsection (3) must be made by statutory instrument subject to annulment in pursuance of a resolution of either House of Parliament.

(6) A person who discloses any information in contravention of this section [is guilty of an offence].

[(6A) A person guilty of an offence under this section is liable—

(a) on conviction on indictment, to imprisonment for a term not exceeding two years or a fine (or both);

(b) on summary conviction—

(i) in England and Wales, to imprisonment for a term not exceeding twelve months or to a fine not exceeding the statutory maximum (or both);

(ii) in Scotland or Northern Ireland, to imprisonment for a term not exceeding six months, or to a fine not exceeding the statutory maximum (or both).]

(7) . . .

(8) Any information which may by virtue of this section be disclosed to a person specified in Schedule 15C may be disclosed to any officer or employee of the person.

(9) This section does not prohibit the disclosure of information if the information is or has been available to the public from any other source.

(10) For the purposes of this section, information obtained by an investigator in consequence of the exercise of his powers under section 453A includes information obtained by a person accompanying the investigator in pursuance of subsection (4) of that section in consequence of that person's accompanying the investigator.

(11) Nothing in this section authorises the making of a disclosure in contravention of [the data protection legislation].]

NOTES

Substituted by the Companies (Audit, Investigations and Community Enterprise) Act 2004, s 25, Sch 2, Pt 3, paras 16, 18, as from 6 April 2005.

Sub-s (6): words in square brackets substituted (for the original paras (a), (b)) by the Companies Act 2006, s 1124, Sch 3, para 3(1), (2), as from 1 October 2007 (except in relation to offences committed before that date (see s 1133 of the 2006 Act at **[1.1303]**)).

Sub-s (6A): inserted by the Companies Act 2006, s 1124, Sch 3, para 3(1), (3), as from 1 October 2007 (except in relation to offences committed before that date (see s 1133 of the 2006 Act at **[1.1303]**)).

Sub-s (7): repealed by the Companies Act 2006, ss 1124, 1295, Sch 3, para 3(1), (4), Sch 16, as from 1 October 2007 (except in relation to offences committed before that date (see s 1133 of the 2006 Act at **[1.1303]**)).

Sub-s (11): words in square brackets substituted by the Data Protection Act 2018, s 211, Sch 19, Pt 1, para 33, as from 25 May 2018 (for transitional provisions and savings relating to the repeal of the Data Protection Act 1998, see Sch 20 to the 2018 Act).

This section has effect in accordance with the Anti-terrorism, Crime and Security Act 2001, s 17. That section, which clarifies and extends a number of information disclosure provisions available to public authorities, permits disclosure to assist any criminal investigation or criminal proceedings being carried out in the UK or abroad or to facilitate determinations of whether or not such investigations or proceedings should begin or end (see Sch 4, Pt 1, para 24 to the 2001 Act).

Orders: the Companies (Disclosure of Information) (Designated Authorities) Order 2006, SI 2006/1644. Article 2 of the Order amended Sch 15D *post* by adding a disclosure for the purpose of enabling or assisting the Gambling Commission to exercise its functions under the Gambling Act 2005 to the list of disclosures that are permitted by virtue of this section and Sch 15D. It was revoked by SI 2013/2329, art 4(2), Schedule, para 37, as from 1 October 2013. Article 3 amends the Table in s 87(4) of the Companies Act 1989 by adding an entry allowing a disclosure to the Gambling Commission for the purpose of its functions under the Gambling Act 2005 to the list of disclosures that are permitted by s 87(1)(b) of the 1989 Act. Also, the Companies (Disclosure of Information) (Specified Persons) Order 2016, SI 2016/741 (which amends Sch 15C *post*).

[5.38]

450 Punishment for destroying, mutilating etc company documents

(1) [An officer of a company . . .] . . . who—

(a) destroys, mutilates or falsifies, or is privy to the destruction, mutilation or falsification of a document affecting or relating to the [company's] property or affairs, or

(b) makes, or is privy to the making of, a false entry in such a document,

is guilty of an offence, unless he proves that he had no intention to conceal the state of affairs of [the company] or to defeat the law.

[(1A) Subsection (1) applies to an officer of an authorised insurance company which is not a body corporate as it applies to an officer of a company.]

(2) Such a person as above mentioned who fraudulently either parts with, alters or makes an omission in any such document or is privy to fraudulent parting with, fraudulent altering or fraudulent making of an omission in, any such document, is guilty of an offence.

[(3) A person guilty of an offence under this section is liable—

(a) on conviction on indictment, to imprisonment for a term not exceeding seven years or a fine (or both);

(b) on summary conviction—

(i) in England and Wales, to imprisonment for a term not exceeding twelve months or to a fine not exceeding the statutory maximum (or both);

(ii) in Scotland or Northern Ireland, to imprisonment for a term not exceeding six months, or to a fine not exceeding the statutory maximum (or both).]

[(4) . . .]

[(5) In this section "document" includes information recorded in any form.]

NOTES

Sub-s (1): words in square brackets substituted by CA 1989, s 66(1), (2), as from 21 February 1990. Words omitted repealed by the Financial Services and Markets Act 2000 (Consequential Amendments and Repeals) Order 2001, SI 2001/3649, art 23(1), (2), as from 1 December 2001.

Sub-s (1A): inserted by SI 2001/3649, art 22(1), (3), as from 1 December 2001.

Sub-s (3): substituted by the Companies Act 2006, s 1124, Sch 3, para 4(1), as from 1 October 2007 (except in relation to offences committed before that date (see s 1133 of the 2006 Act at **[1.1303]**)).

Sub-s (4): originally substituted by CA 1989, s 66(1), (3), as from 21 February 1990. Subsequently repealed by the Companies Act 2006, ss 1124, 1295, Sch 3, para 4(2), Sch 16, as from 1 October 2007 (except in relation to offences committed before that date (see s 1133 of the 2006 Act at **[1.1303]**)).

Sub-s (5): added by CA 1989, s 66(1), (4), as from 21 February 1990.

Deferred Prosecution Agreements: as to the application of Deferred Prosecution Agreements to an offence under this section (ie, an agreement between a designated prosecutor and a person accused of a crime (P) whereby proceedings against P in respect of the alleged offence are automatically suspended as soon as they are instituted if P agrees to comply with certain requirements), see s 45 of, and Sch 17, Pt 1 and Sch 17, Pt 2, para 20 to, the Crime and Courts Act 2013.

[5.39]

[451 Punishment for furnishing false information

(1) A person commits an offence if in purported compliance with a requirement under section 447 to provide information—

(a) he provides information which he knows to be false in a material particular;

(b) he recklessly provides information which is false in a material particular.

[(2) A person guilty of an offence under this section is liable—

(a) on conviction on indictment, to imprisonment for a term not exceeding two years or a fine (or both);

(b) on summary conviction—

(i) in England and Wales, to imprisonment for a term not exceeding twelve months or to a fine not exceeding the statutory maximum (or both);

(ii) in Scotland or Northern Ireland, to imprisonment for a term not exceeding six months, or to a fine not exceeding the statutory maximum (or both).]

(3) . . .]

NOTES

Substituted by the Companies (Audit, Investigations and Community Enterprise) Act 2004, s 25, Sch 2, Pt 3, paras 16, 19, as from 6 April 2005.

Sub-s (2): substituted by the Companies Act 2006, s 1124, Sch 3, para 5(1), as from 1 October 2007 (except in relation to offences committed before that date (see s 1133 of the 2006 Act at **[1.1303]**)).

Sub-s (3): repealed by the Companies Act 2006, ss 1124, 1295, Sch 3, para 5(2), Sch 16, as from 1 October 2007 (except in relation to offences committed before that date (see s 1133 of the 2006 Act at **[1.1303]**)).

[5.40]

[451A Disclosure of information by Secretary of State or inspector

[(1) This section applies to information obtained—

(a) under sections 434 to [446E];

(b) by an inspector in consequence of the exercise of his powers under section 453A.]

(2) The Secretary of State may, if he thinks fit—

(a) disclose any information to which this section applies to any person to whom, or for any purpose for which, disclosure is permitted under section 449, or

(b) authorise or require an inspector appointed under this Part to disclose such information to any such person or for any such purpose.

[(3) Information to which this section applies may also be disclosed by an inspector appointed under this Part to—

(a) another inspector appointed under this Part;

(b) a person appointed under—

(i) section 167 of the Financial Services and Markets Act 2000 (general investigations),

(ii) section 168 of that Act (investigations in particular cases),

(iii) section 169(1)(b) of that Act (investigation in support of overseas regulator),

(iv) section 284 of that Act (investigations into affairs of certain collective investment schemes), or

(v) regulations made as a result of section 262(2)(k) of that Act (investigations into open-ended investment companies),

to conduct an investigation; or

(c) a person authorised to exercise powers under—

(i) section 447 of this Act; or

(ii) section 84 of the Companies Act 1989 (exercise of powers to assist overseas regulatory authority).]

(4) Any information which may by virtue of subsection (3) be disclosed to any person may be disclosed to any officer or servant of that person.

(5) The Secretary of State may, if he thinks fit, disclose any information obtained under section 444 to—

(a) the company whose ownership was the subject of the investigation,

(b) any member of the company,

(c) any person whose conduct was investigated in the course of the investigation,

(d) the auditors of the company, or

(e) any person whose financial interests appear to the Secretary of State to be affected by matters covered by the investigation.]

[(6) For the purposes of this section, information obtained by an inspector in consequence of the exercise of his powers under section 453A includes information obtained by a person accompanying the inspector in pursuance of subsection (4) of that section in consequence of that person's accompanying the inspector.

(7) The reference to an inspector in subsection (2)(b) above includes a reference to a person accompanying an inspector in pursuance of section 453A(4).]

NOTES

Originally inserted by FSA 1986, s 182, Sch 13, para 10. Subsequently substituted by CA 1989, s 68, as from 21 February 1990.

Sub-s (1): substituted by the Companies (Audit, Investigations and Community Enterprise) Act 2004, s 25, Sch 2, Pt 3, paras 16, 20(1), (2), as from 6 April 2005. Figure "446E" in square brackets substituted by the Companies Act 2006, s 1037(2), as from 1 October 2007, with effect where an inspector is appointed under a provision of Pt XIV of this Act on or after that date.

Sub-s (3): substituted by the Financial Services and Markets Act 2000 (Consequential Amendments and Repeals) Order 2001, SI 2001/3649, art 24, as from 1 December 2001.

Sub-ss (6), (7): added by the Companies (Audit, Investigations and Community Enterprise) Act 2004, s 25, Sch 2, Pt 3, paras 16, 20(1), (3), as from 6 April 2005.

Supplementary

[5.41]

452 Privileged information

[(1) Nothing in sections 431 to [446E] compels the disclosure by any person to the Secretary of State or to an inspector appointed by him of information in respect of which in an action in the High Court a claim to legal professional privilege, or in an action in the Court of Session a claim to confidentiality of communications, could be maintained.]

[(1A) Nothing in sections 434, 443 or 446 requires a person (except as mentioned in subsection (1B) below) to disclose information or produce documents in respect of which he owes an obligation of confidence by virtue of carrying on the business of banking unless—

(a) the person to whom the obligation of confidence is owed is the company or other body corporate under investigation,

(b) the person to whom the obligation of confidence is owed consents to the disclosure or production, or

(c) the making of the requirement is authorised by the Secretary of State.

(1B) Subsection (1A) does not apply where the person owing the obligation of confidence is the company or other body corporate under investigation under section 431, 432 or 433.]

[(2) Nothing in sections 447 to 451—

(a) compels the production by any person of a document or the disclosure by any person of information in respect of which in an action in the High Court a claim to legal professional privilege, or in an action in the Court of Session a claim to confidentiality of communications, could be maintained;

(b) authorises the taking of possession of any such document which is in the person's possession.

(3) The Secretary of State must not under section 447 require, or authorise a person to require—

(a) the production by a person carrying on the business of banking of a document relating to the affairs of a customer of his, or

(b) the disclosure by him of information relating to those affairs,

unless one of the conditions in subsection (4) is met.

(4) The conditions are—

(a) the Secretary of State thinks it is necessary to do so for the purpose of investigating the affairs of the person carrying on the business of banking;

(b) the customer is a person on whom a requirement has been imposed under section 447;

(c) the customer is a person on whom a requirement to produce information or documents has been imposed by an investigator appointed by the Secretary of State in pursuance of section 171 or 173 of the Financial Services and Markets Act 2000 (powers of persons appointed under section 167 or as a result of section 168(2) to conduct an investigation).

(5) Despite subsections (1) and (2) a person who is a lawyer may be compelled to disclose the name and address of his client.]

NOTES

Sub-s (1): substituted by the Companies (Audit, Investigations and Community Enterprise) Act 2004, s 25, Sch 2, Pt 3, paras 16, 21(a), as from 6 April 2005. Figure "446E" in square brackets substituted by the Companies Act 2006, s 1037(3), as from 1 October 2007, with effect where an inspector is appointed under a provision of Pt XIV of this Act on or after that date.

Sub-ss (1A), (1B): inserted by CA 1989, s 69(3), as from 21 February 1990.

Sub-ss (2)–(5): substituted (for the original sub-ss (2), (3)) by the Companies (Audit, Investigations and Community Enterprise) Act 2004, s 25, Sch 2, Pt 3, paras 16, 21(b), as from 6 April 2005.

[5.42]

453 Investigation of [overseas] companies

[(1) The provisions of this Part apply to bodies corporate incorporated outside [the United Kingdom] which are carrying on business in [the United Kingdom], or have at any time carried on business there, as they apply to companies under this Act; but subject to the following exceptions, adaptations and modifications.

(1A) The following provisions do not apply to such bodies—

(a) section 431 (investigation on application of company or its members),

(b) . . .

(c) sections 442 to 445 (investigation of company ownership and power to obtain information as to those interested in shares, &c), . . .

(d) . . .

(1B) The other provisions of this Part apply to such bodies subject to such adaptations and modifications as may be specified by regulations made by the Secretary of State.]

(2) Regulations under this section shall be made by statutory instrument subject to annulment in pursuance of a resolution of either House of Parliament.

NOTES

Section heading, sub-s (1): words in square brackets substituted by the Companies Act 2006 (Consequential Amendments, Transitional Provisions and Savings) Order 2009, SI 2009/1941, art 2(1), Sch 1, para 57(1), (7), as from 1 October 2009.

Sub-ss (1), (1B): substituted (together with sub-s (1A)), for original sub-s (1), by CA 1989, s 70, as from 21 February 1990.

Sub-s (1A): substituted as noted above. Para (b) repealed by the Companies Act 2006, ss 1176(3), (4), 1295, Sch 16, as from 6 April 2007, except in relation to proceedings brought under s 438 before that date. Para (d) (and the word immediately preceding it) repealed by s 1295 of, and Sch 16 to, the 2006 Act, as from 1 October 2007.

[5.43]

[453A Power to enter and remain on premises

(1) An inspector or investigator may act under subsection (2) in relation to a company if—

(a) he is authorised to do so by the Secretary of State, and

(b) he thinks that to do so will materially assist him in the exercise of his functions under this Part in relation to the company.

(2) An inspector or investigator may at all reasonable times—
(a) require entry to relevant premises, and
(b) remain there for such period as he thinks necessary for the purpose mentioned in subsection (1)(b).
(3) Relevant premises are premises which the inspector or investigator believes are used (wholly or partly) for the purposes of the company's business.
(4) In exercising his powers under subsection (2), an inspector or investigator may be accompanied by such other persons as he thinks appropriate.
(5) A person who intentionally obstructs a person lawfully acting under subsection (2) or (4) [is guilty of an offence].
[(5A) A person guilty of an offence under this section is liable—
(a) on conviction on indictment, to a fine;
(b) on summary conviction, to a fine not exceeding the statutory maximum.]
(6) . . .
(7) An inspector is a person appointed under section 431, 432 or 442.
(8) An investigator is a person authorised for the purposes of section 447.]

NOTES

Inserted, together with s 453B, by the Companies (Audit, Investigations and Community Enterprise) Act 2004, s 23, as from 6 April 2005.

Sub-s (5): words in square brackets substituted (for the original paras (a), (b)) by the Companies Act 2006, s 1124, Sch 3, para 6(1), (2), as from 1 October 2007 (except in relation to offences committed before that date (see s 1133 of the 2006 Act at **[1.1303]**)).

Sub-s (5A): inserted by the Companies Act 2006, s 1124, Sch 3, para 6(1), (3), as from 1 October 2007 (except in relation to offences committed before that date (see s 1133 of the 2006 Act at **[1.1303]**)).

Sub-s (6): repealed by the Companies Act 2006, ss 1124, 1295, Sch 3, para 6(1), (4), Sch 16, as from 1 October 2007 (except in relation to offences committed before that date (see s 1133 of the 2006 Act at **[1.1303]**)).

[5.44]
[453B Power to enter and remain on premises: procedural

(1) This section applies for the purposes of section 453A.
(2) The requirements of subsection (3) must be complied with at the time an inspector or investigator seeks to enter relevant premises under section 453A(2)(a).
(3) The requirements are—
(a) the inspector or investigator must produce evidence of his identity and evidence of his appointment or authorisation (as the case may be);
(b) any person accompanying the inspector or investigator must produce evidence of his identity.
(4) The inspector or investigator must, as soon as practicable after obtaining entry, give to an appropriate recipient a written statement containing such information as to—
(a) the powers of the investigator or inspector (as the case may be) under section 453A;
(b) the rights and obligations of the company, occupier and the persons present on the premises,
as may be prescribed by regulations.
(5) If during the time the inspector or investigator is on the premises there is no person present who appears to him to be an appropriate recipient for the purposes of subsection (8), the inspector or investigator must as soon as reasonably practicable send to the company—
(a) a notice of the fact and time that the visit took place, and
(b) the statement mentioned in subsection (4).
(6) As soon as reasonably practicable after exercising his powers under section 453A(2), the inspector or investigator must prepare a written record of the visit and—
(a) if requested to do so by the company he must give it a copy of the record;
(b) in a case where the company is not the sole occupier of the premises, if requested to do so by an occupier he must give the occupier a copy of the record.
(7) The written record must contain such information as may be prescribed by regulations.
(8) If the inspector or investigator thinks that the company is the sole occupier of the premises an appropriate recipient is a person who is present on the premises and who appears to the inspector or investigator to be—
(a) an officer of the company, or
(b) a person otherwise engaged in the business of the company if the inspector or investigator thinks that no officer of the company is present on the premises.
(9) If the inspector or investigator thinks that the company is not the occupier or sole occupier of the premises an appropriate recipient is—
(a) a person who is an appropriate recipient for the purposes of subsection (8), and (if different)
(b) a person who is present on the premises and who appears to the inspector or investigator to be an occupier of the premises or otherwise in charge of them.
(10) A statutory instrument containing regulations made under this section is subject to annulment in pursuance of a resolution of either House of Parliament.]

NOTES

Inserted as noted to s 453A at **[5.43]**.

Regulations: the Companies Act 1985 (Power to Enter and Remain on Premises: Procedural) Regulations 2005, SI 2005/684 at **[6.103]**.

[5.45]
[453C Failure to comply with certain requirements

(1) This section applies if a person fails to comply with a requirement imposed by an inspector, the Secretary of State or an investigator in pursuance of either of the following provisions—
(a) section 447;
(b) section 453A.

(2) The inspector, Secretary of State or investigator (as the case may be) may certify the fact in writing to the court.

(3) If, after hearing—

(a) any witnesses who may be produced against or on behalf of the alleged offender;

(b) any statement which may be offered in defence,

the court is satisfied that the offender failed without reasonable excuse to comply with the requirement, it may deal with him as if he had been guilty of contempt of the court.]

NOTES

Inserted by the Companies (Audit, Investigations and Community Enterprise) Act 2004, s 24, as from 6 April 2005.

[5.46]

[453D Offences by bodies corporate

Where an offence under any of sections 448, 449 to 451 and 453A is committed by a body corporate, every officer of the body who is in default also commits the offence.

For this purpose—

(a) any person who purports to act as director, manager or secretary of the body is treated as an officer of the body, and

(b) if the body is a company, any shadow director is treated as an officer of the company.]

NOTES

Inserted by the Companies Act 2006 (Consequential Amendments etc) Order 2008, SI 2008/948, art 3(1), Sch 1, Pt 2, para 82, as from 6 April 2008.

PART XV ORDERS IMPOSING RESTRICTIONS ON SHARES ([SECTION 445])

NOTES

Words in square brackets in the Part heading substituted by the Companies Act 2006 (Commencement No 3, Consequential Amendments, Transitional Provisions and Savings) Order 2007, SI 2007/2194, art 10(1), Sch 4, Pt 1, para 11(1), (2), as from 1 October 2007.

[5.47]

454 Consequence of order imposing restrictions

(1) So long as any shares are directed to be subject to the restrictions of this Part [then, subject to any directions made in relation to an order [pursuant to section 445(1A) or 456(1A)]]—

(a) any transfer of those shares or, in the case of unissued shares, any transfer of the right to be issued with them, and any issue of them, is void;

(b) no voting rights are exercisable in respect of the shares;

(c) no further shares shall be issued in right of them or in pursuance of any offer made to their holder; and

(d) except in a liquidation, no payment shall be made of any sums due from the company on the shares, whether in respect of capital or otherwise.

(2) Where shares are subject to the restrictions of subsection (1)(a), any agreement to transfer the shares or, in the case of unissued shares, the right to be issued with them is void (except [such agreement or right as may be made or exercised under the terms of directions made by the Secretary of State or the court under [section 445(1A) or 456(1A)] or] an agreement to [transfer] the shares on the making of an order under section 456(3)(b) below).

(3) Where shares are subject to the restrictions of subsection (1)(c) or (d), an agreement to transfer any right to be issued with other shares in right of those shares, or to receive any payment on them (otherwise than in a liquidation) is void (except [such agreement or right as may be made or exercised under the terms of directions made by the Secretary of State or the court under [section 445(1A) or 456(1A)] or] an agreement to transfer any such right on the [transfer] of the shares on the making of an order under section 456(3)(b) below).

NOTES

Sub-s (1): words in first (outer) pair of square brackets inserted by the Companies (Disclosure of Interests in Shares) (Orders imposing restrictions on shares) Regulations 1991, SI 1991/1646, reg 6(a), as from 18 July 1991. Words in second (inner) pair of square brackets substituted by the Companies Act 2006 (Commencement No 3, Consequential Amendments, Transitional Provisions and Savings) Order 2007, SI 2007/2194, art 10(1), Sch 4, Pt 1, para 11(1), (3), as from 1 October 2007.

Sub-ss (2), (3): words in first (outer) pair of square brackets inserted by SI 1991/1646, reg 6(b), (c) as from 18 July 1991. Words in second (inner) pair of square brackets substituted by SI 2007/2194, art 10(1), Sch 4, Pt 1, para 11(1), (4), (5), as from 1 October 2007. Word in final pair of square brackets substituted by CA 1989, s 145, Sch 19, para 10(2), as from 7 January 1991.

[5.48]

455 Punishment for attempted evasion of restrictions

(1) [Subject to the terms of any directions made under [section 445(1A) or 456]] a person [commits an offence if he]—

(a) exercises or purports to exercise any right to dispose of any shares which, to his knowledge, are for the time being subject to the restrictions of this Part or of any right to be issued with any such shares, or

(b) votes in respect of any such shares (whether as holder or proxy), or appoints a proxy to vote in respect of them, or

(c) being the holder of any such shares, fails to notify of their being subject to those restrictions any person whom he does not know to be aware of that fact but does know to be entitled (apart from the restrictions) to vote in respect of those shares whether as holder or as proxy, or

(d) being the holder of any such shares, or being entitled to any right to be issued with other shares in right of them, or to receive any payment on them (otherwise than in a liquidation), enters into any agreement which is void under section 454(2) or (3).

(2) [Subject to the terms of any directions made under [section 445(1A) or 456]] if shares in a company are issued in contravention of the restrictions, [an offence is committed by—

(a) the company, and

(b) every officer of the company who is in default].

[(2A) A person guilty of an offence under this section is liable—

(a) on conviction on indictment, to a fine;

(b) on summary conviction, to a fine not exceeding the statutory maximum.]

(3) . . .

NOTES

Sub-s (1): words in first (outer) pair of square brackets inserted by the Companies (Disclosure of Interests in Shares) (Orders imposing restrictions on shares) Regulations 1991, SI 1991/1646, reg 7, as from 18 July 1991. Words in second (inner) pair of square brackets substituted by the Companies Act 2006 (Commencement No 3, Consequential Amendments, Transitional Provisions and Savings) Order 2007, SI 2007/2194, art 10(1), Sch 4, Pt 1, para 11(1), (6), as from 1 October 2007. Words in third pair of square brackets substituted by the Companies Act 2006, s 1124, Sch 3, para 7(1), as from 1 October 2007 (except in relation to offences committed before that date (see s 1133 of the 2006 Act at **[1.1303]**)).

Sub-s (2): words in first (outer) pair of square brackets inserted by SI 1991/1646, reg 7, as from 18 July 1991. Words in second (inner) pair of square brackets substituted by SI 2007/2194, art 10(1), Sch 4, Pt 1, para 11(1), (7), as from 1 October 2007. Words in third pair of square brackets substituted by the Companies Act 2006, s 1124, Sch 3, para 7(2), as from 1 October 2007 (except in relation to offences committed before that date (see s 1133 of the 2006 Act at **[1.1303]**)).

Sub-s (2A): inserted by the Companies Act 2006, s 1124, Sch 3, para 7(3), as from 1 October 2007 (except in relation to offences committed before that date (see s 1133 of the 2006 Act at **[1.1303]**)).

Sub-s (3): repealed by SI 2007/2194, art 10(3), Sch 5, as from 1 October 2007.

[5.49]

456 Relaxation and removal of restrictions

(1) Where shares in a company are by order made subject to the restrictions of this Part, application may be made to the court for an order directing that the shares be no longer so subject.

[(1A) Where the court is satisfied that an order subjecting the shares to the restrictions of this Part unfairly affects the rights of third parties in respect of shares then the court, for the purpose of protecting such rights and subject to such terms as it thinks fit and in addition to any order it may make under subsection (1), may direct on an application made under that subsection that such acts by such persons or descriptions of persons and for such purposes, as may be set out in the order, shall not constitute a breach of the restrictions of Part XV of this Act.

Subsection (3) does not apply to an order made under this subsection.]

(2) If the order applying the restrictions was made by the Secretary of State, or he has refused to make an order disapplying them, the application may be made by any person aggrieved; . . .

(3) Subject as follows, an order of the court or the Secretary of State directing that shares shall cease to be subject to the restrictions may be made only if—

(a) the court or (as the case may be) the Secretary of State is satisfied that the relevant facts about the shares have been disclosed to the company and no unfair advantage has accrued to any person as a result of the earlier failure to make that disclosure, or

(b) the shares are to be [transferred for valuable consideration] and the court (in any case) or the Secretary of State (if the order was made under section . . . 445) approves the [transfer].

(4) [Without prejudice to the power of the court to give directions under subsection (1A),] where shares in a company are subject to the restrictions, the court may on application order the shares to be sold, subject to the court's approval as to the sale, and may also direct that the shares shall cease to be subject to the restrictions.

An application to the court under this subsection may be made by the Secretary of State . . . , or by the company.

(5) Where an order has been made under subsection (4), the court may on application make such further order relating to the sale or transfer of the shares as it thinks fit.

An application to the court under this subsection may be made—

(a) by the Secretary of State . . . , or

(b) by the company, or

(c) by the person appointed by or in pursuance of the order to effect the sale, or

(d) by any person interested in the shares.

(6) An order (whether of the Secretary of State or the court) directing that shares shall cease to be subject to the restrictions of this Part, if it is—

(a) expressed to be made with a view to permitting a transfer of the shares, or

(b) made under subsection (4) of this section,

may continue the restrictions mentioned in paragraphs (c) and (d) of section 454(1), either in whole or in part, so far as they relate to any right acquired or offer made before the transfer.

(7) Subsection (3) does not apply to an order directing that shares shall cease to be subject to any restrictions which have been continued in force in relation to those shares under subsection (6).

NOTES

Sub-s (1A): inserted by the Companies (Disclosure of Interests in Shares) (Orders imposing restrictions on shares) Regulations 1991, SI 1991/1646, reg 8(a), as from 18 July 1991.

Sub-ss (2), (5): words omitted repealed by the Companies Act 2006 (Commencement No 3, Consequential Amendments, Transitional Provisions and Savings) Order 2007, SI 2007/2194, art 10(1), (3), Sch 4, Pt 1, para 11(1), (8), (11), Sch 5, as from 1 October 2007.

Sub-s (3): words in square brackets in para (b) substituted by CA 1989, s 145, Sch 19, para 10(1), as from 7 January 1991. Words omitted repealed by SI 2007/2194, art 10(1), (3), Sch 4, Pt 1, para 11(1), (9), Sch 5, as from 1 October 2007.

Sub-s (4): words in square brackets inserted by SI 1991/1646, reg 8(b), as from 18 July 1991. Words omitted repealed by SI 2007/2194, art 10(1), (3), Sch 4, Pt 1, para 11(1), (10), Sch 5, as from 1 October 2007.

Court . . . may direct: by virtue of SI 1991/1646, reg 9, the power of the court to give a direction under sub-s (1A) above is exercisable in respect of any order made under ss 210(5), 216(1) (both repealed) or s 445(1), including such orders as may be in force on 18 July 1991 (commencement of SI 1991/1646).

[5.50]

457 Further provisions on sale by court order of restricted shares

(1) Where shares are sold in pursuance of an order of the court under section 456(4) the proceeds of sale, less the costs of the sale, shall be paid into court for the benefit of the persons who are beneficially interested in the shares; and any such person may apply to the court for the whole or part of those proceeds to be paid to him.

(2) On application under subsection (1) the court shall (subject as provided below) order the payment to the applicant of the whole of the proceeds of sale together with any interest thereon or, if any other person had a beneficial interest in the shares at the time of their sale, such proportion of those proceeds and interest as is equal to the proportion which the value of the applicant's interest in the shares bears to the total value of the shares.

(3) On granting an application for an order under section 456(4) or (5) the court may order that the applicant's costs be paid out of the proceeds of sale; and if that order is made, the applicant is entitled to payment of his costs out of those proceeds before any person interested in the shares in question receives any part of those proceeds.

PART XVI FRAUDULENT TRADING BY A COMPANY

[5.51]

458 *(S 458 was repealed by CA 2006, s 1295, Sch 16, as from 1 October 2007, except in relation to offences completed before that date (see CO No 3, Sch 3, para 46.)*

PART XVII PROTECTION OF COMPANY'S MEMBERS AGAINST UNFAIR PREJUDICE

[5.52]

459–461 *(Ss 459–461 repealed by CA 2006, s 1295, Sch 16, as from 1 October 2007.)*

PART XVIII FLOATING CHARGES AND RECEIVERS (SCOTLAND)

NOTES

This Part is repealed by the Bankruptcy and Diligence etc (Scotland) Act 2007, s 46(1), as from a day to be appointed (subject to savings). Note that it was not repealed by the Companies Act 2006. Section 46(2), (3) of the 2007 Act provide that nothing in Part 2 of the 2007 Act (except ss 40, 41 of that Act in so far as they concern the ranking of floating charges subsisting immediately before the coming into force of s 46) affects the validity or operation of floating charges subsisting before the coming into force of s 46 and, therefore, despite the repeal of Chapters I and III of Part XVIII of this Act, those provisions will continue to have effect for the purposes of such floating charges.

CHAPTER I FLOATING CHARGES

[5.53]

462 Power of incorporated company to create floating charge

(1) It is competent under the law of Scotland for an incorporated company (whether a company within the meaning of this Act or not), for the purpose of securing any debt or other obligation (including a cautionary obligation) incurred or to be incurred by, or binding upon, the company or any other person, to create in favour of the creditor in the debt or obligation a charge, in this Part referred to as a floating charge, over all or any part of the property (including uncalled capital) which may from time to time be comprised in its property and undertaking.

(2), (3) . . .

(4) References in this Part to the instrument by which a floating charge was created are, in the case of a floating charge created by words in a bond or other written acknowledgment, references to the bond or, as the case may be, the other written acknowledgment.

(5) Subject to this Act, a floating charge has effect in accordance with this Part [and Part III of the Insolvency Act 1986] in relation to any heritable property in Scotland to which it relates, notwithstanding that the instrument creating it is not recorded in the Register of Sasines or, as appropriate, registered in accordance with the Land Registration (Scotland) Act 1979.

NOTES

Repealed by the Bankruptcy and Diligence etc (Scotland) Act 2007, s 46(1), as from a day to be appointed (for savings see the introductory note to this Part).

Sub-s (2): substituted (for the original sub-ss (2), (3)) by CA 1989, s 130(7), Sch 17, para 8. Subsequently repealed by the Law Reform (Miscellaneous Provisions) (Scotland) Act 1990, s 74(1), (2), Sch 8, para 33(6), Sch 9, as from 1 December 1990.

Sub-s (3): substituted as noted above, and repealed again by the Requirements of Writing (Scotland) Act 1995, s 14(2), Sch 5, as from 1 August 1995.

Sub-s (5): words in square brackets inserted by the Insolvency Act 1986, s 439(1), Sch 13, Pt I, as from 29 December 1986.

[5.54]

463 Effect of floating charge on winding up

(1) [Where a company goes into liquidation within the meaning of section 247(2) of the Insolvency Act 1986], a floating charge created by the company attaches to the property then comprised in the company's property and undertaking or, as the case may be, in part of that property and undertaking, but does so subject to the rights of any person who—

(a) has effectually executed diligence on the property or any part of it; or

(b) holds a fixed security over the property or any part of it ranking in priority to the floating charge; or

(c) holds over the property or any part of it another floating charge so ranking.

(2) The provisions of [Part IV of the Insolvency Act (except section 185)] have effect in relation to a floating charge, subject to subsection (1), as if the charge were a fixed security over the property to which it has attached in respect of the principal of the debt or obligation to which it relates and any interest due or to become due thereon.

[(3) Nothing in this section derogates from the provisions of sections 53(7) and 54(6) of the Insolvency Act (attachment of floating charge on appointment of receiver), or prejudices the operation of sections 175 and 176 of that Act (payment of preferential debts in winding up).]

(4) . . . interest accrues, in respect of a floating charge which after 16th November 1972 attaches to the property of the company, until payment of the sum due under the charge is made.

NOTES

Repealed by the Bankruptcy and Diligence etc (Scotland) Act 2007, s 46(1), as from a day to be appointed (for savings see the introductory note to this Part).

Sub-s (1): words in square brackets substituted by CA 1989, s 140(1), as from 3 July 1995.

Sub-s (2): words in square brackets substituted by the Insolvency Act 1986, s 439(1), Sch 13, Pt I, as from 29 December 1986.

Sub-s (3): substituted by the Insolvency Act 1986, s 439(1), Sch 13, Pt I, as from 29 December 1986.

Sub-s (4): words omitted repealed by the Insolvency Act 1986, s 438, Sch 12, as from 29 December 1986.

[5.55]

464 Ranking of floating charges

(1) Subject to subsection (2), the instrument creating a floating charge over all or any part of the company's property under section 462 may contain—

- *(a) provisions prohibiting or restricting the creation of any fixed security or any other floating charge having priority over, or ranking pari passu with, the floating charge; or*
- *(b) [with the consent of the holder of any subsisting floating charge or fixed security which would be adversely affected] provisions regulating the order in which the floating charge shall rank with any other subsisting or future floating charges or fixed securities over that property or any part of it.*

[(1A) Where an instrument creating a floating charge contains any such provision as is mentioned in subsection (1)(a), that provision shall be effective to confer priority on the floating charge over any fixed security or floating charge created after the date of the instrument.]

(2) Where all or any part of the property of a company is subject both to a floating charge and to a fixed security arising by operation of law, the fixed security has priority over the floating charge.

[(3) The order of ranking of the floating charges with any other subsisting or future floating charges or fixed securities over all or any part of the company's property is determined in accordance with the provisions of subsections (4) and (5) except where it is determined in accordance with any provision such as is mentioned in paragraph (a) or (b) of subsection (1).]

(4) Subject to the provisions of this section—

- *(a) a fixed security, the right to which has been constituted as a real right before a floating charge has attached to all or any part of the property of the company, has priority of ranking over the floating charge;*
- *(b) floating charges rank with one another according to the time of registration in accordance with Chapter II of Part XII;*
- *(c) floating charges which have been received by the registrar for registration by the same postal delivery rank with one another equally.*

(5) Where the holder of a floating charge over all or any part of the company's property which has been registered in accordance with Chapter II of Part XII has received intimation in writing of the subsequent registration in accordance with that Chapter of another floating charge over the same property or any part thereof, the preference in ranking of the first-mentioned floating charge is restricted to security for—

- *(a) the holder's present advances;*
- *(b) future advances which he may be required to make under the instrument creating the floating charge or under any ancillary document;*
- *(c) interest due or to become due on all such advances; . . .*
- *(d) any expenses or outlays which may reasonably be incurred by the holder[; and*
- *(e) (in the case of a floating charge to secure a contingent liability other than a liability arising under any further advances made from time to time) the maximum sum to which that contingent liability is capable of amounting whether or not it is contractually limited.]*

(6) This section is subject to [Part XII and to] [sections 175 and 176 of the Insolvency Act] (preferential debts in winding up).

NOTES

Repealed by the Bankruptcy and Diligence etc (Scotland) Act 2007, s 46(1), as from a day to be appointed (for savings see the introductory note to this Part).

Sub-s (1): words in square brackets in para (b) inserted by CA 1989, s 140(2), (3), as from 3 July 1995.

Sub-s (1A): inserted by CA 1989, s 140(2), (4), as from 3 July 1995.

Sub-s (3): substituted by CA 1989, s 140(2), (5), as from 3 July 1995.

Sub-s (5): word omitted from para (c) repealed, and para (e) and the word immediately preceding it added, by CA 1989, ss 140(2), (6), 212, Sch 24, as from 3 July 1995.

Sub-s (6): words in first pair of square brackets inserted by CA 1989, s 140(2), (7), as from a day to be appointed. Words in second pair of square brackets substituted by the Insolvency Act 1986, s 439(1), Sch 13, Pt I, as from 29 December 1986.

[5.56]

465 Continued effect of certain charges validated by Act of 1972

(1) Any floating charge which—

- *(a) purported to subsist as a floating charge on 17th November 1972, and*
- *(b) if it had been created on or after that date, would have been validly created by virtue of the Companies (Floating Charges and Receivers) (Scotland) Act 1972,*

is deemed to have subsisted as a valid floating charge as from the date of its creation.

(2) Any provision which—

(a) is contained in an instrument creating a floating charge or in any ancillary document executed prior to, and still subsisting at, the commencement of that Act,

(b) relates to the ranking of charges, and

(c) if it had been made after the commencement of that Act, would have been a valid provision,

is deemed to have been a valid provision as from the date of its making.

NOTES

Repealed by the Bankruptcy and Diligence etc (Scotland) Act 2007, s 46(1), as from a day to be appointed (for savings see the introductory note to this Part).

[5.57]

466 Alteration of floating charges

(1) [Subsection (4A) applies to an alteration of a floating charge, where the alteration is one which] would be adversely affected by the alteration.

(2) [Without prejudice to any enactment or rule of law regarding the execution of documents,] such an instrument of alteration is validly executed if it is executed—

(a) . . .

(b) where trustees for debenture-holders are acting under and in accordance with a trust deed, by those trustees[; or]

(c) where, in the case of a series of secured debentures, no such trustees are acting, by or on behalf of—

(i) a majority in nominal value of those present or represented by proxy and voting at a meeting of debenture-holders at which the holders of at least one-third in nominal value of the outstanding debentures of the series are present or so represented; or

(ii) where no such meeting is held, the holders of at least one-half in nominal value of the outstanding debentures of the series; . . .

(d) . . .

(3) Section 464 applies to an instrument of alteration under this section as it applies to an instrument creating a floating charge.

(4) Subject to the next subsection, section 410(2) and (3) and section 420 apply to an instrument of alteration under this section which—

(a) prohibits or restricts the creation of any fixed security or any other floating charge having priority over, or ranking pari passu with, the floating charge; or

(b) varies, or otherwise regulates the order of, the ranking of the floating charge in relation to fixed securities or to other floating charges; or

(c) releases property from the floating charge; or

(d) increases the amount secured by the floating charge.

[(4A) Every alteration to a floating charge created by a company is, so far as any security on the company's property or any part of it is conferred by the alteration, void against the liquidator or administrator and any creditor of the company, unless the documents referred to in subsection (4B) are delivered to the registrar for registration by the company or any person interested in the charge before the end of the relevant period allowed for delivery.

(4B) The documents referred to in subsection (4A) are—

(a) a certified copy of the instrument of alteration, and

(b) a statement of particulars including—

(i) the registered name and number of the company;

(ii) the date of creation of the charge;

(iii) a description of the instrument (if any) by which the charge was created or evidenced;

(iv) short particulars of the property or undertaking charged as set out when the charge was registered;

(v) date(s) of execution of the instrument of alteration;

(vi) names and address(es) of the persons who have executed the instrument of alteration.

(4C) In subsection (4A) "the relevant period allowed for delivery" is—

(a) the period of 21 days beginning with the day after the date of execution of the instrument of alteration, or

(b) if an order under section 859F(3) of the Companies Act 2006 (as applied by subsection (4E)) has been made, the period allowed by the order.

(4D) Subsection (4A) is without prejudice to any contract or obligation for repayment of the money secured by the alteration to the charge; and when an alteration becomes void under subsection (4A) the money secured by it immediately becomes payable.

(4E) Sections 859F, 859G, 859I, 859M and 859N of the Companies Act 2006 apply to an alteration to a floating charge to which subsection (4A) applies as they apply to a charge.

(4F) As applied by subsection (4E), those sections apply as if—

(a) references to the documents required or delivered under section 859A or 859B were to the documents referred to in subsection (4B);

(b) references to the period allowed for delivery under the section concerned were to the period referred to in subsection (4C)(a);

(c) references to the delivery of a certified copy of an instrument to the registrar for the purposes of Chapter A1 of Part 25 of the Companies Act 2006 were to the delivery of a certified copy of an instrument of alteration to the registrar for the purposes of this section;

(d) references to registration in accordance with a provision of Chapter A1 of Part 25 of the Companies Act 2006 were to registration in accordance with this section;

(e) references to a section 859D statement of particulars were to the statement of particulars referred to in subsection (4B)(b);

(f) references to registration under section 859A or 859B were to registration under this section;

(g) references to a statement or notice delivered to the registrar in accordance with Chapter A1 of Part 25 of the Companies Act 2006 were to a statement delivered to the registrar in accordance with subsection (4A).]

(5) Section 410(2) and (3) and section 420 apply to an instrument of alteration falling under subsection (4) of this section as if references in the said sections to a charge were references to an alteration to a floating charge, and as if in section 410(2) and (3)—

(a) references to the creation of a charge were references to the execution of such alteration; and

(b) for the words from the beginning of subsection (2) to the word "applies" there were substituted the words "Every alteration to a floating charge created by a company".

(6) Any reference (however expressed) in any enactment, including this Act, to a floating charge is, for the purposes of this section and unless the context otherwise requires, to be construed as including a reference to the floating charge as altered by an [alteration] falling under subsection (4) of this section.

NOTES

Repealed by the Bankruptcy and Diligence etc (Scotland) Act 2007, s 46(1), as from a day to be appointed (for savings see the introductory note to this Part).

Sub-s (1): words in square brackets substituted (for the original words "The instrument creating a floating charge under section 462 or any ancillary document may be altered by the execution of an instrument of alteration by the company, the holder of the charge and the holder of any other charge (including a fixed security) which") by the Companies Act 2006 (Amendment of Part 25) Regulations 2013, SI 2013/600, reg 5, Sch 2, para 1(1), (2), as from 6 April 2013, in relation to charges created on or after that date (see further the transitional provisions note at **[1.982]**).

Sub-s (2): words in square brackets inserted, and words omitted repealed, by CA 1989, ss 130(7), 212, Sch 17, para 9, Sch 24, as from 31 July 1990.

Sub-s (4): repealed by CA 1989, ss 140(8), 212, Sch 24, as from a day to be appointed.

Sub-ss (4A)–(4F): inserted by SI 2013/600, reg 5, Sch 2, para 1(1), (3), as from 6 April 2013, in relation to charges created on or after that date (see further the transitional provisions note at **[1.982]**).

Sub-s (5): repealed by SI 2013/600, reg 5, Sch 2, para 1(1), (4), as from 6 April 2013, in relation to charges created on or after that date (see further the transitional provisions note at **[1.982]**). Note that this subsection was also repealed by CA 1989, ss 140(8), 212, Sch 24, as from a day to be appointed.

Sub-s (6): word in square brackets substituted (for the original words "instrument of alteration") by SI 2013/600, reg 5, Sch 2, para 1(1), (5), as from 6 April 2013, in relation to charges created on or after that date (see further the transitional provisions note at **[1.982]**). Words "falling under subsection (4) of this section" repealed by CA 1989, ss 140(8), 212, Sch 24, as from a day to be appointed.

Temporary modification: the Companies etc (Filing Requirements) (Temporary Modifications) Regulations 2020, SI 2020/645, reg 38 provided for the following temporary modification of this section. By virtue of the Corporate Insolvency and Governance Act 2020, s 39(8), the modification applied from 27 June 2020 to the end of the day on 5 April 2021 (subject to the saving provision in s 39(9) which provides that the expiry of s 39 on 5 April 2021 does not affect the continued operation of any Regulations made under that section for the purpose of determining the length of any period that begins before the expiry):

(1) Section 466(4C)(a) of the Companies Act 1985 (alteration of floating charges) is to have effect as if for the reference to "21 days" there were substituted a reference to "31 days".

(2) Paragraph (1) does not apply in respect of a period allowed for delivery under section 466(4C) of the Companies Act 1985 which has been extended by the court under section 859F of the Companies Act 2006.

Particulars of an instrument of alteration to a floating charge: see form 466 Scot (prescribed by the Companies (Forms) Regulations 1985, SI 1985/854.

467–485 *((Chapter II) repealed, with savings, by the Insolvency Act 1986, ss 437, 438, Schs 11, 12, as from 29 December 1986.)*

CHAPTER III GENERAL

[5.58]

486 Interpretation for Part XVIII generally

(1) In this Part, unless the context otherwise requires, the following expressions have the following meanings respectively assigned to them, that is to say—

"ancillary document" means—

(a) a document which relates to the floating charge and which was executed by the debtor or creditor in the charge before the registration of the charge in accordance with Chapter II of Part XII; or

(b) an instrument of alteration such as is mentioned in section 466 in this Part;

"company", . . . means an incorporated company (whether a company within the meaning of this Act or not);

"fixed security", in relation to any property of a company, means any security, other than a floating charge or a charge having the nature of a floating charge, which on the winding up of the company in Scotland would be treated as an effective security over that property, and (without prejudice to that generality) includes a security over that property, being a heritable security within the meaning of section 9(8) of the Conveyancing and Feudal Reform (Scotland) Act 1970;

. . .

"Register of Sasines" means the appropriate division of the General Register of Sasines.

NOTES

Repealed by the Bankruptcy and Diligence etc (Scotland) Act 2007, s 46(1), as from a day to be appointed (for savings see the introductory note to this Part).

Words omitted repealed by the Insolvency Act 1986, s 438, Sch 12, as from 29 December 1986.

[5.59]

487 Extent of Part XVIII

This Part extends to Scotland only.

NOTES

Repealed by the Bankruptcy and Diligence etc (Scotland) Act 2007, s 46(1), as from a day to be appointed (for savings see the introductory note to this Part).

PART XIX RECEIVERS AND MANAGERS (ENGLAND AND WALES)

[5.60]

488–500 (*Repealed, with savings, by the Insolvency Act 1986, ss 437, 438, Schs 11, 12, as from 29 December 1986.*)

PART XX WINDING UP OF COMPANIES REGISTERED UNDER THIS ACT OR THE FORMER COMPANIES ACTS

[5.61]
501–664

NOTES

This Part has been repealed as follows:

501–650 (Chapters I–V)	Repealed, with savings, by the Insolvency Act 1986, as from 29 Dec 1986.
651 Power of court to declare dissolution of company void	Repealed by CA 2006, as from 1 Oct 2009. Savings: CO No 8, Sch 2, para 89 provides that the repeal of this section (and s 653) does not affect an application made before 1 Oct 2009.
652 Registrar may strike defunct company off register	Repealed by CA 2006, as from 1 Oct 2009.
652A Registrar may strike private company off register on application	Repealed by CA 2006, as from 1 Oct 2009.
652B Duties in connection with making application under section 652A	Repealed by CA 2006, as from 1 Oct 2009.
652C Directors' duties following application under section 652A	Repealed by CA 2006, as from 1 Oct 2009.
652D Sections 652B and 652C: supplementary provisions	Repealed by CA 2006, as from 1 Oct 2009.
652E Sections 652B and 652C: enforcement	Repealed by CA 2006, as from 1 Oct 2009.
652F Other offences connected with section 652A	Repealed by CA 2006, as from 1 Oct 2009.
653 Objection to striking off by person aggrieved	Repealed by CA 2006, as from 1 Oct 2009. For savings see the note to s 651.
654 Property of dissolved company to be bona vacantia	Repealed by CA 2006, as from 1 Oct 2009. Savings and transitional provisions: CO No 8, Sch 2, para 88 provides that (subject to para 88A) CA 2006, ss 1012–1023 (property of dissolved company) apply in relation to the property of a company dissolved on or after 1 Oct 2009, and that the corresponding provisions of this Act continue to apply in relation to the property of a company dissolved before that date.
655 Effect on s 654 of company's revival after dissolution	Repealed by CA 2006, as from 1 Oct 2009.
656 Crown disclaimer of property vesting as bona vacantia	Repealed by CA 2006, as from 1 Oct 2009. For savings see the note to s 654.
657 Effect of Crown disclaimer under s 656	Repealed by CA 2006, as from 1 Oct 2009. For savings see the note to s 654.
658 Liability for rentcharge on company's land after dissolution	Repealed by CA 2006, as from 1 Oct 2009. For savings see the note to s 654.
659–664 (Chapter VII)	Repealed, with savings, by the Insolvency Act 1986, as from 29 Dec 1986. Also repealed by CA 2006, as from 1 Oct 2009.

PART XXI WINDING UP OF UNREGISTERED COMPANIES

[5.62]

665–674 (*Repealed, with savings, by the Insolvency Act 1986, ss 437, 438, Schs 11, 12, as from 29 December 1986. Also repealed by the Companies Act 2006, s 1295, Sch 16, as from 1 October 2009.*)

PART XXII BODIES CORPORATE SUBJECT, OR BECOMING SUBJECT, TO THIS ACT (OTHERWISE THAN BY ORIGINAL FORMATION UNDER PART I)

[5.63]
675–690

NOTES

This Part has been repealed as follows:

675 Companies formed and registered under former Companies Acts	Repealed by CA 2006, as from 1 Oct 2009. Savings: for general savings in relation to existing companies, see CO No 8, Sch 2, para 1. Note in particular that nothing in CA 2006 affects (a) the registration or re-registration of a company under the former Companies Acts, or the continued existence of a company by virtue of such registration or re-registration, or (b) the application in relation to an existing company of: (i) Table B in the Joint Stock Companies Act 1856, (ii) Table A in any of the former Companies Acts, or (iii) the Companies (Tables A to F) Regulations 1985. Note also that s 1297(3) of the 2006 Act (continuity of the law: etc) applies (a) in relation to a company to which s 675(1) of this Act applied as if the company had been formed and registered under Part I of this Act; (b) in relation to a company to which s 676(1) of this Act applied as if the company had been registered under Chapter II of Part XXII of this Act; (c) in relation to a company to which s 677(1) of this Act applied as if the company had been re-registered under Part II of this Act.
676 Companies registered but not formed under former Companies Acts	Repealed by CA 2006, as from 1 Oct 2009. For savings see the note to s 675.
677 Companies re-registered with altered status under former Companies Acts	Repealed by CA 2006, as from 1 Oct 2009. For savings see the note to s 675.
678 Companies registered under Joint Stock Companies Acts	Repealed by CA 2006, as from 1 Oct 2009. For savings see the note to s 675.
679 Northern Ireland and Irish companies	Repealed by CA 2006, as from 1 Oct 2009. For savings see the note to s 675.
680 Companies capable of being registered under this Chapter	Repealed by CA 2006, as from 1 Oct 2009. Savings: CO No 8, Sch 2, para 93 provides that ss 680–690 continue to apply to an application for registration if (a) it is received by the registrar, and (b) the requirements as to registration are met in relation to it, before 1 Oct 2009. Any application for registration under this Act in relation to which the requirements as to registration are not met before that date shall be treated as withdrawn.
681 Procedural requirements for registration	Repealed by CA 2006, as from 1 Oct 2009. For savings see the note to s 680.
682 Change of name on registration	Repealed by CA 2006, as from 1 Oct 2009. For savings see the note to s 680.
683 Definition of "joint stock company"	Repealed by CA 2006, as from 1 Oct 2009. For savings see the note to s 680.
684 Requirements for registration by joint stock companies	Repealed by CA 2006, as from 1 Oct 2009. For savings see the note to s 680.
685 Registration of joint stock company as public company	Repealed by CA 2006, as from 1 Oct 2009. For savings see the note to s 680.
686 Other requirements for registration	Repealed by CA 2006, as from 1 Oct 2009. For savings see the note to s 680.
687 Name of company registering	Repealed by CA 2006, as from 1 Oct 2009. For savings see the note to s 680.
688 Certificate of registration under this Chapter	Repealed by CA 2006, as from 1 Oct 2009. For savings see the note to s 680.
689 Effect of registration	Repealed by CA 2006, as from 1 Oct 2009. For savings see the note to s 680.
690 Power to substitute memorandum and articles for deed of settlement	Repealed by CA 2006, as from 1 Oct 2009. For savings see the note to s 680.

PART XXIII OVERSEA COMPANIES

[5.64]
690A–703R

NOTES

This Part has been repealed as follows:

690A Branch registration under the Eleventh Company Law Directive (89/666/EEC)	Repealed by CA 2006, as from 1 Oct 2009. Transitional provisions and savings: SI 2009/1801, Sch 8 provides for various transitional provisions and savings in connection with the repeal of Chapter I (Registration, etc) and the commencement of the 2009 Regulations (see **[4.309]** et seq).
690B Scope of sections 691 and 692	Repealed by CA 2006, as from 1 Oct 2009. For transitional provisions and savings, see the note to s 690A.
691 Documents to be delivered to	Repealed by CA 2006, as from 1 Oct 2009. For transitional provisions and sav-

registrar	ings, see the note to s 690A.
692 Registration of altered particulars	Repealed by CA 2006, as from 1 Oct 2009. For transitional provisions and savings, see the note to s 690A.
692A Change in registration regime	Repealed by CA 2006, as from 1 Oct 2009. For transitional provisions and savings, see the note to s 690A.
693 Obligation to state name and other particulars	Repealed by CA 2006, as from 1 Oct 2009. For transitional provisions and savings, see the note to s 690A. As to the previous repeal of certain words by FSA 1986, see the notes to Part III ante.
694 Regulation of oversea companies in respect of their names	Repealed by CA 2006, as from 1 Oct 2009. For transitional provisions and savings, see the note to s 690A.
694A Service of documents: companies to which section 690A applies	Repealed by CA 2006, as from 1 Oct 2009. For transitional provisions and savings, see the note to s 690A.
695 Service of documents on oversea company	Repealed by CA 2006, as from 1 Oct 2009. For transitional provisions and savings, see the note to s 690A.
695A Registrar to whom documents to be delivered: companies to which section 690A applies	Repealed by CA 2006, as from 1 Oct 2009. For transitional provisions and savings, see the note to s 690A.
696 Office where documents to be filed	Repealed by CA 2006, as from 1 Oct 2009. For transitional provisions and savings, see the note to s 690A.
697 Penalties for non-compliance	Repealed by CA 2006, as from 1 Oct 2009. For transitional provisions and savings, see the note to s 690A.
698 Definitions	Repealed by CA 2006, as from 1 Oct 2009. For transitional provisions and savings, see the note to s 690A.
699 Channel Islands and Isle of Man companies	Repealed by CA 2006, as from 1 Oct 2009. For transitional provisions and savings, see the note to s 690A.
699A Credit and financial institutions to which the Bank Branches Directive (89/117/EEC) applies	Repealed by CA 2006, as from 1 Oct 2009. Transitional provisions and savings: SI 2009/1801, Sch 8 provides for various transitional provisions and savings in connection with the repeal of Chapter II (Delivery of Accounts and Reports) and the commencement of the 2009 Regulations (see **[4.313]** et seq).
699AA Companies to which the Eleventh Company Law Directive applies	Repealed by CA 2006, as from 1 Oct 2009. For transitional provisions and savings, see the note to s 699A.
699B Scope of sections 700 to 703	Repealed by CA 2006, as from 1 Oct 2009. For transitional provisions and savings, see the note to s 699A.
700 Preparation of accounts and reports by oversea companies	Repealed by CA 2006, as from 1 Oct 2009. For transitional provisions and savings, see the note to s 699A.
701 Oversea company's financial year and accounting reference periods	Repealed by CA 2006, as from 1 Oct 2009. For transitional provisions and savings, see the note to s 699A.
702 Delivery to registrar of accounts and reports of oversea company	Repealed by CA 2006, as from 1 Oct 2009. For transitional provisions and savings, see the note to s 699A.
703 Penalty for non-compliance	Repealed by CA 2006, as from 1 Oct 2009. For transitional provisions and savings, see the note to s 699A.
703A–703N (Chapter III)	Repealed by CA 2006, as from 1 Oct 2009 (without ever coming into force).
703O Scope of Chapter	Repealed by CA 2006, as from 1 Oct 2009.
703P Particulars to be delivered to the registrar: winding up	Repealed by CA 2006, as from 1 Oct 2009. Transitional provisions and savings: see SI 2009/1801, Sch 8, Pt 7, paras 27, 28 at **[4.315]** which provides: (i) sub-s (1) continues to apply in relation to a winding up beginning before 1 Oct 2009; (ii) sub-s (3) continues to apply in relation to an appointment made before that date; (iii) sub-s (5) continues to apply where the event occurred before that date. See also Sch 8, Pt 8 to that Order (at **[4.316]**) for savings as to form or manner in which documents to be delivered.
703Q Particulars to be delivered to the registrar: insolvency proceedings	Repealed by CA 2006, as from 1 Oct 2009. Transitional provisions and savings: see SI 2009/1801, Sch 8, Pt 7, para 29 at **[4.315]** which provides that this section continues to apply where the proceedings began before 1 Oct 2009. See also Sch 8, Pt 8 to that Order (at **[4.316]**) for savings as to form or manner in which documents to be delivered.
703R Penalty for non-compliance	Repealed by CA 2006, as from 1 Oct 2009.

PART XXIV THE REGISTRAR OF COMPANIES, HIS FUNCTIONS AND OFFICES

[5.65]
704–715A

NOTES

This Part has been repealed as follows:

704 Registration offices	Repealed by CA 2006, as from 1 Oct 2009. Savings, etc: CO No 8, Sch 2, paras 94–109 provide for a variety of savings and transitional provisions in relation to the commencement (also on 1 Oct 2009) of Part 35 of CA 2006 (the Registrar of Companies).
705 Companies' registered numbers	Repealed by CA 2006, as from 1 Oct 2009. For savings etc, see the note to s 704.
705A Registration of branches of oversea companies	Repealed by CA 2006, as from 1 Oct 2009. For savings etc, see the note to s 704.
706 Delivery to the registrar of documents in legible form	Repealed by CA 2006, as from 1 Oct 2009. For savings etc, see the note to s 704.
707 Delivery to the registrar of documents otherwise than in legible form	Repealed by SI 2000/3373, as from 22 Dec 2000.
707A The keeping of company records by the registrar	Repealed by CA 2006, as from 1 Jan 2007 (in part), and as from 1 Oct 2009 (otherwise). For general transitional provisions, see the note to s 704.
707B Delivery to the registrar using electronic communications	Repealed by CA 2006, as from 1 Oct 2009. For general transitional provisions see the note to s 704. See also CO No 8, Sch 2, para 115 which provides that any saving in that Schedule for the effect of a provision of this Act requiring a document to be delivered to the registrar extends to this section so far as relating to the provision in question and the delivery of documents under it. See also (in relation to overseas companies) the note to s 690A. Note also that various transitional provisions contained in commencement orders made under CA 2006, s 1300 provide that until s 1068 (Registrar's requirements as to form, authentication and manner of delivery) of the 2006 Act comes fully into force (which it did on 1 Oct 2009) this section applies in relation to documents required or authorised to be delivered to the registrar under various provisions of CA 2006 brought into force by those Orders.
708 Fees payable to registrar	Repealed by CA 2006, as from 6 Apr 2007 (in part), and as from 1 Oct 2009 (otherwise). For general transitional provisions see the note to s 704. See, in particular, CO No 8, Sch 2, para 94 which provides that any Regulations made under this section that are in force immediately before 1 Oct 2009 have effect on or after that date as if made under CA 2006, s 1063 (note that SI 2009/1804, Sch 1, Pt 9, para 36 at **[10.417]** makes similar provisions regarding SIs made under this section that apply to LLPs). Note also that sub-s (5) of this section provided that the registrar may charge a fee for any services provided by him otherwise than in pursuance of an obligation imposed on him by law. CO No 1, Sch 5, Pt 3, para 6(3) provides that the repeal of that subsection shall not prevent the registrar from continuing to charge fees thereunder of which notice had before the repeal been given to those to whom the services in question have been, are being or are to be provided. See also SI 2009/2101 in Appendix 4.
709 Inspection, &c of records kept by registrar	Repealed by CA 2006, as from 1 Jan 2007. As to the previous repeal of s 709(2), (3) by FSA 1986, see the notes to Part III ante.
710 Certificate of incorporation	Repealed by CA 2006, as from 1 Oct 2009. For savings etc, see the note to s 704.
710A Provision and authentication by registrar of documents in non-legible form	Repealed by CA 2006, as from 1 Oct 2009. For general transitional provisions see the note to s 704 and see, in particular, CO No 8, Sch 2, para 111 which provides that the repeal of this section does not affect its application on or after 1 Oct 2009 in relation to saved provisions of this Act.
710B Documents relating to Welsh companies	Repealed by CA 2006, as from 1 Jan 2007. For general transitional provisions see the note to s 704. See also CO No 1, Sch 5, para 1 which provides that regs 4, 5 of the Companies (Welsh Language Forms and Documents) Regulations 1994 continue to have effect notwithstanding the repeal of this section, subject to certain adaptations (note, however, that reg 4 was revoked by SI 2009/1803, as from 1 Oct 2009).
711 Public notice by registrar of receipt and issue of certain documents	Repealed by CA 2006, as from 1 Jan 2007.
711A Exclusion of deemed notice	Repealed by CA 2006, as from 1 Oct 2009 (without ever coming into force).
712 Removal of documents to Public Record Office	Repealed by CA 1989, as from 1 Jul 1991.
713 Enforcement of company's duty to make returns	Repealed by CA 2006, as from 1 Oct 2009. For savings etc, see the note to s 704.
714 Registrar's index of company and corporate names	Repealed by CA 2006, as from 1 Oct 2009. For savings etc, see the note to s 704.
715 Destruction of old records	Repealed by CA 1989, as from 1 Jul 1991.
715A Interpretation	Repealed by CA 2006, as from 1 Oct 2009. For savings, see the note to s 704.

PART XXV MISCELLANEOUS AND SUPPLEMENTARY PROVISIONS

[5.66]
716–734

NOTES

This Part has been repealed as follows. Note that s 726(2) is still in force and that section is reproduced below these notes (at **[5.67]**):

716 Prohibition of partnerships with more than 20 members	Repealed by SI 2002/3203, as from 21 Dec 2002.
717 Limited partnerships: limit on number of members	Repealed by SI 2002/3203, as from 21 Dec 2002.
718 Unregistered companies	Repealed by CA 2006, as from 1 Oct 2009.
719 Power of company to provide for employees on cessation or transfer of business	Repealed by CA 2006, as from 1 Oct 2009. Savings: CO No 8, Sch 2, para 40 provides that CA 2006, s 247 (power to make provision for employees on cessation or transfer of business) applies to provision made on or after 1 Oct 2009 (subject to para (b) below). This section continues to apply (a) to provision made before that date, and (b) to anything sanctioned in accordance with sub-s (3) before that date.
720 Certain companies to publish periodical statement	Repealed by CA 2006, as from 6 Apr 2007.
721 Production and inspection of books where offence suspected	Repealed by CA 2006, as from 1 Oct 2009.
722 Form of company registers, etc	Repealed by CA 2006, as from 1 Oct 2009.
723 Use of computers for company records	Repealed by CA 2006, as from 1 Oct 2009.
723A Obligations of company as to inspections of register, &c	Repealed by CA 2006, as from 1 Oct 2009.
723B Confidentiality orders	Repealed by CA 2006, as from 1 Oct 2009. Savings: see CO No 8, Sch 2, paras 36–39 (Continuation of protection afforded by confidentiality orders under the 1985 Act). See also, in so far as relating to overseas companies, SI 2009/1801, Sch 8, Pt 4 at **[4.312]**.
723C Effect of confidentiality orders	Repealed by CA 2006, as from 1 Oct 2009. For general savings in relation to the continuation of protection afforded by confidentiality orders, see the note to s 723B.
723D Construction of sections 723B and 723C	Repealed by CA 2006, as from 1 Oct 2009. For general savings in relation to the continuation of protection afforded by confidentiality orders, see the note to s 723B.
723E Sections 723B and 723C: offences	Repealed by CA 2006, as from 1 Oct 2009. For general savings in relation to the continuation of protection afforded by confidentiality orders, see the note to s 723B.
723F Regulations under sections 723B to 723E	Repealed by CA 2006, as from 1 Oct 2009. For general savings in relation to the continuation of protection afforded by confidentiality orders, see the note to s 723B.
724 Cross-border operation of receivership provisions	Repealed, with savings, by the Insolvency Act 1986, as from 29 Dec 1986 (also repealed by CA 2006, as from 1 Oct 2009).
725 Service of documents	Repealed by CA 2006, as from 1 Oct 2009.
726 Costs and expenses in actions by certain limited companies	Still in force for certain purposes see **[5.67] immediately below this note.**
727 Power of court to grant relief in certain cases	Repealed by CA 2006, as from 1 Oct 2008.
728 Enforcement of High Court orders	Repealed by CA 2006, as from 1 Oct 2009.
729 Annual report by Secretary of State	Repealed by CA 2006, as from 6 Apr 2007.
730 Punishment of offences	Repealed by CA 2006, as from 1 Oct 2009.
730A Meaning of "officer in default"	Repealed by CA 2006, as from 1 Oct 2009.
731 Summary proceedings	Repealed by CA 2006, as from 1 Oct 2009.
732 Prosecution by public authorities	Repealed by CA 2006, as from 6 Apr 2008. Savings: this section and ss 733, 734 continue to apply in relation to offences committed before 6 Apr 2008 (see CO No 5, Sch 4, Pt 1, para 44 and the introductory notes to this Act).
733 Offences by bodies corporate	Repealed by CA 2006, as from 6 Apr 2008. For savings, see the note to s 732.
734 Criminal proceedings against unincorporated bodies	Repealed by CA 2006, as from 6 Apr 2008. For savings, see the note to s 732.

[5.67]

726 Costs and expenses in actions by certain limited companies

(1) . . .

(2) Where in Scotland a limited company is pursuer in an action or other legal proceeding, the court having jurisdiction in the matter may, if it appears by credible testimony that there is reason to believe that the company will be unable to pay the defender's expenses if successful in his defence, order the company to find caution and sist the proceedings until caution is found.

NOTES

Repealed by the Companies Act 2006, s 1295, Sch 16, as from 1 October 2009 (in so far as relating to sub-s (1)), and as from a day to be appointed (otherwise). See further the note below.

The Companies Act 2006 (Commencement No 8, Transitional Provisions and Savings) Order 2008, SI 2008/2860, Sch 1 originally provided that this section would be completely repealed as from 1 October 2009. That Schedule was amended by the Companies Act 2006 (Consequential Amendments, Transitional Provisions and Savings) Order 2009, SI 2009/1941, art 13(1)(a) (as from 1 October 2009). The amendment substitutes a reference to "s 726(1)" for the original reference to "s 726"; the effect being that sub-s (2) above is not repealed as from 1 October 2009.

See also the Companies Act 2006 (Consequential Amendments, Transitional Provisions and Savings) Order 2009, SI 2009/1941, art 13(3) (at **[4.367]**) which provides that sub-s (2) above applies to a LLP registered under the Limited Liability Partnerships Act 2000 as it applies to a limited company.

PART XXVI INTERPRETATION

[5.68]

735–744A

NOTES

This Part has been repealed as follows:

735 "Company", etc	Repealed by CA 2006, as from 1 Oct 2009.
735A Relationship of this Act to Insolvency Act	Repealed by CA 2006, as from 1 Oct 2009.
735B Relationship of this Act to Part 6 of the Financial Services and Markets Act 2000	Repealed by CA 2006, as from 1 Oct 2009.
736 "Subsidiary", "holding company" and "wholly-owned subsidiary"	Repealed by CA 2006, as from 1 Oct 2009.
736A Provisions supplementing s 736	Repealed by CA 2006, as from 1 Oct 2009.
736B Power to amend ss 736 and 736A	Repealed by CA 2006, as from 1 Oct 2009.
737 "Called-up share capital"	Repealed by CA 2006, as from 1 Oct 2009.
738 "Allotment" and "paid up"	Repealed by CA 2006, as from 1 Oct 2009.
739 "Non-cash asset"	Repealed by CA 2006, as from 1 Oct 2009.
740 "Body corporate" and "corporation"	Repealed by CA 2006, as from 1 Oct 2009.
741 "Director" and "shadow director"	Repealed by CA 2006, as from 1 Oct 2007.
742 Expressions used in connection with accounts	Repealed by CA 2006, as from 1 Oct 2009.
742A Meaning of "offer to the public"	Repealed by CA 2006, as from 6 Apr 2008.
742B Meaning of "banking company"	Repealed by CA 2006, as from 6 Apr 2008.
742C Meaning of "insurance company" and "authorised insurance company"	Repealed by CA 2006, as from 6 Apr 2008.
743 "Employees' share scheme"	Repealed by CA 2006, as from 1 Oct 2009.
743A Meaning of "office copy" in Scotland	Repealed by CA 2006, as from 1 Oct 2009.
744 Expressions used generally in this Act	Repealed by CA 2006, as from 6 Apr 2007 and 6 Apr 2008 (in part), and as from 1 Oct 2009 (otherwise).
744A Index of defined expressions	Repealed by CA 2006, as from 1 Oct 2009.

PART XXVII FINAL PROVISIONS

745 *(Repealed by the Companies Act 2006, s 1295, Sch 16, as from 1 October 2009.)*

[5.69]

[745A "Bank of England"

In this Act references to the Bank of England do not include the Bank acting in its capacity as the Prudential Regulation Authority.]

NOTES

Inserted by the Bank of England and Financial Services (Consequential Amendments) Regulations 2017, SI 2017/80, reg 2, Schedule, Pt 1, para 1, as from 1 March 2017.

[5.70]

746 Commencement

. . . this Act comes into force on 1st July 1985.

NOTES

Repealed by the Companies Act 2006, s 1295, Sch 16, as from a day to be appointed.

Words omitted repealed by CA 1989, s 212, Sch 24, as from 1 April 1990.

[5.71]

747 Citation

This Act may be cited as the Companies Act 1985.

SCHEDULES

SCHEDULES 1–15B

[5.72]

NOTES

These Schedules have been repealed as follows:

Schedule 1—Particulars of Directors etc to be Contained in Statement under Section 10	Repealed by CA 2006, as from 1 Oct 2009. For savings see the note to s 1.
Schedule 2—Interpretation of References to "Beneficial Interest"	
Part I—References in Sections 23, 145, 146 and 148	Repealed by CA 2006, as from 1 Oct 2009. For savings see the note to s 146.
Part II—References in Schedule 5	Repealed by SI 2008/948, as from 6 Apr 2008.
Schedule 3—Mandatory Contents of Prospectus	Repealed, subject to savings in relation to para 2, by FSA 1986, as from the dates, and for the purposes noted in the notes to Part III of this Act ante. In so far as it continued to have effect, it was repealed by CA 2006, as from 1 Oct 2009.
Schedule 4—Form and Content of Company Accounts	
Part I—General rules and formats	Repealed by CA 2006, as from 6 Apr 2008. For savings see the note to s 221.
Part II—Accounting principles and rules	Repealed by CA 2006, as from 6 Apr 2008. For savings see the note to s 221.
Part III—Notes to the accounts	Repealed by CA 2006, as from 6 Apr 2008. For savings see the note to s 221.
Part IV—Special provisions where company is a parent company or subsidiary undertaking	Repealed by CA 2006, as from 6 Apr 2008. For savings see the note to s 221.
Part V—Special provisions where the company is an investment company	Repealed by CA 2006, as from 6 Apr 2008. For savings see the note to s 221.
Part VI	Repealed by CA 1989, as from 1 Apr 1990.
Part VII—Interpretation of Schedule	Repealed by CA 2006, as from 6 Apr 2008. For savings see the note to s 221. Note also that the repeal of Sch 4, Pt VII, paras 88, 89 does not affect the operation of those provisions for the purposes of ss 152(2) or 172(2)(b)(i) of this Act (saving for accounting definitions, see SI 2008/948, art 9(1) at **[4.144]**).
Schedule 4A—Form and Content of Group Accounts	Repealed by CA 2006, as from 6 Apr 2008. For savings see the note to s 221.
Schedule 5—Disclosure of Information: Related Undertakings	Repealed by CA 2006, as from 6 Apr 2008. For savings see the note to s 221.
Schedule 6—Disclosure of Information: Emoluments and Other Benefits of Directors and Others	Repealed by CA 2006, as from 6 Apr 2008. For savings see the note to s 221.
Schedule 7—Matters to be Dealt With in Directors' Report	
Part I—Matters of a general nature	Repealed by CA 2006, as from 6 Apr 2008. For savings see the note to s 221. See also CO No 3, Sch 3, para 41(3) which provides that the repeal of Part XA of this Act does not affect Sch 7, Pt I, para 3(4) (Political donations and expenditure)
Part II—Disclosure required by company acquiring its own shares, etc	Repealed by CA 2006, as from 6 Apr 2008. For savings see the note to s 221.
Part III—Disclosure concerning employment, etc, of disabled persons	Repealed by CA 2006, as from 6 Apr 2008. For savings see the note to s 221.
Part IV	Repealed, in relation to any financial year ending on or after 2 Feb 1996, by SI 1996/189 (subject to transitional provisions in relation to financial years ending on or before 24 Mar 1996.
Part V—Employee involvement	Repealed by CA 2006, as from 6 Apr 2008. For savings see the note to s 221.

Part VI—Policy and practice on payment of creditors	Repealed by CA 2006, as from 6 Apr 2008. For savings see the note to s 221.
Part VII—Disclosure Required by Certain Publicly-Traded Companies	Repealed by CA 2006, as from 6 Apr 2008. For savings see the note to s 221.
Schedule 7ZA—Operating and Financial Review	Repealed by SI 2005/3442, as from 12 Jan 2006.
Schedule 7A—Directors' remuneration report	Repealed by CA 2006, as from 6 Apr 2008. For savings see the note to s 221.
Schedule 7B—Specified Persons, Descriptions of Disclosures Etc for the Purposes of Section 245G	Repealed by CA 2006, as from 6 Apr 2008. For savings see the note to s 221.
Schedule 8—Form and Content of Accounts Prepared by Small Companies	Repealed by CA 2006, as from 6 Apr 2008. For savings see the note to s 221.
Schedule 8A—Form and Content of Abbreviated Accounts of Small Companies Delivered to Registrar	Repealed by CA 2006, as from 6 Apr 2008. For savings see the note to s 221.
Schedule 9—Special provisions for banking companies and groups	Repealed by CA 2006, as from 6 Apr 2008. For savings see the note to s 221.
Schedule 9A—Form and Content of Accounts of Insurance Companies and Groups	Repealed by CA 2006, as from 6 Apr 2008. For savings see the note to s 221.
Schedule 10—Additional matters to be dealt with in directors' report attached to special category accounts	Repealed by SI 1993/3246, as from 19 Dec 1993, subject to transitional provisions and exemptions in relation to certain companies.
Schedule 10A—Parent and Subsidiary Undertakings: Supplementary Provisions	Repealed by CA 2006, as from 6 Apr 2008. For savings see the note to s 221.
Schedule 11—Modifications of Part VIII Where Company's Accounts Prepared in Accordance with Special Provisions for Banking or Insurance Companies	Repealed by CA 2006, as from 6 Apr 2008. For savings see the note to s 263.
Schedule 12—Supplementary provisions in connection with disqualification orders	Repealed by the Company Directors Disqualification Act 1986, as from 29 Dec 1986, subject to transitional provisions and savings.
Schedule 13—Provisions Supplementing and Interpreting ss 324–328	
Part I—Rules for interpretation of the sections and also section 346(4) and (5)	Repealed by CA 2006, as from 1 Oct 2007. Savings: see CO No 3, Sch 3, para 50 which provides that the repeal of Sch 13 does not affect (a) s 17(3)(b) of this Act (directors to disclose interest in contracts), (b) the Industrial and Provident Societies Act 1965, ss 7E, 7F(3), (c) FSMA 2000, s 96B(2)(a).
Part II—Periods within which obligations imposed by section 324 must be fulfilled	Repealed by CA 2006, as from 6 Apr 2007.
Part III—Circumstances in which obligation imposed by section 324 is not discharged	Repealed by CA 2006, as from 6 Apr 2007.
Part IV—Provisions with respect to register of directors' interests to be kept under section 325	Repealed by CA 2006, as from 6 Apr 2007.
Schedule 14—Overseas Branch Registers	Repealed by CA 2006, as from 1 Oct 2009.
Schedule 15—Contents of annual return of a company having a share capital.	Repealed by CA 1989, as from 7 Jan 1991.
Schedule 15A—Written Resolutions of Private Companies	Repealed by CA 2006, as from 1 Oct 2007. For savings see the note to s 366.
Schedule 15B—Provisions Subject to which ss 425–427 have Effect in their Application to Mergers and Divisions of Public Companies	Repealed by CA 2006, as from 6 Apr 2008.

[SCHEDULE 15C SPECIFIED PERSONS

Section 449

[5.73]

1. The Secretary of State.

2. The Department of Enterprise, Trade and Investment for Northern Ireland.

3. The Treasury.

[3A. The Commissioners for Her Majesty's Revenue and Customs.]

4. The Lord Advocate.

5. The Director of Public Prosecutions.

6. The Director of Public Prosecutions for Northern Ireland.

[6A. The Director of the Serious Fraud Office.]

[7. The Financial Conduct Authority.

7A. The Prudential Regulation Authority.

7B. The Bank of England.]

[**7C.** The registrar of companies.

7D. The Gangmasters and Labour Abuse Authority.]

8. A constable.

9. A procurator fiscal.

10. The Scottish Ministers.]

NOTES

Inserted, together with Sch 15D, by the Companies (Audit, Investigations and Community Enterprise) Act 2004, s 25, Sch 2, Pt 3, paras 16, 25, as from 6 April 2005 (for transitional provisions see below).

Paras 3A, 6A, 7C, 7D: inserted by the Companies (Disclosure of Information) (Specified Persons) Order 2016, SI 2016/741, art 2, as from 1 October 2016.

Paras 7–7B: substituted (for the original para 7) by the Financial Services Act 2012, s 114(1), Sch 18, Pt 2, paras 45, 46, as from 1 April 2013.

Transitional provisions: note that the Companies (Audit, Investigations and Community Enterprise) Act 2004 (Commencement) and Companies Act 1989 (Commencement No 18) Order 2004, SI 2004/3322, art 10 provides that new s 449 (under which this Schedule takes effect) applies, and old s 449 does not apply, to information to which old s 449(1) applied immediately before 6 April 2005.

[SCHEDULE 15D DISCLOSURES

Section 449

[5.74]

1. A disclosure for the purpose of enabling or assisting a person authorised under [section 457 of the Companies Act 2006] to exercise his functions.

2. A disclosure for the purpose of enabling or assisting an inspector appointed under Part 14 to exercise his functions.

3. A disclosure for the purpose of enabling or assisting a person authorised under section 447 of this Act or section 84 of the Companies Act 1989 to exercise his functions.

4. A disclosure for the purpose of enabling or assisting a person appointed under section 167 of the Financial Services and Markets Act 2000 (general investigations) to conduct an investigation to exercise his functions.

5. A disclosure for the purpose of enabling or assisting a person appointed under section 168 of the Financial Services and Markets Act 2000 (investigations in particular cases) to conduct an investigation to exercise his functions.

6. A disclosure for the purpose of enabling or assisting a person appointed under section 169(1)(b) of the Financial Services and Markets Act 2000 (investigation in support of overseas regulator) to conduct an investigation to exercise his functions.

7. A disclosure for the purpose of enabling or assisting a person appointed under section 284 of the Financial Services and Markets Act 2000 (investigations into affairs of certain collective investment schemes) to conduct an investigation to exercise his functions.

8. A disclosure for the purpose of enabling or assisting a person appointed under regulations made under sections 262(1) and (2)(k) of the Financial Services and Markets Act 2000 (investigations into open-ended investment companies) to conduct an investigation to exercise his functions.

9. A disclosure for the purpose of enabling or assisting the Secretary of State or the Treasury to exercise any of their functions under any of the following—

[(a) the Companies Acts (as defined in section 2(1) of the Companies Act 2006);]
[(b) Part 5 of the Criminal Justice Act 1993 (insider dealing);]
(c) the Insolvency Act 1986;
(d) the Company Directors Disqualification Act 1986;
[(da) Part 42 of the Companies Act 2006 (statutory auditors);]
[(e) Parts 3 and 7 of the Companies Act 1989 (investigations and powers to obtain information and financial markets and insolvency);]
(f) the Financial Services and Markets Act 2000;
[(g) the Investment Bank Special Administration Regulations 2011];
[(h) the Payment and Electronic Money Institution Insolvency Regulations 2021].

10. A disclosure for the purpose of enabling or assisting the Scottish Ministers to exercise their functions under the enactments relating to insolvency.

11. A disclosure for the purpose of enabling or assisting the Department of Enterprise, Trade and Investment for Northern Ireland to exercise any powers conferred on it by the enactments relating to companies or insolvency.

12. A disclosure for the purpose of enabling or assisting a person appointed or authorised by the Department of Enterprise, Trade and Investment for Northern Ireland under the enactments relating to companies or insolvency to exercise his functions.

[**13.** A disclosure for the purpose of enabling or assisting the Pensions Regulator to exercise the functions conferred on it by or by virtue of any of the following—

(a) the Pension Schemes Act 1993;
(b) the Pensions Act 1995;

(c) the Welfare Reform and Pensions Act 1999;
(d) the Pensions Act 2004;
(e) any enactment in force in Northern Ireland corresponding to any of those enactments.]

[13A. A disclosure for the purpose of enabling or assisting the Board of the Pension Protection Fund to exercise the functions conferred on it by or by virtue of Part 2 of the Pensions Act 2004 or any enactment in force in Northern Ireland corresponding to that Part.]

14. A disclosure for the purpose of enabling or assisting the Bank of England to exercise its functions.

15. A disclosure for the purpose of enabling or assisting the body known as the Panel on Takeovers and Mergers to exercise its functions.

16. A disclosure for the purpose of enabling or assisting organs of the Society of Lloyd's (being organs constituted by or under the Lloyd's Act 1982) to exercise their functions under or by virtue of the Lloyd's Acts 1871 to 1982.

17. A disclosure for the purpose of enabling or assisting the [Competition and Markets Authority] to exercise its functions under any of the following—
(a) the Fair Trading Act 1973;
(b), (c) . . .
(d) the Competition Act 1980;
(e) the Competition Act 1998;
(f) the Financial Services and Markets Act 2000;
(g) the Enterprise Act 2002;
(h), (i) . . .
[(j) the Business Protection from Misleading Marketing Regulations 2008;
(k) the Consumer Protection from Unfair Trading Regulations 2008];
[(l) Parts 3 and 4 of the Enterprise and Regulatory Reform Act 2013];
[(m) Schedule 3 to the Consumer Rights Act 2015].

18. . . .

19. A disclosure with a view to the institution of, or otherwise for the purposes of, proceedings before the Competition Appeal Tribunal.

20. A disclosure for the purpose of enabling or assisting an enforcer under Part 8 of the Enterprise Act 2002 to exercise its functions under that Part.

21. A disclosure for the purpose of enabling or assisting the [Charity Commission to exercise its] functions.

22. A disclosure for the purpose of enabling or assisting the Attorney General to exercise his functions in connection with charities.

[23. A disclosure for the purpose of enabling or assisting the Gambling Commission to exercise its functions under any of the following—
(a) the Gambling Act 2005;
(b) sections 5 to 10 and 15 of the National Lottery etc Act 1993.]

24. A disclosure by the [Gambling Commission] to the National Audit Office for the purpose of enabling or assisting the Comptroller and Auditor General to carry out an examination under Part 2 of the National Audit Act 1983 into the economy, effectiveness and efficiency with which the [Gambling Commission] has used its resources in discharging its functions under sections 5 to 10 of the National Lottery etc Act 1993.

[25. A disclosure for the purposes of enabling or assisting a regulator under Schedule 3 to the Consumer Rights Act 2015 other than the Competition and Markets Authority to exercise its functions under that Schedule.]

26. A disclosure for the purpose of enabling or assisting an enforcement authority under [the Consumer Contracts (Information, Cancellation and Additional Charges) Regulations 2013] to exercise its functions under those Regulations.

27. A disclosure for the purpose of enabling or assisting a local weights and measures authority in England and Wales to exercise its functions under section 230(2) of the Enterprise Act 2002.

[27A. A disclosure for the purpose of enabling or assisting the lead enforcement authority (as defined in section 33(1) of the Estate Agents Act 1979) to exercise its functions under the Estate Agents Act 1979.]

28. A disclosure for the purpose of enabling or assisting the [Financial Conduct Authority or the Prudential Regulation Authority] to exercise its functions under any of the following—
(a) the legislation relating to friendly societies or to industrial and provident societies;
[(aa) the Consumer Credit Act 1974;]
(b) the Building Societies Act 1986;
(c) Part 7 of the Companies Act 1989;
(d) the Financial Services and Markets Act 2000.

29. . . .

30. A disclosure for the purpose of enabling or assisting a body corporate established in accordance with section 212(1) of the Financial Services and Markets Act 2000 (compensation scheme manager) to exercise its functions.

31. (1) A disclosure for the purpose of enabling or assisting a recognised investment exchange[, a recognised clearing house or a recognised CSD] to exercise its functions as such.

(2) Recognised investment exchange[, recognised clearing house and recognised CSD] have the same meaning as in section 285 of the Financial Services and Markets Act 2000.

32. A disclosure for the purpose of enabling or assisting a body designated under section 326(1) of the Financial Services and Markets Act 2000 (designated professional bodies) to exercise its functions in its capacity as a body designated under that section.

33. A disclosure with a view to the institution of, or otherwise for the purposes of, civil proceedings arising under or by virtue of the Financial Services and Markets Act 2000.

34. A disclosure for the purpose of enabling or assisting a body designated by order under [section 1252 of the Companies Act 2006] (delegation of functions of Secretary of State) to exercise its functions under [Part 42 of that Act (statutory auditors)].

35. A disclosure for the purpose of enabling or assisting a recognised supervisory or qualifying body (within the meaning of [Part 42 of the Companies Act 2006]) to exercise its functions as such.

36. A disclosure for the purpose of enabling or assisting an official receiver (including the Accountant in Bankruptcy in Scotland and the Official Assignee in Northern Ireland) to exercise his functions under the enactments relating to insolvency.

37. . . .

38. A disclosure for the purpose of enabling or assisting a body which is for the time being a recognised professional body for the purposes of section 391 of the Insolvency Act 1986 [or Article 350 of the Insolvency (Northern Ireland) Order 1989] (recognised professional bodies) to exercise its functions as such.

39. (1) A disclosure for the purpose of enabling or assisting an overseas regulatory authority to exercise its regulatory functions.

(2) Overseas regulatory authority and regulatory functions have the same meaning as in section 82 of the Companies Act 1989.

40. A disclosure for the purpose of enabling or assisting the Regulator of Community Interest Companies to exercise functions under the Companies (Audit, Investigations and Community Enterprise) Act 2004.

41. A disclosure with a view to the institution of, or otherwise for the purposes of, criminal proceedings.

42. A disclosure with a view to the institution of, or otherwise for the purposes of, proceedings on an application under section 6, 7 or 8 of the Company Directors Disqualification Act 1986 [or Article 9, 10 or 11 of the Company Directors Disqualification (Northern Ireland) Order 2002].

[43. A disclosure with a view to the institution of, or otherwise for the purposes of, proceedings before the Upper Tribunal in respect of—

[(a) a decision of the Financial Conduct Authority;

(aa) a decision of the Prudential Regulation Authority;]

(b) a decision of the Bank of England; or

(c) a decision of a person relating to the assessment of any compensation or consideration under the Banking (Special Provisions) Act 2008 or the Banking Act 2009.]

44. A disclosure for the purposes of proceedings before the Financial Services Tribunal by virtue of the Financial Services and Markets Act 2000 (Transitional Provisions) (Partly Completed Procedures) Order 2001 (SI 2001/3592).

[44A. A disclosure for the purposes of proceedings before [tribunal in relation to a decision of the Pensions Regulator].]

45. A disclosure for the purpose of enabling or assisting a body appointed under section 14 of the Companies (Audit, Investigations and Community Enterprise) Act 2004 (supervision of periodic accounts and reports of issuers of listed securities) to exercise functions mentioned in subsection (2) of that section.

46. [(1)] A disclosure with a view to the institution of, or otherwise for the purposes of, disciplinary proceedings relating to the performance by a [relevant lawyer], auditor, accountant, valuer or actuary of his professional duties.

[(2) "Relevant lawyer" means—

(a) a person who, for the purposes of the Legal Services Act 2007, is an authorised person in relation to an activity which constitutes a reserved legal activity (within the meaning of that Act),

(b) a solicitor or barrister in Northern Ireland, or

(c) a solicitor or advocate in Scotland.]

47. (1) A disclosure with a view to the institution of, or otherwise for the purposes of, disciplinary proceedings relating to the performance by a public servant of his duties.

(2) Public servant means an officer or employee of the Crown or of any public or other authority for the time being designated for the purposes of this paragraph by the Secretary of State by order.

(3) An order under sub-paragraph (2) must be made by statutory instrument subject to annulment in pursuance of a resolution of either House of Parliament.

48. A disclosure for the purpose of the provision of a summary or collection of information framed in such a way as not to enable the identity of any person to whom the information relates to be ascertained.

49. A disclosure in pursuance of any [EU] obligation.

[50. . . .]]

NOTES

Inserted as noted to Sch 15C at **[5.73]**.

Para 1: words in square brackets substituted by the Companies Act 2006 (Consequential Amendments etc) Order 2008, SI 2008/948, art 3(1), Sch 1, Pt 2, para 92, as from 6 April 2008, in relation to disclosures for the purpose of enabling or assisting a person to exercise functions in relation to accounts for financial years beginning on or after that date.

Para 9: sub-paras (a), (b), (e) substituted, and sub-para (da) inserted, by the Companies Act 2006 (Consequential Amendments, Transitional Provisions and Savings) Order 2009, SI 2009/1941, art 2(1), Sch 1, para 58(1), (2), as from 1 October 2009. Sub-para (g) inserted by the Investment Bank Special Administration Regulations 2011, SI 2011/245, reg 27, Sch 6, Pt 3, para 8, as from 8 February 2011. Sub-para (h) inserted by the Payment and Electronic Money Institution Insolvency Regulations 2021, SI 2021/716, reg 47(4), Sch 4, Pt 1, para 1, as from 8 July 2021.

Para 13: substituted by the Pensions Act 2004, s 319, Sch 12, para 5(1), (3)(a), as from 6 April 2005.

Para 13A: inserted by the Pensions Act 2004, s 319(1), Sch 12, para 5(1), (3)(b), as from 6 April 2005.

Para 17: words "Competition and Markets Authority" in square brackets substituted, and sub-para (i) originally added, by the Enterprise and Regulatory Reform Act 2013 (Competition) (Consequential, Transitional and Saving Provisions) Order 2014, SI 2014/892, art 2, Sch 1, Pt 2, para 42(1), (2), as from 1 April 2014. Sub-para (b) repealed by the Financial Services and Markets Act 2000 (Regulated Activities) (Amendment) (No 2) Order 2013, SI 2013/1881, art 28, Schedule, Pt 1, para 1(a), as from 1 April 2014. Sub-para (c) repealed by the Public Bodies (Abolition of the National Consumer Council and Transfer of the Office of Fair Trading's Functions in relation to Estate Agents etc) Order 2014, SI 2014/631, art 5(3), Sch 2, para 2(a), as from 31 March 2014. Sub-para (i) repealed, and sub-para (m) added, by the Consumer Rights Act 2015, s 75, Sch 4, para 28(1), (2), as from 1 October 2015 (for transitional provisions in relation to the continued application of the Unfair Terms in Consumer Contracts Regulations 1999, see the Consumer Rights Act 2015 (Commencement No 3, Transitional Provisions, Savings and Consequential Amendments) Order 2015, SI 2015/1630, art 6). Sub-para (h) repealed, and sub-paras (j), (k) added, by the Consumer Protection from Unfair Trading Regulations 2008, SI 2008/1277, reg 30(1), (3), Sch 2, Pt 1, para 30, Sch 4, Pt 1, as from 26 May 2008.

Para 18: repealed by SI 2014/892, art 2, Sch 1, Pt 2, para 42(1), (3), as from 1 April 2014.

Para 21: words in square brackets substituted by the Charities Act 2006, s 75, Sch 8, paras 74, 76, as from 27 February 2007.

Para 23: substituted by the Public Bodies (Merger of the Gambling Commission and the National Lottery Commission) Order 2013, SI 2013/2329, art 4, Schedule, para 22(a), as from 1 October 2013.

Para 24: words in square brackets substituted by SI 2013/2329, art 4, Schedule, para 22(b), as from 1 October 2013.

Para 25: substituted by the Consumer Rights Act 2015, s 75, Sch 4, para 28(1), (3), as from 1 October 2015 (for transitional provisions in relation to the continued application of the Unfair Terms in Consumer Contracts Regulations 1999, see the Consumer Rights Act 2015 (Commencement No 3, Transitional Provisions, Savings and Consequential Amendments) Order 2015, SI 2015/1630, art 6).

Para 26: words in square brackets substituted by the Consumer Contracts (Information, Cancellation and Additional Charges) Regulations 2013, SI 2013/3134, reg 47, Sch 4, para 3, as from 13 June 2014, in relation to contracts entered into on or after that date.

Para 27A: inserted by SI 2014/631, art 5(3), Sch 2, para 2(b), as from 31 March 2014.

Para 28: words in first pair of square brackets substituted by the Financial Services Act 2012, s 114(1), Sch 18, Pt 2, paras 45, 47(1), (2), as from 1 April 2013. Sub-para (aa) inserted by SI 2013/1881, art 28, Schedule, Pt 1, para 1(b), as from 1 April 2014.

Para 29: repealed by the Financial Services (Banking Reform) Act 2013, s 141, Sch 10, para 1, as from 1 March 2014.

Para 31: words in square brackets substituted by the Central Securities Depositories Regulations 2017, SI 2017/1064, reg 10, Schedule, para 3, as from 28 November 2017.

Paras 34, 35: words in square brackets substituted by SI 2009/1941, art 2(1), Sch 1, para 58(1), (3), (4), as from 1 October 2009.

Para 37: repealed by the Deregulation Act 2015, s 19, Sch 6, Pt 6, para 22(1), (4), as from 1 October 2015.

Paras 38, 42: words in square brackets inserted by SI 2009/1941, art 2(1), Sch 1, para 58(1), (5), (6), as from 1 October 2009.

Para 43: substituted by the Transfer of Tribunal Functions Order 2010, SI 2010/22, art 5(1), Sch 2, para 5(a), as from 6 April 2010. Sub-paras (a), (aa) substituted (for the original sub-para (a)) by the Financial Services Act 2012, s 114(1), Sch 18, Pt 2, paras 45, 47(1), (4), as from 1 April 2013.

Para 44A: inserted by the Pensions Act 2004, s 102(4), Sch 4, Pt 4, para 19, as from 6 April 2005. Words in square brackets substituted by SI 2010/22, art 5(1), Sch 2, para 5(b), as from 6 April 2010.

Para 46: sub-para (1) numbered as such, words in square brackets in that paragraph substituted, and sub-para (2) added, by the Legal Services Act 2007, s 208, Sch 21, para 63, as from 1 January 2010.

Para 49: reference to "EU" in square brackets substituted by the Treaty of Lisbon (Changes in Terminology) Order 2011, SI 2011/1043, art 6, as from 22 April 2011.

Para 50: originally added by the Companies (Disclosure of Information) (Designated Authorities) Order 2006, SI 2006/1644, art 2, as from 1 October 2006. Subsequently repealed by the Public Bodies (Merger of the Gambling Commission and the National Lottery Commission) Order 2013, SI 2013/2329, art 4, Schedule, para 22(c), as from 1 October 2013.

Charity Commissioners: as to the abolition of the office of Charity Commissioner for England and Wales, the establishment of the Charity Commission for England and Wales, and the transfer of the functions, rights, liabilities, etc from the Charity Commissioners for England and Wales to the Charity Commission, see the Charities Act 2006, s 6. Note that s 6 of the 2006 Act was repealed by the Charities Act 2011, s 354(4), Sch 10, as from 14 March 2012. As to the Charity Commission for England and Wales, see now s 13 of the 2011 Act.

SCHEDULES 16–25

[5.75]

NOTES

These Schedules have been repealed as follows:

Schedule 16—Orders in course of winding up pronounced in vacation (Scotland)	Repealed by the Insolvency Act 1986, as from 29 Dec 1986.
Schedule 17—Proceedings of committee of inspection	Repealed by the Insolvency Act 1986, as from 29 Dec 1986.
Schedule 18—Provisions of Part XX not applicable in winding up subject to supervision of the court	Repealed by the Insolvency Act 1986, as from 29 Dec 1986.
Schedule 19—Preference among creditors in company winding up	Repealed by the Insolvency Act 1986, as from 29 Dec 1986.
Schedule 20—Vesting of Disclaimed Property; Protection of Third Parties	
Part I	Repealed by the Insolvency Act 1986, as from 29 Dec 1986.
Part II—Crown Disclaimer Under Section 656 (Scotland Only)	Repealed by CA 2006, as from 1 Oct 2009.For savings see the note to s 654.
Schedule 21—Effect of Registration Under Section 680	Repealed by CA 2006, as from 1 Oct 2009.For savings see the

	note to s 680.
Schedule 21A—Branch Registration Under the Eleventh Company Law Directive (89/666/EEC)	Repealed by CA 2006, as from 1 Oct 2009. For transitional provisions and savings see the note to s 690A.
Schedule 21B—Change in the Registration Regime: Transitional Provisions	Repealed by CA 2006, as from 1 Oct 2009. For transitional provisions and savings see the note to s 690A.
Schedule 21C—Delivery of Reports and Accounts: Credit and Financial Institutions to which the Bank Branches Directive (89/117/EEC) Applies	Repealed by CA 2006, as from 1 Oct 2009. For transitional provisions and savings see the note to s 699A.
Schedule 21D—Delivery of Reports and Accounts: Companies to which the Eleventh Company Law Directive Applies	Repealed by CA 2006, as from 1 Oct 2009. For transitional provisions and savings see the note to s 699A.
Schedule 22—Provisions of this Act applying to unregistered companies	Repealed by CA 2006, as from 1 Oct 2009.
Schedule 23—Form of statement to be published by certain companies under s 720	Repealed by CA 2006, as from 6 Apr 2007.
Schedule 24—Punishment of Offences Under this Act	Repealed by CA 2006, as from 1 Oct 2007, 6 Apr 2008, and 1 Oct 2008 (certain purposes), and as from 1 Oct 2009 (otherwise). Savings: see CO No 3, Sch 3, para 51; CO No 5, art 9(1), (2); CO No 8, art 7 and Sch 2, para 116.
Schedule 25—Companies Act 1981, section 38, as originally enacted.	Repealed by CA 2006, as from 1 Oct 2009.

COMPANY DIRECTORS DISQUALIFICATION ACT 1986

(1986 c 46)

NOTES

This Act is reproduced as amended by the following Acts:

1989	Companies Act 1989.
1992	Friendly Societies Act 1992.
1994	Deregulation and Contracting Out Act 1994.
1999	Youth Justice and Criminal Evidence Act 1999.
2000	Insolvency Act 2000.
2002	Enterprise Act 2002.
2003	Communications Act 2003; Water Act 2003; Railways and Transport Safety Act 2003.
2004	Companies (Audit, Investigations and Community Enterprise) Act 2004; Pensions Act 2004.
2006	National Health Service (Consequential Provisions) Act 2006; Companies Act 2006.
2007	Tribunals, Courts and Enforcement Act 2007.
2009	Banking Act 2009.
2010	Co-operative and Community Benefit Societies and Credit Unions Act 2010.
2012	Health and Social Care Act 2012.
2013	Financial Services (Banking Reform) Act 2013.
2014	Co-operative and Community Benefit Societies Act 2014.
2015	Small Business, Enterprise and Employment Act 2015; Deregulation Act 2015.
2017	Technical and Further Education Act 2017.
2021	Rating (Coronavirus) and Directors Disqualification (Dissolved Companies) Act 2021.
2022	Health and Care Act 2022.

This Act is reproduced as amended by the following SIs:

1996	Open-Ended Investment Companies (Investment Companies with Variable Capital) Regulations 1996, SI 1996/2827.
2001	Open-Ended Investment Companies Regulations 2001, SI 2001/1228; Financial Services and Markets Act 2000 (Consequential Amendments and Repeals) Order 2001, SI 2001/3649.
2003	Enterprise Act 2002 (Insolvency) Order 2003, SI 2003/2096.
2004	Insolvency Act 2000 (Company Directors Disqualification Undertakings) Order 2004, SI 2004/1941.
2007	Companies Act 2006 (Commencement No 3, Consequential Amendments, Transitional Provisions and Savings) Order 2007, SI 2007/2194.
2008	Companies Act 2006 (Consequential Amendments etc) Order 2008, SI 2008/948.
2009	Building Societies (Insolvency and Special Administration) Order 2009, SI 2009/805; Companies Act 2006 (Consequential Amendments, Transitional Provisions and Savings) Order 2009, SI 2009/1941.
2012	Treaty of Lisbon (Changes in Terminology or Numbering) Order 2012, SI 2012/1809; Tribunals, Courts

	and Enforcement Act 2007 (Consequential Amendments) Order 2012, SI 2012/2404.
2013	Financial Services Act 2012 (Mutual Societies) Order 2013, SI 2013/496.
2014	Co-operative and Community Benefit Societies and Credit Unions (Investigations) Regulations 2014, SI 2014/574; Enterprise and Regulatory Reform Act 2013 (Competition) (Consequential, Transitional and Saving Provisions) Order 2014, SI 2014/892.
2015	Office of Rail Regulation (Change of Name) Regulations 2015, SI 2015/1682.
2016	Enterprise and Regulatory Reform Act 2013 (Consequential Amendments) (Bankruptcy) and the Small Business, Enterprise and Employment Act 2015 (Consequential Amendments) Regulations 2016, SI 2016/481; Bankruptcy (Scotland) Act 2016 (Consequential Provisions and Modifications) Order 2016, SI 2016/1034.
2017	Risk Transformation Regulations 2017, SI 2017/1212.
2019	Competition (Amendment etc) (EU Exit) Regulations 2019, SI 2019/93.

Limited liability partnerships: the Limited Liability Partnerships Regulations 2001, SI 2001/1090, reg 4(2) (at **[10.102]**) provides that the provisions of this Act shall apply to limited liability partnerships, except where the context otherwise requires, with the general modifications specified in that paragraph. See also Sch 2, Pt II to the 2001 Regulations (at **[10.110]**) for specific modifications of Sch 1, Pt II to this Act.

UK Economic Interest Groupings (UKEIGs) and EEIG establishments: as to the application of certain provisions of this Act to UKEIGs and EEIG establishments, see the European Economic Interest Grouping Regulations 1989, SI 1989/638, reg 20 (as amended by the European Economic Interest Grouping (Amendment) (EU Exit) Regulations 2018, SI 2018/1299).

Insolvent partnerships: as to the application of certain provisions of this Act to insolvent partnerships, see the Insolvent Partnerships Order 1994, SI 1994/2421, reg 16 (Application of Company Directors Disqualification Act 1986).

Official Receiver: as to the contracting out of certain functions of the Official Receiver conferred by or under this Act, see the Contracting Out (Functions of the Official Receiver) Order 1995, SI 1995/1386.

ARRANGEMENT OF SECTIONS

Preliminary

Disqualification for general misconduct in connection with companies

Disqualification for unfitness

Persons instructing unfit directors

Further provision about disqualification undertakings

Disqualification for competition infringements

Other cases of disqualification

Consequences of contravention

Compensation orders and undertakings

Supplementary provisions

Miscellaneous and general

SCHEDULES

An Act to consolidate certain enactments relating to the disqualification of persons from being directors of companies, and from being otherwise concerned with a company's affairs

[25 July 1986]

Preliminary

[5.76]

1 Disqualification orders: general

(1) In the circumstances specified below in this Act a court may, and under [sections 6 and 9A] shall, make against a person a disqualification order, that is to say an order that [for a period specified in the order—

(a) he shall not be a director of a company, act as receiver of a company's property or in any way, whether directly or indirectly, be concerned or take part in the promotion, formation or management of a company unless (in each case) he has the leave of the court, and

(b) he shall not act as an insolvency practitioner.]

(2) In each section of this Act which gives to a court power or, as the case may be, imposes on it the duty to make a disqualification order there is specified the maximum (and, in [sections 6 and 8ZA], the minimum) period of disqualification which may or (as the case may be) must be imposed by means of the order [and, unless the court otherwise orders, the period of disqualification so imposed shall begin at the end of the period of 21 days beginning with the date of the order].

(3) Where a disqualification order is made against a person who is already subject to such an order [or to a disqualification undertaking], the periods specified in those orders [or, as the case may be, in the order and the undertaking] shall run concurrently.

(4) A disqualification order may be made on grounds which are or include matters other than criminal convictions, notwithstanding that the person in respect of whom it is to be made may be criminally liable in respect of those matters.

NOTES

Sub-s (1): words in first pair of square brackets substituted by the Enterprise Act 2002, s 204(1), (3), as from 20 June 2003. Words in second pair of square brackets substituted by the Insolvency Act 2000, s 5(1), as from 2 April 2001.

Sub-s (2): words in first pair of square brackets substituted by the Small Business, Enterprise and Employment Act 2015, s 111, Sch 7, Pt 1, paras 1, 2, as from 1 October 2015. Words in second pair of square brackets inserted by the Insolvency Act 2000, ss 5(2), 8, Sch 4, Pt I, paras 1, 2, as from 2 April 2001.

Sub-s (3): words in square brackets inserted by the Insolvency Act 2000, ss 5(2), 8, Sch 4, Pt I, paras 1, 2, as from 2 April 2001.

[5.77]

[1A Disqualification undertakings: general

(1) In the circumstances specified in sections [5A, 7, 8, 8ZC and 8ZE] the Secretary of State may accept a disqualification undertaking, that is to say an undertaking by any person that, for a period specified in the undertaking, the person—

(a) will not be a director of a company, act as receiver of a company's property or in any way, whether directly or indirectly, be concerned or take part in the promotion, formation or management of a company unless (in each case) he has the leave of a court, and

(b) will not act as an insolvency practitioner.

(2) The maximum period which may be specified in a disqualification undertaking is 15 years; and the minimum period which may be specified in a disqualification undertaking under section 7 [or 8ZC] is two years.

(3) Where a disqualification undertaking by a person who is already subject to such an undertaking or to a disqualification order is accepted, the periods specified in those undertakings or (as the case may be) the undertaking and the order shall run concurrently.

(4) In determining whether to accept a disqualification undertaking by any person, the Secretary of State may take account of matters other than criminal convictions, notwithstanding that the person may be criminally liable in respect of those matters.]

NOTES

Inserted by the Insolvency Act 2000, s 6(1), (2), as from 2 April 2001.

Sub-s (1): words in square brackets substituted by the Small Business, Enterprise and Employment Act 2015, s 111, Sch 7, Pt 1; paras 1, 3(1), (2), as from 1 October 2015.

Sub-s (2): words in square brackets inserted by the Small Business, Enterprise and Employment Act 2015, s 111, Sch 7, Pt 1, paras 1, 3(1), (3), as from 1 October 2015.

Disqualification for general misconduct in connection with companies

[5.78]

2 Disqualification on conviction of indictable offence

(1) The court may make a disqualification order against a person where he is convicted of an indictable offence (whether on indictment or summarily) in connection with the promotion, formation, management[, liquidation or striking off] of a company [with the receivership of a company's property or with his being an administrative receiver of a company].

[(1A) In subsection (1), "company" includes overseas company.]

(2) "The court" for this purpose means—

(a) any court having jurisdiction to wind up the company in relation to which the offence was committed, or

[(aa) in relation to an overseas company not falling within paragraph (a), the High Court or, in Scotland, the Court of Session, or]

(b) the court by or before which the person is convicted of the offence, or

(c) in the case of a summary conviction in England and Wales, any other magistrates' court acting [in the same local justice] area;

and for the purposes of this section the definition of "indictable offence" in Schedule 1 to the Interpretation Act 1978 applies for Scotland as it does for England and Wales.

(3) The maximum period of disqualification under this section is—

(a) where the disqualification order is made by a court of summary jurisdiction, 5 years, and

(b) in any other case, 15 years.

NOTES

Sub-s (1): words in first pair of square brackets substituted by the Deregulation and Contracting Out Act 1994, s 39, Sch 11, para 6, as from 1 July 1995. Words in second pair of square brackets substituted by the Insolvency Act 2000, s 8, Sch 4, Pt I, paras 1, 3, as from 2 April 2001.

Sub-s (1A): inserted by the Small Business, Enterprise and Employment Act 2015, s 111, Sch 7, Pt 1, paras 1, 4(1), (2), as from 1 October 2015.

Sub-s (2): para (aa) inserted by the Small Business, Enterprise and Employment Act 2015, s 111, Sch 7, Pt 1, paras 1, 4(1), (3), as from 1 October 2015. Words in square brackets in para (c) substituted by the Courts Act 2003, s 109(1), Sch 8, para 300, as from 1 April 2005.

[5.79]

3 Disqualification for persistent breaches of companies legislation

(1) The court may make a disqualification order against a person where it appears to it that he has been persistently in default in relation to provisions of the companies legislation requiring any return, account or other document to be filed with, delivered or sent, or notice of any matter to be given, to the registrar of companies.

(2) On an application to the court for an order to be made under this section, the fact that a person has been persistently in default in relation to such provisions as are mentioned above may (without prejudice to its proof in any other manner) be conclusively proved by showing that in the 5 years ending with the date of the application he has been adjudged guilty (whether or not on the same occasion) of three or more defaults in relation to those provisions.

(3) A person is to be treated under subsection (2) as being adjudged guilty of a default in relation to any provision of that legislation if—

(a) he is convicted (whether on indictment or summarily) of an offence consisting in a contravention of or failure to comply with that provision (whether on his own part or on the part of any company), or

(b) a default order is made against him, that is to say an order under any of the following provisions—
(i) [section 452 of the Companies Act 2006] (order requiring delivery of company accounts),
[(ia) [section 456] of that Act (order requiring preparation of revised accounts),]
(ii) [section 1113 of that Act (enforcement of company's filing obligations)],
(iii) section 41 of the Insolvency Act [1986] (enforcement of receiver's or manager's duty to make returns), or
(iv) section 170 of that Act (corresponding provision for liquidator in winding up),
in respect of any such contravention of or failure to comply with that provision (whether on his own part or on the part of any company).

[(3A) In this section "company" includes overseas company.]

(4) In this section "the court" means[—
(a)] any court having jurisdiction to wind up any of the companies in relation to which the offence or other default has been or is alleged to have been committed[,
(b) in relation to an overseas company not falling within paragraph (a), the High Court or, in Scotland, the Court of Session].

[(4A) In this section "the companies legislation" means the Companies Acts and Parts 1 to 7 of the Insolvency Act 1986 (company insolvency and winding up).]

(5) The maximum period of disqualification under this section is 5 years.

NOTES

Sub-s (3) is amended as follows:

Words in square brackets in sub-paras (b)(i) and (ia) substituted by the Companies Act 2006 (Consequential Amendments etc) Order 2008, SI 2008/948, art 3(1), Sch 1, Pt 2, para 106(1), (2)(a), (b), as from 6 April 2008.

Sub-para (b)(ia) originally inserted by CA 1989, s 23, Sch 10, para 35(2)(b), as from 7 January 1991.

Words in square brackets in sub-para (b)(ii) substituted by the Companies Act 2006 (Consequential Amendments, Transitional Provisions and Savings) Order 2009, SI 2009/1941, art 2(1), Sch 1, para 85(1), (2)(a)(i), as from 1 October 2009.

The year "1986" in square brackets in sub-para (b)(iii) was inserted by SI 2009/1941, art 2(1), Sch 1, para 85(1), (2)(a)(ii), as from 1 October 2009.

Sub-s (3A): inserted by the Small Business, Enterprise and Employment Act 2015, s 111, Sch 7, Pt 1, paras 1, 5(1), (2), as from 1 October 2015.

Sub-s (4): words in square brackets inserted by the Small Business, Enterprise and Employment Act 2015, s 111, Sch 7, Pt 1, paras 1, 5(1), (3), as from 1 October 2015.

Sub-s (4A): inserted by SI 2009/1941, art 2(1), Sch 1, para 85(1), (2)(b), as from 1 October 2009.

[5.80]

4 Disqualification for fraud, etc, in winding up

(1) The court may make a disqualification order against a person if, in the course of the winding up of a company, it appears that he—
(a) has been guilty of an offence for which he is liable (whether he has been convicted or not) under [section 993 of the Companies Act 2006] (fraudulent trading), or
(b) has otherwise been guilty, while an officer or liquidator of the company [receiver of the company's property or administrative receiver of the company], of any fraud in relation to the company or of any breach of his duty as such officer, liquidator, [receiver or administrative receiver].

(2) In this section "the court" means any court having jurisdiction to wind up any of the companies in relation to which the offence or other default has been or is alleged to have been committed; and "officer" includes a shadow director.

(3) The maximum period of disqualification under this section is 15 years.

NOTES

Sub-s (1): words in first pair of square brackets substituted by the Companies Act 2006 (Commencement No 3, Consequential Amendments, Transitional Provisions and Savings) Order 2007, SI 2007/2194, art 10(3), Sch 4, Pt 3, para 46, as from 1 October 2007. Words in second pair of square brackets substituted by the Insolvency Act 2000, s 8, Sch 4, Pt I, paras 1, 4, as from 2 April 2001.

[5.81]

5 Disqualification on summary conviction

(1) An offence counting for the purposes of this section is one of which a person is convicted (either on indictment or summarily) in consequence of a contravention of, or failure to comply with, any provision of the companies legislation requiring a return, account or other document to be filed with, delivered or sent, or notice of any matter to be given, to the registrar of companies (whether the contravention or failure is on the person's own part or on the part of any company).

(2) Where a person is convicted of a summary offence counting for those purposes, the court by which he is convicted (or, in England and Wales, any other magistrates' court acting [in the same local justice] area) may make a disqualification order against him if the circumstances specified in the next subsection are present.

(3) Those circumstances are that, during the 5 years ending with the date of the conviction, the person has had made against him, or has been convicted of, in total not less than 3 default orders and offences counting for the purposes of this section; and those offences may include that of which he is convicted as mentioned in subsection (2) and any other offence of which he is convicted on the same occasion.

(4) For the purposes of this section—
(a) the definition of "summary offence" in Schedule 1 to the Interpretation Act 1978 applies for Scotland as for England and Wales, and
(b) "default order" means the same as in section 3(3)(b).

[(4A) In this section "the companies legislation" means the Companies Acts and Parts 1 to 7 of the Insolvency Act 1986 (company insolvency and winding up).]

[(4B) In this section "company" includes overseas company.]

(5) The maximum period of disqualification under this section is 5 years.

NOTES

Sub-s (2): words in square brackets substituted by the Courts Act 2003, s 109(1), Sch 8, para 300, as from 1 April 2005.

Sub-s (4A): inserted by the Companies Act 2006 (Consequential Amendments, Transitional Provisions and Savings) Order 2009, SI 2009/1941, art 2(1), Sch 1, para 85(1), (3), as from 1 October 2009.

Sub-s (4B): inserted by the Small Business, Enterprise and Employment Act 2015, s 111, Sch 7, Pt 1, paras 1, 6, as from 1 October 2015.

[5.82]

[5A Disqualification for certain convictions abroad

(1) If it appears to the Secretary of State that it is expedient in the public interest that a disqualification order under this section should be made against a person, the Secretary of State may apply to the court for such an order.

(2) The court may, on an application under subsection (1), make a disqualification order against a person who has been convicted of a relevant foreign offence.

(3) A "relevant foreign offence" is an offence committed outside Great Britain—

(a) in connection with—

(i) the promotion, formation, management, liquidation or striking off of a company (or any similar procedure),

(ii) the receivership of a company's property (or any similar procedure), or

(iii) a person being an administrative receiver of a company (or holding a similar position), and

(b) which corresponds to an indictable offence under the law of England and Wales or (as the case may be) an indictable offence under the law of Scotland.

(4) Where it appears to the Secretary of State that, in the case of a person who has offered to give a disqualification undertaking—

(a) the person has been convicted of a relevant foreign offence, and

(b) it is expedient in the public interest that the Secretary of State should accept the undertaking (instead of applying, or proceeding with an application, for a disqualification order),

the Secretary of State may accept the undertaking.

(5) In this section—

"company" includes an overseas company;

"the court" means the High Court or, in Scotland, the Court of Session.

(6) The maximum period of disqualification under an order under this section is 15 years.]

NOTES

Inserted by the Small Business, Enterprise and Employment Act 2015, s 104, as from 1 October 2015.

Note that sub-ss (2), (4) apply in relation to a conviction of a relevant foreign offence which occurs on or after 1 October 2015 regardless of whether the act or omission which constituted the offence occurred before that day.

Disqualification for unfitness

[5.83]

6 Duty of court to disqualify unfit directors . . .

(1) The court shall make a disqualification order against a person in any case where, on an application under this section . . . —

[(a) the court is satisfied—

(i) that the person is or has been a director of a company which has at any time become insolvent (whether while the person was a director or subsequently), or

(ii) that the person has been a director of a company which has at any time been dissolved without becoming insolvent (whether while the person was a director or subsequently), and

(b) the court is satisfied that the person's conduct as a director of that company (either taken alone or taken together with the person's conduct as a director of one or more other companies or overseas companies) makes the person unfit to be concerned in the management of a company].

[(1A) In this section references to a person's conduct as a director of any company or overseas company include, where that company or overseas company has become insolvent, references to that person's conduct in relation to any matter connected with or arising out of the insolvency.]

(2) For the purposes of this section . . . a company becomes insolvent if—

(a) the company goes into liquidation at a time when its assets are insufficient for the payment of its debts and other liabilities and the expenses of the winding up,

[(b) the company enters administration,] or

(c) an administrative receiver of the company is appointed;

. . .

[(2A) For the purposes of this section, an overseas company becomes insolvent if the company enters into insolvency proceedings of any description (including interim proceedings) in any jurisdiction.]

[(3) In this section and section 7(2), "the court" means—

(a) where the company in question is being or has been wound up by the court, that court,

(b) where the company in question is being or has been wound up voluntarily, any court which has or (as the case may be) had jurisdiction to wind it up,

[(c) where neither paragraph (a) nor (b) applies but an administrator or administrative receiver has at any time been appointed in respect of the company in question, any court which has jurisdiction to wind it up;]

[(d) where the company in question has been dissolved without becoming insolvent, a court which at the time it was dissolved had jurisdiction to wind it up.]

(3A) Sections 117 and 120 of the Insolvency Act 1986 (jurisdiction) shall apply for the purposes of subsection (3) as if the references in the definitions of "registered office" to the presentation of the petition for winding up were references—

(a) in a case within paragraph (b) of that subsection, to the passing of the resolution for voluntary winding up, [(b) in a case within paragraph (c) of that subsection, to the appointment of the administrator or (as the case may be) administrative receiver.]

(3B) Nothing in subsection (3) invalidates any proceedings by reason of their being taken in the wrong court; and proceedings—

(a) for or in connection with a disqualification order under this section, or

(b) in connection with a disqualification undertaking accepted under section 7,

may be retained in the court in which the proceedings were commenced, although it may not be the court in which they ought to have been commenced.

(3C) In this section and section 7, "director" includes a shadow director.]

(4) Under this section the minimum period of disqualification is 2 years, and the maximum period is 15 years.

NOTES

Section heading: the words omitted were repealed by the Rating (Coronavirus) and Directors Disqualification (Dissolved Companies) Act 2021, s 2(2)(a), as from 15 December 2021 (for the purposes of the exercise by the Secretary of State or the official receiver of powers under s 7(4) of this Act), and as from 15 February 2022 (otherwise). Note that the amendments made by s 2 of the 2021 Act have effect in relation to conduct of directors of companies occurring, and in relation to companies dissolved, at any time before, as well as after, 15 December 2021 (see the note relating to s 2(14) of the 2021 Act at **[9.633]**).

Sub-s (1): the words omitted were repealed, and paras (a) and (b) were substituted, by the Rating (Coronavirus) and Directors Disqualification (Dissolved Companies) Act 2021, s 2(2)(b), as from 15 December 2021 (for the purposes of the exercise by the Secretary of State or the official receiver of powers under s 7(4) of this Act), and as from 15 February 2022 (otherwise) (for effect, see the first note relating to the 2021 Act above).

Sub-ss (1A), (2A): inserted by the Small Business, Enterprise and Employment Act 2015, s 106(1), (2)(b), (d), as from 1 October 2015, in respect of a person's conduct as a director of an overseas company where that conduct occurs on or after that date.

Sub-s (2): para (b) substituted by the Enterprise Act 2002, s 248(3), Sch 17, paras 40, 41(a), as from 15 September 2003 (for savings and transitional provisions, see the note to the Insolvency Act 1986, s 8 at **[9.147]**). First words omitted repealed by the Small Business, Enterprise and Employment Act 2015, s 111, Sch 7, Pt 1, paras 1, 7, as from 1 October 2015. Second words omitted repealed by s 106(1), (2)(c) of the 2015 Act, as from 1 October 2015, in respect of a person's conduct as a director of an overseas company where that conduct occurs on or after that date.

Sub-ss (3), (3A)–(3C): substituted (for the original sub-s (3)) by the Insolvency Act 2000, s 8, Sch 4, Pt I, paras 1, 5, as from 2 April 2001. These subsections have subsequently been amended as follows—

Sub-ss (3)(c), (3A)(b) were further substituted by the Enterprise Act 2002, s 248(3), Sch 17, paras 40, 41(b), (c), as from 15 September 2003 (for savings and transitional provisions, see the note to the Insolvency Act 1986, s 8 at **[9.147]**).

Sub-s (3)(d) was added by the Rating (Coronavirus) and Directors Disqualification (Dissolved Companies) Act 2021, s 2(2)(c), as from 15 December 2021 (for the purposes of the exercise by the Secretary of State or the official receiver of powers under s 7(4) of this Act), and as from 15 February 2022 (otherwise) (for effect, see the first note relating to the 2021 Act above).

[5.84]

7 [Disqualification orders under section 6: applications and acceptance of undertakings]

(1) If it appears to the Secretary of State that it is expedient in the public interest that a disqualification order under section 6 should be made against any person, an application for the making of such an order against that person may be made—

(a) by the Secretary of State, or

(b) if the Secretary of State so directs in the case of a person who is or has been a director of a company which is being [or has been] wound up by the court in England and Wales, by the official receiver.

(2) Except with the leave of the court, an application for the making under that section of a disqualification order against any person shall not be made after the end of the period of [3 years] beginning with[—

(a) in a case where the person is or has been a director of a company which has become insolvent, the day on which the company became insolvent, or

(b) in a case where the person has been a director of a company which has been dissolved without becoming insolvent, the day on which the company was dissolved.]

[(2A) If it appears to the Secretary of State that the conditions mentioned in section 6(1) are satisfied as respects any person who has offered to give him a disqualification undertaking, he may accept the undertaking if it appears to him that it is expedient in the public interest that he should do so (instead of applying, or proceeding with an application, for a disqualification order).]

(3) . . .

(4) The Secretary of State or the official receiver may require [any person]—

(a) to furnish him with such information with respect to [that person's or another person's conduct as a director of a company which has at any time become insolvent [or been dissolved without becoming insolvent] (whether while the person was a director or subsequently), and]

(b) to produce and permit inspection of such books, papers and other records [as are considered by the Secretary of State or (as the case may be) the official receiver to be relevant to that person's or another person's conduct as such a director],

as the Secretary of State or the official receiver may reasonably require for the purpose of determining whether to exercise, or of exercising, any function of his under this section.

[(5) Subsections (1A) and (2) of section 6 apply for the purposes of this section as they apply for the purposes of that section.]

NOTES

Section heading: substituted by the Small Business, Enterprise and Employment Act 2015, s 107(1), (4), as from 6 April 2016 (for transitional provisions see the note below).

Sub-s (1): words in square brackets inserted by the Insolvency Act 2000, s 8, Sch 4, Pt I, paras 1, 6(a), as from 2 April 2001.

Sub-s (2) is amended as follows:

Words in first pair of square brackets substituted by the Small Business, Enterprise and Employment Act 2015, s 108(1), as from 1 October 2015. Note that this amendment applies only to an application relating to a company which has become insolvent after the commencement of s 108(1) of the 2015 Act and, for these purposes, the Insolvency Act 1986, s 6(2) applies (meaning of "becoming insolvent") (see s 108(2), (3) of the 2015 Act).

Words in second pair of square brackets substituted by the Rating (Coronavirus) and Directors Disqualification (Dissolved Companies) Act 2021, s 2(3)(a), as from 15 December 2021. Note that the amendments made by s 2 of the 2021 Act have effect in relation to conduct of directors of companies occurring, and in relation to companies dissolved, at any time before, as well as after, 15 December 2021 (see the note relating to s 2(14) of the 2021 Act at **[9.633]**).

Sub-s (2A): inserted by the Insolvency Act 2000, s 6(1), (3), as from 2 April 2001.

Sub-s (3): repealed by the Small Business, Enterprise and Employment Act 2015, s 107(1), (3), as from 6 April 2016 (for transitional provisions see the note below).

Sub-s (4) is amended as follows:

The words "or been dissolved without becoming insolvent" in square brackets were inserted by the Rating (Coronavirus) and Directors Disqualification (Dissolved Companies) Act 2021, s 2(3)(b), as from 15 December 2021 (for effect, see the first note relating to the 2021 Act above).

The other words in square brackets were substituted by the Deregulation Act 2015, s 19, Sch 6, Pt 4, para 11, as from 1 October 2015. Note that the Deregulation Act 2015 (Commencement No 3 and Transitional and Saving Provisions) Order 2015, SI 2015/1732, art 5 provides that these amendments do not have effect in respect of a person who is or has been a director of a company that becomes insolvent (within the meaning of s 6(2) *ante*) before 1 October 2015.

Sub-s (5): added by the Small Business, Enterprise and Employment Act 2015, s 111, Sch 7, Pt 1, paras 1, 8, as from 1 October 2015.

Transitional provisions: the Small Business, Enterprise and Employment Act 2015 (Commencement No 4, Transitional and Savings Provisions) Regulations 2016, SI 2016/321, Schedule, Pt 1, paras 1, 2 provide as follows—

"1. The changes made by section 107 of the Act have no effect in respect of an office-holder reporting on the conduct of a person who is or has been a director of an insolvent company in cases where the insolvency date in respect of that company is before 6th April 2016.

2. "Insolvency date" in paragraph 1 has the meaning given in section 7A(10) of the Company Directors Disqualification Act 1986.".

[5.85]

[7A Office-holder's report on conduct of directors

(1) The office-holder in respect of a company which is insolvent must prepare a report (a "conduct report") about the conduct of each person who was a director of the company—

(a) on the insolvency date, or

(b) at any time during the period of 3 years ending with that date.

(2) For the purposes of this section a company is insolvent if—

(a) the company is in liquidation and at the time it went into liquidation its assets were insufficient for the payment of its debts and other liabilities and the expenses of the winding up,

(b) the company has entered administration, or

(c) an administrative receiver of the company has been appointed;

and subsection (1A) of section 6 applies for the purposes of this section as it applies for the purpose of that section.

(3) A conduct report must, in relation to each person, describe any conduct of the person which may assist the Secretary of State in deciding whether to exercise the power under section 7(1) or (2A) in relation to the person.

(4) The office-holder must send the conduct report to the Secretary of State before the end of—

(a) the period of 3 months beginning with the insolvency date, or

(b) such other longer period as the Secretary of State considers appropriate in the particular circumstances.

(5) If new information comes to the attention of an office-holder, the office-holder must send that information to the Secretary of State as soon as reasonably practicable.

(6) "New information" is information which an office-holder considers should have been included in a conduct report prepared in relation to the company, or would have been so included had it been available before the report was sent.

(7) If there is more than one office-holder in respect of a company at any particular time (because the company is insolvent by virtue of falling within more than one paragraph of subsection (2) at that time), subsection (1) applies only to the first of the office-holders to be appointed.

(8) In the case of a company which is at different times insolvent by virtue of falling within one or more different paragraphs of subsection (2)—

(a) the references in subsection (1) to the insolvency date are to be read as references to the first such date during the period in which the company is insolvent, and

(b) subsection (1) does not apply to an office-holder if at any time during the period in which the company is insolvent a conduct report has already been prepared and sent to the Secretary of State.

(9) The "office-holder" in respect of a company which is insolvent is—

(a) in the case of a company being wound up by the court in England and Wales, the official receiver;

(b) in the case of a company being wound up otherwise, the liquidator;

(c) in the case of a company in administration, the administrator;

(d) in the case of a company of which there is an administrative receiver, the receiver.

(10) The "insolvency date"—

(a) in the case of a company being wound up by the court, means the date on which the court makes the winding-up order (see section 125 of the Insolvency Act 1986);

(b) in the case of a company being wound up by way of a members' voluntary winding up, means the date on which the liquidator forms the opinion that the company will be unable to pay its debts in full (together with interest at the official rate) within the period stated in the directors' declaration of solvency under section 89 of the Insolvency Act 1986;

(c) in the case of a company being wound up by way of a creditors' voluntary winding up where no such declaration under section 89 of that Act has been made, means the date of the passing of the resolution for voluntary winding up;

(d) in the case of a company which has entered administration, means the date the company did so;

(e) in the case of a company in respect of which an administrative receiver has been appointed, means the date of that appointment.

(11) For the purposes of subsection (10)(e), any appointment of an administrative receiver to replace an administrative receiver who has died or vacated office pursuant to section 45 of the Insolvency Act 1986 is to be ignored.

(12) In this section—

"court" has the same meaning as in section 6;

"director" includes a shadow director.]

NOTES

Inserted by the Small Business, Enterprise and Employment Act 2015, s 107(1), (2), as from 6 April 2016.

For transitional provisions see the note relating to the Small Business, Enterprise and Employment Act 2015 (Commencement No 4, Transitional and Savings Provisions) Regulations 2016, SI 2016/321 on s 7 *ante*.

[5.86]

8 [Disqualification of director on finding of unfitness]

[(1) If it appears to the Secretary of State . . . that it is expedient in the public interest that a disqualification order should be made against a person who is, or has been, a director or shadow director of a company, he may apply to the court for such an order.

(1A) . . .]

(2) The court may make a disqualification order against a person where, on an application under this section, it is satisfied that his conduct in relation to the company [(either taken alone or taken together with his conduct as a director or shadow director of one or more other companies or overseas companies)] makes him unfit to be concerned in the management of a company.

[(2A) Where it appears to the Secretary of State . . . that, in the case of a person who has offered to give him a disqualification undertaking—

(a) the conduct of the person in relation to a company of which the person is or has been a director or shadow director [(either taken alone or taken together with his conduct as a director or shadow director of one or more other companies or overseas companies)] makes him unfit to be concerned in the management of a company, and

(b) it is expedient in the public interest that he should accept the undertaking (instead of applying, or proceeding with an application, for a disqualification order),

he may accept the undertaking.]

[(2B) Subsection (1A) of section 6 applies for the purposes of this section as it applies for the purposes of that section.]

(3) In this section "the court" means the High Court or, in Scotland, the Court of Session.

(4) The maximum period of disqualification under this section is 15 years.

NOTES

Section heading: words in square brackets substituted by the Small Business, Enterprise and Employment Act 2015, s 109(2), as from 1 October 2015.

Sub-s (1): substituted, together with sub-s (1A) for the original sub-s (1), by the Financial Services and Markets Act 2000 (Consequential Amendments and Repeals) Order 2001, SI 2001/3649, art 39, as from 1 December 2001. Words omitted repealed by the Small Business, Enterprise and Employment Act 2015, s 109(1)(a), as from 1 October 2015.

Sub-s (1A): substituted as noted above. Subsequently repealed by the Small Business, Enterprise and Employment Act 2015, s 109(1)(b), as from 1 October 2015.

Sub-s (2): words in square brackets inserted by the Small Business, Enterprise and Employment Act 2015, s 106(1), (3)(a), as from 1 October 2015, in respect of a person's conduct as a director of an overseas company where that conduct occurs on or after that date.

Sub-s (2A): inserted by the Insolvency Act 2000, s 6(1), (4), as from 2 April 2001. Words omitted repealed by the Small Business, Enterprise and Employment Act 2015, s 109(1)(a), as from 1 October 2015. Words in square brackets inserted by s 106(1), (3)(b) of the 2015 Act, as from 1 October 2015, in respect of a person's conduct as a director of an overseas company where that conduct occurs on or after that date.

Sub-s (2B): inserted by the Small Business, Enterprise and Employment Act 2015, s 106(1), (3)(c), as from 1 October 2015, in respect of a person's conduct as a director of an overseas company where that conduct occurs on or after that date.

[Persons instructing unfit directors

[5.87]

8ZA Order disqualifying person instructing unfit director . . .

(1) The court may make a disqualification order against a person ("P") if, on an application under section 8ZB, it is satisfied—

(a) either—

(i) that a disqualification order under section 6 has been made against a person who is or has been a director (but not a shadow director) of a company, or

(ii) that the Secretary of State has accepted a disqualification undertaking from such a person under section 7(2A), and

(b) that P exercised the requisite amount of influence over the person.

That person is referred to in this section as "the main transgressor".

(2) For the purposes of this section, P exercised the requisite amount of influence over the main transgressor if any of the conduct—

(a) for which the main transgressor is subject to the order made under section 6, or

(b) in relation to which the undertaking was accepted from the main transgressor under section 7(2A),

was the result of the main transgressor acting in accordance with P's directions or instructions.

(3) But P does not exercise the requisite amount of influence over the main transgressor by reason only that the main transgressor acts on advice given by P in a professional capacity.

(4) Under this section the minimum period of disqualification is 2 years and the maximum period is 15 years.

(5) In this section and section 8ZB "the court" has the same meaning as in section 6; and subsection (3B) of section 6 applies in relation to proceedings mentioned in subsection (6) below as it applies in relation to proceedings mentioned in section 6(3B)(a) and (b).

(6) The proceedings are proceedings—

(a) for or in connection with a disqualification order under this section, or

(b) in connection with a disqualification undertaking accepted under section 8ZC.]

NOTES

Inserted, together with the preceding heading and ss 8ZB–8ZE, by the Small Business, Enterprise and Employment Act 2015, s 105, as from 1 October 2015, in relation to a case where (i) the main transgressor's conduct (as mentioned in s 8ZA(2)), and (ii) the exercise by P of the requisite amount of influence (as mentioned in s 8ZA(1), (2)), occur on or after that date.

Section heading: the words omitted were repealed by the Rating (Coronavirus) and Directors Disqualification (Dissolved Companies) Act 2021, s 2(4), as from 15 December 2021 (for the purposes of the exercise by the Secretary of State or the official receiver of powers under s 7(4) of this Act), and as from 15 February 2022 (otherwise). Note that the amendments made by s 2 of the 2021 Act have effect in relation to conduct of directors of companies occurring, and in relation to companies dissolved, at any time before, as well as after, 15 December 2021 (see the note relating to s 2(14) of the 2021 Act at **[9.633]**).

[5.88]

[8ZB Application for order under section 8ZA

(1) If it appears to the Secretary of State that it is expedient in the public interest that a disqualification order should be made against a person under section 8ZA, the Secretary of State may—

(a) make an application to the court for such an order, or

(b) in a case where an application for an order under section 6 against the main transgressor has been made by the official receiver, direct the official receiver to make such an application.

(2) Except with the leave of the court, an application for a disqualification order under section 8ZA must not be made after the end of the period of 3 years beginning with the day on which the company in question became insolvent (within the meaning given by section 6(2)) [or was dissolved without becoming insolvent].

(3) Subsection (4) of section 7 applies for the purposes of this section as it applies for the purposes of that section.]

NOTES

Inserted as noted to s 8ZA at **[5.87]**.

Sub-s (2): words in square brackets inserted by the Rating (Coronavirus) and Directors Disqualification (Dissolved Companies) Act 2021, s 2(5), as from 15 December 2021 (for the purposes of the exercise by the Secretary of State or the official receiver of powers under s 7(4) of this Act), and as from 15 February 2022 (otherwise). Note that the amendments made by s 2 of the 2021 Act have effect in relation to conduct of directors of companies occurring, and in relation to companies dissolved, at any time before, as well as after, 15 December 2021 (see the note relating to s 2(14) of the 2021 Act at **[9.633]**).

[5.89]

[8ZC Disqualification undertaking instead of an order under section 8ZA

(1) If it appears to the Secretary of State that it is expedient in the public interest to do so, the Secretary of State may accept a disqualification undertaking from a person ("P") if—

(a) any of the following is the case—

(i) a disqualification order under section 6 has been made against a person who is or has been a director (but not a shadow director) of a company,

(ii) the Secretary of State has accepted a disqualification undertaking from such a person under section 7(2A), or

(iii) it appears to the Secretary of State that such an undertaking could be accepted from such a person (if one were offered), and

(b) it appears to the Secretary of State that P exercised the requisite amount of influence over the person.

That person is referred to in this section as "the main transgressor".

(2) For the purposes of this section, P exercised the requisite amount of influence over the main transgressor if any of the conduct—

(a) for which the main transgressor is subject to the disqualification order made under section 6,

(b) in relation to which the disqualification undertaking was accepted from the main transgressor under section 7(2A), or

(c) which led the Secretary of State to the conclusion set out in subsection (1)(a)(iii),

was the result of the main transgressor acting in accordance with P's directions or instructions.

(3) But P does not exercise the requisite amount of influence over the main transgressor by reason only that the main transgressor acts on advice given by P in a professional capacity.

(4) Subsection (4) of section 7 applies for the purposes of this section as it applies for the purposes of that section.]

NOTES

Inserted as noted to s 8ZA at **[5.87]**.

[5.90]

[8ZD Order disqualifying person instructing unfit director: other cases

(1) The court may make a disqualification order against a person ("P") if, on an application under this section, it is satisfied—

(a) either—

(i) that a disqualification order under section 8 has been made against a person who is or has been a director (but not a shadow director) of a company, or

(ii) that the Secretary of State has accepted a disqualification undertaking from such a person under section 8(2A), and

(b) that P exercised the requisite amount of influence over the person.

That person is referred to in this section as "the main transgressor".

(2) The Secretary of State may make an application to the court for a disqualification order against P under this section if it appears to the Secretary of State that it is expedient in the public interest for such an order to be made.
(3) For the purposes of this section, P exercised the requisite amount of influence over the main transgressor if any of the conduct—
(a) for which the main transgressor is subject to the order made under section 8, or
(b) in relation to which the undertaking was accepted from the main transgressor under section 8(2A),
was the result of the main transgressor acting in accordance with P's directions or instructions.
(4) But P does not exercise the requisite amount of influence over the main transgressor by reason only that the main transgressor acts on advice given by P in a professional capacity.
(5) Under this section the maximum period of disqualification is 15 years.
(6) In this section "the court" means the High Court or, in Scotland, the Court of Session.]

NOTES

Inserted as noted to s 8ZA at **[5.87]**.

[5.91]

[8ZE Disqualification undertaking instead of an order under section 8ZD

(1) If it appears to the Secretary of State that it is expedient in the public interest to do so, the Secretary of State may accept a disqualification undertaking from a person ("P") if—
(a) any of the following is the case—
(i) a disqualification order under section 8 has been made against a person who is or has been a director (but not a shadow director) of a company,
(ii) the Secretary of State has accepted a disqualification undertaking from such a person under section 8(2A), or
(iii) it appears to the Secretary of State that such an undertaking could be accepted from such a person (if one were offered), and
(b) it appears to the Secretary of State that P exercised the requisite amount of influence over the person.
That person is referred to in this section as "the main transgressor".
(2) For the purposes of this section, P exercised the requisite amount of influence over the main transgressor if any of the conduct—
(a) for which the main transgressor is subject to the disqualification order made under section 8,
(b) in relation to which the disqualification undertaking was accepted from the main transgressor under section 8(2A), or
(c) which led the Secretary of State to the conclusion set out in subsection (1)(a)(iii),
was the result of the main transgressor acting in accordance with P's directions or instructions.
(3) But P does not exercise the requisite amount of influence over the main transgressor by reason only that the main transgressor acts on advice given by P in a professional capacity.]

NOTES

Inserted as noted to s 8ZA at **[5.87]**.

[Further provision about disqualification undertakings]

[5.92]

[8A Variation etc of disqualification undertaking

(1) The court may, on the application of a person who is subject to a disqualification undertaking—
(a) reduce the period for which the undertaking is to be in force, or
(b) provide for it to cease to be in force.
(2) On the hearing of an application under subsection (1), the Secretary of State shall appear and call the attention of the court to any matters which seem to him to be relevant, and may himself give evidence or call witnesses.
[(2A) Subsection (2) does not apply to an application in the case of an undertaking given under section 9B, and in such a case on the hearing of the application whichever of the [Competition and Markets Authority] or a specified regulator (within the meaning of section 9E) accepted the undertaking—
(a) must appear and call the attention of the court to any matters which appear to it or him (as the case may be) to be relevant;
(b) may give evidence or call witnesses.]
[(3) In this section "the court"—
[(za) in the case of an undertaking given under section 8ZC has the same meaning as in section 8ZA;
(zb) in the case of an undertaking given under section 8ZE means the High Court or, in Scotland, the Court of Session;]
(a) in the case of an undertaking given under section 9B means the High Court or (in Scotland) the Court of Session;
(b) in any other case has the same meaning as in section [5A(5),] 7(2) or 8 (as the case may be).]]

NOTES

The heading preceding this section was inserted by the Small Business, Enterprise and Employment Act 2015, s 111, Sch 7, Pt 1, paras 1, 9, as from 1 October 2015.

This section was inserted by the Insolvency Act 2000, s 6(1), (5), as from 2 April 2001.

Sub-s (2A): inserted by the Enterprise Act 2002, s 204(1), (4), as from 20 June 2003. Words in square brackets substituted by the Enterprise and Regulatory Reform Act 2013 (Competition) (Consequential, Transitional and Saving Provisions) Order 2014, SI 2014/892, art 2, Sch 1, Pt 2, paras 52, 53(a), as from 1 April 2014.

Sub-s (3): substituted by the Enterprise Act 2002, s 204(1), (5), as from 20 June 2003. Paras (za), (zb), and the figure in square brackets in para (b), were inserted by the Small Business, Enterprise and Employment Act 2015, s 111, Sch 7, Pt 1, paras 1, 10, as from 1 October 2015.

9 (*Repealed by the Small Business, Enterprise and Employment Act 2015, s 106(1), (4), as from 1 October 2015.*)

[Disqualification for competition infringements

[5.93]

9A Competition disqualification order

(1) The court must make a disqualification order against a person if the following two conditions are satisfied in relation to him.

(2) The first condition is that an undertaking which is a company of which he is a director commits a breach of competition law.

(3) The second condition is that the court considers that his conduct as a director makes him unfit to be concerned in the management of a company.

(4) An undertaking commits a breach of competition law if it engages in conduct which infringes [either of the following]—

(a) the Chapter 1 prohibition (within the meaning of the Competition Act 1998) (prohibition on agreements, etc preventing, restricting or distorting competition);

(b) the Chapter 2 prohibition (within the meaning of that Act) (prohibition on abuse of a dominant position);

(c), (d) . . .

(5) For the purpose of deciding under subsection (3) whether a person is unfit to be concerned in the management of a company the court—

(a) must have regard to whether subsection (6) applies to him;

(b) may have regard to his conduct as a director of a company in connection with any other breach of competition law;

(c) must not have regard to the matters mentioned in Schedule 1.

(6) This subsection applies to a person if as a director of the company—

(a) his conduct contributed to the breach of competition law mentioned in subsection (2);

(b) his conduct did not contribute to the breach but he had reasonable grounds to suspect that the conduct of the undertaking constituted the breach and he took no steps to prevent it;

(c) he did not know but ought to have known that the conduct of the undertaking constituted the breach.

(7) For the purposes of subsection (6)(a) it is immaterial whether the person knew that the conduct of the undertaking constituted the breach.

(8) For the purposes of subsection (4)(a) . . . references to the conduct of an undertaking are references to its conduct taken with the conduct of one or more other undertakings.

(9) The maximum period of disqualification under this section is 15 years.

(10) An application under this section for a disqualification order may be made by the [Competition and Markets Authority] or by a specified regulator.

(11) [Section 60A of the Competition Act 1998 (certain principles etc to be considered or applied from IP completion day)] applies in relation to any question arising by virtue of subsection (4)(a) or (b) above as it applies in relation to any question arising under Part 1 of that Act.]

NOTES

Inserted, together with preceding heading and ss 9B–9E, by the Enterprise Act 2002, s 204(1), (2), as from 20 June 2003.

Sub-s (4): the words in square brackets were substituted, and paras (c) and (d) were repealed, by the Competition (Amendment etc) (EU Exit) Regulations 2019, SI 2019/93, reg 60, Sch 1, para 1(1), (2), as from IP completion day (as defined in the European Union (Withdrawal Agreement) Act 2020, s 39) (for transitional provisions, see the note below).

Sub-s (8): the words omitted were repealed by SI 2019/93, reg 60, Sch 1, para 1(1), (3), as from IP completion day (as defined in the European Union (Withdrawal Agreement) Act 2020, s 39) (for transitional provisions, see the note below).

Sub-s (10): words in square brackets substituted by the Enterprise and Regulatory Reform Act 2013 (Competition) (Consequential, Transitional and Saving Provisions) Order 2014, SI 2014/892, art 2, Sch 1, Pt 2, paras 52, 53(b), as from 1 April 2014.

Sub-s (11): the words in square brackets were substituted by SI 2019/93, reg 60, Sch 1, para 1(1), (4), as from IP completion day (as defined in the European Union (Withdrawal Agreement) Act 2020, s 39). Note that Sch 1, para 1(4) to the 2019 Regulations was amended by the Competition (Amendment etc) (EU Exit) Regulations 2020, SI 2020/1343, reg 13, with effect from immediately before IP completion day; and the effect of the amendment has been incorporated in the text set out above.

Transitional provisions: the Competition (Amendment etc) (EU Exit) Regulations 2019, SI 2019/93, Sch 4, para 36 (as amended by the Competition (Amendment etc.) (EU Exit) Regulations 2020, SI 2020/1343, reg 59) provides that where an undertaking engages in conduct which infringes Article 101 or 102 of the Treaty of the Functioning of the European Union before IP completion day, this section has effect without the amendments made to it by Sch 1, para 1(1)–(3) to those Regulations.

[5.94]

[9B Competition undertakings

(1) This section applies if—

(a) the [Competition and Markets Authority] or a specified regulator thinks that in relation to any person an undertaking which is a company of which he is a director has committed or is committing a breach of competition law,

(b) the [Competition and Markets Authority] or the specified regulator thinks that the conduct of the person as a director makes him unfit to be concerned in the management of a company, and

(c) the person offers to give the [Competition and Markets Authority] or the specified regulator (as the case may be) a disqualification undertaking.

(2) The [Competition and Markets Authority] or the specified regulator (as the case may be) may accept a disqualification undertaking from the person instead of applying for or proceeding with an application for a disqualification order.

(3) A disqualification undertaking is an undertaking by a person that for the period specified in the undertaking he will not—

(a) be a director of a company;

(b) act as receiver of a company's property;

(c) in any way, whether directly or indirectly, be concerned or take part in the promotion, formation or management of a company;

(d) act as an insolvency practitioner.

(4) But a disqualification undertaking may provide that a prohibition falling within subsection (3)(a) to (c) does not apply if the person obtains the leave of the court.

(5) The maximum period which may be specified in a disqualification undertaking is 15 years.

(6) If a disqualification undertaking is accepted from a person who is already subject to a disqualification undertaking under this Act or to a disqualification order the periods specified in those undertakings or the undertaking and the order (as the case may be) run concurrently.

(7) Subsections (4) to (8) of section 9A apply for the purposes of this section as they apply for the purposes of that section but in the application of subsection (5) of that section the reference to the court must be construed as a reference to the [Competition and Markets Authority] or a specified regulator (as the case may be).]

NOTES

Inserted as noted to s 9A at **[5.93]**.

Words in square brackets substituted by the Enterprise and Regulatory Reform Act 2013 (Competition) (Consequential, Transitional and Saving Provisions) Order 2014, SI 2014/892, art 2, Sch 1, Pt 2, paras 52, 53(c), as from 1 April 2014.

[5.95]

[9C Competition investigations

(1) If the [Competition and Markets Authority] or a specified regulator has reasonable grounds for suspecting that a breach of competition law has occurred it or he (as the case may be) may carry out an investigation for the purpose of deciding whether to make an application under section 9A for a disqualification order.

(2) For the purposes of such an investigation sections 26 to 30 of the Competition Act 1998 (c 41) apply to the [Competition and Markets Authority] and the specified regulators as they apply to the [Competition and Markets Authority] for the purposes of an investigation under section 25 of that Act.

(3) Subsection (4) applies if as a result of an investigation under this section the [Competition and Markets Authority] or a specified regulator proposes to apply under section 9A for a disqualification order.

(4) Before making the application the [Competition and Markets Authority] or regulator (as the case may be) must—

(a) give notice to the person likely to be affected by the application, and

(b) give that person an opportunity to make representations.]

NOTES

Inserted as noted to s 9A at **[5.93]**.

Words in square brackets substituted by the Enterprise and Regulatory Reform Act 2013 (Competition) (Consequential, Transitional and Saving Provisions) Order 2014, SI 2014/892, art 2, Sch 1, Pt 2, paras 52, 53(d), as from 1 April 2014.

[5.96]

[9D Co-ordination

(1) The Secretary of State may make regulations for the purpose of co-ordinating the performance of functions under sections 9A to 9C (relevant functions) which are exercisable concurrently by two or more persons.

(2) Section 54(5) to (7) of the Competition Act 1998 (c 41) applies to regulations made under this section as it applies to regulations made under that section and for that purpose in that section—

(a) references to Part 1 functions must be read as references to relevant functions;

(b) references to a regulator must be read as references to a specified regulator;

[(ba) the reference in subsection (6A)(b) to notice under section 31(1) of the Competition Act 1998 that the regulator proposes to make a decision within the meaning given by section 31(2) of that Act is to be read as notice under section 9C(4) that the specified regulator proposes to apply under section 9A for a disqualification order;]

(c) a competent person also includes any of the specified regulators.

(3) The power to make regulations under this section must be exercised by statutory instrument subject to annulment in pursuance of a resolution of either House of Parliament.

(4) Such a statutory instrument may—

(a) contain such incidental, supplemental, consequential and transitional provision as the Secretary of State thinks appropriate;

(b) make different provision for different cases.]

NOTES

Inserted as noted to s 9A at **[5.93]**.

Sub-s (2): para (ba) inserted by the Enterprise and Regulatory Reform Act 2013 (Competition) (Consequential, Transitional and Saving Provisions) Order 2014, SI 2014/892, art 2, Sch 1, Pt 2, paras 52, 54, as from 1 April 2014.

[5.97]

[9E Interpretation

(1) This section applies for the purposes of sections 9A to 9D.

(2) Each of the following is a specified regulator for the purposes of a breach of competition law in relation to a matter in respect of which he or it has a function—

[(a) the Office of Communications;]

(b) the Gas and Electricity Markets Authority;

[(c) the Water Services Regulation Authority;]

(d) [the Office of Rail and Road];

(e) the Civil Aviation Authority;

[(f) Monitor];

[(g) the Payment Systems Regulator established under section 40 of the Financial Services (Banking Reform) Act 2013];

[(h) the Financial Conduct Authority].
(3) The court is the High Court or (in Scotland) the Court of Session.
(4) Conduct includes omission.
(5) Director includes shadow director.]

NOTES

Inserted as noted to s 9A at **[5.93]**.

Sub-s (2): para (a) substituted by the Communications Act 2003, s 406, Sch 17, para 83, as from 29 December 2003. Para (c) substituted by the Water Act 2003, s 101(1), Sch 7, Pt 2, para 25, as from 1 April 2006. Words in square brackets in para (d) substituted by the Office of Rail Regulation (Change of Name) Regulations 2015, SI 2015/1682, reg 2(2), Schedule, Pt 1, para 4(h), as from 16 October 2015. Para (f) was added by the Health and Social Care Act 2012, s 74(4), as from 1 April 2013, and is repealed by the Health and Care Act 2022, s 84, Sch 12, para 1, as from a day to be appointed. Para (g) added by the Financial Services (Banking Reform) Act 2013, s 67(1), as from 1 April 2015. Para (h) added by s 129 of, and Sch 8, Pt 2, para 8 to, the 2013 Act, as from 1 April 2015.

Other cases of disqualification

[5.98]

10 Participation in wrongful trading

(1) Where the court makes a declaration under section 213 or 214 of the Insolvency Act [1986] that a person is liable to make a contribution to a company's assets, then, whether or not an application for such an order is made by any person, the court may, if it thinks fit, also make a disqualification order against the person to whom the declaration relates.
(2) The maximum period of disqualification under this section is 15 years.
[(3) In this section "company" includes overseas company.]

NOTES

Sub-s (1): year "1986" in square brackets inserted by the Companies Act 2006 (Consequential Amendments, Transitional Provisions and Savings) Order 2009, SI 2009/1941, art 2(1), Sch 1, para 85(1), (6), as from 1 October 2009.

Sub-s (3): added by the Small Business, Enterprise and Employment Act 2015, s 111, Sch 7, Pt 1, paras 1, 11, as from 1 October 2015.

[5.99]

11 Undischarged bankrupts

[(1) It is an offence for a person to act as director of a company or directly or indirectly to take part in or be concerned in the promotion, formation or management of a company, without the leave of the court, at a time when any of the circumstances mentioned in subsection (2) apply to the person.
(2) The circumstances are—
(a) the person is an undischarged bankrupt—
(i) in England and Wales or Scotland, or
(ii) in Northern Ireland,
(b) a bankruptcy restrictions order or undertaking is in force in respect of the person under—
(i) the Bankruptcy (Scotland) Act 1985 [or 2016] or the Insolvency Act 1986, or
(ii) the Insolvency (Northern Ireland) Order 1989,
(c) a debt relief restrictions order or undertaking is in force in respect of the person under—
(i) the Insolvency Act 1986, or
(ii) the Insolvency (Northern Ireland) Order 1989,
(d) a moratorium period under a debt relief order applies in relation to the person under—
(i) the Insolvency Act 1986, or
(ii) the Insolvency (Northern Ireland) Order 1989.
(2A) In subsection (1) "the court" means—
(a) for the purposes of subsection (2)(a)(i)—
[(i) the court by which the bankruptcy order was made or (if the order was not made by a court) the court to which a debtor may appeal against a refusal to make a bankruptcy order, or]
(ii) in Scotland, the court by which sequestration of the person's estate was awarded or, if awarded other than by the court, the court which would have jurisdiction in respect of sequestration of the person's estate,
(b) for the purposes of subsection (2)(b)(i)—
(i) the court which made the order,
(ii) in Scotland, if the order has been made other than by the court, the court to which the person may appeal against the order, or
(iii) the court to which the person may make an application for annulment of the undertaking,
(c) for the purposes of subsection (2)(c)(i)—
(i) the court which made the order, or
(ii) the court to which the person may make an application for annulment of the undertaking,
(d) for the purposes of subsection (2)(d)(i), the court to which the person would make an application under section 251M(1) of the Insolvency Act 1986 (if the person were dissatisfied as mentioned there),
(e) for the purposes of paragraphs (a)(ii), (b)(ii), (c)(ii) and (d)(ii) of subsection (2), the High Court of Northern Ireland.]
(3) In England and Wales, the leave of the court shall not be given unless notice of intention to apply for it has been served on the official receiver; and it is the latter's duty, if he is of opinion that it is contrary to the public interest that the application should be granted, to attend on the hearing of the application and oppose it.
[(4) In this section "company" includes a company incorporated outside Great Britain that has an established place of business in Great Britain.]

NOTES

Sub-ss (1), (2), (2A): substituted (for the original sub-ss (1), (2)) by the Small Business, Enterprise and Employment Act 2015, s 113(1), as from 1 October 2015, in respect of a person where (a) a bankruptcy order, a bankruptcy restrictions order, a debt relief restrictions order, (b) a bankruptcy restrictions undertaking, a debt relief restrictions undertaking, or (c) a moratorium period under a debt relief order, is, as the case may be, made, awarded, accepted, granted or commences on or after that date. These subsections have subsequently been amended as follows—

Words in square brackets in sub-s (2)(b)(i) inserted by the Bankruptcy (Scotland) Act 2016 (Consequential Provisions and Modifications) Order 2016, SI 2016/1034, art 7(1), (3), Sch 1, para 5, as from 30 November 2016 (except in relation to (i) a sequestration as regards which the petition is presented, or the debtor application is made before that date; or (ii) a trust deed executed before that date).

Sub-s (2A)(a)(i) substituted by the Enterprise and Regulatory Reform Act 2013 (Consequential Amendments) (Bankruptcy) and the Small Business, Enterprise and Employment Act 2015 (Consequential Amendments) Regulations 2016, SI 2016/481, reg 2(1), Sch 1, para 8, as from 6 April 2016.

Sub-s (4): added by the Companies Act 2006 (Consequential Amendments, Transitional Provisions and Savings) Order 2009, SI 2009/1941, art 2(1), Sch 1, para 85(1), (7), as from 1 October 2009.

[5.100]

12 *Failure to pay under county court administration order*

(1) The following has effect where a court under section 429 of the Insolvency Act revokes an administration order under Part VI of the County Courts Act 1984.

(2) A person to whom *that section applies by virtue of the order under section 429(2)(b)* shall not, except with the leave of the court which made the order, act as director or liquidator of, or directly or indirectly take part or be concerned in the promotion, formation or management of, a company.

NOTES

Section heading: for the words in italics there are substituted the words "Disabilities on revocation of administration order" by the Tribunals, Courts and Enforcement Act 2007, s 106, Sch 16, para 5(1), (2), as from a day to be appointed (except in relation to any case in which an administration order was made, or an application for such an order was made, before the day on which s 106 comes into force).

Sub-s (1): repealed by the Tribunals, Courts and Enforcement Act 2007, ss 106, 146, Sch 16, para 5(1), (3), Sch 23, Pt 5, as from a day to be appointed (subject to the same exception as noted above).

Sub-s (2): for the words in italics there are substituted the words "section 429 of the Insolvency Act applies by virtue of an order under subsection (2) of that section" by the Tribunals, Courts and Enforcement Act 2007, s 106, Sch 16, para 5(1), (4), as from a day to be appointed (subject to the same exception as noted above). Note that the Companies Act 2006 (Consequential Amendments, Transitional Provisions and Savings) Order 2009, SI 2009/1941, art 2(1), Sch 1, para 85(1), (6) provides that "1986" should be inserted after the words "the Insolvency Act" in sub-s (2) of this section (as from 1 October 2009). It is assumed that this amendment should take effect after the substitution noted *ante* comes into force.

[5.101]

[12A Northern Irish disqualification orders

A person subject to a disqualification order under [the Company Directors Disqualification (Northern Ireland) Order 2002]—

(a) shall not be a director of a company, act as receiver of a company's property or in any way, whether directly or indirectly, be concerned or take part in the promotion, formation or management of a company unless (in each case) he has the leave of the High Court of Northern Ireland, and

(b) shall not act as an insolvency practitioner.]

NOTES

Inserted by the Insolvency Act 2000, s 7(1), as from 2 April 2001, except in relation to a person subject to a disqualification order under the Companies (Northern Ireland) Order 1989, Part II made before that date.

Words in square brackets substituted by the Companies Act 2006 (Consequential Amendments, Transitional Provisions and Savings) Order 2009, SI 2009/1941, art 2(1), Sch 1, para 85(1), (8), as from 1 October 2009.

[5.102]

[12B Northern Irish disqualification undertakings

A person subject to a disqualification undertaking under the Company Directors Disqualification (Northern Ireland) Order 2002—

(a) shall not be a director of a company, act as receiver of a company's property or in any way, whether directly or indirectly, be concerned or take part in the promotion, formation or management of a company unless (in each case) he has the leave of the High Court of Northern Ireland, and

(b) shall not act as an insolvency practitioner.]

NOTES

Inserted by the Insolvency Act 2000 (Company Directors Disqualification Undertakings) Order 2004, SI 2004/1941, art 2(1), (2), as from 1 September 2004, in relation to disqualification undertakings under the Company Directors Disqualification (Northern Ireland) Order 2002 accepted on or after that date.

[5.103]

[12C Determining unfitness etc: matters to be taken into account

(1) This section applies where a court must determine—

(a) whether a person's conduct as a director of one or more companies or overseas companies makes the person unfit to be concerned in the management of a company;

(b) whether to exercise any discretion it has to make a disqualification order under any of sections 2 to 4, 5A, 8 or 10;

(c) where the court has decided to make a disqualification order under any of those sections or is required to make an order under section 6, what the period of disqualification should be.

(2) But this section does not apply where the court in question is one mentioned in section 2(2)(b) or (c).

(3) This section also applies where the Secretary of State must determine—

(a) whether a person's conduct as a director of one or more companies or overseas companies makes the person unfit to be concerned in the management of a company;

(b) whether to exercise any discretion the Secretary of State has to accept a disqualification undertaking under section 5A, 7 or 8.

(4) In making any such determination in relation to a person, the court or the Secretary of State must—

(a) in every case, have regard in particular to the matters set out in paragraphs 1 to 4 of Schedule 1;

(b) in a case where the person concerned is or has been a director of a company or overseas company, also have regard in particular to the matters set out in paragraphs 5 to 7 of that Schedule.

(5) In this section "director" includes a shadow director.

(6) Subsection (1A) of section 6 applies for the purposes of this section as it applies for the purposes of that section.

(7) The Secretary of State may by order modify Schedule 1; and such an order may contain such transitional provision as may appear to the Secretary of State to be necessary or expedient.

(8) The power to make an order under this section is exercisable by statutory instrument.

(9) An order under this section may not be made unless a draft of the instrument containing it has been laid before, and approved by a resolution of, each House of Parliament.]

NOTES

Inserted by the Small Business, Enterprise and Employment Act 2015, s 106(1), (5), as from 26 May 2015 (for the purposes of enabling the exercise of any power to make provision by order made by statutory instrument), and as from 1 October 2015 (otherwise). Save where conduct is considered by a court or by the Secretary of State under s 5A of this Act, this section applies to a person's conduct as a director where that conduct occurs on or after 1 October 2015 (see SI 2015/1689, Schedule).

Consequences of contravention

[5.104]

13 Criminal penalties

If a person acts in contravention of a disqualification order or [disqualification undertaking or in contravention] of section 12(2)[, 12A or 12B], or is guilty of an offence under section 11, he is liable—

(a) on conviction on indictment, to imprisonment for not more than 2 years or a fine, or both; and

(b) on summary conviction, to imprisonment for not more than 6 months or a fine not exceeding the statutory maximum, or both.

NOTES

Words in first pair of square brackets inserted by the Insolvency Act 2000, s 8, Sch 4, Pt I, paras 1, 8, as from 2 April 2001. Words in second pair of square brackets substituted by the Insolvency Act 2000 (Company Directors Disqualification Undertakings) Order 2004, SI 2004/1941, art 2(1), (3), as from 1 September 2004, in relation to disqualification undertakings under the Company Directors Disqualification (Northern Ireland) Order 2002 accepted on or after that date.

[5.105]

14 Offences by body corporate

(1) Where a body corporate is guilty of an offence of acting in contravention of a disqualification order [or disqualification undertaking or in contravention of section 12A] [or 12B], and it is proved that the offence occurred with the consent or connivance of, or was attributable to any neglect on the part of any director, manager, secretary or other similar officer of the body corporate, or any person who was purporting to act in any such capacity he, as well as the body corporate, is guilty of the offence and liable to be proceeded against and punished accordingly.

(2) Where the affairs of a body corporate are managed by its members, subsection (1) applies in relation to the acts and defaults of a member in connection with his functions of management as if he were a director of the body corporate.

NOTES

Sub-s (1): words in first pair of square brackets inserted by the Insolvency Act 2000, s 8, Sch 4, Pt I, paras 1, 9, as from 2 April 2001. Words in second pair of square brackets inserted by the Insolvency Act 2000 (Company Directors Disqualification Undertakings) Order 2004, SI 2004/1941, art 2(1), (4), as from 1 September 2004, in relation to disqualification undertakings under the Company Directors Disqualification (Northern Ireland) Order 2002 accepted on or after that date.

[5.106]

15 Personal liability for company's debts where person acts while disqualified

(1) A person is personally responsible for all the relevant debts of a company if at any time—

(a) in contravention of a disqualification order or [disqualification undertaking or in contravention] of section 11[, 12A or 12B] of this Act he is involved in the management of the company, or

[(b) as a person who is involved in the management of the company, he acts or is willing to act on instructions given without the leave of the court by a person whom he knows at that time—

(i) to be the subject of a disqualification order made or disqualification undertaking accepted under this Act or under the Company Directors Disqualification (Northern Ireland) Order 2002, or

(ii) to be an undischarged bankrupt.]

(2) Where a person is personally responsible under this section for the relevant debts of a company, he is jointly and severally liable in respect of those debts with the company and any other person who, whether under this section or otherwise, is so liable.

(3) For the purposes of this section the relevant debts of a company are—

(a) in relation to a person who is personally responsible under paragraph (a) of subsection (1), such debts and other liabilities of the company as are incurred at a time when that person was involved in the management of the company, and

(b) in relation to a person who is personally responsible under paragraph (b) of that subsection, such debts and other liabilities of the company as are incurred at a time when that person was acting or was willing to act on instructions given as mentioned in that paragraph.

(4) For the purposes of this section, a person is involved in the management of a company if he is a director of the company or if he is concerned, whether directly or indirectly, or takes part, in the management of the company.

[(5) For the purposes of this section a person who, as a person involved in the management of a company, has at any time acted on instructions given without the leave of the court by a person whom he knew at that time—

(a) to be the subject of a disqualification order made or disqualification undertaking accepted under this Act or under the Company Directors Disqualification (Northern Ireland) Order 2002, or

(b) to be an undischarged bankrupt,

is presumed, unless the contrary is shown, to have been willing at any time thereafter to act on any instructions given by that person.]

NOTES

Sub-s (1): words in first pair of square brackets inserted by the Insolvency Act 2000, s 8, Sch 4, Pt I, paras 1, 10, as from 2 April 2001. Words in second pair of square brackets substituted by the Insolvency Act 2000 (Company Directors Disqualification Undertakings) Order 2004, SI 2004/1941, art 2(1), (5)(a), as from 1 September 2004, in relation to disqualification undertakings under the Company Directors Disqualification (Northern Ireland) Order 2002 accepted on or after that date. Para (b) substituted by the Companies Act 2006 (Consequential Amendments, Transitional Provisions and Savings) Order 2009, SI 2009/1941, art 2(1), Sch 1, para 85(1), (9)(a), as from 1 October 2009.

Sub-s (5): substituted by SI 2009/1941, art 2(1), Sch 1, para 85(1), (9)(b), as from 1 October 2009.

[Compensation orders and undertakings

[5.107]

15A Compensation orders and undertakings

(1) The court may make a compensation order against a person on the application of the Secretary of State if it is satisfied that the conditions mentioned in subsection (3) are met.

(2) If it appears to the Secretary of State that the conditions mentioned in subsection (3) are met in respect of a person who has offered to give the Secretary of State a compensation undertaking, the Secretary of State may accept the undertaking instead of applying, or proceeding with an application, for a compensation order.

(3) The conditions are that—

(a) the person is subject to a disqualification order or disqualification undertaking under this Act, and

(b) conduct for which the person is subject to the order or undertaking has caused loss to one or more creditors of an insolvent company[, or a company which has been dissolved without becoming insolvent,] of which the person has at any time been a director.

(4) An "insolvent company" is a company that is or has been insolvent and a company becomes insolvent if—

(a) the company goes into liquidation at a time when its assets are insufficient for the payment of its debts and other liabilities and the expenses of the winding up,

(b) the company enters administration, or

(c) an administrative receiver of the company is appointed.

(5) The Secretary of State may apply for a compensation order at any time before the end of the period of two years beginning with the date on which the disqualification order referred to in paragraph (a) of subsection (3) was made, or the disqualification undertaking referred to in that paragraph was accepted.

(6) In the case of a person subject to a disqualification order under section 8ZA or 8ZD, or a disqualification undertaking under section 8ZC or 8ZE, the reference in subsection (3)(b) to conduct is a reference to the conduct of the main transgressor in relation to which the person has exercised the requisite amount of influence.

(7) In this section and sections 15B and 15C "the court" means—

(a) in a case where a disqualification order has been made, the court that made the order,

(b) in any other case, the High Court or, in Scotland, the Court of Session.]

NOTES

Inserted, together with the preceding heading and ss 15B, 15C, by the Small Business, Enterprise and Employment Act 2015, s 110, as from 1 October 2015, in respect of a person's (a) conduct (as mentioned in s 15A(3)(b)), or (b) exercise of the requisite amount of influence (as mentioned in s 15A(6)), occurring on or after that date.

Sub-s (3): words in square brackets in para (b) inserted by the Rating (Coronavirus) and Directors Disqualification (Dissolved Companies) Act 2021, s 2(6), as from 15 December 2021 (for the purposes of the exercise by the Secretary of State or the official receiver of powers under s 7(4) of this Act), and as from 15 February 2022 (otherwise). Note that the amendments made by s 2 of the 2021 Act have effect in relation to conduct of directors of companies occurring, and in relation to companies dissolved, at any time before, as well as after, 15 December 2021 (see the note relating to s 2(14) of the 2021 Act at **[9.633]**).

As to compensation orders made under this section, see the Compensation Orders (Disqualified Directors) Proceedings (England and Wales) Rules 2016, SI 2016/890 at **[10.465]**. As to fees, see the Disqualified Directors Compensation Orders (Fees) (England and Wales) Order 2016, SI 2016/1047, and the Disqualified Directors Compensation Orders (Fees) (Scotland) Order 2016, SI 2016/1048.

[5.108]

[15B Amounts payable under compensation orders and undertakings

(1) A compensation order is an order requiring the person against whom it is made to pay an amount specified in the order—

(a) to the Secretary of State for the benefit of—

(i) a creditor or creditors specified in the order;

(ii) a class or classes of creditor so specified;

(b) as a contribution to the assets of a company so specified.

(2) A compensation undertaking is an undertaking to pay an amount specified in the undertaking—

(a) to the Secretary of State for the benefit of—

(i) a creditor or creditors specified in the undertaking;

(ii) a class or classes of creditor so specified;

(b) as a contribution to the assets of a company so specified.

(3) When specifying an amount the court (in the case of an order) and the Secretary of State (in the case of an undertaking) must in particular have regard to—

(a) the amount of the loss caused;

(b) the nature of the conduct mentioned in section 15A(3)(b);

(c) whether the person has made any other financial contribution in recompense for the conduct (whether under a statutory provision or otherwise).

(4) An amount payable by virtue of subsection (2) under a compensation undertaking is recoverable as if payable under a court order.

(5) An amount payable under a compensation order or compensation undertaking is provable as a bankruptcy debt.]

NOTES

Inserted as noted to s 15A at **[5.107]**.

[5.109]

[15C Variation and revocation of compensation undertakings

(1) The court may, on the application of a person who is subject to a compensation undertaking—

(a) reduce the amount payable under the undertaking, or

(b) provide for the undertaking not to have effect.

(2) On the hearing of an application under subsection (1), the Secretary of State must appear and call the attention of the court to any matters which the Secretary of State considers relevant, and may give evidence or call witnesses.]

NOTES

Inserted as noted to s 15A at **[5.107]**.

Supplementary provisions

[5.110]

16 Application for disqualification order

(1) A person intending to apply for the making of a disqualification order . . . shall give not less than 10 days' notice of his intention to the person against whom the order is sought; and on the hearing of the application the last-mentioned person may appear and himself give evidence or call witnesses.

(2) An application to a court[, other than a court mentioned in section 2(2)(b) or (c),] for the making against any person of a disqualification order under any of sections 2 to [4] may be made by the Secretary of State or the official receiver, or by the liquidator or any past or present member or creditor of any company [or overseas company] in relation to which that person has committed or is alleged to have committed an offence or other default.

(3) On the hearing of any application under this Act made by [a person falling within subsection (4)], the applicant shall appear and call the attention of the court to any matters which seem to him to be relevant, and may himself give evidence or call witnesses.

[(4) The following fall within this subsection—

(a) the Secretary of State;

(b) the official receiver;

(c) the [Competition and Markets Authority];

(d) the liquidator;

(e) a specified regulator (within the meaning of section 9E).]

NOTES

Sub-s (1): words omitted repealed by the Small Business, Enterprise and Employment Act 2015, s 111, Sch 7, Pt 1, paras 1, 12(1), (2), as from 1 October 2015.

Sub-s (2): words in first pair of square brackets substituted, and words in third pair of square brackets inserted, by the Small Business, Enterprise and Employment Act 2015, s 111, Sch 7, Pt 1, paras 1, 12(1), (3), as from 1 October 2015. Figure "4" in second pair of square brackets substituted by the Insolvency Act 2000, s 8, Sch 4, Pt I, paras 1, 11, as from 2 April 2001.

Sub-s (3): words in square brackets substituted by the Enterprise Act 2002, s 204(1), (6), as from 20 June 2003.

Sub-s (4): added by the Enterprise Act 2002, s 204(1), (7), as from 20 June 2003. Words in square brackets substituted by the Enterprise and Regulatory Reform Act 2013 (Competition) (Consequential, Transitional and Saving Provisions) Order 2014, SI 2014/892, art 2, Sch 1, Pt 2, paras 52, 53(e), as from 1 April 2014.

[5.111]

[17 Application for leave under an order or undertaking

(1) Where a person is subject to a disqualification order made by a court having jurisdiction to wind up companies, any application for leave for the purposes of section 1(1)(a) shall be made to that court.

(2) Where—

(a) a person is subject to a disqualification order made under section 2 by a court other than a court having jurisdiction to wind up companies, or

(b) a person is subject to a disqualification order made under section 5,

any application for leave for the purposes of section 1(1)(a) shall be made to any court which, when the order was made, had jurisdiction to wind up the company (or, if there is more than one such company, any of the companies) to which the offence (or any of the offences) in question related.

(3) Where a person is subject to a disqualification undertaking accepted at any time under section [5A,] 7 or 8, any application for leave for the purposes of section 1A(1)(a) shall be made to any court to which, if the Secretary of State had applied for a disqualification order under the section in question at that time, his application could have been made.

[(3ZA) Where a person is subject to a disqualification undertaking accepted at any time under section 8ZC, any application for leave for the purposes of section 1A(1)(a) must be made to any court to which, if the Secretary of State had applied for a disqualification order under section 8ZA at that time, that application could have been made.

(3ZB) Where a person is subject to a disqualification undertaking accepted at any time under section 8ZE, any application for leave for the purposes of section 1A(1)(a) must be made to the High Court or, in Scotland, the Court of Session.]

[(3A) Where a person is subject to a disqualification undertaking accepted at any time under section 9B any application for leave for the purposes of section 9B(4) must be made to the High Court or (in Scotland) the Court of Session.]

(4) But where a person is subject to two or more disqualification orders or undertakings (or to one or more disqualification orders and to one or more disqualification undertakings), any application for leave for the purposes of section 1(1)(a) [1A(1)(a) or 9B(4)] shall be made to any court to which any such application relating to the latest order to be made, or undertaking to be accepted, could be made.

(5) On the hearing of an application for leave for the purposes of section 1(1)(a) or 1A(1)(a), the Secretary of State shall appear and call the attention of the court to any matters which seem to him to be relevant, and may himself give evidence or call witnesses.

[(6) Subsection (5) does not apply to an application for leave for the purposes of section 1(1)(a) if the application for the disqualification order was made under section 9A.

(7) In such a case and in the case of an application for leave for the purposes of section 9B(4) on the hearing of the application whichever of the [Competition and Markets Authority] or a specified regulator (within the meaning of section 9E) applied for the order or accepted the undertaking (as the case may be)—

- (a) must appear and draw the attention of the court to any matters which appear to it or him (as the case may be) to be relevant;
- (b) may give evidence or call witnesses.]]

NOTES

Substituted by the Insolvency Act 2000, s 8, Sch 4, Pt I, paras 1, 12, as from 2 April 2001, subject to transitional provisions in relation to cases where a person subject to a disqualification order, made on the application of the Secretary of State, the official receiver or the liquidator, has applied for leave of the court under this section before that date.

Sub-s (3): figure in square brackets inserted by the Small Business, Enterprise and Employment Act 2015, s 111, Sch 7, Pt 1, paras 1, 13(1), (2), as from 1 October 2015.

Sub-ss (3ZA), (3ZB): inserted by the Small Business, Enterprise and Employment Act 2015, s 111, Sch 7, Pt 1, paras 1, 13(1), (3), as from 1 October 2015.

Sub-s (3A): inserted by the Enterprise Act 2002, s 204(1), (8), as from 20 June 2003.

Sub-s (4): words in square brackets substituted by the Enterprise Act 2002, s 204(1), (9), as from 20 June 2003.

Sub-ss (6), (7): added by the Enterprise Act 2002, s 204(1), (10), as from 20 June 2003. Words in square brackets in sub-s (7) substituted by the Enterprise and Regulatory Reform Act 2013 (Competition) (Consequential, Transitional and Saving Provisions) Order 2014, SI 2014/892, art 2, Sch 1, Pt 2, paras 52, 53(f), as from 1 April 2014.

[5.112]

18 [Register of disqualification orders and undertakings]

(1) The Secretary of State may make regulations requiring officers of courts to furnish him with such particulars as the regulations may specify of cases in which—

- (a) a disqualification order is made, or
- (b) any action is taken by a court in consequence of which such an order [or a disqualification undertaking] is varied or ceases to be in force, or
- (c) leave is granted by a court for a person subject to such an order to do any thing which otherwise the order prohibits him from doing; [or
- (d) leave is granted by a court for a person subject to such an undertaking to do anything which otherwise the undertaking prohibits him from doing]

and the regulations may specify the time within which, and the form and manner in which, such particulars are to be furnished.

(2) The Secretary of State shall, from the particulars so furnished, continue to maintain the register of orders, and of cases in which leave has been granted as mentioned in subsection (1)(c) . . .

[(2A) The Secretary of State must include in the register such particulars as he considers appropriate of—

- (a) disqualification undertakings accepted by him under section [5A, 7, 8, 8ZC or 8ZE];
- (b) disqualification undertakings accepted by the [Competition and Markets Authority] or a specified regulator under section 9B;
- (c) cases in which leave has been granted as mentioned in subsection (1)(d).]

(3) When an order [or undertaking] of which entry is made in the register ceases to be in force, the Secretary of State shall delete the entry from the register and all particulars relating to it which have been furnished to him under this section or any previous corresponding provision [and, in the case of a disqualification undertaking, any other particulars he has included in the register].

(4) The register shall be open to inspection on payment of such fee as may be specified by the Secretary of State in regulations.

[(4A) Regulations under this section may extend the preceding provisions of this section, to such extent and with such modifications as may be specified in the regulations, to disqualification orders . . . [or disqualification undertakings made under the Company Directors Disqualification (Northern Ireland) Order 2002].]

(5) Regulations under this section shall be made by statutory instrument subject to annulment in pursuance of a resolution of either House of Parliament.

NOTES

Section heading: substituted by the Insolvency Act 2000, s 8, Sch 4, Pt I, paras 1, 13(1), (6), as from 2 April 2001.

Sub-ss (1), (3): words in square brackets inserted by the Insolvency Act 2000, s 8, Sch 4, Pt I, paras 1, 13(1), (2), (4), as from 2 April 2001.

Sub-s (2): words omitted repealed by the Companies Act 2006 (Consequential Amendments, Transitional Provisions and Savings) Order 2009, SI 2009/1941, art 2(1), Sch 1, para 85(1), (10)(a), as from 1 October 2009.

Sub-s (2A): originally inserted by the Insolvency Act 2000, s 8, Sch 4, Pt I, paras 1, 13(1), (3), as from 2 April 2001. Subsequently substituted by the Enterprise Act 2002, s 204(1), (11), as from 20 June 2003. Words in square brackets in para (a) substituted by the Small Business, Enterprise and Employment Act 2015, s 111, Sch 7, Pt 1, paras 1, 14, as from 1 October 2015. Words in square brackets in para (b) substituted by the Enterprise and Regulatory Reform Act 2013 (Competition) (Consequential, Transitional and Saving Provisions) Order 2014, SI 2014/892, art 2, Sch 1, Pt 2, paras 52, 53(g), as from 1 April 2014.

Sub-s (4A): inserted by the Insolvency Act 2000, s 8, Sch 4, Pt I, paras 1, 13(1), (5), as from 2 April 2001. Words omitted repealed by SI 2009/1941, art 2(1), Sch 1, para 85(1), (10)(b), as from 1 October 2009. Words in square brackets added by the Insolvency Act 2000 (Company Directors Disqualification Undertakings) Order 2004, SI 2004/1941, art 2(1), (6), as from 1 September 2004, in relation to disqualification undertakings under the Company Directors Disqualification (Northern Ireland) Order 2002 accepted on or after that date.

Regulations: the Companies (Disqualification Orders) Regulations 2009, SI 2009/2471 at **[6.155]**.

[5.113]

19 Special savings from repealed enactments

Schedule 2 to this Act has effect—

(a) in connection with certain transitional cases arising under sections 93 and 94 of the Companies Act 1981, so as to limit the power to make a disqualification order, or to restrict the duration of an order, by reference to events occurring or things done before those sections came into force,

(b) to preserve orders made under section 28 of the Companies Act 1976 (repealed by the Act of 1981), and

(c) to preclude any applications for a disqualification order under section 6 or 8, where the relevant company went into liquidation before 28th April 1986.

Miscellaneous and general

[5.114]

20 Admissibility in evidence of statements

[(1)] In any proceedings (whether or not under this Act), any statement made in pursuance of a requirement imposed by or under sections [5A, 6 to 10, 12C, 15 to 15C] or 19(c) of, or Schedule 1 to, this Act, or by or under rules made for the purposes of this Act under the Insolvency Act [1986], may be used in evidence against any person making or concurring in making the statement.

[(2) However, in criminal proceedings in which any such person is charged with an offence to which this subsection applies—

(a) no evidence relating to the statement may be adduced, and

(b) no question relating to it may be asked,

by or on behalf of the prosecution, unless evidence relating to it is adduced, or a question relating to it is asked, in the proceedings by or on behalf of that person.

(3) Subsection (2) applies to any offence other than—

(a) an offence which is—

(i) created by rules made for the purposes of this Act under the Insolvency Act [1986], and

(ii) designated for the purposes of this subsection by such rules or by regulations made by the Secretary of State;

(b) an offence which is—

(i) created by regulations made under any such rules, and

(ii) designated for the purposes of this subsection by such regulations;

(c) an offence under section 5 of the Perjury Act 1911 (false statements made otherwise than on oath); or

(d) an offence under section 44(2) of the Criminal Law (Consolidation) (Scotland) Act 1995 (false statements made otherwise than on oath).

(4) Regulations under subsection (3)(a)(ii) shall be made by statutory instrument and, after being made, shall be laid before each House of Parliament.]

NOTES

Sub-s (1) numbered as such, and sub-ss (2)–(4) added, by the Youth Justice and Criminal Evidence Act 1999, s 59, Sch 3, para 8, as from 14 April 2000 (in relation to England and Wales), and 1 January 2001 (in relation to Scotland).

Words in square brackets in sub-s (1) substituted by the Small Business, Enterprise and Employment Act 2015, s 111, Sch 7, Pt 1, paras 1, 15, as from 1 October 2015.

Year "1986" in square brackets in sub-ss (1), (3) inserted by the Companies Act 2006 (Consequential Amendments, Transitional Provisions and Savings) Order 2009, SI 2009/1941, art 2(1), Sch 1, para 85(1), (6), as from 1 October 2009.

[5.115]

[20A Legal professional privilege

In proceedings against a person for an offence under this Act nothing in this Act is to be taken to require any person to disclose any information that he is entitled to refuse to disclose on grounds of legal professional privilege (in Scotland, confidentiality of communications).]

NOTES

Inserted by the Companies Act 2006 (Consequential Amendments etc) Order 2008, SI 2008/948, art 3(1), Sch 1, Pt 2, para 106(1), (3), as from 6 April 2008.

[5.116]

21 Interaction with Insolvency Act [1986]

(1) References in this Act to the official receiver, in relation to the winding up of a company or the bankruptcy of an individual, are to any person who, by virtue of section 399 of the Insolvency Act [1986], is authorised to act as the official receiver in relation to that winding up or bankruptcy; and, in accordance with section 401(2) of that Act, references in this Act to an official receiver includes a person appointed as his deputy.

(2) Sections [1A,] [5A, 6 to 10, 12C to 15C], 19(c) and 20 of, and Schedule 1 to, this Act [and sections 1 and 17 of this Act as they apply for the purposes of those provisions] are deemed included in Parts I to VII of the Insolvency Act [1986] for the purposes of the following sections of that Act—

section 411 (power to make insolvency rules);

section 414 (fees orders);

section 420 (orders extending provisions about insolvent companies to insolvent partnerships);

section 422 (modification of such provisions in their application to recognised banks);

. . .

(3) Section 434 of that Act (Crown application) applies to sections [1A,] [5A, 6 to 10, 12C to 15C], 19(c) and 20 of, and Schedule 1 to, this Act [and sections 1 and 17 of this Act as they apply for the purposes of those provisions] as it does to the provisions of that Act which are there mentioned.

[(4) For the purposes of summary proceedings in Scotland, section 431 of that Act applies to summary proceedings for an offence under section 11 or 13 of this Act as it applies to summary proceedings for an offence under Parts I to VII of that Act.]

NOTES

Section heading and sub-s (1): year "1986" in square brackets inserted by the Companies Act 2006 (Consequential Amendments, Transitional Provisions and Savings) Order 2009, SI 2009/1941, art 2(1), Sch 1, para 85(1), (6), as from 1 October 2009.

Sub-s (2) is amended as follows:

Figure "1A," in square brackets inserted by the Insolvency Act 2000, s 8, Sch 4, Pt I, paras 1, 14(1), (2)(a), as from 2 April 2001.

Words "5A, 6 to 10, 12C to 15C" in square brackets substituted by the Small Business, Enterprise and Employment Act 2015, s 111, Sch 7, Pt 1, paras 1, 16, as from 1 October 2015.

Words "and sections 1 and 17 of this Act as they apply for the purposes of those provisions" in square brackets inserted by the Insolvency Act 2000, s 8, Sch 4, Pt I, paras 1, 14(1), (2)(c), as from 2 April 2001.

Year "1986" in square brackets inserted by SI 2009/1941, art 2(1), Sch 1, para 85(1), (6)(a), as from 1 October 2009.

Words omitted repealed by the Companies Act 1989, s 212, Sch 24, as from 1 March 1990.

Sub-s (3): words "5A, 6 to 10, 12C to 15C" in square brackets substituted by the Small Business, Enterprise and Employment Act 2015, s 111, Sch 7, Pt 1, paras 1, 16, as from 1 October 2015. Other figures and words in square brackets inserted by the Insolvency Act 2000, s 8, Sch 4, Pt I, paras 1, 14(1), (3), as from 2 April 2001.

Sub-s (4): added by CA 1989, s 208, as from 1 March 1990.

As to Rules and Orders having effect under this section, see the notes to the sections listed in sub-s (2) above.

[5.117]

[21A Bank insolvency

Section 121 of the Banking Act 2009 provides for this Act to apply in relation to bank insolvency as it applies in relation to liquidation.]

NOTES

Inserted by the Banking Act 2009, s 121(4), as from 21 February 2009.

[5.118]

[21B Bank administration

Section 155 of the Banking Act 2009 provides for this Act to apply in relation to bank administration as it applies in relation to liquidation]

NOTES

Inserted by the Banking Act 2009, s 155(4), as from 21 February 2009.

[5.119]

[21C Building society insolvency and special administration

Section 90E of the Building Societies Act 1986 provides for this Act to apply in relation to building society insolvency and building society special administration as it applies in relation to liquidation.]

NOTES

Inserted by the Building Societies (Insolvency and Special Administration) Order 2009, SI 2009/805, art 12, as from 30 March 2009.

[5.120]

22 Interpretation

(1) This section has effect with respect to the meaning of expressions used in this Act, and applies unless the context otherwise requires.

[(2) "Company" means—

(a) a company registered under the Companies Act 2006 in Great Britain, or

(b) a company that may be wound up under Part 5 of the Insolvency Act 1986 (unregistered companies).]

[(2A) An "overseas company" is a company incorporated or formed outside Great Britain.]

(3) Section 247 in Part VII of the Insolvency Act [1986] (interpretation for the first Group of Parts of that Act) applies as regards references to a company's insolvency and to its going into liquidation; and "administrative receiver" has the meaning given by section 251 of that Act [and references to acting as an insolvency practitioner are to be read in accordance with section 388 of that Act].

(4) "Director" includes any person occupying the position of director, by whatever name called . . .

(5) "Shadow director", in relation to a company, means a person in accordance with whose directions or instructions the directors of the company are accustomed to act[, but so that a person is not deemed a shadow director by reason only that the directors act—

(a) on advice given by that person in a professional capacity;

(b) in accordance with instructions, a direction, guidance or advice given by that person in the exercise of a function conferred by or under an enactment;

(c) in accordance with guidance or advice given by that person in that person's capacity as a Minister of the Crown (within the meaning of the Ministers of the Crown Act 1975)].

[(6) "Body corporate" and "officer" have the same meaning as in the Companies Acts (see section 1173(1) of the Companies Act 2006).]

[(7) "The Companies Acts" has the meaning given by section 2(1) of the Companies Act 2006.]

[(8) Any reference to provisions, or a particular provision, of the Companies Acts or the Insolvency Act 1986 includes the corresponding provisions or provision of corresponding earlier legislation.]

[(9) Subject to the provisions of this section, expressions that are defined for the purposes of the Companies Acts [(see section 1174 of, and Schedule 8 to, the Companies Act 2006)] have the same meaning in this Act.]

[(10) Any reference to acting as receiver—

(a) includes acting as manager or as both receiver and manager, but

(b) does not include acting as administrative receiver;

and "receivership" is to be read accordingly.]

NOTES

Sub-ss (2), (6)–(8): substituted by the Companies Act 2006 (Consequential Amendments, Transitional Provisions and Savings) Order 2009, SI 2009/1941, art 2(1), Sch 1, para 85(1), (11)(a)–(d), as from 1 October 2009.

Sub-s (2A): inserted by the Small Business, Enterprise and Employment Act 2015, s 111, Sch 7, Pt 1, paras 1, 17, as from 1 October 2015.

Sub-s (3): year "1986" in square brackets inserted by SI 2009/1941, art 2(1), Sch 1, para 85(1), (6), as from 1 October 2009. Words in square brackets added by the Insolvency Act 2000, s 8, Sch 4, Pt I, paras 1, 15(1), (2), as from 2 April 2001.

Sub-s (4): words omitted repealed by the Insolvency Act 2000, ss 8, 15(1), Sch 4, Pt I, paras 1, 15(1), (3), Sch 5, as from 2 April 2001.

Sub-s (5): words in square brackets substituted by the Small Business, Enterprise and Employment Act 2015, s 90(2), as from 26 May 2015.

Sub-s (9): substituted by SI 2008/948, art 3(1), Sch 1, Pt 2, para 106(1), (4)(c), as from 6 April 2008. Words in square brackets inserted by SI 2009/1941, art 2(1), Sch 1, para 85(1), (11)(e), as from 1 October 2009.

Sub-s (10): added by the Insolvency Act 2000, s 5(3), as from 2 April 2001.

[5.121]

[22A Application of Act to building societies

(1) This Act applies to building societies as it applies to companies.

(2) References in this Act to a company, or to a director or an officer of a company include, respectively, references to a building society within the meaning of the Building Societies Act 1986 or to a director or officer, within the meaning of that Act, of a building society.

(3) In relation to a building society the definition of "shadow director" in section 22(5) applies with the substitution of "building society" for "company".

[(3A) In relation to a building society, this Act applies as if—

(a) sections 6(1)(a)(ii) and (3)(d) and 7(2)(b) were omitted;

(b) references in sections 7(4)(a), 8ZB(2) and 15A(3)(b) to a company which has been dissolved without becoming insolvent were omitted.]

(4) . . .]

NOTES

Inserted by CA 1989, s 211(3), as from 31 July 1990.

Sub-s (3A): inserted by the Rating (Coronavirus) and Directors Disqualification (Dissolved Companies) Act 2021, s 2(7), as from 15 December 2021 (for the purposes of the exercise by the Secretary of State or the official receiver of powers under s 7(4) of this Act), and as from 15 February 2022 (otherwise). Note that the amendments made by s 2 of the 2021 Act have effect in relation to conduct of directors of companies occurring, and in relation to companies dissolved, at any time before, as well as after, 15 December 2021 (see the note relating to s 2(14) of the 2021 Act at **[9.633]**).

Sub-s (4): repealed by the Small Business, Enterprise and Employment Act 2015, s 111, Sch 7, Pt 1, paras 1, 18, as from 1 October 2015.

[5.122]

[22B Application of Act to incorporated friendly societies

(1) This Act applies to incorporated friendly societies as it applies to companies.

(2) References in this Act to a company, or to a director or an officer of a company include, respectively, references to an incorporated friendly society within the meaning of the Friendly Societies Act 1992 or to a member of the committee of management or officer, within the meaning of that Act, of an incorporated friendly society.

(3) In relation to an incorporated friendly society every reference to a shadow director shall be omitted.

[(3A) In relation to an incorporated friendly society, this Act applies as if[—

(a) sections 6(1)(a)(ii) and (3)(d), 7(2)(b) and 8ZA to 8ZE were omitted;

(b) references in sections 7(4)(a) and 15A(3)(b) to a company which has been dissolved without becoming insolvent were omitted].]

(4) . . .]

NOTES

Inserted by the Friendly Societies Act 1992, s 120(1), Sch 21, Pt I, para 8, as from 1 February 1993.

Sub-s (3A): inserted by the Small Business, Enterprise and Employment Act 2015, s 111, Sch 7, Pt 1, paras 1, 19(a), as from 1 October 2015. Words in square brackets substituted by the Rating (Coronavirus) and Directors Disqualification (Dissolved Companies) Act 2021, s 2(8), as from 15 December 2021 (for the purposes of the exercise by the Secretary of State or the official receiver of powers under s 7(4) of this Act), and as from 15 February 2022 (otherwise) (note that the amendments made by s 2 of the 2021 Act have effect in relation to conduct of directors of companies occurring, and in relation to companies dissolved, at any time before, as well as after, 15 December 2021) (see the note relating to s 2(14) of the 2021 Act at **[9.633]**).

Sub-s (4): repealed by the Small Business, Enterprise and Employment Act 2015, s 111, Sch 7, Pt 1, paras 1, 19(b), as from 1 October 2015.

[5.123]

[22C Application of Act to NHS foundation trusts

(1) This Act applies to NHS foundation trusts as it applies to companies within the meaning of this Act.

(2) References in this Act to a company, or to a director or officer of a company, include, respectively, references to an NHS foundation trust or to a director or officer of the trust; but references to shadow directors are omitted.

[(2A) In relation to an NHS foundation trust, this Act applies as if—

(a) sections 6(1)(a)(ii) and (3)(d) and 7(2)(b) were omitted;

(b) references in sections 7(4)(a), 8ZB(2) and 15A(3)(b) to a company which has been dissolved without becoming insolvent were omitted.]

(3) . . .]

NOTES

Inserted by the Health and Social Care (Community Health and Standards) Act 2003, s 34, Sch 4, paras 67, 68, as from 1 April 2004.

Sub-s (2A): inserted by the Rating (Coronavirus) and Directors Disqualification (Dissolved Companies) Act 2021, s 2(9), as from 15 December 2021 (for the purposes of the exercise by the Secretary of State or the official receiver of powers under s 7(4) of this Act), and as from 15 February 2022 (otherwise). Note that the amendments made by s 2 of the 2021 Act have effect in relation to conduct of directors of companies occurring, and in relation to companies dissolved, at any time before, as well as after, 15 December 2021 (see the note relating to s 2(14) of the 2021 Act at **[9.633]**).

Sub-s (3): repealed by the Small Business, Enterprise and Employment Act 2015, s 111, Sch 7, Pt 1, paras 1, 20, as from 1 October 2015.

22D (*Originally inserted by the Companies Act 2006 (Consequential Amendments, Transitional Provisions and Savings) Order 2009, SI 2009/1941, art 2(1), Sch 1, para 85(1), (13), as from 1 October 2009; and subsequently repealed by the Small Business, Enterprise and Employment Act 2015, s 111, Sch 7, Pt 1, paras 1, 21, as from 1 October 2015.*)

[5.124]

[22E [Application of Act to registered societies]

[(1) In this section "registered society" has the same meaning as in the Co-operative and Community Benefit Societies Act 2014 ("the 2014 Act").]

(2) This Act applies to registered societies as it applies to companies.

(3) Accordingly, in this Act—

(a) references to a company include a registered society, and

(b) references to a director or an officer of a company include a member of the committee or an officer of a registered society.

In paragraph (b) "committee" and "officer" have the same meaning as in [the 2014 Act: see section 149 of that Act].

(4) As they apply in relation to registered societies, the provisions of this Act have effect with the following modifications—

(a) in section 2(1) (disqualification on conviction of indictable offence), the reference to striking off includes cancellation of the registration of a society under [the 2014 Act];

(b) in section 3 (disqualification for persistent breaches) and section 5 (disqualification on summary conviction), references to the companies legislation shall be read as references to the legislation relating to registered societies;

(c) . . .

(d) references to the registrar shall be read as references to the [Financial Conduct Authority];

(e) references to a shadow director shall be disregarded;

[(f) sections 6(1)(a)(ii) and (3)(d), 7(2)(b) and 8ZA to 8ZE are to be disregarded;

(g) references in sections 7(4)(a) and 15A(3)(b) to a company which has been dissolved without becoming insolvent are to be disregarded].

(5) . . .

[(6) "The legislation relating to registered societies" means the Credit Unions Act 1979 and the Co-operative and Community Benefit Societies Act 2014.]]

NOTES

Inserted by the Co-operative and Community Benefit Societies and Credit Unions Act 2010, s 3, as from 6 April 2014.

Section heading: substituted by the Co-operative and Community Benefit Societies Act 2014, s 151, Sch 4, Pt 2, para 38(1), (6), as from 1 August 2014.

Sub-s (1): substituted by the Co-operative and Community Benefit Societies Act 2014, s 151, Sch 4, Pt 2, para 38(1), (2), as from 1 August 2014.

Sub-s (3): words in square brackets substituted by the Co-operative and Community Benefit Societies Act 2014, s 151, Sch 4, Pt 2, para 38(1), (3), as from 1 August 2014.

Sub-s (4) is amended as follows:

Words in first and second pairs of square brackets substituted by the Co-operative and Community Benefit Societies Act 2014, s 151, Sch 4, Pt 2, para 38(1), (4), as from 1 August 2014.

Para (c) was repealed, and para (f) was originally added, by the Small Business, Enterprise and Employment Act 2015, s 111, Sch 7, Pt 1, paras 1, 22(1), (2), as from 1 October 2015.

Words in square brackets in para (d) substituted by the Financial Services Act 2012 (Mutual Societies) Order 2013, SI 2013/496, art 2(c), Sch 1, para 3, as from 1 April 2013.

Paras (f) and (g) were substituted (for the original para (f) as added as noted above) by the Rating (Coronavirus) and Directors Disqualification (Dissolved Companies) Act 2021, s 2(10), as from 15 December 2021 (for the purposes of the exercise by the Secretary of State or the official receiver of powers under s 7(4) of this Act), and as from 15 February 2022 (otherwise) (note that the amendments made by s 2 of the 2021 Act have effect in relation to conduct of directors of companies occurring, and in relation to companies dissolved, at any time before, as well as after, 15 December 2021) (see the note relating to s 2(14) of the 2021 Act at **[9.633]**).

Sub-s (5): repealed by the Small Business, Enterprise and Employment Act 2015, s 111, Sch 7, Pt 1, paras 1, 22(1), (3), as from 1 October 2015.

Sub-s (6): substituted by the Co-operative and Community Benefit Societies Act 2014, s 151, Sch 4, Pt 2, para 38(1), (5), as from 1 August 2014.

[5.125]

[22F Application of Act to charitable incorporated organisations

(1) This Act applies to charitable incorporated organisations ("CIOs") as it applies to companies.

(2) Accordingly, in this Act—

(a) references to a company are to be read as including references to a CIO;

(b) references to a director or an officer of a company are to be read as including references to a charity trustee of a CIO; and

(c) any reference to the Insolvency Act 1986 is to be read as including a reference to that Act as it applies to CIOs.

In paragraph (b) "committee" and "officer" have the same meaning as in the 1965 Act: see section 74(1) of that Act.

(3) As they apply in relation to registered societies, the provisions of this Act have effect with the following modifications—

(a) in section 2(1), the reference to striking off is to be read as including a reference to dissolution;

(b) in section 4(1)(a), the reference to an offence under section 993 of the Companies Act 2006 is to be read as including a reference to an offence under regulation 60 of the Charitable Incorporated Organisations (General) Regulations 2012(fraudulent trading);

[(ba) sections 6(1)(a)(ii) and (3)(d) and 7(2)(b) are to be disregarded;

(bb) references in sections 7(4)(a), 8ZB(2) and 15A(3)(b) to a company which has been dissolved without becoming insolvent are to be disregarded;]

(c) sections 9A to 9E are to be disregarded;

(d) references to any of sections 9A to 9E are to be disregarded;

(e) references to a shadow director are to be disregarded.

(4) . . .

(5) In this section "charity trustees" has the meaning given by section 177 of the Charities Act 2011.]

NOTES

Inserted by the Charitable Incorporated Organisations (Consequential Amendments) Order 2012, SI 2012/3014, art 2, as from 2 January 2013.

Sub-s (3): paras (ba), (bb) inserted by the Rating (Coronavirus) and Directors Disqualification (Dissolved Companies) Act 2021, s 2(11), as from 15 December 2021 (for the purposes of the exercise by the Secretary of State or the official receiver of powers under s 7(4) of this Act), and as from 15 February 2022 (otherwise). Note that the amendments made by s 2 of the 2021 Act have effect in relation to conduct of directors of companies occurring, and in relation to companies dissolved, at any time before, as well as after, 15 December 2021 (see the note relating to s 2(14) of the 2021 Act at **[9.633]**).

Sub-s (4): repealed by the Small Business, Enterprise and Employment Act 2015, s 111, Sch 7, Pt 1, paras 1, 23, as from 1 October 2015.

[5.126]

[22G Application of Act to further education bodies

(1) This Act applies to further education bodies as it applies to companies.

(2) Accordingly, in this Act—

(a) references to a company are to be read as including references to a further education body;

(b) references to a director or an officer of a company are to be read as including references to a member of a further education body;

(c) any reference to the Insolvency Act 1986 is to be read as including a reference to that Act as it applies to further education bodies.

(3) As they apply in relation to further education bodies, the provisions of this Act have effect with the following modifications—

(a) in section 2(1), the reference to striking off is to be read as including a reference to dissolution;

[(aa) sections 6(1)(a)(ii) and (3)(d) and 7(2)(b) are to be disregarded;

(ab) references in sections 7(4)(a), 8ZB(2) and 15A(3)(b) to a company which has been dissolved without becoming insolvent are to be disregarded;]

(b) sections 9A to 9E are to be disregarded;

(c) references to any of sections 9A to 9E are to be disregarded.

(4) In this section—

"further education body" means—

(a) a further education corporation, or

(b) a sixth form college corporation;

"further education corporation" means a body corporate that—

(a) is established under section 15 or 16 of the Further and Higher Education Act 1992, or

(b) has become a further education corporation by virtue of section 33D or 47 of that Act;

"sixth form college corporation" means a body corporate—

(a) designated as a sixth form college corporation under section 33A or 33B of the Further and Higher Education Act 1992, or

(b) established under section 33C of that Act.]

NOTES

Inserted by the Technical and Further Education Act 2017, s 39, as from 31 January 2019.

Sub-s (3): paras (aa), (ab) inserted by the Rating (Coronavirus) and Directors Disqualification (Dissolved Companies) Act 2021, s 2(12), as from 15 December 2021 (for the purposes of the exercise by the Secretary of State or the official receiver of powers under s 7(4) of this Act), and as from 15 February 2022 (otherwise). Note that the amendments made by s 2 of the 2021 Act have effect in relation to conduct of directors of companies occurring, and in relation to companies dissolved, at any time before, as well as after, 15 December 2021 (see the note relating to s 2(14) of the 2021 Act at **[9.633]**).

[5.127]

[22H Application of Act to protected cell companies

(1) In this section—

(a) "protected cell company" means a protected cell company incorporated under Part 4 of the Risk Transformation Regulations 2017 which has its registered office in England and Wales (or Wales) or Scotland; and

(b) a reference to a part of a protected cell company is a reference to the core or a cell of the protected cell company (see regulations 42 and 43 of the Risk Transformation Regulations 2017).

(2) This Act applies to protected cell companies as it applies to companies.

(3) Accordingly, in this Act, references to a company are to be read as including references to a protected cell company.

(4) As they apply in relation to protected cell companies, the provisions of this Act have effect with the following modifications—

[(za) sections 6(1)(a)(ii) and (3)(d) and 7(2)(b) are to be disregarded;

(zb) references in sections 7(4)(a), 8ZB(2) and 15A(3)(b) to a company which has been dissolved without becoming insolvent are to be disregarded;]

(a) references to the administration, insolvency, liquidation or winding up of a company are to be read as references to the administration, insolvency, liquidation or winding up of a part of a protected cell company;

(b) references to striking off are to be read as including references to dissolution;

(c) references to a director of a company which is or has been insolvent are to be read as references to the director of a protected cell company, a part of which is or has been insolvent;

(d) references to a director of a company which is being or has been wound up are to be read as references to the director of a protected cell company, a part of which is being or has been wound up;

(e) references to the court with jurisdiction to wind up a company are to be read as references to the court with jurisdiction to wind up the parts of a protected cell company;

(f) references to the companies legislation are to be read as references to Part 4 of, and Schedules 1 to 3 to, the Risk Transformation Regulations 2017;

(g) references to the Insolvency Act 1986 are to be read as references to that Act as applied by Part 4 of, and Schedules 1 to 3 to, the Risk Transformation Regulations 2017;

(h) references to section 452 and 456 of the Companies Act 2006 are to be read as references to those sections as applied by regulation 163 of the Risk Transformation Regulations 2017;

(i) references to the registrar of companies are to be read as references to the Financial Conduct Authority; and

(j) references to an overseas company include references to a protected cell company incorporated under the Risk Transformation Regulations 2017 which has its registered office in Northern Ireland.

(5) Where two or more parts of a protected cell company are or have been insolvent, then sections 6 to 7A and 8ZA to 8ZC apply in relation to each part separately.

(6) A contribution to the assets of a protected cell company given in accordance with a compensation order under section 15A(1) or a compensation undertaking under section 15A(2) is to be held by the protected cell company on behalf of the part of the protected cell company specified in the order or undertaking.]

NOTES

Inserted by the Risk Transformation Regulations 2017, SI 2017/1212, reg 190, Sch 4, para 3, as from 8 December 2017.

Sub-s (4): paras (za), (zb) inserted by the Rating (Coronavirus) and Directors Disqualification (Dissolved Companies) Act 2021, s 2(13), as from 15 December 2021 (for the purposes of the exercise by the Secretary of State or the official receiver of powers under s 7(4) of this Act), and as from 15 February 2022 (otherwise). Note that the amendments made by s 2 of the 2021 Act have effect in relation to conduct of directors of companies occurring, and in relation to companies dissolved, at any time before, as well as after, 15 December 2021 (see the note relating to s 2(14) of the 2021 Act at **[9.633]**).

[5.128]

23 Transitional provisions, savings, repeals

(1) The transitional provisions and savings in Schedule 3 to this Act have effect, and are without prejudice to anything in the Interpretation Act 1978 with regard to the effect of repeals.

(2) The enactments specified in the second column of Schedule 4 to this Act are repealed to the extent specified in the third column of that Schedule.

[5.129]

24 Extent

(1) This Act extends to England and Wales and to Scotland.

[(2) Subsections (1) to (2A) of section 11 also extend to Northern Ireland.]

NOTES

Sub-s (2): substituted by the Small Business, Enterprise and Employment Act 2015, s 113(2), as from 1 October 2015.

[5.130]

25 Commencement

This Act comes into force simultaneously with the Insolvency Act 1986.

NOTES

The Insolvency Act 1986 came into force on 29 December 1986.

[5.131]

26 Citation

This Act may be cited as the Company Directors Disqualification Act 1986.

SCHEDULES

[SCHEDULE 1
DETERMINING UNFITNESS ETC: MATTERS TO BE TAKEN INTO ACCOUNT

Section 12C

Matters to be taken into account in all cases

[5.132]

1. The extent to which the person was responsible for the causes of any material contravention by a company or overseas company of any applicable legislative or other requirement.

2. Where applicable, the extent to which the person was responsible for the causes of a company or overseas company becoming insolvent.

3. The frequency of conduct of the person which falls within paragraph 1 or 2.

4. The nature and extent of any loss or harm caused, or any potential loss or harm which could have been caused, by the person's conduct in relation to a company or overseas company.

Additional matters to be taken into account where person is or has been a director

5. Any misfeasance or breach of any fiduciary duty by the director in relation to a company or overseas company.

6. Any material breach of any legislative or other obligation of the director which applies as a result of being a director of a company or overseas company.

7. The frequency of conduct of the director which falls within paragraph 5 or 6.

Interpretation

8. Subsections (1A) to (2A) of section 6 apply for the purposes of this Schedule as they apply for the purposes of that section.

9. In this Schedule "director" includes a shadow director.]

NOTES

Substituted by the Small Business, Enterprise and Employment Act 2015, s 106(1), (6), as from 1 October 2015. Note that save where conduct is considered by a court or by the Secretary of State under s 5A of this Act, this Schedule applies to a person's conduct as a director where that conduct occurs on or after 1 October 2015 (see SI 2015/1689, Schedule).

SCHEDULE 2
SAVINGS FROM COMPANIES ACT 1981 SS 93, 94, AND INSOLVENCY ACT 1985 SCHEDULE 9

Section 19

[5.133]

1. Sections 2 and 4(1)(b) do not apply in relation to anything done before 15th June 1982 by a person in his capacity as liquidator of a company or as receiver or manager of a company's property.

2. Subject to paragraph 1—

(a) section 2 applies in a case where a person is convicted on indictment of an offence which he committed (and, in the case of a continuing offence, has ceased to commit) before 15th June 1982; but in such a case a disqualification order under that section shall not be made for a period in excess of 5 years;

(b) that section does not apply in a case where a person is convicted summarily—

  (i) in England and Wales, if he had consented so to be tried before that date, or

  (ii) in Scotland, if the summary proceedings commenced before that date.

3. Subject to paragraph 1, section 4 applies in relation to an offence committed or other thing done before 15th June 1982; but a disqualification order made on the grounds of such an offence or other thing done shall not be made for a period in excess of 5 years.

4. The powers of a court under section 5 are not exercisable in a case where a person is convicted of an offence which he committed (and, in the case of a continuing offence, had ceased to commit) before 15th June 1982.

5. For purposes of section 3(1) and section 5, no account is to be taken of any offence which was committed, or any default order which was made, before 1st June 1977.

6. An order made under section 28 of the Companies Act 1976 has effect as if made under section 3 of this Act; and an application made before 15th June 1982 for such an order is to be treated as an application for an order under the section last mentioned.

7. Where—

(a) an application is made for a disqualification order under section 6 of this Act by virtue of paragraph (a) of subsection (2) of that section, and

(b) the company in question went into liquidation before 28th April 1986 (the coming into force of the provision replaced by section 6),

the court shall not make an order under that section unless it could have made a disqualification order under section 300 of [the Companies Act 1985] as it had effect immediately before the date specified in sub-paragraph (b) above.

8. An application shall not be made under section 8 of this Act in relation to a report made or information or documents obtained before 28th April 1986.

NOTES

Para 7: words in square brackets substituted by the Companies Act 2006 (Consequential Amendments, Transitional Provisions and Savings) Order 2009, SI 2009/1941, art 2(1), Sch 1, para 85(1), (15), as from 1 October 2009.

SCHEDULE 3
TRANSITIONAL PROVISIONS AND SAVINGS

Section 23(1)

[5.134]

1. In this Schedule, "the former enactments" means so much of [the Companies Act 1985], and so much of [the Insolvency Act 1986], as is repealed and replaced by this Act; and "the appointed day" means the day on which this Act comes into force.

2. So far as anything done or treated as done under or for the purposes of any provision of the former enactments could have been done under or for the purposes of the corresponding provision of this Act, it is not invalidated by the repeal of that provision but has effect as if done under or for the purposes of the corresponding provision; and any order, regulation, rule or other instrument made or having effect under any provision of the former enactments shall, insofar as its effect is preserved by this paragraph, be treated for all purposes as made and having effect under the corresponding provision.

3. Where any period of time specified in a provision of the former enactments is current immediately before the appointed day, this Act has effect as if the corresponding provision had been in force when the period began to run; and (without prejudice to the foregoing) any period of time so specified and current is deemed for the purposes of this Act—

(a) to run from the date or event from which it was running immediately before the appointed day, and

(b) to expire (subject to any provision of this Act for its extension) whenever it would have expired if this Act had not been passed;

and any rights, priorities, liabilities, reliefs, obligations, requirements, powers, duties or exemptions dependent on the beginning, duration or end of such a period as above mentioned shall be under this Act as they were or would have been under the former enactments.

4. Where in any provision of this Act there is a reference to another such provision, and the first-mentioned provision operates, or is capable of operating, in relation to things done or omitted, or events occurring or not occurring, in the past (including in particular past acts of compliance with any enactment, failures of compliance, contraventions, offences and convictions of offences) the reference to the other provision is to be read as including a reference to the corresponding provision of the former enactments.

5. Offences committed before the appointed day under any provision of the former enactments may, notwithstanding any repeal by this Act, be prosecuted and punished after that day as if this Act had not passed.

6. A reference in any enactment, instrument or document (whether express or implied, and in whatever phraseology) to a provision of the former enactments (including the corresponding provision of any yet earlier enactment) is to be read, where necessary to retain for the enactment, instrument or document the same force and effect as it would have had but for the passing of this Act, as, or as including, a reference to the corresponding provision by which it is replaced in this Act.

NOTES

Para 1: words in square brackets substituted by the Companies Act 2006 (Consequential Amendments, Transitional Provisions and Savings) Order 2009, SI 2009/1941, art 2(1), Sch 1, para 85(1), (16), as from 1 October 2009.

SCHEDULE 4

(Sch 4 repeals CA 1985, ss 295–299, 301, 302, Sch 2 (the entries relating to ss 295(7), 302(1) only), Sch 12, and IA 1985, ss 12–14, 16, 18, 108(2), Sch 2, Sch 6, paras 1, 2, 7, 14, Sch 9, paras 2, 3.)

COMPANIES ACT 1989

(1989 c 40)

NOTES

This Act is reproduced as amended by the following Acts:

1992	Friendly Societies Act 1992; Trade Union and Labour Relations (Consolidation) Act 1992.
1993	Charities Act 1993; Criminal Justice Act 1993.
1998	Bank of England Act 1998; Competition Act 1998; Northern Ireland Act 1998.
1999	Youth Justice and Criminal Evidence Act 1999.
2002	Enterprise Act 2002.
2004	Finance Act 2004; Companies (Audit, Investigations and Community Enterprise) Act 2004; Pensions Act 2004.
2006	Companies Act 2006.
2007	Bankruptcy and Diligence etc (Scotland) Act 2007; Tribunals, Courts and Enforcement Act 2007; Legal Services Act 2007.
2012	Civil Aviation Act 2012; Financial Services Act 2012.

This Act is reproduced as amended by the following SIs:

1991	Financial Markets and Insolvency Regulations 1991, SI 1991/880.
1992	Transfer of Functions (Financial Services) Order 1992, SI 1992/1315.
1993	Financial Services (Disclosure of Information) (Designated Authorities) (No 7) Order 1993, SI 1993/1826.
1994	Financial Services (Disclosure of Information) (Designated Authorities) (No 8) Order 1994, SI 1994/340.
1995	Public Offers of Securities Regulations 1995, SI 1995/1537.
1998	Financial Markets and Insolvency Regulations 1998, SI 1998/1748.
1999	Scotland Act 1998 (Consequential Modifications) (No 2) Order 1999, SI 1999/1820.
2001	Financial Services and Markets Act 2000 (Dissolution of the Insurance Brokers Registration Council) (Consequential Provisions) Order 2001, SI 2001/1283; Financial Services and Markets Act 2000 (Consequential Amendments and Repeals) Order 2001, SI 2001/3649.
2002	Companies (Disclosure of Information) (Designated Authorities) (No 2) Order 2002, SI 2002/1889.
2003	Companies (Acquisition of Own Shares) (Treasury Shares) Regulations 2003, SI 2003/1116.
2004	Competition Act 1998 and other enactments (Amendment) Regulations 2004, SI 2004/1261.
2005	Regulatory Reform (Execution of Deeds and Documents) Order 2005, SI 2005/1906.
2006	Charities and Trustee Investment (Scotland) Act 2005 (Consequential Provisions and Modifications) Order 2006, SI 2006/242; Companies (Disclosure of Information) (Designated Authorities) Order 2006, SI 2006/1644; Financial Services and Markets Act 2000 (Regulated Activities) (Amendment No 3) Order 2006, SI 2006/3384.
2008	Companies Act 2006 (Consequential Amendments etc) Order 2008, SI 2008/948.
2009	Financial Markets and Insolvency Regulations 2009, SI 2009/853; Companies Act 2006 (Consequential Amendments, Transitional Provisions and Savings) Order 2009, SI 2009/1941.
2010	Transfer of Tribunal Functions Order 2010, SI 2010/22.
2011	Treaty of Lisbon (Changes in Terminology) Order 2011, SI 2011/1043.
2013	Financial Services and Markets Act 2000 (Over the Counter Derivatives, Central Counterparties and Trade Repositories) Regulations 2013, SI 2013/504; Alternative Investment Fund Managers Regulations 2013, SI 2013/1773; Financial Services and Markets Act 2000 (Over the Counter Derivatives, Central Counterparties and Trade Repositories) (No 2) Regulations 2013, SI 2013/1908; Public Bodies (Merger of the Gambling Commission and the National Lottery Commission) Order 2013, SI 2013/2329.
2014	Enterprise and Regulatory Reform Act 2013 (Competition) (Consequential, Transitional and Saving Provisions) Order 2014, SI 2014/892.
2016	Enterprise and Regulatory Reform Act 2013 (Consequential Amendments) (Bankruptcy) and the Small Business, Enterprise and Employment Act 2015 (Consequential Amendments) Regulations 2016, SI 2016/481; Bankruptcy (Scotland) Act 2016 (Consequential Provisions and Modifications) Order 2016, SI 2016/1034.
2017	Bank of England and Financial Services (Consequential Amendments) Regulations 2017, SI 2017/80; Financial Services and Markets Act 2000 (Regulated Activities) (Amendment) Order 2017, SI 2017/488; Deregulation Act 2015 and Small Business, Enterprise and Employment Act 2015 (Consequential Amendments) (Savings) Regulations 2017, SI 2017/540; Central Securities Depositories Regulations 2017, SI 2017/1064; Companies Act 1989 (Financial Markets and Insolvency) (Amendment) Regulations 2017, SI 2017/1247.
2019	Financial Markets and Insolvency (Amendment and Transitional Provision) (EU Exit) Regulations 2019, SI 2019/341.

Commencement: most of this Act came into force between 16 November 1989 (Royal assent) and 3 July 1995, although a limited number of provisions were commenced after 1995, and a few are yet to be brought into force. Extensive transitional provisions and savings were made in connection with the commencement of this Act by the Orders noted to s 215 at **[5.191]**.

Community interest companies: as to the application of this Act (subject to certain modifications) to community interest companies, see the Companies (Audit, Investigations and Community Enterprise) Act 2004. See, in particular, Part 2 of that Act.

Civil Procedure Rules: the Civil Procedure Rules 1998, SI 1998/3132, r 49, states that those Rules apply to proceedings under (a) the Companies Act 1985; (b) the Companies Act 2006; and (c) other legislation relating to companies and limited liability partnerships, subject to the provision of the relevant practice direction which applies to those proceedings.

ARRANGEMENT OF SECTIONS

PART III
INVESTIGATIONS AND POWERS TO OBTAIN INFORMATION

Powers exercisable to assist overseas regulatory authorities

PART V
OTHER AMENDMENTS OF COMPANY LAW

A company's capacity and related matters

Miscellaneous

PART VII
FINANCIAL MARKETS AND INSOLVENCY

Introduction

Recognised bodies

Other exchanges and clearing houses

Market charges

Market property

Supplementary provisions

PART X
MISCELLANEOUS AND GENERAL PROVISIONS

General

An Act to amend the law relating to company accounts; to make new provision with respect to the persons eligible for appointment as company auditors; to amend the Companies Act 1985 and certain other enactments with respect to investigations and powers to obtain information and to confer new powers exercisable to assist overseas regulatory authorities; to make new provision with respect to the registration of company charges and otherwise to amend the law relating to companies; to amend the Fair Trading Act 1973; to enable provision to be made for the payment of fees in connection with the exercise by the Secretary of State, the Director General of Fair Trading and the Monopolies and Mergers Commission of their functions under Part V of that Act; to make provision for safeguarding the operation of certain financial markets; to amend the Financial Services Act 1986; to enable provision to be made for the recording and transfer of title to securities without a written instrument; to amend the Company Directors Disqualification Act 1986, the Company Securities (Insider Dealing) Act 1985, the Policyholders Protection Act 1975 and the law relating to building societies; and for connected purposes

[16 November 1989]

PART I COMPANY ACCOUNTS

1–23 *(Ss 1–22 amended the Companies Act 1985, Pt VII, and were repealed by the Companies Act 2006, s 1295, Sch 16, as from 1 October 2007 (in so far as relating to s 16), and as from 6 April 2008 (otherwise); s 23 introduces Sch 10 to this Act (Consequential amendments on this Part) (as to the repeal of that Schedule, see the Sch 10 note post).)*

PART II ELIGIBILITY FOR APPOINTMENT AS COMPANY AUDITOR

24–54 *(Part II has been repealed as follows: Ss 24, 35, 36, 39, 51 repealed by the Companies Act 2006, s 1295, Sch 16, as from 6 April 2008. Ss 25–28 repealed by CA 2006, s 1295, Sch 16, as from 6 April 2008, except in relation to auditors appointed for financial years beginning before that date (see the Companies Act 2006 (Commencement No 5, Transitional Provisions and Savings) Order 2007, SI 2007/3495, Sch 4, Pt 1, para 37). Ss 29, 40–45, 49 repealed by CA 2006, s 1295, Sch 16, as from 6 April 2008, except in relation to auditors, supervisory bodies or qualifying bodies to whom ss 25–28 and 30–39 of this Act apply (see SI 2007/3495, Sch 4, Pt 1, para 41(1), (2)). Ss 30–34, 48 (and Schs 11, 12) repealed by CA 2006, s 1295, Sch 16, as from 6 April 2008, except in relation to the supervision and qualification of auditors appointed for financial years beginning before that date (see SI 2007/3495, Sch 4, Pt 1, para 38; note also that any declaration by the Secretary of State in force under s 33 (approval of overseas qualifications) immediately before 6 April 2008 continues in force on and after that date as if made under s 1221 of CA 2006). Ss 37, 38 repealed by CA 2006, s 1295, Sch 16, as from 6 April 2008, except in relation to the operation of those sections in relation to functions exercised under this Part on or after that date (see SI 2007/3495, Sch 4, Pt 1, para 39). Ss 46, 46A (and Sch 13) repealed by CA 2006, s 1295, Sch 16, as from 6 April 2008, except in relation to the operation of those provisions in relation to functions exercised under this Part on or after that date (see SI 2007/3495, Sch 4, Pt 1, para 42(1)). S 47 repealed by the Competition Act 1998 and other enactments (Amendment) Regulations 2004, SI 2004/1261, reg 5, Sch 2, para 2(1), (2), as from 1 May 2004. S 50 repealed by CA 2006, s 1295, Sch 16, as from 6 April 2008 (note that this repeal does not affect any amendments made by Regulations under this section that are in force immediately before that date (see the Companies Act 2006 (Consequential Amendments etc) Order 2008, SI 2008/948, art 10 at* **[4.145]***). Ss 52–54 repealed by CA 2006, s 1295, Sch 16, as from 6 April 2008, except in relation to the operation of those sections for the purposes of interpreting provisions of this Act that continue to apply on or after that date.)*

PART III INVESTIGATIONS AND POWERS TO OBTAIN INFORMATION

55–81 *(In so far as these sections are still in force they contain amendments to Part XIV of the Companies Act 1985 (Investigation of Companies and their Affairs; Requisition of Documents), other consequential amendments to the 1985 Act, and amendments to the Insolvency Act 1986, which have been incorporated at the appropriate place (and amendments to the Building Societies Act 1986 (outside the scope of this work)). Note that Pt XIV of the 1985 Act was not repealed by the Companies Act 2006 (see* **[5.17]** *et seq). Though certain sections of Part XIV were repealed by the 2006 Act (as to which, see Sch 16 to that Act at* **[1.1535]***).)*

Powers exercisable to assist overseas regulatory authorities

[5.135]
82 Request for assistance by overseas regulatory authority

(1) The powers conferred by section 83 are exercisable by the Secretary of State for the purpose of assisting an overseas regulatory authority which has requested his assistance in connection with inquiries being carried out by it or on its behalf.

(2) An "overseas regulatory authority" means an authority which in a country or territory outside the United Kingdom exercises—

[(a) any function corresponding to—
  (i) any function of the Secretary of State under the Companies Act 1985 [or the Companies Act 2006];
  (ii) any function of the [FCA, the PRA or the Bank of England] under the Financial Services and Markets Act 2000;
  (iii) . . .

(b) any function in connection with the investigation of, or the enforcement of rules (whether or not having the force of law) relating to, conduct of the kind prohibited by [Part V of the Criminal Justice Act 1993 (insider dealing)], or

(c) any function prescribed for the purposes of this subsection by order of the Secretary of State, being a function which in the opinion of the Secretary of State relates to companies or financial services.

An order under paragraph (c) shall be made by statutory instrument which shall be subject to annulment in pursuance of a resolution of either House of Parliament.

(3) The Secretary of State shall not exercise the powers conferred by section 83 unless [he and the [corresponding UK regulator (if any)] are] satisfied that the assistance requested by the overseas regulatory authority is for the purposes of its regulatory functions.

An authority's "regulatory functions" means any functions falling within subsection (2) and any other functions relating to companies or financial services.

[(3A) In subsection (3), "the corresponding UK regulator" means such one or more of the FCA, PRA and the Bank of England as appears to the Secretary of State to exercise functions corresponding to the regulatory functions for the purposes of which the request is made.]

(4) In deciding whether to exercise those powers the Secretary of State may take into account, in particular—

(a) whether corresponding assistance would be given in that country or territory to an authority exercising regulatory functions in the United Kingdom;

(b) whether the inquiries relate to the possible breach of a law, or other requirement, which has no close parallel in the United Kingdom or involves the assertion of a jurisdiction not recognised by the United Kingdom;

(c) the seriousness of the matter to which the inquiries relate, the importance to the inquiries of the information sought in the United Kingdom and whether the assistance could be obtained by other means;

(d) whether it is otherwise appropriate in the public interest to give the assistance sought.

(5) Before deciding whether to exercise those powers in a case where the overseas regulatory authority is a banking supervisor, the Secretary of State shall consult the [FCA and the PRA].

A "banking supervisor" means an overseas regulatory authority with respect to which the [FCA or the PRA] has notified the Secretary of State, for the purposes of this subsection, that it exercises functions corresponding to those of [the body giving the notification] [in relation to authorised persons with permission under the Financial Services and Markets Act 2000 to accept deposits].

[(5A) In subsection (5), "authorised person" has the meaning given in the Financial Services and Markets Act 2000 and the references to deposits and their acceptance must be read with—

(a) section 22 of that Act;

(b) any relevant order under that section; and

(c) Schedule 2 to that Act.]

(6) The Secretary of State may decline to exercise those powers unless the overseas regulatory authority undertakes to make such contribution towards the costs of their exercise as the Secretary of State considers appropriate.

(7) References in this section to financial services include, in particular, investment business, insurance and banking.

NOTES

Sub-s (2): para (a) substituted by the Financial Services and Markets Act 2000 (Consequential Amendments and Repeals) Order 2001, SI 2001/3649, art 76(1), (2), as from 1 December 2001. Words in square brackets in sub-para (a)(i) inserted by the Companies Act 2006 (Consequential Amendments etc) Order 2008, SI 2008/948, art 3(1), Sch 1, Pt 2, para 157, as from 6 April 2008. Words in square brackets in sub-para (a)(ii) substituted, and sub-para (a)(iii) repealed, by the Financial Services Act 2012, s 114(1), Sch 18, Pt 2, paras 62, 63(1), (2), as from 1 April 2013. Words in square brackets in para (b) substituted by the Criminal Justice Act 1993, s 79(13), Sch 5, Pt I, para 16, as from 1 March 1994.

Sub-s (3): words in first (outer) pair of square brackets substituted by SI 2001/3649, art 76(1), (3), as from 1 December 2001. Words in second (inner) pair of square brackets substituted by the Financial Services Act 2012, s 114(1), Sch 18, Pt 2, paras 62, 63(1), (3), as from 1 April 2013.

Sub-s (3A): inserted by the Financial Services Act 2012, s 114(1), Sch 18, Pt 2, paras 62, 63(1), (4), as from 1 April 2013.

Sub-s (5): words in first, second and third pairs of square brackets substituted by the Financial Services Act 2012, s 114(1), Sch 18, Pt 2, paras 62, 63(1), (5), as from 1 April 2013. Words in fourth pair of square brackets substituted by SI 2001/3649, art 76(1), (4), as from 1 December 2001.

Sub-s (5A): inserted by SI 2001/3649, art 76(1), (5), as from 1 December 2001.

Transfer of functions: by the Transfer of Functions (Financial Services) Order 1992, SI 1992/1315, art 5, Sch 3, para 3, the function of the Secretary of State under sub-s (3) above is exercisable concurrently by the Secretary of State and the Treasury.

[5.136]

83 Power to require information, documents or other assistance

(1) The following powers may be exercised in accordance with section 82, if the Secretary of State considers there is good reason for their exercise.

(2) The Secretary of State may require any person—

(a) to attend before him at a specified time and place and answer questions or otherwise furnish information with respect to any matter relevant to the inquiries,

(b) to produce at a specified time and place any specified documents which appear to the Secretary of State to relate to any matter relevant to the inquiries, and

(c) otherwise to give him such assistance in connection with the inquiries as he is reasonably able to give.

(3) The Secretary of State may examine a person on oath and may administer an oath accordingly.

(4) Where documents are produced the Secretary of State may take copies or extracts from them.

(5) A person shall not under this section be required to disclose information or produce a document which he would be entitled to refuse to disclose or produce on grounds of legal professional privilege in proceedings in the High Court or on grounds of confidentiality as between client and professional legal adviser in proceedings in the Court of Session, except that a lawyer may be required to furnish the name and address of his client.

(6) A statement by a person in compliance with a requirement imposed under this section may be used in evidence against him.

[(6A) However, in criminal proceedings in which that person is charged with an offence to which this subsection applies—

(a) no evidence relating to the statement may be adduced, and

(b) no question relating to it may be asked,

by or on behalf of the prosecution, unless evidence relating to it is adduced, or a question relating to it is asked, in the proceedings by or on behalf of that person.

(6B) Subsection (6A) applies to any offence other than—

(a) an offence under section 85;

(b) an offence under section 2 or 5 of the Perjury Act 1911 (false statements made on oath otherwise than in judicial proceedings or made otherwise than on oath);

(c) an offence under section 44(1) or (2) of the Criminal Law (Consolidation) (Scotland) Act 1995 (false statements made on oath or otherwise than on oath); or

(d) an offence under Article 7 or 10 of the Perjury (Northern Ireland) Order 1979 (false statements made on oath otherwise than in judicial proceedings or made otherwise than on oath).]

(7) Where a person claims a lien on a document, its production under this section is without prejudice to his lien.

(8) In this section "documents" includes information recorded in any form; and, in relation to information recorded otherwise than in legible form, the power to require its production includes power to require the production of a copy of it in legible form.

NOTES

Sub-ss (6A), (6B): inserted by the Youth Justice and Criminal Evidence Act 1999, s 59, Sch 3, para 21, as from 14 April 2000 (in relation to England and Wales), and as from 1 January 2001 (in relation to Scotland).

[5.137]

84 Exercise of powers by officer, &c

(1) The Secretary of State may authorise an officer of his or any other competent person to exercise on his behalf all or any of the powers conferred by section 83.

(2) No such authority shall be granted except for the purpose of investigating—

(a) the affairs, or any aspects of the affairs, of a person specified in the authority, or

(b) a subject-matter so specified,

being a person who, or subject-matter which, is the subject of the inquiries being carried out by or on behalf of the overseas regulatory authority.

(3) No person shall be bound to comply with a requirement imposed by a person exercising powers by virtue of an authority granted under this section unless he has, if required, produced evidence of his authority.

(4) A person shall not by virtue of an authority under this section be required to disclose any information or produce any documents in respect of which he owes an obligation of confidence by virtue of carrying on the business of banking unless—

(a) the imposing on him of a requirement with respect to such information or documents has been specifically authorised by the Secretary of State, or

(b) the person to whom the obligation of confidence is owed consents to the disclosure or production.

In this subsection "documents" has the same meaning as in section 83.

(5) Where the Secretary of State authorises a person other than one of his officers to exercise any powers by virtue of this section, that person shall make a report to the Secretary of State in such manner as he may require on the exercise of those powers and the results of exercising them.

[5.138]

85 Penalty for failure to comply with requirement, &c

(1) A person who without reasonable excuse fails to comply with a requirement imposed on him under section 83 commits an offence and is liable on summary conviction to imprisonment for a term not exceeding six months or to a fine not exceeding level 5 on the standard scale, or both.

(2) A person who in purported compliance with any such requirement furnishes information which he knows to be false or misleading in a material particular, or recklessly furnishes information which is false or misleading in a material particular, commits an offence and is liable—

(a) on conviction on indictment, to imprisonment for a term not exceeding two years or to a fine, or both;

(b) on summary conviction, to imprisonment for a term not exceeding six months or to a fine not exceeding the statutory maximum, or both.

[5.139]

86 Restrictions on disclosure of information

(1) This section applies to information relating to the business or other affairs of a person which—

(a) is supplied by an overseas regulatory authority in connection with a request for assistance, or

(b) is obtained by virtue of the powers conferred by section 83, whether or not any requirement to supply it is made under that section.

(2) Except as permitted by section 87 below, such information shall not be disclosed for any purpose—

(a) by the primary recipient, or

(b) by any person obtaining the information directly or indirectly from him,

without the consent of the person from whom the primary recipient obtained the information and, if different, the person to whom it relates.

(3) The "primary recipient" means, as the case may be—

(a) the Secretary of State,

(b) any person authorised under section 84 to exercise powers on his behalf, and

(c) any officer or servant of any such person.

(4) Information shall not be treated as information to which this section applies if it has been made available to the public by virtue of being disclosed in any circumstances in which, or for any purpose for which, disclosure is not precluded by this section.

(5) A person who contravenes this section commits an offence and is liable—
(a) on conviction on indictment, to imprisonment for a term not exceeding two years or to a fine, or both;
(b) on summary conviction, to imprisonment for a term not exceeding three months or to a fine not exceeding the statutory maximum, or both.

[5.140]

87 Exceptions from restrictions on disclosure

(1) Information to which section 86 applies may be disclosed—
(a) to any person with a view to the institution of, or otherwise for the purposes of, relevant proceedings,
(b) for the purpose of enabling or assisting a relevant authority to discharge any relevant function (including functions in relation to proceedings),
(c) to the Treasury, if the disclosure is made in the interests of investors or in the public interest,
(d) if the information is or has been available to the public from other sources,
(e) in a summary or collection of information framed in such a way as not to enable the identity of any person to whom the information relates to be ascertained, or
(f) in pursuance of any [EU] obligation.

(2) The relevant proceedings referred to in subsection (1)(a) are—
(a) any criminal proceedings,
[(b) civil proceedings arising under or by virtue of the Financial Services and Markets Act 2000 and proceedings before the Upper Tribunal in respect of—
[(i) a decision of the FCA;
(ia) a decision of the PRA;]
(ii) a decision of the Bank of England; or
(iii) a decision of a person relating to the assessment of any compensation or consideration under the Banking (Special Provisions) Act 2008 or the Banking Act 2009,]
(c) disciplinary proceedings relating to—
(i) the exercise by a [relevant lawyer], auditor, accountant, valuer or actuary of his professional duties, or
(ii) the discharge by a public servant of his duties;
[(d) proceedings before [a tribunal in relation to a decision of the Pensions Regulator]].

[(2A) In subsection (2)(c)(i) "relevant lawyer" means—
(a) a person who, for the purposes of the Legal Services Act 2007, is an authorised person in relation to an activity which constitutes a reserved legal activity (within the meaning of that Act),
(b) a solicitor or barrister in Northern Ireland, or
(c) a solicitor or advocate in Scotland.]

(3) In subsection (2)(c)(ii) "public servant" means an officer or servant of the Crown or of any public or other authority for the time being designated for the purposes of that provision by order of the Secretary of State.

(4) The relevant authorities referred to in subsection (1)(b), and the relevant functions in relation to each such authority, are as follows—

Authority	Functions
[The Secretary of State.	Functions under— (a) the enactments relating to companies or insolvency; (b) Part 2, this Part or Part 7 of this Act; (c) the Financial Services and Markets Act 2000.]
[The Treasury	Functions under— (a) this Part or Part 7 of this Act; (b) the Financial Services and Markets Act 2000.]
[An inspector appointed under Part 14 of the Companies Act 1985.	Functions under that Part.]
[A person authorised to exercise powers under section 447 of the Companies Act 1985 or section 84 of this Act.	Functions under that section.]
[A person appointed under— (a) section 167 of the Financial Services and Markets Act 2000 (general investigations), (b) section 168 of that Act (investigations in particular cases), (c) section 169(1)(b) of that Act (investigation in support of overseas regulator), (d) section 284 of that Act (investigations into affairs of certain collective investment schemes), or (e) regulations made as a result of section 262(2)(k) of that Act (investigations into open-ended investment companies), to conduct an investigation.	Functions in relation to the investigation.]
An overseas regulatory authority.	Its regulatory functions (within the meaning of sec-

Authority	Functions
	tion 82 of this Act).
The Department of Economic Development in Northern Ireland or a person appointed or authorised by that Department.	Functions conferred on it or him by the enactments relating to companies or insolvency.
. . .	. . .
. . .	. . .
. . .	. . .
. . .	. . .
[. . .	. . .]
The Bank of England.	[Any of its functions]
[[The FCA or the PRA]	Functions under the enactments relating to friendly societies, under the Building Societies Act 1986 and under the Financial Services and Markets Act 2000.]
[A body corporate established in accordance with section 212(1) of that Act.	Functions under the Financial Services Compensation Scheme, established in accordance with section 213 of that Act.]
[A recognised investment exchange[, recognised clearing house or recognised CSD] (as defined by section 285 of that Act).	Functions in its capacity as an exchange[, clearing house or central securities depository] recognised under that Act.]
[A body designated under section 326(1) of the Financial Services and Markets Act 2000.	Functions in its capacity as a body designated under that section.]
. . .	. . .
[A body designated by order under section 1252 of the Companies Act 2006.	Functions under Part 42 of the Companies Act 2006.]
[A recognised supervisory or qualifying body within the meaning of Part 42 of the Companies Act 2006.	Functions as such a body.]
. . .	. . .
. . .	. . .
The Official Receiver or, in Northern Ireland, the Official Assignee for company liquidations or for bankruptcy.	Functions under the enactments relating to insolvency.
A recognised professional body (within the meaning of section 391 of the Insolvency Act 1986).	Functions in its capacity as such a body under the Insolvency Act 1986.
. . .	. . .
[The Pensions Regulator	Functions conferred by or by virtue of— (a) the Pension Schemes Act 1993, (b) the Pensions Act 1995, (c) the Welfare Reform and Pensions Act 1999, (d) the Pensions Act 2004, or any enactment in force in Northern Ireland corresponding to an enactment mentioned in paragraphs (a) to (d) above.
The Board of the Pension Protection Fund	Functions conferred by or by virtue of Part 2 of the Pensions Act 2004 or any enactment in force in Northern Ireland corresponding to that Part.]
[The Competition and Markets Authority]	Functions under the [Financial Services and Markets Act 2000].
[A person authorised by the Secretary of State under section 245C of the Companies Act 1985.	Functions relating to the securing of compliance by companies with the accounting requirements of that Act.]
. . .	. . .
[The Comptroller and Auditor General	Functions under Part 2 of the National Audit Act 1983.]
[The Scottish Ministers	Functions under the enactments relating to insolvency]
[The Accountant in Bankruptcy	Functions he has under the enactments relating to insolvency.]
[The Regulator of Community Interest Companies.	Functions under the Companies (Audit, Investigations and Community Enterprise) Act 2004."
[The Gambling Commission	[Functions under— the Gambling Act 2005, sections 5 to 10 and 15 of the National Lottery

Authority	Functions
	etc Act 1993.]]

[*Note*: Article 3(4) of the Companies (Disclosure of Information) (Designated Authorities) (No 2) Order 2002 restricts the circumstances in which disclosure for the purpose of enabling or assisting the Comptroller and Auditor General to discharge his relevant functions is permitted.]

(5) The Secretary of State may by order amend the Table in subsection (4) so as to—
- (a) add any public or other authority to the Table and specify the relevant functions of that authority,
- (b) remove any authority from the Table, or
- (c) add functions to, or remove functions from, those which are relevant functions in relation to an authority specified in the Table;

and the order may impose conditions subject to which, or otherwise restrict the circumstances in which, disclosure is permitted.

(6) An order under this section shall be made by statutory instrument which shall be subject to annulment in pursuance of a resolution of either House of Parliament.

NOTES

Sub-s (1): reference to "EU" in square brackets substituted by the Treaty of Lisbon (Changes in Terminology) Order 2011, SI 2011/1043, art 6, as from 22 April 2011.

Sub-s (2) is amended as follows:

Para (b) substituted by the Transfer of Tribunal Functions Order 2010, SI 2010/22, art 5(1), Sch 2, para 9(a), as from 6 April 2010.

Sub-para (b)(i) and (ia) substituted (for the original sub-para (b)(i)), by the Financial Services Act 2012, s 114(1), Sch 18, Pt 2, paras 62, 64(1), (2), as from 1 April 2013.

Words in square brackets in sub-para (c)(i) substituted by the Legal Services Act 2007, s 208, Sch 21, para 82(a), as from 1 January 2010.

Para (d) added by the Pensions Act 2004, s 102, Sch 4, Pt 4, para 20, as from 6 April 2005.

Words in square brackets in para (d) substituted by SI 2010/22, art 5(1), Sch 2, para 9(b), as from 6 April 2010.

Sub-s (2A): inserted by the Legal Services Act 2007, s 208, Sch 21, para 82(b), as from 1 January 2010.

Sub-s (4) is amended as follows:

Entry "The Secretary of State" substituted by SI 2001/3649, art 77(1), (3), (5), as from 1 December 2001.

Entry "The Treasury" inserted by the Transfer of Functions (Financial Services) Order 1992, SI 1992/1315, art 10(1), Sch 4, para 12, as from 7 June 1992. Subsequently substituted by SI 2001/3649, art 77(1), (3), (6), as from 1 December 2001.

Entry beginning "An inspector appointed under Part 14" substituted by SI 2001/3649, art 77(1), (3), (7), as from 1 December 2001.

Entry beginning "A person authorised to exercise powers" and subsequent entry substituted (for the original entry beginning with those words) by SI 2001/3649, art 77(1), (3), (8), as from 1 December 2001.

First, second, third, fourth, fifth, seventh, eighth and tenth entries omitted repealed by SI 2001/3649, art 77(1), (3), (4), as from 1 December 2001

Sixth entry omitted originally inserted by the Friendly Societies Act 1992, s 120, Sch 21, Pt I, para 11, and repealed by SI 2001/3649, 77(1), (3), (4), as from 1 December 2001.

In the entry "The Bank of England" words in square brackets substituted by the Bank of England Act 1998, s 23(1), Sch 5, para 66(1), (3), as from 1 June 1998.

The entry following the entry for the "The Bank of England" was originally inserted (as the entry "The Financial Services Authority") by the Bank of England Act 1998, s 23(1), Sch 5, para 66(1), (3), as from 1 June 1998; and was subsequently substituted by SI 2001/3649, art 77(1), (3), (9), as from 1 December 2001. The words in square brackets in that entry were substituted by the Financial Services Act 2012, s 114(1), Sch 18, Pt 2, paras 62, 64(1), (3), as from 1 April 2013.

Entry "A body corporate established in accordance with section 212(1) of that Act" inserted by SI 2001/3649, art 77(1), (3), (10), as from 1 December 2001.

Entry beginning "A recognised investment exchange" inserted by SI 2001/3649, art 77(1), (3), (10), as from 1 December 2001. Words in square brackets substituted by the Central Securities Depositories Regulations 2017, SI 2017/1064, reg 10, Schedule, para 5(1), (2), as from 28 November 2017.

Entry "A body designated under section 326(1) of the Financial Services and Markets Act 2000" inserted by SI 2001/3649, art 77(1), (3), (10), as from 1 December 2001.

Ninth entry omitted repealed by the Financial Services and Markets Act 2000 (Dissolution of the Insurance Brokers Registration Council) (Consequential Provisions) Order 2001, SI 2001/1283, art 3(4), as from 30 April 2001.

Entries "A body designated by order under section 1252 of the Companies Act 2006" and "A recognised supervisory or qualifying body within the meaning of Part 42 of the Companies Act 2006" substituted by the Companies Act 2006 (Consequential Amendments etc) Order 2008, SI 2008/948, art 3(1), Sch 1, Pt 2, para 158, as from 6 April 2008.

Entries "The Pensions Regulator" and "The Board of the Pension Protection Fund" substituted by the Pensions Act 2004, s 319, Sch 12, para 6, as from 6 April 2005.

In entry "The Competition and Markets Authority" (formerly "The Office of Fair Trading") words in square brackets in column 1 substituted by the Enterprise and Regulatory Reform Act 2013 (Competition) (Consequential, Transitional and Saving Provisions) Order 2014, SI 2014/892, art 2, Sch 1, Pt 2, para 69, as from 1 April 2014. Words in square brackets in column 2 substituted by SI 2001/3649, art 77(1), (3), (11), as from 1 December 2001.

Entry beginning "A person authorised by the Secretary of State" inserted by the Financial Services (Disclosure of Information) (Designated Authorities) (No 7) Order 1993, SI 1993/1826, art 3, as from 16 August 1993.

Entry relating to "the National Lottery" (omitted) originally inserted by the Financial Services (Disclosure of Information) (Designated Authorities) (No 8) Order 1994, SI 1994/340, art 3, as from 10 March 1994; and subsequently repealed by the Public Bodies (Merger of the Gambling Commission and the National Lottery Commission) Order 2013, SI 2013/2329, art 4, Schedule, para 23(a), as from 1 October 2013.

Entry "The Comptroller and Auditor General" inserted by the Companies (Disclosure of Information) (Designated Authorities) (No 2) Order 2002, SI 2002/1889, art 3(1), (2), as from 14 August 2002. See further the note relating to the 2002 Order below.

Entry "The Scottish Ministers" inserted by the Scotland Act 1998 (Consequential Modifications) (No 2) Order 1999, SI 1999/1820, art 4, Sch 2, Pt I, para 96, as from 1 July 1999.

Entry "The Accountant in Bankruptcy" inserted by the Scotland Act 1998 (Consequential Modifications) (No 2) Order 1999, SI 1999/1820, art 4, Sch 2, Pt I, para 96, as from 1 July 1999.

Entry "The Regulator of Community Interest Companies" inserted by the Companies (Audit, Investigations and Community Enterprise) Act 2004, s 25, Sch 2, Pt 3, para 29, as from 1 July 2005.

Entry "The Gambling Commission" inserted by the Companies (Disclosure of Information) (Designated Authorities) Order 2006, SI 2006/1644, art 3, as from 1 October 2006. Words in square brackets substituted by SI 2013/2329, art 4, Schedule, para 23(b), as from 1 October 2013.

Table note: added by SI 2002/1889, art 3(1), (3), as from 14 August 2002.

Note: SI 2002/1889, art 3(4) (as amended by SI 2012/725 and SI 2013/2329) provides as follows—

"(4) Disclosure under section 87(1)(b) of the 1989 Act is permitted by virtue of the amendment made by paragraph (2) only where the disclosure is made by the [Gambling Commission] to [the Comptroller and Auditor General] for the purpose of enabling or assisting the Comptroller and Auditor General to carry out an examination into the economy, efficiency and effectiveness with which the [Gambling Commission] has used its resources in discharging its functions under sections 5 to 10 of the National Lottery etc Act 1993"

Sub-s (1) above has effect in accordance with the Anti-terrorism, Crime and Security Act 2001, s 17. That section, which clarifies and extends a number of information disclosure provisions available to public authorities, permits disclosure to assist any criminal investigation or criminal proceedings being carried out in the UK or abroad or to facilitate determinations of whether or not such investigations or proceedings should begin or end (see Sch 4 to the 2001 Act).

Orders: the Financial Services (Disclosure of Information) (Designated Authorities) (No 7) Order 1993, SI 1993/1826; the Financial Services (Disclosure of Information) (Designated Authorities) (No 8) Order 1994, SI 1994/340; the Companies (Disclosure of Information) (Designated Authorities) (No 2) Order 2002, SI 2002/1889; the Companies (Disclosure of Information) (Designated Authorities) Order 2006, SI 2006/1644.

[5.141]

88 Exercise of powers in relation to Northern Ireland

(1) The following provisions apply where it appears to the Secretary of State that a request for assistance by an overseas regulatory authority may involve the powers conferred by section 83 being exercised in Northern Ireland in relation to matters which are transferred matters within the meaning of the Northern Ireland Constitution Act 1973.

(2) The Secretary of State shall before deciding whether to accede to the request consult the Department of Economic Development in Northern Ireland, and if he decides to accede to the request and it appears to him—

(a) that the powers should be exercised in Northern Ireland, and

(b) that the purposes for which they should be so exercised relate wholly or primarily to transferred matters,

he shall by instrument in writing authorise the Department to exercise in Northern Ireland his powers under section 83.

(3) The following provisions have effect in relation to the exercise of powers by virtue of such an authority with the substitution for references to the Secretary of State of references to the Department of Economic Development in Northern Ireland—

(a) section 84 (exercise of powers by officer, &c),

[(b) section 449 of the Companies Act 1985 and sections 86 and 87 above (restrictions on disclosure of information),] and

(c) section 89 (authority for institution of criminal proceedings);

and references to the Secretary of State in other enactments which proceed by reference to those provisions shall be construed accordingly as being or including references to the Department.

(4) The Secretary of State may after consultation with the Department of Economic Development in Northern Ireland revoke an authority given to the Department under this section.

(5) In that case nothing in the provisions referred to in subsection (3)(b) shall apply so as to prevent the Department from giving the Secretary of State any information obtained by virtue of the authority; and (without prejudice to their application in relation to disclosure by the Department) those provisions shall apply to the disclosure of such information by the Secretary of State as if it had been obtained by him in the first place.

(6) Nothing in this section affects the exercise by the Secretary of State of any powers in Northern Ireland—

(a) in a case where at the time of acceding to the request it did not appear to him that the circumstances were such as to require him to authorise the Department of Economic Development in Northern Ireland to exercise those powers, or

(b) after the revocation by him of any such authority;

and no objection shall be taken to anything done by or in relation to the Secretary of State or the Department on the ground that it should have been done by or in relation to the other.

NOTES

Sub-s (3): para (b) substituted by the Financial Services and Markets Act 2000 (Consequential Amendments and Repeals) Order 2001, SI 2001/3649, art 78, as from 1 December 2001.

[5.142]

89 Prosecutions

Proceedings for an offence under section 85 or 86 shall not be instituted—

(a) in England and Wales, except by or with the consent of the Secretary of State or the Director of Public Prosecutions;

(b) in Northern Ireland, except by or with the consent of the Secretary of State or the Director of Public Prosecutions for Northern Ireland.

[5.143]

90 Offences by bodies corporate, partnerships and unincorporated associations

(1) Where an offence under section 85 or 86 committed by a body corporate is proved to have been committed with the consent or connivance of, or to be attributable to any neglect on the part of, a director, manager, secretary or other similar officer of the body, or a person purporting to act in any such capacity, he as well as the body corporate is guilty of the offence and liable to be proceeded against and punished accordingly.

(2) Where the affairs of a body corporate are managed by its members, subsection (1) applies in relation to the acts and defaults of a member in connection with his functions of management as to a director of a body corporate.

(3) Where an offence under section 85 or 86 committed by a partnership is proved to have been committed with the consent or connivance of, or to be attributable to any neglect on the part of, a partner, he as well as the partnership is guilty of the offence and liable to be proceeded against and punished accordingly.

(4) Where an offence under section 85 or 86 committed by an unincorporated association (other than a partnership) is proved to have been committed with the consent or connivance of, or to be attributable to any neglect on the part of, any officer of the association or any member of its governing body, he as well as the association is guilty of the offence and liable to be proceeded against and punished accordingly.

[5.144]

91 Jurisdiction and procedure in respect of offences

(1) Summary proceedings for an offence under section 85 may, without prejudice to any jurisdiction exercisable apart from this section, be taken against a body corporate or unincorporated association at any place at which it has a place of business and against an individual at any place where he is for the time being.

(2) Proceedings for an offence alleged to have been committed under section 85 or 86 by an unincorporated association shall be brought in the name of the association (and not in that of any of its members), and for the purposes of any such proceedings any rules of court relating to the service of documents apply as in relation to a body corporate.

(3) Section 33 of the Criminal Justice Act 1925 and Schedule 3 to the Magistrates' Courts Act 1980 (procedure on charge of offence against a corporation) apply in a case in which an unincorporated association is charged in England and Wales with an offence under section 85 or 86 as they apply in the case of a corporation.

(4) In relation to proceedings on indictment in Scotland for an offence alleged to have been committed under section 85 or 86 by an unincorporated association, section 74 of the Criminal Procedure (Scotland) Act 1975 (proceedings on indictment against bodies corporate) applies as if the association were a body corporate.

(5) Section 18 of the Criminal Justice Act (Northern Ireland) 1945 and Schedule 4 to the Magistrates' Courts (Northern Ireland) Order 1981 (procedure on charge of offence against a corporation) apply in a case in which an unincorporated association is charged in Northern Ireland with an offence under section 85 or 86 as they apply in the case of a corporation.

(6) A fine imposed on an unincorporated association on its conviction of such an offence shall be paid out of the funds of the association.

PART IV REGISTRATION OF COMPANY CHARGES

92–107 *(Repealed by the Companies Act 2006, ss 1180, 1295, Sch 16, as from 1 October 2009 (without ever coming into force).)*

PART V OTHER AMENDMENTS OF COMPANY LAW

A company's capacity and related matters

108–111 *(Ss 108–110 repealed by the Companies Act 2006, s 1295, Sch 16, as from 1 October 2009; s 111 repealed by the Charities Act 1993, s 98(2), Sch 7, as from 1 August 1993.)*

[5.145]

112 Charitable companies (Scotland)

(1) In the following provisions (which extend to Scotland only)—

(a) "company" means [a company registered under the Companies Act 2006]; and

(b) "charity" means a body [entered in the Scottish Charity Register].

(2) Where a charity is a company or other body corporate having power to alter the instruments establishing or regulating it as a body corporate, no exercise of that power which has the effect of the body ceasing to be a charity shall be valid so as to affect the application of—

(a) any property acquired by virtue of any transfer, contract or obligation previously effected otherwise than for full consideration in money or money's worth, or any property representing property so acquired,

(b) any property representing income which has accrued before the alteration is made, or

(c) the income from any such property as aforesaid.

(3) [Sections 39 and 40 of the Companies Act 2006 (company's capacity and power of directors to bind company)]) do not apply to the acts of a company which is a charity except in favour of a person who—

(a) gives full consideration in money or money's worth in relation to the act in question, and

(b) does not know that the act is not permitted by the company's [constitution] or, as the case may be, is beyond the powers of the directors,

or who does not know at the time the act is done that the company is a charity.

(4) However, where such a company purports to transfer or grant an interest in property, the fact that the act was not permitted by the company's [constitution] or, as the case may be, that the directors in connection with the act exceeded any limitation on their powers under the company's constitution, does not affect the title of a person who subsequently acquires the property or any interest in it for full consideration without actual notice of any such circumstances affecting the validity of the company's act.

(5) In any proceedings arising out of subsection (3) the burden of proving—

(a) that a person knew that an act was not permitted by the company's [constitution] or was beyond the powers of the directors, or

(b) that a person knew that the company was a charity,

lies on the person making that allegation.

(6) Where a company is a charity and its name does not include the word "charity" or the word "charitable", the fact that the company is a charity shall be stated in English in legible characters—

(a) in all business letters of the company,

(b) in all its notices and other official publications,

(c) in all bills of exchange, promissory notes, endorsements, cheques and orders for money or goods purporting to be signed by or on behalf of the company,

(d) in all conveyances purporting to be executed by the company, and

(e) in all its bills of parcels, invoices, receipts and letters of credit.

(7) In subsection (6)(d) "conveyance" means any document for the creation, transfer, variation or extinction of an interest in land.

[(8) If a company fails to comply with subsection (6) it commits an offence.

(9) An officer of a company, or a person acting on its behalf, who—

(a) issues or authorises the issue of any business letter of the company, or any notice or other official publication of the company, in which the statement required by subsection (6) does not appear, or

(b) issues or authorises the issue of any bill, invoice, receipt or letter of credit in which the statement required by subsection (6) does not appear,

commits an offence.

(10) An officer of a company, or a person acting on its behalf, who signs or authorises to be signed on behalf of the company any bill of exchange, promissory note, endorsement, cheque or order for money or goods in which the statement required by subsection (6) does not appear—

(a) commits an offence, and

(b) is personally liable to the holder of the bill of exchange, promissory note, endorsement, cheque or order for money or goods for the amount of it (unless it is duly paid by the company).

(11) A person guilty of an offence under subsection (8), (9) or (10) is liable on summary conviction to a fine not exceeding level 3 on the standard scale.]

NOTES

Sub-s (1): words in square brackets in para (a) substituted by the Companies Act 2006 (Consequential Amendments, Transitional Provisions and Savings) Order 2009, SI 2009/1941, art 2(1), Sch 1, para 103(1), (2)(a), as from 1 October 2009. Words in square brackets in para (b) substituted by the Charities and Trustee Investment (Scotland) Act 2005 (Consequential Provisions and Modifications) Order 2006, SI 2006/242, art 5, Schedule, Pt 1, para 4, as from 1 April 2006.

Sub-s (3)–(5): words in square brackets substituted by SI 2009/1941, art 2(1), Sch 1, para 103(1), (2)(b), (c), as from 1 October 2009.

Sub-ss (8)–(11): substituted (for the original sub-s (8)) by the Companies Act 2006 (Consequential Amendments etc) Order 2008, SI 2008/948, art 4(1), Sch 3, para 6, as from 1 October 2008.

113–129 *(Ss 113, 114(1), 115(2), (3), 117 repealed by the Companies Act 2006, s 1295, Sch 16, as from 1 October 2007. Ss 114(2),118–122, 123(1)–(4) repealed by CA 2006, s 1295, Sch 16, as from 6 April 2008. Ss 115(1), 117, 123(5), 125(1), 126–129 repealed by CA 2006, s 1295, Sch 16, as from 1 October 2009. S 116 inserted ss 379A, 380(4)(bb) of the Companies Act 1985 Act, and was repealed by CA 2006, s 1295, Sch 16, as from 1 October 2009 (in so far as inserting s 379A) and as from a day to be appointed (in so far as inserting s 380(4)(bb)) (note, however, that s 388 is itself repealed as from 1 October 2009). S 124 repealed by the Trade Union and Labour Relations (Consolidation) Act 1992, s 300(1), Sch 1. S 125(2) substituted CA 1985, s 707 (repealed) and is therefore spent.)*

Miscellaneous

[5.146]

130 Company contracts and execution of documents by companies

(1)–(5) . . .

(6) The Secretary of State may make provision by regulations applying sections 36 to 36C of the Companies Act 1985 (company contracts; execution of documents; [execution of deeds;] pre-incorporation contracts, deeds and obligations) to companies incorporated outside Great Britain, subject to such exceptions, adaptations or modifications as may be specified in the regulations.

Regulations under this subsection shall be made by statutory instrument which shall be subject to annulment in pursuance of a resolution of either House of Parliament.

(7) . . .

NOTES

Repealed by the Companies Act 2006, s 1295, Sch 16, as from 1 October 2009 (in so far as relating to sub-ss (1)–(5), (7)), and as from a day to be appointed (otherwise).

Sub-s (6): words in square brackets inserted by the Regulatory Reform (Execution of Deeds and Documents) Order 2005, SI 2005/1906, art 10(1), Sch 1, para 16, as from 15 September 2005, except in relation to any instrument executed before that date.

131–134 *(Ss 131, 132 repealed by the Companies Act 2006, s 1295, Sch 16, as from 1 October 2009. S 133 was partly repealed by the Companies (Acquisition of Own Shares) (Treasury Shares) Regulations 2003, SI 2003/1116, reg 4, Schedule, para 34, as from 1 December 2003 (and was completely repealed by CA 2006, s 1295, Sch 16, as from 1 October 2009). S 134 repealed by CA 2006, s 1295, Sch 16, as from 20 January 2007.)*

[5.147]

135 Orders imposing restrictions on shares

(1) The Secretary of State may by regulations made by statutory instrument make such amendments of the provisions of the Companies Act 1985 [and the Companies Act 2006] relating to orders imposing restrictions on shares as appear to him necessary or expedient—

(a) for enabling orders to be made in a form protecting the rights of third parties;

(b) with respect to the circumstances in which restrictions may be relaxed or removed;

(c) with respect to the making of interim orders by a court.

(2) The provisions referred to in subsection (1) are . . . , section 445 and Part XV of the Companies Act 1985 [and section 794 of the Companies Act 2006].

(3) The regulations may make different provision for different cases and may contain such transitional and other supplementary and incidental provisions as appear to the Secretary of State to be appropriate.

(4) Regulations under this section shall not be made unless a draft of the regulations has been laid before Parliament and approved by resolution of each House of Parliament.

NOTES

Repealed by the Companies Act 2006, s 1295, Sch 16, as from a day to be appointed.

Sub-s (1): words in square brackets inserted by the Companies Act 2006 (Consequential Amendments etc) Order 2008, SI 2008/948, art 3(1), Sch 1, Pt 2, para 159(1), (2), as from 6 April 2008.

Sub-s (2): words omitted repealed, and words in square brackets inserted, by SI 2008/948, art 3, Sch 1, Pt 2, para 159(1), (3), Sch 2, as from 6 April 2008.

Regulations: the Companies (Disclosure of Interests in Shares) (Orders imposing restrictions on shares) Regulations 1991, SI 1991/1646 (which amends various provisions in Part VI (repealed), and Parts XIV, XV of CA 1985).

136–143 *(Ss 136, 142 repealed by the Companies Act 2006, s 1295, Sch 16, as from 1 October 2009. S 137 repealed by CA 2006, s 1295, Sch 16, as from 6 April 2008. S 138 repealed by CA 2006, s 1295, Sch 16, as from 1 October 2007. S 139(1)–(3) repealed CA 2006, s 1295, Sch 16, as from 1 October 2009. S 139(4) amends the Company Directors Disqualification Act 1986, Sch 1, Pt I, at* **[5.132]**. *S 139(5) repealed by the Finance Act 2004, s 326, Sch 42, Part 2 (in relation to payments made on or after 6 April 2007 under contracts relating to construction operations). S 140 amends various provisions in the Companies Act 1985, Pt XVIII (Floating Charges and Receivers (Scotland)) at* **[5.54]** *et seq, and is repealed by the Bankruptcy and Diligence etc (Scotland) Act 2007, s 46(4), as from a day to be appointed (for savings, see the introductory note to Pt XVIII). S 141 repealed by CA 2006, s 1295, Sch 16, as from 1 October 2008 (in part), and as from 1 October 2009 (otherwise). S 143 repealed by CA 2006, s 1295, Sch 16, as from 20 January 2007 (in part), as from 6 April 2007 (in part), as from 1 October 2007 (in part), as from 6 April 2008 (in part), and as from 1 October 2009 (otherwise).)*

[5.148]

144 "Subsidiary", "holding company" and "wholly-owned subsidiary"

(1) . . .

(2) Any reference in any enactment (including any enactment contained in subordinate legislation within the meaning of the Interpretation Act 1978) to a "subsidiary" or "holding company" within the meaning of section 736 of the Companies Act 1985 shall, subject to any express amendment or saving made by or under this Act, be read as referring to a subsidiary or holding company as defined in section 736 as substituted by subsection (1) above.

This applies whether the reference is specific or general, or express or implied.

(3) . . .

(4) Schedule 18 contains amendments and savings consequential on the amendments made by this section; and the Secretary of State may by regulations make such further amendments or savings as appear to him to be necessary or expedient.

(5) Regulations under this section shall be made by statutory instrument which shall be subject to annulment in pursuance of a resolution of either House of Parliament.

(6) So much of section 23(3) of the Interpretation Act 1978 as applies section 17(2)(a) of that Act (presumption as to meaning of references to enactments repealed and re-enacted) to deeds or other instruments or documents does not apply in relation to the repeal and re-enactment by this section of section 736 of the Companies Act 1985.

NOTES

Sub-s (1), (3): repealed by the Companies Act 2006, s 1295, Sch 16, as from 1 October 2009.

Sub-ss (2), (6): repealed by the Companies Act 2006, s 1295, Sch 16, as from a day to be appointed.

Regulations: the Companies and Limited Liability Partnerships (Forms, etc) Amendment Regulations 2013, SI 2013/1947.

145–153 *(S 145 introduces Sch 19 (Minor amendments of CA1985); Pt VII (ie, ss 146–153 (Mergers and related matters)) provides as follows: ss 146–150 amended the Fair Trading Act 1973 and were repealed by the Enterprise Act 2002, s 278(2), Sch 26, as from 20 June 2003 (for all purposes except in relation to the merger of water or sewerage undertakings), and from 29 December 2004 (otherwise); s 151 inserted the Fair Trading Act 1973, s 93B, and was repealed by the Civil Aviation Act 2012, s 76, Sch 9, para 17, as from 1 April 2014; s 152 repealed by the Enterprise Act 2002, s 278(2), Sch 26, as from 29 December 2004; s 153 introduces Sch 20 (Amendments about Mergers and Related Matters).)*

PART VII FINANCIAL MARKETS AND INSOLVENCY

NOTES

Transfer of functions: by the Transfer of Functions (Financial Services) Order 1992, SI 1992/1315, art 2(1)(c), the functions of the Secretary of State under this Part of this Act are transferred to the Treasury. However, by art 4 of, and Sch 2, para 7 to, that Order, the functions of the Secretary of State under ss 158(4), (5), 160(5), 170 (other than the function under s 170(1) of approving an overseas investment exchange) 171–174, 181, 185, and so much of his functions under s 186 as relate to any function under the aforementioned provisions, are to be exercisable jointly by the Secretary of State and the Treasury.

Introduction

[5.149]

154 Introduction

This Part has effect for the purposes of safeguarding the operation of certain financial markets by provisions with respect to—

(a) the insolvency, winding up or default of a person party to transactions in the market (sections 155 to 172),
(b) the effectiveness or enforcement of certain charges given to secure obligations in connection with such transactions (sections 173 to 176), and
(c) rights and remedies in relation to certain property provided as cover for margin in relation to such transactions [or as default fund contribution,] or subject to such a charge (sections 177 to 181).

NOTES

Words in square brackets in para (c) inserted by the Financial Markets and Insolvency Regulations 2009, SI 2009/853, reg 2(1), (2), as from 15 June 2009.

[Recognised bodies]

[5.150]

155 Market contracts

[(1) In this Part—

(a) "clearing member client contract" means a contract between a recognised central counterparty and one or more of the parties mentioned in subsection (1A) which is recorded in the accounts of the recognised central counterparty as a position held for the account of a client, an indirect client or a group of clients or indirect clients;

(b) "clearing member house contract" means a contract between a recognised central counterparty and a clearing member recorded in the accounts of the recognised central counterparty as a position held for the account of a clearing member;

(c) "client trade" means a contract between two or more of the parties mentioned in subsection (1A) which corresponds to a clearing member client contract;

(d) "market contracts" means the contracts to which this Part applies by virtue of subsections (2) to [(3ZA)].]

[(1A) The parties referred to in subsections (1)(a) and (c) are—

(a) a clearing member;

(b) a client; and

(c) an indirect client.]

[(2) Except as provided in subsection (2A), in relation to a recognised investment exchange this Part applies to—

(a) contracts entered into by a member or designated non-member of the exchange [with a person other than the exchange] which are either

(i) contracts made on the exchange or an exchange to whose undertaking the exchange has succeeded whether by amalgamation, merger or otherwise; or

(ii) contracts in the making of which the member or designated non-member was subject to the rules of the exchange or of an exchange to whose undertaking the exchange has succeeded whether by amalgamation, merger or otherwise; . . .

[(b) contracts entered into by the exchange, in its capacity as such, with a member of the exchange or with a recognised clearing house [or with a recognised CSD] or with another recognised investment exchange for the purpose of enabling the rights and liabilities of that member [or recognised body] under a transaction to be settled; and

(c) contracts entered into by the exchange with a member of the exchange or with a recognised clearing house [or with a recognised CSD] or with another recognised investment exchange for the purpose of providing central counterparty clearing services to that member [or recognised body].]

A "designated non-member" means a person in respect of whom action may be taken under the default rules of the exchange but who is not a member of the exchange.

[(2A) Where the exchange in question is a recognised overseas investment exchange, this Part does not apply to a contract that falls within paragraph (a) of subsection (2) (unless it also falls within subsection (3)).]

[(2B) In relation to transactions which are cleared through a recognised central counterparty, this Part applies to—

(a) clearing member house contracts;

(b) clearing member client contracts;

(c) client trades, other than client trades excluded by subsection (2C) [or (2D)]; and

(d) contracts entered into by the recognised central counterparty with a recognised investment exchange [or with a recognised CSD] or a recognised clearing house for the purpose of providing central counterparty clearing services to [that recognised body].

(2C) A client trade is excluded by this subsection from subsection (2B)(c) if—

(a) the clearing member which is a party to the clearing member client contract corresponding to the client trade defaults; and

(b) the clearing member client contract is not transferred to another clearing member within the period specified for this purpose in the default rules of the recognised central counterparty.]]

[(2D) A client trade is also excluded by this subsection from subsection (2B)(c) if—

(a) the client trade was entered into by a client in the course of providing indirect clearing services to an indirect client;

(b) the client defaults; and

(c) the clearing member client contract corresponding to the client trade is not transferred within—

(i) the period specified for this purpose in the default rules of the recognised central counterparty; or

(ii) if no such period is specified in the default rules of the recognised central counterparty, a period of 14 days beginning with the day on which proceedings in respect of the client's insolvency are begun.]

[(3) In relation to a recognised clearing house [which is not a recognised central counterparty,] this Part applies to—

(a) contracts entered into by the clearing house, in its capacity as such, with a member of the clearing house or with a recognised investment exchange [or with a recognised CSD] or with another recognised clearing house for the purpose of enabling the rights and liabilities of that member [or recognised body] under a transaction to be settled; and

(b) contracts entered into by the clearing house with a member of the clearing house or with a recognised investment exchange [or with a recognised CSD] or with another recognised clearing house for the purpose of providing central counterparty clearing services to that member [or recognised body].]

[(3ZA) In relation to a recognised CSD, this Part applies to contracts entered into by the central securities depository with a member of the central securities depository or with a recognised investment exchange or with a recognised clearing house or with another recognised CSD for the purpose of providing authorised central securities depository services to that member or recognised body.]

[(3A) In this section "central counterparty clearing services" means—

(a) the services provided by a recognised investment exchange or a recognised clearing house to the parties to a transaction in connection with contracts between each of the parties and the investment exchange or clearing house (in place of, or as an alternative to, a contract directly between the parties),

(b) the services provided by a recognised clearing house to [a recognised body] in connection with contracts between them, or

(c) the services provided by a recognised investment exchange to [a recognised body] in connection with contracts between them.]

[(3B) The reference in subsection (2D)(c)(ii) to the beginning of insolvency proceedings is to—

(a) [the making of a bankruptcy application or] the presentation of a bankruptcy petition or a petition for sequestration of a client's estate, or

(b) the application for an administration order or the presentation of a winding-up petition or the passing of a resolution for voluntary winding up, or

(c) the appointment of an administrative receiver.

(3C) In subsection (3B)(b) the reference to an application for an administration order is to be taken to include a reference to—

(a) in a case where an administrator is appointed under paragraph 14 or 22 of Schedule B1 to the Insolvency Act 1986 (appointment by floating charge holder, company or directors) following filing with the court of a copy of a notice of intention to appoint under that paragraph, the filing of the copy of the notice, and

(b) in a case where an administrator is appointed under either of those paragraphs without a copy of a notice of intention to appoint having been filed with the court, the appointment of the administrator.]

[(3D) In this Part "authorised central securities depository services" means, in relation to a recognised CSD—

(a) the core services listed in Section A of the Annex to the CSD regulation which that central securities depository is authorised to provide pursuant to Article 16 or 19(1)(a) or (c) of the CSD regulation;

(b) the non-banking-type ancillary services listed in or permitted under Section B of that Annex which that central securities depository is authorised to provide, including services notified under Article 19 of the CSD regulation; and

(c) the banking-type ancillary services listed in or permitted under Section C of that Annex which that central securities depository is authorised to provide pursuant to Article 54(2)(a) of the CSD regulation.]

(4) The Secretary of State may by regulations make further provision as to the contracts to be treated as "market contracts", for the purposes of this Part, in relation to [a recognised body].

(5) The regulations may add to, amend or repeal the provisions of subsections [(2), (3), (3ZA) and (3D)] above.

NOTES

The heading preceding this section was substituted by the Central Securities Depositories Regulations 2017, SI 2017/1064, reg 3(1), (2), as from 28 November 2017.

Sub-s (1): substituted by the Financial Services and Markets Act 2000 (Over the Counter Derivatives, Central Counterparties and Trade Repositories) Regulations 2013, SI 2013/504, reg 4(1), (2)(a), as from 1 April 2013. Figure "(3ZA)" in square brackets substituted by SI 2017/1064, reg 3(1), (3)(a), as from 28 November 2017.

Sub-ss (1A), (2B), (2C): inserted by SI 2013/504, reg 4(1), (2)(b), (c), as from 1 April 2013. Words in square brackets in sub-s (2B)(c) inserted by the Financial Services and Markets Act 2000 (Over the Counter Derivatives, Central Counterparties and Trade Repositories) (No 2) Regulations 2013, SI 2013/1908, reg 2(1), (2)(a), as from 26 August 2013. Words in first pair of square brackets in sub-s (2B)(d) inserted, and words in second pair of square brackets substituted, by SI 2017/1064, reg 3(1), (3)(c), as from 28 November 2017.

Sub-s (2) is amended as follows:

Substituted, together with sub-s (2A), for the original sub-s (2) by the Financial Markets and Insolvency Regulations 1991, SI 1991/880, reg 3, as from 25 April 1991.

Words in square brackets in para (a) inserted by the Financial Markets and Insolvency Regulations 1998, SI 1998/1748, reg 3, as from 11 August 1998.

Word omitted from para (a) repealed, and paras (b), (c) substituted (for the original para (b)) by the Financial Markets and Insolvency Regulations 2009, SI 2009/853, reg 2(1), (3)(a), as from 15 June 2009.

Words in first pair of square brackets in paras (b) and (c) inserted, and words in second pair of square brackets substituted, by SI 2017/1064, reg 3(1), (3)(b), as from 28 November 2017.

Sub-s (2A): substituted as noted above. Further substituted by SI 2009/853, reg 2(1), (3)(b), as from 15 June 2009.

Sub-ss (2D), (3B), (3C): inserted by SI 2013/1908, reg 2(1), (2)(b), (c), as from 26 August 2013. Words in square brackets in sub-s (3B) inserted by the Enterprise and Regulatory Reform Act 2013 (Consequential Amendments) (Bankruptcy) and the Small Business, Enterprise and Employment Act 2015 (Consequential Amendments) Regulations 2016, SI 2016/481, reg 2(1), Sch 1, para 9(1), (2), as from 6 April 2016.

Sub-s (3): substituted by SI 2009/853, reg 2(1), (3)(c), as from 15 June 2009. Words in first pair of square brackets substituted by SI 2013/504, reg 4(1), (2)(d), as from 1 April 2013. Words in first pair of square brackets in paras (a) and (b) inserted, and words in second pair of square brackets substituted, by SI 2017/1064, reg 3(1), (3)(d), as from 28 November 2017.

Sub-ss (3ZA), (3D): inserted by SI 2017/1064, reg 3(1), (3)(e), (g), as from 28 November 2017.

Sub-s (3A): inserted by SI 2009/853, reg 2(1), (3)(d), as from 15 June 2009. Words in square brackets substituted by SI 2017/1064, reg 3(1), (3)(f), as from 28 November 2017.

Sub-ss (4), (5): words in square brackets substituted by SI 2017/1064, reg 3(1), (3)(h), (i), as from 28 November 2017.

Regulations: the Financial Markets and Insolvency Regulations 1991, SI 1991/880 at **[6.8]**; the Financial Markets and Insolvency Regulations 1998, SI 1998/1748; the Financial Markets and Insolvency Regulations 2009, SI 2009/853; the Financial Services and Markets Act 2000 (Over the Counter Derivatives, Central Counterparties and Trade Repositories) Regulations 2013, SI 2013/504; the Financial Services and Markets Act 2000 (Over the Counter Derivatives, Central Counterparties and Trade Repositories) (No 2) Regulations 2013, SI 2013/1908.

[5.151]

[155A Qualifying collateral arrangements and qualifying property transfers

(1) In this Part—

(a) "qualifying collateral arrangements" means the contracts and contractual obligations to which this Part applies by virtue of subsection (2); and

(b) "qualifying property transfers" means the property transfers to which this Part applies by virtue of subsection (4).

(2) In relation to transactions which are cleared through a recognised central counterparty, this Part applies to any contracts or contractual obligations for, or arising out of, the provision of property as margin where—

(a) the margin is provided to a recognised central counterparty and is recorded in the accounts of the recognised central counterparty as an asset held for the account of a client, an indirect client, or a group of clients or indirect clients; or

(b) the margin is provided to a client or clearing member for the purpose of providing cover for exposures arising out of present or future client trades.

(3) In subsection (2)—

(a) "property" has the meaning given by section 436(1) of the Insolvency Act 1986 and

(b) the reference to a contract or contractual obligation for, or arising out of, the provision of property as margin in circumstances falling within paragraph (a) or (b) of that subsection includes a reference to a contract or contractual obligation of that kind which has been amended to reflect the transfer of a clearing member client contract or client trade.

(4) In relation to transactions which are cleared through a recognised central counterparty, this Part applies to—

(a) transfers of property made in accordance with Article 48(7) of the EMIR Level 1 Regulation;

[(aa) transfers of property made in accordance with Article 4(6) and (7) of the EMIR Level 2 Regulation or Article 4(6) and (7) of the MIFIR Level 2 Regulation;]

(b) transfers of property to the extent that they—

(i) are made by a recognised central counterparty to a non-defaulting clearing member instead of, or in place of, a defaulting clearing member;

(ii) represent the termination or close out value of a clearing member client contract which is transferred from a defaulting clearing member to a non-defaulting clearing member; and

(iii) are determined in accordance with the default rules of the recognised central counterparty.

[(c) transfers of property to the extent that they—

(i) are made by a clearing member to a non-defaulting client or another clearing member instead of, or in place of, a defaulting client;

(ii) represent the termination or close out value of a client trade which is transferred from a defaulting client to another clearing member or a non-defaulting client; and

(iii) do not exceed the termination or close out value of the clearing member client contract corresponding to that client trade, as determined in accordance with the default rules of the recognised central counterparty.]]

NOTES

Inserted by the Financial Services and Markets Act 2000 (Over the Counter Derivatives, Central Counterparties and Trade Repositories) Regulations 2013, SI 2013/504, reg 4(1), (3), as from 1 April 2013.

Sub-s (4): paras (aa), (c) inserted by the Financial Services and Markets Act 2000 (Over the Counter Derivatives, Central Counterparties and Trade Repositories) (No 2) Regulations 2013, SI 2013/1908, reg 2(1), (3), as from 26 August 2013. Para (aa) subsequently substituted by the Companies Act 1989 (Financial Markets and Insolvency) (Amendment) Regulations 2017, SI 2017/1247, reg 2(1), (2), as from 3 January 2018.

156 (*Repealed by the Financial Services and Markets Act 2000 (Consequential Amendments and Repeals) Order 2001, SI 2001/3649, art 75(e), as from 1 December 2001.*)

[5.152]

157 Change in default rules

(1) [A recognised body] shall give the [appropriate regulator] at least [three months] notice of any proposal to amend, revoke or add to its default rules; and the [regulator] may within [three months] from receipt of the notice direct [the recognised body] not to proceed with the proposal, in whole or in part.

[(1A) The appropriate regulator may, if it considers it appropriate to do so, agree a shorter period of notice and, in a case where it does so, any direction under this section must be given by it within that shorter period.]

(2) A direction under this section may be varied or revoked.

(3) Any amendment or revocation of, or addition to, the default rules of [a recognised body] in breach of a direction under this section is ineffective.

[(4) "The appropriate regulator"—

(a) in relation to a recognised UK investment exchange, means the FCA, and

(b) in relation to a [recognised clearing house] [or a recognised CSD], means the Bank of England.]

NOTES

Sub-s (1) is amended as follows:

Words "A recognised body" and "the recognised body" in square brackets substituted by the Central Securities Depositories Regulations 2017, SI 2017/1064, reg 3(1), (4)(a), as from 28 November 2017.

Words "appropriate regulator" and "regulator" in square brackets substituted by the Financial Services Act 2012, s 114(1), Sch 18, Pt 2, paras 62, 65(1), (2), as from 1 April 2013.

Words "three months" in square brackets (in both places they occur) substituted by the Financial Services and Markets Act 2000 (Over the Counter Derivatives, Central Counterparties and Trade Repositories) Regulations 2013, SI 2013/504, reg 4(1), (4)(a)(ii), as from 1 April 2013.

Sub-s (1A): inserted by SI 2013/504, reg 4(1), (4)(b), as from 1 April 2013.

Sub-s (3): words in square brackets substituted by SI 2017/1064, reg 3(1), (4)(b), as from 28 November 2017.

Sub-s (4): added by the Financial Services Act 2012, s 114(1), Sch 18, Pt 2, paras 62, 65(1), (3), as from 1 April 2013. Words "recognised clearing house" in square brackets in para (b) substituted by SI 2013/504, reg 4(1), (4)(c), as from 1 April 2013. Words "or a recognised CSD" in square brackets in para (b) substituted by SI 2017/1064, reg 3(1), (4)(c), as from 28 November 2017.

[5.153]

158 Modifications of the law of insolvency

[(1) The general law of insolvency has effect in relation to—

(a) market contracts,

(b) action taken under the rules of [a recognised body other than a recognised central counterparty], with respect to market contracts,

(c) action taken under the rules of a recognised central counterparty to transfer clearing member client contracts, or settle clearing member client contracts or clearing member house contracts, in accordance with the default rules of the recognised central counterparty,

(d) where clearing member [or client] client contracts transferred in accordance with the default rules of a recognised central counterparty were entered into by the clearing member as a principal, action taken to transfer . . . client trades, or groups of client trades, corresponding to those clearing member client contracts,

(e) action taken to transfer qualifying collateral arrangements in conjunction with a transfer of clearing member client contracts as mentioned in paragraph (c) or a transfer of client trades as mentioned in paragraph (d), and

(f) qualifying property transfers,

subject to the provisions of sections 159 to 165.]

(2) So far as those provisions relate to insolvency proceedings in respect of a person other than a defaulter, they apply in relation to—

[(a) proceedings in respect of a recognised investment exchange or a member or designated non-member of a recognised investment exchange,

(aa) proceedings in respect of a recognised clearing house or a member of a recognised clearing house, . . .]

[(ab) proceedings in respect of a recognised CSD or a member of a recognised CSD, and]

(b) proceedings in respect of a party to a market contract [other than a client trade which are] begun after [a recognised body] has taken action under its default rules in relation to a person party to the contract as principal,

but not in relation to any other insolvency proceedings, notwithstanding that rights or liabilities arising from market contracts fall to be dealt with in the proceedings.

(3) The reference in subsection (2)(b) to the beginning of insolvency proceedings is to—

(a) [the making of a bankruptcy application or] the presentation of a bankruptcy petition or a petition for sequestration of a person's estate, or

[(b) the application for an administration order or the presentation of a winding-up petition or the passing of a resolution for voluntary winding up,] or

(c) the appointment of an administrative receiver.

[(3A) In subsection (3)(b) the reference to an application for an administration order shall be taken to include a reference to—

(a) in a case where an administrator is appointed under paragraph 14 or 22 of Schedule B1 to the Insolvency Act 1986 (appointment by floating charge holder, company or directors) following filing with the court of a copy of a notice of intention to appoint under that paragraph, the filing of the copy of the notice, and

(b) in a case where an administrator is appointed under either of those paragraphs without a copy of a notice of intention to appoint having been filed with the court, the appointment of the administrator.]

(4) The Secretary of State may make further provision by regulations modifying the law of insolvency in relation to the matters mentioned in [paragraphs (a) to (d) of] subsection (1).

(5) The regulations may add to, amend or repeal the provisions mentioned in subsection (1), and any other provision of this Part as it applies for the purposes of those provisions, or provide that those provisions have effect subject to such additions, exceptions or adaptations as are specified in the regulations.

NOTES

Sub-s (1): substituted by the Financial Services and Markets Act 2000 (Over the Counter Derivatives, Central Counterparties and Trade Repositories) Regulations 2013, SI 2013/504, reg 4(1), (5)(a), as from 1 April 2013. Words in square brackets in para (b) substituted by the Central Securities Depositories Regulations 2017, SI 2017/1064, reg 3(1), (5)(a), as from 28 November 2017. Words in square brackets in para (d) inserted, and the word omitted from that paragraph repealed, by the Financial Services and Markets Act 2000 (Over the Counter Derivatives, Central Counterparties and Trade Repositories) (No 2) Regulations 2013, SI 2013/1908, reg 2(1), (4), as from 26 August 2013.

Sub-s (2): paras (a), (aa) substituted, for the original para (a), by the Financial Markets and Insolvency Regulations 2009, SI 2009/853, reg 2(1), (4), as from 15 June 2009 (for transitional provisions see the note below). Word omitted from para (aa) repealed, para (ab) inserted, and words in second pair of square brackets in para (b) substituted, by SI 2017/1064, reg 3(1), (5)(a), as from 28 November 2017. Words in first pair of square brackets in para (b) inserted by SI 2013/504, reg 4(1), (5)(b), as from 1 April 2013.

Sub-s (3): words in square brackets in para (a) inserted by the Enterprise and Regulatory Reform Act 2013 (Consequential Amendments) (Bankruptcy) and the Small Business, Enterprise and Employment Act 2015 (Consequential Amendments) Regulations 2016, SI 2016/481, reg 2(1), Sch 1, para 9(1), (3), as from 6 April 2016. Para (b) substituted by the Enterprise Act 2002, s 248(3), Sch 17, paras 43, 44(a), as from 15 September 2003 (for savings and transitional provisions, see the note to the Insolvency Act 1986, s 8 at **[9.147]**).

Sub-s (3A): inserted by the Enterprise Act 2002, s 248(3), Sch 17, paras 43, 44(b), as from 15 September 2003 (for savings and transitional provisions, see the note to the Insolvency Act 1986, s 8 at **[9.147]**).

Sub-s (4): words in square brackets inserted by SI 2013/504, reg 4(1), (5)(c), as from 1 April 2013.

Transitional provisions: the Financial Markets and Insolvency Regulations 2009, SI 2009/853, reg 1(2), (3) (as amended by the Enterprise and Regulatory Reform Act 2013 (Consequential Amendments) (Bankruptcy) and the Small Business, Enterprise and Employment Act 2015 (Consequential Amendments) Regulations 2016, SI 2016/481, reg 2(2), Sch 2, para 11, as from

6 April 2016) provides as follows—

"(2) Regulation 2 paragraphs (4), (5), (6), (7), (8), (9), (10) and (12) apply to insolvency proceedings which relate to any of the insolvency events set out in paragraph (3) which take place on or after the date on which these Regulations come into force.

(3) The insolvency events are—

(a) an application for an administration order;

(b) an application for a bank administration order under Part 3 of the Banking Act 2009;

(c) the filing of a notice of intention to appoint an administrator for an appointment under paragraph 14 or 22 of Schedule B1 to the Insolvency Act 1986;

(d) where no notice of intention to appoint is filed, the appointment of an administrator under paragraph 14 or 22 of Schedule B1 to the Insolvency Act 1986;

[(da) the making of a bankruptcy application;]

(e) the presentation of a bankruptcy petition;

(f) the presentation of a petition for sequestration of a person's estate;

(g) the presentation of a winding up petition;

(h) an application for a bank insolvency order under Part 2 of the Banking Act 2009;

(i) the passing of a resolution for voluntary winding up;

(j) the appointment of an administrative receiver;

(k) the making of an order appointing an interim receiver.".

Regulations: the Financial Markets and Insolvency Regulations 1991, SI 1991/880 at **[6.8]**; the Financial Markets and Insolvency Regulations 2009, SI 2009/853; the Financial Services and Markets Act 2000 (Over the Counter Derivatives, Central Counterparties and Trade Repositories) Regulations 2013, SI 2013/504; the Financial Services and Markets Act 2000 (Over the Counter Derivatives, Central Counterparties and Trade Repositories) (No 2) Regulations 2013, SI 2013/1908.

[5.154]

159 [Proceedings of recognised bodies take precedence over insolvency procedures]

(1) None of the following shall be regarded as to any extent invalid at law on the ground of inconsistency with the law relating to the distribution of the assets of a person on bankruptcy, winding up or sequestration, or [in the administration of a company or other body or] in the administration of an insolvent estate—

(a) a market contract,

(b) the default rules of a [a recognised body],

(c) the rules of [a recognised body other than a recognised central counterparty] as to the settlement of market contracts not dealt with [under its default rules,]

[(d) the rules of a recognised central counterparty on which the recognised central counterparty relies to give effect to the transfer of a clearing member client contract, or the settlement of a clearing member client contract or clearing member house contract, in accordance with its default rules,

(e) a transfer of a clearing member client contract, or the settlement of a clearing member client contract or a clearing member house contract, in accordance with the default rules of a recognised central counterparty,

(f) where a clearing member client contract transferred in accordance with the default rules of a recognised central counterparty was entered into by the clearing member [or client] as principal, a transfer of [a client trade] or group of client trades corresponding to that clearing member client contract,

(g) a transfer of a qualifying collateral arrangement in conjunction with the transfer of clearing member client contract as mentioned in paragraph (e) or of a client trade as mentioned in paragraph (f), or

(h) a qualifying property transfer.]

(2) The powers of a relevant office-holder in his capacity as such, and the powers of the court under the Insolvency Act 1986[, the Bankruptcy (Scotland) Act [2016], Part 10 of the Building Societies Act 1986, Parts 2 and 3 of the Banking Act 2009 or under regulations made under section 233 of that Act,] shall not be exercised in such a way as to prevent or interfere with—

(a) the settlement in accordance with the rules of [a recognised body other than a recognised central counterparty] of a market contract not dealt with under its default rules, . . .

(b) any action taken under the default rules of [a recognised body other than a recognised central counterparty]

[(c) the transfer of a clearing member client contract, or the settlement of a clearing member client contract or a clearing member house contract, in accordance with the default rules of a recognised central counterparty,

(d) where a clearing member client contract transferred in accordance with the default rules of a recognised central counterparty was entered into by the clearing member [or client] as principal, the transfer of [a client trade] or group of client trades corresponding to that clearing member contract,

(e) the transfer of a qualifying collateral arrangement in conjunction with a transfer of a clearing member client contract as mentioned in paragraph (c), or a transfer of a client trade as mentioned in paragraph (d),

(f) any action taken to give effect to any of the matters mentioned in paragraphs (c) to (e), or

(g) any action taken to give effect to a qualifying property transfer.]

This does not prevent a relevant office-holder from afterwards seeking to recover any amount under section 163(4) or 164(4) or prevent the court from afterwards making any such order or decree as is mentioned in section 165(1) or (2) (but subject to subsections (3) and (4) of that section).

(3) Nothing in the following provisions of this Part shall be construed as affecting the generality of the above provisions.

(4) A debt or other liability arising out of a market contract which is the subject of default proceedings may not be proved in a winding up or bankruptcy [or in the administration of a company or other body], or in Scotland claimed in a winding up or sequestration [or in the administration of a company or other body], until the completion of the default proceedings.

A debt or other liability which by virtue of this subsection may not be proved or claimed shall not be taken into account for the purposes of any set-off until the completion of the default proceedings.

[(4A) However, prior to the completion of default proceedings—

(a) where it appears [to the convener] that a sum will be certified under section 162(1) to be payable, subsection (4) shall not prevent any proof or claim including or consisting of an estimate of that sum which has been lodged or, in Scotland, submitted, from being admitted or, in Scotland, accepted, for the purpose only of determining the entitlement of a creditor to vote [in a decision procedure]; and

(b) a creditor whose claim or proof has been lodged and admitted or, in Scotland, submitted and accepted, for the purpose of determining the entitlement of a creditor to vote [in a decision procedure] and which has not been subsequently wholly withdrawn, disallowed or rejected, is eligible as a creditor to be a member of a liquidation committee or, in bankruptcy proceedings in England and Wales, [or in the administration of a company or other body] a creditors' committee.]

(5) For the purposes of [subsections (4) and (4A)] the default proceedings shall be taken to be completed in relation to a person when a report is made under section 162 stating the sum (if any) certified to be due to or from him.

NOTES

Section heading substituted by the Central Securities Depositories Regulations 2017, SI 2017/1064, reg 3(1), (6)(a), as from 28 November 2017.

Sub-s (1) is amended as follows:

Words in first pair of square brackets inserted by the Financial Markets and Insolvency Regulations 2009, SI 2009/853, reg 2(1), (5)(a), as from 15 June 2009 (subject to transitional provisions as noted to s 158 at **[5.153]**).

Words in square brackets in para (b) substituted SI 2017/1064, reg 3(1), (6)(b), as from 28 November 2017.

Words "a recognised body other than a recognised central counterparty" in para (c) substituted SI 2017/1064, reg 3(1), (6)(c), as from 28 November 2017.

Words "under its default rules," in para (c) substituted by the Financial Services and Markets Act 2000 (Over the Counter Derivatives, Central Counterparties and Trade Repositories) Regulations 2013, SI 2013/504, reg 4(1), (6)(a)(ii), as from 1 April 2013.

Paras (d)–(h) inserted by SI 2013/504, reg 4(1), (6)(b), as from 1 April 2013.

Words in first pair of square brackets in para (f) inserted, and words in second pair of square brackets substituted, by the Financial Services and Markets Act 2000 (Over the Counter Derivatives, Central Counterparties and Trade Repositories) (No 2) Regulations 2013, SI 2013/1908, reg 2(1), (5)(a), as from 26 August 2013.

Sub-s (2): the year "2016" in square brackets was substituted by the Bankruptcy (Scotland) Act 2016 (Consequential Provisions and Modifications) Order 2016, SI 2016/1034, art 7(1), (3), Sch 1, para 6(1), (2), as from 30 November 2016 (except in relation to (i) a sequestration as regards which the petition is presented, or the debtor application is made before that date; or (ii) a trust deed executed before that date). Words in square brackets in paras (a) and (b) substituted by SI 2017/1064, reg 3(1), (6)(d), (e), as from 28 November 2017. Words in first pair of square brackets in para (d) inserted, and words in second pair of square brackets substituted, by SI 2013/1908, reg 2(1), (5)(b), as from 26 August 2013. Paras (c)–(g) inserted, other words in square brackets substituted, and words omitted repealed, by SI 2013/504, reg 4(1), (6)(c)–(f), as from 1 April 2013.

Sub-s (4): words in square brackets inserted by the Financial Markets and Insolvency Regulations 2009, SI 2009/853, reg 2(1), (5)(b), as from 15 June 2009 (subject to transitional provisions as noted to s 158 at **[5.153]**).

Sub-s (4A): inserted by the Financial Markets and Insolvency Regulations 1991, SI 1991/880, reg 4(1), (2), as from 25 April 1991. Words in square brackets in para (a) substituted, and words in first pair of square brackets in para (b) substituted, by the Deregulation Act 2015 and Small Business, Enterprise and Employment Act 2015 (Consequential Amendments) (Savings) Regulations 2017, SI 2017/540, reg 2, Sch 1, para 2(1), (2), as from 6 April 2017. Words in second pair of square brackets in para (b) inserted by SI 2009/853, reg 2(1), (5)(c), as from 15 June 2009 (subject to transitional provisions as noted to s 158 at **[5.153]**).

Sub-s (5): words in square brackets substituted by SI 1991/880, reg 4(1), (3), as from 25 April 1991.

[5.155]

160 Duty to give assistance for purposes of default proceedings

(1) It is the duty of—

(a) any person who has or had control of any assets of a defaulter, and

(b) any person who has or had control of any documents of or relating to a defaulter,

to give [a recognised body] such assistance as it may reasonably require for the purposes of its default proceedings.

This applies notwithstanding any duty of that person under the enactments relating to insolvency.

(2) A person shall not under this section be required to provide any information or produce any document which he would be entitled to refuse to provide or produce on grounds of legal professional privilege in proceedings in the High Court or on grounds of confidentiality as between client and professional legal adviser in proceedings in the Court of Session.

(3) Where original documents are supplied in pursuance of this section, [the recognised body] shall return them forthwith after the completion of the relevant default proceedings, and shall in the meantime allow reasonable access to them to the person by whom they were supplied and to any person who would be entitled to have access to them if they were still in the control of the person by whom they were supplied.

(4) The expenses of a relevant office-holder in giving assistance under this section are recoverable as part of the expenses incurred by him in the discharge of his duties; and he shall not be required under this section to take any action which involves expenses which cannot be so recovered, unless [the recognised body] undertakes to meet them.

There shall be treated as expenses of his such reasonable sums as he may determine in respect of time spent in giving the assistance [and for the purpose of determining the priority in which his expenses are payable out of the assets, sums in respect of time spent shall be treated as his remuneration and other sums shall be treated as his disbursements or, in Scotland, outlays].

(5) The Secretary of State may by regulations make further provision as to the duties of persons to give assistance to [a recognised body] for the purposes of its default proceedings, and the duties of [the recognised body] with respect to information supplied to it.

The regulations may add to, amend or repeal the provisions of subsections (1) to (4) above.

(6) In this section "document" includes information recorded in any form.

NOTES

Words "and for the purpose of determining the priority in which his expenses are payable out of the assets, sums in respect of time spent shall be treated as his remuneration and other sums shall be treated as his disbursements or, in Scotland, outlays" in square brackets in sub-s (4) added by the Financial Markets and Insolvency Regulations 1991, SI 1991/880, reg 5, as from 25 April 1991.

All other words in square brackets in this section were substituted by the Central Securities Depositories Regulations 2017, SI 2017/1064, reg 3(1), (7), as from 28 November 2017.

Regulations: the Financial Markets and Insolvency Regulations 1991, SI 1991/880 at **[6.8]**.

[5.156]

161 Supplementary provisions as to default proceedings

(1) If the court is satisfied on an application by a relevant office-holder that a party to a market contract with a defaulter intends to dissipate or apply his assets so as to prevent the officer-holder recovering such sums as may become due upon the completion of the default proceedings, the court may grant such interlocutory relief (in Scotland, such interim order) as it thinks fit.

(2) A liquidator[, administrator] or trustee of a defaulter or, in Scotland, a [trustee in the sequestration of the] estate of the defaulter shall not—

(a) declare or pay any dividend to the creditors, or

(b) return any capital to contributories,

unless he has retained what he reasonably considers to be an adequate reserve in respect of any claims arising as a result of the default proceedings of [the recognised body] concerned.

(3) The court may on an application by a relevant office-holder make such order as it thinks fit altering or dispensing from compliance with such of the duties of his office as are affected by the fact that default proceedings are pending or could be taken, or have been or could have been taken.

(4) Nothing in [section 126, 128, 130, 185 or 285 of, or paragraph [40, 41,] 42 or 43 ([including those paragraphs as applied by paragraph 44]) of Schedule B1 to, the Insolvency Act 1986] (which restrict the taking of certain legal proceedings and other steps), and nothing in any rule of law in Scotland to the like effect as the said section 285, in the Bankruptcy (Scotland) Act [2016] or in the Debtors (Scotland) Act 1987 as to the effect of sequestration, shall affect any action taken by [a recognised body] for the purpose of its default proceedings.

NOTES

Sub-s (2): word in first pair of square brackets inserted by the Financial Markets and Insolvency Regulations 2009, SI 2009/853, reg 2(1), (6)(a), as from 15 June 2009, subject to transitional provisions as noted to s 158 at **[5.153]**. Words in second pair of square brackets substituted by the Bankruptcy (Scotland) Act 2016 (Consequential Provisions and Modifications) Order 2016, SI 2016/1034, art 7(1), (3), Sch 1, para 6(1), (3)(a), as from 30 November 2016 (except in relation to (i) a sequestration as regards which the petition is presented, or the debtor application is made before that date; or (ii) a trust deed executed before that date). Words in final pair of square brackets substituted by the Central Securities Depositories Regulations 2017, SI 2017/1064, reg 3(1), (8)(a), as from 28 November 2017.

Sub-s (4) is amended as follows:

Words in first (outer) pair of square brackets substituted by the Enterprise Act 2002, s 248(3), Sch 17, paras 43, 45, as from 15 September 2003 (for savings and transitional provisions, see the note to the Insolvency Act 1986, s 8 at **[9.147]**).

Figures "40, 41," in square brackets inserted, and words "including those paragraphs as applied by paragraph 44" in square brackets substituted, by SI 2009/853, reg 2(1), (6)(b), as from 15 June 2009, subject to transitional provisions as noted to s 158 at **[5.153]**.

The year "2016" in square brackets was substituted by SI 2016/1034, art 7(1), (3), Sch 1, para 6(1), (3)(b), as from 30 November 2016 (except in relation to (i) a sequestration as regards which the petition is presented, or the debtor application is made before that date; or (ii) a trust deed executed before that date).

Words in final pair of square brackets substituted by SI 2017/1064, reg 3(1), (8)(b), as from 28 November 2017.

[5.157]

162 Duty to report on completion of default proceedings

(1) [Subject to subsection (1A),] [a recognised body] house shall, on the completion of proceedings under its default rules, report to the [appropriate regulator] on its proceedings stating in respect of each creditor or debtor the sum [or sums] certified by them to be payable from or to the defaulter or, as the case may be, the fact that no sum is payable.

[(1A) A recognised overseas investment exchange or recognised overseas clearing house shall not be subject to the obligation under subsection (1) unless it has been notified by the [appropriate regulator] that a report is required for the purpose of insolvency proceedings in any part of the United Kingdom.]

[(1B) The report under subsection (1) need not deal with a clearing member client contract which has been transferred in accordance with the default rules of a recognised central counterparty.]

(2) [The recognised body] may make a single report or may make reports from time to time as proceedings are completed with respect to the transactions affecting particular persons.

(3) [The recognised body] shall supply a copy of every report under this section to the defaulter and to any relevant office-holder acting in relation to him or his estate.

(4) When a report under this section is received by the [[appropriate regulator], it] shall publish notice of that fact in such manner as [it] thinks appropriate for bringing [the report] to the attention of creditors and debtors of the defaulter.

(5) [A recognised body] shall make available for inspection by a creditor or debtor of the defaulter so much of any report by it under this section as relates to the sum (if any) certified to be due to or from him or to the method by which that sum was determined.

(6) Any such person may require [the recognised body], on payment of such reasonable fee as [the recognised body] may determine, to provide him with a copy of any part of a report which he is entitled to inspect.

[(7) "The appropriate regulator"—

(a) in relation to a recognised investment exchange or a recognised overseas investment exchange, means the FCA, and

(b) in relation to a [recognised CSD, a] recognised clearing house or a recognised overseas clearing house, means the Bank of England.]

NOTES

Sub-s (1): words in first pair of square brackets inserted by the Financial Markets and Insolvency Regulations 1991, SI 1991/880, reg 6(1), (2), as from 25 April 1991. Words in second pair of square brackets substituted by the Central Securities Depositories Regulations 2017, SI 2017/1064, reg 3(1), (9)(a), as from 28 November 2017. Words in third pair of square brackets substituted by the Financial Services Act 2012, s 114(1), Sch 18, Pt 2, paras 62, 66(1), (2), as from 1 April 2013. Words in final pair of square brackets inserted by the Financial Services and Markets Act 2000 (Over the Counter Derivatives, Central Counterparties and Trade Repositories) Regulations 2013, SI 2013/504, reg 4(1), (7)(a), as from 1 April 2013.

Sub-s (1A): inserted by SI 1991/880, reg 6(1), (3), as from 25 April 1991. Words in square brackets substituted by the Financial Services Act 2012, s 114(1), Sch 18, Pt 2, paras 62, 66(1), (2), as from 1 April 2013.

Sub-s (1B): inserted by SI 2013/504, reg 4(1), (7)(b), as from 1 April 2013.

Sub-ss (2), (3), (5), (6): words in square brackets substituted by SI 2017/1064, reg 3(1), (9)(b)–(d), as from 28 November 2017.

Sub-s (4): words in first (outer), third and fourth pairs of square brackets substituted by the Financial Services and Markets Act 2000 (Consequential Amendments and Repeals) Order 2001, SI 2001/3649, art 80(1), (4), as from 1 December 2001. Words in second (inner) pair of square brackets substituted by the Financial Services Act 2012, s 114(1), Sch 18, Pt 2, paras 62, 66(1), (3), as from 1 April 2013.

Sub-s (7): added by the Financial Services Act 2012, s 114(1), Sch 18, Pt 2, paras 62, 66(1), (4), as from 1 April 2013. Words in square brackets substituted by SI 2017/1064, reg 3(1), (9)(e), as from 28 November 2017.

[5.158]

163 Net sum payable on completion of default proceedings

[(1) The following provisions apply with respect to a net sum certified by [a recognised body] under its default rules to be payable by or to a defaulter.]

(2) If, in England and Wales, a bankruptcy[, winding-up or administration order has been made], or a resolution for voluntary winding up has been passed, the debt—

(a) is provable in the bankruptcy[, winding up or administration] or, as the case may be, is payable to the relevant officer-holder, and

(b) shall be taken into account, where appropriate, under section 323 of the Insolvency Act 1986 (mutual dealings and set-off) or the corresponding provision applicable in the case of winding up [or administration],

in the same way as a debt due before the commencement of the bankruptcy, the date on which the body corporate goes into liquidation (within the meaning of section 247 of the Insolvency Act 1986)[, or enters administration] or, in the case of a partnership, the date of the winding-up order [or the date on which the partnership enters administration].

(3) If, in Scotland, an award of sequestration or a winding-up [or administration] order has been made, or a resolution for voluntary winding up has been passed, the debt—

(a) may be claimed in the sequestration[, winding up or administration] or, as the case may be, is payable to the relevant office-holder, and

(b) shall be taken into account for the purposes of any rule of law relating to set-off applicable in sequestration[, winding up or administration],

in the same way as a debt due before the date of sequestration (within the meaning of section [22(7) of the Bankruptcy (Scotland) Act 2016]) or the commencement of the winding up (within the meaning of section 129 of the Insolvency Act 1986) [or the date on which the body corporate enters administration].

[(3A) In subsections (2) and (3), a reference to the making of an administration order shall be taken to include a reference to the appointment of an administrator under—

(a) paragraph 14 of Schedule B1 to the Insolvency Act 1986 (appointment by holder of qualifying floating charge); or

(b) paragraph 22 of that Schedule (appointment by company or directors).]

(4) However, where (or to the extent that) a sum is taken into account by virtue of subsection (2)(b) or (3)(b) which arises from a contract entered into at a time when the creditor had notice—

(a) that [a bankruptcy application or] a bankruptcy petition or, in Scotland, a petition for sequestration was pending, . . .

(b) that [a statement as to the affairs of the company had been made out and sent under section 99] of the Insolvency Act 1986 or that a winding-up petition was pending, [or]

[(c) that an application for an administration order was pending or that any person had given notice of intention to appoint an administrator,]

the value of any profit to him arising from the sum being so taken into account (or being so taken into account to that extent) is recoverable from him by the relevant office-holder unless the court directs otherwise.

(5) Subsection (4) does not apply in relation to a sum arising from a contract effected under the default rules of [a recognised body].

(6) Any sum recoverable by virtue of subsection (4) ranks for priority, in the event of the insolvency of the person from whom it is due, immediately before preferential or, in Scotland, preferred debts.

NOTES

Sub-s (1): substituted by the Financial Services and Markets Act 2000 (Over the Counter Derivatives, Central Counterparties and Trade Repositories) Regulations 2013, SI 2013/504, reg 4(1), (8), as from 1 April 2013. Words in square brackets substituted by the Central Securities Depositories Regulations 2017, SI 2017/1064, reg 3(1), (10), as from 28 November 2017.

Sub-s (2): words in first and second pairs of square brackets substituted, and words in other pairs of square brackets inserted, by the Financial Markets and Insolvency Regulations 2009, SI 2009/853, reg 2(1), (7)(a), as from 15 June 2009, subject to transitional provisions as noted to s 158 at **[5.153]**.

Sub-s (3): words "22(7) of the Bankruptcy (Scotland) Act 2016" in square brackets substituted by the Bankruptcy (Scotland) Act 2016 (Consequential Provisions and Modifications) Order 2016, SI 2016/1034, art 7(1), (3), Sch 1, para 6(1), (4), as from 30 November 2016 (except in relation to (i) a sequestration as regards which the petition is presented, or the debtor application is made before that date; or (ii) a trust deed executed before that date). The words ", winding up or administration" (in both places that they occur) were substituted, and the other words in square brackets were inserted, by SI 2009/853, reg 2(1), (7)(b), as from 15 June 2009, subject to transitional provisions as noted to s 158 at **[5.153]**.

Sub-s (3A): inserted by SI 2009/853, reg 2(1), (7)(c), as from 15 June 2009, subject to transitional provisions as noted to s 158 at **[5.153]**.

Sub-s (4): words in square brackets in para (a) inserted by the Enterprise and Regulatory Reform Act 2013 (Consequential Amendments) (Bankruptcy) and the Small Business, Enterprise and Employment Act 2015 (Consequential Amendments) Regulations 2016, SI 2016/481, reg 2(1), Sch 1, para 9(1), (4), as from 6 April 2016. The word omitted from the end of para (a) was repealed, and the word "or" at the end of para (b) was inserted together with para (c), by SI 2009/853, reg 2(1), (7)(d), as from 15 June 2009, subject to transitional provisions as noted to s 158 at **[5.153]**. The first words in square brackets in para (b) were substituted by the Deregulation Act 2015 and Small Business, Enterprise and Employment Act 2015 (Consequential Amendments) (Savings) Regulations 2017, SI 2017/540, reg 2, Sch 1, para 2(1), (3), as from 6 April 2017.

Sub-s (5): words in square brackets substituted by SI 2017/1064, reg 3(1), (10), as from 28 November 2017.

[5.159]

164 Disclaimer of property, rescission of contracts, &c

(1) Sections 178, 186, 315 and 345 of the Insolvency Act 1986 (power to disclaim onerous property and court's power to order rescission of contracts, &c) do not apply in relation to—

(a) a market contract, . . .

[(aa) a qualifying collateral arrangement,

(ab) a transfer of a clearing member client contract, a client trade or a qualifying collateral arrangement, as mentioned in paragraphs (c) to (e) of section 158(1),

(ac) a qualifying property transfer, or]

(b) a contract effected by [the recognised body] for the purpose of realising property provided as margin in relation to market contracts [or as default fund contribution].

In the application of this subsection in Scotland, the reference to sections 178, 315 and 345 shall be construed as a reference to any rule of law having the like effect as those sections.

(2) In Scotland, a [trustee in the sequestration of the] estate of a defaulter or a liquidator is bound by any market contract to which that defaulter is a party and by any contract as is mentioned in subsection (1)(b) above notwithstanding section [110 of the Bankruptcy (Scotland) Act 2016] or any rule of law to the like effect applying in liquidations.

(3) Sections 127 and 284 of the Insolvency Act 1986 (avoidance of property dispositions effected after commencement of winding up[, submission of bankruptcy application] or presentation of bankruptcy petition), and section [87(4) of the Bankruptcy (Scotland) Act 2016] (effect of dealing with debtor relating to estate vested in . . . trustee) do not apply to—

(a) a market contract, or any disposition of property in pursuance of such a contract,

(b) the provision of margin in relation to market contracts,

[(ba) the provision of default fund contribution to [the recognised body],]

[(bb) a qualifying collateral arrangement,

(bc) a transfer of a clearing member client contract, a client trade or a qualifying collateral arrangement, as mentioned in paragraphs (c) to (e) of section 158(1),

(bd) a qualifying property transfer]

(c) a contract effected by [the recognised body] for the purpose of realising property provided as margin in relation to a market contract [or as default fund contribution], or any disposition of property in pursuance of such a contract, or

(d) any disposition of property in accordance with the rules of [the recognised body] as to the application of property provided as margin [or as default fund contribution].

(4) However, where—

(a) a market contract is entered into by a person who has notice that [a bankruptcy application has been submitted or] a petition has been presented for the winding up or bankruptcy or sequestration of the estate of the other party to the contract, or

(b) margin in relation to a market contract [or default fund contribution] is accepted by a person who has notice that [such an application has been made or petition presented] in relation to the person by whom or on whose behalf the margin [or default fund contribution] is provided,

the value of any profit to him arising from the contract or, as the case may be, the amount or value of the margin [or default fund contribution] is recoverable from him by the relevant office-holder unless the court directs otherwise.

[(5) Subsection (4)(a) does not apply where the person entering into the contract is [a recognised body] acting in accordance with its rules, or where the contract is effected under the default rules of such [a recognised body]; but subsection (4)(b) applies in relation to the provision of—

(a) margin in relation to any such contract, unless the contract has been transferred in accordance with the default rules of the central counterparty, or

(b) default fund contribution.]

(6) Any sum recoverable by virtue of subsection (4) ranks for priority, in the event of the insolvency of the person from whom it is due, immediately before preferential or, in Scotland, preferred debts.

NOTES

The word omitted from para (a) of sub-s (1) was repealed, paras (aa)–(ac) of that subsection were inserted, paras (bb)–(bd) of sub-s (3) were inserted, and sub-s (5) was substituted, by the Financial Services and Markets Act 2000 (Over the Counter Derivatives, Central Counterparties and Trade Repositories) Regulations 2013, SI 2013/504, reg 4(1), (9), as from 1 April 2013.

The words "the recognised body" and "a recognised body" in square brackets (in each place that they occur) were substituted by the Central Securities Depositories Regulations 2017, SI 2017/1064, reg 3(1), (11), as from 28 November 2017.

The words "trustee in the sequestration of the" and "42 of the Bankruptcy (Scotland) Act 1985" in square brackets in sub-s (2) were substituted, the words "87(4) of the Bankruptcy (Scotland) Act 2016" in square brackets in sub-s (3) were substituted, and the word omitted was repealed, by the Bankruptcy (Scotland) Act 2016 (Consequential Provisions and Modifications) Order

2016, SI 2016/1034, art 7(1), (3), Sch 1, para 6(1), (5), as from 30 November 2016 (except in relation to (i) a sequestration as regards which the petition is presented, or the debtor application is made before that date; or (ii) a trust deed executed before that date).

The words ", submission of bankruptcy application" in sub-s (3), and the words "a bankruptcy application has been submitted or" in sub-s (4)(a) were inserted, and the words "such an application has been made or petition presented" in subs-s (4)(b) were substituted, by the Enterprise and Regulatory Reform Act 2013 (Consequential Amendments) (Bankruptcy) and the Small Business, Enterprise and Employment Act 2015 (Consequential Amendments) Regulations 2016, SI 2016/481, reg 2(1), Sch 1, para 9(1), (5), as from 6 April 2016.

All other words in square brackets were inserted by the Financial Markets and Insolvency Regulations 2009, SI 2009/853, reg 2(1), (8), as from 15 June 2009, subject to transitional provisions as noted to s 158 at **[5.153]**.

[5.160]

165 Adjustment of prior transactions

(1) No order shall be made in relation to a transaction to which this section applies under—

(a) section 238 or 339 of the Insolvency Act 1986 (transactions at an undervalue),

(b) section 239 or 340 of that Act (preferences), or

(c) section 423 of that Act (transactions defrauding creditors).

(2) As respects Scotland, no decree shall be granted in relation to any such transaction—

(a) under section [98 or 99 of the Bankruptcy (Scotland) Act 2016] or section 242 or 243 of the Insolvency Act 1986 (gratuitous alienations and unfair preferences), or

(b) at common law on grounds of gratuitous alienations or fraudulent preferences.

(3) This section applies to—

(a) a market contract to which a [recognised body] is a party or which is entered into under its default rules, . . .

[(ab) a market contract to which this Part applies by virtue of section 155(2B), and

(b) a disposition of property in pursuance of a market contract referred to in paragraph (a) or (ab).]

(4) Where margin is provided in relation to a market contract and (by virtue of subsection (3)(a)[, (3)(ab)] or otherwise) no such order or decree as is mentioned in subsection (1) or (2) has been, or could be, made in relation to that contract, this section applies to—

(a) the provision of the margin,

[(ab) a qualifying collateral arrangement,]

(b) any contract effected by [the recognised body] in question for the purpose of realising the property provided as margin, and

(c) any disposition of property in accordance with the rules of [the recognised body] [in question] as to the application of property provided as margin.

[(5) This section also applies to—

(a) the provision of default fund contribution to a [recognised body],

(b) any contract effected by a [recognised body] for the purpose of realising the property provided as default fund contribution, . . .

(c) any disposition of property in accordance with the rules of the [recognised body] as to the application of property provided as default fund [contribution,]

[(d) a transfer of a clearing member client contract, a client trade or a qualifying collateral arrangement as mentioned in paragraphs (c) to (e) of section 158(1), and

(e) a qualifying property transfer.]]

NOTES

Sub-s (2): words in square brackets substituted by the Bankruptcy (Scotland) Act 2016 (Consequential Provisions and Modifications) Order 2016, SI 2016/1034, art 7(1), (3), Sch 1, para 6(1), (6), as from 30 November 2016 (except in relation to (i) a sequestration as regards which the petition is presented, or the debtor application is made before that date; or (ii) a trust deed executed before that date).

Sub-s (3): word omitted from para (a) repealed, and paras (ab), (b) substituted (for the original para (b)), by the Financial Services and Markets Act 2000 (Over the Counter Derivatives, Central Counterparties and Trade Repositories) Regulations 2013, SI 2013/504, reg 4(1), (10)(a), (b), as from 1 April 2013. Words "recognised body" in square brackets in para (a) substituted by the Central Securities Depositories Regulations 2017, SI 2017/1064, reg 3(1), (12)(a), as from 28 November 2017.

Sub-s (4): words in first pair of square brackets inserted, and para (ab) inserted, by SI 2013/504, reg 4(1), (10)(c), (d), as from 1 April 2013. Words in square brackets in para (b) and words in first pair of square brackets in para (c) substituted by SI 2017/1064, reg 3(1), (12)(b), as from 28 November 2017. Words in second pair of square brackets in para (c) inserted by the Financial Markets and Insolvency Regulations 2009, SI 2009/853, reg 2(1), (9)(a), as from 15 June 2009, subject to transitional provisions as noted to s 158 at **[5.153]**.

Sub-s (5): added by SI 2009/853, reg 2(1), (9)(b), as from 15 June 2009, subject to transitional provisions as noted to s 158 at **[5.153]**. Words "recognised body" in square brackets in paras (a)–(c) substituted by SI 2017/1064, reg 3(1), (12)(a), as from 28 November 2017. Word omitted from para (b) repealed, word "contribution" in square brackets in para (c) substituted, and paras (d), (e) added by SI 2013/504, reg 4(1), (10)(e)–(g), as from 1 April 2013.

[5.161]

166 Powers . . . to give directions

(1) The powers conferred by this section are exercisable in relation to a recognised UK investment exchange or [recognised clearing house] [or recognised CSD].

(2) Where in any case [a recognised body] has not taken action under its default rules—

(a) if it appears to the [appropriate regulator] that it could take action, [the [regulator]] may direct it to do so, and

(b) if it appears to the [appropriate regulator] that it is proposing to take or may take action, [the [regulator]] may direct it not to do so.

(3) Before giving such a direction the [appropriate regulator] shall consult the [recognised body] house in question; and [it] shall not give a direction unless [it] is satisfied, in the light of that consultation—

(a) in the case of a direction to take action, that failure to take action would involve undue risk to investors or other participants in the market, . . .

(b) in the case of a direction not to take action, that the taking of action would be premature or otherwise undesirable in the interests of investors or other participants in the market,

[(c) in either case, that the direction is necessary having regard to the public interest in the stability of the financial system of the United Kingdom, or

(d) in either case, that the direction is necessary—

(i) to facilitate a proposed or possible use of a power under Part 1 of the Banking Act 2009 (special resolution regime), or

(ii) in connection with a particular exercise of a power under that Part.]

[(3A) The appropriate regulator may give a direction to a relevant office-holder appointed in respect of a defaulting clearing member to take any action, or refrain from taking any action, if the direction is given for the purposes of facilitating—

(a) the transfer of a clearing member client contract, a client trade or a qualifying collateral arrangement, or

(b) a qualifying property transfer.

(3B) The relevant office-holder to whom a direction is given under subsection (3A)—

(a) must comply with the direction notwithstanding any duty on the relevant office-holder under any enactment relating to insolvency, but

(b) is not required to comply with the direction given if the value of the clearing member's estate is unlikely to be sufficient to meet the office-holder's reasonable expenses of complying.

(3C) The expenses of the relevant office-holder in complying with a direction of the regulator under subsection (3A) are recoverable as part of the expenses incurred in the discharge of the office-holder's duties.]

(4) A direction shall specify the grounds on which it is given.

(5) A direction not to take action may be expressed to have effect until the giving of a further direction (which may be a direction to take action or simply revoking the earlier direction).

(6) No direction shall be given not to take action if, in relation to the person in question—

(a) a bankruptcy order or an award of sequestration of his estate has been made, or an interim receiver or interim trustee has been appointed, or

(b) a winding up order has been made, a resolution for voluntary winding up has been passed or an administrator, administrative receiver or provisional liquidator has been appointed;

and any previous direction not to take action shall cease to have effect on the making or passing of any such order, award or appointment.

(7) Where [a recognised body] has taken or been directed to take action under its default rules, the [appropriate regulator] may direct it to do or not to do such things (being things which it has power to do under its default rules) as are specified in the direction.

. . .

[(7A) Where the [recognised body] is acting in accordance with a direction under subsection (2)(a) that was given only by virtue of paragraph (a) of subsection (3), the appropriate regulator shall not give a direction under subsection (7) unless it is satisfied that the direction under that subsection will not impede or frustrate the proper and efficient conduct of the default proceedings.

(7B) Where the [recognised body] has taken action under its default rules without being directed to do so, the appropriate regulator shall not give a direction under subsection (7) unless—

(a) it is satisfied that the direction under that subsection will not impede or frustrate the proper and efficient conduct of the default proceedings, or

(b) it is satisfied that the direction is necessary—

(i) having regard to the public interest in the stability of the financial system of the United Kingdom,

(ii) to facilitate a proposed or possible use of a power under Part 1 of the Banking Act 2009 (special resolution regime), or

(iii) in connection with a particular exercise of a power under that Part.]

(8) A direction under this section is enforceable, on the application of the [regulator which gave the direction], by injunction or, in Scotland, by an order under section 45 of the Court of Session Act 1988; and where [a recognised body] [or a relevant office-holder] has not complied with a direction, the court may make such order as it thinks fit for restoring the position to what it would have been if the direction had been complied with.

[(9) "The appropriate regulator"—

(a) in relation to a recognised UK investment exchange, means the FCA, and

(b) in relation to a [recognised CSD, a] [recognised clearing house] [or a defaulting clearing member], means the Bank of England.]

NOTES

Section heading: words omitted repealed by the Financial Services Act 2012, s 111(1), (9), as from 1 April 2013.

Sub-s (1): words in first pair of square brackets substituted by the Financial Services and Markets Act 2000 (Over the Counter Derivatives, Central Counterparties and Trade Repositories) Regulations 2013, SI 2013/504, reg 4(1), (11)(a), as from 1 April 2013. Words in second pair of square brackets inserted by the Central Securities Depositories Regulations 2017, SI 2017/1064, reg 3(1), (13)(a), as from 28 November 2017.

Sub-s (2): words "a recognised body" in square brackets substituted by SI 2017/1064, reg 3(1), (13)(b), as from 28 November 2017. In each of paras (a), (b), words in first and third (inner) pairs of square brackets substituted by the Financial Services Act 2012, s 111(1)–(3), as from 1 April 2013, and words in second (outer) pair of square brackets substituted by the Financial Services and Markets Act 2000 (Consequential Amendments and Repeals) Order 2001, SI 2001/3649, art 81(1), (2), as from 1 December 2001.

Sub-s (3): words in first pair of square brackets substituted, word omitted from para (a) repealed, and paras (c), (d) inserted by the Financial Services Act 2012, s 111(1), (4), as from 1 April 2013. Words in second pair of square brackets substituted by SI 2017/1064, reg 3(1), (13)(c), as from 28 November 2017. Words in third and fourth pairs of square brackets substituted by the Financial Services and Markets Act 2000 (Consequential Amendments and Repeals) Order 2001, SI 2001/3649, art 81(1), (3), as from 1 December 2001.

Sub-ss (3A)–(3C): inserted by SI 2013/504, reg 4(1), (11)(b), as from 1 April 2013.

Sub-s (7): words "a recognised body" in square brackets substituted by SI 2017/1064, reg 3(1), (13)(b), as from 28 November 2017. Other words in square brackets substituted, and words omitted repealed, by the Financial Services Act 2012, s 111(1), (5), as from 1 April 2013.

Sub-ss (7A), (7B): inserted by the Financial Services Act 2012, s 111(1), (6), as from 1 April 2013. Words in square brackets substituted by SI 2017/1064, reg 3(1), (13)(c), as from 28 November 2017.

Sub-s (8): words in first pair of square brackets substituted by the Financial Services Act 2012, s 111(1), (7), as from 1 April 2013. Words in second pair of square brackets substituted by SI 2017/1064, reg 3(1), (13)(d), as from 28 November 2017. Words in final pair of square brackets substituted by virtue of SI 2013/504, reg 4(1), (11)(c), as from 1 April 2013.

Sub-s (9): added by the Financial Services Act 2012, s 111(1), (8), as from 1 April 2013. Words in first pair of square brackets substituted by SI 2017/1064, reg 3(1), (13)(c), as from 28 November 2017. Words in second pair of square brackets inserted by SI 2013/504, reg 4(1), (11)(e), as from 1 April 2013. Words in final pair of square brackets inserted by the Financial Services and Markets Act 2000 (Over the Counter Derivatives, Central Counterparties and Trade Repositories) (No 2) Regulations 2013, SI 2013/1908, reg 2(1), (6), as from 26 August 2013.

[5.162]

167 Application to determine whether default proceedings to be taken

[(1) This section applies where a relevant insolvency event has occurred in the case of—

(a) a recognised investment exchange or a member or designated non-member of a recognised investment exchange, . . .

(b) a recognised clearing house or a member of a recognised clearing house[; . . .

[(ba) a recognised CSD or a member of a recognised CSD, or]

(c) a client which is providing indirect clearing services to an indirect client.]

[The person referred to in paragraphs (a) to (c)] in whose case a relevant insolvency event has occurred is referred to below as "the person in default".

(1A) For the purposes of this section a "relevant insolvency event" occurs where—

(a) a bankruptcy order is made,

(b) an award of sequestration is made,

(c) an order appointing an interim receiver is made,

(d) an administration or winding up order is made,

(e) an administrator is appointed under paragraph 14 of Schedule B1 to the Insolvency Act 1986 (appointment by holder of qualifying floating charge) or under paragraph 22 of that Schedule (appointment by company or directors),

(f) a resolution for voluntary winding up is passed, or

(g) an order appointing a provisional liquidator is made.

(1B) Where in relation to a person in default [a recognised body] ("[the responsible recognised body]")—

(a) has power under its default rules to take action in consequence of the relevant insolvency event or the matters giving rise to it, but

(b) has not done so,

a relevant office-holder appointed in connection with or in consequence of the relevant insolvency event may apply to the [appropriate regulator].]

(2) The application shall specify [the responsible recognised body] and the grounds on which it is made.

(3) On receipt of the application the [appropriate regulator] shall notify [the responsible recognised body], and unless within three business days after the day on which the notice is received [the responsible recognised body]—

(a) takes action under its default rules, or

(b) notifies the [appropriate regulator] that it proposes to do so forthwith,

then, subject as follows, the provisions of sections 158 to 165 above do not apply in relation to market contracts to which [the person in default] is a party or to anything done by [the responsible recognised body] for the purposes of, or in connection with, the settlement of any such contract.

For this purpose a "business day" means any day which is not a Saturday or Sunday, Christmas Day, Good Friday or a bank holiday in any part of the United Kingdom under the Banking and Financial Dealings Act 1971.

(4) The provisions of sections 158 to 165 are not disapplied if before the end of the period mentioned in subsection (3) the [appropriate regulator] gives [the responsible recognised body] a direction under section 166(2)(a) (direction to take action under default rules).

No such direction may be given after the end of that period.

(5) If [the responsible recognised body] notifies the [appropriate regulator] that it proposes to take action under its default rules forthwith, it shall do so; and that duty is enforceable, on the application of the [appropriate regulator], by injunction or, in Scotland, by an order under section 45 of the Court of Session Act 1988.

[(6) "The appropriate regulator"—

(a) in relation to a recognised investment exchange, means the FCA, and

(b) in relation to a recognised clearing house or recognised CSD, means the Bank of England.]

NOTES

Sub-s (1): substituted (together with sub-ss (1A), (1B) for sub-ss (1), (1A)) by the Financial Markets and Insolvency Regulations 2009, SI 2009/853, reg 2(1), (10)(a), as from 15 June 2009, subject to transitional provisions as noted to s 158 at **[5.153]**. The original sub-s (1A) was inserted by the Enterprise Act 2002, s 248(3), Sch 17, paras 43, 46, as from 15 September 2003. Word omitted from para (a) repealed, and para (c) (and the preceding word) inserted, by the Financial Services and Markets Act 2000 (Over the Counter Derivatives, Central Counterparties and Trade Repositories) (No 2) Regulations 2013, SI 2013/1908, reg 2(1), (7), as from 26 August 2013. Word omitted from para (b) repealed, para (ba) inserted, and words "The person referred to in paragraphs (a) to (c)" in square brackets substituted, by the Central Securities Depositories Regulations 2017, SI 2017/1064, reg 3(1), (14)(a), as from 28 November 2017.

Sub-s (1A): substituted as noted to sub-s (1) above.

Sub-s (1B): substituted as noted to sub-s (1) above. Words in first and second pairs of square brackets substituted by SI 2017/1064, reg 3(1), (14)(b), (c), as from 28 November 2017. Words in final pair of square brackets substituted by the Financial Services Act 2012, s 114(1), Sch 18, Pt 2, paras 62, 67(1), (2), as from 1 April 2013.

Sub-s (2): words in square brackets substituted by SI 2017/1064, reg 3(1), (14)(c), as from 28 November 2017.

Sub-ss (3)–(5): words "appropriate regulator" in square brackets (in each place they occur) substituted by the Financial Services Act 2012, s 114(1), Sch 18, Pt 2, paras 62, 67(1), (2), as from 1 April 2013. Words "the responsible recognised body" in square brackets (in each place they occur) substituted by 2017/1064, reg 3(1), (14)(c), as from 28 November 2017. Other words in square brackets substituted by SI 2009/853, reg 2(1), (10)(c), (d), as from 15 June 2009, subject to transitional provisions as noted to s 158 at **[5.153]**.

Sub-s (6): originally added by the Financial Services Act 2012, s 114(1), Sch 18, Pt 2, paras 62, 67(1), (3), as from 1 April 2013. Subsequently substituted by 2017/1064, reg 3(1), (14)(d), as from 28 November 2017.

168 (*Repealed by the Financial Services and Markets Act 2000 (Consequential Amendments and Repeals) Order 2001, SI 2001/3649, art 75(f), as from 1 December 2001.*)

[5.163]

169 Supplementary provisions

(1) . . .

(2) [Sections 296 and 297 of the Financial Services and Markets Act 2000 apply] in relation to a failure by a recognised investment exchange or recognised clearing house to comply with an obligation under this Part as to a failure to comply with an obligation under that Act.

[(2A) Section 296 of the Financial Services and Markets Act 2000 applies in relation to a failure by a recognised CSD to comply with an obligation under this Part as to a failure to comply with an obligation under that Act.]

(3) Where the recognition of [an investment exchange, clearing house or central securities depository] is revoked under the [Financial Services and Markets Act 2000, the appropriate authority] may, before or after the revocation order, give such directions as [it] thinks fit with respect to the continued application of the provisions of this Part, with such exceptions, additions and adaptations as may be specified in the direction, in relation to cases where a relevant event of any description specified in the directions occurred before the revocation order takes effect.

[(3A) "The appropriate authority" means—

(a) in the case of an overseas investment exchange or clearing house, the Treasury;

[(b) in the case of a UK investment exchange, the FCA, . . .

(c) in the case of a UK clearing house, the Bank of England];[and

(d) in the case of a central securities depository, the Bank of England].]

(4) . . .

(5) [Regulations under section 414 of the Financial Services and Markets Act 2000 (service of notices) may make provision] in relation to a notice, direction or other document required or authorised by or under this Part to be given to or served on any person other than the [Treasury[, the FCA or the Bank of England]].

NOTES

Sub-s (1): repealed by the Financial Services and Markets Act 2000 (Consequential Amendments and Repeals) Order 2001, SI 2001/3649, art 75(g), as from 1 December 2001.

Sub-s (2): words in square brackets substituted by SI 2001/3649, art 83(1)–(3), as from 1 December 2001.

Sub-s (2A): inserted by the Central Securities Depositories Regulations 2017, SI 2017/1064, reg 3(1), (15)(a), as from 28 November 2017.

Sub-s (3): words "an investment exchange, clearing house or central securities depository" in square brackets substituted by SI 2017/1064, reg 3(1), (15)(b), as from 28 November 2017. Other words in square brackets substituted by SI 2001/3649, art 83(1)–(3), as from 1 December 2001.

Sub-s (3A): inserted by SI 2001/3649, art 83(1), (4), as from 1 December 2001. Paras (b), (c) substituted (for the original para (b) and the word immediately preceding it) by the Financial Services Act 2012, s 114(1), Sch 18, Pt 2, paras 62, 68(1), (2), as from 1 April 2013. Word omitted from para (b) repealed, and para (d) (and the preceding word) inserted by SI 2017/1064, reg 3(1), (15)(c), as from 28 November 2017.

Sub-s (4): repealed (without having been brought into force) by SI 2001/3649, art 75(g), as from 1 December 2001.

Sub-s (5): words in first pair and second (outer) pair of square brackets substituted by SI 2001/3649, art 83(1), (5), as from 1 December 2001. Words in third (inner) pair of square brackets substituted by the Financial Services Act 2012, s 114(1), Sch 18, Pt 2, paras 62, 68(1), (3), as from 1 April 2013.

Other exchanges and clearing houses

[5.164]

170 Certain overseas exchanges and clearing houses

[(1) The Secretary of State and the Treasury may by regulations provide that this Part applies in relation to contracts connected with an overseas investment exchange or overseas clearing house which—

(a) is not a recognised investment exchange or recognised clearing house, but

(b) is approved by the Treasury in accordance with such requirements as may be so specified,

as it applies in relation to contracts connected with a recognised investment exchange or recognised clearing house.]

(2) The [Treasury] shall not approve an overseas investment exchange or clearing house unless [they are] satisfied—

(a) that the rules and practices of the body, together with the law of the country in which the body's head office is situated, provide adequate procedures for dealing with the default of persons party to contracts connected with the body, and

(b) that it is otherwise appropriate to approve the body.

(3) The reference in subsection (2)(a) to default is to a person being unable to meet his obligations.

(4) The regulations may apply in relation to the approval of a body under this section such of the provisions of the [Financial Services and Markets Act 2000] as the Secretary of State considers appropriate.

(5) The Secretary of State may make regulations which, in relation to a body which is so approved—

(a) apply such of the provisions of the [Financial Services and Markets Act 2000] as the Secretary of State considers appropriate, and

(b) provide that the provisions of this Part apply with such exceptions, additions and adaptations as appear to the Secretary of State to be necessary or expedient;

and different provision may be made with respect to different bodies or descriptions of body.

(6) Where the regulations apply any provisions of the [Financial Services and Markets Act 2000], they may provide that those provisions apply with such exceptions, additions and adaptations as appear to the Secretary of State to be necessary or expedient.

NOTES

Commencement: 25 March 1991 (certain purposes); not in force (otherwise); see the final note below.

Sub-s (1): substituted by the Financial Markets and Insolvency Regulations 2009, SI 2009/853, reg 2(1), (11), as from 15 June 2009.

Sub-ss (2), (4)–(6): words in square brackets substituted by SI 2001/3649, art 84(1), (3), (4), as from 1 December 2001.

Note: the Companies Act 1989 (Commencement No 9 and Saving and Transitional Provisions) Order 1991, SI 1991/488 provided that this Part (ie, ss 154–191, Schs 21, 22) comes into force on 25 March 1991 in so far as necessary to enable Regulations to be made under ss 155(4), (5), 158(4), (5), 160(5), 173(4), (5), 174(2)–(4), 185, 186, 187(3), Sch 21, para 2(3). The Companies Act 1989 (Commencement No 10 and Saving Provisions) Order 1991, SI 1991/878 brought most of the remaining provisions of this Part into force on 25 April 1991 but, as of 1 August 2022, this section (and ss 172, 178) have not been commenced for other purposes.

[5.165]

[170A [Third] country central counterparties

(1) In this section and section 170B—

(a) "assets" has the meaning given by Article 39(10) of the EMIR Level 1 Regulation;

(b), (c) . . .

(d) "overseas competent authority" means a competent authority responsible for the authorisation or supervision of clearing houses or central counterparties in a country or territory other than the United Kingdom;

(e) "relevant provisions" means any provisions of the default rules of [a] third country central counterparty which—

(i) provide for the transfer of the positions or assets of a defaulting clearing member;

(ii) are not necessary for the purposes of complying with the minimum requirements of Articles 48(5) and (6) of the EMIR Level 1 Regulation; and

(iii) may be relevant to a question falling to be determined in accordance with the law of a part of the United Kingdom;

(f) "relevant requirements" means the requirements specified in paragraph 34(2) (portability of accounts: default rules going beyond requirements of EMIR) of Part 6 of the Schedule to the Financial Services and Markets Act 2000 (Recognition Requirements for Investment Exchanges[, Clearing Houses and Central Securities Depositories]) Regulations 2001;

(g) "UK clearing member" means a clearing member to which the law of a part of the United Kingdom will apply for the purposes of an insolvent reorganisation or winding up[, and

(h) "UK client" means a client—

(i) which offers indirect clearing services, and

(ii) to which the law of a part of the United Kingdom will apply for the purposes of an insolvent reorganisation or winding up.]

(2) This Part applies to transactions cleared through . . . a third country central counterparty by a UK clearing member [or a UK client] as it applies to transactions cleared through a recognised central counterparty, but subject to the modifications in subsections (3) to (5).

(3) For section 157 there is to be substituted—

"157 Change in default rules

(1) [A] third country central counterparty in respect of which an order under section 170B(4) has been made and not revoked must give the Bank of England at least three months' notice of any proposal to amend, revoke or add to its default rules.

(2) The Bank of England may, if it considers it appropriate to do so, agree a shorter period of notice.

(3) Where notice is given to the Bank of England under subsection (1)[, a] third country central counterparty must provide the Bank of England with such information, documents and reports as the Bank of England may require.

(4) Information, documents and reports required under subsection (3) must be provided in English and be given at such times, in such form and at such place, and verified in such a manner, as the Bank of England may direct.".

(4) Section 162 does not apply to . . . a third country central counterparty unless it has been notified by the Bank of England that a report under that section is required for the purposes of insolvency proceedings in any part of the United Kingdom.

(5) In relation to [a] third country central counterparty, references in this Part to the "rules" or "default rules" of the central counterparty are to be taken not to include references to any relevant provisions unless—

(a) the relevant provisions satisfy the relevant requirements; or

(b) the Bank of England has made an order under section 170B(4) recognising that the relevant provisions of its default rules satisfy the relevant requirements and the order has not been revoked.]

NOTES

Inserted, together with 170B, by the Financial Services and Markets Act 2000 (Over the Counter Derivatives, Central Counterparties and Trade Repositories) Regulations 2013, SI 2013/504, reg 4(1), (12), as from 1 April 2013.

Section heading: word in square brackets substituted by the Financial Markets and Insolvency (Amendment and Transitional Provision) (EU Exit) Regulations 2019, SI 2019/341, reg 2(1), (2)(a), as from IP completion day (as defined in the European Union (Withdrawal Agreement) Act 2020, s 39).

Sub-s (1) is amended as follows:

Paras (b) and (c) were repealed, and the word "a" in square brackets in para (e) was substituted, by SI 2019/341, reg 2(1), (2)(b), as from IP completion day (as defined in the European Union (Withdrawal Agreement) Act 2020, s 39).

Words in square brackets in sub-para (f) inserted by the Central Securities Depositories Regulations 2017, SI 2017/1064, reg 3(1), (16), as from 28 November 2017.

Para (h) (and the preceding word) added by the Financial Services and Markets Act 2000 (Over the Counter Derivatives, Central Counterparties and Trade Repositories) (No 2) Regulations 2013, SI 2013/1908, reg 2(1), (8), as from 26 August 2013.

Sub-s (2): words omitted repealed by SI 2019/341, reg 2(1), (2)(c), as from IP completion day (as defined in the European Union (Withdrawal Agreement) Act 2020, s 39). Words in square brackets inserted by SI 2013/1908, reg 2(1), (8), as from 26 August 2013.

Sub-s (3): in s 157 as set out in this subsection, the words in square brackets were substituted by SI 2019/341, reg 2(1), (2)(d), as from IP completion day (as defined in the European Union (Withdrawal Agreement) Act 2020, s 39).

Sub-s (4): words omitted repealed by SI 2019/341, reg 2(1), (2)(e), as from IP completion day (as defined in the European Union (Withdrawal Agreement) Act 2020, s 39).

Sub-s (5): word in square brackets substituted SI 2019/341, reg 2(1), (2)(f), as from IP completion day (as defined in the European Union (Withdrawal Agreement) Act 2020, s 39).

[5.166]

[170B [Third] country central counterparties: procedure

(1) [A] third country central counterparty may apply to the Bank of England for an order recognising that the relevant provisions of its default rules satisfy the relevant requirements.

(2) The application must be made in such manner, and must be accompanied by such information, documents and reports, as the Bank of England may direct.

(3) Information, documents and reports required under subsection (2) must be provided in English and be given at such times, in such form and at such place, and verified in such manner, as the Bank of England may direct.

(4) The Bank of England may make an order recognising that the relevant provisions of the default rules satisfy the relevant requirements.

(5) The Bank of England may by order revoke an order made under subsection (4) if—

(a) the . . . third country central counterparty consents;

(b) the . . . third country central counterparty has failed to pay a fee which is owing to the Bank of England under paragraph 36 of Schedule 17A to the Financial Services and Markets Act 2000;

(c) the . . . third country central counterparty is failing or has failed to comply with a requirement of or imposed under section 157 (as modified by section 170A(3)); or

(d) it appears to the Bank of England that the relevant provisions no longer satisfy the relevant requirements.

(6) An order made under subsection (4) or (5) must state the time and date when it is to have effect.

(7) An order made under subsection (5) may contain such transitional provision as the Bank of England considers appropriate.

(8) The Bank of England must—

(a) maintain a register of orders made under subsection (4) which are in force; and

(b) publish the register in such manner as it appears to the Bank of England to be appropriate.

(9) Section 298 of the Financial Services and Markets Act 2000 applies to a refusal to make an order under subsection (4) or the making of a revocation order under subsection (5)(b), (c) or (d) as it applies to the making of a revocation order under section 297(2) of the Financial Services and Markets Act 2000, but with the following modifications—

(a) for "appropriate regulator" substitute "the Bank of England";

(b) for "recognised body" substitute " . . . third country central counterparty"; and

(c) in subsection (7), for "give a direction under section 296" substitute "make an order under paragraph (b), (c) or (d) of section 170B(5) of the Companies Act 1989".

(10) If the Bank of England refuses to make an order under subsection (4) or makes an order under subsection (5)(b), (c) or (d), the . . . third country central counterparty may refer the matter to the Upper Tribunal.

(11) The Bank of England may rely on information or advice from an overseas competent authority . . . in its determination of an application under subsection (1) or the making of a revocation order under subsection (5)(d).]

NOTES

Inserted as noted to s 170A at **[5.165]**.

The words in square brackets in the section heading and sub-s (1) were substituted, and the words omitted from sub-ss (5), (9)–(11) were repealed, by the Financial Markets and Insolvency (Amendment and Transitional Provision) (EU Exit) Regulations 2019, SI 2019/341, reg 2(1), (3) as from IP completion day (as defined in the European Union (Withdrawal Agreement) Act 2020, s 39).

[5.167]

[170C [Third] country CSDs

(1) This Part applies to transactions settled through . . . a third country CSD by a UK member of the central securities depository as it applies to transactions settled through a recognised CSD, but subject to subsections (2), (3) and (4).

(2) The definition of "authorised central securities depository services" in section 155(3D) applies to third country CSDs as if it read—

""authorised central securities depository services" means, in relation to a third country CSD, those services which that central securities depository is authorised to provide that are equivalent to the services listed in the Annex to the CSD regulation.".

(3) Section 157 does not apply to . . . a third country CSD.

(4) Section 162 does not apply to . . . a third country CSD unless it has been notified by the Bank of England that a report under that section is required for the purposes of insolvency proceedings in any part of the United Kingdom. Where . . . a third country CSD has been so notified, the appropriate regulator for the purposes of section 162 shall be the Bank of England.

(5) In this section "UK member" means a member of . . . a third country CSD to which the law of a part of the United Kingdom will apply for the purposes of an insolvent reorganisation or winding up.]

NOTES

Inserted by the Central Securities Depositories Regulations 2017, SI 2017/1064, reg 3(1), (17), as from 28 November 2017.

The word in square brackets in the section heading was substituted, and all words omitted were repealed, by the Financial Markets and Insolvency (Amendment and Transitional Provision) (EU Exit) Regulations 2019, SI 2019/341, reg 2(1), (4), as from IP completion day (as defined in the European Union (Withdrawal Agreement) Act 2020, s 39).

171 *(Repealed by the Financial Services and Markets Act 2000 (Consequential Amendments and Repeals) Order 2001, SI 2001/3649, art 75(h), as from 1 December 2001.)*

[5.168]

172 Settlement arrangements provided by the Bank of England

(1) The Secretary of State may by regulations provide that this Part applies to contracts of any specified description in relation to which settlement arrangements are provided by the Bank of England, as it applies to contracts connected with [a recognised body].

(2) Regulations under this section may provide that the provisions of this Part apply with such exceptions, additions and adaptations as appear to the Secretary of State to be necessary or expedient.

(3) Before making any regulations under this section, the Secretary of State [and the Treasury shall consult] the Bank of England.

NOTES

Commencement: 25 March 1991 (certain purposes); not in force (otherwise).

Sub-s (1): words in square brackets substituted by the Central Securities Depositories Regulations 2017, SI 2017/1064, reg 3(1), (18), as from 28 November 2017.

Sub-s (3): words in square brackets substituted by the Transfer of Functions (Financial Services) Order 1992, SI 1992/1315, art 10(1), Sch 4, para 13, as from 7 June 1992.

As to the commencement of this section, see the note to s 170 at **[5.164]**.

Market charges

[5.169]

173 Market charges

(1) In this Part "market charge" means a charge whether fixed or floating, granted—

(a) in favour of a recognised investment exchange, for the purpose of securing debts or liabilities arising in connection with the settlement of market contracts,

[(aa) in favour of The Stock Exchange, for the purpose of securing debts or liabilities arising in connection with short term certificates;]

(b) in favour of a recognised clearing house, for the purpose of securing debts or liabilities arising in connection with their ensuring the performance of market contracts, . . .

[(ba) in favour of a recognised CSD, for the purpose of securing debts or liabilities arising in connection with their ensuring the performance of market contracts, or]

(c) in favour of a person who agrees to make payments as a result of the transfer [or allotment] of specified securities made through the medium of a computer-based system established by the Bank of England and The Stock Exchange, for the purpose of securing debts or liabilities of the transferee [or allottee] arising in connection therewith.

(2) Where a charge is granted partly for purposes specified in subsection (1)(a), [(aa),] (b)[, (ba)] or (c) and partly for other purposes, it is a "market charge" so far as it has effect for the specified purposes.

(3) [In subsection (1)—

"short term certificate" means an instrument issued by The Stock Exchange undertaking to procure the transfer of property of a value and description specified in the instrument to or to the order of the person to whom the instrument is issued or his endorsee or to a person acting on behalf of either of them and also undertaking to make appropriate payments in cash, in the event that the obligation to procure the transfer of property cannot be discharged in whole or in part;]

"specified securities" means securities for the time being specified in the list in Schedule 1 to the Stock Transfer Act 1982, and includes any right to such securities; and

"transfer", in relation to any such securities or right, means a transfer of the beneficial interest.

(4) The Secretary of State may by regulations make further provision as to the charges granted in favour of any such person as is mentioned in subsection (1)(a), (b)[, (ba)] or (c) which are to be treated as "market charges" for the purposes of this Part; and the regulations may add to, amend or repeal the provisions of subsections (1) to (3) above.

(5) The regulations may provide that a charge shall or shall not be treated as a market charge if or to the extent that it secures obligations of a specified description, is a charge over property of a specified description or contains provisions of a specified description.

(6) Before making regulations under this section in relation to charges granted in favour of a person within subsection (1)(c), the Secretary of State [and the Treasury shall consult] the Bank of England.

NOTES

Sub-s (1): para (aa), and words in square brackets in para (c), inserted by the Financial Markets and Insolvency Regulations 1991, SI 1991/880, reg 9(a), (b), as from 25 April 1991. Word omitted from para (b) repealed, and para (ba) inserted, by the Central Securities Depositories Regulations 2017, SI 2017/1064, reg 3(1), (19)(a), as from 28 November 2017.

Sub-s (2): the reference "(aa)," in square brackets was inserted by SI 1991/880, reg 9(c), as from 25 April 1991. The reference ", (ba)" in square brackets was inserted by SI 2017/1064, reg 3(1), (19)(b), as from 28 November 2017.

Sub-s (3): words in square brackets substituted by SI 1991/880, reg 9(d), as from 25 April 1991.

Sub-s (4): the reference ", (ba)" in square brackets was inserted by SI 2017/1064, reg 3(1), (19)(b), as from 28 November 2017.

Sub-s (6): words in square brackets substituted by the Transfer of Functions (Financial Services) Order 1992, SI 1992/1315, art 10(1), Sch 4, para 13, as from 7 June 1992.

Regulations: the Financial Markets and Insolvency Regulations 1991, SI 1991/880 at **[6.8]**; the Financial Markets and Insolvency (CGO Service) Regulations 1999, SI 1999/1209.

[5.170]

174 Modifications of the law of insolvency

(1) The general law of insolvency has effect in relation to market charges and action taken in enforcing them subject to the provisions of section 175.

(2) The Secretary of State may by regulations make further provision modifying the law of insolvency in relation to the matters mentioned in subsection (1).

(3) The regulations may add to, amend or repeal the provisions mentioned in subsection (1), and any other provision of this Part as it applies for the purposes of those provisions, or provide that those provisions have effect with such exceptions, additions or adaptations as are specified in the regulations.

(4) The regulations may make different provision for cases defined by reference to the nature of the charge, the nature of the property subject to it, the circumstances, nature or extent of the obligations secured by it or any other relevant factor.

(5) Before making regulations under this section in relation to charges granted in favour of a person within section 173(1)(c), the Secretary of State [and the Treasury shall consult] the Bank of England.

NOTES

Sub-s (5): words in square brackets substituted by the Transfer of Functions (Financial Services) Order 1992, SI 1992/1315, art 10(1), Sch 4, para 13, as from 7 June 1992.

Regulations: the Financial Markets and Insolvency Regulations 1991, SI 1991/880 at **[6.8]**; the Financial Markets and Insolvency (CGO Service) Regulations 1999, SI 1999/1209; the Financial Services and Markets Act 2000 (Over the Counter Derivatives, Central Counterparties and Trade Repositories) Regulations 2013, SI 2013/504.

[5.171]

175 Administration orders, &c

[(1) The following provisions of Schedule B1 to the Insolvency Act 1986 (administration) do not apply in relation to a market charge—

(a) paragraph 43(2) and (3) (restriction on enforcement of security or repossession of goods) (including that provision as applied by paragraph 44 (interim moratorium)), and

(b) paragraphs 70, 71 and 72 (power of administrator to deal with charged or hire-purchase property).

(1A) Paragraph 41(2) of that Schedule (receiver to vacate office at request of administrator) does not apply to a receiver appointed under a market charge.]

(2) However, where a market charge falls to be enforced after [the occurrence of an event to which subsection (2A) applies], and there exists another charge over some or all of the same property ranking in priority to or *pari passu* with the market charge [on the application of any person interested], the court may order that there shall be taken after enforcement of the market charge such steps as the court may direct for the purpose of ensuring that the chargee under the other charge is not prejudiced by the enforcement of the market charge.

[(2A) This subsection applies to—

(a) making an administration application under paragraph 12 of Schedule B1 to the Insolvency Act 1986,

(b) appointing an administrator under paragraph 14 or 22 of that Schedule (appointment by floating charge holder, company or directors),

(c) filing with the court a copy of notice of intention to appoint an administrator under either of those paragraphs.]

(3) The following provisions of the Insolvency Act 1986 (which relate to the powers of receivers) do not apply in relation to a market charge—

(a) section 43 (power of administrative receiver to dispose of charged property), and

(b) section 61 (power of receiver in Scotland to dispose of an interest in property).

(4) Sections 127 and 284 of the Insolvency Act 1986 (avoidance of property dispositions effected after commencement of winding up[, making of bankruptcy application] or presentation of bankruptcy petition), and section [87(4) of the Bankruptcy (Scotland) Act 2016] (effect of dealing with debtor relating to estate vested in . . . trustee), do not apply to a disposition of property as a result of which the property becomes subject to a market charge or any transaction pursuant to which that disposition is made.

[(5) However, if a person who is party to a disposition mentioned in subsection (4) has notice at the time of the disposition that [a bankruptcy application has been made or] a petition has been presented for the winding up or bankruptcy or sequestration of the estate of the party making the disposition, the value of any profit to him arising from the disposition is recoverable from him by the relevant office-holder unless—

(a) the person is a chargee under the market charge,

(b) the disposition is made in accordance with the default rules of a recognised central counterparty for the purposes of transferring a position or asset of a clearing member in default, or

(c) the court directs otherwise.]

[(5A) In subsection (5)(b), "asset" has the meaning given by Article 39(10) of the EMIR Level 1 Regulation.]

(6) Any sum recoverable by virtue of subsection (5) ranks for priority, in the event of the insolvency of the person from whom it is due, immediately before preferential or, in Scotland, preferred debts.

(7) In a case falling within both subsection (4) above (as a disposition of property as a result of which the property becomes subject to a market charge) and section 164(3) (as the provision of margin in relation to a market contract), section 164(4) applies with respect to the recovery of the amount or value of the margin and subsection (5) above does not apply.

NOTES

Sub-ss (1), (1A): substituted, for the original sub-s (1), by the Enterprise Act 2002, s 248(3), Sch 17, paras 43, 47(1), (2), as from 15 September 2003 (for savings and transitional provisions, see the note to the Insolvency Act 1986, s 8 at **[9.147]**).

Sub-s (2): words in first pair of square brackets substituted by the Enterprise Act 2002, s 248(3), Sch 17, paras 43, 47(1), (3), as from 15 September 2003 (for savings and transitional provisions, see the note to the Insolvency Act 1986, s 8 at **[9.147]**). Words in second pair of square brackets inserted by the Financial Markets and Insolvency Regulations 1991, SI 1991/880, reg 18, as from 25 April 1991.

Sub-s (2A): inserted by the Enterprise Act 2002, s 248(3), Sch 17, paras 43, 47(1), (4), as from 15 September 2003 (for savings and transitional provisions, see the note to the Insolvency Act 1986, s 8 at **[9.147]**).

Sub-s (4): words in first pair of square brackets inserted by the Enterprise and Regulatory Reform Act 2013 (Consequential Amendments) (Bankruptcy) and the Small Business, Enterprise and Employment Act 2015 (Consequential Amendments) Regulations 2016, SI 2016/481, reg 2(1), Sch 1, para 9(1), (6)(a), as from 6 April 2016. Words in second pair of square brackets substituted, and word omitted repealed, by the Bankruptcy (Scotland) Act 2016 (Consequential Provisions and Modifications) Order 2016, SI 2016/1034, art 7(1), (3), Sch 1, para 6(1), (7), as from 30 November 2016 (except in relation to (i) a sequestration as regards which the petition is presented, or the debtor application is made before that date; or (ii) a trust deed executed before that date).

Sub-s (5): substituted by the Financial Services and Markets Act 2000 (Over the Counter Derivatives, Central Counterparties and Trade Repositories) Regulations 2013, SI 2013/504, reg 4(1), (13), as from 1 April 2013. Words in square brackets inserted by SI 2016/481, reg 2(1), Sch 1, para 9(1), (6)(b), as from 6 April 2016.

Sub-s (5A): inserted by SI 2013/504, reg 4(1), (14), as from 1 April 2013.

[5.172]

176 Power to make provision about certain other charges

(1) The Secretary of State may by regulations provide that the general law of insolvency has effect in relation to charges of such descriptions as may be specified in the regulations, and action taken in enforcing them, subject to such provisions as may be specified in the regulations.

(2) The regulations may specify any description of charge granted in favour of—

(a) a body approved under section 170 (certain overseas exchanges and clearing houses),

[(aa) . . . a third country CSD,]

(b) a person included in the list maintained by the [. . . [Bank of England]] for the purposes of [section 301 of the Financial Services and Markets Act 2000] (certain money market institutions),

(c) the Bank of England,

[(d) a person who has permission under [Part 4A] of the Financial Services and Markets Act 2000 to carry on a relevant regulated activity, or

(e) an international securities self-regulating organisation approved for the purposes of an order made under section 22 of the Financial Services and Markets Act 2000,]

for the purpose of securing debts or liabilities arising in connection with or as a result of the settlement of contracts or the transfer of assets, rights or interests on a financial market.

(3) The regulations may specify any description of charge granted for that purpose in favour of any other person in connection with exchange facilities or clearing services [or settlement arrangements] provided by a recognised investment exchange or recognised clearing house or by any such body, person, authority or organisation as is mentioned in subsection (2)[, or in connection with authorised central securities depository services (see section 155(3D)) provided by a recognised CSD].

(4) Where a charge is granted partly for the purpose specified in subsection (2) and partly for other purposes, the power conferred by this section is exercisable in relation to the charge so far as it has effect for that purpose.

(5) The regulations may—

(a) make the same or similar provision in relation to the charges to which they apply as is made by or under sections 174 and 175 in relation to market charges, or

(b) apply any of those provisions with such exceptions, additions or adaptations as are specified in the regulations.

[(6) Before making regulations under this section relating to a description of charges defined by reference to their being granted in favour of a person included in the list maintained by the . . . [Bank of England] for the purposes of [section 301 of the Financial Services and Markets Act 2000], or in connection with exchange facilities or clearing services [or settlement arrangements] provided by a person included in that list, the Secretary of State and the Treasury shall consult the [FCA] and the Bank of England.

(6A) Before making regulations under this section relating to a description of charges defined by reference to their being granted in favour of the Bank of England, or in connection with settlement arrangements provided by the Bank, the Secretary of State and the Treasury shall consult the Bank.]

(7) Regulations under this section may provide that they apply or do not apply to a charge if or to the extent that it secures obligations of a specified description, is a charge over property of a specified description or contains provisions of a specified description.

[(8) For the purposes of subsection (2)(d), "relevant regulated activity" means—

(a) dealing in investments as principal or as agent;

(b) arranging deals in investments;

[(ba) operating a multilateral trading facility;]

[(bb) operating an organised trading facility;]

(c) managing investments;

(d) safeguarding and administering investments;

(e) sending dematerialised instructions; . . .

[(ea) managing a UCITS;

(eb) acting as trustee or depositary of a UCITS;

(ec) managing an AIF;

(ed) acting as trustee or depositary of an AIF; or]

(f) establishing etc a collective investment scheme.

(9) Subsection (8) must be read with—

(a) section 22 of the Financial Services and Markets Act 2000;

(b) any relevant order under that section; and

(c) Schedule 2 to that Act.]

NOTES

Sub-s (2) is amended as follows:

Para (aa) inserted by the Central Securities Depositories Regulations 2017, SI 2017/1064, reg 3(1), (20)(a), as from 28 November 2017.

Words omitted from para (aa) repealed by the Financial Markets and Insolvency (Amendment and Transitional Provision) (EU Exit) Regulations 2019, SI 2019/341, reg 2(1), (5), as from IP completion day (as defined in the European Union (Withdrawal Agreement) Act 2020, s 39).

Words in first (outer) pair of square brackets in para (b) substituted by the Bank of England Act 1998, s 23(1), Sch 5, Pt III, paras 46, 48(1), (2), as from 1 June 1998.

Words in second (inner) pair of square brackets in para (b) substituted, and words in square brackets in para (d) substituted, by the Financial Services Act 2012, s 114(1), Sch 18, Pt 2, paras 62, 69(1), (2), as from 1 April 2013.

Words omitted from para (b) repealed, and words in third pair of square brackets substituted, by the Financial Services and Markets Act 2000 (Consequential Amendments and Repeals) Order 2001, SI 2001/3649, art 85(1), (2), as from 1 December 2001. Note that the section heading of the Financial Services and Markets Act 2000, s 301 is "Supervision of certain contracts" and not "certain money market institutions" as stated in sub-s (2)(b) above, therefore it is thought that the words "certain money market institutions" should be deleted from the text of this subsection.

Paras (d), (e) substituted by SI 2001/3649, art 85(1), (3), as from 1 December 2001.

Sub-s (3): words in square brackets inserted by SI 2017/1064, reg 3(1), (20)(b), as from 28 November 2017.

Sub-s (6): substituted, together with sub-s (6A) (for the original sub-s (6)), by the Bank of England Act 1998, s 23(1), Sch 5, Pt III, paras 46, 48(1), (3), as from 1 June 1998. Words omitted repealed, and words in second pair of square brackets substituted, by SI 2001/3649, art 85(1), (4), as from 1 December 2001. Words in first and final pairs of square brackets substituted by the Financial Services Act 2012, s 114(1), Sch 18, Pt 2, paras 62, 69(1), (3), as from 1 April 2013. Words in third pair of square brackets inserted by SI 2017/1064, reg 3(1), (20)(c), as from 28 November 2017.

Sub-s (6A): substituted as noted above.

Sub-s (8): added, together with sub-s (9), by SI 2001/3649, art 85(1), (5), as from 1 December 2001. Para (ba) inserted by the Financial Services and Markets Act 2000 (Regulated Activities) (Amendment No 3) Order 2006, SI 2006/3384, art 32, as from 1 November 2007. Para (bb) inserted by the Financial Services and Markets Act 2000 (Regulated Activities) (Amendment) Order 2017, SI 2017/488, art 14, Schedule, para 2, as from 3 January 2018. The word omitted from para (e) was repealed, and paras (ea)–(ed) were inserted, by the Alternative Investment Fund Managers Regulations 2013, SI 2013/1773, reg 80, Sch 1, Part 2, para 39, as from 22 July 2013.

Sub-s (9): added as noted above.

Market property

[5.173]

177 Application of margin [or default fund contribution] not affected by certain other interests

(1) The following provisions have effect with respect to the application by [a recognised body] of property (other than land) held by [the recognised body] as margin in relation to a market contract [or as default fund contribution].

(2) So far as necessary to enable the property to be applied in accordance with the rules of [the recognised body], it may be so applied notwithstanding any prior equitable interest or right, or any right or remedy arising from a breach of fiduciary duty, unless [the recognised body] had notice of the interest, right or breach of duty at the time the property was provided as margin [or as default fund contribution].

(3) No right or remedy arising subsequently to the property being provided as margin [or as default fund contribution] may be enforced so as to prevent or interfere with the application of the property by [the recognised body] in accordance with its rules.

(4) Where [a recognised body] has power by virtue of the above provisions to apply property notwithstanding an interest, right or remedy, a person to whom [the recognised body] disposes of the property in accordance with its rules takes free from that interest, right or remedy.

NOTES

Words "a recognised body" and "the recognised body" in square brackets (in each place that they occur) substituted by the Central Securities Depositories Regulations 2017, SI 2017/1064, reg 3(1), (21), as from 28 November 2017.

Other words in square brackets inserted by the Financial Markets and Insolvency Regulations 2009, SI 2009/853, reg 2(1), (13), as from 15 June 2009.

[5.174]

178 Priority of floating market charge over subsequent charges

(1) The Secretary of State may by regulations provide that a market charge which is a floating charge has priority over a charge subsequently created or arising, including a fixed charge.

(2) The regulations may make different provision for cases defined, as regards the market charge or the subsequent charge, by reference to the description of charge, its terms, the circumstances in which it is created or arises, the nature of the charge, the person in favour of whom it is granted or arises or any other relevant factor.

NOTES

Commencement: 25 March 1991 (certain purposes); not in force (otherwise).

As to the commencement of this section, see the note to s 170 at **[5.164]**.

[5.175]

179 Priority of market charge over unpaid vendor's lien

Where property subject to an unpaid vendor's lien becomes subject to a market charge, the charge has priority over the lien unless the chargee had actual notice of the lien at the time the property became subject to the charge.

[5.176]

180 Proceedings against market property by unsecured creditors

(1) Where property (other than land) is held by [a recognised body] as margin in relation to market contracts [or as default fund contribution,] or is subject to a market charge, no execution or other legal process for the enforcement of a judgment or order may be commenced or continued, and no distress may be levied, [and no power to use the

procedure in Schedule 12 to the Tribunals, Courts and Enforcement Act 2007 (taking control of goods) may be exercised,] against the property by a person not seeking to enforce any interest in or security over the property, except with the consent of—

(a) in the case of property provided as cover for margin [or as default fund contribution], [the recognised body] in question, or

(b) in the case of property subject to a market charge, the person in whose favour the charge was granted.

(2) Where consent is given the proceedings may be commenced or continued notwithstanding any provision of the Insolvency Act 1986 or the Bankruptcy (Scotland) Act [2016].

(3) Where by virtue of this section a person would not be entitled to enforce a judgment or order against any property, any injunction or other remedy granted with a view to facilitating the enforcement of any such judgment or order shall not extend to that property.

(4) In the application of this section to Scotland, the reference to execution being commenced or continued includes a reference to diligence being carried out or continued, and the reference to distress being levied shall be omitted.

NOTES

Sub-s (1): words "a recognised body" and "the recognised body" in square brackets substituted by the Central Securities Depositories Regulations 2017, SI 2017/1064, reg 3(1), (22), as from 28 November 2017. Words "or as default fund contribution," in square brackets (in both places they occur) inserted by the Financial Markets and Insolvency Regulations 2009, SI 2009/853, reg 2(1), (14), as from 15 June 2009. Words in third pair of square brackets inserted by the Tribunals, Courts and Enforcement Act 2007, s 62(3), Sch 13, para 91, as from 6 April 2014.

Sub-s (2): year "2016" in square brackets substituted by the Bankruptcy (Scotland) Act 2016 (Consequential Provisions and Modifications) Order 2016, SI 2016/1034, art 7(1), (3), Sch 1, para 6(1), (8), as from 30 November 2016 (except in relation to (i) a sequestration as regards which the petition is presented, or the debtor application is made before that date; or (ii) a trust deed executed before that date).

[5.177]

181 Power to apply provisions to other cases

(1) [A power to which this subsection applies includes the] power to apply sections 177 to 180 to any description of property provided as cover for margin in relation to contracts in relation to which the power is exercised or, as the case may be, property subject to charges in relation to which the power is exercised.

(2) The regulations may provide that those sections apply with such exceptions, additions and adaptations as may be specified in the regulations.

[(3) Subsection (1) applies to the powers of the Secretary of State and the Treasury to act jointly under—

(a) sections 170, 172 and 176 of this Act; and

(b) section 301 of the Financial Services and Markets Act 2000 (supervision of certain contracts).]

NOTES

Words in square brackets in sub-s (1) substituted, and sub-s (3) added, by the Financial Services and Markets Act 2000 (Consequential Amendments and Repeals) Order 2001, SI 2001/3649, art 86, as from 1 December 2001.

Supplementary provisions

[5.178]

182 Powers of court in relation to certain proceedings begun before commencement

(1) The powers conferred by this section are exercisable by the court where insolvency proceedings in respect of—

(a) a member of a recognised investment exchange or a recognised clearing house, or

(b) a person by whom a market charge has been granted,

are begun on or after 22nd December 1988 and before the commencement of this section.

That person is referred to in this section as "the relevant person".

(2) For the purposes of this section "insolvency proceedings" means proceedings under Part II, IV, V or IX of the Insolvency Act 1986 (administration, winding up and bankruptcy) or under the Bankruptcy (Scotland) Act [2016]; and references in this section to the beginning of such proceedings are to—

[(za) the making of a bankruptcy application on which a bankruptcy order is made,]

(a) the presentation of a petition on which an administration order, winding-up order, bankruptcy order or award of sequestration is made, or

(b) the passing of a resolution for voluntary winding up.

(3) This section applies in relation to—

(a) in England and Wales, the administration of the insolvent estate of a deceased person, and

(b) in Scotland, the administration by a judicial factor appointed under section 11A of the Judicial Factors (Scotland) Act 1889 of the insolvent estate of a deceased person,

as it applies in relation to insolvency proceedings.

In such a case references to the beginning of the proceedings shall be construed as references to the death of the relevant person.

(4) The court may on an application made, within three months after the commencement of this section, by—

(a) a recognised investment exchange or recognised clearing house, or

(b) a person in whose favour a market charge has been granted,

make such order as it thinks fit for achieving, except so far as assets of the relevant person have been distributed before the making of the application, the same result as if the provisions of Schedule 22 had come into force on 22nd December 1988.

(5) The provisions of that Schedule ("the relevant provisions") reproduce the effect of certain provisions of this Part as they appeared in the Bill for this Act as introduced into the House of Lords and published on that date.

(6) The court may in particular—

(a) require the relevant person or a relevant office-holder—

(i) to return property provided as cover for margin or which was subject to a market charge, or to pay to the applicant or any other person the proceeds of realisation of such property, or

(ii) to pay to the applicant or any other person such amount as the court estimates would have been payable to that person if the relevant provisions had come into force on 22nd December 1988 and market contracts had been settled in accordance with the rules of the recognised investment exchange or recognised clearing house, or a proportion of that amount if the property of the relevant person or relevant office-holder is not sufficient to meet the amount in full;

(b) provide that contracts, rules and dispositions shall be treated as not having been void;

(c) modify the functions of a relevant office-holder, or the duties of the applicant or any other person, in relation to the insolvency proceedings, or indemnify any such person in respect of acts or omissions which would have been proper if the relevant provisions had been in force;

(d) provide that conduct which constituted an offence be treated as not having done so;

(e) dismiss proceedings which could not have been brought if the relevant provisions had come into force on 22nd December 1988, and reverse the effect of any order of a court which could not, or would not, have been made if those provisions had come into force on that date.

(7) An order under this section shall not be made against a relevant office-holder if the effect would be that his remuneration, costs and expenses could not be met.

NOTES

Sub-s (2): year "2016" in square brackets substituted by the Bankruptcy (Scotland) Act 2016 (Consequential Provisions and Modifications) Order 2016, SI 2016/1034, art 7(1), (3), Sch 1, para 6(1), (8), as from 30 November 2016 (except in relation to (i) a sequestration as regards which the petition is presented, or the debtor application is made before that date; or (ii) a trust deed executed before that date). Para (za) inserted by the Enterprise and Regulatory Reform Act 2013 (Consequential Amendments) (Bankruptcy) and the Small Business, Enterprise and Employment Act 2015 (Consequential Amendments) Regulations 2016, SI 2016/481, reg 2(1), Sch 1, para 9(1), (7), as from 6 April 2016.

[5.179]

[182A Recognised central counterparties: disapplication of provisions on mutual credit and set-off

(1) Nothing in the law of insolvency shall enable the setting off against each other of—

(a) positions and assets recorded in an account at a recognised central counterparty and held for the account of a client, an indirect client or a group of clients or indirect clients in accordance with Article 39 of the EMIR Level 1 Regulation[, Article 3(1) of the EMIR Level 2 Regulation or Article 3(1) of the MIFIR Level 2 Regulation]; and

(b) positions and assets recorded in any other account at the recognised central counterparty.

[(2) Nothing in the law of insolvency shall enable the setting off against each other of—

(a) positions and assets recorded in an account at a clearing member and held for the account of an indirect client or a group of indirect clients in accordance with [Article 4(2) of the EMIR Level 2 Regulation or Article 4(2) of the MIFIR Level 2 Regulation]; and

(b) positions and assets recorded in any other account at the clearing member.]]

NOTES

Inserted by the Financial Services and Markets Act 2000 (Over the Counter Derivatives, Central Counterparties and Trade Repositories) Regulations 2013, SI 2013/504, reg 4(1), (15), as from 1 April 2013.

Sub-s (1): words in square brackets in para (a) substituted by the Companies Act 1989 (Financial Markets and Insolvency) (Amendment) Regulations 2017, SI 2017/1247, reg 2(1), (3)(a), as from 3 January 2018.

Sub-s (2): added by the Financial Services and Markets Act 2000 (Over the Counter Derivatives, Central Counterparties and Trade Repositories) (No 2) Regulations 2013, SI 2013/1908, reg 2(1), (9), as from 26 August 2013. Words in square brackets in para (a) substituted by SI 2017/1247, reg 2(1), (3)(b), as from 3 January 2018.

[5.180]

183 Insolvency proceedings in other jurisdictions

(1) The references to insolvency law in section 426 of the Insolvency Act 1986 (co-operation with courts exercising insolvency jurisdiction in other jurisdictions) include, in relation to a part of the United Kingdom, the provisions made by or under this Part and, in relation to a relevant country or territory within the meaning of that section, so much of the law of that country or territory as corresponds to any provisions made by or under this Part.

(2) A court shall not, in pursuance of that section or any other enactment or rule of law, recognise or give effect to—

(a) any order of a court exercising jurisdiction in relation to insolvency law in a country or territory outside the United Kingdom, or

(b) any act of a person appointed in such a country or territory to discharge any functions under insolvency law,

in so far as the making of the order or the doing of the act would be prohibited in the case of a court in the United Kingdom or a relevant office-holder by provisions made by or under this Part.

(3) Subsection (2) does not affect the recognition or enforcement of a judgment required to be recognised or enforced under or by virtue of the Civil Jurisdiction and Judgments Act 1982 . . .

NOTES

Sub-s (3): words omitted repealed by the Financial Markets and Insolvency (Amendment and Transitional Provision) (EU Exit) Regulations 2019, SI 2019/341, reg 2(1), (6), as from IP completion day (as defined in the European Union (Withdrawal Agreement) Act 2020, s 39).

[5.181]

184 Indemnity for certain acts, &c

(1) Where a relevant office-holder takes any action in relation to property of a defaulter which is liable to be dealt with in accordance with the default rules of a [recognised body], and believes and has reasonable grounds for believing that he is entitled to take that action, he is not liable to any person in respect of any loss or damage resulting from his action except in so far as the loss or damage is caused by the office-holder's own negligence.

(2) Any failure by a [recognised body] to comply with its own rules in respect of any matter shall not prevent that matter being treated for the purposes of this Part as done in accordance with those rules so long as the failure does not substantially affect the rights of any person entitled to require compliance with the rules.

(3) No [recognised body], nor any officer or servant or member of the governing body of a [recognised body], shall be liable in damages for anything done or omitted in the discharge or purported discharge of any functions to which this subsection applies unless the act or omission is shown to have been in bad faith.

(4) The functions to which subsection (3) applies are the functions of [the recognised body] so far as relating to, or to matters arising out of—

(a) its default rules, or

(b) any obligations to which it is subject by virtue of this Part.

(5) No person [to whom the exercise of any function of a [recognised body] is delegated under its default rules], nor any officer or servant of such a person, shall be liable in damages for anything done or omitted in the discharge or purported discharge of those functions unless the act or omission is shown to have been in bad faith.

NOTES

Words "recognised body" and "the recognised body" in square brackets substituted by the Central Securities Depositories Regulations 2017, SI 2017/1064, reg 3(1), (23), as from 28 November 2017.

Other words in square brackets in sub-s (5) substituted by the Financial Services and Markets Act 2000 (Consequential Amendments and Repeals) Order 2001, SI 2001/3649, art 87, as from 1 December 2001.

[5.182]

185 Power to make further provision by regulations

(1) The Secretary of State may by regulations make such further provision as appears to him necessary or expedient for the purposes of this Part.

(2) Provision may, in particular, be made—

(a) for integrating the provisions of this Part with the general law of insolvency, and

(b) for adapting the provisions of this Part in their application to overseas investment exchanges and clearing houses.

(3) Regulations under this section may add to, amend or repeal any of the provisions of this Part or provide that those provisions have effect subject to such additions, exceptions or adaptations as are specified in the regulations.

[(4) References in this section to the provisions of this Part include any provision made under section 301 of the Financial Services and Markets Act 2000.]

NOTES

Sub-s (4): added by the Financial Services and Markets Act 2000 (Consequential Amendments and Repeals) Order 2001, SI 2001/3649, art 88, as from 1 December 2001.

Regulations: the Financial Markets and Insolvency Regulations 1991, SI 1991/880 at **[6.8]**; the Financial Markets and Insolvency Regulations 1996, SI 1996/1469; the Financial Markets and Insolvency Regulations 1998, SI 1998/1748; the Financial Markets and Insolvency (CGO Service) Regulations 1999, SI 1999/1209; the Financial Markets and Insolvency Regulations 2009, SI 2009/853; the Financial Services and Markets Act 2000 (Over the Counter Derivatives, Central Counterparties and Trade Repositories) Regulations 2013, SI 2013/504; the Financial Services and Markets Act 2000 (Over the Counter Derivatives, Central Counterparties and Trade Repositories) (No 2) Regulations 2013, SI 2013/1908.

[5.183]

186 Supplementary provisions as to regulations

(1) Regulations under this Part may make different provision for different cases and may contain such incidental, transitional and other supplementary provisions as appear to the Secretary of State to be necessary or expedient.

(2) Regulations under this Part shall be made by statutory instrument which shall be subject to annulment in pursuance of a resolution of either House of Parliament.

[5.184]

187 Construction of references to parties to market contracts

(1) Where a person enters into market contracts in more than one capacity, the provisions of this Part apply (subject as follows) as if the contracts entered into in each different capacity were entered into by different persons.

(2) References in this Part to a market contract to which a person is a party include (subject as follows, and unless the context otherwise requires) contracts to which he is party as agent.

[(2A) Subsections (1) and (2) do not apply to market contracts to which this Part applies by virtue of section 155(2B).]

(3) The Secretary of State may by regulations—

(a) modify or exclude the operation of subsections (1) and (2), and

(b) make provision as to the circumstances in which a person is to be regarded for the purposes of those provisions as acting in different capacities.

NOTES

Sub-s (2A): inserted by the Financial Services and Markets Act 2000 (Over the Counter Derivatives, Central Counterparties and Trade Repositories) Regulations 2013, SI 2013/504, reg 4(1), (16), as from 1 April 2013.

Regulations: the Financial Markets and Insolvency Regulations 1991, SI 1991/880 at **[6.8]**; the Financial Markets and Insolvency (Amendment) Regulations 1992, SI 1992/716; the Financial Markets and Insolvency Regulations 2009, SI 2009/853; the Financial Services and Markets Act 2000 (Over the Counter Derivatives, Central Counterparties and Trade Repositories) Regulations 2013, SI 2013/504; the Financial Services and Markets Act 2000 (Over the Counter Derivatives, Central Counterparties and Trade Repositories) (No 2) Regulations 2013, SI 2013/1908.

[5.185]

188 Meaning of "default rules" and related expressions

(1) In this Part "default rules" means rules of a [recognised body] which provide for the taking of action in the event of a person [(including another [recognised body]] appearing to be unable, or likely to become unable, to meet his obligations in respect of one or more market contracts [connected with [the recognised body] . . . .]

[(1A) In the case of a recognised central counterparty, "default rules" includes—

(a) the default procedures referred to in Article 48 of the EMIR Level 1 Regulation; and

(b) any rules of the recognised central counterparty which provide for the taking of action in accordance with a request or instruction from a clearing member under the default procedures referred to in [Article 4(6) and (7) of the EMIR Level 2 Regulation or Article 4(6) and (7) of the MIFIR Level 2 Regulation] in respect of assets or positions held by the recognised central counterparty for the account of an indirect client or group of indirect clients.]

[(1B) In the case of a recognised CSD, "default rules" includes the default rules and procedures referred to in Article 41 of the CSD regulation.]

(2) References in this Part to a "defaulter" are to a person in respect of whom action has been taken by [a recognised body] under its default rules, whether by declaring him to be a defaulter or otherwise; and references in this Part to "default"[, "defaulting" and "non-defaulting"] shall be construed accordingly.

[(2A) For the purposes of subsection (2), where a recognised central counterparty takes action under the rules referred to in subsection (1A)(b), the action is to be treated as taken in respect of the client providing the indirect clearing services.]

(3) In this Part "default proceedings" means proceedings taken by [a recognised body] under its default rules.

[(3A) In this Part "default fund contribution" means—

(a) contribution by a member or designated non-member of a recognised investment exchange to a fund which—
   (i) is maintained by that exchange for the purpose of covering losses arising in connection with defaults by any of the members of the exchange, or defaults by any of the members or designated non-members of the exchange, and
   (ii) may be applied for that purpose under the default rules of the exchange;
(b) contribution by a member of a recognised clearing house to a fund which—
   (i) is maintained by that clearing house for the purpose of covering losses arising in connection with defaults by any of the members of the clearing house, and
   (ii) may be applied for that purpose under the default rules of the clearing house;
(c) contribution by a recognised clearing house to a fund which—
   [(i) is maintained by another recognised body (A) for the purpose of covering losses arising in connection with defaults by recognised bodies other than A or by any of their members, and]
   (ii) may be applied for that purpose under A's default rules; . . .
(d) contribution by a recognised investment exchange to a fund which—
   [(i) is maintained by another recognised body (A) for the purpose of covering losses arising in connection with defaults by recognised bodies other than A or by any of their members, and]
   (ii) may be applied for that purpose under A's default rules];
[(e) contribution by a member of a recognised CSD to a fund which—
   (i) is maintained by that central securities depository for the purpose of covering losses arising in connection with defaults by any of the members of the central securities depository, and
   (ii) may be applied for that purpose under the default rules of the central securities depository; or
(f) contribution by a recognised CSD to a fund which—
   (i) is maintained by another recognised body (A) for the purpose of covering losses arising in connection with defaults by recognised bodies other than A or by any of their members, and
   (ii) may be applied for that purpose under A's default rules].

(4) If [a recognised body] takes action under its default rules in respect of a person, all subsequent proceedings under its rules for the purposes of or in connection with the settlement of market contracts to which the defaulter is a party shall be treated as done under its default rules.

NOTES

Sub-s (1): words "recognised body" and "the recognised body" in square brackets substituted by the Central Securities Depositories Regulations 2017, SI 2017/1064, reg 3(1), (24)(a), as from 28 November 2017. Words in second (outer) pair of square brackets inserted by the Financial Markets and Insolvency Regulations 2009, SI 2009/853, reg 2(1), (15)(a), as from 15 June 2009. Words in fourth (outer) of square brackets substituted by the Financial Services and Markets Act 2000 (Over the Counter Derivatives, Central Counterparties and Trade Repositories) Regulations 2013, SI 2013/504, reg 4(1), (17)(a), as from 1 April 2013. Words omitted repealed by the Financial Services and Markets Act 2000 (Over the Counter Derivatives, Central Counterparties and Trade Repositories) (No 2) Regulations 2013, SI 2013/1908, reg 2(1), (10)(a), as from 26 August 2013.

Sub-ss (1A), (2A): inserted by SI 2013/1908, reg 2(1), (10)(b), (c), as from 26 August 2013. Words in square brackets in sub-s (1A)(b) substituted by the Companies Act 1989 (Financial Markets and Insolvency) (Amendment) Regulations 2017, SI 2017/1247, reg 2(1), (4), as from 3 January 2018.

Sub-s (1B): inserted by SI 2017/1064, reg 3(1), (24)(b), as from 28 November 2017.

Sub-s (2): words in first pair of square brackets substituted by SI 2017/1064, reg 3(1), (24)(c), as from 28 November 2017. Words in second pair of square brackets inserted by SI 2013/504, reg 4(1), (17)(b), as from 1 April 2013.

Sub-ss (3), (4): words in square brackets substituted by SI 2017/1064, reg 3(1), (24)(c), (e), as from 28 November 2017.

Sub-s (3A): inserted by SI 2009/853, reg 2(1), (15)(b), as from 15 June 2009. Words in square brackets substituted or inserted, and words omitted repealed, by SI 2017/1064, reg 3(1), (24)(d), as from 28 November 2017.

[5.186]

189 Meaning of "relevant office-holder"

(1) The following are relevant office-holders for the purposes of this Part—

(a) the official receiver,
(b) any person acting in relation to a company as its liquidator, provisional liquidator, administrator or administrative receiver,
(c) any person acting in relation to an individual (or, in Scotland, any debtor within the meaning of the Bankruptcy (Scotland) Act [2016]) as his trustee in bankruptcy or interim receiver of his property or as [trustee] or interim trustee in the sequestration of his estate,
(d) any person acting as administrator of an insolvent estate of a deceased person.

(2) In subsection (1)(b) "company" means any company, society, association, partnership or other body which may be wound up under the Insolvency Act 1986.

NOTES

Sub-s (1): year "2016" in square brackets substituted, and word "trustee" in square brackets substituted, by the Bankruptcy (Scotland) Act 2016 (Consequential Provisions and Modifications) Order 2016, SI 2016/1034, art 7(1), (3), Sch 1, para 6(1), (10), as from 30 November 2016 (except in relation to (i) a sequestration as regards which the petition is presented, or the debtor application is made before that date; or (ii) a trust deed executed before that date).

[5.187]

[189A Meaning of "transfer"

(1) In this Part, a reference to a transfer of a clearing member client contract, a client trade or a qualifying collateral arrangement shall be interpreted in accordance with this section.

(2) A transfer of a clearing member client contract or client trade includes—

(a) an assignment;

(b) a novation; and

(c) terminating or closing out the clearing member client contract or client trade and establishing an equivalent position between different parties.

(3) Where a clearing member client contract is recorded in the accounts of a recognised central counterparty as a position held for the account of an indirect client or group of indirect clients, the clearing member client contract is to be treated as having been transferred if the position is transferred to a different account at the recognised central counterparty.

(4) A reference to a transfer of a qualifying collateral arrangement includes an assignment or a novation.]

NOTES

Inserted by the Financial Services and Markets Act 2000 (Over the Counter Derivatives, Central Counterparties and Trade Repositories) (No 2) Regulations 2013, SI 2013/1908, reg 2(1), (11), as from 26 August 2013.

[5.188]

190 Minor definitions

(1) In this Part—

"administrative receiver" has the meaning given by section 251 of the Insolvency Act 1986;

[. . .]

"charge" means any form of security, including a mortgage and, in Scotland, a heritable security;

["clearing member", in relation to a recognised central counterparty, has the meaning given by Article 2(14) of the EMIR Level 1 Regulation;]

["client" has the meaning given by Article 2(15) of the EMIR Level 1 Regulation;]

["CSD regulation" means Regulation (EU) No 909/2014 of the European Parliament and of the Council of 23 July 2014 on improving securities settlement in the European Union and on central securities depositories;]

[. . . "recognised central counterparty", "recognised CSD", "recognised clearing house", "recognised investment exchange"[, "third country central counterparty"] and "third country CSD" have the same meaning as in the Financial Services and Markets Act 2000 (see section 285 of that Act);]

["EMIR Level 1 Regulation" means Regulation (EU) No 648/2012 of the European Parliament and of the Council of 4 July 2012 on OTC derivatives, central counterparties and trade repositories;]

["EMIR Level 2 Regulation" means Commission Delegated Regulation (EU) No 149/2013 of 19 December 2012 supplementing Regulation (EU) No 648/2012 of the European Parliament and of the Council of 4 July 2012 with regard to regulatory technical standards on indirect clearing arrangements, the clearing obligation, the public register, access to a trading venue, non-financial counterparties, risk mitigation for OTC derivatives contracts not cleared by a CCP [as amended by Commission Delegated Regulation (EU) 2017/2155 of 22 September 2017];]

["the FCA" means the Financial Conduct Authority;]

["indirect clearing services" has the same meaning as in the EMIR Level 2 Regulation;]

["indirect client" has the meaning given by Article 1(a) of the EMIR Level 2 Regulation;]

["interim trustee" has the same meaning as in the Bankruptcy (Scotland) Act 2016;]

. . .

["member", in relation to a central securities depository, means a participant of that central securities depository as defined in Article 2(1)(19) of the CSD regulation;]

["member of a clearing house" includes a clearing member of a recognised central counterparty;]

[MIFIR Level 2 Regulation" means Commission Delegated Regulation (EU) 2017/2154 of 22 September 2017 supplementing Regulation (EU) No 600/2014 of the European Parliament and of the Council with regard to regulatory technical standards on indirect clearing arrangements;]

"overseas", in relation to an investment exchange or clearing house [or central securities depository], means having its head office outside the United Kingdom;

["position" has the same meaning as in the EMIR Level 1 Regulation;]

["the PRA" means the Prudential Regulation Authority;]

["recognised body" has the same meaning as in section 313 of the Financial Services and Markets Act 2000;]

["sequestration" means sequestration under the Bankruptcy (Scotland) Act 2016;]

. . .

"set-off", in relation to Scotland, includes compensation;

["The Stock Exchange" means the London Stock Exchange Limited;]

["UK", in relation to an investment exchange, means having its head office in the United Kingdom].

[(2) References in this Part to settlement—

(a) mean, in relation to a market contract, the discharge of the rights and liabilities of the parties to the contract, whether by performance, compromise or otherwise;

(b) include, in relation to a clearing member client contract or a clearing member house contract, a reference to its liquidation for the purposes of Article 48 of the EMIR Level 1 Regulation.]

(3) In this Part the expressions "margin" and "cover for margin" have the same meaning.

[(3A)], (4) . . .

(5) For the purposes of this Part a person shall be taken to have notice of a matter if he deliberately failed to make enquiries as to that matter in circumstances in which a reasonable and honest person would have done so.

This does not apply for the purposes of a provision requiring "actual notice".

[(6) References in this Part to the law of insolvency—

(a) include references to every provision made by or under the Insolvency Act 1986 or the Bankruptcy (Scotland) Act [2016]; and in relation to a building society references to insolvency law or to any provision of the Insolvency Act 1986 are to that law or provision as modified by the Building Societies Act 1986;

(b) are also to be interpreted in accordance with the modifications made by the enactments mentioned in subsection (6B).

(6A) For the avoidance of doubt, references in this Part to administration, administrator, liquidator and winding up are to be interpreted in accordance with the modifications made by the enactments mentioned in subsection (6B).

(6B) The enactments referred to in subsections (6)(b) and (6A) are—

(a) article 3 of, and the Schedule to, the Banking Act 2009 (Parts 2 and 3 Consequential Amendments) Order 2009;

(b) article 18 of, and paragraphs 1(a), (2) and (3) of Schedule 2 to, the Building Societies (Insolvency and Special Administration) Order 2009; and

(c) regulation 27 of, and Schedule 6 to, the Investment Bank Special Administration Regulations 2011.]

(7) In relation to Scotland, references in this Part—

(a) to sequestration include references to the administration by a judicial factor of the insolvent estate of a deceased person, and

(b) to an interim [trustee or to a trustee in the sequestration of an estate] include references to a judicial factor on the insolvent estate of a deceased person,

unless the context otherwise requires.

NOTES

Sub-s (1) is amended as follows:

Definition "the Authority" (omitted) originally inserted by the Financial Services and Markets Act 2000 (Consequential Amendments and Repeals) Order 2001, SI 2001/3649, art 89(1), (2), as from 1 December 2001, and repealed by the Financial Services Act 2012, s 114(1), Sch 18, Pt 2, paras 62, 70(1), (2), as from 1 April 2013.

Definitions "clearing house", "investment and investment exchange" and "recognised" (omitted) repealed by SI 2001/3649, art 89(1), (3), as from 1 December 2001.

Definitions "clearing member", "client", "EMIR Level 1 Regulation", "EMIR Level 2 Regulation", "indirect client", "member of a clearing house", and "position" inserted by the Financial Services and Markets Act 2000 (Over the Counter Derivatives, Central Counterparties and Trade Repositories) Regulations 2013, SI 2013/504, reg 4(1), (18)(a), as from 1 April 2013.

Definitions "CSD regulation", "member" and "recognised body" inserted, by the Central Securities Depositories Regulations 2017, SI 2017/1064, reg 3(1), (25)(a), as from 28 November 2017.

The group of definitions that now begins with the definition "recognised central counterparty" was originally substituted by SI 2017/1064, reg 3(1), (25)(c), as from 28 November 2017. The words omitted from these definitions were repealed, and the words in square brackets were inserted, by the Financial Markets and Insolvency (Amendment and Transitional Provision) (EU Exit) Regulations 2019, SI 2019/341, reg 2(1), (7), as from IP completion day (as defined in the European Union (Withdrawal Agreement) Act 2020, s 39).

Words in square brackets in the definition "EMIR Level 2 Regulation" inserted, and definition "MIFIR Level 2 Regulation" inserted, by the Companies Act 1989 (Financial Markets and Insolvency) (Amendment) Regulations 2017, SI 2017/1247, reg 2(1), (5), as from 3 January 2018.

Definitions "the FCA" and "the PRA" inserted by the Financial Services Act 2012, s 114(1), Sch 18, Pt 2, paras 62, 70(1), (3), (4), as from 1 April 2013.

Definition "indirect clearing services" inserted by the Financial Services and Markets Act 2000 (Over the Counter Derivatives, Central Counterparties and Trade Repositories) (No 2) Regulations 2013, SI 2013/1908, reg 2(1), (12)(a), as from 26 August 2013.

Definition "interim trustee" substituted (for the original definitions "interim trustee" and "permanent trustee") by the Bankruptcy (Scotland) Act 2016 (Consequential Provisions and Modifications) Order 2016, SI 2016/1034, art 7(1), (3), Sch 1, para 6(1), (11)(a)(i), as from 30 November 2016 (except in relation to (i) a sequestration as regards which the petition is presented, or the debtor application is made before that date; or (ii) a trust deed executed before that date).

Words in square brackets in the definition "overseas" inserted by SI 2017/1064, reg 3(1), (25)(b), as from 28 November 2017.

Definition "sequestration" inserted by SI 2016/1034, art 7(1), (3), Sch 1, para 6(1), (11)(a)(ii), as from 30 November 2016 (except in relation to (i) a sequestration as regards which the petition is presented, or the debtor application is made before that date; or (ii) a trust deed executed before that date).

Definition "The Stock Exchange" substituted by SI 2001/3649, art 89(1), (5), as from 1 December 2001.

Definition "UK" substituted by SI 2013/504, reg 4(1), (18)(b)(ii), as from 1 April 2013.

Sub-s (2): substituted by SI 2013/504, reg 4(1), (18)(c), as from 1 April 2013.

Sub-s (3A): originally inserted by SI 2013/504, reg 4(1), (18)(d), as from 1 April 2013, and subsequently repealed by SI 2013/1908, reg 2(1), (12)(b), as from 26 August 2013.

Sub-s (4): repealed by SI 2001/3649, art 89(1), (6), as from 1 December 2001.

Sub-ss (6), (6A)–(6C): substituted (for the original sub-s (6)) by SI 2013/504, reg 4(1), (18)(e), as from 1 April 2013. Year "2016" in square brackets in sub-s (6)(a) substituted by SI 2016/1034, art 7(1), (3), Sch 1, para 6(1), (11)(b), as from 30 November 2016 (except in relation to (i) a sequestration as regards which the petition is presented, or the debtor application is made before that date; or (ii) a trust deed executed before that date).

Sub-s (7): words in square brackets substituted by SI 2016/1034, art 7(1), (3), Sch 1, para 6(1), (11)(c), as from 30 November 2016 (except in relation to (i) a sequestration as regards which the petition is presented, or the debtor application is made before that date; or (ii) a trust deed executed before that date).

[5.189]

191 Index of defined expressions

The following Table shows provisions defining or otherwise explaining expressions used in this Part (other than provisions defining or explaining an expression used only in the same section or paragraph)—

[Defined Expression	Section
administration	Sections 190(6A) and (6B)
administrator	Sections 190(6A) and (6B)
administrative receiver	Section 190(1)
[authorised central securities depository services	Section 155(3D)]
charge	Section 190(1)
clearing member	Section 190(1)
clearing member client contract	Section 155(1)(a)
clearing member house contract	Section 155(1)(b)
client	Section 190(1)
client trade	Section 155(1)(c)
cover for margin	Section 190(3)
[CSD regulation	Section 190(1)]
default fund contribution	Section 188(3A)
default rules (and related expressions)	Section 188
designated non-member	Section 155(2)
[. . .	. . .]
EMIR Level 1 Regulation	Section 190(1)
EMIR Level 2 Regulation	Section 190(1)
the FCA	Section 190(1)
[indirect clearing services	Section 190(1)]
indirect client	Section 190(1)
insolvency law (and similar expressions)	Sections 190(6) and (6B)
interim trustee	Sections 190(1) and 190(7)(b)
liquidator	Sections 190(6A) and (6B)
margin	Section 190(3)
market charge	Section 173
market contract	Section 155
[member (in relation to a central securities depository)	Section 190(1)]
member of a clearing house	Section 190(1)
[MIFIR Level 2 Regulation	Section 190(1)]
notice	Section 190(5)
overseas (in relation to investment exchanges[, clearing houses and central securities depositories]	Section 190(1)
party (in relation to a market contract)	Section 187
. . .	. . .
the PRA	Section 190(1)
qualifying collateral arrangement	Section 155A(1)(a)
qualifying property transfers	Section 155A(1)(b)
[recognised body	Section 190(1)]
recognised central counterparty	Section 190(1)
recognised clearing house	Section 190(1)
[recognised CSD	Section 190(1)]
recognised investment exchange	Section 190(1)
relevant office-holder	Section 189
sequestration	Section 190(7)(a)
set off (in relation to Scotland)	Section 190(1)
settlement and related expressions (in relation to a market contract)	Section 190 (2)
The Stock Exchange	Section 190(1)
[third country central counterparty	Section 190(1)]
[third country CSD	Section 190(1)]
[transfer	Section 189A]
[interim trustee and trustee in the sequestration of an estate (in relation to Scotland)	section 190(1) and (7)(b)]

[Defined Expression	Section
UK (in relation to investment exchanges)	Section 190(1)
winding up	Sections 190(6A) and (6B)]

NOTES

The table was substituted by the Financial Services and Markets Act 2000 (Over the Counter Derivatives, Central Counterparties and Trade Repositories) Regulations 2013, SI 2013/504, reg 4(1), (19), Schedule, as from 1 April 2013.

Entries "authorised central securities depository services", "CSD regulation", "member (in relation to a central securities depository)", "recognised body", "recognised CSD", and "third country CSD" inserted, and words in square brackets in the entry "overseas" inserted, by the Central Securities Depositories Regulations 2017, SI 2017/1064, reg 3(1), (26), as from 28 November 2017.

Entry "EEA CSD" (omitted) originally inserted by SI 2017/1064, reg 3(1), (26), as from 28 November 2017. Subsequently repealed by the Financial Markets and Insolvency (Amendment and Transitional Provision) (EU Exit) Regulations 2019, SI 2019/341, reg 2(1), (8)(a), as from IP completion day (as defined in the European Union (Withdrawal Agreement) Act 2020, s 39).

Entries "indirect clearing services" and "transfer" inserted by the Financial Services and Markets Act 2000 (Over the Counter Derivatives, Central Counterparties and Trade Repositories) (No 2) Regulations 2013, SI 2013/1908, reg 2(1), (13), as from 26 August 2013.

Entry "MIFIR Level 2 Regulation" inserted by the Companies Act 1989 (Financial Markets and Insolvency) (Amendment) Regulations 2017, SI 2017/1247, reg 2(1), (6), as from 3 January 2018.

Entry "permanent trustee" (omitted) repealed, and entry in square brackets beginning "interim trustee and trustee" substituted, by the Bankruptcy (Scotland) Act 2016 (Consequential Provisions and Modifications) Order 2016, SI 2016/1034, art 7(1), (3), Sch 1, para 6(1), (12), as from 30 November 2016 (except in relation to (i) a sequestration as regards which the petition is presented, or the debtor application is made before that date; or (ii) a trust deed executed before that date).

Entry "third country central counterparty" inserted by SI 2019/341, reg 2(1), (8)(b), as from IP completion day (as defined in the European Union (Withdrawal Agreement) Act 2020, s 39).

192–207 *(Ss 192–206 (Pt VIII: Amendments of FSA 1986): ss 192–197 repealed by the Financial Services and Markets Act 2000 (Consequential Amendments and Repeals) Order 2001, SI 2001/3649, art 75(i), as from 1 December 2001; ss 198, 199 repealed by the Public Offers of Securities Regulations 1995, SI 1995/1537, reg 17, Sch 2, Pt II, para 10, as from 19 June 1995; s 200 repealed in part by SI 2001/3649, art 75(j), as from 1 December 2001 and the reminder of the section is effectively spent (it amended the Civil Jurisdiction and Judgments Act 1982 by inserting a reference to FSA 1986, s 188 into Sch 5 to the 1982 Act – that reference has now been superseded by a reference to FSMA 2000, s 415); ss 201–206 repealed by SI 2001/3649, art 75(k), as from 1 December 2001. S 207 (Pt IX: Transfer of Securities) repealed by the Companies Act 2006, s 1295, Sch 16, as from 6 April 2008. Note that by virtue of the Companies Act 2006, s 1297 (continuity of law) the Uncertificated Securities Regulations 2001, SI 2001/3755 (at* **[6.40]***) and the Uncertificated Securities (Amendment) (Eligible Debt Securities) Regulations 2003, SI 2003/1633 which were made under this section now have effect as if made under ss 783, 784(3), 785 and 788 of the 2006 Act.)*

PART X MISCELLANEOUS AND GENERAL PROVISIONS

208–211 *(S 208 adds the Company Directors Disqualification Act 1986, s 21(4) at* **[5.116]***; s 209 repealed by the Criminal Justice Act 1993, s 79(14), Sch 6, Pt I, as from 1 March 1994; s 210 spent (amended the Policyholders Protection Act 1975, Sch 3 (repealed)); s 211 amends the Building Societies Act 1986, s 104, Sch 15 and inserts the Company Directors Disqualification Act 1986, s 22A at* **[5.121]***.)*

General

[5.190]

[211A "Bank of England"

In this Act references to the Bank of England do not include the Bank acting in its capacity as the Prudential Regulation Authority.]

NOTES

Inserted by the Bank of England and Financial Services (Consequential Amendments) Regulations 2017, SI 2017/80, reg 2, Schedule, Pt 1, para 3(a), as from 1 March 2017.

212–214 *(S 212 introduces Sch 24 (Repeals). S 213 (Provisions extending to Northern Ireland) is outside the scope of this work. S 214 repealed by the Financial Services and Markets Act 2000 (Consequential Amendments and Repeals) Order 2001, SI 2001/3649, art 75(m), as from 1 December 2001.)*

[5.191]

215 Commencement and transitional provisions

(1) The following provisions of this Act come into force on Royal Assent—

- (a) in Part V (amendments of company law), section 141 (application to declare dissolution of company void);
- (b) in Part VI (mergers)—
  - (i) sections 147 to 150, and
  - (ii) paragraphs 2 to 12, 14 to 16, 18 to 20, 22 to 25 of Schedule 20, and section 153 so far as relating to those paragraphs;
- (c) in Part VIII (amendments of the Financial Services Act 1986), section 202 (offers of short-dated debentures);
- (d) in Part X (miscellaneous and general provisions), the repeals made by Schedule 24 in sections 71, 74, 88 and 89 of, and Schedule 9 to, the Fair Trading Act 1973, and section 212 so far as relating to those repeals.

(2) The other provisions of this Act come into force on such day as the Secretary of State may appoint by order made by statutory instrument; and different days may be appointed for different provisions and different purposes.

(3) An order bringing into force any provision may contain such transitional provisions and savings as appear to the Secretary of State to be necessary or expedient.

(4) The Secretary of State may also by order under this section amend any enactment which refers to the commencement of a provision brought into force by the order so as to substitute a reference to the actual date on which it comes into force.

NOTES

Transfer of functions: as to the exercise of functions under this section, see the Transfer of Functions (Financial Services) Order 1992, SI 1992/1315, art 2(2)(c).

Financial Services Act 1986: repealed by the Financial Services and Markets Act 2000 (Consequential Amendments and Repeals) Order 2001, SI 2001/3649, art 3(1)(c), as from 1 December 2001.

Orders: the Companies Act 1989 (Commencement No 1) Order 1990, SI 1990/98; the Companies Act 1989 (Commencement No 2) Order 1990, SI 1990/142 (as amended by SI 1990/355); the Companies Act 1989 (Commencement No 3, Transitional Provisions and Transfer of Functions under the Financial Services Act 1986) Order 1990, SI 1990/354; the Companies Act 1989 (Commencement No 4, Transitional and Saving Provisions) Order 1990, SI 1990/355 (as amended by SI 1990/1707, SI 1990/2569, SI 1993/3246); the Companies Act 1989 (Commencement No 5 and Transitional and Saving Provisions) Order 1990, SI 1990/713; the Companies Act 1989 (Commencement No 6 and Transitional and Savings Provisions) Order 1990, SI 1990/1392 (as amended by SI 1990/1707); the Companies Act 1989 (Commencement No 7, Transitional and Saving Provisions) Order 1990, SI 1990/1707; the Companies Act 1989 (Commencement No 8 and Transitional and Saving Provisions) Order 1990, SI 1990/2569; the Companies Act 1989 (Commencement No 9 and Saving and Transitional Provisions) Order 1991, SI 1991/488; the Companies Act 1989 (Commencement No 10 and Saving Provisions) Order 1991, SI 1991/878; the Companies Act 1989 (Commencement No 11) Order 1991, SI 1991/1452; the Companies Act 1989 (Commencement No 12 and Transitional Provision) Order 1991, SI 1991/1996; the Companies Act 1989 (Commencement No 13) Order 1991, SI 1991/2173; the Companies Act 1989 (Commencement No 14 and Transitional Provision) Order 1991, SI 1991/2945; the Companies Act 1989 (Commencement No 15 and Transitional and Savings Provisions) Order 1995, SI 1995/1352; the Companies Act 1989 (Commencement No 16) Order 1995, SI 1995/1591; the Companies Act 1989 (Commencement No 17) Order 1998, SI 1998/1747; the Companies (Audit, Investigations and Community Enterprise) Act 2004 (Commencement) and Companies Act 1989 (Commencement No 18) Order 2004, SI 2004/3322 at **[6.90]**.

[5.192]

216 Short title

This Act may be cited as the Companies Act 1989.

SCHEDULES

SCHEDULES 1–24

(Schs 1–9 repealed by the Companies Act 2006, s 1295, Sch 16, as from 6 April 2008. Sch 10 (Amendments consequential on Part I) contains various amendments to CA 1985 and other legislation which, in so far as relevant to this work, and still in force, are incorporated at the appropriate place. Schs 11, 12 repealed by CA 2006, s 1295, Sch 16, as from 6 April 2008 (except in relation to the supervision and qualification of auditors appointed for financial years beginning before that date, see SI 2007/3495, Sch 4, Pt 1, para 38). Sch 13 repealed by CA 2006, s 1295, Sch 16, as from 6 April 2008 (but this repeal does not affect the operation of this Schedule in relation to functions exercised under Part II of this Act on or after that date, see SI 2007/3495, Sch 4, Pt 1, para 42(1)). Sch 14 repealed by the Competition Act 1998 and other enactments (Amendment) Regulations 2004, SI 2004/1261, reg 5, Sch 2, para 2(1), (2), as from 1 May 2004. Schs 15, 16 repealed by CA 2006, ss 1180, 1295, Sch 16, as from 1 October 2009. Sch 17 repealed by CA 2006, s 1295, Sch 16, as from 6 April 2007 (in part), as from 6 April 2008 (in part), and as from 1 October 2009 (otherwise). Sch 18 ("Subsidiary" and Related Expressions: Consequential Amendments and Savings) was repealed by CA 2006, s 1295, Sch 16, as from 1 October 2007 (in part), and as from 1 October 2009 (in part) and, in so far as still in force, it is now outside the scope of this work. Sch 19 (Minor Amendments of the Companies Act 1985) makes various amendments to CA 1985 which have been incorporated at the appropriate place (note that most of this Schedule is repealed by the Companies Act 2006, s 1295, Sch 16, as from 1 October 2007 (in part), as from 6 April 2008 (in part), and as from 1 October 2009 (otherwise), though a small number of paragraphs remain in force for limited purposes); Sch 20 (Amendments about Mergers and Related Matters) this Schedule has been repealed, or is spent, except in so far as it relates to a minor amendment to the Fair Trading Act 1973, s 132; Schs 21–23 repealed by the Financial Services and Markets Act 2000 (Consequential Amendments and Repeals) Order 2001, SI 2001/3649, art 75(p)–(r), as from 1 December 2001; Sch 24 contains various repeals to the Harbours Act 1964, the Fair Trading Act 1973, CA 1985, the Insolvency Act 1985, the Insolvency Act 1986, the Building Societies Act 1986, the Company Directors Disqualification Act 1986, FSA 1986, the Banking Act 1987, the Criminal Justice (Scotland) Act 1987, ICTA 1988, the Criminal Justice Act 1988, and the Copyright, Designs and Patents Act 1988 and, in so far as relevant to this work, are incorporated at the appropriate place.)

CRIMINAL JUSTICE ACT 1993

(1993 c 36)

NOTES

This Act is reproduced as amended by: the Financial Services and Markets Act 2000 (Consequential Amendments and Repeals) Order 2001, SI 2001/3649; the Companies Act 2006 (Consequential Amendments, Transitional Provisions and Savings) Order 2009, SI 2009/1941; the Financial Services and Markets Act 2000 (Market Abuse) Regulations 2016, SI 2016/680; the Market Abuse (Amendment) (EU Exit) Regulations 2019, SI 2019/310; the Financial Services (Miscellaneous) (Amendment) (EU Exit) (No 3) Regulations 2019, SI 2019/1390; the Financial Services Act 2021.

Only those provisions of this Act relating to company law are reproduced. Provisions not reproduced are not annotated. The provisions of Part V (including Schs 1, 2) came into force on 1 March 1994 (see the Criminal Justice Act 1993 (Commencement No 5) Order 1994, SI 1994/242 which was made under s 78 of this Act). By virtue of s 79 (Short title, extent etc) Part V applies to the whole of the UK.

ARRANGEMENT OF SECTIONS

PART V
INSIDER DEALING

The offence of insider dealing

An Act to make provision about the jurisdiction of courts in England and Wales in relation to certain offences of dishonesty and blackmail; to amend the law about drug trafficking offences and to implement provisions of the Community Council Directive No 91/308/EEC; to amend Part VI of the Criminal Justice Act 1988; to make provision with respect to the financing of terrorism, the proceeds of terrorist-related activities and the investigation of terrorist activities; to amend Part I of the Criminal Justice Act 1991; to implement provisions of the Community Council Directive No 89/592/EEC and to amend and restate the law about insider dealing in securities; to provide for certain offences created by the Banking Coordination (Second Council Directive) Regulations 1992 to be punishable in the same way as offences under sections 39, 40 and 41 of the Banking Act 1987 and to enable regulations implementing Article 15 of the Community Council Directive No 89/646/EEC and Articles 3, 6 and 7 of the Community Council Directive No 92/30/EEC to create offences punishable in that way; to make provision with respect to the penalty for causing death by dangerous driving or causing death by careless driving while under the influence of drink or drugs; to make it an offence to assist in or induce certain conduct which for the purposes of, or in connection with, the provisions of Community law is unlawful in another member State; to provide for the introduction of safeguards in connection with the return of persons under backing of warrants arrangements; to amend the Criminal Procedure (Scotland) Act 1975 and Part I of the Prisoners and Criminal Proceedings (Scotland) Act 1993; and for connected purposes

[27 July 1993]

PART V INSIDER DEALING

The offence of insider dealing

[5.193]

52 The offence

(1) An individual who has information as an insider is guilty of insider dealing if, in the circumstances mentioned in subsection (3), he deals in securities that are price-affected securities in relation to the information.

(2) An individual who has information as an insider is also guilty of insider dealing if—

(a) he encourages another person to deal in securities that are (whether or not that other knows it) price-affected securities in relation to the information, knowing or having reasonable cause to believe that the dealing would take place in the circumstances mentioned in subsection (3); or

(b) he discloses the information, otherwise than in the proper performance of the functions of his employment, office or profession, to another person.

(3) The circumstances referred to above are that the acquisition or disposal in question occurs on a regulated market, or that the person dealing relies on a professional intermediary or is himself acting as a professional intermediary.

(4) This section has effect subject to section 53.

[5.194]

53 Defences

(1) An individual is not guilty of insider dealing by virtue of dealing in securities if he shows—

(a) that he did not at the time expect the dealing to result in a profit attributable to the fact that the information in question was price-sensitive information in relation to the securities, or

(b) that at the time he believed on reasonable grounds that the information had been disclosed widely enough to ensure that none of those taking part in the dealing would be prejudiced by not having the information, or

(c) that he would have done what he did even if he had not had the information.

(2) An individual is not guilty of insider dealing by virtue of encouraging another person to deal in securities if he shows—

(a) that he did not at the time expect the dealing to result in a profit attributable to the fact that the information in question was price-sensitive information in relation to the securities, or

(b) that at the time he believed on reasonable grounds that the information had been or would be disclosed widely enough to ensure that none of those taking part in the dealing would be prejudiced by not having the information, or

(c) that he would have done what he did even if he had not had the information.

(3) An individual is not guilty of insider dealing by virtue of a disclosure of information if he shows—

(a) that he did not at the time expect any person, because of the disclosure, to deal in securities in the circumstances mentioned in subsection (3) of section 52; or

(b) that, although he had such an expectation at the time, he did not expect the dealing to result in a profit attributable to the fact that the information was price-sensitive information in relation to the securities.

(4) Schedule 1 (special defences) shall have effect.

(5) The Treasury may by order amend Schedule 1.

(6) In this section references to a profit include references to the avoidance of a loss.

Interpretation

[5.195]

54 Securities to which Part V applies

(1) This Part applies to any security which—

(a) falls within any paragraph of Schedule 2; and

(b) satisfies any conditions applying to it under an order made by the Treasury for the purposes of this subsection;

and in the provisions of this Part (other than that Schedule) any reference to a security is a reference to a security to which this Part applies.

(2) The Treasury may by order amend Schedule 2.

NOTES

Orders: the Insider Dealing (Securities and Regulated Markets) Order 1994, SI 1994/187 at **[6.21]**.

[5.196]

55 "Dealing" in securities

(1) For the purposes of this Part, a person deals in securities if—

(a) he acquires or disposes of the securities (whether as principal or agent); or

(b) he procures, directly or indirectly, an acquisition or disposal of the securities by any other person.

(2) For the purposes of this Part, "acquire", in relation to a security, includes—

(a) agreeing to acquire the security; and

(b) entering into a contract which creates the security.

(3) For the purposes of this Part, "dispose", in relation to a security, includes—

(a) agreeing to dispose of the security; and

(b) bringing to an end a contract which created the security.

(4) For the purposes of subsection (1), a person procures an acquisition or disposal of a security if the security is acquired or disposed of by a person who is—

(a) his agent,

(b) his nominee, or

(c) a person who is acting at his direction,

in relation to the acquisition or disposal.

(5) Subsection (4) is not exhaustive as to the circumstances in which one person may be regarded as procuring an acquisition or disposal of securities by another.

[5.197]

56 "Inside information", etc

(1) For the purposes of this section and section 57, "inside information" means information which—

(a) relates to particular securities or to a particular issuer of securities or to particular issuers of securities and not to securities generally or to issuers of securities generally;

(b) is specific or precise;

(c) has not been made public; and

(d) if it were made public would be likely to have a significant effect on the price of any securities.

(2) For the purposes of this Part, securities are "price-affected securities" in relation to inside information, and inside information is "price-sensitive information" in relation to securities, if and only if the information would, if made public, be likely to have a significant effect on the price of the securities.

(3) For the purposes of this section "price" includes value.

[5.198]

57 "Insiders"

(1) For the purposes of this Part, a person has information as an insider if and only if—

(a) it is, and he knows that it is, inside information, and

(b) he has it, and knows that he has it, from an inside source.

(2) For the purposes of subsection (1), a person has information from an inside source if and only if—

(a) he has it through—

(i) being a director, employee or shareholder of an issuer of securities; or

(ii) having access to the information by virtue of his employment, office or profession; or

(b) the direct or indirect source of his information is a person within paragraph (a).

[5.199]

58 Information "made public"

(1) For the purposes of section 56, "made public", in relation to information, shall be construed in accordance with the following provisions of this section; but those provisions are not exhaustive as to the meaning of that expression.

(2) Information is made public if—

- (a) it is published in accordance with the rules of a regulated market for the purpose of informing investors and their professional advisers;
- (b) it is contained in records which by virtue of any enactment are open to inspection by the public;
- (c) it can be readily acquired by those likely to deal in any securities—
  - (i) to which the information relates, or
  - (ii) of an issuer to which the information relates; or
- (d) it is derived from information which has been made public.

(3) Information may be treated as made public even though—

- (a) it can be acquired only by persons exercising diligence or expertise;
- (b) it is communicated to a section of the public and not to the public at large;
- (c) it can be acquired only by observation;
- (d) it is communicated only on payment of a fee; or
- (e) it is published only outside the United Kingdom.

[5.200]

59 "Professional intermediary"

(1) For the purposes of this Part, a "professional intermediary" is a person—

- (a) who carries on a business consisting of an activity mentioned in subsection (2) and who holds himself out to the public or any section of the public (including a section of the public constituted by persons such as himself) as willing to engage in any such business; or
- (b) who is employed by a person falling within paragraph (a) to carry out any such activity.

(2) The activities referred to in subsection (1) are—

- (a) acquiring or disposing of securities (whether as principal or agent); or
- (b) acting as an intermediary between persons taking part in any dealing in securities.

(3) A person is not to be treated as carrying on a business consisting of an activity mentioned in subsection (2)—

- (a) if the activity in question is merely incidental to some other activity not falling within subsection (2); or
- (b) merely because he occasionally conducts one of those activities.

(4) For the purposes of section 52, a person dealing in securities relies on a professional intermediary if and only if a person who is acting as a professional intermediary carries out an activity mentioned in subsection (2) in relation to that dealing.

[5.201]

60 Other interpretation provisions

(1) For the purposes of this Part, "regulated market" means any market, however operated, which, by an order made by the Treasury, is identified (whether by name or by reference to criteria prescribed by the order) as a regulated market for the purposes of this Part.

(2) For the purposes of this Part an "issuer", in relation to any securities, means any company, public sector body or individual by which or by whom the securities have been or are to be issued.

(3) For the purposes of this Part—

- (a) "company" means any body (whether or not incorporated and wherever incorporated or constituted) which is not a public sector body; and
- (b) "public sector body" means—
  - (i) the government of the United Kingdom, of Northern Ireland or of any country or territory outside the United Kingdom;
  - (ii) a local authority in the United Kingdom or elsewhere;
  - (iii) any international organisation the members of which include the United Kingdom or another member state;
  - (iv) the Bank of England; or
  - (v) the central bank of any sovereign State.

(4) For the purposes of this Part, information shall be treated as relating to an issuer of securities which is a company not only where it is about the company but also where it may affect the company's business prospects.

NOTES

Orders: the Insider Dealing (Securities and Regulated Markets) Order 1994, SI 1994/187 at **[6.21]**; the Insider Dealing (Securities and Regulated Markets) (Amendment) Order 1996, SI 1996/1561; the Insider Dealing (Securities and Regulated Markets) (Amendment) Order 2000, SI 2000/1923; the Insider Dealing (Securities and Regulated Markets) (Amendment) Order 2002, SI 2002/1874.

Miscellaneous

[5.202]

61 Penalties and prosecution

(1) An individual guilty of insider dealing shall be liable—

- (a) on summary conviction, to a fine not exceeding the statutory maximum or imprisonment for a term not exceeding six months or to both; or
- (b) on conviction on indictment, to a fine or imprisonment for a term not exceeding [ten years] or to both.

(2) Proceedings for offences under this Part shall not be instituted in England and Wales except by or with the consent of—

- (a) the Secretary of State; or
- (b) the Director of Public Prosecutions.

(3) In relation to proceedings in Northern Ireland for offences under this Part, subsection (2) shall have effect as if the reference to the Director of Public Prosecutions were a reference to the Director of Public Prosecutions for Northern Ireland.

NOTES

Sub-s (1): words in square brackets substituted by the Financial Services Act 2021, s 31(1), as from 1 November 2021. Note: (a) this amendment does not apply in relation to offences committed before that date; (b) where an offence is found to have been committed over a period of 2 or more days, or at some time during a period of 2 or more days, it must be taken for the purposes of (a) above to have been committed on the first of those days. See s 31(3), (4) of the 2021 Act. Note also that the previous words were "seven years".

[5.203]

[61A Summary proceedings: venue and time limit for proceedings

(1) Summary proceedings for an offence of insider dealing may (without prejudice to any jurisdiction exercisable apart from this subsection) be brought against an individual at any place at which the individual is for the time being.

(2) An information relating to an offence of insider dealing that is triable by a magistrates' court in England and Wales may be so tried if it is laid—

(a) at any time within three years after the commission of the offence, and

(b) within twelve months after the date on which evidence sufficient in the opinion of the Director of Public Prosecutions or the Secretary of State (as the case may be) to justify the proceedings comes to that person's knowledge.

(3) Summary proceedings in Scotland for an offence of insider dealing—

(a) must not be commenced after the expiration of three years from the commission of the offence;

(b) subject to that, may be commenced at any time—

(i) within twelve months after the date on which evidence sufficient in the Lord Advocate's opinion to justify the proceedings came to that person's knowledge, or

(ii) where such evidence was reported to the Lord Advocate by the Secretary of State, within twelve months after the date on which it came to the knowledge of the latter.

Section 136(3) of the Criminal Procedure (Scotland) Act 1995 (date when proceedings deemed to be commenced) applies for the purposes of this subsection as for the purposes of that section.

(4) A magistrates' court in Northern Ireland has jurisdiction to hear and determine a complaint charging the commission of a summary offence of insider dealing provided that the complaint is made—

(a) within three years from the time when the offence was committed, and

(b) within twelve months from the date on which evidence sufficient in the opinion of the Director of Public Prosecutions for Northern Ireland or the Secretary of State (as the case may be) to justify the proceedings comes to that person's knowledge.

(5) For the purposes of this section a certificate of the Director of Public Prosecutions, the Lord Advocate, the Director of Public Prosecutions for Northern Ireland or the Secretary of State (as the case may be) as to the date on which such evidence as is referred to above came to that person's notice is conclusive evidence.]

NOTES

Inserted by the Companies Act 2006 (Consequential Amendments, Transitional Provisions and Savings) Order 2009, SI 2009/1941, art 2(1), Sch 1, para 141, as from 1 October 2009.

[5.204]

62 Territorial scope of offence of insider dealing

(1) An individual is not guilty of an offence falling within subsection (1) of section 52 unless—

(a) he was within the United Kingdom at the time when he is alleged to have done any act constituting or forming part of the alleged dealing;

(b) the regulated market on which the dealing is alleged to have occurred is one which, by an order made by the Treasury, is identified (whether by name or by reference to criteria prescribed by the order) as being, for the purposes of this Part, regulated in the United Kingdom; or

(c) the professional intermediary was within the United Kingdom at the time when he is alleged to have done anything by means of which the offence is alleged to have been committed.

(2) An individual is not guilty of an offence falling within subsection (2) of section 52 unless—

(a) he was within the United Kingdom at the time when he is alleged to have disclosed the information or encouraged the dealing; or

(b) the alleged recipient of the information or encouragement was within the United Kingdom at the time when he is alleged to have received the information or encouragement.

NOTES

Orders: the Insider Dealing (Securities and Regulated Markets) Order 1994, SI 1994/187 at **[6.21]**; the Insider Dealing (Securities and Regulated Markets) (Amendment) Order 1996, SI 1996/1561; the Insider Dealing (Securities and Regulated Markets) (Amendment) Order 2000, SI 2000/1923; the Insider Dealing (Securities and Regulated Markets) (Amendment) Order 2002, SI 2002/1874.

[5.205]

63 Limits on section 52

(1) Section 52 does not apply to anything done by an individual acting on behalf of a public sector body in pursuit of monetary policies or policies with respect to exchange rates or the management of public debt or foreign exchange reserves.

(2) No contract shall be void or unenforceable by reason only of section 52.

[5.206]

64 Orders

(1) Any power under this Part to make an order shall be exercisable by statutory instrument.

(2) No order shall be made under this Part unless a draft of it has been laid before and approved by a resolution of each House of Parliament.

(3) An order under this Part—

(a) may make different provision for different cases; and

(b) may contain such incidental, supplemental and transitional provisions as the Treasury consider expedient.

SCHEDULES

SCHEDULE 1
SPECIAL DEFENCES

Section 53(4)

Market makers

[5.207]

1. (1) An individual is not guilty of insider dealing by virtue of dealing in securities or encouraging another person to deal if he shows that he acted in good faith in the course of—

(a) his business as a market maker, or

(b) his employment in the business of a market maker.

(2) A market maker is a person who—

(a) holds himself out at all normal times in compliance with the rules of a regulated market or an approved organisation as willing to acquire or dispose of securities; and

(b) is recognised as doing so under those rules.

(3) In this paragraph "approved organisation" means an international securities self-regulating organisation approved [by the Treasury under any relevant order under section 22 of the Financial Services and Markets Act 2000].

Market information

2. (1) An individual is not guilty of insider dealing by virtue of dealing in securities or encouraging another person to deal if he shows that—

(a) the information which he had as an insider was market information; and

(b) it was reasonable for an individual in his position to have acted as he did despite having that information as an insider at the time.

(2) In determining whether it is reasonable for an individual to do any act despite having market information at the time, there shall, in particular, be taken into account—

(a) the content of the information;

(b) the circumstances in which he first had the information and in what capacity; and

(c) the capacity in which he now acts.

3. An individual is not guilty of insider dealing by virtue of dealing in securities or encouraging another person to deal if he shows—

(a) that he acted—

(i) in connection with an acquisition or disposal which was under consideration or the subject of negotiation, or in the course of a series of such acquisitions or disposals; and

(ii) with a view to facilitating the accomplishment of the acquisition or disposal or the series of acquisitions or disposals; and

(b) that the information which he had as an insider was market information arising directly out of his involvement in the acquisition or disposal or series of acquisitions or disposals.

4. For the purposes of paragraphs 2 and 3 market information is information consisting of one or more of the following facts—

(a) that securities of a particular kind have been or are to be acquired or disposed of, or that their acquisition or disposal is under consideration or the subject of negotiation;

(b) that securities of a particular kind have not been or are not to be acquired or disposed of;

(c) the number of securities acquired or disposed of or to be acquired or disposed of or whose acquisition or disposal is under consideration or the subject of negotiation;

(d) the price (or range of prices) at which securities have been or are to be acquired or disposed of or the price (or range of prices) at which the securities whose acquisition or disposal is under consideration or the subject of negotiation may be acquired or disposed of;

(e) the identity of the persons involved or likely to be involved in any capacity in an acquisition or disposal.

[Buy-back programmes and stabilisation

5. [(1)] An individual is not guilty of insider dealing by virtue of dealing in securities or encouraging another person to deal if he shows that he acted in conformity with—

(a) Article 5 of Regulation (EU) No 596/2014 of the European Parliament and of the Council of 16 April 2014 on market abuse (market abuse regulation)[, as that Article has effect at the time mentioned in sub-paragraph (2),] [and—

(i) each EU regulation, originally made under that Article before that time, which is retained direct EU legislation; and

(ii) all subordinate legislation (within the meaning of the Interpretation Act 1978) made under that Article on or after IP completion day];

(b) rules made under section 137Q(1) of the Financial Services and Markets Act 2000.]

[(2) The time is the beginning of the day on which the Market Abuse (Amendment) (EU Exit) Regulations 2019 are made.]

[6. An individual ("A") is not guilty of insider dealing by virtue of dealing, or encouraging another person to deal, in securities through a trading venue in Gibraltar if A shows that A acted in conformity with—

(a) the following as they have effect in Gibraltar law—
   (i) Article 5 of Regulation (EU) No 596/2014 of the European Parliament and of the Council of 16 April 2014 on market abuse (market abuse regulation), and
   (ii) each EU regulation originally made under that Article, and
(b) all other applicable Gibraltar law (if any).

7. An individual ("A") is not guilty of insider dealing by virtue of dealing, or encouraging another person to deal, in securities through a trading venue in an EEA State if A shows that A acted in conformity with—
(a) the following as they apply in the EEA State—
   (i) Article 5 of Regulation (EU) No 596/2014 of the European Parliament and of the Council of 16 April 2014 on market abuse (market abuse regulation), and
   (ii) each EU regulation made under that Article, and
(b) all other applicable law of the EEA State (if any).

8. For the purposes of paragraphs 6 and 7 "trading venue" has the meaning given by Article 2(1)(16) of Regulation (EU) No 600/2014 of the European Parliament and of the Council of 15 May 2014 on markets in financial instruments and amending Regulation (EU) No 648/2012, as substituted by the Markets in Financial Instruments (Amendment) (EU Exit) Regulations 2018 (SI 2018/1403).]

NOTES

Para 1: words in square brackets in sub-para (3) substituted by the Financial Services and Markets Act 2000 (Consequential Amendments and Repeals) Order 2001, SI 2001/3649, art 341(1), (2), as from 1 December 2001.

Para 5 is amended as follows:

Originally substituted by the Financial Services and Markets Act 2000 (Market Abuse) Regulations 2016, SI 2016/680, art 11, as from 3 July 2016.

Sub-para (1) numbered as such, words in first pair of square brackets in para (a) inserted, and sub-para (2) added, by the Market Abuse (Amendment) (EU Exit) Regulations 2019, SI 2019/310, reg 2, as from 19 February 2019.

Words in second pair of square brackets in sub-para (1)(a) substituted by SI 2019/310, reg 4, as from IP completion day (as defined in the European Union (Withdrawal Agreement) Act 2020, s 39). Note that reg 4 of the 2019 Regulations was amended by the Financial Services and Economic and Monetary Policy (Consequential Amendments) (EU Exit) Regulations 2020, SI 2020/1301, Schedule, para 17, as from 20 December 2020; and that the effect of the amendment has been incorporated in the text set out above.

Paras 6–8: added by the Financial Services (Miscellaneous) (Amendment) (EU Exit) (No 3) Regulations 2019, SI 2019/1390, reg 2, as from IP completion day (as defined in the European Union (Withdrawal Agreement) Act 2020, s 39).

SCHEDULE 2
SECURITIES

Section 54

Shares

[5.208]

1. Shares and stock in the share capital of a company ("shares").

Debt securities

2. Any instrument creating or acknowledging indebtedness which is issued by a company or public sector body, including, in particular, debentures, debenture stock, loan stock, bonds and certificates of deposit ("debt securities").

Warrants

3. Any right (whether conferred by warrant or otherwise) to subscribe for shares or debt securities ("warrants").

Depositary receipts

4. (1) The rights under any depositary receipt.

(2) For the purposes of sub-paragraph (1) a "depositary receipt" means a certificate or other record (whether or not in the form of a document)—
(a) which is issued by or on behalf of a person who holds any relevant securities of a particular issuer; and
(b) which acknowledges that another person is entitled to rights in relation to the relevant securities or relevant securities of the same kind.

(3) In sub-paragraph (2) "relevant securities" means shares, debt securities and warrants.

Options

5. Any option to acquire or dispose of any security falling within any other paragraph of this Schedule.

Futures

6. (1) Rights under a contract for the acquisition or disposal of relevant securities under which delivery is to be made at a future date and at a price agreed when the contract is made.

(2) In sub-paragraph (1)—
(a) the references to a future date and to a price agreed when the contract is made include references to a date and a price determined in accordance with terms of the contract; and
(b) "relevant securities" means any security falling within any other paragraph of this Schedule.

Contracts for differences

7. (1) Rights under a contract which does not provide for the delivery of securities but whose purpose or pretended purpose is to secure a profit or avoid a loss by reference to fluctuations in—
(a) a share index or other similar factor connected with relevant securities;
(b) the price of particular relevant securities; or
(c) the interest rate offered on money placed on deposit.

(2) In sub-paragraph (1) "relevant securities" means any security falling within any other paragraph of this Schedule.

NOTES

Modification: the reference in para 2 to securities, instruments or investments creating or acknowledging indebtedness (or creating or acknowledging a present or future indebtedness) includes a reference to uncertificated units of eligible debt securities; see the Uncertificated Securities (Amendment) (Eligible Debt Securities) Regulations 2003, SI 2003/1633, reg 15, Sch 2, para 8(2)(f).

COMPANIES (AUDIT, INVESTIGATIONS AND COMMUNITY ENTERPRISE) ACT 2004

(2004 c 27)

NOTES

This Act is reproduced as amended by the following Acts: the Charities Act 2006; the Companies Act 2006; the Corporation Tax Act 2010; the Charities Act 2011; the Local Audit and Accountability Act 2014; the Co-operative and Community Benefit Societies Act 2014; the Pensions Act 2014; the Small Business, Enterprise and Employment Act 2015; the Data Protection Act 2018.

And by the following Statutory Instruments: the Prospectus Regulations 2005, SI 2005/1433; the Charities and Trustee Investment (Scotland) Act 2005 (Consequential Provisions and Modifications) Order 2006, SI 2006/242; the Companies Act 2006 (Commencement No 2, Consequential Amendments, Transitional Provisions and Savings) Order 2007, SI 2007/1093; the Companies Act 2006 (Commencement No 3, Consequential Amendments, Transitional Provisions and Savings) Order 2007, SI 2007/2194; the Companies Act 2006 (Consequential Amendments etc) Order 2008, SI 2008/948; the Companies Act 2006 (Consequential Amendments, Transitional Provisions and Savings) Order 2009, SI 2009/1941; the Community Interest Company (Amendment) Regulations 2009, SI 2009/1942; the Charities (Pre-consolidation Amendments) Order 2011, SI 2011/1396; the Statutory Auditors and Third Country Auditors (Amendment) Regulations 2011, SI 2011/1856; the Supervision of Accounts and Reports (Prescribed Body) and Companies (Defective Accounts and Directors' Reports) (Authorised Person) Order 2012, SI 2012/1439; the Legal Aid, Sentencing and Punishment of Offenders Act 2012 (Fines on Summary Conviction) Regulations 2015, SI 2015/664; the Statutory Auditors and Third Country Auditors Regulations 2016, SI 2016/649; the Bankruptcy (Scotland) Act 2016 (Consequential Provisions and Modifications) Order 2016, SI 2016/1034; the Bank of England and Financial Services (Consequential Amendments) Regulations 2017, SI 2017/80; the Statutory Auditors and Third Country Auditors (Amendment) (EU Exit) Regulations 2019, SI 2019/177; the Criminal Justice Act 2003 (Commencement No 33) and Sentencing Act 2020 (Commencement No 2) Regulations 2022, SI 2022/500.

Commencement: see s 65 at **[5.268]** and the Orders noted thereto.

Old public companies: as to the application of Part 2 of this Act to old public companies, see the note "Application of this Act to old public companies" in the introductory notes to the Companies Act 2006 *ante*, and note that for these purposes "the Companies Acts" includes Part 2 of this Act (see **[1.2]**).

Offences under this Act: see further the Companies Act 2006, ss 1131 at **[1.1301]**.

ARRANGEMENT OF SECTIONS

PART 1
AUDITORS, ACCOUNTS, DIRECTORS' LIABILITIES AND INVESTIGATIONS

CHAPTER 2 ACCOUNTS AND REPORTS

Supervision of accounts and reports

Bodies concerned with accounting standards etc

CHAPTER 5 SUPPLEMENTARY

PART 2
COMMUNITY INTEREST COMPANIES

Introductory

Requirements

An Act to amend the law relating to company auditors and accounts, to the provision that may be made in respect of certain liabilities incurred by a company's officers, and to company investigations; to make provision for community interest companies; and for connected purposes

[28 October 2004]

PART 1 AUDITORS, ACCOUNTS, DIRECTORS' LIABILITIES AND INVESTIGATIONS

1–7 *(Ss 1–7 (Chap 1) repealed by the Companies Act 2006, s 1295, Sch 16, as from 6 April 2008.)*

CHAPTER 2 ACCOUNTS AND REPORTS

8–13 *(Ss 8–13 repealed by the Companies Act 2006, s 1295, Sch 16, as from 6 April 2008.)*

Supervision of accounts and reports

[5.209]

14 Supervision of periodic accounts and reports of issuers of listed securities

(1) The Secretary of State may make an order appointing a body ("the prescribed body") to exercise the functions mentioned in subsection (2).

(2) The functions are—

(a) keeping under review periodic accounts and reports that are produced by issuers of [transferable] securities and are required to comply with any accounting requirements imposed by [Part 6] rules; and

(b) if the prescribed body thinks fit, informing the [Financial Conduct Authority] of any conclusions reached by the body in relation to any such accounts or report.

(3) A body may be appointed under this section if it is a body corporate or an unincorporated association which appears to the Secretary of State—

(a) to have an interest in, and to have satisfactory procedures directed to, monitoring compliance by issuers of [transferable] securities with accounting requirements imposed by [Part 6] rules in relation to periodic accounts and reports produced by such issuers; and

(b) otherwise to be a fit and proper body to be appointed.

(4) But where the order is to contain any requirements or other provisions specified under subsection (8), the Secretary of State may not appoint a body unless, in addition, it appears to him that the body would, if appointed, exercise its functions as a prescribed body in accordance with any such requirements or provisions.

(5) A body may be appointed either generally or in respect of any of the following, namely—

(a) any particular class or classes of issuers,

(b) any particular class or classes of periodic accounts or reports,

and different bodies may be appointed in respect of different classes within either or both of paragraphs (a) and (b).

(6) In relation to the appointment of a body in respect of any such class or classes, subsections (2) and (3) are to be read as referring to issuers, or (as the case may be) to periodic accounts or reports, of the class or classes concerned.

(7) Where—

(a) a body is so appointed, but

(b) the [Financial Conduct Authority] requests the body to exercise its functions under subsection (2) in relation to any particular issuer of [transferable] securities in relation to whom those functions would not otherwise be exercisable,

the body is to exercise those functions in relation to that issuer as well.

(8) An order under this section may contain such requirements or other provisions relating to the exercise of functions by the prescribed body as appear to the Secretary of State to be appropriate.

(9) If the prescribed body is an unincorporated association, any relevant proceedings may be brought by or against that body in the name of any body corporate whose constitution provides for the establishment of the body.

For this purpose "relevant proceedings" means proceedings brought in or in connection with the exercise of any function by the body as a prescribed body.

(10) Where an appointment is revoked, the revoking order may make such provision as the Secretary of State thinks fit with respect to pending proceedings.

(11) The power to make an order under this section is exercisable by statutory instrument subject to annulment in pursuance of a resolution of either House of Parliament.

(12) In this section [and sections 15A to 15E below]—

[["Part 6 Rules" has] have the meaning given by section 103(1) of the Financial Services and Markets Act 2000 (c 8) (interpretation of Part 6);

["issuer" has the meaning given by section 102A(6) of that Act;]]

"periodic" accounts and reports means accounts and reports which are required by [Part 6] rules to be produced periodically;

["transferable securities" has the meaning given by section 102A(3) of that Act].

NOTES

Sub-s (2): words in first and second pairs of square brackets substituted by the Companies Act 2006, s 1272, Sch 15, Pt 2, paras 13, 14(1), (2), as from 8 November 20060 Other words in square brackets substituted by the Financial Services Act 2012, s 114(1), Sch 18, Pt 2, para 103, as from 1 April 2013.

Sub-s (3): words in square brackets substituted by the Companies Act 2006, s 1272, Sch 15, Pt 2, paras 13, 14(1), (3), as from 8 November 2006.

Sub-s (7): words in first pair of square brackets substituted by the Financial Services Act 2012, s 114(1), Sch 18, Pt 2, para 103, as from 1 April 2013. Word in second pair of square brackets substituted by the Companies Act 2006, s 1272, Sch 15, Pt 2, paras 13, 14(1), (4), as from 8 November 2006.

Sub-s (12): words in first pair of square brackets substituted by the Companies Act 2006 (Consequential Amendments etc) Order 2008, SI 2008/948, art 3(1), Sch 1, Pt 2, para 232(1), as from 6 April 2008. Words in second (outer) pair of square brackets substituted by the Prospectus Regulations 2005, SI 2005/1433, reg 2(3), Sch 3, para 5, as from 1 July 2005. Other words in square brackets substituted, and definition "transferable securities" inserted, by the Companies Act 2006, s 1272, Sch 15, Pt 2, paras 13, 14(1), (5), as from 8 November 2006.

Orders: the Supervision of Accounts and Reports (Prescribed Body) and Companies (Defective Accounts and Directors' Reports) (Authorised Person) Order 2012, SI 2012/1439 (at **[4.429]**); the Supervision of Accounts and Reports (Prescribed Body) and Companies (Defective Accounts and Reports) (Authorised Person) Order 2021, SI 2021/465 at **[4.722]**. Note that the 2021 Order largely revokes the 2012 Order.

[5.210]

[15 Application of sections 15A to 15E

(1) The provisions of sections 15A to 15E have effect in relation to bodies appointed under section 14 (supervision of accounts and reports of issuers of transferable securities).

(2) In those sections—

- (a) "prescribed body" means a body appointed under that section; and
- (b) references to the functions of a prescribed body are to its functions under that section.]

NOTES

This section together with ss 15A–15E were substituted (for the original s 15) by the Companies Act 2006 (Consequential Amendments etc) Order 2008, SI 2008/948, art 3(1), Sch 1, Pt 2, para 232(2), as from 6 April 2008.

[5.211]

[15A Disclosure of information by tax authorities

(1) The Commissioners for Her Majesty's Revenue and Customs may disclose information to a prescribed body for the purposes of its functions.

(2) This section applies despite any statutory or other restriction on the disclosure of information.

Provided that, in the case of personal data . . . , information is not to be disclosed in contravention of [the data protection legislation].

(3) Information disclosed to a prescribed body under this section—

- (a) may only be used for the purposes of its functions, and
- (b) must not be further disclosed except to the person to whom the information relates.

(4) A person who contravenes subsection (3) commits an offence unless—

- (a) the person did not know, and had no reason to suspect, that the information had been disclosed under this section, or
- (b) the person took all reasonable steps and exercised all due diligence to avoid the commission of the offence.

(5) A person guilty of an offence under subsection (4) is liable—

- (a) on conviction on indictment, to imprisonment for a term not exceeding two years or a fine (or both);
- (b) on summary conviction—
  - (i) in England and Wales or Scotland, to imprisonment for a term not exceeding twelve months or to a fine not exceeding the statutory maximum (or both);
  - (ii) in Northern Ireland, to imprisonment for a term not exceeding three months, or to a fine not exceeding the statutory maximum (or both).

(6) In subsection (5)(b)(i) as it applies in relation to England and Wales in the case of an offence committed before [2 May 2022], for "twelve months" substitute "six months".

(7) Sections 400, 401 and 403 of the Financial Services and Markets Act 2000 (supplementary provisions relating to offences) apply in relation to an offence under this section.

[(8) In this section—

"the data protection legislation" has the same meaning as in the Data Protection Act 2018 (see section 3 of that Act);

"personal data" has the same meaning as in Parts 5 to 7 of that Act (see section 3(2) and (14) of that Act).]]

NOTES

Substituted as noted to s 15 at **[5.210]**.

Words omitted from sub-s (2) repealed, words in square brackets in that subsection substituted, and sub-s (8) added, by the Data Protection Act 2018, s 211, Sch 19, Pt 1, paras 100, 101, as from 25 May 2018 (for transitional provisions and savings relating to the repeal of the Data Protection Act 1998, see Sch 20 to the 2018 Act).

Words in square brackets in sub-s (6) substituted by the Criminal Justice Act 2003 (Commencement No 33) and Sentencing Act 2020 (Commencement No 2) Regulations 2022, SI 2022/500, reg 5, Schedule, Pt 1, as from 28 April 2022.

[5.212]

[15B Power of prescribed body to require documents, information and explanations

(1) This section applies where it appears to a prescribed body that there is, or may be, a question whether the periodic accounts and reports produced by an issuer of transferable securities comply with any accounting requirements imposed by Part 6 rules.

(2) The prescribed body may require any of the persons mentioned in subsection (3) to produce any document, or to provide any information or explanations, that the body may reasonably require for the purpose of its functions.

(3) Those persons are—

- (a) the issuer;
- (b) any officer, employee, or auditor of the issuer;
- (c) any persons who fell within paragraph (b) at a time to which the document or information required by the prescribed body relates.

(4) If a person fails to comply with such a requirement, the prescribed body may apply to the court.

(5) If it appears to the court that the person has failed to comply with a requirement under subsection (2), it may order the person to take such steps as it directs for securing that the documents are produced or the information or explanations are provided.

(6) A statement made by a person in response to a requirement under subsection (2) or an order under subsection (5) may not be used in evidence against him in any criminal proceedings.

(7) Nothing in this section compels any person to disclose documents or information in respect of which a claim to legal professional privilege (in Scotland, to confidentiality of communications) could be maintained in legal proceedings.

(8) In this section—

"the court" means the High Court or the Court of Session; and

"document" includes information recorded in any form.]

NOTES

Substituted as noted to s 15 at **[5.210]**.

[5.213]

[15C Restrictions on disclosure of information obtained under compulsory powers

(1) This section applies to information (in whatever form) obtained in pursuance of a requirement or order under section 15B (power of prescribed body to require documents etc) that relates to the private affairs of an individual or to any particular business.

(2) No such information may, during the lifetime of that individual or so long as that business continues to be carried on, be disclosed without the consent of that individual or the person for the time being carrying on that business.

(3) This does not apply—

(a) to disclosure permitted by section 15D (permitted disclosure of information obtained under compulsory powers), or

(b) to the disclosure of information that is or has been available to the public from another source.

(4) A person who discloses information in contravention of this section commits an offence, unless—

(a) the person did not know, and had no reason to suspect, that the information had been disclosed under section 15B, or

(b) the person took all reasonable steps and exercised all due diligence to avoid the commission of the offence.

(5) A person guilty of an offence under this section is liable—

(a) on conviction on indictment, to imprisonment for a term not exceeding two years or a fine (or both);

(b) on summary conviction—

(i) in England and Wales or Scotland, to imprisonment for a term not exceeding twelve months or to a fine not exceeding the statutory maximum (or both);

(ii) in Northern Ireland, to imprisonment for a term not exceeding six months, or to a fine not exceeding the statutory maximum (or both).

(6) In subsection (5)(b)(i) as it applies in relation to England and Wales in the case of an offence committed before [2 May 2022], for "twelve months" substitute "six months".]

NOTES

Substituted as noted to s 15 at **[5.210]**.

Sub-s (6): words in square brackets substituted by the Criminal Justice Act 2003 (Commencement No 33) and Sentencing Act 2020 (Commencement No 2) Regulations 2022, SI 2022/500, reg 5, Schedule, Pt 1, as from 28 April 2022.

[5.214]

[15D Permitted disclosure of information obtained under compulsory powers

(1) The prohibition in section 15C of the disclosure of information obtained in pursuance of a requirement or order under section 15B (power of prescribed body to require documents etc) that relates to the private affairs of an individual or to any particular business has effect subject to the following exceptions.

(2) It does not apply to the disclosure of information for the purpose of facilitating the carrying out by the prescribed body of its functions.

(3) It does not apply to disclosure to—

(a) the Secretary of State,

(b) the Department of Enterprise, Trade and Investment for Northern Ireland,

(c) the Treasury,

(d) the Bank of England [(including the Bank in its capacity as the Prudential Regulation Authority)],

(e) the [Financial Conduct Authority], or

(f) the Commissioners for Her Majesty's Revenue and Customs.

(4) It does not apply to disclosure—

(a) for the purpose of assisting a body designated by an order under section 1252 of the Companies Act 2006 (delegation of functions of the Secretary of State) to exercise its functions under Part 42 of that Act (statutory auditors);

[(aa) for the purposes of facilitating—

(i) the carrying out of inspections under paragraph 1 of Schedule 12 to the Companies Act 2006 (arrangements for independent monitoring of audits of [UK-traded third country companies]); or

(ii) the carrying out of investigations under paragraph 2 of that Schedule (arrangements for independent investigations for disciplinary purposes);]

[(ab) for the purposes of enabling the competent authority to exercise its functions under the Statutory Auditors and Third Country Auditors Regulations 2016 or under Regulation (EU) 537/2014 on specific requirements regarding statutory audit of public interest entities;]

(b) with a view to the institution of, or otherwise for the purposes of, disciplinary proceedings relating to the performance by an accountant or auditor of his professional duties;

(c) for the purpose of enabling or assisting the Secretary of State or the Treasury to exercise any of their functions under any of the following—

(i) the Companies Acts (as defined in section 2 of the Companies Act 2006),

(ii) Part 5 of the Criminal Justice Act 1993 (insider dealing),

(iii) the Insolvency Act 1986 or the Insolvency (Northern Ireland) Order 1989,

(iv) the Company Directors Disqualification Act 1986 or the Company Directors Disqualification (Northern Ireland) Order 2002,

(v) the Financial Services and Markets Act 2000;

(d) for the purpose of enabling or assisting the Department of Enterprise, Trade and Investment for Northern Ireland to exercise any powers conferred on it by the enactments relating to companies, directors' disqualification or insolvency;

(e) for the purpose of enabling or assisting the Bank of England [(acting otherwise than in its capacity as the Prudential Regulation Authority)] to exercise its functions;

(f) for the purpose of enabling or assisting the Commissioners for Her Majesty's Revenue and Customs to exercise their functions;

(g) for the purpose of enabling or assisting the [Financial Conduct Authority or the Prudential Regulation Authority] to exercise its functions under any of the following—

(i) the legislation relating to friendly societies . . . ,

[(ia) the Credit Unions Act 1979,]

(ii) the Building Societies Act 1986,

(iii) Part 7 of the Companies Act 1989,

(iv) the Financial Services and Markets Act 2000;

[(v) the Co-operative and Community Benefit Societies Act 2014;] or

(h) in pursuance of any [retained EU obligation].

(5) It does not apply to disclosure to a body exercising functions of a public nature under legislation in any country or territory outside the United Kingdom that appear to the prescribed body to be similar to its functions for the purpose of enabling or assisting that body to exercise those functions.

(6) In determining whether to disclose information to a body in accordance with subsection (5), the prescribed body must have regard to the following considerations—

(a) whether the use which the other body is likely to make of the information is sufficiently important to justify making the disclosure;

(b) whether the other body has adequate arrangements to prevent the information from being used or further disclosed other than—

(i) for the purposes of carrying out the functions mentioned in that subsection, or

(ii) for other purposes substantially similar to those for which information disclosed to the prescribed body could be used or further disclosed.

(7) Nothing in this section authorises the making of a disclosure in contravention of [the data protection legislation].

[(8) In this section, "the data protection legislation" has the same meaning as in the Data Protection Act 2018 (see section 3 of that Act).]]

NOTES

Substituted as noted to s 15 at **[5.210]**.

Sub-s (3): words in square brackets in para (d) inserted, and words in square brackets in para (e) substituted, by the Bank of England and Financial Services (Consequential Amendments) Regulations 2017, SI 2017/80, reg 2, Schedule, Pt 1, para 14(a), (b), as from 1 March 2017.

Sub-s (4) is amended as follows:

Para (aa) originally inserted by the Supervision of Accounts and Reports (Prescribed Body) and Companies (Defective Accounts and Directors' Reports) (Authorised Person) Order 2012, SI 2012/1439, art 6(1), as from 2 July 2012. Subsequently substituted by the Statutory Auditors and Third Country Auditors Regulations 2016, SI 2016/649, reg 17, Sch 5, para 1(1), (2)(a), as from 17 June 2016 (note that reg 1(11) of the 2016 Regulations provides that this amendment does not apply where Sch 10, paras 23 and 23A to the Companies Act 2006 continue to apply by virtue of savings contained in reg 1(9) of the 2016 Regulations (see **[4.650]**)).

Words in square brackets in sub-para (aa)(i) substituted by the Statutory Auditors and Third Country Auditors (Amendment) (EU Exit) Regulations 2019, SI 2019/177, regs 41, 42(a), as from IP completion day (as defined in the European Union (Withdrawal Agreement) Act 2020, s 39) (for transitional provisions, see Sch 4 to the 2019 Regulations at **[12.88]**).

Para (ab) inserted by SI 2016/649, reg 17, Sch 5, para 1(1), (2)(b), as from 17 June 2016.

Words in square brackets in para (e) inserted, and words in square brackets in para (g) substituted, by SI 2017/80, reg 2, Schedule, Pt 1, para 14(c), (d), as from 1 March 2017.

Words omitted from sub-para (g)(i) repealed, and sub-paras (g)(ia) and (v) inserted, by the Co-operative and Community Benefit Societies Act 2014, s 151, Sch 4, Pt 2, paras 87, 88, as from 1 August 2014.

Words in square brackets in sub-para (h) substituted by SI 2019/177, regs 41, 42(b), as from IP completion day (as defined in the European Union (Withdrawal Agreement) Act 2020, s 39) (for transitional provisions, see Sch 4 to the 2019 Regulations at **[12.88]**).

Words in square brackets in sub-s (7) inserted, and sub-s (8) added, by the Data Protection Act 2018, s 211, Sch 19, Pt 1, paras 100, 102, as from 25 May 2018 (for transitional provisions and savings relating to the repeal of the Data Protection Act 1998, see Sch 20 to the 2018 Act).

[5.215]

[15E Power to amend categories of permitted disclosure

(1) The Secretary of State may by order amend section 15D(3), (4) and (5).

(2) An order under this section must not—

(a) amend subsection (3) of that section (UK public authorities) by specifying a person unless the person exercises functions of a public nature (whether or not he exercises any other function);

(b) amend subsection (4) of that section (purposes for which disclosure permitted) by adding or modifying a description of disclosure unless the purpose for which the disclosure is permitted is likely to facilitate the exercise of a function of a public nature;

(c) amend subsection (5) of that section (overseas regulatory authorities) so as to have the effect of permitting disclosures to be made to a body other than one that exercises functions of a public nature in a country or territory outside the United Kingdom.

(3) The power to make an order under this section is exercisable by statutory instrument subject to annulment in pursuance of a resolution of either House of Parliament.]

NOTES

Substituted as noted to s 15 at **[5.210]**.

Orders: the Supervision of Accounts and Reports (Prescribed Body) and Companies (Defective Accounts and Directors' Reports) (Authorised Person) Order 2012, SI 2012/1439 (at **[4.429]**). Note that this Order is largely revoked by the Supervision of Accounts and Reports (Prescribed Body) and Companies (Defective Accounts and Reports) (Authorised Person) Order 2021, SI 2021/456 at **[4.722]**

Bodies concerned with accounting standards etc

[5.216]

16 Grants to bodies concerned with accounting standards etc

(1) The Secretary of State may make grants to any body carrying on activities concerned with any of the matters set out in subsection (2).

(2) The matters are—

(a) issuing accounting standards;

(b) issuing standards in respect of matters to be contained in reports required to be produced by auditors or company directors;

(c) investigating departures from standards within paragraph (a) or (b) or from the accounting requirements of [the Companies Act 2006] or any requirements of directly applicable [EU] legislation relating to company accounts;

(d) taking steps to secure compliance with such standards or requirements;

(e) keeping under review periodic accounts and reports that are produced by issuers of listed securities and are required to comply with any accounting requirements imposed by listing rules;

[(ea) exercising the functions of the competent authority under the Statutory Auditors and Third Country Auditors Regulations 2016 and under Regulation (EU) 537/2014 on specific requirements regarding statutory audit of public interest entities;]

[(eb) assessing, and reporting to the Secretary of State on, the comparability of the audit regulatory regimes of third countries to the audit regulatory regime of the United Kingdom;

(ec) assessing, and reporting to the Secretary of State on, the adequacy of third country competent authorities, in relation to their ability to co-operate with the competent authority on the exchange of audit working papers and investigation reports;]

(f) establishing, maintaining or carrying out arrangements within [paragraph 21, 22, 23(1)[, 23A(1)] or 24(1) of Schedule 10 to the Companies Act 2006];

(g) exercising functions of the Secretary of State under [Part 42 of that Act];

(h) carrying out investigations into public interest cases arising in connection with the performance of accountancy functions by members of professional accountancy bodies;

(i) holding disciplinary hearings relating to members of such bodies following the conclusion of such investigations;

(j) deciding whether (and, if so, what) disciplinary action should be taken against members of such bodies to whom such hearings related;

(k) supervising the exercise by such bodies of regulatory functions in relation to their members;

[(ka) exercising functions of the Independent Supervisor appointed under Chapter 3 of Part 42 of the Companies Act 2006;]

[(kb) establishing, maintaining or carrying out arrangements within paragraph 1 or 2 of Schedule 12 to the Companies Act 2006;]

[(l) issuing standards to be applied in actuarial work;

(m) issuing standards in respect of matters to be contained in reports or other communications required to be produced or made by actuaries or in accordance with standards within paragraph (l);

(n) investigating departures from standards within paragraph (l) or (m);

(o) taking steps to secure compliance with standards within paragraph (l) or (m);

[(oa) exercising functions under regulations made under section 113(3A) of the Pension Schemes Act 1993 or section 109(3A) of the Pension Schemes (Northern Ireland) Act 1993 (preparing guidance for pensions illustrations);]

(p) carrying out investigations into public interest cases arising in connection with the performance of actuarial functions by members of professional actuarial bodies;

(q) holding disciplinary hearings relating to members of professional actuarial bodies following the conclusion of investigations within paragraph (p);

(r) deciding whether (and, if so, what) disciplinary action should be taken against members of professional actuarial bodies to whom hearings within paragraph (q) related;

(s) supervising the exercise by professional actuarial bodies of regulatory functions in relation to their members;

(t) overseeing or directing any of the matters mentioned above.]

(3) A grant may be made to a body within subsection (1) in respect of any of its activities.

(4) For the purposes of this section—

(a) a body is to be regarded as carrying on any subsidiary activities of the body; and

(b) a body's "subsidiary activities" are activities carried on by any of its subsidiaries or by any body established under its constitution or under the constitution of such a subsidiary.

(5) In this section—

"accountancy functions" means functions performed as an accountant, whether in the capacity of auditor or otherwise;

["audit regulatory regime" in relation to a country or territory, means the system of public oversight, quality assurance, investigations and sanctions for auditors in that country or territory;]

"company" means a company [as defined in section 1(1) of the Companies Act 2006];

["the competent authority" means the Financial Reporting Council Limited;]

["listed securities" and "listing rules" have the meaning given by section 103(1) of the Financial Services and Markets Act 2000 (c 8) (interpretation of Part 6);

"issuer", in relation to listed securities, has the meaning given by section 102A(6)(b) of the Financial Services and Markets Act 2000 (meaning of "securities" etc,);]

"professional accountancy body" means—

(a) a supervisory body which is recognised for the purposes of [Part 42 of the Companies Act 2006], or

(b) a qualifying body, as defined by [section 1220] of that Act, which enforces rules as to the performance of accountancy functions by its members,

and references to the members of professional accountancy bodies include persons who, although not members of such bodies, are subject to their rules in performing accountancy functions;

["professional actuarial body" means—

(a) the Institute of Actuaries, or

(b) the Faculty of Actuaries in Scotland,

and the "members" of a professional actuarial body include persons who, although not members of the body, are subject to its rules in performing actuarial functions;]

"public interest cases" means matters which raise or appear to raise important issues affecting the public interest;

"regulatory functions", in relation to professional accountancy bodies, means any of the following functions—

(a) investigatory or disciplinary functions exercised by such bodies in relation to the performance by their members of accountancy functions,

(b) the setting by such bodies of standards in relation to the performance by their members of accountancy functions, and

(c) the determining by such bodies of requirements in relation to the education and training of their members;

["regulatory functions", in relation to professional actuarial bodies, means any of the following—

(a) investigatory or disciplinary functions exercised by such bodies in relation to the performance by their members of actuarial functions,

(b) the setting by such bodies of standards in relation to the performance by their members of actuarial functions, and

(c) the determining by such bodies of requirements in relation to the education and training of their members;]

"subsidiary" has the meaning given by [section 1159 of the Companies Act 2006];

["third country" means a country or territory other than the United Kingdom;

"third country competent authority" means a body established in a third country exercising functions related to the regulation or oversight of auditors.]

. . .

[(6) In their application to Scotland, subsection (2)(a) to (t) are to be read as referring only to matters provision relating to which would be outside the legislative competence of the Scottish Parliament.]

[(6A) References in this section to Part 42 of the Companies Act 2006 or to paragraph 21, 22, 23(1) or 24(1) of Schedule 10 to that Act include that Part or paragraph as it has effect by virtue of Schedule 5 to the Local Audit and Accountability Act 2014 (which applies Part 42 with modifications in relation to audits of local authorities etc).

(6B) The reference in the definition of "professional accountancy body" in subsection (5) to section 1220 of the Companies Act 2006 includes a reference to section 1219 of that Act as it has effect by virtue of Schedule 5 to the Local Audit and Accountability Act 2014.]

(7) (*Repeals the Companies Act 1985, s 256(3).*)

NOTES

Sub-s (2) is amended as follows:

Words in first pair of square brackets in para (c) substituted by the Companies Act 2006 (Consequential Amendments etc) Order 2008, SI 2008/948, art 3(1), Sch 1, Pt 2, para 233, as from 6 April 2008.

The word "EU" in square brackets in para (c) was substituted by the Treaty of Lisbon (Changes in Terminology) Order 2011, SI 2011/1043, art 6, as from 22 April 2011.

Para (ea) inserted by the Statutory Auditors and Third Country Auditors Regulations 2016, SI 2016/649, reg 17, Sch 5, para 1(1), (3), as from 17 June 2016.

Paras (eb) and (ec) inserted by the Statutory Auditors and Third Country Auditors (Amendment) (EU Exit) Regulations 2019, SI 2019/177, regs 41, 43(a), as from IP completion day (as defined in the European Union (Withdrawal Agreement) Act 2020, s 39) (for transitional provisions, see Sch 4 to the 2019 Regulations at **[12.88]**).

Words in first (outer) pair of square brackets in para (f), and words in square brackets in para (g), substituted by the Companies Act 2006, s 1264, Sch 14, paras 1(1), (2), as from 6 April 2008.

Words in second (inner) pair of square brackets in para (f) inserted by the Statutory Auditors and Third Country Auditors (Amendment) Regulations 2011, SI 2011/1856, reg 2, as from 1 October 2011 (in relation to audits of accounts for periods beginning on or after that date).

Paras (ka) and (kb) inserted by the Companies Act 2006, s 1238, 1247, as from 6 April 2008.

Paras (l)–(t) substituted, for the original para (l), by the Companies Act 2006, s 1274(1), (2), as from 8 November 2006.

Para (oa) inserted by the Pensions Act 2014, s 47, as from 14 July 2014.

Sub-s (5) is amended as follows:

Definitions "audit regulatory regime", "the competent authority", "third country", and "third country competent authority" inserted by SI 2019/177, regs 41, 43(a), as from IP completion day (as defined in the European Union (Withdrawal Agreement) Act 2020, s 39) (for transitional provisions, see Sch 4 to the 2019 Regulations at **[12.88]**).

Words in square brackets in the definitions "company" and "subsidiary" substituted by the Companies Act 2006 (Consequential Amendments, Transitional Provisions and Savings) Order 2009, SI 2009/1941, art 2(1), Sch 1, para 222(1)–(3), as from 1 October 2009.

Definitions "listed securities", "listing rules" and "issuer" substituted (for the original definitions "issuer", "listing rules" and "security") by the Prospectus Regulations 2005, SI 2005/1433, reg 2(3), Sch 3, para 6, as from 1 July 2005.

Words in square brackets in the definition "professional accountancy body" substituted by the Companies Act 2006, s 1264, Sch 14, paras 1(1), (2), as from 6 April 2008.

Definitions "professional actuarial body" and "regulatory functions (in relation to professional actuarial bodies)" inserted by the Companies Act 2006, s 1274(1), (3), as from 8 November 2006.

Definition "the 1986 Order" (omitted) originally inserted by the Companies Act 2006, s 1276(1), (4)(c), as from 8 November 2006; and subsequently repealed by SI 2009/1941, art 2(1), Sch 1, para 222(1), (4), as from 1 October 2009.

Sub-s (6): substituted by the Companies Act 2006, s 1276(1), (2), as from 8 November 2006.

Sub-ss (6A), (6B): inserted by the Local Audit and Accountability Act 2014, s 45, Sch 12, para 67, as from 1 April 2015.

[5.217]

17 Levy to pay expenses of bodies concerned with accounting standards etc

(1) For the purpose of meeting any part of the expenses of a grant-aided body, the Secretary of State may by regulations provide for a levy to be payable to that body ("the specified recipient") by bodies or persons which are specified, or are of a description specified, in the regulations.

(2) For the purposes of this section—

(a) "grant-aided body" means a body to whom the Secretary of State has paid, or is proposing to pay, grant under section 16; and

(b) any expenses of any body carrying on subsidiary activities of the grant-aided body (within the meaning of that section) are to be regarded as expenses of the grant-aided body.

(3) The power to specify (or to specify descriptions of) bodies or persons must be exercised in such a way that the levy is only payable by—

(a) bodies corporate to which[, or persons within subsection (3A) to whom,] the Secretary of State considers that any of the activities of the specified recipient, or any of its subsidiary activities, are relevant to a significant extent, or

(b) bodies or persons who the Secretary of State considers have a major interest in any of those activities being carried on.

[(3A) The following persons are within this subsection—

(a) the administrators of a public service pension scheme (within the meaning of section 1 of the Pension Schemes Act 1993);

(b) the trustees or managers of an occupational or personal pension scheme (within the meaning of that section).]

(4) Regulations under this section may in particular—

(a) specify the rate of the levy and the period in respect of which it is payable at that rate;

(b) make provision as to the times when, and the manner in which, payments are to be made in respect of the levy;

[(c) make different provision for different cases].

(5) In determining the rate of the levy payable in respect of a particular period, the Secretary of State—

(a) must take into account the amount of any grant which is to be or has been made to the specified recipient in respect of that period under section 16;

(b) may take into account estimated as well as actual expenses of that body in respect of that period.

(6) Any amount of levy payable by any body or person is a debt due from the body or person to the specified recipient, and is recoverable accordingly.

(7) The specified recipient must—

(a) keep proper accounts in respect of amounts of levy received, and

(b) prepare in relation to each levy period a statement of account relating to such amounts in such form and manner as is specified in the regulations.

(8) Those accounts must be audited, and the statement certified, by persons appointed by the Secretary of State.

(9) The power to make regulations under this section is exercisable by statutory instrument.

(10) Regulations to which this subsection applies may not be made unless a draft of the regulations has been laid before, and approved by a resolution of, each House of Parliament.

(11) Subsection (10) applies to—

(a) the first regulations under this section, and

(b) any other regulations under this section that would result in any change in the bodies or persons by whom the levy is payable.

(12) Otherwise, any statutory instrument containing regulations under this section is subject to annulment in pursuance of a resolution of either House of Parliament.

[(13) If a draft of any regulations to which subsection (10) applies would, apart from this subsection, be treated for the purposes of the standing orders of either House of Parliament as a hybrid instrument, it is to proceed in that House as if it were not such an instrument.]

NOTES

Sub-ss (3), (4): words in square brackets inserted by the Companies Act 2006, s 1275(1), (2), (4), as from 1 October 2009.

Sub-ss (3A), (13): inserted and added respectively by the Companies Act 2006, s 1275(1), (3), (5), as from 1 October 2009.

18 *(Repealed by the Small Business, Enterprise and Employment Act 2015, s 38(2), as from 1 June 2016. Note that the Small Business, Enterprise and Employment Act 2015 (Commencement No 5 and Saving Provision) Regulations 2016, SI 2016/532, reg 4(2) provides that the repeal of this section does not affect any exemption from liability arising under that section in respect of acts or omissions occurring before 1 June 2016.)*

[5.218]

[18A Power to confer exemption from liability

(1) The Secretary of State may by order or regulations provide for the exemption from liability in subsections (3) and (4) to apply to specified bodies or persons (referred to in this section as "exempt persons").

(2) The order or regulations may provide for the exemption to apply subject to specified conditions or for a specified period.

(3) Neither the exempt person, nor any person who is (or is acting as) a member, officer or member of staff of the exempt person, is to be liable in damages for anything done, or omitted to be done, for the purposes of or in connection with—

(a) the carrying on of those section 16(2) activities of the exempt person that are specified in relation to that person, or

(b) the purported carrying on of any such activities.

(4) Subsection (3) does not apply—

(a) if the act or omission is shown to have been in bad faith, or

(b) so as to prevent an award of damages in respect of the act or omission on the grounds that it was unlawful as a result of section 6(1) of the Human Rights Act 1998 (acts of public authorities incompatible with Convention rights).

(5) In this section—

"section 16(2) activities" means activities concerned with any of the matters within section 16(2);

"specified" means specified in an order or regulations under this section.

(6) Orders and regulations under this section—

(a) are to be made by statutory instrument;

(b) may make different provision for different cases;

(c) may make transitional provision and savings.

(7) A statutory instrument containing an order or regulations under this section is subject to annulment in pursuance of a resolution of either House of Parliament, subject to subsection (8).

(8) An order or regulations under this section may be included in a statutory instrument which may not be made unless a draft of the instrument is laid before, and approved by a resolution of, each House of Parliament.]

NOTES

Inserted by the Small Business, Enterprise and Employment Act 2015, s 38(1), as from 1 January 2016 (for the purposes of enabling the exercise of any power to make provision by regulations or order made by statutory instrument), and as from 1 June 2016 (otherwise).

Regulations: the Companies (Bodies Concerned with Auditing Standards etc) (Exemption from Liability) Regulations 2016, SI 2016/571; the Statutory Auditors and Third Country Auditors Regulations 2016, SI 2016/649 at **[4.650]**; the Statutory Auditors and Third Country Auditors (Amendment) (EU Exit) Regulations 2019, SI 2019/177 at **[12.83]**; the Supervision of Accounts and Reports (Prescribed Body) and Companies (Defective Accounts and Reports) (Authorised Person) Order 2021, SI 2021/456 at **[4.722]**; the International Accounting Standards (Delegation of Functions) (EU Exit) Regulations 2021, SI 2021/609 at **[12.191]**.

19–24 *((Chapters 3, 4): s 19 repealed by the Companies Act 2006, s 1295, Sch 16, as from 1 October 2007 (in part), and as from 6 April 2008 (otherwise); s 20 repealed by CA 2006, s 1295, Sch 16, as from 1 October 2007; s 21 substitutes CA 1985, s 447 at* **[5.33]**; *s 22 inserts CA 1985, s 448A at* **[5.36]**; *s 23 inserts CA 1985, ss 453A, 453B at* **[5.43]**, **[5.44]**; *s 24 inserts CA 1985, s 453C at* **[5.45]**.)

CHAPTER 5 SUPPLEMENTARY

[5.219]

25 Minor and consequential amendments

(1) Schedule 2 (minor and consequential amendments relating to Part 1) has effect.

(2) That Schedule has effect subject to the modifications set out in subsection (3)—

(a) in relation to England and Wales, in the case of an offence committed before [2 May 2022], and

(b) in relation to Scotland.

(3) The modifications are—

(a) the amendment in paragraph 10(2) has effect as if for "12 months" there were substituted "6 months";

(b) the amendment in paragraph 10(3) has effect as if for "12 months", in both places where it occurs, there were substituted "3 months";

(c) the amendment in paragraph 10(4) has effect as if for "12 months" there were substituted "6 months";

(d) the amendment in paragraph 26(2) has effect as if for "12 months" there were substituted "6 months"; and

(e) the amendment in paragraph 26(3) has effect as if for "12 months" there were substituted "6 months".

NOTES

Sub-s (2): words in square brackets in para (a) substituted by the Criminal Justice Act 2003 (Commencement No 33) and Sentencing Act 2020 (Commencement No 2) Regulations 2022, SI 2022/500, reg 5, Schedule, Pt 1, as from 28 April 2022.

PART 2 COMMUNITY INTEREST COMPANIES

Introductory

[5.220]

26 Community interest companies

(1) There is to be a new type of company to be known as the community interest company.

(2) In accordance with this Part—

(a) a company limited by shares or a company limited by guarantee and not having a share capital may be formed as or become a community interest company, and

(b) a company limited by guarantee and having a share capital may become a community interest company.

(3) A community interest company established for charitable purposes is to be treated as not being so established and accordingly—

(a) is not [an English charity or a Northern Ireland charity], and

(b) must not be [entered in the Scottish Charity Register].

NOTES

Sub-s (3): words in square brackets in para (a) substituted by the Companies Act 2006 (Commencement No 2, Consequential Amendments, Transitional Provisions and Savings) Order 2007, SI 2007/1093, art 6(2), Sch 4, Pt 1, para 1, as from 6 April

2007. Words in square brackets in para (b) substituted by the Charities and Trustee Investment (Scotland) Act 2005 (Consequential Provisions and Modifications) Order 2006, SI 2006/242, art 5, Schedule, Pt 1, para 8(1), (2), as from 1 April 2006.

[5.221]

27 Regulator

(1) There is to be an officer known as the Regulator of Community Interest Companies (referred to in this Part as "the Regulator").

(2) The Secretary of State must appoint a person to be the Regulator.

(3) The Regulator has such functions relating to community interest companies as are conferred or imposed by or by virtue of this Act or any other enactment.

(4) The Regulator must adopt an approach to the discharge of those functions which is based on good regulatory practice, that is an approach adopted having regard to—

(a) the likely impact on those who may be affected by the discharge of those functions,
(b) the outcome of consultations with, and with organisations representing, community interest companies and others with relevant experience, and
(c) the desirability of using the Regulator's resources in the most efficient and economic way.

(5) The Regulator may issue guidance, or otherwise provide assistance, about any matter relating to community interest companies.

(6) The Secretary of State may require the Regulator to issue guidance or otherwise provide assistance about any matter relating to community interest companies which is specified by the Secretary of State.

(7) Any guidance issued under this section must be such that it is readily accessible to, and capable of being easily understood by, those at whom it is aimed; and any other assistance provided under this section must be provided in the manner which the Regulator considers is most likely to be helpful to those to whom it is provided.

(8) Schedule 3 (further provisions about the Regulator) has effect.

[5.222]

28 Appeal Officer

(1) There is to be an officer known as the Appeal Officer for Community Interest Companies (referred to in this Part as "the Appeal Officer").

(2) The Secretary of State must appoint a person to be the Appeal Officer.

(3) The Appeal Officer has the function of determining appeals against decisions and orders of the Regulator which under or by virtue of this Act or any other enactment lie to the Appeal Officer.

(4) An appeal to the Appeal Officer against a decision or order of the Regulator may be brought on the ground that the Regulator made a material error of law or fact.

(5) On such an appeal the Appeal Officer must—

(a) dismiss the appeal,
(b) allow the appeal, or
(c) remit the case to the Regulator.

(6) Where a case is remitted the Regulator must reconsider it in accordance with any rulings of law and findings of fact made by the Appeal Officer.

(7) Schedule 4 (further provisions about the Appeal Officer) has effect.

[5.223]

29 Official Property Holder

(1) There is to be an officer known as the Official Property Holder for Community Interest Companies (referred to in this Part as "the Official Property Holder").

(2) The Regulator must appoint a member of the Regulator's staff to be the Official Property Holder.

(3) The Official Property Holder has such functions relating to property of community interest companies as are conferred or imposed by or by virtue of this Act or any other enactment.

(4) Schedule 5 (further provisions about the Official Property Holder) has effect.

Requirements

[5.224]

30 Cap on distributions and interest

(1) Community interest companies must not distribute assets to their members unless regulations make provision authorising them to do so.

(2) If regulations authorise community interest companies to distribute assets to their members, the regulations may impose limits on the extent to which they may do so.

(3) Regulations may impose limits on the payment of interest on debentures issued by, or debts of, community interest companies.

(4) Regulations under this section may make provision for limits to be set by the Regulator.

(5) The Regulator—

(a) may set a limit by reference to a rate determined by any other person (as it has effect from time to time), and
(b) may set different limits for different descriptions of community interest companies.

(6) The Regulator must (in accordance with section 27)—

(a) undertake appropriate consultation before setting a limit, and
(b) in setting a limit, have regard to its likely impact on community interest companies.

(7) Regulations under this section may include power for the Secretary of State to require the Regulator to review a limit or limits.

(8) Where the Regulator sets a limit he must publish notice of it in the Gazette.

NOTES

Regulations: the Community Interest Company Regulations 2005, SI 2005/1788 at **[6.106]**; the Community Interest Company (Amendment) Regulations 2009, SI 2009/1942; the Community Interest Company (Amendment) Regulations

2014, SI 2014/2483.

[5.225]

31 Distribution of assets on winding up

(1) Regulations may make provision for and in connection with the distribution, on the winding up of a community interest company, of any assets of the company which remain after satisfaction of the company's liabilities.

(2) The regulations may, in particular, amend or modify the operation of any enactment or instrument.

NOTES

Regulations: the Community Interest Company Regulations 2005, SI 2005/1788 at **[6.106]**; the Community Interest Company (Amendment) Regulations 2009, SI 2009/1942.

[5.226]

32 [Articles of association]

(1) The [articles] of a community interest company must state that the company is to be a community interest company.

(2) . . .

(3) The [articles] of a community interest company of any description—

(a) must at all times include such provisions as regulations require to be included in the [articles] of every community interest company or a community interest company of that description, and

(b) must not include such provisions as regulations require not to be so included.

(4) The provisions required by regulations under subsection (3)(a) to be included in the [articles] of a community interest company may (in particular) include—

(a) provisions about the transfer and distribution of the company's assets (including their distribution on a winding up),

(b) provisions about the payment of interest on debentures issued by the company or debts of the company,

(c) provisions about membership of the company,

(d) provisions about the voting rights of members of the company,

(e) provisions about the appointment and removal of directors of the company, and

(f) provisions about voting at meetings of directors of the company.

(5) The [articles] of a community interest company are of no effect to the extent that they—

(a) are inconsistent with provisions required to be included in the [articles] of the company by regulations under subsection (3)(a), or

(b) include provisions required not to be included by regulations under subsection (3)(b).

(6) Regulations may make provision for and in connection with restricting the ability of a community interest company [to amend its articles so as to add, remove or alter a statement of the company's objects].

NOTES

All words in square brackets were substituted, and sub-s (2) was repealed, by the Companies Act 2006 (Consequential Amendments, Transitional Provisions and Savings) Order 2009, SI 2009/1941, art 2(1), Sch 1, para 223, as from 1 October 2009.

Regulations: the Community Interest Company Regulations 2005, SI 2005/1788 at **[6.106]**; the Community Interest Company (Amendment) Regulations 2009, SI 2009/1942.

[5.227]

33 Names

(1) The name of a community interest company which is not a public company must end with—

(a) "community interest company", or

(b) "cic".

(2) [In the case of a Welsh company, its name may instead] end with—

(a) "cwmni buddiant cymunedol", or

(b) "cbc",

. . .

(3) The name of a community interest company which is a public company must end with—

(a) "community interest public limited company", or

(b) "community interest plc".

(4) [In the case of a Welsh company, its name may instead] end with—

(a) "cwmni buddiant cymunedol cyhoeddus cyfyngedig", or

(b) "cwmni buddiant cymunedol ccc",

. . .

(5) . . .

(6) Schedule 6 (further provisions about names) has effect.

NOTES

Words in square brackets in sub-ss (2), (4) substituted, and words omitted from those subsections and the whole of sub-s (5) repealed, by the Companies Act 2006 (Consequential Amendments, Transitional Provisions and Savings) Order 2009, SI 2009/1941, art 2(1), Sch 1, para 224, as from 1 October 2009.

[5.228]

34 Community interest company reports

(1) The directors of a community interest company must prepare in respect of each financial year a report about the company's activities during the financial year (a "community interest company report").

(2) [Regulations must make provision] requiring the directors of a community interest company to deliver to the registrar of companies a copy of the community interest company report.

(3) Regulations—

(a) must make provision requiring community interest company reports to include information about the remuneration of directors,
(b) may make provision as to the form of, and other information to be included in, community interest company reports, and
(c) may apply provisions of [. . . the Companies Act 2006] relating to directors' reports to community interest company reports (with any appropriate modifications).

(4) The registrar of companies must forward to the Regulator a copy of each community interest company report delivered to the registrar by virtue of this section.

NOTES

Sub-s (2): words in square brackets substituted by the Companies Act 2006 (Consequential Amendments etc) Order 2008, SI 2008/948, art 3(1), Sch 1, Pt 2, para 234(1), (2)(a), as from 6 April 2008.

Sub-s (3): words in square brackets substituted by the Companies Act 2006 (Commencement No 3, Consequential Amendments, Transitional Provisions and Savings) Order 2007, SI 2007/2194, art 10(1), Sch 4, Pt 3, para 104, as from 1 October 2007. Words omitted therefrom repealed by SI 2008/948, art 3, Sch 1, Pt 2, para 234(1), (2)(b), Sch 2, as from 6 April 2008.

Regulations: the Community Interest Company Regulations 2005, SI 2005/1788 at **[6.106]**; the Community Interest Company (Amendment) Regulations 2012, SI 2012/2335; the Community Interest Company (Amendment) Regulations 2014, SI 2014/2483; the Companies (Miscellaneous Reporting) Regulations 2018, SI 2018/860.

[5.229]
35 Community interest test and excluded companies

(1) This section has effect for the purposes of this Part.
(2) A company satisfies the community interest test if a reasonable person might consider that its activities are being carried on for the benefit of the community.
(3) An object stated in the [articles] of a company is a community interest object of the company if a reasonable person might consider that the carrying on of activities by the company in furtherance of the object is for the benefit of the community.
(4) Regulations may provide that activities of a description prescribed by the regulations are to be treated as being, or as not being, activities which a reasonable person might consider are activities carried on for the benefit of the community.
(5) "Community" includes a section of the community (whether in [the United Kingdom] or anywhere else); and regulations may make provision about what does, does not or may constitute a section of the community.
(6) A company is an excluded company if it is a company of a description prescribed by regulations.

NOTES

Sub-s (3): word in square brackets substituted by the Companies Act 2006 (Consequential Amendments, Transitional Provisions and Savings) Order 2009, SI 2009/1941, art 2(1), Sch 1, para 225, as from 1 October 2009.

Sub-s (5): words in square brackets substituted by the Companies Act 2006 (Commencement No 2, Consequential Amendments, Transitional Provisions and Savings) Order 2007, SI 2007/1093, art 6(2), Sch 4, Pt 1, para 5, as from 6 April 2007.

Regulations: the Community Interest Company Regulations 2005, SI 2005/1788 at **[6.106]**; the Community Interest Company (Amendment) Regulations 2009, SI 2009/1942.

Becoming a community interest company

[5.230]
[36 Formation of company as a community interest company

(1) If a company is to be formed as a community interest company, the documents delivered to the registrar of companies under section 9 of the Companies Act 2006 (registration documents) must be accompanied by the prescribed formation documents.
(2) The "prescribed formation documents" means such declarations or statements as are required by regulations to accompany the application, in such form as may be approved in accordance with the regulations.
(3) On receiving the documents delivered under that section and the prescribed formation documents, the registrar must (instead of registering the documents)—
(a) forward a copy of each of the documents to the Regulator, and
(b) retain the documents pending the Regulator's decision.]

NOTES

Substituted (together with ss 36A, 36B for the original s 36) by the Companies Act 2006 (Consequential Amendments, Transitional Provisions and Savings) Order 2009, SI 2009/1941, art 2(1), Sch 1, para 226, as from 1 October 2009.

Regulations: the Community Interest Company Regulations 2005, SI 2005/1788 at **[6.106]**.

[5.231]
[36A Formation as community interest company: decision on eligibility

(1) The Regulator must decide whether the company is eligible to be formed as a community interest company.
(2) A company is eligible to be formed as a community interest company if—
(a) its articles comply with the requirements imposed by and by virtue of section 32,
(b) its proposed name complies with section 33, and
(c) the Regulator, having regard to the application and accompanying documents and any other relevant considerations, considers that the company—
(i) will satisfy the community interest test, and
(ii) is not an excluded company.

(3) The Regulator must give notice of the decision to the registrar of companies (but the registrar is not required to record it).]

NOTES

Substituted as noted to s 36 at **[5.230]**.

[5.232]

[36B Formation as community interest company: implementation of decision on eligibility

(1) If the Regulator decides that the company is eligible to be formed as a community interest company, the registrar of companies must—

(a) proceed in accordance with sections 14 and 15 of the Companies Act 2006 (registration and issue of certificate of incorporation), and

(b) if the company is entered on the register, retain and record the prescribed formation documents.

(2) The certificate of incorporation must state that the company is a community interest company and is conclusive evidence that the company is a community interest company.

(3) If the Regulator decides that the company is not eligible to be formed as a community interest company, any subscriber to the memorandum of association may appeal to the Appeal Officer against the decision.]

NOTES

Substituted as noted to s 36 at **[5.230]**.

[5.233]

[37 Company becoming a community interest company

(1) If a company is to become a community interest company—

(a) the company must by special resolution—

(i) state that it is to be a community interest company,

(ii) make such alterations of its articles as it considers necessary to comply with requirements imposed by and by virtue of section 32 or otherwise appropriate in connection with becoming a community interest company, and

(iii) change its name to comply with section 33;

(b) the conditions specified below must be met; and

(c) an application must be delivered to the registrar of companies in accordance with section 37C together with the other documents required by that section.

(2) The conditions referred to in subsection (1)(b) are that—

(a) where no application under section 37A for cancellation of the special resolutions has been made—

(i) having regard to the number of members who consented to or voted in favour of the resolutions, no such application may be made, or

(ii) the period within which such an application could be made has expired, or

(b) where such an application has been made—

(i) the application has been withdrawn, or

(ii) an order has been made confirming the resolutions and a copy of that order has been delivered to the registrar.

(3) Section 30 of the Companies Act 2006 (copies of resolutions to be forwarded to the registrar) applies to the special resolutions as follows—

(a) that section is complied with by forwarding copies of the resolutions together with the application in accordance with section 37C,

(b) copies of the resolutions must not be so forwarded before the relevant date, and

(c) subsection (1) of that section has effect in relation to the resolutions as if it referred to 15 days after the relevant date.

(4) The relevant date is—

(a) if an application is made under section 37A for cancellation of the special resolutions—

(i) the date on which the court determines the application (or if there is more than one application, the date on which the last to be determined by the court is determined), or

(ii) such later date as the court may order;

(b) if there is no such application—

(i) if having regard to the number of members who consented to or voted in favour of the resolutions, no such application may be made, the date on which the resolutions were passed or made (or, if the resolutions were passed or made on different days, the date on which the last of them was passed or made);

(ii) in any other case, the end of the period for making such an application.]

NOTES

Substituted (together with ss 37A–37C for the original s 37) by the Companies Act 2006 (Consequential Amendments, Transitional Provisions and Savings) Order 2009, SI 2009/1941, art 2(1), Sch 1, para 226, as from 1 October 2009.

[5.234]

[37A Becoming a community interest company: application to court to cancel resolutions

(1) Where special resolutions have been passed with a view to the company becoming a community interest company, an application to the court for the cancellation of the resolutions may be made—

(a) by the holders of not less in the aggregate than 15% in nominal value of the company's issued share capital or any class of the company's issued share capital (disregarding any shares held by the company as treasury shares);

(b) if the company is not limited by shares, by not less than 15% of its members; or

(c) by the holders of not less than 15% of the company's debentures entitling the holders to object to an alteration of its objects;

but not by a person who has consented to or voted in favour of the resolutions.

(2) The application—

(a) must be made within 28 days after the date on which the resolutions are passed or made (or, if the resolutions are passed or made on different days, the date on which the last of them is passed or made), and
(b) may be made on behalf of the persons entitled to make it by such one or more of their number as they may appoint for the purpose.

(3) On the hearing of the application the court shall make an order either cancelling or confirming the resolutions.

(4) The court may—
(a) make that order on such terms and conditions as it thinks fit,
(b) if it thinks fit adjourn the proceedings in order that an arrangement may be made to the satisfaction of the court for the purchase of the interests of dissentient members, and
(c) give such directions, and make such orders, as it thinks expedient for facilitating or carrying into effect any such arrangement.

(5) The court's order may, if the court thinks fit—
(a) provide for the purchase by the company of the shares of any of its members and for the reduction accordingly of the company's capital; and
(b) make such alteration in the company's articles as may be required in consequence of that provision.

(6) The court's order may, if the court thinks fit, require the company not to make any, or any specified, amendments to its articles without the leave of the court.]

NOTES

Substituted as noted to s 37 at **[5.233]**.

[5.235]

[37B Becoming a community interest company: notice to registrar of court application or order

(1) On making an application under section 37A (application to court to cancel resolutions) the applicants, or the person making the application on their behalf, must immediately give notice to the registrar of companies.

This is without prejudice to any provision of rules of court as to service of notice of the application.

(2) On being served with notice of any such application, the company must immediately give notice to the registrar.

(3) Within 15 days of the making of the court's order on the application, or such longer period as the court may at any time direct, the company must deliver to the registrar a copy of the order.

(4) If a company fails to comply with subsection (2) or (3) an offence is committed by—
(a) the company, and
(b) every officer of the company who is in default.

(5) A person guilty of an offence under this section is liable on summary conviction to a fine not exceeding level 3 on the standard scale and, for continued contravention, a daily default fine not exceeding one-tenth of level 3 on the standard scale.]

NOTES

Substituted as noted to s 37 at **[5.233]**.

[5.236]

[37C Becoming a community interest company: application and accompanying documents

(1) An application to become a community interest company must be accompanied by—
(a) a copy of the special resolutions,
(b) a copy of the company's articles as proposed to be amended, and
(c) the prescribed conversion documents.

(2) The "prescribed conversion documents" means such declarations or statements as are required by regulations to accompany the application, in such form as may be approved in accordance with the regulations.

(3) On receiving an application to become a community interest company together with the other documents required to accompany it, the registrar of companies must (instead of recording the documents and entering a new name on the register)—
(a) forward a copy of each of the documents to the Regulator, and
(b) retain the documents pending the Regulator's decision.]

NOTES

Substituted as noted to s 37 at **[5.233]**.

[5.237]

[38 Becoming a community interest company: decision by Regulator

(1) The Regulator must decide whether the company is eligible to become a community interest company.

(2) A company is eligible to become a community interest company if—
(a) its articles as proposed to be amended comply with the requirements imposed by and by virtue of section 32,
(b) its proposed name complies with section 33, and
(c) the Regulator, having regard to the application and accompanying documents and any other relevant considerations, considers that the company—
(i) will satisfy the community interest test, and
(ii) is not an excluded company.

(3) The Regulator must give notice of the decision to the registrar of companies (but the registrar is not required to record it).]

NOTES

Substituted (together with s 38A for the original s 38) by the Companies Act 2006 (Consequential Amendments, Transitional Provisions and Savings) Order 2009, SI 2009/1941, art 2(1), Sch 1, para 227(2), as from 1 October 2009.

[5.238]

[38A Becoming a community interest company: implementation of decision on eligibility

(1) If the Regulator gives notice of a decision that the company is eligible to become a community interest company, the registrar of companies must—

(a) proceed in accordance with section 80 of the Companies Act 2006 (change of name: registration and issue of new certificate of incorporation), and

(b) if the registrar enters the new name of the company on the register, retain and record the documents mentioned in section 37C(3).

(2) The new certificate of incorporation must state—

(a) that it is issued on the company's conversion to a community interest company,

(b) the date on which it is issued, and

(c) that the company is a community interest company.

(3) On the issue of the certificate—

(a) the company by virtue of the issue of the certificate becomes a community interest company, and

(b) the changes in the company's name and articles take effect.

(4) The certificate is conclusive evidence that the company is a community interest company.

(5) If the Regulator decides that the company is not eligible to become a community interest company, the company may appeal to the Appeal Officer against the decision.]

NOTES

Substituted as noted to s 38 at **[5.237]**.

[5.239]

39 [Becoming a community interest company: English charities]

(1) A [company that is an English charity] may not [become a community interest company] without the prior written consent of the [Charity Commission].

(2) If a [company that is an English charity] contravenes subsection (1), the [Charity Commission] may apply to the High Court for an order quashing any altered certificate of incorporation issued under [section 38A].

(3) If a [company that is an English charity] becomes a community interest company, that does not affect the application of—

(a) any property acquired under any disposition or agreement previously made otherwise than for full consideration in money or money's worth, or any property representing property so acquired,

(b) any property representing income which has previously accrued, or

(c) the income from any such property.

(4) . . .

NOTES

Section heading substituted, words in second pair of square brackets in sub-s (1) substituted, and final words in square brackets in sub-s (2) substituted, by the Companies Act 2006 (Consequential Amendments, Transitional Provisions and Savings) Order 2009, SI 2009/1941, art 2(1), Sch 1, para 228, as from 1 October 2009.

Words "Charity Commission" in square brackets in sub-ss (1) and (2) substituted by the Charities Act 2006, s 75, Sch 8, paras 200, 201, as from 27 February 2007.

All other words in square bracket substituted, and sub-s (4) repealed, by the Companies Act 2006 (Commencement No 2, Consequential Amendments, Transitional Provisions and Savings) Order 2007, SI 2007/1093, art 6(2), Sch 4, Pt 1, para 9, as from 6 April 2007.

[5.240]

40 [Becoming a community interest company: Scottish charities]

(1), (2) . . .

(3) Regulations may repeal subsections (1) and (2); and subsections (4) to (7) have effect on and after the day on which regulations under this subsection come into force.

(4) A [company that is a Scottish charity] may not [become a community interest company] without the prior written consent—

(a) if the company's registered office is situated in Scotland, of the Scottish Charity Regulator, or

(b) if the company's registered office is situated in England and Wales (or Wales), of both the Scottish Charity Regulator and the [Charity Commission].

(5) If a [company that is a Scottish charity] contravenes subsection (4)(a), the Scottish Charity Regulator may apply to the Court of Session for an order quashing any altered certificate of incorporation issued under [section 38A].

(6) If a [company that is a Scottish charity] contravenes subsection (4)(b), the Scottish Charity Regulator or the [Charity Commission] may apply to the High Court for such an order.

(7) If a [company that is a Scottish charity] becomes a community interest company, [it shall continue to be under a duty to apply—

(a) any property previously acquired, or any property representing property previously acquired,

(b) any property representing income which has previously accrued, and

(c) the income from any such property,

in accordance with its purposes as set out in its entry in the Scottish Charity Register immediately before it became a community interest company.]

(8), (9) . . .

NOTES

Section heading: substituted by the Companies Act 2006 (Consequential Amendments, Transitional Provisions and Savings) Order 2009, SI 2009/1941, art 2(1), Sch 1, para 229(1), (2), as from 1 October 2009.

Sub-ss (1), (2): repealed by the Community Interest Company (Amendment) Regulations 2009, SI 2009/1942, reg 2, as from 1 October 2009.

Sub-s (4): words in first pair of square brackets substituted by the Companies Act 2006 (Commencement No 2, Consequential Amendments, Transitional Provisions and Savings) Order 2007, SI 2007/1093, art 6(2), Sch 4, Pt 1, para 10(a), as from 6 April

2007. Words in second pair of square brackets substituted by SI 2009/1941, art 2(1), Sch 1, para 229(1), (3), as from 1 October 2009. Words in final pair of square brackets substituted by the Charities Act 2006, s 75, Sch 8, paras 200, 202, as from 27 February 2007.

Sub-s (5): words in first pair of square brackets substituted by SI 2007/1093, art 6(2), Sch 4, Pt 1, para 10(a), (b), as from 6 April 2007. Words in second pair of square brackets substituted by SI 2009/1941, art 2(1), Sch 1, para 229(1), (4), as from 1 October 2009.

Sub-s (6): words in first pair of square brackets substituted by SI 2007/1093, art 6(2), Sch 4, Pt 1, para 10(a), as from 6 April 2007. Words in second pair of square brackets substituted by the Charities Act 2006, s 75, Sch 8, paras 200, 202, as from 27 February 2007.

Sub-s (7): words in first pair of square brackets substituted by SI 2007/1093, art 6(2), Sch 4, Pt 1, para 10(a), as from 6 April 2007. Words in second pair of square brackets substituted by the Charities and Trustee Investment (Scotland) Act 2005 (Consequential Provisions and Modifications) Order 2006, SI 2006/242, art 5, Schedule, Pt 1, para 8(1), (3)(a), as from 1 April 2006.

Sub-s (8): repealed by SI 2007/1093, art 6(2), Sch 4, Pt 1, para 10(c), as from 6 April 2007.

Sub-s (9): repealed by SI 2006/242, art 5, Schedule, Pt 1, para 8(1), (3)(c), as from 1 April 2006.

Commissioners of Inland Revenue: a reference to the Commissioners of Inland Revenue is now to be taken as a reference to the Commissioners for Her Majesty's Revenue and Customs; see the Commissioners for Revenue and Customs Act 2005, s 50(1), (7).

Regulations: the Community Interest Company Regulations 2005, SI 2005/1788 at **[6.106]**; the Community Interest Company (Amendment) Regulations 2009, SI 2009/1942.

[5.241]

[40A [Becoming a community interest company: Northern Ireland charities]

(1) A company that is a Northern Ireland charity may not become a community interest company.

(2) If a company that is a Northern Ireland charity purports [to become a community interest company], the Commissioners of Her Majesty's Revenue and Customs may apply to the High Court for an order quashing any altered certificate of incorporation under [section 38A].]

NOTES

Inserted by the Companies Act 2006 (Commencement No 2, Consequential Amendments, Transitional Provisions and Savings) Order 2007, SI 2007/1093, art 6(2), Sch 4, Pt 1, para 11, as from 6 April 2007.

Section heading, sub-s (2): words in square brackets substituted by the Companies Act 2006 (Consequential Amendments, Transitional Provisions and Savings) Order 2009, SI 2009/1941, art 2(1), Sch 1, para 230, as from 1 October 2009.

Supervision by Regulator

[5.242]

41 Conditions for exercise of supervisory powers

(1) In deciding whether and how to exercise the powers conferred by sections 42 to 51 the Regulator must adopt an approach which is based on the principle that those powers should be exercised only to the extent necessary to maintain confidence in community interest companies.

(2) No power conferred on the Regulator by—
- (a) section 45 (appointment of director),
- (b) section 46 (removal of director),
- (c) section 47 (appointment of manager), or
- (d) section 48 (property),

is exercisable in relation to a community interest company unless the company default condition is satisfied in relation to the power and the company.

(3) The company default condition is satisfied in relation to a power and a company if it appears to the Regulator necessary to exercise the power in relation to the company because—
- (a) there has been misconduct or mismanagement in the administration of the company,
- (b) there is a need to protect the company's property or to secure the proper application of that property,
- (c) the company is not satisfying the community interest test, or
- (d) if the company has community interest objects, the company is not carrying on any activities in pursuit of those objects.

(4) The power conferred on the Regulator by section 49 (transfer of shares etc) is not exercisable in relation to a community interest company unless it appears to the Regulator that the company is an excluded company.

[5.243]

42 Investigation

(1) The Regulator may—
- (a) investigate the affairs of a community interest company, or
- (b) appoint any person (other than a member of the Regulator's staff) to investigate the affairs of a community interest company on behalf of the Regulator.

(2) Subsection (1)(b) is in addition to paragraph 5 of Schedule 3 (powers of Regulator exercisable by authorised members of staff) and does not affect the application of that paragraph to the Regulator's power under subsection (1)(a).

(3) Schedule 7 (further provision about investigations under this section) has effect.

[5.244]

43 Audit

(1) The Regulator may by order require a community interest company to allow the annual accounts of the company to be audited by a qualified auditor appointed by the Regulator.

(2) A person is a qualified auditor if he is eligible for appointment [as a statutory auditor under Part 42 of the Companies Act 2006].

(3) [Sections 499 to 501 of the Companies Act 2006] (auditor's rights to information) apply in relation to an auditor appointed under this section . . .

(4) On completion of the audit the auditor must make a report to the Regulator on such matters and in such form as the Regulator specifies.
(5) The expenses of the audit, including the remuneration of the auditor, are to be paid by the Regulator.
(6) An audit under this section is in addition to, and does not affect, any audit required by or by virtue of any other enactment.

NOTES

Sub-s (2): words in square brackets substituted by the Companies Act 2006 (Consequential Amendments etc) Order 2008, SI 2008/948, art 3(1), Sch 1, Pt 1, para 31, as from 6 April 2008.

Sub-s (3): words in square brackets substituted by SI 2008/948, art 3(1), Sch 1, Pt 2, para 234(1), (3), as from 6 April 2008. Words omitted repealed by the Companies Act 2006 (Commencement No 3, Consequential Amendments, Transitional Provisions and Savings) Order 2007, SI 2007/2194, art 10(1), (3), Sch 4, Pt 3, para 106, Sch 5, as from 1 October 2007.

[5.245]
44 Civil proceedings
(1) The Regulator may bring civil proceedings in the name and on behalf of a community interest company.
(2) Before instituting proceedings under this section the Regulator must give written notice to the company stating—
  (a) the cause of action,
  (b) the remedy sought, and
  (c) a summary of the facts on which the proceedings are to be based.
(3) Any director of the company may apply to the court for an order—
  (a) that proposed proceedings are not to be instituted under this section, or
  (b) that proceedings instituted under this section are to be discontinued.
(4) On an application under subsection (3) the court may make such order as it thinks fit.
(5) In particular the court may (as an alternative to ordering that proposed proceedings are not to be instituted under this section or that proceedings instituted under this section are to be discontinued) order—
  (a) that the proposed proceedings may be instituted under this section, or the proceedings instituted under this section may be continued, on such terms and conditions as the court thinks fit,
  (b) that any proceedings instituted by the company are to be discontinued, or
  (c) that any proceedings instituted by the company may be continued on such terms and conditions as the court thinks fit.
(6) The Regulator must indemnify the company against any costs (or expenses) incurred by it in connection with proceedings brought under this section.
(7) Any costs (or expenses)—
  (a) awarded to the company in connection with proceedings brought under this section, or
  (b) incurred by the company in connection with the proceedings and which it is agreed should be paid by a defendant (or defender),
are to be paid to the Regulator.

[5.246]
45 Appointment of director
(1) The Regulator may by order appoint a director of a community interest company.
(2) The person appointed may be anyone whom the Regulator thinks appropriate, other than a member of the Regulator's staff.
(3) A person may be appointed as a director of a company under this section—
  (a) whether or not the person is a member of the company, and
  (b) irrespective of any provision made by the [articles] of the company or a resolution of the company . . .
(4) An order appointing a person to be a director of a company under this section must specify the terms on which the director is to hold office; and those terms have effect as if contained in a contract between the director and the company.
(5) The terms specified must include the period for which the director is to hold office, and may include terms as to the remuneration of the director by the company.
(6) A director appointed under this section has all the powers of the directors appointed by the company (including powers exercisable only by a particular director or class of directors).
(7) A director appointed under this section may not be removed by the company, but may be removed by the Regulator at any time.
(8) Where—
  (a) a person is appointed to be a director of the company under this section, or
  (b) a person so appointed ceases to be a director of the company,
the obligation which would otherwise be imposed on the company under [section 167(1)(a) of the Companies Act 2006] (requirement that company notify change among directors to registrar) is instead an obligation of the Regulator.
(9) But if subsection (10) applies, [section 167(1)(a)] applies as if the period within which the Regulator must send a notification to the registrar of companies is 14 days from the date on which the Regulator receives notification under that subsection.
(10) Where a person appointed to be a director of the company under this section ceases to be a director of the company (otherwise than by removal under subsection (7)), the company must give notification of that fact to the Regulator in a form approved by the Regulator before the end of the period of 14 days beginning with the date on which the person ceases to be a director.
[(11) If default is made in complying with subsection (10) an offence is committed by—
  (a) the company, and
  (b) every officer of the company who is in default.
  For this purpose a shadow director is treated as an officer of the company.

(12) A person guilty of an offence under subsection (11) is liable on summary conviction to a fine not exceeding level 5 on the standard scale and, for continued contravention, a daily default fine not exceeding [one-tenth of the greater of £5,000 or level 4 on the standard scale].]

(13) The company may appeal to the Appeal Officer against an order under this section.

NOTES

Sub-s (3): word in square brackets substituted by the Companies Act 2006 (Consequential Amendments, Transitional Provisions and Savings) Order 2009, SI 2009/1941, art 2(1), Sch 1, para 231(1), (2), as from 1 October 2009. Words omitted repealed by the Companies Act 2006 (Consequential Amendments etc) Order 2008, SI 2008/948, art 3, Sch 1, Pt 2, para 234(1), (4), Sch 2, as from 6 April 2008.

Sub-s (8), (9): words in square brackets substituted by SI 2009/1941, art 2(1), Sch 1, para 231(1), (3), (4), as from 1 October 2009.

Sub-s (11): substituted, together with sub-s (12), by SI 2009/1941, art 2(1), Sch 1, para 231(1), (5), as from 1 October 2009.

Sub-s (12): substituted as noted above. Words in square brackets substituted (for the original words "one-tenth of level 5 on the standard scale") by the Legal Aid, Sentencing and Punishment of Offenders Act 2012 (Fines on Summary Conviction) Regulations 2015, SI 2015/664, reg 3, Sch 3, Pt 1, para 8, as from 12 March 2015, in relation to England and Wales only (except in relation to (a) fines for offences committed before 12 March 2015, (b) the operation of restrictions on fines that may be imposed on a person aged under 18, or (c) fines that may be imposed on a person convicted by a magistrates' court who is to be sentenced as if convicted on indictment).

[5.247]

46 Removal of director

(1) The Regulator may by order remove a director of a community interest company.

(2) If a person has been removed under subsection (1)—

- (a) the company may not subsequently appoint him a director of the company, and
- (b) any assignment to the person of the office of director of the company is of no effect (even if approved by special resolution of the company).

(3) The Regulator may by order suspend a director of the company pending a decision whether to remove him.

(4) The maximum period for which a director may be suspended under subsection (3) is one year.

(5) If the Regulator suspends a director under subsection (3) the Regulator may give directions in relation to the performance of the director's functions.

(6) The Regulator may discharge an order made under subsection (1).

(7) The discharge of an order made under subsection (1) does not reinstate the person removed by the order as a director of the company, but on the discharge of the order subsection (2) ceases to apply to the person.

(8) The Regulator must from time to time review any order made under subsection (3) and, if it is appropriate to do so, discharge the order.

(9) Before making an order under subsection (1) or (3) in relation to a director, the Regulator must give at least 14 days' notice to—

- (a) the director, and
- (b) the company.

(10) Where an order is made in relation to a director under subsection (1) or (3) the director may appeal against the order—

- (a) in England and Wales [or Northern Ireland], to the High Court, or
- (b) in Scotland, to the Court of Session.

(11) The Regulator must, before the end of the period of 14 days beginning with the date on which—

- (a) an order under subsection (1) is made or discharged,
- (b) an order under subsection (3) is made or discharged or expires, or
- (c) an order under subsection (1) or (3) is quashed on appeal,

give notification of that event to the registrar of companies in a form approved by the registrar of companies.

(12) Where subsection (11) imposes an obligation to notify the registrar of companies of an event, [section 167(1)(a) of the Companies Act 2006] (requirement that company notify change among directors to registrar) does not apply in respect of the event.

NOTES

Sub-s (10): words in square brackets inserted by the Companies Act 2006 (Commencement No 2, Consequential Amendments, Transitional Provisions and Savings) Order 2007, SI 2007/1093, art 6(2), Sch 4, Pt 1, para 14(a), as from 6 April 2007.

Sub-s (12): words in square brackets substituted by the Companies Act 2006 (Consequential Amendments, Transitional Provisions and Savings) Order 2009, SI 2009/1941, art 2(1), Sch 1, para 232, as from 1 October 2009.

[5.248]

47 Appointment of manager

(1) The Regulator may by order appoint a manager in respect of the property and affairs of a community interest company.

(2) The person appointed may be anyone whom the Regulator thinks appropriate, other than a member of the Regulator's staff.

(3) An order under subsection (1) may make provision as to the functions to be exercised by, and the powers of, the manager.

(4) The order may in particular provide—

- (a) for the manager to have such of the functions of the company's directors as are specified in the order, and
- (b) for the company's directors to be prevented from exercising any of those functions.

(5) In carrying out his functions the manager acts as the company's agent; and a person dealing with the manager in good faith and for value need not inquire whether the manager is acting within his powers.

(6) The appointment of the manager does not affect—

(a) any right of any person to appoint a receiver or manager of the company's property (including any right under section 51 of the Insolvency Act 1986 (c 45) [(power to appoint receiver under law of Scotland)]), or

(b) the rights of a receiver or manager appointed by a person other than the Regulator.

(7) The manager's functions are to be discharged by him under the supervision of the Regulator; and the Regulator must from time to time review the order by which the manager is appointed and, if it is appropriate to do so, discharge it in whole or in part.

(8) In particular, the Regulator must discharge the order on the appointment of a person to act as administrative receiver, administrator, provisional liquidator or liquidator of the company.

(9) The Regulator may apply to the court for directions in relation to any matter arising in connection with the manager's functions or powers.

(10) On an application under subsection (9) the court may give such directions or make such orders as it thinks fit.

(11) The costs of any application under subsection (9) are to be paid by the company.

(12) Regulations may authorise the Regulator—

(a) to require a manager to make reports,

(b) to require a manager to give security (or, in Scotland, to find caution) for the due exercise of the manager's functions, and

(c) to remove a manager in circumstances prescribed by the regulations.

(13) Regulations may—

(a) provide for a manager's remuneration to be payable from the property of the company, and

(b) authorise the Regulator to determine the amount of a manager's remuneration and to disallow any amount of remuneration in circumstances prescribed by the regulations.

(14) The company may appeal to the Appeal Officer against an order under this section.

NOTES

Sub-s (6): words in square brackets inserted by the Companies Act 2006 (Commencement No 2, Consequential Amendments, Transitional Provisions and Savings) Order 2007, SI 2007/1093, art 6(2), Sch 4, Pt 1, para 15, as from 6 April 2007.

Regulations: the Community Interest Company Regulations 2005, SI 2005/1788 at **[6.106]**.

[5.249]

48 Property

(1) The Regulator may by order—

(a) vest in the Official Property Holder any property held by or in trust for a community interest company, or

(b) require persons in whom such property is vested to transfer it to the Official Property Holder.

(2) The Regulator—

(a) may order a person who holds property on behalf of a community interest company, or on behalf of a trustee of a community interest company, not to part with the property without the Regulator's consent, and

(b) may order any debtor of a community interest company not to make any payment in respect of the debtor's liability to the company without the Regulator's consent.

(3) The Regulator may by order restrict—

(a) the transactions which may be entered into by a community interest company, or

(b) the nature or amount of the payments that a community interest company may make,

and the order may in particular provide that transactions may not be entered into or payments made without the Regulator's consent.

(4) The vesting or transfer of property under subsection (1) does not constitute a breach of a covenant or condition against alienation, and no right listed in subsection (5) operates or becomes exercisable as a result of the vesting or transfer.

(5) The rights are—

(a) a right of reverter (or, in Scotland, the right of the fiar on the termination of a liferent),

(b) a right of pre-emption,

(c) a right of forfeiture,

(d) a right of re-entry,

(e) a right of irritancy,

(f) an option, and

(g) any right similar to those listed in paragraphs (a) to (f).

(6) The Regulator must from time to time review any order under this section and, if it is appropriate to do so, discharge the order in whole or in part.

(7) On discharging an order under subsection (1) the Regulator may make any order as to the vesting or transfer of the property, and give any directions, which he considers appropriate.

(8) If a person fails to comply with an order under subsection (1)(b), the Regulator may certify that fact in writing to the court.

(9) If, after hearing—

(a) any witnesses who may be produced against or on behalf of the alleged offender, and

(b) any statement which may be offered in defence,

the court is satisfied that the offender failed without reasonable excuse to comply with the order, it may deal with him as if he had been guilty of contempt of the court.

(10) A person who contravenes an order under subsection (2) or (3) commits an offence, but a prosecution may be instituted[—

(a) in England and Wales, only with the consent of the Regulator or the Director of Public Prosecutions;

(b) in Northern Ireland, only with the consent of the Regulator or the Director of Public Prosecutions for Northern Ireland].

(11) A person guilty of an offence under subsection (10) is liable on summary conviction to a fine not exceeding level 5 on the standard scale.

(12) Subsections (8) to (10) do not prevent the bringing of civil proceedings in respect of a contravention of an order under subsection (1)(b), (2) or (3).

(13) The company and any person to whom the order is directed may appeal to the Appeal Officer against an order under subsection (1) or (2).
(14) The company may appeal to the Appeal Officer against an order under subsection (3).

NOTES

Sub-s (10): words in square brackets substituted by the Companies Act 2006 (Commencement No 2, Consequential Amendments, Transitional Provisions and Savings) Order 2007, SI 2007/1093, art 6(2), Sch 4, Pt 1, para 16, as from 6 April 2007.

[5.250]
49 Transfer of shares etc

(1) If a community interest company has a share capital, the Regulator may by order transfer specified shares in the company to specified persons.
(2) If a community interest company is a company limited by guarantee, the Regulator may by order—
(a) extinguish the interests in the company of specified members of the company (otherwise than as shareholders), and
(b) appoint a new member in place of each member whose interest has been extinguished.
(3) An order under subsection (1) may not transfer any shares in respect of which—
(a) a dividend may be paid, or
(b) a distribution of the company's assets may be made if the company is wound up.
(4) An order under this section in relation to a company—
(a) may only transfer shares to, and appoint as new members, persons who have consented to the transfer or appointment, and
(b) may be made irrespective of any provision made by the [articles] of the company or a resolution of the company in general meeting.
(5) The company and any person from whom shares are transferred by the order may appeal to the Appeal Officer against an order under subsection (1).
(6) The company and any person whose interest is extinguished by the order may appeal to the Appeal Officer against an order under subsection (2).
(7) "Specified", in relation to an order, means specified in the order.

NOTES

Sub-s (4): word in square brackets substituted by the Companies Act 2006 (Consequential Amendments, Transitional Provisions and Savings) Order 2009, SI 2009/1941, art 2(1), Sch 1, para 233, as from 1 October 2009.

[5.251]
50 Petition for winding up

(1) The Regulator may present a petition for a community interest company to be wound up if the court is of the opinion that it is just and equitable that the company should be wound up.
(2) Subsection (1) does not apply if the company is already being wound up by the court.
(3) (*Amends the Insolvency Act 1986, s 124 at* **[9.251]**.)

[5.252]
51 Dissolution and striking off

[(1) If a community interest company has been—
(a) dissolved, or
(b) struck off the register under section 1000 or 1001 of the Companies Act 2006,
the Regulator may apply to the court under section 1029 of that Act for an order restoring the company's name to the register.]
(3) If an application under [section 1003 of the Companies Act 2006 (striking off on application by company)] is made on behalf of a community interest company, [section 1006 of the Companies Act 2006] (persons to be notified of application) is to be treated as also requiring a copy of the application to be given to the Regulator.

NOTES

Sub-s (1): substituted (for the original sub-ss (1), (2)) by the Companies Act 2006 (Consequential Amendments, Transitional Provisions and Savings) Order 2009, SI 2009/1941, art 2(1), Sch 1, para 234(1), (2), as from as from 1 October 2009.

Sub-s (3): words in square brackets substituted by SI 2009/1941, art 2(1), Sch 1, para 234(1), (3), as from 1 October 2009.

Change of status

[5.253]
52 Re-registration

(1) A community interest company is excluded from re-registering under [section 102 of the Companies Act 2006] (re-registration of limited company as unlimited).
(2) If a community interest company which is not a public company re-registers as a public company under [section 90 of the Companies Act 2006], or a community interest company which is a public company re-registers as a private company under [section 97 of the Companies Act 2006], the certificate of incorporation issued under [section 96(2) or 101(2) of the Companies Act 2006] is to contain a statement that the company is a community interest company.
(3) The fact that the certificate of incorporation contains such a statement is conclusive evidence that the company is a community interest company.

NOTES

Sub-ss (1), (2): words in square brackets substituted by the Companies Act 2006 (Consequential Amendments, Transitional Provisions and Savings) Order 2009, SI 2009/1941, art 2(1), Sch 1, para 235, as from 1 October 2009.

[5.254]

53 Ceasing to be a community interest company

A community interest company may not cease to be a community interest company except by dissolution or as provided—

(a) by [sections 54 to 55A] (becoming a charity . . .), or

(b) if regulations are made under section 56 (becoming [a registered society]), by the regulations.

NOTES

Words in square brackets in para (a) substituted by the Companies Act 2006 (Consequential Amendments, Transitional Provisions and Savings) Order 2009, SI 2009/1941, art 2(1), Sch 1, para 236, as from 1 October 2009. Words omitted from para (a) repealed by the Companies Act 2006 (Consequential Amendments etc) Order 2008, SI 2008/948, art 3, Sch 1, Pt 2, para 234(1), (4), Sch 2, as from 6 April 2008. Words in square brackets in para (b) substituted by the Co-operative and Community Benefit Societies Act 2014, s 151, Sch 4, Pt 2, paras 87, 89, as from 1 August 2014.

Note: as to the conversion of community interest companies to Charitable Incorporated Organisations, see the Charities Act 2011, s 234, and the Charitable Incorporated Organisations (Conversion) Regulations 2017, SI 2017/1232 (which were made under s 234 of the 2011 Act).

[5.255]

[54 Ceasing to be a community interest company and becoming a charity

(1) If a company is to cease to be a community interest company and become a charity—

(a) the company must by special resolution—

(i) state that it is to cease to be a community interest company,

(ii) make such alterations of its articles as it considers appropriate, and

(iii) change its name so that it does not comply with section 33;

(b) the conditions specified below must be met; and

(c) an application must be delivered to the registrar of companies in accordance with section 54C together with the other documents required by that section.

(2) The conditions referred to in subsection (1)(b) are that—

(a) where no application under section 54A for cancellation of the special resolutions has been made—

(i) having regard to the number of members who consented to or voted in favour of the resolutions, no such application may be made, or

(ii) the period within which such an application could be made has expired, or

(b) where such an application has been made—

(i) the application has been withdrawn, or

(ii) an order has been made confirming the resolutions and a copy of that order has been delivered to the registrar.

(3) Section 30 of the Companies Act 2006 (copies of resolutions to be forwarded to the registrar) applies to the special resolutions as follows—

(a) that section is complied with by forwarding copies of the resolutions together with the application in accordance with section 54C,

(b) copies of the resolutions must not be so forwarded before the relevant date, and

(c) subsection (1) of that section has effect in relation to the resolutions as if it referred to 15 days after the relevant date.

(4) The relevant date is—

(a) if an application is made under section 54A for cancellation of the resolutions—

(i) the date on which the court determines the application (or if there is more than one application, the date on which the last to be determined by the court is determined), or

(ii) such later date as the court may order;

(b) if there is no such application—

(i) if having regard to the number of members who consented to or voted in favour of the resolutions, no such application may be made, the date on which the resolutions were passed or made (or, if the resolutions were passed or made on different days, the date on which the last of them was passed or made);

(ii) in any other case, the end of the period for making such an application.]

NOTES

Substituted (together with ss 54A–54C for the original s 54) by the Companies Act 2006 (Consequential Amendments, Transitional Provisions and Savings) Order 2009, SI 2009/1941, art 2(1), Sch 1, para 237(1), as from 1 October 2009.

Conversion of community interest companies to Charitable Incorporated Organisations: see the note at **[5.254]**.

[5.256]

[54A Ceasing to be a community interest company and becoming a charity: application to court to cancel resolutions

(1) Where special resolutions have been passed with a view to a company ceasing to be a community interest company and becoming a charity, an application to the court for the cancellation of the resolutions may be made—

(a) by the holders of not less in the aggregate than 15% in nominal value of the company's issued share capital or any class of the company's issued share capital (disregarding any shares held by the company as treasury shares);

(b) if the company is not limited by shares, by not less than 15% of its members; or

(c) by the holders of not less than 15% of the company's debentures entitling the holders to object to an alteration of its objects;

but not by a person who has consented to or voted in favour of the resolutions.

(2) The application—

(a) must be made within 28 days after the date on which the resolutions were passed or made (or, if the resolutions were passed or made on different days, the date on which the last of them was passed or made), and
(b) may be made on behalf of the persons entitled to make it by such one or more of their number as they may appoint for the purpose.

(3) On the hearing of the application the court shall make an order either cancelling or confirming the resolutions.

(4) The court may—
(a) make that order on such terms and conditions as it thinks fit,
(b) if it thinks fit adjourn the proceedings in order that an arrangement may be made to the satisfaction of the court for the purchase of the interests of dissentient members, and
(c) give such directions, and make such orders, as it thinks expedient for facilitating or carrying into effect any such arrangement.

(5) The court's order may, if the court thinks fit—
(a) provide for the purchase by the company of the shares of any of its members and for the reduction accordingly of the company's capital; and
(b) make such alteration in the company's articles as may be required in consequence of that provision.

(6) The court's order may, if the court thinks fit, require the company not to make any, or any specified, amendments to its articles without the leave of the court.]

NOTES

Substituted as noted to s 54 at **[5.255]**.

Conversion of community interest companies to Charitable Incorporated Organisations: see the note at **[5.254]**.

[5.257]

[54B Ceasing to be a community interest company and becoming a charity: notice to registrar of court application or order

(1) On making an application under section 54A (application to court to cancel resolutions) the applicants, or the person making the application on their behalf, must immediately give notice to the registrar of companies.

This is without prejudice to any provision of rules of court as to service of notice of the application.

(2) On being served with notice of any such application, the company must immediately give notice to the registrar.

(3) Within 15 days of the making of the court's order on the application, or such longer period as the court may at any time direct, the company must deliver to the registrar a copy of the order.

(4) If a company fails to comply with subsection (2) or (3) an offence is committed by—
(a) the company, and
(b) every officer of the company who is in default.

(5) A person guilty of an offence under this section is liable on summary conviction to a fine not exceeding level 3 on the standard scale and, for continued contravention, a daily default fine not exceeding one-tenth of level 3 on the standard scale.]

NOTES

Substituted as noted to s 54 at **[5.255]**.

Conversion of community interest companies to Charitable Incorporated Organisations: see the note at **[5.254]**.

[5.258]

[54C Ceasing to be a community interest company and becoming a charity: application and accompanying documents

(1) An application to cease to be a community interest company and become a charity must be accompanied by—
(a) a copy of the special resolutions,
(b) a copy of the company's articles as proposed to be amended, and
(c) the statement required by subsection (2).

(2) The statement required is—
(a) where the company is to become an English charity, a statement by the Charity Commission that, in its opinion, if the proposed changes take effect the company will be an English charity and will not be an exempt charity;
(b) where the company is to become a Scottish charity, a statement by the Scottish Charity Regulator that if the proposed changes take effect the company will be entered in the Scottish Charity Register;
(c) where the company is to become a Northern Ireland charity, a statement by the Commissioners of Her Majesty's Revenue and Customs that the company has claimed exemption under [a relevant provision of Part 11 of the Corporation Tax Act 2010].

(3) In subsection (2)(a) ["exempt charity" has the same meaning as in the Charities Act 2011 (see section 22 of that Act)].

[(3A) For the purposes of subsection (2)(c) all the provisions of Part 11 of the Corporation Tax Act 2010 under which exemption may be claimed are relevant provisions except—
(a) section 480 (exemption for profits of small-scale trades), and
(b) section 481 (exemption from charges under provisions to which section 1173 applies).]

(4) On receiving an application to cease to be a community interest company and become a charity, together with the other documents required to accompany it, the registrar of companies must (instead of recording the documents and entering a new name on the register)—
(a) forward a copy of each of the documents to the Regulator, and
(b) retain the documents pending the Regulator's decision.]

NOTES

Substituted as noted to s 54 at **[5.255]**.

Sub-s (2): words in square brackets in para (c) substituted by the Corporation Tax Act 2010, s 1177, Sch 1, Pt 2, para 439(1), (2) (note that the 2010 Act comes into force on 1 April 2010 and has effect, for corporation tax purposes for accounting periods ending on or after that day, and for income tax and capital gains tax purposes for the tax year 2010–11 and subsequent tax years; see s 1184(1) of the 2010 Act).

Sub-s (3): words in square brackets substituted by the Charities Act 2011, s 354, Sch 7, Pt 2, para 98, as from 15 March 2011.

Sub-s (3A): inserted by the Corporation Tax Act 2010, s 1177, Sch 1, Pt 2, para 439(1), (3) (see the note above with regard to the commencement of this amendment).

Conversion of community interest companies to Charitable Incorporated Organisations: see the note at **[5.254]**.

[5.259]

[55 Ceasing to be a community interest company and becoming a charity: decision by Regulator

(1) The Regulator must decide whether the company is eligible to cease being a community interest company.

(2) A company is eligible to cease being a community interest company if it has complied with sections 54 and 54C and none of the following applies—

- (a) the Regulator has under section 43 appointed an auditor to audit the company's annual accounts and the audit has not been completed,
- (b) civil proceedings instituted by the Regulator in the name of the company under section 44 have not been determined or discontinued,
- (c) a director of the company holds office by virtue of an order under section 45,
- (d) a director of the company is suspended under section 46(3),
- (e) there is a manager in respect of the property and affairs of the company appointed under section 47,
- (f) the Official Property Holder holds property as trustee for the company,
- (g) an order under section 48(2) or (3) is in force in relation to the company,
- (h) a petition has been presented for the company to be wound up.

(3) The Regulator must give notice of the decision to the registrar of companies (but the registrar is not required to record it).]

NOTES

Substituted (together with ss 55A for the original s 55) by the Companies Act 2006 (Consequential Amendments, Transitional Provisions and Savings) Order 2009, SI 2009/1941, art 2(1), Sch 1, para 237(2), as from 1 October 2009.

Conversion of community interest companies to Charitable Incorporated Organisations: see the note at **[5.254]**.

[5.260]

[55A Ceasing to be a community interest company and becoming a charity: consequences of Regulator's decision

(1) If the Regulator gives notice of a decision that the company is eligible to cease being a community interest company, the registrar of companies must—

- (a) proceed in accordance with section 80 of the Companies Act 2006 (change of name: registration and issue of new certificate of incorporation), and
- (b) if the registrar enters the new name of the company on the register, retain and record the documents mentioned in section 54C(4).

(2) The new certificate of incorporation must state—

- (a) that it is issued on the company's ceasing to be a community interest company, and
- (b) the date on which it is issued.

(3) On the issue of the certificate—

- (a) the changes in the company's name and articles take effect, and
- (b) the company ceases to be a community interest company.

(4) If the Regulator decides that the company is not eligible to cease being a community interest company, the company may appeal to the Appeal Officer against the decision.]

NOTES

Substituted as noted to s 55 at **[5.259]**.

Conversion of community interest companies to Charitable Incorporated Organisations: see the note at **[5.254]**.

[5.261]

56 Becoming [a registered society]

(1) Unless regulations make provision to the contrary, a community interest company may not convert itself into a registered society under [section 115 of the Co-operative and Community Benefit Societies Act 2014] [or section 62 of the Industrial and Provident Societies Act (Northern Ireland) 1969].

(2) If regulations make provision allowing the conversion of community interest companies under that section they may include provision modifying that section in its application by virtue of the regulations.

NOTES

Words in square brackets in the section heading substituted, and words in first pair of square brackets in sub-s (1) substituted, by the Co-operative and Community Benefit Societies Act 2014, s 151, Sch 4, Pt 2, paras 87, 90, as from 1 August 2014.

The words in the second pair of square brackets in sub-s (1) were inserted by the Companies Act 2006 (Commencement No 2, Consequential Amendments, Transitional Provisions and Savings) Order 2007, SI 2007/1093, art 6(2), Sch 4, Pt 1, para 21, as from 6 April 2007.

Regulations: the Community Interest Company (Amendment) Regulations 2009, SI 2009/1942.

Supplementary

[5.262]

57 Fees

(1) Regulations may require the payment of such fees in connection with the Regulator's functions as may be specified in the regulations.

(2) The regulations may provide for fees to be paid to the registrar of companies (rather than to the Regulator).

(3) The Regulator may charge a fee for any service which is provided otherwise than in pursuance of an obligation imposed by law, other than the provision of guidance which the Regulator considers to be of general interest.
(4) Fees paid by virtue of this section are to be paid into the Consolidated Fund.

NOTES

Regulations: the Community Interest Company Regulations 2005, SI 2005/1788 at **[6.106]**; the Community Interest Company (Amendment) Regulations 2009, SI 2009/1942.

58 *(Repealed by the Companies Act 2006 (Consequential Amendments, Transitional Provisions and Savings) Order 2009, SI 2009/1941, art 2(1), Sch 1, para 238, as from 1 October 2009.)*

[5.263]
59 Information

(1) Regulations may require the registrar of companies—
  (a) to notify the Regulator of matters specified in the regulations, and
  (b) to provide the Regulator with copies of documents specified in the regulations.

(2), (3) *(Sub-s (2) which inserted the Bankruptcy (Scotland) Act 1985, s 71A, was repealed by the Bankruptcy (Scotland) Act 2016 (Consequential Provisions and Modifications) Order 2016, SI 2016/1034, as from 30 November 2016 (subject to savings); sub-s (3) amended the Data Protection Act 1998, s 31 (which has been repealed with savings).)*

(4) A public authority may disclose to the Regulator, for any purpose connected with the exercise of the Regulator's functions, information received by the authority in connection with its functions.

(5) The Regulator may disclose to a public authority any information received by the Regulator in connection with the functions of the Regulator—
  (a) for a purpose connected with the exercise of those functions, or
  (b) for a purpose connected with the exercise by the authority of its functions.

(6) In deciding whether to disclose information to a public authority in a country or territory outside the United Kingdom the Regulator must have regard to the considerations listed in section 243(6) of the Enterprise Act 2002 (c 40) (overseas disclosures), but as if the reference to information of a kind to which section 237 of that Act applies were to information of the kind the Regulator is considering disclosing.

(7) The powers to disclose information in subsections (4) and (5) are subject to—
  (a) any restriction on disclosure imposed by or by virtue of an enactment, and
  (b) any express restriction on disclosure subject to which information was supplied.

(8) Information may be disclosed under subsection (4) or (5) subject to a restriction on its further disclosure.

(9) A person who discloses information in contravention of a restriction imposed under subsection (8) is guilty of an offence, but a prosecution may be instituted[—
  (a) in England and Wales, only with the consent of the Regulator or the Director of Public Prosecutions;
  (b) in Northern Ireland, only with the consent of the Regulator or the Director of Public Prosecutions for Northern Ireland].

(10) A person guilty of an offence under subsection (9) is liable on summary conviction to a fine not exceeding level 3 on the standard scale.

(11) "Public authority" means a person or body having functions of a public nature.

NOTES

Sub-s (9): words in square brackets substituted by the Companies Act 2006 (Commencement No 2, Consequential Amendments, Transitional Provisions and Savings) Order 2007, SI 2007/1093, art 6(2), Sch 4, Pt 1, para 23, as from 6 April 2007.

Regulations: the Community Interest Company Regulations 2005, SI 2005/1788 at **[6.106]**; the Community Interest Company (Amendment) Regulations 2009, SI 2009/1942.

[5.264]
60 Offences

(1) If an offence under [section 48 or 59 or paragraph 5 of Schedule 7] committed by a body corporate is proved—
  (a) to have been committed with the consent or connivance of an officer, or
  (b) to be attributable to any neglect on the part of an officer,

the officer as well as the body corporate is guilty of the offence and liable to be proceeded against and punished accordingly.

(2) "Officer" means a director, manager, secretary or other similar officer of the body corporate, or a person purporting to act in any such capacity.

(3) "Director"—
  (a) includes a shadow director, and
  (b) if the affairs of a body corporate are managed by its members, means a member of the body.

NOTES

Sub-s (1): words in square brackets substituted by the Companies Act 2006 (Consequential Amendments, Transitional Provisions and Savings) Order 2009, SI 2009/1941, art 2(1), Sch 1, para 239, as from 1 October 2009.

[5.265]
61 Orders made by Regulator

(1) An order made by the Regulator under this Part must be given to the community interest company in relation to which it is made and—
  (a) if the order is under section 46(1) or (3), to the director removed or suspended,
  (b) if the order is under section 48(1)(b) or (2), to the person to whom the order is directed,
  (c) if the order is under section 49(1), to the persons from and to whom shares are transferred,
  (d) if the order is under section 49(2), to the person whose interest is extinguished and any person appointed in his place.

(2) Orders made by the Regulator under or by virtue of this Part may contain any incidental or supplementary provisions the Regulator considers expedient.
(3) When discharging an order made under or by virtue of this Part, the Regulator may make savings and transitional provisions.
(4) A document certified by the Regulator to be a true copy of an order made by the Regulator is evidence of the order without further proof; and a document purporting to be so certified shall, unless the contrary is proved, be taken to be so certified.
(5) Where the Regulator makes an order or decision against which an appeal lies under or by virtue of this Part, the Regulator must give reasons for the order or decision to the persons entitled to appeal against it.

[5.266]
62 Regulations
(1) Any power to make regulations under this Part is exercisable by the Secretary of State by statutory instrument.
(2) Regulations under this Part may make different provision for different cases.
(3) Regulations under this Part may confer or impose functions on the Regulator or any other person specified in the regulations (and, unless made under paragraph 4 of Schedule 4, may provide for appeals to the Appeal Officer from a person on whom functions are conferred by the regulations).
(4) No regulations to which this subsection applies are to be made unless a draft of the statutory instrument containing the regulations (whether or not together with other provisions) has been laid before, and approved by a resolution of, each House of Parliament.
(5) Subsection (4) applies to regulations under—
(a) section 30,
(b) section 31,
(c) section 32,
(d) section 34,
(e) section 35,
(f) section 36,
(g) [section 37C],
(h) section 47, and
(i) section 56.
(6) A statutory instrument containing regulations under this Part is (unless a draft of it has been approved by each House of Parliament under subsection (4)) subject to annulment in pursuance of a resolution of either House of Parliament.

NOTES
Sub-s (5): words in square brackets substituted by the Companies Act 2006 (Consequential Amendments, Transitional Provisions and Savings) Order 2009, SI 2009/1941, art 2(1), Sch 1, para 240, as from 1 October 2009.

[5.267]
63 Interpretation
(1) In this Part—
. . .
. . .
"administrative receiver" has the meaning given[—
(a) in England and Wales or Scotland, by section 251 of the Insolvency Act 1986, and
(b) in Northern Ireland, by Article 5 of the Insolvency (Northern Ireland) Order 1989;]
"the Appeal Officer" has the meaning given by section 28(1),
["charity" means an English charity, a Scottish charity or a Northern Ireland charity, as defined below;]
"community interest object" is to be construed in accordance with section 35(3),
"the community interest test" is to be construed in accordance with section 35(2),
"enactment" includes an Act of the Scottish Parliament,
["English charity" means a charity [as defined by section 1(1) of the Charities Act 2011];]
"excluded company" is to be construed in accordance with section 35(6),
. . .
["Northern Ireland charity" means a charity within the meaning of the Charities Act (Northern Ireland) 1964 (see section 35 of that Act);]
"the Official Property Holder" has the meaning given by section 29(1),
"the Regulator" has the meaning given by section 27(1), and
["Scottish charity" means a body entered in the Scottish Charity Register].
[(2), (3) . . .]

NOTES
Sub-s (1) is amended as follows:
Words in square brackets in definition "administrative receiver" substituted, definition "charity" substituted, and definitions "the 1985 Act" (omitted), "the 1986 Order" (omitted), "English charity", "the Gazette" (omitted), and "Northern Ireland charity" inserted, by the Companies Act 2006 (Commencement No 2, Consequential Amendments, Transitional Provisions and Savings) Order 2007, SI 2007/1093, art 6(2), Sch 4, Pt 1, para 24(1)–(4), as from 6 April 2007.
Definitions omitted repealed by the Companies Act 2006 (Consequential Amendments, Transitional Provisions and Savings) Order 2009, SI 2009/1941, art 2(1), Sch 1, para 241(1), as from 1 October 2009.
Words in square brackets in the definition "English charity" substituted by the Charities Act 2011, s 354, Sch 7, Pt 2, para 99, as from 14 March 2012.
Definition "Scottish charity" substituted by the Charities and Trustee Investment (Scotland) Act 2005 (Consequential Provisions and Modifications) Order 2006, SI 2006/242, art 5, Schedule, Pt 1, para 8(1), (5), as from 1 April 2006.
Sub-ss (2), (3): substituted, for the original sub-s (2), by SI 2007/1093, art 6(2), Sch 4, Pt 1, para 24(1), (5), as from 6 April 2007, and repealed by SI 2009/1941, art 2(1), Sch 1, para 241(2), as from 1 October 2009.

PART 3 SUPPLEMENTARY

64 (*Introduces Schedule 8 to this Act (repeals and revocations).*)

[5.268]

65 Commencement etc

(1) This Act (apart from this section and sections 66 and 67) does not come into force until such day as the Secretary of State may by order made by statutory instrument appoint; and different days may be appointed for different provisions or otherwise for different purposes.

(2) The Secretary of State may by order made by statutory instrument make any transitional provisions or savings which appear appropriate in connection with the commencement of any provision of this Act.

NOTES

Orders: the Companies (Audit, Investigations and Community Enterprise) Act 2004 (Commencement) and Companies Act 1989 (Commencement No 18) Order 2004, SI 2004/3322.

[5.269]

66 Extent

(1) Any amendment made by this Act has the same extent as the provision to which it relates.

(2) Sections 14, 15(1)(b), (3) and (7) and [16 to [18A]] [and Part 2] extend to Northern Ireland.

(3) Subject to that, this Act (apart from section 65, this section and section 67) does not extend to Northern Ireland.

NOTES

Sub-s (2): words in first (outer) pair of square brackets substituted by the Companies Act 2006, s 1276(5), as from 8 November 2006. Figure in second (inner) pair of square brackets substituted by the Small Business, Enterprise and Employment Act 2015, s 38(3), as from 1 June 2016. Words in final pair of square brackets inserted by the Companies Act 2006 (Commencement No 2, Consequential Amendments, Transitional Provisions and Savings) Order 2007, SI 2007/1093, art 6(2), Sch 4, Pt 1, para 25, as from 6 April 2007.

As to the application of this Act to Northern Ireland, see also the Companies Act 2006, s 1284(1) at **[1.1480]**.

[5.270]

67 Short title

This Act may be cited as the Companies (Audit, Investigations and Community Enterprise) Act 2004.

SCHEDULES

SCHEDULES 1, 2

(Sch 1 repealed by the Companies Act 2006, s 1295, Sch 16, as from 6 April 2008; Sch 2 Pt 1 (Amendments Relating to Auditors) and Sch 2, Pt 2 (Amendments Relating to Accounts and Reports) make various amendments to CA 1985, CA 1989, the Companies (Northern Ireland) Order 1986, and the Companies (Northern Ireland) Order 1990, and are repealed by CA 2006, s 1295, Sch 16, as from 1 October 2007 (in part), as from 6 April 2008 (in part), and as from a day to be appointed (otherwise); Sch 2, Pt 3 (Amendments Relating to Investigations) amends Part XIV of CA 1985 (Investigation of Companies and their Affairs; Requisition of Documents at **[5.16]** *et seq), contains other consequential amendments to the 1985 Act, and consequential amendments to the Insolvency Act 1986, the Company Directors Disqualification Act 1986, the Criminal Justice and Police Act 2001, and the Anti-terrorism, Crime and Security Act 2001, and is partly repealed by CA 2006, as from 1 October 2007, 6 April 2008, and as from a day to be appointed.)*

SCHEDULE 3
REGULATOR OF COMMUNITY INTEREST COMPANIES

Section 27

Regulator's terms of appointment

[5.271]

1. (1) The period for which a person is appointed as Regulator must not exceed five years.

(2) A person who has held office as Regulator may be re-appointed, once only, for a further period not exceeding five years.

(3) The Regulator may at any time resign the office by giving notice in writing to the Secretary of State.

(4) The Secretary of State may at any time remove the Regulator on the ground of incapacity or misbehaviour.

(5) Subject to that, the Regulator holds and vacates office on the terms determined by the Secretary of State.

Remuneration and pensions

2. (1) The Secretary of State may pay remuneration and travelling and other allowances to the Regulator.

(2) The Secretary of State may—

- (a) pay a pension, allowance or gratuity to or in respect of a person who is or has been the Regulator, or
- (b) make contributions or payments towards provision for a pension, allowance or gratuity for or in respect of such a person.

Staff

3. (1) The Regulator may, after consulting the Minister for the Civil Service as to numbers and terms and conditions of service, appoint such staff as the Regulator may determine.

(2) The members of staff must include a deputy to the Regulator who is to act as Regulator—

- (a) during any vacancy in that office, or

(b) if the Regulator is absent, subject to suspension or unable to act.

(3) Where a participant in a scheme under section 1 of the Superannuation Act 1972 (c 11) is appointed as the Regulator, the Minister for the Civil Service may determine that the person's term of office as the Regulator is to be treated for the purposes of the scheme as service in the employment by reference to which he was a participant (whether or not any benefits are payable by virtue of paragraph 2(2)).

[**4.** The person appointed to chair the Charity Commission may make available to the Regulator, to assist in the exercise of the Regulator's functions—

(a) any other member of the Commission appointed under paragraph 1(1) of Schedule 1 to the Charities Act 2011, or

(b) any member of staff of the Commission appointed under paragraph 5(1) of that Schedule.]

Delegation of functions

5. Anything which the Regulator is authorised or required to do may be done by a member of the Regulator's staff if authorised by the Regulator (generally or specifically) for that purpose.

Finance

6. The Secretary of State may make payments to the Regulator.

Reports and other information

7. (1) The Regulator must, in respect of each financial year, prepare a report on the exercise of the Regulator's functions during the financial year.

(2) The Regulator must prepare accounts in respect of a financial year if the Secretary of State so directs.

(3) The Regulator must send a copy of the accounts to the Comptroller and Auditor General.

(4) The Comptroller and Auditor General must examine, certify and report on the accounts and send a copy of the report to the Regulator.

(5) The Regulator must include the accounts and the Comptroller and Auditor General's report on them in the report prepared by the Regulator in respect of the financial year to which the accounts relate.

(6) The Regulator must prepare that report as soon as possible after the end of the financial year to which it relates.

(7) The Regulator must send to the Secretary of State a copy of—

(a) each report prepared by the Regulator under sub-paragraph (1), and

(b) each report prepared by the Official Property Holder under paragraph 6 of Schedule 5.

(8) The Secretary of State must lay before each House of Parliament a copy of each of those reports.

(9) The Regulator must supply the Secretary of State with such other reports and information relating to the exercise of the Regulator's functions as the Secretary of State may require.

(10) "Financial year" means—

(a) the period beginning with the date on which a person is first appointed as the Regulator and ending with the next 31st March, and

(b) each successive period of 12 months beginning with 1st April.

Amendments

8, 9. (*Para 8 amended the Parliamentary Commissioner Act 1967, Sch 2 (and is superseded by the Parliamentary Commissioner Order 2005, SI 2005/249, art 2, Sch 1); para 9 amends the House of Commons Disqualification Act 1975, Sch 1, Pt III.*)

NOTES

Para 4: substituted by the Charities Act 2011, s 354(1), Sch 7, Pt 2, para 100, as from 14 March 2012.

SCHEDULE 4
APPEAL OFFICER FOR COMMUNITY INTEREST COMPANIES

Section 28

Appeal Officer's terms of appointment

[5.272]

1. (1) The Appeal Officer holds office for the period determined by the Secretary of State on appointment (or re-appointment).

(2) But—

(a) the Appeal Officer may at any time resign the office by giving notice in writing to the Secretary of State, and

(b) the Secretary of State may at any time remove the Appeal Officer on the ground of incapacity or misbehaviour.

(3) Subject to that, the Appeal Officer holds and vacates office on the terms determined by the Secretary of State.

Remuneration and pensions

2. (1) The Secretary of State may pay remuneration and travelling and other allowances to the Appeal Officer.

(2) The Secretary of State may—

(a) pay a pension, allowance or gratuity to or in respect of a person who is or has been the Appeal Officer, or

(b) make contributions or payments towards provision for a pension, allowance or gratuity for or in respect of such a person.

Finance

3. The Secretary of State may make payments to the Appeal Officer.

Procedure

4. (1) Regulations may make provision about the practice and procedure to be followed by the Appeal Officer.

(2) Regulations under this paragraph may in particular impose time limits for bringing appeals.

Amendments

5, 6. *(Amend the Parliamentary Commissioner Act 1967, Sch 2, and the House of Commons Disqualification Act 1975, Sch 1, Pt III.)*

NOTES

Regulations: the Community Interest Company Regulations 2005, SI 2005/1788 at **[6.106]**.

SCHEDULE 5
OFFICIAL PROPERTY HOLDER FOR COMMUNITY INTEREST COMPANIES

Section 29

Status

[5.273]

1. (1) The Official Property Holder is a corporation sole.

(2) A document purporting to be—

(a) duly executed under the seal of the Official Property Holder, or

(b) signed on behalf of the Official Property Holder,

shall be received in evidence and shall, unless the contrary is proved, be taken to be so executed or signed.

Relationship with Regulator

2. The Regulator must make available to the Official Property Holder such members of the Regulator's staff as the Official Property Holder may require in order to exercise the functions of the office.

Effect of vacancy

3. The Regulator must appoint a member of the Regulator's staff who is to act as Official Property Holder—

(a) during any vacancy in the office, or

(b) if the Official Property Holder is absent, subject to suspension or unable to act.

Property

4. (1) The Official Property Holder holds property vested in or transferred to him as a trustee.

(2) The Official Property Holder may release or deal with the property—

(a) to give effect to any interest in or right over the property of any person (other than the community interest company by which, or in trust for which, the property was held before it was vested or transferred), or

(b) at the request of a person appointed to act as administrative receiver, administrator, provisional liquidator or liquidator of the company.

(3) Subject to sub-paragraph (2), the Official Property Holder may not release or deal with the property except in accordance with directions given by the Regulator.

Finance

5. (1) The Official Property Holder may recover his expenses in respect of property held by him from the property or from the community interest company by which, or in trust for which, the property was held before it was vested in or transferred to the Official Property Holder.

(2) Any expenses of the Official Property Holder not recovered under sub-paragraph (1) are to be met by the Regulator.

Reports

6. (1) As soon as possible after the end of each financial year, the Official Property Holder must prepare a report on the exercise of the Official Property Holder's functions during the financial year.

(2) The Official Property Holder must send a copy of the report to the Regulator.

(3) "Financial year" means—

(a) the period beginning with the date on which a person is first appointed as the Official Property Holder and ending with the next 31st March, and

(b) each successive period of 12 months beginning with 1st April.

SCHEDULE 6

(Sch 6 repealed by a combination of the Companies Act 2006, s 1295, Sch 16, and the Companies Act 2006 (Consequential Amendments, Transitional Provisions and Savings) Order 2009, SI 2009/1941, art 2(2), Sch 2, as from 1 October 2008 (in part), and as from 1 October 2009 (otherwise).)

SCHEDULE 7
COMMUNITY INTEREST COMPANIES: INVESTIGATIONS

Section 42

Power to require documents and information

[5.274]

1. (1) The investigator of a community interest company may require the company or any other person—

(a) to produce such documents (or documents of such description) as the investigator may specify;

(b) to provide such information (or information of such description) as the investigator may specify.

(2) A person on whom a requirement is imposed under sub-paragraph (1) may require the investigator to produce evidence of his authority.

(3) A requirement under sub-paragraph (1) must be complied with at such time and place as may be specified by the investigator.

(4) The production of a document in pursuance of this paragraph does not affect any lien which a person has on the document.

(5) The investigator may take copies of or extracts from a document produced in pursuance of this paragraph.

(6) In relation to information recorded otherwise than in legible form, the power to require production of it includes power to require the production of a copy of it in legible form or in a form from which it can readily be produced in visible and legible form.

(7) In this Schedule—

(a) "the investigator of a community interest company" means a person investigating the company's affairs under section 42, and

(b) "document" includes information recorded in any form.

Privileged information

2. (1) Nothing in paragraph 1 requires a person to produce a document or provide information in respect of which a claim could be maintained—

(a) in an action in the High Court, to legal professional privilege, or

(b) in an action in the Court of Session, to confidentiality of communications,

but a person who is a lawyer may be required to provide the name and address of his client.

(2) Nothing in paragraph 1 requires a person carrying on the business of banking to produce a document, or provide information, relating to the affairs of a customer unless a requirement to produce the document, or provide the information, has been imposed on the customer under that paragraph.

Use of information as evidence

3. (1) A statement made by a person in compliance with a requirement imposed under paragraph 1 may be used in evidence against the person.

(2) But in criminal proceedings—

(a) no evidence relating to the statement may be adduced by or on behalf of the prosecution, and

(b) no question relating to it may be asked by or on behalf of the prosecution,

unless evidence relating to it is adduced or a question relating to it is asked in the proceedings by or on behalf of that person.

(3) However, sub-paragraph (2) does not apply to proceedings in which a person is charged with—

[(a) an offence under paragraph 5 below (false information), or

(b) an offence under section 5 of the Perjury Act 1911, section 44(2) of the Criminal Law (Consolidation) (Scotland) Act 1995 or Article 10 of the Perjury (Northern Ireland) Order 1979 (false statement made otherwise than on oath).]

Failure to comply with requirement

4. (1) This paragraph applies if a person fails to comply with a requirement imposed under paragraph 1.

(2) The investigator may certify that fact in writing to the court.

(3) If, after hearing—

(a) any witnesses who may be produced against or on behalf of the alleged offender, and

(b) any statement which may be offered in defence,

the court is satisfied that the offender failed without reasonable excuse to comply with the requirement, it may deal with him as if he had been guilty of contempt of the court.

False information

5. (1) A person commits an offence if in purported compliance with a requirement under paragraph 1 to provide information, the person—

(a) provides information which the person knows to be false in a material particular, or

(b) recklessly provides information which is false in a material particular,

. . .

[(1A) A prosecution for an offence under sub-paragraph (1) may be instituted—

(a) in England and Wales, only with the consent of the Director of Public Prosecutions;

(b) in Northern Ireland, only with the consent of the Director of Public Prosecutions for Northern Ireland.]

(2) A person guilty of an offence under sub-paragraph (1) is liable—

(a) on conviction on indictment to imprisonment for a term not exceeding two years or a fine or to both,

(b) on summary conviction in England and Wales, to imprisonment for a term not exceeding twelve months or a fine of an amount not exceeding the statutory maximum or to both, and

(c) on summary conviction in Scotland [or Northern Ireland], to imprisonment for a term not exceeding six months or a fine of an amount not exceeding the statutory maximum or to both.

(3) In relation to an offence committed before [2 May 2022] comes into force, sub-paragraph (2)(b) has effect as if for "twelve" there were substituted "six".

NOTES

Para 3: words in square brackets in sub-para (3) substituted by the Companies Act 2006 (Commencement No 2, Consequential Amendments, Transitional Provisions and Savings) Order 2007, SI 2007/1093, art 6(2), Sch 4, Pt 1, para 26(1), (2), as from 6 April 2007.

Para 5: words omitted from sub-para (1) repealed, sub-para (1A) inserted, and words in square brackets in sub-para (2) inserted, by SI 2007/1093, art 6(2), Sch 4, Pt 1, para 26(1), (3), as from 6 April 2007. Words in square brackets in sub-para (3) substituted by the Criminal Justice Act 2003 (Commencement No 33) and Sentencing Act 2020 (Commencement No 2) Regulations 2022, SI 2022/500, reg 5, Schedule, Pt 1, as from 28 April 2022.

SCHEDULE 8

(Sch 8 contains repeals of or in CA 1985, ss 27, 245C, 256, 310, 390A, 734, Schs 4A, 24, IA 1986, Sch 13, and CA 1989, s 48, 63, 65, 67, 69, 120. Other repeals in this Schedule are outside the scope of this work.)

PART 6
OTHER COMPANIES STATUTORY INSTRUMENTS

COMPANIES (TABLES A TO F) REGULATIONS 1985

(SI 1985/805)

NOTES

Made: 22 May 1985.

Authority: Companies Act 1985, ss 3, 8 (repealed by the Companies Act 2006, s 1295, Sch 16, as from 1 October 2009 (for savings see the note below)).

Commencement: 1 July 1985.

Savings: the Companies Act 2006 (Commencement No 8, Transitional Provisions and Savings) Order 2008, SI 2008/2860, Sch 2, para 1(1) provides as follows—

"(1) Nothing in the Companies Act 2006 affects—

(a) the registration or re-registration of a company under the former Companies Acts, or the continued existence of a company by virtue of such registration or re-registration, or

(b) the application in relation to an existing company of—

(i) Table B in the Joint Stock Companies Act 1856,

(ii) Table A in any of the former Companies Acts, or

(iii) the Companies (Tables A to F) Regulations 1985 or the Companies (Tables A to F) Regulations (Northern Ireland) 1986.".

Note that Sch 2, para 2(1) to the 2008 Order provides that ss 7–16 of the Companies Act 2006 (company formation) apply to applications for registration received by the registrar on or after 1 October 2009. Sch 2, para 2(3) further provides that the corresponding provisions of the 1985 Act continue to apply to an application for registration if (a) it is received by the registrar, and (b) the requirements as to registration are met in relation to it, before that date. The corresponding provisions of the 1985 Act include s 3(1) (see the table of origins at **[3.8]**). Note also that Sch 2, para 3(1) to the 2008 Order provides that ss 7 and 8 of the 1985 Act apply, and sections 18–20 of the 2006 Act do not apply, to a company formed and registered under the 1985 Act on an application to which para 2(3) applies (as to which, see above).

Note that Table A of these Regulations is reproduced in Appendix 2 at **[A2]**.

These Regulations are reproduced as amended by: the Companies (Tables A to F) (Amendment) Regulations 2007, SI 2007/2541; the Companies (Tables A to F) (Amendment) Regulations 2008, SI 2008/739.

[6.1]
1

These Regulations may be cited as the Companies (Tables A to F) Regulations 1985 and shall come into operation on 1st July 1985.

[6.2]
2

The regulations in Table A and the forms in Tables B, C, D, E and F in the Schedule to these Regulations shall be the regulations and forms of memorandum and articles of association for the purposes of sections 3 and 8 of the Companies Act 1985.

3 (*Revokes the Companies (Alteration of Table A etc) Regulations 1984, SI 1984/717.*)

SCHEDULE

(Table A reproduced in Appendix 2 at **[A2]**.*)*

TABLE B

A PRIVATE COMPANY LIMITED BY SHARES

Memorandum of Association

[6.3]

1. The company's name is "The South Wales Motor Transport Company cyfyngedig".

2. The company's registered office is to be situated in Wales.

3. The company's objects are the carriage of passengers and goods in motor vehicles between such places as the company may from time to time determine and the doing of all such other things as are incidental or conducive to the attainment of that object.

4. The liability of the members is limited.

5. The company's share capital is £50,000 divided into 50,000 shares of £1 each.

We, the subscribers to this memorandum of association, wish to be formed into a company pursuant to this memorandum; and we agree to take the number of shares shown opposite our respective names.

Names and Addresses of Subscribers	Number of shares taken by each Subscriber
1. Thomas Jones, 138 Mountfield Street, Tredegar.	1
2. Mary Evans, 19 Merthyr Road, Aberystwyth.	1
Total shares taken	2
Dated. . . . . 19.	

Part 6 Other companies SIs

Names and Addresses of Subscribers	Number of shares taken by each Subscriber

Witness to the above signatures,

Anne Brown, "Woodlands", Fieldside Road, Bryn Mawr.

TABLE C

A COMPANY LIMITED BY GUARANTEE AND NOT HAVING A SHARE CAPITAL

Memorandum of Association

[6.4]

[A1. References in these Articles to Table A are to that Table so far as it relates to private companies limited by shares.]

1. The company's name is "The Dundee School Association Limited".

2. The company's registered office is to be situated in Scotland.

3. The company's objects are the carrying on of a school for boys and girls in Dundee and the doing of all such other things as are incidental or conducive to the attainment of that object.

4. The liability of the members is limited.

5. Every member of the company undertakes to contribute such amount as may be required (not exceeding £100) to the company's assets if it should be wound up while he is a member or within one year after he ceases to be a member, for payment of the company's debts and liabilities contracted before he ceases to be a member, and of the costs, charges and expenses of winding up, and for the adjustment of the rights of the contributories among themselves.

We, the subscribers to this memorandum of association, wish to be formed into a company pursuant to this memorandum.

Names and Addresses of Subscribers.

1. Kenneth Brodie, 14 Bute Street, Dundee.

2. Ian Davis, 2 Burns Avenue, Dundee.

Dated . . . . 19. . . . .
Witness to the above signatures.

Anne Brown, 149 Princes Street, Edinburgh.

Articles of Association

Preliminary

1. Regulations 2 to 35 inclusive, 54, 55, 57, 59, 102 to 108 inclusive, 110, 114, 116 and 117 of Table A, shall not apply to the company but the articles hereinafter contained and, subject to the modifications hereinafter expressed, the remaining regulations of Table A shall constitute the articles of association of the company.

Interpretation

2. In regulation 1 of Table A, the definition of "the holder" shall be omitted.

Members

3. The subscribers to the memorandum of association of the company and such other persons as are admitted to membership in accordance with the articles shall be members of the company. No person shall be admitted a member of the company unless he is approved by the directors. Every person who wishes to become a member shall deliver to the company an application for membership in such form as the directors require executed by him.

4. A member may at any time withdraw from the company by giving at least seven clear days' notice to the company. Membership shall not be transferable and shall cease on death.

Notice of General Meetings

5. In regulation 38 of Table A—

(a) in paragraph (b) the words "of the total voting rights at the meeting of all the members" shall be substituted for "in nominal value of the shares giving that right" and

(b) the words "The notice shall be given to all the members and to the directors and auditors" shall be substituted for the last sentence.

Proceedings at General Meetings

6. The words "and at any separate meeting of the holders of any class of shares in the company" shall be omitted from regulation 44 of Table A.

7. Paragraph (d) of regulation 46 of Table A shall be omitted.

Votes of Members

8. On a show of hands every member present in person [or by proxy] shall have one vote. On a poll every member present in person or by proxy shall have one vote.

Directors' Expenses

9. The words "of any class of shares or" shall be omitted from regulation 83 of Table A.

Proceedings of Directors

10. In paragraph (c) of regulation 94 of Table A the word "debentures" shall be substituted for the words "shares, debentures or other securities" in both places where they occur.

Minutes

11. The words "of the holders of any class of shares in the company" shall be omitted from regulation 100 of Table A.

Notices

12. The second sentence of regulation 112 of Table A shall be omitted.

13. The words "or of the holders of any class of shares in the company" shall be omitted from regulation 113 of Table A.

NOTES

Para A1 of the Memorandum of Association was inserted by the Companies (Tables A to F) (Amendment) Regulations 2007, SI 2007/2541, reg 23, with effect from 1 October 2007.

The words in square brackets in Article 8 of the Articles of Association were inserted by the Companies (Tables A to F) (Amendment) Regulations 2008, SI 2008/739, reg 2, with effect from 6 April 2008.

TABLE D

PART I A PUBLIC COMPANY LIMITED BY GUARANTEE AND HAVING A SHARE CAPITAL

Memorandum of Association

[6.5]

1. The company's name is "Gwestai Glyndwr, cwmni cyfyngedig cyhoeddus".

2. The company is to be a public company.

3. The company's registered office is to be situated in Wales.

4. The company's objects are facilitating travelling in Wales by providing hotels and conveyances by sea and by land for the accommodation of travellers and the doing of all such other things as are incidental or conducive to the attainment of those objects.

5. The liability of the members is limited.

6. Every member of the company undertakes to contribute such amount as may be required (not exceeding £100) to the company's assets if it should be wound up while he is a member or within one year after he ceases to be a member, for payment of the company's debts and liabilities contracted before he ceases to be a member, and of the costs, charges and expenses of winding up, and for the adjustment of the rights of the contributories among themselves.

7. The company's share capital is £50,000 divided into 50,000 shares of £1 each.

We, the subscribers to this memorandum of association, wish to be formed into a company pursuant to this memorandum; and we agree to take the number of shares shown opposite our respective names.

Names and Addresses of Subscribers	**Number of shares taken by each Subscriber**
1. Thomas Jones, 138 Mountfield Street, Tredegar.	1
2. Mary Evans, 19 Merthyr Road, Aberystwyth.	1
Total shares taken	2
Dated. . . . . 19.	
Witness to the above signatures,	
Anne Brown, "Woodlands", Fieldside Road, Bryn Mawr.	

PART II A PRIVATE COMPANY LIMITED BY GUARANTEE AND HAVING A SHARE CAPITAL

Memorandum of Association

1. The company's name is "The Highland Hotel Company Limited".

2. The company's registered office is to be situated in Scotland.

3. The company's objects are facilitating travelling in the Highlands of Scotland by providing hotels and conveyances by sea and by land for the accommodation of travellers and the doing of all such other things as are incidental or conducive to the attainment of those objects.

4. The liability of the members is limited.

5. Every member of the company undertakes to contribute such amount as may be required (not exceeding £100) to the company's assets if it should be wound up while he is a member or within one year after he ceases to be a member, for payment of the company's debts and liabilities contracted before he ceases to be a member, and of the costs, charges and expenses of winding up, and for the adjustment of the rights of the contributories among themselves.

6. The company's share capital is £50,000 divided into 50,000 shares of £1 each.

We, the subscribers to this memorandum of association, wish to be formed into a company pursuant to this memorandum; and we agree to take the number of shares shown opposite our respective names.

Names and Addresses of Subscribers	Number of shares taken by each Subscriber
Kenneth Brodie, 14 Bute Street, Dundee.	1
Ian Davis, 2 Burns Avenue, Dundee.	1
Total shares taken	2
Dated. . . . . 19.	
Witness to the above signatures,	
Anne Brown, 149 Princes Street, Edinburgh.	

PART III A COMPANY (PUBLIC OR PRIVATE) LIMITED BY GUARANTEE AND HAVING A SHARE CAPITAL

Articles of Association

The regulations of Table A shall constitute the articles of association of the company.

TABLE E

AN UNLIMITED COMPANY HAVING A SHARE CAPITAL

Memorandum of Association

[6.6]

1. The company's name is "The Woodford Engineering Company".

2. The company's registered office is to be situated in England and Wales.

3. The company's objects are the working of certain patented inventions relating to the application of microchip technology to the improvement of food processing, and the doing of all such other things as are incidental or conducive to the attainment of that object.

We, the subscribers to this memorandum of association, wish to be formed into a company pursuant to this memorandum; and we agree to take the number of shares shown opposite our respective names.

Names and Addresses of Subscribers	Number of shares taken by each Subscriber
1. Brian Smith, 24 Nibley Road, Wotton-under-Edge, Gloucestershire.	3
2. William Green, 278 High Street, Chipping Sodbury, Avon.	5
Total shares taken	8
Dated. . . . . 19.	
Witness to the above signatures,	
Anne Brown, 108 Park Way, Bristol 8.	

Articles of Association

1. Regulations 3, 32, 34 and 35 of Table A shall not apply to the company, but the articles hereinafter contained and, subject to the modification hereinafter expressed, the remaining regulations of Table A shall constitute the articles of association of the company.

2. The company's registered office is to be situated in England and Wales.

3. The share capital of the company is £20,000 divided into 20,000 shares of £1 each.

4. The company may by special resolution—

(a) increase the share capital by such sum to be divided into shares of such amount as the resolution may prescribe;

(b) consolidate and divide all or any of its share capital into shares of a larger amount than its existing shares;

(c) subdivide its shares, or any of them, into shares of a smaller amount than its existing shares;

(d) cancel any shares which at the date of the passing of the resolution have not been taken or agreed to be taken by any person;

(e) reduce its share capital and any share premium account in any way.

NOTES

Article 2 of the Articles of Association was revoked by the Companies (Tables A to F) (Amendment) Regulations 2008, SI 2008/739, reg 3, with effect from 6 April 2008.

TABLE F

A PUBLIC COMPANY LIMITED BY SHARES

Memorandum of Association

[6.7]

1. The company's name is "Western Electronics Public Limited Company".

2. The company is to be a public company.

3. The company's registered office is to be situated in England and Wales.

4. The company's objects are the manufacture and development of such descriptions of electronic equipment, instruments and appliances as the company may from time to time determine, and the doing of all such other things as are incidental or conducive to the attainment of that object.

5. The liability of the members is limited.

6. The company's share capital is £5,000,000 divided into 5,000,000 shares of £1 each.

We, the subscribers of this memorandum of association, wish to be formed into a company pursuant to this memorandum; and we agree to take the number of shares shown opposite our respective names.

Names and Addresses of Subscribers	Number of shares taken by each Subscriber
1. James White, 12 Broadmead, Birmingham.	1
2. Patrick Smith, 145A Huntley House, London Wall, London EC2.	1
Total shares taken	2
Dated. . . . . 19.	
Witness to the above signatures, Anne Brown, 13 Hute Street, London WC2.	

FINANCIAL MARKETS AND INSOLVENCY REGULATIONS 1991

(SI 1991/880)

NOTES

Made: 27 March 1991.

Authority: Companies Act 1989, ss 155(4), (5), 158(4), (5), 160(5), 173(4), (5), 174(2)–(4), 185, 186, 187(3).

Commencement: 25 April 1991.

These Regulations are reproduced as amended by: the Financial Markets and Insolvency (Amendment) Regulations 1992, SI 1992/716; the Financial Markets and Insolvency (CGO Service) Regulations 1999, SI 1999/1209; the Financial Services and Markets Act 2000 (Consequential Amendments and Repeals) Order 2001, SI 2001/3649; the Enterprise Act 2002 (Insolvency) Order 2003, SI 2003/2096; the Financial Markets and Insolvency Regulations 2009, SI 2009/853; the Financial Services Act 2012 (Consequential Amendments and Transitional Provisions) Order 2013, SI 2013/472; the Financial Services and Markets Act 2000 (Over the Counter Derivatives, Central Counterparties and Trade Repositories) Regulations 2013, SI 2013/504; the Central Securities Depositories Regulations 2017, SI 2017/1064; the Financial Markets and Insolvency (Amendment and Transitional Provision) (EU Exit) Regulations 2019, SI 2019/341.

ARRANGEMENT OF REGULATIONS

PART I
GENERAL

PART V
MARKET CHARGES

PART VI
CONSTRUCTION OF REFERENCES TO PARTIES TO MARKET CONTRACTS

PART VIII
LEGAL PROCEEDINGS

PART I GENERAL

[6.8]

1 Citation and commencement

These Regulations may be cited as the Financial Markets and Insolvency Regulations 1991 and shall come into force on 25th April 1991.

[6.9]

2 Interpretation: general

(1) In these Regulations "the Act" means the Companies Act 1989.

[(1A) In these Regulations "the Recognition Requirements Regulations" means the Financial Services and Markets Act 2000 (Recognition Requirements for Investment Exchanges[, Clearing Houses and Central Securities Depositories]) Regulations 2001.]

(2) A reference in any of these Regulations to a numbered regulation shall be construed as a reference to the regulation bearing that number in these Regulations.

(3) A reference in any of these Regulations to a numbered paragraph shall, unless the reference is to a paragraph of a specified regulation, be construed as a reference to the paragraph bearing that number in the regulation in which the reference is made.

NOTES

Para (1A): inserted by the Financial Markets and Insolvency Regulations 2009, SI 2009/853, reg 3(1), (2), as from 15 June 2009. Words in square brackets inserted by the Central Securities Depositories Regulations 2017, SI 2017/1064, reg 10, Schedule, para 20(1), (2), as from 28 November 2017.

3–6 ((*Pts II–IV) amend CA 1989, ss 155, 159, 160, 162 at* **[5.150]**, **[5.154]**, **[5.155]**, **[5.157]**.)

PART V MARKET CHARGES

[6.10]

7 Interpretation of Part V

In this Part of these Regulations, unless the context otherwise requires—

"the Bank" means the Bank of England;

"business day" has the same meaning as in section 167(3) of the Act;

. . .

"CGO" means the Central Gilts Office of the Bank;

"CGO Service" means the computer-based system established by the Bank and The Stock Exchange to facilitate the transfer of specified securities;

"CGO Service charge" means a charge of the kind described in section 173(1)(c) of the Act;

"CGO Service member" means a person who is entitled by contract with [CRESTCo Limited (which is now responsible for operating the CGO Service)] to use the CGO Service;

["clearing member" has the same meaning as in section 190(1) of the Act;]

["client" has the same meaning as in section 190(1) of the Act;]

["default fund contribution" has the same meaning as in section 188(3A) of the Act;]

[. . .]

"former CGO Service member" means a person whose entitlement . . . to use the CGO Service has been terminated or suspended;

["indirect client" has the same meaning as in section 190(1) of the Act;]

"market charge" means a charge which is a market charge for the purposes of Part VII of the Act;

["recognised body" has the same meaning as in section 190(1) of the Act;]

["recognised central counterparty" has the same meaning as in section 190(1) of the Act;]

["recognised CSD" has the same meaning as in section 190(1) of the Act;]

"settlement bank" means a person who has agreed under a contract with [CRESTCo Limited (which is now responsible for operating the CGO Service)] to make payments of the kind mentioned in section 173(1)(c) of the Act;

"specified securities" has the meaning given in section 173(3) of the Act;

"Talisman" means The Stock Exchange settlement system known as Talisman;

"Talisman charge" means a charge granted in favour of The Stock Exchange over property credited to an account within Talisman maintained in the name of the chargor in respect of certain property beneficially owned by the chargor; . . .

["third country CSD" has the same meaning as in section 190(1) of the Act; and]

"transfer" when used in relation to specified securities has the meaning given in section 173(3) of the Act.

NOTES

Definition "CGO" (omitted) revoked, words in square brackets in definitions "CGO Service member" and "settlement bank" substituted, and words omitted from definition "former CGO Service member" revoked, by the Financial Markets and Insolvency (CGO Service) Regulations 1999, SI 1999/1209, reg 3(1), as from 24 May 1999.

Definitions "clearing member", "client", "indirect client", and "recognised central counterparty" inserted by the Financial Services and Markets Act 2000 (Over the Counter Derivatives, Central Counterparties and Trade Repositories) Regulations 2013, SI 2013/504, reg 30(1), (2), as from 1 April 2013.

Definition "default fund contribution" inserted by the Financial Markets and Insolvency Regulations 2009, SI 2009/853, reg 3(1), (3), as from 15 June 2009.

Definition "EEA CSD" (omitted) originally inserted by the Central Securities Depositories Regulations 2017, SI 2017/1064, reg 10, Schedule, para 20(1), (3), as from 28 November 2017; and subsequently revoked by the Financial Markets and Insolvency (Amendment and Transitional Provision) (EU Exit) Regulations 2019, SI 2019/341, reg 11(1), (2), as from IP completion day (as defined in the European Union (Withdrawal Agreement) Act 2020, s 39).

Definitions "recognised body", "recognised CSD", and "third country CSD" inserted, and word omitted from the definition "Talisman Charge" revoked, by SI 2017/1064, reg 10, Schedule, para 20(1), (3), as from 28 November 2017.

[6.11]

8 Charges on land or any interest in land not to be treated as market charges

(1) No charge, whether fixed or floating, shall be treated as a market charge to the extent that it is a charge on land or any interest in land.

(2) For the purposes of paragraph (1), a charge on a debenture forming part of an issue or series shall not be treated as a charge on land or any interest in land by reason of the fact that the debenture is secured by a charge on land or any interest in land.

9 (*Amends CA 1989, s 173 at* **[5.169]**.)

[6.12]

10 Extent to which charge granted in favour of recognised investment exchange to be treated as market charge

(1) A charge granted in favour of a recognised investment exchange other than The Stock Exchange shall be treated as a market charge only to the extent that—

(a) it is a charge over property provided as margin in respect of market contracts entered into by the exchange for the purposes of or in connection with the provision of clearing services [or over property provided as a default fund contribution to the exchange];

(b) in the case of a recognised UK investment exchange, it secures the obligation to pay to the exchange [any sum due to the exchange from a member or designated non-member of the exchange or from a recognised clearing house [or from a recognised CSD] or from another recognised investment exchange in respect of unsettled market contracts to which the member, designated non-member [or recognised body] is a party under the rules referred to in paragraph 12 of the Schedule to the Recognition Requirements Regulations]; and

(c) in the case of a recognised overseas investment exchange, it secures the obligation to reimburse the cost (other than fees and other incidental expenses) incurred by the exchange in settling unsettled market contracts in respect of which the charged property is provided as margin.

(2) A charge granted in favour of The Stock Exchange shall be treated as a market charge only to the extent that—

(a) it is a charge of the kind described in paragraph (1); or

(b) it is a Talisman charge and secures an obligation of either or both of the kinds mentioned in paragraph (3).

(3) The obligations mentioned in this paragraph are—

(a) the obligation of the chargor to reimburse The Stock Exchange for payments (including stamp duty and taxes but excluding Stock Exchange fees and incidental expenses arising from the operation by The Stock Exchange of settlement arrangements) made by The Stock Exchange in settling, through Talisman, market contracts entered into by the chargor; and

(b) the obligation of the chargor to reimburse The Stock Exchange the amount of any payment it has made pursuant to a short term certificate.

(4) In paragraph (3), "short term certificate" means an instrument issued by The Stock Exchange undertaking to procure the transfer of property of a value and description specified in the instrument to or to the order of the person to whom the instrument is issued or his endorsee or to a person acting on behalf of either of them and also undertaking to make appropriate payments in cash, in the event that the obligation to procure the transfer of property cannot be discharged in whole or in part.

NOTES

Para (1): words in square brackets in sub-para (a) inserted, and words in first (outer) pair of square brackets in sub-para (b) substituted, by the Financial Markets and Insolvency Regulations 2009, SI 2009/853, reg 3(1), (4), as from 15 June 2009. Words in second (inner) pair of square brackets in sub-para (b) inserted, and words in third (inner) pair of square brackets substituted, by the Central Securities Depositories Regulations 2017, SI 2017/1064, reg 10, Schedule, para 20(1), (4), as from 28 November 2017.

[6.13]

11 Extent to which charge granted in favour of recognised clearing house to be treated as market charge

A charge granted in favour of a recognised clearing house shall be treated as a market charge only to the extent that—

(a) it is a charge over property provided as margin in respect of market contracts entered into by the clearing house [or over property provided as a default fund contribution to the clearing house];

[(aa) in the case of a recognised central counterparty, it secures the obligation to pay to the recognised central counterparty any sum due to it from a clearing member, a client, an indirect client, a recognised investment exchange[, a recognised CSD] or recognised clearing house in respect of unsettled market contracts to which the clearing member, client, indirect client [or recognised body] is a party;]

(b) [in the case of a recognised clearing house which is not a recognised central counterparty], it secures the obligation to pay to the clearing house [any sum due to the clearing house from a member of the clearing house or from a recognised investment exchange [or from a recognised CSD] or from another recognised clearing house in respect of unsettled market contracts to which the member [or recognised body] is a party under the rules referred to in paragraph 25 of the Schedule to the Recognition Requirements Regulations]; and

(c) in the case of a recognised overseas clearing house, it secures the obligation to reimburse the cost (other than fees or other incidental expenses) incurred by the clearing house in settling unsettled market contracts in respect of which the charged property is provided as margin.

NOTES

Words in square brackets in para (a) inserted, and words in second (outer) pair of square brackets in para (b) substituted, by the Financial Markets and Insolvency Regulations 2009, SI 2009/853, reg 3(1), (5), as from 15 June 2009.

Para (aa) inserted, and words in first pair of square brackets in para (b) substituted, by the Financial Services and Markets Act 2000 (Over the Counter Derivatives, Central Counterparties and Trade Repositories) Regulations 2013, SI 2013/504, reg 30(1), (3), as from 1 April 2013.

Words in first pair of square brackets in para (aa) inserted, words in second pair of square brackets in that sub-paragraph substituted, words in third (inner) pair of square brackets in sub-para (b) inserted, and words in fourth (inner) pair of square brackets substituted, by the Central Securities Depositories Regulations 2017, SI 2017/1064, reg 10, Schedule, para 20(1), (5), as from 28 November 2017.

[6.14]

[11A Extent to which charge granted in favour of recognised CSD to be treated as market charge

(1) A charge granted in favour of a recognised CSD shall be treated as a market charge only to the extent that—

(a) it is a charge over property provided as margin in respect of market contracts entered into by the recognised CSD or over property provided as a default fund contribution to the recognised CSD; and

(b) it secures the obligation to pay to the recognised CSD any sum due to it from a member of the recognised CSD or from a recognised clearing house or from a recognised investment exchange or from another recognised CSD in respect of unsettled market contracts to which the member or recognised body is a party.

(2) A charge granted in favour of [a] third country CSD shall be treated as a market charge only to the extent that—

(a) it is a charge over property provided as margin in respect of market contracts entered into by the . . . third country CSD or over property provided as a default fund contribution to the . . . third country CSD; and

(b) it secures the obligation to reimburse the cost (other than fees or other incidental expenses) incurred by the . . . third country CSD in settling unsettled market contracts in respect of which the charged property is provided as margin.]

NOTES

Inserted by the Central Securities Depositories Regulations 2017, SI 2017/1064, reg 10, Schedule, para 20(1), (6), as from 28 November 2017.

Para (2): word in square brackets substituted, and words omitted revoked, by the Financial Markets and Insolvency (Amendment and Transitional Provision) (EU Exit) Regulations 2019, SI 2019/341, regs 4, 11(3), as from IP completion day (as defined in the European Union (Withdrawal Agreement) Act 2020, s 39).

[6.15]

12 Circumstances in which CGO Service charge to be treated as market charge

A CGO Service charge shall be treated as a market charge only if—

(a) it is granted to a settlement bank by a person for the purpose of securing debts or liabilities of the kind mentioned in section 173(1)(c) of the Act incurred by that person through his use of the CGO Service as a CGO Service member; and

(b) it contains provisions which refer expressly to the [CGO Service].

NOTES

Words in square brackets substituted by the Financial Markets and Insolvency (CGO Service) Regulations 1999, SI 1999/1209, reg 3(2), as from 24 May 1999.

[6.16]

13 Extent to which CGO Service charge to be treated as market charge

A CGO Service charge shall be treated as a market charge only to the extent that—

(a) it is a charge over any one or more of the following—

(i) specified securities held within the CGO Service to the account of a CGO Service member or a former CGO Service member;

(ii) specified securities which were held as mentioned in sub-paragraph (i) above immediately prior to their being removed from the CGO Service consequent upon the person in question becoming a former CGO Service member;

(iii) sums receivable by a CGO Service member or former CGO Service member representing interest accrued on specified securities held within the CGO Service to his account or which were so held immediately prior to their being removed from the CGO Service consequent upon his becoming a former CGO Service member;

(iv) sums receivable by a CGO Service member or former CGO Service member in respect of the redemption or conversion of specified securities which were held within the CGO Service to his account at the time that the relevant securities were redeemed or converted or which were so held immediately prior to their being removed from the CGO Service consequent upon his becoming a former CGO Service member; and

(v) sums receivable by a CGO Service member or former CGO Service member in respect of the transfer by him of specified securities through the medium of the CGO Service; and

(b) it secures the obligation of a CGO Service member or former CGO Service member to reimburse a settlement bank for the amount due from him to the settlement bank as a result of the settlement bank having discharged or become obliged to discharge payment obligations in respect of transfers or allotments of specified securities made to him through the medium of the CGO Service.

[6.17]

14 [Limitation on disapplication of moratorium on certain legal processes under Schedule B1 to the Insolvency Act 1986 (administration) in relation to CGO Service charges]

(1) In this regulation "qualifying period" means the period beginning with the fifth business day before the day on which [an application] for the making of an administration order in relation to the relevant CGO Service member or former CGO Service member is presented and ending with the second business day after the day on which an administration order is made in relation to the relevant CGO Service member or former CGO Service member pursuant to the petition.

[(1A) A reference in paragraph (1) to an application for an administration order shall be treated as including a reference to—

(a) appointing an administrator under paragraph 14 or 22 of Schedule B1 to the Insolvency Act 1986, or

(b) filing with the court a notice of intention to appoint an administrator under either of those paragraphs,

and a reference to "an administration order" shall include the appointment of an administrator under paragraph 14 or 22 of Schedule B1 to the Insolvency Act 1986.]

(2) [The disapplication of paragraph 43(2) of Schedule B1 to the Insolvency Act 1986 (including that provisions as applied by paragraph 44 of that Schedule)] by section 175(1)(a) of the Act shall be limited in respect of a CGO Service charge so that it has effect only to the extent necessary to enable there to be realised, whether through the sale of specified securities or otherwise, a sum equal to whichever is less of the following—

(a) the total amount of payment obligations discharged by the settlement bank in respect of transfers and allotments of specified securities made during the qualifying period to the relevant CGO Service member or former CGO Service member through the medium of the CGO Service less the total amount of payment obligations discharged to the settlement bank in respect of transfers of specified securities made during the qualifying period by the relevant CGO Service member or former CGO Service member through the medium of the CGO Service; and

(b) the amount (if any) described in regulation 13(b) due to the settlement bank from the relevant CGO Service member or former CGO Service member.

NOTES

The regulation heading was substituted, the words in square brackets in paras (1), (2) were substituted, and para (1A) was inserted, by the Enterprise Act 2002 (Insolvency) Order 2003, SI 2003/2096, arts 5, 6, Schedule, Pt 2, paras 47, 48, as from 15 September 2003, except in relation to any case where a petition for an administration order was presented before that date. Note that para 48(b) of the amending Schedule provides: "in paragraph (1) for "a petition" substitute "an application"". It is assumed that the words "the petition" at the end of para (1) should also have been substituted, but SI 2003/2096 made no such provision.

[6.18]

15 Ability of administrator or receiver to recover assets in case of property subject to CGO Service charge or Talisman charge

(1) [The disapplication—

(a) by section 175(1)(b) of the Act, of paragraphs 70, 71 and 72 of Schedule B1 to the Insolvency Act 1986, and

(b) by section 175(3) of the Act, of sections 43 and 61 of the 1986 Act,

shall cease to have effect] in respect of a charge which is either a CGO Service charge or a Talisman charge after the end of the second business day after the day on which an administration order is made or, as the case may be, an administrative receiver or a receiver is appointed, in relation to the grantor of the charge, in relation to property subject to it which—

(a) in the case of a CGO Service charge, is not, on the basis of a valuation in accordance with paragraph (2), required for the realisation of whichever is the less of the sum referred to in regulation 14(2)(a) and the amount referred to in regulation 14(2)(b) due to the settlement bank at the close of business on the second business day referred to above; and

(b) in the case of a Talisman charge is not, on the basis of a valuation in accordance with paragraph (2), required to enable The Stock Exchange to reimburse itself for any payment it has made of the kind referred to in regulation 10(3).

[(1A) A reference in paragraph (1) to "an administration order" shall include the appointment of an administrator under paragraph 14 or 22 of Schedule B1 to the Insolvency Act 1986.]

(2) For the purposes of paragraph (1) the value of property shall, except in a case falling within paragraph (3), be such as may be agreed between whichever is relevant of the administrator, administrative receiver or receiver on the one hand and the settlement bank or The Stock Exchange on the other.

(3) For the purposes of paragraph (1), the value of any investment for which a price for the second business day referred to above is quoted in the Daily Official List of The Stock Exchange shall—

(a) in a case in which two prices are so quoted, be an amount equal to the average of those two prices, adjusted where appropriate to take account of any accrued interest; and

(b) in a case in which one price is so quoted, be an amount equal to that price, adjusted where appropriate to take account of any accrued interest.

NOTES

The words in square brackets in para (1) were substituted, and para (1A) was inserted, by the Enterprise Act 2002 (Insolvency) Order 2003, SI 2003/2096, arts 5, 6, Schedule, Pt 2, paras 47, 49, as from 15 September 2003, except in relation to any case where a petition for an administration order was presented before that date.

PART VI CONSTRUCTION OF REFERENCES TO PARTIES TO MARKET CONTRACTS

[6.19]

16 Circumstances in which member or designated non-member dealing as principal to be treated as acting in different capacities

(1) In this regulation "relevant transaction" means—

[(a) a market contract, effected as principal by a member or designated non-member of a recognised investment exchange or a member of a recognised clearing house [or a member of a recognised CSD], in relation to which money received by the member or designated non-member is—

(i) clients' money for the purposes of rules relating to clients' money, or

(ii) would be clients' money for the purposes of those rules were it not money which, in accordance with those rules, may be regarded as immediately due and payable to the member or designated non-member for its own account; and]

(b) a market contract which would be regarded as a relevant transaction by virtue of sub-paragraph (a) above were it not for the fact that no money is received by the member or designated non-member in relation to the contract

[(1A) In addition "relevant transaction" means a market contract entered into by a recognised clearing house effected as principal in relation to which money is received by the recognised clearing house from a recognised investment exchange [or from a recognised CSD] or from another recognised clearing house.

(1B) In addition "relevant transaction" means a market contract entered into by a recognised investment exchange effected as principal in relation to which money is received by the recognised investment exchange from a recognised clearing house [or from a recognised CSD] or from another recognised investment exchange.

[(1BA) In addition "relevant transaction" means a market contract entered into by a recognised CSD effected as principal in relation to which money is received by the recognised CSD from a recognised clearing house or from a recognised investment exchange or from another recognised CSD.]

[(1C) Where paragraph (1A), (1B) or (1BA) applies, paragraph (1) applies to the recognised clearing house, recognised investment exchange or recognised CSD as it does to a member of the recognised clearing house, recognised investment exchange or recognised CSD, and as if the recognised clearing house, recognised investment exchange or recognised CSD were subject to the rules referred to in paragraph (1)(a)(i).]

[(1D) In paragraph (1), "rules relating to clients' money" are rules made by the Financial Conduct Authority under sections 137A and 137B of the Financial Services and Markets Act 2000.]]

[(2) For the purposes of section 187(1) of the Act (construction of references to parties to market contracts)—

(a) a recognised investment exchange or a member or designated non-member of a recognised investment exchange, . . .

(b) a recognised clearing house or a member of a recognised clearing house, [or

(c) a recognised CSD or a member of a recognised CSD].

shall be treated as effecting relevant transactions in a different capacity from other market contracts it has effected as principal.]

[(3), (4) . . .]

NOTES

Para (1): sub-para (a) substituted by the Financial Markets and Insolvency Regulations 2009, SI 2009/853, reg 3(1), (6)(a), as from 15 June 2009. Words in square brackets in sub-para (a) inserted by the Central Securities Depositories Regulations 2017, SI 2017/1064, reg 10, Schedule, para 20(1), (7)(a), as from 28 November 2017.

Paras (1A), (1B), (1C), (1D): inserted by SI 2009/853, reg 3(1), (6)(b), as from 15 June 2009. Words in square brackets in paras (1A), (1B) inserted, and para (1C) substituted, by SI 2017/1064, reg 10, Schedule, para 20(1), (7)(b), (c), (e), as from 28 November 2017. Para (1D) substituted by the Financial Services Act 2012 (Consequential Amendments and Transitional Provisions) Order 2013, SI 2013/472, art 3, Sch 2, para 9, as from 1 April 2013.

Para (1BA): inserted by SI 2017/1064, reg 10, Schedule, para 20(1), (7)(d), as from 28 November 2017.

Para (2): substituted by SI 2009/853, reg 3(1), (6)(c), as from 15 June 2009. Word omitted from sub-para (a) revoked, and sub-para (c) (and the preceding word) inserted, by SI 2017/1064, reg 10, Schedule, para 20(1), (7)(f), as from 28 November 2017.

Paras (3), (4): originally added by the Financial Services and Markets Act 2000 (Consequential Amendments and Repeals) Order 2001, SI 2001/3649, art 415(1), (3), as from 1 December 2001. Subsequently revoked by SI 2009/853, reg 3(1), (6)(d), as from 15 June 2009.

17 ((*Pt VII) Amended CA 1989, Sch 21 (repealed).*)

PART VIII LEGAL PROCEEDINGS

18 (*Amends CA 1989, s 175 at* **[5.171]**.)

[6.20]

19 Court having jurisdiction in respect of proceedings under Part VII of Act

(1) For the purposes of sections 161, 163, 164, 175(5) and 182 of the Act (various legal proceedings under Part VII of Act) "the court" shall be the court which has last heard an application in the proceedings under the Insolvency Act 1986 or the Bankruptcy (Scotland) Act 1985 in which the relevant office-holder is acting or, as the case may be, any court having jurisdiction to hear applications in those proceedings.

(2) For the purposes of subsection (2) [and (2A)] of section 175 of the Act (administration orders etc), "the court" shall be the court which has made the administration order or, as the case may be, to which the [application] for an administration order has been presented [or the notice of intention to appoint has been filed].

(3) The rules regulating the practice and procedure of the court in relation to applications to the court in England and Wales under sections 161, 163, 164, 175 and 182 of the Act shall be the rules applying in relation to applications to that court under the Insolvency Act 1986.

NOTES

Para (2): words in first and third pairs of square brackets inserted, and word in second pair of square brackets substituted, by the Enterprise Act 2002 (Insolvency) Order 2003, SI 2003/2096, arts 5, 6, Schedule, Pt 2, paras 47, 50, as from 15 September 2003, except in relation to any case where a petition for an administration order was presented before that date.

INSIDER DEALING (SECURITIES AND REGULATED MARKETS) ORDER 1994

(SI 1994/187)

NOTES

Made: 1 February 1994.

Authority: Criminal Justice Act 1993, ss 54(1), 60(1), 62(1), 64(3).

Commencement: 1 March 1994.

This Order is reproduced as amended by: the Insider Dealing (Securities and Regulated Markets) (Amendment) Order 1996, SI 1996/1561; the Insider Dealing (Securities and Regulated Markets) (Amendment) Order 2000, SI 2000/1923; the Insider Dealing (Securities and Regulated Markets) (Amendment) Order 2002, SI 2002/1874; the Financial Services (Miscellaneous) (Amendment) (EU Exit) (No 3) Regulations 2019, SI 2019/1390.

[6.21]

1 Title, commencement and interpretation

This Order may be cited as the Insider Dealing (Securities and Regulated Markets) Order 1994 and shall come into force on the twenty eighth day after the day on which it is made.

[6.22]

2

In this Order a "State within the European Economic Area" means a State which is a member of the [European Union] and the Republics of Austria, Finland and Iceland, the Kingdoms of Norway and Sweden and the Principality of Liechtenstein.

NOTES

Words in square brackets substituted by the Treaty of Lisbon (Changes in Terminology) Order 2011, SI 2011/1043, art 4, as from 22 April 2011.

[6.23]

3 Securities

Articles 4 to 8 set out conditions for the purposes of section 54(1) of the Criminal Justice Act 1993 (securities to which Part V of the Act of 1993 applies).

[6.24]

4

The following condition applies in relation to any security which falls within any paragraph of Schedule 2 to the Act of 1993, [that is—

(a) that it is officially listed in the United Kingdom, in Gibraltar or in a State within the European Economic Area; or

(b) that it is admitted to dealing on, or has its price quoted on or under the rules of, a regulated market].

NOTES

Words in square brackets substituted by the Financial Services (Miscellaneous) (Amendment) (EU Exit) (No 3) Regulations 2019, SI 2019/1390, reg 3, as from IP completion day (as defined in the European Union (Withdrawal Agreement) Act 2020, s 39).

[6.25]

5

The following alternative condition applies in relation to a warrant, that is, that the right under it is a right to subscribe for any share or debt security of the same class as a share or debt security which satisfies the condition in article 4.

[6.26]

6

The following alternative condition applies in relation to a depositary receipt, that is, that the rights under it are in respect of any share or debt security which satisfies the condition in article 4.

[6.27]

7

The following alternative conditions apply in relation to an option or a future, that is, that the option or rights under the future are in respect of—

(a) any share or debt security which satisfies the condition in article 4, or

(b) any depositary receipt which satisfies the condition in article 4 or article 6.

[6.28]

8

The following alternative condition applies in relation to a contract for differences, that is, that the purpose or pretended purpose of the contract is to secure a profit or avoid a loss by reference to fluctuations in—

(a) the price of any shares or debt securities which satisfy the condition in article 4, or
(b) an index of the price of such shares or debt securities.

[6.29]
9 Regulated markets

The following markets are regulated markets for the purposes of Part V of the Act of 1993—

[(a)] any market which is established under the rules of an investment exchange specified in the Schedule to this Order
(b) the market known as OFEX . . .]

NOTES

Para (a) designated as such, and para (b) added, by the Insider Dealing (Securities and Regulated Markets) (Amendment) Order 2000, SI 2000/1923, art 2(1), (2), as from 20 July 2000. Words omitted from para (b) revoked by the Insider Dealing (Securities and Regulated Markets) (Amendment) Order 2002, SI 2002/1874, art 2(1), (2), as from 19 July 2002.

[6.30]
10 United Kingdom regulated markets

The regulated markets which are regulated in the United Kingdom for the purposes of Part V of the Act of 1993 are any market which is established under the rules of—

[(a) the London Stock Exchange Limited;]
(b) LIFFE Administration & Management; . . .
(c) OMLX, the London Securities and Derivatives Exchange Limited [. . .
(d) [virt-x Exchange Limited].]
[(e) [the exchange known as COREDEALMTS]; together with the market known as OFEX . . .]

NOTES

Para (a) substituted, word omitted from para (b) revoked, and para (d) and the word immediately preceding it added, by the Insider Dealing (Securities and Regulated Markets) (Amendment) Order 1996, SI 1996/1561, art 3, as from 1 July 1996. Word omitted from para (c) revoked, and para (e) added, by the Insider Dealing (Securities and Regulated Markets) (Amendment) Order 2000, SI 2000/1923, art 2(1), (3), as from 20 July 2000. Words in square brackets in paras (d), (e) substituted, and words omitted from para (e) revoked, by the Insider Dealing (Securities and Regulated Markets) (Amendment) Order 2002, SI 2002/1874, art 2(1), (3) as from 19 July 2002.

Note that some of the markets listed above have subsequently changed names/been acquired by other entities or otherwise ceased to operate. This regulation has not, however, been updated to reflect those changes.

SCHEDULE
REGULATED MARKETS

Article 9

[6.31]

Any market which is established under the rules of one of the following investment exchanges:

Amsterdam Stock Exchange
Antwerp Stock Exchange
Athens Stock Exchange
Barcelona Stock Exchange
Bavarian Stock Exchange
Berlin Stock Exchange
Bilbao Stock Exchange
Bologna Stock Exchange
. . .
Bremen Stock Exchange
Brussels Stock Exchange
Copenhagen Stock Exchange
[The exchange known as COREDEALMTS]
Dusseldorf Stock Exchange
[The exchange known as EASDAQ]
Florence Stock Exchange
Frankfurt Stock Exchange
Genoa Stock Exchange
. . .
Hamburg Stock Exchange
Hanover Stock Exchange
Helsinki Stock Exchange
[Iceland Stock Exchange]
[The Irish Stock Exchange Limited]
. . .

. . .
Lisbon Stock Exchange
LIFFE Administration & Management
[The London Stock Exchange Limited]
Luxembourg Stock Exchange
Lyon Stock Exchange
Madrid Stock Exchange
. . .
Milan Stock Exchange
. . .
. . .
Naples Stock Exchange
The exchange known as NASDAQ
[The exchange known as the Nouveau Marché]
OMLX, the London Securities and Derivatives Exchange Limited
Oporto Stock Exchange
Oslo Stock Exchange
Palermo Stock Exchange
Paris Stock Exchange
Rome Stock Exchange
. . .
Stockholm Stock Exchange
Stuttgart Stock Exchange
[The exchange known as SWX Swiss Exchange]

[. . .]
Trieste Stock Exchange
Turin Stock Exchange
Valencia Stock Exchange
Venice Stock Exchange
Vienna Stock Exchange
[virt-x Exchange Limited]

NOTES

First to seventh entries omitted revoked, entries "Iceland Stock Exchange" and "The Irish Stock Exchange Limited" substituted, and entries "The London Stock Exchange Limited" and "The exchange known as the Nouveau Marché inserted, by the Insider Dealing (Securities and Regulated Markets) (Amendment) Order 1996, SI 1996/1561, art 4, as from 1 July 1996.

Entry "The exchange known as COREDEALMTS" originally inserted by the Insider Dealing (Securities and Regulated Markets) (Amendment) Order 2000, SI 2000/1923, art 2(1), (4)(a), as from 20 July 2000, and substituted by the Insider Dealing (Securities and Regulated Markets) (Amendment) Order 2002, SI 2002/1874, art 2(1), (4)(a) as from 19 July 2002.

Entry "The exchange known as EASDAQ" inserted, and eighth entry omitted revoked, by SI 2000/1923, art 2(1), (4)(b), (c), as from 20 July 2000.

Entries "The exchange known as SWX Swiss Exchange" and "virt-x Exchange Limited" inserted by SI 2002/1874, art 2(1), (4)(b), (d) as from 19 July 2002.

Final entry omitted originally inserted by SI 1996/1561, art 4, as from 1 July 1996, and revoked by SI 2002/1874, art 2(1), (4)(c) as from 19 July 2002.

See also the final note to art 10 at **[6.30]**.

FINANCIAL MARKETS AND INSOLVENCY REGULATIONS 1996

(SI 1996/1469)

NOTES

Made: 5 June 1996.
Authority: Companies Act 1989, ss 185, 186.
Commencement: 15 July 1996.
These Regulations are reproduced as amended by: the Uncertificated Securities Regulations 2001, SI 2001/3755; the Enterprise Act 2002 (Insolvency) Order 2003, SI 2003/2096; the Enterprise Act 2002 (Insolvency) Order 2004, SI 2004/2312.

ARRANGEMENT OF REGULATIONS

PART I GENERAL

[6.32]
1 Citation and commencement

These Regulations may be cited as the Financial Markets and Insolvency Regulations 1996 and shall come into force on 15th July 1996.

[6.33]
2 Interpretation

(1) In these Regulations—

"the Act" means the Companies Act 1989;

"business day" means any day which is not a Saturday or Sunday, Christmas Day, Good Friday or a bank holiday in any part of the United Kingdom under the Banking and Financial Dealings Act 1971;

"issue", in relation to an uncertificated unit of a security, means to confer on a person title to a new unit;

"register of securities"—

(a) in relation to shares, means a register of members; and

(b) in relation to units of a security other than shares, means [a register, whether maintained by virtue of the Uncertificated Securities Regulations 2001 or otherwise], of persons holding the units;

. . .

"relevant nominee" means a system-member who is a subsidiary undertaking of the Operator designated by him as such in accordance with such rules and practices as are mentioned in [paragraph 25(f) of Schedule 1 to the Uncertificated Securities Regulations 2001];

"settlement bank" means a person who has contracted with an Operator to make payments in connection with transfers, by means of a relevant system, of title to uncertificated units of a security and of interests of system-beneficiaries in relation to such units;

"system-beneficiary" means a person on whose behalf a system-member or former system-member holds or held uncertificated units of a security;

"system-charge" means a charge of a kind to which regulation 3(2) applies;

"system-member" means a person who is permitted by an Operator to transfer by means of a relevant system title to uncertificated units of a security held by him; and "former system-member" means a person whose participation in the relevant system is terminated or suspended;

"transfer", in relation to title to uncertificated units of a security, means [the registration of a transfer of title to those units in the relevant Operator register of securities;] and in relation to an interest of a system-beneficiary in relation to uncertificated units of a security, means the transfer of the interest to another system-beneficiary by means of a relevant system; and

other expressions used in these Regulations which are also used in [the Uncertificated Securities Regulations 2001] have the same meanings as in those Regulations.

(2) For the purposes of these Regulations, a person holds a unit of a security if—

(a) in the case of an uncertificated unit, he is entered on a register of securities in relation to the unit in accordance with [regulation 20, 21 or 22 of the Uncertificated Securities Regulations 2001]; and

(b) in the case of a certificated unit, he has title to the unit.

(3) A reference in any of these Regulations to a numbered regulation shall be construed as a reference to the regulation bearing that number in these Regulations.

(4) A reference in any of these Regulations to a numbered paragraph shall, unless the reference is to a paragraph of a specified regulation, be construed as a reference to the paragraph bearing that number in the regulation in which the reference is made.

NOTES

Para (1): words in square brackets substituted, and the definition "the 1995 Regulations" (omitted) revoked, by the Uncertificated Securities Regulations 2001, SI 2001/3755, reg 51, Sch 7, Pt 2, para 20(a), as from 26 November 2001.

Para (2): words in square brackets substituted by SI 2001/3755, reg 51, Sch 7, Pt 2, para 20(b), as from 26 November 2001.

PART II SYSTEM-CHARGES

[6.34]

3 Application of Part VII of the Act in relation to system-charges

(1) Subject to the provisions of these Regulations, Part VII of the Act shall apply in relation to—

(a) a charge to which paragraph (2) applies ("a system-charge") and any action taken to enforce such a charge; and

(b) any property subject to a system-charge,

in the same way as it applies in relation to a market charge, any action taken to enforce a market charge and any property subject to a market charge.

(2) This paragraph applies in relation to a charge granted in favour of a settlement bank for the purpose of securing debts or liabilities arising in connection with any of the following—

(a) a transfer of uncertificated units of a security to a system-member by means of a relevant system whether the system-member is acting for himself or on behalf of a system-beneficiary;

(b) a transfer, by one system-beneficiary to another and by means of a relevant system, of his interests in relation to uncertificated units of a security held by a relevant nominee where the relevant nominee will continue to hold the units;

(c) an agreement to make a transfer of the kind specified in paragraph (a);

(d) an agreement to make a transfer of the kind specified in paragraph (b); and

(e) an issue of uncertificated units of a security to a system-member by means of a relevant system whether the system-member is acting for himself or on behalf of a system-beneficiary.

(3) In its application, by virtue of these Regulations, in relation to a system-charge, section 173(2) of the Act shall have effect as if the references to "purposes specified" and "specified purposes" were references to any one or more of the purposes specified in paragraph (2).

[6.35]

4 Circumstances in which Part VII applies in relation to system-charge

(1) Part VII of the Act shall apply in relation to a system-charge granted by a system-member and in relation to property subject to such a charge only if—

(a) it is granted to a settlement bank by a system-member for the purpose of securing debts or liabilities arising in connection with any of the transactions specified in regulation 3(2), being debts or liabilities incurred by that system-member or by a system-beneficiary on whose behalf he holds uncertificated units of a security; and

(b) it contains provisions which refer expressly to the relevant system in relation to which the grantor is a system-member.

(2) Part VII of the Act shall apply in relation to a system-charge granted by a system-beneficiary and in relation to property subject to such a charge only if—

(a) it is granted to a settlement bank by a system-beneficiary for the purpose of securing debts or liabilities arising in connection with any of the transactions specified in regulation 3(2), incurred by that system-beneficiary or by a system-member who holds uncertificated units of a security on his behalf; and

(b) it contains provisions which refer expressly to the relevant system in relation to which the system-member who holds the uncertificated units of a security in relation to which the system-beneficiary has the interest is a system-member.

[6.36]

5 Extent to which Part VII applies to a system-charge

Part VII of the Act shall apply in relation to a system-charge only to the extent that—

(a) it is a charge over any one or more of the following—

(i) uncertificated units of a security held by a system-member or a former system-member;

(ii) interests of a kind specified in [regulation 31(2)(b) or 31(4)(b) of the Uncertificated Securities Regulations 2001] in uncertificated units of a security in favour of a system member or a former system-member;

(iii) interests of a system-beneficiary in relation to uncertificated units of a security;

(iv) units of a security which are no longer in uncertificated form because the person holding the units has become a former system-member;

(v) sums or other benefits receivable by a system-member or former system-member by reason of his holding uncertificated units of a security, or units which are no longer in uncertificated form because the person holding the units has become a former system-member;

(vi) sums or other benefits receivable by a system-beneficiary by reason of his having an interest in relation to uncertificated units of a security or in relation to units which are no longer in uncertificated form because the person holding the units has become a former system-member;

(vii) sums or other benefits receivable by a system-member or former system-member by way of repayment, bonus, preference, redemption, conversion or accruing or offered in respect of uncertificated units of a security, or units which are no longer in uncertificated form because the person holding the units has become a former system-member;

(viii) sums or other benefits receivable by a system-beneficiary by way of repayment, bonus, preference, redemption, conversion or accruing or offered in respect of uncertificated units of a security in relation to which he has an interest or in respect of units in relation to which the system-beneficiary has an interest and which are no longer in uncertificated form because the person holding the units has become a former system-member;

(ix) sums or other benefits receivable by a system-member or former system-member in respect of the transfer of uncertificated units of a security by or to him by means of a relevant system;

(x) sums or other benefits receivable by a system-member or former system-member in respect of an agreement to transfer uncertificated units of a security by or to him by means of a relevant system;

(xi) sums or other benefits receivable by a system-beneficiary in respect of the transfer of the interest of a system-beneficiary in relation to uncertificated units of a security by or to him by means of a relevant system or in respect of the transfer of uncertificated units of a security by or to a system-member acting on his behalf by means of a relevant system;

(xii) sums or other benefits receivable by a system-beneficiary in respect of an agreement to transfer the interest of a system-beneficiary in relation to uncertificated units of a security by or to him by means of a relevant system, or in respect of an agreement to transfer uncertificated units of a security by or to a system-member acting on his behalf by means of a relevant system; and

(b) it secures—

(i) the obligation of a system-member or former system-member to reimburse a settlement bank, being an obligation which arises in connection with any of the transactions specified in regulation 3(2) and whether the obligation was incurred by the system-member when acting for himself or when acting on behalf of a system-beneficiary; or

(ii) the obligation of a system-beneficiary to reimburse a settlement bank, being an obligation which arises in connection with any of the transactions specified in regulation 3(2) and whether the obligation was incurred by the system-beneficiary when acting for himself or by reason of a system-member acting on his behalf.

NOTES

Words in square brackets in sub-para (a)(ii) substituted by the Uncertificated Securities Regulations 2001, SI 2001/3755, reg 51, Sch 7, Pt 2, para 20(c), as from 26 November 2001.

[6.37]

6 [Limitation on disapplication of moratorium on certain legal processes under Schedule B1 to the Insolvency Act 1986 (administration) in relation to system-charges]

(1) This regulation applies where an administration order is made in relation to a system-member or former system-member.

[(1A) A reference in paragraph (1) to "an administration order" shall include the appointment of an administrator under paragraph 14 or 22 of Schedule B1 to the Insolvency Act 1986].

(2) [The disapplication of paragraph 43(2) of Schedule B1 to the Insolvency Act 1986 (including that provision as applied by paragraph 44 of that Schedule)] by section 175(1)(a) of the Act shall have effect, in relation to a system-charge granted by a system-member or former system-member, only to the extent necessary to enable there to be realised, whether through the sale of uncertificated units of a security or otherwise, the lesser of the two sums specified in paragraphs (3) and (4).

(3) The first sum of the two sums referred to in paragraph (2) is the net sum of—

(a) all payment obligations discharged by the settlement bank in connection with—

(i) transfers of uncertificated units of a security by means of a relevant system made during the qualifying period to or by the relevant system-member or former system-member, whether acting for himself or on behalf of a system-beneficiary;

Part 6 Other companies SIs

(ii) agreements made during the qualifying period to transfer uncertificated units of a security by means of a relevant system to or from the relevant system-member or former system-member, whether acting for himself or on behalf of a system-beneficiary; and

(iii) issues of uncertificated units of a security by means of a relevant system made during the qualifying period to the relevant system-member or former system-member, whether acting for himself or on behalf of a system-beneficiary; less

(b) all payment obligations discharged to the settlement bank in connection with transactions of any kind described in paragraph (3)(a)(i) and (ii).

(4) The second of the two sums referred to in paragraph (2) is the sum (if any) due to the settlement bank from the relevant system-member or former system-member by reason of an obligation of the kind described in regulation 5(b)(i).

(5) In this regulation and regulation 7, "qualifying period" means the period—

(a) beginning with the fifth business day before the day on which [an application] for the making of the administration order was presented; and

(b) ending with the second business day after the day on which the administration order is made.

[(5A) A reference in paragraph (5) to an application for an administration order shall be treated as including a reference to—

(a) appointing an administrator under [paragraph 14] or 22 of Schedule B1 to the Insolvency Act 1986, or

(b) filing with the court a notice of intention to appoint an administrator under either of those paragraphs,

and a reference to "an administration order" shall include the appointment of an administrator under paragraph 14 or 22 of Schedule B1 to the Insolvency Act 1986.]

NOTES

The regulation heading was substituted, para (1A) was inserted, the words in square brackets in paras (2), (5) were substituted, and para (5A) was added, by the Enterprise Act 2002 (Insolvency) Order 2003, SI 2003/2096, arts 5, 6, Schedule, Pt 2, paras 61, 62, as from 15 September 2003, except in relation to any case where a petition for an administration order was presented before that date.

The words in square brackets in para (5A) were substituted by the Enterprise Act 2002 (Insolvency) Order 2004, SI 2004/2312, art 3, as from 15 October 2004.

[6.38]

7 [Limitation on disapplication of moratorium on certain legal processes under Schedule B1 to the Insolvency Act 1986 (administration) in relation to system-charges granted by a system-beneficiary]

(1) This regulation applies where an administration order is made in relation to a system-beneficiary.

[(1A) A reference in paragraph (1) to "an administration order" shall include the appointment of an administrator under paragraph 14 or 22 of Schedule B1 to the Insolvency Act 1986].

(2) [The disapplication of paragraph 43(2) of Schedule B1 to the Insolvency Act 1986 (including that provision as applied by paragraph 44 of that Schedule)] by section 175(1)(a) of the Act shall have effect, in relation to a system-charge granted by a system-beneficiary, only to the extent necessary to enable there to be realised, whether through the sale of interests of a system-beneficiary in relation to uncertificated units of a security or otherwise, the lesser of the two sums specified in paragraphs (3) and (4).

(3) The first of the two sums referred to in paragraph (2) is the net sum of—

(a) all payment obligations discharged by the settlement bank in connection with—

(i) transfers, to or by the relevant system-beneficiary by means of a relevant system made during the qualifying period, of interests of the system-beneficiary in relation to uncertificated units of a security held by a relevant nominee, where the relevant nominee has continued to hold the units;

(ii) agreements made during the qualifying period to transfer, to or from the relevant system-beneficiary by means of a relevant system, interests of the system-beneficiary in relation to uncertificated units of a security held by a relevant nominee, where the relevant nominee will continue to hold the units;

(iii) transfers, during the qualifying period and by means of a relevant system, of uncertificated units of a security, being transfers made to or by a system-member acting on behalf of the relevant system-beneficiary;

(iv) agreements made during the qualifying period to transfer uncertificated units of a security by means of a relevant system to or from a system-member acting on behalf of the relevant system-beneficiary; and

(v) issues of uncertificated units of a security made during the qualifying period and by means of a relevant system, being issues to a system-member acting on behalf of the relevant system-beneficiary; less

(b) all payment obligations discharged to the settlement bank in connection with transactions of any kind described in paragraph (3)(a)(i) to (iv).

(4) The second of the two sums referred to in paragraph (2) is the sum (if any) due to the settlement bank from the relevant system-beneficiary by reason of an obligation of the kind described in regulation 5(b)(ii).

NOTES

The regulation heading was substituted, para (1A) was inserted, and the words in square brackets in para (2) were substituted, by the Enterprise Act 2002 (Insolvency) Order 2003, SI 2003/2096, arts 5, 6, Schedule, Pt 2, paras 61, 63, as from 15 September 2003, except in relation to any case where a petition for an administration order was presented before that date.

[6.39]

8 Ability of administrator or receiver to recover assets in case of property subject to system-charge

(1) This regulation applies where an administration order is made or an administrator or an administrative receiver or a receiver is appointed, in relation to a system-member, former system-member or system-beneficiary.

[(1A) A reference in paragraph (1) to "an administration order" shall include the appointment of an administrator under paragraph 14 or 22 of Schedule B1 to the Insolvency Act 1986.]

(2) [The disapplication—

(a) by section 175(1)(b) of the Act, of paragraphs 70, 71 and 72 of Schedule B1 to the Insolvency Act 1986, and

(b) by section 175(3) of the Act, of sections 43 and 61 of the 1986 Act,

shall cease to have effect] after the end of the relevant day in respect of any property which is subject to a system-charge granted by the system-member, former system-member or system-beneficiary if on the basis of a valuation in accordance with paragraph (3), the charge is not required for the realisation of the sum specified in paragraph (4) or (5).

(3) For the purposes of paragraph (2), the value of property shall, except in a case falling within paragraph (6), be such as may be agreed between the administrator, administrative receiver or receiver on the one hand and the settlement bank on the other.

(4) Where the system-charge has been granted by a system-member or former system-member, the sum referred to in paragraph (2) is whichever is the lesser of—

(a) the sum referred to in regulation 6(3);

(b) the sum referred to in regulation 6(4) due to the settlement bank at the close of business on the relevant day.

(5) Where the system-charge has been granted by a system-beneficiary, the sum referred to in paragraph (2) is whichever is the lesser of—

(a) the sum referred to in regulation 7(3);

(b) the sum referred to in regulation 7(4) due to the settlement bank at the close of business on the relevant day.

(6) For the purposes of paragraph (2), the value of any property for which a price for the relevant day is quoted in the Daily Official List of The London Stock Exchange Limited shall—

(a) in a case in which two prices are so quoted, be an amount equal to the average of those two prices, adjusted where appropriate to take account of any accrued dividend or interest; and

(b) in a case in which one price is so quoted, be an amount equal to that price, adjusted where appropriate to take account of any accrued dividend or interest.

(7) In this regulation "the relevant day" means the second business day after the day on which the [company enters administration], or the administrative receiver or receiver is appointed.

NOTES

Para (1A): inserted by the Enterprise Act 2002 (Insolvency) Order 2003, SI 2003/2096, arts 5, 6, Schedule, Pt 2, paras 61, 64(a), as from 15 September 2003, except in relation to any case where a petition for an administration order was presented before that date.

Paras (2), (7): words in square brackets substituted by SI 2003/2096, arts 5, 6, Schedule, Pt 2, paras 61, 64(b), (c), as from 15 September 2003, except in relation to any case where a petition for an administration order was presented before that date.

9 *((Pt III) spent; amended CA 1989, s 156 (repealed).)*

UNCERTIFICATED SECURITIES REGULATIONS 2001

(SI 2001/3755)

NOTES

Made: 23 November 2001.

Authority: Companies Act 1989, s 207. Note that s 207 was repealed by the Companies Act 2006, s 1295, Sch 16, as from 6 April 2008. By virtue of s 1297 of that Act at **[1.1494]** (continuity of law) these Regulations have effect as if made under ss 784(3), 785 and 788 of the 2006 Act.

Commencement: 26 November 2001.

These Regulations are reproduced as amended by: the Enterprise Act 2002 (Consequential and Supplemental Provisions) Order 2003, SI 2003/1398; the Uncertificated Securities (Amendment) (Eligible Debt Securities) Regulations 2003, SI 2003/1633; the Enterprise Act 2002 and Media Mergers (Consequential Amendments) Order 2003, SI 2003/3180; the Government Stock (Consequential and Transitional Provision) (No 2) Order 2004, SI 2004/1662; the Local Authorities (Capital Finance) (Further Consequential and Saving Provisions) Order 2004, SI 2004/2044; the Capital Requirements Regulations 2006, SI 2006/3221; the Uncertificated Securities (Amendment) Regulations 2007, SI 2007/124; the Companies Act 2006 (Commencement No 2, Consequential Amendments, Transitional Provisions and Savings) Order 2007, SI 2007/1093; the Companies Act 2006 (Commencement No 3, Consequential Amendments, Transitional Provisions and Savings) Order 2007, SI 2007/2194; the Companies Act 2006 (Consequential Amendments) (Uncertificated Securities) Order 2009, SI 2009/1889; the Capital Requirements (Amendment) Regulations 2010, SI 2010/2628; the Capital Requirements (Amendment) Regulations 2012, SI 2012/917; the Financial Services Act 2012 (Consequential Amendments and Transitional Provisions) Order 2013, SI 2013/472; the Financial Services and Markets Act 2000 (Over the Counter Derivatives, Central Counterparties and Trade Repositories) Regulations 2013, SI 2013/504; the Uncertificated Securities (Amendment) Regulations 2013, SI 2013/632; the Alternative Investment Fund Managers Regulations 2013, SI 2013/1773; the Capital Requirements Regulations 2013, SI 2013/3115; the Financial Services and Markets Act 2000 (Markets in Financial Instruments) Regulations 2017, SI 2017/701; the Uncertificated Securities (Amendment and EU Exit) Regulations 2019, SI 2019/679.

Limited liability partnerships: this Order applies, with modifications, to limited liability partnerships; see the Limited Liability Partnerships Regulations 2001, SI 2001/1090, reg 10, Sch 6, Pt III (at **[10.116]**), and the Interpretation Act 1978, ss 17(2)(a), 23(1), (2).

ARRANGEMENT OF REGULATIONS

PART 1
CITATION, COMMENCEMENT AND INTERPRETATION

PART 1 CITATION, COMMENCEMENT, AND INTERPRETATION

[6.40]

1 Citation and commencement

These Regulations may be cited as the Uncertificated Securities Regulations 2001 and shall come into force on 26th November 2001.

[6.41]

2 Purposes and basic definition

(1) These Regulations enable title to units of a security to be evidenced otherwise than by a certificate and transferred otherwise than by a written instrument, and make provision for certain supplementary and incidental matters; and in these Regulations "relevant system" means a computer-based system, and procedures, which enable title to units of a security to be evidenced and transferred without a written instrument, and which facilitate supplementary and incidental matters.

(2) Where a title to a unit of a security is evidenced otherwise than by a certificate by virtue of these Regulations, the transfer of title to such a unit of a security shall be subject to these Regulations.

[6.42]

3 Interpretation

(1) In these Regulations—

["the 1877 Act" means the Treasury Bills Act 1877;

"the 1950 Act" means the Exchequer and Financial Provisions Act (Northern Ireland) 1950;]

. . .

"the 1986 Act" means the Financial Services Act 1986;

[. . .]

"the 2000 Act" means the Financial Services and Markets Act 2000;

["the 2006 Act" means the Companies Act 2006;];

. . .

. . .

["the 1968 Regulations" means the Treasury Bills Regulations 1968;]

"the 1974 Regulations" means the Local Authority (Stocks and Bonds) Regulations 1974; . . .

[. . .]

"the 1995 Regulations" means the Uncertificated Securities Regulations 1995;

["the 2003 Regulations" means the Uncertificated Securities (Amendment) (Eligible Debt Securities) Regulations 2003;]

["the 2004 Regulations" means the Government Stock Regulations 2004;]

"certificate" means any certificate, instrument or other document of, or evidencing, title to units of a security;

"company" means a company within the meaning of [section 1(1) of the 2006 Act];

["CSD regulation" means Regulation (EU) No 909/2014 of the European Parliament and of the Council of 23 July 2014 on improving securities settlement in the European Union and on central securities depositories;]

"dematerialised instruction" means an instruction sent or received by means of a relevant system;

[. . .]

. . .

["eligible debt security" means—

(a) a security that satisfies the following conditions—

(i) the security is constituted by an order, promise, engagement or acknowledgement to pay on demand, or at a determinable future time, a sum in money to, or to the order of, the holder of one or more units of the security; and

(ii) the current terms of issue of the security provide that its units may only be held in uncertificated form and title to them may only be transferred by means of a relevant system;

(b) an eligible Northern Ireland Treasury Bill; or

(c) an eligible Treasury bill;

"eligible Northern Ireland Treasury Bill" means a security—

(a) constituted by a Northern Ireland Treasury Bill issued in accordance with the 1950 Act as modified by Part 2 of Schedule 1 to the 2003 Regulations; and

(b) whose current terms of issue provide that its units may only be held in uncertificated form and title to them may only be transferred by means of a relevant system;

"eligible Treasury bill" means a security—

(a) constituted by a Treasury bill issued in accordance with the 1877 Act and the 1968 Regulations as modified by Part 1 of Schedule 1 to the 2003 Regulations; and

(b) whose current terms of issue provide that its units may only be held in uncertificated form and title to them may only be transferred by means of a relevant system;]

"enactment" includes an enactment comprised in any subordinate legislation within the meaning of the Interpretation Act 1978, and an enactment comprised in, or in an instrument made under, an Act of the Scottish Parliament;

["general local authority security" means a local authority security that is not an eligible debt security;

"general public sector security" means a public sector security that is not an eligible debt security;

"general UK Government security" means a UK Government security that is not an eligible debt security;]

"generate", in relation to an Operator-instruction, means to initiate the procedures by which the Operator-instruction comes to be sent;

"guidance", in relation to an Operator, means guidance issued by him which is intended to have continuing effect and is issued in writing or other legible form, which if it were a rule, would come within the definition of a rule;

"instruction" includes any instruction, election, acceptance or any other message of any kind;

"interest in a security" means any legal or equitable interest or right in relation to a security, including—

(a) an absolute or contingent right to acquire a security created, allotted or issued or to be created, allotted or issued; and

(b) the interests or rights of a person for whom a security is held on trust or by a custodian or depositary;

"issue", in relation to a new unit of a security, means to confer title to a new unit on a person;

"issuer-instruction" means a properly authenticated dematerialised instruction attributable to a participating issuer;

"issuer register of members" has the meaning given by regulation 20(1)(a);

"issuer register of securities"—

(a) in relation to shares, means an issuer register of members; and

[(b) in relation to units of securities other than—

(i) shares,

(ii) securities in respect of which regulation 22(3) applies, or

(iii) wholly dematerialised securities,

means a register of persons holding the units, maintained by or on behalf of the issuer or, in the case of general public sector securities, by or on behalf of the person specified in regulation 21(3);]

["local authority"—

(a) in relation to a security referred to in paragraph (a)(i) of the definition of "local authority security", has the same meaning as in the 1974 Regulations;

[(b) in relation to a security referred to in paragraph (b) of the definition of "local authority security", has the same meaning as in section 23 of the Local Government Act 2003 ("local authority");]]

["local authority security" means a security which is either—

(a) a security other than an eligible debt security which, when held in certificated form is—

(i) transferable in accordance with regulation 7(1) of the 1974 Regulations and title to which must be registered in accordance with regulation 5 of those Regulations; or

(ii) . . .

(b) an eligible debt security issued by a local authority;]

"officer", in relation to an Operator or a participating issuer, includes—

(a) where the Operator or the participating issuer is a company, such persons as are mentioned in [section 1173(1) of the 2006 Act];

(b) where the Operator or the participating issuer is a partnership, a partner; or in the event that no partner is situated in the United Kingdom, a person in the United Kingdom who is acting on behalf of a partner; and

(c) where the Operator or the participating issuer is neither a company nor a partnership, any member of its governing body; or in the event that no member of its governing body is situated in the United Kingdom, a person in the United Kingdom who is acting on behalf of any member of its governing body;

["Operator" means a person operating or proposing to operate a relevant system subject to these Regulations, who is—

(a) a recognised CSD within the meaning of section 285(1)(e) of the 2000 Act,

(b) . . .

(c) a third country CSD within the meaning of section 285(1)(g) of the 2000 Act;]

"Operator-instruction" means a properly authenticated dematerialised instruction attributable to an Operator;

"Operator register of corporate securities" has the meaning given by regulation 22(2)(a)(i);

["Operator register of eligible debt securities" has the meaning given by regulation 22(3A)(a);

"Operator register of general public sector securities" has the meaning given by regulation 21(1)(a);]

"Operator register of members" has the meaning given by regulation 20(1)(b);

. . .

"Operator register of securities"—

(a) in relation to shares, means an Operator register of members;

(b) in relation to units of a security other than shares, means an Operator register of corporate securities, an Operator register of [general public sector securities, an Operator register of eligible debt securities or, as the case may be, a register maintained by an Operator in accordance with regulation 22(3)(a)];

"Operator's conversion rules" means the rules made and practices instituted by the Operator in order to comply with paragraph 18 of Schedule 1;

"Operator-system" means those facilities and procedures which are part of the relevant system, which are maintained and operated by or for an Operator, by which he generates Operator-instructions and receives dematerialised instructions from system-participants and by which persons change the form in which units of a participating security are held;

"participating issuer" means (subject to paragraph (3)) a person who has issued a security which is a participating security;

"participating security" means a security title to units of which is permitted by an Operator to be transferred by means of a relevant system;

"public sector securities" means UK Government securities and local authority securities;

["record of uncertificated general public sector securities" has the meaning given by regulation 21(2)(a);]

"record of securities" means any of a record of uncertificated corporate securities, a record of uncertificated shares and a record of uncertificated [general public sector securities];

"record of uncertificated corporate securities" has the meaning given by regulation 22(2)(b)(ii);

"record of uncertificated shares" has the meaning given by regulation 20(6)(a);

"register of members" means either or both of an issuer register of members and an Operator register of members;

"register of securities" means either or both of an issuer register of securities and an Operator register of securities;

"relevant system" has the meaning given by regulation 2(1); and "relevant system" includes an Operator-system;

"rules", in relation to an Operator, means rules made or conditions imposed by him with respect to the provision of the relevant system;

"securities" means shares, stock, debentures, debenture stock, loan stock, bonds, units of a collective investment scheme within the meaning of section 235 of the 2000 Act, rights under a depositary receipt within the meaning of paragraph 4 of Schedule 2 to the Criminal Justice Act 1993, and other securities of any description, and interests in a security;

"settlement", [. . .] in relation to a transfer of uncertificated units of a security between two system-members by means of a relevant system, means the delivery of those units to the transferee and, where appropriate, the creation of any associated obligation to make payments, in accordance with the rules and practices of the Operator; and "settle" shall be construed accordingly;

"settlement bank", in relation to a relevant system, means a person who has contracted to make payments in connection with transfers of title to uncertificated units of a security by means of that system;

"share" means share (or stock) in the share capital of a company;

"system-member", in relation to a relevant system, means a person who is permitted by an Operator to transfer by means of that system title to uncertificated units of a security held by him, and shall include, where relevant, two or more persons who are jointly so permitted;

"system-member instruction" means a properly authenticated dematerialised instruction attributable to a system-member;

"system-participant", in relation to a relevant system, means a person who is permitted by an Operator to send and receive properly authenticated dematerialised instructions; and "sponsoring system-participant" means a system-participant who is permitted by an Operator to send properly authenticated dematerialised instructions attributable to another person and to receive properly authenticated dematerialised instructions on another person's behalf;

"system-user", in relation to a relevant system, means a person who as regards that system is a participating issuer, a system-member, system-participant or settlement bank;

"UK Government security" means a security issued by Her Majesty's Government in the United Kingdom or by a Northern Ireland department;

"uncertificated", in relation to a unit of a security, means (subject to Regulation 42(11)(a)) that title to the unit is recorded on the relevant Operator register of securities, and may, by virtue of these Regulations, be transferred by means of a relevant system; and "certificated", in relation to a unit of a security, means that the unit is not an uncertificated unit;

"unit", in relation to a security, means the smallest possible transferable unit of the security (for example a single share);

"wholly dematerialised security" means—

(a) a strip, in relation to any stock or bond, within the meaning of section 47(1B) of the Finance Act 1942; or

(b) a participating security whose terms of issue (or, in the case of shares, where its terms of issue or the articles of association of the company in question) provide that its units may only be held in uncertificated form and title to them may only be transferred by means of a relevant system;

and other expressions have the meanings given to them by the [Companies Acts (as defined by section 2 of the 2006 Act)].

(2) For the purposes of these Regulations—

(a) a dematerialised instruction is properly authenticated if it complies with the specifications referred to in paragraph 5(3) of Schedule 1; or if it was given, and not withdrawn, before these Regulations came into force and was properly authenticated within the meaning of regulation 3(2)(a) of the 1995 Regulations;

(b) a dematerialised instruction is attributable to a person if it is expressed to have been sent by that person, or if it is expressed to have been sent on behalf of that person, in accordance with the rules and specifications referred to in paragraph 5(4) of Schedule 1; and a dematerialised instruction may be attributable to more than one person.

(3) In respect of a participating security which is a [general] public sector security, references in these Regulations to the participating issuer shall, other than in Regulation 41, be taken to be references—

(a) in the case of a local authority security—

(i) to the relevant local authority; or

(ii) if the local authority has appointed another person to act as registrar for the purpose of the 1974 Regulations in respect of that security, to the person so appointed [. . .

(iii) . . .]; and

Part 6 Other companies SIs

(b) in the case of any other [general] public sector security, to [the Registrar of Government Stock].

[(4) In respect of a security which is an eligible debt security, references in these regulations to the issuer or the participating issuer of that security (or units of that security) shall be taken to be references to—

(a) a person ("P") who undertakes as principal to perform the payment obligation constituted by the security in accordance with its current terms of issue; and

(b) any other person who undertakes as principal to perform that obligation in accordance with those terms in the event that P fails to do so.

(5) For the purposes of paragraph (4)(b), a person who undertakes to perform an obligation under a contract of guarantee or other contract of suretyship is not to be regarded as undertaking to perform it as principal.

(6) For the purposes of paragraph (a) of the definition of "eligible debt security" in paragraph (1), a sum of money—

(a) is to be regarded as payable at a determinable future time if it is payable—

(i) at a future time fixed by or in accordance with the current terms of issue of the security; or

(ii) at the expiry of a fixed period after the occurrence of a specified event which is certain to happen, though the time of happening may be uncertain; and

(b) is not to be regarded as payable at a determinable future time if it is payable on a contingency.]

NOTES

Para (1) is amended as follows:

Definitions "the 1877 Act", "the 1950 Act", "the 1968 Regulations", "the 2003 Regulations", "eligible debt security", "eligible Northern Ireland Treasury Bill", "eligible Treasury bill", "general local authority security", "general public sector security", "general UK Government security", "local authority", "Operator register of eligible debt securities" and "Operator register of general public sector securities" inserted, words omitted from definition "the 1974 Regulations", and the definition "Operator register of public sector securities" (omitted) revoked, words in square brackets in definitions "issuer register of securities", "Operator register of securities" and "record of securities" substituted, and definition "record of uncertificated general public sector securities" substituted (for original definition "record of uncertificated public sector securities"), by the Uncertificated Securities (Amendment) (Eligible Debt Securities) Regulations 2003, SI 2003/1633, reg 3, as from 24 June 2003.

Definitions "the 1985 Act" and "the 1986 Order" (omitted) revoked, definition "the 2006 Act" inserted, and the final words in square brackets and the words in square brackets in the definitions "company" and "officer" substituted, by the Companies Act 2006 (Consequential Amendments) (Uncertificated Securities) Order 2009, SI 2009/1889, art 2(1), (2), as from 1 October 2009.

Definitions "the 1989 Act", "the 1990 Regulations" and "dematerialised loan instrument" (omitted) originally inserted by SI 2003/1633, reg 3, as from 24 June 2003; and subsequently revoked by the Local Authorities (Capital Finance) (Further Consequential and Saving Provisions) Order 2004, SI 2004/2044, art 6(1)(a), as from 1 October 2004.

Definition "the 1965 Regulations" (omitted) revoked, and definition "the 2004 Regulations" inserted, by the Government Stock (Consequential and Transitional Provision) (No 2) Order 2004, SI 2004/1662, art 2, Schedule, Pt 3, para 29(1), (2)(a), as from 1 July 2004.

Definition "The Authority" (omitted) revoked by the Financial Services Act 2012 (Consequential Amendments and Transitional Provisions) Order 2013, SI 2013/472, art 3, Sch 2, para 73(a), as from 1 April 2013.

Definition "CSD regulation" inserted by the Uncertificated Securities (Amendment and EU Exit) Regulations 2019, SI 2019/679, reg 4(1), (2)(a), as from 27 March 2019 (for transitional provisions and savings see regs 11, 12 of the 2019 Regulations at **[12.125]** et seq).

Definition "designated agency" (omitted) revoked by the Uncertificated Securities (Amendment) Regulations 2013, SI 2013/632, reg 2(1), (2), as from 1 April 2013.

In the definition "local authority", para (b) was substituted by SI 2004/2044, art 6(1)(b), as from 1 October 2004.

Definition "local authority security" substituted by SI 2003/1633, reg 3, as from 24 June 2003. Sub-para (a)(ii) revoked by SI 2004/2044, art 6(1)(c), as from 1 October 2004.

Definition "Operator" substituted by SI 2019/679, reg 4(1), (2)(b), as from 27 March 2019 (for transitional provisions and savings see regs 11, 12 of the 2019 Regulations at **[12.125]** et seq). Para (b) was revoked by SI 2019/679, reg 14, as from IP completion day (as defined in the European Union (Withdrawal Agreement) Act 2020, s 39).

Words omitted from the definition "settlement" originally inserted by the Uncertificated Securities (Amendment) Regulations 2007, SI 2007/124, reg 2, as from 1 November 2007, and revoked by SI 2019/679, reg 4(1), (2)(c), as from 27 March 2019 (for transitional provisions and savings see regs 11, 12 of the 2019 Regulations at **[12.125]** et seq).

Para (3): the word "general" in square brackets in both places it occurs was inserted by SI 2003/1633, reg 4(1)(a), as from 24 June 2003. Sub-para (a)(iii) and the word immediately preceding it originally inserted by SI 2003/1633, reg 4(1)(b), as from 24 June 2003, and revoked by SI 2004/2044, art 6(1)(d), as from 1 October 2004. Words in final pair of square brackets substituted by SI 2004/1662, art 2, Schedule, Pt 3, para 29(1), (2)(b), as from 1 July 2004.

Paras (4)–(6): added by SI 2003/1633, reg 4(2), as from 24 June 2003.

Note: in the original Queen's Printer's copy of these Regulations there were two definitions of "record of securities" in para (1) above. It is believed that the second one (ie, the one that followed the definition "register of members") should be the definition "*register* of securities". The above text has been changed accordingly, but no correction slip has been issued to confirm this.

Financial Services Act 1986: repealed by the Financial Services and Markets Act 2000 (Consequential Amendments and Repeals) Order 2001, SI 2001/3649, art 3(1)(c), as from 1 December 2001.

Uncertificated Securities Regulations 1995, SI 1995/3272: revoked by these Regulations.

PART 2 THE OPERATOR

Approval and compliance

4 (*Revoked by the Uncertificated Securities (Amendment and EU Exit) Regulations 2019, SI 2019/679, reg 4(1), (3), as from 27 March 2019 (for transitional provisions and savings see regs 11, 12 of the 2019 Regulations at* **[12.125]** *et seq.*)

[6.43]

[5 Operating conditions for relevant system

Schedule 1 contains the requirements which must be satisfied with respect to the Operator, the Operator's rules and practices and the relevant system.]

NOTES

Substituted by the Uncertificated Securities (Amendment and EU Exit) Regulations 2019, SI 2019/679, reg 4(1), (4), as from 27 March 2019 (for transitional provisions and savings see regs 11, 12 of the 2019 Regulations at **[12.125]** et seq).

[6.44]

6 Fees charged by the [Bank of England]

(1) . . .

(2) The [Bank of England] may charge an Operator a periodical fee.

(3) Any fee chargeable by the [Bank of England] under this regulation shall not exceed an amount which reasonably represents the amount of costs incurred—

(a) . . .

(b) in the case of a periodical fee, in satisfying [itself] that the Operator, his rules and practices and the relevant system continue to meet the requirements of Schedule 1 and that the Operator is complying with any obligations imposed on him by or under these Regulations.

(4) For the purposes of paragraph (3), the costs incurred by the [Bank of England] shall be determined on the basis that they include such proportion of the following matters as are properly attributable to the performance of the relevant function—

(a) expenditure on staff, equipment, premises, facilities, research and development;

(b) . . .

(c) any notional interest incurred on any capital expended on or in connection with the performance of the function . . . ; and

(d) any other matter which, in accordance with generally accepted accounting principles, may properly be taken account of in ascertaining the costs properly attributable to the performance of the function.

(5) For the purposes of paragraph (4)(c)—

(a) "notional interest" means any interest which that person might reasonably have been expected to have been liable to pay had the sums expended been borrowed at arm's length; . . .

(b) . . .

[(6) Any fee which is owed to the Bank of England under this regulation may be recovered as a debt due to the Bank of England.]

(7) . . .

NOTES

Para (1) and sub-para (3)(a) were revoked by the Uncertificated Securities (Amendment and EU Exit) Regulations 2019, SI 2019/679, reg 4(1), (5), as from 27 March 2019 (for transitional provisions and savings see regs 11, 12 of the 2019 Regulations at **[12.125]** et seq).

All other amendments to this regulation were made by the Uncertificated Securities (Amendment) Regulations 2013, SI 2013/632, reg 2(1), (5), as from 1 April 2013.

Supervision

7 *(Revoked by the Uncertificated Securities (Amendment and EU Exit) Regulations 2019, SI 2019/679, reg 4(1), (6), as from 27 March 2019 (for transitional provisions and savings see regs 11, 12 of the 2019 Regulations at* **[12.125]** *et seq.)*

[6.45]

8 Compliance orders and directions

(1) This regulation applies if it appears to the [Bank of England] that—

(a) any requirement of Schedule 1 is not satisfied, or is likely not to be satisfied, in relation to an Operator; or

(b) an Operator has failed to comply with any obligation imposed on him by or under these Regulations.

(2) The [Bank of England] may—

(a) make an application to the court; or

(b) subject to paragraph (4), direct the Operator to take specified steps for the purpose of securing—

(i) that the relevant requirement of Schedule 1 is satisfied in relation to the Operator; or

(ii) the Operator's compliance with any obligation of the kind in question.

(3) If on any application by the [Bank of England] under paragraph (2)(a) the court is satisfied that the relevant requirement of Schedule 1 is not satisfied or is likely not to be satisfied, or, as the case may be, that the Operator has failed to comply with the obligation in question, it may order the Operator to take such steps as the court directs for securing that the requirement is satisfied or that the obligation is complied with.

(4) Schedule 3 shall have effect as regards the procedure to be followed before giving a direction under paragraph (2)(b).

(5) A direction under paragraph (2)(b) is enforceable, on the application of the [Bank of England], by an injunction or, in Scotland, by an order for specific performance under section 45 of the Court of Session Act 1988.

(6) The jurisdiction conferred by paragraph (3) shall be exercisable by the High Court and the Court of Session.

(7) The fact that a rule made or condition imposed by an Operator has been altered in response to a direction given by the [Bank of England] under paragraph (2)(b) or an order of the court under paragraph (3) does not prevent it from being subsequently altered or revoked by the Operator.

NOTES

Words in square brackets substituted by the Uncertificated Securities (Amendment) Regulations 2013, SI 2013/632, reg 2(1), (7), as from 1 April 2013.

[6.46]

9 Injunctions and restitution orders

(1) If on the application of the [Bank of England] the court is satisfied—

(a) that there is a reasonable likelihood that any person will contravene a relevant rule; or

(b) that any person has contravened a relevant rule, and that there is a reasonable likelihood that the contravention will continue or be repeated,

the court may make an order restraining (or in Scotland an interdict prohibiting) the contravention.

(2) If on the application of the [Bank of England] the court is satisfied—

(a) that any person has contravened a relevant rule; and

(b) that there are steps which could be taken for remedying the contravention,

the court may make an order requiring that person and any other person who appears to the court to have been knowingly concerned in the contravention to take such steps as the court may direct to remedy it.

(3) No application shall be made by the [Bank of England] under paragraph (1) or (2) in respect of a relevant rule unless it appears to [it] that the Operator of the relevant system is unable or unwilling to take appropriate steps to restrain the contravention or to require the person concerned to take such steps as are mentioned in paragraph (2)(b).

(4) If on the application of the [Bank of England] the court is satisfied that any person may have—

(a) contravened a relevant rule; or

(b) been knowingly concerned in the contravention of a relevant rule,

the court may make an order restraining (or in Scotland an interdict prohibiting) him from disposing of, or otherwise dealing with, any assets of his which it is satisfied he is reasonably likely to dispose of or otherwise deal with.

(5) The court may, on the application of the [Bank of England], make an order under paragraph (6) if it is satisfied that a person has contravened a relevant rule, or been knowingly concerned in the contravention of such a rule, and—

(a) that profits have accrued to him as a result of the contravention; or

(b) that one or more persons have suffered loss or been otherwise adversely affected as a result of the contravention.

(6) The court may order the person concerned to pay to the [Bank of England] such sum as appears to the court to be just having regard—

(a) in a case within subparagraph (a) of paragraph (5), to the profits appearing to the court to have accrued;

(b) in a case within subparagraph (b) of that paragraph, to the extent of the loss or other adverse effect; or

(c) in a case within both of those subparagraphs, to the profits appearing to the court to have accrued and to the extent of the loss or other adverse effect.

(7) Subsections (3) to (5) and (8) of section 382 of the 2000 Act shall apply in relation to an application of the [Bank of England] under paragraph (5) as they have effect in relation to an application of [the appropriate regulator] under subsection (1) of that section; and in those subsections as they so apply—

(a) the references to subsections (1) and (2) shall be taken to be references to paragraphs (5) and (6) respectively;

(b) the references to paragraphs (a) and (b) of subsection (1) shall be taken to be references to subparagraphs (a) and (b) respectively of paragraph (5).

(8) The jurisdiction conferred by this Regulation shall be exercisable by the High Court and the Court of Session.

(9) Nothing in this regulation affects the right of any person other than the [Bank of England] to bring proceedings in respect of matters to which this regulation applies.

(10) In this regulation, "relevant rule" means any provision of the rules of an Operator to which the person in question is subject and which regulate the carrying on by that person of business of any of the following kinds—

(a) dealing in investments as principal;

(b) dealing in investments as agent;

(c) arranging deals in investments;

(d) managing investments;

(e) safeguarding and administering investments;

(f) sending dematerialised instructions;

[(fa) managing a UCITS;

(fb) acting as trustee or depositary of a UCITS;

(fc) managing an AIF;

(fd) acting as trustee or depositary of an AIF;]

(g) establishing etc a collective investment scheme;

(h) advising on investments; or

(i) agreeing to carry on any of the activities mentioned in paragraphs (a) to (h).

(11) In paragraph (2), references to remedying a contravention include references to mitigating its effect.

(12) Paragraph (10) shall be read with—

(a) section 22 of the 2000 Act;

(b) any relevant order under that section; and

(c) Schedule 2 to that Act.

[(13) In this regulation, the "appropriate regulator" means whichever of the Prudential Regulation Authority or the Financial Conduct Authority is the appropriate regulator under section 382 of the 2000 Act.]

NOTES

Words "the appropriate regulator" in square brackets in para (7) substituted, and para (13) added, by the Financial Services Act 2012 (Consequential Amendments and Transitional Provisions) Order 2013, SI 2013/472, art 3, Sch 2, para 73(b), as from 1 April 2013.

Sub-paras (10)(fa)–(fd) were inserted by the Alternative Investment Fund Managers Regulations 2013, SI 2013/1773, reg 81, Sch 2, Part 2, para 15, as from 22 July 2013.

All other words in square brackets in this regulation were substituted by the Uncertificated Securities (Amendment) Regulations 2013, SI 2013/632, reg 2(1), (8), as from 1 April 2013.

[6.47]

10 Provision of information by Operators

[(1) The Bank of England may, in writing, require an Operator to give it such information or documents as it may specify.]

[(2) The Bank of England may also, in writing, require an Operator to give it, at such times or in respect of such periods as it may specify, such information or documents relating to that Operator as it may specify.]

(3) Any information [or documents] required to be given under this regulation shall be only such as the [Bank of England] may reasonably require for the exercise of [its] functions under these Regulations.

(4) The [Bank of England] may require information to be given by a specified time, in a specified form and to be verified in a specified manner.

(5) If an Operator—

(a) alters or revokes any of his rules or guidance; or

(b) makes new rules or issues new guidance,

he shall give written notice to the [Bank of England] without delay.

NOTES

The words "or documents" in square brackets in para (3) were inserted, and all other words in square brackets in this regulation were substituted, by the Uncertificated Securities (Amendment) Regulations 2013, SI 2013/632, reg 2(1), (9), as from 1 April 2013.

[6.48]

[11A Reports by skilled persons

(1) This regulation applies where the Bank of England has required or could require an Operator to provide information or produce documents under regulation 10.

(2) The Bank of England may—

(a) by notice in writing given to the Operator, require the Operator to provide it with a report on any matter relating to such information or documents, or

(b) itself appoint a person to provide it with a report on any matter relating to such information or documents.

(3) When acting under paragraph (2)(a), the Bank of England may require the report to be in such form as may be specified in the notice.

(4) The Bank of England must give notice of an appointment under paragraph (2)(b) to the Operator.

(5) The person appointed to make a report—

(a) must be a person appearing to the Bank of England to have the skills necessary to make a report on the matter concerned, and

(b) where the appointment is to be made by the Operator, must be a person nominated or approved by the Bank of England.

(6) It is the duty of—

(a) the Operator, and

(b) any person who is providing (or who has at any time provided) services to the Operator in relation to the matter concerned,

to give the person appointed to prepare a report all such assistance as the appointed person may reasonably require.

(7) The obligation imposed by paragraph (6) is enforceable, on the application of the Bank of England, by an injunction or, in Scotland, by an order for specific performance under section 45 of the Court of Session Act 1988.

(8) The Bank of England may make rules providing for the expenses incurred by it in relation to an appointment under sub-paragraph (2)(b) to be payable as a fee by the Operator concerned.

(9) Any fee which is owed to the Bank of England under rules made pursuant to paragraph (8) may be recovered as a debt due to the Bank of England.]

NOTES

Substituted, together with reg 11B (for the original reg 11), by the Uncertificated Securities (Amendment) Regulations 2013, SI 2013/632, reg 2(1), (10), as from 1 April 2013.

[6.49]

[11B Appointment of persons to carry out general investigations etc

(1) If it appears to the Bank of England that it is desirable in the interests of the exercise of its functions under these Regulations, the Bank of England may appoint one or more competent persons ("the investigator") to conduct an investigation on its behalf into—

(a) the nature, conduct or state of the business of an Operator;

(b) a particular aspect of that business; or

(c) the ownership or control of an Operator.

(2) An investigator may require the Operator who is the subject of the investigation—

(a) to attend before the investigator at a specified time and place to answer questions; or

(b) otherwise to provide such information as the investigator may require.

(3) An investigator may also require any person to produce at a specified time and place any specified documents or documents of a specified description.

(4) A requirement under paragraph (2) or (3) may be imposed only so far as the investigator concerned reasonably considers the question, provision of information or production of the document to be relevant for the purposes of the investigation.]

NOTES

Substituted as noted to reg 11A at **[6.48]**.

12, 13 (*Revoked by the Uncertificated Securities (Amendment and EU Exit) Regulations 2019, SI 2019/679, reg 4(1), (7), (8), as from 27 March 2019 (for transitional provisions and savings see regs 11, 12 of the 2019 Regulations at* **[12.125]** *et seq.)*

PART 3 PARTICIPATING SECURITIES

Participation by issuers

[6.50]

14 Participation in respect of shares

Where—

(a) an Operator permits title to shares of a class in relation to which regulation 15 applies, or in relation to which a directors' resolution passed in accordance with regulation 16 is effective, to be transferred by means of a relevant system; and

(b) the company in question permits the holding of shares of that class in uncertificated form and the transfer of title to any such shares by means of a relevant system,

title to shares of that class which are recorded on an Operator register of members may be transferred by means of that relevant system.

[6.51]

15

This regulation applies to a class of shares if the company's articles of association are in all respects consistent with—

(a) the holding of shares of that class in uncertificated form;

(b) the transfer of title to shares of that class by means of a relevant system; and

(c) these Regulations.

[6.52]

16

(1) This regulation applies to a class of shares if a company's articles of association in any respect are inconsistent with—

(a) the holding of shares of that class in uncertificated form;

(b) the transfer of title to shares of that class by means of a relevant system; or

(c) any provision of these Regulations.

(2) A company may resolve, subject to paragraph (6)(a), by resolution of its directors (in this Part referred to as a "director's resolution") that title to shares of a class issued or to be issued by it may be transferred by means of a relevant system.

(3) Upon a directors' resolution becoming effective in accordance with its terms, and for as long as it is in force, the articles of association in relation to the class of shares which were the subject of the directors' resolution shall not apply to any uncertificated shares of that class to the extent that they are inconsistent with—

(a) the holding of shares of that class in uncertificated form;

(b) the transfer of title to shares of that class by means of a relevant system; or

(c) any provision of these Regulations.

(4) Unless a company has given notice to every member of the company in accordance with its articles of association of its intention to pass a directors' resolution before the passing of such a resolution, it shall give such notice within 60 days of the passing of the resolution.

(5) Notice given by the company before the coming into force of these Regulations of its intention to pass a directors' resolution which, if it had been given after the coming into force of these Regulations would have satisfied the requirements of paragraph (4), shall be taken to satisfy the requirements of that paragraph.

(6) In respect of a class of shares, the members of a company may by ordinary resolution—

(a) if a directors' resolution has not been passed, resolve that the directors of the company shall not pass a directors' resolution;

(b) if a directors' resolution has been passed but not yet come into effect in accordance with its terms, resolve that it shall not come into effect;

(c) if a directors' resolution has been passed and is effective in accordance with its terms but the class of shares has not yet been permitted by the Operator to be a participating security, resolve that the directors' resolution shall cease to have effect; or

(d) if a directors' resolution has been passed and is effective in accordance with its terms and the class of shares has been permitted by the Operator to be a participating security, resolve that the directors shall take the necessary steps to ensure that title to shares of the class that was the subject of the directors' resolution shall cease to be transferable by means of a relevant system and that the directors' resolution shall cease to have effect,

and the directors shall be bound by the terms of any such ordinary resolution.

[(7) In the event of default in complying with paragraph (4), an offence is committed by every officer of the issuer who is in default.

(7A) A person guilty of such an offence is liable—

(a) on conviction on indictment, to a fine;

(b) on summary conviction, to a fine not exceeding the statutory maximum.]

(8) A company shall not permit the holding of shares in such a class as is referred to in paragraph (1) in uncertificated form, or the transfer of title to shares in such a class by means of a relevant system, unless in relation to that class of shares a directors' resolution is effective.

[(8A) Chapter 3 of Part 3 of [the 2006 Act] (resolutions affecting a company's constitution) applies to—

(a) a directors' resolution passed by virtue of paragraph (2), or

(b) a resolution of a company passed by virtue of paragraph (6) preventing or reversing such a resolution.]

(9) This regulation shall not be taken to exclude the right of the members of a company to amend the articles of association of the company, in accordance with the articles, to allow the holding of any class of its shares in uncertificated form and the transfer of title to shares in such a class by means of a relevant system.

NOTES

Paras (7), (7A): substituted (for the original para (7)) by the Companies Act 2006 (Commencement No 3, Consequential Amendments, Transitional Provisions and Savings) Order 2007, SI 2007/2194, art 10(1), Sch 4, Pt 3, para 97(1), (2), as from 1 October 2007.

Para (8A): inserted by SI 2007/2194, art 10(1), Sch 4, Pt 3, para 97(1), (3), as from 1 October 2007. Words in square brackets substituted by the Companies Act 2006 (Consequential Amendments) (Uncertificated Securities) Order 2009, SI 2009/1889, art 2(1), (3), as from 1 October 2009.

[6.53]

17

(1) A class of shares in relation to which, immediately before the coming into force of these Regulations—

(a) regulation 15 of the 1995 Regulations applied; or

(b) a directors' resolution passed in accordance with regulation 16 of the 1995 Regulations was effective,

shall be taken to be a class of shares in relation to which regulation 15 of these Regulations applies or, as the case may be, a directors' resolution passed in accordance with regulation 16 is effective.

(2) On the coming into force of these Regulations a company's articles of association in relation to any such class of shares, and the terms of issue of any such class of shares, shall cease to apply to the extent that they are inconsistent with any provision of these Regulations.

[6.54]

18 Interpretation of regulations 15, 16 and 17

For the purposes of regulations 15, 16 and 17 any shares with respect to which share warrants to bearer are issued under [section 779 of the 2006 Act] shall be regarded as forming a separate class of shares.

NOTES

Words in square brackets substituted by the Companies Act 2006 (Consequential Amendments) (Uncertificated Securities) Order 2009, SI 2009/1889, art 2(1), (4), as from 1 October 2009.

[6.55]

19 Participation in respect of securities other than shares

(1) Subject to paragraph (2), where—

(a) an Operator permits title to a security other than a share to be transferred by means of a relevant system; and

(b) the issuer permits the holding of units of that security in uncertificated form and the transfer of title to units of that security by means of a relevant system,

title to units of that security which are recorded on an Operator register of securities may be transferred by means of that relevant system.

(2) In relation to any security other than a share, if the law under which it is constituted is not the law of England and Wales, Northern Ireland or Scotland, or if the current terms of its issue are in any respect inconsistent with—

(a) the holding of title to units of that security in uncertificated form;

(b) the transfer of title to units of that security by means of a relevant system; or

(c) subject to paragraph (3), these Regulations,

[an issuer of that security] shall not permit the holding of units of that security in uncertificated form, or the transfer of title to units of that security by means of a relevant system.

(3) On the coming into force of these Regulations the current terms of issue of a relevant participating security shall cease to apply to the extent that they are inconsistent with any provision of these Regulations.

(4) For the purposes of this regulation—

(a) a relevant participating security is a participating security (other than a share) the terms of issue of which, immediately before the coming into force of these Regulations, were in all respects consistent with the 1995 Regulations; and

(b) the terms of issue of a security shall be taken to include the terms prescribed by the issuer on which units of the security are held and title to them is transferred.

NOTES

Para (2): words in square brackets substituted by the Uncertificated Securities (Amendment) (Eligible Debt Securities) Regulations 2003, SI 2003/1633, regs 2, 5, as from 24 June 2004.

Keeping of registers and records

[6.56]

20 Entries on registers and records in respect of shares

(1) In respect of every company which is a participating issuer, there shall be—

(a) a register maintained by the participating issuer, and such a register is referred to in these Regulations as an "issuer register of members"; and

(b) a register maintained by the Operator, and such a register is referred to in these Regulations as an "Operator register of members".

(2) A participating issuer which is a company shall keep and enter up the issuer register of members in accordance with paragraph 2 of Schedule 4.

(3) In respect of every company which is a participating issuer, the Operator shall keep and enter up the Operator register of members in accordance with paragraph 4 of Schedule 4.

(4) References in any enactment or instrument to a company's register of members shall, unless the context otherwise requires, be construed in relation to a company which is a participating issuer as referring to the company's issuer register of members and Operator register of members.

(5) Paragraph (4) does not apply in relation to a company's issuer register of members to the extent that any of the particulars entered in that register in accordance with paragraph 2(1) of Schedule 4 are inconsistent with the company's Operator register of members.

(6) A participating issuer which is a company shall—

(a) maintain a record of the entries made in its Operator register of members; and such a record is referred to in these Regulations as a "record of uncertificated shares"; and

(b) keep and enter up that record in accordance with paragraph 5 of Schedule 4.

(7) Such sanctions as apply to a company and its officers in the event of a default in complying with [section 113 of the 2006 Act] shall apply to—

(a) a company which is a participating issuer and its officers in the event of a default in complying with paragraph (1)(a) or (6)(a), or

(b) an Operator and his officers in the event of a default in complying with paragraph (1)(b).

NOTES

Para (7): words in square brackets substituted by the Companies Act 2006 (Consequential Amendments) (Uncertificated Securities) Order 2009, SI 2009/1889, art 2(1), (5), as from 1 October 2009.

[6.57]

21 Entries on registers and records in respect of [general] public sector securities

(1) In respect of every participating security which is a [general] public sector security the Operator shall—

(a) maintain a register, and such a register is referred to in these Regulations as an "Operator register of [general] public sector securities"; and

(b) keep and enter up the Operator register of [general] public sector securities in accordance with paragraph 12 of Schedule 4.

(2) The person specified in paragraph (3) shall—

(a) maintain a record of the entries made in an Operator register of [general] public sector securities; and such a record is referred to in these Regulations as a "record of uncertificated [general] public sector securities"; and

(b) keep and enter up that record in accordance with paragraph 13 of Schedule 4.

(3) The person referred to in paragraph (2) is [the Registrar of Government Stock], except where the security to which an Operator register of [general] public sector securities relates is a [general] local authority security, in which case it is—

(a) the relevant local authority; or

(b) if the local authority has appointed another person to act as registrar for the purpose of the 1974 Regulations in respect of that security, the person so appointed [. . .

(c) . . .].

(4) Such sanctions as apply to a company and its officers in the event of a default in complying with [section 113 of the 2006 Act] shall apply to an Operator and his officers in the event of a default in complying with paragraph (1)(a).

(5) Such sanctions as apply to the registrar, within the meaning of the 1974 Regulations, in the event of a default in complying with regulation 5 of those Regulations shall apply to a participating issuer and his officers in the event of a default in complying with paragraph (2)(a) in respect of a local authority security [falling within paragraph (a)(i) of the definition of "local authority security" in regulation 3(1)].

[(6) . . .]

NOTES

Regulation heading, paras (1), (2), (5): words in square brackets inserted by the Uncertificated Securities (Amendment) (Eligible Debt Securities) Regulations 2003, SI 2003/1633, regs 6(1), (2), 8(2), as from 24 June 2003.

Para (3): words in first pair of square brackets substituted by the Government Stock (Consequential and Transitional Provision) (No 2) Order 2004, SI 2004/1662, art 2, Schedule, Pt 3, para 29(1), (3), as from 1 July 2004. The word "general" in square brackets (in both places that it occurs) was inserted by SI 2003/1633, regs 6(2), 8(1)(a), (2), as from 24 June 2003. Para (c) and the word immediately preceding it originally inserted by SI 2003/1633, art 8(1)(b), as from 24 June 2003, and subsequently revoked by the Local Authorities (Capital Finance) (Further Consequential and Saving Provisions) Order 2004, SI 2004/2044, art 6(2)(a), as from 1 October 2004.

Para (4): words in square brackets substituted by the Companies Act 2006 (Consequential Amendments) (Uncertificated Securities) Order 2009, SI 2009/1889, art 2(1), (6), as from 1 October 2009.

Para (6): added by SI 2003/1633, reg 8(3), as from 24 June 2003, and revoked by SI 2004/2044, art 6(2)(b), as from 1 October 2004.

[6.58]

22 Entries on registers and records in respect of other securities

(1) Paragraph (2) applies where a participating issuer is required by or under an enactment or instrument to maintain in the United Kingdom a register of persons holding securities (other than shares[, general public sector securities or eligible debt securities]) issued by him.

(2) Where this paragraph applies, then in so far as the register in question relates to any class of security which is a participating security—

(a) the Operator shall—

(i) maintain a register, and such a register is referred to in these Regulations as an "Operator register of corporate securities"; and
(ii) keep and enter up the Operator register of corporate securities in accordance with paragraph 14 of Schedule 4;

(b) the participating issuer—
(i) shall not maintain the register to the extent that it relates to securities held in uncertificated form;
(ii) shall maintain a record of the entries made in any Operator register of corporate securities, and such a record is referred to in these Regulations as a "record of uncertificated corporate securities"; and
(iii) shall keep and enter up that record in accordance with paragraph 15 of Schedule 4.

(3) Where a participating issuer is not required by or under an enactment or instrument to maintain in the United Kingdom in respect of a participating security [(other than an eligible debt security)] issued by him a register of persons holding units of that participating security, the Operator shall—
(a) maintain a register in respect of that participating security; and
(b) record in that register—
(i) the names and addresses of the persons holding units of that security in uncertificated form, and
(ii) how many units of that security each such person holds in that form.

[(3A) In respect of every participating security which is an eligible debt security, the Operator shall—
(a) maintain a register, and such a register is referred to in these Regulations as an "Operator register of eligible debt securities"; and
(b) record in that register—
(i) the names and addresses of the persons holding units of that security; and
(ii) how many units of that security each such person holds.]

(4) Such sanctions as apply to a company and its officers in the event of a default in complying with [section 113 of the 2006 Act] shall apply to an Operator and his officers in the event of a default in complying with paragraph [(2)(a)(i), (3) or (3A)].

(5) Such sanctions as apply in the event of a default in complying with the requirement to maintain a register imposed by the relevant enactment or instrument referred to in paragraph (1) shall apply to a participating issuer and his officers in the event of a default in complying with paragraph (2)(b)(ii).

NOTES

Para (1): words in square brackets substituted by the Uncertificated Securities (Amendment) (Eligible Debt Securities) Regulations 2003, SI 2003/1633, reg 6(3), as from 24 June 2003.

Para (3): words in square brackets inserted by SI 2003/1633, reg 9(1), as from 24 June 2003.

Para (3A): inserted by SI 2003/1633, reg 9(2), as from 24 June 2003.

Para (4): words in first pair of square brackets substituted by the Companies Act 2006 (Consequential Amendments) (Uncertificated Securities) Order 2009, SI 2009/1889, art 2(1), (6), as from 1 October 2009. Words in second pair of square brackets substituted by SI 2003/1633, reg 9(3), as from 24 June 2003.

[6.59]
23 General provisions concerning keeping registers and records

(1) The obligations of an Operator to maintain and to keep and enter up any register of securities, imposed by these Regulations—
(a) shall not give rise to any form of duty or liability on the Operator, except such as is expressly provided for in these Regulations or as arises from fraud or other wilful default, or negligence, on the part of the Operator;
(b) shall not give rise to any form of duty or liability on a participating issuer, other than where the Operator acts on the instructions of that participating issuer, in the absence of fraud or other wilful default, or negligence, on the part of that participating issuer; and
(c) shall not give rise to any form of duty or liability enforceable by civil proceedings for breach of statutory duty.

(2) Without prejudice to paragraph (1) or to any lesser period of limitation and to any rule as to the prescription of rights, liability incurred by a participating issuer or by an Operator arising—
(a) from the making or deletion of an entry in a register of securities or record of securities pursuant to these Regulations; or
(b) from a failure to make or delete any such entry,

shall not be enforceable more than [10 years] after the date on which the entry was made or deleted or, in the case of a failure, the failure first occurred.

(3) No notice of any trust, expressed, implied or constructive, shall be entered on an Operator register of securities, or a part of such a register, or be receivable by an Operator.

(4) Schedule 4 (which provides for the keeping of registers and records of participating securities, and which excludes, or applies with appropriate modifications, certain provisions of [the 2006 Act]) shall have effect.

[(5) Section 120 of the 2006 Act shall not apply with respect to a company which is a participating issuer.]

NOTES

Paras (2), (4): words in square brackets substituted by the Companies Act 2006 (Consequential Amendments) (Uncertificated Securities) Order 2009, SI 2009/1889, art 2(1), (8), as from 1 October 2009.

Para (5): added by SI 2009/1889, art 2(1), (9), as from 1 October 2009.

[6.60]
24 Effect of entries on registers

(1) Subject to regulation 29 and to paragraphs (2) and (3) below, a register of members is prima facie evidence, and in Scotland sufficient evidence unless the contrary is shown, of any matters which are by these Regulations directed or authorised to be inserted in it.

(2) Paragraph (1) does not apply to a company's issuer register of members to the extent that any of the particulars entered in that register in accordance with paragraph 2(1) of Schedule 4 are inconsistent with the company's Operator register of members.

(3) The entry of a person's name and address in a company's issuer register of members shall not be treated as showing that person to be a member of the company unless—

(a) the issuer register of members also shows him as holding shares in the company in certificated form;
(b) the Operator register of members shows him as holding shares in the company in uncertificated form; or
(c) he is deemed to be a member of the company by regulation 32(6)(b).

(4) [Section 127 of the 2006 Act] shall not apply with respect to a company which is a participating issuer.

(5) Subject to regulation 29, an Operator register of [general] public sector securities is prima facie evidence, and in Scotland sufficient evidence unless the contrary is shown, of any matters which are by these Regulations directed or authorised to be inserted in it.

(6) Subject to regulation 29, an entry on an Operator register of corporate securities which records a person as holding units of a security in uncertificated form shall be evidence of such title to the units as would be evidenced if the entry on that register—

(a) were an entry on the part maintained by the participating issuer of such register as is mentioned in regulation 22(1); and
(b) where appropriate, related to units of that security held in certificated form.

(7) Subject to regulation 29, an entry on a register maintained by virtue of regulation 22(3)(a) shall (where the units are capable of being held in certificated form) be prima facie evidence, and in Scotland sufficient evidence unless the contrary is shown, that the person to whom the entry relates has such title to the units of the security which he is recorded as holding in uncertificated form as he would have if he held the units in certificated form.

[(8) Subject to regulation 29, an entry on an Operator register of eligible debt securities shall be prima facie evidence, and in Scotland sufficient evidence unless the contrary is shown, of any matters which are by these Regulations directed or authorised to be inserted in it.]

NOTES

Para (4): words in square brackets substituted by the Companies Act 2006 (Consequential Amendments) (Uncertificated Securities) Order 2009, SI 2009/1889, art 2(1), (10), as from 1 October 2009.

Para (5): word in square brackets inserted by the Uncertificated Securities (Amendment) (Eligible Debt Securities) Regulations 2003, SI 2003/1633, reg 6(4), as from 24 June 2003.

Para (8): added by SI 2003/1633, reg 10, as from 24 June 2003.

[6.61]
25 Rectification of registers of securities

(1) Unless the circumstances described in paragraph (2) apply, a participating issuer shall not rectify an issuer register of securities if such rectification would also require the rectification of an Operator register of securities.

(2) The circumstances referred to in paragraph (1) are that the rectification of an issuer register of securities is effected—

(a) with the consent of the Operator; or
(b) by order of a court in the United Kingdom.

(3) A participating issuer who rectifies an issuer register of securities in order to give effect to an order of a court in the United Kingdom shall immediately give the Operator written notification of the change to the entry, if any rectification of the Operator register of securities may also be required (unless the change to the issuer register is made in response to an Operator-instruction).

(4) An Operator who rectifies an Operator register of securities shall immediately—

(a) generate an Operator-instruction to inform the relevant participating issuer of the change to the entry (unless the change is made in response to an issuer-instruction); and
(b) generate an Operator-instruction to inform the system-members concerned of the change to the entry.

[6.62]
26 Closing registers

Notwithstanding . . . any other enactment, a participating issuer shall not close a register of securities relating to a participating security without the consent of the Operator.

NOTES

Words omitted revoked by the Companies Act 2006 (Consequential Amendments) (Uncertificated Securities) Order 2009, SI 2009/1889, art 2(1), (11), as from 1 October 2009.

[6.63]
27 Registration by an Operator of transfers of securities

(1) Except where relevant units of a security are transferred by means of a relevant system to a person who is to hold them thereafter in certificated form (and subject to paragraphs (2) and (4))—

(a) upon settlement of a transfer of uncertificated units of a security in accordance with his rules;
(b) following receipt of an issuer-instruction notifying him that the circumstances specified in regulation 33(2)(b) have arisen in respect of a transfer of units of a participating security; or
(c) following receipt of an issuer-instruction given under Regulation 42(8)(b),

an Operator shall register on the relevant Operator register of securities the transfer of title to those units of that security.

(2) An Operator shall refuse to register a transfer of title to units of a participating security in accordance with a system-member instruction or an issuer-instruction (as the case may be) if he has actual notice that the transfer is—

(a) prohibited by order of a court in the United Kingdom;

(b) prohibited or avoided by or under an enactment;
(c) a transfer to a deceased person; or
(d) where the participating issuer is constituted under the law of Scotland, prohibited by or under an arrestment.

(3) Notwithstanding that an Operator has received, in respect of a transfer of title to units of a participating security, actual notice of the kind referred to in paragraph (2), the Operator may register that transfer of title on the relevant Operator register of securities if at the time that he received the actual notice it was not practicable for him to halt the process of registration.

(4) Without prejudice to his rules, an Operator may refuse to register a transfer of title to units of a participating security in accordance with a system-member instruction or an issuer-instruction (as the case may be) if the instruction requires a transfer of units—
(a) to an entity which is not a natural or legal person;
(b) to a minor (which, in relation to a participating issuer constituted under the law of Scotland, shall mean a person under 16 years of age);
(c) to be held jointly in the names of more persons than is permitted under the terms of the issue of the security; or
(d) where, in relation to the system-member instruction or the issuer-instruction (as the case may be), the Operator has actual notice of any of the matters specified in regulation 35(5)(a)(i) to (iii).

(5) An Operator shall not register a transfer of title to uncertificated units of a security on an Operator register of securities otherwise than in accordance with paragraph (1) unless he is required to do so by order of a court in the United Kingdom or by or under an enactment.

(6) Paragraph (5) shall not be taken to prevent an Operator from entering on an Operator register of securities a person who is a system-member to whom title to uncertificated units of a security has been transmitted by operation of law.

(7) [Subject to paragraph (7A), immediately upon]—
(a) the registration by an Operator of the transfer of title to units of a participating security in accordance with—
(i) paragraph (1);
(ii) an order of a court in the United Kingdom; or
(iii) a requirement arising by or under an enactment; or
(b) the making or deletion by an Operator of an entry on an Operator register of securities—
(i) following the transmission of title to uncertificated units of a security by operation of law; or
(ii) upon the transfer of uncertificated units of a security to a person who is to hold them thereafter in certificated form,

the Operator shall generate an Operator-instruction to inform the relevant participating issuer of the registration, or of the making or deletion of the entry (as the case may be); and where appropriate the participating issuer shall register the transfer or transmission of title to those units on an issuer register of securities in accordance with regulation 28.

[(7A) Paragraph (7) does not apply in relation to units of an eligible debt security.]

[(8) If an Operator refuses to register a transfer of securities in any of the circumstances specified in paragraphs (2) and (4), the Operator shall, within 2 months of the date on which the relevant system-member instruction or issuer-instruction (as the case may be) was received by the Operator, send an Operator-instruction, or written notification, informing the relevant system-member or participating issuer (as the case may be) of the refusal.]

(9) Such sanctions as apply to a company and its officers in the event of a default in complying with [subsections (1) and (2) of section 771 of the 2006 Act] shall apply to an Operator and his officers in the event of a default in complying with that subsection as applied by paragraph (8).

NOTES

Para (7): words in square brackets substituted by the Uncertificated Securities (Amendment) (Eligible Debt Securities) Regulations 2003, SI 2003/1633, reg 11(a), as from 24 June 2003.

Para (7A): added by SI 2003/1633, reg 11(b), as from 24 June 2003.

Para (8): substituted by the Companies Act 2006 (Consequential Amendments) (Uncertificated Securities) Order 2009, SI 2009/1889, art 2(1), (12)(a), as from 1 October 2009.

Para (9): words in square brackets substituted by SI 2009/1889, art 2(1), (12)(b), as from 1 October 2009.

[6.64]

28 Registration by a participating issuer of transfers of securities upon conversion into certificated form

(1) Paragraphs (2) to (5) apply where relevant units of a security are transferred by means of a relevant system to a person who is to hold them thereafter in certificated form.

(2) Subject to paragraphs (3) and (4), a participating issuer shall (where appropriate) register a transfer of title to relevant units of a security on an issuer register of securities in accordance with an Operator-instruction.

(3) A participating issuer shall refuse to register a transfer of title to relevant units of a security in accordance with an Operator-instruction if he has actual notice that the transfer is—
(a) prohibited by order of a court in the United Kingdom;
(b) prohibited or avoided by or under an enactment;
(c) a transfer to a deceased person; or
(d) where the participating issuer is constituted under the law of Scotland, prohibited by or under an arrestment.

(4) A participating issuer may refuse to register a transfer of title to relevant units of a security in accordance with an Operator-instruction if the instruction requires a transfer of units—
(a) to an entity which is not a natural or legal person;
(b) to a minor (which, in relation to a participating issuer constituted under the law of Scotland, shall mean a person under 16 years of age);
(c) to be held jointly in the names of more persons than is permitted under the terms of the issue of the security; or

(d) where, in relation to the Operator-instruction, the participating issuer has actual notice from the Operator of any of the matters specified in regulation 35(5)(a)(i) to (iii).

(5) A participating issuer shall notify the Operator by issuer-instruction whether he has registered a transfer in response to an Operator-instruction to do so.

(6) A participating issuer shall not register a transfer of title to relevant units of a security on an issuer register of securities unless he is required to do so—

(a) by an Operator-instruction;
(b) by an order of a court in the United Kingdom; or
(c) by or under an enactment.

(7) A unit of a security is a relevant unit for the purposes of this regulation if, immediately before the transfer in question, it was held by the transferor in uncertificated form.

[(8) If a participating issuer refuses to register under paragraph (2) a transfer of securities in any of the circumstances specified in paragraphs (3) and (4), the participating issuer shall, within 2 months of the date on which the Operator-instruction was received by the participating issuer, send to the transferee notice of the refusal.]

(9) Such sanctions as apply to a company and its officers in the event of a default in complying with [subsections (1) and (2) of section 771 of the 2006 Act] shall apply to a participating issuer and his officers in the event of a default in complying with that subsection as applied by paragraph (8).

NOTES

Para (8), and the words in square brackets in para (9), were substituted by the Companies Act 2006 (Consequential Amendments) (Uncertificated Securities) Order 2009, SI 2009/1889, art 2(1), (13), as from 1 October 2009.

[6.65]

29 Registration to be in accordance with regulations 27 and 28

Any purported registration of a transfer of title to an uncertificated unit of a security other than in accordance with regulation 27 or 28 shall be of no effect.

[6.66]

30 Registration of linked transfers

(1) Paragraph (2) applies where an Operator receives two or more system-member instructions requesting him to register two or more transfers of title to uncertificated units of a security, and it appears to the Operator—

(a) either—
 (i) that there are fewer units of the security registered on an Operator register of securities in the name of a person identified in any of the system-member instructions as a transferor than the number of units to be transferred from him under those system-member instructions; or
 (ii) that it has not been established in accordance with paragraph 21(1)(c) of Schedule 1, in relation to any of the transfers taken without regard to the other transfers, that a settlement bank has agreed to make a payment; and
(b) that registration of all of the transfers would result in each of the persons identified in the system-member instructions as a transferor having title to a number of uncertificated units of a security equal to or greater than nil; and
(c) that the combined effect of all the transfers taken together would result in paragraph 21(1)(c) of Schedule 1 being satisfied.

(2) Where this paragraph applies, the Operator may either—

(a) register the combined effect of all the transfers taken together; or
(b) register all the transfers simultaneously,

unless one or more of those transfers may not be registered by virtue of the fact that the Operator has actual notice of any of the circumstances specified in regulation 27(2), or is to be refused registration by virtue of regulation 27(4).

(3) Notwithstanding that an Operator has received, in respect of two or more such system-member instructions as are referred to in paragraph (1), actual notice of the kind referred to in paragraph (2), the Operator may register all the transfers in question or their combined effect if at the time that he received the actual notice it was not practicable for him to halt the process of registration.

[6.67]

31 Position of a transferee prior to entry on an issuer register of securities

(1) Paragraph (2) applies when an Operator deletes an entry on an Operator register of securities in consequence of which—

(a) the Operator must generate an Operator-instruction in accordance with regulation 27(7); and
(b) by virtue of that instruction a participating issuer must register, on an issuer register of securities, a transfer of title to units of a participating security constituted under the law of England and Wales or Northern Ireland.

(2) Where this paragraph applies—

(a) subject to—
 (i) subparagraph (b); and
 (ii) any enactment or rule of law,

 the transferor shall, notwithstanding the deletion of the entry in the Operator register of securities, retain title to the requisite number of units of the relevant participating security until the transferee is entered on the relevant issuer register of securities as the holder thereof; and
(b) the transferee shall acquire an equitable interest in the requisite number of units of that security.

(3) Paragraph (4) applies when an Operator deletes an entry on an Operator register of securities in consequence of which—

(a) the Operator must generate an Operator-instruction in accordance with regulation 27(7); and

(b) by virtue of that instruction a participating issuer must register, on an issuer register of securities, a transfer of title to units of a participating security constituted under the law of Scotland.

(4) Where this paragraph applies—

(a) subject to—

(i) subparagraph (b); and

(ii) any enactment or rule of law,

the transferor shall, notwithstanding the deletion of the entry in the Operator register of securities, retain title to the requisite number of units of the relevant participating security until the transferee is entered on the relevant issuer register of securities as the holder thereof; and

(b) the transferor shall hold the requisite number of units of that security on trust for the benefit of the transferee.

(5) The requisite number for the purposes of this regulation is the number of units which are to be specified in the Operator-instruction which the Operator must generate in accordance with regulation 27(7).

(6) This regulation has effect notwithstanding that the units to which the deletion of the entry in the Operator register of securities relates, or in which an interest arises by virtue of paragraph (2)(b) or (4)(b), or any of them, may be unascertained.

(7) In Scotland—

(a) this regulation has effect notwithstanding that the requirements relating to the creation of a trust under any enactment or rule of law have not been complied with; and

(b) as from the time the trust referred to in paragraph (4)(b) arises, any holder, or any holder thereafter, of a floating charge over any part of the property of the transferor shall be deemed to have received notice of the trust's existence and of the property to which it relates.

(8) Subject to paragraphs (6) and (7), this regulation shall not be construed as conferring a proprietary interest (whether of the kind referred to in paragraph (2)(b) or (4)(b), or of any other kind) in units of a security if the conferring of such an interest at the time specified in these Regulations would otherwise be void by or under any enactment or rule of law.

(9) In this regulation—

(a) "the transferee" means the person to be identified in the Operator-instruction as the transferee; and

(b) "the transferor" means the person to be identified in the Operator-instruction as the transferor.

Conversions and New Issues

[6.68]

32 Conversion of securities into certificated form

(1) Except as provided in regulation 42, a unit of a participating security shall not be converted from uncertificated form into certificated form unless an Operator generates an Operator-instruction to notify the relevant participating issuer that a conversion event has occurred; and in this regulation such an Operator-instruction is referred to as a "rematerialisation notice".

(2) A conversion event occurs—

(a) where such a conversion is permitted by the Operator's conversion rules; or

(b) following receipt by an Operator of a system-member instruction requiring the conversion into certificated form of uncertificated units of a participating security registered in the name of the system-member; or

(c) following receipt by an Operator of written notification from a participating issuer which is a company requiring the conversion into certificated form of uncertificated units of a participating security, issued by that participating issuer and registered in the name of a system-member, and which contains a statement that the conversion is required to enable the participating issuer to deal with the units in question in accordance with provisions in that participating issuer's memorandum or articles or in the terms of issue of the units in question.

(3) An Operator—

(a) may generate a rematerialisation notice following a conversion event occurring in the circumstances specified in paragraph (2)(a);

(b) shall generate a rematerialisation notice following a conversion event occurring in the circumstances specified in paragraph (2)(b) unless the participation in the relevant system, by the system-member in whose name the uncertificated units in question are registered, has been suspended pursuant to the Operator's rules; and

(c) shall generate a rematerialisation notice following a conversion event occurring in the circumstances specified in paragraph (2)(c).

(4) On the generation of a rematerialisation notice, the Operator shall delete any entry in an Operator register of securities which shows the relevant system-member as the holder of the unit or units specified in the rematerialisation notice.

(5) On receipt of a rematerialisation notice, the participating issuer to whom the rematerialisation notice is addressed shall, where relevant, enter the name of the system-member on an issuer register of securities as the holder of the unit or units specified in the rematerialisation notice.

(6) During any period between the deletion of any entry in an Operator register of securities required to be made by paragraph (4) and the making of the entry in an issuer register of securities required to be made by paragraph (5)—

(a) the relevant system-member shall retain title to the units of the security specified in the rematerialisation notice notwithstanding the deletion of any entry in the Operator register of securities; and

(b) where those units are shares, the relevant system-member shall be deemed to continue to be a member of the company.

(7) Following—

(a) the making of an entry in an issuer register of securities in accordance with paragraph (5); or

(b) registration of a transfer of title to units of a security in accordance with regulation 28, the relevant participating issuer shall, where the terms of issue of the security in question provide for a certificate to be issued, issue a certificate in respect of the units of the security to the relevant person.

(8) [Subsection (1) of section 776 of the 2006 Act] shall apply in relation to the issue of a certificate by a participating issuer pursuant to paragraph (7) as it applies in relation to the completion and having ready for delivery by a company of share certificates, debentures or certificates of debenture stock; and in that subsection as it so applies the reference to the date on which a transfer is lodged with the company shall be a reference to the date on which the participating issuer receives the relevant rematerialisation notice in accordance with this regulation, or the relevant Operator-instruction in accordance with regulation 27(7).

(9) Such sanctions as apply to a company and its officers in the event of a default in complying with [subsections (1) and (2) of section 771 of the 2006 Act] shall apply—

- (a) to an Operator and his officers in the event of a default in complying with paragraph (4); and
- (b) to a participating issuer and his officers in the event of a default in complying with paragraph (5).

(10) Such sanctions as apply to a company and its officers in the event of a default in complying with [subsection (1) of section 776 of the 2006 Act] shall apply to a participating issuer and his officers in the event of a default in complying with paragraph (7) in accordance with the requirements laid down in paragraph (8).

NOTES

Paras (8)–(10): words in square brackets substituted by the Companies Act 2006 (Consequential Amendments) (Uncertificated Securities) Order 2009, SI 2009/1889, art 2(1), (14), as from 1 October 2009.

[6.69]

33 Conversion of securities into uncertificated form

(1) A unit of a participating security shall not be converted from certificated form into uncertificated form unless the participating issuer notifies the Operator by means of an issuer-instruction that any of the circumstances specified in paragraph (2) have arisen; and in this regulation such an issuer-instruction is referred to as a "dematerialisation notice".

(2) The circumstances referred to in paragraph (1) are—

- (a) where the unit of the participating security is held by a system-member, that the participating issuer has received—
  - (i) a request in writing from the system-member in the form required by the Operator's conversion rules that the unit be converted from certificated form to uncertificated form; and
  - (ii) subject to paragraph (4), the certificate relating to that unit; or
- (b) where the unit of the participating security is to be registered on an Operator register of securities in the name of a system-member following a transfer of the unit to him, that the participating issuer—
  - (i) subject to paragraph (3), has received (by means of the Operator-system unless the Operator's conversion rules permit otherwise) a proper instrument of transfer in favour of the system-member relating to the unit to be transferred;
  - (ii) subject to paragraph (4), has received (by means of the Operator-system unless the Operator's conversion rules permit otherwise) the certificate relating to that unit; and
  - (iii) may accept by virtue of the Operator's conversion rules that the system-member to whom the unit is to be transferred wishes to hold it in uncertificated form.

(3) The requirement in paragraph (2)(b)(i) that the participating issuer shall have received an instrument of transfer relating to the unit of the participating security shall not apply in a case where for a transfer of a unit of that security no instrument of transfer is required.

(4) The requirements in paragraphs (2)(a)(ii) and (2)(b)(ii) that the participating issuer shall have received a certificate relating to the unit of the participating security shall not apply in a case where the system-member or transferor (as the case may be) does not have a certificate in respect of the unit to be converted into uncertificated form because no certificate has yet been issued to him or is due to be issued to him in accordance with the terms of issue of the relevant participating security.

(5) Subject to paragraphs (3) and (4), a participating issuer shall not give a dematerialisation notice except in the circumstances specified in paragraph (2).

(6) Upon giving a dematerialisation notice, a participating issuer shall delete any entry in any issuer register of securities which evidences title to the unit or units of the participating security in question.

(7) Following receipt of a dematerialisation notice, an Operator shall enter the name of the relevant system-member on an Operator register of securities as the holder of the relevant unit or units of the participating security in question, provided that this obligation shall be subject to regulation 27 if the notice was given in the circumstances specified in paragraph (2)(b).

(8) When a dematerialisation notice is given, the relevant system-member, or the transferor of the unit or units of the security in question, as the case may be, shall (without prejudice to any equitable interest which the transferee may have acquired in the unit or units in question)—

- (a) retain title to the units of the security specified in the dematerialisation notice notwithstanding the deletion of any entry in any issuer register of securities required to be made by paragraph (6); and
- (b) where those units are shares, be deemed to continue to be a member of the company.

(9) Where a dematerialisation notice is given in the circumstances specified in paragraph (2)(b), such title shall be retained, and (where appropriate) such membership shall be deemed to continue, until the time at which the Operator enters the name of the relevant system-member on an Operator register of securities in accordance with paragraph (7).

(10) Within 2 months of receiving a dematerialisation notice, an Operator shall generate an Operator-instruction informing the participating issuer whether an entry has been made in an Operator register of securities in response to the dematerialisation notice.

(11) Such sanctions as apply to a company and its officers in the event of a default in complying with [subsections (1) and (2) of section 771 of the 2006 Act] shall apply—

(a) to a participating issuer and his officers in the event of a default in complying with paragraph (6); and
(b) to an Operator and his officers in the event of a default in complying with paragraph (7) or (10).

NOTES

Para (11): words in square brackets substituted by the Companies Act 2006 (Consequential Amendments) (Uncertificated Securities) Order 2009, SI 2009/1889, art 2(1), (15), as from 1 October 2009.

[6.70]

34 New issues in uncertificated form

(1) For the purposes of an issue of units of a participating security, a participating issuer may require the Operator to enter the name of a person in an Operator register of securities as the holder of new units of that security in uncertificated form if, and only if, that person is a system-member; and provided that compliance with any such requirement shall be subject to the rules of the Operator.

(2) For the purposes of calculating the number of new units to which a system-member is entitled a participating issuer may treat a system-member's holdings of certificated and uncertificated units of a security as if they were separate holdings.

(3) A requirement made by a participating issuer under paragraph (1) may be made by means of an issuer-instruction and shall specify the names of the persons to be entered in the Operator register of securities as the holders of new uncertificated units of the security, and the number of such units to be issued to each of those persons.

(4) An Operator who receives a requirement made by a participating issuer under paragraph (1) shall notify the participating issuer, by Operator-instruction or in writing, if he has not entered the name of any one or more of the persons in question in the Operator register of securities as the holder of new units of the security.

PART 4 DEMATERIALISED INSTRUCTIONS ETC

[6.71]

35 Properly authenticated dematerialised instructions, etc

(1) This regulation has effect for the purpose of determining the rights and obligations of persons to whom properly authenticated dematerialised instructions are attributable and of persons to whom properly authenticated dematerialised instructions are addressed, when such instructions relate to an uncertificated unit of a security, or relate to a right, benefit or privilege attaching to or arising from such a unit, or relate to the details of a holder of such a unit.

(2) Where a properly authenticated dematerialised instruction is expressed to have been sent on behalf of a person by a sponsoring system-participant or the Operator—

(a) the person on whose behalf the instruction is expressed to have been sent shall not be able to deny to the addressee—
 (i) that the properly authenticated dematerialised instruction was sent with his authority; or
 (ii) that the information contained in the properly authenticated dematerialised instruction is correct; and
(b) the sponsoring system-participant or the Operator (as the case may be) shall not be able to deny to the addressee—
 (i) that he has authority to send the properly authenticated dematerialised instruction; or
 (ii) that he has sent the properly authenticated dematerialised instruction.

(3) Where a properly authenticated dematerialised instruction is expressed to have been sent by a person, and the properly authenticated dematerialised instruction is not expressed to have been sent on behalf of another person, the person shall not be able to deny to the addressee—

(a) that the information contained in the properly authenticated dematerialised instruction is correct; or
(b) that he has sent the properly authenticated dematerialised instruction.

(4) An addressee who receives (whether directly, or by means of the facilities of a sponsoring system-participant acting on his behalf) a properly authenticated dematerialised instruction may, subject to paragraph (5), accept that at the time at which the properly authenticated dematerialised instruction was sent or at any time thereafter—

(a) the information contained in the instruction was correct;
(b) the system-participant or the Operator (as the case may be) identified in the instruction as having sent the instruction sent the instruction; and
(c) the instruction, where relevant, was sent with the authority of the person on whose behalf it is expressed to have been sent.

(5) Subject to paragraph (6), an addressee may not accept any of the matters specified in paragraph (4) if at the time he received the properly authenticated dematerialised instruction or at any time thereafter—

(a) he was a person other than a participating issuer or a sponsoring system-participant receiving properly authenticated dematerialised instructions on behalf of a participating issuer, and he had actual notice—
 (i) that any information contained in it was incorrect;
 (ii) that the system-participant or the Operator (as the case may be) expressed to have sent the instruction did not send the instruction; or
 (iii) where relevant, that the person on whose behalf it was expressed to have been sent had not given to the Operator or the sponsoring system-participant (as the case may be), identified in the properly authenticated dematerialised instruction as having sent it, his authority to send the properly authenticated dematerialised instruction on his behalf; or
(b) he was a participating issuer, or a sponsoring system-participant receiving properly authenticated dematerialised instructions on behalf of a participating issuer, and—
 (i) he had actual notice from the Operator of any of the matters specified in subparagraph (a)(i) to (iii); or
 (ii) if the instruction was an Operator-instruction requiring the registration of a transfer of title, he had actual notice of any of the circumstances specified in regulation 28(3); or
(c) he was an Operator and the instruction related to a transfer of units of a security which was in excess of any limit imposed by virtue of paragraph 15 of Schedule 1; or

(d) he was an Operator and he had actual notice of any of the circumstances specified in regulation 27(2) in a case where the instruction was—
   (i) a system-member instruction requesting him to settle a transfer in accordance with his rules; or
   (ii) an issuer-instruction given in the circumstances specified in regulation 33(2)(b) requesting him to register a transfer of title.

(6) Notwithstanding that an addressee has received, in respect of a properly authenticated dematerialised instruction, actual notice of the kind referred to in paragraph (5), the addressee may accept the matters specified in paragraph (4) if at the time that he received the actual notice it was not practicable for him to halt the processing of the instruction.

(7) Subject to paragraph (8), this regulation has effect without prejudice to the liability of any person for causing or permitting a dematerialised instruction—
(a) to be sent without authority; or
(b) to contain information which is incorrect; or
(c) to be expressed to have been sent by a person who did not send it.

(8) Subject to paragraph (9), a person who is permitted by this regulation to accept any matter shall not be liable in damages or otherwise to any person by reason of his having relied on the matter that he was permitted to accept.

(9) The provisions of paragraph (8) do not affect—
(a) any liability of the Operator to pay compensation under regulation 36; or
(b) any liability of a participating issuer under regulation 46 arising by reason of a default in complying with, or contravention of, regulation 28(6).

(10) For the purposes of this regulation—
(a) a properly authenticated dematerialised instruction is expressed to have been sent by a person or on behalf of a person if it is attributable to that person; and
(b) an addressee is the person to whom a properly authenticated dematerialised instruction indicates it is addressed in accordance with the rules and specifications referred to in paragraph 5(5) of Schedule 1.

(11) Nothing in this regulation shall be taken, in respect of any authority, to modify or derogate from the protections to a donee or third person given by or under any enactment or to prohibit a donee or third person so protected from accepting any of the matters specified in paragraph (4).

(12) Paragraphs (2) to (4), (5)(a), (6) to (9) and (11) of this regulation shall apply in relation to a written notification given under regulation 25(3) or 32(2)(c) as if—
(a) each reference to a properly authenticated dematerialised instruction were to such a notification which has been authenticated by the Operator in accordance with rules made and practices instituted by the Operator in order to comply with paragraph 25(g) of Schedule 1;
(b) each reference to information contained in the properly authenticated dematerialised instruction being correct (or incorrect) included, in the case of written notification given under subparagraph (c) of regulation 32(2), a reference to any statement of the sort referred to in that subparagraph being true (or untrue, as the case may be);
(c) each reference to an addressee were a reference to the Operator; and
(d) the reference in paragraph (6) to the processing of the instruction were to acting on the written notification.

[6.72]

36 Liability for forged dematerialised instructions, induced amendments to Operator registers of securities, and induced Operator-instructions

(1) For the purpose of this regulation—
(a) a dematerialised instruction is a forged dematerialised instruction if—
   (i) it was not sent from the computers of a system-participant or the computers comprising an Operator-system; or
   (ii) it was not sent from the computers of the system-participant or the computers comprising an Operator-system (as the case may be) from which it is expressed to have been sent;
(b) an act is a causative act if, not being a dematerialised instruction and not being an act which causes a dematerialised instruction to be sent from the computer of a system-participant, it unlawfully causes the Operator—
   (i) to make, delete or amend an entry on an Operator register of securities; or
   (ii) to send an Operator-instruction to a participating issuer;
(c) an entry on, deletion from, or amendment to an Operator register of securities is an induced amendment if it is an entry on, deletion from, or amendment to an Operator register of securities which results from a causative act or a forged dematerialised instruction; and
(d) an Operator-instruction is an induced Operator-instruction if it is an Operator-instruction to a participating issuer which results from a causative act or a forged dematerialised instruction.

(2) If, as a result of a forged dematerialised instruction (not being one which results in an induced amendment to an Operator register of securities or an induced Operator-instruction), an induced amendment to an Operator register of securities, or an induced Operator-instruction, any one or more of the following events occurs—
(a) the name of any person remains on, is entered on, or is removed or omitted from, a register of securities;
(b) the number of units of a security in relation to which the name of any person is entered on a register of securities is increased, reduced, or remains unaltered;
(c) the description of any units of a security in relation to which the name of any person is entered on a register of securities is changed or remains unaltered,

and that person suffers loss as a result, he may apply to the court for an order that the Operator compensate him for his loss.

(3) It is immaterial for the purposes of subparagraphs (a) to (c) of paragraph (2) whether the event is permanent or temporary.

(4) The court shall not make an order under paragraph (2)—

(a) if the Operator identifies a person as being responsible (whether alone or with others) for the forged dematerialised instruction (not being one which results in an induced amendment to an Operator register of securities or an induced Operator-instruction) or the causative act or forged dematerialised instruction resulting in the induced amendment to the Operator register of securities or the induced Operator-instruction (as the case may be) notwithstanding that it is impossible (for whatever reason) for the applicant to obtain satisfactory compensation from that person; or

(b) if the Operator shows that a participating issuer would be liable under regulation 46 to compensate the applicant for the loss in respect of which the application is made, by reason of the participating issuer's default in complying with, or contravention of, regulation 28(6).

(5) Subject to paragraphs (6) and (7), the court may award to an applicant compensation for—

(a) each forged dematerialised instruction (not being one which results in an induced amendment to an Operator register of securities or an induced Operator-instruction);

(b) each induced amendment to an Operator register of securities; and

(c) each induced Operator-instruction,

resulting in an event mentioned in subparagraph (a), (b) or (c) of paragraph (2).

(6) The court shall not under paragraph (5) award to an applicant—

(a) more than £50,000 for each such forged dematerialised instruction, induced amendment to an Operator register of securities, or induced Operator-instruction;

(b) compensation for both an induced amendment to an Operator register of securities and an induced Operator-instruction if that induced amendment and that induced Operator-instruction resulted from the same causative act or the same forged dematerialised instruction.

(7) In respect of liability arising under this regulation the court shall—

(a) in awarding compensation only order the Operator to pay such amount of compensation as it appears to it to be just and equitable in all the circumstances having regard to the loss sustained by the applicant as a result of the forged dematerialised instruction, induced amendment to the Operator register of securities, or induced Operator-instruction;

(b) in ascertaining the loss, apply the same rules concerning the duty of a person to mitigate his loss as apply to damages recoverable under the common law of England and Wales, Northern Ireland, or Scotland, (as the case may be); and

(c) where it finds that the loss was to any extent caused or contributed to by any act or omission of the applicant, reduce the amount of the award by such proportion as it thinks just and equitable having regard to that finding.

(8) An application to the court for an order under paragraph (2) shall not prejudice any right of the Operator to recover from a third party any sum that he may be ordered to pay.

(9) An event mentioned in subparagraph (a), (b) or (c) of paragraph (2) shall not give rise to any liability on the Operator other than such as is expressly provided for in this regulation, except such as may arise from fraud or other wilful default, or negligence, on the part of the Operator.

(10) Subject to paragraph (9), this regulation does not affect—

(a) any right which any person may have other than under this regulation (not being a right against the Operator); or

(b) any liability which any person other than the Operator may incur other than under this regulation.

(11) Where an application is made under paragraph (2), and the Operator receives from the applicant a request for information or documents relating to—

(a) a forged dematerialised instruction;

(b) an induced amendment to an Operator register of securities; or

(c) an induced Operator-instruction,

in respect of which the application is made, the Operator shall, in so far as he is able, and in so far as the request is reasonable, within one month give the applicant the information and documents.

(12) The applicant shall, in so far as he is able, within one month give the Operator such information or documents as the Operator reasonably requests in connection with an application under paragraph (2) with respect to—

(a) steps taken by the applicant to prevent the giving of any forged dematerialised instruction (whether of the kind referred to in paragraph (2) or of any other kind); and

(b) steps taken by the applicant to mitigate the loss suffered by him,

provided that the applicant need not give information or documents pursuant to this paragraph until the Operator has complied with any request made by virtue of paragraph (11).

(13) Neither the Operator nor the applicant shall be required to disclose any information by virtue of, respectively, paragraph (11) or (12) which would be privileged in the course of civil proceedings, or, in Scotland, which they would be entitled to refuse to disclose—

(a) on grounds of confidentiality as between client and professional legal adviser in proceedings in the Court of Session; or

(b) on grounds of confidentiality of communications made in connection with, or in contemplation of, such proceedings and for the purposes of those proceedings.

(14) The jurisdiction conferred by this regulation shall be exercisable, in the case of a participating security constituted under the law of England and Wales, or Northern Ireland, by the High Court; and in the case of a participating security constituted under the law of Scotland by the Court of Session.

PART 5 MISCELLANEOUS AND SUPPLEMENTAL

Miscellaneous

[6.73]

37 Construction of references to transfers etc

References in any enactment or rule of law to a proper instrument of transfer or to a transfer with respect to securities, or any expression having like meaning, shall be taken to include a reference to an Operator-instruction to a participating issuer to register a transfer of title on the relevant issuer register of securities in accordance with the Operator-instruction.

[6.74]

38 Certain formalities and requirements not to apply

(1) Any requirements in an enactment or rule of law which apply in respect of the transfer of securities otherwise than by means of a relevant system shall not prevent—

(a) an Operator from registering a transfer of title to uncertificated units of a security upon settlement of a transfer of such units in accordance with his rules; or

(b) an Operator-instruction from requiring a participating issuer to register a transfer of title to uncertificated units of a security.

(2) Subject to regulation 32(7), notwithstanding any enactment, instrument or rule of law, a participating issuer shall not issue a certificate in relation to any uncertificated units of a participating security.

(3) A document issued by or on behalf of a participating issuer purportedly evidencing title to an uncertificated unit of a participating security shall not be evidence of title to the unit of the security; and in particular—

(a) [section 768 of the 2006 Act] shall not apply to any document issued with respect to uncertificated shares; and

(b) [regulation 9(3) of the 2004 Regulations] and regulation 6(3) of the 1974 Regulations shall not apply to any document issued with respect to uncertificated units of a public sector security.

(4) Any requirement in or under any enactment to endorse any statement or information on a certificate evidencing title to a unit of a security—

(a) shall not prohibit the conversion into, or issue of, units of the security in uncertificated form; and

(b) in relation to uncertificated units of the security, shall be taken to be a requirement for the relevant participating issuer to provide the holder of the units with the statement or information on request by him.

(5) Sections 53(1)(c) and 136 of the Law of Property Act 1925 (which impose requirements for certain dispositions and assignments to be in writing) shall not apply (if they would otherwise do so) to—

(a) any transfer of title to uncertificated units of a security by means of a relevant system; and

(b) any disposition or assignment of an interest in uncertificated units of a security title to which is held by a relevant nominee.

(6) In paragraph (5) "relevant nominee" means a subsidiary undertaking of an Operator designated by him as a relevant nominee in accordance with such rules and practices as are mentioned in paragraph 25(f) of Schedule 1.

(7) [Section 772 of the 2006 Act] shall not apply in relation to the transfer of uncertificated units of a security by means of a relevant system.

NOTES

Para (3): words in first pair of square brackets substituted by the Companies Act 2006 (Consequential Amendments) (Uncertificated Securities) Order 2009, SI 2009/1889, art 2(1), (16)(a), as from 1 October 2009. Words in second pair of square brackets substituted by the Government Stock (Consequential and Transitional Provision) (No 2) Order 2004, SI 2004/1662, art 2, Schedule, Pt 3, para 29(1), (4), as from 1 July 2004.

Para (7): words in square brackets substituted by SI 2009/1889, art 2(1), (16)(b), as from 1 October 2009.

[6.75]

39 Fees charged by Operators

(1) Subject to paragraph (2), nothing in these Regulations prevents an Operator from charging a fee for carrying out any function under Part 3 of these Regulations.

(2) An Operator may not charge a fee to a participating issuer for maintaining or keeping and entering up an Operator register of securities.

[6.76]

40 Trusts, trustees and personal representatives etc

(1) Unless expressly prohibited from transferring units of a security by means of any computer-based system, a trustee or personal representative shall not be chargeable with a breach of trust or, as the case may be, with default in administering the estate by reason only of the fact that—

(a) for the purpose of acquiring units of a security which he has the power to acquire in connection with the trust or estate, he has paid for the units under arrangements which provide for them to be transferred to him from a system-member but not to be so transferred until after the payment of the price;

(b) for the purpose of disposing of units of a security which he has power to dispose of in connection with the trust or estate, he has transferred the units to a system-member under arrangements which provide that the price is not to be paid to him until after the transfer is made; or

(c) for the purpose of holding units of a security belonging to the trust or estate in uncertificated form and for transferring title to them by means of a relevant system, he has become a system-member.

(2) Notwithstanding [sections 750 and 751 of the 2006 Act], a trustee of a trust deed for securing an issue of debentures shall not be chargeable with a breach of trust by reason only of the fact that he has assented to an amendment of the trust deed only for the purposes of—

(a) allowing the holding of debentures in uncertificated form;

(b) allowing the exercise of rights attaching to the debentures by means of a relevant system; or

(c) allowing the transfer of title to the debentures by means of a relevant system, provided that he has given or caused to be given notice of the amendment in accordance with the trust deed not less than 30 days prior to its becoming effective to all persons registered as holding the debentures on a date not more than 21 days before the dispatch of the notice.

(3) Without prejudice to regulation 23(3) or [section 126 of the 2006 Act], the Operator shall not be bound by or compelled to recognise any express, implied or constructive trust or other interest in respect of uncertificated units of a security, even if he has actual or constructive notice of the said trust or interest.

(4) Paragraph (3) shall not prevent, in the case of a participating issuer constituted under the law of Scotland, an Operator giving notice of a trust to the participating issuer on behalf of a system-member.

NOTES

Paras (2), (3): words in square brackets substituted by the Companies Act 2006 (Consequential Amendments) (Uncertificated Securities) Order 2009, SI 2009/1889, art 2(1), (17), as from 1 October 2009.

[6.77]

41 Notices of meetings etc

(1) For the purposes of determining which persons are entitled to attend or vote at a meeting, and how many votes such persons may cast, the participating issuer may specify in the notice of the meeting a time, not more than 48 hours before the time fixed for the meeting, by which a person must be entered on the relevant register of securities in order to have the right to attend or vote at the meeting.

(2) Changes to entries on the relevant register of securities after the time specified by virtue of paragraph (1) shall be disregarded in determining the rights of any person to attend or vote at the meeting, notwithstanding any provisions in any enactment, articles of association or other instrument to the contrary.

(3) For the purposes of—

(a) serving notices of meetings, whether under [section 310(1) of the 2006 Act], any other enactment, a provision in the articles of association or any other instrument; or

(b) sending copies of the documents required to be sent to any person by [section 423(1) of the 2006 Act],

a participating issuer may determine that persons entitled to receive such notices, or copies of such documents (as the case may be), are those persons entered on the relevant register of securities at the close of business on a day determined by him.

(4) The day determined by a participating issuer under paragraph (3) may not be more than 21 days before the day that the notices of the meeting, or the copies of the documents as the case may be, are sent.

(5) This regulation is without prejudice to the protection afforded—

(a) by paragraph 5(3) of Schedule 4, to a participating issuer which is a company; and

(b) by paragraph 13(4) or 15(3) of Schedule 4, to a participating issuer.

[(6) In calculating the period mentioned in paragraph (1) above no account shall be taken of any part of a day that is not a working day.]

NOTES

Words in square brackets in para (3) substituted, and para (6) added, by the Companies Act 2006 (Consequential Amendments) (Uncertificated Securities) Order 2009, SI 2009/1889, art 2(1), (18), as from 1 October 2009.

[6.78]

42 Notices to minority shareholders

(1) Paragraphs (2) to (4) shall apply in relation to any uncertificated units of a security (other than a wholly dematerialised security) to which a notice given under [section 979 of the [2006 Act]] relates, in place of the provisions of [section 981(7)] of that Act.

(2) Immediately on receipt of a copy sent under [section 981(6)(a) of the [2006 Act]] of a notice given under [section 979] relating to uncertificated units of a participating security (whether or not it also relates to certificated units of the security), a company which is a participating issuer shall—

(a) by issuer-instruction—

(i) inform the Operator that the copy notice has been received, and

(ii) identify the holding of uncertificated units of the participating security to which the notice relates; and

(b) enter the name of the relevant system-member on an issuer register of securities as the holder of those uncertificated units.

(3) On receipt of an issuer-instruction under paragraph (2)(a), the Operator shall delete any entry in an Operator register of securities which shows the relevant system-member as the holder of the uncertificated units of the participating security to which the notice relates.

(4) On registration on an issuer register of securities (in accordance with paragraph (2)(b)) of the relevant system-member as the holder of the uncertificated units of the participating security to which the notice relates, the participating issuer—

(a) shall be under the same obligation to enter the offeror on that register as the holder of those units, in place of the relevant system-member, as it would be if it had received an Operator-instruction under regulation 28(2) requiring it to register a transfer of title to those units in that manner; and regulation 28(9) shall have effect accordingly; and

(b) where the terms of issue of the security in question provide for a certificate to be issued, shall issue to the offeror a certificate in respect of those units.

(5) [Subsection (1) of section 776 of the 2006 Act] shall apply in relation to the issue of a certificate by a participating issuer pursuant to paragraph (4)(b) as it applies in relation to the completion and having ready for delivery by a company of share certificates, debentures or certificates of debenture stock; and in that subsection as it so applies the reference to the date on which a transfer is lodged with the company shall be a reference to the date on which the participating issuer receives the copy notice sent under [section 981(6)(a) of the [2006 Act]].

(6) Such sanctions as apply to a company and its officers in the event of a default in complying with [subsection (1) of section 776 of the 2006 Act] shall apply to a participating issuer and his officers in the event of a default in complying with paragraph (4)(b) in accordance with the requirements laid down in paragraph (5).

(7) Paragraphs (8) to (11) shall apply in relation to any units of a wholly dematerialised security to which a notice given under [section 979 of the [2006 Act]] relates, in place of the provisions of [section 981(7)] of that Act.

(8) Immediately on receipt of a copy sent under [section 981(6)(a) of the [2006 Act]] of a notice given under [section 979] relating to units of a wholly dematerialised security, a company which is a participating issuer shall—

(a) by issuer-instruction—

(i) inform the Operator that the copy notice has been received; and

(ii) identify the holding of units of the wholly dematerialised security to which the notice relates; and

(b) by a further issuer-instruction, inform the Operator of the name of the transferee.

(9) On receipt of an issuer-instruction under paragraph (8)(a), the Operator shall delete any entry in an Operator register of securities which shows the relevant system-member as the holder of the units to which the notice relates.

(10) On receipt of an issuer-instruction under paragraph (8)(b), the Operator shall enter the transferee on the relevant Operator register of securities as the holder of the units to which the notice relates, in place of the relevant system-member.

(11) Where an Operator deletes an entry in an Operator register of securities pursuant to paragraph (9)—

(a) the units of the wholly dematerialised security to which the notice relates shall notwithstanding that deletion, continue to be regarded as uncertificated units for the purposes of these Regulations until the Operator enters the transferee on the relevant Operator register of securities as the holder of those units;

(b) subject to—

(i) subparagraph (c) or (d), as the case may be; and

(ii) any enactment or rule of law,

the relevant system-member shall, notwithstanding that deletion, retain title to the units of the wholly dematerialised security to which the notice relates until the transferee is entered on the relevant Operator register of securities pursuant to paragraph (10);

(c) in the case of a security constituted under the law of England and Wales or Northern Ireland, the transferee shall acquire an equitable interest in the units of the wholly dematerialised security to which the notice relates;

(d) in the case of a security constituted under the law of Scotland, the relevant system-member shall hold the units of the wholly dematerialised security to which the notice relates on trust for the benefit of the transferee.

(12) Such sanctions as apply to a company and its officers in the event of a default in complying with [subsections (1) and (2) of section 771 of the 2006 Act] shall apply—

(a) to a participating issuer and his officers in the event of a default in complying with paragraph (2)(b) or (8); and

(b) to an Operator and his officers in the event of a default in complying with paragraph (3), (9) or (10).

(13) For the purposes of this regulation—

(a) "offeror" has the meaning [in section 991(1) of the [2006 Act];]

(b) "relevant system-member" means the system-member identified in the copy notice sent under [section 981(6)(a) of the [2006 Act]] as the holder of the uncertificated units, or as the case may be the units of the wholly dematerialised security, to which the notice relates; and

(c) "transferee" means the offeror or, if the offeror is not a system-member, the system-member in whose name the units of the wholly dematerialised security to which the notice given under [section 979 of the [2006 Act]] relates are to be registered on the Operator register of securities.

(14) The reference in [section 987(8) of the [2006 Act] to section 981(7)] shall be taken to include a reference to the provisions of paragraphs (4), (8) and (9).

NOTES

Paras (1), (2), (7), (8), (13), (14): the words "2006 Act" in square brackets were substituted by the Companies Act 2006 (Consequential Amendments) (Uncertificated Securities) Order 2009, SI 2009/1889, art 2(1), (19)(a), as from 1 October 2009. All other words in square brackets substituted by the Companies Act 2006 (Commencement No 2, Consequential Amendments, Transitional Provisions and Savings) Order 2007, SI 2007/1093, art 6(1), Sch 3, para 9, as from 6 April 2007.

Para (5): words in first pair of square brackets and third (inner) pair of square brackets substituted by SI 2009/1889, art 2(1), (19)(a), (b), as from 1 October 2009. Words in second (outer) pair of square brackets substituted by SI 2007/1093, art 6(1), Sch 3, para 9, as from 6 April 2007.

Paras (6), (12): words in square brackets substituted by SI 2009/1889, art 2(1), (19)(c), (d), as from 1 October 2009.

[6.79]

43 Irrevocable powers of attorney

(1) This regulation applies where the terms of an offer for all or any uncertificated units of a participating security provide that a person accepting the offer creates an irrevocable power of attorney in favour of the offeror, or a person nominated by the offeror, in the terms set out in the offer.

(2) An acceptance communicated by properly authenticated dematerialised instruction in respect of uncertificated units of a security shall constitute a grant of an irrevocable power of attorney by the system-member accepting the offer in favour of the offeror, or person nominated by the offeror, in the terms set out in the offer.

(3) Where the contract constituted by such offer and acceptance as are referred to in paragraphs (1) and (2) respectively is governed by the law of England and Wales, section 4 of the Powers of Attorney Act 1971 shall apply to a power of attorney constituted in accordance with this regulation.

(4) A declaration in writing by the offeror stating the terms of a power of attorney and that it has been granted by virtue of this regulation and stating the name and address of the grantor shall be prima facie evidence, and in Scotland sufficient evidence unless the contrary is shown, of the grant; and any requirement in any enactment, rule of law, or instrument to produce a copy of the power of attorney, or such a copy certified in a particular manner, shall be satisfied by the production of the declaration or a copy of the declaration certified in that manner.

(5) In the application of this regulation to an offer, acceptance or contract governed by the law of Scotland, any reference to an irrevocable power of attorney shall mean and include reference to an irrevocable mandate, however expressed.

[6.80]

44 Actual notice

For the purpose of determining under these Regulations whether a person has actual notice of a fact, matter or thing that person shall not under any circumstances be taken to be concerned to establish whether or not it exists or has occurred.

[6.81]

45 Participating securities issued in uncertificated form

Nothing in these Regulations shall require—

(a) a participating issuer or its officers to maintain a register which records how many units of a wholly dematerialised security are held in certificated form; or

(b) an Operator or participating issuer, or their officers, to take any action to change a unit of a wholly dematerialised security from uncertificated form to certificated form or vice versa.

Defaults and Contraventions

[6.82]

46 Breaches of statutory duty

(1) A default in complying with, or a contravention of, regulation 16(8), 19(2), 25(1), 26, 28(5) or (6), 32(5), 33(5), or 42(2) or (8) shall be actionable at the suit of a person who suffers loss as a result of the default or contravention, or who is otherwise adversely affected by it, subject to the defences and other incidents applying to actions for breach of statutory duty.

(2) Paragraph (1) shall not affect the liability which any person may incur, nor affect any right which any person may have, apart from paragraph (1).

[6.83]

47 Liability of officers for contraventions

(1) In regulation 16(7), 20(7), 21(5), 22(5), 28(9), 32(9) or (10), 33(11) or 42(6) or (12) an officer of a participating issuer shall be in default in complying with, or in contravention of, the provision mentioned in that regulation if, and only if, he knowingly and wilfully authorised or permitted the default or contravention.

(2) In regulation 20(7), 21(4), 22(4), 27(9), 32(9), 33(11) or 42(12) an officer of an Operator shall be in default in complying with, or in contravention of, the provision mentioned in that regulation if, and only if, he knowingly and wilfully authorised or permitted the default or contravention.

[6.84]

48 Exemption from liability

Regulations 21(5), 28(9), 32(9) and (10), and 33(11) shall not apply to any of the following or its officers—

(a) the Crown;

(b) any person acting on behalf of the Crown;

[(c) the Bank of England;

(d) the Registrar of Government Stock;

(e) any previous Registrar of Government Stock; or

(f) in respect of a security which immediately before it became a participating security was transferable by exempt transfer within the meaning of the Stock Transfer Act 1982, a participating issuer].

NOTES

Paras (c)–(f) substituted (for the original paras (c), (d)) by the Government Stock (Consequential and Transitional Provision) (No 2) Order 2004, SI 2004/1662, art 2, Schedule, Pt 3, para 29(1), (5), as from 1 July 2004.

49 (*Reg 49 (Application to Northern Ireland) outside the scope of this work.*)

Transitory Provisions, Amendments and Revocations

[6.85]

50 Transitory provisions

Schedule 6 (transitory provisions) shall have effect.

[6.86]

51 Minor and consequential amendments

Schedule 7 (minor and consequential amendments) shall have effect.

52 (*Revokes the Government Stock Regulations 1965, SI 1965/1420, regs 4(3), (4), 4A, 4B, 6(5), 17(7), 18(5), 19(2), 20(2), Sch 1, the Local Authority (Stocks and Bonds) Regulations 1974, SI 1974/519, reg 6(6), 6A, 7(1)(b), (4), (5), 8(2), (3), 9(4), 10(3), 16(4), 21(3), Sch 2, the Uncertificated Securities Regulations 1995, SI 1995/3272, the Open-Ended Investment Companies Regulations 2001, SI 2001/1228, reg 47(1), Sch 3, paras 2(2), 5(1)(c), 6(3)(d), Sch 4, para 3, Sch 7, para 12.*)

SCHEDULES

SCHEDULE 1
[REQUIREMENTS FOR OPERATION OF A RELEVANT SYSTEM]

Regulation 5(1)

[6.87]

1–4. . . .

System security

5. [(1) A relevant system must satisfy the requirements of sub-paragraphs (3) to (6).]

(2) . . .

(3) Each dematerialised instruction must be authenticated—

[(a) in accordance with the specifications of the Operator, and those specifications shall provide that each dematerialised instruction is identifiable as being from the computers of the Operator or of a particular system-participant; or]

(b) if it is sent to the Operator by, or by the Operator to, a depositary, a clearing house or an exchange, in accordance with specifications of that depositary, clearing house or exchange to which the Operator has agreed and which provide that each dematerialised instruction—

(i) is identifiable as being from the computers of the Operator or of the depositary, clearing house or exchange which sent it; . . .

(ii) . . .

(4) Each dematerialised instruction must, in accordance with any relevant rules of the Operator and with the specifications of the Operator or the specifications referred to in subparagraph (3)(b) (as the case may be), express by whom it has been sent and, where relevant, on whose behalf it has been sent.

(5) Each dematerialised instruction must, in accordance with any relevant rules of the Operator and with the specifications of the Operator or the specifications referred to in subparagraph (3)(b) (as the case may be), indicate—

(a) where it is sent to a system-participant or the Operator, that it is addressed to that system-participant or the Operator;

(b) where it is sent to a person who is using the facilities of a sponsoring system-participant to receive dematerialised instructions, that it is addressed to that person and the sponsoring system-participant; and

(c) where it is sent to the Operator in order for him to send an Operator-instruction to a system-participant, that it is addressed to the Operator, to the system-participant and, if the system-participant is acting as a sponsoring system-participant, to the relevant person on whose behalf the sponsoring system-participant receives dematerialised instructions; and

(6) The relevant system must minimise the possibility for a system-participant to send a dematerialised instruction on behalf of a person from whom he has no authority.

(7) For the purposes of this paragraph—

"clearing house" means a body or association—

(a) which is a recognised clearing house within section 285(1)(b) of the 2000 Act;

(b) which is authorised under that Act to provide clearing services in the United Kingdom; . . .

[(ba) which is . . . or a third country central counterparty within the meaning of section 285(1) of the 2000 Act; or]

(c) which provides services outside the United Kingdom which are similar in nature to those provided by any such body or association, and which is regulated or supervised in the provision of those services by a regulatory body or agency of government;

"depositary" means [[a CSD or third-country CSD within the meaning of the CSD regulation as amended from time to time] or] a body or association carrying on business outside the United Kingdom with whom an Operator has made arrangements—

(a) to enable system-members to hold (whether directly or indirectly) and transfer title to securities (other than participating securities) by means of facilities provided by that body or association; or

(b) to enable that body or association to permit persons to whom it provides services in the course of its business to hold (whether directly or indirectly) and transfer title to participating securities by means of the Operator's relevant system; and

"exchange" means a body or association—

(a) which is a recognised investment exchange within section 285(1)(a) of the 2000 Act;

(b) which is authorised under that Act to provide a facility for the matching and execution of transactions in securities in the United Kingdom; or

(c) which provides services outside the United Kingdom which are similar in nature to those provided by any such body or association, and which is regulated or supervised in the provision of those services by a regulatory body or agency of government.

System capabilities

6–8. . . .

9. A relevant system must enable an Operator to comply with his obligations to keep all necessary Operator registers of securities in accordance with these Regulations.

10, 11. . . .

12. A relevant system must be able to permit each participating issuer to inspect the entries from time to time appearing in an Operator register of securities [(other than an Operator register of eligible debt securities)] relating to any participating security issued by him.

13. A relevant system must be able to establish, where there is a transfer of uncertificated units of a security to a system-member for value, that a settlement bank has agreed to make payment in respect of the transfer, whether alone or taken together with another transfer for value.

14. A relevant system must ensure that the Operator-system is able to generate Operator- instructions—

(a) requiring participating issuers to amend the appropriate issuer registers of securities kept by them;

(b) informing participating issuers in a way which enables them to amend the appropriate records of securities kept by them; and

(c) informing settlement banks of their payment obligations.

15. A relevant system must—

(a) enable a system-member—
  (i) to grant authority to a sponsoring system-participant to send properly authenticated dematerialised instructions on his behalf; and
  (ii) to limit such authority by reference to the net value of the units of the securities to be transferred in any one day; and
(b) prevent the transfer of units in excess of that limit.

16. For the purposes of paragraph 15(a)(ii), once authority is granted pursuant to a system charge (within the meaning of regulation 3 of the Financial Markets and Insolvency Regulations 1996) a limit of such authority shall not be imposed or changed without the consent of the donee of that authority.

17. Nothing in paragraph 15 or 16 shall be taken, in respect of an authority, to modify or derogate from the protections given by or under any enactment to a donee of the authority or a third person.

18. A relevant system must enable system-members—
(a) to change the form in which they hold units of a participating security; and
(b) where appropriate, to require participating issuers to issue certificates relating to units of a participating security held or to be held by them.

19. Paragraph 18 shall not apply to any wholly dematerialised security.

Operating procedures

20. A relevant system must comprise procedures which provide that it responds only to properly authenticated dematerialised instructions which are attributable to a system-user or an Operator.

21. (1) Subject to subparagraphs (2) to (5), a relevant system must comprise procedures which provide that an Operator only registers a transfer of title to uncertificated units of a security or generates an Operator-instruction requiring a participating issuer to register such a transfer, and only generates an Operator-instruction informing a settlement bank of its payment obligations in respect of such a transfer, if—
(a) it has—
  (i) received a system-member instruction which is attributable to the transferor; or
  (ii) been required to do so by a court in the United Kingdom or by or under an enactment;
(b) it has—
  (i) established that the transferor has title to such number of units as is in aggregate at least equal to the number to be transferred; or
  (ii) established that the transfer is one of two or more transfers which may be registered in accordance with regulation 30(2);
(c) in the case of a transfer to a system-member for value, it has established that a settlement bank has agreed to make payment in respect of the transfer, whether alone or taken together with another transfer for value; and
(d) the transfer is not in excess of any limit which by virtue of paragraph 15(a)(ii) the transferor has set on an authority given by him to a sponsoring system-participant.

(2) Subparagraph (1)(a) shall not prevent the registration by an Operator of a transfer of title to uncertificated units of a security, or the generation of an Operator-instruction, in accordance with procedures agreed between the Operator and the transferor to enable the transfer by means of a relevant system of uncertificated units of a security provided that such transfer is for the purpose of, or relates to, facilitating the provision of financial credit or financial liquidity to the transferor by a settlement bank, the Bank of England, the European Central Bank, any other central bank, or any other body having functions as a monetary authority.

(3) A relevant system must comprise procedures which provide that—
(a) the Operator may amend an Operator register of securities; and
(b) an Operator-instruction requiring a participating issuer to register a transfer of uncertificated units of a security, or informing a settlement bank of its payment obligations in respect of such a transfer, may be generated,

if necessary to correct an error and if in accordance with the rules made and practices instituted by the Operator in order to comply with this Schedule.

(4) A relevant system must comprise procedures which provide that—
(a) the Operator may amend an Operator register of securities; and
(b) an Operator-instruction requiring a participating issuer to register a transfer of units of a wholly dematerialised security, or informing a settlement bank of its payment obligations in respect of such a transfer, may be generated,

if necessary to effect a transfer of such units, on the termination of participation in the relevant system by the system-member by whom those units are held and if in accordance with the rules made and practices instituted by the Operator in order to comply with this Schedule, to a person nominated under the Operator's rules.

(5) Subparagraph (1)(a) shall not prevent the registration by an Operator of a transfer of title to uncertificated units of a security, or the generation of an Operator-instruction, in order to give effect to the procedures referred to in subparagraph (3) or (4).

22. (1) Subject to subparagraph (2), a relevant system must comprise procedures which provide that an Operator-instruction to a participating issuer relating to a right, privilege or benefit attaching to or arising from an uncertificated unit of a security, is generated only if it has—
(a) received a properly authenticated dematerialised instruction attributable to the system-member having the right, privilege or benefit requiring the Operator to generate an Operator-instruction to the participating issuer; or
(b) been required to do so by a court in the United Kingdom or by or under an enactment.

(2) A relevant system must comprise procedures which provide that an Operator-instruction to a participating issuer relating to a right, privilege or benefit attaching to or arising from an uncertificated unit of a security, may be generated if necessary to correct an error and if in accordance with the rules made and practices instituted by an Operator in order to comply with this Schedule.

23, 24. . . .

Rules and Practices

25. An Operator's rules and practices—

(a) . . .

(b) must make provision as to the manner in which a system-member or the relevant participating issuer may change the form in which that system-member holds units of a participating security (other than a wholly dematerialised security);

(c) must make provision for a participating issuer to cease to participate in respect of a participating security so as—

(i) to minimise so far as practicable any disruption to system-members in respect of their ability to transfer the relevant security; and

(ii) to provide the participating issuer with any relevant information held by the Operator relating to the uncertificated units of the relevant security held by system-members;

(d) . . .

(e) must make provision—

(i) as to which of the Operator's records are to constitute an Operator register of securities in relation to a participating security, or a participating security of a particular kind; and

(ii) as to the times at which, and the manner in which, a participating issuer may inspect an Operator register of securities [(other than an Operator register of eligible debt securities)] in accordance with paragraph 12;

(f) if they make provision for the designation of a subsidiary undertaking as a relevant nominee, must require that the relevant nominee maintain adequate records of—

(i) the names of the persons who have an interest in the securities it holds; and

(ii) the nature and extent of their interests; and

(g) must make provision for the authentication by the Operator of any written notification given under regulation 25(3) or 32(2)(c).

26. An Operator's rules and practices must require—

(a) that each system-participant is able to send and receive properly authenticated dematerialised instructions;

(b) that each system-member has arrangements—

(i) for properly authenticated dematerialised instructions attributable to him to be sent;

(ii) for properly authenticated dematerialised instructions to be received by or for him; and

(iii) with a settlement bank for payments to be made, where appropriate, for units of a security transferred by means of the relevant system; and

(c) that each participating issuer is able to respond with sufficient speed to Operator-instructions.

27, 28 . . .

NOTES

Schedule heading: words in square brackets substituted by the Uncertificated Securities (Amendment and EU Exit) Regulations 2019, SI 2019/679, reg 4(1), (9)(a), as from 27 March 2019 (for transitional provisions and savings see regs 11, 12 of the 2019 Regulations at **[12.125]** et seq).

Paras 1–4: revoked by SI 2019/679, reg 4(1), (9)(b), as from 27 March 2019 (for transitional provisions and savings see regs 11, 12 of the 2019 Regulations at **[12.125]** et seq).

Para 5 is amended as follows:

Sub-para (1) substituted by SI 2019/679, reg 4(1), (9)(c)(i), as from 27 March 2019 (for transitional provisions and savings see regs 11, 12 of the 2019 Regulations at **[12.125]** et seq).

Sub-para (2) was revoked by SI 2019/679, reg 4(1), (9)(c)(ii), as from 27 March 2019 (for transitional provisions and savings see regs 11, 12 of the 2019 Regulations at **[12.125]** et seq).

Sub-para (3)(a) was substituted, and sub-para (3)(b)(ii) and the preceding word were revoked, by SI 2019/679, reg 4(1), (9)(c)(iii), as from 27 March 2019 (for transitional provisions and savings see regs 11, 12 of the 2019 Regulations at **[12.125]** et seq).

In the definition "clearing house" in sub-para (7), the word omitted from para (b) was revoked, and para (ba) was inserted, by the Financial Services and Markets Act 2000 (Over the Counter Derivatives, Central Counterparties and Trade Repositories) Regulations 2013, SI 2013/504, reg 36, as from 1 April 2013. The words omitted from para (ba) were revoked by SI 2019/679, reg 14, as from IP completion day (as defined in the European Union (Withdrawal Agreement) Act 2020, s 39).

In the definition "depositary" in sub-para (7), the words in the first (outer) pair square brackets (ie, now only the word "or") were inserted by SI 2019/679, reg 4(1), (9)(c)(iv), as from 27 March 2019 (for transitional provisions and savings see regs 11, 12 of the 2019 Regulations at **[12.125]** et seq). The words in the second (inner) pair of square brackets were substituted by SI 2019/679, reg 14, as from IP completion day (as defined in the European Union (Withdrawal Agreement) Act 2020, s 39).

Paras 6–8, 10, 11: revoked by SI 2019/679, reg 4(1), (9)(d), (e), as from 27 March 2019 (for transitional provisions and savings see regs 11, 12 of the 2019 Regulations at **[12.125]** et seq).

Para 12: words in square brackets inserted by the Uncertificated Securities (Amendment) (Eligible Debt Securities) Regulations 2003, SI 2003/1633, reg 12, as from 24 June 2003.

Paras 23, 24: revoked by SI 2019/679, reg 4(1), (9)(f), as from 27 March 2019 (for transitional provisions and savings see regs 11, 12 of the 2019 Regulations at **[12.125]** et seq).

Para 25: sub-paras (a) and (d) revoked by SI 2019/679, reg 4(1), (9)(g), as from 27 March 2019 (for transitional provisions and savings see regs 11, 12 of the 2019 Regulations at **[12.125]** et seq). Words in square brackets inserted by SI 2003/1633, reg 12, as from 24 June 2003.

Para 27: revoked by SI 2019/679, reg 4(1), (9)(h), as from 27 March 2019 (for transitional provisions and savings see regs 11, 12 of the 2019 Regulations at **[12.125]** et seq).

Para 28: originally added by the Uncertificated Securities (Amendment) Regulations 2007, SI 2007/124, reg 3, as from 1 November 2007. Subsequently revoked by SI 2019/679, reg 4(1), (9)(h), as from 27 March 2019 (for transitional provisions and savings see regs 11, 12 of the 2019 Regulations at **[12.125]** et seq).

SCHEDULE 2

(Revoked by the Uncertificated Securities (Amendment and EU Exit) Regulations 2019, SI 2019/679, reg 4(1), (10), as from 27 March 2019 (for transitional provisions and savings see regs 11, 12 of the 2019 Regulations at **[12.125]** *et seq).*

SCHEDULE 3
[PROCEDURE FOR GIVING DIRECTIONS]

Regulations 5(4), 7(3) and 8(4)

[6.88]

[1. Before—

(a), (b) . . .

(c) giving a direction under regulation 8,

the Bank of England must give written notice of its intention to do so to the Operator.]

2. A notice under paragraph 1 shall—

[(a) state why the Bank of England intends to . . . give the direction; and]

(b) draw attention to the right to make representations conferred by paragraph 3.

[3. Before the end of the period for making representations, the Operator may make representations to the Bank of England.]

[4. The period for making representations is such period as is specified in the notice (which may, in any particular case, be extended by the Bank of England).]

5. In deciding whether to . . . , give the direction . . . the [Bank of England must] have regard to any representations made in accordance with paragraph 3.

[6. (1) When the Bank of England has decided whether to—

(a), (b) . . .

(c) give the direction;

it must give the Operator written notice of its decision [and the reasons for its decision].]

7, 8. . . .

[9. If the Bank of England decides to give the direction, the Operator may refer the matter to the Upper Tribunal.

10. Part 9 of the 2000 Act (hearings and appeals) applies to a reference to the Upper Tribunal under paragraph 9 as it applies to a reference to the Upper Tribunal under the 2000 Act, with the following modifications—

(a) a reference is a "disciplinary reference" for the purposes of section 133 of the 2000 Act if it is in respect of a decision to give a direction under this Schedule;

(b) section 133(1)(a) and (c) of the 2000 Act does not apply.]

NOTES

Schedule heading: words in square brackets substituted by the Uncertificated Securities (Amendment and EU Exit) Regulations 2019, SI 2019/679, reg 4(1), (11)(a), as from 27 March 2019 (for transitional provisions and savings see regs 11, 12 of the 2019 Regulations at **[12.125]** et seq).

Paras 1, 2, 5: words omitted revoked by SI 2019/679, reg 4(1), (11)(b)–(d), as from 27 March 2019 (for transitional provisions and savings see regs 11, 12 of the 2019 Regulations at **[12.125]** et seq).

Para 6: sub-paras (a) and (b) revoked, and words in square brackets inserted, by SI 2019/679, reg 4(1), (11)(e), as from 27 March 2019 (for transitional provisions and savings see regs 11, 12 of the 2019 Regulations at **[12.125]** et seq).

Paras 7, 8: revoked by SI 2019/679, reg 4(1), (11)(g), as from 27 March 2019 (for transitional provisions and savings see regs 11, 12 of the 2019 Regulations at **[12.125]** et seq).

Paras 9, 10: added by SI 2019/679, reg 4(1), (11)(f), as from 27 March 2019 (for transitional provisions and savings see regs 11, 12 of the 2019 Regulations at **[12.125]** et seq).

All other amendments to this Schedule were made by the Uncertificated Securities (Amendment) Regulations 2013, SI 2013/632, reg 2(1), (15), as from 1 April 2013.

SCHEDULE 4
KEEPING OF REGISTERS AND RECORDS OF PARTICIPATING SECURITIES

Regulation 23(4)

Interpretation

[6.89]

1. In this Schedule—

"uncertificated shares" means shares title to which may be transferred by means of a relevant system; and

"certificated shares" means shares which are not uncertificated shares; and "uncertificated stock" means stock title to which may be transferred by means of a relevant system; and "certificated stock" means stock which is not uncertificated stock.

Registers of members

2. (1) Every participating issuer which is a company shall enter in its issuer register of members—

(a) the names and addresses of the members;

(b) the date on which each person was registered as a member; and

(c) the date at which any person ceased to be a member.

(2) With the names and addresses of the members there shall be entered a statement—

(a) of the certificated shares held by each member, distinguishing each share by its number (so long as the share has a number) and, where the company has more than one class of issued shares, by its class; and

(b) of the amount paid or agreed to be considered as paid on the certificated shares of each member.

(3) Where the company has converted any of its shares into stock and given notice of the conversion to the registrar of companies, the issuer register of members shall show the amount and class of the certificated stock held by each member, instead of the amount of shares and the particulars relating to shares specified in subparagraph (2).

(4) Subject to subparagraph (5), [section 113 of the 2006 Act] shall not apply to a company which is a participating issuer, other than as respects any overseas branch register.

(5) [Section 113(7) and (8) of the 2006 Act] shall apply to a participating issuer which is a company which makes default in complying with this paragraph and every officer of it who is in default as if such a default were a default in complying with [section 113] of the Act.

(6) An entry relating to a former member of the company may be removed from the issuer register of members after the expiration of [10 years] beginning with the day on which he ceased to be a member.

(7) For the purposes of this paragraph references to an issuer register of members shall not be taken to include an overseas branch register.

3. [Section 123 of the 2006 Act] shall apply to a participating issuer which is a private company limited by shares as if references therein to the company's register of members were references to its issuer register of members.

4. (1) In relation to every participating issuer which is a company, an Operator of a relevant system shall, in respect of any class of shares which is a participating security for the purposes of that system, enter on an Operator register of members—

(a) the names and addresses of the members who hold uncertificated shares in the company;

(b) with those names and addresses a statement of the uncertificated shares held by each member and, where the company has more than one class of issued uncertificated shares, distinguishing each share by its class; and

(c) where the company has converted any of its shares into stock and given notice of the conversion to the registrar of companies, the Operator register of members shall show the amount and class of uncertificated stock held by each member, instead of the amount of shares and the particulars relating to shares specified in subparagraph (b).

(2) An entry relating to a member of a company who has ceased to hold any uncertificated shares in the company may be removed from the Operator register of members after the expiration of [10 years] beginning with the day on which he ceased to hold any such shares.

(3) For the purposes of this paragraph references to an Operator register of members shall not be taken to include an overseas branch register.

(4) Members of a company who hold shares in uncertificated form may not be entered as holders of those shares on an overseas branch register.

Records of uncertificated shares

5. (1) Every participating issuer which is a company shall enter in its record of uncertificated shares—

(a) the same particulars, so far as practicable, as are required by paragraph 4(1) to be entered in the Operator register of members; and

(b) a statement of the amount paid or agreed to be considered as paid on the uncertificated shares of each member.

(2) A company to which this paragraph applies shall, unless it is impracticable to do so by virtue of circumstances beyond its control, ensure that the record of uncertificated shares is regularly reconciled with the Operator register of members.

(3) Provided that it has complied with subparagraph (2), a company shall not be liable in respect of any act or thing done or omitted to be done by or on behalf of the company in reliance upon the assumption that the particulars entered in any record of uncertificated shares which the company is required to keep by these Regulations accord with the particulars entered in its Operator register of members.

(4) [Section 113(7) and (8) of the 2006 Act] shall apply to a participating issuer which is a company which makes default in complying with this paragraph and every officer of it who is in default as if such a default were a default in complying with [section 113] of that Act.

Location of issuer register of members and records of uncertificated shares, and ancillary matters

6. (1) Subject to subparagraph (2), a company's issuer register of members and its record of uncertificated shares shall be [kept available for inspection] at its registered office, [or at a place specified in regulations made under section 1136 of the 2006 Act].

(a), (b) . . .

but the issuer register of members must not be [kept available for inspection], in the case of a company registered in England and Wales, at any place elsewhere than in England and Wales or, in the case of a company registered in Scotland, at any place elsewhere than in Scotland.

(2) A company's issuer register of members and its record of uncertificated shares shall at all times be [kept available for inspection] at the same place.

(3) Subject as follows, every participating issuer which is a company shall send notice . . . to the registrar of companies of the place where its issuer register of members and its record of uncertificated shares are [kept available for inspection], and of any change in that place, provided that any notice sent by such a company in accordance with [section 114(2) of the 2006 Act], and which has effect on the coming into force of these Regulations, shall be treated as being a notice sent in compliance with this subparagraph.

(4) The notice need not be sent if the issuer register of members and the record of uncertificated shares have at all times since they came into existence been [kept available for inspection] at the company's registered office.

(5) Subject to subparagraph (6), [section 114 of the 2006 Act] shall not apply to a company which is a participating issuer.

(6) [Section 114 (6) of the 2006 Act] shall apply to a participating issuer which is a company which makes default in complying with subparagraph (2) at any time, or makes default for 14 days in complying with subparagraph (3), and every officer of it who is in default as if such a default were a default in complying with [section 114(2)] of that Act.

7. (1) Every participating issuer which is a company having more than 50 members shall, unless the particulars required by paragraph 2(1) to be entered in the issuer register of members are kept in such a form as to constitute in themselves an index, keep an index of the names of the members of the company and shall, within 14 days after the date on which any alteration is made in the issuer register of members or the Operator register of members, make any necessary alteration in the index.

(2) The index shall in respect of each member contain a sufficient indication to enable the account of that member in the issuer register of members and, in the case of a member who holds uncertificated shares in the company, in the record of uncertificated shares, to be readily found.

(3) The index shall be at all times [kept available for inspection] at the same place as the issuer register of members and the record of uncertificated shares.

(4) Subject to subparagraph (5), [section 115 of the 2006 Act] shall not apply to a company which is a participating issuer.

(5) [Section 115(5) and (6) of the 2006 Act] shall apply to a participating issuer which is a company which makes default in complying with this paragraph and every officer of it who is in default as if such a default were a default in complying with [section 115] of that Act.

8. [Section 122 of the 2006 Act] shall apply to a company which is a participating issuer as if references in that section to the company's register of members were references instead to its issuer register of members.

9. [Sections 115 to 118 of the 2006 Act] shall apply to a company which is a participating issuer as if—

(a) references in those provisions to the company's register of members were references to its issuer register of members and its record of uncertificated shares; and

(b) references in [section 116] to the company's [index of members' names] were references to the index required to be kept by paragraph 7,

and references to [the 2006 Act in the Companies (Fees for Inspection and Copying of Company Records) Regulations 2007 and the Companies (Fees for Inspection and Copying of Company Records) Regulations 2008] shall be construed accordingly.

10. Where under [paragraph 6(1)], a company's issuer register of members and record of uncertificated shares is [kept available for inspection] at the office of some person other than the company, and by reason of any default of his the company fails to comply with—

paragraph 6(2) (record of uncertificated shares to be [kept available for inspection] with issuer register of members);

paragraph 6(3) (notice to registrar);

paragraph 7(3) (index to be [kept available for inspection] with issuer register of members and record of uncertificated shares); or

[section 116 of the 2006 Act (rights to inspect and require copies)],

or with any requirement of the [the 2006 Act] as to the production of the register of members or any part thereof, that other person is liable to the same penalties as if he were an officer of the company who was in default, and the power of the court under [section 118(3) of the 2006 Act] extends to the making of orders against that other and his officers and servants.

11. Where, under [section 125 of the 2006 Act], the court orders rectification of the register of members of a company which is a participating issuer, it shall not order the payment of any damages under subsection (2) of that section to the extent that such rectification relates to the company's Operator register of members and does not arise from an act or omission of the Operator on the instructions of that company or from fraud or other wilful default, or negligence, on the part of that company.

Registers of [general] public sector securities

12. (1) Where an Operator of a relevant system is required to maintain an Operator register of [general] public sector securities that register shall comprise the following particulars which the Operator shall enter on it, namely—

(a) the names and address of the persons holding units of the relevant participating security in uncertificated form; and

(b) how many units of that security each such person holds in that form.

[(2) The following provisions of the 2004 Regulations shall not apply in respect of units of general UK Government securities held in uncertificated form—

regulations 7 to 9;
regulations 12 to 14;
regulations 16 to 24;
regulation 28; and
regulations 30 to 31.]

(3) The following provisions of the 1974 Regulations shall not apply in respect of units of [general] local authority securities held in uncertificated form—

regulations 5 and 6;
regulations 8 to 14;
regulation 16; and
regulation 21.

Records of uncertificated [general] public sector securities

13. (1) The participating issuer shall enter in a record of uncertificated [general] public sector securities the same particulars, so far as is practicable, as are required by paragraph 12(1) to be entered in the relevant Operator register of [general] public sector securities.

(2) In respect of every participating security which is a [general] UK Government security, the record of uncertificated [general] public sector securities shall be kept [by the Registrar of Government Stock].

(3) The participating issuer shall, unless it is impracticable to do so by virtue of circumstances beyond his control, ensure that the record of uncertificated [general] public sector securities is regularly reconciled with the Operator register of [general] public sector securities.

(4) Provided that he has complied with subparagraph (3), a participating issuer shall not be liable in respect of any act or thing done or omitted to be done by him or on his behalf in reliance upon the assumption that the particulars entered in any record of uncertificated [general] public sector securities which he is required to keep by these Regulations accord with particulars entered in the Operator register of [general] public sector securities to which the record relates.

(5) The provisions of the Bankers' Books Evidence Act 1879 shall apply for the purpose of proving any entry in the record of uncertificated [general] public sector securities as if the participating issuer were a bank and a banker within the meaning of that Act, and as if such entry in the record, or, where the information recorded therein is not in readable form and is later transcribed into readable form, the transcribed version of such entry, were an entry in a banker's book.

Registers of corporate securities

14. (1) Where an Operator of a relevant system is required to maintain an Operator register of corporate securities, that register shall comprise the following particulars which the Operator shall enter on it, namely—

(a) the names and addresses of the persons holding units of the relevant participating security in uncertificated form; and

(b) how many units of that security each such person holds in that form.

(2) [Sections 743 to 748 of the 2006 Act] shall not apply to any part of an Operator register of corporate securities.

Records of uncertificated corporate securities

15. (1) A participating issuer shall enter in a record of uncertificated corporate securities the same particulars, so far as practicable, as are required by paragraph 14(1) to be entered in the relevant Operator register of corporate securities.

(2) A participating issuer to which this paragraph applies shall, unless it is impracticable to do so by virtue of circumstances beyond its control, ensure that the record of uncertificated corporate securities is regularly reconciled with the Operator register of corporate securities.

(3) Provided that it has complied with subparagraph (2), a participating issuer shall not be liable in respect of any act or thing done or omitted to be done by it or on its behalf in reliance upon the assumption that the particulars entered in any record of uncertificated corporate securities which the participating issuer is required to keep by these Regulations accord with particulars entered in any Operator register of corporate securities relating to it.

(4) In the case of a participating issuer which is a company, the record of uncertificated corporate securities shall be kept at the same place as the part of any register of debenture holders maintained by the company would be required to be kept.

(5) [Sections 744(1) to (4) and 746 of the 2006 Act] shall apply in relation to a record of uncertificated corporate securities maintained by a participating issuer which is a company, so far as that record relates to debentures, [as they apply] or would apply to any register of debenture holders maintained by the company; and references to [the 2006 Act in the Companies (Fees for Inspection and Copying of Company Records) Regulations 2007 and the Companies (Fees for Inspection and Copying of Company Records) Regulations 2008] shall be construed accordingly.

(6) Any provision of an enactment or instrument which requires a register of persons holding securities (other than shares or public sector securities) to be open to inspection shall also apply to the record of uncertificated corporate securities relating to any units of those securities which are participating securities.

Miscellaneous

16. (1) . . .

(2) [Every register which an Operator is required to maintain by virtue of these Regulations] [(other than an Operator register of eligible debt securities)] which relates to securities issued by a company shall be deemed to be kept—

(a) in the case of a company registered in England and Wales, in England and Wales; or

(b) in the case of a company registered in Scotland, in Scotland.

17. (1) An entry in a register of securities or in a record of securities relating to a person who no longer holds the securities which are the subject of the entry may be removed from the register or the record (as the case may be) after the expiration of 20 years beginning with the day on which the person ceased to hold any of those securities.

(2) Subparagraph (1) does not apply in respect of an entry in a register of members.

18. [Sections 1134, 1135 and 1138 of the 2006 Act] shall apply—

(a) to any register, record or index required to be kept by any person in accordance with these Regulations as they apply to any register, record or index required by the Companies Acts to be kept by a company; and

(b) to an Operator and its officers as they apply to a company and its officers.

19. (1) Such sanctions as apply to a company and its officers in the event of a default in complying with [section 113 of the 2006 Act] shall apply to an Operator and his officers in the event of a default in complying with paragraph 4, 12 or 14.

(2) Such sanctions as apply to the registrar, within the meaning of the 1974 Regulations, in the event of a default in complying with regulation 5 of those Regulations shall apply to a participating issuer and his officers in the event of a default in complying with paragraph 13 in respect of a local authority security [falling within paragraph (a)(i) of the definition of "local authority security" in regulation 3(1)].

[(2A) . . .]

(3) Such sanctions as apply in the event of a default in complying with the requirement to maintain a register imposed by the relevant enactment or instrument referred to in Regulation 22(1) shall apply to—

- (a) a participating issuer other than a company; and
- (b) a participating issuer which is a company, in relation to so much of the record of uncertificated corporate securities as does not relate to debentures,

and his officers in the event of a default in complying with paragraph 15.

(4) Subparagraphs (2) and (3) shall not apply to any of the following or its officers—

- (a) the Crown;
- (b) any person acting on behalf of the Crown;
- [(c) the Bank of England;
- (d) the Registrar of Government Stock;
- (e) any previous Registrar of Government Stock; or
- (f) in respect of a security which immediately before it became a participating security was transferable by exempt transfer within the meaning of the Stock Transfer Act 1982, a participating issuer].

20. An officer of a participating issuer shall be in default in complying with, or in contravention of paragraph 2, 5, 6, 7, 13 or 15, or [section 1138 of the 2006 Act] as applied by paragraph 18, if, and only if, he knowingly and wilfully authorised or permitted the default or contravention.

21. An officer of an Operator shall be in default in complying with, or in contravention of, the provisions referred to in paragraph 19(1) of this Schedule, or of [section 1138 of the 2006 Act] as applied by paragraph 18, if, and only if, he knowingly and wilfully authorised or permitted the default or contravention.

NOTES

Paras 2–5, 8–11, 14, 15, 18, 20, 21: words in square brackets substituted by the Companies Act 2006 (Consequential Amendments) (Uncertificated Securities) Order 2009, SI 2009/1889, art 2(1), (21)(a)–(f), (o)–(v), (y), (aa), (bb), as from 1 October 2009.

Para 6: words in square brackets substituted, and words omitted revoked, by SI 2009/1889, art 2(1), (21)(g)–(k), as from 1 October 2009.

Para 7: words in square brackets substituted by SI 2009/1889, art 2(1), (21)(l)–(n), as from 1 October 2009. Note that art 2(1), (21)(n) actually provided "in paragraph 7(5), for "Section 354(4)" substitute "Section 115(5) and (6)". It is believed that references to the '1985 Act' and '2006 Act' were inadvertently omitted from this sub-paragraph.

Para 12: word "general" in square brackets (in every place that it occurs) substituted by the Uncertificated Securities (Amendment) (Eligible Debt Securities) Regulations 2003, SI 2003/1633, regs 6(5)(a), (b), 7, 8(4)(a), as from 24 June 2003. Sub-para (2) substituted by the Government Stock (Consequential and Transitional Provision) (No 2) Order 2004, SI 2004/1662, art 2, Schedule, Pt 3, para 29(1), (6)(a), as from 1 July 2004.

Para 13: word "general" in square brackets (in every place that it occurs) substituted by SI 2003/1633, regs 6(5)(c), (d), 7, as from 24 June 2003. Final words in square brackets in sub-para (2) substituted by SI 2004/1662, art 2, Schedule, Pt 3, para 29(1), (6)(b), as from 1 July 2004.

Para 16: sub-para (1) revoked, and words in first pair of square brackets in sub-para (2) substituted, by SI 2009/1889, art 2(1), (21)(w), (x), as from 1 October 2009. Words in second pair of square brackets in sub-para (2) inserted by SI 2003/1633, reg 13, as from 24 June 2003.

Para 19: words in square brackets in sub-para (1) substituted by SI 2009/1889, art 2(1), (21)(z), as from 1 October 2009. Words in square brackets in sub-para (2) and the whole of sub-para (2A) originally inserted by SI 2003/1633, reg 8(4)(b), (c), as from 24 June 2003. Sub-para (2A) subsequently revoked by the Local Authorities (Capital Finance) (Further Consequential and Saving Provisions) Order 2004, SI 2004/2044, art 6(3), as from 1 October 2004. Sub-para (4)(c)–(f) substituted, for original sub-para (4)(c), (d), by SI 2004/1662, art 2, Schedule, Pt 3, para 29(1), (6)(c), as from 1 July 2004.

SCHEDULES 5–7

(Sch 5 revoked by the Companies Act 2006 (Consequential Amendments) (Uncertificated Securities) Order 2009, SI 2009/1889, art 2(1), (22), as from 1 October 2009; Sch 6 contains transitory modifications of these Regulations which had effect until the date upon which the Financial Services and Markets Act 2000, s 19 came into force (this was 1 December 2001 and this Schedule is now regarded as spent); Sch 7 (minor and consequential amendments to statutes and secondary legislation); in so far as these are relevant to this work, they have been incorporated at the appropriate place.)

COMPANIES (AUDIT, INVESTIGATIONS AND COMMUNITY ENTERPRISE) ACT 2004 (COMMENCEMENT) AND COMPANIES ACT 1989 (COMMENCEMENT NO 18) ORDER 2004

(SI 2004/3322)

NOTES

Made: 9 December 2004.

Authority: CA 1989, s 215(2); Companies (Audit, Investigations and Community Enterprise) Act 2004, s 65.

ARRANGEMENT OF ARTICLES

[6.90]
1 Citation and interpretation

(1) This Order may be cited as the Companies (Audit, Investigations and Community Enterprise) Act 2004 (Commencement) and Companies Act 1989 (Commencement No 18) Order 2004.

(2) In this Order—

"the 1985 Act" means the Companies Act 1985; and

"the 2004 Act" means the Companies (Audit, Investigations and Community Enterprise) Act 2004.

(3) References in articles 3 to 11 to sections are references to those sections of the 1985 Act; and the references in article 3 to Schedule 4A and in article 7 to Schedule 24 are references to those Schedules to that Act.

(4) References in this Order to old sections of the 1985 Act are references to the sections in question as they had effect before their amendment by the 2004 Act; and references to new sections of that Act are references to the sections in question as inserted by the 2004 Act.

[6.91]
2 Commencement

(1) Section 46 of and Schedule 13 to the Companies Act 1989 and the provisions of the 2004 Act set out in Schedule 1 hereto shall come into force on 1st January 2005.

(2) The provisions of the 2004 Act set out in Schedule 2 hereto shall, subject to articles 4 to 13 below, come into force on 6th April 2005.

(3) The provisions of the 2004 Act set out in Schedule 3 hereto shall come into force on 1st July 2005.

(4) The provisions of the 2004 Act set out in Schedule 4 hereto shall, subject to article 3 below, come into force on 1st October 2005.

[6.92]
3 Transitional provision for section 7 of the 2004 Act

New section 390B, and the repeal of old section 390A(3) and of words in paragraph 1(1) of Schedule 4A relating thereto, shall have no effect in relation to the accounts of a company for a financial year beginning before 1st October 2005.

[6.93]
4 Transitional provision for section 9 of the 2004 Act

New sections 234(2A) and 234ZA shall not apply in relation to any report of the directors of a company prepared under section 234 concerning a financial year beginning before 1st April 2005 or ending before 6th April 2005.

[6.94]
5 Transitional provision for section 19 of the 2004 Act

New section 309A shall have no effect in relation to provisions made before 29th October 2004 which are not void under old section 310.

[6.95]
6 Authorisations under old section 447 of the 1985 Act effective immediately before 6th April 2005

An authorisation under old section 447(3) which was effective immediately before 6th April 2005 shall have effect on and after 6th April 2005 as though it were an authorisation under new section 447(3).

[6.96]
7 Outstanding requirements under old section 447 of the 1985 Act

(1) An outstanding requirement imposed under old section 447 shall be treated, on and after 6th April 2005, as a requirement imposed under new section 447, whether or not the requirement could have been imposed under new section 447.

(2) But old section 447(6) and (7) shall apply, and section 453C shall not apply, in relation to a failure to comply with such an outstanding requirement.

(3) The following shall continue to have effect for the purposes of paragraph (2):

- (a) the references to section 447 in sections 732, 733 and 734; and
- (b) the entry in Schedule 24 relating to old section 447(6).

(4) Where a person provides information on or after 6th April 2005 in purported compliance with an outstanding requirement and in doing so commits an offence under section 451, the court, on summary conviction of that person for that offence, may not impose a term of imprisonment greater than six months.

(5) For the purposes of this article, an outstanding requirement is a requirement imposed under old section 447, either in directions given by the Secretary of State or by a person authorised by the Secretary of State, which—

- (a) was imposed before 6th April 2005;
- (b) was required to be complied with on or after that date; and
- (c) had not been complied with before that date.

[6.97]

8 Power to take copies of or extracts from documents produced under old section 447 of the 1985 Act before 6th April 2005

The powers in new section 447(7) are exercisable on and after 6th April 2005 in relation to any document produced before that date in pursuance of old section 447.

[6.98]

9 Use in evidence of statements made in compliance with requirements under section 447 of the 1985 Act

(1) Subsections (8) to (8B) of old section 447 continue to have effect on and after 6th April 2005 in relation to any statement made before that date as if the reference in subsection (8B)(a) to section 451 were a reference to old or new section 451.

(2) In its application to any statement made on or after 6th April 2005 by a person in compliance with an outstanding requirement imposed under old section 447 or a requirement imposed under new section 447, section 447A has effect as if the relevant offences in section 447A(3) included the offences under old sections 451 and 447(6).

[6.99]

10 Security of information obtained under old section 447 of the 1985 Act

New section 449 applies, and old section 449 does not apply, to information to which old section 449(1) applied immediately before 6th April 2005.

[6.100]

11 Power to enter and remain on premises: persons authorised under old section 447 of the 1985 Act

For the purposes of sections 453A and 453B, and for the purposes of section 453C as it relates to section 453A, an investigator includes a person authorised for the purposes of old section 447 whose authorisation was effective immediately before 6th April 2005.

[6.101]

12 Use of information obtained under the 1985 Act for the purposes of proceedings under section 8 of the Company Directors Disqualification Act 1986

The references to sections 447 and 448 of the 1985 Act in section 8(1A)(b)(i) of the Company Directors Disqualification Act 1986 are references to either the old or the new sections.

[6.102]

13 Use of information obtained under Part 14 of the 1985 Act for the purposes of proceedings under section 124A of the Insolvency Act 1986

The reference to information obtained under Part 14 of the 1985 Act in section 124A(1)(a) of the Insolvency Act 1986, insofar as it is a reference to information obtained under section 447 or 448 of the 1985 Act, is a reference to information obtained either the old or the new section.

SCHEDULES 1–4

(Sch 1 brings the following provisions of the 2004 Act into force on 1 January 2005: ss 3–5, 10, 13, 14, 16–18, 25 (in respect of the provisions of Sch 2 mentioned below), 27, 64 (in respect of the provisions of Sch 8 mentioned below), Sch 2, paras 1, 3, 4, Sch 3, and Sch 8 (in respect of the entries relating to the 1985 Act, ss 245C(6), 256(3), CA 1989, s 48(3), the Companies (Northern Ireland) Order 1990, the Competition Act 1998, the Competition Act 1998 (Competition Commission) Transitional, Consequential and Supplemental Provisions Order 1999, and the Enterprise Act 2002); Sch 2 brings the following provisions of the 2004 Act into force on 6 April 2005: ss 1, 2, 6, 8, 9, 11, 12, 15, 19–24, 25 (in respect of the provisions of Sch 2 mentioned below), 64 (in respect of the provisions of Sch 8 mentioned below), Sch 1, Sch 2, paras 2, 5–24, 25 (except in respect of paras 40 and 45 of new Sch 15D to the 1985 Act), 26–28, 30, 31, and Sch 8 (in respect of the entries relating to the 1985 Act, ss 310, 734(1), Sch 24, IA 1986, IA 1986, CA 1989, ss 63, 65, 67, 69, 120, the Friendly Societies Act 1992, the Pensions Act 1995, the Bank of England Act 1998, and the Youth Justice and Criminal Evidence Act 1999); Sch 3 brings the following provisions of the 2004 Act into force on 1 July 2005: ss 25 (so far as not already in force), 26, 28–63, 64 (in respect of the provisions of Sch 8 mentioned below), Sch 2 (so far as not already in force), Schs 4–7, and Sch 8 (in respect of the entry relating to the 1985 Act, s 27(4)); Sch 4 brings the following provisions of the 2004 Act into force on 1 October 2005: ss 7, 64 (so far as not already in force), Sch 8 (so far as not already in force).)

COMPANIES ACT 1985 (POWER TO ENTER AND REMAIN ON PREMISES: PROCEDURAL) REGULATIONS 2005

(SI 2005/684)

NOTES

Made: 9 March 2005.

Authority: Companies Act 1985, s 453B(4), (7).

Commencement: 6 April 2005.

Limited liability partnerships: these Regulations apply, with modifications, to limited liability partnerships; see the Limited Liability Partnerships Regulations 2001, SI 2001/1090, reg 10, Sch 6, Pt I (at **[10.114]**).

[6.103]

1 Citation, commencement and interpretation

(1) These Regulations may be cited as the Companies Act 1985 (Power to Enter and Remain on Premises: Procedural) Regulations 2005 and shall come into force on 6 April 2005.

(2) In these Regulations "the 1985 Act" means the Companies Act 1985.

(3) References in regulations 2 and 3 to sections are references to those sections of the 1985 Act.

[6.104]

2 Prescribed contents of the written statement given under section 453B(4) or sent under section 453B(5)

The written statement which section 453B(4) requires the inspector or investigator to give to an appropriate recipient (or which section 453B(5), where it applies, requires him to send to the company) must contain the following information—

(a) a statement that the inspector or investigator has been appointed or (as the case may be) authorised by the Secretary of State to carry out an investigation and a reference to the enactment under which that appointment or authorisation was made;

(b) a statement that the inspector or investigator has been authorised by the Secretary of State under section 453A to exercise the powers in that section;

(c) a description of the conditions which are required by section 453A(1) to be satisfied before an inspector or investigator can act under section 453A(2);

(d) a description of the powers in sub-section 453A(2);

(e) a statement that the inspector or investigator must, at the time he seeks to enter premises under section 453A, produce evidence of his identity and evidence of his appointment or authorisation (as the case may be);

(f) a statement that any person accompanying the inspector or investigator when the inspector or investigator seeks to enter the premises must, at that time, produce evidence of his identity;

(g) a statement that entry to premises under section 453A may be refused to an inspector, investigator or other person who fails to produce the evidence referred to (in the case of an inspector or investigator) in paragraph (e) or (in the case of any other person) in paragraph (f);

(h) a statement that the company, occupier and the persons present on the premises may be required by the inspector or investigator, while he is on the premises, to comply with any powers the inspector or investigator may have by virtue of his appointment or authorisation (as the case may be) to require documents or information;

(i) a statement that the inspector or investigator is not permitted to use any force in exercising his powers under section 453A and is not permitted during the course of his visit to search the premises or to seize any document or other thing on the premises;

(j) a description of the effect of section 453C as it relates to a requirement imposed by an inspector or investigator under section 453A;

(k) a statement that it is an offence under section 453A(5) intentionally to obstruct an inspector, investigator or other person lawfully acting under section 453A;

(l) a description of the inspector's or investigator's obligations under section 453B(6) and (7) to prepare a written record of the visit and to give a copy of the record, when requested, to the company and any other occupier of the premises; and

(m) information about how any person entitled under section 453B(6) to receive a copy of that record can request it.

[6.105]

3 Prescribed contents of the written record prepared under section 453B(6)

The written record which section 453B(6) requires an inspector or investigator to prepare must contain the following information—

(a) the name by which the company in relation to which the powers under section 453A were exercised was registered at the time of the authorisation under section 453A(1)(a);

(b) the company's registered number at that time;

(c) the postal address of the premises visited;

(d) the name of the inspector or investigator who visited the premises and the name of any person accompanying him;

(e) the date and time when the inspector or investigator entered the premises and the duration of his visit;

(f) the name (if known by the inspector or investigator) of the person to whom the inspector or investigator and any person accompanying him produced evidence of their identity under section 453B(3);

(g) the name (if known by the inspector or investigator) of the person to whom the inspector or investigator produced evidence of his appointment or authorisation (as the case may be) as required by section 453B(3);

(h) if the inspector or investigator does not know the name of the person to whom he produced evidence of his identity and appointment or authorisation as required by section 453B(3), an account of how he produced that evidence under that section;

(i) if the inspector or investigator does not know the name of the person to whom any person accompanying the inspector or investigator produced evidence of his identity under section 453B(3), an account of how that evidence was produced under that section;

(j) the name (if known by the inspector or investigator) of the person who admitted the inspector or investigator to the premises or, if the inspector or investigator does not know that person's name, an account of how he was admitted to the premises;

(k) the name (if known by the inspector or investigator) of every appropriate recipient to whom the inspector or investigator, while on the premises, gave a written statement of powers, rights and obligations as required by section 453B(4);

(l) if the inspector or investigator does not know the name of a person referred to in paragraph (k), an account of how the written statement was given to that person;

(m) the name (if known by the inspector or investigator) of any person physically present on the premises (to the inspector's or investigator's knowledge) at any time during the inspector's or investigator's visit (other than another inspector or investigator, a person accompanying the inspector or investigator or a person referred to in paragraph (k)) and with whom the inspector or investigator communicated in relation to the inspector's or investigator's presence on the premises;

(n) a record of any apparent failure by any person during the course of the inspector's or investigator's visit to the premises to comply with any requirement imposed by the inspector or investigator under Part 14 of the 1985 Act; and

(o) a record of any conduct by any person during the course of the inspector's or investigator's visit to the premises which the inspector or investigator believes amounted to the intentional obstruction of him, or anyone accompanying him, in the lawful exercise of the power to enter and remain on the premises under section 453A.

COMMUNITY INTEREST COMPANY REGULATIONS 2005

(SI 2005/1788)

NOTES

Made: 30 June 2005.

Authority: Companies (Audit, Investigations and Community Enterprise) Act 2004, ss 30(1)–(4), (7), 31, 32(3), (4), (6), 34(3), 35(4)–(6), 36(2), 37(7), 47(12), (13), 57(1), (2), 58, 59(1), 62(2), (3), Sch 4, para 4.

Commencement: 1 July 2005.

These Regulations are reproduced as amended by: the Charities and Trustee Investment (Scotland) Act 2005 (Consequential Provisions and Modifications) Order 2006, SI 2006/242; the Companies Act 2006 (Commencement No 2, Consequential Amendments, Transitional Provisions and Savings) Order 2007, SI 2007/1093; the Companies Act 2006 (Consequential Amendments etc) Order 2008, SI 2008/948; the Community Interest Company (Amendment) Regulations 2009, SI 2009/1942; the Housing and Regeneration Act 2008 (Consequential Provisions) (No 2) Order 2010, SI 2010/671; the Community Interest Company (Amendment) Regulations 2012, SI 2012/2335; the Financial Services Act 2012 (Mutual Societies) Order 2013, SI 2013/496; the Co-operative and Community Benefit Societies and Credit Unions Act 2010 (Consequential Amendments) Regulations 2014, SI 2014/1815; the Community Interest Company (Amendment) Regulations 2014, SI 2014/2483; the Companies (Miscellaneous Reporting) Regulations 2018, SI 2018/860.

ARRANGEMENT OF REGULATIONS

PART 4
PRESCRIBED DOCUMENTS

PART 5
ALTERATION OF OBJECTS

PART 6
RESTRICTIONS ON DISTRIBUTIONS AND INTEREST

PART 7
COMMUNITY INTEREST COMPANY REPORT

PART 8
MANAGERS

PART 9
THE REGISTRAR OF COMPANIES

PART 10
FEES

PART 11
THE APPEAL OFFICER

SCHEDULES

PART 1 CITATION, COMMENCEMENT AND INTERPRETATION

[6.106]

1 Citation and commencement

These Regulations may be cited as the Community Interest Company Regulations 2005 and shall come into force on 1 July 2005.

[6.107]

2 Interpretation

In these Regulations—

["the 1965 Act" means the Industrial and Provident Societies Act 1965;]

["the 1969 Northern Ireland Act" means the Industrial and Provident Societies Act (Northern Ireland) 1969;]

. . .

[. . .]

"the 2004 Act" means the Companies (Audit, Investigations and Community Enterprise) Act 2004;

["the 2006 Act" means the Companies Act 2006;]

"aggregate dividend cap" means a cap set under regulation 22 for the purposes of determining maximum aggregate dividends;

"appellant" means, in respect of an appeal to the Appeal Officer, the person bringing the appeal;

. . .

"applicable interest cap" has the meaning given in regulation 21(3);

"asset-locked body" means—

(a) a community interest company, [a charity or a [permitted society]]; or

(b) a body established outside [the United Kingdom] that is equivalent to [either of those];

["the Authority" means the [Financial Conduct Authority];]

"community interest statement" means a statement in a form approved by the Regulator which—

(a) contains a declaration that the company will carry on its activities for the benefit of the community or a section of the community; and

(b) indicates how it is proposed that the company's activities will benefit the community (or a section of the community);

"distributable profits" means, in relation to a company, its accumulated, realised profits, so far as not previously utilised by distribution or capitalisation, less its accumulated, realised losses, so far as not previously written off in a reduction or reorganisation of capital duly made . . .

"election" means any election to public office held in [the United Kingdom] or elsewhere;

"employee" means a person who has entered into or works under (or, where the employment has ceased, worked under)—

(a) a contract of service or apprenticeship; or

(b) a contract for services under which it is agreed that a specified individual is to perform services, whether express or implied, and (if it is express) whether oral or in writing;

"employer" means the person by whom an employee is (or, where the employment has ceased, was) employed;

"exempt dividend" has the meaning given in regulation 17(3);

["governmental authority" includes—

(a) any national, regional or local government in the United Kingdom or elsewhere;

(b) the [European Union];

(c) any inter-governmental organisation; and

(d) any organisation which is able to make rules or adopt decisions which are legally binding on any governmental authority falling within sub-paragraph (a), (b) or (c);

or any of their organs, institutions or agencies;]

"interest cap" means a cap set under regulation 22 for the purpose of determining the maximum rate of interest payable under regulation 21;

"manager" means a person appointed by order under section 47(1) of the 2004 Act;

"maximum aggregate dividend" has the meaning given to it in regulation 19;

. . .

"paid up value" means, in respect of any share in a company, the sum of—

(a) so much of the share's nominal value as has been paid up; and

(b) any premium on that share paid to the company;

["permitted society" means a registered society which has a restriction on the use of its assets in accordance with regulation 4 of the Community Benefit Societies (Restriction on Use of Assets) Regulations 2006 or regulation 4 of the Community Benefit Societies (Restriction on Use of Assets) Regulations (Northern Ireland) 2006;]

"performance-related rate" means any rate which is linked to the company's profits or turnover or to any item in the balance sheet of the company;

"political party" includes any person standing, or proposing to stand, as a candidate at any election, and any person holding public office following his election to that office;

"political campaigning organisation" means any person carrying on, or proposing to carry on activities—

(a) to promote, or oppose, changes in any law applicable in [the United Kingdom] or elsewhere, or any policy of a governmental or public authority (unless such activities are incidental to other activities carried on by that person); or

(b) which could reasonably be regarded as intended to affect public support for a political party, or to influence voters in relation to any election or referendum (unless such activities are incidental to other activities carried on by that person);

["public authority" includes—

(a) a court or tribunal; and

(b) any person certain of whose functions are functions of a public nature,

whether in the United Kingdom or elsewhere;]

["quoted company" has the meaning given by section 385 of the 2006 Act;]

"referendum" includes any national or regional referendum or other poll held in pursuance of any provision made by or under the law of any state on one or more questions or propositions specified in or in accordance with any such provision;

["registered society" means—

(a) a registered society within the meaning given by section 1(1) of the Co-operative and Community Benefit Societies Act 2014; or

(b) a society registered or deemed to be registered under the Industrial and Provident Societies Act (Northern Ireland) 1969;]

"relevant company" means a community interest company which is a company limited by shares or a company limited by guarantee with a share capital;

. . .

"subsidiary" has the meaning [given to it by section 1159 of the 2006 Act]; . . .

. . .

NOTES

Definitions "the 1965 Act", "the 1969 Northern Ireland Act", "the Authority" inserted by the Community Interest Company (Amendment) Regulations 2009, SI 2009/1942, reg 3(1), (2), as from 1 October 2009.

Definition "the 1985 Act" (omitted) revoked by SI 2009/1942, reg 3(1), (3), as from 1 October 2009.

Definition "the 1986 Order" (omitted) originally inserted by the Companies Act 2006 (Commencement No 2, Consequential Amendments, Transitional Provisions and Savings) Order 2007, SI 2007/1093, art 6(2), Sch 4, Pt 2, para 27(a), as from 6 April 2007; and subsequently revoked by SI 2009/1942, reg 3(1), (3), as from 1 October 2009.

Definition "the 2006 Act" inserted by the Companies Act 2006 (Consequential Amendments etc) Order 2008, SI 2008/948, art 3(1), Sch 1, Pt 2, para 242(1), (2), as from 6 April 2008.

Definitions "applicable share dividend cap", "maximum dividend per share", "share dividend cap", "unused dividend capacity" (all omitted) revoked, and the word omitted from the definition "subsidiary" revoked, by the Community Interest Company (Amendment) Regulations 2014, SI 2014/2483, regs 2, 3, as from 1 October 2014, in relation to any dividend declared, or proposed to be declared, on or after that date.

Words in first (outer) pair of square brackets in definition "asset-locked body" substituted by SI 2009/1942, reg 3(1), (4), as from 1 October 2009. Words in second (inner) pair of square brackets substituted by the Co-operative and Community Benefit Societies and Credit Unions Act 2010 (Consequential Amendments) Regulations 2014, SI 2014/1815, reg 2, Schedule, para 16(1), (4)(a), as from 1 August 2014. Other words in square brackets substituted by SI 2007/1093, art 6(2), Sch 4, Pt 2, para 27(b), as from 6 April 2007.

Words in square brackets in definition "the Authority" substituted by the Financial Services Act 2012 (Mutual Societies) Order 2013, SI 2013/496, art 2(c), Sch1, para 14, as from 1 April 2013.

Words omitted from the definition "distributable profits" revoked by SI 2008/948, art 3(1), Sch 1, Pt 2, para 242(1), (2), as from 6 April 2008.

Words in square brackets in definition "election" substituted by SI 2007/1093, art 6(2), Sch 4, Pt 2, para 27(d), as from 6 April 2007.

Definition "governmental authority" substituted by SI 2009/1942, reg 3(1), (5), as from 1 October 2009. Words in square brackets in para (b) substituted by the Treaty of Lisbon (Changes in Terminology) Order 2011, SI 2011/1043, art 4, as from 22 April 2011.

Definition "permitted society" substituted (for the original definition "permitted industrial and provident society"), and definition "registered society" inserted, by SI 2014/1815, reg 2, Schedule, para 16(1), (2), as from 1 August 2014.

Words in square brackets in definition "political campaigning organisation" substituted by SI 2007/1093, art 6(2), Sch 4, Pt 2, para 27(f), as from 6 April 2007.

Definition "public authority" substituted by SI 2009/1942, reg 3(1), (6), as from 1 October 2009.

Definition "quoted company" inserted by the Companies (Miscellaneous Reporting) Regulations 2018, SI 2018/860, regs 20, 21, as from 7 August 2018, in relation to community interest company reports for financial years ending on or after that date.

Words in square brackets in definition "subsidiary" substituted by SI 2009/1942, reg 3(1), (7), as from 1 October 2009.

Industrial and Provident Societies Act 1965: repealed by the Co-operative and Community Benefit Societies Act 2014.

PART 2 THE COMMUNITY INTEREST TEST AND EXCLUDED COMPANIES

[6.108]

3 Political activities not to be treated as being carried on for the benefit of the community

(1) For the purposes of the community interest test the following activities are to be treated as not being activities which a reasonable person might consider are activities carried on for the benefit of the community:

(a) the promotion of, or the opposition to, changes in—

(i) any law applicable in [the United Kingdom] or elsewhere; or

(ii) the policy adopted by any governmental or public authority in relation to any matter;

(b) the promotion of, or the opposition (including the promotion of changes) to, the policy which any governmental or public authority proposes to adopt in relation to any matter; and

(c) activities which can reasonably be regarded as intended or likely to—

(i) provide or affect support (whether financial or otherwise) for a political party or political campaigning organisation; or

(ii) influence voters in relation to any election or referendum.

(2) But activities of the descriptions prescribed in paragraph (1) are to be treated as being activities which a reasonable person might consider are activities carried on for the benefit of the community if—

(a) they can reasonably be regarded as incidental to other activities, which a reasonable person might consider are being carried on for the benefit the community; and

(b) those other activities cannot reasonably be regarded as incidental to activities of any of the descriptions prescribed in paragraph (1).

NOTES

Para (1): words in square brackets substituted by the Companies Act 2006 (Commencement No 2, Consequential Amendments, Transitional Provisions and Savings) Order 2007, SI 2007/1093, art 6(2), Sch 4, Pt 2, para 28, as from 6 April 2007.

[6.109]

4 Other activities not to be treated as being carried on for the benefit of the community

For the purposes of the community interest test, an activity is to be treated as not being an activity which a reasonable person might consider is an activity carried on for the benefit of the community if, or to the extent that, a reasonable person might consider that that activity benefits only the members of a particular body or the employees of a particular employer.

[6.110]

[5 Section of the community

For the purposes of the community interest test, any group of individuals may constitute a section of the community if—

(a) they share a common characteristic which distinguishes them from other members of the community; and
(b) a reasonable person might consider that they constitute a section of the community.]

NOTES

Substituted by the Community Interest Company (Amendment) Regulations 2009, SI 2009/1942, reg 4, as from 1 October 2009.

[6.111]

6 Excluded companies

For the purposes of section 35(6) of the 2004 Act, the following are excluded companies:

(a) a company which is (or when formed would be) a political party;
(b) a company which is (or when formed would be) a political campaigning organisation; or
(c) a company which is (or when formed would be) a subsidiary of a political party or of a political campaigning organisation.

[PART 2A CONVERSION TO [A REGISTERED SOCIETY]

NOTES

Part 2A (reg 6A only) was inserted by the Community Interest Company (Amendment) Regulations 2009, SI 2009/1942, reg 5, as from 1 October 2009.

Words in square brackets in the Part heading substituted by the Co-operative and Community Benefit Societies and Credit Unions Act 2010 (Consequential Amendments) Regulations 2014, SI 2014/1815, reg 2, Schedule, para 16(1), (5), as from 1 August 2014.

[6.112]

6A Becoming [a registered society]

Pursuant to section 56 of the 2004 Act, a community interest company may convert itself into a [permitted society] and section 53 of the 1965 Act and section 62 of the 1969 Northern Ireland Act apply to community interest companies, modified so that they read as follows—

(a) section 53 of the 1965 Act—

"53 Conversion of company into registered society

(1) A company registered under the Companies Acts which is a community interest company may, by special resolution, determine to convert itself into a registered society which has a restriction on use of assets in accordance with the provisions of the Community Benefit Societies (Restriction on Use of Assets) Regulations 2006; and for this purpose, in any case where the nominal value of the company's shares held by any member other than a registered society exceeds the maximum for the time being permitted by section 6(1) of this Act in the case of a member of a registered society the resolution may provide for the conversion of the shares representing that excess into a transferable loan stock bearing such rate of interest as may be fixed, and repayable on such conditions only as are determined by the resolution.

(2) Any such resolution as aforesaid shall be accompanied by a copy of the rules of the society therein referred to and shall appoint three persons, being members of the company, who, together with a director, shall sign the rules and who may either—

(a) be authorised to accept any alterations made by the Authority therein without further consulting the company; or
(b) be required to lay any such alterations before the company in general meeting for acceptance as the resolution may direct.

(2A) The following documents shall be sent to the registrar of companies—

(a) a copy of the resolution;
(b) a copy of the rules of the society therein referred to; and
(c) a statement by the Authority that, in its opinion, if those rules take effect, the company will become a registered society which has a restriction on use of assets in accordance with the provisions of the Community Benefit Societies (Restriction on Use of Assets) Regulations 2006,

and, on receiving them, the registrar of companies must forward each of the documents to the Regulator.

(2B) The Regulator must decide whether the company is eligible to cease being a community interest company.

(2C) The company is eligible to cease being a community interest company if none of the following applies—

(a) the Regulator has under section 43 of the 2004 Act appointed an auditor to audit the company's annual accounts and the audit has not been completed,

(b) civil proceedings instituted by the Regulator in the name of the company under section 44 of the 2004 Act have not been determined or discontinued,

(c) a director of the company holds office by virtue of an order under section 45 of the 2004 Act,

(d) a director of the company is suspended under section 46(3) of the 2004 Act,

(e) there is a manager in respect of the property and affairs of the company appointed under section 47 of the 2004 Act,

(f) the Official Property Holder holds property as trustee for the company,

(g) an order under section 48(2) or (3) of the 2004 Act is in force in relation to the company,

(h) a petition has been presented for the company to be wound up.

(2D) The Regulator must give notice of the decision to the company.

(2E) The Authority shall register the community interest company as a registered society under this Act if the following conditions are met—

(a) a copy of the resolution aforesaid and a copy of the rules aforesaid is delivered to the Authority;

(b) a copy of the decision of the Regulator that the company is eligible to cease being a community interest company is delivered to the Authority;

(c) the company has a restriction on use of assets in accordance with the provisions of the Community Benefit Societies (Restriction on Use of Assets) Regulations 2006.

(3) The Authority upon the registration of the society under this Act, shall give to it, in addition to an acknowledgement of registration under section 2(3) of this Act, a certificate similarly sealed or signed that the rules of the society referred to in the resolution have been registered.

(4) A copy of any such resolution as aforesaid together with a copy of the notice of the decision issued by the Regulator and the certificate issued as aforesaid by the Authority shall be sent to the registrar of companies and, upon his registering that resolution and certificate (but not the notice of the decision issued by the Regulator), the conversion shall take effect.

(5) The name under which any community interest company is registered under this section as a registered society shall not include any of the following words, expressions or abbreviations—

(a) "company",

(b) "community interest company" or (with or without full stops) the abbreviation "cic",

(c) "cwmni buddiant cymunedol" or (with or without full stops) the abbreviation "cbc",

(d) "community interest public limited company" or (with or without full stops) the abbreviation "community interest plc", or

(e) "cwmni buddiant cymunedol cyhoeddus cyfyngedig" or (with or without full stops) the abbreviation "cwmni buddiant cymunedol ccc".

(6) Subject to the next following subsection, upon the conversion of a community interest company into a registered society under this section, the registration of the company under the Companies Acts shall become void and shall be cancelled by the registrar of companies.

(7) The registration of a community interest company as a registered society shall not affect any right or claim for the time being subsisting against the company or any penalty for the time being incurred by the company; and—

(a) for the purpose of enforcing any such right, penalty or claim the company may be sued and proceeded against in the same manner as if it had not been registered as a society;

(b) any such right or claim and the liability to any such penalty shall have priority as against the property of the registered society over all other rights or claims against or liabilities of the society.

(8) In this section—

"the 2004 Act" means the Companies (Audit, Investigations and Community Enterprise) Act 2004;

"the Official Property Holder" has the meaning given in section 29 of the 2004 Act; and

"the Regulator" has the meaning given in section 27 of the 2004 Act.",

(b) *(Para (b) sets out s 62 of the Industrial and Provident Societies Act (Northern Ireland) 1969 as it applies to community interest companies, and is outside the scope of this work.)*

NOTES

Part 2A (reg 6A only) was inserted by the Community Interest Company (Amendment) Regulations 2009, SI 2009/1942, reg 5, as from 1 October 2009.

Words in square brackets (including those in the regulation heading) substituted by the Co-operative and Community Benefit Societies and Credit Unions Act 2010 (Consequential Amendments) Regulations 2014, SI 2014/1815, reg 2, Schedule, para 16(1), (5), as from 1 August 2014.

1965 Act, ie the Industrial and Provident Societies Act 1965: repealed by the Co-operative and Community Benefit Societies Act 2014.

PART 3 REQUIREMENTS CONCERNING THE [ARTICLES OF ASSOCIATION]

NOTES

Words in square brackets in the Part heading substituted by the Community Interest Company (Amendment) Regulations 2009, SI 2009/1942, reg 6(1), as from 1 October 2009.

Saving for provisions relating to community interest companies: the Companies Act 2006 (Commencement No 2, Consequential Amendments, Transitional Provisions and Savings) Order 2007, SI 2007/1093, Sch 6, para 4 provides that a community interest company in relation to which regs 7–9 of these Regulations were complied with immediately before 6 April 2007 need not alter its memorandum or articles to take account of any amendment made by that Order.

[6.113]
[7 Company without share capital

A community interest company which is a company limited by guarantee without a share capital must include in its articles the provisions prescribed by Schedule 1, but if the company is a community interest company immediately prior to 1st October 2009 it may continue to comply with Schedule 1, as Schedule 1 read immediately prior to that date.]

NOTES

Substituted by the Community Interest Company (Amendment) Regulations 2009, SI 2009/1942, reg 7, as from 1 October 2009 (for savings, see the note following the Part heading above).

[6.114]
[8 Company with share capital

A community interest company which is a company limited by shares or a company limited by guarantee with a share capital must include in its articles either—

(a) the provisions prescribed by Schedule 2; or
(b) the provisions prescribed by Schedule 3,

but if the company is a community interest company immediately prior to 1st October 2009 it may continue to comply with Schedule 2 or Schedule 3 (as the case may be), as Schedule 2 or Schedule 3 read immediately prior to that date.]

NOTES

Substituted by the Community Interest Company (Amendment) Regulations 2009, SI 2009/1942, reg 8, as from 1 October 2009 (for savings, see the note following the Part heading above).

[6.115]
9 Alternative provisions

(1) For paragraph 1(4)(a) of the provisions prescribed by Schedule 1, 2 or 3 a community interest company may substitute—

""charitable body" means [a charity or an equivalent body established outside the United Kingdom;]"

(2) If a community interest company makes the substitution permitted by paragraph (1), it must also for every reference to "asset-locked body" in paragraph 1(2) of the provisions prescribed by Schedule 1, 2 or 3 substitute a reference to "charitable body".

NOTES

Para (1): words in square brackets substituted by the Companies Act 2006 (Commencement No 2, Consequential Amendments, Transitional Provisions and Savings) Order 2007, SI 2007/1093, art 6(2), Sch 4, Pt 2, para 29, as from 6 April 2007 (for savings, see the note following the Part heading above).

[6.116]
10 Declaration of dividends

A relevant company must not include in its . . . articles any provision which purports to permit a dividend to be declared otherwise than by an ordinary or special resolution of its members.

NOTES

Words omitted revoked by the Community Interest Company (Amendment) Regulations 2009, SI 2009/1942, reg 6(2), as from 1 October 2009.

PART 4 PRESCRIBED DOCUMENTS

[6.117]
11 Prescribed formation documents

(1) For the purposes of section 36 of the 2004 Act, the prescribed formation documents are—

(a) a community interest statement signed by each person who is to be a first director of the company; and
(b) a declaration that the company, when formed, will not be an excluded company.

(2) The declaration referred to in paragraph (1)(b) must be in a form approved by the Regulator and must be made by each person who is to be a first director of the company.

[6.118]
12 Prescribed conversion documents

(1) For the purposes of section 37 of the 2004 Act, the prescribed conversion documents are—

(a) a community interest statement signed by each person who is a director of the company;
(b) a declaration that the company is not an excluded company; and
[(c) either—
(i) a declaration that the company is not a charity, . . .
(ii) in the case of a company that is an English charity, a declaration that [the Charity Commission] have given the company the written consent required by section 39 of the 2004 Act][, or]
[(iii) in the case of a company that is a Scottish charity, a declaration that the Scottish Charity Regulator, and, where applicable, the Charity Commission, has given the company the written consent required by section 40 of the 2004 Act]].

(2) The declarations referred to in sub-paragraphs (b) and (c) of paragraph (1) must be in a form approved by the Regulator and must be made by each person who is a director of the company.

NOTES

Para (1): sub-para (c) substituted by the Companies Act 2006 (Commencement No 2, Consequential Amendments, Transitional Provisions and Savings) Order 2007, SI 2007/1093, art 6(2), Sch 4, Pt 2, para 30, as from 6 April 2007. All other amendments to this sub-paragraph were made by the Community Interest Company (Amendment) Regulations 2009, SI 2009/1942, reg 9, as from 1 October 2009.

PART 5 ALTERATION OF OBJECTS

[6.119]

13 Requirement for Regulator's approval

An alteration of the [articles] of a community interest company with respect to the statement of the company's objects does not have effect except in so far as it is approved by the Regulator.

NOTES

Word in square brackets substituted by the Community Interest Company (Amendment) Regulations 2009, SI 2009/1942, reg 10, as from 1 October 2009.

[6.120]

14 Documents to be delivered to registrar of companies

(1) If [notice under section 31(2)(a) of the 2006 Act (notice of amendment of articles so as to add, remove or alter a statement of the company's objects) is given to the registrar of companies], the company must also deliver—

(a) a community interest statement; and

(b) a statement, in a form approved by the Regulator, of the steps that have been taken to bring the proposed alteration to the notice of persons affected by the company's activities.

(2) The community interest statement and the statement under paragraph (1)(b) must be signed by each person who is a director of the company.

NOTES

Para (1): words in square brackets substituted by the Community Interest Company (Amendment) Regulations 2009, SI 2009/1942, reg 11, as from 1 October 2009.

[6.121]

15 Decisions etc

(1) On receiving [notice under section 31(2)(a) of the 2006 Act], the community interest statement delivered under regulation 14(1)(a) and the statement delivered under regulation 14(1)(b), the registrar of companies must—

(a) forward a copy of each of the documents to the Regulator; and

(b) retain the documents pending the Regulator's decision.

(2) The Regulator must decide whether to approve the proposed alteration of the [articles] of the community interest company with respect to the statement of the company's objects.

(3) The Regulator may approve the proposed alteration if he considers that—

(a) the statement of the company's objects as altered by the special resolution will comply with the requirements imposed by and by virtue of section 32 of the 2004 Act;

(b) the company will satisfy the community interest test; and

(c) the company has taken reasonable steps to bring the proposed alteration to the notice of persons affected by its activities.

(4) In considering whether the company will satisfy the community interest test, the Regulator shall have regard to—

(a) the statement of the company's objects as altered by the special resolution;

(b) the community interest statement; and

(c) any other relevant considerations.

(5) The Regulator must give notice of the decision to the registrar (but the registrar is not required to record it).

(6) The registrar shall not—

[(a) register the notice under section 31(2)(a) of the 2006 Act;

(b) register any copy of the amended articles delivered pursuant to section 26(1) of that Act;]

(c) cause notice of that alteration to be published pursuant to [section 1077 of the Companies Act 2006] (public notice by registrar of receipt of documents),

unless and until the Regulator has given notice of a decision to approve the proposed alteration.

(7) If the Regulator gives notice of a decision to approve the proposed alteration, the registrar shall also—

(a) record the community interest statement; and

(b) record the statement delivered under regulation 14(1)(b).

(8) If the Regulator decides not to approve the proposed alteration of the memorandum of the community interest company with respect to the statement of the company's objects, the company may appeal to the Appeal Officer against the decision.

NOTES

Paras (1), (2): words in square brackets substituted by the Community Interest Company (Amendment) Regulations 2009, SI 2009/1942, reg 12(a), (b), as from 1 October 2009.

Para (6): sub-paras (a), (b) substituted by SI 2009/1942, reg 12(c), as from 1 October 2009. Words in square brackets in sub-para (c) substituted by SI 2007/1093, art 6(2), Sch 4, Pt 2, para 32(d), as from 6 April 2007.

[6.122]

16 Exemptions

Regulations 13 to 15 do not apply where a community interest company is to cease being a community interest company by becoming a charity or . . . and the special resolution to alter the [articles] of the company with respect to the statement of its objects is forwarded to the registrar of companies in accordance with section 54 of the 2004 Act.

NOTES

Words omitted revoked by the Companies Act 2006 (Commencement No 2, Consequential Amendments, Transitional Provisions and Savings) Order 2007, SI 2007/1093, art 6(2), Sch 4, Pt 2, para 33, as from 6 April 2007. Word in square brackets substituted by the Community Interest Company (Amendment) Regulations 2009, SI 2009/1942, reg 13, as from 1 October 2009.

PART 6 RESTRICTIONS ON DISTRIBUTIONS AND INTEREST

[6.123]

17 Declaration of dividends

(1) A relevant company may declare a dividend to its members only—

(a) to the extent that its . . . articles permit it to do so;

(b) if an ordinary or special resolution of the company's members has approved the declaration of the dividend; and

[(c) if the declaration of the dividend does not cause the total amount of all the dividends declared on shares in the relevant company for the financial year for which it is declared to exceed the maximum aggregate dividend for that financial year.]

(2) Paragraph (1)(c) does not apply to a dividend if, or to the extent that, it is an exempt dividend.

(3) A dividend declared on a share in a relevant company is an exempt dividend if one of the conditions specified in paragraph (4) and one of the conditions specified in paragraph (5) is satisfied in respect of it.

(4) The conditions specified in this paragraph are—

(a) that the dividend is declared on a share which is held by an asset-locked body (but this condition is not satisfied in respect of a share which the directors recommending the dividend are aware is being held on trust for a person who is not an asset-locked body);

(b) that the dividend is declared on a share which is held on behalf of an asset-locked body (or is believed by the directors recommending the dividend to be so held).

(5) The conditions specified in this paragraph are—

(a) that the Regulator has consented to the declaration of the dividend;

(b) that the asset-locked body by or on behalf of which the share on which the dividend is declared is held (or on behalf of which the directors declaring the dividend believe that it is held) is named in the memorandum or articles of the company as a possible recipient of the assets of the company.

(6) If a relevant company has made the substitutions prescribed in regulation 9(2), references to "asset-locked body" in this article shall have effect as if there were substituted for them references to "charitable body", with the meaning prescribed in regulation 9(1).

NOTES

Para (1): words omitted from sub-para (a) revoked by the Community Interest Company (Amendment) Regulations 2009, SI 2009/1942, reg 14, as from 1 October 2009. Sub-para (c) substituted by the Community Interest Company (Amendment) Regulations 2014, SI 2014/2483, regs 2, 4, as from 1 October 2014, in relation to any dividend declared, or proposed to be declared, on or after that date.

18 (*Revoked by the Community Interest Company (Amendment) Regulations 2014, SI 2014/2483, regs 2, 5, as from 1 October 2014, in relation to any dividend declared, or proposed to be declared, on or after that date.*)

[6.124]

19 Maximum aggregate dividend

The maximum aggregate dividend for a financial year of a relevant company is declared when the total amount of all dividends declared on its shares for that year, less the amount of any exempt dividends, equals (when expressed as a percentage of the relevant company's distributable profits) the aggregate dividend cap which had effect in relation to that company on the first day of the financial year in respect of which the dividends are declared.

20 (*Revoked by the Community Interest Company (Amendment) Regulations 2014, SI 2014/2483, regs 2, 6, as from 1 October 2014, in relation to any dividend declared, or proposed to be declared, on or after that date.*)

[6.125]

21 The interest cap

(1) This regulation applies to debentures issued by, and debts of, a community interest company in respect of which—

(a) a performance-related rate of interest is payable; and

(b) the agreement to pay interest at a performance-related rate was entered into by the company on or after the date on which it became a community interest company.

(2) In connection with debentures and debts of the kind specified in paragraph (1), a community interest company shall not be liable to pay, and shall not pay, interest at a higher rate than the applicable interest cap.

(3) The applicable interest cap is the interest cap which had effect at the time that the agreement to pay interest at a performance-related rate was made.

(4) Where the expression of the interest cap includes reference to a rate or figure determined by any person other than the company, the Regulator or the Secretary of State [(in Northern Ireland, the Department of Enterprise, Trade and Investment for Northern Ireland)], the interest payable on any debt or debenture to which the interest cap applies shall be calculated by reference to that rate or figure as it had effect at the beginning of the first day of the financial year in which the interest became due.

(5) Nothing in paragraph (2) shall be taken as releasing a community interest company from liability to pay, or as preventing a community interest company from paying—

(a) interest which accrued before the company became a community interest company; or

(b) arrears of interest which if it had been paid at the time it became due would not have breached paragraph (2).

NOTES

Para (4): words in square brackets inserted by the Companies Act 2006 (Commencement No 2, Consequential Amendments, Transitional Provisions and Savings) Order 2007, SI 2007/1093, art 6(2), Sch 4, Pt 2, para 35, as from 6 April 2007.

[6.126]

22 Initial level and subsequent variation of [dividend cap] and interest cap

(1) Subject to paragraph (3)—

(a) . . .

(b) the aggregate dividend cap shall be 35 per cent of a relevant company's distributable profits; and

(c) the interest cap shall be that percentage of the average amount of a community interest company's debt, or the sum outstanding under a debenture issued by it, during the 12 month period immediately preceding the date on which the interest on that debt or debenture becomes due (determined in accordance with Schedule 4) which is 4 percentage points higher than the Bank of England's base lending rate.

(2) For the purposes of paragraph (1), the Bank of England's base lending rate is the base lending rate most recently set by the Monetary Policy Committee of the Bank of England in connection with its responsibilities under Part II of the Bank of England Act 1998.

(3) The Regulator may from time to time, with the approval of the Secretary of State, set a new . . . aggregate dividend cap, or interest cap.

(4) A new cap set under paragraph (3)—

(a) shall not take effect from a date less than three months after it is published; and

(b) subject to paragraphs [(6) and] (7), may result in a change to both the level of any cap and the way in which it is expressed.

(5) . . .

(6) The aggregate dividend cap must be expressed as a percentage of distributable profits.

(7) The interest cap must be expressed as a percentage of the average amount of a debt, or the sum outstanding under a debenture, during the 12 month period immediately preceding the date on which the interest on that debt or debenture becomes due (determined in accordance with Schedule 4).

(8) The Secretary of State may from time to time require the Regulator to review any cap set under this regulation.

NOTES

All amendments to this regulation were made by the Community Interest Company (Amendment) Regulations 2014, SI 2014/2483, regs 2, 7, as from 1 October 2014, in relation to any dividend declared, or proposed to be declared, on or after that date.

[6.127]

23 Distribution of assets on a winding up

(1) This regulation applies where—

(a) a community interest company is wound up under the Insolvency Act 1986 [or the Insolvency (Northern Ireland) Order 1989]; and

(b) some property of the company (the "residual assets") remains after satisfaction of the company's liabilities.

(2) Subject to paragraph (3), the residual assets shall be distributed to those members of the community interest company (if any) who are entitled to share in any distribution of assets on the winding up of the company according to their rights and interests in the company.

(3) No member shall receive under paragraph (2) an amount which exceeds the paid up value of the shares which he holds in the company.

(4) If any residual assets remain after any distribution to members under paragraph (2) (the "remaining residual assets"), they shall be distributed in accordance with paragraphs (5) and (6).

(5) If the . . . articles of the company specify an asset-locked body to which any remaining residual assets of the company should be distributed, then, unless either of the conditions specified in sub-paragraphs (b) and (c) of paragraph (6) is satisfied, the remaining residual assets shall be distributed to that asset-locked body in such proportions or amounts as the Regulator shall direct.

(6) If—

(a) the . . . articles of the company do not specify an asset-locked body to which any remaining residual assets of the company should be distributed;

(b) the Regulator is aware that the asset-locked body to which the . . . articles of the company specify that the remaining residual assets of the company should be distributed is itself in the process of being wound up; or

(c) the Regulator—

(i) has received representations from a member or director of the company stating, with reasons, that the asset-locked body to which the . . . articles of the company specify that the remaining residual assets of the company should be distributed is not an appropriate recipient of the company's remaining residual assets; and

(ii) has agreed with those representations,

then the remaining residual assets shall be distributed to such asset-locked bodies, and in such proportions or amounts, as the Regulator shall direct.

(7) In considering any direction to be made under this regulation, the Regulator must—

(a) consult the directors and members of the company, to the extent that he considers it practicable and appropriate to do so; and

(b) have regard to the desirability of distributing assets in accordance with any relevant provisions of the company's . . . articles.

(8) The Regulator must give notice of any direction under this regulation to the company and the liquidator.

(9) This regulation has effect notwithstanding anything in the Insolvency Act 1986 [or the Insolvency (Northern Ireland) Order 1989].

(10) This regulation has effect subject to the provisions of the Housing Act 1996[, Part 2 of the Housing and Regeneration Act 2008] and the Housing (Scotland) Act 2001.

(11) Any member or director of the company may appeal to the Appeal Officer against a direction of the Regulator made under this regulation.

NOTES

Paras (1), (9): words in square brackets inserted by the Companies Act 2006 (Commencement No 2, Consequential Amendments, Transitional Provisions and Savings) Order 2007, SI 2007/1093, art 6(2), Sch 4, Pt 2, para 36, as from 6 April 2007.

Paras (5)–(7): words omitted revoked by the Community Interest Company (Amendment) Regulations 2009, SI 2009/1942, reg 15, as from 1 October 2009.

Para (10): words in square brackets inserted by the Housing and Regeneration Act 2008 (Consequential Provisions) (No 2) Order 2010, SI 2010/671, art 4, Sch 1, para 42, as from 1 April 2010.

[6.128]

24 Redemption and purchase of shares

A relevant company may not distribute assets to its members by way of the redemption or purchase of the company's own shares, unless the amount to be paid by the company in respect of any such share does not exceed the paid up value of the share.

[6.129]

25 Reduction of share capital

A relevant company may not distribute assets to its members by way of a reduction of the company's share capital unless—

(a) the reduction is made by extinguishing or reducing the liability of any of the members on any of the company's shares in respect of share capital not paid up; or

(b) the amount to be paid by the company to members in paying off paid up share capital does not exceed the paid up value of their respective shares.

PART 7 COMMUNITY INTEREST COMPANY REPORT

[6.130]

26 General

(1) Every community interest company report shall contain—

(a) a fair and accurate description of the manner in which the company's activities during the financial year have benefited the community;

(b) a description of the steps, if any, which the company has taken during the financial year to consult persons affected by the company's activities, and the outcome of any such consultation; and

[(c) directors' remuneration information].

[(1A) In paragraph (1)(c) "directors' remuneration information" means—

(a) in the case of a company to which the Small Companies and Groups (Accounts and Directors' Report) Regulations 2008 apply, the information specified in Schedule 4A to these Regulations;

(b) in the case of a company to which the Large and Medium-sized Companies and Groups (Accounts and Reports) Regulations 2008 apply, the information specified in Schedule 5 to those Regulations, save that the information specified in Part 2 of that Schedule need only be given in the case of a company which is not a quoted company.]

(2) If, during a financial year, a community interest company has transferred any of its assets other than for full consideration—

(a) to any asset-locked body (other than by way of an exempt dividend); or

(b) for the benefit of the community other than by way of transfer to an asset-locked body,

its community interest report for that financial year shall specify the amount, or contain a fair estimate of the value, of such transfer.

[(3) If—

(a) a community interest company has provided the information required by paragraph (1)(c) in its copy of the annual accounts for the year delivered to the registrar of companies under section 441 of the 2006 Act; and

(b) its community interest company report contains a statement that details of the remuneration of the directors of the company during the financial year may be found in the notes to the annual accounts of the company,

the community interest report need not contain the information required by paragraph (1)(c).

(4) Paragraphs (1)(c) and (3) have effect for financial years ending on or after 1st October 2009.]

NOTES

Para (1): sub-para (c) substituted by the Companies (Miscellaneous Reporting) Regulations 2018, SI 2018/860, regs 20, 22(a), as from 7 August 2018, in relation to community interest company reports for financial years ending on or after that date.

Para (1A): inserted by SI 2018/860, regs 20, 22(b), as from 7 August 2018, in relation to community interest company reports for financial years ending on or after that date.

Paras (3), (4): added by SI 2009/1942, reg 16(1), (3), as from 1 October 2009. Note that there was an original para (3), which was revoked by SI 2008/948, art 3, Sch 1, Pt 2, para 242(1), (3), Sch 2, as from 6 April 2008.

[6.131]
[27 Information about dividends

(1) This regulation applies to the community interest company report of any community interest company which has declared, or whose directors propose to declare, a dividend for the financial year to which the report relates.

(2) The report must state the amount of any dividend declared, or proposed to be declared, by the company on each of its shares for the financial year to which the report relates.

(3) The report must also explain how the declaration or proposed declaration of any dividend declared, or proposed to be declared, by the company in respect of the financial year to which the report relates complies, or will comply, with regulations 17 and 19.

(4) The explanation provided under paragraph (3) must include details of—
- (a) in the case of an exempt dividend, why it is an exempt dividend; and
- (b) in the case of any other dividend, the maximum aggregate dividend

and how each of these has been determined.]

NOTES

Substituted by the Community Interest Company (Amendment) Regulations 2014, SI 2014/2483, regs 2, 8, as from 1 October 2014, in relation to any dividend declared, or proposed to be declared, on or after that date.

[6.132]
28 Information about debts or debentures on which a performance-related rate is payable

(1) Where a community interest company has at any time during the financial year a debt outstanding, or a debenture in issue, to which regulation 21 applies, its community interest company report must state—
- (a) the rate of interest payable on that debt or debenture as calculated over a 12 month period ending with the most recent date on which interest became payable in respect of that debt or debenture during the financial year; and
- (b) the applicable interest cap applying to that debt or debenture,

and how each of these has been determined.

(2) Where the company has at any time during the financial year a debt outstanding, or a debenture in issue, to which regulation 21 does not apply, but on which a performance-related rate is payable, its community interest company report must state—
- (a) the rate of interest payable on that debt or debenture as calculated over a 12 month period ending with the most recent date on which interest became payable in respect of that debt or debenture during the financial year; and
- (b) why regulation 21 does not apply to that debt or debenture.

[6.133]
[29 Application of provisions relating to directors' report

The following provisions of the 2006 Act apply to the community interest company report as they apply to the directors' report—

section 419 (approval and signing);
sections 423 to 425, 430 to 433 and 436 (publication);
sections 437 and 438 (public companies: laying before general meeting);
. . .
section 454 (voluntary revision).]

NOTES

Substituted by the Companies Act 2006 (Consequential Amendments etc) Order 2008, SI 2008/948, art 3(1), Sch 1, Pt 2, para 242(1), (4), as from 6 April 2008.

Words omitted revoked by the Community Interest Company (Amendment) Regulations 2012, SI 2012/2335, reg 2(1), (2), as from 1 October 2012, in relation to community interest company reports for financial years ending on or after that date.

PART 8 MANAGERS

[6.134]
[29A Delivery of community interest company report to the registrar of companies

(1) The directors of a community interest company must deliver to the registrar of companies for each financial year a copy of the community interest company report.

(2) For these purposes, sections 441 to 443, 445(1) and (5), 446(1) and (3), 447(1) and (3) and 451 to 453 of the 2006 Act apply to a community interest company report as they apply to a directors' report.

(3) Sections 444(1) and (6) and 444A(1) and (3) apply to a community interest company report as they apply to a directors' report with the following modifications—
- (a) section 444(1) has effect as if the directors of a community interest company subject to the small companies regime must deliver a copy of the community interest company report for each financial year to the registrar; and
- (b) section 444A(1) has effect as if the directors of a community interest company which is entitled to the small companies exemption in relation to the directors' report for a financial year must deliver a copy of the community interest company report for that year to the registrar.]

NOTES

Inserted by the Community Interest Company (Amendment) Regulations 2012, SI 2012/2335, reg 2(1), (3), as from 1 October 2012 (in relation to community interest company reports for financial years ending on or after that date).

[6.135]

30 Remuneration

(1) The Regulator is authorised to determine the amount of a manager's remuneration.

(2) The remuneration of a manager shall be payable out of the income of the community interest company in respect of which the manager was appointed.

(3) The Regulator is authorised to disallow any amount of remuneration of a manager if—

(a) the time specified in the notice referred to in regulation 32(2) has expired; and

(b) the Regulator—

(i) has considered such representations, if any, as are duly made in response to such a notice; and

(ii) is satisfied that the manager has failed in such manner as is set out in sub-paragraph (a)(i) or (ii) of regulation 32(1) and specified in such a notice.

[6.136]

31 Security

The Regulator is authorised to require the manager to give security to him for the due discharge of the manager's functions within such time and in such form as the Regulator may specify.

[6.137]

32 Failure and removal

(1) Where—

(a) it appears to the Regulator that a manager has failed—

(i) to give security within such time or in such form as the Regulator has specified; or

(ii) satisfactorily to discharge any function imposed on the manager by or by virtue of the order by which the manager was appointed or by regulation 33; and

(b) the Regulator wishes to consider exercising his powers under regulation 30(3) or paragraph (3) of this regulation,

the Regulator shall give the manager, whether in person or by post, a written notice complying with paragraph (2).

(2) A notice given to a manager under paragraph (1) shall inform the manager of—

(a) any failure under paragraph (1)(a) in respect of which the notice is issued;

(b) the Regulator's power under regulation 30(3) to authorise the disallowance of any amount of remuneration if satisfied as to any such failure;

(c) the Regulator's power under paragraph (3) to remove the manager if satisfied as to any such failure; and

(d) the manager's right to make representations to the Regulator in respect of any such alleged failure within such reasonable time as is specified in the notice.

(3) The Regulator may remove a manager (whether or not he also exercises the power conferred by regulation 30(3)) if—

(a) the time specified in the notice referred to in paragraph (2) has expired; and

(b) the Regulator—

(i) has considered such representations, if any, as are duly made in response to such a notice; and

(ii) is satisfied that the manager has failed in such manner as is set out in paragraph (1)(a)(i) or (ii) and specified in such notice.

[6.138]

33 Reports

The manager must make such reports to the Regulator as the Regulator may from time to time require on such matters and in such form as the Regulator specifies.

PART 9 THE REGISTRAR OF COMPANIES

[6.139]

34 Modifications and amendments

[(1) The registrar of companies shall not cause to be published in the Gazette notice pursuant to section 1077 of the Companies Act 2006 of the receipt of documents under section 37C(3) or 54C(4) of the 2004 Act unless the registrar records those documents pursuant to section 38A(1)(b) or 55A(1)(b) of the 2004 Act.]

(2)–(4) . . .

NOTES

Para (1): substituted by the Community Interest Company (Amendment) Regulations 2009, SI 2009/1942, reg 17(a), as from 1 October 2009.

Para (2): amended CA 1985, ss 715A (repealed) and is therefore spent.

Para (3): revoked by the Companies Act 2006 (Commencement No 2, Consequential Amendments, Transitional Provisions and Savings) Order 2007, SI 2007/1093, art 6(2), Sch 4, Pt 2, para 39(b), as from 6 April 2007.

Para (4): revoked by SI 2009/1942, reg 17(b), as from 1 October 2009.

[6.140]

35 Documents

(1) The registrar of companies shall, on receiving any notice under section 109(1) of the Insolvency Act 1986 [or Article 95 of the Insolvency (Northern Ireland) Order 1989] (notice by liquidator of his appointment) in relation to a community interest company, provide a copy of that notice to the Regulator.

(2) The registrar of companies shall, on receiving any copy of a winding-up order forwarded under section 130(1) of the Insolvency Act 1986 [or Article 110 of the Insolvency (Northern Ireland) Order 1989] (consequences of a winding-up order) in relation to a community interest company, provide the Regulator with a copy of that winding-up order.

NOTES

Words in square brackets inserted by the Companies Act 2006 (Commencement No 2, Consequential Amendments, Transitional Provisions and Savings) Order 2007, SI 2007/1093, art 6(2), Sch 4, Pt 2, para 40, as from 6 April 2007.

PART 10 FEES

[6.141]

36 Fees payable by a community interest company

The fees set out in the second column of Schedule 5—

(a) shall be the fees payable in connection with the Regulator's functions in relation to the matters set out in the first column of that Schedule;

(b) shall be payable as stated in the third column of that Schedule; and

(c) shall be paid to the registrar of companies.

PART 11 THE APPEAL OFFICER

[6.142]

37 Time limits

(1) Unless paragraph (2) applies, an appeal to the Appeal Officer must be made by sending a notice of appeal to the Regulator so that it is received within two months of the date upon which the appellant was given reasons for the disputed order or decision in accordance with section 61(5) of the 2004 Act.

(2) When an appeal is brought against a direction of the Regulator made under regulation 23, it must be made by sending a notice of appeal to the Regulator so that it is received within three weeks of the date upon which notice of the disputed direction was given to the community interest company in accordance with regulation 23(8).

(3) On receiving the notice of appeal, the Regulator must—

(a) send an acknowledgement of its receipt to the appellant together with a copy of any statement made under paragraph (4); and

(b) forward the notice of appeal to the Appeal Officer endorsed with the date of receipt.

(4) Where paragraph (2) applies, the Regulator must forward with the notice of appeal a statement—

(a) of the date upon which notice of the disputed direction or decision was given to the community interest company in accordance with regulation 23(8); or

(b) that no such notice was given.

[6.143]

38 Notice of appeal

(1) The notice of appeal must state—

(a) the name and address of the appellant; and

(b) an address for service in [the United Kingdom].

(2) Unless regulation 37(2) applies, the notice of appeal must—

(a) specify as precisely as the appellant is able the date or dates on which the appellant was given reasons by the Regulator for the disputed order or decision; or

(b) include a statement that no such reasons were given.

(3) The notice of appeal must contain—

(a) a statement of the grounds for the appeal;

(b) details of the disputed order, decision or direction;

(c) a succinct presentation of the arguments supporting each of the grounds of appeal; and

(d) a schedule listing all the documents annexed to the notice of appeal.

(4) There shall be annexed to the notice of appeal—

(a) in the case of a disputed order or decision, a copy of any reasons given by the Regulator under section 61(5) of the 2004 Act; and

(b) as far as practicable a copy of every document on which the appellant relies.

(5) The notice of appeal must be signed and dated by the appellant, or on his behalf by his duly authorised officer or his legal representative.

NOTES

Para (1): words in square brackets substituted by the Companies Act 2006 (Commencement No 2, Consequential Amendments, Transitional Provisions and Savings) Order 2007, SI 2007/1093, art 6(2), Sch 4, Pt 2, para 41, as from 6 April 2007.

[6.144]

39 Appeal procedure etc

(1) The Regulator may make a written response to the notice of appeal.

(2) Any such written response must be sent to the Appeal Officer so that it is received by him within two weeks of the date on which the Regulator received the notice of appeal or such further time as the Appeal Officer may allow.

(3) The Appeal Officer must send a copy of the written response to the appellant.

(4) The Appeal Officer may give the appellant and the Regulator the opportunity to make further written or oral representations.

(5) The Appeal Officer may specify the time and manner in which such further representations are to be made.

(6) The Appeal Officer may—

(a) make enquiries of any person;

(b) receive representations from any person;

(c) hold any meeting or hearing; and

(d) subject to these Regulations, follow such practice and procedure,

as he thinks fit, having regard to the just, expeditious and economical conduct of the appeal.

(7) The Appeal Officer may specify the time and place at which any meeting or hearing is to be held.

[6.145]

40 Determination of appeal

In determining an appeal, the Appeal Officer shall have regard to all matters that appear to him to be relevant.

[6.146]

41 Dismissal of appeal

(1) The Appeal Officer may dismiss an appeal at any stage if he considers that—

(a) the notice of appeal discloses no valid ground of appeal;

(b) the notice of appeal fails to comply with the requirements of regulation 38; or

(c) the appellant is not entitled to bring the appeal.

(2) The Appeal Officer must dismiss an appeal if he considers that the appeal was not brought within the time limits imposed by regulation 37 unless he is satisfied that the circumstances are exceptional.

(3) The Appeal Officer may dismiss an appeal at any stage at the request of the appellant.

[6.147]

42 Reasons

(1) The Appeal Officer must give reasons for a decision to—

(a) dismiss an appeal;

(b) allow an appeal; or

(c) remit a case to the Regulator.

(2) The reasons must be given to the Regulator and to the person bringing the appeal.

(3) The Appeal Officer must make such arrangements for the publication of the decisions listed in paragraph (1) and his reasons for them as he considers appropriate.

SCHEDULES

SCHEDULE 1
PROVISIONS PRESCRIBED FOR THE . . . ARTICLES OF A COMMUNITY INTEREST COMPANY LIMITED BY GUARANTEE WITHOUT A SHARE CAPITAL

Regulation 7

[6.148]

1. (1) The company shall not transfer any of its assets other than for full consideration.

(2) Provided the conditions in sub-paragraph (3) are satisfied, sub-paragraph (1) shall not apply to—

(a) the transfer of assets to any specified asset-locked body, or (with the consent of the Regulator) to any other asset-locked body; and

(b) the transfer of assets made for the benefit of the community other than by way of a transfer of assets to an asset-locked body.

(3) The conditions are that the transfer of assets must comply with any restrictions on the transfer of assets for less than full consideration which may be set out elsewhere in the memorandum or articles of the company.

(4) In this paragraph—

(a) "asset-locked body" means—

(i) a community interest company, [a charity, or a [permitted society]]; or

(ii) a body established outside the United Kingdom that is equivalent to [either of those];

(b) "community" is to be construed in accordance with section 35(5) of the Companies (Audit, Investigations and Community Enterprise) Act 2004;

[(ba) "permitted society" means a registered society which has a restriction on the use of its assets in accordance with regulation 4 of the Community Benefit Societies (Restriction on Use of Assets) Regulations 2006 or regulation 4 of the Community Benefit Societies (Restriction on Use of Assets) Regulations (Northern Ireland) 2006;

(bb) "registered society" means—

(i) a registered society within the meaning given by section 1(1) of the Co-operative and Community Benefit Societies Act 2014; or

(ii) a society registered or deemed to be registered under the Industrial and Provident Societies Act (Northern Ireland) 1969;]

(c) . . .

(d) "the Regulator" means the Regulator of Community Interest Companies;

[(e) . . .]

(f) "specified" means specified in the memorandum or articles of association of the company for the purposes of this paragraph; and

(g) "transfer" includes every description of disposition, payment, release or distribution, and the creation or extinction of an estate or interest in, or a right over, any property.

2. (1) The subscribers to the memorandum are the first members of the company.

(2) Such other persons as are admitted to membership in accordance with the articles shall be members of the company.

(3) No person shall be admitted a member of the company unless he is approved by the directors.

(4) Every person who wishes to become a member shall deliver to the company an application for membership in such form (and containing such information) as the directors require and executed by him.

(5) Membership is not transferable to anyone else.

(6) Membership is terminated if:

(a) the member dies or ceases to exist; or
(b) otherwise in accordance with the articles.

3. (1) A person who is not a member of the company shall not have any right to vote at a general meeting of the company; but this is without prejudice to any right to vote on a resolution affecting the rights attached to a class of the company's debentures.

(2)–(5) . . .

4. (1) Questions arising at a meeting of directors shall be decided by a majority of votes . . .

(2) . . .

(3) Except as provided by sub-paragraphs (1) and (2) in all proceedings of directors each director must not have more than one vote.

NOTES

Schedule heading: words omitted revoked by the Community Interest Company (Amendment) Regulations 2009, SI 2009/1942, reg 18, as from 1 October 2009.

Para 1 is amended as follows:

Words in first (outer) pair of square brackets in sub-para (4)(a)(i) substituted, and original sub-para (ba) inserted, by SI 2009/1942, regs 19, 20, as from 1 October 2009.

Words in second (inner) pair of square brackets in sub-para (4)(a)(i) substituted, and sub-paras (ba), (bb) substituted (for the original sub-para (ba) as inserted as noted above) by the Co-operative and Community Benefit Societies and Credit Unions Act 2010 (Consequential Amendments) Regulations 2014, SI 2014/1815, reg 2, Schedule, para 16(1), (3), (4)(c), as from 1 August 2014.

Words in square brackets in sub-para (4)(a)(ii) substituted, and sub-paras (4)(c), (e) revoked, by the Companies Act 2006 (Commencement No 2, Consequential Amendments, Transitional Provisions and Savings) Order 2007, SI 2007/1093, art 6(2), Sch 4, Pt 2, para 42(a)–(c), as from 6 April 2007 (sub-para (4)(e) was previously substituted by the Charities and Trustee Investment (Scotland) Act 2005 (Consequential Provisions and Modifications) Order 2006, SI 2006/242, art 5, Schedule, Pt 2, para 12, as from 1 April 2006).

Para 3: sub-paras (2)–(5) revoked by SI 2009/1942, reg 21, as from 1 October 2009.

Para 4: words omitted from sub-para (1), and the whole of sub-para (2), revoked by SI 2009/1942, reg 22, as from 1 October 2009.

SCHEDULE 2
PROVISIONS PRESCRIBED FOR THE . . . ARTICLES OF A COMMUNITY INTEREST COMPANY LIMITED BY SHARES, OR LIMITED BY GUARANTEE WITH A SHARE CAPITAL

Regulation 8(a)

[6.149]

1. (1) The company shall not transfer any of its assets other than for full consideration.

(2) Provided the conditions in sub-paragraph (3) are satisfied, sub-paragraph (1) shall not apply to—

(a) the transfer of assets to any specified asset-locked body, or (with the consent of the Regulator) to any other asset-locked body; and
(b) the transfer of assets made for the benefit of the community other than by way of a transfer of assets to an asset-locked body.

(3) The conditions are that the transfer of assets must comply with any restrictions on the transfer of assets for less than full consideration which may be set out elsewhere in the memorandum or articles of the company.

(4) In this paragraph—

(a) "asset-locked body" means—
  (i) a community interest company, [a charity, or [permitted society]]; or
  (ii) a body established outside [the United Kingdom] that is equivalent to [either of those];
(b) "community" is to be construed in accordance with section 35(5) of the Companies (Audit, Investigations and Community Enterprise) Act 2004;
[(ba) "permitted society" means a registered society which has a restriction on the use of its assets in accordance with regulation 4 of the Community Benefit Societies (Restriction on Use of Assets) Regulations 2006 or regulation 4 of the Community Benefit Societies (Restriction on Use of Assets) Regulations (Northern Ireland) 2006;
(bb) "registered society" means—
  (i) a registered society within the meaning given by section 1(1) of the Co-operative and Community Benefit Societies Act 2014; or
  (ii) a society registered or deemed to be registered under the Industrial and Provident Societies Act (Northern Ireland) 1969;]
(c) . . .
(d) "the Regulator" means the Regulator of Community Interest Companies;
[(e) . . .]
(f) "specified" means specified in the memorandum or articles of association of the company for the purposes of this paragraph; and
(g) "transfer" includes every description of disposition, payment, release or distribution, and the creation or extinction of an estate or interest in, or a right over, any property.

2. (1) The directors may refuse to register the transfer of a share to a person of whom they do not approve.

(2) They may also refuse to register the transfer unless it is lodged at the registered office of the company or at such other place as the directors may appoint and is accompanied by such evidence as the directors may reasonably require to show the right of the transferor to make the transfer, and by such other information as they may reasonably require.

(3) If the directors refuse to register such a transfer, they shall within two months after the date on which the transfer was lodged with the company send to the transferee notice of the refusal.

(4) The provisions of this paragraph apply in addition to any restrictions on the transfer of a share which may be set out elsewhere in the memorandum or articles of the company.

3. (1) A person who is not a member of the company shall not have any right to vote at a general meeting of the company; but this is without prejudice to any right to vote on a resolution affecting the rights attached to a class of the company's debentures.

(2)–(5) . . .

4. (1) Questions arising at a meeting of directors shall be decided by a majority of votes . . .

(2) . . .

(3) Except as provided by sub-paragraphs (1) and (2) in all proceedings of directors each director must not have more than one vote.

NOTES

Schedule heading: words omitted revoked by the Community Interest Company (Amendment) Regulations 2009, SI 2009/1942, reg 18, as from 1 October 2009.

Para 1 is amended as follows:

Words in first (outer) pair of square brackets in sub-para (4)(a)(i) substituted, and original sub-para (ba) inserted, by SI 2009/1942, regs 19, 20, as from 1 October 2009.

Words in second (inner) pair of square brackets in sub-para (4)(a)(i) substituted, and sub-paras (ba), (bb) substituted (for the original sub-para (ba) as inserted as noted above) by the Co-operative and Community Benefit Societies and Credit Unions Act 2010 (Consequential Amendments) Regulations 2014, SI 2014/1815, reg 2, Schedule, para 16(1), (3), (4)(c), as from 1 August 2014.

Words in square brackets in sub-para (4)(a)(ii) substituted, and sub-paras (4)(c), (e) revoked, by the Companies Act 2006 (Commencement No 2, Consequential Amendments, Transitional Provisions and Savings) Order 2007, SI 2007/1093, art 6(2), Sch 4, Pt 2, para 43(a)–(c), as from 6 April 2007 (sub-para (4)(e) was previously substituted by the Charities and Trustee Investment (Scotland) Act 2005 (Consequential Provisions and Modifications) Order 2006, SI 2006/242, art 5, Schedule, Pt 2, para 12, as from 1 April 2006).

Para 3: sub-paras (2)–(5) revoked by SI 2009/1942, reg 21, as from 1 October 2009.

Para 4: words omitted from sub-para (1), and the whole of sub-para (2), revoked by SI 2009/1942, reg 22, as from 1 October 2009.

SCHEDULE 3
ALTERNATIVE PROVISIONS PRESCRIBED FOR THE . . . ARTICLES OF A COMMUNITY INTEREST COMPANY LIMITED BY SHARES, OR LIMITED BY GUARANTEE WITH A SHARE CAPITAL

Regulation 8(b)

[6.150]

1. (1) The company shall not transfer any of its assets other than for full consideration.

(2) Provided the conditions in sub-paragraph (3) are satisfied, sub-paragraph (1) shall not apply to—

(a) the transfer of assets to any specified asset-locked body, or (with the consent of the Regulator) to any other asset-locked body;

(b) the transfer of assets made for the benefit of the community other than by way of a transfer of assets to an asset-locked body;

(c) the payment of dividends in respect of shares in the company;

(d) the distribution of assets on a winding up;

(e) payments on the redemption or purchase of the company's own shares;

(f) payments on the reduction of share capital; and

(g) the extinguishing or reduction of the liability of members in respect of share capital not paid up on the reduction of share capital.

(3) The conditions are that the transfer of assets—

(a) must comply with any restrictions on the transfer of assets for less than full consideration which may be set out elsewhere in the memorandum or articles of the company; and

(b) must not exceed any limits imposed by, or by virtue of, Part 2 of the Companies (Audit, Investigations and Community Enterprise) Act 2004.

(4) In this paragraph—

(a) "asset-locked body" means—

(i) a community interest company, [a charity, or [permitted society]]; or

(ii) a body established outside [the United Kingdom] that is equivalent to [either of those];

(b) "community" is to be construed in accordance with section 35(5) of the Companies (Audit, Investigations and Community Enterprise) Act 2004;

[(ba) "permitted society" means a registered society which has a restriction on the use of its assets in accordance with regulation 4 of the Community Benefit Societies (Restriction on Use of Assets) Regulations 2006 or regulation 4 of the Community Benefit Societies (Restriction on Use of Assets) Regulations (Northern Ireland) 2006;

(bb) "registered society" means—

(i) a registered society within the meaning given by section 1(1) of the Co-operative and Community Benefit Societies Act 2014; or

(ii) a society registered or deemed to be registered under the Industrial and Provident Societies Act (Northern Ireland) 1969;]

(c) . . .

(d) "the Regulator" means the Regulator of Community Interest Companies;

[(e) . . .]

(f) "specified" means specified in the memorandum or articles of association of the company for the purposes of this paragraph; and

(g) "transfer" includes every description of disposition, payment, release or distribution, and the creation or extinction of an estate or interest in, or a right over, any property.

2. (1) The directors may refuse to register the transfer of a share to a person of whom they do not approve.

(2) They may also refuse to register the transfer unless it is lodged at the registered office of the company or at such other place as the directors may appoint and is accompanied by such evidence as the directors may reasonably require to show the right of the transferor to make the transfer, and by such other information as they may reasonably require.

(3) If the directors refuse to register such a transfer, they shall within two months after the date on which the transfer was lodged with the company send to the transferee notice of the refusal.

(4) The provisions of this paragraph apply in addition to any restrictions on the transfer of a share which may be set out elsewhere in the memorandum or articles of the company.

3. (1) A person who is not a member of the company shall not have any right to vote at a general meeting of the company; but this is without prejudice to any right to vote on a resolution affecting the rights attached to a class of the company's debentures.

(2)–(5) . . .

4. (1) Questions arising at a meeting of directors shall be decided by a majority of votes . . .

(2) . . .

(3) Except as provided by sub-paragraphs (1) and (2) in all proceedings of directors each director must not have more than one vote.

NOTES

Schedule heading: words omitted revoked by the Community Interest Company (Amendment) Regulations 2009, SI 2009/1942, reg 18, as from 1 October 2009.

Para 1 is amended as follows:

Words in first (outer) pair of square brackets in sub-para (4)(a)(i) substituted, and original sub-para (ba) inserted, by SI 2009/1942, regs 19, 20, as from 1 October 2009.

Words in second (inner) pair of square brackets in sub-para (4)(a)(i) substituted, and sub-paras (ba), (bb) substituted (for the original sub-para (ba) as inserted as noted above) by the Co-operative and Community Benefit Societies and Credit Unions Act 2010 (Consequential Amendments) Regulations 2014, SI 2014/1815, reg 2, Schedule, para 16(1), (3), (4)(c), as from 1 August 2014.

Words in square brackets in sub-para (4)(a)(ii) substituted, and sub-paras (4)(c), (e) revoked, by the Companies Act 2006 (Commencement No 2, Consequential Amendments, Transitional Provisions and Savings) Order 2007, SI 2007/1093, art 6(2), Sch 4, Pt 2, para 44(a)–(c), as from 6 April 2007 (sub-para (4)(e) was previously substituted by the Charities and Trustee Investment (Scotland) Act 2005 (Consequential Provisions and Modifications) Order 2006, SI 2006/242, art 5, Schedule, Pt 2, para 12, as from 1 April 2006).

Para 3: sub-paras (2)–(5) revoked by SI 2009/1942, reg 21, as from 1 October 2009.

Para 4: words omitted from sub-para (1), and the whole of sub-para (2), revoked by SI 2009/1942, reg 22, as from 1 October 2009.

SCHEDULE 4
CALCULATION OF THE AVERAGE DEBT OR SUM OUTSTANDING UNDER A DEBENTURE DURING A 12 MONTH PERIOD

Regulation 22(7)

[6.151]

1. (1) The average amount of a debt or sum outstanding under a debenture during any 12 month period is the amount which satisfies the calculation set out in sub-paragraph (2).

(2) The calculation referred to in sub-paragraph (1) is A divided by B where:

A is the aggregate of the amount of the debt or the sum outstanding under the debenture as at the end of each day during the 12 month period; and

B is the number of days during that 12 month period.

(3) For the purposes of A in sub-paragraph (2) there shall be excluded any sums which represent interest which has accrued on that debt or debenture within that 12 month period.

(4) For the purposes of A in sub-paragraph (2) where the debt or debenture did not exist at the end of any day during the 12 month period, the amount of the debt or the sum outstanding under the debenture as at the end of that day shall be treated as being zero for the purposes of the calculation in A.

2. Where the amount of the debt or the sum outstanding under the debenture is not known as at the end of any particular date, the directors of the community interest company may, for the purposes of the calculation referred to in paragraph 1, substitute for the debt or the sum outstanding under the debenture such amount or sum as they estimate to be the amount of the debt or the sum outstanding under the debenture as at the end of that particular date.

[SCHEDULE 4A
INFORMATION ABOUT DIRECTORS' BENEFITS

Regulation 26

PART 1 INFORMATION REQUIRED TO BE DISCLOSED

Total amount of directors' remuneration etc

[6.152]

1. (1) There must be shown the overall total of the following amounts—

(a) the amount of remuneration paid to or receivable by directors in respect of qualifying services,

(b) the amount of money paid to or receivable by directors, and the net value of assets (other than money, share options or shares) received or receivable by directors, under long term incentive schemes in respect of qualifying services, and

(c) the value of any company contributions—

(i) paid, or treated as paid, to a pension scheme in respect of directors' qualifying services, and

(ii) by reference to which the rate or amount of any money purchase benefits that may become payable will be calculated.

(2) There must be shown the number of directors (if any) to whom retirement benefits are accruing in respect of qualifying services—

(a) under money purchase schemes, and

(b) under defined benefit schemes.

Payments for loss of office

2. (1) There must be shown the aggregate amount of any payments for loss of office.

(2) "Payment for loss of office" has the same meaning as in section 215 of the 2006 Act.

Sums paid to third parties in respect of directors' services

3. (1) There must be shown the aggregate amount of any consideration paid to or receivable by third parties for making available the services of any person—

(a) as a director of the company, or

(b) while director of the company—

(i) as director of any of its subsidiary undertakings, or

(ii) otherwise in connection with the management of the affairs of the company or any of its subsidiary undertakings.

(2) In sub-paragraph (1)—

(a) the reference to consideration includes benefits otherwise than in cash, and

(b) in relation to such consideration the reference to its amount is to the estimated money value of the benefit.

The nature of any such consideration must be disclosed.

(3) For the purposes of this paragraph a "third party" means a person other than—

(a) the director, a person connected with the director, or body corporate controlled by the director, or

(b) the company or any of its subsidiary undertakings.]

NOTES

Inserted by the Companies (Miscellaneous Reporting) Regulations 2018, SI 2018/860, regs 20, 23, Schedule, as from 7 August 2018, in relation to community interest company reports for financial years ending on or after that date.

[PART 2 SUPPLEMENTARY PROVISIONS

General nature of obligations

[6.153]

4. (1) This Schedule requires information to be given only so far as it is contained in the company's books and papers or the company has the right to obtain it from the persons concerned.

(2) For the purposes of this Schedule information is treated as shown if it is capable of being readily ascertained from other information which is shown.

Provisions as to amounts to be shown

5. (1) The following provisions apply with respect to the amounts to be shown under this Schedule.

(2) The amount in each case includes all relevant sums, whether paid by or receivable from the company, any of the company's subsidiary undertakings or any other person.

(3) References to amounts paid to or receivable by a person include amounts paid to or receivable by a person connected with that person or a body corporate controlled by the person (but not so as to require an amount to be counted twice).

(4) Except as otherwise provided, the amounts to be shown for any financial year are—

(a) the sums receivable in respect of that year (whenever paid), or

(b) in the case of sums not receivable in respect of a period, the sums paid during that year.

(5) Sums paid by way of expenses allowance that are charged to United Kingdom income tax after the end of the relevant financial year must be shown in a note to the first accounts in which it is practicable to show them and must be distinguished from the amounts to be shown apart from this provision.

(6) Where it is necessary to do so for the purpose of making any distinction required in complying with this Schedule, the directors may apportion payments between the matters in respect of which they have been paid or are receivable in such manner as they think appropriate.

Exclusion of sums liable to be accounted for to company etc

6. (1) The amounts to be shown under this Schedule do not include any sums that are to be accounted for—

Part 6 Other companies SIs

(a) to the company or any of its subsidiary undertakings, or

(b) by virtue of sections 219 and 222(3) of the 2006 Act (payments in connection with share transfers: duty to account), to persons who sold their shares as a result of the offer made.

(2) Where—

(a) any such sums are not shown in a note to the accounts for the relevant financial year on the ground that the person receiving them is liable to account for them, and

(b) the liability is afterwards wholly or partly released or is not enforced within a period of two years,

those sums, to the extent to which the liability is released or not enforced, must be shown in a note to the first accounts in which it is practicable to show them and must be distinguished from the amounts to be shown apart from this provision.

Meaning of "remuneration"

7. (1) In this Schedule "remuneration" of a director includes—

(a) salary, fees and bonuses, sums paid by way of expenses allowance (so far as they are chargeable to United Kingdom income tax), and

(b) subject to sub-paragraph (2), the estimated money value of any other benefits received by the director otherwise than in cash.

(2) The expression "remuneration" does not include—

(a) the value of any share options granted to a director or the amount of any gains made on the exercise of any such options,

(b) any company contributions paid, or treated as paid, in respect of the director under any pension scheme or any benefits to which the director is entitled under any such scheme, or

(c) any money or other assets paid to or received or receivable by the director under any long term incentive scheme.

Meaning of "long term incentive scheme"

8. (1) In this Schedule "long term incentive scheme" means an agreement or arrangement—

(a) under which money or other assets may become receivable by a director, and

(b) which includes one or more qualifying conditions with respect to service or performance which cannot be fulfilled within a single financial year.

(2) For this purpose the following must be disregarded—

(a) bonuses the amount of which falls to be determined by reference to service or performance within a single financial year,

(b) compensation for loss of office, payments for breach of contract and other termination payments, and

(c) retirement benefits.

Meaning of "shares" and "share option" and related expressions

9. In this Schedule—

(a) "shares" means shares (whether allotted or not) in the company, or any undertaking which is a group undertaking in relation to the company, and includes a share warrant as defined by section 779(1) of the 2006 Act, and

(b) "share option" means a right to acquire shares.

Meaning of "pension scheme" and related expressions

10. (1) In this Schedule—

"pension scheme" means a retirement benefits scheme within the meaning given by section 150(1) of the Finance Act 2004 which is—

(a) one in which the company participates, or

(b) one to which the company paid a contribution during the financial year, and

"retirement benefits" means relevant benefits within the meaning given by section 393B of the Income Tax (Earnings and Pensions) Act 2003 read as if subsection (2) were omitted.

(2) In this Schedule, "company contributions", in relation to a pension scheme and a director, means any payments (including insurance premiums) made, or treated as made, to the scheme in respect of the director by a person other than the director.

(3) In this Schedule, in relation to a director—

"defined benefits" means retirement benefits payable under a pension scheme that are not money purchase benefits,

"defined benefit scheme" means a pension scheme that is not a money purchase scheme,

"money purchase benefits" means retirement benefits payable under a pension scheme the rate or amount of which is calculated by reference to payments made, or treated as made, by the director or by any other person in respect of the director and which are not average salary benefits, and

"money purchase scheme" means a pension scheme under which all of the benefits that may become payable to or in respect of the director are money purchase benefits.

(4) Where a pension scheme provides for any benefits that may become payable to or in respect of any director to be whichever are the greater of—

(a) money purchase benefits as determined by or under the scheme, and

(b) defined benefits as so determined,

the company may assume for the purposes of this paragraph that those benefits will be money purchase benefits, or defined benefits, according to whichever appears more likely at the end of the financial year.

(5) For the purpose of determining whether a pension scheme is a money purchase or defined benefit scheme, any death in service benefits provided for by the scheme are to be disregarded.

References to subsidiary undertakings

11. (1) Any reference in this Schedule to a subsidiary undertaking of the company, in relation to a person who is or was, while a director of the company, a director also, by virtue of the company's nomination (direct or indirect) of any other undertaking, includes that undertaking, whether or not it is or was in fact a subsidiary undertaking of the company.

(2) Any reference to a subsidiary undertaking of the company—

(a) for the purposes of paragraph 1 (remuneration etc) is to an undertaking which is a subsidiary undertaking at the time the services were rendered, and

(b) for the purposes of paragraph 2 (compensation for loss of office) is to a subsidiary undertaking immediately before the loss of office as director.

Other minor definitions

12. (1) In this Schedule—

"net value", in relation to any assets received or receivable by a director, means value after deducting any money paid or other value given by the director in respect of those assets;

"qualifying services", in relation to any person, means the person's services as a director of the company, and that person's services while director of the company—

(a) as director of any of its subsidiary undertakings, or

(b) otherwise in connection with the management of the affairs of the company or any of its subsidiary undertakings.

(2) For the purposes of this Schedule, remuneration paid or receivable or share options granted in respect of a person's accepting office as a director are treated as emoluments paid or receivable or share options granted in respect of the person's services as a director.]

NOTES

Inserted by the Companies (Miscellaneous Reporting) Regulations 2018, SI 2018/860, regs 20, 23, Schedule, as from 7 August 2018, in relation to community interest company reports for financial years ending on or after that date.

SCHEDULE 5
FEES PAYABLE TO THE REGISTRAR OF COMPANIES

Regulation 36

[6.154]

[Matter in relation to which fee is payable	**Amount of fee**	**When payable**
Decision under section 36A(1) of the 2004 Act as to whether a company is eligible to be formed as a community interest company	£15.00	On delivery to the registrar under section 9 of the 2006 Act, section 36 of the 2004 Act and regulation 11 of the documents constituting an application to form a community interest company
Decision under section 38(1) of the 2004 Act as to whether a company is eligible to become a community interest company	£15.00	On delivery to the registrar under section 30 of the 2006 Act, section 37 of the 2004 Act and regulation 12 of the documents constituting an application to the registrar to become a community interest company
Consideration of a community interest company report forwarded by the registrar under section 34(4) of the 2004 Act	£15.00	On delivery of the report to the registrar]

NOTES

Substituted by the Community Interest Company (Amendment) Regulations 2009, SI 2009/1942, reg 23, as from 1 October 2009.

COMPANIES (DISQUALIFICATION ORDERS) REGULATIONS 2009

(SI 2009/2471)

NOTES

Made: 8 September 2009.

Authority: Company Directors Disqualification Act 1986, s 18.

Commencement: 1 October 2009.

These Regulations are reproduced as amended by: the Small Business, Enterprise and Employment Act 2015 (Consequential Amendments) (Insolvency and Company Directors Disqualification) Regulations 2015, SI 2015/1651.

ARRANGEMENT OF REGULATIONS

Part 6 Other companies SIs

[6.155]

1 Citation and commencement

These Regulations may be cited as the Companies (Disqualification Orders) Regulations 2009 and come into force on 1st October 2009.

[6.156]

2 Definitions

(1) In these Regulations—

"the Act" means the Company Directors Disqualification Act 1986;

["disqualification order" means an order of the court under any of sections 2 to 5, 5A, 6, 8, 8ZA, 8ZD, 9A and 10 of the Act;]

["disqualification undertaking" means an undertaking accepted by the Secretary of State under section 5A, 7, 8, 8ZC, 8ZE or 9B of the Act;]

"grant of leave" means a grant by the court of leave under section 17 of the Act to any person in relation to a disqualification order or a disqualification undertaking.

For the purposes of regulations 5 and 9, "leave granted"—

(a) in relation to a disqualification order granted under Part 2 of the Companies (Northern Ireland) Order 1989 means leave granted by a court for a person subject to such an order to do anything which otherwise the order prohibits that person from doing; and

(b) in relation to a disqualification undertaking accepted under the Company Directors Disqualification (Northern Ireland) Order 2002 means leave granted by a court for a person subject to such an undertaking to do anything which otherwise the undertaking prohibits that person from doing.

NOTES

Definitions in square brackets substituted by the Small Business, Enterprise and Employment Act 2015 (Consequential Amendments) (Insolvency and Company Directors Disqualification) Regulations 2015, SI 2015/1651, regs 4(1), (2), as from 1 October 2015.

[6.157]

3 Revocations

The following instruments are revoked—

(a) the Companies (Disqualification Orders) Regulations 2001;

(b) the Companies (Disqualification Orders) (Amendment No 2) Regulations 2002; and

(c) the Companies (Disqualification Orders) (Amendment) Regulations 2004.

[6.158]

4 Transitional provisions

Other than regulation 9, these Regulations apply—

(a) in relation to a disqualification order made after the coming into force of these Regulations; and

(b) in relation to—

(i) a grant of leave made after the coming into force of these Regulations; or

(ii) any action taken by a court after the coming into force of these Regulations in consequence of which a disqualification order or a disqualification undertaking is varied or ceases to be in force,

whether the disqualification order or disqualification undertaking to which the grant of leave or the action relates was made by the court or accepted by the Secretary of State before or after the coming into force of these Regulations.

[6.159]

5

Regulation 9 applies to—

(a) particulars of disqualification orders made and leave granted under Part 2 of the Companies (Northern Ireland) Order 1989 received by the Secretary of State on or after 1st October 2009 other than particulars of disqualification orders made and leave granted under that Order which relate to disqualification orders made by the courts of Northern Ireland before 2nd April 2001; and

(b) particulars of undertakings accepted under the Company Directors Disqualification (Northern Ireland) Order 2002 on or after 1st October 2009, and to leave granted under that Order in relation to such undertakings.

[6.160]

6 Particulars to be furnished by officers of the court

(1) The following officers of the court must furnish to the Secretary of State the particulars specified in regulation 7(a) to (c) in the form and manner there specified—

(a) where a disqualification order is made by the Crown Court, the Court Manager;

(b) where a disqualification order or grant of leave is made by the High Court, the Court Manager;

(c) where a disqualification order or grant of leave is made by a County Court, the Court Manager;

(d) where a disqualification order is made by a Magistrates' Court, the designated officer for a Magistrates' Court;

(e) where a disqualification order is made by the High Court of Justiciary, the Deputy Principal Clerk of Justiciary;

(f) where a disqualification order or grant of leave is made by a Sheriff Court, the Sheriff Clerk;

(g) where a disqualification order or grant of leave is made by the Court of Session, the Deputy Principal Clerk of Session;

(h) where a disqualification order or grant of leave is made by the Court of Appeal, the Court Manager; and
(i) where a disqualification order or grant of leave is made by the Supreme Court, the Registrar of the Supreme Court.

(2) Where—
(a) a disqualification order has been made by any of the courts mentioned in paragraph (1), or
(b) a disqualification undertaking has been accepted by the Secretary of State,
and subsequently any action is taken by a court in consequence of which that order or that undertaking is varied or ceases to be in force, the officer specified in paragraph (1) of the court which takes such action must furnish to the Secretary of State the particulars specified in regulation 7(d) in the form and manner there specified.

[6.161]
7

The form in which the particulars are to be furnished is—
(a) that set out in Schedule 1 to these Regulations with such variations as circumstances require when the person against whom the disqualification order is made is an individual, and the particulars contained therein are the particulars specified for that purpose;
(b) that set out in Schedule 2 to these Regulations with such variations as circumstances require when the person against whom the disqualification order is made is a body corporate, and the particulars contained therein are the particulars specified for that purpose;
(c) that set out in Schedule 3 to these Regulations with such variations as circumstances require when a grant of leave is made by the court in relation to a disqualification order or a disqualification undertaking, and the particulars contained therein are the particulars specified for that purpose;
(d) that set out in Schedule 4 to these Regulations with such variations as circumstances require when any action is taken by a court in consequence of which a disqualification order or a disqualification undertaking is varied or ceases to be in force, and the particulars contained therein are the particulars specified for that purpose.

[6.162]
8

The time within which the officer specified in regulation 6(1) is to furnish the Secretary of State with the said particulars is the period of 14 days beginning with the day on which the disqualification order or grant of leave is made or on which action is taken by a court in consequence of which the disqualification order or disqualification undertaking is varied or ceases to be in force.

[6.163]
9 Extension of certain of the provisions of section 18 of the Act to orders made, undertakings accepted and leave granted in Northern Ireland

(1) Section 18(2) of the Act is extended to the particulars furnished to the Secretary of State of disqualification orders made and leave granted under Part 2 of the Companies (Northern Ireland) Order 1989.

(2) Section 18(2A) of the Act is extended to the particulars of disqualification undertakings accepted under and leave granted in relation to disqualification undertakings under the Company Directors Disqualification (Northern Ireland) Order 2002.

(3) Section 18(3) of the Act is extended to all entries in the register and particulars relating to them furnished to the Secretary of State in respect of orders made under Part 2 of the Companies (Northern Ireland) Order 1989 or disqualification undertakings accepted under the Company Directors Disqualification (Northern Ireland) Order 2002.

SCHEDULES

SCHEDULES 1–4

NOTES

Regulation 7 of these Regulations (at **[6.161]**) specifies the form and manner in which certain particulars must be furnished to the Secretary of State. Schs 1 to 4 contain the forms to be used when furnishing such particulars. Those forms are not reproduced here, but their names and numbers are listed below. Note that the forms in Schs 1 and 2 were substituted by the Small Business, Enterprise and Employment Act 2015 (Consequential Amendments) (Insolvency and Company Directors Disqualification) Regulations 2015, SI 2015/1651, as from 1 October 2015:

Form No	*Description*
DQO1	Disqualification order against an individual
DQO2	Disqualification order against a corporate body or firm
DQO3	Grant of leave in relation to a disqualification order or disqualification undertaking
DQO4	Variation or cessation of a disqualification order or disqualification undertaking

9

PART 7
FINANCIAL SERVICES PRIMARY LEGISLATION

FINANCIAL SERVICES AND MARKETS ACT 2000

(2000 c 8)

NOTES

Only those provisions of this Act of most relevance to company law are reproduced in this Handbook. The Parts of, and Schedules to, this Act not reproduced are listed below (note also that certain sections contained in Parts that are included in this Handbook may also be omitted because they are outside the scope of this work)—

- Part IX—Hearings and Appeals (ss 132–137);
- Part 9B—Ring-fencing (ss 142A–142Z1);
- Part 9C—Prudential Regulation of FCA Investment Firms (ss 143A–143Z);
- Part 9D—Prudential Regulation of Credit Institutions etc (ss 144A–144H);
- Part XIII—Incoming Firms: Intervention by FCA or PRA (only s 195 of which is in force);
- Part XIV—Disciplinary Measures (ss 204A–211);
- Part XV—The Financial Services Compensation Scheme (ss 212–224A);
- Part 15A—Power to Require FSCS Manager to Act in Relation to Other Schemes (ss 224B–224F);
- Part XVI—The Ombudsman Scheme (ss 225–234B);
- Part 16A—Consumer Protection and Competition (ss 234C–234O);
- Part 17A—Transformer Vehicles (s 284A);
- Part XIX—Lloyd's (ss 314–324);
- Part 20B—Illegal Money Lending (ss 333S, 333T);
- Part 20C—Politically Exposed Persons: Money Laundering and Terrorist Financing (s 333U);
- Part XXI—Mutual Societies (ss 334–339);
- Part XXX—Supplemental (ss 426–433);
- Schedule 1ZB—The Prudential Regulation Authority;
- Schedule 2A—Gibraltar-Based Persons Carrying on Activities in the UK;
- Schedule 2B—UK-Based Persons Carrying on Activities in Gibraltar;
- Schedule 17—The Ombudsman Scheme;
- Schedule 18—Mutuals;
- Schedule 20—Minor and Consequential Amendments;
- Schedule 21—Transitional provisions and Savings;
- Schedule 22—Repeals.

The Act is reproduced in full in *Butterworths Securities & Financial Services Law Handbook*.

Transitional provisions relating to exiting the European Union: the United Kingdom left the European Union on exit day, as defined in the European Union (Withdrawal) Act 2018, s 20 at **[12.28]** (ie, 11pm on 31 January 2020). The implementation period provided for by the EU/UK Withdrawal Agreement came to an end on IP completion day, as defined in the European Union (Withdrawal Agreement) Act 2020, s 39 at **[12.53]** (ie, 11pm on 31 December 2020). Various Regulations made under the European Union (Withdrawal) Act 2018 contain transitional provisions relating to: exemptions from the general prohibition; temporary permissions to carry on regulated activities; the performance of regulated activities; restrictions on financial promotion, etc. They also contain savings provisions and modify the application of this Act and subordinate legislation made under it. See Part 12 *post* (Exiting the EU Materials)

Modification of this Act and the FCA's and PRA's functions under it: various Regulations and Orders made under this Act designate the FCA or the PRA for the purposes of those Regulations and Orders and consequently modify this Act and the appropriate regulator's functions etc for the purposes of those Regulations and Orders. The majority of these are outside the scope of this work but see, for example: the Open-Ended Investment Companies Regulations 2001, SI 2001/1228 at **[8.339]**; the Alternative Investment Fund Managers Regulations 2013, SI 2013/1773; and the Proxy Advisors (Shareholders' Rights) Regulations 2019, SI 2019/926 at **[10.1296]**.

Commencement: The main provisions of this Act came into force on 1 December 2001, ie, the date on which s 19 (the general prohibition) came into force (see s 432 and Orders made under that section).

Extent: this Act extends to the whole of the United Kingdom with the exception of Chapter IV of Part XVII which does not extend to Northern Ireland; see s 430 (not printed).

Application of Act to Limited liability partnerships: ss 215(3), (4), (6), 356, 359(1)–(4), 361–365, 367, 370, and 371 of this Act apply to limited liability partnerships (except where the context otherwise requires and subject to certain modifications); see the Limited Liability Partnerships Regulations 2001, SI 2001/1090, reg 6 at **[10.104]**.

Application of Act to certain overseas investment exchanges and clearing houses: see the Companies Act 1989, s 170 at **[5.164]**.

Application of Act to banks and building socities: various Orders made under the Banking (Special Provisions) Act 2008 and Banking Act 2009 apply and modify certain provisions of this Act in relation to the banks and building societies that are the subject of the Orders.

Application of Act to other bodies: note that the application of this Act to certain other bodies (*eg* co-operative and community benefit societies, etc) is not noted as it is considered outside the scope of this work.

Exemption from requirement for contract for sale etc of land to be in writing: a contract regulated under this Act, other than a regulated mortgage contract, a regulated home reversion plan, a regulated home purchase plan or a regulated sale and rent back agreement, is exempt from the Law of Property (Miscellaneous Provisions) Act 1989, s 2 (contracts for sale etc of land to be made by writing); see s 2(5) of that Act.

Transitional provisions in relation to Gibraltar-based firms and activities: see the Gibraltar (Miscellaneous Amendments) (EU Exit) Regulations 2019, SI 2019/680, reg 11 at **[12.129]**.

The Provisions of this Act included in this work are reproduced as amended by the following Acts:

2000	Regulation of Investigatory Powers Act 2000.
2001	Criminal Justice and Police Act 2001.
2002	Enterprise Act 2002.
2003	Criminal Justice Act 2003.
2005	Regulation of Financial Services (Land Transactions) Act 2005.
2006	Consumer Credit Act 2006; Companies Act 2006; Investment Exchanges and Clearing Houses Act 2006.
2008	Dormant Bank and Building Society Accounts Act 2008.

2009	Banking Act 2009.
2010	Financial Services Act 2010.
2011	Charities Act 2011.
2012	Financial Services Act 2012.
2013	Financial Services (Banking Reform) Act 2013.
2014	Co-operative and Community Benefit Societies Act 2014; Pensions Act 2014.
2015	Pension Schemes Act 2015.
2016	Bank of England and Financial Services Act 2016; Investigatory Powers Act 2016.
2017	Digital Economy Act 2017.
2018	Financial Guidance and Claims Act 2018; Data Protection Act 2018; Civil Liability Act 2018.
2020	Corporate Insolvency and Governance Act 2020; Sentencing Act 2020.
2021	Pension Schemes Act 2021; Financial Services Act 2021.
2022	Dormant Assets Act 2022.

The Provisions of this Act included in this work are reproduced as amended by the following SIs:

2000	Banking Consolidation Directive (Consequential Amendments) Regulations 2000, SI 2000/2952.
2002	Electronic Commerce Directive (Financial Services and Markets) Regulations 2002, SI 2002/1775.
2003	Insurance Mediation Directive (Miscellaneous Amendments) Regulations 2003, SI 2003/1473; Collective Investment Schemes (Miscellaneous Amendments) Regulations 2003, SI 2003/2066.
2004	Life Assurance Consolidation Directive (Consequential Amendments) Regulations 2004, SI 2004/3379.
2005	Financial Services and Markets Act 2000 (Market Abuse) Regulations 2005, SI 2005/381; Prospectus Regulations 2005, SI 2005/1433.
2006	Charities and Trustee Investment (Scotland) Act 2005 (Consequential Provisions and Modifications) Order 2006, SI 2006/242; Taxation of Pension Schemes (Consequential Amendments) Order 2006, SI 2006/745; Takeovers Directive (Interim Implementation) Regulations 2006, SI 2006/1183; Financial Services and Markets Act 2000 (Markets in Financial Instruments) (Modification of Powers) Regulations 2006, SI 2006/2975; Capital Requirements Regulations 2006, SI 2006/3221.
2007	Financial Services (EEA State) Regulations 2007, SI 2007/108; Financial Services and Markets Act 2000 (Markets in Financial Instruments) Regulations 2007, SI 2007/126; Companies Act 2006 (Commencement No 2, Consequential Amendments, Transitional Provisions and Savings) Order 2007, SI 2007/1093; Regulatory Reform (Financial Services and Markets Act 2000) Order 2007, SI 2007/1973; Reinsurance Directive Regulations 2007, SI 2007/3253.
2008	Companies Act 2006 (Consequential Amendments etc) Order 2008, SI 2008/948; Financial Services and Markets Act 2000 (Amendments to Part 7) Regulations 2008, SI 2008/1468.
2009	Financial Services and Markets Act 2000 (Controllers) Regulations 2009, SI 2009/534; Companies Act 2006 (Consequential Amendments, Transitional Provisions and Savings) Order 2009, SI 2009/1941; Financial Services and Markets Act 2000 (Amendment) Regulations 2009, SI 2009/2461.
2010	Transfer of Tribunal Functions Order 2010, SI 2010/22; Financial Services and Markets Act 2000 (Liability of Issuers) Regulations 2010, SI 2010/1192.
2011	Companies Act 2006 (Consequential Amendments and Transitional Provisions) Order 2011, SI 2011/1265; Undertakings for Collective Investment in Transferable Securities Regulations 2011, SI 2011/1613.
2012	Financial Services (Omnibus 1 Directive) Regulations 2012, SI 2012/916; Prospectus Regulations 2012, SI 2012/1538; Financial Services and Markets Act 2000 (Regulated Activities) (Amendment) Order 2012, SI 2012/1906; Financial Services and Markets Act 2000 (Short Selling) Regulations 2012, SI 2012/2554.
2013	Financial Services and Markets Act 2000 (Over the Counter Derivatives, Central Counterparties and Trade Repositories) Regulations 2013, SI 2013/504; Financial Services and Markets Act 2000 (Threshold Conditions) Order 2013, SI 2013/555; Financial Services Act 2012 (Consequential Amendments) Order 2013, SI 2013/636; Financial Services and Markets Act 2000 (Regulated Activities) (Amendment) Order 2013, SI 2013/655; Prospectus Regulations 2013, SI 2013/1125; Collective Investment in Transferable Securities (Contractual Scheme) Regulations 2013, SI 2013/1388; Alternative Investment Fund Managers Regulations 2013, SI 2013/1773; Alternative Investment Fund Managers (Amendment) Regulations 2013, SI 2013/1797; Financial Services and Markets Act 2000 (Regulated Activities) (Amendment) (No 2) Order 2013, SI 2013/1881; Financial Services and Markets Act 2000 (Over the Counter Derivatives, Central Counterparties and Trade Repositories) (No 2) Regulations 2013, SI 2013/1908; Capital Requirements Regulations 2013, SI 2013/3115.
2014	Financial Services and Markets Act 2000 (Regulated Activities) (Amendment) Order 2014, SI 2014/366; Enterprise and Regulatory Reform Act 2013 (Competition) (Consequential, Transitional and Saving Provisions) Order 2014, SI 2014/892; Alternative Investment Fund Managers Order 2014, SI 2014/1292; Central Securities Depositories Regulations 2014, SI 2014/2879; Payments to Governments and Miscellaneous Provisions Regulations 2014, SI 2014/3293; Bank Recovery and Resolution (No 2) Order 2014, SI 2014/3348; Bank Recovery and Resolution Order 2014, SI 2014/3329.
2015	Solvency 2 Regulations 2015, SI 2015/575; Legal Aid, Sentencing and Punishment of Offenders Act 2012 (Fines on Summary Conviction) Regulations 2015, SI 2015/664; Financial Services and Markets Act 2000 (Miscellaneous Provisions) Order 2015, SI 2015/853; Mortgage Credit Directive Order 2015, SI 2015/910; Transparency Regulations 2015, SI 2015/1755; Financial Services and Markets Act 2000 (Misconduct and Appropriate Regulator) Order 2015, SI 2015/1864; European Long-term Investment Funds Regulations 2015, SI 2015/1882.
2016	Undertakings for Collective Investment in Transferable Securities Regulations 2016, SI 2016/225; Enter-

	prise and Regulatory Reform Act 2013 (Consequential Amendments) (Bankruptcy) and the Small Business, Enterprise and Employment Act 2015 (Consequential Amendments) Regulations 2016, SI 2016/481; Financial Services and Markets Act 2000 (Market Abuse) Regulations 2016, SI 2016/680; Financial Services and Markets Act 2000 (Transparency of Securities Financing Transactions and of Reuse) Regulations 2016, SI 2016/715; Bankruptcy (Scotland) Act 2016 (Consequential Provisions and Modifications) Order 2016, SI 2016/1034; Financial Services and Markets (Disclosure of Information to the European Securities and Markets Authority etc and Other Provisions) Regulations 2016, SI 2016/1095; Bank Recovery and Resolution Order 2016, SI 2016/1239.
2017	Deregulation Act 2015, the Small Business, Enterprise and Employment Act 2015 and the Insolvency (Amendment) Act (Northern Ireland) 2016 (Consequential Amendments and Transitional Provisions) Regulations 2017, SI 2017/400; Legislative Reform (Private Fund Limited Partnerships) Order 2017, SI 2017/514; Financial Services and Markets Act 2000 (Markets in Financial Instruments) Regulations 2017, SI 2017/701; Payment Services Regulations 2017, SI 2017/752; Central Securities Depositories Regulations 2017, SI 2017/1064; Packaged Retail and Insurance-based Investment Products Regulations 2017, SI 2017/1127; Risk Transformation Regulations 2017, SI 2017/1212; Financial Services and Markets Act 2000 (Markets in Financial Instruments) (No 2) Regulations 2017, SI 2017/1255.
2018	Financial Services and Markets Act 2000 (Benchmarks) Regulations 2018, SI 2018/135; Small Business, Enterprise and Employment Act 2015 (Consequential Amendments, Savings and Transitional Provisions) Regulations 2018, SI 2018/208; Insurance Distribution (Regulated Activities and Miscellaneous Amendments) Order 2018, SI 2018/546; Money Market Funds Regulations 2018, SI 2018/698; Financial Services and Markets Act 2000 (Prospectus and Markets in Financial Instruments) Regulations 2018, SI 2018/786; Financial Regulators' Powers (Technical Standards etc) (Amendment etc) (EU Exit) Regulations 2018, SI 2018/1115; EEA Passport Rights (Amendment, etc, and Transitional Provisions) (EU Exit) Regulations 2018, SI 2018/1149; Central Counterparties (Amendment, etc, and Transitional Provision) (EU Exit) Regulations 2018, SI 2018/1184; Financial Services and Markets Act 2000 (Claims Management Activity) Order 2018, SI 2018/1253; Securitisation Regulations 2018, SI 2018/1288; Short Selling (Amendment) (EU Exit) Regulations 2018, SI 2018/1321.
2019	Market Abuse (Amendment) (EU Exit) Regulations 2019, SI 2019/310; Collective Investment Schemes (Amendment etc) (EU Exit) Regulations 2019, SI 2019/325; Financial Guidance and Claims Act 2018 (Naming and Consequential Amendments) Regulations 2019, SI 2019/383; Financial Services and Markets Act 2000 (Amendment) (EU Exit) Regulations 2019, SI 2019/632; Investment Exchanges, Clearing Houses and Central Securities Depositories (Amendment) (EU Exit) Regulations 2019, SI 2019/662; Public Record, Disclosure of Information and Co-operation (Financial Services) (Amendment) (EU Exit) Regulations 2019, SI 2019/681; Official Listing of Securities, Prospectus and Transparency (Amendment etc) (EU Exit) Regulations 2019, SI 2019/707; Financial Services (Miscellaneous) (Amendment) (EU Exit) Regulations 2019, SI 2019/710; Financial Services and Markets Act 2000 (Prospectus) Regulations 2019, SI 2019/1043; Financial Services (Electronic Money, Payment Services and Miscellaneous Amendments) (EU Exit) Regulations 2019, SI 2019/1212; Prospectus (Amendment etc) (EU Exit) Regulations 2019, SI 2019/1234; Electronic Commerce and Solvency 2 (Amendment etc) (EU Exit) Regulations 2019, SI 2019/1361.
2020	Over the Counter Derivatives, Central Counterparties and Trade Repositories (Amendment, etc, and Transitional Provision) (EU Exit) Regulations 2020, SI 2020/646; Bearer Certificates (Collective Investment Schemes) Regulations 2020, SI 2020/1346; Bank Recovery and Resolution (Amendment) (EU Exit) Regulations 2020, SI 2020/1350; Securities Financing Transactions, Securitisation and Miscellaneous Amendments (EU Exit) Regulations 2020, SI 2020/1385; Financial Holding Companies (Approval etc) and Capital Requirements (Capital Buffers and Macro-prudential Measures) (Amendment) (EU Exit) Regulations 2020, SI 2020/1406.
2021	Recognised Auction Platforms (Amendment and Miscellaneous Provisions) Regulations 2021, SI 2021/494; Financial Services Act 2021 (Prudential Regulation of Credit Institutions and Investment Firms) (Consequential Amendments and Miscellaneous Provisions) Regulations 2021, SI 2021/1376; Financial Services and Markets Act 2000 (Consequential Amendments of References to Rules) Regulations 2021, SI 2021/1388.
2022	Financial Services and Markets Act 2000 (Regulated Activities) (Amendment) Order 2022, SI 2022/466; Criminal Justice Act 2003 (Commencement No 33) and Sentencing Act 2020 (Commencement No 2) Regulations 2022, SI 2022/500; Financial Services Act 2021 (Prudential Regulation of Credit Institutions and Investment Firms) (Consequential Amendments and Miscellaneous Provisions) Regulations 2022, SI 2022/838.

ARRANGEMENT OF SECTIONS

PART 1A
THE REGULATORS

CHAPTER 1 THE FINANCIAL CONDUCT AUTHORITY

The Financial Conduct Authority

The FCA's general duties

Interpretation of terms used in relation to FCA's general duties

PART 4A
PERMISSION TO CARRY ON REGULATED ACTIVITIES

Application for permission

Variation and cancellation of Part 4A permission

Imposition and variation of requirements

Exercise of power in support of overseas regulator

Connected persons

Persons whose interests are protected

Procedure

References to the Tribunal

Interpretation

PART V
PERFORMANCE OF REGULATED ACTIVITIES

Prohibition orders

Approval

Statement of policy

Procedure

Miscellaneous

PART 8A
SHORT SELLING

Power to require information

Breach of short selling regulation etc

PART 9A
RULES AND GUIDANCE

CHAPTER 1 RULE-MAKING POWERS

General rule-making powers of the FCA and the PRA

CHAPTER III AUTHORISED UNIT TRUST SCHEMES

CHAPTER 3A AUTHORISED CONTRACTUAL SCHEMES

CHAPTER VI INVESTIGATIONS

PART XVIII
RECOGNISED INVESTMENT EXCHANGES, CLEARING HOUSES AND CSDS

CHAPTER I EXEMPTION

General

Applications for recognition

Publication of information by recognised investment exchange

Supervision

Power to disallow excessive regulatory provision

Other matters

CHAPTER 1A CONTROL OVER RECOGNISED INVESTMENT EXCHANGE

Notices of acquisitions of control over recognised investment exchanges

Acquiring and increasing control

Assessment procedure

Enforcement procedures

Supplemental provisions concerning insurers

Settlement finality

PART XXV
INJUNCTIONS AND RESTITUTION

Injunctions

Restitution orders

Restitution required by [FCA or PRA]

PART XXVI
NOTICES

Warning notices

Decision notices

Conclusion of proceedings

Publication

Third party rights and access to evidence

The FCA's and PRA's procedures

PART XXVII
OFFENCES

Miscellaneous offences

Bodies corporate and partnerships

Institution of proceedings

PART XXVIII
MISCELLANEOUS

PART XXIX
INTERPRETATION

SCHEDULES

An Act to make provision about the regulation of financial services and markets; to provide for the transfer of certain statutory functions relating to building societies, friendly societies, industrial and provident societies and certain other mutual societies; and for connected purposes

[14 June 2000]

[PART 1A THE REGULATORS

NOTES

Transitional provisions etc in connection with the commencement of the Financial Services Act 2012: for transitional provisions in relation to the commencement of this Part, see the Financial Services Act 2012 (Transitional Provisions) (Miscellaneous Provisions) Order 2013, SI 2013/442. Part 2 of that Order contains transitional provisions in respect of the Financial Conduct Authority and the Prudential Regulation Authority. Article 2 makes provision in respect of the board of the Financial Services Authority (which is renamed as the Financial Conduct Authority by FSMA 2000 (as amended by the 2012 Act)). Article 3 makes provision in respect of the FCA's first annual report, and article 4 makes provision in respect of the PRA's first annual report. Articles 5 and 6 make provision in respect of the Consumer and Practitioner Panels. Article 7 makes provision in respect of references to "consumers" in certain provisions of FSMA 2000.

CHAPTER 1 THE FINANCIAL CONDUCT AUTHORITY

The Financial Conduct Authority

[7.1]

1A The Financial Conduct Authority

(1) The body corporate previously known as the Financial Services Authority is renamed as the Financial Conduct Authority.

(2) The Financial Conduct Authority is in this Act referred to as "the FCA".

(3) The FCA is to have the functions conferred on it by or under this Act.

(4) The FCA must comply with the requirements as to its constitution set out in Schedule 1ZA.

(5) Schedule 1ZA also makes provision about the status of the FCA and the exercise of certain of its functions.

(6) References in this Act or any other enactment to functions conferred on the FCA by or under this Act include references to functions conferred on the FCA by or under—

(a) the Insolvency Act 1986,
(b) the Banking Act 2009,
(c) the Financial Services Act 2012, . . .
[(cza) the Financial Guidance and Claims Act 2018,]
[(czb) the Civil Liability Act 2018,]
[(ca) the Alternative Investment Fund Managers Regulations 2013, . . .]
(d) a [qualifying provision] that is specified, or of a description specified, for the purposes of this subsection by the Treasury by order], [or
(e) regulations made by the Treasury under section 8 of the European Union (Withdrawal) Act 2018].

NOTES

This section was substituted (together with the rest of Part 1A (ie, ss 1A–1T, 2A–2O, 3A–3S) for the original Part I (ss 1–18)) by the Financial Services Act 2012, s 6(1), as from 24 January 2013 (sub-ss (2), (6), and sub-ss (4), (5) certain purposes), and as from 1 April 2013 (otherwise) (for transitional provisions and savings in relation to the transfer of the FSA's functions, property, rights and liabilities, see s 119 of, and Schs 20, 21 to, the 2012 Act).

Sub-s (6): the word omitted from para (c) was repealed, and para (ca) was inserted, by the Alternative Investment Fund Managers Regulations 2013, SI 2013/1773, reg 80, Sch 1, Part 1, paras 1, 2, as from 22 July 2013. Para (cza) was inserted by the Financial Guidance and Claims Act 2018, s 25, Sch 3, paras 5, 6, as from 1 October 2018. Para (czb) was inserted by the Civil Liability Act 2018, s 11(10)(a), as from 20 December 2018. The word omitted from para (ca) was repealed, and para (e) and the preceding word were added, by the Financial Regulators' Powers (Technical Standards etc) (Amendment etc) (EU Exit) Regulations 2018, SI 2018/1115, reg 7(1), (2), as from 26 October 2018. Words in square brackets in para (d) substituted by the Financial Services and Markets Act 2000 (Amendment) (EU Exit) Regulations 2019, SI 2019/632, regs 2, 3, as from IP completion day (as defined in the European Union (Withdrawal Agreement) Act 2020, s 39) (for transitional provisions see SI 2019/710, reg 37 at **[12.110]**).

Orders and Regulations: the Financial Services and Markets Act 2000 (Qualifying Provisions) Order 2013, SI 2013/419; the Financial Services and Markets Act 2000 (Qualifying Provisions) (No 2) Order 2013, SI 2013/3116; the Financial Services and Markets Act 2000 (Transparency of Securities Financing Transactions and of Reuse) Regulations 2016, SI 2016/715; the

Alternative Investment Fund Managers (Amendment) Regulations 2018, SI 2018/134; the Insurance Distribution (Regulated Activities and Miscellaneous Amendments) Order 2018, SI 2018/546.

[The FCA's general duties

[7.2]

1B The FCA's general duties

(1) In discharging its general functions the FCA must, so far as is reasonably possible, act in a way which—

(a) is compatible with its strategic objective, and

(b) advances one or more of its operational objectives.

(2) The FCA's strategic objective is: ensuring that the relevant markets (see section 1F) function well.

(3) The FCA's operational objectives are—

(a) the consumer protection objective (see section 1C);

(b) the integrity objective (see section 1D);

(c) the competition objective (see section 1E).

(4) The FCA must, so far as is compatible with acting in a way which advances the consumer protection objective or the integrity objective, discharge its general functions in a way which promotes effective competition in the interests of consumers.

(5) In discharging its general functions the FCA must have regard to—

(a) the regulatory principles in section 3B, and

(b) the importance of taking action intended to minimise the extent to which it is possible for a business carried on—

(i) by an authorised person or a recognised investment exchange, or

(ii) in contravention of the general prohibition,

to be used for a purpose connected with financial crime.

(6) For the purposes of this Chapter, the FCA's general functions are—

(a) its function of making rules under this Act (considered as a whole),

[(aa) its function of making technical standards in accordance with Chapter 2A of Part 9A;]

(b) its function of preparing and issuing codes under this Act (considered as a whole),

(c) its functions in relation to the giving of general guidance under this Act (considered as a whole), and

(d) its function of determining the general policy and principles by reference to which it performs particular functions under this Act.

(7) Except to the extent that an order under section 50 of the Financial Services Act 2012 (orders relating to mutual societies functions) so provides, the FCA's general functions do not include functions that are transferred functions within the meaning of section 52 of that Act.

[(7A) . . .]

(8) "General guidance" has the meaning given in section 139B(5).]

NOTES

Substituted as noted to s 1A at **[7.1]**.

Sub-s (6): para (aa) inserted by the Financial Regulators' Powers (Technical Standards etc) (Amendment etc) (EU Exit) Regulations 2018, SI 2018/1115, reg 7(1), (3), as from 26 October 2018.

Sub-s (7A): originally inserted by the Pension Schemes Act 2015, s 47, Sch 3, paras 1, 3, as from 3 March 2015. subsequently repealed by the Financial Guidance and Claims Act 2018, s 25, Sch 3, paras 5, 7, as from 1 January 2019.

Note: sub-s (4) does not apply to certain credit-related rules made or guidance given by the FCA; see the Financial Services and Markets Act 2000 (Regulated Activities) (Amendment) (No 2) Order 2013, SI 2013/1881, art 61.

[7.3]

[1C The consumer protection objective

(1) The consumer protection objective is: securing an appropriate degree of protection for consumers.

(2) In considering what degree of protection for consumers may be appropriate, the FCA must have regard to—

(a) the differing degrees of risk involved in different kinds of investment or other transaction;

(b) the differing degrees of experience and expertise that different consumers may have;

(c) the needs that consumers may have for the timely provision of information and advice that is accurate and fit for purpose;

(d) the general principle that consumers should take responsibility for their decisions;

(e) the general principle that those providing regulated financial services should be expected to provide consumers with a level of care that is appropriate having regard to the degree of risk involved in relation to the investment or other transaction and the capabilities of the consumers in question;

(f) the differing expectations that consumers may have in relation to different kinds of investment or other transaction;

(g) . . .

(h) any information which the scheme operator of the ombudsman scheme has provided to the FCA pursuant to section 232A.]

NOTES

Substituted as noted to s 1A at **[7.1]**.

Sub-s (2): para (g) repealed by the Financial Guidance and Claims Act 2018, s 25, Sch 3, paras 5, 8, as from 6 April 2021.

[7.4]

[1D The integrity objective

(1) The integrity objective is: protecting and enhancing the integrity of the UK financial system.

(2) The "integrity" of the UK financial system includes—

(a) its soundness, stability and resilience,

(b) its not being used for a purpose connected with financial crime,

(c) its not being affected by [contraventions by persons of Article 14 (prohibition of insider dealing and of unlawful disclosure of inside information) or Article 15 (prohibition of market manipulation) of the market abuse regulation],
(d) the orderly operation of the financial markets, and
(e) the transparency of the price formation process in those markets.]

NOTES

Substituted as noted to s 1A at **[7.1]**.

Sub-s (2): words in square brackets in para (c) substituted by the Financial Services and Markets Act 2000 (Market Abuse) Regulations 2016, SI 2016/680, reg 10(1), (2), as from 3 July 2016.

[7.5]
[1E The competition objective

(1) The competition objective is: promoting effective competition in the interests of consumers in the markets for—
(a) regulated financial services, or
(b) services provided by a recognised investment exchange in carrying on regulated activities in respect of which it is by virtue of section 285(2) exempt from the general prohibition.

(2) The matters to which the FCA may have regard in considering the effectiveness of competition in the market for any services mentioned in subsection (1) include—
(a) the needs of different consumers who use or may use those services, including their need for information that enables them to make informed choices,
(b) the ease with which consumers who may wish to use those services, including consumers in areas affected by social or economic deprivation, can access them,
(c) the ease with which consumers who obtain those services can change the person from whom they obtain them,
(d) the ease with which new entrants can enter the market, and
(e) how far competition is encouraging innovation.]

NOTES

Substituted as noted to s 1A at **[7.1]**.

[Interpretation of terms used in relation to FCA's general duties

[7.6]
1F Meaning of "relevant markets" in strategic objective

In section 1B(2) "the relevant markets" means—
(a) the financial markets,
(b) the markets for regulated financial services (see section 1H(2)), and
(c) the markets for services that are provided by persons other than authorised persons in carrying on regulated activities but are provided without contravening the general prohibition.

NOTES

Substituted as noted to s 1A at **[7.1]**.

[7.7]
[1G Meaning of "consumer"

(1) In sections 1B to 1E "consumers" means persons . . .—
(a) [who] use, have used or may use—
(i) regulated financial services, or
(ii) services that are provided by persons other than authorised persons but are provided in carrying on regulated activities,
(b) [who] have relevant rights or interests in relation to any of those services,
(c) [who] have invested, or may invest, in financial instruments, . . .
(d) [who] have relevant rights or interests in relation to financial instruments[, . . .
(e) [who] have rights, interests or obligations that are affected by the level of a regulated benchmark][; or
(f) in respect of whom a person carries on an activity which is specified in article 89G of the Financial Services and Markets Act 2000 (Regulated Activities) Order 2001 (seeking out etc claims) whether that activity, as carried on by that person, is a regulated activity, or is, by reason of an exclusion provided for under the 2001 Order or the 2000 Act, not a regulated activity].

(2) A person ("P") has a "relevant right or interest" in relation to any services within subsection (1)(a) if P has a right or interest—
(a) which is derived from, or is otherwise attributable to, the use of the services by others, or
(b) which may be adversely affected by the use of the services by persons acting on P's behalf or in a fiduciary capacity in relation to P.

(3) If a person is providing a service within subsection (1)(a) as trustee, the persons who are, have been or may be beneficiaries of the trust are to be treated as persons who use, have used or may use the service.

(4) A person who deals with another person ("B") in the course of B providing a service within subsection (1)(a) is to be treated as using the service.

(5) A person ("P") has a "relevant right or interest" in relation to any financial instrument if P has—
(a) a right or interest which is derived from, or is otherwise attributable to, investment in the instrument by others, or
(b) a right or interest which may be adversely affected by the investment in the instrument by persons acting on P's behalf or in a fiduciary capacity in relation to P.]

NOTES

Substituted as noted to s 1A at **[7.1]**.

Sub-s (1): first word omitted and word omitted from para (d) repealed, words in square brackets in paras (a)–(e) inserted, and para (f) and the preceding word added, by the Financial Services and Markets Act 2000 (Claims Management Activity) Order

2018, SI 2018/1253, art 91(1), (2), as from 1 April 2019 (for provision specifying that the 2018 Order also comes into force on 29 November 2018 for the purposes of the FCA and FOS making rules and issuing guidance, and for transitional provisions in relation to carrying on a claims management activity, etc, see arts 1, 39–89 of the 2018 Order). The word omitted from para (c) was repealed, and para (e) (and the word immediately preceding it) was inserted, by the Financial Services and Markets Act 2000 (Regulated Activities) (Amendment) Order 2013, SI 2013/655, art 3(1), (2), as from 2 April 2013.

Note: the definition of "consumers" is extended for the purposes of this section and ss 1Q and 391(6) (as from 1 April 2014) by the Financial Services and Markets Act 2000 (Regulated Activities) (Amendment) (No 2) Order 2013, SI 2013/1881, art 65. Ie, "consumers" includes persons (a) who before 1 April 2014 used a relevant credit service, (b) who have rights or interests which are derived from, or are otherwise attributable to, the use of any such services by other persons, or (c) who have rights or interests which may be adversely affected by the use of any such services by persons acting on their behalf or in a fiduciary capacity in relation to them. See also as to the meaning of "consumers", art 89E of the Regulated Activities Order at **[8.234]**; and art 89 of the Financial Services and Markets Act 2000 (Claims Management Activity) Order 2018, SI 2018/1253 (which provides that for the purposes of this section and ss 404E and 425A, "consumer" includes a person: (a) who before 1 April 2019 received services from persons authorised, or by any person providing services for which an authorisation was required, under the Compensation Act 2006, s 5; (b) who has rights or interests which are derived from, or are otherwise attributable to, the use of any such services by other persons; (c) who has rights or interests which may be adversely affected by the use of any such services by a person acting on their behalf or in a fiduciary capacity in relation to them; or (d) in respect of whom a person carries on an activity specified in article 89G of the Financial Services and Markets Act 2000 (Regulated Activities) Order 2001, whether that activity is a regulated activity or is, by reason of an exclusion provided for under the 2001 Order or under the 2000 Act, not a regulated activity). The Financial Services Act 2012 (Transitional provisions) (Enforcement) Order 2013, SI 2013/441, art 33 and the Financial Services Act 2012 (Transitional Provisions) (Miscellaneous Provisions) Order 2013, SI 2013/442, art 7 also provides that. for the purposes of this section, ss 1Q, 391(6)(b) (and s 68 of the Financial Services Act 2012), "consumers" includes persons: (a) who used any of the services provided before section 19 came into force by (i) persons who were then regulated persons in carrying on relevant activities, or (ii) a credit union in the course of accepting deposits; (b) who have rights or interests which are derived from, or are otherwise attributable to, the use of any such services by other persons; or (c) who have rights or interests which may be adversely affected by the use of any such services by persons acting on their behalf or in a fiduciary capacity in relation to them.

[7.8]

[1H Further interpretative provisions for sections 1B to 1G

(1) The following provisions have effect for the interpretation of sections 1B to 1G.

(2) "Regulated financial services" means services provided—

(a) by authorised persons in carrying on regulated activities;

(b) . . .

(c) by authorised persons in communicating, or approving the communication by others of, invitations to engage in investment activity [or to engage in claims management activity];

(d) by authorised persons who are investment firms, or [qualifying credit institutions], in providing relevant ancillary services;

(e) by persons acting as appointed representatives;

(f) by payment service providers in providing payment services;

(g) by electronic money issuers in issuing electronic money;

(h) by sponsors to issuers of securities;

(i) by primary information providers to persons who issue financial instruments.

(3) "Financial crime" includes any offence involving—

(a) fraud or dishonesty,

(b) misconduct in, or misuse of information relating to, a financial market,

(c) handling the proceeds of crime, or

(d) the financing of terrorism.

(4) "Offence" includes an act or omission which would be an offence if it had taken place in the United Kingdom.

(5) "Issuer", except in the expression "electronic money issuer", has the meaning given in section 102A(6).

(6) "Financial instrument" has the meaning given in section 102A(4).

(7) "Securities" has the meaning given in section 102A(2).

[(7A) "Regulated benchmark" means a benchmark, as defined in section 22 . . . [(6A)], in relation to which any provision made under section 22(1A) . . . [(c)] has effect.]

(8) In this section—

. . .

. . .

. . .

"electronic money" has the same meaning as in the Electronic Money Regulations 2011;

"electronic money issuer" means a person who is an electronic money issuer as defined in regulation 2(1) of the Electronic Money Regulations 2011 other than a person falling within paragraph (f), (g) or (j) of the definition;

["engage in claims management activity" has the meaning given in section 21;]

"engage in investment activity" has the meaning given in section 21;

"financial instrument" has the meaning given in section 102A(4);

"payment services" has the same meaning as in the Payment Services Regulations [2017];

"payment service provider" means a person who is a payment service provider as defined in regulation 2(1) of the Payment Services Regulations [2017] other than a person falling within paragraph [(i) or (j)] of the definition;

"primary information provider" has the meaning given in section 89P(2);

"relevant ancillary service" means any service of a kind mentioned in [Part 3A of Schedule 2 to the Financial Services and Markets Act 2000 (Regulated Activities) Order 2001] the provision of which does not involve the carrying on of a regulated activity;

"sponsor" has the meaning given in section 88(2).]

NOTES

Substituted as noted to s 1A at **[7.1]**.

Para (b) of sub-s (2), and the first two definitions omitted from sub-s (8), were repealed by the Financial Services and Markets Act 2000 (Regulated Activities) (Amendment) (No 2) Order 2013, SI 2013/1881, art 10(1), (2), as from 1 April 2014.

The words in square brackets in sub-s (2)(c) and the definition "engage in claims management activity" in sub-s (8) were inserted by the Financial Guidance and Claims Act 2018, s 27(1), (2), as from 6 October 2018. For transitional provisions in relation to the transfer of regulation of claims management services to the FCA, see Sch 5 to the 2018 Act.

Words in square brackets in sub-s (2)(d) substituted by the Financial Services and Markets Act 2000 (Amendment) (EU Exit) Regulations 2019, SI 2019/632, regs 2, 4(1), (2), as from IP completion day (as defined in the European Union (Withdrawal Agreement) Act 2020, s 39).

Sub-s (7A) was inserted by the Financial Services and Markets Act 2000 (Regulated Activities) (Amendment) Order 2013, SI 2013/655, art 3(1), (3), as from 2 April 2013. The words in square brackets were inserted, and the words omitted were repealed, by the Financial Services and Markets Act 2000 (Benchmarks) Regulations 2018, SI 2018/135, reg 37, as from 27 February 2018 (in relation to the insertion of the words in square brackets), and as from 1 May 2020 (in relation to the repeal of the omitted words).

The third definition omitted from sub-s (8) was repealed, and the words in square brackets in the definition "relevant ancillary service" were substituted, by SI 2019/632, regs 2, 4(1), (3), as from IP completion day (as defined in the European Union (Withdrawal Agreement) Act 2020, s 39).

Words in square brackets in the definitions "payment services" and "payment service provider" substituted by the Payment Services Regulations 2017, SI 2017/752, reg 156, Sch 8, Pt 1, para 2(1), (2), as from 13 January 2018 (for general transitional provisions, see regs 149–154 of, and Sch 8, Pt 1, para 2(1), (11) to, the 2017 Regulations).

[7.9]

[1I Meaning of "the UK financial system"

In this Act "the UK financial system" means the financial system operating in the United Kingdom and includes—

(a) financial markets and exchanges,
(b) regulated activities [(including regulated claims management activities)], and
(c) other activities connected with financial markets and exchanges.]

NOTES

Substituted as noted to s 1A at **[7.1]**.

Para (b): words in square brackets inserted by the Financial Services and Markets Act 2000 (Claims Management Activity) Order 2018, SI 2018/1253, art 91(1), (3), as from 1 April 2019 (for provision specifying that the 2018 Order also comes into force on 29 November 2018 for the purposes of the FCA and FOS making rules and issuing guidance, and for transitional provisions in relation to carrying on a claims management activity, etc, see arts 1, 39–89 of the 2018 Order).

[Modifications applying if core activity not regulated by PRA

[7.10]

1IA Modifications applying if core activity not regulated by PRA

(1) If and so long as any regulated activity is a core activity (see section 142B) without also being a PRA-regulated activity (see section 22A), the provisions of this Chapter are to have effect subject to the following modifications.

(2) Section 1B is to have effect as if—

(a) in subsection (3), after paragraph (c) there were inserted—

"(d) in relation to the matters mentioned in section 1EA(2), the continuity objective (see section 1EA).", and

(b) in subsection (4), for "or the integrity objective," there were substituted ", the integrity objective or (in relation to the matters mentioned in section 1EA(2)) the continuity objective,".

(3) After section 1E there is to be taken to be inserted—

"1EA Continuity objective

(1) In relation to the matters mentioned in subsection (2), the continuity objective is: protecting the continuity of the provision in the United Kingdom of core services (see section 142C).

(2) Those matters are—

(a) Part 9B (ring-fencing);
(b) ring-fenced bodies (see section 142A);
(c) any body corporate incorporated in the United Kingdom that has a ring-fenced body as a member of its group;
(d) applications under Part 4A which, if granted, would result, or would be capable of resulting, in a person becoming a ring-fenced body.

(3) The FCA's continuity objective is to be advanced primarily by—

(a) seeking to ensure that the business of ring-fenced bodies is carried on in a way that avoids any adverse effect on the continuity of the provision in the United Kingdom of core services,
(b) seeking to ensure that the business of ring-fenced bodies is protected from risks (arising in the United Kingdom or elsewhere) that could adversely affect the continuity of the provision in the United Kingdom of core services, and
(c) seeking to minimise the risk that the failure of a ring-fenced body or of a member of a ring-fenced body's group could adversely affect the continuity of the provision in the United Kingdom of core services.

(4) In subsection (3)(c), "failure" is to be read in accordance with section 2J(3) to (4)."]

NOTES

Inserted, together with the preceding heading, by the Financial Services (Banking Reform) Act 2013, s 2, as from 1 January 2019.

[Power to amend objectives

[7.11]
1J Power to amend objectives
The Treasury may by order amend any of the following provisions—
- (a) in section 1E(1), paragraphs (a) and (b),
- (b) section 1G, and
- (c) section 1H(2) and (5) to (8).]

NOTES
Substituted as noted to s 1A at **[7.1]**.

[Recommendations

[7.12]
1JA Recommendations by Treasury in connection with general duties
(1) The Treasury may at any time by notice in writing to the FCA make recommendations to the FCA about aspects of the economic policy of Her Majesty's Government to which the FCA should have regard when considering—
- (a) how to act in a way which is compatible with its strategic objective,
- (b) how to advance one or more of its operational objectives,
- (c) how to discharge the duty in section 1B(4) (duty to promote effective competition in the interests of consumers),
- (d) the application of the regulatory principles in section 3B, and
- (e) the matter mentioned in section 1B(5)(b) (importance of taking action to minimise the extent to which it is possible for a business to be used for a purpose connected with financial crime).

(2) The Treasury must make recommendations under subsection (1) at least once in each Parliament.
(3) The Treasury must—
- (a) publish in such manner as they think fit any notice given under subsection (1), and
- (b) lay a copy of it before Parliament.]

NOTES
Inserted, together with the preceding heading, by the Bank of England and Financial Services Act 2016, s 19, as from 6 July 2016.

[Guidance about objectives

[7.13]
1K Guidance about objectives
(1) The general guidance given by the FCA under section 139A must include guidance about how it intends to advance its operational objectives in discharging its general functions in relation to different categories of authorised person or regulated activity.
(2) Before giving or altering any guidance complying with subsection (1), the FCA must consult the PRA.]

NOTES
Substituted as noted to s 1A at **[7.1]**.

[Supervision, monitoring and enforcement

[7.14]
1L Supervision, monitoring and enforcement
(1) The FCA must maintain arrangements for supervising authorised persons.
(2) The FCA must maintain arrangements designed to enable it to determine whether persons other than authorised persons are complying—
- (a) with requirements imposed on them by or under this Act, in cases where the FCA is the appropriate regulator for the purposes of Part 14 (disciplinary measures), . . .
- [(aa) with requirements imposed on them by the Alternative Investment Fund Managers Regulations 2013, or]
- (b) with requirements imposed on them by any [qualifying provision] that is specified, or of a description specified, for the purposes of this subsection by the Treasury by order.

(3) The FCA must also maintain arrangements for enforcing compliance by persons other than authorised persons with relevant requirements, within the meaning of Part 14, in cases where the FCA is the appropriate regulator for the purposes of any provision of that Part.]

NOTES
Substituted as noted to s 1A at **[7.1]**.

Sub-s (2): the word omitted from para (a) was repealed, and para (aa) was inserted, by the Alternative Investment Fund Managers Regulations 2013, SI 2013/1773, reg 80, Sch 1, Part 1, paras 1, 3, as from 22 July 2013. Words in square brackets in para (b) substituted by the Financial Services and Markets Act 2000 (Amendment) (EU Exit) Regulations 2019, SI 2019/632, regs 2, 5, as from IP completion day (as defined in the European Union (Withdrawal Agreement) Act 2020, s 39) (for transitional provisions see SI 2019/710, reg 37 at **[12.110]**).

Orders and Regulations: the Financial Services and Markets Act 2000 (Qualifying Provisions) Order 2013, SI 2013/419; the Financial Services and Markets Act 2000 (Qualifying Provisions) (No 2) Order 2013, SI 2013/3116; the Financial Services and Markets Act 2000 (Transparency of Securities Financing Transactions and of Reuse) Regulations 2016, SI 2016/715; the Alternative Investment Fund Managers (Amendment) Regulations 2018, SI 2018/134; the Insurance Distribution (Regulated Activities and Miscellaneous Amendments) Order 2018, SI 2018/546.

[Arrangements for consulting practitioners and consumers

[7.15]
1M The FCA's general duty to consult
The FCA must make and maintain effective arrangements for consulting practitioners and consumers on the extent to which its general policies and practices are consistent with its general duties under section 1B [. . .].]

NOTES

Substituted as noted to s 1A at **[7.1]**.

The words omitted were originally inserted by the Pension Schemes Act 2015, s 47, Sch 3, paras 1, 4, as from 3 March 2015; and were subsequently repealed by the Financial Guidance and Claims Act 2018, s 25, Sch 3, paras 5, 9, as from 1 January 2019.

[7.16]

[1N The FCA Practitioner Panel

(1) Arrangements under section 1M must include the establishment and maintenance of a panel of persons (to be known as "the FCA Practitioner Panel") to represent the interests of practitioners.

(2) The FCA must appoint one of the members of the FCA Practitioner Panel to be its chair.

(3) The Treasury's approval is required for the appointment or dismissal of the chair.

(4) The FCA must appoint to the FCA Practitioner Panel such—

(a) persons representing authorised persons, and

(b) persons representing recognised investment exchanges,

as it considers appropriate.

(5) The FCA may appoint to the FCA Practitioner Panel such other persons as it considers appropriate.]

NOTES

Substituted as noted to s 1A at **[7.1]**.

[7.17]

[1O The Smaller Business Practitioner Panel

(1) Arrangements under section 1M must include the establishment and maintenance of a panel of persons (to be known as "the Smaller Business Practitioner Panel") to represent the interests of eligible practitioners.

(2) "Eligible practitioners" means authorised persons of a description specified in a statement maintained by the FCA.

(3) The FCA must appoint one of the members of the Smaller Business Practitioner Panel to be its chair.

(4) The Treasury's approval is required for the appointment or dismissal of the chair.

(5) The FCA must appoint to the Smaller Business Practitioner Panel such—

(a) individuals who are eligible practitioners, and

(b) persons representing eligible practitioners,

as it considers appropriate.

(6) The FCA may appoint to the Smaller Business Practitioner Panel such other persons as it considers appropriate.

(7) In making the appointments, the FCA must have regard to the desirability of ensuring the representation of eligible practitioners carrying on a range of regulated activities.

(8) The FCA may revise the statement maintained under subsection (2).

(9) The FCA must—

(a) give the Treasury a copy of the statement or revised statement without delay, and

(b) publish the statement as for the time being in force in such manner as it thinks fit.]

NOTES

Substituted as noted to s 1A at **[7.1]**.

[7.18]

[1P The Markets Practitioner Panel

(1) Arrangements under section 1M must include the establishment and maintenance of a panel of persons (to be known as "the Markets Practitioner Panel") to represent the interests of practitioners who are likely to be affected by the exercise by the FCA of its functions relating to markets, including its functions under Parts 6, 8A and 18.

(2) The FCA must appoint one of the members of the Markets Practitioner Panel to be its chair.

(3) The Treasury's approval is required for the appointment or dismissal of the chair.

(4) The FCA must appoint to the Markets Practitioner Panel such persons to represent the interests of persons within subsection (5) as it considers appropriate.

(5) The persons within this subsection are—

(a) authorised persons,

(b) persons who issue financial instruments,

(c) sponsors, as defined in section 88(2),

(d) recognised investment exchanges, and

(e) primary information providers, as defined in section 89P(2).

(6) The FCA may appoint to the Markets Practitioner Panel such other persons as it considers appropriate.]

NOTES

Substituted as noted to s 1A at **[7.1]**.

[7.19]

[1Q The Consumer Panel

(1) Arrangements under section 1M must include the establishment and maintenance of a panel of persons (to be known as "the Consumer Panel") to represent the interests of consumers.

(2) The FCA must appoint one of the members of the Consumer Panel to be its chair.

(3) The Treasury's approval is required for the appointment or dismissal of the chair.

(4) The FCA may appoint to the Consumer Panel such consumers, or persons representing the interests of consumers, as it considers appropriate.

(5) The FCA must secure that membership of the Consumer Panel is such as to give a fair degree of representation to those who are using, or are or may be contemplating using, services otherwise than in connection with businesses carried on by them.

[(5A) If it appears to the Consumer Panel that any matter being considered by it is relevant to the extent to which the general policies and practices of the PRA are consistent with the PRA's general duties under sections 2B to 2H, it may communicate to the PRA any views relating to that matter.

(5B) The PRA may arrange to meet any of the FCA's expenditure on the Consumer Panel which is attributable to the Panel's functions under subsection (5A).]

(6) Sections 425A and 425B (meaning of "consumers") apply for the purposes of this section, but the references to consumers in this section do not include consumers who are authorised persons.]

NOTES

Substituted as noted to s 1A at **[7.1]**.

Sub-ss (5A), (5B): inserted by the Financial Services (Banking Reform) Act 2013, s 132, as from 1 March 2014.

Consumers: as to the meaning of this, see the note on s 1G at **[7.7]**.

[7.20]

[1R Duty to consider representations made by the Panels

(1) The FCA must consider representations that are made to it in accordance with arrangements made under section 1M.

(2) The FCA must from time to time publish in such manner as it thinks fit responses to the representations.]

NOTES

Substituted as noted to s 1A at **[7.1]**.

[Reviews

[7.21]

1S Reviews

(1) The Treasury may appoint an independent person to conduct a review of the economy, efficiency and effectiveness with which the FCA has used its resources in discharging its functions.

(2) A review may be limited by the Treasury to such functions of the FCA (however described) as the Treasury may specify in appointing the person to conduct it.

(3) A review is not to be concerned with the merits of the FCA's general policy or principles in complying with its general duties under section 1B(1) and (4) [. . .].

(4) On completion of a review, the person conducting it must make a written report to the Treasury—

(a) setting out the result of the review, and

(b) making such recommendations (if any) as the person considers appropriate.

(5) A copy of the report must be—

(a) laid before Parliament, and

(b) published in such manner as the Treasury consider appropriate.

(6) Any expenses reasonably incurred in the conduct of the review are to be met by the Treasury out of money provided by Parliament.

(7) "Independent" means appearing to the Treasury to be independent of the FCA.]

NOTES

Substituted as noted to s 1A at **[7.1]**.

Sub-s (3): the words omitted were originally inserted by the Pension Schemes Act 2015, s 47, Sch 3, paras 1, 5, as from 3 March 2015; and were subsequently repealed by the Financial Guidance and Claims Act 2018, s 25, Sch 3, paras 5, 10, as from 1 January 2019.

[7.22]

[1T Right to obtain documents and information

(1) A person conducting a review under section 1S—

(a) has a right of access at any reasonable time to all such documents as the person may reasonably require for the purposes of the review, and

(b) may require any person holding or accountable for any such document to provide such information and explanation as are reasonably necessary for that purpose.

(2) Subsection (1) applies only to documents in the custody of or under the control of the FCA.

(3) An obligation imposed on a person as a result of the exercise of the powers conferred by subsection (1) is enforceable by injunction or, in Scotland, by an order for specific performance under section 45 of the Court of Session Act 1988.]

NOTES

Substituted as noted to s 1A at **[7.1]**.

[CHAPTER 2 THE PRUDENTIAL REGULATION AUTHORITY

The Prudential Regulation Authority

[7.23]

[2A The Prudential Regulation Authority

(1) The "Prudential Regulation Authority" is the Bank of England.

(2) The Bank's functions as the Prudential Regulation Authority—

(a) are to be exercised by the Bank acting through its Prudential Regulation Committee (see Part 3A of the Bank of England Act 1998), and

(b) are not exercisable by the Bank in any other way.

(3) References in this Act or any other enactment to the Prudential Regulation Authority do not include the Bank of England acting otherwise than in its capacity as the Prudential Regulation Authority.
(4) References in this Act to the Bank of England do not (unless otherwise provided) include the Bank acting in its capacity as the Prudential Regulation Authority.
(5) Subsections (3) and (4) do not apply to this section.
(6) Subsection (4) does not apply for the interpretation of references to the court of directors of the Bank of England, or to a Deputy Governor or committee of the Bank.
(7) The Prudential Regulation Authority is referred to in this Act as the PRA.]

NOTES

Substituted as noted to s 1A at **[7.1]**.

Further substituted by new ss 2A, 2AB, by the Bank of England and Financial Services Act 2016, s 12, as from 1 March 2017.

Orders: see the note to s 2AB at **[7.24]**.

[7.24]
[2AB Functions of the PRA
(1) The PRA is to have the functions conferred on it by or under this Act.
(2) Schedule 1ZB makes provision about functions of the PRA.
(3) References in this Act or any other enactment to functions conferred on the PRA by or under this Act include references to functions conferred on the PRA by or under—
(a) the Insolvency Act 1986,
(b) the Banking Act 2009,
(c) the Financial Services Act 2012, . . .
(d) a [qualifying provision] that is specified, or of a description specified, for the purposes of this subsection by the Treasury by order, [or
(e) regulations made by the Treasury under section 8 of the European Union (Withdrawal) Act 2018].]

NOTES

Substituted as noted to s 2A at **[7.23]**.

Sub-s (3): word omitted from para (c) repealed, and para (e) (and the preceding word) added, by the Financial Regulators' Powers (Technical Standards etc) (Amendment etc) (EU Exit) Regulations 2018, SI 2018/1115, reg 7(1), (4), as from 26 October 2018. Words in square brackets in para (d) substituted by the Financial Services and Markets Act 2000 (Amendment) (EU Exit) Regulations 2019, SI 2019/632, regs 2, 6, as from IP completion day (as defined in the European Union (Withdrawal Agreement) Act 2020, s 39) (for transitional provisions see SI 2019/710, reg 37 at **[12.110]**).

Orders: the Financial Services and Markets Act 2000 (Qualifying Provisions) Order 2013, SI 2013/419; the Financial Services and Markets Act 2000 (Qualifying Provisions) (No 2) Order 2013, SI 2013/3116; the Financial Services and Markets Act 2000 (Qualifying EU Provisions) (Amendment) Order 2016, SI 2016/936. Note that these were originally made under s 2A ante, but now have effect under this section following the substitution noted above; see the transitional provisions in the Bank of England and Financial Services Act 2016, Sch 3.

[The PRA's general duties

[7.25]
2B The PRA's general objective
(1) In discharging its general functions the PRA must, so far as is reasonably possible, act in a way which advances its general objective.
(2) The PRA's general objective is: promoting the safety and soundness of PRA-authorised persons.
(3) That objective is to be advanced primarily by—
(a) seeking to ensure that the business of PRA-authorised persons is carried on in a way which avoids any adverse effect on the stability of the UK financial system, . . .
(b) seeking to minimise the adverse effect that the failure of a PRA-authorised person could be expected to have on the stability of the UK financial system[, and
(c) discharging its general functions in relation to the matters mentioned in subsection (4A) in a way that seeks to—
(i) ensure that the business of ring-fenced bodies is carried on in a way that avoids any adverse effect on the continuity of the provision in the United Kingdom of core services,
(ii) ensure that the business of ring-fenced bodies is protected from risks (arising in the United Kingdom or elsewhere) that could adversely affect the continuity of the provision in the United Kingdom of core services, and
(iii) minimise the risk that the failure of a ring-fenced body or of a member of a ring-fenced body's group could affect the continuity of the provision in the United Kingdom of core services].
(4) The adverse effects mentioned in [subsection (3)(a) and (b)] may, in particular, result from the disruption of the continuity of financial services.
[(4A) The matters referred to in subsection (3)(c) are—
(a) Part 9B (ring-fencing);
(b) ring-fenced bodies (see section 142A);
(c) any body corporate incorporated in the United Kingdom that has a ring-fenced body as a member of its group;
(d) applications under Part 4A which, if granted, would result, or would be capable of resulting, in a person becoming a ring-fenced body.]
(5) In this Act "PRA-authorised person" means an authorised person who has permission—
(a) given under Part 4A, or
(b) resulting from any other provision of this Act,
to carry on regulated activities that consist of or include one or more PRA-regulated activities (see section 22A).
(6) Subsection (1) is subject to sections 2C and 2D.]

NOTES

Substituted as noted to s 1A at **[7.1]**.

The word omitted from sub-s (3)(a) was repealed, sub-s (3)(c) (and the word preceding it) was inserted, the words in square brackets in sub-s (4) were substituted, and sub-s (4A) was inserted, by the Financial Services (Banking Reform) Act 2013, s 1(1)–(4), as from 1 January 2019.

[7.26]

[2C Insurance objective

(1) In discharging its general functions so far as relating to a PRA-regulated activity relating to the effecting or carrying out of contracts of insurance or PRA-authorised persons carrying on that activity, the PRA must, so far as is reasonably possible, act in a way—

(a) which is compatible with its general objective and its insurance objective, and

(b) which the PRA considers most appropriate for the purpose of advancing those objectives.

(2) The PRA's insurance objective is: contributing to the securing of an appropriate degree of protection for those who are or may become policyholders.

(3) This section applies only if the effecting or carrying out of contracts of insurance as principal is to any extent a PRA-regulated activity.]

NOTES

Substituted as noted to s 1A at **[7.1]**.

[7.27]

[2D Power to provide for additional objectives

(1) Subsection (2) applies to an order under section 22A which—

(a) is made at any time after the coming into force of the first order under that section, and

(b) contains a statement by the Treasury that, in their opinion, the effect (or one of the effects) of the proposed order is that an activity would become a PRA-regulated activity.

(2) An order to which this subsection applies may specify an additional objective ("the specified objective") in relation to specified activities that become PRA-regulated activities by virtue of the order ("the additional activities").

(3) In discharging its general functions so far as relating to the additional activities or PRA-authorised persons carrying on those activities, the PRA must, so far as is reasonably possible, act in a way—

(a) which is compatible with its general objective and the specified objective, and

(b) which the PRA considers most appropriate for the purpose of advancing those objectives.]

NOTES

Substituted as noted to s 1A at **[7.1]**.

[7.28]

[2E Strategy

(1) The PRA must—

(a) determine its strategy in relation to its objectives, and

(b) from time to time review, and if necessary revise, the strategy.

(2) Before determining or revising its strategy, the PRA must consult the court of directors of the Bank of England about a draft of the strategy or of the revisions.

(3) The PRA must determine its strategy within 12 months of the coming into force of this section.

(4) The PRA must carry out and complete a review of its strategy before the end of each relevant period.

(5) The relevant period is 12 months beginning with the date on which the previous review was completed, except that in the case of the first review the relevant period is the period of 12 months beginning with the date on which the strategy was determined under subsection (3).

(6) The PRA must publish its strategy.

(7) If the strategy is revised the PRA must publish the revised strategy.

(8) Publication under subsection (6) or (7) is to be in such manner as the PRA thinks fit.]

NOTES

Substituted as noted to s 1A at **[7.1]**.

[7.29]

[2F Interpretation of references to objectives

In this Act, a reference, in relation to any function of the PRA, to the objectives of the PRA is a reference to its general objective but—

(a) so far as the function is exercisable in relation to the activity of effecting or carrying out contracts of insurance, or PRA-authorised persons carrying on that activity, is a reference to its general objective and its insurance objective;

(b) so far as the function is exercisable in relation to an activity to which an objective specified by order by virtue of section 2D(2) relates, or PRA-authorised persons carrying on that activity, is a reference to its general objective and the objective specified by the order.]

NOTES

Substituted as noted to s 1A at **[7.1]**.

[7.30]

[2G Limit on effect of sections 2B to 2D

Nothing in sections 2B to 2D is to be regarded as requiring the PRA to ensure that no PRA-authorised person fails.]

NOTES

Substituted as noted to s 1A at **[7.1]**.

[7.31]

[2H Secondary competition objective and duty to have regard to regulatory principles

(1) When discharging its general functions in a way that advances its objectives (see section 2F), the PRA must so far as is reasonably possible act in a way which, as a secondary objective, facilitates effective competition in the markets for services provided by PRA-authorised persons in carrying on regulated activities.

(2) In discharging its general functions, the PRA must also have regard to the regulatory principles in section 3B.]

NOTES

Substituted as noted to s 1A at **[7.1]**.

Further substituted by the Financial Services (Banking Reform) Act 2013, s 130(1), as from 1 March 2014.

[7.32]

[2I Guidance about objectives

(1) The PRA must give, and from time to time review, guidance about how it intends to advance its objectives in discharging its general functions in relation to different categories of PRA-authorised person or PRA-regulated activity.

(2) Before giving or altering any guidance complying with subsection (1), the PRA must consult the FCA.

(3) The PRA must publish the guidance as for the time being in force.]

NOTES

Substituted as noted to s 1A at **[7.1]**.

[7.33]

[2J Interpretation of Chapter 2

(1) For the purposes of this Chapter, the PRA's general functions are—

(a) its function of making rules under this Act (considered as a whole),

[(aa) its function of making technical standards in accordance with Chapter 2A of Part 9A;]

(b) its function of preparing and issuing codes under this Act (considered as a whole), and

(c) its function of determining the general policy and principles by reference to which it performs particular functions under this Act.

(2) Except to the extent that an order under section 50 of the Financial Services Act 2012 (orders relating to mutual societies functions) so provides, the PRA's general functions do not include functions that are transferred functions within the meaning of section 52 of that Act.

(3) For the purposes of this Chapter, the cases in which [an authorised] person ("P") is to be regarded as failing include those where—

(a) P enters insolvency,

(b) any of the stabilisation options in Part 1 of the Banking Act 2009 is achieved in relation to P, or

(c) P falls to be taken for the purposes of the compensation scheme to be unable, or likely to be unable, to satisfy claims against P.

[(3A) For the purposes of this Chapter, the cases in which a person ("P") other than an authorised person is to be regarded as failing include any case where P enters insolvency.]

(4) In [subsections (3)(a) and (3A)] "insolvency" includes—

(a) bankruptcy,

(b) liquidation,

(c) bank insolvency,

(d) administration,

(e) bank administration,

(f) receivership,

(g) a composition between P and P's creditors, and

(h) a scheme of arrangement of P's affairs.]

NOTES

Substituted as noted to s 1A at **[7.1]**.

Sub-s (1)(aa) inserted by the Financial Regulators' Powers (Technical Standards etc) (Amendment etc) (EU Exit) Regulations 2018, SI 2018/1115, reg 7(1), (5), as from 26 October 2018.

The words in square brackets in sub-ss (3) and (4) were substituted, and sub-s (3A) was inserted, by the Financial Services (Banking Reform) Act 2013, s 1(5), as from 1 January 2019.

[Supervision

[7.34]

2K Arrangements for supervision of PRA-authorised persons

The PRA must maintain arrangements for supervising PRA-authorised persons.]

NOTES

Substituted as noted to s 1A at **[7.1]**.

[Arrangements for consulting practitioners

[7.35]

2L The PRA's general duty to consult

The PRA must make and maintain effective arrangements for consulting PRA-authorised persons or, where appropriate, persons appearing to the PRA to represent the interests of such persons on the extent to which its general policies and practices are consistent with its general duties under sections 2B to 2H.]

NOTES

Substituted as noted to s 1A at **[7.1]**.

[7.36]

[2M The PRA Practitioner Panel

(1) Arrangements under section 2L must include the establishment and maintenance of a panel of persons (to be known as "the PRA Practitioner Panel") to represent the interests of practitioners.

(2) The PRA must appoint one of the members of the PRA Practitioner Panel to be its chair.

(3) The Treasury's approval is required for the appointment or dismissal of the chair.

(4) The PRA must appoint to the PRA Practitioner Panel such persons representing PRA-authorised persons as it considers appropriate.

(5) The PRA may appoint to the PRA Practitioner Panel such other persons as it considers appropriate.]

NOTES

Substituted as noted to s 1A at **[7.1]**.

[7.37]

[2N Duty to consider representations

(1) The PRA must consider representations that are made to it in accordance with arrangements made under section 2L.

(2) The PRA must from time to time publish in such manner as it thinks fit responses to the representations.]

NOTES

Substituted as noted to s 1A at **[7.1]**.

2O, 2P (*Substituted as noted to s 1A ante. Subsequently repealed by the Bank of England and Financial Services Act 2016, s 16, Sch 2, Pt 2, paras 26, 27, as from 1 March 2017.*)

[CHAPTER 3 FURTHER PROVISIONS RELATING TO FCA AND PRA

Introductory

[7.38]

3A Meaning of "regulator"

(1) This section has effect for the interpretation of this Act.

(2) The FCA and the PRA are the "regulators", and references to a regulator are to be read accordingly.

(3) Subsection (2) does not affect—

(a) the meaning of the following expressions—
"home state regulator";
"host state regulator";
"overseas regulator";
["Gibraltar regulator"];

(b) the meaning of "the appropriate regulator" in Part 18 ([recognised investment exchanges, clearing houses and CSDs])[; or

(c) the meaning of "regulator" in sections 410A and 410B (fees to meet certain expenses of Treasury)].]

NOTES

Substituted as noted to s 1A at **[7.1]**.

Sub-s (3): word omitted from para (a) repealed, and para (c) (and the preceding word) added, by the Financial Services (Banking Reform) Act 2013, s 135(2), as from 1 March 2014. Words "Gibraltar regulator" in square brackets in para (a) inserted by the Financial Services Act 2021, s 22, Sch 8, para 2, as from a day to be appointed. Words in square brackets in para (b) substituted by the Central Securities Depositories Regulations 2017, SI 2017/1064, reg 2(1), (2), as from 28 November 2017.

[Regulatory principles

[7.39]

3B Regulatory principles to be applied by both regulators

(1) In relation to the regulators, the regulatory principles referred to in section 1B(5)(a) and [2H(2)] are as follows—

(a) the need to use the resources of each regulator in the most efficient and economic way;

(b) the principle that a burden or restriction which is imposed on a person, or on the carrying on of an activity, should be proportionate to the benefits, considered in general terms, which are expected to result from the imposition of that burden or restriction;

(c) the desirability of sustainable growth in the economy of the United Kingdom in the medium or long term;

(d) the general principle that consumers should take responsibility for their decisions;

(e) the responsibilities of the senior management of persons subject to requirements imposed by or under this Act, including those affecting consumers, in relation to compliance with those requirements;

(f) the desirability where appropriate of each regulator exercising its functions in a way that recognises differences in the nature of, and objectives of, businesses carried on by different persons [(including different kinds of person such as mutual societies and other kinds of business organisation)] subject to requirements imposed by or under this Act;

(g) the desirability in appropriate cases of each regulator publishing information relating to persons on whom requirements are imposed by or under this Act, or requiring such persons to publish information, as a means of contributing to the advancement by each regulator of its objectives;

(h) the principle that the regulators should exercise their functions as transparently as possible.

(2) "Consumer" has the meaning given in section 1G.

(3) "Objectives", in relation to the FCA, means operational objectives.

[(3A) Mutual society" has the same meaning as in section 138K.]

(4) The Treasury may by order amend subsection (2).]

NOTES

Substituted as noted to s 1A at **[7.1]**.

Sub-s (1): figure "2H(2)" in square brackets substituted by the Financial Services (Banking Reform) Act 2013, s 130(2), as from 1 March 2014. Words in square brackets in para (f) inserted by the Bank of England and Financial Services Act 2016, s 20(1), (2), as from 6 July 2016.

Sub-s (3A): inserted by the Bank of England and Financial Services Act 2016, s 20(1), (3), as from 6 July 2016.

[Corporate governance

[7.40]

3C Duty to follow principles of good governance

In managing its affairs, [the FCA] must have regard to such generally accepted principles of good corporate governance as it is reasonable to regard as applicable to it.]

NOTES

Substituted as noted to s 1A at **[7.1]**.

Words in square brackets substituted by the Bank of England and Financial Services Act 2016, s 16, Sch 2, Pt 2, paras 26, 29, as from 1 March 2017.

[Relationship between FCA and PRA

[7.41]

3D Duty of FCA and PRA to ensure co-ordinated exercise of functions

(1) The regulators must co-ordinate the exercise of their respective functions conferred by or under this Act with a view to ensuring—

(a) that each regulator consults the other regulator (where not otherwise required to do so) in connection with any proposed exercise of a function in a way that may have a material adverse effect on the advancement by the other regulator of any of its objectives;

(b) that where appropriate each regulator obtains information and advice from the other regulator in connection with the exercise of its functions in relation to matters of common regulatory interest in cases where the other regulator may be expected to have relevant information or relevant expertise;

(c) that where either regulator exercises functions in relation to matters of common regulatory interest, both regulators comply with their respective duties under section 1B(5)(a) or 2H(1)(a), so far as relating to the regulatory principles in section 3B(1)(a) and (b).

(2) The duty in subsection (1) applies only to the extent that compliance with the duty—

(a) is compatible with the advancement by each regulator of any of its objectives, and

(b) does not impose a burden on the regulators that is disproportionate to the benefits of compliance.

(3) A function conferred on either regulator by or under this Act relates to matters of common regulatory interest if—

(a) the other regulator exercises similar or related functions in relation to the same persons,

(b) the other regulator exercises functions which relate to different persons but relate to similar subject-matter, or

(c) its exercise could affect the advancement by the other regulator of any of its objectives.

(4) "Objectives", in relation to the FCA, means operational objectives.]

NOTES

Substituted as noted to s 1A at **[7.1]**.

[7.42]

[3E Memorandum of understanding

(1) The regulators must prepare and maintain a memorandum which describes in general terms—

(a) the role of each regulator in relation to the exercise of functions conferred by or under this Act which relate to matters of common regulatory interest, and

(b) how the regulators intend to comply with section 3D in relation to the exercise of such functions.

(2) The memorandum may in particular contain provisions about how the regulators intend to comply with section 3D in relation to—

(a) applications for Part 4A permission;

(b) the variation of permission;

(c) the imposition of requirements;

(d) the obtaining and disclosure of information;

(e) cases where a PRA-authorised person is a member of a group whose other members include one or more other authorised persons (whether or not PRA-authorised persons);

(f) . . .

(g) the making of rules;

(h) directions under section 138A (modification or waiver of rules);

(i) powers to appoint competent persons under Part 11 (information gathering and investigations) to conduct investigations on their behalf;

(j) functions under Part 12 (control over authorised persons);

(k) . . .

(l) functions under Part 19 (Lloyd's);

(m) functions under section 347 (record of authorised persons etc);

(n) functions under Part 24 (insolvency);

(o) fees payable to either regulator.

(3) The memorandum must contain provision about the co-ordination by the regulators of—

(a) . . .

(b) their relations with regulatory bodies outside the United Kingdom, and

(c) the exercise of their functions in relation to the compensation scheme.

Part 7 Financial Services Acts

(4) The regulators must review the memorandum at least once in each calendar year.

(5) The regulators must give the Treasury a copy of the memorandum and any revised memorandum.

(6) The Treasury must lay before Parliament a copy of any document received by them under this section.

(7) The regulators must ensure that the memorandum as currently in force is published in the way appearing to them to be best calculated to bring it to the attention of the public.

(8) The memorandum need not relate to any aspect of compliance with section 3D if the regulators consider—

(a) that publication of information about that aspect would be against the public interest, or

(b) that that aspect is a technical or operational matter not affecting the public.

(9) The reference in subsection (1)(a) to matters of common regulatory interest is to be read in accordance with section 3D(3).]

NOTES

Substituted as noted to s 1A at **[7.1]**.

Sub-s (2): paras (f) and (k) repealed by the EEA Passport Rights (Amendment, etc, and Transitional Provisions) (EU Exit) Regulations 2018, SI 2018/1149, reg 3, Schedule, Pt 1, paras 1, 2, as from IP completion day (as defined in the European Union (Withdrawal Agreement) Act 2020, s 39).

Sub-s (3): para (a) repealed by the Financial Services and Markets Act 2000 (Amendment) (EU Exit) Regulations 2019, SI 2019/632, regs 2, 7, as from IP completion day (as defined in the European Union (Withdrawal Agreement) Act 2020, s 39).

[7.43]

[3F With-profits insurance policies

(1) The regulators must prepare and maintain a memorandum which describes in general terms—

(a) the role of each regulator in relation to the exercise of functions conferred by or under this Act so far as they relate to with-profits insurers, and

(b) how the regulators intend to comply with section 3D in relation to the exercise of those functions so far as they relate to the effecting or carrying out of with-profits policies by with-profits insurers.

(2) The memorandum required by this section may be combined with the memorandum required by section 3E.

(3) If the memorandum required by this section is contained in a separate document, the PRA and the FCA must publish the memorandum as currently in force in such manner as they think fit.

(4) Subsections (1) to (3) apply only if the effecting or carrying out of with-profits policies is a PRA-regulated activity.

(5) For the purposes of this section—

(a) a "with-profits policy" is a contract of insurance under which the policyholder is eligible to receive a financial benefit at the discretion of the insurer;

(b) a "with-profits insurer" is a PRA-authorised person who has a Part 4A permission, or permission resulting from any other provision of this Act, relating to the effecting or carrying out of with-profits policies (whether or not the permission also relates to contracts of insurance of other kinds).

(6) The Treasury may by order amend the definition of "with-profits policy" applying for the purposes of this section.]

NOTES

Substituted as noted to s 1A at **[7.1]**.

[7.44]

[3G Power to establish boundary between FCA and PRA responsibilities

(1) The Treasury may by order specify matters that, in relation to the exercise by either regulator of its functions relating to PRA-authorised persons, are to be, or are to be primarily, the responsibility of one regulator rather than the other.

(2) The order may—

(a) provide that one regulator is or is not to have regard to specified matters when exercising specified functions;

(b) require one regulator to consult the other.]

NOTES

Substituted as noted to s 1A at **[7.1]**.

[7.45]

[3H Parliamentary control of orders under section 3G

(1) No order may be made under section 3G unless—

(a) a draft of the order has been laid before Parliament and approved by a resolution of each House, or

(b) subsection (3) applies.

(2) Subsection (3) applies if an order under section 3G contains a statement that the Treasury are of the opinion that, by reason of urgency, it is necessary to make the order without a draft being so laid and approved.

(3) Where this subsection applies the order—

(a) must be laid before Parliament after being made, and

(b) ceases to have effect at the end of the relevant period unless before the end of that period the order is approved by a resolution of each House of Parliament (but without that affecting anything done under the order or the power to make a new order).

(4) The "relevant period" is a period of 28 days beginning with the day on which the order is made.

(5) In calculating the relevant period no account is to be taken of any time during which Parliament is dissolved or prorogued or during which both Houses are adjourned for more than 4 days.]

NOTES

Substituted as noted to s 1A at **[7.1]**.

[Power of PRA to restrain proposed action by FCA

[7.46]

3I Power of PRA to require FCA to refrain from specified action

(1) Where the first, second and third conditions are met, the PRA may give a direction under this section to the FCA.

(2) The first condition is that the FCA is proposing—

- (a) to exercise any of its regulatory powers in relation to PRA-authorised persons generally, a class of PRA-authorised persons or a particular PRA-authorised person, or
- (b) to exercise any of its insolvency powers in relation to—
  - (i) a PRA-authorised person,
  - (ii) an appointed representative whose principal, or one of whose principals, is a PRA-authorised person, or
  - (iii) a person who is carrying on a PRA-regulated activity in contravention of the general prohibition.

(3) In subsection (2)—

- (a) "regulatory powers", in relation to the FCA, means its powers in relation to the regulation of authorised persons, other than its powers in relation to consent for the purposes of section 55F or 55I[, a power conferred on it by sections 234I to 234M] or its powers under Part 24;
- (b) "insolvency powers", in relation to the FCA, means its powers under Part 24.

(4) The second condition is that the PRA is of the opinion that the exercise of the power in the manner proposed may—

- (a) threaten the stability of the UK financial system, . . .
- (b) result in the failure of a PRA-authorised person in a way that would adversely affect the UK financial system[, or
- (c) threaten the continuity of core services provided in the United Kingdom.]

(5) The third condition is that the PRA is of the opinion that the giving of the direction is necessary in order to avoid the possible consequence falling within subsection (4).

(6) A direction under this section is a direction requiring the FCA not to exercise the power or not to exercise it in a specified manner.

(7) The direction may be expressed to have effect during a specified period or until revoked.

(8) The FCA is not required to comply with a direction under this section if or to the extent that in the opinion of the FCA compliance would be incompatible with any . . . international obligation of the United Kingdom.

(9) The reference in subsection (4)(b) to the "failure" of a PRA-authorised person is to be read in accordance with section 2J(3) and (4).]

NOTES

Substituted as noted to s 1A at **[7.1]**.

Sub-s (3): words in square brackets inserted by the Financial Services (Banking Reform) Act 2013, s 129, Sch 8, Pt 1, para 4, as from 1 November 2014.

Sub-s (4): the word omitted from para (a) was repealed, and para (c) (and the preceding word) was added, by the Financial Services (Banking Reform) Act 2013, s 3, as from 1 January 2019.

Sub-s (8): words omitted repealed by the Financial Services and Markets Act 2000 (Amendment) (EU Exit) Regulations 2019, SI 2019/632, regs 2, 8, as from IP completion day (as defined in the European Union (Withdrawal Agreement) Act 2020, s 39).

[7.47]

[3J Power of PRA in relation to with-profits policies

(1) Where the first, second and third conditions are met, the PRA may give a direction under this section to the FCA.

(2) The first condition is that the FCA is proposing to exercise any of its regulatory powers in relation to with-profits insurers, a class of with-profits insurers or a particular with-profits insurer.

(3) In subsection (2) "regulatory powers", in relation to the FCA, means its powers in relation to the regulation of authorised persons, including its powers under Part 24 (insolvency) but not its powers in relation to consent for the purposes of section 55F or 55I.

(4) The second condition is that the proposed exercise of the power relates to the provision of financial benefits under with-profits policies at the discretion of the insurer, or affects or may affect the amount, timing or distribution of financial benefits that are so provided or the entitlement to future benefits that are so provided.

(5) The third condition is that the PRA is of the opinion that the giving of the direction is desirable in order to advance the PRA's general objective or its insurance objective.

(6) A direction under this section is a direction requiring the FCA not to exercise the power or not to exercise it in a specified manner.

(7) The direction may be expressed to have effect during a specified period or until revoked.

(8) The FCA is not required to comply with a direction under this section if or to the extent that in the opinion of the FCA compliance would be incompatible with any . . . international obligation of the United Kingdom.

(9) Subsections (1) to (8) apply only if the effecting or carrying out of with-profits policies is a PRA-regulated activity.

(10) In this section "with-profits insurer" and "with-profits policy" have the same meaning as they have for the purposes of section 3F.]

NOTES

Substituted as noted to s 1A at **[7.1]**.

Sub-s (8): words omitted repealed by the Financial Services and Markets Act 2000 (Amendment) (EU Exit) Regulations 2019, SI 2019/632, regs 2, 9, as from IP completion day (as defined in the European Union (Withdrawal Agreement) Act 2020, s 39).

[7.48]

[3K Revocation of directions under section 3I or 3J

(1) The PRA may at any time by notice to the FCA revoke a direction under section 3I or 3J.

(2) The revocation of a direction under section 3I or 3J does not affect the validity of anything previously done in accordance with it.]

NOTES

Substituted as noted to s 1A at **[7.1]**.

[7.49]

[3L Further provisions about directions under section 3I or 3J

(1) Before giving a direction under section 3I or 3J, the PRA must consult the FCA.

(2) A direction under section 3I or 3J must be given or confirmed in writing, and must be accompanied by a statement of the reasons for giving it.

(3) A notice revoking a direction under section 3I or 3J must be given or confirmed in writing.

(4) The PRA must—

(a) publish the direction and statement, or the notice, in such manner as it thinks fit, and

(b) where the direction or notice relates to a particular authorised person or a particular with-profits insurer, give a copy of the direction and statement, or the notice, to that person.

(5) The PRA must give the Treasury a copy of—

(a) a direction under section 3I;

(b) a statement relating to such a direction;

(c) a notice revoking such a direction.

(6) The Treasury must lay before Parliament any document received by them under subsection (5).

(7) Subsection (4) does not apply where the PRA, after consulting the Treasury, decides that compliance with that subsection would be against the public interest, and at any time when this subsection excludes the application of subsection (4) in relation to a direction under section 3I, subsection (6) also does not apply.

(8) Where the PRA decides that compliance with subsection (4) would be against the public interest, it must from time to time review that decision and if it subsequently decides that compliance is no longer against the public interest it must—

(a) comply with that subsection, and

(b) in the case of a direction under section 3I, notify the Treasury for the purposes of subsection (6).]

NOTES

Substituted as noted to s 1A at **[7.1]**.

[Directions relating to consolidated supervision

[7.50]

3M Directions relating to consolidated supervision of groups

(1) This section applies where one of the regulators ("the supervising regulator"), but not the other, is the competent authority for the purpose of consolidated supervision that is required in relation to some or all of the members of a group ("the relevant group") in pursuance of—

[(a) any implementing provision contained in subordinate legislation (within the meaning of the Interpretation Act 1978) made otherwise than by any of the following—

(i) statutory instrument, and

(ii) statutory rule for the purposes of the Statutory Rules (Northern Ireland) Order 1979 (SI 1979/1573 (NI 12)); . . .

(b) any other implementing provision (as amended from time to time)];

[(c) Part 9C rules;

(d) CRR rules; or

(e) rules made under section 192XA].

(2) "Consolidated supervision" includes supplementary supervision.

[(2A) "Implementing provision" means an enactment that immediately before IP completion day implemented provisions of any of the relevant directives.]

(3) The "relevant directives" are—

(a) the [capital requirements directive];

(b) Directive 2002/87/EC of the European Parliament and of the Council on the supplementary supervision of credit institutions, insurance undertakings and investment firms in a financial conglomerate;

(c) . . .

(d) Directive 2009/138/EC of the European Parliament and the Council of 25 November 2009 on the taking-up and pursuit of the business of Insurance and Reinsurance (Solvency II);

[(e) Directive 2014/59/EU of the European Parliament and of the Council of 15th May 2014 establishing a framework for the recovery and resolution of credit institutions and investment firms].

(4) The supervising regulator may, if it considers it necessary to do so for the effective consolidated supervision of the relevant group, give the other regulator a direction under this section.

(5) A direction under this section is a direction requiring the other regulator to exercise, or not to exercise, a relevant function in a specified manner in relation to authorised persons who are members of the relevant group.

(6) The direction may relate to members of the relevant group other than the members in respect of which consolidated supervision is required.

(7) A "relevant function", in relation to either regulator, is a function conferred by or under this Act which relates to the regulation of authorised persons, but does not include—

(a) the regulator's function of making rules under this Act;

(b) its function of preparing and issuing codes under this Act;

(c) its function of determining the general policy and principles by reference to which it performs particular functions;

(d) the FCA's functions in relation to the giving of general guidance;

(e) the PRA's functions in relation to the giving of guidance under section 2I;

(f) the FCA's functions in relation to consent for the purposes of section 55F or 55I.

(8) The direction may not require the regulator to which it is given ("the directed regulator") to do anything that it has no power to do, but the direction is relevant to the exercise of any discretion conferred on the directed regulator.

(9) The directed regulator must comply with the direction as soon as practicable, but this is subject to subsections (10) and (11).

(10) The directed regulator is not required to comply with a direction under this section if or to the extent that in its opinion compliance would be incompatible with any . . . international obligation of the United Kingdom.

(11) Directions given by the FCA under this section are subject to any directions given to the FCA under section 3I or 3J.]

NOTES

Substituted as noted to s 1A at **[7.1]**.

Sub-s (1): para (a) substituted by the Financial Services and Markets Act 2000 (Amendment) (EU Exit) Regulations 2019, SI 2019/632, regs 2, 10(1), (2), as from IP completion day (as defined in the European Union (Withdrawal Agreement) Act 2020, s 39). The word omitted from para (a) was repealed, and paras (c)–(e) were inserted, by the Financial Services Act 2021 (Prudential Regulation of Credit Institutions and Investment Firms) (Consequential Amendments and Miscellaneous Provisions) Regulations 2021, SI 2021/1376, reg 4(2), as from 1 January 2022.

Sub-s (2A): inserted by SI 2019/632, regs 2, 10(1), (3), as from IP completion day (as defined in the European Union (Withdrawal Agreement) Act 2020, s 39). Note that reg 10(3) of the 2019 Regulations was amended by the Financial Services and Economic and Monetary Policy (Consequential Amendments) (EU Exit) Regulations 2020, SI 2020/1301, reg 3, Schedule, para 33(a), as from 30 December 2020 (and the effect of the amendment has been incorporated in the text set out above).

Sub-s (3): words in square brackets in para (a) substituted, and para (c) repealed, by the Capital Requirements Regulations 2013, SI 2013/3115, reg 46(1), Sch 2, Pt 1, paras 1, 3, as from 1 January 2014. Para (e) added by the Bank Recovery and Resolution Order 2014, SI 2014/3329, arts 112, 113, as from 1 January 2015.

Sub-s (10): words omitted repealed by SI 2019/632, regs 2, 10(1), (4), as from IP completion day (as defined in the European Union (Withdrawal Agreement) Act 2020, s 39).

[7.51]

[3N Revocation of directions under section 3M

(1) The supervising regulator may at any time by notice to the other regulator revoke a direction under section 3M.

(2) The revocation of the direction does not affect the validity of anything previously done in accordance with it.

(3) Expressions defined for the purposes of section 3M have the same meaning in this section.]

NOTES

Substituted as noted to s 1A at **[7.1]**.

[7.52]

[3O Further provisions about directions under section 3M

(1) Before giving a direction under section 3M, the supervising regulator must consult the other regulator.

(2) A direction under section 3M must be given or confirmed in writing, and must be accompanied by a statement of the reasons for giving it.

(3) A notice revoking a direction under section 3M must be given or confirmed in writing.

(4) The regulator to which a direction under section 3M is given must give a copy of the direction and statement to each of the authorised persons to whom the direction relates.

(5) The supervising regulator must publish the direction and statement, or the notice, in such manner as it thinks fit.

(6) But subsection (4) or (5) does not apply in a case where the regulator on which the duty is imposed considers that compliance with that subsection would be against the public interest.

(7) In a case where a regulator decides that compliance with subsection (4) or (5) would be against the public interest, the regulator must from time to time review that decision and if it subsequently decides that compliance is no longer against the public interest it must comply with the subsection.

(8) Expressions defined for the purposes of section 3M have the same meaning in this section.]

NOTES

Substituted as noted to s 1A at **[7.1]**.

[7.53]

[3P Consultation by regulator complying with direction

(1) If the directed regulator is required by this Act to consult any person other than the supervising regulator before exercising the relevant function to which the direction relates, the directed regulator must give the supervising regulator copies of any written representations received from the persons consulted.

(2) Expressions defined for the purposes of section 3M have the same meaning in this section.]

NOTES

Substituted as noted to s 1A at **[7.1]**.

[Co-operation with Bank of England

[7.54]

3Q Co-operation by FCA . . . with Bank of England

(1) [The FCA] must take such steps as it considers appropriate to co-operate with the Bank of England in connection with—

(a) the pursuit by the Bank of its Financial Stability Objective, and

(b) the Bank's compliance with its duties under sections 58 and 59 of the Financial Services Act 2012 (duty to notify Treasury of possible need for public funds and of subsequent changes).

(2) Co-operation under subsection (1) may include the sharing of information that the [FCA] is not prevented from disclosing.]

NOTES

Substituted as noted to s 1A at **[7.1]**.

The words omitted from the section heading were repealed, and the words in square brackets in sub-ss (1), (2) were substituted, by the Bank of England and Financial Services Act 2016, s 16, Sch 2, Pt 2, paras 26, 30, as from 1 March 2017.

[Arrangements for provision of services

[7.55]

3R Arrangements for provision of services

(1) The regulators may enter into arrangements with each other for the provision of services by one of them to the other.

(2) [The FCA] may enter into arrangements with the Bank of England for the provision of services—

(a) by the Bank to the [FCA], or

(b) by the [FCA] to the Bank.

(3) Either regulator may enter into arrangements with any of the bodies specified in subsection (4) for the provision of services by the regulator to that body.

(4) Those bodies are—

[(a) the [Money and Pensions Service] (see Part 1 of the Financial Guidance and Claims Act 2018),]

(b) the scheme manager (see section 212(1)), and

(c) the scheme operator (see section 225(2)).

(5) The FCA may enter into arrangements with—

(a) a local weights and measures authority in England, Wales or Scotland, or

(b) the Department of Enterprise, Trade and Investment in Northern Ireland,

for the provision by the authority or department to the FCA of services which relate to activities to which this subsection applies.

(6) Subsection (5) applies to activities that are regulated activities by virtue of—

(a) an order made under section 22(1) in relation to an investment of a kind falling within paragraph 23 or 23B of Schedule 2, or

(b) an order made under section 22(1A)(a).

(7) Arrangements under this section are to be on such terms as may be agreed by the parties.]

NOTES

Substituted as noted to s 1A at **[7.1]**.

Sub-s (2): words in square brackets substituted by the Bank of England and Financial Services Act 2016, s 16, Sch 2, Pt 2, paras 26, 31, as from 1 March 2017.

Sub-s (4): para (a) substituted by the Financial Guidance and Claims Act 2018, s 25, Sch 3, paras 5, 11, as from 1 October 2018. Words "Money and Pensions Service" in square brackets substituted by the Financial Guidance and Claims Act 2018 (Naming and Consequential Amendments) Regulations 2019, SI 2019/383, reg 3, Schedule, Pt 1, para 7(a), as from 6 April 2019.

. . .

3S *(S 3S (The consumer financial education body) was originally substituted as noted to s 1A ante. Subsequently repealed, together with the preceding heading, by the Financial Guidance and Claims Act 2018, s 25, Sch 3, paras 5, 12, as from 6 April 2021.)*

[Interpretation

[7.56]

3T Interpretation

In this Part "enactment" includes—

(a) an enactment contained in subordinate legislation within the meaning of the Interpretation Act 1978;

(b) an enactment contained in, or in an instrument made under, an Act of the Scottish Parliament;

(c) an enactment contained in, or in an instrument made under, a Measure or Act of the National Assembly for Wales;

(d) an enactment contained in, or in an instrument made under, Northern Ireland legislation.]

NOTES

Inserted by the Bank of England and Financial Services Act 2016, s 16, Sch 2, Pt 2, paras 26, 32, as from 6 July 2016.

National Assembly for Wales: see further, in relation to the renaming of the National Assembly for Wales as the Senedd Cymru or the Welsh Parliament, the Senedd and Elections (Wales) Act 2020, s 2 (with effect from 6 May 2020). See also ss 3–9 of the 2020 Act in relation to the renaming of Acts of the National Assembly for Wales, Members of the National Assembly for Wales, etc.

PART II REGULATED AND PROHIBITED ACTIVITIES

NOTES

Transitional provisions etc in connection with the original commencement of this Act: ss 26(1), (2) and 27(1), (2) (and, subject to certain modifications, s 28 below) apply to certain agreements entered into in contravention of the Financial Services Act 1986, s 3 (repealed by the Financial Services and Markets Act 2000 (Consequential Amendments and Repeals) Order 2001, SI 2001/3649, art 3(1)(c)), or the Insurance Companies Act 1982, s 2 (repealed by art 3(1)(b) of that Order) as they apply to an agreement in contravention of the general prohibition; see the Financial Services and Markets Act 2000 (Transitional Provisions and Savings) (Civil Remedies, Discipline, Criminal Offences etc) (No 2) Order 2001, SI 2001/3083, art 5(1), (3), (4), (6).

The general prohibition

[7.57]

19 The general prohibition

(1) No person may carry on a regulated activity in the United Kingdom, or purport to do so, unless he is—

(a) an authorised person; or
(b) an exempt person.

(2) The prohibition is referred to in this Act as the general prohibition.

Requirement for permission

[7.58]

20 Authorised persons acting without permission

(1) If an authorised person [other than a PRA-authorised person] carries on a regulated activity in the United Kingdom, or purports to do so, otherwise than in accordance with permission—

[(a) given to that person under Part 4A, or]
(b) resulting from any other provision of this Act,

he is to be taken to have contravened a requirement imposed on him by the [FCA] under this Act.

[(1A) If a PRA-authorised person carries on a regulated activity in the United Kingdom, or purports to do so, otherwise than in accordance with permission given to the person under Part 4A or resulting from any other provision of this Act, the person is to be taken to have contravened—

(a) a requirement imposed by the FCA, and
(b) a requirement imposed by the PRA.]

[(2) A contravention within subsection (1) or (1A)—

(a) does not, except as provided by section 23(1A), make a person guilty of an offence,
(b) does not, except as provided by section 26A, make any transaction void or unenforceable, and
(c) does not, except as provided by subsection (3), give rise to any right of action for breach of statutory duty.]

(3) In prescribed cases [a contravention within subsection (1) or (1A)] is actionable at the suit of a person who suffers loss as a result of the contravention, subject to the defences and other incidents applying to actions for breach of statutory duty.

[(4) Subsections (1) and (1A) are subject to section 39(1D).

(5) References in this Act to an authorised person acting in contravention of this section are references to the person acting in a way that results in a contravention within subsection (1) or (1A).]

NOTES

Sub-s (1): words in first pair of square brackets inserted, and para (a) and the word "FCA" in square brackets substituted, by the Financial Services Act 2012, s 37(1), Sch 9, Pt 1, para 1, Pt 2, para 2(1), (2), as from 1 April 2013.

Sub-ss (1A), (4), (5): inserted and added respectively by the Financial Services Act 2012, s 37(1), Sch 9, Pt 1, para 1, Pt 2, para 2(1), (3), (6), as from 1 April 2013.

Sub-s (2): substituted by the Financial Services Act 2012, s 37(1), Sch 9, Pt 1, para 1, Pt 2, para 2(1), (4), as from 1 April 2013.

Sub-s (3): words in square brackets substituted by the Financial Services Act 2012, s 37(1), Sch 9, Pt 1, para 1, Pt 2, para 2(1), (5), as from 1 April 2013.

Regulations: the Financial Services and Markets Act 2000 (Rights of Action) Regulations 2001, SI 2001/2256.

Financial promotion

[7.59]

21 Restrictions on financial promotion

(1) A person ("A") must not, in the course of business, communicate an invitation or inducement—

[(a)] to engage in investment activity[, or
(b) to engage in claims management activity].

(2) But subsection (1) does not apply if—

(a) A is an authorised person; or
(b) the content of the communication is approved for the purposes of this section by an authorised person.

(3) In the case of a communication originating outside the United Kingdom, subsection (1) applies only if the communication is capable of having an effect in the United Kingdom.

(4) The Treasury may by order specify circumstances in which a person is to be regarded for the purposes of subsection (1) as—

(a) acting in the course of business;
(b) not acting in the course of business.

(5) The Treasury may by order specify circumstances (which may include compliance with financial promotion rules) in which subsection (1) does not apply.

(6) An order under subsection (5) may, in particular, provide that subsection (1) does not apply in relation to communications—

(a) of a specified description;
(b) originating in a specified country or territory outside the United Kingdom;
(c) originating in a country or territory which falls within a specified description of country or territory outside the United Kingdom; or
(d) originating outside the United Kingdom.

(7) The Treasury may by order repeal subsection (3).

(8) "Engaging in investment activity" means—

(a) entering or offering to enter into an agreement the making or performance of which by either party constitutes a controlled activity; or
(b) exercising any rights conferred by a controlled investment to acquire, dispose of, underwrite or convert a controlled investment.

(9) An activity is a controlled activity if—

(a) it is an activity of a specified kind or one which falls within a specified class of activity; and
(b) it relates to an investment of a specified kind, or to one which falls within a specified class of investment.

(10) An investment is a controlled investment if it is an investment of a specified kind or one which falls within a specified class of investment.

[(10A) "Engaging in claims management activity" means entering into or offering to enter into an agreement the making or performance of which by either party constitutes a controlled claims management activity.

(10B) An activity is a "controlled claims management activity" if—

(a) it is an activity of a specified kind,

(b) it is, or relates to, claims management services, and

(c) it is carried on in Great Britain.]

(11) Schedule 2 (except paragraph 26) applies for the purposes of subsections (9) and (10) with references to section 22 being read as references to each of those subsections.

(12) Nothing in Schedule 2, as applied by subsection (11), limits the powers conferred by subsection (9) or (10).

[(12A) Paragraph 25 of Schedule 2 applies for the purposes of subsection (10B) with the references to section 22 in sub-paragraph (3) of that paragraph being read as references to subsection (10B).]

(13) "Communicate" includes causing a communication to be made.

(14) "Investment" includes any asset, right or interest.

(15) "Specified" means specified in an order made by the Treasury.

NOTES

Sub-s (1): para (a) designated as such, and para (b) and the preceding word added, by the Financial Guidance and Claims Act 2018, s 27(1), (3)(a), as from 6 October 2018 (for transitional provisions in relation to the transfer of regulation of claims management services to the FCA, see Sch 5 to the 2018 Act).

Sub-ss (10A), (10B), (12A): inserted by the Financial Guidance and Claims Act 2018, s 27(1), (3)(b), (c), as from 6 October 2018 (for transitional provisions in relation to the transfer of regulation of claims management services to the FCA, see Sch 5 to the 2018 Act).

Orders: the Financial Services and Markets Act 2000 (Miscellaneous Provisions) Order 2001, SI 2001/3650; the Financial Services and Markets Act 2000 (Financial Promotion and Miscellaneous Amendments) Order 2002, SI 2002/1310; the Financial Services and Markets Act 2000 (Commencement of Mortgage Regulation) (Amendment) Order 2002, SI 2002/1777; the Financial Services and Markets Act 2000 (Promotion of Collective Investment Schemes etc) (Exemptions) (Amendment) Order 2003, SI 2003/2067; the Financial Services and Markets Act 2000 (Financial Promotion and Promotion of Collective Investment Schemes) (Miscellaneous Amendments) Order 2005, SI 2005/270; the Financial Services and Markets Act 2000 (Financial Promotion) Order 2005, SI 2005/1529 at **[8.443]**; the Financial Services and Markets Act 2000 (Financial Promotion) (Amendment) Order 2005, SI 2005/3392; the Financial Services and Markets Act 2000 (Financial Promotion) (Amendment) Order 2007, SI 2007/1083; the Financial Services and Markets Act 2000 (Financial Promotion) (Amendment No 2) Order 2007, SI 2007/2615; the Financial Services and Markets Act 2000 (Financial Promotion) (Amendment) Order 2010, SI 2010/905; the Financial Services and Markets Act 2000 (Miscellaneous Provisions) (No 2) Order 2015, SI 2015/352; the Financial Services and Markets Act 2000 (Miscellaneous Provisions) Order 2015, SI 2015/853; the Mortgage Credit Directive Order 2015, SI 2015/910; the Financial Services and Markets Act 2000 (Regulated Activities) (Amendment) Order 2016, SI 2016/392; the Financial Services and Markets Act 2000 (Regulated Activities) (Amendment) Order 2016, SI 2016/392; the Financial Services and Markets Act 2000 (Regulated Activities) (Amendment) Order 2017, SI 2017/488; the Financial Services and Markets Act 2000 (Claims Management Activity) Order 2018, SI 2018/1253; the Financial Services and Markets Act 2000 (Regulated Activities) (Amendment) Order 2021, SI 2021/90; the Recognised Auction Platforms (Amendment and Miscellaneous Provisions) Regulations 2021, SI 2021/494.

Regulated activities

[7.60]

22 [Regulated activities]

(1) An activity is a regulated activity for the purposes of this Act if it is an activity of a specified kind which is carried on by way of business and—

(a) relates to an investment of a specified kind; or

(b) in the case of an activity of a kind which is also specified for the purposes of this paragraph, is carried on in relation to property of any kind.

[(1A) An activity is also a regulated activity for the purposes of this Act if it is an activity of a specified kind which is carried on by way of business and relates to—

(a) information about a person's financial standing, . . . [or]

(b) . . .

[(c) administering a benchmark].]

[(1B) An activity is also a regulated activity for the purposes of this Act if it is an activity of a specified kind which—

(a) is carried on by way of business in Great Britain, and

(b) is, or relates to, claims management services.]

(2) Schedule 2 makes provision supplementing this section.

(3) Nothing in Schedule 2 limits the powers conferred by [subsections (1) to (1B)].

(4) "Investment" includes any asset, right or interest.

(5) "Specified" means specified in an order made by the Treasury.

[(6) . . .]

[(6A) For the purposes of subsection (1A)(c), "benchmark" has the meaning given by Article 3 of the EU Benchmarks Regulation 2016, and "administering" a benchmark means acting as an administrator of that benchmark within the meaning of that Article.]

NOTES

Sub-ss (1A) and (6) were inserted and added respectively, and the section heading was substituted, by the Financial Services Act 2012, s 7(1), as from 24 January 2013.

The original word "or" omitted from sub-s (1A)(a) was repealed, sub-s (1A)(c) was inserted, and sub-s (6A) was added, by the Financial Services and Markets Act 2000 (Benchmarks) Regulations 2018, SI 2018/135, reg 38, as from 27 February 2018.

The new word "or" in square brackets in sub-s (1A)(a) was inserted, and sub-ss (1A)(b) and (6) were repealed by SI 2018/135, reg 39, as from 1 May 2020.

Sub-s (1B) was inserted, and the words in square brackets in sub-s (3) were substituted, by the Financial Guidance and Claims Act 2018, s 27(1), (4), as from 6 October 2018 (for transitional provisions in relation to the transfer of regulation of claims management services to the FCA, see Sch 5 to the 2018 Act).

See further, in relation to Orders made under this section, the Financial Services Act 2012, s 107 (Power to make further provision about regulation of consumer credit).

Orders and Regulations: the Financial Services and Markets Act 2000 (Regulated Activities) Order 2001, SI 2001/544 at **[8.1]**; the Financial Services and Markets Act 2000 (Regulated Activities) (Amendment) Order 2001, SI 2001/3544; the Financial Services and Markets Act 2000 (Regulated Activities) (Amendment) Order 2002, SI 2002/682; the Financial Services and Markets Act 2000 (Financial Promotion and Miscellaneous Amendments) Order 2002, SI 2002/1310; the Financial Services and Markets Act 2000 (Regulated Activities) (Amendment) (No 2) Order 2002, SI 2002/1776; the Financial Services and Markets Act 2000 (Commencement of Mortgage Regulation) (Amendment) Order 2002, SI 2002/1777; the Financial Services and Markets Act 2000 (Regulated Activities) (Amendment) (No 1) Order 2003, SI 2003/1475; the Financial Services and Markets Act 2000 (Regulated Activities) (Amendment) (No 2) Order 2003, SI 2003/1476; the Financial Services and Markets Act 2000 (Regulated Activities) (Amendment) (No 3) Order 2003, SI 2003/2822; the Financial Services and Markets Act 2000 (Regulated Activities) (Amendment) Order 2004, SI 2004/1610; the Financial Services and Markets Act 2000 (Regulated Activities) (Amendment) (No 2) Order 2004, SI 2004/2737; the Financial Services and Markets Act 2000 (Regulated Activities) (Amendment) Order 2005, SI 2005/593; the Financial Services and Markets Act 2000 (Regulated Activities) (Amendment) (No 2) Order 2005, SI 2005/1518; the Financial Services and Markets Act 2000 (Regulated Activities) (Amendment) Order 2006, SI 2006/1969; the Financial Services and Markets Act 2000 (Regulated Activities) (Amendment) (No 2) Order 2006, SI 2006/2383; the Financial Services and Markets Act 2000 (Regulated Activities) (Amendment No 3) Order 2006, SI 2006/3384; the Financial Services and Markets Act 2000 (Regulated Activities) (Amendment) Order 2007, SI 2007/1339; the Financial Services and Markets Act 2000 (Reinsurance Directive) Order 2007, SI 2007/3254; the Financial Services and Markets Act 2000 (Regulated Activities) (Amendment) (No 2) Order 2007, SI 2007/3510; the Financial Services and Markets Act 2000 (Regulated Activities) (Amendment) Order 2009, SI 2009/1342; the Financial Services and Markets Act 2000 (Regulated Activities) (Amendment) (No 2) Order 2009, SI 2009/1389; the Financial Services and Markets Act 2000 (Regulated Activities) (Amendment) Order 2010, SI 2010/86; the Financial Services and Markets Act 2000 (Regulated Activities) (Amendment) Order 2011, SI 2011/133; the Financial Services and Markets Act 2000 (Regulated Activities) (Amendment) Order 2012, SI 2012/1906; the Financial Services and Markets Act 2000 (Regulated Activities) (Amendment) Order 2013, SI 2013/655; the Financial Services and Markets Act 2000 (Regulated Activities) (Amendment) (No 2) Order 2013, SI 2013/1881; the Financial Services and Markets Act 2000 (Regulated Activities) (Amendment) Order 2014, SI 2014/366; the Alternative Investment Fund Managers Order 2014, SI 2014/1292; the Alternative Investment Fund Managers (Amendment) Order 2014, SI 2014/1313; the Financial Services and Markets Act 2000 (Regulated Activities) (Amendment) (No 2) Order 2014, SI 2014/1448; the Financial Services and Markets Act 2000 (Regulated Activities) (Amendment) (No 3) Order 2014, SI 2014/1470; the Financial Services and Markets Act 2000 (Miscellaneous Provisions) (No 2) Order 2015, SI 2015/352; the Financial Services and Markets Act 2000 (Regulated Activities) (Amendment) Order 2015, SI 2015/369; the Financial Services and Markets Act 2000 (Regulated Activities) (Amendment) (Pensions Guidance Exclusions) Order 2015, SI 2015/489; the Financial Services and Markets Act 2000 (Regulated Activities) (Amendment) (No 2) Order 2015, SI 2015/731; the Electronic Commerce Directive (Financial Services and Markets) (Amendment) Order 2015, SI 2015/852; the Financial Services and Markets Act 2000 (Miscellaneous Provisions) Order 2015, SI 2015/853; the Mortgage Credit Directive Order 2015, SI 2015/910; the Mortgage Credit Directive (Amendment) Order 2015, SI 2015/1557; the Financial Services and Markets Act 2000 (Regulated Activities) (Amendment) (No 3) Order 2015, SI 2015/1863; the Financial Services and Markets Act 2000 (Regulated Activities) (Amendment) Order 2016, SI 2016/392; the Financial Services and Markets Act 2000 (Regulated Activities) (Amendment) Order 2017, SI 2017/488; the Financial Services and Markets Act 2000 (Regulated Activities) (Amendment) (No 2) Order 2017, SI 2017/500; the Risk Transformation Regulations 2017, SI 2017/1212; the Financial Services and Markets Act 2000 (Markets in Financial Instruments) (No 2) Regulations 2017, SI 2017/1255; the Alternative Investment Fund Managers (Amendment) Regulations 2018, SI 2018/134; the Insurance Distribution (Regulated Activities and Miscellaneous Amendments) Order 2018, SI 2018/546; the Financial Services and Markets Act 2000 (Regulated Activities) (Amendment) Order 2018, SI 2018/831; the Financial Services and Markets Act 2000 (Claims Management Activity) Order 2018, SI 2018/1253; the Financial Services and Markets Act 2000 (Regulated Activities) (Amendment) Order 2019, SI 2019/1067; the Financial Services and Markets Act 2000 (Regulated Activities) (Coronavirus) (Amendment) Order 2020, SI 2020/480; the Financial Services and Markets Act 2000 (Regulated Activities) (Amendment) Order 2021, SI 2021/90; the Recognised Auction Platforms (Amendment and Miscellaneous Provisions) Regulations 2021, SI 2021/494; the Financial Services and Markets Act 2000 (Regulated Activities) (Amendment) Order 2022, SI 2022/466; the Financial Services and Markets Act 2000 (Regulated Activities) (Amendment) (No 2) Order 2022, SI 2022/726.

[7.61]

[22A Designation of activities requiring prudential regulation by PRA

(1) The Treasury may by order specify the regulated activities that are "PRA-regulated activities" for the purposes of this Act.

(2) An order under subsection (1) may—

- (a) provide for exceptions;
- (b) confer powers on the Treasury or either regulator;
- (c) authorise the making of rules or other instruments by either regulator for purposes of, or connected with, any relevant provision;
- (d) make provision in respect of any information or document which in the opinion of the Treasury or either regulator is relevant for purposes of, or connected with, any relevant provision;
- (e) make such consequential, transitional, or supplemental provision as the Treasury consider appropriate for purposes of, or connected with, any relevant provision.

(3) Provision made as a result of subsection (2)(e) may amend any primary or subordinate legislation, including any provision of, or made under, this Act.

(4) "Relevant provision" means this section or any provision made under this section.]

NOTES

Inserted, together with s 22B, by the Financial Services Act 2012, s 9, as from 24 January 2013.

Orders and Regulations: the Financial Services and Markets Act 2000 (PRA-regulated Activities) Order 2013, SI 2013/556; the Risk Transformation Regulations 2017, SI 2017/1212.

[7.62]

[22B Parliamentary control in relation to certain orders under section 22A

(1) This section applies to the first order made under section 22A(1).

(2) This section also applies to any subsequent order made under section 22A(1) which—

(a) contains a statement by the Treasury that, in their opinion, the effect (or one of the effects) of the proposed order would be—

(i) that an activity would become a PRA-regulated activity, or

(ii) that a PRA-regulated activity would become a regulated activity that is not a PRA-regulated activity, or

(b) amends primary legislation.

(3) No order to which this section applies may be made unless—

(a) a draft of the order has been laid before Parliament and approved by a resolution of each House, or

(b) subsection (5) applies.

(4) Subsection (5) applies if an order to which this section applies contains a statement that the Treasury are of the opinion that, by reason of urgency, it is necessary to make the order without a draft being so laid and approved.

(5) Where this subsection applies the order—

(a) must be laid before Parliament after being made, and

(b) ceases to have effect at the end of the relevant period unless before the end of that period the order is approved by a resolution of each House of Parliament (but without that affecting anything done under the order or the power to make a new order).

(6) The "relevant period" is a period of 28 days beginning with the day on which the order is made.

(7) In calculating the relevant period no account is to be taken of any time during which Parliament is dissolved or prorogued or during which both Houses are adjourned for more than 4 days.]

NOTES

Inserted as noted to s 22A at **[7.61]**.

Offences

[7.63]

23 Contravention of the general prohibition [or section 20(1) or (1A)]

(1) A person who contravenes the general prohibition is guilty of an offence and liable—

(a) on summary conviction, to imprisonment for a term not exceeding six months or a fine not exceeding the statutory maximum, or both;

(b) on conviction on indictment, to imprisonment for a term not exceeding two years or a fine, or both.

[(1A) An authorised person ("A") is guilty of an offence if A carries on a credit-related regulated activity in the United Kingdom, or purports to do so, otherwise than in accordance with permission—

(a) given to that person under Part 4A, or

(b) resulting from any other provision of this Act.

(1B) In this Act "credit-related regulated activity" means a regulated activity of a kind designated by the Treasury by order.

(1C) The Treasury may designate a regulated activity under subsection (1B) only if the activity involves a person—

(a) entering into or administering an agreement under which the person provides another person with credit,

(b) exercising or being able to exercise the rights of the lender under an agreement under which another person provides a third party with credit, or

(c) taking steps to procure payment of debts due under an agreement under which another person is provided with credit.

(1D) But a regulated activity may not be designated under subsection (1B) if the agreement in question is one under which the obligation of the borrower is secured on land.

(1E) "Credit" includes any cash loan or other financial accommodation.

(1F) A person guilty of an offence under subsection (1A) is liable—

(a) on summary conviction, to imprisonment for a term not exceeding the applicable maximum term or a fine not exceeding the statutory maximum, or both;

(b) on conviction on indictment, to imprisonment for a term not exceeding two years, or a fine, or both.

(1G) The "applicable maximum term" is—

(a) in England and Wales, 12 months (or 6 months, if the offence was committed before [2 May 2022]);

(b) in Scotland, 12 months;

(c) in Northern Ireland, 6 months.]

(2) In this Act "an authorisation offence" means an offence under this section.

(3) In proceedings for an authorisation offence it is a defence for the accused to show that he took all reasonable precautions and exercised all due diligence to avoid committing the offence.

[(4) Subsection (1A) is subject to section 39(1D).

(5) No proceedings may be brought against a person in respect of an offence under subsection (1A) in a case where either regulator has taken action under section 205, 206 or 206A in relation to the alleged contravention within section 20(1) or (1A).]

NOTES

The words in square brackets in the section heading were added, and sub-ss (1A)–(1G) and sub-ss (4), (5) were inserted and added respectively, by the Financial Services Act 2012, s 37(1), Sch 9, Pt 1, para 1, Pt 2, para 3, as from 1 April 2013.

The words in square brackets in sub-s (1G) were substituted by the Criminal Justice Act 2003 (Commencement No 33) and Sentencing Act 2020 (Commencement No 2) Regulations 2022, SI 2022/500, reg 5, Schedule, Pt 1, as from 28 April 2022.

Deferred Prosecution Agreements: as to the application of Deferred Prosecution Agreements to an offence under this section and ss 25, 85, 346, 398 (ie, an agreement between a designated prosecutor and a person accused of a crime (P) whereby proceedings against P in respect of the alleged offence are automatically suspended as soon as they are instituted if P agrees to comply with certain requirements), see s 45 of, and Sch 17, Pt 1 and Sch 17, Pt 2, para 22 to, the Crime and Courts Act 2013.

Orders: the Financial Services and Markets Act 2000 (Consumer Credit) (Designated Activities) Order 2014, SI 2014/334.

[7.64]

[23A Parliamentary control in relation to certain orders under section 23

(1) This section applies to the first order made under section 23(1B).

(2) This section also applies to any subsequent order made under section 23(1B) which contains a statement by the Treasury that, in their opinion, the effect (or one of the effects) of the proposed order would be that an activity would become a credit-related regulated activity.

(3) An order to which this section applies may not be made unless a draft of the order has been laid before Parliament and approved by a resolution of each House.]

NOTES

Inserted by the Financial Services Act 2012, s 37(1), Sch 9, Pt 1, para 1, Pt 2, para 4, as from 1 April 2013.

[7.65]

24 False claims to be authorised or exempt

(1) A person who is neither an authorised person nor, in relation to the regulated activity in question, an exempt person is guilty of an offence if he—

(a) describes himself (in whatever terms) as an authorised person;

(b) describes himself (in whatever terms) as an exempt person in relation to the regulated activity; or

(c) behaves, or otherwise holds himself out, in a manner which indicates (or which is reasonably likely to be understood as indicating) that he is—

(i) an authorised person; or

(ii) an exempt person in relation to the regulated activity.

(2) In proceedings for an offence under this section it is a defence for the accused to show that he took all reasonable precautions and exercised all due diligence to avoid committing the offence.

(3) A person guilty of an offence under this section is liable on summary conviction to imprisonment for a term not exceeding six months or a fine not exceeding level 5 on the standard scale, or both.

(4) But where the conduct constituting the offence involved or included the public display of any material, the maximum fine for the offence is level 5 on the standard scale multiplied by the number of days for which the display continued.

NOTES

Sub-s (4): repealed by the Legal Aid, Sentencing and Punishment of Offenders Act 2012 (Fines on Summary Conviction) Regulations 2015, SI 2015/664, regs 4(4), 5, Sch 5, para 7, as from 12 March 2015, in relation to England and Wales only (except in relation to (a) fines for offences committed before 12 March 2015, (b) the operation of restrictions on fines that may be imposed on a person aged under 18, or (c) fines that may be imposed on a person convicted by a magistrates' court who is to be sentenced as if convicted on indictment).

Deferred Prosecution Agreements: see the note to s 23 at **[7.63]**.

[7.66]

25 Contravention of section 21

(1) A person who contravenes section 21(1) is guilty of an offence and liable—

(a) on summary conviction, to imprisonment for a term not exceeding six months or a fine not exceeding the statutory maximum, or both;

(b) on conviction on indictment, to imprisonment for a term not exceeding two years or a fine, or both.

(2) In proceedings for an offence under this section it is a defence for the accused to show—

(a) that he believed on reasonable grounds that the content of the communication was prepared, or approved for the purposes of section 21, by an authorised person; or

(b) that he took all reasonable precautions and exercised all due diligence to avoid committing the offence.

Enforceability of agreements

[7.67]

26 Agreements made by unauthorised persons

(1) An agreement made by a person in the course of carrying on a regulated activity in contravention of the general prohibition is unenforceable against the other party.

(2) The other party is entitled to recover—

(a) any money or other property paid or transferred by him under the agreement; and

(b) compensation for any loss sustained by him as a result of having parted with it.

(3) "Agreement" means an agreement—

(a) made after this section comes into force; and

(b) the making or performance of which constitutes, or is part of, the regulated activity in question.

(4) This section does not apply if the regulated activity is accepting deposits.

[7.68]

[26A Agreements relating to credit

(1) An agreement that is made by an authorised person in contravention of section 20 is unenforceable against the other party if the agreement is entered into in the course of carrying on a credit-related regulated activity involving matters falling within section 23(1C)(a).

(2) The other party is entitled to recover—

(a) any money or other property paid or transferred by that party under the agreement, and

(b) compensation for any loss sustained by that party as a result of having parted with it.

(3) In subsections (1) and (2) "agreement" means an agreement—

(a) which is made after this section comes into force, and

(b) the making or performance of which constitutes, or is part of, the credit-related regulated activity.

(4) If the administration of an agreement involves the carrying on of a credit-related regulated activity, the agreement may not be enforced by a person for the time being exercising the rights of the lender under the agreement unless that person—

[(a)] has permission, given under Part 4A or resulting from any other provision of this Act, in relation to that activity,

[(b) is an appointed representative in relation to that activity,

(c) is an exempt person in relation to that activity, or

(d) is a person to whom, as a result of Part 20, the general prohibition does not apply in relation to that activity].

(5) If the taking of steps to procure payment of debts due under an agreement involves the carrying on of a credit-related regulated activity, the agreement may not be enforced by a person for the time being exercising the rights of the lender under the agreement unless—

[(a)] the agreement is enforced in accordance with permission—

[(i)] given under Part 4A to the person enforcing the agreement, or

[(ii)] resulting from any other provision of this Act,]

[(b) that person is an appointed representative in relation to that activity,

(c) that person is an exempt person in relation to that activity, or

(d) that person is a person to whom, as a result of Part 20, the general prohibition does not apply in relation to that activity].]

NOTES

Inserted by the Financial Services Act 2012, s 37(1), Sch 9, Pt 1, para 1, Pt 2, para 5, as from 1 April 2013.

Sub-s (4): para (a) designated as such, and paras (b)–(d) added, by the Bank of England and Financial Services Act 2016, s 27(1), (2), as from 6 July 2016.

Sub-s (5): para (a) designated as such, and paras (b)–(d) added, by the Bank of England and Financial Services Act 2016, s 27(1), (3), as from 6 July 2016. Note that the existing paras (a) and (b) were also designated as sub-paras (i) and (ii) of para (a) by this amendment.

[7.69]

27 Agreements made through unauthorised persons

[(1) This section applies to an agreement that—

(a) is made by an authorised person ("the provider") in the course of carrying on a regulated activity,

(b) is not made in contravention of the general prohibition,

(c) if it relates to a credit-related regulated activity, is not made in contravention of section 20, and

(d) is made in consequence of something said or done by another person ("the third party") in the course of—

(i) a regulated activity carried on by the third party in contravention of the general prohibition, or

(ii) a credit-related regulated activity carried on by the third party in contravention of section 20.

[(1ZA) But this section does not apply to a regulated credit agreement or a regulated consumer hire agreement unless the provider knows before the agreement is made that the third party had some involvement in the making of the agreement or matters preparatory to its making.]

(1A) [An agreement to which this section applies] is unenforceable against the other party.]

(2) The other party is entitled to recover—

(a) any money or other property paid or transferred by him under the agreement; and

(b) compensation for any loss sustained by him as a result of having parted with it.

(3) "Agreement" means an agreement—

(a) made after this section comes into force; and

(b) the making or performance of which constitutes, or is part of, the regulated activity in question carried on by the provider.

(4) This section does not apply if the regulated activity is accepting deposits.

[(5) For the purposes of subsection (1ZA)—

"regulated consumer hire agreement" has the meaning given by article 60N of the Financial Services and Markets Act 2000 (Regulated Activities) Order 2001 (SI 2001/544);

"regulated credit agreement" has the meaning given by article 60B of that Order.]

NOTES

Sub-s (1): substituted, together with sub-s (1A) (for the original sub-s (1)), by the Financial Services Act 2012, s 37(1), Sch 9, Pt 1, para 1, Pt 2, para 6, as from 1 April 2013.

Sub-s (1ZA): inserted by the Bank of England and Financial Services Act 2016, s 28(1), (2), as from 6 July 2016.

Sub-s (1A): substituted as noted above. Words in square brackets substituted by the Bank of England and Financial Services Act 2016, s 28(1), (3), as from 6 July 2016.

Sub-s (5): added by the Bank of England and Financial Services Act 2016, s 28(1), (4), as from 6 July 2016.

[7.70]

28 Agreements made unenforceable by section 26 or 27[: general cases]

(1) This section applies to an agreement which is unenforceable because of section 26 or 27[, other than an agreement entered into in the course of carrying on a credit-related regulated activity].

(2) The amount of compensation recoverable as a result of that section is—

(a) the amount agreed by the parties; or

(b) on the application of either party, the amount determined by the court.

(3) If the court is satisfied that it is just and equitable in the circumstances of the case, it may allow—

(a) the agreement to be enforced; or

(b) money and property paid or transferred under the agreement to be retained.

(4) In considering whether to allow the agreement to be enforced or (as the case may be) the money or property paid or transferred under the agreement to be retained the court must—

(a) if the case arises as a result of section 26, have regard to the issue mentioned in subsection (5); or

(b) if the case arises as a result of section 27, have regard to the issue mentioned in subsection (6).

(5) The issue is whether the person carrying on the regulated activity concerned reasonably believed that he was not contravening the general prohibition by making the agreement.

(6) The issue is whether the provider knew that the third party was (in carrying on the regulated activity) contravening the general prohibition.

(7) If the person against whom the agreement is unenforceable—

(a) elects not to perform the agreement, or

(b) as a result of this section, recovers money paid or other property transferred by him under the agreement,

he must repay any money and return any other property received by him under the agreement.

(8) If property transferred under the agreement has passed to a third party, a reference in section 26 or 27 or this section to that property is to be read as a reference to its value at the time of its transfer under the agreement.

(9) The commission of an authorisation offence does not make the agreement concerned illegal or invalid to any greater extent than is provided by section 26 or 27.

NOTES

Section heading, sub-s (1): words in square brackets inserted by the Financial Services Act 2012, s 37(1), Sch 9, Pt 1, para 1, Pt 2, para 7, as from a 1 April 2013.

[7.71]

[28A Credit-related agreements made unenforceable by section 26, 26A or 27

(1) This section applies to an agreement that—

(a) is entered into in the course of carrying on a credit-related regulated activity, and

(b) is unenforceable because of section 26, 26A or 27.

(2) The amount of compensation recoverable as a result of that section is—

(a) the amount agreed by the parties, or

(b) on the application of either party, the amount specified in a written notice given by the FCA to the applicant.

(3) If on application by the relevant firm the FCA is satisfied that it is just and equitable in the circumstances of the case, it may by written notice to the applicant allow—

(a) the agreement to be enforced, or

(b) money paid or property transferred under the agreement to be retained.

(4) In considering whether to allow the agreement to be enforced or (as the case may be) the money or property paid or transferred under the agreement to be retained the FCA must—

(a) if the case arises as a result of section 26 or 26A, have regard to the issue mentioned in subsection (5), or

(b) if the case arises as a result of section 27, have regard to the issue mentioned in subsection (6).

(5) The issue is whether the relevant firm reasonably believed that by making the agreement the relevant firm was neither contravening the general prohibition nor contravening section 20.

(6) The issue is whether the provider knew that the third party was (in carrying on the credit-related regulated activity) either contravening the general prohibition or contravening section 20.

(7) An application to the FCA under this section by the relevant firm may relate to specified agreements or to agreements of a specified description or made at a specified time.

(8) "The relevant firm" means—

(a) in a case falling within section 26, the person in breach of the general prohibition;

(b) in a case falling within section 26A or 27, the authorised person concerned.

(9) If the FCA thinks fit, it may when acting under subsection (2)(b) or (3)—

(a) limit the determination in its notice to specified agreements, or agreements of a specified description or made at a specified time;

(b) make the determination in its notice conditional on the doing of specified acts by the applicant.]

NOTES

Inserted, together with s 28B, by the Financial Services Act 2012, s 37(1), Sch 9, Pt 1, para 1, Pt 2, para 8, as from 1 April 2013.

[7.72]

[28B Decisions under section 28A: procedure

(1) A notice under section 28A(2)(b) or (3) must—

(a) give the FCA's reasons for its determination, and

(b) give an indication of—

(i) the right to have the matter referred to the Tribunal that is conferred by subsection (3), and

(ii) the procedure on such a reference.

(2) The FCA must, so far as it is reasonably practicable to do so, give a copy of the notice to any other person who appears to it to be affected by the determination to which the notice relates.

(3) A person who is aggrieved by the determination of an application under section 28A(2)(b) or (3) may refer the matter to the Tribunal.]

NOTES

Inserted as noted to s 28A at **[7.71]**.

[7.73]

29 Accepting deposits in breach of general prohibition

(1) This section applies to an agreement between a person ("the depositor") and another person ("the deposit-taker") made in the course of the carrying on by the deposit-taker of accepting deposits in contravention of the general prohibition.

(2) If the depositor is not entitled under the agreement to recover without delay any money deposited by him, he may apply to the court for an order directing the deposit-taker to return the money to him.

(3) The court need not make such an order if it is satisfied that it would not be just and equitable for the money deposited to be returned, having regard to the issue mentioned in subsection (4).

(4) The issue is whether the deposit-taker reasonably believed that he was not contravening the general prohibition by making the agreement.

(5) "Agreement" means an agreement—

(a) made after this section comes into force; and

(b) the making or performance of which constitutes, or is part of, accepting deposits.

[7.74]

30 Enforceability of agreements resulting from unlawful communications

(1) In this section—

"unlawful communication" means a communication in relation to which there has been a contravention of section 21(1);

"controlled agreement" means an agreement the making or performance of which by either party constitutes a controlled activity for the purposes of that section; and

"controlled investment" has the same meaning as in section 21.

(2) If in consequence of an unlawful communication a person enters as a customer into a controlled agreement, it is unenforceable against him and he is entitled to recover—

(a) any money or other property paid or transferred by him under the agreement; and

(b) compensation for any loss sustained by him as a result of having parted with it.

(3) If in consequence of an unlawful communication a person exercises any rights conferred by a controlled investment, no obligation to which he is subject as a result of exercising them is enforceable against him and he is entitled to recover—

(a) any money or other property paid or transferred by him under the obligation; and

(b) compensation for any loss sustained by him as a result of having parted with it.

(4) But the court may allow—

(a) the agreement or obligation to be enforced, or

(b) money or property paid or transferred under the agreement or obligation to be retained,

if it is satisfied that it is just and equitable in the circumstances of the case.

(5) In considering whether to allow the agreement or obligation to be enforced or (as the case may be) the money or property paid or transferred under the agreement to be retained the court must have regard to the issues mentioned in subsections (6) and (7).

(6) If the applicant made the unlawful communication, the issue is whether he reasonably believed that he was not making such a communication.

(7) If the applicant did not make the unlawful communication, the issue is whether he knew that the agreement was entered into in consequence of such a communication.

(8) "Applicant" means the person seeking to enforce the agreement or obligation or retain the money or property paid or transferred.

(9) Any reference to making a communication includes causing a communication to be made.

(10) The amount of compensation recoverable as a result of subsection (2) or (3) is—

(a) the amount agreed between the parties; or

(b) on the application of either party, the amount determined by the court.

(11) If a person elects not to perform an agreement or an obligation which (by virtue of subsection (2) or (3)) is unenforceable against him, he must repay any money and return any other property received by him under the agreement.

(12) If (by virtue of subsection (2) or (3)) a person recovers money paid or property transferred by him under an agreement or obligation, he must repay any money and return any other property received by him as a result of exercising the rights in question.

(13) If any property required to be returned under this section has passed to a third party, references to that property are to be read as references to its value at the time of its receipt by the person required to return it.

PART III AUTHORISATION AND EXEMPTION

NOTES

Transitional provisions etc in connection with the original commencement of this Act: see the Financial Services and Markets Act 2000 (Transitional Provisions) (Authorised Persons etc) Order 2001, SI 2001/2636. That Order sets out the transitional arrangements for ensuring that people who had been authorised to carry on particular business under the various regulatory regimes replaced by this Act are treated as authorised persons with the appropriate permission for the purposes of this Act. The regulatory regimes covered by the Order are the Financial Services Act 1986, the Banking Act 1987, the Insurance Companies Act 1982, the Friendly Societies Act 1992, the Building Societies Act 1986, the Banking Coordination (Second Council Directive) Regulations 1992 (SI 1992/3218) and the Investment Services Regulations 1995 (SI 1995/3275).

Authorisation

[7.75]

31 Authorised persons

(1) The following persons are authorised for the purposes of this Act—

(a) a person who has a [Part 4A permission] to carry on one or more regulated activities;

[(aa) a Gibraltar-based person who has a Schedule 2A permission to carry on one or more regulated activities;]

(b), (c) . . .

(d) a person who is otherwise authorised by a provision of, or made under, this Act.

(2) In this Act "authorised person" means a person who is authorised for the purposes of this Act.

NOTES

Sub-s (1): words in square brackets in para (a) substituted by the Financial Services Act 2012, s 11(1), as from 1 April 2013. Para (aa) inserted by the Financial Services Act 2021, s 22(2), as from a day to be appointed. Paras (b), (c) repealed by the EEA Passport Rights (Amendment, etc, and Transitional Provisions) (EU Exit) Regulations 2018, SI 2018/1149, reg 2(1)–(3), as from IP completion day (as defined in the European Union (Withdrawal Agreement) Act 2020, s 39).

[7.76]

32 Partnerships and unincorporated associations

(1) If a firm is authorised—

(a) it is authorised to carry on the regulated activities concerned in the name of the firm; and

(b) its authorisation is not affected by any change in its membership.

(2) If an authorised firm is dissolved, its authorisation continues to have effect in relation to any [individual or] firm which succeeds to the business of the dissolved firm.

[(3) For the purposes of this section, an individual or firm is to be regarded as succeeding to the business of a dissolved firm only if succession is to the whole or substantially the whole of the business of the former firm.]

(4) "Firm" means—

(a) a partnership; or

(b) an unincorporated association of persons.

(5) "Partnership" does not include a partnership which is constituted under the law of any place outside the United Kingdom and is a body corporate.

NOTES

Para (2): words in square brackets inserted by the Regulatory Reform (Financial Services and Markets Act 2000) Order 2007, SI 2007/1973, arts 2, 3(a), as from 12 July 2007.

Para (3): substituted by SI 2007/1973, arts 2, 3(b), as from 12 July 2007.

[7.77]

[32A Gibraltar-based persons

(1) The Treasury must, for each reporting period, prepare a report about the operation of Schedule 2A during the period.

(2) The report must, among other things, consider whether the conditions in paragraphs 7, 8 and 9 of Schedule 2A continue to be satisfied in connection with each regulated activity which is an approved activity for the purposes of that Schedule.

(3) The Treasury must consult the FCA and the PRA during the preparation of the report.

(4) The Treasury must lay a copy of the report before Parliament as soon as reasonably practicable after the end of the reporting period.

(5) The reporting periods are—

(a) the period of two years beginning with the day on which Schedule 2A comes fully into force, and

(b) each subsequent period of two years.]

NOTES

Commencement: to be appointed.

Inserted by the Financial Services Act 2021, s 22(3), as from a day to be appointed.

Ending of authorisation

[7.78]

33 Withdrawal of authorisation . . .

(1) This section applies if—

(a) an authorised person's [Part 4A permission] [or Schedule 2A permission] is cancelled; and

(b) as a result, there is no regulated activity for which he has permission.

(2) The [appropriate regulator] must give a direction withdrawing that person's status as an authorised person.

[(2A) In subsection (2) "the appropriate regulator" means—

(a) in the case of a PRA-authorised person, the PRA, and

(b) in any other case, the FCA.]

NOTES

Section heading: the words omitted were repealed by the Financial Services Act 2012, s 114(1), Sch 18, Pt 1, paras 1, 2, as from 1 April 2013.

Sub-s (1): the words "or Schedule 2A permission" in square brackets are inserted by the Financial Services Act 2021, s 22, Sch 8, para 3, as from a day to be appointed. The other words in square brackets were substituted by the Financial Services Act 2012, s 114(1), Sch 18, Pt 1, paras 1, 2, as from 1 April 2013.

Sub-s (2): words in square brackets substituted by the Financial Services Act 2012, s 114(1), Sch 18, Pt 1, paras 1, 2, as from 1 April 2013.

Sub-s (2A): added by the Financial Services Act 2012, s 114(1), Sch 18, Pt 1, paras 1, 2, as from 1 April 2013.

34, 35 *(Ss 34 (EEA firms) and 35 (Treaty firms) were repealed by the EEA Passport Rights (Amendment, etc, and Transitional Provisions) (EU Exit) Regulations 2018, SI 2018/1149, reg 3, Schedule, Pt 1, paras 1, 3, 4, as from IP completion day (as defined in the European Union (Withdrawal Agreement) Act 2020, s 39).)*

[7.79]

[36 Authorised open-ended investment companies

Schedule 5 makes provision about authorised open-ended investment companies.]

NOTES

Commencement: IP completion day (as defined in the European Union (Withdrawal Agreement) Act 2020, s 39).

Substituted by the Collective Investment Schemes (Amendment etc) (EU Exit) Regulations 2019, SI 2019/325, regs 3, 4, as from IP completion day (as defined in the European Union (Withdrawal Agreement) Act 2020, s 39).

[UK-based persons carrying on activities in Gibraltar

[7.80]

36A UK-based persons carrying on activities in Gibraltar

Schedule 2B makes provision about the carrying on of activities corresponding to regulated activities in Gibraltar by UK-based persons.]

NOTES

Commencement: to be appointed.

Inserted, together with the preceding heading, by the Financial Services Act 2021, s 22(4), as from a day to be appointed.

37 *(S 37 (Exercise of EEA rights by UK firms) repealed by the EEA Passport Rights (Amendment, etc, and Transitional Provisions) (EU Exit) Regulations 2018, SI 2018/1149, reg 2(1), (4), as from IP completion day (as defined in the European Union (Withdrawal Agreement) Act 2020, s 39).)*

Exemption

[7.81]

38 Exemption orders

(1) The Treasury may by order ("an exemption order") provide for—

(a) specified persons, or

(b) persons falling within a specified class,

to be exempt from the general prohibition.

(2) But a person cannot be an exempt person as a result of an exemption order if he has a [Part 4A permission].

(3) An exemption order may provide for an exemption to have effect—

(a) in respect of all regulated activities;

(b) in respect of one or more specified regulated activities;

(c) only in specified circumstances;

(d) only in relation to specified functions;

(e) subject to conditions.

(4) "Specified" means specified by the exemption order.

NOTES

Sub-s (2): words in square brackets substituted by the Financial Services Act 2012, s 114(1), Sch 18, Pt 1, paras 1, 4, as from 1 April 2013.

Orders: the Financial Services and Markets Act 2000 (Exemption) Order 2001, SI 2001/1201 at **[8.326]**; the Financial Services and Markets Act 2000 (Exemption) (Amendment) Order 2001, SI 2001/3623; the Financial Services and Markets Act 2000 (Financial Promotion and Miscellaneous Amendments) Order 2002, SI 2002/1310; the Financial Services and Markets Act 2000 (Exemption) (Amendment) Order 2003, SI 2003/47; the Financial Services and Markets Act 2000 (Exemption) (Amendment) (No 2) Order 2003, SI 2003/1675; the Financial Services and Markets Act 2000 (Exemption) (Amendment) Order 2005, SI 2005/592; the Financial Services and Markets Act 2000 (Exemption) (Amendment) Order 2007, SI 2007/125; the Financial Services and Markets Act 2000 (Exemption) (Amendment No 2) Order 2007, SI 2007/1821; the Financial Services and Markets Act 2000 (Exemption) (Amendment) Order 2008, SI 2008/682; the Financial Services and Markets Act 2000 (Exemption) (Amendment) Order 2009, SI 2009/118; the Financial Services and Markets Act 2000 (Exemption) (Amendment) (No 2) Order 2009, SI 2009/264; the Financial Services and Markets Act 2000 (Exemption) (Amendment) Order 2011, SI 2011/1626; the Financial Services and Markets Act 2000 (Exemption) (Amendment No 2) Order 2011, SI 2011/2716; the Financial Services and Markets Act 2000 (Exemption) (Amendment) Order 2012, SI 2012/763; the Financial Services and Markets Act 2000 (Consumer Credit) (Miscellaneous Provisions) (No 2) Order 2014, SI 2014/506; the Financial Services and Markets Act 2000 (Miscellaneous Provisions) (No 2) Order 2015, SI 2015/352; the Financial Services and Markets Act 2000 (Exemption) (Amendment) Order 2015, SI 2015/447; the Mortgage Credit Directive Order 2015, SI 2015/910; the Financial Services and Markets Act 2000 (Regulated Activities) (Amendment) Order 2016, SI 2016/392; the Financial Services and Markets Act 2000 (Exemption) (Amendment) Order 2020, SI 2020/322; the Financial Services and Markets Act 2000 (Exemption) (Amendment) Order 2021, SI 2021/1127; the Financial Services and Markets Act 2000 (Exemption) (Amendment) Order 2022, SI 2022/100; the Financial Services and Markets Act 2000 (Regulated Activities) (Amendment) Order 2022, SI 2022/466.

[7.82]

39 Exemption of appointed representatives

(1) If a person (other than an authorised person)—

(a) is a party to a contract with an authorised person ("his principal") which—

(i) permits or requires him to carry on business of a prescribed description, and

(ii) complies with such requirements as may be prescribed, and

(b) is someone for whose activities in carrying on the whole or part of that business his principal has accepted responsibility in writing,

he is exempt from the general prohibition in relation to any regulated activity comprised in the carrying on of that business for which his principal has accepted responsibility.

[(1ZA) But a person is not exempt as a result of subsection (1) if subsection (1A)[, (1AA)] or (1BA) applies to the person.]

[(1A) [This subsection applies to a person]—

(a) if his principal is an investment firm[, a [qualifying credit institution], or [a firm which has a Part 4A permission to carry on regulated activities as an exempt investment firm within the meaning of regulation 8 of the Financial Services and Markets Act 2000 (Markets in Financial Instruments) Regulations 2017 (SI 2017/701)]], and

(b) so far as the business for which his principal has accepted responsibility is investment services business,

unless he is entered on the applicable register.

[(1AA) This subsection applies to a person—

(a) if the person's principal is an investment firm or a [qualifying credit institution], and

(b) so far as the business for which the person's principal has accepted responsibility is selling, or advising clients on, structured deposits . . . ,

unless the person is entered on the applicable register.]

(1B) [In subsections (1A) and (1AA)] the "applicable register" is [the record maintained by the FCA by virtue of section 347(1)(ha)].]

[(1BA) This subsection applies to a person ("A")—

(a) if A's principal is a mortgage intermediary, and
(b) so far as the business for which A's principal has accepted responsibility is of a kind [that]—
(i) [is] specified in article 25A (arranging regulated mortgage contracts), article 36A (credit broking), article 53A (advising on regulated mortgage contracts) or article 53DA (advising on regulated credit agreements the purpose of which is to acquire land) of the Financial Services and Markets Act 2000 (Regulated Activities) Order 2001; and
[(ii) relates to mortgage agreements entered into on or after 21st March 2016,]

unless A meets the requirements of subsection (1BB).

(1BB) The requirements of this subsection are—
(a) that A is entered on the record maintained by the FCA by virtue of section 347(1)(hb);
(b) that A's principal is a person who has a Part 4A permission to carry on one or more of the regulated activities mentioned in subsection (1BA)(b)(i); and
(c) that A's principal is not a tied mortgage intermediary.]

[(1C) Subsection (1D) applies where an authorised person ("A")—
(a) has permission under Part 4A, or permission resulting from any other provision of this Act, only in relation to one or more qualifying activities,
(b) is a party to a contract with another authorised person (A's "principal") which—
(i) permits or requires A to carry on business of a prescribed description ("the relevant business"), and
(ii) complies with such requirements as may be prescribed, and
(c) is someone for whose activities in carrying on the whole or part of the relevant business A's principal has accepted responsibility in writing.

(1D) Sections 20(1) and (1A) and 23(1A) do not apply in relation to the carrying on by A of a relevant additional activity.

(1E) In subsections (1C) and (1D)—
(a) "qualifying activity" means a regulated activity which is of a prescribed kind and relates—
(i) to rights under a contract of the kind mentioned in paragraph 23 of Schedule 2, other than one under which the obligation of the borrower to repay is secured on land, or
(ii) to rights under a contract of the kind mentioned in paragraph 23B of that Schedule;
(b) "relevant additional activity" means a regulated activity which—
(i) is not one to which A's permission relates, and
(ii) is comprised in the carrying on of the business for which A's principal has accepted responsibility.]

[(2) In this Act "appointed representative" means—
(a) a person who is exempt as a result of subsection (1), or
(b) a person carrying on a regulated activity in circumstances where, as a result of subsection (1D), sections 20(1) and (1A) and 23(1A) do not apply.]

(3) The principal of an appointed representative is responsible, to the same extent as if he had expressly permitted it, for anything done or omitted by the representative in carrying on the business for which he has accepted responsibility.

[(4) In determining whether an authorised person has complied with—
(a) a provision contained in or made under this Act, or
(b) a [qualifying provision] that is specified, or of a description specified, for the purposes of this subsection by the Treasury by order,

anything which a relevant person has done or omitted as respects business for which the authorised person has accepted responsibility is to be treated as having been done or omitted by the authorised person.]

(5) "Relevant person" means a person who at the material time is or was an appointed representative by virtue of being a party to a contract with the authorised person.

(6) Nothing in subsection (4) is to cause the knowledge or intentions of an appointed representative to be attributed to his principal for the purpose of determining whether the principal has committed an offence, unless in all the circumstances it is reasonable for them to be attributed to him.

[(7) A person carries on "investment services business" if, under the full and unconditional responsibility of only one investment firm on whose behalf the person acts, the person—
(a) promotes investment services or ancillary services to the firm's clients or prospective clients,
(b) receives and transmits instructions or orders from clients in respect of investment services or financial instruments,
(c) places financial instruments, or
(d) provides advice to clients or prospective clients in respect of investment services or financial instruments.]

[(8) In this section—

"ancillary services" means any of the services and activities listed in Part 3A of Schedule 2 to the Financial Services and Markets Act 2000 (Regulated Activities) Order 2001 (SI 2001/544);

"financial instruments" means those instruments specified in Part 1 of Schedule 2 to the Financial Services and Markets Act 2000 (Regulated Activities) Order 2001;

"investment services" means any of the services and activities listed in Part 3 of Schedule 2 to the Financial Services and Markets Act 2000 (Regulated Activities) Order 2001, relating to any of the instruments listed in Part 1 of that Schedule;

"structured deposit" has the meaning given by Article 2.1.23 of the markets in financial instruments regulation.]

NOTES

Sub-s (1ZA): inserted by the Mortgage Credit Directive Order 2015, SI 2015/910, Sch 1, para 1(1), (2)(a), (c), as from 21 March 2016. Figure in square brackets inserted by the Financial Services and Markets Act 2000 (Markets in Financial Instruments) Regulations 2017, SI 2017/701, reg 50(1), Sch 2, paras 1, 2(1), (2), as from 3 January 2018 (note that various provisions of the 2017 Regulations came into force on earlier dates for the purposes of making rules, giving notices and consent, etc (for details see reg 1 of the 2017 Regulations)).

Sub-s (1A): inserted, together with sub-s (1B), by the Financial Services and Markets Act 2000 (Markets in Financial Instruments) Regulations 2007, SI 2007/126, reg 3(5), Sch 5, paras 1, 2(a), (c), as from 1 April 2007 (certain purposes), and as from 1 November 2007 (otherwise). Subsequently amended as follows—

Words in first pair of square brackets substituted by SI 2015/910, Sch 1, para 1(1), (2)(b), as from 21 March 2016.

Words in first (outer) pair of square brackets in para (a) substituted by SI 2017/701, reg 50(1), Sch 2, paras 1, 2(1), (3), as from 3 January 2018 (as to the commencement of the 2017 Regulations, see further the note relating to them above).

Words in second and third (inner) pairs of square brackets in para (a) substituted by the Financial Services and Markets Act 2000 (Amendment) (EU Exit) Regulations 2019, SI 2019/632, regs 11, 12(1), (2), as from IP completion day (as defined in the European Union (Withdrawal Agreement) Act 2020, s 39).

Sub-s (1AA): inserted by SI 2017/701, reg 50(1), Sch 2, paras 1, 2(1), (4), as from 3 January 2018 (as to the commencement of the 2017 Regulations, see further the note relating to them above). Words in square brackets in para (a) substituted, and words omitted from para (b) repealed, by SI 2019/632, regs 11, 12(1), (3), as from IP completion day (as defined in the European Union (Withdrawal Agreement) Act 2020, s 39).

Sub-s (1B): inserted as noted above. The words in the first pair of square brackets were inserted by SI 2017/701, reg 50(1), Sch 2, paras 1, 2(1), (5), as from 3 January 2018 (as to the commencement of the 2017 Regulations, see further the note relating to them above). The words in the second pair of square brackets were substituted by SI 2019/632, regs 11, 12(4), as from IP completion day (as defined in the European Union (Withdrawal Agreement) Act 2020, s 39).

Sub-ss (1BA), (1BB): inserted by SI 2015/910, Sch 1, para 1(1), (2)(a), (c), as from 21 March 2016. In sub-s (1BA) the words "that" and "is" in square brackets in para (b) were inserted, and sub-para (b)(ii) was substituted by SI 2019/632, regs 11, 12(5), as from IP completion day (as defined in the European Union (Withdrawal Agreement) Act 2020, s 39).

Sub-ss (1C)–(1E): inserted by the Financial Services Act 2012, s 10(1), (2), as from 1 April 2013.

Sub-s (2): substituted by the Financial Services Act 2012, s 10(1), (3), as from 1 April 2013.

Sub-s (4): substituted by the Financial Services Act 2012, s 114(1), Sch 18, Pt 1, paras 1, 5(1), (3), as from 24 January 2013 (for the purposes of making orders), and as from 1 April 2013 (otherwise). Words in square brackets in para (b) substituted by SI 2019/632, regs 11, 12(6), as from IP completion day (as defined in the European Union (Withdrawal Agreement) Act 2020, s 39) (for transitional provisions see SI 2019/710, reg 37 at **[12.110]**).

Sub-ss (7), (8): added by SI 2007/126, reg 3(5), Sch 5, paras 1, 2(a), (c), as from 1 April 2007 (certain purposes), and as from 1 November 2007 (otherwise). Subsequently substituted by SI 2019/632, regs 11, 12(7), (8), as from IP completion day (as defined in the European Union (Withdrawal Agreement) Act 2020, s 39).

Regulations and Orders: the Financial Services and Markets Act 2000 (Appointed Representatives) Regulations 2001, SI 2001/1217; the Financial Services and Markets Act 2000 (Appointed Representatives) (Amendment) Regulations 2001, SI 2001/2508; the Financial Services and Markets Act 2000 (Appointed Representatives) (Amendment) Regulations 2004, SI 2004/453; the Financial Services and Markets Act 2000 (Appointed Representatives) (Amendment) Regulations 2006, SI 2006/3414; the Financial Services and Markets Act 2000 (Markets in Financial Instruments) (Amendment) Regulations 2007, SI 2007/763; the Financial Services and Markets Act 2000 (Qualifying Provisions) Order 2013, SI 2013/419; the Financial Services and Markets Act 2000 (Qualifying Provisions) (No 2) Order 2013, SI 2013/3116; the Financial Services and Markets Act 2000 (Appointed Representatives) (Amendment) Regulations 2014, SI 2014/206; the Financial Services and Markets Act 2000 (Regulated Activities) (Amendment) Order 2016, SI 2016/392; the Financial Services and Markets Act 2000 (Qualifying EU Provisions) (Amendment) Order 2016, SI 2016/936; the Alternative Investment Fund Managers (Amendment) Regulations 2018, SI 2018/134; the Insurance Distribution (Regulated Activities and Miscellaneous Amendments) Order 2018, SI 2018/546; the Financial Services and Markets Act 2000 (Regulated Activities) (Amendment) Order 2021, SI 2021/90; the Recognised Auction Platforms (Amendment and Miscellaneous Provisions) Regulations 2021, SI 2021/494.

[7.83]

[39A Certain tied agents operating outside United Kingdom

(1) This section applies to an authorised person whose relevant office is in the United Kingdom if—

(a) he is a party to a contract with a person (other than an authorised person) who is [established in the United Kingdom; and]

(b) the contract is a relevant contract.

(2) A contract is a "relevant contract" if it satisfies conditions A to C

(3) Condition A is that the contract permits or requires the person mentioned in subsection (1)(a) (the "agent") to carry on investment services business.

(4) Condition B is that [the FCA is satisfied that no such business is, or is likely to be, carried on by the agent in the United Kingdom].

(5) Condition C is that the business is of a description that, if carried on in the United Kingdom, would be prescribed for the purposes of section 39(1)(a)(i).

(6) An authorised person to whom this section applies who—

(a) enters into or continues to perform a relevant contract with an agent which does not comply with the applicable requirements,

(b) enters into or continues to perform a relevant contract without accepting or having accepted responsibility in writing for the agent's activities in carrying on investment services business,

[(c) enters into a relevant contract with an agent who is not entered on—

(i) the record maintained by the FCA by virtue of section 347(1)(ha), or

(ii) . . .]

(d) continues to perform a relevant contract with an agent when he knows or ought to know that the agent is not entered on that record [. . .],

is to be taken for the purposes of this Act to have contravened a requirement imposed on him by or under this Act.

(7) The "applicable requirements" are the requirements prescribed for the purposes of subsection (1)(a)(ii) of section 39 which have effect in the case of a person to whom subsection (1A) of that section applies.

[(8) Section 39(7) applies for the purposes of this section.]

(9) In this section—

"competent authority" has the meaning given in [Article 4.1.26] of the markets in financial instruments directive;

"relevant office" means—

(a) in relation to a body corporate, its registered office or, if it has no registered office, its head office, and

(b) in relation to a person other than a body corporate, the person's head office.]

NOTES

Inserted by the Financial Services and Markets Act 2000 (Markets in Financial Instruments) Regulations 2007, SI 2007/126, reg 3(5), Sch 5, paras 1, 3, as from 1 April 2007 (certain purposes), and as from 1 November 2007 (otherwise).

Sub-s (1): words in square brackets substituted by the Financial Services and Markets Act 2000 (Amendment) (EU Exit) Regulations 2019, SI 2019/632, regs 11, 13(1), (2), as from IP completion day (as defined in the European Union (Withdrawal Agreement) Act 2020, s 39). For transitional provisions, see the note below, and note that the original text read as follows—

"established—
(i) in the United Kingdom, or
(ii) in an EEA State which does not permit investment firms authorised by the competent authority of the State to appoint tied agents; and".

Sub-s (4): words in square brackets substituted by SI 2019/632, regs 11, 13(1), (3), as from IP completion day (as defined in the European Union (Withdrawal Agreement) Act 2020, s 39). For transitional provisions, see the final note below, and note that the original text (as amended by the Financial Services Act 2012, s 114(1), Sch 18, Pt 1, paras 1, 6, as from 1 April 2013) read as follows—

"either—
(a) it is a condition of the contract that such business may only be carried on by the agent in an EEA State other than the United Kingdom; or
(b) in a case not falling within paragraph (a), the [FCA] is satisfied that no such business is, or is likely to be, carried on by the agent in the United Kingdom.".

Sub-s (6): para (c) was substituted, and words omitted from para (d) were originally inserted, by the Financial Services and Markets Act 2000 (Markets in Financial Instruments) Regulations 2017, SI 2017/701, reg 50(1), Sch 2, paras 1, 3(1), (2), as from 3 January 2018 (note that various provisions of the 2017 Regulations came into force on earlier dates for the purposes of making rules, giving notices and consent, etc (for details see reg 1 of the 2017 Regulations)). Sub-para (c)(ii) and the words omitted from sub-para (d) were repealed by SI 2019/632, regs 11, 13(1), (4), (5), as from IP completion day (as defined in the European Union (Withdrawal Agreement) Act 2020, s 39).

Sub-s (8): substituted by SI 2019/632, regs 11, 13(1), (6), as from IP completion day (as defined in the European Union (Withdrawal Agreement) Act 2020, s 39).

Sub-s (9): the definition "competent authority" in italics was repealed by SI 2019/632, regs 11, 13(1), (7), as from IP completion day (as defined in the European Union (Withdrawal Agreement) Act 2020, s 39); for transitional provisions, see the final note below. The words in square brackets in the repealed definition were substituted by SI 2017/701, reg 50(1), Sch 2, paras 1, 3(1), (4), as from 3 January 2018.

Transitional provisions: the Financial Services and Markets Act 2000 (Amendment) (EU Exit) Regulations 2019, SI 2019/632, reg 13(8)–(10) provide as follows—

"(8) The amendments made by paragraphs (2), (3) and (7) do not apply during the three-year transitional period in relation to contracts entered into before [IP completion day].

(9) In relation to such contracts, section 39A(6)(d) has effect during the three-year transitional period as if "or on the register of tied agents of an EEA State maintained pursuant to Article 29 of Directive 2014/65/EU of the European Parliament and of the Council of 15 May 2014 on markets in financial instruments" were inserted after "entered on that record".

(10) In paragraphs (8) and (9) "the three-year transitional period" means the period that—
(a) begins with [IP completion day], and
(b) ends at the end of the period of three years starting with the first day after [IP completion day].".

Note that the words "IP completion day" in square brackets in the text set out above were substituted by the Financial Services and Economic and Monetary Policy (Consequential Amendments) (EU Exit) Regulations 2020, SI 2020/1301, reg 3, Schedule, para 33(b), as from 30 December 2020.

[PART 4A PERMISSION TO CARRY ON REGULATED ACTIVITIES

NOTES

Transitional provisions etc in connection with the commencement of the Financial Services Act 2012: For transitional provisions in relation to the commencement of this Part, see the Financial Services Act 2012 (Transitional Provisions) (Permission and Approval) Order 2013, SI 2013/440. Part 2 of that Order (Permission to Carry on Regulated Activities) contains transitional provisions in relation to permission under this Act to carry on regulated activity, including (a) provision for things done by or in relation to the FSA before1 April 2013 to be treated as if done by or in relation to the PRA, or the PRA and the FCA, and (b) provision in respect of applications for permission, requirements on permission, variation of permission and cancellation of permission.

See also the Financial Services Act 2012 (Transitional Provisions) (Enforcement) Order 2013, SI 2013/441. Articles 26–29 contain transitional provisions in relation to various warning notices and decision notices given by the FSA under the original Part IV of this Act before 1 April 2013.

Transitional provisions etc in connection with the original commencement of this Act: see the Financial Services and Markets Act 2000 (Transitional Provisions) (Authorised Persons etc) Order 2001, SI 2001/2636 which, inter alia, provides that persons who were authorised or exempted from the need for authorisation under provisions of the previous regulatory regimes were to be treated, as from 1 December 2001, as having permission under the original Pt IV of this Act (Permission to Carry on Regulated Activities) to carry on the activities they were lawfully able to carry on immediately before that date by reason of that authorisation or exemption. Note that the original Part IV was substituted by a new Part 4A by the Financial Services Act 2012.

See also the Financial Services and Markets Act 2000 (Interim Permissions) Order 2001, SI 2001/3374. This Order conferred an interim permission on certain applicants who applied to the FSA for permission under the original Part IV of this Act and whose application was pending on the date when the main provisions of the Act came into force (1 December 2001).

See also, the Financial Services and Markets Act 2000 (Consequential and Transitional Provisions) (Miscellaneous) (No 2) Order 2001, SI 2001/2659 (transitional provisions in consequence of the Financial Services and Markets Act 2000 (Commencement No 5) Order (SI 2001/2632). That Order brings into force the provisions of the Act relating to (among other things) the making of applications under the Act for permission or authorisation coming into force on 1 December 2001).

Transitional provisions (newly regulated activities etc): as to interim and temporary permissions, interim approvals (etc) and the application of the this Act, subject to transitional provisions, to various activities that have become regulated activities following the amendment of the Financial Services and Markets Act 2000 (Regulated Activities) Order 2001, SI 2001/544, see the note "Transitional provisions (interim and temporary permissions and interim approvals)" in the introductory notes to the Regulated Activities Order which precede paragraph **[8.1]** *post*.

Miscellaneous: note that the Corporate Insolvency and Governance Act 2020, s 12 (suspension of liability for wrongful trading: Great Britain), does not apply if at any relevant time during the relevant period (as defined by s 12(2) thereof) the company concerned has permission under this Part to carry on a regulated activity and it is not subject to a requirement imposed under this Act to refrain from holding money for clients; see s 12(6) of the 2020 Act.

Application for permission

[7.84]

55A Application for permission

(1) An application for permission to carry on one or more regulated activities may be made to the appropriate regulator by—

(a) an individual,

(b) a body corporate,

(c) a partnership, or

(d) an unincorporated association.

(2) "The appropriate regulator", in relation to an application under this section, means [(subject to subsection (2B))]—

(a) the PRA, in a case where—

(i) the regulated activities to which the application relates consist of or include a PRA-regulated activity, or

(ii) the applicant is a PRA-authorised person otherwise than by virtue of a Part 4A permission;

(b) the FCA, in any other case.

[(2A) An application under this section for permission to carry on the regulated activity specified in article 63S of the Financial Services and Markets Act 2000 (Regulated Activities) Order 2001 may not include an application for permission to carry on any other regulated activity.

(2B) The appropriate regulator, in relation to an application under this section for permission to carry on the regulated activity specified in article 63S of the Financial Services and Markets Act 2000 (Regulated Activities) Order 2001, is the FCA.]

(3) An authorised person who has a permission under this Part which is in force may not apply for permission under this section.

(4) . . .

(5) A permission given by the appropriate regulator under this Part or having effect as if so given is referred to in this Act as "a Part 4A permission.]

NOTES

This section was substituted (together with the rest of Part 4A (originally, ss 55A–55Z4) for the original Part IV (ss 40–55)) by the Financial Services Act 2012, s 11(2), as from 1 April 2013.

Words in square brackets in sub-s (2) inserted, and sub-ss (2A), (2B) inserted, by the Financial Services and Markets Act 2000 (Benchmarks) Regulations 2018, SI 2018/135, reg 40(1), (2), as from 27 February 2018.

Sub-s (4) was repealed by the EEA Passport Rights (Amendment, etc, and Transitional Provisions) (EU Exit) Regulations 2018, SI 2018/1149, reg 3, Schedule, Pt 1, paras 1, 5, as from IP completion day (as defined in the European Union (Withdrawal Agreement) Act 2020, s 39).

[7.85]

[55B The threshold conditions

(1) "The threshold conditions", in relation to a regulated activity, means the conditions set out in or specified under Schedule 6, as read with any threshold condition code made by either regulator under section 137O.

(2) Any reference in this Part to the threshold conditions for which either regulator is responsible is to be read as a reference to the conditions set out in or specified under Schedule 6 that are expressed to be relevant to the discharge by that regulator of its functions, as read with any threshold condition code made by that regulator under section 137O.

(3) In giving or varying permission, imposing or varying a requirement, or giving consent, under any provision of this Part, each regulator must ensure that the person concerned will satisfy, and continue to satisfy, in relation to all of the regulated activities for which the person has or will have permission, the threshold conditions for which that regulator is responsible.

(4) But the duty imposed by subsection (3) does not prevent a regulator, having due regard to that duty, from taking such steps as it considers are necessary, in relation to a particular person, in order to advance—

(a) in the case of the FCA, any of its operational objectives;

(b) in the case of the PRA, any of its objectives.

[(5) The duty imposed by subsection (3) does not apply in relation to the regulated activity specified in article 63S of the Financial Services and Markets Act 2000 (Regulated Activities) Order 2001 (administering a benchmark).]]

NOTES

Substituted as noted to s 55A at **[7.84]**.

Sub-s (5): added by the Financial Services and Markets Act 2000 (Benchmarks) Regulations 2018, SI 2018/135, reg 40(1), (3), as from 27 February 2018.

[7.86]

[55C Power to amend Schedule 6

(1) The Treasury may by order amend Parts 1 and 2 of Schedule 6 by altering, adding or repealing provisions, or by substituting for those Parts as they have effect for the time being provisions specified in the order.

(2) Different provision may be made under this section—

(a) in relation to the discharge of the functions of each regulator;

(b) in relation to different regulated activities;

(c) in relation to persons who carry on, or seek to carry on, activities that consist of or include a PRA-regulated activity and in relation to other persons.]

NOTES

Substituted as noted to s 55A at **[7.84]**.

Orders and Regulations: the Financial Services and Markets Act 2000 (Threshold Conditions) Order 2013, SI 2013/555; the Financial Services and Markets Act 2000 (Miscellaneous Provisions) Order 2015, SI 2015/853; the Risk Transformation Regulations 2017, SI 2017/1212.

[7.87]

[55D Firms based outside [the United Kingdom]

(1) This section applies in relation to a person ("the [non-UK] firm")—

(a) who is a body incorporated in, or formed under the law of, or is an individual who is a national of, any country or territory outside the [United Kingdom], and

(b) who is carrying on a regulated activity in any country or territory outside the United Kingdom in accordance with the law of that country or territory ("the overseas state").

(2) In determining whether the [non-UK] firm is satisfying or will satisfy, and continue to satisfy, any one or more of the threshold conditions for which a UK regulator is responsible, the UK regulator may have regard to any opinion notified to it by a regulatory authority in the overseas state ("the overseas regulator") which relates to the [non-UK] firm and appears to the UK regulator to be relevant to compliance with those conditions.

(3) In considering how much weight (if any) to attach to the opinion, the UK regulator must have regard to the nature and scope of the supervision exercised in relation to the [non-UK] firm by the overseas regulator.

(4) In this section "UK regulator" means the FCA or the PRA.]

NOTES

Substituted as noted to s 55A at **[7.84]**.

All words in square brackets were substituted by the Financial Services and Markets Act 2000 (Amendment) (EU Exit) Regulations 2019, SI 2019/632, regs 14, 15, as from IP completion day (as defined in the European Union (Withdrawal Agreement) Act 2020, s 39).

[7.88]

[55E Giving permission: the FCA

(1) This section applies where the FCA is the appropriate regulator in relation to an application for permission under section 55A.

(2) The FCA may give permission for the applicant to carry on the regulated activity or activities to which the application relates or such of them as may be specified in the permission.

(3) If the applicant is a member of a group which includes a PRA-authorised person, the FCA must consult the PRA before determining the application.

[(3A) The FCA must consult the PRA before determining an application for permission to carry on the regulated activity specified in article 63S of the Financial Services and Markets Act 2000 (Regulated Activities) Order 2001 (administering a benchmark) made by a person who is a PRA-authorised person otherwise than by virtue of a Part 4A permission.]

(4) If it gives permission, the FCA must specify the permitted regulated activity or activities, described in such manner as the FCA considers appropriate.

(5) The FCA may—

(a) incorporate in the description of a regulated activity such limitations (for example as to circumstances in which the activity may, or may not, be carried on) as it considers appropriate;

(b) specify a narrower or wider description of regulated activity than that to which the application relates;

(c) give permission for the carrying on of a regulated activity which is not included among those to which the application relates and is not a PRA-regulated activity.]

NOTES

Substituted as noted to s 55A at **[7.84]**.

Sub-s (3A): inserted by the Financial Services and Markets Act 2000 (Benchmarks) Regulations 2018, SI 2018/135, reg 40(1), (4), as from 27 February 2018.

[7.89]

[55F Giving permission: the PRA

(1) This section applies where the PRA is the appropriate regulator in relation to an application for permission under section 55A.

(2) The PRA may with the consent of the FCA give permission for the applicant to carry on the regulated activity or activities to which the application relates or such of them as may be specified in the permission.

(3) If it gives permission, the PRA must specify the permitted regulated activity or activities, described in such manner as the PRA considers appropriate.

(4) The PRA may—

(a) incorporate in the description of a regulated activity such limitations (for example as to circumstances in which the activity may, or may not, be carried on) as it considers appropriate;

(b) specify a narrower or wider description of regulated activity than that to which the application relates;

(c) give permission for the carrying on of a regulated activity which is not included among those to which the application relates.

(5) Consent given by the FCA for the purposes of this section may be conditional on the manner in which the PRA exercises its powers under subsections (3) and (4).

(6) Subsections (3) and (4)(b) and (c) do not enable the PRA to give permission that relates only to activities that are not PRA-regulated activities, except where the applicant is a PRA-authorised person otherwise than by virtue of a Part 4A permission.]

NOTES

Substituted as noted to s 55A at **[7.84]**.

[7.90]

[55G Giving permission: special cases

(1) "The applicant" means an applicant for permission under section 55A.

(2) If the applicant—

(a) in relation to a particular regulated activity, is exempt from the general prohibition as a result of section 39(1) or an order made under section 38(1), but

(b) has applied for permission in relation to another regulated activity,

the application is to be treated as relating to all the regulated activities which, if permission is given, the applicant will carry on.

(3) If the applicant—

(a) in relation to a particular regulated activity, is exempt from the general prohibition as a result of [. . . section 285], but

(b) has applied for permission in relation to another regulated activity,

the application is to be treated as relating only to that other regulated activity.

(4) If the applicant—

(a) is a person to whom, in relation to a particular regulated activity, the general prohibition does not apply as a result of Part 19, but

(b) has applied for permission in relation to another regulated activity,

the application is to be treated as relating only to that other regulated activity.

(5) Subsection (6) applies where either regulator ("the responsible regulator") receives an application for permission under section 55A which is in the regulator's opinion similar to an application which was previously made to the other regulator and was either—

(a) treated by the other regulator as not being a valid application to that regulator because of the regulated activities to which it related, or

(b) refused by the other regulator after being considered.

(6) The responsible regulator must have regard to the desirability of minimising—

(a) the additional work for the applicant in dealing with the new application, and

(b) the time taken to deal with the new application.]

NOTES

Substituted as noted to s 55A at **[7.84]**.

Sub-s (3): words in square brackets substituted by the Financial Services and Markets Act 2000 (Over the Counter Derivatives, Central Counterparties and Trade Repositories) Regulations 2013, SI 2013/504, reg 3(1), (2), as from 1 April 2013. Words omitted repealed by the Central Securities Depositories Regulations 2017, SI 2017/1064, reg 2(1), (3), as from 28 November 2017.

[Variation and cancellation of Part 4A permission

[7.91]

55H Variation by FCA at request of authorised person

(1) . . .

(2) The FCA may, on the application of [an authorised person who has a Part 4A permission but is not a PRA-authorised person], vary the permission by—

(a) adding a regulated activity, other than a PRA-regulated activity, to those to which the permission relates;

(b) removing a regulated activity from those to which the permission relates;

(c) varying the description of a regulated activity to which the permission relates.

(3) The FCA may, on the application of [an authorised person who has a Part 4A permission but is not a PRA-authorised person], cancel the permission.

[(3A) The FCA may, on the application of a PRA-authorised person with a Part 4A permission, vary the permission by—

(a) adding to the regulated activities to which the permission relates the regulated activity specified in article 63S of the Financial Services and Markets Act 2000 (Regulated Activities) Order 2001 (administering a benchmark),

(b) removing that regulated activity from those to which the permission relates, or

(c) varying the description of that regulated activity.

(3B) The FCA must consult the PRA before exercising its power under subsection (3A).]

(4) The FCA may refuse an application under this section if it appears to it that it is desirable to do so in order to advance any of its operational objectives.

[(4A) The FCA may also refuse an application under this section if it appears to the FCA that the authorised person would not comply with requirements in Part 5 of the Alternative Investment Fund Managers Regulations 2013 (AIFs which acquire control of non-listed companies and issuers) that would apply to the authorised person.]

(5) If [on an application under subsection (2) or (3)] the applicant is a member of a group which includes a PRA-authorised person, the FCA must consult the PRA before determining the application.

(6) If as a result of a variation of a Part 4A permission under this section there are no longer any regulated activities for which the authorised person concerned has permission, the FCA must, once it is satisfied that it is no longer necessary to keep the permission in force, cancel it.

(7) The FCA's power to vary a Part 4A permission under this section extends to including in the permission as varied any provision that could be included if a fresh permission were being given by it in response to an application under section 55A.]

NOTES

Substituted as noted to s 55A at **[7.84]**.

Sub-s (1) was repealed, the words in square brackets in sub-ss (2), (3) were substituted, sub-ss (3A), (3B) were inserted, and the words in square brackets in sub-s (5) were inserted, by the Financial Services and Markets Act 2000 (Benchmarks) Regulations 2018, SI 2018/135, reg 40(1), (5), as from 27 February 2018.

Sub-s (4A) was inserted by the Alternative Investment Fund Managers Regulations 2013, SI 2013/1773, reg 80, Sch 1, Part 1, paras 1, 4, as from 22 July 2013.

[7.92]

[55I Variation by PRA at request of authorised person

(1) On the application of a PRA-authorised person with a Part 4A permission, the PRA may with the consent of the FCA vary the permission by—

(a) adding a regulated activity to those to which the permission relates;

(b) removing a regulated activity from those to which the permission relates;

(c) varying the description of a regulated activity to which the permission relates;

[but the PRA may not under this subsection add, remove or vary the description of the regulated activity specified in article 63S of the Financial Services and Markets Act 2000 (Regulated Activities) Order 2001 (administering a benchmark)].

(2) On the application of a PRA-authorised person with a Part 4A permission, the PRA may, after consulting the FCA, cancel the permission[, but the PRA may not under this subsection cancel a permission where the only regulated activity to which the permission relates is the regulated activity in article 63S of the Financial Services and Markets Act 2000 (Regulated Activities) Order 2001 (administering a benchmark)].

(3) On the application of an authorised person other than a PRA-authorised person, the PRA may with the consent of the FCA vary the permission by adding to the regulated activities to which the permission relates one or more regulated activities which include a PRA-regulated activity[, but the PRA may not under this subsection add the regulated activity specified in article 63S of the Financial Services and Markets Act 2000 (Regulated Activities) Order 2001 (administering a benchmark)].

(4) The PRA may refuse an application under this section if it appears to it that it is desirable to do so in order to advance any of its objectives.

(5) The FCA may withhold its consent to a proposed variation under this section if it appears to it that it is desirable to do so in order to advance one or more of its operational objectives.

(6) If as a result of a variation of a Part 4A permission under this section there are no longer any regulated activities for which the authorised person concerned has permission, the PRA must, once it is satisfied after consulting the FCA that it is no longer necessary to keep the permission in force, cancel it.

(7) The PRA's power to vary a Part 4A permission under this section extends to including in the permission as varied any provision that could be included if a fresh permission were being given by it in response to an application under section 55A.

(8) Consent given by the FCA for the purposes of subsection (1) may be conditional on the manner in which the PRA exercises its powers under section 55F(3) and (4) (as a result of subsection (7)).]

NOTES

Substituted as noted to s 55A at **[7.84]**.

Sub-ss (1)–(3): words in square brackets inserted by the Financial Services and Markets Act 2000 (Benchmarks) Regulations 2018, SI 2018/135, reg 40(1), (6), as from 27 February 2018.

[7.93]

[55J Variation or cancellation on initiative of regulator

(1) Either regulator may exercise its power under this section in relation to an authorised person with a Part 4A permission ("A") if it appears to the regulator that—

(a) A is failing, or is likely to fail, to satisfy the threshold conditions for which the regulator is responsible,

(b) A has failed, during a period of at least 12 months, to carry on a regulated activity to which the Part 4A permission relates, . . .

(c) it is desirable to exercise the power in order to advance—

(i) in the case of the FCA, one or more of its operational objectives,

(ii) in the case of the PRA, any of its objectives[; or

(d) in the case of the FCA, A has failed to comply with a requirement in Part 5 of the Alternative Investment Fund Managers Regulations 2013 (AIFs which acquire control of non-listed companies and issuers), or it is for some other reason desirable to exercise the power for the purposes of ensuring compliance with such a requirement.]

(2) The FCA's power under this section is the power—

(a) to vary the Part 4A permission by—

(i) adding a regulated activity other than a PRA-regulated activity to those to which the permission relates,

(ii) removing a regulated activity from those to which the permission relates, or

(iii) varying the description of a regulated activity to which the permission relates in a way which, if it is a PRA-regulated activity, does not, in the opinion of the FCA, widen the description, or

(b) to cancel the Part 4A permission.

(3) The PRA's power under this section is the power—

(a) in the case of a PRA-authorised person, to vary the Part 4A permission in any of the ways mentioned in section 55I(1) or to cancel it;

(b) in the case of an authorised person who is not a PRA-authorised person, to vary the Part 4A permission by adding a PRA-regulated activity to those to which the permission relates and, if the PRA does so, to vary the Part 4A permission in any of the other ways mentioned in section 55I(1).

(4) The FCA—

(a) must consult the PRA before exercising its power under this section in relation to—

(i) a PRA-authorised person, or

(ii) a member of a group which includes a PRA-authorised person, and

(b) in the case of a PRA-authorised person, may exercise the power so as to add a new activity to those to which the permission relates or to widen the description of a regulated activity to which the permission relates, only with the consent of the PRA[,

but paragraph (b) does not apply in relation to the regulated activity specified in article 63S of the Financial Services and Markets Act 2000 (Regulated Activities) Order 2001 (administering a benchmark)].

(5) The PRA—

(a) must consult the FCA before exercising its power under this section, and

(b) may exercise the power so as to add a new activity to those to which the permission relates or to widen the description of a regulated activity to which the permission relates, only with the consent of the FCA.

(6) Without prejudice to the generality of subsections (1) to (3), a regulator may, in relation to an authorised person who is an investment firm, exercise its power under this section to cancel the Part 4A permission if it appears to it that any of the conditions in section 55K is met.

[(6A) Without prejudice to the generality of subsections (1) to (3), the FCA may, in relation to an authorised person who is a full-scope UK AIFM, exercise its power under this section to cancel the Part 4A permission if it appears to it that any of the following conditions is met—

(a) the person has failed, during a period of at least six months, to carry on the regulated activity of managing an AIF;

(b) the person obtained the Part 4A permission to carry on the regulated activity of managing an AIF by making a false statement or by any other irregular means;

(c) in a case where the Part 4A permission includes permission to [carry on the management of portfolios of investments in accordance with mandates given by investors on a discretionary, and client-by-client, basis], the person no longer complies with [Part 9C rules];

(d) the person no longer meets the conditions that a person must meet in order to obtain a Part 4A permission to carry on the regulated activity of managing an AIF;

(e) the person has seriously or systematically infringed—

[(i) an AIFMD requirement;]

(ii), (iii). . .

[(iv) an ELTIF requirement; or]

[(v) an MMF requirement].

[(6AA) For the purposes of subsection (6A)(e)—

(a) an AIFMD requirement is a provision of—

(i) the Alternative Investment Fund Managers Regulations 2013,

(ii) any EU regulation, originally made under the alternative investment fund managers directive, which is retained direct EU legislation,

(iii) any provision made by or under this Act that immediately before IP completion day implemented provisions of the alternative investment fund managers directive (as that implementing provision is amended from time to time), or

(iv) any subordinate legislation (within the meaning of the Interpretation Act 1978) which is made under a power substituted for a power of an EU entity to make a directly applicable regulation under the alternative investment fund managers directive by regulations made under section 8 of the European Union (Withdrawal) Act 2018;

(b) an ELTIF requirement is a provision of—

(i) Regulation (EU) No 2015/760 of the European Parliament and of the Council of 29th April 2015 on European Long-term Investment Funds ("the ELTIF Regulation"),

(ii) any EU regulation, originally made under the ELTIF Regulation, which is retained direct EU legislation, or

(iii) any subordinate legislation (within the meaning of the Interpretation Act 1978) made under the ELTIF Regulation on or after exit day;

(c) an MMF requirement is a provision of—

(i) the MMF Regulation,

(ii) any EU regulation, originally made under the MMF Regulation, which is retained direct EU legislation, or

(iii) any subordinate legislation (within the meaning of the Interpretation Act 1978) made under the MMF Regulation on or after exit day.]

[(6B) Without prejudice to the generality of subsections (1) to (3), the FCA may, in relation to an authorised person who is a mortgage intermediary and who has a Part 4A permission to carry on a relevant mortgage activity, exercise its power under this section to cancel the Part 4A permission or to vary the Part 4A permission by removing a relevant mortgage activity from the activities to which the permission relates, if it appears to the FCA that any of the following conditions is met—

(a) during a period of at least six months, the person has not carried on a relevant mortgage activity;

(b) the person obtained the Part 4A permission to carry on a relevant mortgage activity by making a false statement or by any other irregular means;

(c) the person no longer meets the conditions which the person was . . . required to meet in order to be granted a Part 4A permission to carry on a relevant mortgage activity; or

(d) the person has seriously or systematically infringed any provision made by or under this Act which [sets] the operating conditions for mortgage intermediaries . . .

(6C) In subsection (6B) "relevant mortgage activity" means—

(a) an activity of a kind specified in article 25A (arranging regulated mortgage contracts), article 53A (advising on regulated mortgage contracts) or article 53DA (advising on regulated credit agreements the purpose of which is to acquire land) of the Financial Services and Markets Act 2000 (Regulated Activities) Order 2001, or

(b) an activity of a kind specified in article 36A of that Order (credit broking) which is referred to in Article 33(1)(a) of the mortgages directive.]

(7) . . .

[(7ZA) Without prejudice to the generality of subsections (1) and (2), if it appears to the FCA that there has been a serious failure, by a person with permission to carry on the regulated activity specified in article 51ZA of the Financial Services and Markets Act (Regulated Activities) Order 2001 (managing a [UK] UCITS), to comply with the requirements imposed—

(a) by or under this Act in pursuance of the UCITS Directive, . . .

(b) by the Undertakings for Collective Investment in Transferable Securities Regulations 2011, [or]

[(c) an MMF requirement,]

the FCA may exercise its powers under this section to vary the Part 4A permission of the person concerned by removing that activity from those to which the permission relates, or to cancel the person's Part 4A permission.]

[(7ZB) Without prejudice to the generality of subsections (1) and (2), the FCA may, in relation to an authorised person who is an investment firm, exercise its power under this section if it appears to it that the authorised person has failed to comply with a requirement [imposed by—

(a) the market abuse regulation,

(b) any EU regulation, originally made under the market abuse regulation, which is retained direct EU legislation, or

(c) any subordinate legislation (within the meaning of the Interpretation Act 1978) made under the market abuse regulation on or after IP completion day].]

[(7ZC) Without prejudice to the generality of subsections (1) and (2), if it appears to the FCA, in relation to a person who has a permission to carry on the regulated activity specified in article 63S of the Financial Services and Markets Act 2000 (Regulated Activities) Order 2001 (administering a benchmark), that the conditions in Article 35(1) of the EU Benchmarks Regulation 2016 are met, the FCA may exercise its powers under this section—

(a) to vary the Part 4A permission by removing that activity from those to which the permission relates, or

(b) to cancel the Part 4A permission.]

[(7A) Without prejudice to the generality of subsections (1) and (3), if it appears to the PRA that there has been a serious failure by a PRA-authorised person who is an insurance undertaking or reinsurance undertaking to comply with requirements imposed by or under this Act in pursuance of the Solvency 2 Directive, the PRA may exercise its powers under this section to cancel the undertaking's Part 4A permission.

(7B) If it appears to the PRA that the conditions in section 55KA are met in relation to a PRA-authorised person who is an insurance undertaking, reinsurance undertaking or third-country insurance undertaking, the PRA must—

(a) in relation to the undertaking's Part 4A permission so far as the permission relates to the regulated activity of effecting contracts of insurance as principal ("activity A"), exercise the PRA's powers under this section by varying the permission—

(i) where the permission relates to activity A in relation to both contracts of long-term insurance and contracts of general insurance and the conditions in section 55KA are met only in relation to the business of the undertaking so far as relating to contracts of one of those kinds, so as to remove activity A so far as relating to contracts of that kind from the regulated activities to which the permission relates, and

(ii) in any other case, so as to remove activity A from the regulated activities to which the permission relates;

(b) in relation to the undertaking's Part 4A permission so far as the permission relates to the regulated activity of carrying out contracts of insurance as principal ("activity B"), exercise the PRA's powers under this section, if it appears to the PRA to be necessary to do so to protect the interests of the undertaking's policyholders, by varying the Part 4A permission—

(i) where the permission relates to activity B in relation to both contracts of long-term insurance and contracts of general insurance and the conditions in section 55KA are met only in relation to the business of the undertaking so far as relating to contracts of one of the those kinds, so as to remove activity B so far as relating to contracts of that kind from the regulated activities to which the permission relates, and

(ii) in any other case, so as to remove activity B from the regulated activities to which the permission relates.

(7C) If the effect of a variation required by subsection (7B) is to remove all the regulated activities to which the Part 4A permission relates, the PRA must instead cancel the permission.]

(8) If, as a result of a variation of a Part 4A permission under this section, there are no longer any regulated activities for which the authorised person concerned has permission, the regulator responsible for the variation must, once it is satisfied that it is no longer necessary to keep the permission in force, cancel it.

(9) Before cancelling under subsection (8) a Part 4A permission which relates to a person who (before the variation) was a PRA-authorised person, the regulator must consult the other regulator.

(10) The power of either regulator to vary a Part 4A permission under this section extends to including in the permission as varied any provision that could be included if a fresh permission were being given in response to an application to that regulator under section 55A.

(11) Consent given by one regulator for the purpose of subsection (4)(b) or (5)(b) may be conditional on the manner in which the other regulator exercises its powers under section 55E(4) and (5) or 55F(3) and (4) (as a result of subsection (10)).

(12) The power of the FCA or the PRA under this section is referred to in this Part as its own-initiative variation power.

[(13) In this section "enactment" has the meaning given by section 3T.]]

NOTES

Substituted as noted to s 55A at **[7.84]**.

Sub-s (1): the word omitted from para (b) was repealed, and para (d) (and the preceding word) was inserted, by the Alternative Investment Fund Managers Regulations 2013, SI 2013/1773, reg 80, Sch 1, Pt 1, para 5(a), as from 22 July 2013.

Sub-s (4): words in square brackets inserted by the Financial Services and Markets Act 2000 (Benchmarks) Regulations 2018, SI 2018/135, reg 40(1), (7)(a), as from 27 February 2018.

Part 7 Financial Services Acts

Sub-s (6A): inserted by SI 2013/1773, reg 80, Sch 1, Part 1, para 5(b), as from 22 July 2013; and subsequently amended as follows—

The words in the first pair of square brackets in para (c) were substituted by the Financial Services and Markets Act 2000 (Amendment) (EU Exit) Regulations 2019, SI 2019/632, regs 14, 16(1), (2)(a)(i), as from IP completion day (as defined in the European Union (Withdrawal Agreement) Act 2020, s 39).

The words in the second pair of square brackets in para (c) were substituted by the Financial Services Act 2021 (Prudential Regulation of Credit Institutions and Investment Firms) (Consequential Amendments and Miscellaneous Provisions) Regulations 2021, SI 2021/1376, reg 4(3), as from 1 January 2022.

Sub-para (e)(i) was substituted, and sub-paras (e)(ii) and (iii) were repealed, by SI 2019/632, regs 14, 16(1), (2)(b)(i), (ii), as from IP completion day (as defined in the European Union (Withdrawal Agreement) Act 2020, s 39).

Sub-para (e)(iv) was added by the European Long-term Investment Funds Regulations 2015, SI 2015/1882, reg 3(1), (2), as from 3 December 2015. It was substituted by SI 2019/632, regs 14, 16(1), (2)(b)(iii), as from IP completion day (as defined in the European Union (Withdrawal Agreement) Act 2020, s 39.

Sub-para (e)(v) was added by the Money Market Funds Regulations 2018, SI 2018/698, reg 2(1), (2)(a), as from 21 July 2018. It was substituted by SI 2019/632, regs 14, 16(1), (2)(b)(iv), as from IP completion day (as defined in the European Union (Withdrawal Agreement) Act 2020, s 39.

Sub-s (6AA): inserted by SI 2019/632, regs 14, 16(1), (3), as from IP completion day (as defined in the European Union (Withdrawal Agreement) Act 2020, s 39). Note that reg 16(3) of the 2019 Regulations was amended by the Financial Services and Economic and Monetary Policy (Consequential Amendments) (EU Exit) Regulations 2020, SI 2020/1301, reg 3, Schedule, para 33(c), as from 30 December 2020 (and the effect of the amendment has been incorporated in the text set out above).

Sub-s (6B): inserted, together with sub-s (6C), by the Mortgage Credit Directive Order 2015, SI 2015/910, Sch 1, para 1(1), (3), as from 21 March 2016. Word in square brackets substituted, and words omitted repealed, by SI 2019/632, regs 14, 16(1), (4), as from IP completion day (as defined in the European Union (Withdrawal Agreement) Act 2020, s 39).

Sub-s (6C): inserted as noted to sub-s (6B) above.

Sub-s (7): repealed by SI 2019/632, regs 14, 16(1), (5), as from IP completion day (as defined in the European Union (Withdrawal Agreement) Act 2020, s 39).

Sub-s (7ZA): inserted by the Undertakings for Collective Investment in Transferable Securities Regulations 2016, SI 2016/225, reg 2(1), (2), as from 18 March 2016. The word omitted from para (a) was repealed, the word in square brackets in para (b) was inserted, and para (c) was added, by SI 2018/698, reg 2(1), (2)(b), as from 21 July 2018. The first word in square brackets was added, and para (c) was substituted, by SI 2019/632, regs 14, 16(1), (6), as from IP completion day (as defined in the European Union (Withdrawal Agreement) Act 2020, s 39).

Sub-s (7ZB): inserted by the Financial Services and Markets Act 2000 (Market Abuse) Regulations 2016, SI 2016/680, reg 10(1), (3), as from 3 July 2016. Words in square brackets substituted by SI 2019/632, regs 14, 16(1), (7), as from IP completion day (as defined in the European Union (Withdrawal Agreement) Act 2020, s 39). Note that reg 16(7) of the 2019 Regulations was amended by the Financial Services and Economic and Monetary Policy (Consequential Amendments) (EU Exit) Regulations 2020, SI 2020/1301, reg 3, Schedule, para 33(c), as from 30 December 2020 (and the effect of the amendment has been incorporated in the text set out above).

Sub-s (7ZC): inserted by SI 2018/135, reg 40(1), (7)(b), as from 27 February 2018.

Sub-ss (7A)–(7C): inserted by the Solvency 2 Regulations 2015, SI 2015/575, reg 59, Sch 1, Pt 1, paras 1, 2, as from 1 January 2016.

Sub-s (13): added by SI 2019/632, regs 14, 16(1), (8), as from IP completion day (as defined in the European Union (Withdrawal Agreement) Act 2020, s 39).

[7.94]

[55JA Variation or cancellation on initiative of FCA: additional power

(1) Schedule 6A confers an additional power on the FCA to vary or cancel an FCA-authorised person's Part 4A permission.

(2) In this section and that Schedule "FCA-authorised person" means an authorised person who is not a PRA-authorised person.]

NOTES

Commencement: 1 July 2021.

Inserted by the Financial Services Act 2021, s 28, Sch 11, para 2, as from 1 July 2021.

[7.95]

[55K Investment firms: particular conditions that enable cancellation

(1) The conditions referred to in section 55J(6) are as follows—

(a) that the firm has failed, during a period of at least 6 months, to carry on a regulated activity which is an investment service or activity for which it has a Part 4A permission;

(b) that the firm obtained the Part 4A permission by making a false statement or by other irregular means;

(c) that the firm no longer satisfies the requirements for authorisation . . . in relation to a regulated activity which is an investment service or activity for which it has a Part 4A permission;

(d) that the firm has seriously and systematically infringed [any retained direct EU legislation, or any provision made by or under this Act, which sets the operating conditions] in relation to a regulated activity which is an investment service or activity for which it has a Part 4A permission;

[(e) that the firm has seriously or systematically infringed the markets in financial instruments regulation].

(2) For the purposes of this section a regulated activity is an investment service or activity if it falls within the definition of "investment services and activities" in section 417(1).]

NOTES

Substituted as noted to s 55A at **[7.84]**.

Sub-s (1) is amended as follows:

The words omitted from para (c) were repealed, and the words in square brackets in para (d) were substituted, by the Financial Services and Markets Act 2000 (Amendment) (EU Exit) Regulations 2019, SI 2019/632, regs 14, 17, as from IP completion day (as defined in the European Union (Withdrawal Agreement) Act 2020, s 39).

Para (e) was added by the Financial Services and Markets Act 2000 (Markets in Financial Instruments) Regulations 2017, SI 2017/701, reg 50(1), Sch 2, paras 1, 4, as from 3 January 2018 (note that various provisions of the 2017 Regulations came into force on earlier dates for the purposes of making rules, giving notices and consent, etc (for details see reg 1 of the 2017 Regulations)).

[7.96]

[55KA Insurance undertakings, reinsurance undertakings and third-country insurance undertakings: particular conditions that enable cancellation

(1) The conditions referred to in section 55J(7B) are—

(a) that the insurance undertaking, reinsurance undertaking or third-country insurance undertaking has failed to comply with the appropriate capital requirement; and

(b) that any of the following applies—

(i) the insurance undertaking, reinsurance undertaking or third-country insurance undertaking has failed to submit[, in accordance with requirements imposed by or under this Act, a finance scheme for restoring compliance with the appropriate capital requirement];

(ii) the insurance undertaking, reinsurance undertaking or third-country insurance undertaking has submitted to the PRA a finance scheme that is manifestly inadequate; or

(iii) after the PRA has approved a finance scheme submitted to it, the undertaking has failed to comply with the finance scheme within a period of three months beginning with the date when the undertaking first became aware that it had failed to comply with the appropriate capital requirement to which the scheme relates.

(2) In subsection (1) "the appropriate capital requirement" means—

(a) except in a case within paragraph (b) or (c), the minimum capital requirement;

(b) in the case of an insurance undertaking or reinsurance undertaking whose Part 4A permission relates to both contracts of long-term insurance and to contracts of general insurance, requirements imposed by or under this Act in pursuance of Article 74(2) of the Solvency 2 Directive;

(c) in the case of a third-country insurance undertaking whose Part 4A permission relates both to contracts of long-term insurance and to contracts of general insurance, requirements imposed by or under this Act in pursuance of Articles 74(2) and 166 of the Solvency 2 Directive.]

NOTES

Inserted by the Solvency 2 Regulations 2015, SI 2015/575, reg 59, Sch 1, Pt 1, paras 1, 3, as from 1 January 2016.

Sub-s (1): words in square brackets substituted by the Financial Services and Markets Act 2000 (Amendment) (EU Exit) Regulations 2019, SI 2019/632, regs 14, 18, as from IP completion day (as defined in the European Union (Withdrawal Agreement) Act 2020, s 39).

[Imposition and variation of requirements

[7.97]

55L Imposition of requirements by FCA

(1) Where a person has applied (whether to the FCA or the PRA) for a Part 4A permission or the variation of a Part 4A permission, the FCA may impose on that person such requirements, taking effect on or after the giving or variation of the permission, as the FCA considers appropriate.

(2) The FCA may exercise its power under subsection (3) in relation to an authorised person with a Part 4A permission (whether given by it or by the PRA) ("A") if it appears to the FCA that—

(a) A is failing, or is likely to fail, to satisfy the threshold conditions for which the FCA is responsible,

(b) A has failed, during a period of at least 12 months, to carry on a regulated activity to which the Part 4A permission relates, or

(c) it is desirable to exercise the power in order to advance one or more of the FCA's operational objectives.

(3) The FCA's power under this subsection is a power—

(a) to impose a new requirement,

(b) to vary a requirement imposed by the FCA under this section, or

(c) to cancel such a requirement.

(4) The FCA's power under subsection (3) is referred to in this Part as its own-initiative requirement power.

(5) The FCA may, on the application of an authorised person with a Part 4A permission—

(a) impose a new requirement,

(b) vary a requirement imposed by the FCA under this section, or

(c) cancel such a requirement.

(6) The FCA may refuse an application under subsection (5) if it appears to it that it is desirable to do so in order to advance any of its operational objectives.

(7) The FCA must consult the PRA before imposing or varying a requirement which relates to—

(a) a person who is, or will on the granting of an application for Part 4A permission be, a PRA-authorised person, or

(b) a person who is a member of a group which includes a PRA-authorised person.]

NOTES

Substituted as noted to s 55A at **[7.84]**.

[7.98]

[55M Imposition of requirements by PRA

(1) Where—

(a) a person has applied for a Part 4A permission in relation to activities which consist of or include a PRA-regulated activity,

(b) a PRA-authorised person has applied for a Part 4A permission or the variation of a Part 4A permission, or

(c) an authorised person other than a PRA-authorised person has applied for a Part 4A permission to be varied by adding to the regulated activities to which it relates one or more regulated activities which include a PRA-regulated activity, the PRA may impose on that person such requirements, taking effect on or after the giving or variation of the permission, as the PRA considers appropriate.

(2) The PRA may exercise its power under subsection (3) in relation to a PRA-authorised person with a Part 4A permission ("P") if it appears to the PRA that—

(a) P is failing, or is likely to fail, to satisfy the threshold conditions for which the PRA is responsible,

(b) P has failed, during a period of at least 12 months, to carry on a regulated activity to which the Part 4A permission relates, or

(c) it is desirable to exercise the power in order to advance any of the PRA's objectives.

(3) The PRA's power under this subsection is a power—

(a) to impose a new requirement,

(b) to vary a requirement imposed by the PRA under this section, or

(c) to cancel such a requirement.

(4) The PRA's power under subsection (3) is referred to in this Part as its own-initiative requirement power.

(5) The PRA may, on the application of a PRA-authorised person with a Part 4A permission—

(a) impose a new requirement,

(b) vary a requirement imposed by the PRA under this section, or

(c) cancel such a requirement.

(6) The PRA may refuse an application under subsection (5) if it appears to it that it is desirable to do so in order to advance any of its objectives.

[(6A) The PRA may not exercise its powers under this section to impose a requirement relating to the regulated activity specified in article 63S of the Financial Services and Markets Act 2000 (Regulated Activities) Order 2001 (administering a benchmark).]

(7) The PRA must consult the FCA before imposing or varying a requirement.]

NOTES

Substituted as noted to s 55A at **[7.84]**.

Sub-s (6A): inserted by the Financial Services and Markets Act 2000 (Benchmarks) Regulations 2018, SI 2018/135, reg 40(1), (8), as from 27 February 2018.

[7.99]

[55N Requirements under section 55L or 55M: further provisions

(1) A requirement may, in particular, be imposed—

(a) so as to require the person concerned to take specified action, or

(b) so as to require the person concerned to refrain from taking specified action.

(2) A requirement may extend to activities which are not regulated activities.

(3) A requirement may be imposed by reference to the person's relationship with—

(a) the person's group, or

(b) other members of the person's group.

(4) A requirement may be expressed to expire at the end of such period as the regulator imposing it may specify, but the imposition of a requirement that expires at the end of a specified period does not affect the regulator's power to impose a new requirement.

(5) A requirement may refer to the past conduct of the person concerned (for example, by requiring the person concerned to review or take remedial action in respect of past conduct).

(6) In this section "requirement" means a requirement imposed under section 55L or 55M.]

NOTES

Substituted as noted to s 55A at **[7.84]**.

[7.100]

[55O Imposition of requirements on acquisition of control

(1) This section applies if it appears to the appropriate regulator that—

(a) a person has acquired control over a UK authorised person who has a Part 4A permission, but

(b) there are no grounds for exercising its own-initiative requirement power.

(2) If it appears to the appropriate regulator that the likely effect of the acquisition of control on the UK authorised person, or on any of its activities, is uncertain, the appropriate regulator may—

(a) impose on the UK authorised person a requirement that could be imposed by that regulator under section 55L or 55M (as the case may be) on the giving of permission, or

(b) vary a requirement imposed by that regulator under that section on the UK authorised person.

(3) "The appropriate regulator" means—

(a) in a case where the UK authorised person is a PRA-authorised person, the FCA or the PRA;

(b) in any other case, the FCA.

(4) This section does not affect any duty of the appropriate regulator to consult or obtain the consent of the other regulator in connection with the imposition of the requirement.

(5) Any reference to a person having acquired control is to be read in accordance with Part 12.]

NOTES

Substituted as noted to s 55A at **[7.84]**.

[7.101]

[55P Prohibitions and restrictions

(1) This section applies if—

(a) on a person being given a Part 4A permission, either regulator imposes an assets requirement on that person,

(b) an assets requirement is imposed on an authorised person, or

(c) an assets requirement previously imposed on such a person is varied.

(2) A person on whom an assets requirement is imposed is referred to in this section as "A".

(3) The "appropriate regulator" is the regulator which imposed the requirement.

(4) "Assets requirement" means a requirement under section 55L or 55M—

(a) prohibiting the disposal of, or other dealing with, any of A's assets (whether in the United Kingdom or elsewhere) or restricting such disposals or dealings, or

(b) that all or any of A's assets, or all or any assets belonging to consumers but held by A or to A's order, must be transferred to and held by a trustee approved by the appropriate regulator.

(5) If the appropriate regulator—

(a) imposes a requirement of the kind mentioned in subsection (4)(a), and

(b) gives notice of the requirement to any institution with whom A keeps an account,

the notice has the effects mentioned in subsection (6).

(6) Those effects are that—

(a) the institution does not act in breach of any contract with A if, having been instructed by A (or on A's behalf) to transfer any sum or otherwise make any payment out of A's account, it refuses to do so in the reasonably held belief that complying with the instruction would be incompatible with the requirement, and

(b) if the institution complies with such an instruction, it is liable to pay to the appropriate regulator an amount equal to the amount transferred from, or otherwise paid out of, A's account in contravention of the requirement.

(7) If the appropriate regulator imposes a requirement of the kind mentioned in subsection (4)(b), no assets held by a person as trustee in accordance with the requirement may, while the requirement is in force, be released or dealt with except with the consent of the appropriate regulator.

(8) If, while a requirement of the kind mentioned in subsection (4)(b) is in force, A creates a charge over any assets of A held in accordance with the requirement, the charge is (to the extent that it confers security over the assets) void against the liquidator and any of A's creditors.

(9) Assets held by a person as trustee ("T") are to be taken to be held by T in accordance with any requirement mentioned in subsection (4)(b) only if—

(a) A has given T written notice that those assets are to be held by T in accordance with the requirement, or

(b) they are assets into which assets to which paragraph (a) applies have been transposed by T on the instructions of A.

(10) A person who contravenes subsection (7) is guilty of an offence and liable on summary conviction to a fine not exceeding level 5 on the standard scale.

(11) "Charge" includes a mortgage (or in Scotland a security over property).

(12) Subsections (7) and (9) do not affect any equitable interest or remedy in favour of a person who is a beneficiary of a trust as a result of a requirement of the kind mentioned in subsection (4)(b).]

NOTES

Substituted as noted to s 55A at **[7.84]**.

55PA (*Originally inserted by the Solvency 2 Regulations 2015, SI 2015/575, reg 59, Sch 1, Pt 1, paras 1, 4, as from 1 January 2016. Subsequently repealed by the Financial Services and Markets Act 2000 (Amendment) (EU Exit) Regulations 2019, SI 2019/632, regs 14, 19, as from IP completion day (as defined in the European Union (Withdrawal Agreement) Act 2020, s 39).*)

[7.102]

[55PB Requirements relating to general meetings

(1) This section applies where—

(a) either regulator has imposed a general meeting requirement on an authorised person who is a bank, building society or investment firm,

(b) the authorised person has not complied with the general meeting requirement, and

(c) the appropriate regulator considers that the authorised person has infringed, or is likely in the near future to infringe—

(i) a relevant requirement within the meaning of section 204A; or

(ii) one or more of Articles 3 to 7, 14 to 17 or 24 to 26 of Regulation (EU) No 600/2014 of 15th May 2014 of the European Parliament and of the Council on Markets in Financial Instruments.

(2) A general meeting requirement is a requirement under section 55L or 55M that the authorised person call a general meeting of its shareholders or members.

(3) The appropriate regulator may call a general meeting of the shareholders or members of the authorised person.

(4) The appropriate regulator may propose business for consideration and decision at the general meeting.

(5) The meeting must be called in the same manner, as far as practicable, as that in which meetings are required to be called by the board of directors (or the equivalent management body) of the authorised person.

(6) For the purposes of this section—

"bank" has the meaning given in section 2 of the Banking Act 2009;

"building society" has the meaning given in the Building Societies Act 1986;

"investment firm" has the meaning given in [Article 4(1)(2) of the capital requirements regulation];

"the appropriate regulator" means the regulator who imposed the general meeting requirement.]

NOTES

Inserted by the Bank Recovery and Resolution Order 2016, SI 2016/1239, arts 30, 31, as from 16 December 2016.

Sub-s (6): words in square brackets in the definition "investment firm" substituted by the Financial Services Act 2021 (Prudential Regulation of Credit Institutions and Investment Firms) (Consequential Amendments and Miscellaneous Provisions) Regulations 2021, SI 2021/1376, reg 4(4), as from 1 January 2022.

[Exercise of power in support of overseas regulator

[7.103]

55Q Exercise of power in support of overseas regulator

(1) Either UK regulator's own-initiative powers may be exercised in respect of an authorised person at the request of, or for the purpose of assisting, an overseas regulator of a prescribed kind.

(2) . . .

(3) Subsection (1) does not affect any duty of one UK regulator to consult or obtain the consent of the other UK regulator in relation to the exercise of its own-initiative powers.

(4) . . .

(5) In deciding whether or not to [exercise its own-initiative powers in response to a request, the UK regulator] may take into account in particular—

(a) whether in the country or territory of the overseas regulator concerned, corresponding assistance would be given to a United Kingdom regulatory authority;

(b) whether the case concerns the breach of a law, or other requirement, which has no close parallel in the United Kingdom or involves the assertion of a jurisdiction not recognised by the United Kingdom;

(c) the seriousness of the case and its importance to persons in the United Kingdom;

(d) whether it is otherwise appropriate in the public interest to give the assistance sought.

(6) The UK regulator may decide not to exercise its own-initiative powers, in response to a request, unless the overseas regulator concerned undertakes to make such contribution towards the cost of their exercise as the UK regulator considers appropriate.

(7) . . .

(8) In [subsections (5) and] (6) "request" means a request of a kind mentioned in subsection (1).

(9) In this section—

(a) "UK regulator" means the FCA or the PRA;

(b) "overseas regulator" means a regulator outside the United Kingdom;

(c) "own-initiative powers", in relation to the FCA or the PRA, means its own-initiative variation power and its own-initiative requirement power.]

NOTES

Substituted as noted to s 55A at **[7.84]**.

Sub-s (2): repealed by the EEA Passport Rights (Amendment, etc, and Transitional Provisions) (EU Exit) Regulations 2018, SI 2018/1149, reg 3, Schedule, Pt 1, paras 1, 6, as from IP completion day (as defined in the European Union (Withdrawal Agreement) Act 2020, s 39).

Sub-ss (4), (7): repealed by the Financial Services and Markets Act 2000 (Amendment) (EU Exit) Regulations 2019, SI 2019/632, regs 14, 20(1), (2), (4), as from IP completion day (as defined in the European Union (Withdrawal Agreement) Act 2020, s 39).

Sub-ss (5), (8): words in square brackets substituted by SI 2019/632, regs 14, 20(1), (3), (5), as from IP completion day (as defined in the European Union (Withdrawal Agreement) Act 2020, s 39).

Regulations: no regulations have been made under this section, but by virtue of the Interpretation Act 1978, s 17(2)(b), the Financial Services and Markets Act 2000 (Own-initiative Power) (Overseas Regulators) Regulations 2001, SI 2001/2639 have effect as if made under this section.

[Connected persons

[7.104]

55R Persons connected with an applicant

(1) In considering—

(a) an application for a Part 4A permission,

(b) whether to vary or cancel a Part 4A permission,

(c) whether to impose or vary a requirement under this Part, or

(d) whether to give any consent required by any provision of this Part,

the regulator concerned may have regard to any person appearing to it to be, or likely to be, in a relationship with the applicant or a person given permission which is relevant.

(2), (3) . . .

[(3A), (3B) . . .]

[(4)–(6) . . .]

[(7)–(9) . . .]

NOTES

Substituted as noted to s 55A at **[7.84]**.

Sub-ss (2), (3): repealed by the EEA Passport Rights (Amendment, etc, and Transitional Provisions) (EU Exit) Regulations 2018, SI 2018/1149, reg 3, Schedule, Pt 1, paras 1, 7, as from IP completion day (as defined in the European Union (Withdrawal Agreement) Act 2020, s 39).

Sub-ss (3A), (3B): originally inserted by SI 2017/701, reg 50(1), Sch 2, paras 1, 5(1), (3), as from 3 January 2018. Subsequently repealed by SI 2018/1149, reg 3, Schedule, Pt 1, paras 1, 7, as from IP completion day (as defined in the European Union (Withdrawal Agreement) Act 2020, s 39).

Sub-ss (4)–(6): originally added by the Capital Requirements Regulations 2013, SI 2013/3115, reg 46(1), Sch 2, Pt 1, paras 1, 6, as from 1 January 2014. Subsequently repealed by the Financial Services and Markets Act 2000 (Amendment) (EU Exit) Regulations 2019, SI 2019/632, regs 14, 21, as from IP completion day (as defined in the European Union (Withdrawal Agreement) Act 2020, s 39).

Sub-ss (7)–(9): originally added by SI 2017/701, reg 50(1), Sch 2, paras 1, 5(1), (4), as from 3 January 2018. Subsequently repealed by SI 2019/632, regs 14, 21, as from IP completion day (as defined in the European Union (Withdrawal Agreement) Act 2020, s 39).

55S *(S 55S (Duty of FCA or PRA to consider other Permissions) was originally substituted as noted to s 55A at* **[7.84]**. *Subsequently repealed by the Financial Services and Markets Act 2000 (Amendment) (EU Exit) Regulations 2019, SI 2019/632, regs 14, 22, as from IP completion day (as defined in the European Union (Withdrawal Agreement) Act 2020, s 39).)*

[Persons whose interests are protected

[7.105]

55T Persons whose interests are protected

For the purpose of any provision of this Part which refers to the FCA's operational objectives, or the PRA's objectives in relation to the exercise of a power in relation to a particular person, it does not matter whether there is a relationship between that person and the persons whose interests will be protected by the exercise of the power.]

NOTES

Substituted as noted to s 55A at **[7.84]**.

[Procedure

[7.106]

55U Applications under this Part

(1) An application for a Part 4A permission must—
- (a) contain a statement of the regulated activity or regulated activities which the applicant proposes to carry on and for which the applicant wishes to have permission, and
- (b) give the address of a place in the United Kingdom for service on the applicant of any notice or other document which is required or authorised to be served on the applicant under this Act.

(2) An application for the variation of a Part 4A permission must contain a statement—
- (a) of the desired variation, and
- (b) of the regulated activity or regulated activities which the applicant proposes to carry on if the permission is varied.

(3) An application for the variation of a requirement imposed under section 55L or 55M or for the imposition of a new requirement must contain a statement of the desired variation or requirement.

(4) An application under this Part must—
- (a) be made in such manner as the regulator to which it is to be made may direct, and
- (b) contain, or be accompanied by, such other information as that regulator may reasonably require.

(5) At any time after the application is received and before it is determined, the appropriate regulator may require the applicant to provide it with such further information as it reasonably considers necessary to enable it to determine the application or, as the case requires, to decide whether to give consent.

(6) In subsection (5), the "appropriate regulator" means—
- (a) in a case where the application is made to the FCA, the FCA;
- (b) in a case where the application is made to the PRA, the FCA or the PRA.

(7) Different directions may be given, and different requirements imposed, in relation to different applications or categories of application.

(8) Each regulator may require an applicant to provide information which the applicant is required to provide to it under this section in such form, or to verify it in such a way, as the regulator may direct.

(9) The PRA must consult the FCA before—
- (a) giving a direction under this section in relation to a class of applications, or
- (b) imposing a requirement under this section in relation to a class of applications.]

NOTES

Substituted as noted to s 55A at **[7.84]**.

See further the Financial Services and Markets Act 2000 (Consumer Credit) (Miscellaneous Provisions) Order 2014, SI 2014/208, art 2 which provides that sub-ss (4), (5), (7) and (8) of this section apply to an application made under s 28A of this Act (credit-related agreements made unenforceable by ss 26, 26A or 27) as if the application were an application made to the FCA under Part 4A of this Act. It further provides that where a person ("A") has the right to exercise rights under an agreement entered into by another person ("B"), s 28A *ante* applies as if the references to the relevant firm in sub-ss (3) and (7) of that section include a reference to A. See also the Financial Services and Markets Act 2000 (Regulated Activities) (Amendment) Order 2014, SI 2014/366, art 4 which provides that those subsections also apply to an application made under the Consumer Credit Act 1974, ss 60(3), 64(4), 101(8) and 160.

[7.107]

[55V Determination of applications

(1) An application under this Part must be determined by the regulator to which it is required to be made ("the appropriate regulator") before the end of the period of 6 months beginning with the date on which it received the completed application.

(2) The appropriate regulator may determine an incomplete application if it considers it appropriate to do so; and it must in any event determine such an application within 12 months beginning with the date on which it received the application.

(3) Where the application cannot be determined by the appropriate regulator without the consent of the other regulator, the other regulator's decision must also be made within the period required by subsection (1) or (2).

(4) The applicant may withdraw the application, by giving the appropriate regulator written notice, at any time before the appropriate regulator determines it.

(5) If the appropriate regulator grants an application—
- (a) for Part 4A permission,
- (b) for the variation or cancellation of a Part 4A permission,
- (c) for the variation or cancellation of a requirement imposed under section 55L or 55M, or
- (d) for the imposition of a new requirement under either of those sections,

it must give the applicant written notice.

Part 7 Financial Services Acts

(6) The notice must state the date from which the permission, variation, cancellation or requirement has effect.
(7) A notice under this section which is given by the PRA and relates to the grant of an application for Part 4A permission or for the variation of a Part 4A permission must state that the FCA has given its consent to the grant of the application.]
[(8) In the case of an application for permission under this Part which—
(a) relates to the regulated activity of managing an AIF, and
(b) would if granted result in the applicant becoming a full-scope UK AIFM,
this section has effect subject to *regulation 5* of the Alternative Investment Fund Managers Regulations 2013 and, accordingly, subsections (1) to (3) do not apply.
[(9) In the case of an application which—
(a) is for a Part 4A permission or a variation of a Part 4A permission, and
(b) relates only to the undertaking of insurance distribution activity,
subsection (1) has effect as if the reference to "6 months" were to "3 months".
(10) In this section, "insurance distribution activity" has the meaning given in article 92 of the Financial Services and Markets Act 2000 (Regulated Activities) Order 2001.]]

NOTES
Substituted as noted to s 55A at **[7.84]**.
Sub-s (8): added by the Alternative Investment Fund Managers Regulations 2013, SI 2013/1773, reg 80, Sch 1, Part 1, paras 1, 6, as from 22 July 2013. For the words in italics there are substituted the words "regulations 5 and 5A" by the Alternative Investment Fund Managers (Amendment) Regulations 2013, SI 2013/1797, reg 3, Sch 1, para 1(1), (2), as from a day to be appointed.
Sub-ss (9), (10): added by the Insurance Distribution (Regulated Activities and Miscellaneous Amendments) Order 2018, SI 2018/546, arts 9, 10(2), as from 1 October 2018.

[7.108]
[55W Applications under this Part: communications between regulators
The PRA must as soon as practicable notify the FCA of the receipt or withdrawal of—
(a) an application for permission under section 55A,
(b) an application under section 55I, or
(c) an application under section 55M(5).]

NOTES
Substituted as noted to s 55A at **[7.84]**.

[7.109]
[55X Determination of applications: warning notices and decision notices
(1) If a regulator proposes—
(a) to give a Part 4A permission but to exercise its power under section 55E(5)(a) or (b) or 55F(4)(a) or (b),
(b) to give a Part 4A permission but to exercise its power under section 55L(1) or 55M(1) in connection with the application for permission,
(c) to vary a Part 4A permission on the application of an authorised person but to exercise its power under section 55E(5)(a) or (b) or 55F(4)(a) or (b),
(d) to vary a Part 4A permission but to exercise its power under section 55L(1) or 55M(1) in connection with the application for variation, or
(e) in the case of the FCA, to exercise its power under section 55L(1) in connection with an application to the PRA for a Part 4A permission or the variation of a Part 4A permission,
it must give the applicant a warning notice.
(2) If a regulator proposes to refuse an application made under this Part, it must . . . give the applicant a warning notice.
(3) . . .
(4) If a regulator decides—
(a) to give a Part 4A permission but to exercise its power under section 55E(5)(a) or (b) or 55F(4)(a) or (b),
(b) to give a Part 4A permission but to exercise its power under section 55L(1) or 55M(1) in connection with the giving of the permission,
(c) to vary a Part 4A permission on the application of an authorised person but to exercise its power under section 55E(5)(a) or (b) or 55F(4)(a) or (b),
(d) to vary a Part 4A permission on the application of an authorised person but to exercise its power under section 55L(1) or 55M(1) in connection with the variation,
(e) in the case of the FCA, to exercise its power under section 55L(1) in connection with an application to the PRA for a Part 4A permission or the variation of a Part 4A permission, or
(f) to refuse an application under this Part,
it must give the applicant a decision notice.
[(5) This section does not apply to applications to which section 55XA applies.]]

NOTES
Substituted as noted to s 55A at **[7.84]**.
Sub-s (2): words omitted repealed by the EEA Passport Rights (Amendment, etc, and Transitional Provisions) (EU Exit) Regulations 2018, SI 2018/1149, reg 3, Schedule, Pt 1, paras 1, 8(1), (2), as from IP completion day (as defined in the European Union (Withdrawal Agreement) Act 2020, s 39).
Sub-s (3): repealed by SI 2018/1149, reg 3, Schedule, Pt 1, paras 1, 8(1), (3), as from IP completion day (as defined in the European Union (Withdrawal Agreement) Act 2020, s 39).
Sub-s (5): added by the Financial Services and Markets Act 2000 (Benchmarks) Regulations 2018, SI 2018/135, reg 40(1), (9), as from 27 February 2018.

[7.110]

[55XA Applications relating to administering a benchmark

(1) If the FCA decides—

- (a) to give a Part 4A permission to carry on the regulated activity specified in article 63S of the RAO (administering a benchmark) but to exercise its power in section 55E(5)(a) or (b) in connection with the application for permission,
- (b) to give a Part 4A permission to carry on the regulated activity specified in article 63S of the RAO (administering a benchmark) but to exercise its power in section 55L(1) in connection with the application for permission,
- (c) to vary a Part 4A permission to include permission to carry on the regulated activity specified in article 63S of the RAO (administering a benchmark) on the application of an authorised person but to exercise its power in section 55E(5)(a) or (b) in connection with the application for variation,
- (d) to vary a Part 4A permission to include permission to carry on the regulated activity specified in article 63S of the RAO (administering a benchmark) on the application of an authorised person but to exercise its power in section 55L(1) in connection with the application for variation,
- (e) to refuse an application for a Part 4A permission to carry on the regulated activity specified in article 63S of the RAO (administering a benchmark), or
- (f) to refuse an application for a variation of a Part 4A permission to include permission to carry on the regulated activity specified in article 63S of the RAO (administering a benchmark),

it must give the applicant a written notice.

(2) A written notice under subsection (1) must—

- (a) give details of the decision made by the FCA,
- (b) state the FCA's reasons for the decision,
- (c) state whether the decision takes effect immediately or on such date as may be specified in the notice,
- (d) inform the applicant that the applicant may either—
  - (i) request a review of the decision, and make written representations for the purpose of the review, within such period as may be specified in the notice, or
  - (ii) refer the matter to the Tribunal within such period as may be specified in the notice, and
- (e) indicate the procedure on a reference to the Tribunal.

(3) If the applicant requests a review of the decision made by the FCA ("the original decision"), the FCA must consider any written representations made by the applicant and review the original decision.

(4) On a review under subsection (3) the FCA may make any decision ("the new decision") the FCA could have made on the application.

(5) The FCA must give the applicant written notice of its decision on the review.

(6) If the new decision is to do any of the things mentioned in subsection (1)(a) to (f), the written notice under subsection (5) must—

- (a) give details of the new decision made by the FCA,
- (b) state the FCA's reasons for the new decision,
- (c) inform the applicant that the applicant may, within such period as may be specified in the notice, refer the new decision to the Tribunal, and
- (d) indicate the procedure on a reference to the Tribunal.

(8) In this section "the RAO" means the Financial Services and Markets Act 2000 (Regulated Activities) Order 2001.]

NOTES

Inserted by the Financial Services and Markets Act 2000 (Benchmarks) Regulations 2018, SI 2018/135, reg 40(1), (10), as from 27 February 2018.

[7.111]

[55Y Exercise of own-initiative power: procedure

(1) This section applies to an exercise of either regulator's own-initiative variation power or own-initiative requirement power in relation to an authorised person ("A").

(2) A variation of a permission or the imposition or variation of a requirement takes effect—

- (a) immediately, if the notice given under subsection (4) states that that is the case,
- (b) on such date as may be specified in the notice, or
- (c) if no date is specified in the notice, when the matter to which the notice relates is no longer open to review.

(3) A variation of a permission, or the imposition or variation of a requirement, may be expressed to take effect immediately (or on a specified date) only if the regulator concerned, having regard to the ground on which it is exercising its own-initiative variation power or own-initiative requirement power, reasonably considers that it is necessary for the variation, or the imposition or variation of the requirement, to take effect immediately (or on that date).

(4) If either regulator proposes to vary a Part 4A permission or to impose or vary a requirement, or varies a Part 4A permission or imposes or varies a requirement, with immediate effect, it must give A written notice.

(5) The notice must—

- (a) give details of the variation of the permission or the requirement or its variation,
- (b) state the regulator's reasons for the variation of the permission or the imposition or variation of the requirement,
- (c) inform A that A may make representations to the regulator within such period as may be specified in the notice (whether or not A has referred the matter to the Tribunal),
- (d) inform A of when the variation of the permission or the imposition or variation of the requirement takes effect, and
- (e) inform A of A's right to refer the matter to the Tribunal.

(6) The regulator may extend the period allowed under the notice for making representations.

(7) If, having considered any representations made by A, the regulator decides—

(a) to vary the permission, or impose or vary the requirement, in the way proposed, or
(b) if the permission has been varied or the requirement imposed or varied, not to rescind the variation of the permission or the imposition or variation of the requirement,

it must give A written notice.

(8) If, having considered any representations made by A, the regulator decides—

(a) not to vary the permission, or impose or vary the requirement, in the way proposed,
(b) to vary the permission or requirement in a different way, or impose a different requirement, or
(c) to rescind a variation or requirement which has effect,

it must give A written notice.

(9) A notice under subsection (7) must inform A of A's right to refer the matter to the Tribunal.

(10) A notice under subsection (8)(b) must comply with subsection (5).

(11) If a notice informs A of A's right to refer a matter to the Tribunal, it must give an indication of the procedure on such a reference.

(12) For the purposes of subsection (2)(c), whether a matter is open to review is to be determined in accordance with section 391(8).]

NOTES

Substituted as noted to s 55A at **[7.84]**.

[7.112]

[55Z Cancellation of Part 4A permission: procedure

(1) If a regulator proposes to cancel an authorised person's Part 4A permission otherwise than at the person's request, it must give the person a warning notice.

(2) If a regulator decides to cancel an authorised person's Part 4A permission otherwise than at the person's request, it must give the person a decision notice.]

NOTES

Substituted as noted to s 55A at **[7.84]**.

55Z1–55Z2A *(S 55Z1 (Notification of ESMA) and s 55Z2 (Notification of EBA) were substituted as noted to s 55A at* **[7.84]***. S 55Z2A (Notification of the European Bodies) was inserted by the Capital Requirements Regulations 2013, SI 2013/3115, reg 46(1), Sch 2, Pt 1, paras 1, 8, as from 1 January 2014. They were repealed by the Financial Services and Markets Act 2000 (Amendment) (EU Exit) Regulations 2019, SI 2019/632, regs 14, 23, as from IP completion day (as defined in the European Union (Withdrawal Agreement) Act 2020, s 39).)*

[References to the Tribunal

[7.113]

55Z3 Right to refer matters to the Tribunal

(1) An applicant who is aggrieved by the determination of an application made under this Part may refer the matter to the Tribunal.

(2) An authorised person who is aggrieved by the exercise by either regulator of its own-initiative variation power or its own-initiative requirement power may refer the matter to the Tribunal.

[(3) Where there is a review under section 55XA(3) of a determination within section 55XA(1), subsection (1) applies only in relation to the determination made on the review.]]

NOTES

Substituted as noted to s 55A at **[7.84]**.

Sub-s (3): added by the Financial Services and Markets Act 2000 (Benchmarks) Regulations 2018, SI 2018/135, reg 40(1), (11), as from 27 February 2018.

[Interpretation

[7.114]

55Z4 Interpretation of Part 4A

In this Part—

"own-initiative requirement power", in relation to the FCA or the PRA, is to be read in accordance with section 55L(4) or 55M(4);

"own-initiative variation power", in relation to the FCA or the PRA, is to be read in accordance with section 55J(12).]

NOTES

Substituted as noted to s 55A at **[7.84]**.

PART V PERFORMANCE OF REGULATED ACTIVITIES

NOTES

Transitional provisions etc in connection with the commencement of the Financial Services Act 2012: For transitional provisions in respect of the approval for a person to perform functions which are specified in rules made by a regulator, see the Financial Services Act 2012 (Transitional Provisions) (Permission and Approval) Order 2013, SI 2013/440, art 13 (Approval for particular arrangements). See also the Financial Services Act 2012 (Transitional Provisions) (Enforcement) Order 2013, SI 2013/441, which make provision for the imposition of penalties and disciplinary measures under this Act in relation to the performance of controlled functions before 1 April 2013 (see arts 2 and 3 of the 2013 Order).

Transitional provisions etc in connection with the original commencement of this Act: the Financial Services and Markets Act 2000 (Transitional Provisions) (Authorised Persons etc) Order 2001, SI 2001/2636, Pt VI makes transitional provisions for people working for authorised persons who will be covered by the regime for approved persons in Pt V of this Act after commencement. Where someone is working for an authorised person before commencement in a post for which they would need to be approved under Pt V after commencement, that person is treated has having been approved for the purpose of working in that post. This deemed approval applies unless the person was working before commencement in contravention of certain provisions of the regulatory rules or of rules made by a self-regulating organisation. The Part also carries forward approvals given under the Insurance Companies Act 1982 and the Banking Act 1987 where the person approved did not take up the appointment before commencement. See also, with regard to disciplinary powers. the Financial Services and Markets Act 2000 (Transitional Provisions and Savings) (Civil Remedies, Discipline, Criminal Offences etc) (No 2) Order 2001, SI 2001/3083, art 9.

Other transitional and savings: see also the Financial Services (Banking Reform) Act 2013 (Transitional and Savings Provisions) Order 2015, SI 2015/492 which makes transitional and savings provisions in connection with the commencement of the Financial Services (Banking Reform) Act 2013, Part 4, which amends this Part. Article 2 (Requirement to give notice in relation to an approved person) makes provision about the conditions that must be met for a person who, before the 7 March 2016, has an approval to perform controlled functions in relation to a firm to continue to have approval on and after the 7 March 2016. Article 3 (Conditions for continuation of an approval) sets out additional conditions for the continuation of an approval. Article 4 (Treatment of a continuing approval) makes provision about the treatment, on and after 7 March 2016, of a continuing approval for the purposes of this Part. In particular, it specifies what functions the approval is to be treated as relating to. Article 5 (Regulators' power to impose requirements for an article 2 notice) confers power on either regulator to impose further requirements about the form and content of a notice given in accordance with art 2. Article 6 (Revision of an article 2 notice) requires a notice given in accordance with art 2 (or any revision of that notice) to be updated if there is a change relating to information given in, or accompanying, the notice. Article 7 (Application of section 63ZA to a continuing approval) makes provision to an authorised person to apply for the regulators to impose a condition on a continuing approval (or, if a condition has already been imposed, to vary or remove that condition). Article 8 (Application of section 62A to a statement provided under article 2(3)(c)) requires that a statement of management responsibilities given under art 2 must be updated if there is any significant change in those responsibilities after 7 March 2016. Article 9 (Steps taken under section 63) ensures that any steps taken by either regulator before 7 March 2016 in connection with the withdrawal of an approval continue to have effect on and after 7 March 2016. Article 10 (Period for consideration of an application to perform controlled functions) suspends the period of time which the regulators have to consider such an application until the firm making the application has provided to the regulators a notice in accordance with art 11. Articles 10A and 10B (as inserted by SI 2015/1660) contain supplementary definitions for the purposes of art 10. Article 11 (Conditions for continuation of an application to perform controlled functions) sets out the conditions for the continuation of an application on and after 7 March 2016, including provision of a notice referred to in art 10. Article 12 (Continuation of an application to perform controlled functions) makes provision for the treatment of an application that continues on and after 7 March 2016. In particular, it specifies what functions the application is to be treated as relating to. Article 13 (Regulators' power to impose requirements for an article 11 notice) confers power on either regulator to impose further requirements about the form and content of an art 11 notice. Article 14 (Revision of an article 11 notice) requires a notice given in accordance with art 11 to be updated if there is a change relating to information given in, or accompanying, the notice. Article 15 (Application of section 62A to a statement provided under article 11(d)) requires that a statement of responsibilities given under art 11 must be updated if there is any significant change in those responsibilities after 7 March 2016. Article 16 (Determination of a continuing application) allows the PRA or the FCA, when determining an application which continues after 7 March 2016, to have regard to anything they could have had regard to if the application had been made on or after that date. Article 17 (Power for the regulators to specify equivalent functions) allows the regulators to specify which controlled functions that are specified on or after 7 March 2016 are, for the purposes of the 2015 Order, to be treated as equivalent to controlled functions that are specified before 7 March 2016. Article 18 (Prohibition orders) provides that amendments made by the Financial Services (Banking Reform) Act 2013 to s 59 of this Act (or any rules made by the regulators) do not affect any prohibition made by either regulator before 7 March 2016 (and makes similar provision in relation to warning, decision and final notices given by a regulator in connection with a prohibition). Article 19 (Power to impose penalties) ensures that the regulators' powers to impose a penalty on a person for performing a controlled function without approval before 7 March 2016 is not affected by any rules made by the regulator which alter or replace the controlled function in question. Article 20 (Rules and requirements imposed by a regulator under the 2015 Order) ensures that the regulators' powers to impose a penalty on a person for performing a controlled function without approval before 7 March 2016 is not affected by any rules made by the regulator which alter or replace the controlled function in question. Article 21 (Giving of notices, documents etc under this Order) provides that Regulations under s 414 of this Act (service of notices) apply in relation to any notice, direction or document of any kind required to be given under any provision of the 2015 Order (however that requirement is expressed) as if those provisions were provisions of this Act. Article 22 (Consultation) provides that where any provision in Part 9A of this Act imposes on either regulator, in connection with the making or issuing of any rules or other instrument or document under Part 5 of this Act or under the 2015 Order (a) a requirement (however expressed) to publish a draft of the rules, instrument or other document with or without other material and to invite representations about it, or (b) a requirement (however expressed) to consult particular persons, then the requirement may be satisfied by things done (wholly or in part) before the commencement of the 2015 Order. Article 23 (Enforcement of this Order) provides that a contravention of a requirement imposed by or under the 2015 Order is to be treated for the purposes of Part 14 of this Act (disciplinary measures) as a contravention of a relevant requirement within the meaning of s 204A(2) (meaning of "relevant requirement" and "appropriate regulator").

Prohibition orders

[7.115]

56 Prohibition orders

[(1) The FCA may make a prohibition order if it appears to it that an individual is not a fit and proper person to perform functions in relation to a regulated activity carried on by—

(a) an authorised person,

(b) a person who is an exempt person in relation to that activity, or

(c) a person to whom, as a result of Part 20, the general prohibition does not apply in relation to that activity.

(1A) The PRA may make a prohibition order if it appears to it that an individual is not a fit and proper person to perform functions in relation to a regulated activity carried on by—

(a) a PRA-authorised person, or

(b) a person who is an exempt person in relation to a PRA-regulated activity carried on by the person.]

(2) [A "prohibition order" is an order] prohibiting the individual from performing a specified function, any function falling within a specified description or any function.

(3) A prohibition order may relate to—

(a) a specified regulated activity, any regulated activity falling within a specified description or all regulated activities;

[(b) all persons falling within subsection (3A) or a particular paragraph of that subsection or all persons within a specified class of person falling within a particular paragraph of that subsection.]

[(3A) A person falls within this subsection if the person is—
(a) an authorised person,
(b) an exempt person, or
(c) a person to whom, as a result of Part 20, the general prohibition does not apply in relation to a regulated activity.]
(4) An individual who performs or agrees to perform a function in breach of a prohibition order is guilty of an offence and liable on summary conviction to a fine not exceeding level 5 on the standard scale.
(5) In proceedings for an offence under subsection (4) it is a defence for the accused to show that he took all reasonable precautions and exercised all due diligence to avoid committing the offence.
(6) [A person falling within subsection (3A)] must take reasonable care to ensure that no function of his, in relation to the carrying on of a regulated activity, is performed by a person who is prohibited from performing that function by a prohibition order.
(7) [The regulator that has made a prohibition order] may, on the application of the individual named in [the order], vary or revoke it.
[(7A) If—
(a) the FCA proposes to vary or revoke a prohibition order, and
(b) as a result of the proposed variation or revocation, an individual—
(i) will no longer be prohibited from performing a function of interest to the PRA, or
(ii) will be prohibited from performing such a function,
the FCA must consult the PRA before varying or revoking the order.
(7B) A function is of interest to the PRA if it is performed in relation to a regulated activity carried on by—
(a) a PRA-authorised person, or
(b) a person who is an exempt person in relation to a PRA-regulated activity carried on by the person.
(7C) The PRA must consult the FCA before varying or revoking a prohibition order.]
(8) . . .
(9) "Specified" means specified in the prohibition order.

NOTES

All amendments to this section were made by the Financial Services Act 2012, s 13(1)–(9), as from 1 April 2013.

[7.116]
57 Prohibition orders: procedure and right to refer to Tribunal
(1) If [a regulator] proposes to make a prohibition order it must give the individual concerned a warning notice.
(2) The warning notice must set out the terms of the prohibition.
(3) If [a regulator] decides to make a prohibition order it must give the individual concerned a decision notice.
(4) The decision notice must—
(a) name the individual to whom the prohibition order applies;
(b) set out the terms of the order; and
(c) be given to the individual named in the order.
(5) A person against whom a decision to make a prohibition order is made may refer the matter to the Tribunal.
[(6) If—
(a) the FCA proposes to make a prohibition order, and
(b) as a result of the proposed order, an individual will be prohibited from performing a function of interest to the PRA,
the FCA must consult the PRA before giving a warning notice under this section.
(7) A function is of interest to the PRA if it is performed in relation to a regulated activity carried on by—
(a) a PRA-authorised person, or
(b) a person who is an exempt person in relation to a PRA-regulated activity carried on by the person.
(8) The PRA must consult the FCA before giving a warning notice under this section.]

NOTES

Words in square brackets in sub-ss (1), (3) substituted, and sub-ss (6)–(8) added, by the Financial Services Act 2012, s 13(10)–(12), as from 1 April 2013.

[7.117]
58 Applications relating to prohibitions: procedure and right to refer to Tribunal
(1) This section applies to an application for the variation or revocation of a prohibition order.
(2) If the [appropriate regulator] decides to grant the application, it must give the applicant written notice of its decision.
(3) If the [appropriate regulator] proposes to refuse the application, it must give the applicant a warning notice.
(4) If the [appropriate regulator] decides to refuse the application, it must give the applicant a decision notice.
(5) If the [appropriate regulator] gives the applicant a decision notice, he may refer the matter to the Tribunal.
[(6) The "appropriate regulator" means the regulator to which the application is made.]

NOTES

Words in square brackets in sub-ss (2)–(5) substituted, and sub-s (6) added, by the Financial Services Act 2012, s 15, Sch 5, paras 1, 2, as from 1 April 2013.

Approval

[7.118]
59 Approval for particular arrangements
(1) An authorised person ("A") must take reasonable care to ensure that no person performs a controlled function under an arrangement entered into by A in relation to the carrying on by A of a regulated activity, unless [that person is acting in accordance with an approval given by the appropriate regulator under this section].

(2) An authorised person ("A") must take reasonable care to ensure that no person performs a controlled function under an arrangement entered into by a contractor of A in relation to the carrying on by A of a regulated activity, unless [that person is acting in accordance with an approval given by the appropriate regulator under this section].

[(3) Controlled function"—

(a) in relation to the carrying on of a regulated activity by a PRA-authorised person, means a function of a description specified in rules made by the FCA or the PRA, and

(b) in relation to the carrying on of a regulated activity by any other authorised person, means a function of a description specified in rules made by the FCA.

(4) "The appropriate regulator"—

(a) in relation to a controlled function which is of a description specified in rules made by the FCA, means the FCA, and

(b) in relation to a controlled function which is of a description specified in rules made by the PRA, means the PRA with the consent of the FCA.

(5) . . .

[(6) The PRA may specify a description of function under subsection (3)(a) only if, in relation to the carrying on of a regulated activity by a PRA-authorised person, it is satisfied that the function is a senior management function as defined in section 59ZA.]

[(6A) If the FCA is satisfied that a function of a description specified in rules made by the FCA under subsection (3)(a) or (b) is a senior management function as defined in section 59ZA, the FCA must designate the function in the rules as a senior management function.]

[(6B), (6C) . . .]

(7)–(7B) . . .

[(7C) A regulator may not exercise the power in subsection (3) so as to provide for a function to be a controlled function in relation to the carrying on of the regulated activity of managing an AIF by an AIFM which—

(a) is also an AIF;

(b) does not manage any AIF other than itself;

(c) is a body corporate; and

(d) is not a collective investment scheme.]

(8), (9) . . .

(10) "Arrangement"—

(a) means any kind of arrangement for the performance of a function of A which is entered into by A or any contractor of his with another person; and

(b) includes, in particular, that other person's appointment to an office, his becoming a partner or his employment (whether under a contract of service or otherwise).

(11) . . .

NOTES

Words in square brackets in sub-ss (1) and (2) substituted by the Financial Services (Banking Reform) Act 2013, s 35, Sch 3, para 1, as from 7 March 2016.

Sub-ss (3)–(7B) substituted (for the original sub-ss (3)–(7)) by the Financial Services Act 2012, s 14(1), as from 24 January 2013 (for the purpose of making rules), and as from 1 April 2013 (otherwise).

Sub-ss (5), (7)–(7B) and (11) repealed, sub-s (6) substituted, and sub-ss (6A)–(6C) inserted, by the Financial Services (Banking Reform) Act 2013, s 18, as from 25 July 2014 (for the purpose of the making of rules), and as from 7 March 2016 (otherwise).

Sub-ss (6A) substituted, and sub-ss (6B), (6C) repealed, by the Bank of England and Financial Services Act 2016, s 21, Sch 4, paras 1, 2. Note that s 21 and Sch 4 come into force as follows: (i) 13 September 2018 (for the purpose of making rules, giving directions, imposing requirements and making statements of policy by the appropriate regulator for insurers); (ii) 10 December 2018 (for all other purposes for insurers (except in relation to Sch 4, para 11)), and 10 December 2019 (Sch 4, para 11 for insurers); (iii) 18 July 2019 (for the purpose of the making of rules, the giving of directions, the imposition of requirements and the issuing of statements of policy by the FCA for remaining purposes); (iv) 9 August 2019 (for remaining purposes in relation to authorised persons who are not solo-regulated firms); (v) 9 December 2019 (for remaining purposes in relation to solo-regulated firms other than benchmark firms (except as provided for by (vii) below)); (vi) 7 December 2020 (for remaining purposes in relation to benchmark firms (except as provided for by (viii) below)); (vii) 31 March 2021 (in relation to the employee certification provisions for remaining purposes in relation to solo-regulated firms other than benchmark firms); (viii) 7 December 2021 (in relation to the employee certification provisions for remaining purposes in relation to benchmark firms). For transitional provisions in connection with (i)–(iii) above, see the Bank of England and Financial Services Act 2016 (Commencement No 5 and Transitional Provisions) Regulations 2018, SI 2018/990; and for transitional provisions in connection with the other commencement dates, see the Bank of England and Financial Services Act 2016 (Commencement No 6 and Transitional Provisions) Regulations 2019, SI 2019/1136.

Sub-s (7C): inserted by the Alternative Investment Fund Managers Regulations 2013, SI 2013/1773, reg 80, Sch 1, Part 1, paras 1, 7, as from 22 July 2013.

Sub-s (8): repealed by the Financial Services and Markets Act 2000 (Amendment) (EU Exit) Regulations 2019, SI 2019/632, regs 24, 25, as from IP completion day (as defined in the European Union (Withdrawal Agreement) Act 2020, s 39).

Sub-s (9): repealed by the Financial Services Act 2012, s 15, Sch 5, paras 1, 3, as from 1 April 2013.

[7.119]

[59ZA Senior management functions

(1) This section has effect for determining whether a function is for the purposes of section 59(6) or (6A) a senior management function.

(2) A function is a "senior management function", in relation to the carrying on of a regulated activity by an authorised person, if—

(a) the function will require the person performing it to be responsible for managing one or more aspects of the authorised person's affairs, so far as relating to the activity, and

(b) those aspects involve, or might involve, a risk of serious consequences—

(i) for the authorised person, or

(ii) for business or other interests in the United Kingdom.

(3) In subsection (2)(a) the reference to managing one or more aspects of an authorised person's affairs includes a reference to taking decisions, or participating in the taking of decisions, about how one or more aspects of those affairs should be carried on.]

NOTES

Inserted by the Financial Services (Banking Reform) Act 2013, s 19, as from 25 July 2014.

[7.120]

[59ZB Designated senior management functions

For the purposes of this Part the following are "designated senior management functions"—

(a) a function of a description specified in rules made by the FCA under section 59(3)(a) or (b) which is designated as a senior management function by the FCA under section 59(6A);

(b) a function of a description specified in rules made by the PRA under section 59(3)(a).]

NOTES

Commencement: see the note below.

Inserted by the Bank of England and Financial Services Act 2016, s 21, Sch 4, paras 1, 3. Note that s 21 and Sch 4 come into force as follows: (i) 13 September 2018 (for the purpose of making rules, giving directions, imposing requirements and making statements of policy by the appropriate regulator for insurers); (ii) 10 December 2018 (for all other purposes for insurers (except in relation to Sch 4, para 11)), and 10 December 2019 (Sch 4, para 11 for insurers); (iii) 18 July 2019 (for the purpose of the making of rules, the giving of directions, the imposition of requirements and the issuing of statements of policy by the FCA for remaining purposes); (iv) 9 August 2019 (for remaining purposes in relation to authorised persons who are not solo-regulated firms); (v) 9 December 2019 (for remaining purposes in relation to solo-regulated firms other than benchmark firms (except as provided for by (vii) below)); (vi) 7 December 2020 (for remaining purposes in relation to benchmark firms (except as provided for by (viii) below)); (vii) 31 March 2021 (in relation to the employee certification provisions for remaining purposes in relation to solo-regulated firms other than benchmark firms); (viii) 7 December 2021 (in relation to the employee certification provisions for remaining purposes in relation to benchmark firms). For transitional provisions in connection with (i)–(iii) above, see the Bank of England and Financial Services Act 2016 (Commencement No 5 and Transitional Provisions) Regulations 2018, SI 2018/990; and for transitional provisions in connection with the other commencement dates, see the Bank of England and Financial Services Act 2016 (Commencement No 6 and Transitional Provisions) Regulations 2019, SI 2019/1136.

[7.121]

[59A Specifying functions as controlled functions: supplementary

(1) The FCA must—

(a) keep under review the exercise of its power under section 59(3)(a) to specify any [senior management function as a controlled function, and

(b) exercise that power in a way that it considers will minimise the likelihood that approvals fall to be given by both the FCA and the PRA in respect of the performance by a person of [senior management] functions in relation to the carrying on of a regulated activity by the same PRA-authorised person.

(2) The FCA and the PRA must each consult the other before exercising any power under section 59(3)(a).

(3) Any reference in this section to the exercise of a power includes its exercise by way of amendment or revocation of provision previously made in the exercise of the power.

[(3A) Senior management function" has the meaning given by section 59ZA.]

(4) "Approval" means an approval under section 59.

(5) Any expression which is used both in this section and section 59 has the same meaning in this section as in that section.]

NOTES

Inserted, together with s 59B, by the Financial Services Act 2012, s 14(2), as from 1 April 2013.

Words in square brackets in sub-s (1) substituted, and sub-s (3A) inserted, by the Financial Services (Banking Reform) Act 2013, s 35, Sch 3, para 2, as from 25 July 2014 (for the purpose of the making of rules), and as from 7 March 2016 (otherwise).

[7.122]

[59AB Specifying functions as controlled functions: transitional provision

(1) In relation to rules made by the FCA or the PRA under section 59, the power conferred by section 137T(c) to make transitional provision includes in particular power—

(a) to provide for anything done under this Part in relation to controlled functions of a particular description to be treated as having been done in relation to controlled functions of a different description;

(b) to provide for anything done under this Part (including any application or order made, any requirement imposed and any approval or notice given) to cease to have effect, to continue to have effect, or to continue to have effect with modifications, or subject to time limits or conditions;

(c) to provide for rules made by the regulator making the rules under section 59 to apply with modifications;

(d) to make saving provision.

(2) The Treasury may by regulations make whatever incidental, consequential, transitional, supplemental or saving provision the Treasury consider appropriate in connection with the making of rules by the FCA or the PRA under section 59.

(3) Regulations under subsection (2) may—

(a) confer functions on the FCA or the PRA (including the function of making rules);

(b) modify, exclude or apply (with or without modifications) any primary or subordinate legislation (including any provision of, or made under, this Act).]

NOTES

Inserted by the Bank of England and Financial Services Act 2016, s 22(1), (2), as from 6 July 2016.

[7.123]

[59B Role of FCA in relation to PRA decisions

(1) The FCA may arrange with the PRA that in such cases as may be described in the arrangements the PRA may give approval under section 59 without obtaining the consent of the FCA.

(2) Arrangements under this section must be in writing, and must specify the date on which they come into force.

(3) The regulators must publish any arrangements under this section in such manner as they think fit.

(4) Section 59(4)(b) has effect subject to any arrangements in force under this section.]

NOTES

Inserted as noted to s 59A at **[7.121]**.

[7.124]

60 Applications for approval

(1) An application for the [appropriate regulator's] approval under section 59 may be made by the authorised person concerned.

(2) The application must—

(a) be made in such manner as the [appropriate regulator] may direct; and

(b) contain, or be accompanied by, such information as the [appropriate regulator] may reasonably require.

[(2A) If—

(a) the application is for the approval of a person to perform a designated senior management function, . . .

(b) . . .

the appropriate regulator must require the application to contain, or be accompanied by, a statement setting out the aspects of the affairs of the authorised person concerned which it is intended that the person will be responsible for managing in performing the function.

(2B) A statement provided under subsection (2A) is known as a "statement of responsibilities".

(2C) . . .]

[(3) At any time after the application is received and before it is determined, the appropriate regulator may require the applicant to provide it with such further information as it reasonably considers necessary to enable it to determine the application or, as the case requires, to decide whether to give consent.]

(4) The [appropriate regulator] may require an applicant to present information which he is required to give under this section in such form, or to verify it in such a way, as the [appropriate regulator] may direct.

(5) Different directions may be given, and different requirements imposed, in relation to different applications or categories of application.

(6) "The authorised person concerned" includes a person who has applied for permission under [Part 4A] and will be the authorised person concerned if permission is given.

[(6A) . . .]

[(7) The PRA must consult the FCA before—

(a) giving a direction under subsection (2)(a) in relation to a class of applicants, or

(b) imposing a requirement under subsection (2)(b) on a class of applicants.

(8) The PRA must as soon as practicable notify the FCA of the receipt or withdrawal of an application to the PRA, unless the case is one in which by virtue of arrangements under section 59B the consent of the FCA is not required.

(9) "The appropriate regulator"—

(a) in relation to a controlled function which is of a description specified in rules made by the FCA, means the FCA;

(b) in relation to a controlled function which is of a description specified in rules made by the PRA, means the PRA, and for the purposes of subsection (3) also includes the FCA in cases where the consent of the FCA is required.]

NOTES

Words in square brackets in sub-ss (1), (2), (4), (6) substituted, sub-s (3) substituted, and sub-ss (7)–(9) added, by the Financial Services Act 2012, s 15, Sch 5, paras 1, 4, as from 24 January 2013 (in so far as relating to the giving of directions or the imposition of requirements), and as from 1 April 2013 (otherwise).

Sub-ss (2A)–(2C), (6A): inserted by the Financial Services (Banking Reform) Act 2013, s 20, as from 25 July 2014 (for the purpose of giving directions or imposing requirements), and as from 7 March 2016 (otherwise). In sub-s (2A), para (b) and the preceding word were repealed, and sub-ss (2C) and (6A) were repealed, by the Bank of England and Financial Services Act 2016, s 21, Sch 4, paras 1, 4. Note that s 21 and Sch 4 come into force as follows: (i) 13 September 2018 (for the purpose of making rules, giving directions, imposing requirements and making statements of policy by the appropriate regulator for insurers); (ii) 10 December 2018 (for all other purposes for insurers (except in relation to Sch 4, para 11)), and 10 December 2019 (Sch 4, para 11 for insurers); (iii) 18 July 2019 (for the purpose of the making of rules, the giving of directions, the imposition of requirements and the issuing of statements of policy by the FCA for remaining purposes); (iv) 9 August 2019 (for remaining purposes in relation to authorised persons who are not solo-regulated firms); (v) 9 December 2019 (for remaining purposes in relation to solo-regulated firms other than benchmark firms (except as provided for by (vii) below)); (vi) 7 December 2020 (for remaining purposes in relation to benchmark firms (except as provided for by (viii) below)); (vii) 31 March 2021 (in relation to the employee certification provisions for remaining purposes in relation to solo-regulated firms other than benchmark firms); (viii) 7 December 2021 (in relation to the employee certification provisions for remaining purposes in relation to benchmark firms). For transitional provisions in connection with (i)–(iii) above, see the Bank of England and Financial Services Act 2016 (Commencement No 5 and Transitional Provisions) Regulations 2018, SI 2018/990; and for transitional provisions in connection with the other commencement dates, see the Bank of England and Financial Services Act 2016 (Commencement No 6 and Transitional Provisions) Regulations 2019, SI 2019/1136.

[7.125]

[60A Vetting of candidates by . . . authorised persons

(1) Before [an] authorised person may make an application for a regulator's approval under section 59, the authorised person must be satisfied that the person in respect of whom the application is made ("the candidate") is a fit and proper person to perform the function to which the application relates.

(2) In deciding that question, the authorised person must have regard, in particular, to whether the candidate, or any person who may perform a function on the candidate's behalf—

(a) has obtained a qualification,

(b) has undergone, or is undergoing, training,

(c) possesses a level of competence, or

(d) has the personal characteristics,

required by general rules made by the regulator in relation to persons performing functions of the kind to which the application relates.

(3) . . .]

NOTES

Inserted by the Financial Services (Banking Reform) Act 2013, s 21, as from 7 March 2016.

The word omitted from the section heading was repealed, the word in square brackets in sub-s (1) was substituted, and sub-s (3) was repealed, by the Bank of England and Financial Services Act 2016, s 21, Sch 4, paras 1, 5. Note that s 21 and Sch 4 come into force as follows: (i) 13 September 2018 (for the purpose of making rules, giving directions, imposing requirements and making statements of policy by the appropriate regulator for insurers); (ii) 10 December 2018 (for all other purposes for insurers (except in relation to Sch 4, para 11)), and 10 December 2019 (Sch 4, para 11 for insurers); (iii) 18 July 2019 (for the purpose of the making of rules, the giving of directions, the imposition of requirements and the issuing of statements of policy by the FCA for remaining purposes); (iv) 9 August 2019 (for remaining purposes in relation to authorised persons who are not solo-regulated firms); (v) 9 December 2019 (for remaining purposes in relation to solo-regulated firms other than benchmark firms (except as provided for by (vii) below)); (vi) 7 December 2020 (for remaining purposes in relation to benchmark firms (except as provided for by (viii) below)); (vii) 31 March 2021 (in relation to the employee certification provisions for remaining purposes in relation to solo-regulated firms other than benchmark firms); (viii) 7 December 2021 (in relation to the employee certification provisions for remaining purposes in relation to benchmark firms). For transitional provisions in connection with (i)–(iii) above, see the Bank of England and Financial Services Act 2016 (Commencement No 5 and Transitional Provisions) Regulations 2018, SI 2018/990; and for transitional provisions in connection with the other commencement dates, see the Bank of England and Financial Services Act 2016 (Commencement No 6 and Transitional Provisions) Regulations 2019, SI 2019/1136.

[7.126]

61 Determination of applications

[(1) The regulator to which an application for approval is made under section 60 may grant the application only if—

(a) it is satisfied that the person in respect of whom the application is made ("the candidate") is a fit and proper person to perform the function to which the application relates, or

(b) in a case where the application is for approval to perform a designated senior management function [(a "senior] management application"), it is satisfied that the condition in paragraph (a) will be met if the application is granted subject to one or more conditions (as to which, see subsection (2B)).]

(2) In [determining the application], [the regulator] may have regard (among other things) to whether the candidate, or any person who may perform a function on his behalf—

(a) has obtained a qualification,

(b) has undergone, or is undergoing, training, . . .

(c) possesses a level of competence, [or

(d) has the personal characteristics,]

required by general rules [made by that regulator] in relation to persons performing functions of the kind to which the application relates.

[(2A) Subsections (1) and (2) apply in relation to the giving by the FCA of any required consent as they apply in relation to the grant of the application.]

[(2B) The regulator to which a . . . senior management application is made under section 60 may in particular—

(a) grant the application subject to any conditions that the regulator considers appropriate, and

(b) grant the application so as to give approval only for a limited period.

(2C) A regulator may exercise the power under paragraph (a) or (b) of subsection (2B) only if—

(a) where the regulator is the FCA, it appears to the FCA that it is desirable to do so in order to advance one or more of its operational objectives, and

(b) where the regulator is the PRA, it appears to the PRA that it is desirable to do so in order to advance any of its objectives.

(2D) Consent given by the FCA for the granting of the application may be conditional on the manner in which the PRA exercises its power under subsection (2B).]

(3) [The regulator to which an application is made under section 60 must, before the end of the period for consideration, determine] whether—

(a) to grant the application; or

(b) to give a warning notice under section 62(2).

[(3ZA) In the case of a . . . senior management application, the reference in subsection (3)(a) to granting the application is a reference to granting it without imposing conditions or limiting the period for which the approval has effect.]

[(3A) The period for consideration"—

(a) in any case where the application under section 60 is made by a person applying for permission under Part 4A (see section 60(6)), means whichever ends last of—

(i) the period within which the application for that permission must be determined under section 55V(1) or (2), and

(ii) the period of 3 months beginning with the date on which the regulator receives the application under section 60, and

(b) in any other case, means the period of 3 months beginning with the date on which the regulator receives the application under section 60.]

(4) If [a regulator] imposes a requirement under section 60(3), the period for consideration stops running on the day on which the requirement is imposed but starts running again—

(a) on the day on which the required information is received by [a regulator]; or

(b) if the information is not provided on a single day, on the last of the days on which it is received by [a regulator].

(5) A person who makes an application under section 60 may withdraw his application by giving written notice to the [regulator to which the application was made] at any time before the [regulator] determines it, but only with the consent of—

(a) the candidate; and

(b) the person by whom the candidate is to be retained to perform the function concerned, if not the applicant.

[(6), (7) . . .]

NOTES

Sub-s (1): substituted by the Financial Services (Banking Reform) Act 2013, s 23(1), (2), as from 7 March 2016. Words in square brackets substituted by the Bank of England and Financial Services Act 2016, s 21, Sch 4, paras 1, 6(1), (2). Note that s 21 and Sch 4 come into force as follows: (i) 13 September 2018 (for the purpose of making rules, giving directions, imposing requirements and making statements of policy by the appropriate regulator for insurers); (ii) 10 December 2018 (for all other purposes for insurers (except in relation to Sch 4, para 11)), and 10 December 2019 (Sch 4, para 11 for insurers); (iii) 18 July 2019 (for the purpose of the making of rules, the giving of directions, the imposition of requirements and the issuing of statements of policy by the FCA for remaining purposes); (iv) 9 August 2019 (for remaining purposes in relation to authorised persons who are not solo-regulated firms); (v) 9 December 2019 (for remaining purposes in relation to solo-regulated firms other than benchmark firms (except as provided for by (vii) below)); (vi) 7 December 2020 (for remaining purposes in relation to benchmark firms (except as provided for by (viii) below)); (vii) 31 March 2021 (in relation to the employee certification provisions for remaining purposes in relation to solo-regulated firms other than benchmark firms); (viii) 7 December 2021 (in relation to the employee certification provisions for remaining purposes in relation to benchmark firms). For transitional provisions in connection with (i)–(iii) above, see the Bank of England and Financial Services Act 2016 (Commencement No 5 and Transitional Provisions) Regulations 2018, SI 2018/990; and for transitional provisions in connection with the other commencement dates, see the Bank of England and Financial Services Act 2016 (Commencement No 6 and Transitional Provisions) Regulations 2019, SI 2019/1136.

Sub-s (2): words in first pair of square brackets substituted by the Financial Services (Banking Reform) Act 2013, s 23(1), (3), as from 7 March 2016. Words in second pair of square brackets substituted, and words in final pair of square brackets inserted, by the Financial Services Act 2012, s 15, Sch 5, paras 1, 5(1), (3), as from 1 April 2013. Word omitted from para (b) repealed, and para (d) (and the preceding word) inserted, by the Financial Services (Banking Reform) Act 2013, s 22, as from 7 March 2016.

Sub-ss (2A), (3A): inserted by the Financial Services Act 2012, s 15, Sch 5, paras 1, 5(1), (4), (6), as from 1 April 2013.

Sub-ss (2B)–(2D), (3ZA) and (6), (7): inserted and added respectively by the Financial Services (Banking Reform) Act 2013, s 23(1), (4)–(6), as from 7 March 2016. The words omitted from sub-ss (2B) and (3ZA) were repealed, and sub-ss (6) and (7) were repealed, by the Bank of England and Financial Services Act 2016, s 21, Sch 4, paras 1, 6(1), (3), (4) (as to the commencement of s 21 and Sch 4, and for transitional provisions etc, see the note relating to the 2016 Act above).

Sub-ss (3)–(5): words in square brackets substituted by the Financial Services Act 2012, s 15, Sch 5, paras 1, 5(1), (5), (7), (8), as from 1 April 2013.

[7.127]

62 Applications for approval: procedure and right to refer to Tribunal

(1) [If the regulator to which an application is made under section 60 ("an application") decides to grant the application, it] must give written notice of its decision to each of the interested parties.

(2) If [the regulator to which an application is made] proposes to refuse [the application][, or to grant the application subject to conditions or for a limited period (or both)], it must give a warning notice to each of the interested parties.

(3) If [the regulator to which an application is made] decides to refuse [the application][, or to grant the application subject to conditions or for a limited period (or both)], it must give a decision notice to each of the interested parties.

(4) If [the regulator to which an application is made] decides to refuse [the application][, or to grant the application subject to conditions or for a limited period (or both)], each of the interested parties may refer the matter to the Tribunal.

(5) "The interested parties", in relation to an application, are—

(a) the applicant;

(b) the person in respect of whom the application is made ("A"); and

(c) the person by whom A's services are to be retained, if not the applicant.

NOTES

The words ", or to grant the application subject to conditions or for a limited period (or both)" in square brackets in sub-ss (2)–(4) were inserted by the Financial Services (Banking Reform) Act 2013, s 23(7), as from 7 March 2016.

All other words in square brackets in this section were substituted by the Financial Services Act 2012, s 15, Sch 5, paras 1, 6, as from 1 April 2013.

[7.128]

[62A Changes in responsibilities of senior managers

(1) This section applies where—

(a) an authorised person has made an application to the appropriate regulator for approval under section 59 for a person to perform a designated senior management function,

(b) the application contained, or was accompanied by, a statement of responsibilities under section 60(2A), and

(c) the application has been granted.

(2) If, since the granting of the application, there has been any significant change in the aspects of the authorised person's affairs which the person is responsible for managing in performing the function, the authorised person must provide the appropriate regulator with a revised statement of responsibilities.

(3) The appropriate regulator may require the authorised person—

(a) to provide information which the person is required to give under this section in such form as the appropriate regulator may direct, or

(b) to verify such information in such a way as the appropriate regulator may direct.

(4) In this section—

"the appropriate regulator" has the same meaning as in section 60[, except that the reference in section 60(9)(b) to subsection (3) is to be treated as a reference to subsection (2) of this section];

. . .]

NOTES

Inserted by the Financial Services (Banking Reform) Act 2013, s 24, as from 7 March 2016.

Sub-s (4) is amended as follows:

Words in square brackets in the definition "the appropriate regulator" inserted by the Bank of England and Financial Services Act 2016, s 23(1), (2), as from 6 July 2016.

Definition "designated senior management function" (omitted) repealed by the Bank of England and Financial Services Act 2016, s 21, Sch 4, paras 1, 7. Note that s 21 and Sch 4 come into force as follows: (i) 13 September 2018 (for the purpose of making rules, giving directions, imposing requirements and making statements of policy by the appropriate regulator for insurers); (ii) 10 December 2018 (for all other purposes for insurers (except in relation to Sch 4, para 11)), and 10 December 2019 (Sch 4, para 11 for insurers); (iii) 18 July 2019 (for the purpose of the making of rules, the giving of directions, the imposition of requirements and the issuing of statements of policy by the FCA for remaining purposes); (iv) 9 August 2019 (for remaining purposes in relation to authorised persons who are not solo-regulated firms); (v) 9 December 2019 (for remaining purposes in relation to solo-regulated firms other than benchmark firms (except as provided for by (vii) below)); (vi) 7 December 2020 (for remaining purposes in relation to benchmark firms (except as provided for by (viii) below)); (vii) 31 March 2021 (in relation to the employee certification provisions for remaining purposes in relation to solo-regulated firms other than benchmark firms); (viii) 7 December 2021 (in relation to the employee certification provisions for remaining purposes in relation to benchmark firms). For transitional provisions in connection with (i)–(iii) above, see the Bank of England and Financial Services Act 2016 (Commencement No 5 and Transitional Provisions) Regulations 2018, SI 2018/990; and for transitional provisions in connection with the other commencement dates, see the Bank of England and Financial Services Act 2016 (Commencement No 6 and Transitional Provisions) Regulations 2019, SI 2019/1136.

[7.129]

63 Withdrawal of approval

[(1) The FCA may withdraw an approval under section 59 given by the FCA or the PRA in relation to the performance by a person of a function if the FCA considers that the person is not a fit and proper person to perform the function.

(1A) The PRA may withdraw an approval under section 59 in relation to the performance by a person ("A") of a function if—

(a) the PRA gave the approval, or the FCA gave the approval and the function is a [relevant senior management function] performed in relation to the carrying on by a PRA-authorised person of a regulated activity, and

(b) the PRA considers that A is not a fit and proper person to perform the function.

[(1B) In subsection (1A) "relevant senior management function" means a function which the PRA is satisfied is a senior management function as defined in section 59ZA (whether or not the function has been designated as such by the FCA).]

(1C) Before one regulator withdraws an approval given by the other regulator, it must consult the other regulator.]

(2) When considering whether to withdraw [an approval, the FCA or the PRA may take into account any matter which could be taken into account in] considering an application made under section 60 in respect of the performance of the function to which the approval relates [(on the assumption, if it is not the case, that the application was one falling to be considered by it)].

[(2A) At least once a year each . . . authorised person must, in relation to every person in relation to whom an approval has been given on the application of the authorised person—

(a) consider whether there are any grounds on which a regulator could withdraw the approval under this section, and

(b) if the authorised person is of the opinion that there are such grounds, notify the regulator of those grounds.

. . .]

(3) If [a regulator] proposes to withdraw [an approval], it must give each of the interested parties a warning notice.

(4) If [a regulator] decides to withdraw [an approval], it must give each of the interested parties a decision notice.

(5) If [a regulator] decides to withdraw [an approval], each of the interested parties may refer the matter to the Tribunal.

(6) "The interested parties", in relation to an approval, are—

(a) the person on whose application it was given ("A");

(b) the person in respect of whom it was given ("B"); and

(c) the person by whom B's services are retained, if not A.

NOTES

Sub-ss (1)–(1C): substituted (for the original sub-s (1)) by the Financial Services Act 2012, s 14(3), as from 1 April 2013. Words in square brackets in sub-s (1A) substituted, and sub-s (1B) further substituted, by the Financial Services (Banking Reform) Act 2013, s 35, Sch 3, para 3, as from 7 March 2016.

Sub-s (2): words in first pair of square brackets substituted, and words in second pair of square brackets inserted, by the Financial Services Act 2012, s 15, Sch 5, paras 1, 7(1), (2), as from 1 April 2013.

Sub-s (2A): inserted by the Financial Services (Banking Reform) Act 2013, s 25, as from 7 March 2016. Words omitted repealed by the Bank of England and Financial Services Act 2016, s 21, Sch 4, paras 1, 8. Note that s 21 and Sch 4 come into force as follows: (i) 13 September 2018 (for the purpose of making rules, giving directions, imposing requirements and making statements of policy by the appropriate regulator for insurers); (ii) 10 December 2018 (for all other purposes for insurers (except in relation to Sch 4, para 11)), and 10 December 2019 (Sch 4, para 11 for insurers); (iii) 18 July 2019 (for the purpose of the making of rules, the giving of directions, the imposition of requirements and the issuing of statements of policy by the FCA for remaining purposes); (iv) 9 August 2019 (for remaining purposes in relation to authorised persons who are not solo-regulated firms); (v) 9 December 2019 (for remaining purposes in relation to solo-regulated firms other than benchmark firms (except as provided for by (vii) below)); (vi) 7 December 2020 (for remaining purposes in relation to benchmark firms (except as provided for by (viii) below)); (vii) 31 March 2021 (in relation to the employee certification provisions for remaining purposes in relation to solo-regulated firms other than benchmark firms); (viii) 7 December 2021 (in relation to the employee certification provisions for remaining purposes in relation to benchmark firms). For transitional provisions in connection with (i)–(iii) above, see the

Bank of England and Financial Services Act 2016 (Commencement No 5 and Transitional Provisions) Regulations 2018, SI 2018/990; and for transitional provisions in connection with the other commencement dates, see the Bank of England and Financial Services Act 2016 (Commencement No 6 and Transitional Provisions) Regulations 2019, SI 2019/1136.

Sub-ss (3)–(5): words in square brackets substituted by the Financial Services Act 2012, s 15, Sch 5, paras 1, 7(1), (3), as from 1 April 2013.

[7.130]

[63ZA Variation of senior manager's approval at request of . . . authorised person

(1) Where an [approval under section 59 has effect] subject to conditions, the authorised person concerned may apply to the appropriate regulator to vary the approval by—

(a) varying a condition,

(b) removing a condition, or

(c) imposing a new condition.

[(1A) Where an approval under section 59 has effect for a limited period, the authorised person concerned may apply to the appropriate regulator to vary the approval by—

(a) varying the period for which the approval is to have effect, or

(b) removing the limit on the period for which the approval is to have effect.]

(2) "The appropriate regulator"—

(a) in the case of an application for variation of an approval in a way described in subsection (1)(a) or (b), means

[(i)] whichever of the FCA or the PRA imposed the condition concerned[, or

(ii) if the condition has been varied before (under this section or section 63ZB), whichever of the FCA or the PRA last varied it;]

(b) in the case of an application for variation of an approval in the way described in subsection (1)(c), means the regulator who gave the approval;

[(c) in the case of an application for variation of an approval in a way described in subsection (1A), means—

(i) whichever of the FCA or the PRA imposed the limit on the period for which the approval has effect, or

(ii) if the limit has been varied before (under this section or section 63ZB), whichever of the FCA or the PRA last varied it].

(3) The PRA must consult the FCA before determining an application under this section, unless the application relates to the variation or removal of a condition [or a limit on the period for which an approval has effect, which was imposed (or last varied)] by the PRA in exercise of its power under section 63ZB.

(4) The regulator to which an application is made under this section must, before the end of the period for consideration, determine whether—

(a) to grant the application; or

(b) to give a warning notice under section 62(2).

(5) "The period for consideration" means the period of 3 months beginning with the date on which the regulator receives the application.

(6) The FCA may refuse an application under this section if it appears to the FCA that it is desirable to do so in order to advance one or more of its operational objectives.

(7) The PRA may refuse an application under this section if it appears to the PRA that it is desirable to do so in order to advance any of its objectives.

[(7A) An application may not be made under this section for the variation or removal of a condition, or a limit on the period for which an approval has effect, where the condition or limit has effect by virtue of section 66.]

(8) The following provisions apply to an application made under this section for variation of an approval as they apply to an application for approval made under section 60—

section 60(2) to (8),

section 61(4) and (5),

section 62[, but as if in subsections (2), (3) and (4) the words ", or to grant the application subject to conditions or for a limited period (or both)" were omitted].]

NOTES

Inserted, together with ss 63ZB, 63ZC, by the Financial Services (Banking Reform) Act 2013, s 26, as from 7 March 2016.

Section heading: word omitted repealed by the Bank of England and Financial Services Act 2016, s 21, Sch 4, paras 1, 9. Note that s 21 and Sch 4 come into force as follows: (i) 13 September 2018 (for the purpose of making rules, giving directions, imposing requirements and making statements of policy by the appropriate regulator for insurers); (ii) 10 December 2018 (for all other purposes for insurers (except in relation to Sch 4, para 11)), and 10 December 2019 (Sch 4, para 11 for insurers); (iii) 18 July 2019 (for the purpose of the making of rules, the giving of directions, the imposition of requirements and the issuing of statements of policy by the FCA for remaining purposes); (iv) 9 August 2019 (for remaining purposes in relation to authorised persons who are not solo-regulated firms); (v) 9 December 2019 (for remaining purposes in relation to solo-regulated firms other than benchmark firms (except as provided for by (vii) below)); (vi) 7 December 2020 (for remaining purposes in relation to benchmark firms (except as provided for by (viii) below)); (vii) 31 March 2021 (in relation to the employee certification provisions for remaining purposes in relation to solo-regulated firms other than benchmark firms); (viii) 7 December 2021 (in relation to the employee certification provisions for remaining purposes in relation to benchmark firms). For transitional provisions in connection with (i)–(iii) above, see the Bank of England and Financial Services Act 2016 (Commencement No 5 and Transitional Provisions) Regulations 2018, SI 2018/990; and for transitional provisions in connection with the other commencement dates, see the Bank of England and Financial Services Act 2016 (Commencement No 6 and Transitional Provisions) Regulations 2019, SI 2019/1136.

Sub-ss (1), (3): words in square brackets substituted by the Bank of England and Financial Services Act 2016, s 23(1), (3)(a), (e), as from 6 July 2016.

Sub-ss (1A), (7A): inserted by the Bank of England and Financial Services Act 2016, s 23(1), (3)(b), (f), as from 6 July 2016.

Sub-s (2): sub-para (a)(i) designated as such, sub-para (a)(ii) (and the preceding word) inserted, and para (c) inserted, by the Bank of England and Financial Services Act 2016, s 23(1), (3)(c), (d), as from 6 July 2016.

Sub-s (8): words in square brackets inserted by the Bank of England and Financial Services Act 2016, s 23(1), (3)(g), as from 6 July 2016.

[7.131]

[63ZB Variation of senior manager's approval on initiative of regulator

(1) The FCA may vary an approval under section 59 given by the FCA or the PRA for the performance of a designated senior management function in relation to the carrying on of a regulated activity by [an] authorised person if the FCA considers that it is desirable to do so in order to advance one or more of its operational objectives.

(2) The PRA may vary an approval under section 59 for the performance of a designated senior management function in relation to the carrying on of a regulated activity by [an] authorised person if—

- (a) either—
  - (i) the PRA gave the approval, or
  - (ii) the FCA gave the approval and the . . . authorised person is a PRA-authorised person, and
- (b) the PRA considers that it is desirable to do so in order to advance any of its objectives.

(3) A regulator may vary an approval by—

- (a) imposing a condition,
- (b) varying a condition,
- (c) removing a condition, . . .
- (d) [where the approval has effect for an unlimited period,] limiting the period for which the approval is to have effect[, or
- (e) where the approval has effect for a limited period, varying that period or removing the limit on the period for which the approval is to have effect].

(4) Before one regulator varies an approval given by the other regulator, it must consult the other regulator.

[(4A) Before one regulator varies an approval which was last varied by the other regulator, it must consult the other regulator.]

(5), (6) . . .]

NOTES

Inserted as noted to s 63ZA at **[7.130]**.

The words in square brackets in sub-s (1) and (2) were substituted, the word omitted from sub-s (2) was repealed, and sub-ss (5) and (6) were repealed, by the Bank of England and Financial Services Act 2016, s 21, Sch 4, paras 1, 10. Note that s 21 and Sch 4 come into force as follows: (i) 13 September 2018 (for the purpose of making rules, giving directions, imposing requirements and making statements of policy by the appropriate regulator for insurers); (ii) 10 December 2018 (for all other purposes for insurers (except in relation to Sch 4, para 11)), and 10 December 2019 (Sch 4, para 11 for insurers); (iii) 18 July 2019 (for the purpose of the making of rules, the giving of directions, the imposition of requirements and the issuing of statements of policy by the FCA for remaining purposes); (iv) 9 August 2019 (for remaining purposes in relation to authorised persons who are not solo-regulated firms); (v) 9 December 2019 (for remaining purposes in relation to solo-regulated firms other than benchmark firms (except as provided for by (vii) below)); (vi) 7 December 2020 (for remaining purposes in relation to benchmark firms (except as provided for by (viii) below)); (vii) 31 March 2021 (in relation to the employee certification provisions for remaining purposes in relation to solo-regulated firms other than benchmark firms); (viii) 7 December 2021 (in relation to the employee certification provisions for remaining purposes in relation to benchmark firms). For transitional provisions in connection with (i)–(iii) above, see the Bank of England and Financial Services Act 2016 (Commencement No 5 and Transitional Provisions) Regulations 2018, SI 2018/990; and for transitional provisions in connection with the other commencement dates, see the Bank of England and Financial Services Act 2016 (Commencement No 6 and Transitional Provisions) Regulations 2019, SI 2019/1136.

The word omitted from para (c) of sub-s (3) was repealed, the words in square brackets in para (d) of sub-s (3) were inserted, para (e) of that subsection (and the preceding word) was inserted, and sub-s (4A) was inserted, by the Bank of England and Financial Services Act 2016, s 23(1), (4), as from 6 July 2016.

[7.132]

[63ZC Exercise of power under section 63ZB: procedure

(1) This section applies to an exercise, by either regulator, of the power to vary an approval under section 63ZB.

(2) A variation takes effect—

- (a) immediately, if the notice given under subsection (4) states that that is the case,
- (b) on such date as is specified in the notice, or
- (c) if no date is specified in the notice, when the matter to which the notice relates is no longer open to review.

(3) A variation may be expressed to take effect immediately (or on a specified date) only if the regulator concerned, having regard to the ground on which it is exercising the power to vary, reasonably considers that it is necessary for the variation to take effect immediately (or on that date).

(4) If either regulator proposes to vary an approval or varies an approval with immediate effect, it must give each of the interested parties written notice.

(5) The notice must—

- (a) give details of the variation,
- (b) state the regulator's reasons for the variation,
- (c) inform the interested parties that each of them may make representations to the regulator within such period as may be specified in the notice (whether or not any of the interested parties has referred the matter to the Tribunal),
- (d) inform the interested parties of when the variation takes effect, and
- (e) inform the interested parties of the right of each of them to refer the matter to the Tribunal.

(6) "The interested parties", in relation to an approval, are—

- (a) the person on whose application it was given ("A"),
- (b) the person in respect of whom it was given ("B"), and
- (c) the person by whom B's services are retained, if not A.

(7) The regulator giving the notice may extend the period allowed under the notice for making representations.

(8) If having considered the representations made by the interested parties, the regulator decides—

- (a) to vary the approval, or
- (b) if the variation has taken effect, not to rescind it,

it must give each of the interested parties written notice.

(9) If having considered the representations made by the interested parties, the regulator decides—
- (a) not to vary the approval,
- (b) to vary the approval in a different way, or
- (c) if the variation has taken effect, to rescind it,

it must give each of the interested parties written notice.

(10) A notice under subsection (8) must inform the interested parties of the right of each of them to refer the matter to the Tribunal.

(11) A notice under subsection (9)(b) must comply with subsection (5).

(12) If a notice informs the interested parties of the right to refer a matter to the Tribunal, it must give an indication of the procedure on such a reference.

(13) For the purposes of subsection (2)(c), whether a matter is open to review is to be determined in accordance with section 391(8).

(14) "Approval" means an approval under section 59.]

NOTES

Inserted as noted to s 63ZA at **[7.130]**.

[7.133]

[63ZD Statement of policy relating to conditional approval and variation

(1) Each regulator must prepare and issue a statement of its policy with respect to—
- (a) its giving of approval under section 59 subject to conditions or for a limited period only, and
- (b) its variation under section 63ZA or 63ZB of an approval given under section 59.

(2) A regulator may at any time alter or replace a statement issued by it under this section.

(3) If a statement issued under this section is altered or replaced by a regulator, the regulator must issue the altered or replacement statement.

(4) A statement issued under this section must be published by the regulator concerned in the way appearing to the regulator to be best calculated to bring it to the attention of the public.

(5) A regulator may charge a reasonable fee for providing a person with a copy of a statement published under this section.

(6) A regulator must, without delay, give the Treasury a copy of any statement which it publishes under this section.]

NOTES

Inserted, together with s 63ZE, by the Financial Services (Banking Reform) Act 2013, s 27, as from 25 July 2014.

[7.134]

[63ZE Statement of policy: procedure

(1) Before issuing a statement of policy under section 63ZD, a regulator ("the issuing regulator") must—
- (a) consult the other regulator, and
- (b) publish a draft of the proposed statement in the way appearing to the issuing regulator to be best calculated to bring it to the attention of the public.

(2) The duty of the FCA to consult the PRA under subsection (1)(a) applies only in so far as the statement of policy applies to persons whose approval under section 59 relates to the performance of a function designated by the FCA as a senior management function under section 59(6A) in relation to the carrying on by PRA-authorised persons of regulated activities.

(3) The draft must be accompanied by notice that representations about the proposal may be made to the issuing regulator within a specified time.

(4) Before issuing the proposed statement, the issuing regulator must have regard to any representations made to it in accordance with subsection (3).

(5) If the issuing regulator issues the proposed statement it must publish an account, in general terms, of—
- (a) the representations made to it in accordance with subsection (3), and
- (b) its response to them.

(6) If the statement differs from the draft published under subsection (1) in a way which is in the opinion of the issuing regulator significant, the issuing regulator—
- (a) must before issuing it carry out any consultation required by subsection (1)(a), and
- (b) must (in addition to complying with subsection (5)) publish details of the difference.

(7) The issuing regulator may charge a reasonable fee for providing a person with a draft published under subsection (1)(b).

(8) This section also applies to a proposal to alter or replace a statement.]

NOTES

Inserted as noted to s 63ZD at **[7.133]**.

[Performance of controlled functions without approval

[7.135]

63A Power to impose penalties

(1) If the [appropriate regulator] is satisfied that—
- (a) a person ("P") has at any time performed a controlled function without approval, and
- (b) at that time P knew, or could reasonably be expected to have known, that P was performing a controlled function without approval,

it may impose a penalty on P of such amount as it considers appropriate.

(2) For the purposes of this section P performs a controlled function without approval at any time if at that time—
- (a) P performs a controlled function under an arrangement entered into by an authorised person ("A"), or by a contractor of A, in relation to the carrying on by A of a regulated activity; and
- [(b) P, when performing the function, is not acting in accordance with an approval given under section 59.]

Part 7 Financial Services Acts

(3) The [appropriate regulator] may not impose a penalty under this section after the end of the limitation period unless, before the end of that period, it has given a warning notice to the person concerned under section 63B(1).

(4) "The limitation period" means the [relevant period] beginning with the first day on which the [appropriate regulator] knew that the person concerned had performed a controlled function without approval.

(5) For this purpose the [appropriate regulator] is to be treated as knowing that a person has performed a controlled function without approval if it has information from which that can reasonably be inferred.

[(5A) The appropriate regulator"—

(a) in relation to a controlled function which is of a description specified in rules made by the FCA, means the FCA, and

(b) in relation to a controlled function which is of a description specified in rules made by the PRA, means the PRA.]

[(5B) The relevant period" is—

(a) in relation to the performance of a controlled function without approval before the day on which this subsection comes into force, the period of 3 years, and

(b) in relation to the performance of a controlled function without approval on or after that day, the period of 6 years.]

(6) Any [other] expression which is used both in this section and section 59 has the same meaning in this section as in that section.]

NOTES

Inserted, together with the preceding heading and ss 63B–63D, by the Financial Services Act 2010, s 11, as from 8 June 2010.

Words "appropriate regulator" in square brackets (in each place that they occur) substituted, and sub-s (5A) and the word in square brackets in sub-s (6) inserted, by the Financial Services Act 2012, s 15, Sch 5, paras 1, 8, as from 1 April 2013.

Sub-s (2)(b) substituted by the Financial Services (Banking Reform) Act 2013, s 35, Sch 3, para 4, as from 7 March 2016.

Words "relevant period" in square brackets in sub-s (4) substituted, and sub-s (5B) inserted, by the Financial Services (Banking Reform) Act 2013, s 28(1)–(3), as from 25 July 2014.

[7.136]

[63B Procedure and right to refer to Tribunal

(1) If [a regulator] proposes to impose a penalty on a person under section 63A, it must give the person a warning notice.

(2) A warning notice must state the amount of the penalty.

(3) If [a regulator] decides to impose a penalty on a person under section 63A, it must give the person a decision notice.

(4) A decision notice must state the amount of the penalty.

(5) If [a regulator] decides to impose a penalty on a person under section 63A, the person may refer the matter to the Tribunal.]

NOTES

Inserted as noted to s 63A at **[7.135]**.

Words in square brackets substituted by the Financial Services Act 2012, s 15, Sch 5, paras 1, 9, as from 1 April 2013.

[7.137]

[63C Statement of policy

(1) [Each regulator] must prepare and issue a statement of its policy with respect to—

(a) the imposition of penalties under section 63A; and

(b) the amount of penalties under that section.

(2) [Each regulator's] policy in determining whether a penalty should be imposed, and what the amount of a penalty should be, must include having regard to—

(a) the conduct of the person on whom the penalty is to be imposed;

(b) the extent to which the person could reasonably be expected to have known that a controlled function was performed without approval;

(c) the length of the period during which the person performed a controlled function without approval; and

(d) whether the person on whom the penalty is to be imposed is an individual.

(3) [Each regulator's] policy in determining whether a penalty should be imposed on a person must also include having regard to the appropriateness of taking action against the person instead of, or in addition to, taking action against an authorised person.

(4) A statement issued under this section must include an indication of the circumstances in which [the regulator that has issued the statement] would expect to be satisfied that a person could reasonably be expected to have known that the person was performing a controlled function without approval.

(5) [A regulator] may at any time alter or replace a statement issued [by it] under this section.

(6) If a statement issued under this section is altered or [replaced by a regulator, the regulator] must issue the altered or replaced statement.

(7) [A regulator] must, without delay, give the Treasury a copy of any statement which it publishes under this section.

(8) A statement issued under this section [by a regulator] must be published by the [regulator] in the way appearing to the [regulator] to be best calculated to bring it to the attention of the public.

(9) The [regulator] may charge a reasonable fee for providing a person with a copy of the statement.

(10) In exercising, or deciding whether to exercise, its power under section 63A in the case of any particular person, [a regulator] must have regard to any statement of policy published [by it] under this section and in force at a time when the person concerned performed a controlled function without approval.]

NOTES

Inserted as noted to s 63A at **[7.135]**.

All amendments to this section were made by the Financial Services Act 2012, s 15, Sch 5, paras 1, 10, as from 24 January 2013 (in so far as relating to the preparation and issue of a statement of policy), and as from 1 April 2013 (otherwise).

[7.138]

[63D Statement of policy: procedure

(1) Before [a regulator issues] a statement under section 63C, the [regulator] must publish a draft of the proposed statement in the way appearing to the [regulator] to be best calculated to bring it to the attention of the public.

(2) The draft must be accompanied by notice that representations about the proposal may be made to the [regulator] within a specified time.

(3) Before issuing the proposed statement, the [regulator] must have regard to any representations made to it in accordance with subsection (2).

(4) If the [regulator] issues the proposed statement it must publish an account, in general terms, of—

(a) the representations made to it in accordance with subsection (2); and

(b) its response to them.

(5) If the statement differs from the draft published under subsection (1) in a way which is, in the opinion of the [regulator], significant, the [regulator] must (in addition to complying with subsection (4)) publish details of the difference.

(6) [A regulator] may charge a reasonable fee for providing a person with a copy of a draft published [by it] under subsection (1).

(7) This section also applies to a proposal to alter or replace a statement.]

NOTES

Inserted as noted to s 63A at **[7.135]**.

All amendments to this section were made by the Financial Services Act 2012, s 15, Sch 5, paras 1, 11, as from 24 January 2013 (in so far as relating to the preparation and issue of a statement of policy), and as from 1 April 2013 (otherwise).

[Certification of employees

[7.139]

63E Certification of employees by . . . authorised persons

(1) [An] authorised person ("A") must take reasonable care to ensure that no employee of A performs a specified function under an arrangement entered into by A in relation to the carrying on by A of a regulated activity, unless the employee has a valid certificate issued by A under section 63F.

(2) "Specified function"—

(a) in relation to the carrying on of a regulated activity by a PRA-authorised person, means a function of a description specified in rules made by the FCA or the PRA, and

(b) in relation to the carrying on of a regulated activity by any other authorised person, means a function of a description specified in rules made by the FCA.

(3) The FCA may specify a description of function under subsection (2)(a) or (b) only if, in relation to the carrying on of a regulated activity by [an] authorised person of a particular description—

(a) the function is not a controlled function in relation to the carrying on of that activity by [an] authorised person of that description, but

(b) the FCA is satisfied that the function is nevertheless a significant-harm function.

(4) The PRA may specify a description of function under subsection (2)(a) only if, in relation to the carrying on of a regulated activity by a . . . PRA-authorised person of a particular description—

(a) the function is not a controlled function in relation to the carrying on of that activity by a . . . PRA-authorised person of that description, but

(b) the PRA is satisfied that the function is nevertheless a significant-harm function.

(5) A function is a "significant-harm function", in relation to the carrying on of a regulated activity by an authorised person, if—

(a) the function will require the person performing it to be involved in one or more aspects of the authorised person's affairs, so far as relating to the activity, and

(b) those aspects involve, or might involve, a risk of significant harm to the authorised person or any of its customers.

(6) Each regulator must—

(a) keep under review the exercise of its power under subsection (2) to specify any significant-harm function as a specified function, and

(b) exercise that power in a way that it considers will minimise the risk of employees of . . . authorised persons performing significant-harm functions which they are not fit and proper persons to perform.

(7) . . .

(8) In this section—

"controlled function" has the meaning given by section 59(3);

["customer"—

(a) in relation to an authorised person, means a person who is using, or who is or may be contemplating using, any of the services provided by the authorised person; and

(b) in relation to an authorised person carrying on a regulated claims management activity, also means (so far as not included in paragraph (a)) a person who has or may have a claim within the meaning of section 419A in respect of which the authorised person is carrying on a regulated claims management activity;]

. . .

(9) In this section any reference to an employee of a person ("A") includes a reference to a person who—

(a) personally provides, or is under an obligation personally to provide, services to A under an arrangement made between A and the person providing the services or another person, and

(b) is subject to (or to the right of) supervision, direction or control by A as to the manner in which those services are provided.

(10) . . .]

NOTES

Inserted, together with the preceding heading and s 63F, by the Financial Services (Banking Reform) Act 2013, s 29, as from 25 July 2014 (for the purpose of the making of rules), and as from 7 March 2017 (otherwise).

The words omitted from the section heading and sub-ss (4) and (6) were repealed, the words in square brackets in sub-ss (1) and (3) were substituted, the definition "relevant PRA-authorised person" omitted from sub-s (8) was repealed, and sub-s (10) was repealed, by the Bank of England and Financial Services Act 2016, s 21, Sch 4, paras 1, 11. Note that s 21 and Sch 4 come into force as follows: (i) 13 September 2018 (for the purpose of making rules, giving directions, imposing requirements and making statements of policy by the appropriate regulator for insurers); (ii) 10 December 2018 (for all other purposes for insurers (except in relation to Sch 4, para 11)), and 10 December 2019 (Sch 4, para 11 for insurers); (iii) 18 July 2019 (for the purpose of the making of rules, the giving of directions, the imposition of requirements and the issuing of statements of policy by the FCA for remaining purposes); (iv) 9 August 2019 (for remaining purposes in relation to authorised persons who are not solo-regulated firms); (v) 9 December 2019 (for remaining purposes in relation to solo-regulated firms other than benchmark firms (except as provided for by (vii) below)); (vi) 7 December 2020 (for remaining purposes in relation to benchmark firms (except as provided for by (viii) below)); (vii) 31 March 2021 (in relation to the employee certification provisions for remaining purposes in relation to solo-regulated firms other than benchmark firms); (viii) 7 December 2021 (in relation to the employee certification provisions for remaining purposes in relation to benchmark firms). For transitional provisions in connection with (i)–(iii) above, see the Bank of England and Financial Services Act 2016 (Commencement No 5 and Transitional Provisions) Regulations 2018, SI 2018/990; and for transitional provisions in connection with the other commencement dates, see the Bank of England and Financial Services Act 2016 (Commencement No 6 and Transitional Provisions) Regulations 2019, SI 2019/1136.

Sub-s (7) was repealed by the Financial Services and Markets Act 2000 (Amendment) (EU Exit) Regulations 2019, SI 2019/632, regs 24, 26, as from IP completion day (as defined in the European Union (Withdrawal Agreement) Act 2020, s 39).

The definition "customer" in sub-s (8) was substituted by the Financial Services and Markets Act 2000 (Claims Management Activity) Order 2018, SI 2018/1253, art 91(1), (4), as from 1 April 2019 (for provision specifying that the 2018 Order also comes into force on 29 November 2018 for the purposes of the FCA and FOS making rules and issuing guidance, and for transitional provisions in relation to carrying on a claims management activity, etc, see arts 1, 39–89 of the 2018 Order.

[7.140]

[63F Issuing of certificates

(1) [An] authorised person may issue a certificate to a person under this section only if the authorised person is satisfied that the person is a fit and proper person to perform the function to which the certificate relates.

(2) In deciding whether the person is a fit and proper person to perform the function, the . . . authorised person must have regard, in particular, to whether the person—

- (a) has obtained a qualification,
- (b) has undergone, or is undergoing, training,
- (c) possesses a level of competence, or
- (d) has the personal characteristics,

required by general rules made by the appropriate regulator in relation to employees performing functions of that kind.

(3) In subsection (2) "the appropriate regulator" means—

- (a) in relation to employees of PRA-authorised persons, the FCA or the PRA, and
- (b) in relation to employees of any other authorised person, the FCA.

(4) A certificate issued by [an] authorised person to a person under this section must—

- (a) state that the authorised person is satisfied that the person is a fit and proper person to perform the function to which the certificate relates, and
- (b) set out the aspects of the affairs of the authorised person in which the person will be involved in performing the function.

(5) A certificate issued under this section is valid for a period of 12 months beginning with the day on which it is issued.

(6) If, after having considered whether a person is a fit and proper person to perform a specified function, [an] authorised person decides not to issue a certificate to the person under this section, the authorised person must give the person a notice in writing stating—

- (a) what steps (if any) the authorised person proposes to take in relation to the person as a result of the decision, and
- (b) the reasons for proposing to take those steps.

(7) [An] authorised person must maintain a record of every employee who has a valid certificate issued by it under this section.

(8) Expressions used in this section and in section 63E have the same meaning in this section as they have in that section.]

NOTES

Inserted by the Financial Services (Banking Reform) Act 2013, s 29, as from 25 July 2014 (for the purpose of the making of rules), and as from 7 March 2016 (otherwise).

Words in square brackets in sub-s (1), (4), (6) and (7) substituted, and word omitted from sub-s (2) repealed, by the Bank of England and Financial Services Act 2016, s 21, Sch 4, paras 1, 12. Note that s 21 and Sch 4 come into force as follows: (i) 13 September 2018 (for the purpose of making rules, giving directions, imposing requirements and making statements of policy by the appropriate regulator for insurers); (ii) 10 December 2018 (for all other purposes for insurers (except in relation to Sch 4, para 11)), and 10 December 2019 (Sch 4, para 11 for insurers); (iii) 18 July 2019 (for the purpose of the making of rules, the giving of directions, the imposition of requirements and the issuing of statements of policy by the FCA for remaining purposes); (iv) 9 August 2019 (for remaining purposes in relation to authorised persons who are not solo-regulated firms); (v) 9 December 2019 (for remaining purposes in relation to solo-regulated firms other than benchmark firms (except as provided for by (vii) below)); (vi) 7 December 2020 (for remaining purposes in relation to benchmark firms (except as provided for by (viii) below)); (vii) 31 March 2021 (in relation to the employee certification provisions for remaining purposes in relation to solo-regulated firms other than benchmark firms); (viii) 7 December 2021 (in relation to the employee certification provisions for remaining purposes in relation to benchmark firms). For transitional provisions in connection with (i)–(iii) above, see the Bank of England and Financial Services Act 2016 (Commencement No 5 and Transitional Provisions) Regulations 2018, SI 2018/990; and for transitional provisions in connection with the other commencement dates, see the Bank of England and Financial Services Act 2016 (Commencement No 6 and Transitional Provisions) Regulations 2019, SI 2019/1136.

64 (*Repealed by the Financial Services (Banking Reform) Act 2013, s 30(1), (2), as from 25 July 2014 (for the purpose of the making of rules), and as from 7 March 2016 (otherwise).*)

[Conduct of approved persons and others

[7.141]

64A Rules of conduct

(1) If it appears to the FCA to be necessary or expedient for the purpose of advancing one or more of its operational objectives, the FCA may make rules about the conduct of the following persons—

(a) persons in relation to whom either regulator has given its approval under section 59;

(b) persons who are employees of [authorised persons];

[(c) persons who are directors of authorised persons.]

(2) If it appears to the PRA to be necessary or expedient for the purpose of advancing any of its objectives, the PRA may make rules about the conduct of the following persons—

(a) persons in relation to whom it has given its approval under section 59;

(b) persons in relation to whom the FCA has given its approval under section 59 in respect of the performance by them of a relevant senior management function in relation to the carrying on by a PRA-authorised person of a regulated activity;

(c) persons who are employees of . . . PRA-authorised persons;

[(d) persons who are directors of PRA-authorised persons.]

(3) In subsection (2)—

. . .

"relevant senior management function" means a function which the PRA is satisfied is a senior management function as defined in section 59ZA (whether or not the function has been designated as such by the FCA).

(4) Rules made under this section must relate to the conduct of persons in relation to the performance by them of qualifying functions.

(5) In subsection (4) "qualifying function", in relation to a person, means a function relating to the carrying on of activities (whether or not regulated activities) by—

(a) in the case of an approved person, the person on whose application approval was given, . . .

[(ab) in the case of a person who is a director of an authorised person but is not an approved person, that authorised person, and]

(b) in any other case, the person's employer.

(6) In this section any reference to an employee of a person ("P") includes a reference to a person who—

(a) personally provides, or is under an obligation personally to provide, services to P under an arrangement made between P and the person providing the services or another person, and

(b) is subject to (or to the right of) supervision, direction or control by P as to the manner in which those services are provided,

and "employer" is to be read accordingly.

[(7) In this section "director", in relation to an authorised person, means a member of the board of directors, or if there is no such board, the equivalent body responsible for the management of the authorised person concerned.]]

NOTES

Inserted, together with the preceding heading and s 64B, by the Financial Services (Banking Reform) Act 2013, s 30(3), as from 25 July 2014 (for the purpose of the making of rules), and as from 7 March 2016 (otherwise).

The words in square brackets in sub-s (1)(b) were substituted, and the word omitted from sub-s (2)(c) and the definition "relevant PRA-authorised person" omitted from sub-s (3) were repealed, by the Bank of England and Financial Services Act 2016, s 21, Sch 4, paras 1, 13. Note that s 21 and Sch 4 come into force as follows: (i) 13 September 2018 (for the purpose of making rules, giving directions, imposing requirements and making statements of policy by the appropriate regulator for insurers); (ii) 10 December 2018 (for all other purposes for insurers (except in relation to Sch 4, para 11)), and 10 December 2019 (Sch 4, para 11 for insurers); (iii) 18 July 2019 (for the purpose of the making of rules, the giving of directions, the imposition of requirements and the issuing of statements of policy by the FCA for remaining purposes); (iv) 9 August 2019 (for remaining purposes in relation to authorised persons who are not solo-regulated firms); (v) 9 December 2019 (for remaining purposes in relation to solo-regulated firms other than benchmark firms (except as provided for by (vii) below)); (vi) 7 December 2020 (for remaining purposes in relation to benchmark firms (except as provided for by (viii) below)); (vii) 31 March 2021 (in relation to the employee certification provisions for remaining purposes in relation to solo-regulated firms other than benchmark firms); (viii) 7 December 2021 (in relation to the employee certification provisions for remaining purposes in relation to benchmark firms). For transitional provisions in connection with (i)–(iii) above, see the Bank of England and Financial Services Act 2016 (Commencement No 5 and Transitional Provisions) Regulations 2018, SI 2018/990; and for transitional provisions in connection with the other commencement dates, see the Bank of England and Financial Services Act 2016 (Commencement No 6 and Transitional Provisions) Regulations 2019, SI 2019/1136.

Sub-ss (1)(c), (2)(d), (5)(ab) were inserted, the word omitted from sub-s (5)(a) was repealed, and sub-s (7) was added, by the Bank of England and Financial Services Act 2016, s 24(1), (2), as from 6 July 2016.

[7.142]

[64B Rules of conduct: responsibilities of . . . authorised persons

(1) This section applies where a regulator makes rules under section 64A ("conduct rules").

(2) Every . . . authorised person must—

(a) notify all relevant persons of the conduct rules that apply in relation to them, and

(b) take all reasonable steps to secure that those persons understand how those rules apply in relation to them.

(3) The steps which [an] authorised person must take to comply with subsection (2)(b) include, in particular, the provision of suitable training.

(4) In this section "relevant person", in relation to an authorised person, means—

(a) any person in relation to whom an approval is given under section 59 on the application of the authorised person, . . .
(b) any employee of the authorised person[, and
(c) any person who is a director of the authorised person].

(5) . . .

(6) In this section "employee", in relation to an authorised person, has the same meaning as in section 64A.

[(6A) In this section "director", in relation to an authorised person, has the same meaning as in section 64A.]

(7) . . .]

NOTES

Inserted as noted to s 64A at **[7.141]**.

The words omitted from the section heading and sub-s (2) were repealed, the word in square brackets in sub-s (3) was substituted, and sub-s (7) was repealed, by the Bank of England and Financial Services Act 2016, s 21, Sch 4, paras 1, 14. Note that s 21 and Sch 4 come into force as follows: (i) 13 September 2018 (for the purpose of making rules, giving directions, imposing requirements and making statements of policy by the appropriate regulator for insurers); (ii) 10 December 2018 (for all other purposes for insurers (except in relation to Sch 4, para 11)), and 10 December 2019 (Sch 4, para 11 for insurers); (iii) 18 July 2019 (for the purpose of the making of rules, the giving of directions, the imposition of requirements and the issuing of statements of policy by the FCA for remaining purposes); (iv) 9 August 2019 (for remaining purposes in relation to authorised persons who are not solo-regulated firms); (v) 9 December 2019 (for remaining purposes in relation to solo-regulated firms other than benchmark firms (except as provided for by (vii) below)); (vi) 7 December 2020 (for remaining purposes in relation to benchmark firms (except as provided for by (viii) below)); (vii) 31 March 2021 (in relation to the employee certification provisions for remaining purposes in relation to solo-regulated firms other than benchmark firms); (viii) 7 December 2021 (in relation to the employee certification provisions for remaining purposes in relation to benchmark firms). For transitional provisions in connection with (i)–(iii) above, see the Bank of England and Financial Services Act 2016 (Commencement No 5 and Transitional Provisions) Regulations 2018, SI 2018/990; and for transitional provisions in connection with the other commencement dates, see the Bank of England and Financial Services Act 2016 (Commencement No 6 and Transitional Provisions) Regulations 2019, SI 2019/1136.

The word omitted from sub-s (4)(a) was repealed, sub-s (4)(c) (and the preceding word) was inserted, sub-s (5) was repealed (without ever coming into force), and sub-s (6A) was inserted, by the Bank of England and Financial Services Act 2016, s 24(1), (3), as from 6 July 2016.

[7.143]

[64C Requirement for . . . authorised persons to notify regulator of disciplinary action

(1) If—

(a) [an] authorised person takes disciplinary action in relation to a relevant person, and
(b) the reason, or one of the reasons, for taking that action is a reason specified in rules made by the appropriate regulator for the purposes of this section,

the . . . authorised person must notify that regulator of that fact.

(2) "Disciplinary action", in relation to a person, means any of the following—

(a) the issuing of a formal written warning;
(b) the suspension or dismissal of the person;
(c) the reduction or recovery of any of the person's remuneration.

(3) "The appropriate regulator" means—

(a) in relation to . . . PRA-authorised persons, the FCA or the PRA;
(b) in relation to any other . . . authorised persons, the FCA.

(4) "Relevant person" has the same meaning as in section 64B.

(5) . . .]

NOTES

Inserted by the Financial Services (Banking Reform) Act 2013, s 31, as from 25 July 2014 (for the purpose of the making of rules), and as from 7 March 2016 (otherwise).

Words in square brackets in sub-s (1) substituted, and all words omitted repealed, by the Bank of England and Financial Services Act 2016, s 21, Sch 4, paras 1, 15. Note that s 21 and Sch 4 come into force as follows: (i) 13 September 2018 (for the purpose of making rules, giving directions, imposing requirements and making statements of policy by the appropriate regulator for insurers); (ii) 10 December 2018 (for all other purposes for insurers (except in relation to Sch 4, para 11)), and 10 December 2019 (Sch 4, para 11 for insurers); (iii) 18 July 2019 (for the purpose of the making of rules, the giving of directions, the imposition of requirements and the issuing of statements of policy by the FCA for remaining purposes); (iv) 9 August 2019 (for remaining purposes in relation to authorised persons who are not solo-regulated firms); (v) 9 December 2019 (for remaining purposes in relation to solo-regulated firms other than benchmark firms (except as provided for by (vii) below)); (vi) 7 December 2020 (for remaining purposes in relation to benchmark firms (except as provided for by (viii) below)); (vii) 31 March 2021 (in relation to the employee certification provisions for remaining purposes in relation to solo-regulated firms other than benchmark firms); (viii) 7 December 2021 (in relation to the employee certification provisions for remaining purposes in relation to benchmark firms). For transitional provisions in connection with (i)–(iii) above, see the Bank of England and Financial Services Act 2016 (Commencement No 5 and Transitional Provisions) Regulations 2018, SI 2018/990; and for transitional provisions in connection with the other commencement dates, see the Bank of England and Financial Services Act 2016 (Commencement No 6 and Transitional Provisions) Regulations 2019, SI 2019/1136.

65 (*Repealed by the Financial Services (Banking Reform) Act 2013, s 30(1), (2), as from 25 July 2014 (for the purpose of the making of rules), and as from 7 March 2016 (otherwise).*)

[7.144]

66 Disciplinary powers

(1) [A regulator] may take action against a person under this section [(whether or not it has given its approval in relation to the person)] if—

(a) it appears to the [regulator] that he is guilty of misconduct; and
(b) the [regulator] is satisfied that it is appropriate in all the circumstances to take action against him.

[(1A) For provision about when a person is guilty of misconduct for the purposes of action by a regulator—

(a) see section 66A, in the case of action by the FCA, and

(b) see section 66B, in the case of action by the PRA.]

[(2), (2A) . . .]

(3) If the [regulator] is entitled to take action under this section against a person, [it may do one or more of the following]—

(a) impose a penalty on him of such amount as it considers appropriate;

[(aa) suspend, for such period as it considers appropriate, any approval of the performance by him of any function to which the approval relates;]

[(ab) impose, for such period as it considers appropriate, any conditions in relation to any such approval which it considers appropriate;

(ac) limit the period for which any such approval is to have effect;]

(b) publish a statement of his misconduct.

[(3A) The period for which a suspension or [condition] is to have effect may not exceed two years.

(3B) A suspension[, condition or limitation] may have effect in relation to part of a function.

(3C) A [condition] may, in particular, be imposed so as to require any person to take, or refrain from taking, specified action.

(3D) [The regulator taking action under this section] may—

(a) withdraw a suspension[, condition or limitation]; . . .

(b) vary a suspension or [condition] so as to reduce the period for which it has effect or otherwise to limit its effect;

[(c) vary a limitation so as to increase the period for which the approval is to have effect].]

(4) [A regulator] may not take action under this section after the end of the [relev . . . ant period] beginning with the first day on which [the regulator] knew of the misconduct, unless proceedings in respect of it against the person concerned were begun before the end of that period.

(5) For the purposes of subsection (4)—

(a) [a regulator] is to be treated as knowing of misconduct if it has information from which the misconduct can reasonably be inferred; and

(b) proceedings against a person in respect of misconduct are to be treated as begun when a warning notice is given to him under section 67(1).

[(5ZA) The relevant period" is—

(a) in relation to misconduct which occurs before the day on which this subsection comes into force, the period of 3 years, and

(b) in relation to misconduct which occurs on or after that day, the period of 6 years.]

[(5A) Approval" means an approval given under section 59.]

(6), (7) . . .

[(8) In relation to any time while a suspension is in force under subsection (3)(aa) in relation to part of a function, any reference in section 59 or 63A to the performance of a function includes the performance of part of a function.

(9) If at any time a [condition] imposed under subsection (3)(ab) is contravened, the approval in relation to the person concerned is to be treated for the purposes of sections 59 and 63A as if it had been withdrawn at that time.]

NOTES

Sub-s (1): words in square brackets substituted or inserted by the Financial Services Act 2012, s 15, Sch 5, paras 1, 14(1), (2), as from 1 April 2013.

Sub-s (1A): inserted by the Financial Services (Banking Reform) Act 2013, s 32(1)(a), as from 7 March 2016.

Sub-ss (2), (2A): substituted (for the original sub-s (2)) by the Financial Services Act 2012, s 15, Sch 5, paras 1, 14(1), (3), as from 24 January 2013 (for the purposes of making orders), and as from 1 April 2013 (otherwise). Subsequently repealed by the Financial Services (Banking Reform) Act 2013, s 32(1)(b), as from 7 March 2016.

Sub-s (3) is amended as follows:

Word in first pair of square brackets substituted by the Financial Services Act 2012, s 15, Sch 5, paras 1, 14(1), (4), as from 1 April 2013.

Words in second pair of square brackets substituted, and paras (aa), (ab) inserted, by the Financial Services Act 2010, s 12(1), (2), as from 8 June 2010.

Paras (ab), (ac) substituted (for para (ab) as inserted as noted above) by the Financial Services (Banking Reform) Act 2013, s 35, Sch 3, para 5(1), (2), as from 7 March 2016.

Sub-ss (3A)–(3D) were inserted by the Financial Services Act 2010, ss 12(1), (3), as from 8 June 2010, and have subsequently been amended as follows:

Words in square brackets in sub-ss (3A)–(3C) substituted by the Financial Services (Banking Reform) Act 2013, s 35, Sch 3, para 5(1), (3)–(5), as from 7 March 2016.

Words in first pair of square brackets in sub-s (3D) substituted by the Financial Services Act 2012, s 15, Sch 5, paras 1, 14(1), (5), as from 1 April 2013.

Other words in square brackets in sub-s (3D) substituted or inserted, and word omitted repealed, by the Financial Services (Banking Reform) Act 2013, s 35, Sch 3, para 5(1), (6), as from 7 March 2016.

Sub-s (4): words in first and third pairs of square brackets substituted by the Financial Services Act 2012, s 15, Sch 5, paras 1, 14(1), (6), as from 1 April 2013. Words in second pair of square brackets substituted by the Financial Services (Banking Reform) Act 2013, s 28(4), (5), as from 25 July 2014.

Sub-s (5): words in square brackets substituted by the Financial Services Act 2012, s 15, Sch 5, paras 1, 14(1), (7), as from 1 April 2013.

Sub-s (5ZA): inserted by the Financial Services (Banking Reform) Act 2013, s 28(4), (6), as from 25 July 2014.

Sub-s (5A): inserted by the Financial Services Act 2010, s 24(1), (2), Sch 2, Pt 1, paras 1, 8(1), (2), as from 8 June 2010.

Sub-ss (6), (7): repealed by the Financial Services (Banking Reform) Act 2013, s 32(1)(b), as from 7 March 2016.

Sub-ss (8), (9): added by the Financial Services Act 2010, s 24(1), (2), Sch 2, Pt 1, paras 1, 8(1), (4), as from 8 June 2010. Word in square brackets in sub-s (9) substituted by the Financial Services (Banking Reform) Act 2013, s 35, Sch 3, para 5(1), (7), as from 7 March 2016.

Orders: the Financial Services and Markets Act 2000 (Qualifying Provisions) Order 2013, SI 2013/419; the Financial Services and Markets Act 2000 (Qualifying Provisions) (No 2) Order 2013, SI 2013/3116.

[7.145]

[66A Misconduct: action by the FCA

(1) For the purposes of action by the FCA under section 66, a person is guilty of misconduct if any of conditions A to C is met in relation to the person.

(2) Condition A is that—

(a) the person has at any time failed to comply with rules made by the FCA under section 64A, and

(b) at that time the person was—

(i) an approved person, . . .

(ii) an employee of [an] authorised person[, or

(iii) a director of an authorised person].

(3) Condition B is that—

(a) the person has at any time been knowingly concerned in a contravention of a relevant requirement by an authorised person, and

(b) at that time the person was—

(i) an approved person in relation to the authorised person, . . .

(ii) . . . an employee of the authorised person[, or

(iii) a director of the authorised person].

(4) In this section "relevant requirement" means a requirement—

(a) imposed by or under this Act, . . .

[(aa) imposed by the Alternative Investment Fund Managers Regulations 2013, . . . ;]

[(ab) imposed by the Undertakings for Collective Investment in Transferable Securities Regulations 2011, or]

(b) imposed by any [qualifying provision] specified, or of a description specified, for the purposes of this subsection by the Treasury by order.

(5) Condition C is that—

(a) the person has at any time been a senior manager in relation to [an] authorised person,

(b) there has at that time been (or continued to be) a contravention of a relevant requirement by the authorised person, . . .

(c) the senior manager was at that time responsible for the management of any of the authorised person's activities in relation to which the contravention occurred[, and

(d) the senior manager did not take such steps as a person in the senior manager's position could reasonably be expected to take to avoid the contravention occurring (or continuing)].

(6) . . .

(7) For the purposes of subsection (5)—

"senior manager", in relation to [an] authorised person, means a person who has approval under section 59 to perform a designated senior management function in relation to the carrying on by the authorised person of a regulated activity;

. . .

(8) In this section—

"approved person"—

(a) means a person in relation to whom an approval is given under section 59, and

(b) in relation to an authorised person, means a person in relation to whom such approval is given on the application of the authorised person;

["director", in relation to an authorised person, has the same meaning as in section 64A;]

"employee", in relation to a person, has the same meaning as in section 64A.

(9) . . .]

NOTES

Inserted, together with s 66B, by the Financial Services (Banking Reform) Act 2013, s 32(2), as from 7 March 2016 (sub-s (1) in so far as it applies to Conditions A and B, and sub-ss (2)–(4), (8), (9)); 10 May 2016 (otherwise).

Sub-s (2): the word omitted from sub-para (b)(i) was repealed, and sub-para (b)(iii) (and the preceding word) was inserted, by the Bank of England and Financial Services Act 2016, s 25(1), (2)(a), (b), as from 6 July 2016. The word "an" in square brackets in sub-para (b)(ii) was substituted by the Bank of England and Financial Services Act 2016, s 21, Sch 4, paras 1, 16(1), (2). Note that s 21 and Sch 4 come into force as follows: (i) 13 September 2018 (for the purpose of making rules, giving directions, imposing requirements and making statements of policy by the appropriate regulator for insurers); (ii) 10 December 2018 (for all other purposes for insurers (except in relation to Sch 4, para 11)), and 10 December 2019 (Sch 4, para 11 for insurers); (iii) 18 July 2019 (for the purpose of the making of rules, the giving of directions, the imposition of requirements and the issuing of statements of policy by the FCA for remaining purposes); (iv) 9 August 2019 (for remaining purposes in relation to authorised persons who are not solo-regulated firms); (v) 9 December 2019 (for remaining purposes in relation to solo-regulated firms other than benchmark firms (except as provided for by (vii) below)); (vi) 7 December 2020 (for remaining purposes in relation to benchmark firms (except as provided for by (viii) below)); (vii) 31 March 2021 (in relation to the employee certification provisions for remaining purposes in relation to solo-regulated firms other than benchmark firms); (viii) 7 December 2021 (in relation to the employee certification provisions for remaining purposes in relation to benchmark firms). For transitional provisions in connection with (i)–(iii) above, see the Bank of England and Financial Services Act 2016 (Commencement No 5 and Transitional Provisions) Regulations 2018, SI 2018/990; and for transitional provisions in connection with the other commencement dates, see the Bank of England and Financial Services Act 2016 (Commencement No 6 and Transitional Provisions) Regulations 2019, SI 2019/1136.

Sub-s (3): the word omitted from sub-para (b)(i) was repealed, and sub-para (b)(iii) (and the preceding word) was inserted, by the Bank of England and Financial Services Act 2016, s 25(1), (2)(c), (d), as from 6 July 2016. The words omitted from sub-para (b)(ii) were repealed by the Bank of England and Financial Services Act 2016, s 21, Sch 4, paras 1, 16(1), (3) (as to the commencement of s 21 and Sch 4, and for transitional provisions etc, see the note relating to the 2016 Act above).

Sub-s (4): word omitted from para (a) repealed, and para (aa) inserted, by the Financial Services and Markets Act 2000 (Misconduct and Appropriate Regulator) Order 2015, SI 2015/1864, art 2, as from 7 March 2016. Word omitted from para (aa) repealed, and para (ab) inserted, by the Undertakings for Collective Investment in Transferable Securities Regulations 2016, SI 2016/225, reg 2(1), (3), as from 18 March 2016. Words in square brackets in para (b) substituted by the Financial Services and Markets Act 2000 (Amendment) (EU Exit) Regulations 2019, SI 2019/632, regs 24, 27, as from IP completion day (as defined in the European Union (Withdrawal Agreement) Act 2020, s 39) (for transitional provisions see SI 2019/710, reg 37 at **[12.110]**).

Sub-s (5): word in square brackets in para (a) substituted by the Bank of England and Financial Services Act 2016, s 21, Sch 4, paras 1, 16(1), (4) (as to the commencement of s 21 and Sch 4, and for transitional provisions etc, see the note relating to the 2016 Act above). The word omitted from para (b) was repealed, and para (d) (and the preceding word) was inserted, by the Bank of England and Financial Services Act 2016, s 25(1), (2)(e), (f), as from 10 May 2016.

Sub-s (6): repealed by the Bank of England and Financial Services Act 2016, s 25(1), (2)(g), as from 10 May 2016.

Sub-s (7): the word in square brackets in the definition "senior manager" was substituted, and the definition "designated senior management function" (omitted) was repealed, by the Bank of England and Financial Services Act 2016, s 21, Sch 4, paras 1, 16(1), (5) (as to the commencement of s 21 and Sch 4, and for transitional provisions etc, see the note relating to the 2016 Act above).

Sub-s (8): definition "director" in square brackets inserted by the Bank of England and Financial Services Act 2016, s 25(1), (2)(h), as from 6 July 2016.

Sub-s (9): repealed by the Bank of England and Financial Services Act 2016, s 21, Sch 4, paras 1, 16(1), (6) (as to the commencement of s 21 and Sch 4, and for transitional provisions etc, see the note relating to it above).

Regulations: the Alternative Investment Fund Managers (Amendment) Regulations 2018, SI 2018/134; the Insurance Distribution (Regulated Activities and Miscellaneous Amendments) Order 2018, SI 2018/546.

[7.146]

[66B Misconduct: action by the PRA

(1) For the purposes of action by the PRA under section 66, a person is guilty of misconduct if any of conditions A to C is met in relation to the person.

(2) Condition A is that—

(a) the person has at any time failed to comply with rules made by the PRA under section 64A, and

(b) at that time the person was—

(i) an approved person, . . .

(ii) an employee of a . . . PRA-authorised person[, or

(iii) a director of a PRA-authorised person].

(3) Condition B is that—

(a) the person has at any time been knowingly concerned in a contravention of a relevant requirement by a PRA-authorised person, and

(b) at that time the person was—

(i) an approved person in respect of the performance of a relevant senior management function in relation to the carrying on by the PRA-authorised person of a regulated activity, . . .

[(ii) an employee of the PRA-authorised person][, or

(iii) a director of the PRA-authorised person].

(4) In this section "relevant requirement" means a requirement—

(a) imposed by or under this Act, or

(b) imposed by any [qualifying provision] specified, or of a description specified, for the purposes of this subsection by the Treasury by order.

(5) Condition C is that—

(a) the person has at any time been a senior manager in relation to a . . . PRA-authorised person,

(b) there has at that time been (or continued to be) a contravention of a relevant requirement by the authorised person, . . .

(c) the senior manager was at that time responsible for the management of any of the authorised person's activities in relation to which the contravention occurred [, and

(d) the senior manager did not take such steps as a person in the senior manager's position could reasonably be expected to take to avoid the contravention occurring (or continuing)].

(6) . . .

(7) For the purposes of subsection (5)—

"senior manager", in relation to a . . . PRA-authorised person, means a person who has approval under section 59 to perform a designated senior management function in relation to the carrying on by the authorised person of a regulated activity;

. . .

(8) In this section—

"approved person"—

(a) means a person in relation to whom—

(i) the PRA has given its approval under section 59, or

(ii) the FCA has given its approval under section 59 in respect of the performance by the person of a relevant senior management function in relation to the carrying on by a PRA-authorised person of a regulated activity, and

(b) in relation to an authorised person, means a person in relation to whom approval under section 59 is given on the application of the authorised person;

["director", in relation to an authorised person, has the same meaning as in section 64A;]

"employee", in relation to a person, has the same meaning as in section 64A;

. . .

"relevant senior management function" means a function which the PRA is satisfied is a senior management function as defined in section 59ZA (whether or not the function has been designated as such by the FCA).

(9) . . .]

NOTES

Inserted, together with s 66A, by the Financial Services (Banking Reform) Act 2013, s 32(2), as from 7 March 2016 (sub-s (1) in so far as it applies to Conditions A and B, and sub-ss (2)–(4), (8), (9)); 10 May 2016 (otherwise).

Part 7 Financial Services Acts

Sub-s (2): the word omitted from sub-para (b)(i) was repealed, and sub-para (b)(iii) (and the preceding word) was inserted, by the Bank of England and Financial Services Act 2016, s 25(1), (3)(a), (b), as from 6 July 2016. The word omitted from sub-para (b)(ii) was repealed by the Bank of England and Financial Services Act 2016, s 21, Sch 4, paras 1, 17(1), (2). Note that s 21 and Sch 4 come into force as follows: (i) 13 September 2018 (for the purpose of making rules, giving directions, imposing requirements and making statements of policy by the appropriate regulator for insurers); (ii) 10 December 2018 (for all other purposes for insurers (except in relation to Sch 4, para 11)), and 10 December 2019 (Sch 4, para 11 for insurers); (iii) 18 July 2019 (for the purpose of the making of rules, the giving of directions, the imposition of requirements and the issuing of statements of policy by the FCA for remaining purposes); (iv) 9 August 2019 (for remaining purposes in relation to authorised persons who are not solo-regulated firms); (v) 9 December 2019 (for remaining purposes in relation to solo-regulated firms other than benchmark firms (except as provided for by (vii) below)); (vi) 7 December 2020 (for remaining purposes in relation to benchmark firms (except as provided for by (viii) below)); (vii) 31 March 2021 (in relation to the employee certification provisions for remaining purposes in relation to solo-regulated firms other than benchmark firms); (viii) 7 December 2021 (in relation to the employee certification provisions for remaining purposes in relation to benchmark firms). For transitional provisions in connection with (i)–(iii) above, see the Bank of England and Financial Services Act 2016 (Commencement No 5 and Transitional Provisions) Regulations 2018, SI 2018/990; and for transitional provisions in connection with the other commencement dates, see the Bank of England and Financial Services Act 2016 (Commencement No 6 and Transitional Provisions) Regulations 2019, SI 2019/1136.

Sub-s (3): the word omitted from sub-para (b)(i) was repealed, and sub-para (b)(iii) (and the preceding word) was inserted, by the Bank of England and Financial Services Act 2016, s 25(1), (3)(c), (d), as from 6 July 2016. Sub-para (b)(ii) was substituted by the Bank of England and Financial Services Act 2016, s 21, Sch 4, paras 1, 17(1), (3) (as to the commencement of s 21 and Sch 4, and for transitional provisions etc, see the note relating to the 2016 Act above).

Sub-s (4): words in square brackets in para (b) substituted by the Financial Services and Markets Act 2000 (Amendment) (EU Exit) Regulations 2019, SI 2019/632, regs 24, 28, as from IP completion day (as defined in the European Union (Withdrawal Agreement) Act 2020, s 39) (for transitional provisions see SI 2019/710, reg 37 at **[12.110]**).

Sub-s (5): the word omitted from para (a) was repealed by the Bank of England and Financial Services Act 2016, s 21, Sch 4, paras 1, 17(1), (4) (as to the commencement of s 21 and Sch 4, and for transitional provisions etc, see the note relating to the 2016 Act above). The word omitted from para (b) was repealed, and para (d) (and the preceding word) was inserted, by the Bank of England and Financial Services Act 2016, s 25(1), (3)(e), (f), as from 10 May 2016.

Sub-s (6): repealed by the Bank of England and Financial Services Act 2016, s 25(1), (3)(g), as from 10 May 2016.

Sub-s (7): the word omitted from the definition "senior manager" was repealed, and the definition "designated senior management function" (omitted) was repealed, by the Bank of England and Financial Services Act 2016, s 21, Sch 4, paras 1, 17(1), (5) (as to the commencement of s 21 and Sch 4, and for transitional provisions etc, see the note relating to the 2016 Act above).

Sub-s (8): definition "director" in square brackets inserted by the Bank of England and Financial Services Act 2016, s 25(1), (3)(h), as from 6 July 2016. Definition "relevant PRA-authorised person" (omitted) repealed by the Bank of England and Financial Services Act 2016, s 21, Sch 4, paras 1, 17(1), (6) (as to the commencement of s 21 and Sch 4, and for transitional provisions etc, see the note relating to the 2016 Act above).

Sub-s (9): repealed by the Bank of England and Financial Services Act 2016, s 21, Sch 4, paras 1, 17(1), (7) (as to the commencement of s 21 and Sch 4, and for transitional provisions etc, see the note relating to the 2016 Act above).

Orders: the Financial Services and Markets Act 2000 (Qualifying EU Provisions) (Amendment) Order 2016, SI 2016/936.

[7.147]

67 Disciplinary measures: procedure and right to refer to Tribunal

(1) If [a regulator] proposes to take action against a person under section 66, it must give him a warning notice[; and if it proposes to take action under subsection (3)(aa)[, (ab) or (ac)] of that section, it must also give each of the other interested parties a warning notice].

(2) A warning notice about a proposal to impose a penalty must state the amount of the penalty.

[(2A) A warning notice about a proposal—

(a) to suspend an approval, or

(b) to impose a [condition] in relation to the performance of a function,

must state the period for which the suspension or [condition] is to have effect.]

[(2B) A warning notice about a proposal to limit the period for which an approval is to have effect must state the length of that period.]

(3) A warning notice about a proposal to publish a statement must set out the terms of the statement.

(4) If [a regulator] decides to take action against a person under section 66, it must give him a decision notice[; and if it decides to take action under subsection (3)(aa)[, (ab) or (ac)] of that section, it must also give each of the other interested parties a decision notice].

(5) A decision notice about the imposition of a penalty must state the amount of the penalty.

[(5A) A decision notice about—

(a) the suspension of an approval, or

(b) the imposition of a [condition] in relation to the performance of a function,

must state the period for which the suspension or [condition] is to have effect.]

[(5B) A decision notice about limiting the period for which an approval is to have effect must state the length of that period.]

(6) A decision notice about the publication of a statement must set out the terms of the statement.

(7) If [a regulator] decides to take action against a person under section 66, he may refer the matter to the Tribunal[; and if [the regulator] decides to take action under section 66(3)(aa)[, (ab) or (ac)], each of the other interested parties may also refer the matter to the Tribunal].

[(8) Approval" means an approval given under section 59.

(9) "Other interested parties", in relation to [a person ("A") in relation to whom approval has been given], are—

(a) the person on whose application the approval was given ("B"); and

(b) the person by whom A's services are retained, if not B.

. . .]

NOTES

Sub-ss (1), (4): words "a regulator" in square brackets substituted by the Financial Services Act 2012, s 15, Sch 5, paras 1, 15(1), (2), as from 1 April 2013. Words in second (outer) pair of square brackets added by the Financial Services Act 2010, s 24(1), (2), Sch 2, Pt 1, paras 1, 9(1), (2), (4), as from 8 June 2010. Words ", (ab) or (ac)" in third (inner) pair of square brackets substituted by the Financial Services (Banking Reform) Act 2013, s 35, Sch 3, para 6(1), (2), (5), as from 7 March 2016.

Sub-ss (2A), (5A): inserted by the Financial Services Act 2010, s 24(1), (2), Sch 2, Pt 1, paras 1, 9(1), (3), (5), as from 8 June 2010. Words in square brackets substituted by the Financial Services (Banking Reform) Act 2013, s 35, Sch 3, para 6(1), (3), (6), as from 7 March 2016.

Sub-ss (2B), (5B): inserted by the Financial Services (Banking Reform) Act 2013, s 35, Sch 3, para 6(1), (4), (7), as from 7 March 2016.

Sub-s (7): words in first pair of square brackets and in third (inner) pair of square brackets substituted by the Financial Services Act 2012, s 15, Sch 5, paras 1, 15(1), (3), as from 1 April 2013. Words in second (outer) pair of square brackets added by the Financial Services Act 2010, s 24(1), (2), Sch 2, Pt 1, paras 1, 9(1), (6), as from 8 June 2010. Words ", (ab) or (ac)" in square brackets substituted by the Financial Services (Banking Reform) Act 2013, s 35, Sch 3, para 6(1), (8), as from 7 March 2016.

Sub-ss (8), (9): added by the Financial Services Act 2010, s 24(1), (2), Sch 2, Pt 1, paras 1, 9(1), (7), as from 8 June 2010. Words in square brackets in sub-s (9) substituted, and words omitted repealed, by the Financial Services Act 2012, s 15, Sch 5, paras 1, 15(1), (4), as from 1 April 2013.

[7.148]

68 Publication

After a statement under section 66 is published, [the regulator publishing it] must send a copy of it to the person concerned and to any person to whom a copy of the decision notice was given.

NOTES

Words in square brackets substituted by the Financial Services Act 2012, s 15, Sch 5, paras 1, 16, as from 1 April 2013.

[7.149]

69 Statement of policy

(1) [Each regulator must] prepare and issue a statement of its policy with respect to—

[(a) the imposition of penalties, suspensions[, conditions or limitations] under section 66;

(b) the amount of penalties under that section; . . .

(c) the period for which suspensions or [conditions] under that section are to have effect][; and

(d) the period for which approvals under section 59 are to have effect as a result of a limitation under section 66].

(2) [A regulator's] policy in determining what the amount of a penalty should be[, or what the period for which a suspension or restriction is to have effect should be,] must include having regard to—

(a) the seriousness of the misconduct in question in relation to the nature of the principle or requirement concerned;

(b) the extent to which that misconduct was deliberate or reckless; and

(c) whether [the person against whom action is to be taken] is an individual.

(3) [A regulator] may at any time alter or replace a statement issued [by it] under this section.

(4) If a statement issued under this section is altered or [replaced by a regulator, the regulator] must issue the altered or replacement statement.

(5) [A regulator] must, without delay, give the Treasury a copy of any statement which it publishes under this section.

(6) A statement issued under this section [by a regulator] must be published by [the regulator] in the way appearing to [the regulator] to be best calculated to bring it to the attention of the public.

(7) The [regulator] may charge a reasonable fee for providing a person with a copy of the statement.

(8) In exercising, or deciding whether to exercise, its power under section 66 in the case of any particular misconduct, [a regulator] must have regard to any statement of policy published [by it] under this section and in force at the time when the misconduct in question occurred.

NOTES

Sub-s (1)(a)–(c) were substituted (for the original sub-s (1)(a), (b)), the words ", or what the period for which a suspension or restriction is to have effect should be," in square brackets in sub-s (2) were inserted, and the words "the person against whom action is to be taken" in that subsection were substituted, by the Financial Services Act 2010, s 24(1), (2), Sch 2, Pt 1, paras 1, 10, as from 8 June 2010.

The words ", conditions or limitations" in square brackets in sub-s (1)(a) were substituted, the word omitted from sub-s (1)(b) was repealed, the word "conditions" in square brackets sub-s (1)(c) was substituted, and sub-s (1)(d) (and the preceding word) was inserted, by the Financial Services (Banking Reform) Act 2013, s 35, Sch 3, para 7, as from 25 July 2014.

All other words in square brackets in this section were substituted or inserted by the Financial Services Act 2012, s 15, Sch 5, paras 1, 17, as from 24 January 2013 (in so far as relating to the preparation and issue of a statement of policy), and as from 1 April 2013 (otherwise).

[7.150]

70 Statements of policy: procedure

(1) Before [a regulator issues] a statement under section 69, the [regulator] must publish a draft of the proposed statement in the way appearing to the [regulator] to be best calculated to bring it to the attention of the public.

(2) The draft must be accompanied by notice that representations about the proposal may be made to the [regulator] within a specified time.

(3) Before issuing the proposed statement, the [regulator] must have regard to any representations made to it in accordance with subsection (2).

(4) If the [regulator] issues the proposed statement it must publish an account, in general terms, of—

(a) the representations made to it in accordance with subsection (2); and

(b) its response to them.

(5) If the statement differs from the draft published under subsection (1) in a way which is, in the opinion of the [regulator], significant, the [regulator] must (in addition to complying with subsection (4)) publish details of the difference.

(6) [A regulator] may charge a reasonable fee for providing a person with a copy of a draft published [by it] under subsection (1).

(7) This section also applies to a proposal to alter or replace a statement.

NOTES

Words in square brackets substituted by the Financial Services Act 2012, s 15, Sch 5, paras 1, 18, as from 24 January 2013 (in so far as relating to the preparation and issue of a statement of policy), and as from 1 April 2013 (otherwise).

Breach of statutory duty

[7.151]

71 Actions for damages

(1) A contravention of section 56(6) or 59(1) or (2) is actionable at the suit of a private person who suffers loss as a result of the contravention, subject to the defences and other incidents applying to actions for breach of statutory duty.

(2) In prescribed cases, a contravention of that kind which would be actionable at the suit of a private person is actionable at the suit of a person who is not a private person, subject to the defences and other incidents applying to actions for breach of statutory duty.

(3) "Private person" has such meaning as may be prescribed.

NOTES

Regulations: the Financial Services and Markets Act 2000 (Rights of Action) Regulations 2001, SI 2001/2256.

[. . .

71A *(Originally inserted, together with the preceding heading, by the Financial Services (Banking Reform) Act 2013, s 33, as from 25 July 2014. Subsequently repealed by the Bank of England and Financial Services Act 2016, s 21, Sch 4, paras 1, 18. Note that s 21 and Sch 4 come into force as follows: (i) 13 September 2018 (for the purpose of making rules, giving directions, imposing requirements and making statements of policy by the appropriate regulator for insurers); (ii) 10 December 2018 (for all other purposes for insurers (except in relation to Sch 4, para 11)), and 10 December 2019 (Sch 4, para 11 for insurers); (iii) 18 July 2019 (for the purpose of the making of rules, the giving of directions, the imposition of requirements and the issuing of statements of policy by the FCA for remaining purposes); (iv) 9 August 2019 (for remaining purposes in relation to authorised persons who are not solo-regulated firms); (v) 9 December 2019 (for remaining purposes in relation to solo-regulated firms other than benchmark firms (except as provided for by (vii) below)); (vi) 7 December 2020 (for remaining purposes in relation to benchmark firms (except as provided for by (viii) below)); (vii) 31 March 2021 (in relation to the employee certification provisions for remaining purposes in relation to solo-regulated firms other than benchmark firms); (viii) 7 December 2021 (in relation to the employee certification provisions for remaining purposes in relation to benchmark firms). For transitional provisions in connection with (i)–(iii) above, see the Bank of England and Financial Services Act 2016 (Commencement No 5 and Transitional Provisions) Regulations 2018, SI 2018/990; and for transitional provisions in connection with the other commencement dates, see the Bank of England and Financial Services Act 2016 (Commencement No 6 and Transitional Provisions) Regulations 2019, SI 2019/1136.)*

[Removal of directors and senior executives and appointment of temporary manager

[7.152]

71B Removal of directors and senior executives

(1) If the appropriate regulator is satisfied that the conditions in section 71D(1) and (2) are met in relation to a relevant firm, the appropriate regulator may require the firm to remove—

- (a) any person who is a director of the firm;
- (b) any person who is a senior executive of the firm.

(2) If the appropriate regulator imposes a requirement under subsection (1), the regulator may also require the relevant firm—

- (a) to replace a director or senior executive who has been removed, and
- (b) to take any step needed to give effect to the replacement, including, where necessary, calling a general meeting of the firm's shareholders or members.

[(3) If the appropriate regulator is satisfied that the condition in section 71D(4A) is met in relation to a person who is a director of an institution, of a financial holding company or of a mixed financial holding company, the appropriate regulator may require that institution, financial holding company or mixed financial holding company to remove that person from the board of directors.]]

NOTES

Sections 71B–71I (and the preceding heading) were inserted by the Bank Recovery and Resolution Order 2016, SI 2016/1239, arts 30, 32, as from 16 December 2016.

Sub-s (3): added by the Financial Holding Companies (Approval etc) and Capital Requirements (Capital Buffers and Macro-prudential Measures) (Amendment) (EU Exit) Regulations 2020, SI 2020/1406, reg 2(2), as from 29 December 2020.

[7.153]

[71C Temporary manager

(1) If the appropriate regulator is satisfied—

- (a) in the case of a relevant firm, that the conditions in section 71D(1), (2) and (4) are met in relation to that firm, or
- (b) in the case of a parent undertaking which is not a relevant firm, that the conditions in section 71D(1) and (4) are met in relation to that parent undertaking,

the appropriate regulator may appoint a person to act (or one or more persons to act jointly) as a temporary manager of that firm or that parent undertaking.

(2) Where the appropriate regulator makes an appointment under subsection (1) in relation to a parent undertaking which is not a relevant firm, the regulator may also require the undertaking to remove—

(a) all of its directors;

(b) all of its senior executives.

(3) A temporary manager may be appointed under subsection (1)—

(a) to replace the directors of a relevant firm or a parent undertaking where they have been removed in compliance with a requirement imposed under section 71B or subsection (2), or

(b) to work with the directors of a relevant firm or a parent undertaking.

(4) A temporary manager has the functions specified in the instrument of appointment (see section 71F).

(5) The functions which may be specified include (amongst other things)—

(a) ascertaining the financial position of the relevant firm or the parent undertaking;

(b) managing the business or part of the business of the relevant firm or the parent undertaking in order to preserve or restore the financial position of the firm or the parent undertaking;

(c) taking measures to restore the prudent management of the relevant firm or the parent undertaking;

(d) any function of the directors.

(6) The temporary manager may, with the consent of the appropriate regulator—

(a) require the directors to call a general meeting of the shareholders or members of the relevant firm or the parent undertaking, or

(b) in the case where all of the directors have been removed in compliance with a requirement imposed under section 71B or subsection (2), call a general meeting of the shareholders or members of the relevant firm or the parent undertaking.

(7) The temporary manager may propose business for consideration at the general meeting.

(8) If the temporary manager is being appointed to work with the directors, the appropriate regulator—

(a) may require the directors not to exercise specified functions during the period of appointment;

(b) may require the directors to consult the temporary manager, or obtain the consent of the temporary manager, before taking specified decisions or specified action.

"Specified" means specified in the requirement.]

NOTES

Inserted as noted to s 71B at **[7.152]**.

[7.154]

[71D Sections 71B and 71C: conditions

(1) The condition in this subsection is met in relation to a relevant firm or a parent undertaking if—

(a) there is a deterioration in the financial situation of the relevant firm or the parent undertaking which is a significant deterioration, or

(b) there is a serious infringement by the relevant firm or the parent undertaking of—

(i) a relevant requirement, or

(ii) its memorandum or articles of association or other constituent instrument.

(2) The condition in this subsection is met in relation to a relevant firm if it is not reasonably likely that the deterioration would be reversed or the infringement would be brought to an end by [any measure defined as a "relevant measure" by article 107 of the Bank Recovery and Resolution (No 2) Order 2014 (SI 2014/3348)] which could be taken by the appropriate regulator under the provisions listed in subsection (3).

(3) The provisions mentioned in subsection (2) are—

(a) section 55J (variation or cancellation on initiative of regulator),

(b) section 55L (imposition of requirements by FCA),

(c) section 55M (imposition of requirements by PRA),

(d) section 55PB (requirements relating to general meetings),

(e) section 56 (prohibition orders),

(f) section 63 (withdrawal of approval),

(g) section 63ZA (variation of senior manager's approval at request of authorised person),

(h) section 63ZB (variation of senior manager's approval on initiative of regulator),

(i) section 63A (power to impose penalties),

(j) section 66 (disciplinary powers),

(k) Part 12A (powers exercisable in relation to parent undertakings), or

(l) Part 14 (disciplinary measures).

(4) The condition in this subsection is met if the following action would not be sufficient to reverse the deterioration or bring the infringement to an end—

(a) in the case of a relevant firm, the imposition of one or more requirements under section 71B (removal and replacement of directors and senior executives); or

(b) in the case of a parent undertaking which is not a relevant firm, the exercise of any of the appropriate regulator's powers under Part 12A.

[(4A) The condition in this subsection is met in relation to a director of an institution, of a financial holding company or of a mixed financial holding company, if the director—

(a) is no longer of sufficiently good repute to perform their duties,

(b) no longer possesses sufficient knowledge, skills, experience, honesty, integrity or independence of mind to perform their duties, or

(c) is no longer able to commit sufficient time to perform their duties.]

(5) For the purposes of this section—

(a) "relevant requirement" has the meaning given in section 204A;

(b) a deterioration in the financial situation of the relevant firm or the parent undertaking is significant if—

(i) in the case of a relevant firm, or a parent undertaking which is an authorised person, it no longer satisfies, or is likely to fail to satisfy, the threshold conditions relating to its financial resources which apply to it under Schedule 6;

(ii) in the case of a parent undertaking which is not an authorised person, the deterioration threatens the viability of the parent undertaking.]

NOTES

Inserted as noted to s 71B at **[7.152]**.

Sub-s (2): words in square brackets substituted by the Financial Services and Markets Act 2000 (Amendment) (EU Exit) Regulations 2019, SI 2019/632, regs 24, 29, as from IP completion day (as defined in the European Union (Withdrawal Agreement) Act 2020, s 39).

Sub-s (4A): inserted by the Financial Holding Companies (Approval etc) and Capital Requirements (Capital Buffers and Macro-prudential Measures) (Amendment) (EU Exit) Regulations 2020, SI 2020/1406, reg 2(3), as from 29 December 2020.

[7.155]

[71E Temporary manager: further provisions in relation to the appointment

(1) Before appointing a person to act as a temporary manager, the appropriate regulator must be satisfied that the person—

(a) has the qualifications, ability and knowledge to carry out the functions to be given to the temporary manager, and

(b) would not be subject to any conflict of interest as a result of the appointment.

(2) A person may not be appointed to act as a temporary manager for a period longer than one year, but is eligible for re-appointment (or further re-appointment) if subsection 71C(1) continues to apply in relation to the relevant firm or parent undertaking.

(3) The appropriate regulator may vary the terms of the appointment of a temporary manager, or remove the temporary manager, at any time.

(4) A temporary manager is not liable for damages in respect of anything done in good faith for the purposes of or in connection with the functions of the appointment (subject to section 8 of the Human Rights Act 1998).]

NOTES

Inserted as noted to s 71B at **[7.152]**.

[7.156]

[71F Temporary manager: instrument of appointment

(1) The power in section 71C(1) is to be exercised by an instrument of appointment.

(2) The instrument of appointment must—

(a) specify the functions of the temporary manager,

(b) specify the date on which the appointment of the temporary manager has effect,

(c) specify the period for which the temporary manager is appointed, and

(d) make provision for the resignation and replacement of the person who is appointed as the temporary manager.

(3) The instrument of appointment may—

(a) require the temporary manager to consult the appropriate regulator or other specified person before exercising specified functions,

(b) specify particular matters on which the appropriate regulator or other specified person must be consulted, and

(c) provide that the temporary manager is not to exercise specified functions without the consent of the appropriate regulator or other specified person.

(4) The instrument of appointment may require the temporary manager to make reports to the appropriate regulator, at specified times or intervals, on—

(a) the financial position of the relevant firm or the parent undertaking,

(b) the actions taken by the temporary manager during the course of the temporary manager's appointment,

(c) any other specified matters.

(5) In subsections (3) and (4), "specified" means specified in the instrument of appointment.

(6) The instrument of appointment may provide for the payment of remuneration and allowances to a temporary manager.

(7) Provision under subsection (6) may provide that the amounts are—

(a) to be paid by the appropriate regulator, or

(b) to be determined by the appropriate regulator and paid by the relevant firm or the parent undertaking.

(8) If a temporary manager—

(a) is appointed to replace the directors of the relevant firm or the parent undertaking, or

(b) is appointed to work with the directors of the relevant firm or the parent undertaking and has the power to represent that firm or parent undertaking,

the appropriate regulator must publish the instrument of appointment on its website.]

NOTES

Inserted as noted to s 71B at **[7.152]**.

[7.157]

[71G Right to refer matters to the Tribunal

(1) A relevant firm which is aggrieved by—

(a) the imposition of a requirement on that firm under section 71B, or

(b) the appointment, or the terms of the appointment, of a person to act as a temporary manager of that firm under section 71C(1),

may refer the matter to the Tribunal.

[(1A) An institution, financial holding company or mixed financial holding company which is aggrieved by the imposition of a requirement on that institution or holding company under section 71B(3) may refer the matter to the Tribunal.]

(2) A parent undertaking which is aggrieved by—

(a) the imposition of a requirement on that parent undertaking under section 71C(2), or

(b) the appointment, or the terms of the appointment, of a person to act as a temporary manager of that parent undertaking under section 71C(1),

may refer the matter to the Tribunal.

(3) A director (or a former director) of a relevant firm or a parent undertaking who is aggrieved by the imposition of a requirement on that director under section 71C(8) may refer the matter to the Tribunal.

(4) A director or senior executive (or a former director or senior executive) of a relevant firm or a parent undertaking who is aggrieved by the imposition of a requirement on that firm or parent undertaking under section [71B(1) or (2)] or 71C(2) may refer the matter to the Tribunal.

[(5) A director (or former director) of an institution, a financial holding company or a mixed financial holding company who is aggrieved by the imposition of a requirement on that institution or holding company under section 71B(3) may refer the matter to the Tribunal.]]

NOTES

Inserted as noted to s 71B at **[7.152]**.

Sub-s (1A) was inserted, the words in square brackets in sub-s (4) were substituted, and sub-s (5) was added, by the Financial Holding Companies (Approval etc) and Capital Requirements (Capital Buffers and Macro-prudential Measures) (Amendment) (EU Exit) Regulations 2020, SI 2020/1406, reg 2(4), as from 29 December 2020.

[7.158]

[71H Removal of directors and senior executives and appointment of temporary manager: procedure

(1) A requirement under section 71B or 71C(2) or (8) or the appointment of a temporary manager under section 71C(1) may be expressed to take effect immediately or on a specified date only if the appropriate regulator, having regard to the grounds for imposing the requirement or making the appointment, reasonably considers that it is necessary for the requirement or the appointment to take effect immediately or on that date.

(2) If either regulator proposes to impose a requirement on a relevant firm[, institution, financial holding company or mixed financial holding company] under section 71B or a parent undertaking under section 71C(2), or imposes such a requirement with immediate effect, it must give written notice—

(a) to that firm[, institution, holding company] or parent undertaking, and

(b) to each of the directors or senior executives to whom the requirement relates ("the interested parties").

(3) If either regulator—

(a) proposes to appoint a person to act as a temporary manager under section 71C or to vary the terms on which such a person is appointed, or

(b) makes such an appointment or variation with immediate effect,

the regulator must give written notice to the relevant firm or the parent undertaking concerned.

(4) If either regulator proposes to impose a requirement on the directors under section 71C(8), or imposes such a requirement with immediate effect, the regulator must give written notice to each director.

(5) A notice given under subsection (2) must—

(a) give details of the requirement,

(b) identify each of the directors or senior executives to whom the requirement relates,

(c) give the regulator's reasons for imposing the requirement—

(i) in the case of a notice given to the relevant firm[, the financial holding company, the mixed financial holding company] or the parent undertaking, in relation to each interested party;

(ii) in the case of a notice given to an interested party, in relation to that interested party,

(d) inform the relevant firm[, the financial holding company, the mixed financial holding company] or the parent undertaking and the interested parties that each of them may make representations to the regulator within such period as may be specified in the notice (whether or not the matter has been referred to the Tribunal),

(e) state when the requirement takes effect, and

(f) inform the relevant firm[, the financial holding company, the mixed financial holding company] or the parent undertaking and each of the interested parties of their right to refer the matter to the Tribunal.

(6) A notice given under subsection (3) must—

(a) state when the appointment or variation takes effect, and be accompanied by the instrument, or revised instrument, of appointment,

(b) give the regulator's reasons for making the appointment or variation,

(c) inform the relevant firm or the parent undertaking that it may make representations to the regulator within such period as may be specified in the notice (whether or not the matter has been referred to the Tribunal), and

(d) inform the relevant firm or the parent undertaking of its right to refer the matter to the Tribunal.

(7) A notice given under subsection (4) must—

(a) give details of the requirement,

(b) give the regulator's reasons for imposing the requirement,

(c) state when the requirement takes effect,

(d) inform the director that the director may make representations to the regulator within such period as may be specified in the notice (whether or not the matter has been referred to the Tribunal), and

(e) inform the director of the director's right to refer the matter to the Tribunal.

(8) The regulator may extend the period allowed by the notice given under subsection (2), (3) or (4) for making representations.

(9) If, having considered any representations made by a person to whom notice (the "original notice") has been given under subsection (2), (3) or (4), the regulator decides—

(a) to impose the requirement, make the appointment or vary the terms of an appointment in accordance with the original notice, or

(b) not to rescind the imposition of any such requirement or the making of any such appointment or variation which has already taken effect,

the regulator must give written notice to each person to whom the original notice was given.

(10) A notice under subsection (9) must inform the person to whom it is given of the right of that person to refer the matter to the Tribunal and give an indication of the procedure on such a reference.

(11) If, having considered any representations made by a person to whom notice (the "original notice") has been given under subsection (2), (3) or (4), the regulator decides—

(a) to impose a requirement, make an appointment or a vary the terms of an appointment in a way that is different from the requirement, appointment or variation described in the original notice,

(b) not to impose the requirement, make the appointment or vary the terms of an appointment in accordance with the original notice, or

(c) to rescind the imposition of any such requirement, or the making of any such appointment or variation that has already taken effect,

the regulator must give written notice to each person to whom the original notice was given.

(12) A notice under subsection (11)(a) about the imposition of a requirement under section 71B or 71C(2) must comply with subsection (5).

(13) A notice under subsection (11)(a) about the appointment of a person as a temporary manager or the variation of the terms of the appointment of a person as a temporary manager must comply with subsection (6).

(14) A notice under subsection (11)(a) about the imposition of a requirement under section 71C(8) must comply with subsection (7).

(15) In this section, any reference to "appointment" includes "re-appointment".]

NOTES

Inserted as noted to s 71B at **[7.152]**.

Sub-ss (2), (5): words in square brackets inserted by the Financial Holding Companies (Approval etc) and Capital Requirements (Capital Buffers and Macro-prudential Measures) (Amendment) (EU Exit) Regulations 2020, SI 2020/1406, reg 2(5), as from 29 December 2020.

[7.159]

[71I Sections 71B to 71H: interpretation

(1) For the purposes of sections 71B to 71H "relevant firm" means—

(a) a bank as defined in section 2 of the Banking Act 2009,

(b) a building society as defined in section 119 of the Building Societies Act 1986, or

(c) an investment firm as defined in [Article 4(1)(2) of the capital requirements regulation].

(2) For the purposes of sections 71C to 71H, "parent undertaking" means an institution, financial holding company or mixed financial holding company which—

(a) is incorporated in, or formed under the law of, any part of the United Kingdom,

(b) is [a UK parent], and

(c) either—

(i) has a subsidiary which is an institution, or

(ii) holds a participation (within the meaning given by Article 4.1(35) of the capital requirements regulation) in an institution.

(3) For the purposes of subsection (2), an institution, financial holding company or mixed financial holding company is [a UK parent] if it is not itself the subsidiary of an institution, financial holding company or mixed financial holding company set up in [the United Kingdom].

(4) In [sections 71B to 71H and this section]—

"institution" means a credit institution or an investment firm as defined in [article 2(1) of the Bank Recovery and Resolution (No 2) Order 2014];

"financial holding company" and "mixed financial holding company" have the meanings given in Article 4.1(20) and 4.1(21) of the capital requirements regulation.

(5) For the purposes of sections 71B to 71H—

"appropriate regulator" means—

(a) in relation to a PRA-authorised person, the PRA,

(b) in relation to any other authorised person, the FCA,

(c) in relation to a parent undertaking that is not an authorised person—

(i) the PRA, where the PRA is the consolidating supervisor in relation to that undertaking;

(ii) the FCA, where the FCA is the consolidating supervisor in relation to that undertaking;

[(d) in relation to a financial holding company or mixed financial holding company which is not a parent undertaking—

(i) the PRA, where the holding company is approved by the PRA under Part 12B;

(ii) the FCA in all other cases;]

"consolidating supervisor" means the competent authority responsible for the exercise of supervision on the basis of the consolidated situation (within the meaning of Article 4.1(47) of the capital requirements regulation) of an institution which is [a UK parent];

"director" includes, in relation to an undertaking which has no board of directors, a member of the equivalent management body responsible for the management of the undertaking concerned;

. . .

"senior executive", in relation to a relevant firm or a parent undertaking, means a person who—

(a) exercises executive functions within that firm or that undertaking; and

(b) is responsible, and directly accountable to the directors, for the day to day management of that firm or that undertaking.]

NOTES

Inserted as noted to s 71B at **[7.152]**.

The words in square brackets in sub-s (1)(c) were substituted by the Financial Services Act 2021 (Prudential Regulation of Credit Institutions and Investment Firms) (Consequential Amendments and Miscellaneous Provisions) Regulations 2021, SI 2021/1376, reg 4(5), as from 1 January 2022.

The first words in square brackets in sub-s (4) were substituted, and para (d) of the definition "appropriate regulator" in sub-s (5) was added, by the Financial Holding Companies (Approval etc) and Capital Requirements (Capital Buffers and Macro-prudential Measures) (Amendment) (EU Exit) Regulations 2020, SI 2020/1406, reg 2(6), as from 29 December 2020.

All other amendments to this section were made by the Financial Services and Markets Act 2000 (Amendment) (EU Exit) Regulations 2019, SI 2019/632, regs 24, 30, as from IP completion day (as defined in the European Union (Withdrawal Agreement) Act 2020, s 39).

[Application of this Part to Gibraltar-based persons

[7.160]

71J Application of this Part to Gibraltar-based persons

(1) This section applies to an authorised person that—

(a) has a Schedule 2A permission, but

(b) does not have a Part 4A permission.

(2) The person is only required to comply with the provisions listed in subsection (3) if the person has a branch in the United Kingdom.

(3) Those provisions are—

(a) section 59(1) or (2) (approval for particular arrangements), or

(b) section 63E(1) (certification of employees).

(4) In this section, "branch" has the same meaning as in Schedule 2A (see paragraph 3 of that Schedule).]

NOTES

Commencement: to be appointed.

Inserted, together with the preceding heading, by the Financial Services Act 2021, s 22, Sch 8, para 4, as from a day to be appointed.

PART VI OFFICIAL LISTING

NOTES

Transitional provisions etc in connection with the Prospectus Regulation: the Financial Services and Markets Act 2000 (Prospectus) Regulations 2019, SI 2019/1043 make provision in connection with the implementation of the Prospectus Regulation (Regulation 2017/1129/EU of the European Parliament and of the Council of 14 June 2017 on the prospectus to be published when securities are offered to the public or admitted to trading on a regulated market), including the amendment of this Part. Regulation 40 of the 2019 Regulations contains transitional provisions in relation to a prospectus approved by the FCA, in accordance with this Part before 21 July 2019. See reg 40 at **[8.574]**, and note that that regulation expired on 21 July 2020 or, if earlier, the date on which, in accordance with prospectus rules, the period of validity of the prospectus expired.

Transitional provisions etc in connection with the commencement of the Financial Services Act 2012: see the Financial Services Act 2012 (Transitional Provisions) (Enforcement) Order 2013, SI 2013/441, art 4 which provides that s 88A(2)(a)–(c) and (7) (disciplinary powers: contravention of section 88(3)(c) or (e)) do not apply in respect of a contravention of rules made by the FSA under s 88(3)(c) (sponsors) which occurred (and ceased to occur) before the 1 April 2013.

Transitional provisions etc in connection with the original commencement of this Act: see the Financial Services and Markets Act 2000 (Official Listing of Securities) (Transitional Provisions) Order 2001, SI 2001/2957 which makes transitional provisions in relation to the listing of securities under this Part instead of the Financial Services Act 1986, Pt IV (repealed). The FSA continued to be the competent authority for listing under this Act (as it had been under the 1986 Act since 1 May 2000 by virtue of the Official Listing of Securities (Change of Competent Authority) Regulations 2000 (SI 2000/968)). Note, however, that the FCA assumed that responsibility on 1 April 2013. Securities admitted to the official list prior to commencement continue to be listed after commencement by virtue of s 74(1) of this Act and the definition of "official list" in s 103(1). The 2001 Order makes certain further transitional provisions. Many reflect the fact that, while s 142(9) of the 1986 Act permitted securities to be admitted to the official list either in accordance with Part IV of the 1986 Act ("Part IV securities") or else outside the statutory provisions ("non-Part IV securities"), this Act brings all official listing within this Part.

72, 73 (*Repealed by the Financial Services Act 2012, s 16(1), (14)(a), as from 1 April 2013*).

[Rules]

NOTES

The preceding heading was inserted by the Financial Services Act 2012, s 16(1), (4), as from 24 January 2013.

[7.161]

[73A Part 6 Rules

(1) The [FCA] may make rules ("Part 6 rules") for the purposes of this Part.

(2) Provisions of Part 6 rules expressed to relate to the official list are referred to in this Part as "listing rules".

(3) . . .

[(4) Provisions of Part 6 rules expressed to relate to transferable securities are referred to in this Part as "prospectus rules".

(5) In relation to prospectus rules, the purposes of this Part include the purposes of the prospectus [regulation].]

[(6) Transparency rules and corporate governance rules are not listing rules . . . or prospectus rules, but are Part 6 rules.]]

NOTES

Inserted by the Financial Services and Markets Act 2000 (Market Abuse) Regulations 2005, SI 2005/381, reg 4, Sch 1, para 2, as from 17 March 2005.

Sub-s (1): word in square brackets substituted by the Financial Services Act 2012, s 16(1)–(3), as from 24 January 2013.

Sub-s (3): repealed by the Financial Services and Markets Act 2000 (Market Abuse) Regulations 2016, SI 2016/680, reg 8(1), (2)(a), as from 3 July 2016.

Sub-ss (4), (5): added by the Prospectus Regulations 2005, SI 2005/1433, reg 2(1), Sch 1, para 1, as from 1 July 2005. The word "regulation" in square brackets in sub-s (5) was substituted by the Financial Services and Markets Act 2000 (Prospectus) Regulations 2019, SI 2019/1043, regs 3, 4, as from 21 July 2019.

Sub-s (6): added by the Companies Act 2006, s 1272, Sch 15, Pt 1, paras 1, 3, as from 8 November 2006. Words omitted repealed by SI 2016/680, reg 8(1), (2)(b), as from 3 July 2016.

Rule making power of FCA: note that s 16 of the Financial Services Act 2012 amends this Part so that functions under it are exercisable by the FCA. The Financial Services Act 2012 (Commencement No 1) Order 2013, SI 2013/113, Schedule, Pt 3 provides that these amendments come into force on 24 January 2013 for the purpose of making rules. By virtue of the Schedule to the Financial Services Act 2012 (Commencement No 2) Order 2013, SI 2013/423, s 16 came into force for all other purposes on 1 April 2013.

The official list

[7.162]

74 The official list

(1) The [FCA] must maintain the official list.

(2) The [FCA] may admit to the official list such securities and other things as it considers appropriate.

(3) But—

(a) nothing may be admitted to the official list except in accordance with this Part; and

(b) the Treasury may by order provide that anything which falls within a description or category specified in the order may not be admitted to the official list.

(4) . . .

(5) In the following provisions of this Part—

. . .

"listing" means being included in the official list in accordance with this Part.

NOTES

Sub-ss (1), (2): words in square brackets substituted by the Financial Services Act 2012, s 16(1)–(3), as from 1 April 2013.

Sub-s (4): repealed by the Financial Services and Markets Act 2000 (Market Abuse) Regulations 2005, SI 2005/381, reg 4, Sch 1, para 3, as from 17 March 2005.

Sub-s (5): definition "security" (omitted) repealed by the Prospectus Regulations 2005, SI 2005/1433, reg 2(1), Sch 1, para 2, as from 1 July 2005.

Note: the Financial Services and Markets Act 2000 (Official Listing of Securities) Regulations 2001, SI 2001/2956 at **[8.434]** prescribes certain bodies whose securities may not be considered for listing under this Part. Note also that a share transfer instrument or order under the Banking Act 2009, Pt 1 may provide for the listing of securities under this section to be discontinued or suspended; see s 19(2) of that Act.

Listing

[7.163]

75 Applications for listing

(1) Admission to the official list may be granted only on an application made to the [FCA] in such manner as may be required by listing rules.

(2) No application for listing may be entertained by the [FCA] unless it is made by, or with the consent of, the issuer of the securities concerned.

(3) No application for listing may be entertained by the [FCA] in respect of securities which are to be issued by a body of a prescribed kind.

(4) The [FCA] may not grant an application for listing unless it is satisfied that—

(a) the requirements of listing rules (so far as they apply to the application), and

(b) any other requirements imposed by [the FCA] in relation to the application,

are complied with.

(5) An application for listing may be refused if, for a reason relating to the issuer, the [FCA] considers that granting it would be detrimental to the interests of investors.

(6) An application for listing securities which are already [listed in a country or territory outside the United Kingdom] may be refused if the issuer has failed to comply with any obligations to which he is subject as a result of that listing.

NOTES

Word "FCA" in square brackets in every place it occurs substituted by the Financial Services Act 2012, s 16(1)–(3), as from 1 April 2013.

Sub-s (6): words in square brackets substituted by the Official Listing of Securities, Prospectus and Transparency (Amendment etc) (EU Exit) Regulations 2019, SI 2019/707, regs 3, 5, as from IP completion day (as defined in the European Union (Withdrawal Agreement) Act 2020, s 39).

Regulations: the Financial Services and Markets Act 2000 (Official Listing of Securities) Regulations 2001, SI 2001/2956 at **[8.434]**; the Financial Services and Markets Act 2000 (Official Listing of Securities) (Amendment) Regulations 2001, SI 2001/3439.

[7.164]

76 Decision on application

(1) The [FCA] must notify the applicant of its decision on an application for listing—

(a) before the end of the period of six months beginning with the date on which the application is received; or

(b) if within that period [the FCA] has required the applicant to provide further information in connection with the application, before the end of the period of six months beginning with the date on which that information is provided.

(2) If [FCA] fails to comply with subsection (1), it is to be taken to have decided to refuse the application.

(3) If the [FCA] decides to grant an application for listing, it must give the applicant written notice.

(4) If the [FCA] proposes to refuse an application for listing, it must give the applicant a warning notice.

(5) If the [FCA] decides to refuse an application for listing, it must give the applicant a decision notice.

(6) If the [FCA] decides to refuse an application for listing, the applicant may refer the matter to the Tribunal.

(7) If securities are admitted to the official list, their admission may not be called in question on the ground that any requirement or condition for their admission has not been complied with.

NOTES

Words in square brackets substituted by the Financial Services Act 2012, s 16(1)–(3), as from 1 April 2013.

[7.165]

77 Discontinuance and suspension of listing

(1) The [FCA] may, in accordance with listing rules, discontinue the listing of any securities if satisfied that there are special circumstances which preclude normal regular dealings in them.

(2) The [FCA] may, in accordance with listing rules, suspend the listing of any securities.

[(2A) The [FCA] may discontinue under subsection (1) or suspend under subsection (2) the listing of any securities on its own initiative or on the application of the issuer of those securities.]

(3) If securities are suspended under subsection (2) they are to be treated, for the purposes of [section 96 and paragraph 23(6) of Schedule 1ZA], as still being listed.

[(3A) If securities have been suspended by the Bank of England under section 19, 39B or 48L of the Banking Act 2009, the FCA may, following consultation with the Bank of England, cancel the suspension.]

(4) This section applies to securities whenever they were admitted to the official list.

(5) If the [FCA] discontinues or suspends the listing of any securities, [on its own initiative,] the issuer may refer the matter to the Tribunal.

NOTES

Sub-s (2A) was inserted, and the words "on its own initiative," in square brackets in sub-s (5) were inserted, by the Regulatory Reform (Financial Services and Markets Act 2000) Order 2007, SI 2007/1973, arts 2, 5, as from 12 July 2007.

Sub-s (3A) was inserted by the Bank Recovery and Resolution Order 2014, SI 2014/3329, arts 112, 114, as from 1 January 2015.

All other words in square brackets were substituted by the Financial Services Act 2012, s 16(1), (3), (5), as from 1 April 2013.

[7.166]

78 Discontinuance or suspension: procedure

(1) A discontinuance or suspension [by the [FCA] on its own initiative] takes effect—
  (a) immediately, if the notice under subsection (2) states that that is the case;
  (b) in any other case, on such date as may be specified in that notice.

(2) If [on its own initiative] the [FCA]—
  (a) proposes to discontinue or suspend the listing of securities, or
  (b) discontinues or suspends the listing of securities with immediate effect,

it must give the issuer of the securities written notice.

(3) The notice must—
  (a) give details of the discontinuance or suspension;
  (b) state the [FCA's] reasons for the discontinuance or suspension and for choosing the date on which it took effect or takes effect;
  (c) inform the issuer of the securities that he may make representations to the [FCA] within such period as may be specified in the notice (whether or not he has referred the matter to the Tribunal);
  (d) inform him of the date on which the discontinuance or suspension took effect or will take effect; and
  (e) inform him of his right to refer the matter to the Tribunal.

(4) The [FCA] may extend the period within which representations may be made to it.

(5) If, having considered any representations made by the issuer of the securities, the [FCA] decides—
  (a) to discontinue or suspend the listing of the securities, or
  (b) if the discontinuance or suspension has taken effect, not to cancel it,

the [FCA] must give the issuer of the securities written notice.

(6) A notice given under subsection (5) must inform the issuer of the securities of his right to refer the matter to the Tribunal.

(7) If a notice informs a person of his right to refer a matter to the Tribunal, it must give an indication of the procedure on such a reference.

(8) If the [FCA] decides—
  (a) not to discontinue or suspend the listing of the securities, or
  (b) if the discontinuance or suspension has taken effect, to cancel it,

the [FCA] must give the issuer of the securities written notice.

(9) The effect of cancelling a discontinuance is that the securities concerned are to be readmitted, without more, to the official list.

[(10) If—
  (a) the FCA has suspended the listing of securities on its own initiative, or securities have been suspended by the Bank of England under section 19, 39B or 48L of the Banking Act 2009, and
  (b) the FCA proposes to refuse an application by the issuer of the securities for the cancellation of the suspension,

the FCA must give the issuer a warning notice.]

(11) The [FCA] must, having considered any representations made in response to the warning notice—
  (a) if it decides to refuse the application, give the issuer of the securities a decision notice;
  (b) if it grants the application, give him written notice of its decision.

(12) If the [FCA] decides to refuse an application for the cancellation of the suspension of listed securities, the applicant may refer the matter to the Tribunal.

(13) "Discontinuance" means a discontinuance of listing under section 77(1).

(14) "Suspension" means a suspension of listing under section 77(2) [and in subsections (10) and (12), includes a suspension of listing under section 19, 39B or 48L of the Banking Act 2009].

NOTES

Words "FCA" and "FCA's" in square brackets (in each place that they occur) substituted by the Financial Services Act 2012, s 16(1)–(3), as from 1 April 2013.

Sub-s (10) was substituted, and the words in square brackets in sub-s (14) were inserted, by the Bank Recovery and Resolution Order 2014, SI 2014/3329, arts 112, 115, as from 1 January 2015.

All other words in square brackets were inserted by the Regulatory Reform (Financial Services and Markets Act 2000) Order 2007, SI 2007/1973, arts 2, 6, as from 12 July 2007.

[7.167]
[78A Discontinuance or suspension at the request of the issuer: procedure

(1) A discontinuance or suspension by the [FCA on the application of the issuer of the securities takes effect—

[(a) immediately, if the notification under subsection (2) so provides;

(b) in any other case, on such date as may be provided for in that notification.]

(2) If the [FCA] discontinues or suspends the listing of securities on the application of the issuer of the securities it must [notify the issuer (whether in writing or otherwise)].

[(3) The notification must—

(a) notify the issuer of the date on which the discontinuance or suspension took effect or will take effect, and

(b) notify the issuer of such other matters (if any) as are specified in listing rules.]

(4) If the [FCA] proposes to refuse an application by the issuer of the securities for the discontinuance or suspension of the listing of the securities, it must give him a warning notice.

(5) The [FCA] must, having considered any representations made in response to the warning notice, if it decides to refuse the application, give the issuer of the securities a decision notice.

(6) If the [FCA] decides to refuse an application by the issuer of the securities for the discontinuance or suspension of the listing of the securities, the issuer may refer the matter to the Tribunal.

(7) If the [FCA] has suspended the listing of securities on the application of the issuer of the securities and proposes to refuse an application by the issuer for the cancellation of the suspension, it must give him a warning notice.

(8) The [FCA] must, having considered any representations made in response to the warning notice—

(a) if it decides to refuse the application for the cancellation of the suspension, give the issuer of the securities a decision notice;

(b) if it grants the application, give him written notice of its decision.

(9) If the [FCA] decides to refuse an application for the cancellation of the suspension of listed securities, the applicant may refer the matter to the Tribunal.

(10) "Discontinuance" means a discontinuance of listing under section 77(1).

(11) "Suspension" means a suspension of listing under section 77(2).]

NOTES

Inserted by the Regulatory Reform (Financial Services and Markets Act 2000) Order 2007, SI 2007/1973, arts 2, 7, as from 12 July 2007.

Word "FCA" in square brackets (in each place that it occurs) substituted by the Financial Services Act 2012, s 16(1)–(3), as from 1 April 2013.

Sub-s (1)(a), (b) and sub-s (3) were substituted, and the words in the second pair of square brackets in sub-s (2) were substituted, by the Financial Services Act 2012, s 17(1), (2), as from 19 March 2013 (for the purpose of making rules), and as from 1 April 2013 (otherwise).

Listing particulars

[7.168]
79 Listing particulars and other documents

(1) Listing rules may provide that securities . . . of a kind specified in the rules may not be admitted to the official list unless—

(a) listing particulars have been submitted to, and approved by, the [FCA] and published; or

(b) in such cases as may be specified by listing rules, such document (other than listing particulars or a prospectus of a kind required by listing rules) as may be so specified has been published.

(2) "Listing particulars" means a document in such form and containing such information as may be specified in listing rules.

(3) For the purposes of this Part, the persons responsible for listing particulars are to be determined in accordance with regulations made by the Treasury.

[(3A) Listing rules made under subsection (1) may not specify securities of a kind for which an approved prospectus is required as a result of section 85.]

(4) Nothing in this section affects the [FCA's] general power to make listing rules.

NOTES

Words omitted from sub-s (1) repealed, and sub-s (3A) inserted, by the Prospectus Regulations 2005, SI 2005/1433, reg 2(1), Sch 1, para 3, as from 1 July 2005.

Words "FCA" and "FCA's" in square brackets substituted by the Financial Services Act 2012, s 16(1)–(3), as from 1 April 2013.

Regulations: the Financial Services and Markets Act 2000 (Official Listing of Securities) Regulations 2001, SI 2001/2956 at **[8.434]**.

[7.169]
80 General duty of disclosure in listing particulars

(1) Listing particulars submitted to the [FCA] under section 79 must contain all such information as investors and their professional advisers would reasonably require, and reasonably expect to find there, for the purpose of making an informed assessment of—

(a) the assets and liabilities, financial position, profits and losses, and prospects of the issuer of the securities; and

(b) the rights attaching to the securities.

(2) That information is required in addition to any information required by—

(a) listing rules, or

(b) the [FCA],

as a condition of the admission of the securities to the official list.

(3) Subsection (1) applies only to information—

(a) within the knowledge of any person responsible for the listing particulars; or
(b) which it would be reasonable for him to obtain by making enquiries.

(4) In determining what information subsection (1) requires to be included in listing particulars, regard must be had (in particular) to—
(a) the nature of the securities and their issuer;
(b) the nature of the persons likely to consider acquiring them;
(c) the fact that certain matters may reasonably be expected to be within the knowledge of professional advisers of a kind which persons likely to acquire the securities may reasonably be expected to consult; and
(d) any information available to investors or their professional advisers as a result of requirements imposed on the issuer of the securities by a recognised investment exchange, by listing rules or by or under any other enactment.

NOTES

Words in square brackets substituted by the Financial Services Act 2012, s 16(1)–(3), as from 1 April 2013.

[7.170]

81 Supplementary listing particulars

(1) If at any time after the preparation of listing particulars which have been submitted to the [FCA] under section 79 and before the commencement of dealings in the securities concerned following their admission to the official list—
(a) there is a significant change affecting any matter contained in those particulars the inclusion of which was required by—
(i) section 80,
(ii) listing rules, or
(iii) the [FCA], or
(b) a significant new matter arises, the inclusion of information in respect of which would have been so required if it had arisen when the particulars were prepared,

the issuer must, in accordance with listing rules, submit supplementary listing particulars of the change or new matter to the [FCA], for its approval and, if they are approved, publish them.

(2) "Significant" means significant for the purpose of making an informed assessment of the kind mentioned in section 80(1).

(3) If the issuer of the securities is not aware of the change or new matter in question, he is not under a duty to comply with subsection (1) unless he is notified of the change or new matter by a person responsible for the listing particulars.

(4) But it is the duty of any person responsible for those particulars who is aware of such a change or new matter to give notice of it to the issuer.

(5) Subsection (1) applies also as respects matters contained in any supplementary listing particulars previously published under this section in respect of the securities in question.

NOTES

Words in square brackets substituted by the Financial Services Act 2012, s 16(1)–(3), as from 1 April 2013.

[7.171]

82 Exemptions from disclosure

(1) The [FCA] may authorise the omission from listing particulars of any information, the inclusion of which would otherwise be required by section 80 or 81, on the ground—
(a) that its disclosure would be contrary to the public interest;
(b) that its disclosure would be seriously detrimental to the issuer; or
(c) in the case of securities of a kind specified in listing rules, that its disclosure is unnecessary for persons of the kind who may be expected normally to buy or deal in securities of that kind.

(2) But—
(a) no authority may be granted under subsection (1)(b) in respect of essential information; and
(b) no authority granted under subsection (1)(b) extends to any such information.

(3) The Secretary of State or the Treasury may issue a certificate to the effect that the disclosure of any information (including information that would otherwise have to be included in listing particulars for which they are themselves responsible) would be contrary to the public interest.

(4) The [FCA] is entitled to act on any such certificate in exercising its powers under subsection (1)(a).

(5) This section does not affect any powers of the [FCA] under listing rules made as a result of section 101(2).

(6) "Essential information" means information which a person considering acquiring securities of the kind in question would be likely to need in order not to be misled about any facts which it is essential for him to know in order to make an informed assessment.

(7) "Listing particulars" includes supplementary listing particulars.

NOTES

Words in square brackets substituted by the Financial Services Act 2012, s 16(1)–(3), as from 1 April 2013.

83 *(Repealed by the Prospectus Regulations 2005, SI 2005/1433, reg 2(1), Sch 1, para 4, as from 1 July 2005.)*

[Transferable securities: public offers and admission to trading

[7.172]

84 Matters which may be dealt with by prospectus rules

(1) Prospectus rules may make provision as to—
(a) the required form and content of a prospectus . . . ;
(b) the cases in which a summary need not be included in a prospectus;
(c) the languages which may be used in a prospectus . . . ;
(d) the determination of the persons responsible for a prospectus;

(e) the manner in which applications to the [FCA] for the approval of a prospectus are to be made.

[(1A) In subsection (1) "prospectus" includes any part of a prospectus, and in particular includes a summary and a supplement.]

(2) Prospectus rules may also make provision as to—

(a) the period of validity of a prospectus;

(b) the disclosure of the maximum price or of the criteria or conditions according to which the final offer price is to be determined, if that information is not contained in a prospectus;

(c) the disclosure of the amount of the transferable securities which are to be offered to the public or of the criteria or conditions according to which that amount is to be determined, if that information is not contained in a prospectus;

(d) the required form and content of other summary documents (including the languages which may be used in such a document);

(e) the ways in which a prospectus that has been approved by the [FCA] may be made available to the public;

(f) the disclosure, publication or other communication of such information as the [FCA] may reasonably stipulate;

(g) the principles to be observed in relation to advertisements in connection with an offer of transferable securities to the public or admission of transferable securities to trading on a regulated market and the enforcement of those principles;

(h) the suspension of trading in transferable securities where continued trading would be detrimental to the interests of investors;

[(i) the exercise of entitlements under Article 4 of the prospectus regulation . . .].

(3) . . .

(4) Prospectus rules may make provision for the purpose of dealing with matters arising out of or related to any provision of the prospectus [regulation].

(5), (6) . . .

(7) Nothing in this section affects the [FCA's] general power to make prospectus rules.]

NOTES

Sections 84–87, 87A–87R substituted (together with the preceding heading) for original ss 84–87, by the Prospectus Regulations 2005, SI 2005/1433, reg 2(1), Sch 1, para 5, as from 1 July 2005.

Sub-s (1): words in square brackets substituted by the Financial Services Act 2012, s 16(1)–(3), as from 1 April 2013. The words omitted were repealed by the Financial Services and Markets Act 2000 (Prospectus) Regulations 2019, SI 2019/1043, regs 3, 5(1), (2), as from 21 July 2019.

Sub-s (1A): inserted by SI 2019/1043, regs 3, 5(1), (3), as from 21 July 2019.

Sub-s (2) is amended as follows:

The words in square brackets in paras (e) and (f) were substituted by the Financial Services Act 2012, s 16(1)–(3), as from 1 April 2013.

Para (i) was substituted by SI 2019/1043, regs 3, 5(1), (4), as from 21 July 2019.

The words omitted from para (i) were repealed by the Prospectus (Amendment etc) (EU Exit) Regulations 2019, SI 2019/1234, regs 2, 3, as from IP completion day (as defined in the European Union (Withdrawal Agreement) Act 2020, s 39); for transitional provisions, see regs 74, 75 of the 2019 Regulations at **[12.165]** et seq.

Sub-s (3): repealed by the Prospectus Regulations 2012, SI 2012/1538, reg 3(1), as from 1 July 2012.

Sub-s (4): the word "regulation" in square brackets was substituted by SI 2019/1043, regs 3, 5(1), (5), as from 21 July 2019.

Sub-ss (5), (6): repealed by SI 2019/1043, regs 3, 5(1), (6), as from 21 July 2019.

[7.173]

[85 Prohibition of dealing etc in transferable securities without approved prospectus

(1) It is unlawful for transferable securities to which this subsection applies to be offered to the public in the United Kingdom unless an approved prospectus has been made available to the public before the offer is made.

(2) It is unlawful to request the admission of transferable securities to which this subsection applies to trading on a regulated market situated or operating in the United Kingdom unless an approved prospectus has been made available to the public before the request is made.

(3) A person who contravenes subsection (1) or (2) is guilty of an offence and liable—

(a) on summary conviction, to imprisonment for a term not exceeding 3 months or a fine not exceeding the statutory maximum or both;

(b) on conviction on indictment, to imprisonment for a term not exceeding 2 years or a fine or both.

(4) A contravention of subsection (1) or (2) is actionable, at the suit of a person who suffers loss as a result of the contravention, subject to the defences and other incidents applying to actions for breach of statutory duty.

(5) Subsection (1) applies to all transferable securities other than—

[(a) those listed in Article 1(2) of the prospectus regulation;

(b) any offered in an offer falling within Article 1(3) of the prospectus regulation].

(6) Subsection (2) applies to all transferable securities [other than those listed in Article 1(2) of the prospectus regulation].

[(6A) Schedule 11A makes provision that applies for the purposes of Article 1(2)(e) of the prospectus regulation.]

(7) "Approved prospectus" means, in relation to transferable securities to which this section applies, a prospectus approved by the [FCA].

[(8) . . .]

NOTES

Substituted as noted to s 84 at **[7.172]**.

Sub-s (5): paras (a), (b) substituted by the Financial Services and Markets Act 2000 (Prospectus) Regulations 2019, SI 2019/1043, regs 3, 6(1), (2), as from 21 July 2019.

Sub-s (6): words in square brackets substituted by SI 2019/1043, regs 3, 6(1), (3), as from 21 July 2019.

Sub-s (6A): inserted by SI 2019/1043, regs 3, 6(1), (4), as from 21 July 2019.

Sub-s (7): word in square brackets substituted by the Official Listing of Securities, Prospectus and Transparency (Amendment etc) (EU Exit) Regulations 2019, SI 2019/707, regs 3, 7, as from IP completion day (as defined in the European Union (Withdrawal Agreement) Act 2020, s 39).

Sub-s (8): originally added by SI 2019/1043, regs 3, 6(1), (5), as from 21 July 2019. Subsequently repealed by the Prospectus (Amendment etc) (EU Exit) Regulations 2019, SI 2019/1234, regs 2, 4, as from IP completion day (as defined in the European Union (Withdrawal Agreement) Act 2020, s 39); for transitional provisions, see regs 74, 75 of the 2019 Regulations at **[12.165]** et seq.

Deferred Prosecution Agreements: see the note to s 23 at **[7.63]**.

[7.174]

[86 Exempt offers to the public [and admissions to trading]

(1) A person does not contravene section 85(1) if—

[(aa) the offer falls within Article 1(4) of the prospectus regulation; or]

(e) the total consideration for the transferable securities being offered [in the United Kingdom] cannot exceed [8,000,000] euros (or an equivalent amount)[; . . .

(f) . . .]

[(1A) . . .]

[(1B) . . .]

(2) Where—

(a) a person [("the client") who is not a qualified investor (as defined in *the first sentence of* Article 2(e) of the prospectus regulation)] has engaged a qualified investor falling within [paragraph 3(a) of Schedule 1 to the markets in financial instruments regulation] to act as his agent, and

(b) the terms on which the qualified investor is engaged enable him to make decisions concerning the acceptance of offers of transferable securities on the client's behalf without reference to the client,

an offer made to or directed at the qualified investor is not to be regarded for the purposes of subsection (1) as also having been made to or directed at the client.

(3) For the purposes of [subsection (1)], the making of an offer of transferable securities to—

(a) trustees of a trust,

(b) members of a partnership in their capacity as such, or

(c) two or more persons jointly,

is to be treated as the making of an offer to a single person.

(4) In determining whether subsection (1)(e) is satisfied in relation to an offer ("offer A"), offer A is to be taken together with any other offer of transferable securities of the same class made by the same person which—

(a) was open at any time within the period of 12 months ending with the date on which offer A is first made; and

(b) had previously satisfied subsection (1)(e).

[(4A) A person does not contravene section 85(2) if the admission to trading falls within Article 1(5) of the prospectus regulation.]

(5) For the purposes of this section, an amount (in relation to an amount denominated in euros) is an "equivalent amount" if it is an amount of equal value denominated wholly or partly in another currency or unit of account.

(6) The equivalent is to be calculated at the latest practicable date before (but in any event not more than 3 working days before) the date on which the offer is first made.

[(7) . . .]

[(8)–(10) . . .]

NOTES

Substituted as noted to s 84 at **[7.172]**.

Section heading: words in square brackets inserted by the Financial Services and Markets Act 2000 (Prospectus) Regulations 2019, SI 2019/1043, regs 3, 7(1), (2), as from 21 July 2019.

Sub-s (1) is amended as follows:

Para (aa) was substituted (for the original paras (a)–(d)) by SI 2019/1043, regs 3, 7(1), (3)(a), as from 21 July 2019.

The words "in the United Kingdom" in square brackets in para (e) were substituted by the Official Listing of Securities, Prospectus and Transparency (Amendment etc) (EU Exit) Regulations 2019, SI 2019/707, regs 3, 8(1), (2)(a), as from IP completion day (as defined in the European Union (Withdrawal Agreement) Act 2020, s 39).

The figure "8,000,000" in square brackets in para (e) was substituted by the Financial Services and Markets Act 2000 (Prospectus and Markets in Financial Instruments) Regulations 2018, SI 2018/786, reg 2(1), (2), as from 21 July 2018.

Para (f) and word immediately preceding it (now omitted) were inserted by SI 2012/1538, reg 2(1)(d), as from 1 July 2012. They were repealed by SI 2019/1043, regs 3, 7(1), (3)(b), as from 21 July 2019.

Sub-s (1A): originally inserted by SI 2012/1538, reg 2(2), as from 1 July 2012. Subsequently repealed by SI 2019/1043, regs 3, 7(1), (4), as from 21 July 2019.

Sub-s (1B): originally inserted by SI 2013/1125, reg 2, as from 31 May 2013.Subsequently repealed by SI 2019/1043, regs 3, 7(1), (4), as from 21 July 2019.

Sub-s (2) is amended as follows:

The words in the first pair of square brackets were substituted by SI 2019/1043, regs 3, 7(1), (5), as from 21 July 2019.

The words omitted were repealed by the Prospectus (Amendment etc) (EU Exit) Regulations 2019, SI 2019/1234, regs 2, 5, as from IP completion day (as defined in the European Union (Withdrawal Agreement) Act 2020, s 39); for transitional provisions, see regs 74, 75 of the 2019 Regulations at **[12.165]** et seq.

The words in the second pair of square brackets were substituted by SI 2019/707, regs 3, 8(1), (5), as from IP completion day (as defined in the European Union (Withdrawal Agreement) Act 2020, s 39).

Sub-s (3): words in square brackets substituted by SI 2019/1043, regs 3, 7(1), (6), as from 21 July 2019.

Sub-s (4A): inserted by SI 2019/1043, regs 3, 7(1), (8), as from 21 July 2019.

Sub-s (7): substituted by SI 2012/1538, reg 3(2)(b), as from 1 July 2012. Subsequently repealed by SI 2019/1043, regs 3, 7(1), (7), as from 21 July 2019.

Sub-ss (8)–(10): inserted by SI 2012/1538, reg 3(2)(c), as from 1 July 2012. Subsequently repealed by SI 2019/1043, regs 3, 7(1), (7), as from 21 July 2019.

[7.175]
[87 Election to have prospectus

(1), (2) . . .

(3) Listing rules made under section 79 do not apply to securities [for which a prospectus is drawn up voluntarily in exercise of entitlement to do so under Article 4 of the prospectus regulation].

(4) . . .

NOTES

Substituted as noted to s 84 at **[7.172]**.

Sub-ss (1), (2) and (4) were repealed, and the words in square brackets in sub-s (3) were substituted, by the Financial Services and Markets Act 2000 (Prospectus) Regulations 2019, SI 2019/1043, regs 3, 8, as from 21 July 2019.

[Approval of prospectus

[7.176]
87A Criteria for approval of prospectus by [FCA]

(1) The [FCA] may not approve a prospectus unless it is satisfied that—

(a) . . .

(b) the prospectus contains the [information required by Article 6(1) or 14(2) of the prospectus regulation], and

(c) all of the other requirements imposed by or in accordance with this Part[, the prospectus regulation or prospectus rules] have been complied with (so far as those requirements apply to a prospectus for the transferable securities in question).

[(2) The necessary information is—

(a) the information required by Article 6(1) of the prospectus regulation, or

(b) in a case within Article 14(1) of that regulation, the information required by Article 14(2) of that regulation.]

[(2A) If, in the case of transferable securities to which section 87 applies, the prospectus states that the guarantor is a specified . . . State, the prospectus is not required to include other information about the guarantor.]

(3)–(5) . . .

[(6) . . .]

(7) . . .

[(7A) . . .]

(8) "Prospectus" . . . includes a supplementary prospectus.

[(9), (10) . . .]

NOTES

Substituted as noted to s 84 at **[7.172]**.

Word "FCA" in square brackets (in each place that it occurs) substituted by the Financial Services Act 2012, s 16(1), (6), as from 1 April 2013. Other amendments to this section are as follows:

Sub-s (1) is amended as follows:

Para (a) repealed by the Official Listing of Securities, Prospectus and Transparency (Amendment etc) (EU Exit) Regulations 2019, SI 2019/707, regs 3, 10(1), (2), as from IP completion day (as defined in the European Union (Withdrawal Agreement) Act 2020, s 39).

The words in square brackets in paras (b) and (c) were substituted by the Financial Services and Markets Act 2000 (Prospectus) Regulations 2019, SI 2019/1043, regs 3, 9(1)–(3), as from 21 July 2019.

Sub-s (2): substituted by SI 2019/1043, regs 3, 9(1), (4), as from 21 July 2019.

Sub-s (2A): inserted by the Prospectus Regulations 2012, SI 2012/1538, regs 2(3), 4, as from 1 July 2012. Word omitted repealed by SI 2019/707, regs 3, 10(3), as from IP completion day (as defined in the European Union (Withdrawal Agreement) Act 2020, s 39).

Sub-ss (3)–(5): repealed by SI 2019/1043, regs 3, 9(1), (5), as from 21 July 2019.

Sub-s (6): substituted by SI 2012/1538, regs 2(3), 4, as from 1 July 2012. Subsequently repealed by SI 2019/1043, regs 3, 9(1), (5), as from 21 July 2019.

Sub-s (7): repealed by SI 2019/1043, regs 3, 9(1), (5), as from 21 July 2019.

Sub-s (7A): originally inserted by SI 2012/1538, regs 2(3), 4, as from 1 July 2012. Subsequently repealed by the Payments to Governments and Miscellaneous Provisions Regulations 2014, SI 2014/3293, reg 2(2), as from 17 December 2014.

Sub-s (8): words omitted repealed by SI 2019/1043, regs 3, 9(1), (6), as from 21 July 2019.

Sub-ss (9), (10): originally added by SI 2012/1538, regs 2(3), 4, as from 1 July 2012. Subsequently repealed by SI 2019/1043, regs 3, 9(1), (7), as from 21 July 2019.

[7.177]
[87B Exemptions from disclosure

(1) . . .

(2) The Secretary of State or the Treasury may issue a certificate to the effect that the disclosure of any information would be contrary to the public interest.

(3) The [FCA] is entitled to act on any such certificate in exercising its powers under [Article 18(1)(a) of the prospectus regulation].

(4) This section does not affect any powers of the [FCA] under prospectus rules.

(5) . . .]

NOTES

Substituted as noted to s 84 at **[7.172]**.

Sub-ss (1) and (5) were repealed, and the words in the second pair of square brackets in sub-s (3) were substituted, by the Financial Services and Markets Act 2000 (Prospectus) Regulations 2019, SI 2019/1043, regs 3, 10, as from 21 July 2019.

Word "FCA" in square brackets (in each place that it occurs) substituted by the Financial Services Act 2012, s 16(1)–(3), as from 1 April 2013.

[7.178]

[87C Consideration of application for approval

(1)–(3) . . .

(4) The [FCA] may by notice in writing require a person who has applied for approval of a prospectus to provide—

(a) specified documents or documents of a specified description, or

(b) specified information or information of a specified description.

(5) . . .

(6) Subsection (4) applies only to information and documents reasonably required in connection with the exercise by the [FCA] of its functions in relation to the application.

(7) The [FCA] may require any information provided under this section to be provided in such form as it may reasonably require.

(8) The [FCA] may require—

(a) any information provided, whether in a document or otherwise, to be verified in such manner, or

(b) any document produced to be authenticated in such manner,

as it may reasonably require.

(9) . . . subsections (4) and (6) to (8) apply to [an application for approval of a supplementary prospectus] as they apply to an application for approval of a prospectus.

(10), (11) . . .]

NOTES

Substituted as noted to s 84 at **[7.172]**.

Sub-ss (1)–(3), (5), (10) and (11) were repealed, the words omitted from sub-s (9) were repealed, and the words "an application for approval of a supplementary prospectus" in square brackets in that subsection were substituted, by the Financial Services and Markets Act 2000 (Prospectus) Regulations 2019, SI 2019/1043, regs 3, 11, as from 21 July 2019.

Word "FCA" in square brackets (in each place that it occurs) substituted by the Financial Services Act 2012, s 16(1)–(3), as from 1 April 2013.

[7.179]

[87D Procedure for decision [to refuse an] application for approval

(1) . . .

[(1A) . . .]

(2) If the [FCA] proposes to refuse to approve a prospectus, it must give the applicant written notice.

(3) The notice must state the [FCA's] reasons for the proposed refusal.

(4) If the [FCA] decides to refuse to approve a prospectus, it must give the applicant written notice.

(5) The notice must—

(a) give the [FCA's] reasons for refusing the application; and

(b) inform the applicant of his right to refer the matter to the Tribunal.

(6) If the [FCA] refuses to approve a prospectus, the applicant may refer the matter to the Tribunal.

(7) In this section "prospectus" includes a supplementary prospectus.]

NOTES

Substituted as noted to s 84 at **[7.172]**.

The words in square brackets in the section heading were substituted by the Financial Services and Markets Act 2000 (Prospectus) Regulations 2019, SI 2019/1043, regs 3, 12(1), (2), as from 21 July 2019.

Sub-ss (1) and (1A) were repealed by SI 2019/1043, regs 3, 12(1), (3), as from 21 July 2019. Sub-s(1A) was originally inserted by the Financial Services and Markets (Disclosure of Information to the European Securities and Markets Authority etc and Other Provisions) Regulations 2016, SI 2016/1095, reg 3(1), (2), as from 8 December 2016.

Words "FCA" and "FCA's" in square brackets (in each place that they occur) substituted by the Financial Services Act 2012, s 16(1)–(3), as from 1 April 2013.

87E, 87F, 87FA, 87FB *(Ss 87E and 87F were substituted as noted to s 84 at* **[7.172]**; *they were subsequently repealed by the Financial Services and Markets Act 2000 (Prospectus) Regulations 2019, SI 2019/1043, regs 3, 13, as from 21 July 2019. Ss 87FA and 87FB were inserted by the Payments to Governments and Miscellaneous Provisions Regulations 2014, SI 2014/3293, reg 3, as from 17 December 2014; and subsequently repealed by the Financial Services and Markets Act 2000 (Prospectus) Regulations 2019, SI 2019/1043, regs 3, 14, as from 21 July 2019).)*

[Supplementary prospectus

[7.180]

87G Supplementary prospectus

(1)–(3) . . .

[(3A) . . .]

(4) . . .

(5) Any person [who is responsible for a prospectus approved by the FCA and] who is aware of any new factor, [material mistake or material inaccuracy] which may require the submission of a supplementary prospectus in accordance with [Article 23 of the prospectus regulation] must give notice of it to—

(a) the issuer of the transferable securities to which the prospectus relates, and

(b) the person on whose application the prospectus was approved.

(6), (7) . . .

NOTES

Substituted as noted to s 84 at **[7.172]**.

Sub-ss (1)–(3), (3A), (4), (6) and (7) were repealed by the Financial Services and Markets Act 2000 (Prospectus) Regulations 2019, SI 2019/1043, regs 3, 15(1), (2), (4), as from 21 July 2019. Note that sub-s (3A) was originally inserted by the Prospectus Regulations 2012, SI 2012/1538, reg 5(1), as from 1 July 2012.

The words in square brackets in sub-s (5) were substituted by SI 2019/1043, regs 3, 15(1), (3), as from 21 July 2019.

. . .

87H, 87I (*Substituted as noted to s 84 at* **[7.172]**. *Subsequently repealed by the Financial Services and Markets Act 2000 (Prospectus) Regulations 2019, SI 2019/1043, regs 3, 16, as from 21 July 2019.*)

[Transferable securities: powers of [FCA]

[7.181]

87J Requirements imposed as condition of approval

(1) As a condition of approving a prospectus, the [FCA] may by notice in writing—

(a) require the inclusion in the prospectus of such supplementary information necessary for investor protection as the [FCA] may specify;

(b) require a person controlling, or controlled by, the applicant to provide specified information or documents;

(c) require an auditor or manager of the applicant to provide specified information or documents;

(d) require a financial intermediary commissioned to assist either in carrying out the offer to the public of the transferable securities to which the prospectus relates or in requesting their admission to trading on a regulated market, to provide specified information or documents.

(2) "Specified" means specified in the notice.

(3) "Prospectus" includes a supplementary prospectus.]

NOTES

Substituted as noted to s 84 at **[7.172]**.

Word "FCA" in square brackets (in each place that it occurs (including in the heading preceding this section)) substituted by the Financial Services Act 2012, s 16(1)–(3), as from 1 April 2013.

[7.182]

[87JA Power to suspend scrutiny of prospectus

(1) Where the FCA has received an application for approval of a prospectus, it may suspend its scrutiny of the prospectus on the ground that—

(a) before receiving the application, it had imposed a prohibition or restriction under Article 42 of the markets in financial instruments regulation in relation to any financial activity or practice of the applicant;

(b) in considering the application, it has decided to impose a prohibition or restriction under that Article in relation to the transferable securities to which the prospectus relates or any financial activity or practice of the applicant;

(c) before receiving the application, it had found that a financial activity or practice of the applicant had contravened product intervention rules; or

(d) in considering the application, it has decided that the approval of the prospectus would be likely to result in a contravention of product intervention rules.

(2) The FCA must resume its consideration of the application for approval of the prospectus—

(a) where it suspended scrutiny of the prospectus on the ground specified in subsection (1)(a) or (b)—

(i) upon revoking the prohibition or restriction under Article 42(6) of the markets in financial instruments regulation; or

(ii) when it is satisfied that the prohibition or restriction does not have, or no longer has, any bearing on the approval of the prospectus;

(b) where it suspended scrutiny of the prospectus on the ground specified in subsection (1)(c), when it is satisfied that the contravention of product intervention rules does not have, or no longer has, any bearing on the approval of the prospectus;

(c) where it suspended scrutiny of the prospectus on the ground specified in subsection (1)(d), when it is satisfied that its approval of the prospectus would not result in a contravention of product intervention rules;

(d) upon giving notice under section 87O(5) revoking its decision to suspend scrutiny of the prospectus;

(e) where its decision to suspend scrutiny of the prospectus is quashed on a reference to the Tribunal or in other legal proceedings, on the date of the judgment of the Tribunal or of the court concerned.

(3) "Product intervention rules" has the same meaning as in section 137D.]

NOTES

Commencement: 21 July 2019.

Inserted by the Financial Services and Markets Act 2000 (Prospectus) Regulations 2019, SI 2019/1043, regs 3, 17, as from 21 July 2019.

[7.183]

[87JB Power to refuse approval of a prospectus

(1) Where the FCA is satisfied that a person has repeatedly and seriously infringed provision within subsection (2) (whether or not each infringement is of the same provision), the FCA may decide that, for a period not exceeding 5 years, the FCA will not accept from the person any application for approval of a prospectus.

(2) The provisions referred to in subsection (1) are—

(a) any provision of this Part so far as relating to prospectuses;

(b) any provision of prospectus rules;

(c) any provision of the prospectus regulation;

(d) any provision made in accordance with the prospectus regulation.

(3) If the FCA proposes that for a period it will not accept any application from a person for approval of a prospectus, the FCA must give the person a warning notice specifying the length of the proposed period.

(4) If the FCA decides for a period that it will not accept any application from a person for approval of a prospectus—

(a) the FCA must give the person a decision notice;

(b) the period starts with the date of the notice;

(c) the person may refer that matter to the Tribunal; and

(d) the notice must—
 (i) be dated;
 (ii) specify the length of the period;
 (iii) state that the period begins with the date of the notice; and
 (iv) state that the person may refer the matter to the Tribunal.

(5) If the FCA decides not to accept any application from a person for the approval of a prospectus for a specified period, the person may refer the matter to the Tribunal.]

NOTES

Commencement: 21 July 2019.

Inserted by the Financial Services and Markets Act 2000 (Prospectus) Regulations 2019, SI 2019/1043, regs 3, 17, as from 21 July 2019.

[7.184]

[87K Power to suspend[, restrict] or prohibit offer to the public

(1) This section applies where a person ("the offeror") has made an offer of transferable securities to the public . . . ("the offer").

(2) If the [FCA] has reasonable grounds for suspecting that an applicable provision has been infringed, it may—
 (a) require the offeror to suspend the offer for a period not exceeding 10 working days;
 (b) require a person not to advertise the offer, or to take such steps as [the FCA] may specify to suspend any existing advertisement of the offer, for a period not exceeding 10 working days.

(3) If the [FCA] has reasonable grounds for suspecting that it is likely that an applicable provision will be infringed, it may require the offeror to withdraw the offer.

(4) If the [FCA] finds that an applicable provision has been infringed, it may require the offeror to withdraw the offer.

(5) "An applicable provision" means—
 (a) a provision of this Part,
 (b) a provision contained in prospectus rules,
 [(c) any provision of, or made in accordance with, the prospectus regulation,]

applicable in relation to the offer.

[(6) The FCA may require the offeror to suspend or restrict the offer on the ground that—
 (a) before the offer was made, the FCA had imposed a prohibition or restriction under Article 42 of the markets in financial instruments regulation in relation to any financial activity or practice of the offeror;
 (b) the FCA has decided to impose a prohibition or restriction under that Article in relation to the transferable securities to which the offer relates or any financial activity or practice of the offeror;
 (c) before the offer was made, the FCA had found that a financial activity or practice of the offeror had contravened product intervention rules; or
 (d) the FCA has decided that the offer, if not suspended or restricted, would be likely to result in a contravention of product intervention rules.

(7) A requirement imposed under subsection (6) ceases to have effect—
 (a) where it was imposed on the ground specified in subsection (6)(a) or (b)—
 (i) upon revocation of the prohibition or restriction under Article 42(6) of the markets in financial instruments regulation; or
 (ii) when the FCA notifies the offeror that it is satisfied that the prohibition or restriction does not have, or no longer has, any bearing on the transferable securities to which the offer relates;
 (b) where it was imposed on the ground specified in subsection (6)(c), when the FCA notifies the offeror that it is satisfied that the contravention of product intervention rules does not have, or no longer has, any bearing on the transferable securities to which the offer relates;
 (c) where it was imposed on the ground specified in subsection (6)(d), when the FCA notifies the offeror that it is satisfied that the offer, if no longer suspended or restricted, would not result in a contravention of product intervention rules;
 (d) upon the FCA giving notice under section 87O(5) revoking its decision to impose the requirement;
 (e) where the FCA's decision to impose the requirement is quashed on a reference to the Tribunal or in other legal proceedings, on the date of the judgment of the Tribunal or of the court concerned.

(8) "Product intervention rules" has the same meaning as in section 137D.]]

NOTES

Substituted as noted to s 84 at **[7.172]**.

The words "FCA" and "the FCA" in square brackets (in each place that they occur) were substituted by the Financial Services Act 2012, s 16(1)–(3), as from 1 April 2013.

Section heading: word in square brackets inserted by the Financial Services and Markets Act 2000 (Prospectus) Regulations 2019, SI 2019/1043, regs 3, 18(1), (2), as from 21 July 2019.

Sub-s (1): words omitted repealed by the Payments to Governments and Miscellaneous Provisions Regulations 2014, SI 2014/3293, reg 2(3), as from 17 December 2014.

Sub-s (5): para (c) was substituted by SI 2019/1043, regs 3, 18(1), (3), as from 21 July 2019.

Sub-ss (6)–(8): added by SI 2019/1043, regs 3, 18(1), (4), as from 21 July 2019.

[7.185]

[87L Power to suspend[, restrict] or prohibit admission to trading on a regulated market

(1) This section applies where a person has requested the admission of transferable securities to trading on a regulated market . . .

(2) If the [FCA] has reasonable grounds for suspecting that an applicable provision has been infringed and the securities have not yet been admitted to trading on the regulated market in question, it may—
 (a) require the person requesting admission to suspend the request for a period not exceeding 10 working days;

Part 7 Financial Services Acts

(b) require a person not to advertise the securities to which it relates, or to take such steps as [the FCA] may specify to suspend any existing advertisement in connection with those securities, for a period not exceeding 10 working days.

(3) If the [FCA] has reasonable grounds for suspecting that an applicable provision has been infringed and the securities have been admitted to trading on the regulated market in question, it may—

(a) require the market operator to suspend trading in the securities for a period not exceeding 10 working days;

(b) require a person not to advertise the securities, or to take such steps as [the FCA] may specify to suspend any existing advertisement in connection with those securities, for a period not exceeding 10 working days.

(4) If the [FCA] finds that an applicable provision has been infringed, it may require the market operator to prohibit trading in the securities on the regulated market in question.

(5) "An applicable provision" means—

(a) a provision of this Part,

(b) a provision contained in prospectus rules,

[(c) any provision of, or made in accordance with, the prospectus regulation,]

applicable in relation to the admission of the transferable securities to trading on the regulated market in question.

[(6) Subsections (7) and (8) apply where—

(a) before the request was made for the admission of the securities to trading on the regulated market in question ("the request"), the FCA had imposed a prohibition or restriction under Article 42 of the markets in financial instruments regulation in relation to any financial activity or practice of the person who made the request;

(b) the FCA has decided to impose a prohibition or restriction under that Article in relation to the securities or any financial activity or practice of the person who made the request;

(c) before the request was made, the FCA had found that a financial activity or practice of the person who made the request had contravened product intervention rules; or

(d) the FCA has decided that the admission of the securities to trading on the regulated market in question, if not suspended or restricted, would be likely to result in a contravention of product intervention rules.

(7) Where the securities have not yet been admitted to trading on the regulated market in question, the FCA may—

(a) require the person who made the request to suspend or restrict the request;

(b) require a person not to advertise the securities, or to take such steps as the FCA may specify to suspend any existing advertising in connection with the securities.

(8) Where the securities have been admitted to trading on the regulated market in question, the FCA may—

(a) require the market operator to suspend or restrict trading in the securities;

(b) require a person not to advertise the securities, or to take such steps as the FCA may specify to suspend any existing advertising in connection with the securities.

(9) A requirement imposed under subsection (7) or (8) ceases to have effect—

(a) where it was imposed on the ground mentioned in subsection (6)(a) or (b)—

(i) upon revocation of the prohibition or restriction under Article 42(6) of the markets in financial instruments regulation; or

(ii) when the FCA notifies the person who made the request that it is satisfied that the prohibition or restriction does not have, or no longer has, any bearing on the securities;

(b) where it was imposed on the ground mentioned in subsection (6)(c), when the FCA notifies the person who made the request that it is satisfied that the contravention of product intervention rules does not have, or no longer has, any bearing on the securities;

(c) where it was imposed on the ground mentioned in subsection (6)(d), when the FCA notifies the person who made the request that it is satisfied that the admission of the securities to trading on the regulated market in question, if no longer suspended or restricted, would not result in a contravention of product intervention rules;

(d) upon the FCA giving notice under section 87O(5) revoking its decision to impose the requirement;

(e) where the FCA's decision to impose the requirement is quashed on a reference to the Tribunal or in other legal proceedings, on the date of the judgment of the Tribunal or of the court concerned.

(10) "Product intervention rules" has the same meaning as in section 137D.

(11) Where the FCA considers that the financial or other situation of a person at whose request transferable securities have been admitted to trading on a regulated market is such that trading would be detrimental to the interests of investors, it may require the market operator to suspend trading in the securities.]]

NOTES

Substituted as noted to s 84 at **[7.172]**.

The words "FCA" and "the FCA" in square brackets (in each place that they occur) were substituted by the Financial Services Act 2012, s 16(1)–(3), as from 1 April 2013.

Section heading: word in square brackets inserted by the Financial Services and Markets Act 2000 (Prospectus) Regulations 2019, SI 2019/1043, regs 3, 19(1), (2), as from 21 July 2019.

Sub-s (1): words omitted repealed by the Payments to Governments and Miscellaneous Provisions Regulations 2014, SI 2014/3293, reg 2(4), as from 17 December 2014.

Sub-s (5): para (c) substituted by SI 2019/1043, regs 3, 19(1), (3), as from 21 July 2019.

Sub-ss (6)–(11): added by SI 2019/1043, regs 3, 19(1), (4), as from 21 July 2019.

[7.186]

[87LA Power of FCA to suspend or prohibit trading on a trading facility

(1) This section applies in relation to the trading of transferable securities on a trading facility.

(2) If—

(a) the FCA has reasonable grounds for suspecting that an applicable provision has been infringed, and

(b) the securities have not yet been traded on the trading facility in question,

the FCA may require the person who proposes to trade the securities to suspend taking any action to implement the proposal for a period not exceeding 10 working days.

(3) If—

(a) the FCA has reasonable grounds for suspecting that an applicable provision has been infringed, and
(b) the securities have been traded on the trading facility in question,
the FCA may require the operator of the facility to suspend trading in the securities for a period not exceeding 10 working days.
(4) If the FCA finds that an applicable provision has been infringed, it may require the operator of the trading facility in question to prohibit trading in the securities on that facility.
(5) In this section—
"applicable provision" means—
(a) a provision of this Part,
(b) a provision contained in prospectus rules, or
(c) any provision of, or made in accordance with, the prospectus regulation;
["trading facility" means a UK multilateral trading facility or a UK organised trading facility;
"UK multilateral trading facility" has the meaning given in Article 2(1)(14A) of the markets in financial instruments regulation;
"UK organised trading facility" has the meaning given in Article 2(1)(15A) of the markets in financial instruments regulation].]

NOTES

Commencement: 21 July 2019.

Inserted by the Financial Services and Markets Act 2000 (Prospectus) Regulations 2019, SI 2019/1043, regs 3, 20, as from 21 July 2019.

Sub-s (5): definitions in square brackets substituted by the Prospectus (Amendment etc) (EU Exit) Regulations 2019, SI 2019/1234, regs 2, 6, as from IP completion day (as defined in the European Union (Withdrawal Agreement) Act 2020, s 39); for transitional provisions, see regs 74, 75 of the 2019 Regulations at **[12.165]** et seq.

[7.187]

[87M Public censure of issuer

(1) If the [FCA] finds that—
(a) an issuer of transferable securities,
(b) a person offering transferable securities to the public, or
(c) a person requesting the admission of transferable securities to trading on a regulated market,
is failing or has failed to comply with his obligations under an applicable provision, it may publish a statement to that effect.
(2) If the [FCA] proposes to publish a statement, it must give the person a warning notice setting out the terms of the proposed statement.
(3) If, after considering any representations made in response to the warning notice, the [FCA] decides to make the proposed statement, it must give the person a decision notice setting out the terms of the statement.
(4) "An applicable provision" means—
(a) a provision of this Part,
(b) a provision contained in prospectus rules,
[(c) any provision of, or made in accordance with, the prospectus regulation,]
applicable to a prospectus in relation to the transferable securities in question.
(5) "Prospectus" includes a supplementary prospectus [and also includes, where final terms (see Article 8 of the prospectus regulation) are contained in a separate document that is neither a prospectus nor a supplementary prospectus, that separate document].]

NOTES

Substituted as noted to s 84 at **[7.172]**.

Sub-ss (1)–(3): word "FCA" in square brackets (in each place that it occurs) substituted by the Financial Services Act 2012, s 16(1)–(3), as from 1 April 2013.

Sub-s (4): para (c) substituted by SI 2019/1043, regs 3, 21(1), (2), as from 21 July 2019.

Sub-s (5): words in square brackets inserted by SI 2019/1043, regs 3, 21(1), (3), as from 21 July 2019.

[7.188]

[87N Right to refer matters to the Tribunal

(1) A person to whom a decision notice is given under section 87M may refer the matter to the Tribunal.
(2) A person to whom a notice is given under section 87O may refer the matter to the Tribunal.]

NOTES

Substituted as noted to s 84 at **[7.172]**.

[7.189]

[87O [Procedure under sections 87JA, 87K, 87L and 87LA]

(1) A requirement under section 87K[, 87L or 87LA, or a suspension under section 87JA(1),] takes effect—
(a) immediately, if the notice under subsection (2) states that that is the case;
(b) in any other case, on such date as may be specified in that notice.
(2) If the [FCA]—
(a) proposes to exercise the powers in section [87JA, 87K, 87L or 87LA] in relation to a person, or
(b) exercises any of those powers in relation to a person with immediate effect,
it must give that person written notice.
(3) The notice must—
(a) give details of the [FCA's] action or proposed action;
(b) state the [FCA's] reasons for taking the action in question and choosing the date on which it took effect or takes effect;
(c) inform the recipient that he may make representations to the [FCA] within such period as may be specified by the notice (whether or not he has referred the matter to the Tribunal);

(d) inform him of the date on which the action took effect or takes effect; and
(e) inform him of his right to refer the matter to the Tribunal.

(4) The [FCA] may extend the period within which representations may be made to it.

(5) If, having considered any representations made to it, the [FCA] decides to maintain, vary or revoke its earlier decision, it must give written notice to that effect to the person mentioned in subsection (2).

(6) A notice given under subsection (5) must inform that person, where relevant, of his right to refer the matter to the Tribunal.

(7) If a notice informs a person of his right to refer a matter to the Tribunal, it must give an indication of the procedure on such a reference.

(8) If a notice under this section relates to the exercise of the power conferred by section 87L(3), the notice must also be given to the person at whose request the transferable securities were admitted to trading on the regulated market.]

NOTES

Substituted as noted to s 84 at **[7.172]**.

The section heading was substituted, the words in the first pair of square brackets in sub-s (1) were substituted, and the words in the second pair of square brackets in sub-s (2) were substituted, by the Financial Services and Markets Act 2000 (Prospectus) Regulations 2019, SI 2019/1043, regs 3, 22, as from 21 July 2019.

The words "FCAs" and "FCA's" in square brackets (in each place that they occur) were substituted by the Financial Services Act 2012, s 16(1)–(3), as from 1 April 2013.

87P–87R *(Ss 87P–87R were substituted as noted to s 84 at* **[7.172]**. *S 87P was subsequently repealed by the Official Listing of Securities, Prospectus and Transparency (Amendment etc) (EU Exit) Regulations 2019, SI 2019/707, regs 3, 18, as from IP completion day (as defined in the European Union (Withdrawal Agreement) Act 2020, s 39). Ss 87Q and 87R were subsequently repealed by the Financial Services and Markets Act 2000 (Prospectus) Regulations 2019, SI 2019/1043, regs 3, 24, as from 21 July 2019.)*

Sponsors

[7.190]

88 Sponsors

(1) Listing rules may require a person to make arrangements with a sponsor for the performance by the sponsor of such services in relation to him as may be specified in the rules.

(2) "Sponsor" means a person approved by the [FCA] for the purposes of the rules.

(3) Listing rules made by virtue of subsection (1) may—

(a) provide for the [FCA] to maintain a list of sponsors;
(b) specify services which must be performed by a sponsor;
(c) impose requirements on a sponsor in relation to the provision of services or specified services;
(d) specify the circumstances in which a person is qualified for being approved as a sponsor;
[(e) provide for limitations or other restrictions to be imposed on the services to which an approval relates (whether or not the approval has already been granted);
(f) provide for the approval of a sponsor to be suspended on the application of the sponsor.]

(4) If the [FCA] proposes—

(a) to refuse a person's application [under sponsor rules],
[(aa) to impose limitations or other restrictions on the services to which a person's approval relates,] or
(b) to cancel a person's approval as a sponsor [otherwise than at his request],

it must give him a warning notice.

(5) If, after considering any representations made in response to the warning notice, the [FCA] decides—

(a) to grant the application [under sponsor rules],
[(aa) not to impose limitations or other restrictions on the services to which a person's approval relates,] or
(b) not to cancel the approval,

it must give the person concerned, and any person to whom a copy of the warning notice was given, written notice of its decision.

(6) If, after considering any representations made in response to the warning notice, the [FCA] decides—

(a) to refuse to grant the application [under sponsor rules],
[(aa) to impose limitations or other restrictions on the services to which a person's approval relates,] or
(b) to cancel the approval,

it must give the person concerned a decision notice.

(7) A person to whom a decision notice is given under this section may refer the matter to the Tribunal.

[(8) In this section any reference to an application under sponsor rules means—

(a) an application for approval as a sponsor,
(b) an application for the suspension of an approval as a sponsor,
(c) an application for the withdrawal of the suspension of an approval as a sponsor, or
(d) an application for the withdrawal or variation of a limitation or other restriction on the services to which a sponsor's approval relates.]

NOTES

Word "FCA" in square brackets (in each place that it occurs) substituted by the Financial Services Act 2012, s 16(1)–(3), as from 1 April 2013.

Sub-s (3): paras (e), (f) inserted by the Financial Services Act 2012, s 18(1), (2)(a), (3), as from 19 March 2013 (for the purpose of making rules), and as from 1 April 2013 (otherwise). Note that the power to make provision under para (e) (as inserted by s 18(1), (2)(a)) includes power to make provision in relation to persons who were approved as sponsors before the coming into force of sub-s (2)(a).

Sub-s (4): words "under sponsor rules" in square brackets substituted, and para (aa) inserted, by the Financial Services Act 2012, s 18(1), (2)(b), (c), as from 1 April 2013. Words in square brackets in para (b) inserted by the Regulatory Reform (Financial Services and Markets Act 2000) Order 2007, SI 2007/1973, arts 2, 9, as from 12 July 2007.

Sub-ss (5), (6): words "under sponsor rules" in square brackets substituted, and para (aa) inserted, by the Financial Services Act 2012, s 18(1), (2)(d)–(g), as from 1 April 2013.

Sub-s (8): added by the Financial Services Act 2012, s 18(1), (2)(h), as from 1 April 2013.

[7.191]

[88A Disciplinary powers: contravention of s 88(3)(c) or (e)

(1) The FCA may take action against a sponsor under this section if it considers that the sponsor has contravened a requirement or restriction imposed on the sponsor by rules made as a result of section 88(3)(c) or (e).

(2) If the FCA is entitled to take action under this section against a sponsor, it may do one or more of the following—

(a) impose a penalty on the sponsor of such amount as it considers appropriate;

(b) suspend, for such period as it considers appropriate, the sponsor's approval;

(c) impose, for such period as it considers appropriate, such limitations or other restrictions in relation to the performance of services to which the sponsor's approval relates as it considers appropriate;

(d) publish a statement to the effect that the sponsor has contravened a requirement or restriction imposed on the sponsor by rules made as a result of section 88(3)(c) or (e).

(3) The period for which a suspension or restriction is to have effect may not exceed 12 months.

(4) A suspension may relate only to the performance in specified circumstances of a service to which the approval relates.

(5) A restriction may, in particular, be imposed so as to require the sponsor to take, or refrain from taking, specified action.

(6) The FCA may—

(a) withdraw a suspension or restriction; or

(b) vary a suspension or restriction so as to reduce the period for which it has effect or otherwise to limit its effect.

(7) The FCA may not take action against a sponsor under this section after the end of the limitation period unless, before the end of that period, it has given a warning notice to the sponsor under section 88B(1).

(8) "The limitation period" means the period of 3 years beginning with the first day on which the FCA knew that the sponsor had contravened the requirement or restriction.

(9) For this purpose the FCA is to be treated as knowing that a sponsor has contravened a requirement or restriction if it has information from which that can reasonably be inferred.]

NOTES

Sections 88A–88F were substituted (for the original s 89) by the Financial Services Act 2012, s 18(1), (4), as from 19 March 2013 (for the purpose of making rules), and as from 1 April 2013 (otherwise).

[7.192]

[88B Action under s 88A: procedure and right to refer to Tribunal

(1) If the FCA proposes to take action against a sponsor under section 88A, it must give the sponsor a warning notice.

(2) A warning notice about a proposal to impose a penalty must state the amount of the penalty.

(3) A warning notice about a proposal—

(a) to suspend an approval, or

(b) to impose a restriction in relation to the performance of a service,

must state the period for which the suspension or restriction is to have effect.

(4) A warning notice about a proposal to publish a statement must set out the terms of the statement.

(5) If the FCA decides to take action against a sponsor under section 88A, it must give the sponsor a decision notice.

(6) A decision notice about the imposition of a penalty must state the amount of the penalty.

(7) A decision notice about—

(a) the suspension of an approval, or

(b) the imposition of a restriction in relation to the performance of a service,

must state the period for which the suspension or restriction is to have effect.

(8) A decision notice about the publication of a statement must set out the terms of the statement.

(9) If the FCA decides to take action against a sponsor under section 88A, the sponsor may refer the matter to the Tribunal.]

NOTES

Substituted as noted to s 88A at **[7.191]**.

[7.193]

[88C Action under s 88A: statement of policy

(1) The FCA must prepare and issue a statement of its policy with respect to—

(a) the imposition of penalties, suspensions or restrictions under section 88A,

(b) the amount of penalties under that section, and

(c) the period for which suspensions or restrictions under that section are to have effect.

(2) The FCA's policy in determining what the amount of a penalty should be, or what the period for which a suspension or restriction is to have effect should be, must include having regard to—

(a) the seriousness of the contravention in question in relation to the nature of the requirement concerned,

(b) the extent to which that contravention was deliberate or reckless, and

(c) whether the sponsor concerned is an individual.

(3) The FCA may at any time alter or replace a statement issued under this section.

(4) If a statement issued under this section is altered or replaced, the FCA must issue the altered or replacement statement.

(5) In exercising, or deciding whether to exercise, its power under section 88A in the case of any particular contravention, the FCA must have regard to any statement of policy published under this section and in force at a time when the contravention in question occurred.

(6) A statement issued under this section must be published by the FCA in the way appearing to the FCA to be best calculated to bring it to the attention of the public.

(7) The FCA may charge a reasonable fee for providing a person with a copy of the statement.

(8) The FCA must, without delay, give the Treasury a copy of any statement which it publishes under this section.]

NOTES

Substituted as noted to s 88A at **[7.191]**.

[7.194]

[88D Statement of policy under s 88C: procedure

(1) Before issuing a statement under section 88C, the FCA must publish a draft of the proposed statement in the way appearing to the FCA to be best calculated to bring it to the attention of the public.

(2) The draft must be accompanied by notice that representations about the proposal may be made to the FCA within a specified time.

(3) Before issuing the proposed statement, the FCA must have regard to any representations made to it in accordance with subsection (2).

(4) If the FCA issues the proposed statement it must publish an account, in general terms, of—

(a) the representations made to it in accordance with subsection (2), and

(b) its response to them.

(5) If the statement differs from the draft published under subsection (1) in a way which is, in the opinion of the FCA, significant, the FCA must (in addition to complying with subsection (4)) publish details of the difference.

(6) The FCA may charge a reasonable fee for providing a person with a copy of a draft published under subsection (1).

(7) This section also applies to a proposal to alter or replace a statement.]

NOTES

Substituted as noted to s 88A at **[7.191]**.

[7.195]

[88E Powers exercisable to advance operational objectives

(1) The FCA may take action against a sponsor under this section if it considers that it is desirable to do so in order to advance one or more of its operational objectives.

(2) If the FCA is entitled to take action under this section against a sponsor, it may—

(a) suspend, for such period as it considers appropriate, the sponsor's approval, or

(b) impose, for such period as it considers appropriate, such limitations or other restrictions in relation to the performance of services to which the sponsor's approval relates as it considers appropriate.

(3) A suspension may relate only to the performance in specified circumstances of a service to which the approval relates.

(4) A restriction may, in particular, be imposed so as to require the sponsor to take, or refrain from taking, specified action.

(5) The FCA may—

(a) withdraw a suspension or restriction, or

(b) vary a suspension or restriction so as to reduce the period for which it has effect or otherwise to limit its effect.

(6) A person against whom the FCA takes action under this section may refer the matter to the Tribunal.

NOTES

Substituted as noted to s 88A at **[7.191]**.

[7.196]

[88F Action under s 88E: procedure

(1) Action against a sponsor under section 88E takes effect—

(a) immediately, if the notice given under subsection (3) so provides, or

(b) on such later date as may be specified in the notice.

(2) If the FCA—

(a) proposes to take action against a sponsor under that section, or

(b) takes action against a sponsor under that section with immediate effect,

it must give the sponsor written notice.

(3) The notice must—

(a) give details of the action,

(b) state the FCA's reasons for taking the action and for its determination as to when the action takes effect,

(c) inform the sponsor that the sponsor may make representations to the FCA within such period as may be specified in the notice (whether or not the matter has been referred to the Tribunal),

(d) inform the sponsor of when the action takes effect,

(e) inform the sponsor of the right to refer the matter to the Tribunal, and

(f) give an indication of the procedure on such a reference.

(4) The FCA may extend the period allowed under the notice for making representations.

(5) If the FCA decides—

(a) to take the action in the way proposed, or

(b) if the action has taken effect, not to rescind it,

the FCA must give the sponsor written notice.

(6) If the FCA decides—

(a) not to take the action in the way proposed,

(b) to take action under section 88E that differs from the action originally proposed, or

(c) to rescind action which has taken effect,

the FCA must give the sponsor written notice.

(7) A notice under subsection (5) must—

(a) inform the sponsor of the right to refer the matter to the Tribunal, and

(b) give an indication of the procedure on such a reference.

(8) A notice under subsection (6)(b) must comply with subsection (3).]

NOTES

Substituted as noted to s 88A at **[7.191]**.

[Transparency obligations

[7.197]

89A Transparency rules

[(1) The FCA may make rules—

(a) imposing requirements in relation to the disclosure of periodic or ongoing information about issuers whose securities are admitted to trading on a regulated market, and

(b) dealing with matters arising out of or relating to such requirements.]

(2) The rules may include provision for dealing with any matters [dealt with in the transparency obligations directive or with any matters that, when the United Kingdom was a member State, would have been matters] arising out of or related to any provision of the transparency obligations directive.

(3) The [FCA] may also make rules—

(a) for the purpose of ensuring that voteholder information in respect of voting shares traded on a UK market other than a regulated market is made public or notified to the [FCA];

(b) . . .

(4) Rules under this section may, in particular, make provision—

(a) specifying how the proportion of—

(i) the total voting rights in respect of shares in an issuer, or

(ii) the total voting rights in respect of a particular class of shares in an issuer,

held by a person is to be determined;

(b) specifying the circumstances in which, for the purposes of any determination of the voting rights held by a person ("P") in respect of voting shares in an issuer, any voting rights held . . . by another person in respect of voting shares in the issuer are to be regarded as held by P;

(c) specifying the nature of the information which must be included in any notification;

(d) about the form of any notification;

(e) requiring any notification to be given within a specified period;

(f) specifying the manner in which any information is to be made public and the period within which it must be made public;

(g) specifying circumstances in which any of the requirements imposed by rules under this section does not apply.

[(4A) The provision that may be made by virtue of subsection (4)(g) includes (but is not limited to) provision, in the case of an issuer whose registered office is situated in a country or territory outside the United Kingdom, allowing exemption from specified provisions of rules under this section if—

(a) the law of that country or territory is considered by the FCA to lay down equivalent requirements, or

(b) the issuer complies with the requirements of the law of a country or territory that the FCA considers as equivalent.]

(5) Rules under this section are referred to in this Part as "transparency rules".

(6) Nothing in sections 89B to 89G affects the generality of the power to make rules under this section.]

NOTES

Inserted, together with the preceding heading and ss 89B–89G, by the Companies Act 2006, s 1266(1), as from 8 November 2006.

Sub-s (1) was substituted, the words in square brackets in sub-s (2) were inserted, and sub-s (4A) was inserted, by the Official Listing of Securities, Prospectus and Transparency (Amendment etc) (EU Exit) Regulations 2019, SI 2019/707, regs 3, 19, as from IP completion day (as defined in the European Union (Withdrawal Agreement) Act 2020, s 39).

The word "FCA" in square brackets (in each place that it occurs in sub-s (3)) was substituted by the Financial Services Act 2012, s 16(1)–(3), as from 1 April 2013.

Words omitted from sub-ss (3), (4) repealed by the Transparency Regulations 2015, SI 2015/1755, reg 2(1), as from 1 November 2015 (for the purpose of making rules under Part 6), and as from 26 November 2015 (otherwise).

[7.198]

[89B Provision of voteholder information

(1) Transparency rules may make provision for voteholder information in respect of voting shares to be notified, in circumstances specified in the rules—

(a) to the issuer, or

(b) to the public,

or to both.

(2) Transparency rules may make provision for voteholder information notified to the issuer to be notified at the same time to the [FCA].

(3) In this Part "voteholder information" in respect of voting shares means information relating to the proportion of voting rights held by a person in respect of the shares.

(4) Transparency rules may require notification of voteholder information relating to a [person in accordance with the following provisions].

(5) Transparency rules . . . may require notification of voteholder information relating to a person only where there is a notifiable change in the proportion of—

(a) the total voting rights in respect of shares in the issuer, or

(b) the total voting rights in respect of a particular class of share in the issuer,

held by the person.

(6) For this purpose there is a "notifiable change" in the proportion of voting rights held by a person when the proportion changes—

(a) from being a proportion less than a designated proportion to a proportion equal to or greater than that designated proportion,

(b) from being a proportion equal to a designated proportion to a proportion greater or less than that designated proportion, or

(c) from being a proportion greater than a designated proportion to a proportion equal to or less than that designated proportion.

(7) In subsection (6) "designated" means designated by the rules.]

NOTES

Inserted as noted to s 89A at **[7.197]**.

Sub-s (2): word "FCA" in square brackets substituted by the Financial Services Act 2012, s 16(1)–(3), as from 1 April 2013.

Sub-s (4): words in square brackets substituted by the Official Listing of Securities, Prospectus and Transparency (Amendment etc) (EU Exit) Regulations 2019, SI 2019/707, regs 3, 20(1), (2), as from IP completion day (as defined in the European Union (Withdrawal Agreement) Act 2020, s 39).

Sub-s (5): words omitted repealed by SI 2019/707, regs 3, 20(1), (3), as from IP completion day (as defined in the European Union (Withdrawal Agreement) Act 2020, s 39).

[7.199]

[89C Provision of information by issuers of transferable securities

(1) Transparency rules may make provision requiring the issuer of transferable securities, in circumstances specified in the rules—

(a) to make public information to which this section applies, or

(b) to notify to the [FCA] information to which this section applies,

or to do both.

(2) In the case of every issuer, this section applies to—

[(a) an annual financial report which complies with subsection (5) and with such other requirements as may be specified;

(aa) in the case of an issuer which is—

(i) a mining or quarrying undertaking, or

(ii) a logging undertaking,

reports complying with specified requirements on payments to governments;] [and]

(b) information relating to the rights attached to the transferable securities, including information about the terms and conditions of those securities which could indirectly affect those rights; . . .

(c) . . .

(3) In the case of an issuer of debt securities, this section also applies to [a half-yearly financial report which covers the first 6 months of the financial year and complies with subsection (6) and with such other requirements as may be specified].

(4) In the case of an issuer of shares, this section also applies to—

(a) [a half-yearly financial report which covers the first 6 months of the financial year and complies with subsection (6) and with such other requirements as may be specified];

(b) . . .

(c) voteholder information—

(i) notified to the issuer, or

(ii) relating to the proportion of voting rights held by the issuer in respect of shares in the issuer;

(d) information relating to the issuer's capital; and

(e) information relating to the total number of voting rights in respect of shares or shares of a particular class.

[(5) An issuer's annual financial report must include—

(a) audited financial statements complying with specified requirements,

(b) a management report complying with specified requirements, and

(c) statements which—

(i) relate to the financial statements and the management report,

(ii) are made by the persons responsible within the issuer, and

(iii) comply with specified requirements.

(6) An issuer's half-yearly financial report must include—

(a) a condensed set of financial statements complying with specified requirements,

(b) an interim management report complying with specified requirements, and

(c) statements which—

(i) relate to the condensed set of financial statements and the interim management report,

(ii) are made by the persons responsible within the issuer, and

(iii) comply with specified requirements.

(7) In subsection (2)(aa), "mining or quarrying undertaking", "logging undertaking", "payment" and "government" have the same meanings as in the Reports on Payments to Governments Regulations 2014.

(8) In this section "specified" means specified in, or referred to in, transparency rules.]]

NOTES

Inserted as noted to s 89A at **[7.197]**.

Sub-s (1): word "FCA" in square brackets substituted by the Financial Services Act 2012, s 16(1)–(3), as from 1 April 2013.

Sub-s (2) is amended as follows:

Paras (a) and (aa) were substituted by the Official Listing of Securities, Prospectus and Transparency (Amendment etc) (EU Exit) Regulations 2019, SI 2019/707, regs 3, 21(1), (2), as from IP completion day (as defined in the European Union (Withdrawal Agreement) Act 2020, s 39). Para (aa) was originally inserted by the Payments to Governments and Miscellaneous Provisions Regulations 2014, SI 2014/3293, reg 4(a), as from 17 December 2014.

Word in square brackets in para (aa) inserted, and para (c) (and the preceding word) repealed, by the Transparency Regulations 2015, SI 2015/1755, reg 2(2), as from 1 November 2015 (for the purpose of making rules under Part 6), and as from 26 November 2015 (otherwise).

Sub-s (3): words in square brackets substituted by SI 2019/707, regs 3, 21(1), (3), as from IP completion day (as defined in the European Union (Withdrawal Agreement) Act 2020, s 39).

Sub-s (4): words in square brackets in para (a) substituted by SI 2019/707, regs 3, 21(1), (3), as from IP completion day (as defined in the European Union (Withdrawal Agreement) Act 2020, s 39). Para (b) repealed by SI 2014/3293, reg 4(b), as from 17 December 2014.

Sub-ss (5)–(8): added by SI 2019/707, regs 3, 21(1), (4), as from IP completion day (as defined in the European Union (Withdrawal Agreement) Act 2020, s 39).

[7.200]

[89D Notification of voting rights held by issuer

(1) Transparency rules may require notification of voteholder information relating to the proportion of voting rights held by an issuer in respect of voting shares in [the issuer in accordance with the following provisions].

(2) Transparency rules . . . may require notification of voteholder information relating to the proportion of voting rights held by an issuer in respect of voting shares in the issuer only where there is a notifiable change in the proportion of—

(a) the total voting rights in respect of shares in the issuer, or

(b) the total voting rights in respect of a particular class of share in the issuer,

held by the issuer.

(3) For this purpose there is a "notifiable change" in the proportion of voting rights held by a person when the proportion changes—

(a) from being a proportion less than a designated proportion to a proportion equal to or greater than that designated proportion,

(b) from being a proportion equal to a designated proportion to a proportion greater or less than that designated proportion, or

(c) from being a proportion greater than a designated proportion to a proportion equal to or less than that designated proportion.

(4) In subsection (3) "designated" means designated by the rules.]

NOTES

Inserted as noted to s 89A at **[7.197]**.

Words in square brackets in sub-s (1) substituted, and words omitted from sub-s (2) repealed, by the Official Listing of Securities, Prospectus and Transparency (Amendment etc) (EU Exit) Regulations 2019, SI 2019/707, regs 3, 22, as from IP completion day (as defined in the European Union (Withdrawal Agreement) Act 2020, s 39).

89E *(Inserted as noted to s 89A at* **[7.197]**. *Repealed by the Transparency Regulations 2015, SI 2015/1755, reg 2(3), as from 1 November 2015 (for the purpose of making rules under Part 6), and as from 26 November 2015 (otherwise).)*

[7.201]

[89F Transparency rules: interpretation etc

(1) For the purposes of sections 89A to 89G—

(a) the voting rights in respect of any voting shares are the voting rights attached to those shares, [and]

(b) a person is to be regarded as holding the voting rights in respect of the shares—

(i) if, by virtue of those shares, he is a shareholder within the meaning of Article 2.1(e) of the transparency obligations directive;

(ii) if, and to the extent that, he is entitled to acquire, dispose of or exercise those voting rights in one or more of the cases mentioned in Article 10(a) to (h) of the transparency obligations directive;

[(iii) if he holds, directly or indirectly, a financial instrument which satisfies the conditions set out in Article 13(1)(a) or (b) of the transparency obligations directive].

(c) . . .

[(1A) The FCA must establish, publish and periodically update an indicative list of financial instruments that are subject to notification requirements by virtue of subsection (1)(b)(iii), taking into account developments on financial markets.

(1B) Publication of the indicative list is to be in such manner as the FCA considers appropriate.]

(2) . . .

(3) For the purposes of sections 89A to 89G two or more persons may, at the same time, each be regarded as holding the same voting rights.

(4) In those sections—

. . .

. . .

"UK market" means a market that is situated or operating in the United Kingdom;

"voting shares" means shares of an issuer to which voting rights are attached.]

NOTES

Inserted as noted to s 89A at **[7.197]**.

The word in square brackets in sub-s (1)(a) was added, sub-s (1)(b)(iii) was substituted, sub-ss (1)(c) and (2) were repealed, and the definitions omitted from sub-s (4) were repealed, by the Transparency Regulations 2015, SI 2015/1755, reg 2(4), as from 1 November 2015 (for the purpose of making rules under Part 6), and as from 26 November 2015 (otherwise).

Sub-ss (1A), (1B) were inserted by the Official Listing of Securities, Prospectus and Transparency (Amendment etc) (EU Exit) Regulations 2019, SI 2019/707, regs 3, 23, as from IP completion day (as defined in the European Union (Withdrawal Agreement) Act 2020, s 39).

[7.202]

[89G Transparency rules: other supplementary provisions

(1) Transparency rules may impose the same obligations on a person who has applied for the admission of transferable securities to trading on a regulated market without the issuer's consent as they impose on an issuer of transferable securities.

(2) Transparency rules that require a person to make information public may include provision authorising the [FCA] to make the information public in the event that the person fails to do so.
(3) The [FCA] may make public any information notified to [the FCA] in accordance with transparency rules.
(4) Transparency rules may make provision by reference to any provision of any rules made by the Panel on Takeovers and Mergers under Part 28 of the Companies Act 2006.
(5) Sections 89A to 89F and this section are without prejudice to any other power conferred by this Part to make Part 6 rules.]

NOTES

Inserted as noted to s 89A at **[7.197]**.

Words in square brackets substituted by the Financial Services Act 2012, s 16(1)–(3), as from 1 April 2013.

[Power of [FCA] to call for information

[7.203]

89H [FCA's] power to call for information

(1) The [FCA] may by notice in writing given to a person to whom this section applies require him—
(a) to provide specified information or information of a specified description, or
(b) to produce specified documents or documents of a specified description.
(2) This section applies to—
(a) an issuer in respect of whom transparency rules have effect;
(b) a voteholder;
(c) an auditor of—
(i) an issuer to whom this section applies, or
(ii) a voteholder;
(d) a person who controls a voteholder;
(e) a person controlled by a voteholder;
(f) a director or other similar officer of an issuer to whom this section applies;
(g) a director or other similar officer of a voteholder or, where the affairs of a voteholder are managed by its members, a member of the voteholder.
(3) This section applies only to information and documents reasonably required in connection with the exercise by the [FCA] of functions conferred on it by or under sections 89A to 89G (transparency rules).
(4) Information or documents required under this section must be provided or produced—
(a) before the end of such reasonable period as may be specified, and
(b) at such place as may be specified.
(5) If a person claims a lien on a document, its production under this section does not affect the lien.]

NOTES

Inserted, together with the preceding heading and ss 89I, 89J, by the Companies Act 2006, s 1267, as from 8 November 2006.

Words in square brackets (including those in the section heading and in the heading preceding this section) substituted by the Financial Services Act 2012, s 16(1)–(3), as from 1 April 2013.

[7.204]

[89I Requirements in connection with call for information

(1) The [FCA] may require any information provided under section 89H to be provided in such form as it may reasonably require.
(2) The [FCA] may require—
(a) any information provided, whether in a document or otherwise, to be verified in such manner as it may reasonably require;
(b) any document produced to be authenticated in such manner as it may reasonably require.
(3) If a document is produced in response to a requirement imposed under section 89H, the [FCA] may—
(a) take copies of or extracts from the document; or
(b) require the person producing the document, or any relevant person, to provide an explanation of the document.
(4) In subsection (3)(b) "relevant person", in relation to a person who is required to produce a document, means a person who—
(a) has been or is a director or controller of that person;
(b) has been or is an auditor of that person;
(c) has been or is an actuary, accountant or lawyer appointed or instructed by that person; or
(d) has been or is an employee of that person.
(5) If a person who is required under section 89H to produce a document fails to do so, the [FCA] may require him to state, to the best of his knowledge and belief, where the document is.]

NOTES

Inserted as noted to s 89H at **[7.203]**.

Word "FCA" in square brackets (in each place that it occurs) substituted by the Financial Services Act 2012, s 16(1)–(3), as from 1 April 2013.

[7.205]

[89J Power to call for information: supplementary provisions

(1) The [FCA] may require an issuer to make public any information provided to [the FCA] under section 89H.
(2) If the issuer fails to comply with a requirement under subsection (1), the [FCA] may, after seeking representations from the issuer, make the information public.
(3) In sections 89H and 89I (power of [FCA] to call for information)—
"control" and "controlled" have the meaning given by subsection (4) below;
"specified" means specified in the notice;
"voteholder" means a person who—

(a) holds voting rights in respect of any voting shares for the purposes of sections 89A to 89G (transparency rules), . . .

(b) . . .

(4) For the purposes of those sections a person ("A") controls another person ("B") if—

(a) A holds a majority of the voting rights in B,

(b) A is a member of B and has the right to appoint or remove a majority of the members of the board of directors (or, if there is no such board, the equivalent management body) of B,

(c) A is a member of B and controls alone, pursuant to an agreement with other shareholders or members, a majority of the voting rights in B, or

(d) A has the right to exercise, or actually exercises, dominant influence or control over B.

(5) For the purposes of subsection (4)(b)—

(a) any rights of a person controlled by A, and

(b) any rights of a person acting on behalf of A or a person controlled by A,

are treated as held by A.]

NOTES

Inserted as noted to s 89H at **[7.203]**.

Words in square brackets substituted by the Financial Services Act 2012, s 16(1)–(3), as from 1 April 2013.

Words omitted from the definition "voteholder" in sub-s (3) repealed by the Transparency Regulations 2015, SI 2015/1755, reg 2(5), as from 1 November 2015 (for the purpose of making rules under Part 6), and as from 26 November 2015 (otherwise).

[Powers exercisable in case of infringement of transparency obligation

[7.206]

89K Public censure of issuer

(1) If the [FCA] finds that an issuer of securities admitted to trading on a regulated market is failing or has failed to comply with an applicable transparency obligation, it may publish a statement to that effect.

(2) If the [FCA] proposes to publish a statement, it must give the issuer a warning notice setting out the terms of the proposed statement.

(3) If, after considering any representations made in response to the warning notice, the [FCA] decides to make the proposed statement, it must give the issuer a decision notice setting out the terms of the statement.

(4) A notice under this section must inform the issuer of his right to refer the matter to the Tribunal (see section 89N) and give an indication of the procedure on such a reference.

(5) In this section "transparency obligation" means an obligation [under qualifying transparency legislation].

[(5A) In this Part "qualifying transparency legislation" means—

(a) transparency rules,

(b) any EU regulation, originally made under the transparency obligations directive, that is retained direct EU legislation,

(c) regulations made by the Treasury under regulation 71 of the Official Listing of Securities, Prospectus and Transparency (Amendment etc) (EU Exit) Regulations 2019 for a purpose specified in paragraphs 10 to 20 of Schedule 2 to those Regulations, or

(d) technical standards made by the FCA under regulation 72 of those Regulations for a purpose specified in paragraphs 31 to 35 of that Schedule.]

(6) . . .

NOTES

Inserted, together with the preceding heading and ss 89L–89N, by the Companies Act 2006, s 1268, as from 8 November 2006.

Word "FCA" in square brackets (in each place that it occurs) substituted by the Financial Services Act 2012, s 16(1)–(3), as from 1 April 2013.

Words in square brackets in sub-s (5) substituted, sub-s (5A) inserted, and sub-s (6) repealed, by the Official Listing of Securities, Prospectus and Transparency (Amendment etc) (EU Exit) Regulations 2019, SI 2019/707, regs 3, 24, as from IP completion day (as defined in the European Union (Withdrawal Agreement) Act 2020, s 39).

[7.207]

[89L Power to suspend or prohibit trading of securities

(1) This section applies to securities admitted to trading on a regulated market.

(2) If the [FCA] has reasonable grounds for suspecting that an applicable transparency obligation has been infringed by an issuer, it may—

(a) suspend trading in the securities for a period not exceeding 10 days,

(b) prohibit trading in the securities, or

(c) make a request to the operator of the market on which the issuer's securities are traded—

(i) to suspend trading in the securities for a period not exceeding 10 days, or

(ii) to prohibit trading in the securities.

(3) If the [FCA] has reasonable grounds for suspecting that [an applicable transparency obligation] has been infringed by a voteholder of an issuer, it may—

(a) prohibit trading in the securities, or

(b) make a request to the operator of the market on which the issuer's securities are traded to prohibit trading in the securities.

(4) If the [FCA] finds that an applicable transparency obligation has been infringed, it may require the market operator to prohibit trading in the securities.

(5) In this section "transparency obligation" means an obligation [under qualifying transparency legislation].

(6) . . .

NOTES

Inserted as noted to s 89K at **[7.206]**.

Word "FCA" in square brackets (in each place that it occurs) substituted by the Financial Services Act 2012, s 16(1)–(3), as from 1 April 2013.

Words "an applicable transparency obligation" in square brackets in sub-s (3) substituted, words in square brackets in sub-s (5) substituted, and sub-s (6) repealed, by the Official Listing of Securities, Prospectus and Transparency (Amendment etc) (EU Exit) Regulations 2019, SI 2019/707, regs 3, 25, as from IP completion day (as defined in the European Union (Withdrawal Agreement) Act 2020, s 39).

[7.208]
[89M Procedure under section 89L

(1) A requirement under section 89L takes effect—
- (a) immediately, if the notice under subsection (2) states that that is the case;
- (b) in any other case, on such date as may be specified in the notice.

(2) If the [FCA]—
- (a) proposes to exercise the powers in section 89L in relation to a person, or
- (b) exercises any of those powers in relation to a person with immediate effect,

it must give that person written notice.

(3) The notice must—
- (a) give details of the [FCA's] action or proposed action;
- (b) state the [FCA's] reasons for taking the action in question and choosing the date on which it took effect or takes effect;
- (c) inform the recipient that he may make representations to the [FCA] within such period as may be specified by the notice (whether or not he had referred the matter to the Tribunal);
- (d) inform him of the date on which the action took effect or takes effect;
- (e) inform him of his right to refer the matter to the Tribunal (see section 89N) and give an indication of the procedure on such a reference.

(4) The [FCA] may extend the period within which representations may be made to it.

(5) If, having considered any representations made to it, the [FCA] decides to maintain, vary or revoke its earlier decision, it must give written notice to that effect to the person mentioned in subsection (2).]

NOTES

Inserted as noted to s 89K at **[7.206]**.

Words in square brackets substituted by the Financial Services Act 2012, s 16(1)–(3), as from 1 April 2013.

[7.209]
[89N Right to refer matters to the Tribunal

A person—
- (a) to whom a decision notice is given under section 89K (public censure), or
- (b) to whom a notice is given under section 89M (procedure in connection with suspension or prohibition of trading),

may refer the matter to the Tribunal.]

NOTES

Inserted as noted to s 89K at **[7.206]**.

[7.210]
[89NA Voting rights suspension orders

(1) The court may, on the application of the FCA and in accordance with this section, make a voting rights suspension order in respect of a person who is a voteholder in relation to shares in a particular company which are admitted to trading on a regulated market and identified in the application.

(2) A voting rights suspension order is an order which suspends the person's exercise of voting rights attaching to the shares to which the order relates.

(3) The court may make a voting rights suspension order in respect of a person only if it is satisfied—
- (a) that the person has contravened one or more relevant transparency provisions in respect of any of the shares identified in the application or any other shares in the same company which are admitted to trading on a regulated market, and
- (b) that the contravention is serious enough to make it appropriate to make the order.

(4) For the purposes of subsection (3)(b), the court may, in particular, have regard to—
- (a) whether the contravention was deliberate or repeated;
- (b) the time taken for the contravention to be remedied;
- (c) whether the voteholder ignored warnings or requests for compliance from the FCA;
- (d) the size of the holding of shares to which the contravention relates;
- (e) any impact of the contravention on the integrity of the UK financial system;
- (f) the effect of the contravention on any company merger or takeover.

(5) A voting rights suspension order may be made in relation to some or all of the shares to which the application relates.

(6) A voting rights suspension order may be made for a specified period or an indefinite period.

(7) A voting rights suspension order takes effect—
- (a) on the date specified in the order, or
- (b) if no date is specified, at the time it is made.

(8) Where a voting rights suspension order has been made, the FCA, the person to whom it applies or the company which issued the shares to which it relates, may apply to the court for—
- (a) a variation of the order so as to alter the period for which it has effect or the shares in relation to which it has effect, or
- (b) the discharge of the order.

(9) The FCA must consult the PRA before making an application to the court under this section in relation to—

(a) a person who is a PRA-authorised person, or
(b) shares issued by a PRA-authorised person.

(10) The jurisdiction conferred by this section is exercisable—
(a) in England and Wales and Northern Ireland, by the High Court, and
(b) in Scotland, by the Court of Session.

(11) In this section—

"relevant transparency provision" means—

(a) a provision of the transparency rules which [implemented] Article 9, 10, 12, 13 or 13a of the transparency obligations directive, . . .
[(b) a provision, originally made under any of those Articles, that is retained direct EU legislation,
(c) a provision of regulations made by the Treasury under regulation 71 of the Official Listing of Securities, Prospectus and Transparency (Amendment etc) (EU Exit) Regulations 2019 for a purpose specified in paragraphs 13 to 16 of Schedule 2 to those Regulations, or
(d) a provision of technical standards made by the FCA under regulation 72 of those Regulations for a purpose specified in paragraphs 32 to 35 of that Schedule;]

"voteholder" has the meaning given by section 89J(3).]

NOTES

Inserted by the Transparency Regulations 2015, SI 2015/1755, reg 4(1), as from 26 November 2015.

Sub-s (11): in the definition "relevant transparency provision", the words in square brackets were substituted, and the word omitted was repealed, by the Official Listing of Securities, Prospectus and Transparency (Amendment etc) (EU Exit) Regulations 2019, SI 2019/707, regs 3, 26, as from IP completion day (as defined in the European Union (Withdrawal Agreement) Act 2020, s 39).

[Corporate governance

[7.211]

89O Corporate governance rules

[(1) The FCA may make rules ("corporate governance rules") relating to the corporate governance of issuers who have requested or approved admission of their securities to trading on a regulated market.]

(2) "Corporate governance", in relation to an issuer, includes—
(a) the nature, constitution or functions of the organs of the issuer;
(b) the manner in which organs of the issuer conduct themselves;
(c) the requirements imposed on organs of the issuer;
(d) the relationship between the different organs of the issuer;
(e) the relationship between the organs of the issuer and the members of the issuer or holders of the issuer's securities.

(3), (4) . . .

(5) This section is without prejudice to any other power conferred by this Part to make Part 6 rules.]

NOTES

Inserted, together with the preceding heading, by the Companies Act 2006, s 1269, as from 8 November 2006.

Sub-s (1): substituted by the Official Listing of Securities, Prospectus and Transparency (Amendment etc) (EU Exit) Regulations 2019, SI 2019/707, regs 3, 27(1), (2), as from IP completion day (as defined in the European Union (Withdrawal Agreement) Act 2020, s 39).

Sub-s (3), (4): repealed by SI 2019/707, regs 3, 27(1), (3), as from IP completion day (as defined in the European Union (Withdrawal Agreement) Act 2020, s 39).

[Primary information providers

[7.212]

89P Primary information providers

(1) Part 6 rules may require issuers of financial instruments to use primary information providers for the purpose of giving information of a specified description to a market of a specified description.

(2) "Primary information provider" means a person approved by the FCA for the purposes of this section.

(3) "Specified" means specified in the Part 6 rules.

(4) Part 6 rules made by virtue of subsection (1) may—
(a) provide for the FCA to maintain a list of providers;
(b) impose requirements on a provider in relation to the giving of information or of information of a specified description;
(c) specify the circumstances in which a person is qualified for being approved as a provider;
(d) provide for limitations or other restrictions to be imposed on the giving of information to which an approval relates (whether or not the approval has already been granted);
(e) provide for the approval of a provider to be suspended on the application of the provider.

(5) If the FCA proposes—
(a) to refuse a person's application under information provider rules,
(b) to impose limitations or other restrictions on the giving of information to which a person's approval relates, or
(c) to cancel a person's approval as a provider otherwise than at the person's request,

it must give the person a warning notice.

(6) If the FCA decides—
(a) to grant the application under information provider rules,
(b) not to impose limitations or other restrictions on the giving of information to which a person's approval relates, or
(c) not to cancel the approval,

it must give the person concerned written notice of its decision.

(7) If the FCA decides—
(a) to refuse to grant the application under information provider rules,

(b) to impose limitations or other restrictions on the giving of information to which a person's approval relates, or
(c) to cancel the approval,
it must give the person concerned a decision notice.
(8) A person to whom a decision notice is given under this section may refer the matter to the Tribunal.
(9) In this section any reference to an application under information provider rules means—
(a) an application for approval as a provider,
(b) an application for the suspension of an approval as a provider,
(c) an application for the withdrawal of the suspension of an approval as a provider, or
(d) an application for the withdrawal or variation of a limitation or other restriction on the giving of information to which a provider's approval relates.]

NOTES

Inserted, together with the preceding heading and ss 89Q–89V, by the Financial Services Act 2012, s 19(1), as from 24 January 2013 (for the purpose of making rules), and as from 1 April 2013 (otherwise).

[7.213]
[89Q Disciplinary powers: contravention of s 89P(4)(b) or (d)
(1) The FCA may take action against a provider under this section if it considers that the provider has contravened a requirement or restriction imposed on the provider by rules made as a result of section 89P(4)(b) or (d).
(2) If the FCA is entitled to take action under this section against a provider, it may do one or more of the following—
(a) impose a penalty on the provider of such amount as it considers appropriate;
(b) suspend, for such period as it considers appropriate, the provider's approval;
(c) impose, for such period as it considers appropriate, such limitations or other restrictions in relation to the giving by the provider of information as it considers appropriate;
(d) publish a statement to the effect that the provider has contravened a requirement or restriction imposed on the provider by rules made as a result of section 89P(4)(b) or (d).
(3) The period for which a suspension or restriction is to have effect may not exceed 12 months.
(4) A suspension may relate only to the giving of information in specified circumstances.
(5) A restriction may, in particular, be imposed so as to require the provider to take, or refrain from taking, specified action.
(6) The FCA may—
(a) withdraw a suspension or restriction, or
(b) vary a suspension or restriction so as to reduce the period for which it has effect or otherwise to limit its effect.
(7) The FCA may not take action against a provider under this section after the end of the limitation period unless, before the end of that period, it has given a warning notice to the provider under section 89R(1).
(8) "The limitation period" means the period of 3 years beginning with the first day on which the FCA knew that the provider had contravened the requirement or restriction.
(9) For this purpose the FCA is to be treated as knowing that a provider has contravened a requirement or restriction if it has information from which that can reasonably be inferred.]

NOTES

Inserted as noted to s 88P at **[7.212]**.

[7.214]
[89R Action under s 89Q: procedure and right to refer to Tribunal
(1) If the FCA proposes to take action against a provider under section 89Q, it must give the provider a warning notice.
(2) A warning notice about a proposal to impose a penalty must state the amount of the penalty.
(3) A warning notice about a proposal—
(a) to suspend an approval, or
(b) to impose a restriction in relation to the giving of information,
must state the period for which the suspension or restriction is to have effect.
(4) A warning notice about a proposal to publish a statement must set out the terms of the statement.
(5) If the FCA decides to take action against a provider under section 89Q, it must give the provider a decision notice.
(6) A decision notice about the imposition of a penalty must state the amount of the penalty.
(7) A decision notice about—
(a) the suspension of an approval, or
(b) the imposition of a restriction in relation to the giving of information,
must state the period for which the suspension or restriction is to have effect.
(8) A decision notice about the publication of a statement must set out the terms of the statement.
(9) If the FCA decides to take action against a provider under section 89Q, the provider may refer the matter to the Tribunal.]

NOTES

Inserted as noted to s 88P at **[7.212]**.

[7.215]
[89S Action under s 89Q: statement of policy
(1) The FCA must prepare and issue a statement of its policy with respect to—
(a) the imposition of penalties, suspensions or restrictions under section 89Q,
(b) the amount of penalties under that section,
(c) the period for which suspensions or restrictions under that section are to have effect, and
(d) the matters in relation to which suspensions or restrictions under that section are to have effect.

(2) The FCA's policy in determining what the amount of a penalty should be, or what the period for which a suspension or restriction is to have effect should be, must include having regard to—

(a) the seriousness of the contravention in question in relation to the nature of the requirement concerned,

(b) the extent to which that contravention was deliberate or reckless, and

(c) whether the provider concerned is an individual.

(3) The FCA may at any time alter or replace a statement issued under this section.

(4) If a statement issued under this section is altered or replaced, the FCA must issue the altered or replacement statement.

(5) In exercising, or deciding whether to exercise, its power under section 89Q in the case of any particular contravention, the FCA must have regard to any statement of policy published under this section and in force at a time when the contravention in question occurred.

(6) A statement issued under this section must be published by the FCA in the way appearing to the FCA to be best calculated to bring it to the attention of the public.

(7) The FCA may charge a reasonable fee for providing a person with a copy of the statement.

(8) The FCA must, without delay, give the Treasury a copy of any statement which it publishes under this section.]

NOTES

Inserted as noted to s 88P at **[7.212]**.

[7.216]

[89T Statement of policy under s 89S: procedure

(1) Before issuing a statement under section 89S, the FCA must publish a draft of the proposed statement in the way appearing to the FCA to be best calculated to bring it to the attention of the public.

(2) The draft must be accompanied by notice that representations about the proposal may be made to the FCA within a specified time.

(3) Before issuing the proposed statement, the FCA must have regard to any representations made to it in accordance with subsection (2).

(4) If the FCA issues the proposed statement it must publish an account, in general terms, of—

(a) the representations made to it in accordance with subsection (2); and

(b) its response to them.

(5) If the statement differs from the draft published under subsection (1) in a way which is, in the opinion of the FCA, significant, the FCA must (in addition to complying with subsection (4)) publish details of the difference.

(6) The FCA may charge a reasonable fee for providing a person with a copy of a draft published under subsection (1).

(7) This section also applies to a proposal to alter or replace a statement.]

NOTES

Inserted as noted to s 88P at **[7.212]**.

[7.217]

[89U Powers exercisable to advance operational objectives

(1) The FCA may take action against a provider under this section if it considers that it is desirable to do so in order to advance one or more of its operational objectives.

(2) If the FCA is entitled to take action under this section against a provider, it may—

(a) suspend, for such period as it considers appropriate, the provider's approval, or

(b) impose, for such period as it considers appropriate, such limitations or other restrictions in relation to the giving by the provider of information as it considers appropriate.

(3) A suspension may relate only to the giving of information in specified circumstances.

(4) A restriction may, in particular, be imposed so as to require the provider to take, or refrain from taking, specified action.

(5) The FCA may—

(a) withdraw a suspension or restriction, or

(b) vary a suspension or restriction so as to reduce the period for which it has effect or otherwise to limit its effect.

(6) A person against whom the FCA takes action under this section may refer the matter to the Tribunal.]

NOTES

Inserted as noted to s 88P at **[7.212]**.

[7.218]

[89V Action under s 89U: procedure

(1) Action against a provider under section 89U takes effect—

(a) immediately, if the notice given under subsection (2) so provides, or

(b) on such later date as may be specified in the notice.

(2) If the FCA—

(a) proposes to take action against a provider under that section, or

(b) takes action against a provider under that section with immediate effect,

it must give the provider written notice.

(3) The notice must—

(a) give details of the action,

(b) state the FCA's reasons for taking the action and for its determination as to when the action takes effect,

(c) inform the provider that the provider may make representations to the FCA within such period as may be specified in the notice (whether or not the matter has been referred to the Tribunal),

(d) inform the provider of when the action takes effect,

(e) inform the provider of the right to refer the matter to the Tribunal, and

(f) give an indication of the procedure on such a reference.

(4) The FCA may extend the period allowed under the notice for making representations.
(5) If the FCA decides—
(a) to take the action in the way proposed, or
(b) if the action has taken effect, not to rescind it,
the FCA must give the provider written notice.
(6) If the FCA decides—
(a) not to take the action in the way proposed,
(b) to take action under section 89U that differs from the action originally proposed, or
(c) to rescind action which has taken effect,
the FCA must give the provider written notice.
(7) A notice under subsection (5) must—
(a) inform the provider of the right to refer the matter to the Tribunal, and
(b) give an indication of the procedure on such a reference.
(8) A notice under subsection (6)(b) must comply with subsection (3).]

NOTES

Inserted as noted to s 88P at **[7.212]**.

[7.219]
[89W Storage of regulated information

(1) The FCA must ensure that there is at least one mechanism for the central storage of regulated information . . .
[(1A) The mechanism must comply with minimum quality standards of security, certainty as to the information source, time recording and easy access by end users (see provision made under regulation 71 of the Official Listing of Securities, Prospectus and Transparency (Amendment etc) (EU Exit) Regulations 2019 for the purpose specified in paragraph 19(b) of Schedule 2 to those Regulations).
(1B) The mechanism must be aligned with the procedure for filing the regulated information with the FCA.]
[(2) In this section "regulated information" means information which an issuer, or a person who has applied for the admission of securities to trading on a regulated market without the issuer's consent, is required to disclose under—
(a) listing rules,
(b) qualifying transparency legislation, or
(c) Articles 17 to 19 of the market abuse regulation.]]

NOTES

Inserted by the Transparency Regulations 2015, SI 2015/1755, reg 3, as from 1 November 2015.
The words omitted from sub-s (1) were repealed, sub-ss (1A), (1B) were inserted, and sub-s (2) was substituted, by the Official Listing of Securities, Prospectus and Transparency (Amendment etc) (EU Exit) Regulations 2019, SI 2019/707, regs 3, 28, as from IP completion day (as defined in the European Union (Withdrawal Agreement) Act 2020, s 39).

[Compensation for false or misleading statements etc]

[7.220]
90 [Compensation for statements in listing particulars or prospectus]

(1) Any person responsible for listing particulars is liable to pay compensation to a person who has—
(a) acquired securities to which the particulars apply; and
(b) suffered loss in respect of them as a result of—
(i) any untrue or misleading statement in the particulars; or
(ii) the omission from the particulars of any matter required to be included by section 80 or 81.
(2) Subsection (1) is subject to exemptions provided by Schedule 10.
(3) If listing particulars are required to include information about the absence of a particular matter, the omission from the particulars of that information is to be treated as a statement in the listing particulars that there is no such matter.
(4) Any person who fails to comply with section 81 is liable to pay compensation to any person who has—
(a) acquired securities of the kind in question; and
(b) suffered loss in respect of them as a result of the failure.
(5) Subsection (4) is subject to exemptions provided by Schedule 10.
(6) This section does not affect any liability which may be incurred apart from this section.
(7) References in this section to the acquisition by a person of securities include references to his contracting to acquire them or any interest in them.
(8) No person shall, by reason of being a promoter of a company or otherwise, incur any liability for failing to disclose information which he would not be required to disclose in listing particulars in respect of a company's securities—
(a) if he were responsible for those particulars; or
(b) if he is responsible for them, which he is entitled to omit by virtue of section 82.
(9) The reference in subsection (8) to a person incurring liability includes a reference to any other person being entitled as against that person to be granted any civil remedy or to rescind or repudiate an agreement.
(10) "Listing particulars", in subsection (1) and Schedule 10, includes supplementary listing particulars.
[(11) This section applies in relation to a prospectus as it applies to listing particulars, with the following modifications—
(a) references in this section or in Schedule 10 to listing particulars, supplementary listing particulars or sections 80, 81 or 82 are to be read, respectively, as references to a prospectus, supplementary prospectus and [Articles 6 and 14(2), Article 23 and Article 18 of the prospectus regulation];
(b) references in Schedule 10 to admission to the official list are to be read as references to admission to trading on a regulated market;
(c) in relation to a prospectus, "securities" means "transferable securities".

[(11A) In subsection (11)(a) "supplementary prospectus" includes, where final terms (see Article 8 of the prospectus regulation) are contained in a separate document that is neither a prospectus nor a supplementary prospectus, that separate document.]

[(12) A person is not to be subject to civil liability solely on the basis of a summary in a prospectus unless the summary, when read with the rest of the prospectus—

(a) is misleading, inaccurate or inconsistent; or

(b) does not provide key information [specified by Article 7 of the prospectus regulation],

and in this subsection a summary includes any translation of it.]]

NOTES

The section heading and the heading preceding this section were substituted by the Companies Act 2006, s 1272, Sch 15, Pt 1, paras 1, 4, 5, as from 8 November 2006.

Sub-s (11): added by the Prospectus Regulations 2005, SI 2005/1433, reg 2(1), Sch 1, para 6(1), (2), as from 1 July 2005. Words in square brackets substituted by the Financial Services and Markets Act 2000 (Prospectus) Regulations 2019, SI 2019/1043, regs 3, 25(1), (2), as from 21 July 2019.

Sub-s (11A): inserted by SI 2019/1043, regs 3, 25(1), (3), as from 21 July 2019.

Sub-s (12): added by SI 2005/1433, reg 2(1), Sch 1, para 6(1), (2), as from 1 July 2005. Subsequently substituted by the Prospectus Regulations 2012, SI 2012/1538, reg 7, as from 1 July 2012. Words in square brackets substituted by SI 2019/1043, regs 3, 25(1), (4), as from 21 July 2019.

[7.221]

[90ZA Liability for key investor information

(1) A person is not to be subject to civil liability solely on the basis of the key investor information produced in relation to a collective investment scheme or a sub-fund of such a scheme in accordance with rules or other provisions [originally made in implementation of] Chapter IX of the UCITS directive, or of any translation of that information, unless the key investor information is misleading, inaccurate or inconsistent with the relevant parts of the prospectus published for that collective investment scheme or sub-fund in accordance with rules made by [the FCA] under section 248 [or 261J] of this Act.

(2) In this section, a reference to a sub-fund of a collective investment scheme is a reference to a part of the property of the collective investment scheme which forms a separate pool where—

(a) the collective investment scheme provides arrangements for separate pooling of the contributions of the participants and the profits and income out of which payments are made to them; and

(b) the participants are entitled to exchange rights in one pool for rights in another.]

NOTES

Inserted by the Undertakings for Collective Investment in Transferable Securities Regulations 2011, SI 2011/1613, reg 2(1), (3), as from 1 July 2011.

Sub-s (1): words in first pair of square brackets substituted by the Official Listing of Securities, Prospectus and Transparency (Amendment etc) (EU Exit) Regulations 2019, SI 2019/707, regs 3, 29, as from IP completion day (as defined in the European Union (Withdrawal Agreement) Act 2020, s 39). Words in second pair of square brackets substituted by the Financial Services Act 2012, s 16(1)–(3), as from 1 April 2013. Words in third pair of square brackets inserted by the Collective Investment in Transferable Securities (Contractual Scheme) Regulations 2013, SI 2013/1388, reg 3(1), (2), as from 6 June 2013.

[7.222]

[90A Liability of issuers in connection with published information

Schedule 10A makes provision about the liability of issuers of securities to pay compensation to persons who have suffered loss as a result of—

(a) a misleading statement or dishonest omission in certain published information relating to the securities, or

(b) a dishonest delay in publishing such information.]

NOTES

This section was originally inserted, together with s 90B, by the Companies Act 2006, s 1270, as from 8 November 2006. It was subsequently substituted by the Financial Services and Markets Act 2000 (Liability of Issuers) Regulations 2010, SI 2010/1192, reg 2(1), (2), as from 1 October 2010.

[7.223]

[90B Power to make further provision about liability for published information

(1) The Treasury may by regulations make provision about the liability of issuers of securities traded on a regulated market, and other persons, in respect of information published to holders of securities, to the market or to the public generally.

(2) Regulations under this section may amend any primary or subordinate legislation, including any provision of, or made under, this Act.]

NOTES

Inserted as noted to s 90A at **[7.222]**.

Regulations: the Financial Services and Markets Act 2000 (Liability of Issuers) Regulations 2010, SI 2010/1192.

Penalties

[7.224]

91 [Penalties for breach of Part 6 rules]

[[(1) If the [FCA] considers that—

(a) an issuer of listed securities, or

(b) an applicant for listing,

has contravened any provision of listing rules, it may impose on him a penalty of such amount as it considers appropriate.

(1ZA) . . .]

[(1A) If the [FCA] considers that—

(a) an issuer of transferable securities,
(b) a person offering transferable securities to the public or requesting their admission to trading on a regulated market,
(c) an applicant for the approval of a prospectus in relation to transferable securities,
(d) a person on whom a requirement has been imposed under section 87K or 87L, or
(e) any other person to whom [any provision of, or made in accordance with, the prospectus regulation applies],

has contravened a provision of this Part or of prospectus rules, or a provision [of or] made in accordance with the [prospectus regulation,] or a requirement imposed on him under such a provision, it may impose on him a penalty of such amount as it considers appropriate.]

[(1B) If the [FCA] considers—
(a) that a person has contravened—
  (i) a provision of [qualifying transparency legislation], or
  (ii) a provision of corporate governance rules, or
(b) that a person on whom a requirement has been imposed under section 89L (power to suspend or prohibit trading of securities in case of infringement of applicable transparency obligation), has contravened that requirement,

it may impose on the person a penalty of such amount as it considers appropriate.]

(2) If, in the case of a contravention [by a person] referred to in subsection [(1), . . . (1A) or [(1B)(a)(ii) or (b)]] [("P")], the [FCA] considers that [another person] who was at the material time a director of [P] was knowingly concerned in the contravention, it may impose upon him a penalty of such amount as it considers appropriate.]

[(2A) If—
(a) a person has contravened a provision mentioned in subsection (1B)(a)(i), and
(b) the FCA considers that another person ("A"), who was at the material time a relevant officer of the person, was knowingly concerned in the contravention,

the FCA may impose upon A a penalty of such amount as it considers appropriate.

(2B) In subsection (2A) "relevant officer" of a person means—

(3) If the [FCA] is entitled to impose a penalty on a person under this section in respect of a particular matter it may, instead of imposing a penalty on him in respect of that matter, publish a statement censuring him.

(4) Nothing in this section prevents the [FCA] from taking any other steps which it has power to take under this Part.

(5) A penalty under this section is payable to the [FCA].

(6) The [FCA] may not take action against a person under this section after the end of the period of [3 years] beginning with the first day on which it knew of the contravention unless proceedings against that person, in respect of the contravention, were begun before the end of that period.

(7) For the purposes of subsection (6)—
(a) the [FCA] is to be treated as knowing of a contravention if it has information from which the contravention can reasonably be inferred; and
(b) proceedings against a person in respect of a contravention are to be treated as begun when a warning notice is given to him under section 92.

NOTES

Section heading: substituted by the Prospectus Regulations 2005, SI 2005/1433, reg 2(1), Sch 1, para 7(1), (4), as from 1 July 2005.

The word "FCA" in square brackets (in each place that it occurs) was substituted by the Financial Services Act 2012, s 16(1)–(3), as from 1 April 2013. Other amendments to this section are as follows:

Sub-s (1): originally substituted (together with sub-s (2)) by the Financial Services and Markets Act 2000 (Market Abuse) Regulations 2005, SI 2005/381, reg 4, Sch 1, para 4, as from 1 July 2005. Further substituted (by new sub-ss (1) and (1ZA)) by the Companies Act 2006, s 1272, Sch 15, Pt 1, paras 1, 6(1), (2), as from 8 November 2006.

Sub-s (1ZA): substituted as noted above. Subsequently repealed by the Financial Services and Markets Act 2000 (Market Abuse) Regulations 2016, SI 2016/680, reg 8(1), (3)(a), as from 3 July 2016.

Sub-s (1A): inserted by SI 2005/1433, reg 2(1), Sch 1, para 7(1), (2), as from 1 July 2005. Words in square brackets substituted by the Financial Services and Markets Act 2000 (Prospectus) Regulations 2019, SI 2019/1043, regs 3, 26, as from 21 July 2019.

Sub-s (1B): inserted by the Companies Act 2006, s 1272, Sch 15, Pt 1, paras 1, 6(1), (3), as from 8 November 2006. Words "qualifying transparency legislation" in square brackets substituted by the Official Listing of Securities, Prospectus and Transparency (Amendment etc) (EU Exit) Regulations 2019, SI 2019/707, regs 3, 30(1), (3), as from IP completion day (as defined in the European Union (Withdrawal Agreement) Act 2020, s 39).

Sub-s (2): substituted as noted above. Words in square brackets beginning with "(1)" substituted by the Companies Act 2006, s 1272, Sch 15, Pt 1, paras 1, 6(1), (4), as from 8 November 2006. Words omitted repealed by SI 2016/680, reg 8(1), (3)(b), as from 3 July 2016. Words "(1B)(a)(ii) or (b)" in square brackets substituted by the Transparency Regulations 2015, SI 2015/1755, reg 4(2)(a), as from 26 November 2015. Other words in square brackets (with the exception of the word "FCA") substituted by SI 2005/1433, reg 2(1), Sch 1, para 6(1), (3), as from 1 July 2005.

Sub-ss (2A), (2B): inserted by SI 2015/1755, reg 4(2)(b), as from 26 November 2015.

Sub-s (6): words "3 years" in square brackets substituted by the Financial Services Act 2012, s 20, as from 1 April 2013.

[7.225]

92 Procedure

(1) If the [FCA] proposes to take action against a person under section 91, it must give him a warning notice.

(2) A warning notice about a proposal to impose a penalty must state the amount of the proposed penalty.

(3) A warning notice about a proposal to publish a statement must set out the terms of the proposed statement.

(4) If the [FCA] decides to take action against a person under section 91, it must give him a decision notice.

(5) A decision notice about the imposition of a penalty must state the amount of the penalty.

(6) A decision notice about the publication of a statement must set out the terms of the statement.

(7) If the [FCA] decides to take action against a person under section 91, he may refer the matter to the Tribunal.

NOTES

Words in square brackets substituted by the Financial Services Act 2012, s 16(1)–(3), as from 1 April 2013.

[7.226]

93 Statement of policy

(1) The [FCA] must prepare and issue a statement ("its policy statement") of its policy with respect to—

(a) the imposition of penalties under section 91; and

(b) the amount of penalties under that section.

(2) The [FCA's] policy in determining what the amount of a penalty should be must include having regard to—

(a) the seriousness of the contravention in question in relation to the nature of the requirement contravened;

(b) the extent to which that contravention was deliberate or reckless; and

(c) whether the person on whom the penalty is to be imposed is an individual.

(3) The [FCA] may at any time alter or replace its policy statement.

(4) If its policy statement is altered or replaced, the [FCA] must issue the altered or replacement statement.

(5) In exercising, or deciding whether to exercise, its power under section 91 in the case of any particular contravention, the [FCA] must have regard to any policy statement published under this section and in force at the time when the contravention in question occurred.

(6) The [FCA] must publish a statement issued under this section in the way appearing to the [FCA] to be best calculated to bring it to the attention of the public.

(7) The [FCA] may charge a reasonable fee for providing a person with a copy of the statement.

(8) The [FCA] must, without delay, give the Treasury a copy of any policy statement which it publishes under this section.

NOTES

Words in square brackets substituted by the Financial Services Act 2012, s 16(1)–(3), as from 1 April 2013.

[7.227]

94 Statements of policy: procedure

(1) Before issuing a statement under section 93, the [FCA] must publish a draft of the proposed statement in the way appearing to the [FCA] to be best calculated to bring it to the attention of the public.

(2) The draft must be accompanied by notice that representations about the proposal may be made to the [FCA] within a specified time.

(3) Before issuing the proposed statement, the [FCA] must have regard to any representations made to it in accordance with subsection (2).

(4) If the [FCA] issues the proposed statement it must publish an account, in general terms, of—

(a) the representations made to it in accordance with subsection (2); and

(b) its response to them.

(5) If the statement differs from the draft published under subsection (1) in a way which is, in the opinion of the [FCA], significant, the [FCA] must (in addition to complying with subsection (4)) publish details of the difference.

(6) The [FCA] may charge a reasonable fee for providing a person with a copy of a draft published under subsection (1).

(7) This section also applies to a proposal to alter or replace a statement.

NOTES

Words in square brackets substituted by the Financial Services Act 2012, s 16(1)–(3), as from 1 April 2013.

95 (*Repealed by the Financial Services Act 2012, s 21, as from 1 April 2013.*)

Miscellaneous

[7.228]

96 Obligations of issuers of listed securities

(1) Listing rules may—

(a) specify requirements to be complied with by issuers of listed securities; and

(b) make provision with respect to the action that may be taken by the [FCA] in the event of non-compliance.

(2) If the rules require an issuer to publish information, they may include provision authorising the [FCA] to publish it in the event of his failure to do so.

(3) This section applies whenever the listed securities were admitted to the official list.

NOTES

Words in square brackets substituted by the Financial Services Act 2012, s 16(1)–(3), as from 1 April 2013.

96A–96C (*Inserted by the Financial Services and Markets Act 2000 (Market Abuse) Regulations 2005, SI 2005/381, reg 4, Sch 1, para 6, as from 17 March 2005. Repealed by the Financial Services and Markets Act 2000 (Market Abuse) Regulations 2016, SI 2016/680, reg 8(1), (4), as from 3 July 2016.*)

[7.229]

97 Appointment by [FCA] of persons to carry out investigations

(1) Subsection (2) applies if it appears to the [FCA] that there are circumstances suggesting that—

[(a) there may have been a contravention of—

(i) a provision of this Part or of Part 6 rules, . . .

[(ii) any other provision of qualifying transparency legislation, or]

[(iii) any provision of, or made in accordance with, the prospectus regulation;]

(b) a person who was at the material time a director of a person mentioned in section 91(1), . . . [or (1A), or section 91(1B) (ignoring paragraph (a)(i) of that provision),] has been knowingly concerned in a contravention by that person of—

(i) a provision of this Part or of Part 6 rules, . . .

[(ii) any other provision of qualifying transparency legislation, or]

[(iii) any provision of, or made in accordance with, the prospectus regulation;]

[(ba) a person who was at the material time a relevant officer of a person mentioned in section 91(1B) (ignoring paragraphs (a)(ii) and (b) of that provision) has been knowingly concerned in a contravention [by that person of qualifying transparency legislation];]

(c), (d) . . .

(2) The [FCA] may appoint one or more competent persons to conduct an investigation on its behalf.

(3) Part XI applies to an investigation under subsection (2) as if—

(a) the investigator were appointed under section 167(1);

(b) references to the investigating authority in relation to him were to the [FCA];

(c) references to the offences mentioned in section 168 were to [the offences under section 85];

(d) references to an authorised person were references to the person under investigation.

[(4) In this section "relevant officer" has the meaning given by section 91(2B).]

NOTES

Word "FCA" in square brackets (in each place that it occurs) substituted by the Financial Services Act 2012, s 16(1)–(3), as from 1 April 2013. Other amendments to this section are as follows—

Sub-s (1) is amended as follows:

Paras (a), (b) substituted by the Companies Act 2006, s 1272, Sch 15, Pt 1, paras 1, 8, as from 8 November 2006.

The word omitted from sub-para (a)(i) was repealed by the Financial Services and Markets Act 2000 (Prospectus) Regulations 2019, SI 2019/1043, regs 3, 27(1), (2)(a), (b), as from 21 July 2019.

Sub-para (a)(ii) was substituted by the Official Listing of Securities, Prospectus and Transparency (Amendment etc) (EU Exit) Regulations 2019, SI 2019/707, regs 3, 31(a), as from IP completion day (as defined in the European Union (Withdrawal Agreement) Act 2020, s 39). Note that reg 31(a) of the 2019 Regulations was substituted by the Prospectus (Amendment etc) (EU Exit) Regulations 2019, SI 2019/1234, regs 2, 18, with effect from immediately before IP completion day.

Sub-para (a)(iii) was inserted by SI 2019/1043, regs 3, 27(1), (2)(c), as from 21 July 2019.

Figure omitted from para (b) repealed by the Financial Services and Markets Act 2000 (Market Abuse) Regulations 2016, SI 2016/680, reg 8(1), (5), as from 3 July 2016.

Words in first pair of square brackets in para (b) substituted by the Transparency Regulations 2015, SI 2015/1755, reg 4(3)(a), as from 26 November 2015.

The word omitted from sub-para (b)(i) was repealed by SI 2019/1043, regs 3, 27(1), (3)(a), (b), as from 21 July 2019.

Sub-para (b)(ii) was substituted by SI 2019/707, regs 3, 31(b), as from IP completion day (as defined in the European Union (Withdrawal Agreement) Act 2020, s 39). Note that reg 31(b) of the 2019 Regulations was substituted by the Prospectus (Amendment etc) (EU Exit) Regulations 2019, SI 2019/1234, regs 2, 18, with effect from immediately before IP completion day.

Sub-para (b)(iii) was inserted by SI 2019/1043, regs 3, 27(1), (3)(c), as from 21 July 2019.

Para (ba) was inserted by SI 2015/1755, reg 4(3)(a), as from 26 November 2015. Words in square brackets substituted by SI 2019/707, regs 3, 31(c), as from IP completion day (as defined in the European Union (Withdrawal Agreement) Act 2020, s 39).

Para (c) repealed by the Financial Services and Markets Act 2000 (Market Abuse) Regulations 2005, SI 2005/381, reg 4, Sch 1, para 7, as from 1 July 2005.

Para (d) repealed by SI 2019/1043, regs 3, 27(1), (4), as from 21 July 2019.

Sub-s (3): words in square brackets in para (c) substituted by SI 2019/1043, regs 3, 27(1), (4), as from 21 July 2019.

Sub-s (4): added by SI 2015/1755, reg 4(3)(b), as from 26 November 2015.

[7.230]

[97A Reporting of infringements

(1) This section applies to a person—

(a) who is the employer of any employees, and

(b) who—

(i) provides regulated financial services,

(ii) carries on regulated activities in reliance on the exemption in section 327, or

(iii) is a recognised investment exchange, a recognised clearing house, a recognised CSD . . . or a third country central counterparty.

(2) The person must have in place appropriate internal procedures for the person's employees to report, through an independent channel, contraventions and potential contraventions of—

(a) the prospectus regulation, . . .

[(b) any EU regulation, originally made under the prospectus regulation, which is retained EU law, or

(c) any subordinate legislation (within the meaning of the Interpretation Act 1978) made under the prospectus regulation on or after IP completion day].

(3) In this section—

"employer" and "employee" have the same meaning given in section 230(1) to (5) of the Employment Rights Act 1996;

"regulated financial services" has the meaning given by section 1H.".

NOTES

Commencement: 21 July 2019.

Inserted by the Financial Services and Markets Act 2000 (Prospectus) Regulations 2019, SI 2019/1043, regs 3, 28, as from 21 July 2019.

The words omitted from sub-s (1) and sub-s (2)(a) were repealed, and sub-s (2)(b), (c) were substituted (for the original sub-s (2)(b)), by the Prospectus (Amendment etc) (EU Exit) Regulations 2019, SI 2019/1234, regs 2, 7, as from IP completion day (as defined in the European Union (Withdrawal Agreement) Act 2020, s 39); for transitional provisions, see regs 74, 75 of the 2019 Regulations at **[12.165]** et seq. Note that reg 7 of the 2019 Regulations was amended by the Financial Services and Economic and Monetary Policy (Consequential Amendments) (EU Exit) Regulations 2020, SI 2020/1301, reg 3, Schedule, para 48(a), as from 30 December 2020 (and the effect of the amendment has been incorporated in the text set out above).

98–100A *(S 98 repealed by the Prospectus Regulations 2005, SI 2005/1433, reg 2(1), Sch 1, para 9, as from 1 July 2005. Ss 99, 100 repealed by the Financial Services Act 2012, s 16(1), (14)(c), (d), as from 1 April 2013. S 100A was originally inserted by the Companies Act 2006, s 1271, as from 8 November 2006, and was repealed by the Official Listing of Securities, Prospectus and Transparency (Amendment etc) (EU Exit) Regulations 2019, SI 2019/707, regs 3, 32, as from IP completion day (as defined in the European Union (Withdrawal Agreement) Act 2020, s 39).)*

[7.231]

101 [Part 6 rules]: general provisions

(1) . . .

(2) [Part 6 rules] may authorise the [FCA] to dispense with or modify the application of the rules in particular cases and by reference to any circumstances.

(3)–(8) . . .

NOTES

The words "Part 6 rules" in the section heading and in sub-s (2) were substituted by the Financial Services and Markets Act 2000 (Market Abuse) Regulations 2005, SI 2005/381, reg 4, Sch 1, para 10, as from 1 July 2005. Note that SI 2005/381 actually makes no provision for the section name to be amended, but in consequence of the other amendment, it is believed that it should be.

Sub-ss (1), (3)–(8) were repealed, and the word "FCA" in square brackets in sub-s (2) was substituted, by the Financial Services Act 2012, s 16(1)–(3), (14)(e), as from 1 April 2013.

102 *(Repealed by the Financial Services Act 2012, s 16(1), (14)(f), as from 1 April 2013.)*

[Interpretative provisions

[7.232]

102A Meaning of "securities" etc

(1) This section applies for the purposes of this Part.

(2) "Securities" means (except in section 74(2) and the expression "transferable securities") anything which has been, or may be, admitted to the official list.

(3) "Transferable securities" means anything which is a transferable security for the purposes of [the markets in financial instruments [regulation]], other than money-market instruments for the purposes of that [regulation] which have a maturity of less than 12 months.

[(3A) "Debt securities" means bonds or other forms of transferable securitised debts, with the exception of—

(a) transferable securities which are equivalent to shares, and

(b) transferable securities which, if converted or if the rights conferred by them are exercised, give rise to a right to acquire—

(i) shares, or

(ii) transferable securities equivalent to shares.]

[(4) "Financial instrument" [means those instruments specified in Part 1 of Schedule 2 to the Financial Services and Markets Act 2000 (Regulated Activities) Order 2001].]

(5) . . .

(6) "Issuer"—

(a) in relation to an offer of transferable securities to the public or admission of transferable securities to trading on a regulated market for which an approved prospectus is required [under the prospectus regulation], means a legal person who issues or proposes to issue the transferable securities in question,

[(aa) in relation to transparency rules, means a . . . person whose securities are admitted to trading on a regulated market or whose voting shares are admitted to trading on a UK market other than a regulated market, and in the case of depository receipts [admitted to trading on a regulated market, the issuer is the issuer of the securities represented by the depository receipt, whether or not those securities are admitted to trading on a regulated market],]

(b) in relation to anything else which is or may be admitted to the official list, has such meaning as may be prescribed by the Treasury, and

(c) in any other case, means a person who issues financial instruments.]

NOTES

Sections 102A–102C, 103 substituted (together with the preceding heading) for the original s 103, by the Prospectus Regulations 2005, SI 2005/1433, reg 2(1), Sch 1, para 11, as from 1 July 2005.

Sub-s (3): words in first (outer) pair of square brackets substituted by the Financial Services and Markets Act 2000 (Markets in Financial Instruments) Regulations 2017, SI 2017/701, reg 50(1), Sch 2, paras 1, 7(1), (2), as from 3 January 2018 (note that various provisions of the 2017 Regulations came into force on earlier dates for the purposes of making rules, giving notices and consent, etc (for details see reg 1 of the 2017 Regulations)). Other words in square brackets substituted by the Official Listing of Securities, Prospectus and Transparency (Amendment etc) (EU Exit) Regulations 2019, SI 2019/707, regs 3, 33(1), (2), as from IP completion day (as defined in the European Union (Withdrawal Agreement) Act 2020, s 39).

Sub-s (3A): originally inserted by the Companies Act 2006, s 1272, Sch 15, Pt 1, paras 1, 10(1), (2), as from 8 November 2006. Subsequently substituted by SI 2019/707, regs 3, 33(1), (3), as from IP completion day (as defined in the European Union (Withdrawal Agreement) Act 2020, s 39).

Sub-s (4): substituted by the Financial Services and Markets Act 2000 (Market Abuse) Regulations 2016, SI 2016/680, reg 8(1), (6), as from 3 July 2016. Words in square brackets substituted by SI 2019/707, regs 3, 33(1), (4), as from IP completion day (as defined in the European Union (Withdrawal Agreement) Act 2020, s 39).

Sub-s (5): repealed by the Financial Services and Markets Act 2000 (Prospectus) Regulations 2019, SI 2019/1043, regs 3, 30(1), (2), as from 21 July 2019.

Sub-s (6): words in square brackets in para (a) substituted by SI 2019/1043, regs 3, 30(1), (2), as from 21 July 2019. Para (aa) inserted by the Companies Act 2006, s 1272, Sch 15, Pt 1, paras 1, 10(1), (4), as from 8 November 2006. Word omitted from para (aa) repealed, and words in square brackets in that paragraph substituted, by the Transparency Regulations 2015, SI 2015/1755, reg 5(1), as from 1 November 2015 (for the purpose of making rules under Part 6), and as from 26 November 2015 (otherwise).

[7.233]

[102B Meaning of "offer of transferable securities to the public" etc

(1) For the purposes of this Part there is an offer of transferable securities to the public if there is a communication to any person which presents sufficient information on—

(a) the transferable securities to be offered, and

(b) the terms on which they are offered,

to enable an investor to decide to buy or subscribe for the securities in question.

(2) For the purposes of this Part, to the extent that an offer of transferable securities is made to a person in the United Kingdom it is an offer of transferable securities to the public in the United Kingdom.

(3) The communication may be made—

(a) in any form;

(b) by any means.

(4) Subsection (1) includes the placing of securities through a financial intermediary.

(5) Subsection (1) does not include a communication in connection with trading on—

(a) a regulated market[, as defined in Article 2(1)(13) of the markets in financial instruments regulation];

(b) a multilateral trading facility; or

[(c) a prescribed market].

[(5A) The Treasury may make regulations to specify (whether by name or description) the markets which are prescribed markets for the purposes of subsection (5)(c).]

[(6) "Multilateral trading facility" has the same meaning as in the markets in financial instruments regulation (see Article 2(1)(14) of that Regulation).]

NOTES

Substituted as noted to s 102A at **[7.232]**.

Sub-s (5): words in square brackets in para (a) inserted by the Official Listing of Securities, Prospectus and Transparency (Amendment etc) (EU Exit) Regulations 2019, SI 2019/707, regs 3, 34(1), (2), as from IP completion day (as defined in the European Union (Withdrawal Agreement) Act 2020, s 39). Para (c) substituted by the Financial Services and Markets Act 2000 (Market Abuse) Regulations 2016, SI 2016/680, reg 8(1), (7)(a), as from 3 July 2016.

Sub-s (5A): inserted by SI 2016/680, reg 8(1), (7)(b), as from 3 July 2016.

Sub-s (6): substituted by SI 2019/707, regs 3, 34(1), (3), as from IP completion day (as defined in the European Union (Withdrawal Agreement) Act 2020, s 39).

102C *(S 102C (Meaning of "home State" in relation to transferable securities) originally substituted as noted to s 102A at* **[7.232]***, and further substituted by the Transparency Regulations 2015, SI 2015/1755, reg 5(2), as from 1 November 2015 (for the purpose of making rules under Part 6), and as from 26 November 2015 (otherwise). Subsequently repealed by the Official Listing of Securities, Prospectus and Transparency (Amendment etc) (EU Exit) Regulations 2019, SI 2019/707, regs 3, 35, as from IP completion day (as defined in the European Union (Withdrawal Agreement) Act 2020, s 39).)*

[7.234]

[103 Interpretation of this Part

(1) In this Part, save where the context otherwise requires—

. . .

. . .

"listed securities" means anything which has been admitted to the official list;

"listing" has the meaning given in section 74(5);

"listing particulars" has the meaning given in section 79(2);

"listing rules" has the meaning given in section 73A;

"market operator" means a person who manages or operates the business of a regulated market;

"offer of transferable securities to the public" has the meaning given in section 102B;

"the official list" means the list maintained by the [FCA] as that list has effect for the time being;

"Part 6 rules" has the meaning given in section 73A;

. . .

["the prospectus regulation" means Regulation (EU) No 2017/1129 of the European Parliament and of the Council of 14 June 2017 on the prospectus to be published when securities are offered to the public or admitted to trading on a regulated market, and repealing Directive 2003/71/EC;]

"prospectus rules" has the meaning given in section 73A;

["qualifying transparency legislation" has the meaning given in section 89K(5A);]

["regulated market" (except in section 102B and Schedule 10A) means a UK regulated market, as defined in Article 2(1)(13A) of the markets in financial instruments regulation;]

["supplementary prospectus" means a supplement to a prospectus (and here "supplement" has the same meaning as in Article 23 of the prospectus regulation);]

["the transparency obligations directive" means Directive 2004/109/EC of the European Parliament and of the Council relating to the harmonisation of transparency requirements in relation to information about issuers whose securities are admitted to trading on a regulated market [as amended by Directive 2010/73/EU of the European Parliament and of the Council of 24 November 2010 and by Directive 2010/78/EU of the European Parliament and of the Council of 24 November 2010] [and by Directive 2013/50/EU of the European Parliament and of the Council of 22 October 2013];]

["transparency rules" has the meaning given by section 89A(5);

"voteholder information" has the meaning given by section 89B(3);]

"working day" means any day other that a Saturday, a Sunday, Christmas Day, Good Friday or a day which is a bank holiday under the Banking and Financial Dealings Act 1971 (c 80) in any part of the United Kingdom.

[(1A) . . .]

(2), (3) . . .

NOTES

Substituted as noted to s 102A at **[7.232]**.

Sub-s (1) is amended as follows:

Definitions "disclosure rules" and "inside information" (omitted) repealed by the Financial Services and Markets Act 2000 (Market Abuse) Regulations 2016, SI 2016/680, reg 8(1), (9), as from 3 July 2016.

Word in square brackets in the definition "the official list" substituted by the Financial Services Act 2012, s 16(1)–(3), as from 1 April 2013.

Definition "the prospectus directive" (omitted) repealed by the Financial Services and Markets Act 2000 (Prospectus) Regulations 2019, SI 2019/1043, regs 3, 32(a), as from 21 July 2019.

Definition "the prospectus regulation" inserted by SI 2019/1043, regs 3, 32(a), as from 21 July 2019.

Definition "qualifying transparency legislation" inserted by the Official Listing of Securities, Prospectus and Transparency (Amendment etc) (EU Exit) Regulations 2019, SI 2019/707, regs 3, 36(a), as from IP completion day (as defined in the European Union (Withdrawal Agreement) Act 2020, s 39).

Definition "regulated market" substituted by SI 2019/707, regs 3, 36(b), as from IP completion day (as defined in the European Union (Withdrawal Agreement) Act 2020, s 39).

Definition "supplementary prospectus" substituted by SI 2019/1043, regs 3, 32(b), as from 21 July 2019.

Definitions "the transparency obligations directive", "transparency rules", and "voteholder information" inserted by the Companies Act 2006, ss 1265, 1272, Sch 15, Pt 1, paras 1, 11(1), (3), as from 8 November 2006. Words in first pair of square brackets in the definition "the transparency obligations directive" added by SI 2012/1538, reg 9, as from 1 July 2012. Words in second pair of square brackets added by SI 2015/1755, reg 5(3)(a)(ii), as from 1 November 2015 (for the purpose of making rules under Part 6), and as from 26 November 2015 (otherwise).

Sub-s (1A): originally inserted by SI 2014/3293, reg 5(1), (3), as from 17 December 2014. Subsequently repealed by SI 2015/1755, reg 5(3)(b), as from 1 November 2015 (for the purpose of making rules under Part 6), and as from 26 November 2015 (otherwise).

Sub-ss (2), (3): repealed by the Financial Services Act 2012, s 16(1), (14)(g), as from 1 April 2013.

PART VII CONTROL OF BUSINESS TRANSFERS

NOTES

Transitional provisions etc in connection with the commencement of the Financial Services Act 2012: for transitional provisions in relation to the control of business transfers, see Part 3 of the Financial Services Act 2012 (Transitional Provisions) (Miscellaneous Provisions) Order 2013, SI 2013/442. Article 8 contains transitional provisions regarding scheme reports; arts 9 and 10 deal with the sanction of the court for business transfer schemes; art 11 concerns the appointment of an actuary in relation to reduction of benefits.

Transitional provisions etc in connection with the original commencement of this Act: see the Financial Services and Markets Act 2000 (Transitional Provisions and Savings) (Business Transfers) Order 2001, SI 2001/3639. That Order makes savings and transitional provision for applications under the Insurance Companies Act 1982, Sch 2C (repealed) for approval of a transfer of the whole or part of the long term business carried on by an insurance company or approval of the transfer of rights and obligations under contracts of general insurance (including transfers of business to or from members of Lloyd's). In relation to any application that was made but not determined before 1 December 2001, the relevant provisions of Sch 2C were saved, subject to the general modifications in art 2 of the Order and the specific modifications in arts 3 and 5.

[7.235]

[103A Meaning of "the appropriate regulator"

(1) In this Part "the appropriate regulator" means—

(a) in relation to [a ring-fencing transfer scheme or a scheme (other than a ring-fencing transfer scheme)] in respect of which [the transferor concerned] is a PRA-authorised person, the PRA;

(b) in any other case, the FCA.

(2) In this Part, "[the transferor concerned]"—

(a) in the case of an insurance business transfer scheme, is to be read in accordance with section 105(2);

(b) in the case of a banking business transfer scheme, is to be read in accordance with section 106(2);

(c) in the case of a reclaim fund business transfer scheme, means the reclaim fund to whose business the scheme relates;

[(d) in the case of a ring-fencing transfer scheme, means the body to whose business the scheme relates].]

NOTES

Inserted by the Financial Services Act 2012, s 22, Sch 6, paras 1,2, as from 1 April 2013.

Sub-s (2)(d) added, and all other words in square brackets substituted, by the Financial Services (Banking Reform) Act 2013, s 6, Sch 1, paras 1–3, as from 1 March 2014.

[7.236]

104 Control of business transfers

No insurance business transfer scheme . . . is to have effect unless an order has been made in relation to it under section 111(1).

NOTES

Commencement: 1 December 2001 (for the purpose of insurance business transfer schemes); to be appointed (otherwise). See further the final note below.

Words omitted repealed by the Financial Services Act 2012, s 22(1), as from 1 April 2013.

Note that this provision was never originally brought into force in relation to banking business transfer schemes (see the Financial Services and Markets Act 2000 (Commencement No 7) Order 2001, SI 2001/3538) but, following the repeal of the words "or banking business transfer scheme" as noted above, this section is now effectively in force for all purposes.

[7.237]

105 Insurance business transfer schemes

(1) A scheme is an insurance business transfer scheme if it—

(a) satisfies [the condition] set out in subsection (2);

(b) results in the business transferred being carried on from an establishment of the transferee in [the United Kingdom or Gibraltar]; and

(c) is not an excluded scheme.

[(2) The condition is that the whole or part of the business carried on in the United Kingdom by an authorised person who has permission to effect or carry out contracts of insurance ("the transferor concerned") is to be transferred to another body ("the transferee")]

(3) A scheme is an excluded scheme for the purposes of this section if it falls within any of the following cases:

CASE 1

Where [the transferor concerned] is a friendly society.

. . .

CASE 3

Where—

(a) [the transferor concerned] is a UK authorised person;

(b) the business to be transferred under the scheme is carried on in one or more countries or territories [outside the United Kingdom] and does not include policies of insurance . . . against risks arising in [the United Kingdom]; and

(c) the scheme has been approved by a court in a country or territory [outside the United Kingdom] or by the authority responsible for the supervision of that business in a country or territory in which it is carried on.

CASE 4

Where[—

(a) the business to be transferred under the scheme is the whole of the business of [the transferor concerned];]

(b) all the policyholders are controllers of the firm or of firms within the same group as the firm which is the transferee, and

[(c)] all of the policyholders who will be affected by the transfer have consented to it.

[CASE 5

Where—

(a) the business of [the transferor concerned] consists solely of the effecting or carrying out of contracts of reinsurance;

(b) the business to be transferred is the whole or part of that business;

(c) the scheme does not fall within Case 4;

(d) all of the policyholders who will be affected by the transfer have consented to it; and

(e) a certificate has been obtained under paragraph 2 of Schedule 12 in relation to the proposed transfer.]

(4) The parties to a scheme which falls within Case . . . [3, 4 or 5] may apply to the court for an order sanctioning the scheme as if it were an insurance business transfer scheme.

[(5) If the scheme involves a compromise or arrangement falling within Part 27 of the Companies Act 2006 (mergers and divisions of public companies), the provisions of that Part (and [Part 26 or 26A of that Act, as the case may be]) apply accordingly but this does not affect the operation of this Part in relation to the scheme.]

(8) "UK authorised person" means a body which is an authorised person and which—

(a) is incorporated in the United Kingdom; or

(b) is an unincorporated association formed under the law of any part of the United Kingdom.

(9) "Establishment" means, in relation to a person, his head office or a branch of his.

NOTES

Words "the transferor concerned" in square brackets (in each place that they occur) substituted by the Financial Services (Banking Reform) Act 2013, s 6, Sch 1, paras 1, 2, as from 1 March 2014. Other amendments to this section are as follows:

Sub-s (1): words in square brackets substituted by the Financial Services and Markets Act 2000 (Amendment) (EU Exit) Regulations 2019, SI 2019/632, regs 31, 32(1), (2), as from IP completion day (as defined in the European Union (Withdrawal Agreement) Act 2020, s 39). Note that reg 32(2) of the 2019 Regulations was amended by the Gibraltar (Miscellaneous Amendments) (EU Exit) Regulations 2019, SI 2019/680, reg 9(1), (2), with effect from immediately before IP completion day (and the effect of the amendment has been incorporated in the text set out above).

Sub-s (2): substituted by SI 2019/632, regs 31, 32(1), (3), as from IP completion day (as defined in the European Union (Withdrawal Agreement) Act 2020, s 39).

Sub-s (3) is amended as follows:

Case 2 was repealed by SI 2019/632, regs 31, 32(1), (3), as from IP completion day (as defined in the European Union (Withdrawal Agreement) Act 2020, s 39).

The words in the second, third and fourth pairs of square brackets in Case 3 were substituted by SI 2019/632, regs 31, 32(1), (4), as from IP completion day (as defined in the European Union (Withdrawal Agreement) Act 2020, s 39).

The words omitted from Case 3 were repealed by SI 2007/3253, reg 2(1), Sch 1, paras 1, 2(1)(c), as from 10 December 2007.

In Case 4, para (a) was substituted by SI 2007/3253, reg 2(1), Sch 1, paras 1, 2(1)(d)(i), as from 10 December 2007.

In Case 4, para (c) was designated as such by SI 2007/3253, reg 2(1), Sch 1, paras 1, 2(1)(d)(ii), as from 10 December 2007.

Case 5 was inserted by SI 2007/3253, reg 2(1), Sch 1, paras 1, 2(1)(e), as from 10 December 2007.

Sub-s (4): the figure omitted was repealed by SI 2019/632, regs 31, 32(1), (5), as from IP completion day (as defined in the European Union (Withdrawal Agreement) Act 2020, s 39). The words in square brackets were substituted by SI 2007/3253, reg 2(1), Sch 1, paras 1, 2(1)(f), as from 10 December 2007.

Sub-s (5): substituted (for original sub-ss (5)–(7)) by the Companies Act 2006 (Consequential Amendments etc) Order 2008, SI 2008/948, art 3(1), Sch 1, Pt 2, para 211(1), as from 6 April 2008. Words in square brackets substituted by the Corporate Insolvency and Governance Act 2020, s 7, Sch 9, Pt 2, paras 17, 18, as from 26 June 2020.

[7.238]

106 Banking business transfer schemes

(1) A scheme is a banking business transfer scheme if it—

(a) satisfies one of the conditions set out in subsection (2);

(b) is one under which the whole or part of the business to be transferred includes the accepting of deposits; and

(c) is not an excluded scheme [or a ring-fencing transfer scheme].

(2) The conditions are that—

(a) the whole or part of the business carried on by a UK authorised person who has permission to accept deposits ("[the transferor concerned]") is to be transferred to another body ("the transferee");

(b) the whole or part of the business carried on in the United Kingdom by an authorised person who is not a UK authorised person but who has permission to accept deposits ("[the transferor concerned]") is to be transferred to another body which will carry it on in the United Kingdom ("the transferee").

(3) A scheme is an excluded scheme for the purposes of this section if—

(a) [the transferor concerned] is a building society or a credit union; or

[(b) the scheme is a compromise or arrangement to which Part 27 of the Companies Act 2006 (mergers and divisions of public companies) applies.]

(4) For the purposes of subsection (2)(a) it is immaterial whether or not the business to be transferred is carried on in the United Kingdom.

(5) "UK authorised person" has the same meaning as in section 105.

(6) "Building society" has the meaning given in the Building Societies Act 1986.

(7) "Credit union" means a credit union within the meaning of—

(a) the Credit Unions Act 1979;

(b) the Credit Unions (Northern Ireland) Order 1985.

NOTES

The words "the transferor concerned" (in each place that they occur) were substituted by the Financial Services (Banking Reform) Act 2013, s 6, Sch 1, paras 1, 2, as from 1 March 2014.

The words in square brackets in sub-s (1)(c) were inserted by the Financial Services (Banking Reform) Act 2013, s 6, Sch 1, paras 1, 4, as from 1 March 2014.

Sub-s (3)(b) was substituted by the Companies Act 2006 (Consequential Amendments etc) Order 2008, SI 2008/948, art 3(1), Sch 1, Pt 2, para 211(2), as from 6 April 2008.

[7.239]

[106A Reclaim fund business transfer scheme

(1) A scheme is a reclaim fund business transfer scheme if, under the scheme, the whole or part of the business carried on by a reclaim fund is to be transferred to one or more other reclaim funds.

(2) "Reclaim fund" has the meaning given by section 5(1) of the Dormant Bank and Building Society Accounts Act 2008.]

NOTES

Inserted by the Dormant Bank and Building Society Accounts Act 2008, s 15, Sch 2, para 2, as from 12 March 2009.

[7.240]

[106B Ring-fencing transfer scheme

(1) A scheme is a ring-fencing transfer scheme if it—

(a) is one under which the whole or part of the business carried on—

(i) by a UK authorised person, or

(ii) by a qualifying body,

is to be transferred to another body ("the transferee"),

(b) is to be made for one or more of the purposes mentioned in subsection (3), and

(c) is not an excluded scheme or an insurance business transfer scheme.

(2) "Qualifying body" means a body which—

(a) is incorporated in the United Kingdom,

(b) is a member of the group of a UK authorised person, and

(c) is not itself an authorised person.

(3) The purposes are—

(a) enabling a UK authorised person to carry on core activities as a ring-fenced body in compliance with the ring-fencing provisions;

(b) enabling the transferee to carry on core activities as a ring-fenced body in compliance with the ring-fencing provisions;

(c) making provision in connection with the implementation of proposals that would involve a body corporate whose group includes the body corporate to whose business the scheme relates becoming a ring-fenced body while one or more other members of its group are not ring-fenced bodies;

(d) making provision in connection with the implementation of proposals that would involve a body corporate whose group includes the transferee becoming a ring-fenced body while one or more other members of the transferee's group are not ring-fenced bodies.

(4) A scheme is an excluded scheme for the purposes of this section if—

(a) the body to whose business the scheme relates is a building society or credit union, or

(b) the scheme is a compromise or arrangement to which Part 27 of the Companies Act 2006 (mergers and divisions of public companies) applies.

(5) For the purposes of subsection (1)(a) it is immaterial whether or not the business to be transferred is carried on in the United Kingdom.

(6) "UK authorised person" has the same meaning as in section 105.

(7) "Building society" and "credit union" have the same meanings as in section 106.

(8) "The ring-fencing provisions" means ring-fencing rules and the duty imposed as a result of section 142G.]

NOTES

Inserted by the Financial Services (Banking Reform) Act 2013, s 6, Sch 1, paras 1, 5, as from 1 March 2014.

[7.241]

107 Application for order sanctioning transfer scheme

(1) An application may be made to the court for an order sanctioning an insurance business transfer scheme[, a banking business transfer scheme[, a reclaim fund business transfer scheme or a ring-fencing transfer scheme]].

(2) An application may be made by—

(a) [the transferor concerned];

(b) the transferee; or

(c) both.

[(2A) An application relating to a ring-fencing transfer scheme may be made only with the consent of the PRA.

(2B) In deciding whether to give consent, the PRA must have regard to the scheme report prepared under section 109A in relation to the ring-fencing transfer scheme.]

(3) The application must be made—

(a) if [the transferor concerned] and the transferee are registered or have their head offices in the same jurisdiction, to the court in that jurisdiction;

(b) if [the transferor concerned] and the transferee are registered or have their head offices in different jurisdictions, to the court in either jurisdiction;

(c) if the transferee is not registered in the United Kingdom and does not have his head office there, to the court which has jurisdiction in relation to [the transferor concerned].

(4) "Court" means—

(a) the High Court; or

(b) in Scotland, the Court of Session.

NOTES

The words "the transferor concerned" (in each place that they occur) were substituted by the Financial Services (Banking Reform) Act 2013, s 6, Sch 1, paras 1, 2, as from 1 March 2014.

The words in the first (outer) pair of square brackets in sub-s (1) were substituted by the Dormant Bank and Building Society Accounts Act 2008, s 15, Sch 2, para 3, as from 12 March 2009.

The words in the second (inner) pair of square brackets in sub-s (1) were substituted, and sub-ss (2A), (2B) were inserted, by the Financial Services (Banking Reform) Act 2013, s 6, Sch 1, paras 1, 6, as from 1 March 2014.

[7.242]

108 Requirements on applicants

(1) The Treasury may by regulations impose requirements on applicants under section 107.

(2) The court may not determine an application under that section if the applicant has failed to comply with a prescribed requirement.

(3) The regulations may, in particular, include provision—

(a) as to the persons to whom, and periods within which, notice of an application must be given;

(b) enabling the court to waive a requirement of the regulations in prescribed circumstances.

NOTES

Regulations: the Financial Services and Markets Act 2000 (Control of Business Transfers) (Requirements on Applicants) Regulations 2001, SI 2001/3625; the Financial Services and Markets Act 2000 (Reinsurance Directive) Regulations 2007, SI 2007/3255; the Financial Services and Markets Act 2000 (Control of Business Transfers) (Requirements on Applicants) (Amendment) Regulations 2008, SI 2008/1467; the Financial Services and Markets Act 2000 (Control of Business Transfers) (Requirements on Applicants) (Amendment) Regulations 2009, SI 2009/1390.

[7.243]

109 [Scheme reports: insurance business transfer schemes]

(1) An application under section 107 in respect of an insurance business transfer scheme must be accompanied by a report on the terms of the scheme ("a scheme report").

(2) A scheme report may be made only by a person—

(a) appearing to the [appropriate regulator] to have the skills necessary to enable him to make a proper report; and

(b) nominated or approved for the purpose by the [appropriate regulator].

(3) A scheme report must be made in a form approved by the [appropriate regulator].

[(4) Where the appropriate regulator is the PRA, it must consult the FCA before—

(a) nominating or approving a person under subsection (2)(b), or

(b) approving a form under subsection (3).

(5) Subsection (6) applies where the appropriate regulator is the FCA and either—

(a) the transferee is a PRA-authorised person, or

(b) [the transferor concerned] or the transferee has as a member of its immediate group a PRA-authorised person.

(6) The FCA must consult the PRA before—

(a) nominating or approving a person under subsection (2)(b), or

(b) approving a form under subsection (3).]

NOTES

The section heading and the words in square brackets in sub-s (5) were substituted by the Financial Services (Banking Reform) Act 2013, s 6, Sch 1, paras 1, 2, 7, as from 1 March 2014.

The words in square brackets in sub-ss (2), (3) were substituted, and sub-ss (4)–(6) were added, by the Financial Services Act 2012, s 22, Sch 6, paras 1, 3, as from 1 April 2013.

[7.244]

[109A Scheme reports: ring-fencing transfer schemes

(1) An application under section 106B in respect of a ring-fencing transfer scheme must be accompanied by a report on the terms of the scheme (a "scheme report").

(2) A scheme report may be made only by a person—

(a) appearing to the PRA to have the skills necessary to enable the person to make a proper report, and

(b) nominated or approved for the purpose by the PRA.

(3) A scheme report must be made in a form approved by the PRA.

(4) A scheme report must state—

(a) whether persons other than the transferor concerned are likely to be adversely affected by the scheme, and

(b) if so, whether the adverse effect is likely to be greater than is reasonably necessary in order to achieve whichever of the purposes mentioned in section 106B(3) is relevant.

(5) The PRA must consult the FCA before—

(a) nominating or approving a person under subsection (2)(b), or

(b) approving a form under subsection (3).]

NOTES

Inserted by the Financial Services (Banking Reform) Act 2013, s 6, Sch 1, paras 1, 8, as from 1 March 2014.

[7.245]

110 Right to participate in proceedings

[(1)] On an application under section 107 [relating to an insurance business transfer scheme, a banking business transfer scheme or a reclaim fund business transfer scheme], the following are also entitled to be heard—

[(a) the FCA,

(aa) in the case of a scheme falling within subsection (2), the PRA, and]

(b) any person (including an employee of [the transferor concerned] or of the transferee) who alleges that he would be adversely affected by the carrying out of the scheme.

[(2) A scheme falls within this subsection if—

(a) [the transferor concerned] or the transferee is a PRA-authorised person, or

(b) [the transferor concerned] or the transferee has as a member of its immediate group a PRA-authorised person.]

[(3) Subsections (4) and (5) apply where an application under section 107 relates to a ring-fencing transfer scheme.

(4) The following are also entitled to be heard—

(a) the PRA,

(b) where the transferee is an authorised person, the FCA, and

(c) any person ("P") (including an employee of the transferor concerned or of the transferee) who alleges that P would be adversely affected by the carrying out of the scheme.

(5) P is not entitled to be heard by virtue of subsection (4)(c) unless before the hearing P has—

(a) filed (in Scotland, lodged) with the court a written statement of the representations that P wishes the court to consider, and

(b) served copies of the statement on the PRA and the transferor concerned.]

NOTES

Sub-s (1) numbered as such, paras (a), (aa) substituted (for the original para (a)), and sub-s (2) added, by the Financial Services Act 2012, s 22, Sch 6, paras 1, 4, as from 1 April 2013.

The words in the first pair of square brackets in sub-s (1) were inserted, the words "the transferor concerned" in square brackets (in each place they occur) were substituted, and sub-ss (3)–(5) were added, by the Financial Services (Banking Reform) Act 2013, s 6, Sch 1, paras 1, 2, 9, as from 1 March 2014.

[7.246]

111 Sanction of the court for business transfer schemes

(1) This section sets out the conditions which must be satisfied before the court may make an order under this section sanctioning an insurance business transfer scheme[, a banking business transfer scheme[, a reclaim fund business transfer scheme or a ring-fencing transfer scheme]].

(2) The court must be satisfied that—

(a) [in the case of an insurance business transfer scheme or a banking business transfer scheme,] the appropriate [certificate has] been obtained (as to which see Parts I and II of Schedule 12);

[(aa) in the case of a reclaim fund business transfer scheme, the appropriate certificate has been obtained (as to which see Part 2A of that Schedule);]

[(ab) in the case of a ring-fencing transfer scheme, the appropriate certificates have been obtained (as to which see Part 2B of that Schedule);]

(b) the transferee has the authorisation required (if any) to enable the business, or part, which is to be transferred to be carried on in the place to which it is to be transferred (or will have it before the scheme takes effect).

(3) The court must consider that, in all the circumstances of the case, it is appropriate to sanction the scheme.

NOTES

Sub-s (1): words in first (outer) pair of square brackets substituted by the Dormant Bank and Building Society Accounts Act 2008, s 15, Sch 2, para 4(1), (2), as from 12 March 2009. Words in second (inner) pair of square brackets substituted by the Financial Services (Banking Reform) Act 2013, s 6, Sch 1, paras 1, 10(1), (2), as from 1 March 2014.

Sub-s (2): words in first pair of square brackets in para (a) inserted, and para (aa) inserted, by the Dormant Bank and Building Society Accounts Act 2008, s 15, Sch 2, para 4(1), (3), as from 12 March 2009. Words in second pair of square brackets in para (a) substituted by the Financial Services and Markets Act 2000 (Amendment) (EU Exit) Regulations 2019, SI 2019/632, regs 31, 33(1), as from IP completion day (as defined in the European Union (Withdrawal Agreement) Act 2020, s 39). Para (ab) inserted by the Financial Services (Banking Reform) Act 2013, s 6, Sch 1, paras 1, 10(1), (3), as from 1 March 2014.

[7.247]

112 Effect of order sanctioning business transfer scheme

(1) If the court makes an order under section 111(1), it may by that or any subsequent order make such provision (if any) as it thinks fit—

(a) for the transfer to the transferee of the whole or any part of the undertaking concerned and of any property or liabilities of [the transferor concerned];

(b) for the allotment or appropriation by the transferee of any shares, debentures, policies or other similar interests in the transferee which under the scheme are to be allotted or appropriated to or for any other person;

(c) for the continuation by (or against) the transferee of any pending legal proceedings by (or against) [the transferor concerned];

(d) with respect to such incidental, consequential and supplementary matters as are, in its opinion, necessary to secure that the scheme is fully and effectively carried out.

(2) An order under subsection (1)(a) may—

(a) transfer property or liabilities whether or not [the transferor concerned] otherwise has the capacity to effect the transfer in question;

(b) make provision in relation to property which was held by [the transferor concerned] as trustee;

(c) make provision as to future or contingent rights or liabilities of [the transferor concerned], including provision as to the construction of instruments (including wills) under which such rights or liabilities may arise;

(d) make provision as to the consequences of the transfer in relation to any [occupational pension scheme (within the meaning of section 150(5) of the Finance Act 2004)] operated by or on behalf of [the transferor concerned].

[(2A) Subsection (2)(a) is to be taken to include power to make provision in an order—

(a) for the transfer of property or liabilities which would not otherwise be capable of being transferred or assigned;

(b) for a transfer of property or liabilities to take effect as if there were—

(i) no such requirement to obtain a person's consent or concurrence, and

(ii) no such contravention, liability or interference with any interest or right,

as there would otherwise be (in the case of a transfer apart from this section) by reason of any provision falling within subsection (2B).

(2B) A provision falls within this subsection to the extent that it has effect (whether under an enactment or agreement or otherwise) in relation to the terms on which [the transferor concerned] is entitled to the property or subject to the liabilities in question.

(2C) Nothing in subsection (2A) or (2B) is to be read as limiting the scope of subsection (1).]

(3) If an order under subsection (1) makes provision for the transfer of property or liabilities—

(a) the property is transferred to and vests in, and

(b) the liabilities are transferred to and become liabilities of,

the transferee as a result of the order.

(4) But if any property or liability included in the order is governed by the law of any country or territory outside the United Kingdom, the order may require [the transferor concerned], if the transferee so requires, to take all necessary steps for securing that the transfer to the transferee of the property or liability is fully effective under the law of that country or territory.

(5) Property transferred as the result of an order under subsection (1) may, if the court so directs, vest in the transferee free from any charge which is (as a result of the scheme) to cease to have effect.

(6) An order under subsection (1) which makes provision for the transfer of property is to be treated as an instrument of transfer for the purposes of [section 770(1) of the Companies Act 2006] and any other enactment requiring the delivery of an instrument of transfer for the registration of property.

(7) . . .

(8) If the court makes an order under section 111(1) in relation to an insurance business transfer scheme, it may by that or any subsequent order make such provision (if any) as it thinks fit—

(a) for dealing with the interests of any person who, within such time and in such manner as the court may direct, objects to the scheme;

(b) for the dissolution, without winding up, of [the transferor concerned];

(c) for the reduction, on such terms and subject to such conditions (if any) as it thinks fit, of the benefits payable under—

(i) any description of policy, or

(ii) policies generally,

entered into by [the transferor concerned] and transferred as a result of the scheme.

(9) . . .

(10) The transferee must, if an insurance or banking business transfer scheme [or ring-fencing transfer scheme] is sanctioned by the court, deposit two office copies of the order made under subsection (1) with the [appropriate regulator] within 10 days of the making of the order.

(11) But the [appropriate regulator] may extend that period.

(12) "Property" includes property, rights and powers of any description.

(13) "Liabilities" includes duties.

(14) "Shares" and "debentures" have the same meaning as in [the Companies Acts (see sections 540 and 738 of the Companies Act 2006).]

(15) "Charge" includes a mortgage (or, in Scotland, a security over property).

NOTES

The words "the transferor concerned" (in each place that they occur) were substituted by the Financial Services (Banking Reform) Act 2013, s 6, Sch 1, paras 1, 2, as from 1 March 2014. This section is also amended as follows:

Sub-s (2): words "occupational pension scheme (within the meaning of section 150(5) of the Finance Act 2004)" in square brackets substituted by the Taxation of Pension Schemes (Consequential Amendments) Order 2006, SI 2006/745, art 17, as from 6 April 2006.

Sub-ss (2A)–(2C): inserted by the Financial Services and Markets Act 2000 (Amendments to Part 7) Regulations 2008, SI 2008/1468, reg 2(1), as from 30 June 2008.

Sub-s (6): words in square brackets substituted by the Companies Act 2006 (Consequential Amendments etc) Order 2008, SI 2008/948, art 3(1), Sch 1, Pt 2, para 211(3)(a), as from 6 April 2008.

Sub-s (7): repealed by SI 2008/948, art 3, Sch 1, Pt 2, para 211(3)(b), Sch 2, as from 6 April 2008.

Sub-s (9): repealed by the Financial Services and Markets Act 2000 (Amendment) (EU Exit) Regulations 2019, SI 2019/632, regs 31, 33(2), as from IP completion day (as defined in the European Union (Withdrawal Agreement) Act 2020, s 39).

Sub-s (10): words in first pair of square brackets inserted by the Financial Services (Banking Reform) Act 2013, s 6, Sch 1, paras 1, 11, as from 1 March 2014. Words in second pair of square brackets substituted by the Financial Services Act 2012, s 22, Sch 6, paras 1, 5, as from 1 April 2013.

Sub-s (11): words in square brackets substituted by the Financial Services Act 2012, s 22, Sch 6, paras 1, 5, as from 1 April 2013.

Sub-s (14): words in square brackets substituted by SI 2008/948, art 3(1), Sch 1, Pt 2, para 211(3)(c), as from 6 April 2008.

[7.248]

[112ZA Duty of regulator to provide copy of order

(1) Where the PRA receives under section 112(10) a copy of an order it must, without delay, give a copy of it to the FCA.

(2) Where the FCA receives under section 112(10) a copy of an order it must, without delay, give a copy of it to the PRA if the order relates to a scheme in respect of which—

(a) the transferee is a PRA-authorised person, or

(b) [the transferor concerned] or the transferee has as a member of its immediate group a PRA-authorised person.]

NOTES

Inserted by the Financial Services Act 2012, s 22, Sch 6, paras 1, 6, as from 1 April 2013.

Sub-s (2): words in square brackets substituted by the Financial Services (Banking Reform) Act 2013, s 6, Sch 1, paras 1, 2, as from 1 March 2014.

[7.249]

[112A Rights to terminate etc

(1) Subsection (2) applies where (apart from that subsection) a person would be entitled, in consequence of anything done or likely to be done by or under this Part in connection with an insurance business transfer scheme[, a banking business transfer scheme or a ring-fencing transfer scheme]—

(a) to terminate, modify, acquire or claim an interest or right; or

(b) to treat an interest or right as terminated or modified.

(2) The entitlement—

(a) is not enforceable in relation to that interest or right until after an order has been made under section 112(1) in relation to the scheme; and

(b) is then enforceable in relation to that interest or right only insofar as the order contains provision to that effect.

(3) Nothing in subsection (1) or (2) is to be read as limiting the scope of section 112(1).]

NOTES

Inserted by the Financial Services and Markets Act 2000 (Amendments to Part 7) Regulations 2008, SI 2008/1468, reg 2(3), as from 30 June 2008.

Sub-s (1): words in square brackets substituted by the Financial Services (Banking Reform) Act 2013, s 6, Sch 1, paras 1, 12, as from 1 March 2014.

[7.250]

113 Appointment of actuary in relation to reduction of benefits

(1) This section applies if an order has been made under section 111(1).

(2) The court making the order may, on the application of [either regulator], appoint an independent actuary—

(a) to investigate the business transferred under the scheme; and

(b) to report to the [regulator which made the application] on any reduction in the benefits payable under policies entered into by [the transferor concerned] that, in the opinion of the actuary, ought to be made.

[(3) An application under subsection (2) may be made by the PRA only if—

(a) [the transferor concerned] or the transferee is a PRA-authorised person, or

(b) [the transferor concerned] or the transferee has as a member of its immediate group a PRA-authorised person.]

NOTES

Words "the transferor concerned" (in each place that they occur) substituted by the Financial Services (Banking Reform) Act 2013, s 6, Sch 1, paras 1, 2, as from 1 March 2014.

Other words in square brackets in sub-s (2) substituted, and sub-s (3) added, by the Financial Services Act 2012, s 22, Sch 6, paras 1, 7, as from 1 April 2013.

114, 114A *(S 114 (Rights of certain policyholders) repealed by the Financial Services and Markets Act 2000 (Amendment) (EU Exit) Regulations 2019, SI 2019/632, regs 31, 33(3), as from IP completion day (as defined in the European Union (Withdrawal Agreement) Act 2020, s 39). S 114A (Notice of transfer of reinsurance contracts) was originally inserted by the Reinsurance Directive Regulations 2007, SI 2007/3253, reg 2(1), Sch 1, paras 1, 2(1), (3), as from 10 December 2007, and was also repealed by SI 2019/632, regs 31, 33(3), as from IP completion day.)*

Business transfers outside the United Kingdom

[7.251]

115 Certificates for purposes of insurance business transfers overseas

Part III of Schedule 12 makes provision about certificates which the [appropriate regulator] may issue in relation to insurance business transfers taking place outside the United Kingdom.

NOTES

Words in square brackets substituted by the Financial Services Act 2012, s 22, Sch 6, paras 1, 8, as from 1 April 2013.

116 *(S 116 (Effect of insurance business transfers authorised in other EEA States) repealed by the Financial Services and Markets Act 2000 (Amendment) (EU Exit) Regulations 2019, SI 2019/632, regs 31, 33(3), as from IP completion day (as defined in the European Union (Withdrawal Agreement) Act 2020, s 39).)*

Modifications

[7.252]

117 Power to modify this Part

The Treasury may by regulations—

(a) provide for prescribed provisions of this Part to have effect in relation to prescribed cases with such modifications as may be prescribed;

(b) make such amendments to any provision of this Part as they consider appropriate for the more effective operation of that or any other provision of this Part.

NOTES

Regulations: the Financial Services and Markets Act 2000 (Motor Insurance) Regulations 2007, SI 2007/2403; the Financial Services and Markets Act 2000 (Amendments to Part 7) Regulations 2008, SI 2008/1468.

PART VIII [PROVISIONS RELATING TO MARKET ABUSE]

NOTES

Part heading substituted by the Financial Services and Markets Act 2000 (Market Abuse) Regulations 2016, SI 2016/680, reg 9(1), (2), as from 3 July 2016.

118, 118A–118C, 119–122 (*Repealed by the Financial Services and Markets Act 2000 (Market Abuse) Regulations 2016, SI 2016/680, reg 9(1), (3), as from 3 July 2016. Ss 118A–118C were originally inserted by the Financial Services and Markets Act 2000 (Market Abuse) Regulations 2005, SI 2005/381, reg 5, Sch 2, para 1, as from 1 July 2005.*)

[Powers to require information and supplemental provisions

[7.253]

122A Power to require information from issuers

(1) The FCA may require an issuer, a person discharging managerial responsibilities or a person closely associated with a person discharging managerial responsibilities to provide—

(a) any information the FCA reasonably requires for the purpose of protecting—

(i) the interests of users of financial markets and exchanges in the United Kingdom; or

(ii) the orderly operation of financial markets and exchanges in the United Kingdom; or

(b) any information or explanation the FCA reasonably requires to verify whether Article 17 (public disclosure of inside information) or Article 19 (managers' transactions) of the market abuse regulation is being, or has been, complied with.

(2) Information required under this section must be provided—

(a) before the end of such reasonable period as may be specified by the FCA; and

(b) at such place as may be specified by the FCA.

(3) The FCA may require any information provided under this section to be provided in such form as it may reasonably require.

(4) The FCA may require any information provided, whether in a document or otherwise, to be verified in such manner as it may reasonably require.

(5) In this section—

"person closely associated" has the meaning given in Article 3.1(26) of the market abuse regulation (see section 131AC (meaning of "persons closely associated" in the market abuse regulation)); and

"person discharging managerial responsibilities" has the meaning given in Article 3.1(25) of the market abuse regulation.

(6) For the meaning of "issuer" in this Part, see section 131AB.]

NOTES

Sections 122A–122I (and the preceding headings) were inserted by the Financial Services and Markets Act 2000 (Market Abuse) Regulations 2016, SI 2016/680, reg 9(1), (4), as from 3 July 2016.

[7.254]

[122B General power to require information

(1) The FCA may, by notice in writing, require a person—

(a) to provide specified information or information of a specified description; or

(b) to produce specified documents or documents of a specified description.

(2) This section applies only to information and documents that the FCA reasonably requires for the purpose of the exercise by it of functions under the market abuse regulation or [under supplementary market abuse legislation].

(3) Information or documents required under this section must be provided or produced—

(a) before the end of such reasonable period as may be specified; and

(b) at such place as may be specified.

(4) The FCA may require any information provided under this section to be provided in such form as it may reasonably require.

(5) The FCA may require—

(a) any information provided, whether in a document or otherwise, to be verified in such manner as it may reasonably require; or

(b) any document produced to be authenticated in such manner as it may reasonably require.

[(6) The FCA may exercise its powers under this section at the request of an overseas regulator where the regulator makes the request in the exercise of its relevant functions.

(6A) In subsection (6)—

"overseas regulator" means—

(a) the competent authority of an EEA State for the purposes of the market abuse regulation, as that regulation has effect in the European Union (the "EU version of the market abuse regulation"); or

(b) an authority of any other country or territory outside the United Kingdom which exercises functions corresponding to those of a competent authority under the EU version of the market abuse regulation;

"relevant functions" means—

(a) in relation to the competent authority of an EEA State, its functions under—

(i) the EU version of the market abuse regulation; or

(ii) a directly applicable EU regulation made under the EU version of the market abuse regulation;

(b) in relation to an authority of any other country or territory outside the United Kingdom, its functions corresponding to the functions referred to in paragraph (a).]

(8) In this section "specified" means specified in the notice.]

NOTES

Inserted as noted to s 122A at **[7.253]**.

Sub-s (2): words in square brackets substituted by the Market Abuse (Amendment) (EU Exit) Regulations 2019, SI 2019/310, reg 5(1), (2), as from IP completion day (as defined in the European Union (Withdrawal Agreement) Act 2020, s 39).

Sub-ss (6), (6A): substituted (for the original sub-ss (6), (7)) by SI 2019/310, reg 5(1), (2)(b), as from IP completion day (as defined in the European Union (Withdrawal Agreement) Act 2020, s 39).

[7.255]

[122C Power to require information: supplementary

(1) If a document is produced in response to a requirement imposed under section 122B, the FCA may—

(a) take copies of, or extracts from, the document; or

(b) require the person producing the document, or any relevant person, to provide an explanation of the document.

(2) In subsection (1)(b) "relevant person", in relation to a person who is required to produce a document, means a person who—

(a) has been, is, or is proposed to be, a director or controller of that person;

(b) has been or is an auditor of that person;

(c) has been or is an actuary, accountant or lawyer appointed or instructed by that person; or

(d) has been or is an employee of that person.

(3) If a person who is required under section 122B to produce a document fails to do so, the FCA may require the person to state, to the best of the person's knowledge and belief, where the document is.

(4) A lawyer may be required under section 122B to provide the name and address of the lawyer's client.

(5) A person ("P") may not be required under section 122A or 122B to disclose information or produce a document in respect of which P owes an obligation of confidence by virtue of carrying on the business of banking unless condition A, B or C is met.

(6) Condition A is met if the FCA suspects that P or a member of P's group—

(a) has contravened Article 14 (prohibition of insider dealing and of unlawful disclosure of inside information) or Article 15 (prohibition of market manipulation) of the market abuse regulation; or

(b) has contravened, or been knowingly concerned in the contravention of—

(i) a provision of the market abuse regulation other than Article 14 or 15 of that regulation; or

(ii) a provision of a supplementary EU regulation.

(7) Condition B is met if the FCA suspects that the person to whom the obligation of confidence is owed or a member of that person's group—

(a) has contravened Article 14 or Article 15 of the market abuse regulation; or

(b) has contravened, or been knowingly concerned in the contravention of—

(i) a provision of the market abuse regulation other than Article 14 or 15 of that regulation; or

(ii) a provision of a supplementary EU regulation.

(8) Condition C is met if the person to whom the obligation of confidence is owed consents to the disclosure or production.

(9) If a person claims a lien on a document, its production under section 122B does not affect the lien].

NOTES

Inserted as noted to s 122A at **[7.253]**.

[7.256]

[122D Entry of premises under warrant

(1) A justice of the peace may issue a warrant under this section if satisfied on information on oath given by or on behalf of the FCA that there are reasonable grounds for believing that the conditions in subsection (2) are met.

(2) The conditions are—

(a) that a person on whom a requirement has been imposed under section 122B or 122C has failed (wholly or in part) to comply with it; and

(b) that on the premises specified in the warrant—

(i) there are documents which have been required; or

(ii) there is information which has been required.

(3) A warrant under this section shall authorise a constable—

(a) to enter the premises specified in the warrant;

(b) to search the premises and take possession of any documents or information appearing to be documents or information of a kind in respect of which a warrant under this section was issued ("the relevant kind") or to take, in relation to any such documents or information, any other steps which may appear to be necessary for preserving them or preventing interference with them;

(c) to take copies of, or extracts from, any documents or information appearing to be of the relevant kind;

(d) to require any person on the premises to provide an explanation of any document or information appearing to be of the relevant kind or to state where it may be found; and

(e) to use such force as may be reasonably necessary.

(4) A warrant under this section may be executed by any constable.

(5) The warrant may authorise persons to accompany any constable who is executing it.

(6) The powers in subsection (3) may be exercised by a person authorised by the warrant to accompany a constable; but that person may exercise those powers only in the company of, and under the supervision of, a constable.

(7) In England and Wales, sections 15(5) to (8) and 16(3) to (12) of the Police and Criminal Evidence Act 1984 (execution of search warrants and safeguards) apply to warrants issued under this section.

(8) In Northern Ireland, Articles 17(5) to (8) and 18(3) to (12) of the Police and Criminal Evidence (Northern Ireland) Order 1989 (SI 1989/1341 (NI 12)) apply to warrants issued under this section.

(9) In the application of this section to Scotland—

(a) for the reference to a justice of the peace substitute a reference to a justice of the peace or a sheriff; and

(b) for the references to information on oath substitute references to evidence on oath.

(10) The FCA may give information under subsection (1) or under section 176(1) at the request of an [overseas] regulator where the regulator makes the request in the exercise of its [relevant functions].

[(10A) In subsection (10), "overseas regulator" and "relevant functions" have the meaning given in section 122B(6A).]

(11) . . .]

NOTES

Inserted as noted to s 122A at **[7.253]**.

Words in square brackets in sub-s (10) substituted, sub-s (10A) inserted, and sub-s (11) repealed, by the Market Abuse (Amendment) (EU Exit) Regulations 2019, SI 2019/310, reg 5(1), (3), as from IP completion day (as defined in the European Union (Withdrawal Agreement) Act 2020, s 39).

[7.257]

[122E Retention of documents taken under section 122D

(1) Any document of which possession is taken under section 122D ("a seized document") may be retained so long as it is necessary to retain it (rather than copies of it) in the circumstances.

(2) A person claiming to be the owner of a seized document may apply to a magistrates' court or (in Scotland) the sheriff for an order for the delivery of the document to the person appearing to the court or sheriff to be the owner.

(3) If, on an application under subsection (2), the court or (in Scotland) the sheriff cannot ascertain who is the owner of the seized document the court or sheriff (as the case may be) may make such order as the court or sheriff thinks fit.

(4) An order under subsection (2) or (3) does not affect the right of any person to take legal proceedings against any person in possession of a seized document for the recovery of the document.

(5) Any right to bring proceedings (as described in subsection (4)) may only be exercised within 6 months of the date of the order made under subsection (2) or (3).]

NOTES

Inserted as noted to s 122A at **[7.253]**.

[7.258]

[122F Offences

(1) If a person ("A") fails to comply with a requirement imposed on A under section 122B or 122C the FCA may certify that fact in writing to the court.

(2) If the court is satisfied that A failed without reasonable excuse to comply with the requirement, it may deal with A (and where A is a body corporate, any director or other officer) as if A (or as the case may be the director or officer) were in contempt.

(3) A person ("B") who, in purported compliance with a requirement imposed on B under section 122B or 122C—

(a) provides information which B knows to be false or misleading in a material particular; or

(b) recklessly provides information which is false or misleading in a material particular;

is guilty of an offence.

(4) A person guilty of an offence under subsection (3) is liable—

(a) on summary conviction—

(i) in England and Wales, to imprisonment for a term not exceeding three months or a fine, or both;

(ii) in Scotland, to imprisonment for a term not exceeding three months or a fine not exceeding the statutory maximum, or both;

(iii) in Northern Ireland, to imprisonment for a term not exceeding three months or a fine not exceeding the statutory maximum, or both;

(b) on conviction on indictment, to imprisonment for a term not exceeding two years or a fine, or both.

(5) Any person who intentionally obstructs the exercise of any rights conferred by a warrant under section 122D is guilty of an offence and liable on summary conviction—

(a) in England and Wales, to imprisonment for a term not exceeding three months or a fine, or both;

(b) in Scotland, to imprisonment for a term not exceeding three months or a fine not exceeding level 5 on the standard scale, or both;

(c) in Northern Ireland, to imprisonment for a term not exceeding three months or a fine not exceeding level 5 on the standard scale, or both.

(6) In this section—

(a) "court" means—

(i) the High Court;

(ii) in Scotland, the Court of Session;

(b) "officer", in relation to a limited liability partnership, means a member of the partnership.]

NOTES

Inserted as noted to s 122A at **[7.253]**.

[7.259]

122G Publication of information and corrective statements by issuers

(1) If condition A or B is met, the FCA may require an issuer [or emission allowance market participant] to publish—

(a) specified information; or

(b) a specified statement.

(2) Condition A is met if the FCA considers that the publication of the information or statement is necessary for the purpose of protecting—

(a) the interests of users of financial markets and exchanges in the United Kingdom; or

(b) the orderly operation of financial markets and exchanges in the United Kingdom.

(3) Condition B is met if—

(a) the information or statement corrects false or misleading information made public, or a false or misleading impression given to the public, by that person; and

(b) the FCA considers that the publication of the information is necessary for the purpose of the exercise by it of functions under the market abuse regulation or [under supplementary market abuse legislation].

(4) Information or statements required to be published under this section must be published—

(a) before the end of such reasonable period as may be specified; and

(b) by any method as may be specified.

(5) If a person fails to comply with a requirement to publish information or a statement under this section, the FCA may publish the information or statement.

(6) But before doing so, the FCA must give that person an opportunity to make representations to it regarding its decision to publish the information or statement under subsection (5).

[(7) In this section—

"emission allowance market participant" has the same meaning as in Article [3.1.20] (definitions) of the market abuse regulation; and

"specified" means specified by the FCA.]

(8) For the meaning of "issuer", see section 131AB].

NOTES

Inserted as noted to s 122A at **[7.253]**.

Words in square brackets in sub-s (1) inserted, and sub-s (7) substituted, by the Financial Services and Markets Act 2000 (Markets in Financial Instruments) Regulations 2017, SI 2017/701, reg 50(1), Sch 2, paras 1, 9, as from 3 January 2018 (note that various provisions of the 2017 Regulations came into force on earlier dates for the purposes of making rules, giving notices and consent, etc (for details see reg 1 of the 2017 Regulations)).

Words in square brackets in sub-s (3) substituted by the Market Abuse (Amendment) (EU Exit) Regulations 2019, SI 2019/310, reg 5(1), (4), as from IP completion day (as defined in the European Union (Withdrawal Agreement) Act 2020, s 39).

Figure in square brackets in definition "emission allowance market participant" in sub-s (7) substituted by SI 2019/310, reg 3, as from 19 February 2019.

[7.260]

[122H Publication of corrective statements generally

(1) If condition A or B is met, the FCA may, by notice in writing, require a person to publish—

(a) specified information; or

(b) a specified statement

correcting false or misleading information made public, or a false or misleading impression given to the public, by that person.

(2) Condition A is met if the FCA considers that the publication of the information or statement is necessary for the purpose of protecting—

(a) the interests of users of financial markets and exchanges in the United Kingdom; or

(b) the orderly operation of financial markets and exchanges in the United Kingdom.

(3) Condition B is met if the FCA considers that the publication of the information or statement is necessary for the purpose of the exercise by it of functions under the market abuse regulation or [under supplementary market abuse legislation].

(4) Information or statements required to be published under this section must be published—

(a) before the end of such reasonable period as may be specified; and

(b) by any method as may be specified.

(5) If a person fails to comply with a requirement to publish information or a statement under this section the FCA may publish the information or statement.

(6) But before doing so, the FCA must give that person an opportunity to make representations to it regarding its decision to publish the information or statement under subsection (5).

(7) In this section "specified" means specified in the notice.]

NOTES

Inserted as noted to s 122A at **[7.253]**.

Sub-s (3): words in square brackets substituted by the Market Abuse (Amendment) (EU Exit) Regulations 2019, SI 2019/310, reg 5(1), (5), as from IP completion day (as defined in the European Union (Withdrawal Agreement) Act 2020, s 39).

[7.261]

[122HA Publication of corrective statements relating to benchmarks

(1) If condition A or B is met, the FCA may, by notice in writing, require a person to publish—

(a) specified information, or

(b) a specified statement,

correcting false or misleading information made public, or a false or misleading impression given to the public, by that person.

(2) Condition A is met if the FCA considers that the publication of the information or statement is necessary for the purpose of protecting the interests of users of regulated benchmarks.
(3) Condition B is met if the FCA considers that the publication of the information or statement is necessary for the purpose of the exercise by it of its functions under Article 41(1)(j) of the EU Benchmarks Regulation 2016.
(4) Information or statements required to be published under this section must be published—
(a) before the end of such reasonable period as may be specified; and
(b) by any such method as may be specified.
(5) If a person fails to comply with a requirement to publish information or a statement under this section the FCA may publish the information or statement.
(6) But before doing so, the FCA must give that person an opportunity to make representations to it regarding its decision to publish the information or statement under subsection (5).
(7) In this section—
"specified" means specified in the notice, and
"regulated benchmark" means a regulated benchmark as defined in section 425A(7).]

NOTES

Inserted by the Financial Services and Markets Act 2000 (Benchmarks) Regulations 2018, SI 2018/135, reg 41, as from 27 February 2018.

[7.262]
[122I Power to suspend trading in financial instruments

(1) The FCA may suspend trading of a financial instrument where it considers it necessary for the purpose of the exercise by it of functions under the market abuse regulation or [under supplementary market abuse legislation].
(2) If the FCA does so the issuer of the financial instrument may refer the matter to the Tribunal.
[(2A) But subsection (2) does not apply if the financial instrument is an emission allowance.]
(3) The FCA may—
(a) cancel a suspension under subsection (1); and
(b) impose such conditions for the cancellation to take effect as it considers appropriate.
(4) The provisions relating to suspension of listing of securities in section 78 (discontinuance or suspension: procedure) apply to a suspension of trading in a financial instrument [other than an emission allowance] under subsection (1) and for the purposes of this section—
(a) the references in section 78 to listing are to be read as references to trading; and
(b) the references in section 78 to securities are to be read as references to financial instruments.
[(4A) A suspension of trading in a financial instrument that is an emission allowance takes effect—
(a) immediately, if the FCA states that is the case; or
(b) on such later date as the FCA specify.]
(5) For the meaning of "issuer" in this Part, see section 131AB.]

NOTES

Inserted as noted to s 122A at **[7.253]**.

Sub-s (1): words in square brackets substituted by the Market Abuse (Amendment) (EU Exit) Regulations 2019, SI 2019/310, reg 5(1), (6), as from IP completion day (as defined in the European Union (Withdrawal Agreement) Act 2020, s 39).

Sub-ss (2A), (4A): inserted by the Financial Services and Markets Act 2000 (Markets in Financial Instruments) Regulations 2017, SI 2017/701, reg 50(1), Sch 2, paras 1, 10, as from 3 January 2018 (note that various provisions of the 2017 Regulations came into force on earlier dates for the purposes of making rules, giving notices and consent, etc (for details see reg 1 of the 2017 Regulations)).

Sub-s (4): words in square brackets inserted by SI 2017/701, reg 50(1), Sch 2, paras 1, 10, as from 3 January 2018 (as to the commencement of the 2017 Regulations, see further the note relating to them above).

[7.263]
[122IA Power to suspend auctioning of auctioned products on a recognised auction platform

(1) The FCA may suspend the auctioning of a relevant auctioned product at an auction conducted by a recognised auction platform where it considers it necessary for the purpose of the exercise by it of functions under the market abuse regulation or [any supplementary market abuse legislation].
(2) If the FCA does so the recognised auction platform may refer the matter to the Tribunal.
(3) A suspension by the FCA takes place—
(a) immediately, if the FCA specify this is the case, or
(b) on such later date as the FCA specify.
(4) The FCA may—
(a) cancel a suspension under subsection (1), and
(b) impose such conditions for the cancellation to take effect as it considers appropriate.
(5) The provisions relating to the suspension and removal of financial instruments from trading set out in—
(a) section 313B(2) to (4) (suspension or removal of financial instruments from trading: procedure), and
(b) sections 313BA (procedure following consideration of representations) to 313BC (decisions on applications for revocation by institutions),

apply, with the modifications set out in subsection (6), to a suspension of the auctioning of a relevant auctioned product at an auction conducted by a recognised auction platform.
(6) The modifications referred to in subsection (5) are—
(a) references to a requirement imposed on an institution under section 313A are to be read as references to the suspension of the auctioning of the relevant auctioned product;
(b) references to an institution are to be read as references to the recognised auction platform;
(c) in section 313B, the omission of—
(i) subsection (2)(a)(ii);
(ii) in subsection (3A)(d), the words "or the issuer of the financial instrument in question" and "or the issuer";

(iii) in subsection (3A)(f), the words "or the issuer of the financial instrument in question;
(d) the omission of section 313BA(5)(b) and (8);
(e) the omission of section 313BB(6)(b); and
(f) the omission of section 313BC(3)(b) and (6)(b).

(7) In this section "relevant auctioned product" means an auctioned product[, within the meaning of regulation 4 of the Greenhouse Gas Emissions Trading Scheme Auctioning Regulations 2021].]

NOTES

Inserted by the Financial Services and Markets Act 2000 (Markets in Financial Instruments) Regulations 2017, SI 2017/701, reg 50(1), Sch 2, paras 1, 11, as from 3 January 2018 (note that various provisions of the 2017 Regulations came into force on earlier dates for the purposes of making rules, giving notices and consent, etc (for details see reg 1 of the 2017 Regulations)).

Sub-ss (1), (7): words in square brackets substituted by the Recognised Auction Platforms (Amendment and Miscellaneous Provisions) Regulations 2021, SI 2021/494, reg 2(2), as from 22 April 2021.

[Administrative sanctions

[7.264]

123 Power to impose penalties or issue censure

(1) The FCA may exercise its power under subsection (2) if it is satisfied that—
(a) a person has contravened Article 14 (prohibition of insider dealing and of unlawful disclosure of inside information) or Article 15 (prohibition of market manipulation) of the market abuse regulation;
(b) a person has contravened, or been knowingly concerned in the contravention of—
(i) a provision of the market abuse regulation other than Article 14 or 15 of that regulation; or
(ii) a provision of [any supplementary market abuse legislation]; or
(c) a person other than an authorised person has contravened any requirement—
(i) imposed on that person under section 122A, 122B, 122C, 122G, 122H, [122HA,] 122I, [122IA,] 123A or 123B; or
(ii) relating to the market abuse regulation or [any supplementary market abuse legislation] imposed on that person under Part 11.

(2) The FCA's power under this subsection is a power to impose a penalty of such amount as it considers appropriate on the person.

(3) The FCA may, instead of imposing a penalty on a person, publish a statement censuring the person.]

NOTES

Substituted (together with ss 123A–123C and the preceding heading) for the original s 123 by the Financial Services and Markets Act 2000 (Market Abuse) Regulations 2016, SI 2016/680, reg 9(1), (5), as from 3 July 2016.

Sub-s (1) is amended as follows:

Words in square brackets in sub-paras (b)(ii) and (c)(ii) substituted by the Market Abuse (Amendment) (EU Exit) Regulations 2019, SI 2019/310, reg 5(1), (8)(a), as from IP completion day (as defined in the European Union (Withdrawal Agreement) Act 2020, s 39).

Figure "122HA," in square brackets in sub-para (c)(i) inserted by the Financial Services and Markets Act 2000 (Benchmarks) Regulations 2018, SI 2018/135, reg 42(1), as from 27 February 2018.

Figure "122IA," in square brackets in sub-para (c)(i) inserted by the Financial Services and Markets Act 2000 (Markets in Financial Instruments) Regulations 2017, SI 2017/701, reg 50(1), Sch 2, paras 1, 12, as from 3 January 2018 (note that various provisions of the 2017 Regulations came into force on earlier dates for the purposes of making rules, giving notices and consent, etc (for details see reg 1 of the 2017 Regulations)).

[7.265]

[123A Power to prohibit individuals from managing or dealing

(1) The FCA may exercise its power under subsection (2) if it is satisfied that an individual—
(a) has contravened Article 14 (prohibition of insider dealing and of unlawful disclosure of inside information) or Article 15 (prohibition of market manipulation) of the market abuse regulation;
(b) has contravened, or been knowingly concerned in the contravention of—
(i) a provision of the market abuse regulation other than Article 14 or 15 of that regulation; or
(ii) a provision of [any supplementary market abuse legislation]; or
(c) has contravened a requirement imposed on that individual under this section or section 122A, 122B, 122C, 122G, 122H, [122HA,] 122I[, 122IA] or 123B.

(2) The FCA's power under this subsection is a power to impose [one or more] of the following—
(a) a temporary prohibition on the individual holding an office or position involving responsibility for taking decisions about the management of an investment firm;
(b) a temporary prohibition on the individual acquiring or disposing of financial instruments, whether on his or her own account or the account of a third party and whether directly or indirectly;
[(c) a temporary prohibition on the individual making a bid, on his or her own account or the account of a third party, directly or indirectly, at an auction conducted by a recognised auction platform.]

(3) If the FCA is satisfied that an individual has contravened Article 14 or 15 of the market abuse regulation the FCA may impose a permanent prohibition on the individual holding an office or position involving responsibility for taking decisions about the management of an investment firm.

(4) A prohibition imposed under subsection (2) may be expressed to expire at the end of such period as the FCA may specify, but the imposition of a prohibition that expires at the end of a specified period does not affect the FCA's power to impose a new prohibition under subsection (2).

(5) A prohibition imposed under subsection (2)(a) or (3) may be expressed to prohibit an individual holding an office or position involving responsibility for taking decisions about the management of—
(a) a named investment firm;
(b) an investment firm of a specified description; or
(c) any investment firm.

(6) An investment firm must take reasonable care to ensure that no individual who is subject to a prohibition under subsection (2)(a) or (3) on the holding of an office or position involving responsibility for taking decisions about the management of the firm holds such an office or position.

(7) The FCA may vary or revoke a prohibition imposed under this section.

[(8) For the meaning of "recognised auction platform" in this Part, see section 131AB.]]

NOTES

Substituted as noted to s 123 at **[7.264]**.

Sub-s (1) is amended as follows:

Words in square brackets in sub-para (b)(ii) substituted by the Market Abuse (Amendment) (EU Exit) Regulations 2019, SI 2019/310, reg 5(1), (9)(a), as from IP completion day (as defined in the European Union (Withdrawal Agreement) Act 2020, s 39).

Figure "122HA," in square brackets in para (c) inserted by the Financial Services and Markets Act 2000 (Benchmarks) Regulations 2018, SI 2018/135, reg 42(2), as from 27 February 2018.

Figure ", 122IA" in square brackets in para (c) inserted by the Financial Services and Markets Act 2000 (Markets in Financial Instruments) Regulations 2017, SI 2017/701, reg 50(1), Sch 2, paras 1, 13(1), (2), as from 3 January 2018 (note that various provisions of the 2017 Regulations came into force on earlier dates for the purposes of making rules, giving notices and consent, etc (for details see reg 1 of the 2017 Regulations)).

Sub-s (2): words in first pair of square brackets substituted, and para (c) added, by SI 2017/701, reg 50(1), Sch 2, paras 1, 13(1), (3), as from 3 January 2018 (as to the commencement of the 2017 Regulations, see further the note relating to them above).

Sub-s (8): added by SI 2017/701, reg 50(1), Sch 2, paras 1, 13(1), (4), as from 3 January 2018 (as to the commencement of the 2017 Regulations, see further the note relating to them above).

[7.266]

[123B Suspending permission to carry on regulated activities etc

(1) The FCA may exercise its power under subsection (2) if it is satisfied that an authorised person—

(a) has contravened Article 14 (prohibition of insider dealing and of unlawful disclosure of inside information) or Article 15 (prohibition of market manipulation) of the market abuse regulation;

(b) has contravened, or been knowingly concerned in the contravention of—

(i) a provision of the market abuse regulation other than Article 14 and 15 of that regulation;

(ii) a provision of [any supplementary market abuse legislation]; or

(c) has contravened a requirement imposed on that person under this section or section 122A, 122B, 122C, 122G, 122H, [122HA,] 122I[, 122IA] or 123A.

(2) The FCA's power under this subsection is a power to do either or both of the following—

(a) to suspend, for such period as it considers appropriate, any permission which the person has to carry on a regulated activity;

(b) to impose, for such period as it considers appropriate, such limitations or other restrictions in relation to the carrying on of a regulated activity by the person as it considers appropriate.

(3) In subsection (2) "permission" means any permission that the authorised person has, whether given (or treated as given) by the FCA or the PRA or conferred by any provision of this Act.

(4) The period for which a suspension or restriction is to have effect may not exceed 12 months.

(5) A suspension may relate only to the carrying on of an activity in specified circumstances.

(6) A restriction may, in particular, be imposed so as to require the person concerned to take, or refrain from taking, specified action.

(7) The FCA may—

(a) withdraw a suspension or restriction; or

(b) vary a suspension or restriction so as to reduce the period for which it has effect or otherwise to limit its effect.

(8) The power under this section may (but need not) be exercised so as to have effect in relation to all the regulated activities that the person concerned carries on.]

NOTES

Substituted as noted to s 123 at **[7.264]**.

Sub-s (1) is amended as follows:

Words in square brackets in sub-para (b)(ii) substituted by the Market Abuse (Amendment) (EU Exit) Regulations 2019, SI 2019/310, reg 5(1), (10)(a), as from IP completion day (as defined in the European Union (Withdrawal Agreement) Act 2020, s 39).

Figure "122HA," in square brackets in para (c) inserted by the Financial Services and Markets Act 2000 (Benchmarks) Regulations 2018, SI 2018/135, reg 42(2), as from 27 February 2018.

Figure ", 122IA" in square brackets in para (c) inserted by the Financial Services and Markets Act 2000 (Markets in Financial Instruments) Regulations 2017, SI 2017/701, reg 50(1), Sch 2, paras 1, 14, as from 3 January 2018 (note that various provisions of the 2017 Regulations came into force on earlier dates for the purposes of making rules, giving notices and consent, etc (for details see reg 1 of the 2017 Regulations)).

[7.267]

[123C Exercise of administrative sanctions

Any one or more of the powers under sections 123, 123A and 123B may be exercised in relation to the same contravention.]

NOTES

Substituted as noted to s 123 at **[7.264]**.

Statement of policy

[7.268]

124 Statement of policy

[(1) The FCA must prepare and issue a statement of its policy with respect to the type and level of administrative sanctions it may impose on a relevant person.

(2) The FCA's policy in determining the type and level of administrative sanctions to be imposed must take into account all relevant circumstances including, where appropriate, the matters referred to in Article 31(1) of the market abuse regulation [or Article 43(1) of the EU Benchmarks Regulation 2016].]

(3) . . .

(4) The [FCA] may at any time alter or replace a statement issued under this section.

(5) If a statement issued under this section is altered or replaced, the [FCA] must issue the altered or replacement statement.

[(6) When imposing, or deciding whether to impose, an administrative sanction on a relevant person the FCA must have regard to any statement published under this section in force at the time of the contravention.]

(7) A statement issued under this section must be published by the [FCA] in the way appearing to the [FCA] to be best calculated to bring it to the attention of the public.

(8) The [FCA] may charge a reasonable fee for providing a person with a copy of a statement published under this section.

(9) The [FCA] must, without delay, give the Treasury a copy of any statement which it publishes under this section.

[(10) In this section—

"administrative sanction" means—

- (a) a penalty or statement of censure imposed or published under section 123;
- (b) a prohibition imposed under section 123A; or
- (c) a suspension or restriction imposed under section 123B; and

"relevant person" means a person—

- (a) who has contravened Article 14 (prohibition of insider dealing and of unlawful disclosure of inside information) or Article 15 (prohibition of market manipulation) of the market abuse regulation;
- (b) who has contravened, or been knowingly concerned in the contravention of—
  - (i) a provision of the market abuse regulation other than Article 14 or 15 of that regulation; or
  - (ii) a provision of [any supplementary market abuse legislation]; or
- (c) who has contravened—
  - (i) any requirement imposed on the person under section 122A, 122B, 122C, 122G, 122H, [122HA,] 122I, [. . .] 123A or 123B; or
  - (ii) in the case of a person other than an authorised person, any requirement relating to the market abuse regulation or [any supplementary market abuse legislation] imposed on the person under Part 11.]

NOTES

Sub-ss (1), (2) and (6) were substituted, sub-s (3) was repealed, and sub-s (10) was added, by the Financial Services and Markets Act 2000 (Market Abuse) Regulations 2016, SI 2016/680, reg 9(1), (6), as from 3 July 2016.

Words in square brackets in sub-s (2) substituted, and figure "122HA," in square brackets in sub-para (c)(i) of the definition "relevant person" in sub-s (10) inserted by the Financial Services and Markets Act 2000 (Benchmarks) Regulations 2018, SI 2018/135, reg 42(3), as from 27 February 2018.

Words in square brackets in sub-paras (b)(ii) and (c)(ii) of the definition "relevant person" in sub-s (10) substituted by the Market Abuse (Amendment) (EU Exit) Regulations 2019, SI 2019/310, reg 5(1), (11)(a), as from IP completion day (as defined in the European Union (Withdrawal Agreement) Act 2020, s 39).

The figure omitted from sub-para (c)(i) of the definition "relevant person" in sub-s (10) was originally inserted by the Financial Services and Markets Act 2000 (Markets in Financial Instruments) Regulations 2017, SI 2017/701, reg 50(1), Sch 2, paras 1, 15, as from 3 January 2018; and was subsequently repealed by SI 2019/310, reg 5(1), (10)(b), as from IP completion day (as defined in the European Union (Withdrawal Agreement) Act 2020, s 39).

Other words in square brackets substituted by the Financial Services Act 2012, s 37(1), Sch 9, Pt 1, para 1, Pt 3, para 9(1), (2), as from 1 April 2013.

[7.269]

125 Statement of policy: procedure

(1) Before issuing a statement of policy under section 124, the [FCA] must publish a draft of the proposed statement in the way appearing to the [FCA] to be best calculated to bring it to the attention of the public.

(2) The draft must be accompanied by notice that representations about the proposal may be made to the [FCA] within a specified time.

(3) Before issuing the proposed statement, the [FCA] must have regard to any representations made to it in accordance with subsection (2).

(4) If the [FCA] issues the proposed statement it must publish an account, in general terms, of—

- (a) the representations made to it in accordance with subsection (2); and
- (b) its response to them.

(5) If the statement differs from the draft published under subsection (1) in a way which is, in the opinion of the [FCA], significant, the [FCA] must (in addition to complying with subsection (4)) publish details of the difference.

(6) The [FCA] may charge a reasonable fee for providing a person with a copy of a draft published under subsection (1).

(7) This section also applies to a proposal to alter or replace a statement.

NOTES

Words in square brackets substituted by the Financial Services Act 2012, s 37(1), Sch 9, Pt 1, para 1, Pt 3, para 9(1), (2), as from 1 April 2013.

Procedure

[7.270]

126 Warning notices

[(1) If the FCA proposes—

- (a) to impose a penalty on a person under section 123(2);
- (b) to publish a statement censuring a person under section 123(3);

(c) to impose a temporary prohibition on an individual under section 123A(2)(a);
(d) to impose a temporary prohibition on an individual under section 123A(2)(b);
(e) to impose a permanent prohibition on an individual under section 123A(3); or
(f) to impose a suspension or restriction in relation to a person under section 123B;

it must give the person a warning notice.]

(2) A warning notice about a proposal to impose a penalty [under section 123] must state the amount of the proposed penalty.

(3) A warning notice about a proposal to publish a statement [under section 123] must set out the terms of the proposed statement.

[(4) A warning notice about a proposal to impose a prohibition under section 123A must set out the terms of the proposed prohibition.

(5) A warning notice about a proposal to impose a suspension or restriction under section 123B must state the period for which the suspension or restriction is to have effect.]

NOTES

Sub-s (1) was substituted, the words in square brackets in sub-ss (2), (3) were inserted, and sub-ss (4), (5) were added, by the Financial Services and Markets Act 2000 (Market Abuse) Regulations 2016, SI 2016/680, reg 9(1), (7), as from 3 July 2016.

[7.271]

127 Decision notices and right to refer to Tribunal

[(1) If the FCA decides—
(a) to impose a penalty on a person under section 123(2);
(b) to publish a statement censuring a person under section 123(3);
(c) to impose a temporary prohibition on an individual under section 123A(2)(a);
(d) to impose a temporary prohibition on an individual under section 123A(2)(b);
(e) to impose a permanent prohibition on an individual under section 123A(3);
(f) to impose a suspension or restriction in relation to a person under section 123B;

it must give the person a decision notice.]

(2) A decision notice about the imposition of a penalty [under section 123] must state the amount of the penalty.

(3) A decision notice about the publication of a statement [under section 123] must set out the terms of the statement.

[(3A) A decision notice about the imposition of a prohibition under section 123A must set out the terms of the prohibition.

(3B) A decision notice about the imposition of a suspension or restriction under section 123B must state the period for which the suspension or restriction is to have effect.]

[(4) If the FCA decides—
(a) to impose a penalty on a person under section 123(2);
(b) to publish a statement censuring a person under section 123(3);
(c) to impose a prohibition on an individual under section 123A; or
(d) to impose a suspension or restriction in relation to a person under section 123B;

that person may refer the matter to the Tribunal.]

NOTES

Sub-ss (1) and (4) were substituted, the words in square brackets in sub-ss (2) and (3) were inserted, and sub-ss (3A), (3B) were inserted, by the Financial Services and Markets Act 2000 (Market Abuse) Regulations 2016, SI 2016/680, reg 9(1), (8), as from 3 July 2016.

[7.272]

[127A Consultation with the PRA in relation to administrative sanctions

(1) The FCA must consult the PRA before giving a warning notice under section 126(1)(a), (b), (d) or (f) or a decision notice under section 127(1)(a), (b), (d) or (f) in relation to a person who—
(a) is a PRA-authorised person; or
(b) is a member of a PRA-authorised person's immediate group.

(2) The FCA must consult the PRA before giving a warning notice under section 126(1)(c) or (e) or a decision notice under section 127(1)(c) or (e) if as a result of the prohibition in question an individual would be prohibited from holding an office or position involving responsibility for taking decisions about the management of a PRA-authorised investment firm.

(3) The FCA must consult the PRA before varying or revoking a prohibition under section 123A(2)(a) or (3) if as a result of the proposed variation or revocation an individual would no longer be prohibited from holding an office or position involving responsibility for taking decisions about the management of a PRA-authorised investment firm.

(4) In this section "PRA-authorised investment firm" means an investment firm which is a PRA-authorised person and carries on a regulated activity.]

NOTES

Inserted by the Financial Services and Markets Act 2000 (Market Abuse) Regulations 2016, SI 2016/680, reg 9(1), (9), as from 3 July 2016.

Miscellaneous

[7.273]

128 Suspension of investigations

(1) If the [FCA] considers it desirable or expedient because of the exercise or possible exercise of a [relevant power], it may direct a recognised investment exchange[, recognised clearing house or recognised CSD]—
(a) to terminate, suspend or limit the scope of any inquiry which the exchange[, clearing house or central securities depository] is conducting under its rules; or
(b) not to conduct an inquiry which the exchange[, clearing house or central securities depository] proposes to conduct under its rules.

(2) A direction under this section—

(a) must be given to the exchange[, clearing house or central securities depository] concerned by notice in writing; and

(b) is enforceable, on the application of the [FCA], by injunction or, in Scotland, by an order under section 45 of the Court of Session Act 1988.

[(3) In this section "relevant power" means the FCA's power—

(a) to impose a penalty or publish a statement of censure under section 123;

(b) to impose a prohibition under section 123A;

(c) to impose a suspension or restriction under section 123B;

(d) to appoint a person to conduct an investigation under section 168 in a case falling within subsection (2)(d) of that section; or

(e) to appoint a person to conduct an investigation under section 169 (investigation etc in support of an overseas regulator) in a case falling within subsection (2A) of that section.]

NOTES

Word "FCA" in square brackets in sub-ss (1) and (2) substituted by the Financial Services Act 2012, s 37(1), Sch 9, Pt 1, para 1, Pt 3, para 9(1), (2), as from 1 April 2013.

Words "relevant power" in square brackets in sub-s (1) substituted, and sub-s (3) substituted, by the Financial Services and Markets Act 2000 (Market Abuse) Regulations 2016, SI 2016/680, reg 9(1), (10), as from 3 July 2016.

Other words in square brackets in sub-ss (1), (2) substituted by the Central Securities Depositories Regulations 2017, SI 2017/1064, reg 2(1), (4), as from 28 November 2017.

[7.274]

[129 Power of court to impose administrative sanctions in cases of market abuse

(1) The FCA may, on an application to the court under [Part 25 which relates to the market abuse regulation], request the court to consider whether it is appropriate to impose one or more of the following on the person to whom the application relates—

(a) a penalty;

(b) if the person concerned is an individual, a temporary prohibition or a permanent prohibition; or

(c) a suspension or restriction.

(2) The court may, if it considers it appropriate, make an order which does one or more of the following—

(a) requires the person concerned to pay to the FCA a penalty of such amount as the court considers appropriate;

(b) if the person concerned is an individual, imposes a temporary prohibition or a permanent prohibition on that individual; or

(c) imposes a suspension or restriction on the person concerned.

(3) But the court may impose a permanent prohibition only where it is satisfied the person concerned has contravened Article 14 (prohibition of insider dealing and of unlawful disclosure of inside information) or Article 15 (prohibition of market manipulation) of the market abuse regulation.

(4) Section 123A(4) to (6) apply to a prohibition imposed by an order made under subsection (2) as they do to a prohibition under section 123A, but with—

(a) references to a prohibition under section 123A having effect as references to a prohibition under this section; and

(b) references to the FCA having effect as references to the court which makes the order under this section.

(5) Section 123B(4) to (6) and (8) apply to a suspension or restriction imposed by an order under subsection (2) as they do to a suspension or restriction imposed under section 123B.

(6) The court may—

(a) vary or revoke a prohibition imposed under this section;

(b) withdraw a suspension or restriction imposed under this section; or

(c) vary a suspension or a restriction imposed under this section so as to reduce the period for which it has effect or otherwise to limit its effect.

(7) In this section—

. . .

"permanent prohibition" means a permanent prohibition on an individual holding an office or position involving responsibility for taking decisions about the management of an investment firm;

"suspension or restriction" means—

(a) a suspension of any permission which a person has to carry on a regulated activity for such period as the court considers appropriate ; or

(b) such limitations or other restrictions as the court considers appropriate in relation to the carrying on of a regulated activity by a person for such period as the court considers appropriate;

"temporary prohibition" means a temporary prohibition on an individual—

(a) holding an office or position involving responsibility for taking decisions about the management of an investment firm; . . .

(b) acquiring or disposing of financial instruments, whether on his or her own account or the account of a third party and whether directly or indirectly[; or

(c) making a bid, on his or her own account or the account of a third party, directly or indirectly, at an auction conducted by a recognised auction platform.]

[(8) For the meaning of "recognised auction platform" in this Part, see section 131AB.]]

[(9) An application under Part 25 relates to the market abuse regulation if—

(a) it is made under section 380 or 382 and the relevant requirement for the purposes of that section is a requirement imposed by the market abuse regulation or [by supplementary market abuse legislation]; or

(b) it is made under section 381 or 383.]

NOTES

Substituted by the Financial Services and Markets Act 2000 (Market Abuse) Regulations 2016, SI 2016/680, reg 9(1), (11), as from 3 July 2016.

Sub-s (1): words in square brackets substituted by the Financial Services and Markets Act 2000 (Markets in Financial Instruments) (No 2) Regulations 2017, SI 2017/1255, reg 3(1), (2)(a), as from 3 January 2018.

Sub-s (7): definition "market abuse requirement" (omitted) repealed by SI 2017/1255, reg 3(1), (2)(b), as from. The word omitted from para (a) of the definition "temporary prohibition" was repealed, and para (c) and the preceding word were added, by the Financial Services and Markets Act 2000 (Markets in Financial Instruments) Regulations 2017, SI 2017/701, reg 50(1), Sch 2, paras 1, 16(1), (2), as from (note that various provisions of the 2017 Regulations came into force on earlier dates for the purposes of making rules, giving notices and consent, etc (for details see reg 1 of the 2017 Regulations)).

Sub-s (8): added by SI 2017/701, reg 50(1), Sch 2, paras 1, 16(1), (3), as from (as to the commencement of the 2017 Regulations, see further the note relating to them above).

Sub-s (9): added by the Financial Services and Markets Act 2000 (Markets in Financial Instruments) (No 2) Regulations 2017, SI 2017/1255, reg 3(1), (2)(c), as from 3 January 2018. Words in square brackets substituted by SI 2019/310, reg 5(1), (12)(c), as from IP completion day (as defined in the European Union (Withdrawal Agreement) Act 2020, s 39).

[7.275]

130 Guidance

[(1) The Treasury may from time to time issue written guidance for the purpose of helping relevant authorities to determine the action to be taken in cases where—

(a) it appears a person has contravened Article 14 (prohibition of insider dealing and of unlawful disclosure of inside information) or Article 15 (prohibition of market manipulation) of the market abuse regulation; and

(b) in so doing the person appears to have committed an offence under Part 7 of the Financial Services Act 2012 or Part 5 of the Criminal Justice Act 1993 (insider dealing).]

(2) The Treasury must obtain the consent of the Attorney General and the Secretary of State before issuing any guidance under this section.

(3) In this section "relevant authorities"—

(a) in relation to England and Wales, means the Secretary of State, the [FCA], the Director of the Serious Fraud Office and the Director of Public Prosecutions;

(b) in relation to Northern Ireland, means the Secretary of State, the [FCA], the Director of the Serious Fraud Office and the Director of Public Prosecutions for Northern Ireland.

(4) Subsections (1) to (3) do not apply to Scotland.

(5) In relation to Scotland, the Lord Advocate may from time to time, after consultation with the Treasury, issue written guidance for the purpose of helping the [FCA] to determine the action to be taken in cases [mentioned in subsection (1)].

NOTES

Sub-s (1) substituted, and words in second pair of square brackets in sub-s (5) substituted, by the Financial Services and Markets Act 2000 (Market Abuse) Regulations 2016, SI 2016/680, reg 9(1), (12), as from 3 July 2016.

Word "FCA" in square brackets (in each place that it occurs) substituted by the Financial Services Act 2012, s 37(1), Sch 9, Pt 1, para 1, Pt 3, para 9(1), (2), as from 1 April 2013.

Attorney General: any function of the Attorney General may be exercised by the Solicitor General; see the Law Officers Act 1997, s 1.

130A (*Originally inserted by the Financial Services and Markets Act 2000 (Market Abuse) Regulations 2005, SI 2005/381, reg 5, Sch 2, para 3, as from 1 July 2005; and subsequently repealed by the Financial Services and Markets Act 2000 (Market Abuse) Regulations 2016, SI 2016/680, reg 9(1), (13), as from 3 July 2016.*)

[7.276]

131 Effect on transactions

The imposition of a penalty under this Part does not make any transaction void or unenforceable.

[7.277]

[131A Protected Disclosures

(1) A disclosure which satisfies the following three conditions is not to be taken to breach any restriction on the disclosure of information (however imposed).

(2) The first condition is that the information or other matter—

(a) causes the person making the disclosure (the discloser) to know or suspect, or

[(b) gives him reasonable grounds for knowing or suspecting that another person has engaged in market abuse,] [that another person has contravened Article 14 (prohibition of insider dealing and of unlawful disclosure of inside information) or Article 15 (prohibition of market manipulation) of the market abuse regulation.]

(3) The second condition is that the information or other matter disclosed came to the discloser in the course of his trade, profession, business or employment.

(4) The third condition is that the disclosure is made . . . to a nominated officer as soon as is practicable after the information or other matter comes to the discloser.

(5) A disclosure to a nominated officer is a disclosure which is made to a person nominated by the discloser's employer to receive disclosures under this section, and is made in the course of the discloser's employment and in accordance with the procedure established by the employer for the purpose.

(6) For the purposes of this section, references to a person's employer include any body, association or organisation (including a voluntary organisation) in connection with whose activities the person exercises a function (whether or not for gain or reward) and references to employment must be construed accordingly.]

NOTES

Inserted by the Financial Services and Markets Act 2000 (Market Abuse) Regulations 2005, SI 2005/381, reg 5, Sch 2, para 4, as from 1 July 2005.

Sub-s (2): para (b) substituted, and words in final pair of square brackets added, by the Financial Services and Markets Act 2000 (Market Abuse) Regulations 2016, SI 2016/680, reg 9(1), (14)(a), as from 3 July 2016.

Sub-s (4): words omitted repealed by SI 2016/680, reg 9(1), (14)(b), as from 3 July 2016.

[7.278]

[131AA Reporting of infringements

(1) This section applies to employers who—

(a) provide regulated financial services;

(b) carry on regulated activities in reliance on the exemption in section 327; or

(c) are recognised bodies . . . or third country central counterparties.

(2) Employers must have in place appropriate internal procedures for their employees to report contraventions of the market abuse regulation or any supplementary [market abuse legislation].

(3) In this section—

"employee" and "employer" have the meaning given in section 230 of the Employment Rights Act 1996;

"recognised body" has the meaning given in section 313;

"regulated financial services" has the meaning given in section 1H.

NOTES

Inserted, together with ss 131AB–131AE, by the Financial Services and Markets Act 2000 (Market Abuse) Regulations 2016, SI 2016/680, reg 9(1), (15), as from 3 July 2016.

Sub-s (1): words omitted from para (c) repealed by the Market Abuse (Amendment) (EU Exit) Regulations 2019, SI 2019/310, reg 5(1), (13)(a), as from IP completion day (as defined in the European Union (Withdrawal Agreement) Act 2020, s 39).

Sub-s (2): words in square brackets substituted by SI 2019/310, reg 5(1), (13)(b), as from IP completion day (as defined in the European Union (Withdrawal Agreement) Act 2020, s 39).

[7.279]

[131AB Interpretation

[(1)] In this Part—

. . .

["emission allowance" [means emission allowance as described in paragraph 11 of Part 1 of Schedule 2 to the Financial Services and Markets Act 2000 (Regulated Activities) Order 2001];]

["financial instrument" means any instrument specified in Part 1 of Schedule 2 to the Financial Services and Markets Act 2000 (Regulated Activities) Order, read with Part 2 of that Schedule;]

"issuer" has the meaning given in Article 3.1(21) of the market abuse regulation; and

["recognised auction platform" has the meaning given in regulation 1(3) of the Recognised Auction Platform Regulations 2011 (SI 2011/2699);]

. . .]

[(2) The following are supplementary market abuse legislation for the purposes of this Part—

(a) an EU regulation, originally made under the market abuse regulation, which is retained direct EU legislation; and

(b) subordinate legislation (within the meaning of the Interpretation Act 1978) made under the market abuse regulation on or after IP completion day.]

NOTES

Inserted as noted to s 131AA at **[7.278]**.

Sub-s (1) numbered as such by the Market Abuse (Amendment) (EU Exit) Regulations 2019, SI 2019/310, reg 5(1), (14)(a), as from IP completion day (as defined in the European Union (Withdrawal Agreement) Act 2020, s 39); and amended as follows:

Definition "EEA regulator" (omitted) repealed by SI 2019/310, reg 5(1), (14)(b)(i), as from IP completion day (as defined in the European Union (Withdrawal Agreement) Act 2020, s 39).

Definition "emission allowance" inserted by the Financial Services and Markets Act 2000 (Markets in Financial Instruments) Regulations 2017, SI 2017/701, reg 50(1), Sch 2, paras 1, 17(b), as from 3 January 2018 (note that various provisions of the 2017 Regulations came into force on earlier dates for the purposes of making rules, giving notices and consent, etc (for details see reg 1 of the 2017 Regulations)). Words in square brackets in that definition substituted by the Recognised Auction Platforms (Amendment and Miscellaneous Provisions) Regulations 2021, SI 2021/494, reg 2(3), as from 22 April 2021.

Definition "financial instrument" substituted by SI 2019/310, reg 5(1), (14)(b)(ii), as from IP completion day (as defined in the European Union (Withdrawal Agreement) Act 2020, s 39).

Definition "recognised auction platform" inserted by SI 2017/701, reg 50(1), Sch 2, paras 1, 17(b), as from 3 January 2018 (for further details regarding the commencement of the 2017 Regulations, see the note relating to them above).

Definition "supplementary EU regulation" (omitted) repealed by SI 2019/310, reg 5(1), (14)(b)(iv), as from IP completion day (as defined in the European Union (Withdrawal Agreement) Act 2020, s 39).

Sub-s (2): added by SI 2019/310, reg 5(1), (14)(c), as from IP completion day (as defined in the European Union (Withdrawal Agreement) Act 2020, s 39). Note that reg 5(14)(c) of the 2019 Regulations was amended by the Financial Services and Economic and Monetary Policy (Consequential Amendments) (EU Exit) Regulations 2020, SI 2020/1301, reg 3, Schedule, para 17(b), as from 30 December 2020 (and the effect of the amendment has been incorporated in the text set out above).

[7.280]

[131AC Meaning of "persons closely associated" in the market abuse regulation

(1) In Article 3.1(26)(a) (definitions) of the market abuse regulation "partner considered to be equivalent to a spouse" includes a civil partner.

(2) In Article 3.1(26)(b) of the market abuse regulation "dependent child" means a child who—

(a) is under the age of 18 years;

(b) is unmarried; and

(c) does not have a civil partner.

(3) In this section "child" includes a stepchild.]

NOTES

Inserted as noted to s 131AA at **[7.278]**.

[7.281]

[131AD Individual liability in respect of legal persons under Articles 8 and 12 of the market abuse regulation

(1) An individual participates in a decision by a body corporate for the purposes of Article 8.5 (insider dealing) or Article 12.4 (market manipulation) of the market abuse regulation where—

(a) the individual was an officer of the body corporate when the decision was made; and

(b) the FCA are satisfied that the individual was knowingly concerned in the decision.

(2) In this section "officer", in relation to a body corporate, means—

(a) a director, member of the committee of management, chief executive, manager, secretary or other similar officer of the body, or a person purporting to act in any such capacity; or

(b) an individual who is a controller of the body.]

NOTES

Inserted as noted to s 131AA at **[7.278]**.

[7.282]

[131AE Liability for contraventions of Article 14 or 15 of the market abuse regulation

For the purposes of any enactment a person contravenes Article 14 (prohibition of insider dealing and of unlawful disclosure of inside information) or Article 15 (prohibition of market manipulation) whether the contravention is by that person alone or by that person and one or more other persons jointly or in concert.]

NOTES

Inserted as noted to s 131AA at **[7.278]**.

[PART 8A SHORT SELLING

. . .

131B–131D (*Part 8A (originally ss 131B–131F and 131G–131K) was inserted by the Financial Services Act 2010, s 8, as from 8 June 2010. Ss 131B–131D (and the preceding heading) were repealed by the Financial Services and Markets Act 2000 (Short Selling) Regulations 2012, SI 2012/2554, reg 2(1), (2), as from 1 November 2012, subject to savings in reg 7 of the 2012 Regulations which provides that this repeal does not affect the liability of any person to provide disclosure of a disclosable short position for the purposes of the Financial Stability and Market Confidence Sourcebook Instrument 2010 where (a) that person held the disclosable short position before 1 November 2012, and (b) disclosure is due to be provided on that date (and for these purposes "disclosure" has the meaning given by Financial Stability and Market Confidence Sourcebook Instrument 2010 and "disclosable short position" has the meaning given by the Short Selling Instrument 2008).*)

[Power to require information

[7.283]

131E Power to require information

(1) The [FCA] may, by notice in writing, require a person . . . —

(a) to provide specified information or information of a specified description; or

(b) to produce specified documents or documents of a specified description.

(2) This section applies only to information and documents that the [FCA] reasonably requires for the purpose of [the exercise by it of functions under the short selling regulation] [or to respond to a request referred to in subsection (5A)].

(3) Information or documents required under this section must be provided or produced—

(a) before the end of such reasonable period as may be specified; and

(b) at such place as may be specified.

(4) The [FCA] may require any information provided under this section to be provided in such form as it may reasonably require.

(5) The [FCA] may require—

(a) any information provided, whether in a document or otherwise, to be verified in such manner as it may reasonably require; or

(b) any document produced to be authenticated in such manner as it may reasonably require.

[(5A) The [FCA's] powers under this section may be exercised on a request made in the exercise of [relevant functions] by—

[(a) an overseas regulator, or]

(b) ESMA.

(5B) . . .]

[(6) In this section—

"overseas regulator" means—

(a) the competent authority of an EEA State for the purposes of the short selling regulation, as that regulation has effect in the European Union (the "EU short selling regulation"); or

(b) the authority of a third country which is not an EEA State which exercises functions corresponding to those of a competent authority under the EU short selling regulation;

"relevant functions" means—

(a) in relation to a competent authority of an EEA State, its functions under the EU short selling regulation;

(b) in relation to ESMA, its functions under the EU short selling regulation;

(c) in relation to an authority of a third country which is not an EEA state, its functions corresponding to the functions referred to in paragraph (a);

"specified" means specified in the notice.]

(7) . . .]

NOTES

Part 8A (originally ss 131B–131F and 131G–131K) was inserted by the Financial Services Act 2010, s 8, as from 8 June 2010.

The words "FCA" and "FCA's" in square brackets (in each place that they occur) were substituted by the Financial Services Act 2012, s 25, as from 1 April 2013. Other amendments to this section are as follows:

Sub-s (1): words omitted repealed by the Financial Services and Markets Act 2000 (Short Selling) Regulations 2012, SI 2012/2554, reg 2(1), (3)(a), as from 1 November 2012

Sub-s (2): the words in the second pair of square brackets were substituted by SI 2012/2554, reg 2(1), (3)(b), as from 1 November 2012. The words in the third pair of square brackets were inserted by the Short Selling (Amendment) (EU Exit) Regulations 2018, SI 2018/1321, reg 2(1), (2)(a), as from IP completion day (as defined in the European Union (Withdrawal Agreement) Act 2020, s 39).

Sub-ss (5A), (5B): originally inserted by SI 2012/2554, reg 2(1), (3)(c), as from 1 November 2012. Words in second pair of square brackets in sub-s (5A) substituted, para (a) of that subsection substituted, and sub-s (5B) repealed, by SI 2018/1321, reg 2(1), (2)(b), (c), as from IP completion day (as defined in the European Union (Withdrawal Agreement) Act 2020, s 39).

Sub-s (6): substituted by SI 2018/1321, reg 2(1), (2)(d), as from IP completion day (as defined in the European Union (Withdrawal Agreement) Act 2020, s 39).

Sub-s (7): repealed by SI 2012/2554, reg 2(1), (3)(d), as from 1 November 2012.

[7.284]

[131F Power to require information: supplementary

(1) . . .

(2) If a document is produced in response to a requirement imposed under section 131E, the [FCA] may—

(a) take copies of or extracts from the document; or

(b) require the person producing the document, or any relevant person, to provide an explanation of the document.

(3) In subsection (2)(b) "relevant person", in relation to a person who is required to produce a document, means a person who—

(a) has been or is or is proposed to be a director or controller of that person;

(b) has been or is an auditor of that person;

(c) has been or is an actuary, accountant or lawyer appointed or instructed by that person; or

(d) has been or is an employee of that person.

(4) If a person who is required under section 131E to produce a document fails to do so, the [FCA] may require the person to state, to the best of the person's knowledge and belief, where the document is.

(5) A lawyer may be required under section 131E to provide the name and address of the lawyer's client.

(6) A person ("P") may not be required under section 131E to disclose information or produce a document in respect of which P owes an obligation of confidence by virtue of carrying on the business of banking unless—

[(a) the [FCA] suspects that P or a member of P's group has contravened any provision of the short selling regulation;

(b) the [FCA] suspects that the person to whom the obligation of confidence is owed or a member of that person's group has contravened any provision of the short selling regulation; or]

(c) the person to whom the obligation of confidence is owed consents to the disclosure or production.

[(6A) Where the FCA is exercising its powers under section 131E in response to a request from an overseas regulator or ESMA, references to the short selling regulation are to be read as including the EU short selling regulation, within the meaning of section 131E(6).]

(7) If a person claims a lien on a document, its production under section 131E does not affect the lien.]

NOTES

Inserted as noted to s 131E at **[7.283]**.

Word "FCA" in square brackets (in each place that it occurs) substituted by the Financial Services Act 2012, s 25, as from 1 April 2013. Other amendments to this section are as follows:

Sub-s (1) was repealed, and sub-s (6)(a), (b) were substituted, by the Financial Services and Markets Act 2000 (Short Selling) Regulations 2012, SI 2012/2554, reg 2(1), (4), as from 1 November 2012.

Sub-s (6A): inserted the Short Selling (Amendment) (EU Exit) Regulations 2018, SI 2018/1321, reg 2(1), (3), as from IP completion day (as defined in the European Union (Withdrawal Agreement) Act 2020, s 39).

[7.285]

[131FA Investigations in support of [overseas] regulator

[(1) The FCA may appoint one or more competent persons to investigate any matter if it is requested to do so by—

(a) the competent authority of an EEA state acting in the exercise of its functions under the short selling regulation, as that regulation has effect in the European Union; or

(b) an authority of a third country which is not an EEA state which is acting in the exercise of functions corresponding to those referred to in paragraph (a).]

(2) . . .

(3) Sections 170 to 177 (which relate to investigations) apply in relation to an investigator appointed under subsection (1) as they apply in relation to an investigator appointed under section 168(5).

(4) The [FCA] may direct an investigator appointed under subsection (1) to permit a representative of [the authority making the request under subsection (1) ("the requesting regulator")] to attend, and take part in, any interview conducted for the purposes of the investigation.

(5) The [FCA] is not to give a direction under subsection (4) unless it is satisfied that any information obtained by the [requesting] regulator as a result of the interview will be subject to safeguards equivalent to those contained in Part 23.

(6) The [FCA] must prepare a statement of its policy with respect to the conduct of interviews in relation to which a direction under subsection (4) has been given.

(7) The statement requires the approval of the Treasury.

(8) If the Treasury approve the statement, the [FCA] must publish it.

(9) No direction may be given under subsection (4) before the statement has been published.
(10) The [FCA] may at any time alter or replace a statement issued under subsection (6), and subsections (7) and (8) apply to an altered statement or to a replacement statement.]

NOTES

Inserted, together with ss 131FB, 131FC, by the Financial Services and Markets Act 2000 (Short Selling) Regulations 2012, SI 2012/2554, reg 2(1), (5), as from 1 November 2012.

Word "FCA" in square brackets (in each place that it occurs) substituted by the Financial Services Act 2012, s 25, as from 1 April 2013.

All other amendments to this section were made by the Short Selling (Amendment) (EU Exit) Regulations 2018, SI 2018/1321, reg 2(1), (4), as from IP completion day (as defined in the European Union (Withdrawal Agreement) Act 2020, s 39).

[7.286]
[131FB Entry of premises under warrant

(1) A justice of the peace may issue a warrant under this section if satisfied on information on oath given by or on behalf of the [FCA] that there are reasonable grounds for believing that the conditions in subsection (2) are satisfied.
(2) The conditions are—
- (a) that a relevant person on whom a requirement has been imposed under section 131E or 131F has failed (wholly or in part) to comply with it; and
- (b) that on the premises specified in the warrant—
  - (i) there are documents which have been required; or
  - (ii) there is information which has been required.

(3) A warrant under this section shall authorise a constable—
- (a) to enter the premises specified in the warrant;
- (b) to search the premises and take possession of any documents or information appearing to be documents or information of a kind in respect of which a warrant under this section was issued ("the relevant kind") or to take, in relation to any such documents or information, any other steps which may appear to be necessary for preserving them or preventing interference with them;
- (c) to take copies of, or extracts from, any documents or information appearing to be of the relevant kind;
- (d) to require any person on the premises to provide an explanation of any document or information appearing to be of the relevant kind or to state where it may be found; and
- (e) to use such force as may be reasonably necessary.

(4) A warrant under this section may be executed by any constable.
(5) The warrant may authorise persons to accompany any constable who is executing it.
(6) The powers in subsection (3) may be exercised by a person authorised by the warrant to accompany a constable; but that person may exercise those powers only in the company of, and under the supervision of, a constable.
(7) In England and Wales, sections 15(5) to (8) and 16(3) to (12) of the Police and Criminal Evidence Act 1984 (execution of search warrants and safeguards) apply to warrants issued under this section.
(8) In Northern Ireland, Articles 17(5) to (8) and 18(3) to (12) of the Police and Criminal Evidence (Northern Ireland) Order 1989 apply to warrants issued under this section.
(9) In the application of this section to Scotland—
- (a) for the reference to a justice of the peace substitute a reference to a justice of the peace or a sheriff; and
- (b) for the references to information on oath substitute references to evidence on oath.

(10) The [FCA] may give information under subsection (1) or under section 176(1) at the request of an [overseas] regulator where the regulator makes the request in the exercise of [relevant functions].
(11) . . .
(12) In this section—

["overseas regulator" and "relevant functions" have the meanings given in section 131E(6);]

"relevant person" means—
- (a) an authorised person,
- (b) a person who has been an authorised person,
- (c) a person who is for the purposes of section 165 connected with an authorised person or with a person within paragraph (b).]

NOTES

Inserted as noted to s 131FA at **[7.285]**.

Word "FCA" in square brackets (in each place that it occurs) substituted by the Financial Services Act 2012, s 25, as from 1 April 2013.

The second and third words in square brackets in sub-s (10) were substituted, sub-s (11) was repealed, and the definitions in square brackets in subs (12) were substituted, by the Short Selling (Amendment) (EU Exit) Regulations 2018, SI 2018/1321, reg 2(1), (5), as from IP completion day (as defined in the European Union (Withdrawal Agreement) Act 2020, s 39).

[7.287]
[131FC Retention of documents taken under section 131FB

(1) Any document of which possession is taken under section 131FB ("a seized document") may be retained so long as it is necessary to retain it (rather than copies of it) in the circumstances.
(2) A person claiming to be the owner of a seized document may apply to a magistrates' court or (in Scotland) the sheriff for an order for the delivery of the document to the person appearing to the court or sheriff to be the owner.
(3) If on an application under subsection (2) the court or (in Scotland) the sheriff cannot ascertain who is the owner of the seized document the court or sheriff (as the case may be) may make such order as the court or sheriff thinks fit.
(4) An order under subsection (2) or (3) does not affect the right of any person to take legal proceedings against any person in possession of a seized document for the recovery of the document.
(5) Any right to bring proceedings (as described in subsection (4)) may only be exercised within 6 months of the date of the order made under subsection (2) or (3).]

NOTES

Inserted as noted to s 131FA at **[7.285]**.

[Breach of short selling [regulation] etc

[7.288]

131G Power to impose penalty or issue censure

(1) This section applies if the [FCA] is satisfied that a person has contravened—

(a) any provision of [the short selling regulation]; or

(b) any requirement imposed on the person under section 131E or 131F.

(2) The [FCA] may impose a penalty of such amount as it considers appropriate on—

(a) the person who contravened the provision or requirement; or

(b) any person who was knowingly concerned in the contravention.

(3) It may, instead of imposing a penalty on a person, publish a statement censuring the person.

(4) The [FCA] may not take action against a person under this section after the end of the limitation period unless, before the end of that period, it has given a warning notice to the person under section 131H.

(5) "The limitation period" means the period of three years beginning with the first day on which the [FCA] knew of the contravention.

(6) For this purpose the [FCA] is to be treated as knowing of a contravention if it has information from which the contravention can reasonably be inferred.]

NOTES

Inserted as noted to s 131E at **[7.283]**.

Word "FCA" in square brackets (in each place that it occurs) substituted by the Financial Services Act 2012, s 25, as from 1 April 2013.

Words in square brackets in sub-s (1)(a) and in the heading preceding this section substituted by the Financial Services and Markets Act 2000 (Short Selling) Regulations 2012, SI 2012/2554, reg 2(1), (6), (7), as from 1 November 2012.

[7.289]

[131H Procedure and right to refer to Tribunal

(1) If the [FCA] proposes to take action against a person under section 131G, it must give the person a warning notice.

(2) A warning notice about a proposal to impose a penalty must state the amount of the penalty.

(3) A warning notice about a proposal to publish a statement must set out the terms of the statement.

(4) If the [FCA] decides to take action against a person under section 131G, it must give the person a decision notice.

(5) A decision notice about the imposition of a penalty must state the amount of the penalty.

(6) A decision notice about the publication of a statement must set out the terms of the statement.

(7) If the [FCA] decides to take action against a person under section 131G, the person may refer the matter to the Tribunal.]

NOTES

Inserted as noted to s 131E at **[7.283]**.

Word "FCA" in square brackets (in each place that it occurs) substituted by the Financial Services Act 2012, s 25, as from 1 April 2013.

[7.290]

[131I Duty on publication of statement

After a statement under section 131G(3) is published, the [FCA] must send a copy of the statement to—

(a) the person in respect of whom it is made; and

(b) any person to whom a copy of the decision notice was given under section 393(4).]

NOTES

Inserted as noted to s 131E at **[7.283]**.

Word in square brackets substituted by the Financial Services Act 2012, s 25, as from 1 April 2013.

[7.291]

[131J Imposition of penalties under section 131G: statement of policy

(1) The [FCA] must prepare and issue a statement of its policy with respect to—

(a) the imposition of penalties under section 131G; and

(b) the amount of penalties under that section.

(2) The [FCA's] policy in determining what the amount of a penalty should be must include having regard to—

(a) the seriousness of the contravention;

(b) the extent to which the contravention was deliberate or reckless; and

(c) whether the person on whom the penalty is to be imposed is an individual.

(3) The [FCA] may at any time alter or replace a statement issued under this section.

(4) If a statement issued under this section is altered or replaced, the [FCA] must issue the altered or replaced statement.

(5) The [FCA] must, without delay, give the Treasury a copy of any statement which it publishes under this section.

(6) A statement issued under this section must be published by the [FCA] in the way appearing to the [FCA] to be best calculated to bring it to the attention of the public.

(7) The [FCA] may charge a reasonable fee for providing a person with a copy of the statement.

(8) In exercising, or deciding whether to exercise, a power under section 131G in the case of any particular contravention, the [FCA] must have regard to any statement of policy published under this section and in force at a time when the contravention occurred.]

NOTES

Inserted as noted to s 131E at **[7.283]**.

Words in square brackets substituted by the Financial Services Act 2012, s 25, as from 1 April 2013.

[7.292]

[131K Statement of policy: procedure

(1) Before issuing a statement under section 131J, the [FCA] must publish a draft of the proposed statement in the way appearing to the [FCA] to be best calculated to bring it to the attention of the public.

(2) The draft must be accompanied by notice that representations about the proposal may be made to the [FCA] within a specified time.

(3) Before issuing the proposed statement, the [FCA] must have regard to any representations made to it in accordance with subsection (2).

(4) If the [FCA] issues the proposed statement it must publish an account, in general terms, of—

(a) the representations made to it in accordance with subsection (2); and

(b) its response to them.

(5) If the statement differs from the draft published under subsection (1) in a way which is, in the opinion of the [FCA], significant, the [FCA] must (in addition to complying with subsection (4)) publish details of the difference.

(6) The [FCA] may charge a reasonable fee for providing a person with a copy of a draft published under subsection (1).

(7) This section also applies to a proposal to alter or replace a statement.]

NOTES

Inserted as noted to s 131E at **[7.283]**.

Word "FCA" in square brackets (in each place that it occurs) substituted by the Financial Services Act 2012, s 25, as from 1 April 2013.

[7.293]

[131L Offences

(1) If a relevant person ("A") fails to comply with a requirement imposed on A under section 131E or 131F the [FCA] may certify that fact in writing to the court.

(2) If the court is satisfied that A failed without reasonable excuse to comply with the requirement, it may deal with A (and where A is a body corporate, any director or officer) as if A (or as the case may be the director or officer) were in contempt; and "officer", in relation to a limited liability partnership, means a member of the limited liability partnership.

(3) A relevant person ("B") who, in purported compliance with a requirement imposed on B under section 131E or 131F—

(a) provides information which B knows to be false or misleading in a material particular, or

(b) recklessly provides information which is false or misleading in a material particular,

is guilty of an offence.

(4) A person guilty of an offence under subsection (3) is liable—

(a) on summary conviction, to imprisonment for a term not exceeding three months or a fine not exceeding the statutory maximum, or both;

(b) on conviction on indictment, to imprisonment for a term not exceeding two years or a fine, or both.

(5) Any person who intentionally obstructs the exercise of any rights conferred by a warrant under section 131FB is guilty of an offence and liable on summary conviction to imprisonment for a term not exceeding three months or a fine not exceeding level 5 on the standard scale, or both.

(6) In relation to any contravention by a person, the [FCA] may not exercise both—

(a) its powers under section 131G(2), and

(b) its powers under subsection (1).

(7) In this section—

"court" means—

(a) the High Court;

(b) in Scotland, the Court of Session;

"relevant person" means—

(a) an authorised person,

(b) a person who has been an authorised person,

(c) a person who is for the purposes of section 165 connected with an authorised person or with a person within paragraph (b).]

NOTES

Inserted by the Financial Services and Markets Act 2000 (Short Selling) Regulations 2012, SI 2012/2554, reg 2(1), (8), as from 1 November 2012.

Words in square brackets in sub-ss (1), (6) substituted by the Financial Services Act 2012, s 25, as from 1 April 2013.

132–137 *(Part IX—Hearings and Appeals omitted due to space considerations; see further, the introductory notes to this Act.)*

[PART 9A RULES AND GUIDANCE

CHAPTER 1 RULE-MAKING POWERS

General rule-making powers of the FCA and the PRA

[7.294]

137A The FCA's general rules

(1) The FCA may make such rules applying to authorised persons—

(a) with respect to the carrying on by them of regulated activities, or
(b) with respect to the carrying on by them of activities which are not regulated activities,

as appear to the FCA to be necessary or expedient for the purpose of advancing one or more of its operational objectives.

(2) Rules made under this section are referred to in this Act as the FCA's general rules.

(3) The FCA's general rules may make provision applying to authorised persons even though there is no relationship between the authorised persons to whom the rules will apply and the persons whose interests will be protected by the rules.

(4) The FCA's general rules may contain requirements which take into account, in the case of an authorised person who is a member of a group, any activity of another member of the group.

(5) . . .

[(6) The FCA's general rules may not modify, amend or revoke any retained direct EU legislation (except retained direct EU legislation which takes the form of FCA rules).]

[(7) Subsection (6) is subject to sections 143C(4) and 143D(6).]]

NOTES

This section was substituted (together with the rest of Part 9A (ie, ss 137A–137T, 138A–138O, 139A, 139B, 140A–140H, 141A) for the original Part X (ss 138–164)) by the Financial Services Act 2012, s 24(1), as from 24 January 2013 (for the purpose of making rules), and as from 1 April 2013 (otherwise).

Sub-s (5): repealed by the EEA Passport Rights (Amendment, etc, and Transitional Provisions) (EU Exit) Regulations 2018, SI 2018/1149, reg 3, Schedule, Pt 1, paras 1, 9, as from IP completion day (as defined in the European Union (Withdrawal Agreement) Act 2020, s 39).

Sub-s (6): added by the Financial Regulators' Powers (Technical Standards etc) (Amendment etc) (EU Exit) Regulations 2018, SI 2018/1115, reg 7(1), (6), as from 26 October 2018.

Sub-s (7): added by the Financial Services Act 2021, s 2, Sch 2, Pt 2, para 4, as from 1 July 2021; for transitional provisions, see Sch 2, Pt 3 to the 2021 Act.

Rules: the Industrial Assurance (Premium Receipt Books) Regulations 1948, SI 1948/2770 have effect as if made as rules under this section by virtue of the Industrial Assurance and Friendly Societies Act 1948, s 8(2) (repealed), the Financial Services and Markets Act 2000 (Transitional Provisions and Savings) (Rules) Order 2001, SI 2001/1534, and the Interpretation Act 1978, s 17(2)(b).

[7.295]

[137AA The FCA's general rules: Gibraltar

(1) The FCA's general rules may not make provision prohibiting a Gibraltar-based person from carrying on, or holding itself out as carrying on, an activity which it has a Schedule 2A permission to carry on in the United Kingdom.

(2) Subsection (1) does not apply to rules described in section 137C, 137D or 137FD.

(3) The Treasury may by regulations impose other limitations on what provision applying to Gibraltar-based persons with a Schedule 2A permission to carry on a regulated activity may be made in the FCA's general rules, but may not impose limitations relating to rules described in section 137C, 137D or 137FD.

(4) Before making regulations under subsection (3), the Treasury must consult the FCA.]

NOTES

Commencement: to be appointed.

Inserted by the Financial Services Act 2021, s 22, Sch 8, para 5, as from a day to be appointed.

[7.296]

[137B FCA general rules: clients' money, right to rescind etc

(1) Rules relating to the handling of money held by an authorised person in specified circumstances ("clients' money") may—

(a) make provision which results in that clients' money being held on trust in accordance with the rules,
(b) treat 2 or more accounts as a single account for specified purposes (which may include the distribution of money held in the accounts),
(c) authorise the retention by the authorised person of interest accruing on the clients' money, and
(d) make provision as to the distribution of such interest which is not to be retained by the authorised person.

(2) An institution with which an account is kept in pursuance of rules relating to the handling of clients' money does not incur any liability as constructive trustee if the money is wrongfully paid from the account, unless the institution permits the payment—

(a) with knowledge that it is wrongful, or
(b) having deliberately failed to make enquiries in circumstances in which a reasonable and honest person would have done so.

(3) Rules may—

(a) confer rights on persons to rescind agreements with, or withdraw offers to, authorised persons within a specified period, and
(b) make provision, in respect of authorised persons and persons exercising those rights, for the restitution of property and the making or recovery of payments where those rights are exercised.

(4) "Rules" means general rules of the FCA.

(5) "Specified" means specified in the rules.]

NOTES

Substituted as noted to s 137A at **[7.294]**.

[7.297]

[137C FCA general rules: cost of credit and duration of credit agreements

(1) The power of the FCA to make general rules includes power to make rules prohibiting authorised persons from—

(a) entering into a regulated credit agreement that provides for—

Part 7 Financial Services Acts

(i) the payment by the borrower of charges of a specified description, or
(ii) the payment by the borrower over the duration of the agreement of charges that, taken with the charges paid under one or more other agreements which are treated by the rules as being connected with it, exceed, or are capable of exceeding, a specified amount;
(b) imposing charges of a specified description or exceeding a specified amount on a person who is the borrower under a regulated credit agreement;
(c) entering into a regulated credit agreement that—
(i) is capable of remaining in force after the end of a specified period,
(ii) when taken with one or more other regulated credit agreements which are treated by the rules as being connected with it, would be capable of remaining in force after the end of a specified period, or
(iii) is treated by the rules as being connected with a number of previous regulated credit agreements that exceeds a specified maximum;
(d) exercising the rights of the lender under a regulated credit agreement (as a person for the time being entitled to exercise them) in a way that enables the agreement to remain in force after the end of a specified period or enables the imposition on the borrower of charges within paragraph (a)(i) or (ii).

[(1A) The FCA must make rules by virtue of subsection (1)(a)(ii) and (b) in relation to one or more specified descriptions of regulated credit agreement appearing to the FCA to involve the provision of high-cost short-term credit, with a view to securing an appropriate degree of protection for borrowers against excessive charges.

(1B) Before the FCA publishes a draft of any rules to be made by virtue of subsection (1)(a)(ii) or (b), it must consult the Treasury.]

(2) "Charges" means charges payable, by way of interest or otherwise, in connection with the provision of credit under the regulated credit agreement, whether or not the agreement itself makes provision for them and whether or not the person to whom they are payable is a party to the regulated credit agreement or an authorised person.

(3) "The borrower" includes—
(a) any person providing a guarantee or indemnity under the regulated credit agreement, and
(b) a person to whom the rights and duties of the borrower under the regulated credit agreement or a person falling within paragraph (a) have passed by assignment or operation of law.

(4) In relation to an agreement entered into or obligation imposed in contravention of the rules, the rules may—
(a) provide for the agreement or obligation to be unenforceable against any person or specified person;
(b) provide for the recovery of any money or other property paid or transferred under the agreement or other obligation by any person or specified person;
(c) provide for the payment of compensation for any loss sustained by any person or specified person as a result of paying or transferring any money or other property under the agreement or obligation.

(5) The provision that may be made as a result of subsection (4) includes provision corresponding to that made by section 30 (enforceability of agreements resulting from unlawful communications).

(6) A credit agreement is a contract of the kind mentioned in paragraph 23 of Schedule 2, other than one under which the obligation of the borrower to repay is secured on land: and a credit agreement is a "regulated credit agreement" if any of the following is a regulated activity—
(a) entering into or administering the agreement;
(b) exercising or being able to exercise the rights of the lender under the agreement.

(7) In this section—
(a) "specified amount" means an amount specified in or determined in accordance with the rules;
(b) "specified period" means a period of a duration specified in or determined in accordance with the rules;
(c) "specified person" means a person of a description specified in the rules;
(d) subject to that, "specified" means specified in the rules.]

NOTES

Substituted as noted to s 137A at **[7.294]**.

Sub-ss (1A), (1B): inserted by the Financial Services (Banking Reform) Act 2013, s 131(1), as from 18 February 2014.

[7.298]

[137D FCA general rules: product intervention

(1) The power of the FCA to make general rules includes power to make such rules ("product intervention rules") prohibiting authorised persons from doing anything mentioned in subsection (2) as appear to it to be necessary or expedient for the purpose of advancing—
(a) the consumer protection objective or the competition objective, or
(b) if the Treasury by order provide for this paragraph to apply, the integrity objective.

(2) Those prohibited things are—
(a) entering into specified agreements with any person or specified person;
(b) entering into specified agreements with any person or specified person unless requirements specified in the rules have been satisfied;
(c) doing anything that would or might result in the entering into of specified agreements by persons or specified persons, or the holding by them of a beneficial or other kind of economic interest in specified agreements;
(d) doing anything within paragraph (c) unless requirements specified in the rules have been satisfied.

(3) "Specified agreements" means agreements of a description specified in general rules made by the FCA.

(4) "Specified persons" means persons of a description specified in general rules made by the FCA.

(5) It is of no relevance—
(a) whether the entering into of a specified agreement itself constitutes the carrying on of a regulated activity, or
(b) whether, in a case within subsection (2)(c) or (d), the specified agreements are with the authorised persons concerned or anyone else.

(6) The requirements that may be specified under subsection (2)(b) or (d) include in particular—
(a) requirements as to the terms and conditions that are to be, or are not to be, included in specified or other agreements, and

(b) requirements limiting invitations or inducements to enter into specified or other agreements to those made to specified persons.

(7) In relation to contraventions of product intervention rules, the rules may—

(a) provide for a relevant agreement or obligation to be unenforceable against any person or specified person;

(b) provide for the recovery of any money or other property paid or transferred under a relevant agreement or obligation by any person or specified person;

(c) provide for the payment of compensation for any loss sustained by any person or specified person as a result of paying or transferring any money or other property under a relevant agreement or obligation.

(8) "A relevant agreement or obligation" means—

(a) a specified agreement;

(b) an agreement entered into in contravention of any rule made as a result of subsection (2)(c) or (d);

(c) an obligation to which a person is subject as a result of exercising a right conferred by an agreement within paragraph (a) or (b) of this subsection.

(9) The provision that may be made as a result of subsection (7) includes provision corresponding to that made by section 30 (enforceability of agreements resulting from unlawful communications).

(10) In this section—

(a) any reference to entering into an agreement includes inviting or inducing persons to enter into an agreement, and

(b) any reference to an agreement includes an arrangement.]

NOTES

Substituted as noted to s 137A at **[7.294]**.

Orders: the Financial Services and Markets Act 2000 (Regulated Activities) (Amendment) Order 2017, SI 2017/488 (art 13 of which provides that the integrity objective (see s 1D *ante*) applies for the purposes of this section).

[7.299]

[137E Orders under s 137D(1)(b)

(1) No order may be made under section 137D(1)(b) unless—

(a) a draft of the order has been laid before Parliament and approved by a resolution of each House, or

(b) subsection (3) applies.

(2) Subsection (3) applies if an order under section 137D(1)(b) contains a statement that the Treasury are of the opinion that, by reason of urgency, it is necessary to make the order without a draft being so laid and approved.

(3) Where this subsection applies the order—

(a) must be laid before Parliament after being made, and

(b) ceases to have effect at the end of the relevant period unless before the end of that period the order is approved by a resolution of each House of Parliament (but without that affecting anything done under the order or the power to make a new order).

(4) The "relevant period" is a period of 28 days beginning with the day on which the order is made.

(5) In calculating the relevant period no account is to be taken of any time during which Parliament is dissolved or prorogued or during which both Houses are adjourned for more than 4 days.]

NOTES

Substituted as noted to s 137A at **[7.294]**.

[7.300]

[137F Rules requiring participation in benchmark

(1) The power of the FCA to make general rules includes power to make rules requiring authorised persons to take specified steps in connection with the setting by a specified person of a specified benchmark.

(2) The rules may in particular—

(a) require authorised persons to whom the rules apply to provide information of a specified kind, or expressions of opinion as to specified matters, to persons determined in accordance with the rules;

(b) make provision about the form in which and the time by which any information or expression of opinion is to be provided;

(c) make provision by reference to any code or other document published by the person responsible for the setting of the benchmark or by any other person determined in accordance with the rules, as the code or other document has effect from time to time.

(3) Rules making provision of the kind mentioned in subsection (2)(c) may provide that the code or other document is to be capable of affecting obligations imposed by the rules only if specified requirements are met in relation to it.

(4) In this section—

["benchmark" means a benchmark within the meaning of section 22 . . . (6A);]

"specified" means specified in or determined in accordance with the rules.]

NOTES

Substituted as noted to s 137A at **[7.294]**.

Sub-s (4): definition "benchmark" substituted by the Financial Services and Markets Act 2000 (Benchmarks) Regulations 2018, SI 2018/135, reg 43(a), as from 27 February 2018. The words omitted from that definition were repealed by reg 43(b) of the 2018 Regulations, as from 1 May 2020.

[7.301]

[137FA FCA general rules: disclosure of information about pension scheme transaction costs etc

(1) The FCA must make general rules requiring information about some or all of the transaction costs of a relevant scheme to be given to some or all of the persons mentioned in subsection (2).

(2) Those persons are—

(a) members of the scheme,

(b) spouses or civil partners of members, and

(c) persons within the application of the scheme and qualifying or prospectively qualifying for its benefits.

(3) The FCA must make general rules requiring the publication of information about—

(a) some or all of the transaction costs of a relevant scheme, and

(b) some or all of the [other] administration charges imposed on members of a relevant scheme.

(4) Rules made by virtue of subsection (3) may require other relevant information to be published along with information about transaction costs or [other] administration charges in relation to a scheme.

(5) "Other relevant information" means other information which would or may assist in making comparisons between those costs or charges and costs or charges in relation to other schemes.

(6) Before the FCA publishes a draft of any rules to be made by virtue of this section, it must consult—

(a) the Secretary of State, and

(b) the Treasury.

(7) In determining what provision to include in the rules, the FCA must have regard to any regulations about the disclosure or publication of transaction costs or [other] administration charges that are for the time being in force under section 113 of the Pension Schemes Act 1993.

(8) In this section—

"administration charge" has the meaning given by paragraph 1(5) of Schedule 18 to the Pensions Act 2014;

["money purchase benefit" has the meaning given by section 181(1) of the Pension Schemes Act 1993;]

"money purchase scheme" has the meaning given by section 181(1) of the Pension Schemes Act 1993;

"personal pension scheme" has the meaning given by section 1 of the Pension Schemes Act 1993;

"relevant scheme" means a *money purchase scheme* that is—

(a) a personal pension scheme where direct payment arrangements (within the meaning of section 111A of the Pension Schemes Act 1993) exist in respect of one or more members of the scheme who are workers, or

(b) a personal pension scheme which is or has been registered under section 2 of the Welfare Reform and Pensions Act 1999 (stakeholder pension schemes);

"worker" means a person—

(a) who is a worker for the purposes of Part 1 of the Pensions Act 2008, or

(b) to whom a provision of Part 1 of that Act applies as if the person were a worker because of a provision of Chapter 8 of that Part;

but for the purposes of paragraph (b), ignore section 92 of that Act.]

NOTES

Inserted by the Pensions Act 2014, s 44(2), as from 18 September 2017.

Sub-ss (3), (4), (7): word "other" in square brackets inserted by the Pension Schemes Act 2021, s 127(4), as from 1 October 2021.

Sub-s (8): definition "money purchase benefit" inserted, definition "money purchase scheme" repealed, and for the words in italics in the definition "relevant scheme" there are substituted the words "scheme under which all the benefits that may be provided are money purchase benefits and", by the Pension Schemes Act 2015, s 46, Sch 2, paras 20, 21, as from a day to be appointed.

[7.302]

[137FAA FCA general rules: pensions dashboards

(1) The FCA must make general rules imposing requirements on specified authorised persons with respect to—

(a) providing pensions information by means of—

(i) a qualifying pensions dashboard service;

(ii) the pensions dashboard service provided by the Money and Pensions Service;

(b) facilitating the provision of pensions information by means of—

(i) a qualifying pensions dashboard service;

(ii) the pensions dashboard service provided by the Money and Pensions Service.

(2) In this section "pensions information" means, in relation to a personal or stakeholder pension scheme, information of a description specified in rules made by virtue of subsection (1), which may include in particular—

(a) information relating to—

(i) the constitution of the scheme,

(ii) the administration and finances of the scheme,

(iii) the rights and obligations that arise or may arise under the scheme,

(iv) the pensions and other benefits an entitlement to which would be likely to accrue to a member, or be capable of being secured by a member, in respect of the rights that may arise under the scheme, and

(v) other matters relevant to personal or stakeholder pension schemes in general or to personal or stakeholder pension schemes of a description to which the scheme belongs;

(b) information as regards the position of an individual in relation to the scheme.

(3) Rules made by virtue of subsection (1) may, in particular, impose requirements about—

(a) the persons to whom pensions information must be provided;

(b) the circumstances in which pensions information must be provided;

(c) the steps to be taken before pensions information may be provided;

(d) the manner and form in which pensions information must be provided;

(e) the time within which pensions information must be provided;

(f) the way in which pensions information must be held.

(4) Rules made by virtue of subsection (1) may require specified authorised persons to comply with standards, specifications or technical requirements published from time to time by—

(a) the Secretary of State,

(b) the Money and Pensions Service, or

(c) a person specified or of a description specified in the rules.

(5) Rules made by virtue of subsection (1) may include provision under which a determination may fall to be made by—

(a) the Secretary of State,
(b) the Money and Pensions Service, or
(c) a person specified or of a description specified in the rules.

(6) Rules made by virtue of subsection (1) may require specified authorised persons to provide information specified in the rules about their carrying out of requirements specified in the rules to—
(a) the FCA,
(b) the Money and Pensions Service, or
(c) a person specified or of a description specified in the rules.

(7) Rules made by virtue of subsection (1) may require specified authorised persons to have regard, in complying with requirements specified in the rules, to guidance issued from time to time by a person specified or of a description specified in the rules.

(8) In determining what provision to include in the rules, the FCA must have regard to any regulations that are for the time being in force under—
(a) section 238D of the Pensions Act 2004, or
(b) Article 215D of the Pensions (Northern Ireland) Order 2005 (SI 2005/255 (NI 1)).]

NOTES
Commencement: to be appointed.
Inserted by the Pension Schemes Act 2021, s 121(2), as from a day to be appointed.

[7.303]
[137FAB Pensions dashboards: further provision

(1) General rules made by virtue of section 137FAA(1) may make provision about—
(a) how pensions information is to be provided, including provision about the use of intermediaries;
(b) the involvement of specified authorised persons in the arrangements for dealing with requests for information about pensions.

(2) The provision made by virtue of subsection (1) may, in particular, require—
(a) the use of electronic communications;
(b) the use of facilities or services specified or of a description specified in the rules;
(c) the provision of assistance in connection with the establishment, maintenance or management of such facilities or services;
(d) participation in, or compliance with, arrangements for establishing, maintaining or managing such facilities or services.

(3) The facilities and services for which provision may be made by virtue of subsection (2)(b) may include facilities or services with functions relating to—
(a) the transmission of information,
(b) verifying the identity of a person,
(c) identifying the occupational or personal pension scheme or schemes (as defined in section 1 of the Pension Schemes Act 1993 or the Pension Schemes (Northern Ireland) Act 1993) under which pensions are payable to or in respect of a particular individual,
(d) authenticating information transmitted by means of electronic communications, or
(e) ensuring the security of information transmitted by means of electronic communications.

(4) Rules made by virtue of subsection (2)(b) may impose requirements as regards a facility or service, including requirements about—
(a) compliance with standards, specifications or technical requirements published from time to time by—
  (i) the Secretary of State,
  (ii) the Money and Pensions Service, or
  (iii) a person specified or of a description specified in the rules;
(b) the provider of the facility or service being a person approved from time to time by—
  (i) the Secretary of State,
  (ii) the Money and Pensions Service, or
  (iii) a person specified or of a description specified in the rules.

(5) Rules made by virtue of subsection (2)(d) may, in particular, require specified authorised persons—
(a) to cooperate with the Money and Pensions Service or a person specified or of a description specified in the rules;
(b) to coordinate activities with the Money and Pensions Service or a person specified or of a description specified in the rules.

(6) Except as provided by subsection (7), general rules made by virtue of section 137FAA(1) may provide for the processing of personal data in accordance with the rules not to be in breach of—
(a) any obligation of confidence owed by the person processing the personal data, or
(b) any other restriction on the processing of personal data (however imposed).

(7) General rules made by virtue of section 137FAA(1) are not to be read as authorising or requiring such processing of personal data as would contravene the data protection legislation (but in determining whether particular processing of data would do so, take into account the power conferred or duty imposed by the provision of the rules in question).]

NOTES
Commencement: to be appointed.
Inserted by the Pension Schemes Act 2021, s 121(2), as from a day to be appointed.

[7.304]
[137FAC Sections 137FAA and 137FAB: supplementary

(1) Before the FCA publishes a draft of any general rules to be made by virtue of section 137FAA, it must consult—
(a) the Secretary of State, and
(b) the Treasury.

Part 7 Financial Services Acts

(2) Section 137FAA is not to be treated as requiring the FCA to make general rules by virtue of section 137FAA that come into force before regulations made under section 238D of the Pensions Act 2004 come into force.
(3) Section 137FAA is not to be treated as requiring the FCA to exercise the power to make general rules by virtue of section 137FAA in relation to every case to which the power extends.
(4) A reference in sections 137FAA and 137FAB to the Money and Pensions Service includes a reference to a person with whom arrangements are made under section 5(1), (2) or (3) of the Financial Guidance and Claims Act 2018.
(5) In sections 137FAA and 137FAB—

"the data protection legislation" has the same meaning as in the Data Protection Act 2018 (see section 3 of that Act);

"pensions dashboard service" means—

(a) a pensions dashboard service within the meaning of section 238A of the Pensions Act 2004, or
(b) a pensions dashboard service within the meaning of Article 215A of the Pensions (Northern Ireland) Order 2005 (SI 2005/255 (NI 1));

"personal data" has the same meaning as in the Data Protection Act 2018 (see section 3 of that Act);

"personal pension scheme" means a personal pension scheme within the meaning of an order under section 22 (except in section 137FAB(3)(c));

"qualifying pensions dashboard service" means a pensions dashboard service that satisfies—

(a) such requirements as may be prescribed by regulations under section 238A of the Pensions Act 2004, or
(b) such requirements as may be prescribed by regulations under Article 215A of the Pensions (Northern Ireland) Order 2005;

"specified authorised person" means an authorised person of a description specified in general rules made by virtue of section 137FAA;

"stakeholder pension scheme" has the meaning given by—

(a) section 1 of the Welfare Reform and Pensions Act 1999, in relation to England and Wales and Scotland;
(b) Article 3 of the Welfare Reform and Pensions (Northern Ireland) Order 1999 (SI 1999/3147 (NI 11)), in relation to Northern Ireland.]

NOTES

Commencement: to be appointed.
Inserted by the Pension Schemes Act 2021, s 121(2), as from a day to be appointed.

[7.305]

[137FB FCA general rules: disclosure of information about the availability of pensions guidance

(1) The FCA must make general rules requiring information about the availability of pensions guidance to be given by the trustees or managers of a relevant pension scheme to members of the scheme, and survivors of members of the scheme, with subsisting rights in respect of any flexible benefits.
[(1A) The FCA must also make general rules requiring the trustees or managers of a relevant pension scheme to take the steps mentioned in subsections (1B) and (1C) in relation to an application from a member or survivor—

(a) to transfer any rights accrued under the scheme, or
(b) to start receiving benefits provided by the scheme.

(1B) As part of the application process, the trustees or managers must ensure that—

(a) the member or survivor is referred to appropriate pensions guidance, and
(b) the member or survivor is provided with an explanation of the nature and purpose of such guidance.

(1C) Before proceeding with the application, the trustees or managers must ensure that the member or survivor has either received appropriate pensions guidance or has opted out of receiving such guidance.
(1D) The rules may—

(a) specify what constitutes appropriate pensions guidance;
(b) make further provision about how the trustees or managers must comply with the duties in subsections (1B) and (1C) (such as provision about methods of communication and time limits);
(c) make further provision about how, and to whom, a member or survivor may indicate that they have received or opted out of receiving appropriate pensions guidance for the purposes of subsection (1C);
(d) specify what the duties of the trustees or managers are in the situation where a member or survivor does not respond to a communication that is made for the purposes of complying with the duty in subsection (1C);
(e) provide for exceptions to the duties in subsections (1B) and (1C) in specified cases.]

(2) Before the FCA publishes a draft of any rules to be made by virtue of [subsection (1)], it must consult—

(a) the Secretary of State, and
(b) the Treasury.

[(2A) Before the FCA publishes a draft of any rules to be made by virtue of subsection (1A), it must consult—

(a) the Secretary of State, and
(b) the Money and Pensions Service.]

(3) In determining what provision to include in [rules to be made by virtue of subsection (1)], the FCA must have regard to any regulations that are for the time being in force under section 113 of the Pension Schemes Act 1993 concerning the giving of information about the availability of pensions guidance to members of pension schemes, and survivors of members of pension schemes, with subsisting rights in respect of any flexible benefits.
[(3A) In determining what provision to include in rules to be made by virtue of subsection (1A), the FCA must have regard to any regulations that are for the time being in force under section 113B of the Pension Schemes Act 1993 (occupational pension schemes: requirements to refer members to guidance etc).]
(4) In this section—

"flexible benefit" has the meaning given by section 74 of the Pension Schemes Act 2015;

["pensions guidance" means information or guidance provided by any person in pursuance of the requirements mentioned in section 4 of the Financial Guidance and Claims Act 2018 (information etc about flexible benefits under pension schemes);]

"relevant pension scheme" means a pension scheme set up by a person with permission under this Act to establish—

(a) a personal pension scheme within the meaning of an order under section 22, or

(b) a stakeholder pension scheme within the meaning of such an order;

"subsisting right" has the meaning given by section 76 of the Pension Schemes Act 2015;

"survivor" has the meaning given by section 76 of the Pension Schemes Act 2015."

NOTES

Inserted by the Pension Schemes Act 2015, s 47, Sch 3, paras 1, 6, as from 3 March 2015 (for further provision with regard to the FCA's duty to consult, see Sch 3, para 18 to the 2015 Act).

Sub-ss (1A)–(1D): inserted by the Financial Guidance and Claims Act 2018, s 18(1), (2), as from 5 July 2021 (for the purpose of making rules), and as from 1 June 2022 (otherwise).

Sub-s (2): words in square brackets substituted by the Financial Guidance and Claims Act 2018, s 18(1), (3), as from 5 July 2021.

Sub-s (2A): inserted by the Financial Guidance and Claims Act 2018, s 18(1), (4), as from 5 July 2021. Note that this s 18(4) of the 2018 Act was amended by the Financial Guidance and Claims Act 2018 (Naming and Consequential Amendments) Regulations 2019, SI 2019/383, reg 3, Schedule, Pt 1, para 11, as from 6 April 2019; and the effect of the amendment has been incorporated in the text set out above.

Sub-s (3): words in square brackets substituted by the Financial Guidance and Claims Act 2018, s 18(1), (5), as from 5 July 2021.

Sub-s (3A): inserted by the Financial Guidance and Claims Act 2018, s 18(1), (6), as from 5 July 2021.

Sub-s (4): the definition "pensions guidance" was substituted by the Financial Guidance and Claims Act 2018, s 18(1), (7), as from 1 January 2019.

[7.306]

[137FBA FCA general rules: advice about transferring or otherwise dealing with annuity payments

(1) The FCA must make general rules requiring specified authorised persons to check that an individual—

(a) who has a right to payments under a relevant annuity, and

(b) if the Treasury make regulations under subsection (3), who is not an exempt person by virtue of those regulations,

has received appropriate advice before transferring or otherwise dealing with the right to those payments.

(2) The reference in subsection (1) to a right to payments under a relevant annuity does not include a contingent right to such payments.

(3) The Treasury may by regulations provide that an individual whose financial circumstances meet criteria specified in the regulations is an exempt person for the purposes of subsection (1)(b).

(4) Regulations made under subsection (3) may (amongst other things) specify criteria based on the proportion of the individual's financial resources that is represented by the payments under the relevant annuity or the value of that annuity.

(5) The rules made by virtue of subsection (1) may include provision—

(a) about what specified authorised persons must do to check that an individual has received appropriate advice for the purposes of those rules;

(b) about when the check must be carried out.

(6) For the purposes of this section—

(a) "relevant annuity" means an annuity specified (by type, value or otherwise) as a relevant annuity in regulations made by the Treasury;

(b) "appropriate advice" means advice specified (by reference to the person giving the advice or otherwise) as appropriate advice in regulations made by the Treasury;

(c) "specified authorised person" means an authorised person of a description specified in rules made by virtue of subsection (1).

(7) If regulations under subsection (3) or (6)(a) make provision about the value of an annuity, the regulations may also make provision about the basis on which the value of an annuity is to be calculated.]

NOTES

Inserted by the Bank of England and Financial Services Act 2016, s 33(1), (2), as from 6 July 2016.

[7.307]

[137FBB FCA general rules: early exit pension charges

(1) The FCA must make general rules prohibiting authorised persons from—

(a) imposing specified early exit charges on members of relevant pension schemes, and

(b) including in relevant pension schemes provision for the imposition of specified early exit charges on members of such schemes.

(2) The rules must be made with a view to securing, so far as is reasonably possible, an appropriate degree of protection for members of relevant pension schemes against early exit charges being a deterrent on taking, converting or transferring benefits under the schemes.

(3) The rules may specify early exit charges by reference to charges of a specified class or description, or by reference to charges which exceed a specified amount.

(4) The rules made by virtue of subsection (1)(a) must prohibit the imposition of the charges after those rules come into force, whether the relevant pension scheme was established before or after those rules (or this section) came into force.

(5) In relation to a charge which is imposed, or provision for the imposition of a charge which is included in a pension scheme, in contravention of the rules, the rules may (amongst other things)—

(a) provide for the obligation to pay the charge to be unenforceable or unenforceable to a specified extent;

(b) provide for the recovery of amounts paid in respect of the charge;

(c) provide for the payment of compensation for any losses incurred as a result of paying amounts in respect of the charge.

(6) Subject to subsection (8) an early exit charge, in relation to a member of a pension scheme, is a charge which—

(a) is imposed under the scheme when a member who has reached normal minimum pension age takes the action mentioned in subsection (7), but

(b) is only imposed, or only imposed to that extent, if the member takes that action before the member's expected retirement date.

(7) The action is the member taking benefits under the scheme, converting benefits under the scheme into different benefits or transferring benefits under the scheme to another pension scheme.

(8) The Treasury may by regulations specify matters that are not to be treated as early exit charges for the purposes of this section.

(9) For the purposes of this section—

"charge", in relation to a member of a pension scheme, includes a reduction in the value of the member's benefits under the scheme;

"expected retirement date", in relation to a member of a pension scheme, means the date determined by, or in accordance with, the scheme as the date on which the member's benefits under the scheme are expected to be taken;

"normal minimum pension age" has the same meaning as in section 279(1) of the Finance Act 2004;

"relevant pension scheme" has the same meaning as in section 137FB;

and a reference to benefits includes all or any part of those benefits.]

NOTES

Inserted by the Bank of England and Financial Services Act 2016, s 35(1), (2), as from 6 July 2016.

Regulations: the Financial Services and Markets Act 2000 (Early Exit Pension Charges) Regulations 2016, SI 2016/1079.

[7.308]

[137FC FCA rules: disclosure of information about the availability of financial guidance

(1) The FCA must make general rules requiring specified authorised persons to provide information about the availability of financial guidance to the descriptions of persons specified in the rules.

(2) The rules may specify the circumstances in which the duty to provide the information applies.

(3) Before the FCA publishes a draft of any rules to be made by virtue of this section, it must consult—

(a) the Secretary of State,

(b) the Treasury, and

(c) the [Money and Pensions Service].

(4) In this section—

"financial guidance" means information, guidance or advice provided in pursuance of the [Money and Pensions Service's] pensions guidance, debt advice or money guidance function (see section 3 of the Financial Guidance and Claims Act 2018);

"specified authorised person" means an authorised person of a description specified in rules made by virtue of this section.]

NOTES

Inserted by the Financial Guidance and Claims Act 2018, s 20, as from 1 January 2019.

Sub-ss (3), (4): words "Money and Pensions Service" in square brackets substituted by the Financial Guidance and Claims Act 2018 (Naming and Consequential Amendments) Regulations 2019, SI 2019/383, reg 3, Schedule, Pt 1, para 7(b), as from 6 April 2019.

[7.309]

[137FD FCA general rules: charges for claims management services

(1) The power of the FCA to make general rules includes power to make rules prohibiting authorised persons from—

(a) entering into a specified regulated claims management agreement that provides for the payment by a person of charges which, taken with charges payable under an agreement treated by the rules as being connected with the regulated claims management agreement (if any), are specified charges, and

(b) imposing specified charges on a person in connection with the provision of a service which is, or which is provided in connection with, a specified regulated claims management activity.

(2) The FCA must make rules by virtue of subsection (1) in relation to all regulated claims management agreements, and all regulated claims management activities, which concern claims in relation to financial products or services.

(3) The rules must be made with a view to securing an appropriate degree of protection against excessive charges for the provision of a service which is, or which is provided in connection with, a regulated claims management activity.

(4) The rules may specify charges by reference to charges of a specified class or description, or by reference to charges which exceed, or are capable of exceeding, a specified amount.

(5) In relation to an agreement entered into, or charge imposed, in contravention of the rules, the rules may (amongst other things)—

(a) provide for the agreement, or obligation to pay the charge, to be unenforceable or unenforceable to a specified extent;

(b) provide for the recovery of amounts paid under the agreement or obligation;

(c) provide for the payment of compensation for any losses incurred as a result of paying amounts under the agreement or obligation.

(6) The provision that may be made under subsection (5) includes provision corresponding to that made by section 30 (enforceability of agreements resulting from unlawful communications).

(7) In this section—

(a) "regulated claims management agreement" means an agreement, the entering into or performing of which by either party is a regulated claims management activity, and

(b) "specified" means specified in the rules, but "specified amount" means an amount specified in or determined in accordance with the rules.]

NOTES

Inserted by the Financial Guidance and Claims Act 2018, s 28(1), (2), as from 29 March 2019.

[7.310]

[137G The PRA's general rules

(1) The PRA may make such rules applying to PRA-authorised persons—

(a) with respect to the carrying on by them of regulated activities, or

(b) with respect to the carrying on by them of activities which are not regulated activities,

as appear to the PRA to be necessary or expedient for the purpose of advancing any of its objectives.

(2) Rules made under this section are referred to in this Act as the PRA's general rules.

(3) The PRA's general rules may make provision applying to PRA-authorised persons even though there is no relationship between the PRA-authorised persons to whom the rules will apply and the persons whose interests will be protected by the rules.

(4) The PRA's general rules may contain requirements which take into account, in the case of a PRA-authorised person who is a member of a group, any activity of another member of the group.

(5) . . .

[(6) The PRA's general rules may not modify, amend or revoke any retained direct EU legislation (except retained direct EU legislation which takes the form of PRA rules).]

[(7) Subsection (6) is subject to section 144H(2).]

NOTES

Substituted as noted to s 137A at **[7.294]**.

Sub-s (5): repealed by the EEA Passport Rights (Amendment, etc, and Transitional Provisions) (EU Exit) Regulations 2018, SI 2018/1149, reg 3, Schedule, Pt 1, paras 1, 10, as from IP completion day (as defined in the European Union (Withdrawal Agreement) Act 2020, s 39).

Sub-s (6): added by the Financial Regulators' Powers (Technical Standards etc) (Amendment etc) (EU Exit) Regulations 2018, SI 2018/1115, reg 7(1), (7), as from 26 October 2018.

Sub-s (7): added by the Financial Services Act 2021, s 5, Sch 3, Pt 3, para 7, as from 9 June 2021.

PRA Rules: see the Solvency 2 and Insurance (Amendment, etc) (EU Exit) Regulations 2019, SI 2019/407, reg 4 which provides that the provisions of Commission Delegated Regulation 2015/35/EU supplementing Directive 2009/138/EC of the European Parliament and of the Council on the taking-up and pursuit of the business of Insurance and Reinsurance (Solvency 2), specified in Schedule 3 to those Regulations are deemed to be rules made by the PRA under this section.

[7.311]

[137GA The PRA's general rules: Gibraltar

(1) The PRA's general rules may not make provision prohibiting a Gibraltar-based person from carrying on, or holding itself out as carrying on, an activity which it has a Schedule 2A permission to carry on in the United Kingdom.

(2) The Treasury may by regulations impose other limitations on what provision applying to Gibraltar-based persons with a Schedule 2A permission to carry on a regulated activity may be made in the PRA's general rules.

(3) Before making regulations under subsection (2), the Treasury must consult the PRA.]

NOTES

Commencement: to be appointed.

Inserted by the Financial Services Act 2021, s 22, Sch 8, para 6, as from a day to be appointed.

[7.312]

[137H General rules about remuneration

(1) This section applies where either regulator exercises its power to make general rules so as to make rules prohibiting persons, or persons of a specified description, from being remunerated in a specified way.

(2) The rules may—

(a) provide that any provision of an agreement that contravenes such a prohibition is void, and

(b) provide for the recovery of any payment made, or other property transferred, in pursuance of a provision that is void by virtue of paragraph (a).

(3) A provision that, at the time the rules are made, is contained in an agreement made before that time may not be rendered void under subsection (2)(a) unless it is subsequently amended so as to contravene a prohibition referred to in that subsection.]

NOTES

Substituted as noted to s 137A at **[7.294]**.

[7.313]

[137I Remuneration policies: Treasury direction to consider compliance

(1) This section applies where either regulator exercises its power to make general rules so as to make rules requiring authorised persons, or authorised persons of a description specified in the rules, to act in accordance with a remuneration policy.

(2) A "remuneration policy" is a policy about the remuneration by an authorised person of—

(a) officers,

(b) employees, or

(c) other persons,

of a description specified in the rules.

(3) The Treasury may direct the regulator to consider whether the remuneration policies of authorised persons specified in the direction (or of authorised persons of a description so specified) comply with requirements imposed by rules made by that regulator as to the contents of the policies.

(4) Before giving a direction under subsection (3), the Treasury must consult the regulator concerned.

(5) If the regulator considers that a remuneration policy of an authorised person fails to make provision which complies with the requirements mentioned in subsection (3), the regulator must take such steps as it considers appropriate to deal with the failure.

(6) The steps that the regulator may take include requiring the remuneration policy to be revised.

(7) "Authorised person", in relation to the PRA, means PRA-authorised person.]

NOTES

Substituted as noted to s 137A at **[7.294]**.

[7.314]

[137J Rules about recovery plans: duty to consult

(1) Before either regulator prepares a draft of any general rules that require [a] relevant person (or [a] relevant person of a specified description) to prepare a recovery plan, the regulator must consult [the Treasury].

[(1A) The FCA must also consult the Bank of England.]

[(2) "Relevant person" means—

(a) an institution authorised in the UK; or

(b) a qualifying parent undertaking within the meaning given by section 192B.

(3) A "recovery plan" is a document which provides for measures to be taken—

(a) by an institution authorised in the UK which is not part of a group, following a significant deterioration of the financial position of the institution, in order to restore its financial position; or

(b) in relation to a group, to achieve the stabilisation of the group as a whole, or of any institution within the group, where the group or institution is in a situation of financial stress, in order to address or remove the causes of the financial stress and restore the financial position of the group or institution.

(4) For the purposes of subsection (3)(a) the definition of "group" in section 421 applies with the omission of subsection (1)(e) and (f) of that section.]

(6) In this section—

"authorised person", in relation to the PRA, means PRA-authorised person;

["institution" means—

(a) a credit institution, other than an entity mentioned in Article 2.5 of the capital requirements directive; or

[(b) a designated investment firm as defined in Article 4(1)(2AA) of the capital requirements regulation;]]

"institution authorised in the UK" means [an authorised person who is]—

(a) a bank within the meaning given by section 2 of the Banking Act 2009;

(b) a building society within the meaning given in section 119 of the Building Societies Act 1986; or

(c) an investment firm within the meaning given by section 258A of the Banking Act 2009;]

"specified" means specified in the rules.]

NOTES

Substituted as noted to s 137A at **[7.294]**.

The words "the Treasury" in square brackets in sub-s (1) were substituted, and sub-s (1A) was inserted, by the Bank of England and Financial Services Act 2016, s 16, Sch 2, Pt 2, paras 26, 33, as from 1 March 2017.

The other words in square brackets in sub-s (1) were substituted, sub-ss (2)–(4) were substituted (for the original sub-ss (2)–(5)), and the definitions "institution" and "institution authorised in the UK" in sub-s (6) were inserted, by the Bank Recovery and Resolution (No 2) Order 2014, SI 2014/3348, art 226, Sch 3, Pt 1, paras 1, 2, as from 10 January 2015.

The definition "institution" in sub-s (6) was substituted, and the words in square brackets in the definition "institution authorised in the UK" in that subsection were substituted, by the Financial Services and Markets Act 2000 (Amendment) (EU Exit) Regulations 2019, SI 2019/632, regs 34, 35, as from IP completion day (as defined in the European Union (Withdrawal Agreement) Act 2020, s 39).

Para (b) of the definition "institution" in sub-s (6) was substituted by the Financial Services Act 2021 (Prudential Regulation of Credit Institutions and Investment Firms) (Consequential Amendments and Miscellaneous Provisions) Regulations 2021, SI 2021/1376, reg 4(6), as from 1 January 2022.

[7.315]

[137K [Rules about resolution packs: duty to consult]

(1) Before [either regulator] prepares a draft of any general rules that require [a] relevant person (or [a] relevant person of a specified description) to prepare a [resolution pack], [the regulator] must consult [the Treasury].

[(1A) The FCA must also consult the Bank of England.]

[(2) "Relevant person" has the same meaning as in section 137J(2).]

(3) A "[resolution pack]" is a document containing information within subsection (4) or (5).

(4) Information is within this subsection if it relates to action to be taken in the event of—

(a) circumstances arising in which it is likely that the business (or any part of the business) of an authorised person will fail, or

(b) the failure of the business (or any part of the business) of an authorised person.

(5) Information is within this subsection if it would facilitate anything falling to be done by any person in consequence of that failure.

(6) An example of information within subsection (5) is information that, in the event of that failure, would facilitate—

(a) planning by the Treasury in relation to the possible exercise of any of its powers under Part 1 of the Banking Act 2009, or

(b) planning by the Bank of England in relation to the possible exercise of any of its powers under Part 1, 2 or 3 of that Act.]

[(7) In this section "authorised person", in relation to the PRA, means PRA-authorised person.]

NOTES

Substituted as noted to s 137A at **[7.294]**.

The words "the Treasury" in square brackets in sub-s (1) were substituted, and sub-s (1A) was inserted, by the Bank of England and Financial Services Act 2016, s 16, Sch 2, Pt 2, paras 26, 34, as from 1 March 2017.

The section heading was substituted, the other words in square brackets in sub-s (1) were substituted, sub-s (2) was substituted, the words in square brackets in sub-s (3) were substituted, and sub-s (7) was added, by the Bank Recovery and Resolution (No 2) Order 2014, SI 2014/3348, art 226, Sch 3, Pt 1, paras 1, 3, as from 10 January 2015.

[7.316]

[137L Interpretation of sections 137J and 137K

(1) This section has effect for the interpretation of sections 137J and 137K.

(2) References to the taking of action include the taking of action by—

(a) the authorised person,

(b) any other person in the same group as the authorised person, or

(c) a partnership of which the authorised person is a member.

(3) In subsection (2)(b) the definition of "group" in section 421 applies with the omission of subsection (1)(e) and (f) of that section.

(4) References to the business of an authorised person include the business of—

(a) any person in the same group as the authorised person, and

(b) a partnership of which the authorised person is a member.

(5) For the purposes of section 137K the cases in which the business (or any part of the business) of the authorised person ("A") is to be regarded as having failed include those where—

(a) A enters insolvency,

(b) any of the stabilisation options in Part 1 of the Banking Act 2009 is achieved in relation to A, or

(c) A falls to be taken for the purposes of the compensation scheme to be unable, or likely to be unable, to satisfy claims against A.

(6) In subsection (5)(a) "insolvency" includes—

(a) bankruptcy,

(b) liquidation,

(c) bank insolvency,

(d) administration,

(e) bank administration,

(f) receivership,

(g) a composition between A and A's creditors, and

(h) a scheme of arrangement of A's affairs.]

NOTES

Substituted as noted to s 137A at **[7.294]**.

137M (*Originally substituted as noted to s 137A ante. Subsequently repealed by the Bank Recovery and Resolution (No 2) Order 2014, SI 2014/3348, art 226, Sch 3, Pt 1, paras 1, 4, as from 10 January 2015.*).

[7.317]

[137N Recovery plans and [resolution packs]: restriction on duty of confidence

(1) A contractual or other requirement imposed on a person ("P") to keep information in confidence does not apply if—

(a) the information is or may be relevant to anything required to be done as a result of a requirement imposed by general rules made by either regulator to prepare a recovery plan or a [resolution pack],

(b) an authorised person or a skilled person requests or requires P to provide the information for the purpose of securing that those things are done, and

(c) the regulator in question has approved the making of the request or the imposition of the requirement before it is made or imposed.

(2) An authorised person [or a qualifying parent undertaking] may provide information (whether received under subsection (1) or otherwise) that would otherwise be subject to a contractual or other requirement to keep it in confidence if it is provided for the purposes of anything required to be done as a result of a requirement imposed by general rules to prepare a recovery plan or a [resolution pack].

(3) In this section, references to preparing a recovery plan or a [resolution pack] include—

(a) keeping [that plan or pack] up to date, and

(b) collecting specified information for the purposes of [that plan or pack].

(4) In this section, references to a skilled person are to a person appointed in accordance with section 166A.

(5) In this section—

"authorised person", in relation to rules of the PRA, means a PRA-authorised person;

["qualifying parent undertaking" means—

(a) a qualifying parent undertaking within the meaning given by section 192B; . . .

(b) . . .]

"specified" means specified in the rules.]

NOTES

Substituted as noted to s 137A at **[7.294]**.

All words in square brackets (including those in the section heading) were substituted or inserted by the Bank Recovery and Resolution (No 2) Order 2014, SI 2014/3348, art 226, Sch 3, Pt 1, paras 1, 5, as from 10 January 2015.

In the definition "qualifying parent undertaking" in sub-s (5), para (b) and the preceding word were repealed by the Financial Services and Markets Act 2000 (Amendment) (EU Exit) Regulations 2019, SI 2019/632, regs 34, 36, as from IP completion day (as defined in the European Union (Withdrawal Agreement) Act 2020, s 39).

[Specific rule-making powers

[7.318]

137O Threshold condition code

(1) Either regulator may make rules supplementing any of the conditions for the time being set out in or specified under Schedule 6 that is expressed to be relevant to the discharge of that regulator's functions.

(2) Rules made under this section by a regulator are referred to as that regulator's "threshold condition code".

(3) A threshold condition code may in particular—

(a) specify requirements which a person must satisfy in order to be regarded as satisfying a particular condition in relation to any regulated activities;

(b) specify matters which are, or may be, or are not, relevant in determining whether a person satisfies a particular condition in relation to any regulated activities.

(4) Except where a regulator's threshold condition code so provides, it is not to be regarded as limiting the matters that are, or may be, relevant in determining whether a person satisfies a particular condition in relation to any regulated activities.

(5) A threshold condition code cannot impose obligations that are enforceable against authorised persons otherwise than through the threshold conditions.]

NOTES

Substituted as noted to s 137A at **[7.294]**.

[7.319]

[137P Control of information rules

(1) Either regulator may make rules ("control of information rules") about the disclosure and use of information held by an authorised person ("A").

(2) Control of information rules may—

(a) require the withholding of information which A would otherwise be required to disclose to a person ("B") for or with whom A does business in the course of carrying on any regulated or other activity;

(b) specify circumstances in which A may withhold information which A would otherwise be required to disclose to B;

(c) require A not to use for the benefit of B information—

(i) which is held by A, and

(ii) which A would otherwise be required to use for the benefit of B;

(d) specify circumstances in which A may decide not to use for the benefit of B information within paragraph (c).]

NOTES

Substituted as noted to s 137A at **[7.294]**.

[7.320]

[137Q Price stabilising rules

(1) The FCA may make rules ("price stabilising rules") as to—

(a) the circumstances and manner in which,

(b) the conditions subject to which, and

(c) the time when or the period during which,

action may be taken for the purpose of stabilising the price of investments of specified kinds.

(2) Price stabilising rules—

(a) are to be made so as to apply only to authorised persons;

[(aa) must not apply to transactions, orders, behaviour, actions or omissions to which the market abuse regulation applies;]

(b) may make different provision in relation to different kinds of investment.

[(3) The FCA may make rules which, for the purposes of the relevant exemption provisions, treat a person who acts or engages in conduct in conformity with specified provisions as acting, or engaging in that conduct, in conformity with the relevant provisions of Article 5 (exemption for buy-back programmes and stabilisation) of the market abuse regulation.

(3A) "Specified provisions" means such provisions—

(a) corresponding to the relevant provisions of Article 5 of the market abuse regulation, and

(b) made by a body or authority outside the [United Kingdom] as may be specified in rules made by the FCA,

as may be specified in rules made by the FCA.]

(4) "The relevant exemption provisions" are the following provisions of the Financial Services Act 2012—

(a) [section 90(9)(d)];

(b) [section 91(4)(c)].

[(5) In this section references to Article 5 of the market abuse regulation include—

(a) any technical standards originally adopted or made under that Article which are retained direct EU legislation, and

(b) any technical standards made under that Article by the FCA.]]

NOTES

Substituted as noted to s 137A at **[7.294]**.

Sub-s (2): para (aa) inserted by the Financial Services and Markets Act 2000 (Market Abuse) Regulations 2016, SI 2016/680, reg 10(1), (5), as from 3 July 2016.

Sub-ss (3), (3A): substituted (for the original sub-s (3)) by SI 2016/680, reg 10(1), (5), as from 3 July 2016. Words in square brackets in sub-s (3A) substituted by the Financial Services and Markets Act 2000 (Amendment) (EU Exit) Regulations 2019, SI 2019/632, regs 34, 37, as from IP completion day (as defined in the European Union (Withdrawal Agreement) Act 2020, s 39).

Sub-s (4): words in square brackets substituted by SI 2016/680, reg 10(1), (5), as from 3 July 2016.

Sub-s (5): originally added by SI 2016/680, reg 10(1), (5), as from 3 July 2016. Subsequently substituted by SI 2019/632, regs 34, 37, as from IP completion day (as defined in the European Union (Withdrawal Agreement) Act 2020, s 39).

[7.321]

[137R Financial promotion rules

(1) The FCA may make rules applying to authorised persons about the communication by them, or their approval of the communication by others, of invitations or inducements—

(a) to engage in investment activity, . . .

[(aa) to engage in claims management activity, or]

(b) to participate in a collective investment scheme.

(2) Rules under this section may, in particular, make provision about the form and content of communications.

(3) Subsection (1) applies only to communications which—

(a) if made by a person other than an authorised person, without the approval of an authorised person, would contravene section 21(1), and

(b) may be made by an authorised person without contravening section 238(1).

(4) But subsection (3) does not prevent the FCA from making rules under subsection (1) in relation to a communication that would not contravene section 21(1) if made by a person other than an authorised person, without the approval of an authorised person, if the conditions set out in subsection (5) are satisfied.

(5) Those conditions are—

(a) that the communication would not contravene subsection (1) of section 21 because it is a communication to which that subsection does not apply as a result of an order under subsection (5) of that section,

(b) that the FCA considers that any of the [listed requirements] apply to the communication, and

(c) that the FCA considers that the rules are necessary to secure that the communication satisfies such of the [listed requirements] as the FCA considers apply to the communication.

[(5A) In subsection (5) "the listed requirements" means—

(a) requirements under the law of any part of the United Kingdom that appear to the FCA to correspond to requirements of—

(i) Articles 24 (general principles and information to clients) and 25 (assessment of suitability and appropriateness and reporting to clients) of the markets in financial instruments directive,

(ii) Commission Delegated Directive (EU) 2017/593 of 7 April 2016, so far as adopted under those Articles,

(iii) Article 77 of the UCITS directive,

(iv) Articles 10 and 11 of the mortgages directive,

(v) Article 17 of the insurance distribution directive, or

(vi) Article 44a of the recovery and resolution directive (as defined in paragraph (c)), and

(b) requirements of any retained direct EU legislation originally made under Article 24(13) or 25(8) of the markets in financial instruments directive;

(c) In paragraph (a)(vi), "recovery and resolution directive" means Directive 2014/59/EU of the European Parliament and of the Council of 15 May 2014 establishing a framework for the recovery and resolution of credit institutions and investment firms, as it had effect immediately before IP completion day.]

(6) "Engage in investment activity" [and "engage in claims management activity" have] the same meaning as in section 21.

(7) The Treasury may by order impose limitations on the power to make rules under this section.]

NOTES

Substituted as noted to s 137A at **[7.294]**.

Sub-s (1): the word omitted from para (a) was repealed, and para (aa) was inserted, by the Financial Guidance and Claims Act 2018, s 27(1), (5)(a), as from 6 October 2018 (for transitional provisions in relation to the transfer of regulation of claims management services to the FCA, see Sch 5 to the 2018 Act).

Sub-s (5): words in square brackets substituted by the Financial Services and Markets Act 2000 (Amendment) (EU Exit) Regulations 2019, SI 2019/632, regs 34, 38(1)–(3), as from IP completion day (as defined in the European Union (Withdrawal Agreement) Act 2020, s 39).

Sub-s (5A): inserted by SI 2019/632, regs 34, 38(1), (4), as from IP completion day (as defined in the European Union (Withdrawal Agreement) Act 2020, s 39). Note that reg 38 the 2019 Regulations was amended by the Bank Recovery and Resolution (Amendment) (EU Exit) Regulations 2020, SI 2020/1350, reg 79(2), as from 28 December 2020; and the effect of the amendments has been incorporated in the text set out above.

Sub-s (6): words in square brackets substituted by the Financial Guidance and Claims Act 2018, s 27(1), (5)(b), as from 6 October 2018 (for transitional provisions in relation to the transfer of regulation of claims management services to the FCA, see Sch 5 to the 2018 Act).

[7.322]

[137S Financial promotion rules: directions given by FCA

(1) The FCA may give a direction under this section if—

(a) an authorised person has made, or proposes to make, a communication or has approved, or proposes to approve, another person's communication, and

(b) the FCA considers that there has been, or is likely to be, a contravention of financial promotion rules in respect of the communication or approval.

(2) A direction under this section may require the authorised person—

(a) to withdraw the communication or approval;

(b) to refrain from making the communication or giving the approval (whether or not it has previously been made or given);

(c) to publish details of the direction;

(d) to do anything else specified in the direction in relation to the communication or approval.

(3) A requirement in a direction under this section to refrain from making or approving a communication includes a requirement to refrain from making or approving another communication where—

(a) the other communication is in all material respects the same as, or substantially the same as, the communication to which the direction relates, and
(b) in all the circumstances a reasonable person would think that another direction would be given under this section in relation to the other communication.

(4) The requirements contained in a direction under this section have effect as follows—
(a) a requirement to publish details of the direction has effect at such time (if any) as the FCA gives a notice under subsection (8)(a);
(b) any other requirement takes effect immediately.

(5) If the FCA gives a direction under this section to an authorised person—
(a) it must give written notice to the authorised person, and
(b) if the direction relates to the approval by the authorised person of another person's communication, it must also give written notice to that other person.

(6) The notice must—
(a) give details of the direction,
(b) inform the person to whom the notice is given that the direction takes effect immediately,
(c) state the FCA's reasons for giving the direction, and
(d) inform the person to whom the notice is given that the person may make representations to the FCA within such period as may be specified in the notice (which may be extended by the FCA).

(7) The FCA may amend the direction if, having considered any representations made by a person to whom notice is given under subsection (5), it considers it appropriate to do so.

(8) If, having considered any such representations, the FCA decides not to revoke the direction—
(a) the FCA must give separate written notice to the persons mentioned in subsection (5)(a) or (b), and
(b) any such person may refer the matter to the Tribunal.

(9) A notice under subsection (8)(a) must—
(a) give details of the direction and of any amendment of it,
(b) state the FCA's reasons for deciding not to revoke the direction and, if relevant, for amending it,
(c) inform the person to whom the notice is given of the person's right to refer the matter to the Tribunal, and
(d) give an indication of the procedure on such a reference.

(10) If, having considered any representations made by a person to whom notice is given under subsection (5), the FCA decides to revoke the direction, it must give separate written notice to those persons.

(11) After the period for making representations in relation to a direction given under this section has ended, the FCA may publish such information about the direction as it considers appropriate (even if the direction is revoked).

(12) Nothing in this section requires a notice to be given to a person mentioned in subsection (5)(b) if the FCA considers it impracticable to do so.]

NOTES

Substituted as noted to s 137A at **[7.294]**.

[7.323]

[137SA Rules to recover expenses relating to the [Money and Pensions Service]

(1) The Secretary of State may, from time to time, notify the FCA of the amount of—
(a) the expenses incurred, or expected to be incurred, by the Secretary of State under section 11 of the Financial Guidance and Claims Act 2018 (financial assistance from Secretary of State to [Money and Pensions Service]), and
(b) any other expenses incurred, or expected to be incurred, by the Secretary of State in connection with the operation of the [Money and Pensions Service],

that the Secretary of State considers should be recovered under this section.

(2) Where the Secretary of State has notified the FCA of an amount of expenses under subsection (1), the FCA must make rules for imposing levies with a view to recovering—
(a) the amount notified, and
(b) expenses incurred by the FCA in connection with its functions under this section.

(3) The rules must require the payment to the FCA of specified sums, or sums calculated in a specified way, by—
(a) authorised persons, electronic money issuers or payment service providers, or
(b) any specified class of authorised person, electronic money issuer or payment service provider.

(4) Before the FCA publishes a draft of rules to be made under this section it must consult the Secretary of State.

(5) The rules may be made only with the consent of the Secretary of State.

(6) The Secretary of State may notify the FCA of matters that will be taken into account when deciding whether or not to give consent under subsection (5).

(7) The FCA must have regard to any matters notified under subsection (6) before publishing a draft of rules to be made under this section.

(8) The FCA must pay the Secretary of State the sums it receives under rules made under this section, apart from those paid to recover the expenses mentioned in subsection (2)(b) (which the FCA may keep).

(9) Subsection (10) applies where—
(a) the Secretary of State has notified the FCA under subsection (1) of an amount which included expenses expected to be incurred,
(b) the FCA has made rules to recover the amount, and paid sums received under the rules to the Secretary of State, but
(c) the expenses expected to be incurred were not in fact incurred.

(10) The Secretary of State need not arrange for the sums received under the rules to be paid back, but must, when next notifying an amount to the FCA under subsection (1), take into account the fact that the sums received included an amount representing expenses that were not in fact incurred.

(11) In this section—

"electronic money issuer" means a person who is an electronic money issuer for the purposes of the Electronic Money Regulations 2011 (SI 2011/99) as a result of falling within any of paragraphs (a) to (e) and (h) to (j) of the definition in regulation 2(1);

"payment service provider" means a person who is a payment service provider for the purposes of the Payment Services Regulations 2017 (SI 2017/752) as a result of falling within any of paragraphs (a) to (h) of the definition in regulation 2(1).]

NOTES

Inserted by the Financial Guidance and Claims Act 2018, s 13(1), as from 10 May 2018. For transitional provisions in relation to the FCA's consultation requirements, and the recovery of expenses, see s 13(2), (3) of the 2018 Act.

Section heading and sub-s (1): words "Money and Pensions Service" in square brackets substituted by the Financial Guidance and Claims Act 2018 (Naming and Consequential Amendments) Regulations 2019, SI 2019/383, reg 3, Schedule, Pt 1, para 7(c), as from 6 April 2019.

[7.324]

[137SB Rules to recover debt advice expenses incurred by the devolved authorities

(1) The Treasury may, from time to time, notify the FCA of the amount of the expenses incurred, or expected to be incurred, by the devolved authorities in connection with the provision of information and advice on debt to members of the public in Scotland, Wales and Northern Ireland.

(2) Where the Treasury have notified the FCA of an amount of expenses under subsection (1), the FCA must make rules for imposing levies with a view to recovering—

- (a) the amount notified, and
- (b) expenses incurred by the FCA in connection with its functions under this section.

(3) The rules must require the payment to the FCA of specified sums, or sums calculated in a specified way, by—

- (a) authorised persons, electronic money issuers or payment service providers, or
- (b) any specified class of authorised person, electronic money issuer or payment service provider.

(4) Before the FCA publishes a draft of rules to be made under this section it must consult the Treasury.

(5) The rules may be made only with the consent of the Treasury.

(6) The Treasury may notify the FCA of matters that will be taken into account when deciding whether or not to give consent under subsection (5).

(7) The FCA must have regard to any matters notified under subsection (6) before publishing a draft of rules to be made under this section.

(8) The FCA must pay the Treasury the sums it receives under rules made under this section, apart from those paid to recover the expenses mentioned in subsection (2)(b) (which the FCA may keep).

(9) Subsection (10) applies where—

- (a) the Treasury have notified the FCA under subsection (1) of an amount which included expenses expected to be incurred,
- (b) the FCA has made rules to recover the amount, and paid sums received under the rules to the Treasury, but
- (c) the expenses expected to be incurred were not in fact incurred.

(10) The Treasury need not arrange for the sums received under the rules to be paid back, but must, when next notifying an amount to the FCA under subsection (1), take into account the fact that the sums received included an amount representing expenses that were not in fact incurred.

(11) In this section—

the "devolved authorities" means—

- (a) the Scottish Ministers,
- (b) the Welsh Ministers, and
- (c) the Department for Communities in Northern Ireland;

"electronic money issuer" and "payment service provider" have the same meanings as in section 137SA.]

NOTES

Inserted by the Financial Guidance and Claims Act 2018, s 14(1), as from 1 October 2018. For transitional provisions in relation to the FCA's consultation requirements, and the recovery of expenses, see s 14(2), (3) of the 2018 Act.

[Supplementary powers

[7.325]

137T General supplementary powers

Rules made by either regulator—

- (a) may make different provision for different cases and may, in particular, make different provision in respect of different descriptions of authorised persons, activity or investment,
- (b) may make provision by reference to rules made by the other regulator, as those rules have effect from time to time, and
- (c) may contain such incidental, supplemental, consequential and transitional provision as the regulator making the rule considers appropriate.]

NOTES

Substituted as noted to s 137A at **[7.294]**.

[CHAPTER 2 RULES: MODIFICATION, WAIVER, CONTRAVENTION AND PROCEDURAL PROVISIONS

NOTES

Transitional provisions etc in connection with the commencement of the Financial Services Act 2012: see the Financial Services Act 2012 (Transitional Provisions) (Rules and Miscellaneous Provisions) Order 2013, SI 2013/161, arts 8–11. Article 8 makes provision in relation to FCA consultation requirements. Article 9 provides that where (a) immediately before 1 April 2013, a direction has effect for the purpose of s 148 of this Act (modification or waiver of rules), and (b) the instrument by which the pre-commencement rules were made is designated in accordance with this Order, then: (i) the direction is to be treated as if it had been given under s 138A(1) (modification or waiver of rules) by the relevant regulator in respect of the post-commencement rules; (ii) any direction published by the FSA before 1 April 2013 for the purposes of s 148(6) is to be treated as if it had been published by the relevant regulator for the purposes of s 138B (publication of directions under s 138A); (iii) but s 138B does not apply to the direction if the FSA was satisfied, before 1 April 2013, that it was inappropriate or unnecessary to publish the direction. Article 9 also provides that where (a) immediately before 1 April 2013, a direction has effect for the purpose of s 294 (modification or waiver of rules) in relation to a recognised clearing house; and (b) the instrument by which the pre-commencement rules were made is designated in accordance with this Order by the Bank of England, then the direction is to be treated as if it had been given by the Bank of England in relation to the recognised clearing house in respect of the post-commencement rules. Article 10 provides that if, before1 April 2013, the FSA (a) received an application under s 148(2), and (b) had not determined the application, then the application is to be treated as if it had been made under s 138A(1) to the relevant regulator in respect of the post-commencement rules. Article 10 further provides that if (a) before 1 April 2013, the FSA received an application under s 294(1) in respect of a recognised clearing house, and (b) had not determined the application, then the application is to be treated as if it had been made to the Bank of England in relation to the recognised clearing house in respect of the post-commencement rules. Note that article 11 sets out definitions relevant to arts 9 and 10. See also, in relation to PRA consultation requirements, the Financial Services Act 2012 (Transitional Provisions) (Miscellaneous Provisions) Order 2013, SI 2013/442, art 70.

Modification or waiver of rules

[7.326]

138A Modification or waiver of rules

(1) Either regulator may, on the application or with the consent of a person who is subject to rules made by that regulator, direct that all or any of those rules—

(a) are not to apply to that person, or

(b) are to apply to that person with such modifications as may be specified in the direction.

(2) Subsection (1) does not apply to—

[(za) rules made by either regulator under section 64A (rules of conduct);]

(a) rules made by either regulator under section 137O (threshold condition code);

(b) rules made by the FCA under section 247 (trust scheme rules)[, section 248 (scheme particulars rules), section 261I (contractual scheme rules) or section 261J (contractual scheme particulars rules)].

(3) An application must be made in such manner as the regulator may direct.

(4) A regulator may not give a direction unless it is satisfied that—

(a) compliance by the person with the rules, or with the rules as unmodified, would be unduly burdensome or would not achieve the purpose for which the rules were made, and

(b) the direction would not adversely affect the advancement of any of the regulator's objectives.

(5) In subsection (4)(b) "objectives", in relation to the FCA, means operational objectives.

(6) A direction may be given subject to conditions.

(7) The regulator may—

(a) revoke a direction, or

(b) vary it on the application, or with the consent, of the person to whom it relates.

(8) "Direction" means a direction under this section.]

NOTES

Substituted as noted to s 137A at **[7.294]**.

Sub-s (2): para (za) inserted by the Financial Services (Banking Reform) Act 2013, s 35, Sch 3, para 8, as from 25 July 2014. Words in square brackets in para (b) substituted by the Collective Investment in Transferable Securities (Contractual Scheme) Regulations 2013, SI 2013/1388, reg 3(1), (4), as from 6 June 2013.

[7.327]

[138B Publication of directions under section 138A

(1) Subject to subsection (2), a direction must be published by the regulator concerned in the way appearing to the regulator to be best calculated for bringing it to the attention of—

(a) persons likely to be affected by it, and

(b) persons who are, in the opinion of the regulator, likely to make an application for a similar direction.

(2) Subsection (1) does not apply if the regulator is satisfied that it is inappropriate or unnecessary to publish the direction.

(3) In deciding whether it is satisfied as mentioned in subsection (2), the regulator must—

(a) consider whether the publication of the direction would be detrimental to the stability of the UK financial system,

(b) take into account whether the direction relates to a rule contravention of which is actionable in accordance with section 138D,

(c) consider whether publication of the direction would prejudice, to an unreasonable degree, the commercial interests of the person concerned or any other member of the person's immediate group, and

(d) consider whether its publication would be contrary to an international obligation of the United Kingdom.

(4) The FCA must consult the PRA before publishing or deciding not to publish a direction which relates to—

(a) a PRA-authorised person, or

(b) an authorised person who has as a member of its immediate group a PRA-authorised person.

(5) For the purposes of paragraphs (c) and (d) of subsection (3), the regulator must consider whether it would be possible to publish the direction without either of the consequences mentioned in those paragraphs by publishing it without disclosing the identity of the person concerned.

(6) "Direction" means a direction under section 138A.]

NOTES

Substituted as noted to s 137A at **[7.294]**.

[Contravention of rules

[7.328]

138C Evidential provisions

(1) If a particular rule made by either regulator so provides, contravention of the rule does not give rise to any of the consequences provided for by other provisions of this Act.

(2) A rule made by a regulator which so provides must also provide—

(a) that contravention may be relied on as tending to establish contravention of such other rule made by that regulator as may be specified, or

(b) that compliance may be relied on as tending to establish compliance with such other rule made by that regulator as may be specified.

(3) A rule may include the provision mentioned in subsection (1) only if the regulator making the rule considers that it is appropriate for it also to include the provision required by subsection (2).

(4) In this section "rule" does not include a rule made under—

(a) section 137O (threshold condition code);

(b) section 192J (provision of information by parent undertakings).]

NOTES

Substituted as noted to s 137A at **[7.294]**.

[7.329]

[138D Actions for damages

(1) A rule made by the PRA may provide that contravention of the rule is actionable at the suit of a private person who suffers loss as a result of the contravention, subject to the defences and other incidents applying to actions for breach of statutory duty.

(2) A contravention by an authorised person of a rule made by the FCA is actionable at the suit of a private person who suffers loss as a result of the contravention, subject to the defences and other incidents applying to actions for breach of statutory duty.

(3) If rules made by the FCA so provide, subsection (2) does not apply to a contravention of a specified provision of the rules.

(4) In prescribed cases, a contravention of a rule which by virtue of subsection (1) or (2) would be actionable at the suit of a private person is actionable at the suit of a person who is not a private person, subject to the defences and other incidents applying to actions for breach of statutory duty.

(5) In subsections (1), (2) and (3) "rule" does not include—

[(za) rules made by either regulator under section 64A (rules of conduct);]

(a) Part 6 rules;

(b) rules under section 137O (threshold condition code);

(c) rules under section 192J (provision of information by parent undertakings);

(d) a rule requiring an authorised person to have or maintain financial resources.

(6) "Private person" has such meaning as may be prescribed.]

NOTES

Substituted as noted to s 137A at **[7.294]**.

Sub-s (5): para (za) inserted by the Financial Services (Banking Reform) Act 2013, s 35, Sch 3, para 9, as from 25 July 2014.

Regulations: the Financial Services and Markets Act 2000 (Rights of Action) Regulations 2001, SI 2001/2256, and the Financial Services and Markets Act 2000 (Fourth Motor Insurance Directive) Regulations 2002, SI 2002/2706 have effect as if made under this section by virtue of the Interpretation Act 1978, s 17(2)(b).

[7.330]

[138E Limits on effect of contravening rules

(1) A person is not guilty of an offence by reason of a contravention of a rule made by either regulator.

(2) No such contravention makes any transaction void or unenforceable.

(3) Subsection (2) does not apply in relation to—

(a) rules made by the FCA under section 137C, . . .

(b) product intervention rules made by the FCA under section 137D[, . . .

(c) rules made by the FCA under section 137FBB][; or

(d) rules made by the FCA under section 137FD].]

NOTES

Substituted as noted to s 137A at **[7.294]**.

Sub-s (3): the word omitted from para (a) was repealed, and para (c) (and the preceding word) was inserted, by the Bank of England and Financial Services Act 2016, s 35(1), (3), as from 6 July 2016. Word omitted from para (b) repealed, and para (d) (and the preceding word) inserted, by the Financial Guidance and Claims Act 2018, s 28(1), (3), as from 29 March 2019.

[Procedural provisions

[7.331]

138F Notification of rules

[(1)] If either regulator makes, alters or revokes any rules, that regulator must without delay give written notice [to the Treasury].

[(1A) The FCA must also give written notice to the Bank of England.]

[(2) Subsection [(1A)] does not apply to rules made under or by virtue of section [137FAA,] 137FB, [137FBA,] [137FC,] [137SA,] [137SB,] . . . [or 333T].]]

NOTES

Substituted as noted to s 137A at **[7.294]**.

Sub-s (1) numbered as such, and sub-s (2) added, by the Pension Schemes Act 2015, s 47, Sch 3, paras 1, 7, as from 3 March 2015.

The words "to the Treasury", in sub-s (1) were substituted, sub-s (1A) was inserted, and the figure "(1A)" in square brackets in sub-s (2) was substituted, by the Bank of England and Financial Services Act 2016, s 16, Sch 2, Pt 2, paras 26, 35, as from 1 March 2017.

Figure "137FAA," in square brackets in sub-s (2) inserted by the Pension Schemes Act 2021, s 121(3), as from a day to be appointed.

Figure "137FBA," in square brackets in sub-s (2) inserted by the Bank of England and Financial Services Act 2016, s 33(1), (3), as from 6 July 2016.

The figures "137FC,", "137SA,", and "137SB," in sub-s (2) were inserted, and the words omitted were repealed, by the Financial Guidance and Claims Act 2018, s 25, Sch 3, paras 5, 13, as from 10 May 2018 (in so far as relating to the insertion of the figure "137SA,"), as from 1 October 2018 (in so far as relating to the insertion of the figure "137SB,"), and as from 1 January 2019 (otherwise).

Words "or 333T" in square brackets in sub-s (2) substituted by virtue of the Bank of England and Financial Services Act 2016, s 29(1), (3), as from 6 July 2016.

[7.332]
[138G Rule-making instruments

(1) Any power conferred on either regulator to make rules is exercisable in writing.

(2) An instrument by which rules are made by either regulator ("a rule-making instrument") must specify the provision under which the rules are made.

(3) To the extent that a rule-making instrument does not comply with subsection (2), it is void.

(4) A rule-making instrument must be published by the regulator making the rule in the way appearing to that regulator to be best calculated to bring it to the attention of the public.

(5) The regulator making the rule may charge a reasonable fee for providing a person with a copy of a rule-making instrument.

(6) A person is not to be taken to have contravened any rule made by a regulator if the person shows that at the time of the alleged contravention the rule-making instrument concerned had not been made available in accordance with this section.]

NOTES

Substituted as noted to s 137A at **[7.294]**.

[7.333]
[138H Verification of rules

(1) The production of a printed copy of a rule-making instrument purporting to be made by a regulator—

(a) on which is endorsed a certificate signed by a member of staff of that regulator who is authorised by the regulator for that purpose, and

(b) which contains the required statements,

is evidence (or in Scotland sufficient evidence) of the facts stated in the certificate.

(2) The required statements are—

(a) that the instrument was made by the FCA or the PRA (as the case may be),

(b) that the copy is a true copy of the instrument, and

(c) that on a specified date the instrument was made available to the public in accordance with section 138G(4).

(3) A certificate purporting to be signed as mentioned in subsection (1) is to be taken to have been properly signed unless the contrary is shown.

(4) A person who wishes in any legal proceedings to rely on a rule-making instrument may require the regulator that made the rule to endorse a copy of the instrument with a certificate of the kind mentioned in subsection (1).]

NOTES

Substituted as noted to s 137A at **[7.294]**.

Rule-making instrument: designating instruments made in accordance with the Financial Services Act 2012 (Transitional Provisions) (Rules and Miscellaneous Provisions) Order 2013, SI 2013/161 and the Financial Services and Markets Act 2000 (Regulated Activities) (Amendment) (No 2) Order 2013, SI 2013/1881 are to be treated as rule-making instruments for the purposes of this section (see arts 3 and 64 of those Orders).

[7.334]
[138I Consultation by the FCA

(1) Before making any rules, the FCA must—

(a) consult the PRA, and

(b) after doing so, publish a draft of the proposed rules in the way appearing to the FCA to be best calculated to bring them to the attention of the public.

(2) The draft must be accompanied by—

(a) a cost benefit analysis,

(b) an explanation of the purpose of the proposed rules,

(c) any statement prepared under section 138K(2),

(d) an explanation of the FCA's reasons for believing that making the proposed rules is compatible with its duties under section 1B(1) and (5)(a), and

(e) notice that representations about the proposals may be made to the FCA within a specified time.

(3) Before making the proposed rules, the FCA must have regard to any representations made to it in accordance with subsection (2)(e).

(4) If the FCA makes the proposed rules, it must publish an account, in general terms, of—

(a) the representations made to it in accordance with subsection (2)(e), and

(b) its response to them.

(5) If the rules differ from the draft published under subsection (1)(b) in a way which is, in the opinion of the FCA, significant the FCA must publish—

(a) details of the difference (in addition to complying with subsection (4)) together with a cost benefit analysis, and
(b) any statement prepared under section 138K(4).

(6) The requirements to carry out a cost benefit analysis under this section do not apply in relation to rules made under—
(a) section 136(2);
[(aa) section 137FB;]
[(ab) section 137FBA;]
[(ac) section 137FC;]
[(ad) section 137SA;]
[(ae) section 137SB;]
(b) subsection (1) of section 213 as a result of subsection (4) of that section;
(c) section 234;
[(ca) . . .
(cb) . . .]
[(cc) section 333T;]
(d) paragraph 23 of Schedule 1ZA;
(e) . . .

(7) "Cost benefit analysis" means—
(a) an analysis of the costs together with an analysis of the benefits that will arise—
(i) if the proposed rules are made, or
(ii) if subsection (5) applies, from the rules that have been made, and
(b) subject to subsection (8), an estimate of those costs and of those benefits.

(8) If, in the opinion of the FCA—
(a) the costs or benefits referred to in subsection (7) cannot reasonably be estimated, or
(b) it is not reasonably practicable to produce an estimate,

the cost benefit analysis need not estimate them, but must include a statement of the FCA's opinion and an explanation of it.

(9) The FCA may charge a reasonable fee for providing a person with a copy of a draft published under subsection (1)(b).

[(9A) This section does not apply to rules made by the FCA under section 271E.]

(10) Subsection (1)(a) does not apply[—
(a) rules made by the FCA under section 137FB, [137FBA,] [137FC,] [137SA,] [137SB,] . . . [or 333T], or
(b)] to rules made by the FCA in relation to recognised investment exchanges under Part 18.

(11) This section is subject to section 138L.]

NOTES

Substituted as noted to s 137A at **[7.294]**.

Sub-s (6) is amended as follows:

Para (aa) inserted by the Pension Schemes Act 2015, s 47, Sch 3, paras 1, 8(a), as from 3 March 2015.

Para (ab) inserted by the Bank of England and Financial Services Act 2016, s 33(1), (4)(a), as from 6 July 2016.

Paras (ac), (ad), (ae) inserted by the Financial Guidance and Claims Act 2018, s 25, Sch 3, paras 5, 14(1), (2)(a)–(c), as from 10 May 2018 (in so far as relating to the insertion of para (ad)), as from 1 October 2018 (in so far as relating to the insertion of para (ae)), and as from 1 January 2019 (in relation to the insertion of para (ac)).

Paras (ca), (cb) originally inserted by the Pension Schemes Act 2015, s 47, Sch 3, paras 1, 8(b), as from 3 March 2015. These paragraphs, and para (e), were repealed by the Financial Guidance and Claims Act 2018, s 25, Sch 3, paras 5, 14(1), (2)(d), as from 1 January 2019.

Para (cc) inserted by the Bank of England and Financial Services Act 2016, s 29(1), (4)(a), as from 6 July 2016.

Sub-s (9A): inserted by the Financial Services Act 2021, s 24, Sch 9, Pt 2, para 3, as from 23 February 2022.

Sub-s (10) is amended as follows:

Words in first (outer) pair of square brackets inserted by the Pension Schemes Act 2015, s 47, Sch 3, paras 1, 8(c), as from 3 March 2015.

Figure "137FBA," in square brackets inserted by the Bank of England and Financial Services Act 2016, s 33(1), (4)(b), as from 6 July 2016.

The figures "137FC,", "137SA,", and "137SB," in square brackets were inserted, and the figures omitted were repealed, by the Financial Guidance and Claims Act 2018, s 25, Sch 3, paras 5, 14(1), (3), as from 10 May 2018 (in so far as relating to the insertion of the figure "137SA,"), as from 1 October 2018 (in so far as relating to the insertion of the figure "137SB,"), and as from 1 January 2019 (otherwise).

Words ", or 333T" in square brackets substituted by virtue of the Bank of England and Financial Services Act 2016, s 29(1), (4)(b), as from 6 July 2016.

[7.335]

[138J Consultation by the PRA

(1) Before making any rules, the PRA must—
(a) consult the FCA, and
(b) after doing so, publish a draft of the proposed rules in the way appearing to the PRA to be best calculated to bring them to the attention of the public.

(2) The draft must be accompanied by—
(a) a cost benefit analysis,
(b) an explanation of the purpose of the proposed rules,
(c) any statement prepared under section 138K(2),
(d) an explanation of the PRA's reasons for believing that making the proposed rules is compatible with its duties under—
(i) section 2B(1) or, as the case requires, section 2C(1) or 2D(3), and
(ii) section 2H, and

(e) notice that representations about the proposals may be made to the PRA within a specified time.

(3) Before making the proposed rules, the PRA must have regard to any representations made to it in accordance with subsection (2)(e).

(4) If the PRA makes the proposed rules, it must publish an account, in general terms, of—

(a) the representations made to it in accordance with subsection (2)(e), and

(b) its response to them.

(5) If the rules differ from the draft published under subsection (1)(b) in a way which is, in the opinion of the PRA, significant the PRA must publish—

(a) details of the difference (in addition to complying with subsection (4)) together with a cost benefit analysis, and

(b) any statement prepared under section 138K(4).

(6) The requirements to carry out a cost benefit analysis under this section do not apply in relation to rules made under—

(a) section 136(2);

(b) subsection (1) of section 213 as a result of subsection (4) of that section;

(c) section 234;

(d) paragraph 31 of Schedule 1ZB;

(e) . . .

(7) "Cost benefit analysis" means—

(a) an analysis of the costs together with an analysis of the benefits that will arise—

(i) if the proposed rules are made, or

(ii) if subsection (5) applies, from the rules that have been made, and

(b) subject to subsection (8), an estimate of those costs and of those benefits.

(8) If, in the opinion of the PRA—

(a) the costs or benefits referred to in subsection (7) cannot reasonably be estimated, or

(b) it is not reasonably practicable to produce an estimate,

the cost benefit analysis need not estimate them, but must include a statement of the PRA's opinion and an explanation of it.

(9) The PRA may charge a reasonable fee for providing a person with a copy of a draft published under subsection (1)(b).

(10) This section is subject to [sections 138L and 144E(3)].]

NOTES

Substituted as noted to s 137A at **[7.294]**.

Sub-s (6): para (e) repealed by the Financial Guidance and Claims Act 2018, s 25, Sch 3, paras 5, 15, as from 6 April 2021.

Sub-s (10): words in square brackets substituted by the Financial Services Act 2021, s 5, Sch 3, Pt 3, para 12, as from 9 June 2021.

[7.336]

[138K Consultation: mutual societies

(1) Subsection (2) applies where a regulator proposes to make a rule ("the proposed rule") which would apply both to—

(a) authorised persons which are mutual societies, and

(b) other authorised persons.

(2) The regulator must prepare a statement setting out—

(a) its opinion whether or not the impact of the proposed rule on persons within subsection (1)(a) will be significantly different from its impact on persons within subsection (1)(b), and

(b) if so, details of the difference.

(3) Subsection (4) applies where a regulator makes a rule which—

(a) applies both to—

(i) authorised persons which are mutual societies, and

(ii) other authorised persons, and

(b) differs from the draft of the proposed rule published under section 138I(1)(b) or section 138J(1)(b) (as the case may be).

(4) The regulator must prepare a statement setting out—

(a) its opinion whether or not the impact of the rule is significantly different from the impact of the proposed rule on—

(i) the persons within subsection (3)(a)(i), and

(ii) those persons as compared with persons within subsection (3)(a)(ii), and

(b) if so, details of the difference.

(5) A "mutual society" is—

(a) a building society within the meaning of the Building Societies Act 1986;

(b) a friendly society within the meaning of the Friendly Societies Act 1992;

(c) a registered society within the meaning of [the Co-operative and Community Benefit Societies Act 2014];

(d) . . .

(6) . . .

[(7) This section is subject to section 144E(3).]]

NOTES

Substituted as noted to s 137A at **[7.294]**.

Sub-s (5): words in square brackets substituted by the Co-operative and Community Benefit Societies Act 2014, s 151, Sch 4, Pt 2, paras 68, 69, as from 1 August 2014. Para (d) repealed by the Financial Services and Markets Act 2000 (Amendment) (EU Exit) Regulations 2019, SI 2019/632, regs 34, 39, as from IP completion day (as defined in the European Union (Withdrawal Agreement) Act 2020, s 39).

Sub-s (6): repealed by SI 2019/632, regs 34, 39, as from IP completion day (as defined in the European Union (Withdrawal Agreement) Act 2020, s 39).

Sub-s (7): added by the Financial Services Act 2021, s 5, Sch 3, Pt 3, para 13, as from 9 June 2021.

[7.337]

[138L Consultation: general exemptions

(1) Sections 138I(1)(b) and (2) to (5) and 138K do not apply in relation to rules made by the FCA if the FCA considers that the delay involved in complying with them would be prejudicial to the interests of consumers, as defined in section 425A.

(2) Sections 138J(1)(b) and (2) to (5) and 138K do not apply in relation to rules made by the PRA if the PRA considers that the delay involved in complying with them would—

(a) be prejudicial to the safety and soundness of PRA-authorised persons, or

(b) in a case where section 2C applies, be prejudicial to securing the appropriate degree of protection for policyholders.

(3) The provisions listed in subsection (4) do not apply if the regulator concerned considers that, making the appropriate comparison—

(a) there will be no increase in costs, or

(b) there will be an increase in costs but that increase will be of minimal significance.

(4) Those provisions are—

(a) subsections (2)(a) and (5)(a) of section 138I;

(b) subsections (2)(a) and (5)(a) of section 138J.

(5) The "appropriate comparison" means—

(a) in relation to section 138I(2)(a) or 138J(2)(a), a comparison between the overall position if the rules are made and the overall position if the rules are not made;

(b) in relation to section 138I(5)(a) or 138J(5)(a), a comparison between the overall position after the making of the rules and the overall position before they were made.]

NOTES

Substituted as noted to s 137A at **[7.294]**.

[7.338]

[138M Consultation: exemptions for temporary product intervention rules

(1) Sections 138I(1)(b) and (2) to (5) and 138K do not apply in relation to product intervention rules made by the FCA if it considers that it is necessary or expedient not to comply with them for the purpose of advancing—

(a) the consumer protection objective or the competition objective, or

(b) if an order under section 137D(1)(b) is in force, the integrity objective.

(2) Any rules made as a result of subsection (1) ("temporary product intervention rules") are to cease to have effect at the end of the period specified in the rules.

(3) The longest period that may be specified is the period of 12 months beginning with the day on which the rules come into force.

(4) Nothing in subsection (2) prevents the FCA from revoking temporary product intervention rules before the end of the period mentioned there.

(5) If the FCA has made temporary product intervention rules ("the initial rules"), it may not make further temporary product intervention rules containing the same, or substantially the same, provision as that contained in the initial rules until the prohibited period has ended.

(6) "The prohibited period" means the period of 12 months beginning with the day on which the period mentioned in subsection (2) ends (whether or not the initial rules have been revoked before the end of the period mentioned there).]

NOTES

Substituted as noted to s 137A at **[7.294]**.

[7.339]

[138N Temporary product intervention rules: statement of policy

(1) The FCA must prepare and issue a statement of its policy with respect to the making of temporary product intervention rules.

(2) The FCA may at any time alter or replace a statement issued under this section.

(3) If a statement issued under this section is altered or replaced, the FCA must issue the altered or replacement statement.

(4) The FCA must, without delay, give the Treasury a copy of any statement which it publishes under this section.

(5) A statement issued under this section must be published by the FCA in the way appearing to the FCA to be best calculated to bring it to the attention of the public.

(6) The FCA may charge a reasonable fee for providing a person with a copy of the statement.]

NOTES

Substituted as noted to s 137A at **[7.294]**.

[7.340]

[138O Statement of policy under section 138N: procedure

(1) Before issuing a statement under section 138N, the FCA must publish a draft of the proposed statement in the way appearing to the FCA to be best calculated to bring it to the attention of the public.

(2) The draft must be accompanied by notice that representations about the proposal may be made to the FCA within a specified time.

(3) Before issuing the proposed statement, the FCA must have regard to any representations made to it in accordance with subsection (2).

(4) If the FCA issues the proposed statement it must publish an account, in general terms, of—
(a) the representations made to it in accordance with subsection (2), and
(b) its response to them.
(5) If the statement differs from the draft published under subsection (1) in a way which is, in the opinion of the FCA, significant, the FCA must (in addition to complying with subsection (4)) publish details of the difference.
(6) The FCA may charge a reasonable fee for providing a person with a copy of a draft published under subsection (1).
(7) This section also applies to a proposal to alter or replace a statement.]

NOTES

Substituted as noted to s 137A at **[7.294]**.

[CHAPTER 2A TECHNICAL STANDARDS

[7.341]

138P Technical standards

(1) This Chapter applies where a power for the FCA, the PRA, the Bank of England, or any combination of them to make technical standards is substituted for the power of an EU entity to make EU tertiary legislation ("the original EU power") by regulations made under section 8 of the European Union (Withdrawal) Act 2018.
(2) The power to make technical standards includes power to modify, amend or revoke—
(a) any technical standards made by the regulator under that power;
(b) any EU tertiary legislation made by an EU entity under the original EU power which forms part of retained EU law.
(3) Where power to make a technical standard for the same purposes (as set out in the provision creating the power) and applying to the same persons or class of persons has been given to more than one regulator, no regulator may exercise the power without the consent of the other regulator or regulators.
(4) Before a regulator makes a technical standard in which another regulator has an interest, it must consult the other regulator.
(5) For the purposes of subsection (4)—
(a) the PRA has an interest in a technical standard which—
(i) applies to PRA-authorised persons or other persons connected to them, or
(ii) may affect the exercise of the PRA's functions under or by virtue of this Act or under retained EU law;
(b) the FCA has an interest in all technical standards which a regulator or the Payment Systems Regulator has power to amend;
(c) the Bank of England has an interest in technical standards which—
(i) apply to central counterparties, to financial counterparties or non-financial counterparties within the meaning of the EMIR regulation or to central securities depositories, or
(ii) may affect the exercise of the Bank's functions under or by virtue of this Act, the Banking Act 2009 or retained EU law.
(6) For the purposes of this Chapter—
(a) "EU tertiary legislation" has the meaning given in section 20 of the European Union (Withdrawal) Act 2018;
(b) "regulator" means the FCA, the PRA or the Bank of England;
(c) a person is connected with another person in the circumstances set out in section 165(11);
[(d) "the EMIR regulation" has the meaning given in section 313.]]

NOTES

Chapter 2A (ss 138P–138S) was inserted by the Financial Regulators' Powers (Technical Standards etc) (Amendment etc) (EU Exit) Regulations 2018, SI 2018/1115, reg 7(1), (8), as from 26 October 2018.

Sub-s (6): para (d) added by the Over the Counter Derivatives, Central Counterparties and Trade Repositories (Amendment, etc, and Transitional Provision) (EU Exit) Regulations 2020, SI 2020/646, reg 2(1), (2), as from 25 June 2020.

[7.342]

[138Q Standards instruments

(1) The power to make technical standards is to be exercised by the regulator by making an instrument under this section (a "standards instrument").
(2) A standards instrument must specify the provision under which the instrument is being made.
(3) To the extent that a standards instrument does not comply with subsection (2), it is void.
(4) A standards instrument must be published by the regulator making the instrument in the way appearing to the regulator to be best calculated to bring it to the attention of the public.
(5) The Treasury must lay before Parliament a copy of each standards instrument made under this section.
(6) The regulator making the instrument may charge a reasonable fee for providing a person with a copy of a standards instrument.]

NOTES

Inserted as noted to s 138P at **[7.341]**.

[7.343]

[138R Treasury approval

(1) A standards instrument may be made only if it has been approved by the Treasury.
(2) The Treasury may refuse to approve a standards instrument if subsection (3) or (5) applies.
(3) This subsection applies if it appears to the Treasury that the instrument would—
(a) have implications for public funds (within the meaning of section 78(2) of the Banking Act 2009); or
(b) prejudice any current or proposed negotiations for an international agreement between the United Kingdom and one or more other countries, international organisations or institutions.
(4) For the purposes of subsection (3), "international organisations" includes the European Union.

(5) This subsection applies if it appears to the Treasury that they may direct the regulator not to make the standards instrument under section 410 (international obligations).

(6) The Treasury must notify the regulator in writing whether or not they approve a standards instrument within four weeks after the day on which that instrument is submitted to the Treasury for approval ("the relevant period").

(7) Provision of a draft standards instrument to the Treasury for consultation does not amount to submission of the instrument for approval.

(8) If the Treasury do not approve the instrument, they must—

(a) set out in the notice given under subsection (6) the Treasury's reasons for not approving the instrument;

(b) lay before Parliament—

(i) a copy of that notice;

(ii) a copy of any statement made by the regulator as to its reasons for wishing to make the instrument.

(9) If the Treasury do not give notice under subsection (6) before the end of the relevant period, the Treasury is deemed to have approved the standards instrument.]

NOTES

Inserted as noted to s 138P at **[7.341]**.

[7.344]

[138S Application of Chapters 1 and 2

(1) The sections listed in subsection (2) apply, subject to the modifications specified in that subsection, to—

(a) technical standards made by the FCA or the PRA as they apply to rules made by the FCA or the PRA;

(b) technical standards made by the Bank of England, as they apply to rules made by the Bank under this Act in accordance with paragraph 10(1), (3) and (4) of Schedule 17A to this Act.

(2) The sections referred to in subsection (1) are—

(a) section 137T (general supplementary powers), as if—

(i) the reference in paragraph (a) to authorised persons were a reference to persons,

(ii) the reference in paragraph (b) to rules included a reference to technical standards;

(b) section 138C (evidential provisions);

(c) section 138E (limit on effect of contravening rules);

(d) section 138F (notification of rules);

(e) section 138H (verification of rules), treating the reference in subsection (2)(c) to section 138G(4) of the Act as a reference to section 138Q(4);

(f) section 138I (consultation by the FCA), as if—

(i) subsection (1)(a) were omitted, and

(ii) references to making rules were references to submitting a standards instrument to the Treasury for approval;

(g) section 138J (consultation by the PRA), as if—

(i) subsection (1)(a) were omitted, and

(ii) references to making rules were references to submitting a standards instrument to the Treasury for approval;

(h) section 138K (consultation: mutual societies);

[(i) section 138L (consultation: general exemptions), as if—

(i) in subsection (1), for "425A" there were substituted "1G";

(ii) references to making rules were references to submitting a standards instrument to the Treasury for approval].]

NOTES

Inserted as noted to s 138P at **[7.341]**.

Sub-s (2): para (i) substituted by the Financial Services (Electronic Money, Payment Services and Miscellaneous Amendments) (EU Exit) Regulations 2019, SI 2019/1212, reg 2(1), (2), as from 6 September 2019.

[CHAPTER 3 GUIDANCE

[7.345]

139A Power of the FCA to give guidance

(1) The FCA may give guidance consisting of such information and advice as it considers appropriate—

(a) with respect to the operation of specified parts of this Act and of any rules made by the FCA;

(b) with respect to any other matter relating to functions of the FCA;

(c) with respect to any other matters about which it appears to the FCA to be desirable to give information or advice.

[(1A) . . .]

(2) The FCA may give financial or other assistance to persons giving information or advice of a kind which the FCA could give under this section.

(3) Subsection (5) applies where the FCA proposes to give guidance to FCA-regulated persons generally, or to a class of FCA-regulated persons, in relation to rules to which those persons are subject.

(4) Subsection (5) also applies in relation to guidance which the FCA proposes to give to persons generally, or to a class of person, in relation to its functions under the short selling regulation [or the market abuse regulation[, any retained EU direct legislation originally made under the market abuse regulation or any subordinate legislation (within the meaning of the Interpretation Act 1978) made on or after IP completion day under the market abuse regulation]].

(5) Where this subsection applies, subsections (1), (2)(e) and (3) of section 138I (consultation) apply to the proposed guidance as they apply to proposed rules, unless the FCA considers that the delay in complying with those provisions would be prejudicial to the interests of consumers.

(6) The FCA may—

(a) publish its guidance,

(b) offer copies of its published guidance for sale at a reasonable price, and

(c) if it gives guidance in response to a request made by any person, make a reasonable charge for that guidance.

(7) In this Chapter, references to guidance given by the FCA include references to any recommendations made by the FCA to FCA-regulated persons generally, or to any class of FCA-regulated person.

(8) "Consumers" has the meaning given in section 1G.

(9) "FCA-regulated person" means—

(a) an authorised person, or

(b) any person who is otherwise subject to rules made by the FCA.]

NOTES

Substituted as noted to s 137A at **[7.294]**.

Sub-s (1A): originally inserted by the Pension Schemes Act 2015, s 47, Sch 3, paras 1, 9, as from 3 March 2015. Subsequently repealed by the Financial Guidance and Claims Act 2018, s 25, Sch 3, paras 5, 16, as from 1 January 2019.

Sub-s (4) is amended as follows:

Words in first (outer) pair of square brackets inserted by the Financial Services and Markets Act 2000 (Market Abuse) Regulations 2016, SI 2016/680, reg 10(1), (6), as from 3 July 2016.

Words in second (inner) pair of square brackets substituted by the Financial Services and Markets Act 2000 (Amendment) (EU Exit) Regulations 2019, SI 2019/632, regs 34, 40, as from IP completion day (as defined in the European Union (Withdrawal Agreement) Act 2020, s 39). Note that reg 40 of the 2019 Regulations was amended by the Financial Services and Economic and Monetary Policy (Consequential Amendments) (EU Exit) Regulations 2020, SI 2020/1301, reg 3, Schedule, para 33(d), as from 30 December 2020; and the effect of the amendment has been incorporated in the text set out above.

[7.346]

[139B Notification of FCA guidance to the Treasury

(1) On giving any general guidance, the FCA must give written notice to the Treasury without delay.

(2) If the FCA alters any of its guidance, it must give written notice to the Treasury without delay.

(3) The notice under subsection (2) must include details of the alteration.

(4) If the FCA revokes any of its general guidance, it must give written notice to the Treasury without delay.

(5) "General guidance" means guidance given by the FCA under section 139A which is—

(a) given to persons generally, to FCA-regulated persons generally or to a class of FCA-regulated person,

(b) intended to have continuing effect, and

(c) given in writing or other legible form.

(6) "FCA-regulated person" has the same meaning as in section 139A.]

NOTES

Substituted as noted to s 137A at **[7.294]**.

[CHAPTER 4 COMPETITION SCRUTINY

[7.347]

140A Interpretation

(1) In this Chapter—

["the CMA" means the Competition and Markets Authority.]

"market in the United Kingdom" includes—

(a) so far as it operates in the United Kingdom or a part of the United Kingdom, any market which operates there and in another country or territory or in a part of another country or territory, and

(b) any market which operates only in a part of the United Kingdom;

. . .

"practices", in relation to each regulator, means practices adopted by that regulator in the exercise of functions under this Act;

"regulating provisions" means—

"regulating provisions" means—

(a) in relation to the FCA, any—

(i) rules of the FCA;

(ii) general guidance (as defined by section 139B(5) [. . .]);

(iii), (iv). . .

[(v), (vi). . .]

(b) in relation to the PRA, any—

(i) rules of the PRA;

(ii), (iii). . .

(2) . . .

(3) For the purposes of this Chapter, any reference to a feature of a market in the United Kingdom for goods or services is to be read as a reference to—

(a) the structure of the market concerned or any aspect of that structure,

(b) any conduct (whether or not in the market concerned) of one or more than one person who supplies or acquires goods or services in the market concerned, or

(c) any conduct relating to the market concerned of customers of any person who supplies or acquires goods or services.

(4) In subsection (3) "conduct" includes any failure to act (whether or not intentional) and any other unintentional conduct.]

NOTES

Substituted as noted to s 137A at **[7.294]**.

Sub-s (1) is amended as follows:

Definition "the CMA" inserted, and definition "the OFT" (omitted) repealed, by the Enterprise and Regulatory Reform Act 2013 (Competition) (Consequential, Transitional and Saving Provisions) Order 2014, SI 2014/892, art 2, Sch 1, Pt 2, paras 120, 121(1), (2), as from 1 April 2014.

The words omitted from sub-para (a)(ii) of the definition "regulating provisions" were originally inserted, and sub-paras (a)(v), (vi) of that definition were originally inserted, by the Pension Schemes Act 2015, s 47, Sch 3, paras 1, 10, as from 3 March 2015. All of these words were repealed by the Financial Guidance and Claims Act 2018, s 25, Sch 3, paras 5, 17, as from 1 January 2019.

Sub-para (a)(iv) of the definition "regulating provisions" was repealed by the Financial Services and Markets Act 2000 (Market Abuse) Regulations 2016, SI 2016/680, reg 10(1), (7), as from 3 July 2016.

The other words omitted from the definition "regulating provisions" were repealed by the Financial Services (Banking Reform) Act 2013, s 35, Sch 3, para 10, as from 7 March 2016.

Sub-s (2): repealed by SI 2014/892, art 2, Sch 1, Pt 2, paras 120, 121(1), (3), as from 1 April 2014 (for transitional provisions see the note above).

[7.348]

[140B Advice about effect of regulating provision or practice

(1) In this Chapter, any reference to the giving of "section 140B advice" to a regulator is to be read in accordance with this section.

[(2) The CMA gives "section 140B advice" to a regulator if—

(a) it gives advice to the regulator under section 7 of the Enterprise Act 2002 (provision of competition advice to Ministers etc) and the advice states that in the opinion of the CMA one or more of the things mentioned in subsection (4) may cause, or contribute to, the effect mentioned in subsection (5), or might be expected to do so in the future;

(b) a report published by it under section 136 of the Enterprise Act 2002 (investigations and reports on market investigation reference) contains—

(i) a decision that one or more of the things mentioned in subsection (4) may cause, or contribute to, the effect mentioned in subsection (5), and

(ii) a recommendation that any action should be taken by that regulator.]

(3) . . .

(4) Those things are—

(a) a regulating provision or practice of the regulator,

(b) two or more regulating provisions or practices (of that regulator or of both regulators) taken together,

(c) a particular combination of regulating provision or practices (of that regulator or of both regulators), or

(d) a feature, or combination of features, of a [one or more markets] in the United Kingdom that could be dealt with by regulating provision or practices (of that regulator or of both regulators).

(5) That effect is the prevention, restriction or distortion of competition in connection with the supply or acquisition of any goods or services in the United Kingdom or a part of the United Kingdom.]

NOTES

Substituted as noted to s 137A at **[7.294]**.

Sub-s (2) substituted, sub-s (3) repealed, and words in square brackets in sub-s (4)(d) substituted, by the Enterprise and Regulatory Reform Act 2013 (Competition) (Consequential, Transitional and Saving Provisions) Order 2014, SI 2014/892, art 2, Sch 1, Pt 2, paras 120, 122, as from 1 April 2014.

[7.349]

[140C Consultation with regulator

Before giving section 140B advice, [the CMA] must consult the regulator to which the advice is to be given.]

NOTES

Substituted as noted to s 137A at **[7.294]**.

Words in square brackets substituted by the Enterprise and Regulatory Reform Act 2013 (Competition) (Consequential, Transitional and Saving Provisions) Order 2014, SI 2014/892, art 2, Sch 1, Pt 2, paras 120, 123, as from 1 April 2014.

[7.350]

[140D Investigation powers of [CMA]

[(1)] Where the [CMA] is deciding whether to exercise its power under section 7 of the Enterprise Act 2002 to give advice which, if given, would be section 140B advice, section 174 of that Act has effect as if—

[(a) for subsection (1) there were substituted—

"(1) For the purposes of this section, a permitted purpose is assisting the CMA in deciding whether to exercise its power under section 7 to give advice which for the purposes of Chapter 4 of Part 9A of the Financial Services and Markets Act 2000 would be section 140B advice.", and

(b) subsection (9A) were omitted.]

[(2) Where the CMA has exercised any of its powers under section 174 of the Enterprise Act 2002, as applied by subsection (1), section 174B of that Act has effect as if, after subsection (9), there were inserted—

"(10) Where the section 174 power is exercised for the purpose of assisting the CMA in deciding whether to exercise its power under section 7 to give advice which for the purposes of Chapter 4 of Part 9A of the Financial Services and Markets Act 2000 would be section 140B advice, the relevant day is the day when the CMA publishes that advice.]

NOTES

Substituted as noted to s 137A at **[7.294]**.

Sub-s (1) was numbered as such, sub-s (2) was added, and all other words in square brackets were substituted, by the Enterprise and Regulatory Reform Act 2013 (Competition) (Consequential, Transitional and Saving Provisions) Order 2014, SI 2014/892, art 2, Sch 1, Pt 2, paras 120, 124, as from 1 April 2014; and see also Sch 2, para 4 to that Order which provides that these amendments do not apply in relation to any notice given before 1 April 2014 under s 174 of the Enterprise Act 2002 Act as applied by this Act.

[7.351]

[140E Publication by CMA of section 140B advice

Where the giving of advice under section 7 of the Enterprise Act 2002 to either regulator constitutes the giving of section 140B advice, the CMA must publish that advice in such manner as it thinks fit.]

NOTES

Originally substituted as noted to s 137A at **[7.294]**. Further substituted by the Enterprise and Regulatory Reform Act 2013 (Competition) (Consequential, Transitional and Saving Provisions) Order 2014, SI 2014/892, art 2, Sch 1, Pt 2, paras 120, 125, as from 1 April 2014.

[7.352]

[140F Duty of [CMA] to send report to regulator

(1) Where the publication of a report of the [CMA] under section 142 of the Enterprise Act 2002 constitutes the giving of section 140B advice to either regulator, the [CMA] must give a copy of the report to that regulator.

(2) The day on which the copy is given is the day on which the regulator is to be taken to receive the section 140B advice.]

NOTES

Substituted as noted to s 137A at **[7.294]**.

Words in square brackets substituted by the Enterprise and Regulatory Reform Act 2013 (Competition) (Consequential, Transitional and Saving Provisions) Order 2014, SI 2014/892, art 2, Sch 1, Pt 2, paras 120, 126, as from 1 April 2014.

[7.353]

[140G Duty of regulator to publish response

(1) A regulator must, within 90 days after the day on which it receives section 140B advice, publish a response stating how it proposes to deal with the advice and in particular—

(a) whether it has decided to take any action, or to take no action, in response to the advice,

(b) if it has decided to take action, what action it proposes to take, and

(c) its reasons for its proposals.

(2) Publication is to be in such manner as the regulator thinks fit.]

NOTES

Substituted as noted to s 137A at **[7.294]**.

[7.354]

[140H Role of the Treasury

(1) This section applies where—

(a) [the CMA] has given section 140B advice and the regulator has published a response under section 140G, and

(b) the [CMA] remains of the opinion that one or more of the things mentioned in section 140B(4) may cause or contribute to, the effect mentioned in section 140B(5).

(2) The [CMA] may refer the section 140B advice to the Treasury by sending the Treasury—

(a) a copy of the section 140B advice and of the response, and

(b) a request to consider the advice and the response.

(3) In referring the section 140B advice, the [CMA] may give advice to the Treasury as to what action, if any, ought to be taken by the regulator.

(4) If section 140B advice is referred to them, the Treasury may give a direction to the regulator to which the advice was given requiring the regulator to take such action as may be specified in the direction.

(5) In considering whether to give a direction and, if so, what action to specify, the Treasury must have regard to—

(a) any advice the [CMA] has given under subsection (3),

(b) any action which the section 140B advice suggests that the regulator should take, and

(c) the response of the regulator to the section 140B advice.

(6) The direction may not require the regulator to do anything that it has no power to do, but the existence of the direction is relevant to the exercise of any discretion conferred on the regulator.

(7) Before giving a direction under this section, the Treasury must consult the regulator to which it is to be given.

(8) If the Treasury give a direction under this section they must—

(a) publish in such manner as they think fit a statement giving details of the direction and of their reasons for giving it, and

(b) lay a copy of the statement before Parliament.]

NOTES

Substituted as noted to s 137A at **[7.294]**.

All words in square brackets were substituted by the Enterprise and Regulatory Reform Act 2013 (Competition) (Consequential, Transitional and Saving Provisions) Order 2014, SI 2014/892, art 2, Sch 1, Pt 2, paras 120, 127, as from 1 April 2014.

[CHAPTER 5 POWER TO MAKE CONSEQUENTIAL AMENDMENTS

[7.355]

141A Power to make consequential amendments of references to rules etc

(1) This section applies if—

(a) a provision of primary or subordinate legislation (whenever passed or made) contains a reference (however expressed) to rules of either regulator or to guidance of the FCA,

(b) it appears to the Treasury or the Secretary of State that the reference requires amendment in consequence of the exercise by that regulator of its power under this Part to make, alter or revoke its rules or the exercise by the FCA of its power to make, alter or revoke its guidance.

(2) The Treasury or the Secretary of State may by order make such amendment of the legislation referred to in subsection (1)(a) as appears to them to be necessary or expedient in consequence of the exercise by the regulator of the power mentioned in subsection (1)(b).

(3) The power conferred by subsection (2) includes power—

(a) to replace a reference to the rules of one regulator with a reference to the rules of the other regulator or to the rules of both regulators;

(b) to replace a reference to the rules of both regulators with a reference to the rules of one regulator.

(4) In subsection (1)(a) "subordinate legislation" does not include rules of either regulator.

[(5) A regulator's power under Part 2 of the Powers Regulations to amend its rules is treated for the purposes of this section as a power under this Part; and for this purpose "the Powers Regulations" means the Financial Regulators' Powers (Technical Standards etc.) (Amendment etc.) (EU Exit) Regulations 2018 (SI 2018/1115).]]

NOTES

Substituted as noted to s 137A at **[7.294]**.

Sub-s (5): added by the Financial Services and Markets Act 2000 (Amendment) (EU Exit) Regulations 2019, SI 2019/632, regs 34, 41, as from IP completion day (as defined in the European Union (Withdrawal Agreement) Act 2020, s 39).

Regulations: the Markets in Financial Instruments (Capital Markets) (Amendment) Regulations 2021, SI 2021/774; the Financial Services and Markets Act 2000 (Consequential Amendments of References to Rules) Regulations 2021, SI 2021/1388; the Financial Services and Markets Act 2000 (Consequential Amendments of References to Rules and Miscellaneous Amendments) Regulations 2022, SI 2022/854.

142A–142Z1, 143A–143Z, 144A–144H *(Part 9B—Ring-fencing (ss 142A–142Z1), Part 9C—Prudential regulation of FCA Investment Firms (ss 143A–143Z), and Part 9D—Prudential regulation of Credit Institutions etc (ss 144A–144H) are omitted due to space considerations; see further, the introductory notes to this Act. Note that Part 10 (originally ss 138–164) was replaced by the new Part 9A as noted ante)*

PART XI INFORMATION GATHERING AND INVESTIGATIONS

NOTES

Transitional provisions etc in connection with the commencement of the Financial Services Act 2012: For transitional provisions in relation to information gathering and investigations, and in respect of legally privileged information, see Part 5 of the Financial Services Act 2012 (Transitional Provisions) (Miscellaneous Provisions) Order 2013, SI 2013/442. Articles 15 and 16 contain transitional provisions in relation to cases where the FSA exercised its power to require information under s 165 or s 165A respectively before 1 April 2013; art 17 contains safeguards in respect of the exercise of the power under s 165A; art 18 deals with reports by skilled persons; art 19 concerns the appointment of persons to carry out investigations; art 20 deals with requests from overseas regulators made before 1 April 2013; art 21 concerns the power to enter premises under s 176; art 22 contains transitional provisions with regard to legal professional privilege.

Transitional provisions etc in connection with the original commencement of this Act: ss 165, 166, 167 are modified by the Financial Services and Markets Act 2000 (Transitional Provisions and Savings) (Civil Remedies, Discipline, Criminal Offences etc) (No 2) Order 2001, SI 2001/3083, arts 15–17, so that the powers conferred by those sections are exercisable in respect of any person who was, before 1 December 2001, a regulated person but who is not, and never has been, an authorised person under this Act. See also art 18 of the 2021 Order which modifies s 168 so it applies where there are circumstances suggesting that a person has contravened, or committed an offence under, certain enactments, provisions or rules before commencement.

Powers to gather information

[7.356]

165 [Regulators'] power to require information[: authorised persons etc]

(1) [Either regulator] may, by notice in writing given to an authorised person, require him—

(a) to provide specified information or information of a specified description; or

(b) to produce specified documents or documents of a specified description.

(2) The information or documents must be provided or produced—

(a) before the end of such reasonable period as may be specified; and

(b) at such place as may be specified.

(3) An officer who has written authorisation from the [regulator] to do so may require an authorised person without delay—

(a) to provide the officer with specified information or information of a specified description; or

(b) to produce to him specified documents or documents of a specified description.

(4) This section applies only to—

[(a)] information and documents reasonably required in connection with the exercise by [either regulator] of functions conferred on it by or under this Act[, and

(b) in relation to the exercise by the PRA of the powers conferred by subsections (1) and (3), information and documents reasonably required by the Bank of England in connection with the exercise by the Bank of its functions in pursuance of its financial stability objective].

(5) [The regulator in question] may require any information provided under this section to be provided in such form as it may reasonably require.

(6) [The regulator in question] may require—

(a) any information provided, whether in a document or otherwise, to be verified in such manner, or

(b) any document produced to be authenticated in such manner,

as it may reasonably require.

(7) The powers conferred by subsections (1) and (3) may also be exercised—

(a) by either regulator, to impose requirements on a person who is connected with an authorised person;

(b) by the FCA, to impose requirements on an operator, trustee or depositary of a scheme recognised under section . . . [271A or] 272 who is not an authorised person;

(c) by the FCA, to impose requirements on a recognised investment exchange;

(d) by the FCA, to impose requirements on a person who is connected with a recognised investment exchange;]

[(da) by the FCA, to impose requirements on a person who provides, or has provided, a service to an FCA investment firm or to a relevant parent undertaking of such a firm;]

[(e) by either regulator, to impose requirements on a person who provides any service to an insurance undertaking, reinsurance undertaking or third-country insurance undertaking.]

(8) "Authorised person" includes a person who was at any time an authorised person but who has ceased to be an authorised person.

[(8A) "Financial stability objective" means the objective set out in section 2A of the Bank of England Act 1998.]

(9) "Officer" means an officer of [the regulator exercising the power] and includes a member of [that regulator's] staff or an agent of [that regulator].

(10) "Specified" means—

(a) in subsections (1) and (2), specified in the notice; and

(b) in subsection (3), specified in the authorisation.

(11) For the purposes of this section, a person is connected with [another person] ("A") if he is or has at any relevant time been—

(a) a member of A's group;

(b) a controller of A;

(c) any other member of a partnership of which A is a member; . . .

(d) in relation to A, a person mentioned in Part I of Schedule 15 [(reading references in that Part to the authorised person as references to A)][; or

(e) involved in the administration of any trust arrangement relating to a funeral plan contract entered into or carried out by A].

[(12) In subsection (7)(b), the reference to a scheme that is recognised includes a scheme a part of which is recognised.]

[(13) In this section, "funeral plan contract" has the same meaning as in article 59(2) of the Financial Services and Markets Act 2000 (Regulated Activities) Order 2001.]

NOTES

The words in the second pair of square brackets in the section heading were inserted by the Financial Services Act 2010, s 24(1), (2), Sch 2, Pt 1, paras 1, 15, as from 8 June 2010.

Para (a) of sub-s (4) was designated as such, para (b) and the preceding word were added, and sub-s (8A) was added, by the Bank of England and Financial Services Act 2016, s 16, Sch 2, Pt 2, paras 26, 36, as from 1 March 2017.

The words omitted from sub-s (7)(b) were repealed by the Alternative Investment Fund Managers Regulations 2013, SI 2013/1773, reg 80, Sch 1, Part 1, paras 1, 9, as from 22 July 2013.

The words in square brackets sub-s (7)(b) were inserted by the Financial Services Act 2021, s 24, Sch 9, Pt 2, para 4(2), as from 23 February 2022.

Para (da) of sub-s (7) was inserted by the Financial Services Act 2021, s 2, Sch 2, Pt 2, para 5, as from 1 July 2021; for transitional provisions, see Sch 2, Pt 3 to the 2021 Act.

Para (e) of sub-s (7) was inserted by the Solvency 2 Regulations 2015, SI 2015/575, reg 59, Sch 1, Pt 1, paras 1, 7, as from 1 January 2016.

The word omitted from sub-s (11)(c) was repealed, sub-s (11)(e) and the preceding word were added, and sub-s (13) was added, by the Financial Services and Markets Act 2000 (Regulated Activities) (Amendment) Order 2022, SI 2022/466, art 6(2), as from 16 May 2022 (for the purposes of enabling the FCA to make rules, and to give guidance), and as from 29 July 2022 (for all other purposes).

The words in square brackets in sub-s (11)(d) were added by the Financial Services Act 2012, s 41, Sch 12, Pt 1, para 1, as from 1 April 2013.

Sub-s (12) added by the Financial Services Act 2021, s 24, Sch 9, Pt 2, para 4(3), as from 23 February 2022.

Authorised person: as from 1 April 2014, this section has effect as if each reference to "authorised person" (except in sub-s (7)) included a reference to a person who at any time held a standard licence under the Consumer Credit Act 1974; see the Financial Services and Markets Act 2000 (Regulated Activities) (Amendment) (No 2) Order 2013, SI 2013/1881, art 50(1).

[7.357]

[165A [PRA's] power to require information: financial stability

(1) The [PRA] may, by notice in writing given to a person to whom this section applies, require the person—

(a) to provide specified information or information of a specified description; or

(b) to produce specified documents or documents of a specified description.

(2) This section applies to—

(a) a person who has a legal or beneficial interest in any of the assets of a relevant investment fund;

(b) a person who is responsible for the management of a relevant investment fund;

(c) a person (a "service provider") who provides any service to an authorised person;

(d) a person prescribed by an order made by the Treasury or any person of a description prescribed by such an order (and see also section 165C);

(e) a person who is connected with a person to whom this section applies as a result of any of the above paragraphs.

(3) This section applies only to—

[(a)] information and documents that the [PRA] considers are, or might be, relevant to the stability of one or more aspects of the UK financial system[, and

(b) information and documents reasonably required by the Bank of England in connection with the exercise by the Bank of its functions in pursuance of its financial stability objective].

(4) A notice may be given to a service provider, or to a person who is connected with a service provider, only if the [PRA] considers that—

(a) the service or the way in which it (or any part of it) is provided, or

(b) any failure to provide the service (or any part of it),

poses, or would be likely to pose, a serious threat to the stability of the UK financial system.

(5) Information or documents required under this section must be provided or produced—

(a) before the end of such reasonable period as may be specified; and

(b) at such place as may be specified.

(6) The [PRA] may require any information provided under this section to be provided in such form as it may reasonably require.

(7) The [PRA] may require—

(a) any information provided, whether in a document or otherwise, to be verified in such manner as it may reasonably require; or

(b) any document produced to be authenticated in such manner as it may reasonably require.

[(7A) "Financial stability objective" means the objective set out in section 2A of the Bank of England Act 1998.]

(8) In this section—

"management" includes any of the activities listed in [Schedule 6 to the Financial Services and Markets Act 2000 (Regulated Activities) Order 2001];

"relevant investment fund" means an investment fund whose assets consist of or include financial instruments which—

(a) are traded in the United Kingdom; or

(b) were issued by a body incorporated in the United Kingdom;

"service" includes facility;

"specified" means specified in the notice.

(9) For the purposes of the definition of "relevant investment fund"—

(a) arrangements may constitute an investment fund even if there is only one person participating in the arrangements; and

(b) the reference to financial instruments has the [same meaning as in the Financial Services and Markets Act 2000 (Regulated Activities) Order 2001 (see article 3(1) of that Order)].

(10) For the purposes of this section a person is connected with another person ("A") if the person is or has at any relevant time been—

(a) a member of A's group;

(b) a controller of A;

(c) any other member of a partnership of which A is a member; or

(d) in relation to A, a person mentioned in Part 1 of Schedule 15 (reading references in that Part to the authorised person as references to A).]

NOTES

Inserted, together with ss 165B, 165C, by the Financial Services Act 2010, s 18(1), (2), as from 8 June 2010.

Words "PRA" and "PRA's" in square brackets (in each place that they occur) substituted by the Financial Services Act 2012, s 41, Sch 12, Pt 1, para 2, as from 1 April 2013.

Para (a) of sub-s (3) was designated as such, para (b) and the preceding word were added, and sub-s (7A) was added, by the Bank of England and Financial Services Act 2016, s 16, Sch 2, Pt 2, paras 26, 37, as from 1 March 2017.

Words in square brackets in the definition "management" in sub-s (8), and in sub-s (9)(b), substituted by the Financial Services and Markets Act 2000 (Amendment) (EU Exit) Regulations 2019, SI 2019/632, regs 42, 43, as from IP completion day (as defined in the European Union (Withdrawal Agreement) Act 2020, s 39).

Note that the Banking Act 2009, s 250 provides that the PRA shall collect information that it thinks is or may be relevant to the stability of individual financial institutions, or one or more aspects of the financial systems of the UK. The Authority may perform that function by the exercise of the power in section 165 or 165A.

[7.358]

[165B Safeguards etc in relation to exercise of power under section 165A

(1) If the [PRA] proposes to impose a requirement on a person under section 165A, it must give the person a notice in writing warning the person that the [PRA] is proposing to impose the requirement.

(2) The notice under subsection (1) must—

(a) give the [PRA's] reasons for proposing to impose the requirement; and

(b) specify a reasonable period within which the person may make representations to the [PRA].

(3) The [PRA] must then decide, within a reasonable period, whether to impose the requirement.

(4) Subsections (1) to (3) do not apply in any case where the [PRA] is satisfied that it is necessary for the information or documents to be provided or produced without delay.

(5) If the [PRA] imposes a requirement on a person under section 165A, the notice under that section must give the [PRA's] reasons for imposing the requirement.

(6) The [PRA] must prepare a statement of its policy with respect to the exercise of the power conferred by section 165A.

(7) The statement requires the approval of the Treasury.

(8) If the Treasury approve the statement, the [PRA] must publish it.

(9) The power conferred by section 165A may not be exercised before the statement has been published.]

NOTES

Inserted as noted to s 165A at **[7.357]**.

Words "PRA" and "PRA's" in square brackets (in each place that they occur) substituted by the Financial Services Act 2012, s 41, Sch 12, Pt 1, para 3, as from 1 April 2013.

[7.359]

[165C Orders under section 165A(2)(d)

[(1) The Treasury may make an order under section 165A(2)(d) only if either or both of the following conditions is met in relation to the provision made by the order.

(1A) Condition A is that the Treasury consider that—

(a) the activities carried on by the prescribed person or persons of the prescribed description, or the way in which those activities (or any part of them) are carried on, or

(b) any failure to carry on those activities (or any part of them),

pose, or would be likely to pose, a serious threat to the stability of the UK financial system.

(1B) Condition B is that the provision implements all or part of a recommendation made by the Financial Policy Committee of the Bank of England under section 9P of the Bank of England Act 1998.]

(2) Subject as follows, an order under section 165A(2)(d) may not be made unless a draft of the order has been laid before, and approved by a resolution of, each House of Parliament.

(3) Subsection (2) does not apply in any case where the Treasury are satisfied that it is necessary to make an order under section 165A(2)(d) without laying a draft for approval.

(4) In that case, the order—

(a) must be laid before Parliament after being made; and

(b) ceases to have effect at the end of the relevant period unless before the end of that period it is approved by a resolution of each House of Parliament.

(5) If an order ceases to have effect as a result of subsection (4)(b) that does not affect—

(a) anything done under it; or

(b) the power to make a new one.

(6) "Relevant period" means a period of 28 days beginning with the day on which the order is made.

(7) In calculating the relevant period no account is to be taken of any time during which Parliament is dissolved or prorogued or during which both Houses are adjourned for more than four days.

(8) If a statutory instrument containing an order under section 165A(2)(d) would, apart from this subsection, be treated as a hybrid instrument for the purposes of the Standing Orders of either House of Parliament, it is to proceed in that House as if it were not a hybrid instrument.]

NOTES

Inserted as noted to s 165A at **[7.357]**.

Sub-ss (1)–(1B): substituted (for the original sub-s (1)) by the Financial Services Act 2012, s 41, Sch 12, Pt 1, para 4, as from 1 April 2013.

[7.360]

[166 Reports by skilled persons

(1) This section applies where either regulator has required or could require a person to whom subsection (2) applies ("the person concerned") to provide information or produce documents with respect to any matter ("the matter concerned").

(2) This subsection applies to—

(a) an authorised person ("A"),

(b) any other member of A's group,

(c) a partnership of which A is a member, or

(d) a person who has at any relevant time been a person falling within paragraph (a), (b) or (c),

who is, or was at the relevant time, carrying on a business.

(3) The regulator mentioned in subsection (1) may either—

(a) by notice in writing given to the person concerned, require the person concerned to provide the regulator with a report on the matter concerned, or

(b) itself appoint a person to provide the regulator with a report on the matter concerned.

(4) When acting under subsection (3)(a), the regulator may require the report to be in such form as may be specified in the notice.

(5) The regulator must give notice of an appointment under subsection (3)(b) to the person concerned.

(6) The person appointed to make a report—

(a) must be a person appearing to the regulator to have the skills necessary to make a report on the matter concerned, and

(b) where the appointment is to be made by the person concerned, must be a person nominated or approved by the regulator.

(7) It is the duty of—

(a) the person concerned, and

(b) any person who is providing (or who has at any time provided) services to the person concerned in relation to the matter concerned,

to give the person appointed to prepare a report all such assistance as the appointed person may reasonably require.

(8) The obligation imposed by subsection (7) is enforceable, on the application of the regulator in question, by an injunction or, in Scotland, by an order for specific performance under section 45 of the Court of Session Act 1988.

(9) A regulator may make rules providing for expenses incurred by it in relation to an appointment under subsection (3)(b) to be payable as a fee by the person concerned.

(10) The powers conferred by this section may also be exercised by the FCA in relation to a person to whom subsection (11)[, (12) or (13)] applies, (and references to the person concerned are to be read accordingly).

(11) This subsection applies to—

(a) a recognised investment exchange ("A"),

(b) any other member of A's group,

(c) a partnership of which A is a member, or

(d) a person who has at any time been a person falling within paragraph (a), (b) or (c),

who is, or was at the relevant time, carrying on a business.

[(12) This subsection applies to a person who provides, or has provided, a service to an FCA investment firm or to a relevant parent undertaking of such a firm.]

[(13) This subsection applies to a person who is or has at any relevant time been involved in the administration of any trust arrangement relating to a funeral plan contract entered into or carried out by an authorised person.

(14) In this section, "funeral plan contract" has the same meaning as in article 59(2) of the Financial Services and Markets Act 2000 (Regulated Activities) Order 2001.]]

NOTES

Substituted by the Financial Services Act 2012, s 41, Sch 12, Pt 1, para 5, as from 24 January 2013 (for the purpose of making rules), and as from 1 April 2013 (otherwise).

The words in square brackets in sub-s (10) were inserted, and sub-s (12) was added, by the Financial Services Act 2021, s 2, Sch 2, Pt 2, para 6, as from 1 July 2021; for transitional provisions, see Sch 2, Pt 3 to the 2021 Act.

Words in square brackets in sub-s (10) substituted, and sub-ss (13) and (14) added, by the Financial Services and Markets Act 2000 (Regulated Activities) (Amendment) Order 2022, SI 2022/466, art 6(3), as from 16 May 2022 (for the purposes of enabling the FCA to make rules, and to give guidance), and as from 29 July 2022 (for all other purposes).

[7.361]

[166A Appointment of skilled person to collect and update information

(1) This section applies if either regulator considers that an authorised person has contravened a requirement in rules made by that regulator to collect, and keep up to date, information of a description specified in the rules.

(2) The regulator may either—

(a) require the authorised person to appoint a skilled person to collect or update the information, or

(b) itself appoint a skilled person to do so.

(3) References in this section to a skilled person are to a person—

(a) appearing to the regulator to have the skills necessary to collect or update the information in question, and

(b) where the appointment is to be made by the authorised person, nominated or approved by the regulator.

(4) The regulator must give notice of an appointment under subsection (2)(b) to the authorised person.

(5) The skilled person may require any person to provide all such assistance as the skilled person may reasonably require to collect or update the information in question.

(6) A requirement imposed under subsection (5) is enforceable, on the application of the regulator in question, by an injunction or, in Scotland, by an order for specific performance under section 45 of the Court of Session Act 1988.

(7) A contractual or other requirement imposed on a person ("P") to keep any information in confidence does not apply if—

(a) the information is or may be relevant to anything required to be done as a result of this section,

(b) an authorised person or a skilled person requests or requires P to provide the information for the purpose of securing that those things are done, and

(c) the regulator in question has approved the making of the request or the imposition of the requirement before it is made or imposed.

(8) An authorised person may provide information (whether received under subsection (7) or otherwise) that would otherwise be subject to a contractual or other requirement to keep it in confidence if it is provided for the purposes of anything required to be done as a result of this section.

(9) A regulator may make rules providing for expenses incurred by it in relation to an appointment under subsection (2)(b) to be payable as a fee by the authorised person.

(10) In this section "authorised person", in relation to the PRA, means PRA-authorised person.]

NOTES

Inserted by the Financial Services Act 2012, s 41, Sch 12, Pt 1, para 6, as from 24 January 2013 (for the purpose of making rules), and as from 1 April 2013 (otherwise).

Appointment of investigators

[7.362]

167 Appointment of persons to carry out general investigations

(1) If it appears to [an investigating authority] that there is good reason for doing so, the investigating authority may appoint one or more competent persons to conduct an investigation on its behalf into—

(a) the nature, conduct or state of the business of [a person to whom subsection (1A) applies or] an appointed representative;

(b) a particular aspect of that business; or

(c) the ownership or control of [a person to whom subsection (1A) applies].

[(1A) This subsection applies to the following persons—

(a) a recognised investment exchange;

(b) an authorised person;

(c) a relevant parent undertaking of an FCA investment firm;

(d) a person who provides a service to an FCA investment firm or to a relevant parent undertaking of such a firm.]

(2) If a person appointed under subsection (1) thinks it necessary for the purposes of his investigation, he may also investigate the business of a person who is or has at any relevant time been—

(a) a member of the group of which the person under investigation ("A") is part; . . .

(b) a partnership of which A is a member[; or;]

[(c) where A is an insurance undertaking, reinsurance undertaking or third-country insurance undertaking, a person who provides services to A].

(3) If a person appointed under subsection (1) decides to investigate the business of any person under subsection (2) he must give that person written notice of his decision.

[(3A) . . .]

[(4A) The power conferred by this section may be exercised in relation to a person who has at any time been an authorised person or a person described in subsection (1A)(c) or (d) but only in relation to—

(a) business carried on at any time when the person was an authorised person or a person described in subsection (1A)(c) or (d), or

(b) the ownership or control of the person at such a time.

(4B) The power conferred by this section may be exercised in relation to a person who has at any time been an appointed representative but only in relation to business carried on at any time when the person was an appointed representative.]

(5) "Business" includes any part of a business even if it does not consist of carrying on regulated activities.

[(5A) Investigating authority" means—

(a) in relation to a recognised investment exchange, the Secretary of State or the FCA;

(b) in relation to an authorised person or former authorised person, the FCA or the PRA;

(c) in relation to an appointed representative or former appointed representative, the FCA or the PRA;

[(d) in relation to a person who is, or has at any time been, a person described in subsection (1A)(c) or (d) who is not an authorised person, the FCA].]

[(6) References in subsection (1) to a recognised investment exchange do not include references to an overseas investment exchange (as defined by section 313(1)).]

NOTES

Sub-s (1): words in first pair of square brackets substituted by the Financial Services Act 2012, s 41, Sch 12, Pt 1, para 7(1), (2), as from 1 April 2013. Words in square brackets in paras (a) and (c) substituted by the Financial Services Act 2021, s 2, Sch 2, Pt 2, para 7(2), as from 1 July 2021; for transitional provisions, see Sch 2, Pt 3 to the 2021 Act.

Sub-s (1A): inserted by the Financial Services Act 2021, s 2, Sch 2, Pt 2, para 7(3), as from 1 July 2021; for transitional provisions, see Sch 2, Pt 3 to the 2021 Act.

Sub-s (2): word omitted from para (a) repealed, and para (c) (and the preceding word in square brackets) inserted, by the Solvency 2 Regulations 2015, SI 2015/575, reg 59, Sch 1, Pt 1, paras 1, 8(1), (2), as from 1 January 2016.

Sub-s (3A): originally inserted by SI 2015/575, reg 59, Sch 1, Pt 1, paras 1, 8(1), (3), as from 1 January 2016. Subsequently repealed by the Financial Services and Markets Act 2000 (Amendment) (EU Exit) Regulations 2019, SI 2019/632, regs 42, 44, as from IP completion day (as defined in the European Union (Withdrawal Agreement) Act 2020, s 39).

Sub-ss (4), (4A): substituted (for the original sub-s (4)) by the Financial Services Act 2021, s 2, Sch 2, Pt 2, para 7(4), as from 1 July 2021; for transitional provisions, see Sch 2, Pt 3 to the 2021 Act.

Sub-s (5A): inserted by the Financial Services Act 2012, s 41, Sch 12, Pt 1, para 7(1), (3), as from 1 April 2013. Para (d) added by the Financial Services Act 2021, s 2, Sch 2, Pt 2, para 7(5), as from 1 July 2021; for transitional provisions, see Sch 2, Pt 3 to the 2021 Act.

Sub-s (6): added by SI 2007/126, reg 3(5), Sch 5, paras 1, 7(b), as from 1 April 2007 (certain purposes), and as from 1 November 2007 (otherwise).

[7.363]

168 Appointment of persons to carry out investigations in particular cases

(1) Subsection (3) applies if it appears to an investigating authority that there are circumstances suggesting that—

(a) . . .

(b) a person may be guilty of an offence under section [122F,] 177, [191F], 346 or 398(1) . . .

(2) Subsection (3) also applies if it appears to an investigating authority that there are circumstances suggesting that—

(a) an offence under section 24(1) [. . .] [or under Part 7 of the Financial Services Act 2012] or under Part V of the Criminal Justice Act 1993 may have been committed;

(b) there may have been a breach of the general prohibition;

[(ba) an authorised person may have contravened section 20 in relation to a credit-related regulated activity;]

(c) there may have been a contravention of section 21 or 238; or

[(d) a person has contravened Article 14 (prohibition of insider dealing and of unlawful disclosure of inside information) or Article 15 (prohibition of market manipulation) of the market abuse regulation].

(3) The investigating authority may appoint one or more competent persons to conduct an investigation on its behalf.

(4) Subsection (5) applies if it appears to [an investigating authority] that there are circumstances suggesting that—

(a) a person may have contravened section 20;

(b) a person may be guilty of an offence under prescribed regulations relating to money laundering;

[(ba) a person may be guilty of an offence under Schedule 7 to the Counter-Terrorism Act 2008 (terrorist financing or money laundering);]

(c) [a person] may have contravened a rule made by the [investigating authority];

[(ca) a recognised investment exchange may have contravened the recognition requirements (within the meaning of Part 18);]

(d) an individual may not be a fit and proper person to perform functions in relation to a regulated activity carried on by an authorised or exempt person;

(e) an individual may have performed or agreed to perform a function in breach of a prohibition order;

(f) [a person] may have failed to comply with section 56(6);

(g) an authorised person may have failed to comply with section 59(1) or (2);

(h) a person in relation to whom [a regulator] has given its approval under section 59 may not be a fit and proper person to perform the function to which that approval relates; . . .

[(ha) a person may have performed a controlled function without approval for the purposes of section 63A;]

(i) a person may be guilty of misconduct for the purposes of section 66[; . . .

[(ia) a person may have failed to comply with section 143R;

(ib) an individual may have performed or agreed to perform a function in breach of a Part 9C prohibition order;

(ic) a person may have failed to comply with section 143S(6);]

(j) a person may have contravened any provision made by or under this Act for the purpose of implementing the markets in financial instruments directive . . .]; [. . .

[(ja) a person may have contravened—

(i) any provision made by or under this Act for the purpose of implementing the alternative investment fund managers directive; . . .

(ii) any provision made by the Alternative Investment Fund Managers Regulations 2013; or]

[(iii) any provision made by or under this Act for the purpose of implementing the UCITS Directive; or

(iv) any provision made by the Undertakings for Collective Investment in Transferable Securities Regulations 2011; . . .]

[(jb) a person may have contravened—

(i) any provision made by or under this Act for the purposes of the market abuse regulation; or

(ii) a requirement imposed on that person under sections 122A to 122C, 122G to 122I, 123A or 123B;

(jc) a person may have been knowingly concerned in the contravention of—

(i) a provision of the market abuse regulation other than Article 14 (prohibition of insider dealing) or 15 (prohibition of market manipulation) of that regulation; or

(ii) [any retained EU direct legislation originally made under the market abuse regulation or any subordinate legislation (within the meaning of the Interpretation Act 1978) made on or after IP completion day] under the market abuse regulation; or]

[(k) a person may have contravened a [qualifying provision] that is specified, or of a description specified, for the purposes of this subsection by the Treasury by order].

(5) The [investigating authority] may appoint one or more competent persons to conduct an investigation on its behalf.

[(6) Investigating authority" means—

(a) in subsections (1) to (3), the FCA, the PRA or the Secretary of State;

(b) in subsections (4) and (5), the FCA or the PRA.]

NOTES

Sub-s (1): para (a) repealed, and figure in second pair of square brackets in para (b) substituted, by the Financial Services Act 2012, s 41, Sch 12, Pt 1, para 8(1), (2), as from 1 April 2013. Figure in first pair of square brackets in para (b) inserted by the Financial Services and Markets Act 2000 (Market Abuse) Regulations 2016, SI 2016/680, reg 10(1), (8)(a), as from 3 July 2016. Words omitted from para (b) repealed by the EEA Passport Rights (Amendment, etc, and Transitional Provisions) (EU Exit) Regulations 2018, SI 2018/1149, reg 3, Schedule, Pt 1, paras 1, 11, as from IP completion day (as defined in the European Union (Withdrawal Agreement) Act 2020, s 39).

Sub-s (2): words omitted from para (a) originally inserted by the Pension Schemes Act 2015, s 47, Sch 3, paras 1, 11, as from 3 March 2015. Subsequently repealed by the Financial Guidance and Claims Act 2018, s 25, Sch 3, paras 5, 18, as from 1 January 2019. Words in square brackets in para (a) substituted, and para (ba) inserted, by the Financial Services Act 2012, s 41, Sch 12, Pt 1, para 8(1), (3), as from 1 April 2013. Para (d) substituted by SI 2016/680, reg 10(1), (8)(b), as from 3 July 2016.

Sub-s (4) is amended as follows

Words "an investigating authority" in square brackets substituted by the Financial Services Act 2012, s 41, Sch 12, Pt 1, para 8(1), (4)(a), as from 1 April 2013.

Para (ba) inserted by the Counter-Terrorism Act 2008, s 62, Sch 7, Pt 7, para 33(3), as from 27 November 2008.

Words "a person" in square brackets in para (c) substituted, and para (ha) inserted, by the Financial Services Act 2010, s 24(1), (2), Sch 2, Pt 1, paras 1, 16, as from 8 April 2010 (in the case of the amendment to para (c)), and as from 8 June 2010 (in the case of the insertion of para (ha)).

Words "investigating authority" in square brackets in para (c) substituted by the Financial Services Act 2012, s 41, Sch 12, Pt 1, para 8(1), (4)(b), as from 1 April 2013.

Para (ca) inserted by the Financial Services Act 2012, s 41, Sch 12, Pt 1, para 8(1), (4)(c), as from 1 April 2013.

Words "a person" in square brackets in para (f) substituted by the Financial Services Act 2012, s 41, Sch 12, Pt 1, para 8(1), (4)(d), as from 1 April 2013.

Words "a regulator" in square brackets in para (h) substituted by the Financial Services Act 2012, s 41, Sch 12, Pt 1, para 8(1), (4)(e), as from 1 April 2013.

Word omitted from para (h) repealed, and para (j) and the word immediately preceding it inserted, by the Financial Services and Markets Act 2000 (Markets in Financial Instruments) Regulations 2007, SI 2007/126, reg 3(5), Sch 5, paras 1, 8, as from 1 April 2007 (certain purposes), and as from 1 November 2007 (otherwise).

Word omitted from para (i) repealed, and para (k) and the word immediately preceding it inserted, by the Financial Services and Markets Act 2000 (Short Selling) Regulations 2012, SI 2012/2554, reg 2(1), (11), as from 1 November 2012.

Paras (ia)–(ic) inserted by the Financial Services Act 2021, s 2, Sch 2, Pt 2, para 8(1), as from 1 July 2021; for transitional provisions, see Sch 2, Pt 3 to the 2021 Act.

First words omitted from para (j) repealed by the Financial Services Act 2012, s 41, Sch 12, Pt 1, para 8(1), (4)(f), as from 1 April 2013.

The second word omitted from para (j) was repealed, and para (ja) was inserted, by the Alternative Investment Fund Managers Regulations 2013, SI 2013/1773, reg 80, Sch 1, Part 1, paras 1, 10, as from 22 July 2013.

The word omitted from sub-para (ja)(i) was repealed, and sub-paras (ja)(iii), (iv) were added, by the Undertakings for Collective Investment in Transferable Securities Regulations 2016, SI 2016/225, reg 2(1), (4), as from 18 March 2016.

The word omitted from sub-para (ja)(iv) was repealed, and the original para (jb) was inserted, by SI 2016/680, reg 10(1), (8)(c), as from 3 July 2016.

Paras (jb), (jc) substituted (for the original para (jb)) by the Financial Services and Markets Act 2000 (Markets in Financial Instruments) (No 2) Regulations 2017, SI 2017/1255, reg 3(1), (4), as from 3 January 2018. Words in square brackets in sub-para (jc)(ii) substituted by the Financial Services and Markets Act 2000 (Amendment) (EU Exit) Regulations 2019, SI 2019/632, regs 42, 45(a), as from IP completion day (as defined in the European Union (Withdrawal Agreement) Act 2020, s 39) (for transitional provisions see SI 2019/710, reg 37 at **[12.110]**). Note that reg 45(a) of the 2019 Regulations was amended by the Financial Services and Economic and Monetary Policy (Consequential Amendments) (EU Exit) Regulations 2020, SI 2020/1301, reg 3, Schedule, para 33(e), as from 30 December 2020; and the effect of the amendment has been incorporated in the text set out above.

Para (k) substituted by the Financial Services Act 2012, s 41, Sch 12, Pt 1, para 8(1), (4)(g), as from 24 January 2013 (for the purposes of making orders), and as from 1 April 2013 (otherwise). Words in square brackets substituted by SI 2019/632, regs 42, 45(b), as from IP completion day (as defined in the European Union (Withdrawal Agreement) Act 2020, s 39) (for transitional provisions see SI 2019/710, reg 37 at **[12.110]**).

Sub-s (5): words in square brackets substituted by the Financial Services Act 2012, s 41, Sch 12, Pt 1, para 8(1), (5), as from 1 April 2013.

Sub-s (6): substituted by the Financial Services Act 2012, s 41, Sch 12, Pt 1, para 8(1), (5), as from 1 April 2013.

Offence: as from 1 April 2014, this section applies as if sub-s (1) included a reference to an offence under the Consumer Credit Act 1974; see the Financial Services and Markets Act 2000 (Regulated Activities) (Amendment) (No 2) Order 2013, SI 2013/1881, art 50(2)(a).

Circumstances suggesting, etc (sub-s (4)): as from 1 April 2014, sub-s (4) has effect as if it included a reference to circumstances suggesting that a person may have, before that date, failed to comply with a requirement imposed on that person under the Consumer Credit Act 1974, ss 33A, 33B or 36A; see the Financial Services and Markets Act 2000 (Regulated Activities) (Amendment) (No 2) Order 2013, SI 2013/1881, art 50(2)(b).

Note: the Money Laundering, Terrorist Financing and Transfer of Funds (Information on the Payer) Regulations 2017, SI 2017/692 are prescribed for the purposes of sub-s (4)(b) above by reg 2 of those Regulations.

Extension of powers (civil sanctions): where, by virtue of sub-s (4)(b) above, a Minister of the Crown (or the Welsh Ministers) has the power by statutory instrument to make provision creating a criminal offence and the power has been or is being exercised so as to create the offence, then that power is extended so as to include the power to confer on certain persons the power to impose civil sanctions in relation to the offence; see the Regulatory Enforcement and Sanctions Act 2008, s 62, Sch 7

Regulations and Orders: the Financial Services and Markets Act 2000 (Qualifying Provisions) Order 2013, SI 2013/419; the Financial Services and Markets Act 2000 (Qualifying Provisions) (No 2) Order 2013, SI 2013/3116; the Financial Services and Markets Act 2000 (Transparency of Securities Financing Transactions and of Reuse) Regulations 2016, SI 2016/715; the Financial Services and Markets Act 2000 (Qualifying EU Provisions) (Amendment) Order 2016, SI 2016/936; the Money Laundering, Terrorist Financing and Transfer of Funds (Information on the Payer) Regulations 2017, SI 2017/692; the Oversight of Professional Body Anti-Money Laundering and Counter Terrorist Financing Supervision Regulations 2017, SI 2017/1301; the Alternative Investment Fund Managers (Amendment) Regulations 2018, SI 2018/134; the Insurance Distribution (Regulated Activities and Miscellaneous Amendments) Order 2018, SI 2018/546.

Assistance to overseas regulators

[7.364]

169 Investigations etc in support of overseas regulator

(1) At the request of an overseas regulator, [a regulator] may—

- (a) exercise the power conferred by section 165; or
- (b) appoint one or more competent persons to investigate any matter.

(2) An investigator has the same powers as an investigator appointed under section 168(3) (as a result of subsection (1) of that section).

[(2A) But where the investigator is—

- (a) appointed by the FCA, and
- (b) the appointment is in response to a request to the FCA to investigate a possible contravention by a person of Article 14 (prohibition of insider dealing and of unlawful disclosure of inside information) or Article 15 (prohibition of market manipulation) of the market abuse regulation,

the investigator has the same powers as an investigator appointed under section 168(3) (as a result of subsection (2) of that section).]

(3) . . .

(4) In deciding whether or not to exercise its investigative power, the [regulator] may take into account in particular—

- (a) whether in the country or territory of the overseas regulator concerned, corresponding assistance would be given to a United Kingdom regulatory authority;
- (b) whether the case concerns the breach of a law, or other requirement, which has no close parallel in the United Kingdom or involves the assertion of a jurisdiction not recognised by the United Kingdom;
- (c) the seriousness of the case and its importance to persons in the United Kingdom;
- (d) whether it is otherwise appropriate in the public interest to give the assistance sought.

(5) The [regulator] may decide that it will not exercise its investigative power unless the overseas regulator undertakes to make such contribution towards the cost of its exercise as the [regulator] considers appropriate.

(6) . . .

(7) If [a regulator] has appointed an investigator in response to a request from an overseas regulator, it may direct the investigator to permit a representative of that regulator to attend, and take part in, any interview conducted for the purposes of the investigation.

(8) A direction under subsection (7) is not to be given unless the [regulator] is satisfied that any information obtained by an overseas regulator as a result of the interview will be subject to safeguards equivalent to those contained in Part XXIII.

(9) [Each regulator] must prepare a statement of its policy with respect to the conduct of interviews in relation to which a direction under subsection (7) has been given.

(10) The statement requires the approval of the Treasury.

(11) If the Treasury approve the statement, the [regulator] must publish it.

(12) No direction may be given under subsection (7) before the statement has been published.

(13) "Overseas regulator" has the same meaning as in section 195.

(14) "Investigative power" means one of the powers mentioned in subsection (1).

(15) "Investigator" means a person appointed under subsection (1)(b).

NOTES

Sub-ss (1), (4), (5), (7)–(9), (11): words in square brackets substituted by the Financial Services Act 2012, s 41, Sch 12, Pt 1, para 9(1), (2), (6), as from 24 January 2013 (in so far as relating to the preparation of a statement of policy), and as from 1 April 2013 (otherwise).

Sub-s (2A): inserted by the Financial Services and Markets Act 2000 (Market Abuse) Regulations 2016, SI 2016/680, reg 10(1), (9), as from 3 July 2016.

Sub-ss (3), (6): repealed by the Financial Services and Markets Act 2000 (Amendment) (EU Exit) Regulations 2019, SI 2019/632, regs 42, 46, as from IP completion day (as defined in the European Union (Withdrawal Agreement) Act 2020, s 39) (for transitional provisions see SI 2019/710, reg 37 at **[12.110]**).

[7.365]

[169A Support of overseas regulator with respect to financial stability

(1) At the request of an overseas regulator, the [PRA] may exercise a corresponding section 165A power.

(2) An "overseas regulator" means an authority in a country or territory outside the United Kingdom which exercises functions with respect to the stability of the financial system operating in that country or territory.

(3) A "corresponding section 165A power" means a power corresponding to the one conferred by section 165A, but reading references in that section to the stability of the UK financial system as references to the stability of the financial system operating in the country or territory of the overseas regulator.

(4) The following provisions apply in relation to the exercise of the corresponding section 165A power—

- (a) section 165B(1) to (5); and
- (b) section [169(4)(a) and (d) and (5)].

(5) In this section "the financial system" includes—
(a) financial markets and exchanges;
(b) activities that would be regulated activities if carried on in the United Kingdom; and
(c) other activities connected with financial markets and exchanges.]

NOTES

Inserted by the Financial Services Act 2010, s 18(1), (3), as from 8 June 2010.

Sub-s (1): word in square brackets substituted by the Financial Services Act 2012, s 41, Sch 12, Pt 1, para 10, as from 1 April 2013.

Sub-s (4): words in square brackets in para (b) substituted by the Financial Services and Markets Act 2000 (Amendment) (EU Exit) Regulations 2019, SI 2019/632, regs 42, 47, as from IP completion day (as defined in the European Union (Withdrawal Agreement) Act 2020, s 39).

Conduct of investigations

[7.366]

170 Investigations: general

(1) This section applies if an investigating authority appoints one or more competent persons ("investigators") under section 167 or 168(3) or (5) to conduct an investigation on its behalf.

(2) The investigating authority must give written notice of the appointment of an investigator to the person who is the subject of the investigation ("the person under investigation").

(3) Subsections (2) and (9) do not apply if—
(a) the investigator is appointed as a result of section 168(1) or (4) and the investigating authority believes that the notice required by subsection (2) or (9) would be likely to result in the investigation being frustrated; or
(b) the investigator is appointed as a result of subsection (2) of section 168.

(4) A notice under subsection (2) must—
(a) specify the provisions under which, and as a result of which, the investigator was appointed; and
(b) state the reason for his appointment.

(5) Nothing prevents the investigating authority from appointing a person who is a member of its staff as an investigator.

(6) An investigator must make a report of his investigation to the investigating authority.

(7) The investigating authority may, by a direction to an investigator, control—
(a) the scope of the investigation;
(b) the period during which the investigation is to be conducted;
(c) the conduct of the investigation; and
(d) the reporting of the investigation.

(8) A direction may, in particular—
(a) confine the investigation to particular matters;
(b) extend the investigation to additional matters;
(c) require the investigator to discontinue the investigation or to take only such steps as are specified in the direction;
(d) require the investigator to make such interim reports as are so specified.

(9) If there is a change in the scope or conduct of the investigation and, in the opinion of the investigating authority, the person subject to investigation is likely to be significantly prejudiced by not being made aware of it, that person must be given written notice of the change.

(10) "Investigating authority", in relation to an investigator, means—
[(a) the FCA, if the FCA appointed the investigator;
(aa) the PRA, if the PRA appointed the investigator;
(b) the Secretary of State, if the Secretary of State appointed the investigator].

NOTES

Sub-s (10): paras (a), (aa), (b) substituted (for the original paras (a), (b)) by the Financial Services Act 2012, s 41, Sch 12, Pt 1, para 10, as from 1 April 2013.

[7.367]

171 Powers of persons appointed under section 167

(1) [An investigator may require a person to whom subsection (1A) applies—]
(a) to attend before the investigator at a specified time and place and answer questions; or
(b) otherwise to provide such information as the investigator may require.

[(1A) This subsection applies to the following persons—
(a) the person who is the subject of the investigation ("the person under investigation");
(b) any person connected with the person under investigation;
(c) where the person under investigation is an FCA investment firm, a person who provides, or has provided, a service to the firm or to a relevant parent undertaking of the firm;
(d) where the person under investigation is a relevant parent undertaking of an FCA investment firm, a person who provides, or has provided, a service to the parent undertaking or to the firm.]

(2) An investigator may also require any person to produce at a specified time and place any specified documents or documents of a specified description.

(3) A requirement under subsection (1) or (2) may be imposed only so far as the investigator concerned reasonably considers the question, provision of information or production of the document to be relevant to the purposes of the investigation.

[(3A) Where the investigation relates to a recognised investment exchange, an investigator has the additional powers conferred by sections 172 and 173 (and for this purpose references in those sections to an investigator are to be read accordingly).]

(4) For the purposes of this section and section 172, a person is connected with the person under investigation ("A") if he is or has at any relevant time been—

Part 7 Financial Services Acts

(a) a member of A's group;
(b) a controller of A;
(c) a partnership of which A is a member; or
(d) in relation to A, a person mentioned in Part I or II of Schedule 15.

(5) "Investigator" means a person conducting an investigation under section 167.
(6) "Specified" means specified in a notice in writing.
[(7) The reference in subsection (3A) to a recognised investment exchange does not include a reference to an overseas investment exchange (as defined by section 313(1)).]

NOTES

Sub-s (1): words in square brackets substituted by the Financial Services Act 2021, s 2, Sch 2, Pt 2, para 8(3), as from 1 July 2021; for transitional provisions, see Sch 2, Pt 3 to the 2021 Act.

Sub-s (1A): inserted by the Financial Services Act 2021, s 2, Sch 2, Pt 2, para 8(4), as from 1 July 2021; for transitional provisions, see Sch 2, Pt 3 to the 2021 Act.

Sub-ss (3A), (7): inserted and added respectively by the Financial Services and Markets Act 2000 (Markets in Financial Instruments) Regulations 2007, SI 2007/126, reg 3(5), Sch 5, paras 1, 9, as from 1 April 2007 (certain purposes), and as from 1 November 2007 (otherwise).

[7.368]

172 Additional power of persons appointed as a result of section 168(1) or (4)

(1) An investigator has the powers conferred by section 171.
(2) An investigator may also require a person who is neither the subject of the investigation ("the person under investigation") nor a person connected with the person under investigation—
(a) to attend before the investigator at a specified time and place and answer questions; or
(b) otherwise to provide such information as the investigator may require for the purposes of the investigation.

(3) A requirement may only be imposed under subsection (2) if the investigator is satisfied that the requirement is necessary or expedient for the purposes of the investigation.
(4) "Investigator" means a person appointed as a result of subsection (1) or (4) of section 168.
(5) "Specified" means specified in a notice in writing.

[7.369]

173 Powers of persons appointed as a result of section 168(2)

(1) Subsections (2) to (4) apply if an investigator considers that any person ("A") is or may be able to give information which is or may be relevant to the investigation.
(2) The investigator may require A—
(a) to attend before him at a specified time and place and answer questions; or
(b) otherwise to provide such information as he may require for the purposes of the investigation.

(3) The investigator may also require A to produce at a specified time and place any specified documents or documents of a specified description which appear to the investigator to relate to any matter relevant to the investigation.
(4) The investigator may also otherwise require A to give him all assistance in connection with the investigation which A is reasonably able to give.
(5) "Investigator" means a person appointed under subsection (3) of section 168 (as a result of subsection (2) of that section).

[7.370]

174 Admissibility of statements made to investigators

(1) A statement made to an investigator by a person in compliance with an information requirement is admissible in evidence in any proceedings, so long as it also complies with any requirements governing the admissibility of evidence in the circumstances in question.
(2) But in criminal proceedings in which that person is charged with an offence to which this subsection applies or in proceedings in relation to action to be taken against that person under section 123 [to which this subsection applies]—
(a) no evidence relating to the statement may be adduced, and
(b) no question relating to it may be asked,

by or on behalf of the prosecution or (as the case may be) [a regulator], unless evidence relating to it is adduced, or a question relating to it is asked, in the proceedings by or on behalf of that person.
(3) Subsection (2) applies to any offence other than one—
(a) under section 177(4) or 398;
(b) under section 5 of the Perjury Act 1911 (false statements made otherwise than on oath);
(c) under section 44(2) of the Criminal Law (Consolidation) (Scotland) Act 1995 (false statements made otherwise than on oath); or
(d) under Article 10 of the Perjury (Northern Ireland) Order 1979.

[(3A) Subsection (2) applies to proceedings in relation to action to be taken under section 123(2) or (3) against a person who may have contravened Article 14 (prohibition of insider dealing and of unlawful disclosure of inside information) or Article 15 (prohibition of market manipulation) of the market abuse regulation.]
(4) "Investigator" means a person appointed under section 167 or 168(3) or (5)[, or a person appointed under section 169 who has the powers conferred by virtue of subsection (2A) of that section].
(5) "Information requirement" means a requirement imposed by an investigator under section 171, 172, 173 or 175.

NOTES

Words in first pair of square brackets in sub-s (2) inserted, sub-s (3A) inserted, and words in square brackets in sub-s (4) inserted, by the Financial Services and Markets Act 2000 (Market Abuse) Regulations 2016, SI 2016/680, reg 10(1), (10), as from 3 July 2016.

Words in second pair of square brackets in sub-s (2) substituted by the Financial Services Act 2012, s 41, Sch 12, Pt 1, para 12, as from 1 April 2013.

[7.371]

175 Information and documents: supplemental provisions

(1) If [either regulator] or an investigator has power under this Part to require a person to produce a document but it appears that the document is in the possession of a third person, that power may be exercised in relation to the third person.

(2) If a document is produced in response to a requirement imposed under this Part, the person to whom it is produced may—

(a) take copies or extracts from the document; or

(b) require the person producing the document, or any relevant person, to provide an explanation of the document.

[(2A) A document so produced may be retained for so long as the person to whom it is produced considers that it is necessary to retain it (rather than copies of it) for the purposes for which the document was requested.

(2B) If the person to whom a document is so produced has reasonable grounds for believing—

(a) that the document may have to be produced for the purposes of any legal proceedings, and

(b) that it might otherwise be unavailable for those purposes,

it may be retained until the proceedings are concluded.]

(3) If a person who is required under this Part to produce a document fails to do so, the [regulator] or an investigator may require him to state, to the best of his knowledge and belief, where the document is.

(4) A lawyer may be required under this Part to furnish the name and address of his client.

(5) No person may be required under this Part to disclose information or produce a document in respect of which he owes an obligation of confidence by virtue of carrying on the business of banking unless—

(a) he is the person under investigation or a member of that person's group;

(b) the person to whom the obligation of confidence is owed is the person under investigation or a member of that person's group;

(c) the person to whom the obligation of confidence is owed consents to the disclosure or production; or

(d) the imposing on him of a requirement with respect to such information or document has been specifically authorised by the investigating authority.

[(5A) Nothing in this Part is to be read as enabling a person to secure the disclosure by a telecommunications operator or postal operator of communications data without the consent of the operator.

(5B) In subsection (5A) "communications data", "postal operator" and "telecommunications operator" have the same meanings as in the Investigatory Powers Act 2016 (see sections 261 and 262 of that Act).]

(6) If a person claims a lien on a document, its production under this Part does not affect the lien.

(7) "Relevant person", in relation to a person who is required to produce a document, means a person who—

(a) has been or is or is proposed to be a director or controller of that person;

(b) has been or is an auditor of that person;

(c) has been or is an actuary, accountant or lawyer appointed or instructed by that person; or

(d) has been or is an employee of that person.

(8) "Investigator" means a person appointed under section 167 or 168(3) or (5).

NOTES

Words in square brackets in sub-ss (1), (3) substituted, and sub-ss (2A), (2B) inserted, by the Financial Services Act 2012, s 41, Sch 12, Pt 1, para 13, as from 1 April 2013.

Sub-ss (5A), (5B): inserted by the Investigatory Powers Act 2016, s 12(1), Sch 2, para 9, as from 22 July 2020.

[7.372]

176 Entry of premises under warrant

(1) A justice of the peace may issue a warrant under this section if satisfied on information on oath given by or on behalf of the Secretary of State, [either regulator] or an investigator that there are reasonable grounds for believing that the first, second or third set of conditions is satisfied.

(2) The first set of conditions is—

(a) that a person on whom an information requirement has been imposed has failed (wholly or in part) to comply with it; and

(b) that on the premises specified in the warrant—

(i) there are documents which have been required; or

(ii) there is information which has been required.

(3) The second set of conditions is—

(a) that the premises specified in the warrant are premises of [a person to whom subsection (3A) applies];

(b) that there are on the premises documents or information in relation to which an information requirement could be imposed; and

(c) that if such a requirement were to be imposed—

(i) it would not be complied with; or

(ii) the documents or information to which it related would be removed, tampered with or destroyed.

[(3A) This subsection applies to the following persons—

(a) an authorised person;

(b) an appointed representative;

(c) a relevant parent undertaking of an FCA investment firm;

(4) The third set of conditions is—

(a) that an offence mentioned in section 168 for which the maximum sentence on conviction on indictment is two years or more has been (or is being) committed by any person;

(b) that there are on the premises specified in the warrant documents or information relevant to whether that offence has been (or is being) committed;

(c) that an information requirement could be imposed in relation to those documents or information; and

(d) that if such a requirement were to be imposed—
(i) it would not be complied with; or
(ii) the documents or information to which it related would be removed, tampered with or destroyed.

(5) A warrant under this section shall authorise a constable—
(a) to enter the premises specified in the warrant;
(b) to search the premises and take possession of any documents or information appearing to be documents or information of a kind in respect of which a warrant under this section was issued ("the relevant kind") or to take, in relation to any such documents or information, any other steps which may appear to be necessary for preserving them or preventing interference with them;
(c) to take copies of, or extracts from, any documents or information appearing to be of the relevant kind;
(d) to require any person on the premises to provide an explanation of any document or information appearing to be of the relevant kind or to state where it may be found; and
(e) to use such force as may be reasonably necessary.

[(5A) A warrant under this section may be executed by any constable.

(5B) The warrant may authorise persons to accompany any constable who is executing it.

(5C) The powers in subsection (5) may be exercised by a person authorised by the warrant to accompany a constable; but that person may exercise those powers only in the company of, and under the supervision of, a constable.]

(6) In England and Wales, sections 15(5) to (8) and section [16(3) to (12)] of the Police and Criminal Evidence Act 1984 (execution of search warrants and safeguards) apply to warrants issued under this section.

(7) In Northern Ireland, Articles 17(5) to (8) and [18(3) to (12)] of the Police and Criminal Evidence (Northern Ireland) Order 1989 apply to warrants issued under this section.

(8) . . .

(9) In the application of this section to Scotland—
(a) for the references to a justice of the peace substitute references to a justice of the peace or a sheriff; and
(b) for the references to information on oath substitute references to evidence on oath.

(10) "Investigator" means a person appointed under section 167 or 168(3) or (5).

(11) "Information requirement" means a requirement imposed—
(a) by [a regulator] under section [87C, 87J,] 165[, 165A, 169A] or 175; or
(b) by an investigator under section 171, 172, 173 or 175.

NOTES

The words in square brackets in sub-ss (1), (6), (7) were substituted, sub-ss (5A)–(5C) were inserted, sub-s (8) was repealed, and the words "a regulator" in square brackets in subs (11) were substituted, by the Financial Services Act 2012, s 41, Sch 12, Pt 1, para 14, as from 1 April 2013.

The words in square brackets in sub-s (3)(a) were substituted, and sub-s (3A) was inserted, by the Financial Services Act 2021, s 2, Sch 2, Pt 2, para 9, as from 1 July 2021; for transitional provisions, see Sch 2, Pt 3 to the 2021 Act.

Figures "87C, 87J" in square brackets in sub-s (11)(a) inserted by the Prospectus Regulations 2005, SI 2005/1433, reg 2(1), Sch 1, para 12, as from 1 July 2005.

Figures ", 165A, 169A" in square brackets in sub-s (11)(a) inserted by the Financial Services Act 2010, s 24(1), (2), Sch 2, Pt 1, paras 1, 17, as from 8 June 2010.

Additional powers of seizure: the power of seizure conferred by sub-s (5) above is a power of seizure to which the Criminal Justice and Police Act 2001, s 50 (additional powers of seizure from premises) applies; see s 50 of, and Sch 1, Pt 1, para 69 to, the 2001 Act.

[7.373]

[176A Retention of documents taken under section 176

(1) Any document of which possession is taken under section 176 ("a seized document") may be retained so long as it is necessary to retain it (rather than copies of it) in the circumstances.

(2) A person claiming to be the owner of a seized document may apply to a magistrates' court or (in Scotland) the sheriff for an order for the delivery of the document to the person appearing to the court or sheriff to be the owner.

(3) If on an application under subsection (2) the court or (in Scotland) the sheriff cannot ascertain who is the owner of the seized document the court or sheriff (as the case may be) may make such order as the court or sheriff thinks fit.

(4) An order under subsection (2) or (3) does not affect the right of any person to take legal proceedings against any person in possession of a seized document for the recovery of the document.

(5) Any right to bring proceedings (as described in subsection (4)) may only be exercised within 6 months of the date of the order made under subsection (2) or (3).]

NOTES

Inserted by the Financial Services Act 2012, s 41, Sch 12, Pt 1, para 15, as from 1 April 2013.

Offences

[7.374]

177 Offences

(1) If a person other than the investigator ("the defaulter") fails to comply with a requirement imposed on him under this Part the person imposing the requirement may certify that fact in writing to the court.

(2) If the court is satisfied that the defaulter failed without reasonable excuse to comply with the requirement, it may deal with the defaulter (and in the case of a body corporate, any director or [other] officer) as if he were in contempt[; and "officer", in relation to a limited liability partnership, means a member of the limited liability partnership].

(3) A person who knows or suspects that an investigation is being or is likely to be conducted under this Part is guilty of an offence if—
(a) he falsifies, conceals, destroys or otherwise disposes of a document which he knows or suspects is or would be relevant to such an investigation, or
(b) he causes or permits the falsification, concealment, destruction or disposal of such a document,

unless he shows that he had no intention of concealing facts disclosed by the documents from the investigator.

(4) A person who, in purported compliance with a requirement imposed on him under this Part—

(a) provides information which he knows to be false or misleading in a material particular, or
(b) recklessly provides information which is false or misleading in a material particular,

is guilty of an offence.

(5) A person guilty of an offence under subsection (3) or (4) is liable—

(a) on summary conviction, to imprisonment for a term not exceeding six months or a fine not exceeding the statutory maximum, or both;
(b) on conviction on indictment, to imprisonment for a term not exceeding two years or a fine, or both.

(6) Any person who intentionally obstructs the exercise of any rights conferred by a warrant under section 176 is guilty of an offence and liable on summary conviction to imprisonment for a term not exceeding *three months* or a fine not exceeding level 5 on the standard scale, or both.

[(7) In this section—

"court" means—

(a) the High Court;
(b) in Scotland, the Court of Session;

"investigator appointed by the FCA" means an investigator appointed by the FCA under section 167, 168 or 169;

"officer of the FCA" means an officer authorised by the FCA for the purposes of section 165(3).]

NOTES

Sub-s (2): word in first pair of square brackets inserted by the Financial Services Act 2012, s 114(1), Sch 18, Pt 1, paras 1, 8, as from 1 April 2013. Words in second pair of square brackets added by the Limited Liability Partnerships Regulations 2001, SI 2001/1090, reg 9, Sch 5, para 21, as from 6 April 2001.

Sub-s (6): for the words in italics there are substituted the words "51 weeks" by the Criminal Justice Act 2003, s 280(2), Sch 26, para 54(1), (2), as from a day to be appointed.

Sub-s (7): substituted by the Financial Services and Markets Act 2000 (Market Abuse) Regulations 2016, SI 2016/680, reg 10(1), (11), as from 3 July 2016.

[Interpretation

[7.375]

177A Interpretation of Part 11

In this Part—

"FCA investment firm" has the meaning given in section 143A;

"relevant parent undertaking", in relation to an FCA investment firm, means an authorised parent undertaking or a non-authorised parent undertaking (as defined in section 143B).]

NOTES

Commencement: 1 July 2021.

Inserted, together with the preceding heading, by the Financial Services Act 2021, s 2, Sch 2, Pt 2, para 10, as from 1 July 2021; for transitional provisions, see Sch 2, Pt 3 to the 2021 Act.

PART XII CONTROL OVER AUTHORISED PERSONS

NOTES

Transitional provisions etc in connection with the commencement of the Financial Services Act 2012: for transitional provisions in relation to control over authorised persons, see Part 6 of the Financial Services Act 2012 (Transitional Provisions) (Miscellaneous Provisions) Order 2013, SI 2013/442. Articles 24–27 contain transitional provisions in relation to cases where, before 1 April 2013, the FSA (a) received a notice given under s 178 (obligation to notify: acquisition of control), and (b) the notice would have been required to be given to the PRA as the appropriate regulator (within the meaning of s 178) had the notice been given on that date. Article 28 concerns restriction notices given by the FSA under s 191B before 1 April 2013. Article 29 concerns cases where the FSA received a notice given under s 191D (obligation to notify: dispositions of control) before that date. Article 30 contain transitional provisions in relation to s 191F(6) (offences under this Part). See also the Financial Services Act 2012 (Transitional Provisions) (Enforcement) Order 2013, SI 2013/441, art 30 (control over authorised persons).

Transitional provisions etc in connection with the original commencement of this Act: see the Financial Services and Markets Act 2000 (Transitional Provisions) (Controllers) Order 2001, SI 2001/2637 which makes transitional provisions for people who are subject to a regime requiring them to notify a significant shareholding in an authorised person and who will fall within this Part. The Order deals both with the status after commencement of people who have been approved as shareholder controllers under existing regimes and with partly completed procedures. See also s 192 at **[7.400]** with regard to the Treasury's power to change the definition of "control".

[Notices of acquisitions of control over UK authorised persons

[7.376]

178 Obligation to notify the [appropriate regulator]: acquisitions of control

(1) A person who decides to acquire or increase control over a UK authorised person must give the [appropriate regulator] notice in writing before making the acquisition.

(2) For the purposes of calculations relating to this section, the holding of shares or voting power by a person ("A1") includes any shares or voting power held by another ("A2") if A1 and A2 are acting in concert.

[(2ZA) This section does not apply if the only regulated activity for which the UK authorised person has a Part 4A permission is the regulated activity specified in article 63S of the Financial Services and Markets Act 2000 (Regulated Activities) Order 2001 (administering a benchmark).]

[(2A) In this Part, "the appropriate regulator" means—

(a) where the UK authorised person is a PRA-authorised person, the PRA;
(b) in any other case, the FCA.]

(3) In this Part, a notice given under this section is a "section 178 notice" and a person giving notice is a "section 178 notice-giver".]

NOTES

Sections 178–191G were substituted (for the original ss 178–191) by the Financial Services and Markets Act 2000 (Controllers) Regulations 2009, SI 2009/534, reg 3, Sch 1, as from 21 March 2009.

Words in square brackets in the section heading and in sub-s (1) substituted, and sub-s (2A) inserted, by the Financial Services Act 2012, s 26(1)–(3), as from 1 April 2013.

Sub-s (2ZA): inserted by the Financial Services and Markets Act 2000 (Benchmarks) Regulations 2018, SI 2018/135, reg 44, as from 27 February 2018.

[7.377]

[179 Requirements for section 178 notices

(1) A section 178 notice must be in such form, include such information and be accompanied by such documents as the [appropriate regulator] may reasonably require.

(2) [Each regulator] must publish a list of its requirements as to the form, information and accompanying documents for a section 178 notice.

(3) The [appropriate regulator] may impose different requirements for different cases and may vary or waive requirements in particular cases.]

NOTES

Substituted as noted to s 178 at **[7.376]**.

Words in square brackets substituted by the Financial Services Act 2012, s 26(1), (2), (4), as from 1 April 2013.

[7.378]

[180 Acknowledgment of receipt

(1) The [appropriate regulator] must acknowledge receipt of a completed section 178 notice in writing before the end of the second working day following receipt.

(2) If the [appropriate regulator] receives an incomplete section 178 notice it must inform the section 178 notice-giver as soon as reasonably practicable.]

NOTES

Substituted as noted to s 178 at **[7.376]**.

Words in square brackets substituted by the Financial Services Act 2012, s 26(1), (2), as from 1 April 2013.

[Acquiring control and other changes of holding

[7.379]

181 Acquiring control

(1) For the purposes of this Part, a person ("A") acquires control over a UK authorised person ("B") if any of the cases in subsection (2) begin to apply.

(2) The cases are where A holds—

(a) 10% or more of the shares in B or in a parent undertaking of B ("P");
(b) 10% or more of the voting power in B or P; or
(c) shares or voting power in B or P as a result of which A is able to exercise significant influence over the management of B.]

NOTES

Substituted as noted to s 178 at **[7.376]**.

[7.380]

[182 Increasing control

(1) For the purposes of this Part, a person ("A") increases control over a UK authorised person ("B") whenever—

(a) the percentage of shares which A holds in B or in a parent undertaking of B ("P") increases by any of the steps mentioned in subsection (2);
(b) the percentage of voting power A holds in B or P increases by any of the steps mentioned in subsection (2); or
(c) A becomes a parent undertaking of B.

(2) The steps are—

(a) from less than 20% to 20% or more;
(b) from less than 30% to 30% or more;
(c) from less than 50% to 50% or more.]

NOTES

Substituted as noted to s 178 at **[7.376]**.

[7.381]

[183 Reducing or ceasing to have control

(1) For the purposes of this Part, a person ("A") reduces control over a UK authorised person ("B") whenever—

(a) the percentage of shares which A holds in B or in a parent undertaking of B ("P") decreases by any of the steps mentioned in subsection (2);
(b) the percentage of voting power which A holds in B or P decreases by any of the steps mentioned in subsection (2); or
(c) A ceases to be a parent undertaking of B.

(2) The steps are—

(a) from 50% or more to less than 50%;
(b) from 30% or more to less than 30%;
(c) from 20% or more to less than 20%.

(3) For the purposes of this Part, a person ("A") ceases to have control over a UK authorised person ("B") if A ceases to be in the position of holding—

(a) 10% or more of the shares in B or in a parent undertaking of B ("P");

(b) 10% or more of the voting power in B or P; or

(c) shares or voting power in B or P as a result of which A is able to exercise significant influence over the management of B.]

NOTES

Substituted as noted to s 178 at **[7.376]**.

Regulations: see the note to s 188 *post*. Note also that the Alternative Investment Fund Managers Regulations 2013, SI 2013/1773 were purportedly made under this section, however, following its substitution as noted above, this section no longer contains any Regulation making powers.

[7.382]

[184 Disregarded holdings

(1) For the purposes of sections 181 to 183, shares and voting power that a person holds in a UK authorised person ("B") or in a parent undertaking of B ("P") are disregarded in the following circumstances.

(2) Shares held only for the purposes of clearing and settling within a short settlement cycle are disregarded.

(3) Shares held by a custodian or its nominee in a custodian capacity are disregarded, provided that the custodian or nominee is only able to exercise voting power represented by the shares in accordance with instructions given in writing.

(4) Shares representing no more than 5% of the total voting power in B or P held by an investment firm are disregarded, provided that it—

(a) holds the shares in the capacity of a market maker (as defined in [article 2.1.6 of the markets in financial instruments regulation]);

[(b) has a Part 4A permission to carry on one or more investment services and activities;]

(c) neither intervenes in the management of B or P nor exerts any influence on B or P to buy the shares or back the share price.

(5) Shares held by a [qualifying credit institution] or investment firm in its trading book are disregarded, provided that—

(a) the shares represent no more than 5% of the total voting power in B or P; and

(b) . . . the voting power is not used to intervene in the management of B or P.

(6) Shares held by a [qualifying credit institution] or an investment firm are disregarded, provided that—

(a) the shares are held as a result of performing the investment services and activities of—

(i) underwriting a share issue; or

(ii) placing shares on a firm commitment basis . . . ; and

(b) the [qualifying credit institution] or investment firm—

(i) does not exercise voting power represented by the shares or otherwise intervene in the management of the issuer; and

(ii) retains the holding for a period of less than one year.

(7) Where a management company (as defined in [section 237(2]) and its parent undertaking both hold shares or voting power, each may disregard holdings of the other, provided that each exercises its voting power independently of the other.

(8) But subsection (7) does not apply if the management company—

[(a) manages holdings for its parent undertaking or a controlled undertaking of the parent undertaking;]

(b) has no discretion as to the exercise of the voting power attached to such holdings; and

(c) may only exercise the voting power in relation to such holdings under direct or indirect instruction from—

(i) the parent undertaking; or

[(ii) a controlled undertaking of the parent undertaking].

(9) Where an investment firm and its parent undertaking both hold shares or voting power, the parent undertaking may disregard holdings managed by the investment firm on a client by client basis and the investment firm may disregard holdings of the parent undertaking, provided that the investment firm—

(a) has permission to provide portfolio management;

(b) exercises its voting power independently from the parent undertaking; and

(c) may only exercise the voting power under instructions given in writing, or has appropriate mechanisms in place for ensuring that individual portfolio management services are conducted independently of any other services.

[(9A) Shares acquired for stabilisation purposes in accordance with [the market abuse regulation and the Commission Delegated Regulation (EU) No 1052/2016 of 8 March 2016 supplementing Regulation (EU) No 596/2014 of the European Parliament and the Council with regard to the regulatory technical standards for conditions applicable to buy-back programmes and stabilisation measures] are disregarded, provided that the voting power attached to those shares is not exercised or otherwise used to intervene in the management of B or P.]

[(10) For the purposes of this section, an undertaking is a controlled undertaking of the parent undertaking if it is controlled by the parent undertaking; and for this purpose the question of whether one undertaking controls another is to be determined in accordance with section 89J(4) and (5).]]

NOTES

Substituted as noted to s 178 at **[7.376]**.

Sub-s (4): words in square brackets in para (a) substituted, and para (b) substituted, by the Financial Services and Markets Act 2000 (Amendment) (EU Exit) Regulations 2019, SI 2019/632, regs 48, 49(a), as from IP completion day (as defined in the European Union (Withdrawal Agreement) Act 2020, s 39).

Sub-s (5): words in square brackets substituted by SI 2019/632, regs 48, 49(b), as from IP completion day (as defined in the European Union (Withdrawal Agreement) Act 2020, s 39). Words omitted from para (b) repealed by the Transparency Regulations 2015, SI 2015/1755, reg 6(1), as from 1 November 2015 (for the purpose of making rules under Part 9A), and as from 31 May 2016 (otherwise)

Sub-s (6): words in square brackets substituted, and words omitted repealed, by SI 2019/632, regs 48, 49(c), as from IP completion day (as defined in the European Union (Withdrawal Agreement) Act 2020, s 39).

Sub-s (7): words in square brackets substituted by SI 2019/632, regs 48, 49(d), as from IP completion day (as defined in the European Union (Withdrawal Agreement) Act 2020, s 39).

Sub-s (8): para (a) and sub-para (c)(ii) were substituted by the Capital Requirements Regulations 2013, SI 2013/3115, reg 46(1), Sch 2, Pt 1, paras 1, 10, as from 1 January 2014.

Sub-s (9A): inserted by SI 2015/1755, reg 6(1), as from 1 November 2015 (for the purpose of making rules under Part 9A), and as from 31 May 2016 (otherwise). Words in square brackets substituted by SI 2019/632, regs 48, 49(e), as from 23 March 2019.

Sub-s (10): added by SI 2013/3115, reg 46(1), Sch 2, Pt 1, paras 1, 10, as from 1 January 2014.

[Assessment procedure

[7.383]

185 Assessment: general

(1) Where the [appropriate regulator] receives a section 178 notice, it must—

(a) determine whether to approve the acquisition to which it relates unconditionally; or

(b) propose to—

(i) approve the acquisition subject to conditions (see section 187); or

(ii) object to the acquisition.

(2) The [appropriate regulator] must—

(a) consider the suitability of the section 178 notice-giver and the financial soundness of the acquisition in order to ensure the sound and prudent management of the UK authorised person;

(b) have regard to the likely influence that the section 178 notice-giver will have on the UK authorised person; and

(c) disregard the economic needs of the market.

(3) The [appropriate regulator] may only object to an acquisition—

(a) if there are reasonable grounds for doing so on the basis of the matters set out in section 186; or

(b) if the information provided by the section 178 notice-giver is incomplete.]

NOTES

Substituted as noted to s 178 at **[7.376]**.

Words in square brackets substituted by the Financial Services Act 2012, s 26(1), (2), as from 1 April 2013.

[7.384]

[186 Assessment criteria

The matters specified in section 185(3)(a) are—

(a) the reputation of the section 178 notice-giver;

(b) the reputation[, knowledge, skills] and experience of any person who will direct the business of the UK authorised person as a result of the proposed acquisition;

(c) the financial soundness of the section 178 notice-giver, in particular in relation to the type of business that the UK authorised person pursues or envisages pursuing;

(d) whether the UK authorised person will be able to comply with its prudential requirements (including the threshold conditions in relation to all of the regulated activities for which it has or will have permission);

(e) if the UK authorised person is to become part of a group as a result of the acquisition, whether that group has a structure which makes it possible to—

(i) exercise effective supervision;

(ii) exchange information among regulators; and

(iii) determine the allocation of responsibility among regulators; and

(f) whether there are reasonable grounds to suspect that in connection with the proposed acquisition—

(i) money laundering or terrorist financing ([as defined in regulation 3(1) of the Money Laundering, Terrorist Financing and Transfer of Funds (Information on the Payer) Regulations 2017]) is being or has been committed or attempted; or

(ii) the risk of such activity could increase.]

NOTES

Substituted as noted to s 178 at **[7.376]**.

Words in square brackets in para (b) inserted by the Capital Requirements Regulations 2013, SI 2013/3115, reg 46(1), Sch 2, Pt 1, paras 1, 11, as from 1 January 2014.

Words in square brackets in para (f) substituted by the Financial Services and Markets Act 2000 (Amendment) (EU Exit) Regulations 2019, SI 2019/632, regs 48, 50, as from IP completion day (as defined in the European Union (Withdrawal Agreement) Act 2020, s 39).

[7.385]

[187 Approval with conditions

(1) The [appropriate regulator] may impose conditions on its approval of an acquisition.

[(2) The appropriate regulator may only impose conditions where—

(a) if it did not impose those conditions, it would propose to object to the acquisition, or

(b) it is required to do so by a direction under section 187A(3)(b) or section 187B(3).]

(3) The [appropriate regulator] may not impose conditions requiring a particular level of holding to be acquired.

(4) The [appropriate regulator] may vary or cancel the conditions.]

NOTES

Substituted as noted to s 178 at **[7.376]**.

Words in square brackets in sub-ss (1), (3), (4) substituted, and sub-s (2) substituted, by the Financial Services Act 2012, s 26(1), (2), (5), as from 1 April 2013.

[7.386]

[187A Assessment: consultation by PRA with FCA

(1) The PRA must consult the FCA before acting under section 185.

(2) The FCA may make representations to the PRA in relation to any of the matters set out in sections 185(2) and 186.

(3) If the FCA considers that on the basis of the matters set out in section 186(f) there are reasonable grounds to object to the acquisition, the FCA may—

(a) direct the PRA to object to the acquisition, or

(b) direct the PRA not to approve the acquisition unless it does so subject to conditions specified in the direction (with or without other conditions).

(4) Before giving a direction under subsection (3), the FCA must notify the PRA of its proposal to do so.

(5) In order to comply with the obligation under subsection (1), the PRA must provide the FCA with—

(a) copies of—

(i) the section 178 notice, and

(ii) any document included with that notice,

(b) any further information provided pursuant to section 190, and

(c) any other information in the possession of the PRA which—

(i) in the opinion of the PRA, is relevant to the application, or

(ii) is reasonably requested by the FCA.

[(5A) Where the PRA notifies the FCA that it [is required by section 189(1ZB)] to act in a timely manner, the FCA may take action under subsection (2), (3) or (4) after the time it receives that notification only if that action is taken as soon as reasonably practicable after that time.]

(6) If the PRA acts under section 185(1)(b), it must indicate to the section 178 notice-giver any representations or directions received from the FCA.

(7) Directions given by the FCA under this section are subject to any directions given to the FCA under section 3I or 3J.]

NOTES

Inserted, together with ss 187B, 187C, by the Financial Services Act 2012, s 6(1), (6), as from 1 April 2013.

Sub-s (5A): inserted by the Bank Recovery and Resolution Order 2014, SI 2014/3329, arts 112, 117, as from 1 January 2015. Words in square brackets substituted by the Bank of England and Financial Services Act 2016, s 16, Sch 2, Pt 2, paras 26, 38, as from 1 March 2017.

[7.387]

[187B Assessment: consultation by FCA with PRA

(1) The FCA must consult the PRA before acting under section 185 if—

(a) the UK authorised person to which the section 178 notice relates has as a member of its immediate group a PRA-authorised person, or

(b) the section 178 notice-giver is a PRA-authorised person.

(2) The PRA may make representations to the FCA in relation to any of the matters set out in sections 185(2) and 186.

(3) If the PRA considers that on the basis of relevant matters there are reasonable grounds to object to the acquisition, the PRA may direct the FCA not to approve the acquisition unless it does so subject to conditions specified in the direction (with or without other conditions).

(4) In subsection (3) "relevant matters"—

(a) means the matters in paragraphs (d) and (e)(i) of section 186, and

(b) in a case falling within subsection (1)(b) of this section, also includes the matter in paragraph (c) of section 186.

(5) In order to comply with the obligation under subsection (1), the FCA must provide the PRA with—

(a) copies of—

(i) the section 178 notice, and

(ii) any document included with that notice,

(b) any further information provided pursuant to section 190, and

(c) any other information in the possession of the FCA which—

(i) in the opinion of the FCA, is relevant to the application, or

(ii) is reasonably requested by the PRA.

(6) If the FCA acts under section 185(1)(b), it must indicate to the section 178 notice-giver any representations or directions received from the PRA.]

NOTES

Inserted as noted to s 187A at **[7.386]**.

[7.388]

[187C Variation etc of conditions

(1) Where the PRA has imposed conditions required by a direction given by the FCA under section 187A(3)—

(a) the FCA may direct the PRA to exercise its power under section 187(4) to vary or cancel any of those conditions;

(b) the PRA must consult the FCA before it exercises that power in relation to those conditions otherwise than in accordance with a direction under paragraph (a).

(2) Where the FCA has imposed conditions required by a direction given by the PRA under section 187B(3)—

(a) the PRA may direct the FCA to exercise its power under section 187(4) to vary or cancel any of those conditions;

(b) the FCA must consult the PRA before it exercises that power in relation to those conditions otherwise than in accordance with a direction under paragraph (a).]

NOTES

Inserted as noted to s 187A at **[7.386]**.

188 *(S 188 (Assessment: consultation with EC competent authorities) was substituted as noted to s 178 at* **[7.376]**. *Subsequently repealed by the Financial Services and Markets Act 2000 (Amendment) (EU Exit) Regulations 2019, SI 2019/632, regs 48, 51, as from IP completion day (as defined in the European Union (Withdrawal Agreement) Act 2020, s 39).)*

[7.389]

[189 Assessment: Procedure

(1) The [appropriate regulator] must act under section 185 within a period of 60 working days beginning with the day on which the [appropriate regulator] acknowledges receipt of the section 178 notice ("the assessment period").

[(1A) [Where the appropriate regulator is the FCA and] the section 178 notice relates to an acquisition or increase of control over a [qualifying credit institution], investment firm or banking group company, the Bank of England, acting in the exercise of its functions under sections 6A to 6C of the Banking Act 2009 or under the special resolution regime under Part 1 of that Act, may direct the appropriate regulator to act under this Part in a timely manner, and to shorten the assessment period so far as reasonably practicable.

[(1ZB) Where the appropriate regulator is the PRA and—

(a) the section 178 notice relates to an acquisition or increase of control over a [qualifying credit institution], investment firm or banking group company, and

(b) the [qualifying credit institution], investment firm or banking group company is one in relation to which the Bank of England is exercising its functions under sections 6A to 6C of the Banking Act 2009 or the special resolution regime under Part 1 of that Act,

the PRA must act under this Part in a timely manner, and shorten the assessment period so far as reasonably practicable.]

(1B) In [subsections (1A) and (1ZB)]—

. . .

"banking group company" has the meaning given in section 81D of [the Banking Act 2009].]

(2) The assessment period may be interrupted, no more than once, in accordance with section 190.

(3) The [appropriate regulator] must inform the section 178 notice-giver in writing of—

(a) the duration of the assessment period;

(b) its expiry date; and

(c) any change to the expiry date by virtue of section 190.

(4) The [appropriate regulator] must, within two working days of acting under section 185 (and in any event no later than the expiry date of the assessment period)—

(a) notify the section 178 notice-giver that it has determined to approve the acquisition unconditionally; or

(b) give a warning notice stating that it proposes to—

(i) approve the acquisition subject to conditions; or

(ii) object to the acquisition.

(5) Where the [appropriate regulator] gives a warning notice stating that it proposes to approve the acquisition subject to conditions—

(a) it must, in the warning notice, specify those conditions; and

(b) the conditions take effect as interim conditions.

(6) [Unless section 190A applies] the [appropriate regulator] is treated as having approved the acquisition if, at the expiry of the assessment period, it has neither—

(a) given notice under subsection (4); nor

(b) informed the section 178 notice-giver that the section 178 notice is incomplete.

(7) If the [appropriate regulator] decides to approve an acquisition subject to conditions or to object to an acquisition it must give the section 178 notice-giver a decision notice.

(8) Following receipt of a decision notice under this section, the section 178 notice-giver may refer the [appropriate regulator's] decision to the Tribunal.]

NOTES

Substituted as noted to s 178 at **[7.376]**.

Sub-ss (1A), (1B) were inserted by the Bank Recovery and Resolution Order 2014, SI 2014/3329, arts 112, 118, as from 1 January 2015.

The words "Where the appropriate regulator is the FCA and" in square brackets in sub-s (1A) were substituted, sub-s (1ZB) was inserted, the words in square brackets in sub-s (1B) were substituted, and the definition "bank" (omitted) was repealed, by the Bank of England and Financial Services Act 2016, s 16, Sch 2, Pt 2, paras 26, 39, as from 1 March 2017.

The words "qualifying credit institution" in square brackets in sub-ss (1A), (1ZB)(a) and (1ZB)(b) were substituted by the Financial Services and Markets Act 2000 (Amendment) (EU Exit) Regulations 2019, SI 2019/632, regs 48, 52, as from IP completion day (as defined in the European Union (Withdrawal Agreement) Act 2020, s 39).

The words "Unless section 190A applies" in square brackets in sub-s (6) were inserted by the Bank Recovery and Resolution Order 2016, SI 2016/1239, arts 30, 33(1), as from 16 December 2016.

All other words in square brackets in this section were substituted by the Financial Services Act 2012, s 26(1), (2), as from 1 April 2013.

[7.390]

[190 Requests for further information

(1) The [appropriate regulator] may, no later than the 50th working day of the assessment period, in writing ask the section 178 notice-giver to provide any further information necessary to complete its assessment.

[(1A) But where a direction has been given by the Bank of England under section 189(1A) [or section 189(1ZB) applies], the appropriate regulator must, as soon as reasonably practicable, ask the section 178 notice-giver to provide any further information necessary to complete its assessment.]

(2) On the first occasion that the [appropriate regulator] asks for further information, the assessment period is interrupted from the date of the request until the date the [appropriate regulator] receives the requested information ("the interruption period").

(3) But the interruption period may not exceed 20 working days, unless subsection (4) applies.

(4) The interruption period may not exceed 30 working days if the notice-giver—

(a) is situated or regulated outside the [United Kingdom or Gibraltar]; or

[(b) is not subject to supervision under the laws of the United Kingdom (or any part of the United Kingdom) or Gibraltar relied on immediately before IP completion day to implement—

(i) the UCITS directive;

(ii) the Solvency 2 Directive;

(iii) the markets in financial instruments directive; or

(iv) the capital requirements directive.

including rules made by the appropriate regulator under this Act, in force on IP completion day, and, as amended from to time, in all other cases].

(5) The [appropriate regulator] may make further requests for information (but a further request does not result in a further interruption of the assessment period).

(6) The [appropriate regulator] must acknowledge in writing receipt of further information before the end of the second working day following receipt.]

NOTES

Substituted as noted to s 178 at **[7.376]**.

Sub-s (1A) was inserted by the Bank Recovery and Resolution Order 2014, SI 2014/3329, arts 112, 119, as from 1 January 2015.

Words in square brackets in sub-s (1A) inserted by the Bank of England and Financial Services Act 2016, s 16, Sch 2, Pt 2, paras 26, 40, as from 1 March 2017.

Sub-s (4) is amended as follows:

The words "United Kingdom or Gibraltar" in square brackets in para (a) were substituted by the Financial Services and Markets Act 2000 (Amendment) (EU Exit) Regulations 2019, SI 2019/632, regs 48, 53(a), as from IP completion day (as defined in the European Union (Withdrawal Agreement) Act 2020, s 39). Note that reg 53(a) of the 2019 Regulations was amended by the Gibraltar (Miscellaneous Amendments) (EU Exit) Regulations 2019, SI 2019/680, reg 9(1), (3)(a), with effect from immediately before IP completion day; and the effect of the amendment has been incorporated in the text set out above.

Para (b) was substituted by SI 2019/632, regs 48, 53(b), as from IP completion day (as defined in the European Union (Withdrawal Agreement) Act 2020, s 39). Note that reg 53(b) of the 2019 Regulations was amended by the Gibraltar (Miscellaneous Amendments) (EU Exit) Regulations 2019, SI 2019/680, reg 9(1), (3)(b) (with effect from immediately before IP completion day), and by the Financial Services and Economic and Monetary Policy (Consequential Amendments) (EU Exit) Regulations 2020, SI 2020/1301, reg 3, Schedule, para 33(f) (as from 30 December 2020); and the effect of these amendments has been incorporated in the text set out above.

All other words in square brackets in this section were substituted by the Financial Services Act 2012, s 26(1), (2), as from 1 April 2013.

[7.391]

[190A Assessment and resolution

(1) This section applies if—

(a) the appropriate regulator receives a section 178 notice in relation to a [qualifying credit institution], investment firm or banking group company,

(b) as a result of a direction under section 189(1A) or the application of section 189(1ZB), the appropriate regulator is required to act under this Part in a timely manner in relation to that notice, and

(c) the appropriate regulator does not complete the assessment required by section 185 before a relevant transfer instrument has been made by the Bank of England which transfers shares issued by, or voting power in, that [qualifying credit institution], investment firm or banking group company.

(2) The transfer of shares or voting takes effect in accordance with the terms of the relevant transfer instrument, but the right of the person who acquires shares under that instrument ("the acquirer") to exercise the voting power represented by those shares is suspended.

(3) During the suspension, the voting power represented by the shares in question may be exercised by the Bank (and only by the Bank).

(4) If the appropriate regulator issues a decision notice under section 189(7) objecting to the acquisition, the Bank may direct the acquirer to sell the shares within a period specified by the Bank in the direction ("the sale period").

(5) In determining the sale period, the Bank must take account of prevailing market conditions.

(6) The suspension provided for in subsection (2) ends—

(a) if the appropriate regulator gives notice under section 189(4)(a) or (b)(i) that it approves the acquisition, on the date of that notice, or

(b) if the Bank gives a direction under subsection (4), on the earlier of the day on which the sale period ends and the day on which the shares are sold.

(7) In this section a "relevant transfer instrument" means an instrument made by the Bank acting in the exercise of its functions under sections 6A to 6C of the Banking Act 2009 or under the special resolution regime under Part 1 of that Act, which transfers, or has the effect of transferring, shares issued by, or voting power in, the [qualifying credit institution], investment firm or banking group company.]

NOTES

Inserted by the Bank Recovery and Resolution Order 2016, SI 2016/1239, arts 30, 33(2), as from 16 December 2016.

Sub-ss (1), (7): words in square brackets substituted by the Financial Services and Markets Act 2000 (Amendment) (EU Exit) Regulations 2019, SI 2019/632, regs 48, 54, as from IP completion day (as defined in the European Union (Withdrawal Agreement) Act 2020, s 39).

[7.392]

[191 Duration of approval

(1) Approval of an acquisition (whether granted unconditionally or subject to conditions) is effective for such period as the [appropriate regulator] may specify in writing.

(2) Where the [appropriate regulator] has specified a period under subsection (1), it may extend the period.

(3) Where the [appropriate regulator] has not specified a period, the approval is effective for one year beginning with the date—

(a) of the notice given under section 189(4)(a) or (b)(i);

(b) on which the [appropriate regulator] is treated as having given approval under section 189(6);192 or

(c) of a decision on a reference to the Tribunal which results in the person receiving approval.]

NOTES

Substituted as noted to s 178 at **[7.376]**.

Words in square brackets substituted by the Financial Services Act 2012, s 26(1), (2), as from 1 April 2013.

[Enforcement procedures

[7.393]

191A Objection by the [appropriate regulator]

(1) The [appropriate regulator] may object to a person's control over a UK authorised person in any of the circumstances specified in subsection (2).

(2) The circumstances are that the [appropriate regulator] reasonably believes that—

(a) the person acquired or increased control without giving notice under section 178(1) in circumstances where notice was required;

(b) the person is in breach of a condition imposed under section 187; or

(c) there are grounds for objecting to control on the basis of the matters in section 186.

(3) The [appropriate regulator]—

(a) must take into account whether influence exercised by the person is likely to operate to the detriment of the sound and prudent management of the UK authorised person; and

(b) may take into account whether the person has co-operated with any information requests made or requirements imposed by the [appropriate regulator].

(4) If the [appropriate regulator] proposes to object to a person's control over a UK authorised person, it must give that person a warning notice.

[(4A) Where the appropriate regulator is the PRA, it must consult the FCA before giving a warning notice under this section.

(4B) Where the appropriate regulator is the FCA, it must consult the PRA before giving a warning notice under this section if—

(a) the UK authorised person has as a member of its immediate group a PRA-authorised person, or

(b) the person to whom the warning notice is to be given is a PRA-authorised person.]

(5) . . .

(6) If the [appropriate regulator] decides to object to a person's control over a UK authorised person, it must give that person a decision notice.

(7) A person to whom the [appropriate regulator] gives a decision notice under this section may refer the matter to the Tribunal.]

NOTES

Substituted as noted to s 178 at **[7.376]**.

Words "appropriate regulator" in square brackets (in each place that they occur) substituted, and sub-ss (4A), (4B) inserted, by the Financial Services Act 2012, s 26(1), (2), (7), as from 1 April 2013.

Sub-s (5) was repealed by the Financial Services and Markets Act 2000 (Amendment) (EU Exit) Regulations 2019, SI 2019/632, regs 48, 55, as from IP completion day (as defined in the European Union (Withdrawal Agreement) Act 2020, s 39).

Regulations: note that the Alternative Investment Fund Managers Regulations 2013, SI 2013/1773, the Financial Conglomerates and Other Financial Groups Regulations 2004, SI 2004/1862, the Collective Investment Schemes (Miscellaneous Amendments) Regulations 2003, SI 2003/2066, and the Financial Services and Markets Act 2000 (Reinsurance Directive) Regulations 2007, SI 2007/3255 were originally made under ss 183 and 188 of this Act (prior to the substitution of those sections as noted to s 178 *ante*) and now have effect under this section (and still had effect under s 188 prior to its repeal as noted *ante*).

[7.394]

[191B Restriction notices

(1) The [appropriate regulator] may give notice in writing (a "restriction notice") to a person in the following circumstances.

(2) The circumstances are that—

(a) the person has control over a UK authorised person by virtue of holding shares or voting power; and

(b) in relation to the shares or voting power, the [appropriate regulator] has given the person a warning notice or a decision notice under section 189 or 191A or a final notice which confirms a decision notice given under section 189 or 191A.

[(2A) Where the appropriate regulator is the PRA, it must consult the FCA before giving a restriction notice under this section.

(2B) Where the appropriate regulator is the FCA, it must consult the PRA before giving a restriction notice under this section if—

(a) the UK authorised person has as a member of its immediate group a PRA-authorised person, or

(b) the person to whom the restriction notice is to be given is a PRA-authorised person.]

(3) In a restriction notice, the [appropriate regulator] may direct that shares or voting power to which the notice relates are, until further notice, subject to one or more of the following restrictions—

(a) except by court order, an agreement to transfer or a transfer of any such shares or voting power or, in the case of unissued shares, any agreement to transfer or transfer of the right to be issued with them, is void;
(b) no voting power is to be exercisable;
(c) no further shares are to be issued in pursuance of any right of the holder of any such shares or voting power or in pursuance of any offer made to their holder;
(d) except in a liquidation, no payment is to be made of any sums due from the body corporate on any such shares, whether in respect of capital or otherwise.

[(3A) Subsection (3)(a) and (b) does not apply where the voting power represented by the shares in question is suspended under section 190A(2).]

(4) A restriction notice takes effect—
(a) immediately; or
(b) on such date as may be specified in the notice.

(5) A restriction notice does not extinguish rights which would be enjoyable but for the notice.

(6) A copy of the restriction notice must be served on—
(a) the UK authorised person in question; and
(b) in the case of shares or voting power held in a parent undertaking of a UK authorised person, the parent undertaking.

(7) A person to whom the [appropriate regulator] gives a restriction notice may refer the matter to the Tribunal.]

NOTES

Substituted as noted to s 178 at **[7.376]**.

Words "appropriate regulator" in square brackets (in each place that they occur) substituted, and sub-ss (2A), (2B) inserted, by the Financial Services Act 2012, s 26(1), (2), (8), as from 1 April 2013.

Sub-s (3A): inserted by the Bank Recovery and Resolution Order 2016, SI 2016/1239, arts 30, 33(3), as from 16 December 2016.

[7.395]

[191C Orders for sale of shares

(1) The court may, on the application of the [appropriate regulator], order the sale of shares or the disposition of voting power in the following circumstances.

(2) The circumstances are that—
(a) a person has control over a UK authorised person by virtue of holding the shares or voting power; and
(b) the acquisition or continued holding of the shares or voting power by that person is in contravention of a final notice which confirms a decision notice given under section 189 or section 191A.

[(2A) Where the appropriate regulator is the PRA, it must consult the FCA before making an application to the court under this section.

(2B) Where the appropriate regulator is the FCA, it must consult the PRA before making an application to the court under this section if—
(a) the UK authorised person has as a member of its immediate group a PRA-authorised person, or
(b) the person holding the shares or voting power is a PRA-authorised person.]

(3) Where the court orders the sale of shares or disposition of voting power it may—
(a) if a restriction notice has been given in relation to the shares or voting power, order that the restrictions cease to apply; and
(b) make any further order.

(4) Where the court makes an order under this section, it must take into account the level of holding that the person would have been entitled to acquire, or to continue to hold, without contravening the final notice.

(5) If shares are sold or voting power disposed of in pursuance of an order under this section, any proceeds, less the costs of the sale or disposition, must be paid into court for the benefit of the persons beneficially interested in them; and any such person may apply to the court for payment of a whole or part of the proceeds.

(6) The jurisdiction conferred by this section may be exercised by the High Court and the Court of Session.

[(7) The appropriate regulator must obtain the consent of the Bank of England before making an application under this section in relation to shares if the Bank has the power to direct the sale of those shares under section 190A(4).

(8) The appropriate regulator may not make an application under this section in relation to shares if the Bank of England has given a direction for the sale of those shares under section 190A(4).]]

NOTES

Substituted as noted to s 178 at **[7.376]**.

Words in square brackets in sub-s (1) substituted, and sub-ss (2A), (2B) inserted, by the Financial Services Act 2012, s 26(1), (2), (9), as from 1 April 2013.

Sub-ss (7), (8): added by the Bank Recovery and Resolution Order 2016, SI 2016/1239, arts 30, 33(4), as from 16 December 2016.

[Notice of reductions of control of UK authorised persons

[7.396]

191D Obligation to notify the [appropriate regulator]: dispositions of control

(1) A person who decides to reduce or cease to have control over a UK authorised person must give the [appropriate regulator] notice in writing before making the disposition.

[(1A) The PRA must give the FCA a copy of any notice it receives under this section.

(1B) The FCA must give the PRA a copy of any notice it receives under this section which—
(a) relates to a UK authorised person who has as a member of its immediate group a PRA-authorised person, or
(b) is given by a PRA-authorised person.]

(2) For the purposes of calculations relating to this section, the holding of shares or voting power by a person ("A1") includes any shares or voting power held by another ("A2") if A1 and A2 are acting in concert.]

NOTES

Substituted as noted to s 178 at **[7.376]**.

Words "appropriate regulator" in square brackets (in each place that they occur) substituted, and sub-ss (1A), (1B) inserted, by the Financial Services Act 2012, s 26(1), (2), (10), as from 1 April 2013.

[7.397]

[191E Requirements for notices under section 191D

(1) A notice under section 191D must be in such form, include such information and be accompanied by such documents as the [appropriate regulator] may reasonably require.

(2) [Each regulator] must publish a list of its requirements as to the form, information and accompanying documents for a notice under section 191D.

(3) The [appropriate regulator] may impose different requirements for different cases and may vary or waive requirements in particular cases.]

NOTES

Substituted as noted to s 178 at **[7.376]**.

Words in square brackets substituted by the Financial Services Act 2012, s 26(1), (2), (11), as from 1 April 2013.

[Offences

[7.398]

191F Offences under this Part

(1) A person who fails to comply with an obligation to notify the [appropriate regulator] under section 178(1) or 191D(1) is guilty of an offence.

(2) A person who gives notice to the [appropriate regulator] under section 178(1) and makes the acquisition to which the notice relates before the expiry date of the assessment period is guilty of an offence unless the [appropriate regulator] has approved the acquisition or given a warning notice under section 189(4)(b)(i) [or section 190A applies].

(3) A person who contravenes an interim condition in a warning notice given under section 189(4)(b)(i) or a condition in a decision notice given under section 189(7) or a final notice which confirms a decision notice under that section is guilty of an offence.

(4) A person who makes an acquisition in contravention of a warning notice given under section 189(4)(b)(ii) or a decision notice given under section 189(7) or a final notice which confirms a decision notice under that section is guilty of an offence.

[(4A) A person who fails to comply with a direction given by the Bank of England under section 190A(4) is guilty of an offence.]

(5) A person who makes an acquisition after the [appropriate regulator's] approval for the acquisition has ceased to be effective by virtue of section 191 is guilty of an offence.

(6) A person who provides information to the [appropriate regulator] which is false in a material particular is guilty of an offence.

(7) A person who breaches a direction contained in a restriction notice given under section 191B is guilty of an offence.

(8) A person guilty of an offence under subsection (1) to (3) or (5) to (7) is liable—

(a) on summary conviction to a fine not exceeding the statutory maximum; or

(b) on conviction on indictment, to a fine.

(9) A person guilty of an offence under subsection (4) [or (4A)] is liable—

(a) on summary conviction, to a fine not exceeding the statutory maximum; or

(b) on conviction on indictment, to imprisonment for a term not exceeding two years or a fine, or both.]

NOTES

Substituted as noted to s 178 at **[7.376]**.

The words "or section 190A applies" in square brackets in sub-s (2) and "or (4A)" in square brackets in sub-s (9) were inserted, and sub-s (4A) was inserted, by the Bank Recovery and Resolution Order 2016, SI 2016/1239, arts 30, 33(5), as from 16 December 2016.

All other words in square brackets in this section were substituted by the Financial Services Act 2012, s 26(1), (2), as from 1 April 2013.

[Interpretation

[7.399]

191G Interpretation

(1) In this Part—

"acquisition" means the acquisition of control or of an increase in control over a UK authorised person;

["the appropriate regulator" is to be read in accordance with section 178(2A);]

. . .

["qualifying credit institution" includes a credit institution which is authorised under the law of Gibraltar relied on immediately before IP completion day to implement the capital requirements directive;]

"shares" has the same meaning as in section 422;

"UK authorised person" means an authorised person who—

(a) is a body incorporated in, or an unincorporated association formed under the law of, any part of the United Kingdom; and

(b) is not a person authorised as a result of paragraph 1 of Schedule 5[, or a person treated as having a Part 4A permission to carry on a regulated activity by virtue of regulation 71 of the Collective Investment Schemes (Amendment etc.) (EU Exit) Regulations 2019]; and

"voting power" has the same meaning as in section 422.

(2) For the purposes of this Part, a "working day" is a day other than—

(a) a Saturday or a Sunday; or

(b) a day which is a bank holiday in England and Wales under the Banking and Financial Dealings Act 1971.]

NOTES

Substituted as noted to s 178 at **[7.376]**.

Sub-s (1) is amended as follows:

Definition "the appropriate regulator" inserted by the Financial Services Act 2012, s 26(1), (12), as from 1 April 2013.

The definition "credit institution" (omitted) was repealed, and the words in square brackets in the definition "UK authorised person" were inserted, by the Financial Services and Markets Act 2000 (Amendment) (EU Exit) Regulations 2019, SI 2019/632, regs 48, 56(a), (b), as from IP completion day (as defined in the European Union (Withdrawal Agreement) Act 2020, s 39).

Definition "qualifying credit institution" inserted by SI 2019/632, regs 48, 56(c), as from IP completion day (as defined in the European Union (Withdrawal Agreement) Act 2020, s 39). Note that reg 56(c) of the 2019 Regulations was added by the Gibraltar (Miscellaneous Amendments) (EU Exit) Regulations 2019, SI 2019/680, reg 9(1), (4), with effect from immediately before IP completion day. Note also that the Gibraltar (Miscellaneous Amendments) (EU Exit) Regulations 2019, SI 2019/680, reg 9(4) was itself amended by the Financial Services and Economic and Monetary Policy (Consequential Amendments) (EU Exit) Regulations 2020, SI 2020/1301, reg 3, Schedule, para 40(d), as from 30 December 2020; and the effect of the amendment has been incorporated in the text set out above.

The words in square brackets in the definition "credit institution" were substituted by the Capital Requirements Regulations 2013, SI 2013/3115, reg 46(1), Sch 2, Pt 1, paras 1, 13, as from 1 January 2014.

Miscellaneous

[7.400]

192 Power to change definitions of control etc

The Treasury may by order—

(a) provide for exemptions from the obligations to notify imposed by sections 178 and [191D];

(b) amend section [181] by varying, or removing, any of the cases in which a person is treated as [acquiring] control over a UK authorised person or by adding a case;

(c) amend section [182] by varying, or removing, any of the cases in which a person is treated as increasing control over a UK authorised person or by adding a case;

(d) amend section [183] by varying, or removing, any of the cases in which a person is treated as [reducing or ceasing to have] control over a UK authorised person or by adding a case;

(e) amend section 422 by varying, or removing, any of the cases in which a person is treated as being a controller of a person or by adding a case.

NOTES

Words and figures in square brackets substituted by the Financial Services and Markets Act 2000 (Controllers) Regulations 2009, SI 2009/534, reg 4, as from 21 March 2009.

Orders: the Financial Services and Markets Act 2000 (Regulated Activities) (Amendment) (No 2) Order 2003, SI 2003/1476; the Financial Services and Markets Act 2000 (Controllers) (Exemption) Order 2009, SI 2009/774 at **[8.555]**.

[PART 12A POWERS EXERCISABLE IN RELATION TO PARENT UNDERTAKINGS

Introductory

[7.401]

192A Meaning of "qualifying authorised person"

(1) In this Part "qualifying authorised person" means an authorised person satisfying the following conditions.

(2) Condition A is that the authorised person is a body corporate incorporated in the United Kingdom.

(3) Condition B is that the authorised person is—

(a) a PRA-authorised person, or

(b) an investment firm.

(4) The Treasury may by order—

(a) amend subsection (3) so as to add to or restrict the descriptions of authorised person who can be qualifying authorised persons, or

(b) provide that while the order is in force subsection (3) is not to have effect.

(5) Except as provided by subsection (6), an order under subsection (4) is not to be made unless a draft of the order has been laid before Parliament and approved by a resolution of each House.

(6) An order under subsection (4) may be made without a draft having been laid and approved as mentioned in subsection (5) if the order contains a statement that the Treasury are of the opinion that, by reason of urgency, it is necessary to make the order without a draft being so laid and approved.

(7) An order under subsection (4) made in accordance with subsection (6)—

(a) must be laid before Parliament after being made, and

(b) ceases to have effect at the end of the relevant period unless before the end of that period the order is approved by a resolution of each House of Parliament (but without affecting anything done under the order or the power to make a new order).

(8) The "relevant period" is a period of 28 days beginning with the day on which the order is made.

(9) In calculating the relevant period no account is to be taken of any time during which Parliament is dissolved or prorogued or during which both Houses are adjourned for more than 4 days.]

NOTES

Inserted (together with the rest of Part 12A (originally ss 192A–192J,192K–192N)) by the Financial Services Act 2012, s 27, as from 24 January 2013 (for the purposes of making orders), and as from 1 April 2013 (otherwise).

[7.402]

[192B Meaning of "qualifying parent undertaking"

(1) The parent undertaking of a qualifying authorised person or recognised UK investment exchange is for the purposes of this Part a "qualifying parent undertaking" if the following conditions are satisfied in relation to it.

(2) Condition A is that the parent undertaking is a body corporate which—

(a) is incorporated in the United Kingdom, or

(b) has a place of business in the United Kingdom.

(3) Condition B is that the parent undertaking is not itself an authorised person, a recognised investment exchange[, a recognised clearing house or a recognised CSD].

(4) Condition C is that the parent undertaking is a financial institution of a kind prescribed by the Treasury by order.

(5) "Recognised UK investment exchange" means a recognised investment exchange that is not an overseas investment exchange as defined in section 313(1).

(6) The Treasury may by order—

(a) amend subsection (4) by omitting the words "a financial institution", and

(b) make any amendment of subsection (2) that they consider desirable in connection with an amendment made under paragraph (a).]

NOTES

Inserted as noted to s 192A at **[7.401]**.

Sub-s (3): words in square brackets substituted by the Central Securities Depositories Regulations 2017, SI 2017/1064, reg 2(1), (6), as from 28 November 2017.

Orders: the Financial Services and Markets Act 2000 (Prescribed Financial Institutions) Order 2013, SI 2013/165; the Bank Recovery and Resolution (No 2) Order 2014, SI 2014/3348 at **[8.564]**.

[Power of direction

[7.403]

192C Power to direct qualifying parent undertaking

(1) The appropriate regulator may give a direction under this section to a qualifying parent undertaking if either the general condition or the consolidated supervision condition is satisfied.

(2) The general condition is that the appropriate regulator considers that it is desirable to give the direction in order to advance—

(a) in the case of the FCA, one or more of its operational objectives;

(b) in the case of the PRA, any of its objectives.

(3) The consolidated supervision condition is that—

(a) the appropriate regulator is the competent authority for the purpose of consolidated supervision that is required, in relation to some or all of the members of the group of a qualifying authorised person, [in pursuance of—

(i) any implementing provision contained in subordinate legislation (within the meaning of the Interpretation Act 1978) made otherwise than by any of the following—

(aa) statutory instrument, and

(bb) statutory rule for the purposes of the Statutory Rules (Northern Ireland) Order 1979 (SI 1979/1573 (NI 12)); . . .

(ii) any other implementing provision (as amended from time to time)], and

[(iii) Part 9C rules;

(iv) CRR rules; or

(v) rules made under section 192XA, and]

(b) the appropriate regulator considers that the giving of the direction is desirable for the purpose of the effective consolidated supervision of the group.

[(4) In subsection (3)(a)—

"consolidated supervision" includes supplemental supervision;

"implementing provision" has the same meaning as in section 3M.]

(5) In deciding whether to give a direction under this section, a regulator must have regard—

(a) to the desirability where practicable of exercising its powers in relation to authorised persons or recognised investment exchanges rather than its powers under this section, and

(b) to the principle that a burden or restriction which is imposed on a person should be proportionate to the benefits, considered in general terms, which are expected to result from its imposition.

(6) "The appropriate regulator" means—

(a) where a direction relates to a qualifying authorised person or recognised investment exchange who is a PRA-authorised person, the FCA or the PRA;

(b) in any other case, the FCA.]

NOTES

Inserted as noted to s 192A at **[7.401]**.

Sub-s (3): words in first pair of square brackets substituted by the Financial Services and Markets Act 2000 (Amendment) (EU Exit) Regulations 2019, SI 2019/632, regs 57, 58(1), (2), as from IP completion day (as defined in the European Union (Withdrawal Agreement) Act 2020, s 39). Word omitted from sub-para (a)(i)(bb) revoked, and sub-paras (a)(iii)–(v) inserted, by the Financial Services Act 2021 (Prudential Regulation of Credit Institutions and Investment Firms) (Consequential Amendments and Miscellaneous Provisions) Regulations 2022, SI 2022/838, reg 3, as from 17 August 2022.

Sub-s (4): substituted by SI 2019/632, regs 57, 58(1), (3), as from IP completion day (as defined in the European Union (Withdrawal Agreement) Act 2020, s 39).

[7.404]

[192D Requirements that may be imposed

(1) A direction under section 192C may require the parent undertaking—

(a) to take specified action, or

(b) to refrain from taking specified action.

(2) A requirement may be imposed by reference to the parent undertaking's relationship with—

(a) its group, or

(b) other members of its group.

(3) A requirement may refer to the past conduct of the parent undertaking (for example, by requiring the parent undertaking to review or take remedial action in respect of past conduct).

(4) A requirement imposed by the direction may be expressed to expire at the end of a specified period, but the imposition of a requirement that expires at the end of a specified period does not affect the power to give a further direction imposing a new requirement.

(5) The direction—

(a) may be revoked by the regulator which gave it by written notice to the body to which it is given, and

(b) ceases to be in force if the body to which it is given ceases to be a qualifying parent undertaking.]

NOTES

Inserted as noted to s 192A at **[7.401]**.

[7.405]

[192E Direction: procedure

(1) If a regulator proposes to give a direction under section 192C, or gives such a direction with immediate effect, it must give written notice to—

(a) the parent undertaking to which the direction is given (or to be given) ("P"), and

(b) any authorised person or recognised investment exchange who will, in the opinion of the regulator, be significantly affected by the direction.

(2) In the following provisions of this section "notified person" means a person to whom notice under subsection (1) is given.

(3) A direction under section 192C takes effect—

(a) immediately, if the notice under subsection (1) states that that is the case,

(b) on such other date as may be specified in the notice, or

(c) if no date is specified in the notice, when the matter to which the notice relates is no longer open to review.

(4) A direction may be expressed to take effect immediately (or on a specified date) only if the regulator reasonably considers that it is necessary for the direction to take effect immediately (or on that date).

(5) The notice under subsection (1) must—

(a) give details of the direction,

(b) state the regulator's reasons for the direction and for its determination as to when the direction takes effect,

(c) inform the notified person that the person may make representations to the regulator within such period as may be specified in the notice (whether or not the notified person has referred the matter to the Tribunal), and

(d) inform the notified person of the person's right to refer the matter to the Tribunal.

(6) The regulator may extend the period allowed under the notice for making representations.

(7) If, having considered any representations made by any notified person, the regulator decides—

(a) to give the direction proposed, or

(b) if the direction has been given, not to revoke the direction,

it must give each of the notified persons written notice.

(8) If, having considered any representations made by any notified person, the regulator decides—

(a) not to give the direction proposed,

(b) to give a different direction, or

(c) to revoke a direction which has effect,

it must give each of the notified persons written notice.

(9) A notice given under subsection (7) must inform the notified person of the person's right to refer the matter to the Tribunal.

(10) A notice under subsection (8)(b) must comply with subsection (5).

(11) If a notice informs the notified person of the person's right to refer a matter to the Tribunal, it must give an indication of the procedure on such a reference.

(12) For the purposes of subsection (3)(c), whether a matter is open to review is to be determined in accordance with section 391(8).]

NOTES

Inserted as noted to s 192A at **[7.401]**.

[7.406]

[192F Consultation between regulators

(1) Before the PRA gives a notice under section 192E(1) or (8)(b), it must consult the FCA.

(2) Before the FCA gives a notice under section 192E(1) or (8)(b) in relation to the parent undertaking of a PRA-authorised person, the FCA must consult the PRA.

(3) Before [the FCA] gives a notice under section 192E(1) or (8)(b) in relation to the parent undertaking of a recognised clearing house [or a recognised CSD], [it] must consult the Bank of England.]

NOTES

Inserted as noted to s 192A at **[7.401]**.

Sub-s (3): words in first and third pairs of square brackets substituted by the Bank of England and Financial Services Act 2016, s 16, Sch 2, Pt 2, paras 26, 41, as from 1 March 2017. Words in second pair of square brackets inserted by the Central Securities Depositories Regulations 2017, SI 2017/1064, reg 2(1), (7), as from 28 November 2017.

[7.407]

[192G References to Tribunal

(1) A notified person who is aggrieved by the exercise by either regulator of its powers in relation to directions under section 192C may refer the matter to the Tribunal.

(2) "Notified person" is to be read in accordance with subsection (2) of section 192E, except that it includes a person to whom a notice under subsection (1) of that section ought to have been given.]

NOTES

Inserted as noted to s 192A at **[7.401]**.

[7.408]

[192H Statement of policy: directions under section 192C

(1) Each regulator must prepare and issue a statement of policy with respect to the giving of directions under section 192C.

(2) A regulator may at any time alter or replace a statement issued under this section.

(3) If a statement issued under this section is altered or replaced, the regulator must issue the altered or replacement statement.

(4) In exercising or deciding whether to exercise its power under section 192C in any particular case, a regulator must have regard to any statement published under this section and for the time being in force.

(5) A statement under this section must be published by the regulator concerned in the way appearing to the regulator to be best calculated to bring it to the attention of the public.

(6) A regulator may charge a reasonable fee for providing a person with a copy of a statement published under this section.

(7) A regulator must, without delay, give the Treasury a copy of any statement which the regulator publishes under this section.]

NOTES

Inserted as noted to s 192A at **[7.401]**.

[7.409]

[192I Statement of policy relating to directions: procedure

(1) Before issuing a statement of policy under section 192H, a regulator ("the issuing regulator") must—

(a) consult the other regulator and[, where the issuing regulator is the FCA,] the Bank of England, and

(b) publish a draft of the proposed statement in the way appearing to the issuing regulator to be best calculated to bring it to the attention of the public.

(2) The draft must be accompanied by notice that representations about the proposal may be made to the issuing regulator within a specified time.

(3) Before issuing the proposed statement, the issuing regulator must have regard to any representations made to it in accordance with subsection (2).

(4) If the issuing regulator issues the proposed statement it must publish an account, in general terms, of—

(a) the representations made to it in accordance with subsection (2), and

(b) its response to them.

(5) If the statement differs from the draft published under subsection (2) in a way which is, in the opinion of the issuing regulator, significant, the issuing regulator—

(a) must before issuing it consult the other regulator again, and

(b) must (in addition to complying with subsection (4)), publish details of the difference.

(6) The issuing regulator may charge a reasonable fee for providing a person with a draft published under subsection (1)(b).

(7) This section also applies to a proposal to alter or replace a statement.]

NOTES

Inserted as noted to s 192A at **[7.401]**.

Sub-s (1): words in square brackets inserted by the Bank of England and Financial Services Act 2016, s 16, Sch 2, Pt 2, paras 26, 42, as from 1 March 2017.

[Rules requiring provision of information by parent undertakings

[7.410]

192J Rules requiring provision of information by parent undertakings

(1) The appropriate regulator may make rules requiring qualifying parent undertakings—

(a) to provide to the regulator information of a specified description;

(b) to produce to the regulator documents of a specified description.

(2) The rules may only specify a description of information or documents that is relevant to the exercise by the regulator of its functions.

(3) The rules may make provision—

(a) as to the time within which information must be provided or documents produced;

(b) about the form in which any information is to provided;

(c) about the place where any documents are to be produced;

(d) requiring information provided to be verified in a specified manner;

(e) requiring documents produced to be authenticated in a specified manner.

(4) "The appropriate regulator" means—

(a) in relation to the parent undertaking of a qualifying authorised person who is a PRA-authorised person, the FCA or the PRA;

(b) in any other case, the FCA.]

NOTES

Inserted as noted to s 192A at **[7.401]**.

[Rules applying to parent undertakings of ring-fenced bodies

[7.411]

192JA Rules applying to parent undertakings of ring-fenced bodies

(1) The appropriate regulator may make such rules applying to bodies corporate falling within subsection (2) as appear to the regulator to be necessary or expedient for the group ring-fencing purposes.

(2) A body corporate falls within this subsection if—

(a) it is incorporated in the United Kingdom or has a place of business in the United Kingdom,

(b) it is a parent undertaking of a ring-fenced body, and

(c) it is not itself an authorised person.

(3) The "group ring-fencing purposes" are the purposes set out in section 142H(4).

(4) "The appropriate regulator" means—

(a) in relation to the parent undertaking of a ring-fenced body that is a PRA-authorised person, the PRA;

(b) in any other case, the FCA.]

NOTES

Inserted, together with the preceding heading, by the Financial Services (Banking Reform) Act 2013, s 133(1), as from 21 April 2016.

[Rules requiring parent undertakings to facilitate resolution

[7.412]

192JB Rules requiring parent undertakings to facilitate resolution

[(1) The appropriate regulator may make rules requiring a qualifying parent undertaking to make arrangements that in the opinion of the regulator—

(a) would facilitate the preparation, maintenance, implementation and review of a recovery plan in relation to the group of the qualifying parent undertaking,

(b) are required in relation to the provision of financial support to other members of the group of the qualifying parent undertaking which encounter or are likely to encounter financial difficulties, or

(c) would allow or facilitate the exercise of the resolution powers in relation to the qualifying parent undertaking or any of its subsidiary undertakings in the event of a situation arising where all or part of the business of the parent undertaking or the subsidiary undertaking encounters or is likely to encounter financial difficulties.]

[(1A) A "recovery plan" in relation to a group, is a document which provides for measures to be taken to achieve the stabilisation of the group as a whole, or any institution within the group, where the group or institution is in a situation of financial stress, in order to address or remove the causes of the financial stress and restore the financial position of the group or the institution.]

(2) The "resolution powers" are—

(a) the powers conferred on the Treasury and the Bank of England by or under Parts 1 to 3 of the Banking Act 2009, and

(b) any similar powers exercisable by an authority outside the United Kingdom.

(3) The arrangements that may be required include arrangements relating to—

(a) the issue of debt instruments by the parent undertaking;

(b) the provision to a subsidiary undertaking ("S") or a transferee by the parent undertaking, or by any other subsidiary undertaking of the parent undertaking, of such services and facilities as would be required to enable S or the transferee to operate the business, or part of the business, effectively;

[(c) the review of a recovery plan by the [PRA];

(d) the entry by the parent undertaking into a group financial support agreement and provision of financial support by the parent undertaking in accordance with that agreement].

[(4) In subsection (3)—

(a) . . .

[(b) "group financial support agreement" means an agreement for the provision of financial support, by a member of the group of the parent undertaking, to an institution in the group which, at any time after the agreement is concluded, comes to need financial support;]

(c) "transferee" means a person to whom all or part of the business of the parent undertaking or the subsidiary undertaking could be transferred as a result of the exercise of the resolution powers.]

(5) "Debt instrument" has the same meaning as in section 142Y.

(6) "The appropriate regulator" means—

(a) where the subsidiary undertakings of the qualifying parent undertaking include a ring-fenced body that is a PRA-authorised person, the PRA;

(b) where the subsidiary undertakings of the qualifying parent undertaking include one or more PRA-authorised persons but do not include any authorised person that is not a PRA-authorised person, the PRA;

(c) where the subsidiary undertakings of the qualifying parent undertaking do not include any PRA-authorised person, the FCA;

(d) in any other case, the PRA or the FCA.]

NOTES

Inserted, together with the preceding heading, by the Financial Services (Banking Reform) Act 2013, s 133(1), as from 31 December 2014.

Sub-ss (1) and (4) were substituted, and sub-s (1A) and sub-s (3)(c), (d) were inserted, by the Bank Recovery and Resolution Order 2014, SI 2014/3329, arts 112, 120, as from 1 January 2015.

The word in square brackets in sub-s (3)(c) was substituted, and sub-s (4)(a) was repealed, by the Financial Services Act 2021 (Prudential Regulation of Credit Institutions and Investment Firms) (Consequential Amendments and Miscellaneous Provisions) Regulations 2021, SI 2021/1376, reg 4(7), as from 1 January 2022.

Sub-s (4)(b) was substituted by the Financial Services and Markets Act 2000 (Amendment) (EU Exit) Regulations 2019, SI 2019/632, regs 57, 59, as from IP completion day (as defined in the European Union (Withdrawal Agreement) Act 2020, s 39).

[Failure to comply with direction or breach of rules

[7.413]

192K Power to impose penalty or issue censure

(1) This section applies if a regulator is satisfied that a person who is or has been a qualifying parent undertaking ("P") has contravened—

(a) a requirement of a direction given to P by that regulator under section 192C, . . .

(b) a provision of rules made by that regulator under section 192J [or 192JB], [or] [(c) a requirement imposed by a [qualifying provision] specified, or of a description specified, for the purposes of this subsection by the Treasury by order].

[(1A) This section also applies if a regulator is satisfied that a person ("P") who is or has been a parent undertaking of a ring-fenced body has contravened a provision of rules made by that regulator under section 192JA.]

(2) The regulator may impose a penalty of such amount as it considers appropriate on—

(a) P, or

(b) any person who was knowingly concerned in the contravention.

(3) The regulator may, instead of imposing a penalty on a person, publish a statement censuring the person.

[(3A) The regulator may impose, for such period as it considers appropriate, restrictions (including a temporary ban) on the exercise by any member of the management body or senior management of, or other person who works for, a qualifying parent undertaking of any functions in a PRA-authorised person, an investment firm or a qualifying parent undertaking.

(3B) The regulator may only impose restrictions under subsection (3A) on a person who was, at any time, knowingly concerned in the contravention.]

(4) The regulator may not take action against a person under this section after the end of the limitation period unless, before the end of that period, it has given a warning notice to the person under section 192L.

(5) "The limitation period" means the period of 3 years beginning with the first day on which the regulator knew of the contravention.

(6) For this purpose a regulator is to be treated as knowing of a contravention if it has information from which the contravention can reasonably be inferred.

[(7) In this section—

"management body" means the board of directors, or if there is no such board, the equivalent body responsible for the management of the undertaking concerned;

"member of the senior management" means a person who—

(a) exercises executive functions within a qualifying parent undertaking, and

(b) is responsible, and directly accountable to the management body, for the day to day management of that qualifying parent undertaking.

(8) A regulator which imposes a restriction on any person under subsection (3A) may—

(a) vary the restriction so as to reduce the period for which it has effect or otherwise to limit its effect, or

(b) cancel the restriction.]]

NOTES

Inserted as noted to s 192A at **[7.401]**.

The word omitted from sub-s (1)(a) was repealed, sub-s (1)(c) (and the preceding word) was inserted, and sub-ss (3A), (3B) and (7), (8) were inserted and added respectively, by the Bank Recovery and Resolution Order 2014, SI 2014/3329, arts 112, 121, as from 1 January 2015.

Words "or 192JB" in square brackets in sub-s (1) inserted, and sub-s (1A) inserted, by the Financial Services (Banking Reform) Act 2013, s 133(2), as from 31 December 2014 (in so far as relating to the sub-s (1) amendment), and as from 1 January 2019 (in so far as inserting sub-s (1A)).

Words in square brackets in sub-s (1)(c) substituted by the Financial Services and Markets Act 2000 (Amendment) (EU Exit) Regulations 2019, SI 2019/632, regs 57, 60, as from IP completion day (as defined in the European Union (Withdrawal Agreement) Act 2020, s 39) (for transitional provisions see SI 2019/710, reg 37 at **[12.110]**).

[7.414]

[192L Procedure and right to refer to Tribunal

(1) If a regulator proposes to take action against a person under section 192K, it must give the person a warning notice.

(2) A warning notice about a proposal to impose a penalty must state the amount of the penalty.

(3) A warning notice about a proposal to publish a statement must set out the terms of the statement.

[(3A) A warning notice about a proposal to impose a restriction under section 192K(3A) must state—

(a) the terms of the restriction, and

(b) the period for which the restriction is to have effect.]

(4) If the regulator decides to take action against a person under section 192K, it must give the person a decision notice.

(5) A decision notice about the imposition of a penalty must state the amount of the penalty.

(6) A decision notice about the publication of a statement must set out the terms of the statement.

[(6B) A decision notice about the imposition of a restriction under section 192K(3A) must state—

(a) the terms of the restriction, and

(b) the period for which the restriction is to have effect.]

(7) If the regulator decides to take action against a person under section 192K, the person may refer the matter to the Tribunal.]

NOTES

Inserted as noted to s 192A at **[7.401]**.

Sub-ss (3A), (6A), (6B): inserted by the Bank Recovery and Resolution Order 2014, SI 2014/3329, arts 112, 122, as from 1 January 2015.

[7.415]

[192M Duty on publication of statement

After a statement under section 192K(3) is published, the regulator must send a copy of the statement to—

(a) the person in respect of whom it is made, and

(b) any person to whom a copy of the decision notice was given under section 393(4).]

NOTES

Inserted as noted to s 192A at **[7.401]**.

[7.416]

[192N Imposition of penalties under section 192K: statement of policy

(1) Each regulator must prepare and issue a statement of policy with respect to—

(a) the imposition of penalties under section 192K, and

(b) the amount of penalties under that section.

(2) A regulator's policy in determining what the amount of a penalty should be must include having regard to—

(a) the seriousness of the contravention,

(b) the extent to which the contravention was deliberate or reckless, and

(c) whether the person on whom the penalty is to be imposed is an individual.

(3) A regulator may at any time alter or replace a statement issued under this section.

(4) If a statement issued under this section is altered or replaced, the regulator must issue the altered or replacement statement.

(5) In exercising, or deciding whether to exercise, a power under section 192K(2) in the case of any particular contravention, a regulator must have regard to any statement of policy published under this section and in force at a time when the contravention occurred.

(6) A statement under this section must be published by the regulator concerned in the way appearing to the regulator to be best calculated to bring it to the attention of the public.

(7) A regulator may charge a reasonable fee for providing a person with a copy of the statement published under this section.

(8) A regulator must, without delay, give the Treasury a copy of any statement which it publishes under this section.

(9) Section 192I applies in relation to a statement under this section as it applies in relation to a statement under section 192H.]

NOTES

Inserted as noted to s 192A at **[7.401]**.

[PART 12B APPROVAL OF CERTAIN HOLDING COMPANIES

[Interpretation]

NOTES

The above heading in square brackets was inserted by the Financial Services Act 2021, s 5, Sch 3, Pt 2, para 3, as from 9 June 2021 (for transitional provisions, see Sch 3, Pt 4 to the 2021 Act).

[7.417]

192O Interpretation

(1) In this Part—

. . .

["on a consolidated basis" means on the basis of the consolidated situation;

"consolidated situation" means the situation that results from an entity being treated, for the purposes of the capital requirements regulation or CRR rules (as appropriate), as if that entity and one or more other entities formed a single entity;]

"designated investment firm" means an investment firm which is for the time being designated by the PRA under article 3 of the Financial Services and Markets Act 2000 (PRA-regulated Activities) Order 2013;

"Directive 2013/36/EU UK law" means—

(a) before IP completion day, the law of the United Kingdom which is relied on by the United Kingdom to implement the capital requirements directive and its implementing measures ("the relevant EU provisions"); and

(b) after IP completion day, the law of the United Kingdom which was relied on immediately before that date to implement the relevant EU provisions as it has effect—

(i) on [1 January 2022], in the case of rules made by the FCA or by the PRA under this Act, and

(ii) as amended from time to time, in all other cases,

. . .

["EU tertiary legislation" has the meaning given in section 20 of the European Union (Withdrawal) Act 2018;]

"financial holding company" has the meaning given in Article 4(1)(20) of the capital requirements regulation;

"financial institution" has the meaning given in Article 4(1)(26) of the capital requirements regulation;

"institution" means a credit institution or an investment firm;

"investment firm" has the meaning given in Article 4(1)(2) of the capital requirements regulation;

"mixed financial holding company" has the meaning given in Article 4(1)(21) of the capital requirements regulation;

"parent institution" means an institution which is a parent undertaking;

"parent undertaking" has the meaning given in section 420;

. . .

["section 192XA rules" means rules made under section 192XA;]

["on a sub-consolidated basis" means—

(a) on the basis of the consolidated situation of a parent institution, financial holding company or mixed financial holding company, excluding a sub-group of entities, or

(b) on the basis of the consolidated situation of a parent institution, financial holding company or mixed financial holding company that is not the ultimate parent institution, financial holding company or mixed financial holding company;]

"subsidiary institution" means an institution which is a subsidiary undertaking.

(2) A "parent financial holding company" or "parent mixed financial holding company" means a financial holding company or a mixed financial holding company which—

(a) is a UK parent financial holding company or a UK parent mixed financial holding company, within the meaning given in Article 4(1)(30) and 4(1)(32) respectively of the capital requirements regulation; or

(b) is required, whether by the PRA by direction under section 192C or otherwise, to comply with the capital requirements regulation[, CRR rules] and Directive 2013/36/EU UK law on a sub-consolidated basis.

[(3) In this Part, references to instruments made under the capital requirements regulation include EU tertiary legislation made under that regulation which forms part of retained EU law.]]

NOTES

Commencement: 29 December 2020.

Part 12B was inserted by the Financial Holding Companies (Approval etc) and Capital Requirements (Capital Buffers and Macro-prudential Measures) (Amendment) (EU Exit) Regulations 2020, SI 2020/1406, reg 2(7), as from 28 December 2020 (to the extent necessary for making rules under s 192V), and as from 29 December 2020 (otherwise). For transitional provisions, see the note below.

Sub-s (1) is amended as follows:

Definition "consolidated basis" (omitted) repealed, definitions "on a consolidated basis" and "consolidated situation" inserted, and definition "on a sub-consolidated basis" substituted, by the Financial Services Act 2021 (Prudential Regulation of Credit Institutions and Investment Firms) (Consequential Amendments and Miscellaneous Provisions) Regulations 2021, SI 2021/1376, reg 4(8)(a), as from 1 January 2022.

The words omitted from the definition "Directive 2013/36/EU UK law" were repealed, and the definition "EU tertiary legislation" was inserted, by the Financial Services Act 2021, s 5, Sch 3, Pt 3, para 14(2), as from 9 June 2021.

Words in square brackets in para (b) of the definition "Directive 2013/36/EU UK law" substituted Financial Services and Markets Act 2000 (Consequential Amendments of References to Rules) Regulations 2021, SI 2021/1388, reg 2(4), as from 1 January 2022.

The definition "section 192V rules" (omitted) was repealed, and the definition "section 192XA rules" was inserted, by the Financial Services Act 2021, s 5, Sch 3, Pt 2, para 4, as from 9 June 2021 (for transitional provisions, see Sch 3, Pt 4 to the 2021 Act).

Sub-s (2): words in square brackets in para (b) inserted by SI 2021/1376, reg 4(8)(b), as from 1 January 2022.

Sub-s (3): added by the Financial Services Act 2021, s 5, Sch 3, Pt 3, para 14(3), as from 9 June 2021.

Transitional provisions: the Financial Holding Companies (Approval etc) and Capital Requirements (Capital Buffers and Macro-prudential Measures) (Amendment) (EU Exit) Regulations 2020, SI 2020/1406, reg 5 provides as follows—

"5 Transitional provisions

(1) Paragraphs (2) to (7) apply to a company ("C") which—

(a) is established in the United Kingdom as a parent financial holding company or a parent mixed financial holding company on 29th December 2020; and

(b) requires approval or confirmation of an exemption from the Prudential Regulation Authority ("PRA") under section 192P of the Financial Services and Markets Act 2000 ("FSMA").

(2) C is to be treated as having an approval to be established in the United Kingdom as a parent financial holding company or parent mixed financial holding company (as the case may be).

(3) C's approval under paragraph (2) lapses—

(a) on 28th June 2021, if C has not submitted an application to the PRA under section 192Q of FSMA before that date; or

(b) on the earlier of—

(i) the day on which C's application under section 192Q of FSMA is finally determined, or

(ii) 31st December 2021.

(4) For the purposes of this regulation, an application is finally determined—

(a) when the application is withdrawn;

(b) when the PRA approves C, or confirms that C is exempt from the requirement for approval, under section 192R of FSMA;

(c) where the PRA refuses approval, or rejects an application for confirmation of exemption, and the matter is not referred to the Tribunal, when the time for referring the matter to the Tribunal has expired;

(d) where the PRA refuses approval, or rejects an application for confirmation of exemption, and the matter is referred to the Tribunal, the date on which the reference is determined by the Tribunal or has otherwise ended.

(5) The PRA may designate one or more financial holding companies, mixed financial holding companies or institutions within the group of which the holding company or institution forms part as being responsible for ensuring that the group complies with the requirements laid down in Directive 2013/36/EU UK law and in the capital requirements regulation on a consolidated or sub-consolidated basis until such time as C's application has been finally determined.

(6) For the purposes of sections 71B to 71H of FSMA, in relation to a holding company designated under paragraph (5) which is not a parent undertaking, "appropriate regulator" means the PRA.

(7) For the purposes of this regulation—

(a) "consolidated basis", "Directive 2013/36/EU UK law", "financial holding company", "mixed financial holding company", "institution", "parent financial holding company", "parent mixed financial holding company" and "sub-consolidated basis" have the meanings given in section 192O of FSMA (inserted by regulation 2(7));

(b) "capital requirements regulation" has the meaning given in section 417 of FSMA;

(c) "group" has the meaning given in section 421 of FSMA.

(8) In relation to rules made under section 192V of FSMA, the requirements of section 138J of that Act (consultation) may be satisfied by things done before 28th December 2020 as well as by things done on or after that date.".

[Approval]

NOTES

The above heading in square brackets was inserted by the Financial Services Act 2021, s 5, Sch 3, Pt 2, para 5, as from 9 June 2021 (for transitional provisions, see Sch 3, Pt 4 to the 2021 Act).

[7.418]

[192P Requirement for approval

(1) No company may be established in the United Kingdom as a parent financial holding company or a parent mixed financial holding company unless—

(a) the company is approved by the PRA;

(b) the PRA has confirmed that the company is exempt from the requirement for approval under subsection (2); or

(c) the subsidiary undertakings of the company do not include—
(i) a credit institution, or
(ii) a designated investment firm.

(2) A company is exempt from the requirement for approval if—
(a) it is a parent financial holding company and its principal activity is to acquire holdings in subsidiary undertakings; or
(b) it is a parent mixed financial holding company and its principal activity with respect to institutions and financial institutions is to acquire holdings in subsidiary undertakings,

and all of the conditions in subsection (3) are satisfied.

(3) The conditions in this subsection are satisfied if—
(a) the Bank of England has not identified the company as a resolution entity (within the meaning of section 3 of the Banking Act 2009) in a group resolution plan under Part 5 of the Bank Recovery and Resolution (No 2) Order 2014;
(b) a credit institution or a designated investment firm which is a subsidiary undertaking in the same group as the company—
(i) has been designated by the PRA as responsible to ensure the group's compliance with prudential requirements on a consolidated or sub-consolidated basis, and
(ii) has the power required to discharge those obligations effectively, whether under contractual arrangements with other companies in the group or otherwise;
(c) the company does not take any management, operational or financial decisions affecting—
(i) the group as a whole, or
(ii) any of its subsidiary undertakings which are institutions or financial institutions;
(d) the PRA is satisfied that there is no impediment to the effective supervision of the group on a consolidated or sub-consolidated basis.

(4) For the purposes of this section, a company is established in the United Kingdom if the company is incorporated in, or formed under the law of, any part of the United Kingdom.]

NOTES

Commencement: 29 December 2020.

Part 12B was inserted as noted to s 192O at **[7.417]**.

[7.419]

[192Q Application for approval or exemption

(1) An application for—
(a) the PRA's approval for the purposes of section 192P(1)(a); or
(b) confirmation of exemption from the requirement for approval,

must be made by the company concerned.

(2) The application must—
(a) be made in such manner as the PRA may direct; and
(b) contain or be accompanied by the information referred to in subsection (3).

(3) The information referred to in subsection (2) is—
(a) a description of the structural organisation of the group of which the company is part, indicating—
(i) its subsidiary undertakings and parent undertakings, and
(ii) the location and type of activity undertaken by each of the entities within the group;
(b) the identity of at least two individuals who are directors of the company;
(c) a description as to how each director of the company complies with the requirements that they are of sufficiently good repute, and possess sufficient knowledge, skills and experience, to perform their duties as directors;
(d) where one of the subsidiary undertakings of the company is a credit institution or a designated investment firm—
(i) the identity of any persons who hold, whether directly or indirectly, qualifying holdings (within the meaning of Article 4(1)(36) of the capital requirements regulation), in the credit institution or designated investment firm, and the amounts of those holdings, or
(ii) if no person holds a qualifying holding in the credit institution or designated investment firm, the identity of the 20 largest shareholders in the credit institution or designated investment firm and the amount of their shareholdings;
(e) a description of the internal organisation and the distribution of tasks with the group.

(4) The PRA may, by notice in writing, require the company to provide any further information necessary to enable the PRA to assess whether the conditions referred to in section 192P(2) and (3) or section 192R are fulfilled.]

NOTES

Commencement: 29 December 2020.

Part 12B was inserted as noted to s 192O at **[7.417]**.

[7.420]

[192R Grant of approval

(1) When the PRA receives an application from a company under section 192Q, it must decide whether—
(a) to approve the company,
(b) to confirm that the company qualifies for an exemption under section 192P(2) and (3), or
(c) to take one or more of the measures in section 192T.

(2) The PRA may only approve the company under this section where conditions A, B and C are satisfied.

(3) Condition A is that the internal arrangements and distribution of tasks within the group of which the company is part are—

(a) adequate for the purpose of complying with the requirements imposed by Directive 2013/36/EU UK law[, CRR rules] . . . and the capital requirements regulation on a consolidated or sub-consolidated basis . . .

[(aa) adequate for the purpose of complying with section 192XA rules, and]

(b) effective to—

(i) co-ordinate all the subsidiary undertakings of the company, including, where necessary, through an adequate distribution of tasks among subsidiary institutions;

(ii) prevent or manage intra-group conflicts; and

(iii) enforce the group-wide policies set by the company throughout the group.

(4) Condition B is that the structural organisation of the group of which the company is part does not obstruct or otherwise prevent the effective supervision of the subsidiary institutions and parent institutions as concerns the individual, consolidated and, where appropriate, sub-consolidated obligations to which they are subject.

(5) In assessing whether Condition B is satisfied, the PRA must take into account—

(a) the position of the company within the group;

(b) the shareholding structure of the company, and the group of which it is part; and

(c) the role of the company within the group.

(6) Condition C is that—

(a) the PRA has received the information as to the identity of the shareholders of any credit institution in the group, and the amount of their shareholdings, which is required under Directive 2013/36/EU UK law; and

(b) the directors of the company are of sufficiently good repute, and possess sufficient knowledge, skills and experience to perform their duties as directors.

(7) Where the PRA proposes to refuse approval, or to reject an application for confirmation of exemption, it must give the company a warning notice within four months beginning with—

(a) the date on which it received the application under section 192Q; or

(b) if later (subject to subsection (8) and section 387), the date on which it received any further information requested under section 192Q(4).

(8) When the PRA decides to refuse approval, or to reject an application for an exemption, it must give the company a decision notice within six months of the date on which it received which the application under section 192Q.]

NOTES

Commencement: 29 December 2020.

Part 12B was inserted as noted to s 192O at **[7.417]**.

Sub-s (3): words in square brackets in para (a) inserted by the Financial Services Act 2021 (Prudential Regulation of Credit Institutions and Investment Firms) (Consequential Amendments and Miscellaneous Provisions) Regulations 2021, SI 2021/1376, reg 4(9), as from 1 January 2022. The words omitted from para (a) were repealed, and para (aa) was inserted, by the Financial Services Act 2021, s 5, Sch 3, Pt 3, para15, as from 9 June 2021.

[7.421]

[192S Regulator's duty to monitor

(1) The PRA must monitor whether—

(a) a company approved under section 192R continues to satisfy the conditions in section 192R(3) to (6); and

(b) a company which it has confirmed is exempt from the requirement for approval under section 192P continues to satisfy the conditions for exemption set out in section 192P(2) and (3).

(2) A company which is subject to the requirement for approval under section 192P(1), or exempt from that requirement under section 192P(2), must give the PRA notice in writing of—

(a) any change in the structural organisation of the group; and

(b) any other information required by rules made under section 192J.]

NOTES

Commencement: 29 December 2020.

Part 12B was inserted as noted to s 192O at **[7.417]**.

[7.422]

[192T Measures

(1) Where the PRA determines that the conditions in section 192R are not met, or have ceased to be met, by a company which is subject to the requirement for approval under section 192P(1), the PRA must take appropriate measures in relation to the company—

(a) to ensure the continuity and integrity of the consolidated or sub-consolidated supervision of the group of which the company is part (the "relevant group"); . . .

(b) to ensure that the relevant group complies with the requirements in Directive 2013/36/EU UK law[, CRR rules] . . . and the capital requirements regulation on a consolidated or sub-consolidated basis; [and

(c) to ensure that the relevant group complies with section 192XA rules].

(2) Measures taken under subsection (1) may include a direction—

(a) suspending the exercise by the company of voting rights attached to the shares of specified subsidiary institutions held by the company;

(b) requiring the company to transfer its holdings in its subsidiary institutions to its shareholders;

(c) designating another financial holding company, mixed financial holding company or institution within the group as being responsible for a period specified in the direction for ensuring that the group complies with the requirements laid down in Directive 2013/36/EU UK law[, in CRR rules] . . . and in the capital requirements regulation on a consolidated or sub-consolidated basis [and with section 192XA rules];

(d) restricting or prohibiting distributions or interest payments to shareholders;

(e) requiring the company to divest from, or reduce its holdings in, institutions or financial institutions;

(f) requiring the company to submit a plan setting out how it proposes to correct any deficiencies in its compliance with the conditions in section 192R.

(3) Where the PRA determines that a company which it has confirmed is exempt from the requirement for approval under section 192P no longer satisfies the conditions for exemption under section 192P(3), it must direct that company to apply for approval for the purposes of section 192P(1)(a).]

NOTES

Commencement: 29 December 2020.

Part 12B was inserted as noted to s 192O at **[7.417]**.

Sub-s (1): the words omitted from paras (a) and (b) were repealed, and para (c) and the preceding word were inserted, by the Financial Services Act 2021, s 5, Sch 3, Pt 3, para 16(2), as from 9 June 2021. Words in square brackets in para (b) inserted by the Financial Services Act 2021 (Prudential Regulation of Credit Institutions and Investment Firms) (Consequential Amendments and Miscellaneous Provisions) Regulations 2021, SI 2021/1376, reg 4(10), as from 1 January 2022.

Sub-s (2): the words omitted from para (c) were repealed, and the words in square brackets in that paragraph were inserted, by the Financial Services Act 2021, s 5, Sch 3, Pt 3, para 16(3), as from 9 June 2021. Words in square brackets in para (c) inserted by the Financial Services Act 2021 (Prudential Regulation of Credit Institutions and Investment Firms) (Consequential Amendments and Miscellaneous Provisions) Regulations 2021, SI 2021/1376, reg 4(10), as from 1 January 2022.

[7.423]

[192U Directions: procedure

(1) If the PRA proposes to give a direction under section 192T, or gives such a direction with immediate effect, it must give written notice to—

(a) the financial holding company or mixed financial holding company to which the direction is given (or to be given); and

(b) any authorised person or recognised investment exchange who will, in the opinion of the PRA, be significantly affected by the direction.

(2) In the following provisions of this section "notified person" means a person to whom notice under subsection (1) is given.

(3) A direction under section 192T takes effect—

(a) immediately, if the notice under subsection (1) states that that is the case;

(b) on such other date as may be specified in the notice; or

(c) if no date is specified in the notice, when the matter to which the notice relates is no longer open to review.

(4) A direction may be expressed to take effect immediately (or on a specified date) only if the PRA reasonably considers that it is necessary for the direction to take effect immediately (or on that date).

(5) The notice under subsection (1) must—

(a) give details of the direction;

(b) state the PRA's reasons for the direction and for its determination as to when the direction takes effect;

(c) inform the notified person that the person may make representations to the PRA within such period as may be specified in the notice (whether or not the notified person has referred the matter to the Tribunal); and

(d) inform the notified person of the person's right to refer the matter to the Tribunal.

(6) The PRA may extend the period allowed under the notice for making representations.

(7) If, having considered any representations made by any notified person, the PRA decides—

(a) to give the direction proposed; or

(b) if the direction has been given, not to revoke the direction,

it must give each of the notified persons written notice.

(8) If, having considered any representations made by any notified person, the PRA decides—

(a) not to give the direction proposed,

(b) to give a different direction, or

(c) to revoke a direction which has effect,

it must give each of the notified persons written notice.

(9) A notice given under subsection (7) must inform the notified person of the person's right to refer the matter to the Tribunal.

(10) A notice under subsection (8)(b) must comply with subsection (5).

(11) If a notice informs the notified person of the person's right to refer a matter to the Tribunal, it must give an indication of the procedure on such a reference.

(12) For the purposes of subsection (3)(c), whether a matter is open to review is to be determined in accordance with section 391(8).]

NOTES

Commencement: 29 December 2020.

Part 12B was inserted as noted to s 192O at **[7.417]**.

192V *(Part 12B was inserted as noted to s 192O ante. This section was repealed by the Financial Services Act 2021, s 5, Sch 3, Pt 2, para 6, as from 9 June 2021 (for transitional provisions, see Sch 3, Pt 4 to the 2021 Act).)*

[7.424]

[192W Consultation between regulators

The PRA must consult the FCA before—

(a) approving an application under section 192Q; or

(b) giving a notice under section 192U(1) or (8)(b) to the financial holding company or mixed financial company of a group which includes an institution which is not a PRA-authorised person.]

NOTES

Commencement: 29 December 2020.

Part 12B was inserted as noted to s 192O at **[7.417]**.

[7.425]

[192X References to Tribunal

(1) A reference may be made to the Tribunal by—

(a) a company which is aggrieved by the decision of the PRA under section 192R to refuse approval, or to reject an application for an exemption; or

(b) a notified person who is aggrieved by the exercise by the PRA of its powers in relation to directions under section 192T.

(2) "Notified person" means a person to whom notice under section 192U(1) has been given, or ought to have been given.]

NOTES

Commencement: 29 December 2020.

Part 12B was inserted as noted to s 192O at **[7.417]**.

[Rules

[7.426]

192XA Rules applying to holding companies

(1) The PRA may make rules described in subsection (2) applying to financial holding companies and mixed financial holding companies that are—

(a) approved under section 192R, or

(b) designated under section 192T(2)(c),

where it appears to the PRA to be necessary or expedient to make the rules for the purpose of advancing any of its objectives.

(2) Those rules are—

(a) rules imposing requirements to be complied with by holding companies on a consolidated or sub-consolidated basis;

(b) rules imposing requirements which, in the PRA's opinion, are likely to mitigate group risk;

(c) rules imposing reporting requirements related to requirements described in paragraph (a) or (b);

(d) rules imposing public disclosure requirements related to requirements described in paragraph (a) or (b);

(e) rules imposing requirements in respect of governance arrangements;

(f) rules imposing requirements in respect of remuneration policies and practices.

(3) Subject to subsection (4), rules made under this section may not modify, amend or revoke any retained direct EU legislation, except retained direct EU legislation which takes the form of PRA rules.

(4) Rules made under this section may include provision that modifies the capital requirements regulation or an instrument made under that regulation (but may not amend or revoke provisions of that regulation or such an instrument).

(5) Rules made under this section may make provision by reference to the capital requirements regulation, to instruments made under that regulation or to Directive 2013/36/EU UK law, as amended from time to time.

(6) Section 137H (rules about remuneration) applies where the PRA makes rules under this section prohibiting persons, or persons of a specified description, from being remunerated in a specified way as it applies where the PRA makes general rules imposing such a prohibition.

(7) Section 137I (Treasury direction to consider compliance with remuneration policies) applies where the PRA makes rules under this section requiring financial holding companies or mixed financial holding companies, or a specified description of such companies, to act in accordance with a remuneration policy as it applies where the PRA makes general rules imposing such requirements on authorised persons, but as if—

(a) the references in that section to authorised persons were references to financial holding companies or mixed financial holding companies, and

(b) subsection (7) of that section were omitted.

(8) Section 141A (power to make consequential amendments of references to rules etc) applies to the exercise by the PRA of its power to make, alter or revoke rules under this section as it applies in relation to the exercise by the PRA of its power to make, alter or revoke rules under Part 9A.

(9) In this section—

"governance arrangements" includes organisational structure, lines of responsibility and internal control mechanisms;

"group risk" means the risk that the financial position of a financial holding company or mixed financial holding company or of a member of its group may be adversely affected—

(a) by its relationships, whether financial or non-financial, with other members of the group, or

(b) by matters which affect the financial position of the group, or of a group which forms part of that group, taken as a whole (including, for example, reputational contagion).]

NOTES

Commencement: 9 June 2021.

Inserted, together with the preceding heading and ss 192XB, 192XC, by the Financial Services Act 2021, s 5, Sch 3, Pt 2, para 7, as from 9 June 2021 (for transitional provisions, see Sch 3, Pt 4 to the 2021 Act).

[7.427]

[192XB Procedural provision

(1) For provision about the making of section 192XA rules that are CRR rules, see Part 9D.

(2) The following provisions of Part 9D apply in relation to section 192XA rules that are not CRR rules as if they were CRR rules—

(a) section 144C (matters to consider when making rules);

(b) section 144D (explanation to accompany consultation on rules);

(c) section 144E(1) and (4) to (7) (exceptions from sections 144C and 144D).]

NOTES

Commencement: 9 June 2021.

Inserted as noted to s 192XA at **[7.426]**.

[7.428]

[192XC Disapplication or modification of rules in individual cases

(1) This section applies to a section 192XA rule if, or to the extent that, section 192XA rules provide for it to apply to the rule.

(2) The PRA may, on the application of or with the consent of a person who is subject to section 192XA rules, give the person a permission that enables the person—

(a) not to apply the section 192XA rule, or

(b) to apply the section 192XA rule with the modifications specified in the permission.

(3) The PRA may—

(a) give permission under this section subject to conditions, and

(b) revoke or vary permission under this section.]

NOTES

Commencement: 9 June 2021.

Inserted as noted to s 192XA at **[7.426]**.

[Disciplinary measures]

NOTES

The preceding heading in square brackets was inserted by the Financial Services Act 2021, s 5, Sch 3, Pt 2, para 7, as from 9 June 2021 (for transitional provisions, see Sch 3, Pt 4 to the 2021 Act).

[7.429]

[192Y Power to impose penalty or issue censure

(1) This section applies if the PRA is satisfied that a company which is or has been a financial holding company or a mixed financial holding company ("the company") has contravened a requirement imposed by—

(a) this Part;

(b) a direction given to the company by the PRA under section 192T;

(c) . . .

[(ca) section 192XA rules; or]

[(d) the capital requirements regulation or an instrument made under that regulation].

(2) The PRA may impose a penalty of such amount as it considers appropriate on—

(a) the company; or

(b) any person who was knowingly concerned in the contravention.

(3) The PRA may, instead of imposing a penalty on a person, publish a statement censuring the person.

(4) The PRA may not take action against a person under this section after the end of the limitation period unless, before the end of that period, it has given a warning notice to the person under section 192Z.

(5) "The limitation period" means the period of 3 years beginning with the first day on which the PRA knew of the contravention.

(6) For this purpose the PRA is to be treated as knowing of a contravention if it has information from which the contravention can reasonably be inferred.]

NOTES

Commencement: 29 December 2020.

Part 12B was inserted as noted to s 192O at **[7.417]**.

Sub-s (1) is amended as follows:

Para (c) was repealed, and para (ca) was inserted, by the Financial Services Act 2021, s 5, Sch 3, Pt 3, para 17, as from 9 June 2021.

Para (d) was substituted by the Financial Services Act 2021, s 5, Sch 3, Pt 2, para 8, as from 9 June 2021 (for transitional provisions, see Sch 3, Pt 4 to the 2021 Act).

[7.430]

[192Z Procedure and right to refer to Tribunal

(1) If a regulator proposes to take action against a person under section 192Y, it must give the person a warning notice.

(2) A warning notice about a proposal to impose a penalty must state the amount of the penalty.

(3) A warning notice about a proposal to publish a statement must set out the terms of the statement.

(4) If the regulator decides to take action against a person under section 192Y, it must give the person a decision notice.

(5) A decision notice about the imposition of a penalty must state the amount of the penalty.

(6) A decision notice about the publication of a statement must set out the terms of the statement.

(7) If the regulator decides to take action against a person under section 192Y, the person may refer the matter to the Tribunal.]

NOTES

Commencement: 29 December 2020.

Part 12B was inserted as noted to s 192O at **[7.417]**.

[7.431]

[192Z1 Duty on publication of statement

After a statement under section 192Y(3) is published, the regulator must send a copy of the statement to—

(a) the person in respect of whom it is made; and

(b) any person to whom a copy of the decision notice was given under section 393(4).]

NOTES

Commencement: 29 December 2020.
Part 12B was inserted as noted to s 192O at **[7.417]**.

[7.432]

[192Z2 Directions and penalties: statement of policy

(1) The PRA must prepare and issue a statement of policy with respect to—
  (a) the taking of measures, including directions, under section 192T;
  (b) the imposition of penalties under section 192Y;
  (c) the amount of penalties under that section.

(2) The PRA's policy in determining what the amount of a penalty should be must include having regard to—
  (a) the seriousness of the contravention;
  (b) the extent to which the contravention was deliberate or reckless; and
  (c) whether the person on whom the penalty is to be imposed is an individual.

(3) The PRA may at any time alter or replace a statement issued under this section.

(4) If a statement issued under this section is altered or replaced, the PRA must issue the altered or replacement statement.

(5) In imposing, or deciding whether to impose a penalty under section 192Y(2) in the case of any particular contravention, the PRA must have regard to any statement of policy published under this section and in force at a time when the contravention occurred.

(6) A statement under this section must be published by the PRA in the way appearing to the PRA to be best calculated to bring it to the attention of the public.

(7) The PRA may charge a reasonable fee for providing a person with a copy of the statement published under this section.

(8) The PRA must, without delay, give the Treasury a copy of any statement which it publishes under this section.]

NOTES

Commencement: 29 December 2020.
Part 12B was inserted as noted to s 192O at **[7.417]**.

[7.433]

[192Z3 Statement of policy relating to directions: procedure

(1) Before issuing a statement of policy under section 192Z2, the PRA must—
  (a) consult the FCA; and
  (b) publish a draft of the proposed statement in the way appearing to the PRA to be best calculated to bring it to the attention of the public.

(2) The draft must be accompanied by notice that representations about the proposal may be made to the PRA within a specified time.

(3) Before issuing the proposed statement, the PRA must have regard to any representations made to it in accordance with subsection (2).

(4) If the PRA issues the proposed statement it must publish an account, in general terms, of—
  (a) the representations made to it in accordance with subsection (2); and
  (b) its response to them.

(5) If the statement differs from the draft published under subsection (2) in a way which is, in the opinion of the PRA, significant, the PRA must—
  (a) consult the FCA again before issuing it; and
  (b) in addition to complying with subsection (4), publish details of the difference.

(6) The PRA may charge a reasonable fee for providing a person with a draft published under subsection (1)(b).

(7) This section also applies to a proposal to alter or replace a statement.]

NOTES

Commencement: 29 December 2020.
Part 12B was inserted as noted to s 192O at **[7.417]**.

193–234O *(Part XIII—Incoming Firms: Intervention by FCA or PRA (ss 193–203 and Sch 16) was, with the exception of s 195(3) and (4), repealed by the EEA Passport Rights (Amendment, etc, and Transitional Provisions) (EU Exit) Regulations 2018, SI 2018/1149, reg 3, Schedule, Pt 1, paras 1, 12, as from IP completion day (as defined in the European Union (Withdrawal Agreement) Act 2020, s 39). Part 13A (Enhanced supervision of firms exercising rights under the Insurance Distribution Directive) was originally inserted by the Insurance Distribution (Regulated Activities and Miscellaneous Amendments) Order 2018, SI 2018/546, arts 9, 14, as from 1 October 2018, and was repealed by SI 2018/1149, reg 3, Schedule, Pt 1, paras 1, 13, as from IP completion day. Part XIV—Disciplinary Measures (ss 204A–211); Part XV—The Financial Services Compensation Scheme (ss 212–224A); Part 15A—Power to Require FSCS Manager to Act in Relation to Other Schemes (ss 224B–224F); Part XVI—The Ombudsman Scheme (ss 225–234A and Sch 17); and Part 16A—Consumer Protection and Competition (ss 234C–234O) are omitted due to space considerations; see further, the introductory notes to this Act.)*

PART XVII COLLECTIVE INVESTMENT SCHEMES

NOTES

Transitional provisions etc in connection with the commencement of the Financial Services Act 2012: see the Financial Services Act 2012 (Transitional Provisions) (Enforcement) Order 2013, SI 2013/441. Article 12 provides that if a failure for the purposes of s 249 (disciplinary measures) of an auditor to comply with a duty imposed on the auditor by trust scheme rules occurred (and ceased to occur) before the 1 April 2013, then s 249(1) applies as if sub-paras (b) and (c) were omitted.

Transitional provisions etc in connection with the original commencement of this Act: the Financial Services and Markets Act 2000 (Transitional Provisions) (Authorised Persons etc) Order 2001, SI 2001/2636, Pt V provides that collective investment schemes that were authorised or recognised under the Financial Services Act 1986, Pt I, Chapter VIII immediately before 1 December 2001 are to be treated as from that date as if authorised and recognised under Pt XVII of this Act. Directions imposed on schemes under the 1986 Act have effect, as from 1 December 2001, as directions imposed under Pt XVII of this Act.

CHAPTER I INTERPRETATION

[7.434]

235 Collective investment schemes

(1) In this Part "collective investment scheme" means any arrangements with respect to property of any description, including money, the purpose or effect of which is to enable persons taking part in the arrangements (whether by becoming owners of the property or any part of it or otherwise) to participate in or receive profits or income arising from the acquisition, holding, management or disposal of the property or sums paid out of such profits or income.

(2) The arrangements must be such that the persons who are to participate ("participants") do not have day-to-day control over the management of the property, whether or not they have the right to be consulted or to give directions.

(3) The arrangements must also have either or both of the following characteristics—

(a) the contributions of the participants and the profits or income out of which payments are to be made to them are pooled;

(b) the property is managed as a whole by or on behalf of the operator of the scheme.

(4) If arrangements provide for such pooling as is mentioned in subsection (3)(a) in relation to separate parts of the property, the arrangements are not to be regarded as constituting a single collective investment scheme unless the participants are entitled to exchange rights in one part for rights in another.

(5) The Treasury may by order provide that arrangements do not amount to a collective investment scheme—

(a) in specified circumstances; or

(b) if the arrangements fall within a specified category of arrangement.

NOTES

Orders: the Financial Services and Markets Act 2000 (Collective Investment Schemes) Order 2001, SI 2001/1062 at **[8.311]**; the Financial Services and Markets Act 2000 (Miscellaneous Provisions) Order 2001, SI 2001/3650; the Financial Services and Markets Act 2000 (Collective Investment Schemes) (Amendment) Order 2005, SI 2005/57; the Financial Services and Markets Act 2000 (Collective Investment Schemes) (Amendment) Order 2007, SI 2007/800; the Financial Services and Markets Act 2000 (Collective Investment Schemes) (Amendment) Order 2008, SI 2008/1641; the Financial Services and Markets Act 2000 (Collective Investment Schemes) (Amendment) (No 2) Order 2008, SI 2008/1813; the Financial Services and Markets Act 2000 (Collective Investment Schemes) (Amendment) Order 2015, SI 2015/754; the Financial Services and Markets Act 2000 (Collective Investment Schemes) (Amendment) Order 2015, SI 2015/2061; the Financial Services and Markets Act 2000 (Regulated Activities) (Amendment) Order 2021, SI 2021/90; the Financial Services and Markets Act 2000 (Collective Investment Schemes) (Amendment) Order 2021, SI 2021/566; the Financial Services and Markets Act 2000 (Regulated Activities) (Amendment) Order 2022, SI 2022/466.

[7.435]

[235A Contractual schemes

(1) In this Part "contractual scheme" means—

(a) a co-ownership scheme; or

(b) a partnership scheme.

(2) In this Part "co-ownership scheme" means a collective investment scheme which satisfies the conditions in subsection (3).

(3) The conditions are—

(a) that the arrangements constituting the scheme are contractual;

(b) that they are set out in a deed that is entered into between the operator and a depositary and meets the requirements of subsection (4);

(c) that the scheme does not constitute a body corporate, a partnership or a limited partnership;

(d) that the property subject to the scheme is held by, or to the order of, a depositary; and

(e) that either—

(i) the property is beneficially owned by the participants as tenants in common (or, in Scotland, is the common property of the participants); or

(ii) where the arrangements constituting the scheme provide for such pooling as is mentioned in section 235(3)(a) in relation to separate parts of the property, each part is beneficially owned by the participants in that part as tenants in common (or, in Scotland, is the common property of the participants in that part).

(4) The deed—

(a) must contain a statement that the arrangements are intended to constitute a co-ownership scheme as defined in section 235A of the Financial Services and Markets Act 2000;

(b) must make provision for the issue and redemption of units;

(c) must—

(i) prohibit the transfer of units,

(ii) allow units to be transferred only if specified conditions are met, or

(iii) where the arrangements constituting the scheme provide for such pooling as is mentioned in section 235(3)(a) in relation to separate parts of the property, in relation to each separate part make provision falling within sub-paragraph (i) or (ii);

(d) must authorise the operator—

(i) to acquire, manage and dispose of property subject to the scheme; and

(ii) to enter into contracts which are binding on participants for the purposes of, or in connection with, the acquisition, management or disposal of property subject to the scheme; and

(e) must make provision requiring the operator and depositary to wind up the scheme in specified circumstances.

(5) In this Part "partnership scheme" means a collective investment scheme which satisfies the conditions in subsection (6).

(6) The conditions are—

(a) that the scheme is a limited partnership;

[(aa) that the limited partnership is not designated under section 8(2) of the Limited Partnerships Act 1907 as a private fund limited partnership;]

(b) that the limited partnership—

(i) at any time has only one general partner; and

(ii) on formation has only one limited partner, who is a person nominated by the general partner ("the nominated partner");

(c) that the arrangements constituting the partnership are set out in a deed that is entered into between the general partner and the nominated partner;

(d) that the deed prohibits such pooling as is mentioned in section 235(3)(a) in relation to separate parts of the property; and

(e) that the deed provides that if an authorisation order is made in respect of the limited partnership under section 261D(1)—

(i) the property subject to the scheme is to be held by, or to the order of, a person appointed to be a depositary;

(ii) the limited partners, other than the nominated partner, are to be the participants in the scheme; and

(iii) the partnership is not dissolved on any person ceasing to be a limited partner provided that there remains at least one limited partner.

(7) In this section "general partner", "limited partner" and "limited partnership" have the same meaning as in the Limited Partnerships Act 1907.

(8) In this Part "contractual scheme deed" means—

(a) in relation to a co-ownership scheme, the deed referred to in subsection (3)(b); and

(b) in relation to a partnership scheme, the deed referred to in subsection (6)(c).]

NOTES

Inserted by the Collective Investment in Transferable Securities (Contractual Scheme) Regulations 2013, SI 2013/1388, reg 3(1), (5), as from 6 June 2013.

Sub-s (6): para (aa) inserted by the Legislative Reform (Private Fund Limited Partnerships) Order 2017, SI 2017/514, art 3, as from 6 April 2017.

[7.436]

236 Open-ended investment companies

(1) In this Part "an open-ended investment company" means a collective investment scheme which satisfies both the property condition and the investment condition.

(2) The property condition is that the property belongs beneficially to, and is managed by or on behalf of, a body corporate ("BC") having as its purpose the investment of its funds with the aim of—

(a) spreading investment risk; and

(b) giving its members the benefit of the results of the management of those funds by or on behalf of that body.

(3) The investment condition is that, in relation to BC, a reasonable investor would, if he were to participate in the scheme—

(a) expect that he would be able to realize, within a period appearing to him to be reasonable, his investment in the scheme (represented, at any given time, by the value of shares in, or securities of, BC held by him as a participant in the scheme); and

(b) be satisfied that his investment would be realized on a basis calculated wholly or mainly by reference to the value of property in respect of which the scheme makes arrangements.

(4) In determining whether the investment condition is satisfied, no account is to be taken of any actual or potential redemption or repurchase of shares or securities under—

[(a) Chapters 3 to 7 of Part 18 of the Companies Act 2006;]

(c) . . . or

(d) provisions in force in a country or territory . . . which the Treasury have, by order, designated as corresponding provisions.

(5) The Treasury may by order amend the definition of "an open-ended investment company" for the purposes of this Part.

NOTES

Sub-s (4): para (a) substituted (for the original paras (a), (b)) by the Companies Act 2006 (Consequential Amendments, Transitional Provisions and Savings) Order 2009, SI 2009/1941, art 2(1), Sch 1, para 181(1), (3), as from 1 October 2009. Words omitted repealed by the Collective Investment Schemes (Amendment etc) (EU Exit) Regulations 2019, SI 2019/325, regs 3, 5, as from IP completion day (as defined in the European Union (Withdrawal Agreement) Act 2020, s 39).

[7.437]

[236A Meaning of "UCITS"

(1) For the purposes of this Act, and subject to subsection (4), "UCITS" means an undertaking established in the United Kingdom or an EEA State—

(a) with the sole object of collective investment, operating on the principle of risk-spreading, in transferable securities or other liquid financial assets mentioned in subsection (3), of capital raised from the public; and

(b) with units which are, at the request of holders, repurchased or redeemed, directly or indirectly, out of the undertaking's assets.

(2) A UCITS may consist of several sub-funds (see section 237(4)).

(3) The transferable securities or other liquid financial assets referred to in subsection (1)(a) are—

(a) in the case of an undertaking established in the United Kingdom, those permitted by section 2 of chapter 5 of the Collective Investment Schemes sourcebook; or

(b) in the case of an undertaking established in an EEA State, those referred to in Article 50(1) of the UCITS directive.

(4) For the purposes of subsection (1)(b), action taken by the undertaking to ensure that the price of its units on an investment exchange does not significantly vary from their net asset value is to be regarded as equivalent to the repurchase or redemption of units at the request of holders.

(5) An undertaking is not a UCITS if it is any of the following—

(a) a collective investment undertaking of the closed-ended type;

(b) a collective investment undertaking which raises capital without promoting the sale of its units to the public within the relevant area or any part of it;

(c) an open-ended investment company, or other collective investment undertaking, the units of which may, under its fund rules or instruments of incorporation, be sold only to the public in countries or territories outside the relevant area.

(6) In subsection (5) "the relevant area" means—

(a) in the case of an undertaking established in the United Kingdom, the United Kingdom;

(b) in the case of an undertaking established in an EEA State, the EEA States.]

NOTES

Commencement: IP completion day (as defined in the European Union (Withdrawal Agreement) Act 2020, s 39).

Inserted by the Collective Investment Schemes (Amendment etc) (EU Exit) Regulations 2019, SI 2019/325, regs 3, 6, as from IP completion day (as defined in the European Union (Withdrawal Agreement) Act 2020, s 39).

[7.438]

237 Other definitions

(1) In this Part "unit trust scheme" means a collective investment scheme under which the property is held on trust for the participants[, except that it does not include a contractual scheme].

(2) In this Part—

"trustee", in relation to a unit trust scheme, means the person holding the property in question on trust for the participants;

"depositary", in relation to—

(a) a collective investment scheme which is constituted by a body incorporated by virtue of regulations under section 262, or

(b) any other collective investment scheme which is not a unit trust scheme,

means any person to whom the property subject to the scheme is entrusted for safekeeping;

["management company" means an undertaking, as defined in section 1161 of the Companies Act 2006, whose regular business is the management of UK UCITS;]

["the operator"—

(a) in relation to a unit trust scheme with a separate trustee, means the manager;

[(aa) in relation to a co-ownership scheme, means the operator appointed under the terms of the contractual scheme deed;

(ab) in relation to a partnership scheme, means the general partner;] [. . .]

(b) in relation to an open-ended investment company, means that company; . . . [and

(ba) in relation to a recognised scheme, means the legal entity with overall responsibility for the management and performance of the functions of the scheme].

(c) . . .]

["working day" has the meaning given in section 191G(2)].

(3) In this Part—

"an authorised unit trust scheme" means a unit trust scheme which is authorised for the purposes of this Act by an authorisation order in force under section 243;

["an authorised contractual scheme" means a contractual scheme which is authorised for the purposes of this Act by an authorisation order in force under section 261D(1);]

"an authorised open-ended investment company" means a body incorporated by virtue of regulations under section 262 in respect of which an authorisation order is in force under any provision made in such regulations by virtue of subsection (2)(l) of that section;

["the Collective Investment Schemes sourcebook" means the Collective Investment Schemes sourcebook made under this Act by the FCA, as it has effect on IP completion day];

["EEA UCITS" means a UCITS which is authorised pursuant to Article 5 of the UCITS directive in an EEA State;]

[. . .]

["feeder UCITS" means—

(a) a UK UCITS which has been approved by the FCA to invest 85% or more of the total property which is subject to the collective investment scheme constituted by the UK UCITS in units of—

(i) another UK UCITS,

(ii) a sub-fund of another UK UCITS,

(iii) an EEA UCITS, or

(iv) a sub-fund of an EEA UCITS, or

(b) a sub-fund of a UK UCITS which has been approved by the FCA to invest 85% or more of the sub-fund's separate pool of the property of the UK UCITS in units of—

(i) another UK UCITS,

(ii) another sub-fund of a UK UCITS,

(iii) an EEA UCITS, or

(iv) a sub-fund of an EEA UCITS;

"master UCITS", in relation to a feeder UCITS, means (as the case may be)—

(a) the other UK UCITS mentioned in paragraph (a)(i) or (b)(i) of the definition of "feeder UCITS",

(b) the EEA UCITS mentioned in paragraph (a)(iii) or (b)(iii) of that definition, or

(c) the sub-fund mentioned in paragraph (a)(ii) or (iv) or (b)(ii) or (iv) of that definition;]

["feeder UCITS" means—

(a) a UK UCITS which has been approved by the FCA to invest 85% or more of the total property which is subject to the collective investment scheme constituted by the UK UCITS in units of—

(i) another UK UCITS,

(ii) a sub-fund of another UK UCITS,

(iii) an EEA UCITS, or

(iv) a sub-fund of an EEA UCITS, or

(b) a sub-fund of a UK UCITS which has been approved by the FCA to invest 85% or more of the sub-fund's separate pool of the property of the UK UCITS in units of—

(i) another UK UCITS,

(ii) another sub-fund of a UK UCITS,

(iii) an EEA UCITS, or

(iv) a sub-fund of an EEA UCITS;

"master UCITS", in relation to a feeder UCITS, means (as the case may be)—

(a) the other UK UCITS mentioned in paragraph (a)(i) or (b)(i) of the definition of "feeder UCITS",

(b) the EEA UCITS mentioned in paragraph (a)(iii) or (b)(iii) of that definition, or

(c) the sub-fund mentioned in paragraph (a)(ii) or (iv) or (b)(ii) or (iv) of that definition;]

"a recognised scheme" means [a section 271A scheme or] a scheme recognised under section . . . 272 [(and see also section 282C)];

["a section 271A scheme" means a scheme recognised under section 271A (and see also section 271S);]

["UCITS-related direct EU legislation" means—

(a) Commission Regulation (EU) 2010/583 of 1 July 2010 implementing Directive 2009/65/EC of the European Parliament and of the Council as regards key investor information and conditions to be met when providing key investor information or the prospectus in a durable medium other than paper or by means of a website, or

(b) Commission Delegated Regulation (EU) 2016/438 of 17 December 2015 supplementing Directive 2009/65/EC of the European Parliament and of the Council with regard to obligations of depositaries;]

[. . .

"UK UCITS" means a UCITS which is an authorised unit trust scheme[, an authorised contractual scheme] or an authorised open-ended investment company].

[(4) In this Part, references to a sub-fund of a UCITS are references to a part of the property of the UCITS which forms a separate pool where—

(a) the UCITS provides arrangements for separate pooling of the contributions of the participants and the profits and income out of which payments are made to them; and

(b) the participants are entitled to exchange rights in one pool for rights in another.]

[(5) In this Part "umbrella co-ownership scheme" means an authorised contractual scheme which satisfies the conditions in subsection (6).

(6) The conditions are—

(a) that the scheme is a co-ownership scheme;

(b) that the arrangements constituting the scheme provide for such pooling as is mentioned in section 235(3)(a) in relation to separate parts of the property; and

(c) that the participants are entitled under the terms of the scheme to exchange rights in one part for rights in another.

(7) In this Part "sub-scheme", in relation to an umbrella co-ownership scheme, means the arrangements constituting the scheme so far as they relate to a separate part of the property.

(8) In this Part "stand-alone co-ownership scheme" means an authorised contractual scheme which—

(a) is a co-ownership scheme; and

(b) is not an umbrella co-ownership scheme.]

NOTES

Sub-s (1): words in square brackets inserted by the Collective Investment in Transferable Securities (Contractual Scheme) Regulations 2013, SI 2013/1388, reg 3(1), (6)(a), as from 6 June 2013.

Sub-s (2) is amended as follows:

Definition "management company" originally inserted by the Undertakings for Collective Investment in Transferable Securities Regulations 2011, SI 2011/1613, reg 2(1), (14)(a)(i), as from 1 July 2011. Subsequently substituted by the Collective Investment Schemes (Amendment etc) (EU Exit) Regulations 2019, SI 2019/325, regs 3, 7(1), (2)(a), as from IP completion day (as defined in the European Union (Withdrawal Agreement) Act 2020, s 39).

Definition "the operator" substituted by SI 2011/1613, reg 2(1), (14)(a)(ii), as from 1 July 2011. Paras (aa), (ab) were inserted by SI 2013/1388, reg 3(1), (6)(b), as from 6 June 2013. The word omitted from para (ab) was originally inserted, and para (c) and the preceding word were repealed, by SI 2019/325, regs 3, 7(1), (2)(b), as from IP completion day (as defined in the European Union (Withdrawal Agreement) Act 2020, s 39). The word omitted from para (ab) was subsequently repealed, and para (ba) and the preceding word were inserted, by the Financial Services Act 2021, s 24, Sch 9, Pt 2, para 5, as from 23 February 2022.

Definition "working day" inserted by SI 2011/1613, reg 2(1), (14)(a)(iii), as from 1 July 2011.

Sub-s (3) is amended as follows:

Definition "an authorised contractual scheme" inserted by SI 2013/1388, reg 3(1), (6)(c)(i), as from 6 June 2013.

Definition "the Collective Investment Schemes sourcebook" inserted by SI 2019/325, regs 3, 7(1), (3)(a), as from IP completion day (as defined in the European Union (Withdrawal Agreement) Act 2020, s 39). Note that the reg 7(3)(a) of the 2019 Regulations was amended by the Financial Services and Economic and Monetary Policy (Consequential Amendments) (EU Exit) Regulations 2020, SI 2020/1301, reg 3, Schedule, para 18(a), as from 30 December 2020 (and the effect of the amendment has been incorporated in the text set out above).

New definition "EEA UCITS" inserted by SI 2019/325, regs 3, 7(1), (3)(a), as from IP completion day (as defined in the European Union (Withdrawal Agreement) Act 2020, s 39) (see further the note immediately below).

Original definition "EEA UCITS"(omitted) originally inserted by SI 2011/1613, reg 2(1), (14)(b)(i), as from 1 July 2011, and subsequently repealed by the Money Market Funds Regulations 2018, SI 2018/698, reg 2(1), (4), as from 21 July 2018.

Definition "feeder UCITS" originally inserted by SI 2011/1613, reg 2(1), (14)(b)(i), as from 1 July 2011. Subsequently substituted (together with the definition "master UCITS") by SI 2019/325, regs 3, 7(1), (3)(b), as from IP completion day (as defined in the European Union (Withdrawal Agreement) Act 2020, s 39).

Words in square brackets in the definition "a recognised scheme" inserted by the Financial Services Act 2021, ss 24(1), 25(6), as from 23 February 2022. The words omitted from the definition were repealed by a combination of the Alternative Investment Fund Managers Regulations 2013, SI 2013/1773, reg 80, Sch 1, Part 1, paras 1, 16, as from 22 July 2013, and SI 2019/325, regs 3, 7(1), (3)(c), as from IP completion day (as defined in the European Union (Withdrawal Agreement) Act 2020, s 39).

Definition "a section 271A scheme" inserted by the Financial Services Act 2021, s 24(1), as from 23 February 2022.

Definitions "UCITS" and "UK UCITS" originally inserted by SI 2011/1613, reg 2(1), (14)(b)(ii), as from 1 July 2011. Definition "UCITS" (omitted) subsequently repealed by SI 2018/698, reg 2(1), (4), as from 21 July 2018. Words in square brackets in definition "UK UCITS" inserted by SI 2013/1388, reg 3(1), (6)(c)(ii), as from 6 June 2013.

Definition "UCITS-related direct EU legislation" inserted by SI 2019/325, regs 3, 7(1), (3)(d), as from IP completion day (as defined in the European Union (Withdrawal Agreement) Act 2020, s 39).

Sub-s (4): added by SI 2011/1613, reg 2(1), (14)(c), as from 1 July 2011.

Sub-ss (5)–(8): added by SI 2013/1388, reg 3(1), (6)(d), as from 6 June 2013.

CHAPTER II RESTRICTIONS ON PROMOTION

[7.439]

238 Restrictions on promotion

(1) An authorised person must not communicate an invitation or inducement to participate in a collective investment scheme.

(2) But that is subject to the following provisions of this section and to section 239.

(3) Subsection (1) applies in the case of a communication originating outside the United Kingdom only if the communication is capable of having an effect in the United Kingdom.

(4) Subsection (1) does not apply in relation to—

(a) an authorised unit trust scheme;

[(aa) an authorised contractual scheme;]

(b) a scheme constituted by an authorised open-ended investment company; or

(c) a recognised scheme.

(5) Subsection (1) does not apply to anything done in accordance with rules made by the [FCA] for the purpose of exempting from that subsection the promotion otherwise than to the general public of schemes of specified descriptions.

(6) The Treasury may by order specify circumstances in which subsection (1) does not apply.

(7) An order under subsection (6) may, in particular, provide that subsection (1) does not apply in relation to communications—

(a) of a specified description;

(b) originating in a specified country or territory outside the United Kingdom;

(c) originating in a country or territory which falls within a specified description of country or territory outside the United Kingdom; or

(d) originating outside the United Kingdom.

(8) The Treasury may by order repeal subsection (3).

(9) "Communicate" includes causing a communication to be made.

(10) "Promotion otherwise than to the general public" includes promotion in a way designed to reduce, so far as possible, the risk of participation by persons for whom participation would be unsuitable.

(11) "Participate", in relation to a collective investment scheme, means become a participant (within the meaning given by section 235(2)) in the scheme.

NOTES

Sub-s (4): para (aa) inserted by the Collective Investment in Transferable Securities (Contractual Scheme) Regulations 2013, SI 2013/1388, reg 3(1), (7), as from 6 June 2013.

Sub-s (5): word in square brackets substituted by the Financial Services Act 2012, s 114(1), Sch 18, Pt 1, paras 1, 9, as from 1 April 2013.

Orders: the Financial Services and Markets Act 2000 (Promotion of Collective Investment Schemes) (Exemptions) Order 2001, SI 2001/1060 at **[8.277]**; the Financial Services and Markets Act 2000 (Financial Promotion and Miscellaneous Amendments) Order 2002, SI 2002/1310; the Financial Services and Markets Act 2000 (Promotion of Collective Investment Schemes etc) (Exemptions) (Amendment) Order 2003, SI 2003/2067; the Financial Services and Markets Act 2000 (Financial Promotion and Promotion of Collective Investment Schemes) (Miscellaneous Amendments) Order 2005, SI 2005/270; the Financial Services and Markets Act 2000 (Promotion of Collective Investment Schemes) (Exemptions) (Amendment) Order 2005, SI 2005/1532.

[7.440]

239 Single property schemes

(1) The Treasury may by regulations make provision for exempting single property schemes from section 238(1).

(2) For the purposes of subsection (1) a single property scheme is a scheme which has the characteristics mentioned in subsection (3) and satisfies such other requirements as are prescribed by the regulations conferring the exemption.

(3) The characteristics are—

(a) that the property subject to the scheme (apart from cash or other assets held for management purposes) consists of—

(i) a single building (or a single building with ancillary buildings) managed by or on behalf of the operator of the scheme, or

(ii) a group of adjacent or contiguous buildings managed by him or on his behalf as a single enterprise, with or without ancillary land and with or without furniture, fittings or other contents of the building or buildings in question; and

(b) that the units of the participants in the scheme are either dealt in on a recognised investment exchange or offered on terms such that any agreement for their acquisition is conditional on their admission to dealings on such an exchange.

(4) If regulations are made under subsection (1), the [FCA] may make rules imposing duties or liabilities on the operator and (if any) the trustee or depositary of a scheme exempted by the regulations.

(5) The rules may include, to such extent as the [FCA] thinks appropriate, provision for purposes corresponding to those for which provision can be made under section 248 in relation to authorised unit trust schemes.

NOTES

Sub-ss (4), (5): words in square brackets substituted by the Financial Services Act 2012, s 114(1), Sch 18, Pt 1, paras 1, 9, as from 1 April 2013.

[7.441]

240 Restriction on approval of promotion

(1) An authorised person may not approve for the purposes of section 21 the content of a communication relating to a collective investment scheme if he would be prohibited by section 238(1) from effecting the communication himself or from causing it to be communicated.

(2) For the purposes of determining in any case whether there has been a contravention of section 21(1), an approval given in contravention of subsection (1) is to be regarded as not having been given.

[7.442]

241 Actions for damages

If an authorised person contravenes a requirement imposed on him by section 238 or 240, [section 138D] applies to the contravention as it applies to a contravention mentioned in [section 138D(2)].

NOTES

Words in square brackets substituted by the Financial Services Act 2012 (Consequential Amendments) Order 2013, SI 2013/636, art 2, Schedule, para 6, as from 1 April 2013.

[CHAPTER 2A PROHIBITION ON ISSUE OF BEARER UNITS

[7.443]

241A Bearer units no longer to be issued

(1) No bearer units in a collective investment scheme may be issued, converted or cancelled after 1 January 2021.

(2) Subsection (1) applies in relation to a collective investment scheme even if the arrangements constituting the scheme purport to authorise the issue, conversion or cancellation of bearer units in the scheme.

(3) In this section "bearer units", in relation to a collective investment scheme, means units in the scheme evidenced by a certificate, or any other documentary evidence of title, which indicates—

(a) that the holder of the document is entitled to the units specified in it; and

(b) that no entry identifying the holder of those units will be made in any register, or other record, of participants in the scheme.

(4) Subsection (1) does not apply to a collective investment scheme constituted by an open-ended investment company, but regulation 48 of the Open-Ended Investment Companies Regulations 2001 (SI 2001/1228) makes corresponding provision.]

NOTES

Commencement: 1 January 2021.

Inserted, together with the preceding heading, by the Bearer Certificates (Collective Investment Schemes) Regulations 2020, SI 2020/1346, reg 2. as from 1 January 2021; for transitional provisions see the Schedule to the 2020 Regulations at **[8.578]**.

CHAPTER III AUTHORISED UNIT TRUST SCHEMES

Applications for authorisation

[7.444]

242 Applications for authorisation of unit trust schemes

[(1) The manager and trustee, or proposed manager and trustee, of a unit trust scheme may apply to the FCA for—

(a) an order declaring the scheme to be an authorised unit trust scheme;

(b) an order declaring the scheme to be an authorised money market fund.]

(2) The manager and trustee (or proposed manager and trustee) must be different persons.

(3) [An application]—

(a) must be made in such manner as the [FCA] may direct; and

(b) must contain or be accompanied by such information as the [FCA] may reasonably require for the purpose of determining the application.

(4) At any time after receiving an application and before determining it, the [FCA] may require the applicants to provide it with such further information as it reasonably considers necessary to enable it to determine the application.

(5) Different directions may be given, and different requirements imposed, in relation to different applications.

(6) The [FCA] may require applicants to present information which they are required to give under this section in such form, or to verify it in such a way, as the [FCA] may direct.

NOTES

Word "FCA" in square brackets (in each place that it occurs) substituted by the Financial Services Act 2012, s 114(1), Sch 18, Pt 1, paras 1, 9, as from 1 April 2013. Other amendments to this section are as follows:

Sub-s (1): substituted by the Money Market Funds Regulations 2018, SI 2018/698, reg 2(1), (5)(a), as from 21 July 2018.

Sub-s (3): words in square brackets substituted by SI 2018/698, reg 2(1), (5)(b), as from 21 July 2018.

[7.445]

243 Authorisation orders[: authorised unit trust schemes]

(1) If, on an application under section [242(1)(a)] in respect of a unit trust scheme, the [FCA]—

(a) is satisfied that the scheme complies with the requirements set out in this section,

(b) is satisfied that the scheme complies with the requirements of the trust scheme rules, and

(c) has been provided with a copy of the trust deed and a certificate signed by a solicitor to the effect that it complies with such of the requirements of this section or those rules as relate to its contents,

the [FCA] may make an order declaring the scheme to be an authorised unit trust scheme.

(2) If the [FCA] makes an order under subsection (1), it must give written notice of the order to the applicant.

(3) . . .

(4) The manager and the trustee must be persons who are independent of each other.

[(5) The manager and the trustee must each be a body corporate incorporated in the United Kingdom *or another EEA State* and the affairs of each must be administered in the [United Kingdom].

[(5A) The manager and the trustee must each have a place of business in the United Kingdom.]]

(6) . . .

(7) The manager and the trustee must each be an authorised person and the manager must have permission to act as manager and the trustee must have permission to act as trustee.

[(7A) The manager must be a fit and proper person to manage the unit trust scheme to which the application relates.]

(8) The name of the scheme must not be undesirable or misleading.

(9) The purposes of the scheme must be reasonably capable of being successfully carried into effect.

(10) The participants must be entitled to have their units redeemed in accordance with the scheme at a price—

(a) related to the net value of the property to which the units relate; and

(b) determined in accordance with the scheme.

(11) But a scheme is to be treated as complying with subsection (10) if it requires the manager to ensure that a participant is able to sell his units on an investment exchange at a price not significantly different from that mentioned in that subsection.

NOTES

The words in square brackets in the section heading were inserted, the figure in square brackets in sub-s (1) was substituted, and sub-s (3) was repealed, by the Money Market Funds Regulations 2018, SI 2018/698, reg 2(1), (6), as from 21 July 2018.

Word "FCA" in square brackets (in each place that it occurs in sub-ss (1), (2)) substituted by the Financial Services Act 2012, s 114(1), Sch 18, Pt 1, paras 1, 9, as from 1 April 2013.

Sub-ss (5), (5A) were substituted (for the original sub-s (5)), and sub-s (7A) was inserted, by the Undertakings for Collective Investment in Transferable Securities Regulations 2011, SI 2011/1613, reg 2(1), (15), as from 1 July 2011.

The words in italics in sub-s (5) were repealed, the words in square brackets in that subsection were substituted (for the original words "country in which it is incorporated"), and sub-s (5A) was further substituted, by the Collective Investment Schemes (Amendment etc) (EU Exit) Regulations 2019, SI 2019/325, regs 3, 8(1)–(3), as from IP completion day (as defined in the European Union (Withdrawal Agreement) Act 2020, s 39). Note that reg 73(1) of the 2019 Regulations provides that these amendments do not prevent an authorised unit trust scheme from having as its manager or trustee a qualifying EEA firm, and do not apply to an authorised unit trust scheme whose manager or trustee is a qualifying EEA firm. The original sub-s (5A) read as follows—

"(5A) The trustee must have a place of business in the United Kingdom, and the manager must have a place of business in the United Kingdom or in another EEA State.".

Sub-s (6) was repealed by SI 2019/325, regs 3, 8(1), (4), as from IP completion day (as defined in the European Union (Withdrawal Agreement) Act 2020, s 39).

[7.446]

[243A Authorisation orders: authorised money market funds

(1) If, on an application under section 242(1)(b) in respect of a unit trust scheme, conditions A and B are met the FCA may make an order declaring the scheme to be an authorised money market fund.

(2) Condition A is that the FCA is satisfied that the scheme will be able to comply with the requirements imposed on a money market fund under the MMF Regulation.

(3) Condition B is that—

(a) the scheme is an authorised unit trust scheme, or

(b) the scheme—

(i) is the subject of an application under section 242(1)(a), and

(ii) the conditions in section 243(1)(a) to (c) are met in relation to that application.

(4) If the FCA makes an order under subsection (1), it must give written notice of the order to the applicant.

(5) In this Chapter "authorisation order" means—

(a) an order under section 243(1), or

(b) an order under subsection (1) of this section.]

NOTES

Inserted by the Money Market Funds Regulations 2018, SI 2018/698, reg 2(1), (7), as from 21 July 2018.

[7.447]

244 Determination of applications

(1) [Subject to subsection (1A),] an application under section [242(1)(a)] must be determined by the [FCA] before the end of the period of six months beginning with the date on which it receives the completed application.

[(1A) An application under [section 242(1)(a) in respect of a unit trust scheme which is a UCITS, or an application under section 242(1)(b),] must be determined by the [FCA] before the end of two months beginning with the date on which it receives the application.]

(2) The [FCA] may determine an incomplete application if it considers it appropriate to do so; and it must in any event determine such an application within twelve months beginning with the date on which it first receives the application.

(3) The applicant may withdraw his application, by giving the [FCA] written notice, at any time before the [FCA] determines it.

NOTES

Word "FCA" in square brackets (in each place that it occurs) substituted by the Financial Services Act 2012, s 114(1), Sch 18, Pt 1, paras 1, 9, as from 1 April 2013.

Words "Subject to subsection (1A)," in square brackets in sub-s (1) inserted, and sub-s (1A) inserted, by the Undertakings for Collective Investment in Transferable Securities Regulations 2011, SI 2011/1613, reg 2(1), (16), as from 1 July 2011.

Figure in square brackets in sub-s (1) substituted, and words in square brackets in sub-s (1A) substituted, by the Money Market Funds Regulations 2018, SI 2018/698, reg 2(1), (8), as from 21 July 2018.

Applications refused

[7.448]

245 Procedure when refusing an application

(1) If the [FCA] proposes to refuse an application made under section 242 it must give each of the applicants a warning notice.

(2) If the [FCA] decides to refuse the application—

- (a) it must give each of the applicants a decision notice; and
- (b) either applicant may refer the matter to the Tribunal.

NOTES

Words in square brackets substituted by the Financial Services Act 2012, s 114(1), Sch 18, Pt 1, paras 1, 9, as from 1 April 2013.

Certificates

[7.449]

246 Certificates

(1) If the manager or trustee of a unit trust scheme which complies with the conditions necessary for it to [be a UK UCITS] so requests, the [FCA] may issue a certificate to the effect that the scheme complies with those conditions.

(2) Such a certificate may be issued on the making of an authorisation order in respect of the scheme or at any subsequent time.

NOTES

Sub-s (1): words in first pair of square brackets by the Collective Investment Schemes (Amendment etc) (EU Exit) Regulations 2019, SI 2019/325, regs 3, 9, as from IP completion day (as defined in the European Union (Withdrawal Agreement) Act 2020, s 39). The word "FCA" in square brackets was substituted by the Financial Services Act 2012, s 114(1), Sch 18, Pt 1, paras 1, 9, as from 1 April 2013.

Rules

[7.450]

247 Trust scheme rules

(1) The [FCA] may make rules ("trust scheme rules") as to—

- (a) the constitution, management and operation of authorised unit trust schemes;
- (b) the powers, duties, rights and liabilities of the manager and trustee of any such scheme;
- (c) the rights and duties of the participants in any such scheme; and
- (d) the winding up of any such scheme.

(2) Trust scheme rules may, in particular, make provision—

- (a) as to the issue and redemption of the units under the scheme;
- (b) as to the expenses of the scheme and the means of meeting them;
- (c) for the appointment, removal, powers and duties of an auditor for the scheme;
- (d) for restricting or regulating the investment and borrowing powers exercisable in relation to the scheme;
- (e) requiring the keeping of records with respect to the transactions and financial position of the scheme and for the inspection of those records;
- (f) requiring the preparation of periodical reports with respect to the scheme and the provision of those reports to the participants and to the [FCA]; and
- (g) with respect to the amendment of the scheme.

(3) Trust scheme rules may make provision as to the contents of the trust deed, including provision requiring any of the matters mentioned in subsection (2) to be dealt with in the deed.

(4) But trust scheme rules are binding on the manager, trustee and participants independently of the contents of the trust deed and, in the case of the participants, have effect as if contained in it.

(5) If—

- (a) a modification is made of the statutory provisions in force in [the United Kingdom] relating to companies,
- (b) the modification relates to the rights and duties of persons who hold the beneficial title to any shares in a company without also holding the legal title, and
- (c) it appears to the Treasury that, for the purpose of assimilating the law relating to authorised unit trust schemes to the law relating to companies as so modified, it is expedient to modify the rule-making powers conferred on the [FCA] by this section,

the Treasury may by order make such modifications of those powers as they consider appropriate.

NOTES

Word "FCA" in square brackets (in each place that it occurs) substituted by the Financial Services Act 2012, s 114(1), Sch 18, Pt 1, paras 1, 9, as from 1 April 2013.

Words "the United Kingdom" in square brackets in sub-s (5) substituted by the Companies Act 2006 (Consequential Amendments and Transitional Provisions) Order 2011, SI 2011/1265, art 12(1), (2), as from 12 May 2011.

[7.451]

248 Scheme particulars rules

(1) The [FCA] may make rules ("scheme particulars rules") requiring the manager of an authorised unit trust scheme—

(a) to submit scheme particulars to the [FCA]; and

(b) to publish scheme particulars or make them available to the public on request.

(2) "Scheme particulars" means particulars in such form, containing such information about the scheme and complying with such requirements, as are specified in scheme particulars rules.

(3) Scheme particulars rules may require the manager of an authorised unit trust scheme to submit, and to publish or make available, revised or further scheme particulars if there is a significant change affecting any matter—

(a) which is contained in scheme particulars previously published or made available; and

(b) whose inclusion in those particulars was required by the rules.

(4) Scheme particulars rules may require the manager of an authorised unit trust scheme to submit, and to publish or make available, revised or further scheme particulars if—

(a) a significant new matter arises; and

(b) the inclusion of information in respect of that matter would have been required in previous particulars if it had arisen when those particulars were prepared.

(5) Scheme particulars rules may provide for the payment, by the person or persons who in accordance with the rules are treated as responsible for any scheme particulars, of compensation to any qualifying person who has suffered loss as a result of—

(a) any untrue or misleading statement in the particulars; or

(b) the omission from them of any matter required by the rules to be included.

(6) "Qualifying person" means a person who—

(a) has become or agreed to become a participant in the scheme; or

(b) although not being a participant, has a beneficial interest in units in the scheme.

(7) Scheme particulars rules do not affect any liability which any person may incur apart from the rules.

NOTES

Sub-s (1): word "FCA" in square brackets (in each place that it occurs) substituted by the Financial Services Act 2012, s 114(1), Sch 18, Pt 1, paras 1, 9, as from 1 April 2013.

[7.452]

249 [Disciplinary measures]

(1) If it appears to the [FCA] that an auditor has failed to comply with a duty imposed on him by trust scheme rules, [it may do one or more of the following—

(a) disqualify the auditor from being the auditor of any authorised unit trust scheme[, authorised contractual scheme] or authorised open-ended investment company;

(b) publish a statement to the effect that it appears to the FCA that the auditor has failed to comply with the duty;

(c) impose on the auditor a penalty, payable to the FCA, of such amount as the FCA considers appropriate.]

[(2) Sections 345B to 345E have effect in relation to the taking of action under subsection (1) as they have effect in relation to the taking of action under section 345(2).]

NOTES

The section heading was substituted, and the words in the first pair of square brackets and in the second (outer) pair of square brackets in sub-s (1) were substituted, by the Financial Services Act 2012, s 114(1), Sch 18, Pt 1, paras 1, 9, 10(1), (2), (4), as from 1 April 2013.

Words ", authorised contractual scheme" in sub-s (1) inserted by the Collective Investment in Transferable Securities (Contractual Scheme) Regulations 2013, SI 2013/1388, reg 3(1), (8), as from 6 June 2013.

Sub-s (2) was substituted by the Financial Services Act 2012, s 114(1), Sch 18, Pt 1, paras 1, 10(1), (3), as from 24 January 2013 (in so far as relating to the preparation and issue of a statement of policy under s 345D as applied by this subsection), and as from 1 April 2013 (otherwise).

[7.453]

250 Modification or waiver of rules

(1) In this section "rules" means—

(a) trust scheme rules; or

(b) scheme particulars rules.

(2) The [FCA] may, on the application or with the consent of any person to whom any rules apply, direct that all or any of the rules—

(a) are not to apply to him as respects a particular scheme; or

(b) are to apply to him, as respects a particular scheme, with such modifications as may be specified in the direction.

(3) The [FCA] may, on the application or with the consent of the manager and trustee of a particular scheme acting jointly, direct that all or any of the rules—

(a) are not to apply to the scheme; or

(b) are to apply to the scheme with such modifications as may be specified in the direction.

(4) [Section 138A and subsections (1) to (3), (5) and (6) of section 138B] have effect in relation to a direction under subsection (2) as they have effect in relation to a direction under [section 138A(1)] but with the following modifications—

(a) . . .

(b) any reference to the [person] is to be read as a reference to the person mentioned in subsection (2); and

(c) [section 138B(3)(c)] is to be read, in relation to a participant of the scheme, as if the word "commercial" were omitted.

(5) [Section 138A and subsections (1) to (3), (5) and (6) of section 138B] have effect in relation to a direction under subsection (3) as they have effect in relation to a direction under [section 138A(1)] but with the following modifications—

(a) [subsection (4)(a) of section 138A] is to be read as if the words "by the . . . person" were omitted;

(b) [section 138B(3)(c) and the definition of "immediate group" in section 421ZA as it applies to that section] are to be read as if references to the . . . person were references to each of the manager and the trustee of the scheme;

(c) [section 138B(3)(c)] is to be read, in relation to a participant of the scheme, as if the word "commercial" were omitted;

(d) [section 138B(5)] is to be read as if the reference to the . . . person concerned were a reference to the scheme concerned and to its manager and trustee; and

(e) [section 138A(7)] is to be read as if the reference to the . . . person were a reference to the manager and trustee of the scheme acting jointly.

NOTES

Sub-ss (2), (3): words in square brackets substituted by the Financial Services Act 2012, s 114(1), Sch 18, Pt 1, paras 1, 9, as from 1 April 2013

Sub-s (4): para (a) repealed, and word in square brackets in para (b) substituted, by the Regulatory Reform (Financial Services and Markets Act 2000) Order 2007, SI 2007/1973, arts 2, 11(a), (b), as from 12 July 2007. Other words in square brackets substituted by the Financial Services Act 2012, s 114(1), Sch 18, Pt 1, paras 1, 11(1), (2), as from 1 April 2013.

Sub-s (5): words in square brackets substituted by the Financial Services Act 2012, s 114(1), Sch 18, Pt 1, paras 1, 11(1), (3), as from 1 April 2013. Words omitted repealed by SI 2007/1973, arts 2, 11(c), as from 12 July 2007.

Alterations

[7.454]

251 Alteration of schemes and changes of manager or trustee

[(A1) This section applies where the manager of an authorised unit trust scheme proposes—

(a) to make an alteration to the scheme, other than an alteration—

(i) to which section 252A applies; or

(ii) to which Part 4 of the Undertakings for Collective Investment in Transferable Securities Regulations 2011 (mergers) applies; or

(b) to replace its trustee.

(1) The manager must give written notice of the proposal to the [FCA].]

(2) Any notice given in respect of a proposal to alter the scheme involving a change in the trust deed must be accompanied by a certificate signed by a solicitor to the effect that the change will not affect the compliance of the deed with the trust scheme rules.

(3) The trustee of an authorised unit trust scheme must give written notice to the [FCA] of any proposal to replace the manager of the scheme.

(4) Effect is not to be given to any proposal of which notice has been given under subsection (1) or (3) unless—

(a) the [FCA], by written notice, has given its approval to the proposal; or

(b) one month, beginning with the date on which the notice was given, has expired without the manager or trustee having received from the [FCA] a warning notice under section 252 in respect of the proposal.

(5) The [FCA] must not approve a proposal to replace the manager or the trustee of an authorised unit trust scheme unless it is satisfied that, if the proposed replacement is made, the scheme will continue to comply with the requirements of section 243(4) to (7).

NOTES

Word "FCA" in square brackets (in each place that it occurs) substituted by the Financial Services Act 2012, s 114(1), Sch 18, Pt 1, paras 1, 9, as from 1 April 2013.

Sub-ss (A1), (1) were substituted (for the original sub-s (1)) by the Undertakings for Collective Investment in Transferable Securities Regulations 2011, SI 2011/1613, reg 2(1), (17), as from 1 July 2011.

[7.455]

252 Procedure when refusing approval [of a proposal under section 251]

(1) If the [FCA] proposes to refuse approval of a proposal [under section 251] to replace the trustee or manager of an authorised unit trust scheme, it must give a warning notice to the person by whom notice of the proposal was given under section 251(1) or (3).

(2) If the [FCA] proposes to refuse approval of a proposal [under section 251] to alter an authorised unit trust scheme it must give separate warning notices to the manager and the trustee of the scheme.

(3) To be valid the warning notice must be received by that person before the end of one month beginning with the date on which notice of the proposal was given.

(4) If, having given a warning notice to a person, the [FCA] decides to refuse approval—

(a) it must give him a decision notice; and

(b) he may refer the matter to the Tribunal.

NOTES

The words in square brackets in the section heading were substituted, and the words "under section 251" in square brackets in sub-ss (1), (2) were inserted, by the Undertakings for Collective Investment in Transferable Securities Regulations 2011, SI 2011/1613, reg 2(1), (18), as from 1 July 2011.

Word "FCA" in square brackets (in each place that it occurs) substituted by the Financial Services Act 2012, s 114(1), Sch 18, Pt 1, paras 1, 9, as from 1 April 2013.

[7.456]

[252A Proposal to convert to a non-feeder UCITS

(1) This section applies where the manager of an authorised unit trust scheme which is a feeder UCITS proposes to make an alteration to the scheme which—

(a) involves a change in the trust deed, and

(b) will enable the scheme to convert into a [UK] UCITS which is not a feeder UCITS.

(2) The manager must give written notice of the proposal to the [FCA].

(3) Any notice given in respect of such a proposal must be accompanied by—

(a) a certificate signed by a solicitor to the effect that the change will not affect the compliance of the deed with the trust scheme rules; and

(b) the specified information.

(4) The [FCA] must, within 15 working days after the date on which it received the notice under subsection (2), give—

(a) written notice to the manager of the scheme that the [FCA] approves the proposed amendments to the trust deed, or

(b) separate warning notices to the manager and trustee of the scheme that the [FCA] proposes to refuse approval of the proposed amendments.

(5) Effect is not to be given to any proposal of which notice has been given under subsection (2) unless the [FCA], by written notice, has given its approval to the proposal.

(6) If, having given a warning notice to a person, the [FCA] decides to refuse approval—

(a) it must give that person a decision notice; and

(b) that person may refer the matter to the Tribunal.

(7) Subsection (8) applies where—

(a) the notice given under subsection (2) relates to a proposal to amend the trust deed of a feeder UCITS to enable it to convert into a [UK] UCITS which is not a feeder UCITS following the winding-up of its master UCITS; and

(b) the proceeds of the winding-up are to be paid to the feeder UCITS before the date on which the feeder UCITS proposes to start investing in accordance with the new investment objectives and policy provided for in its amended trust deed and scheme rules.

(8) Where this subsection applies, the [FCA] may only approve the proposal subject to the conditions set out in section 283A(5) and (6).

(9) In this section, "specified" means—

[(a) specified in rule 11.6.3(2) of the Collective Investment Schemes sourcebook, or

(b) specified in UCITS-related direct EU legislation].]

NOTES

Inserted by the Undertakings for Collective Investment in Transferable Securities Regulations 2011, SI 2011/1613, reg 2(1), (19), as from 1 July 2011.

Word "FCA" in square brackets (in each place that it occurs) substituted by the Financial Services Act 2012, s 114(1), Sch 18, Pt 1, paras 1, 9, as from 1 April 2013.

The words in square brackets in sub-ss (1)(b) and (7)(a) were inserted, and paras (a), (b) of sub-s (9) were substituted, by the Collective Investment Schemes (Amendment etc) (EU Exit) Regulations 2019, SI 2019/325, regs 3, 10, as from IP completion day (as defined in the European Union (Withdrawal Agreement) Act 2020, s 39).

Exclusion clauses

[7.457]

253 Avoidance of exclusion clauses

Any provision of the trust deed of an authorised unit trust scheme is void in so far as it would have the effect of exempting the manager or trustee from liability for any failure to exercise due care and diligence in the discharge of his functions in respect of the scheme.

Ending of authorisation

[7.458]

254 Revocation of authorisation order otherwise than by consent

(1) An authorisation order may be revoked by an order made by the [FCA] if it appears to the [FCA] that—

(a) one or more of the requirements for the making of the order are no longer satisfied;

(b) the manager or trustee of the scheme concerned has contravened a requirement imposed on him by or under this Act;

(c) the manager or trustee of the scheme has, in purported compliance with any such requirement, knowingly or recklessly given the [FCA] information which is false or misleading in a material particular;

(d) no regulated activity is being carried on in relation to the scheme and the period of that inactivity began at least twelve months earlier; or

(e) none of paragraphs (a) to (d) applies, but it is desirable to revoke the authorisation order in order to protect the interests of participants or potential participants in the scheme.

(2) For the purposes of subsection (1)(e), the [FCA] may take into account any matter relating to—

(a) the scheme;

(b) the manager or trustee;

(c) any person employed by or associated with the manager or trustee in connection with the scheme;

(d) any director of the manager or trustee;

(e) any person exercising influence over the manager or trustee;

(f) any body corporate in the same group as the manager or trustee;

(g) any director of any such body corporate;

(h) any person exercising influence over any such body corporate.

NOTES

Words in square brackets substituted by the Financial Services Act 2012, s 114(1), Sch 18, Pt 1, paras 1, 9, as from 1 April 2013.

[7.459]
255 Procedure

(1) If the [FCA] proposes to make an order under section 254 revoking an authorisation order ("a revoking order"), it must give separate warning notices to the manager and the trustee of the scheme.

(2) If the [FCA] decides to make a revoking order, it must without delay give each of them a decision notice and either of them may refer the matter to the Tribunal.

NOTES

Words in square brackets substituted by the Financial Services Act 2012, s 114(1), Sch 18, Pt 1, paras 1, 9, as from 1 April 2013.

[7.460]
256 Requests for revocation of authorisation order

(1) An authorisation order may be revoked by an order made by the [FCA] at the request of the manager or trustee of the scheme concerned.

(2) If the [FCA] makes an order under subsection (1), it must give written notice of the order to the manager and trustee of the scheme concerned.

(3) The [FCA] may refuse a request to make an order under this section if it considers that—

(a) the public interest requires that any matter concerning the scheme should be investigated before a decision is taken as to whether the authorisation order should be revoked; or

(b) revocation would not be in the interests of the participants . . .

(4) If the [FCA] proposes to refuse a request under this section, it must give separate warning notices to the manager and the trustee of the scheme.

(5) If the [FCA] decides to refuse the request, it must without delay give each of them a decision notice and either of them may refer the matter to the Tribunal.

NOTES

Words in square brackets substituted by the Financial Services Act 2012, s 114(1), Sch 18, Pt 1, paras 1, 9, as from 1 April 2013.

Words omitted repealed by the Collective Investment Schemes (Amendment etc) (EU Exit) Regulations 2019, SI 2019/325, regs 3, 11, as from IP completion day (as defined in the European Union (Withdrawal Agreement) Act 2020, s 39).

Powers of intervention

[7.461]
257 Directions

(1) The [FCA] may give a direction under this section if it appears to the [FCA] that—

(a) one or more of the requirements for the making of an authorisation order are no longer satisfied;

[(b) the manager or trustee of an authorised unit trust scheme has contravened, or is likely to contravene, a requirement imposed—

(i) by or under this Act; . . .

(ii) by [UCITS-related direct EU legislation]; [or]

[(iii) by the MMF Regulation or any directly applicable regulation or decision made under that Regulation [which constitutes retained direct EU legislation];]]

(c) the manager or trustee of such a scheme has, in purported compliance with any such requirement, knowingly or recklessly given the [FCA] information which is false or misleading in a material particular; or

(d) none of paragraphs (a) to (c) applies, but it is desirable to give a direction in order to protect the interests of participants or potential participants in such a scheme.

(2) A direction under this section may—

(a) require the manager of the scheme to cease the issue or redemption, or both the issue and redemption, of units under the scheme;

(b) require the manager and trustee of the scheme to wind it up.

(3) If the authorisation order is revoked, the revocation does not affect any direction under this section which is then in force.

(4) A direction may be given under this section in relation to a scheme in the case of which the authorisation order has been revoked if a direction under this section was already in force at the time of revocation.

(5) If a person contravenes a direction under this section, [section 138D] applies to the contravention as it applies to a contravention mentioned in that section.

(6) The [FCA] may, either on its own initiative or on the application of the manager or trustee of the scheme concerned, revoke or vary a direction given under this section if it appears to the [FCA]—

(a) in the case of revocation, that it is no longer necessary for the direction to take effect or continue in force;

(b) in the case of variation, that the direction should take effect or continue in force in a different form.

NOTES

Word "FCA" in square brackets (in each place that it occurs in sub-ss (1), (6)) substituted by the Financial Services Act 2012, s 114(1), Sch 18, Pt 1, paras 1, 9, as from 1 April 2013.

Sub-s (1)(b) was substituted by the Undertakings for Collective Investment in Transferable Securities Regulations 2011, SI 2011/1613, reg 2(1), (20), as from 1 July 2011.

The word omitted from sub-s (1)(b)(i) was repealed, the word "or" in square brackets in sub-s (1)(b)(ii) was inserted, and sub-s (1)(b)(iii) was inserted, by the Money Market Funds Regulations 2018, SI 2018/698, reg 2(1), (9), as from 21 July 2018.

The words in the first pair of square brackets in sub-s (1)(b)(ii) were substituted, and the words "which constitutes retained direct EU legislation" in square brackets in sub-s (1)(b)(iii) were inserted, by the Collective Investment Schemes (Amendment etc) (EU Exit) Regulations 2019, SI 2019/325, regs 3, 12, as from IP completion day (as defined in the European Union (Withdrawal Agreement) Act 2020, s 39).

Words in square brackets in sub-s (5) substituted by the Financial Services Act 2012, s 114(1), Sch 18, Pt 1, paras 1, 12, as from 1 April 2013.

[7.462]

258 Applications to the court

(1) If the [FCA] could give a direction under section 257, it may also apply to the court for an order—
 (a) removing the manager or the trustee, or both the manager and the trustee, of the scheme; and
 (b) replacing the person or persons removed with a suitable person or persons nominated by the [FCA].

(2) The [FCA] may nominate a person for the purposes of subsection (1)(b) only if it is satisfied that, if the order was made, the requirements of section 243(4) to (7) would be complied with.

(3) If it appears to the [FCA] that there is no person it can nominate for the purposes of subsection (1)(b), it may apply to the court for an order—
 (a) removing the manager or the trustee, or both the manager and the trustee, of the scheme; and
 (b) appointing an authorised person to wind up the scheme.

(4) On an application under this section the court may make such order as it thinks fit.

(5) The court may, on the application of the [FCA], rescind any such order as is mentioned in subsection (3) and substitute such an order as is mentioned in subsection (1).

(6) The [FCA] must give written notice of the making of an application under this section to the manager and trustee of the scheme concerned.

(7) The jurisdiction conferred by this section may be exercised by—
 (a) the High Court;
 (b) in Scotland, the Court of Session.

NOTES

Words in square brackets substituted by the Financial Services Act 2012, s 114(1), Sch 18, Pt 1, paras 1, 9, as from 1 April 2013.

[7.463]

[258A Winding up or merger of master UCITS

(1) Subsection (2) applies if a master UCITS which has one or more feeder UCITS which are authorised unit trust schemes is wound up, whether as a result of a direction given by the [FCA] under section 257 [or 261X], an order of the court under section 258 [or 261Y], rules made by the [FCA] or otherwise.

(2) The [FCA] must direct the manager and trustee of any authorised unit trust scheme which is a feeder UCITS of the master UCITS to wind up the feeder UCITS unless—
 (a) the [FCA] approves under section 283A the investment by the feeder UCITS of at least 85% of the total property which is subject to the collective investment scheme constituted by the feeder UCITS in units of another UCITS or master UCITS; or
 (b) the [FCA] approves under section 252A an amendment of the trust deed of the feeder UCITS which would enable it to convert into a [UK] UCITS which is not a feeder UCITS.

(3) Subsection (4) applies if a master UCITS which has one or more feeder UCITS which are authorised unit trust schemes—
 (a) merges with another UCITS, or
 (b) is divided into two or more UCITS.

(4) The [FCA] must direct the manager and trustee of any authorised unit trust scheme which is a feeder UCITS of the master UCITS to wind up the scheme unless—
 (a) the [FCA] approves under section 283A the investment by the scheme of at least 85% of the total property which is subject to the collective investment scheme constituted by the feeder UCITS in the units of—
  (i) the master UCITS which results from the merger;
  (ii) one of the UCITS resulting from the division; or
  (iii) another UCITS or master UCITS;
 (b) the [FCA] approves under section 252A an amendment of the trust deed of the scheme which would enable it to convert into a [UK] UCITS which is not a feeder UCITS.]

NOTES

Inserted by the Undertakings for Collective Investment in Transferable Securities Regulations 2011, SI 2011/1613, reg 2(1), (21), as from 1 July 2011.

Word "FCA" in square brackets (in each place that it occurs) substituted by the Financial Services Act 2012, s 114(1), Sch 18, Pt 1, paras 1, 9, as from 1 April 2013.

Words "or 261X" and "or 261Y" in square brackets in sub-s (1) inserted by the Collective Investment in Transferable Securities (Contractual Scheme) Regulations 2013, SI 2013/1388, reg 3(1), (9), as from 6 June 2013.

Word "UK" in square brackets in sub-ss (2)(b), (4)(b) inserted by the Collective Investment Schemes (Amendment etc) (EU Exit) Regulations 2019, SI 2019/325, regs 3, 13, as from IP completion day (as defined in the European Union (Withdrawal Agreement) Act 2020, s 39).

[7.464]

259 Procedure on giving directions under section 257 [or 258A] and varying them on [FCA's] own initiative

(1) A direction [under section 257 or 258A] takes effect—
 (a) immediately, if the notice given under subsection (3) states that that is the case;
 (b) on such date as may be specified in the notice; or
 (c) if no date is specified in the notice, when the matter to which it relates is no longer open to review.

(2) A direction [under section 257] may be expressed to take effect immediately (or on a specified date) only if the [FCA], having regard to the ground on which it is exercising its power under [that section], considers that it is necessary for the direction to take effect immediately (or on that date).

(3) If the [FCA] proposes to give a direction under [section 257 or 258A, or gives a direction under either section] with immediate effect, it must give separate written notice to the manager and the trustee of the scheme concerned.

(4) The notice must—

(a) give details of the direction;

(b) inform the person to whom it is given of when the direction takes effect;

(c) state the [FCA's] reasons for giving the direction and for its determination as to when the direction takes effect;

(d) inform the person to whom it is given that he may make representations to the [FCA] within such period as may be specified in it (whether or not he has referred the matter to the Tribunal); and

(e) inform him of his right to refer the matter to the Tribunal.

(5) If the direction imposes a requirement under section 257(2)(a), the notice must state that the requirement has effect until—

(a) a specified date; or

(b) a further direction.

(6) If the direction [is given under section 257(2)(b) or section 258A(2) or (4)], the scheme must be wound up—

(a) by a date specified in the notice; or

(b) if no date is specified, as soon as practicable.

(7) The [FCA] may extend the period allowed under the notice for making representations.

(8) If, having considered any representations made by a person to whom the notice was given, the [FCA] decides—

(a) to give the direction in the way proposed, or

(b) if it has been given, not to revoke the direction,

it must give separate written notice to the manager and the trustee of the scheme concerned.

(9) If, having considered any representations made by a person to whom the notice was given, the [FCA] decides—

(a) not to give the direction in the way proposed,

(b) to give the direction in a way other than that proposed, or

(c) to revoke a direction which has effect,

it must give separate written notice to the manager and the trustee of the scheme concerned.

(10) A notice given under subsection (8) must inform the person to whom it is given of his right to refer the matter to the Tribunal.

(11) A notice under subsection (9)(b) must comply with subsection (4).

(12) If a notice informs a person of his right to refer a matter to the Tribunal, it must give an indication of the procedure on such a reference.

(13) This section applies to the variation of a direction on the [FCA's] own initiative as it applies to the giving of a direction.

(14) For the purposes of subsection (1)(c), whether a matter is open to review is to be determined in accordance with section 391(8).

NOTES

The words in the first pair of square brackets in the section heading and in sub-s (1) were inserted, and the words in square brackets in sub-s (6) were substituted, by the Undertakings for Collective Investment in Transferable Securities Regulations 2011, SI 2011/1613, reg 2(1), (22), as from 1 July 2011.

The words in the first pair of square brackets in sub-s (2) were inserted, the words in the third pair of square brackets in that subsection were substituted, and the words in the second pair of square brackets in sub-s (3) were substituted, by the Collective Investment in Transferable Securities (Contractual Scheme) Regulations 2013, SI 2013/1388, reg 3(1), (10), as from 6 June 2013.

Words "FCA" and "FCA's" in square brackets (in each place that they occur) substituted by the Financial Services Act 2012, s 114(1), Sch 18, Pt 1, paras 1, 9, as from 1 April 2013.

[7.465]

260 Procedure: refusal to revoke or vary direction

(1) If on an application under section 257(6) for a direction to be revoked or varied the [FCA] proposes—

(a) to vary the direction otherwise than in accordance with the application, or

(b) to refuse to revoke or vary the direction,

it must give the applicant a warning notice.

(2) If the [FCA] decides to refuse to revoke or vary the direction—

(a) it must give the applicant a decision notice; and

(b) the applicant may refer the matter to the Tribunal.

NOTES

Words in square brackets substituted by the Financial Services Act 2012, s 114(1), Sch 18, Pt 1, paras 1, 9, as from 1 April 2013.

[7.466]

261 Procedure: revocation of direction and grant of request for variation

(1) If the [FCA] decides on its own initiative to revoke a direction under section 257 it must give separate written notices of its decision to the manager and trustee of the scheme.

(2) If on an application under section 257(6) for a direction to be revoked or varied the [FCA] decides to revoke the direction or vary it in accordance with the application, it must give the applicant written notice of its decision.

(3) A notice under this section must specify the date on which the decision takes effect.

(4) The [FCA] may publish such information about the revocation or variation, in such way, as it considers appropriate.

NOTES

Words in square brackets substituted by the Financial Services Act 2012, s 114(1), Sch 18, Pt 1, paras 1, 9, as from 1 April 2013.

261A (*Originally inserted, together with s 261B, by the Undertakings for Collective Investment in Transferable Securities Regulations 2011, SI 2011/1613, reg 2(1), (23), as from 1 July 2011. Subsequently repealed by the Collective Investment Schemes (Amendment etc) (EU Exit) Regulations 2019, SI 2019/325, regs 3, 14, as from IP completion day (as defined in the European Union (Withdrawal Agreement) Act 2020, s 39).*)

[7.467]

[261B Information for feeder UCITS

(1) The [FCA] must immediately inform the operator of any authorised unit trust scheme which is a feeder UCITS of an authorised unit trust scheme[, an authorised contractual scheme] or an authorised open-ended investment company (the master UCITS) of—

(a) any failure of which the [FCA] becomes aware by the master UCITS to comply with a provision made [by or under any enactment] in implementation of Chapter VIII of the UCITS directive;

(b) any warning notice or decision notice given to the master UCITS in relation to a contravention of any provision made in implementation of Chapter VIII of the UCITS directive by or under any enactment or in rules of the [FCA];

(c) any information reported to the [FCA] pursuant to rules of the [FCA] made to implement Article 106(1) of the UCITS directive which relates to the master UCITS, or to one or more of its directors, or its management company, trustee, depositary or auditor.

(2), (3) . . .

NOTES

Inserted as noted to s 261A *ante*.

Word "FCA" in square brackets (in each place that it occurs) substituted by the Financial Services Act 2012, s 114(1), Sch 18, Pt 1, paras 1, 9, as from 1 April 2013.

Words ", an authorised contractual scheme" in square brackets in sub-s (1) inserted by the Collective Investment in Transferable Securities (Contractual Scheme) Regulations 2013, SI 2013/1388, reg 3(1), (11), as from 6 June 2013.

Words "by or under any enactment" in square brackets in sub-s (1) inserted, and sub-ss (2), (3) repealed, by the Collective Investment Schemes (Amendment etc) (EU Exit) Regulations 2019, SI 2019/325, regs 3, 15, as from IP completion day (as defined in the European Union (Withdrawal Agreement) Act 2020, s 39).

[CHAPTER 3A AUTHORISED CONTRACTUAL SCHEMES

Applications for authorisation

[7.468]

261C Applications for authorisation of contractual schemes

[(1) The operator and depositary, or proposed operator and depositary, of a contractual scheme may apply to the FCA for—

(a) an order declaring the scheme to be an authorised contractual scheme;

(b) an order declaring the scheme to be an authorised money market fund.]

(2) [An application under subsection (1)(a)]—

(a) must be made in such manner as the FCA may direct;

(b) must state the name and the registered office, or if it does not have a registered office, the head office, of the operator or proposed operator and of the depositary or proposed depositary; and

(c) in the case of a partnership scheme, must be accompanied by a copy of the certificate of registration as a limited partnership under the Limited Partnerships Act 1907.

[(2A) An application under subsection (1)(b) must—

(a) be made in such a manner as the FCA may direct, and

(b) contain or be accompanied by such information as the FCA may reasonably require for the purpose of determining the application.]

(3) At any time after receiving an application and before determining it, the FCA may require the applicants to provide it with such further information as it reasonably considers necessary to enable it to determine the application.

(4) Different directions may be given, and different requirements imposed, in relation to different applications.

(5) The FCA may require applicants to present information which they are required to give under this section in such form, or to verify it in such a way, as the FCA may direct.]

NOTES

Chapter 3A (ss 261C–261Z5) was inserted by the Collective Investment in Transferable Securities (Contractual Scheme) Regulations 2013, SI 2013/1388, reg 3(1), (12), as from 6 June 2013.

Sub-s (1): substituted by the Money Market Funds Regulations 2018, SI 2018/698, reg 2(1), (10)(a), as from 21 July 2018.

Sub-s (2): words in square brackets substituted by SI 2018/698, reg 2(1), (10)(b), as from 21 July 2018.

Sub-s (2A): inserted by SI 2018/698, reg 2(1), (10)(c), as from 21 July 2018.

[7.469]

[261D Authorisation orders[: authorised contractual schemes]

(1) If, on an application under section [261C(1)(a)] in respect of a contractual scheme, the FCA—

(a) is satisfied that the scheme complies with the requirements set out in this section and section 261E,

(b) is satisfied that the scheme complies with the requirements of contractual scheme rules, and

(c) has been provided with a copy of the contractual scheme deed and a certificate signed by a solicitor to the effect that it complies with such of the requirements of this section or those rules as relate to its contents,

the FCA may make an order declaring the scheme to be an authorised contractual scheme.

(2) If the FCA makes an order under subsection (1), it must give written notice of the order to the applicants.

(3) . . .

(4) The operator and the depositary must be persons who are independent of each other.

(5) The operator and the depositary must each be a body corporate incorporated in the United Kingdom *or another EEA State*, and the affairs of each must be administered in the [United Kingdom].

[(6) The operator and the depositary must each have a place of business in the United Kingdom.]

(7) . . .

(8) The operator and the depositary must each be an authorised person, and the operator must have [such permission as may be necessary to act as operator] and the depositary must have permission to act as depositary.

(9) The operator must be a fit and proper person to manage the scheme to which the application relates.

(10) The name of the scheme must not be undesirable or misleading.

(11) The purposes of the scheme must be reasonably capable of being successfully carried into effect.]

NOTES

Inserted as noted to s 261C at **[7.468]**.

The words in square brackets in the section heading were inserted, the figure in square brackets in sub-s (1) was substituted, and sub-s (3) was repealed, by the Money Market Funds Regulations 2018, SI 2018/698, reg 2(1), (11), as from 21 July 2018.

The words in italics in sub-s (5) were repealed, the words in square brackets in that subsection were substituted (for the original words "country in which it is incorporated"), and sub-s (6) was substituted, by the Collective Investment Schemes (Amendment etc) (EU Exit) Regulations 2019, SI 2019/325, regs 3, 16(1)–(3), as from IP completion day (as defined in the European Union (Withdrawal Agreement) Act 2020, s 39). Note that reg 73(2) of the 2019 Regulations provides that these amendments do not prevent an authorised contractual scheme from having as its manager or depositary a qualifying EEA firm, and do not apply to an authorised contractual scheme whose manager or depositary is a qualifying EEA firm. The original sub–s (6) read as follows—

> "(6) The depositary must have a place of business in the United Kingdom, and the operator must have a place of business in the United Kingdom or in another EEA State.".

Sub-s (7) repealed by SI 2019/325, regs 3, 16(1), (4), as from IP completion day (as defined in the European Union (Withdrawal Agreement) Act 2020, s 39).

Sub-s (8): words in square brackets substituted by the Alternative Investment Fund Managers Regulations 2013, SI 2013/1773, reg 80, Sch 1, Part 1, paras 1, 17, as from 22 July 2013.

[7.470]

[261E [Authorised contractual schemes]: holding of units

(1) The participants in a contractual scheme must be entitled to have their units redeemed in accordance with the scheme at a price—

(a) related to the net value of the property to which the units relate; and

(b) determined in accordance with the scheme.

(2) The scheme must not allow units in the scheme to be issued to anyone other than—

(a) a professional investor;

(b) a large investor; or

(c) a person who already holds units in the scheme.

(3) The scheme must require the operator, if it becomes aware that units have become vested in a person to whom as a result of subsection (2) the units could not have been issued, to redeem the units as soon as practicable.

(4) In subsection (2)—

"professional investor" means a person who falls within one of the categories [(a) to (d) of paragraph 3 of Schedule 1 to the markets in financial instruments regulation]; and

"large investor" means a person who, in exchange for units in the scheme, makes a payment of, or contributes property with a value of, not less than £1,000,000.]

NOTES

Inserted as noted to s 261C at **[7.468]**.

Words in square brackets in the section heading substituted by the Money Market Funds Regulations 2018, SI 2018/698, reg 2(1), (12), as from 21 July 2018.

Sub-s (4): words in square brackets in the definition "professional investor" substituted by the Collective Investment Schemes (Amendment etc) (EU Exit) Regulations 2019, SI 2019/325, regs 3, 17, as from IP completion day (as defined in the European Union (Withdrawal Agreement) Act 2020, s 39).

[7.471]

[261EA Authorisation orders: authorised money market funds

(1) If, on an application under section 261C(1)(b) in respect of a contractual scheme, conditions A and B are met the FCA may make an order declaring the scheme to be an authorised money market fund.

(2) Condition A is that the FCA is satisfied that the scheme will be able to comply with the requirements imposed on a money market fund under the MMF Regulation.

(3) Condition B is that—

(a) the scheme is an authorised contractual scheme, or

(b) the scheme—

(i) is the subject of an application under section 261C(1)(a), and

(ii) the conditions in section 261D(1)(a) to (c) are met in relation to that application.

(4) If the FCA makes an order under subsection (1), it must give written notice of the order to the applicant.

(5) In this Chapter "authorisation order" means—

(a) an order under section 261D(1), or

(b) an order under subsection (1) of this section.]

NOTES

Inserted by the Money Market Funds Regulations 2018, SI 2018/698, reg 2(1), (13), as from 21 July 2018.

[7.472]

[261F Determination of applications

(1) Subject to subsection (2), an application under section [261C(1)(a)] must be determined by the FCA before the end of the period of six months beginning with the date on which it receives the completed application.

(2) An application under section [261C(1)(a) in respect of a contractual scheme which is a UCITS, or an application under section 261C(1)(b),] must be determined by the FCA before the end of two months beginning with the date on which it receives the application.

(3) The FCA may determine an incomplete application if it considers it appropriate to do so; and it must in any event determine such an application within twelve months beginning with the date on which it first receives the application.

(4) The applicants may withdraw the application, by giving the FCA written notice, at any time before the FCA determines it.]

NOTES

Inserted as noted to s 261C at **[7.468]**.

The figure in square brackets in sub-(1) was substituted, and the words in square brackets in sub-s (2) were substituted, by the Money Market Funds Regulations 2018, SI 2018/698, reg 2(1), (14), as from 21 July 2018.

[Applications refused

[7.473]

261G Procedure when refusing an application

(1) If the FCA proposes to refuse an application made under section 261C, it must give each of the applicants a warning notice.

(2) If the FCA decides to refuse the application—

(a) it must give each of the applicants a decision notice; and

(b) either applicant may refer the matter to the Tribunal.]

NOTES

Inserted as noted to s 261C at **[7.468]**.

[Certificates

[7.474]

261H Certificates

(1) If the operator of a contractual scheme which complies with the conditions necessary for it to [be a UK UCITS] so requests, the FCA may issue a certificate to the effect that the scheme complies with those conditions.

(2) Such a certificate may be issued on the making of an authorisation order in respect of the scheme or at any subsequent time.]

NOTES

Inserted as noted to s 261C at **[7.468]**.

Sub-s (1): words in square brackets substituted by the Collective Investment Schemes (Amendment etc) (EU Exit) Regulations 2019, SI 2019/325, regs 3, 18, as from IP completion day (as defined in the European Union (Withdrawal Agreement) Act 2020, s 39).

[Rules

[7.475]

261I Contractual scheme rules

(1) The FCA may by rules ("contractual scheme rules") make in relation to authorised contractual schemes provision corresponding to that which may be made under section 247 in relation to authorised unit trust schemes.

(2) For the purposes of subsection (1), section 247 is to be read with the following modifications—

(a) a reference to trust scheme rules is to be read as a reference to contractual scheme rules;

(b) a reference to authorised unit trust schemes is to be read as a reference to authorised contractual schemes;

(c) a reference to the manager is to be read as a reference to the operator;

(d) a reference to the trustee is to be read as a reference to the depositary; and

(e) a reference to the trust deed is to be read as a reference to the contractual scheme deed.

(3) The Treasury's power by order under section 247(5) to modify the FCA's power to make trust scheme rules shall also be exercisable in relation to the FCA's power to make contractual scheme rules.

(4) For the purposes of subsection (3), section 247(5) is to be read as if the reference to authorised unit trust schemes were a reference to authorised contractual schemes.]

NOTES

Inserted as noted to s 261C at **[7.468]**.

[7.476]

[261J Contractual scheme particulars rules

(1) The FCA may by rules ("contractual scheme particulars rules") make in relation to authorised contractual schemes provision corresponding to that which may be made under section 248 in relation to authorised unit trust schemes.

(2) For the purposes of subsection (1), section 248 is to be read with the following modifications—

(a) a reference to scheme particulars rules is to be read as a reference to contractual scheme particulars rules;

(b) a reference to scheme particulars is to be read as a reference to contractual scheme particulars; and

(c) a reference to the manager of an authorised unit trust scheme is to be read as a reference to the operator of an authorised contractual scheme.]

NOTES

Inserted as noted to s 261C at **[7.468]**.

[7.477]

[261K Disciplinary measures

(1) If it appears to the FCA that an auditor has failed to comply with a duty imposed on the auditor by contractual scheme rules, it may do one or more of the following—

(a) disqualify the auditor from being the auditor of any authorised unit trust scheme, authorised contractual scheme or authorised open-ended investment company;

(b) publish a statement to the effect that it appears to the FCA that the auditor has failed to comply with the duty;

(c) impose on the auditor a penalty, payable to the FCA, of such amount as the FCA considers appropriate.

(2) Sections 345B to 345E have effect in relation to the taking of action under subsection (1) as they have effect in relation to the taking of action under section 345(2).]

NOTES

Inserted as noted to s 261C at **[7.468]**.

[7.478]

[261L Modification or waiver of rules

(1) In this section "rules" means—

(a) contractual scheme rules; or

(b) contractual scheme particulars rules.

(2) The FCA may, on the application or with the consent of any person to whom rules apply, direct that all or any of the rules—

(a) are not to apply to that person as respects a particular scheme; or

(b) are to apply to that person, as respects a particular scheme, with such modifications as may be specified in the direction.

(3) The FCA may, on the application or with the consent of the operator and depositary of a particular scheme acting jointly, direct that all or any of the rules—

(a) are not to apply to the scheme; or

(b) are to apply to the scheme with such modifications as may be specified in the direction.

(4) Section 138A and subsections (1) to (3), (5) and (6) of section 138B have effect in relation to a direction under subsection (2) as they have effect in relation to a direction under section 138A(1) but with the following modifications—

(a) any reference to the person is to be read as a reference to the person mentioned in subsection (2); and

(b) section 138B(3)(c) is to be read, in relation to a participant in the scheme, as if the word "commercial" were omitted.

(5) Section 138A and subsections (1) to (3), (5) and (6) of section 138B have effect in relation to a direction under subsection (3) as they have effect in relation to a direction under section 138A(1) but with the following modifications—

(a) subsection (4)(a) of section 138A is to be read as if the words "by the person" were omitted;

(b) section 138B(3)(c) and the definition of "immediate group" in section 421ZA as it applies to that section are to be read as if references to the person were references to each of the operator and the depositary of the scheme;

(c) section 138B(3)(c) is to be read, in relation to a participant in the scheme, as if the word "commercial" were omitted;

(d) section 138B(5) is to be read as if the reference to the person concerned were a reference to the scheme concerned and to its operator and depositary; and

(e) section 138A(7) is to be read as if the reference to the person were a reference to the operator and depositary of the scheme acting jointly.]

NOTES

Inserted as noted to s 261C at **[7.468]**.

[Co-ownership schemes: rights and liabilities of participants

[7.479]

261M Contracts

(1) In this section "authorised contract" means a contract which the operator of a co-ownership scheme is authorised to enter into on behalf of the relevant participants for the purposes of, or in connection with, the acquisition, management or disposal of property subject to the scheme (but does not include a contract by which a person becomes a participant in the scheme).

(2) The relevant participants are—

(a) in the case of a contract relating to a stand-alone co-ownership scheme, the participants in the scheme;

(b) in the case of a contract relating to an umbrella co-ownership scheme, the participants in the sub-scheme of the umbrella co-ownership scheme to which the contract relates.

(3) The operator on behalf of the relevant participants may—

(a) exercise rights under an authorised contract;

(b) bring and defend proceedings for the resolution of any matter relating to an authorised contract; and

(c) take action in relation to the enforcement of any judgment given in such proceedings.

(4) The relevant participants may not themselves do any of the things mentioned in subsection (3), but this does not affect their rights as against the operator.

(5) A person who enters into a contract which purports to be an authorised contract is deemed to have actual knowledge of the scope of the authority given to the operator by the contractual scheme deed.

(6) The validity of an authorised contract is not to be called into question on the ground that a participant lacks capacity to authorise the operator to enter into such a contract.

(7) An authorised contract must make provision for any property which is acquired under or by virtue of the contract to be held by, or to the order of, the depositary of the scheme concerned.]

NOTES

Inserted as noted to s 261C at **[7.468]**.

[7.480]

[261N Effect of becoming or ceasing to be a participant

(1) A person who at any time becomes a participant in a relevant scheme acquires the rights and becomes subject to the liabilities to which the other participants in the relevant scheme are entitled or subject at that time under, or in connection with, authorised contracts.

(2) A person who ceases to be a participant in a relevant scheme ceases to have any of the rights and to be subject to any of the liabilities to which a participant in the relevant scheme is entitled or subject under, or in connection with, authorised contracts.

(3) In this section—

(a) "authorised contract" has the meaning given in section 261M(1); and

(b) each of the following is a "relevant scheme"—

(i) a stand-alone co-ownership scheme; and

(ii) a sub-scheme of an umbrella co-ownership scheme.]

NOTES

Inserted as noted to s 261C at **[7.468]**.

[7.481]

[261O Limited liability

(1) The debts of a relevant scheme are to be paid by the operator out of the property subject to the relevant scheme.

(2) The participants in a relevant scheme are not liable for the debts of the relevant scheme beyond the amount of the property subject to the relevant scheme which is available to the operator to meet the debts.

(3) In this section—

(a) a reference to the debts of a relevant scheme is a reference to debts and obligations incurred under, or in connection with, authorised contracts;

(b) "authorised contract" has the meaning given in section 261M(1); and

(c) "relevant scheme" has the meaning given in section 261N(3).]

NOTES

Inserted as noted to s 261C at **[7.468]**.

[7.482]

[261P Segregated liability in relation to umbrella co-ownership schemes

(1) The property subject to a sub-scheme of an umbrella co-ownership scheme must not be used to discharge any liabilities of, or meet any claims against, any person other than the participants in that sub-scheme.

(2) Any provision contained in any contract, agreement or other document is void in so far as it is inconsistent with subsection (1), and any transaction involving the application of property in contravention of that subsection is void.

(3) The FCA may give a direction under section 261X(2) in relation to a sub-scheme of an umbrella co-ownership scheme as if the sub-scheme were an authorised contractual scheme, but this subsection does not enable the FCA to apply to the court for an order under section 261Y in relation to a sub-scheme of an umbrella co-ownership scheme.

(4) Where such a direction is given, the reference in section 261Z1(6) to the scheme is to be read as a reference to the sub-scheme concerned.]

NOTES

Inserted as noted to s 261C at **[7.468]**.

[Alterations

[7.483]

261Q Alteration of contractual schemes and changes of operator or depositary

(1) This section applies where the operator of an authorised contractual scheme proposes to make an alteration to the scheme, other than an alteration—

(a) to which section 261S applies; or

(b) to which Part 4 of the Undertakings for Collective Investment in Transferable Securities Regulations 2011 (mergers) applies.

(2) The operator must give written notice of the proposal to the FCA.

(3) Any notice given in respect of a proposal to alter the scheme involving a change in the contractual scheme deed must be accompanied by a certificate signed by a solicitor to the effect that the change will not affect the compliance of the deed with the contractual scheme rules.

(4) The operator of an authorised contractual scheme must give written notice to the FCA of any proposal to replace the depositary of the scheme.

(5) The depositary of an authorised contractual scheme must give written notice to the FCA of any proposal to replace the operator of the scheme.

(6) Effect is not to be given to any proposal of which notice has been given under subsection (2), (4) or (5) unless—

(a) the FCA, by written notice, has given its approval to the proposal; or

(b) one month, beginning with the date on which the notice was given, has expired without the operator or the depositary having received from the FCA a warning notice under section 261R in respect of the proposal.

(7) The FCA must not approve a proposal to replace the operator or the depositary of an authorised contractual scheme unless it is satisfied that, if the proposed replacement is made, the scheme will continue to comply with the requirements of section 261D(4) to (9).]

NOTES

Inserted as noted to s 261C at **[7.468]**.

[7.484]

[261R Procedure when refusing approval of a proposal under section 261Q

(1) If the FCA proposes to refuse approval of a proposal under section 261Q to replace the depositary or operator of an authorised contractual scheme, it must give a warning notice to the person by whom notice of the proposal was given under section 261Q(4) or (5).

(2) If the FCA proposes to refuse approval of a proposal under section 261Q to alter an authorised contractual scheme, it must give separate warning notices to the operator and the depositary of the scheme.

(3) To be valid the warning notice must be received by the person to whom it is given before the end of one month beginning with the date on which notice of the proposal was given.

(4) If, having given a warning notice to a person, the FCA decides to refuse approval—

- (a) it must give that person a decision notice; and
- (b) that person may refer the matter to the Tribunal.]

NOTES

Inserted as noted to s 261C at **[7.468]**.

[7.485]

[261S Proposal to convert to a non-feeder UCITS

(1) This section applies where the operator of an authorised contractual scheme which is a feeder UCITS proposes to make an alteration to the scheme which—

- (a) involves a change in the contractual scheme deed, and
- (b) will enable the scheme to convert into a [UK] UCITS which is not a feeder UCITS.

(2) The operator must give written notice of the proposal to the FCA.

(3) Any notice given in respect of such a proposal must be accompanied by—

- (a) a certificate signed by a solicitor to the effect that the change will not affect the compliance of the deed with the contractual scheme rules; and
- (b) the specified information.

(4) The FCA must, within 15 working days after the date on which it received the notice under subsection (2), give—

- (a) written notice to the operator of the scheme that the FCA approves the proposed amendments to the contractual scheme deed, or
- (b) separate warning notices to the operator and depositary of the scheme that the FCA proposes to refuse approval of the proposed amendments.

(5) Effect is not to be given to any proposal of which notice has been given under subsection (2) unless the FCA, by written notice, has given its approval to the proposal.

(6) If, having given a warning notice to a person, the FCA decides to refuse approval—

- (a) it must give that person a decision notice; and
- (b) that person may refer the matter to the Tribunal.

(7) Subsection (8) applies where—

- (a) the notice given under subsection (2) relates to a proposal to amend the contractual scheme deed of a feeder UCITS to enable it to convert into a [UK] UCITS which is not a feeder UCITS following the winding-up of its master UCITS; and
- (b) the proceeds of the winding-up are to be paid to the feeder UCITS before the date on which the feeder UCITS proposes to start investing in accordance with the new investment objectives and policy provided for in its amended contractual scheme deed and contractual scheme rules.

(8) Where this subsection applies, the FCA may only approve the proposal subject to the conditions set out in section 283A(5) and (6).

(9) In this section "specified" means—

- [(a) specified in rule 11.6.3(2) of the Collective Investment Schemes sourcebook, or
- (b) specified in UCITS-related direct EU legislation].]

NOTES

Inserted as noted to s 261C at **[7.468]**.

Words in square brackets in sub-ss (1)(b), (7)(a) inserted, and sub-s (9)(a), (b) substituted, by the Collective Investment Schemes (Amendment etc) (EU Exit) Regulations 2019, SI 2019/325, regs 3, 19, as from IP completion day (as defined in the European Union (Withdrawal Agreement) Act 2020, s 39).

[Exclusion clauses

[7.486]

261T Avoidance of exclusion clauses

Any provision—

- (a) of the contractual scheme deed of an authorised contractual scheme, or
- (b) in the case of an authorised contractual scheme which is a partnership scheme, of the contract under which the depositary of the scheme is appointed,

is void in so far as it would have the effect of exempting the operator or the depositary from liability for any failure to exercise due care and diligence in the discharge of its functions in respect of the scheme.]

NOTES

Inserted as noted to s 261C at **[7.468]**.

[Ending of authorisation

[7.487]

261U Revocation of authorisation order otherwise than by consent

(1) An authorisation order may be revoked by an order made by the FCA if it appears to the FCA that—

(a) one or more of the requirements for the making of the order are no longer satisfied;

(b) the operator or depositary of the scheme concerned has contravened a requirement imposed on the operator or depositary by or under this Act;

(c) the operator or depositary of the scheme has, in purported compliance with any such requirement, knowingly or recklessly given the FCA information which is false or misleading in a material particular;

(d) no regulated activity is being carried on in relation to the scheme and the period of that inactivity began at least twelve months earlier; or

(e) none of paragraphs (a) to (d) applies, but it is desirable to revoke the authorisation order in order to protect the interests of participants or potential participants in the scheme.

(2) For the purposes of subsection (1)(e), the FCA may take into account any matter relating to—

(a) the scheme;

(b) the operator or depositary;

(c) any person employed by or associated with the operator or depositary in connection with the scheme;

(d) any director of the operator or depositary;

(e) any person exercising influence over the operator or depositary;

(f) any body corporate in the same group as the operator or depositary;

(g) any director of any such body corporate;

(h) any person exercising influence over any such body corporate.]

NOTES

Inserted as noted to s 261C at **[7.468]**.

[7.488]

[261V Procedure for revoking authorisation order

(1) If the FCA proposes to make an order under section 261U revoking an authorisation order ("a revoking order"), it must give separate warning notices to the operator and the depositary of the scheme.

(2) If the FCA decides to make a revoking order, it must without delay give each of them a decision notice and either of them may refer the matter to the Tribunal.]

NOTES

Inserted as noted to s 261C at **[7.468]**.

[7.489]

[261W Requests for revocation of authorisation order

(1) An authorisation order may be revoked by an order made by the FCA at the request of the operator or depositary of the scheme concerned.

(2) If the FCA makes an order under subsection (1), it must give written notice of the order to the operator and depositary of the scheme concerned.

(3) The FCA may refuse a request to make an order under this section if it considers that—

(a) the public interest requires that any matter concerning the scheme should be investigated before a decision is taken as to whether the authorisation order should be revoked; or

(b) revocation would not be in the interests of the participants . . .

(4) If the FCA proposes to refuse a request under this section, it must give separate warning notices to the operator and the depositary of the scheme.

(5) If the FCA decides to refuse the request, it must without delay give each of them a decision notice and either of them may refer the matter to the Tribunal.]

NOTES

Inserted as noted to s 261C at **[7.468]**.

Sub-s (3): words omitted repealed by the Collective Investment Schemes (Amendment etc) (EU Exit) Regulations 2019, SI 2019/325, regs 3, 20, as from IP completion day (as defined in the European Union (Withdrawal Agreement) Act 2020, s 39).

[Powers of intervention

[7.490]

261X Directions

(1) The FCA may give a direction under this section if it appears to the FCA that—

(a) one or more of the requirements for the making of an authorisation order are no longer satisfied;

(b) the operator or depositary of an authorised contractual scheme has contravened, or is likely to contravene, a requirement imposed—

(i) by or under this Act; . . .

(ii) by [UCITS-related direct EU legislation]; [or]

[(iii) by the MMF Regulation or any directly applicable regulation or decision made under that Regulation [which constitutes retained direct EU legislation];]

(c) the operator or depositary of such a scheme has, in purported compliance with any such requirement, knowingly or recklessly given the FCA information which is false or misleading in a material particular; or

(d) none of paragraphs (a) to (c) applies, but it is desirable to give a direction in order to protect the interests of participants or potential participants in such a scheme.

(2) A direction under this section may—

(a) require the operator of the scheme to cease the issue or redemption, or both the issue and redemption, of units under the scheme;

(b) require the operator and depositary of the scheme to wind it up.

Part 7 Financial Services Acts

(3) If the authorisation order is revoked, the revocation does not affect any direction under this section which is then in force.

(4) A direction may be given under this section in relation to a scheme in the case of which the authorisation order has been revoked.

(5) If a person contravenes a direction under this section, section 138D applies to the contravention as it applies to a contravention mentioned in that section.

(6) The FCA may revoke or vary a direction given under this section, either on its own initiative or on the application of a person to whom the direction was given, if it appears to the FCA—

(a) in the case of revocation, that it is no longer necessary for the direction to take effect or continue in force;

(b) in the case of variation, that the direction should take effect or continue in force in a different form.]

NOTES

Inserted as noted to s 261C at **[7.468]**.

Sub-s (1): the word omitted from sub-para (b)(i) was repealed, the word "or" in square brackets in sub-para (b)(ii) was inserted, and sub-para (b)(iii) was inserted, by the Money Market Funds Regulations 2018, SI 2018/698, reg 2(1), (15), as from 21 July 2018. The words "UCITS-related direct EU legislation" in sub-para (b)(ii) were substituted, and the words "which constitutes retained direct EU legislation" in sub-para (b)(iii) were inserted, by the Collective Investment Schemes (Amendment etc) (EU Exit) Regulations 2019, SI 2019/325, regs 3, 21, as from IP completion day (as defined in the European Union (Withdrawal Agreement) Act 2020, s 39).

[7.491]

[261Y Applications to the court

(1) If the FCA could give a direction under section 261X, it may also apply to the court for an order—

(a) removing the operator or the depositary, or both the operator and the depositary, of the scheme; and

(b) replacing the person or persons removed with a suitable person or persons nominated by the FCA.

(2) The FCA may nominate a person for the purposes of subsection (1)(b) only if it is satisfied that, if the order was made, the requirements of section 261D(4) to (9) would be complied with.

(3) If it appears to the FCA that there is no person it can nominate for the purposes of subsection (1)(b), it may apply to the court for an order—

(a) removing the operator or the depositary, or both the operator and the depositary, of the scheme; and

(b) appointing an authorised person to wind up the scheme.

(4) On an application under this section the court may make such order as it thinks fit.

(5) The court may, on the application of the FCA, rescind any such order as is mentioned in subsection (3) and substitute such an order as is mentioned in subsection (1).

(6) The FCA must give written notice of the making of an application under this section to the operator and depositary of the scheme concerned.

(7) The jurisdiction conferred by this section may be exercised by—

(a) the High Court;

(b) in Scotland, the Court of Session.]

NOTES

Inserted as noted to s 261C at **[7.468]**.

[7.492]

[261Z Winding up or merger of master UCITS

(1) Subsection (2) applies if a master UCITS which has one or more feeder UCITS which are authorised contractual schemes is wound up, whether as a result of a direction given by the FCA under section 257 or 261X, an order of the court under section 258 or 261Y, rules made by the FCA or otherwise.

(2) The FCA must direct the operator and depositary of any authorised contractual scheme which is a feeder UCITS of the master UCITS to wind up the feeder UCITS unless—

(a) the FCA approves under section 283A the investment by the feeder UCITS of at least 85% of the total property which is subject to the collective investment scheme constituted by the feeder UCITS in units of another UCITS or master UCITS; or

(b) the FCA approves under section 261S an amendment of the contractual scheme deed of the feeder UCITS which would enable it to convert into a [UK] UCITS which is not a feeder UCITS.

(3) Subsection (4) applies if a master UCITS which has one or more feeder UCITS which are authorised contractual schemes—

(a) merges with another UCITS, or

(b) is divided into two or more UCITS.

(4) The FCA must direct the operator and depositary of any authorised contractual scheme which is a feeder UCITS of the master UCITS to wind up the scheme unless—

(a) the FCA approves under section 283A the investment by the scheme of at least 85% of the total property which is subject to the collective investment scheme constituted by the feeder UCITS in the units of—

(i) the master UCITS which results from the merger;

(ii) one of the UCITS resulting from the division; or

(iii) another UCITS or master UCITS;

(b) the FCA approves under section 261S an amendment of the contractual scheme deed of the scheme concerned which would enable it to convert into a [UK] UCITS which is not a feeder UCITS.]

NOTES

Inserted as noted to s 261C at **[7.468]**.

Sub-ss (2), (4): word in square brackets inserted by the Collective Investment Schemes (Amendment etc) (EU Exit) Regulations 2019, SI 2019/325, regs 3, 22, as from IP completion day (as defined in the European Union (Withdrawal Agreement) Act 2020, s 39).

[7.493]

[261Z1 Procedure on giving directions under section 261X or 261Z and varying them on FCA's own initiative

(1) A direction under section 261X or 261Z takes effect—

(a) immediately, if the notice given under subsection (3) states that that is the case;

(b) on such date as may be specified in the notice; or

(c) if no date is specified in the notice, when the matter to which it relates is no longer open to review.

(2) A direction under section 261X may be expressed to take effect immediately (or on a specified date) only if the FCA, having regard to the ground on which it is exercising its power under that section, considers that it is necessary for the direction to take effect immediately (or on that date).

(3) If the FCA proposes to give a direction under section 261X or 261Z, or gives a direction under either section with immediate effect, it must give separate written notice to the operator and the depositary of the scheme concerned.

(4) The notice must—

(a) give details of the direction;

(b) inform the person to whom it is given of when the direction takes effect;

(c) state the FCA's reasons for giving the direction and for its determination as to when the direction takes effect;

(d) inform the person to whom it is given that representations may be made to the FCA within such period as may be specified in it (whether or not the matter has been referred to the Tribunal); and

(e) inform the person to whom it is given of the right to refer the matter to the Tribunal.

(5) If the direction imposes a requirement under section 261X(2)(a), the notice must state that the requirement has effect until—

(a) a specified date; or

(b) a further direction.

(6) If the direction is given under section 261X(2)(b) or section 261Z(2) or (4), the scheme must be wound up—

(a) by a date specified in the notice; or

(b) if no date is specified, as soon as practicable.

(7) The FCA may extend the period allowed under the notice for making representations.

(8) If, having considered any representations made by a person to whom the notice was given, the FCA decides—

(a) to give the direction in the way proposed, or

(b) if it has been given, not to revoke the direction,

it must give separate written notice to the operator and the depositary of the scheme concerned.

(9) If, having considered any representations made by a person to whom the notice was given, the FCA decides—

(a) not to give the direction in the way proposed,

(b) to give the direction in a way other than that proposed, or

(c) to revoke a direction which has effect,

it must give separate written notice to the operator and the depositary of the scheme concerned.

(10) A notice given under subsection (8) must inform the persons to whom it is given of the right to refer the matter to the Tribunal.

(11) A notice under subsection (9)(b) must comply with subsection (4).

(12) If a notice informs a person of the right to refer a matter to the Tribunal, it must give an indication of the procedure on such a reference.

(13) This section applies to the variation of a direction on the FCA's own initiative as it applies to the giving of a direction.

(14) For the purposes of subsection (1)(c), whether a matter is open to review is to be determined in accordance with section 391(8).]

NOTES

Inserted as noted to s 261C at **[7.468]**.

[7.494]

[261Z2 Procedure: refusal to revoke or vary direction

(1) If on an application under section 261X(6) for a direction to be revoked or varied the FCA proposes—

(a) to vary the direction otherwise than in accordance with the application, or

(b) to refuse to revoke or vary the direction,

it must give the applicant a warning notice.

(2) If the FCA decides to refuse to revoke or vary the direction—

(a) it must give the applicant a decision notice; and

(b) the applicant may refer the matter to the Tribunal.]

NOTES

Inserted as noted to s 261C at **[7.468]**.

[7.495]

[261Z3 Procedure: revocation of direction and grant of request for variation

(1) If the FCA decides on its own initiative to revoke a direction under section 261X it must give separate written notice of its decision to the operator and the depositary of the scheme.

(2) If on an application under section 261X(6) for a direction to be revoked or varied the FCA decides to revoke the direction or vary it in accordance with the application, it must give the applicant written notice of its decision.

(3) A notice under this section must specify the date on which the decision takes effect.

(4) The FCA may publish such information about the revocation or variation, in such way, as it considers appropriate.]

NOTES

Inserted as noted to s 261C at **[7.468]**.

261Z4 *(S 261Z4 (Information for home state regulator) originally inserted as noted to s 261C ante. Subsequently repealed by the Collective Investment Schemes (Amendment etc) (EU Exit) Regulations 2019, SI 2019/325, regs 3, 23, as from IP completion day (as defined in the European Union (Withdrawal Agreement) Act 2020, s 39).)*

[7.496]

[261Z5 Information for feeder UCITS

(1) The FCA must immediately inform the operator of any authorised contractual scheme which is a feeder UCITS of an authorised unit trust scheme, an authorised contractual scheme or an authorised open-ended investment company (the master UCITS) of—

(a) any failure of which the FCA becomes aware by the master UCITS to comply with a provision made [by or under any enactment] in implementation of Chapter VIII of the UCITS directive;

(b) any warning notice or decision notice given to the master UCITS in relation to a contravention of any provision made in implementation of Chapter VIII of the UCITS directive by or under any enactment or in rules of the FCA;

(c) any information reported to the FCA pursuant to rules of the FCA made to implement Article 106(1) of the UCITS directive which relates to the master UCITS, or to one or more of its directors, or its management company, trustee, depositary or auditor.

(2), (3) . . .]

NOTES

Inserted as noted to s 261C at **[7.468]**.

Words in square brackets in sub-s (1) inserted, and sub-ss (2), (3) repealed, by the Collective Investment Schemes (Amendment etc) (EU Exit) Regulations 2019, SI 2019/325, regs 3, 24, as from IP completion day (as defined in the European Union (Withdrawal Agreement) Act 2020, s 39).

CHAPTER IV OPEN-ENDED INVESTMENT COMPANIES

[7.497]

262 Open-ended investment companies

(1) The Treasury may by regulations make provision for—

(a) facilitating the carrying on of collective investment by means of open-ended investment companies;

(b) regulating such companies.

(2) The regulations may, in particular, make provision—

(a) for the incorporation and registration in [the United Kingdom] of bodies corporate;

(b) for a body incorporated by virtue of the regulations to take such form as may be determined in accordance with the regulations;

(c) as to the purposes for which such a body may exist, the investments which it may issue and otherwise as to its constitution;

(d) as to the management and operation of such a body and the management of its property;

(e) as to the powers, duties, rights and liabilities of such a body and of other persons, including—

(i) the directors or sole director of such a body;

(ii) its depositary (if any);

(iii) its shareholders, and persons who hold the beneficial title to shares in it without holding the legal title;

(iv) its auditor; and

(v) any persons who act or purport to act on its behalf;

(f) as to the merger of one or more such bodies and the division of such a body;

(g) for the appointment and removal of an auditor for such a body;

(h) as to the winding up and dissolution of such a body;

(i) for such a body, or any director or depositary of such a body, to be required to comply with directions given by the [FCA];

(j) enabling the [FCA] to apply to a court for an order removing and replacing any director or depositary of such a body;

(k) for the carrying out of investigations by persons appointed by the [FCA] or the Secretary of State;

(l) corresponding to any provision made in relation to unit trust schemes by Chapter III of this Part.

(3) Regulations under this section may—

(a) impose criminal liability;

(b) confer functions on the [FCA];

(c) in the case of provision made by virtue of subsection (2)(l), authorise the making of rules by the [FCA];

(d) confer jurisdiction on any court or on the Tribunal;

(e) provide for fees to be charged by the [FCA] in connection with the carrying out of any of its functions under the regulations (including fees payable on a periodical basis);

(f) modify, exclude or apply (with or without modifications) any primary or subordinate legislation (including any provision of, or made under, this Act);

(g) make consequential amendments, repeals and revocations of any such legislation;

(h) modify or exclude any rule of law.

(4) The provision that may be made by virtue of subsection (3)(f) includes provision extending or adapting any power to make subordinate legislation.

(5) Regulations under this section may, in particular—

(a) revoke the Open-Ended Investment Companies (Investment Companies with Variable Capital) Regulations 1996; and

(b) provide for things done under or in accordance with those regulations to be treated as if they had been done under or in accordance with regulations under this section.

NOTES

Words "the United Kingdom" in square brackets in sub-s (2)(a) substituted by the Companies Act 2006 (Consequential Amendments and Transitional Provisions) Order 2011, SI 2011/1265, art 12(1), (3), as from 12 May 2011.

Word "FCA" in square brackets (in each place that it occurs) substituted by the Financial Services Act 2012, s 114(1), Sch 18, Pt 1, paras 1, 9, as from 1 April 2013.

Open-Ended Investment Companies (Investment Companies with Variable Capital) Regulations 1996 (SI 1996/2827): revoked, subject to transitional provisions and savings, by the Open-Ended Investment Companies Regulations 2001, SI 2001/1228, reg 85.

Regulations: the Open-Ended Investment Companies Regulations 2001, SI 2001/1228 at **[8.339]**; the Open-Ended Investment Companies (Amendment) Regulations 2005, SI 2005/923; the Open-Ended Investment Companies (Amendment) Regulations 2009, SI 2009/553; the Undertakings for Collective Investment in Transferable Securities Regulations 2011, SI 2011/1613; the Open-Ended Investment Companies (Amendment) Regulations 2011, SI 2011/3049; the Alternative Investment Fund Managers Regulations 2013, SI 2013/1773; the Bearer Certificates (Collective Investment Schemes) Regulations 2020, SI 2020/1346 at **[8.576]**.

263 *(Spent; this section amended the Companies Act 1985, s 716 (s 716 was repealed by the Regulatory Reform (Removal of 20 Member Limit in Partnerships etc) Order 2002, SI 2002/3203, art 2, as from 21 December 2002). This section is also repealed by the Companies Act 2006, s 1295, Sch 16, as from a day to be appointed.)*

CHAPTER V RECOGNISED OVERSEAS SCHEMES

264–269 *(Ss 264–269 (Schemes constituted in other EEA States) were repealed (together with the preceding heading) by the Collective Investment Schemes (Amendment etc) (EU Exit) Regulations 2019, SI 2019/325, regs 3, 25, as from IP completion day (as defined in the European Union (Withdrawal Agreement) Act 2020, s 39). Note that s 265 was previously repealed by the Undertakings for Collective Investment in Transferable Securities Regulations 2011, SI 2011/1613, reg 2(1), (25), as from 1 July 2011.)*

. . .

270 Schemes authorised in designated countries or territories

(Repealed subject to transitional provisions as noted below.)

NOTES

This section was repealed (together with the preceding heading and s 271) by the Alternative Investment Fund Managers Regulations 2013, SI 2013/1773, reg 80, Sch 1, Part 1, paras 1, 18, as from 22 July 2013.

Orders: the Financial Services and Markets Act 2000 (Collective Investment Schemes) (Designated Countries and Territories) Order 2003, SI 2003/1181 (which designated Jersey, Guernsey and the Isle of Man). Also, the Financial Services (Designated Countries and Territories) (Overseas Collective Investment Schemes) (Bermuda) Order 1988, SI 1988/2284 (made under FSA 1986, s 87) which continued in force and had effect as if made under sub-s (1) above by virtue of the Financial Services and Markets Act 2000 (Transitional Provisions) (Authorised Persons etc) Order 2001, SI 2001/2636, art 67(1). Note that the 2003 Order was revoked by the Alternative Investment Fund Managers Regulations 2013, SI 2013/1773, s 81, Sch 2, Part 2, para 16, as from 22 July 2013, and that the 1988 Order lapsed on the repeal of this section as noted above. For transitional provisions, see the note below.

Transitional provisions: the Alternative Investment Fund Managers Regulations 2013, SI 2013/1773, Sch 1, Part 3, para 45 (Transitional provisions in respect of recognised overseas schemes) provides as follows—

"(1) A collective investment scheme which immediately before 22nd July 2013 was recognised by virtue of section 270 of the Act (schemes authorised in designated countries or territories) is to be treated on and after that date as if it were recognised pursuant to an order under section 272 of the Act (individually recognised overseas schemes), and may be revoked in accordance with the provisions applying to such an order.

(2) Sub-paragraphs (3) to (5) apply in relation to a collective investment scheme which immediately before 22nd July 2013 was recognised by virtue of section 270 of the Act or pursuant to an order under section 272 of the Act.

(3) The operator of the scheme is to be treated for the purposes of section 277A(2) of the Act (regular provision of information relating to compliance with requirements for recognition) as if it had provided information to the FCA pursuant to a direction under section 277A(1) of the Act on 21st July 2013.

(4) If the FCA gives a direction under section 277(5) (alteration of schemes and changes of operator, trustee or depositary) or 277A(1) of the Act pursuant to which requires the operator is required to provide information to the FCA before 22nd July 2014, and the operator has not provided such information before 5th August 2014, the scheme will cease to be recognised on 5th August 2014.

(5) If the operator of the scheme gives written notice of a proposed alteration to the FCA under section 277(1) of the Act after 21st July 2013 but before 22nd July 2014, section 277(2) of the Act applies to that proposal as if the reference in section 277(2)(b) to a period of one month referred to a period of three months.

(6) In this paragraph "the operator" has the meaning given in section 237(2) of the Act (other definitions).".

271 *(S 271 (Procedure) was repealed, subject to transitional provisions, as noted to s 270 ante.)*

[Schemes authorised in approved countries

[7.498]

271A Schemes authorised in approved countries

(1) A collective investment scheme which is authorised under the law of a country or territory outside the United Kingdom is a recognised scheme if—

(a) regulations made by the Treasury approving the country or territory for the purposes of this section are in force,

(b) the scheme is of a description specified in the regulations in relation to which the country or territory is approved,

(c) the operator of the scheme has applied to the FCA for recognition of the scheme,

Part 7 Financial Services Acts

(d) the FCA has made (and has not revoked) an order granting the application, and

(e) no direction under section 271L (suspension of recognition) has effect in relation to the scheme.

(2) In making regulations under this section, the Treasury may have regard to any matter that they consider relevant (and see the restrictions in sections 271B and 271C).]

NOTES

Commencement: 23 February 2022.

Inserted, together with ss 271B–271S, by the Financial Services Act 2021, s 24(2), Sch 9, Pt 1, as from 23 February 2022.

[7.499]

[271B Approval of country: equivalent protection afforded to participants

(1) The Treasury may not make regulations under section 271A approving a country or territory and specifying a description of collective investment scheme unless satisfied that the equivalent protection test is met.

(2) The equivalent protection test is met if the protection afforded to participants or potential participants in the schemes by the law and practice of the country or territory is at least equivalent to that afforded to participants or potential participants in comparable authorised schemes by the law and practice of the United Kingdom under which such schemes are authorised and supervised.

(3) In this section—

"comparable authorised schemes" means whichever of the following the Treasury consider to be the most appropriate—

(a) authorised unit trust schemes;

(b) authorised contractual schemes which are co-ownership schemes;

(c) authorised contractual schemes which are partnership schemes;

(d) authorised open-ended investment companies;

(e) any two or more of the kinds of collective investment scheme mentioned in paragraphs (a) to (d);

"participants" means participants in the United Kingdom.]

NOTES

Commencement: 23 February 2022.

Inserted as noted to s 271A at **[7.498]**.

[7.500]

[271C Approval of country: regulatory co-operation

(1) The Treasury may not make regulations under section 271A approving a country or territory and specifying a description of collective investment scheme unless satisfied that adequate arrangements exist, or will exist, for co-operation between the FCA and the overseas regulator.

(2) In this section, "the overseas regulator" means the authority responsible for the authorisation and supervision of schemes of that description in the country or territory.]

NOTES

Commencement: 23 February 2022.

Inserted as noted to s 271A at **[7.498]**.

[7.501]

[271D Report by the FCA in relation to approval

(1) When considering whether to make, vary or revoke regulations under section 271A approving a country or territory and specifying a description of collective investment scheme, the Treasury may ask the FCA to prepare a report on—

(a) the law and practice of the country or territory under which such schemes are authorised and supervised, or particular aspects of such law and practice, and

(b) any existing or proposed arrangements for co-operation between the FCA and the overseas regulator.

(2) A request for a report under subsection (1) must be made in writing.

(3) If the Treasury ask for a report under subsection (1), the FCA must provide the Treasury with the report.

(4) In this section, "the overseas regulator" has the same meaning as in section 271C.]

NOTES

Commencement: 23 February 2022.

Inserted as noted to s 271A at **[7.498]**.

[7.502]

[271E Power to impose requirements on schemes

(1) The Treasury may by regulations—

(a) provide that a section 271A scheme of a description specified in the regulations must comply with requirements specified in the regulations, and

(b) impose requirements on the operator of such a scheme.

(2) In making regulations under this section in relation to a description of section 271A scheme, the Treasury must have regard to any requirements imposed in relation to comparable authorised schemes by or under this Act.

(3) Regulations under this section may describe requirements by reference to—

(a) rules made or to be made by the FCA, or

(b) other enactments.

(4) The power under subsection (3) includes power to make provision by reference to rules or other enactments as amended from time to time.

(5) The FCA may make, amend or revoke a rule if it considers it necessary or appropriate to do so for the purposes of a requirement imposed (or varied or withdrawn) by regulations under this section which is described by reference to a rule made or to be made by the FCA.

(6) If, for the purposes of a requirement imposed (or varied or withdrawn) by regulations under this section which is described by reference to a rule made or to be made by the FCA, the Treasury consider that it is necessary or appropriate for the FCA to make, amend or revoke a rule, they may direct the FCA to do so.
(7) If the Treasury give a direction under subsection (6), the FCA must comply with the direction within such time as the Treasury may specify in the direction.
(8) The references in paragraphs (5) and (6) to the amendment or revocation of rules are to the amendment or revocation of rules made by the FCA.
(9) Section 141A (power to make consequential amendments of references to rules) applies in relation to the FCA's power to make, amend or revoke rules under this section as it applies in relation to its power to make, amend or revoke rules under Part 9A.
(10) In this section—
"comparable authorised schemes" has the same meaning as in section 271B;
"enactment" includes—
(a) retained direct EU legislation,
(b) an enactment comprised in subordinate legislation,
(c) an enactment comprised in, or in an instrument made under, a Measure or Act of Senedd Cymru,
(d) an enactment comprised in, or in an instrument made under, an Act of the Scottish Parliament, and
(e) an enactment comprised in, or in an instrument made under, Northern Ireland legislation;
"subordinate legislation" has the same meaning as in the Interpretation Act 1978 (see section 21 of that Act).]

NOTES
Commencement: 23 February 2022.
Inserted as noted to s 271A at **[7.498]**.

[7.503]
[271F Application for recognition to the FCA
(1) An application for recognition of a collective investment scheme under section 271A—
(a) must be made in such manner as the FCA may direct,
(b) must contain the address of a place in the United Kingdom for service of notices, or other documents, required or authorised to be served on the operator under this Act, and
(c) must contain or be accompanied by such information as the FCA may reasonably require for the purpose of determining the application.
(2) Where requirements imposed by regulations under section 271E would apply to the scheme or its operator if the application were granted, the application must contain an explanation of how each requirement would be satisfied.
(3) At any time after the application is received and before it is determined, the FCA may require the applicant to provide it with such further information as it reasonably considers necessary to enable it to determine the application.
(4) The FCA may require the applicant to present information provided under this section in such form, or to verify the information in such a way, as the FCA may direct.
(5) Different directions may be given, and different requirements imposed, in relation to different applications.]

NOTES
Commencement: 23 February 2022.
Inserted as noted to s 271A at **[7.498]**.

[7.504]
[271G Determination of applications
(1) The FCA—
(a) may only make an order under section 271A granting an application under that section if it is satisfied that the conditions in subsection (2) are met, and
(b) if it is so satisfied, must make such an order unless it is permitted to refuse the application under subsection (3) or required to do so under subsection (4).
(2) Those conditions are—
(a) that the scheme is authorised in a country or territory which is approved by the Treasury in regulations under section 271A,
(b) that the scheme is of a description of scheme specified in the regulations,
(c) that adequate arrangements exist for co-operation between the FCA and the overseas regulator, and
(d) that, where requirements imposed by regulations under section 271E would apply to the scheme or its operator if the application were granted, each such requirement would be satisfied.
(3) The FCA may refuse an application under section 271A if it appears to the FCA that the operator of the scheme—
(a) has contravened a requirement imposed on them by or under this Act, or would contravene such a requirement if the application were granted, or
(b) has, in purported compliance with such a requirement, knowingly or recklessly given the FCA information which is false or misleading in a material particular.
(4) The FCA must refuse an application under section 271A if it considers it desirable to do so in order to protect the interests of participants or potential participants in the scheme in the United Kingdom.
(5) Where the FCA receives an application under section 271A which is complete, it must give the applicant a notice under section 271H(1) or (2) before the end of the period of two months beginning with the day on which the FCA receives the application.
(6) An application under section 271A is complete if the FCA considers that the application satisfies section 271F(1) and (2).
(7) Where the FCA receives an application under section 271A which is not complete, it must—
(a) notify the operator of the scheme that it does not consider that the application satisfies section 271F(1) or (2) (as applicable), and
(b) identify the information needed to complete the application.

Part 7 Financial Services Acts

(8) In this section, "the overseas regulator" has the same meaning as in section 271C.]

NOTES

Commencement: 23 February 2022.
Inserted as noted to s 271A at **[7.498]**.

[7.505]
[271H Procedure when determining an application

(1) If the FCA decides to make an order under section 271A granting an application under that section, it must give written notice of its decision to the applicant.
(2) If the FCA proposes to refuse an application under section 271A, it must give the applicant a warning notice.
(3) If the FCA decides to refuse the application, it must give the applicant a decision notice.
(4) If the FCA gives the applicant a decision notice under subsection (3), the applicant may refer the matter to the Tribunal, except where the FCA refuses the application on the ground that it is not satisfied that a condition in section 271G(2)(a) or (c) is met.]

NOTES

Commencement: 23 February 2022.
Inserted as noted to s 271A at **[7.498]**.

[7.506]
[271I Obligations on operator of a section 271A scheme

(1) The operator of a section 271A scheme must notify the FCA if the operator becomes aware that it has contravened, or expects to contravene, a requirement imposed on it by or under this Act.
(2) The operator of a section 271A scheme must notify the FCA of any change to—
(a) the name or address of the operator of the scheme,
(b) the name or address of any trustee or depositary of the scheme,
(c) the name or address of any representative of the operator in the United Kingdom, and
(d) the address of the place in the United Kingdom for service of notices, or other documents, required or authorised to be served on the operator under this Act.
(3) A notification under subsection (1) or (2) must be made in writing as soon as reasonably practicable.]

NOTES

Commencement: 23 February 2022.
Inserted as noted to s 271A at **[7.498]**.

[7.507]
[271J Provision of information to the FCA

(1) The operator of a section 271A scheme must provide to the FCA such information as the FCA may direct, at such times as the FCA may direct, for the purpose of determining whether—
(a) the conditions set out in section 271G(2)(a) to (c) are met, and
(b) any requirements relating to the scheme or its operator imposed by or under this Act are satisfied.
(2) The FCA may require the operator to present information provided under this section in such form, or to verify the information in such a way, as the FCA may direct.
(3) Different directions may be given in relation to different schemes or different descriptions of scheme.]

NOTES

Commencement: 23 February 2022.
Inserted as noted to s 271A at **[7.498]**.

[7.508]
[271K Rules as to scheme particulars

(1) The FCA may make rules in relation to section 271A schemes for purposes corresponding to those for which rules may be made under section 248 in relation to authorised unit trust schemes.
(2) For the purposes of subsection (1), a reference in section 248 to the manager of an authorised unit trust scheme is to be read as a reference to the operator of a section 271A scheme.
(3) Rules made under this section do not affect any liability which a person may incur apart from the rules.]

NOTES

Commencement: 23 February 2022.
Inserted as noted to s 271A at **[7.498]**.

[7.509]
[271L Suspension of recognition

(1) The FCA may direct that a section 271A scheme is not to be a recognised scheme—
(a) for a specified period,
(b) until the occurrence of a specified event, or
(c) until specified conditions are complied with.
(2) The FCA may give a direction under subsection (1) only if—
(a) the FCA is no longer satisfied that the conditions set out in section 271G(2)(a) to (c) are met,
(b) it appears to the FCA that a requirement relating to the scheme or its operator imposed by or under this Act has not been satisfied, or is likely not to be satisfied,
(c) it appears to the FCA that the operator of the scheme has, in purported compliance with any such requirement, knowingly or recklessly given the FCA information which is false or misleading in a material particular, or
(d) although none of paragraphs (a) to (c) applies, the FCA considers it desirable to do so in order to protect the interests of participants or potential participants in the United Kingdom.]

NOTES

Commencement: 23 February 2022.

Inserted as noted to s 271A at **[7.498]**.

[7.510]

[271M Procedure when suspending recognition

(1) A direction under section 271L takes effect—

(a) immediately, if the notice given under subsection (3) states that to be the case,

(b) on a day specified in the notice, or

(c) if no day is specified in the notice, when the matter to which it relates is no longer open to review.

(2) A direction under section 271L may be expressed to take effect immediately or on a specified day only if the FCA, having regard to its reason for giving the direction, reasonably considers that it is necessary for the direction to take effect immediately or on that day (as appropriate).

(3) If the FCA proposes to give a direction under section 271L, or gives such a direction with immediate effect, it must give written notice to—

(a) the operator of the scheme, and

(b) the trustee or depositary of the scheme (if any).

(4) The notice must—

(a) set out details of the direction,

(b) set out when the direction takes effect,

(c) state the FCA's reasons for giving the direction and for its determination as to when the direction takes effect,

(d) state that the recipient of the notice may make representations to the FCA within such period as may be specified in the notice (whether or not the matter has been referred to the Tribunal), and

(e) set out the recipient's right to refer the matter to the Tribunal.

(5) The FCA may extend the period allowed under the notice for making representations.

(6) The FCA must give written notice to the operator and (if any) the trustee or depositary of the scheme concerned if, having considered any representations made, the FCA decides—

(a) to give the direction in the way proposed, or

(b) if it has been given, not to revoke the direction.

(7) The FCA must give written notice to the operator and (if any) the trustee or depositary of the scheme concerned if, having considered any representations made, the FCA decides—

(a) not to give the direction in the way proposed,

(b) to give the direction in a way other than that proposed, or

(c) where the direction has been given, to revoke it.

(8) A notice under subsection (6) must set out the recipient's right to refer the matter to the Tribunal.

(9) A notice under subsection (7)(b) must comply with subsection (4).

(10) Where a notice sets out the right of the recipient to refer a matter to the Tribunal, it must give an indication of the procedure on such a reference.

(11) This section applies to the variation of a direction as it applies to the giving of a direction.

(12) For the purposes of subsection (1)(c), whether a matter is open to review is to be determined in accordance with section 391(8).]

NOTES

Commencement: 23 February 2022.

Inserted as noted to s 271A at **[7.498]**.

[7.511]

[271N Revocation of recognition on the FCA's initiative

(1) The FCA may revoke an order made under section 271A in relation to a collective investment scheme if—

(a) the FCA is no longer satisfied that the conditions set out in section 271G(2)(a) to (c) are met,

(b) it appears to the FCA that a requirement relating to the scheme or its operator imposed by or under this Act has not been satisfied,

(c) it appears to the FCA that the operator of the scheme has, in purported compliance with any such requirement, knowingly or recklessly given the FCA information which is false or misleading in a material particular, or

(d) although none of paragraphs (a) to (c) applies, the FCA considers it desirable to revoke the order to protect the interests of participants or potential participants in the United Kingdom.

(2) If the FCA proposes to revoke an order made under section 271A, it must give a warning notice to—

(a) the operator of the scheme, and

(b) the trustee or depositary of the scheme (if any).

(3) If the FCA decides to revoke the order—

(a) it must without delay give a decision notice to the operator and (if any) the trustee or depositary of the scheme, and

(b) the operator, trustee or depository may refer the matter to the Tribunal.]

NOTES

Commencement: 23 February 2022.

Inserted as noted to s 271A at **[7.498]**.

[7.512]

[271O Requests for revocation of recognition

(1) The FCA may revoke an order made under section 271A in relation to a collective investment scheme at the request of the scheme's operator.

(2) If the FCA decides to do so, it must give written notice to the operator and (if any) the trustee or depositary of the scheme.

(3) The FCA may refuse a request under this section if it considers that—

(a) the public interest requires that any matter concerning the scheme should be investigated before a decision is taken as to whether the order should be revoked, or

(b) revocation would not be in the interests of participants in the scheme.

(4) If the FCA proposes to refuse a request under this section, it must give a warning notice to the operator and (if any) the trustee or depositary of the scheme.

(5) If the FCA decides to refuse the request—

(a) it must without delay give a decision notice to the operator and (if any) the trustee or depositary of the scheme, and

(b) the operator, trustee or depositary may refer the matter to the Tribunal.]

NOTES

Commencement: 23 February 2022.

Inserted as noted to s 271A at **[7.498]**.

[7.513]

[271P Obligations on operator where recognition is revoked or suspended

(1) This section applies where—

(a) the FCA gives a decision notice under section 271N(3), or a written notice under section 271O(2), in relation to a section 271A scheme, or

(b) a direction given by the FCA under section 271L(1) in relation to a section 271A scheme takes effect.

(2) The operator of the scheme must notify such persons as the FCA may direct that the FCA has revoked an order under section 271A for recognition of the scheme or given a direction under section 271L in relation to the scheme (as applicable).

(3) A notification under subsection (2) that relates to a direction under section 271L must set out the terms of the direction.

(4) A notification under subsection (2) must—

(a) contain such information as the FCA may direct, and

(b) be made in such form and manner as the FCA may direct.

(5) Different directions may be given under subsection (2) or (4) in relation to—

(a) different schemes or different descriptions of scheme;

(b) different persons or descriptions of persons to whom a notification under subsection (2) must be given.]

NOTES

Commencement: 23 February 2022.

Inserted as noted to s 271A at **[7.498]**.

[7.514]

[271Q Effect of variation or revocation of Treasury regulations

(1) This section applies, in relation to a section 271A scheme, where the Treasury vary or revoke regulations under section 271A and, as a result, the scheme ceases to be a recognised scheme because—

(a) the country or territory in which the scheme is authorised is no longer approved for the purposes of that section, or

(b) the scheme is no longer of a description of scheme specified in regulations under that section.

(2) Where this section applies, the order given by the FCA under section 271A in relation to the scheme is revoked.

(3) The Treasury may by regulations make provision, in relation to a scheme which has ceased to be recognised under section 271A by virtue of this section—

(a) requiring an application under section 272 by such a scheme to be made during a period specified in the regulations or in a direction given by the FCA, and

(b) modifying or disapplying section 275(1) and (2) (time limits for determining applications under section 272) for the purposes of an application under section 272 relating to such a scheme.]

NOTES

Commencement: 23 February 2022.

Inserted as noted to s 271A at **[7.498]**.

[7.515]

[271R Public censure

(1) This section applies where the FCA considers that—

(a) a requirement imposed by regulations under section 271E has been contravened,

(b) rules made under section 271K have been contravened,

(c) the operator of a section 271A scheme has contravened section 271I, 271J or 271P, or

(d) the operator of a section 271A scheme has contravened a rule made, or a requirement imposed, under section 283.

(2) The FCA may publish a statement to that effect.

(3) Where the FCA proposes to publish a statement under subsection (2) relating to a scheme or the operator of a scheme, it must give the operator a warning notice setting out the terms of the statement.

(4) If the FCA decides to publish the statement—

(a) it must give the operator, without delay, a decision notice setting out the terms of the statement, and

(b) the operator may refer the matter to the Tribunal.

(5) After a statement under subsection (2) is published, the FCA must send a copy of it to the operator and to any person to whom a copy of the decision notice was given under section 393(4).]

NOTES

Commencement: 23 February 2022.

Inserted as noted to s 271A at **[7.498]**.

[7.516]

[271S Recognition of parts of schemes under section 271A

(1) Section 271A(1) applies in relation to a part of a collective investment scheme as it applies in relation to such a scheme.

(2) Accordingly, the following include a part of a scheme recognised under section 271A—

(a) the reference to a scheme recognised under section 271A in the definition of "section 271A scheme" in section 237(3), and

(b) other references to such a scheme (however expressed) in or in provision made under this Part of this Act (unless the contrary intention appears).

(3) Provisions of or made under this Part of this Act have effect in relation to parts of schemes recognised, or seeking recognition, under section 271A with appropriate modifications.

(4) The Treasury may by regulations—

(a) make provision about what are, or are not, appropriate modifications for the purposes of subsection (3);

(b) make provision so that a relevant enactment has effect in relation to parts of schemes recognised, or seeking recognition, under section 271A with such modifications as the Treasury consider appropriate;

(c) make provision so that a relevant enactment does not have effect in relation to such parts of schemes.

(5) Regulations under subsection (4)(b) or (c) may amend, repeal or revoke an enactment.

(6) In this section—

"enactment" has the same meaning as in section 271E;

"relevant enactment" means an enactment passed or made before the day on which subsection (1) comes into force that makes provision in relation to collective investment schemes recognised, or seeking recognition, under section 271A.]

NOTES

Commencement: 23 February 2022.

Inserted as noted to s 271A at **[7.498]**.

Individually recognised overseas schemes

[7.517]

272 Individually recognised overseas schemes

(1) The [FCA] may, on the application of the operator of a collective investment scheme which—

(a) is managed in a country or territory outside the United Kingdom, [. . .]

(b), (c) . . .

[(ca) does not have the benefit of section 271A, and]

(d) appears to the [FCA] to satisfy the requirements set out in [subsections (2) to (15)],

make an order declaring the scheme to be a recognised scheme.

[(1A) For the purposes of subsection (1)(ca), a collective investment scheme has the benefit of section 271A if—

(a) it is authorised under the law of a country or territory which is for the time being approved by regulations under section 271A, and

(b) it falls within a description of schemes specified in the regulations.]

(2) Adequate protection must be afforded to participants in the scheme.

(3) The arrangements for the scheme's constitution and management must be adequate.

(4) The powers and duties of the operator and, if the scheme has a trustee or depositary, of the trustee or depositary must be adequate.

(5) In deciding whether the matters mentioned in subsection (3) or (4) are adequate, the [FCA] must have regard to—

(a) any rule of law, and

(b) any matters which are . . . the subject of rules,

applicable in relation to comparable authorised schemes.

(6) "Comparable authorised schemes" means whichever of the following the [FCA] considers the most appropriate, having regard to the nature of scheme in respect of which the application is made—

(a) authorised unit trust schemes;

[(aa) authorised contractual schemes which are co-ownership schemes;

(ab) authorised contractual schemes which are partnership schemes;]

(b) authorised open-ended investment companies;

[(c) any two or more of the kinds of collective investment scheme mentioned in paragraphs (a) to (b)].

(7) The scheme must take the form of an open-ended investment company or (if it does not take that form) the operator must be a body corporate.

(8) The operator of the scheme must—

(a) if an authorised person, have permission to act as operator;

(b) if not an authorised person, be a fit and proper person to act as operator.

(9) The trustee or depositary (if any) of the scheme must—

(a) if an authorised person, have permission to act as trustee or depositary;

(b) if not an authorised person, be a fit and proper person to act as trustee or depositary.

(10) The operator and the trustee or depositary (if any) of the scheme must be able and willing to co-operate with the [FCA] by the sharing of information and in other ways.

(11) The name of the scheme must not be undesirable or misleading.

(12) The purposes of the scheme must be reasonably capable of being successfully carried into effect.

(13) The participants must be entitled to have their units redeemed in accordance with the scheme at a price related to the net value of the property to which the units relate and determined in accordance with the scheme.

(14) But a scheme is to be treated as complying with subsection (13) if it requires the operator to ensure that a participant is able to sell his units on an investment exchange at a price not significantly different from that mentioned in that subsection.

(15) Subsection (13) is not to be read as imposing a requirement that the participants must be entitled to have their units redeemed (or sold as mentioned in subsection (14)) immediately following a demand to that effect.

NOTES

Word "FCA" in square brackets (in each place that it occurs) substituted by the Financial Services Act 2012, s 114(1), Sch 18, Pt 1, paras 1, 9, as from 1 April 2013.

The word omitted from sub-s (1)(a) was repealed, sub-s (1)(ca) was inserted, and the words in square brackets in sub-s (1)(d) were substituted, by the Financial Services Act 2021, s 25(3)(a), as from 23 February 2022.

Sub-s (1)(c) was repealed by the Alternative Investment Fund Managers Regulations 2013, SI 2013/1773, reg 80, Sch 1, Part 1, paras 1, 19, as from 22 July 2013 (for transitional provisions see the note to s 270 *ante*).

The word omitted from sub-s (1)(a) was originally inserted, and sub-s (1)(b) was repealed, by the Collective Investment Schemes (Amendment etc) (EU Exit) Regulations 2019, SI 2019/325, regs 3, 26, as from IP completion day (as defined in the European Union (Withdrawal Agreement) Act 2020, s 39).

Sub-s (1A) was inserted by the Financial Services Act 2021, s 25(3)(b), as from 23 February 2022.

The words omitted from sub-s (5) were repealed by the Financial Services Act 2021, s 25(3)(c), as from 23 February 2022.

Paras (aa), (ab) of sub-s (6) were inserted, and para (c) of that subsection was substituted, by the Collective Investment in Transferable Securities (Contractual Scheme) Regulations 2013, SI 2013/1388, reg 3(1), (14), as from 6 June 2013.

[7.518]

273 Matters that may be taken into account

For the purposes of subsections (8)(b) and (9)(b) of section 272, the [FCA] may take into account any matter relating to—

(a) any person who is or will be employed by or associated with the operator, trustee or depositary in connection with the scheme;
(b) any director of the operator, trustee or depositary;
(c) any person exercising influence over the operator, trustee or depositary;
(d) any body corporate in the same group as the operator, trustee or depositary;
(e) any director of any such body corporate;
(f) any person exercising influence over any such body corporate.

NOTES

Word "FCA" in square brackets substituted by the Financial Services Act 2012, s 114(1), Sch 18, Pt 1, paras 1, 9, as from 1 April 2013.

[7.519]

274 Applications for recognition of individual schemes

(1) An application under section 272 for an order declaring a scheme to be a recognised scheme must be made to the [FCA] by the operator of the scheme.

(2) The application—

(a) must be made in such manner as the [FCA] may direct;
(b) must contain the address of a place in the United Kingdom for the service on the operator of notices or other documents required or authorised to be served on him under this Act;
(c) must contain or be accompanied by such information as the [FCA] may reasonably require for the purpose of determining the application.

(3) At any time after receiving an application and before determining it, the [FCA] may require the applicant to provide it with such further information as it reasonably considers necessary to enable it to determine the application.

(4) Different directions may be given, and different requirements imposed, in relation to different applications.

(5) The [FCA] may require an applicant to present information which he is required to give under this section in such form, or to verify it in such a way, as the [FCA] may direct.

NOTES

Words in square brackets substituted by the Financial Services Act 2012, s 114(1), Sch 18, Pt 1, paras 1, 9, as from 1 April 2013.

[7.520]

275 Determination of applications

(1) An application under section 272 must be determined by the [FCA] before the end of the period of six months beginning with the date on which it receives the completed application.

(2) The [FCA] may determine an incomplete application if it considers it appropriate to do so; and it must in any event determine such an application within twelve months beginning with the date on which it first receives the application.

(3) If the [FCA] makes an order under section 272(1), it must give written notice of the order to the applicant.

NOTES

Words in square brackets substituted by the Financial Services Act 2012, s 114(1), Sch 18, Pt 1, paras 1, 9, as from 1 April 2013.

[7.521]

276 Procedure when refusing an application

(1) If the [FCA] proposes to refuse an application made under section 272 it must give the applicant a warning notice.

(2) If the [FCA] decides to refuse the application—

(a) it must give the applicant a decision notice; and
(b) the applicant may refer the matter to the Tribunal.

NOTES

Words in square brackets substituted by the Financial Services Act 2012, s 114(1), Sch 18, Pt 1, paras 1, 9, as from 1 April 2013.

[7.522]

277 Alteration of schemes and changes of operator, trustee or depositary

(1) The operator of a scheme recognised by virtue of section 272 must give written notice to the [FCA] of any proposed alteration to the scheme [which, if made, would be a material alteration].

(2) Effect is not to be given to any such proposal unless—

- (a) the [FCA], by written notice, has given its approval to the proposal; or
- (b) one month, beginning with the date on which notice was given under subsection (1), has expired without the [FCA] having given written notice to the operator that it has decided to refuse approval.

(3) . . . Before any replacement of the operator, trustee or depositary of such a scheme, notice of the proposed replacement must be given to the [FCA]—

- (a) by the operator, trustee or depositary (as the case may be); or
- (b) by the person who is to replace him.

[(3A) A notice under subsection (3) must be given—

- (a) at least one month before the proposed replacement, or
- (b) if that is not reasonably practicable, as soon as is reasonably practicable in the period of one month before the proposed replacement.

(3B) The operator of such a scheme must give written notice to the FCA, as soon as reasonably practicable, of any change to—

- (a) the name or address of the operator of the scheme,
- (b) the name or address of any trustee or depositary of the scheme,
- (c) the name or address of any representative of the operator in the United Kingdom, and
- (d) the address of the place in the United Kingdom for service of notices, or other documents, required or authorised to be served on the operator under this Act.]

[(4) If a change is made, or is to be made, to the law which applies to such a scheme in the country or territory in which it is managed and the change affects or will affect any of the matters mentioned at section 272(2) to (4), the operator of the scheme must give written notice of the change to the FCA—

- (a) at least one month before the change takes effect; or
- (b) if that is not reasonably practicable, as soon as it is reasonably practicable to do so.

(5) A notice under this section—

- (a) must be given in such manner as the FCA may direct; and
- (b) where the notice is given under subsection (1) or (3), must include such information as the FCA may direct for the purpose of determining whether the requirements for the making of an order under section 272 in respect of the scheme would continue to be satisfied following the alteration or replacement that is the subject of the notice.]

[(6) The FCA may make rules specifying when a proposed alteration is a material alteration for the purposes of subsection (1).]

NOTES

Sub-s (1): word "FCA" in square brackets substituted by the Financial Services Act 2012, s 114(1), Sch 18, Pt 1, paras 1, 9, as from 1 April 2013. Words in second pair of square brackets inserted by the Financial Services Act 2021, s 25(4)(a), as from 1 January 2023.

Sub-s (2): word "FCA" in square brackets (in each place that it occurs) substituted by the Financial Services Act 2012, s 114(1), Sch 18, Pt 1, paras 1, 9, as from 1 April 2013.

Sub-s (3): the words omitted were repealed by the Financial Services Act 2021, s 25(4)(b), as from 23 February 2022. Word "FCA" in square brackets substituted by the Financial Services Act 2012, s 114(1), Sch 18, Pt 1, paras 1, 9, as from 1 April 2013.

Sub-ss (3A), (3B): inserted by the Financial Services Act 2021, s 25(4)(c), as from 23 February 2022.

Sub-ss (4), (5): added by the Alternative Investment Fund Managers Regulations 2013, SI 2013/1773, reg 80, Sch 1, Part 1, paras 1, 20, as from 22 July 2013 (for transitional provisions, see the note to s 270 *ante*).

Sub-s (6): added by the Financial Services Act 2021, s 25(4)(d), as from 23 February 2022.

[7.523]

[277A Regular provision of information relating to compliance with requirements for recognition

(1) The operator of a scheme recognised by virtue of section 272 must provide to the FCA such information as the FCA may direct, at such times as the FCA may direct, for the purpose of determining whether the requirements for the making of an order under section 272 in respect of the scheme continue to be satisfied.

(2) A direction under subsection (1) may not require information to be provided within the period of 12 months beginning with the date on which information was last required to be provided to the FCA in respect of the scheme pursuant to a requirement under section 274(2)(c) or a direction under subsection (1) or section 277(5)(b).

(3) The information must be provided in such manner as the FCA may direct.]

NOTES

Inserted by the Alternative Investment Fund Managers Regulations 2013, SI 2013/1773, reg 80, Sch 1, Part 1, paras 1, 21, as from 22 July 2013 (for transitional provisions, see the note to s 270 *ante*).

. . .

[7.524]

278 Rules as to scheme particulars

The [FCA] may make rules imposing duties or liabilities on the operator of a scheme recognised under section . . . 272 for purposes corresponding to those for which rules may be made under section 248 in relation to authorised unit trust schemes.

NOTES

The heading preceding this section and the words omitted from the text were repealed by the Alternative Investment Fund Managers Regulations 2013, SI 2013/1773, reg 80, Sch 1, Part 1, paras 1, 22, 23, as from 22 July 2013.

Word "FCA" in square brackets substituted by the Financial Services Act 2012, s 114(1), Sch 18, Pt 1, paras 1, 9, as from 1 April 2013.

[7.525]

279 Revocation of recognition

The [FCA] may . . . revoke an order under section 272 if it appears to the [FCA]—

(a) that the operator, trustee or depositary of the scheme has contravened a requirement imposed on him by or under this Act;

(b) that the operator, trustee or depositary of the scheme has, in purported compliance with any such requirement, knowingly or recklessly given the [FCA] information which is false or misleading in a material particular;

(c) . . . that one or more of the requirements for the making of the order are no longer satisfied; or

(d) that none of paragraphs (a) to (c) applies, but it is undesirable in the interests of the participants or potential participants that the scheme should continue to be recognised.

NOTES

Word "FCA" in square brackets (in each place that it occurs) substituted by the Financial Services Act 2012, s 114(1), Sch 18, Pt 1, paras 1, 9, as from 1 April 2013.

Words omitted repealed by the Alternative Investment Fund Managers Regulations 2013, SI 2013/1773, reg 80, Sch 1, Part 1, paras 1, 24, as from 22 July 2013.

[7.526]

280 Procedure

(1) If the [FCA] proposes to [make an order under section 279] revoking a recognition order, it must give a warning notice to the operator and (if any) the trustee or depositary of the scheme.

(2) If the [FCA] decides to . . . make an order under that section—

(a) it must without delay give a decision notice to the operator and (if any) the trustee or depositary of the scheme; and

(b) the operator or the trustee or depositary may refer the matter to the Tribunal.

NOTES

Word "FCA" in square brackets (in each place that it occurs) substituted by the Financial Services Act 2012, s 114(1), Sch 18, Pt 1, paras 1, 9, as from 1 April 2013.

Words in second pair of square brackets in sub-s (1) substituted, and words omitted from sub-s (2) repealed, by the Alternative Investment Fund Managers Regulations 2013, SI 2013/1773, reg 80, Sch 1, Part 1, paras 1, 25, as from 22 July 2013.

[7.527]

281 Directions

(1) In this section a "relevant recognised scheme" means a scheme recognised under section . . . 272.

(2) If it appears to the [FCA] that—

(a) the operator, trustee or depositary of a relevant recognised scheme has contravened, or is likely to contravene, a requirement imposed on him by or under this Act,

(b) the operator, trustee or depositary of such a scheme has, in purported compliance with any such requirement, knowingly or recklessly given the [FCA] information which is false or misleading in a material particular,

(c) one or more of the requirements for the recognition of [such a scheme] are no longer satisfied, or

(d) none of paragraphs (a) to (c) applies, but the exercise of the power conferred by this section is desirable in order to protect the interests of participants or potential participants in a relevant recognised scheme who are in the United Kingdom,

it may direct that the scheme is not to be a recognised scheme for a specified period or until the occurrence of a specified event or until specified conditions are complied with.

NOTES

Word "FCA" in square brackets (in each place that it occurs) substituted by the Financial Services Act 2012, s 114(1), Sch 18, Pt 1, paras 1, 9, as from 1 April 2013.

Words omitted from sub-s (1) repealed, and words in square brackets in sub-s (2)(c) substituted, by the Alternative Investment Fund Managers Regulations 2013, SI 2013/1773, reg 80, Sch 1, Part 1, paras 1, 26, as from 22 July 2013.

[7.528]

282 Procedure on giving directions under section 281 and varying them otherwise than as requested

(1) A direction takes effect—

(a) immediately, if the notice given under subsection (3) states that that is the case;

(b) on such date as may be specified in the notice; or

(c) if no date is specified in the notice, when the matter to which it relates is no longer open to review.

(2) A direction may be expressed to take effect immediately (or on a specified date) only if the [FCA], having regard to the ground on which it is exercising its power under section 281, considers that it is necessary for the direction to take effect immediately (or on that date).

(3) If the [FCA] proposes to give a direction under section 281, or gives such a direction with immediate effect, it must give separate written notice to the operator and (if any) the trustee or depositary of the scheme concerned.

(4) The notice must—

(a) give details of the direction;

(b) inform the person to whom it is given of when the direction takes effect;

(c) state the [FCA's] reasons for giving the direction and for its determination as to when the direction takes effect;

(d) inform the person to whom it is given that he may make representations to the [FCA] within such period as may be specified in it (whether or not he has referred the matter to the Tribunal); and

(e) inform him of his right to refer the matter to the Tribunal.

(5) The [FCA] may extend the period allowed under the notice for making representations.

(6) If, having considered any representations made by a person to whom the notice was given, the [FCA] decides—

(a) to give the direction in the way proposed, or

(b) if it has been given, not to revoke the direction,

it must give separate written notice to the operator and (if any) the trustee or depositary of the scheme concerned.

(7) If, having considered any representations made by a person to whom the notice was given, the [FCA] decides—

(a) not to give the direction in the way proposed,

(b) to give the direction in a way other than that proposed, or

(c) to revoke a direction which has effect,

it must give separate written notice to the operator and (if any) the trustee or depositary of the scheme concerned.

(8) A notice given under subsection (6) must inform the person to whom it is given of his right to refer the matter to the Tribunal.

(9) A notice under subsection (7)(b) must comply with subsection (4).

(10) If a notice informs a person of his right to refer a matter to the Tribunal, it must give an indication of the procedure on such a reference.

(11) This section applies to the variation of a direction on the [FCA's] own initiative as it applies to the giving of a direction.

(12) For the purposes of subsection (1)(c), whether a matter is open to review is to be determined in accordance with section 391(8).

NOTES

Words in square brackets substituted by the Financial Services Act 2012, s 114(1), Sch 18, Pt 1, paras 1, 9, as from 1 April 2013.

[7.529]

[282A Obligations on operator where recognition is revoked or suspended

(1) This section applies where—

(a) the FCA gives a decision notice under section 280(2) in relation to a scheme recognised under section 272, or

(b) a direction given by the FCA under section 281(2) in relation to such a scheme takes effect.

(2) The operator of the scheme must notify such persons as the FCA may direct that the FCA has revoked an order under section 272 for recognition of the scheme or given a direction under section 281 in relation to the scheme (as applicable).

(3) A notification under subsection (2) that relates to a direction under section 281 must set out the terms of the direction.

(4) A notification under subsection (2) must—

(a) contain such information as the FCA may direct, and

(b) be made in such form and manner as the FCA may direct.

(5) Different directions may be given under subsection (2) or (4) in relation to—

(a) different schemes or different descriptions of schemes;

(b) different persons or descriptions of persons to whom a notification under subsection (2) must be given.]

NOTES

Commencement: 23 February 2022.

Inserted, together with ss 282B, 282C, by the Financial Services Act 2021, s 25(5), as from 23 February 2022.

[7.530]

[282B Public censure

(1) This section applies where the FCA considers that—

(a) rules made under section 278 have been contravened,

(b) the operator of a scheme recognised under section 272 has contravened section 277, 277A or 282A, or

(c) the operator of a scheme recognised under section 272 has contravened a rule made, or a requirement imposed, under section 283.

(2) The FCA may publish a statement to that effect.

(3) Where the FCA proposes to publish a statement under subsection (2) in relation to a scheme or the operator of a scheme, it must give the operator a warning notice setting out the terms of the statement.

(4) If the FCA decides to publish the statement—

(a) it must give the operator, without delay, a decision notice setting out the terms of the statement, and

(b) the operator may refer the matter to the Tribunal.

(5) After a statement under subsection (2) is published, the FCA must send a copy of it to the operator and to any person to whom a copy of the decision notice was given under section 393(4).]

NOTES

Commencement: 23 February 2022.

Inserted as noted to s 282A at **[7.529]**.

[7.531]

[282C Recognition of parts of schemes under section 272

(1) Section 272(1) applies in relation to a part of a collective investment scheme as it applies in relation to such a scheme.

(2) Accordingly, the following include a part of a scheme recognised under section 272—

(a) the reference to a scheme recognised under section 272 in the definition of "recognised scheme" in section 237(3), and

(b) other references to such a scheme (however expressed) in or in provision made under this Part of this Act (unless the contrary intention appears).

(3) Provisions of or made under this Part of this Act have effect in relation to parts of schemes recognised, or seeking recognition, under section 272 with appropriate modifications.

(4) The Treasury may by regulations—

(a) make provision about what are, or are not, appropriate modifications for the purposes of subsection (3);

(b) make provision so that a relevant enactment has effect in relation to parts of schemes recognised, or seeking recognition, under section 272 with such modifications as the Treasury consider appropriate;

(c) make provision so that a relevant enactment does not have effect in relation to such parts of schemes.

(5) Regulations under subsection (4)(b) or (c) may amend, repeal or revoke an enactment.

(6) In this section—

"enactment" has the same meaning as in section 271E;

"relevant enactment" means an enactment passed or made before the day on which subsection (1) comes into force that makes provision in relation to collective investment schemes recognised, or seeking recognition, under section 272.]

NOTES

Commencement: 23 February 2022.

Inserted as noted to s 282A at **[7.529]**.

Facilities and information in UK

[7.532]

283 Facilities and information in UK

(1) The [FCA] may make rules requiring operators of recognised schemes to maintain in the United Kingdom, or in such part or parts of it as may be specified, such facilities as the [FCA] thinks desirable in the interests of participants and as are specified in rules.

(2) The [FCA] may by notice in writing require the operator of any recognised scheme to include such explanatory information as is specified in the notice in any communication of his which—

(a) is a communication of an invitation or inducement of a kind mentioned in section 21(1); and

(b) names the scheme.

(3) In the case of a communication originating outside the United Kingdom, subsection (2) only applies if the communication is capable of having an effect in the United Kingdom.

NOTES

Words in square brackets substituted by the Financial Services Act 2012, s 114(1), Sch 18, Pt 1, paras 1, 9, as from 1 April 2013.

[CHAPTER 5A MASTER-FEEDER STRUCTURES

[7.533]

283A Master-feeder structures

(1) The operator of a UK UCITS may not invest a higher proportion of the property which is subject to the collective investment scheme constituted by that UCITS in units of another UCITS than is permitted by [rule 5.2.11(9) of the Collective Investment Schemes sourcebook] unless the investment is approved by the [FCA] in accordance with this section.

(2) An application for approval under subsection (1) of an investment must be made by the operator of the UK UCITS in such manner, and accompanied by such information, as is required by rules made by the [FCA].

(3) The [FCA] must grant an application made under subsection (2) if it is satisfied—

(a) [that the UK UCITS], its operator, trustee or depositary and auditor and the UCITS in which it proposes to invest, and its operator, have complied with—

(i) the requirements laid down in [the Chapter 8 provisions,] and

(ii) any other requirements imposed by the [FCA] in relation to the application;

(b) in a case where the application is made by the operator of a feeder UCITS in respect of the investment of the proceeds of the winding-up of its master UCITS, that the proceeds of the winding up are to be paid to the feeder UCITS before the date on which the investment is to be made.

[(3A) In subsection (3)(a)(i) "the Chapter 8 provisions" means—

(a) in relation to a UK UCITS or its operator, trustee or depositary, or auditor, any provision made by or under an enactment in implementation of Chapter 8 of the UCITS directive, and

(b) in relation to an EEA UCITS or its operator, Chapter 8 of the UCITS directive.]

(4) In a case within subsection (3)(b), approval must be subject to the conditions in subsections (5) and (6).

(5) The first condition is that the feeder UCITS is to receive the proceeds of the winding-up—

(a) in cash; or

(b) wholly or partly in assets other than cash in a case where the feeder UCITS so elects and each of the following so permits—

(i) the decision of the master UCITS that it should be wound up;

(ii) the trust deed[, contractual scheme deed] or instrument of incorporation of the feeder UCITS; and

(iii) either the agreement between the feeder UCITS and its master UCITS, or the internal conduct of business rules operated by the feeder UCITS and the master UCITS in accordance with rules made by the [FCA].

(6) The second condition is that cash received by the feeder UCITS in accordance with paragraph (5)(a) may not be reinvested before the date on which the feeder UCITS proposes to invest in the new UCITS, except for the purpose of efficient cash management.

(7) The [FCA] must, within 15 working days of the date on which the [FCA] had received all the information required in relation to the application, give written notice to the operator—

(a) that the [FCA] approves its application, or

(b) that the [FCA] objects to the application.

(8) Following receipt of notice that the [FCA] objects to the application, the operator may refer the [FCA's] decision to the Tribunal.]

NOTES

Chapter 5A (ss 283A, 283B) was inserted by the Undertakings for Collective Investment in Transferable Securities Regulations 2011, SI 2011/1613, reg 2(1), (26), as from 1 July 2011.

Words "FCA" and "FCA's" in square brackets (in each place that they occur) substituted by the Financial Services Act 2012, s 114(1), Sch 18, Pt 1, paras 1, 9, as from 1 April 2013.

The other words in square brackets in sub-ss (1) and (3) were substituted, and sub-s (3A) was inserted, by the Collective Investment Schemes (Amendment etc) (EU Exit) Regulations 2019, SI 2019/325, regs 3, 27, as from IP completion day (as defined in the European Union (Withdrawal Agreement) Act 2020, s 39).

The other words in square brackets in sub-s (5) were inserted by the Collective Investment in Transferable Securities (Contractual Scheme) Regulations 2013, SI 2013/1388, reg 3(1), (15), as from 6 June 2013.

[7.534]

[283B Reports on derivative instruments

(1) An authorised person who is the management company in relation to a [UK] UCITS must report to the [FCA] at specified intervals of not more than 12 months about any investment in derivative instruments during the specified period to which the report relates.

(2) The report must be in the specified form and contain the specified information.

(3) The [FCA] must review the regularity and completeness of the information provided by each management company under subsection (1).

(4) In this section, "specified" means specified—

[(a) in rules 6.12.3 and 6.12.3A, and annex 2R to chapter 6, of the Collective Investment Schemes sourcebook, or

(b) in UCITS-related direct EU legislation].]

NOTES

Inserted as noted to s 283A at **[7.533]**.

Word "FCA" in square brackets (in each place that it occurs) substituted by the Financial Services Act 2012, s 114(1), Sch 18, Pt 1, paras 1, 9, as from 1 April 2013.

Word "UK" in square brackets in sub-s (1) inserted, and subs (4)(a) and (b) substituted, by the Collective Investment Schemes (Amendment etc) (EU Exit) Regulations 2019, SI 2019/325, regs 3, 28, as from IP completion day (as defined in the European Union (Withdrawal Agreement) Act 2020, s 39).

CHAPTER VI INVESTIGATIONS

[7.535]

284 Power to investigate

(1) An investigating authority may appoint one or more competent persons to investigate on its behalf—

(a) the affairs of, or of the manager or trustee of, any authorised unit trust scheme,

(b) the affairs of, or of the operator, trustee or depositary of, any recognised scheme so far as relating to activities carried on in the United Kingdom, or

(c) the affairs of, or of the operator, trustee or depositary of, any other collective investment scheme except a body incorporated by virtue of regulations under section 262,

if it appears to the investigating authority that it is in the interests of the participants or potential participants to do so or that the matter is of public concern.

(2) A person appointed under subsection (1) to investigate the affairs of, or of the manager, trustee, operator or depositary of, any scheme (scheme "A"), may also, if he thinks it necessary for the purposes of that investigation, investigate—

(a) the affairs of, or of the manager, trustee, operator or depositary of, any other such scheme as is mentioned in subsection (1) whose manager, trustee, operator or depositary is the same person as the manager, trustee, operator or depositary of scheme A;

(b) the affairs of such other schemes and persons (including bodies incorporated by virtue of regulations under section 262 and the directors and depositaries of such bodies) as may be prescribed.

(3) If the person appointed to conduct an investigation under this section ("B") considers that a person ("C") is or may be able to give information which is relevant to the investigation, B may require C—

(a) to produce to B any documents in C's possession or under his control which appear to B to be relevant to the investigation,

(b) to attend before B, and

(c) otherwise to give B all assistance in connection with the investigation which C is reasonably able to give,

and it is C's duty to comply with that requirement.

(4) Subsections (5) to (9) of section 170 apply if an investigating authority appoints a person under this section to conduct an investigation on its behalf as they apply in the case mentioned in subsection (1) of that section.

(5) Section 174 applies to a statement made by a person in compliance with a requirement imposed under this section as it applies to a statement mentioned in that section.

(6) Subsections (2) to (4) and (6) of section 175 and section 177 have effect as if this section were contained in Part XI.

(7) Subsections (1) to (9) of section 176 apply in relation to a person appointed under subsection (1) as if—

(a) references to an investigator were references to a person so appointed;

(b) references to an information requirement were references to a requirement imposed under section 175 or under subsection (3) by a person so appointed;

(c) the premises mentioned in subsection (3)(a) were the premises of a person whose affairs are the subject of an investigation under this section or of an appointed representative of such a person.

(8) No person may be required under this section to disclose information or produce a document in respect of which he owes an obligation of confidence by virtue of carrying on the business of banking unless subsection (9) or (10) applies.

(9) This subsection applies if—

(a) the person to whom the obligation of confidence is owed consents to the disclosure or production; or

(b) the imposing on the person concerned of a requirement with respect to information or a document of a kind mentioned in subsection (8) has been specifically authorised by the investigating authority.

(10) This subsection applies if the person owing the obligation of confidence or the person to whom it is owed is—

(a) the manager, trustee, operator or depositary of any collective investment scheme which is under investigation;

(b) the director of a body incorporated by virtue of regulations under section 262 which is under investigation;

(c) any other person whose own affairs are under investigation.

(11) "Investigating authority" means [the FCA] or the Secretary of State.

NOTES

Sub-s (11): words "the FCA" in square brackets substituted by the Financial Services Act 2012, s 114(1), Sch 18, Pt 1, paras 1, 17, as from 1 April 2013.

The business of banking: this phrase is not defined in this Act and it is not clear whether it applies to all those who have permission or authorisation to accept deposits.

284A *(Part 17A—Transformer Vehicles (s 284A) omitted due to space considerations; see further, the introductory notes to this Act.)*

PART XVIII [RECOGNISED INVESTMENT EXCHANGES, CLEARING HOUSES AND CSDS]

NOTES

Part heading substituted by the Central Securities Depositories Regulations 2017, SI 2017/1064, reg 2(1), (8), as from 28 November 2017.

Transitional provisions etc in connection with the commencement of the Financial Services Act 2012: for transitional provisions in relation to recognised investment exchanges and clearing houses, see Part 8 of the Financial Services Act 2012 (Transitional Provisions) (Miscellaneous Provisions) Order 2013, SI 2013/442. Article 32 concerns exemption for recognised investment exchanges under s 285(2)(b). Article 33 deals with applications made to the FSA by a clearing house under s 288 before 1 April 2013. Article 34 concerns recognition orders made by the FSA under s 290 or s 292 before 1 April 2013. Article 35 concerns notification requirements. Article 36 deals with directions given by the FSA to a recognised clearing house under s 296(2) before 1 April 2013. Article 37 concerns orders made by the FSA under s 297 (revoking recognition) before 1 April 2013. Article 38 concerns the procedure for directions and procedure under s 298. Article 39 contains transitional provisions in relation to complaints about recognised bodies under s 299. Article 40 concerns directions given before 1 April 2013 under s 300A(2) (power to disallow excessive regulatory provision). Article 41 deals with notices under s 300B (duty to notify proposal to make regulatory provision). Article 42 concerns notices under s 300C(3) given by the FSA before 1 April 2013. Article 43 deals with the supervision of certain contracts under s 301(2).

See also the Financial Services Act 2012 (Transitional Provisions) (Enforcement) Order 2013, SI 2013/441. Article 13 provides that ss 312E–312I do not apply to a contravention by recognised clearing houses and recognised investment exchanges that occurred (and ceased to occur) before1 April 2013.

Other transitional provisions (recognised central counterparties): the Financial Services and Markets Act 2000 (Over the Counter Derivatives, Central Counterparties and Trade Repositories) Regulations 2013, SI 2013/504, regs 50–54 (as amended) provide for transitional provisions in relation to a "CCP RCH" (ie, a person which immediately before 15 March 2013 was a recognised clearing house or recognised investment exchange providing clearing services as a central counterparty in the UK). During the "transition period" certain amendments made to this Act (and to other legislation) by the 2013 Regulations do not apply. In relation to a CCP RCH established in the UK, the transition period begins on 1 April 2013 and ends immediately after (i) the Bank of England determines its application under s 288(1) *post* in accordance with Article 17 of the EMIR regulation, or (ii) the end of the six month period specified in the first sub-paragraph of Article 89(3) of the EMIR regulation, if the CCP RCH has not made an application under s 288(1) before the end of that period. The 2013 Regulations also provide for transitional provisions for a CCP RCH established in an EEA State other than the UK, for a CCP RCH established in a State which is not an EEA State, and for an overseas person.

CHAPTER I EXEMPTION

General

[7.536]

285 [Exemption for recognised bodies etc]

(1) In this Act—

(a) "recognised investment exchange" means an investment exchange in relation to which a recognition order is in force;

[(b) "recognised clearing house" means—

(i) a central counterparty in relation to which a recognition order is in force (in this Part referred to as a "recognised central counterparty"), or

(ii) a clearing house which provides clearing services in the United Kingdom without doing so as a central counterparty, and in relation to which a recognition order is in force;

(c) . . .

[(d) "third country central counterparty" means a person established in a country other than the United Kingdom who has been recognised by the Bank of England as a central counterparty pursuant to Article 25 of the EMIR Regulation;]

[(e) "recognised CSD" means a central securities depository in relation to which a recognition order is in force;

[(g) "third country CSD" means a central securities depository, established in a country other than the United Kingdom, which is recognised by the Bank of England pursuant to Article 25 of the CSD regulation].]

(2) A recognised investment exchange is exempt from the general prohibition as respects any regulated activity—

(a) which is carried on as a part of the exchange's business as an investment exchange; or

[(b) which is carried on for the purposes of, or in connection with, the provision by the exchange of services designed to facilitate the provision of clearing services by another person.]

(3) [A recognised clearing house which is not a recognised central counterparty] is exempt from the general prohibition as respects any regulated [activity—

(a) which is carried on for the purposes of, or in connection with, the provision of clearing services by the clearing house, or

(b) which is carried on for the purposes of, or in connection with, the provision by the clearing house of services designed to facilitate the provision of clearing services by another person.]

[(3ZA) Subsections (2) and (3) do not apply in respect of the regulated activity specified in article 63S of the Financial Services and Markets Act 2000 (Regulated Activities) Order 2001 (administering a benchmark).]

[(3A) A recognised central counterparty is exempt from the general prohibition as respects any regulated activity which is carried on for the purposes of, or in connection with, the services or activities specified in its recognition order.

(3B) . . .

(3C) A third country central counterparty is exempt from the general prohibition as respects any regulated activity which is carried on for the purposes of, or in connection with, the services or activities specified in its recognition by [the Bank of England] pursuant to Article 25 of the EMIR regulation.]

[(3D) A recognised CSD is exempt from the general prohibition as respects any regulated activity which is carried on for the purposes of, or in connection with—

(a) the core services listed in Section A of the Annex to the CSD regulation which the central securities depository is authorised to provide pursuant to Article 16 or 19(1)(a) or (c) of that regulation, or

(b) any non-banking-type ancillary services listed in or permitted under Section B of that Annex which the central securities depository is authorised to provide, including services notified under Article 19 of the CSD regulation.

(3E), (3F) . . .

(3G) A third country CSD is exempt from the general prohibition as respects any regulated activity which is carried on for the purposes of, or in connection with, the services and activities covered by its recognition by [the Bank of England] pursuant to Article 25 of the CSD regulation.

(3H) But a recognised CSD, . . . or a third country CSD is not exempt from the general prohibition as respects any regulated activity which is carried on for the purposes of, or in connection with, any banking-type ancillary service listed in or permitted under Section C of the Annex to the CSD regulation.]

[(4) The Treasury may by order amend paragraph (b) of subsection (2) or (3).]

NOTES

Section heading substituted, and sub-s (1)(e)–(g) inserted, by the Central Securities Depositories Regulations 2017, SI 2017/1064, reg 2(1), (9), as from 28 November 2017.

Sub-s (1)(b)–(d) substituted (for the original sub-s (1)(b) and the word "and" at the end of sub-s (1)(a)), words in first pair of square brackets in sub-s (3) substituted, and sub-ss (3A)–(3C) inserted, by the Financial Services and Markets Act 2000 (Over the Counter Derivatives, Central Counterparties and Trade Repositories) Regulations 2013, SI 2013/504, reg 3(1), (3), as from 1 April 2013.

Sub-s (1)(c) was repealed, and sub-s(1)(d) was substituted, by the Central Counterparties (Amendment, etc, and Transitional Provision) (EU Exit) Regulations 2018, SI 2018/1184, regs 2, 3(1), (2), as from IP completion day (as defined in the European Union (Withdrawal Agreement) Act 2020, s 39) (for transitional provision in relation to the provision of clearing services in the UK by CCPs who are established outside of the UK, see Part 6 of the 2018 Regulations).

Sub-s (1)(g) substituted (for the original sub-s (1)(f) and (g)) by the Investment Exchanges, Clearing Houses and Central Securities Depositories (Amendment) (EU Exit) Regulations 2019, SI 2019/662, regs 4, 5(1), (2)(a), as from IP completion day (as defined in the European Union (Withdrawal Agreement) Act 2020, s 39.

Sub-s (2)(b) substituted, words in second pair of square brackets in sub-s (3) substituted, and sub-s (4) added, by the Financial Services Act 2012, s 28, as from 1 April 2013.

Sub-s (3ZA) was inserted by the Financial Services and Markets Act 2000 (Benchmarks) Regulations 2018, SI 2018/135, reg 45, as from 27 February 2018.

Sub-s (3B) was inserted as noted above. Subsequently repealed by SI 2018/1184, regs 2, 3(1), (3), as from IP completion day (as defined in the European Union (Withdrawal Agreement) Act 2020, s 39) (for transitional provision in relation to the provision of clearing services in the UK by CCPs who are established outside of the UK, see Part 6 of the 2018 Regulations).

Sub-s (3C) was inserted as noted above. Words in square brackets substituted by SI 2018/1184, regs 2, 3(1), (4), as from IP completion day (as defined in the European Union (Withdrawal Agreement) Act 2020, s 39) (for transitional provision in relation to the provision of clearing services in the UK by CCPs who are established outside of the UK, see Part 6 of the 2018 Regulations).

Sub-ss (3D)–(3H) inserted by SI 2017/1064, reg 2(1), (9), as from 28 November 2017. Sub-ss (3E) and (3F) were repealed, the words in square brackets in sub-s (3G) were substituted, and the words omitted from sub-s (3H) were repealed, by SI 2019/662, regs 4, 5(1), (2)(b)–(d), as from IP completion day (as defined in the European Union (Withdrawal Agreement) Act 2020, s 39).

Note: this section is modified in its application to a recognised investment exchange that is also a recognised auction platform so that the reference in sub-s (2) to the exchange's business as an investment exchange includes a reference to its business as an auction platform; see the Recognised Auction Platforms Regulations 2011, SI 2011/2699, reg 7, Sch 2, para 1.

[7.537]

[285A [Powers exercisable in relation to recognised bodies]

(1) For the purposes of this Part, the FCA is "the appropriate regulator" in relation to recognised investment exchanges.

(2) For the purposes of this Part, the Bank of England is "the appropriate regulator" in relation to recognised clearing houses [and recognised CSDs].

(3) In Schedule 17A—

(a) Part 1 makes provision for a memorandum of understanding between the appropriate regulators[, and between the FCA and the PRA,] with respect to the exercise of their functions in relation to recognised [bodies]

(b) Part 2 applies certain provisions of this Act in relation to the Bank of England in consequence of the conferring of functions on the Bank under this Part of this Act;

(c) Part 3 makes provision relating to the winding up, administration or insolvency of [recognised clearing houses] [and recognised CSDs]; and

(d) Part 4 makes provision about fees.]

NOTES

Inserted by the Financial Services Act 2012, s 29(1), as from 24 January 2013 (for the purposes of making orders under Sch 17A and in so far as relating to the preparation of a memorandum, the making of rules or the preparation and issue of a statement of policy under that Schedule), and as from 1 April 2013 (otherwise).

Section heading: substituted by the Central Securities Depositories Regulations 2017, SI 2017/1064, reg 2(1), (10)(a), as from 28 November 2017.

Sub-s (2): words in square brackets substituted by the Investment Exchanges, Clearing Houses and Central Securities Depositories (Amendment) (EU Exit) Regulations 2019, SI 2019/662, regs 4, 5(3), as from IP completion day (as defined in the European Union (Withdrawal Agreement) Act 2020, s 39).

Sub-s (3): words in first pair of square brackets in para (a) substituted by the Bank of England and Financial Services Act 2016, s 16, Sch 2, Pt 2, paras 26, 43, as from 1 March 2017. Words in first pair of square brackets in para (c) substituted by the Financial Services and Markets Act 2000 (Over the Counter Derivatives, Central Counterparties and Trade Repositories) Regulations 2013, SI 2013/504, reg 3(1), (4), as from 1 April 2013. Word in second pair of square brackets in para (a) substituted, and words in second pair of square brackets in para (c) inserted, by SI 2017/1064, reg 2(1), (10)(c), as from 28 November 2017.

[7.538]

286 Qualification for recognition

(1) The Treasury may make regulations setting out the requirements—

(a) which must be satisfied by an investment exchange[, clearing house or central securities depository] if it is to qualify as a body in respect of which [the appropriate regulator] may make a recognition order under this Part; and

(b) which, if a recognition order is made, it must continue to satisfy if it is to remain a recognised body.

(2) But if regulations contain provision as to the default rules of an investment exchange[, clearing house or central securities depository], or as to proceedings taken under such rules by such a body, they require the approval of the Secretary of State.

(3) "Default rules" means rules of an investment exchange[, clearing house or central securities depository] which provide for the taking of action in the event of a person's appearing to be unable, or likely to become unable, to meet his obligations in respect of one or more market contracts connected with the exchange[, clearing house or central securities depository].

(4) "Market contract" means—

(a) a contract to which Part VII of the Companies Act 1989 applies as a result of section 155 of that Act or a contract to which Part V of the Companies (No 2) (Northern Ireland) Order 1990 applies as a result of Article 80 of that Order; and

(b) such other kind of contract as may be prescribed.

[(4A)–(4E) . . .]

[(4F) Regulations under subsection (1) may confer power on the appropriate regulator to make rules for the purposes of the regulations or of any specified provision made by the regulations.]

(5) Requirements resulting from this section are referred to in this Part as "recognition requirements".

[(6) In the case of an investment exchange, requirements resulting from this section are in addition to requirements which must be satisfied by the exchange as a result of section 290(1A) before [the FCA] may make a recognition order declaring the exchange to be a recognised investment exchange.]

NOTES

Sub-s (1): words in first pair of square brackets substituted by the Central Securities Depositories Regulations 2017, SI 2017/1064, reg 2(1), (11)(a), as from 28 November 2017. Words in second pair of square brackets substituted by the Financial Services Act 2012, s 35, Sch 8, paras 1, 2(1), (2), as from 1 April 2013.

Sub-ss (2), (3): words in square brackets substituted by SI 2017/1064, reg 2(1), (11)(b), (c), as from 28 November 2017.

Sub-ss (4A)–(4E): originally inserted by the Financial Services and Markets Act 2000 (Markets in Financial Instruments) (Modification of Powers) Regulations 2006, SI 2006/2975, regs 2, 8, as from 6 December 2006. Subsequently repealed by the Financial Services and Markets Act 2000 (Markets in Financial Instruments) Regulations 2017, SI 2017/701, reg 50(1), Sch 2, paras 1, 29, as from 3 January 2018.

Sub-s (4F): inserted by the Financial Services Act 2012, s 30, as from 24 January 2013.

Sub-s (6): added by the Financial Services and Markets Act 2000 (Markets in Financial Instruments) Regulations 2007, SI 2007/126, reg 3(2), Sch 2, paras 1, 2, as from 1 April 2007 (certain purposes), and as from 1 November 2007 (otherwise). Words in square brackets substituted by the Financial Services Act 2012, s 35, Sch 8, paras 1, 2(1), (3), as from 1 April 2013.

Regulations: the Financial Services and Markets Act 2000 (Recognition Requirements for Investment Exchanges, Clearing Houses and Central Securities Depositories) Regulations 2001, SI 2001/995; the Financial Services and Markets Act 2000 (Recognition Requirements for Investment Exchanges and Clearing Houses) (Amendment) Regulations 2006, SI 2006/3386; the Financial Markets and Insolvency Regulations 2009, SI 2009/853; the Financial Services and Markets Act 2000 (Over the Counter Derivatives, Central Counterparties and Trade Repositories) Regulations 2013, SI 2013/504; the Financial Services and Markets Act 2000 (Over the Counter Derivatives, Central Counterparties and Trade Repositories) (No 2) Regulations 2013, SI 2013/1908; the Financial Services and Markets Act 2000 (Markets in Financial Instruments) Regulations 2017, SI 2017/701; the Central Securities Depositories Regulations 2017, SI 2017/1064; the Investment Exchanges, Clearing Houses and Central Securities Depositories (Amendment) (EU Exit) Regulations 2019, SI 2019/662; the Recognised Auction Platforms (Amendment and Miscellaneous Provisions) Regulations 2021, SI 2021/494; the Markets in Financial Instruments (Capital Markets) (Amendment) Regulations 2021, SI 2021/774.

Applications for recognition

[7.539]

287 Application by an investment exchange

(1) Any body corporate or unincorporated association may apply to [the FCA] for an order declaring it to be a recognised investment exchange for the purposes of this Act.

(2) The application must be made in such manner as [the FCA] may direct and must be accompanied by—

(a) a copy of the applicant's rules;
(b) a copy of any guidance issued by the applicant;
(c) the required particulars; and
(d) such other information as [the FCA] may reasonably require for the purpose of determining the application.

(3) The required particulars are—

(a) particulars of any arrangements which the applicant has made, or proposes to make, for the provision [by another person] of clearing services in respect of transactions effected on the exchange;
(b) if the applicant proposes to provide [services falling within section 285(2)(b)] in respect of transactions other than those effected on the exchange, particulars of the criteria which the applicant will apply when determining to whom it will provide those services[;
(c) a programme of operations which includes the types of business the applicant proposes to undertake and the applicant's proposed organisational structure;
(d) such particulars of the persons who effectively direct the business and operations of the exchange as [the FCA] may reasonably require;
(e) such particulars of the ownership of the exchange, and in particular of the identity and scale of interests of the persons who are in a position to exercise significant influence over the management of the exchange, whether directly or indirectly, as [the FCA] may reasonably require].

[(4) Subsection (3)(c) to (e) does not apply to an application by an overseas applicant.]

NOTES

Sub-ss (1), (2): words in square brackets substituted by the Financial Services Act 2012, s 35, Sch 8, paras 1, 3(1), (2), as from 1 April 2013.

Sub-s (3): words in square brackets in para (a) inserted, and words in square brackets in paras (b), (d) and (e) substituted, by the Financial Services Act 2012, s 35, Sch 8, paras 1, 3(1), (3), as from 1 April 2013. Paras (c)–(e) added by the Financial Services and Markets Act 2000 (Markets in Financial Instruments) Regulations 2007, SI 2007/126, reg 3(2), Sch 2, paras 1, 3(a), as from 1 April 2007 (certain purposes), and as from 1 November 2007 (otherwise).

Sub-s (4): added by SI 2007/126, reg 3(2), Sch 2, paras 1, 3(b), as from 1 April 2007 (certain purposes), and as from 1 November 2007 (otherwise).

Transitional provisions: see the Financial Services (Miscellaneous) (Amendment) (EU Exit) Regulations 2019, SI 2019/710, reg 38 (Transitional provision: recognition of overseas investment exchanges) at **[12.163]**.

287A *(Originally inserted by the Financial Services and Markets Act 2000 (Markets in Financial Instruments) Regulations 2017, SI 2017/701, reg 50(1), Sch 2, paras 1, 30, as from 3 January 2018. Subsequently repealed by the Investment Exchanges, Clearing Houses and Central Securities Depositories (Amendment) (EU Exit) Regulations 2019, SI 2019/662, regs 4, 5(4), as from IP completion day (as defined in the European Union (Withdrawal Agreement) Act 2020, s 39).)*

[7.540]

288 Application by a clearing house

[(A1) This section applies only in relation to an application by a clearing house.]

[(1) A body corporate or unincorporated association which is established in the United Kingdom may, where it intends to provide clearing services as a central counterparty, apply to the Bank of England in accordance with Article 17 of the EMIR regulation for an order granting authorisation for the purposes of that Article and declaring it to be a recognised central counterparty for the purposes of this Act.

(1A) A body corporate or unincorporated association may, where it intends to provide clearing services in the United Kingdom without doing so as a central counterparty, apply to the Bank of England for an order declaring it to be for the purposes of this Act a recognised clearing house which is not a recognised central counterparty.]

(2) [An application under subsection (1A)] must be made in such manner as [the Bank of England] may direct and must be accompanied by—

(a) a copy of the applicant's rules;
(b) a copy of any guidance issued by the applicant;
(c) the required particulars; and
(d) such other information as [the Bank] may reasonably require for the purpose of determining the application.

(3) The required particulars are—

(a) if the applicant makes, or proposes to make, clearing arrangements with a recognised investment exchange, particulars of those arrangements;
(b) if the applicant proposes to provide clearing services [or services falling within section 285(3)(b)] for persons other than recognised investment exchanges, particulars of the criteria which it will apply when determining to whom it will provide those services.

NOTES

Sub-s (A1) was inserted by the Central Securities Depositories Regulations 2017, SI 2017/1064, reg 2(1), (12), as from 28 November 2017.

Sub-ss (1), (1A) were substituted (for the original sub-s (1)), and the words in the first pair of square brackets in sub-s (2) were substituted, by the Financial Services and Markets Act 2000 (Over the Counter Derivatives, Central Counterparties and Trade Repositories) Regulations 2013, SI 2013/504, reg 3(1), (5), as from 1 April 2013.

The other words in square brackets in sub-s (2) were substituted, and words in square brackets in sub-s (3) were inserted, by the Financial Services Act 2012, s 35, Sch 8, paras 1, 4, as from 1 April 2013.

[7.541]

[288A Application by a central securities depository

Where a legal person which is established in the United Kingdom intends—

(a) to operate a securities settlement system referred to in point (3) of Section A of the Annex to the CSD regulation, and

(b) to provide at least one other core service listed in Section A of that Annex,

it may apply to the Bank of England in accordance with Article 17 of the CSD regulation[, and any technical standards originally made or adopted under that Article which are retained direct EU legislation and any technical standards made under that Article by the Bank on or after IP completion day,] for an order granting authorisation for the purposes of Article 16 of that regulation and declaring it to be a recognised CSD for the purposes of this Act.]

NOTES

Inserted by the Central Securities Depositories Regulations 2017, SI 2017/1064, reg 2(1), (13), as from 28 November 2017.

Words in square brackets substituted by the Investment Exchanges, Clearing Houses and Central Securities Depositories (Amendment) (EU Exit) Regulations 2019, SI 2019/662, regs 4, 5(5), as from IP completion day (as defined in the European Union (Withdrawal Agreement) Act 2020, s 39). Note that reg 5(5) of the 2019 Regulations was amended by the Financial Services and Economic and Monetary Policy (Consequential Amendments) (EU Exit) Regulations 2020, SI 2020/1301, reg 3, Schedule, para 37(b), as from 30 December 2020 (and the effect of the amendment has been incorporated in the text set out above).

[7.542]

289 Applications: supplementary

(1) At any time after receiving an application and before determining it, [the appropriate regulator] may require the applicant to provide such further information as it reasonably considers necessary to enable it to determine the application.

(2) Information which [the appropriate regulator] requires in connection with an application must be provided in such form, or verified in such manner, as [the appropriate regulator] may direct.

(3) Different directions may be given, or requirements imposed, by [the appropriate regulator] with respect to different applications.

[(4) In relation to an application under section 288(1), this section does not apply to information which can be required under Article 17 of the EMIR regulation.]

[(5) In relation to an application under section 288A, this section applies only in relation to information which the Bank of England may require in connection with recognition requirements which do not [derive from any of the following—

(a) the CSD Regulation;

(b) any EU regulation, originally made under the CSD regulation, which is retained direct EU legislation;

(c) any subordinate legislation (within the meaning of the Interpretation Act 1978) made under the CSD regulation on or after IP completion day].]

NOTES

Sub-ss (1)–(3): words in square brackets substituted by the Financial Services Act 2012, s 35, Sch 8, paras 1, 5, as from 1 April 2013.

Sub-s (4): added by the Financial Services and Markets Act 2000 (Over the Counter Derivatives, Central Counterparties and Trade Repositories) Regulations 2013, SI 2013/504, reg 3(1), (6), as from 1 April 2013.

Sub-s (5): added by the Central Securities Depositories Regulations 2017, SI 2017/1064, reg 2(1), (14), as from 28 November 2017. Words in square brackets substituted by the Investment Exchanges, Clearing Houses and Central Securities Depositories (Amendment) (EU Exit) Regulations 2019, SI 2019/662, regs 4, 5(6), as from IP completion day (as defined in the European Union (Withdrawal Agreement) Act 2020, s 39). Note that reg 5(6) of the 2019 Regulations was amended by the Financial Services and Economic and Monetary Policy (Consequential Amendments) (EU Exit) Regulations 2020, SI 2020/1301, reg 3, Schedule, para 37(b), as from 30 December 2020 (and the effect of the amendment has been incorporated in the text set out above).

[7.543]

290 Recognition orders

[(1) If it appears to the appropriate regulator that the applicant satisfies the recognition requirements applicable in its case, the regulator may—

(a) where the application is made under section 287, make a recognition order declaring the applicant to be a recognised investment exchange;

(b) where the application is made under section 288(1) and Article 17 of the EMIR regulation allows authorisation to be granted, make a recognition order ("a central counterparty recognition order") granting authorisation for the purposes of that Article and declaring the applicant to be a recognised central counterparty; . . .

(c) where the application is made under section 288(1A), make a recognition order declaring the applicant to be a recognised clearing house which is not a recognised central counterparty][; or

(d) where the application is made under section 288A, make a recognition order (a "CSD recognition order") granting authorisation for the purposes of Article 16 of the CSD regulation and declaring the applicant to be a recognised CSD].

[(1A) In the case of an application for an order declaring the applicant to be a recognised investment exchange, the reference in subsection (1) to the recognition requirements applicable in its case includes a reference to requirements contained in any of the following—

(a) any EU regulation, originally made under the markets in financial instruments directive, which is retained direct EU legislation;
(b) any EU regulation, originally made under the markets in financial instruments regulation, which is retained direct EU legislation;
(c) any subordinate legislation (within the meaning of the Interpretation Act 1978) made under the markets in financial instruments regulation on or after IP completion day].

(1B) In the case mentioned in subsection (1A), the application must be determined by [the FCA] before the end of the period of six months beginning with the date on which it receives the completed application.
(1C) Subsection (1B) does not apply in the case of an application by an overseas applicant.]
[(1D) A central counterparty recognition order must specify the services or activities linked to clearing which the applicant may provide or perform and the classes of financial instruments covered by the order.]
[(1E) A CSD recognition order must specify—
(a) the core services listed in Section A of the Annex to the CSD regulation which the applicant is authorised to provide pursuant to Article 16 or 19(1)(a) or (c) of that regulation, and
(b) any non-banking-type ancillary services listed in or permitted under Section B of that Annex which the applicant is authorised to provide, including services notified under Article 19 of the CSD regulation.

(1F) A CSD recognition order must also record the terms of any of the following authorisations granted to the CSD under the CSD regulation or notifications made by the CSD under that regulation—
(a) an authorisation under Article 19(1) of the CSD regulation to outsource a core service under Article 30 of that regulation,
(b) an authorisation under Article 19(1)(d) of the CSD regulation (settlement of cash leg of securities settlement system in the books of another settlement agent),
(c) an authorisation under Article 19(1)(e) of the CSD regulation (setting up interoperable link),
(d) a notification under Article 19(5) of the CSD regulation (other CSD links),
(e) an authorisation under Article 54 or 56 of the CSD regulation to provide (in accordance with Article 54(2)(a) or (b)) any banking-type ancillary service listed in or permitted under Section C of the Annex to that regulation, and
(f) an authorisation to provide investment services and activities in addition to the services explicitly listed in Sections A and B of the Annex to the CSD regulation.]

(2) . . .
(3) In considering an application [made under section 287 or 288(1A)], [the appropriate regulator] may have regard to any information which it considers is relevant to the application.
(4) A recognition order must specify a date on which it is to take effect.
[(4A) If the Bank of England has not made a decision in relation to an application under section 288A within six months of that application being complete, the applicant may refer the matter to the Tribunal.
(4B) For the purposes of subsection (4A), an application is "complete" when the Bank of England informs the applicant that it is complete pursuant to Article 17(3) of the CSD regulation.]
(5) Section 298 has effect in relation to a decision to refuse to make a recognition order [in respect of an investment exchange or a clearing house which is not a central counterparty]—
(a) as it has effect in relation to a decision to revoke such an order; and
(b) as if references to a recognised body were references to the applicant.

[(5A) Section 298 has effect in relation to a decision to refuse an application under section 288A—
(a) as it has effect in relation to a decision to make a revocation order under section 297(1B); and
(b) as if references to a recognised body were references to the applicant.]

(6) . . .
[(7) Where—
(a) a body corporate or unincorporated association has made an application under section 288(1), and
(b) the Bank of England has determined that application in accordance with Article 17 of the EMIR regulation, any previous recognition order under section 290(1)(c) or 292(2)(b) shall cease to be valid.]

NOTES

Sub-s (1) was substituted, sub-ss (1D), (7) were inserted and added respectively, and the words in the first pair of square brackets in sub-s (3) and the words in square brackets in sub-s (5) were inserted, by the Financial Services and Markets Act 2000 (Over the Counter Derivatives, Central Counterparties and Trade Repositories) Regulations 2013, SI 2013/504, reg 3(1), (7), as from 1 April 2013.

Word omitted from sub-s (1)(b) repealed, and sub-s (1)(d) (and the preceding word) and sub-ss (1E), (1F), (4A), (4B), (5A) inserted, by the Central Securities Depositories Regulations 2017, SI 2017/1064, reg 2(1), (15), as from 28 November 2017.

Sub-ss (1A)–(1C) were originally inserted by the Financial Services and Markets Act 2000 (Markets in Financial Instruments) Regulations 2007, SI 2007/126, reg 3(2), Sch 2, paras 1, 4, as from 1 April 2007 (certain purposes), and as from 1 November 2007 (otherwise). Sub-s (1A) was subsequently substituted by the Investment Exchanges, Clearing Houses and Central Securities Depositories (Amendment) (EU Exit) Regulations 2019, SI 2019/662, regs 4, 5(7), as from IP completion day (as defined in the European Union (Withdrawal Agreement) Act 2020, s 39). Note that reg 5(7) of the 2019 Regulations was amended by the Financial Services and Economic and Monetary Policy (Consequential Amendments) (EU Exit) Regulations 2020, SI 2020/1301, reg 3, Schedule, para 37(b), as from 30 December 2020 (and the effect of the amendment has been incorporated in the text set out above)

The words in square brackets in sub-ss (1B) and the words in the second pair of square brackets in sub-s (3) were substituted, and sub-ss (2), (6) were repealed, by the Financial Services Act 2012, s 35, Sch 8, paras 1, 6, as from 1 April 2013.

[7.544]

[290ZA Variation of central counterparty recognition order

(1) On an application made to it in accordance with Article 15 of the EMIR regulation, the Bank of England may in accordance with Article 17 of that regulation vary a central counterparty recognition order by specifying an additional service or activity or class of financial instruments.
(2) Where Article 20(5) of the EMIR regulation applies, the Bank of England may vary a central counterparty recognition order by removing a service or activity or class of financial instruments from those specified in the order.

(3) The Bank of England may at any time vary a central counterparty recognition order for the purpose of correcting an error in, or omission from, the order.

NOTES

Inserted by the Financial Services and Markets Act 2000 (Over the Counter Derivatives, Central Counterparties and Trade Repositories) Regulations 2013, SI 2013/504, reg 3(1), (8), as from 1 April 2013.

[7.545]

[290ZB Variation of CSD recognition order

(1) Where the Bank of England—

(a) grants an authorisation in accordance with Article 19(1), 54 or 56 of the CSD regulation,

(b) receives a notification under Article 19 of that regulation, or

(c) decides to withdraw authorisation for a service, activity or financial instrument in accordance with Article 20(4) or 57(4) of that regulation,

the Bank of England must vary the CSD recognition order accordingly.

(2) Where an authorisation to provide investment services and activities in addition to the services explicitly listed in Sections A and B of the Annex to the CSD regulation is granted, varied or withdrawn, the Bank of England must vary the CSD recognition order accordingly.

(3) The Bank of England may at any time vary a CSD recognition order for the purpose of correcting an error in, or omission from, the order.]

NOTES

Inserted by the Central Securities Depositories Regulations 2017, SI 2017/1064, reg 2(1), (16), as from 28 November 2017.

[7.546]

[290A Refusal of recognition on ground of excessive regulatory provision

(1) [The appropriate regulator must] not make a recognition order if it appears to [it that] an existing or proposed regulatory provision of the applicant in connection with—

(a) the applicant's business as an investment exchange, . . .

(b) the provision by the applicant of clearing services, [or

(c) the provision by the applicant of services falling within section 285(2)(b) or (3)(b),]

imposes or will impose an excessive requirement on the persons affected (directly or indirectly) by it.

(2) The reference in section 290(1) (making of recognition order) to satisfying the applicable recognition requirements shall be read accordingly.

(3) Expressions used in subsection (1) above that are defined for the purposes of section 300A (power of [appropriate regulator] to disallow excessive regulatory provision) have the same meaning as in that section.

(4) The provisions of section 300A(3) and (4) (determination whether regulatory provision excessive) apply for the purposes of this section as for the purposes of section 300A.

(5) Section 298 has effect in relation to a decision under this section to refuse a recognition order—

(a) as it has effect in relation to a decision to revoke such an order, and

(b) as if references to a recognised body were references to the applicant.

[(6) This section does not apply to an application for recognition as an overseas investment exchange, an overseas clearing house[, a recognised central counterparty or a recognised CSD].]]

NOTES

Inserted by the Investment Exchanges and Clearing Houses Act 2006, s 4, as from 20 December 2006.

The words in the first and second pairs of square brackets in sub-s (1) and the words in square brackets in sub-s (3) were substituted, the word omitted from sub-s (1)(a) was repealed, and sub-s (1)(c) and the preceding word were added, by the Financial Services Act 2012, s 35, Sch 8, paras 1, 7, as from 1 April 2013.

Sub-s (6) was substituted by the Financial Services and Markets Act 2000 (Over the Counter Derivatives, Central Counterparties and Trade Repositories) Regulations 2013, SI 2013/504, reg 3(1), (9), as from 1 April 2013.

Words in square brackets in sub-s (6) substituted by the Central Securities Depositories Regulations 2017, SI 2017/1064, reg 2(1), (17), as from 28 November 2017.

Note: this section does not apply to a recognised investment exchange in its capacity as a recognised auction platform; see the Recognised Auction Platforms Regulations 2011, SI 2011/2699, reg 7, Sch 2, para 9.

[7.547]

291 Liability in relation to recognised body's regulatory functions

(1) A recognised body and its officers and staff are not to be liable in damages for anything done or omitted in the discharge of the recognised body's regulatory functions unless it is shown that the act or omission was in bad faith.

(2) But subsection (1) does not prevent an award of damages made in respect of an act or omission on the ground that the act or omission was unlawful as a result of section 6(1) of the Human Rights Act 1998.

(3) "Regulatory functions" means the functions of the recognised body so far as relating to, or to matters arising out of, the obligations to which the body is subject under or by virtue of this Act.

NOTES

This section is modified in its application to a recognised investment exchange that is also a recognised auction platform so that the reference in sub-s (3) to the obligations to which the body is subject under or by virtue of this Act is to be read as including a reference to the obligations to which it is subject under the Recognised Auction Platforms Regulations 2011 or under the UK auctioning Regulations; see the Recognised Auction Platforms Regulations 2011, SI 2011/2699, reg 7, Sch 2, para 2 (as amended by the Recognised Auction Platforms (Amendment and Miscellaneous Provisions) Regulations 2021, SI 2021/494, reg 6, as from 22 April 2021).

[7.548]

292 Overseas investment exchanges and overseas clearing houses

(1) An application under section 287 or [288(1A)] by an overseas applicant must contain the address of a place in the United Kingdom for the service on the applicant of notices or other documents required or authorised to be served on it under this Act.

(2) If it appears to [the appropriate regulator] that an overseas applicant satisfies the requirements of subsection (3) it may make a recognition order declaring the applicant to be—

(a) a recognised investment exchange;

(b) a recognised clearing house [which is not a central counterparty].

(3) The requirements are that—

[(a) investors are afforded protection equivalent to that which they would be afforded if the body concerned were required to comply with—

(i) recognition requirements, other than any such requirements which are expressed in regulations under section 286 not to apply for the purposes of this paragraph, and

[(ii) requirements contained in any of the following—

(aa) any EU regulation, originally made under the markets in financial instruments directive, which is retained direct EU legislation;

(bb) any EU regulation, originally made under the markets in financial instruments regulation, which is retained direct EU legislation;

(cc) any subordinate legislation (within the meaning of the Interpretation Act 1978) made under the markets in financial instruments regulation on or after IP completion day;]

(b) there are adequate procedures for dealing with a person who is unable, or likely to become unable, to meet his obligations in respect of one or more market contracts connected with the investment exchange or clearing house;

(c) the applicant is able and willing to co-operate with [the appropriate regulator] by the sharing of information and in other ways;

(d) adequate arrangements exist for co-operation between [the appropriate regulator] and those responsible for the supervision of the applicant in the country or territory in which the applicant's head office is situated.

(4) In considering whether it is satisfied as to the requirements mentioned in subsection (3)(a) and (b), [the appropriate regulator] is to have regard to—

(a) the relevant law and practice of the country or territory in which the applicant's head office is situated;

(b) the rules and practices of the applicant.

(5) In relation to an overseas applicant and a body or association declared to be a recognised investment exchange or recognised clearing house by a recognition order made by virtue of subsection (2)—

(a) the reference in section 313(2) to recognition requirements is to be read as a reference to matters corresponding to the matters in respect of which provision is made in the recognition requirements;

(b) sections 296(1) and 297(2) have effect as if the requirements mentioned in section 296(1)(a) and section 297(2)(a) were those of subsection (3)(a), (b), and (c) of this section;

(c) section 297(2) has effect as if the grounds on which a recognition order may be revoked under that provision included the ground that in the opinion of [the appropriate regulator] arrangements of the kind mentioned in subsection (3)(d) no longer exist.

[(6) Where a recognised clearing house is . . . recognised as a third country central counterparty, any previous recognition order under section 290(1)(c) or 292(2)(b) shall cease to be valid.]

NOTES

The figure in square brackets in sub-s (1) was substituted, the words in square brackets in sub-s (2)(b) were inserted, and sub-s (6) was added, by the Financial Services and Markets Act 2000 (Over the Counter Derivatives, Central Counterparties and Trade Repositories) Regulations 2013, SI 2013/504, reg 3(1), (10), as from 1 April 2013.

The words "the appropriate regulator" (in each place that they occur) were substituted by the Financial Services Act 2012, s 35, Sch 8, paras 1, 8, as from 1 April 2013.

Sub-s (3)(a) was substituted by the Financial Services and Markets Act 2000 (Markets in Financial Instruments) Regulations 2017, SI 2017/701, reg 50(1), Sch 2, paras 1, 32, as from 3 January 2018 (note that various provisions of the 2017 Regulations came into force on earlier dates for the purposes of making rules, giving notices and consent, etc (for details see reg 1 of the 2017 Regulations)). Sub-s (3)(a)(ii) was further substituted by the Investment Exchanges, Clearing Houses and Central Securities Depositories (Amendment) (EU Exit) Regulations 2019, SI 2019/662, regs 4, 5(8), as from IP completion day (as defined in the European Union (Withdrawal Agreement) Act 2020, s 39). Note that reg 5(8) of the 2019 Regulations was amended by the Financial Services and Economic and Monetary Policy (Consequential Amendments) (EU Exit) Regulations 2020, SI 2020/1301, reg 3, Schedule, para 37(b), as from 30 December 2020 (and the effect of the amendment has been incorporated in the text set out above).

The words omitted from sub-s (6) were repealed by the Central Counterparties (Amendment, etc, and Transitional Provision) (EU Exit) Regulations 2018, SI 2018/1184, regs 2, 4, as from IP completion day (as defined in the European Union (Withdrawal Agreement) Act 2020, s 39) (for transitional provision in relation to the provision of clearing services in the UK by CCPs who are established outside of the UK, see Part 6 of the 2018 Regulations).

[Publication of information by recognised investment exchange

[7.549]

292A Publication of information by recognised investment exchange

(1) A recognised investment exchange must as soon as practicable after a recognition order is made in respect of it publish such particulars of the ownership of the exchange as the [FCA] may reasonably require.

(2) The particulars published under subsection (1) must include particulars of the identity and scale of interests of the persons who are in a position to exercise significant influence over the management of the exchange, whether directly or indirectly.

(3) If an ownership transfer takes place in relation to a recognised investment exchange, the exchange must as soon as practicable after becoming aware of the transfer publish such particulars relating to the transfer as the [FCA] may reasonably require.

(4) "Ownership transfer", in relation to an exchange, means a transfer of ownership which gives rise to a change in the persons who are in a position to exercise significant influence over the management of the exchange, whether directly or indirectly.

(5) A recognised investment exchange must publish such particulars of any decision it makes to suspend or remove a financial instrument from trading on a regulated market operated by it as the [FCA] may reasonably require.

(6) The [FCA] may determine the manner of publication under subsections (1), (3) and (5) and the timing of publication under subsection (5).

(7) This section does not apply to an overseas investment exchange.]

NOTES

Inserted, together with the preceding heading, by the Financial Services and Markets Act 2000 (Markets in Financial Instruments) Regulations 2007, SI 2007/126, reg 3(2), Sch 2, paras 1, 5, as from 1 April 2007 (certain purposes), and as from 1 November 2007 (otherwise).

Word "FCA" in square brackets (in each place that it occurs) substituted by the Financial Services Act 2012, s s 35, Sch 8, paras 1, 9, as from 1 April 2013.

Note: this section is modified in its application to a recognised investment exchange that is also a recognised auction platform so that (a) the reference in sub-s (1) to a recognition order is to be read as including a reference to a recognition order under reg 2 of the Recognised Auction Platforms Regulations 2011, and (b) the references in sub-ss (2), (4) to the management of the exchange are to be read as including references to the management of the auction platform; see the Recognised Auction Platforms Regulations 2011, SI 2011/2699, reg 7, Sch 2, para 3.

Supervision

[7.550]

293 Notification requirements

(1) The [appropriate regulator] may make rules requiring a recognised body to give it—

(a) notice of such events relating to the body as may be specified; and

(b) such information in respect of those events as may be specified.

(2) The rules may also require a recognised body to give the [appropriate regulator], at such times or in respect of such periods as may be specified, such information relating to the body as may be specified.

(3) An obligation imposed by the rules extends only to a notice or information which the [appropriate regulator] may reasonably require for the exercise of its functions under this Act [or [for the purposes of] Directive 2016/1148/EU of the European Parliament and of the Council of 6 July 2016 concerning measures for a high common level of security network and information systems across the Union] [as that directive had effect immediately before IP completion day].

(4) The rules may require information to be given in a specified form and to be verified in a specified manner.

(5) If a recognised body—

(a) alters or revokes any of its rules or guidance, or

(b) makes new rules or issues new guidance,

it must give written notice to the [appropriate regulator] without delay.

[(5A) In relation to a recognised CSD, in subsection (5), "guidance" means guidance issued, or any recommendation made, in writing or other legible form and intended to have continuing effect, by the recognised CSD to—

(a) all or any class of its members, or

(b) persons using or seeking to use its services,

with respect to any of the services or activities specified in its recognition order.]

(6) If a recognised investment exchange makes a change—

(a) in the arrangements it makes for the provision [by another person] of clearing services in respect of transactions effected on the exchange, or

(b) in the criteria which it applies when determining to whom it will provide [services falling within section 285(2)(b)],

it must give written notice to [the FCA and the Bank of England] without delay.

(7) If a recognised clearing house makes a change—

(a) in the recognised investment exchanges for whom it provides clearing services [or services falling within section 285(3)(b)], or

(b) in the criteria which it applies when determining to whom (other than recognised investment exchanges) it will provide clearing services [or services falling within section 285(3)(b)],

it must give written notice to [the Bank of England and the FCA] without delay.

[(7A) In subsections (1) and (2), "recognised body" includes [a third country CSD, in relation to any services referred to in the Annex to the CSD regulation which the third country CSD provides in the United Kingdom].]

(8) Subsections (5) to (7) do not apply to an overseas investment exchange or an overseas clearing house.

(9) "Specified" means specified in [the appropriate regulator's] rules.

NOTES

The words in the second (outer) pair of square brackets in sub-s (3) were inserted, and sub-ss (5A) and (7A) were inserted, by the Central Securities Depositories Regulations 2017, SI 2017/1064, reg 2(1), (18), as from 28 November 2017.

The words in the third (inner) pair of square brackets in sub-s (3) were substituted by the Financial Services and Markets Act 2000 (Benchmarks) Regulations 2018, SI 2018/135, reg 67, as from 27 February 2018.

The words in the final pair of square brackets in sub-s (3) were inserted by the Investment Exchanges, Clearing Houses and Central Securities Depositories (Amendment) (EU Exit) Regulations 2019, SI 2019/662, regs 4, 5(9)(a), as from IP completion day (as defined in the European Union (Withdrawal Agreement) Act 2020, s 39). Note that reg 5(9)(a) of the 2019 Regulations was amended by the Financial Services and Economic and Monetary Policy (Consequential Amendments) (EU Exit) Regulations 2020, SI 2020/1301, reg 3, Schedule, para 37(b), as from 30 December 2020 (and the effect of the amendment has been incorporated in the text set out above).

The words in square brackets in sub-s (7A) were substituted by SI 2019/662, regs 4, 5(9)(b), as from IP completion day (as defined in the European Union (Withdrawal Agreement) Act 2020, s 39).

All other words in square brackets in this section were substituted or inserted by the Financial Services Act 2012, s s 35, Sch 8, paras 1, 10, as from 24 January 2013 (for the purpose of making rules), and as from 1 April 2013 (otherwise).

Note: this section is modified in its application to a recognised investment exchange that is also a recognised auction platform so that the reference in sub-s (6)(a) to transactions effected on the exchange is to be read as including a reference to transactions effected on the auction platform; see the Recognised Auction Platforms Regulations 2011, SI 2011/2699, reg 7, Sch 2, para 4.

[7.551]

[293A Information: compliance with [specified] requirements

[(1)] The appropriate regulator may require a recognised body to give the appropriate regulator such information as the appropriate regulator reasonably requires in order to satisfy itself that the body is complying with any [qualifying provision] that is specified, or of a description specified, for the purposes of this section by the Treasury by order.

[(2) The Bank of England may require [a third country CSD] which provides any services referred to in the Annex to the CSD regulation in the United Kingdom to give the Bank reports on those services and statistical information relating to those services, at such times or in respect of such periods as may be specified by the Bank.

(3) A requirement under subsection (2) extends only to information which the Bank may reasonably require for the exercise of its functions under the CSD regulation or [any EU regulation originally made under the CSD regulation which is retained direct EU legislation, or any subordinate legislation (within the meaning of the Interpretation Act 1978) made under the CSD regulation on or after IP completion day].]]

NOTES

Inserted by the Financial Services and Markets Act 2000 (Markets in Financial Instruments) Regulations 2007, SI 2007/126, reg 3(2), Sch 2, paras 1, 6, as from 1 April 2007 (certain purposes), and as from 1 November 2007 (otherwise).

Substituted by the Financial Services Act 2012, s s 35, Sch 8, paras 1, 11, as from 24 January 2013 (for the purposes of making orders), and as from 1 April 2013 (otherwise).

Sub-s (1) numbered as such, and sub-ss (2), (3) added, by the Central Securities Depositories Regulations 2017, SI 2017/1064, reg 2(1), (19), as from 28 November 2017.

All other amendments to this section were made by the Investment Exchanges, Clearing Houses and Central Securities Depositories (Amendment) (EU Exit) Regulations 2019, SI 2019/662, regs 4, 5(10), as from IP completion day (as defined in the European Union (Withdrawal Agreement) Act 2020, s 39) (for transitional provisions see SI 2019/710, reg 37 at **[12.110]**). Note that reg 5(10) of the 2019 Regulations was amended by the Financial Services and Economic and Monetary Policy (Consequential Amendments) (EU Exit) Regulations 2020, SI 2020/1301, reg 3, Schedule, para 37(b), as from 30 December 2020 (and the effect of the amendment has been incorporated in the text set out above).

Orders and Regulations: the Financial Services and Markets Act 2000 (Qualifying Provisions) Order 2013, SI 2013/419; the Financial Services and Markets Act 2000 (Transparency of Securities Financing Transactions and of Reuse) Regulations 2016, SI 2016/715.

[7.552]

294 Modification or waiver of rules

(1) The [appropriate regulator] may, on the application or with the consent of a recognised body, direct that rules made under section 293 or 295—

- (a) are not to apply to the body; or
- (b) are to apply to the body with such modifications as may be specified in the direction.

(2) An application must be made in such manner as the [appropriate regulator] may direct.

(3) Subsections (4) to (6) apply to a direction given under subsection (1).

(4) The [appropriate regulator] may not give a direction unless it is satisfied that—

- (a) compliance by the recognised body with the rules, or with the rules as unmodified, would be unduly burdensome or would not achieve the purpose for which the rules were made; and
- (b) the direction would not result in undue risk to persons whose interests the rules are intended to protect.

(5) A direction may be given subject to conditions.

(6) The [appropriate regulator] may—

- (a) revoke a direction; or
- (b) vary it on the application, or with the consent, of the recognised body to which it relates.

[(7) In this section, "recognised body", in relation to rules made under section 293, includes [a third country CSD].]

NOTES

Sub-ss (1), (2), (4), (6): words in square brackets substituted by the Financial Services Act 2012, s 35, Sch 8, paras 1, 12, as from 1 April 2013.

Sub-s (7): added by the Central Securities Depositories Regulations 2017, SI 2017/1064, reg 2(1), (20), as from 28 November 2017. Words in square brackets substituted by the Investment Exchanges, Clearing Houses and Central Securities Depositories (Amendment) (EU Exit) Regulations 2019, SI 2019/662, regs 4, 5(11), as from IP completion day (as defined in the European Union (Withdrawal Agreement) Act 2020, s 39).

[7.553]

295 Notification: overseas investment exchanges and overseas clearing houses

(1) At least once a year, every overseas investment exchange and overseas clearing house must provide [the appropriate regulator] with a report.

(2) The report must contain a statement as to whether any events have occurred which are [likely to affect the appropriate regulator's assessment of whether it is satisfied as to the requirements set out in section 292(3)]

(3) The report must also contain such information as may be specified in rules made by [the appropriate regulator].

(4) . . .

NOTES

Words in square brackets substituted, and sub-s (4) repealed, by the Financial Services Act 2012, s 35, Sch 8, paras 1, 13, as from 24 January 2013 (for the purpose of making rules), and as from 1 April 2013 (otherwise).

[7.554]

[295A On-site inspection of [United Kingdom branches of third country] CSDs

(1) For the purposes of [Article 25(11) of the CSD regulation], the Bank of England may, on giving reasonable notice and at any reasonable time, carry out an on-site inspection of any branch maintained by [a third country CSD] in the United Kingdom.

(2) . . .

(3) The Bank of England's power under subsection (1) is enforceable, on the application of the Bank of England, by an injunction or, in Scotland, by an order for specific performance under section 45 of the Court of Session Act 1988.]

NOTES

Inserted by the Central Securities Depositories Regulations 2017, SI 2017/1064, reg 2(1), (21), as from 28 November 2017.

Words in square brackets in sub-s (1) substituted, and sub-s (2) repealed, by the Investment Exchanges, Clearing Houses and Central Securities Depositories (Amendment) (EU Exit) Regulations 2019, SI 2019/662, regs 4, 5(12), as from IP completion day (as defined in the European Union (Withdrawal Agreement) Act 2020, s 39).

[7.555]

296 [Appropriate regulator's] power to give directions

(1) This section applies if it appears to [the appropriate regulator] that a recognised body—

(a) has failed, or is likely to fail, to satisfy the recognition requirements; or

(b) has failed to comply with any other obligation imposed on it by or under this Act.

[(1A) This section also applies [if it appears to the appropriate regulator that a recognised body] has failed, or is likely to fail, to comply with any obligation imposed on it by [or under] [any qualifying provision] [specified (or of a description specified) [for the purposes of this subsection] in an order made by the Treasury].]

[(1B) . . .]

[(1C) This section also applies if it appears to the Bank of England that a Tier 2 third country central counterparty has failed to comply with an obligation imposed on it by or under this Act, or by or under the EMIR regulation.]

(2) [The regulator concerned] may direct [the recognised body . . .] to take specified steps for the purpose of securing the body's compliance with—

(a) the recognition requirements; or

(b) any obligation of the kind in question.

[(2ZA) Where this section applies by virtue of subsection (1C), the Bank of England may direct the Tier 2 third country central counterparty to take specified steps for the purpose of securing compliance with the obligations referred to in that subsection.]

[(2A) In the case of [a recognised body other than an overseas investment exchange or overseas clearing house], those steps may include—

(a) the granting to [the regulator concerned] of access to the premises of [the body] for the purpose of inspecting—

(i) those premises; or

(ii) any documents on the premises which appear to [the regulator concerned] to be relevant for the purpose mentioned in subsection (2);

(b) the suspension of the carrying on of any regulated activity by [the body] for the period specified in the direction.]

[(2B) . . .]

[(2C) In the case of a Tier 2 third country central counterparty, those steps may include—

(a) the granting to the Bank of England of access to any premises of the Tier 2 third country central counterparty for the purposes of inspecting—

(i) those premises; or

(ii) any documents on the premises which appear to the Bank of England to be relevant for the purposes mentioned in subsection (2ZA);

(b) the suspension for the period specified in the direction of the carrying on in the United Kingdom by the Tier 2 third country central counterparty of any activity in respect of which the third country central counterparty is exempt from the general prohibition.

(2D) The Bank of England may not inspect the premises or documents on the premises of a Tier 2 third country central counterparty without first informing the relevant third country competent authority, and inspections must be conducted in accordance with cooperation arrangements established under Article 25.7 of the EMIR regulation.

(2E) In subsection (2D), relevant third country competent authority means a regulatory authority of a country other than the United Kingdom which is responsible for the authorisation and supervision of central counterparties in its territory.]

(3) A direction under this section [(except a direction made under subsection (2ZA))] is enforceable, on the application of [the regulator concerned], by an injunction or, in Scotland, by an order for specific performance under section 45 of the Court of Session Act 1988.

(4) The fact that a rule made by a recognised body has been altered in response to a direction given by [an appropriate regulator] does not prevent it from being subsequently altered or revoked by the recognised body.

NOTES

Section heading: words "Appropriate regulator's" in square brackets substituted by the Financial Services Act 2012, s 35, Sch 8, paras 1, 14, as from 24 January 2013 (for the purposes of making orders), and as from 1 April 2013 (otherwise).

Sub-s (1): words "the appropriate regulator" in square brackets substituted by the Financial Services Act 2012, s 35, Sch 8, paras 1, 14, as from 24 January 2013 (for the purposes of making orders), and as from 1 April 2013 (otherwise).

Sub-s (1A) was inserted by the Financial Services and Markets Act 2000 (Markets in Financial Instruments) Regulations 2007, SI 2007/126, reg 3(2), Sch 2, paras 1, 7, as from 1 April 2007 (certain purposes), and as from 1 November 2007 (otherwise); and has subsequently been amended as follows—

Words "if it appears to the appropriate regulator that a recognised body" in square brackets substituted by the Financial Services Act 2012, s 35, Sch 8, paras 1, 14, as from 24 January 2013 (for the purposes of making orders), and as from 1 April 2013 (otherwise).

Words "or under" in square brackets inserted by the Central Securities Depositories Regulations 2017, SI 2017/1064, reg 2(1), (22), as from 28 November 2017.

The words "any qualifying provision" and "for the purposes of this subsection" in square brackets were substituted and inserted respectively by the Investment Exchanges, Clearing Houses and Central Securities Depositories (Amendment) (EU Exit) Regulations 2019, SI 2019/662, regs 4, 5(13), as from IP completion day (as defined in the European Union (Withdrawal Agreement) Act 2020, s 39).

The words in square brackets beginning with the words "specified (or of a description specified)" and ending with the words "in an order made by the Treasury" were substituted by virtue of the Financial Services Act 2012, s 35, Sch 8, paras 1, 14, as from 24 January 2013 (for the purposes of making orders), and as from 1 April 2013 (otherwise).

Sub-s (1B): originally inserted by SI 2017/1064, reg 2(1), (22), as from 28 November 2017. Subsequently repealed by SI 2019/662, regs 4, 5(13), as from IP completion day (as defined in the European Union (Withdrawal Agreement) Act 2020, s 39).

Sub-s (1C): inserted by the Over the Counter Derivatives, Central Counterparties and Trade Repositories (Amendment, etc, and Transitional Provision) (EU Exit) Regulations 2020, SI 2020/646, reg 2(1), (3), as from IP completion day (as defined in the European Union (Withdrawal Agreement) Act 2020, s 39).

Sub-s (2) is amended as follows:

Words "The regulator concerned" in square brackets substituted by the Financial Services Act 2012, s 35, Sch 8, paras 1, 14, as from 24 January 2013 (for the purposes of making orders), and as from 1 April 2013 (otherwise).

Words in second pair of square brackets substituted by SI 2017/1064, reg 2(1), (22), as from 28 November 2017.

Words omitted repealed by SI 2019/662, regs 4, 5(1), (13), as from IP completion day (as defined in the European Union (Withdrawal Agreement) Act 2020, s 39).

Sub-s (2ZA): inserted SI 2020/646, reg 2(1), (3), as from IP completion day (as defined in the European Union (Withdrawal Agreement) Act 2020, s 39).

Sub-s (2A): inserted by SI 2007/126, reg 3(2), Sch 2, paras 1, 7, as from 1 April 2007 (certain purposes), and as from 1 November 2007 (otherwise). All words in square brackets in this subsection were substituted by the Financial Services Act 2012, s 35, Sch 8, paras 1, 14, as from 24 January 2013 (for the purposes of making orders), and as from 1 April 2013 (otherwise).

Sub-s (2B): originally inserted by SI 2017/1064, reg 2(1), (22), as from 28 November 2017. Subsequently repealed by SI 2019/662, regs 4, 5(13), as from IP completion day (as defined in the European Union (Withdrawal Agreement) Act 2020, s 39).

Sub-ss (2C)–(2E): inserted by SI 2020/646, reg 2(1), (3), as from IP completion day (as defined in the European Union (Withdrawal Agreement) Act 2020, s 39).

Sub-s (3): words in first pair of square brackets inserted by SI 2020/646, reg 2(1), (3), as from IP completion day (as defined in the European Union (Withdrawal Agreement) Act 2020, s 39). Words in second pair of square brackets substituted by the Financial Services Act 2012, s 35, Sch 8, paras 1, 14, as from 24 January 2013 (for the purposes of making orders), and as from 1 April 2013 (otherwise).

Sub-s (4): words in square brackets substituted by the Financial Services Act 2012, s 35, Sch 8, paras 1, 14, as from 24 January 2013 (for the purposes of making orders), and as from 1 April 2013 (otherwise).

Application: this section and s 297 apply in relation to a failure by a recognised investment exchange or recognised clearing house to comply with an obligation under the Companies Act 1989, Pt VII, as to a failure to comply with an obligation under this Act; see s 169(2) of the 1989 Act. This section (only) also applies in relation to a failure by a recognised CSD to comply with an obligation under the Companies Act 1989, Pt VII, as to a failure to comply with an obligation under this Act; see s 169(2A) of the 1989 Act.

Orders and Regulations: the Financial Services and Markets Act 2000 (Qualifying Provisions) Order 2013, SI 2013/419; the Financial Services and Markets Act 2000 (Transparency of Securities Financing Transactions and of Reuse) Regulations 2016, SI 2016/715.

[7.556]

[296A Additional power to direct [recognised central counterparties]

(1) The Bank of England may direct a [recognised central counterparty] to take, or refrain from taking, specified action if the Bank is satisfied that it is necessary to give the direction, having regard to the public interest in—

(a) protecting and enhancing the stability of the UK financial system,

(b) maintaining public confidence in the stability of the UK financial system,

(c) maintaining the continuity of the . . . clearing services provided by the [recognised central counterparty], and

(d) maintaining and enhancing the financial resilience of the [recognised central counterparty].

(2) The direction may, in particular—

(a) specify the time for compliance with the direction,

(b) require the rules of the [recognised central counterparty] to be amended, and

(c) override such rules (whether generally or in their application to a particular case).

(3) The direction may not require the [recognised central counterparty]—

(a) to take any steps for the purpose of securing its compliance with—

(i) the recognition requirements, or

(ii) any obligation of a kind mentioned in section 296(1)(b) or (1A), or

(b) to accept a transfer of property, rights or liabilities of another [recognised central counterparty].

(4) If the direction is given in reliance on section 298(7) the Bank must, within a reasonable time of giving the direction, give the [recognised central counterparty] a statement of its reasons—

(a) for giving the direction, and

(b) for relying on section 298(7).

(5) The direction is enforceable, on the application of the Bank, by an injunction or, in Scotland, by an order for specific performance under section 45 of the Court of Session Act 1988.

(6) The Bank may revoke a direction given under this section.]

NOTES

Inserted by the Financial Services Act 2012, s 31, as from 1 April 2013.

Words in square brackets substituted, and words omitted repealed, by the Financial Services and Markets Act 2000 (Over the Counter Derivatives, Central Counterparties and Trade Repositories) Regulations 2013, SI 2013/504, reg 3(1), (11), as from 1 April 2013.

[7.557]
297 Revoking recognition
(1) A recognition order [in respect of a recognised investment exchange or in respect of a recognised clearing house which is not a recognised central counterparty] may be revoked by an order made by [the appropriate regulator] at the request, or with the consent, of the recognised body concerned.
[(1A) A central counterparty recognition order may be revoked by an order made by the Bank of England in accordance with Article 20 of the EMIR regulation.]
[(1B) A CSD recognition order may be revoked by an order made by the Bank of England in accordance with Article 20 of the CSD regulation.]
(2) If it appears to [the appropriate regulator] that a recognised body [which is not a recognised central counterparty] [or a recognised CSD]—
(a) is failing, or has failed, to satisfy the recognition requirements, or
(b) is failing, or has failed, to comply with any other obligation imposed on it by or under this Act,
it may make an order revoking the recognition order for that body even though the body does not wish the order to be made.
[(2A) If it appears to [the appropriate regulator] that a recognised body [which is not a recognised central counterparty] [or a recognised CSD] . . . —
(a) has not carried on the business of an investment exchange [or (as the case may be) of a clearing house] during the period of twelve months beginning with the day on which the recognition order took effect in relation to it,
(b) has not carried on the business of an investment exchange [or (as the case may be) of a clearing house] at any time during the period of six months ending with the relevant day, or
(c) has failed, or is likely to fail, to comply with any obligation imposed on it by [any qualifying provision] [specified (or of a description specified) [for the purposes of this subsection] in an order made by the Treasury],
it may make an order revoking the recognition order for that body even though the body does not wish the order to be made.
(2B) The "relevant day", for the purposes of paragraph (b) of subsection (2A), is the day on which the power to make an order under that subsection is exercised.
(2C) Subsection (2A) does not apply to an overseas investment exchange [or overseas clearing house].]
[(2D) If it appears to the Bank of England that a recognised central counterparty [or a recognised CSD] has failed, or is likely to fail, to comply with an obligation imposed on it by or under Article 4 or 15 of the SFT regulation it may make an order revoking the recognition order for that body even though the body does not wish the order to be made.]
(3) An order under this section ("a revocation order") must specify the date on which it is to take effect.
(4) In the case of a revocation order made under subsection (2) [or (2A)], the specified date must not be earlier than the end of the period of three months beginning with the day on which the order is made.
(5) A revocation order may contain such transitional provisions as [the appropriate regulator] thinks necessary or expedient.
[(6) . . .]

NOTES
Sub-s (1): words in first pair of square brackets substituted by the Financial Services and Markets Act 2000 (Over the Counter Derivatives, Central Counterparties and Trade Repositories) Regulations 2013, SI 2013/504, reg 3(1), (12)(a), as from 1 April 2013. Words in second pair of square brackets substituted by the Financial Services Act 2012, s 35, Sch 8, paras 1, 15(1), (2), as 1 April 2013.
Sub-s (1A): inserted by SI 2013/504, reg 3(1), (12)(b), as from 1 April 2013.
Sub-s (1B): inserted by the Central Securities Depositories Regulations 2017, SI 2017/1064, reg 2(1), (23)(a), as from 28 November 2017.
Sub-s (2): words in first pair of square brackets substituted by the Financial Services Act 2012, s 35, Sch 8, paras 1, 15(1), (2), as 1 April 2013. Words in second pair of square brackets substituted by SI 2013/504, reg 3(1), (12)(c), as from 1 April 2013. Words in third pair of square brackets inserted by SI 2017/1064, reg 2(1), (23)(b), as from 28 November 2017.
Sub-s (2A): inserted, together with sub-ss (2B), (2C), by the Financial Services and Markets Act 2000 (Markets in Financial Instruments) Regulations 2007, SI 2007/126, reg 3(2), Sch 2, paras 1, 8(a), as from 1 April 2007 (certain purposes), and as from 1 November 2007 (otherwise). This subsection has been subsequently amended as follows—
Words "the appropriate regulator" in square brackets substituted by the Financial Services Act 2012, s 35, Sch 8, paras 1, 15(1), (3), as from 24 January 2013 (for the purposes of making orders), and as from 1 April 2013 (otherwise).
Words "which is not a recognised central counterparty" in square brackets inserted by SI 2013/504, reg 3(1), (12)(d), as from 1 April 2013.
Words "or a recognised CSD" in square brackets inserted by SI 2017/1064, reg 2(1), (23)(b), as from 28 November 2017.
Words omitted repealed by the Financial Services Act 2012, s 35, Sch 8, paras 1, 15(1), (3), as from 24 January 2013 (for the purposes of making orders), and as from 1 April 2013 (otherwise).
Words "or (as the case may be) of a clearing house" in square brackets in paras (a), (b) inserted by the Financial Services Act 2012, s 35, Sch 8, paras 1, 15(1), (3), as from 24 January 2013 (for the purposes of making orders), and as from 1 April 2013 (otherwise).
Words "any qualifying provision" in square brackets in para (c) substituted by the Investment Exchanges, Clearing Houses and Central Securities Depositories (Amendment) (EU Exit) Regulations 2019, SI 2019/662, regs 4, 5(14)(a), as from IP completion day (as defined in the European Union (Withdrawal Agreement) Act 2020, s 39).
Words in square brackets in para (c) beginning with the words "specified (or of a description specified)" substituted by virtue of the Financial Services Act 2012, s 35, Sch 8, paras 1, 15(1), (3), as from 24 January 2013 (for the purposes of making orders), and as from 1 April 2013 (otherwise).
Words "for the purposes of this subsection" in square brackets in para (c) inserted by SI 2019/662, regs 4, 5(14)(a), as from IP completion day (as defined in the European Union (Withdrawal Agreement) Act 2020, s 39).
Sub-s (2B): inserted as noted above.

Sub-s (2C): inserted as noted above. Words in square brackets inserted by the Financial Services Act 2012, s 35, Sch 8, paras 1, 15(1), (4), as from 1 April 2013.

Sub-s (2D): inserted by the Financial Services and Markets Act 2000 (Transparency of Securities Financing Transactions and of Reuse) Regulations 2016, SI 2016/715, reg 29, Sch 1, para 1(1), (2), as from 13 July 2016. Words in square brackets inserted by SI 2017/1064, reg 2(1), (23)(b), as from 28 November 2017.

Sub-s (4): words in square brackets inserted by SI 2007/126, reg 3(2), Sch 2, paras 1, 8(b), as from 1 April 2007 (certain purposes), and as from 1 November 2007 (otherwise).

Sub-s (5): words in square brackets substituted by the Financial Services Act 2012, s 35, Sch 8, paras 1, 15(1), (5), as 1 April 2013.

Sub-s (6): originally added by the Financial Services (Omnibus 1 Directive) Regulations 2012, SI 2012/916, reg 2(1), (10), as from 16 April 2012. Subsequently repealed by SI 2019/662, regs 4, 5(14)(b), as from IP completion day (as defined in the European Union (Withdrawal Agreement) Act 2020, s 39).

Application: see the note to s 296 at **[7.555]**.

Orders and Regulations: the Financial Services and Markets Act 2000 (Qualifying Provisions) Order 2013, SI 2013/419; the Financial Services and Markets Act 2000 (Transparency of Securities Financing Transactions and of Reuse) Regulations 2016, SI 2016/715.

[7.558]

298 Directions and revocation: procedure

(1) Before giving a direction under section 296 [or 296A], or making a revocation order under section [297(1B), (2)][, (2A) or (2D)], [the appropriate regulator] must—

(a) give written notice of its intention to do so to the recognised body concerned;

(b), (c) . . .

(2) A notice under subsection (1) must—

(a) state why [the appropriate regulator] intends to give the direction or make the order; and

(b) draw attention to the right to make representations conferred by subsection (3).

(3) Before the end of the period for making representations—

(a) the recognised body,

(b), (c) . . .

may make representations to [the appropriate regulator].

[(4) The period for making representations is such period as is specified in the notice (which may, in any particular case, be extended by the appropriate regulator).]

(5) In deciding whether to—

(a) give a direction, or

(b) make a revocation order,

[the appropriate regulator] must have regard to any representations made in accordance with subsection (3).

(6) When [the appropriate regulator] has decided whether to give a direction under section 296 [or 296A] or to make the proposed revocation order, it must—

(a) give the recognised body written notice of its decision[; and

(aa) in the case of a direction under section 296 given to a recognised CSD . . . or a revocation order under section 297(1B), give the recognised CSD . . . reasons for its decision].

(b) . . .

[(6A) If the appropriate regulator—

(a) gives a direction under section 296 to a recognised body because it has failed, or is likely to fail, to comply with an obligation imposed on it by or under Article 4 or 15 of the SFT regulation;

[(aa) gives any other direction under section 296 to a recognised CSD;

(ab) . . .

(ac) makes a revocation order under section 297(1B);]

(b) makes a revocation order under section 297(2A)(c) because a recognised body has failed, or is likely to fail, to comply with an obligation imposed on it by or under Article 4 or 15 of the SFT regulation; or

(c) makes a revocation order under section 297(2D),

the body concerned may refer the matter to the Tribunal.]

(7) If [the appropriate regulator] [reasonably considers it necessary] to do so, it may give a direction under section 296 [or 296A]—

(a) without following the procedure set out in this section; or

(b) if [the appropriate regulator] has begun to follow that procedure, regardless of whether the period for making representations has expired.

[(7A) Subsection (7) does not apply in relation to a direction given to a recognised CSD . . . under section 296.

(7B) . . .]

(8) If [the appropriate regulator] has, in relation to a particular matter, followed the procedure set out in subsections (1) to (5), it need not follow it again if, in relation to that matter, it decides to take action other than that specified in its notice under subsection (1).

[(9) . . .]

NOTES

Sub-s (1) is amended as follows:

Words in first pair of square brackets inserted, and words in final pair of square brackets substituted, by the Financial Services Act 2012, s 35, Sch 8, paras 1, 16(a), (b), as from 1 April 2013.

Figure in second pair of square brackets substituted by the Central Securities Depositories Regulations 2017, SI 2017/1064, reg 2(1), (24)(a), as from 28 November 2017.

Words in third pair of square brackets substituted by the Financial Services and Markets Act 2000 (Transparency of Securities Financing Transactions and of Reuse) Regulations 2016, SI 2016/715, reg 29, Sch 1, para 1(1), (3)(a), as from 13 July 2016.

Paras (b), (c) repealed by the Financial Services Act 2012, s 32(1), (2), as from 1 April 2013.

Sub-ss (2), (5), (8): words in square brackets substituted by the Financial Services Act 2012, s 35, Sch 8, paras 1, 16(b), as from 1 April 2013.

Sub-s (3): paras (b), (c) repealed by the Financial Services Act 2012, s 32(1), (3), as from 1 April 2013. Words in square brackets substituted by s 35 of, and Sch 8, paras 1, 16(b) to, the 2012 Act, as from 1 April 2013.

Sub-s (4): substituted by the Financial Services Act 2012, s 32(1), (4), as from 1 April 2013.

Sub-s (6): words in first pair of square brackets substituted, and words in second pair of square brackets inserted, by the Financial Services Act 2012, s 35, Sch 8, paras 1, 16(a), (b), as from 1 April 2013. Para (aa) and the preceding word inserted by SI 2017/1064, reg 2(1), (24)(b), as from 28 November 2017. The words omitted from para (aa) were repealed by the Investment Exchanges, Clearing Houses and Central Securities Depositories (Amendment) (EU Exit) Regulations 2019, SI 2019/662, regs 4, 5(15)(a), as from IP completion day (as defined in the European Union (Withdrawal Agreement) Act 2020, s 39). Para (b) was repealed by s 32(1), (5) of the 2012 Act, as from 1 April 2013.

Sub-s (6A): inserted by SI 2016/715, reg 29, Sch 1, para 1(1), (3)(b), as from 13 July 2016. Paras (aa)–(ac) inserted by SI 2017/1064, reg 2(1), (24)(c), as from 28 November 2017. Para (ab) subsequently repealed by SI 2019/662, regs 4, 5(15)(b), as from IP completion day (as defined in the European Union (Withdrawal Agreement) Act 2020, s 39).

Sub-s (7): words in first and final pairs of square brackets substituted, and words in third pair of square brackets inserted, by the Financial Services Act 2012, s 35, Sch 8, paras 1, 16(a), (b), as from 1 April 2013. Words in second pair of square brackets substituted by s 32(1), (6) of the 2012 Act, as from 1 April 2013.

Sub-ss (7A), (7B), (9): originally inserted and added respectively by SI 2017/1064, reg 2(1), (24)(d), (e), as from 28 November 2017. The words omitted from sub-s (7A) were repealed, and sub-ss (7B) and (9) were repealed, by SI 2019/662, regs 4, 5(15)(c)–(e), as from IP completion day (as defined in the European Union (Withdrawal Agreement) Act 2020, s 39).

[7.559]

299 Complaints about recognised bodies

(1) The [appropriate regulator] must make arrangements for the investigation of any relevant complaint about a recognised body.

(2) "Relevant complaint" means a complaint which the [appropriate regulator] considers is relevant to the question of whether the body concerned should remain a recognised body.

NOTES

Words in square brackets substituted by the Financial Services Act 2012, s 35, Sch 8, paras 1, 17, as from 1 April 2013.

Note: this section is modified in its application to a recognised investment exchange that is also a recognised auction platform so that the reference in sub-s (2) to whether the body concerned should remain a recognised body is to be read as including whether it should remain a recognised auction platform; see the Recognised Auction Platforms Regulations 2011, SI 2011/2699, reg 7, Sch 2, para 6.

[7.560]

300 Extension of functions of Tribunal

(1) If the Treasury are satisfied that the condition mentioned in subsection (2) is satisfied, they may by order confer functions on the Tribunal with respect to disciplinary proceedings—

(a) of one or more investment exchanges in relation to which a recognition order under section 290 is in force or of such investment exchanges generally, . . .

(b) of one or more clearing houses in relation to which a recognition order under that section is in force or of such clearing houses generally[, or

(c) of one or more central securities depositories in relation to which a recognition order under that section is in force or of such central securities depositories generally].

(2) The condition is that it is desirable to exercise the power conferred under subsection (1) with a view to ensuring that—

(a) decisions taken in disciplinary proceedings with respect to which functions are to be conferred on the Tribunal are consistent with—

(i) decisions of the Tribunal in cases arising under Part VIII; and

(ii) decisions taken in other disciplinary proceedings with respect to which the Tribunal has functions as a result of an order under this section; or

(b) the disciplinary proceedings are in accordance with the Convention rights.

(3) An order under this section may modify or exclude any provision made by or under this Act with respect to proceedings before the Tribunal.

(4) "Disciplinary proceedings" means proceedings under the rules of an investment exchange[, clearing house or central securities depository] in relation to [a contravention of Article 14 (prohibition of insider dealing and of unlawful disclosure of inside information) or Article 15 (prohibition of market manipulation) of the market abuse regulation by a person subject to the rules].

(5) "The Convention rights" has the meaning given in section 1 of the Human Rights Act 1998.

NOTES

Sub-s (1): word omitted from para (a) repealed, and para (c) (and the preceding word) inserted, by the Central Securities Depositories Regulations 2017, SI 2017/1064, reg 2(1), (25)(a), as from 28 November 2017.

Sub-s (4): words in first pair of square brackets substituted by SI 2017/1064, reg 2(1), (25)(b), as from 28 November 2017. Words in second pair of square brackets substituted by the Financial Services and Markets Act 2000 (Market Abuse) Regulations 2016, SI 2016/680, reg 10(1), (13), as from 3 July 2016.

Note: this section is modified in its application to a recognised investment exchange that is also a recognised auction platform so that (a) the reference in sub-s (1)(a) to a recognition order under s 290 is to be read as including a reference to a recognition order under reg 2 of the Recognised Auction Platforms Regulations 2011, and (b) the references in sub-s (4) to the rules of an investment exchange is to be read as including a reference to rules made in relation to an auction platform; see the Recognised Auction Platforms Regulations 2011, SI 2011/2699, reg 7, Sch 2, para 7.

[Power to disallow excessive regulatory provision

[7.561]

300A Power of [appropriate regulator] to disallow excessive regulatory provision

(1) This section applies where a recognised body proposes to make any regulatory provision in connection [with—

(a) its business as an investment exchange,

(b) the provision by it of clearing services, or
(c) the provision by it of services falling within section 285(2)(b) or (3)(b).]

(2) If it appears to the [appropriate regulator]—
(a) that the proposed provision will impose a requirement on persons affected (directly or indirectly) by it, and
(b) that the requirement is excessive,

the [appropriate regulator] may direct that the proposed provision must not be made.

(3) A requirement is excessive if—
(a) it is not required under . . . any enactment or rule of law in the United Kingdom, and
(b) either—
(i) it is not justified as pursuing a reasonable regulatory objective, or
(ii) it is disproportionate to the end to be achieved.

(4) In considering whether a requirement is excessive the [appropriate regulator] must have regard to all the relevant circumstances, including—
(a) the effect of existing legal and other requirements,
(b) the global character of financial services and markets and the international mobility of activity,
(c) the desirability of facilitating innovation, and
(d) the impact of the proposed provision on market confidence.

(5) In this section "requirement" includes any obligation or burden.

(6) Any provision made in contravention of a direction under this section is of no effect.]

NOTES

Inserted, together with the preceding heading, by the Investment Exchanges and Clearing Houses Act 2006, s 1, as from 20 December 2006. Note that by virtue of s 5(3) of the 2006 Act, ss 300A–300E (a) do not apply to regulatory provision made before that day, and (b) apply to regulatory provision proposed on or after that day, whenever originally proposed.

All words in square brackets were substituted by the Financial Services Act 2012, s 35, Sch 8, paras 1, 18, as from 1 April 2013.

The words omitted from sub-s (3)(a) were repealed by the Investment Exchanges, Clearing Houses and Central Securities Depositories (Amendment) (EU Exit) Regulations 2019, SI 2019/662, regs 4, 5(16), as from IP completion day (as defined in the European Union (Withdrawal Agreement) Act 2020, s 39).

Note: this section does not apply to a recognised investment exchange in its capacity as a recognised auction platform; see the Recognised Auction Platforms Regulations 2011, SI 2011/2699, reg 7, Sch 2, para 9.

[7.562]

[300B Duty to notify proposal to make regulatory provision

(1) A recognised body that proposes to make any regulatory provision must give written notice of the proposal to the [appropriate regulator] without delay.

(2) The [appropriate regulator] may by rules under section 293 (notification requirements)—
(a) specify descriptions of regulatory provision in relation to which, or circumstances in which, the duty in subsection (1) above does not apply, or
(b) provide that the duty applies only to specified descriptions of regulatory provision or in specified circumstances.

(3) The [appropriate regulator] may also by rules under that section—
(a) make provision as to the form and contents of the notice required, and
(b) require the body to provide such information relating to the proposal as may be specified in the rules or as the [appropriate regulator] may reasonably require.]

NOTES

Inserted, together with ss 300C–300E, by the Investment Exchanges and Clearing Houses Act 2006, s 2, as from 20 December 2006. Note that by virtue of s 5(3) of the 2006 Act, ss 300A–300E (a) do not apply to regulatory provision made before that day, and (b) apply to regulatory provision proposed on or after that day, whenever originally proposed.

Words in square brackets substituted by the Financial Services Act 2012, s 35, Sch 8, paras 1, 19, as from 24 January 2013 (for the purpose of making rules), and as from 1 April 2013 (otherwise).

Note: this section does not apply to a recognised investment exchange in its capacity as a recognised auction platform; see the Recognised Auction Platforms Regulations 2011, SI 2011/2699, reg 7, Sch 2, para 9.

[7.563]

[300C Restriction on making provision before [appropriate regulator] decides whether to act

(1) Where notice of a proposal to make regulatory provision is required to be given to the [appropriate regulator] under section 300B, the provision must not be made—
(a) before that notice is given, or
(b) subject to the following provisions of this section, before the end of the initial period.

(2) The initial period is—
(a) the period of 30 days beginning with the day on which the [appropriate regulator] receives notice of the proposal, or
(b) if any consultation period announced by the body in relation to the proposal ends after that 30-day period, the end of the consultation period.

(3) If before the end of the initial period the [appropriate regulator] notifies the body that it is calling in the proposal, the provisions of section 300D (consideration by [appropriate regulator] whether to disallow proposed provision) apply as to when the provision may be made.

(4) If—
(a) before the end of the initial period the [appropriate regulator] notifies the body that it is not calling in the proposal, or
(b) the initial period ends without the [appropriate regulator] having notified the body that it is calling in the proposal,

the body may then make the proposed provision.

(5) Any provision made in contravention of this section is of no effect.]

NOTES

Inserted as noted to s 300B at **[7.562]**.

Words in square brackets substituted by the Financial Services Act 2012, s 35, Sch 8, paras 1, 20, as from 1 April 2013.

Note: this section does not apply to a recognised investment exchange in its capacity as a recognised auction platform; see the Recognised Auction Platforms Regulations 2011, SI 2011/2699, reg 7, Sch 2, para 9.

[7.564]

[300D Consideration by [appropriate regulator] whether to disallow proposed provision

(1) This section applies where the [appropriate regulator] notifies a recognised body that it is calling in a proposal to make regulatory provision.

(2) The [appropriate regulator] must publish a notice—

(a) giving details of the proposed provision,

(b) stating that it has called in the proposal in order to consider whether to disallow it, and

(c) specifying a period during which representations with respect to that question may be made to it.

(3) The [appropriate regulator] may extend the period for making representations.

(4) The [appropriate regulator] must notify the body of its decision whether to disallow the provision not later than 30 days after the end of the period for making representations, and must publish the decision and the reasons for it.

(5) The body must not make the provision unless and until—

(a) the [appropriate regulator] notifies it of its decision not to disallow it, or

(b) the 30-day period specified in subsection (4) ends without the [appropriate regulator] having notified any decision.

(6) If [the appropriate regulator] notifies the body of its decision to disallow the provision and that decision is questioned in legal proceedings—

(a) the body must not make the provision until those proceedings, and any proceedings on appeal, are finally determined,

(b) if [the appropriate regulator's] decision is quashed and the matter is remitted to it for reconsideration, the court may give directions as to the period within which [the regulator concerned] is to complete its reconsideration, and

(c) the body must not make the provision until—

(i) [the appropriate regulator] notifies it of its decision on reconsideration not to disallow the provision, or

(ii) the period specified by the court ends without [the appropriate regulator] having notified any decision.

(7) Any provision made in contravention of subsection (5) or (6) is of no effect.]

NOTES

Inserted as noted to s 300B at **[7.562]**.

Words in square brackets substituted by the Financial Services Act 2012, s 35, Sch 8, paras 1, 21, as from 1 April 2013.

Note: this section does not apply to a recognised investment exchange in its capacity as a recognised auction platform; see the Recognised Auction Platforms Regulations 2011, SI 2011/2699, reg 7, Sch 2, para 9.

[7.565]

[300E Power to disallow excessive regulatory provision: supplementary

(1) In sections 300A to 300D—

(a) "regulatory provision" means any rule, guidance, arrangements, policy or practice, and

(b) references to making provision shall be read accordingly as including, as the case may require, issuing guidance, entering into arrangements or adopting a policy or practice.

(2) For the purposes of those sections a variation of a proposal is treated as a new proposal.

(3) Those sections do not apply to an overseas investment exchange[, overseas clearing house[, recognised central counterparty or recognised CSD]].]

NOTES

Inserted as noted to s 300B at **[7.562]**.

Sub-s (3): words in first (outer) pair of square brackets substituted by the Financial Services and Markets Act 2000 (Over the Counter Derivatives, Central Counterparties and Trade Repositories) Regulations 2013, SI 2013/504, reg 3(1), (13), as from 1 April 2013. Words in second (inner) pair of square brackets substituted by the Central Securities Depositories Regulations 2017, SI 2017/1064, reg 2(1), (26), as from 28 November 2017.

Note: this section does not apply to a recognised investment exchange in its capacity as a recognised auction platform; see the Recognised Auction Platforms Regulations 2011, SI 2011/2699, reg 7, Sch 2, para 9.

Other matters

[7.566]

301 Supervision of certain contracts

(1) The Secretary of State and the Treasury, acting jointly, may by regulations provide for—

(a) Part VII of the Companies Act 1989 (financial markets and insolvency), and

(b) Part V of the Companies (No 2) (Northern Ireland) Order 1990,

to apply to relevant contracts as it applies to contracts connected with a recognised body.

(2) "Relevant contracts" means contracts of a prescribed description in relation to which settlement arrangements are provided by a person for the time being included in a list ("the list") maintained by [the Bank of England] for the purposes of this section.

(3) Regulations may be made under this section only if the Secretary of State and the Treasury are satisfied, having regard to the extent to which the relevant contracts concerned are contracts of a kind dealt in by persons supervised by [the FCA or the Bank of England], that it is appropriate for the arrangements mentioned in subsection (2) to be supervised by [the Bank].

(4) The approval of the Treasury is required for—
   (a) the conditions set by the [Bank of England] for admission to the list; and
   (b) the arrangements for admission to, and removal from, the list.

(5) If the Treasury withdraw an approval given by them under subsection (4), all regulations made under this section and then in force are to be treated as suspended.

(6) But if—
   (a) the [Bank of England] changes the conditions or arrangements (or both), and
   (b) the Treasury give a fresh approval under subsection (4),

the suspension of the regulations ends on such date as the Treasury may, in giving the fresh approval, specify.

(7) The [Bank of England] must—
   (a) publish the list as for the time being in force; and
   (b) provide a certified copy of it to any person who wishes to refer to it in legal proceedings.

(8) A certified copy of the list is evidence (or in Scotland sufficient evidence) of the contents of the list.

(9) A copy of the list which purports to be certified by or on behalf of the [Bank of England] is to be taken to have been duly certified unless the contrary is shown.

(10) Regulations under this section may, in relation to a person included in the list—
   (a) apply (with such exceptions, additions and modifications as appear to the Secretary of State and the Treasury to be necessary or expedient) such provisions of, or made under, this Act as they consider appropriate;
   (b) provide for the provisions of Part VII of the Companies Act 1989 and Part V of the Companies (No 2) (Northern Ireland) Order 1990 to apply (with such exceptions, additions or modifications as appear to the Secretary of State and the Treasury to be necessary or expedient).

NOTES

Words in square brackets substituted by the Financial Services Act 2012, s 35, Sch 8, paras 1, 22, as from 1 April 2013.

As to the extension of the power under this section to apply the Companies Act 1989, Pt VII, see s 181 thereof. As to the Secretary of State's power to make further provision by Regulations for the purposes of this section, see s 185 thereof.

[CHAPTER 1A CONTROL OVER RECOGNISED INVESTMENT EXCHANGE

Notices of acquisitions of control over recognised investment exchanges

[7.567]

301A Obligation to notify [the FCA]: acquisitions of control

(1) A person who decides to acquire or increase control over a recognised investment exchange must give [the FCA] notice in writing before making the acquisition.

(2) A person who acquires or increases control over a recognised investment exchange in circumstances where notice is not required under subsection (1) must give [the FCA] notice in writing before the end of 14 days beginning with—
   (a) the day the person acquired or increased the control; or
   (b) if later, the day on which the person first became aware that the control had been acquired or increased.

(3) For the purposes of calculations relating to this section, the holding of shares or voting power by a person ("A1") includes any shares or voting power held by another ("A2") if A1 and A2 are acting in concert.

(4) A notice given under this section is a "section 301A notice" and a person giving notice is a "section 301A notice-giver".

[(5) Nothing in this Chapter applies to an overseas investment exchange.]]

NOTES

The original Chapter 1A (ie, ss 301A–301G) was inserted by the Financial Services and Markets Act 2000 (Markets in Financial Instruments) Regulations 2007, SI 2007/126, reg 3(2), Sch 2, paras 1, 10, as from 1 April 2007 (certain purposes), and as from 1 November 2007 (otherwise). It was subsequently substituted (by new ss 301A–301M) by the Financial Services and Markets Act 2000 (Controllers) Regulations 2009, SI 2009/534, reg 5, Sch 2, as from 21 March 2009.

Sub-s (5) was added by the Financial Services and Markets Act 2000 (Over the Counter Derivatives, Central Counterparties and Trade Repositories) (No 2) Regulations 2013, SI 2013/1908, reg 5, as from 26 August 2013.

All other words in square brackets were substituted by the Financial Services Act 2012, s 35, Sch 8, paras 1, 23, as from 1 April 2013.

[7.568]

[301B Requirements for section 301A notices

(1) A section 301A notice must be in such form, include such information and be accompanied by such documents as the [FCA] may reasonably require.

(2) The [FCA] must publish a list of its requirements as to the form, information and accompanying documents for a section 301A notice.

(3) The [FCA] may impose different requirements for different cases and may vary or waive requirements in particular cases.]

NOTES

Chapter 1A was inserted and subsequently substituted as noted to s 301A at **[7.567]**.

Words in square brackets substituted by the Financial Services Act 2012, s 35, Sch 8, paras 1, 24, as from 1 April 2013.

[7.569]

[301C Acknowledgment of receipt

(1) The [FCA] must acknowledge receipt of a section 301A notice in writing before the end of the second working day following receipt.

(2) If the [FCA] receives an incomplete section 301A notice it must inform the section 301A notice-giver as soon as reasonably practicable.]

NOTES

Chapter 1A was inserted and subsequently substituted as noted to s 301A at **[7.567]**.

Words in square brackets substituted by the Financial Services Act 2012, s 35, Sch 8, paras 1, 25, as from 1 April 2013.

[Acquiring and increasing control

[7.570]

301D Acquiring and increasing control

(1) For the purposes of this Chapter, a person ("A") acquires control over a recognised investment exchange ("B") if any of the cases in subsection (2) begin to apply.

(2) The cases are where A holds—

- (a) 20% or more of the shares in B or in a parent undertaking of B ("P");
- (b) 20% or more of the voting power in B or P; or
- (c) shares or voting power in B or P as a result of which A is able to exercise significant influence over the management of B.

(3) For the purposes of this Chapter, a person ("A") increases control over a recognised investment exchange ("B") whenever—

- (a) the percentage of shares which A holds in B or in a parent undertaking of B ("P") increases from less than 50% to 50% or more;
- (b) the percentage of voting power A holds in B or P increases from less than 50% to 50% or more; or
- (c) A becomes a parent undertaking of B.]

NOTES

Chapter 1A was inserted and subsequently substituted as noted to s 301A at **[7.567]**.

[7.571]

[301E Disregarded holdings

(1) For the purpose of section 301D, shares and voting power that a person holds in a recognised investment exchange ("B") or in a parent undertaking of B ("P") are disregarded in the following circumstances.

(2) Shares held only for the purposes of clearing and settling within a short settlement cycle are disregarded.

(3) Shares held by a custodian or its nominee in a custodian capacity are disregarded, provided that the custodian or nominee is only able to exercise voting power represented by the shares in accordance with instructions given in writing.

(4) Shares representing no more than 5% of the total voting power in B or P held by an investment firm are disregarded, provided that it—

- (a) holds the shares in the capacity of a market maker (as defined [Article 2(1)(6) of the markets in financial instruments regulation];
- [(b) has a Part 4A permission to carry on a regulated activity which is any of the investment services or activities; and]
- (c) neither intervenes in the management of B or P nor exerts any influence on B or P to buy the shares or back the share price.

(5) Shares held by a [qualifying credit institution] or investment firm in its trading book are disregarded, provided that—

- (a) the shares represent no more than 5% of the total voting power in B or P; and
- (b) . . . the voting power is not exercised nor otherwise used to intervene in the management of B or P.

(6) Shares held by a [qualifying credit institution] or an investment firm are disregarded, provided that—

- (a) the shares are held as a result of performing the investment services and activities of—
  - (i) underwriting a share issue; or
  - (ii) placing shares on a firm commitment basis . . . ; and
- (b) the [qualifying credit institution] or investment firm—
  - (i) does not exercise voting power represented by the shares or otherwise intervene in the management of the issuer; and
  - (ii) retains the holding for a period of less than one year.

(7) Where a management company (as defined in [section 237(2)]) and its parent undertaking both hold shares or voting power, each may disregard holdings of the other, provided that each exercises its voting power independently of the other.

(8) But subsection (7) does not apply if the management company—

- [(a) manages holdings for its parent undertaking or a controlled undertaking of the parent undertaking;]
- (b) has no discretion as to the exercise of the voting power attached to such holdings; and
- (c) may only exercise the voting power in relation to such holdings under direct or indirect instruction from—
  - (i) the parent undertaking; or
  - [(ii) a controlled undertaking of the parent undertaking].

(9) Where an investment firm and its parent undertaking both hold shares or voting power, the parent undertaking may disregard holdings managed by the investment firm on a client by client basis and the investment firm may disregard holdings of the parent undertaking, provided that the investment firm—

- (a) has permission to provide portfolio management;
- (b) exercises its voting power independently from the parent undertaking; and
- (c) may only exercise the voting power under instructions given in writing, or has appropriate mechanisms in place for ensuring that individual portfolio management services are conducted independently of any other services.

[(9A) Shares acquired for stabilisation purposes in accordance with [the market abuse regulation and Commission Delegated Regulation (EU) No 1052/2016 of 8 March 2016 supplementing Regulation (EU) No 596/2014 of the European Parliament and the Council with regard to the regulatory technical standards for conditions applicable to buy-back programmes and stabilisation measures] are disregarded, provided that the voting power attached to those shares is not exercised or otherwise used to intervene in the management of B or P.]

[(10) For the purposes of this section, an undertaking is a controlled undertaking of the parent undertaking if it is controlled by the parent undertaking; and for this purpose the question of whether one undertaking controls another is to be determined in accordance with section 89J(4) and (5).]]

NOTES

Chapter 1A was inserted and subsequently substituted as noted to s 301A at **[7.567]**.

Sub-s (4): words in square brackets in para (a) substituted, and para (b) substituted, by the Investment Exchanges, Clearing Houses and Central Securities Depositories (Amendment) (EU Exit) Regulations 2019, SI 2019/662, regs 4, 6(1), (2)(a), as from IP completion day (as defined in the European Union (Withdrawal Agreement) Act 2020, s 39).

Sub-s (5): words in square brackets substituted by SI 2019/662, regs 4, 6(1), (2)(b), as from IP completion day (as defined in the European Union (Withdrawal Agreement) Act 2020, s 39). The words omitted from para (b) were repealed by the Transparency Regulations 2015, SI 2015/1755, reg 6(2), as from 1 November 2015 (for the purpose of making rules under Part 9A), and as from 31 May 2016 (otherwise).

Sub-s (6): words in square brackets substituted, and words omitted repealed, by SI 2019/662, regs 4, 6(1), (2)(c), as from IP completion day (as defined in the European Union (Withdrawal Agreement) Act 2020, s 39).

Sub-s (7): the words in square brackets were substituted by SI 2019/662, regs 4, 6(1), (2)(d), as from IP completion day (as defined in the European Union (Withdrawal Agreement) Act 2020, s 39).

Sub-s (8): paras (a) and (c)(ii) substituted by the Capital Requirements Regulations 2013, SI 2013/3115, reg 46(1), Sch 2, Pt 1, paras 1, 17, as from 1 January 2014.

Sub-s (9A): inserted by SI 2015/1755, reg 6(2), as from 1 November 2015 (for the purpose of making rules under Part 9A), and as from 31 May 2016 (otherwise). Words in square brackets substituted by SI 2019/662, reg 2(a), as from 26 March 2019.

Sub-s (10): added by SI 2013/3115, reg 46(1), Sch 2, Pt 1, paras 1, 17, as from 1 January 2014.

[Assessment procedure

[7.572]

301F Assessment: general

(1) Where the [FCA] receives a section 301A notice, it must—

(a) determine whether to approve the acquisition to which it relates; or

(b) propose to object to the acquisition.

(2) In making its determination the [FCA] must—

(a) consider the suitability of the section 301A notice-giver and the financial soundness of the acquisition in order to ensure the sound and prudent management of the recognised investment exchange in question; and

(b) have regard to the likely influence that the section 301A notice-giver will have on the recognised investment exchange.

(3) The [FCA] may only object to an acquisition if it is not satisfied that the approval requirement is met.

(4) The approval requirement is that the acquisition in question by the notice-giver does not pose a threat to the sound and prudent management of any financial market operated by the recognised investment exchange.]

NOTES

Chapter 1A was inserted and subsequently substituted as noted to s 301A at **[7.567]**.

Word "FCA" in square brackets (in each place that it occurs) substituted by the Financial Services Act 2012, s 35, Sch 8, paras 1, 26, as from 1 April 2013.

Note: this section is modified in its application to a recognised investment exchange that is also a recognised auction platform so that the reference in sub-s (4) to any financial market operated by the recognised investment exchange is to be read as including a reference to any auction platform operated by it; see the Recognised Auction Platforms Regulations 2011, SI 2011/2699, reg 7, Sch 2, para 8.

[7.573]

[301G Assessment: Procedure

(1) The [FCA] must act under section 301F within a period three months from the date the [FCA] receives the completed section 301A notice ("the assessment period").

(2) The [FCA] must inform the section 301A notice-giver in writing of—

(a) the duration of the assessment period; and

(b) its expiry date.

(3) The [FCA] must, within two working days of acting under section 301F (and in any event no later than the expiry date of the assessment period)—

(a) notify the section 301A notice-giver that it has determined to approve the acquisition; or

(b) in the case of a proposed objection to an acquisition, give a warning notice.

(4) The [FCA] is treated as having approved the acquisition if, at the expiry of the assessment period, it has neither—

(a) given notice under subsection (3); nor

(b) informed the section 301A notice-giver that the notice is incomplete.

(5) If the [FCA] decides to object to an acquisition it must give the section 301A notice-giver a decision notice.

(6) Following receipt of a decision notice under this section, the section 301A notice-giver may refer [the FCA's] decision to the Tribunal.]

NOTES

Chapter 1A was inserted and subsequently substituted as noted to s 301A at **[7.567]**.

Words in square brackets substituted by the Financial Services Act 2012, s 35, Sch 8, paras 1, 27, as from 1 April 2013.

[7.574]

[301H Duration of approval

(1) Approval of an acquisition is effective for such period as [the FCA] may specify in writing.

(2) Where [the FCA] has specified a period under subsection (1), it may extend the period.

(3) Where [the FCA] has not specified a period, the approval is effective for one year beginning with the date—

(a) of the notice given under section 301G(3)(a);

(b) on which [the FCA] is treated as having given approval under section 301G(5); or

(c) of a decision on a reference to the Tribunal which results in the person receiving approval.]

NOTES

Chapter 1A was inserted and subsequently substituted as noted to s 301A at **[7.567]**.
Words in square brackets substituted by the Financial Services Act 2012, s 35, Sch 8, paras 1, 28, as from 1 April 2013.

[Enforcement procedures

[7.575]

301I Objections by the [FCA]

(1) The [FCA] may object to a person's control over a recognised investment exchange in any of the circumstances specified in subsection (2).

(2) The circumstances are that the [FCA] reasonably believes that—

(a) the person acquired or increased control without giving notice under section 301A in circumstances where notice was required; and

(b) there are grounds for objecting to control on the basis of the approval requirement in section 301F(4).

(3) If the [FCA] proposes to object to a person's control over a recognised investment exchange, it must give that person a warning notice.

(4) If the [FCA] decides to object to a person's control over a UK authorised person, it must give that person a decision notice.

(5) A person to whom the [FCA] gives a decision notice under this section may refer the matter to the Tribunal.]

NOTES

Chapter 1A was inserted and subsequently substituted as noted to s 301A at **[7.567]**.
Words in square brackets substituted by the Financial Services Act 2012, s 35, Sch 8, paras 1, 29, as from 1 April 2013.

[7.576]

[301J Restriction notices

(1) The [FCA] may give notice in writing (a "restriction notice") to a person in the following circumstances.

(2) The circumstances are that—

(a) the person has control over a recognised investment exchange by virtue of holding shares or voting power; and

(b) in relation to the shares or voting power, the [FCA] has given the person a warning notice or a decision notice under section 301G or 301I or a final notice which confirms a decision notice given under section 301G or 301I.

(3) In a restriction notice, the [FCA] may direct that shares or voting power to which the notice relates are, until further notice, subject to one or more of the following restrictions—

(a) except by court order, an agreement to transfer or a transfer of any such shares or voting power or, in the case of unissued shares, any agreement to transfer or transfer of the right to be issued with them, is void;

(b) no voting power is to be exercisable;

(c) no further shares are to be issued in pursuance of any right of the holder of any such shares or voting power or in pursuance of any offer made to their holder;

(d) except in a liquidation, no payment is to be made of any sums due from the body corporate on any such shares, whether in respect of capital or otherwise.

(4) A restriction notice takes effect—

(a) immediately; or

(b) on such date as may be specified in the notice.

(5) A restriction notice does not extinguish rights which would be enjoyable but for the notice.

(6) A copy of the restriction notice must be served on—

(a) the recognised investment exchange in question; and

(b) in the case of shares or voting power held in a parent undertaking of a recognised investment exchange, the parent undertaking.

(7) A person to whom the [FCA] gives a restriction notice may refer the matter to the Tribunal.]

NOTES

Chapter 1A was inserted and subsequently substituted as noted to s 301A at **[7.567]**.
Words in square brackets substituted by the Financial Services Act 2012, s 35, Sch 8, paras 1, 30, as from 1 April 2013.

[7.577]

[301K Orders for sale of shares

(1) The court may, on the application of [the FCA], order the sale of shares or the disposition of voting power in the following circumstances.

(2) The circumstances are that—

(a) a person has control over a recognised investment exchange by virtue of holding the shares or voting power; and

(b) the acquisition or continued holding of the shares or voting power by that person is in contravention of a final notice which confirms a decision notice given under section 301G or section 301I.

(3) Where the court orders the sale of shares or disposition of voting power it may—

(a) if a restriction notice has been given in relation to the shares or voting power, order that the restrictions cease to apply; and

(b) make any further order.

(4) Where the court makes an order under this section, it must take into account the level of holding that the person would have been entitled to acquire, or to continue to hold, without contravening the final notice.

(5) If shares are sold or voting power disposed of in pursuance of an order under this section, any proceeds, less the costs of the sale or disposition, must be paid into court for the benefit of the persons beneficially interested in them; and any such person may apply to the court for payment of a whole or part of the proceeds.

(6) The jurisdiction conferred by this section may be exercised by the High Court and the Court of Session.]

NOTES

Chapter 1A was inserted and subsequently substituted as noted to s 301A at **[7.567]**.

Sub-s (1): words in square brackets substituted by the Financial Services Act 2012, s 35, Sch 8, paras 1, 31, as from 1 April 2013.

[Offences

[7.578]

301L Offences under this Chapter

(1) A person who fails to comply with an obligation to notify [the FCA] under section 301A(1) or (2) is guilty of an offence.

(2) A person who gives notice [the FCA] under section 301A(1) and makes the acquisition to which the notice relates before the expiry date of the assessment period is guilty of an offence unless [the FCA] has approved the acquisition.

(3) A person who makes an acquisition in contravention of a warning notice or a decision notice given under section 301G or a final notice which confirms a decision notice under that section is guilty of an offence.

(4) A person who makes an acquisition after [the FCA's] approval for the acquisition has ceased to be effective by virtue of section 301H is guilty of an offence.

(5) A person who provides information to [the FCA] which is false in a material particular is guilty of an offence.

(6) A person who breaches a direction contained in a restriction notice given under section 301J is guilty of an offence.

(7) A person guilty of an offence under subsection (1), (2) or (4) to (6) is liable—

(a) on summary conviction to a fine not exceeding the statutory maximum; or

(b) on conviction on indictment, to a fine.

(8) A person guilty of an offence under subsection (3) is liable—

(a) on summary conviction, to a fine not exceeding the statutory maximum; or

(b) on conviction on indictment, to imprisonment for a term not exceeding two years or a fine, or both.

(9) It is a defence for a person charged with an offence under subsection (1) in relation to section 301A(2) to show that the person had, at the time of the alleged offence, no knowledge of the act or circumstances by virtue of which the duty to notify [the FCA] arose.]

NOTES

Chapter 1A was inserted and subsequently substituted as noted to s 301A at **[7.567]**.

Words in square brackets substituted by the Financial Services Act 2012, s 35, Sch 8, paras 1, 32, as from 1 April 2013.

[Interpretation

[7.579]

301M Interpretation

(1) In this Chapter—

"acquisition" means the acquisition of control or of an increase in control over a recognised investment exchange;

. . .

"shares" and "voting power" have the same meaning as in section 422.

(2) For the purposes of this Chapter, a "working day" is a day other than—

(a) a Saturday or a Sunday; or

(b) a day which is a bank holiday in England and Wales under the Banking and Financial Dealings Act 1971.]

NOTES

Chapter 1A was inserted and subsequently substituted as noted to s 301A at **[7.567]**.

Sub-s (1): definition "credit institution" (omitted) repealed by the Investment Exchanges, Clearing Houses and Central Securities Depositories (Amendment) (EU Exit) Regulations 2019, SI 2019/662, regs 4, 6(3), as from IP completion day (as defined in the European Union (Withdrawal Agreement) Act 2020, s 39).

302–312, 312A–312D (*Ss 302–310 (Chapter II) and ss 311, 312 (Chapter III) were repealed by the Financial Services Act 2012, s 34, as from 1 April 2013. Ss 312A–312D (Chapter 3A Passport Rights) were originally inserted by the Financial Services and Markets Act 2000 (Markets in Financial Instruments) Regulations 2007, SI 2007/126, reg 3(2), Sch 2, paras 1, 15, as from 1 April 2007 (certain purposes), and as from 1 November 2007 (otherwise); and were subsequently repealed by the Investment Exchanges, Clearing Houses and Central Securities Depositories (Amendment) (EU Exit) Regulations 2019, SI 2019/662, regs 4, 7, as from IP completion day (as defined in the European Union (Withdrawal Agreement) Act 2020, s 39).*)

[CHAPTER 3B DISCIPLINARY MEASURES

[7.580]

312E Public censure

(1) If the appropriate regulator considers that a recognised body has contravened a relevant requirement imposed on the body, it may publish a statement to that effect.

[(1A) . . .]

(2) Where the FCA is the appropriate regulator, a requirement is a "relevant requirement" for the purposes of this Chapter if it is—

(a) a requirement that is imposed by or under any provision of this Part that relates to a recognised investment exchange,

(b) a requirement that is imposed under any other provision of this Act by the FCA that relates to a recognised investment exchange,

(c) a requirement that is imposed by a [qualifying provision] specified, or of a description specified, for the purposes of this subsection by the Treasury by order, or

(d) a requirement that is imposed by this Act and whose contravention constitutes an offence that the FCA has power to prosecute under this Act (see section 401).

(3) Where the Bank of England is the appropriate regulator, a requirement is a "relevant requirement" for the purposes of this Chapter if it is—

(a) a requirement that is imposed by or under any provision of this Part that relates to a recognised clearing house[, third country central counterparty or a recognised CSD],

(b) a requirement that is imposed under any other provision of this Act by the Bank,

(c) a requirement that is imposed by [or under] a [qualifying provision] specified, or of a description specified, for the purposes of this subsection by the Treasury by order, or

(d) a requirement that is imposed by this Act and whose contravention constitutes an offence that the Bank has power to prosecute under this Act (see section 401, as applied by paragraph 31 of Schedule 17A).]

NOTES

Chapter 3B (originally ss 312E, 312F, 312G–312K) was inserted by the Financial Services Act 2012, s 33, as from 24 January 2013 (for the purposes of making orders), and as from 1 April 2013 (otherwise).

Sub-s (1A): originally inserted by the Central Securities Depositories Regulations 2017, SI 2017/1064, reg 2(1), (27)(a), as from 28 November 2017. Subsequently repealed by the Investment Exchanges, Clearing Houses and Central Securities Depositories (Amendment) (EU Exit) Regulations 2019, SI 2019/662, regs 4, 8(1), (2)(a), as from IP completion day (as defined in the European Union (Withdrawal Agreement) Act 2020, s 39).

Sub-s (2): words in square brackets substituted by SI 2019/662, regs 4, 8(1), (2)(b), as from IP completion day (as defined in the European Union (Withdrawal Agreement) Act 2020, s 39) (for transitional provisions see SI 2019/710, reg 37 at **[12.110]**).

Sub-s (3) is amended as follows:

Words in square brackets in para (a) and words in second pair of square brackets in para (c) substituted by SI 2019/662, regs 4, 8(1), (2)(c), as from IP completion day (as defined in the European Union (Withdrawal Agreement) Act 2020, s 39) (for transitional provisions see SI 2019/710, reg 37 at **[12.110]**). Note that reg 8 of the 2019 Regulations was amended by the Over the Counter Derivatives, Central Counterparties and Trade Repositories (Amendment, etc, and Transitional Provision) (EU Exit) Regulations 2020, SI 2020/646, reg 11, as from 25 June 2020 (and the effect of the amendment has been incorporated in the text set out above).

Words in first pair of square brackets in para (c) inserted by SI 2017/1064, reg 2(1), (27)(b), as from 28 November 2017.

Orders and Regulations: the Financial Services and Markets Act 2000 (Qualifying Provisions) Order 2013, SI 2013/419; the Financial Services and Markets Act 2000 (Transparency of Securities Financing Transactions and of Reuse) Regulations 2016, SI 2016/715.

[7.581]

[312F Financial penalties

[(1)] If the appropriate regulator considers that a recognised body has contravened a relevant requirement imposed on the body, it may impose on the body a penalty, in respect of the contravention, of such amount as it considers appropriate.

[(2) . . .]]

NOTES

Inserted as noted to s 312E at **[7.580]**.

Sub-s (1) numbered as such, and sub-s (2) added, by the Central Securities Depositories Regulations 2017, SI 2017/1064, reg 2(1), (28), as from 28 November 2017.

Sub-s (2) was repealed by the Investment Exchanges, Clearing Houses and Central Securities Depositories (Amendment) (EU Exit) Regulations 2019, SI 2019/662, regs 4, 8(3), as from IP completion day (as defined in the European Union (Withdrawal Agreement) Act 2020, s 39).

[7.582]

[312FA Central securities depositories: further disciplinary measures

(1) If the Bank of England considers that a contravention by a recognised CSD of a relevant requirement occurred with the consent or connivance of, or was attributable to any neglect on the part of, a member of the management body or other person who effectively controls the business of the recognised CSD, the Bank of England may do one or both of the following—

(a) publish a statement to that effect;

(b) impose on that person a penalty, in respect of the contravention, of such amount as it considers appropriate.

(2) If the Bank of England considers that a member of the management body or other person who effectively controls the business of a recognised CSD is responsible for a contravention by the central securities depository of a relevant requirement, it may do one or more of the following—

(a) publish a statement to that effect;

(b) impose on that person a penalty, in respect of the contravention, of such amount as it considers appropriate;

(c) prohibit that person from holding an office or position involving responsibility for taking decisions about the management of the recognised CSD.

(3) A prohibition under subsection (2)(c) may apply—

(a) for a specified period,

(b) until further notice, or

(c) for repeated serious contraventions, permanently.

(4) The Bank of England may, on the application of the person subject to a prohibition under subsection (2)(c), vary or revoke the prohibition.

(5) . . .]

NOTES

Inserted by the Central Securities Depositories Regulations 2017, SI 2017/1064, reg 2(1), (29), as from 28 November 2017.

Sub-s (5): repealed by the Investment Exchanges, Clearing Houses and Central Securities Depositories (Amendment) (EU Exit) Regulations 2019, SI 2019/662, regs 4, 8(4), as from IP completion day (as defined in the European Union (Withdrawal Agreement) Act 2020, s 39).

[7.583]

[312G Proposal to take disciplinary measures

[(1) If the appropriate regulator proposes to impose a sanction—

(a) on a recognised body under section 312E or 312F, or

(b) on a person under section 312FA,

it must give the body or person (as the case may be) a warning notice.]

(2) A warning notice about a proposal to publish a statement must set out the terms of the statement.

(3) A warning notice about a proposal to impose a penalty must state the amount of the penalty.

[(4) A warning notice about a proposal to impose a prohibition must specify the extent of the prohibition.

(5) . . .]]

NOTES

Inserted as noted to s 312E at **[7.580]**.

Sub-s (1) substituted, and sub-ss (4), (5) added, by the Central Securities Depositories Regulations 2017, SI 2017/1064, reg 2(1), (30), as from 28 November 2017.

Sub-s (5) was subsequently repealed by the Investment Exchanges, Clearing Houses and Central Securities Depositories (Amendment) (EU Exit) Regulations 2019, SI 2019/662, regs 4, 8(5), as from IP completion day (as defined in the European Union (Withdrawal Agreement) Act 2020, s 39).

[7.584]

[312H Decision notice

[(1) If the appropriate regulator decides to impose a sanction—

(a) on a recognised body under section 312E or 312F, or

(b) on a person under section 312FA,

it must give the body or person (as the case may be) a decision notice.]

(2) In the case of a statement, the decision notice must set out the terms of the statement.

(3) In the case of a penalty, the decision notice must state the amount of the penalty.

[(3A) In the case of a prohibition, the decision notice must specify the extent of the prohibition.

(3B) The sanction which the appropriate regulator decides to impose may differ from that proposed in the warning notice.]

[(4) If the appropriate regulator decides to impose a sanction—

(a) on a recognised body under section 312E or 312F, or

(b) on a person under section 312FA,

the body or person (as the case may be) may refer the matter to the Tribunal.]

[(5) . . .]]

NOTES

Inserted as noted to s 312E at **[7.580]**.

Sub-ss (1), (4) substituted, and sub-ss (3A), (3B) and (5) inserted and added respectively, by the Central Securities Depositories Regulations 2017, SI 2017/1064, reg 2(1), (31), as from 28 November 2017.

Sub-s (5) was subsequently repealed by the Investment Exchanges, Clearing Houses and Central Securities Depositories (Amendment) (EU Exit) Regulations 2019, SI 2019/662, regs 4, 8(6), as from IP completion day (as defined in the European Union (Withdrawal Agreement) Act 2020, s 39).

[7.585]

[312I Publication

After an appropriate regulator publishes a statement under section 312E [or 312FA], it must send a copy of the statement to—

(a) the recognised body [. . . or person] concerned, and

(b) any person to whom a copy of the decision notice was given under section 393(4).]

NOTES

Inserted as noted to s 312E at **[7.580]**.

Words in square brackets inserted by the Central Securities Depositories Regulations 2017, SI 2017/1064, reg 2(1), (32), as from 28 November 2017.

Words omitted repealed by the Investment Exchanges, Clearing Houses and Central Securities Depositories (Amendment) (EU Exit) Regulations 2019, SI 2019/662, regs 4, 8(7), as from IP completion day (as defined in the European Union (Withdrawal Agreement) Act 2020, s 39).

[7.586]

[312J Statement of policy

(1) Each appropriate regulator must prepare and issue a statement of its policy with respect to—

(a) the imposition of penalties under [sections 312F and 312FA and prohibitions under section 312FA], . . .

(b) the amount of penalties under [those sections][; and

(c) the period for which prohibitions under section 312FA are to have effect].

(2) An appropriate regulator's policy in determining what the amount of a penalty should be[, or what the period for which a prohibition is to have effect should be,] must include having regard to—

(a) the seriousness of the contravention in question in relation to the nature of the requirement concerned, . . .

(b) the extent to which that contravention was deliberate or reckless[; and

(c) whether the person against whom action is to be taken is an individual].

(3) An appropriate regulator may at any time alter or replace a statement issued by it under this section.

(4) If a statement issued by an appropriate regulator under this section is altered or replaced, the regulator must issue the altered or replacement statement.

(5) In exercising, or deciding whether to exercise, its power under section 312F [or 312FA] in the case of any particular contravention, an appropriate regulator must have regard to any statement of policy published by it under this section and in force at a time when the contravention in question occurred.

(6) A statement issued by an appropriate regulator under this section must be published by the regulator in the way appearing to the regulator to be best calculated to bring it to the attention of the public.

(7) An appropriate regulator may charge a reasonable fee for providing a person with a copy of the statement.

(8) An appropriate regulator must, without delay, give the Treasury a copy of any statement which it publishes under this section.]

NOTES

Inserted as noted to s 312E at **[7.580]**.

All words in square brackets were substituted or inserted, and all words omitted were repealed, by the Central Securities Depositories Regulations 2017, SI 2017/1064, reg 2(1), (33), as from 28 November 2017.

[7.587]

[312K Statement of policy: procedure

(1) Before issuing a statement under section 312J, an appropriate regulator must publish a draft of the proposed statement in the way appearing to the regulator to be best calculated to bring it to the attention of the public.

(2) The draft must be accompanied by notice that representations about the proposal may be made to the regulator within a specified time.

(3) Before issuing the proposed statement, the regulator must have regard to any representations made to it in accordance with subsection (2).

(4) If the regulator issues the proposed statement it must publish an account, in general terms, of—

(a) the representations made to it in accordance with subsection (2), and

(b) its response to them.

(5) If the statement differs from the draft published under subsection (1) in a way which is, in the opinion of the regulator, significant, the regulator must (in addition to complying with subsection (4)) publish details of the difference.

(6) An appropriate regulator may charge a reasonable fee for providing a person with a copy of a draft published under subsection (1).

(7) This section also applies to a proposal to alter or replace a statement.]

NOTES

Inserted as noted to s 312E at **[7.580]**.

CHAPTER IV

Interpretation

[7.588]

313 Interpretation of Part XVIII

(1) In this Part—

"application" means an application for a recognition order made under section 287[, 288 or 288A];

"applicant" means a [person who] has applied for a recognition order;

[. . .]

["central counterparty" means a body corporate or unincorporated association which interposes itself between the counterparties to the contracts traded on one or more financial markets, becoming the buyer to every seller and the seller to every buyer;]

["central counterparty recognition order" means a recognition order made under section 290(1)(b);]

["clearing", in relation to a central counterparty, means the process of establishing positions, including the calculation of net obligations and ensuring that financial instruments, cash, or both, are available to secure the exposures arising from those positions; and "clearing services", in relation to a central counterparty, is to be read accordingly;]

["CSD recognition order" means a recognition order made under section 290(1)(d);]

[. . .]

["the EMIR regulation" means Regulation (EU) 648/2012 of the European Parliament and of the Council of 4 July 2012 on OTC derivatives, central counterparties and trade repositories [as it forms part of retained EU law], and any [reference to requirements contained in or to functions under the EMIR regulation includes a reference (as the case may be) to requirements contained in or to functions under—

(a) any EU regulation, originally made under the EMIR regulation, which is retained direct EU legislation; or

(b) any subordinate legislation (within the meaning of the Interpretation Act 1978) made under the EMIR regulation on or after IP completion day];]

["multilateral trading facility" means a UK multilateral trading facility as defined by Article 2(1)(14A) of the markets in financial instruments regulation;]

[. . .]

["organised trading facility" means a UK organised trading facility as defined by Article 2(1)(15A) of the markets in financial instruments regulation;]

"overseas applicant" means a body corporate or association which has neither its head office nor its registered office in the United Kingdom and which has applied for a recognition order;

["overseas clearing house" means a body corporate or association which is not a central counterparty and has neither its head office nor its registered office in the United Kingdom and in relation to which a recognition order is in force;]

"overseas investment exchange" means a body corporate or association which has neither its head office nor its registered office in the United Kingdom and in relation to which a recognition order is in force;

"recognised body" means a recognised investment exchange[, a recognised clearing house or a recognised CSD][, and in Chapter 3B also includes a third country central counterparty];

["recognised central counterparty" has the meaning given in section 285;]

"recognised clearing house" has the meaning given in section 285;

["recognised CSD" has the meaning given in section 285;]

"recognised investment exchange" has the meaning given in section 285;

"recognition order" means an order made under section 290 or 292;

"recognition requirements" has the meaning given by section 286;

["regulated market" means a UK regulated market as defined by Article 2(1)(13A) of the markets in financial instruments regulation;]

"remedial direction" has the meaning given in section 308(8);

"revocation order" has the meaning given in section 297;

["Tier 2 third country central counterparty" means a third country central counterparty which has been determined by the Bank of England to be systemically important or likely to become systemically important in accordance with Article 25.2a of the EMIR regulation;]

["trading venue" means a multilateral trading facility, a regulated market or an organised trading facility].

[. . .]

[(1A) For the purposes of this Part, a clearing house does not include a central securities depository.]

(2) References in this Part to rules of an investment exchange (or a clearing house [or central securities depository]) are to rules made, or conditions imposed, by the investment exchange (or the clearing house [or central securities depository]) with respect to—

(a) recognition requirements;
(b) admission of persons to, or their exclusion from the use of, its facilities; or
(c) matters relating to its constitution.

(3) References in this Part to guidance issued by an investment exchange are references to guidance issued, or any recommendation made, in writing or other legible form and intended to have continuing effect, by the investment exchange to—

(a) all or any class of its members or users, or
(b) persons seeking to become members of the investment exchange or to use its facilities,

with respect to any of the matters mentioned in subsection (2)(a) to (c).

(4) References in this Part to guidance issued by a clearing house are to guidance issued, or any recommendation made, in writing or other legible form and intended to have continuing effect, by the clearing house to—

(a) all or any class of its members, or
(b) persons using or seeking to use its services,

with respect to the provision by it or its members of clearing services [or services falling within section 285(3)(b)].

NOTES

Sub-s (1) is amended a follows:

Words in square brackets in the definitions "application" and "applicant" substituted by the Central Securities Depositories Regulations 2017, SI 2017/1064, reg 2(1), (34)(a)(i), (ii), as from 28 November 2017.

Definitions "central counterparty clearing services" and "UK clearing house" (omitted) originally inserted by the Financial Services Act 2012, s 35, Sch 8, paras 1, 36(1), (2), as from 1 April 2013; and subsequently repealed by the Financial Services and Markets Act 2000 (Over the Counter Derivatives, Central Counterparties and Trade Repositories) Regulations 2013, SI 2013/504, reg 3(1), (14), as from the same date without coming into force.

Definitions "central counterparty", "central counterparty recognition order", "clearing", and "recognised central counterparty" inserted, and definition "overseas clearing house" substituted, by SI 2013/504, reg 3(1), (14), as from 1 April 2013.

Definitions "CSD recognition order" and "recognised CSD" inserted by SI 2017/1064, reg 2(1), (34)(a)(iv), as from 28 November 2017.

Definition "EEA CSD" (omitted) originally inserted by SI 2017/1064, reg 2(1), (34)(a)(iv), as from 28 November 2017; and subsequently repealed by the Investment Exchanges, Clearing Houses and Central Securities Depositories (Amendment) (EU Exit) Regulations 2019, SI 2019/662, regs 4, 9(a), as from IP completion day (as defined in the European Union (Withdrawal Agreement) Act 2020, s 39).

Definition "the EMIR regulation" inserted by SI 2013/504, reg 3(1), (14), as from 1 April 2013. Words in first pair of square brackets in that definition substituted by the Securities Financing Transactions, Securitisation and Miscellaneous Amendments (EU Exit) Regulations 2020, SI 2020/1385, reg 38(2), with effect from immediately before IP completion day (as defined in the European Union (Withdrawal Agreement) Act 2020, s 39). Words in second pair of square brackets substituted by SI 2019/662, regs 4, 9(b), as from IP completion day (as defined in the European Union (Withdrawal Agreement) Act 2020, s 39). Note that reg 9(b) of the 2019 Regulations was amended by the Financial Services and Economic and Monetary Policy (Consequential Amendments) (EU Exit) Regulations 2020, SI 2020/1301, reg 3, Schedule, para 37(c), as from 30 December 2020 (and the effect of the amendment has been incorporated in the text set out above).

Definition "multilateral trading facility" originally inserted by the Financial Services and Markets Act 2000 (Markets in Financial Instruments) Regulations 2007, SI 2007/126, reg 3(2), Sch 2, paras 1, 16, as from 1 April 2007 (certain purposes), and as from 1 November 2007 (otherwise). Subsequently substituted by SI 2019/662, regs 4, 9(c), as from IP completion day (as defined in the European Union (Withdrawal Agreement) Act 2020, s 39).

Definition "OFT" (omitted) substituted by the Enterprise Act 2002, s 278(1), Sch 25, para 40(1), (15), as from 1 April 2003, and subsequently repealed by the Enterprise and Regulatory Reform Act 2013 (Competition) (Consequential, Transitional and Saving Provisions) Order 2014, SI 2014/892, art 2, Sch 1, Pt 2, paras 120, 129, as from 1 April 2014 (for transitional provisions in relation to the abolition of the OFT and the Competition Commission and the continuity of functions, etc, see art 3 of that Order).

Definition "organised trading facility" originally inserted by SI 2017/701, reg 50(1), Sch 2, paras 1, 38, as from 3 January 2018 (as to the commencement of the 2017 Regulations, see further the note relating to them above). Subsequently substituted by SI 2019/662, regs 4, 9(d), as from IP completion day (as defined in the European Union (Withdrawal Agreement) Act 2020, s 39).

Words in first pair of square brackets in the definition "recognised body" substituted by SI 2017/1064, reg 2(1), (34)(a)(i), (iii), as from 28 November 2017. Words in second pair of square brackets inserted by the Over the Counter Derivatives, Central Counterparties and Trade Repositories (Amendment, etc, and Transitional Provision) (EU Exit) Regulations 2020, SI 2020/646, reg 2(1), (4)(a), as from IP completion day (as defined in the European Union (Withdrawal Agreement) Act 2020, s 39).

Definition "regulated market" originally inserted by SI 2007/126, reg 3(2), Sch 2, paras 1, 16, as from 1 April 2007 (certain purposes), and as from 1 November 2007 (otherwise). Subsequently substituted by SI 2019/662, regs 4, 9(e), as from IP completion day (as defined in the European Union (Withdrawal Agreement) Act 2020, s 39).

Definition "Tier 2 third country central counterparty" inserted by SI 2020/646, reg 2(1), (4)(b), as from IP completion day (as defined in the European Union (Withdrawal Agreement) Act 2020, s 39)

Definition "trading venue" inserted by SI 2017/701, reg 50(1), Sch 2, paras 1, 38, as from 3 January 2018 (as to the commencement of the 2017 Regulations, see further the note relating to them above).

Sub-s (1A): inserted by SI 2017/1064, reg 2(1), (34)(b), as from 28 November 2017.

Sub-s (2): words in square brackets inserted by SI 2017/1064, reg 2(1), (34)(c), as from 28 November 2017.

Sub-s (4): words in square brackets inserted by the Financial Services Act 2012, s 35, Sch 8, paras 1, 36(1), (3), as from 1 April 2013.

[PART 18A SUSPENSION AND REMOVAL OF FINANCIAL INSTRUMENTS FROM TRADING

[7.589]

313A [FCA's] power to require suspension or removal of financial instruments from trading

(1) The [FCA] may, for the purpose of protecting—

(a) the interests of investors, or

(b) the orderly functioning of the financial markets,

require an institution [or a class of institutions] to suspend or remove a financial instrument from trading.

[(2) If the [FCA] exercises the power conferred by subsection (1), the matter may be referred to the Tribunal by—

(a) the institution or, as the case may be, any institution in the class, or

(b) the issuer of the financial instrument (if any).]

(3) In this section, "trading" includes trading otherwise than on a [trading venue].]

NOTES

Part 18A (originally ss 313A, 313B, 313C, 313D) was inserted by the Financial Services and Markets Act 2000 (Markets in Financial Instruments) Regulations 2007, SI 2007/126, reg 3(3), Sch 3, as from 1 April 2007 (certain purposes), and as from 1 November 2007 (otherwise).

Words "FCA" and "FCA's" in square brackets (in each place that they occur) substituted by the Financial Services Act 2012, s 36, as from 1 April 2013.

Words "or a class of institutions" in square brackets in sub-s (1) inserted, and sub-s (2) substituted, by the Financial Services and Markets Act 2000 (Amendments to Part 18A etc) Regulations 2010, SI 2010/1193, reg 2, as from 9 April 2010.

Words in square brackets in sub-s (3) substituted by the Financial Services and Markets Act 2000 (Markets in Financial Instruments) Regulations 2017, SI 2017/701, reg 50(1), Sch 2, paras 1, 39, as from 3 January 2018 (note that various provisions of the 2017 Regulations came into force on earlier dates for the purposes of making rules, giving notices and consent, etc (for details see reg 1 of the 2017 Regulations)).

[7.590]

[313B Suspension or removal of financial instruments from trading: procedure

(1) A requirement imposed on an institution under section 313A (a "relevant requirement") takes effect—

(a) immediately, if the notice given under subsection (2) states that this is the case;

(b) in any other case, on such date as may be specified in the notice.

(2) If the [FCA] proposes to impose a relevant requirement on an institution, [or a class of institutions,] or imposes such a requirement with immediate effect, it must [give notice—

(a) by written notice to—

(i) the institution or, as the case may be, each institution in the class, and

(ii) the issuer of the financial instrument in question (if any); or

(b) by publishing a notice by means of a regulatory information service].

(3) [A notice given under subsection (2)(a)] must—

(a) give details of the relevant requirement;

(b) state the [FCA's] reasons for imposing the requirement and choosing the date on which it took effect or takes effect;

(c) inform the recipient that he may make representations to the [FCA] within such period as may be specified by the notice (whether or not he has referred the matter to the Tribunal);

(d) inform him of the date on which the requirement took effect or takes effect; and

(e) inform him of his right to refer the matter to the Tribunal and give an indication of the procedure on such a reference.

[(3A) A notice published under subsection (2)(b) must—

(a) give details of the relevant requirement;

(b) specify the institution, or the class of institutions, to which it applies;

(c) state the [FCA's] reasons for imposing the requirement and choosing the date on which it took effect or takes effect;

(d) state that any institution to which the requirement applies or the issuer of the financial instrument in question may make representations to the [FCA] within such period as may be specified by the notice (whether or not the institution or the issuer has referred the matter to the Tribunal);

(e) state the date on which the requirement took effect or takes effect; and

(f) state that any institution to which the requirement applies or the issuer of the financial instrument in question has a right to refer the matter to the Tribunal, and give an indication of the procedure on such a reference.]

(4) The [FCA] may extend the period within which representations may be made to it.

(5)–(12) . . .]

NOTES

Inserted as noted to s 313A at **[7.589]**.

Words "FCA" and "FCA's" in square brackets (in each place that they occur) substituted by the Financial Services Act 2012, s 36, as from 1 April 2013. Other amendments to this section are as follows:

Sub-s (2): words in second pair of square brackets inserted, and words in third pair of square brackets substituted, by the Financial Services and Markets Act 2000 (Amendments to Part 18A etc) Regulations 2010, SI 2010/1193, reg 3(1), (2), as from 9 April 2010.

Sub-s (3): words in first pair of square brackets substituted by SI 2010/1193, reg 3(1), (3), as from 9 April 2010.

Sub-s (3A): inserted by SI 2010/1193, reg 3(1), (4), as from 9 April 2010.

Sub-ss (5)–(12): repealed by SI 2010/1193, reg 3(1), (5), as from 9 April 2010.

[7.591]

[313BA Procedure following consideration of representations

(1) This section applies where, within the period specified under section 313B(3), (3A) or (4), representations are made to the [FCA] in relation to a requirement that it has proposed to impose or has imposed under section 313A.

(2) The [FCA] must decide whether to impose the requirement or (in the case of a requirement that has been imposed) whether to revoke it.

(3) In the case of a requirement that the [FCA] has proposed to impose on a class of institutions, the [FCA] may decide to impose the requirement—

(a) on the class;

(b) on the class apart from one or more specified members of it; or

(c) only on one or more specified members of the class.

(4) In the case of a requirement that the [FCA] has imposed on a class of institutions, the [FCA] may decide to revoke it in relation to—

(a) the class;

(b) the class apart from one or more specified members of it; or

(c) one or more specified members of the class only.

(5) The [FCA] must give written notice of its decision to—

(a) any institution which has made representations, and

(b) the issuer of the financial instrument in question (if any).

(6) In the case of a requirement that the [FCA] has proposed to impose or has imposed on a class, the [FCA] must also give notice of its decision by publishing it by means of a regulatory information service unless the decision is—

(a) to impose the requirement on the class, or

(b) not to revoke the requirement in relation to the class or any member of it.

(7) An institution to which notice is required to be given under subsection (5) may refer the matter to the Tribunal if the [FCA's] decision is that the requirement will be imposed on, or will continue to apply to, the institution.

(8) An issuer to whom notice is required to be given under subsection (5) may refer the matter to the Tribunal if the [FCA's] decision is that the requirement will be imposed on, or will continue to apply to, the institution or (in the case of a requirement relating to a class) any of the institutions in the class.

(9) A notice given under subsection (5) must inform the recipient if the recipient has a right to refer the matter to the Tribunal.]

NOTES

Inserted, together with ss 313BB–313BE, by the Financial Services and Markets Act 2000 (Amendments to Part 18A etc) Regulations 2010, SI 2010/1193, reg 4, as from 9 April 2010.

Words in square brackets substituted by the Financial Services Act 2012, s 36, as from 1 April 2013.

[7.592]

[313BB Revocation of requirements: applications by institutions

(1) This section applies where the [FCA] has imposed a requirement on an institution or a class of institutions under section 313A.

(2) The institution or any of the institutions in the class may apply to the [FCA] for the revocation of the requirement.

(3) The [FCA] must decide whether to revoke the requirement.

(4) In the case of a requirement imposed on a class of institutions, the [FCA] may decide to revoke it in relation to—

(a) the class;

(b) the class apart from one or more specified members of it; or

(c) one or more specified members of the class only.

(5) The [FCA] must give a warning notice if—

(a) in the case of a requirement imposed on an institution, the [FCA] proposes not to revoke the requirement, or

(b) in the case of a requirement imposed on a class, the [FCA] proposes to make a decision which would have the effect that the requirement continues to apply to the applicant (whether or not it would have the effect that it continues to apply to other members of the class).

(6) The warning notice must be given to—

(a) the applicant, and

(b) the issuer of the financial instrument in question (if any).]

NOTES

Inserted as noted to s 313BA at **[7.591]**.

Words in square brackets substituted by the Financial Services Act 2012, s 36, as from 1 April 2013.

[7.593]

[313BC Decisions on applications for revocation by institutions

(1) This section applies where, having considered any representations made in response to a warning notice, the [FCA] has decided whether to grant an application for revocation made under section 313BB.

(2) The [FCA] must give written notice in accordance with subsection (3) if—
- (a) in the case of a requirement imposed on an institution, the [FCA] decides to revoke the requirement, or
- (b) in the case of a requirement imposed on a class, the [FCA] makes a decision which has the effect that the requirement will no longer apply to the applicant (whether or not it will continue to apply to other members of the class).

(3) The written notice must be given to—
- (a) the applicant, and
- (b) the issuer of the financial instrument in question (if any).

(4) If the [FCA] is required to give written notice under subsection (2) in relation to a requirement imposed on a class, the [FCA] must also give notice of its decision by publishing it by means of a regulatory information service.

(5) The [FCA] must give a decision notice in accordance with subsection (6) if—
- (a) in the case of a requirement imposed on an institution, the [FCA] decides not to revoke the requirement, or
- (b) in the case of a requirement imposed on a class, the [FCA] makes a decision which has the effect that the requirement will continue to apply to the applicant (whether or not it will continue to apply to other members of the class).

(6) The decision notice must be given to—
- (a) the applicant, and
- (b) the issuer of the financial instrument in question (if any).

(7) If the [FCA] is required to give a decision notice in relation to a requirement imposed on a class, the [FCA] must also give notice of its decision by publishing it by means of a regulatory information service.

(8) If the [FCA] gives a decision notice, the recipient may refer the matter to the Tribunal.]

NOTES

Inserted as noted to s 313BA at **[7.591]**.

Words in square brackets substituted by the Financial Services Act 2012, s 36, as from 1 April 2013.

[7.594]

[313BD Revocation of requirements: applications by issuers

(1) This section applies where the [FCA] has imposed a requirement on an institution or a class of institutions under section 313A.

(2) The issuer of the financial instrument may apply to the [FCA] for the revocation of the requirement.

(3) The [FCA] must decide whether to revoke the requirement.

(4) In the case of a requirement imposed on a class of institutions, the [FCA] may decide to revoke it in relation to—
- (a) the class;
- (b) the class apart from one or more specified members of it; or
- (c) one or more specified members of the class only.

(5) The [FCA] must give the issuer a warning notice if—
- (a) in the case of a requirement imposed on an institution, the [FCA] proposes not to revoke the requirement, or
- (b) in the case of a requirement imposed on a class, the [FCA] proposes not to revoke the requirement or to revoke it in relation to—
  - (i) the class apart from one or more specified members of it, or
  - (ii) one or more specified members of the class only.]

NOTES

Inserted as noted to s 313BA at **[7.591]**.

Words in square brackets substituted by the Financial Services Act 2012, s 36, as from 1 April 2013.

[7.595]

[313BE Decisions on applications for revocation by issuers

(1) This section applies where, having considered any representations made in response to a warning notice, the [FCA] has decided whether to grant an application for revocation made under section 313BD.

(2) The [FCA] must give written notice to the issuer if the [FCA] decides to revoke the requirement.

(3) If the [FCA] is required to give written notice under subsection (2) in relation to a requirement imposed on a class, the [FCA] must also give notice of its decision by publishing it by means of a regulatory information service.

(4) The [FCA] must give the issuer a decision notice if—
- (a) in the case of a requirement imposed on an institution, the [FCA] decides not to revoke the requirement, or
- (b) in the case of a requirement imposed on a class, the [FCA] decides not to revoke the requirement or makes a decision to revoke the requirement in relation to—
  - (i) the class apart from one or more specified members of it, or
  - (ii) one or more specified members of the class only.

(5) If the [FCA] is required to give a decision notice under subsection (4)(b), it must also give notice of its decision by publishing it by means of a regulatory information service.

(6) If the [FCA] gives a decision notice under subsection (4), the issuer may refer the matter to the Tribunal.]

NOTES

Inserted as noted to s 313BA at **[7.591]**.

Words in square brackets substituted by the Financial Services Act 2012, s 36, as from 1 April 2013.

313C (*Originally inserted as noted to s 313A ante. Subsequently repealed by the Financial Services and Markets Act 2000 (Markets in Financial Instruments) Regulations 2017, SI 2017/701, reg 50(1), Sch 2, paras 1, 40, as from 3 January 2018.*)

[7.596]

[313CA Suspension or removal of financial instruments from trading: notification and trading on other venues

(1) The FCA must take the steps in subsection (2) to (4) if it imposes a requirement on an institution under section 313A to—

(a) suspend or remove a financial instrument from trading; or

(b) suspend or remove a derivative which relates, or is referenced, to the financial instrument from trading to support the objectives of a suspension or removal mentioned in paragraph (a).

(2) The FCA must require any trading venue or systematic internaliser which falls under its jurisdiction and trades the same instrument or derivative to suspend or remove the instrument or derivative from trading if a suspension or removal mentioned in subsection (1) was due to—

(a) suspected market abuse;

(b) a take-over bid; or

(c) the non-disclosure of inside information about the issuer or the instrument.

(3) But the FCA is not obliged to impose a requirement under subsection (2) if it could cause significant damage to the interests of investors or the orderly functioning of the market.

[(4) The FCA must publish a decision of any of the following kinds in such a manner as the FCA considers appropriate—

(a) a decision to impose a requirement under section 313A;

(b) a decision to revoke a requirement imposed under section 313A;

(c) a decision to impose, or to revoke or not to impose, a requirement under subsection (2).

(5) Subsection (4) does not require a decision to be published if it has already been published under section 313B(2)(b) or 313BE(5).]]

NOTES

Inserted by the Financial Services and Markets Act 2000 (Markets in Financial Instruments) Regulations 2017, SI 2017/701, reg 50(1), Sch 2, paras 1, 41, as from 3 January 2018 (note that various provisions of the 2017 Regulations came into force on earlier dates for the purposes of making rules, giving notices and consent, etc (for details see reg 1 of the 2017 Regulations)).

Sub-ss (4), (5): substituted (for the original sub-s (4)) by the Investment Exchanges, Clearing Houses and Central Securities Depositories (Amendment) (EU Exit) Regulations 2019, SI 2019/662, reg 10(1), (2), as from IP completion day (as defined in the European Union (Withdrawal Agreement) Act 2020, s 39).

[7.597]

[313CB Suspension or removal of a financial instrument from a trading by a trading venue: FCA duties

(1) The FCA must take the steps in subsections (2), (4), and (5) if a person specified in subsection (6) operating a trading venue in the United Kingdom informs the FCA it has made a decision—

(a) to suspend or remove a financial instrument from trading on the trading venue because the instrument no longer complies with the venue's rules, or

(b) to suspend or remove a derivative which relates, or is referenced, to the financial instrument from trading on the trading venue to support the objectives of a suspension or removal mentioned in paragraph (a).

(2) The FCA must require any other trading venue or any systematic internaliser which falls under its jurisdiction and trades the same instrument or derivative to suspend or remove the instrument or derivative from trading if a suspension or removal mentioned in subsection (1) was due to—

(a) suspected market abuse;

(b) a take-over bid; or

(c) the non-disclosure of inside information about the issuer or the instrument.

(3) But the FCA is not obliged to impose a requirement under subsection (2) if it could cause significant damage to the interests of investors or the orderly functioning of the market.

(4) The FCA must revoke a requirement imposed under subsection (2) if the person mentioned in subsection (1) informs the FCA it has lifted the suspension mentioned in that subsection.

[(5) The FCA must publish any decision to impose, or to revoke or not to impose, a requirement under subsection (2) in such a manner as the FCA considers appropriate.]

(6) The specified persons for the purposes of subsection (6) are—

(a) a recognised investment exchange,

(b) an investment firm with a Part 4A permission to carry on a regulated activity which is any of the investment services and activities,

[(c) a qualifying credit institution that has Part 4A permission to carry on the regulated activity of accepting deposits].]

NOTES

Inserted by the Financial Services and Markets Act 2000 (Markets in Financial Instruments) Regulations 2017, SI 2017/701, reg 50(1), Sch 2, paras 1, 41, as from 3 January 2018 (note that various provisions of the 2017 Regulations came into force on earlier dates for the purposes of making rules, giving notices and consent, etc (for details see reg 1 of the 2017 Regulations)).

Sub-s (5): substituted by the Investment Exchanges, Clearing Houses and Central Securities Depositories (Amendment) (EU Exit) Regulations 2019, SI 2019/662, reg 10(1), (3)(a), as from IP completion day (as defined in the European Union (Withdrawal Agreement) Act 2020, s 39).

Sub-s (6): para (c) substituted by SI 2019/662, reg 10(1), (3)(b), as from IP completion day (as defined in the European Union (Withdrawal Agreement) Act 2020, s 39).

313CC *(S 313CC (Suspension or removal of a financial instrument from trading in another EEA state: FCA duties) originally inserted by the Financial Services and Markets Act 2000 (Markets in Financial Instruments) Regulations 2017, SI 2017/701, reg 50(1), Sch 2, paras 1, 41, as from 3 January 2018. Subsequently repealed by the Investment Exchanges, Clearing Houses and Central Securities Depositories (Amendment) (EU Exit) Regulations 2019, SI 2019/662, reg 10(1), (4), as from IP completion day (as defined in the European Union (Withdrawal Agreement) Act 2020, s 39).)*

[7.598]

[313D Interpretation of Part 18A

[(1)] In this Part—

[. . .]

["derivative" means a derivative referred to in [paragraphs 4 to 10 of Part 1 of Schedule 2 to the Financial Services and Markets Act 2000 (Regulated Activities) Order 2001 (SI 2001/544)];]

["financial instrument" means an instrument specified in Part 1 of Schedule 2 to the Financial Services and Markets Act 2000 (Regulated Activities) Order 2001;]

"institution" means—

(a) a recognised investment exchange, other than an overseas investment exchange (within the meaning of Part 18);

(b) an investment firm;

[(c) a qualifying credit institution that has Part 4A permission to carry on the regulated activity of accepting deposits, when carrying out investment services or activities; or

(d) a qualifying credit institution other than one that has Part 4A permission to carry on the regulated activity of accepting deposits;]

. . . ;

"issuer", in relation to a financial instrument, means the person who issued the instrument;

["market abuse" means a contravention of Article 14 (prohibition of insider dealing and of unlawful disclosure of inside information) or 15 (prohibition of market manipulation) of the market abuse regulation;]

. . .

["non-disclosure of inside information" means a failure to disclose inside information, as defined by Article 7 (inside information) of the market abuse regulation, in contravention of Article 17 (public disclosure of inside information) of that Regulation;]

["regulated information" has the meaning given in Article 2(1)(k) of the transparency obligations directive (as defined in section 103 of this Act);]

["regulatory information service" means—

(a) a service approved by the [FCA] to disseminate regulated information in accordance with rules made under section 89A of this Act, . . .

(b) . . .]

. . .

["systematic internaliser" has the meaning given in Article 2(1)(12) of the markets in financial instruments regulation;]

["trading venue" means a UK trading venue, as defined by Article 2(1)(16A) of the markets in financial instruments regulation].

[(2) In this Part a trading venue or systematic internaliser falls under the FCA's jurisdiction if—

[(a) it is established in the United Kingdom; or]

(b) in the case of a systematic internaliser [which] does not fall within the FCA's jurisdiction by virtue of paragraph (a)—

(i) it has established a branch (as defined by [Article 2(1)(20) of the markets in financial instruments regulation]) in the United Kingdom; and

(ii) the FCA considers that it is necessary to impose a requirement on the systematic internaliser under [section 313CA(2) or 313CB(2)].]

NOTES

Inserted as noted to s 313A at **[7.589]**.

Sub-s (1) was numbered as such by the Financial Services and Markets Act 2000 (Markets in Financial Instruments) Regulations 2017, SI 2017/701, reg 50(1), Sch 2, paras 1, 42(1), (2), as from 3 January 2018 (note that various provisions of the 2017 Regulations came into force on earlier dates for the purposes of making rules, giving notices and consent, etc (for details see reg 1 of the 2017 Regulations)). This subsection has been amended as follows:

Definition "competent authority" (omitted) originally inserted by SI 2017/701, reg 50(1), Sch 2, paras 1, 42(1), (3), as from 3 January 2018. Subsequently repealed by the Investment Exchanges, Clearing Houses and Central Securities Depositories (Amendment) (EU Exit) Regulations 2019, SI 2019/662, reg 10(1), (5)(a)(i), as from IP completion day (as defined in the European Union (Withdrawal Agreement) Act 2020, s 39).

Definition "derivative" inserted by SI 2017/701, reg 50(1), Sch 2, paras 1, 42(1), (3), as from 3 January 2018 (as to the commencement of the 2017 Regulations, see further the note relating to them above). Words in square brackets substituted by SI 2019/662, reg 10(1), (5)(a)(ii), as from IP completion day (as defined in the European Union (Withdrawal Agreement) Act 2020, s 39).

Definition "financial instrument" substituted by SI 2019/662, reg 10(1), (5)(a)(iii), as from IP completion day (as defined in the European Union (Withdrawal Agreement) Act 2020, s 39).

Paras (c) and (d) of the definition "institution" were substituted by SI 2019/662, reg 10(1), (5)(a)(iv), as from IP completion day (as defined in the European Union (Withdrawal Agreement) Act 2020, s 39). The words omitted were repealed by the EEA Passport Rights (Amendment, etc, and Transitional Provisions) (EU Exit) Regulations 2018, SI 2018/1149, reg 3, Schedule, Pt 1, paras 1, 18, as from IP completion day (as defined in the European Union (Withdrawal Agreement) Act 2020, s 39).

Definition "market abuse" inserted by SI 2017/701, reg 50(1), Sch 2, paras 1, 42(1), (3), as from 3 January 2018 (as to the commencement of the 2017 Regulations, see further the note relating to them above).

Definitions "multilateral trading facility" and "regulated market" (omitted) repealed by SI 2017/701, reg 50(1), Sch 2, paras 1, 42(1), (3), as from 3 January 2018 (as to the commencement of the 2017 Regulations, see further the note relating to them above).

Definition "non-disclosure of inside information" inserted by SI 2017/701, reg 50(1), Sch 2, paras 1, 42(1), (3), as from 3 January 2018 (as to the commencement of the 2017 Regulations, see further the note relating to them above).

Definition "regulated information" inserted by the Financial Services and Markets Act 2000 (Amendments to Part 18A etc) Regulations 2010, SI 2010/1193, reg 6, as from 9 April 2010.

Definition "regulatory information service" inserted by SI 2010/1193, reg 6, as from 9 April 2010. Word in square brackets substituted by the Financial Services Act 2012, s 36, as from 1 April 2013. Para (b) and the preceding word were repealed by SI 2019/662, reg 10(1), (5)(a)(v), as from IP completion day (as defined in the European Union (Withdrawal Agreement) Act 2020, s 39).

Definition "systematic internaliser" originally inserted by SI 2017/701, reg 50(1), Sch 2, paras 1, 42(1), (3), as from 3 January 2018 (as to the commencement of the 2017 Regulations, see further the note relating to them above). Subsequently substituted by SI 2019/662, reg 10(1), (5)(a)(vi), as from IP completion day (as defined in the European Union (Withdrawal Agreement) Act 2020, s 39).

Definition "trading venue" originally inserted by SI 2017/701, reg 50(1), Sch 2, paras 1, 42(1), (3), as from 3 January 2018 (as to the commencement of the 2017 Regulations, see further the note relating to them above). Subsequently substituted by SI 2019/662, reg 10(1), (5)(a)(vi), as from IP completion day (as defined in the European Union (Withdrawal Agreement) Act 2020, s 39).

Sub-s (2): added by SI 2017/701, reg 50(1), Sch 2, paras 1, 42(1), (4), as from 3 January 2018 (as amended by the Financial Services and Markets Act 2000 (Markets in Financial Instruments) (No 2) Regulations 2017, SI 2017/1255, regs 11, 35, as from 2 January 2018) (as to the commencement of SI 2017/701, see further the note relating to it above). This subsection has been amended as follows:

Para (a) substituted by SI 2019/662, reg 10(1), (5)(b)(i), as from IP completion day (as defined in the European Union (Withdrawal Agreement) Act 2020, s 39)

Word in first pair of square brackets in para (b) inserted by the Investment Exchanges, Clearing Houses and Central Securities Depositories (Amendment) (EU Exit) Regulations 2019, SI 2019/662, reg 2(b), as from 26 March 2019.

Words in square brackets in sub-paras (b)(i), (ii) substituted by SI 2019/662, reg 10(1), (5)(b)(ii), as from IP completion day (as defined in the European Union (Withdrawal Agreement) Act 2020, s 39).

314–324 *(Part XIX—Lloyd's (ss 314–324) omitted due to space considerations; see further, the introductory notes to this Act.)*

PART XX PROVISION OF FINANCIAL SERVICES BY MEMBERS OF THE PROFESSIONS

[7.599]

325 [FCA's] general duty

(1) The [FCA] must keep itself informed about—

(a) the way in which designated professional bodies supervise and regulate the carrying on of exempt regulated activities by members of the professions in relation to which they are established;

(b) the way in which such members are carrying on exempt regulated activities.

(2) In this Part—

"exempt regulated activities" means regulated activities which may, as a result of this Part, be carried on by members of a profession which is supervised and regulated by a designated professional body without breaching the general prohibition; and

"members", in relation to a profession, means persons who are entitled to practise the profession in question and, in practising it, are subject to the rules of the body designated in relation to that profession, whether or not they are members of that body.

(3) The [FCA] must keep under review the desirability of exercising any of its powers under this Part.

(4) Each designated professional body must co-operate with the [FCA], by the sharing of information and in other ways, in order to enable the [FCA] to perform its functions under this Part.

NOTES

Words in square brackets substituted by the Financial Services Act 2012, s 46, Sch 16, para 1, as from 1 April 2013.

[7.600]

326 Designation of professional bodies

(1) The Treasury may by order designate bodies for the purposes of this Part.

(2) A body designated under subsection (1) is referred to in this Part as a designated professional body.

(3) The Treasury may designate a body under subsection (1) only if they are satisfied that—

(a) the basic condition, and

(b) one or more of the additional conditions,

are met in relation to it.

(4) The basic condition is that the body has rules applicable to the carrying on by members of the profession in relation to which it is established of regulated activities which, if the body were to be designated, would be exempt regulated activities.

(5) The additional conditions are that—

(a) the body has power under any enactment to regulate the practice of the profession;

(b) being a member of the profession is a requirement under any enactment for the exercise of particular functions or the holding of a particular office;

(c) the body has been recognised for the purpose of any enactment other than this Act and the recognition has not been withdrawn;

(d) . . .

(6) "Enactment" includes an Act of the Scottish Parliament, Northern Ireland legislation and subordinate legislation (whether made under an Act, an Act of the Scottish Parliament or Northern Ireland legislation).

(7) "Recognised" means recognised by—

(a) a Minister of the Crown;

(b) the Scottish Ministers;

(c) a Northern Ireland Minister;

(d) a Northern Ireland department or its head.

NOTES

Sub-s (5): para (d) repealed by the Financial Services and Markets Act 2000 (Amendment) (EU Exit) Regulations 2019, SI 2019/632, regs 62, 63, as from IP completion day (as defined in the European Union (Withdrawal Agreement) Act 2020, s 39).

Orders: the Financial Services and Markets Act 2000 (Designated Professional Bodies) Order 2001, SI 2001/1226 at **[8.337]**; the Financial Services and Markets Act 2000 (Designated Professional Bodies) (Amendment) Order 2004, SI 2004/3352; the Financial Services and Markets Act 2000 (Designated Professional Bodies) (Amendment) Order 2006, SI 2006/58.

[7.601]

327 Exemption from the general prohibition

(1) The general prohibition does not apply to the carrying on of a regulated activity by a person ("P") if—

(a) the conditions set out in subsections (2) to (7) are satisfied; . . .

[(aa) where the activity is the provision of a service listed in [Part 3 of Schedule 2 to the Financial Services and Markets Act 2000 (Regulated Activities) Order 2001] relating to a financial instrument, the condition set out in subsection (7A) is also satisfied; and]

(b) there is not in force—

(i) a direction under section 328, or

(ii) an order under section 329,

which prevents this subsection from applying to the carrying on of that activity by him.

(2) P must be—

(a) a member of a profession; or

(b) controlled or managed by one or more such members.

(3) P must not receive from a person other than his client any pecuniary reward or other advantage, for which he does not account to his client, arising out of his carrying on of any of the activities.

(4) The manner of the provision by P of any service in the course of carrying on the activities must be incidental to the provision by him of professional services.

(5) P must not carry on, or hold himself out as carrying on, a regulated activity other than—

(a) one which rules made as a result of section 332(3) allow him to carry on; or

(b) one in relation to which he is an exempt person.

(6) The activities must not be of a description, or relate to an investment of a description, specified in an order made by the Treasury for the purposes of this subsection.

(7) The activities must be the only regulated activities carried on by P (other than regulated activities in relation to which he is an exempt person).

[(7A) The condition mentioned in subsection (1)(aa) is that—

(a) the service is provided in an incidental manner in the course of a professional activity . . . ; and

(b) the professional activity concerned is the provision of professional services.

(7B) In subsection (7A) a service is provided in an incidental manner in the course of a professional activity . . . if the applicable conditions are satisfied.

(7C) The applicable conditions for the purposes of subsection (7B) are those set out in [paragraph 6(a) to (c) of Schedule 3 to the Financial Services and Markets Act 2000 (Regulated Activities) Order 2001].]

(8) "Professional services" means services—

(a) which do not constitute carrying on a regulated activity, and

(b) the provision of which is supervised and regulated by a designated professional body.

[(9) The exemption in this section does not apply to the carrying on of a regulated claims management activity in Great Britain.]

NOTES

Sub-s (1): word omitted from para (a) repealed, and para (aa) inserted, by the Financial Services and Markets Act 2000 (Markets in Financial Instruments) Regulations 2017, SI 2017/701, reg 50(1), Sch 2, paras 1, 43(1), (2), as from 3 January 2018 (note that various provisions of the 2017 Regulations came into force on earlier dates for the purposes of making rules, giving notices and consent, etc (for details see reg 1 of the 2017 Regulations)). Words in square brackets in para (aa) substituted by the Financial Services and Markets Act 2000 (Amendment) (EU Exit) Regulations 2019, SI 2019/632, regs 62, 64(a), as from IP completion day (as defined in the European Union (Withdrawal Agreement) Act 2020, s 39).

Sub-ss (7A)–(7C): inserted by SI 2017/701, reg 50(1), Sch 2, paras 1, 43(1), (3), as from 3 January 2018 (as to the commencement of the 2017 Regulations, see further the note relating to them above). The words omitted from sub-ss (7A) and (7B) were repealed, and the words in square brackets in sub-s (7C) were substituted, by SI 2019/632, regs 62, 64(b)–(d), as from IP completion day (as defined in the European Union (Withdrawal Agreement) Act 2020, s 39).

Sub-s (9): added by the Financial Services and Markets Act 2000 (Claims Management Activity) Order 2018, SI 2018/1253, art 91(1), (5), as from 1 April 2019 (for provision specifying that the 2018 Order also comes into force on 29 November 2018 for the purposes of the FCA and FOS making rules and issuing guidance, and for transitional provisions in relation to carrying on a claims management activity, etc, see arts 1, 39–89 of the 2018 Order).

Orders: the Financial Services and Markets Act 2000 (Professions) (Non-Exempt Activities) Order 2001, SI 2001/1227; the Financial Services and Markets Act 2000 (Miscellaneous Provisions) Order 2001, SI 2001/3650; the Financial Services and Markets Act 2000 (Commencement of Mortgage Regulation) (Amendment) Order 2002, SI 2002/1777.

[7.602]

328 Directions in relation to the general prohibition

(1) The [FCA] may direct that section 327(1) is not to apply to the extent specified in the direction.

(2) A direction under subsection (1)—

(a) must be in writing;

(b) may be given in relation to different classes of person or different descriptions of regulated activity.

(3) A direction under subsection (1) must be published in the way appearing to the [FCA] to be best calculated to bring it to the attention of the public.

(4) The [FCA] may charge a reasonable fee for providing a person with a copy of the direction.

(5) The [FCA] must, without delay, give the Treasury a copy of any direction which it gives under this section.

[(6) The [FCA] may exercise the power conferred by subsection (1) only if it is satisfied . . . —

(a) that it is desirable to do so in order to protect the interests of clients; . . .

(b) . . .

(7) In considering whether it is [satisfied of the matter specified in subsection (6)(a)], the [FCA] must have regard amongst other things to the effectiveness of any arrangements made by any designated professional body—

(a) for securing compliance with rules made under section 332(1);

(b) for dealing with complaints against its members in relation to the carrying on by them of exempt regulated activities;

(c) in order to offer redress to clients who suffer, or claim to have suffered, loss as a result of misconduct by its members in their carrying on of exempt regulated activities;

(d) for co-operating with the [FCA] under section 325(4).

(8) In this Part "clients" means—

(a) persons who use, have used or are or may be contemplating using, any of the services provided by a member of a profession in the course of carrying on exempt regulated activities;

(b) persons who have rights or interests which are derived from, or otherwise attributable to, the use of any such services by other persons; or

(c) persons who have rights or interests which may be adversely affected by the use of any such services by persons acting on their behalf or in a fiduciary capacity in relation to them.

(9) If a member of a profession is carrying on an exempt regulated activity in his capacity as a trustee, the persons who are, have been or may be beneficiaries of the trust are to be treated as persons who use, have used or are or may be contemplating using services provided by that person in his carrying on of that activity.

NOTES

The word "FCA" in square brackets (in each place that it occurs) was substituted by the Financial Services Act 2012, s 46, Sch 16, para 2, as from 1 April 2013.

Sub-s (6) and the words in the first pair of square brackets in sub-s (7) were substituted by the Insurance Mediation Directive (Miscellaneous Amendments) Regulations 2003, SI 2003/1473, reg 9, as from 14 January 2005.

The words omitted from sub-s (6) were repealed by the Financial Services and Markets Act 2000 (Amendment) (EU Exit) Regulations 2019, SI 2019/632, regs 62, 65, as from IP completion day (as defined in the European Union (Withdrawal Agreement) Act 2020, s 39).

See also as to the meaning of "client", art 89E of the Regulated Activities Order at **[8.234]**

[7.603]

329 Orders in relation to the general prohibition

(1) Subsection (2) applies if it appears to the [FCA] that a person to whom, as a result of section 327(1), the general prohibition does not apply is not a fit and proper person to carry on regulated activities in accordance with that section.

(2) The [FCA] may make an order disapplying section 327(1) in relation to that person to the extent specified in the order.

(3) The [FCA] may, on the application of the person named in an order under subsection (1), vary or revoke it.

(4) "Specified" means specified in the order.

(5) If a partnership is named in an order under this section, the order is not affected by any change in its membership.

(6) If a partnership named in an order under this section is dissolved, the order continues to have effect in relation to any partnership which succeeds to the business of the dissolved partnership.

(7) For the purposes of subsection (6), a partnership is to be regarded as succeeding to the business of another partnership only if—

(a) the members of the resulting partnership are substantially the same as those of the former partnership; and

(b) succession is to the whole or substantially the whole of the business of the former partnership.

NOTES

Words in square brackets substituted by the Financial Services Act 2012, s 46, Sch 16, para 3, as from 1 April 2013.

[7.604]

330 Consultation

(1) Before giving a direction under section 328(1), the [FCA] must publish a draft of the proposed direction.

(2) The draft must be accompanied by—

(a) a cost benefit analysis; and

(b) notice that representations about the proposed direction may be made to the [FCA] within a specified time.

(3) Before giving the proposed direction, the [FCA] must have regard to any representations made to it in accordance with subsection (2)(b).

(4) If the [FCA] gives the proposed direction it must publish an account, in general terms, of—

(a) the representations made to it in accordance with subsection (2)(b); and

(b) its response to them.

(5) If the direction differs from the draft published under subsection (1) in a way which is, in the opinion of the [FCA], significant—

(a) the [FCA] must (in addition to complying with subsection (4)) publish details of the difference; and

(b) those details must be accompanied by a cost benefit analysis.

(6) Subsections (1) to (5) do not apply if the [FCA] considers that the delay involved in complying with them would prejudice the interests of consumers.

(7) Neither subsection (2)(a) nor subsection (5)(b) applies if the [FCA] considers—

(a) that, making the appropriate comparison, there will be no increase in costs; or

(b) that, making that comparison, there will be an increase in costs but the increase will be of minimal significance.

(8) The [FCA] may charge a reasonable fee for providing a person with a copy of a draft published under subsection (1).

(9) When the [FCA] is required to publish a document under this section it must do so in the way appearing to it to be best calculated to bring it to the attention of the public.

[(10) Cost benefit analysis" means—

(a) an analysis of the costs together with an analysis of the benefits that will arise—

(i) if the proposed direction is given, or

(ii) if subsection (5)(b) applies, from the direction that has been given, and

(b) subject to subsection (10A), an estimate of those costs and of those benefits.

(10A) If, in the opinion of the FCA—

(a) the costs or benefits referred to in subsection (10) cannot reasonably be estimated, or

(b) it is not reasonably practicable to produce an estimate,

the cost benefit analysis need not estimate them, but must include a statement of the FCA's opinion and an explanation of it.]

(11) "The appropriate comparison" means—

(a) in relation to subsection (2)(a), a comparison between the overall position if the direction is given and the overall position if it is not given;

(b) in relation to subsection (5)(b), a comparison between the overall position after the giving of the direction and the overall position before it was given.

NOTES

The word "FCA" in square brackets (in each place that it occurs) was substituted, and sub-ss (10), (10A) were substituted (for the original sub-s (10)), by the Financial Services Act 2012, s 46, Sch 16, para 4, as from 1 April 2013.

[7.605]

331 Procedure on making or varying orders under section 329

(1) If the [FCA] proposes to make an order under section 329, it must give the person concerned a warning notice.

(2) The warning notice must set out the terms of the proposed order.

(3) If the [FCA] decides to make an order under section 329, it must give the person concerned a decision notice.

(4) The decision notice must—

(a) name the person to whom the order applies;

(b) set out the terms of the order; and

(c) be given to the person named in the order.

(5) Subsections (6) to (8) apply to an application for the variation or revocation of an order under section 329.

(6) If the [FCA] decides to grant the application, it must give the applicant written notice of its decision.

(7) If the [FCA] proposes to refuse the application, it must give the applicant a warning notice.

(8) If the [FCA] decides to refuse the application, it must give the applicant a decision notice.

(9) A person—

(a) against whom the [FCA] have decided to make an order under section 329, or

(b) whose application for the variation or revocation of such an order the [FCA] had decided to refuse,

may refer the matter to the Tribunal.

(10) The [FCA] may not make an order under section 329 unless—

(a) the period within which the decision to make to the order may be referred to the Tribunal has expired and no such reference has been made; or

(b) if such a reference has been made, the reference has been determined.

NOTES

Words in square brackets substituted by the Financial Services Act 2012, s 46, Sch 16, para 5, as from 1 April 2013.

[7.606]

332 Rules in relation to persons to whom the general prohibition does not apply

(1) The [FCA] may make rules applicable to persons to whom, as a result of section 327(1), the general prohibition does not apply.

(2) The power conferred by subsection (1) is to be exercised for the purpose of ensuring that clients are aware that such persons are not authorised persons.

(3) A designated professional body must make rules—

(a) applicable to members of the profession in relation to which it is established who are not authorised persons; and

(b) governing the carrying on by those members of regulated activities (other than regulated activities in relation to which they are exempt persons).

(4) Rules made in compliance with subsection (3) must be designed to secure that, in providing a particular professional service to a particular client, the member carries on only regulated activities which arise out of, or are complementary to, the provision by him of that service to that client.

(5) Rules made by a designated professional body under subsection (3) require the approval of the [FCA].

NOTES

Word "FCA" in square brackets in sub-ss (1), (5) substituted by the Financial Services Act 2012, s 46, Sch 16, para 6, as from 1 April 2013.

[7.607]

333 False claims to be a person to whom the general prohibition does not apply

(1) A person who—

(a) describes himself (in whatever terms) as a person to whom the general prohibition does not apply, in relation to a particular regulated activity, as a result of this Part, or

(b) behaves, or otherwise holds himself out, in a manner which indicates (or which is reasonably likely to be understood as indicating) that he is such a person,

is guilty of an offence if he is not such a person.

(2) In proceedings for an offence under this section it is a defence for the accused to show that he took all reasonable precautions and exercised all due diligence to avoid committing the offence.

(3) A person guilty of an offence under this section is liable on summary conviction to imprisonment for a term not exceeding six months or a fine not exceeding level 5 on the standard scale, or both.

(4) But where the conduct constituting the offence involved or included the public display of any material, the maximum fine for the offence is level 5 on the standard scale multiplied by the number of days for which the display continued.

333A–339 *(Part 20A—Pensions Guidance (ss 333A–333R), Part 20B—Illegal Money Lending (ss 333S, 333T), Part 20C—Politically exposed persons: money laundering and terrorist financing (s 333U), and Part XXI—Mutual Societies (ss 334–339 and Sch 18) omitted due to space considerations; see further, the introductory notes to this Act.)*

PART XXII AUDITORS AND ACTUARIES

NOTES

Transitional provisions etc in connection with the commencement of the Financial Services Act 2012: see the Financial Services Act 2012 (Transitional Provisions) (Enforcement) Order 2013, SI 2013/441. Article 14 makes transitional provision in relation to persons disqualified before 1 April 2013 from being the auditor of, or acting as the actuary for, an authorised person or class of authorised person.

Transitional provisions etc in connection with the original commencement of this Act: (1) the Financial Services and Markets Act 2000 (Transitional Provisions) (Authorised Persons etc) Order 2001, SI 2001/2636, art 78 provides for the disqualification under this s 345 (as originally enacted) of an auditor who, at 1 December 2001, had been disqualified pursuant to the Financial Services Act 1986, s 111(3) or the Insurance Companies Act 1982, s 21A(5) (both repealed); (2) the Financial Services and Markets Act 2000 (Transitional Provisions and Savings) (Civil Remedies, Discipline, Criminal Offences etc) (No 2) Order 2001, SI 2001/3083, art 19, provides that s 345 (as originally enacted) had effect as if the reference to a duty imposed on an auditor under the Act included a reference to a duty imposed (whether before or, where applicable, after commencement) on an auditor under any of the following enactments: FSA 1986, s 109, Banking Act 1987, s 47, Insurance Companies Act 1982, s 21A, Building Societies Act 1986, s 82, Friendly Societies Act 1992, s 79.

[[General duties of regulator]

NOTES

The preceding heading was substituted by the Financial Services (Banking Reform) Act 2013, s 134(1), (3), as from 1 March 2014.

[7.608]

339A General duties of PRA in relation to auditors

(1) The arrangements maintained by the PRA under section 2K (supervision of PRA-authorised persons) must include arrangements for—

(a) the sharing with auditors of PRA-authorised persons of information that the PRA is not prevented from disclosing, and

(b) the exchange of opinions with auditors of PRA-authorised persons.

(2) The PRA must issue and maintain a code of practice describing how it will comply with subsection (1).

(3) The PRA may at any time alter or replace a code issued under this section.

(4) If a code is altered or replaced, the PRA must issue the altered or replacement code.

(5) When the PRA issues a code under this section the PRA must—

(a) give a copy of the code to the Treasury, and

(b) publish the code in such manner as the PRA thinks fit.

(6) The Treasury must lay before Parliament a copy of the code.

(7) "Auditor" means an auditor appointed under or as a result of a statutory provision.]

NOTES

Inserted, together with the preceding heading, by the Financial Services Act 2012, s 42, Sch 13 paras 1, 2, as from 24 January 2013 (in so far as relating to the issue of a code of practice), and as from 1 April 2013 (otherwise).

[7.609]

[339B Duty to meet auditors of certain institutions

(1) The FCA must make arrangements for meetings to take place at least once a year between—

(a) the FCA, and

(b) the auditor of any PRA-authorised person to which section 339C applies.

(2) The PRA must make arrangements for meetings to take place at least once a year between—

(a) the PRA, and

(b) the auditor of any PRA-authorised person to which section 339C applies.

(3) The annual report of each regulator must include the number of meetings that have taken place during the period to which the report relates between the regulator and auditors of PRA-authorised persons to which section 339C applies.

(4) In subsection (3) "the annual report" means—

(a) in relation to the FCA, every report which it is required by paragraph 11 of Schedule 1ZA to make to the Treasury, and

(b) in relation to the PRA, every report which it is required by paragraph 19 of Schedule 1ZB to make to the Treasury.

(5) In this section "auditor" means an auditor appointed under or as a result of a statutory provision.]

NOTES

Inserted, together with s 339C, by the Financial Services (Banking Reform) Act 2013, s 134(1), (2), as from 1 March 2014.

[7.610]

[339C PRA-authorised persons to which this section applies

(1) This section applies to a PRA-authorised person which—

(a) is a UK institution,

(b) meets condition A or B,

(c) is not an insurer or a credit union, and

(d) is, in the opinion of the PRA, important to the stability of the UK financial system.

(2) Condition A is that the person has permission under Part 4A to carry on the regulated activity of accepting deposits.

(3) Condition B is that—

(a) the person is an investment firm that has permission under Part 4A to carry on the regulated activity of dealing in investments as principal, and

(b) when carried on by the person, that activity is a PRA-regulated activity.

(4) In this section—

(a) "UK institution" means an institution which is incorporated in, or formed under the law of any part of, the United Kingdom;

(b) "insurer" means an institution which is authorised under this Act to carry on the regulated activity of effecting or carrying out contracts of insurance as principal;

(c) "credit union" means a credit union as defined by section 31 of the Credit Unions Act 1979 or a credit union as defined by Article 2(2) of the Credit Unions (Northern Ireland) Order 1985.

(5) Subsections (2), (3) and (4)(b) are to be read in accordance with Schedule 2, taken together with any order under section 22.]

NOTES

Inserted as noted to s 339B at **[7.609]**.

Appointment

[7.611]

340 Appointment

(1) [The appropriate regulator may make rules requiring] an authorised person, or an authorised person falling within a specified class—

(a) to appoint an auditor, or

(b) to appoint an actuary,

if he is not already under an obligation to do so imposed by another enactment.

(2) [The appropriate regulator may make rules requiring] an authorised person, or an authorised person falling within a specified class—

(a) to produce periodic financial reports; and

(b) to have them reported on by an auditor or an actuary.

[(3A) The PRA—

(a) must make rules imposing on auditors of PRA-authorised persons such duties as may be specified in relation to co-operation with the PRA in connection with the supervision by the PRA of PRA-authorised persons, and

(b) may make rules—

(i) imposing such other duties on auditors of PRA-authorised persons as may be specified, and

(ii) imposing such duties on actuaries acting for PRA-authorised persons as may be specified.

(3B) The FCA may make rules imposing on auditors of, or actuaries acting for, authorised persons such duties as may be specified.]

(4) Rules under subsection (1) may make provision—

(a) specifying the manner in which and time within which an auditor or actuary is to be appointed;

(b) requiring the [regulator making the rules] to be notified of an appointment;

(c) enabling the [regulator making the rules] to make an appointment if no appointment has been made or notified;

(d) as to remuneration;

(e) as to the term of office, removal and resignation of an auditor or actuary.

(5) An auditor or actuary appointed as a result of rules under subsection (1), or on whom duties are imposed by rules under subsection [(3A) or (3B)]—

(a) must act in accordance with such provision as may be made by rules; and

(b) is to have such powers in connection with the discharge of his functions as may be provided by rules.

[(5A) In subsections (1) and (2) "the appropriate regulator" means—

(a) in the case of a PRA-authorised person, the PRA;

(b) in any other case, the FCA.]

(6) In subsections (1) to [(3A) or (3B)] "auditor" or "actuary" means an auditor, or actuary, who satisfies such requirements as to qualifications, experience and other matters (if any) as may be specified.

(7) "Specified" means specified in rules.

[(8) The powers conferred by this section enable only the making of such rules as appear to the regulator making them to be necessary or expedient—

(a) in the case of the FCA, for the purpose of advancing one or more of its operational objectives, or

(b) in the case of the PRA, for the purpose of advancing any of its objectives.]

NOTES

Sub-ss (3A), (3B) were substituted (for the original sub-s (3)), sub-ss (5A) and (8) were inserted and added respectively, and the words in square brackets in sub-ss (1), (2), (4), (5), (6) were substituted, by the Financial Services Act 2012, s 42, Sch 13, paras 1, 3, as from 1 April 2013.

Information

[7.612]

341 Access to books etc

(1) An appointed auditor of, or an appointed actuary acting for, an authorised person—
- (a) has a right of access at all times to the authorised person's books, accounts and vouchers; and
- (b) is entitled to require from the authorised person's officers such information and explanations as he reasonably considers necessary for the performance of his duties as auditor or actuary.

(2) "Appointed" means appointed under or as a result of this Act.

[7.613]

342 Information given by auditor or actuary to [a regulator]

(1) This section applies to a person who is, or has been, an auditor of an authorised person [or recognised investment exchange,] appointed under or as a result of a statutory provision.

(2) This section also applies to a person who is, or has been, an actuary acting for an authorised person and appointed under or as a result of a statutory provision.

(3) An auditor or actuary does not contravene any duty to which he is subject merely because he gives to [a regulator]—
- (a) information on a matter of which he has, or had, become aware in his capacity as auditor of, or actuary acting for, the authorised person [or recognised investment exchange], or
- (b) his opinion on such a matter,

if he is acting in good faith and he reasonably believes that the information or opinion is relevant to any functions of [that regulator].

(4) Subsection (3) applies whether or not the auditor or actuary is responding to a request from the [regulator].

(5) The Treasury may make regulations prescribing circumstances in which an auditor or actuary must communicate matters to [a regulator] as mentioned in subsection (3).

(6) It is the duty of an auditor or actuary to whom any such regulations apply to communicate a matter to [a regulator] in the circumstances prescribed by the regulations.

[(6A) If the authorised person concerned is a credit institution or an investment firm, and an auditor or actuary communicates a matter to a regulator in accordance with the regulations, the matter must be disclosed simultaneously to the management body of the authorised person, unless there are compelling reasons not to do so.]

(7) The matters to be communicated to [a regulator] in accordance with the regulations may include matters relating to persons other than the authorised person [or recognised investment exchange] concerned.

[(8) In subsection (6A) ["investment firm" has] the same meaning as in Article 4(1) of the capital requirements regulation.]

NOTES

Sub-s (6A): inserted by the Capital Requirements Regulations 2013, SI 2013/3115, reg 46(1), Sch 2, Pt 1, paras 1, 20, as from 1 January 2014.

Sub-s (8): added by SI 2013/3115, reg 46(1), Sch 2, Pt 1, paras 1, 20, as from 1 January 2014. Words in square brackets substituted by the Financial Services and Markets Act 2000 (Amendment) (EU Exit) Regulations 2019, SI 2019/632, regs 66, 67, as from IP completion day (as defined in the European Union (Withdrawal Agreement) Act 2020, s 39).

All other words in square brackets in this section were substituted or inserted by the Financial Services Act 2012, s 42, Sch 13, paras 1, 4, as from 1 April 2013.

Regulations: the Financial Services and Markets Act 2000 (Communications by Auditors) Regulations 2001, SI 2001/2587; the Financial Services and Markets Act 2000 (Communications by Actuaries) Regulations 2003, SI 2003/1294.

[7.614]

343 Information given by auditor or actuary to [a regulator]: persons with close links

(1) This section applies to a person who—
- (a) is, or has been, an auditor of an authorised person [or recognised investment exchange,] appointed under or as a result of a statutory provision; and
- (b) is, or has been, an auditor of a person ("CL") who has close links with the authorised person [or recognised investment exchange].

(2) This section also applies to a person who—
- (a) is, or has been, an actuary acting for an authorised person and appointed under or as a result of a statutory provision; and
- (b) is, or has been, an actuary acting for a person ("CL") who has close links with the authorised person.

(3) An auditor or actuary does not contravene any duty to which he is subject merely because he gives to [a regulator]—
- (a) information on a matter concerning the authorised person [or recognised investment exchange] of which he has, or had, become aware in his capacity as auditor of, or actuary acting for, CL, or
- (b) his opinion on such a matter,

if he is acting in good faith and he reasonably believes that the information or opinion is relevant to any functions of [that regulator].

(4) Subsection (3) applies whether or not the auditor or actuary is responding to a request from the [regulator].

(5) The Treasury may make regulations prescribing circumstances in which an auditor or actuary must communicate matters to [a regulator] as mentioned in subsection (3).

(6) It is the duty of an auditor or actuary to whom any such regulations apply to communicate a matter to [a regulator] in the circumstances prescribed by the regulations.

[(6A) If the authorised person concerned is a credit institution or an investment firm, and an auditor or actuary communicates a matter to a regulator in accordance with the regulations, the matter must be disclosed simultaneously to the management body of the authorised person, unless there are compelling reasons not to do so.]

(7) The matters to be communicated to [a regulator] in accordance with the regulations may include matters relating to persons other than the authorised person [or recognised investment exchange] concerned.

(8) CL has close links with the authorised person [or recognised investment exchange] concerned ("A") if CL is—

(a) a parent undertaking of A;
(b) a subsidiary undertaking of A;
(c) a parent undertaking of a subsidiary undertaking of A; or
(d) a subsidiary undertaking of a parent undertaking of A.

(9) . . .

[(10) In subsection (6A) ["investment firm" has] the same meaning as in Article 4(1) of the capital requirements regulation.]

NOTES

Sub-s (6A): inserted by the Capital Requirements Regulations 2013, SI 2013/3115, reg 46(1), Sch 2, Pt 1, paras 1, 21, as from 1 January 2014.

Sub-s (9): repealed by the Financial Services and Markets Act 2000 (Amendment) (EU Exit) Regulations 2019, SI 2019/632, regs 66, 68(a), as from IP completion day (as defined in the European Union (Withdrawal Agreement) Act 2020, s 39).

Sub-s (10): added by SI 2013/3115, reg 46(1), Sch 2, Pt 1, paras 1, 21, as from 1 January 2014. Words in square brackets substituted by SI 2019/632, regs 66, 68(b), as from IP completion day (as defined in the European Union (Withdrawal Agreement) Act 2020, s 39).

All other words in square brackets in this section were inserted or substituted by the Financial Services Act 2012, s 42, Sch 13, paras 1, 5, as from 1 April 2013.

Regulations: the Financial Services and Markets Act 2000 (Communications by Auditors) Regulations 2001, SI 2001/2587; the Financial Services and Markets Act 2000 (Communications by Actuaries) Regulations 2003, SI 2003/1294.

[7.615]

344 Duty of auditor or actuary resigning etc to give notice

(1) This section applies to an auditor or actuary to whom section 342 applies.

(2) He must without delay notify the [appropriate regulator] if he—

(a) is removed from office by an authorised person [or recognised investment exchange];
(b) resigns before the expiry of his term of office with such a person; or
(c) is not re-appointed by such a person.

(3) If he ceases to be an auditor of, or actuary acting for, such a person, he must without delay notify the [appropriate regulator]—

(a) of any matter connected with his so ceasing which he thinks ought to be drawn to the [regulator's] attention; or
(b) that there is no such matter.

[(4) In this section "the appropriate regulator" means—

(a) in the case of an auditor of, or an actuary acting for, a PRA-authorised person, the PRA;
(b) in any other case, the FCA.]

NOTES

The words "appropriate regulator" and "regulator's" in square brackets were substituted, the words in square brackets in sub-s (2)(a) were inserted, and sub-s (4) was added, by the Financial Services Act 2012, s 42, Sch 13, paras 1, 6, as from 1 April 2013.

[Disciplinary measures

[7.616]

345 Disciplinary measures: FCA

(1) Subsection (2) applies if it appears to the FCA that an auditor or actuary to whom section 342 applies—

(a) has failed to comply with a duty imposed on the auditor or actuary by rules made by the FCA, or
(b) has failed to comply with a duty imposed under this Act to communicate information to the FCA.

(2) The FCA may do one or more of the following—

(a) disqualify the auditor or actuary from being the auditor of, or (as the case may be) from acting as an actuary for, any authorised person or any particular class of authorised person;
(b) disqualify the auditor from being the auditor of any recognised investment exchange or any particular class of recognised investment exchange;
(c) publish a statement to the effect that it appears to the FCA that the auditor or (as the case may be) actuary has failed to comply with the duty;
(d) impose on the auditor or actuary a penalty, payable to the FCA, of such amount as the FCA considers appropriate.

(3) If an auditor or actuary has been disqualified by the PRA under section 345A(4)(a), the FCA may disqualify the auditor or actuary, so long as the disqualification under that provision remains in force, from being the auditor of, or (as the case may be) from acting as an actuary for—

(a) any FCA-authorised person,
(b) any particular class of FCA-authorised person,
(c) any recognised investment exchange, or
(d) any particular class of recognised investment exchange.

(4) In subsection (3) "FCA-authorised person" means an authorised person who is not a PRA-authorised person.

(5) Where under subsection (2) or (3) the FCA disqualifies a person from being the auditor of an authorised person or recognised investment exchange or class of authorised person or recognised investment exchange and that authorised person or recognised investment exchange is also, or any person within that class is also, a recognised clearing house [or a recognised CSD], the FCA must—

(a) notify the Bank of England, and
(b) notify the disqualified person that it has made a notification under paragraph (a).

(6) The FCA may remove any disqualification imposed under paragraph (a) or (b) of subsection (2) if satisfied that the disqualified person will in future comply with the duty in question.

(7) The FCA may at any time remove any disqualification imposed under subsection (3).]

NOTES

Substituted, together with the preceding heading and ss 345A–345E (for the original s 345) by the Financial Services Act 2012, s 42, Sch 13 paras 1, 7, as from 1 April 2013.

Sub-s (5): words in square brackets inserted by the Central Securities Depositories Regulations 2017, SI 2017/1064, reg 2(1), (35), as from 28 November 2017.

[7.617]

[345A Disciplinary measures: PRA

(1) The following provisions of this section have effect only if the Treasury, by order made after consultation with the PRA, so provide.

(2) Subsection (3) applies if it appears to the PRA that an auditor or actuary to whom section 342 applies—
(a) has failed to comply with a duty imposed on the auditor or actuary by rules made by the PRA, or
(b) has failed to comply with a duty imposed under this Act to communicate information to the PRA.

(3) The PRA may exercise one or more of the specified powers.

(4) The specified powers are such one or more of the following as may be specified in the order under subsection (1)—
(a) to disqualify the auditor or actuary from being the auditor of, or (as the case may be) from acting as an actuary for, any PRA-authorised person or any particular class of PRA-authorised person;
(b) to publish a statement to the effect that it appears to the PRA that the auditor or (as the case may be) actuary has failed to comply with the duty;
(c) to impose on the auditor or actuary a penalty, payable to the PRA, of such amount as the PRA considers appropriate.

(5) Where the PRA disqualifies a person under subsection (4)(a) it must—
(a) notify the FCA, and
(b) notify the person concerned that it has made a notification under paragraph (a).

(6) . . .

(7) The PRA may remove any disqualification imposed under subsection (4)(a) if satisfied that the disqualified person will in future comply with the duty in question.]

NOTES

Substituted as noted to s 345 at **[7.616]**.

Sub-s (6): repealed by the Bank of England and Financial Services Act 2016, s 16, Sch 2, Pt 2, paras 26, 44, as from 1 March 2017.

Orders: the Financial Services and Markets Act 2000 (Regulation of Auditors and Actuaries) (PRA Specified Powers) Order 2015, SI 2015/61 which provides that for the purpose of sub-s (3) above, all the powers of the PRA described in sub-s (4) above are specified (as from 20 February 2015).

[7.618]

[345B Procedure and right to refer to Tribunal

(1) If the FCA proposes to act under section 345(2) or the PRA proposes to act under section 345A(3), it must give the auditor or actuary to whom the action would relate a warning notice.

(2) A warning notice about a proposal to impose a penalty must state the amount of the penalty.

(3) A warning notice about a proposal to publish a statement must set out the terms of the statement.

(4) If the FCA decides to act under section 345(2) or the PRA decides to act under section 345A(3), it must give the auditor or actuary to whom the action would relate a decision notice.

(5) A decision notice about the imposition of a penalty must state the amount of the penalty.

(6) A decision notice about the publication of a statement must set out the terms of the statement.

(7) If the FCA decides to act under section 345(2) or the PRA decides to act under section 345A(3), the auditor or actuary concerned may refer the matter to the Tribunal.]

NOTES

Substituted as noted to s 345 at **[7.616]**.

[7.619]

[345C Duty on publication of statement

After a statement under section 345(2)(c) or 345A(4)(b) is published, the regulator that published it must send a copy of the statement to—
(a) the auditor or actuary, and
(b) any person to whom a copy of the decision notice was given under section 393(4).]

NOTES

Substituted as noted to s 345 at **[7.616]**.

[7.620]

[345D Imposition of penalties on auditors or actuaries: statement of policy

(1) The FCA must prepare and issue a statement of its policy with respect to—
(a) the imposition of penalties under section 345(2)(d), and
(b) the amount of penalties under that provision.

(2) If by virtue of an order under section 345A(1), the PRA has power to impose penalties under section 345A(4)(c), the PRA must prepare and issue a statement of its policy with respect to—

(a) the imposition of penalties under section 345A(4)(c), and
(b) the amount of penalties under that provision.

(3) A regulator's policy in determining what the amount of a penalty should be must include having regard to—
(a) the seriousness of the contravention, and
(b) the extent to which the contravention was deliberate or reckless.

(4) A regulator may at any time alter or replace a statement issued under this section.

(5) If a statement issued under this section is altered or replaced, the regulator must issue the altered or replacement statement.

(6) A regulator must, without delay, give the Treasury a copy of any statement which it publishes under this section.

(7) A statement issued under this section must be published by the regulator in the way appearing to the regulator to be best calculated to bring it to the attention of the public.

(8) In deciding whether to exercise a power under section 345(2)(d) in the case of any particular contravention, the FCA must have regard to any statement of policy published by it under this section and in force at a time when the contravention occurred.

(9) In deciding whether to exercise a power under section 345A(4)(c) in the case of any particular contravention, the PRA must have regard to any statement of policy published by it under this section and in force at a time when the contravention occurred.

(10) A regulator may charge a reasonable fee for providing a person with a copy of the statement.]

NOTES

Substituted as noted to s 345 at **[7.616]**.

[7.621]

[345E Statements of policy: procedure

(1) Before a regulator issues a statement under section 345D, the regulator must publish a draft of the proposed statement in the way appearing to the regulator to be best calculated to bring it to the attention of the public.

(2) The draft must be accompanied by notice that representations about the proposal may be made to the regulator within a specified time.

(3) Before issuing the proposed statement, the regulator must have regard to any representations made to it in accordance with subsection (2).

(4) If the regulator issues the proposed statement it must publish an account, in general terms, of—
(a) the representations made to it in accordance with subsection (2), and
(b) its response to them.

(5) If the statement differs from the draft published under subsection (1) in a way which is, in the opinion of the regulator, significant, the regulator must (in addition to complying with subsection (4)) publish details of the difference.

(6) A regulator may charge a reasonable fee for providing a person with a copy of a draft under subsection (1).

(7) This section also applies to a proposal to alter or replace a statement.]

NOTES

Substituted as noted to s 345 at **[7.616]**.

Offence

[7.622]

346 Provision of false or misleading information to auditor or actuary

(1) An authorised person who knowingly or recklessly gives an appointed auditor or actuary information which is false or misleading in a material particular is guilty of an offence and liable—
(a) on summary conviction, to imprisonment for a term not exceeding six months or a fine not exceeding the statutory maximum, or both;
(b) on conviction on indictment, to imprisonment for a term not exceeding two years or a fine, or both.

(2) Subsection (1) applies equally to an officer, controller or manager of an authorised person.

(3) "Appointed" means appointed under or as a result of this Act.

NOTES

Deferred Prosecution Agreements: see the note to s 23 at **[7.63]**.

PART XXIII PUBLIC RECORD, DISCLOSURE OF INFORMATION AND CO-OPERATION

The public record

[7.623]

347 The record of authorised persons etc

(1) The [FCA] must maintain a record of every—
(a) person who appears to the [FCA] to be an authorised person;
(b) authorised unit trust scheme;
[(ba) authorised contractual scheme;]
(c) authorised open-ended investment company;
(d) recognised scheme;
(e) recognised investment exchange;
(f) . . .
(g) individual to whom a prohibition order [or Part 9C prohibition order] relates;
(h) approved person; . . .
[(ha) person to whom subsection (2A) applies; . . .]
[(hb) appointed representative to whom subsection (2B) applies;]
[(hc) appointed representative to whom subsection (2C) applies; and]

(i) person falling within such other class (if any) as the [FCA] may determine.

(2) The record must include such information as the [FCA] considers appropriate and at least the following information—

(a) in the case of a person appearing to the [FCA] to be an authorised person—
  (i) information as to the services which he holds himself out as able to provide; and
  (ii) any address of which the [FCA] is aware at which a notice or other document may be served on him;

(b) in the case of an authorised unit trust scheme, the name and address of the manager and trustee of the scheme;

[(ba) in the case of an authorised contractual scheme, the name and address of the operator and depositary of the scheme;]

(c) in the case of an authorised open-ended investment company, the name and address of—
  (i) the company;
  (ii) if it has only one director, the director; and
  (iii) its depositary (if any);

(d) in the case of a recognised scheme, the name and address of—
  (i) the operator of the scheme; and
  (ii) any representative of the operator in the United Kingdom;

(e) in the case of a recognised investment exchange . . . , the name and address of the exchange . . . ;

(f) in the case of an individual to whom a prohibition order relates—
  (i) his name; and
  (ii) details of the effect of the order;

(g) in the case of a person who is an approved person—
  (i) his name;
  (ii) the name of the [authorised person concerned];
  (iii) if the approved person is performing a controlled function under an arrangement with a contractor of the [authorised person concerned], the name of the contractor;
  [(iv) . . . whether or not the person is a senior manager;]

[(h) in the case of an approved person who is a senior manager in relation to [an] authorised person—
  (i) whether a final notice has been given to the person under section 390; and
  (ii) if so, any information about the matter to which the notice relates which has been published under section 391(4)];

[(i) in the case of a mortgage intermediary—
  (i) the names of the persons within the management who are responsible for the activities specified by article 25A (arranging regulated mortgage contracts), article 36A (credit broking), article 53A (advising on regulated mortgage contracts) and article 53DA (advising on regulated credit agreements the purpose of which is to acquire land) of the Financial Services and Markets Act 2000 (Regulated Activities) Order 2001; and
  (ii) whether the mortgage intermediary is a tied mortgage intermediary or not;

(j) in the case of an appointed representative to whom subsection (2B) applies, the name of the mortgage intermediary on whose behalf the appointed representative acts].

[(2A) This subsection applies to—

(a) an appointed representative to whom subsection (1A) [or (1AA)] of section 39 applies for whom the applicable register (as defined by subsection (1B) of that section) is the record maintained by virtue of subsection (1)(ha) above; [and]

(b) a person mentioned in subsection (1)(a) of section 39A if—
  (i) the contract with an authorised person to which he is party complies with the applicable requirements (as defined by subsection (7) of that section), and
  (ii) the authorised person has accepted responsibility in writing for the person's activities in carrying on investment services business (as defined by subsection (8) of that section); . . .

(c) . . .]

[(2B) This subsection applies to an appointed representative to whom section 39(1BA) applies or to whom that subsection would apply if the requirements of section 39(1BB) were not met.]

[(2C) This subsection applies to an appointed representative of an authorised person who has a Part 4A permission by virtue of regulation 4 or 7 of the Financial Services and Markets Act 2000 (Markets in Financial Instruments) Regulations 2017 (SI 2017/701).

(3) If it appears to the [FCA] that a person in respect of whom there is an entry in the record as a result of one of the paragraphs of subsection (1) has ceased to be a person to whom that paragraph applies, the [FCA] may remove the entry from the record.

[(3A) But if a person ceases to be a person to whom one of the paragraphs of subsection (1) applies as a [result of a cancellation of that person's Part 4A permission under section 55J because one or more of the conditions in section 55K(1)(b) to (d) was met, the power] conferred by subsection (3) is not exercisable for a period of five years from the date on which the person ceased to be a person to whom subsection (1) applied.

(3B) Where the power conferred by subsection (3) is not exercisable in respect of an entry in the record as a result of subsection (3A) the FCA must—

(a) make a note in the record that it considers the person to whom the entry relates has ceased to be person to whom one of the paragraphs of subsection (1) applies as a result of a cancellation of that person's Part 4A permission for a reason mentioned in subsection (3A)(a) or (b); and

(b) state why it considers that is the case.]

(4) But if the [FCA] decides not to remove the entry, it must—

(a) make a note to that effect in the record; and

(b) state why it considers that the person has ceased to be a person to whom that paragraph applies [in any case where it has not already done so under subsection (3B)].

[(4A) If the FCA cancels or varies the Part 4A permission of a mortgage intermediary and as a result the person to whom the entry relates no longer has a Part 4A permission to carry on a relevant mortgage activity within the meaning of section 55J(6C), the FCA must delete mention of such permission from the record without undue delay.]

(5) The [FCA] must—

(a) make the record available for inspection by members of the public in a legible form at such times and in such place or places as the [FCA] may determine; and

(b) provide a certified copy of the record, or any part of it, to any person who asks for it—

(i) on payment of the fee (if any) fixed by the [FCA]; and

(ii) in a form (either written or electronic) in which it is legible to the person asking for it.

(6) The [FCA] may—

(a) publish the record, or any part of it;

(b) exploit commercially the information contained in the record, or any part of that information.

(7) "Authorised unit trust scheme", ["authorised contractual scheme",] "authorised open-ended investment company" and "recognised scheme" have the same meaning as in Part XVII, and associated expressions are to be read accordingly.

(8) "Approved person" means a person in relation to whom the [FCA or the PRA] has given its approval under section 59 and "controlled function" and "arrangement" have the same meaning as in that section.

[(8A) In this section—

[. . .]

. . .

"senior manager", in relation to [an] authorised person, means a person who has approval under section 59 to perform a designated senior management function in relation to the carrying on by the authorised person of a regulated activity, and

"designated senior management function" [has the meaning given by section 59ZB].]

[(9) "The authorised person concerned", in relation to an approved person, means the person on whose application approval was given.]

NOTES

Word "FCA" in square brackets (in each place that it occurs) substituted by the Financial Services Act 2012, s 41, Sch 12, Pt 2, para 16, as from 1 April 2013. Other amendments to this section are as follows—

Sub-s (1) is amended as follows:

Para (ba) inserted by the Collective Investment in Transferable Securities (Contractual Scheme) Regulations 2013, SI 2013/1388, reg 3(1), (16), as from 6 June 2013.

Para (f) repealed by the Financial Services Act 2012, s 41, Sch 12, Pt 2, para 16, as from 1 April 2013.

The words in square brackets in para (g) were inserted by the Financial Services Act 2021, s 2, Sch 2, Pt 2, para 11, as from 1 July 2021; for transitional provisions, see Sch 2, Pt 3 to the 2021 Act.

The word omitted from para (h) was repealed, and para (ha) was inserted, by the Financial Services and Markets Act 2000 (Markets in Financial Instruments) Regulations 2007, SI 2007/126, reg 3(5), Sch 5, paras 1, 12, as from 1 April 2007 (certain purposes), and as from 1 November 2007 (otherwise).

The word omitted from para (ha) was repealed, and para (hb) was inserted, by the Mortgage Credit Directive Order 2015, SI 2015/910, Sch 1, para 1(1), (7), as from 21 March 2016.

Para (hc) was substituted for the word "and" that originally occurred at the end of para (hb) by the Financial Services and Markets Act 2000 (Markets in Financial Instruments) Regulations 2017, SI 2017/701, reg 50(1), Sch 2, paras 1, 44, as from 31 July 2017 (to enable entries to be added, removed, or altered in the record the FCA maintains under sub-s (1)), and as from 3 January 2018 (otherwise).

Sub-s (2) is amended as follows:

Para (ba) inserted by SI 2013/1388, reg 3(1), (16), as from 6 June 2013.

Words omitted from para (e) repealed by the Financial Services Act 2012, s 41, Sch 12, Pt 2, para 16, as from 1 April 2013.

Words in square brackets in sub-paras (g)(ii), (iii) substituted by the Financial Services (Banking Reform) Act 2013, s 35, Sch 3, para 11, as from 7 March 2016.

Sub-para (g)(iv) and para (h) inserted by the Financial Services (Banking Reform) Act 2013, s 34, as from 7 March 2016.

The words omitted from sub-para (g)(iv) were repealed, and the word in square brackets in para (h) was substituted, by the Bank of England and Financial Services Act 2016, s 21, Sch 4, paras 1, 19. Note that s 21 and Sch 4 come into force as follows: (i) 13 September 2018 (for the purpose of making rules, giving directions, imposing requirements and making statements of policy by the appropriate regulator for insurers); (ii) 10 December 2018 (for all other purposes for insurers (except in relation to Sch 4, para 11)), and 10 December 2019 (Sch 4, para 11 for insurers); (iii) 18 July 2019 (for the purpose of the making of rules, the giving of directions, the imposition of requirements and the issuing of statements of policy by the FCA for remaining purposes); (iv) 9 August 2019 (for remaining purposes in relation to authorised persons who are not solo-regulated firms); (v) 9 December 2019 (for remaining purposes in relation to solo-regulated firms other than benchmark firms (except as provided for by (vii) below)); (vi) 7 December 2020 (for remaining purposes in relation to benchmark firms (except as provided for by (viii) below)); (vii) 31 March 2021 (in relation to the employee certification provisions for remaining purposes in relation to solo-regulated firms other than benchmark firms); (viii) 7 December 2021 (in relation to the employee certification provisions for remaining purposes in relation to benchmark firms). For transitional provisions in connection with (i)–(iii) above, see the Bank of England and Financial Services Act 2016 (Commencement No 5 and Transitional Provisions) Regulations 2018, SI 2018/990; and for transitional provisions in connection with the other commencement dates, see the Bank of England and Financial Services Act 2016 (Commencement No 6 and Transitional Provisions) Regulations 2019, SI 2019/1136.

Paras (i), (j) inserted by SI 2015/910, Sch 1, para 1(1), (7), as from 21 March 201.

Sub-s (2A): inserted by SI 2007/126, reg 3(5), Sch 5, paras 1, 12, as from 1 April 2007 (certain purposes), and as from 1 November 2007 (otherwise). This subsection has subsequently been amended as follows:

The words "or (1AA)" in square brackets in para (a) were inserted by SI 2017/701, reg 50(1), Sch 2, paras 1, 44, as from 31 July 2017 (to enable entries to be added, removed, or altered in the record the FCA maintains under sub-s (1)), and as from 3 January 2018 (otherwise).

The word "and" in square brackets at the end of para (a) was inserted, and para (c) and the preceding word were repealed, by the Public Record, Disclosure of Information and Co-operation (Financial Services) (Amendment) (EU Exit) Regulations 2019, SI 2019/681, reg 2(1), (2), as from IP completion day (as defined in the European Union (Withdrawal Agreement) Act 2020, s 39).

Sub-s (2B): inserted by SI 2015/910, Sch 1, para 1(1), (7), as from 21 March 2016.

Sub-s (2C): inserted by SI 2017/701, reg 50(1), Sch 2, paras 1, 44, as from 31 July 2017 (to enable entries to be added, removed, or altered in the record the FCA maintains under sub-s (1)), and as from 3 January 2018 (otherwise).

Sub-ss (3A), (3B): inserted by SI 2017/701, reg 50(1), Sch 2, paras 1, 44, as from 31 July 2017 (to enable entries to be added, removed, or altered in the record the FCA maintains under sub-s (1)), and as from 3 January 2018 (otherwise). Words in square brackets in sub-s (3A) substituted by SI 2019/681, reg 2(1), (2), as from IP completion day (as defined in the European Union (Withdrawal Agreement) Act 2020, s 39).

Sub-s (4): words "in any case where it has not already done so under subsection (3B)" inserted by SI 2017/701, reg 50(1), Sch 2, paras 1, 44, as from 31 July 2017 (to enable entries to be added, removed, or altered in the record the FCA maintains under sub-s (1)), and as from 3 January 2018 (otherwise).

Sub-s (4A): inserted by SI 2015/910, Sch 1, para 1(1), (7), as from 21 March 2016.

Sub-s (7): words in square brackets inserted by SI 2013/1388, reg 3(1), (16), as from 6 June 2013.

Sub-s (8): words "FCA or the PRA" in square brackets substituted by the Financial Services Act 2012, s 41, Sch 12, Pt 2, para 16, as from 1 April 2013.

Sub-s (8A): inserted by the Financial Services (Banking Reform) Act 2013, s 34, as from 7 March 2016. This subsection has subsequently been amended as follows:

The definition "exempt investment firm" (omitted) was originally inserted by SI 2017/701, reg 50(1), Sch 2, paras 1, 44, as from 31 July 2017 (to enable entries to be added, removed, or altered in the record the FCA maintains under sub-s (1)), and as from 3 January 2018 (otherwise); and was subsequently repealed by SI 2019/681, reg 2(1), (2), as from IP completion day (as defined in the European Union (Withdrawal Agreement) Act 2020, s 39).

All other amendments to sub-s (8A) were made by the Bank of England and Financial Services Act 2016, s 21, Sch 4, paras 1, 19 (as to the commencement of this amendment, see the first note relating to the 2016 Act above).

Sub-s (9): substituted by the Financial Services (Banking Reform) Act 2013, s 34, as from 7 March 2016.

[7.624]

[347A Duty of PRA to disclose information relevant to the record

(1) The PRA must, for the purpose of assisting the FCA to comply with its duty under section 347—

(a) notify the FCA if the information included in the record as required under section 347(2)(a) appears to the PRA to be incomplete or inaccurate,

(b) if it makes a prohibition order relating to an individual, provide the FCA with information falling within section 347(2)(f) in relation to that order,

(c) where it is the appropriate regulator in relation to an approved person, provide the FCA with information falling within section 347(2)(g) in relation to that approved person, and

(d) where the FCA has notified the PRA that it considers it appropriate to include in the record information of a certain description, disclose to the FCA such information of that description as the PRA has in its possession.

(2) The duty to provide information under this section does not apply to information which the PRA reasonably believes is in the possession of the FCA.

(3) Subsection (1) does not require or authorise the disclosure of information whose disclosure is prohibited by or under section 348.

(4) This section is without prejudice to any other power to disclose information.

(5) In this section references to the "record" are to the record maintained under section 347.]

NOTES

Inserted by the Financial Services Act 2012, s 41, Sch 12, Pt 2, para 17, as from 1 April 2013.

Disclosure of information

[7.625]

348 Restrictions on disclosure of confidential information by [FCA, PRA] etc

(1) Confidential information must not be disclosed by a primary recipient, or by any person obtaining the information directly or indirectly from a primary recipient, without the consent of—

(a) the person from whom the primary recipient obtained the information; and

(b) if different, the person to whom it relates.

(2) In this Part "confidential information" means information which—

(a) relates to the business or other affairs of any person;

(b) was received by the primary recipient for the purposes of, or in the discharge of, any functions of the [FCA, the PRA] . . . or the Secretary of State under any provision made by or under this Act; and

(c) is not prevented from being confidential information by subsection (4).

(3) It is immaterial for the purposes of subsection (2) whether or not the information was received—

(a) by virtue of a requirement to provide it imposed by or under this Act;

(b) for other purposes as well as purposes mentioned in that subsection.

(4) Information is not confidential information if—

(a) it has been made available to the public by virtue of being disclosed in any circumstances in which, or for any purposes for which, disclosure is not precluded by this section; or

(b) it is in the form of a summary or collection of information so framed that it is not possible to ascertain from it information relating to any particular person.

(5) Each of the following is a primary recipient for the purposes of this Part—

[(a) the FCA;

(aa) the [Bank of England];]

(b) . . .

(c) the Secretary of State;

[(zd) a person appointed to act as a temporary manager by the FCA or the PRA under section 71C;]

(d) a person appointed [to collect or update information under section [166A] or] to make a report under section 166;

(e) any person who is or has been employed by a person mentioned in paragraphs (a) to (c);

[(ea) a person who is or has been engaged to provide services to a person mentioned in those paragraphs;]

(f) any auditor or expert instructed by a person mentioned in those paragraphs.

(6) In subsection (5)(f) "expert" includes—

(a) a competent person appointed by [the FCA] under section 97;

(b) a competent person appointed by the [FCA, the PRA] or the Secretary of State to conduct an investigation under Part XI;

(c) . . .

[(7) Nothing in this section applies to information received by a primary recipient for the purposes of, or in the discharge of, any functions of the FCA under the Competition Act 1998 or the Enterprise Act 2002 by virtue of Part 16A of this Act.

(For provision about the disclosure of such information, see Part 9 of the Enterprise Act 2002.)]

[(8) In this section references to the Bank of England include the Bank acting in its capacity as the PRA.]

NOTES

The words "Bank of England" in square brackets in sub-s (5)(aa) were substituted, and sub-s (8) was added, by the Bank of England and Financial Services Act 2016, s 16, Sch 2, Pt 2, paras 26, 45, as from 1 March 2017 (for transitional provisions, see Sch 3, para 6 to the 2016 Act).

In sub-s (5), para (zd) was inserted by the Bank Recovery and Resolution Order 2016, SI 2016/1239, arts 30, 34, as from 16 December 2016.

The words in the first (outer) pair of square brackets in sub-s (5)(d) were inserted by the Financial Services Act 2010, s 24(1), (2), Sch 2, Pt 1, paras 1, 26, as from 8 June 2010.

Sub-s (7) was added by the Financial Services (Banking Reform) Act 2013, s 129, Sch 8, Pt 1, para 5, as from a 1 November 2014.

All other words in square brackets in this section were substituted, and the words omitted were repealed, by the Financial Services Act 2012, s 41, Sch 12, Pt 2, para 18, as from 1 April 2013.

[7.626]

349 Exceptions from section 348

(1) Section 348 does not prevent a disclosure of confidential information which is—

(a) made for the purpose of facilitating the carrying out of a public function; and

(b) permitted by regulations made by the Treasury under this section.

(2) The regulations may, in particular, make provision permitting the disclosure of confidential information or of confidential information of a prescribed kind—

(a) by prescribed recipients, or recipients of a prescribed description, to any person for the purpose of enabling or assisting the recipient to discharge prescribed public functions;

(b) by prescribed recipients, or recipients of a prescribed description, to prescribed persons, or persons of prescribed descriptions, for the purpose of enabling or assisting those persons to discharge prescribed public functions;

(c) by the [FCA or the PRA] to the Treasury or the Secretary of State for any purpose;

(d) by any recipient if the disclosure is with a view to or in connection with prescribed proceedings.

(3) The regulations may also include provision—

(a) making any permission to disclose confidential information subject to conditions (which may relate to the obtaining of consents or any other matter);

(b) restricting the uses to which confidential information disclosed under the regulations may be put.

[(3A) Section 348 does not apply to—

(a) the disclosure by [the Panel on Takeovers and Mergers] of confidential information disclosed to it by the [FCA or the PRA] in reliance on subsection (1);

(b) the disclosure of such information by a person obtaining it directly or indirectly from [the Panel on Takeovers and Mergers].

(3B) . . .]

(4) In relation to confidential information, each of the following is a "recipient"—

(a) a primary recipient;

(b) a person obtaining the information directly or indirectly from a primary recipient.

(5) "Public functions" includes—

(a) functions conferred by or in accordance with any provision contained in any enactment or subordinate legislation;

(b) . . .

(c) similar functions [to those referred to in paragraph (a)] conferred on persons by or under provisions having effect as part of the law of a country or territory outside the United Kingdom;

(d) functions exercisable in relation to prescribed disciplinary proceedings.

(6) "Enactment" includes—

(a) an Act of the Scottish Parliament;

(b) Northern Ireland legislation.

(7) "Subordinate legislation" has the meaning given in the Interpretation Act 1978 and also includes an instrument made under an Act of the Scottish Parliament or under Northern Ireland legislation.

[(8) . . .]

NOTES

Sub-s (2): words in square brackets substituted by the Financial Services Act 2012, s 41, Sch 12, Pt 2, para 19(1), (2), as from 1 April 2013.

Sub-ss (3A), (3B): originally inserted by the Companies Act 2006, s 964(1), (4), as from 6 April 2007. Words in second pair of square brackets in sub-s (3A) substituted by the Financial Services Act 2012, s 41, Sch 12, Pt 2, para 19(1), (3), (4), as from 1 April 2013. Other words in square brackets in sub-s (3A) substituted, and sub-s (3B) repealed, by the Public Record, Disclosure of Information and Co-operation (Financial Services) (Amendment) (EU Exit) Regulations 2019, SI 2019/681, reg 2(1), (3)(a), (b), as from IP completion day (as defined in the European Union (Withdrawal Agreement) Act 2020, s 39).

Sub-s (5): para (b) repealed, and words in square brackets in para (c) inserted, by SI 2019/681, reg 2(1), (3)(c), (d), as from IP completion day (as defined in the European Union (Withdrawal Agreement) Act 2020, s 39).

Sub-s (8): originally added by the Takeovers Directive (Interim Implementation) Regulations 2006, SI 2006/1183, reg 18(3), (5), as from 20 May 2006. Subsequently repealed by the Companies Act 2006 (Commencement No 2, Consequential Amendments, Transitional Provisions and Savings) Order 2007, SI 2007/1093, art 7, Sch 5, as from 6 April 2007.

Regulations: the Financial Services and Markets Act 2000 (Disclosure of Confidential Information) Regulations 2001, SI 2001/2188; the Financial Services and Markets Act 2000 (Disclosure of Confidential Information) (Amendment) Regulations 2001, SI 2001/3437; the Financial Services and Markets Act 2000 (Disclosure of Confidential Information) (Amendment) (No 2) Regulations 2001, SI 2001/3624; the Electronic Commerce Directive (Financial Services and Markets) Regulations 2002, SI 2002/1775; the Financial Services and Markets Act 2000 (Disclosure of Confidential Information) (Amendment) Regulations 2003, SI 2003/693; the Insurance Mediation Directive (Miscellaneous Amendments) Regulations 2003, SI 2003/1473; the Collective Investment Schemes (Miscellaneous Amendments) Regulations 2003, SI 2003/2066; the Financial Services and Markets Act 2000 (Disclosure of Confidential Information) (Amendment) (No 2) Regulations 2003, SI 2003/2174; the Financial Services and Markets Act 2000 (Disclosure of Confidential Information) (Amendment) (No 3) Regulations 2003, SI 2003/2817; the Financial Services and Markets Act 2000 (Disclosure of Confidential Information) (Amendment) Regulations 2005, SI 2005/3071; the Financial Services and Markets Act 2000 (Disclosure of Confidential Information) (Amendment) Regulations 2006, SI 2006/3413; the Financial Services and Markets Act 2000 (Markets in Financial Instruments) (Amendment) Regulations 2007, SI 2007/763; the Financial Services and Markets Act 2000 (Reinsurance Directive) Regulations 2007, SI 2007/3255; the Financial Services and Markets Act 2000 (Disclosure of Confidential Information) (Amendment) Regulations 2009, SI 2009/2877; the Credit Rating Agencies Regulations 2010, SI 2010/906; the Financial Services and Markets Act 2000 (Disclosure of Confidential Information) (Amendment) Regulations 2012, SI 2012/3019; the Alternative Investment Fund Managers Regulations 2013, SI 2013/1773; the Capital Requirements Regulations 2013, SI 2013/3115; the Financial Services and Markets Act 2000 (Disclosure of Confidential Information) (Amendment) Regulations 2014, SI 2014/883; the Financial Services and Markets Act 2000 and the Financial Services (Banking Reform) Act 2013 (Disclosure of Confidential Information) (Amendment) Regulations 2017, SI 2017/456; the Public Record, Disclosure of Information and Co-operation (Financial Services) (Amendment) (EU Exit) Regulations 2019, SI 2019/681; the Financial Services (Miscellaneous) (Amendment) (EU Exit) (No 3) Regulations 2019, SI 2019/1390; the Financial Holding Companies (Approval etc) and Capital Requirements (Capital Buffers and Macro-prudential Measures) (Amendment) (EU Exit) Regulations 2020, SI 2020/1406; the Recognised Auction Platforms (Amendment and Miscellaneous Provisions) Regulations 2021, SI 2021/494.

[7.627]
350 Disclosure of information by the Inland Revenue

[(1) No obligation as to secrecy imposed by statute or otherwise prevents the disclosure of Revenue information to—

(a) the FCA or the PRA, if the disclosure is made for the purpose of assisting or enabling that regulator to discharge its functions under this or any other Act, or

(b) the Secretary of State, if the disclosure is made for the purpose of assisting in the investigation of a matter under section 168 or with a view to the appointment of an investigator under that section.]

(2) A disclosure may only be made under subsection (1) by or under the authority of the Commissioners of Inland Revenue.

(3) Section 348 does not apply to Revenue information.

(4) Information obtained as a result of [subsection (1)(b)] may not be used except—

(a) for the purpose of deciding whether to appoint an investigator under section 168;

(b) in the conduct of an investigation under section 168;

(c) in criminal proceedings brought against a person under this Act or the Criminal Justice Act 1993 as a result of an investigation under section 168;

(d) for the purpose of taking action under this Act against a person as a result of an investigation under section 168;

(e) in proceedings before the Tribunal as a result of action taken as mentioned in paragraph (d).

(5) Information obtained as a result of subsection (1) may not be disclosed except—

(a) by or under the authority of the Commissioners of Inland Revenue;

(b) in proceedings mentioned in subsection (4)(c) or (e) or with a view to their institution.

(6) Subsection (5) does not prevent the disclosure of information obtained as a result of subsection (1) to a person to whom it could have been disclosed under subsection (1).

(7) "Revenue information" means information held by a person which it would be an offence under section 182 of the Finance Act 1989 for him to disclose.

NOTES

Sub-s (1) was substituted, and the words in square brackets in sub-s (4) were substituted, by the Financial Services Act 2012, s 41, Sch 12, Pt 2, para 20, as from 1 April 2013.

Commissioners of Inland Revenue: a reference to the Commissioners of Inland Revenue is now to be taken as a reference to the Commissioners for Her Majesty's Revenue and Customs; see the Commissioners for Revenue and Customs Act 2005, s 50(1), (7).

Application: the Commissioners for Her Majesty's Revenue and Customs may supply information in accordance with this section only if the information was obtained or is held in the exercise of a function relating to matters to which the Commissioners for Revenue and Customs Act 2005, s 7 applies; see s 17(6) of, and Sch 2, Pt 2, para 18 to, that Act

351 (*Repealed by the Financial Services Act 2012, s 41, Sch 12, Pt 2, para 21, as from 1 April 2013.*)

[7.628]
[351A Disclosure under the UCITS directive

(1) This section applies in relation to a disclosure made by a person who falls within subsection (2) for the purpose of compliance with requirements set out in rules made by [the FCA or the PRA] to implement Chapter VIII of the UCITS directive.

(2) The following persons fall within this subsection—

(a) the auditor of an authorised unit trust scheme [or authorised contractual scheme] that is a master UCITS;

(b) the trustee of an authorised unit trust scheme that is a master UCITS;

[(ba) the depositary of an authorised contractual scheme that is a master UCITS;]

(c) the auditor of an authorised unit trust scheme [or authorised contractual scheme] that is a feeder UCITS;
(d) the trustee of an authorised unit trust scheme that is a feeder UCITS; . . .
[(da) the depositary of an authorised contractual scheme that is a feeder UCITS; or]
[(e) a person acting on behalf of a person within any of paragraphs (a) to (da)].

(3) A disclosure to which this section applies is not to be taken as a contravention of any duty to which the person making the disclosure is subject.

(4) In this section, "authorised unit trust scheme", ["authorised contractual scheme",] "master UCITS" and "feeder UCITS" have the meaning given in section 237.]

NOTES

Inserted by the Undertakings for Collective Investment in Transferable Securities Regulations 2011, SI 2011/1613, reg 2(1), (28), as from 1 July 2011.

The words in square brackets in sub-s (1) were substituted by the Financial Services Act 2012, s 41, Sch 12, Pt 2, para 22, as from 1 April 2013.

The words in square brackets in subs (2)(a), (c) and sub-s (4) were inserted, sub-s (2)(ba), (da) were inserted, the word omitted from sub-s (2)(d) was repealed, and sub-s (2)(e) was substituted, by the Collective Investment in Transferable Securities (Contractual Scheme) Regulations 2013, SI 2013/1388, reg 3(1), (17), as from 6 June 2013.

[7.629]

352 Offences

(1) A person who discloses information in contravention of section 348 or 350(5) is guilty of an offence.

(2) A person guilty of an offence under subsection (1) is liable—
(a) on summary conviction, to imprisonment for a term not exceeding three months or a fine not exceeding the statutory maximum, or both;
(b) on conviction on indictment, to imprisonment for a term not exceeding two years or a fine, or both.

(3) A person is guilty of an offence if, in contravention of any provision of regulations made under section 349, he uses information which has been disclosed to him in accordance with the regulations.

(4) A person is guilty of an offence if, in contravention of subsection (4) of section 350, he uses information which has been disclosed to him in accordance with that section.

(5) A person guilty of an offence under subsection (3) or (4) is liable on summary conviction to imprisonment for a term not exceeding *three months* or a fine not exceeding level 5 on the standard scale, or both.

(6) In proceedings for an offence under this section it is a defence for the accused to prove—
(a) that he did not know and had no reason to suspect that the information was confidential information or that it had been disclosed in accordance with section 350;
(b) that he took all reasonable precautions and exercised all due diligence to avoid committing the offence.

NOTES

Sub-s (5): for the words in italics there are substituted the words "51 weeks" by the Criminal Justice Act 2003, s 280(2), Sch 26, para 54(1), (3), as from a day to be appointed.

[7.630]

353 Removal of other restrictions on disclosure

(1) The Treasury may make regulations permitting the disclosure of any information, or of information of a prescribed kind—
(a) by prescribed persons for the purpose of assisting or enabling them to discharge prescribed functions under this Act or any rules or regulations made under it;
(b) by prescribed persons, or persons of a prescribed description, to the [FCA or the PRA] for the purpose of assisting or enabling [either of them] to discharge prescribed functions;
[(c) . . .]

(2) Regulations under this section may not make any provision in relation to the disclosure of confidential information by primary recipients or by any person obtaining confidential information directly or indirectly from a primary recipient.

(3) If a person discloses any information as permitted by regulations under this section the disclosure is not to be taken as a contravention of any duty to which he is subject.

NOTES

Sub-s (1): words in square brackets in para (b) substituted by the Financial Services Act 2012, s 41, Sch 12, Pt 2, para 23, as from 1 April 2013. Para (c) originally inserted by the Consumer Credit Act 2006, s 61(9), as from 16 June 2006, and subsequently repealed by the Financial Services and Markets Act 2000 (Regulated Activities) (Amendment) (No 2) Order 2013, SI 2013/1881, art 10(1), (13), as from 1 April 2014.

Regulations: the Financial Services and Markets Act 2000 (Disclosure of Information by Prescribed Persons) Regulations 2001, SI 2001/1857; the Financial Services and Markets Act 2000 (Disclosure of Information by Prescribed Persons) (Amendment) Regulations 2005, SI 2005/272.

[Information received from Bank of England

[7.631]

353A Information received from Bank of England

(1) [The FCA] must not disclose to any person specially protected information.

(2) "Specially protected information" is information in relation to which the first and second conditions are met.

(3) The first condition is that [the FCA received the information from the Bank of England]

(4) The second condition is that the Bank notified the [FCA] that the Bank held the information for the purpose of its functions with respect to any of the following—
(a) monetary policy;
(b) financial operations intended to support financial institutions for the purposes of maintaining stability;
(c) the provision of private banking services and related services.

(5) The notification referred to in subsection (4) must be—

(a) in writing, and

(b) given before, or at the same time as, the Bank discloses the information.

(6) The prohibition in subsection (1) does not apply—

(a) . . .

(b) where the Bank has consented to disclosure of the information;

(c) to information which has been made available to the public by virtue of being disclosed in any circumstances in which, or for any purposes for which, disclosure is not precluded by this section;

(d) . . .

(7) In this section references to disclosure by or to [the FCA] or by the Bank include references to disclosure by or to—

(a) persons who are, or are acting as,—

(i) officers of, or members of the staff of, the [FCA], or

(ii) officers, employees or agents of the Bank, or

(b) auditors, experts, contractors or investigators appointed by the [FCA] or the Bank under powers conferred by this Act or otherwise.

(8) References to disclosure by [the FCA] do not include references to disclosure between persons who fall within any paragraph of subsection (7)(a) or (b) in relation to [the FCA].

(9) [The FCA] must take such steps as are reasonable in the circumstances to prevent the disclosure of specially protected information, in cases not excluded by subsection (6), by those who are or have been—

(a) its officers or members of staff (including persons acting as its officers or members of staff);

(b) auditors, experts, contractors or investigators appointed by the [FCA] under powers conferred by this Act or otherwise;

(c) persons to whom the [FCA] has delegated any of its functions.

[(10) In this section references to the Bank of England include the Bank acting in its capacity as the PRA.]]

NOTES

Inserted, together with the preceding heading, by the Financial Services Act 2012, s 41, Sch 12, Pt 2, para 24, as from 1 April 2013.

Sub-s (6): para (d) repealed by the Public Record, Disclosure of Information and Co-operation (Financial Services) (Amendment) (EU Exit) Regulations 2019, SI 2019/681, reg 2(1), (4), as from IP completion day (as defined in the European Union (Withdrawal Agreement) Act 2020, s 39).

All other amendments to this section were made by the Bank of England and Financial Services Act 2016, s 16, Sch 2, Pt 2, paras 26, 46, as from 1 March 2017.

Co-operation

[7.632]

[354A FCA's duty to co-operate with others

(1) The FCA must take such steps as it considers appropriate to co-operate with other persons (whether in the United Kingdom or elsewhere) who have functions—

(a) similar to those of the FCA, or

(b) in relation to the prevention or detection of financial crime.

(2) The persons referred to in subsection (1) do not include the Bank of England or the PRA (but see sections 3D and 3Q).

[(2A) Subsection (1) does not apply in relation to the Competition and Markets Authority in a case where the FCA has made a reference under section 131 of the Enterprise Act 2002 as a result of section 234I (but see section 234L).]

(3) The FCA must take such steps as it considers appropriate to co-operate with—

(a) the Panel on Takeovers and Mergers;

(b) . . .

(c) any . . . person or body that exercises functions of a public nature, under legislation in any country or territory outside the United Kingdom, that appear to the FCA to be similar to those of the Panel on Takeovers and Mergers.

(4) Co-operation may include the sharing of information which the FCA is not prevented from disclosing.

(5) "Financial crime" has the meaning given in section 1H(3).]

NOTES

Sections 354A–354C were substituted (for the original s 354) by the Financial Services Act 2012, s 41, Sch 12, Pt 2, para 25, as from 1 April 2013.

Sub-s (2A): inserted by the Financial Services (Banking Reform) Act 2013, s 129, Sch 8, Pt 1, para 6, as from 1 April 2015.

Sub-s (3): para (b) and the word omitted from para (c) were repealed by the Public Record, Disclosure of Information and Co-operation (Financial Services) (Amendment) (EU Exit) Regulations 2019, SI 2019/681, reg 2(1), (5), as from IP completion day (as defined in the European Union (Withdrawal Agreement) Act 2020, s 39).

[7.633]

[354B PRA's duty to co-operate with others

(1) The PRA must take such steps as it considers appropriate to co-operate with—

(a) other persons (whether in the United Kingdom or elsewhere) who have functions similar to those of the PRA, and

(b) other bodies that have functions relevant to financial stability.

(2) The persons referred to in subsection (1) do not include the [FCA (but see section 3D)].

(3) Co-operation may include the sharing of information which the PRA is not prevented from disclosing.]

NOTES

Substituted as noted to s 354A at **[7.632]**.

Sub-s (2): words in square brackets substituted by the Bank of England and Financial Services Act 2016, s 16, Sch 2, Pt 2, paras 26, 47, as from 1 March 2017.

Part 7 Financial Services Acts

345C–345H *(S 354C was originally substituted as noted to s 354A ante; and was subsequently repealed by the Bank of England and Financial Services Act 2016, s 16, Sch 2, Pt 2, paras 26, 48, as from 1 March 2017. Ss 345D–345H (Provision of information to ESMA, the Commission and other EEA States) and the preceding heading were originally inserted by the Financial Services and Markets (Disclosure of Information to the European Securities and Markets Authority etc and Other Provisions) Regulations 2016, SI 2016/1095, reg 3, as from 8 December 2016 (ss 345D–345G), and by the Insurance Distribution (Regulated Activities and Miscellaneous Amendments) Order 2018, SI 2018/546, arts 9, 15, as from 1 October 2018 (s 345H), and were subsequently repealed by the Public Record, Disclosure of Information and Co-operation (Financial Services) (Amendment) (EU Exit) Regulations 2019, SI 2019/681, reg 2(1), (6), as from IP completion day (as defined in the European Union (Withdrawal Agreement) Act 2020, s 39).)*

PART XXIV INSOLVENCY

NOTES

Transitional provisions etc in connection with the commencement of the Financial Services Act 2012: for transitional provisions in relation to this Part, see Part 10 of the Financial Services Act 2012 (Transitional Provisions) (Miscellaneous Provisions) Order 2013, SI 2013/442. Article 45 concerns the powers of the FCA and the PRA to participate in proceedings under s 358 (trust deeds for creditors in Scotland). Article 46 contains transitional provisions for cases where an administrator made a report to the FSA in accordance with s 361(2) before 1 April 2013. Article 47 contains transitional provisions in relation to cases where a notice or other document was sent to the FSA in accordance with s 362(3) (powers to participate in proceedings) before that date. Article 48 deals with cases where the FSA had consented for the purposes of s 362A(2) to the appointment of an administrator. Article 49 contains transitional provisions in relation to reports sent to the FSA in accordance with s 363(4). Article 50 concerns reports made to the FSA by a receiver in accordance with s 364. Article 51 concerns notices or other documents sent to the FSA in accordance with s 365(4). Article 52 contains transitional provisions in relation to the voluntary winding-up of an insurer. Article 53 concerns petitions served on the FSA in accordance with s 369(1) (insurers: service of petition etc). Article 54 concerns petitions served on the FSA in accordance with s 369A(1) (reclaim funds: service of petition etc) and applications served in accordance with s 369(2). Article 55 deals with a liquidator's report served on the FSA in accordance with s 370. Article 56 concerns notices or other documents sent to the FSA in accordance with s 371(3). Article 57 contains transitional provisions in relation to reports made to the FSA by an insolvency practitioner in accordance with s 373(1). Article 58 concerns reports sent to the FSA in accordance with s 374(3). Article 59 provides that in s 375(1A) (right to apply for an order), the reference to a PRA-regulated activity includes an activity which would have been a PRA-regulated activity if it had been carried on, on 1 April 2013. Article 60 contains transitional provisions in relation to cases where the court appointed an independent actuary for the purposes of s 376(10) (continuation of contracts of long-term insurance where insurer in liquidation) on the application of the FSA.

Transitional provisions etc in connection with the original commencement of this Act: as to the application of s 367 to a body that had been an authorised institution within the meaning of the Banking Act 1987 (repealed), or which, before 1 December 2001, contravened s 3 of the 1987 Act (restriction on acceptance of deposits), see the Financial Services and Markets Act 2000 (Transitional Provisions and Savings) (Civil Remedies, Discipline, Criminal Offences etc) (No 2) Order 2001, SI 2001/3083, art 12.

Interpretation

[7.634]

355 Interpretation of this Part

(1) In this Part—

. . .

"the 1986 Act" means the Insolvency Act 1986;

"the 1989 Order" means the Insolvency (Northern Ireland) Order 1989;

["the 2016 Act" means the Bankruptcy (Scotland) Act 2016;]

"body" means a body of persons—

(a) over which the court has jurisdiction under any provision of, or made under, the 1986 Act (or the 1989 Order); but

(b) which is not a building society, a friendly society or [a registered society]; and

"court" means—

(a) the court having jurisdiction for the purposes of the 1985 Act or the 1986 Act; or

(b) in Northern Ireland, the High Court;

["creditors' decision procedure" has the meaning given by section 379ZA(11) of the 1986 Act;]

["PRA-regulated person" means a person who—

(a) is or has been a PRA-authorised person,

(b) is or has been an appointed representative whose principal (or one of whose principals) is, or was, a PRA-authorised person, or

(c) is carrying on or has carried on a PRA-regulated activity in contravention of the general prohibition];

["qualifying decision procedure" has the meaning given by section 246ZE(11) of the 1986 Act].

(2) In this Part "insurer" has such meaning as may be specified in an order made by the Treasury.

NOTES

Sub-s (1) is amended as follows:

Definition "the 1985 Act" (omitted) repealed, and definition "the 1989 Order" inserted, by the Bankruptcy (Scotland) Act 2016 (Consequential Provisions and Modifications) Order 2016, SI 2016/1034, art 7(1), (3), Sch 1, para 20(1), (4), as from 30 November 2016 (except in relation to (i) a sequestration as regards which the petition is presented, or the debtor application is made before that date; or (ii) a trust deed executed before that date).

Words in square brackets in the definition "body" substituted by the Co-operative and Community Benefit Societies Act 2014, s 151, Sch 4, Pt 2, paras 68, 70, as from 1 August 2014.

Definitions "creditors' decision procedure" and "qualifying decision procedure" inserted by the Small Business, Enterprise and Employment Act 2015 (Consequential Amendments, Savings and Transitional Provisions) Regulations 2018, SI 2018/208, reg 4(1), (2), as from 13 March 2018.

Definition "PRA-regulated person" inserted by the Financial Services Act 2012, s 44, Sch 14, paras 1, 2, as from 1 April 2013.

Orders: the Financial Services and Markets Act 2000 (Insolvency) (Definition of "Insurer") Order 2001, SI 2001/2634. As amended, the Order provides that for the purposes of this Part, "insurer" means any person who is carrying on a regulated activity of the kind specified by art 10(1) or (2) of the Regulated Activities Order (effecting and carrying out contracts of insurance) but who is not: (a) exempt from the general prohibition in respect of that regulated activity; (b) a friendly society; or (c) a person who effects or carries out contracts of insurance all of which fall within paras 14 to 18 of Part I of Schedule 1 to the RAO in the course of, or for the purposes of, a banking business.

[Arrangements and reconstructions: companies in financial difficulty

[7.635]

355A Powers of FCA and PRA to participate in proceedings

(1) This section applies where Part 26A of the Companies Act 2006 ("the 2006 Act") (arrangements and reconstructions: companies in financial difficulty) applies in relation to a company which—

- (a) is, or has been, an authorised person or recognised investment exchange;
- (b) is, or has been, any of the following—
  - (i) an electronic money institution;
  - (ii) an authorised payment institution;
  - (iii) a small payment institution;
  - (iv) a registered account information service provider;
- (c) is, or has been, an appointed representative; or
- (d) is carrying on, or has carried on, a regulated activity in contravention of the general prohibition.

(2) A relevant applicant must give notice to the appropriate regulator of—

- (a) any application which the relevant applicant intends to make under section 901C(1) of the 2006 Act, and
- (b) any application which the relevant applicant believes a creditor or member of the company has made, or intends to make, under section 901C(1) of that Act in relation to the company.

(3) A relevant applicant may not make an application under section 901C(1) of the 2006 Act in relation to a company that is a PRA-regulated person without the consent of the PRA.

(4) In this section "relevant applicant", in relation to a company, means—

- (a) the company;
- (b) if the company is being wound up, the liquidator;
- (c) if the company is in administration, the administrator.

(5) The appropriate regulator is entitled to be heard at any hearing of an application made under section 901C or 901F of the 2006 Act in relation to the company.

(6) Any notice or other document required to be sent to a creditor of the company must also be sent to the appropriate regulator.

(7) A person appointed for the purpose by the appropriate regulator is entitled—

- (a) to attend any meeting of creditors of the company summoned under section 901C of the 2006 Act;
- (b) to make representations as to any matter for decision at such a meeting.

(8) In this section—

"the appropriate regulator" means—

- (a) where the company is a PRA-regulated person, each of the FCA and the PRA, except that the reference in subsection (7) to a person appointed by the appropriate regulator is to be read as a reference to a person appointed by either the FCA or the PRA;
- (b) in any other case, the FCA;

"authorised payment institution", "small payment institution" and "registered account information service provider" have the same meaning as in the Payment Services Regulations 2017 (SI 2017/752) (see regulation 2 of those Regulations);

"electronic money institution" has the same meaning as in the Electronic Money Regulations 2011 (SI 2011/99) (see regulation 2 of those Regulations).]

NOTES

Commencement: 26 June 2020.

Inserted, together with the preceding heading and s 355B, by the Corporate Insolvency and Governance Act 2020, s 7, Sch 9, Pt 2, paras 17, 20(1), (2), as from 26 June 2020.

[7.636]

[355B Enforcement of requirements imposed by section 355A

(1) For the purpose of enforcing a requirement imposed on a company by section 355A(2) or (3), the appropriate regulator may exercise any of the following powers (so far as it would not otherwise be exercisable)—

- (a) the power to publish a statement under section 205 (public censure);
- (b) the power to impose a financial penalty under section 206.

(2) Accordingly, sections 205 and 206, and so much of this Act as relates to either of those sections, have effect in relation to a requirement imposed by section 355A(2) or (3) as if—

- (a) any reference to an authorised person included (so far as would not otherwise be the case) a reference to a company falling within any of paragraphs (a) to (d) of section 355A(1),
- (b) any reference to a relevant requirement included (so far as would not otherwise be the case) a reference to a requirement imposed by section 355A(2) or (3), and
- (c) "the appropriate regulator" had the same meaning as in section 355A.

(3) In this section "the appropriate regulator" has the same meaning as in section 355A.]

NOTES

Commencement: 26 June 2020.

Inserted as noted to s 355A at **[7.635]**.

Part 7 Financial Services Acts

Voluntary arrangements

[7.637]

356 [Powers of FCA and PRA] to participate in proceedings: company voluntary arrangements

[(1) Where a voluntary arrangement has effect under Part I of the 1986 Act in respect of a company or insolvent partnership which is an authorised person, [or recognised investment exchange, the appropriate regulator] may apply to the court under section 6 or 7 of that Act.

(2) Where a voluntary arrangement has been approved under Part II of the 1989 Order in respect of a company or insolvent partnership which is an authorised person, [or recognised investment exchange, the appropriate regulator] may apply to the court under Article 19 or 20 of that Order.]

(3) If a person other than [a regulator] makes an application to the court in relation to the company or insolvent partnership under [any] of those provisions, [the appropriate regulator] is entitled to be heard at any hearing relating to the application.

[(4) The appropriate regulator" means—

(a) in the case of a PRA-authorised person—

(i) for the purposes of subsections (1) and (2), the FCA or the PRA, and

(ii) for the purposes of subsection (3), each of the FCA and the PRA;

(b) in any other case, the FCA.

(5) If either regulator makes an application to the court under any of those provisions in relation to a PRA-authorised person, the other regulator is entitled to be heard at any hearing relating to the application.]

NOTES

Section heading: words in square brackets substituted by the Financial Services Act 2012, s 44, Sch 14, paras 1, 3(1), (5), as from 1 April 2013.

Sub-ss (1), (2): substituted by the Insolvency Act 2000, s 15(3)(a), (b), as from 1 January 2003. Words in square brackets substituted by the Financial Services Act 2012, s 44, Sch 14, paras 1, 3(1), (2), as from 1 April 2013.

Sub-s (3): words in first and third pairs of square brackets substituted by the Financial Services Act 2012, s 44, Sch 14, paras 1, 3(1), (3), as from 1 April 2013. Word in second pair of square brackets substituted by the Insolvency Act 2000, s 15(3)(c), as from 1 January 2003.

Sub-ss (4), (5): added by the Financial Services Act 2012, s 44, Sch 14, paras 1, 3(1), (4), as from 1 April 2013.

[7.638]

357 [Powers of FCA and PRA] to participate in proceedings: individual voluntary arrangements

(1) The [appropriate regulator] is entitled to be heard on an application by an individual who is an authorised person under section 253 of the 1986 Act (or Article 227 of the 1989 Order).

(2) Subsections [(2A)] to (6) apply if such an order is made on the application of such a person.

[(2A) Where under section 257 of the 1986 Act the individual's creditors are asked to decide whether to approve the proposed voluntary arrangement—

(a) notice of the creditors' decision procedure must be given to the appropriate regulator; and

(b) the appropriate regulator or a person appointed by the appropriate regulator is entitled to participate in (but not vote in) the creditors' decision procedure by which the decision is made.

(2B) Notice of the decision made by the creditors' decision procedure is to be given to the appropriate regulator by the nominee or the nominee's replacement under section 256(3) or 256A(4) of the 1986 Act.]

(3) A person appointed for the purpose by the [appropriate regulator] is entitled to attend any meeting of creditors of the debtor summoned under [Article 231 of the 1989 Order].

(4) Notice of the result of a meeting so summoned is to be given to the [appropriate regulator] by the chairman of the meeting.

(5) The [appropriate regulator] may apply to the court—

(a) under section 262 of the 1986 Act (or Article 236 of the 1989 Order); or

(b) under section 263 of the 1986 Act (or Article 237 of the 1989 Order).

(6) If a person other than [a regulator] makes an application to the court under any provision mentioned in subsection (5), [the appropriate regulator] is entitled to be heard at any hearing relating to the application.

[(7) The appropriate regulator" means—

[(a) in the case of a PRA-authorised person, each of the FCA and the PRA, except that the references in subsections (2A)(b) and (3) to a person appointed by the appropriate regulator are to be read as references to a person appointed by either the FCA or the PRA;]

(b) in any other case, the FCA.

(8) If either regulator makes an application to the court under any of the provisions mentioned in subsection (5) in relation to a PRA-authorised person, the other regulator is entitled to be heard at any hearing relating to the application.]

NOTES

The words in square brackets in the section heading and in sub-ss (1), (4)–(6) were substituted, the words in the first pair of square brackets in sub-s (3) were substituted, and sub-ss (7), (8) were added, by the Financial Services Act 2012, s 44, Sch 14, paras 1, 4, as from 1 April 2013.

The figure "(2A)" in square brackets in sub-s (2) was substituted, sub-ss (2A) and (2B) were inserted, the words in the second pair of square brackets in sub-s (3) were substituted, and sub-s (7)(a) was substituted, by the Small Business, Enterprise and Employment Act 2015 (Consequential Amendments, Savings and Transitional Provisions) Regulations 2018, SI 2018/208, reg 4(1), (3), as from 13 March 2018 (subject to transitional provisions as noted below).

Transitional provisions: the Small Business, Enterprise and Employment Act 2015 (Consequential Amendments, Savings and Transitional Provisions) Regulations 2018, SI 2018/208, regs 16, 17 provide as follows:

"16 Interpretation of Part 4

In this Part—

"the 1986 Act" means the Insolvency Act 1986;

"the 2000 Act" means the Financial Services and Markets Act 2000;

"the 2009 Act" means the Banking Act 2009; and

"relevant meeting" means a meeting of creditors which is to be held on or after the date on which Parts 2 and 3 of these Regulations come into force, and was—

(a) called, summoned or otherwise required before 6th April 2017 under a provision of the 1986 Act or the Insolvency Rules 1986;

(b) requisitioned by a creditor before 6th April 2017 under a provision of the 1986 Act or the Insolvency Rules 1986; or

(c) called or summoned under section 106, 146 or 331 of the 1986 Act as a result of—

(i) a final report to creditors sent before 6th April 2017 under rule 4.49D of the Insolvency Rules 1986 (final report to creditors in liquidation);

(ii) a final report to creditors and bankrupt sent before that date under rule 6.78B of those Rules (final report to creditors and bankrupt).

17 Transitional provisions for regulation 4

Where a relevant meeting is to be held in proceedings relating to an application by an individual who is an authorised person under section 253 of the 1986 Act (application for interim order where insolvent debtor intends to make a proposal for a voluntary arrangement), section 357 of the 2000 Act applies in relation to the meeting without the amendments made by regulation 4(3).".

[7.639]

358 [Powers of FCA and PRA] to participate in proceedings: trust deeds for creditors in Scotland

(1) This section applies where a trust deed has been granted by or on behalf of a debtor who is an authorised person [or recognised investment exchange].

(2) The trustee must, as soon as practicable after he becomes aware that the debtor is an authorised person [or recognised investment exchange], send to the [appropriate regulator]—

(a) in every case, a copy of the trust deed;

(b) where any other document or information is sent to every creditor known to the trustee in pursuance of [section 170 of the 2016] Act, a copy of such document or information.

(3) . . .

(4) The [appropriate regulator] must be given the same notice as the creditors of any meeting of creditors held in relation to the trust deed.

(5) A person appointed for the purpose by [the appropriate regulator] is entitled to attend and participate in (but not to vote at) any such meeting of creditors as if [that regulator] were a creditor under the deed.

(6) This section does not affect any right [a regulator] has as a creditor of a debtor who is an authorised person [or recognised investment exchange].

[(6A) The appropriate regulator" means—

(a) in the case of a PRA-authorised person—

(i) for the purposes of subsections (2) . . . and (4), each of the FCA and the PRA, and

(ii) for the purposes of subsection (5), the FCA or the PRA;

(b) in any other case, the FCA.]

(7) Expressions used in this section and in the [2016] Act have the same meaning in this section as in that Act.

NOTES

The words "section 170 of the 2016" in square brackets in sub-s (2)(b) were substituted, sub-s (3) was repealed, the figure omitted from sub-s (6A)(a)(i) was repealed, and the year "2016" in square brackets in sub-s (7) was substituted, by the Bankruptcy (Scotland) Act 2016 (Consequential Provisions and Modifications) Order 2016, SI 2016/1034, art 7(1), (3), Sch 1, para 20(1), (5), as from 30 November 2016 (except in relation to (i) a sequestration as regards which the petition is presented, or the debtor application is made before that date; or (ii) a trust deed executed before that date).

The words "or recognised investment exchange" in square brackets in sub-ss (1), (2), (6) were inserted, sub-s (6A) was inserted, and all other words in square brackets in this section were substituted, by the Financial Services Act 2012, s 44, Sch 14, paras 1, 5, as from 1 April 2013.

Administration orders

[7.640]

[359 Administration order

(1) The [FCA] may make an administration application under Schedule B1 to the 1986 Act [or Schedule B1 to the 1989 Order] in relation to a company or insolvent partnership which—

(a) is or has been an authorised person [or recognised investment exchange],

(b) is or has been an appointed representative, or

(c) is carrying on or has carried on a regulated activity in contravention of the general prohibition.

[(1A) The PRA may make an administration application under Schedule B1 to the 1986 Act or Schedule B1 to the 1989 Order in relation to a company or insolvent partnership which is a PRA-regulated person.]

(2) Subsection (3) applies in relation to an administration application made (or a petition presented) by [a regulator] by virtue of this section.

(3) Any of the following shall be treated for the purpose of paragraph 11(a) of Schedule B1 to the 1986 Act [or paragraph 12(a) of Schedule B1 to the 1989 Order] as unable to pay its debts—

(a) a company or partnership in default on an obligation to pay a sum due and payable under an agreement, . . .

(b) an authorised deposit taker in default on an obligation to pay a sum due and payable in respect of a relevant deposit[, and

(c) an authorised reclaim fund in default on an obligation to pay a sum payable as a result of a claim made by virtue of section 1(2)(b) or 2(2)(b) of the Dormant Bank and Building Society Accounts Act 2008].

(4) In this section—

"agreement" means an agreement the making or performance of which constitutes or is part of a regulated activity carried on by the company or partnership, "authorised deposit taker" means a person with a [Part 4A] permission to accept deposits (but not a person who has a [Part 4A] permission to accept deposits only for the purpose of carrying on another regulated activity in accordance with that permission),

["authorised reclaim fund" [has the same meaning as in the Dormant Assets Acts 2008 to 2022 (see section 26 of the Dormant Assets Act 2022)];]

"company" means a company—

(a) in respect of which an administrator may be appointed under Schedule B1 to the 1986 Act, or

[(b) in respect of which an administrator may be appointed under Schedule B1 to the 1989 Order,] and

"relevant deposit" shall, ignoring any restriction on the meaning of deposit arising from the identity of the person making the deposit, be construed in accordance with—

(a) section 22,

(b) any relevant order under that section, and

(c) Schedule 2.

(5) The definition of "authorised deposit taker" in subsection (4) shall be construed in accordance with—

(a) section 22,

(b) any relevant order under that section, and

(c) Schedule 2.]

NOTES

Substituted by the Enterprise Act 2002, s 248(3), Sch 17, paras 53, 55, as from 15 September 2003 (for savings and transitional provisions in relation to a petition for an administration order presented before that date, and in relation to special administration regimes (within the meaning of the Enterprise Act 2002, s 249), see the note to the Insolvency Act 1986, s 8 at **[9.147]**).

Sub-s (1): word in first pair of square brackets substituted, and words in the third pair of square brackets inserted, by the Financial Services Act 2012, s 44, Sch 14, paras 1, 6(1), (2), as from 1 April 2013. Words in second pair of square brackets substituted by the Insolvency (Northern Ireland) Order 2005, SI 2005/1455, art 3(3), Sch 2, paras 56, 58(1), (2), as from 27 March 2006.

Sub-s (1A): inserted by the Financial Services Act 2012, s 44, Sch 14, paras 1, 6(1), (3), as from 1 April 2013.

Sub-s (2): words in square brackets substituted by the Financial Services Act 2012, s 44, Sch 14, paras 1, 6(1), (4), as from 1 April 2013.

Sub-s (3): words in first pair of square brackets substituted by SI 2005/1455, art 3(3), Sch 2, paras 56, 58(1), (3), as from 27 March 2006. Word omitted from para (a) repealed, and para (c) and the word immediately preceding it added, by the Dormant Bank and Building Society Accounts Act 2008, s 15, Sch 2, para 6(1), (2), as from 12 March 2009.

Sub-s (4) is amended as follows:

Words in square brackets in the definition "authorised deposit taker" substituted by the Financial Services Act 2012, s 44, Sch 14, paras 1, 6(1), (5), as from 1 April 2013.

Definition "authorised reclaim fund" inserted by the Dormant Bank and Building Society Accounts Act 2008, s 15, Sch 2, para 6(1), (3), as from 12 March 2009. Words in square brackets substituted by the Dormant Assets Act 2022, s 32(3), Sch 1, para 2(2), as from 6 June 2022.

Words in square brackets in definition "company" substituted by SI 2005/1455, art 3(3), Sch 2, paras 56, 58(1), (4), as from 27 March 2006.

[7.641]

360 Insurers

(1) The Treasury may by order provide that such provisions of Part II of the 1986 Act (or Part III of the 1989 Order) as may be specified are to apply in relation to insurers with such modifications as may be specified.

(2) An order under this section—

(a) may provide that such provisions of this Part as may be specified are to apply in relation to the administration of insurers in accordance with the order with such modifications as may be specified; and

(b) requires the consent of the Secretary of State.

(3) "Specified" means specified in the order.

NOTES

Orders: the Financial Services and Markets Act 2000 (Administration Orders Relating to Insurers) (Amendment) Order 2003, SI 2003/2134; the Financial Services and Markets Act 2000 (Transitional Provisions, Repeals and Savings) (Financial Services Compensation Scheme) (Amendment) Order 2004, SI 2004/952; the Financial Services and Markets Act 2000 (Administration Orders Relating to Insurers) (Northern Ireland) Order 2007, SI 2007/846; the Financial Services and Markets Act 2000 (Administration Orders Relating to Insurers) Order 2010, SI 2010/3023; the Financial Services and Markets (Insolvency) (Amendment of Miscellaneous Enactments) Regulations 2019, SI 2019/755.

[7.642]

[361 Administrator's duty to report to [FCA and PRA]

(1) This section applies where a company or partnership is—

(a) in administration within the meaning of Schedule B1 to the 1986 Act, or

[(b) in administration within the meaning of Schedule B1 to the 1989 Order].

[(2) If the administrator thinks that the company or partnership is carrying on, or has carried on—

(a) a regulated activity in contravention of the general prohibition, or

(b) a credit-related regulated activity in contravention of section 20,

the administrator must report the matter to the appropriate regulator without delay.]

[(2A) The appropriate regulator" means—

(a) where the regulated activity is a PRA-regulated activity, the FCA and the PRA;

(b) in any other case, the FCA.]

[(3) Subsection (2) does not apply where—

(a) the administration arises out of an administration order made on an application made or petition presented by a regulator, and

(b) the regulator's application or petition depended on a contravention by the company or partnership of the general prohibition.]

NOTES

Substituted by the Enterprise Act 2002, s 248(3), Sch 17, paras 53, 56, as from 15 September 2003 (for savings and transitional provisions in relation to a petition for an administration order presented before that date, and in relation to special administration regimes (within the meaning of the Enterprise Act 2002, s 249), see the note to the Insolvency Act 1986, s 8 at **[9.147]**).

Section heading: words in square brackets substituted by the Financial Services Act 2012, s 44, Sch 14, paras 1, 7(1), (5), as from 1 April 2013.

Sub-s (1): para (b) substituted by the Insolvency (Northern Ireland) Order 2005, SI 2005/1455, art 3(3), Sch 2, paras 56, 59, as from 27 March 2006.

Sub-ss (2), (3): substituted by the Financial Services Act 2012, s 44, Sch 14, paras 1, 7(1), (2), (4), as from 1 April 2013.

Sub-s (2A): inserted by the Financial Services Act 2012, s 44, Sch 14, paras 1, 7(1), (3), as from 1 April 2013.

[7.643]

362 [Powers of FCA and PRA] to participate in proceedings

(1) This section applies if a person . . . [makes an administration application under Schedule B1 to the 1986 Act] [or Schedule B1 to the 1989 Order] in relation to a company or partnership which—

(a) is, or has been, an authorised person [or recognised investment exchange];

(b) is, or has been, an appointed representative; or

(c) is carrying on, or has carried on, a regulated activity in contravention of the general prohibition.

[(1A) This section also applies in relation to—

(a) the appointment under paragraph 14 or 22 of Schedule B1 to the 1986 Act [or paragraph 15 or 23 of Schedule B1 to the 1989 Order] of an administrator of a company of a kind described in subsection (1)(a) to (c), or

(b) the filing with the court of a copy of notice of intention to appoint an administrator under [any] of those paragraphs.]

[(1B) This section also applies in relation to—

(a) the appointment under paragraph 22 of Schedule B1 to the 1986 Act (as applied by order under section 420 of the 1986 Act), or under paragraph 23 of Schedule B1 to the 1989 Order (as applied by order under Article 364 of the 1989 Order), of an administrator of a partnership of a kind described in subsection (1)(a) to (c), or

(b) the filing with the court of a copy of notice of intention to appoint an administrator under either of those paragraphs (as so applied).]

(2) The [appropriate regulator] is entitled to be heard—

(a) at the hearing of the [administration application . . .]; and

(b) at any other hearing of the court in relation to the company or partnership under Part II of the 1986 Act (or Part III of the 1989 Order).

(3) Any notice or other document required to be sent to a creditor of the company or partnership must also be sent to the [appropriate regulator].

[(4) The [appropriate regulator] may apply to the court under paragraph 74 of Schedule B1 to the 1986 Act [or paragraph 75 of Schedule B1 to the 1989 Order].

(4A) In respect of an application under subsection (4)—

(a) paragraph 74(1)(a) and (b) shall have effect as if for the words "harm the interests of the applicant (whether alone or in common with some or all other members or creditors)" there were substituted the words "harm the interests of some or all members or creditors", and

[(b) paragraph 75(1)(a) and (b) of Schedule B1 to the 1989 Order shall have effect as if for the words "harm the interests of the applicant (whether alone or in common with some or all other members or creditors)" there were substituted the words "harm the interests of some or all members or creditors".]]

(5) A person appointed for the purpose by the [appropriate regulator] is entitled—

(a) to attend any meeting of creditors of the company or partnership summoned under any enactment;

(b) to attend any meeting of a committee established under [paragraph 57 of Schedule B1 to the 1986 Act] [or paragraph 58 of Schedule B1 to the 1989 Order]; and

(c) to make representations as to any matter for decision at such a meeting.

[(5A) The appropriate regulator or a person appointed by the appropriate regulator is entitled to participate in (but not vote in) a qualifying decision procedure by which a decision about any matter is sought from the creditors of the company or partnership.]

(6) If, during the course of the administration of a company, a compromise or arrangement [in relation to which Part 26 of the Companies Act 2006 applies] is proposed between the company and its creditors, or any class of them, the [appropriate regulator] may apply to the court under [section 896 or 899 of [that Act]].

[(6A) If, during the course of the administration of a company, a compromise or arrangement in relation to which Part 26A of the Companies Act 2006 applies is proposed between the company and its creditors, or any class of them, the appropriate regulator may apply to the court under section 901C or 901F of that Act.]

[(7) "The appropriate regulator" means—

(a) where the company or partnership is a PRA-regulated person, each of the FCA and the PRA, except that the references in subsections (5) and (5A) to a person appointed by the appropriate regulator are to be read as references to a person appointed by either the FCA or the PRA;

(b) in any other case, the FCA.].

[(8) But where the administration application was made by a regulator "the appropriate regulator" does not include that regulator.]

NOTES

Section heading: words in square brackets substituted by the Financial Services Act 2012, s 44, Sch 14, paras 1, 8(1), (6), as from 1 April 2013.

Sub-s (1): words omitted repealed, and words in square brackets in para (a) inserted, by the Financial Services Act 2012, s 44, Sch 14, paras 1, 8(1), (2), as from 1 April 2013. Words in first pair of square brackets substituted by the Enterprise Act 2002,

Part 7 Financial Services Acts

s 248(3), Sch 17, paras 53, 57(a), as from 15 September 2003 (for savings and transitional provisions in relation to a petition for an administration order presented before that date, and in relation to special administration regimes (within the meaning of the Enterprise Act 2002, s 249), see the note to the Insolvency Act 1986, s 8 at **[9.147]**). Words in second pair of square brackets substituted by the Insolvency (Northern Ireland) Order 2005, SI 2005/1455, art 3(3), Sch 2, paras 56, 60(1), (2), as from 27 March 2006.

Sub-s (1A): inserted by the Enterprise Act 2002, s 248(3), Sch 17, paras 53, 57(b), as from 15 September 2003 (subject to savings and transitional provisions as noted above). Words in square brackets in para (a) inserted, and word in square brackets in para (b) substituted, by SI 2005/1455, art 3(3), Sch 2, paras 56, 60(1), (3), as from 27 March 2006.

Sub-s (1B): inserted by the Financial Services Act 2012, s 44, Sch 14, paras 1, 8(1), (3), as from 1 April 2013.

Sub-s (2): words in first pair of square brackets substituted by the Financial Services Act 2012, s 44, Sch 14, paras 1, 8(1), (4), as from 1 April 2013. Words in second pair of square brackets substituted by the Enterprise Act 2002, s 248(3), Sch 17, paras 53, 57(c), as from 15 September 2003 (subject to savings and transitional provisions as noted above). Words omitted repealed by SI 2005/1455, arts 3(3), 31, Sch 2, paras 56, 60(1), (4), Sch 9, as from 27 March 2006.

Sub-s (3): words in square brackets substituted by the Financial Services Act 2012, s 44, Sch 14, paras 1, 8(1), (4), as from 1 April 2013.

Sub-s (4): substituted, together with sub-s (4A) for the original sub-s (4), by the Enterprise Act 2002, s 248(3), Sch 17, paras 53, 57(d), as from 15 September 2003 (subject to savings and transitional provisions as noted above). Words in first pair of square brackets substituted by the Financial Services Act 2012, s 44, Sch 14, paras 1, 8(1), (4), as from 1 April 2013. Words in second pair of square brackets substituted by SI 2005/1455, art 3(3), Sch 2, paras 56, 60(1), (5), as from 27 March 2006.

Sub-s (4A): substituted as noted above. Para (b) substituted by SI 2005/1455, art 3(3), Sch 2, paras 56, 60(1), (6), as from 27 March 2006.

Sub-s (5): words in first pair of square brackets substituted by the Financial Services Act 2012, s 44, Sch 14, paras 1, 8(1), (4), as from 1 April 2013. Words in second pair of square brackets substituted by the Enterprise Act 2002, s 248(3), Sch 17, paras 53, 57(e), as from 15 September 2003 (subject to savings and transitional provisions as noted above); words in third pair of square brackets substituted by SI 2005/1455, art 3(3), Sch 2, paras 56, 60(1), (7), as from 27 March 2006.

Sub-s (5A): inserted by the Small Business, Enterprise and Employment Act 2015 (Consequential Amendments, Savings and Transitional Provisions) Regulations 2018, SI 2018/208, reg 4(1), (4)(a), as from 13 March 2018.

Sub-s (6) is amended as follows:

Words in first pair of square brackets inserted, and words in fourth (inner) pair of square brackets substituted, by the Corporate Insolvency and Governance Act 2020, s 7, Sch 9, Pt 2, paras 17, 20(1), (3)(a), as from 26 June 2020.

Words in second pair of square brackets substituted by the Financial Services Act 2012, s 44, Sch 14, paras 1, 8(1), (4), as from 1 April 2013.

Words in third (outer) pair of square brackets substituted by the Companies Act 2006 (Consequential Amendments etc) Order 2008, SI 2008/948, art 3(1), Sch 1, Pt 2, para 211(4), as from 6 April 2008.

Sub-s (6A): inserted by the Corporate Insolvency and Governance Act 2020, s 7, Sch 9, Pt 2, paras 17, 20(1), (3)(b), as from 26 June 2020.

Sub-s (7): originally added by the Financial Services Act 2012, s 44, Sch 14, paras 1, 8(1), (5), as from 1 April 2013. Subsequently substituted by SI 2018/208, reg 4(1), (4)(b), as from 13 March 2018.

Sub-s (8): added by the Financial Services Act 2012, s 44, Sch 14, paras 1, 8(1), (5), as from 1 April 2013.

[7.644]

[362A Administrator appointed by company or directors

(1) This section applies in relation to a company [or partnership] of a kind described in section 362(1)(a) to (c).

[(2) An administrator of the company or partnership may not be appointed under a provision specified in subsection (2A) without the consent of the appropriate regulator.

(2A) Those provisions are—

(a) paragraph 22 of Schedule B1 to the 1986 Act (including that paragraph as applied in relation to partnerships by order under section 420 of that Act);

(b) paragraph 23 of Schedule B1 to the 1989 Order (including that paragraph as applied in relation to partnerships by order under article 364 of that Order).

(2B) "The appropriate regulator" means—

(a) where the company or partnership is a PRA-regulated person, the PRA, and

(b) in any other case, the FCA.]

(3) Consent under subsection (2)—

(a) must be in writing, and

(b) must be filed with the court along with the notice of intention to appoint under paragraph 27 of [Schedule B1 to the 1986 Act or paragraph 28 of Schedule B1 to the 1989 Order].

(4) In a case where no notice of intention to appoint is required—

(a) subsection (3)(b) shall not apply, but

(b) consent under subsection (2) must accompany the notice of appointment filed under paragraph 29 of [Schedule B1 to the 1986 Act or paragraph 30 of Schedule B1 to the 1989 Order].]

NOTES

Inserted by the Enterprise Act 2002, s 248(3), Sch 17, paras 53, 58, as from 15 September 2003 (for savings and transitional provisions in relation to a petition for an administration order presented before that date, and in relation to special administration regimes (within the meaning of the Enterprise Act 2002, s 249), see the note to the Insolvency Act 1986, s 8 at **[9.147]**).

Sub-s (1): words in square brackets inserted by the Financial Services Act 2012, s 44, Sch 14, paras 1, 9(1), (2), as from 1 April 2013.

Sub-ss (2)–(2B): substituted (for the original sub-s (2)) by the Financial Services Act 2012, s 44, Sch 14, paras 1, 9(1), (3), as from 1 April 2013.

Sub-ss (3), (4): words in square brackets substituted by the Insolvency (Northern Ireland) Order 2005, SI 2005/1455, art 3(3), Sch 2, paras 56, 61(1), (3), (4), as from 27 March 2006.

Receivership

[7.645]

363 [Powers of FCA and PRA] to participate in proceedings

(1) This section applies if a receiver has been appointed in relation to a company which—

(a) is, or has been, an authorised person [or recognised investment exchange];
(b) is, or has been, an appointed representative; or
(c) is carrying on, or has carried on, a regulated activity in contravention of the general prohibition.

(2) The [appropriate regulator] is entitled to be heard on an application made under section 35 or 63 of the 1986 Act (or Article 45 of the 1989 Order).

(3) The [appropriate regulator] is entitled to make an application under section 41(1)(a) or 69(1)(a) of the 1986 Act (or Article 51(1)(a) of the 1989 Order).

(4) A report under section 48(1) or 67(1) of the 1986 Act (or Article 58(1) of the 1989 Order) must be sent by the person making it to the [appropriate regulator].

(5) A person appointed for the purpose by the [appropriate regulator] is entitled—
(a) to attend any meeting of creditors of the company summoned under any enactment;
(b) to attend any meeting of a committee established under section 49 or 68 of the 1986 Act (or Article 59 of the 1989 Order); and
(c) to make representations as to any matter for decision at such a meeting.

[(6) The appropriate regulator" means—
(a) for the purposes of subsections (2) to (4)—
(i) where the company is a PRA-regulated person, each of the FCA and the PRA, and
(ii) in any other case, the FCA;
(b) for the purposes of subsection (5)—
(i) where the company is a PRA-regulated person, the FCA or the PRA, and
(ii) in any other case, the FCA.]

NOTES

Words in square brackets in sub-s (1)(a) inserted, sub-s (6) added, and other words in square brackets substituted, by the Financial Services Act 2012, s 44, Sch 14, paras 1, 10, as from 1 April 2013.

[7.646]

364 Receiver's duty to report to [FCA and PRA]

If—
(a) a receiver has been appointed in relation to a company, and
(b) it appears to the receiver that the company is carrying on, or has carried on, a regulated activity in contravention of the general prohibition [or a credit-related regulated activity in contravention of section 20],

the receiver must report the matter [without delay to the FCA and, if the regulated activity concerned is a PRA-regulated activity, to the PRA].

NOTES

The words in square brackets in the section heading, and the words in the final pair of square brackets were substituted, and the words in square brackets in para (b) were inserted, by the Financial Services Act 2012, s 44, Sch 14, paras 1, 11, as from 1 April 2013.

Voluntary winding up

[7.647]

365 [Powers of FCA and PRA] to participate in proceedings

(1) This section applies in relation to a company which—
(a) is being wound up voluntarily;
(b) is an authorised person [or recognised investment exchange]; and
(c) is not an insurer effecting or carrying out contracts of long-term insurance.

(2) The [appropriate regulator] may apply to the court under section 112 of the 1986 Act (or Article 98 of the 1989 Order) in respect of the company.

(3) The [appropriate regulator] is entitled to be heard at any hearing of the court in relation to the voluntary winding up of the company.

(4) Any notice or other document required to be sent to a creditor of the company must also be sent to the [appropriate regulator].

(5) A person appointed for the purpose by the [appropriate regulator] is entitled—
(a) to attend any meeting of creditors of the company summoned under any enactment;
(b) to attend any meeting of a committee established under section 101 of the 1986 Act (or Article 87 of the 1989 Order); and
(c) to make representations as to any matter for decision at such a meeting.

[(5A) The appropriate regulator or a person appointed by the appropriate regulator is entitled to participate in (but not vote in) a qualifying decision procedure by which a decision about any matter is sought from the creditors of the company.]

(6) The voluntary winding up of the company does not bar the right of the [appropriate regulator] to have it wound up by the court.

(7) If, during the course of the winding up of the company, a compromise or arrangement [in relation to which Part 26 of the Companies Act 2006 applies] is proposed between the company and its creditors, or any class of them, the [appropriate regulator] may apply to the court under [section 896 or 899 of [that Act]].

[(7A) If, during the course of the winding up of the company, a compromise or arrangement in relation to which Part 26A of the Companies Act 2006 applies is proposed between the company and its creditors, or any class of them, the appropriate regulator may apply to the court under section 901C or 901F of that Act.]

[(8) "The appropriate regulator" means—
(a) where the company is a PRA-authorised person, each of the FCA and the PRA, except that the references in subsections (5) and (5A) to a person appointed by the appropriate regulator are to be read as references to a person appointed by either the FCA or the PRA;
(b) in any other case, the FCA.]

NOTES

Sub-s (5A) was inserted, and sub-s (8) was substituted, by the Small Business, Enterprise and Employment Act 2015 (Consequential Amendments, Savings and Transitional Provisions) Regulations 2018, SI 2018/208, reg 4(1), (5), as from 13 March 2018. Note that sub-s (8) was originally added by the Financial Services Act 2012, s 44, Sch 14, paras 1, 12, as from 1 April 2013.

The words in the third (outer) pair of square brackets in sub-s (7) (ie, "section 896 or 899") were substituted by the Companies Act 2006 (Consequential Amendments etc) Order 2008, SI 2008/948, art 3(1), Sch 1, Pt 2, para 211(4), as from 6 April 2008.

The words "in relation to which Part 26 of the Companies Act 2006 applies" and "that Act" in square brackets in sub-s (7) were inserted and substituted respectively, and sub-s (7A) was inserted, by the Corporate Insolvency and Governance Act 2020, s 7, Sch 9, Pt 2, paras 17, 20(1), (4), as from 26 June 2020.

The words in square brackets in sub-s (1)(b) were inserted, and all other words in square brackets in this section were substituted, by the Financial Services Act 2012, s 44, Sch 14, paras 1, 12, as from 1 April 2013.

[7.648]

366 Insurers effecting or carrying out long-term contracts or insurance

(1) An insurer effecting or carrying out contracts of long-term insurance may not be wound up voluntarily without the consent of the [PRA].

(2) If notice of a general meeting of such an insurer is given, specifying the intention to propose a resolution for voluntary winding up of the insurer, a director of the insurer must notify the [PRA] as soon as practicable after he becomes aware of it.

(3) A person who fails to comply with subsection (2) is guilty of an offence and liable on summary conviction to a fine not exceeding level 5 on the standard scale.

[(4) A winding up resolution may not be passed—

(a) as a written resolution (in accordance with Chapter 2 of Part 13 of the Companies Act 2006), or

(b) at a meeting called in accordance with section 307(4) to (6) or 337(2) of that Act (agreement of members to calling of meeting at short notice).]

(5) A copy of a winding-up resolution forwarded to the registrar of companies in accordance with [section 30 of the Companies Act 2006] must be accompanied by a certificate issued by the [PRA] stating that it consents to the voluntary winding up of the insurer.

(6) If subsection (5) is complied with, the voluntary winding up is to be treated as having commenced at the time the resolution was passed.

(7) If subsection (5) is not complied with, the resolution has no effect.

(8) "Winding-up resolution" means a resolution for voluntary winding up of an insurer effecting or carrying out contracts of long-term insurance.

[(9) Before giving or refusing consent under subsection (1), the PRA must consult the FCA.

(10) In the event that the activity of effecting or carrying out long-term contracts of insurance as principal is not to any extent a PRA-regulated activity—

(a) references to the PRA in subsections (1), (2) and (5) are to be read as references to the FCA, and

(b) subsection (9) does not apply.]

NOTES

Sub-ss (1), (2): words in square brackets substituted by the Financial Services Act 2012, s 44, Sch 14, paras 1, 13(1), (2), as from 1 April 2013.

Sub-s (4): substituted by the Companies Act 2006 (Commencement No 3, Consequential Amendments, Transitional Provisions and Savings) Order 2007, SI 2007/2194, art 10(1), Sch 4, Pt 3, para 93(1), (2), as from 1 October 2007.

Sub-s (5): words in first pair of square brackets substituted by SI 2007/2194, art 10(1), Sch 4, Pt 3, para 93(1), (3), as from 1 October 2007. Word in second pair of square brackets substituted by the Financial Services Act 2012, s 44, Sch 14, paras 1, 13(1), (2), as from 1 April 2013.

Sub-ss (9), (10): added by the Financial Services Act 2012, s 44, Sch 14, paras 1, 13(1), (3), as from 1 April 2013.

Winding up by the court

[7.649]

367 Winding-up petitions

(1) The [FCA] may present a petition to the court for the winding up of a body which—

(a) is, or has been, an authorised person [or recognised investment exchange];

(b) is, or has been, an appointed representative; or

(c) is carrying on, or has carried on, a regulated activity in contravention of the general prohibition.

[(1A) The PRA may present a petition to the court for the winding up of a body which is a PRA-regulated person.]

(2) In [subsections (1) and (1A)] "body" includes any partnership.

(3) On such a petition, the court may wind up the body if—

[(za) in the case of an insurance undertaking or reinsurance undertaking, the PRA has cancelled the body's Part 4A permission pursuant to section 55J(7C);]

(a) the body is unable to pay its debts within the meaning of section 123 or 221 of the 1986 Act (or Article 103 or 185 of the 1989 Order); or

(b) the court is of the opinion that it is just and equitable that it should be wound up.

(4) If a body is in default on an obligation to pay a sum due and payable under an agreement, it is to be treated for the purpose of subsection (3)(a) as unable to pay its debts.

(5) "Agreement" means an agreement the making or performance of which constitutes or is part of a regulated activity carried on by the body concerned.

(6) Subsection (7) applies if a petition is presented under subsection (1) [or (1A)] for the winding up of a partnership—

(a) on the ground mentioned in subsection (3)(b); or

(b) in Scotland, on a ground mentioned in subsection (3)(a) or (b).

(7) The court has jurisdiction, and the 1986 Act (or the 1989 Order) has effect, as if the partnership were an unregistered company as defined by section 220 of that Act (or Article 184 of that Order).

NOTES

The word in the first pair of square brackets in sub-s (1) and the words in square brackets in sub-s (2) were substituted, the words in the second pair of square brackets in sub-s (1) and the words in square brackets in sub-s (6) were inserted, and sub-s (1A) was inserted, by the Financial Services Act 2012, s 44, Sch 14, paras 1, 14, as from 1 April 2013.

Para (za) of sub-s (3) was inserted by the Solvency 2 Regulations 2015, SI 2015/575, reg 59, Sch 1, Pt 1, paras 1, 13, as from 1 January 2016.

[7.650]

[367A Winding-up petitions: Gibraltar-based persons

(1) A regulator may not present a petition to the court under section 367 for the winding up of a Gibraltar-based person who has a Schedule 2A permission unless either regulator has been asked to do so by the Gibraltar regulator.

(2) If a regulator receives a request from the Gibraltar regulator to present a petition to the court under section 367 for the winding up of a Gibraltar-based person who has a Schedule 2A permission, it must—

(a) notify the other regulator of the request, and

(b) provide the other regulator with such information relating to the request as it thinks fit.

(3) In this section, "the Gibraltar regulator" has the meaning given in Schedule 2A (see paragraph 2 of that Schedule).]

NOTES

Commencement: to be appointed.

Inserted by the Financial Services Act 2021, s 22, Sch 8, para 10, as from a day to be appointed.

368 *(Repealed by the EEA Passport Rights (Amendment, etc, and Transitional Provisions) (EU Exit) Regulations 2018, SI 2018/1149, reg 3, Schedule, Pt 1, paras 1, 19, as from IP completion day (as defined in the European Union (Withdrawal Agreement) Act 2020, s 39).)*

[7.651]

369 Insurers: service of petition etc on [FCA and PRA]

(1) If a person other than [a regulator] presents a petition for the winding up of an authorised person with permission to effect or carry out contracts of insurance, the petitioner must serve a copy of the petition [on the appropriate regulator].

(2) If a person other than [a regulator] applies to have a provisional liquidator appointed under section 135 of the 1986 Act (or Article 115 of the 1989 Order) in respect of an authorised person with permission to effect or carry out contracts of insurance, the applicant must serve a copy of the application [on the appropriate regulator].

[(3) The appropriate regulator" means—

(a) in relation to a PRA-authorised person, the FCA and the PRA, and

(b) in any other case, the FCA.

(4) If either regulator—

(a) presents a petition for the winding up of a PRA-authorised person with permission to effect or carry out contracts of insurance, or

(b) applies to have a provisional liquidator appointed under section 135 of the 1986 Act (or Article 115 of the 1989 Order) in respect of a PRA-authorised person with permission to effect or carry out contracts of insurance,

that regulator must serve a copy of the petition or application (as the case requires) on the other regulator.]

NOTES

Sub-ss (3), (4) were added, and all other words in square brackets in this section were substituted, by the Financial Services Act 2012, s 44, Sch 14, paras 1, 16, as from 1 April 2013.

[7.652]

[369A Reclaim funds: service of petition etc on [FCA and PRA]

(1) If a person [other than a regulator] presents a petition for the winding up of an authorised reclaim fund, the petitioner must serve a copy of the petition [on the appropriate regulator].

(2) If a person [other than a regulator] applies to have a provisional liquidator appointed under section 135 of the 1986 Act (or Article 115 of the 1989 Order) in respect of an authorised reclaim fund, the applicant must serve a copy of the application [on the appropriate regulator].

(3) In this section "authorised reclaim fund" [has the same meaning as in the Dormant Assets Acts 2008 to 2022 (see section 26 of the Dormant Assets Act 2022)].

[(4) The appropriate regulator" means—

(a) in relation to an authorised reclaim fund that is a PRA-authorised person, the FCA and the PRA, and

(b) in relation to any other authorised reclaim fund, the FCA.

(5) If either regulator—

(a) presents a petition for the winding up of an authorised reclaim fund that is a PRA-authorised person, or

(b) applies to have a provisional liquidator appointed under section 135 of the 1986 Act (or Article 115 of the 1989 Order) in respect of an authorised reclaim fund that is a PRA-authorised person,

that regulator must serve a copy of the petition or application (as the case requires) on the other regulator.]]

NOTES

Inserted by the Dormant Bank and Building Society Accounts Act 2008, s 15, Sch 2, para 7, as from 12 March 2009.

Sub-s (3): words in square brackets substituted by the Dormant Assets Act 2022, s 32(3), Sch 1, para 2(3), as from 6 June 2022.

Sub-ss (4), (5) were added, and all other words in square brackets in this section were substituted, by the Financial Services Act 2012, s 44, Sch 14, paras 1, 17, as from 1 April 2013.

[7.653]

[370 Liquidator's duty to report to FCA and PRA

(1) If—

(a) a company is being wound up voluntarily or a body is being wound up on a petition presented by any person, and

(b) it appears to the liquidator that the company or body is carrying on, or has carried on—

(i) a regulated activity in contravention of the general prohibition, or

(ii) a credit-related regulated activity in contravention of section 20,

the liquidator must report the matter without delay to the FCA and, if the regulated activity concerned is a PRA-regulated activity, to the PRA.

(2) Subsection (1) does not apply where—

(a) a body is being wound up on a petition presented by a regulator, and

(b) the regulator's petition depended on a contravention by the body of the general prohibition.]

NOTES

Substituted by the Financial Services Act 2012, s 44, Sch 14, paras 1, 18, as from 1 April 2013.

This section is modified in relation to a relevant scheme (ie, a stand-alone co-ownership scheme and a sub-scheme of an umbrella co-ownership scheme (as defined in s 237)) which is being wound up on a petition presented by any person so that (a) in sub-ss (1)(a) and (2)(a) the reference to a body is to be read as a reference to the relevant scheme, and (b) in sub-ss (1)(b) and (2)(b) the reference to the body is to be read as a reference to the operator or the depositary of the relevant scheme; see the Collective Investment in Transferable Securities (Contractual Scheme) Regulations 2013, SI 2013/1388 reg 17.

[7.654]

371 [Powers of FCA and PRA] to participate in proceedings

(1) This section applies if a person . . . presents a petition for the winding up of a body which—

(a) is, or has been, an authorised person [or recognised investment exchange];

(b) is, or has been, an appointed representative; or

(c) is carrying on, or has carried on, a regulated activity in contravention of the general prohibition.

(2) The [appropriate regulator] is entitled to be heard—

(a) at the hearing of the petition; and

(b) at any other hearing of the court in relation to the body under or by virtue of Part IV or V of the 1986 Act (or Part V or VI of the 1989 Order).

(3) Any notice or other document required to be sent to a creditor of the body must also be sent to the [appropriate regulator].

(4) A person appointed for the purpose by the [appropriate regulator] is entitled—

(a) to attend any meeting of creditors of the body;

(b) to attend any meeting of a committee established for the purposes of Part IV or V of the 1986 Act under section 101 of that Act or under section 141 or 142 of that Act;

(c) to attend any meeting of a committee established for the purposes of Part V or VI of the 1989 Order under Article 87 of that Order or under Article 120 of that Order; and

(d) to make representations as to any matter for decision at such a meeting.

[(4A) The appropriate regulator or a person appointed by the appropriate regulator is entitled to participate in (but not vote in) a qualifying decision procedure by which a decision about any matter is sought from the creditors of the body.]

(5) If, during the course of the winding up of a company, a compromise or arrangement [in relation to which Part 26 of the Companies Act 2006 applies] is proposed between the company and its creditors, or any class of them, the [appropriate regulator] may apply to the court under [section 896 or 899 of [that Act]].

[(5A) If, during the course of the winding up of a company, a compromise or arrangement in relation to which Part 26A of the Companies Act 2006 applies is proposed between the company and its creditors, or any class of them, the appropriate regulator may apply to the court under section 901C or 901F of that Act.]

[[(6) "The appropriate regulator" means—

(a) where the body is a PRA-regulated person, each of the FCA and the PRA, except that the references in subsections (4) and (4A) to a person appointed by the appropriate regulator are to be read as references to a person appointed by either the FCA or the PRA;

(b) in any other case, the FCA.]

(7) But where the petition was presented by a regulator "the appropriate regulator" does not include the regulator which presented the petition.]

NOTES

The words in the third (outer) pair of square brackets in sub-s (5) (ie, "section 896 or 899") were substituted by the Companies Act 2006 (Consequential Amendments etc) Order 2008, SI 2008/948, art 3(1), Sch 1, Pt 2, para 211(4), as from 6 April 2008.

The words "in relation to which Part 26 of the Companies Act 2006 applies" and "that Act" in square brackets in sub-s (5) were inserted and substituted respectively, and sub-s (5A) was inserted, by the Corporate Insolvency and Governance Act 2020, s 7, Sch 9, Pt 2, paras 17, 20(1), (5), as from 26 June 2020.

Sub-s (4A) was inserted, and sub-s (6) was substituted, by the Small Business, Enterprise and Employment Act 2015 (Consequential Amendments, Savings and Transitional Provisions) Regulations 2018, SI 2018/208, reg 4(1), (6), as from 13 March 2018. Note that sub-s (6) was originally added by the Financial Services Act 2012, s 44, Sch 14, paras 1, 19, as from 1 April 2013.

The words omitted from sub-s (1) were repealed, the words in square brackets in that subsection were inserted, sub-s (7) was added, and all other words in square brackets in this section were substituted, by the Financial Services Act 2012, s 44, Sch 14, paras 1, 19, as from 1 April 2013.

Bankruptcy

[7.655]

372 Petitions

(1) The [FCA] may present a petition to the court—

(a) under section 264 of the 1986 Act (or Article 238 of the 1989 Order) for a bankruptcy order to be made against an individual; or

(b) under section [2 or 5 of the 2016] Act for the sequestration of the estate of an individual.

[(1A) The PRA may present a petition to the court—

(a) under section 264 of the 1986 Act (or Article 238 of the 1989 Order) for a bankruptcy order to be made against an individual who is a PRA-regulated person;

(b) under section [2 or 5 of the 2016] Act for the sequestration of the estate of an individual who is a PRA-regulated person.]

(2) But [a petition may be presented by virtue of subsection (1) or (1A)] only on the ground that—

(a) the individual appears to be unable to pay a regulated activity debt; or

(b) the individual appears to have no reasonable prospect of being able to pay a regulated activity debt.

(3) An individual appears to be unable to pay a regulated activity debt if he is in default on an obligation to pay a sum due and payable under an agreement.

(4) An individual appears to have no reasonable prospect of being able to pay a regulated activity debt if—

(a) [a regulator] has served on him a demand requiring him to establish to the satisfaction of [that regulator] that there is a reasonable prospect that he will be able to pay a sum payable under an agreement when it falls due;

(b) at least three weeks have elapsed since the demand was served; and

(c) the demand has been neither complied with nor set aside in accordance with rules.

(5) A demand made under subsection (4)(a) is to be treated for the purposes of the 1986 Act (or the 1989 Order) as if it were a statutory demand under section 268 of that Act (or Article 242 of that Order).

(6) For the purposes of a petition presented in accordance with subsection (1)(b) [or (1A)(b)]—

(a) [the regulator by which the petition is presented] is to be treated as a qualified creditor; and

(b) a ground mentioned in subsection (2) constitutes apparent insolvency.

(7) "Individual" means an individual—

(a) who is, or has been, an authorised person; or

(b) who is carrying on, or has carried on, a regulated activity in contravention of the general prohibition.

(8) "Agreement" means an agreement the making or performance of which constitutes or is part of a regulated activity carried on by the individual concerned.

(9) "Rules" means—

(a) in England and Wales, rules made under section 412 of the 1986 Act;

(b) in Scotland, rules made by order by the Treasury, after consultation with the Scottish Ministers, for the purposes of this section; and

(c) in Northern Ireland, rules made under Article 359 of the 1989 Order.

NOTES

The words "2 or 5 of the 2016" in square brackets in sub-ss (1)(b) and (1A)(b) were substituted by the Bankruptcy (Scotland) Act 2016 (Consequential Provisions and Modifications) Order 2016, SI 2016/1034, art 7(1), (3), Sch 1, para 20(1), (6), as from 30 November 2016 (except in relation to (i) a sequestration as regards which the petition is presented, or the debtor application is made before that date; or (ii) a trust deed executed before that date).

Sub-s (1A) and the words "or (1A)(b)" in square brackets in sub-s (6) were inserted, and all other words in square brackets in this section were substituted, by the Financial Services Act 2012, s 44, Sch 14, paras 1, 20, as from 1 April 2013.

Rules: the Bankruptcy (Financial Services and Markets Act 2000) (Scotland) Rules 2001, SI 2001/3591.

[7.656]

373 Insolvency practitioner's duty to report [to FCA and PRA]

(1) If—

(a) a bankruptcy order or sequestration award is in force in relation to an individual . . . , and

(b) it appears to the insolvency practitioner that the individual is carrying on, or has [carried on—

(i) a regulated activity in contravention of the general prohibition, or

(ii) a credit-related regulated activity in contravention of section 20,]

the insolvency practitioner must report the matter [without delay to the FCA and, if the regulated activity concerned is a PRA-regulated activity, to the PRA].

[(1A) Subsection (1) does not apply where—

(a) the bankruptcy order or sequestration award is in force by virtue of a petition presented by a regulator, and

(b) the regulator's petition depended on a contravention by the individual of the general prohibition.]

(2) "Bankruptcy order" means a bankruptcy order under Part IX of the 1986 Act (or Part IX of the 1989 Order).

(3) "Sequestration award" means an award of sequestration under section [22 of the 2016] Act.

(4) "Individual" includes an entity mentioned in section 374(1)(c).

NOTES

The words in square brackets in the section heading and in sub-s (1) were substituted, the words omitted from sub-s (1) were repealed, and sub-s (1A) was inserted, by the Financial Services Act 2012, s 44, Sch 14, paras 1, 21, as from 1 April 2013.

Sub-s (3): words in square brackets substituted by the Bankruptcy (Scotland) Act 2016 (Consequential Provisions and Modifications) Order 2016, SI 2016/1034, art 7(1), (3), Sch 1, para 20(1), (7), as from 30 November 2016 (except in relation to (i) a sequestration as regards which the petition is presented, or the debtor application is made before that date; or (ii) a trust deed executed before that date).

[7.657]

374 [Powers of FCA and PRA] to participate in proceedings

(1) This section applies if a person . . . presents a petition to the court—

(a) under section 264 of the 1986 Act (or Article 238 of the 1989 Order) for a bankruptcy order to be made against an individual;
(b) under section [2 or 5 of the 2016] Act for the sequestration of the estate of an individual; or
(c) under section 6 of the [2016] Act for the sequestration of the estate belonging to or held for or jointly by the members of an entity mentioned in subsection (1) of that section.

(2) The [appropriate regulator] is entitled to be heard—
(a) at the hearing of the petition; and
(b) at any other hearing in relation to the individual or entity under—
(i) Part IX of the 1986 Act;
(ii) Part IX of the 1989 Order; or
(iii) the [2016] Act.

(3) [In the case of a petition presented under Article 238 of the 1989 Order, a copy of the report prepared under Article 248 of that Order] must also be sent to the [appropriate regulator].

(4) A person appointed for the purpose by the [appropriate regulator] is entitled—
(a) to attend any meeting of creditors of the individual or entity;
(b) to attend any meeting of a committee established under section 301 of the 1986 Act (or Article 274 of the 1989 Order);
(c) to attend any meeting of commissioners held under paragraph [26 or 27 of Schedule 6 to the 2016] Act; and
(d) to make representations as to any matter for decision at such a meeting.

[(4A) The appropriate regulator or a person appointed by the appropriate regulator is entitled to participate in (but not vote in) a creditors' decision procedure by which a decision about any matter is sought from the creditors of the individual or entity.]

(5) "Individual" means an individual who—
(a) is, or has been, an authorised person; or
(b) is carrying on, or has carried on, a regulated activity in contravention of the general prohibition.

(6) "Entity" means an entity which—
(a) is, or has been, an authorised person; or
(b) is carrying on, or has carried on, a regulated activity in contravention of the general prohibition.

[[(7) "The appropriate regulator" means—
(a) where the individual or entity is a PRA-regulated person, each of the FCA and the PRA, except that the references in subsections (4) and (4A) to a person appointed by the appropriate regulator are to be read as references to a person appointed by either the FCA or the PRA;
(b) in any other case, the FCA.]

(8) But where the petition was presented by a regulator "the appropriate regulator" does not include the regulator which presented the petition.]

NOTES

The words "2 or 5 of the 2016" in square brackets in sub-s (1)(b) were substituted, the year "2016" in square brackets in sub-s (1)(c) and sub-s (2)(b)(iii) was substituted, and the words "26 or 27 of Schedule 6 to the 2016" in square brackets in sub-s (4)(c) were substituted, by the Bankruptcy (Scotland) Act 2016 (Consequential Provisions and Modifications) Order 2016, SI 2016/1034, art 7(1), (3), Sch 1, para 20(1), (8), as from 30 November 2016 (except in relation to (i) a sequestration as regards which the petition is presented, or the debtor application is made before that date; or (ii) a trust deed executed before that date).

Words in first pair of square brackets in sub-s (3) inserted by the Enterprise and Regulatory Reform Act 2013 (Consequential Amendments) (Bankruptcy) and the Small Business, Enterprise and Employment Act 2015 (Consequential Amendments) Regulations 2016, SI 2016/481, reg 2(1), Sch 1, para 13, as from 6 April 2016.

Sub-s (4A) was inserted, and sub-s (7) was substituted, by the Small Business, Enterprise and Employment Act 2015 (Consequential Amendments, Savings and Transitional Provisions) Regulations 2018, SI 2018/208, reg 4(1), (7), as from 13 March 2018. Note that sub-s (7) was originally added by the Financial Services Act 2012, s 44, Sch 14, paras 1, 22, as from 1 April 2013.

Words omitted from sub-s (1) repealed, sub-s (8) added, and all other words in square brackets in this section substituted, by the Financial Services Act 2012, s 44, Sch 14, paras 1, 22, as from 1 April 2013.

Provisions against debt avoidance

[7.658]

375 [Right of FCA and PRA] to apply for an order

(1) The [FCA] may apply for an order under section 423 of the 1986 Act (or Article 367 of the 1989 Order) in relation to a debtor if—
(a) at the time the transaction at an undervalue was entered into, the debtor was carrying on a regulated activity (whether or not in contravention of the general prohibition); and
(b) a victim of the transaction is or was party to an agreement entered into with the debtor, the making or performance of which constituted or was part of a regulated activity carried on by the debtor.

[(1A) The PRA may apply for an order under section 423 of the 1986 Act (or Article 367 of the 1989 Order) in relation to a debtor if—
(a) at the time the transaction at an undervalue was entered into, the debtor was carrying on a PRA-regulated activity (whether or not in contravention of the general prohibition); and
(b) a victim of the transaction is or was party to an agreement entered into with the debtor, the making or performance of which constituted or was part of a PRA-regulated activity carried on by the debtor.]

(2) An application made under this section is to be treated as made on behalf of every victim of the transaction to whom subsection (1)(b) [or subsection (1A)(b) (as the case may be)] applies.

(3) Expressions which are given a meaning in Part XVI of the 1986 Act (or Article 367, 368 or 369 of the 1989 Order) have the same meaning when used in this section.

NOTES

Words in square brackets in the section heading and in sub-s (1) substituted, and sub-s (1A) and the words in square brackets in sub-s (2) inserted, by the Financial Services Act 2012, s 44, Sch 14, paras 1, 23, as from 1 April 2013.

Supplemental provisions concerning insurers

[7.659]

376 Continuation of contracts of long-term insurance where insurer in liquidation

(1) This section applies in relation to the winding up of an insurer which effects or carries out contracts of long-term insurance.

(2) Unless the court otherwise orders, the liquidator must carry on the insurer's business so far as it consists of carrying out the insurer's contracts of long-term insurance with a view to its being transferred as a going concern to a person who may lawfully carry out those contracts.

(3) In carrying on the business, the liquidator—

(a) may agree to the variation of any contracts of insurance in existence when the winding up order is made; but

(b) must not effect any new contracts of insurance.

(4) If the liquidator is satisfied that the interests of the creditors in respect of liabilities of the insurer attributable to contracts of long-term insurance effected by it require the appointment of a special manager, he may apply to the court.

(5) On such an application, the court may appoint a special manager to act during such time as the court may direct.

(6) The special manager is to have such powers, including any of the powers of a receiver or manager, as the court may direct.

(7) Section 177(5) of the 1986 Act (or Article 151(5) of the 1989 Order) applies to a special manager appointed under subsection (5) as it applies to a special manager appointed under section 177 of the 1986 Act (or Article 151 of the 1989 Order).

(8) If the court thinks fit, it may reduce the value of one or more of the contracts of long-term insurance effected by the insurer.

(9) Any reduction is to be on such terms and subject to such conditions (if any) as the court thinks fit.

(10) The court may, on the application of an official, appoint an independent actuary to investigate the insurer's business so far as it consists of carrying out its contracts of long-term insurance and to report to the official—

(a) on the desirability or otherwise of that part of the insurer's business being continued; and

(b) on any reduction in the contracts of long-term insurance effected by the insurer that may be necessary for successful continuation of that part of the insurer's business.

(11) "Official" means—

(a) the liquidator;

(b) a special manager appointed under subsection (5); or

(c) the [PRA].

[(11A) The PRA must—

(a) consult the FCA before making an application under subsection (10), and

(b) provide the FCA with a copy of any actuary's report made to the PRA under that subsection.

(11B) In the event that the activity of effecting or carrying out long-term contracts of insurance as principal is not to any extent a [PRA-regulated] activity—

(a) the reference in subsection (11)(c) to the PRA is to be read as a reference to the FCA, and

(b) subsection (11A) does not apply.]

(12) The liquidator may make an application in the name of the insurer and on its behalf under Part VII without obtaining the permission that would otherwise be required by [Article 142 of, and Schedule 2 to, the 1989 Order].

NOTES

Word in square brackets in the sub-s (11)(c) substituted, and sub-ss (11A), (11B) inserted, by the Financial Services Act 2012, s 44, Sch 14, paras 1, 24, as from 1 April 2013.

Words in square brackets in sub-s (11B) substituted by the Financial Services (Banking Reform) Act 2013, s 141, Sch 10, para 2, as from 1 March 2014.

Words in square brackets in sub-s (12) substituted by the Deregulation Act 2015, the Small Business, Enterprise and Employment Act 2015 and the Insolvency (Amendment) Act (Northern Ireland) 2016 (Consequential Amendments and Transitional Provisions) Regulations 2017, SI 2017/400, reg 4, as from 7 April 2017.

[7.660]

377 Reducing the value of contracts instead of winding up

(1) This section applies in relation to an insurer which has been proved to be unable to pay its debts.

(2) If the court thinks fit, it may reduce the value of one or more of the insurer's contracts instead of making a winding up order.

(3) Any reduction is to be on such terms and subject to such conditions (if any) as the court thinks fit.

[7.661]

378 Treatment of assets on winding up

(1) The Treasury may by regulations provide for the treatment of the assets of an insurer on its winding up.

(2) The regulations may, in particular, provide for—

(a) assets representing a particular part of the insurer's business to be available only for meeting liabilities attributable to that part of the insurer's business;

(b) separate general meetings of the creditors to be held in respect of liabilities attributable to a particular part of the insurer's business.

[7.662]

379 Winding-up rules

(1) Winding-up rules may include provision—

(a) for determining the amount of the liabilities of an insurer to policyholders of any class or description for the purpose of proof in a winding up; and

(b) generally for carrying into effect the provisions of this Part with respect to the winding up of insurers.

(2) Winding-up rules may, in particular, make provision for all or any of the following matters—

(a) the identification of assets and liabilities;

(b) the apportionment, between assets of different classes or descriptions, of—
  (i) the costs, charges and expenses of the winding up; and
  (ii) any debts of the insurer of a specified class or description;
(c) the determination of the amount of liabilities of a specified description;
(d) the application of assets for meeting liabilities of a specified description;
(e) the application of assets representing any excess of a specified description.

(3) "Specified" means specified in winding-up rules.

(4) "Winding-up rules" means rules made under section 411 of the 1986 Act (or Article 359 of the 1989 Order).

(5) Nothing in this section affects the power to make winding-up rules under the 1986 Act or the 1989 Order.

NOTES

Rules: the Insurers (Winding Up) Rules 2001, SI 2001/3635; the Insurers (Winding Up) (Scotland) Rules 2001, SI 2001/4040; the Bankruptcy (Financial Services and Markets Act 2000) Rules 2001 and the Insurers (Winding Up) Rules 2001 (Amendment) Rules 2019, SI 2019/754; the Insolvency (Scotland) Rules 2018 (Miscellaneous Amendments) Rules 2019, SI 2019/1059.

[Settlement finality

[7.663]

379A Power to apply settlement finality regime to payment institutions

(1) The Treasury may by regulations made by statutory instrument provide for the application to payment institutions, as participants in payment or securities settlement systems, of provision in subordinate legislation—
(a) modifying the law of insolvency or related law in relation to such systems, or
(b) relating to the securing of rights and obligations.

(2) "Payment institution" means—
(a) an authorised payment institution or small payment institution within the meaning of the Payment Services Regulations [2017], or
(b) a person whose head office, registered office or place of residence, as the case may be, is outside the United Kingdom and whose functions correspond to those of an institution within paragraph (a).

(3) "Payment or securities settlement system" means arrangements between a number of participants for or in connection with the clearing or execution of instructions by participants relating to any of the following—
(a) the placing of money at the disposal of a recipient;
(b) the assumption or discharge of a payment obligation;
(c) the transfer of the title to, or an interest in, securities.

(4) "Subordinate legislation" has the same meaning as in the Interpretation Act 1978.

(5) Regulations under this section may—
(a) make consequential, supplemental or transitional provision;
(b) amend subordinate legislation.

(6) A statutory instrument containing regulations under this section is subject to annulment in pursuance of a resolution of either House of Parliament.]

NOTES

Inserted, together with the preceding heading, by the Digital Economy Act 2017, s 112, as from 27 April 2017.

Sub-s (2): year "2017" in square brackets substituted by the Payment Services Regulations 2017, SI 2017/752, reg 156, Sch 8, Pt 1, para 2(1), (6), as from 13 August 2017 (for general transitional provisions, see regs 149–154 of, and Sch 8, Pt 1, para 2(1), (11) to, the 2017 Regulations).

Regulations: the Payment Systems and Services and Electronic Money (Miscellaneous Amendments) Regulations 2017, SI 2017/1173.

PART XXV INJUNCTIONS AND RESTITUTION

NOTES

Transitional provisions etc in connection with the commencement of the Financial Services Act 2012: see the Financial Services Act 2012 (Transitional Provisions) (Enforcement) Order 2013, SI 2013/441. Article 15 contains transitional provisions in relation to injunctions. Article 16 contains transitional provisions in relation to restitution orders. Article 17 contains transitional provisions in relation to the power to require restitution. Article 18 contains transitional provisions in relation to injunctions and restitution in respect of certain post-1 April 2013 contraventions.

Transitional provisions etc in connection with the original commencement of this Act: any requirement, condition or prohibition imposed before 1 December 2001 by or under certain specified provisions is to be treated as a relevant requirement for the purposes of ss 380(2), 382, and any restriction or requirement imposed by or under certain other provisions is to be treated as a relevant requirement for the purposes of s 380(3)(a); see, in general, the Financial Services and Markets Act 2000 (Transitional Provisions and Savings) (Civil Remedies, Discipline, Criminal Offences etc) (No 2) Order 2001, SI 2001/3083, arts 2, 4. See also art 3 of the 2001 Order, in relation to the FSA's power to require restitution under s 384.

Injunctions

[7.664]

380 Injunctions

(1) If, on the application of the [appropriate regulator] or the Secretary of State, the court is satisfied—
(a) that there is a reasonable likelihood that any person will contravene a relevant requirement, or
(b) that any person has contravened a relevant requirement and that there is a reasonable likelihood that the contravention will continue or be repeated,

the court may make an order restraining (or in Scotland an interdict prohibiting) the contravention.

(2) If on the application of the [appropriate regulator] or the Secretary of State the court is satisfied—
(a) that any person has contravened a relevant requirement, and
(b) that there are steps which could be taken for remedying the contravention,

the court may make an order requiring that person, and any other person who appears to have been knowingly concerned in the contravention, to take such steps as the court may direct to remedy it.

(3) If, on the application of the [appropriate regulator] or the Secretary of State, the court is satisfied that any person may have—

(a) contravened a relevant requirement, or

(b) been knowingly concerned in the contravention of such a requirement,

it may make an order restraining (or in Scotland an interdict prohibiting) him from disposing of, or otherwise dealing with, any assets of his which it is satisfied he is reasonably likely to dispose of or otherwise deal with.

(4) The jurisdiction conferred by this section is exercisable by the High Court and the Court of Session.

(5) In subsection (2), references to remedying a contravention include references to mitigating its effect.

(6) "Relevant requirement"—

(a) in relation to an application by the [appropriate regulator], means a requirement—

[(i) which is imposed by or under this Act or by a [qualifying provision] specified, or of a description specified, for the purposes of this subsection by the Treasury by order]; . . .

(ii) which is imposed by or under any other Act and whose contravention constitutes an offence [mentioned in section 402(1)][; . . .

(iii) which is imposed by the Alternative Investment Fund Managers Regulations 2013;][. . .

(iv) which is imposed by Part 7 of the Financial Services Act 2012 (offences relating to financial services) and whose contravention constitutes an offence under that Part;][. . .]

[(v) which is imposed by a provision made in accordance with the transparency obligations directive (within the meaning of section 103(1));][or

(vi) which is imposed by the Undertakings for Collective Investment in Transferable Securities Regulations 2011].

(b) in relation to an application by the Secretary of State, means a requirement which is imposed by or under this Act and whose contravention constitutes an offence which the Secretary of State has power to prosecute under this Act.

(7) In the application of subsection (6) to Scotland—

(a) . . .

(b) in paragraph (b) omit "which the Secretary of State has power to prosecute under this Act".

[(8) The PRA is the "appropriate regulator" in the case of a contravention of—

(a) a requirement that is imposed by the PRA under any provision of this Act,

(b) a requirement under section 56(6) where the authorised person concerned is a PRA-authorised person and the prohibition order concerned is made by the PRA, or

(c) a requirement under section 59(1) or (2) where the authorised person concerned is a PRA-authorised person and the approval concerned falls to be given by the PRA.

(9) In the case of a contravention of a requirement that is imposed by a [qualifying provision], "the appropriate regulator" is whichever of the PRA or the FCA (or both) is specified by the Treasury by order in relation to the [qualifying provision] for the purposes of this section.

(10) In the case of a contravention of a requirement where the contravention constitutes an offence under this Act, the "appropriate regulator" is whichever of the PRA or the FCA has power to prosecute the offence (see section 401).

(11) The FCA is the "appropriate regulator" in the case of a contravention of any other requirement.

(12) The Treasury may by order amend the definition of "appropriate regulator".]

NOTES

Sub-ss (1)–(3): words in square brackets substituted by the Financial Services Act 2012, s 37(1), Sch 9, Pt 1, para 1, Pt 5, para 19(1), (2), as from 1 April 2013.

Sub-s (6) is amended as follows:

Words in square brackets in sub-para (a)(i) substituted by the Financial Services and Markets Act 2000 (Amendment) (EU Exit) Regulations 2019, SI 2019/632, regs 69, 70(1), (2), as from IP completion day (as defined in the European Union (Withdrawal Agreement) Act 2020, s 39) (for transitional provisions see SI 2019/710, reg 37 at **[12.110]**).

The word omitted from sub-para (a)(i) was repealed, and sub-para (a)(iii) and the preceding word were inserted, by the Alternative Investment Fund Managers Regulations 2013, SI 2013/1773, reg 80, Sch 1, Part 1, paras 1, 27, as from 22 July 2013.

The word omitted from sub-para (a)(ii) was repealed, the word omitted from sub-para (a)(iv) was repealed, and sub-para (a)(vi) and the preceding word were added, by the Undertakings for Collective Investment in Transferable Securities Regulations 2016, SI 2016/225, reg 2(1), (6), as from 18 March 2016.

The word omitted from sub-para (a)(iii) was repealed, the word omitted from sub-para (a)(iv) was originally inserted, and sub-para (a)(v) was inserted, by the Transparency Regulations 2015, SI 2015/1755, reg 4(4), as from 26 November 2015.

Sub-para (a)(iv) and the preceding word were inserted by the Financial Services (Banking Reform) Act 2013, s 141, Sch 10, para 3(1), (2), as from 1 April 2014. Note that this sub-paragraph was incorrectly added as a second sub-para (a)(iii) and was renumbered as sub-para (a)(iv) by SI 2016/225, reg 2(1), (6).

All other words in square brackets in this subsection were substituted by the Financial Services Act 2012, s 37(1), Sch 9, Pt 1, para 1, Pt 5, para 19(1), (3), as from 1 April 2013.

Sub-s (7): para (a) repealed by the Financial Services Act 2012, s 37(1), Sch 9, Pt 1, para 1, Pt 5, para 19(1), (4), as from 1 April 2013.

Sub-ss (8)–(12): added by the Financial Services Act 2012, s 37(1), Sch 9, Pt 1, para 1, Pt 5, para 19(1), (5), as from 24 January 2013 (for the purposes of making orders), and as from 1 April 2013 (otherwise). Words in square brackets in sub-s (9) substituted by SI 2019/632, regs 69, 70(1), (3), as from IP completion day (as defined in the European Union (Withdrawal Agreement) Act 2020, s 39) (for transitional provisions see SI 2019/710, reg 37 at **[12.110]**).

Note: for the purposes of this section, a requirement imposed by the FCA under the Central Securities Depositories Regulations 2014, SI 2014/2879 is a "relevant requirement" for the purposes of this section (see reg 3(8) of those Regulations).

Orders and Regulations: the Financial Services and Markets Act 2000 (Qualifying Provisions) Order 2013, SI 2013/419; the Financial Services and Markets Act 2000 (Qualifying Provisions) (No 2) Order 2013, SI 2013/3116; the Financial Services and Markets Act 2000 (Transparency of Securities Financing Transactions and of Reuse) Regulations 2016, SI 2016/715; the Financial Services and Markets Act 2000 (Qualifying EU Provisions) (Amendment) Order 2016, SI 2016/936; the Alternative Investment Fund Managers (Amendment) Regulations 2018, SI 2018/134; the Insurance Distribution (Regulated Activities and Miscellaneous Amendments) Order 2018, SI 2018/546.

[7.665]
381 Injunctions in cases of market abuse

(1) If, on the application of the [FCA], the court is satisfied—

(a) that there is a reasonable likelihood that any person will [contravene Article 14 (prohibition of insider dealing and of unlawful disclosure of inside information) or Article 15 (prohibition of market manipulation) of the market abuse regulation], or

(b) that any person is or has [contravened Article 14 or 15 of the market abuse regulation] and that there is a reasonable likelihood that the [contravention] will continue or be repeated,

the court may make an order restraining (or in Scotland an interdict prohibiting) the [contravention].

(2) If on the application of the [FCA] the court is satisfied—

(a) that any person is or has [contravened Article 14 or 15 of the market abuse regulation], and

(b) that there are steps which could be taken for remedying the [contravention],

the court may make an order requiring him to take such steps as the court may direct to remedy it.

(3) Subsection (4) applies if, on the application of the [FCA], the court is satisfied that any person—

(a) may be [contravening Article 14 or 15 of the market abuse regulation]; or

(b) may have [contravened Article 14 or 15 of the market abuse regulation].

(4) The court [may] make an order restraining (or in Scotland an interdict prohibiting) the person concerned from disposing of, or otherwise dealing with, any assets of his which it is satisfied that he is reasonably likely to dispose of, or otherwise deal with.

(5) The jurisdiction conferred by this section is exercisable by the High Court and the Court of Session.

(6) In subsection (2), references to remedying any [contravention] include references to mitigating its effect.

NOTES

Word "FCA" in square brackets in sub-ss (1)–(3) substituted, and word in square brackets in sub-s (4) inserted, by the Financial Services Act 2012, s 37(1), Sch 9, Pt 1, para 1, Pt 5, para 20, as from 1 April 2013.

All other words in square brackets substituted by the Financial Services and Markets Act 2000 (Market Abuse) Regulations 2016, SI 2016/680, reg 10(1), (14), as from 3 July 2016.

Restitution orders

[7.666]
382 Restitution orders

(1) The court may, on the application of the [appropriate regulator] or the Secretary of State, make an order under subsection (2) if it is satisfied that a person has contravened a relevant requirement, or been knowingly concerned in the contravention of such a requirement, and—

(a) that profits have accrued to him as a result of the contravention; or

(b) that one or more persons have suffered loss or been otherwise adversely affected as a result of the contravention.

(2) The court may order the person concerned to pay to the [regulator concerned] such sum as appears to the court to be just having regard—

(a) in a case within paragraph (a) of subsection (1), to the profits appearing to the court to have accrued;

(b) in a case within paragraph (b) of that subsection, to the extent of the loss or other adverse effect;

(c) in a case within both of those paragraphs, to the profits appearing to the court to have accrued and to the extent of the loss or other adverse effect.

(3) Any amount paid to the [regulator concerned] in pursuance of an order under subsection (2) must be paid by it to such qualifying person or distributed by it among such qualifying persons as the court may direct.

(4) On an application under subsection (1) the court may require the person concerned to supply it with such accounts or other information as it may require for any one or more of the following purposes—

(a) establishing whether any and, if so, what profits have accrued to him as mentioned in paragraph (a) of that subsection;

(b) establishing whether any person or persons have suffered any loss or adverse effect as mentioned in paragraph (b) of that subsection and, if so, the extent of that loss or adverse effect; and

(c) determining how any amounts are to be paid or distributed under subsection (3).

(5) The court may require any accounts or other information supplied under subsection (4) to be verified in such manner as it may direct.

(6) The jurisdiction conferred by this section is exercisable by the High Court and the Court of Session.

(7) Nothing in this section affects the right of any person other than the [appropriate regulator] or the Secretary of State to bring proceedings in respect of the matters to which this section applies.

(8) "Qualifying person" means a person appearing to the court to be someone—

(a) to whom the profits mentioned in subsection (1)(a) are attributable; or

(b) who has suffered the loss or adverse effect mentioned in subsection (1)(b).

(9) "Relevant requirement"—

(a) in relation to an application by the [appropriate regulator], means a requirement—

[(i) which is imposed by or under this Act or by a [qualifying provision] specified, or of a description specified, for the purposes of this subsection by the Treasury by order]; . . .

(ii) which is imposed by or under any other Act and whose contravention constitutes an offence [mentioned in section 402(1)]; [. . .

(iii) which is imposed by the Alternative Investment Fund Managers Regulations 2013;][or

(iv) which is imposed by Part 7 of the Financial Services Act 2012 (offences relating to financial services) and whose contravention constitutes an offence under that Part;]

(b) in relation to an application by the Secretary of State, means a requirement which is imposed by or under this Act and whose contravention constitutes an offence which the Secretary of State has power to prosecute under this Act.

(10) In the application of subsection (9) to Scotland—

(a) . . .

(b) in paragraph (b) omit "which the Secretary of State has power to prosecute under this Act".

[(11) The PRA is the "appropriate regulator" in the case of a contravention of—

(a) a requirement that is imposed by the PRA under any provision of this Act,

(b) a requirement under section 56(6) where the authorised person concerned is a PRA-authorised person and the prohibition order concerned is made by the PRA, or

(c) a requirement under section 59(1) or (2) where the authorised person concerned is a PRA-authorised person and the approval concerned falls to be given by the PRA.

(12) In the case of a contravention of a requirement that is imposed by a [qualifying provision], "the appropriate regulator" is whichever of the PRA or the FCA (or both) is specified by the Treasury by order in relation to the [qualifying provision] for the purposes of this section.

(13) In the case of a contravention of a requirement where the contravention constitutes an offence under this Act, the "appropriate regulator" is the regulator which has power to prosecute the offence (see section 401).

(14) The FCA is the "appropriate regulator" in the case of a contravention of any other requirement.

(15) The Treasury may by order amend the definition of "appropriate regulator".]

NOTES

Sub-ss (1)–(3), (7): words in square brackets substituted by the Financial Services Act 2012, s 37(1), Sch 9, Pt 1, para 1, Pt 5, para 21(1)–(4), as from 1 April 2013.

Sub-s (9) is amended as follows:

Words in square brackets in sub-para (a)(i) substituted by the Financial Services and Markets Act 2000 (Amendment) (EU Exit) Regulations 2019, SI 2019/632, regs 69, 71(1), (2), as from IP completion day (as defined in the European Union (Withdrawal Agreement) Act 2020, s 39) (for transitional provisions see SI 2019/710, reg 37 at **[12.110]**).

The word omitted from sub-para (a)(i) was repealed, and sub-para (a)(iii) and the preceding word were inserted, by the Alternative Investment Fund Managers Regulations 2013, SI 2013/1773, reg 80, Sch 1, Part 1, paras 1, 27, as from 22 July 2013.

Sub-para (a)(iv) and the preceding word were inserted, and the word omitted from sub-para (a)(ii) was repealed, by the Financial Services (Banking Reform) Act 2013, s 141, Sch 10, para 3(1), (3), as from 1 April 2014.

All other words in square brackets in this subsection were substituted by the Financial Services Act 2012, s 37(1), Sch 9, Pt 1, para 1, Pt 5, para 21(1), (5), as from 1 April 2013.

Sub-s (10): para (a) repealed by the Financial Services Act 2012, s 37(1), Sch 9, Pt 1, para 1, Pt 5, para 21(1), (6), as from 1 April 2013.

Sub-ss (11)–(15): added by the Financial Services Act 2012, s 37(1), Sch 9, Pt 1, para 1, Pt 5, para 21(1), (7), as from 24 January 2013 (for the purposes of making orders), and as from 1 April 2013 (otherwise). Words in square brackets in sub-s (12) substituted by SI 2019/632, regs 69, 71(1), (3), as from IP completion day (as defined in the European Union (Withdrawal Agreement) Act 2020, s 39) (for transitional provisions see SI 2019/710, reg 37 at **[12.110]**).

Note: for the purposes of this section, a requirement imposed by the FCA under the Central Securities Depositories Regulations 2014, SI 2014/2879 is a "relevant requirement" for the purposes of this section (see reg 3(8) of those Regulations).

Orders and Regulations: the Financial Services and Markets Act 2000 (Qualifying Provisions) Order 2013, SI 2013/419; the Financial Services and Markets Act 2000 (Qualifying Provisions) (No 2) Order 2013, SI 2013/3116; the Financial Services and Markets Act 2000 (Qualifying EU Provisions) (Amendment) Order 2016, SI 2016/936; the Alternative Investment Fund Managers (Amendment) Regulations 2018, SI 2018/134; the Insurance Distribution (Regulated Activities and Miscellaneous Amendments) Order 2018, SI 2018/546.

[7.667]

383 Restitution orders in cases of market abuse

[(1) The court may, on the application of the FCA, make an order under subsection (4) if it is satisfied that—

(a) a person ("the person concerned") has contravened Article 14 (prohibition of insider dealing and of unlawful disclosure of inside information) or Article 15 (prohibition of market manipulation) of the market abuse regulation; and

(b) the condition mentioned in subsection (2) is fulfilled.]

(2) The condition is—

(a) that profits have accrued to the person concerned as a result; or

(b) that one or more persons have suffered loss or been otherwise adversely affected as a result.

(3) . . .

(a) the person concerned believed, on reasonable grounds, that his behaviour did not fall within paragraph (a) or (b) of subsection (1); or

(b) he took all reasonable precautions and exercised all due diligence to avoid behaving in a way which fell within paragraph (a) or (b) of subsection (1).

(4) The court may order the person concerned to pay to the [FCA] such sum as appears to the court to be just having regard—

(a) in a case within paragraph (a) of subsection (2), to the profits appearing to the court to have accrued;

(b) in a case within paragraph (b) of that subsection, to the extent of the loss or other adverse effect;

(c) in a case within both of those paragraphs, to the profits appearing to the court to have accrued and to the extent of the loss or other adverse effect.

(5) Any amount paid to the [FCA] in pursuance of an order under subsection (4) must be paid by it to such qualifying person or distributed by it among such qualifying persons as the court may direct.

(6) On an application under subsection (1) the court may require the person concerned to supply it with such accounts or other information as it may require for any one or more of the following purposes—

(a) establishing whether any and, if so, what profits have accrued to him as mentioned in subsection (2)(a);

(b) establishing whether any person or persons have suffered any loss or adverse effect as mentioned in subsection (2)(b) and, if so, the extent of that loss or adverse effect; and

(c) determining how any amounts are to be paid or distributed under subsection (5).

(7) The court may require any accounts or other information supplied under subsection (6) to be verified in such manner as it may direct.

(8) The jurisdiction conferred by this section is exercisable by the High Court and the Court of Session.

(9) Nothing in this section affects the right of any person other than the [FCA] to bring proceedings in respect of the matters to which this section applies.

(10) "Qualifying person" means a person appearing to the court to be someone—

(a) to whom the profits mentioned in paragraph (a) of subsection (2) are attributable; or

(b) who has suffered the loss or adverse effect mentioned in paragraph (b) of that subsection.

NOTES

Sub-s (1) substituted, and sub-s (3) repealed, by the Financial Services and Markets Act 2000 (Market Abuse) Regulations 2016, SI 2016/680, reg 10(1), (15), as from 3 July 2016.

Word "FCA" in square brackets in sub-ss (4), (5), (9) substituted by the Financial Services Act 2012, s 37(1), Sch 9, Pt 1, para 1, Pt 5, para 22, as from 1 April 2013.

Restitution required by [FCA or PRA]

[7.668]

384 Power of [FCA or PRA] to require restitution

(1) [The appropriate regulator] may exercise the power in subsection (5) if it is satisfied that an authorised person [or recognised investment exchange] ("the person concerned") has contravened a relevant requirement, or been knowingly concerned in the contravention of such a requirement, and—

(a) that profits have accrued to him as a result of the contravention; or

(b) that one or more persons have suffered loss or been otherwise adversely affected as a result of the contravention.

[(2) The FCA may exercise the power in subsection (5) if it is satisfied that—

(a) a person ("the person concerned") has contravened Article 14 (prohibition of insider dealing and of unlawful disclosure of inside information) or Article 15 (prohibition of market manipulation) of the market abuse regulation; and

(b) the condition mentioned in subsection (3) is fulfilled.]

(3) The condition is—

(a) that profits have accrued to the person concerned as a result of the [contravention of Article 14 or 15 of the market abuse regulation]; or

(b) that one or more persons have suffered loss or been otherwise adversely affected as a result of the [contravention of Article 14 or 15 of the market abuse regulation].

(4) . . .

(5) The power referred to in subsections (1) and (2) is a power to require the person concerned, in accordance with such arrangements as the [regulator exercising the power ("the regulator concerned")] considers appropriate, to pay to the appropriate person or distribute among the appropriate persons such amount as appears to the [regulator concerned] to be just having regard—

(a) in a case within paragraph (a) of subsection (1) or (3), to the profits appearing to the [regulator concerned] to have accrued;

(b) in a case within paragraph (b) of subsection (1) or (3), to the extent of the loss or other adverse effect;

(c) in a case within paragraphs (a) and (b) of subsection (1) or (3), to the profits appearing to the [regulator concerned] to have accrued and to the extent of the loss or other adverse effect.

(6) "Appropriate person" means a person appearing to the [regulator concerned] to be someone—

(a) to whom the profits mentioned in paragraph (a) of subsection (1) or (3) are attributable; or

(b) who has suffered the loss or adverse effect mentioned in paragraph (b) of subsection (1) or (3).

(7) "Relevant requirement" means—

(a) a requirement imposed by or under this Act [or by [a [qualifying provision] specified, or of a description specified, for the purposes of this subsection by the Treasury by order]]; . . .

(b) a requirement which is imposed by or under any other Act and whose contravention constitutes an offence [mentioned in section 402(1)][; . . .

(c) a requirement imposed by the Alternative Investment Fund Managers Regulations 2013][or

(d) a requirement which is imposed by Part 7 of the Financial Services Act 2012 (offences relating to financial services) and whose contravention constitutes an offence under that Part].

(8) . . .

[(9) The PRA is the "appropriate regulator" in the case of a contravention of—

(a) a requirement that is imposed by the PRA under any provision of this Act,

(b) a requirement under section 56(6) where the authorised person concerned is a PRA-authorised person and the prohibition order concerned is made by the PRA, or

(c) a requirement under section 59(1) or (2) where the authorised person concerned is a PRA-authorised person and the approval concerned falls to be given by the PRA.

(10) In the case of a contravention of a requirement that is imposed by a [qualifying provision], "the appropriate regulator" is whichever of the PRA or the FCA (or both) is specified by the Treasury by order in relation to the [qualifying provision] for the purposes of this section.

(11) In the case of a contravention of a requirement where the contravention constitutes an offence under this Act, the "appropriate regulator" is the regulator which has power to prosecute the offence (see section 401).

(12) The FCA is the "appropriate regulator" in the case of a contravention of any other requirement.

(13) The Treasury may by order amend the definition of "appropriate regulator".]

NOTES

In the heading preceding this section, and in the section heading, the words in square brackets were substituted by the Financial Services Act 2012, s 37(1), Sch 9, Pt 1, para 1, Pt 5, para 23(1), (9), (10), as from 1 April 2013.

Sub-s (1): word in first pair of square brackets substituted, and words in second pair of square brackets inserted, by the Financial Services Act 2012, s 37(1), Sch 9, Pt 1, para 1, Pt 5, para 23(1), (2), as from 1 April 2013.

Sub-s (2): substituted by the Financial Services and Markets Act 2000 (Market Abuse) Regulations 2016, SI 2016/680, reg 10(1), (16)(a), as from 3 July 2016.

Sub-s (3): words in square brackets substituted by SI 2016/680, reg 10(1), (16)(b), as from 3 July 2016.

Sub-s (4): repealed by SI 2016/680, reg 10(1), (16)(c), as from 3 July 2016.

Sub-ss (5), (6): words in square brackets substituted by the Financial Services Act 2012, s 37(1), Sch 9, Pt 1, para 1, Pt 5, para 23(1), (3)–(5), as from 1 April 2013.

Sub-s (7) is amended as follows:

Words in first (outer) pair of square brackets in para (a) inserted by the Financial Services and Markets Act 2000 (Markets in Financial Instruments) Regulations 2007, SI 2007/126, reg 3(5), Sch 5, paras 1, 15, as from 1 April 2007 (certain purposes), and as from 1 November 2007 (otherwise).

Words in second (inner) pair of square brackets in para (a), and words in square brackets in para (b), substituted by the Financial Services Act 2012, s 37(1), Sch 9, Pt 1, para 1, Pt 5, para 23(1), (6), as from 24 January 2013 (for the purposes of making orders), and as from 1 April 2013 (otherwise).

Words in third (inner) pair of square brackets in para (a) substituted by the Financial Services and Markets Act 2000 (Amendment) (EU Exit) Regulations 2019, SI 2019/632, regs 69, 72(1), (2), as from IP completion day (as defined in the European Union (Withdrawal Agreement) Act 2020, s 39) (for transitional provisions see SI 2019/710, reg 37 at **[12.110]**).

The word omitted from para (a) was repealed, and para (c) and the preceding word were inserted, by the Alternative Investment Fund Managers Regulations 2013, SI 2013/1773, reg 80, Sch 1, Part 1, paras 1, 29, as from 22 July 2013.

Para (d) and the preceding word were inserted, and the word omitted from para (b) was repealed, by the Financial Services (Banking Reform) Act 2013, s 141, Sch 10, para 3(4), as from 1 April 2014

Sub-s (8): repealed by the Financial Services Act 2012, s 37(1), Sch 9, Pt 1, para 1, Pt 5, para 23(1), (7), as from 1 April 2013.

Sub-ss (9)–(13): added by the Financial Services Act 2012, s 37(1), Sch 9, Pt 1, para 1, Pt 5, para 23(1), (8), as from 24 January 2013 (for the purposes of making orders), and as from 1 April 2013 (otherwise). Words in square brackets in sub-s (10) substituted by SI 2019/632, regs 69, 72(1), (3), as from IP completion day (as defined in the European Union (Withdrawal Agreement) Act 2020, s 39) (for transitional provisions see SI 2019/710, reg 37 at **[12.110]**).

Orders and Regulations: the Financial Services and Markets Act 2000 (Qualifying Provisions) Order 2013, SI 2013/419; the Financial Services and Markets Act 2000 (Qualifying Provisions) (No 2) Order 2013, SI 2013/3116; the Financial Services and Markets Act 2000 (Qualifying EU Provisions) (Amendment) Order 2016, SI 2016/936; the Alternative Investment Fund Managers (Amendment) Regulations 2018, SI 2018/134; the Insurance Distribution (Regulated Activities and Miscellaneous Amendments) Order 2018, SI 2018/546.

[7.669]

385 Warning notices

(1) If [a regulator] proposes to exercise the power under section 384(5) in relation to a person, it must give him a warning notice.

(2) A warning notice under this section must specify the amount which [the regulator] proposes to require the person concerned to pay or distribute as mentioned in section 384(5).

NOTES

Words in square brackets substituted by the Financial Services Act 2012, s 37(1), Sch 9, Pt 1, para 1, Pt 5, para 24, as from 1 April 2013.

[7.670]

386 Decision notices

(1) If the [regulator] decides to exercise the power under section 384(5), it must give a decision notice to the person in relation to whom the power is exercised.

(2) The decision notice must—

(a) state the amount that he is to pay or distribute as mentioned in section 384(5);

(b) identify the person or persons to whom that amount is to be paid or among whom that amount is to be distributed; and

(c) state the arrangements in accordance with which the payment or distribution is to be made.

(3) If the [regulator] decides to exercise the power under section 384(5), the person in relation to whom it is exercised may refer the matter to the Tribunal.

NOTES

Words in square brackets substituted by the Financial Services Act 2012, s 37(1), Sch 9, Pt 1, para 1, Pt 5, para 25, as from 1 April 2013.

PART XXVI NOTICES

NOTES

Transitional provisions etc in connection with the commencement of the Financial Services Act 2012: See the Financial Services Act 2012 (Transitional Provisions) (Enforcement) Order 2013, SI 2013/441. Articles 19–32 make provision for various notices and other matters given or imposed by the Financial Services Authority before 1 April 2013 to be treated as if given or imposed by the Prudential Regulation Authority, or by the Prudential Regulation Authority and the Financial Conduct Authority. See, in particular, art 19 (warning notices), art 20 (written notices) and art 21 (decision notices). Article 33 disapplies provisions relating to the publication of warning notices under s 390 in relation to warning notices given before that date.

Warning notices

[7.671]

387 Warning notices

(1) A warning notice must—

(a) state the action which the [regulator giving the notice ("the regulator concerned")] proposes to take;

(b) be in writing;

(c) give reasons for the proposed action;

(d) state whether section 394 applies; and

(e) if that section applies, describe its effect and state whether any secondary material exists to which the person concerned must be allowed access under it.

[(1A) Where the PRA is the regulator concerned and the FCA proposes to refuse consent for the purposes of section 55F, 55I or 59 or to give conditional consent as mentioned in section 55F(5)[, 55I(8) or 61(2D)], the warning notice given by the PRA must—

(a) state that fact, and

(b) give the reasons for the FCA's proposal.]

(2) [A warning] notice must specify a reasonable period (which may not be less than [14 days]) within which the person to whom it is given may make representations to the [regulator concerned].

(3) [The regulator concerned] may extend the period specified in the notice.

[(3A) Where the PRA receives any representations in response to a warning notice given by it under section 55X(1) or (2) or 62(2) in a case falling within subsection (1A) it must—

(a) if the representations are in writing, give a copy to the FCA, or

(b) if they are not in writing and have not been given directly to the FCA by the person making them, provide the FCA with a record of them.]

(4) [The regulator concerned] must then decide, within a reasonable period, whether to give the person concerned a decision notice.

NOTES

Sub-ss (1A), (3A) were inserted, and all other words in square brackets in this section (with the exception of the words ", 55I(8) or 61(2D)" in sub-s (1A)) were substituted, by the Financial Services Act 2012, s 37(1), Sch 9, Pt 1, para 1, Pt 6, para 26, as from 1 April 2013.

Words in square brackets in sub-s (1A) substituted by the Financial Services (Banking Reform) Act 2013, s 35, Sch 3, para 12, as from 7 March 2016.

Decision notices

[7.672]

388 Decision notices

(1) A decision notice must—

(a) be in writing;

(b) give [the reasons of the regulator giving the notice ("the regulator concerned")] for the decision to take the action to which the notice relates;

(c) state whether section 394 applies;

(d) if that section applies, describe its effect and state whether any secondary material exists to which the person concerned must be allowed access under it; and

(e) give an indication of—

(i) any right to have the matter referred to the Tribunal which is given by this Act; and

(ii) the procedure on such a reference.

[(1A) Where the PRA is the regulator concerned and the FCA has decided to refuse consent for the purposes of section 55F, 55I or 59 or to give conditional consent as mentioned in section 55F(5)[, 55I(8) or 61(2D)], the decision notice given by the PRA must—

(a) state that fact, and

(b) give the reasons for the FCA's decision.]

(2) If the decision notice was preceded by a warning notice, the action to which the decision notice relates must be action under the same Part as the action proposed in the warning notice.

(3) [The regulator concerned] may, before it takes the action to which a decision notice ("the original notice") relates, give the person concerned a further decision notice which relates to different action in respect of the same matter.

(4) [The regulator concerned] may give a further decision notice as a result of subsection (3) only if the person to whom the original notice was given consents.

(5) If the person to whom a decision notice is given under subsection (3) had the right to refer the matter to which the original decision notice related to the Tribunal, he has that right as respects the decision notice under subsection (3).

NOTES

Words in square brackets in sub-ss (1), (3), (4) substituted, and sub-s (1A) inserted, by the Financial Services Act 2012, s 37(1), Sch 9, Pt 1, para 1, Pt 6, para 27, as from 1 April 2013.

Words in square brackets in sub-s (1A) substituted by the Financial Services (Banking Reform) Act 2013, s 35, Sch 3, para 13, as from 7 March 2016.

Conclusion of proceedings

[7.673]

389 Notices of discontinuance

(1) If [a regulator] decides not to take—

(a) the action proposed in a warning notice [given by it], or

(b) the action to which a decision notice [given by it] relates,

it must give a notice of discontinuance to the person to whom the warning notice or decision notice was given.

(2) But subsection (1) does not apply if the discontinuance of the proceedings concerned results in the granting of an application made by the person to whom the warning or decision notice was given.

(3) A notice of discontinuance must identify the proceedings which are being discontinued.

NOTES

Words in first pair of square brackets in sub-s (1) substituted, and words in square brackets in paras (a), (b) of that subsection inserted, by the Financial Services Act 2012, s 37(1), Sch 9, Pt 1, para 1, Pt 6, para 28, as from 1 April 2013.

[7.674]

390 Final notices

(1) If [a regulator] has given a person a decision notice and the matter was not referred to the Tribunal within the [time required by Tribunal Procedure Rules], [the regulator] must, on taking the action to which the decision notice relates, give the person concerned and any person to whom the decision notice was copied a final notice.

(2) If [a regulator] has given a person a decision notice and the matter was referred to the Tribunal, [the regulator] must, on taking action in accordance with any directions given by—

(a) the Tribunal, or

[(b) a court on an appeal against the decision of the Tribunal,]

give that person and any person to whom the decision notice was copied [the notice required by subsection (2A)].

[(2A) The notice required by this subsection is—

(a) in a case where the regulator is acting in accordance with a direction given by the Tribunal under section 133(6)(b), or by the court on an appeal from a decision by the Tribunal under section 133(6), a further decision notice, and

(b) in any other case, a final notice.]

(3) A final notice about a statement must—

(a) set out the terms of the statement;

(b) give details of the manner in which, and the date on which, the statement will be published.

(4) A final notice about an order must—

(a) set out the terms of the order;

(b) state the date from which the order has effect.

(5) A final notice about a penalty must—

(a) state the amount of the penalty;

(b) state the manner in which, and the period within which, the penalty is to be paid;

(c) give details of the way in which the penalty will be recovered if it is not paid by the date stated in the notice.

(6) A final notice about a requirement to make a payment or distribution in accordance with section 384(5) must state—

(a) the persons to whom,

(b) the manner in which, and

(c) the period within which,

it must be made.

(7) In any other case, the final notice must—

(a) give details of the action being taken;

(b) state the date on which the action is to be taken.

(8) The period stated under subsection (5)(b) or (6)(c) may not be less than 14 days beginning with the date on which the final notice is given.

(9) If all or any of the amount of a penalty payable under a final notice is outstanding at the end of the period stated under subsection (5)(b), [the regulator giving the notice] may recover the outstanding amount as a debt due to it.

(10) If all or any of a required payment or distribution has not been made at the end of a period stated in a final notice under subsection (6)(c), the obligation to make the payment is enforceable, on the application of [the regulator giving the notice], by injunction or, in Scotland, by an order under section 45 of the Court of Session Act 1988.

NOTES

Sub-s (1): words in first and third pairs of square brackets substituted by the Financial Services Act 2012, s 37(1), Sch 9, Pt 1, para 1, Pt 6, para 29(1), (2), as from 1 April 2013. Words in second pair of square brackets substituted by the Transfer of Tribunal Functions Order 2010, SI 2010/22, art 5(1), Sch 2, paras 43, 47(a), as from 6 April 2010.

Sub-s (2): words in first, second and final pairs of square brackets substituted by the Financial Services Act 2012, s 37(1), Sch 9, Pt 1, para 1, Pt 6, para 29(1), (3), as from 1 April 2013. Para (b) substituted by SI 2010/22, art 5(1), Sch 2, paras 43, 47, as from 6 April 2010.

Sub-s (2A): inserted by the Financial Services Act 2012, s 37(1), Sch 9, Pt 1, para 1, Pt 6, para 29(1), (4), as from 1 April 2013.

Sub-ss (9), (10): words in square brackets substituted by the Financial Services Act 2012, s 37(1), Sch 9, Pt 1, para 1, Pt 6, para 29(1), (5), as from 1 April 2013.

Publication

[7.675]

391 Publication

[(1) In the case of a warning notice falling within subsection (1ZB)—

(a) neither the regulator giving the notice nor a person to whom it is given or copied may publish the notice,

(b) a person to whom the notice is given or copied may not publish any details concerning the notice unless the regulator giving the notice has published those details, and

(c) after consulting the persons to whom the notice is given or copied, the regulator giving the notice may publish such information about the matter to which the notice relates as it considers appropriate.

(1ZA) In the case of a warning notice not falling within subsection (1ZB), neither the regulator giving the notice nor a person to whom it is given or copied may publish the notice or any details concerning it.

(1ZB) A warning notice falls within this subsection if it is given under—

(a) section 63B;

(b) section 67;

(c) section 87M;

(d) section 88B;

(e) section 89K;

(f) section 89R;

(g) section 92;

(h) section 126;

(i) section 131H;
[(ia) section 142N;]
[(ib) section 143T;
(ic) section 143X;]
(j) section 192L;
(k) section 207;
(l) section 312G;
(m) section 345B (whether as a result of section 345(2) or 345A(3) or section 249(1) [or 261K(1)]).]

[(1A) A person to whom a decision notice is given or copied may not publish the notice or any details concerning it unless the [regulator giving the notice] has published the notice or those details.]

(2) A notice of discontinuance must state that, if the person to whom the notice is given consents, the [regulator giving the notice] may publish such information as it considers appropriate about the matter to which the discontinued proceedings related.

(3) A copy of a notice of discontinuance must be accompanied by a statement that, if the person to whom the notice is copied consents, the [regulator giving the notice] may publish such information as it considers appropriate about the matter to which the discontinued proceedings related, so far as relevant to that person.

(4) [The regulator giving a decision or final notice] must publish such information about the matter to which [the notice] relates as it considers appropriate.

[(4A) Subsection (4) is subject to [sections 391A[, 391B[, 391C [391D, 391E and 391F]]]].]

(5) When a supervisory notice takes effect, the [regulator giving the notice] must publish such information about the matter to which the notice relates as it considers appropriate.

[(5A) Subsection (5) does not apply in relation to a notice given in accordance with section 137S(5) or (8)(a) (but see section 137S(11)).]

[(6) The FCA may not publish information under this section if, in its opinion, publication of the information would be—
(a) unfair to the person with respect to whom the action was taken (or was proposed to be taken),
(b) prejudicial to the interests of consumers, or
(c) detrimental to the stability of the UK financial system.

(6A) The PRA may not publish information under this section if, in its opinion, publication of the information would be—
(a) unfair to the person with respect to whom the action was taken (or was proposed to be taken),
(b) prejudicial to the safety and soundness of PRA-authorised persons, or
(c) in a case where section 2C applies, prejudicial to securing the appropriate degree of protection for policyholders.]

(7) Information is to be published under this section in such manner as the [a regulator] considers appropriate.

[(7A), (7B) . . .]

(8) For the purposes of determining when a supervisory notice takes effect, a matter to which the notice relates is open to review if—
(a) the period during which any person may refer the matter to the Tribunal is still running;
(b) the matter has been referred to the Tribunal but has not been dealt with;
(c) the matter has been referred to the Tribunal and dealt with but the period during which an appeal may be brought against the Tribunal's decision is still running; or
(d) such an appeal has been brought but has not been determined.

[(8A) Where a decision notice or final notice relates to any decision or action under a provision of this Act in relation to the contravention of a [CSD requirement], this section has effect subject to Article 62 of the CSD regulation (publication of decisions).]

[(8AA) A "CSD requirement" is a requirement imposed by—
(a) the CSD regulation,
(b) any EU regulation, originally made under the CSD regulation, which is retained direct EU legislation, or
(c) any subordinate legislation (within the meaning of the Interpretation Act 1978) made under the CSD regulation on or after IP completion day.]

[(8B) Where a decision notice or final notice relates to any decision or action under a provision of this Act in relation to the contravention of a [market abuse requirement], this section has effect subject to Article 34 of the market abuse regulation (publication of decisions).]

[(8BA) A "market abuse requirement" is a requirement imposed by—
(a) the market abuse regulation,
(b) any EU regulation, originally made under the market abuse regulation, which is retained direct EU legislation, or
(c) any subordinate legislation (within the meaning of the Interpretation Act 1978) made under the market abuse regulation on or after IP completion day.]

[(8C) Where a decision notice, final notice or supervisory notice relates to any decision or action under a provision of this Act in relation to the contravention of a requirement imposed by or under Article 4 or 15 of the SFT regulation, this section has effect subject to Article 26 of the SFT regulation (publication of decisions).]

[(8D) Where a decision notice, final notice or supervisory notice relates to any decision or action under a provision of this Act in relation to the contravention of a requirement imposed by—
(a) Regulation (EU) No 1286/2014 of the European Parliament and of the Council of 26 November 2014 on key information documents for packaged retail and insurance-based investment products (the "PRIIPs regulation") . . .
(b) any [EU regulation, originally] made under the PRIIPs regulation, [which is retained direct EU legislation,] [or
(c) any subordinate legislation (within the meaning of the Interpretation Act 1978) made under the PRIIPs regulation on or after IP completion day,]

this section has effect subject to Article 29 of the PRIIPs regulation (publication of decisions).]

[(8E) Where a decision notice or final notice relates to any decision or action under a provision of this Act in relation to the contravention of a requirement [imposed by—

(a) the EU Benchmarks Regulation 2016,

(b) any EU regulation, originally made under the EU Benchmarks Regulation 2016, which is retained direct EU legislation, or

(c) any subordinate legislation (within the meaning of the Interpretation Act 1978) made under the EU Benchmarks Regulation on or after IP completion day,

this section] has effect subject to Article 45 of the EU Benchmarks Regulation 2016 (publication of decisions).]

[(8F) . . .]

[(8G) Where a decision notice or final notice relates to any decision or action under a provision of this Act in relation to the contravention of a requirement [imposed by—

(a) the prospectus regulation,

(b) any EU regulation, originally made under the prospectus regulation, which is retained EU law, or

(c) any subordinate legislation (within the meaning of the Interpretation Act 1978) made under the prospectus regulation on or after IP completion day,

this section] has effect subject to Article 42 of the prospectus regulation (publication of decisions).]

(9) "Notice of discontinuance" means a notice given under section 389.

(10) "Supervisory notice" has the same meaning as in section 395.

[(11) Section 425A (meaning of "consumers") applies for the purposes of this section.]

NOTES

Sub-ss (1)–(1ZB): substituted (for the original sub-s (1)) by the Financial Services Act 2012, s 37(1), Sch 9, Pt 1, para 1, Pt 6, para 30(1), (2), as from 1 April 2013. These subsections have subsequently been amended as follows—

Sub-s (1ZB)(ia) inserted by the Financial Services (Banking Reform) Act 2013, s 4(3), as from 1 January 2019.

Sub-s (1ZB)(ib), (ic) inserted by the Financial Services Act 2021, s 2, Sch 2, Pt 2, para 12, as from 1 July 2021; for transitional provisions, see Sch 2, Pt 3 to the 2021 Act.

Words in square brackets in sub-s (1ZB)(m) inserted by the Collective Investment in Transferable Securities (Contractual Scheme) Regulations 2013, SI 2013/1388, reg 3(1), (18), as from 6 June 2013.

Sub-s (1A): inserted by the Financial Services Act 2010, s 13(1), (3), as from 12 October 2010. Words in square brackets substituted by the Financial Services Act 2012, s 37(1), Sch 9, Pt 1, para 1, Pt 6, para 30(1), (3), as from 1 April 2013.

Sub-ss (2)–(5), (7): words in square brackets substituted by the Financial Services Act 2012, s 37(1), Sch 9, Pt 1, para 1, Pt 6, para 30(1), (3)–(5), (7), as from 1 April 2013.

Sub-s (4A): inserted by the Capital Requirements Regulations 2013, SI 2013/3115, reg 46(1), Sch 2, Pt 1, paras 1, 22, as from 1 January 2014; and subsequently amended as follows—

Words in first (outer) pair of square brackets substituted by the Transparency Regulations 2015, SI 2015/1755, reg 4(5), as from 26 November 2015.

Words in second (inner) pair of square brackets substituted by the Undertakings for Collective Investment in Transferable Securities Regulations 2016, SI 2016/225, reg 2(1), (7), as from 18 March 2016.

Words in third (inner) pair of square brackets substituted by the Financial Services and Markets Act 2000 (Markets in Financial Instruments) Regulations 2017, SI 2017/701, reg 50(1), Sch 2, paras 1, 45(a), as from 3 January 2018 (note that various provisions of the 2017 Regulations came into force on earlier dates for the purposes of making rules, giving notices and consent, etc (for details see reg 1 of the 2017 Regulations)).

Words in fourth (inner) pair of square brackets substituted by the Financial Services and Markets Act 2000 (Prospectus) Regulations 2019, SI 2019/1043, regs 3, 33(1)(a), as from 21 July 2019.

Sub-s (5A): inserted by the Financial Services Act 2012, s 24(2), as from 1 April 2013.

Sub-ss (6), (6A): substituted (for the original sub-s (6)) by the Financial Services Act 2012, s 37(1), Sch 9, Pt 1, para 1, Pt 6, para 30(1), (6), as from 1 April 2013.

Sub-ss (7A), (7B): originally inserted by the Financial Services (Omnibus 1 Directive) Regulations 2012, SI 2012/916, reg 2(1), (13), as from 16 April 2012. Subsequently repealed by the Financial Services and Markets Act 2000 (Amendment) (EU Exit) Regulations 2019, SI 2019/632, regs 73, 74(1), (2), as from IP completion day (as defined in the European Union (Withdrawal Agreement) Act 2020, s 39).

Sub-s (8A): inserted by the Central Securities Depositories Regulations 2014, SI 2014/2879, reg 6(1), (2), as from 21 November 2014. Words in square brackets substituted by SI 2019/632, regs 73, 74(1), (3), as from IP completion day (as defined in the European Union (Withdrawal Agreement) Act 2020, s 39).

Sub-s (8AA): inserted by SI 2019/632, regs 73, 74(1), (4), as from IP completion day (as defined in the European Union (Withdrawal Agreement) Act 2020, s 39). Note that reg 74(4) of the 2019 Regulations was amended by the Financial Services and Economic and Monetary Policy (Consequential Amendments) (EU Exit) Regulations 2020, SI 2020/1301, reg 3, Schedule, para 33(g), as from 30 December 2020 (and the effect of the amendment has been incorporated in the text set out above).

Sub-s (8B): inserted by SI 2016/680, reg 10(1), (17)(b), as from 3 July 2016. Words in square brackets substituted by SI 2019/632, regs 73, 74(1), (5), as from IP completion day (as defined in the European Union (Withdrawal Agreement) Act 2020, s 39).

Sub-s (8BA): inserted by SI 2019/632, regs 73, 74(1), (6), as from IP completion day (as defined in the European Union (Withdrawal Agreement) Act 2020, s 39). Note that reg 74(6) of the 2019 Regulations was amended by the Financial Services and Economic and Monetary Policy (Consequential Amendments) (EU Exit) Regulations 2020, SI 2020/1301, reg 3, Schedule, para 33(g), as from 30 December 2020 (and the effect of the amendment has been incorporated in the text set out above).

Sub-s (8C): inserted by the Financial Services and Markets Act 2000 (Transparency of Securities Financing Transactions and of Reuse) Regulations 2016, SI 2016/715, reg 29, Sch 1, para 1(1), (4), as from 13 July 2016.

Sub-s (8D): inserted by the Packaged Retail and Insurance-based Investment Products Regulations 2017, SI 2017/1127, reg 12, Sch 2, para 1, as from 1 January 2018. All amendments to this subsection were made by SI 2019/632, regs 73, 74(1), (7), as from IP completion day (as defined in the European Union (Withdrawal Agreement) Act 2020, s 39). Note that reg 74(7) of the 2019 Regulations was amended by the Financial Services and Economic and Monetary Policy (Consequential Amendments) (EU Exit) Regulations 2020, SI 2020/1301, reg 3, Schedule, para 33(g), as from 30 December 2020 (and the effect of the amendment has been incorporated in the text set out above).

Sub-s (8E): inserted by the Financial Services and Markets Act 2000 (Benchmarks) Regulations 2018, SI 2018/135, reg 46, as from 27 February 2018. Words in square brackets substituted by SI 2019/632, regs 73, 74(1), (8), as from IP completion day (as defined in the European Union (Withdrawal Agreement) Act 2020, s 39). Note that SI 2019/632, reg 74(8) was amended by the Financial Services and Economic and Monetary Policy (Consequential Amendments) (EU Exit) Regulations 2020, SI 2020/1301, reg 3, Schedule, para 33(g), as from 30 December 2020 (and the effect of the amendment has been incorporated in the text set out above).

Sub-s (8F): originally inserted by the Securitisation Regulations 2018, SI 2018/1288, reg 28, Sch 2, para 1, as from 1 January 2019. Subsequently repealed by SI 2019/632, regs 73, 74(1), (9), as from IP completion day (as defined in the European Union (Withdrawal Agreement) Act 2020, s 39).

Sub-s (8G): inserted by SI 2019/1043, regs 3, 33(1)(b), as from 21 July 2019. Words in square brackets substituted by the Prospectus (Amendment etc) (EU Exit) Regulations 2019, SI 2019/1234, regs 2, 8, as from IP completion day (as defined in the European Union (Withdrawal Agreement) Act 2020, s 39); for transitional provisions, see regs 74, 75 of the 2019 Regulations at **[12.165]** et seq. Note that reg 8 of the 2019 Regulations was amended by the Financial Services and Economic and Monetary Policy (Consequential Amendments) (EU Exit) Regulations 2020, SI 2020/1301, reg 3, Schedule, para 48(b), as from 30 December 2020 (and the effect of the amendment has been incorporated in the text set out above)

Sub-s (11): substituted by the Financial Services Act 2010, s 24(1), (2), Sch 2, Pt 1, paras 1, 28, as from 8 April 2010.

Consumers: as to the meaning of this, see the note on s 1G at **[7.7]**.

Note that the Financial Services Act 2012, s 37(2)(a) provides that if the Treasury consider that it is in the public interest to do so, it may by order amend this section by substituting for subsections (1)–(1ZB) the following—

"(1) Neither the regulator giving a warning notice nor a person to whom it is given or copied may publish the notice or any details concerning it.".

[7.676]

[391A [Publication: special provisions relating to [capital requirements]]

(1) This section applies where a decision notice or final notice relates to the imposition of a penalty [for breach of—

(a) a provision made in or under this Act for the purpose of implementing the capital requirements directive, or

(b) a provision of the capital requirements regulation].

(2) Where a regulator publishes information under section 391(4) about a matter to which a decision notice relates and the person to whom the notice is given refers the matter to the Tribunal, the regulator must, without undue delay, publish on its official website information about the status of the appeal and its outcome.

(3) Subject to subsection (4), where a regulator gives a final notice, the regulator must publish information on the type and nature of the breach and the identity of the person on whom the penalty is imposed.

(4) Information about a matter to which a final notice relates must be published anonymously where—

(a) the penalty is imposed on an individual and, following an obligatory prior assessment, publication of personal data is found to be disproportionate;

(b) publication would jeopardise the stability of financial markets or an ongoing criminal investigation; or

(c) publication would cause, insofar as it can be determined, disproportionate damage to the persons involved.

(5) Where subsection (4) applies, the regulator may make such arrangements as to the publication of information (including as to the timing of publication) as are necessary to preserve the anonymity of the person on whom the penalty is imposed.

(6) Where a regulator publishes information in accordance with subsections (2) to (5), the regulator must—

(a) publish the information on its official website; [and]

(b) ensure the information remains on its official website for at least five years, unless the information is personal data and [the data protection legislation] requires the information to be retained for a different period . . .

(c) . . .]

NOTES

Inserted by the Capital Requirements Regulations 2013, SI 2013/3115, reg 46(1), Sch 2, Pt 1, paras 1, 23, as from 1 January 2014.

Section heading: substituted by the Transparency Regulations 2015, SI 2015/1755, reg 4(6), as from 26 November 2015. Words in square brackets therein substituted by the Financial Services and Markets Act 2000 (Amendment) (EU Exit) Regulations 2019, SI 2019/632, regs 73, 75(1), (2), as from IP completion day (as defined in the European Union (Withdrawal Agreement) Act 2020, s 39).

Sub-s (1): words in square brackets substituted by SI 2019/632, regs 73, 75(1), (3), as from IP completion day (as defined in the European Union (Withdrawal Agreement) Act 2020, s 39).

Sub-s (6): the word in square brackets at the end of para (a) was inserted, and para (c) and the preceding word were repealed, by SI 2019/632, regs 73, 75(1), (4), as from IP completion day (as defined in the European Union (Withdrawal Agreement) Act 2020, s 39). Words in square brackets in para (b) substituted by the Data Protection Act 2018, s 211, Sch 19, Pt 1, paras 48, 50, as from 25 May 2018 (for transitional provisions and savings relating to the repeal of the Data Protection Act 1998, see Sch 20 to the 2018 Act).

[7.677]

[391B Publication: special provisions relating to [transparency obligations]

(1) This section applies where a decision notice, final notice or notice under section 89M relates to the imposition of a sanction or measure [for breach of a provision made in or under this Act for the purpose of implementing the transparency obligations directive].

(2) Where the FCA publishes information under section 391(4) or subsection (3) about a matter to which a decision notice or a notice under section 89M relates and the person to whom the notice is given refers the matter to the Tribunal—

(a) the FCA must include information to that effect in the publication at the time of the publication, or,

(b) if the matter is referred to the Tribunal after the publication, the FCA must update the publication or publish that information separately.

(3) Subject to subsection (4), where the FCA gives a final notice or a notice under section 89M, it must publish information on the type and nature of the breach and the identity of the person on whom the sanction or measure is imposed.

(4) Information about a matter to which a final notice or a notice under section 89M relates may be published anonymously where—

(a) the sanction is imposed on an individual and, following an obligatory prior assessment, publication of personal data is found to be disproportionate;

(b) failing to publish anonymously would seriously jeopardise the stability of the financial system or an ongoing official investigation; or

(c) failing to publish anonymously would cause, insofar as it can be determined, disproportionate and serious damage to the persons involved.

(5) Where subsection (4) applies, the FCA may make such arrangements as to the publication of information (including as to the timing of publication) as are necessary to preserve the anonymity of the person on whom the sanction or measure is imposed.

(6) In this section, the "transparency obligations directive" has the same meaning as in section 103(1).]

NOTES

Inserted by the Transparency Regulations 2015, SI 2015/1755, reg 4(7), as from 26 November 2015.

Section heading, sub-s (1): words in square brackets substituted by the Financial Services and Markets Act 2000 (Amendment) (EU Exit) Regulations 2019, SI 2019/632, regs 73, 76, as from IP completion day (as defined in the European Union (Withdrawal Agreement) Act 2020, s 39).

[7.678]

[391C Publication: special provisions relating to [UCITS]

(1) This section applies where a supervisory notice, decision notice or final notice relates to the imposition of a sanction or measure [for breach of a provision made in or under this Act for the purpose of implementing the UCITS directive].

(2) Where the FCA publishes information under section 391(4) or (5) about a matter to which a decision notice or supervisory notice relates and the person to whom the notice is given refers the matter to the Tribunal, the FCA must, without undue delay, publish on its official website information about the status of the appeal and its outcome.

(3) Subject to subsection (4), where the FCA gives a final notice, it must, without undue delay, publish on its official website information on the type and nature of the breach and the identity of the person on whom the sanction or measure is imposed.

(4) Subject to subsection (6), information about a matter to which a final notice relates must be published anonymously where—

(a) the sanction or measure is imposed on an individual and, following an obligatory prior assessment, publication of personal data is found to be disproportionate;

(b) failing to publish anonymously would jeopardise the stability of financial markets or an ongoing investigation; or

(c) failing to publish anonymously would cause, insofar as it can be determined, disproportionate damage to the persons involved.

(5) Where subsection (4) applies, the FCA may make such arrangements as to the publication of information (including as to the timing of publication) as are necessary to preserve the anonymity of the person on whom the sanction or measure is imposed.

(6) Information about a matter to which a final notice relates must not be published where anonymous publication under subsection (4) is considered by the FCA to be insufficient to ensure—

(a) that the stability of the financial markets would not be put in jeopardy; or

(b) that the publication would be proportionate with regard to sanctions or measures which are considered by the FCA to be of a minor nature.

(7) Where the FCA publishes information in accordance with subsections (2) to (5), the FCA must—

(a) ensure the information remains on its official website for at least five years, unless the information is personal data and [the data protection legislation] requires the information to be retained for a different period; . . .

(b) . . .]

NOTES

Inserted by the Undertakings for Collective Investment in Transferable Securities Regulations 2016, SI 2016/225, reg 2(1), (8), as from 18 March 2016.

Section heading, sub-s (1): words in square brackets substituted by the Financial Services and Markets Act 2000 (Amendment) (EU Exit) Regulations 2019, SI 2019/632, regs 73, 77(1)–(3), as from IP completion day (as defined in the European Union (Withdrawal Agreement) Act 2020, s 39).

Sub-s (7): words in square brackets in para (a) substituted by the Data Protection Act 2018, s 211, Sch 19, Pt 1, paras 48, 51, as from 25 May 2018 (for transitional provisions and savings relating to the repeal of the Data Protection Act 1998, see Sch 20 to the 2018 Act). Para (b) and the preceding word repealed by SI 2019/632, regs 73, 77(1), (4), as from IP completion day (as defined in the European Union (Withdrawal Agreement) Act 2020, s 39).

[7.679]

[391D Publication: special provisions relating to [markets in financial instruments]

(1) This section applies where a supervisory notice, decision notice or final notice relates to the imposition of a sanction or measure [for breach of—

(a) a provision made in or under this Act for the purpose of implementing the markets in financial instruments directive, or

(b) a provision of the markets in financial instruments regulation].

(2) Where a regulator publishes information under section 391(4) or (5) about a matter to which a supervisory notice or decision notice relates and the person to whom the notice is given refers the matter to the Tribunal, the regulator must, without undue delay, publish on its official website information about the status of the appeal and its outcome.

(3) Subject to subsections (4), (5), and (8) where a regulator gives a final notice, it must, without undue delay, publish on its official website information on the type and nature of the breach and the identity of the person on whom the sanction or measure is imposed.

(4) Subject to subsection (7) and (8), information about a matter to which a final notice relates must be published in accordance with subsection (5) where—

(a) a regulator considers it to be disproportionate to publish the identity of a legal person on whom the sanction or measure is imposed following an assessment by the regulator of the proportionality of publishing the person's identity;

(b) a regulator considers it to be disproportionate to publish the personal data of an individual on whom the sanction or measure is imposed following an assessment by the regulator of the proportionality of publishing the personal data; or

(c) the publication of information under subsection (3) would jeopardise the stability of the financial markets or an ongoing investigation.

(5) Where subsection (4) applies, a regulator must—

(a) defer the publication of the information about a matter to which a final notice relates until such time as subsection (4) ceases to apply; or

(b) publish the information on an anonymous basis if publication on that basis would ensure the effective protection of any anonymised personal data in the information.

(6) Where subsection (5)(b) applies, the regulator may make such arrangements as to the publication of information (including as to the timing of publication) as are necessary to preserve the anonymity of the person on whom the sanction or measure is imposed.

(7) The regulator may make arrangements for the postponed publication of any personal data that is anonymised in information it publishes under subsection (5)(b) if—

(a) publication of the data is postponed for a reasonable period of time; and

(b) the regulator considers that subsection (5)(b) will no longer apply in respect of that data at the time of the postponed publication.

(8) Information about a matter to which a final notice relates must not be published if publication in accordance with subsection (5) is considered by the regulator insufficient to ensure—

(a) that the stability of the financial markets would not be put in jeopardy; or

(b) that the publication of the information would be proportionate with regard to sanctions or measures which are considered by the regulator to be of a minor nature.

(9) Where a regulator publishes information in accordance with subsections (2) to (7), the regulator must—

(a) ensure the information remains on its official website for at least five years, unless the information is personal data and [the data protection legislation] requires the information to be retained for a different period; . . .

(b) . . .]

NOTES

Inserted by the Financial Services and Markets Act 2000 (Markets in Financial Instruments) Regulations 2017, SI 2017/701, reg 50(1), Sch 2, paras 1, 46, as from 3 January 2018 (note that various provisions of the 2017 Regulations came into force on earlier dates for the purposes of making rules, giving notices and consent, etc (for details see reg 1 of the 2017 Regulations)).

Section heading, sub-s (1): words in square brackets substituted by the Financial Services and Markets Act 2000 (Amendment) (EU Exit) Regulations 2019, SI 2019/632, regs 73, 78(1)–(3), as from IP completion day (as defined in the European Union (Withdrawal Agreement) Act 2020, s 39).

Sub-s (9): words in square brackets in para (a) substituted by the Data Protection Act 2018, s 211, Sch 19, Pt 1, paras 48, 52, as from 25 May 2018 (for transitional provisions and savings relating to the repeal of the Data Protection Act 1998, see Sch 20 to the 2018 Act). Para (b) and the preceding word repealed by SI 2019/632, regs 73, 78(1), (4), as from IP completion day (as defined in the European Union (Withdrawal Agreement) Act 2020, s 39).

[7.680]

[391E Publication: special provisions relating to [insurance distribution]

(1) This section applies where a supervisory notice, decision notice or final notice relates to the imposition of a sanction or measure [for breach of a provision made in or under this Act for the purpose of implementing the insurance distribution directive].

(2) Where a regulator publishes information under section 391(4) or (5) about a matter to which a decision notice or supervisory notice relates and the person to whom the notice is given refers the matter to the Tribunal, the regulator must, without undue delay, publish on its official website information about the status of the appeal and its outcome.

(3) Subject to subsection (4), where the regulator gives a final notice, it must, without undue delay, publish on its official website information on the type and nature of the breach and the identity of the person on whom the sanction or measure is imposed.

(4) The regulator may publish the information anonymously, defer publication of the information or withhold some, or all, of the information where—

(a) following an obligatory prior assessment, the regulator considers that publication of the identity of the person, or any personal data, would be disproportionate; or

(b) the regulator considers that publication would jeopardise the stability of financial markets or an ongoing investigation.

(5) . . .

(6) In this section "supervisory notice" has the same meaning as in section 395.]

NOTES

Inserted by the Insurance Distribution (Regulated Activities and Miscellaneous Amendments) Order 2018, SI 2018/546, arts 9, 16, as from 1 October 2018.

Section heading, sub-s (1): words in square brackets substituted by the Financial Services and Markets Act 2000 (Amendment) (EU Exit) Regulations 2019, SI 2019/632, regs 73, 79(1)–(3), as from IP completion day (as defined in the European Union (Withdrawal Agreement) Act 2020, s 39).

Sub-s (5): repealed by SI 2019/632, regs 73, 79(1), (4), as from IP completion day (as defined in the European Union (Withdrawal Agreement) Act 2020, s 39).

[7.681]

[391F Publication: special provisions relating to the prospectus regulation

(1) Subsection (2) applies where a decision notice or final notice relates to the imposition of a sanction or measure [for an infringement of the prospectus regulation], and—

(a) following an assessment by the FCA of the proportionality of publishing personal data of a person on whom the sanction or measure is imposed, the FCA considers it disproportionate to do so, or

(b) publication of personal data of a person on whom the sanction or measure is imposed would jeopardise the stability of financial markets or an ongoing investigation.

(2) The FCA—

(a) if publication on an anonymous basis of information about the matter to which the notice relates would ensure the effective protection of the personal data, must publish the information on an anonymous basis;

(b) otherwise, must defer publication of the information until the conditions in subsection (1) cease to be met,

but this is subject to subsection (4).

(3) The FCA may make such arrangements as to the publication of information under subsection (2)(a) (including as to the timing of publication) as the FCA considers necessary to ensure effective protection of the personal data.

(4) The FCA must not publish the notice, or information about the matter to which the notice relates, if actions under subsection (2) are considered by the FCA to be insufficient to ensure—

(a) that the stability of the financial markets would not be put in jeopardy; or

(b) that, in cases involving sanctions or measures considered by the FCA to be of a minor nature, information is published only where it is proportionate to do so.

(5) In this section, "personal data", in relation to a person who is not an individual, means the person's identity.]

NOTES

Commencement: 21 July 2019.

Inserted by the Financial Services and Markets Act 2000 (Prospectus) Regulations 2019, SI 2019/1043, regs 3, 33(2), as from 21 July 2019.

Sub-s (1): words in square brackets substituted by the Prospectus (Amendment etc) (EU Exit) Regulations 2019, SI 2019/1234, regs 2, 9, as from IP completion day (as defined in the European Union (Withdrawal Agreement) Act 2020, s 39); for transitional provisions, see regs 74, 75 of the 2019 Regulations at **[12.165]** et seq.

Third party rights and access to evidence

[7.682]

392 Application of sections 393 and 394

Sections 393 and 394 apply to—

(a) a warning notice given in accordance with section [55Z(1)], 57(1), 63(3), [63B(1),] 67(1), 88(4)(b),[88B(1)], 92(1), 126(1), [131H(1),] [142T(1),] [143N(1), 143T(1), 143U(2), 143X(1),] [192L(1)][, 192R(8), 192Z(1)] 207(1), 255(1), [261V(1),] [271N(2), 271R(3),] 280(1), [282B(3),] [312G(1),] 331(1), [345B(1) (whether as a result of section 345(2), 345A(3)] or section 249(1) [or 261K(1)])[, 385(1) or 412B(4) or (8)] [or paragraph 38, 42 or 69 of Schedule 2A or paragraph 11, 16 or 20 of Schedule 2B] [or paragraph 5(6) of Schedule 6A];

(b) a decision notice given in accordance with section [55Z(2)], 57(3), 63(4), [63B(3),] 67(4), 88(6)(b), [88B(5)], 92(4), 127(1), [131H(4),] [142T(4),] [143N(2), 143T(3), 143U(2), 143X(5),] [192L(4),][, 192R(9), 192Z(4)] 208(1), 255(2), [261V(2),] [271N(3), 271R(4),] 280(2), [282B(4),] [312H(1),] 331(3), [345B(4) (whether as a result of section 345(2), 345A(3)] or section 249(1) [or 261K(1)])[, 386(1) or 412B(5) or (9)] [or paragraph 38, 42 or 69 of Schedule 2A or paragraph 11, 16 or 20 of Schedule 2B] [or paragraph 5(7) of Schedule 6A].

NOTES

Figures "55Z(1)", "55Z(2)", "192L(1)" and "192L(4)," in square brackets inserted by the Financial Services Act 2012, s 37(1), Sch 9, Pt 1, para 1, Pt 6, para 31, as from 1 April 2013.

Figures "63B(1),", "131H(1),", "63B(3),", and "131H(4)," in square brackets inserted by the Financial Services Act 2010, s 24(1), (2), Sch 2, Pt 1, paras 1, 29, as from 8 June 2010.

Figures "88B(1)" and "88B(5)" in square brackets substituted by the Financial Services Act 2012, s 18(1), (5), as from 1 April 2013.

Figures "142T(1)," and "142T(4)," in square brackets inserted by the Financial Services (Banking Reform) Act 2013, s 4(4), as from 1 January 2019.

Figures "143N(1), 143T(1), 143U(2), 143X(1)," and "143N(2), 143T(3), 143U(2), 143X(5)," in square brackets inserted by the Financial Services Act 2021, s 2, Sch 2, Pt 2, para 13, as from 1 July 2021; for transitional provisions, see Sch 2, Pt 3 to the 2021 Act.

Figures ", 192R(8), 192Z(1)" and ", 192R(9), 192Z(4)" in square brackets inserted by the Financial Holding Companies (Approval etc) and Capital Requirements (Capital Buffers and Macro-prudential Measures) (Amendment) (EU Exit) Regulations 2020, SI 2020/1406, reg 2(8), as from 29 December 2020.

Figures and words "261V(1),", "or 261K(1)", "261V(2)," and "or 261K(1)" in square brackets inserted by the Collective Investment in Transferable Securities (Contractual Scheme) Regulations 2013, SI 2013/1388, reg 3(1), (19), as from 6 June 2013.

Figures "271N(2), 271R(3)," and "271N(3), 271R(4)," in square brackets inserted by the Financial Services Act 2021, s 24, Sch 9, Pt 2, para 6, as from 23 February 2022.

Figures "282B(3)," and "282B(4)," in square brackets inserted by the Financial Services Act 2021, s 25(7), as from 23 February 2022.

Figures "312G(1)," and "312H(1)," in square brackets inserted by the Financial Services Act 2012, s 35, Sch 8, paras 1, 37, as from 1 April 2013.

Words "345B(1) (whether as a result of section 345(2), 345A(3)" and "345B(4) (whether as a result of section 345(2), 345A(3)" in square brackets substituted by the Financial Services Act 2012, s 42, Sch 13, para 8, as from 1 April 2013.

Words ", 385(1) or 412B(4) or (8)" and ", 386(1) or 412B(5) or (9)" in square brackets substituted by the Financial Services and Markets Act 2000 (Markets in Financial Instruments) Regulations 2007, SI 2007/126, reg 3(5), Sch 5, paras 1, 16, as from 1 April 2007 (certain purposes (see reg 1(2)), and as from 1 November 2007 (otherwise).

The penultimate words in square brackets in paras (a) and (b) are inserted by the Financial Services Act 2021, s 22, Sch 8, para 11, as from a day to be appointed.

The final words in square brackets in paras (a) and (b) were inserted by the Financial Services Act 2021, s 28, Sch 11, para 5, as from 1 July 2021.

[7.683]

393 Third party rights

(1) If any of the reasons contained in a warning notice to which this section applies relates to a matter which—

(a) identifies a person ("the third party") other than the person to whom the notice is given, and

(b) in the opinion of the [regulator giving the notice], is prejudicial to the third party,

a copy of the notice must be given to the third party.

(2) Subsection (1) does not require a copy to be given to the third party if the [regulator giving the notice]—

(a) has given him a separate warning notice in relation to the same matter; or

(b) gives him such a notice at the same time as it gives the warning notice which identifies him.

(3) The notice copied to a third party under subsection (1) must specify a reasonable period (which may not be less than [14 days]) within which he may make representations to [the regulator giving the notice].

(4) If any of the reasons contained in a decision notice to which this section applies relates to a matter which—

(a) identifies a person ("the third party") other than the person to whom the decision notice is given, and

(b) in the opinion of [the regulator giving the notice], is prejudicial to the third party,

a copy of the notice must be given to the third party.

(5) If the decision notice was preceded by a warning notice, a copy of the decision notice must (unless it has been given under subsection (4)) be given to each person to whom the warning notice was copied.

(6) Subsection (4) does not require a copy to be given to the third party if [the regulator giving the notice]—

(a) has given him a separate decision notice in relation to the same matter; or

(b) gives him such a notice at the same time as it gives the decision notice which identifies him.

(7) Neither subsection (1) nor subsection (4) requires a copy of a notice to be given to a third party if [the regulator giving the notice] considers it impracticable to do so.

(8) Subsections (9) to (11) apply if the person to whom a decision notice is given has a right to refer the matter to the Tribunal.

(9) A person to whom a copy of the notice is given under this section may refer to the Tribunal—

(a) the decision in question, so far as it is based on a reason of the kind mentioned in subsection (4); or

(b) any opinion expressed by [the regulator giving the notice] in relation to him.

(10) The copy must be accompanied by an indication of the third party's right to make a reference under subsection (9) and of the procedure on such a reference.

(11) A person who alleges that a copy of the notice should have been given to him, but was not, may refer to the Tribunal the alleged failure and—

(a) the decision in question, so far as it is based on a reason of the kind mentioned in subsection (4); or

(b) any opinion expressed by [the regulator giving the notice] in relation to him.

(12) Section 394 applies to a third party as it applies to the person to whom the notice to which this section applies was given, in so far as the material [to which access must be given] under that section relates to the matter which identifies the third party.

(13) A copy of a notice given to a third party under this section must be accompanied by a description of the effect of section 394 as it applies to him.

(14) Any person to whom a warning notice or decision notice was copied under this section must be given a copy of a notice of discontinuance applicable to the proceedings to which the warning notice or decision notice related.

NOTES

All words in square brackets in this section were substituted by the Financial Services Act 2012, s 37(1), Sch 9, Pt 1, para 1, Pt 6, para 32, as from 1 April 2013.

[7.684]

394 Access to [FCA or PRA] material

(1) If [a regulator] gives a person ("A") a notice to which this section applies, it must—

(a) allow him access to the material on which it relied in taking the decision which gave rise to the obligation to give the notice;

(b) allow him access to any secondary material which[, in the regulator's opinion,] might undermine that decision.

(2) But [the regulator giving the notice] does not have to allow A access to material under subsection (1) if the material is excluded material or it—

(a) relates to a case involving a person other than A; and

(b) was taken into account by [the regulator giving the notice] in A's case only for purposes of comparison with other cases.

(3) [The regulator giving the notice] may refuse A access to particular material which it would otherwise have to allow him access to if, in its opinion, allowing him access to the material—

(a) would not be in the public interest; or

(b) would not be fair, having regard to—

(i) the likely significance of the material to A in relation to the matter in respect of which he has been given a notice to which this section applies; and

(ii) the potential prejudice to the commercial interests of a person other than A which would be caused by the material's disclosure.

(4) If [the regulator giving the notice] does not allow A access to material because it is excluded material consisting of a protected item, it must give A written notice of—

(a) the existence of the protected item; and

(b) [the regulator's] decision not to allow him access to it.

(5) If [the regulator giving the notice] refuses under subsection (3) to allow A access to material, it must give him written notice of—

(a) the refusal; and

(b) the reasons for it.

(6) "Secondary material" means material, other than material falling within paragraph (a) of subsection (1) which—

(a) was considered by [the regulator giving the notice] in reaching the decision mentioned in that paragraph; or

(b) was obtained by [the regulator giving the notice in connection with the matter to which that notice] relates but which was not considered by it in reaching that decision.

(7) "Excluded material" means material which—

[(a) is material the disclosure of which for the purposes of or in connection with any legal proceedings is prohibited by [section 56 of the Investigatory Powers Act 2016]; or]

(c) is a protected item (as defined in section 413).

NOTES

Sub-s (7)(a) was substituted (for the original sub-s (7)(a), (b)) by the Regulation of Investigatory Powers Act 2000, s 82(1), Sch 4, para 11, as from 2 October 2000.

The words in square brackets in sub-s (7)(a) were substituted by the Investigatory Powers Act 2016, s 271(1), Sch 10, Pt 2, para 43, as from 27 June 2018.

All other words in square brackets in this section were substituted by the Financial Services Act 2012, s 37(1), Sch 9, Pt 1, para 1, Pt 6, para 33, as from 1 April 2013.

The [FCA's and PRA's] procedures

[7.685]

395 The [FCA's and PRA's] procedures

[(1) Each regulator must determine the procedure that it proposes to follow in relation to the following—

(a) a decision which gives rise to an obligation to give a supervisory notice,

(b) in the case of the FCA, a decision which—

(i) gives rise to an obligation for it to give a warning notice or decision notice, or

(ii) gives rise to an obligation for the PRA to include a statement under section 387(1A) in a warning notice or a statement under section 388(1A) in a decision notice,

(c) in the case of the PRA, a decision which gives rise to an obligation for it to give a warning notice or decision notice, other than a decision which depends entirely on a decision of the FCA of the kind mentioned in paragraph (b)(ii), and

(d) a decision under section 391(1)(c) to publish information about the matter to which a warning notice relates.]

(2) That procedure must be designed to secure, among other things [that—

(a) a decision falling within any of paragraphs (a) to (c) of subsection (1) is taken—

(i) by a person not directly involved in establishing the evidence on which the decision is based, or

(ii) by 2 or more persons who include a person not directly involved in establishing that evidence,

(b) a decision falling within paragraph (d) of subsection (1) is taken—

(i) by a person other than the person by whom the decision was first proposed, or

(ii) by 2 or more persons not including the person by whom the decision was first proposed, and

(c) a decision falling within paragraph (d) of subsection (1) is taken in accordance with a procedure which is, as far as possible, the same as that applicable to a decision which gives rise to an obligation to give a warning notice and which falls within paragraph (b) or (c) of subsection (1).]

(3) But the procedure may permit a decision which gives rise to an obligation to give a supervisory notice to be [taken otherwise than as mentioned in subsection (2) if the person taking the decision is of a level of seniority laid down by the procedure and—

(a) in the case of procedure proposed by the FCA, the FCA considers that, in the particular case, it is necessary in order to advance one or more of its operational objectives, or

(b) in the case of procedure proposed by the PRA, the PRA considers that, in the particular case, it is necessary in order to advance any of its objectives].

(4) A level of seniority laid down by the procedure for the purposes of subsection (3)(b) must be appropriate to the importance of the decision.

(5) [Each regulator] must issue a statement of [its procedure].

(6) The statement must be published in the way appearing to [the regulator issuing it] to be best calculated to bring [the statement] to the attention of the public.

(7) [The regulator issuing the statement] may charge a reasonable fee for providing a person with a copy of the statement.

(8) [The regulator issuing a statement under this section] must, without delay, give the Treasury a copy of [the statement].

(9) When [a regulator gives] a supervisory notice, or a warning notice or decision notice [other than a warning notice or decision notice relating to a decision of the PRA that is required by a decision of the FCA of the kind mentioned in subsection (1)(b)(ii)], [the regulator] must follow its stated procedure.

[(9A) When the FCA takes a decision falling within subsection (1)(b)(ii), it must follow its stated procedure.]

(10) If [a regulator] changes [its procedure] in a material way, it must publish a revised statement.

(11) [A regulator's] failure in a particular case to follow its procedure as set out in the latest published statement does not affect the validity of a notice given in that case.

(12) But subsection (11) does not prevent the Tribunal from taking into account any such failure in considering a matter referred to it.

(13) "Supervisory notice" means a notice [or notification] given in accordance with *section*—

[(za) [section] 55XA(1) or (5) (where subsection (6) applies);]

[(a) [section] 55Y(4), (7) or (8)(b);]

[(aa) [section] 63ZC(4), (8) or (9)(b);]

[(ab) [section] 71H(2), (3), (4), (9) or (11)(a);]

(b) [section] 78(2) or (5);
[(bza) [section] 78A(2) or (8)(b);]
[(bzb) section 88F(2), (5) or (6)(b);]
[(bzc) section 89V(2), (5) or (6)(b);]
[(ba) . . .]
[(bb) [section] 87O(2) or (5);]
[(bbza) [section] 122I;]
[(bbzb) section 122IA;]
[(bba) section 137S(5) or (8)(a);]
[(bbb) section 143O(3), (6) or (8)(b);]
[(bc) [section] 191B(1);]
[(bd) section 192U(1), (7) or (8);]
(c) [section] 197(3), (6) or (7)(b);
(d) [section] 259(3), (8) or (9)(b);
[(da) [section] 261Z1(3), (8) or (9)(b);]
(e) . . .
[(ea) section 271M(3), (6) or (7)(b);]
(f) [section] 282(3), (6) or (7)(b);
[(fa) [section] 301J(1);]
(g) [section] 321(2) or (5);
[(h) a provision of Schedule 2A listed in subsection (14);
(i) paragraph 18(3), (6) or (8)(b) of Schedule 2B].

[(14) The provisions of Schedule 2A mentioned in subsection (13)(h) are—
(a) paragraph 29(3), (6) or (8)(b);
(b) paragraph 50(3), (6) or (8)(b);
(c) paragraph 60(3) or (6).]

NOTES

Sub-s (9A) and the words in the second pair of square brackets in sub-s (9) were inserted, and all other words in square brackets in sub-ss (1)–(12) and in the section heading and in the heading preceding this section were substituted, by the Financial Services Act 2012, s 37(1), Sch 9, Pt 1, para 1, Pt 6, para 34(1)–(12), (14), (15), as from 24 January 2013 (in so far as relating to the determination of a procedure and the issue of a statement of the procedure), and as from 1 April 2013 (otherwise).

Sub-s (13) is amended as follows:

For the word "section" in italics there is substituted the words "any of the following", and the word "section" in square brackets (in each place that it occurs) is inserted, by the Financial Services Act 2021, s 22, Sch 8, para 12(2)(a), (b), as from a day to be appointed.

Words in first pair of square brackets inserted by the Financial Services Act 2012, s 17(1), (3), as from 1 April 2013.

Para (za) inserted by the Financial Services and Markets Act 2000 (Benchmarks) Regulations 2018, SI 2018/135, reg 47, as from 27 February 2018.

Para (a) substituted by the Financial Services Act 2012, s 37(1), Sch 9, Pt 1, para 1, Pt 6, para 34(1), (13), as from 1 April 2013.

Para (aa) inserted by the Financial Services (Banking Reform) Act 2013, s 35, Sch 3, para 14, as from 7 March 2016.

Para (ab) inserted by the Bank Recovery and Resolution Order 2016, SI 2016/1239, arts 30, 35, as from 16 December 2016.

Para (bza) inserted by the Regulatory Reform (Financial Services and Markets Act 2000) Order 2007, SI 2007/1973, arts 2, 8, as from 12 July 2007.

Paras (bzb), (bzc), (bba) inserted by the Financial Services Act 2012, ss 18(1), (6), 19(2), 24(3), as from 24 January 2013 (in so far as relating to para (bba)), and as from 1 April 2013 (otherwise).

Para (ba) originally inserted by the Financial Services and Markets Act 2000 (Market Abuse) Regulations 2005, SI 2005/381, reg 7, as from 1 July 2005. Subsequently repealed by the Financial Services and Markets Act 2000 (Market Abuse) Regulations 2016, SI 2016/680, reg 10(1), (18)(a), as from 3 July 2016.

Para (bb) inserted by the Prospectus Regulations 2005, SI 2005/1433, reg 2(1), Sch 1, para 14, as from 1 July 2005.

Para (bbza) inserted by SI 2016/680, reg 10(1), (18)(b), as from 3 July 2016.

Para (bbzb) inserted by the Financial Services and Markets Act 2000 (Markets in Financial Instruments) Regulations 2017, SI 2017/701, reg 50(1), Sch 2, paras 1, 47, as from 3 January 2018 (note that various provisions of the 2017 Regulations came into force on earlier dates for the purposes of making rules, giving notices and consent, etc (for details see reg 1 of the 2017 Regulations)).

Para (bbb) inserted by the Financial Services Act 2021, s 2, Sch 2, Pt 2, para 14, as from 1 July 2021; for transitional provisions, see Sch 2, Pt 3 to the 2021 Act.

Paras (bc), (fa) inserted by the Financial Services and Markets Act 2000 (Controllers) Regulations 2009, SI 2009/534, reg 6, as from 21 March 2009.

Para (bd) inserted by the Financial Holding Companies (Approval etc) and Capital Requirements (Capital Buffers and Macro-prudential Measures) (Amendment) (EU Exit) Regulations 2020, SI 2020/1406, reg 2(9), as from 29 December 2020.

Para (da) inserted by the Collective Investment in Transferable Securities (Contractual Scheme) Regulations 2013, SI 2013/1388, reg 3(1), (20), as from 6 June 2013.

Para (e) repealed by the Collective Investment Schemes (Amendment etc) (EU Exit) Regulations 2019, SI 2019/325, regs 3, 29, as from IP completion day (as defined in the European Union (Withdrawal Agreement) Act 2020, s 39).

Para (ea) inserted by the Financial Services Act 2021, s 24, Sch 9, Pt 2, para 7, as from 23 February 2022.

Paras (h) and (i) are inserted by the Financial Services Act 2021, s 22, Sch 8, para 12(2)(c), as from a day to be appointed.

Sub-s (14): added by the Financial Services Act 2021, s 22, Sch 8, para 12(3), as from a day to be appointed.

Note that the Financial Services Act 2012, s 37(2)(b) provides that if the Treasury consider that it is in the public interest to do so, it may by order amend this section by repealing sub-ss (1)(d), (2)(b), (c).

[7.686]

396 Statements under section 395: consultation

(1) Before issuing a statement of [its] procedure under section 395, [the regulator] must publish a draft of the proposed statement in the way appearing to [it] to be best calculated to bring [the draft] to the attention of the public.

(2) The draft must be accompanied by notice that representations about the proposal may be made to the [regulator publishing the draft] within a specified time.

(3) [Before a regulator issues the proposed statement of its procedure, it] must have regard to any representations made to it in accordance with subsection (2).

(4) If the [regulator issues the proposed statement of its procedure,] it must publish an account, in general terms, of—

(a) the representations made to it in accordance with subsection (2); and

(b) its response to them.

(5) If the [statement of the regulator's procedure differs from the draft published by it] under subsection (1) in a way which is[, in its opinion,] significant, [it must] (in addition to complying with subsection (4)) publish details of the difference.

(6) [The regulator publishing a draft under subsection (1)] may charge a reasonable fee for providing a person with a copy of [the draft].

(7) This section also applies to a proposal to revise a statement of policy.

NOTES

The word in the first pair of square brackets in sub-s (1) was inserted, and all other words in square brackets in this section were substituted, by the Financial Services Act 2012, s 37(1), Sch 9, Pt 1, para 1, Pt 6, para 35, as from 24 January 2013 (in so far as relating to the determination of a procedure and the issue of a statement of the procedure), and as from 1 April 2013 (otherwise).

PART XXVII OFFENCES

NOTES

Meaning of "offence" for the purposes of this Part : as from 1 April 2014, references in this Part to an offence include references to an offence under Part 11 of this Act as modified by the Financial Services and Markets Act 2000 (Regulated Activities) (Amendment) (No 2) Order 2013, SI 2013/1881; see art 50(3) of that Order.

Transitional provisions etc in connection with the commencement of the Financial Services Act 2012: see the Financial Services Act 2012 (Transitional Provisions) (Enforcement) Order 2013, SI 2013/441, art 34 which provides that where (a) an act or omission occurred before1 April 2013, (b) the FSA had not, before that date, instituted proceedings for an offence in relation to the act or omission, and the PRA would have been the appropriate regulator within the meaning of s 401(3A) in respect of proceedings for an offence in relation to the act or omission had the act or omission occurred on that date, then that section applies as if it defined both the FCA and the PRA as the appropriate regulator in respect of proceedings for the offence.

Transitional provisions etc in connection with the original commencement of this Act: ss 401 and 403 have effect as if offences committed before 1 December 2001 under certain provisions (the Insurance Companies Act 1982, the Financial Services Act 1986, the Banking Act 1987, and certain related provisions) were an offence under this Act; see the Financial Services and Markets Act 2000 (Transitional Provisions and Savings) (Civil Remedies, Discipline, Criminal Offences etc) (No 2) Order 2001, SI 2001/3083, art 13.

Miscellaneous offences

397 (*S 397 (Misleading statements and practices) was repealed by the Financial Services Act 2012, s 95, as from 1 April 2013 (see now Part 7 of the Financial Services Act 2012 at* **[7.750]** *et seq).*)

[7.687]

398 Misleading [FCA or PRA]: residual cases

(1) A person who, in purported compliance with any requirement [falling within subsection (1A)] knowingly or recklessly gives [a regulator] information which is false or misleading in a material particular is guilty of an offence.

[(1A) A requirement falls within this subsection if it is imposed by or under—

(a) this Act;

(b) the Alternative Investment Fund Managers Regulations 2013;

[(ba) the Financial Services and Markets Act 2000 (Markets in Financial Instruments) Regulations 2017 (SI 2017/701);]

(c) the short selling regulation;

(d) Regulation (EU) No 345/2013 of the European Parliament and the Council of 17 April 2013 on European venture capital funds; . . .

(e) Regulation (EU) No 346/2013 of the European Parliament and the Council of 17 April 2013 on European social entrepreneurship funds[; . . .]

[(ea) any EU regulation, originally made under the markets in financial instruments directive, which is retained direct EU legislation;

(eb) any of the following—

(i) the markets in financial instruments regulation,

(ii) any EU regulation, originally made under the markets in financial instruments regulation, which is retained direct EU legislation, and

(iii) any subordinate legislation (within the meaning of the Interpretation Act 1978) made under the markets in financial instruments regulation on or after IP completion day;]

[(f) Regulation (EU) No 2015/760 of the European Parliament and of the Council of 29th April 2015 on European Long-term Investment Funds[; . . .]

[(g) the market abuse regulation;] [. . .]

[(h) the EU Benchmarks Regulation 2016][; . . .]

[(i) the MMF Regulation][; or]

[(j) the prospectus regulation (as defined by section 103)].]

(2) Subsection (1) applies only to a requirement in relation to which no other provision of this Act creates an offence in connection with the giving of information.

(3) A person guilty of an offence under this section is liable—

(a) on summary conviction, to a fine not exceeding the statutory maximum;

(b) on conviction on indictment, to a fine.

NOTES

Section heading: words in square brackets substituted by the Financial Services Act 2012, s 37(1), Sch 9, Pt 1, para 1, Pt 7, para 36(1), (3), as from 1 April 2013.

Sub-s (1): words in first pair of square brackets substituted by the Alternative Investment Fund Managers Regulations 2013, SI 2013/1773, reg 80, Sch 1, Part 1, paras 1, 30(a), as from 22 July 2013. Words in second pair of square brackets substituted by the Financial Services Act 2012, s 37(1), Sch 9, Pt 1, para 1, Pt 7, para 36(1), (2), as from 1 April 2013.

Sub-s (1A): inserted by SI 2013/1773, reg 80, Sch 1, Part 1, paras 1, 30(b), as from 22 July 2013; and subsequently amended as follows—

Para (ba) inserted by the Financial Services and Markets Act 2000 (Markets in Financial Instruments) Regulations 2017, SI 2017/701, reg 50(1), Sch 2, paras 1, 48, as from 3 January 2018 (note that various provisions of the 2017 Regulations came into force on earlier dates for the purposes of making rules, giving notices and consent, etc (for details see reg 1 of the 2017 Regulations)). Note also that the inserted paragraph was amended by the Financial Services and Markets Act 2000 (Markets in Financial Instruments) (No 2) Regulations 2017, SI 2017/1255, regs 11, 36, as from 2 January 2018 (and the effect of the amendment has been incorporated in the text set out above).

The word omitted from para (d) was repealed, the word omitted from para (e) was originally inserted, and para (f) was added, by the European Long-term Investment Funds Regulations 2015, SI 2015/1882, reg 3(1), (4), as from 3 December 2015.

The word omitted from para (e) was repealed, and para (g) and the preceding word were inserted, by the Financial Services and Markets Act 2000 (Market Abuse) Regulations 2016, SI 2016/680, reg 10(1), (19), as from 3 July 2016.

Para (ea), (eb) originally inserted by SI 2017/701, reg 50(1), Sch 2, paras 1, 48, as from 3 January 2018. Subsequently substituted by the Financial Services and Markets Act 2000 (Amendment) (EU Exit) Regulations 2019, SI 2019/632, reg 80, as from IP completion day (as defined in the European Union (Withdrawal Agreement) Act 2020, s 39). Note that reg 80 of the 2019 Regulations was amended by the Financial Services and Economic and Monetary Policy (Consequential Amendments) (EU Exit) Regulations 2020, SI 2020/1301, reg 3, Schedule, para 33(h), as from 30 December 2020 (and the effect of the amendment has been incorporated in the text set out above).

The word omitted from para (f) was repealed, and para (h) and the preceding word were inserted, by the Financial Services and Markets Act 2000 (Benchmarks) Regulations 2018, SI 2018/135, reg 48, as from 27 February 2018.

The word omitted from para (g) was repealed, and para (i) and the preceding word were inserted, by the Money Market Funds Regulations 2018, SI 2018/698, reg 2(1), (16), as from 21 July 2018.

The word omitted from para (h) was repealed, and para (j) and the preceding word were inserted, by the Financial Services and Markets Act 2000 (Prospectus) Regulations 2019, SI 2019/1043, regs 3, 34, as from 21 July 2019.

Deferred Prosecution Agreements: see the note to s 23 at **[7.63]**.

[7.688]

399 Misleading [the CMA]

Section 44 of the Competition Act 1998 (offences connected with the provision of false or misleading information) applies in relation to any function of [the Competition and Markets Authority] under this Act as if it were a function under Part I of that Act.

NOTES

Words in square brackets substituted by the Enterprise and Regulatory Reform Act 2013 (Competition) (Consequential, Transitional and Saving Provisions) Order 2014, SI 2014/892, art 2, Sch 1, Pt 2, paras 120, 130, as from 1 April 2014.

Bodies corporate and partnerships

[7.689]

400 Offences by bodies corporate etc

(1) If an offence under this Act committed by a body corporate is shown—

(a) to have been committed with the consent or connivance of an officer, or

(b) to be attributable to any neglect on his part,

the officer as well as the body corporate is guilty of the offence and liable to be proceeded against and punished accordingly.

(2) If the affairs of a body corporate are managed by its members, subsection (1) applies in relation to the acts and defaults of a member in connection with his functions of management as if he were a director of the body.

(3) If an offence under this Act committed by a partnership is shown—

(a) to have been committed with the consent or connivance of a partner, or

(b) to be attributable to any neglect on his part,

the partner as well as the partnership is guilty of the offence and liable to be proceeded against and punished accordingly.

(4) In subsection (3) "partner" includes a person purporting to act as a partner.

(5) "Officer", in relation to a body corporate, means—

(a) a director, member of the committee of management, chief executive, manager, secretary or other similar officer of the body, or a person purporting to act in any such capacity; and

(b) an individual who is a controller of the body.

(6) If an offence under this Act committed by an unincorporated association (other than a partnership) is shown—

(a) to have been committed with the consent or connivance of an officer of the association or a member of its governing body, or

(b) to be attributable to any neglect on the part of such an officer or member,

that officer or member as well as the association is guilty of the offence and liable to be proceeded against and punished accordingly.

[(6A) References in this section to an offence under this Act include a reference to an offence under Part 7 of the Financial Services Act 2012 (offences relating to financial services).]

(7) Regulations may provide for the application of any provision of this section, with such modifications as the Treasury consider appropriate, to a body corporate or unincorporated association formed or recognised under the law of a territory outside the United Kingdom.

NOTES

Sub-s (6A): inserted by the Financial Services Act 2012, s 37(1), Sch 9, Pt 1, para 1, Pt 7, para 37, as from 1 April 2013.

Institution of proceedings

[7.690]

401 Proceedings for offences

[(1) In this section "offence" means—

(a) an offence under this Act,

(b) an offence under subordinate legislation made under this Act, or

(c) an offence under Part 7 of the Financial Services Act 2012 (offences relating to financial services).]

(2) Proceedings for an offence may be instituted in England and Wales only—

(a) by the [appropriate regulator] or the Secretary of State; or

(b) by or with the consent of the Director of Public Prosecutions.

(3) Proceedings for an offence may be instituted in Northern Ireland only—

(a) by the [appropriate regulator] or the Secretary of State; or

(b) by or with the consent of the Director of Public Prosecutions for Northern Ireland.

[(3A) For the purposes of subsections (2)(a) and (3)(a), the PRA is the "appropriate regulator" in respect of each of the following offences—

(a) an offence under section 55P(10) where the contravention is of a requirement imposed by the PRA;

(b) an offence under section 56(4) where the prohibition order is made by the PRA;

(c) an offence under section 177(3) where the investigation is being, or is likely to be, conducted on behalf of the PRA;

(d) an offence under section 177(4) where the requirement is imposed by the PRA;

(e) an offence under section 177(6) where the warrant is issued as a result of information on oath given by the PRA or a person appointed by the PRA to conduct an investigation on its behalf;

(f) an offence under section 191F(1) where the notice should have been given to the PRA;

(g) an offence under any of section 191F(2) to [(4) and (5) to] (7) where the notice, approval or information was given to or by the PRA;

(h) an offence under section 366(3), unless the activity of effecting or carrying out long-term contracts of insurance is not to any extent a PRA-regulated activity;

(i) an offence under section 398(1) where the information was given to the PRA.

[(3AB) For the purposes of subsections (2)(a) and (3)(a), the Bank of England is the "appropriate regulator" in respect of an offence under section 191F(4A).]

(3B) For the purposes of subsections (2)(a) and (3)(a), the FCA is the "appropriate regulator" in respect of any other offence.]

(4) . . .

(5) In exercising its power to institute proceedings for an offence, the [appropriate regulator] must comply with any conditions or restrictions imposed in writing by the Treasury.

(6) Conditions or restrictions may be imposed under subsection (5) in relation to—

(a) proceedings generally; or

(b) such proceedings, or categories of proceedings, as the Treasury may direct.

NOTES

Sub-s (1) was substituted, the words in square brackets in sub-ss (2), (3), (5) were substituted, and sub-ss (3A), (3B) were inserted, by the Financial Services Act 2012, s 37(1), Sch 9, Pt 1, para 1, Pt 7, para 38, as from 1 April 2013.

The words in square brackets in sub-s (3A)(g) were inserted, and sub-s (3AB) was inserted, by the Bank Recovery and Resolution Order 2016, SI 2016/1239, arts 30, 33(6), as from 16 December 2016.

Sub-s (4) was repealed by the Financial Services and Markets Act 2000 (Regulated Activities) (Amendment) (No 2) Order 2013, SI 2013/1881, art 10(1), (14), as from 1 April 2014.

[7.691]

402 Power of [FCA] to institute proceedings for certain other offences

(1) Except in Scotland, the [FCA] may institute proceedings for an offence under—

(a) Part V of the Criminal Justice Act 1993 (insider dealing); . . .

(b) prescribed regulations relating to money laundering; [or

(c) Schedule 7 to the Counter-Terrorism Act 2008 (terrorist financing or money laundering)].

(2) In exercising its power to institute proceedings for any such offence, the [FCA] must comply with any conditions or restrictions imposed in writing by the Treasury.

(3) Conditions or restrictions may be imposed under subsection (2) in relation to—

(a) proceedings generally; or

(b) such proceedings, or categories of proceedings, as the Treasury may direct.

NOTES

Word "FCA" in square brackets (in each place that it occurs) substituted by the Financial Services Act 2012, s 37(1), Sch 9, Pt 1, para 1, Pt 7, para 39, as from 1 April 2013.

Word omitted from sub-s (1)(b) repealed, and sub-s (1)(c) (and the word immediately preceding it) inserted, by the Counter-Terrorism Act 2008, s 62, Sch 7, Pt 7, para 33(4), as from 27 November 2008.

Note that sub-s (1) applies as if it included a reference to offences committed under the Consumer Credit Act 1974 Act before 1 April 2014; see the Financial Services and Markets Act 2000 (Regulated Activities) (Amendment) (No 2) Order 2013, SI 2013/1881, art 49.

Note: the Money Laundering, Terrorist Financing and Transfer of Funds (Information on the Payer) Regulations 2017, SI 2017/692 are prescribed for the purposes of sub-s (1)(b) above by reg 2 of those Regulations. The 2017 Regulations revoke the Money Laundering Regulations 2007, SI 2007/2157 and the Transfer of Funds (Information on the Payer) Regulations 2007, SI 2007/3298.

Regulations: the Money Laundering, Terrorist Financing and Transfer of Funds (Information on the Payer) Regulations 2017, SI 2017/692; the Oversight of Professional Body Anti-Money Laundering and Counter Terrorist Financing Supervision Regulations 2017, SI 2017/1301.

[7.692]
403 Jurisdiction and procedure in respect of offences

(1) A fine imposed on an unincorporated association on its conviction of an offence is to be paid out of the funds of the association.

(2) Proceedings for an offence alleged to have been committed by an unincorporated association must be brought in the name of the association (and not in that of any of its members).

(3) Rules of court relating to the service of documents are to have effect as if the association were a body corporate.

(4) In proceedings for an offence brought against an unincorporated association—

(a) section 33 of the Criminal Justice Act 1925 and Schedule 3 to the Magistrates' Courts Act 1980 (procedure) apply as they do in relation to a body corporate;

(b) section 70 of the Criminal Procedure (Scotland) Act 1995 (procedure) applies as if the association were a body corporate;

(c) section 18 of the Criminal Justice (Northern Ireland) Act 1945 and Schedule 4 to the Magistrates' Courts (Northern Ireland) Order 1981 (procedure) apply as they do in relation to a body corporate.

(5) Summary proceedings for an offence may be taken—

(a) against a body corporate or unincorporated association at any place at which it has a place of business;

(b) against an individual at any place where he is for the time being.

(6) Subsection (5) does not affect any jurisdiction exercisable apart from this section.

(7) "Offence" means an offence under this Act [or an offence under Part 7 of the Financial Services Act 2012 (offences relating to financial services)].

NOTES

Sub-s (7): words in square brackets inserted by the Financial Services Act 2012, s 37(1), Sch 9, Pt 1, para 1, Pt 7, para 40, as from 1 April 2013.

PART XXVIII MISCELLANEOUS

404–411 *(Ss 404–404G (Consumer redress schemes), ss 405–409 (Third countries), s 410 (International obligations), and ss 410A, 410B (Fees to meet Treasury expenses) are omitted due to space considerations (see further, the introductory notes to this Act); s 411 has been repealed. Note also that ss 405–408 were repealed by the Financial Services and Markets Act 2000 (Markets in Financial Instruments) Regulations 2017, SI 2017/701, reg 50(1), Sch 2, paras 1, 49, as from 3 January 2018. Note also that s 409 (Gibraltar) is repealed the Financial Services Act 2021, s 22, Sch 8, para 13, as from a day to be appointed.)*

Gaming contracts

[7.693]
412 Gaming contracts

(1) No contract to which this section applies is void or unenforceable because of—

(a) . . . Article 170 of the Betting, Gaming, Lotteries and Amusements (Northern Ireland) Order 1985; or

(b) . . .

(2) This section applies to a contract if—

(a) it is entered into by either or each party by way of business;

(b) the entering into or performance of it by either party constitutes an activity of a specified kind or one which falls within a specified class of activity; and

(c) it relates to an investment of a specified kind or one which falls within a specified class of investment.

(3) Part II of Schedule 2 applies for the purposes of subsection (2)(c), with the references to section 22 being read as references to that subsection.

(4) Nothing in Part II of Schedule 2, as applied by subsection (3), limits the power conferred by subsection (2)(c).

(5) "Investment" includes any asset, right or interest.

(6) "Specified" means specified in an order made by the Treasury.

NOTES

Sub-s (1): words omitted from para (a) repealed, and para (b) repealed, by the Gambling Act 2005, ss 334(1)(e), 356, (2), Sch 17, as from 1 September 2007.

Orders: the Financial Services and Markets Act 2000 (Gaming Contracts) Order 2001, SI 2001/2510.

412A, 412B (*Inserted by the Financial Services and Markets Act 2000 (Markets in Financial Instruments) Regulations 2007, SI 2007/126, reg 3(5), Sch 5, paras 1, 18, as from 1 April 2007 (certain purposes), and as from 1 November 2007 (otherwise). Repealed by the Financial Services and Markets Act 2000 (Markets in Financial Instruments) Regulations 2017, SI 2017/701, reg 50(1), Sch 2, paras 1, 50, as from 3 January 2018.*)

Limitation on powers to require documents

[7.694]
413 Protected items

(1) A person may not be required under this Act to produce, disclose or permit the inspection of protected items.

(2) "Protected items" means—

(a) communications between a professional legal adviser and his client or any person representing his client which fall within subsection (3);

(b) communications between a professional legal adviser, his client or any person representing his client and any other person which fall within subsection (3) (as a result of paragraph (b) of that subsection);
(c) items which—
(i) are enclosed with, or referred to in, such communications;
(ii) fall within subsection (3); and
(iii) are in the possession of a person entitled to possession of them.

(3) A communication or item falls within this subsection if it is made—
(a) in connection with the giving of legal advice to the client; or
(b) in connection with, or in contemplation of, legal proceedings and for the purposes of those proceedings.

(4) A communication or item is not a protected item if it is held with the intention of furthering a criminal purpose.

Service of notices

[7.695]

414 Service of notices

(1) The Treasury may by regulations make provision with respect to the procedure to be followed, or rules to be applied, when a provision of or made under this Act requires a notice, direction or document of any kind to be given or authorises the imposition of a requirement.

(2) The regulations may, in particular, make provision—
(a) as to the manner in which a document must be given;
(b) as to the address to which a document must be sent;
(c) requiring, or allowing, a document to be sent electronically;
(d) for treating a document as having been given, or as having been received, on a date or at a time determined in accordance with the regulations;
(e) as to what must, or may, be done if the person to whom a document is required to be given is not an individual;
(f) as to what must, or may, be done if the intended recipient of a document is outside the United Kingdom.

(3) Subsection (1) applies however the obligation to give a document is expressed (and so, in particular, includes a provision which requires a document to be served or sent).

(4) Section 7 of the Interpretation Act 1978 (service of notice by post) has effect in relation to provisions made by or under this Act subject to any provision made by regulations under this section.

NOTES

Regulations: the Financial Services and Markets Act 2000 (Service of Notices) Regulations 2001, SI 2001/1420; the Electronic Commerce Directive (Financial Services and Markets) Regulations 2002, SI 2002/1775; the Financial Services and Markets Act 2000 (Service of Notices) (Amendment) Regulations 2005, SI 2005/274.

Jurisdiction

[7.696]

415 Jurisdiction in civil proceedings

(1) Proceedings arising out of any act or omission (or proposed act or omission) of—
[(a) the FCA,
(aa) the PRA,
(ab) the Bank of England,]
(b) . . .
(c) the scheme manager, or
(d) the scheme operator,

in the discharge or purported discharge of any of its functions under this Act may be brought before the High Court or the Court of Session.

(2) The jurisdiction conferred by subsection (1) is in addition to any other jurisdiction exercisable by those courts.

NOTES

Sub-s (1): paras (a)–(ab) substituted (for the original para (a)), and para (b) repealed, by the Financial Services Act 2012, ss 16(1), (14)(j), 114(1), Sch 18, Pt 1, paras 1, 24, as from 1 April 2013.

[Powers [under the Act]

[7.697]

415A Powers [under the Act]

Any power which the [FCA, the PRA or the Bank of England] has under any provision of this Act is not limited in any way by any other power which it has under any other provision of this Act.]

NOTES

Inserted, together with the preceding heading, by the Financial Services Act 2010, s 24(1), (2), Sch 2, Pt 1, paras 1, 30, as from 8 April 2010.

The words in square brackets in this section and in the heading preceding it were substituted by the Financial Services Act 2012, s 114(1), Sch 18, Pt 1, paras 1, 25(1), (2), as from 1 April 2013.

[Consultation

[7.698]

415B Consultation in relation to taking certain enforcement action

(1) The FCA must consult the PRA before taking a qualifying step in relation to a person who—
(a) is a PRA-authorised person, or
(b) has a qualifying relationship with a PRA-authorised person.

(2) The PRA must consult the FCA before taking a qualifying step.

(3) In this section any reference to the taking of a qualifying step is a reference to—
(a) the giving of a warning notice or decision notice under section 63B (performance of controlled functions without approval),

(b) the giving of a warning notice or decision notice under section 67 (disciplinary powers in relation to approved person),
(c) . . .
(d) the giving of a warning notice or decision notice under section 131H (short selling),
(e) the giving of a warning notice under section 207 or a decision notice under section 208 (breaches of requirements imposed by or under Act etc),
(f) the giving of a warning notice under section 312G or a decision notice under section 312H (recognised bodies),
(g) the making of an application to the court under section 380, 381, 382 or 383 (injunctions or restitution), or
(h) the giving of a warning notice under section 385 or a decision notice under section 386 (power of FCA or PRA to require restitution).

(4) A person has a qualifying relationship with a PRA-authorised person ("A") for the purposes of this section if—
(a) the person is a member of A's immediate group, or
(b) in the case of a qualifying step within subsection (3)(a) or (b), the person performs a [relevant senior management] function under an arrangement entered into by A, or by a contractor of A, in relation to the carrying on by A of a regulated activity.

. . .

[(5) In subsection (4)—
"arrangement" has the same meaning as in section 59;
"relevant senior management function" means a function which the FCA is satisfied is a senior management function as defined in section 59ZA (whether or not it [is a designated senior management function as defined by section 59ZB)].]]

NOTES

Inserted, together with the preceding heading, by the Financial Services Act 2012, s 37(1), Sch 9, Pt 1, para 1, Pt 8, para 41, as from 1 April 2013.

Sub-s (3)(c) repealed by the Financial Services and Markets Act 2000 (Market Abuse) Regulations 2016, SI 2016/680, reg 10(1), (20), as from 3 July 2016.

Words in square brackets in sub-s (4) substituted, words omitted from that subsection repealed, and sub-s (5) added, by the Financial Services (Banking Reform) Act 2013, s 35, Sch 3, para 15, as from 7 March 2016.

Words in square brackets in the definition "relevant senior management function" in sub-s (5) substituted by the Bank of England and Financial Services Act 2016, s 21, Sch 4, paras 1, 20. Note that s 21 and Sch 4 come into force as follows: (i) 13 September 2018 (for the purpose of making rules, giving directions, imposing requirements and making statements of policy by the appropriate regulator for insurers); (ii) 10 December 2018 (for all other purposes for insurers (except in relation to Sch 4, para 11)), and 10 December 2019 (Sch 4, para 11 for insurers); (iii) 18 July 2019 (for the purpose of the making of rules, the giving of directions, the imposition of requirements and the issuing of statements of policy by the FCA for remaining purposes); (iv) 9 August 2019 (for remaining purposes in relation to authorised persons who are not solo-regulated firms); (v) 9 December 2019 (for remaining purposes in relation to solo-regulated firms other than benchmark firms (except as provided for by (vii) below)); (vi) 7 December 2020 (for remaining purposes in relation to benchmark firms (except as provided for by (viii) below)); (vii) 31 March 2021 (in relation to the employee certification provisions for remaining purposes in relation to solo-regulated firms other than benchmark firms); (viii) 7 December 2021 (in relation to the employee certification provisions for remaining purposes in relation to benchmark firms). For transitional provisions in connection with (i)–(iii) above, see the Bank of England and Financial Services Act 2016 (Commencement No 5 and Transitional Provisions) Regulations 2018, SI 2018/990; and for transitional provisions in connection with the other commencement dates, see the Bank of England and Financial Services Act 2016 (Commencement No 6 and Transitional Provisions) Regulations 2019, SI 2019/1136.

416 *(S 416 (Provisions relating to industrial assurance and certain other enactments) omitted due to space considerations (see further, the introductory notes to this Act).)*

PART XXIX INTERPRETATION

[7.699]

417 Definitions

(1) In this Act [and in any order or regulations made under this Act]—
["AIF" has the meaning given in regulation 3 of the Alternative Investment Fund Managers Regulations 2013;]
"appointed representative" has the meaning given in section 39(2);
"auditors and actuaries rules" means rules made under section 340;
"authorisation offence" has the meaning given in section 23(2);
"authorised open-ended investment company" has the meaning given in section 237(3);
"authorised person" has the meaning given in section 31(2);
. . .
["Bank of England" is to be read in accordance with section 2A(4) to (6);]
"body corporate" includes a body corporate constituted under the law of a country or territory outside the United Kingdom;
["capital requirements directive" means Directive 2013/36/EU of the European Parliament and of the Council of 26 June 2013 on access to the activity of credit institutions and the prudential supervision of credit institutions and investment firms, amending Directive 2002/87/EC and repealing Directives 2006/48/EC and 2006/49/EC[, as it had effect immediately before IP completion day];]
["capital requirements regulation" means Regulation (EU) No 575/2013 of the European Parliament and of the Council of 26 June 2013 on prudential requirements for credit institutions and investment firms and amending Regulation (EU) No 648/2012[, as it [forms part of retained EU law];]
["central securities depository" [means a CSD or third-country CSD as defined in] Article 2(1) of the CSD regulation;]
"chief executive"—

(a) in relation to a body corporate whose principal place of business is within the United Kingdom, means an employee of that body who, alone or jointly with one or more others, is responsible under the immediate authority of the directors, for the conduct of the whole of the business of that body; and

(b) in relation to a body corporate whose principal place of business is outside the United Kingdom, means the person who, alone or jointly with one or more others, is responsible for the conduct of its business within the United Kingdom;

["claim", in relation to the Financial Services Compensation Scheme under Part XV, is to be construed in accordance with section 214(1B);]

"collective investment scheme" has the meaning given in section 235;

"the Commission" means the European Commission . . . ;

"the compensation scheme" has the meaning given in section 213(2);

"control of information rules" has the meaning given in [section 137P];

["core activities" has the meaning given in section 142B;

"core services" has the meaning given in section 142C;]

["credit institution" means an undertaking the business of which is to take deposits or other repayable funds from the public and to grant credits for its own account;]

["credit-related regulated activity" has the meaning given in section 23(1B);]

["CRR rules" has the meaning given in section 144A;]

["the CSD regulation" means Regulation (EU) No 909/2014 of the European Parliament and of the Council of 23 July 2014 on improving securities settlement in the European Union and on central securities depositories[, as it [forms part of retained EU law]];]

["the data protection legislation" has the same meaning as in the Data Protection Act 2018 (see section 3 of that Act);]

"director", in relation to a body corporate, includes—

(a) a person occupying in relation to it the position of a director (by whatever name called); and

(b) a person in accordance with whose directions or instructions (not being advice given in a professional capacity) the directors of that body are accustomed to act;

"documents" includes information recorded in any form and, in relation to information recorded otherwise than in legible form, references to its production include references to producing a copy of the information in legible form[, or in a form from which it can readily be produced in visible and legible form];

[. . .]

[. . .]

[. . .]

["ESMA" means the European Securities and Markets Authority established by Regulation (EU) No 1095/2010 of the European Parliament and of the Council of 24 November 2010 establishing a European Supervisory Authority (European Securities and Markets Authority);]

["the EU Benchmarks Regulation 2016" means Regulation EU 2016/1011 of the European Parliament and of the Council of 8 June 2016 on indices used as benchmarks in financial instruments and financial contracts or to measure the performance of investment funds and amending Directives 2008/48/EC and 2014/17/EU and Regulation (EU) No 596/2014[, as it forms part of retained EU law];]

["excluded activities" has the meaning given in section 142D;]

"exempt person", in relation to a regulated activity, means a person who is exempt from the general prohibition in relation to that activity as a result of an exemption order made under section 38(1) or as a result of section 39(1) or [. . . 285];

["the FCA" means the Financial Conduct Authority;]

"financial promotion rules" means rules made under [section 137R];

"friendly society" means an incorporated or registered friendly society;

["full-scope UK AIFM" has the meaning given in regulation 2(1) of the Alternative Investment Fund Managers Regulations 2013;]

"general prohibition" has the meaning given in section 19(2);

["general rules"—

(a) in relation to the FCA, has the meaning given in section 137A(2), and

(b) in relation to the PRA, has the meaning given in section 137G(2);]

["Gibraltar-based person" has the meaning given in paragraph 1 of Schedule 2A (read with Part 14 of that Schedule);]

"incorporated friendly society" means a society incorporated under the Friendly Societies Act 1992;

. . .

[. . .]

["insurance undertaking" means an undertaking which—

(a) has its head office in the United Kingdom,

(b) has a Part 4A permission to carry on one or more regulated activities, and

(c) would require authorisation in accordance with Article 14 of the Solvency 2 Directive if the United Kingdom were a member State;]

["investment services and activities" means any of the services and activities listed in Part 3 of Schedule 2 to the Financial Services and Markets Act 2000 (Regulated Activities) Order 2001 (SI 2001/544), relating to any of the instruments listed in Part 1 of that Schedule;]

. . .

["market abuse regulation" means Regulation (EU) No 596/2014 of the European Parliament and of the Council of 16 April 2014 on market abuse (market abuse regulation) and repealing Directive 2003/6/EC of the European Parliament and of the Council and Commission Directives 2003/124/EC, 2003/125/EC and 2004/72/EC[, as it [forms part of retained EU law]];]

["markets in financial instruments regulation" means Regulation (EU) No 600/2014 of the European Parliament and of the Council of 15 May 2004 on markets in financial [instruments, as it forms part of retained EU law];]

["minimum capital requirement" means—

(a) in relation to an insurance undertaking or reinsurance undertaking, requirements imposed by or under this Act in pursuance of Section 5 of Chapter 6 of Title 1 of the Solvency 2 Directive;

(b) in relation to a third-country insurance undertaking, requirements imposed by or under this Act in pursuance of those provisions and Article 166 of the Solvency 2 Directive;]

"Minister of the Crown" has the same meaning as in the Ministers of the Crown Act 1975;

["MMF Regulation" means Regulation (EU) 2017/1131 of the European Parliament and of the Council of 14 June 2017 on money market funds[, as it forms part of retained EU law];]

. . .

[. . .]

[. . .]

. . .

"the ombudsman scheme" has the meaning given in section 225(3);

"open-ended investment company" has the meaning given in section 236;

["Part 4A permission" has the meaning given in section 55A(5);]

["Part 9C prohibition order" has the meaning given in section 143S;

"Part 9C rules" has the meaning given in section 143F;]

"partnership" includes a partnership constituted under the law of a country or territory outside the United Kingdom;

["the PRA" means the Prudential Regulation Authority;]

["PRA-authorised person" has the meaning given in section 2B(5);]

["PRA-regulated activity" has the meaning given in section 22A;]

"prescribed" (where not otherwise defined) means prescribed in regulations made by the Treasury;

"price stabilising rules" means rules made under [section 137Q];

["principal" in relation to an appointed representative, is to be read in accordance with section 39;]

"private company" has [the same meaning as in the Companies Acts (see section 4 of the Companies Act 2006)];

"prohibition order" [(except in the expression "Part 9C prohibition order")] has the meaning given in section 56(2);

["qualifying credit institution" means a credit institution which—

(a) is a person who—

(i) has Part 4A permission to carry on the regulated activity of accepting deposits, or

(ii) satisfies the conditions for being given permission under Part 4A to carry on that activity, or

(iii) is a body corporate incorporated in the United Kingdom and would satisfy those conditions—

(aa) were its head office in the United Kingdom, or

(bb) if it has a registered office, were its registered office, or its registered office and its head office, in the United Kingdom,

(b) is not a friendly society, and

(c) is not a society registered as a credit union under—

(i) the Co-operative and Community Benefit Societies Act 2014,

(ii) the Credit Unions (Northern Ireland) Order 1985 (SI 1985/1205 (NI 12)), or

(iii) the Co-operative and Community Benefit Societies Act (Northern Ireland) 1969 (c 24 (NI));]

["recognised CSD",] "recognised clearing house" and "recognised investment exchange" have the meaning given in section 285;

"registered friendly society" means a society which is—

(a) a friendly society within the meaning of section 7(1)(a) of the Friendly Societies Act 1974; and

(b) registered within the meaning of that Act;

["registered society" (except where otherwise indicated) means—

(a) a registered society within the meaning of the Co-operative and Community Benefit Societies Act 2014, or

(b) a society registered or deemed to be registered under the Industrial and Provident Societies Act (Northern Ireland) 1969;]

"regulated activity" has the meaning given in section 22;

["regulated claims management activity" means activity of a kind specified in an order under section 22(1B) (regulated activities: claims management services);]

"regulating provisions" has the meaning given in [section 140A];

["regulator" has the meaning given in section 3A(2);]

. . .

. . .

["reinsurance undertaking" means an undertaking which—

(a) has its head office in the United Kingdom,

(b) has a Part 4A permission to carry on one or more regulated activities,

(c) effects or carries out contracts of insurance that are limited to reinsurance contracts, and

(d) would require authorisation in accordance with Article 14 of the Solvency 2 Directive if the United Kingdom were a member State;]

["ring-fenced body" has the meaning given in section 142A;

"ring-fencing rules" has the meaning given in section 142H;]

["rule" means a rule made by the FCA or the PRA under this Act;]

"rule-making instrument" has the meaning given in [section 138G];

["Schedule 2A permission" has the meaning given in paragraph 12(4) of Schedule 2A;

"Schedule 2B permission" has the meaning given in paragraph 7(6) of Schedule 2B;]

"the scheme manager" has the meaning given in section 212(1);

"the scheme operator" has the meaning given in section 225(2);

"scheme particulars rules" has the meaning given in section 248(1);

"Seventh Company Law Directive" means the European Council Seventh Company Law Directive of 13 June 1983 on consolidated accounts (No 83/349/EEC);

["SFT regulation" means Regulation (EU) 2015/2365 of the European Parliament and of the Council of 25 November 2015 on transparency of securities financing transactions and of reuse and amending Regulation (EU) No 648/2012;]

["short selling regulation" means Regulation (EU) No 236/2012 of the European Parliament and of the Council of 14 March 2012 on short selling and certain aspects of credit default swaps[, as it [forms part of retained EU law]];]

["solvency capital requirement" means—

(a) in relation to an insurance undertaking or reinsurance undertaking, requirements imposed by or under this Act in pursuance of Section 4 of Chapter 6 of Title 1 of the Solvency 2 Directive;

(b) in relation to a third-country insurance undertaking, requirements imposed by or under this Act in pursuance of those provisions and Article 166 of the Solvency 2 Directive;]

["Takeovers Directive" means Directive 2004/25/EC of the European Parliament and of the Council;]

[. . .]

["third-country insurance undertaking" means an undertaking that has received [from the PRA or the FCA authorisation under any enactment (including an enactment contained in subordinate legislation within the meaning of the Interpretation Act 1978), or any rule made under this Act by the PRA or the FCA, that implemented Article 162 of the Solvency 2 Directive];]

["threshold conditions", in relation to a regulated activity, has the meaning given in section 55B(1);]

. . .

["the Tribunal" means the Upper Tribunal;]

"trust scheme rules" has the meaning given in section 247(1);

["UCITS" has the meaning given in [section 236A];]

"UK authorised person" has the meaning given in [section 191G(1)];

["the UK financial system" has the meaning given in [section 1I];] and

"unit trust scheme" has the meaning given in section 237.

[(1A) . . .]

(2) In the application of this Act to Scotland, references to a matter being actionable at the suit of a person are to be read as references to the matter being actionable at the instance of that person.

(3) For the purposes of any provision of this Act [(other than a provision of Part 6)] authorising or requiring a person to do anything within a specified number of days no account is to be taken of any day which is a public holiday in any part of the United Kingdom.

[(4) . . .]

NOTES

Sub-s (1) is amended as follows:

Words in first pair of square brackets inserted by the Financial Services and Markets Act 2000 (Amendment) (EU Exit) Regulations 2019, SI 2019/632, regs 84, 85(1), (2), as from IP completion day (as defined in the European Union (Withdrawal Agreement) Act 2020, s 39).

Definitions "AIF" and "full-scope UK AIFM" inserted by the Alternative Investment Fund Managers Regulations 2013, SI 2013/1773, reg 80, Sch 1, Part 1, paras 1, 31, as from 22 July 2013.

Definitions "the Authority", "money laundering rules", "notice of control", "regulatory objectives", and "regulatory provisions" (all omitted) repealed by the Financial Services Act 2012, s 49(1)(a), (g), (h), (o), as from 1 April 2013.

Definition "Bank of England" inserted by the Bank of England and Financial Services Act 2016, s 16, Sch 2, Pt 2, paras 26, 49, as from 1 March 2017.

Definition "capital requirements directive" inserted by the Capital Requirements Regulations 2013, SI 2013/3115, reg 46(1), Sch 2, Pt 1, paras 1, 24, as from 1 January 2014. Words in square brackets inserted by the Financial Holding Companies (Approval etc) and Capital Requirements (Capital Buffers and Macro-prudential Measures) (Amendment) (EU Exit) Regulations 2020, SI 2020/1406, reg 2(10), as from 29 December 2020.

Definition "capital requirements regulation" inserted by SI 2013/3115, reg 46(1), Sch 2, Pt 1, paras 1, 24, as from 1 January 2014. Words in first (outer) pair of square brackets inserted by SI 2019/632, regs 84, 85(1), (3), as from 23 March 2019. Words in second (inner) pair of square brackets substituted by the Securities Financing Transactions, Securitisation and Miscellaneous Amendments (EU Exit) Regulations 2020, SI 2020/1385, reg 38(3)(a)(i), with effect from immediately before IP completion day (as defined in the European Union (Withdrawal Agreement) Act 2020, s 39).

Definition "central securities depository" inserted by the Central Securities Depositories Regulations 2017, SI 2017/1064, reg 2(1), (38)(a), as from 28 November 2017. Words in square brackets substituted by SI 2019/632, regs 84, 85(1), (4), as from IP completion day (as defined in the European Union (Withdrawal Agreement) Act 2020, s 39).

Definition "claim" inserted by the Banking Act 2009, s 174(2), as from 21 February 2009.

Words omitted from the definition "the Commission" repealed by the Enterprise and Regulatory Reform Act 2013 (Competition) (Consequential, Transitional and Saving Provisions) Order 2014, SI 2014/892, art 2, Sch 1, Pt 2, paras 120, 131, as from 1 April 2014.

Words in square brackets in the definition "control of information rules" substituted by the Financial Services Act 2012, s 49(1)(b), as from 1 April 2013.

Definitions "core activities", "core services", and "excluded activities" inserted by the Financial Services (Banking Reform) Act 2013, s 4(5), as from 1 January 2019.

Definition "credit institution" inserted by SI 2019/632, regs 84, 85(1), (5), as from IP completion day (as defined in the European Union (Withdrawal Agreement) Act 2020, s 39).

Definitions "credit-related regulated activity", "the FCA", "the PRA", "PRA-authorised person", "PRA-regulated activity", "principal", and "regulator" inserted by the Financial Services Act 2012, s 49(1)(c), (d), (j), (l), (n), as from 25 January 2013 (in so far as relating to the definitions "the FCA", "the PRA", "PRA-authorised person", "PRA-regulated activity", and "regulator"), and as from 1 April 2013 (otherwise).

Definition "CRR rules" inserted by the Financial Services Act 2021, s 5, Sch 3, Pt 3, para 18, as from 9 June 2021.

Definition "the CSD regulation" inserted by the Central Securities Depositories Regulations 2014, SI 2014/2879, reg 6(1), (3), as from 21 November 2014. Words in first (outer) pair of square brackets inserted by SI 2019/632, regs 84, 85(1), (6), as from 23 March 2019. Words in second (inner) pair of square brackets substituted by SI 2020/1385, reg 38(3)(a)(ii), with effect from immediately before IP completion day (as defined in the European Union (Withdrawal Agreement) Act 2020, s 39).

Definition "the data protection legislation" inserted by the Data Protection Act 2018, s 211, Sch 19, Pt 1, paras 48, 53, as from 25 May 2018 (for transitional provisions and savings relating to the repeal of the Data Protection Act 1998, see Sch 20 to the 2018 Act).

Words in square brackets in the definition "documents" inserted by the Criminal Justice and Police Act 2001, s 70, Sch 2, Pt 2, para 16(1), (2)(f), as from 1 April 2003.

Definitions "EBA" and "ESMA" inserted by the Financial Services (Omnibus 1 Directive) Regulations 2012, SI 2012/916, reg 2(1), (14), as from 16 April 2012. Definition "EBA" (now omitted) repealed by SI 2019/632, regs 84, 85(1), (13), as from IP completion day (as defined in the European Union (Withdrawal Agreement) Act 2020, s 39).

Definition "EIOPA" (omitted) originally inserted by the Insurance Distribution (Regulated Activities and Miscellaneous Amendments) Order 2018, SI 2018/546, art 18(2), as from 1 October 2018. Subsequently repealed by SI 2019/632, regs 84, 85(1), (13), as from IP completion day (as defined in the European Union (Withdrawal Agreement) Act 2020, s 39).

Definitions "electronic commerce directive" and "information society service" (omitted) originally inserted by the Electronic Commerce Directive (Financial Services and Markets) Regulations 2002, SI 2002/1775, reg 13(1), (2)(a), (b), as from 21 August 2002. Subsequently repealed by the Electronic Commerce and Solvency 2 (Amendment etc) (EU Exit) Regulations 2019, SI 2019/1361, reg 3, as from IP completion day (as defined in the European Union (Withdrawal Agreement) Act 2020, s 39).

Definition "the EU Benchmarks Regulation 2016" inserted by the Financial Services and Markets Act 2000 (Benchmarks) Regulations 2018, SI 2018/135, reg 49(1), as from 27 February 2018. Words in square brackets inserted by SI 2020/1385, reg 38(3)(a)(iii), with effect from immediately before IP completion day (as defined in the European Union (Withdrawal Agreement) Act 2020, s 39).

Words in square brackets in the definition "exempt person" originally substituted by the Financial Services and Markets Act 2000 (Over the Counter Derivatives, Central Counterparties and Trade Repositories) Regulations 2013, SI 2013/504, reg 3(1), (15), as from 1 April 2013. Words omitted therefrom repealed by SI 2017/1064, reg 2(1), (38)(b), as from 28 November 2017.

Words in square brackets in the definition "financial promotion rules" substituted by the Financial Services Act 2012, s 49(1)(e), as from 1 April 2013.

Definition "general rules" substituted by the Financial Services Act 2012, s 49(1)(f), as from 1 April 2013.

Definition "Gibraltar-based person" inserted by the Financial Services Act 2021, s 22, Sch 8, para 14, as from a day to be appointed.

Definition "industrial and provident society" (omitted) repealed, and definition "registered society" inserted, by the Co-operative and Community Benefit Societies Act 2014, s 151, Sch 4, Pt 2, paras 68, 71, as from 1 August 2014.

Definition "insurance undertaking" originally inserted by the Solvency 2 Regulations 2015, SI 2015/575, reg 59, Sch 1, Pt 1, paras 1, 15, as from 31 March 2015. Subsequently substituted by SI 2019/632, regs 84, 85, as from IP completion day (as defined in the European Union (Withdrawal Agreement) Act 2020, s 39).

Definition "investment services and activities" originally inserted by the Financial Services and Markets Act 2000 (Markets in Financial Instruments) Regulations 2007, SI 2007/126, reg 3(5), Sch 5, paras 1, 19, as from 1 April 2007 (certain purposes), and as from 1 November 2007 (otherwise). Subsequently substituted by SI 2020/1385, reg 38(3)(a)(iv), with effect from immediately before IP completion day (as defined in the European Union (Withdrawal Agreement) Act 2020, s 39).

Definition "market abuse" (omitted) repealed, and definition "market abuse regulation" inserted, by the Financial Services and Markets Act 2000 (Market Abuse) Regulations 2016, SI 2016/680, reg 10(1), (21), as from 3 July 2016. Words in first (outer) pair of square brackets in the definition "market abuse regulation" inserted by SI 2019/632, regs 84, 85(1), (8), as from 23 March 2019. Words in second (inner) pair of square brackets substituted by SI 2020/1385, reg 38(3)(a)(v), with effect from immediately before IP completion day (as defined in the European Union (Withdrawal Agreement) Act 2020, s 39).

Definition "markets in financial instruments regulation" inserted by SI 2017/701, reg 50(1), Sch 2, paras 1, 51(1), (2), as from 3 January 2018 (as to the commencement of the 2017 Regulations, see further the note relating to them above). Words in square brackets substituted by SI 2020/1385, reg 38(3)(a)(vi), with effect from immediately before IP completion day (as defined in the European Union (Withdrawal Agreement) Act 2020, s 39).

Definition "minimum capital requirement" inserted by SI 2015/575, reg 59, Sch 1, Pt 1, paras 1, 15, as from 31 March 2015.

Definition "MMF Regulation" inserted by the Money Market Funds Regulations 2018, SI 2018/698, reg 2(1), (17), as from 21 July 2018. Words in square brackets inserted by SI 2020/1385, reg 38(3)(a)(vii), with effect from immediately before IP completion day (as defined in the European Union (Withdrawal Agreement) Act 2020, s 39).

Definitions "mortgage creditor", "mortgage intermediary" and "tied mortgage intermediary" (all omitted) originally inserted by the Mortgage Credit Directive Order 2015, SI 2015/910, Sch 1, para 1(1), (8), as from 21 March 2016. All three definitions were repealed by SI 2019/632, regs 84, 85(1), (13), as from IP completion day (as defined in the European Union (Withdrawal Agreement) Act 2020, s 39).

Definition "Part 4A permission" substituted (for the original definition "Part IV permission") by the Financial Services Act 2012, s 49(1)(i), as from 1 April 2013.

Definitions "Part 9C prohibition order" and "Part 9C rules" inserted by the Financial Services Act 2021, s 2, Sch 2, Pt 2, para 15(2), as from 1 July 2021; for transitional provisions, see Sch 2, Pt 3 to the 2021 Act.

Words in square brackets in the definition "price stabilising rules" substituted by the Financial Services Act 2012, s 49(1)(k), as from 1 April 2013.

Words in square brackets in the definition "private company" substituted by the Companies Act 2006 (Consequential Amendments, Transitional Provisions and Savings) Order 2009, SI 2009/1941, art 2(1), Sch 1, para 181(1), (4), as from 1 October 2009.

Words in square brackets in the definition "prohibition order" inserted by the Financial Services Act 2021, s 2, Sch 2, Pt 2, para 15(3), as from 1 July 2021; for transitional provisions, see Sch 2, Pt 3 to the 2021 Act.

Definition "qualifying credit institution" inserted by SI 2019/632, regs 84, 85(1), (9), as from IP completion day (as defined in the European Union (Withdrawal Agreement) Act 2020, s 39).

Words "recognised CSD," in square brackets added to the existing definitions "recognised clearing house" and "recognised investment exchange" by SI 2017/1064, reg 2(1), (38)(c), as from 28 November 2017.

Definition "regulated claims management activity" inserted by the Financial Guidance and Claims Act 2018, s 27(1), (10), as from 6 October 2018 (for transitional provisions in relation to the transfer of regulation of claims management services to the FCA, see Sch 5 to the 2018 Act).

Words in square brackets in the definition "regulating provisions" substituted by the Financial Services Act 2012, s 49(1)(m), as from 1 April 2013.

Definition "reinsurance undertaking" originally inserted by SI 2015/575, reg 59, Sch 1, Pt 1, paras 1, 15, as from 31 March 2015. Subsequently substituted by SI 2019/632, regs 84, 85, as from IP completion day (as defined in the European Union (Withdrawal Agreement) Act 2020, s 39).

Definitions "ring-fenced body", and "ring-fencing rules" inserted by the Financial Services (Banking Reform) Act 2013, s 4(5), as from 1 January 2019.

Definition "rule" substituted by the Financial Services Act 2012, s 49(1)(p), as from 1 April 2013.

Words in square brackets in the definition "rule-making instrument" substituted by the Financial Services Act 2012, s 49(1)(q), as from 1 April 2013.

Definitions "Schedule 2A permission" and "Schedule 2B permission" inserted by the Financial Services Act 2021, s 22, Sch 8, para 14, as from a day to be appointed.

Definition "SFT regulation" inserted by the Financial Services and Markets Act 2000 (Transparency of Securities Financing Transactions and of Reuse) Regulations 2016, SI 2016/715, reg 29, Sch 1, para 1(1), (5), as from 13 July 2016.

Definition "short selling regulation" inserted by the Financial Services and Markets Act 2000 (Short Selling) Regulations 2012, SI 2012/2554, reg 2(1), (15), as from 1 November 2012. Words in first (outer) pair of square brackets inserted by SI 2019/632, regs 84, 85(1), (11), as from 23 March 2019. Words in second (inner) pair of square brackets substituted by SI 2020/1385, reg 38(3)(a)(viii), with effect from immediately before IP completion day (as defined in the European Union (Withdrawal Agreement) Act 2020, s 39).

Definition "solvency capital requirement" inserted by SI 2015/575, reg 59, Sch 1, Pt 1, paras 1, 15, as from 31 March 2015.

Definition "Takeovers Directive" inserted by the Companies Act 2006, s 964(1), (6), as from 6 April 2007.

Definition "third-country insurance undertaking" inserted by 2015, SI 2015/575, reg 59, Sch 1, Pt 1, paras 1, 15, as from 31 March 2015. Words in square brackets substituted by SI 2019/632, regs 84, 85, as from IP completion day (as defined in the European Union (Withdrawal Agreement) Act 2020, s 39).

Definition "threshold conditions" substituted by the Financial Services Act 2012, s 49(1)(r), as from 1 April 2013.

Definition "the Treaty" (omitted) repealed by the Electronic Commerce and Solvency 2 (Amendment etc) (EU Exit) Regulations 2019, SI 2019/1361, reg 3, as from IP completion day (as defined in the European Union (Withdrawal Agreement) Act 2020, s 39).

Definition "the Tribunal" inserted by the Transfer of Tribunal Functions Order 2010, SI 2010/22, art 5(1), Sch 2, paras 43, 48, as from 6 April 2010.

Definition "UCITS" inserted by SI 2018/698, reg 2(1), (17), as from 21 July 2018. Words in square brackets substituted by the Collective Investment Schemes (Amendment etc) (EU Exit) Regulations 2019, SI 2019/325, regs 3, 30, as from IP completion day (as defined in the European Union (Withdrawal Agreement) Act 2020, s 39).

Words in square brackets in the definition "UK authorised person" substituted by the Financial Services Act 2012, s 49(1)(s), as from 1 April 2013.

Definition "the UK financial system" inserted by the Financial Services Act 2010, s 24(1), (2), Sch 2, Pt 1, paras 1, 31, as from 8 April 2010. Words in square brackets substituted by the Financial Services Act 2012, s 49(1)(t), as from 1 April 2013.

Sub-s (1A): originally inserted by SI 2019/632, regs 84, 85(14), as from 23 March 2019. Subsequently repealed by SI 2020/1385, reg 38(3)(b), with effect from immediately before IP completion day (as defined in the European Union (Withdrawal Agreement) Act 2020, s 39).

Sub-s (3): words in square brackets inserted by the Prospectus Regulations 2005, SI 2005/1433, reg 2(1), Sch 1, para 15, as from 1 July 2005.

Sub-s (4): originally added by SI 2002/1775, reg 13(1), (2)(c), as from 21 August 2002. Subsequently repealed SI 2019/1361, reg 3, as from IP completion day (as defined in the European Union (Withdrawal Agreement) Act 2020, s 39).

[7.700]

418 Carrying on regulated activities in the United Kingdom

(1) [In the cases] described in this section, a person who—

(a) is carrying on a regulated activity, but

(b) would not otherwise be regarded as carrying it on in the United Kingdom,

is, for the purposes of this Act, to be regarded as carrying it on in the United Kingdom.

(2), (3) . . .

(4) The third case is where—

(a) his registered office (or if he does not have a registered office his head office) is in the United Kingdom;

(b) the day-to-day management of the carrying on of the regulated activity is the responsibility of—

(i) his registered office (or head office); or

(ii) another establishment maintained by him in the United Kingdom.

(5) The fourth case is where—

(a) his head office is not in the United Kingdom; but

(b) the activity is carried on from an establishment maintained by him in the United Kingdom.

[(5A) . . .]

[(5AA) The sixth case is where—

(a) the regulated activity being carried on by the person is the regulated activity of managing an AIF;

(b) the AIF being managed—

(i) has its registered office in [the United Kingdom]; or

(ii) is marketed in [the United Kingdom];

(c) the person's registered office is in the United Kingdom or, if the person does not have a registered office, the person's head office is in the United Kingdom; and

(d) the activity is carried on from an establishment maintained in a country or territory outside [the United Kingdom].];

[(5B) The seventh case is where—

(a) the regulated activity being carried on by the person is the regulated activity of managing an AIF,

(b) the AIF being managed—

(i) has its registered office in the United Kingdom, or

(ii) is marketed in the United Kingdom,

(c) if the AIF being managed is marketed in the United Kingdom, it is marketed otherwise than in accordance with regulation 59 of the Alternative Investment Fund Managers Regulations 2013, and

(d) the person does not have a registered office in the United Kingdom.]

[(5C) The eighth case is where—
(a) the person's head office or registered office is in the United Kingdom, and
(b) the person is carrying on a restricted activity (as defined in paragraph 3 of Schedule 2B) in Gibraltar.]
(6) [For the purposes of the preceding subsections] it is irrelevant where the person with whom the activity is carried on is situated.
[(7) . . .]
[(8) For the purposes of this section, an AIF is "marketed" when—
(a) the person managing the AIF ("the AIFM") makes a direct or indirect offering or placement of units or shares of the AIF to or with an investor domiciled or with a registered office in the United Kingdom, or
(b) another person makes such an offering or placement at the initiative of, or on behalf of, the AIFM.]

NOTES

Sub-s (1): words in square brackets substituted by the Financial Services and Markets Act 2000 (Amendment) (EU Exit) Regulations 2019, SI 2019/632, regs 84, 86(1), (2), as from IP completion day (as defined in the European Union (Withdrawal Agreement) Act 2020, s 39).

Sub-ss (2), (3): repealed by SI 2019/632, regs 84, 86(1), (3), as from IP completion day (as defined in the European Union (Withdrawal Agreement) Act 2020, s 39).

Sub-s (5A): originally inserted by the Electronic Commerce Directive (Financial Services and Markets) Regulations 2002, SI 2002/1775, reg 13(1), (3)(b), as from 21 August 2002. Subsequently repealed by the Electronic Commerce and Solvency 2 (Amendment etc) (EU Exit) Regulations 2019, SI 2019/1361, reg 4, as from IP completion day (as defined in the European Union (Withdrawal Agreement) Act 2020, s 39).

Sub-s (5AA): inserted by the Alternative Investment Fund Managers Order 2014, SI 2014/1292, art 2(b), as from 16 June 2014. Words in square brackets substituted by SI 2019/632, regs 84, 86(1), (4), as from IP completion day (as defined in the European Union (Withdrawal Agreement) Act 2020, s 39).

Sub-s (5B): inserted by the Alternative Investment Fund Managers (Amendment) Regulations 2013, SI 2013/1797, reg 3, Sch 1, para 1(1), (4)(b), as from a day to be appointed. Note that Schedule 1, para 1(4)(b) to the 2013 Regulations was amended by SI 2014/1292, art 5(b) (as from 16 June 2014), and by the Alternative Investment Fund Managers (Amendment etc) (EU Exit) Regulations 2019, SI 2019/328, regs 16, 20 (as from IP completion day (as defined in the European Union (Withdrawal Agreement) Act 2020, s 39)); and the effect of the amendments has been incorporated in the text above. Sub-s (5B)(c) is repealed by reg 4 of, and Sch 2, Pt 1, para 1 to, the 2013 Regulations as from a day to be appointed.

Sub-s (5C): inserted by the Financial Services Act 2021, s 22, Sch 8, para 15, as from a day to be appointed.

Sub-s (6): words in square brackets substituted by SI 2019/632, regs 84, 86(1), (5), as from IP completion day (as defined in the European Union (Withdrawal Agreement) Act 2020, s 39).

Sub-s (7): originally added by the Financial Services and Markets Act 2000 (Regulated Activities) (Amendment) Order 2012, SI 2012/1906, art 3(1), (15), as from 20 July 2012. Subsequently repealed by SI 2019/632, regs 84, 86(1), (6), as from IP completion day (as defined in the European Union (Withdrawal Agreement) Act 2020, s 39).

Sub-s (8): originally added by SI 2014/1292, art 2(d), as from 16 June 2014. Subsequently substituted by SI 2019/632, regs 84, 86(1), (7), as from IP completion day (as defined in the European Union (Withdrawal Agreement) Act 2020, s 39).

[7.701]
419 Carrying on regulated activities by way of business

(1) The Treasury may by order make provision—
(a) as to the circumstances in which a person who would otherwise not be regarded as carrying on a regulated activity by way of business is to be regarded as doing so;
(b) as to the circumstances in which a person who would otherwise be regarded as carrying on a regulated activity by way of business is to be regarded as not doing so.
(2) An order under subsection (1) may be made so as to apply—
(a) generally in relation to all regulated activities;
(b) in relation to a specified category of regulated activity; or
(c) in relation to a particular regulated activity.
(3) An order under subsection (1) may be made so as to apply—
(a) for the purposes of all provisions;
(b) for a specified group of provisions; or
(c) for a specified provision.
(4) "Provision" means a provision of, or made under, this Act.
(5) Nothing in this section is to be read as affecting the provisions of section 428(3).

NOTES

Orders: the Financial Services and Markets Act 2000 (Carrying on Regulated Activities by Way of Business) Order 2001, SI 2001/1177 at **[8.315]**; the Financial Services and Markets Act 2000 (Carrying on Regulated Activities by Way of Business) (Amendment) Order 2005, SI 2005/922; the Financial Services and Markets Act 2000 (Carrying on Regulated Activities by Way of Business) (Amendment) Order 2011, SI 2011/2304; the Financial Services and Markets Act 2000 (Carrying on Regulated Activities by Way of Business) (Amendment) Order 2014, SI 2014/3340; the Financial Services and Markets Act 2000 (Regulated Activities) (Amendment) Order 2017, SI 2017/488; the Financial Services and Markets Act 2000 (Carrying on Regulated Activities by Way of Business) (Amendment) Order 2018, SI 2018/394; the Financial Services and Markets Act 2000 (Regulated Activities) (Amendment) Order 2018, SI 2018/831.

[7.702]
[419A Claims management services

(1) In this Act "claims management services" means advice or other services in relation to the making of a claim.
(2) In subsection (1) "other services" includes—
(a) financial services or assistance,
(b) legal representation,
(c) referring or introducing one person to another, and
(d) making inquiries,

but giving, or preparing to give, evidence (whether or not expert evidence) is not, by itself, a claims management service.

(3) In this section "claim" means a claim for compensation, restitution, repayment or any other remedy or relief in respect of loss or damage or in respect of an obligation, whether the claim is made or could be made—

(a) by way of legal proceedings,

(b) in accordance with a scheme of regulation (whether voluntary or compulsory), or

(c) in pursuance of a voluntary undertaking.

(4) The Treasury may by order provide that a claim for a specified benefit is to be treated as a claim for the purposes of this section.

(5) The Treasury may specify a benefit under subsection (4) only if it appears to the Treasury to be a social security benefit, payable under the law of any part of the United Kingdom, designed to provide compensation for industrial injury.]

NOTES

Inserted, together with s 419B, by the Financial Guidance and Claims Act 2018, s 27(1), (11), as from 6 October 2018 (for transitional provisions in relation to the transfer of regulation of claims management services to the FCA, see Sch 5 to the 2018 Act).

Orders: the Financial Services and Markets Act 2000 (Claims Management Activity) Order 2018, SI 2018/1253.

[7.703]

[419B Carrying on claims management activity in Great Britain

(1) The Treasury may by order make provision as to the circumstances in which a person is, or is not, to be treated as carrying on—

(a) a regulated claims management activity, or

(b) an activity of a kind specified in an order under section 21(10B),

in Great Britain.

(2) Subsections (2) to (5) of section 419 apply in relation to an order under subsection (1) as they apply in relation to an order under subsection (1) of that section, but as if the references to regulated activities in subsection (2) of that section were references to regulated claims management activities or, as the case may be, to activities of a kind specified in an order under section 21(10B).]

NOTES

Inserted as noted to s 419A at **[7.702]**.

Orders: the Financial Services and Markets Act 2000 (Claims Management Activity) Order 2018, SI 2018/1253.

[7.704]

420 Parent and subsidiary undertaking

(1) In this Act, except in relation to an incorporated friendly society, "parent undertaking" and "subsidiary undertaking" have the same meaning as in [the Companies Acts (see section 1162 of, and Schedule 7 to, the Companies Act 2006)].

(2) But—

(a) "parent undertaking" also includes an individual who would be a parent undertaking for the purposes of those provisions if he were taken to be an undertaking (and "subsidiary undertaking" is to be read accordingly);

(b) "subsidiary undertaking" also includes, in relation to a body incorporated in or formed under the law of an EEA State . . . , an undertaking which is a subsidiary undertaking within the meaning of any rule of law in force in that State for purposes connected with implementation of the [Directive 2013/34/EU of the European Parliament and of the Council of 26 June 2013 on the annual financial statements, consolidated financial statements and related reports of certain types of undertakings, amending Directive 2006/43/EC of the European Parliament and of the Council and repealing Council Directives 78/660/EEC and 83/349/EEC] (and "parent undertaking" is to be read accordingly).

(3) In this Act "subsidiary undertaking", in relation to an incorporated friendly society, means a body corporate of which the society has control within the meaning of section 13(9)(a) or (aa) of the Friendly Societies Act 1992 (and "parent undertaking" is to be read accordingly).

NOTES

Sub-s (1): words in square brackets substituted by the Companies Act 2006 (Consequential Amendments etc) Order 2008, SI 2008/948, art 3(1), Sch 1, Pt 2, para 212(1), as from 6 April 2008.

Sub-s (2): the words omitted from para (b) were repealed, and the words in square brackets were substituted, by the Financial Services and Markets Act 2000 (Amendment) (EU Exit) Regulations 2019, SI 2019/632, regs 84, 87, as from IP completion day (as defined in the European Union (Withdrawal Agreement) Act 2020, s 39) (in the case of the repealed words), and as from 23 March 2019 (in the case of the substitution of the words in square brackets).

[7.705]

421 Group

(1) In this Act "group", in relation to a person ("A"), means A and any person who is—

(a) a parent undertaking of A;

(b) a subsidiary undertaking of A;

(c) a subsidiary undertaking of a parent undertaking of A;

(d) a parent undertaking of a subsidiary undertaking of A;

(e) an undertaking in which A or an undertaking mentioned in paragraph (a), (b), (c) or (d) has a participating interest;

(f) if A or an undertaking mentioned in paragraph (a) or (d) is a building society, an associated undertaking of the society; or

(g) if A or an undertaking mentioned in paragraph (a) or (d) is an incorporated friendly society, a body corporate of which the society has joint control (within the meaning of section 13(9)(c) or (cc) of the Friendly Societies Act 1992).

(2) "Participating interest" [has the meaning given in section 421A]; but also includes an interest held by an individual which would be a participating interest for the purposes of those provisions if he were taken to be an undertaking.
(3) "Associated undertaking" has the meaning given in section 119(1) of the Building Societies Act 1986.

NOTES

Sub-s (2): words in square brackets substituted by the Companies Act 2006 (Consequential Amendments etc) Order 2008, SI 2008/948, art 3(1), Sch 1, Pt 2, para 212(2), as from 6 April 2008.

[7.706]
[421ZA Immediate group

In this Act "immediate group", in relation to a person ("A"), means—
- (a) A;
- (b) a parent undertaking of A;
- (c) a subsidiary undertaking of A;
- (d) a subsidiary undertaking of a parent undertaking of A;
- (e) a parent undertaking of a subsidiary undertaking of A.]

NOTES

Inserted by the Financial Services Act 2012, s 48(2), as from 24 January 2013.

[7.707]
[421A Meaning of "participating interest"

(1) In section 421 a "participating interest" means an interest held by an undertaking in the shares of another undertaking which it holds on a long-term basis for the purpose of securing a contribution to its activities by the exercise of control or influence arising from or related to that interest.
(2) A holding of 20% or more of the shares of an undertaking is presumed to be a participating interest unless the contrary is shown.
(3) The reference in subsection (1) to an interest in shares includes—
- (a) an interest which is convertible into an interest in shares, and
- (b) an option to acquire shares or any such interest;

And an interest or option falls within paragraph (a) or (b) notwithstanding that the shares to which it relates are, until the conversion or the exercise of the option, unissued.
(4) For the purposes of this section an interest held on behalf of an undertaking shall be treated as held by it.
(5) In this section "undertaking" has the same meaning as in the Companies Acts (see section 1161(1) of the Companies Act 2006).]

NOTES

Inserted by the Companies Act 2006 (Consequential Amendments etc) Order 2008, SI 2008/948, art 3(1), Sch 1, Pt 2, para 212(3), as from 6 April 2008.

[7.708]
[422 Controller

(1) In this Act "controller", in relation to an undertaking ("B"), means a person ("A") who falls within any of the cases in subsection (2).
(2) The cases are where A holds—
- (a) 10% or more of the shares in B or in a parent undertaking of B ("P");
- (b) 10% or more of the voting power in B or P; or
- (c) shares or voting power in B or P as a result of which A is able to exercise significant influence over the management of B.

(3) For the purposes of calculations relating to this section, the holding of shares or voting power by a person ("A1") includes any shares or voting power held by another ("A2") if A1 and A2 are acting in concert.
(4) In this section "shares"—
- (a) in relation to an undertaking with a share capital, means allotted shares;
- (b) in relation to an undertaking with capital but no share capital, means rights to share in the capital of the undertaking;
- (c) in relation to an undertaking without capital, means interests—
  - (i) conferring any right to share in the profits, or liability to contribute to the losses, of the undertaking; or
  - (ii) giving rise to an obligation to contribute to the debts or expenses of the undertaking in the event of a winding up.

(5) In this section "voting power"—
- (a) includes, in relation to a person ("H")—
  - (i) voting power held by a third party with whom H has concluded an agreement, which obliges H and the third party to adopt, by concerted exercise of the voting power they hold, a lasting common policy towards the management of the undertaking in question;
  - (ii) voting power held by a third party under an agreement concluded with H providing for the temporary transfer for consideration of the voting power in question;
  - (iii) voting power attaching to shares which are lodged as collateral with H, provided that H controls the voting power and declares an intention to exercise it;
  - (iv) voting power attaching to shares in which H has a life interest;
  - (v) voting power which is held, or may be exercised within the meaning of subparagraphs (i) to (iv), by a [controlled undertaking] of H;
  - (vi) voting power attaching to shares deposited with H which H has discretion to exercise in the absence of specific instructions from the shareholders;

(vii) voting power held in the name of a third party on behalf of H;

(viii) voting power which H may exercise as a proxy where H has discretion about the exercise of the voting power in the absence of specific instructions from the shareholders; and

(b) in relation to an undertaking which does not have general meetings at which matters are decided by the exercise of voting rights, means the right under the constitution of the undertaking to direct the overall policy of the undertaking or alter the terms of its constitution.

[(6) For the purposes of this section, an undertaking "B" is a controlled undertaking of H if any of the conditions in section 89J(4)(a) to (d) (read with section 89J(5)) is met (reading references in those provisions to A as references to H).]]

NOTES

The original s 422 was substituted by new ss 422, 422A by the Financial Services and Markets Act 2000 (Controllers) Regulations 2009, SI 2009/534, reg 7, Sch 3, as from 21 March 2009.

The words in square brackets in sub-s (5)(a)(v) were substituted, and sub-s (6) was added, by the Capital Requirements Regulations 2013, SI 2013/3115, reg 46(1), Sch 2, Pt 1, paras 1, 25, as from 1 January 2014.

[7.709]

[422A Disregarded holdings

(1) For the purposes of section 422, shares and voting power that a person holds in an undertaking ("B") or in a parent undertaking of B ("P") are disregarded in the following circumstances.

(2) Shares held only for the purposes of clearing and settling within a short settlement cycle are disregarded.

(3) Shares held by a custodian or its nominee in a custodian capacity are disregarded, provided that the custodian or nominee is only able to exercise voting power attached to the shares in accordance with instructions given in writing.

(4) Shares representing no more than 5% of the total voting power in B or P held by an investment firm are disregarded, provided that it—

(a) holds the shares in the capacity of a market maker (as defined in [article 2.1.6 of the markets in financial instruments regulation]);

[(b) has a Part 4A permission to carry on one or more investment services and activities;]

(c) neither intervenes in the management of B or P nor exerts any influence on B or P to buy the shares or back the share price.

(5) Shares held by a [qualifying credit institution] or investment firm in its trading book are disregarded, provided that—

(a) the shares represent no more than 5% of the total voting power in B or P; and

(b) . . . the voting power is not used to intervene in the management of B or P.

(6) Shares held by a [qualifying credit institution] or an investment firm are disregarded, provided that—

(a) the shares are held as a result of performing the investment services and activities of—

(i) underwriting shares; or

(ii) placing shares on a firm commitment basis . . . ; and

(b) the [qualifying credit institution] or investment firm—

(i) does not exercise voting power represented by the shares or otherwise intervene in the management of the issuer; and

(ii) retains the holding for a period of less than one year.

(7) Where a management company (as defined in [section 237(2)] and its parent undertaking both hold shares or voting power, each may disregard holdings of the other, provided that each exercises its voting power independently of the other.

(8) But subsection (7) does not apply if the management company—

[(a) manages holdings for its parent undertaking or a controlled undertaking of its parent undertaking;]

(b) has no discretion to exercise the voting power attached to such holdings; and

(c) may only exercise the voting power in relation to such holdings under direct or indirect instruction from—

(i) its parent undertaking; or

[(ii) a controlled undertaking of the parent undertaking].

(9) Where an investment firm and its parent undertaking both hold shares or voting power, the parent undertaking may disregard holdings managed by the investment firm on a client by client basis and the investment firm may disregard holdings of the parent undertaking, provided that the investment firm—

(a) has permission to provide portfolio management;

(b) exercises its voting power independently from the parent undertaking; and

(c) may only exercise the voting power under instructions given in writing, or has appropriate mechanisms in place for ensuring that individual portfolio management services are conducted independently of any other services.

[(9A) Shares acquired for stabilisation purposes in accordance with [the market abuse regulation and Commission Delegated Regulation (EU) No 1052/2016 of 8 March 2016 supplementing Regulation (EU) No 596/2014 of the European Parliament and the Council with regard to the regulatory technical standards for conditions applicable to buy-back programmes and stabilisation measures] are disregarded, provided that the voting power attached to those shares is not exercised or otherwise used to intervene in the management of B or P.]

[(10) For the purposes of this section "qualifying credit institution" includes a credit institution which is authorised under the law of Gibraltar relied on immediately before IP completion day to implement the capital requirements directive.]

[(11) For the purposes of this section, an undertaking is a controlled undertaking of the parent undertaking if it is controlled by the parent undertaking; and for this purpose the question of whether one undertaking controls another is to be determined in accordance with section 89J(4) and (5).]]

NOTES

Substituted as noted to s 422 at **[7.708]**.

Sub-s (4): words in square brackets in para (a) substituted, and para (b) substituted, by the Financial Services and Markets Act 2000 (Amendment) (EU Exit) Regulations 2019, SI 2019/632, regs 84, 88(a), as from IP completion day (as defined in the European Union (Withdrawal Agreement) Act 2020, s 39).

Sub-s (5): words in square brackets substituted by SI 2019/632, regs 84, 88(b), as from IP completion day (as defined in the European Union (Withdrawal Agreement) Act 2020, s 39). Words omitted from para (b) repealed by the Transparency Regulations 2015, SI 2015/1755, reg 6(3)(a), as from 1 November 2015 (for the purpose of making rules under Part 9A), and as from 31 May 2016 (otherwise).

Sub-s (6): words in square brackets substituted, and words omitted repealed, by SI 2019/632, regs 84, 88(c), as from IP completion day (as defined in the European Union (Withdrawal Agreement) Act 2020, s 39).

Sub-s (7): words in square brackets substituted by SI 2019/632, regs 84, 88(d), as from IP completion day (as defined in the European Union (Withdrawal Agreement) Act 2020, s 39).

Sub-s (8): paras (a) and (c)(ii) were substituted by the Capital Requirements Regulations 2013, SI 2013/3115, reg 46(1), Sch 2, Pt 1, paras 1, 26(a), (b), as from 1 January 2014.

Sub-s (9A): inserted by SI 2015/1755, reg 6(3)(b), as from 1 November 2015 (for the purpose of making rules under Part 9A), and as from 31 May 2016 (otherwise). Words in square brackets substituted by SI 2019/632, regs 84, 88(e), as from 23 March 2019.

Sub-s (10): substituted by SI 2019/632, regs 84, 88(f), as from IP completion day (as defined in the European Union (Withdrawal Agreement) Act 2020, s 39). Note that SI 2019/632, reg 88(f) originally provided for the repeal of this subsection but that paragraph was substituted by the Gibraltar (Miscellaneous Amendments) (EU Exit) Regulations 2019, SI 2019/680, reg 9(1), (5), with effect from immediately before IP completion day. The substituted para (f) provides for the substitution of sub-s (10) instead of its repeal. Note also that the Gibraltar (Miscellaneous Amendments) (EU Exit) Regulations 2019, SI 2019/680, reg 9(5) was itself amended by the Financial Services and Economic and Monetary Policy (Consequential Amendments) (EU Exit) Regulations 2020, SI 2020/1301, reg 3, Schedule, para 40(d), as from 30 December 2020 (and the effect of the amendment has been incorporated in the text set out above).

Sub-s (11): added by SI 2013/3115, reg 46(1), Sch 2, Pt 1, paras 1, 26(d), as from 1 January 2014.

[7.710]

423 Manager

(1) In this Act, except in relation to a unit trust scheme or a registered friendly society, "manager" means an employee who—

- (a) under the immediate authority of his employer is responsible, either alone or jointly with one or more other persons, for the conduct of his employer's business; or
- (b) under the immediate authority of his employer or of a person who is a manager by virtue of paragraph (a) exercises managerial functions or is responsible for maintaining accounts or other records of his employer.

(2) If the employer is not an individual, references in subsection (1) to the authority of the employer are references to the authority—

- (a) in the case of a body corporate, of the directors;
- (b) in the case of a partnership, of the partners; and
- (c) in the case of an unincorporated association, of its officers or the members of its governing body.

(3) "Manager", in relation to a body corporate, means a person (other than an employee of the body) who is appointed by the body to manage any part of its business and includes an employee of the body corporate (other than the chief executive) who, under the immediate authority of a director or chief executive of the body corporate, exercises managerial functions or is responsible for maintaining accounts or other records of the body corporate.

[7.711]

[423A Mortgage agreements etc

(1) In this Act—

"mortgage agreement" means an agreement to which subsection (2) applies, but to which subsection (3) does not apply, under which a mortgage creditor grants or promises to grant, to a consumer, a credit in the form of a deferred payment, loan or other similar financial accommodation;

"mortgage creditor" means a person who grants or promises to grant—

- (a) in the course of the person's trade, business or profession, and
- (b) under an agreement to which subsection (2) applies but to which subsection (3) does not apply,

credit in the form of a deferred payment, loan or other similar financial accommodation;

"mortgage intermediary" means a person who, in the course of the person's trade, business or profession, and acting neither as a mortgage creditor or notary nor in an introductory capacity, does any of the following for any agreed form of financial consideration—

- (a) presenting or offering mortgage agreements to consumers;
- (b) assisting consumers by undertaking preparatory work or other pre-contractual administration in respect of mortgage agreements (otherwise than as referred to in paragraph (a));
- (c) concluding mortgage agreements with consumers on behalf of mortgage creditors;

"tied mortgage intermediary" means a mortgage intermediary who acts on behalf of and under the full and unconditional responsibility of—

- (a) only one mortgage creditor,
- (b) only one group of mortgage creditors, or
- (c) a number of mortgage creditors or groups of mortgage creditors which does not represent the majority of the market.

(2) This subsection applies to the following agreements—

- (a) an agreement secured by a mortgage on, or (in Scotland) a heritable security over, residential immovable property, or by any other charge or right over or related to such property;
- (b) an agreement the purpose of which is to acquire or retain property rights in land or in an existing or projected building.

(3) This subsection applies to the following agreements—

- (a) an agreement under which the creditor—

(i) contributes a lump sum, periodic payments or other forms of credit disbursement in return for a sum deriving from the future sale of a residential immovable property or a right relating to residential immovable property, and

(ii) will not seek repayment of the credit until the occurrence of one or more specified life events of the consumer, unless the consumer breaches contractual obligations so as to allow the creditor to terminate the agreement;

(b) an agreement under which credit is granted by an employer to its employees as a secondary activity where the agreement is offered free of interest or at an annual rate lower than that prevailing on the market and not offered to the public generally;

(c) an agreement under which credit is granted free of interest and without any other charges except those that recover costs directly related to the securing of the credit;

(d) an agreement in the form of an overdraft facility under which the credit has to be repaid within one month;

(e) an agreement which is the outcome of a settlement reached in or before a court or other statutory authority;

(f) an agreement which—

(i) relates to the deferred payment, free of charge, of an existing debt, and

(ii) is not secured by a mortgage, by another comparable security commonly used in the United Kingdom on residential immovable property or by a right related to residential immovable property.

(4) In this section—

"acting in an introductory capacity" means merely introducing (directly or indirectly) a consumer to a mortgage creditor or mortgage intermediary;

"annual rate" means the total cost to the borrower expressed as an annual percentage of the total amount of credit;

"consumer" means an individual who is acting for purposes outside those of any trade, business or profession carried on by the individual;

"group of mortgage creditors" means a group of mortgage creditors that are to be consolidated for the purposes of drawing up consolidated accounts in accordance with—

(a) the requirements of Part 15 of the Companies Act 2006, if the parent undertaking (within the meaning of that Act) is a company, or

(b) if it is not, the legal requirements that apply to the drawing up of consolidated accounts for the parent undertaking;

"specified" means specified in rules made by the FCA.

(5) A reference in this section to any immovable property, land or building—

(a) in relation to an agreement entered into before IP completion day, is a reference to any immovable property, land or building in the United Kingdom or within the territory of an EEA State;

(b) in relation to an agreement entered into on or after IP completion day, is a reference to any immovable property, land or building in the United Kingdom.]

NOTES

Commencement: IP completion day (as defined in the European Union (Withdrawal Agreement) Act 2020, s 39).

Inserted by the Financial Services and Markets Act 2000 (Amendment) (EU Exit) Regulations 2019, SI 2019/632, regs 84, 89, as from IP completion day (as defined in the European Union (Withdrawal Agreement) Act 2020, s 39). Note that reg 89 of the 2019 Regulations was amended by the Financial Services and Economic and Monetary Policy (Consequential Amendments) (EU Exit) Regulations 2020, SI 2020/1301, reg 3, Schedule, para 33(i), as from 30 December 2020; and the effect of the amendments has been incorporated in the text set out above.

[7.712]

424 Insurance

(1) In this Act, references to—

(a) contracts of insurance,

(b) reinsurance,

(c) contracts of long-term insurance,

(d) contracts of general insurance,

are to be read with section 22 and Schedule 2.

(2) In this Act "policy" and "policyholder", in relation to a contract of insurance, have such meaning as the Treasury may by order specify.

(3) The law applicable to a contract of insurance, the effecting of which constitutes the carrying on of a regulated activity, is to be determined, if it is of a prescribed description, in accordance with regulations made by the Treasury.

NOTES

Regulations and Orders: the Financial Services and Markets Act 2000 (Meaning of "Policy" and "Policyholder") Order 2001, SI 2001/2361; the Financial Services and Markets Act 2000 (Law Applicable to Contracts of Insurance) Regulations 2001, SI 2001/2635; the Financial Services and Markets Act 2000 (Law Applicable to Contracts of Insurance) (Amendment) Regulations 2001, SI 2001/3542; the Financial Services and Markets Act 2000 (Motor Insurance) Regulations 2007, SI 2007/2403; the Financial Services and Markets Act 2000 (Law Applicable to Contracts of Insurance) Regulations 2009, SI 2009/3075.

[7.713]

[424A Investment firm

(1) In this Act [(except as otherwise provided)], "investment firm" has the meaning given in [paragraph 2.1A of the markets in financial instruments regulation].

(2) Subsection (1) is subject to [subsection (5)].

[(3) . . .]

(4) . . .

(5) References in this Act to an "investment firm" do not include references to—

[(a) a person excluded from the definition of "investment firm" in Article 3(1) of the Financial Services and Markets Act 2000 (Regulated Activities) Order 2001 (SI 2001/544) by paragraph (a) or (b) of that definition; or

(b) a firm which has a Part 4A permission to carry on regulated activities as an exempt investment firm within the meaning of regulation 8 of the Financial Services and Markets Act 2000 (Markets in Financial Instruments) Regulations 2017 (SI 2017/701)].]

NOTES

Inserted by the Financial Services and Markets Act 2000 (Markets in Financial Instruments) (Modification of Powers) Regulations 2006, SI 2006/2975, regs 2, 10, as from 6 December 2006.

Sub-s (1): words in first pair of square brackets inserted by the Financial Services Act 2021, s 2, Sch 2, Pt 2, para 16, as from 1 July 2021; for transitional provisions, see Sch 2, Pt 3 to the 2021 Act. Words in second pair of square brackets substituted by the Financial Services and Markets Act 2000 (Amendment) (EU Exit) Regulations 2019, SI 2019/632, regs 84, 90(1), (2), as from IP completion day (as defined in the European Union (Withdrawal Agreement) Act 2020, s 39).

Sub-s (2): words in square brackets substituted by SI 2019/632, regs 84, 90(1), (3), as from IP completion day (as defined in the European Union (Withdrawal Agreement) Act 2020, s 39).

Sub-s (3): originally substituted by the Financial Services and Markets Act 2000 (Markets in Financial Instruments) Regulations 2007, SI 2007/126, reg 3(5), Sch 5, paras 1, 21, as from 1 April 2007 (certain purposes), and as from 1 November 2007 (otherwise). Subsequently repealed by SI 2019/632, regs 84, 90(1), (4), as from IP completion day (as defined in the European Union (Withdrawal Agreement) Act 2020, s 39).

Sub-s (4): repealed by SI 2019/632, regs 84, 90(1), (4), as from IP completion day (as defined in the European Union (Withdrawal Agreement) Act 2020, s 39).

Sub-s (5): paras (a) and (b) substituted by SI 2019/632, regs 84, 90(1), (5), as from IP completion day (as defined in the European Union (Withdrawal Agreement) Act 2020, s 39).

[7.714]

425 Expressions relating to authorisation . . . in the single market

(1) In this Act—

[(a) ["alternative investment fund managers directive",] "[capital requirements directive]", [. . .] [. . .] . . . "EEA firm", "EEA right", "EEA State", ["emission allowance auctioning regulation",] . . . . [. . .] "[insurance distribution directive]", . . . ["markets in financial instruments directive",] ["mortgages directive",] "single market directives"[, "Solvency 2 Directive"][, "tied agent"] and "UCITS directive" have the meaning given in Schedule 3; . . .]

[(aa) . . . and]

(b) "home state regulator", in relation to an EEA firm, has the meaning given in Schedule 3.

(2) . . .

NOTES

The word omitted from the section heading, and all of sub-s (2), were repealed by the EEA Passport Rights (Amendment, etc, and Transitional Provisions) (EU Exit) Regulations 2018, SI 2018/1149, reg 3, Schedule, Pt 1, paras 1, 20, as from IP completion day (as defined in the European Union (Withdrawal Agreement) Act 2020, s 39).

Para (a) of sub-s (1) was substituted by the Collective Investment Schemes (Miscellaneous Amendments) Regulations 2003, SI 2003/2066, reg 2(1), as from 13 February 2004; and is further amended as follows:

Words ""alternative investment fund managers directive"," in square brackets inserted by the Alternative Investment Fund Managers Regulations 2013, SI 2013/1773, reg 80, Sch 1, Pt 1, paras 1, 32(a), as from 22 July 2013.

Words "capital requirements directive" in square brackets substituted by the Capital Requirements Regulations 2013, SI 2013/3115, reg 46(1), Sch 2, Pt 1, paras 1, 27, as from 1 January 2014.

First words omitted originally inserted by the Life Assurance Consolidation Directive (Consequential Amendments) Regulations 2004, SI 2004/3379, reg 6(1), (5), as from 11 January 2005. Subsequently repealed by the Solvency 2 Regulations 2015, SI 2015/575, reg 59, Sch 1, Pt 1, paras 1, 16(a), as from 1 January 2016.

Second words omitted originally inserted by SI 2013/1773, reg 80, Sch 1, Pt 1, paras 1, 32(b), as from 22 July 2013. Subsequently repealed by the Financial Services (Miscellaneous) (Amendment) (EU Exit) Regulations 2019, SI 2019/710, reg 3, as from IP completion day (as defined in the European Union (Withdrawal Agreement) Act 2020, s 39).

Third words omitted repealed by SI 2019/710, reg 3, as from IP completion day (as defined in the European Union (Withdrawal Agreement) Act 2020, s 39).

Words ""emission allowance auctioning regulation"," in square brackets inserted by the Financial Services and Markets Act 2000 (Regulated Activities) (Amendment) Order 2012, SI 2012/1906, art 3(1), (16), as from 20 July 2012.

Fourth words omitted repealed by SI 2004/3379, reg 6(1), (5), as from 11 January 2005.

Fifth and sixth words omitted repealed by SI 2015/575, reg 59, Sch 1, Pt 1, paras 1, 16(a), as from 1 January 2016.

Seventh words omitted originally inserted by the Reinsurance Directive Regulations 2007, SI 2007/3253, reg 2(1), Sch 1, paras 1, 5, as from 10 December 2007. Subsequently repealed by SI 2015/575, reg 59, Sch 1, Pt 1, paras 1, 16(a), as from 1 January 2016.

Words "insurance distribution directive" in square brackets substituted by the Insurance Distribution (Regulated Activities and Miscellaneous Amendments) Order 2018, SI 2018/546, art 18(3), as from 1 October 2018.

Eighth words omitted repealed by the Financial Services and Markets Act 2000 (Markets in Financial Instruments) Regulations 2007, SI 2007/126, reg 3(5), Sch 5, paras 1, 22(a), as from 1 April 2007 (certain purposes), and as from 1 November 2007 (otherwise).

Words ""markets in financial instruments directive"," in square brackets inserted by the Financial Services and Markets Act 2000 (Markets in Financial Instruments) (Modification of Powers) Regulations 2006, SI 2006/2975, regs 2, 11, as from 6 December 2006.

Words ""mortgages directive"," in square brackets inserted by the Mortgage Credit Directive Order 2015, SI 2015/910, Sch 1, para 1(1), (9), as from 21 March 2016.

Words ", "Solvency 2 Directive"" in square brackets inserted by the Solvency 2 Regulations 2015, SI 2015/575, reg 59, Sch 1, Pt 1, paras 1, 16(b), as from 1 January 2016.

Words ", "tied agent"" in square brackets inserted by SI 2007/126, reg 3(5), Sch 5, paras 1, 22(b), as from 1 April 2007 (certain purposes), and as from 1 November 2007 (otherwise).

The word omitted from the end of para (a) was repealed, and para (aa) was inserted, by the Money Market Funds Regulations 2018, SI 2018/698, reg 2(1), (18), as from 21 July 2018. Para (aa) (but not the word "and" at the end) was subsequently repealed by the Collective Investment Schemes (Amendment etc) (EU Exit) Regulations 2019, SI 2019/325, regs 3, 31, as from IP completion day (as defined in the European Union (Withdrawal Agreement) Act 2020, s 39).

[7.715]

[425A Consumers: regulated activities etc carried on by authorised persons

(1) This section has effect for the purposes of the provisions of this Act which apply this section.

(2) "Consumers" means persons . . . —

(a) [who] use, have used or may use any of the services within subsection (3); . . .

(b) [who] have relevant rights or interests in relation to any of those services[; . . .

(c) whose rights, interests or obligations are affected by the level of a regulated benchmark][; or

(d) in respect of whom a person carries on an activity which is specified in article 89G of the Financial Services and Markets Act 2000 (Regulated Activities) Order 2001 (seeking out etc claims) whether that activity, as carried on by that person, is a regulated activity or is, by reason of an exclusion provided for under the 2001 Order or the 2000 Act, not a regulated activity].

(3) The services within this subsection are services provided by—

(a) authorised persons in carrying on regulated activities;

(b) authorised persons who are investment firms, or [qualifying credit institutions], in providing relevant ancillary services; or

(c) persons acting as appointed representatives.

(4) A person ("P") has a "relevant right or interest" in relation to any services within subsection (3) if P has a right or interest—

(a) which is derived from, or is otherwise attributable to, the use of the services by others; or

(b) which may be adversely affected by the use of the services by persons acting on P's behalf or in a fiduciary capacity in relation to P.

(5) If a person is providing a service within subsection (3) as a trustee, the persons who are, have been or may be beneficiaries of the trust are to be treated as persons who use, have used or may use the service.

(6) A person who deals with another person ("A") in the course of A providing a service within subsection (3) is to be treated as using the service.

(7) In this section—

. . .

["regulated benchmark" means a benchmark, as defined in section 22 . . . [(6A)], in relation to which any provision made under section 22(1A) . . . [(c)] has effect;]

"relevant ancillary service" means any service of a kind mentioned in [Part 3A of Schedule 2 to the Financial Services and Markets Act 2000 (Regulated Activities) Order 2001 (SI 2001/544)] the provision of which does not involve the carrying on of a regulated activity.]

NOTES

Inserted, together with s 425B, by the Financial Services Act 2010, s 24(1), (2), Sch 2, Pt 1, paras 1, 32, as from 8 April 2010.

Sub-s (2): first words omitted and words omitted from para (b) repealed, words in square brackets in paras (a), (b) inserted, and para (d) and the preceding word added, by the Financial Services and Markets Act 2000 (Claims Management Activity) Order 2018, SI 2018/1253, art 91(1), (7), as from 1 April 2019 (for provision specifying that the 2018 Order also comes into force on 29 November 2018 for the purposes of the FCA and FOS making rules and issuing guidance, and for transitional provisions in relation to carrying on a claims management activity, etc, see arts 1, 39–89 of the 2018 Order). The word omitted from para (a) was repealed, and para (c) (and the word immediately preceding it) was inserted, by the Financial Services and Markets Act 2000 (Regulated Activities) (Amendment) Order 2013, SI 2013/655, art 3(1), (4)(a), (b), as from 2 April 2013.

Sub-s (3): words in square brackets substituted by the Financial Services and Markets Act 2000 (Amendment) (EU Exit) Regulations 2019, SI 2019/632, regs 84, 91(1), (2), as from IP completion day (as defined in the European Union (Withdrawal Agreement) Act 2020, s 39).

Sub-s (7) is amended as follows:

Definition "credit institution" (omitted) repealed by SI 2019/632, regs 84, 91(1), (3)(a), as from IP completion day (as defined in the European Union (Withdrawal Agreement) Act 2020, s 39).

Definition "regulated benchmark" inserted by SI 2013/655, art 3(1), (4)(c), as from 2 April 2013. The words in square brackets in that definition were inserted by the Financial Services and Markets Act 2000 (Benchmarks) Regulations 2018, SI 2018/135, reg 49(2)(a), (b), as from 27 February 2018. The words omitted were repealed by reg 49(2)(c), (d) of the 2018 Regulations, as from 1 May 2020.

Words in square brackets in the definition "relevant ancillary service" substituted by SI 2019/632, regs 84, 91(1), (3)(b), as from IP completion day (as defined in the European Union (Withdrawal Agreement) Act 2020, s 39).

See also as to the meaning of "consumers", the note to s 1G at **[7.7]**.

[7.716]

[425B Consumers: regulated activities carried on by others

(1) This section has effect for the purposes of the provisions of this Act which apply this section.

(2) "Consumers" means persons who, in relation to regulated activities carried on otherwise than by authorised persons, would be consumers as defined by section 425A if the activities were carried on by authorised persons.]

NOTES

Inserted as noted to s 425A at **[7.715]**.

[7.717]

[425C "Qualifying provision"

[(1)] In this Act "qualifying provision" means a provision of any of the following—

(a) retained direct EU legislation;

(b) technical standards made in accordance with Chapter 2A of Part 9A;

[(ba) other subordinate legislation made under retained direct EU legislation;]

(c) subordinate legislation . . . made by virtue of regulations made under section 8 of the European Union (Withdrawal) Act 2018.

[(2) In this section, "subordinate legislation" has the same meaning as in the Interpretation Act 1978 (see section 21 of that Act).]]

NOTES

Commencement: IP completion day (as defined in the European Union (Withdrawal Agreement) Act 2020, s 39).

Originally inserted by the Financial Services Act 2012, s 48(3), as from 24 January 2013.

Subsequently substituted by the Financial Services and Markets Act 2000 (Amendment) (EU Exit) Regulations 2019, SI 2019/632, regs 84, 92, as from IP completion day (as defined in the European Union (Withdrawal Agreement) Act 2020, s 39). For transitional provisions see the Financial Services (Miscellaneous) (Amendment) (EU Exit) Regulations 2019, SI 2019/710, reg 37 at **[12.110]**.

Sub-s (1) was numbered as such, para (ba) of that subsection was inserted, the words omitted from para (c) of that subsection were repealed, and sub-s (2) was added, by the Financial Services Act 2021, s 43(2), as from 1 July 2021.

426–433 *(Part XXX—Supplemental (ss 426–433 and Schs 20–22) omitted due to space considerations; see further, the introductory notes to this Act.)*

SCHEDULES

[SCHEDULE 1ZA
THE FINANCIAL CONDUCT AUTHORITY

Section 1A

NOTES

Transitional provisions etc in connection with the commencement of the Financial Services Act 2012: For transitional provisions in relation to the commencement of this Schedule, see Part 2 (arts 2–7) of the Financial Services Act 2012 (Transitional Provisions) (Miscellaneous Provisions) Order 2013, SI 2013/442.

Note that only relevant paragraphs of this Schedule are reproduced below. Omitted paragraphs are not annotated.

PART 1 GENERAL

Interpretation

[7.718]

1. In this Schedule—

"the Bank" means the Bank of England;

"functions", in relation to the FCA, means functions conferred on the FCA by or under any provision of this Act (see section 1A(6) which affects the meaning of references to such functions).

Constitution

2. (1) The constitution of the FCA must provide for the FCA to have a governing body.

(2) The governing body must consist of—

(a) a chair appointed by the Treasury,
(b) a chief executive appointed by the Treasury,
(c) the Bank's Deputy Governor for prudential regulation,
(d) 2 members appointed jointly by the Secretary of State and the Treasury, and
(e) at least one other member appointed by the Treasury.

(3) The members referred to in sub-paragraph (2)(a), (c) and (d) are to be non-executive members.

(4) In exercising its powers under sub-paragraph (2)(e) to appoint executive or non-executive members, the Treasury must secure that the majority of members of the governing body are non-executive members.

(5) An employee of the FCA may not be appointed as a non-executive member.

(6) In the following provisions of this Schedule an "appointed member" means a member of the governing body appointed under sub-paragraph (2)(a), (b), (d) or (e).

[2A. (1) The term of office of a person appointed as chief executive under paragraph 2(2)(b) must not begin before—

(a) the person has, in connection with the appointment, appeared before the Treasury Committee of the House of Commons, or
(b) (if earlier) the end of the period of 3 months beginning with the day on which the appointment is made.

[(1A) Appointment as chief executive under paragraph 2(2)(b) is to be for a period of 5 years.]

(2) [Sub-paragraphs (1) and (1A) do] not apply if the person is appointed as chief executive on an acting basis, pending a further appointment being made.

(3) The reference to the Treasury Committee of the House of Commons—

(a) if the name of that Committee is changed, is a reference to that Committee by its new name, and
(b) if the functions of that Committee (or substantially corresponding functions) become functions of a different Committee of the House of Commons, is to be treated as a reference to the Committee by which the functions are exercisable.

(4) Any question arising under sub-paragraph (3) is to be determined by the Speaker of the House of Commons.]

[2B. (1) A person may not be appointed as chief executive under paragraph 2(2)(b) more than twice.

(2) For this purpose an appointment as chief executive on an acting basis, pending a further appointment being made, is to be ignored.]

Arrangements for discharging functions

8. (1) The FCA may make arrangements for any of its functions to be discharged by a committee, sub-committee, officer or member of staff of the FCA, but subject to the following provisions.

(2) In exercising its legislative functions, the FCA must act through its governing body.

(3) For that purpose, the following are the FCA's legislative functions—

(a) making rules [under this Act or under retained direct EU legislation];

(b) . . .

(c) issuing statements under—

(i) section [63ZD,] 63C, . . . 69, 88C, 89S, 93, 124, 131J, 138N, [142V,] 192H, 192N, 210 [or 312J],

(ii) section 345D (whether as a result of section 345(2)[, section 249(1) or 261K(1)]), or

(iii) section 80 of the Financial Services Act 2012;

(d) giving directions under section 316, 318 or 328;

[(e) . . .];

[(f) making technical standards in accordance with Chapter 2A of Part 9A;

(g) making EU Exit instruments under the Financial Regulators' Powers (Technical Standards) (Amendment etc) (EU Exit) Regulations 2018].

[(3A) In exercising its functions under sections 9(2) and 10 of the Financial Guidance and Claims Act 2018 (approving and reviewing standards set by [Money and Pensions Service]), the FCA must act through its governing body.]

(4) The function of issuing general guidance (as defined in section 139B(5) [. . .]) may not be discharged by an officer or member of staff of the FCA.

[(5) In respect of the exercise of a function under Part 1 of the Competition Act 1998, the power in sub-paragraph (1) is subject to provision in rules made under section 51 of that Act by virtue of paragraph 1A of Schedule 9 to that Act.]

NOTES

This Schedule was substituted (together with Sch 1ZB for the original Sch 1) by the Financial Services Act 2012, s 6(2), Sch 3, as from 24 January 2013 (in so far as relating to the preparation of a scheme under para 21 of this Schedule or the making of rules), as from 19 February 2013 (paras 2, 3 for the purposes of making appointments), and as from 1 April 2013 (otherwise); for transitional provisions and savings in relation to the transfer of the FSA's functions, property, rights and liabilities, see s 119 of, and Schs 20, 21 to, the 2012 Act.

Para 2A: inserted by the Bank of England and Financial Services Act 2016, s 18, as from 6 July 2016. Sub-para (1A) was inserted, and the words in square brackets in sub-para (2) were substituted, by the Financial Services Act 2021, s 42(2), as from 29 June 2021.

Para 2B: inserted by the Financial Services Act 2021, s 42(3), as from 29 June 2021.

Para 8 is amended as follows:

The words in square brackets in sub-para (3)(a) were inserted by the Financial Services Act 2021, s 43(3), as from 1 July 2021.

Sub-para (3)(b) repealed by the Financial Services and Markets Act 2000 (Market Abuse) Regulations 2016, SI 2016/680, reg 10(1), (22), as from 3 July 2016.

The figure omitted from sub-para (3)(c)(i) was repealed, and the figure "63ZD," in square brackets in that sub-paragraph was inserted, by the Financial Services (Banking Reform) Act 2013, s 35, Sch 3, para 16, as from 25 July 2014 (in so far as relating to the insertion of the figure "63ZD,"), and as from 7 March 2016 (otherwise).

The figure "142V," in square brackets in sub-para (3)(c)(i) was inserted by the Financial Services (Banking Reform) Act 2013, s 4(6), as from 1 January 2019.

The words "or 312J" in square brackets in sub-para (3)(c)(i) were substituted, sub-para (3)(e) and the words omitted from sub-para (4) were repealed, and sub-para (3A) was inserted, by the Financial Guidance and Claims Act 2018, s 25, Sch 3, paras 5, 21(1), (2), as from 1 October 2018 (in so far as relating to the insertion of sub-para (3A)), and as from 1 January 2019 (otherwise). Note that sub-para (3)(e) was originally inserted, and the words in square brackets in sub-para (4) were originally inserted, by the Pension Schemes Act 2015, s 47, Sch 3, paras 1, 13, as from 3 March 2015.

The words in square brackets in sub-para (3)(c)(ii) were inserted by the Collective Investment in Transferable Securities (Contractual Scheme) Regulations 2013, SI 2013/1388, reg 3(1), (21), as from 6 June 2013.

Sub-paras (3)(f), (g) were added by the Financial Regulators' Powers (Technical Standards etc) (Amendment etc) (EU Exit) Regulations 2018, SI 2018/1115, reg 7(1), (9)(a), as from 26 October 2018.

Words "Money and Pensions Service" in square brackets in sub-para (3A) substituted by the Financial Guidance and Claims Act 2018 (Naming and Consequential Amendments) Regulations 2019, SI 2019/383, reg 3, Schedule, Pt 1, para 7(d), as from 6 April 2019.

Sub-para (5) added by the Financial Services (Banking Reform) Act 2013, s 129, Sch 8, Pt 1, para 7(1), (2), as from 1 November 2014.

Para 11: sub-para (1)(ha) inserted by the Financial Services (Banking Reform) Act 2013, s 131(2), as from 18 February 2014. Sub-para (1)(hb) originally inserted by the Pension Schemes Act 2015, s 47, Sch 3, paras 1, 14, as from 3 March 2015. Sub-para (1)(hb) and the word omitted from sub-para (1)(i) repealed, and sub-para (1)(ia) inserted, by the Financial Guidance and Claims Act 2018, s 25, Sch 3, paras 5, 21(1), (3), as from 1 October 2018 (in so far as relating to the repeal in sub-para (1)(i), and the insertion of sub-para (1)(ia)), and as from 1 January 2019 (otherwise).

Rule-making instrument: designating instruments made in accordance with the Financial Services Act 2012 (Transitional Provisions) (Rules and Miscellaneous Provisions) Order 2013, SI 2013/161 and the Financial Services and Markets Act 2000 (Regulated Activities) (Amendment) (No 2) Order 2013, SI 2013/1881 are to be treated as rule-making instruments for the purposes of para 8(2) above (see arts 3 and 64 of those Orders respectively).

[PART 4 MISCELLANEOUS

Exemption from liability in damages

[7.719]

25. (1) None of the following is to be liable in damages for anything done or omitted in the discharge, or purported discharge, of the FCA's functions—

(a) the FCA;

(b) any person ("P") who is, or is acting as, a member, officer or member of staff of the FCA;

(c) any person who could be held vicariously liable for things done or omitted by P, but only in so far as the liability relates to P's conduct.

[(1A) In sub-paragraph (1) the reference to the FCA's functions includes its functions under Part 5 of the Financial Services (Banking Reform) Act 2013 (regulation of payment systems).]

(2) Anything done or omitted by a person mentioned in sub-paragraph (1)(a) or (b) while acting, or purporting to act, as a result of an appointment under any of sections 166 to 169 is to be taken for the purposes of sub-paragraph (1) to have been done or omitted in the discharge, or as the case may be purported discharge, of the FCA's functions.

(3) Sub-paragraph (1) does not apply—
- (a) if the act or omission is shown to have been in bad faith, or
- (b) so as to prevent an award of damages made in respect of an act or omission on the ground that the act or omission was unlawful as a result of section 6(1) of the Human Rights Act 1998.

NOTES

Substituted as noted to Part 1 of this Schedule at **[7.718]**.

Para 25: sub-para (1A) inserted by the Financial Services (Banking Reform) Act 2013, s 109(1), as from 1 March 2014.

SCHEDULES 1ZB, 1A

(Sch 1ZB—The Prudential Regulation Authority is omitted due to space considerations; see further, the introductory notes to this Act. Sch 1A—Further Provision about the Consumer Financial Education Body (as inserted by the Financial Services Act 2010) was repealed by the Financial Guidance and Claims Act 2018, s 25, Sch 3, paras 5, 22, as from 6 April 2021.)

SCHEDULE 2
REGULATED ACTIVITIES

Section 22(2)

NOTES

The regulated activities for the purposes of s 22 of this Act are set out in the Financial Services and Markets Act 2000 (Regulated Activities) Order 2001, SI 2001/544 at **[8.1]**.

PART I [REGULATED ACTIVITIES: GENERAL]

General

[7.720]

1. The matters with respect to which provision may be made under section 22(1) in respect of activities include, in particular, those described in general terms in this Part of this Schedule.

Dealing in investments

2. (1) Buying, selling, subscribing for or underwriting investments or offering or agreeing to do so, either as a principal or as an agent.

(2) In the case of an investment which is a contract of insurance, that includes carrying out the contract.

Arranging deals in investments

3. Making, or offering or agreeing to make—
- (a) arrangements with a view to another person buying, selling, subscribing for or underwriting a particular investment;
- (b) arrangements with a view to a person who participates in the arrangements buying, selling, subscribing for or underwriting investments.

Deposit taking

4. Accepting deposits.

Safekeeping and administration of assets

5. (1) Safeguarding and administering assets belonging to another which consist of or include investments or offering or agreeing to do so.

(2) Arranging for the safeguarding and administration of assets belonging to another, or offering or agreeing to do so.

Managing investments

6. Managing, or offering or agreeing to manage, assets belonging to another person where—
- (a) the assets consist of or include investments; or
- (b) the arrangements for their management are such that the assets may consist of or include investments at the discretion of the person managing or offering or agreeing to manage them.

Investment advice

7. Giving or offering or agreeing to give advice to persons on—
- (a) buying, selling, subscribing for or underwriting an investment; or
- (b) exercising any right conferred by an investment to acquire, dispose of, underwrite or convert an investment.

Establishing collective investment schemes

8. Establishing, operating or winding up a collective investment scheme, including acting as—
- (a) trustee of a unit trust scheme;
- (b) depositary of a collective investment scheme other than a unit trust scheme; or
- (c) sole director of a body incorporated by virtue of regulations under section 262.

Using computer-based systems for giving investment instructions

9. (1) Sending on behalf of another person instructions relating to an investment by means of a computer-based system which enables investments to be transferred without a written instrument.

(2) Offering or agreeing to send such instructions by such means on behalf of another person.

(3) Causing such instructions to be sent by such means on behalf of another person.

(4) Offering or agreeing to cause such instructions to be sent by such means on behalf of another person.

NOTES

Part heading: words in square brackets substituted by the Dormant Bank and Building Society Accounts Act 2008, s 15, Sch 2, para 1(1), (2), as from 12 March 2009.

[PART 1A REGULATED ACTIVITIES: RECLAIM FUNDS

Activities of reclaim funds

[7.721]

9A. (1) The matters with respect to which provision may be made under section 22(1) in respect of activities include, in particular, any of the activities of a reclaim fund.

(2) "Reclaim fund" has the meaning given by section 5(1) of the Dormant Bank and Building Society Accounts Act 2008.]

NOTES

Part 1A was inserted by the Dormant Bank and Building Society Accounts Act 2008, s 15, Sch 2, para 1(1), (3), as from 12 March 2009.

PART II INVESTMENTS

General

[7.722]

10. The matters with respect to which provision may be made under section 22(1) in respect of investments include, in particular, those described in general terms in this Part of this Schedule.

Securities

11. (1) Shares or stock in the share capital of a company.

(2) "Company" includes—

(a) any body corporate (wherever incorporated), and

(b) any unincorporated body constituted under the law of a country or territory outside the United Kingdom, other than an open-ended investment company.

Instruments creating or acknowledging indebtedness

12. Any of the following—

(a) debentures;

(b) debenture stock;

(c) loan stock;

(d) bonds;

(e) certificates of deposit;

(f) any other instruments creating or acknowledging a present or future indebtedness.

Government and public securities

13. (1) Loan stock, bonds and other instruments—

(a) creating or acknowledging indebtedness; and

(b) issued by or on behalf of a government, local authority or public authority.

(2) "Government, local authority or public authority" means—

(a) the government of the United Kingdom, of Northern Ireland, or of any country or territory outside the United Kingdom;

(b) a local authority in the United Kingdom or elsewhere;

(c) any international organisation the members of which include the United Kingdom . . .

Instruments giving entitlement to investments

14. (1) Warrants or other instruments entitling the holder to subscribe for any investment.

(2) It is immaterial whether the investment is in existence or identifiable.

Certificates representing securities

15. Certificates or other instruments which confer contractual or property rights—

(a) in respect of any investment held by someone other than the person on whom the rights are conferred by the certificate or other instrument; and

(b) the transfer of which may be effected without requiring the consent of that person.

Units in collective investment schemes

16. (1) Shares in or securities of an open-ended investment company.

(2) Any right to participate in a collective investment scheme.

Options

17. Options to acquire or dispose of property.

Futures

18. Rights under a contract for the sale of a commodity or property of any other description under which delivery is to be made at a future date.

Contracts for differences

19. Rights under—

(a) a contract for differences; or

(b) any other contract the purpose or pretended purpose of which is to secure a profit or avoid a loss by reference to fluctuations in—

(i) the value or price of property of any description; or

(ii) an index or other factor designated for that purpose in the contract.

Contracts of insurance

20. Rights under a contract of insurance, including rights under contracts falling within head C of Schedule 2 to the Friendly Societies Act 1992.

Participation in Lloyd's syndicates

21. (1) The underwriting capacity of a Lloyd's syndicate.

(2) A person's membership (or prospective membership) of a Lloyd's syndicate.

Deposits

22. Rights under any contract under which a sum of money (whether or not denominated in a currency) is paid on terms under which it will be repaid, with or without interest or a premium, and either on demand or at a time or in circumstances agreed by or on behalf of the person making the payment and the person receiving it.

[Loans and other forms of credit

23. (1) Rights under any contract under which one person provides another with credit.

(2) "Credit" includes any cash loan or other financial accommodation.

(3) "Cash" includes money in any form.

(4) It is immaterial for the purposes of sub-paragraph (1) whether or not the obligation of the borrower is secured on property of any kind.]

[Other finance arrangements involving land

23A. (1) Rights under any arrangement for the provision of finance under which the person providing the finance either—

(a) acquires a major interest in land from the person to whom the finance is provided, or

(b) disposes of a major interest in land to that person,

as part of the arrangement.

(2) References in sub-paragraph (1) to a "major interest" in land are to—

(a) in relation to land in England or Wales—

(i) an estate in fee simple absolute, or

(ii) a term of years absolute,

whether subsisting at law or in equity;

(b) in relation to land in Scotland—

(i) the interest of an owner of land, or

(ii) the tenant's right over or interest in a property subject to a lease;

(c) in relation to land in Northern Ireland—

(i) any freehold estate, or

(ii) any leasehold estate,

whether subsisting at law or in equity.

(3) It is immaterial for the purposes of sub-paragraph (1) whether either party acquires or (as the case may be) disposes of the interest in land—

(a) directly, or

(b) indirectly.]

[Contracts for hire of goods

23B. (1) Rights under a contract for the bailment or (in Scotland) hiring of goods to a person other than a body corporate.

(2) "Goods" has the meaning given in section 61(1) of the Sale of Goods Act 1979.

(3) It is immaterial for the purposes of sub-paragraph (1) whether the rights of the person to whom the goods are bailed or hired have been assigned to a body corporate.]

Rights in investments

24. Any right or interest in anything which is an investment as a result of any other provision made under section 22(1).

NOTES

Para 13: words omitted from sub-para (2)(c) repealed by the Financial Services and Markets Act 2000 (Amendment) (EU Exit) Regulations 2019, SI 2019/632, reg 95, as from IP completion day (as defined in the European Union (Withdrawal Agreement) Act 2020, s 39).

Para 23: substituted by the Financial Services Act 2012, s 7(2), (3), as from 24 January 2013.

Para 23A: inserted by the Regulation of Financial Services (Land Transactions) Act 2005, s 1, as from 19 February 2006.

Para 23B: inserted by the Financial Services Act 2012, s 7(2), (4), as from 24 January 2013.

Modifications to para 12(e): (i) a reference to a certificate of deposit includes a reference to uncertificated units of an eligible debt security where the issue of those units corresponds, in accordance with the current terms of issue of the security, to the issue of a certificate of deposit which is a certificate of deposit for the purposes of that enactment; (ii) a reference to an amount stated in a certificate of deposit includes a reference to a principal amount stated in, or determined in accordance with, the current terms of issue of an eligible debt security of the kind referred to in (i) above; see the Uncertificated Securities (Amendment) (Eligible Debt Securities) Regulations 2003, SI 2003/1633, reg 15, Sch 2, para 6.

Modifications to para 12(f): the reference to securities, instruments or investments creating or acknowledging indebtedness (or creating or acknowledging a present or future indebtedness) includes a reference to uncertificated units of eligible debt securities; see SI 2003/1633, reg 15, Sch 2, para 8.

[PART 2A REGULATED ACTIVITIES RELATING TO INFORMATION ABOUT PERSONS' FINANCIAL STANDING

General

[7.723]

24A. The matters with respect to which provision may be made under section 22(1A)(a) include, in particular, those described in general terms in this Part of this Schedule.

Providing credit reference services

24B. Furnishing persons with information that—

(a) is relevant to the financial standing of persons other than bodies corporate, and
(b) is collected for that purpose by the person furnishing it.

Providing credit information services

24C. (1) Taking steps on behalf of a person other than a body corporate in connection with information relevant to that person's financial standing that is or may be held by a [person who is carrying on a regulated activity].

(2) . . .

24D. Giving advice to a person other than a body corporate in relation to the taking of any steps of the kind mentioned in paragraph 24C(1).]

NOTES

Inserted, together with Part 2B of this Schedule, by the Financial Services Act 2012, s 7(2), (5), as from 24 January 2013.

Para 24C: words in square brackets in sub-para (1) substituted, and sub-para (2) repealed, by the Financial Services and Markets Act 2000 (Regulated Activities) (Amendment) (No 2) Order 2013, SI 2013/1881, art 10(1), (17), as from 1 April 2014.

[PART 2B

(Inserted as noted to Part 2A ante. Repealed by the Financial Services and Markets Act 2000 (Benchmarks) Regulations 2018, SI 2018/135, reg 50, as from 1 May 2020.)

PART III SUPPLEMENTAL PROVISIONS

The order-making power

[7.724]

25. (1) An order under section 22(1) [to (1B)] may—

(a) provide for exemptions;
(b) confer powers on the Treasury or [either regulator];
(c) authorise the making of regulations or other instruments by the Treasury for purposes of, or connected with, any relevant provision;
(d) authorise the making of rules or other instruments by [either regulator] for purposes of, or connected with, any relevant provision;
(e) make provision in respect of any information or document which, in the opinion of the Treasury or [either regulator], is relevant for purposes of, or connected with, any relevant provision;
(f) make such consequential, transitional or supplemental provision as the Treasury consider appropriate for purposes of, or connected with, any relevant provision[, including provision which applies (with or without modification) provision in this Act or other primary or subordinate legislation that relates to investment activity or financial services to a regulated activity that does not relate to investment activity or financial services].

(2) Provision made as a result of sub-paragraph (1)(f) may amend any primary or subordinate legislation, including any provision of, or made under, this Act.

(3) "Relevant provision" means any provision—

(a) of section 22 or this Schedule; or
(b) made under that section or this Schedule.

[Parliamentary control

26. (1) This paragraph applies to any order made under section 22(1) [to (1B)] which contains a statement by the Treasury that, in their opinion, the effect (or one of the effects) of the proposed order would be that an activity which is not a regulated activity would become a regulated activity.

(2) No order to which this paragraph applies may be made unless—

(a) a draft of the order has been laid before Parliament and approved by a resolution of each House, or
(b) sub-paragraph (4) applies.

(3) Sub-paragraph (4) applies if an order to which this paragraph applies also contains a statement that the Treasury are of the opinion that, by reason of urgency, it is necessary to make the order without a draft being so laid and approved.

(4) Where this sub-paragraph applies the order—

(a) must be laid before Parliament after being made, and
(b) ceases to have effect at the end of the relevant period unless before the end of that period the order is approved by a resolution of each House of Parliament (but without that affecting anything done under the order or the power to make a new order).

(5) The "relevant period" is a period of 28 days beginning with the day on which the order is made.

(6) In calculating the relevant period no account is to be taken of any time during which Parliament is dissolved or prorogued or during which both Houses are adjourned for more than 4 days.]

Interpretation

27. (1) In this Schedule—

"buying" includes acquiring for valuable consideration;

"offering" includes inviting to treat;

"property" includes currency of the United Kingdom or any other country or territory; and

"selling" includes disposing for valuable consideration.

(2) In sub-paragraph (1) "disposing" includes—

(a) in the case of an investment consisting of rights under a contract—

(i) surrendering, assigning or converting those rights; or

(ii) assuming the corresponding liabilities under the contract;

(b) in the case of an investment consisting of rights under other arrangements, assuming the corresponding liabilities under the contract or arrangements;

(c) in the case of any other investment, issuing or creating the investment or granting the rights or interests of which it consists.

(3) In this Schedule references to an instrument include references to any record (whether or not in the form of a document).

NOTES

Para 25: words in first pair of square brackets in sub-para (1) substituted, and words in square brackets in sub-para (1)(f) inserted, by the Financial Guidance and Claims Act 2018, s 27(1), (13)(a), as from 6 October 2018 (for transitional provisions in relation to the transfer of regulation of claims management services to the FCA, see Sch 5 to the 2018 Act). Words in square brackets in sub-paras (1)(b), (d), (e) substituted by the Financial Services Act 2012, 8(1), (2), as from 24 January 2013.

Para 26: substituted by the Financial Services Act 2012, s 8(1), (3), as from 24 January 2013. Words in square brackets in sub-para (1) substituted by the Financial Guidance and Claims Act 2018, s 27(1), (13)(b), as from 6 October 2018 (for transitional provisions in relation to the transfer of regulation of claims management services to the FCA, see Sch 5 to the 2018 Act).

Orders: as to Orders made under para 25 above, see that section at **[7.60]**.

SCHEDULES 2A, 2B

(Schedule 2A—Gibraltar-Based Persons Carrying on Activities in the UK, and Schedule 2B—UK-Based Persons Carrying on Activities in Gibraltar are omitted due to space considerations.)

SCHEDULE 3
EEA PASSPORT RIGHTS

Sections 31(1)(b) and 37

NOTES

Transitional provisions etc in connection with the commencement of the Financial Services Act 2012: for transitional provisions see Chapter 1 of Part 5 of the Financial Services Act 2012 (Transitional Provisions) (Permission and Approval) Order 2013, SI 2013/440. Article 15 concerns cases where, before 1 April 2013, an EEA firm satisfied the establishment conditions in para 13 of this Schedule (establishment) or the services conditions in para 14 (services). Article 16 contains transitional provisions in relation to requests made, before 1 April 2013, to the FSA under s 34(2). Article 17 contains tops in relation to an EEA firm which, before that date, was seeking to establish a branch as mentioned in para 12(1) (firms qualifying for authorisation). Article 18 applies to EEA firms which, before that date, were seeking to provide services as mentioned in para 12(2). Article 19 and 20 contain transitional provisions in relation to cases where the FSA received a notice of intention within the meaning of para 19(2) (establishment) and para 20(1) (services) respectively.

Transitional provisions etc in connection with the original commencement of this Act: the Financial Services and Markets Act 2000 (Transitional Provisions) (Authorised Persons etc) Order 2001, SI 2001/2636, Pt II, Chapter II, provides that EEA firms with "passports" before 1 December 2001 under the Insurance Companies Act 1982, the Banking Coordination (Second Council Directive) Regulations 1992, SI 1992/3218, or the Investment Services Regulations 1995, SI 1995/3275, are to be treated after that date as having complied with the procedures in this Schedule. In relation to UK firms with "passports" before 1 December 2001, see art 77 of the 2001 Order. The 1982 Act was repealed, and SI 1992/3218 and SI 1995/3275 were revoked, by the Financial Services and Markets Act 2000 (Consequential Amendments and Repeals) Order 2001, SI 2001/3649, art 3(1)(b), (2)(a), (c).

Note (repeal of this Schedule): ss 31(1)(b) and 37 of this Act (the enabling provisions of this Schedule) were both repealed by the EEA Passport Rights (Amendment, etc, and Transitional Provisions) (EU Exit) Regulations 2018, SI 2018/1149, reg 2, as from IP completion day (as defined in the European Union (Withdrawal Agreement) Act 2020, s 39). That regulation also specifically repeals Parts II and III of this Schedule, but it does not repeal this Part.

PART I DEFINED TERMS

The single market directives

[7.725]

1. "The single market directives" means—

[(a) the capital requirements directive;]

[(c) the Solvency 2 Directive;]

[(ca) . . .]

(d) the [markets in financial instruments directive][; . . .

(e) [the insurance distribution directive]][; . . .

(f) the UCITS directive][; . . .

(g) the alternative investment fund managers directive] [; and

(h) the mortgages directive.]

. . .

[2. . . .]

[The Solvency 2 Directive

3. "The Solvency 2 Directive" means Directive 2009/138/EC of the European Parliament and of the Council of 25 November 2009 on the taking-up and pursuit of the business of Insurance and Reinsurance (Solvency II).].

[. . .

3A. . . .]

. . .

4. . . .

[The insurance distribution directive

4A. "The insurance distribution directive" means Directive (EU) 2016/97 of the European Parliament and of the Council of 20 January 2016 on insurance distribution (recast) as amended by Directive (EU) 2018/411 of the European Parliament and of the Council of 14 March 2018.]

[The UCITS directive

4B. "The UCITS directive" means the Directive of the European Parliament and of the Council of 13 July 2009 on the coordination of laws, regulations and administrative provisions relating to undertakings for collective investment in transferable securities (No 2009/65/EC)[, as amended by Directive 2014/91/EU of the European Parliament and of the Council of 23rd July 2014].]

[The markets in financial instruments directive

4C. "The markets in financial instruments directive" means Directive 2014/65/EU of the European Parliament and of the Council of 15 May 2014 on markets in financial instruments.]]

[The emission allowance auctioning regulation

4D. "The emission allowance auctioning regulation" means Commission Regulation (EU) No 1031/2010 of 12 November 2010 on the timing, administration and other aspects of auctioning of greenhouse gas emission allowances pursuant to Directive 2003/87/EC of the European Parliament and of the Council of 13 October 2003 establishing a scheme for greenhouse gas emission allowance trading within the Community.]

[The alternative investment fund managers directive

4E. "The alternative investment fund managers directive" means Directive 2011/61/EU of the European Parliament and of the Council of 8 June 2011 on Alternative Investment Fund Managers.]

[The mortgages directive

4F. "The mortgages directive" means Directive 2014/17/EU of the European Parliament and of the Council of 4th February 2014 on credit agreements for consumers relating to residential immovable property and amending Directives 2008/48/EC and 2013/36/EU and Regulation (EU) No 1093/2010.]

EEA firm

5. "EEA firm" means any of the following if it does not have its [relevant office] in the United Kingdom—

(a) an investment firm (as defined in [Article 4.1.1 of the markets in financial instruments directive]) which is authorised (within the meaning of [Article 5]) by its home state regulator;

[(b) a credit institution (as defined in Article 4(1)(1) of the capital requirements regulation) which is authorised (within the meaning of Article 8 of the capital requirements directive) by its home state regulator;]

[(c) a financial institution (as defined in Article 4(1)(26) of the capital requirements regulation) which is a subsidiary of the kind mentioned in Article 34 of the capital requirements directive and which fulfils the conditions of that Article;]

[(d) an undertaking pursuing the activity of direct insurance (within the meaning of Article 2 of the Solvency 2 Directive) which has received authorisation under Article 14 of that directive from its home state regulator;

(da) an undertaking pursuing the activity of reinsurance (within the meaning of Article 2 of the Solvency 2 Directive) as a reinsurance undertaking which has received authorisation under Article 14 of that directive from its home state regulator;]

[(e) an insurance intermediary (as defined in Article 2.1(3) of the insurance distribution directive), an ancillary insurance intermediary (as defined in Article 2.1(4) of that directive) or a reinsurance intermediary (as defined in Article 2.1(5) of that directive), which is registered with its home state regulator under Article 3 of that directive;]

[(f) a management company (as defined in paragraph 11B) which is authorised (within the meaning of Article 6 of the UCITS directive) by its home state regulator]][; . . .

(g) a person who has received authorisation under Article 18.2 of the emission allowance auctioning regulation]][; . . .

(h) an AIFM (as defined in Article 4.1(b) of the alternative investment fund managers directive) which is authorised (in accordance with *Article 6.1 of* that directive) by its home state regulator] [; or

(i) a mortgage intermediary which is admitted (in accordance with Article 29(1) of the mortgages directive) by its home state regulator to carry out all or part of the credit intermediation activities set out in Article 4(5) of that directive or to provide advisory services (as defined in Article 4(21) of that directive).]

[5A. In paragraph 5, "relevant office" means—

(a) in relation to a firm falling within sub-paragraph (e) [or (i)] of that paragraph which has a registered office, its registered office;

[(aa) in relation to a firm falling within sub-paragraph (h) of that paragraph, its registered office;]

(b) in relation to any other firm, its head office.]

. . .

[6. . . .]

EEA right

7. "EEA right" means the entitlement of a person to establish a branch, or provide services, in an EEA State other than that in which he has his [relevant office]—

(a) in accordance with the Treaty as applied in the EEA; and
(b) subject to the conditions of the relevant single market directive [or, as the case may be, the emission allowance auctioning regulation].

[7A. In paragraph 7, "relevant office" means—

(a) in relation to a person who has a registered office and whose entitlement is subject to the conditions of the [insurance distribution directive] [or the mortgages directive], his registered office;
[(aa) in relation to a person whose entitlement is subject to the conditions of the alternative investment fund managers directive, its registered office;]
(b) in relation to any other person, his head office.]

EEA State

[8. "EEA State" has the meaning given by Schedule 1 to the Interpretation Act 1978.]

Home state regulator

9. "Home state regulator" means the competent authority (within the meaning of the relevant single market directive [or, as the case may be, the emission allowance auctioning regulation]) of an EEA State (other than the United Kingdom) in relation to the EEA firm concerned.

UK firm

10. "UK firm" means a person whose [relevant office] is in the UK and who has an EEA right to carry on activity in an EEA State other than the United Kingdom.

[10A. In paragraph 10, "relevant office" means—

(a) in relation to a firm whose EEA right derives from the [insurance distribution directive] and which has a registered office, its registered office;
[(aa) in relation to a firm whose EEA right derives from the alternative investment fund managers directive, its registered office;]
(b) in relation to any other firm, its head office.]

[UK investment firm

10B. "UK investment firm" means a UK firm—

(a) which is an investment firm, and
(b) whose EEA right derives from the markets in financial instruments directive.]

11. "Host state regulator" means the competent authority (within the meaning of the relevant single market directive [or, as the case may be, the emission allowance auctioning regulation]) of an EEA State (other than the United Kingdom) in relation to a UK firm's exercise of EEA rights there.

[Tied agent

11A. "Tied agent" has the meaning given in Article [4.1.29] of the markets in financial instruments directive.]

[Management company

11B. "Management company" has the meaning given in Article 2.1(b) of the UCITS directive.]

. . .

11C. . . .]

[. . .

11D. . . .]

NOTES

Para 1 is amended as follows:

Sub-para (a) was substituted (for the original sub-paras (a), (b)) by the Banking Consolidation Directive (Consequential Amendments) Regulations 2000, SI 2000/2952, reg 8(1), (5)(a), as from 22 November 2000; and was further substituted by the Capital Requirements Regulations 2013, SI 2013/3115, reg 46(1), Sch 2, Pt 1, paras 1, 29(1), (2), as from 1 January 2014.

Sub-para (c) substituted by the Solvency 2 Regulations 2015, SI 2015/575, reg 59, Sch 1, Pt 1, paras 1, 17(1), (2)(a), as from 1 January 2016.

Sub-para (ca) originally inserted by the Reinsurance Directive Regulations 2007, SI 2007/3253, reg 2(1), Sch 1, paras 1, 6(a), as from 10 December 2007; and subsequently repealed by SI 2015/575, reg 59, Sch 1, Pt 1, paras 1, 17(1), (2)(b), as from 1 January 2016.

Words in square brackets in sub-para (d) substituted by the Financial Services and Markets Act 2000 (Markets in Financial Instruments) Regulations 2007, SI 2007/126, reg 3(4), Sch 4, paras 1, 2, as from 1 April 2007 (certain purposes), and as from 1 November 2007 (otherwise).

Word omitted from sub-para (d) repealed, and sub-para (f) and the word immediately preceding it inserted, by the Collective Investment Schemes (Miscellaneous Amendments) Regulations 2003, SI 2003/2066, reg 2(2)(a), as from 13 February 2004.

Sub-para (e) and the word immediately preceding it inserted by the Insurance Mediation Directive (Miscellaneous Amendments) Regulations 2003, SI 2003/1473, reg 2(2)(a), as from 14 January 2005.

Words "the insurance distribution directive" in square brackets in sub-para (e) substituted by the Insurance Distribution (Regulated Activities and Miscellaneous Amendments) Order 2018, SI 2018/546, arts 9, 17(1), (2), as from 1 October 2018.

The word omitted from sub-para (e) was repealed, and sub-para (g) and the preceding word were inserted, by the Alternative Investment Fund Managers Regulations 2013, SI 2013/1773, reg 80, Sch 1, Part 1, paras 1, 34(1), (2), as from 22 July 2013.

The word omitted from sub-para (f) was repealed, and sub-para (h) and the preceding word were inserted, by the Mortgage Credit Directive Order 2015, SI 2015/910, Sch 1, para 1(1), (10)(a), as from 21 March 2016.

Para 2: originally substituted by the Capital Requirements Regulations 2006, SI 2006/3221, reg 29(1), Sch 3, para 2(1), (2), as from 1 January 2007; and subsequently repealed by SI 2013/3115, reg 46(1), Sch 2, Pt 1, paras 1, 29(1), (3), as from 1 January 2014.

Para 3: substituted by SI 2015/575, reg 59, Sch 1, Pt 1, paras 1, 17(1), (3), as from 1 January 2016.

Para 3A: originally inserted by SI 2007/3253, reg 2(1), Sch 1, paras 1, 6(b), as from 10 December 2007; and subsequently repealed by SI 2015/575, reg 59, Sch 1, Pt 1, paras 1, 17(1), (4), as from 1 January 2016.

Para 4: repealed by SI 2007/126, reg 3(4), Sch 4, paras 1, 3, as from 1 April 2007 (certain purposes), and as from 1 November 2007 (otherwise).

Para 4A: originally inserted by SI 2003/1473, reg 2(2)(b), as from 14 January 2005; and subsequently substituted by SI 2018/546, arts 9, 17(1), (3), as from 1 October 2018.

Para 4B: originally inserted by SI 2003/2066, reg 2(2)(b), as from 13 February 2004; and subsequently substituted by the Undertakings for Collective Investment in Transferable Securities Regulations 2011, SI 2011/1613, reg 2(1), (33)(a), as from 1 July 2011. Words in square brackets inserted by the Undertakings for Collective Investment in Transferable Securities Regulations 2016, SI 2016/225, reg 2(1), (9), as from 18 March 2016.

Para 4C: originally inserted by the Financial Services and Markets Act 2000 (Markets in Financial Instruments) (Modification of Powers) Regulations 2006, SI 2006/2975, regs 2, 13, as from 6 December 2006. Subsequently substituted by the Financial Services and Markets Act 2000 (Markets in Financial Instruments) Regulations 2017, SI 2017/701, reg 50(1), Sch 2, paras 1, 54(1), (2), as from 3 January 2018 (note that various provisions of the 2017 Regulations came into force on earlier dates for the purposes of making rules, giving notices and consent, etc (for details see reg 1 of the 2017 Regulations)).

Para 4D: inserted by the Financial Services and Markets Act 2000 (Regulated Activities) (Amendment) Order 2012, SI 2012/1906, art 4(1), (2), as from 20 July 2012.

Para 4E: inserted by SI 2013/1773, reg 80, Sch 1, Part 1, paras 1, 34(1), (3), (8), as from 22 July 2013.

Para 4F: inserted by SI 2015/910, Sch 1, para 1(1), (10)(b), as from 21 March 2016.

Para 5 is amended as follows:

Words in first pair of square brackets substituted, and sub-para (e) (and the word immediately preceding it) inserted, by SI 2003/1473, reg 2(2)(c), as from 14 January 2005.

Words in square brackets in sub-para (a) substituted by SI 2007/126, reg 3(4), Sch 4, paras 1, 4, as from 1 April 2007 (certain purposes), and as from 1 November 2007 (otherwise).

Sub-paras (b), (c) substituted by SI 2013/3115, reg 46(1), Sch 2, Pt 1, paras 1, 29(1), (4), as from 1 January 2014.

Sub-paras (d), (da) substituted by SI 2015/575, reg 59, Sch 1, Pt 1, paras 1, 17(1), (5), as from 1 January 2016. Sub-para (da) was originally inserted by SI 2007/3253, reg 2(1), Sch 1, paras 1, 6(c), as from 10 December 2007.

Sub-para (e) substituted by SI 2018/546, arts 9, 17(1), (4), as from 1 October 2018.

Sub-para (f) and the word immediately preceding it inserted by SI 2003/2066, reg 2(2)(c), as from 13 February 2004.

Sub-para (f) subsequently substituted by SI 2011/1613, reg 2(1), (33)(b), as from 1 July 2011.

The word omitted from sub-para (f) was repealed, and sub-para (h) and the preceding word were inserted, by SI 2013/1773, reg 80, Sch 1, Part 1, paras 1, 34(1), (4), as from 22 July 2013.

Sub-para (g) and the word immediately preceding it inserted by SI 2012/1906, art 4(1), (3), as from 20 July 2012.

The word omitted from sub-para (g) was repealed, and sub-para (i) and the preceding word were added, by SI 2015/910, Sch 1, para 1(1), (10)(c), as from 21 March 2016.

Words in italics in sub-para (h) repealed by the Alternative Investment Fund Managers (Amendment) Regulations 2013, SI 2013/1797, reg 3, Sch 1, para 1(1), (5)(a), as from a day to be appointed.

Para 5A: inserted by SI 2003/1473, reg 2(2)(d), as from 14 January 2005. Words in square brackets in sub-para (a) inserted by SI 2015/910, Sch 1, para 1(1), (10)(d), as from 21 March 2016. Sub-para (aa) inserted by SI 2013/1773, reg 80, Sch 1, Part 1, paras 1, 34(1), (5), as from 22 July 2013.

Para 6: substituted by SI 2003/1473, reg 2(2)(e), as from 14 January 2005. Subsequently repealed by the Financial Services (Miscellaneous) (Amendment) (EU Exit) Regulations 2019, SI 2019/710, reg 3, as from IP completion day (as defined in the European Union (Withdrawal Agreement) Act 2020, s 39).

Para 7: words in first pair of square brackets substituted by SI 2003/1473, reg 2(2)(f), as from 14 January 2005. Words in second pair of square brackets inserted by SI 2012/1906, art 4(1), (4), as from 20 July 2012.

Para 7A: inserted by SI 2003/1473, reg 2(2)(g), as from 14 January 2005. Words in first pair of square brackets in sub-para (a) substituted by SI 2018/546, arts 9, 17(1), (6), as from 1 October 2018. Words in second pair of square brackets in sub-para (a) inserted by SI 2015/910, Sch 1, para 1(1), (10)(e), as from 21 March 2016. Sub-para (aa) originally inserted by SI 2013/1773, reg 80, Sch 1, Part 1, paras 1, 34(1), (6), as from 22 July 2013. Sub-para (aa) is substituted by the SI 2013/1797, reg 3, Sch 1, para 1(1), (5)(b), as from a day to be appointed, as follows (note that Sch 1, para 1(5)(b) was amended by the Alternative Investment Fund Managers (Amendment etc) (EU Exit) Regulations 2019, SI 2019/328, regs 16, 20 (as from IP completion day (as defined in the European Union (Withdrawal Agreement) Act 2020, s 39)) and that the amendment has been incorporated in the text below)—

"(aa) in relation to a person whose entitlement derives from the alternative investment fund managers directive—

(i) if the person's registered office is in an EEA State, its registered office;

(ii) if the person's registered office is not in an EEA State, the registered office or branch of its legal representative (as defined in Article 4(1)(u) of the alternative investment fund managers directive);".

Para 8: substituted by the Financial Services (EEA State) Regulations 2007, SI 2007/108, reg 2, as from 13 February 2007.

Paras 9, 11: words in square brackets inserted by SI 2012/1906, art 4(1), (4), as from 20 July 2012.

Para 10: words in square brackets substituted by SI 2003/1473, reg 2(2)(h), as from 14 January 2005.

Para 10A: inserted by SI 2003/1473, reg 2(2)(i), as from 14 January 2005. Words in square brackets in sub-para (a) substituted by SI 2018/546, arts 9, 17(1), (7), as from 1 October 2018. Sub-para (aa) originally inserted by SI 2013/1773, reg 80, Sch 1, Part 1, paras 1, 34(1), (7), as from 22 July 2013. Sub-para (aa) is substituted by the SI 2013/1797, reg 3, Sch 1, para 1(1), (5)(c), as from a day to be appointed, as follows—

"(aa) in relation to a firm whose EEA right derives from the alternative investment fund managers directive—

(i) if the firm's registered office is in an EEA State, its registered office;

(ii) if the firm's registered office is not in an EEA State, the registered office or branch of its legal representative (as defined in Article 4(1)(u) of the alternative investment fund managers directive);".

Paras 10B, 11A: inserted by SI 2007/126, reg 3(4), Sch 4, paras 1, 5, 6, as from 1 April 2007 (certain purposes), and as from 1 November 2007 (otherwise). Figure in square brackets in para 11A substituted by SI 2017/701, reg 50(1), Sch 2, paras 1, 54(1), (3), as from 3 January 2018 (as to the commencement of the 2017 Regulations, see further the note relating to them above).

Paras 11B, 11C: originally inserted by SI 2011/1613, reg 2(1), (33)(c), as from 1 July 2011. Para 11C subsequently repealed by the Money Market Funds Regulations 2018, SI 2018/698, reg 2(1), (19), as from 21 July 2018.

Para 11D: originally inserted by SI 2013/1773, reg 80, Sch 1, Part 1, paras 1, 34(1), (3), (8), as from 22 July 2013. Subsequently repealed by SI 2019/710, reg 3, as from IP completion day (as defined in the European Union (Withdrawal Agreement) Act 2020, s 39).

PARTS II III

(Part II (Firms qualifying for authorisation) and Part III (Exercise of Passport Rights by UK Firms) were repealed by the EEA Passport Rights (Amendment, etc, and Transitional Provisions) (EU Exit) Regulations 2018, SI 2018/1149, reg 2(1), (5)(a), as from IP completion day (as defined in the European Union (Withdrawal Agreement) Act 2020, s 39). For savings in relation to the continued application of these Parts to Gibraltar-based firms, see the Financial Services and Markets Act 2000 (Gibraltar) Order 2001 (as amended by the Financial Services (Gibraltar) (Amendment) (EU Exit) Regulations 2019).)

SCHEDULE 4

(Sch 4 (Treaty Rights) was repealed by the EEA Passport Rights (Amendment, etc, and Transitional Provisions) (EU Exit) Regulations 2018, SI 2018/1149, reg 2(1), (6), as from IP completion day (as defined in the European Union (Withdrawal Agreement) Act 2020, s 39.)

SCHEDULE 5
PERSONS CONCERNED IN COLLECTIVE INVESTMENT SCHEMES

Section 36

Authorisation

[7.726]

1. (1), (2) . . .

(3) An authorised open-ended investment company is an authorised person.

[(4) A body—

(a) incorporated by virtue of regulations made under section 1 of the Open-Ended Investment Companies Act (Northern Ireland) 2002 in respect of which an authorisation order is in force, and

[(b) which is a UCITS as defined in section 236A,]

is an authorised person.

(5) "Authorisation order" means an order made under (or having effect as made under) any provision of those regulations which is made by virtue of section 1(2)(1) of that Act (provision corresponding to Chapter 3 of Part 17 of the Act).]

Permission

2. (1) . . .

(2) A person authorised as a result of paragraph 1(3) [or (4)] has permission to carry on, so far as it is a regulated activity [other than the activity of managing an AIF]—

(a) the operation of the scheme;

(b) any activity in connection with, or for the purposes of, the operation of the scheme.

NOTES

Para 1: sub-paras (1) and (2) were repealed, and sub-para (4)(b) was substituted, by the Collective Investment Schemes (Amendment etc) (EU Exit) Regulations 2019, SI 2019/325, regs 3, 32(1), (2), as from IP completion day (as defined in the European Union (Withdrawal Agreement) Act 2020, s 39). Sub-paras (4), (5) were previously added by the Collective Investment Schemes (Miscellaneous Amendments) Regulations 2003, SI 2003/2066, reg 10(a), as from 13 February 2004.

Para 2: sub-para (1) was repealed by SI 2019/325, regs 3, 32(1), (3), as from IP completion day (as defined in the European Union (Withdrawal Agreement) Act 2020, s 39). Words in first pair of square brackets in sub-para (2) inserted by SI 2003/2066, reg 10(b), as from 13 February 2004. Words in second pair of square brackets inserted by the Alternative Investment Fund Managers Regulations 2013, SI 2013/1773, reg 80, Sch 1, Part 1, paras 1, 35, as from 22 July 2013.

SCHEDULE 6
THRESHOLD CONDITIONS

[Section 55B]

[PART 1 INTRODUCTION

[7.727]

1A. (1) In this Schedule—

"assets" includes contingent assets;

"consolidated supervision" has the same meaning as in section 3M;

"consumers" has the meaning given in section 425A;

"financial crime" is to be read with section 1H(3);

"functions", in relation to the FCA or the PRA, means functions conferred on that regulator by or under this Act;

["implementing provisions" has the same meaning as in section 3M;]

"liabilities" includes contingent liabilities;

"relevant directives" has the same meaning as in section 3M;

["relevant implementing provisions" means—

(a) any implementing provision contained in subordinate legislation (within the meaning of the Interpretation Act 1978) made otherwise than by any of the following—

(i) statutory instrument, and

(ii) statutory rule for the purposes of the Statutory Rules (Northern Ireland) Order 1979 (SI 1979/1573 (NI 12)); or

(b) any other implementing provision (as amended from time to time));]

"Society" means the society incorporated by Lloyd's Act 1871 by the name of Lloyd's;

"subsidiary undertaking" includes all the instances mentioned in Article 1(1) and (2) of the Seventh Company Law Directive in which an entity may be a subsidiary of an undertaking.

(2) For the purposes of this Schedule, the "non-financial resources" of a person include any systems, controls, plans or policies that the person maintains, any information that the person holds and the human resources that the person has available.

(3) In this Schedule, References to "integrity" of the UK financial system are to be read in accordance section 1D(2).

(4) References to the failure of a person are to be read in accordance with section 2J(3) and (4).]

NOTES

The enabling authority of this Schedule was substituted (it was previously s 41) and Parts 1 and 1B–1G were substituted for the original Parts I, II, by the Financial Services and Markets Act 2000 (Threshold Conditions) Order 2013, SI 2013/555, art 2, as from 1 April 2013.

Para 1A: definitions "implementing provisions" and "relevant implementing provisions" in sub-para (1) inserted by the Financial Services and Markets Act 2000 (Amendment) (EU Exit) Regulations 2019, SI 2019/632, regs 96, 97, as from IP completion day (as defined in the European Union (Withdrawal Agreement) Act 2020, s 39).

[PART 1B PART 4A PERMISSION: AUTHORISED PERSONS WHO ARE NOT PRA-AUTHORISED PERSONS

[7.728]

2A. Introduction

If the person concerned ("A") carries on, or is seeking to carry on, regulated activities which do not consist of or include a PRA-regulated activity, the threshold conditions that are relevant to the discharge by the FCA of its functions in relation to A are the conditions set out in paragraphs 2B to 2F.

2B. Location of offices

(1) Unless sub-paragraph (3)[, (4)(a) or (7)] applies, if A is a body corporate incorporated in the United Kingdom—

(a) A's head office, and

(b) if A has a registered office, that office,

must be in the United Kingdom.

(2) If A is not a body corporate but A's head office is in the United Kingdom, A must carry on business in the United Kingdom.

(3) If—

(a) A is seeking to carry on, or is carrying on, a regulated activity which is any of the investment services and activities,

(b) A is a body corporate with no registered office, and

(c) A's head office is in the United Kingdom,

A must carry on business in the United Kingdom.

(4) If A is seeking to carry on, or is carrying on, an insurance [distribution] activity—

(a) where A is a body corporate incorporated in the United Kingdom, A's registered office, or if A has no registered office, A's head office, must be in the United Kingdom;

(b) where A is an individual, A is to be treated for the purposes of sub-paragraph (2) as having a head office in the United Kingdom if A is resident in the United Kingdom.

(5) "Insurance [distribution] activity" means any of the following activities—

(a) dealing in rights under a contract of insurance as agent;

(b) arranging deals in rights under a contract of insurance;

(c) assisting in the administration and performance of a contract of insurance;

(d) advising on buying or selling rights under a contract of insurance;

(e) agreeing to do any of the activities specified in paragraphs (a) to (d).

(6) Sub-paragraph (5) must be read with—

(a) section 22,

(b) any relevant order under that section, and

(c) Schedule 2.

[(7) If A is seeking to carry on, or is carrying on, the regulated activity of managing an AIF and is, or upon being granted Part 4A permission to carry on that regulated activity would be, *a full-scope UK AIFM, A's head office and registered office must be in the United Kingdom*.]

2C. Effective supervision

(1) A must be capable of being effectively supervised by the FCA having regard to all the circumstances including—

(a) the nature (including the complexity) of the regulated activities that A carries on or seeks to carry on;

(b) the complexity of any products that A provides or will provide in carrying on those activities;

(c) the way in which A's business is organised;

(d) if A is a member of a group, whether membership of the group is likely to prevent the FCA's effective supervision of A;

(e) whether A is subject to consolidated supervision required under any [relevant implementing provisions];

(f) if A has close links with another person ("CL")—

(i) the nature of the relationship between A and CL,

Part 7 Financial Services Acts

(ii) whether those links are or that relationship is likely to prevent the FCA's effective supervision of A, and

(iii) if CL is subject to the laws, regulations or administrative provisions of a [country or territory outside the United Kingdom] ("the foreign provisions"), whether those foreign provisions, or any deficiency in their enforcement, would prevent the FCA's effective supervision of A.

[(1A) Paragraphs (a), (b) and (e) of sub-paragraph (1) do not apply where the only regulated activities that the person carries on, or seeks to carry on, are—

(a) relevant credit activities, and

(b) if any, activities to which, by virtue of section 39(1D), sections 20(1) and (1A) and 23(1A) do not apply when carried on by the person.]

(2) A has close links with CL if—

(a) CL is a parent undertaking of A,

(b) CL is a subsidiary undertaking of A,

(c) CL is a parent undertaking of a subsidiary undertaking of A,

(d) CL is a subsidiary undertaking of a parent undertaking of A,

(e) CL owns or controls 20% or more of the voting rights or capital of A, or

(f) A owns or controls 20% or more of the voting rights or capital of CL.

2D. Appropriate resources

(1) The resources of A must be appropriate in relation to the regulated activities that A carries on or seeks to carry on.

(2) The matters which are relevant in determining whether A has appropriate resources include—

(a) the nature and scale of the business carried on, or to be carried on, by A;

(b) the risks to the continuity of the services provided by, or to be provided by, A;

(c) A's membership of a group and any effect which that membership may have.

(3) [Except in a case within sub-paragraph (3A), the matters] which are relevant in determining whether A has appropriate financial resources include—

(a) the provision A makes and, if A is a member of a group, which other members of the group make, in respect of liabilities;

(b) the means by which A manages and, if A is a member of a group, by which other members of the group manage, the incidence of risk in connection with A's business.

[(3A) Where the only regulated activities that A carries on or seeks to carry on are—

(a) relevant credit activities, and

(b) if any, activities to which, by virtue of section 39(1D), sections 20(1) and (1A) and 23(1A) do not apply when carried on by A,

A has adequate financial resources if A is capable of meeting A's debts as they fall due.]

(4) The matters which are relevant in determining whether A has appropriate non-financial resources include—

(a) the skills and experience of those who manage A's affairs;

(b) whether A's non-financial resources are sufficient to enable A to comply with—

(i) requirements imposed or likely to be imposed on A by the FCA in the exercise of its functions, or

(ii) any other requirement in relation to whose contravention the FCA would be the appropriate regulator for the purpose of any provision of Part 14 of this Act.

2E. Suitability

A must be a fit and proper person having regard to all the circumstances, including—

(a) A's connection with any person;

(b) the nature (including the complexity) of the regulated activities that A carries on or seeks to carry on;

(c) the need to ensure that A's affairs are conducted in an appropriate manner, having regard in particular to the interests of consumers and the integrity of the UK financial system;

(d) whether A has complied and is complying with requirements imposed by the FCA in the exercise of its functions, or requests made by the FCA, relating to the provision of information to the FCA and, where A has so complied or is so complying, the manner of that compliance;

(e) whether those who manage A's affairs have adequate skills and experience and have acted and may be expected to act with probity;

(f) whether A's business is being, or is to be, managed in such a way as to ensure that its affairs will be conducted in a sound and prudent manner;

(g) the need to minimise the extent to which it is possible for the business carried on by A, or to be carried on by A, to be used for a purpose connected with financial crime.

2F. Business model

(1) A's business model (that is, A's strategy for doing business) must be suitable for a person carrying on the regulated activities that A carries on or seeks to carry on.

(2) The matters which are relevant in determining whether A satisfies the condition in sub-paragraph (1) include—

(a) whether the business model is compatible with A's affairs being conducted, and continuing to be conducted, in a sound and prudent manner;

(b) the interests of consumers;

(c) the integrity of the UK financial system.

[(3) This paragraph does not apply where the only regulated activities that the person carries on, or seeks to carry on, are—

(a) relevant credit activities, and

(b) if any, activities to which, by virtue of section 39(1D), sections 20(1) and (1A) and 23(1A) do not apply when carried on by the person.]

[2G. Interpretation

(1) In this Part of this Schedule, each of the following is a "relevant credit activity"—

(a) an activity of the kind specified by article 36A of the Regulated Activities Order (credit broking) when carried on in the case specified in sub-paragraph (3), (4) or (5),

(b) an activity of the kind specified by article 39D of that Order (debt adjusting) when carried on—

(i) in the case specified in sub-paragraph (3), by a person who also carries on an activity of the kind specified by paragraph (a),

[(ii) by a person in connection with an activity of the kind specified by paragraph (d) or (e) which the person also carries on,]

(iii) by a not-for-profit body,

(c) an activity of the kind specified by article 39E of that Order (debt-counselling) when carried on—

(i) in the case specified in sub-paragraph (3), by a person who also carries on an activity of the kind specified by paragraph (a),

[(ii) by a person in connection with an activity of the kind specified by paragraph (d) or (e) which the person also carries on,]

(iii) by a not-for-profit body,

(d) an activity of the kind specified by article 60B of that Order (regulated credit agreements) if—

(i) it is carried on by a supplier,

(ii) no charge (by way of interest or otherwise) is payable by the borrower in connection with the provision of credit under the regulated credit agreement, and

(iii) the regulated credit agreement is not a hire-purchase agreement or a conditional sale agreement,

[(da) an activity of the kind specified by article 60B of that Order (regulated credit agreements) if carried on by a local authority,]

(e) an activity of the kind specified by article 60N of that Order (regulated consumer hire agreements),

(f) an activity of the kind specified by article 89A of that Order (providing credit information services) where carried on by a person [in connection with an activity of the kind specified by any of paragraphs (a) to (e) which the person also carries on], or

(g) an activity of the kind specified by article 64 of that Order (agreeing to carry on specified kinds of activity) so far as relevant to any of the activities specified in paragraphs (a) to (f).

(2) [Except where the activity is carried on by a not-for-profit body,] an activity is not a relevant credit activity for the purposes of—

(a) paragraph (a) to (e) of sub-paragraph (1), and

(b) paragraph (g) of that sub-paragraph so far at it relates to activities of the kind specified by any of those paragraphs,

if it relates to an agreement under which the obligation of the borrower to repay [or the hirer to pay] is secured, or is to be secured, by a legal mortgage on land.

(3) The case specified in this sub-paragraph is where a supplier (other than a domestic premises supplier) carries on the activity for the purposes of, or in connection with, the sale of goods or supply of services by the supplier to a customer (who need not be the borrower under the credit agreement or the hirer under the consumer hire agreement).

[(3A) For the purposes of sub-paragraph (3), "domestic premises supplier" means a supplier who—

(a) sells, offers to sell or agrees to sell goods, or

(b) offers to supply services or contracts to supply services,

to customers who are individuals while the supplier, or the supplier's representative, is physically present at the dwelling of the individual (but see sub-paragraph (3B)).

(3B) A supplier who acts as described in sub-paragraph (3A) on an occasional basis only will not be a domestic premises supplier unless the supplier indicates to the public at large, or any section of the public, the supplier's willingness to attend (in person or through a representative) the dwelling of potential customers in order to carry on any of the activities mentioned in sub-paragraph (3A)(a) or (b).]

(4) The case specified in this sub-paragraph is where the activity relates to a green deal plan.

[(5) The case specified in this sub-paragraph is where the activity relates to a consumer hire agreement or a hire-purchase agreement.]

(6) For the purposes of this paragraph—

"borrower" includes—

(a) any person providing a guarantee or indemnity under an agreement, and

(b) a person to whom the rights and duties of the borrower under an agreement or a person falling within paragraph (a) have passed by assignment or operation of law;

"conditional sale agreement" has the meaning given by article 60L of the Regulated Activities Order;

["consumer hire agreement" has the meaning given by article 60N(3) of the Regulated Activities Order;]

"customer" means a person to whom a supplier sells goods or supplies services or agrees to do so;

. . .

"green deal plan" has the meaning given by section 1 of the Energy Act 2011;

"hire-purchase agreement" has the meaning given by the Regulated Activities Order;

["local authority" means—

(a) in England and Wales, a local authority within the meaning of the Local Government Act 1972, the Greater London Authority, the Common Council of the City of London or the Council of the Isles of Scilly;

(b) in Scotland, a local authority within the meaning of the Local Government (Scotland) Act 1973; and

(c) in Northern Ireland, a district council within the meaning of the Local Government Act (Northern Ireland) 1972;]

"not-for-profit body" means a body which, by virtue of its constitution or any enactment—

(a) is required (after payment of outgoings) to apply the whole of its income and any capital it expends for charitable or public purposes, and

(b) is prohibited from directly or indirectly distributing amongst its members any part of its assets (otherwise than for charitable or public purposes);

"Regulated Activities Order" means the Financial Services and Markets Act 2000 (Regulated Activities) Order 2001;

"regulated credit agreement" has the meaning given by the Regulated Activities Order;

"supplier" means a person whose main business is to sell goods or supply services and not to carry on a regulated activity, other than an activity of the kind specified by article 60N of the Regulated Activities Order (regulated consumer hire agreements).]]

NOTES

Substituted as noted to Part 1 of this Schedule at **[7.727]**.

Para 2B: words in square brackets in sub-para (1) substituted, and sub-para (7) added, by the Alternative Investment Fund Managers Regulations 2013, SI 2013/1773, reg 80, Sch 1, Part 1, paras 1, 36, as from 22 July 2013. Words in square brackets in sub-paras (4) and (5) substituted by the Insurance Distribution (Regulated Activities and Miscellaneous Amendments) Order 2018, SI 2018/546, art 18(4), as from 1 October 2018. For the words in italics in sub-para (7) there are substituted the following words by the Alternative Investment Fund Managers (Amendment) Regulations 2013, SI 2013/1797, reg 3, Sch 1, para 1(1), (6), as from a day to be appointed (note that Sch 1, para 1(6) to the 2013 Regulations was amended by the Alternative Investment Fund Managers (Amendment etc) (EU Exit) Regulations 2019, SI 2019/328, regs 16, 20 (as from IP completion day (as defined in the European Union (Withdrawal Agreement) Act 2020, s 39)) and that the effect of the amendment has been incorporated in the text below)—

"a full-scope UK AIFM—

(a) A's head office and registered office must be in the United Kingdom, or

(b) A's registered office must be in a third country.".

Para 2C: words in square brackets in sub-paras (1)(e) and (f)(iii) substituted by the Financial Services and Markets Act 2000 (Amendment) (EU Exit) Regulations 2019, SI 2019/632, regs 96, 98, as from IP completion day (as defined in the European Union (Withdrawal Agreement) Act 2020, s 39). Sub-para (1A) originally inserted by the Financial Services and Markets Act 2000 (Regulated Activities) (Amendment) (No 2) Order 2013, SI 2013/1881, art 10(1), (19)(a), as from 1 April 2014. Sub-para (1A) subsequently substituted by the Financial Services and Markets Act 2000 (Regulated Activities) (Amendment) Order 2014, SI 2014/366, art 5(1), (2), as from 1 April 2014.

Para 2D: words in square brackets in sub-para (3) substituted, and sub-para (3A) inserted, by SI 2013/1881, art 10(1), (19)(b), as from 1 April 2014. Sub-para (3A) subsequently substituted by SI 2014/366, art 5(1), (3), as from 1 April 2014.

Para 2F: sub-para (3) added by SI 2013/1881, art 10(1), (19)(c), as from 1 April 2014. Subsequently substituted by SI 2014/366, art 5(1), (4), as from 1 April 2014.

Para 2G: added by SI 2013/1881, art 10(1), (19)(d), as from 1 April 2014. Sub-paras (3A), (3B) inserted, sub-para (5) substituted, definition "consumer hire agreement" in sub-para (6) inserted, and definition "domestic premises supplier" (omitted) repealed, by the Financial Services and Markets Act 2000 (Miscellaneous Provisions) Order 2015, SI 2015/853, art 2, as from 24 March 2015. All other words in square brackets in this paragraph were substituted or inserted by SI 2014/366, art 5(1), (5), as from 1 April 2014.

[PART 1C PART 4A PERMISSION: CONDITIONS FOR WHICH FCA IS RESPONSIBLE IN RELATION TO PRA-AUTHORISED PERSONS

[7.729]

3A. Introduction

If the person concerned ("B") carries on, or is seeking to carry on, regulated activities which consist of or include a PRA-regulated activity, the threshold conditions which are relevant to the discharge by the FCA of its functions in relation to B are the conditions set out in paragraphs 3B to 3E.

3B. Effective supervision

(1) B must be capable of being effectively supervised by the FCA having regard to all the circumstances including—

(a) the nature (including the complexity) of the regulated activities that B carries on or seeks to carry on;

(b) the complexity of any products that B provides or will provide in carrying on those activities;

(c) the way in which B's business is organised;

(d) if B is a member of a group, whether membership of the group is likely to prevent the FCA's effective supervision of B;

(e) whether B is subject to consolidated supervision required under any [relevant implementing provisions];

(f) if B has close links with another person ("CL")—

(i) the nature of the relationship between B and CL,

(ii) whether those links are or that relationship is likely to prevent the FCA's effective supervision of B, and

(iii) if CL is subject to the laws, regulations or administrative provisions of a [country or territory outside the United Kingdom] ("the foreign provisions"), whether those foreign provisions, or any deficiency in their enforcement, would prevent the FCA's effective supervision of B.

(2) B has close links with CL if—

(a) CL is a parent undertaking of B,

(b) CL is a subsidiary undertaking of B,

(c) CL is a parent undertaking of a subsidiary undertaking of B,

(d) CL is a subsidiary undertaking of a parent undertaking of B,

(e) CL owns or controls 20% or more of the voting rights or capital of B, or

(f) B owns or controls 20% or more of the voting rights or capital of CL.

3C. Appropriate non-financial resources

(1) The non-financial resources of B must be appropriate in relation to the regulated activities that B carries on or seeks to carry on, having regard to the operational objectives of the FCA.

(2) The matters which are relevant in determining whether the condition in sub-paragraph (1) is met include—

(a) the nature and scale of the business carried on, or to be carried on, by B;
(b) the risks to the continuity of the services provided by, or to be provided by, B;
(c) B's membership of a group and any effect which that membership may have;
(d) the skills and experience of those who manage B's affairs;
(e) whether B's non-financial resources are sufficient to enable B to comply with—
  (i) requirements imposed or likely to be imposed on B by the FCA in the exercise of its functions, or
  (ii) any other requirement in relation to whose contravention the FCA would be the appropriate regulator for the purpose of any provision of Part 14 of this Act.

3D. Suitability

(1) B must be a fit and proper person, having regard to the operational objectives of the FCA.

(2) The matters which are relevant in determining whether B satisfies the condition in sub-paragraph (1) include—

(a) B's connection with any person;
(b) the nature (including the complexity) of the regulated activities that B carries on or seeks to carry on;
(c) the need to ensure that B's affairs are conducted in an appropriate manner, having regard in particular to the interests of consumers and the integrity of the UK financial system;
(d) whether B has complied and is complying with requirements imposed by the FCA in the exercise its functions, or requests made by the FCA, relating to the provision of information to the FCA and, where B has so complied or is so complying, the manner of that compliance;
(e) whether those who manage B's affairs have adequate skills and experience and have acted and may be expected to act with probity;
(f) the need to minimise the extent to which it is possible for the business carried on by B, or to be carried on by B, to be used for a purpose connected with financial crime.

3E. Business model

B's business model (that is, B's strategy for doing business) must be suitable for a person carrying on the regulated activities that B carries on or seeks to carry on, having regard to the FCA's operational objectives.]

NOTES

Substituted as noted to Part 1 of this Schedule at **[7.727]**.

Para 3B: words in square brackets in sub-paras (1)(e) and (1)(f)(iii) substituted by the Financial Services and Markets Act 2000 (Amendment) (EU Exit) Regulations 2019, SI 2019/632, regs 96, 99, as from IP completion day (as defined in the European Union (Withdrawal Agreement) Act 2020, s 39).

[PART 1D PART 4A PERMISSION: CONDITIONS FOR WHICH THE PRA IS RESPONSIBLE IN RELATION TO INSURERS ETC

[7.730]

4A. Introduction

(1) If the person concerned ("C") carries on, or is seeking to carry on, regulated activities which consist of or include a PRA-regulated activity relating to the effecting or carrying out of contracts of insurance, the threshold conditions which are relevant to the discharge by the PRA of its functions in relation to C are the conditions set out in paragraphs 4B to 4F.

(2) If the person concerned ("C") carries on, or is seeking to carry on, regulated activities which consist of or include a PRA-regulated activity relating to managing the underwriting capacity of a Lloyd's syndicate as a managing agent at Lloyd's, the conditions which are relevant to the discharge by the PRA of its functions in relation to C are the conditions set out in paragraphs 4C to 4F except for sub-paragraphs (5)(d) and (5)(e) of paragraph 4D which are not relevant for that purpose.

(3) If the person concerned ("C") carries on, or is seeking to carry on, regulated activities which consist of or include a PRA-regulated activity relating to the arranging, by the Society, of deals in contracts of insurance written at Lloyd's, the conditions which are relevant to the discharge by the PRA of its functions in relation to C are the conditions set out in paragraphs 4C to 4F, subject to sub-paragraph (4).

(4) Paragraph 4D has effect in relation to persons of the kind specified by sub-paragraph (3) as if—

(a) for paragraph (d) and (e) of sub-paragraph (5) there were substituted—

"(d) the effect that the carrying on of business by C might be expected to have on the stability of the UK financial system or on those who are or may become policyholders of members of C;
(e) the effect that the failure of C might be expected to have on the stability of the UK financial system or on those who are or may become policyholders of members of C;", and

(b) sub-paragraph (6) were omitted.

[(5) If the person concerned ("C") carries on, or is seeking to carry on, regulated activities which consist of or include a PRA-regulated activity relating to an assumption of risk falling within article 13A of the Financial Services and Markets Act 2000 (Regulated Activities) Order 2001, the threshold conditions which are relevant to the discharge by the PRA of its functions in relation to C are the conditions set out in paragraphs 4B to 4F, subject to sub-paragraph (6).

(6) Paragraphs 4B to 4F have effect in relation to persons of the kind specified by sub-paragraph (5) as if—

[(a) the persons are undertakings, whether incorporated or not, other than an existing insurance or reinsurance undertaking, which assume risks from insurance or reinsurance undertakings and which fully fund their exposure to such risks through the proceeds of a debt issuance or any other financing mechanism where the repayment rights of the providers of such debt or financing mechanism are subordinated to the reinsurance obligations of such an undertaking;

(b) the persons are not insurance undertakings;]

(c) references to contracts of insurance are references to contracts for the assumption of risk; and

[(7) In paragraph (6)(a), references to undertakings which assume risks from insurance or reinsurance undertakings include references to undertakings which assume risks from third country insurance or reinsurance undertakings and Gibraltarian insurance or reinsurance undertakings; and for these purposes "third country insurance undertakings", "third country reinsurance undertakings", "Gibraltarian insurance undertakings" and "Gibraltarian reinsurance undertakings" have the same meaning as in the Solvency 2 Regulations 2015 (SI 2015/575), as amended under the European Union (Withdrawal) Act 2018 (see, in particular, regulation 2(1)).]

4B. Legal status

C must be—

(a) a body corporate (other than a limited liability partnership),

(b) a registered friendly society, or

(c) a member of Lloyd's.

4C. Location of offices

(1) If C is a body corporate incorporated in the United Kingdom—

(a) C's head office, and

(b) if C has a registered office, that office,

must be in the United Kingdom.

(2) If C is not a body corporate but C's head office is in the United Kingdom, C must carry on business in the United Kingdom.

4D. Business to be conducted in a prudent manner

(1) The business of C must be conducted in a prudent manner.

(2) To satisfy the condition in sub-paragraph (1), C must in particular have appropriate financial and non-financial resources.

(3) To have appropriate financial resources C must satisfy the following conditions—

(a) C's assets must be appropriate given C's liabilities, and

(b) the liquidity of C's resources must be appropriate given C's liabilities and when they fall due or may fall due.

(4) To have appropriate non-financial resources C must satisfy the following conditions—

(a) C must be willing and able to value C's assets and liabilities appropriately,

(b) C must have resources to identify, monitor, measure and take action to remove or reduce risks to the safety and soundness of C,

(c) C must have resources to identify, monitor, measure and take action to remove or reduce risks to the accuracy of C's valuation of C's assets and liabilities,

(d) the effectiveness with which C's business is managed must meet a reasonable standard of effectiveness, and

(e) C's non-financial resources must be sufficient to enable C to comply with—

(i) requirements imposed or likely to be imposed on C by the PRA in the exercise of its functions, and

(ii) any other requirement in relation to whose contravention the PRA would be the appropriate regulator for the purpose of any provision of Part 14 of this Act.

(5) The matters which are relevant in determining whether C satisfies the condition in sub-paragraph (1) or (2) include—

(a) the nature (including the complexity) of the regulated activities that C carries on or seeks to carry on;

(b) the nature and scale of the business carried on or to be carried on by C;

(c) the risks to the continuity of the services provided by, or to be provided by, C;

(d) the effect that the carrying on of the business of effecting or carrying out contracts of insurance by C might be expected to have on the stability of the UK financial system or on those who are or may become C's policyholders;

(e) the effect that C's failure or C being closed to new business might be expected to have on the stability of the UK financial system or on those who are or may become C's policyholders;

(f) C's membership of a group and any effect which that membership may have.

(6) C is "closed to new business" for the purposes of this paragraph if C has ceased to effect contracts of insurance or has substantially reduced the number of such contracts which C effects.

4E. Suitability

(1) C must be a fit and proper person, having regard to the PRA's objectives.

(2) The matters which are relevant in determining whether C satisfies the condition in sub-paragraph (1) include—

(a) whether C has complied and is complying with requirements imposed by the PRA in the exercise of its functions, or requests made by the PRA relating to the provision of information to the PRA and, if C has so complied or is so complying, the manner of that compliance;

(b) whether those who manage C's affairs have adequate skills and experience and have acted and may be expected to act with probity.

4F. Effective supervision

(1) C must be capable of being effectively supervised by the PRA.

(2) The matters which are relevant in determining whether C satisfies the condition in sub-paragraph (1) include—

(a) the nature (including the complexity) of the regulated activities that C carries on or seeks to carry on;

(b) the complexity of any products that C provides or will provide in carrying on those activities;

(c) the way in which C's business is organised;

(d) if C is a member of a group, whether membership of the group is likely to prevent the PRA's effective supervision of C;
(e) whether C is subject to consolidated supervision required under any [relevant implementing provisions];
(f) if C has close links with another person ("CL")—
(i) the nature of the relationship between C and CL,
(ii) whether those links are or that relationship is likely to prevent the PRA's effective supervision of C, and
(iii) if CL is subject to the laws, regulations or administrative provisions of a [country or territory outside the United Kingdom] ("the foreign provisions"), whether those foreign provisions, or any deficiency in their enforcement, would prevent the PRA's effective supervision of C.

(3) C has close links with CL if—
(a) CL is a parent undertaking of C,
(b) CL is a subsidiary undertaking of C,
(c) CL is a parent undertaking of a subsidiary undertaking of C,
(d) CL is a subsidiary undertaking of a parent undertaking of C,
(e) CL owns or controls 20% or more of the voting rights or capital of C, or
(f) C owns or controls 20% or more of the voting rights or capital of CL.]

NOTES

Substituted as noted to Part 1 of this Schedule at **[7.727]**.

Para 4A: sub-paras (5), (6) added by the Risk Transformation Regulations 2017, SI 2017/1212, reg 4(1), (2)(a), as from 8 December 2017. Sub-paras (6)(a) and (b) subsequently substituted, and sub-para (7) added, by the Financial Services and Markets Act 2000 (Amendment) (EU Exit) Regulations 2019, SI 2019/632, regs 96, 100, as from IP completion day (as defined in the European Union (Withdrawal Agreement) Act 2020, s 39). Note that reg 100 of the 2019 Regulations was amended by the Risk Transformation and Solvency 2 (Amendment) (EU Exit) Regulations 2019, SI 2019/1233, reg 5, with effect from immediately before IP completion day (and the effect of the amendment has been incorporated above).

Para 4F: words in square brackets in sub-paras (2)(e) and (f)(iii) substituted by SI 2019/632, regs 96, 101, as from IP completion day (as defined in the European Union (Withdrawal Agreement) Act 2020, s 39).

[PART 1E PART 4A PERMISSION: CONDITIONS FOR WHICH THE PRA IS RESPONSIBLE IN RELATION TO OTHER PRA-AUTHORISED PERSONS

[7.731]

5A. Introduction

If the person concerned ("D") carries on, or is seeking to carry on, PRA-regulated activities which do not consist of or include a regulated activity relating to—
(a) the effecting or carrying out of contracts of insurance,
(b) managing the underwriting capacity of a Lloyd's syndicate as a managing agent at Lloyds, . . .
(c) arranging, by the Society, of deals in contracts of insurance written at Lloyd's, [or]
[(d) an assumption of risk falling within article 13A of the Financial Services and Markets Act 2000 (Regulated Activities) Order 2001,]

the threshold conditions which are relevant to the discharge by the PRA of its functions in relation to D are the conditions set out in paragraphs 5B to 5F.

5B. Legal status

If D carries on or is seeking to carry on a regulated activity which consists of or includes accepting deposits or issuing electronic money, D must be—
(a) a body corporate, or
(b) a partnership.

5C. Location of offices

(1) If D is a body corporate incorporated in the United Kingdom—
(a) D's head office, and
(b) if D has a registered office, that office,

must be in the United Kingdom.

(2) If D is not a body corporate but D's head office is in the United Kingdom, D must carry on business in the United Kingdom.

5D. Business to be conducted in a prudent manner

(1) The business of D must be conducted in a prudent manner.

(2) To satisfy the condition in sub-paragraph (1), D must in particular have appropriate financial and non-financial resources.

(3) To have appropriate financial resources D must satisfy the following conditions—
(a) D's assets must be appropriate given D's liabilities, and
(b) the liquidity of D's resources must be appropriate given D's liabilities and when they fall due or may fall due.

(4) To have appropriate non-financial resources D must satisfy the following conditions—
(a) D must be willing and able to value D's assets and liabilities appropriately,
(b) D must have resources to identify, monitor, measure and take action to remove or reduce risks to the safety and soundness of D,
(c) D must have resources to identify, monitor, measure and take action to remove or reduce risks to the accuracy of D's valuation of D's assets and liabilities,
(d) the effectiveness with which D's business is managed must meet a reasonable standard of effectiveness, and
(e) D's non-financial resources must be sufficient to enable D to comply with—
(i) requirements imposed or likely to be imposed on D by the PRA in the exercise of its functions, and

(ii) any other requirement in relation to whose contravention the PRA would be the appropriate regulator for the purpose of any provision of Part 14 of this Act.

(5) The matters which are relevant in determining whether D satisfies the condition in sub-paragraph (1) or (2) include—

(a) the nature (including the complexity) of the regulated activities that D carries on or seeks to carry on;
(b) the nature and scale of the business carried on or to be carried on by D;
(c) the risks to the continuity of the services provided or to be provided by D;
(d) the effect that the carrying on of the business carried on or to be carried on by D might be expected to have on the stability of the UK financial system;
(e) the effect that D's failure might be expected to have on the stability of the UK financial system;
(f) D's membership of a group and any effect which that membership may have.

5E. Suitability

(1) D must be a fit and proper person, having regard to the PRA's objectives.

(2) The matters which are relevant in determining whether D satisfies the condition in sub-paragraph (1) include—

(a) whether D has complied and is complying with requirements imposed by the PRA in the exercise of its functions, or requests made by the PRA relating to the provision of information to the PRA and, if D has so complied or is so complying, the manner of that compliance;
(b) whether those who manage D's affairs have adequate skills and experience and have acted and may be expected to act with probity.

5F. Effective supervision

(1) D must be capable of being effectively supervised by the PRA.

(2) The matters which are relevant in determining whether D satisfies the condition in sub-paragraph (1) include—

(a) the nature (including the complexity) of the regulated activities that D carries on or seeks to carry on;
(b) the complexity of any products that D provides or will provide in carrying on those activities;
(c) the way in which D's business is organised;
(d) if D is a member of a group, whether membership of the group is likely to prevent the PRA's effective supervision of D;
(e) whether D is subject to consolidated supervision required under any [relevant implementing provisions];
(f) if D has close links with another person ("CL")—
 (i) the nature of the relationship between D and CL,
 (ii) whether those links are or that relationship is likely to prevent the PRA's effective supervision of D, and
 (iii) if CL is subject to the laws, regulations or administrative provisions of a [country or territory outside the United Kingdom] ("the foreign provisions"), whether those foreign provisions, or any deficiency in their enforcement, would prevent the PRA's effective supervision of D.

(3) D has close links with CL if—

(a) CL is a parent undertaking of D,
(b) CL is a subsidiary undertaking of D,
(c) CL is a parent undertaking of a subsidiary undertaking of D,
(d) CL is a subsidiary undertaking of a parent undertaking of D,
(e) CL owns or controls 20% or more of the voting rights or capital of D, or
(f) D owns or controls 20% or more of the voting rights or capital of CL.]

NOTES

Substituted as noted to Part 1 of this Schedule at **[7.727]**.

Para 5A: word omitted from sub-para (b) repealed, word in square brackets in sub-para (c) inserted, and sub-para (d) added, by the Risk Transformation Regulations 2017, SI 2017/1212, reg 4(1), (2)(b), as from 8 December 2017.

Para 5F: words in square brackets in sub-paras (2)(e) and (f)(iii) substituted by the Financial Services and Markets Act 2000 (Amendment) (EU Exit) Regulations 2019, SI 2019/632, regs 96, 102, as from IP completion day (as defined in the European Union (Withdrawal Agreement) Act 2020, s 39).

PARTS 1F, 1G

(These Parts were originally substituted as noted to Part 1 of this Schedule ante. Part 1F (Authorisation Under Schedule 3), and Part 1G (Authorisation Under Schedule 4) were subsequently repealed by the EEA Passport Rights (Amendment, etc, and Transitional Provisions) (EU Exit) Regulations 2018, SI 2018/1149, reg 3, Schedule, Pt 1, paras 1, 23(1), (2), as from IP completion day (as defined in the European Union (Withdrawal Agreement) Act 2020, s 39).)

PART III ADDITIONAL CONDITIONS

[7.732]

8. (1) If this paragraph applies to the person concerned, he must, for the purposes of such provisions of this Act as may be specified, satisfy specified additional conditions.

(2) This paragraph applies to a person who—

(a) has his head office outside the [United Kingdom]; and
(b) appears to [such of the FCA or the PRA as may be specified,] to be seeking to carry on a regulated activity relating to insurance business.

(3) "Specified" means specified in, or in accordance with, an order made by the Treasury.

9. . . .

NOTES

Para 8: words in square brackets in sub-para (2)(a) substituted by the Financial Services and Markets Act 2000 (Amendment) (EU Exit) Regulations 2019, SI 2019/632, regs 96, 103, as from IP completion day (as defined in the European Union (Withdrawal Agreement) Act 2020, s 39). Words in square brackets in sub-para (2)(b) substituted by the Financial Services Act 2012, s 114(1), Sch 18, Pt 1, paras 1, 26, as from 1 April 2013.

Para 9: repealed by the Financial Services Act 2012, s 11(3), as from 1 April 2013.

Orders: the Financial Services and Markets Act 2000 (Variation of Threshold Conditions) Order 2001, SI 2001/2507; the Financial Services and Markets Act 2000 (Variation of Threshold Conditions) Order 2002, SI 2002/2707; the Financial Services and Markets Act 2000 (Variation of Threshold Conditions) (Amendment) Order 2005, SI 2005/680.

[SCHEDULE 6A
VARIATION OR CANCELLATION OF PART 4A PERMISSION ON INITIATIVE OF FCA: ADDITIONAL POWER

Section 55JA

Additional power

[7.733]

1. (1) If it appears to the FCA that an FCA-authorised person with a Part 4A permission is carrying on no regulated activity to which the permission relates, the FCA may exercise its power under this paragraph.

(2) The FCA's power under this paragraph is the power—

- (a) to vary the Part 4A permission by—
  - (i) removing a regulated activity from those to which the permission relates, or
  - (ii) varying the description of a regulated activity to which the permission relates, or
- (b) to cancel the Part 4A permission.

(3) The circumstances in which the FCA may form the view that an authorised person is carrying on no regulated activity include (but are not limited to) circumstances where the person fails—

- (a) to pay any periodic fee or levy as is required by the FCA Handbook, or
- (b) to provide such information to the FCA as is required by the FCA Handbook.

(4) "The FCA Handbook" means the Handbook made by the FCA under this Act (as that Handbook is amended from time to time).

(5) If, as a result of a variation of a permission under this paragraph, there are no longer any regulated activities for which the person has permission, the FCA must, once it is satisfied that it is no longer necessary to keep the permission in force, cancel it.

(6) The power to vary a permission under this paragraph extends to including in the permission as varied any provision that could be included if a fresh permission were being given in response to an application to the FCA under section 55A.

(7) The FCA's power under this paragraph must be exercised in accordance with paragraph 2.

Procedure etc

2. (1) The FCA may exercise its power under paragraph 1 in relation to an authorised person with a Part 4A permission only if the following conditions are met.

(2) The first condition is that the FCA has given a notice in writing to the person—

- (a) stating that it appears to the FCA that the person is carrying on no regulated activity to which the permission relates,
- (b) inviting the person to respond in a specified manner, and
- (c) warning of the potential consequences that may arise under this Schedule of a failure to do so.

(3) The second condition is that—

- (a) at least 14 days beginning with the date on which the notice was given have elapsed, and
- (b) the person has failed to respond in the specified manner.

(4) The third condition is that the FCA has given a further notice in writing to the person setting out—

- (a) in a case where the FCA proposes to vary the permission—
  - (i) the proposed variation,
  - (ii) the date on which the FCA proposes to vary the permission (and, if different, the date on which the variation is to take effect), and
  - (iii) any specified steps the person may take that would (if taken) result in the FCA deciding not to vary the permission as proposed;
- (b) in a case where the FCA proposes to cancel the permission—
  - (i) the date on which the FCA proposes to cancel the permission (and, if different, the date on which the cancellation is to take effect), and
  - (ii) any specified steps the person may take that would (if taken) result in the FCA deciding not to cancel the permission.

(5) The fourth condition is that the date specified in the notice under sub-paragraph (4) is not earlier than the end of the period of 14 days beginning with the date on which the notice is given.

(6) Where the FCA decides to publicise a notice given under this paragraph (or any details relating to it), it may do so in such manner as it considers appropriate.

Notice of decision

3. (1) Where the FCA decides to vary or cancel an authorised person's Part 4A permission under paragraph 1, the FCA must give the person a notice in writing setting out—

- (a) in a case where the FCA varies the permission, the variation,
- (b) the date on which the variation or cancellation takes effect, and

(c) the person's power to make an application under paragraph 4.

(2) Where the FCA—
- (a) has given the person a notice under paragraph 2(4), but
- (b) decides not to vary or cancel the permission (whether or not because the specified steps referred to in that notice have been taken),

the FCA must give the person a notice in writing of that decision.

(3) A notice given under this paragraph may include such other information as the FCA considers appropriate.

(4) Where the FCA decides to publicise a notice given under this paragraph (or any details relating to it), it may do so in such manner as it considers appropriate.

Application for decision to be annulled

4. (1) This paragraph applies where the FCA decides to vary or cancel an authorised person's Part 4A permission under paragraph 1.

(2) If the person is aggrieved by the FCA's decision, the person may apply to the FCA to have the decision annulled.

(3) An application under this paragraph must be made before the end of the period of 12 months beginning with the day on which the variation or cancellation took effect.

(4) An application under this paragraph must be determined before the end of the period of 6 months beginning with the date on which the FCA received the completed application.

(5) The applicant may withdraw the application, by giving the FCA written notice, at any time before the FCA determines it.

(6) The FCA may direct that an application under this paragraph must—
- (a) contain specified information, or
- (b) take a specified form.

Annulment etc

5. (1) This paragraph applies where the FCA receives an application under paragraph 4 in relation to a decision to vary or cancel an authorised person's Part 4A permission under paragraph 1.

(2) The FCA may—
- (a) annul the decision unconditionally,
- (b) annul the decision subject to such conditions as it considers appropriate, or
- (c) refuse to annul the decision.

(3) The FCA may annul the decision (unconditionally or subject to conditions) only if satisfied that, in all the circumstances, it is just and reasonable to do so.

(4) The FCA's power under sub-paragraph (2)(b) includes the power—
- (a) to remove or describe differently a regulated activity specified in the permission, and
- (b) to withdraw or vary an approval given under section 59 that has effect in relation to the carrying on of a regulated activity specified in the permission,

provided that the activity in question was one to which the permission related immediately before the decision was taken.

(5) Where the FCA annuls the decision it must give the person a notice in writing setting out—
- (a) where the annulment is subject to conditions, the conditions, and
- (b) the date on which the annulment takes effect.

(6) If the FCA proposes to refuse to annul the decision it must give the person a warning notice.

(7) If the FCA decides to refuse to annul the decision it must give the person a decision notice.

Effect

6. (1) Where the FCA—
- (a) varies or cancels an authorised person's Part 4A permission under paragraph 1, but
- (b) that decision is subsequently annulled under paragraph 5,

the variation or cancellation is treated as if it had not taken place, subject as follows.

(2) The FCA does not become subject to any statutory obligation by virtue of sub-paragraph (1).

(3) Where, by virtue of sub-paragraph (1)—
- (a) a person becomes subject to a statutory obligation, and
- (b) the FCA has functions in relation to the obligation,

the FCA may, in exercising those functions, treat the person as if the person had not become subject to the obligation.

(4) If the FCA treats a person as not having become subject to an obligation, it must notify the person of that fact in such manner as it considers appropriate.

(5) In a case where paragraph 5(4)(a) applies—
- (a) the permission is treated as if it had been varied in accordance with the FCA's own-initiative variation power, and
- (b) that variation is treated as if it took effect on the date on which the annulment took effect.

(6) In a case where paragraph 5(4)(b) applies—
- (a) the approval is treated as if it had been withdrawn in accordance with section 63 or varied in accordance with section 63ZB (as the case may be), and
- (b) that withdrawal or variation is treated as if it took effect on the date on which the annulment took effect.

(7) In this paragraph "statutory obligation" means any obligation arising under or by virtue of this Act or any other enactment.

(8) In sub-paragraph (7) "enactment" includes—
- (a) the enactments listed in section 3T, and

(b) any retained direct EU legislation.

Right to refer matter to Tribunal

7. (1) This paragraph applies where the FCA—

(a) decides to vary or cancel an authorised person's Part 4A permission under paragraph 1,

(b) receives an application from the person under paragraph 4 in respect of that decision, and

(c) has disposed of that application under paragraph 5(2).

(2) Either party may refer the matter to the Tribunal.

(3) In determining a reference made under this paragraph, the Tribunal may give such directions, and may make such provision, as it considers reasonable for placing the person and other persons in the same position (as nearly as may be) as if the permission had not been varied or cancelled.

Supplementary

8. (1) Nothing in this Schedule affects the generality of any other provision made under or by virtue of this Act that confers power on the FCA to vary or cancel an authorised person's Part 4A permission.

(2) Nothing in paragraph 6(5) and (6) gives rise to a right to make a reference to the Tribunal.

(3) Sections 55U to 55X (applications made under Part 4A: procedure) do not apply in relation to an application made under paragraph 4.

(4) Section 55Z (cancellation of Part 4A permission: procedure) does not apply in relation to a proposal, or decision, to cancel an authorised person's Part 4A permission under paragraph 1.

(5) Section 55Z3(1) (right to refer matters to the Tribunal) does not apply in relation to the determination of an application under paragraph 4.

(6) In this Schedule "specified" means specified in a direction given by the FCA under this Schedule.

(7) A direction made by the FCA under this Schedule may make different provision for different cases.

(8) The FCA may revoke or amend a direction it makes under this Schedule.]

NOTES

Commencement: 1 July 2021.

Inserted by the Financial Services Act 2021, s 28, Sch 11, para 3, as from 1 July 2021.

SCHEDULES 7–9

(Schs 7, 8 repealed by the Financial Services Act 2012, s 16(1), (14)(k), (l), as from 1 April 2013. Sch 9 repealed by the Prospectus Regulations 2005, SI 2005/1433, reg 2(1), Sch 1, para 16, as from 1 July 2005.)

SCHEDULE 10
COMPENSATION: EXEMPTIONS

Section 90(2) and (5)

Statements believed to be true

[7.734]

1. (1) In this paragraph "statement" means—

(a) any untrue or misleading statement in listing particulars; or

(b) the omission from listing particulars of any matter required to be included by section 80 or 81.

(2) A person does not incur any liability under section 90(1) for loss caused by a statement if he satisfies the court that, at the time when the listing particulars were submitted to the [FCA], he reasonably believed (having made such enquiries, if any, as were reasonable) that—

(a) the statement was true and not misleading, or

(b) the matter whose omission caused the loss was properly omitted,

and that one or more of the conditions set out in sub-paragraph (3) are satisfied.

(3) The conditions are that—

(a) he continued in his belief until the time when the securities in question were acquired;

(b) they were acquired before it was reasonably practicable to bring a correction to the attention of persons likely to acquire them;

(c) before the securities were acquired, he had taken all such steps as it was reasonable for him to have taken to secure that a correction was brought to the attention of those persons;

(d) he continued in his belief until after the commencement of dealings in the securities following their admission to the official list and they were acquired after such a lapse of time that he ought in the circumstances to be reasonably excused.

Statements by experts

2. (1) In this paragraph "statement" means a statement included in listing particulars which—

(a) purports to be made by, or on the authority of, another person as an expert; and

(b) is stated to be included in the listing particulars with that other person's consent.

(2) A person does not incur any liability under section 90(1) for loss in respect of any securities caused by a statement if he satisfies the court that, at the time when the listing particulars were submitted to the [FCA], he reasonably believed that the other person—

(a) was competent to make or authorise the statement, and

(b) had consented to its inclusion in the form and context in which it was included,

and that one or more of the conditions set out in sub-paragraph (3) are satisfied.

(3) The conditions are that—

(a) he continued in his belief until the time when the securities were acquired;

(b) they were acquired before it was reasonably practicable to bring the fact that the expert was not competent, or had not consented, to the attention of persons likely to acquire the securities in question;
(c) before the securities were acquired he had taken all such steps as it was reasonable for him to have taken to secure that that fact was brought to the attention of those persons;
(d) he continued in his belief until after the commencement of dealings in the securities following their admission to the official list and they were acquired after such a lapse of time that he ought in the circumstances to be reasonably excused.

Corrections of statements

3. (1) In this paragraph "statement" has the same meaning as in paragraph 1.

(2) A person does not incur liability under section 90(1) for loss caused by a statement if he satisfies the court—
(a) that before the securities in question were acquired, a correction had been published in a manner calculated to bring it to the attention of persons likely to acquire the securities; or
(b) that he took all such steps as it was reasonable for him to take to secure such publication and reasonably believed that it had taken place before the securities were acquired.

(3) Nothing in this paragraph is to be taken as affecting paragraph 1.

Corrections of statements by experts

4. (1) In this paragraph "statement" has the same meaning as in paragraph 2.

(2) A person does not incur liability under section 90(1) for loss caused by a statement if he satisfies the court—
(a) that before the securities in question were acquired, the fact that the expert was not competent or had not consented had been published in a manner calculated to bring it to the attention of persons likely to acquire the securities; or
(b) that he took all such steps as it was reasonable for him to take to secure such publication and reasonably believed that it had taken place before the securities were acquired.

(3) Nothing in this paragraph is to be taken as affecting paragraph 2.

Official statements

5. A person does not incur any liability under section 90(1) for loss resulting from—
(a) a statement made by an official person which is included in the listing particulars, or
(b) a statement contained in a public official document which is included in the listing particulars,
if he satisfies the court that the statement is accurately and fairly reproduced.

False or misleading information known about

6. A person does not incur any liability under section 90(1) or (4) if he satisfies the court that the person suffering the loss acquired the securities in question with knowledge—
(a) that the statement was false or misleading,
(b) of the omitted matter, or
(c) of the change or new matter,
as the case may be.

Belief that supplementary listing particulars not called for

7. A person does not incur any liability under section 90(4) if he satisfies the court that he reasonably believed that the change or new matter in question was not such as to call for supplementary listing particulars.

Meaning of "expert"

8. "Expert" includes any engineer, valuer, accountant or other person whose profession, qualifications or experience give authority to a statement made by him.

NOTES

Paras 1, 2: word "FCA" in square brackets substituted by the Financial Services Act 2012, s 16(1), (13), as from 1 April 2013.

[SCHEDULE 10A
LIABILITY OF ISSUERS IN CONNECTION WITH PUBLISHED INFORMATION

Section 90A

PART 1 SCOPE OF THIS SCHEDULE

Securities to which this Schedule applies

[7.735]

1. (1) This Schedule applies to securities that are, with the consent of the issuer, admitted to trading on a securities market, where—
(a) the market is situated or operating in the United Kingdom, or
(b) the United Kingdom is the issuer's home State.

(2) For the purposes of this Schedule—
(a) an issuer of securities is not taken to have consented to the securities being admitted to trading on a securities market by reason only of having consented to their admission to trading on another market as a result of which they are admitted to trading on the first-mentioned market;
(b) an issuer who has accepted responsibility (to any extent) for any document prepared for the purposes of the admission of the securities to trading on a securities market (such as a prospectus or listing particulars) is taken to have consented to their admission to trading on that market.

[(3) For the purposes of this Schedule the United Kingdom is the home State of an issuer if—
(a) the transparency rules impose requirements on the issuer in relation to the securities, or

(b) the issuer has its registered office (or, if it does not have a registered office, its head office) in the United Kingdom.]

Published information to which this Schedule applies

2. (1) This Schedule applies to information published by the issuer of securities to which this Schedule applies—

(a) by recognised means, or

(b) by other means where the availability of the information has been announced by the issuer by recognised means.

(2) It is immaterial whether the information is required to be published (by recognised means or otherwise).

(3) The following are "recognised means"—

(a) a recognised information service;

(b) other means required or authorised to be used to communicate information to the market in question, or to the public, when a recognised information service is unavailable.

(4) A "recognised information service" means—

(a) in relation to a securities market situated or operating in the [United Kingdom], a service used for the dissemination of information in accordance with [Article 21 of the transparency obligations directive];

(b) in relation to a securities market situated or operating outside the [United Kingdom], a service used for the dissemination of information corresponding to that required to be disclosed under [transparency rules]; or

(c) in relation to any securities market, any other service used by issuers of securities for the dissemination of information required to be disclosed by the rules of the market.]

NOTES

Inserted by the Financial Services and Markets Act 2000 (Liability of Issuers) Regulations 2010, SI 2010/1192, reg 2(1), (3), Schedule, as from 1 October 2010.

Para 1: sub-para (3) substituted by the Official Listing of Securities, Prospectus and Transparency (Amendment etc) (EU Exit) Regulations 2019, SI 2019/707, regs 3, 37(1), (2), as from IP completion day (as defined in the European Union (Withdrawal Agreement) Act 2020, s 39).

Para 2: words in square brackets substituted by SI 2019/707, regs 3, 37(1), (2), as from IP completion day (as defined in the European Union (Withdrawal Agreement) Act 2020, s 39).

[PART 2 LIABILITY IN CONNECTION WITH PUBLISHED INFORMATION

Liability of issuer for misleading statement or dishonest omission

[7.736]

3. (1) An issuer of securities to which this Schedule applies is liable to pay compensation to a person who—

(a) acquires, continues to hold or disposes of the securities in reliance on published information to which this Schedule applies, and

(b) suffers loss in respect of the securities as a result of—

(i) any untrue or misleading statement in that published information, or

(ii) the omission from that published information of any matter required to be included in it.

(2) The issuer is liable in respect of an untrue or misleading statement only if a person discharging managerial responsibilities within the issuer knew the statement to be untrue or misleading or was reckless as to whether it was untrue or misleading.

(3) The issuer is liable in respect of the omission of any matter required to be included in published information only if a person discharging managerial responsibilities within the issuer knew the omission to be a dishonest concealment of a material fact.

(4) A loss is not regarded as suffered as a result of the statement or omission unless the person suffering it acquired, continued to hold or disposed of the relevant securities—

(a) in reliance on the information in question, and

(b) at a time when, and in circumstances in which, it was reasonable for him to rely on it.

4. An issuer of securities to which this Schedule applies is not liable under paragraph 3 to pay compensation to a person for loss suffered as a result of an untrue or misleading statement in, or omission from, published information to which this Schedule applies if—

(a) the published information is contained in listing particulars or a prospectus (or supplementary listing particulars or a supplementary prospectus), and

(b) the issuer is liable under section 90 (compensation for statements in listing particulars or prospectus) to pay compensation to the person in respect of the statement or omission.

Liability of issuer for dishonest delay in publishing information

5. (1) An issuer of securities to which this Schedule applies is liable to pay compensation to a person who—

(a) acquires, continues to hold or disposes of the securities, and

(b) suffers loss in respect of the securities as a result of delay by the issuer in publishing information to which this Schedule applies.

(2) The issuer is liable only if a person discharging managerial responsibilities within the issuer acted dishonestly in delaying the publication of the information.

Meaning of dishonesty

6. For the purposes of paragraphs 3(3) and 5(2) a person's conduct is regarded as dishonest if (and only if)—

(a) it is regarded as dishonest by persons who regularly trade on the securities market in question, and

(b) the person was aware (or must be taken to have been aware) that it was so regarded.

Exclusion of certain other liabilities

7. (1) The issuer is not subject—

(a) to any liability other than that provided for by paragraph 3 in respect of loss suffered as a result of reliance by any person on—
   (i) an untrue or misleading statement in published information to which this Schedule applies, or
   (ii) the omission from any such published information of any matter required to be included in it;
(b) to any liability other than that provided for by paragraph 5 in respect of loss suffered as a result of delay in the publication of information to which this Schedule applies.

(2) A person other than the issuer is not subject to any liability, other than to the issuer, in respect of any such loss.

(3) This paragraph does not affect—
(a) civil liability—
   (i) under section 90 (compensation for statements in listing particulars or prospectus),
   (ii) under rules made by virtue of section 954 of the Companies Act 2006 (compensation),
   (iii) for breach of contract,
   (iv) under the Misrepresentation Act 1967, or
   (v) arising from a person's having assumed responsibility, to a particular person for a particular purpose, for the accuracy or completeness of the information concerned;
(b) liability to a civil penalty; or
(c) criminal liability.

(4) This paragraph does not affect the powers conferred by sections 382 and 384 (powers of the court to make a restitution order and of the Authority to require restitution).

(5) References in this paragraph to liability, in relation to a person, include a reference to another person being entitled as against that person to be granted any civil remedy or to rescind or repudiate an agreement.]

NOTES

Inserted as noted to Part 1 of this Schedule at **[7.735]**.

[PART 3 SUPPLEMENTARY PROVISIONS

Interpretation

[7.737]

8. (1) In this Schedule—
[(a) "securities" means transferable securities as defined in Article 2(1)(24) of the markets in financial instruments regulation, other than money market instruments as defined in Article 2(1)(25A) of that regulation that have a maturity of less than 12 months (and includes instruments outside the United Kingdom);]
(b) "securities market" means—
   [(i) a regulated market as defined in Article 2(1)(13) of the markets in financial instruments regulation, or
   (ii) a multilateral trading facility as defined in Article 2(1)(14) of that regulation].

(2) References in this Schedule to the issuer of securities are—
(a) in relation to a depositary receipt, derivative instrument or other financial instrument representing securities where the issuer of the securities represented has consented to the admission of the instrument to trading as mentioned in paragraph 1(1), to the issuer of the securities represented;
(b) in any other case, to the person who issued the securities.

(3) References in this Schedule to the acquisition or disposal of securities include—
(a) acquisition or disposal of any interest in securities, or
(b) contracting to acquire or dispose of securities or of any interest in securities,

except where what is acquired or disposed of (or contracted to be acquired or disposed of) is a depositary receipt, derivative instrument or other financial instrument representing securities.

(4) References to continuing to hold securities have a corresponding meaning.

(5) For the purposes of this Schedule the following are persons "discharging managerial responsibilities" within an issuer—
(a) any director of the issuer (or person occupying the position of director, by whatever name called);
(b) in the case of an issuer whose affairs are managed by its members, any member of the issuer;
(c) in the case of an issuer that has no persons within paragraph (a) or (b), any senior executive of the issuer having responsibilities in relation to the information in question or its publication.

(6) The following definitions (which apply generally for the purposes of Part 6 of this Act) do not apply for the purposes of this Schedule:
(a) section 102A(1), (2) and (6) (meaning of "securities" and "issuer");
(b) . . .]

NOTES

Inserted as noted to Part 1 of this Schedule at **[7.735]**.

Para 8: words in square brackets in sub-para (1) substituted, and sub-para (6)(b) repealed, by the Official Listing of Securities, Prospectus and Transparency (Amendment etc) (EU Exit) Regulations 2019, SI 2019/707, regs 3, 37(1), (4), as from IP completion day (as defined in the European Union (Withdrawal Agreement) Act 2020, s 39).

[SCHEDULE 11

(Sch 11 repealed by the Prospectus Regulations 2005, SI 2005/1433, reg 2(1), Sch 1, para 16, as from 1 July 2005.)

[SCHEDULE 11A
TRANSFERABLE SECURITIES

Section [85(6A)]

NOTES

The enabling authority of this Schedule was substituted by the Financial Services and Markets Act 2000 (Prospectus) Regulations 2019, SI 2019/1043, regs 3, 35(1), (4), as from 21 July 2019.

PART 1

(This Schedule was inserted by the Prospectus Regulations 2005, SI 2005/1433, reg 2(2), Sch 2, as from 1 July 2005. Part 1 was repealed by the Financial Services and Markets Act 2000 (Prospectus) Regulations 2019, SI 2019/1043, regs 3, 35(1), (2), as from 21 July 2019.)

[PART 2

[7.738]

7. (1) . . .

(2) [The bodies recognised for the purposes of Article 1(2)(e) of the prospectus regulation are]—

(a) a charity[—

(i) as defined by section 1(1) of the Charities Act 2011, or

(ii) within the meaning of] section 35 of the Charities Act (Northern Ireland) 1964 (c 33 (NI));

[(b) a body entered in the Scottish Charity Register;]

(c) a housing association within the meaning of—

(i) section 5(1) of the Housing Act 1985 (c 68),

(ii) section 1 of the Housing Associations Act 1985 (c 69), or

(iii) Article 3 of the Housing (Northern Ireland) Order 1992 (SI 1992/1725 (NI 15));

[(d) a registered society that—

(i) is registered under the Co-operative and Community Benefit Societies Act 2014 as a community benefit society,

(ii) is a pre-commencement society within the meaning of that Act that was registered in accordance with section 2(2)(a)(ii) of that Act, or

(iii) is registered in accordance with section 1(2)(b) of the Industrial and Provident Societies Act (Northern Ireland) 1969;]

(e) . . .

8, 9. . . .

NOTES

Inserted by the Prospectus Regulations 2005, SI 2005/1433, reg 2(2), Sch 2, as from 1 July 2005.

Para 7: sub-para (1) was repealed, and the words in the first pair of square brackets in sub-para (2) were substituted, by the Financial Services and Markets Act 2000 (Prospectus) Regulations 2019, SI 2019/1043, regs 3, 35(1), (3)(a), (b), as from 21 July 2019. Words in square brackets in sub-para (2)(a) substituted by the Charities Act 2011, s 354, Sch 7, Pt 2, para 86, as from 14 March 2012. Sub-para (2)(b) substituted by the Charities and Trustee Investment (Scotland) Act 2005 (Consequential Provisions and Modifications) Order 2006, SI 2006/242, art 5, Schedule, Pt 1, para 7, as from 1 April 2006. Sub-para (2)(d) substituted by the Co-operative and Community Benefit Societies Act 2014, s 151, Sch 4, Pt 2, paras 68, 72, as from 1 August 2014. Sub-para (2)(e) repealed by the Official Listing of Securities, Prospectus and Transparency (Amendment etc) (EU Exit) Regulations 2019, SI 2019/707, regs 3, 38(1), (6), as from IP completion day (as defined in the European Union (Withdrawal Agreement) Act 2020, s 39).

Paras 8, 9: repealed by SI 2019/1043, regs 3, 35(1), (3)(c), as from 21 July 2019.

[SCHEDULE 11B

(Sch 11B (Connected persons) was originally inserted by the Financial Services and Markets Act 2000 (Amendment) Regulations 2009, SI 2009/2461, reg 2(2), Schedule, as from 1 October 2009, and was repealed by the Financial Services and Markets Act 2000 (Market Abuse) Regulations 2016, SI 2016/680, reg 8(1), (10), as from 3 July 2016.)

SCHEDULE 12
TRANSFER SCHEMES: CERTIFICATES

NOTES

Transitional provisions etc in connection with the commencement of the Financial Services Act 2012: see the Financial Services Act 2012 (Transitional Provisions) (Miscellaneous Provisions) Order 2013, SI 2013/442, art 9.

Sections 111(2) and 115

PART I INSURANCE BUSINESS TRANSFER SCHEMES

[7.739]

[**1.** For the purposes of section 111(2) the appropriate certificate, in relation to an insurance business transfer scheme, is a certificate under paragraph 2.]

Certificates as to margin of solvency

2. (1) A certificate under this paragraph is to be given—

(a) by the relevant authority; or

(b) in a case in which there is no relevant authority, by the [appropriate regulator].

(2) A certificate given under sub-paragraph (1)(a) is one certifying that, taking the proposed transfer into account—

(a) the transferee possesses, or will possess before the scheme takes effect, the necessary margin of solvency; or

(b) there is no necessary margin of solvency applicable to the transferee.

Part 7 Financial Services Acts

(3) A certificate under sub-paragraph (1)(b) is one certifying that the [appropriate regulator] has received from the authority which it considers to be the authority responsible for supervising persons who effect or carry out contracts of insurance in the place to which the business is to be transferred [certification] that, taking the proposed transfer into account—

(a) the transferee possesses or will possess before the scheme takes effect the margin of solvency required under the law applicable in that place; or
(b) there is no such margin of solvency applicable to the transferee.

(4) "Necessary margin of solvency" means the margin of solvency required in relation to the transferee, taking the proposed transfer into account, under the law which it is the responsibility of the relevant authority to apply.

(5) "Margin of solvency" means the excess of the value of the assets of the transferee over the amount of its liabilities.

(6) "Relevant authority" means—

(a) . . .
[(aa) . . .]
(b) if the transferee is a Swiss general insurer, the authority responsible in Switzerland for supervising persons who effect or carry out contracts of insurance;
(c) if the transferee is an authorised person not falling within [paragraph . . .] . . . (b)[—
   (i) the PRA, if the transferee is a PRA-authorised person with a Part 4A permission . . . ;
   (ii) the FCA, if the transferee is a person with a Part 4A permission . . . but is not a PRA-authorised person.]

(7) In sub-paragraph (6), any reference to a transferee of a particular description includes a reference to a transferee who will be of that description if the proposed scheme takes effect.

[(7A) . . .]

(8) "Swiss general insurer" means a body—

(a) whose head office is in Switzerland;
(b) which has permission to carry on regulated activities consisting of the effecting and carrying out of contracts of general insurance; and
(c) whose permission is not restricted to the effecting or carrying out of contracts of reinsurance.

[(9) . . .]

. . .

3, 3A, 4, 5, 5A, 6. . . .

NOTES

Para 1: substituted by the Financial Services and Markets Act 2000 (Amendment) (EU Exit) Regulations 2019, SI 2019/632, regs 104, 105, as from IP completion day (as defined in the European Union (Withdrawal Agreement) Act 2020, s 39).

Para 2 is amended as follows:

All the omitted words were repealed by SI 2019/632, regs 104, 106, as from IP completion day (as defined in the European Union (Withdrawal Agreement) Act 2020, s 39). Note that reg 106(2) of the 2019 Regulations was amended by the Gibraltar (Miscellaneous Amendments) (EU Exit) Regulations 2019, SI 2019/680, reg 9(1), (6), with effect from immediately before IP completion day (and the effect of the amendment has been incorporated).

Words "appropriate regulator" in square brackets in sub-paras (1)(b) and (3) substituted, words in second pair of square brackets in sub-para (6)(c) substituted, and word in second pair of square brackets in sub-para (3) inserted, by the Financial Services Act 2012, s 22, Sch 6, paras 9, 11, as from 1 April 2013.

Words in square brackets in sub-para (6)(a) inserted, sub-paras (6)(aa), (7A) and (9) inserted, and words in first pair of square brackets in sub-para (6)(c) substituted, by SI 2007/3253, reg 2(1), Sch 1, paras 1, 2(5)(e), as from 10 December 2007.

Sub-paras (6)(aa), (7A) and (9) subsequently substituted by SI 2015/575, reg 59, Sch 1, Pt 1, paras 1, 18(1), (3), as from 1 January 2016.

Paras 3, 3A, 4, 5, 5A, 6: repealed by SI 2019/632, regs 104, 107, as from IP completion day (as defined in the European Union (Withdrawal Agreement) Act 2020, s 39). Para 3A was originally inserted by SI 2015/575, reg 59, Sch 1, Pt 1, paras 1, 18(1), (5), as from 1 January 2016. Para 5A was originally inserted by SI 2007/3253, reg 2(1), Sch 1, paras 1, 2(5)(f), as from 10 December 2007.

Regulations: the Financial Services and Markets Act 2000 (Control of Business Transfers) (Requirements on Applicants) Regulations 2001, SI 2001/3625.

PART II BANKING BUSINESS TRANSFER SCHEMES

[7.740]

[**7.** For the purposes of section 111(2) the appropriate certificate, in relation to a banking business transfer scheme, is a certificate under paragraph 8.]

Certificates as to financial resources

8. (1) A certificate under this paragraph is one given by the relevant authority and certifying that, taking the proposed transfer into account, the transferee possesses, or will possess before the scheme takes effect, adequate financial resources.

(2) "Relevant authority" means—

[(a) if the transferee is a PRA-authorised person with a Part 4A permission . . . , the PRA;
(aa) if the transferee is a person with Part 4A permission . . . but is not a PRA-authorised person, the FCA;]
(b) . . .
(c) if the transferee does not fall within paragraph [(a) or (aa)], the authority responsible for the supervision of the transferee's business in the place in which the transferee has its head office.

(3) In sub-paragraph (2), any reference to a transferee of a particular description of person includes a reference to a transferee who will be of that description if the proposed banking business transfer scheme takes effect.

9. . . .

NOTES

Para 7: substituted by the Financial Services and Markets Act 2000 (Amendment) (EU Exit) Regulations 2019, SI 2019/632, regs 104, 108, as from IP completion day (as defined in the European Union (Withdrawal Agreement) Act 2020, s 39).

Para 8: sub-paras (2)(a), (aa) substituted (for the original sub-para (2)(a)) by the Financial Services Act 2012, s 22, Sch 6, paras 9, 16, as from 1 April 2013. The words omitted from sub-paras (2)(a), (aa) were repealed, sub-para (2)(b) was repealed, and the words in square brackets in sub-para (2)(c) were substituted, by SI 2019/632, regs 104, 109, as from IP completion day (as defined in the European Union (Withdrawal Agreement) Act 2020, s 39).

Para 9: repealed SI 2019/632, regs 104, 110, as from IP completion day (as defined in the European Union (Withdrawal Agreement) Act 2020, s 39).

[PART 2A RECLAIM FUND BUSINESS TRANSFER SCHEMES

Certificate as to financial resources

[7.741]

9A. [(1)] For the purposes of section 111(2) the appropriate certificate, in relation to a reclaim fund business transfer scheme, is a certificate given by the [appropriate regulator] certifying that, taking the proposed transfer into account, the transferee possesses, or will possess before the scheme takes effect, adequate financial resources.

[(2) In this paragraph the "relevant regulator" means—

(a) if the transferee is a PRA-authorised person, the PRA;

(b) in any other case, the FCA.]

NOTES

Inserted by the Dormant Bank and Building Society Accounts Act 2008, s 15, Sch 2, para 5, as from 12 March 2009.

Sub-para (1) numbered as such, words in square brackets substituted in that paragraph, and sub-para (2) added, by the Financial Services Act 2012, s 22, Sch 6, paras 9, 18, as from 1 April 2013.

[PART 2B RING-FENCING TRANSFER SCHEMES

[Appropriate certificates

[7.742]

9B. For the purposes of section 111(2) the appropriate certificates, in relation to a ring-fencing transfer scheme, are—

(a) a certificate given by the PRA certifying its approval of the application, and

(b) a certificate under paragraph 9C.]

Certificate as to financial resources

9C. (1) A certificate under this paragraph is one given by the relevant authority and certifying that, taking the proposed transfer into account, the transferee possesses, or will possess before the scheme takes effect, adequate financial resources.

(2) "Relevant authority" means—

(a) if the transferee is a PRA-authorised person with a Part 4A permission . . . , the PRA;

(b) . . .

(c) if the transferee does not fall within paragraph (a) . . . but is subject to regulation in a country or territory outside the United Kingdom, the authority responsible for the supervision of the transferee's business in the place in which the transferee has its head office;

(d) in any other case, the FCA.

(3) In sub-paragraph (2), any reference to a transferee of a particular description includes a reference to a transferee who will be of that description if the proposed ring-fencing transfer scheme takes effect.

. . .

9D. . . .]

NOTES

Inserted by the Financial Services (Banking Reform) Act 2013, s 6, Sch 1, paras 1, 13, as from 1 March 2014.

Para 9B: substituted by the Financial Services and Markets Act 2000 (Amendment) (EU Exit) Regulations 2019, SI 2019/632, regs 104, 111, as from IP completion day (as defined in the European Union (Withdrawal Agreement) Act 2020, s 39).

Para 9C: words omitted repealed by SI 2019/632, regs 104, 112, as from IP completion day (as defined in the European Union (Withdrawal Agreement) Act 2020, s 39).

Para 9D: repealed by SI 2019/632, regs 104, 113, as from IP completion day (as defined in the European Union (Withdrawal Agreement) Act 2020, s 39).

PART III INSURANCE BUSINESS TRANSFERS EFFECTED OUTSIDE THE UNITED KINGDOM

[7.743]

10. (1) This paragraph applies to a proposal to execute under provisions corresponding to Part VII in a country or territory other than the United Kingdom an instrument transferring all the rights and obligations of the transferor under general or long-term insurance policies, or under such descriptions of such policies as may be specified in the instrument, to the transferee if [the condition in sub-paragraph (4)] is met in relation to it.

(2) . . .

[(3) . . .

(4) The transferor is a Swiss general insurer and the transferee is [a UK authorised person as defined in section 105(8)].]

Part 7 Financial Services Acts

(5) In relation to a proposed transfer to which this paragraph applies, the [regulator which supervises the transferee's margin of solvency] may, if it is satisfied that the transferee possesses the necessary margin of solvency, issue a certificate to that effect.

(6) "Necessary margin of solvency" means the margin of solvency which the transferee, taking the proposed transfer into account, is required by the [FCA or the PRA] to maintain.

(7) "Swiss general insurer" has the same meaning as in paragraph 2.

(8) "General policy" means a policy evidencing a contract which, if it had been effected by the transferee, would have constituted the carrying on of a regulated activity consisting of the effecting of contracts of general insurance.

(9) "Long-term policy" means a policy evidencing a contract which, if it had been effected by the transferee, would have constituted the carrying on of a regulated activity consisting of the effecting of contracts of long-term insurance.

NOTES

Para 10 is amended as follows:

Words in square brackets sub-paras (1) and (4) substituted, sub-paras (2) and (3) repealed, by the Financial Services and Markets Act 2000 (Amendment) (EU Exit) Regulations 2019, SI 2019/632, regs 104, 114, as from IP completion day (as defined in the European Union (Withdrawal Agreement) Act 2020, s 39).

Sub-paras (3), (4) were previously substituted by the Solvency 2 Regulations 2015, SI 2015/575, reg 59, Sch 1, Pt 1, paras 1, 18(1), (7), as from 1 January 2016.

Words in square brackets in sub-paras (5) and (6) substituted by the Financial Services Act 2012, s 22, Sch 6, paras 9, 19, as from 1 April 2013.

SCHEDULES 13, 14

(Sch 13 repealed by the Transfer of Tribunal Functions Order 2010, SI 2010/22, art 5(1), Sch 2, paras 43, 49, as from 6 April 2010. Sch 14 repealed by the Financial Services Act 2012, s 24(4), as from 1 April 2013.)

SCHEDULE 15
INFORMATION AND INVESTIGATIONS: CONNECTED PERSONS

Sections 165(11) and 171(4)

PART I RULES FOR SPECIFIC BODIES

Corporate bodies

[7.744]

1. If the authorised person ("BC") is a body corporate, a person who is or has been—

(a) an officer or manager of BC or of a parent undertaking of BC;
(b) an employee of BC;
(c) an agent of BC or of a parent undertaking of BC.

Partnerships

2. If the authorised person ("PP") is a partnership, a person who is or has been a member, manager, employee or agent of PP.

Unincorporated associations

3. If the authorised person ("UA") is an unincorporated association of persons which is neither a partnership nor an unincorporated friendly society, a person who is or has been an officer, manager, employee or agent of UA.

Friendly societies

4. (1) If the authorised person ("FS") is a friendly society, a person who is or has been an officer, manager or employee of FS.

(2) In relation to FS, "officer" and "manager" have the same meaning as in section 119(1) of the Friendly Societies Act 1992.

Building societies

5. (1) If the authorised person ("BS") is a building society, a person who is or has been an officer or employee of BS.

(2) In relation to BS, "officer" has the same meaning as it has in section 119(1) of the Building Societies Act 1986.

Individuals

6. If the authorised person ("IP") is an individual, a person who is or has been an employee or agent of IP.

Application to sections 171 and 172

7. For the purposes of sections 171 and 172, if the person under investigation is not an authorised person the references in this Part of this Schedule to an authorised person are to be taken to be references to the person under investigation.

PART II ADDITIONAL RULES

[7.745]

8. A person who is, or at the relevant time was, the partner, manager, employee, agent, appointed representative, banker, auditor, actuary or solicitor of—

(a) the person under investigation ("A");
(b) a parent undertaking of A;
(c) a subsidiary undertaking of A;
(d) a subsidiary undertaking of a parent undertaking of A; or
(e) a parent undertaking of a subsidiary undertaking of A.

SCHEDULES 16, 17

(Sch 16 repealed by the Financial Services and Markets Act 2000 (Regulated Activities) (Amendment) (No 2) Order 2013, 2013/1881, art 10(1), (20), as from 26 July 2013 (certain purposes), and as from 1 April 2014 (otherwise). Sch 17 omitted due to space considerations (see further, the introductory notes to this Act).)

[SCHEDULE 17A
FURTHER PROVISION IN RELATION TO EXERCISE OF PART 18 FUNCTIONS BY BANK OF ENGLAND

Section 285A

PART 1 CO-OPERATION BETWEEN APPROPRIATE REGULATORS

Memorandum of understanding between appropriate regulators and PRA

[7.746]

1. (1) The appropriate regulators must prepare and maintain a memorandum describing how they intend to work together in exercising their functions in relation to persons who are recognised bodies.

(2) The memorandum must in particular make provision about—

(a) the need for each party when exercising a function in relation to any person ("A") who is a recognised body, or any member of A's group, to have regard to the exercise (or possible exercise) of any function by the other party in relation to A or any member of A's group;

(b) the role of each party in cases where they are both exercising functions in relation to the same persons;

(c) the obtaining and disclosure of information;

(d) the co-ordination by the parties of the exercise of their powers to appoint competent persons under Part 11 (information gathering and investigations) to conduct investigations on their behalf.

(3) In this paragraph any reference to a function is to any function whether conferred by or under any provision of this Part of this Act or any other provision of this Act or otherwise.

2. (1) The [FCA] and the PRA must prepare and maintain a memorandum describing how they intend to work together in exercising their functions in relation to persons who are recognised bodies and who—

(a) are PRA-authorised persons; or

(b) are members of a group of which a member is a PRA-authorised person.

(2) The memorandum must in particular make provision about—

(a) the need for each party when exercising a function in relation to any person ("A") who is a recognised body, or any member of A's group, to have regard to the exercise (or possible exercise) of any function by the other party in relation to A or any member of A's group;

(b) the role of each party in cases where they are both exercising functions in relation to the same persons;

(c) the obtaining and disclosure of information;

(d) the co-ordination by the parties of the exercise of their powers to appoint competent persons under Part 11 (information gathering and investigations) to conduct investigations on their behalf.

(3) In this paragraph any reference to a function is to any function whether conferred by or under any provision of this Part of this Act or any other provision of this Act or otherwise.

3. The parties to a memorandum under paragraph 1 or 2 must review the memorandum at least once in each calendar year.

4. The parties to a memorandum under paragraph 1 or 2 must give the Treasury a copy of the memorandum and any revised memorandum.

5. The Treasury must lay before Parliament a copy of any document received by them under paragraph 4.

6. The parties to a memorandum under paragraph 1 or 2 must ensure that the memorandum as currently in force is published in the way appearing to them to be best calculated to bring it to the attention of the public.

Notification by FCA of action in relation to recognised clearing houses

7. The FCA must notify the Bank of England of any direction given by it under section 128 to a recognised clearing house [or a recognised CSD] (market abuse: suspension of investigations).

8. The FCA must notify the Bank of England of any requirement imposed by it under section 313A on a recognised clearing house (power to require suspension or removal of financial instruments from trading).]

NOTES

Inserted by the Financial Services Act 2012, s 29(2), Sch 7, as from 24 January 2013 (for the purposes of making orders and in so far as relating to the preparation of a memorandum, the making of rules or the preparation and issue of a statement of policy), and as from 1 April 2013 (otherwise).

Para 2: word in square brackets substituted by the Bank of England and Financial Services Act 2016, s 16, Sch 2, Pt 2, paras 26, 51(1), (2), as from 1 March 2017.

Para 7: words in square brackets inserted by the Central Securities Depositories Regulations 2017, SI 2017/1064, reg 2(1), (39)(a), as from 28 November 2017.

[PART 2 APPLICATION OF PROVISIONS OF THIS ACT IN RELATION TO BANK OF ENGLAND

NOTES

Transitional provisions etc in connection with the commencement of the Financial Services Act 2012: see the Financial Services Act 2012 (Transitional Provisions) (Miscellaneous Provisions) Order 2013, SI 2013/442, art 70.

Introduction

[7.747]

9. (1) The provisions of this Act mentioned in this Part of this Schedule are to apply in relation to the Bank of England in accordance with the provision made by this Part of this Schedule.

(2) In any case where sub-paragraph (1) applies—

(a) any reference in this Act to the FCA or the PRA which is contained in, or relates to, any of those provisions (however expressed) is to be read as a reference to the Bank; and

(b) this Act has effect with any other necessary modifications.

Rules

10. (1) The following provisions of Part 9A of this Act are to apply in relation to rules made by the Bank under any provision made by or under this Act—

(a) section 137T (general supplementary powers);

(b) sections 138A and 138B (modification or waiver of rules), but with the omission of subsection (4)(b) of section 138A and subsection (4) of section 138B;

(c) section 138C (evidential provisions);

(d) section 138D (actions for damages), but with the omission of subsection (2);

(e) section 138E (limits on effect of contravening rules);

(f) section 138F (notification of rules);

(g) section 138G (rule-making instruments);

(h) section 138H (verification of rules);

(i) section 138J (consultation), but with the omission of subsections (1)(a), (2)(c) and (5)(b); and

(j) section 138L (consultation: general exemptions), but with the omission of [subsection (1)].

(2) Any reference in any of those provisions to an authorised person is to be read as a reference to a recognised clearing house[. . . or a recognised CSD].

(3) Section 138J(2)(d) has effect in relation to rules proposed to be made by the Bank as if the reference to the compatibility of the proposed rules with the provisions mentioned in section 138J(2)(d) were a reference to their compatibility with the Bank's financial stability objective.

(4) Section 138L(2) has effect as if for paragraphs (a) and (b) there were substituted "be prejudicial to financial stability".

[(5) Rules made by the Bank under any provision made by or under this Act may not modify, amend or revoke any retained direct EU legislation (except retained direct EU legislation which takes the form of rules made by the Bank).]

Information gathering and investigations

11. (1) The powers conferred by section 165(1) and (3) (power to require information) are exercisable by the Bank or (as the case may be) its officers to impose requirements on—

(a) a recognised clearing house;

[(aa) a recognised CSD;

[(ab) a third country CSD, in relation to any services referred to in the Annex to the CSD regulation which the third country CSD provides in the United Kingdom;]

[(ac) a third country central counterparty and any person to whom that central counterparty has outsourced operational functions, services or activities;]

(b) a person who for the purposes of section 165 is connected with a recognised clearing house[, a third country central counterparty] [[or a recognised CSD] (as the case may be)].

(2) The information or documents that the Bank may require to be provided or produced are limited to—

(a) information or documents reasonably required in connection with the exercise by the Bank of functions conferred on it by or under this Part of this Act;

(b) information or documents reasonably required in connection with the exercise by the Bank of any of its other functions in pursuance of its financial stability objective; . . .

(c) information or documents which the Bank reasonably considers may enable or assist the FCA in discharging functions conferred on the FCA by or under this Act[; and

[(d) information or documents reasonably required in connection with the exercise by the Bank of its functions—

(i) under—

(aa) the EMIR regulation,

(bb) the CSD regulation,

(cc) any EU regulation originally made under the CSD Regulation which is retained direct EU legislation, or

(dd) any subordinate legislation made under the CSD Regulation on or after IP completion day;

(ii) in connection with Article 4 or 15 of the SFT regulation; or

(iii) under any subordinate legislation made under the SFT regulation on or after IP completion day].

(3) In consequence of the provision made by sub-paragraph (2), section 165(4) is not to apply in relation to section 165(1) and (3) as applied by this paragraph.

12. The power conferred by section 166 (reports by skilled person) is exercisable by the Bank as if references in that section to an authorised person were to a [recognised clearing house, third country central counterparty or a recognised CSD].

13. (1) The powers conferred by section 167 (appointment of persons to carry out general investigations) are exercisable by the Bank as if references in that section to an authorised person were to any recognised clearing house other than an overseas clearing house [or to any Tier 2 third country central counterparty] [or to any recognised CSD].

[(1A) . . .]

(2) In addition to the powers conferred by section 171, a person conducting an investigation under section 167 as a result of this paragraph is to have the powers conferred by sections 172 and 173 (and for this purpose the references in those sections to an investigator are to be read accordingly).

14. (1) The power conferred by section 168(5) (appointment of persons to carry out investigations in particular cases) is exercisable by the Bank.

(2) That power is exercisable if it appears to the Bank that there are circumstances suggesting that—

(a) a clearing house [or a central securities depository] may be guilty of an offence under section 398(1) or an offence under prescribed regulations relating to money laundering;

(b) a clearing house [or a central securities depository] may have contravened a rule made by the Bank under this Part of this Act;

(c) a clearing house [or a central securities depository] may have contravened the recognition requirements;

(d) a clearing house [or a central securities depository] may have contravened any [qualifying provision] that is specified, or of a description specified, for the purposes of this sub-paragraph by the Treasury by order;

(e) a clearing house [or a central securities depository] may have breached the general prohibition;

[(f) . . .]

[(g) a third country central counterparty may be guilty of an offence under section 398(1);

(h) a Tier 2 third country central counterparty may have contravened the requirements of the EMIR regulation].

(3) In addition to the powers conferred by section 171, a person conducting an investigation under section 168(5) as a result of this paragraph is to have the powers conferred by sections 172 and 173 (and for this purpose the references in those sections to an investigator are to be read accordingly).

15. An overseas regulator may, in accordance with section 169, request the Bank to exercise the power conferred by section 165 (as applied by paragraph 11 of this Schedule).

16. The power to give information under section 176(1) (entry of premises under warrant) is exercisable by the Bank, or an investigator appointed by the Bank, as if the reference to the second set of conditions were omitted.

Powers in relation to parent undertakings

17. (1) The following provisions of Part 12A of this Act are to apply in relation to the Bank—

(a) section 192C (power to direct qualifying parent undertaking);

(b) section 192D (requirements that may be imposed);

(c) section 192E (direction: procedure);

(d) section 192G (references to Tribunal);

(e) section 192H (statement of policy);

(f) section 192I (statement of policy: procedure);

(g) section 192J (rules requiring provision of information);

(h) sections 192K to 192N (enforcement).

(2) For the purposes of those provisions section 192B (meaning of "qualifying parent undertaking") is to apply as if the reference in subsection (1) to a qualifying authorised person or recognised UK investment exchange were a reference to a recognised clearing house other than an overseas clearing house [or to a recognised CSD].

(3) Section 192C has effect as if—

(a) the general condition in subsection (2) were that the Bank considers that it is desirable to give the direction for the purpose of the effective regulation of one or more recognised clearing houses [or recognised CSDs] in the group of the qualifying parent undertaking,

(b) subsections (3) and (4) were omitted, and

(c) the reference in subsection (5)(a) to authorised persons or recognised investment exchanges were a reference to recognised clearing houses [or recognised CSDs].

(4) Section 192E has effect as if the reference in subsection (1) to an authorised person or recognised investment exchange were a reference to a recognised clearing house [or a recognised CSD].

(5) Section 192I has effect as if [subsection (1)(a) required consultation with the FCA].

(6) Before the Bank gives a notice under section 192E(1) or (8)(b)—

(a) if the notice relates to the parent undertaking of an authorised person or recognised investment exchange, the Bank must consult the FCA, and

(b) . . .

Auditors

18. (1) Section 342 (information given by auditor to a regulator) applies in relation to a relevant auditor as if—

(a) the references in that section to a recognised investment exchange were to a recognised clearing house [or a recognised CSD],

(b) in the case of an auditor of a recognised clearing house [or a recognised CSD] which is also an authorised person or recognised investment exchange, the references to a regulator included the Bank, and

(c) in the case of an auditor of a recognised clearing house [or a recognised CSD] not falling within paragraph (b), the references to a regulator were to the Bank.

(2) A "relevant auditor" is a person who is, or has been, an auditor of a recognised clearing house [or a recognised CSD] appointed under or as a result of a statutory provision[, the EMIR regulation or the CSD regulation].

19. (1) Section 343 (information given by auditor: person with close links) applies in relation to a relevant auditor as if—

(a) the references in that section to a recognised investment exchange were to a recognised clearing house [or a recognised CSD],

(b) in the case of an auditor of a recognised clearing house [or a recognised CSD] which is an authorised person or which is a recognised investment exchange, the references to a regulator included the Bank, and

Part 7 Financial Services Acts

(c) in the case of an auditor of a recognised clearing house [or a recognised CSD] not falling within paragraph (b), the references to a regulator were to the Bank.

(2) A "relevant auditor" is a person who—

(a) is, or has been, an auditor of a recognised clearing house [or a recognised CSD] appointed under or as a result of a statutory provision[, the EMIR regulation or the CSD regulation], and

(b) is, or has been, an auditor of a person who has close links with the recognised clearing house [or the recognised CSD].

20. Section 344 (duty of auditor resigning to give notice) applies to an auditor to whom section 342 applies (whether by virtue of paragraph 18 or otherwise) as if—

(a) the references in that section to a recognised investment exchange were to a recognised clearing house [or a recognised CSD],

(b) in the case of an auditor of a recognised clearing house [or a recognised CSD] which is neither an authorised person nor a recognised investment exchange, the reference in the definition of "the appropriate regulator" to the FCA were a reference to the Bank,

(c) in the case of an auditor of a recognised clearing house [or a recognised CSD] which is a PRA-authorised person, the reference in the definition of "the appropriate regulator" to the PRA were a reference to the PRA and the Bank, and

(d) in the case, not falling within paragraph (c), of an auditor of a recognised clearing house [or a recognised CSD] which is an authorised person or which is a recognised investment exchange, the reference in the definition of "the appropriate regulator" to the FCA were a reference to the FCA and the Bank.

21. Sections 345A to 345E apply to auditors to whom section 342 applies only by virtue of paragraph 18 as if—

(a) the references in those sections to an auditor or actuary to whom section 342 applies were to an auditor to whom section 342 applies by virtue of paragraph 18,

(b) the references in those sections to a PRA-authorised person were to a recognised clearing house [or a recognised CSD],

(c) in a case where the Bank disqualifies a person from being an auditor of a recognised clearing house [or a recognised CSD] that is also a recognised investment exchange, section 345A(5)(a) required the Bank to notify the FCA, and

(d) the references in sections 345D and 345E to a regulator included the Bank.

Public record and disclosure of information

22. Section 347 (record of authorised persons, recognised investment exchanges, etc), so far as it relates to recognised investment exchanges, applies in relation to the Bank as if references in that section to a recognised investment exchange were to a recognised clearing house[, third country central counterparty][, a third country CSD] [or a recognised CSD].

23. [(1)] Sections 348 to 350 and 353 (disclosure of information) apply in relation to information received by the Bank for the purposes of, or in the discharge of, any of its functions relating to recognised clearing houses [or recognised CSDs] [or any of its functions under the EMIR regulation][, the CSD regulation [, any EU regulation originally made under the CSD regulation which is retained direct EU legislation, or any subordinate legislation made under the CSD regulation on or after IP completion day]].

[(2) Paragraph 9(2)(a) does not apply to the reference to the PRA in section 348(8).]

[Co-operation

23A. Section 354B (co-operation) applies in relation to the Bank for the purposes of, or in the discharge of, any of its functions under—

(a) the EMIR regulation;

(b) the CSD regulation;

(c) the SFT regulation;

(d) any EU regulation, originally made under the CSD regulation or the SFT regulation, which is retained direct EU legislation; or

(e) any subordinate legislation (within the meaning of the Interpretation Act 1978) made under the CSD regulation, or the SFT regulation, on or after IP completion day.]

Insolvency

24. (1) The following provisions of Part 24 of this Act are to apply in relation to the Bank—

[(za) sections 355A and 355B (powers to participate in proceedings under Part 26A of the Companies Act 2006);]

(a) section 356 (powers to participate in proceedings: company voluntary arrangements);

(b) section 358 (powers to participate in proceedings: trust deeds for creditors in Scotland);

(c) section 359 (administration order);

(d) section 362 (powers to participate in administration proceedings);

(e) section 362A (consent to appointment of administrator);

(f) section 363 (powers to participate in proceedings: receivership);

(g) section 365 (powers to participate in proceedings: voluntary winding-up);

(h) section 367 (winding-up petitions);

(i) section 371 (powers to participate in proceedings: winding-up).

(2) Those provisions are to apply as if any reference to an authorised person or recognised investment exchange [(other than the reference to "an authorised person" in section 355B(2)(a))] were a reference to a recognised clearing house [or a recognised CSD].

25. [(1)] In the case of any regulated activity which is carried on for the purposes of, or in connection with, the provision of clearing services, the reference to the FCA in section 375(1) is to be read as including a reference to the Bank.

[(2) In the case of any regulated activity which is carried on for the purposes of, or in connection with, the provision of any service mentioned in section 285(3D), the reference to the FCA in section 375(1) is to be read as including a reference to the Bank.]

Injunctions and restitution

26. (1) The power to make an application under section 380(1), (2) or (3) (injunctions) is exercisable by the Bank.

(2) For the purposes of the application, any reference in that section to a relevant requirement is to—

(a) a requirement that is imposed by or under any provision of this Part of this Act that relates to a recognised clearing house [[or a recognised CSD] (and for this purpose a prohibition imposed under section 312FA(2)(c) (prohibition on person holding office etc with a central securities depository) is treated as a requirement)];

(b) a requirement that is imposed under any other provision of this Act by the Bank;

(c) a requirement that is imposed by any [qualifying provision] that is specified, or of a description specified, for the purposes of this sub-paragraph by the Treasury by order; or

(d) a requirement that is imposed by this Act and whose contravention constitutes an offence that the Bank has power to prosecute under this Act (see section 401, as applied by paragraph 31).

27. (1) The power to make an application under section 382(1) (restitution order) is exercisable by the Bank.

(2) For the purposes of the application, any reference in that section to a relevant requirement is to be read in accordance with paragraph 26(2) of this Schedule [(subject to sub-paragraph (3))].

[(3) The power to make an application under section 382(1) is not exercisable by the Bank in respect of the contravention of a requirement imposed by or under Article 4 or 15 of the SFT regulation.]

28. (1) The power conferred by section 384(5) (power of FCA to require restitution order) is exercisable by the Bank.

(2) That power is exercisable if the Bank is satisfied that a recognised clearing house [or a recognised CSD] has contravened a relevant requirement, or been knowingly concerned in the contravention of a relevant requirement, and—

(a) that profits have accrued to the recognised clearing house [or the recognised CSD] as a result of the contravention; or

(b) that one or more persons have suffered loss or been otherwise adversely affected as a result of the contravention.

(3) For the purposes of that power, "relevant requirement" is to be read in accordance with paragraph 26(2) of this Schedule[(subject to sub-paragraph (3A))].

[(3A) The power conferred by section 384(5) is not exercisable by the Bank in respect of the contravention of a requirement imposed by or under Article 4 or 15 of the SFT regulation].]

(4) Where this paragraph applies, section 384(5) and (6) are to have effect as if—

(a) any reference to the person concerned were a reference to the recognised clearing house [or the recognised CSD]; and

(b) any reference to subsection (1) were a reference to sub-paragraph (2) of this paragraph.

Notices

29. The provisions of Part 26 of this Act (notices) apply in relation to a warning or decision notice given by the Bank under section 192L, 312G or 312H as they apply in relation to such a notice given by the FCA under that section.

Offences

30. Section 398 (misleading the FCA: residual cases) applies to information given to the Bank in purported compliance with—

(a) a requirement that is imposed by or under any provision of Part 18 of this Act that relates to a recognised clearing house[, a third country central counterparty][, a recognised CSD or an EEA CSD];

(b) a requirement that is imposed under any other provision of this Act by the Bank; or

(c) a requirement that is imposed by any [qualifying provision] specified, or of a description specified, for the purposes of this paragraph by the Treasury by order.

31. (1) Section 401 (proceedings for an offence) applies to the Bank as if for the purposes of subsections (2)(a) and (3)(a) of that section the Bank were an appropriate regulator in respect of each of the following offences—

(a) an offence under section 177(3) where the investigation is being, or is likely to be, conducted on behalf of the Bank;

(b) an offence under section 177(4) where the requirement is imposed by the Bank;

(c) an offence under section 177(6) where the warrant is issued as a result of information on oath given by the Bank or a person appointed by it to conduct an investigation on its behalf;

(d) an offence under section 398(1) where the information was given to the Bank.

(2) Section 401(3B) has effect subject to the provision made by this paragraph (so that the FCA is not the appropriate regulator for the purposes of subsections (2)(a) and (3)(a) in respect of the above offences).

Records

32. Paragraph 17 of Schedule 1ZB (records) applies in relation to the recording of decisions made by the Bank in the exercise of its functions relating to recognised clearing houses[, third country central counterparties][, recognised CSDs and [third country CSDs]].

Annual report

33. Paragraph 19 of Schedule 1ZB (annual report by PRA) applies in relation to the Bank, but—

(a) as if for paragraphs (a) to (f) of sub-paragraph (1) there were substituted—

"(a) the discharge of its functions relating to recognised clearing houses[, third country central counterparties][, recognised CSDs and [third country CSDs]],

(b) the extent to which, in its opinion, in discharging those functions its financial stability objective has been met,", and

(b) as if sub-paragraph (3) were omitted.]

NOTES

Inserted as noted to Part 1 of this Schedule at **[7.746]**.

Para 10: words in square brackets in sub-para (1)(j) substituted by the Financial Services (Banking Reform) Act 2013, s 141, Sch 10, para 5, as from 1 March 2014. Words in square brackets in sub-para (2) inserted by the Central Securities Depositories Regulations 2017, SI 2017/1064, reg 2(1), 39(b), as from 28 November 2017. Words omitted from sub-para (2) repealed by the Investment Exchanges, Clearing Houses and Central Securities Depositories (Amendment) (EU Exit) Regulations 2019, SI 2019/662, regs 11, 12, as from IP completion day (as defined in the European Union (Withdrawal Agreement) Act 2020, s 39). Sub-para (5) added by the Financial Regulators' Powers (Technical Standards etc) (Amendment etc) (EU Exit) Regulations 2018, SI 2018/1115, reg 7(1), (11)(a), as from 26 October 2018.

Para 11 is amended as follows:

Sub-paras (1)(aa), (ab) inserted by SI 2017/1064, reg 2(1), 39(c), as from 28 November 2017. Sub-para (1)(ab) further substituted by the Financial Services and Markets Act 2000 (Amendment) (EU Exit) Regulations 2019, SI 2019/632, regs 115, 116(a)(i), as from IP completion day (as defined in the European Union (Withdrawal Agreement) Act 2020, s 39).

Sub-para (1)(ac) and the words ", a third country central counterparty" in square brackets in sub-para (1)(b) were inserted by the Over the Counter Derivatives, Central Counterparties and Trade Repositories (Amendment, etc, and Transitional Provision) (EU Exit) Regulations 2020, SI 2020/646, reg 2(1), (5)(a), as from IP completion day (as defined in the European Union (Withdrawal Agreement) Act 2020, s 39).

Words in second (outer) pair of square brackets in sub-para (1)(b) inserted by SI 2017/1064, reg 2(1), 39(c), as from 28 November 2017. Words in third (inner) pair of square brackets in sub-para (1)(b) substituted by SI 2019/632, regs 115, 116(a)(ii), as from IP completion day (as defined in the European Union (Withdrawal Agreement) Act 2020, s 39).

Word omitted from sub-para (2)(b) repealed, and sub-para (2)(d) (and the preceding word) added, by the Financial Services and Markets Act 2000 (Over the Counter Derivatives, Central Counterparties and Trade Repositories) Regulations 2013, SI 2013/504, reg 3(1), (16)(a), as from 1 April 2013.

Sub-para (2)(d) was substituted by SI 2019/632, regs 115, 116(b), as from IP completion day (as defined in the European Union (Withdrawal Agreement) Act 2020, s 39). Note that reg 116(b) of the 2019 Regulations was amended by the Financial Services and Economic and Monetary Policy (Consequential Amendments) (EU Exit) Regulations 2020, SI 2020/1301, reg 3, Schedule, para 33(j), as from 30 December 2020 (and the effect of the amendments has been incorporated in the text set out above).

Para 12: words in square brackets substituted by SI 2019/662, regs 11, 13(1), as from IP completion day (as defined in the European Union (Withdrawal Agreement) Act 2020, s 39). Note that reg 13 of the 2019 Regulations was amended by the Over the Counter Derivatives, Central Counterparties and Trade Repositories (Amendment, etc, and Transitional Provision) (EU Exit) Regulations 2020, SI 2020/646, reg 11, as from 25 June 2020 (and the effect of that amendment has been incorporated in the text set out above).

Para 13: words in first pair of square brackets in sub-para (1) inserted by SI 2020/646, reg 2(1), (5)(b), as from IP completion day (as defined in the European Union (Withdrawal Agreement) Act 2020, s 39). Words in second pair of square brackets in sub-para (1) inserted, and sub-para (1A) originally inserted, by SI 2017/1064, reg 2(1), 39(e), as from 28 November 2017. Sub-para (1A) was subsequently repealed by SI 2019/662, regs 11, 13(2), as from IP completion day (as defined in the European Union (Withdrawal Agreement) Act 2020, s 39).

Para 14: words in square brackets in sub-para (d) substituted, and sub-para (f) repealed, by SI 2019/662, regs 11, 13(3), as from IP completion day (as defined in the European Union (Withdrawal Agreement) Act 2020, s 39) (for transitional provisions see SI 2019/710, reg 37 at **[12.110]**). Sub-paras (2)(g) and (h) were inserted by SI 2020/646, reg 2(1), (5)(c), as from IP completion day (as defined in the European Union (Withdrawal Agreement) Act 2020, s 39). All other words in square brackets were inserted by SI 2017/1064, reg 2(1), 39(f), as from 28 November 2017.

Para 17: words in square brackets in sub-paras (2)–(4) inserted by SI 2017/1064, reg 2(1), 39(g), as from 28 November 2017. Words in square brackets in sub-para (5) substituted, and sub-para (6)(b) repealed, by the Bank of England and Financial Services Act 2016, s 16, Sch 2, Pt 2, paras 26, 51(1), (3), as from 1 March 2017.

Paras 18, 19: words in square brackets inserted or substituted by SI 2017/1064, reg 2(1), 39(h), (i), as from 28 November 2017.

Paras 20, 21: words in square brackets inserted by SI 2017/1064, reg 2(1), 39(j)–(l), as from 28 November 2017.

Para 22: words ", third country central counterparty" in square brackets inserted by the Central Counterparties (Amendment, etc, and Transitional Provision) (EU Exit) Regulations 2018, SI 2018/1184, regs 2, 5(a), as from IP completion day (as defined in the European Union (Withdrawal Agreement) Act 2020, s 39) (for transitional provision in relation to the provision of clearing services in the UK by CCPs who are established outside of the UK, see Part 6 of the 2018 Regulations). Words ", a third country CSD" in square brackets inserted by SI 2019/632, regs 115, 117(1), as from IP completion day (as defined in the European Union (Withdrawal Agreement) Act 2020, s 39). Words "or a recognised CSD" in square brackets inserted by SI 2017/1064, reg 2(1), 39(j)–(l), as from 28 November 2017.

Para 23 is amended as follows:

Sub-para (1) numbered as such, and sub-para (2) added, by the Bank of England and Financial Services Act 2016, s 16, Sch 2, Pt 2, paras 26, 51(1), (4), as from 1 March 2017.

Words "or recognised CSDs" in square brackets in sub-para (1) inserted by SI 2017/1064, reg 2(1), 39(m), as from 28 November 2017.

Words "or any of its functions under the EMIR regulation" in square brackets in sub-para (1) inserted by SI 2013/504, reg 3(1), (16)(d), as from 1 April 2013.

Words in third (outer) pair of square brackets in sub-para (1) inserted by SI 2014/2879, reg 6(1), (4)(b), as from 21 November 2014.

Words in fourth (inner) pair of square brackets in sub-para (1) substituted by SI 2019/632, regs 115, 117(2), as from IP completion day (as defined in the European Union (Withdrawal Agreement) Act 2020, s 39). Note that reg 117(2) of the 2019 Regulations was amended by the Financial Services and Economic and Monetary Policy (Consequential Amendments) (EU Exit) Regulations 2020, SI 2020/1301, reg 3, Schedule, para 33(k), as from 30 December 2020 (and the effect of the amendment has been incorporated in the text set out above).

Para 23A: inserted by SI 2019/662, regs 11, 14, as from IP completion day (as defined in the European Union (Withdrawal Agreement) Act 2020, s 39). Note that reg 14 of the 2019 Regulations was amended by the Financial Services and Economic and Monetary Policy (Consequential Amendments) (EU Exit) Regulations 2020, SI 2020/1301, reg 3, Schedule, para 37(d), as from 30 December 2020 (and the effect of the amendment has been incorporated in the text set out above).

Para 24: sub-para (1)(za) inserted, and words in first pair of square brackets in sub-para (2) inserted, by the Corporate Insolvency and Governance Act 2020, s 7, Sch 9, Pt 2, paras 17, 19, as from 26 June 2020. Words in second pair of square brackets in sub-para (2) inserted by SI 2017/1064, reg 2(1), 39(n), as from 28 November 2017.

Para 25: sub-para (1) numbered as such, and sub-para (2) added, by SI 2017/1064, reg 2(1), 39(o), as from 28 November 2017.

Para 26: words in first (outer) pair of square brackets in sub-para (2)(a) inserted by SI 2017/1064, reg 2(1), 39(p), as from 28 November 2017. Words in second (inner) pair of square brackets in sub-para (2)(a) substituted, and words in square brackets in sub-para (2)(c) substituted, by SI 2019/662, regs 11, 15(1), as from IP completion day (as defined in the European Union (Withdrawal Agreement) Act 2020, s 39) (for transitional provisions see SI 2019/710, reg 37 at **[12.110]**).

Para 27: words in square brackets in sub-para (2) inserted, and sub-para (3) added, by SI 2016/715, reg 29, Sch 1, para 1(1), (6)(b), as from 13 July 2016.

Para 28: words in square brackets in sub-paras (2), (4) substituted by SI 2019/662, regs 11, 15(2), as from IP completion day (as defined in the European Union (Withdrawal Agreement) Act 2020, s 39). Words in square brackets in sub-para (3) inserted, and sub-para (3A) inserted, by SI 2016/715, reg 29, Sch 1, para 1(1), (6)(c), as from 13 July 2016.

Para 30: words in first pair of square brackets inserted by SI 2020/646, reg 2(1), (5)(d), as from IP completion day (as defined in the European Union (Withdrawal Agreement) Act 2020, s 39). Words in second and third pairs of square brackets substituted by SI 2019/632, regs 115, 118, as from IP completion day (as defined in the European Union (Withdrawal Agreement) Act 2020, s 39) (for transitional provisions see SI 2019/710, reg 37 at **[12.110]**).

Paras 32, 33: words in first pair of square brackets inserted by SI 2018/1184, regs 2, 5(b), (c), as from IP completion day (as defined in the European Union (Withdrawal Agreement) Act 2020, s 39) (for transitional provision in relation to the provision of clearing services in the UK by CCPs who are established outside of the UK, see Part 6 of the 2018 Regulations). Words in second (outer) pair of square brackets inserted by SI 2017/1064, reg 2(1), 39(s), (t), as from 28 November 2017. Words in third (inner) pair of square brackets substituted by SI 2019/662, regs 11, 16, 17, as from IP completion day (as defined in the European Union (Withdrawal Agreement) Act 2020, s 39).

Orders and Regulations: the Financial Services and Markets Act 2000 (Prescribed Financial Institutions) Order 2013, SI 2013/165; the Financial Services and Markets Act 2000 (Qualifying Provisions) Order 2013, SI 2013/419; the Financial Services and Markets Act 2000 (Transparency of Securities Financing Transactions and of Reuse) Regulations 2016, SI 2016/715.

[PART 3 WINDING UP, ADMINISTRATION OR INSOLVENCY OF [RECOGNISED CLEARING HOUSES]

Notice to Bank of England of preliminary steps

[7.748]

34. (1) An application for an administration order in respect of a [recognised clearing house] [or a recognised CSD] may not be determined unless the conditions below are satisfied.

(2) A petition for a winding up order in respect of a [recognised clearing house] [or a recognised CSD] may not be determined unless the conditions below are satisfied.

(3) A resolution for voluntary winding up of a [recognised clearing house] [or a recognised CSD] may not be made unless the conditions below are satisfied.

(4) An administrator of a [recognised clearing house] [or a recognised CSD] may not be appointed unless the conditions below are satisfied.

(5) Condition 1 is that the Bank of England has been notified—

- (a) by the applicant for an administration order, that the application has been made,
- (b) by the petitioner for a winding up order, that the petition has been presented,
- (c) by the [recognised clearing house] [or the recognised CSD], that a resolution for voluntary winding up may be made, or
- (d) by the person proposing to appoint an administrator, of the proposed appointment.

(6) Condition 2 is that a copy of the notice complying with Condition 1 has been filed (in Scotland, lodged) with the court (and made available for public inspection by the court).

(7) Condition 3 is that—

- (a) the period of 2 weeks, beginning with the day on which the notice is received, has ended, or
- (b) the Bank of England has informed the person who gave the notice that—
  - (i) it has no objection to the order, resolution or appointment being made, and
  - (ii) it does not intend to exercise a stabilisation power under Part 1 of the Banking Act 2009.

(8) Arranging for the giving of notice in order to satisfy Condition 1 can be a step with a view to minimising the potential loss to a [recognised clearing house's] [or a recognised CSD's] creditors for the purpose of section 214 of the Insolvency Act 1986 (wrongful trading).

(9) In this paragraph "the court" means—

- (a) in England and Wales, the High Court,
- (b) in Scotland, the Court of Session, and
- (c) in Northern Ireland, the High Court.

Power to give directions to insolvency practitioner

35. (1) This paragraph applies where a person has been appointed to act as an insolvency practitioner (within the meaning of section 388 of the Insolvency Act 1986 or Article 3 of the Insolvency (Northern Ireland) Order 1989) in relation to a company which is, or has been, a [recognised clearing house] [or a recognised CSD].

(2) The Bank of England may give directions to the person if satisfied that it is desirable to give the directions, having regard to the public interest in—

- (a) protecting and enhancing the stability of the UK financial system,
- (b) protecting and enhancing public confidence in the stability of the UK financial system, . . .

(c) [in the case of a company which is, or has been, a recognised clearing house,] maintaining the continuity of . . . clearing services[, and]

[(d) in the case of a company which is, or has been, a recognised CSD, maintaining the continuity of the services referred to in section 285(3D)].

(3) Before giving directions the Bank of England must consult—

(a) the Treasury, [and]

(b) . . .

(c) the FCA.

(4) Directions are enforceable, on an application by the Bank of England, by an injunction or, in Scotland, by an order for specific performance under section 45 of the Court of Session Act 1988.

(5) A person is not liable for damages in respect of action or inaction in accordance with directions.

(6) The immunity does not extend to action or inaction—

(a) in bad faith, or

(b) in contravention of section 6(1) of the Human Rights Act 1998.]

NOTES

Inserted as noted to Part 1 of this Schedule at **[7.746]**.

The words in square brackets in the Part heading were substituted by the Financial Services and Markets Act 2000 (Over the Counter Derivatives, Central Counterparties and Trade Repositories) Regulations 2013, SI 2013/504, reg 3(1), (16)(e), as from 1 April 2013.

Para 34: words "recognised clearing house" in square brackets in each place they occur substituted by SI 2013/504, reg 3(1), (16)(f), as from 1 April 2013. Other words in square brackets inserted by the Central Securities Depositories Regulations 2017, SI 2017/1064, reg 2(1), 39(u), as from 28 November 2017.

Para 35 is amended as follows:

Words "recognised clearing house" in square brackets in sub-para (1) substituted, and words omitted from sub-para (2)(c) repealed, by SI 2013/504, reg 3(1), (16)(g), as from 1 April 2013.

Word "and" in square brackets in sub-para (3)(a) inserted, and sub-para (3)(b) repealed, by the Bank of England and Financial Services Act 2016, s 16, Sch 2, Pt 2, paras 26, 51(1), (5)(a), as from 1 March 2017; for transitional provision and savings see s 17, Sch 3.

All other amendments to this Part were made by the Central Securities Depositories Regulations 2017, SI 2017/1064, reg 2(1), 39(u), as from 28 November 2017.

[PART 4 FEES

[7.749]

36. (1) The Bank of England may, in connection with the discharge of any of its qualifying functions, require recognised clearing houses . . . [, third country central counterparties, recognised CSDs . . . or settlement internalisers (as defined in point (11) of Article 2(1) of the CSD regulation)] to pay fees to the Bank.

(2) The "qualifying functions" of the Bank are—

(a) its functions under or as a result of this Part of this Act, . . .

(b) its functions under or as a result of a [qualifying provision] that is specified, or of a description specified, for the purposes of this sub-paragraph by the Treasury by order[; . . .

[(ba) its functions under or as a result of regulations made under section 8 of the European Union (Withdrawal) Act 2018; and]

(c) its functions under or as a result of Part 7 of the Companies Act 1989.]

(3) The power of the Bank to set fees includes power to set fees for the purpose of meeting expenses incurred by it or the FCA—

(a) in preparation for the exercise of functions by the Bank under this Part of this Act, . . .

(b) for the purpose of facilitating the exercise by the Bank of those functions or otherwise in connection with their exercise by it[, or]

[(c) in preparation for the exercise of functions by the Bank under Article 9(1) of the CSD regulation].

(4) It is irrelevant when the expenses were incurred (and, in particular, it is irrelevant if expenses were incurred by the FCA at a time when it was known as the Financial Services Authority).

37. Any fee which is owed to the Bank under paragraph 36 may be recovered as a debt due to the Bank.]

NOTES

Inserted as noted to Part 1 of this Schedule at **[7.746]**.

Para 36 is amended as follows:

First words omitted from sub-para (1) repealed by the Central Counterparties (Amendment, etc, and Transitional Provision) (EU Exit) Regulations 2018, SI 2018/1184, regs 2, 5(d), as from IP completion day (as defined in the European Union (Withdrawal Agreement) Act 2020, s 39) (for transitional provision in relation to the provision of clearing services in the UK by CCPs who are established outside of the UK, see Part 6 of the 2018 Regulations).

Words in square brackets in sub-para (1) substituted, word omitted from sub-para (3)(a) repealed, and sub-para (3)(c) (and the preceding word) inserted, by the Central Securities Depositories Regulations 2017, SI 2017/1064, reg 2(1), 39(w), as from 28 November 2017.

Second words omitted from sub-para (1) repealed by the Financial Services and Markets Act 2000 (Amendment) (EU Exit) Regulations 2019, SI 2019/632, regs 115, 119(a), as from IP completion day (as defined in the European Union (Withdrawal Agreement) Act 2020, s 39).

Word omitted from sub-para (2)(a) repealed, and sub-para (2)(c) (and the preceding word) inserted, by the Financial Services and Markets Act 2000 (Over the Counter Derivatives, Central Counterparties and Trade Repositories) Regulations 2013, SI 2013/504, reg 3(1), (16)(h), as from 1 April 2013.

Words in square brackets in sub-para (2)(b) substituted by SI 2019/632, regs 115, 119(b), as from IP completion day (as defined in the European Union (Withdrawal Agreement) Act 2020, s 39) (for transitional provisions see SI 2019/710, reg 37 at **[12.110]**).

Word omitted from sub-para (2)(b) repealed, and sub-para (2)(ba) inserted, by the Financial Regulators' Powers (Technical Standards etc) (Amendment etc) (EU Exit) Regulations 2018, SI 2018/1115, reg 7(1), (11)(b), as from 26 October 2018.

Orders and Regulations: the Financial Services and Markets Act 2000 (Qualifying Provisions) Order 2013, SI 2013/419; the Financial Services and Markets Act 2000 (Transparency of Securities Financing Transactions and of Reuse) Regulations 2016, SI 2016/715.

SCHEDULES 18–22

(Schedules 18, 20–22 are omitted due to space considerations (see further, the introductory notes to this Act); Sch 19 was repealed by the Enterprise Act 2002, ss 247(k), 278(2), Sch 26, as from 23 June 2003.)

FINANCIAL SERVICES ACT 2012

(2012 c 21)

NOTES

Only Part 7 of this Act (Offences Relating to Financial Services) is reproduced here. By virtue of s 121 (Extent) this Act applies to the whole of the UK.

This Act is reproduced as amended by: the Financial Services and Markets Act 2000 (Market Abuse) Regulations 2016, SI 2016/680; the Bank of England (Amendment) (EU Exit) Regulations 2018, SI 2018/1297; the Sentencing Act 2020; the Financial Services Act 2021; the Criminal Justice Act 2003 (Commencement No 33) and Sentencing Act 2020 (Commencement No 2) Regulations 2022, SI 2022/500.

ARRANGEMENT OF SECTIONS

PART 7
OFFENCES RELATING TO FINANCIAL SERVICES

An Act to amend the Bank of England Act 1998, the Financial Services and Markets Act 2000 and the Banking Act 2009; to make other provision about financial services and markets; to make provision about the exercise of certain statutory functions relating to building societies, friendly societies and other mutual societies; to amend section 785 of the Companies Act 2006; to make provision enabling the Director of Savings to provide services to other public bodies; and for connected purposes

[19 December 2012]

1–88 *(Ss 1–5 (Part 1: Bank of England) contain various amendments to the Bank of England Act 1998; ss 6–49 (Part 2: Amendments of the Financial Services and Markets Act 2000) amend FSMA 2000 at* **[7.1]** *et seq (these sections also establish the Financial Conduct Authority and the Prudential Regulation Authority – see Part 1A of the 2000 Act at* **[7.1]** *et seq); ss 50–57 (Part 3: Mutual Societies) are outside the scope of this work; ss 58–67 (Part 4: Collaboration Between Treasury and Bank of England, FCA or PRA) are outside the scope of this work; ss 68–83 (Part 5: Inquiries and Investigations) are outside the scope of this work; ss 84–88 (Part 6: Investigation of Complaints Against Regulators) are outside the scope of this work.)*

PART 7 OFFENCES RELATING TO FINANCIAL SERVICES

[7.750]

89 Misleading statements

(1) Subsection (2) applies to a person ("P") who—

(a) makes a statement which P knows to be false or misleading in a material respect,

(b) makes a statement which is false or misleading in a material respect, being reckless as to whether it is, or

(c) dishonestly conceals any material facts whether in connection with a statement made by P or otherwise.

(2) P commits an offence if P makes the statement or conceals the facts with the intention of inducing, or is reckless as to whether making it or concealing them may induce, another person (whether or not the person to whom the statement is made)—

(a) to enter into or offer to enter into, or to refrain from entering or offering to enter into, a relevant agreement, or

(b) to exercise, or refrain from exercising, any rights conferred by a relevant investment.

(3) In proceedings for an offence under subsection (2) brought against a person to whom that subsection applies as a result of paragraph (a) of subsection (1), it is a defence for the person charged ("D") to show that the statement was made in conformity with—

(a) price stabilising rules,

(b) control of information rules, or

[(c) the relevant provisions of Article 5 (exemption for buy-back programmes and stabilisation) of the market abuse regulation].

(4) Subsections (1) and (2) do not apply unless—
  (a) the statement is made in or from, or the facts are concealed in or from, the United Kingdom or arrangements are made in or from the United Kingdom for the statement to be made or the facts to be concealed,
  (b) the person on whom the inducement is intended to or may have effect is in the United Kingdom, or
  (c) the agreement is or would be entered into or the rights are or would be exercised in the United Kingdom.

NOTES

Sub-s (3): para (c) substituted by the Financial Services and Markets Act 2000 (Market Abuse) Regulations 2016, SI 2016/680, reg 15(1), (2), as from 3 July 2016.

[7.751]
90 Misleading impressions

(1) A person ("P") who does any act or engages in any course of conduct which creates a false or misleading impression as to the market in or the price or value of any relevant investments commits an offence if—
  (a) P intends to create the impression, and
  (b) the case falls within subsection (2) or (3) (or both).
(2) The case falls within this subsection if P intends, by creating the impression, to induce another person to acquire, dispose of, subscribe for or underwrite the investments or to refrain from doing so or to exercise or refrain from exercising any rights conferred by the investments.
(3) The case falls within this subsection if—
  (a) P knows that the impression is false or misleading or is reckless as to whether it is, and
  (b) P intends by creating the impression to produce any of the results in subsection (4) or is aware that creating the impression is likely to produce any of the results in that subsection.
(4) Those results are—
  (a) the making of a gain for P or another, or
  (b) the causing of loss to another person or the exposing of another person to the risk of loss.
(5) References in subsection (4) to gain or loss are to be read in accordance with subsections (6) to (8).
(6) "Gain" and "loss"—
  (a) extend only to gain or loss in money or other property of any kind;
  (b) include such gain or loss whether temporary or permanent.
(7) "Gain" includes a gain by keeping what one has, as well as a gain by getting what one does not have.
(8) "Loss" includes a loss by not getting what one might get, as well as a loss by parting with what one has.
(9) In proceedings brought against any person ("D") for an offence under subsection (1) it is a defence for D to show—
  (a) to the extent that the offence results from subsection (2), that D reasonably believed that D's conduct would not create an impression that was false or misleading as to the matters mentioned in subsection (1),
  (b) that D acted or engaged in the conduct—
    (i) for the purpose of stabilising the price of investments, and
    (ii) in conformity with price stabilising rules,
  (c) that D acted or engaged in the conduct in conformity with control of information rules, or
  [(d) that D acted or engaged in the conduct in conformity with the relevant provisions of Article 5 (exemption for buy-back programmes and stabilisation) of the market abuse regulation].
(10) This section does not apply unless—
  (a) the act is done, or the course of conduct is engaged in, in the United Kingdom, or
  (b) the false or misleading impression is created there.
[(11) See section 137Q(3) of FSMA 2000 regarding the power of the FCA to make rules for the purposes of subsection (9)(d).]

NOTES

Sub-s (9)(d) substituted, and sub-s (11) added, by the Financial Services and Markets Act 2000 (Market Abuse) Regulations 2016, SI 2016/680, reg 15(1), (3), as from 3 July 2016.

[7.752]
91 Misleading statements etc in relation to benchmarks

(1) A person ("A") who makes to another person ("B") a false or misleading statement commits an offence if—
  (a) A makes the statement in the course of arrangements for the setting of a relevant benchmark,
  (b) A intends that the statement should be used by B for the purpose of the setting of a relevant benchmark, and
  (c) A knows that the statement is false or misleading or is reckless as to whether it is.
(2) A person ("C") who does any act or engages in any course of conduct which creates a false or misleading impression as to the price or value of any investment or as to the interest rate appropriate to any transaction commits an offence if—
  (a) C intends to create the impression,
  (b) the impression may affect the setting of a relevant benchmark,
  (c) C knows that the impression is false or misleading or is reckless as to whether it is, and
  (d) C knows that the impression may affect the setting of a relevant benchmark.
(3) In proceedings for an offence under subsection (1), it is a defence for the person charged ("D") to show that the statement was made in conformity with—
  (a) . . .
  (b) control of information rules, or
  [(c) the relevant provisions of Article 5 (exemption for buy-back programmes and stabilisation) of the market abuse regulation].
(4) In proceedings brought against any person ("D") for an offence under subsection (2) it is a defence for D to show—
  (a) that D acted or engaged in the conduct—

(i) for the purpose of stabilising the price of investments, and
(ii) in conformity with price stabilising rules,

(b) that D acted or engaged in the conduct in conformity with control of information rules, or

[(c) that D acted or engaged in the conduct in conformity with the relevant provisions of Article 5 (exemption for buy-back programmes and stabilisation) of the market abuse regulation].

(5) Subsection (1) does not apply unless the statement is made in or from the United Kingdom or to a person in the United Kingdom.

(6) Subsection (2) does not apply unless—

(a) the act is done, or the course of conduct is engaged in, in the United Kingdom, or
(b) the false or misleading impression is created there.

[(7) See section 137Q(3) of FSMA 2000 regarding the power of the FCA to make rules for the purposes of subsection (4)(c).]

NOTES

Sub-s (3)(a) was repealed, sub-ss (3)(c), (4)(c) were substituted, and sub-s (7) was added, by the Financial Services and Markets Act 2000 (Market Abuse) Regulations 2016, SI 2016/680, reg 15(1), (4), as from 3 July 2016.

[7.753]

92 Penalties

(1) A person guilty of an offence under this Part is liable—

(a) on summary conviction, to imprisonment for a term not exceeding the applicable maximum term or a fine not exceeding the statutory maximum, or both;
(b) on conviction on indictment, to imprisonment for a term not exceeding [10 years] or a fine, or both.

(2) For the purpose of subsection (1)(a) "the applicable maximum term" is—

(a) in England and Wales, 12 months (or 6 months, if the offence was committed before [2 May 2022]);
(b) in Scotland, 12 months;
(c) in Northern Ireland, 6 months.

NOTES

Sub-s (1): words in square brackets substituted by the Financial Services Act 2021, s 31(2), as from 1 November 2021. Note that this amendment does not apply in relation to offences committed before that date (see s 31(3), (4) of the 2021 Act). Note also that the previous words were "7 years".

Sub-s (2): words in square brackets substituted by the Criminal Justice Act 2003 (Commencement No 33) and Sentencing Act 2020 (Commencement No 2) Regulations 2022, SI 2022/500, reg 5, Schedule, Pt 1, as from 28 April 2022.

[7.754]

93 Interpretation of Part 7

(1) This section has effect for the interpretation of this Part.

(2) "Investment" includes any asset, right or interest.

(3) "Relevant agreement" means an agreement—

(a) the entering into or performance of which by either party constitutes an activity of a kind specified in an order made by the Treasury, and
(b) which relates to a relevant investment.

(4) "Relevant benchmark" means a benchmark of a kind specified in an order made by the Treasury.

(5) "Relevant investment" means an investment of a kind specified in an order made by the Treasury.

(6) Schedule 2 to FSMA 2000 (except paragraphs 25 and 26) applies for the purposes of subsections (3) and (5) with references to section 22 of that Act being read as references to each of those subsections.

(7) Nothing in Schedule 2 to FSMA 2000, as applied by subsection (6), limits the power conferred by subsection (3) or (5).

(8) "Price stabilising rules" and "control of information rules" have the same meaning as in FSMA 2000.

[(8A) "Market abuse regulation" means Regulation (EU) No 596/2014 of the European Parliament and of the Council of 16 April 2014 on market abuse (market abuse regulation) and repealing Directive 2003/6/EC of the European Parliament and of the Council and Commission Directives 2003/124/EC, 2003/125/EC and 2004/72/EC.

[(8B) References to Article 5 of the market abuse regulation include—

(a) any EU regulation, originally made under that Article, which is retained direct EU legislation, and
(b) any subordinate legislation (within the meaning of the Interpretation Act 1978) made under that Article on or after IP completion day.]

(9) In this section "benchmark" has the meaning given in section 22(6) of FSMA 2000.

NOTES

Sub-ss (8A), (8B): inserted by the Financial Services and Markets Act 2000 (Market Abuse) Regulations 2016, SI 2016/680, reg 15(1), (5), as from 3 July 2016. Sub-s (8B) was subsequently substituted by the Bank of England (Amendment) (EU Exit) Regulations 2018, SI 2018/1297, reg 8(1), (5), as from IP completion day (as defined in the European Union (Withdrawal Agreement) Act 2020, s 39). Note that the Bank of England (Amendment) (EU Exit) Regulations 2018, SI 2018/1297, reg 8(5) was amended by the Financial Services and Economic and Monetary Policy (Consequential Amendments) (EU Exit) Regulations 2020, SI 2020/1301, reg 3, Schedule, para 7(a), as from 30 December 2020 (and the effect of the amendment has been incorporated in the text set out above).

Orders: the Financial Services Act 2012 (Misleading Statements and Impressions) Order 2013, SI 2013/637 at **[8.560]**; the Financial Services and Markets Act 2000 (Regulated Activities) (Amendment) Order 2015, SI 2015/369.

[7.755]

94 Affirmative procedure for certain orders

(1) This section applies to the first order made under section 93.

(2) This section also applies to any subsequent order made under that section which contains a statement by the Treasury that the effect of the proposed order would include one or more of the following—

(a) that an activity which is not specified for the purposes of subsection (3)(a) of that section would become one so specified,
(b) that an investment which is not a relevant investment would become a relevant investment;
(c) that a benchmark which is not a relevant benchmark would become a relevant benchmark.

(3) A statutory instrument containing (alone or with other provisions) an order to which this section applies may not be made unless a draft of the instrument has been laid before Parliament and approved by a resolution of each House.

[7.756]
95 Consequential repeal
(*Repeals FSMA 2000, s 397 (which relates to misleading statements and practices and is superseded by the provisions of this Part).*)

96–123 (*Ss 96–106 (Part 8: Amendments of the Banking Act 2009) amends the Banking Act 2009; ss 107–113 (Part 9: Miscellaneous) amends the Consumer Credit Act 1974, the Companies Act 1989 at* **[5.161]**, *the Companies Act 2006, s 785 at* **[1.869]**, *and makes provision with regard to penalties received by FSA and the Bank of England, and the with regard to Director of Savings; ss 114–123 (Part 10: General) makes provision with regard to interpretation, transitional provisions in relation to the transfer of the FSA's functions, property, etc, and citation, commencement and extent.*)

SCHEDULES 1–21

(*Sch 1 (Bank of England Financial Policy Committee) and Sch 2 (Further Amendments Relating to the Bank of England) amend the Bank of England Act 1998 and contain other amendments that are outside the scope of this work; Sch 3 (Financial Conduct Authority and Prudential Regulation Authority: Schedules to be Substituted as Schedules 1ZA and 1ZB to FSMA 2000) sets out the new Schs 1ZA and 1ZB that are substituted for the existing Sch 1 to the 2000 Act (see* **[7.718]** *et seq); Sch 4 (EEA Passport Rights and Treaty Rights), Sch 5 (Performance of Regulated Activities), Sch 6 (Control of Business Transfers), Sch 7 (Application of Provisions of FSMA 2000 to the Bank of England etc), Sch 8 (Sections 28 to 34: Minor and Consequential Amendments), Sch 9 (Discipline and Enforcement), Sch 10 (The Financial Services Compensation Scheme), Sch 11 (The Financial Ombudsman Service), Sch 12 (Amendments of Parts 11 and 23 of FSMA 2000), Sch 13 (Auditors and Actuaries), Sch 14 (Amendments of Part 24 of FSMA 2000: Insolvency), Sch 15 (The Consumer Financial Education Body), and Sch 16 (Provision of Financial Services by Members of the Professions) all amend FSMA 2000 at* **[7.1]** *et seq; Sch 17 (Amendments of the Banking Act 2009 Related to Part 2 of this Act) amends the Banking Act 2009; Sch 18 (Further Minor and Consequential Amendments) contains minor amendments to FSMA 2000, the Companies Act 1985, the Insolvency Act 1986, the Companies Act 1989, the Criminal Justice Act 1993, the Companies (Audit, Investigations and Community Enterprise) Act 2004, and the Companies Act 2006, which have been incorporated at the appropriate place in this Handbook (and contains amendments to other Acts of Parliament, Acts of the Scottish Parliament, Northern Ireland legislation and Measures of the National Assembly for Wales that are outside the scope of this work); Sch 19 (Repeals) contains minor and consequential repeals; Sch 20 (Transitional Provisions) and Sch 21 (Transfer Schemes) contain transitional provisions with regard to the renaming of the Financial Services Authority as the Financial Conduct Authority, and the transfer of the property, rights and liabilities of the FSA.*)

FINANCIAL SERVICES ACT 2021

(2021 c 22)

An Act to make provision about financial services and markets; to make provision about debt respite schemes; to make provision about Help-to-Save accounts; and for connected purposes

[29 April 2021]

NOTES

Most of this Act concerns matters that are outside the scope of this work, and only ss 29 and 41 are included below. Provisions not included are not annotated. The vast majority of this Act contains amendments to other UK legislation and Retained EU legislation. The enactments amended are as follows—

– FSMA 2000 at **[7.1]**. Note that certain amendments are considered to be outside the scope of this work – for example, the insertion of a new Part 9C (Prudential Regulation of FCA Investment Firms) and Part 9D (Prudential Regulation of Credit Institutions etc), and new Schedules 2A (Gibraltar-Based Persons Carrying on Activities in the UK) and 2B (UK-Based Persons Carrying on Activities in Gibraltar). Only amendments relevant to this Handbook have been incorporated.
– Financial Services Act 2012 (the provisions amended are outside the scope of this work).
– Criminal Justice Act 1993 at **[5.193]** et seq.
– Bank of England Act 1998 (outside the scope of this work).
– Anti-terrorism, Crime and Security Act 2001 (outside the scope of this work).
– Proceeds of Crime Act 2002 (outside the scope of this work).
– Banking Act 2009 (outside the scope of this work).
– Sanctions and Anti-Money Laundering Act 2018 (outside the scope of this work).
– Financial Guidance and Claims Act 2018 (outside the scope of this work).
– Financial Services and Markets Act 2000 (Gibraltar) Order 2001 (outside the scope of this work).
– Alternative Investment Fund Managers Regulations 2013 (the provisions amended are outside the scope of this work).
– Capital Requirements Regulations 2013 (outside the scope of this work).
– Capital Requirements (Country-by-Country Reporting) Regulations 2013 (outside the scope of this work).
– Collective Investment Schemes (Amendment etc) (EU Exit) Regulations 2019 (outside the scope of this work).
– Retained European Market Infrastructure Regulation (outside the scope of this work).
– Retained Capital Requirements Regulation (outside the scope of this work).
– Retained Markets in Financial Instruments Regulation (outside the scope of this work).

– Retained Market Abuse Regulation (outside the scope of this work).
– Retained PRIIPs Regulation (outside the scope of this work).
– Retained Benchmarks Regulation (outside the scope of this work).
– Retained Money Market Funds Regulation (outside the scope of this work).

Sections 29 and 41 apply to the whole of the United Kingdom (see s 48 (Extent) not reproduced).

By virtue of s 49 (Commencement etc) (not reproduced), s 29 comes into force on such day as the Treasury may by regulations appoint; and s 41 came into force on 29 April 2021. In relation to s 29, see the Financial Services Act 2021 (Commencement No 2) Regulations 2021 which brought the section into force on 1 July 2021.

Rules about level of care provided by authorised persons

[7.757]

29 FCA rules about level of care provided to consumers by authorised persons

(1) The Financial Conduct Authority must carry out a public consultation about whether it should make general rules providing that authorised persons owe a duty of care to consumers.

(2) The consultation must include consultation about—

(a) whether the Financial Conduct Authority should make other provision in general rules about the level of care that must be provided to consumers by authorised persons, either instead of or in addition to a duty of care,

(b) whether a duty of care should be owed, or other provision should apply, to all consumers or to particular classes of consumer, and

(c) the extent to which a duty of care, or other provision, would advance the Financial Conduct Authority's consumer protection objective (see section 1C of the Financial Services and Markets Act 2000).

(3) The Financial Conduct Authority—

(a) must carry out the consultation, and publish its analysis of the responses, before 1 January 2022, and

(b) must, before 1 August 2022, make such general rules about the level of care that must be provided to consumers, or particular classes of consumer, by authorised persons as it considers appropriate, having regard to that analysis.

(4) The duties to consult under this section may be satisfied by consultation carried out after 1 January 2021 but before this section comes into force (as well as by consultation carried out after this section comes into force).

(5) In this section—

"authorised person" has the same meaning as in the Financial Services and Markets Act 2000 (see section 31 of that Act);

"consumer" has the meaning given in section 1G of that Act;

"general rules" means rules made under section 137A of that Act.

NOTES

Commencement: 1 July 2021.

Miscellaneous

[7.758]

41 Regulations about financial collateral arrangements

(1) The Financial Collateral Arrangements (No 2) Regulations 2003 (SI 2003/3226) as originally made, and all amendments made to them, have effect, and are to be treated as having had effect, despite any lack of power to make the regulations and amendments.

(2) Accordingly, the validity of anything done under or in reliance on those regulations (whether as originally made or as amended) is to be treated as unaffected by any such lack of power.

(3)–(6) *(Amend the Banking Act 2009 (outside the scope of this work).)*

NOTES

Commencement: 29 April 2021.

Note that the 2003 Regulations are at **[10.121]**.

PART 8
FINANCIAL SERVICES
STATUTORY INSTRUMENTS

FINANCIAL SERVICES AND MARKETS ACT 2000 (REGULATED ACTIVITIES) ORDER 2001

(SI 2001/544)

NOTES

Made: 26 February 2001.

Authority: Financial Services and Markets Act 2000, ss 22(1), (5), 426, 428(3), Sch 2, para 25.

Commencement: 1 December 2001 (being the date on which the Financial Services and Markets Act 2000, s 19 came into force) and subject as follows; 1 January 2002 (arts 59, 60, 87); 31 October 2004 (arts 61–63, 88, 90, 91).

This Order is reproduced as amended by:

2001	Financial Services and Markets Act 2000 (Regulated Activities) (Amendment) Order 2001, SI 2001/3544.
2002	Financial Services and Markets Act 2000 (Regulated Activities) (Amendment) Order 2002, SI 2002/682; Financial Services and Markets Act 2000 (Financial Promotion and Miscellaneous Amendments) Order 2002, SI 2002/1310; Financial Services and Markets Act 2000 (Regulated Activities) (Amendment) (No 2) Order 2002, SI 2002/1776; Financial Services and Markets Act 2000 (Commencement of Mortgage Regulation) (Amendment) Order 2002, SI 2002/1777.
2003	Financial Services and Markets Act 2000 (Regulated Activities) (Amendment) (No 1) Order 2003, SI 2003/1475; Financial Services and Markets Act 2000 (Regulated Activities) (Amendment) (No 2) Order 2003, SI 2003/1476; Financial Services and Markets Act 2000 (Regulated Activities) (Amendment) (No 3) Order 2003, SI 2003/2822.
2004	Financial Services and Markets Act 2000 (Regulated Activities) (Amendment) Order 2004, SI 2004/1610; Financial Services and Markets Act 2000 (Regulated Activities) (Amendment) (No 2) Order 2004, SI 2004/2737.
2005	Financial Services and Markets Act 2000 (Regulated Activities) (Amendment) Order 2005, SI 2005/593; Financial Services and Markets Act 2000 (Regulated Activities) (Amendment) (No 2) Order 2005, SI 2005/1518; Civil Partnership Act 2004 (Amendments to Subordinate Legislation) Order 2005, SI 2005/2114.
2006	Financial Services and Markets Act 2000 (Regulated Activities) (Amendment) Order 2006, SI 2006/1969; Financial Services and Markets Act 2000 (Regulated Activities) (Amendment) (No 2) Order 2006, SI 2006/2383; Financial Services and Markets Act 2000 (Regulated Activities) (Amendment No 3) Order 2006, SI 2006/3384.
2007	Companies Act 2006 (Commencement No 2, Consequential Amendments, Transitional Provisions and Savings) Order 2007, SI 2007/1093; Financial Services and Markets Act 2000 (Regulated Activities) (Amendment) Order 2007, SI 2007/1339; Financial Services and Markets Act 2000 (Reinsurance Directive) Order 2007, SI 2007/3254; Financial Services and Markets Act 2000 (Regulated Activities) (Amendment) (No 2) Order 2007, SI 2007/3510.
2008	Companies Act 2006 (Consequential Amendments etc) Order 2008, SI 2008/948.
2009	Payment Services Regulations 2009, SI 2009/209; Solicitors' Recognised Bodies (Amendment) Order 2009, SI 2009/500; Financial Services and Markets Act 2000 (Regulated Activities) (Amendment) Order 2009, SI 2009/1342; Financial Services and Markets Act 2000 (Regulated Activities) (Amendment) (No 2) Order 2009, SI 2009/1389.
2010	Financial Services and Markets Act 2000 (Regulated Activities) (Amendment) Order 2010, SI 2010/86; Timeshare, Holiday Products, Resale and Exchange Contracts Regulations 2010, SI 2010/2960.
2011	Electronic Money Regulations 2011, SI 2011/99; Financial Services and Markets Act 2000 (Regulated Activities) (Amendment) Order 2011, SI 2011/133; Companies Act 2006 (Consequential Amendments and Transitional Provisions) Order 2011, SI 2011/1265; Public Services Reform (Scotland) Act 2010 (Consequential Modifications of Enactments) Order 2011, SI 2011/2581; Legislative Reform (Industrial and Provident Societies and Credit Unions) Order 2011, SI 2011/2687.
2012	Financial Services and Markets Act 2000 (Regulated Activities) (Amendment) Order 2012, SI 2012/1906.
2013	Financial Services Act 2012 (Consequential Amendments and Transitional Provisions) Order 2013, SI 2013/472; Financial Services and Markets Act 2000 (Over the Counter Derivatives, Central Counterparties and Trade Repositories) Regulations 2013, SI 2013/504; Financial Services and Markets Act 2000 (Regulated Activities) (Amendment) Order 2013, SI 2013/655; Alternative Investment Fund Managers Regulations 2013, SI 2013/1773; Alternative Investment Fund Managers (Amendment) Regulations 2013, SI 2013/1797; Financial Services and Markets Act 2000 (Regulated Activities) (Amendment) (No 2) Order 2013, SI 2013/1881.
2014	Financial Services and Markets Act 2000 (Regulated Activities) (Amendment) Order 2014, SI 2014/366; Financial Services and Markets Act 2000 (Regulated Activities) (Amendment) (No 2) Order 2014, SI 2014/1448; Financial Services and Markets Act 2000 (Regulated Activities) (Amendment) (No 3) Order 2014, SI 2014/1740; Co-operative and Community Benefit Societies and Credit Unions Act 2010 (Consequential Amendments) Regulations 2014, SI 2014/1815; Financial Services and Markets Act 2000 (Regulated Activities) (Green Deal) (Amendment) Order 2014, SI 2014/1850.
2015	Financial Services and Markets Act 2000 (Miscellaneous Provisions) (No 2) Order 2015, SI 2015/352; Financial Services and Markets Act 2000 (Regulated Activities) (Amendment) Order 2015, SI 2015/369; Financial Services and Markets Act 2000 (Regulated Activities) (Amendment) (Pensions Guidance Exclusions) Order 2015, SI 2015/489; Solvency 2 Regulations 2015, SI 2015/575; Financial Services and Markets Act 2000 (Regulated Activities) (Amendment) (No 2) Order 2015, SI 2015/731; Financial Services and Markets Act 2000 (Miscellaneous Provisions) Order 2015, SI 2015/853; Mortgage Credit Directive Order 2015, SI 2015/910; Financial Services and Markets Act 2000 (Regulated Activities) (Amendment) (No 3) Order 2015, SI 2015/1863.
2016	Financial Services and Markets Act 2000 (Regulated Activities) (Amendment) Order 2016, SI 2016/392; Financial Services and Markets Act 2000 (Transparency of Securities Financing Transactions and of Reuse)

	Regulations 2016, SI 2016/715.
2017	Financial Services and Markets Act 2000 (Regulated Activities) (Amendment) Order 2017, SI 2017/488; Financial Services and Markets Act 2000 (Regulated Activities) (Amendment) (No 2) Order 2017, SI 2017/500; Money Laundering, Terrorist Financing and Transfer of Funds (Information on the Payer) Regulations 2017, SI 2017/692; Financial Services and Markets Act 2000 (Markets in Financial Instruments) Regulations 2017, SI 2017/701; Payment Services Regulations 2017, SI 2017/752; Central Securities Depositories Regulations 2017, SI 2017/1064; Risk Transformation Regulations 2017, SI 2017/1212; Financial Services and Markets Act 2000 (Markets in Financial Instruments) (No 2) Regulations 2017, SI 2017/1255.
2018	Alternative Investment Fund Managers (Amendment) Regulations 2018, SI 2018/134; Financial Services and Markets Act 2000 (Benchmarks) Regulations 2018, SI 2018/135; Insurance Distribution (Regulated Activities and Miscellaneous Amendments) Order 2018, SI 2018/546; EEA Passport Rights (Amendment, etc, and Transitional Provisions) (EU Exit) Regulations 2018, SI 2018/1149; Financial Services and Markets Act 2000 (Claims Management Activity) Order 2018, SI 2018/1253; Securitisation Regulations 2018, SI 2018/1288; Markets in Financial Instruments (Amendment) (EU Exit) Regulations 2018, SI 2018/1403.
2019	Financial Services and Markets Act 2000 (Amendment) (EU Exit) Regulations 2019, SI 2019/632; Securitisation (Amendment) (EU Exit) Regulations 2019, SI 2019/660; Uncertificated Securities (Amendment and EU Exit) Regulations 2019, SI 2019/679; Financial Services (Miscellaneous) (Amendment) (EU Exit) Regulations 2019, SI 2019/710; Financial Services and Markets Act 2000 (Regulated Activities) (Amendment) Order 2019, SI 2019/1067; Electronic Commerce and Solvency 2 (Amendment etc) (EU Exit) Regulations 2019, SI 2019/1361.
2020	Financial Services and Markets Act 2000 (Regulated Activities) (Coronavirus) (Amendment) Order 2020, SI 2020/480; Securities Financing Transactions, Securitisation and Miscellaneous Amendments (EU Exit) Regulations 2020, SI 2020/1385; Financial Holding Companies (Approval etc) and Capital Requirements (Capital Buffers and Macro-prudential Measures) (Amendment) (EU Exit) Regulations 2020, SI 2020/1406.
2021	Financial Services and Markets Act 2000 (Regulated Activities) (Amendment) Order 2021, SI 2021/90; Recognised Auction Platforms (Amendment and Miscellaneous Provisions) Regulations 2021, SI 2021/494.
2022	Dormant Assets Act 2022; Financial Services and Markets Act 2000 (Regulated Activities) (Amendment) Order 2022, SI 2022/466; Financial Services and Markets Act 2000 (Regulated Activities) (Amendment) (No 2) Order 2022, SI 2022/726.

References to the "European Community", "Community", etc: see the Treaty of Lisbon (Changes in Terminology) Order 2011, SI 2011/1043, which provides (with effect from 22 April 2011): (1) that for references to the "European Communities" or to the "European Community" (including references to "the Communities", "the Community", "the EC" or "the EEC") substitute references to the European Union; and (2) that "EU" should be substituted for the word "Community" (subject to certain exceptions) in references to "Community treaties", "Community customs duty", "Community institution", "Community instrument", "Community obligation", "enforceable Community right", "Community law", "Community legislation", and "Community provision". Also, where such a term is preceded by the word "a", for "a" substitute "an".

Transitional provisions (interim and temporary permissions and interim approvals): see the Financial Services and Markets Act 2000 (Interim Permissions) Order 2001, SI 2001/3374. That Order conferred an interim permission on certain applicants who applied to the FSA for permission under the original Part IV of the 2000 Act and whose application was pending on the date when the main provisions of the Act came into force (1 December 2001). Note that the original Part IV of the 2000 Act has now been substituted by a new Part 4A by the Financial Services Act 2012. See the notes to Part 4A (preceding s 55A of the 2000 Act at **[7.84]**) with regard to transitional provisions etc relating to the commencement of the 2012 Act.

For transitional provisions relating to interim permissions and interim approvals to various activities that have become regulated activities following the amendment of this Order, see below:

— the Financial Services and Markets Act 2000 (Transitional Provisions) (Mortgages) Order 2004, SI 2004/2615 (in relation to certain mortgage mediation activities)

— the Financial Services and Markets Act 2000 (Regulated Activities) (Amendment) (No 2) Order 2004, SI 2004/2737 (in relation to advice on stakeholder products)

— the Financial Services and Markets Act 2000 (Transitional Provisions) (General Insurance Intermediaries) Order 2004, SI 2004/3351 (in relation to certain general insurance mediation activities)

— the Financial Services and Markets Act 2000 (Regulated Activities) (Amendment) Order 2006, SI 2006/1969 (in relation to establishing, operating or winding up a personal pension scheme, or activities which relate to the specified investment of rights under a personal pension scheme)

— the Financial Services and Markets Act 2000 (Regulated Activities) (Amendment) (No 2) Order 2006, SI 2006/2383 at (in relation to administering, arranging or advising on regulated home reversion plans or regulated home purchase plans)

— the Financial Services and Markets Act 2000 (Regulated Activities) (Amendment) (No 2) Order 2007, SI 2007/3510 (in relation to provision of travel insurance in certain circumstances)

— the Financial Services and Markets Act 2000 (Regulated Activities) (Amendment) Order 2009, SI 2009/1342 (in relation to entering into, administering, arranging and advising on regulated sale and rent back agreements

— the Financial Services and Markets Act 2000 (Regulated Activities) (Amendment) Order 2013, SI 2013/655 and the Financial Services and Markets Act 2000 (Regulated Activities) (Amendment) Order 2015, SI 2015/369 (in relation to providing information in relation to and administering specified benchmarks)

— the Financial Services and Markets Act 2000 (Regulated Activities) (Amendment) (No 2) Order 2013, SI 2013/1881 (in relation to credit broking, operating an electronic system in relation to lending, debt adjusting, debt-counselling, debt-collecting, debt administration, entering into etc a regulated credit agreement, entering into etc a regulated consumer hire agreement, providing credit information services and providing credit references).

— the Financial Services and Markets Act 2000 (Regulated Activities) (Amendment) (No 2) Order 2015, SI 2015/731, and the Financial Services and Markets Act 2000 (Regulated Activities) (Transitional Provisions) Order 2015, SI 2015/732 (in relation to advising on conversion or transfer of pension benefits).

— the Financial Services and Markets Act 2000 (Regulated Activities) (Amendment) Order 2016, SI 2016/392 (in relation to the extension of the activities of operating an electronic system in relation to lending, and advising on investments).

— the Financial Services and Markets Act 2000 (Regulated Activities) (Amendment) Order 2017, SI 2017/488 (in relation to the operation of an organised trading facility; dealing in investments as agent, arranging deals in investments, managing investments, and advising on investments in relation to structured deposits; emission allowances; certain derivatives relating to currencies and binary contracts, etc).

— the Financial Services and Markets Act 2000 (Benchmarks) Regulations 2018, SI 2018/135 (in relation to administering a regulated benchmark, etc)

— the Financial Services and Markets Act 2000 (Claims Management Activity) Order 2018, SI 2018/1253 (in relation to carrying on a regulated claims management activity).

See also the Mortgage Credit Directive Order 2015, SI 2015/910 (interim permissions in relation to entering (etc) into a regulated mortgage contract or a regulated credit agreement as lender, credit broking agreements, and arranging regulated mortgage contracts).

See also the Alternative Investment Fund Managers Order 2014, SI 2014/1292, art 7 which provides a process whereby fund managers that have applied for permission to carry on the new regulated activities of managing an AIF or managing a UCITS before 16 June 2014, and that will require permission to carry on insurance mediation activities after art 6 of that Order comes into force (ie, 22 July 2014), may notify the FCA of this fact and obtain such permission without the need to make a new application for a variation of permission. Note that art 6 of the 2014 Order amends art 4(4A)(b) of this Order *post*.

See also the Financial Services and Markets Act 2000 (Regulated Activities) (Green Deal) (Amendment) Order 2014, SI 2014/1850, art 12. That article contains transitional provisions in connection with the application of the provisions of the Consumer Credit Act 1974 to a green deal plan which (a) is made in the period starting with 1 April 2014 and ending on 14 July 2014, and (b) is not a regulated credit agreement for the purposes of Chapter 14A of this Order at the time it is made, but (c) becomes on the coming into force of the 2014 Order a regulated credit agreement for those purposes in consequence of provision made by the 2014 Order (an "interim plan").

Transitional provisions in relation to Gibraltar-based firms and activities: see the Gibraltar (Miscellaneous Amendments) (EU Exit) Regulations 2019, SI 2019/680, reg 11 at **[12.129]**.

ARRANGEMENT OF ARTICLES

CHAPTER III INSURANCE

The activities

Exclusions

Supplemental

CHAPTER 3A INSURANCE RISK TRANSFORMATION

CHAPTER IV DEALING IN INVESTMENTS AS PRINCIPAL

The activity

Exclusions

CHAPTER V DEALING IN INVESTMENTS AS AGENT

The activity

Exclusions

CHAPTER 5A BIDDING IN EMISSIONS AUCTIONS

The activity

Exclusions

CHAPTER VI ARRANGING DEALS IN INVESTMENTS

The activities

Exclusions

Exclusion

CHAPTER XIV FUNERAL PLAN CONTRACTS

The activity

Exclusions

CHAPTER 14A REGULATED CREDIT AGREEMENTS

The activities

Exclusions

Supplemental

CHAPTER 14B REGULATED CONSUMER HIRE AGREEMENTS

The Activities

Exclusion

Supplemental

CHAPTER XV REGULATED MORTGAGE CONTRACTS

The activities

Exclusions

CHAPTER 15A REGULATED HOME REVERSION PLANS

The activities

Exclusions

PART I GENERAL

[8.1]

1 Citation

This Order may be cited as the Financial Services and Markets Act 2000 (Regulated Activities) Order 2001.

[8.2]

2 Commencement

(1) Except as provided by paragraph (2), this Order comes into force on the day on which section 19 of the Act comes into force.

(2) This Order comes into force—

(a) for the purposes of articles 59, 60 and 87 (funeral plan contracts) on 1st January 2002; and

(b) for the purposes of articles 61 to 63, 88, 90 and 91 (regulated mortgage contracts) [on such a day as the Treasury may specify].

[(3) Any day specified under paragraph 2(b) must be caused to be notified in the London, Edinburgh and Belfast Gazettes published not later than one week before that day.]

NOTES

Para (2): words in square brackets in sub-para (b) substituted by the Financial Services and Markets Act 2000 (Commencement of Mortgage Regulation) (Amendment) Order 2002, SI 2002/1777, art 2(1), (2), as from 30 August 2002.

Para (3): added by SI 2002/1777, art 2(1), (3), as from 30 August 2002.

FSMA 2000, s 19 came into force on 1 December 2001 (see the Financial Services and Markets Act 2000 (Commencement No 7) Order 2001, SI 2001/3538).

On such a day as the Treasury may specify: 31 October 2004 (see the London Gazette, 14 July 2003).

[8.3]

3 Interpretation

(1) In this Order—

"the Act" means the Financial Services and Markets Act 2000;

["acting as an insolvency practitioner" is to be read with section 388 of the Insolvency Act 1986 or, as the case may be, article 3 of the Insolvency (Northern Ireland) Order 1989 and, in any provision of this Order which provides for activities to be excluded from a specified activity, references to things done by a person acting—

(a) as an insolvency practitioner, or

(b) in reasonable contemplation of that person's appointment as an insolvency practitioner,

include anything done by the person's firm in connection with that person so acting;]

["AIFM" has the meaning given by regulation 4 of the Alternative Investment Fund Managers Regulations 2013;]

["agreement provider" has the meaning given by article 63J(3);

"agreement seller" has the meaning given by article 63J(3);]

["aircraft operator" has the meaning given in article 6 of the trading scheme order;]

["alternative investment fund managers directive" means Directive 2011/61/EU of the European Parliament and of the Council of 8 June 2011 on Alternative Investment Fund Managers;]

"annuities on human life" does not include superannuation allowances and annuities payable out of any fund applicable solely to the relief and maintenance of persons engaged, or who have been engaged, in any particular profession, trade or employment, or of the dependants of such persons;

["assignment", in relation to a credit agreement, has the meaning given by article 60L;]

["auction platform" means a platform on which auctions of greenhouse gas emissions allowances are held in accordance with the emission allowance auctioning regulation [or the UK auctioning regulations];]

["borrower"—

(a) in relation to a credit agreement other than a regulated mortgage contract[,] an article 36H agreement (within the meaning given by article 36H) [or an agreement that is a green deal plan], has the meaning given by article 60L;
(b) in relation to an article 36H agreement (within the meaning given by that article) other than a regulated mortgage contract, [has the meaning given by article 36H];
[(c) in relation to a credit agreement that is a green deal plan, has the meaning given by article 60LB].]

"buying" includes acquiring for valuable consideration;

"close relative" in relation to a person means—
(a) his spouse [or civil partner];
(b) his children and step children, his parents and step-parents, his brothers and sisters and his step-brothers and step-sisters; and
(c) the spouse [or civil partner] of any person within sub-paragraph (b);

["the Commission Regulation" means [Commission Delegated Regulation of 25.4.2016 supplementing Directive 2014/65/EU of the European Parliament and of the Council as regards organisational requirements and operating conditions for investment firms and defined terms for the purposes of that Directive];]

["consumer hire agreement" has the meaning given by article 60N;]

"contract of general insurance" means any contract falling within Part I of Schedule 1;

"contract of insurance" means any contract of insurance which is a contract of long-term insurance or a contract of general insurance, and includes—
(a) fidelity bonds, performance bonds, administration bonds, bail bonds, customs bonds or similar contracts of guarantee, where these are—
(i) effected or carried out by a person not carrying on a banking business;
(ii) not effected merely incidentally to some other business carried on by the person effecting them; and
(iii) effected in return for the payment of one or more premiums;
(b) tontines;
(c) capital redemption contracts or pension fund management contracts, where these are effected or carried out by a person who—
(i) does not carry on a banking business; and
(ii) otherwise carries on a regulated activity of the kind specified by article 10(1) or (2);
(d) contracts to pay annuities on human life;
(e) contracts of a kind referred to in [Article 2(3)(b)(v) of the Solvency 2 Directive]); and
[(f) contracts relating to the length of human life that are regulated by or under any enactment relating to social security, in so far as they are effected or carried out at their own risk by undertakings with permission to effect or carry out contracts of long-term insurance as principals;]

but does not include a funeral plan contract . . . ;

"contract of long-term insurance" means any contract falling within Part II of Schedule 1;

"contractually based investment" means—
(a) rights under a qualifying contract of insurance;
(b) any investment of the kind specified by any of articles 83, 84, 85 and 87; or
(c) any investment of the kind specified by article 89 so far as relevant to an investment falling within (a) or (b);

["credit agreement"—
(a) in relation to an agreement other than a green deal plan, has the meaning given by article 60B;
(b) in relation to a green deal plan, has the meaning given by article 60LB;]

[. . .]

"deposit" has the meaning given by article 5 [except where the definition given in article 60L applies];

[. . .]

[. . .]

["electronic money" has the meaning given by regulation 2(1) of the Electronic Money Regulations 2011;]

["emission allowance trading directive" means Directive 2003/87/EC of the European Parliament and of the Council of 13 October 2003 establishing a scheme for greenhouse gas emission allowances trading within the Community;]

["emission allowance auctioning regulation" means Commission Regulation (EU) No 1031/2010 of 12 November 2010 on the timing, administration and other aspects of auctioning of greenhouse gas emission allowances pursuant to the emission allowance trading directive;]

["EU Securitisation Regulation 2017" means Regulation (EU) 2017/2402 of the European Parliament and of the Council of 12 December 2017 laying down a general framework for securitisation and creating a specific framework for simple, transparent and standardised securitisation, and amending Directives 2009/65/EC, 2009/138/EC and 2011/61/EU and Regulations (EC) No 1060/2009 and (EU) No 648/2012 [as it forms part of retained EU law];]

["financial instrument" means any instrument listed in [Part 1 of Schedule 2] read with [Articles 5 to 8, 10 and 11] of the Commission Regulation (the text of which is set out in Part 2 of Schedule 2);]

["full-scope UK AIFM" has the meaning given by regulation 2(1) of the Alternative Investment Fund Managers Regulations 2013;]

"funeral plan contract" has the meaning given by article 59;

["green deal plan" has the meaning given by section 1 of the Energy Act 2011;]

["greenhouse gas emissions allowances" mean "allowances" as defined in Article 3(a) of the emission allowance trading directive [or in article 4(1) of the trading scheme order];]

["hire-purchase agreement" has the meaning given by article 60L;]

["hirer" is to be read with the definition of "consumer hire agreement" in article 60N;]

[. . .]

["home purchase provider" has the meaning given by article 63F(3);
"home purchaser" has the meaning given by article 63F(3);]
["home State"—
(a) in relation to a qualifying credit institution, means the State in which the institution has been granted authorisation;
(b) in relation to a legal person (other than a qualifying credit institution) that has a registered office under the person's national law, means the State in which that office is located;
(c) in relation to any other person, means the State in which the person's head office is located;]
"instrument" includes any record whether or not in the form of a document;
["investment firm" means a person whose regular occupation or business is the provision or performance of investment services and activities on a professional basis, other than—
(a) a person excluded by Schedule 3, read with the Commission Regulation and with Commission Delegated Regulation (EU) 2017/592 of 1 December 2016 supplementing Directive 2014/65/EU of the European Parliament and of the Council with regard to regulatory technical standards for the criteria to establish when an activity is considered to be ancillary to the main business;
(b) a person whose home State is not the United Kingdom and who would be excluded by Schedule 3, read with the Commission Regulation and with Commission Delegated Regulation (EU) 2017/592, if the person's registered office (or head office, in the case of a person that is not a body corporate or a person that is a body corporate but has no registered office) was in the United Kingdom;].
[. . .]
"joint enterprise" means an enterprise into which two or more persons ("the participators") enter for commercial purposes related to a business or businesses (other than the business of engaging in a regulated activity) carried on by them; and, where a participator is a member of a group, each other member of the group is also to be regarded as a participator in the enterprise;
["lender"—
(a) in relation to a credit agreement other than a regulated mortgage contract[,] an article 36H agreement (within the meaning given by article 36H) [or an agreement that is a green deal plan], has the meaning given by article 60L;
(b) in relation to an article 36H agreement (within the meaning given by that article) other than a regulated mortgage contract, [has the meaning given by article 36H];
[(c) in relation to a credit agreement that is a green deal plan, has the meaning given by article 60LB;]]
"local authority" means—
(a) in England and Wales, a local authority within the meaning of the Local Government Act 1972, the Greater London Authority, the Common Council of the City of London or the Council of the Isles of Scilly;
(b) in Scotland, a local authority within the meaning of the Local Government (Scotland) Act 1973;
(c) in Northern Ireland, a district council within the meaning of the Local Government Act (Northern Ireland) 1972;
["management company" has the meaning given by section 237(2) of the Act;]
"managing agent" means a person who is permitted by the Council of Lloyd's in the conduct of his business as an underwriting agent to perform for a member of Lloyd's one or more of the following functions—
(a) underwriting contracts of insurance at Lloyd's;
(b) reinsuring such contracts in whole or in part;
(c) paying claims on such contracts;
["market operator" means—other than a person falling within paragraph (1A);"
(a) a person that manages or operates the business of a UK regulated market (including a person who does so as the UK regulated market itself), or
(b) a person that would fall within paragraph (a) if the person had its registered office (or, if it does not have one, its head office) in the United Kingdom;]
["markets in financial instruments directive" means Directive 2014/65/EU of the European Parliament and of the Council of 15 May 2014 on markets in financial instruments (recast);]
["markets in financial instruments regulation" means Regulation (EU) No 600/2014 of the European Parliament and of the Council of 15 May 2014 on markets in financial instruments [as it forms part of retained EU law];]
["multilateral trading facility" or "MTF" means—
(a) a UK multilateral trading facility (within the meaning of Article 2.1.14A of the markets in financial instruments regulation) operated by an investment firm, a qualifying credit institution or a market operator, or
(b) a facility which—
(i) is operated by an investment firm, qualifying credit institution or market operator whose home State is not the United Kingdom, and
(ii) if its operator's home State was the United Kingdom, would be a UK multilateral trading facility (within the meaning of Article 2.1.14A of the markets in financial instruments regulation);]
["occupational pension scheme" has the meaning given by section 1 of the Pension Schemes Act 1993 but with paragraph (b) of the definition omitted;]
["operator" has the same meaning as in the [trading scheme order];]
["organised trading facility" or "OTF" means—
(a) a UK organised trading facility (within the meaning of Article 2.1.15A of the markets in financial instruments regulation) operated by an investment firm, a qualifying credit institution or a market operator, or
(b) a facility which—

(i) is operated by an investment firm, qualifying credit institution or market operator whose home State is not the United Kingdom, and

(ii) if its operator's home State was the United Kingdom, would be a UK organised trading facility (within the meaning of Article 2.1.15A of the markets in financial instruments regulation);]

"overseas person" means a person who—

(a) carries on activities of the kind specified by any of articles 14, 21, 25, [25A,] [25B, 25C,] [25D,] [25DA,] [25E,] 37[, 39A], 40, 45, 51, 52[, 53, 53A [, 53B, 53C, [53D,] 61, 63B[, 63F and 63J]]] or, so far as relevant to any of those articles, article 64 (or activities of a kind which would be so specified but for the exclusion in article 72); but

(b) does not carry on any such activities, or offer to do so, from a permanent place of business maintained by him in the United Kingdom;

["owner", in relation to a hire purchase agreement, has the meaning given by article 60N;]

"pension fund management contract" means a contract to manage the investments of pension funds (other than funds solely for the benefit of the officers or employees of the person effecting or carrying out the contract and their dependants or, in the case of a company, partly for the benefit of officers and employees and their dependants of its subsidiary or holding company or a subsidiary of its holding company); and for the purposes of this definition, "subsidiary" and "holding company" are to be construed in accordance with [section 1159 of the Companies Act 2006];

["the person's firm", in relation to a person acting as an insolvency practitioner or in reasonable contemplation of that person's appointment as an insolvency practitioner, means—

(a) the person's employer;

(b) where the person is a partner in a partnership other than a limited liability partnership, that partnership;

(c) where the person is a member of a limited liability partnership, that partnership;]

["personal pension scheme" means a scheme or arrangement which is not an occupational pension scheme or a stakeholder pension scheme and which is comprised in one or more instruments or agreements, having or capable of having effect so as to provide benefits to or in respect of people—

(a) on retirement,

(b) on having reached a particular age, or

(c) on termination of service in an employment;]

["plan provider" has the meaning given by paragraph (3) of article 63B, read with paragraphs (7) and (8) of that article;]

["portfolio management" has the meaning given by Article 2.7 of the Commission Regulation;]

"property" includes currency of the United Kingdom or any other country or territory;

"qualifying contract of insurance" means a contract of long-term insurance which is not—

(a) a reinsurance contract; nor

(b) a contract in respect of which the following conditions are met—

(i) the benefits under the contract are payable only on death or in respect of incapacity due to injury, sickness or infirmity;

(ii) . . .

(iii) the contract has no surrender value, or the consideration consists of a single premium and the surrender value does not exceed that premium; and

(iv) the contract makes no provision for its conversion or extension in a manner which would result in it ceasing to comply with any of the above conditions;

["qualifying credit institution" means a credit institution which—

(a) is a person who—

(i) has Part 4A permission to carry on the regulated activity of accepting deposits, or

(ii) satisfies the conditions for being given permission under Part 4A to carry on that activity, or

(iii) is a body corporate incorporated in the United Kingdom and would satisfy those conditions—

(aa) were its head office in the United Kingdom, or

(bb) if it has a registered office, were its registered office, or its registered office and its head office, in the United Kingdom,

(b) is not a friendly society,

(c) is not a society registered as a credit union under—

(i) i)the Co-operative and Community Benefit Societies Act 2014,

(ii) the Credit Unions (Northern Ireland) Order 1985, or

(iii) the Co-operative and Community Benefit Societies Act (Northern Ireland) 1969, and

(d) is not a person excluded from the definition of "investment firm" by Schedule 3, read with the Commission Regulation and with Commission Delegated Regulation (EU) 2017/592 of 1 December 2016 supplementing Directive 2014/65/EU of the European Parliament and the Council with regard to regulatory technical standards for the criteria to establish when an activity is considered to be ancillary to the main business;]

["reception", "transmission" and "submission" have the same meaning in relation to a bid at an auction for an investment of the kind specified in article 82A as in the emission allowance auctioning regulation [or the UK auctioning regulations];]

["regulated consumer hire agreement" has the meaning given by article 60N;]

["regulated credit agreement" has the meaning given by article 60B;]

["regulated home purchase plan" has the meaning given by article 63F(3);

"regulated home reversion plan" has the meaning given by article 63B(3);]

"regulated mortgage contract" has the meaning given by article 61(3);

["regulated sale and rent back agreement" has the meaning given by article 63J(3);]

["relevant investment" means—

(a) rights under a qualifying contract of insurance;

(b) rights under any other contract of insurance;

(c) any investment of the kind specified by any of articles 83, 84, 85 and 87; or

(d) any investment of the kind specified by article 89 so far as relevant to an investment falling within (a) or (c);]

["relevant recipient of credit" has the meaning given by article 60L;]

["restricted-use credit agreement" has the meaning given in article 60L;]

["reversion seller" has the meaning given by article 63B(3);]

["securitisation repository" means a person registered with [FCA (as the competent authority)] under Article 10 of the EU Securitisation Regulation 2017;]

"security" means (except where the context otherwise requires) any investment of the kind specified by any of articles 76 to 82 [or by article 82B] or, so far as relevant to any such investment, article 89;

"selling", in relation to any investment, includes disposing of the investment for valuable consideration, and for these purposes "disposing" includes—

(a) in the case of an investment consisting of rights under a contract—

(i) surrendering, assigning or converting those rights; or

(ii) assuming the corresponding liabilities under the contract;

(b) in the case of an investment consisting of rights under other arrangements, assuming the corresponding liabilities under the arrangements; and

(c) in the case of any other investment, issuing or creating the investment or granting the rights or interests of which it consists;

["small registered UK AIFM" has the meaning given by regulation 2(1) of the Alternative Investment Fund Managers Regulations 2013;]

"stakeholder pension scheme" has the meaning given by section 1 of the Welfare Reform and Pensions Act 1999 [in relation to Great Britain and has the meaning given by article 3 of the Welfare Reform and Pensions (Northern Ireland) Order 1999 in relation to Northern Ireland];

["structured deposit" means a deposit which is fully repayable at maturity on terms under which interest or a premium will be paid or is at risk, according to a formula involving factors such as—

(a) an index or combination of indices, excluding variable rate deposits whose return is directly linked to an interest rate index such as Euribor or Libor;

(b) a financial instrument or combination of financial instruments;

(c) a commodity or combination of commodities or other physical or non-physical non-fungible assets; or

(d) a foreign exchange rate or combination of foreign exchange rates;]

"syndicate" means one or more persons, to whom a particular syndicate number has been assigned by or under the authority of the Council of Lloyd's, carrying out or effecting contracts of insurance written at Lloyd's;

["trade repository" means—

(a) a person registered with [the FCA] under Article 55 of Regulation (EU) 648/2012 of the European Parliament and of the Council of 4 July 2012 on OTC derivatives, central counterparties and trade repositories or a person recognised by [the FCA] under Article 77 of that Regulation; or

(b) a person registered with [the FCA] under Article 5 of the SFT regulation or a person recognised by [the FCA] under Article 19 of that Regulation;]

["trading scheme order" means the Greenhouse Gas Emissions Trading Scheme Order 2020;]

[. . .]

[. . .]

["UK auctioning regulations" means the Greenhouse Gas Emissions Trading Scheme Auctioning Regulations 2021;]

["UK regulated market" has the meaning given by Article 2.1.13A of the markets in financial instruments regulation;]

["UK UCITS" has the meaning given by section 237(3) of the Act;]

"voting shares", in relation to a body corporate, means shares carrying voting rights attributable to share capital which are exercisable in all circumstances at any general meeting of that body corporate.

[(1A) A person falls within this paragraph if—

(a) the person is excluded from the definition of "investment firm" by Schedule 3, read with the Commission Regulation and with Commission Delegated Regulation (EU) 2017/592 of 1 December 2016 supplementing Directive 2014/65/EU of the European Parliament and of the Council with regard to regulatory technical standards for the criteria to establish when an activity is considered to be ancillary to the main business, or

(b) the person is one whose home State is not the United Kingdom and who would be excluded from that definition by Schedule 3, read with the Commission Regulation and with Commission Delegated Regulation (EU) 2017/592, if the person had its registered office (or, if it does not have one, its head office) in the United Kingdom.]

(2) For the purposes of this Order, a transaction is entered into through a person if he enters into it as agent or arranges, in a manner constituting the carrying on of an activity of the kind specified by article 25(1)[, 25A(1), 25B(1)[, 25C(1) or 25E(1)]], for it to be entered into by another person as agent or principal.

(3) For the purposes of this Order, a contract of insurance is to be treated as falling within Part II of Schedule 1, notwithstanding the fact that it contains related and subsidiary provisions such that it might also be regarded as falling within Part I of that Schedule, if its principal object is that of a contract falling within Part II and it is effected or carried out by an authorised person who has permission to effect or carry out contracts falling within paragraph I of Part II of Schedule 1.

[(4) In this Order any reference to a sourcebook is to a sourcebook in the Handbook of Rules and Guidance published by the FCA containing rules made by the FCA under the Act, as the sourcebook has effect on [IP completion day].]

NOTES

Para (1) is amended as follows:

Definitions "acting as an insolvency practitioner" and "the person's firm" inserted by the Financial Services and Markets Act 2000 (Regulated Activities) (Amendment) Order 2014, SI 2014/366, art 2(1), (2), as from 1 April 2014 (note that the 2014 Order came into force on 14 February 2014 for the purpose of the FCA making rules, giving guidance etc, and came into force on 1 April 2014, immediately after SI 2013/1881 (and SI 2013/1882) come into force, in so far as not already in force).

Definitions "AIFM", "EEA AIFM", "full-scope UK AIFM", "small registered UK AIFM", "UCITS" and "UK AIF" inserted by the Alternative Investment Fund Managers Regulations 2013, SI 2013/1773, reg 81, Sch 2, Part 1, para 1(1), (2), as from 22 July 2013. Definitions "EEA AIFM", "UCITS", and "UK AIF" (all omitted) subsequently revoked by the Financial Services and Markets Act 2000 (Amendment) (EU Exit) Regulations 2019, SI 2019/632, regs 120, 121(1), (2), as from IP completion day (as defined in the European Union (Withdrawal Agreement) Act 2020, s 39).

Definitions "agreement provider", "agreement seller", and "regulated sale and rent back agreement" inserted by the Financial Services and Markets Act 2000 (Regulated Activities) (Amendment) Order 2009, SI 2009/1342, arts 2, 3(1)(a), (b), as from 1 July 2009 (other than for the purposes of enabling applications to be made for a Part IV permission, or a variation of a Part IV permission, in relation to activities of the kind specified by arts 25E, 53D or 63J or, so far as relevant to any such activity, art 64 of this Order), and as from 30 June 2010 (otherwise).

Definition "aircraft operator" originally inserted by the Financial Services and Markets Act 2000 (Regulated Activities) (Amendment) Order 2012, SI 2012/1906, art 2(1), (2)(b), as from 20 July 2012. Subsequently substituted by the Recognised Auction Platforms (Amendment and Miscellaneous Provisions) Regulations 2021, SI 2021/494, reg 3(2)(b), as from 22 April 2021.

Definition "auction platform" inserted by SI 2012/1906, art 2(1), (2)(b), as from 20 July 2012. Words in square brackets inserted by SI 2021/494, reg 3(2)(c), as from 22 April 2021.

Definitions "alternative investment fund managers directive", "markets in financial instruments directive", "markets in financial instruments regulation", and "structured deposit" inserted by the Financial Services and Markets Act 2000 (Regulated Activities) (Amendment) Order 2017, SI 2017/488, art 2(1), (12), as from 1 April 2017 (for the purposes of (i) enabling applications to be made for a Part 4A permission, for a variation of a Part 4A permission or for an approval under FSMA 2000, s 59, or (ii) enabling such applications to be determined, in relation to any specified activity or any specified investment amended or inserted by the 2017 Order), and as from 3 January 2018 (otherwise) (for transitional provisions, see arts 15, 16 of the 2017 Order). Words in square brackets in the definition "markets in financial instruments regulation" inserted by the Securities Financing Transactions, Securitisation and Miscellaneous Amendments (EU Exit) Regulations 2020, SI 2020/1385, reg 40(3), with effect from immediately before IP completion day (as defined in the European Union (Withdrawal Agreement) Act 2020, s 39).

Definitions "assignment", "borrower", "consumer hire agreement", "credit agreement", "hire-purchase agreement", "hirer", "lender", "owner", "regulated consumer hire agreement", "regulated credit agreement", "relevant recipient of credit", and "restricted-use credit agreement" inserted, and words in square brackets in definition "deposit" inserted, by the Financial Services and Markets Act 2000 (Regulated Activities) (Amendment) (No 2) Order 2013, SI 2013/1881, arts 2, 3(1), (2), as from 1 April 2014.

In the definitions "borrower" and "lender", the comma in square brackets was substituted (for the original word "or"), the words in square brackets in para (a) were inserted, and para (c) was inserted, by the Financial Services and Markets Act 2000 (Regulated Activities) (Green Deal) (Amendment) Order 2014, SI 2014/1850, arts 2, 3(1), (2), (5), as from 15 July 2014. The words in square brackets in para (b) of those definitions were substituted by the Financial Services and Markets Act 2000 (Regulated Activities) (Amendment) Order 2016, SI 2016/392, art 2(1), (2), as from 17 March 2016. With regard to the definition "lender", note that the original insertion by SI 2013/1881 as noted above, contained paragraphs (c) and (d) rather than paragraphs (a) and (b). It was assumed that this was a typographical error and the paragraphs have been numbered as (a) and (b) in the definition set out above. Note also that SI 2014/1850, art 3 did not correct this error but instead provided that a new paragraph (e) should be inserted after the existing paragraph (d). This new paragraph has been numbered as paragraph (c) in the above definition.

Words in square brackets in the definition "close relative" inserted by the Civil Partnership Act 2004 (Amendments to Subordinate Legislation) Order 2005, SI 2005/2114, art 2(16), Sch 16, Pt 1, para 1(1), (2), as from 5 December 2005.

Definition "the Commission Regulation" inserted by the Financial Services and Markets Act 2000 (Regulated Activities) (Amendment No 3) Order 2006, SI 2006/3384, arts 2, 3(b), as from 1 April 2007 (for the purposes of enabling applications to be made for (i) a Pt IV permission, (ii) a variation of a Pt IV permission, and (iii) the Authority's approval under s 59 of the 2000 Act, in relation to an activity of the kind specified by art 25D of this Order, or in relation to an investment of the kind specified by arts 83, 84 or 85 of this Order), and as from 1 November 2007 (otherwise). Words in square brackets in the definition "the Commission Regulation" substituted by SI 2017/488, art 2(1), as from 1 April 2017 (certain purposes), and as from 3 January 2018 (otherwise) (for details and for transitional provisions, see the first note relating to the 2017 Regulations above).

Words in square brackets in para (e) of the definition "contract of insurance" substituted by the Solvency 2 Regulations 2015, SI 2015/575, reg 60, Sch 2, para 11(1), (2), as from 1 January 2016. Para (f) was substituted by SI 2019/632, regs 120, 121(1), (3), as from IP completion day (as defined in the European Union (Withdrawal Agreement) Act 2020, s 39). The words omitted from that paragraph were revoked by the Financial Services and Markets Act 2000 (Regulated Activities) (Amendment) Order 2021, SI 2021/90, art 2(2); note that this Order comes into force (1) on 28 January 2021 (for the purposes of (a) enabling the FCA to make or approve rules and to give guidance and directions; (b) enabling applications to be made etc for: (i) a Part 4A permission under s 55A of FSMA 2000; (ii) a variation of a Part 4A permission under s 55H of that Act; and (iii) approval under Part 5 of the Act; (c) enabling the FCA to exercise any of its powers under Part 4A or Part 5 of that Act in relation to any activity which becomes a regulated activity by virtue of this Order; and (d) enabling the scheme operator to make rules and to give guidance); and (2) for all other purposes 29 July 2022 (see art 1 of the 2021 Order, and see Part 3 of that Order for transitional provisions).

Definition "credit agreement" substituted, and definition "green deal plan" inserted, by SI 2014/1850, arts 2, 3(1), (3), (4), as from 15 July 2014.

Definition "credit institution" (omitted) originally inserted by SI 2006/3384, arts 2, 3(b), as from 1 April 2007 (certain purposes), and as from 1 November 2007 (otherwise). Subsequently revoked by SI 2019/632, regs 120, 121(1), (2), as from IP completion day (as defined in the European Union (Withdrawal Agreement) Act 2020, s 39).

Definition "designated guidance provider" (omitted) originally inserted by the Financial Services and Markets Act 2000 (Regulated Activities) (Amendment) (Pensions Guidance Exclusions) Order 2015, SI 2015/489, art 2(1), (2), as from 26 March 2015. Subsequently revoked by the Financial Services and Markets Act 2000 (Regulated Activities) (Amendment) (No 2) Order 2022, SI 2022/726, art 2(2), as from 21 July 2022.

Definition "electronic money" originally inserted by the Financial Services and Markets Act 2000 (Regulated Activities) (Amendment) Order 2002, SI 2002/682, art 2, as from 27 April 2002. Subsequently substituted by SI 2011/99, reg 79, Sch 4, Pt 2, para 12(a)(ii), as from 30 April 2011.

Definition "emission allowance auctioning regulation" inserted by SI 2012/1906, art 2(1), (2)(b), as from 20 July 2012.

Definition "emission allowance trading directive" inserted by SI 2012/1906, art 2(1), (2)(b), as from 20 July 2012.

Definitions "EU Securitisation Regulation 2017" and "securitisation repository" inserted by the Securitisation Regulations 2018, SI 2018/1288, reg 28, Sch 2, para 2(1), (2), as from 1 January 2019. Words in square brackets in the definition "EU Securitisation Regulation 2017" inserted by SI 2020/1385, reg 40(2), with effect from immediately before IP completion day (as defined in the European Union (Withdrawal Agreement) Act 2020, s 39). Words in square brackets in the definition "securitisation repository" substituted by the Securitisation (Amendment) (EU Exit) Regulations 2019, SI 2019/660, reg 57, as from IP completion day (as defined in the European Union (Withdrawal Agreement) Act 2020, s 39).

Definition "financial instrument" inserted by SI 2006/3384, arts 2, 3(b), as from 1 April 2007 (certain purposes), and as from 1 November 2007 (otherwise) (for more detail, see the note relating to the definition "the Commission Regulation" above). Words in first pair of square brackets substituted by SI 2019/632, regs 120, 121(1), (4), as from IP completion day (as defined in the European Union (Withdrawal Agreement) Act 2020, s 39). Words in second pair of square brackets substituted by SI 2017/488, art 2(1), (4), as from 1 April 2017 (certain purposes), and as from 3 January 2018 (otherwise) (for details and for transitional provisions, see the first note relating to the 2017 Regulations above).

Definition "greenhouse gas emissions allowances" inserted by SI 2012/1906, art 2(1), (2)(b), as from 20 July 2012. Words in square brackets inserted by SI 2021/494, reg 3(2)(d), as from 22 April 2021.

Definition "home Member State" (omitted) originally inserted by SI 2006/3384, arts 2, 3(b), as from 1 April 2007 (certain purposes), and as from 1 November 2007. Subsequently revoked by SI 2019/632, regs 120, 121(1), (5), as from IP completion day (as defined in the European Union (Withdrawal Agreement) Act 2020, s 39).

Definitions "home purchase provider", "home purchaser", "plan provider", "regulated home purchase plan", "regulated home reversion plan", and "reversion seller" inserted by the Financial Services and Markets Act 2000 (Regulated Activities) (Amendment) (No 2) Order 2006, SI 2006/2383, arts 2, 3(1)(a), (c)–(e), as from 6 November 2006 (for the purposes of enabling applications to be made for (i) a Pt IV permission, or a variation of a Pt IV permission, in relation to activities of the kind specified by arts 25B, 25C, 53B, 53C, 63B or 63F or, so far as relevant to any such activity, art 64 of this Order; or (ii) the Authority's approval under FSMA 2000, s 59 in relation to any of those activities), and as from 6 April 2007 (otherwise).

Definition "home State" inserted by SI 2019/632, regs 120, 121(1), (5), as from IP completion day (as defined in the European Union (Withdrawal Agreement) Act 2020, s 39).

Definition "investment firm" originally inserted by SI 2006/3384, arts 2, 3(b), as from 1 April 2007 (certain purposes), and as from 1 November 2007 (otherwise). Subsequently substituted by SI 2019/632, regs 120, 121(1), (6), as from IP completion day (as defined in the European Union (Withdrawal Agreement) Act 2020, s 39).

Definition "investment services and activities" (omitted) originally inserted by SI 2006/3384, as from 1 April 2007 (certain purposes), and as from 1 November 2007 (otherwise). Subsequently revoked by SI 2019/632, regs 120, 121(1), (2), as from IP completion day (as defined in the European Union (Withdrawal Agreement) Act 2020, s 39).

Definition "management company" originally inserted by the Financial Services and Markets Act 2000 (Regulated Activities) (Amendment No 3) Order 2006, SI 2006/3384, arts 2, 3(b), as from 1 April 2007 (certain purposes), and as from 1 November 2007 (otherwise). Subsequently substituted by SI 2019/632, regs 120, 121(1), (7), as from IP completion day (as defined in the European Union (Withdrawal Agreement) Act 2020, s 39).

Definition "market operator" originally inserted by SI 2006/3384, arts 2, 3(b), as from 1 April 2007 (certain purposes), and as from 1 November 2007 (otherwise). Subsequently substituted by SI 2019/632, regs 120, 121(1), (8), as from IP completion day (as defined in the European Union (Withdrawal Agreement) Act 2020, s 39).

Definition "multilateral trading facility" originally inserted by SI 2006/3384, arts 2, 3(b), as from 1 April 2007 (certain purposes), and as from 1 November 2007 (otherwise). Subsequently substituted by SI 2019/632, regs 120, 121(1), (9), as from IP completion day (as defined in the European Union (Withdrawal Agreement) Act 2020, s 39).

Definition "occupational pension scheme" substituted by the Financial Services and Markets Act 2000 (Regulated Activities) (Amendment) Order 2006, SI 2006/1969, art 2(1), (2)(a), as from 1 October 2006 (for the purposes of enabling applications to be made for Pt IV permission or for a variation of Pt IV permission in relation to the regulated activity specified by art 52(b) of this Order (as amended by SI 2006/1969) or in relation to an investment specified by art 82(2) of this Order (as so amended)), and as from 6 April 2007 (otherwise).

Definition "operator" inserted by SI 2012/1906, art 2(1), (2)(b), as from 20 July 2012. Words in square brackets substituted by SI 2021/494, reg 3(2)(e), as from 22 April 2021.

Definition organised trading facility" originally inserted by SI 2017/488, art 2(1), (12), as from 1 April 2017 (certain purposes), and as from 3 January 2018 (otherwise). Subsequently substituted by SI 2019/632, regs 120, 121(1), (10), as from IP completion day (as defined in the European Union (Withdrawal Agreement) Act 2020, s 39).

Definition "overseas person" is amended as follows:

Figure "25A," in square brackets inserted by the Financial Services and Markets Act 2000 (Regulated Activities) (Amendment) (No 1) Order 2003, SI 2003/1475, art 3(a), as from 31 October 2004.

Figures "25B, 25C," in square brackets inserted by SI 2006/2383, arts 2, 3(1)(b)(i), as from the same dates and for the same purposes, etc, as mentioned in the note relating to this Order above.

Figure "25D," in square brackets inserted by SI 2006/3384, arts 2, 3(a), as from 1 April 2007 (certain purposes), and as from 1 November 2007 (otherwise) (for details, see the note relating to the definition "the Commission Regulation" above).

Figure "25DA," in square brackets inserted by SI 2017/488, art 2(1), (10), as from 1 April 2017 (certain purposes), and as from 3 January 2018 (otherwise) (for details and for transitional provisions, see the first note relating to the 2017 Regulations above).

Figure "25E," in square brackets inserted by SI 2009/1342, arts 2, 3(1)(c)(i), as from the same dates and for the same purposes, etc, as mentioned in the note relating to this Order above.

Figure ", 39A" in square brackets inserted by SI 2003/1476, arts 2, 3(1)(a), as from 31 October 2004 (in so far as relating to contracts of long-term care insurance), and as from 14 January 2005 (otherwise).

Figures "51ZA, 51ZB, 51ZC, 51ZD, 51ZE" in square brackets substituted by SI 2013/1773, reg 81(1), Sch 2, Pt 1, para 1(1), (2)(a), as from 22 July 2013.

Words in square brackets beginning with the figures ", 53, 53A" substituted by SI 2003/1475, art 3(b), as from 31 October 2004.

Words in square brackets beginning with the figures ", 53B, 53C" substituted by SI 2006/2383, arts 2, 3(1)(b)(ii), as from the same dates and for the same purposes as mentioned in the note relating to this Order above.

Figure "53D," in square brackets inserted by SI 2009/1342, arts 2, 3(1)(c)(ii), as from the same dates and for the same purposes, etc, as mentioned in the note relating to this Order above.

Words ", 63F and 63J" in square brackets substituted by SI 2009/1342, arts 2, 3(1)(c)(iii), as from the same dates and for the same purposes, etc, as mentioned in the note relating to this Order above.

Words in square brackets in definition "pension fund management contract" substituted by the Companies Act 2006 (Consequential Amendments and Transitional Provisions) Order 2011, SI 2011/1265, art 13(1), (2), as from 12 May 2011.

Definition "personal pension scheme" inserted by SI 2006/1969, art 2(1), (2)(a), as from the same dates and for the same purposes, etc, as mentioned in the note relating to this Order above.

Definitions "portfolio management" and "qualifying credit institution" inserted by SI 2019/632, regs 120, 121(1), (11), as from IP completion day (as defined in the European Union (Withdrawal Agreement) Act 2020, s 39).

In definition "qualifying contract of insurance" sub-para (b)(ii) revoked by the Financial Services and Markets Act 2000 (Regulated Activities) (Amendment) Order 2007, SI 2007/1339, arts 2, 3, as from 6 June 2007.

Definitions "reception", "transmission" and "submission" inserted by SI 2012/1906, art 2(1), (2)(b), as from 20 July 2012. Words in square brackets inserted by SI 2021/494, reg 3(2)(f), as from 22 April 2021.

Definition "relevant investment" inserted by SI 2003/1476, art 3(1)(b), as from 31 October 2004 (in so far as relating to contracts of long-term care insurance), and as from 14 January 2005 (otherwise).

Words in square brackets in definition "security" inserted by SI 2017/488, art 2(1), (11), as from 1 April 2017 (certain purposes), and as from 3 January 2018 (otherwise) (for details and for transitional provisions, see the first note relating to the 2017 Regulations above).

Words in square brackets in definition "stakeholder pension scheme" added by SI 2005/593, art 2(1), (2)(b), as from 6 April 2005.

Definition "trade repository" substituted by the Financial Services and Markets Act 2000 (Transparency of Securities Financing Transactions and of Reuse) Regulations 2016, SI 2016/715, reg 30, Sch 2, para 1(1), (2), as from 13 July 2016. Words in square brackets substituted by SI 2019/632, regs 120, 121(1), (12), as from IP completion day (as defined in the European Union (Withdrawal Agreement) Act 2020, s 39).

Definitions "trading scheme order" and "UK auctioning regulations" inserted by SI 2021/494, reg 3(2)(a), as from 22 April 2021.

Definitions "UK regulated market" and "UK UCITS" inserted by SI 2019/632, regs 120, 121(1), (13), as from IP completion day (as defined in the European Union (Withdrawal Agreement) Act 2020, s 39).

Para (1A): inserted by SI 2019/632, regs 120, 121(14), as from IP completion day (as defined in the European Union (Withdrawal Agreement) Act 2020, s 39).

Para (2): words in first (outer) pair of square brackets inserted by SI 2006/2383, arts 2, 3(2), as from the same dates and for the same purposes, etc, as mentioned in the note relating to this Order above. Words in second (inner) pair of square brackets substituted by SI 2009/1342, arts 2, 3(2), as from the same dates and for the same purposes, etc, as mentioned in the note relating to this Order above.

Para (4): added by SI 2019/632, regs 120, 121(15), as from IP completion day (as defined in the European Union (Withdrawal Agreement) Act 2020, s 39). Note that reg 121(15) of the 2019 Regulations was amended by the Financial Services and Economic and Monetary Policy (Consequential Amendments) (EU Exit) Regulations 2020, SI 2020/1301, reg 3, Schedule, para 33(l), as from 30 December 2020 (and the effect of the amendment has been incorporated in the text set out above).

Close relative: as to the meaning of "step-children", and related expressions, see the Civil Partnership Act 2004, s 246 (as applied to this Order by the Civil Partnership Act 2004 (Relationships Arising Through Civil Partnership) Order 2005, SI 2005/3137, art 3, Schedule).

PART II SPECIFIED ACTIVITIES

CHAPTER I GENERAL

[8.4]

4 Specified activities: general

(1) The following provisions of this Part specify kinds of activity for the purposes of [section 22(1)] of the Act (and accordingly any activity of one of those kinds, which is carried on by way of business, and relates to an investment of a kind specified by any provision of Part III and applicable to that activity, is a regulated activity for the purposes of the Act).

(2) The kinds of activity specified by articles [[51ZA, 51ZB, 51ZC, 51ZD, 51ZE], 52 and 63N] are also specified for the purposes of section 22(1)(b) of the Act (and accordingly any activity of one of those kinds, when carried on by way of business, is a regulated activity when carried on in relation to property of any kind).

[(2A) The kinds of activity specified by Part 3A are specified for the purposes of section 22(1A)(a) of the Act (and accordingly any activity of one of those kinds, when carried on by way of business, is a regulated activity).]

[(2B) The kinds of activity specified in Part 3B are specified for the purposes of section 22(1B) of the Act (and accordingly any activity of one of those kinds, when carried on by way of business in Great Britain, is a regulated activity).]

(3) Subject to paragraph (4), each provision specifying a kind of activity is subject to the exclusions applicable to that provision (and accordingly any reference in this Order to an activity of the kind specified by a particular provision is to be read subject to any such exclusions).

[(4) Where an investment firm or [qualifying credit institution]—

(a) provides or performs investment services and activities on a professional basis, and
(b) in doing so would be treated as carrying on an activity of a kind specified by a provision of this Part but for an exclusion in any of articles 15, 16, [18,] 19, 22, 23, 29, [34,] 38, 67, 68, 69, 70 and 72E,

that exclusion is to be disregarded and, accordingly, the investment firm or [qualifying credit institution] is to be treated as carrying on an activity of the kind specified by the provision in question.]

[(4A) Where a person, other than an ancillary insurance intermediary carrying out insurance distribution activities falling within Article 1.3 of the insurance distribution directive (the text of which is set out in Part 1 of Schedule 4)—

(a) for remuneration, takes up or pursues insurance distribution, or reinsurance distribution, in relation to a risk or commitment located in [the United Kingdom], and

(b) in doing so would be treated as carrying on an activity of a specified kind by a provision of this Part but for an exclusion in any of articles 30, 66, 67 and 72AA,

that exclusion is to be disregarded (and accordingly that person is to be treated as carrying on an activity of the kind specified by the provision in question).]

[(4AA) In its application to any activity relating to a contract of insurance entered into before IP completion day, paragraph (4A)(a) has effect as if "or an EEA State" were inserted after "the United Kingdom.]

[(4B) Where—

(a) a person is a mortgage creditor or a mortgage intermediary; and

(b) in acting as a mortgage creditor or a mortgage intermediary [in respect of an agreement entered into, or to be entered into, on or after 21st March 2016], that person would be treated as carrying on an activity of a kind specified by article 25A (arranging regulated mortgage contracts), 36A (credit broking), 53A (advising on regulated mortgage contracts), 53DA (advising on regulated credit agreements for the acquisition of land), 60B (regulated credit agreements) or 61 (entering into and administering regulated mortgage contracts), but for an exclusion or exemption provided for by this Order,

that exclusion or exemption is to be disregarded (and accordingly that person is to be treated as carrying on an activity of the kind specified by the provision in question) to the extent that such exclusion or exemption [neither relates to an agreement to which section 423A(3) of the Act applies nor falls within the scope of any of the derogations set out in Article 3(3) of the mortgages directive (as it had effect immediately before IP completion day)].]

[(5) In this article—

"ancillary insurance intermediary" has the meaning given by Article 2.1(4) of the insurance distribution directive, the text of which is set out in Part 4 of Schedule 4[, read with the modifications set out in paragraph 3 of Part 6 of that Schedule];

"insurance distribution" has the meaning given by Articles 2.1(1) and 2.2 of the insurance distribution directive, the text of which is set out in Parts 2 and 5 of Schedule 4, respectively[read with the modification set out in paragraph 4 of Part 6 of that Schedule]; and

"reinsurance distribution" has the meaning given by Articles 2.1(2) and 2.2 of the insurance distribution directive, the text of which is set out in Parts 3 and 5 of Schedule 4, respectively[, read with the modifications set out in paragraphs 2 and 4 of Part 6 of that Schedule].]

NOTES

Para (1): words in square brackets substituted by the Financial Services and Markets Act 2000 (Regulated Activities) (Amendment) (No 2) Order 2013, SI 2013/1881, arts 2, 3(3)(a), as from 1 April 2014.

Para (2): words in first (outer) square brackets substituted by the Financial Services and Markets Act 2000 (Regulated Activities) (Amendment) (No 2) Order 2009, SI 2009/1389, arts 2, 3, as from 13 July 2009. Figures in second (inner) pair of square brackets substituted by the Alternative Investment Fund Managers Regulations 2013, SI 2013/1773, reg 81, Sch 2, Part 1, para 1(1), (3), as from 22 July 2013.

Para (2A): inserted by SI 2013/1881, arts 2, 3(3)(b), as from 1 April 2014.

Para (2B): inserted by the Financial Services and Markets Act 2000 (Claims Management Activity) Order 2018, SI 2018/1253, arts 3, 4, as from 1 April 2019 (for provision specifying that the 2018 Order also comes into force on 29 November 2018 for the purposes of the FCA and FOS making rules and issuing guidance, and for transitional provisions in relation to carrying on a claims management activity, etc, see arts 1, 39–89 of the 2018 Order).

Para (4): substituted by the Financial Services and Markets Act 2000 (Regulated Activities) (Amendment No 3) Order 2006, SI 2006/3384, arts 2, 4(a), as from 1 April 2007 (for the purposes of enabling applications to be made for (i) a Part IV permission, (ii) a variation of a Part IV permission, and (iii) the Authority's approval under s 59 of the 2000 Act, in relation to an activity of the kind specified by art 25D of this Order, or in relation to an investment of the kind specified by arts 83, 84 or 85 of this Order), and as from 1 November 2007 (otherwise). Words "qualifying credit institution" in square brackets (in both places that they occur) substituted by the Financial Services and Markets Act 2000 (Amendment) (EU Exit) Regulations 2019, SI 2019/632, regs 120, 122(1), (2), as from IP completion day (as defined in the European Union (Withdrawal Agreement) Act 2020, s 39). Figures in square brackets in sub-para (b) inserted by the Financial Services and Markets Act 2000 (Regulated Activities) (Amendment) Order 2017, SI 2017/488, art 12(1), (2), as from 1 April 2017 (for the purposes of (i) enabling applications to be made for a Part 4A permission, for a variation of a Part 4A permission or for an approval under FSMA 2000, s 59, or (ii) enabling such applications to be determined, in relation to any specified activity or any specified investment amended or inserted by the 2017 Order), and as from 3 January 2018 (otherwise) (for transitional provisions, see arts 15, 16 of the 2017 Order).

Para (4A): originally inserted by the Financial Services and Markets Act 2000 (Regulated Activities) (Amendment) (No 2) Order 2003, SI 2003/1476, art 3(2)(a), as from 31 October 2004 (in so far as relating to contracts of long-term care insurance), and as from 14 January 2005 (otherwise). Subsequently substituted by the Insurance Distribution (Regulated Activities and Miscellaneous Amendments) Order 2018, SI 2018/546, arts 2, 3(a), as from 1 October 2018. Words in square brackets substituted by SI 2019/632, regs 120, 122(1), (3), as from IP completion day (as defined in the European Union (Withdrawal Agreement) Act 2020, s 39).

Para (4AA): inserted by SI 2019/632, regs 120, 122(1), (4), as from IP completion day (as defined in the European Union (Withdrawal Agreement) Act 2020, s 39). Note that reg 122(4) of the 2019 Regulations was amended by the Financial Services and Economic and Monetary Policy (Consequential Amendments) (EU Exit) Regulations 2020, SI 2020/1301, reg 3, Schedule, para 33(m), as from 30 December 2020 (and the effect of the amendment has been incorporated in the text set out above).

Para (4B) was inserted by the Mortgage Credit Directive Order 2015, SI 2015/910, Sch 1, Pt 2, para 4(1), (3), as from 21 March 2016, and subsequently has been amended as follows:

Words in square brackets in sub-para (b) inserted by the Financial Services and Markets Act 2000 (Regulated Activities) (Amendment) Order 2016, SI 2016/392, art 2(1), (3), as from 21 March 2016.

Words in second pair of square brackets substituted by SI 2019/632, regs 120, 122(1), (5), as from IP completion day (as defined in the European Union (Withdrawal Agreement) Act 2020, s 39). Note that reg 122(5) of the 2019 Regulations was amended by the Financial Services and Economic and Monetary Policy (Consequential Amendments) (EU Exit) Regulations 2020, SI 2020/1301, reg 3, Schedule, para 33(m), as from 30 December 2020 (and the effect of the amendment has been incorporated in the text set out above).

Para (5): substituted by SI 2018/546, arts 2, 3(b), as from 1 October 2018. Words in square brackets inserted by SI 2019/632, regs 120, 122(1), (6), as from IP completion day (as defined in the European Union (Withdrawal Agreement) Act 2020, s 39).

CHAPTER II ACCEPTING DEPOSITS

The activity

[8.5]

5 Accepting deposits

(1) Accepting deposits is a specified kind of activity if—

(a) money received by way of deposit is lent to others; or

(b) any other activity of the person accepting the deposit is financed wholly, or to a material extent, out of the capital of or interest on money received by way of deposit.

(2) In paragraph (1), "deposit" means a sum of money, other than one excluded by any of [articles 6 to 9A], paid on terms—

(a) under which it will be repaid, with or without interest or premium, and either on demand or at a time or in circumstances agreed by or on behalf of the person making the payment and the person receiving it; and

(b) which are not referable to the provision of property (other than currency) or services or the giving of security.

(3) For the purposes of paragraph (2), money is paid on terms which are referable to the provision of property or services or the giving of security if, and only if—

(a) it is paid by way of advance or part payment under a contract for the sale, hire or other provision of property or services, and is repayable only in the event that the property or services is or are not in fact sold, hired or otherwise provided;

(b) it is paid by way of security for the performance of a contract or by way of security in respect of loss which may result from the non-performance of a contract; or

(c) without prejudice to sub-paragraph (b), it is paid by way of security for the delivery up or return of any property, whether in a particular state of repair or otherwise.

NOTES

Para (2): words in square brackets substituted by the Financial Services and Markets Act 2000 (Regulated Activities) (Amendment) Order 2002, SI 2002/682, art 3(1), as from 27 April 2002.

Exclusions

[8.6]

6 Sums paid by certain persons

(1) A sum is not a deposit for the purposes of article 5 if it is—

(a) paid by any of the following persons—

(i) the Bank of England . . . ;

(ii) an authorised person who has permission to accept deposits, or to effect or carry out contracts of insurance;

(iii) . . .

[(iv) National Savings and Investments;]

(v) a municipal bank, that is to say a company which was, immediately before the coming into force of this article, exempt from the prohibition in section 3 of the Banking Act 1987 by virtue of section 4(1) of, and paragraph 4 of Schedule 2 to, that Act;

(vi) Keesler Federal Credit Union;

(vii) a body of persons certified as a school bank by the National Savings Bank or by an authorised person who has permission to accept deposits;

(viii) a local authority;

(xi) any body which by virtue of any enactment has power to issue a precept to a local authority in England and Wales or a requisition to a local authority in Scotland, or to the expenses of which, by virtue of any enactment, a local authority in the United Kingdom is or can be required to contribute (and in this paragraph, "enactment" includes an enactment comprised in, or in an instrument made under, an Act of the Scottish Parliament);

(x)

(xi) the European Investment Bank;

(xii) the International Bank for Reconstruction and Development;

(xiii) the International Finance Corporation;

(xiv) the International Monetary Fund;

(xv) the African Development Bank;

(xvi) the Asian Development Bank;

(xvii) the Caribbean Development Bank;

(xviii) the Inter-American Development Bank;

(xix) the European Bank for Reconstruction and Development;

[(xx) the Council of Europe Development Bank;]

(b) paid by a person other than one mentioned in sub-paragraph (a) in the course of carrying on a business consisting wholly or to a significant extent of lending money;

(c) paid by one company to another at a time when both are members of the same group or when the same individual is a majority shareholder controller of both of them; or

(d) paid by a person who, at the time when it is paid, is a close relative of the person receiving it or who is, or is a close relative of, a director or manager of that person or who is, or is a close relative of, a controller of that person.

(2) For the purposes of paragraph (1)(c), an individual is a majority shareholder controller of a company if he is a controller of the company by virtue of paragraph (a), (c), (e) or (g) of section 422(2) of the Act, and if in his case the greatest percentage of those referred to in those paragraphs is 50 or more.

(3) In the application of sub-paragraph (d) of paragraph (1) to a sum paid by a partnership, that sub-paragraph is to have effect as if, for the reference to the person paying the sum, there were substituted a reference to each of the partners.

NOTES

Para (1) is amended as follows:

Words omitted from sub-para (a)(i) revoked by the Financial Services and Markets Act 2000 (Amendment) (EU Exit) Regulations 2019, SI 2019/632, regs 120, 123(1), (2), as from IP completion day (as defined in the European Union (Withdrawal Agreement) Act 2020, s 39).

Sub-para (a)(iii) revoked by the EEA Passport Rights (Amendment, etc, and Transitional Provisions) (EU Exit) Regulations 2018, SI 2018/1149, reg 3, Schedule, Pt 3, para 49(1), (2), as from IP completion day (as defined in the European Union (Withdrawal Agreement) Act 2020, s 39).

Sub-para (a)(iv) substituted by the Financial Holding Companies (Approval etc) and Capital Requirements (Capital Buffers and Macro-prudential Measures) (Amendment) (EU Exit) Regulations 2020, SI 2020/1406, reg 3, as from 29 December 2020.

Sub-para (a)(x) revoked by SI 2019/632, regs 120, 123(1), (3), as from IP completion day (as defined in the European Union (Withdrawal Agreement) Act 2020, s 39).

Sub-para (a)(xx) substituted by the Financial Services and Markets Act 2000 (Financial Promotion and Miscellaneous Amendments) Order 2002, SI 2002/1310, art 4(1), as from 5 June 2002.

Banking Act 1987: repealed by the Financial Services and Markets Act 2000 (Consequential Amendments and Repeals) Order 2001, SI 2001/3649.

[8.7]
7 Sums received by solicitors etc

(1) A sum is not a deposit for the purposes of article 5 if it is received by a practising solicitor acting in the course of his profession.

(2) In paragraph (1), "practising solicitor" means—

(a) a solicitor who is qualified to act as such under section 1 of the Solicitors Act 1974, article 4 of the Solicitors (Northern Ireland) Order 1976 or section 4 of the Solicitors (Scotland) Act 1980;

(b) a recognised body;

(c) a registered foreign lawyer in the course of providing professional services as a member of a multi-national partnership; [or]

(d) [a Swiss lawyer who is a registered European lawyer]; . . .

(e) . . .

(3) In this article—

(a) "a recognised body" means a body . . . recognised by—

(i) the Council of the Law Society under section 9 of the Administration of Justice Act 1985;

(ii) the Incorporated Law Society of Northern Ireland under article 26A of the Solicitors (Northern Ireland) Order 1976; or

(iii) the Council of the Law Society of Scotland under section 34 of the Solicitors (Scotland) Act 1980;

(b) "registered foreign lawyer" has the meaning given by section 89 of the Courts and Legal Services Act 1990 or, in Scotland, section 65 of the Solicitors (Scotland) Act 1980;

(c) "multi-national partnership" has the meaning given by section 89 of the Courts and Legal Services Act 1990 but, in Scotland, is a reference to a "multi-national practice" within the meaning of section 60A of the Solicitors (Scotland) Act 1980; . . .

(d) "registered European lawyer" has the meaning given by regulation 2(1) of the European Communities (Lawyer's Practice) Regulations 2000 or regulation 2(1) of the European Communities (Lawyer's Practice) (Scotland) Regulation 2000; [and]

[(e) "Swiss lawyer" means a national of the United Kingdom or a Swiss national who—

(i) immediately before IP completion day was authorised in Switzerland to pursue professional activities under the professional title of Avocat, Advokat, Rechtsanwalt, Anwalt, Fürsprecher, Fürsprech or Avvocato, or

(ii) had started training towards but not yet obtained their professional qualifications before IP completion day in order to be authorised in Switzerland to pursue professional activities under one of the professional titles referred to in paragraph (i) but who completed their qualifications and were so authorised before the end of the period of four years beginning with IP completion day.]

NOTES

Para (2): the word "or" in square brackets at the end of sub-para (c) was inserted, the words in square brackets in sub-para (d) were substituted, and sub-para (e) and the preceding word were revoked, by the Financial Services (Miscellaneous) (Amendment) (EU Exit) Regulations 2019, SI 2019/710, reg 6(a), as from IP completion day (as defined in the European Union (Withdrawal Agreement) Act 2020, s 39). Note that reg 6 of the 2019 Regulations was substituted by the Services of Lawyers and Lawyer's Practice (Revocation etc) (EU Exit) Regulations 2020, SI 2020/1342, reg 12, Schedule, Pt 2, para 19 (with effect from immediately before IP completion day), and the effect of this amendment has been incorporated in the text set out above (for transitional provisions, see regs 4–12 of the 2020 Regulations).

Para (3): the word omitted from the definition "a recognised body" was revoked by the Solicitors' Recognised Bodies (Amendment) Order 2009, SI 2009/500, art 3, as from 31 March 2009. The word omitted from sub-para (c) was revoked, and sub-para (e) and the preceding word were inserted, by SI 2019/710, reg 6(b), as from IP completion day (as defined in the European Union (Withdrawal Agreement) Act 2020, s 39). Note that reg 6 of the 2019 Regulations was substituted by SI 2020/1342, reg 12, Schedule, Pt 2, para 19 (with effect from immediately before IP completion day), and the effect of this amendment has been incorporated in the text set out above (for transitional provisions, see regs 4–12 of the 2020 Regulations).

See further, the Legal Services Act 2007 (Designation as a Licensing Authority) (No 2) Order 2011, SI 2011/2866, Sch 3 (Statutory Instruments which apply to licensed bodies with additions, omissions and modifications), which provides that para (1) above has effect as if the reference to a "practising solicitor" includes a reference to a licensed body in relation to such of its activities as are regulated by the Law Society in accordance with a licence issued to it under Part 5 of the Legal Services Act 2007.

European Communities (Lawyer's Practice) Regulations 2000; European Communities (Lawyer's Practice) (Scotland) Regulation 2000: revoked by the Services of Lawyers and Lawyer's Practice (Revocation etc) (EU Exit) Regulations 2020, SI 2020/1342, as from IP completion day (as defined in the European Union (Withdrawal Agreement) Act 2020, s 39).

[8.8]

8 Sums received by persons authorised to deal etc

A sum is not a deposit for the purposes of article 5 if it is received by a person who is—

(a) an authorised person with permission to carry on an activity of the kind specified by any of articles 14, 21, 25, 37, [51ZA, 51ZB, 51ZC, 51ZD, 51ZE] and 52, or

(b) an exempt person in relation to any such activity,

in the course of, or for the purpose of, [carrying on any such activity (or any activity which would be such an activity but for any exclusion made by this Part)] with or on behalf of the person by or on behalf of whom the sum is paid.

NOTES

Figures in first pair of square brackets substituted by the Alternative Investment Fund Managers Regulations 2013, SI 2013/1773, reg 81, Sch 2, Part 1, para 1(1), (3), as from 22 July 2013. Words in second pair of square brackets substituted by the Financial Services and Markets Act 2000 (Regulated Activities) (Amendment) Order 2001, SI 2001/3544, arts 2, 3, as from 1 December 2001.

[8.9]

9 Sums received in consideration for the issue of debt securities

(1) Subject to paragraph (2), a sum is not a deposit for the purposes of article 5 if it is received by a person as consideration for the issue by him of any investment of the kind specified by article 77 or 78.

(2) The exclusion in paragraph (1) does not apply to the receipt by a person of a sum as consideration for the issue by him of commercial paper unless—

(a) the commercial paper is issued to persons—

(i) whose ordinary activities involve them in acquiring, holding, managing or disposing of investments (as principal or agent) for the purposes of their businesses; or

(ii) who it is reasonable to expect will acquire, hold, manage or dispose of investments (as principal or agent) for the purposes of their businesses; and

(b) the redemption value of the commercial paper is not less than £100,000 (or an amount of equivalent value denominated wholly or partly in a currency other than sterling), and no part of the commercial paper may be transferred unless the redemption value of that part is not less than £100,000 (or such an equivalent amount).

[(3) In paragraph (2), "commercial paper" means an investment of the kind specified by article 77 or 78 having a maturity of less than one year from the date of issue.]

NOTES

Para (3): substituted by the Financial Services and Markets Act 2000 (Regulated Activities) (Amendment) Order 2002, SI 2002/682, art 12, as from 27 April 2002.

[8.10]

[9A Sums received in exchange for electronic money

A sum is not a deposit for the purposes of article 5 if it is immediately exchanged for electronic money.]

NOTES

Inserted by the Financial Services and Markets Act 2000 (Regulated Activities) (Amendment) Order 2002, SI 2002/682, art 3(2), as from 27 April 2002.

[8.11]

[9AA . . . [. . . Managers of [UK UCITS] and AIFs]

Article 5 is subject to the [exclusion] in . . . [. . . article 72AA (managers of [UK UCITS] and AIFs)].]

NOTES

Inserted by the Financial Services and Markets Act 2000 (Regulated Activities) (Amendment) (No 2) Order 2002, SI 2002/1776, art 3(1), (2), as from 21 August 2002.

The Article heading is amended as follows:

The words omitted were revoked by the Electronic Commerce and Solvency 2 (Amendment etc) (EU Exit) Regulations 2019, SI 2019/1361, reg 5(1), (3), as from IP completion day (as defined in the European Union (Withdrawal Agreement) Act 2020, s 39) (for transitional provisions, see the note in relation to art 72A of this Order *post*).

The words in the first (outer) pair of square brackets were inserted by the Alternative Investment Fund Managers Regulations 2013, SI 2013/1773, reg 81, Sch 2, Part 1, para 1(1), (4), as from 22 July 2013.

The words in the second (inner) pair of square brackets were substituted by the Financial Services and Markets Act 2000 (Amendment) (EU Exit) Regulations 2019, SI 2019/632, regs 120, 148(2), as from IP completion day (as defined in the European Union (Withdrawal Agreement) Act 2020, s 39).

The Article text is amended as follows:

The word "exclusion" in square brackets was substituted, and the words omitted were revoked, by SI 2019/1361, reg 5(1), (3), as from IP completion day (as defined in the European Union (Withdrawal Agreement) Act 2020, s 39) (for transitional provisions, see the note in relation to art 72A of this Order *post*).

The words in second (outer) pair of square brackets were inserted by SI 2013/1773, reg 81, Sch 2, Part 1, para 1(1), (4), as from 22 July 2013.

The words "UK UCITS" were substituted by SI 2019/632, regs 120, 148(2), as from IP completion day (as defined in the European Union (Withdrawal Agreement) Act 2020, s 39).

[8.12]
[9AB Funds received for payment services

(1) A sum is not a deposit for the purposes of article 5 if it is received by an authorised payment institution, an EEA authorised payment institution[, a small payment institution, an electronic money institution or an EEA authorised electronic money institution] from a payment service user with a view to the provision of payment services.

(2) For the purposes of paragraph (1), "authorised payment institution", "EEA authorised payment institution", "small payment institution", "payment services" and "payment service user" have the meanings given in the Payment Services Regulations [2017] [and "electronic money institution" and "EEA authorised electronic money institution" have the meanings given in the Electronic Money Regulations 2011].]

NOTES

Inserted by the Payment Services Regulations 2009, SI 2009/209, reg 126, Sch 6, Pt 2, para 4(a), as from 1 November 2009.

Para (1): words in square brackets substituted by the Electronic Money Regulations 2011, SI 2011/99, reg 79, Sch 4, Pt 2, para 12(b)(i), as from 30 April 2011.

Para (2): year "2017" in square brackets substituted by the Payment Services Regulations 2017, SI 2017/752, reg 156, Sch 8, Pt 3, para 8(a), as from 13 January 2018. Words in square brackets inserted by SI 2011/99, reg 79, Sch 4, Pt 2, para 12(b)(ii), as from 30 April 2011.

[8.13]
[9AC Local authorities

Article 5 is subject to the exclusion in article 72G (local authorities).]

NOTES

Inserted by the Financial Services and Markets Act 2000 (Regulated Activities) (Amendment) Order 2014, SI 2014/366, art 2(1), (3), as from 1 April 2014.

[CHAPTER IIA ELECTRONIC MONEY

The activity

[8.14]
9B Issuing electronic money

Issuing electronic money [by—

(a) a [qualifying credit institution], a credit union or a municipal bank; or

(b) a person who is deemed to have been granted authorisation under regulation 74 of the Electronic Money Regulations 2011 or who falls within regulation 76(1) of those Regulations,]

is a specified kind of activity.]

NOTES

Inserted, together with arts 9C–9K and the preceding heading, by the Financial Services and Markets Act 2000 (Regulated Activities) (Amendment) Order 2002, SI 2002/682, art 4, as from 27 April 2002.

Words in first (outer) pair of square brackets inserted by the Electronic Money Regulations 2011, SI 2011/99, reg 79, Sch 4, Pt 2, para 12(c), as from 30 April 2011.

Words "qualifying credit institution" in square brackets substituted by the Financial Services and Markets Act 2000 (Amendment) (EU Exit) Regulations 2019, SI 2019/632, regs 120, 124, as from IP completion day (as defined in the European Union (Withdrawal Agreement) Act 2020, s 39).

[8.15]
[9BA

Articles 9C to 9I and 9K apply only in the case of a person falling within regulation 76(1) of the Electronic Money Regulations 2011.

NOTES

Inserted by the Electronic Money Regulations 2011, SI 2011/99, reg 79, Sch 4, Pt 2, para 12(c), as from 30 April 2011.

[Exclusions

[8.16]
9C Persons certified as small issuers etc

(1) There is excluded from article 9B the issuing of electronic money by a person to whom [the FCA] has given a certificate under this article (provided the certificate has not been revoked).

(2) An application for a certificate may be made by—

(a) a body corporate, or

(b) a partnership,

(other than a credit institution . . .) which has its head office in the United Kingdom.

(3) [The FCA] must, on the application of such a person ("A"), give A a certificate if it appears to [the FCA] that paragraph (4), (5) or (6) applies.

(4) This paragraph applies if—

(a) A does not issue electronic money except on terms that the electronic device on which the monetary value is stored is subject to a maximum storage amount of not more than 150 euro; and

(b) A's total liabilities with respect to the issuing of electronic money do not (or will not) usually exceed 5 million euro and do not (or will not) ever exceed 6 million euro.

(5) This paragraph applies if—

(a) the condition in paragraph (4)(a) is met;

(b) A's total liabilities with respect to the issuing of electronic money do not (or will not) exceed 10 million euro; and

(c) electronic money issued by A is accepted as a means of payment only by—

(i) subsidiaries of A which perform operational or other ancillary functions related to electronic money issued or distributed by A; or

(ii) other members of the same group as A (other than subsidiaries of A).

(6) This paragraph applies if—

(a) the conditions in paragraphs (4)(a) and (5)(b) are met; and

(b) electronic money issued by A is accepted as a means of payment, in the course of business, by not more than one hundred persons where—

(i) those persons accept such electronic money only at locations within the same premises or limited local area; or

(ii) those persons have a close financial or business relationship with A, such as a common marketing or distribution scheme.

(7) For the purposes of paragraph (6)(b)(i), locations are to be treated as situated within the same premises or limited local area if they are situated within—

(a) a shopping centre, airport, railway station, bus station, or campus of a university, polytechnic, college, school or similar educational establishment; or

(b) an area which does not exceed four square kilometres;

but sub-paragraphs (a) and (b) are illustrative only and are not to be treated as limiting the scope of paragraph (6)(b)(i).

(8) For the purposes of paragraph (6)(b)(ii), persons are not to be treated as having a close financial or business relationship with A merely because they participate in arrangements for the acceptance of electronic money issued by A.

(9) In this article, references to amounts in euro include references to equivalent amounts in sterling.

(10) A person to whom a certificate has been given under this article (and whose certificate has not been revoked) is referred to in this Chapter as a "certified person".]

NOTES

Inserted as noted to art 9B at **[8.14]**.

Paras (1), (3): words in square brackets substituted by the Financial Services Act 2012 (Consequential Amendments and Transitional Provisions) Order 2013, SI 2013/472, art 3, Sch 2, para 35(a), (b), as from 1 April 2013.

Para (2): words omitted revoked by the Financial Services and Markets Act 2000 (Amendment) (EU Exit) Regulations 2019, SI 2019/632, regs 120, 125, as from IP completion day (as defined in the European Union (Withdrawal Agreement) Act 2020, s 39).

[8.17]

[9D Applications for certificates

The following provisions of the Act apply to applications to [the FCA] for certificates under 9C (and the determination of such applications) as they apply to applications for [Part 4A] permissions (and the determination of such applications)—

[(a) section 55U(1)(b) and (4) to (8);

(b) section 55V;

(c) section 55X(2) and (4)(f); and

(d) section 55Z3(1).]]

NOTES

Inserted as noted to art 9B at **[8.14]**.

Words in square brackets substituted by the Financial Services Act 2012 (Consequential Amendments and Transitional Provisions) Order 2013, SI 2013/472, arts 3, 4, Sch 2, para 35(a), (c), as from 1 April 2013.

[8.18]

[9E Revocation of certificate on [FCA's] own initiative

(1) [The FCA] may revoke a certificate given to a person ("A") under article 9C if—

(a) it appears to it that A does not meet the relevant conditions, or has failed to meet the relevant conditions at any time since the certificate was given; or

(b) the person to whom the certificate was given has contravened any rule or requirement to which he is subject as a result of article 9G.

(2) For the purposes of paragraph (1), A meets the relevant conditions at any time if, at that time, paragraph (4), (5) or (6) of article 9C applies.

(3) Sections [55Z and 55Z3(2)] of the Act apply to the revocation of a certificate under paragraph (1) as they apply to the cancellation of a [Part 4A] permission on [the FCA's] own initiative, as if references in those sections to an authorised person were references to a certified person.]

NOTES

Inserted as noted to art 9B at **[8.14]**.

Words in square brackets substituted by the Financial Services Act 2012 (Consequential Amendments and Transitional Provisions) Order 2013, SI 2013/472, arts 3, 4, Sch 2, para 35(a), (d), as from 1 April 2013.

[8.19]

[9F Revocation of certificate on request

(1) A certified person ("B") may apply to [the FCA] for his certificate to be revoked, and [the FCA] must then revoke the certificate and give B written notice that it has done so.

(2) An application under paragraph (1) must be made in such manner as [the FCA] may direct.

(3) If—

(a) B has made an application under [Part 4A] of the Act for permission to carry on a regulated activity of the kind specified by article 9B (or for variation of an existing permission so as to add a regulated activity of that kind), and

(b) on making an application for revocation of his certificate under paragraph (1), he requests that the revocation be conditional on the granting of his application under [Part 4A] of the Act,

the revocation of B's certificate is to be conditional on the granting of his application under [Part 4A] of the Act.]

NOTES

Inserted as noted to art 9B at **[8.14]**.

Words in square brackets substituted by the Financial Services Act 2012 (Consequential Amendments and Transitional Provisions) Order 2013, SI 2013/472, arts 3, 4, Sch 2, para 35(a), as from 1 April 2013.

[8.20]

[9G Obtaining information from certified persons etc

(1) [The FCA] may make rules requiring certified persons to provide information to [the FCA] about their activities so far as relating to the issuing of electronic money, including the amount of their liabilities with respect to the issuing of electronic money.

(2) [Section 138A] of the Act (modification or waiver of rules) applies in relation to rules made under paragraph (1) as if references in that section to an authorised person were references to a certified person.

(3) [Section 138D] of the Act (actions for damages) applies in relation to a rule made under paragraph (1) as if the reference in subsection (1) of that section to an authorised person were a reference to a certified person.

(4) [The FCA] may, by notice in writing given to a certified person, require him—

(a) to provide specified information or information of a specified description; or

(b) to produce specified documents or documents of a specified description.

(5) Paragraph (4) applies only to information or documents reasonably required for the purposes of determining whether the certified person meets, or has met, the relevant conditions.

(6) Subsections (2), (5) and (6) of section 165 of the Act ([Regulator's] power to require information) apply to a requirement imposed under paragraph (4) as they apply to a requirement imposed under that section.

(7) Section 166 of the Act (reports by skilled persons) has effect as if—

(a) . . .

(b) the reference in section 166(2)(a) of the Act to an authorised person included a reference to a certified person.

(8) Subsection (4) of section 168 of the Act (appointment of persons to carry out investigations in particular cases) has effect as if it provided for subsection (5) of that section to apply if it appears to [the FCA] that there are circumstances suggesting that a certified person may not meet, or may not have met, the relevant conditions.

(9) Sections 175 (information and documents: supplemental provisions), 176 (entry of premises under warrant) and 177 (offences) of the Act apply to a requirement imposed under paragraph (4) as they apply to a requirement imposed under section 165 of the Act (the reference in section 176(3)(a) to an authorised person being read as a reference to a certified person).

(10) In this article—

(a) "specified", in paragraph (4), means specified in the notice mentioned in that paragraph;

(b) a certified person ("A") meets the relevant conditions at any time if, at that time, paragraph (4), (5) or (6) of article 9C applies.]

NOTES

Inserted as noted to art 9B at **[8.14]**.

Words in square brackets substituted, and sub-para (7)(a) revoked, by the Financial Services Act 2012 (Consequential Amendments and Transitional Provisions) Order 2013, SI 2013/472, art 3, Sch 2, para 35(a), (e) as from 1 April 2013.

[Supplemental

[8.21]

9H Rules prohibiting the issue of electronic money at a discount

(1) [The FCA] may make rules applying to authorised persons with permission to carry on an activity of the kind specified by article 9B, prohibiting the issue of electronic money having a monetary value greater than the funds received.

(2) [Section 138A] of the Act (modification or waiver of rules) applies in relation to rules made under paragraph (1).]

NOTES

Inserted as noted to art 9B at **[8.14]**.

Words in square brackets substituted by the Financial Services Act 2012 (Consequential Amendments and Transitional Provisions) Order 2013, SI 2013/472, art 3, Sch 2, para 35(a), (f), as from 1 April 2013.

[8.22]

[9I False claims to be a certified person

A person who is not a certified person is to be treated as guilty of an offence under section 24 of the Act (false claims to be authorised or exempt) if he—

(a) describes himself (in whatever terms) as a certified person;

(b) behaves, or otherwise holds himself out, in a manner which indicates (or which is reasonably likely to be understood as indicating) that he is a certified person.]

NOTES

Inserted as noted to art 9B at **[8.14]**.

[8.23]

[9J Exclusion of electronic money from the compensation scheme

The compensation scheme established under Part XV of the Act is not to provide for the compensation of persons in respect of claims made in connection with any activity of the kind specified by article 9B.]

NOTES

Inserted as noted to art 9B at **[8.14]**.

[8.24]

[9K Record of certified persons

The record maintained by [the FCA] under section 347 of the Act (public record of authorised persons etc) must include every certified person.]

NOTES

Inserted as noted to art 9B at **[8.14]**.

Words in square brackets substituted by the Financial Services Act 2012 (Consequential Amendments and Transitional Provisions) Order 2013, SI 2013/472, art 3, Sch 2, para 35(a), as from 1 April 2013.

9L *(Inserted by the Payment Services Regulations 2009, SI 2009/209, reg 126, Sch 6, Pt 2, para 4(b), as from 1 November 2009, and subsequently revoked by the Electronic Money Regulations 2011, SI 2011/99, reg 79, Sch 4, Pt 2, para 12(e), as from 30 April 2011.)*

CHAPTER III INSURANCE

The activities

[8.25]

10 Effecting and carrying out contracts of insurance

(1) Effecting a contract of insurance as principal is a specified kind of activity.

(2) Carrying out a contract of insurance as principal is a specified kind of activity.

Exclusions

11 *(Revoked by the EEA Passport Rights (Amendment, etc, and Transitional Provisions) (EU Exit) Regulations 2018, SI 2018/1149, reg 3, Schedule, Pt 3, para 49(1), (3), as from IP completion day (as defined in the European Union (Withdrawal Agreement) Act 2020, s 39).)*

[8.26]

12 Breakdown insurance

(1) There is excluded from article 10(1) or (2) the effecting or carrying out, by a person who does not otherwise carry on an activity of the kind specified by that article, of a contract of insurance which—

(a) is a contract under which the benefits provided by that person ("the provider") are exclusively or primarily benefits in kind in the event of accident to or breakdown of a vehicle; and

(b) contains the terms mentioned in paragraph (2).

(2) Those terms are that—

(a) the assistance takes either or both of the forms mentioned in paragraph (3)(a) and (b);

(b) the assistance is not available outside the United Kingdom and the Republic of Ireland except where it is provided without the payment of additional premium by a person in the country concerned with whom the provider has entered into a reciprocal agreement; and

(c) assistance provided in the case of an accident or breakdown occurring in the United Kingdom or the Republic of Ireland is, in most circumstances, provided by the provider's servants.

(3) The forms of assistance are—

(a) repairs to the relevant vehicle at the place where the accident or breakdown has occurred; this assistance may also include the delivery of parts, fuel, oil, water or keys to the relevant vehicle;

(b) removal of the relevant vehicle to the nearest or most appropriate place at which repairs may be carried out, or to—

(i) the home, point of departure or original destination within the United Kingdom of the driver and passengers, provided the accident or breakdown occurred within the United Kingdom;

(ii) the home, point of departure or original destination within the Republic of Ireland of the driver and passengers, provided the accident or breakdown occurred within the Republic of Ireland or within Northern Ireland;

(iii) the home, point of departure or original destination within Northern Ireland of the driver and passengers, provided the accident or breakdown occurred within the Republic of Ireland;

and this form of assistance may include the conveyance of the driver or passengers of the relevant vehicle, with the vehicle, or (where the vehicle is to be conveyed only to the nearest or most appropriate place at which repairs may be carried out) separately, to the nearest location from which they may continue their journey by other means.

(4) A contract does not fail to meet the condition in paragraph (1)(a) solely because the provider may reimburse the person entitled to the assistance for all or part of any sums paid by him in respect of assistance either because he failed to identify himself as a person entitled to the assistance or because he was unable to get in touch with the provider in order to claim the assistance.

(5) In this article—

"the assistance" means the benefits to be provided under a contract of the kind mentioned in paragraph (1);

"breakdown" means an event—

(a) which causes the driver of the relevant vehicle to be unable to start a journey in the vehicle or involuntarily to bring the vehicle to a halt on a journey because of some malfunction of the vehicle or failure of it to function, and

(b) after which the journey cannot reasonably be commenced or continued in the relevant vehicle;

"the relevant vehicle" means the vehicle (including a trailer or caravan) in respect of which the assistance is required.

[8.27]

[12A . . . [. . . Managers of [UK UCITS] and AIFs]

Article 10 is subject to the [exclusion] in . . . [. . . article 72AA (managers of [UK UCITS] and AIFs)].]

NOTES

Inserted by the Financial Services and Markets Act 2000 (Regulated Activities) (Amendment) (No 2) Order 2002, SI 2002/1776, art 3(1), (2), as from 21 August 2002.

The Article heading is amended as follows:

The words omitted were revoked by the Electronic Commerce and Solvency 2 (Amendment etc) (EU Exit) Regulations 2019, SI 2019/1361, reg 5(1), (3), as from IP completion day (as defined in the European Union (Withdrawal Agreement) Act 2020, s 39) (for transitional provisions, see the note in relation to art 72A of this Order *post*).

The words in the first (outer) pair of square brackets were inserted by the Alternative Investment Fund Managers Regulations 2013, SI 2013/1773, reg 81, Sch 2, Part 1, para 1(1), (4), as from 22 July 2013.

The words in the second (inner) pair of square brackets were substituted by the Financial Services and Markets Act 2000 (Amendment) (EU Exit) Regulations 2019, SI 2019/632, regs 120, 148(2), as from IP completion day (as defined in the European Union (Withdrawal Agreement) Act 2020, s 39).

The Article text is amended as follows:

The word "exclusion" in square brackets was substituted, and the words omitted were revoked, by SI 2019/1361, reg 5(1), (3), as from IP completion day (as defined in the European Union (Withdrawal Agreement) Act 2020, s 39) (for transitional provisions, see the note in relation to art 72A of this Order *post*).

The words in second (outer) pair of square brackets were inserted by SI 2013/1773, reg 81, Sch 2, Part 1, para 1(1), (4), as from 22 July 2013.

The words "UK UCITS" were substituted by SI 2019/632, regs 120, 148(2), as from IP completion day (as defined in the European Union (Withdrawal Agreement) Act 2020, s 39).

[8.28]

[12B Transformer vehicles: insurance risk transformation

A transformer vehicle does not carry on an activity of a kind specified by article 10 by assuming a risk from an undertaking, provided the assumption of the risk is a specified kind of activity falling within article 13A (transformer vehicles: insurance risk transformation).]

NOTES

Inserted by the Risk Transformation Regulations 2017, SI 2017/1212, reg 5(1), (2), as from 8 December 2017.

Supplemental

[8.29]

13 Application of sections 327 and 332 of the Act to insurance market activities

(1) In sections 327(5) and (7) and 332(3)(b) of the Act (exemption from the general prohibition for members of the professions, and rules in relation to such persons), the references to "a regulated activity" and "regulated activities" do not include—

(a) any activity of the kind specified by article 10(1) or (2), where—

(i) P is a member of the Society; and

(ii) by virtue of section 316 of the Act (application of the Act to Lloyd's underwriting), the general prohibition does not apply to the carrying on by P of that activity; or

(b) any activity of the kind specified by article 10(2), where—

(i) P is a former underwriting member; and

(ii) the contract of insurance in question is one underwritten by P at Lloyd's.

(2) In paragraph (1)—

"member of the Society" has the same meaning as in Lloyd's Act 1982; and

"former underwriting member" has the meaning given by section 324(1) of the Act.

[CHAPTER 3A INSURANCE RISK TRANSFORMATION

[8.30]

13A Transformer vehicles: insurance risk transformation

It is a specified kind of activity for a transformer vehicle to assume a risk from an undertaking where—

(a) the undertaking assumes a risk under a contract of insurance ("the underlying risk"); and

(b) the assumption of risk by the transformer vehicle has the legal or economic effect of transferring some or all of the underlying risk to the transformer vehicle.]

NOTES

Inserted (together with the preceding heading) by the Risk Transformation Regulations 2017, SI 2017/1212, reg 5(1), (3), as from 8 December 2017.

CHAPTER IV DEALING IN INVESTMENTS AS PRINCIPAL

The activity

[8.31]

14 Dealing in investments as principal

[(1)] Buying, selling, subscribing for or underwriting securities or contractually based investments (other than investments of the kind specified by article 87, or article 89 so far as relevant to that article) as principal is a specified kind of activity.

[(2) Paragraph (1) does not apply to a kind of activity to which article 25D [or 25DA] applies.]

NOTES

Para (1) numbered as such, and para (2) added, by the Financial Services and Markets Act 2000 (Regulated Activities) (Amendment No 3) Order 2006, SI 2006/3384, arts 2, 5, as from 1 April 2007 (for the purposes of enabling applications to be made for (i) a Part IV permission, (ii) a variation of a Part IV permission, and (iii) the Authority's approval under s 59 of the 2000 Act, in relation to an activity of the kind specified by art 25D of this Order, or in relation to an investment of the kind specified by arts 83, 84 or 85 of this Order), and as from 1 November 2007 (otherwise).

Para (2): words in square brackets inserted by the Financial Services and Markets Act 2000 (Regulated Activities) (Amendment) Order 2017, SI 2017/488, art 12(1), (3), as from 1 April 2017 (for the purposes of (i) enabling applications to be made for a Part 4A permission, for a variation of a Part 4A permission or for an approval under FSMA 2000, s 59, or (ii) enabling such applications to be determined, in relation to any specified activity or any specified investment amended or inserted by the 2017 Order), and as from 3 January 2018 (otherwise) (for transitional provisions, see arts 15, 16 of the 2017 Order).

Exclusions

[8.32]

15 Absence of holding out etc

(1) Subject to paragraph (3), a person ("A") does not carry on an activity of the kind specified by article 14 by entering into a transaction which relates to a security or is the assignment (or, in Scotland, the assignation) of a qualifying contract of insurance (or an investment of the kind specified by article 89, so far as relevant to such a contract), unless—

- (a) A holds himself out as willing, as principal, to buy, sell or subscribe for investments of the kind to which the transaction relates at prices determined by him generally and continuously rather than in respect of each particular transaction;
- (b) A holds himself out as engaging in the business of buying investments of the kind to which the transaction relates, with a view to selling them;
- (c) A holds himself out as engaging in the business of underwriting investments of the kind to which the transaction relates; or
- (d) A regularly solicits members of the public with the purpose of inducing them, as principals or agents, to enter into transactions constituting activities of the kind specified by article 14, and the transaction is entered into as a result of his having solicited members of the public in that manner.

(2) In paragraph (1)(d), "members of the public" means any persons other than—

- (a) authorised persons or persons who are exempt persons in relation to activities of the kind specified by article 14;
- (b) members of the same group as A;
- (c) persons who are or who propose to become participators with A in a joint enterprise;
- (d) any person who is solicited by A with a view to the acquisition by A of 20 per cent or more of the voting shares in a body corporate;
- (e) if A (either alone or with members of the same group as himself) holds more than 20 per cent of the voting shares in a body corporate, any person who is solicited by A with a view to—
  - (i) the acquisition by A of further shares in the body corporate; or
  - (ii) the disposal by A of shares in the body corporate to the person solicited or to a member of the same group as the person solicited;
- (f) any person who—
  - (i) is solicited by A with a view to the disposal by A of shares in a body corporate to the person solicited or to a member of the same group as that person; and
  - (ii) either alone or with members of the same group holds 20 per cent or more of the voting shares in the body corporate;
- (g) any person whose head office is outside the United Kingdom, who is solicited by an approach made or directed to him at a place outside the United Kingdom and whose ordinary business involves him in carrying on activities of the kind specified by any of articles 14, 21, 25, 37, 40, 45, [51ZA, 51ZB, 51ZC, 51ZD, 51ZE], 52 and 53 or (so far as relevant to any of those articles) article 64, or would do so apart from any exclusion from any of those articles made by this Order.

(3) This article does not apply where A enters into the transaction as bare trustee or, in Scotland, as nominee for another person and is acting on that other person's instructions (but the exclusion in article 66(1) applies if the conditions set out there are met).

[(4) This article is subject to article 4(4).]

NOTES

Para (2): figures in square brackets in sub-para (g) substituted by the Alternative Investment Fund Managers Regulations 2013, SI 2013/1773, reg 81, Sch 2, Part 1, para 1(1), (3), as from 22 July 2013.

Para (4): added by the Financial Services and Markets Act 2000 (Regulated Activities) (Amendment No 3) Order 2006, SI 2006/3384, arts 2, 6, as from 1 April 2007 (for the purposes of enabling applications to be made for (i) a Part IV permission, (ii) a variation of a Part IV permission, and (iii) the Authority's approval under s 59 of the 2000 Act, in relation to an activity of the kind specified by art 25D of this Order, or in relation to an investment of the kind specified by arts 83, 84 or 85 of this Order), and as from 1 November 2007 (otherwise).

[8.33]
16 Dealing in contractually based investments

[(1)] A person who is not an authorised person does not carry on an activity of the kind specified by article 14 by entering into a transaction relating to a contractually based investment—

(a) with or through an authorised person, or an exempt person acting in the course of a business comprising a regulated activity in relation to which he is exempt; or
(b) through an office outside the United Kingdom maintained by a party to the transaction, and with or through a person whose head office is situated outside the United Kingdom and whose ordinary business involves him in carrying on activities of the kind specified by any of articles 14, 21, 25, 37, 40, 45, [51ZA, 51ZB, 51ZC, 51ZD, 51ZE], 52 and 53 or, so far as relevant to any of those articles, article 64 (or would do so apart from any exclusion from any of those articles made by this Order).

[(2) This article is subject to article 4(4).]

NOTES

Para (1) numbered as such, and para (2) added, by the Financial Services and Markets Act 2000 (Regulated Activities) (Amendment No 3) Order 2006, SI 2006/3384, arts 2, 7, as from 1 April 2007 (for the purposes of enabling applications to be made for (i) a Part IV permission, (ii) a variation of a Part IV permission, and (iii) the Authority's approval under s 59 of the 2000 Act, in relation to an activity of the kind specified by art 25D of this Order, or in relation to an investment of the kind specified by arts 83, 84 or 85 of this Order), and as from 1 November 2007 (otherwise).

Figures in square brackets in sub-para (1)(b) substituted by the Alternative Investment Fund Managers Regulations 2013, SI 2013/1773, reg 81, Sch 2, Part 1, para 1(1), (3), as from 22 July 2013.

[8.34]
17 Acceptance of instruments creating or acknowledging indebtedness

(1) A person does not carry on an activity of the kind specified by article 14 by accepting an instrument creating or acknowledging indebtedness in respect of any loan, credit, guarantee or other similar financial accommodation or assurance which he has made, granted or provided.

(2) The reference in paragraph (1) to a person accepting an instrument includes a reference to a person becoming a party to an instrument otherwise than as a debtor or a surety.

NOTES

Modification: references in para (1) to securities, instruments or investments creating or acknowledging indebtedness (or creating or acknowledging a present or future indebtedness) includes a reference to uncertificated units of eligible debt securities; see the Uncertificated Securities (Amendment) (Eligible Debt Securities) Regulations 2003, SI 2003/1633, reg 15, Sch 2, para 8.

Modification: references in para (2) to a person becoming party to an instrument includes a reference to a person assuming rights and obligations in respect of uncertificated units of an eligible debt security in accordance with its current terms of issue; see the Uncertificated Securities (Amendment) (Eligible Debt Securities) Regulations 2003, SI 2003/1633, reg 15, Sch 2, para 9.

[8.35]
18 Issue by a company of its own shares etc

(1) There is excluded from article 14 the issue by a company of its own shares or share warrants, and the issue by any person of his own debentures or debenture warrants.

(2) In this article—

(a) "company" means any body corporate other than an open-ended investment company;
(b) "shares" and "debentures" include any investment of the kind specified by article 76[, 77 or 77A];
(c) "share warrants" and "debenture warrants" mean any investment of the kind specified by article 79 which relates to shares in the company concerned or, as the case may be, debentures issued by [the person concerned].

[(3) This article is subject to article 4(4).]

NOTES

Para (2): words in square brackets in sub-para (b) substituted by the Financial Services and Markets Act 2000 (Regulated Activities) (Amendment) Order 2010, SI 2010/86, art 4, Schedule, para 5(a), as from 24 February 2010. Words in square brackets in sub-para (c) substituted by the Financial Services and Markets Act 2000 (Regulated Activities) (Amendment) Order 2001, SI 2001/3544, arts 2, 4, as from 1 December 2001.

Para (3): added by the Financial Services and Markets Act 2000 (Regulated Activities) (Amendment) Order 2017, SI 2017/488, art 12(1), (4), as from 1 April 2017 (for the purposes of (i) enabling applications to be made for a Part 4A permission, for a variation of a Part 4A permission or for an approval under FSMA 2000, s 59, or (ii) enabling such applications to be determined, in relation to any specified activity or any specified investment amended or inserted by the 2017 Order), and as from 3 January 2018.

[8.36]
[18A Dealing by a company in its own shares

(1) A company does not carry on an activity of the kind specified by article 14 by purchasing its own shares where [section 724 of the Companies Act 2006] (Treasury shares) applies to the shares purchased.

(2) A company does not carry on an activity of the kind specified by article 14 by dealing in its own shares held as treasury shares, in accordance with [section 727 (Treasury shares: disposal) or 729 (Treasury shares: cancellation) of that Act].

(3) In this article "shares held as treasury shares" has the same meaning as in that Act.]

NOTES

Inserted by the Financial Services and Markets Act 2000 (Regulated Activities) (Amendment) (No 3) Order 2003, SI 2003/2822, arts 2, 3, as from 1 December 2003.

Paras (1), (2): words in square brackets substituted by the Companies Act 2006 (Consequential Amendments and Transitional Provisions) Order 2011, SI 2011/1265, art 13(1), (3), as from 12 May 2011.

[8.37]

19 Risk management

(1) A person ("B") does not carry on an activity of the kind specified by article 14 by entering as principal into a transaction with another person ("C") if—

- (a) the transaction relates to investments of the kind specified by any of articles 83 to 85 (or article 89 so far as relevant to any of those articles);
- (b) neither B nor C is an individual;
- (c) the sole or main purpose for which B enters into the transaction (either by itself or in combination with other such transactions) is that of limiting the extent to which a relevant business will be affected by any identifiable risk arising otherwise than as a result of the carrying on of a regulated activity; and
- (d) the relevant business consists mainly of activities other than—
  - (i) regulated activities; or
  - (ii) activities which would be regulated activities but for any exclusion made by this Part.

(2) In paragraph (1), "relevant business" means a business carried on by—

- (a) B;
- (b) a member of the same group as B; or
- (c) where B and another person are, or propose to become, participators in a joint enterprise, that other person.

[(3) This article is subject to article 4(4).]

NOTES

Para (3): added by the Financial Services and Markets Act 2000 (Regulated Activities) (Amendment No 3) Order 2006, SI 2006/3384, arts 2, 8, as from 1 April 2007 (for the purposes of enabling applications to be made for (i) a Part IV permission, (ii) a variation of a Part IV permission, and (iii) the Authority's approval under s 59 of the 2000 Act, in relation to an activity of the kind specified by art 25D of this Order, or in relation to an investment of the kind specified by arts 83, 84 or 85 of this Order), and as from 1 November 2007 (otherwise).

[8.38]

[19A Transformer vehicles: insurance risk transformation

A transformer vehicle does not carry on an activity of a kind specified by article 14 by assuming a risk from an undertaking, provided the assumption of the risk is a specified kind of activity falling within article 13A (transformer vehicles: insurance risk transformation).]

NOTES

Inserted by the Risk Transformation Regulations 2017, SI 2017/1212, reg 5(1), (4), as from 8 December 2017.

[8.39]

20 Other exclusions

Article 14 is also subject to the exclusions in articles 66 (trustees etc), 68 (sale of goods and supply of services), 69 (groups and joint enterprises), 70 (sale of body corporate), 71 (employee share schemes)[, 72 (overseas persons)] . . . [, 72AA (managers of [UK UCITS] and AIFs) and 72H (insolvency practitioners)].

NOTES

Words in first pair of square brackets substituted by the Financial Services and Markets Act 2000 (Regulated Activities) (Amendment) (No 2) Order 2002, SI 2002/1776, art 3(1), (4), as from 21 August 2002.

Words omitted revoked by the Electronic Commerce and Solvency 2 (Amendment etc) (EU Exit) Regulations 2019, SI 2019/1361, reg 5(1), (3), as from IP completion day (as defined in the European Union (Withdrawal Agreement) Act 2020, s 39) (for transitional provisions, see the note in relation to art 72A of this Order *post*).

Words in second (outer) pair of square brackets substituted by the Financial Services and Markets Act 2000 (Regulated Activities) (Amendment) Order 2014, SI 2014/366, art 2(1), (4), as from 1 April 2014 (note that the 2014 Order came into force on 14 February 2014 for the purpose of the FCA making rules, giving guidance etc, and came into force on 1 April 2014, immediately after SI 2013/1881 (and SI 2013/1882) come into force, in so far as not already in force).

Words "UK UCITS" in square brackets substituted by the Financial Services and Markets Act 2000 (Amendment) (EU Exit) Regulations 2019, SI 2019/632, regs 120, 148(2), as from IP completion day (as defined in the European Union (Withdrawal Agreement) Act 2020, s 39).

CHAPTER V DEALING IN INVESTMENTS AS AGENT

The activity

[8.40]

21 Dealing in investments as agent

[(1)] Buying, selling, subscribing for or underwriting securities[, structured deposits] or [relevant investments] . . . as agent is a specified kind of activity.

[(2) Paragraph (1) does not apply to a kind of activity to which article 25D [or 25DA] applies.]

NOTES

Para (1) numbered as such, and para (2) added, by the Financial Services and Markets Act 2000 (Regulated Activities) (Amendment No 3) Order 2006, SI 2006/3384, arts 2, 9, as from 1 April 2007 (for the purposes of enabling applications to be made for (i) a Part IV permission, (ii) a variation of a Part IV permission, and (iii) the Authority's approval under s 59 of the 2000 Act, in relation to an activity of the kind specified by art 25D of this Order, or in relation to an investment of the kind specified by arts 83, 84 or 85 of this Order), and as from 1 November 2007 (otherwise).

Words in first pair of square brackets in para (1), and words in square brackets in para (2), inserted by the Financial Services and Markets Act 2000 (Regulated Activities) (Amendment) Order 2017, SI 2017/488, arts 4(1), 12(1), (3), as from 1 April 2017 (for the purposes of (i) enabling applications to be made for a Part 4A permission, for a variation of a Part 4A permission or for an approval under FSMA 2000, s 59, or (ii) enabling such applications to be determined, in relation to any specified activity or any specified investment amended or inserted by the 2017 Order), and as from 3 January 2018 (otherwise).

Words in second pair of square brackets in para (1) substituted by the Financial Services and Markets Act 2000 (Regulated Activities) (Amendment) (No 2) Order 2003, SI 2003/1476, art 4(1), as from 31 October 2004 (in so far as relating to contracts of long-term care insurance), and as from 14 January 2005 (otherwise).

The words omitted from para (1) were revoked by the Financial Services and Markets Act 2000 (Regulated Activities) (Amendment) Order 2021, SI 2021/90, art 2(3); note that this Order comes into force (1) on 28 January 2021 (for the purposes of (a) enabling the FCA to make or approve rules and to give guidance and directions; (b) enabling applications to be made etc for: (i) a Part 4A permission under s 55A of FSMA 2000; (ii) a variation of a Part 4A permission under s 55H of that Act; and (iii) approval under Part 5 of the Act; (c) enabling the FCA to exercise any of its powers under Part 4A or Part 5 of that Act in relation to any activity which becomes a regulated activity by virtue of this Order; and (d) enabling the scheme operator to make rules and to give guidance); and (2) for all other purposes 29 July 2022 (see art 1 of the 2021 Order, and see Part 3 for transitional provisions).

Exclusions

[8.41]

22 Deals with or through authorised persons

(1) A person who is not an authorised person does not carry on an activity of the kind specified by article 21 by entering into a transaction as agent for another person ("the client") with or through an authorised person if—

(a) the transaction is entered into on advice given to the client by an authorised person; or

(b) it is clear, in all the circumstances, that the client, in his capacity as an investor, is not seeking and has not sought advice from the agent as to the merits of the client's entering into the transaction (or, if the client has sought such advice, the agent has declined to give it but has recommended that the client seek such advice from an authorised person).

[(2) But the exclusion in paragraph (1) does not apply if—

(a) the transaction relates to a contract of insurance; or

(b) the agent receives from any person other than the client any pecuniary reward or other advantage, for which he does not account to the client, arising out of his entering into the transaction.]

[(3) This article is subject to article 4(4).]

NOTES

Para (2): substituted by the Financial Services and Markets Act 2000 (Regulated Activities) (Amendment) (No 2) Order 2003, SI 2003/1476, art 4(2), as from 31 October 2004 (in so far as relating to contracts of long-term care insurance), and as from 14 January 2005 (otherwise).

Para (3): added by the Financial Services and Markets Act 2000 (Regulated Activities) (Amendment No 3) Order 2006, SI 2006/3384, arts 2, 10, as from 1 April 2007 (for the purposes of enabling applications to be made for (i) a Part IV permission, (ii) a variation of a Part IV permission, and (iii) the Authority's approval under s 59 of the 2000 Act, in relation to an activity of the kind specified by art 25D of this Order, or in relation to an investment of the kind specified by arts 83, 84 or 85 of this Order), and as from 1 November 2007 (otherwise).

[8.42]

23 Risk management

(1) A person ("B") does not carry on an activity of the kind specified by article 21 by entering as agent for a relevant person into a transaction with another person ("C") if—

(a) the transaction relates to investments of the kind specified by any of articles 83 to 85 (or article 89 so far as relevant to any of those articles);

(b) neither B nor C is an individual;

(c) the sole or main purpose for which B enters into the transaction (either by itself or in combination with other such transactions) is that of limiting the extent to which a relevant business will be affected by any identifiable risk arising otherwise than as a result of the carrying on of a regulated activity; and

(d) the relevant business consists mainly of activities other than—

(i) regulated activities; or

(ii) activities which would be regulated activities but for any exclusion made by this Part.

(2) In paragraph (1), "relevant person" means—

(a) a member of the same group as B; or

(b) where B and another person are, or propose to become, participators in a joint enterprise, that other person;

and "relevant business" means a business carried on by a relevant person.

[(3) This article is subject to article 4(4).]

NOTES

Para (3): added by the Financial Services and Markets Act 2000 (Regulated Activities) (Amendment No 3) Order 2006, SI 2006/3384, arts 2, 11, as from 1 April 2007 (for the purposes of enabling applications to be made for (i) a Part IV permission, (ii) a variation of a Part IV permission, and (iii) the Authority's approval under s 59 of the 2000 Act, in relation to an activity of the kind specified by art 25D of this Order, or in relation to an investment of the kind specified by arts 83, 84 or 85 of this Order), and as from 1 November 2007 (otherwise).

[8.43]

24 Other exclusions

Article 21 is also subject to the exclusions in articles 67 (profession or non-investment business), 68 (sale of goods and supply of services), 69 (groups and joint enterprises), 70 (sale of body corporate), 71 (employee share schemes)[, 72 (overseas persons)[, . . . 72B (activities carried on by a provider of relevant goods or services)]][, 72AA (managers of [UK UCITS] and AIFs)][, 72D (large risks contracts where risk situated [outside the United Kingdom]), 72G (local authorities) and 72H (insolvency practitioners)].

NOTES

Words in first (outer) pair of square brackets substituted by the Financial Services and Markets Act 2000 (Regulated Activities) (Amendment) (No 2) Order 2002, SI 2002/1776, art 3(1), (5), as from 21 August 2002.

Words in second (inner) pair of square brackets substituted by the Financial Services and Markets Act 2000 (Regulated Activities) (Amendment) (No 2) Order 2003, SI 2003/1476, art 4(3), as from 31 October 2004 (in so far as relating to contracts of long-term care insurance), and as from 14 January 2005 (otherwise).

The words omitted were revoked by the Electronic Commerce and Solvency 2 (Amendment etc) (EU Exit) Regulations 2019, SI 2019/1361, reg 5(1), (3), as from IP completion day (as defined in the European Union (Withdrawal Agreement) Act 2020, s 39) (for transitional provisions, see the note in relation to art 72A of this Order *post*).

Words in third (outer) pair of square brackets substituted by the Alternative Investment Fund Managers Regulations 2013, SI 2013/1773, reg 81, Sch 2, Part 1, para 1(1), (7), as from 22 July 2013.

The words "UK UCITS" in the fourth (inner) pair of square brackets were substituted by the Financial Services and Markets Act 2000 (Amendment) (EU Exit) Regulations 2019, SI 2019/632, regs 120, 148(2), as from IP completion day (as defined in the European Union (Withdrawal Agreement) Act 2020, s 39).

The words in the fifth (outer) pair of square brackets were substituted by the Financial Services and Markets Act 2000 (Regulated Activities) (Amendment) Order 2014, SI 2014/366, art 2(1), (5), as from 1 April 2014 (note that the 2014 Order came into force on 14 February 2014 for the purpose of the FCA making rules, giving guidance etc, and came into force on 1 April 2014, immediately after SI 2013/1881 (and SI 2013/1882) come into force, in so far as not already in force).

The words "outside the United Kingdom" in the sixth (inner) square brackets were substituted by SI 2019/632, regs 120, 149(5), as from IP completion day (as defined in the European Union (Withdrawal Agreement) Act 2020, s 39).

[CHAPTER 5A BIDDING IN EMISSIONS AUCTIONS

The activity

[8.44]

24A Bidding in emissions auctions

(1) The reception, transmission or submission of a bid at an auction of an investment of the kind specified by article 82A conducted—

(a) on a recognised auction platform [in accordance with the UK auctioning regulations], or

(b) on [an] auction platform which has been appointed under the emission allowance auctioning regulation [in accordance with that regulation],

is a specified kind of activity.

(2) An activity which falls within paragraph (1) (or would do so but for the exclusions in article 24B) does not form part of any other activity specified under any other article of this Order.

(3) In this article, "recognised auction platform" has the meaning given in regulation 1(3) of the Recognised Auction Platform Regulations 2011.]

NOTES

Chapter 5a (arts 24A, 24B) was inserted by the Financial Services and Markets Act 2000 (Regulated Activities) (Amendment) Order 2012, SI 2012/1906, art 2(1), (3), as from 20 July 2012.

Para (1): the words in square brackets were inserted or substituted by the Recognised Auction Platforms (Amendment and Miscellaneous Provisions) Regulations 2021, SI 2021/494, reg 3(3), as from 22 April 2021.

[Exclusions

[8.45]

24B Miscellaneous exclusions

(1) There is excluded from article 24A any activity carried on by—

(a) an operator or an aircraft operator having an operator holding account, in either case bidding on its own account, including any parent undertaking, subsidiary undertaking or [affiliated undertaking] forming part of the same group of undertakings as the operator or the aircraft operator;

(b) business groupings of persons listed in sub-paragraph (a) bidding on their own account or acting as an agent on behalf of their members; or

(c) public bodies or state-owned entities of the Member States [or of the United Kingdom] that control any of the persons listed in sub-paragraph (a).

(2) . . .

(3) In this article, the expressions "parent undertaking", "subsidiary undertaking", "[affiliated undertaking]", "business grouping", "public bodies" and "state-owned entities" have the same meaning as in the [UK auctioning regulations].]

NOTES

Inserted as noted to reg 24A at **[8.44]**.

All amendments to this article were made by the Recognised Auction Platforms (Amendment and Miscellaneous Provisions) Regulations 2021, SI 2021/494, reg 3(4), as from 22 April 2021.

CHAPTER VI ARRANGING DEALS IN INVESTMENTS

The activities

[8.46]

25 Arranging deals in investments

(1) Making arrangements for another person (whether as principal or agent) to buy, sell, subscribe for or underwrite a particular investment which is—

(a) a security,

(b) a [relevant investment], . . .

(c) an investment of the kind specified by article 86, or article 89 so far as relevant to that article, [or

(d) a structured deposit,]

is a specified kind of activity.

(2) Making arrangements with a view to a person who participates in the arrangements buying, selling, subscribing for or underwriting investments falling within paragraph (1)(a), (b)[, (c) or (d)] (whether as principal or agent) is also a specified kind of activity.

[(3) Paragraphs (1) and (2) do not apply to a kind of activity to which article 25D [or 25DA] applies.]

NOTES

Para (1): words in square brackets in sub-para (b) substituted by the Financial Services and Markets Act 2000 (Regulated Activities) (Amendment) (No 2) Order 2003, SI 2003/1476, art 5(1), as from 31 October 2004 (in so far as relating to contracts of long-term care insurance), and as from 14 January 2005 (otherwise). Word omitted from sub-para (b) revoked, and sub-para (d) and the preceding word inserted, by the Financial Services and Markets Act 2000 (Regulated Activities) (Amendment) Order 2017, SI 2017/488, art 4(2)(a), as from 1 April 2017 (for the purposes of (i) enabling applications to be made for a Part 4A permission, for a variation of a Part 4A permission or for an approval under FSMA 2000, s 59, or (ii) enabling such applications to be determined, in relation to any specified activity or any specified investment amended or inserted by the 2017 Order), and as from 3 January 2018 (otherwise).

Para (2): words in square brackets substituted by SI 2017/488, art 4(2)(b), as from 1 April 2017 (certain purposes), and as from 3 January 2018 (otherwise) (for details, see the first note relating to the 2017 Regulations above).

Para (3): added by the Financial Services and Markets Act 2000 (Regulated Activities) (Amendment No 3) Order 2006, SI 2006/3384, arts 2, 12, as from 1 April 2007 (for the purposes of enabling applications to be made for (i) a Part IV permission, (ii) a variation of a Part IV permission, and (iii) the Authority's approval under s 59 of the 2000 Act, in relation to an activity of the kind specified by art 25D of this Order, or in relation to an investment of the kind specified by arts 83, 84 or 85 of this Order), and as from 1 November 2007 (otherwise). Words in square brackets substituted by SI 2017/488, art 12(1), (3), as from 1 April 2017 (certain purposes), and as from 3 January 2018 (otherwise) (for details, see the first note relating to the 2017 Regulations above).

[8.47]

[25A Arranging regulated mortgage contracts

(1) Making arrangements—

(a) for another person to enter into a regulated mortgage contract as borrower; or

(b) for another person to vary the terms of a regulated mortgage contract [falling within paragraph (1A)] entered into by him as borrower . . . , in such a way as to vary his obligations under that contract,

is a specified kind of activity.

[(1A) A regulated mortgage contract falls within this paragraph if—

(a) the contract was entered into on or after 31st October 2004; or

(b) the contract—

(i) was entered into before 31st October 2004; and

(ii) was a regulated credit agreement immediately before 21st March 2016.]

(2) Making arrangements with a view to a person who participates in the arrangements entering into a regulated mortgage contract as borrower is also a specified kind of activity.

[(2A) Making arrangements to enter into a regulated mortgage contract with a borrower on behalf of a lender is also a specified kind of activity.]

(3) In this article ["borrower" and "lender" have the meanings] given by article 61(3)(a)(i).]

NOTES

Inserted by the Financial Services and Markets Act 2000 (Regulated Activities) (Amendment) (No 1) Order 2003, SI 2003/1475, art 4, as from 31 October 2004.

Words in square brackets in para (1) inserted, words omitted from that paragraph revoked, and para (1A) inserted, by the Financial Services and Markets Act 2000 (Regulated Activities) (Amendment) Order 2016, SI 2016/392, art 2(1), (4), as from 21 March 2016.

Para (2A) inserted, and words in square brackets in para (3) substituted, by the Mortgage Credit Directive Order 2015, SI 2015/910, Sch 1, Pt 2, para 4(1), (4), as from 21 March 2016.

[8.48]

[25B Arranging regulated home reversion plans

(1) Making arrangements—

(a) for another person to enter into a regulated home reversion plan as reversion seller or as plan provider; or

(b) for another person to vary the terms of a regulated home reversion plan, entered into on or after 6th April 2007 by him as reversion seller or as plan provider, in such a way as to vary his obligations under that plan,

is a specified kind of activity.

(2) Making arrangements with a view to a person who participates in the arrangements entering into a regulated home reversion plan as reversion seller or as plan provider is also a specified kind of activity.]

NOTES

Inserted, together with art 25C, by the Financial Services and Markets Act 2000 (Regulated Activities) (Amendment) (No 2) Order 2006, SI 2006/2383, arts 2, 4, as from 6 November 2006 (for the purposes of enabling applications to be made for (i) a Pt IV permission, or a variation of a Pt IV permission, in relation to activities of the kind specified by arts 25B, 25C, 53B, 53C, 63B or 63F or, so far as relevant to any such activity, art 64 of this Order; or (ii) the Authority's approval under FSMA 2000, s 59 in relation to any of those activities), and as from 6 April 2007 (otherwise).

[8.49]

[25C Arranging regulated home purchase plans

(1) Making arrangements—

(a) for another person to enter into a regulated home purchase plan as home purchaser; or

(b) for another person to vary the terms of a regulated home purchase plan, entered into on or after 6th April 2007 by him as home purchaser, in such a way as to vary his obligations under that plan,

is a specified kind of activity.

(2) Making arrangements with a view to a person who participates in the arrangements entering into a regulated home purchase plan as home purchaser is also a specified kind of activity.]

NOTES

Inserted as noted to art 25B at **[8.48]**.

[8.50]

[25D Operating a multilateral trading facility

(1) The operation of a multilateral trading facility on which MiFID instruments are traded is a specified kind of activity.

(2) In paragraph (1), "MiFID instrument" means any investment—

(a) of the kind specified by article 76, 77, [77A,] 78, 79, 80, 81, [82B,] 83, 84 or 85; or

(b) of the kind specified by article 89 so far as relevant to an investment falling within sub-paragraph (a),

that is a financial instrument.]

NOTES

Inserted by the Financial Services and Markets Act 2000 (Regulated Activities) (Amendment No 3) Order 2006, SI 2006/3384, arts 2, 13, as from 1 April 2007 (for the purposes of enabling applications to be made for (i) a Part IV permission, (ii) a variation of a Part IV permission, and (iii) the Authority's approval under s 59 of the 2000 Act, in relation to an activity of the kind specified by art 25D of this Order, or in relation to an investment of the kind specified by arts 83, 84 or 85 of this Order), and as from 1 November 2007 (otherwise).

Para (2): figure "77A" in square brackets inserted by the Financial Services and Markets Act 2000 (Regulated Activities) (Amendment) Order 2010, SI 2010/86, art 4, Schedule, para 5(b), as from 24 February 2010. Figure "82B" in square brackets inserted by the Financial Services and Markets Act 2000 (Regulated Activities) (Amendment) Order 2017, SI 2017/488, art 12(1), (5), as from 1 April 2017 (for the purposes of (i) enabling applications to be made for a Part 4A permission, for a variation of a Part 4A permission or for an approval under FSMA 2000, s 59, or (ii) enabling such applications to be determined, in relation to any specified activity or any specified investment amended or inserted by the 2017 Order), and as from 3 January 2018 (otherwise).

[8.51]

[25DA Operating an organised trading facility

(1) The operation of an organised trading facility on which non-equity MiFID instruments are traded is a specified kind of activity.

(2) In paragraph (1) a "non-equity MiFID instrument" means any investment—

(a) of the kind specified by article 77, 77A, 78, 79, 80, 81, 82B, 83, 84 or 85; or

(b) of the kind specified by article 89 so far as relevant to an investment falling within sub-paragraph (a),

that is a bond, a structured finance product (within the meaning of Article 2.1.28 of the markets in financial instruments regulation), an emission allowance, or a derivative (within the meaning of Article 2.1.29 of the markets in financial instruments regulation).]

NOTES

Inserted by the Financial Services and Markets Act 2000 (Regulated Activities) (Amendment) Order 2017, SI 2017/488, art 3, as from 1 April 2017 (for the purposes of (i) enabling applications to be made for a Part 4A permission, for a variation of a Part 4A permission or for an approval under FSMA 2000, s 59, or (ii) enabling such applications to be determined, in relation to any specified activity or any specified investment amended or inserted by the 2017 Order), and as from 3 January 2018 (otherwise).

[8.52]

[25E Arranging regulated sale and rent back agreements

(1) Making arrangements—

(a) for another person to enter into a regulated sale and rent back agreement as an agreement seller or as an agreement provider; or

(b) for another person ("A") to vary the terms of a regulated sale and rent back agreement, entered into on or after 1st July 2009 by A as agreement seller or agreement provider, in such a way as to vary A's obligations under that agreement,

is a specified kind of activity.

(2) Making arrangements with a view to a person who participates in the arrangements entering into a regulated sale and rent back agreement as agreement seller or agreement provider is also a specified kind of activity.]

NOTES

Inserted by the Financial Services and Markets Act 2000 (Regulated Activities) (Amendment) Order 2009, SI 2009/1342, arts 2, 4, as from 1 July 2009 (other than for the purposes of enabling applications to be made for a Part IV permission, or a variation of a Part IV permission, in relation to activities of the kind specified by arts 25E, 53D or 63J or, so far as relevant to any such activity, art 64 of this Order), and as from 30 June 2010 (for those purposes).

Exclusions

[8.53]

26 Arrangements not causing a deal

There are excluded from [articles 25(1), 25A(1), 25B(1)[, 25C(1) and 25E(1)]] arrangements which do not or would not bring about the transaction to which the arrangements relate.

NOTES

Words in first (outer) pair of square brackets substituted by the Financial Services and Markets Act 2000 (Regulated Activities) (Amendment) (No 2) Order 2006, SI 2006/2383, arts 2, 5, as from 6 November 2006 (for the purposes of enabling applications to be made for (i) a Pt IV permission, or a variation of a Pt IV permission, in relation to activities of the kind specified by arts 25B, 25C, 53B, 53C, 63B or 63F or, so far as relevant to any such activity, art 64 of this Order; or (ii) the Authority's approval under FSMA 2000, s 59 in relation to any of those activities), and as from 6 April 2007 (otherwise).

Words in second (inner) pair of square brackets substituted by the Financial Services and Markets Act 2000 (Regulated Activities) (Amendment) Order 2009, SI 2009/1342, arts 2, 5, as from 1 July 2009 (other than for the purposes of enabling applications to be made for a Part IV permission, or a variation of a Part IV permission, in relation to activities of the kind specified by arts 25E, 53D or 63J or, so far as relevant to any such activity, art 64 of this Order), and as from 30 June 2010 (for those purposes).

[8.54]
27 Enabling parties to communicate

A person does not carry on an activity of the kind specified by [article 25(2), 25A(2), 25B(2)[, 25C(2) or 25E(2)]] merely by providing means by which one party to a transaction (or potential transaction) is able to communicate with other such parties.

NOTES

Words in first (outer) pair of square brackets substituted by the Financial Services and Markets Act 2000 (Regulated Activities) (Amendment) (No 2) Order 2006, SI 2006/2383, arts 2, 6, as from 6 November 2006 (for the purposes of enabling applications to be made for (i) a Pt IV permission, or a variation of a Pt IV permission, in relation to activities of the kind specified by arts 25B, 25C, 53B, 53C, 63B or 63F or, so far as relevant to any such activity, art 64 of this Order; or (ii) the Authority's approval under FSMA 2000, s 59 in relation to any of those activities), and as from 6 April 2007 (otherwise).

Words in second (inner) pair of square brackets substituted by the Financial Services and Markets Act 2000 (Regulated Activities) (Amendment) Order 2009, SI 2009/1342, arts 2, 6, as from 1 July 2009 (other than for the purposes of enabling applications to be made for a Part IV permission, or a variation of a Part IV permission, in relation to activities of the kind specified by arts 25E, 53D or 63J or, so far as relevant to any such activity, art 64 of this Order), and as from 30 June 2010 (for those purposes).

[8.55]
28 Arranging transactions to which the arranger is a party

(1) There are excluded from article 25(1) any arrangements for a transaction into which the person making the arrangements enters or is to enter as principal or as agent for some other person.

(2) There are excluded from article 25(2) any arrangements which a person makes with a view to transactions into which he enters or is to enter as principal or as agent for some other person.

[(3) But the exclusions in paragraphs (1) and (2) do not apply to arrangements made for or with a view to a transaction which relates to a contract of insurance, unless the person making the arrangements either—

(a) is the only policyholder; or
(b) as a result of the transaction, would become the only policyholder.]

NOTES

Para (3): added by the Financial Services and Markets Act 2000 (Regulated Activities) (Amendment) (No 2) Order 2003, SI 2003/1476, art 5(2), as from 31 October 2004 (in so far as relating to contracts of long-term care insurance), and as from 14 January 2005 (otherwise).

[8.56]
[28A Arranging contracts[, plans or agreements] to which the arranger is a party]

[(1) There are excluded from [articles 25A(1), 25B(1)[, 25C(1) and 25E(1)]] any arrangements—

(a) for a [contract][, plan or agreement] into which the person making the arrangements enters or is to enter; or
(b) for a variation of a [contract][, plan or agreement] to which that person is (or is to become) a party.

(2) There are excluded from [articles 25A(2), 25B(2)][, 25C(2) and 25E(2)] any arrangements which a person makes with a view to contracts[, plans or agreements] into which he enters or is to enter.]

NOTES

Inserted by the Financial Services and Markets Act 2000 (Regulated Activities) (Amendment) (No 1) Order 2003, SI 2003/1475, art 7, as from 31 October 2004.

Article heading: words in square brackets substituted by the Financial Services and Markets Act 2000 (Regulated Activities) (Amendment) Order 2009, SI 2009/1342, arts 2, 7(1), as from 1 July 2009 (other than for the purposes of enabling applications to be made for a Part IV permission, or a variation of a Part IV permission, in relation to activities of the kind specified by arts 25E, 53D or 63J or, so far as relevant to any such activity, art 64 of this Order), and as from 30 June 2010 (for those purposes).

Para (1): words in first (outer), third (outer) and fifth (outer) pairs of square brackets substituted by the Financial Services and Markets Act 2000 (Regulated Activities) (Amendment) (No 2) Order 2006, SI 2006/2383, arts 2, 7(1)(a), as from 6 November 2006 (for the purposes of enabling applications to be made for (i) a Pt IV permission, or a variation of a Pt IV permission, in relation to activities of the kind specified by arts 25B, 25C, 53B, 53C, 63B or 63F or, so far as relevant to any such activity, art 64 of this Order; or (ii) the Authority's approval under FSMA 2000, s 59 in relation to any of those activities), and as from 6 April 2007 (otherwise). Words in second (inner), fourth (inner) and sixth (inner) pairs of square brackets substituted by SI 2009/1342, arts 2, 7(2)(a), as from 1 July 2009 (certain purposes), and as from 30 June 2010 (otherwise) (for purposes, see the first note relating to this Order above).

Para (2): words in first pair of square brackets substituted by SI 2006/2383, arts 2, 7(1)(b)(i), as from 6 November 2006 (certain purposes), and as from 6 April 2007 (otherwise) (for purposes, see the first note relating to this Order above). Words in second and third pairs of square brackets substituted by SI 2009/1342, arts 2, 7(2)(b), as from 1 July 2009 (certain purposes), and as from 30 June 2010 (otherwise) (for purposes, see the first note relating to this Order above).

[8.57]

29 Arranging deals with or through authorised persons

(1) There are excluded from [articles 25(1) and (2), [25A(1), (2) and (2A)], 25B(1) and (2)[, 25C(1) and (2) and 25E(1) and (2)]] arrangements made by a person ("A") who is not an authorised person for or with a view to a transaction which is or is to be entered into by a person ("the client") with or though an authorised person if—

(a) the transaction is or is to be entered into on advice to the client by an authorised person; or

(b) it is clear, in all the circumstances, that the client, in his capacity as an [investor, borrower, reversion seller, plan provider, home purchaser, agreement provider or (as the case may be) agreement seller], is not seeking and has not sought advice from A as to the merits of the client's entering into the transaction (or, if the client has sought such advice, A has declined to give it but has recommended that the client seek such advice from an authorised person).

[(2) But the exclusion in paragraph (1) does not apply if—

(a) the transaction relates, or would relate, to a contract of insurance; or

(b) A receives from any person other than the client any pecuniary reward or other advantage, for which he does not account to the client, arising out of his making the arrangements.]

[(3) This article is subject to article 4(4) [and (4B)].]

NOTES

Para (1): words in first (outer) pair of square brackets substituted by the Financial Services and Markets Act 2000 (Regulated Activities) (Amendment) (No 2) Order 2006, SI 2006/2383, arts 2, 8, as from 6 November 2006 (for the purposes of enabling applications to be made for (i) a Pt IV permission, or a variation of a Pt IV permission, in relation to activities of the kind specified by arts 25B, 25C, 53B, 53C, 63B or 63F or, so far as relevant to any such activity, art 64 of this Order; or (ii) the Authority's approval under FSMA 2000, s 59 in relation to any of those activities), and as from 6 April 2007 (otherwise). Words in second (inner) pair of square brackets substituted by the Mortgage Credit Directive Order 2015, SI 2015/910, Sch 1, Pt 2, para 4(1), (5)(a), as from 21 March 2016. Other words in square brackets substituted by the Financial Services and Markets Act 2000 (Regulated Activities) (Amendment) Order 2009, SI 2009/1342, arts 2, 8, as from 1 July 2009 (other than for the purposes of enabling applications to be made for a Part IV permission, or a variation of a Part IV permission, in relation to activities of the kind specified by arts 25E, 53D or 63J or, so far as relevant to any such activity, art 64 of this Order), and as from 30 June 2010 (for those purposes).

Para (2): substituted by the Financial Services and Markets Act 2000 (Regulated Activities) (Amendment) (No 2) Order 2003, SI 2003/1476, art 5(3), as from 31 October 2004 (in so far as relating to contracts of long-term care insurance), and as from 14 January 2005 (otherwise).

Para (3): added by the Financial Services and Markets Act 2000 (Regulated Activities) (Amendment No 3) Order 2006, SI 2006/3384, arts 2, 14, as from 1 April 2007 (for the purposes of enabling applications to be made for (i) a Part IV permission, (ii) a variation of a Part IV permission, and (iii) the Authority's approval under s 59 of the 2000 Act, in relation to an activity of the kind specified by art 25D of this Order, or in relation to an investment of the kind specified by arts 83, 84 or 85 of this Order), and as from 1 November 2007 (otherwise). Words in square brackets inserted by SI 2015/910,Sch 1, Pt 2, para 4(1), (5)(b), as from 21 March 2016.

[8.58]

[29A Arrangements made in the course of administration by authorised person

[(1)] A person who is not an authorised person ("A") does not carry on an activity of the kind specified by article 25A(1)(b) as a result of—

(a) anything done by an authorised person ("B") in relation to a regulated mortgage contract which B is administering pursuant to an arrangement of the kind mentioned in article 62(a); or

(b) anything A does in connection with the administration of a regulated mortgage contract in circumstances falling within article 62(b).

[(2) A person who is not an authorised person ("A") does not carry on an activity of the kind specified by article 25B(1)(b) as a result of—

(a) anything done by an authorised person ("B") in relation to a regulated home reversion plan which B is administering pursuant to an arrangement of the kind mentioned in article 63C(a); or

(b) anything A does in connection with the administration of a regulated home reversion plan in circumstances falling within article 63C(b).

(3) A person who is not an authorised person ("A") does not carry on an activity of the kind specified by article 25C(1)(b) as a result of—

(a) anything done by an authorised person ("B") in relation to a regulated home purchase plan which B is administering pursuant to an arrangement of the kind mentioned in article 63G(a); or

(b) anything A does in connection with the administration of a regulated home purchase plan in circumstances falling within article 63G(b).]]

[(4) A person who is not an authorised person ("A") does not carry on an activity of the kind specified by article 25E(1)(b) as a result of—

(a) anything done by an authorised person ("B") in relation to a regulated sale and rent back agreement which B is administering pursuant to an arrangement of the kind mentioned in article 63K(a); or

(b) anything A does in connection with the administration of a regulated sale and rent back agreement in circumstances falling within article 63K(b).]

NOTES

Inserted by the Financial Services and Markets Act 2000 (Regulated Activities) (Amendment) (No 1) Order 2003, SI 2003/1475, art 9, as from 31 October 2004.

Para (1) numbered as such, and paras (2), (3) added, by the Financial Services and Markets Act 2000 (Regulated Activities) (Amendment) (No 2) Order 2006, SI 2006/2383, arts 2, 9, as from 6 November 2006 (for the purposes of enabling applications to be made for (i) a Pt IV permission, or a variation of a Pt IV permission, in relation to activities of the kind specified by arts 25B, 25C, 53B, 53C, 63B or 63F or, so far as relevant to any such activity, art 64 of this Order; or (ii) the Authority's approval under FSMA 2000, s 59 in relation to any of those activities), and as from 6 April 2007 (otherwise).

Para (4): added by the Financial Services and Markets Act 2000 (Regulated Activities) (Amendment) Order 2009, SI 2009/1342, arts 2, 9, as from 1 July 2009 (other than for the purposes of enabling applications to be made for a Part IV permission, or a variation of a Part IV permission, in relation to activities of the kind specified by arts 25E, 53D or 63J or, so far as relevant to any such activity, art 64 of this Order), and as from 30 June 2010 (for those purposes).

[8.59]

30 Arranging transactions in connection with lending on the security of insurance policies

(1) There are excluded from article 25(1) and (2) arrangements made by a money-lender under which either—

[(a) a relevant authorised person or a person acting on his behalf will introduce to the money-lender persons with whom the relevant authorised person has entered, or proposes to enter, into a relevant transaction, or will advise such persons to approach the money-lender, with a view to the money-lender lending money on the security of any contract effected pursuant to a relevant transaction;]

(b) a relevant authorised person gives an assurance to the money-lender as to the amount which, on the security of any contract effected pursuant to a relevant transaction, will or may be received by the money-lender should the money-lender lend money to a person introduced to him pursuant to the arrangements.

(2) In paragraph (1)—

"money-lender" means a person who is—

(a) a money-lending company within the meaning of [section 209 of the Companies Act 2006];

(b) a body corporate incorporated under the law of, or of any part of, the United Kingdom relating to building societies; or

(c) a person whose ordinary business includes the making of loans or the giving of guarantees in connection with loans;

"relevant authorised person" means an authorised person who has permission to effect [contracts of insurance] or to sell investments of the kind specified by article 89, so far as relevant to such contracts;

"relevant transaction" means the effecting of a [contract of insurance] or the sale of an investment of the kind specified by article 89, so far as relevant to such contracts.

[(3) This article is subject to article 4(4A).]

NOTES

Para (1): sub-para (a) substituted by the Financial Services and Markets Act 2000 (Regulated Activities) (Amendment) Order 2001, SI 2001/3544, arts 2, 5, as from 1 December 2001.

Para (2): words in square brackets in the definition "money-lender" substituted by the Companies Act 2006 (Consequential Amendments and Transitional Provisions) Order 2011, SI 2011/1265, art 13(1), (4), as from 12 May 2011. Words in square brackets in the definitions "relevant authorised person" and "relevant transaction" substituted by the Financial Services and Markets Act 2000 (Regulated Activities) (Amendment) (No 2) Order 2003, SI 2003/1476, art 5(4), as from 31 October 2004 (in so far as relating to contracts of long-term care insurance), and as from 14 January 2005 (otherwise).

Para (3): added by the Financial Services and Markets Act 2000 (Regulated Activities) (Amendment No 3) Order 2006, SI 2006/3384, arts 2, 15, as from 1 April 2007 (for the purposes of enabling applications to be made for (i) a Part IV permission, (ii) a variation of a Part IV permission, and (iii) the Authority's approval under s 59 of the 2000 Act, in relation to an activity of the kind specified by art 25D of this Order, or in relation to an investment of the kind specified by arts 83, 84 or 85 of this Order), and as from 1 November 2007 (otherwise).

[8.60]

31 Arranging the acceptance of debentures in connection with loans

(1) There are excluded from article 25(1) and (2) arrangements under which a person accepts or is to accept, whether as principal or agent, an instrument creating or acknowledging indebtedness in respect of any loan, credit, guarantee or other similar financial accommodation or assurance which is, or is to be, made, granted or provided by that person or his principal.

(2) The reference in paragraph (1) to a person accepting an instrument includes a reference to a person becoming a party to an instrument otherwise than as a debtor or a surety.

NOTES

Modification: references in para (1) to securities, instruments or investments creating or acknowledging indebtedness (or creating or acknowledging a present or future indebtedness) includes a reference to uncertificated units of eligible debt securities; see the Uncertificated Securities (Amendment) (Eligible Debt Securities) Regulations 2003, SI 2003/1633, reg 15, Sch 2, para 8.

Modification: references in para (2) to a person becoming party to an instrument includes a reference to a person assuming rights and obligations in respect of uncertificated units of an eligible debt security in accordance with its current terms of issue; see the Uncertificated Securities (Amendment) (Eligible Debt Securities) Regulations 2003, SI 2003/1633, reg 15, Sch 2, para 9.

[8.61]

32 Provision of finance

There are excluded from article 25(2) arrangements having as their sole purpose the provision of finance to enable a person to buy, sell, subscribe for or underwrite investments.

[8.62]

33 Introducing

There are excluded from [articles 25(2), 25A(2), 25B(2)[, 25C(2) and 25E(2)]] arrangements where—

(a) they are arrangements under which persons ("clients") will be introduced to another person;

(b) the person to whom introductions are to be made is—

(i) an authorised person;

(ii) an exempt person acting in the course of a business comprising a regulated activity in relation to which he is exempt; or

(iii) a person who is not unlawfully carrying on regulated activities in the United Kingdom and whose ordinary business involves him in engaging in an activity of the kind specified by any of articles 14, 21, 25, [25A,] [25B, 25C,] [25E,] 37[, 39A], 40, 45, [51ZA, 51ZB, 51ZC, 51ZD, 51ZE], [52, 53[, 53A, 53B][, 53C and 53D]] (or, so far as relevant to any of those articles, article 64), or would do so apart from any exclusion from any of those articles made by this Order; . . .

(c) the introduction is made with a view to the provision of independent advice or the independent exercise of discretion in relation to investments generally or in relation to any class of investments to which the arrangements relate[; and

[(d) The arrangements—

(i) are made with a view to a person entering into a transaction which does not relate to a contract of insurance, or

(ii) are of the type specified in article 33B (provision of information—contracts of insurance)]].

NOTES

Words in first (outer) pair of square brackets substituted by the Financial Services and Markets Act 2000 (Regulated Activities) (Amendment) (No 2) Order 2006, SI 2006/2383, arts 2, 10(a), as from 6 November 2006 (for the purposes of enabling applications to be made for (i) a Pt IV permission, or a variation of a Pt IV permission, in relation to activities of the kind specified by arts 25B, 25C, 53B, 53C, 63B or 63F or, so far as relevant to any such activity, art 64 of this Order; or (ii) the Authority's approval under FSMA 2000, s 59 in relation to any of those activities), and as from 6 April 2007 (otherwise).

Words in second (inner) pair of square brackets substituted by the Financial Services and Markets Act 2000 (Regulated Activities) (Amendment) Order 2009, SI 2009/1342, arts 2, 10(a), as from 1 July 2009 (other than for the purposes of enabling applications to be made for a Part IV permission, or a variation of a Part IV permission, in relation to activities of the kind specified by arts 25E, 53D or 63J or, so far as relevant to any such activity, art 64 of this Order), and as from 30 June 2010 (otherwise).

Figure "25A," in square brackets in sub-para (b)(iii) inserted, and words in the antepenultimate (outer) pair of square brackets in that paragraph (ie, beginning with "52,") substituted, by the Financial Services and Markets Act 2000 (Regulated Activities) (Amendment) (No 1) Order 2003, SI 2003/1475, art 10, as from 31 October 2004.

Figures "25B, 25C," in square brackets in sub-para (b)(iii) inserted, and words in penultimate (inner) pair of square brackets (ie, beginning with ", 53A,") substituted, by SI 2006/2383, arts 2, 10(b), as from 6 November 2006 (certain purposes), and as from 6 April 2007 (otherwise) (for purposes, see the first note relating to the Order above).

Figure "25E," in square brackets in sub-para (b)(iii) inserted by SI 2009/1342, arts 2, 10(b)(i), as from 1 July 2009 (certain purposes), and as from 30 June 2010 (otherwise) (for purposes, see the first note relating to this Order above).

Figure ", 39A" in square brackets in sub-para (b)(iii) inserted, word omitted from that paragraph revoked, and para (d) and the word immediately preceding it originally added, by the Financial Services and Markets Act 2000 (Regulated Activities) (Amendment) (No 2) Order 2003, SI 2003/1476, art 5(5), as from 31 October 2004 (in so far as relating to contracts of long-term care insurance), and as from 14 January 2005 (otherwise).

Figures "51ZA, 51ZB, 51ZC, 51ZD, 51ZE" in square brackets substituted by the Alternative Investment Fund Managers Regulations 2013, SI 2013/1773, reg 81, Sch 2, Part 1, para 1(1), (3), as from 22 July 2013.

Words in final (inner) pair of square brackets in sub-para (b)(iii) (ie, ", 53C and 53D") substituted by SI 2009/1342, arts 2, 10(b)(ii), as from 1 July 2009 (certain purposes), and as from 30 June 2010 (otherwise) (for purposes, see the first note relating to this Order above).

Para (d) substituted by the Insurance Distribution (Regulated Activities and Miscellaneous Amendments) Order 2018, SI 2018/546, arts 2, 4, as from 1 October 2018.

[8.63]

[33A Introducing to authorised persons etc

(1) There are excluded from article 25A(2) arrangements where—

(a) they are arrangements under which a client is introduced to a person ("N") who is—

(i) an authorised person who has permission to carry on a regulated activity of the kind specified by any of articles 25A, 53A, and 61(1),

(ii) an appointed representative who may carry on a regulated activity of the kind specified by either of articles 25A and 53A without contravening the general prohibition, or

(iii) an overseas person who carries on activities specified by any of articles 25A, 53A and 61(1); and

(b) the conditions mentioned in paragraph (2) are satisfied.

[(1A) There are excluded from article 25B(2) arrangements where—

(a) they are arrangements under which a client is introduced to a person ("N") who is—

(i) an authorised person who has permission to carry on a regulated activity of the kind specified by any of articles 25B, 53B and 63B(1),

(ii) an appointed representative who may carry on a regulated activity of the kind specified by either of articles 25B and 53B without contravening the general prohibition, or

(iii) an overseas person who carries on activities specified by any of articles 25B, 53B and 63B(1); and

(b) the conditions mentioned in paragraph (2) are satisfied.

(1B) There are excluded from article 25C(2) arrangements where—

(a) they are arrangements under which a client is introduced to a person ("N") who is—

(i) an authorised person who has permission to carry on a regulated activity of the kind specified by any of articles 25C, 53C and 63F(1),

(ii) an appointed representative who may carry on a regulated activity of the kind specified by either of articles 25C and 53C without contravening the general prohibition, or

(iii) an overseas person who carries on activities specified by any of articles 25C, 53C and 63F(1); and

(b) the conditions mentioned in paragraph (2) are satisfied.]

[(1C) There are excluded from article 25E(2) arrangements where—

(a) they are arrangements under which a client is introduced to a person ("N") who is—

(i) an authorised person who has permission to carry on a regulated activity of the kind specified by any of articles 25E, 53D and 63J(1),

(ii) an appointed representative who may carry on a regulated activity of the kind specified by either of articles 25E or 53D without contravening the general prohibition, or

(iii) an overseas person who carries on activities specified by any of articles 25E, 53D and 63J(1); and

(b) the conditions mentioned in paragraph (2) are satisfied.]

(2) Those conditions are—

(a) that the person making the introduction ("P") does not receive any money, other than money payable to P on his own account, paid by the client for or in connection with any transaction which the client enters into with or through N as a result of the introduction; and

(b) that before making the introduction P discloses to the client such of the information mentioned in paragraph (3) as applies to P.

(3) That information is—

(a) that P is a member of the same group as N;

(b) details of any payment which P will receive from N, by way of fee or commission, for introducing the client to N;

(c) an indication of any other reward or advantage received or to be received by P that arises out of his introducing clients to N.

[(4) In this article, "client" means—

(a) for the purposes of paragraph (1), a borrower within the meaning given by article 61(3)(a)(i), or a person who is or may be contemplating entering into a regulated mortgage contract as such a borrower;

(b) for the purposes of paragraph (1A), a reversion seller, a plan provider or a person who is or may be contemplating entering into a regulated home reversion plan as a reversion seller or as a plan provider;

(c) for the purposes of paragraph (1B), a home purchaser or a person who is or may be contemplating entering into a regulated home purchase plan as a home purchaser;

[(d) for the purposes of paragraph (1C), an agreement provider, an agreement seller or a person who is or may be contemplating entering into a regulated sale and rent back agreement as an agreement provider or agreement seller.]]

NOTES

Inserted by the Financial Services and Markets Act 2000 (Regulated Activities) (Amendment) (No 1) Order 2003, SI 2003/1475, art 11, as from 31 October 2004.

Paras (1A), (1B): inserted by the Financial Services and Markets Act 2000 (Regulated Activities) (Amendment) (No 2) Order 2006, SI 2006/2383, arts 2, 11(a), as from 6 November 2006 (for the purposes of enabling applications to be made for (i) a Pt IV permission, or a variation of a Pt IV permission, in relation to activities of the kind specified by arts 25B, 25C, 53B, 53C, 63B or 63F or, so far as relevant to any such activity, art 64 of this Order; or (ii) the Authority's approval under FSMA 2000, s 59 in relation to any of those activities), and as from 6 April 2007 (otherwise).

Para (1C): inserted by the Financial Services and Markets Act 2000 (Regulated Activities) (Amendment) Order 2009, SI 2009/1342, arts 2, 11(a), as from 1 July 2009 (other than for the purposes of enabling applications to be made for a Part IV permission, or a variation of a Part IV permission, in relation to activities of the kind specified by arts 25E, 53D or 63J or, so far as relevant to any such activity, art 64 of this Order), and as from 30 June 2010 (for those purposes).

Para (4): substituted by SI 2006/2383, arts 2, 11(b), as from 6 November 2006 (certain purposes), and as from 6 April 2007 (otherwise) (for purposes, see the first note relating to the Order above). Sub-para (d) inserted by SI 2009/1342, arts 2, 11(b), as from 1 July 2009 (certain purposes), and as from 30 June 2010 (otherwise) (for purposes, see the first note relating to this Order above).

[8.64]

[33B Provision of information—contracts of insurance

(1) There is excluded from article 25(1) and (2) (arranging deals in investments) the making of arrangements for, or with a view to, a transaction for the sale or purchase of a contract of insurance, where that activity meets the conditions specified in paragraphs (2) and (3).

(2) The conditions specified in this paragraph are that the activity—

(a) consists of the provision of information about a potential policyholder to a relevant insurer or an insurance or reinsurance intermediary, or

(b) consists of the provision of information to a potential policyholder about—

(i) a contract of insurance, or

(ii) a relevant insurer or insurance or reinsurance intermediary.

(3) The condition specified in this paragraph is that the provider of the information does not take any step other than the provision of information to assist in the conclusion of a contract of insurance.

(4) In this article—

["insurance intermediary" means a person other than—who, for remuneration, takes up or pursues the activity of insurance distribution;"

(a) an insurance or reinsurance undertaking or an employee of such an undertaking, or

(b) an ancillary insurance intermediary;

"reinsurance intermediary" means a person other than—who, for remuneration, takes up or pursues the activity of reinsurance distribution;"

(a) a reinsurance undertaking, or

(b) an employee of a reinsurance undertaking;]

"relevant insurer" has the meaning given in article 39B(2) (claims management on behalf of an insurer etc).

[(5) In paragraph (4)—

"ancillary insurance intermediary", "insurance distribution" and "reinsurance distribution" have the same meaning as in article 4;

"remuneration" means any commission, fee, charge or other payment, including an economic benefit of any kind or any other financial or non-financial advantage or incentive offered or given.]]

NOTES

Inserted by the Insurance Distribution (Regulated Activities and Miscellaneous Amendments) Order 2018, SI 2018/546, arts 2, 5, as from 1 October 2018.

Definitions "insurance intermediary" and "reinsurance intermediary" in para (4) substituted, and para (5) added, by the Financial Services and Markets Act 2000 (Amendment) (EU Exit) Regulations 2019, SI 2019/632, regs 120, 128, as from IP completion day (as defined in the European Union (Withdrawal Agreement) Act 2020, s 39).

[8.65]

34 Arrangements for the issue of shares etc

(1) There are excluded from article 25(1) and (2)—

(a) arrangements made by a company for the purposes of issuing its own shares or share warrants; and

(b) arrangements made by any person for the purposes of issuing his own debentures or debenture warrants;

and for the purposes of article 25(1) and (2), a company is not, by reason of issuing its own shares or share warrants, and a person is not, by reason of issuing his own debentures or debenture warrants, to be treated as selling them.

(2) In paragraph (1), "company", "shares", "debentures", "share warrants" and "debenture warrants" have the meanings given by article 18(2).

[(3) This article is subject to article 4(4).]

NOTES

Para (3): added by the Financial Services and Markets Act 2000 (Regulated Activities) (Amendment) Order 2017, SI 2017/488, art 12(1), (6), as from 1 April 2017 (for the purposes of (i) enabling applications to be made for a Part 4A permission, for a variation of a Part 4A permission or for an approval under FSMA 2000, s 59, or (ii) enabling such applications to be determined, in relation to any specified activity or any specified investment amended or inserted by the 2017 Order), and as from 3 January 2018 (otherwise).

[8.66]

35 International securities self-regulating organisations

(1) There are excluded from article 25(1) and (2) any arrangements made for the purposes of carrying out the functions of a body or association which is approved under this article as an international securities self-regulating organisation, whether the arrangements are made by the organisation itself or by a person acting on its behalf.

(2) The Treasury may approve as an international securities self-regulating organisation any body corporate or unincorporated association with respect to which the conditions mentioned in paragraph (3) appear to them to be met if, having regard to such matters affecting international trade, overseas earnings and the balance of payments or otherwise as they consider relevant, it appears to them that to do so would be desirable and not result in any undue risk to investors.

(3) The conditions are that—

(a) the body or association does not have its head office in the United Kingdom;

(b) the body or association is not eligible for recognition under section 287 or 288 of the Act (applications by investment exchanges and clearing houses) on the ground that (whether or not it has applied, and whether or not it would be eligible on other grounds) it is unable to satisfy the requirements of one or both of paragraphs (a) and (b) of section 292(3) of the Act (requirements for overseas investment exchanges and overseas clearing houses);

[(ba) the body or association is also not eligible to become . . . a third country central counterparty (as defined in section 285(1)(d) of the Act);]

[(bb) the body or association is also not eligible to become . . . a third country CSD (as defined in section 285(1)(g) of the Act);]

(c) the body or association is able and willing to co-operate with [the FCA and the PRA] by the sharing of information and in other ways;

(d) adequate arrangements exist for co-operation between [the FCA and the PRA] and those responsible for the supervision of the body or association in the country or territory in which its head office is situated;

(e) the body or association has a membership composed of persons falling within any of the following categories, that is to say, authorised persons, exempt persons, and persons whose head offices are outside the United Kingdom and whose ordinary business involves them in engaging in activities which are activities of a kind specified by this Order (or would be apart from any exclusion made by this Part); and

(f) the body or association facilitates and regulates the activity of its members in the conduct of international securities business.

(4) In paragraph (3)(f), "international securities business" means the business of buying, selling, subscribing for or underwriting investments (or agreeing to do so), either as principal or agent, where—

(a) the investments are securities or [relevant investments] and are of a kind which, by their nature, and the manner in which the business is conducted, may be expected normally to be bought or dealt in by persons sufficiently expert to understand the risks involved; and

(b) either the transaction is international or each of the parties may be expected to be indifferent to the location of the other;

and, for the purposes of this definition, it is irrelevant that the investments may ultimately be bought otherwise than in the course of such business by persons not so expert.

(5) Any approval under this article is to be given by notice in writing; and the Treasury may by a further notice in writing withdraw any such approval if for any reason it appears to them that it is not appropriate to it to continue in force.

NOTES

Para (3): sub-para (ba) inserted by the Financial Services and Markets Act 2000 (Over the Counter Derivatives, Central Counterparties and Trade Repositories) Regulations 2013, SI 2013/504, reg 33(1), (3), as from 1 April 2013. Sub-para (bb) inserted by the Central Securities Depositories Regulations 2017, SI 2017/1064, reg 10, Schedule, para 23(1), (2), as from 28 November 2017. The words omitted from sub-paras (ba), (bb) were revoked by the Financial Services and Markets Act 2000 (Amendment) (EU Exit) Regulations 2019, SI 2019/632, regs 120, 129, as from IP completion day (as defined in the European Union (Withdrawal Agreement) Act 2020, s 39). The other words in square brackets in this paragraph were substituted by the Financial Services Act 2012 (Consequential Amendments and Transitional Provisions) Order 2013, SI 2013/472, art 3, Sch 2, para 35(g), as from 1 April 2013.

Para (4): words in square brackets in sub-para (a) substituted by the Financial Services and Markets Act 2000 (Regulated Activities) (Amendment) (No 2) Order 2003, SI 2003/1476, art 5(6), as from 31 October 2004 (in so far as relating to contracts of long-term care insurance), and as from 14 January 2005 (otherwise).

[8.67]
[35A Trade repositories

[(1)] A trade repository does not carry on an activity of the kind specified by article 25(2) by carrying on its functions of centrally collecting and maintaining records of—

[(a)] derivatives under Regulation (EU) 648/2012 of the European Parliament and of the Council of 4 July 2012 on OTC derivatives, central counterparties and trade repositories[; or

(b) securities financing transactions under the SFT regulation].

[(2) The reference in paragraph (1)(a) to Regulation (EU) 648/2012 is a reference to that instrument as it [forms part of retained EU law].]

NOTES

Inserted by the Financial Services and Markets Act 2000 (Over the Counter Derivatives, Central Counterparties and Trade Repositories) Regulations 2013, SI 2013/504, reg 33(1), (4), as from 1 April 2013.

Para (1) numbered as such and para (2) added, by the Financial Services and Markets Act 2000 (Amendment) (EU Exit) Regulations 2019, SI 2019/632, regs 120, 130, as from 23 March 2019.

In para (1), the letter "(a)" in square brackets was inserted, and para (b) and the preceding word were added, by the Financial Services and Markets Act 2000 (Transparency of Securities Financing Transactions and of Reuse) Regulations 2016, SI 2016/715, reg 30, Sch 2, para 1(1), (3), as from 13 July 2016.

The words in square brackets in para (2) were substituted by the Securities Financing Transactions, Securitisation and Miscellaneous Amendments (EU Exit) Regulations 2020, SI 2020/1385, reg 71, Schedule, para 1, with effect from immediately before IP completion day (as defined in the European Union (Withdrawal Agreement) Act 2020, s 39).

[8.68]
[35AB Securitisation repositories

A securitisation repository does not carry on an activity of the kind specified by article 25(2) by carrying on its functions of centrally collecting and maintaining records of securitisations under the EU Securitisation Regulation 2017.]

NOTES

Inserted by the Securitisation Regulations 2018, SI 2018/1288, reg 28, Sch 2, para 2(1), (3), as from 1 January 2019.

[8.69]
[35B Providing pensions guidance . . .

(1) A person does not carry on an activity of the kind specified in article 25(1) or (2) by reason of providing pensions guidance . . .

[(2) For the purposes of paragraph (1), pensions guidance means—

(a) information or guidance provided by the Money and Pensions Service in carrying out its pensions guidance function (see section 3 of the Financial Guidance and Claims Act 2018);

(b) information or guidance provided by another person with whom arrangements under section 5(1), (2) or (3) of the Financial Guidance and Claims Act 2018 are made to carry out the Money and Pensions Service's pensions guidance function.]

NOTES

Inserted by the Financial Services and Markets Act 2000 (Regulated Activities) (Amendment) (Pensions Guidance Exclusions) Order 2015, SI 2015/489, art 2(1), (3), as from 26 March 2015.

Words omitted revoked, and para (2) substituted, by the Financial Services and Markets Act 2000 (Regulated Activities) (Amendment) (No 2) Order 2022, SI 2022/726, art 2(3), as from 21 July 2022.

[8.70]
36 Other exclusions

[(1)] Article 25 is also subject to the exclusions in articles 66 (trustees etc), 67 (profession or non-investment business), 68 (sale of goods and supply of services), 69 (groups and joint enterprises), 70 (sale of body corporate), 71 (employee share schemes)[, 72 (overseas persons)[. . . , 72B (activities carried on by a provider of relevant goods or services), 72C (provision of information about contracts of insurance on an incidental basis)[, article 72AA (managers of [UK UCITS] and AIFs)[, 72D (large risks contracts where risk situated [outside the United Kingdom]), 72G (local authorities) and 72H (insolvency practitioners)]]]].

[(2) [Articles 25A, 25B[, 25C and 25E] are] also subject to the exclusions in articles 66 (trustees etc), 67 (profession or non-investment business), 72 (overseas persons)[. . .][, 72AA (managers of [UK UCITS] and AIFs) and 72G (local authorities)].]

[(2A) Article 25A is also subject to the exclusion in article 72I (registered consumer buy-to-let mortgage firms).]

[(3) Article 25D is also subject to [the exclusions in articles 72 (overseas persons)[, 72AA (managers of [UK UCITS] and AIFs) and 72H (insolvency practitioners)]].]

NOTES

Para (1) was numbered as such by the Financial Services and Markets Act 2000 (Regulated Activities) (Amendment) (No 1) Order 2003, SI 2003/1475, art 12(a), as from 31 October 2004. It has subsequently been amended as follows:

Words in first (outer) pair of square brackets substituted by the Financial Services and Markets Act 2000 (Regulated Activities) (Amendment) (No 2) Order 2002, SI 2002/1776, art 3(1), (6), as from 21 August 2002.

Words in second (inner) pair of square brackets substituted by the Financial Services and Markets Act 2000 (Regulated Activities) (Amendment) (No 2) Order 2003, SI 2003/1476, art 5(7), as from 31 October 2004 (in so far as relating to contracts of long-term care insurance), and as from 14 January 2005 (otherwise).

The words omitted were revoked by the Electronic Commerce and Solvency 2 (Amendment etc) (EU Exit) Regulations 2019, SI 2019/1361, reg 5(1), (3), as from IP completion day (as defined in the European Union (Withdrawal Agreement) Act 2020, s 39) (for transitional provisions, see the note in relation to art 72A of this Order *post*).

Words in third (inner) pair of square brackets (ie, beginning ", article 72A") substituted by the Alternative Investment Fund Managers Regulations 2013, SI 2013/1773, reg 81, Sch 2, Part 1, para 1(1), (7), as from 22 July 2013.

The words "UK UCITS" in the fourth (inner) pair of square brackets were substituted by the Financial Services and Markets Act 2000 (Amendment) (EU Exit) Regulations 2019, SI 2019/632, regs 120, 148(2), as from IP completion day (as defined in the European Union (Withdrawal Agreement) Act 2020, s 39).

Words in fifth (inner) pair of square brackets (ie, beginning ", 72D") substituted by the Financial Services and Markets Act 2000 (Regulated Activities) (Amendment) Order 2014, SI 2014/366, art 2(1), (6)(a), as from 1 April 2014 (note that the 2014 Order came into force on 14 February 2014 for the purpose of the FCA making rules, giving guidance etc, and came into force on 1 April 2014, immediately after SI 2013/1881 (and SI 2013/1882) come into force, in so far as not already in force).

Words in sixth (inner) pair of square brackets (ie, the words "outside the United Kingdom") substituted by SI 2019/632, regs 120, 149(5), as from IP completion day (as defined in the European Union (Withdrawal Agreement) Act 2020, s 39).

Para (2) was added by SI 2003/1475, art 12(b), as from 31 October 2004. It has subsequently been amended as follows:

Words in first (outer) pair of square brackets substituted by the Financial Services and Markets Act 2000 (Regulated Activities) (Amendment) (No 2) Order 2006, SI 2006/2383, arts 2, 12, as from 6 November 2006 (for the purposes of enabling applications to be made for (i) a Pt IV permission, or a variation of a Pt IV permission, in relation to activities of the kind specified by arts 25B, 25C, 53B, 53C, 63B or 63F or, so far as relevant to any such activity, art 64 of this Order; or (ii) the Authority's approval under FSMA 2000, s 59 in relation to any of those activities), and as from 6 April 2007 (otherwise).

Words in second (inner) pair of square brackets substituted by the Financial Services and Markets Act 2000 (Regulated Activities) (Amendment) Order 2009, SI 2009/1342, arts 2, 12, as from 1 July 2009 (other than for the purposes of enabling applications to be made for a Part IV permission, or a variation of a Part IV permission, in relation to activities of the kind specified by arts 25E, 53D or 63J or, so far as relevant to any such activity, art 64 of this Order), and as from 30 June 2010 (otherwise).

The omitted words were originally substituted by virtue of SI 2013/1773, reg 81, Sch 2, Part 1, para 1(1), (6), as from 22 July 2013; and were subsequently revoked by SI 2019/1361, reg 5(1), (3), as from IP completion day (as defined in the European Union (Withdrawal Agreement) Act 2020, s 39) (for transitional provisions, see the note in relation to art 72A of this Order *post*).

Words in fourth (inner) pair of square brackets (ie, beginning ", 72AA") substituted by SI 2014/366, art 2(1), (6)(b), as from 1 April 2014 (as to the commencement of the 2014 Order, see the note above).

Words "UK UCITS" in square brackets substitute by SI 2019/632, regs 120, 148(2), as from IP completion day (as defined in the European Union (Withdrawal Agreement) Act 2020, s 39).

Para (2A): inserted by the Mortgage Credit Directive Order 2015, SI 2015/910, Sch 1, Pt 2, para 4(1), (6), as from 21 March 2016.

Para (3): added by the Financial Services and Markets Act 2000 (Regulated Activities) (Amendment No 3) Order 2006, SI 2006/3384, arts 2, 16, as from 1 April 2007 (for the purposes of enabling applications to be made for (i) a Pt IV permission, (ii) a variation of a Pt IV permission, and (iii) the Authority's approval under s 59 of the 2000 Act, in relation to an activity of the kind specified by art 25D of this Order, or in relation to an investment of the kind specified by arts 83, 84 or 85 of this Order), and as from 1 November 2007 (otherwise). It has subsequently been amended as follows:

Words in first (outer) pair of square brackets substituted by SI 2013/1773, reg 81, Sch 2, Part 1, para 1(1), (8), as from 22 July 2013.

Words in second (inner) pair of square brackets substituted by SI 2014/366, art 2(1), (6)(c), as from 1 April 2014 (as to the commencement of the 2014 Order, see the note above).

Words "UK UCITS" in square brackets substituted by SI 2019/632, regs 120, 148(2), as from IP completion day (as defined in the European Union (Withdrawal Agreement) Act 2020, s 39).

[CHAPTER 6A CREDIT BROKING

The Activity

[8.71]

36A Credit broking

(1) Each of the following is a specified kind of activity—

(a) effecting an introduction of an individual or relevant recipient of credit who wishes to enter into a credit agreement to a person ("P") with a view to P entering into by way of business as lender a regulated credit agreement (or an agreement which would be a regulated credit agreement but for any of the relevant provisions);

(b) effecting an introduction of an individual or relevant recipient of credit who wishes to enter into a consumer hire agreement to a person ("P") with a view to P entering into by way of business as owner a regulated consumer hire agreement or an agreement which would be a regulated consumer hire agreement but for article 60O (exempt agreements: exemptions relating to the nature of the agreement) or 60Q (exempt agreements: exemptions relating to the nature of the hirer);

(c) effecting an introduction of an individual or relevant recipient of credit who wishes to enter into a credit agreement or consumer hire agreement (as the case may be) to a person who carries on an activity of the kind specified in sub-paragraph (a) or (b) by way of business;

(d) presenting or offering an agreement which would (if entered into) be a regulated credit agreement (or an agreement which would be a regulated credit agreement but for any of the relevant provisions);

(e) assisting an individual or relevant recipient of credit by undertaking preparatory work with a view to that person entering into a regulated credit agreement (or an agreement which would be a regulated credit agreement but for any of the relevant provisions);

(f) entering into a regulated credit agreement (or an agreement which would be a regulated credit agreement but for any of the relevant provisions) on behalf of a lender.

(2) Paragraph (1) does not apply in so far as the activity is an activity of the kind specified by article 36H (operating an electronic system in relation to lending).

(3) For the purposes of paragraph (1) it is immaterial whether the credit agreement or consumer hire agreement is subject to the law of a country outside the United Kingdom.

(4) For the purposes of this article, the "relevant provisions" are the following provisions—

(a) article 60C (exempt agreements: exemptions relating to the nature of the agreement);

(b) article 60D (exempt agreements: exemptions relating to the purchase of land for non-residential purposes);

(c) article 60E (exempt agreements: exemptions relating to the nature of the lender)[, except for paragraph (5) of that article];

(d) article 60G (exempt agreements: exemptions relating to the total charge for credit);

(e) article 60H (exempt agreements: exemptions relating to the nature of the borrower).]

NOTES

Chapter 6A (arts 36A–36G) was inserted by the Financial Services and Markets Act 2000 (Regulated Activities) (Amendment) (No 2) Order 2013, SI 2013/1881, arts 2, 4, as from 1 April 2014.

Para (4): words in square brackets in sub-para (c) inserted by the Financial Services and Markets Act 2000 (Regulated Activities) (Amendment) (No 2) Order 2014, SI 2014/1448, art 2, as from 27 June 2014.

[Exclusions

[8.72]

36B Introducing by individuals in the course of canvassing off trade premises

(1) There are excluded from article 36A activities carried on by an individual by canvassing off trade premises—

(a) a restricted-use credit agreement used to finance a transaction between the lender or a member of the lender's group and the borrower whether forming part of that agreement or not, or

(b) a regulated consumer hire agreement.

(2) But paragraph (1) does not apply if A carries on any other activity of a kind specified by article 36A(1)(a) to (c).

(3) A canvasses a restricted-use credit agreement or a regulated consumer hire agreement off trade premises for the purposes of this article if—

(a) A solicits the entry of an individual or relevant recipient of credit ("B") into such an agreement by making oral representations to B during a visit by A to any place (not excluded by paragraph (4)) where B is, and

(b) that visit is made by A for the purpose of making such oral representations.

(4) A place is excluded from paragraph (3) if it is a place where a business is carried on (whether on a permanent or temporary basis) by—

(a) the lender or owner,

(b) the supplier under the restricted-use credit agreement,

(c) A,

(d) a person who employs A or has appointed A as an agent, or

(e) B.]

NOTES

Inserted as noted to art 36A at **[8.71]**.

[8.73]

[36C Activities for which no fee is paid

(1) There are excluded from sub-paragraphs (d), (e) and (f) of article 36A(1) activities carried on by a person for which that person does not receive a fee.

(2) For the purposes of this article, "fee" includes pecuniary consideration or any other form of financial consideration.]

NOTES

Inserted as noted to art 36A at **[8.71]**.

[8.74]

[36D Transaction to which the broker is a party

There are excluded from article 36A activities in relation to a regulated credit agreement (or an agreement which would be a regulated credit agreement but for the exclusions in articles 60C to 60H) or a regulated consumer hire agreement (or an agreement which would be a regulated consumer hire agreement but for the exclusions in articles 60O to 60Q) into which the person carrying on the activity enters or is to enter as lender or owner.]

NOTES

Inserted as noted to art 36A at **[8.71]**.

[8.75]

[36E Activities in relation to certain agreements relating to land

(1) There are excluded from article 36A activities carried on with a view to an individual or a relevant recipient of credit entering into an investment property loan, as defined in article 61A(6) (mortgage contracts which are not regulated mortgage contracts).

(2) There are excluded from article 36A activities of a kind specified by article 25A (arranging regulated mortgage contracts) or 25C (arranging regulated home purchase plans).

(3) There are excluded from article 36A other activities not excluded by paragraph (1) or (2) which consist of effecting an introduction with a view to an individual or relevant recipient of credit entering into a relevant agreement, if the person to whom the introduction is made is an authorised person who has permission to—

(a) enter into such an agreement as lender or home purchase provider (as the case may be), or

(b) make an introduction to an authorised person who has permission to enter into such an agreement as lender or home purchase provider (as the case may be).

(4) In paragraph (3) "relevant agreement" means a regulated mortgage contract or a regulated home purchase plan.]

NOTES

Originally inserted as noted to art 36A at **[8.71]**.

Subsequently substituted by the Mortgage Credit Directive Order 2015, SI 2015/910, Sch 1, Pt 2, para 4(1), (7), as from 21 March 2016.

[8.76]

[36F Activities carried on by members of the legal profession etc

(1) There are excluded from article 36A (credit broking) activities carried on by—

(a) a barrister or advocate acting in that capacity;

(b) a solicitor (within the meaning of the Solicitors Act 1974) in the course of providing advocacy services or litigation services;

(c) a solicitor (within the meaning of the Solicitors (Scotland) Act 1980) in the course of providing advocacy services or litigation services;

(d) a solicitor (within the meaning of the Solicitors (Northern Ireland) Order 1976) in the course of providing advocacy services or litigation services;

(e) a relevant person (other than a person falling within sub-paragraph (a) to (d)) in the course of providing advocacy services or litigation services.

(2) In paragraph (1)—

"advocacy services" means any services which it would be reasonable to expect a person who is exercising, or contemplating exercising, a right of audience in relation to any proceedings, or contemplated proceedings, to provide for the purpose of those proceedings or contemplated proceedings;

"litigation services" means any services which it would be reasonable to expect a person who is exercising, or contemplating exercising, a right to conduct litigation in relation to any proceedings, or contemplated proceedings, to provide for the purpose of those proceedings or contemplated proceedings;

"relevant person" means a person who, for the purposes of the Legal Services Act 2007, is an authorised person in relation to an activity which constitutes the exercise of a right of audience or the conduct of litigation (within the meaning of that Act).]

NOTES

Originally inserted as noted to art 36A at **[8.71]**.

Subsequently substituted by the Financial Services and Markets Act 2000 (Miscellaneous Provisions) Order 2015, SI 2015/853, art 3(1), (2), as from 24 March 2015.

[8.77]

[36FA Activities carried on by registered social landlords

(1) There are excluded from article 36A (credit broking) activities carried on by a registered social landlord, for which the registered social landlord does not receive a fee.

(2) The exclusion in paragraph (1) only applies to activities relating to the introduction of an individual who wishes to enter into a credit agreement, to—

(a) a credit union;

(b) a community benefit society;

(c) a community interest company limited by guarantee;

(d) a registered charity, or a subsidiary of a registered charity;

(e) a subsidiary of a registered social landlord.

(3) For the purposes of this article, "fee" includes pecuniary consideration or any other form of financial consideration.

(4) In this article—

"community benefit society" means a registered society within the meaning of the Co-operative and Community Benefit Societies Act 2014 or a registered society within the meaning of the Co-operative and Community Benefit Societies Act (Northern Ireland) 1969;

"community interest company limited by guarantee" means a community interest company limited by guarantee within the meaning of section 26 of the Companies (Audit, Investigations and Community Enterprise) Act 2004;

"credit union" means a credit union within the meaning of—

(a) the Credit Unions Act 1979;

(b) the Credit Unions (Northern Ireland) Order 1985;

"registered charity" means

(a) in England and Wales, a charity registered under section 30(1) of the Charities Act 2011;

(b) in Scotland, a charity registered within the meaning of section 13(1) of the Charities and Trustee Investment (Scotland) Act 2005

(c) in Northern Ireland, a charity registered under section 16(2) of the Charities Act (Northern Ireland) 2008;

"registered social landlord" means—

(a) in England, a private registered provider within the meaning of section 80(3) of the Housing and Regeneration Act 2008;

(b) in Wales, a registered social landlord within the meaning of Part 1 of the Housing Act 1996;

(c) in Scotland, a registered social landlord within the meaning of the Housing (Scotland) Act 2010;

(d) in Northern Ireland, a housing association within the meaning of Part 2 of the Housing (Northern Ireland) Order 1992;

"subsidiary" means a subsidiary as defined by section 1159 of the Companies Act 2006.]

NOTES

Commencement: 23 July 2019.

Inserted by the Financial Services and Markets Act 2000 (Regulated Activities) (Amendment) Order 2019, SI 2019/1067, art 2, as from 23 July 2019.

[8.78]

[36G [Other exclusions]

Article 36A is also subject to [the exclusions in articles . . . 72G (local authorities) and 72I (registered consumer buy-to-let mortgage firms)].]

NOTES

Inserted as noted to art 36A at **[8.71]**.

Article heading substituted by the Financial Services and Markets Act 2000 (Regulated Activities) (Amendment) Order 2014, SI 2014/366, art 2(1), (7), (8), as from 1 April 2014.

Other words in square brackets substituted by the Mortgage Credit Directive Order 2015, SI 2015/910, Sch 1, Pt 2, para 4(1), (8), as from 21 March 2016.

The words omitted were revoked by the Electronic Commerce and Solvency 2 (Amendment etc) (EU Exit) Regulations 2019, SI 2019/1361, reg 5(1), (3), as from IP completion day (as defined in the European Union (Withdrawal Agreement) Act 2020, s 39) (for transitional provisions, see the note in relation to art 72A of this Order *post*).

[CHAPTER 6B OPERATING AN ELECTRONIC SYSTEM IN RELATION TO LENDING

The Activity

[8.79]

36H Operating an electronic system in relation to lending

(1) Where the [conditions in paragraphs (2), (2A) and (2C) are] satisfied, operating an electronic system which enables the operator ("A") to facilitate persons ("B" and "C") becoming the lender and borrower under an article 36H agreement is a specified kind of activity.

(2) The condition [in this paragraph] is that the system operated by A is capable of determining which agreements should be made available to each of B and C (whether in accordance with general instructions provided to A by B or C or otherwise).

[(2A) The condition in this paragraph is that A, or another person ("X") acting under an arrangement with A or at A's direction, undertakes to—

(a) receive payments in respect of [either interest or capital or both] due under the article 36H agreement from C, and

(b) make payments in respect of [either interest or capital or both] due under the article 36H agreement to B.

(2B) For the purposes of paragraph (2A)—

(a) an agreement by A to appoint X to perform the activities in that paragraph is to be treated as an undertaking by A within the meaning of that paragraph;

(b) it is immaterial that—

(i) payments may be subject to conditions;

(ii) A, or X, may be entitled to retain a portion or the entirety of any payment received from C.

(2C) The condition in this paragraph is that A, or another person ("X") acting under an arrangement with A or at A's direction, undertakes to perform, or A undertakes to appoint or direct another person to perform either or both of the following activities—

(a) taking steps to procure the payment of a debt under the article 36H agreement;

(b) exercising or enforcing rights under the article 36H agreement on behalf of B.]

[(2D) Where A carries on an activity of the kind specified in paragraph (1), it is a specified kind of activity for A to operate an electronic system where—

(a) that system enables A to facilitate a person ("B") assuming the rights of the lender under an article 36H agreement by assignment or operation of law, and

(b) the conditions in paragraphs (2), (2A) and (2C) are satisfied where C is the borrower under the agreement in sub-paragraph (a).]

(3) The following are specified kinds of activities if carried on by A in the course of, or in connection with, the carrying on by A of the activity specified by paragraph (1) [or (2D)]—

(a) presenting or offering article 36H agreements to [either B or C] with a view to B becoming the lender under the article 36H agreement [or] C becoming the borrower under the article 36H agreement,

(b) furnishing information relevant to the financial standing of a person ("Y") with a view to assisting in the determination as to whether another person should—

(i) enter into, as the lender, an article 36H agreement with Y, or

(ii) assume the rights of the lender under an article 36H agreement under which Y is the borrower,

(c) taking steps to procure the payment of a debt due under an article 36H agreement,

(d) [taking steps to perform duties, or exercise or enforce] rights under an article 36H agreement on behalf of the lender,

(e) [taking steps with a view to] ascertaining whether a credit information agency (within the meaning given by article 89A(6)) holds information relevant to the financial standing of an individual or relevant person,

(f) [taking steps with a view to] ascertaining the contents of such information,

(g) [taking steps with a view to] securing the correction of, the omission of anything from, or the making of any other kind of modification of, such information, . . .

(h) [taking steps with a view to] securing that a credit information agency which holds such information—

(i) stops holding the information, or

(ii) does not provide it to any other person[, or

(i) giving advice in relation to the taking of any of the steps in sub-paragraphs (e) to (h)].

[(4) [Subject to article 60C(4C),] an "article 36H agreement" is an agreement by which one person provides another person with credit and in relation to which—

(a) the condition in paragraph (4A) is satisfied, and
(b) the condition in either paragraph (5) or (6) is satisfied, or was satisfied at the time the agreement was entered into.

(4A) The condition in this paragraph is that A does not provide credit, assume the rights (by assignment or operation of law) of a person who provided credit, or receive credit under the agreement.]

(5) The condition in this paragraph is that the lender is an individual or relevant person.

(6) The condition in this paragraph is that the borrower is an individual or relevant person and—

(a) the lender provides the borrower with credit less than or equal to £25,000, or
(b) the agreement is not entered into by the borrower wholly or predominantly for the purposes of a business carried on, or intended to be carried on, by the borrower.

(7) Paragraphs (5) and (6) of article 60C (exempt agreements: exemptions relating to the nature of the agreement) apply for the purposes of paragraph (6)(b).

(8) It is immaterial for the purposes of this article whether the lender is carrying on a regulated activity.

[(9) In this article—

"assignment", in relation to Scotland, means assignation;

"borrower" means a person who receives credit under an article 36H agreement or a person to whom the rights and duties of a borrower under such an agreement have passed by assignment or operation of law;

"credit" has the meaning given by article 60L;

"lender" means—

(a) a person providing credit under an article 36H agreement, or
(b) a person who by assignment or operation of law has assumed the rights of a person who provided credit under such an agreement;

"relevant person" means—

(a) a partnership consisting of two or three persons not all of whom are bodies corporate, or
(b) an unincorporated body of persons which does not consist entirely of bodies corporate and is not a partnership.]

[(10) For the purposes of the application of section 22(1) of the Act (regulated activities) to an activity of a kind specified by this article, article 88D (credit agreement), and article 73 (investments: general) in so far as it relates to that article, [have] effect as if the reference to a credit agreement in article 88D includes a reference to an article 36H agreement.]]

NOTES

Chapter 6B (originally arts 36H, 36I, 36J) was inserted by the Financial Services and Markets Act 2000 (Regulated Activities) (Amendment) (No 2) Order 2013, SI 2013/1881, arts 2, 4, as from 1 April 2014.

Words in square brackets in para (1) substituted, words in square brackets in para (2) inserted, and paras (2A)–(2C) and (10) inserted and added respectively, by the Financial Services and Markets Act 2000 (Regulated Activities) (Amendment) Order 2014, SI 2014/366, art 2(1), (9), as from 1 April 2014.

Words in square brackets in para (2A) substituted, para (2D) inserted, words in square brackets in para (3) substituted or inserted, paras (4), (4A) substituted (for the original para (4)), para (9) substituted, and word in square brackets in para (10) substituted, by the Financial Services and Markets Act 2000 (Regulated Activities) (Amendment) Order 2016, SI 2016/392, art 2(1), (5), as from 17 March 2016.

The words in square brackets at the beginning of para (4) were inserted by the Financial Services and Markets Act 2000 (Regulated Activities) (Coronavirus) (Amendment) Order 2020, SI 2020/480, art 2(1), (2), as from 4 May 2020 (for transitional provisions, see the note relating to the 2020 Order on art 60C at **[8.143]**.)

[Exclusion

36I (*Article 36I (Information society services) was originally inserted as noted to art 36H at* **[8.79]**. *Subsequently revoked by the Electronic Commerce and Solvency 2 (Amendment etc) (EU Exit) Regulations 2019, SI 2019/1361, reg 5(1), (3), as from IP completion day (as defined in the European Union (Withdrawal Agreement) Act 2020, s 39) (for transitional provisions see the note in relation to art 72A of this Order post).*)

[8.80]

[36IA Activities in relation to debentures and bonds

There is excluded from article 36H (operating an electronic system in relation to lending) any activity of a kind specified by article 14 (dealing in investments as principal), 25 (arranging deals in investments), 37 (managing investments) or 53 (advising on investments).]

NOTES

Inserted by the Financial Services and Markets Act 2000 (Regulated Activities) (Amendment) Order 2014, SI 2014/366, art 2(1), (10), as from 1 April 2014 (note that the 2014 Order came into force on 14 February 2014 for the purpose of the FCA making rules, giving guidance etc, and came into force on 1 April 2014, immediately after SI 2013/1881 (and SI 2013/1882) come into force, in so far as not already in force).

[Supplemental

[8.81]

36J Meaning of "consumer"

(1) For the purposes of sections 1G, 404E and 425A of the Act (meaning of "consumer"), a person ("C") is only to be regarded as a person who uses, may use, has, may have used or has or may have contemplated using, services provided by authorised persons in carrying on a regulated activity of the kind specified by article 36H or article 64 in so far as relevant to that activity if—

(a) C is, may be, has been or may have been the lender under a relevant agreement and is an individual or relevant person, or

(b) C is, may be, has been or may have been the borrower under a relevant agreement, C is an individual or relevant person and one of the conditions in paragraph (2) is satisfied, or

(c) C meets the following conditions—

(i) C is, was or would be the lender under a relevant agreement, and

(ii) C is not, was not or would not be, as a result, carrying on a regulated activity.

(2) The conditions in this paragraph are that—

(a) the lender provides, provided or would provide the borrower with credit (within the meaning given by article 60L) less than or equal to £25,000, or

(b) the agreement is not, was not or would not be entered into by the borrower wholly or predominantly for the purposes of a business carried on, or intended to be carried on, by the borrower.

(3) Paragraphs (5) and (6) of article 60C (exempt agreements: exemptions relating to the nature of the agreement) apply for the purposes of paragraph (2)(b).

(4) In paragraph (1)—

"relevant agreement" means an agreement between one person ("the borrower") and another person ("the lender") by which the lender provides the borrower with credit (within the meaning given by article 60L);

"relevant person" has the meaning given in article 36H.]

NOTES

Inserted as noted to art 36H at **[8.79]**.

CHAPTER VII MANAGING INVESTMENTS

The activity

[8.82]

37 Managing investments

Managing assets belonging to another person, in circumstances involving the exercise of discretion, is a specified kind of activity if—

(a) the assets consist of or include any investment which is a security[, structured deposit] or a contractually based investment; or

(b) the arrangements for their management are such that the assets may consist of or include such investments, and either the assets have at any time since 29th April 1988 done so, or the arrangements have at any time (whether before or after that date) been held out as arrangements under which the assets would do so.

NOTES

Words in square brackets inserted by the Financial Services and Markets Act 2000 (Regulated Activities) (Amendment) Order 2017, SI 2017/488, art 4(3), as from 1 April 2017 (for the purposes of (i) enabling applications to be made for a Part 4A permission, for a variation of a Part 4A permission or for an approval under FSMA 2000, s 59, or (ii) enabling such applications to be determined, in relation to any specified activity or any specified investment amended or inserted by the 2017 Order), and as from 3 January 2018 (otherwise).

Exclusions

[8.83]

38 Attorneys

[(1)] A person does not carry on an activity of the kind specified by article 37 if—

(a) he is a person appointed to manage the assets in question under a power of attorney; and

(b) all routine or day-to-day decisions, so far as relating to investments of a kind mentioned in article 37(a), are taken on behalf of that person by—

(i) an authorised person with permission to carry on activities of the kind specified by article 37; . . .

(ii) a person who is an exempt person in relation to activities of that kind[; or

(iii) an overseas person.]

[(2) This article is subject to article 4(4).]

NOTES

Para (1) numbered as such, and para (2) added, by the Financial Services and Markets Act 2000 (Regulated Activities) (Amendment No 3) Order 2006, SI 2006/3384, arts 2, 17, as from 1 April 2007 (for the purposes of enabling applications to be made for (i) a Part IV permission, (ii) a variation of a Part IV permission, and (iii) the Authority's approval under s 59 of the 2000 Act, in relation to an activity of the kind specified by art 25D of this Order, or in relation to an investment of the kind specified by arts 83, 84 or 85 of this Order), and as from 1 November 2007 (otherwise). Note that the Queen's Printer's copy of SI 2006/3384 does not actually specify that the words "This article is subject to article 4(4)" should be numbered as paragraph (2) even though it does provide that the original text should be numbered as paragraph (1). It is assumed that this is an error.

Word omitted from sub-para (1)(b)(i) revoked, and sub-para (1)(b)(iii) and the word immediately preceding it added, by the Financial Services and Markets Act 2000 (Regulated Activities) (Amendment) Order 2001, SI 2001/3544, arts 2, 6, as from 1 December 2001.

[8.84]

39 Other exclusions

Article 37 is also subject to the exclusions in articles 66 (trustees etc), 68 (sale of goods and supply of services)[, 69 (groups and joint enterprises)] . . . [, 72AA (managers of [UK UCITS] and AIFs)][, 72C (provision of information about contracts of insurance on an incidental basis) and 72H (insolvency practitioners)].

NOTES

Words in first pair of square brackets substituted by the Financial Services and Markets Act 2000 (Regulated Activities) (Amendment) (No 2) Order 2002, SI 2002/1776, art 3(1), (7), as from 21 August 2002.

The words omitted were revoked by the Electronic Commerce and Solvency 2 (Amendment etc) (EU Exit) Regulations 2019, SI 2019/1361, reg 5(1), (3), as from IP completion day (as defined in the European Union (Withdrawal Agreement) Act 2020, s 39) (for transitional provisions, see the note in relation to art 72A of this Order *post*).

Words in second pair of square brackets substituted by the Alternative Investment Fund Managers Regulations 2013, SI 2013/1773, reg 81, Sch 2, Part 1, para 1(1), (9), as from 22 July 2013.

The words "UK UCITS" in square brackets were substituted by the Financial Services and Markets Act 2000 (Amendment) (EU Exit) Regulations 2019, SI 2019/632, regs 120, 148(2), as from IP completion day (as defined in the European Union (Withdrawal Agreement) Act 2020, s 39).

Words in fourth pair of square brackets substituted by the Financial Services and Markets Act 2000 (Regulated Activities) (Amendment) Order 2014, SI 2014/366, art 2(1), (11), as from 1 April 2014.

[CHAPTER VIIA ASSISTING IN THE ADMINISTRATION AND PERFORMANCE OF A CONTRACT OF INSURANCE

The Activity

[8.85]

39A Assisting in the administration and performance of a contract of insurance

Assisting in the administration and performance of a contract of insurance is a specified kind of activity.]

NOTES

Chapter VIIA (arts 39A–39C) was inserted by the Financial Services and Markets Act 2000 (Regulated Activities) (Amendment) (No 2) Order 2003, SI 2003/1476, art 7, as from 31 October 2004 (in so far as relating to contracts of long-term care insurance), and as from 14 January 2005 (otherwise).

[Exclusions

[8.86]

39B Claims management on behalf of an insurer etc

(1) A person does not carry on an activity of the kind specified by article 39A if he acts in the course of carrying on the activity of—

(a) expert appraisal;
(b) loss adjusting on behalf of a relevant insurer; or
(c) managing claims on behalf of a relevant insurer,

and that activity is carried on in the course of carrying on any profession or business.

(2) In this article—

(a) "relevant insurer" means—
  (i) a person who has [Part 4A] permission to carry on an activity of the kind specified by article 10;
  (ii) a person to whom the general prohibition does not apply by virtue of section 316(1)(a) of the Act (members of the Society of Lloyd's);
  (iii) . . . or
  (iv) a relevant reinsurer;
(b) "relevant reinsurer" means a person whose main business consists of accepting risks ceded by—
  (i) a person falling within sub-paragraph (i), (ii) or (iii) of the definition of "relevant insurer"; . . .
  [(ii) . . . or
  (iii) a person established outside the United Kingdom . . . who carries on an activity of the kind specified by article 10 by way of business].]

NOTES

Inserted as noted to art 39A at **[8.85]**.

Para (2): words in square brackets in sub-para (a)(i) substituted by the Financial Services Act 2012 (Consequential Amendments and Transitional Provisions) Order 2013, SI 2013/472, art 4, as from 1 April 2013. Word omitted from sub-para (b)(i) revoked, and sub-paras (b)(ii), (iii) substituted (for the original sub-para (b)(ii)) by the Financial Services and Markets Act 2000 (Reinsurance Directive) Order 2007, SI 2007/3254, reg 2, as from 10 December 2007. All other words omitted were revoked by the EEA Passport Rights (Amendment, etc, and Transitional Provisions) (EU Exit) Regulations 2018, SI 2018/1149, reg 3, Schedule, Pt 3, para 49(1), (4), as from IP completion day (as defined in the European Union (Withdrawal Agreement) Act 2020, s 39).

[8.87]

[39C Other exclusions

Article 39A is also subject to the exclusions in articles 66 (trustees etc), 67 (profession or non-investment business) . . . , 72B (activities carried on by a provider of relevant goods or services), 72C (provision of information about contracts of insurance on an incidental basis)[, article 72AA (managers of [UK UCITS] and AIFs)[, 72D (large risks contracts where risk situated [outside the United Kingdom]), 72G (local authorities) and 72H (insolvency practitioners)]].]

NOTES

Inserted as noted to art 39A at **[8.85]**.

The words omitted were revoked by the Electronic Commerce and Solvency 2 (Amendment etc) (EU Exit) Regulations 2019, SI 2019/1361, reg 5(1), (3), as from IP completion day (as defined in the European Union (Withdrawal Agreement) Act 2020, s 39) (for transitional provisions, see the note in relation to art 72A of this Order *post*).

Words in first (outer) pair of square brackets substituted by the Alternative Investment Fund Managers Regulations 2013, SI 2013/1773, reg 81, Sch 2, Part 1, para 1(1), (7), as from 22 July 2013.

The words "UK UCITS" and "outside the United Kingdom" in square brackets were substituted by the Financial Services and Markets Act 2000 (Amendment) (EU Exit) Regulations 2019, SI 2019/632, regs 120, 148(2), 149(5), as from IP completion day (as defined in the European Union (Withdrawal Agreement) Act 2020, s 39).

The words in square brackets beginning ", 72D" were substituted by the Financial Services and Markets Act 2000 (Regulated Activities) (Amendment) Order 2014, SI 2014/366, art 2(1), (12), as from 1 April 2014.

[CHAPTER 7B ACTIVITIES IN RELATION TO DEBT

The Activities

[8.88]

39D Debt adjusting

(1) When carried on in relation to debts due under a credit agreement—

(a) negotiating with the lender, on behalf of the borrower, terms for the discharge of a debt,

(b) taking over, in return for payments by the borrower, that person's obligation to discharge a debt, or

(c) any similar activity concerned with the liquidation of a debt,

is a specified kind of activity.

(2) When carried on in relation to debts due under a consumer hire agreement—

(a) negotiating with the owner, on behalf of the hirer, terms for the discharge of a debt,

(b) taking over, in return for payments by the hirer, that person's obligation to discharge a debt, or

(c) any similar activity concerned with the liquidation of a debt,

is a specified kind of activity.]

NOTES

Chapter 7B (originally arts 39D–39K, 39L, 39M) was inserted by the Financial Services and Markets Act 2000 (Regulated Activities) (Amendment) (No 2) Order 2013, SI 2013/1881, arts 2, 5, as from 1 April 2014.

[8.89]

[39E Debt-counselling

(1) Giving advice to a borrower about the liquidation of a debt due under a credit agreement is a specified kind of activity.

(2) Giving advice to a hirer about the liquidation of a debt due under a consumer hire agreement is a specified kind of activity.]

NOTES

Inserted as noted to art 39D at **[8.88]**.

[8.90]

[39F Debt-collecting

(1) Taking steps to procure the payment of a debt due under a credit agreement or a relevant article 36H agreement is a specified kind of activity.

(2) Taking steps to procure the payment of a debt due under a consumer hire agreement is a specified kind of activity.

(3) Paragraph (1) does not apply in so far as the activity is an activity of the kind specified by article 36H (operating an electronic system in relation to lending).

(4) In this article, "relevant article 36H agreement" means an article 36H agreement (within the meaning of article 36H) which has been entered into with the facilitation of an authorised person with permission to carry on a regulated activity of the kind specified by that article.]

NOTES

Inserted as noted to art 39D at **[8.88]**.

Transitional provisions: see the note to art 60C at **[8.143]**.

[8.91]

[39G Debt administration

(1) Subject to paragraph (3), taking steps—

(a) to perform duties under a credit agreement or relevant article 36H agreement on behalf of the lender, or

(b) to exercise or enforce rights under such an agreement on behalf of the lender,

is a specified kind of activity

(2) Subject to paragraph (3), taking steps—

(a) to perform duties under a consumer hire agreement on behalf of the owner, or

(b) to exercise or enforce rights under such an agreement on behalf of the owner,

is a specified kind of activity.

(3) Paragraphs (1) and (2) do not apply in so far as the activity is an activity of the kind specified by article 36H (operating an electronic system in relation to lending) or article 39F (debt-collecting).

(4) In this article, "relevant article 36H agreement" means an article 36H agreement (within the meaning of article 36H) which has been entered into with the facilitation of an authorised person with permission to carry on a regulated activity of the kind specified by that article.]

NOTES

Inserted as noted to art 39D at **[8.88]**.

[Exclusions

[8.92]

39H Activities where person has a connection to the agreement

(1) There are excluded from articles 39D(1), 39E(1) and 39F(1) activities carried on by a person who is—

(a) the lender under the agreement,

(b) the supplier in relation to that agreement,

(c) a person carrying on an activity of the kind specified by article 36A by way of business and who has acquired the business of the person who was the supplier in relation to the agreement, or

(d) a person who would be carrying on an activity of the kind specified by article 36A by way of business but for the exclusion in article 36B where the agreement was made in consequence of an introduction (by that person or another person) to which article 36B applies.

[(1A) In so far as it applies to article 39F(1), the exclusion in paragraph (1)(a) does not apply to a lender under a credit agreement which is an exempt agreement by virtue of article 60C(4A).]

(2) There are excluded from articles 39D(2), 39E(2) and 39F(2) activities carried on by a person who is—

(a) the owner under the consumer hire agreement, or

(b) a person who would be carrying on an activity of the kind specified by article 36A by way of business but for the exclusion in article 36B where the agreement was made in consequence of an introduction (by that person or another person) to which article 36B applies.

(3) There is excluded from article 39G(1) steps taken under or in relation to an agreement [by] a person who is, in relation to that agreement, a person falling within paragraph (1)(a) to (d).

(4) There is excluded from article 39G(2) steps taken under or in relation to a consumer hire agreement [by] a person who is, in relation to that agreement, a person falling within paragraph (2)(a) or (b).

(5) In paragraph (1), "supplier", in relation to an agreement, means—

(a) a person, other than the lender, whose transaction with the borrower is, or is to be, financed by the agreement, or

(b) a person to whom the rights and duties of a person falling within sub-paragraph (a) have been passed by assignment or operation of law.]

NOTES

Inserted as noted to art 39D at **[8.88]**.

Para (1A): inserted by the Financial Services and Markets Act 2000 (Regulated Activities) (Coronavirus) (Amendment) Order 2020, SI 2020/480, art 2(1), (3), as from 4 May 2020 (for transitional provisions, see the note relating to the 2020 Order on art 60C at **[8.143]**).

Paras (3), (4): words in square brackets substituted by the Financial Services and Markets Act 2000 (Regulated Activities) (Amendment) Order 2014, SI 2014/366, art 2(1), (13), as from 1 April 2014.

[8.93]

[39I Activities carried on by certain energy suppliers

(1) There are excluded from articles 39D, 39E, 39F and 39G activities carried on by a relevant energy supplier acting in that capacity in relation to debts due under a green deal plan associated with the supplier.

(2) A green deal plan is associated with a supplier if the payments under the plan are to be made to the supplier.

(3) In this article—

(a) . . .

(b) "relevant energy supplier" has the meaning given in regulations made for the purpose of section 2(9) of [the Energy Act 2011].]

NOTES

Inserted as noted to art 39D at **[8.88]**.

Para (3): sub-para (a) revoked, and words in square brackets in sub-para (b) substituted, by the Financial Services and Markets Act 2000 (Regulated Activities) (Green Deal) (Amendment) Order 2014, SI 2014/1850, arts 2, 4, as from 15 July 2014.

[8.94]

[39J Activities carried on in relation to a relevant agreement in relation to land

There [is] excluded from articles 39D, 39E, 39F and 39G [any activity that relates] to a regulated mortgage contract or a regulated home purchase plan [to the extent that the activity constitutes an activity of the kind specified by a provision of Part 2 of this Order other than articles 39D, 39E, 39F and 39G, where entering into that contract as lender constitutes an activity of the kind specified by article 61 or entering into that plan as home purchase provider constitutes an activity of the kind under article 63F].]

NOTES

Inserted as noted to art 39D at **[8.88]**.

Words in first and second pairs of square brackets substituted, and words in third pair of square brackets inserted, by the Financial Services and Markets Act 2000 (Regulated Activities) (Amendment) Order 2014, SI 2014/366, art 2(1), (14), as from 1 April 2014.

[8.95]

[39K Activities carried on by members of the legal profession etc

(1) There are excluded from articles 39D, 39E, 39F and 39G activities carried on by—

(a) a barrister or advocate acting in that capacity;

(b) a solicitor (within the meaning of the Solicitors Act 1974) in the course of providing advocacy services or litigation services;

(c) a solicitor (within the meaning of the Solicitors (Scotland) Act 1980) in the course of providing advocacy services or litigation services;

(d) a solicitor (within the meaning of the Solicitors (Northern Ireland) Order 1976) in the course of providing advocacy services or litigation services;

(e) a relevant person (other than a person falling within sub-paragraph (a) to (d)) in the course of providing advocacy services or litigation services.

(2) In paragraph (1)—

"advocacy services" means any services which it would be reasonable to expect a person who is exercising, or contemplating exercising, a right of audience in relation to any proceedings, or contemplated proceedings, to provide for the purpose of those proceedings or contemplated proceedings;

"litigation services" means any services which it would be reasonable to expect a person who is exercising, or contemplating exercising, a right to conduct litigation in relation to any proceedings, or contemplated proceedings, to provide for the purpose of those proceedings or contemplated proceedings;

"relevant person" means a person who, for the purposes of the Legal Services Act 2007, is an authorised person in relation to an activity which constitutes the exercise of a right of audience or the conduct of litigation (within the meaning of that Act).]

NOTES

Originally inserted as noted to art 39D at **[8.88]**.

Subsequently substituted by the Financial Services and Markets Act 2000 (Miscellaneous Provisions) Order 2015, SI 2015/853, art 3(1), (3), as from 24 March 2015.

[8.96]

[39KA Activities carried on by reason of providing pensions guidance . . .

(1) There are excluded from article 39E activities carried on by reason of providing pensions guidance . . .

[(2) For the purposes of paragraph (1), pensions guidance means—

(a) information or guidance provided by the Money and Pensions Service in carrying out its pensions guidance function (see section 3 of the Financial Guidance and Claims Act 2018);

(b) information or guidance provided by another person with whom arrangements under section 5(1), (2) or (3) of the Financial Guidance and Claims Act 2018 are made to carry out the Money and Pensions Service's pensions guidance function.]

NOTES

Inserted by the Financial Services and Markets Act 2000 (Regulated Activities) (Amendment) (Pensions Guidance Exclusions) Order 2015, SI 2015/489, art 2(1), (4), as from 26 March 2015.

Words omitted revoked, and para (2) substituted, by the Financial Services and Markets Act 2000 (Regulated Activities) (Amendment) (No 2) Order 2022, SI 2022/726, art 2(4), as from 21 July 2022.

[8.97]

[39L [Other exclusions]

Articles 39D, 39E, 39F and 39G are also subject to the [exclusions] in . . . [article 72G (local authorities) and article 72H (insolvency practitioners)].]

NOTES

Inserted as noted to art 39D at **[8.88]**.

Article heading and word in first pair of square brackets substituted, and words in second pair of square brackets inserted, by the Financial Services and Markets Act 2000 (Regulated Activities) (Amendment) Order 2014, SI 2014/366, art 2(1), (15), (16), as from 1 April 2014.

The words omitted were revoked by the Electronic Commerce and Solvency 2 (Amendment etc) (EU Exit) Regulations 2019, SI 2019/1361, reg 5(1), (3), as from IP completion day (as defined in the European Union (Withdrawal Agreement) Act 2020, s 39) (for transitional provisions, see the note in relation to art 72A of this Order *post*).

[Supplemental

[8.98]

39M Meaning of "consumer" etc

(1) For the purposes of sections 1G, 404E and 425A of the Act (meaning of "consumer"), in so far as those provisions relate to a person ("A") carrying on a regulated activity of the kind specified by article 39F (debt-collecting) or 39G (debt administration), or article 64 (agreeing to carry on specified kinds of activity) so far as relevant to that activity the following are to be treated as a "consumer"—

(a) the borrower under the agreement or the hirer under the consumer hire agreement;

(b) someone who has been the borrower or hirer under that agreement;

(c) a person who is treated by A as a person falling within sub-paragraph (a) or (b).

(2) For the purposes of section 328(8) of the Act (meaning of "clients") in so far as that provision relates to a person ("A") carrying on a regulated activity of the kind specified by article 39F or 39G, the following are to be treated as a "client"—

(a) the borrower under the agreement or the hirer under the consumer hire agreement;

(b) someone who has been the borrower or hirer under that agreement;

(c) a person who is treated by A as a person falling within sub-paragraph (a) or (b).

(3) In this article, "borrower" includes (in addition to those persons included in the definition in article 60L)—

(a) any person providing a guarantee or indemnity under the agreement, and

(b) a person to whom the rights and duties of a person falling within sub-paragraph (a) have passed by assignment or operation of law.]

NOTES

Inserted as noted to art 39D at **[8.88]**.

CHAPTER VIII SAFEGUARDING AND ADMINISTERING INVESTMENTS

The activity

[8.99]

40 Safeguarding and administering investments

(1) The activity consisting of both—

(a) the safeguarding of assets belonging to another, and

(b) the administration of those assets,

or arranging for one or more other persons to carry on that activity, is a specified kind of activity if the condition in sub-paragraph (a) or (b) of paragraph (2) is met.

(2) The condition is that—

(a) the assets consist of or include any investment which is a security or a contractually based investment; or

(b) the arrangements for their safeguarding and administration are such that the assets may consist of or include such investments, and either the assets have at any time since 1st June 1997 done so, or the arrangements have at any time (whether before or after that date) been held out as ones under which such investments would be safeguarded and administered.

(3) For the purposes of this article—

(a) it is immaterial that title to the assets safeguarded and administered is held in uncertificated form;

(b) it is immaterial that the assets safeguarded and administered may be transferred to another person, subject to a commitment by the person safeguarding and administering them, or arranging for their safeguarding and administration, that they will be replaced by equivalent assets at some future date or when so requested by the person to whom they belong.

Exclusions

[8.100]

41 Acceptance of responsibility by third party

(1) There are excluded from article 40 any activities which a person carries on pursuant to arrangements which—

(a) are ones under which a qualifying custodian undertakes to the person to whom the assets belong a responsibility in respect of the assets which is no less onerous than the qualifying custodian would have if the qualifying custodian were safeguarding and administering the assets; and

(b) are operated by the qualifying custodian in the course of carrying on in the United Kingdom an activity of the kind specified by article 40.

(2) In paragraph (1), "qualifying custodian" means a person who is—

(a) an authorised person who has permission to carry on an activity of the kind specified by article 40, or

(b) an exempt person acting in the course of a business comprising a regulated activity in relation to which he is exempt.

[8.101]

42 Introduction to qualifying custodians

(1) There are excluded from article 40 any arrangements pursuant to which introductions are made by a person ("P") to a qualifying custodian with a view to the qualifying custodian providing in the United Kingdom a service comprising an activity of the kind specified by article 40, where the qualifying person (or other person who is to safeguard and administer the assets in question) is not connected with P.

(2) For the purposes of paragraph (1)—

(a) "qualifying custodian" has the meaning given by article 41(2); and

(b) a person is connected with P if either he is a member of the same group as P, or P is remunerated by him.

[8.102]

[42A Depositaries of [UK UCITS] and AIFs

A person does not carry on an activity of the kind specified by article 40 if the person carries on the activity in relation to—

(a) [a UK UCITS], and the person has a Part 4A permission to carry on the activity specified in article 51ZB in respect of that UCITS; or

(b) an AIF, and the person has a Part 4A permission to carry on the activity specified in article 51ZD in respect of that AIF.]

NOTES

Inserted by the Alternative Investment Fund Managers Regulations 2013, SI 2013/1773, reg 81, Sch 2, Part 1, para 1(1), (10), as from 22 July 2013.

Words in square brackets substituted by the Financial Services and Markets Act 2000 (Amendment) (EU Exit) Regulations 2019, SI 2019/632, regs 120, 131, as from IP completion day (as defined in the European Union (Withdrawal Agreement) Act 2020, s 39).

[8.103]

43 Activities not constituting administration

The following activities do not constitute the administration of assets for the purposes of article 40—

(a) providing information as to the number of units or the value of any assets safeguarded;

(b) converting currency;

(c) receiving documents relating to an investment solely for the purpose of onward transmission to, from or at the direction of the person to whom the investment belongs.

[8.104]

44 Other exclusions

Article 40 is also subject to the exclusions in articles 66 (trustees etc), 67 (profession or non-investment business), 68 (sale of goods and supply of services), 69 (groups and joint enterprises)[, 71 (employee share schemes)] . . . [, 72AA (managers of [UK UCITS] and AIFs)][, 72C (provisions of information about contracts of insurance on an incidental basis) and 72H (insolvency practitioners)].

NOTES

Words in first pair of square brackets substituted by the Financial Services and Markets Act 2000 (Regulated Activities) (Amendment) (No 2) Order 2002, SI 2002/1776, art 3(1), (8), as from 21 August 2002.

The words omitted were revoked by the Electronic Commerce and Solvency 2 (Amendment etc) (EU Exit) Regulations 2019, SI 2019/1361, reg 5(1), (3), as from IP completion day (as defined in the European Union (Withdrawal Agreement) Act 2020, s 39) (for transitional provisions, see the note in relation to art 72A of this Order *post*).

Words in second pair of square brackets substituted by the Alternative Investment Fund Managers Regulations 2013, SI 2013/1773, reg 81, Sch 2, Part 1, para 1(1), (9), as from 22 July 2013.

The words "UK UCITS" in square brackets were substituted by the Financial Services and Markets Act 2000 (Amendment) (EU Exit) Regulations 2019, SI 2019/632, regs 120, 148(2), as from IP completion day (as defined in the European Union (Withdrawal Agreement) Act 2020, s 39).

Words in final pair of square brackets substituted by the Financial Services and Markets Act 2000 (Regulated Activities) (Amendment) Order 2014, SI 2014/366, art 2(1), (17), as from 1 April 2014.

CHAPTER IX SENDING DEMATERIALISED INSTRUCTIONS

The activities

[8.105]

45 Sending dematerialised instructions

(1) Sending, on behalf of another person, dematerialised instructions relating to a security [or a contractually based investment] is a specified kind of activity, where those instructions are sent by means of a relevant system [within the meaning of the 2001 Regulations].

(2) Causing dematerialised instructions relating to a security [or a contractually based investment] to be sent [on behalf of another person] by means of such a system is also a specified kind of activity where the person causing them to be sent is a system-participant.

(3) In this Chapter—

[(a) "the 2001 Regulations" means the Uncertificated Securities Regulations 2001;]

(b) "dematerialised instruction", . . . "settlement bank" and "system-participant" have the meaning given by regulation 3 of the [2001] Regulations.

NOTES

Para (1): words in first pair of square brackets inserted by the Financial Services and Markets Act 2000 (Regulated Activities) (Amendment) Order 2002, SI 2002/682, art 13(1), as from 27 April 2002. Words in second pair of square brackets substituted by the Uncertificated Securities (Amendment and EU Exit) Regulations 2019, SI 2019/679, reg 6(a), as from 27 March 2019 (for transitional provisions and savings see regs 11, 12 of the 2019 Regulations at **[12.125]** et seq).

Para (2): words in first pair of square brackets inserted by SI 2002/682, art 13(2), as from 27 April 2002. Words in second pair of square brackets inserted by the Financial Services and Markets Act 2000 (Regulated Activities) (Amendment) Order 2001, SI 2001/3544, arts 2, 7, as from 1 December 2001.

Para (3): words in square brackets substituted by SI 2002/682, art 13(3), as from 27 April 2002. The word omitted was revoked by SI 2019/679, reg 6(a), as from 27 March 2019 (for transitional provisions and savings see regs 11, 12 of the 2019 Regulations at **[12.125]** et seq).

Exclusions

[8.106]

46 Instructions on behalf of participating issuers

There is excluded from article 45 the act of sending, or causing to be sent, a dematerialised instruction where the person on whose behalf the instruction is sent or caused to be sent is a participating issuer within the meaning of the [2001] Regulations.

NOTES

Year in square brackets substituted by the Financial Services and Markets Act 2000 (Regulated Activities) (Amendment) Order 2002, SI 2002/682, art 13(4), as from 27 April 2002.

[8.107]

47 Instructions on behalf of settlement banks

There is excluded from article 45 the act of sending, or causing to be sent, a dematerialised instruction where the person on whose behalf the instruction is sent or caused to be sent is a settlement bank in its capacity as such.

[8.108]

48 Instructions in connection with takeover offers

(1) There is excluded from article 45 of the act of sending, or causing to be sent, a dematerialised instruction where the person on whose behalf the instruction is sent or caused to be sent is an offeror making a takeover offer.

(2) In this article—

(a) "offeror" means, in the case of a takeover offer made by two or more persons jointly, the joint offers or any of them;

(b) "takeover offer" means—

(i) an offer to acquire shares (which in this sub-paragraph has the same meaning as in [section 974 of the Companies Act 2006]) in a body corporate incorporated in the United Kingdom which is a takeover offer within the meaning of [Chapter 3 of Part 28] of that Act (or would be such an offer if that Part of that Act applied in relation to any body corporate);

(ii) an offer to acquire all or substantially all the shares, or all the shares of a particular class, in a body corporate incorporated outside the United Kingdom; or

(iii) an offer made to all the holders of shares, or shares of a particular class, in a body corporate to acquire a specified proportion of those shares;

but in determining whether an offer falls within paragraph (ii) there are to be disregarded any shares which the offeror or any associate of his (within the meaning of [section 988 of the Companies Act 2006]) holds or has contracted to acquire; and in determining whether an offer falls within paragraph (iii) the offeror, any such associate and any person whose shares the offeror or any such associate has contracted to acquire is not to be regarded as a holder of shares.

NOTES

Para (2): words in square brackets in sub-para (b) substituted the Companies Act 2006 (Commencement No 2, Consequential Amendments, Transitional Provisions and Savings) Order 2007, SI 2007/1093, art 6(1), Sch 3, para 8, as from 6 April 2007.

[8.109]

49 Instructions in the course of providing a network

There is excluded from article 45 the act of sending, or causing to be sent, a dematerialised instruction as a necessary part of providing a network, the purpose of which is to carry dematerialised instructions which are at all time properly authenticated (within the meaning of the [2001] Regulations).

NOTES

Figure in square brackets substituted by the Financial Services and Markets Act 2000 (Regulated Activities) (Amendment) Order 2002, SI 2002/682, art 13(4), as from 27 April 2002.

[8.110]

50 Other exclusions

Article 45 is also subject to the exclusions in articles 66 (trustees etc)[, 69 (groups and joint enterprises)] . . . [, 72AA (managers of [UK UCITS] and AIFs) and 72H (insolvency practitioners)].

NOTES

Words in first pair of square brackets substituted by the Financial Services and Markets Act 2000 (Regulated Activities) (Amendment) (No 2) Order 2002, SI 2002/1776, art 3(1), (9), as from 21 August 2002.

Words omitted revoked by the Electronic Commerce and Solvency 2 (Amendment etc) (EU Exit) Regulations 2019, SI 2019/1361, reg 5(1), (3), as from IP completion day (as defined in the European Union (Withdrawal Agreement) Act 2020, s 39) (for transitional provisions, see the note in relation to art 72A of this Order *post*).

Words in second pair of square brackets substituted by the Financial Services and Markets Act 2000 (Regulated Activities) (Amendment) Order 2014, SI 2014/366, art 2(1), (18), as from 1 April 2014.

The words "UK UCITS" in square brackets were substituted by the Financial Services and Markets Act 2000 (Amendment) (EU Exit) Regulations 2019, SI 2019/632, regs 120, 148(2), as from IP completion day (as defined in the European Union (Withdrawal Agreement) Act 2020, s 39).

CHAPTER X COLLECTIVE INVESTMENT . . .

NOTES

The word "Schemes" was revoked from the preceding heading by the Alternative Investment Fund Managers Regulations 2013, SI 2013/1773, reg 81, Sch 2, Part 1, para 1(1), (11), as from 22 July 2013.

The activities

[8.111]

[51ZA Managing [a UK UCITS]

(1) Managing a [a UK UCITS] is a specified kind of activity.

[(2) A person manages a UK UCITS when the person carries on collective portfolio management of it.

(2A) In paragraph (2) "collective portfolio management" includes investment management, administration and marketing; and "administration" here means—

- (a) legal and fund management accounting services;
- (b) customer inquiries;
- (c) valuation and pricing (including tax returns);
- (d) regulatory compliance monitoring;
- (e) maintenance of unit-holder register;
- (f) distribution of income;
- (g) unit issues and redemptions;
- (h) contract settlements (including certificate dispatch);
- (i) record keeping.]

(3) If a person manages [a UK UCITS] and also carries on other activities in connection with or for the purposes of the management of that UCITS, such other activities are also included in the activity specified in paragraph (1).]

NOTES

Articles 51ZA–51ZG were substituted (for the original art 51 and the heading that preceded art 51A) by the Alternative Investment Fund Managers Regulations 2013, SI 2013/1773, reg 81, Sch 2, Part 1, para 1(1), (12), as from 22 July 2013.

All amendments to this Article were made by the Financial Services and Markets Act 2000 (Amendment) (EU Exit) Regulations 2019, SI 2019/632, regs 120, 132(1)–(4), as from IP completion day (as defined in the European Union (Withdrawal Agreement) Act 2020, s 39).

[8.112]

[51ZB Acting as trustee or depositary of [a UK UCITS]

(1) Acting as—

- (a) the trustee of an authorised unit trust scheme, or
- (b) the depositary of an open-ended investment company or authorised contractual scheme,

where the scheme or company is [a UK UCITS], is a specified kind of activity.

(2) In paragraph (1), "authorised contractual scheme", "authorised unit trust scheme", "trustee" and "depositary" have the meanings given by section 237 of the Act (other definitions).]

NOTES

Substituted as noted to art 51ZA at **[8.111]**.

Words "a UK UCITS" in square brackets substituted by the Financial Services and Markets Act 2000 (Amendment) (EU Exit) Regulations 2019, SI 2019/632, regs 120, 133(1), as from IP completion day (as defined in the European Union (Withdrawal Agreement) Act 2020, s 39).

[8.113]

[51ZC Managing an AIF

(1) Managing an AIF is a specified kind of activity.

(2) A person manages an AIF when the person performs at least risk management or portfolio management for the AIF.

(3) A person does not manage an AIF if the functions they perform for the AIF have been delegated to it by another person, provided that such other person is not an AIFM that has delegated such functions to the extent that it is a letter-box entity.

(4) Paragraph (5) applies if a person manages an AIF, and also carries on—

(a) one or more of the additional activities listed in paragraph 2 of Annex 1 to the alternative investment fund managers directive (the text of which is set out in Schedule 7) for that AIF; or

(b) one or more other activities in connection with or for the purposes of the management of that AIF.

(5) The additional or other activities are included in the activity specified in paragraph (1).

(6) Any expression used in this article which is not defined in this Order and is used in the alternative investment fund managers directive has the same meaning as in that directive.]

NOTES

Substituted as noted to art 51ZA at **[8.111]**.

[8.114]

[51ZD Acting as trustee or depositary of an AIF

(1) Acting as—

(a) the depositary of an AIF falling within paragraph (2),

(b) the trustee of an authorised unit trust scheme which is an AIF that does not fall within paragraph (2), or

(c) the depositary of an open-ended investment company or authorised contractual scheme which is an AIF that does not fall within paragraph (2),

is a specified kind of activity.

(2) An AIF falls within this paragraph if it is—

(a) an AIF managed by a full-scope UK AIFM;

(b) . . .

(3) In paragraph (1)(a) "depositary" means—

[(a) a person appointed as a depositary by the AIFM in compliance with a requirement imposed by rule 3.11.10, 3.11.12 or 3.11.33 of the Investment Funds sourcebook; or]

(b) an Article 36 custodian as defined in regulation 57(5)(a) of the Alternative Investment Fund Managers Regulations 2013.

(4) In paragraph (1)(b) "authorised unit trust scheme" and "trustee" have the meanings given by section 237 of the Act.

(5) In paragraph (1)(c) "authorised contractual scheme" and "depositary" have the meanings given by section 237 of the Act.

(6) Until 22nd July 2017, an AIF also falls within paragraph (2) if the FCA or an authority in another EEA State has permitted a person with its registered office or a branch in the United Kingdom to be appointed as a depositary of the AIF in accordance with Article 61.5 of the alternative investment fund managers directive.]

NOTES

Substituted as noted to art 51ZA at **[8.111]**.

Para (2): sub-para (b) and the preceding word were revoked by the Financial Services and Markets Act 2000 (Amendment) (EU Exit) Regulations 2019, SI 2019/632, regs 120, 134(1), (2), as from IP completion day (as defined in the European Union (Withdrawal Agreement) Act 2020, s 39).

Para (3): sub-para (a) was substituted by SI 2019/632, regs 120, 134(1), (3), as from IP completion day (as defined in the European Union (Withdrawal Agreement) Act 2020, s 39).

[8.115]

[51ZE Establishing etc a collective investment scheme

Establishing, operating or winding up a collective investment scheme is a specified kind of activity.]

NOTES

Substituted as noted to art 51ZA at **[8.111]**.

Exclusions

[8.116]

[51ZF Persons excluded from managing an AIF

There is excluded from article 51ZC the activity of managing an AIF if the person carrying on the activity is listed or described in Schedule 8].

NOTES

Substituted as noted to art 51ZA at **[8.111]**.

[8.117]

[51ZG Operating a collective investment scheme in relation to [a UK UCITS] or an AIF

(1) A person does not carry on an activity of the kind specified by article 51ZE if the person carries on the activity—

(a) in relation to [a UK UCITS], and—

(i) at the time the person carries on the activity, the UCITS is managed by a person with a Part 4A permission to carry on the activity specified by article 51ZA in respect of that UCITS; or

(ii) no more than the permitted period has passed since the UCITS was managed by a person with such a Part 4A permission; or

(b) in relation to an AIF, and—

(i) at the time the person carries on the activity, the AIF is managed by—

(aa) a person with a Part 4A permission to carry on the activity specified by article 51ZC in respect of that AIF; or

(bb) a person registered as a small registered UK AIFM because the conditions in regulation 10(4) of the Alternative Investment Fund Managers Regulations 2013 are met in respect of that AIF; or

(ii) no more than the permitted period has passed since the AIF was managed by a person with such a Part 4A permission or registration.

(2) In this article "the permitted period" means a period calculated as follows—

(a) subject to sub-paragraphs (b) and (c), the period is 30 days;

(b) if, before the end of the period, the FCA receives notice of the action being taken to appoint a person with a Part 4A permission or registration to manage [the UK UCITS or the AIF], the period is extended by a further 30 days, and may be so extended a second time;

(c) if, before the end of the period calculated in accordance with sub-paragraphs (a) and (b), the FCA receives notice of a proposal in respect of [the UK UCITS or the AIF] for a new manager under section 251(3) of the Act, a new operator under section 261Q(5) of the Act or a new director under regulation 21(1)(e) of the Open-Ended Investment Company Regulations 2001, the period is further extended until the earlier of—

(i) the date on which the FCA gives written notice of its approval to the proposal;

(ii) the date on which the FCA gives a decision notice refusing the proposal; or

(iii) one month after the date on which notice of the proposal was given.]

NOTES

Substituted as noted to art 51ZA at **[8.111]**.

All words in square brackets were substituted by the Financial Services and Markets Act 2000 (Amendment) (EU Exit) Regulations 2019, SI 2019/632, regs 120, 135, as from IP completion day (as defined in the European Union (Withdrawal Agreement) Act 2020, s 39).

[8.118]

[51A [Other exclusions]

[Articles 51ZA, 51ZB, 51ZC, 51ZD, and 51ZE are also] subject to the [exclusions] in [articles] [72AA (managers of [UK UCITS] and AIFs) and 72H (insolvency practitioners)].]

NOTES

Inserted by the Financial Services and Markets Act 2000 (Regulated Activities) (Amendment) (No 2) Order 2002, SI 2002/1776, art 3(1), (10), as from 21 August 2002.

The Article heading was substituted, and the words in square brackets beginning "72AA" were substituted, by the Financial Services and Markets Act 2000 (Regulated Activities) (Amendment) Order 2014, SI 2014/366, art 2(1), (19), (20), as from 1 April 2014.

The words "Articles 51ZA, 51ZB, 51ZC, 51ZD, and 51ZE are also" and "exclusions" in square brackets were substituted, by the Alternative Investment Fund Managers Regulations 2013, SI 2013/1773, reg 81, Sch 2, Part 1, para 1(1), (4), (13), as from 22 July 2013.

The word "articles" in square brackets was substituted by the Electronic Commerce and Solvency 2 (Amendment etc) (EU Exit) Regulations 2019, SI 2019/1361, reg 5(1), (3), as from IP completion day (as defined in the European Union (Withdrawal Agreement) Act 2020, s 39) (for transitional provisions, see the note in relation to art 72A of this Order *post*).

The words "UK UCITS" in square brackets were substituted by the Financial Services and Markets Act 2000 (Amendment) (EU Exit) Regulations 2019, SI 2019/632, regs 120, 148(2), as from IP completion day (as defined in the European Union (Withdrawal Agreement) Act 2020, s 39).

CHAPTER XI . . . PENSION SCHEMES

The activities

[8.119]

[52 Establishing etc a pension scheme

The following are specified kinds of activity—

(a) establishing, operating or winding up a stakeholder pension scheme;

(b) establishing, operating or winding up a personal pension scheme.]

NOTES

The word omitted from the Chapter heading preceding this article was revoked, and this article was substituted, by the Financial Services and Markets Act 2000 (Regulated Activities) (Amendment) Order 2006, SI 2006/1969, art 2(1), (3), (4), as from 1 October 2006 (for the purposes of enabling applications to be made for Part IV permission or for a variation of Part IV permission in relation to the regulated activity specified by art 52(b) of this Order (as so substituted)), and as from 6 April 2007 (otherwise).

[Exclusion

[8.120]

52A [Other exclusions]

Article 52 is subject to the [exclusions] in [articles] [72AA (managers of [UK UCITS] and AIFs) and 72H (insolvency practitioners)].]

NOTES

Inserted by the Financial Services and Markets Act 2000 (Regulated Activities) (Amendment) (No 2) Order 2002, SI 2002/1776, art 3(1), (11), as from 21 August 2002.

The Article heading was substituted, and the words in square brackets beginning "72AA" were substituted, by the Financial Services and Markets Act 2000 (Regulated Activities) (Amendment) Order 2014, SI 2014/366, art 2(1), (21), (22), as from 1 April 2014.

The word "exclusions" in square brackets was substituted by the Alternative Investment Fund Managers Regulations 2013, SI 2013/1773, reg 81, Sch 2, Part 1, para 1(1), (4), as from 22 July 2013.

The word "articles" in square brackets was substituted by the Electronic Commerce and Solvency 2 (Amendment etc) (EU Exit) Regulations 2019, SI 2019/1361, reg 5(1), (3), as from IP completion day (as defined in the European Union (Withdrawal Agreement) Act 2020, s 39) (for transitional provisions, see the note in relation to art 72A of this Order *post*).

The words "UK UCITS" in square brackets were substituted by the Financial Services and Markets Act 2000 (Amendment) (EU Exit) Regulations 2019, SI 2019/632, regs 120, 148(2), as from IP completion day (as defined in the European Union (Withdrawal Agreement) Act 2020, s 39).

[CHAPTER XIA PROVIDING BASIC ADVICE ON STAKEHOLDER PRODUCTS

The Activity

[8.121]

52B Providing basic advice on stakeholder products

(1) Providing basic advice to a retail consumer on a stakeholder product is a specified kind of activity.

(2) For the purposes of paragraph (1), a person ("P") provides basic advice when—

(a) he asks a retail consumer questions to enable him to assess whether a stakeholder product is appropriate for that consumer; and

(b) relying on the information provided by the retail consumer P assesses that a stakeholder product is appropriate for the retail consumer and—

(i) describes that product to that consumer;

(ii) gives a recommendation of that product to that consumer; and

(c) the retail consumer has indicated to P that he has understood the description and the recommendation in sub-paragraph (b).

(3) In this article—

"retail consumer" means any person who is advised by P on the merits of opening or buying a stakeholder product in the course of a business carried on by P and who does not receive the advice in the course of a business carried on by him;

"stakeholder product" means—

(a) an account which qualifies as a stakeholder child trust fund within the meaning given by the Child Trust Funds Regulations 2004;

[(b) rights under a stakeholder pension scheme;]

(c) an investment of a kind specified in regulations made by the Treasury.]

NOTES

Inserted, together with the preceding headings, by the Financial Services and Markets Act 2000 (Regulated Activities) (Amendment) (No 2) Order 2004, SI 2004/2737, arts, 2, 3, as from 6 April 2005.

Para (3): in definition "stakeholder product", para (b) substituted by the Financial Services and Markets Act 2000 (Regulated Activities) (Amendment) Order 2005, SI 2005/593, art 2(3), as from 6 April 2005.

Regulations: the Financial Services and Markets 2000 (Stakeholder Products) Regulations 2004, SI 2004/2738 (which define the term "stakeholder product" for the purposes of this article).

[Exclusion

[8.122]

52C Providing pensions guidance . . .

(1) A person does not carry on an activity of the kind specified in article 52B by reason of providing pensions guidance . . .

[(2) For the purposes of paragraph (1), pensions guidance means—

(a) information or guidance provided by the Money and Pensions Service in carrying out its pensions guidance function (see section 3 of the Financial Guidance and Claims Act 2018);

(b) information or guidance provided by another person with whom arrangements under section 5(1), (2) or (3) of the Financial Guidance and Claims Act 2018 are made to carry out the Money and Pensions Service's pensions guidance function.]

NOTES

Inserted, together with the preceding heading, by the Financial Services and Markets Act 2000 (Regulated Activities) (Amendment) (Pensions Guidance Exclusions) Order 2015, SI 2015/489, art 2(1), (5), as from 26 March 2015.

Words omitted revoked, and para (2) substituted, by the Financial Services and Markets Act 2000 (Regulated Activities) (Amendment) (No 2) Order 2022, SI 2022/726, art 2(5), as from 21 July 2022.

CHAPTER XII ADVISING ON INVESTMENTS

The activity

[8.123]

53 Advising on investments

[(1)] Advising a person is a specified kind of activity if the advice is—

(a) given to the person in his capacity as an investor or potential investor, or in his capacity as agent for an investor or a potential investor; and

(b) advice on the merits of his doing any of the following (whether as principal or agent)—

(i) buying, selling, subscribing for[, exchanging, redeeming, holding] or underwriting a particular investment which is a security[, structured deposit] or a [relevant investment], or

(ii) exercising [or not exercising] any right conferred by such an investment to buy, sell, subscribe for[, exchange or redeem] such an investment.

[(1A) Paragraph (1) does not apply to a person who is appropriately authorised except to the extent that they are providing a personal recommendation.

(1B) A person is appropriately authorised when they are authorised for the purposes of the Act to carry on an activity of a kind specified by a provision of this Order which is not the activity specified by paragraph (1) and is not the activity of agreeing to carry on the activity specified by paragraph (1).

(1C) Subject to paragraph (1D), a personal recommendation is a recommendation—

(a) made to a person in their capacity as an investor or potential investor, or in their capacity as agent for an investor or a potential investor;

(b) which constitutes a recommendation to them to do any of the following (whether as principal or agent)—

(i) buy, sell, subscribe for, exchange, redeem, hold or underwrite a particular investment which is a security[, structured deposit] or a relevant investment; or

(ii) exercise or not exercise any right conferred by such an investment to buy, sell, subscribe for, exchange or redeem such an investment; and

(c) that is—

(i) presented as suitable for the person to whom it is made; or

(ii) based on a consideration of the circumstances of that person.

(1D) A recommendation is not a personal recommendation if it is issued exclusively to the public.]

[(2) Advising a person is a specified kind of activity if the advice is—

(a) given to the person in that person's capacity as a lender or potential lender under a relevant article 36H agreement, or in that person's capacity as an agent for a lender or potential lender under such an agreement; and

(b) advice on the merits of that person doing any of the following (whether as principal or agent)—

(i) entering into a relevant article 36H agreement as a lender or assuming the rights of a lender under such an agreement by assignment or operation of law,

(ii) providing instructions to an operator with a view to entering into a relevant article 36H agreement as a lender or assuming the rights of a lender under such an agreement by assignment or operation of law, where the instructions involve—

(aa) accepting particular parameters for the terms of the agreement presented by an operator,

(bb) choosing between options governing the parameters of the terms of the agreement presented by an operator, or

(cc) specifying the parameters of the terms of the agreement by other means,

(iii) enforcing or exercising the lender's rights under a relevant article 36H agreement, or

(iv) assigning rights under a relevant article 36H agreement.

(3) Paragraph (2) does not apply in so far as—

(a) the advice is given in relation to a relevant article 36H agreement which has been facilitated by the person giving the advice, in the course of carrying on an activity of a kind specified by article 36H and is given by—

(i) an authorised person with permission to carry on a regulated activity of the kind specified by article 36H(1) (operating an electronic system in relation to lending),

(ii) an appointed representative in relation to that activity,

(iii) an exempt person in relation to that activity, or

(iv) a person to whom, as a result of Part 20 of the Act, the general prohibition does not apply in relation to that activity;

(b) the advice is given in the course of carrying on an activity of a kind specified by article 39F (debt-collecting) by a person carrying on that activity not in contravention of the general prohibition; or

(c) the advice is given in the course of carrying on an activity of a kind specified by article 39G (debt administration) by a person carrying on that activity not in contravention of the general prohibition.

(4) In this article—

"operator" means a person carrying on an activity of the kind specified by article 36H(1) or (2D), and

"relevant article 36H agreement" means an article 36H agreement (within the meaning of article 36H (operating an electronic system in relation to lending)) which has been, or may be, entered into with the facilitation of a person carrying on an activity of the kind specified by article 36H(1) or (2D).

(5) For the purposes of the application of section 22(1) of the Act (regulated activities) to an activity of a kind specified by paragraph (2) of this article, article 88D (credit agreement), and article 73 (investments: general) in so far as it relates to that article, have effect as if the reference to a credit agreement in article 88D includes a reference to a relevant article 36H agreement.]

NOTES

Para (1) numbered as such, and paras (2)–(5) added, by the Financial Services and Markets Act 2000 (Regulated Activities) (Amendment) Order 2016, SI 2016/392, art 2(1), (6), as from 17 March 2016.

Words in first pair and fourth pairs of square brackets in para (1) inserted, and words in final pair of square brackets substituted, by the Financial Services and Markets Act 2000 (Regulated Activities) (Amendment) (No 2) Order 2017, SI 2017/500, art 2(1)–(3), as from 3 January 2018.

Words in second pair of square brackets in para (1) inserted by the Financial Services and Markets Act 2000 (Regulated Activities) (Amendment) Order 2017, SI 2017/488, art 4(4), as from 1 April 2017 (for the purposes of (i) enabling applications to be made for a Part 4A permission, for a variation of a Part 4A permission or for an approval under FSMA 2000, s 59, or (ii) enabling such applications to be determined, in relation to any specified activity or any specified investment amended or inserted by the 2017 Order), and as from 3 January 2018 (otherwise).

Words in third pair of square brackets in para (1) substituted by the Financial Services and Markets Act 2000 (Regulated Activities) (Amendment) (No 2) Order 2003, SI 2003/1476, art 9(1), as from 31 October 2004 (in so far as relating to contracts of long-term care insurance), and as from 14 January 2005 (otherwise).

Paras (1A)–(1D) were inserted by SI 2017/500, art 2(1), (4), as from 3 January 2018. The words in square brackets in sub-para (1C)(b)(i) were inserted by the Financial Services and Markets Act 2000 (Markets in Financial Instruments) Regulations 2017, SI 2017/701, reg 50(2), Sch 3, para 2, as from 3 January 2018.

[8.124]
[53A Advising on regulated mortgage contracts

(1) Advising a person is a specified kind of activity if the advice—
 (a) is given to the person in his capacity as a borrower or potential borrower; and
 (b) is advice on the merits of his doing any of the following—
  (i) entering into a particular regulated mortgage contract, or
  (ii) varying the terms of a regulated mortgage contract [falling within paragraph (1A)] entered into by him . . . in such a way as to vary his obligations under that contract.

[(1A) A regulated mortgage contract falls within this paragraph if—
 (a) the contract was entered into on or after 31st October 2004; or
 (b) the contract—
  (i) was entered into before 31st October 2004; and
  (ii) was a regulated credit agreement immediately before 21st March 2016.]

(2) In this article, "borrower" has the meaning given by article 61(3)(a)(i).]

NOTES

Inserted by the Financial Services and Markets Act 2000 (Regulated Activities) (Amendment) (No 1) Order 2003, SI 2003/1475, art 13, as from 31 October 2004.

Words in square brackets in para (1) inserted, words omitted from that paragraph revoked, and para (1A) inserted, by the Financial Services and Markets Act 2000 (Regulated Activities) (Amendment) Order 2016, SI 2016/392, art 2(1), (7), as from 21 March 2016.

[8.125]
[53B Advising on regulated home reversion plans

Advising a person is a specified kind of activity if the advice—
 (a) is given to the person in his capacity as—
  (i) a reversion seller or potential reversion seller, or
  (ii) a plan provider or potential plan provider; and
 (b) is advice on the merits of his doing either of the following—
  (i) entering into a particular regulated home reversion plan, or
  (ii) varying the terms of a regulated home reversion plan, entered into on or after 6th April 2007 by him, in such a way as to vary his obligations under that plan.]

NOTES

Inserted, together with art 53C, by the Financial Services and Markets Act 2000 (Regulated Activities) (Amendment) (No 2) Order 2006, SI 2006/2383, arts 2, 13, as from 6 November 2006 (for the purposes of enabling applications to be made for (i) a Pt IV permission, or a variation of a Pt IV permission, in relation to activities of the kind specified by arts 25B, 25C, 53B, 53C, 63B or 63F or, so far as relevant to any such activity, art 64 of this Order; or (ii) the Authority's approval under FSMA 2000, s 59 in relation to any of those activities), and as from 6 April 2007 (otherwise).

[8.126]
[53C Advising on regulated home purchase plans

Advising a person is a specified kind of activity if the advice—
 (a) is given to the person in his capacity as a home purchaser or potential home purchaser; and
 (b) is advice on the merits of his doing either of the following—
  (i) entering into a particular regulated home purchase plan, or
  (ii) varying the terms of a regulated home purchase plan, entered into on or after 6th April 2007 by him, in such a way as to vary his obligations under that plan.]

NOTES

Inserted as noted to art 53B at **[8.125]**.

[8.127]
[53D Advising on regulated sale and rent back agreements

Advising a person is a specified kind of activity if the advice—
 (a) is given to the person ("A") in A's capacity as—
  (i) an agreement seller or potential agreement seller, or
  (ii) an agreement provider or potential agreement provider; and
 (b) is advice on the merits of A doing either of the following—
  (i) entering into a particular regulated sale and rent back agreement; or

(ii) varying the terms of a regulated sale and rent back agreement entered into on or after 1st July 2009 by A as agreement seller or agreement provider, in such a way so as to vary A's obligations under that agreement.]

NOTES

Inserted by the Financial Services and Markets Act 2000 (Regulated Activities) (Amendment) Order 2009, SI 2009/1342, arts 2, 13, as from 1 July 2009 (other than for the purposes of enabling applications to be made for a Part IV permission, or a variation of a Part IV permission, in relation to activities of the kind specified by arts 25E, 53D or 63J or, so far as relevant to any such activity, art 64 of this Order), and as from 30 June 2010 (for those purposes).

[8.128]

[53DA Advising on regulated credit agreements for the acquisition of land

(1) Advising a person ("P") is a specified kind of activity if—

(a) the advice is given to P in P's capacity as a recipient of credit, or potential recipient of credit, under a regulated credit agreement;

(b) P intends to use the credit to acquire or retain property rights in land or in an existing or projected building; and

(c) the advice consists of the provision of personal recommendations to P in respect of one or more transactions relating to regulated credit agreements [entered into, or to be entered into, on or after 21st March 2016].

[(2) In this article—

(a) a reference to any land or building—

(i) in relation to an agreement entered into before IP completion day, is a reference to any land or building in the United Kingdom or within the territory of an EEA State;

(ii) in relation to an agreement entered into on or after IP completion day, is a reference to any land or building in the United Kingdom;

(b) "regulated credit agreement" has the meaning given by article 60B(3).]]

NOTES

Inserted by the Mortgage Credit Directive Order 2015, SI 2015/910, Sch 1, Pt 2, para 4(1), (9), as from 21 March 2016.

Para (1): words in square brackets inserted by the Financial Services and Markets Act 2000 (Regulated Activities) (Amendment) Order 2016, SI 2016/392, art 2(1), (8), as from 21 March 2016.

Para (2): substituted by the Financial Services and Markets Act 2000 (Amendment) (EU Exit) Regulations 2019, SI 2019/632, regs 120, 136, as from IP completion day (as defined in the European Union (Withdrawal Agreement) Act 2020, s 39). Note that reg 136 of the 2019 Regulations was amended by the Financial Services and Economic and Monetary Policy (Consequential Amendments) (EU Exit) Regulations 2020, SI 2020/1301, reg 3, Schedule, para 33(n), as from 30 December 2020 (and the effect of the amendment has been incorporated in the text set out above).

[8.129]

[53E Advising on conversion or transfer of pension benefits

(1) Advising a person ("P") is a specified kind of activity if—

(a) the advice is given to P in P's capacity as—

(i) a member of a pension scheme; or

(ii) a survivor of a member of a pension scheme;

(b) P has subsisting rights in respect of any safeguarded benefits; and

(c) the advice is advice on the merits of P requiring the trustee or manager of the pension scheme to—

(i) convert any of the safeguarded benefits into different benefits that are flexible benefits under the scheme;

(ii) make a transfer payment in respect of any of the safeguarded benefits with a view to acquiring a right or entitlement to flexible benefits for P under another pension scheme; or

(iii) pay a lump sum that would be an uncrystallised funds pension lump sum in respect of any of the safeguarded benefits.

(2) In this article—

"flexible benefit" means—

(a) a money purchase benefit;

(b) a cash balance benefit; or

(c) a benefit, other than a money purchase benefit or cash balance benefit, calculated by reference to an amount available for the provision of benefits to or in respect of the member (whether the amount so available is calculated by reference to payments made by the member or any other person in respect of the member or any other factor);

"pension scheme" has the meaning given by section 1(5) of the Pension Schemes Act 1993 or section 1(5) of the Pension Schemes (Northern Ireland) Act 1993;

"safeguarded benefits" means benefits other than—

(a) money purchase benefits; and

(b) cash balance benefits;

"subsisting right"—

(a) in relation to a member of a pension scheme, means—

(i) any right which has accrued to or in respect of the member to future benefits under the scheme; or

(ii) any entitlement to benefits under the scheme; and

(b) in relation to a survivor of a member of a pension scheme means any right to future benefits, or entitlement to benefits, which the survivor has under the scheme in respect of the member;

"survivor", in relation to a member of a pension scheme, means a person who has survived the member and has a right to future benefits, or is entitled to benefits, under the scheme in respect of the member;

"trustees or managers" means—

(a) in relation to a scheme established under a trust, the trustees; and

(b) in relation to any other scheme, the managers; and

"uncrystallised funds pension lump sum" has the meaning given by paragraph 4A of Schedule 29 to the Finance Act 2004.

(3) Paragraphs (4) to (9) apply for the interpretation of "flexible benefit" and "safeguarded benefits".

(4) "Cash balance benefit", in relation to a member of a pension scheme or a survivor of a member, means a benefit calculated by reference to an amount available for the provision of benefits to or in respect of the member ("the available amount") where there is a promise about that amount.

(5) But a benefit is not a "cash balance benefit" if, under the scheme—

(a) a pension may be provided from the available amount to or in respect of the member; and

(b) there is a promise about the rate of that pension.

(6) The promise mentioned in paragraph (4) includes, in particular, a promise about the change in the value of, or the return from, payments made by the member or any other person in respect of the member.

(7) The promise mentioned in paragraph (5)(b) includes a promise that—

(a) the available amount will be sufficient to provide a pension of a particular rate;

(b) the rate of a pension will represent a particular proportion of the available amount.

(8) A benefit is not excluded from the definition of "cash balance benefit" by paragraph (5) merely because under the scheme there is a promise that—

(a) the rate or amount of the benefit payable in respect of a deceased member will be a particular proportion of the rate or amount of the benefit which was (or would have been) payable to the member; or

(b) the amount of a lump sum payable to a member, or in respect of a deceased member, will represent a particular proportion of the available amount.

(9) "Money purchase benefits"—

(a) in relation to a pension scheme governed by the law of England and Wales or Scotland, has the meaning given by section 181 of the Pension Schemes Act 1993; and

(b) in relation to a pensions scheme governed by the law of Northern Ireland, has the meaning given by section 176 of the Pension Schemes (Northern Ireland) Act 1993.]

NOTES

Inserted by the Financial Services and Markets Act 2000 (Regulated Activities) (Amendment) (No 2) Order 2015, SI 2015/731, art 2(1), (2), as from 6 April 2015.

Exclusions

[8.130]

54 Advice given in newspapers etc

(1) There is excluded from [articles 53, 53A, 53B[, 53C[, 53D[, 53DA] and 53E]]] the giving of advice in writing or other legible form if the advice is contained in a newspaper, journal, magazine, or other periodical publication, or is given by way of a service comprising regularly updated news or information, if the principal purpose of the publication or service, taken as a whole and including any advertisements or other promotional material contained in it, is neither—

(a) that of giving advice of a kind mentioned in article 53[, 53A, 53B[, 53C[, 53D[, 53DA] or 53E],] as the case may be]; nor

[(b) that of leading or enabling persons—

(i) to buy, sell, subscribe for or underwrite securities[structured deposits,] or [relevant investments], or (as the case may be),

[(ia) to enter into a relevant article 36H agreement (within the meaning of that article) as a lender, to assume the rights of a lender under such an agreement by assignment or operation of law, or to assign rights under such an agreement,]

(ii) to enter as borrower into regulated mortgage contracts, or vary the terms of regulated mortgage contracts entered into by them as borrower;

[(iii) to enter as reversion seller or plan provider into regulated home reversion plans, or vary the terms of regulated home reversion plans entered into by them as reversion seller or plan provider,

(iv) to enter as home purchaser into regulated home purchase plans, or vary the terms of regulated home purchase plans entered into by them as home purchaser][;

(v) to enter as agreement seller or agreement provider into regulated sale and rent back agreements, or vary the terms of regulated sale and rent back agreements entered into by them as agreement seller or agreement provider]];

[(va) to enter as a recipient of credit into a regulated credit agreement the purpose of which is to acquire or retain property rights in land [in the United Kingdom] or in an existing or projected building [in the United Kingdom],]

[(vi) to require the trustee or manager of a pension scheme to take any of the actions referred to in article 53E(1)(c)].

(2) There is also excluded from [articles 53, 53A, 53B[, 53C[, 53D[, 53DA] and 53E]]] the giving of advice in any service consisting of the broadcast or transmission of television or radio programmes, if the principal purpose of the service, taken as a whole and including any advertisements or other promotional material contained in it, is neither of those mentioned in paragraph (1)(a) and (b).

[(2A) Paragraphs (1) and (2) do not apply to advice which is a personal recommendation falling within article 53(1A).]

(3) [The FCA] may, on the application of the proprietor of any such publication or service as is mentioned in paragraph (1) or (2), certify that it is of the nature described in that paragraph, and may revoke any such certificate if it considers that it is no longer justified.

(4) A certificate given under paragraph (3) and not revoked is conclusive evidence of the matters certified.

NOTES

Para (1) is amended as follows:

Words in square brackets beginning with the words "articles 53, 53A, 53B" substituted by the Financial Services and Markets Act 2000 (Regulated Activities) (Amendment) (No 2) Order 2006, SI 2006/2383, arts 2, 14(a)(i), as from 6 November 2006 (for the purposes of enabling applications to be made for (i) a Pt IV permission, or a variation of a Pt IV permission, in relation to activities of the kind specified by arts 25B, 25C, 53B, 53C, 63B or 63F or, so far as relevant to any such activity, art 64 of this Order; or (ii) the Authority's approval under FSMA 2000, s 59 in relation to any of those activities), and as from 6 April 2007 (otherwise).

Words in square brackets beginning with ", 53C" substituted by the Financial Services and Markets Act 2000 (Regulated Activities) (Amendment) Order 2009, SI 2009/1342, arts 2, 14(a), as from 1 July 2009 (other than for the purposes of enabling applications to be made for a Part IV permission, or a variation of a Part IV permission, in relation to activities of the kind specified by arts 25E, 53D or 63J or, so far as relevant to any such activity, art 64 of this Order), and as from 30 June 2010 (otherwise).

Words ", 53D and 53E" in square brackets (in both places they occur) substituted by the Financial Services and Markets Act 2000 (Regulated Activities) (Amendment) (No 2) Order 2015, SI 2015/731, art 2(1), (3)(a)(i), (ii), as from 6 April 2015.

Figure ", 53DA" in square brackets (in both places it occurs) inserted by the Mortgage Credit Directive Order 2015, SI 2015/910, Sch 1, Pt 2, para 4(1), (10)(a), as from 21 March 2016.

In sub-para (a) words in square brackets beginning with the words ", 53A, 53B" substituted by SI 2006/2383, arts 2, 14(a)(ii), as from 6 November 2006 (certain purposes), and as from 6 April 2007 (otherwise) (see the first note relating to the 2006 Order above).

In sub-para (a) words in square brackets beginning with the reference to ", 53C" substituted by SI 2009/1342, arts 2, 14(b), as from 1 July 2009 (certain purposes), and as from 30 June 2010 (otherwise) (see the first note relating to the 2009 Order above).

Sub-para (b) substituted, by the Financial Services and Markets Act 2000 (Regulated Activities) (Amendment) (No 1) Order 2003, SI 2003/1475, art 14, as from 31 October 2004.

Words in first pair of square brackets in sub-para (b)(i) inserted by the Financial Services and Markets Act 2000 (Markets in Financial Instruments) (No 2) Regulations 2017, SI 2017/1255, reg 4(1), (2), as from 3 January 2018.

Words in second pair of square brackets in sub-para (b)(i) substituted by the Financial Services and Markets Act 2000 (Regulated Activities) (Amendment) (No 2) Order 2003, SI 2003/1476, art 9(2), as from 31 October 2004 (in so far as relating to contracts of long-term care insurance), and as from 14 January 2005 (otherwise).

Sub-para (b)(ia) inserted by the Financial Services and Markets Act 2000 (Regulated Activities) (Amendment) Order 2016, SI 2016/392, art 2(1), (9), as from 6 April 2016.

Sub-paras (b)(iii), (iv) inserted by SI 2006/2383, arts 2, 14(a)(iii), as from 6 November 2006 (certain purposes), and as from 6 April 2007 (otherwise) (see the first note relating to the 2006 Order above).

Sub-para (b)(v) inserted by SI 2009/1342, arts 2, 14(c), as from 1 July 2009 (certain purposes), and as from 30 June 2010 (otherwise) (see the first note relating to the 2009 Order above).

Sub-para (b)(va) inserted by SI 2015/910, Sch 1, Pt 2, para 4(1), (10)(b), as from 21 March 2016. The words in square brackets were inserted by the Financial Services and Markets Act 2000 (Amendment) (EU Exit) Regulations 2019, SI 2019/632, regs 120, 137(1), as from IP completion day (as defined in the European Union (Withdrawal Agreement) Act 2020, s 39). Note that reg 137(2) (as amended by the Financial Services and Economic and Monetary Policy (Consequential Amendments) (EU Exit) Regulations 2020, SI 2020/1301, reg 3, Schedule, para 33(o)) provides that this amendment does not apply in relation to any advice published or given before IP completion day.

Sub-para (b)(vi) inserted by SI 2015/731, art 2(1), (3)(a)(iii), as from 6 April 2015.

Para (2) is amended as follows:

Words in square brackets beginning with the words "articles 53, 53A, 53B" substituted by SI 2006/2383, arts 2, 14(b), as from 6 November 2006 (certain purposes), and as from 6 April 2007 (otherwise) (see the first note relating to the 2006 Order above).

Words in square brackets beginning with the reference to ", 53C" substituted by SI 2009/1342, arts 2, 14(d), as from 1 July 2009 (certain purposes), and as from 30 June 2010 (otherwise) (see the first note relating to the 2009 Order above).

Words ", 53D and 53E" in square brackets substituted by SI 2015/731, art 2(1), (3)(b), as from 6 April 2015.

Figure ", 53DA" in square brackets inserted by SI 2015/910, Sch 1, Pt 2, para 4(1), (10)(a), as from 21 March 2016.

Para (2A): inserted by the Financial Services and Markets Act 2000 (Regulated Activities) (Amendment) (No 2) Order 2017, SI 2017/500, art 3, as from 3 January 2018.

Para (3): words in square brackets substituted by the Financial Services Act 2012 (Consequential Amendments and Transitional Provisions) Order 2013, SI 2013/472, art 3, Sch 2, para 35(a), as from 1 April 2013.

[8.131]

[54A Advice given in the course of administration by authorised person

[(1)] A person who is not an authorised person ("A") does not carry on an activity of the kind specified by article 53A by reason of—

(a) anything done by an authorised person ("B") in relation to a regulated mortgage contract which B is administering pursuant to arrangements of the kind mentioned in article 62(a); or

(b) anything A does in connection with the administration of a regulated mortgage contract in circumstances falling within article 62(b).

[(2) A person who is not an authorised person ("A") does not carry on an activity of the kind specified by article 53B by reason of—

(a) anything done by an authorised person ("B") in relation to a regulated home reversion plan which B is administering pursuant to arrangements of the kind mentioned in article 63C(a); or

(b) anything A does in connection with the administration of a regulated home reversion plan in circumstances falling within article 63C(b).

(3) A person who is not an authorised person ("A") does not carry on an activity of the kind specified by article 53C by reason of—

(a) anything done by an authorised person ("B") in relation to a regulated home purchase plan which B is administering pursuant to arrangements of the kind mentioned in article 63G(a); or

(b) anything A does in connection with the administration of a regulated home purchase plan in circumstances falling within article 63G(b).]]

[(4) A person who is not an authorised person ("A") does not carry on an activity of the kind specified by article 53D by reason of

(a) anything done by an authorised person ("B") in relation to a regulated sale and rent back agreement which B is administering pursuant to arrangements of the kind mentioned in article 63K(a); or

(b) anything A does in connection with the administration of a regulated sale and rent back agreement in circumstances falling within article 63K(b).

[(5) A person who is not an authorised person ("A") does not carry on an activity of the kind specified by article 53DA by reason of—

(a) anything done by an authorised person ("B") in relation to a regulated credit agreement which B is administering pursuant to arrangements of the kind mentioned in article 60I(a) (arranging administration by authorised person); or

(b) anything A does in connection with the administration of a regulated credit agreement in circumstances falling within article 60I(b).]]

NOTES

Inserted by the Financial Services and Markets Act 2000 (Regulated Activities) (Amendment) (No 1) Order 2003, SI 2003/1475, art 15, as from 31 October 2004.

Para (1) numbered as such, and paras (2), (3) added, by the Financial Services and Markets Act 2000 (Regulated Activities) (Amendment) (No 2) Order 2006, SI 2006/2383, arts 2, 15, as from 6 November 2006 (for the purposes of enabling applications to be made for (i) a Pt IV permission, or a variation of a Pt IV permission, in relation to activities of the kind specified by arts 25B, 25C, 53B, 53C, 63B or 63F or, so far as relevant to any such activity, art 64 of this Order; or (ii) the Authority's approval under FSMA 2000, s 59 in relation to any of those activities), and as from 6 April 2007 (otherwise).

Para (4): added by the Financial Services and Markets Act 2000 (Regulated Activities) (Amendment) Order 2009, SI 2009/1342, arts 2, 15, as from 1 July 2009 (other than for the purposes of enabling applications to be made for a Part IV permission, or a variation of a Part IV permission, in relation to activities of the kind specified by arts 25E, 53D or 63J or, so far as relevant to any such activity, art 64 of this Order), and as from 30 June 2010 (for those purposes).

Para (5): added by the Mortgage Credit Directive Order 2015, SI 2015/910, Sch 1, Pt 2, para 4(1), (11), as from 21 March 2016.

[8.132]

[54B Advice given by reason of providing pensions guidance . . .

(1) A person does not carry on an activity of the kind specified in article 53, 53A, 53B, 53C or 53D by reason of providing pensions guidance . . .

[(2) For the purposes of paragraph (1), pensions guidance means—

(a) information or guidance provided by the Money and Pensions Service in carrying out its pensions guidance function (see section 3 of the Financial Guidance and Claims Act 2018);

(b) information or guidance provided by another person with whom arrangements under section 5(1), (2) or (3) of the Financial Guidance and Claims Act 2018 are made to carry out the Money and Pensions Service's pensions guidance function.]

NOTES

Inserted by the Financial Services and Markets Act 2000 (Regulated Activities) (Amendment) (Pensions Guidance Exclusions) Order 2015, SI 2015/489, art 2(1), (6), as from 26 March 2015.

Words omitted revoked, and para (2) substituted, by the Financial Services and Markets Act 2000 (Regulated Activities) (Amendment) (No 2) Order 2022, SI 2022/726, art 2(6), as from 21 July 2022.

[8.133]

55 Other exclusions

[(1)] Article 53 is also subject to the exclusions in articles 66 (trustees etc), 67, (profession or non-investment business), 68 (sale of goods and supply of services), 69 (groups and joint enterprises), 70 (sale of body corporate)[, 72 (overseas persons)][. . . 72B (activities carried on by a provider of relevant goods or services)][, article 72AA (managers of [UK UCITS] and AIFs)][, 72D (large risks contracts where risk situated [outside the United Kingdom]), 72G (local authorities) and 72H (insolvency practitioners)].

[(2) [Articles 53A, 53B, [53C, 53D and 53DA] are] also subject to the exclusions in articles 66 (trustees etc), 67 (profession or non-investment business) . . . [, 72AA (managers of [UK UCITS] and AIFs)][, 72G (local authorities) and 72I (registered consumer buy-to-let mortgage firms)].]

NOTES

Para (1): numbered as such by the Financial Services and Markets Act 2000 (Regulated Activities) (Amendment) (No 1) Order 2003, SI 2003/1475, art 16(a), as from 31 October 2004; and amended as follows:

Words in first pair of square brackets substituted by the Financial Services and Markets Act 2000 (Regulated Activities) (Amendment) (No 2) Order 2002, SI 2002/1776, art 3(1), (12), as from 21 August 2002.

Words in second pair of square brackets substituted by the Financial Services and Markets Act 2000 (Regulated Activities) (Amendment) (No 2) Order 2003, SI 2003/1476, art 9(3), as from 31 October 2004 (in so far as relating to contracts of long-term care insurance), and as from 14 January 2005 (otherwise).

Words omitted revoked by the Electronic Commerce and Solvency 2 (Amendment etc) (EU Exit) Regulations 2019, SI 2019/1361, reg 5(1), (3), as from IP completion day (as defined in the European Union (Withdrawal Agreement) Act 2020, s 39) (for transitional provisions, see the note in relation to art 72A of this Order *post*).

Words in third (outer) pair of square brackets substituted by the Alternative Investment Fund Managers Regulations 2013, SI 2013/1773, reg 81, Sch 2, Part 1, para 1(1), (7), as from 22 July 2013.

The words "UK UCITS" in the fourth (inner) pair of square brackets were substituted by the Financial Services and Markets Act 2000 (Amendment) (EU Exit) Regulations 2019, SI 2019/632, regs 120, 148(2), 149(5), as from IP completion day (as defined in the European Union (Withdrawal Agreement) Act 2020, s 39).

Words in fifth (outer) pair of square brackets substituted by the Financial Services and Markets Act 2000 (Regulated Activities) (Amendment) Order 2014, SI 2014/366, art 2(1), (23)(a), as from 1 April 2014 (note that the 2014 Order came into force on 14 February 2014 for the purpose of the FCA making rules, giving guidance etc, and came into force on 1 April 2014, immediately after SI 2013/1881 (and SI 2013/1882) come into force, in so far as not already in force).

The words "outside the United Kingdom" in the sixth (inner) pair of square brackets were substituted by SI 2019/632, regs 120, 148(2), 149(5), as from IP completion day (as defined in the European Union (Withdrawal Agreement) Act 2020, s 39).

Para (2): added by SI 2003/1475, art 16(b), as from 31 October 2004; and subsequently amended as follows:

Words in first (outer) pair of square brackets substituted by the Financial Services and Markets Act 2000 (Regulated Activities) (Amendment) (No 2) Order 2006, SI 2006/2383, arts 2, 16, as from 6 November 2006 (for the purposes of enabling applications to be made for (i) a Pt IV permission, or a variation of a Pt IV permission, in relation to activities of the kind specified by arts 25B, 25C, 53B, 53C, 63B or 63F or, so far as relevant to any such activity, art 64 of this Order; or (ii) the Authority's approval under FSMA 2000, s 59 in relation to any of those activities), and as from 6 April 2007 (otherwise).

Words in second (inner) pair of square brackets substituted, and words in final pair of square brackets substituted, by the Mortgage Credit Directive Order 2015, SI 2015/910, Sch 1, Pt 2, para 4(1), (12), as from 21 March 2016.

Words omitted revoked by SI 2019/1361, reg 5(1), (3), as from IP completion day (as defined in the European Union (Withdrawal Agreement) Act 2020, s 39) (for transitional provisions, see the note in relation to art 72A of this Order *post*).

Words in third (outer) pair of square brackets substituted by SI 2014/366, art 2(1), (23)(b), as from 1 April 2014 (see the first note relating to the 2014 Order above).

The words "UK UCITS" in the fourth (inner) pair of square brackets were substituted by SI 2019/632, regs 120, 148(2), as from IP completion day (as defined in the European Union (Withdrawal Agreement) Act 2020, s 39).

CHAPTER XIII LLOYD'S

The activities

[8.134]

56 Advice on syndicate participation at Lloyd's

Advising a person to become, or continue or cease to be, a member of a particular Lloyd's syndicate is a specified kind of activity.

[8.135]

57 Managing the underwriting capacity of a Lloyd's syndicate

Managing the underwriting capacity of a Lloyd's syndicate as a managing agent at Lloyd's is a specified kind of activity.

[8.136]

58 Arranging deals in contracts of insurance written at Lloyd's

The arranging, by the society incorporated by Lloyd's Act 1871 by the name of Lloyd's, of deals in contracts of insurance written at Lloyd's, is a specified kind of activity.

[Exclusion

[8.137]

58A . . . [. . . Managers of [UK UCITS] and AIFs]

Articles 56 to 58 are subject to the [exclusion] in . . . [. . . article 72AA (managers of [UK UCITS] and AIFs)].]

NOTES

Inserted, together with the preceding heading, by the Financial Services and Markets Act 2000 (Regulated Activities) (Amendment) (No 2) Order 2002, SI 2002/1776, art 3(1), (13), as from 21 August 2002.

The Article heading is amended as follows:

The words omitted were revoked by the Electronic Commerce and Solvency 2 (Amendment etc) (EU Exit) Regulations 2019, SI 2019/1361, reg 5(1), (3), as from IP completion day (as defined in the European Union (Withdrawal Agreement) Act 2020, s 39) (for transitional provisions, see the note in relation to art 72A of this Order *post*).

The words in the first (outer) pair of square brackets were inserted by the Alternative Investment Fund Managers Regulations 2013, SI 2013/1773, reg 81, Sch 2, Part 1, para 1(1), (4), as from 22 July 2013.

The words in the second (inner) pair of square brackets were substituted by the Financial Services and Markets Act 2000 (Amendment) (EU Exit) Regulations 2019, SI 2019/632, regs 120, 148(2), as from IP completion day (as defined in the European Union (Withdrawal Agreement) Act 2020, s 39).

The Article text is amended as follows:

The word "exclusion" in square brackets was substituted, and the words omitted were revoked, by SI 2019/1361, reg 5(1), (3), as from IP completion day (as defined in the European Union (Withdrawal Agreement) Act 2020, s 39) (for transitional provisions, see the note in relation to art 72A of this Order *post*).

The words in second (outer) pair of square brackets were inserted by SI 2013/1773, reg 81, Sch 2, Part 1, para 1(1), (4), as from 22 July 2013.

The words "UK UCITS" were substituted by SI 2019/632, regs 120, 148(2), as from IP completion day (as defined in the European Union (Withdrawal Agreement) Act 2020, s 39).

CHAPTER XIV FUNERAL PLAN CONTRACTS

The activity

[8.138]

59 Funeral plan contracts

(1) Entering as provider into a funeral plan contract is a specified kind of activity.

[(1A) Carrying out a funeral plan contract as provider is a specified kind of activity.]

(2) A "funeral plan contract" is a contract . . . under which—

(a) a person ("the customer") makes one or more payments to another person ("the provider"); and

(b) the provider undertakes to provide, or secure that another person provides, a funeral in the United Kingdom for the customer (or some other person who is living at the date when the contract is entered into) on his death;

unless, at the time of entering into the contract, the customer and the provider intend or expect the funeral to occur within one month.

[(2A) For the purposes of paragraph (1A), "provider" includes a person who has assumed the undertaking referred to in paragraph (2)(b) as a result of the novation, assignment or transfer by operation of law of an existing funeral plan contract.]

[(3) Where—

(a) a person ("A") has a funeral plan contract ("the contract") with a customer under which A has given or assumed the undertaking referred to in paragraph (2)(b);
(b) another person ("B") intends to give an equivalent or substantially similar undertaking ("the proposed undertaking") to that customer;
(c) A and B intend that B's proposed undertaking will replace A's undertaking;
(d) paragraph (4) or (5) applies; and
(e) A and B have notified the FCA in writing—
  (i) that they consider the conditions in sub-paragraphs (a) to (d) to be met; and
  (ii) of a date, on or after 29th July 2022, from which A and B agree to regard B's undertaking as having replaced A's undertaking for the purpose of the operation of this article;

for the purposes of paragraph (1A), B is to be treated as if B were carrying out the contract as provider from the date specified in the notification to the FCA under sub-paragraph (e)(ii).

(4) This paragraph applies if—

(a) A and B intend that, in order for B's proposed undertaking to replace A's undertaking under the contract, B should assume A's undertaking by novation;
(b) A has taken reasonable steps to secure the customer's written consent to the proposed novation; and
(c) the customer has neither provided that consent nor objected, in either case within a reasonable period.

(5) This paragraph applies if it appears to A and B that it would not be reasonably practicable for B to assume A's undertaking referred to in paragraph (2)(b) by novation, assignment or operation of law, or for the conditions in paragraph (4) to be met, before the first day paragraph (1A) applies in relation to activities carried on by A in accordance with articles 1 and 1A of the Financial Services and Markets Act 2000 (Regulated Activities) (Amendment) Order 2021.

(6) If—

(a) paragraph (3) applies; and
(b) the proposed undertaking referred to in paragraph (3)(b) is given to the customer;

then that undertaking is to be treated as if it were a "funeral plan contract" for the purposes of paragraph (2).]

NOTES

Paras (1A) and (2A) were inserted, and the words omitted from para (2) were revoked, by the Financial Services and Markets Act 2000 (Regulated Activities) (Amendment) Order 2021, SI 2021/90, art 2(4); note that this Order comes into force (1) on 28 January 2021 (for the purposes of (a) enabling the FCA to make or approve rules and to give guidance and directions; (b) enabling applications to be made etc for: (i) a Part 4A permission under s 55A of FSMA 2000; (ii) a variation of a Part 4A permission under s 55H of that Act; and (iii) approval under Part 5 of the Act; (c) enabling the FCA to exercise any of its powers under Part 4A or Part 5 of that Act in relation to any activity which becomes a regulated activity by virtue of this Order; and (d) enabling the scheme operator to make rules and to give guidance); and (2) for all other purposes 29 July 2022 (see art 1 of the 2021 Order, and see Part 3 for transitional provisions; note also that art 1A of the 2021 Order provides further transitional provisions in relation to the insertion of para (1A) above, in certain cases where the FCA received a provider's application before 1 March 2022).

Paras (3)–(6): added by the Financial Services and Markets Act 2000 (Regulated Activities) (Amendment) Order 2022, SI 2022/466, art 2(2), as from 16 May 2022 (for the purposes of enabling the FCA to make rules, and to give guidance), and as from 29 July 2022 (for all other purposes).

[Exclusions]

NOTES

The preceding heading was substituted by the Financial Services and Markets Act 2000 (Regulated Activities) (Amendment) (No 2) Order 2002, art 3(1), (14), as from 21 August 2002.

60 *(Revoked by the Financial Services and Markets Act 2000 (Regulated Activities) (Amendment) Order 2021, SI 2021/90, art 2(5); note that this Order comes into force (1) on 28 January 2021 (for the purposes of (a) enabling the FCA to make or approve rules and to give guidance and directions; (b) enabling applications to be made etc for: (i) a Part 4A permission under s 55A of FSMA 2000; (ii) a variation of a Part 4A permission under s 55H of that Act; and (iii) approval under Part 5 of the Act; (c) enabling the FCA to exercise any of its powers under Part 4A or Part 5 of that Act in relation to any activity which becomes a regulated activity by virtue of this Order; and (d) enabling the scheme operator to make rules and to give guidance); and (2) for all other purposes on 29 July 2022 (see art 1 of the 2021 Order, and see Part 3 of that Order for transitional provisions.)*

[8.139]

[60ZA Local authorities

Article 59 is subject to the exclusion in article 72G (local authorities).]

NOTES

Commencement: see the note below.

Inserted by the Financial Services and Markets Act 2000 (Regulated Activities) (Amendment) Order 2021, SI 2021/90, art 2(6); note that this Order comes into force (1) on 28 January 2021 (for the purposes of (a) enabling the FCA to make or approve rules and to give guidance and directions; (b) enabling applications to be made etc for: (i) a Part 4A permission under s 55A of FSMA 2000; (ii) a variation of a Part 4A permission under s 55H of that Act; and (iii) approval under Part 5 of the Act;

(c) enabling the FCA to exercise any of its powers under Part 4A or Part 5 of that Act in relation to any activity which becomes a regulated activity by virtue of this Order; and (d) enabling the scheme operator to make rules and to give guidance); and (2) for all other purposes on 29 July 2022 (see art 1 of the 2021 Order, and see Part 3 of that Order for transitional provisions).

[8.140]
[60A . . . [. . . Managers of [UK UCITS] and AIFs]

Article 59 is subject to the [exclusion] in . . . [. . . article 72AA (managers of [UK UCITS] and AIFs)].]

NOTES

Inserted by the Financial Services and Markets Act 2000 (Regulated Activities) (Amendment) (No 2) Order 2002, SI 2002/1776, art 3(1), (15), as from 21 August 2002.

The Article heading is amended as follows:

The words omitted were revoked by the Electronic Commerce and Solvency 2 (Amendment etc) (EU Exit) Regulations 2019, SI 2019/1361, reg 5(1), (3), as from IP completion day (as defined in the European Union (Withdrawal Agreement) Act 2020, s 39) (for transitional provisions, see the note in relation to art 72A of this Order *post*).

The words in the first (outer) pair of square brackets were inserted by the Alternative Investment Fund Managers Regulations 2013, SI 2013/1773, reg 81, Sch 2, Part 1, para 1(1), (4), as from 22 July 2013.

The words in the second (inner) pair of square brackets were substituted by the Financial Services and Markets Act 2000 (Amendment) (EU Exit) Regulations 2019, SI 2019/632, regs 120, 148(2), as from IP completion day (as defined in the European Union (Withdrawal Agreement) Act 2020, s 39).

The Article text is amended as follows:

The word "exclusion" in square brackets was substituted, and the words omitted were revoked, by SI 2019/1361, reg 5(1), (3), as from IP completion day (as defined in the European Union (Withdrawal Agreement) Act 2020, s 39) (for transitional provisions, see the note in relation to art 72A of this Order *post*).

The words in second (outer) pair of square brackets were inserted by SI 2013/1773, reg 81, Sch 2, Part 1, para 1(1), (4), as from 22 July 2013.

The words "UK UCITS" were substituted by SI 2019/632, regs 120, 148(2), as from IP completion day (as defined in the European Union (Withdrawal Agreement) Act 2020, s 39).

[8.141]
[60AA Insolvency practitioners

Article 59(1A) is subject to the exclusion in article 72H (insolvency practitioners).]

NOTES

Commencement: 16 May 2022 (for the purposes of enabling the FCA to make rules, and to give guidance); 29 July 2022 (otherwise)

Inserted by the Financial Services and Markets Act 2000 (Regulated Activities) (Amendment) Order 2022, SI 2022/466, art 2(3), as from 16 May 2022 (for the purposes of enabling the FCA to make rules, and to give guidance), and as from 29 July 2022 (otherwise).

[CHAPTER 14A REGULATED CREDIT AGREEMENTS

The Activities

[8.142]
60B Regulated credit agreements

(1) Entering into a regulated credit agreement as lender is a specified kind of activity.

(2) It is a specified kind of activity for the lender or another person to exercise, or to have the right to exercise, the lender's rights and duties under a regulated credit agreement.

(3) In this article—

["credit agreement"—

(a) in relation to an agreement other than a green deal plan, means an agreement between an individual or relevant recipient of credit ("A") and any other person ("B") under which B provides A with credit of any amount;

(b) in relation to a green deal plan, has the meaning given by article 60LB;]

["exempt agreement" means a credit agreement which is an exempt agreement under articles 60C to 60H, but where only part of a credit agreement falls within a provision of articles 60C to 60H, only that part is an exempt agreement under those articles;]

["regulated credit agreement" means—

(a) in the case of an agreement entered into on or after 1st April 2014, any credit agreement which is not an exempt agreement; or

(b) in the case of an agreement entered into before 1st April 2014, a credit agreement which—

(i) was a regulated agreement within the meaning of section 189(1) of the Consumer Credit Act 1974 when the agreement was entered into; or

(ii) became such a regulated agreement after being varied or supplemented by another agreement before [1st April 2014,

and would not be an exempt agreement pursuant to article 60C(2) on 21st March 2016 if the agreement were entered into on that date]].]

NOTES

Chapter 14A (originally arts 60B–60J, 60K, 60L, 60M) was inserted by the Financial Services and Markets Act 2000 (Regulated Activities) (Amendment) (No 2) Order 2013, SI 2013/1881, arts 2, 6, as from 1 April 2014.

Para (3) is amended as follows:

Definition "credit agreement" substituted by the Financial Services and Markets Act 2000 (Regulated Activities) (Green Deal) (Amendment) Order 2014, SI 2014/1850, arts 2, 5, as from 15 July 2014.

Definition "exempt agreement" substituted by the Financial Services and Markets Act 2000 (Miscellaneous Provisions) Order 2015, SI 2015/853, art 3(1), (4), as from 24 March 2015.

Definition "regulated credit agreement" substituted by the Financial Services and Markets Act 2000 (Regulated Activities) (Amendment) Order 2016, SI 2016/392, art 2(1), (10)(a), as from 20 March 2016.

Words in square brackets in definition "regulated credit agreement" substituted by SI 2016/392, art 2(1), (10)(b), as from 21 March 2016.

Transitional provisions: see the note to art 60C at **[8.143]**.

[8.143]

[60C Exempt agreements: exemptions relating to the nature of the agreement

(1) A credit agreement is an exempt agreement for the purposes of this Chapter in the following cases.

[(2) A credit agreement is an exempt agreement if—

(a) by entering into the agreement as lender, a person is or was carrying on an activity of a kind specified by article 61(1) (entering into regulated mortgage contracts); . . .

(b) by entering into the agreement as home purchase provider, a person is or was carrying on an activity of a kind specified by article 63F(1) (entering into regulated home purchase plans)[; or

(c) . . . by administering the agreement on 21st March 2016 a person is carrying on an activity of a kind specified by article 61(2) (administering regulated mortgage contracts).]]

(3) A credit agreement is an exempt agreement if—

(a) the lender provides the borrower with credit exceeding £25,000, and

(b) the agreement is entered into by the borrower wholly or predominantly for the purposes of a business carried on, or intended to be carried on, by the borrower.

(4) A credit agreement is an exempt agreement if—

(a) the lender provides the borrower with credit of £25,000 or less,

(b) the agreement is entered into by the borrower wholly for the purposes of a business carried on, or intended to be carried on, by the borrower, and

[(c) the agreement is a green deal plan made in relation to a property that is not a domestic property (as defined by article 60LB).]

[(4A) A credit agreement is an exempt agreement if—

(a) the lender provides the borrower with credit of £25,000 or less,

(b) the agreement is entered into by the borrower wholly for the purposes of a business carried on, or intended to be carried on, by the borrower, and

(c) the agreement is entered into by the lender and the borrower under the Bounce Back Loan Scheme.

(4B) For the purposes of paragraph (4A), "Bounce Back Loan Scheme" means the scheme of that name operated from 4th May 2020 by the British Business Bank plc on behalf of the Secretary of State.

(4C) An agreement exempt under paragraph (4A) may not also be an article 36H agreement by virtue of paragraph (4) of that article.]

(5) For the purposes of paragraph (3), if an agreement includes a declaration which—

(a) is made by the borrower,

(b) provides that the agreement is entered into by the borrower wholly or predominantly for the purposes of a business carried on, or intended to be carried on, by the borrower, and

(c) complies with rules made by the FCA for the purpose of this article,

the agreement is to be presumed to have been entered into by the borrower wholly or predominantly for the purposes specified in sub-paragraph (b) unless paragraph (6) applies.

(6) This paragraph applies if, when the agreement is entered into—

(a) the lender (or, if there is more than one lender, any of the lenders), or

(b) any person who has acted on behalf of the lender (or, if there is more than one lender, any of the lenders) in connection with the entering into of the agreement,

knows or has reasonable cause to suspect that the agreement is not entered into by the borrower wholly or predominantly for the purposes of a business carried on, or intended to be carried on, by the borrower.

(7) Paragraphs (5) and (6) also apply for the purposes of paragraph (4) but with the omission of the words "or predominantly".

(8) A credit agreement is an exempt agreement if it is made in connection with trade in goods or services—

(a) between the United Kingdom and a country outside the United Kingdom,

(b) within a country [outside the United Kingdom], or

(c) between countries outside the United Kingdom, and

the credit is provided to the borrower in the course of a business carried on by the borrower.]

NOTES

Inserted as noted to art 60B at **[8.142]**.

Para (2): substituted by the Financial Services and Markets Act 2000 (Regulated Activities) (Amendment) (No 3) Order 2015, SI 2015/1863, art 2(1), (2), as from 5 November 2015 (the purposes of enabling the making and determination of applications for a permission, or for variation of a permission, to be given under Part 4A of the Financial Services and Markets Act 2000), and as from 1 January 2016 (otherwise). The word omitted from sub-para (a) was revoked, and sub-para (c) and the preceding word were inserted, by art 2(1), (3) of the 2015 Order, as from 5 November 2015 (for the purposes of enabling the making and determination of applications for a permission, or for variation of a permission, to be given under Part 4A of the Financial Services and Markets Act 2000), and as from 21 March 2016 (otherwise). The words omitted from sub-para (c) were revoked by the Financial Services and Markets Act 2000 (Regulated Activities) (Amendment) Order 2016, SI 2016/392, art 2(1), (11), as from 21 March 2016.

Para (4): sub-para (c) substituted by the Financial Services and Markets Act 2000 (Regulated Activities) (Green Deal) (Amendment) Order 2014, SI 2014/1850, arts 2, 6, as from 15 July 2014.

Paras (4A)–(4C): inserted by the Financial Services and Markets Act 2000 (Regulated Activities) (Coronavirus) (Amendment) Order 2020, SI 2020/480, art 2(1), (4), as from 4 May 2020 (for transitional provisions, see the note below).

Para (8): words in square brackets in sub-para (b) inserted by the Financial Services and Markets Act 2000 (Regulated Activities) (Amendment) Order 2014, SI 2014/366, art 2(1), (24), as from 1 April 2014.

Transitional provisions: the Financial Services and Markets Act 2000 (Regulated Activities) (Coronavirus) (Amendment) Order 2020, SI 2020/480, art 3 provides as follows (note that the Order came into force on 4 May 2020)—

"3 Transitional provisions

(1) Subject to paragraph (2), a person who immediately before the date this Order comes into force had permission under Part 4A of the Act to carry on an activity of the kind specified under article 60B(2) of the Regulated Activities Order is, from the date on which this Order comes into force, to be treated as having a Part 4A permission under the Act to carry on an activity of the kind specified by article 39F(1) of the Regulated Activities Order in relation to an exempt agreement specified in article 60C(4A) of the Regulated Activities Order.

(2) Paragraph (1) applies where the person is a lender who enters into an exempt agreement as specified in article 60C(4A) of the Regulated Activities Order.

(3) Paragraph (1) does not affect the ability of the FCA or the PRA to vary or cancel a Part 4A permission under the Act.

(4) Where, by virtue of paragraph (1), a person is treated as having a Part 4A permission of the kind specified by article 39F(1) of the Regulated Activities Order, section 347(2) of the Act (the record of authorised persons etc) does not require the FCA to amend the record maintained under that section in respect of that permission, but this does not prevent the FCA from doing so."

[8.144]

[60D Exempt agreements: exemption relating to the purchase of land for non-residential purposes

(1) A credit agreement is an exempt agreement for the purposes of this Chapter if, at the time it is entered into, any sums due under it are secured by a legal [or equitable] mortgage on land and the condition in paragraph (2) is satisfied.

(2) The condition is that less than 40% of the land is used, or is intended to be used, as or in connection with a dwelling—

(a) by the borrower or a related person of the borrower, or

(b) in the case of credit provided to trustees, by an individual who is a beneficiary of the trust or a related person of a beneficiary.

(3) For the purposes of paragraph (2)—

(a) the area of any land which comprises a building or other structure containing two or more storeys is to be taken to be the aggregate of the floor areas of each of those stories;

(b) "related person" in relation to a person ("B") who is the borrower or (in the case of credit provided to trustees) a beneficiary of the trust, means—

(i) B's spouse or civil partner,

(ii) a person (whether or not of the opposite sex) whose relationship with B has the characteristics of the relationship between husband and wife, or

(iii) B's parent, brother, sister, child, grandparent or grandchild.

[(4) This article does not apply to an agreement if—

(a) the agreement is entered into on or after 21st March 2016,

(b) under the agreement a mortgage creditor grants or promises to grant a credit in the form of a deferred payment, loan or other similar financial accommodation,

(c) the credit is granted or promised to an individual who is acting for purposes outside those of any trade, business or profession carried on by the individual,

(d) the purpose of the agreement is to acquire or retain property rights in land or in an existing or projected building, and

(e) the agreement does not meet the conditions in paragraphs (i) to (iii) of article 61(3)(a) (regulated mortgage contracts).

(5) A reference in paragraph (4)(d) to any land or building—

(a) in relation to an agreement entered into before IP completion day, is a reference to any land or building in the United Kingdom or within the territory of an EEA State;

(b) in relation to an agreement entered into on or after IP completion day, is a reference to any land or building in the United Kingdom.]]

NOTES

Inserted as noted to art 60B at **[8.142]**.

Para (1): words in square brackets inserted by the Financial Services and Markets Act 2000 (Regulated Activities) (Amendment) Order 2014, SI 2014/366, art 2(1), (25), as from 1 April 2014.

Paras (4), (5): substituted (for the original para (4)) by the Financial Services and Markets Act 2000 (Amendment) (EU Exit) Regulations 2019, SI 2019/632, regs 120, 138, as from IP completion day (as defined in the European Union (Withdrawal Agreement) Act 2020, s 39). Note that reg 138 of the 2019 Regulations was amended by the Financial Services and Economic and Monetary Policy (Consequential Amendments) (EU Exit) Regulations 2020, SI 2020/1301, reg 3, Schedule, para 33(p), as from 30 December 2020 (and the effect of the amendment has been incorporated in the text set out above).

[8.145]

[60E Exempt agreements: exemptions relating to the nature of the lender

(1) A credit agreement is an exempt agreement for the purposes of this Chapter in the following cases.

(2) [Subject to article 60HA, a relevant credit agreement] relating to the purchase of land is an exempt agreement if the lender is—

(a) specified, or of a description specified, in rules made by the FCA under paragraph (3), or

(b) a local authority.

(3) The FCA may make rules specifying any of the following for the purpose of paragraph (2)—

(a) an authorised person with permission to effect or carry out contracts of insurance;

(b) a friendly society;

(c) an organisation of employers or organisation of workers;

(d) a charity;

(e) an improvement company (within the meaning given by section 7 of the Improvement of Land Act 1899);

(f) a body corporate named or specifically referred to in any public general Act;
(g) a body corporate named or specifically referred to in, or in an order made under, a relevant housing provision;
(h) a building society (within the meaning of the Building Societies Act 1986);
(i) an authorised person with permission to accept deposits.

(4) Rules under paragraph (3) may—
(a) specify a particular person or class of persons;
(b) be limited so as to apply only to agreements or classes of agreement specified in the rules.

(5) [Subject to article 60HA, a relevant credit agreement] is an exempt agreement if it is—
(a) secured by a legal [or equitable] mortgage on land,
(b) that land is used or is intended to be used as or in connection with a dwelling, and
(c) the lender is a housing authority.

(6) A credit agreement is an exempt agreement if—
(a) the lender is an investment firm or a [qualifying credit institution], and
(b) the agreement is entered into for the purpose of allowing the borrower to carry out a transaction relating to one or more financial instruments.

(7) In this article—
"housing authority" means—
(a) in England and Wales, the Homes and Communities Agency, the Welsh Ministers[, a company which is a wholly-owned subsidiary of the Welsh Ministers,] [a registered social landlord within the meaning of Part 1 of the Housing Act 1996,] or a private registered provider (within the meaning of Part 2 of the Housing and Regeneration Act 2008);
(b) in Scotland, the Scottish Ministers or a registered social landlord (within the meaning of the Housing (Scotland) Act 2010;
(c) in Northern Ireland, the Northern Ireland Housing Executive [or a housing association within the meaning of Part 2 of the Housing (Northern Ireland) Order 1992];

"relevant credit agreement relating to the purchase of land" means—
(a) a borrower-lender-supplier agreement financing—
(i) the purchase of land, or
(ii) provision of dwellings on land,
and secured by a legal [or equitable] mortgage on that land,
(b) a borrower-lender agreement secured by a legal mortgage on land, or
(c) a borrower-lender-supplier agreement financing a transaction which is a linked transaction in relation to—
(i) an agreement falling within sub-paragraph (a), or
(ii) an agreement falling within sub-paragraph (b) financing—
(aa) the purchase of land,
(bb) the provision of dwellings on land,
and secured by a legal mortgage on the land referred to in sub-paragraph (a) or the land referred to in paragraph (ii);

"relevant housing provision" means any of the following—
(a) section 156(4) or 447(2)(a) of the Housing Act 1985,
(b) section 156(4) of that Act as it has effect by virtue of section 17 of the Housing Act 1996 (the right to acquire), or
(c) article 154(1)(a) of the Housing (Northern Ireland) Order 1981.

[(7A) In paragraph (7), in the definition of "housing authority", in paragraph (a), "wholly-owned subsidiary" has the same meaning as in section 1159 (meaning of "subsidiary" etc) of the Companies Act 2006.

(7B) For the purpose of paragraph (7A), the Welsh Ministers are to be treated as a body corporate.]

(8) For the purposes of the definition of "relevant credit agreement relating to the purchase of land", a transaction is, unless paragraph (9) applies, a "linked transaction" in relation to a credit agreement ("the principal agreement") if—
(a) it is (or will be) entered into by the borrower under the principal agreement or by a relative of the borrower,
(b) it does not relate to the provision of security,
(c) it does not form part of the principal agreement, and
(d) one of the following conditions is satisfied—
(i) the transaction is entered into in compliance with a term of the principal agreement;
(ii) the principal agreement is a borrower-lender-supplier agreement and the transaction is financed, or to be financed, by the principal agreement;
(iii) the following conditions are met—
(aa) the other party is a person to whom paragraph (10) applies,
(bb) the other party initiated the transaction by suggesting it to the borrower or the relative of the borrower, and
(cc) the borrower or the relative of the borrower enters into the transaction to induce the lender to enter into the principal agreement or for another purpose related to the principal agreement or to a transaction financed or to be financed by the principal agreement.

(9) This paragraph applies if the transaction is—
(a) a contract of insurance,
(b) a contract which contains a guarantee of goods, or
(c) a transaction which comprises, or is effected under—
(i) an agreement for the operation of an account (including any savings account) for the deposit of money, or

(ii) an agreement for the operation of a current account, under which the customer ("C") may, by means of cheques or similar orders payable to C or to any other person, obtain or have the use of money held or made available by the person with whom the account is kept.

(10) The persons to whom this paragraph applies are—

(a) the lender;

(b) the lender's associate;

(c) a person who, in the negotiation of the transaction, is represented by a person who carries on an activity of the kind specified by article 36A (credit broking) by way of business who is or was also a negotiator in negotiations for the principal agreement;

(d) a person who, at the time the transaction is initiated, knows that the principal agreement has been made or contemplates that it might be made.]

NOTES

Inserted as noted to art 60B at **[8.142]**.

The words in square brackets in para (2) were substituted by the Mortgage Credit Directive Order 2015, SI 2015/910, Sch 1, Pt 2, para 4(1), (15)(a), as from 21 March 2016.

The words in square brackets in para (5), and the words "or equitable" in square brackets in the definition "housing authority" in para (7), were inserted by the Financial Services and Markets Act 2000 (Regulated Activities) (Amendment) Order 2014, SI 2014/366, art 2(1), (26), as from 1 April 2014. The words "Subject to article 60HA, a relevant credit agreement" in square brackets in para (5) were substituted by SI 2015/910, Sch 1, Pt 2, para 4(1), (15)(b), as from 21 March 2016. See also the note below.

Note that SI 2015/910, Sch 1, Pt 2, para 4(1), (15)(b) actually provides as follows—

"(b) in paragraph (5) for "A relevant credit agreement" substitute "Subject to article 60HA, a relevant credit agreement".".

However, the words "A relevant credit agreement" did not occur in para (5) and it is assumed that the intention was to substitute the words "A credit agreement" which did appear in the paragraph.

Words in square brackets in para (6) substituted by the Financial Services and Markets Act 2000 (Amendment) (EU Exit) Regulations 2019, SI 2019/632, regs 120, 139, as from IP completion day (as defined in the European Union (Withdrawal Agreement) Act 2020, s 39).

The words ", a company which is a wholly-owned subsidiary of the Welsh Ministers" in square brackets in the definition "housing authority" in para (7) were inserted, and paras (7A), (7B) were inserted, by the Financial Services and Markets Act 2000 (Regulated Activities) (Amendment) (No 3) Order 2014, SI 2014/1740, art 2, as from 28 July 2014.

The words "a registered social landlord within the meaning of Part 1 of the Housing Act 1996," and "or a housing association within the meaning of Part 2 of the Housing (Northern Ireland) Order 1992" in the definition "housing authority" in para (7) were inserted by the Financial Services and Markets Act 2000 (Regulated Activities) (Amendment) Order 2016, SI 2016/392, art 2(1), (13), as from 20 March 2016.

[8.146]

[60F Exempt agreements: exemptions relating to number of repayments to be made

(1) A credit agreement is an exempt agreement for the purposes of this Chapter in the following cases.

(2) A credit agreement is an exempt agreement if—

(a) the agreement is a borrower-lender-supplier agreement for fixed-sum credit[, other than a green deal plan],

(b) the number of payments to be made by the borrower is not more than [twelve],

(c) those payments are required to be made within a period of 12 months or less (beginning on the date of the agreement),

(d) the credit is—

(i) secured on land, or

(ii) provided without interest or other . . . charges, and

(e) paragraph (7) does not apply to the agreement.

(3) A credit agreement is an exempt agreement if—

(a) the agreement is a borrower-lender-supplier agreement for running-account credit,

(b) the borrower is to make payments in relation to specified periods which must be, unless the agreement is secured on land, of 3 months or less,

(c) the number of payments to be made by the borrower in repayment of the whole amount of credit provided in each such period is not more than one,

(d) the credit is—

(i) secured on land, or

(ii) provided without interest or other significant charges, and

(e) paragraph (7) does not apply to the agreement.

(4) [Subject to article 60HA, a credit agreement] is an exempt agreement if—

(a) the agreement is a borrower-lender-supplier agreement financing the purchase of land,

(b) the number of payments to be made by the borrower is not more than four, and

(c) the credit is—

(i) secured on land, or

(ii) provided without interest or other charges.

(5) A credit agreement is an exempt agreement if—

(a) the agreement is a borrower-lender-supplier agreement for fixed-sum credit,

(b) the credit is to finance a premium under a contract of insurance relating to land or anything on land,

(c) the lender is the lender under a credit agreement secured by a legal [or equitable] mortgage on that land,

(d) the credit is to be repaid within the period (which must be 12 months or less) to which the premium relates,

(e) in the case of an agreement secured on land, there is no charge forming part of the total charge for credit under the agreement other than interest at a rate not exceeding the rate of interest from time to time payable under the agreement mentioned at sub-paragraph (c),

(f) in the case of an agreement which is not secured on land, the credit is provided without interest or other charges, and
(g) the number of payments to be made by the borrower is not more than twelve.

(6) A credit agreement is an exempt agreement if—
(a) the agreement is a borrower-lender-supplier agreement for fixed-sum credit,
(b) the lender is the lender under a credit agreement secured by a legal [or equitable] mortgage on land,
(c) the agreement is to finance a premium under a contract of whole life insurance which provides, in the event of the death of the person on whose life the contract is effected before the credit referred to in sub-paragraph (b) has been repaid, for payment of a sum not exceeding the amount sufficient to meet the amount which, immediately after that credit has been advanced, would be payable to the lender in respect of that credit (including interest from time to time payable under that agreement),
(d) in the case of an agreement secured on land, there is no charge forming part of the total charge for credit under the agreement other than interest at a rate not exceeding the rate of interest from time to time payable under the agreement mentioned at sub-paragraph (b),
(e) in the case of an agreement which is not secured on land, the credit is provided without interest or other charges, and
(f) the number of payments to be made by the borrower is not more than twelve.

(7) This paragraph applies to—
(a) agreements financing the purchase of land;
(b) agreements which are conditional sale agreements or hire-purchase agreements;
(c) agreements secured by a pledge (other than a pledge of documents of title or of bearer bonds).

[(8) In this article, "payment" means any payment which comprises or includes—
(a) the repayment of capital, or
(b) the payment of interest or any other charge which forms part of the total charge for credit.]

NOTES

Inserted as noted to art 60B at **[8.142]**.

Words in square brackets in sub-para (2)(a) inserted by the Financial Services and Markets Act 2000 (Regulated Activities) (Green Deal) (Amendment) Order 2014, SI 2014/1850, arts 2, 7, as from 15 July 2014.

Word in square brackets in sub-para (2)(b) substituted by the Financial Services and Markets Act 2000 (Miscellaneous Provisions) (No 2) Order 2015, SI 2015/352, art 2(a), as from 18 March 2015.

The word omitted from sub-para (2)(d)(ii) was revoked, and the words in square brackets in sub-paras (5)(c), (6)(b) were inserted, by the Financial Services and Markets Act 2000 (Regulated Activities) (Amendment) Order 2014, SI 2014/366, art 2(1), (27), as from 1 April 2014.

Words in square brackets in para (4) substituted by the Mortgage Credit Directive Order 2015, SI 2015/910, Sch 1, Pt 2, para 4(1), (16), as from 21 March 2016.

Para (8) was substituted by the Financial Services and Markets Act 2000 (Miscellaneous Provisions) Order 2015, SI 2015/853, art 3(1), (5), as from 24 March 2015.

[8.147]

[60G Exempt agreements: exemptions relating to the total charge for credit

(1) A credit agreement is an exempt agreement for the purposes of this Chapter in the following cases.

(2) A credit agreement is an exempt agreement if—
(a) it is a borrower-lender agreement, . . .
(b) the lender is a credit union and the rate of the total charge for credit does not exceed 42.6 per cent[, and
[(c) paragraph (2A) applies to the agreement.]

[(2A) This paragraph applies to the agreement if—
(a) the agreement is not [one to which subsection (2) of section 423A of the Act applies]; . . .
(b) the agreement is [one to which that subsection applies] and—
(i) the agreement is [one to which subsection (3) of that section applies],
(ii) the agreement is a bridging loan . . . , or
(iii) in relation to the agreement—
(aa) the borrower receives timely information on the main features, risks and costs of the agreement at the pre-contractual stage, and
(bb) any advertising of the agreement is fair, clear and not misleading[; or
(c) the agreement was entered into before 21st March 2016].]

(3) [Subject to paragraph (8), a credit agreement] is an exempt agreement if—
(a) it is a borrower-lender agreement,
(b) it is an agreement of a kind offered to a particular class of individual or relevant recipient of credit and not offered to the public generally,
(c) it provides that the only charge included in the total charge for credit is interest,
(d) interest under the agreement may not at any time be more than the sum of one per cent and the highest of the base rates published by the banks specified in paragraph (7) on the date 28 days before the date on which the interest is charged, and
(e) paragraph (5) does not apply to the agreement.

(4) [Subject to paragraph (8), a credit agreement] is an exempt agreement if—
(a) it is a borrower-lender agreement,
(b) it is an agreement of a kind offered to a particular class of individual or relevant recipient of credit and not offered to the public generally,
(c) it does not provide for or permit an increase in the rate or amount of any item which is included in the total charge for credit,

(d) the total charge for credit under the agreement is not more than the sum of one per cent and the highest of the base rates published by the banks specified in paragraph (7) on the date 28 days before the date on which the charge is imposed, and

(e) paragraph (5) does not apply to the agreement.

(5) This paragraph applies to an agreement if—

(a) the total amount to be repaid by the borrower to discharge the borrower's indebtedness may vary according to a formula which is specified in the agreement and which has effect by reference to movements in the level of any index or other factor, or

[(b) the agreement—

(i) is not—

(aa) secured on land, or

[(bb) offered by a lender to a borrower as an incident of the borrower's employment with the lender or with an undertaking in the same group as the lender;] and

(ii) does not meet the general interest test.]

(6) For the purposes of [paragraphs (5) and (8)], an agreement meets the general interest test if—

(a) the agreement is offered under an enactment with a general interest purpose, and

(b) the terms on which the credit is provided are more favourable to the borrower than those prevailing on the market, either because the rate of interest is lower than that prevailing on the market, or because the rate of interest is no higher than that prevailing on the market but the other terms on which credit is provided are more favourable to the borrower.

(7) The banks specified in this paragraph are—

(a) the Bank of England;

(b) Bank of Scotland;

(c) Barclays Bank plc;

(d) Clydesdale Bank plc;

(e) Co-operative Bank Public Limited Company;

(f) Coutts & Co;

(g) National Westminster Bank Public Limited Company;

(h) the Royal Bank of Scotland plc.

[(8) A credit agreement [to which subsection (2) of section 423A of the Act applies] [which is entered into on or after 21st March 2016] is an exempt agreement pursuant to paragraph (3) or (4) only if—

(a) the agreement meets the general interest test;

(b) the borrower receives timely information on the main features, risks and costs of the agreement at the pre-contractual stage; and

(c) any advertising of the agreement is fair, clear and not misleading.]

[(9) In this article "bridging loan" means a mortgage agreement that—

(a) is of no fixed duration or is due to be repaid within 12 months, and

(b) is used by a consumer, within the meaning given by section 423A(4) of the Act, as a temporary financing solution while transitioning to another financial arrangement for the immovable property concerned.]]

NOTES

Inserted as noted to art 60B at **[8.142]**.

Para (2): word omitted from sub-para (a) revoked, and sub-para (c) (and the preceding word) inserted, by the Mortgage Credit Directive Order 2015, SI 2015/910, Sch 1, Pt 2, para 4(1), (17)(a), as from 21 March 2016.

Para (2A): inserted by SI 2015/910, Sch 1, Pt 2, para 4(1), (17)(b), as from 21 March 2016. Word omitted from sub-para (a) revoked, and sub-para (c) (and the preceding word) added, by the Financial Services and Markets Act 2000 (Regulated Activities) (Amendment) Order 2016, SI 2016/392, art 2(1), (14)(a), as from 21 March 2016. Words in square brackets in sub-paras (a) and (b) substituted, and words omitted from sub-para (b) revoked, by the Financial Services and Markets Act 2000 (Amendment) (EU Exit) Regulations 2019, SI 2019/632, regs 120, 140(1)–(3), as from IP completion day (as defined in the European Union (Withdrawal Agreement) Act 2020, s 39).

Paras (3), (4): words in square brackets substituted by SI 2015/910, Sch 1, Pt 2, para 4(1), (17)(c), (d), as from 21 March 2016.

Para (5): sub-para (b) substituted by the Financial Services and Markets Act 2000 (Regulated Activities) (Amendment) Order 2014, SI 2014/366, art 2(1), (28), as from 1 April 2014. Sub-para (b)(i)(bb) further substituted by the Financial Services and Markets Act 2000 (Miscellaneous Provisions) (No 2) Order 2015, SI 2015/352, art 2(b), as from 18 March 2015.

Para (6): words in square brackets substituted by SI 2015/910, Sch 1, Pt 2, para 4(1), (17)(e), as from 21 March 2016.

Para (8): added by SI 2015/910, Sch 1, Pt 2, para 4(1), (17)(f), as from 21 March 2016. Words in first pair of square brackets by SI 2019/632, regs 120, 140(1), (4), as from IP completion day (as defined in the European Union (Withdrawal Agreement) Act 2020, s 39). Words in second pair of square brackets inserted SI 2016/392, art 2(1), (14)(b), as from 21 March 2016.

Para (9): added by SI 2019/632, regs 120, 140(1), (5), as from IP completion day (as defined in the European Union (Withdrawal Agreement) Act 2020, s 39).

[8.148]

[60H Exempt agreements: exemptions relating to the nature of the borrower

[(1)] [[A] credit agreement] is an exempt agreement for the purposes of this Chapter if—

(a) the borrower is an individual,

(b) the agreement is either—

(i) secured on land, or

[(ii) for credit which exceeds £60,260 and[, if entered into on or after 21st March 2016,] is for a purpose other than—

(aa) the renovation of residential property, . . .

(bb) . . .]

(c) the agreement includes a declaration made by the borrower which provides that the borrower agrees to forgo the protection and remedies that would be available to the borrower if the agreement were a regulated credit agreement and which complies with rules made by the FCA for the purposes of this paragraph,
(d) a statement has been made in relation to the income or assets of the borrower which complies with rules made by the FCA for the purposes of this paragraph,
(e) the connection between the statement and the agreement complies with any rules made by the FCA for the purposes of this paragraph (including as to the period of time between the making of the statement and the agreement being entered into), and
(f) a copy of the statement was provided to the lender before the agreement was entered into.

[(1A) Article 4(4B) does not apply to an agreement which is exempt under paragraph (1), the purpose of which is to acquire or retain property rights in land or in an existing or projected building, and—
(a) a declaration has been made by the borrower which either—
(i) provides that the borrower is UK resident, or
(ii) provides that the borrower is treated as present in the United Kingdom,
(b) a copy of that declaration was provided to the lender before the agreement was entered into, and
(c) the agreement is entered into on or after 21st July 2022.

(1B) For the purposes of paragraph (1A), a borrower is "UK resident" if—
(a) the borrower is present in the United Kingdom on at least 183 days during the continuous period of 365 days ending with the date the agreement is entered into, or
(b) the spouse or civil partner of the borrower—
(i) is living with the borrower on the date the agreement was entered into, and
(ii) is present in the United Kingdom on at least 183 days during the continuous period of 365 days ending with the date the agreement is entered into.

(1C) For the purposes of paragraph (1A), a borrower is treated as present in the United Kingdom if, on the date the agreement was entered into, the borrower—
(a) is in Crown employment, and
(b) is present in a country or territory outside the United Kingdom for the purpose of performing activities in the course of that employment, or
(c) is the spouse or civil partner of an individual who—
(i) is in Crown employment,
(ii) is present in a country or territory outside the United Kingdom for the purpose of performing activities in the course of that employment, and
(d) is living with their spouse or civil partner.

(1D) References in this article to a borrower being present in the United Kingdom on a day are to the borrower being present in the United Kingdom at the end of that day.

(1E) Individuals who are married to, or are civil partners of, each other are treated, for the purposes of this article, as living together unless—
(a) they are separated under an order of a court of competent jurisdiction,
(b) they are separated by deed of separation, or
(c) they are in fact separated in circumstances in which the separation is likely to be permanent.

(1F) For the purposes of this article, "Crown employment" means employment under or for the purposes of a government department or any officer or body exercising on behalf of the Crown functions conferred by a statutory provision.]

[(2) . . .]]

NOTES

Inserted as noted to art 60B at **[8.142]**.

Para (1) numbered as such by the Mortgage Credit Directive Order 2015, SI 2015/910, Sch 1, Pt 2, para 4(1), (18), as from 21 March 2016; and amended as follows—

Sub-para (b)(ii) and the words in the first (outer) pair of square brackets were substituted by SI 2015/910, Sch 1, Pt 2, para 4(1), (18), as from 21 March 2016.

The word "A" in the second (inner) pair of square brackets was substituted by the Financial Services and Markets Act 2000 (Regulated Activities) (Amendment) (No 2) Order 2022, SI 2022/726, art 2(7)(a), as from 21 July 2022.

The words ", if entered into on or after 21st March 2016," in square brackets in sub-para (b)(ii) were inserted by the Financial Services and Markets Act 2000 (Regulated Activities) (Amendment) Order 2016, SI 2016/392, art 2(1), (15). as from 21 March 2016.

Sub-para (b)(ii)(bb) and the preceding word were revoked by the Financial Services and Markets Act 2000 (Amendment) (EU Exit) Regulations 2019, SI 2019/632, regs 120, 141, as from IP completion day (as defined in the European Union (Withdrawal Agreement) Act 2020, s 39).

Paras (1A)–(1F): inserted SI 2022/726, art 2(7)(b), as from 21 July 2022.

Para (2): originally added by SI 2015/910, Sch 1, Pt 2, para 4(1), (18), as from 21 March 2016. Subsequently revoked by SI 2019/632, regs 120, 141, as from IP completion day (as defined in the European Union (Withdrawal Agreement) Act 2020, s 39).

[8.149]

[60HA Exempt agreements: [provision qualifying articles [60E and 60F]]

(1) A credit agreement [entered into on or after 21st March 2016] is not an exempt agreement pursuant to article 60E(2) or (5) [or 60F(4) if it is a mortgage agreement to which paragraph (2) does not apply].

(2) This paragraph applies [to an agreement] if—
(a) . . .
(b) the agreement is a bridging loan within the meaning of [given by article 60G(9)]; or
(c) the agreement is a restricted public loan in respect of which—

(i) the borrower receives timely information on the main features, risks and costs at the pre-contractual stage; and

(ii) any advertising is fair, clear and not misleading.

(3) In paragraph (2)(c) "restricted public loan" means a credit agreement that is—

(a) offered to a particular class of borrower and not offered to the public generally;

(b) offered under an enactment with a general interest purpose; and

(c) provided on terms which are more favourable to the borrower than those prevailing on the market, because it meets one of the following conditions—

(i) it is interest free;

(ii) the rate of interest is lower than that prevailing on the market; or

(iii) the rate of interest is no higher than that prevailing on the market but the other terms on which credit is provided are more favourable to the borrower.]

NOTES

Inserted by the Mortgage Credit Directive Order 2015, SI 2015/910, Sch 1, Pt 2, para 4(1), (19), as from 21 March 2016.

Article heading: words in first (outer) pair of square brackets substituted by the Financial Services and Markets Act 2000 (Amendment) (EU Exit) Regulations 2019, SI 2019/632, regs 120, 142(1), (2), as from IP completion day (as defined in the European Union (Withdrawal Agreement) Act 2020, s 39). Words in second (inner) pair of square brackets substituted by the Financial Services and Markets Act 2000 (Regulated Activities) (Amendment) (No 2) Order 2022, SI 2022/726, art 2(8), as from 21 July 2022.

Para (1): words in first pair of square brackets inserted by the Financial Services and Markets Act 2000 (Regulated Activities) (Amendment) Order 2016, SI 2016/392, art 2(1), (16). as from 21 March 2016. Words in second pair of square brackets substituted by SI 2019/632, regs 120, 142(1), (3), as from IP completion day (as defined in the European Union (Withdrawal Agreement) Act 2020, s 39).

Para (2): the words in the first pair of square brackets were inserted, sub-para (a) was revoked, and the words in the second pair of square brackets were substituted, by SI 2019/632, regs 120, 142(1), (4), as from IP completion day (as defined in the European Union (Withdrawal Agreement) Act 2020, s 39).

[Exclusions

[8.150]

60I Arranging administration by authorised person

A person ("A") who is not an authorised person does not carry on an activity of the kind specified by article 60B(2) in relation to a regulated credit agreement where A—

(a) arranges for another person, who is an authorised person with permission to carry on an activity of that kind, to exercise or to have the right to exercise the lender's rights and duties under the agreement, or

(b) exercises or has the right to exercise the lender's rights and duties under the agreement during a period of not more than one month beginning with the day on which any such arrangement comes to an end.]

NOTES

Inserted as noted to art 60B at **[8.142]**.

[8.151]

[60J Administration pursuant to agreement with authorised person

A person who is not an authorised person does not carry on an activity of the kind specified by article 60B(2) in relation to regulated credit agreement if that person exercises or has the right to exercise the lender's rights and duties under the agreement pursuant to an agreement with an authorised person who has permission to carry on an activity of the kind specified by article 60B(2).]

NOTES

Inserted as noted to art 60B at **[8.142]**.

[8.152]

[60JA Payment institutions

(1) There are excluded from article 60B activities carried on by a person who is an EEA authorised payment institution exercising passport rights in the United Kingdom in accordance with Article [18(4)] of the payment services directive.

(2) Terms used in this article have the meanings given in Payment Services Regulations [2017].]

NOTES

Inserted, together with art 60JB, by the Financial Services and Markets Act 2000 (Regulated Activities) (Amendment) Order 2014, SI 2014/366, art 2(1), (29), as from 1 April 2014.

This article was revoked by the Financial Services and Markets Act 2000 (Amendment) (EU Exit) Regulations 2019, SI 2019/632, regs 120, 143(1), as from IP completion day (as defined in the European Union (Withdrawal Agreement) Act 2020, s 39). For savings, see reg 143(2)–(3) of the 2019 Regulations (as amended by the Financial Services (Electronic Money, Payment Services and Miscellaneous Amendments) (EU Exit) Regulations 2019, SI 2019/1212) which provide as follows—

"(2) In relation to a person who has transitional authorisation by virtue of paragraph 14 of Schedule 3 to the Electronic Money, Payment Services and Payment Systems (Amendment and Transitional Provisions) (EU Exit) Regulations 2018 ("the 2018 Regulations"), the amendment made by paragraph (1) does not apply during the transition period (within the meaning given by paragraph 22 of that Schedule).

(2A) In relation to a person who has a continued authorisation for a limited purpose in accordance with paragraph 26 of Schedule 3 to the 2018 Regulations or is exempt from the prohibition in regulation 138(1) of Payment Services Regulations 2017 by virtue of paragraph 36 of Schedule 3 to the 2018 Regulations, the amendment made by paragraph (1) does not apply during the extension period (within the meaning given by paragraph 31 of that Schedule) or the period of exemption (within the meaning given by paragraph 36 of that Schedule).

(3) Despite the repeal of Schedule 5 to the Payment Services Regulations 2017 by the 2018 Regulations, that Schedule has effect, with any necessary modifications, in relation to a case where the amendment made by paragraph (1) does not apply because of paragraph (2) or (2A).".

Figure in square brackets in para (1), and year "2017" in square brackets in para (2), substituted by the Payment Services Regulations 2017, SI 2017/752, reg 156, Sch 8, Pt 3, para 8(b), as from 13 January 2018.

[8.153]
[60JB Electronic money institutions

(1) There are excluded from article 60B activities carried on by a person who is an EEA authorised electronic money institution exercising passport rights in the United Kingdom in accordance with Article [18(4)] of the payment services directive as applied by Article 6 of the electronic money directive.

(2) Terms used in this article have the meanings given in the Electronic Money Regulations 2011.]

NOTES

Inserted as noted to art 60JA at **[8.152]**.

This article was revoked by the Financial Services and Markets Act 2000 (Amendment) (EU Exit) Regulations 2019, SI 2019/632, regs 120, 144(1), as from IP completion day (as defined in the European Union (Withdrawal Agreement) Act 2020, s 39). For savings, see reg 144(2)–(3) of the 2019 Regulations (as amended by the Financial Services (Electronic Money, Payment Services and Miscellaneous Amendments) (EU Exit) Regulations 2019, SI 2019/1212) which provide as follows—

"(2) In relation to a person who has transitional authorisation by virtue of paragraph 2 of Schedule 3 to the Electronic Money, Payment Services and Payment Systems (Amendment and Transitional Provisions) (EU Exit) Regulations 2018 ("the 2018 Regulations"), the amendment made by paragraph (1) does not apply during the transition period (within the meaning given by paragraph 10 of that Schedule).

(2A) In relation to a person who has continued authorisation for limited purposes in accordance with paragraph 12B of Schedule 3 to the 2018 Regulations or is exempt from the prohibition in regulation 63(1) of Electronic Money Regulations 2011 by virtue of paragraph 12L of Schedule 3 to the 2018 Regulations, the amendment made by paragraph (1) does not apply during the extension period (within the meaning given by paragraph 12G of that Schedule) or the period of exemption (within the meaning given by paragraph 12L of that Schedule).

(3) Despite the repeal of Schedule 2A to the Electronic Money Regulations 2011 by the 2018 Regulations, that Schedule has effect, with any necessary modifications, in relation to a case where the amendment made by paragraph (1) does not apply because of paragraph (2) or (2A).".

Para (1): figure in square brackets substituted by the Payment Services Regulations 2017, SI 2017/752, reg 156, Sch 8, Pt 3, para 8(c), as from 13 January 2018.

[8.154]
[60K [Other exclusions]

Article 60B is also subject to [the exclusions in articles . . . 72G (local authorities) and 72I (registered consumer buy-to-let mortgage firms)].]

NOTES

Inserted as noted to art 60B at **[8.142]**.

Article heading substituted by the Financial Services and Markets Act 2000 (Regulated Activities) (Amendment) Order 2014, SI 2014/366, art 2(1), (30), (31), as from 1 April 2014.

Words in square brackets substituted by the Mortgage Credit Directive Order 2015, SI 2015/910, Sch 1, Pt 2, para 4(1), (20), as from 21 March 2016.

The words omitted were revoked by the Electronic Commerce and Solvency 2 (Amendment etc) (EU Exit) Regulations 2019, SI 2019/1361, reg 5(1), (3), as from IP completion day (as defined in the European Union (Withdrawal Agreement) Act 2020, s 39) (for transitional provisions, see the note in relation to art 72A of this Order *post*).

[Supplemental

[8.155]
60L Interpretation of Chapter 14A etc

(1) In this Chapter—

"assignment", in relation to Scotland, means assignation;

"associate" means, in relation to a person ("P")—

(a) where P is an individual, any person who is or who has been—
  (i) P's spouse or P's civil partner;
  (ii) a relative of P, of P's spouse or of P's civil partner;
  (iii) the spouse or civil partner of a relative of P or P's spouse or civil partner;
  (iv) if P is a member of a partnership, any of P's partners and the spouse or civil partner of any such person;

(b) where P is a body corporate—
  (i) any person who is a controller ("C") of P, and
  (ii) any other person for whom C is a controller;

"borrower" means [(except in relation to green deal plans: see instead article 60LB)] a person who receives credit under a credit agreement or a person to whom the rights and duties of a borrower under a credit agreement have passed by assignment or operation of law;

"borrower-lender agreement" means—

(a) a credit agreement—
  (i) to finance a transaction between the borrower and a person ("the supplier") other than the lender, and
  (ii) which is not made by the lender under pre-existing arrangements, or in contemplation of future arrangements, between the lender and the supplier,

(b) a credit agreement to refinance any existing indebtedness of the borrower, whether to the lender or another person, or

(c) a credit agreement which is—

(i) an unrestricted-use credit agreement, and

(ii) not made by the lender—

(aa) under pre-existing arrangements between the lender and a person other than the borrower ("the supplier"), and

(bb) in the knowledge that the credit is to be used to finance a transaction between the borrower and the supplier;

"borrower-lender-supplier agreement" means—

(a) a credit agreement to finance a transaction between the borrower and the lender, whether forming part of that agreement or not;

(b) a credit agreement—

(i) to finance a transaction between the borrower and a person ("the supplier") other than the lender, and

(ii) which is made by the lender under pre-existing arrangements, or in contemplation of future arrangements, between the lender and the supplier, or

(c) a credit agreement which is—

(i) an unrestricted-use credit agreement, and

(ii) made by the lender under pre-existing arrangements between the lender and a person ("the supplier") other than the borrower in the knowledge that the credit is to be used to finance a transaction between the borrower and the supplier;

"conditional sale agreement" means an agreement for the sale of goods or land under which the purchase price or part of it is payable by instalments, and the property in the goods or land is to remain with the seller (notwithstanding that the buyer is to be in possession of the goods or land) until such conditions as to the payment of instalments or otherwise as may be specified in the agreement are fulfilled;

"credit" includes a cash loan and any other form of financial accommodation;

["credit agreement"—

(a) in relation to an agreement other than a green deal plan, has the meaning given by article 60B;

(b) in relation to a green deal plan, has the meaning given by article 60LB;]

"credit union" means a credit union within the meaning of—

(a) the Credit Unions Act 1979;

(b) the Credit Unions (Northern Ireland) Order 1985;

"deposit" (except where specified otherwise) means any sum payable by a borrower by way of deposit or down-payment, or credited or to be credited to the borrower on account of any deposit or down-payment, whether the sum is to be or has been paid to the lender or any other person, or is to be or has been discharged by a payment of money or a transfer or delivery of goods or other means;

"exempt agreement" has the meaning given by article 60B;

"finance" includes financing in whole or in part, and "refinance" is to be read accordingly;

"fixed-sum credit" means a facility under a credit agreement whereby the borrower is enabled to receive credit (whether in one amount or by instalments) but which is not running-account credit;

"hire-purchase agreement" means an agreement—

(a) which is not a conditional sale agreement,

(b) under which goods are bailed or (in Scotland) hired to a person ("P") in return for periodical payments by P, and

(c) the property in the goods will pass to P if the terms of the agreement are complied with and one or more of the following occurs—

(i) the exercise by P of an option to purchase the goods;

(ii) the doing by any party to the agreement of any other act specified in the agreement;

(iii) the happening of any event specified in the agreement;

"legal [or equitable] mortgage" includes [a legal or equitable] charge and, in Scotland, a heritable security;

"lender" means [(except in relation to green deal plans: see instead article 60LB)]—

(a) the person providing credit under a credit agreement, or

(b) a person who exercises or has the right to exercise the rights and duties of a person who provided credit under such an agreement;

"payment" (except in article 60F) means a payment comprising or including an amount in respect of credit;

"regulated credit agreement" has the meaning given by article 60B;

"relative" means brother, sister, uncle, aunt, nephew, niece, lineal ancestor or lineal descendent;

"relevant recipient of credit" means—

(a) a partnership consisting of two or three persons not all of whom are bodies corporate, or

(b) an unincorporated body of persons which does not consist entirely of bodies corporate and is not a partnership;

"restricted-use credit agreement" means a credit agreement—

(a) to finance a transaction between the borrower and the lender, whether forming part of that agreement or not,

(b) to finance a transaction between the borrower and a person ("the supplier") other than the lender, or

(c) to refinance any existing indebtedness of the borrower's, whether to the lender or another person;

"running-account credit" means a facility under a credit agreement under which the borrower or another person is enabled to receive from time to time from the lender or a third party cash, goods or services to an amount or value such that, taking into account payments made by or to the credit of the borrower, the credit limit (if any) is not at any time exceeded;

"security" in relation to a credit agreement, means a mortgage, charge, pledge, bond, debenture, indemnity, guarantee, bill, note or other right provided by the borrower or at the implied or express request of the borrower to secure the carrying out of the obligations of the borrower under the agreement;

"total charge for credit" has the meaning given in rules made by the FCA under article 60M;

"total price" means the total sum payable by the debtor under a hire-purchase agreement, including any sum payable on the exercise of an option to purchase but excluding any sum payable as a penalty or as compensation or damages for a breach of the agreement;

"unrestricted-use credit agreement" means a credit agreement which is not a restricted-use credit agreement.

[(1A) For the purposes of this Chapter, a credit agreement that is a green deal plan is to be treated as—

(a) a borrower-lender-supplier agreement falling within paragraph (a) of the definition of "borrower-lender-supplier agreement";

(b) a restricted-use credit agreement falling within paragraph (a) of the definition of "restricted-use credit agreement".]

(2) For the purposes of the definition of "restricted-use credit agreement"—

(a) a credit agreement does not fall within the definition if the credit is in fact provided in such a way as to leave the borrower free to use it as the borrower chooses, even though certain uses would contravene that or any other agreement; and

(b) an agreement may fall within paragraph (b) of the definition even though the identity of the supplier is unknown at the time the agreement is made.

(3) For the purposes of the definition of "borrower-lender agreement" [and the definition of "borrower-lender-supplier agreement"], a credit agreement is, subject to paragraph (6), entered into under pre-existing arrangements between a lender and a supplier if it is entered into in accordance with, or in connection with, arrangements previously made between the lender (or the lender's associate) and the supplier (or the supplier's associate) unless the arrangements fall within paragraph (5).

(4) For the purposes of the definition of "borrower-lender agreement" [and the definition of "borrower-lender-supplier agreement"], a credit agreement is entered into in contemplation of future arrangements between a lender and a supplier if it is entered into in the expectation that arrangements will subsequently be made between the lender (or the lender's associate) and the supplier (or the supplier's associate) for the supply of cash, goods or services to be financed by the credit agreement unless the arrangements fall within paragraph (5).

(5) Arrangements fall within this paragraph if they are—

(a) for the making, in circumstances specified in the credit agreement, of payments to the supplier by the lender ("L") and L indicates that L is willing to make, in such circumstances, payments of the kind to suppliers generally, or

(b) for the electronic transfer of funds from a current account held with an authorised person with permission to accept deposits (within the meaning given by article 3).

(6) If a lender is an associate of the supplier's, the credit agreement is to be treated as entered into under pre-existing arrangements between the lender and the supplier unless the lender can show that this is not the case.

(7) For the purposes of the definition of "running-account credit", "credit limit" means, as respects any period, the maximum debit balance which, under a credit agreement, is allowed to stand on the account during that period, disregarding any term of the agreement allowing that maximum to be exceeded on a temporary basis.

(8) For the purposes of this Chapter, a person by whom goods are bailed or (in Scotland) hired to an individual or relevant recipient of credit under a hire-purchase agreement is to be taken to be providing that individual or person with fixed-sum credit to finance the transaction of an amount equal to the total price of the goods less the aggregate of the deposit (if any) and the total charge for credit.

(9) For the purposes of this Chapter, where credit is provided otherwise than in sterling, it is to be treated as provided in sterling of an equivalent amount.

[(10) For the purposes of this Chapter, where a provision specifies an amount of credit, running-account credit shall be taken not to exceed the amount specified in that provision ("the specified amount") if—

(a) the credit limit does not exceed the specified amount; or

(b) the credit limit exceeds the specified amount, or there is no credit limit, and—

(i) the borrower is not enabled to draw at any one time an amount which, so far as it represents credit, exceeds the specified amount; or

(ii) the agreement provides that, if the debit balance rises above a given amount (not exceeding the specified amount), the rate of the total charge for credit increases or any other condition favouring the lender or the lender's associate comes into operation; or

(iii) at the time the agreement is made it is probable, having regard to the terms of the agreement and any other relevant considerations, that the debit balance will not at any time rise above the specified amount.

(11) For the purposes of this Chapter, an item entering into the total charge for credit is not to be treated as credit even though time is allowed for its payment.]]

NOTES

Inserted as noted to art 60B at **[8.142]**.

The words "(except in relation to green deal plans: see instead article 60LB)" in the definitions "borrower" and "lender" in para (1) were inserted, the definition "credit agreement" in that paragraph was substituted, and para (1A) was inserted, by the Financial Services and Markets Act 2000 (Regulated Activities) (Green Deal) (Amendment) Order 2014, SI 2014/1850, arts 2, 8, as from 15 July 2014.

The other words in square brackets in para (1), and the words in square brackets in paras (3), (4), were inserted by the Financial Services and Markets Act 2000 (Regulated Activities) (Amendment) Order 2014, SI 2014/366, art 2(1), (32), as from 1 April 2014.

Paras (10), (11) were added by the Financial Services and Markets Act 2000 (Miscellaneous Provisions) Order 2015, SI 2015/853, art 3(1), (6), as from 24 March 2015.

[8.156]

[60LA Meaning of consumer etc

(1) For the purposes of sections 1G, 404E and 425A of the Act (meaning of "consumer"), in so far as those provisions relate to a person ("A") carrying on a regulated activity of the kind specified by—

(a) article 60B (regulated credit agreements), or

(b) article 64 (agreeing to carry on specified kinds of activity) in so far as that article relates to article 60B,

a person who is treated by A as a person who is or has been the borrower under a regulated credit agreement is to be treated as a "consumer".

(2) For the purposes of section 328(8) of the Act (meaning of "clients") in so far as that provision relates to a person ("A") carrying on a regulated activity of the kind specified by—

(a) article 60B (regulated credit agreements), or

(b) article 64 (agreeing to carry on specified kinds of activity) in so far as that article relates to article 60B,

a person who is treated by A as a person who is or has been the borrower under a regulated credit agreement is to be treated as a "client".

(3) In this article, "borrower" includes (in addition to those persons included in the definition in article 60L [or, where the credit agreement is a green deal plan, article 60LB])—

(a) any person providing a guarantee or indemnity under a regulated credit agreement, and

(b) a person to whom the rights and duties of a person falling within sub-paragraph (a) have passed by assignment or operation of law.]

NOTES

Inserted by the Financial Services and Markets Act 2000 (Regulated Activities) (Amendment) Order 2014, SI 2014/366, art 2(1), (33), as from 1 April 2014.

Para (3): words in square brackets inserted by the Financial Services and Markets Act 2000 (Regulated Activities) (Green Deal) (Amendment) Order 2014, SI 2014/1850, arts 2, 9, as from 15 July 2014.

[8.157]

[60LB Green deal plans

(1) A green deal plan is to be treated as a credit agreement for the purposes of this Order if (and only if)—

(a) the property in relation to the plan is a domestic property at the time when the plan is commenced, or

(b) if sub-paragraph (a) does not apply, the occupier or owner of the property who makes the arrangement for the plan is an individual or relevant recipient of credit.

(2) In the application of this Order to a green deal credit agreement—

(a) the lender is to be treated as being—

(i) the green deal provider (within the meaning of Chapter 1 of Part 1 of the Energy Act 2011) for the plan, or

(ii) a person who exercises or has the right to exercise the rights and duties of the green deal provider under the plan,

(b) credit is to be treated as advanced under the agreement of an amount equal to the amount of the improvement costs, and

(c) the advance of credit is to be treated as made on the completion of the installation of the energy efficiency improvements to the property (but this sub-paragraph is subject to any term of the green deal plan providing that part of the advance is to be treated as made on completion of any part of the installation).

(3) A reference in a provision of this Order listed in the first column of the table in Schedule 4A to the borrower is, in the application of the provision in relation to a green deal credit agreement, to be read as a reference to—

(a) a person who at the relevant time falls (or fell) within the description or descriptions specified in the corresponding entry in the second column of the table, or

(b) if more than one description is specified and at the relevant time different persons fall (or fell) within the descriptions, each of those persons,

and except as provided by this paragraph, a person is not and is not to be treated as the borrower in relation to the agreement.

(4) References in Schedule 4A to the "improver", "first bill payer", "current bill payer" and "previous bill payer" are to be read as follows—

(a) a person is the "improver" if the person—

(i) is the owner or occupier of the property, and

(ii) is the person who makes (or has made or proposes to make) the arrangement for the green deal plan;

(b) a person is the "first bill payer" if the person is liable to pay the energy bills for the property at the time when the green deal plan is commenced;

(c) a person is the "current bill payer" if the person is liable by virtue of section 1(6)(a) of the Energy Act 2011 to pay instalments under the plan as a result of being for the time being liable to pay the energy bills for the property;

(d) a person is a "previous bill payer" if, as a result of previously falling within sub-paragraph (c) for an earlier period, the person has an outstanding payment liability under the plan in respect of that period.

(5) In this article—

"domestic property" means a building or part of a building that is occupied as a dwelling or (if not occupied) is intended to be occupied as a dwelling;

"energy bill" has the same meaning as in section 1 of the Energy Act 2011;

"energy efficiency improvements" has the meaning given by section 2(4) of the Energy Act 2011;

"green deal credit agreement" means a green deal plan that is to be treated as a credit agreement for the purposes of this Order by virtue of paragraph (1);

"improvement costs", in relation to a green deal plan, are the costs of the energy efficiency improvements to the property which are to be paid by instalments under the plan after the time when credit is to be treated as being advanced by virtue of paragraph (2) (but ignoring any interest or other charges for credit in determining those costs);

"occupier" and "owner" have the same meanings as in Chapter 1 of Part 1 of the Energy Act 2011;

"property", in relation to a green deal plan, means the property to which the energy efficiency improvements under the plan are or are intended to be made.

(6) For the purposes of this article—

(a) a green deal plan is commenced when—

(i) the occupier or owner of the property signs in the prescribed manner a document in relation to the plan in accordance with section 61(1) of the Consumer Credit Act 1974 (requirements as to form and content of regulated agreements), or

(ii) if the occupier or owner of the property does not sign such a document, the green deal plan is made;

(b) a person is liable to pay the energy bills for a property at any time if the person would be treated as the bill payer for the property at that time for the purposes of Chapter 1 of Part 1 of the Energy Act 2011 (see section 2(3) and (10)).".

NOTES

Inserted by the Financial Services and Markets Act 2000 (Regulated Activities) (Green Deal) (Amendment) Order 2014, SI 2014/1850, arts 2, 10, as from 15 July 2014.

[8.158]

[60M Total charge for credit

(1) The FCA may make rules specifying how the total charge for credit to the borrower under a credit agreement is to be determined for the purposes of this Chapter.

(2) Rules made under paragraph (1) may in particular—

(a) specify how the total charge for credit to a person who is, or is to become, the borrower under a credit agreement is to be determined;

(b) specify what items are to be included in determining the total charge for credit and how the value of those items is to be determined;

(c) specify the method of calculating the rate of the total charge for credit;

(d) provide for the whole or part of the amount payable by the borrower or a relative of the borrower under a linked transaction (within the meaning given by article 60E(8)) to be included in the total charge for credit, whether or not the lender is a party to the transaction or derives a benefit from it.]

NOTES

Inserted as noted to art 60B at **[8.142]**.

[CHAPTER 14B REGULATED CONSUMER HIRE AGREEMENTS

The Activities

[8.159]

60N Regulated consumer hire agreements

(1) Entering into a regulated consumer hire agreement as owner is a specified kind of activity.

(2) It is a specified kind of activity for the owner or another person to exercise, or to have the right to exercise, the owner's rights and duties under a regulated consumer hire agreement.

(3) In this Chapter—

"consumer hire agreement" means an agreement between a person ("the owner") and an individual or relevant recipient of credit ("the hirer") for the bailment or, in Scotland, the hiring, of goods to the hirer which—

(a) is not a hire-purchase agreement, and

(b) is capable of subsisting for more than three months;

"exempt agreement" means a consumer hire agreement which is an exempt agreement under articles 60O to 60Q;

"owner" means—

(a) the person who bails or, in Scotland, hires, goods under a . . . consumer hire agreement, or

(b) a person who exercises or has the right to exercise the rights and duties of a person who bailed or, in Scotland, hired, goods under such an agreement;

["regulated consumer hire agreement" means—

(a) in the case of an agreement entered into on or after 1st April 2014, any consumer hire agreement which is not an exempt agreement; or

(b) in the case of an agreement entered into before 1st April 2014, a consumer hire agreement which—

(i) was a regulated agreement within the meaning of section 189(1) of the Consumer Credit Act 1974 when the agreement was entered into; or

(ii) became such a regulated agreement after being varied or supplemented by another agreement before 1st April 2014].]

NOTES

Chapter 14B (originally arts 60N–60R) was inserted by the Financial Services and Markets Act 2000 (Regulated Activities) (Amendment) (No 2) Order 2013, SI 2013/1881, arts 2, 6, as from 1 April 2014.

Para (3): word omitted from the definition "owner" revoked by the Financial Services and Markets Act 2000 (Regulated Activities) (Amendment) Order 2014, SI 2014/366, art 2(1), (34), as from 1 April 2014. Definition "regulated consumer hire agreement" substituted by the Financial Services and Markets Act 2000 (Regulated Activities) (Amendment) Order 2016, SI 2016/392, art 2(1), (17), as from 20 March 2016.

[8.160]

[60O Exempt agreements: exemptions relating to nature of agreement

(1) An agreement is an exempt agreement for the purposes of this Chapter if—

(a) the hirer is required by the agreement to make payments exceeding £25,000, and

(b) the agreement is entered into by the hirer wholly or predominantly for the purposes of a business carried on, or intended to be carried on, by the hirer.

(2) For the purposes of paragraph (1), if an agreement includes a declaration which—

(a) is made by the hirer,

(b) provides that the agreement is entered into by the hirer wholly or predominantly for the purposes of a business carried on, or intended to be carried on, by the hirer, and

(c) complies with rules made by the FCA for the purposes of this article,

the agreement is to be presumed to have been entered into by the hirer wholly or predominantly for the purpose in sub-paragraph (b) unless paragraph (3) applies.

(3) This paragraph applies if, when the agreement is entered into—

(a) the owner (or, if there is more than one owner, any of the owners), or

(b) any person who has acted on behalf of the owner (or, if there is more than one owner, any of the owners), in connection with the entering into of the agreement,

knows or has reasonable cause to suspect that the agreement is not entered into by the hirer wholly or predominantly for the purposes of a business carried on, or intended to be carried on, by the hirer.

(4) For the purposes of this article, where credit is provided otherwise than in sterling, it is to be treated as provided in sterling of an equivalent amount.]

NOTES

Inserted as noted to art 60N at **[8.159]**.

[8.161]

[60P Exempt agreements: exemptions relating to supply of essential services

An agreement is an exempt agreement for the purposes of this Chapter if—

(a) the owner is a body corporate which is authorised by or under an enactment to supply gas, electricity or water, and

(b) the subject of the agreement is a meter or metering equipment which is used (or is to be used) in connection with the supply of gas, electricity or water.]

NOTES

Inserted as noted to art 60N at **[8.159]**.

[8.162]

[60Q Exempt agreements: exemptions relating to the nature of the hirer

An agreement is an exempt agreement for the purposes of this Chapter if—

(a) the hirer is an individual,

(b) the agreement includes a declaration made by the hirer which provides that the hirer agrees to forgo the protection and remedies that would be available to the hirer if the agreement were a regulated consumer hire agreement and which complies with rules made by the FCA for the purposes of this paragraph,

(c) a statement has been made in relation to the income or assets of the hirer which complies with rules made by the FCA for the purposes of this paragraph,

(d) the connection between the statement and the agreement complies with any rules made by the FCA for the purposes of this paragraph (including as to the period of time between the making of the statement and the agreement being entered into), and

(e) a copy of the statement was provided to the owner before the agreement was entered into.]

NOTES

Inserted as noted to art 60N at **[8.159]**.

[Exclusion

[8.163]

60R [Other exclusions]

Article 60N is subject to . . . [. . . the exclusion in article 72G (local authorities)].]

NOTES

Inserted as noted to art 60N at **[8.159]**.

Article heading substituted, and words in square brackets inserted, by the Financial Services and Markets Act 2000 (Regulated Activities) (Amendment) Order 2014, SI 2014/366, art 2(1), (35), (36), as from 1 April 2014.

The words omitted were revoked by the Electronic Commerce and Solvency 2 (Amendment etc) (EU Exit) Regulations 2019, SI 2019/1361, reg 5(1), (3), as from IP completion day (as defined in the European Union (Withdrawal Agreement) Act 2020, s 39) (for transitional provisions, see the note in relation to art 72A of this Order *post*).

[Supplemental

[8.164]

60S Meaning of consumer etc

(1) For the purposes of sections 1G, 404E and 425A of the Act (meaning of "consumer"), in so far as those provisions relate to a person ("A") carrying on a regulated activity of the kind specified by—

(a) article 60N (regulated consumer hire agreements), or

(b) article 64 (agreeing to carry on specified kinds of activity) in so far as that article relates to article 60N, a person who is treated by A as a person who is or has been the hirer under a regulated consumer hire agreement is to be treated as a "consumer".

(2) For the purposes of section 328(8) of the Act (meaning of "clients") in so far as that provision relates to a person ("A") carrying on a regulated activity of the kind specified by—

(a) article 60N (regulated consumer hire agreements), or

(b) article 64 (agreeing to carry on specified kinds of activity) in so far as that article relates to article 60N,

a person who is treated by A as a person who is or has been the hirer under a regulated consumer hire agreement is to be treated as a "client".

(3) In this article, "hirer" includes (in addition to those persons defined as "the hirer" in the definition of "consumer hire agreement" in article 60N(3))—

(a) any person providing a guarantee or indemnity under a consumer hire agreement, and

(b) a person to whom the rights and duties of a person falling within sub-paragraph (a) have passed by assignment or operation of law.]

NOTES

Inserted, together with the preceding heading, by the Financial Services and Markets Act 2000 (Regulated Activities) (Amendment) Order 2014, SI 2014/366, art 2(1), (37), as from 1 April 2014.

CHAPTER XV REGULATED MORTGAGE CONTRACTS

The activities

[8.165]

61 Regulated mortgage contracts

(1) Entering into a regulated mortgage contract as lender is a specified kind of activity.

(2) Administering a regulated mortgage contract is also a specified kind of activity [where—

(a) the contract was entered into by way of business on or after 31st October 2004; or

(b) the contract—

(i) was entered into by way of business before 31st October 2004, and

(ii) was a regulated credit agreement immediately before 21st March 2016.]

(3) In this Chapter—

[(a) [subject to paragraph (5),] a contract is a "regulated mortgage contract" if, at the time it is entered into, the following conditions are met—

[(i) the contract is one under which a person ("the lender") provides credit to an individual or to trustees ("the borrower");

(ii) the contract provides for the obligation of the borrower to repay to be secured by a mortgage on land . . . ;

(iii) at least 40% of that land is used, or is intended to be used—

(aa) in the case of credit provided to an individual, as or in connection with a dwelling; or

(bb) in the case of credit provided to a trustee which is not an individual, as or in connection with a dwelling by an individual who is a beneficiary of the trust, or by a related person]

[but such a contract is not a regulated mortgage contract if it [falls within article 61A(1) or (2)];]]

(b) "administering" a regulated mortgage contract means either or both of—

(i) notifying the borrower of changes in interest rates or payments due under the contract, or of other matters of which the contract requires him to be notified; and

(ii) taking any necessary steps for the purposes of collecting or recovering payments due under the contract from the borrower;

but a person is not to be treated as administering a regulated mortgage contract merely because he has, or exercises, a right to take action for the purposes of enforcing the contract (or to require that such action is or is not taken);

(c) "credit" includes a cash loan, and any other form of financial accommodation.

(4) For the purposes of [paragraph 3(a)]—

[(a) "mortgage" includes a charge and (in Scotland) a heritable security;]

[(aa) "land"—

(i) in relation to a contract entered into before IP completion day, means land in the United Kingdom or within the territory of an EEA State;

(ii) in relation to a contract entered into on or after IP completion day, means land in the United Kingdom;]

(b) the area of any land which comprises a building or other structure containing two or more storeys is to be taken to be the aggregate of the floor areas of each of those storeys;

(c) "related person", in relation to the borrower or (in the case of credit provided to trustees) a beneficiary of the trust, means—

(i) that person's spouse [or civil partner];

(ii) a person (whether or not of the opposite sex) whose relationship with that person has the characteristics of the relationship between husband and wife; or

(iii) that person's parent, brother, sister, child, grandparent or grandchild; . . .

[(d) . . .]

[(5) In this Chapter, a contract entered into before 21st March 2016 is a "regulated mortgage contract" only if—

(a) at the time it was entered into, entering into the contract was an activity of the kind specified by paragraph (1), or

(b) the contract is a consumer credit back book mortgage contract within the meaning of article 2 of the Mortgage Credit Directive Order 2015.]

NOTES

Para (2): words in square brackets substituted by the Financial Services and Markets Act 2000 (Regulated Activities) (Amendment) (No 3) Order 2015, SI 2015/1863, art 2(1), (4), as from 5 November 2015 (the purposes of enabling the making and determination of applications for a permission, or for variation of a permission, to be given under Part 4A of the Financial Services and Markets Act 2000), and as from 21 March 2016 (otherwise).

Para (3) is amended as follows:

Sub-para (a) substituted by the Financial Services and Markets Act 2000 (Regulated Activities) (Amendment) Order 2001, SI 2001/3544, arts 2, 8(b), as from 1 September 2002.

Sub-para (a)(i)–(iii) further substituted by the Mortgage Credit Directive Order 2015, SI 2015/910, Sch 1, Pt 2, para 4(1), (21)(a)(i), as from 21 March 2016.

Words "subject to paragraph (5)," in square brackets in sub-para (a) inserted by the Financial Services and Markets Act 2000 (Regulated Activities) (Amendment) Order 2016, SI 2016/392, art 2(1), (18)(a), as from 21 March 2016.

The words omitted from sub-para (a)(ii) were revoked by the Financial Services and Markets Act 2000 (Amendment) (EU Exit) Regulations 2019, SI 2019/632, regs 120, 145(1), (2), as from IP completion day (as defined in the European Union (Withdrawal Agreement) Act 2020, s 39).

Words in penultimate (outer) pair of square brackets in sub-para (a) inserted by the Financial Services and Markets Act 2000 (Regulated Activities) (Amendment) (No 2) Order 2006, SI 2006/2383, arts 2, 17, as from 6 November 2006 (for the purposes of enabling applications to be made for (i) a Pt IV permission, or a variation of a Pt IV permission, in relation to activities of the kind specified by arts 25B, 25C, 53B, 53C, 63B or 63F or, so far as relevant to any such activity, art 64 of this Order; or (ii) the Authority's approval under FSMA 2000, s 59 in relation to any of those activities), and as from 6 April 2007 (otherwise).

Words "falls within article 61A(1) or (2)" in final (inner) pair of square brackets in sub-para (a) substituted by SI 2015/910, Sch 1, Pt 2, para 4(1), (21)(a)(ii), as from 21 March 2016.

Para (4) is amended as follows:

Words in first pair of square brackets substituted by SI 2001/3544, arts 2, 8(c), as from 1 September 2002.

Sub-para (a) substituted by SI 2015/910, Sch 1, Pt 2, para 4(1), (21)(b), as from 21 March 2016.

Sub-para (aa) inserted by SI 2019/632, regs 120, 145(1), (3), as from IP completion day (as defined in the European Union (Withdrawal Agreement) Act 2020, s 39). Note that reg 145(3) of the 2019 Regulations was amended by the Financial Services and Economic and Monetary Policy (Consequential Amendments) (EU Exit) Regulations 2020, SI 2020/1301, reg 3, Schedule, para 33(q), as from 30 December 2020 (and the effect of the amendment has been incorporated in the text set out above).

Words in square brackets in sub-para (c)(i) inserted by the Civil Partnership Act 2004 (Amendments to Subordinate Legislation) Order 2005, SI 2005/2114, art 2(16), Sch 16, Pt 1, para 1(1), (3), as from 5 December 2005.

Sub-para (d) originally substituted by the Timeshare, Holiday Products, Resale and Exchange Contracts Regulations 2010, SI 2010/2960, reg 36(3), Sch 6, para 7(1), (2), as from 23 February 2011.

Sub-para (d) (and the preceding word) subsequently revoked by SI 2015/910, Sch 1, Pt 2, para 4(1), (21)(c), as from 21 March 2016.

Para (5): added by SI 2016/392, art 2(1), (18)(b), as from 21 March 2016.

[8.166]

[61A Mortgage contracts which are not regulated mortgage contracts

(1) A contract falls within this paragraph if it is—

(a) a regulated home purchase plan;

(b) a limited payment second charge bridging loan;

(c) a second charge business loan;

(d) an investment property loan; . . .

(e) an exempt consumer buy-to-let mortgage contract; [. . .

(f) an exempt equitable mortgage bridging loan][; or

(g) an exempt housing authority loan].

(2) A contract falls within this paragraph if—

(a) it is a limited interest second charge credit union loan;

(b) the borrower receives timely information on the main features, risks and costs of the contract at the pre-contractual stage; and

(c) any advertising of the contract is fair, clear and not misleading.

(3) For the purposes of this article, if an agreement includes a declaration which—

(a) is made by the borrower, and

(b) includes—

(i) a statement that the agreement is entered into by the borrower wholly or predominantly for the purposes of a business carried on, or intended to be carried on, by the borrower,

(ii) a statement that the borrower understands that the borrower will not have the benefit of the protection and remedies that would be available to the borrower under the Act if the agreement were a regulated mortgage contract under the Act, and

(iii) a statement that the borrower is aware that if the borrower is in any doubt as to the consequences of the agreement not being regulated by the Act, then the borrower should seek independent legal advice,

the agreement is to be presumed to have been entered into by the borrower wholly or predominantly for the purposes specified in sub-paragraph (b)(i) unless paragraph (4) applies.

(4) This paragraph applies if, when the agreement is entered into—

(a) the lender (or, if there is more than one lender, any of the lenders), or

(b) any person who has acted on behalf of the lender (or, if there is more than one lender, any of the lenders) in connection with the entering into of the agreement,

knows or has reasonable cause to suspect that the agreement is not entered into by the borrower wholly or predominantly for the purposes of a business carried on, or intended to be carried on, by the borrower.

(5) For the purposes of this article a borrower is to be regarded as entering into an agreement for the purposes of a business carried on, or intended to be carried on, by the borrower if the agreement is a buy-to-let mortgage contract and—

(a)
- (i) the borrower previously purchased, or is entering into the contract in order to finance the purchase by the borrower of, the land subject to the mortgage;
- (ii) at the time of the purchase the borrower intended that the land would be occupied as a dwelling on the basis of a rental agreement and would not at any time be occupied as a dwelling by the borrower or by a related person, or where the borrower has not yet purchased the land the borrower has such an intention at the time of entering into the contract; and
- (iii) where the borrower has purchased the land, since the time of the purchase the land has not at any time been occupied as a dwelling by the borrower or by a related person; or

(b) the borrower is the owner of land, other than the land subject to the mortgage, which is—
- (i) occupied as a dwelling on the basis of a rental agreement and is not occupied as a dwelling by the borrower or by a related person; or
- (ii) secured by a mortgage under a buy-to-let mortgage contract.

(6) For the purposes of this article—

"borrower" and "lender" have the meaning set out in article 61(3) (regulated mortgage contracts);

"borrower-lender agreement", "borrower-lender-supplier agreement", "credit union" and "total charge for credit" have the meanings set out in article 60L (interpretation of Chapter 14A);

"bridging loan" has the meaning given by [article 60G(9)];

"buy-to-let mortgage contract" has the meaning given in article 4 of the Mortgage Credit Directive Order 2015 (interpretation of Part 3);

"exempt consumer buy-to-let mortgage contract" is a contract that, at the time it is entered into, is a consumer buy-to-let mortgage contract within the meaning of article 4 of the Mortgage Credit Directive Order 2015 and—
- (a) is [an agreement to which section 423A(3) of the Act applies]; or
- (b) is a bridging loan;

["exempt equitable mortgage bridging loan" is a contract that—
- (a) is a bridging loan;
- (b) is secured by an equitable mortgage on land; and
- (c) is an exempt agreement within the meaning of article 60B(3) (regulated credit agreements) by virtue of article 60E(2) (exempt agreements: exemptions relating to the nature of the lender);]

["exempt housing authority loan" is a contract that—
- (a) provides for credit to be granted by a housing authority within the meaning of article 60E (exempt agreements: exemptions relating to the nature of the lender); and
- (b) if it is entered into on or after 21st March 2016—
  - [(i) is an agreement to which section 423A(3) of the Act applies,]
  - (ii) is a bridging loan, or
  - (iii) is a restricted public loan within the meaning of article 60HA (exempt agreements: [provision qualifying articles 60E, 60F and 60H]), in respect of which the borrower receives timely information on the main features, risks and costs at the pre-contractual stage, and any advertising is fair, clear and not misleading]

"investment property loan" is a contract that, at the time it is entered into, meets the conditions in paragraphs (i) to (iii) of article 61(3)(a) and the following conditions—
- (a) less than 40% of the land subject to the mortgage is used, or intended to be used, as or in connection with a dwelling by the borrower or (in the case of credit provided to trustees) by an individual who is a beneficiary of the trust, or by a related person; and
- (b) the agreement is entered into by the borrower wholly or predominantly for the purposes of a business carried on, or intended to be carried on, by the borrower;

"limited payment second charge bridging loan" is a contract that, at the time it is entered into, meets the conditions in paragraphs (i) to (iii) of article 61(3)(a) and the following conditions—
- (a) it is a borrower-lender-supplier agreement financing the purchase of land;
- (b) it is used by the borrower as a temporary financing solution while transitioning to another financial arrangement for the land subject to the mortgage;
- (c) the mortgage ranks in priority behind one or more other mortgages affecting the land in question; and
- (d) the number of payments to be made by the borrower under the contract is not more than four;

"limited interest second charge credit union loan" is a contract that, at the time it is entered into, meets the conditions in paragraphs (i) to (iii) of article 61(3)(a) and the following conditions—
- (a) it is a borrower-lender agreement;
- (b) the mortgage ranks in priority behind one or more other mortgages affecting the land in question;
- (c) the lender is a credit union; and
- (d) the rate of the total charge for credit does not exceed 42.6 per cent;

"payment" has the meaning set out in article 60F(8) (exempt agreement: exemptions relating to number of repayments to be made);

"regulated home purchase plan" has the meaning set out in article 63F(3)(a) (entering into and administering regulated home purchase plans);

"related person" in relation to the borrower or (in the case of credit provided to trustees) a beneficiary of the trust, means—
- (a) that person's spouse or civil partner;
- (b) a person (whether or not of the opposite sex) whose relationship with that person has the characteristics of the relationship between husband and wife; or
- (c) that person's parent, brother, sister, child, grandparent or grandchild;

"second charge business loan" is a contract that, at the time it is entered into, meets the conditions in paragraphs (i) to (iii) of article 61(3)(a) and the following conditions—

(a) the lender provides the borrower with credit exceeding £25,000;
(b) the mortgage ranks in priority behind one or more other mortgages affecting the land in question; and
(c) the agreement is entered into by the borrower wholly or predominantly for the purposes of a business carried on, or intended to be carried on, by the borrower.]

NOTES

Inserted by the Mortgage Credit Directive Order 2015, SI 2015/910, Sch 1, Pt 2, para 4(1), (22), as from 21 March 2016.

The word omitted from sub-para (1)(d) was revoked, sub-para (1)(f) and the preceding word were added, and the definition "exempt equitable mortgage bridging loan" in para (6) was added, by the Financial Services and Markets Act 2000 (Regulated Activities) (Amendment) (No 3) Order 2015, SI 2015/1863, art 2(1), (5), as from 5 November 2015 (the purposes of enabling the making and determination of applications for a permission, or for variation of a permission, to be given under Part 4A of the Financial Services and Markets Act 2000), and as from 21 March 2016 (otherwise).

The word omitted from sub-para (1)(e) was revoked, sub-para (1)(g) and the preceding word were added, and the definition "exempt housing authority loan" in para (6) was inserted, by the Financial Services and Markets Act 2000 (Regulated Activities) (Amendment) Order 2016, SI 2016/392, art 2(1), (19), as from 21 March 2016.

In para (6), the words in square brackets in the definitions "bridging loan", "exempt consumer buy-to-let mortgage contract", and "exempt housing authority loan" were substituted by the Financial Services and Markets Act 2000 (Amendment) (EU Exit) Regulations 2019, SI 2019/632, regs 120,146, as from IP completion day (as defined in the European Union (Withdrawal Agreement) Act 2020, s 39).

Exclusions

[8.167]

62 Arranging administration by authorised person

A person who is not an authorised person does not carry on an activity of the kind specified by article 61(2) in relation to a regulated mortgage contract where he—

(a) arranges for another person, being an authorised person with permission to carry on an activity of that kind, to administer the contract; or
(b) administers the contract himself during a period of not more than one month beginning with the day on which any such arrangement comes to an end.

[8.168]

63 Administration pursuant to agreement with authorised person

A person who is not an authorised person does not carry on an activity of the kind specified by article 61(2) in relation to a regulated mortgage contract where he administers the contract pursuant to an agreement with an authorised person who has permission to carry on an activity of that kind.

[8.169]

[63A Other exclusions

Article 61 is also subject to the exclusions in articles 66 (trustees etc), 72 (overseas persons) . . . [, 72AA (managers of [UK UCITS] and AIFs)[, 72G (local authorities) and 72I (registered consumer buy-to-let mortgage firms)]].]

NOTES

Originally inserted by the Financial Services and Markets Act 2000 (Regulated Activities) (Amendment) (No 2) Order 2002, SI 2002/1776, art 3(1), (16), as from 21 August 2002. Subsequently substituted by the Financial Services and Markets Act 2000 (Regulated Activities) (Amendment) (No 1) Order 2003, SI 2003/1475, art 17, as from 31 October 2004.

Words omitted revoked by the Electronic Commerce and Solvency 2 (Amendment etc) (EU Exit) Regulations 2019, SI 2019/1361, reg 5(1), (3), as from IP completion day (as defined in the European Union (Withdrawal Agreement) Act 2020, s 39) (for transitional provisions, see the note in relation to art 72A of this Order *post*).

Words in first (outer) pair of square brackets substituted by the Financial Services and Markets Act 2000 (Regulated Activities) (Amendment) Order 2014, SI 2014/366, art 2(1), (38), as from 1 April 2014.

Words "UK UCITS" in second (inner) pair of square brackets substituted by the Financial Services and Markets Act 2000 (Amendment) (EU Exit) Regulations 2019, SI 2019/632, regs 120, 148(2), as from IP completion day (as defined in the European Union (Withdrawal Agreement) Act 2020, s 39).

Words in third (inner) pair of square brackets substituted by the Mortgage Credit Directive Order 2015, SI 2015/910, Sch 1, Pt 2, para 4(1), (23), as from 21 March 2016.

[CHAPTER 15A REGULATED HOME REVERSION PLANS

The activities

[8.170]

63B Entering into and administering regulated home reversion plans

(1) Entering into a regulated home reversion plan as plan provider is a specified kind of activity.

(2) Administering a regulated home reversion plan is also a specified kind of activity where the plan was entered into on or after 6th April 2007.

(3) In this Chapter—

(a) a "regulated home reversion plan" is an arrangement comprised in one or more instruments or agreements, in relation to which the following conditions are met at the time it is entered into—
  (i) the arrangement is one under which a person (the "plan provider") buys all or part of a qualifying interest in land (other than timeshare accommodation) in the United Kingdom from an individual or trustees (the "reversion seller");
  (ii) the reversion seller (if he is an individual) or an individual who is a beneficiary of the trust (if the reversion seller is a trustee), or a related person, is entitled under the arrangement to occupy at least 40% of the land in question as or in connection with a dwelling, and intends to do so; and
  (iii) the arrangement specifies one or more qualifying termination events, on the occurrence of which that entitlement will end;

(b) "administering" a regulated home reversion plan means any of—
(i) notifying the reversion seller of changes in payments due under the plan, or of other matters of which the plan requires him to be notified;
(ii) taking any necessary steps for the purposes of making payments to the reversion seller under the plan; and
(iii) taking any necessary steps for the purposes of collecting or recovering payments due under the plan from the reversion seller,

but a person is not to be treated as administering a regulated home reversion plan merely because he has, or exercises, a right to take action for the purposes of enforcing the plan (or to require that such action is or is not taken).

(4) For the purposes of paragraph (3)—
(a) the reference to a "qualifying interest" in land—
(i) in relation to land in England or Wales, is to an estate in fee simple absolute or a term of years absolute, whether subsisting at law or in equity;
(ii) in relation to land in Scotland, is to the interest of an owner in land or the tenant's right over or interest in a property subject to a lease;
(iii) in relation to land in Northern Ireland, is to any freehold estate or any leasehold estate, whether subsisting at law or in equity;
(b) "timeshare accommodation" has the meaning given by section 1 of the Timeshare Act 1992;
(c) "related person" in relation to the reversion seller or, where the reversion seller is a trustee, a beneficiary of the trust, means—
(i) that person's spouse or civil partner;
(ii) a person (whether or not of the opposite sex) whose relationship with that person has the characteristics of the relationship between husband and wife; or
(iii) that person's parent, brother, sister, child, grandparent or grandchild; and
(d) "qualifying termination event", in relation to a person's entitlement to occupy land, means—
(i) the person becomes a resident of a care home;
(ii) the person dies;
(iii) the end of a specified period of at least twenty years beginning with the day on which the reversion seller entered into the arrangement.

(5) For the purposes of paragraph (3)(a)(ii), the area of any land which comprises a building or other structure containing two or more storeys is to be taken to be the aggregate of the floor areas of each of those storeys.

(6) For the purposes of the definition of "qualifying termination event" in paragraph (4), "care home"—
(a) in relation to England . . . , has the meaning given by section 3 of the Care Standards Act 2000;
[(aa) in relation to Wales, means a place at which a care home service, within the meaning of Part 1 of the Regulation and Inspection of Social Care (Wales) Act 2016, is provided wholly or mainly to persons aged 18 or over;]
(b) in relation to Scotland, means accommodation provided by a ["care home service" within the meaning of paragraph 2 of schedule 12 to the Public Services Reform (Scotland) Act 2010];
(c) in relation to Northern Ireland, means—
(i) a residential care home within the meaning of article 10 of the Health and Personal Social Services (Quality, Improvement and Regulation) (Northern Ireland) Order 2003; or
(ii) a nursing home within the meaning of article 11 of that Order.

(7) In this Order—
(a) references to entering into a regulated home reversion plan as plan provider include acquiring any obligations or rights (including his interest in land) of the plan provider, under such a plan; but
(b) in relation to a person who acquires any such obligations or rights, an activity is a specified kind of activity for the purposes of articles 25B(1)(b) and 53B(b)(ii) and paragraph (2) only if the plan was entered into by the plan provider (rather than the obligations or rights acquired) on or after 6th April 2007.

(8) Accordingly, references in this Order to a plan provider, other than in paragraph (7), include a person who acquires any such obligations or rights.]

NOTES

Chapters 15A, 15B (arts 63B–63I) were inserted by the Financial Services and Markets Act 2000 (Regulated Activities) (Amendment) (No 2) Order 2006, SI 2006/2383, arts 2, 18, as from 6 November 2006 (for the purposes of enabling applications to be made for (i) a Pt IV permission, or a variation of a Pt IV permission, in relation to activities of the kind specified by arts 25B, 25C, 53B, 53C, 63B or 63F or, so far as relevant to any such activity, art 64 of this Order; or (ii) the Authority's approval under FSMA 2000, s 59 in relation to any of those activities), and as from 6 April 2007 (otherwise).

Para (6): words omitted from sub-para (a) revoked, and sub-para (aa) inserted, by the Alternative Investment Fund Managers (Amendment) Regulations 2018, SI 2018/134, reg 4, as from 2 April 2018. Words in square brackets in sub-para (b) substituted by the Public Services Reform (Scotland) Act 2010 (Consequential Modifications of Enactments) Order 2011, SI 2011/2581, art 2, Sch 3, para 32, as from 28 October 2011.

[Exclusions

[8.171]

63C Arranging administration by authorised person

A person who is not an authorised person does not carry on an activity of the kind specified by article 63B(2) in relation to a regulated home reversion plan where he—
(a) arranges for another person, being an authorised person with permission to carry on an activity of that kind, to administer the plan; or
(b) administers the plan himself during a period of not more than one month beginning with the day on which any such arrangement comes to an end.]

NOTES

Inserted as noted to art 63B at **[8.170]**.

[8.172]

[63D Administration pursuant to agreement with authorised person

A person who is not an authorised person does not carry on an activity of the kind specified by article 63B(2) in relation to a regulated home reversion plan where he administers the plan pursuant to an agreement with an authorised person who has permission to carry on an activity of that kind.]

NOTES

Inserted as noted to art 63B at **[8.170]**.

[8.173]

[63E Other exclusions

Article 63B is also subject to the exclusions in articles 66 (trustees etc), 72 (overseas persons) . . . [, 72AA (managers of [UK UCITS] and AIFs) and 72G (local authorities)].]

NOTES

Inserted as noted to art 63B at **[8.170]**.

Words omitted revoked by the Electronic Commerce and Solvency 2 (Amendment etc) (EU Exit) Regulations 2019, SI 2019/1361, reg 5(1), (3), as from IP completion day (as defined in the European Union (Withdrawal Agreement) Act 2020, s 39) (for transitional provisions, see the note in relation to art 72A of this Order *post*).

Words in first (outer) pair of square brackets substituted by the Financial Services and Markets Act 2000 (Regulated Activities) (Amendment) Order 2014, SI 2014/366, art 2(1), (39), as from 1 April 2014 (note that the 2014 Order came into force on 14 February 2014 for the purpose of the FCA making rules, giving guidance etc, and came into force on 1 April 2014, immediately after SI 2013/1881 (and SI 2013/1882) come into force, in so far as not already in force).

Words "UK UCITS" in second (inner) pair of square brackets substituted by the Financial Services and Markets Act 2000 (Amendment) (EU Exit) Regulations 2019, SI 2019/632, regs 120, 148(2), as from IP completion day (as defined in the European Union (Withdrawal Agreement) Act 2020, s 39).

[CHAPTER 15B REGULATED HOME PURCHASE PLANS

The activities

[8.174]

63F Entering into and administering regulated home purchase plans

(1) Entering into a regulated home purchase plan as home purchase provider is a specified kind of activity.

(2) Administering a regulated home purchase plan is also a specified kind of activity where the plan was entered into by way of business on or after 6th April 2007.

(3) In this Chapter—

(a) a "regulated home purchase plan" is an arrangement comprised in one or more instruments or agreements, in relation to which the following conditions are met at the time it is entered into—

(i) the arrangement is one under which a person (the "home purchase provider") buys a qualifying interest or an undivided share of a qualifying interest in land (other than timeshare accommodation) in the United Kingdom;

(ii) where an undivided share of a qualifying interest in land is bought, the interest is held on trust for the home purchase provider and the individual or trustees mentioned in paragraph (iii) as beneficial tenants in common;

(iii) the arrangement provides for the obligation of an individual or trustees (the "home purchaser") to buy the interest bought by the home purchase provider over the course of or at the end of a specified period; and

(iv) the home purchaser (if he is an individual) or an individual who is a beneficiary of the trust (if the home purchaser is a trustee), or a related person, is entitled under the arrangement to occupy at least 40% of the land in question as or in connection with a dwelling during that period, and intends to do so;

(b) "administering" a regulated home purchase plan means either or both of—

(i) notifying the home purchaser of changes in payments due under the plan, or of other matters of which the plan requires him to be notified; and

(ii) taking any necessary steps for the purposes of collecting or recovering payments due under the plan from the home purchaser;

but a person is not to be treated as administering a regulated home purchase plan merely because he has, or exercises, a right to take action for the purposes of enforcing the plan or to require that such action is or is not taken.

(4) Article 63B(4)(a) to (c) applies for the purposes of paragraph (3)(a) with references to the "reversion seller" being read as references to the "home purchaser".

(5) Article 63B(5) applies for the purposes of paragraph (3)(a)(iv) with the reference to "paragraph (3)(a)(ii)" being read as a reference to "paragraph (3)(a)(iv)".]

NOTES

Inserted as noted to art 63B at **[8.170]**.

[Exclusions

[8.175]
63G Arranging administration by authorised person

A person who is not an authorised person does not carry on an activity of the kind specified by article 63F(2) in relation to a regulated home purchase plan where he—

(a) arranges for another person, being an authorised person with permission to carry on an activity of that kind, to administer the plan; or

(b) administers the plan himself during a period of not more than one month beginning with the day on which any such arrangement comes to an end.]

NOTES

Inserted as noted to art 63B at **[8.170]**.

[8.176]
[63H Administration pursuant to agreement with authorised person

A person who is not an authorised person does not carry on an activity of the kind specified by article 63F(2) in relation to a regulated home purchase plan where he administers the plan pursuant to an agreement with an authorised person who has permission to carry on an activity of that kind.]

NOTES

Inserted as noted to art 63B at **[8.170]**.

[8.177]
[63I Other exclusions

Article 63F is also subject to the exclusions in articles 66 (trustees etc), 72 (overseas persons) . . . [, 72AA (managers of [UK UCITS] and AIFs) and 72G (local authorities)].]

NOTES

Inserted as noted to art 63B at **[8.170]**.

Words omitted revoked by the Electronic Commerce and Solvency 2 (Amendment etc) (EU Exit) Regulations 2019, SI 2019/1361, reg 5(1), (3), as from IP completion day (as defined in the European Union (Withdrawal Agreement) Act 2020, s 39) (for transitional provisions, see the note in relation to art 72A of this Order *post*).

Words in first (outer) pair of square brackets substituted by the Financial Services and Markets Act 2000 (Regulated Activities) (Amendment) Order 2014, SI 2014/366, art 2(1), (40), as from 1 April 2014.

Words "UK UCITS" in second (inner) pair of square brackets substituted by the Financial Services and Markets Act 2000 (Amendment) (EU Exit) Regulations 2019, SI 2019/632, regs 120, 148(2), as from IP completion day (as defined in the European Union (Withdrawal Agreement) Act 2020, s 39).

[CHAPTER 15C REGULATED SALE AND RENT BACK AGREEMENTS THE ACTIVITIES

The activities

[8.178]
63J Entering into and administering regulated sale and rent back agreements

(1) Entering into a regulated sale and rent back agreement as an agreement provider is a specified kind of activity.

(2) Administering a regulated sale and rent back agreement is also a specified kind of activity when the agreement was entered into on or after 1st July 2009.

(3) In this Chapter—

(a) a "regulated sale and rent back agreement" is an arrangement comprised in one or more instruments or agreements, in relation to which the following conditions are met at the time it is entered into—

(i) the arrangement is one under which a person (the "agreement provider") buys all or part of the qualifying interest in land (other than timeshare accommodation) in the United Kingdom from an individual or trustees (the "agreement seller "); and

(ii) the agreement seller (if the agreement seller is an individual) or an individual who is the beneficiary of the trust (if the agreement seller is a trustee), or a related person, is entitled under the arrangement to occupy at least 40% of the land in question as or in connection with a dwelling, and intends to do so;

but such an arrangement is not a regulated sale and rent back agreement if it is a regulated home reversion plan;

(b) "administering" a regulated sale and rent back agreement means any of—

(i) notifying the agreement seller of changes in payments due under the agreement, or of other matters of which the agreement requires the agreement seller to be notified;

(ii) taking any necessary steps for the purpose of making payments to the agreement seller under the agreement; and

(iii) taking any necessary steps for the purposes of collecting or recovering payments due under the agreement from the agreement seller,

but a person is not to be treated as administering a regulated sale and rent back agreement because that person has, or exercises, a right to take action for the purposes of enforcing the agreement (or to require that such action is or is not taken).

(4) For the purposes of paragraph (3)—

(a) the reference to a "qualifying interest" in land—

(i) in relation to land in England and Wales, is to an estate in fee simple absolute or a term of years absolute, whether subsisting at law or in equity;

(ii) in relation to land in Scotland, is to the interest of an owner in land or the tenant's right over or interest in a property subject to a lease;

(iii) in relation to land in Northern Ireland, is to any freehold estate or any leasehold estate, whether subsisting at law or in equity;

[(b) "timeshare accommodation" means overnight accommodation which is the subject of a timeshare contract within the meaning of the Timeshare, Holiday Products, Resale and Exchange Contracts Regulations 2010; and]

(c) "related person" in relation to the agreement seller or, where the agreement seller is a trustee, a beneficiary of the trust, means—

(i) that person's spouse or civil partner;

(ii) a person (whether or not of the opposite sex) whose relationship with that person has the characteristic of the relationship between husband and wife;

(iii) that person's parent, brother, sister, child, grandparent or grandchild.

(5) For the purposes of paragraph (3)(a)(ii), the area of any land which compromises a building or other structure containing two or more storeys is to be taken to be the aggregate of the floor areas of each of those storeys.

(6) In this Order—

(a) references to entering into a regulated sale and rent back agreement as agreement provider include acquiring any obligations or rights of the agreement provider, including the agreement provider's interest in land or interests under one or more of the instruments or agreements referred to in paragraph (3)(a); but

(b) in relation to a person who acquires any such obligations or rights, an activity is a specified kind of activity for the purposes of articles 25E(1)(b) and 53D(b)(ii) and paragraph (2) only if the agreement was entered into by the agreement provider (rather than the obligations or rights acquired) on or after 1st July 2009.

(7) Accordingly, references in this Order to an agreement provider, other than in paragraph (6), include a person who acquires any such obligations or rights.]

NOTES

Chapter 15C (arts 63J–63M) was inserted by the Financial Services and Markets Act 2000 (Regulated Activities) (Amendment) Order 2009, SI 2009/1342, arts 2, 17, as from 1 July 2009 (other than for the purposes of enabling applications to be made for a Part IV permission, or a variation of a Part IV permission, in relation to activities of the kind specified by arts 25E, 53D or 63J or, so far as relevant to any such activity, art 64 of this Order), and as from 30 June 2010 (for those purposes).

Para (4): sub-para (b) substituted by the Timeshare, Holiday Products, Resale and Exchange Contracts Regulations 2010, SI 2010/2960, reg 36(3), Sch 6, para 7(1), (3), as from 23 February 2011.

[Exclusions

[8.179]

63K Arranging administration by authorised person

A person who is not an authorised person does not carry on an activity of the kind specified by article 63J(2) in relation to a regulated sale and rent back agreement where that person—

(a) arranges for another person, being an authorised person with permission to carry on an activity of that kind, to administer the agreement; or

(b) administers the agreement during a period of not more than one month beginning with the day on which any such arrangement comes to an end.]

NOTES

Inserted as noted to art 63J at **[8.178]**.

[8.180]

[63L Administration pursuant to agreement with authorised person

A person who is not an authorised person does not carry on an activity of the kind specified by article 63J(2) in relation to a regulated sale and rent back agreement where that person administers the agreement pursuant to an agreement with an authorised person who has permission to carry on activity of that kind.]

NOTES

Inserted as noted to art 63J at **[8.178]**.

[8.181]

[63M Other exclusions

Article 63J is also subject to the exclusions in article 66 (trustees etc), 72 (overseas persons) . . . [, 72AA (managers of [UK UCITS] and AIFs) and 72G (local authorities)].]

NOTES

Inserted as noted to art 63J at **[8.178]**.

Words omitted revoked by the Electronic Commerce and Solvency 2 (Amendment etc) (EU Exit) Regulations 2019, SI 2019/1361, reg 5(1), (3), as from IP completion day (as defined in the European Union (Withdrawal Agreement) Act 2020, s 39) (for transitional provisions, see the note in relation to art 72A of this Order *post*).

Words in first (outer) pair of square brackets substituted by the Financial Services and Markets Act 2000 (Regulated Activities) (Amendment) Order 2014, SI 2014/366, art 2(1), (41), as from 1 April 2014.

Words "UK UCITS" in second (inner) pair of square brackets substituted by the Financial Services and Markets Act 2000 (Amendment) (EU Exit) Regulations 2019, SI 2019/632, regs 120, 148(2), as from IP completion day (as defined in the European Union (Withdrawal Agreement) Act 2020, s 39).

[CHAPTER 15D ACTIVITIES OF RECLAIM FUNDS

The activities

[8.182]

63N Dormant account funds

(1) The following are specified kinds of activity—

(a) the meeting of repayment claims by a reclaim fund;

(b) the management of dormant [assets] funds (including the investment of such funds) by a reclaim fund;

[(c) dealing with unwanted asset money].

(2) In this article—

. . .

["dealing with unwanted asset money" means—

(a) the acceptance of transfers of amounts as mentioned in section 21(2)(b) of the Dormant Assets Act 2022, and

(b) dealing with those funds (so far as they are not needed for either of the purposes mentioned in section 5(1)(c)(ii) or (iii) of the Dormant Bank and Building Society Accounts Act 2008) with a view to their transfer to the body or bodies for the time being specified in section 16 of the Dormant Bank and Building Society Accounts Act 2008;]

["dormant assets funds", "reclaim fund"] and "repayment claims" have the same meaning as in section 5 of that Act;

["management of dormant assets funds" means—

(a) the acceptance of transfers of amounts as mentioned in section 1(1)(a) or 2(1)(a) of the Dormant Bank and Building Society Accounts Act 2008 or 2(1)(a), 5(1)(a), 8(1)(a), 12(1)(a) or 14(1)(a) of the Dormant Assets Act 2022,

(b)] the management of those funds in such a way as to enable the reclaim fund to meet whatever repayment claims it is prudent to anticipate[, and

(c) dealing with those funds with a view to the transfer of amounts to the body or bodies for the time being specified in section 16 of the Dormant Bank and Building Society Accounts Act 2008].]

NOTES

Chapter 15D (art 63N) was inserted by the Financial Services and Markets Act 2000 (Regulated Activities) (Amendment) (No 2) Order 2009, SI 2009/1389, arts 2, 4, as from 13 July 2009.

All amendments to this Article were made by the Dormant Assets Act 2022, s 32(3), Sch 1, para 3, as from 6 June 2022.

[CHAPTER 15E SPECIFIED BENCHMARKS

The activities

63O–63R (*Chapter 15E (originally arts 63O–63R only) was inserted by the Financial Services and Markets Act 2000 (Regulated Activities) (Amendment) Order 2013, SI 2013/655, arts 4, 5, as from 2 April 2013, subject to various transitional provisions relating to interim permissions, etc in arts 7–10 of that Order. Arts 63O–63R were revoked by the Financial Services and Markets Act 2000 (Benchmarks) Regulations 2018, SI 2018/135, reg 53, as from 1 May 2020, subject to transitional provisions in Part 7 of those Regulations.*)

[8.183]

[63S Administering a benchmark

(1) Administering a benchmark is a specified kind of activity.

(2) In paragraph (1) "administering a benchmark" means acting as an administrator of a benchmark within the meaning of Article 3 of Regulation EU 2016/1011 of the European Parliament and of the Council of 8 June 2016 on indices used as benchmarks in financial instruments and financial contracts or to measure the performance of investment funds and amending Directives 2008/48/EC and 2014/17/EU and Regulation (EU) No 596/2014.]

NOTES

Inserted, together with art 63T, by the Financial Services and Markets Act 2000 (Benchmarks) Regulations 2018, SI 2018/135, reg 51, as from 27 February 2018, subject to transitional provisions in Part 7 of those Regulations.

[8.184]

[63T Administration of a benchmark by the FCA

The FCA does not carry on the activity of the kind specified by article 63S(1) in relation to a benchmark where the FCA administers the benchmark itself.]

NOTES

Inserted as noted to art 63S at **[8.183]**.

CHAPTER XVI AGREEING TO CARRY ON ACTIVITIES

The activity

[8.185]

64 Agreeing to carry on specified kinds of activity

Agreeing to carry on an activity of the kind specified by any other provision of this Part[, Part 3A or Part 3B] (other than article 5, [9B,] 10, [25D,] [25DA,] [[51ZA, 51ZB, 51ZC, 51ZD, 51ZE], 52, 63N] [and 63S]) is a specified kind of activity.

NOTES

Words ", Part 3A or Part 3B" in square brackets substituted by the Financial Services and Markets Act 2000 (Claims Management Activity) Order 2018, SI 2018/1253, arts 3, 5, as from 1 April 2019 (for provision specifying that the 2018 Order also comes into force on 29 November 2018 for the purposes of the FCA and FOS making rules and issuing guidance, and for transitional provisions in relation to carrying on a claims management activity, etc, see arts 1, 39–89 of the 2018 Order).

Figure "9B," in second pair of square brackets inserted by the Financial Services and Markets Act 2000 (Regulated Activities) (Amendment) Order 2002, SI 2002/682, art 5, as from 27 April 2002.

Figure "25D," in third pair of square brackets inserted by the Financial Services and Markets Act 2000 (Regulated Activities) (Amendment No 3) Order 2006, SI 2006/3384, arts 2, 18, as from 1 April 2007 (for the purposes of enabling applications to be made for (i) a Part IV permission, (ii) a variation of a Part IV permission, and (iii) the Authority's approval under s 59 of the 2000 Act, in relation to an activity of the kind specified by art 25D of this Order, or in relation to an investment of the kind specified by arts 83, 84 or 85 of this Order), and as from 1 November 2007 (otherwise).

Figure "25DA," in fourth pair of square brackets inserted by the Financial Services and Markets Act 2000 (Regulated Activities) (Amendment) Order 2017, SI 2017/488, art 12(1), (7), as from 1 April 2017 (for the purposes of (i) enabling applications to be made for a Part 4A permission, for a variation of a Part 4A permission or for an approval under FSMA 2000, s 59, or (ii) enabling such applications to be determined, in relation to any specified activity or any specified investment amended or inserted by the 2017 Order), and as from 3 January 2018 (otherwise).

Words in fifth (outer) pair of square brackets substituted by the Financial Services and Markets Act 2000 (Regulated Activities) (Amendment) (No 2) Order 2009, SI 2009/1389, arts 2, 5, as from 13 July 2009.

Figures "51ZA, 51ZB, 51ZC, 51ZD, 51ZE" in sixth (inner) pair of square brackets substituted by the Alternative Investment Fund Managers Regulations 2013, SI 2013/1773, reg 81, Sch 2, Part 1, para 1(1), (14), as from 22 July 2013.

Words "and 63S" inserted by the Financial Services and Markets Act 2000 (Benchmarks) Regulations 2018, SI 2018/135, reg 52, as from 27 February 2018.

[Exclusions

[8.186]

65 Overseas persons etc

Article 64 is subject to the exclusions in articles 72 (overseas persons)[. . .), 72G (local authorities) and 72H (insolvency practitioners)].]

NOTES

Substituted, together with the preceding heading, by the Financial Services and Markets Act 2000 (Regulated Activities) (Amendment) (No 2) Order 2002, SI 2002/1776, art 3(1), (17), as from 21 August 2002.

Words in square brackets substituted by the Financial Services and Markets Act 2000 (Regulated Activities) (Amendment) Order 2014, SI 2014/366, art 2(1), (42), as from 1 April 2014.

Words omitted revoked by the Electronic Commerce and Solvency 2 (Amendment etc) (EU Exit) Regulations 2019, SI 2019/1361, reg 5(1), (3), as from IP completion day (as defined in the European Union (Withdrawal Agreement) Act 2020, s 39) (for transitional provisions, see the note in relation to art 72A of this Order *post*).

CHAPTER XVII EXCLUSIONS APPLYING TO SEVERAL SPECIFIED KINDS OF ACTIVITY

[8.187]

66 Trustees, nominees and personal representatives

(1) A person ("X") does not carry on an activity of the kind specified by article 14 where he enters into a transaction as bare trustee or, in Scotland, as nominee for another person ("Y") and—

(a) X is acting on Y's instructions; and

(b) X does not hold himself out as providing a service of buying and selling securities or contractually based investments.

(2) Subject to paragraph (7), there are excluded from [articles 25(1) and (2)[, [25A(1), (2) and (2A)], 25B(1) and (2)][, 25C(1) and (2) and 25E (1) and (2)]] arrangements made by a person acting as trustee or personal representative for or with a view to a transaction which is or is to be entered into—

(a) by that person and a fellow trustee or personal representative (acting in their capacity as such); or

(b) by a beneficiary under the trust, will or intestacy.

(3) Subject to paragraph (7), there is excluded from article 37 any activity carried on by a person acting as trustee or personal representative, unless—

(a) he holds himself out as providing a service comprising an activity of the kind specified by article 37; or

(b) the assets in question are held for the purposes of an occupational pension scheme, and, by virtue of article 4 of the Financial Services and Markets Act 2000 (Carrying on Regulated Activities by Way of Business) Order 2001, he is to be treated as carrying on that activity by way of business.

[(3A) Subject to paragraph (7), there is excluded from article 39A any activity carried on by a person acting as trustee or personal representative, unless he holds himself out as providing a service comprising an activity of the kind specified by article 39A.]

(4) Subject to paragraph (7), there is excluded from article 40 any activity carried on by a person acting as trustee or personal representative, unless he holds himself out as providing a service comprising an activity of the kind specified by article 40.

[(4A) There is excluded from article 40 any activity carried on by a person acting as trustee which consists of arranging for one or more other persons to safeguard and administer trust assets where—

(a) that other person is a qualifying custodian; or

(b) that safeguarding and administration is also arranged by a qualifying custodian.

In this paragraph, "qualifying custodian" has the meaning given by article 41(2).]

(5) A person does not, by sending or causing to be sent a dematerialised instruction (within the meaning of article 45), carry on an activity of the kind specified by that article if the instruction relates to an investment which that person holds as trustee or personal representative.

(6) Subject to paragraph (7), there is excluded from [articles 53[, 53A, 53B], [53C, 53D and 53DA]] the giving of advice by a person acting as trustee or personal representative where he gives the advice to—

(a) a fellow trustee or personal representative for the purposes of the trust or the estate; or

(b) a beneficiary under the trust, will or intestacy concerning his interest in the trust fund or estate.

[(6A) Subject to paragraph (7), a person acting as trustee or personal representative does not carry on an activity of the kind specified by article 61(1) or (2) where the borrower under the regulated mortgage contract in question is a beneficiary under the trust, will or intestacy.]

[(6B) Subject to paragraph (7), a person acting as trustee or personal representative does not carry on an activity of the kind specified by article 63B(1) or (2) where the reversion seller under the regulated home reversion plan in question is a beneficiary under the trust, will or intestacy.

(6C) Subject to paragraph (7), a person acting as trustee or personal representative does not carry on an activity of the kind specified by article 63F(1) or (2) where the home purchaser under the regulated home purchase plan in question is a beneficiary under the trust, will or intestacy.]

[(6D) Subject to paragraph (7), a person acting as a trustee or personal representative does not carry on an activity of the kind specified by article 63J(1) or (2) where the agreement seller under the regulated sale and rent back agreement is a beneficiary under the trust, will or intestacy.]

(7) Paragraphs (2), (3)[, (3A)], [(4), (6)[, (6A), (6B)][, (6C) and (6D)]] do not apply if the person carrying on the activity is remunerated for what he does in addition to any remuneration he receives as trustee or personal representative, and for these purposes a person is not to be regarded as receiving additional remuneration merely because his remuneration is calculated by reference to time spent.

[(8) This article is subject to article 4(4A) [and (4B)].]

NOTES

Para (2) is amended as follows:

Words in first (outer) pair of square brackets substituted by the Financial Services and Markets Act 2000 (Regulated Activities) (Amendment) (No 1) Order 2003, SI 2003/1475, art 18(a), as from 31 October 2004.

Words in second (inner) pair of square brackets substituted by the Financial Services and Markets Act 2000 (Regulated Activities) (Amendment) (No 2) Order 2006, SI 2006/2383, arts 2, 19(a), as from 6 November 2006 (for the purposes of enabling applications to be made for (i) a Pt IV permission, or a variation of a Pt IV permission, in relation to activities of the kind specified by arts 25B, 25C, 53B, 53C, 63B or 63F or, so far as relevant to any such activity, art 64 of this Order; or (ii) the Authority's approval under FSMA 2000, s 59 in relation to any of those activities), and as from 6 April 2007 (otherwise).

Words in third (inner) pair of square brackets substituted by the Mortgage Credit Directive Order 2015, SI 2015/910, Sch 1, Pt 2, para 4(1), (24)(a), as from 21 March 2016.

Words in fourth (inner) pair of square brackets substituted by the Financial Services and Markets Act 2000 (Regulated Activities) (Amendment) Order 2009, SI 2009/1342, arts 2, 18(a), as from 1 July 2009 (other than for the purposes of enabling applications to be made for a Part IV permission, or a variation of a Part IV permission, in relation to activities of the kind specified by arts 25E, 53D or 63J or, so far as relevant to any such activity, art 64 of this Order), and as from 30 June 2010 (otherwise).

Para (3A): inserted by the Financial Services and Markets Act 2000 (Regulated Activities) (Amendment) (No 2) Order 2003, SI 2003/1476, art 10(1)(a), as from 31 October 2004 (in so far as relating to contracts of long-term care insurance), and as from 14 January 2005 (otherwise).

Para (4A): inserted by the Financial Services and Markets Act 2000 (Regulated Activities) (Amendment) Order 2005, SI 2005/593, art 2(4), as from 6 April 2005.

Para (6): words in first (outer) pair of square brackets substituted by SI 2003/1475, art 18(b), as from 31 October 2004. Words in second (inner) pair of square brackets substituted by SI 2006/2383, arts 2, 19(b), as from 6 November 2006 (certain purposes), and as from 6 April 2007 (otherwise) (see the first note relating to the 2006 Order above). Words in third (inner) pair of square brackets substituted by SI 2015/910, Sch 1, Pt 2, para 4(1), (24)(b), as from 21 March 2016.

Para (6A): inserted by SI 2003/1475, art 18(c), as from 31 October 2004.

Paras (6B), (6C): inserted by SI 2006/2383, arts 2, 19(c), as from 6 November 2006 (certain purposes), and as from 6 April 2007 (otherwise) (see the first note relating to the 2006 Order above).

Para (6D): inserted by SI 2009/1342, arts 2, 18(c), as from 1 July 2009 (certain purposes), and as from 30 June 2010 (otherwise) (see the first note relating to the 2009 Order above).

Para (7): figure in first pair of square brackets inserted by SI 2003/1476, art 10(1)(b), as from 31 October 2004 (in so far as relating to contracts of long-term care insurance), and as from 14 January 2005 (otherwise). Words in second (outer) pair of square brackets substituted by SI 2003/1475, art 18(d), as from 31 October 2004. Words in third (inner) pair of square brackets substituted by SI 2006/2383, arts 2, 19(d), as from 6 November 2006 (certain purposes), and as from 6 April 2007 (otherwise) (see the first note relating to the 2006 Order above). Words in fourth (inner) pair of square brackets substituted by SI 2009/1342, arts 2, 18(d), as from 1 July 2009 (certain purposes), and as from 30 June 2010 (otherwise) (see the first note relating to the 2009 Order above).

Para (8): added by the Financial Services and Markets Act 2000 (Regulated Activities) (Amendment No 3) Order 2006, SI 2006/3384, arts 2, 19, as from 1 April 2007 (for the purposes of enabling applications to be made for (i) a Part IV permission, (ii) a variation of a Part IV permission, and (iii) the Authority's approval under s 59 of the 2000 Act, in relation to an activity of the kind specified by art 25D of this Order, or in relation to an investment of the kind specified by arts 83, 84 or 85 of this Order), and as from 1 November 2007 (otherwise). Words in square brackets inserted by SI 2015/910, Sch 1, Pt 2, para 4(1), (24)(c), as from 21 March 2016.

[8.188]

67 Activities carried on in the course of a profession or non-investment business

(1) There is excluded from articles 21, 25(1) and (2)[, 25A], [25B, 25C,] [25E,] [39A, 40] [53[, 53A, 53B]], [53C, 53D and 53DA] any activity which—

(a) is carried on in the course of carrying on any profession or business which does not otherwise consist of [the carrying on of regulated activities in the United Kingdom]; and

(b) may reasonably be regarded as a necessary part of other services provided in the course of that profession or business.

(2) But the exclusion in paragraph (1) does not apply if the activity in question is remunerated separately from the other services.

[(3) This article is subject to article [4(4), (4A) and (4B)].]

NOTES

Para (1) is amended as follows:

Figure ", 25A" in square brackets inserted, and words in fifth (outer) pair of square brackets (ie, beginning ", 53") substituted, by the Financial Services and Markets Act 2000 (Regulated Activities) (Amendment) (No 1) Order 2003, SI 2003/1475, art 19, as from 31 October 2004.

Figures "25B, 25C," in square brackets inserted by the Financial Services and Markets Act 2000 (Regulated Activities) (Amendment) (No 2) Order 2006, SI 2006/2383, arts 2, 20(a), as from 6 November 2006 (for the purposes of enabling applications to be made for (i) a Pt IV permission, or a variation of a Pt IV permission, in relation to activities of the kind specified by arts 25B, 25C, 53B, 53C, 63B or 63F or, so far as relevant to any such activity, art 64 of this Order; or (ii) the Authority's approval under FSMA 2000, s 59 in relation to any of those activities), and as from 6 April 2007 (otherwise).

Figure "25E," in square brackets inserted by the Financial Services and Markets Act 2000 (Regulated Activities) (Amendment) Order 2009, SI 2009/1342, arts 2, 19, as from 1 July 2009 (other than for the purposes of enabling applications to be made for a Part IV permission, or a variation of a Part IV permission, in relation to activities of the kind specified by arts 25E, 53D or 63J or, so far as relevant to any such activity, art 64 of this Order), and as from 30 June 2010 (otherwise).

Figures "39A, 40" in square brackets substituted by the Financial Services and Markets Act 2000 (Regulated Activities) (Amendment) (No 2) Order 2003, SI 2003/1476, art 10(2), as from 31 October 2004 (in so far as relating to contracts of long-term care insurance), and as from 14 January 2005 (otherwise).

Figures ", 53A, 53B" in square brackets substituted by SI 2006/2383, arts 2, 20(b), as from 6 November 2006 (certain purposes), and as from 6 April 2007 (otherwise) (see the first note relating to the 2006 Order above).

Words "53C, 53D and 53DA" in square brackets substituted by the Mortgage Credit Directive Order 2015, SI 2015/910, Sch 1, Pt 2, para 4(1), (25)(a), as from 21 March 2016.

Words in square brackets in sub-para (a) substituted by the Financial Services and Markets Act 2000 (Regulated Activities) (Amendment) Order 2001, SI 2001/3544, arts 2, 9, as from 1 December 2001.

Para (3): added by the Financial Services and Markets Act 2000 (Regulated Activities) (Amendment No 3) Order 2006, SI 2006/3384, arts 2, 20, as from 1 April 2007 (for the purposes of enabling applications to be made for (i) a Part IV permission, (ii) a variation of a Part IV permission, and (iii) the Authority's approval under s 59 of the 2000 Act, in relation to an activity of the kind specified by art 25D of this Order, or in relation to an investment of the kind specified by arts 83, 84 or 85 of this Order), and as from 1 November 2007 (otherwise). Words in square brackets substituted by SI 2015/910, Sch 1, Pt 2, para 4(1), (25)(b), as from 21 March 2016.

[8.189]

68 Activities carried on in connection with the sale of goods or supply of services

(1) Subject to paragraphs (9), (10) and (11), this article concerns certain activities carried on for the purposes of or in connection with the sale of goods or supply of services by a supplier to a customer, where—

"supplier" means a person whose main business is to sell goods or supply services and not to carry on any activities of the kind specified by any of articles 14, 21, 25, 37[, 39A], 40, 45, [51ZA, 51ZB, 51ZC, 51ZD, 51ZE], 52 and 53 and, where the supplier is a member of a group, also means any other member of that group; and

"customer" means a person, other than an individual, to whom a supplier sells goods or supplies services, or agrees to do so, and, where the customer is a member of a group, also means any other member of that group;

and in this article "related sale or supply" means a sale of goods or supply of services to the customer otherwise than by the supplier, but for or in connection with the same purpose as the sale or supply mentioned above.

(2) There is excluded from article 14 any transaction entered into by a supplier with a customer, if the transaction is entered into for the purposes of or in connection with the sale of goods or supply of services, or a related sale or supply.

(3) There is excluded from article 21 any transaction entered into [by a supplier as agent for a customer], if the transaction is entered into for the purposes of or in connection with the sale of goods or supply of services, or a related sale or supply, and provided that—

(a) where the investment to which the transaction relates is a security, the supplier does not hold himself out (other than to the customer) as engaging in the business of buying securities of the kind to which the transaction relates with a view to selling them, and does not regularly solicit members of the public for the purpose of inducing them (as principals or agents) to buy, sell, subscribe for or underwrite securities;

(b) where the investment to which the transaction relates is a contractually based investment, the supplier enters into the transaction—

(i) with or through an authorised person, or an exempt person acting in the course of a business comprising a regulated activity in relation to which he is exempt; or

(ii) through an office outside the United Kingdom maintained by a party to the transaction, and with or through a person whose head office is situated outside the United Kingdom and whose ordinary business involves him in carrying on activities of the kind specified by any of articles 14, 21, 25, 37, 40, 45, [51ZA, 51ZB, 51ZC, 51ZD, 51ZE], 52 and 53 or, so far as relevant to any of those articles, article 64, or would do so apart from any exclusion from any of those articles made by this Order.

(4) In paragraph (3)(a), "members of the public" has the meaning given by article 15(2), references to "A" being read as references to the supplier.

(5) There are excluded from article 25(1) and (2) arrangements made by a supplier for, or with a view to, a transaction which is or is to be entered into by a customer for the purposes of or in connection with the sale of goods or supply of services, or a related sale or supply.

(6) There is excluded from article 37 any activity carried on by a supplier where the assets in question—

(a) are those of a customer; and

(b) are managed for the purposes of or in connection with the sale of goods or supply of services, or a related sale or supply.

(7) There is excluded from article 40 any activity carried on by a supplier where the assets in question are or are to be safeguarded and administered for the purposes of or in connection with the sale of goods or supply of services, or a related sale or supply.

(8) There is excluded from article 53 the giving of advice by a supplier to a customer for the purposes of or in connection with the sale of goods or supply of services, or a related sale or supply, or to a person with whom the customer proposes to enter into a transaction for the purposes of or in connection with such a sale or supply or related sale or supply.

(9) Paragraphs (2), (3) and (5) do not apply in the case of a transaction for the sale or purchase of a [contract of insurance], an investment of the kind specified by article 81, or an investment of the kind specified by article 89 so far as relevant to such a contract or such an investment.

(10) Paragraph (6) does not apply where the assets managed consist of qualifying contracts of insurance, investments of the kind specified by article 81, or investments of the kind specified by article 89 so far as relevant to such contracts or such investments.

(11) Paragraph (8) does not apply in the case of advice in relation to an investment which is a [contract of insurance], is of the kind specified by article 81, or is of the kind specified by article 89 so far as relevant to such a contract or such an investment.

[(12) This article is subject to article 4(4).]

NOTES

Para (1): figure in first pair of square brackets in the definition "supplier" inserted by the Financial Services and Markets Act 2000 (Regulated Activities) (Amendment) (No 2) Order 2003, SI 2003/1476, art 10(3)(a), as from 31 October 2004 (in so far as relating to contracts of long-term care insurance), and as from 14 January 2005 (otherwise). Figures in second pair of square brackets in that definition substituted by the Alternative Investment Fund Managers Regulations 2013, SI 2013/1773, reg 81, Sch 2, Part 1, para 1(1), (14), as from 22 July 2013.

Para (3): words in first pair of square brackets substituted by the Financial Services and Markets Act 2000 (Regulated Activities) (Amendment) Order 2001, SI 2001/3544, arts 2, 10, as from 1 December 2001. Figures in second pair of square brackets substituted by SI 2013/1773, reg 81, Sch 2, Part 1, para 1(1), (14), as from 22 July 2013.

Paras (9), (11): words in square brackets substituted by SI 2003/1476, art 10(3)(b), (c), as from 31 October 2004 (in so far as relating to contracts of long-term care insurance), and as from 14 January 2005 (otherwise).

Para (12): added by the Financial Services and Markets Act 2000 (Regulated Activities) (Amendment No 3) Order 2006, SI 2006/3384, arts 2, 21, as from 1 April 2007 (for the purposes of enabling applications to be made for (i) a Part IV permission, (ii) a variation of a Part IV permission, and (iii) the Authority's approval under s 59 of the 2000 Act, in relation to an activity of the kind specified by art 25D of this Order, or in relation to an investment of the kind specified by arts 83, 84 or 85 of this Order), and as from 1 November 2007 (otherwise).

[8.190]
69 Groups and joint enterprises

(1) There is excluded from article 14 any transaction into which a person enters as principal with another person if that other person is also acting as principal and—

(a) they are members of the same group; or

(b) they are, or propose to become, participators in a joint enterprise and the transaction is entered into for the purposes of or in connection with that enterprise.

(2) There is excluded from article 21 any transaction into which a person enters as agent for another person if that other person is acting as principal, and the condition in paragraph (1)(a) or (b) is met, provided that—

(a) where the investment to which the transaction relates is a security, the agent does not hold himself out (other than to members of the same group or persons who are or propose to become participators with him in a joint enterprise) as engaging in the business of buying securities of the kind to which the transaction relates with a view to selling them, and does not regularly solicit members of the public for the purpose of inducing them (as principals or agents) to buy, sell, subscribe for or underwrite securities;

(b) where the investment to which the transaction relates is a contractually based investment, the agent enters into the transaction—

(i) with or through an authorised person, or an exempt person acting in the course of a business comprising a regulated activity in relation to which he is exempt; or

(ii) through an office outside the United Kingdom maintained by a party to the transaction, and with or through a person whose head office is situated outside the United Kingdom and whose ordinary business involves him in carrying on activities of the kind specified by any of articles 14, 21, 25, 37, 40, 45, [51ZA, 51ZB, 51ZC, 51ZD, 51ZE], 52 and 53 or, so far as relevant to any of those articles, article 64, or would do so apart from any exclusion from any of those articles made by this Order.

(3) In paragraph (2)(a), "members of the public" has the meaning given by article 15(2), references to "A" being read as references to the agent.

(4) There are excluded from article 25(1) and (2) arrangements made by a person if—

(a) he is a member of a group and the arrangements in question are for, or with a view to, a transaction which is or is to be entered into, as principal, by another member of the same group; or

(b) he is or proposes to become a participator in a joint enterprise, and the arrangements in question are for, or with a view to, a transaction which is or is to be entered into, as principal, by another person who is or proposes to become a participator in that enterprise, for the purposes of or in connection with that enterprise.

(5) There is excluded from article 37 any activity carried on by a person if—

(a) he is a member of a group and the assets in question belong to another member of the same group; or

(b) he is or proposes to become a participator in a joint enterprise with the person to whom the assets belong, and the assets are managed for the purposes of or in connection with that enterprise.

(6) There is excluded from article 40 any activity carried on by a person if—

(a) he is a member of a group and the assets in question belong to another member of the same group; or

(b) he is or proposes to become a participator in a joint enterprise, and the assets in question—

(i) belong to another person who is or proposes to become a participator in that joint enterprise; and

(ii) are or are to be safeguarded and administered for the purposes of or in connection with that enterprise.

(7) A person who is a member of a group does not carry on an activity of the kind specified by article 45 where he sends a dematerialised instruction, or causes one to be sent, on behalf of another member of the same group, if the investment to which the instruction relates is one in respect of which a member of the same group is registered as holder in the appropriate register of securities, or will be so registered as a result of the instruction.

(8) In paragraph (7), "dematerialised instruction" and "register of securities" have the meaning given by regulation 3 of the Uncertificated Securities Regulations [2001].

(9) There is excluded from article 53 the giving of advice by a person if—

(a) he is a member of a group and gives the advice in question to another member of the same group; or

(b) he is, or proposes to become, a participator in a joint enterprise and the advice in question is given to another person who is, or proposes to become, a participator in that enterprise for the purposes of or in connection with that enterprise.

[(10) Paragraph (2) does not apply to a transaction for the sale or purchase of a contract of insurance.

(11) Paragraph (4) does not apply to arrangements for, or with a view to, a transaction for the sale or purchase of a contract of insurance.

(12) Paragraph (9) does not apply where the advice relates to a transaction for the sale or purchase of a contract of insurance.]

[(13) This article is subject to article 4(4).]

NOTES

Para (2): figures "51ZA, 51ZB, 51ZC, 51ZD, 51ZE" in square brackets in sub-para (b)(ii) substituted by the Alternative Investment Fund Managers Regulations 2013, SI 2013/1773, reg 81, Sch 2, Part 1, para 1(1), (14), as from 22 July 2013.

Para (8): figure in square brackets substituted by the Financial Services and Markets Act 2000 (Regulated Activities) (Amendment) Order 2002, SI 2002/682, art 13(4), as from 27 April 2002.

Paras (10)–(12): added by the Financial Services and Markets Act 2000 (Regulated Activities) (Amendment) (No 2) Order 2003, SI 2003/1476, art 10(4), as from 31 October 2004 (in so far as relating to contracts of long-term care insurance), and as from 14 January 2005 (otherwise).

Para (13): added by the Financial Services and Markets Act 2000 (Regulated Activities) (Amendment No 3) Order 2006, SI 2006/3384, arts 2, 22, as from 1 April 2007 (for the purposes of enabling applications to be made for (i) a Part IV permission, (ii) a variation of a Part IV permission, and (iii) the Authority's approval under s 59 of the 2000 Act, in relation to an activity of the kind specified by art 25D of this Order, or in relation to an investment of the kind specified by arts 83, 84 or 85 of this Order), and as from 1 November 2007 (otherwise).

[8.191]

70 Activities carried on in connection with the sale of a body corporate

(1) A person does not carry on an activity of the kind specified by article 14 by entering as principal into a transaction if—

(a) the transaction is one to acquire or dispose of shares in a body corporate other than an open-ended investment company, or is entered into for the purposes of such an acquisition or disposal; and

(b) either—

(i) the conditions set out in paragraph (2) are met; or

(ii) those conditions are not met, but the object of the transaction may nevertheless reasonably be regarded as being the acquisition of day to day control of the affairs of the body corporate.

(2) The conditions mentioned in paragraph (1)(b) are that—

(a) the shares consist of or include 50 per cent or more of the voting shares in the body corporate; or

(b) the shares, together with any already held by the person acquiring them, consist of or include at least that percentage of such shares; and

(c) in either case, the acquisition or disposal is between parties each of whom is a body corporate, a partnership, a single individual or a group of connected individuals.

(3) In paragraph (2)(c), "a group of connected individuals" means—

(a) in relation to a party disposing of shares in a body corporate, a single group of persons each of whom is—

(i) a director or manager of the body corporate;

(ii) a close relative of any such director or manager;

(iii) a person acting as trustee for any person falling within paragraph (i) or (ii); and

(b) in relation to a party acquiring shares in a body corporate, a single group of persons each of whom is—

(i) a person who is or is to be a director or manager of the body corporate;

(ii) a close relative of any such person; or

(iii) a person acting as trustee for any person falling within paragraph (i) or (ii).

(4) A person does not carry on an activity of the kind specified by article 21 by entering as agent into a transaction of the kind described in paragraph (1).

(5) There are excluded from article 25(1) and (2) arrangements made for, or with a view to, a transaction of the kind described in paragraph (1).

(6) There is excluded from article 53 the giving of advice in connection with a transaction (or proposed transaction) of the kind described in paragraph (1).

[(7) Paragraphs (4), (5) and (6) do not apply in the case of a transaction for the sale or purchase of a contract of insurance.]

[(8) This article is subject to article 4(4).]

NOTES

Para (7): added by the Financial Services and Markets Act 2000 (Regulated Activities) (Amendment) (No 2) Order 2003, SI 2003/1476, art 10(5), as from 31 October 2004 (in so far as relating to contracts of long-term care insurance), and as from 14 January 2005 (otherwise).

Para (8): added by the Financial Services and Markets Act 2000 (Regulated Activities) (Amendment No 3) Order 2006, SI 2006/3384, arts 2, 23, as from 1 April 2007 (for the purposes of enabling applications to be made for (i) a Part IV permission, (ii) a variation of a Part IV permission, and (iii) the Authority's approval under s 59 of the 2000 Act, in relation to an activity of the kind specified by art 25D of this Order, or in relation to an investment of the kind specified by arts 83, 84 or 85 of this Order), and as from 1 November 2007 (otherwise).

[8.192]
71 Activities carried on in connection with employee share schemes

(1) A person ("C"), a member of the same group as C or a relevant trustee does not carry on an activity of the kind specified by article 14 by entering as principal into a transaction the purpose of which is to enable or facilitate—

(a) transactions in shares in, or debentures issued by, C between, or for the benefit of, any of the persons mentioned in paragraph (2); or
(b) the holding of such shares or debentures by, or for the benefit of, such persons.

(2) The persons referred to in paragraph (1) are—

(a) the bona fide employees or former employees of C or of another member of the same group as C;
(b) the wives, husbands, widows, widowers, [civil partners, surviving civil partners,] or children or step-children under the age of eighteen of such employees or former employees.

(3) C, a member of the same group as C or a relevant trustee does not carry on an activity of the kind specified by article 21 by entering as agent into a transaction of the kind described in paragraph (1).

(4) There are excluded from article 25(1) or (2) arrangements made by C, a member of the same group as C or a relevant trustee if the arrangements in question are for, or with a view to, a transaction of the kind described in paragraph (1).

(5) There is excluded from article 40 any activity if the assets in question are, or are to be, safeguarded and administered by C, a member of the same group as C or a relevant trustee for the purpose of enabling or facilitating transactions of the kind described in paragraph (1).

(6) In this article—

(a) "shares" and "debentures" include—
    (i) any investment of the kind specified by article 76[, 77 or 77A];
    (ii) any investment of the kind specified by article 79 or 80 so far as relevant to articles 76[, 77 and 77A]; and
    (iii) any investment of the kind specified by article 89 so far as relevant to investments of the kind mentioned in paragraph (i) or (ii);
(b) "relevant trustee" means a person who, in pursuance of the arrangements made for the purpose mentioned in paragraph (1), holds, as trustee, shares in or debentures issued by C.

NOTES

Para (2): words in square brackets in sub-para (b) inserted by the Civil Partnership Act 2004 (Amendments to Subordinate Legislation) Order 2005, SI 2005/2114, art 2(16), Sch 16, Pt 1, para 1(1), (4), as from 5 December 2005.

Para (6): words in square brackets substituted by the Financial Services and Markets Act 2000 (Regulated Activities) (Amendment) Order 2010, SI 2010/86, art 4, Schedule, para 5(c), (d), as from 24 February 2010.

Step-children, etc: as to the meaning of this, and related expressions, see the Civil Partnership Act 2004, s 246 (as applied to this Order by the Civil Partnership Act 2004 (Relationships Arising Through Civil Partnership) Order 2005, SI 2005/3137, art 3, Schedule).

[8.193]
72 Overseas persons

(1) An overseas person does not carry on an activity of the kind specified by article 14[, 25D or 25DA] by—

(a) entering into a transaction as principal with or though an authorised person, or an exempt person acting in the course of a business comprising a regulated activity in relation to which he is exempt; or
(b) entering into a transaction as principal with a person in the United Kingdom, if the transaction is the result of a legitimate approach.

(2) An overseas person does not carry on an activity of the kind specified by article 21[, 25D or 25DA] by—

(a) entering into a transaction as agent for any person with or through an authorised person or an exempt person acting in the course of a business comprising a regulated activity in relation to which he is exempt; or
(b) entering into a transaction with another party ("X") as agent for any person ("Y"), other than with or through an authorised person or such an exempt person, unless—
    (i) either X or Y is in the United Kingdom; and
    (ii) the transaction is the result of an approach (other than a legitimate approach) made by or on behalf of, or to, whichever of X or Y is in the United Kingdom.

(3) There are excluded from article 25(1)[, 25D or 25DA] arrangements made by an overseas person with an authorised person, or an exempt person acting in the course of a business comprising a regulated activity in relation to which he is exempt.

(4) There are excluded from article 25(2)[, 25D or 25DA] arrangements made by an overseas person with a view to transactions which are, as respects transactions in the United Kingdom, confined to—

(a) transactions entered into by authorised persons as principal or agent; and
(b) transactions entered into by exempt persons, as principal or agent, in the course of business comprising regulated activities in relation to which they are exempt.

(5) There is excluded from article 53 the giving of advice by an overseas person as a result of a legitimate approach.

[(5A) An overseas person does not carry on an activity of the kind specified by article 25A(1)(a), [25A(2A),] 25B(1)(a)[, 25C(1)(a) or 25E(1)(a)] if each person who may be contemplating entering into the relevant type of agreement in the relevant capacity is non-resident.

(5B) There are excluded from articles 25A(1)(b), 25B(1)(b)[, 25C(1)(b) and 25E(1)(b)] arrangements made by an overseas person to vary the terms of a qualifying agreement.

(5C) There are excluded from articles 25A(2), 25B(2)[, 25C(2) and 25E(2)], arrangements made by an overseas person which are made solely with a view to non-resident persons who participate in those arrangements entering, in the relevant capacity, into the relevant type of agreement.

(5D) An overseas person does not carry on an activity of the kind specified in article 61(1), 63B(1)[, 63F(1) or 63J(1)] by entering into a qualifying agreement.

(5E) An overseas person does not carry on an activity of the kind specified in article 61(2), 63B(2)[, 63F(2) or 63J(2)] where he administers a qualifying agreement.

(5F) In paragraphs (5A) to (5E)—

(a) "non-resident" means not normally resident in the United Kingdom;

(b) "qualifying agreement" means—

(i) in relation to articles 25A and 61, a regulated mortgage contract where the borrower (or each borrower) is non-resident when he enters into it;

(ii) in relation to articles 25B and 63B, a regulated home reversion plan where the reversion seller (or each reversion seller) is non-resident when he enters into it;

(iii) in relation to articles 25C and 63F, a regulated home purchase plan where the home purchaser (or each home purchaser) is non-resident when he enters into it;

[(iv) in relation to articles 25E and 63J, a regulated sale and rent back agreement where the agreement seller (or each agreement seller) is non-resident when the agreement seller enters into it;]

(c) "the relevant capacity" means—

(i) in the case of a regulated mortgage contract, as borrower;

(ii) in the case of a regulated home reversion plan, as reversion seller or plan provider;

(iii) in the case of a regulated home purchase plan, as home purchaser;

[(iv) in the case of a regulated sale and rent back agreement, as agreement seller or agreement provider;]

(d) "the relevant type of agreement" means—

(i) in relation to article 25A, a regulated mortgage contract;

(ii) in relation to article 25B, a regulated home reversion plan;

(iii) in relation to article 25C, a regulated home purchase plan[;

(iv) in relation to article 25E, a regulated sale and rent back agreement]].

(6) There is excluded from article 64 any agreement made by an overseas person to carry on an activity of the kind specified by article 25(1) or (2), 37[, 39A], 40 or 45 if the agreement is the result of a legitimate approach.

(7) In this article, "legitimate approach" means—

(a) an approach made to the overseas person which has not been solicited by him in any way, or has been solicited by him in a way which does not contravene section 21 of the Act; or

(b) an approach made by or on behalf of the overseas person in a way which does not contravene that section.

[(8) Paragraphs (1) to (5) do not apply where the overseas person is an investment firm or [qualifying credit institution]—

(a) who is providing or performing investment services and activities on a professional basis; and

(b) whose home . . . State is the United Kingdom.]

[(9) Paragraphs (1) to (5) do not apply where the overseas person is providing clearing services as a central counterparty (within the meaning of section 313(1) of the Act).]

[(9A) Paragraphs (1) to (5) do not apply—

(a) where the overseas person is a central securities depository which provides the services referred to in Article . . . 25(2) of the CSD regulation in the United Kingdom (including through a branch in the United Kingdom); . . .

(b) . . .]

[(10) Paragraphs (5A) and (5C) do not apply where the overseas person is a mortgage intermediary whose home . . . State is the United Kingdom.]

[(10A) This article does not apply in the following two cases.]

[(11) [The first case is] where the overseas person is—

(a) a third-country firm, as defined by Article 4.1.57 ("definitions") of the markets in financial instruments directive ("third country firm");

(b) established in a country subject to an equivalence decision; and

(c) carrying on an activity a third country firm established in that third country may carry on by virtue of the equivalence decision under—

(i) Article 46.1 of the markets in financial instruments regulation (general provisions) if it is registered by ESMA in the register of third country firms established in accordance with Article 48 of that Regulation (register);

(ii) Article 47.3 of the markets in financial instruments regulation (equivalence decision) if it has a branch in an EEA State other than the United Kingdom and is authorised in that State in accordance with Article 39 of the markets in financial instruments directive (establishment of a branch); or

(iii) Article 46.5 of the markets in financial instruments regulation.

[(11A) The second case is where the overseas person is—

(a) a third-country firm, as defined by Article 2.1.42 of the markets in financial instruments regulation;

(b) established in a county that is the subject of an equivalence determination; and

(c) carrying on an activity a third country firm established in that third country may carry on, by virtue of the equivalence determination, under—

(i) Article 46.1 of the markets in financial instruments regulation, if it is registered by the FCA in the register of third country firms established in accordance with Article 48 of that regulation, or

(ii) Article 46.5 of that regulation.]

(12) For the purposes of [paragraphs (11) and (11A)]—

(a) "equivalence decision" means a decision adopted by the Commission [before IP completion day] in relation to a country under Article 47.1 of the markets in financial instruments regulation which has not been withdrawn by a subsequent decision adopted by the Commission [before IP completion day] under that Article . . .

(b) a country is subject to an equivalence decision if a period of more than three years has elapsed since the adoption of the decision by the Commission, beginning on the day after the date of the adoption of the decision.

[(c) "equivalence determination" means a determination made by the Treasury—

(i) in regulations under Article 47.1 of the markets in financial instruments regulation and not revoked; or

(ii) by direction under regulation 2 of the Equivalence Determinations for Financial Services and Miscellaneous Provisions (Amendment etc) (EU Exit) Regulations 2019 and not revoked;

(d) a country is the subject of an equivalence determination if a period of more than three years has elapsed since—

(i) the date on which the equivalence determination came into force, or

(ii) where two or more equivalence determinations have been made in succession in relation to the country concerned, the date on which the first equivalence determination came into force;

(e) for the purposes of sub-paragraph (d), an equivalence determination is not made in succession to an earlier determination if the earlier determination ceased to have effect before the later determination came into force.]]

NOTES

Paras (1)–(4): words in square brackets substituted by the Financial Services and Markets Act 2000 (Regulated Activities) (Amendment) Order 2017, SI 2017/488, art 5(1), (2), as from 1 April 2017 (for the purposes of (i) enabling applications to be made for a Part 4A permission, for a variation of a Part 4A permission or for an approval under FSMA 2000, s 59, or (ii) enabling such applications to be determined, in relation to any specified activity or any specified investment amended or inserted by the 2017 Order), and as from 3 January 2018 (otherwise).

Paras (5A)–(5F): originally inserted by the Financial Services and Markets Act 2000 (Regulated Activities) (Amendment) (No 1) Order 2003, SI 2003/1475, art 20, as from 31 October 2004. Subsequently substituted by the Financial Services and Markets Act 2000 (Regulated Activities) (Amendment) (No 2) Order 2006, SI 2006/2383, arts 2, 21, as from 6 November 2006 (for the purposes of enabling applications to be made for (i) a Pt IV permission, or a variation of a Pt IV permission, in relation to activities of the kind specified by arts 25B, 25C, 53B, 53C, 63B or 63F or, so far as relevant to any such activity, art 64 of this Order; or (ii) the Authority's approval under FSMA 2000, s 59 in relation to any of those activities), and as from 6 April 2007 (otherwise). These paragraphs have subsequently been amended as follows—

Figure "25A(2A)," in square brackets in para (5A) inserted by the Mortgage Credit Directive Order 2015, SI 2015/910, Sch 1, Pt 2, para 4(1), (26)(a), as from 21 March 2016.

Other words in square brackets in paras (5A)–(5E) substituted by the Financial Services and Markets Act 2000 (Regulated Activities) (Amendment) Order 2009, SI 2009/1342, arts 2, 20(a)–(e), as from 1 July 2009 (other than for the purposes of enabling applications to be made for a Part IV permission, or a variation of a Part IV permission, in relation to activities of the kind specified by arts 25E, 53D or 63J or, so far as relevant to any such activity, art 64 of this Order), and as from 30 June 2010 (for those purposes).

In para (5F), sub-paras (b)(iv), (c)(iv), and (d)(iv) inserted by SI 2009/1342, arts 2, 20(f)–(h), as from 1 July 2009 (certain purposes), and as from 30 June 2010 (otherwise) (see the first note relating to the 2009 Order above).

Para (6): figure in square brackets inserted by the Financial Services and Markets Act 2000 (Regulated Activities) (Amendment) (No 2) Order 2003, SI 2003/1476, art 10(6), as from 31 October 2004 (in so far as relating to contracts of long-term care insurance), and as from 14 January 2005 (otherwise).

Para (8): added by the Financial Services and Markets Act 2000 (Regulated Activities) (Amendment No 3) Order 2006, SI 2006/3384, arts 2, 24(e), as from 1 April 2007 (for the purposes of enabling applications to be made for (i) a Part IV permission, (ii) a variation of a Part IV permission, and (iii) the Authority's approval under s 59 of the 2000 Act, in relation to an activity of the kind specified by art 25D of this Order, or in relation to an investment of the kind specified by arts 83, 84 or 85 of this Order), and as from 1 November 2007 (otherwise). Words in square brackets substituted, and word omitted from sub-para (b) revoked, by the Financial Services and Markets Act 2000 (Amendment) (EU Exit) Regulations 2019, SI 2019/632, regs 120, 147(1)–(3), as from IP completion day (as defined in the European Union (Withdrawal Agreement) Act 2020, s 39).

Para (9): added by the Financial Services and Markets Act 2000 (Over the Counter Derivatives, Central Counterparties and Trade Repositories) Regulations 2013, SI 2013/504, reg 33(1), (5), as from 1 April 2013.

Para (9A): inserted by the Central Securities Depositories Regulations 2017, SI 2017/1064, reg 10, Schedule, para 23(1), (3), as from 28 November 2017. Words omitted revoked by SI 2019/632, regs 120, 147(1), (4), as from IP completion day (as defined in the European Union (Withdrawal Agreement) Act 2020, s 39).

Para (10): added by SI 2015/910, Sch 1, Pt 2, para 4(1), (26)(b), as from 21 March 2016. Word omitted revoked by SI 2019/632, regs 120, 147(1), (3), as from IP completion day (as defined in the European Union (Withdrawal Agreement) Act 2020, s 39).

Para (10A): inserted by SI 2019/632, regs 120, 147(1), (5), as from IP completion day (as defined in the European Union (Withdrawal Agreement) Act 2020, s 39).

Para (11): added, together with para (12), by SI 2017/488, art 5(1), (3), as from 1 April 2017 (certain purposes), and as from 3 January 2018 (otherwise) (for details, see the first note relating to the 2017 Regulations above). Words in square bracket substituted by SI 2019/632, regs 120, 147(1), (6), as from IP completion day (as defined in the European Union (Withdrawal Agreement) Act 2020, s 39).

Para (11A): inserted by SI 2019/632, regs 120, 147(1), (7), as from IP completion day (as defined in the European Union (Withdrawal Agreement) Act 2020, s 39). Note that reg 147(7) of the 2019 Regulations was amended by the Financial Services (Miscellaneous) (Amendment) (EU Exit) Regulations 2019, SI 2019/710, reg 19, with effect from immediately before IP completion day; and the effect of the amendment has been incorporated in the text set out above.

Para (12): added as noted to para (11) above. The words in the first pair of square brackets were substituted, the words in square brackets in sub-para (a) were inserted, the word omitted from sub-para (a) was revoked, and sub-paras (c)–(e) were inserted, by SI 2019/632, regs 120, 147(1), (8), as from IP completion day (as defined in the European Union (Withdrawal Agreement) Act 2020, s 39). Note that reg 147(8) of the 2019 Regulations was amended by the Financial Services (Miscellaneous) (Amendment) (EU Exit) Regulations 2019, SI 2019/710, reg 19 (with effect from immediately before IP completion day), and by the Financial Services and Economic and Monetary Policy (Consequential Amendments) (EU Exit) Regulations 2020, SI 2020/1301, reg 3, Schedule, para 33(r) (as from 30 December 2020); and the effect of the amendments has been incorporated in the text set out above.

72A *(Art 72A (Information society services) was originally inserted by the Financial Services and Markets Act 2000 (Regulated Activities) (Amendment) (No 2) Order 2002, SI 2002/1776, art 2, as from 21 August 2002. It was subsequently revoked by the Electronic Commerce and Solvency 2 (Amendment etc) (EU Exit) Regulations 2019, SI 2019/1361, reg 5(1), (2), as from IP completion day (as defined in the European Union (Withdrawal Agreement) Act 2020, s 39). See further Part 4 of the 2019 Regulations (Transitional Provisions: Temporary Exclusion from General Prohibition) which contains transitional provisions in connection with the revocation of this article. It provides a regime by which a person providing information society services to which this article applied immediately before IP completion day to persons in the UK from an establishment in an EEA State can continue to provide such services while those services are run down.)*

[8.194]

[72AA Managers of [UK UCITS] and AIFs

(1) This article applies to a person with a Part 4A permission to carry on the activity of the kind specified by article 51ZA or 51ZC.

(2) Activities carried on by the person in connection with or for the purposes of managing [a UK UCITS] or, as the case may be, managing an AIF, are excluded from the activities specified by this Part, other than the activities mentioned in paragraph (1).]

NOTES

Inserted by the Alternative Investment Fund Managers Regulations 2013, SI 2013/1773, reg 81, Sch 2, Part 1, para 1(1), (16), as from 22 July 2013.

Words in square brackets substituted by the Financial Services and Markets Act 2000 (Amendment) (EU Exit) Regulations 2019, SI 2019/632, regs 120, 148(1), as from IP completion day (as defined in the European Union (Withdrawal Agreement) Act 2020, s 39).

[8.195]

[72B Activities carried on by a provider of relevant goods or services

(1) In this article—

"connected contract of insurance" means a contract of insurance which—

(a) is not a contract of long-term insurance;

(b) . . .

[(c) has a premium of—

(i) 600 euro or less (calculated on a pro rata annual basis), or

(ii) where the insurance is complementary to a service being provided by the provider and the duration of that service is equal to or less than three months, 200 euro or less,

or equivalent amounts of sterling or another currency;]

(d) covers the risk of—

(i) breakdown, loss of, or damage to, non-motor goods supplied by the provider; . . .

[(ia) the non-use of services supplied by the provider; or]

[(ii) damage to, or loss of, baggage and other risks linked to the travel booked with the provider ("travel risks") in circumstances where—

(aa) the travel booked with the provider relates to attendance at an event organised or managed by that provider and the party seeking insurance is not an individual (acting in his private capacity) or a small business; or

(bb) the travel booked with the provider is only the hire of an aircraft, vehicle or vessel which does not provide sleeping accommodation;]

(e) does not cover any liability risks (except, in the case of a contract which covers travel risks, where that cover is ancillary to the main cover provided by the contract); [and]

(f) is complementary to the non-motor goods being supplied or service being provided by the provider; . . .

(g) . . . ;

"non-motor goods" means goods which are not mechanically propelled road vehicles;

"provider" means a person who supplies [non-motor goods or services] or provides services related to travel in the course of carrying on a profession or business which does not otherwise consist of the carrying on of regulated activities.

[For these purposes, the transfer of possession of an aircraft, vehicle or vessel under an agreement for hire which is not—

(a) a hire-purchase agreement . . . , or

(b) any other agreement which contemplates that the property in those goods will also pass at some time in the future,

is the provision of a service related to travel, not a supply of goods.]

["small business" means—

(a) subject to paragraph (b) a sole trader, body corporate, partnership or an unincorporated association which had a turnover in the last financial year of less than £1,000,000;

(b) where the business concerned is a member of a group within the meaning of [section 474(1) of the Companies Act 2006], reference to its turnover means the combined turnover of the group;

"turnover" means the amounts derived from the provision of goods and services falling within the business's ordinary activities, after deduction of trade discounts, value added tax and any other taxes based on the amounts so derived].

(2) There is excluded from article 21 any transaction for the sale or purchase of a connected contract of insurance into which a provider enters as agent.

(3) There are excluded from article 25(1) and (2) any arrangements made by a provider for, or with a view to, a transaction for the sale or purchase of a connected contract of insurance.

(4) There is excluded from article 39A any activity carried on by a provider where the contract of insurance in question is a connected contract of insurance.

(5) There is excluded from article 53 the giving of advice by a provider in relation to a transaction for the sale or purchase of a connected contract of insurance.

(6) For the purposes of this article, a contract of insurance which covers travel risks is not to be treated as a contract of long-term insurance, notwithstanding the fact that it contains related and subsidiary provisions such that it might be regarded as a contract of long-term insurance, if the cover to which those provisions relate is ancillary to the main cover provided by the contract.]

NOTES

Inserted, together with arts 72C, 72D, by the Financial Services and Markets Act 2000 (Regulated Activities) (Amendment) (No 2) Order 2003, SI 2003/1476, art 11, as from 31 October 2004 (in so far as relating to contracts of long-term care insurance), and as from 14 January 2005 (otherwise).

Para (1) is amended as follows:

In the definition "connected contract of insurance", para (b) was revoked, para (c) was substituted, the word omitted from sub-para (d)(i) was revoked, sub-para (d)(ia) was inserted, the word in square brackets in para (e) was inserted, and para (g) and the preceding word were revoked, by the Insurance Distribution (Regulated Activities and Miscellaneous Amendments) Order 2018, SI 2018/546, arts 2, 6(a), as from 1 October 2018.

In the definition "connected contract of insurance", sub-para (d)(ii) was substituted by the Financial Services and Markets Act 2000 (Regulated Activities) (Amendment) (No 2) Order 2007, SI 2007/3510, art 2(1), (2), as from 30 June 2008 (for the purposes of enabling applications to be made, pursuant to this amendment, for (i) a Pt IV permission, or a variation of a Pt IV permission, in relation to activities of the kind specified by arts 21, 25(1), 25(2), 39A, 53 or, so far as relevant to any such activity, art 64 of this Order, or (ii) the Authority's approval under s 59 of FSMA 2000 in relation to any of those activities), and as from 1 January 2009 (otherwise).

Words in first pair of square brackets in the definition "provider" substituted by SI 2018/546, arts 2, 6(b), as from 1 October 2018.

Words in second pair of square brackets in definition "provider" inserted, and definitions "small business" and "turnover" added, by SI 2007/3510, art 2(1), (3), as from the same dates and for the same purposes as noted above.

Words omitted from the definition "provider" revoked by the Financial Services and Markets Act 2000 (Regulated Activities) (Amendment) (No 2) Order 2013, SI 2013/1881, arts 2, 9(1), as from 1 April 2014.

Words in square brackets in definition "small business" substituted by the Companies Act 2006 (Consequential Amendments and Transitional Provisions) Order 2011, SI 2011/1265, art 13(1), (5), as from 12 May 2011.

[8.196]
[72C Provision of information on an incidental basis

(1) There is excluded from articles 25(1) and (2) the making of arrangements for, or with a view to, a transaction for the sale or purchase of a contract of insurance or an investment of the kind specified by article 89, so far as relevant to such a contract, where that activity meets the conditions specified in paragraph (4).

(2) There is excluded from articles 37 and 40 any activity—

(a) where the assets in question are rights under a contract of insurance or an investment of the kind specified by article 89, so far as relevant to such a contract; and

(b) which meets the conditions specified in paragraph (4).

(3) There is excluded from article 39A any activity which meets the conditions specified in paragraph (4).

(4) The conditions specified in this paragraph are that the activity—

(a) consists of the provision of information to the policyholder or potential policyholder;

(b) is carried on by a person in the course of carrying on a profession or business which does not otherwise consist of the carrying on of regulated activities; and

(c) may reasonably be regarded as being incidental to that profession or business.]

NOTES

Inserted as noted to art 72B at **[8.195]**.

[8.197]
[72D Large risks contracts where risk situated outside [the United Kingdom]

(1) There is excluded from articles 21, 25(1) and (2), 39A and 53 any activity which is carried on in relation to a large risks contract of insurance, to the extent that the risk or commitment covered by the contract is not situated in [the United Kingdom].

(2) In this article, a "large risks contract of insurance" is a contract of insurance the principal object of which is to cover—

(a) risks falling within paragraph 4 (railway rolling stock), 5 (aircraft), 6 (ships), 7 (goods in transit), 11 (aircraft liability) or 12 (liability of ships) of Part 1 of Schedule 1;

(b) risks falling within paragraph 14 (credit) or 15 (suretyship) of that Part provided that the risks relate to a business carried on by the policyholder; or

(c) risks falling within paragraph 3 (land vehicles), 8 (fire and natural forces), 9 (damage to property), 10 (motor vehicle liability), 13 (general liability) or 16 (miscellaneous financial loss) of that Part provided that the risks relate to a business carried on by the policyholder and that the condition specified in paragraph (3) is met in relation to that business.

(3) The condition specified in this paragraph is that at least two of the three following criteria were met in the most recent financial year for which information is available—

(a) the balance sheet total of the business [(within the meaning of section 382(5) or 465(5) of the Companies Act 2006)] exceeded 6.2 million euro,

(b) the net turnover [(within the meaning given to "turnover" by section 474(1) of the Companies Act 2006)] exceeded 12.8 million euro,

(c) the number of employees [(within the meaning given by sections 382(6) and 465(6) of the Companies Act 2006)] exceeded 250,

and for a financial year which is a company's financial year but not in fact a year, the net turnover of the policyholder shall be proportionately adjusted.

(4) For the purposes of paragraph (3), where the policyholder is a member of a group for which consolidated accounts . . . are drawn up, the question whether the condition specified by that paragraph is met is to be determined by reference to those accounts.]

NOTES

Inserted as noted to art 72B at **[8.195]**.

Article heading, para (1): words in square brackets substituted by the Financial Services and Markets Act 2000 (Amendment) (EU Exit) Regulations 2019, SI 2019/632, regs 120, 149(1)–(3), as from IP completion day (as defined in the European Union (Withdrawal Agreement) Act 2020, s 39).

Para (3): words in square brackets substituted by the Companies Act 2006 (Consequential Amendments and Transitional Provisions) Order 2011, SI 2011/1265, art 13(1), (6), as from 12 May 2011.

Para (4): words omitted revoked by SI 2019/632, regs 120, 149(1), (4), as from IP completion day (as defined in the European Union (Withdrawal Agreement) Act 2020, s 39).

[8.198]

[72E Business Angel-led Enterprise Capital Funds

(1) A body corporate of a type specified in paragraph (7) does not carry on the activity of the kind specified by article 21 by entering as agent into a transaction on behalf of the participants of a Business Angel-led Enterprise Capital Fund.

(2) There are excluded from article 25(1) and (2) arrangements, made by a body corporate of a type specified in paragraph (7), for or with a view to a transaction which is or is to be entered into by or on behalf of the participants in a Business Angel-led Enterprise Capital Fund.

(3) There is excluded from article 37 any activity, carried on by a body corporate of a type specified in paragraph (7), which consists in the managing of assets belonging to the participants in a Business Angel-led Enterprise Capital Fund.

(4) There is excluded from article 40 any activity, carried on by a body corporate of a type specified in paragraph (7), in respect of assets belonging to the participants in a Business Angel-led Enterprise Capital Fund.

(5) A body corporate of a type specified in paragraph (7) does not carry on the activity of the kind specified in article [51ZA, 51ZC or 51ZE] where it carries on the activity of establishing, operating or winding up a Business Angel-led Enterprise Capital Fund.

(6) A body corporate of a type specified in paragraph (7) does not carry on the activity of the kind specified in article 53 where it is advising the participants in a Business Angel-led Enterprise Capital Fund on investments to be made by or on behalf of the participants of that Business Angel-led Enterprise Capital Fund.

(7) The type of body corporate specified is a limited company—

(i) which operates a Business Angel-led Enterprise Capital Fund; and

(ii) the members of which are participants in the Business Angel-led Enterprise Capital Fund operated by that limited company and between them have invested at least 50 per cent of the total investment in that Business Angel-led Enterprise Capital Fund excluding any investment made by the Secretary of State.

(8) For the purposes of paragraph (7), "a limited company" means a body corporate with limited liability which is a company or firm formed [under the law of any part of the United Kingdom] and having its registered office, central administration or principal place of business [in the United Kingdom].

(9) Nothing in this article has the effect of excluding a body corporate from the application of the [Money Laundering, Terrorist Financing and Transfer of Funds (Information on the Payer) Regulations 2017], in so far as those Regulations would have applied to it but for this article.

(10) Nothing in this article has the effect of excluding a body corporate from the application of section 397 of the Act (misleading statements and practices), in so far as that section would have applied to it but for this article.]

[(11) This article is subject to article 4(4).]

NOTES

Inserted, together with art 72F, by the Financial Services and Markets Act 2000 (Regulated Activities) (Amendment) (No 2) Order 2005, SI 2005/1518, art 2(1), (3), as from 1 October 2005.

Para (5): figures "51ZA, 51ZC or 51ZE" in square brackets substituted by the Alternative Investment Fund Managers Regulations 2013, SI 2013/1773, reg 81, Sch 2, Part 1, para 1(1), (15), as from 22 July 2013.

Para (8): words in square brackets substituted by the Financial Services and Markets Act 2000 (Amendment) (EU Exit) Regulations 2019, SI 2019/632, regs 120, 150, as from IP completion day (as defined in the European Union (Withdrawal Agreement) Act 2020, s 39).

Para (9): words in square brackets substituted by the Money Laundering, Terrorist Financing and Transfer of Funds (Information on the Payer) Regulations 2017, SI 2017/692, reg 109, Sch 7, Pt 2, para 17, as from 26 June 2017.

Para (11): added by the Financial Services and Markets Act 2000 (Regulated Activities) (Amendment No 3) Order 2006, SI 2006/3384, arts 2, 25, as from 1 April 2007 (for the purposes of enabling applications to be made for (i) a Part IV permission, (ii) a variation of a Part IV permission, and (iii) the Authority's approval under s 59 of the 2000 Act, in relation to an activity of the kind specified by art 25D of this Order, or in relation to an investment of the kind specified by arts 83, 84 or 85 of this Order), and as from 1 November 2007 (otherwise).

[8.199]
[72F Interpretation

(1) For the purposes of this article and of article 72E—

"Business Angel-led Enterprise Capital Fund" means a collective investment scheme which—

(a) is established for the purpose of enabling participants to participate in or receive profits or income arising from the acquisition, holding, management or disposal of investments falling within one or more of—

(i) article 76, being shares in an unlisted company;

(ii) article 77, being instruments creating or acknowledging indebtedness in respect of an unlisted company; and

[(iia) article 77A, being rights under an alternative finance investment bond issued by an unlisted company;]

(iii) article 79, being warrants or other instruments entitling the holder to subscribe for shares in an unlisted company;

(b) has only the following as its participants—

(i) the Secretary of State;

(ii) a body corporate of a type specified in article 72E(7); and

(iii) one or more persons each of whom at the time they became a participant was—

(aa) a sophisticated investor;

(bb) a high net worth individual;

(cc) a high net worth company;

(dd) a high net worth unincorporated association;

(ee) a trustee of a high value trust; or

(ff) a self-certified sophisticated investor;

(c) is prevented, by the arrangements by which it is established, from—

(i) acquiring investments, other than those falling within paragraphs (i) to (iii) of sub-paragraph (a); and

(ii) acquiring investments falling within paragraphs (i) to (iii) of sub-paragraph (a) in an unlisted company, where the aggregated cost of those investments exceeds £2 million, unless that acquisition is necessary to prevent or reduce the dilution of an existing share-holding in that unlisted company;

"high net worth company" means a body corporate which—

(a) falls within article 49(2)(a) of the Financial Services and Markets Act 2000 (Financial Promotion) Order 2001 (high net worth companies, unincorporated associations etc); and

(b) has executed a document [(in a manner which binds the company)] in the following terms:

"This company is a high net worth company and falls within article 49(2)(a) of the Financial Services and Markets Act 2000 (Financial Promotion) Order 2001. We understand that any Business Angel-led Enterprise Capital Fund (within the meaning of article 72F of the Financial Services and Markets Act 2000 (Regulated Activities) Order 2001), in which this company participates, or any person who operates that Business Angel-led Enterprise Capital Fund, in which this company participates, will not be authorised under the Financial Services and Markets Act 2000 (and so will not have to satisfy the threshold conditions set out in Part I of Schedule 6 to that Act and will not be subject to Financial Services Authority rules such as those on holding client money). We understand that this means that redress through the Financial Services Authority, the Financial Ombudsman Scheme or the Financial Services Compensation Scheme will not be available. We also understand the risks associated in investing in a Business Angel-led Enterprise Capital Fund and are aware that it is open to us to seek advice from someone who is authorised under the Financial Services and Markets Act 2000 and who specialises in advising on this kind of investment."

"high net worth individual" means an individual who—

(a) is a "certified high net worth individual" within the meaning of article 48(2) of the Financial Services and Markets Act 2000 (Financial Promotion) Order 2001 (certified high net worth individuals); and

(b) has signed a statement in the following terms:

"I declare that I am a certified high net worth individual within the meaning of article 48(2) of the Financial Services and Markets Act 2000 (Financial Promotion) Order 2001 and that I understand that any Business Angel-led Enterprise Capital Fund (within the meaning of article 72F of the Financial Services and Markets Act 2000 (Regulated Activities) Order 2001), in which I participate, or any person who operates that Business Angel-led Enterprise Capital Fund, in which I participate, will not be authorised under the Financial Services and Markets Act 2000 (and so will not have to satisfy the threshold conditions set out in Part I of Schedule 6 to that Act and will not be subject to Financial Services Authority rules such as those on holding client money). I understand that this means that redress through the Financial Services Authority, the Financial Ombudsman Scheme or the Financial Services Compensation Scheme will not be available. I also understand the risks associated in investing in a Business Angel-led Enterprise Capital Fund and am aware that it is open to me to seek advice from someone who is authorised under the Financial Services and Markets Act 2000 and who specialises in advising on this kind of investment.";

"high net worth unincorporated association" means an unincorporated association—

(a) which falls within article 49(2)(b) of the Financial Services and Markets Act 2000 (Financial Promotion) Order 2001; and

(b) on behalf of which an officer of that association or a member of its governing body has signed a statement in the following terms:

"This unincorporated association is a high net worth unincorporated association and falls within article 49(2)(b) of the Financial Services and Markets Act 2000 (Financial Promotion) Order 2001. I understand that any Business Angel-led Enterprise Capital Fund (within the meaning of article 72F of the Financial Services and Markets Act 2000 (Regulated Activities) Order 2001), in which this association participates, or any person who operates that Business Angel-led Enterprise Capital Fund, in which this association participates, will not be authorised under the Financial Services and Markets Act 2000 (and so will not have to satisfy the threshold conditions set out in Part I of Schedule 6 to that Act and will not be subject to Financial Services Authority rules such as those on holding client money). I understand that this means that redress through the Financial Services Authority, the Financial Ombudsman Scheme or the Financial Services Compensation Scheme will not be available. I also understand the risks associated in investing in a Business Angel-led Enterprise Capital Fund and am aware that it is open to the association to seek advice from someone who is authorised under the Financial Services and Markets Act 2000 and who specialises in advising on this kind of investment.";

"high value trust" means a trust—

(a) where the aggregate value of the cash and investments which form a part of the trust's assets (before deducting the amount of its liabilities) is £10 million or more;

(b) on behalf of which a trustee has signed a statement in the following terms:

"This trust is a high value trust. I understand that any Business Angel-led Enterprise Capital Fund (within the meaning of article 72F of the Financial Services and Markets Act 2000 (Regulated Activities) Order 2001), in which this trust participates, or any person who operates that Business Angel-led Enterprise Capital Fund, in which this trust participates, will not be authorised under the Financial Services and Markets Act 2000 (and so will not have to satisfy the threshold conditions set out in Part I of Schedule 6 to that Act and will not be subject to Financial Services Authority rules such as those on holding client money). I understand that this means that redress through the Financial Services Authority, the Financial Ombudsman Scheme or the Financial Services Compensation Scheme will not be available. I also understand the risks associated in investing in a Business Angel-led Enterprise Capital Fund and am aware that it is open to the trust to seek advice from someone who is authorised under the Financial Services and Markets Act 2000 and who specialises in advising on this kind of investment.";

"self-certified sophisticated investor" means an individual who—

(a) is a "self-certified sophisticated investor" within the meaning of article 50A of the Financial Services and Markets Act 2000 (Financial Promotion) Order 2001;

(b) has signed a statement in the following terms:

"I declare that I am a self-certified sophisticated investor within the meaning of article 50A of the Financial Services and Markets Act 2000 (Financial Promotion) Order 2001 and that I understand that any Business Angel-led Enterprise Capital Fund (within the meaning of article 72F of the Financial Services and Markets Act 2000 (Regulated Activities) Order 2001), in which I participate, or any person who operates that Business Angel-led Enterprise Capital Fund, in which I participate, will not be authorised under the Financial Services and Markets Act 2000 (and so will not have to satisfy the threshold conditions set out in Part I of Schedule 6 to that Act and will not be subject to Financial Services Authority rules such as those on holding client money). I understand that this means that redress through the Financial Services Authority, the Financial Ombudsman Scheme or the Financial Services Compensation Scheme will not be available. I also understand the risks associated in investing in a Business Angel-led Enterprise Capital Fund and am aware that it is open to me to seek advice from someone who is authorised under the Financial Services and Markets Act 2000 and who specialises in advising on this kind of investment.";

"sophisticated investor" means an individual who—

(a) is a "certified sophisticated investor" within the meaning of article 50(1) of the Financial Services and Markets Act 2000 (Financial Promotion) Order 2001; and

(b) has signed a statement in the following terms:

"I declare that I am a certified sophisticated investor within the meaning of article 50(1) of the Financial Services and Markets Act 2000 (Financial Promotion) Order 2001 and that I understand that any Business Angel-led Enterprise Capital Fund (within the meaning of article 72F of the Financial Services and Markets Act 2000 (Regulated Activities) Order 2001), in which I participate, or any person who operates that Business Angel-led Enterprise Capital Fund, in which I participate, will not be authorised under the Financial Services and Markets Act 2000 (and so will not have to satisfy the threshold conditions set out in Part I of Schedule 6 to that Act and will not be subject to Financial Services Authority rules such as those on holding client money). I understand that this means that redress through the Financial Services Authority, the Financial Ombudsman Scheme or the Financial Services Compensation Scheme will not be available. I also understand the risks associated in investing in a Business Angel-led Enterprise Capital Fund and am aware that it is open to me to seek advice from someone who is authorised under the Financial Services and Markets Act 2000 and who specialises in advising on this kind of investment.";

"unlisted company" has the meaning given by article 3 of the Financial Services and Markets Act 2000 (Financial Promotion) Order 2001.

(2) References in this Article and in Article 72E to a participant in a Business Angel-led Enterprise Capital Fund, doing things on behalf of such a participant and property belonging to such a participant are, respectively, references to that participant in that capacity, to doing things on behalf of that participant in that capacity or to the property of that participant held in that capacity.]

NOTES

Inserted as noted to art 72E at **[8.198]**.

Para (1): sub-para (iia) of the definition "Business Angel-led Enterprise Capital Fund" inserted by the Financial Services and Markets Act 2000 (Regulated Activities) (Amendment) Order 2010, SI 2010/86, art 4, Schedule, para 5(e), as from 24 February 2010. Words in square brackets in definition "high net worth company" substituted by the Financial Services and Markets Act 2000 (Regulated Activities) (Amendment) (No 2) Order 2006, SI 2006/2383, arts 2, 22, as from 6 November 2006 (for the purposes of enabling applications to be made for (i) a Pt IV permission, or a variation of a Pt IV permission, in relation to activities of the kind specified by arts 25B, 25C, 53B, 53C, 63B or 63F or, so far as relevant to any such activity, art 64 of this Order; or (ii) the Authority's approval under FSMA 2000, s 59 in relation to any of those activities), and as from 6 April 2007 (otherwise).

[8.200]

[72G Local authorities

(1) There is excluded from article 5 any activity which is carried on by a local authority.

(2) There is excluded from articles 21, 25(1) and (2), 39A and 53 any activity carried on by a local authority which relates to a contract of insurance which is not a qualifying contract of insurance.

(3) There is excluded from articles [25A(1)(b), 25A(2)], 25B, 25C, 25E, 36A, 39D, 39E, 39F, 39G, . . . 53B, 53C, 53D, 60N, . . . 63B, 63F, 63J or 89A any activity which is carried on by a local authority.

[(3A) There is excluded from article 25A(1)(b) and (2) any activity which is carried on by a company which is a wholly-owned subsidiary of a local authority.

(3B) There is excluded from articles 25A(1)(a) and (2A), 53A, 53DA and 61 any activity which is carried on by a local authority, or a company which is a wholly-owned subsidiary of a local authority, in so far as the contract . . . —

[(a) was entered into before 21st March 2016; or
(b) is entered into on or after 21st March 2016 and—
  [(i) is an agreement to which section 423A(3) of the Act applies;]
  (ii) is a bridging loan; or
  (iii) is a restricted public loan in relation to which the requirements of paragraph (6) are met].

[(3C) There is excluded from article 59(1) and (1A) any activity which is carried on by a local authority.]

[(4) There is excluded from article 60B—

[(a) any activity which is carried on by a local authority—
  (i) in relation to a credit agreement which was entered into before 21st March 2016, or which is entered into on or after that date for a purpose other than acquiring or retaining property rights in land or in an existing or projected building; and
  (ii) in so far as the activity is carried on in relation to a credit agreement [falling within paragraph (6A) or within section 423A(2)(a) or (b) or (3)(b), (d), (e) or (f) of the Act];]
(b) any activity which is carried on by a local authority [in relation to a credit agreement entered into on or after 21st March 2016], the purpose of which is to acquire or retain property rights in land or in an existing or projected building, in so far as the credit agreement meets one of the following conditions—
  [(i) it is an agreement to which section 423A(3) of the Act applies;]
  (ii) it is a bridging loan; or
  (iii) it is a restricted public loan in relation to which the requirements of paragraph (6) are met.]

[(4A) A reference in paragraph (4) to any land or building—

(a) in relation to an agreement entered into before IP completion day, is a reference to any land or building in the United Kingdom or within the territory of an EEA State;
(b) in relation to an agreement entered into on or after IP completion day, is a reference to any land or building in the United Kingdom.]

(5) There is excluded from article 64 any agreement made by a local authority to carry on an activity of the kind excluded by paragraphs (2) to (4).

[(6) The requirements of this paragraph are that—

(a) the borrower receives timely information on the main features, risks and costs of the loan at the pre-contractual stage; and
(b) any advertising of the loan is fair, clear and not misleading.

[(6A) The following credit agreements fall within this paragraph—

(a) an agreement involving a total amount of credit of less than 200 euro;
(b) an agreement that involves a total amount of credit of more than 75,000 euro, other than an unsecured credit agreement the purpose of which is the renovation of a residential immovable property;
(c) a hiring or leasing agreement under which an obligation to purchase the object of the agreement is not laid down either by the agreement itself or by any separate agreement;
(d) an agreement under which the credit is granted free of interest and without any other charges;
(e) an agreement under which the credit has to be repaid within three months and only insignificant charges are payable;
(f) an agreement concluded with an investment firm or a credit institution for the purposes of allowing an investor to carry out a transaction relating to one or more of the instruments listed in Part 1 of Schedule 2, where the investment firm or credit institution granting the credit is involved in that transaction;
(g) an agreement under which the consumer's liability is strictly limited to an item that the consumer is requested to deposit, upon the conclusion of the agreement, as security in the creditor's safe-keeping;

(h) an agreement that relates to a restricted public loan.

(6B) For the purposes of subsection (6A)(c), an obligation to purchase the object of the agreement is deemed to exist if the creditor decides that it does.]

(7) In this article—

"bridging loan" has the meaning given by [article 60G(9)];

"borrower" means a person receiving credit;

["consumer" means an individual who is acting for purposes outside those of any trade, business or profession carried on by the individual;]

. . .

"credit" includes a cash loan and any other form of financial accommodation;

"restricted public loan" means credit that is—

(a) offered to a particular class of borrower and not offered to the public generally;

(b) offered under an enactment with a general interest purpose; and

(c) provided on terms which are more favourable to the borrower than those prevailing on the market, because the credit meets one of the following conditions—

(i) it is interest free;

(ii) the rate of interest is lower than that prevailing on the market; or

(iii) the rate of interest is no higher than that prevailing on the market but the other terms on which the credit is provided are more favourable to the borrower; and

"wholly-owned subsidiary" has the same meaning as in section 1159 (meaning of "subsidiary" etc) of the Companies Act 2006 and, for the purposes of this definition, a local authority is to be treated as a body corporate.]]

NOTES

Inserted, together with art 72H, by the Financial Services and Markets Act 2000 (Regulated Activities) (Amendment) Order 2014, SI 2014/366, art 2(1), (43), as from 1 April 2014.

Para (3): figure in square brackets substituted, and figures omitted revoked, by the Mortgage Credit Directive Order 2015, SI 2015/910, Sch 1, Pt 2, para 4(1), (27)(a), as from 21 March 2016.

Para (3A): inserted, together with para (3B), by SI 2015/910, Sch 1, Pt 2, para 4(1), (27)(b), as from 21 March 2016.

Para (3B): inserted as noted above. Word omitted revoked, and sub-paras (a), (b) substituted (for the original sub-paras (a)–(c)), by the Financial Services and Markets Act 2000 (Regulated Activities) (Amendment) Order 2016, SI 2016/392, art 2(1), (20)(a), as from 21 March 2016. Sub-para (b)(i) further substituted by the Financial Services and Markets Act 2000 (Amendment) (EU Exit) Regulations 2019, SI 2019/632, regs 120, 151(1), (2), as from IP completion day (as defined in the European Union (Withdrawal Agreement) Act 2020, s 39).

Para (3C): inserted by the Financial Services and Markets Act 2000 (Regulated Activities) (Amendment) Order 2021, SI 2021/90, art 2(7); note that this Order comes into force (1) on 28 January 2021 (for the purposes of (a) enabling the FCA to make or approve rules and to give guidance and directions; (b) enabling applications to be made etc for: (i) a Part 4A permission under s 55A of FSMA 2000; (ii) a variation of a Part 4A permission under s 55H of that Act; and (iii) approval under Part 5 of the Act; (c) enabling the FCA to exercise any of its powers under Part 4A or Part 5 of that Act in relation to any activity which becomes a regulated activity by virtue of this Order; and (d) enabling the scheme operator to make rules and to give guidance); and (2) for all other purposes on 29 July 2022 (see art 1 of the 2021 Order, and see Part 3 of that Order for transitional provisions).

Para (4): substituted by SI 2015/910, Sch 1, Pt 2, para 4(1), (27)(c), as from 21 March 2016. Sub-para (a) substituted, and words in first pair of square brackets in sub-para (b) inserted, by SI 2016/392, art 2(1), (20)(b), as from 21 March 2016. Words in square brackets in sub-para (a)(ii) substituted, and sub-para (b)(i) substituted, by SI 2019/632, regs 120, 151(1), (3), (4), as from IP completion day (as defined in the European Union (Withdrawal Agreement) Act 2020, s 39).

Para (4A): inserted by SI 2019/632, regs 120, 151(1), (5), as from IP completion day (as defined in the European Union (Withdrawal Agreement) Act 2020, s 39). Note that reg 151(5) of the 2019 Regulations was amended by the Financial Services and Economic and Monetary Policy (Consequential Amendments) (EU Exit) Regulations 2020, SI 2020/1301, reg 3, Schedule, para 33(s), as from 30 December 2020 (and the effect of the amendment has been incorporated in the text set out above).

Para (6): added, together with para (7), by SI 2015/910, Sch 1, Pt 2, para 4(1), (27)(b), (d), as from 21 March 2016.

Paras (6A), (6B): inserted by SI 2019/632, regs 120, 151(1), (6), as from IP completion day (as defined in the European Union (Withdrawal Agreement) Act 2020, s 39).

Para (7): added as noted to para (6) above. Words in square brackets in the definition "bridging loan" substituted, definition "consumer" inserted, and definition "consumer credit directive" (omitted) revoked, by SI 2019/632, regs 120, 151(1), (7), as from IP completion day (as defined in the European Union (Withdrawal Agreement) Act 2020, s 39).

[8.201]

[72H Insolvency practitioners

(1) There is excluded from the provisions listed in paragraph (2) any activity carried on by a person acting as an insolvency practitioner.

(2) The provisions are—

(a) article 14 (dealing in investments as principal);

(b) article 21 (dealing in investments as agent);

(c) article 25 (arranging deals in investments);

(d) article 25D (operating a multilateral trading facility);

[(da) article 25DA (operating an organised trading facility);];

(e) article 37 (managing investments);

(f) article 39A (assisting in the administration and performance of a contract of insurance);

(g) article 39D (debt adjusting);

(h) article 39E (debt-counselling);

(i) article 39F (debt-collecting);

(j) article 39G (debt administration);

(k) article 40 (safeguarding and administering investments);

(l) article 45 (sending dematerialised instructions);
(m) article 51ZA (managing [a UK UCITS]);
(n) article 51ZB (acting as trustee or depositary of [a UK UCITS]);
(o) article 51ZC (managing an AIF);
(p) article 51ZD (acting as trustee or depositary of an AIF);
(q) article 51ZE (establishing etc a collective investment scheme);
(r) article 52 (establishing etc a pension scheme);
(s) article 53 (advising on investments);
[(sa) article 59(1A) (carrying out a funeral plan contract as provider);]
(t) article 89A (providing credit information services).

(3) There is excluded from articles 39D, 39E and 89A any activity carried on by a person acting in reasonable contemplation of that person's appointment as an insolvency practitioner.

(4) There is excluded from article 64 any agreement made by a person acting as an insolvency practitioner to carry on an activity of the kind excluded by paragraph (1).

(5) There is excluded from article 64 any agreement made by a person acting in reasonable contemplation of that person's appointment as an insolvency practitioner to carry on an activity of the kind excluded by paragraph (3).]

NOTES

Inserted as noted to art 72G at **[8.200]**.

Para (2) is amended as follows:

Sub-para (da) inserted by the Financial Services and Markets Act 2000 (Regulated Activities) (Amendment) Order 2017, SI 2017/488, art 12(1), (8), as from 1 April 2017 (for the purposes of (i) enabling applications to be made for a Part 4A permission, for a variation of a Part 4A permission or for an approval under FSMA 2000, s 59, or (ii) enabling such applications to be determined, in relation to any specified activity or any specified investment amended or inserted by the 2017 Order), and as from 3 January 2018 (otherwise).

Words in square brackets in sub-paras (m) and (n) substituted by the Financial Services and Markets Act 2000 (Amendment) (EU Exit) Regulations 2019, SI 2019/632, regs 120, 132(5), 133(2), as from IP completion day (as defined in the European Union (Withdrawal Agreement) Act 2020, s 39).

Sub-para (sa) inserted by the Financial Services and Markets Act 2000 (Regulated Activities) (Amendment) Order 2022, SI 2022/466, art 2(4), as from 16 May 2022 (for the purposes of enabling the FCA to make rules, and to give guidance), and as from 29 July 2022 (for all other purposes).

[8.202]

[72I Registered consumer buy-to-let mortgage firms

(1) There is excluded from articles 25A, 36A, 53A, 53DA, 60B and 61 any consumer buy-to-let mortgage business [which relates to an agreement entered into on or after 21st March 2016 and is] carried on by a registered consumer buy-to-let mortgage firm.

(2) In this article "consumer buy-to-let mortgage business" and "registered consumer buy-to-let mortgage firm" have the meanings given in article 4 of the Mortgage Credit Directive Order 2015 (interpretation of Part 3).]

NOTES

Inserted by the Mortgage Credit Directive Order 2015, SI 2015/910, Sch 1, Pt 2, para 4(1), (28), as from 21 March 2016.

Words in square brackets inserted by the Financial Services and Markets Act 2000 (Regulated Activities) (Amendment) Order 2016, SI 2016/392, art 2(1), (21), as from 21 March 2016.

[8.203]

[72J Persons seeking to use the exemption under Article 2.1(j) of the markets in financial instruments directive

(1) An activity which falls within Article 2.1(j)(i) or (ii) (exemptions) of the markets in financial instruments directive ("an Article 2.1(j) activity") is excluded from the activities specified by articles 14, 21 and 25 if during a calendar year the person carrying on the activity—

(a) cannot perform the market threshold calculation to establish if the Article 2.1(j) activity falls within the exemption under Article 2.1(j) of the markets in financial instruments directive because the relevant data is not publicly available from an official source;
(b) carries on the Article 2.1(j) activity during a period of 8 weeks beginning with the day after the day on which the relevant data is made publicly available from an official source; or
(c) has made an application to the appropriate regulator for a Part 4A permission to carry on a regulated activity specified by articles 14, 21 and 25 which constitutes the Article 2.1(j) activity and the application has not been determined or withdrawn.

(2) The exclusion in paragraph (1) does not apply to an Article 2.1(j) activity carried on by a person who is an authorised person in relation to an activity which constitutes the Article 2.1(j) activity.

(3) In this paragraph—

"market threshold calculation" means the calculation of the size of trading activities referred to in Article 2 of the delegated regulation that must be carried out annually in the first quarter of a calendar year under the procedure set out in Article 4 (procedure for calculation) of that delegated regulation;

"official source" means an EU institution or a regulator;

"relevant data" means any data or other information that enables a calculation to be made of the overall market trading activity in an asset class under the procedure in Article 2.3 (overall market threshold) of the delegated regulation;

"the appropriate regulator" in relation to an application for a Part 4A permission means the appropriate regulator in relation to that application for the purposes of section 55A (application for permission) of the Act; and "the delegated regulation" means Commission Delegated Regulation (EU) 2017/592 of 1 December 2016 supplementing Directive 2014/65/EU of the European Parliament and the Council with regard to regulatory technical standards for the criteria to establish when an activity is considered to be ancillary to the main business.]

NOTES

Inserted by the Financial Services and Markets Act 2000 (Markets in Financial Instruments) (No 2) Regulations 2017, SI 2017/1255, reg 4(1), (3), as from 3 January 2018.

PART III SPECIFIED INVESTMENTS

[8.204]
73 Investments: general

The following kinds of investment are specified for the purposes of section 22 of the Act.

[8.205]
74 Deposits

A deposit.

[8.206]
[74A Electronic money

Electronic money.]

NOTES

Inserted by the Financial Services and Markets Act 2000 (Regulated Activities) (Amendment) Order 2002, SI 2002/682, art 6, as from 27 April 2002.

[8.207]
75 Contracts of insurance

Rights under a contract of insurance.

[8.208]
76 Shares etc

(1) Shares or stock in the share capital of—

(a) any body corporate (wherever incorporated), and

(b) any unincorporated body constituted under the law of a country or territory outside the United Kingdom.

(2) Paragraph (1) includes—

(a) any shares of a class defined as deferred shares for the purposes of section 119 of the Building Societies Act 1986 [or section 31A of the Credit Unions Act 1979]; and

(b) any transferable shares in a body incorporated under the law of, or any part of, the United Kingdom relating to [co-operative and community benefit societies,] industrial and provident societies or credit unions, or in a body constituted under the law of another EEA State for purposes equivalent to those of such a body.

(3) But subject to paragraph (2) there are excluded from paragraph (1) shares or stock in the share capital of—

(a) an open-ended investment company;

(b) a building society incorporated under the law of, or any part of, the United Kingdom;

(c) a body incorporated under the law of, or any part of, the United Kingdom relating to [co-operative and community benefit societies,] industrial and provident societies or credit unions;

(d) any body constituted under the law of an EEA State for purposes equivalent to those of a body falling within sub-paragraph (b) or (c).

NOTES

Para (2): words in square brackets in sub-para (a) inserted by the Legislative Reform (Industrial and Provident Societies and Credit Unions) Order 2011, SI 2011/2687, art 22, as from 8 January 2012. Words in square brackets in sub-para (b) inserted by the Co-operative and Community Benefit Societies and Credit Unions Act 2010 (Consequential Amendments) Regulations 2014, SI 2014/1815, reg 2, Schedule, para 8, as from 1 August 2014.

Para (3): words in square brackets in sub-para (c) inserted by SI 2014/1815, reg 2, Schedule, para 8, as from 1 August 2014.

[8.209]
77 Instruments creating or acknowledging indebtedness

(1) Subject to paragraph (2), such of the following as do not fall within [article . . . 78]—

(a) debentures;

(b) debenture stock;

(c) loan stock;

(d) bonds;

(e) certificates of deposit;

(f) any other instrument creating or acknowledging indebtedness.

(2) If and to the extent that they would otherwise fall within paragraph (1), there are excluded from that paragraph—

(a) an instrument acknowledging or creating indebtedness for, or for money borrowed to defray, the consideration payable under a contract for the supply of goods or services;

(b) a cheque or other bill of exchange, a banker's draft or a letter of credit (but not a bill of exchange accepted by a banker);

(c) a banknote, a statement showing a balance on a current, deposit or savings account, a lease or other disposition of property, or a heritable security; and

(d) a contract of insurance;

[(e) . . .]

(3) An instrument excluded from paragraph (1) of article 78 by paragraph (2)(b) of that article is not thereby to be taken to fall within paragraph (1) of this article.

NOTES

Para (1): words in square brackets substituted by the Financial Services and Markets Act 2000 (Regulated Activities) (Amendment) Order 2010, SI 2010/86, art 2(1), (2)(a), as from 24 February 2010. Words omitted revoked by the Financial Services and Markets Act 2000 (Regulated Activities) (Amendment) Order 2011, SI 2011/133, art 2(1), (2)(a), as from 16 February 2011 (note also (i) art 4 of the 2011 Order which provides that, from 16 February 2011, the instruments falling within article 77 or 77A of the this Order (or paragraphs 15 or 15A of Schedule 1 to the Financial Promotion Order), in each case as amended by this Order, include instruments already in existence at that date; and (ii) the Finance Act 2011, s 89 which provides that this amendment is to be treated for all tax purposes as having come into force on 24 February 2010 unless an election is made to the contrary).

Para (2): sub para (e) added by SI 2010/86, art 2(1), (2)(b), as from 24 February 2010. Subsequently revoked by SI 2011/133, art 2(1), (2)(b), as from 16 February 2011 (subject to the same transitional provisions in art 4 as noted above).

Modification: references in para (1) to securities, instruments or investments creating or acknowledging indebtedness (or creating or acknowledging a present or future indebtedness) includes a reference to uncertificated units of eligible debt securities; see the Uncertificated Securities (Amendment) (Eligible Debt Securities) Regulations 2003, SI 2003/1633, reg 15, Sch 2, para 8.

[8.210]

[77A Alternative finance investment bonds

(1) Rights under an alternative finance investment bond, to the extent that they do not fall within article [77 or] 78.

(2) For the purposes of this article, arrangements constitute an alternative finance investment bond if—

(a) the arrangements provide for a person ("the bond-holder") to pay a sum of money ("the capital") to another ("the bond-issuer");

(b) the arrangements identify assets, or a class of assets, which the bond-issuer will acquire for the purpose of generating income or gains directly or indirectly ("the bond assets");

(c) the arrangements specify a period at the end of which they cease to have effect ("the bond term");

(d) the bond-issuer undertakes under the arrangements—

(i) to make a repayment in respect of the capital ("the redemption payment") to the bond-holder during or at the end of the bond term (whether or not in instalments); and

(ii) to pay to the bond-holder other payments on one or more occasions during or at the end of the bond term ("the additional payments");

(e) the amount of the additional payments does not exceed an amount which would, at the time at which the bond is issued, be a reasonable commercial return on a loan of the capital; and

[(f) the arrangements are—

(i) a security that is admitted to the official list in accordance with Part 6 of the Act,

(ii) a security that is admitted to an official list in the EEA (in accordance with the provisions of Directive 2001/34/EC of the European Parliament and of the Council on the admission of securities to official stock exchange listing and on information to be published on those securities) and has been so admitted since before IP completion day,

(iii) a security that is admitted to trading on a recognised investment exchange or a UK trading venue, or

(iv) a security that is admitted to trading on an EU trading venue and has been so admitted since before IP completion day].

(3) For the purposes of paragraph (2)—

(a) the bond-issuer may acquire the bond assets before or after the arrangements take effect;

(b) the bond assets may be property of any kind, including rights in relation to property owned by someone other than the bond-issuer;

(c) the identification of the bond assets mentioned in paragraph (2)(b) and the undertakings mentioned in paragraph (2)(d) may (but need not) be described as, or accompanied by a document described as, a declaration of trust;

(d) the reference to a period in paragraph (2)(c) includes any period specified to end upon the redemption of the bond by the bond-issuer;

(e) the bond-holder may (but need not) be entitled under the arrangements to terminate them, or participate in terminating them, before the end of the bond term;

(f) the amount of the additional payments may be—

(i) fixed at the beginning of the bond term;

(ii) determined wholly or partly by reference to the value of or income generated by the bond assets; or

(iii) determined in some other way;

(g) if the amount of the additional payments is not fixed at the beginning of the bond term, the reference in paragraph (2)(e) to the amount of the additional payments is a reference to the maximum amount of the additional payments;

(h) the amount of the redemption payment may (but need not) be subject to reduction in the event of a fall in the value of the bond assets or in the rate of income generated by them; and

(i) entitlement to the redemption payment may (but need not) be capable of being satisfied (whether or not at the option of the bond-issuer or the bond-holder) by the issue or transfer of shares or other securities.

[(3A) In sub-paragraph (2)(f)—

"EU trading venue" has the meaning given by Article 2.1.16B of the markets in financial instruments regulation;

"UK trading venue" has the meaning given by Article 2.1.16A of that regulation.]

(4) An instrument excluded from paragraph (1) of article 78 by paragraph (2)(b) of that article is not thereby taken to fall within paragraph (1) of this article.]

NOTES

Inserted by the Financial Services and Markets Act 2000 (Regulated Activities) (Amendment) Order 2010, SI 2010/86, art 2(1), (3), as from 24 February 2010.

Para (1): words in square brackets inserted by the Financial Services and Markets Act 2000 (Regulated Activities) (Amendment) Order 2011, SI 2011/133, art 2(1), (3), as from 16 February 2011 (see also the note relating to the 2011 Order on art 77 at **[8.209]**).

Para (2): sub-para (f) substituted by the Financial Services and Markets Act 2000 (Amendment) (EU Exit) Regulations 2019, SI 2019/632, regs 120, 152(1), (2), as from IP completion day (as defined in the European Union (Withdrawal Agreement) Act 2020, s 39). Note that SI 2019/632, reg 152(2) was amended by the Financial Services and Economic and Monetary Policy (Consequential Amendments) (EU Exit) Regulations 2020, SI 2020/1301, reg 3, Schedule, para 33(t), as from 30 December 2020 (and the effect of the amendment has been incorporated in the text set out above).

Para (3A): inserted by SI 2019/632, regs 120, 152(1), (3), as from IP completion day (as defined in the European Union (Withdrawal Agreement) Act 2020, s 39).

The reference in this article to an alternative finance investment bond includes a reference to uncertificated units of eligible debt securities; see the Uncertificated Securities (Amendment) (Eligible Debt Securities) Regulations 2003, SI 2003/1633, Schedule, para 8(3).

[8.211]

78 Government and public securities

(1) Subject to paragraph (2), loan stock, bonds and other instruments creating or acknowledging indebtedness, issued by or on behalf of any of the following—

(a) the government of the United Kingdom;
(b) the Scottish Administration;
(c) the Executive Committee of the Northern Ireland Assembly;
(d) the National Assembly for Wales;
(e) the government of any country or territory outside the United Kingdom;
(f) a local authority in the United Kingdom or elsewhere; or
(g) a body the members of which comprise—
  (i) states including the United Kingdom . . . ; or
  (ii) bodies whose members comprise states including the United Kingdom . . .

(2) [Subject to paragraph (3),] there are excluded from paragraph (1)—

(a) so far as applicable, the instruments mentioned in article 77(2)(a) to (d);
(b) any instrument creating or acknowledging indebtedness in respect of—
  (i) money received by the Director of Savings as deposits or otherwise in connection with the business of the National Savings Bank;
  (ii) money raised under the National Loans Act 1968 under the auspices of the Director of Savings or treated as so raised by virtue of section 11(3) of the National Debt Act 1972.

[(3) Paragraph (2)(a) does not exclude an instrument which meets the requirements set out in sub-paragraphs (a) to (e) of article 77A(2).]

NOTES

Para (1): words omitted from sub-paras (g)(i), (ii) revoked by the Financial Services and Markets Act 2000 (Amendment) (EU Exit) Regulations 2019, SI 2019/632, regs 120, 153, as from IP completion day (as defined in the European Union (Withdrawal Agreement) Act 2020, s 39).

Para (2): words in square brackets inserted by the Financial Services and Markets Act 2000 (Regulated Activities) (Amendment) Order 2010, SI 2010/86, art 2(1), (4), as from 24 February 2010.

Para (3): added by SI 2010/86, art 2(1), (5), as from 24 February 2010.

Modification: references in this article to securities, instruments or investments creating or acknowledging indebtedness (or creating or acknowledging a present or future indebtedness) includes a reference to uncertificated units of eligible debt securities; see the Uncertificated Securities (Amendment) (Eligible Debt Securities) Regulations 2003, SI 2003/1633, reg 15, Sch 2, para 8.

National Assembly for Wales: see further, in relation to the renaming of the National Assembly for Wales as the Senedd Cymru or the Welsh Parliament, the Senedd and Elections (Wales) Act 2020, s 2 (with effect from 6 May 2020). See also ss 3–9 of the 2020 Act in relation to the renaming of Acts of the National Assembly for Wales, Members of the National Assembly for Wales, etc.

[8.212]

79 Instruments giving entitlements to investments

(1) Warrants and other instruments entitling the holder to subscribe for any investment of the kind specified by article 76, 77[, 77A] or 78.

(2) It is immaterial whether the investment to which the entitlement relates is in existence or identifiable.

(3) An investment of the kind specified by this article is not to be regarded as falling within article 83, 84 or 85.

NOTES

Para (1): figure in square brackets inserted by the Financial Services and Markets Act 2000 (Regulated Activities) (Amendment) Order 2010, SI 2010/86, art 4, Schedule, para 5(f), as from 24 February 2010.

[8.213]

80 Certificates representing certain securities

(1) Subject to paragraph (2), certificates or other instruments which confer contractual or property rights (other than rights consisting of an investment of the kind specified by article 83)—

(a) in respect of any investment of the kind specified by any of articles 76 to 79, being an investment held by a person other than the person on whom the rights are conferred by the certificate or instrument; and
(b) the transfer of which may be effected without the consent of that person.

(2) There is excluded from paragraph (1) any certificate or other instrument which confers rights in respect of two or more investments issued by different persons, or in respect of two or more different investments of the kind specified by article 78 and issued by the same person.

[8.214]
81 Units in a collective investment scheme

Units in a collective investment scheme (within the meaning of Part XVII of the Act).

[8.215]
[82 Rights under a pension scheme

(1) Rights under a stakeholder pension scheme.

(2) Rights under a personal pension scheme.

[(3) Rights or interests under a pension scheme which provides safeguarded benefits (within the meaning given in article 53E(2)).

(4) specifies a kind of investment in relation to the kind of activity specified in article 53E (advising on conversion or transfer of pension benefits), and not in relation to any other specified kind of activity.]]

NOTES

Substituted by the Financial Services and Markets Act 2000 (Regulated Activities) (Amendment) Order 2006, SI 2006/1969, art 2(1), (5), as from 1 October 2006 (for the purposes of enabling applications to be made for Part IV permission or for a variation of Part IV permission in relation to an investment specified by art 82(2) of this Order (as so substituted)), and as from 6 April 2007 (otherwise).

Paras (3), (4): added by the Financial Services and Markets Act 2000 (Regulated Activities) (Amendment) (No 2) Order 2015, SI 2015/731, art 2(1), (4), as from 6 April 2015.

[8.216]
[82A Greenhouse gas emissions allowances

Greenhouse gas emissions allowances which are auctioned as financial instruments or as two-day spots within the meaning of Article 3.3 of the emission allowance auctioning regulation [or regulation 2(1) of the UK auctioning regulations].]

NOTES

Inserted by the Financial Services and Markets Act 2000 (Regulated Activities) (Amendment) Order 2012, SI 2012/1906, art 2(1), (4), as from 20 July 2012.

Words in square brackets inserted by the Recognised Auction Platforms (Amendment and Miscellaneous Provisions) Regulations 2021, SI 2021/494, reg 3(5), as from 22 April 2021.

[8.217]
[82B Emission allowances

[(1) Subject to paragraph (2)—

(a) emission allowances consisting of any units recognised for compliance (by an EEA State) with the requirements of the emission allowance trading directive; and

(b) allowances created under article 18 of the trading scheme order and transferable in accordance with that order.]

(2) Paragraph (1) only applies to emission allowances in relation to which—

[(a) an investment firm or qualifying credit institution is providing or performing investment services and activities on a professional basis,

(b) a management company which has a Part 4A permission to do so is providing the investment service specified in paragraph 4 or 5 of Part 3 of Schedule 2 or the ancillary service specified in paragraph 1 of Part 3A of that Schedule,

(c) a market operator is providing the investment service specified in paragraph 8 or 9 of Part 3 of that Schedule, or

(d) a full-scope UK AIFM which has a Part 4A permission to do so is providing the investment service specified in paragraph 1, 4 or 5 of Part 3 of that Schedule or the ancillary service specified in paragraph 1 of Part 3A of that Schedule].]

NOTES

Inserted by the Financial Services and Markets Act 2000 (Regulated Activities) (Amendment) Order 2017, SI 2017/488, art 6, as from 1 April 2017 (for the purposes of (i) enabling applications to be made for a Part 4A permission, for a variation of a Part 4A permission or for an approval under FSMA 2000, s 59, or (ii) enabling such applications to be determined, in relation to any specified activity or any specified investment amended or inserted by the 2017 Order), and as from 3 January 2018 (otherwise).

Para (1): substituted by the Recognised Auction Platforms (Amendment and Miscellaneous Provisions) Regulations 2021, SI 2021/494, reg 3(6), as from 22 April 2021.

Para (2): sub-paras (a)–(d) substituted by the Financial Services and Markets Act 2000 (Amendment) (EU Exit) Regulations 2019, SI 2019/632, regs 120, 155, as from IP completion day (as defined in the European Union (Withdrawal Agreement) Act 2020, s 39).

[8.218]
83 Options

[(1)] Options to acquire or dispose of—

(a) a security or contractually based investment (other than one of a kind specified by this article);

(b) currency of the United Kingdom or any other country or territory;

(c) palladium, platinum, gold or silver; . . .

(d) an option to acquire or dispose of an investment of the kind specified by this article by virtue of paragraph (a), (b) or (c);

[(e) subject to paragraph (4), an option to acquire or dispose of an option to which [paragraph 5, 6, 7 or 10 of Part 1 of Schedule 2 (read with Articles 5, 6, 7, and 8 of the Commission Regulation) applies]].

[(2) Subject to paragraph (4), options—

(a) to which paragraph (1) does not apply;

(b) which relate to commodities;

(c) which may be settled physically; and

(d) either—

(i) to which paragraph 5 or 6 of . . . Part 1 of Schedule 2 [(read with Articles 5 and 6 of the Commission Regulation)], applies, or

(ii) which in accordance with Article [7] of the Commission Regulation (the text of which is set out in Part 2 of Schedule 2) are to be considered as having the characteristics of other derivative financial instruments and not being for commercial purposes, and to which paragraph 7 of [Part 1 of that Schedule] applies.

(3) Subject to paragraph (4), options—

(a) to which paragraph (1) does not apply;

(b) which may be settled physically; and

(c) to which paragraph 10 of [Part 1 of Schedule 2] (read with [Articles 7 and 8 of] the Commission Regulation) applies.

(4) Paragraphs (1)(e), (2) and (3) only apply to options in relation to which—

[(a) an investment firm or qualifying credit institution is providing or performing investment services and activities on a professional basis,

(b) a management company which has a Part 4A permission to do so is providing the investment service specified in paragraph 4 or 5 of Part 3 of Schedule 2 or the ancillary service specified in paragraph 1 of Part 3A of that Schedule,

(c) a market operator is providing the investment service specified in paragraph 8 or 9 of Part 3 of that Schedule, or

(d) a full-scope UK AIFM which has a Part 4A permission to do so is providing the investment service specified in paragraph 1, 4 or 5 of Part 3 of that Schedule or the ancillary service specified in paragraph 1 of Part 3A of that Schedule.]

(5) . . .]

NOTES

Para (1): numbered as such, word omitted from sub-para (c) revoked, and sub-para (e) inserted, by the Financial Services and Markets Act 2000 (Regulated Activities) (Amendment No 3) Order 2006, SI 2006/3384, arts 2, 26(a), (b), as from 1 April 2007 (for the purposes of enabling applications to be made for (i) a Pt IV permission, (ii) a variation of a Pt IV permission, and (iii) the Authority's approval under s 59 of the 2000 Act, in relation to an activity of the kind specified by art 25D of this Order, or in relation to an investment of the kind specified by arts 83, 84 or 85 of this Order), and as from 1 November 2007 (otherwise). Words in square brackets in sub-para (e) substituted by the Financial Services and Markets Act 2000 (Amendment) (EU Exit) Regulations 2019, SI 2019/632, regs 120, 156(1), (2), as from IP completion day (as defined in the European Union (Withdrawal Agreement) Act 2020, s 39).

Paras (2)–(5) were added by SI 2006/3384, arts 2, 26(c), as from the same dates and for the same purposes as noted above; and have subsequently been amended as follows:

Words omitted from sub-para (2)(d)(i) revoked, and words in square brackets in sub-para (2)(d)(ii) substituted by SI 2019/632, regs 120, 156(1), (3), as from IP completion day (as defined in the European Union (Withdrawal Agreement) Act 2020, s 39).

Words in square brackets in sub-para (2)(d)(i) inserted, and figure in square brackets in sub-para (2)(d)(ii) substituted, by SI 2017/488, art 7(1), (3), as from 1 April 2017 (for the purposes of (i) enabling applications to be made for a Part 4A permission, for a variation of a Part 4A permission or for an approval under FSMA 2000, s 59, or (ii) enabling such applications to be determined, in relation to any specified activity or any specified investment amended or inserted by the 2017 Order), and as from 3 January 2018 (otherwise).

Words in first pair of square brackets in sub-para (3)(c) substituted by SI 2019/632, regs 120, 156(1), (4), as from IP completion day (as defined in the European Union (Withdrawal Agreement) Act 2020, s 39).

Words in second pair of square brackets in sub-para (3)(c) inserted by SI 2017/488, art 7(1), (4), as from 1 April 2017 (certain purposes), and as from 3 January 2018 (otherwise) (for details, see the first note relating to the 2017 Regulations above).

Sub-paras (4)(a)–(d) substituted by SI 2019/632, regs 120, 156(1), (5), as from IP completion day (as defined in the European Union (Withdrawal Agreement) Act 2020, s 39).

Para (5): revoked by SI 2019/632, regs 120, 156(1), (6), as from IP completion day (as defined in the European Union (Withdrawal Agreement) Act 2020, s 39).

[8.219]

84 Futures

(1) Subject to paragraph (2), rights under a contract for the sale of a commodity or property of any other description under which delivery is to be made at a future date and at a price agreed on when the contract is made.

[(1A) Subject to paragraph (1D), futures—

(a) to which paragraph (1) does not apply;

(b) which relate to commodities;

(c) which may be settled physically; and

(d) to which paragraph 5 or 6 of [Part 1 of Schedule 2] [(read with Articles 5 and 6 of the Commission Regulation)] applies.

(1B) Subject to paragraph (1D), futures and forwards—

(a) to which paragraph (1) does not apply;

(b) which relate to commodities;

(c) which may be settled physically;

(d) which in accordance with Article [7] of the Commission Regulation (the text of which is set out in Part 2 of Schedule 2) are to be considered as having the characteristics of other derivative financial instruments and not being for commercial purposes; and

(e) to which paragraph 7 of [Part 1 of Schedule 2] applies.

(1C) Subject to paragraph (1D), futures—

(a) to which paragraph (1) does not apply;

(b) which may be settled physically; and

(c) to which paragraph 10 of [Part 1 of Schedule 2] (read with [Articles 7 and 8 of] the Commission Regulation) applies.

[(1CA) Subject to paragraph (1D), any other derivative contract, relating to currencies to which paragraph 4 of [Part 1 of Schedule 2] read with Article 10 of the Commission Regulation ([the text of which is set out in Part 2 of Schedule 2]) applies.

(1D) Paragraph (1A), (1B)[, (1C) and (1CA)] only apply to futures[, forwards or derivative contracts] in relation to which—

[(a) an investment firm or qualifying credit institution is providing or performing investment services and activities on a professional basis,

(b) a management company which has a Part 4A permission to do so is providing the investment service specified in paragraph 4 or 5 of Part 3 of Schedule 2 or the ancillary service specified in paragraph 1 of Part 3A of that Schedule,

(c) a market operator is providing the investment service specified in paragraph 8 or 9 of Part 3 of that Schedule, or

(d) a full-scope UK AIFM which has a Part 4A permission to do so is providing the investment service specified in paragraph 1, 4 or 5 of Part 3 of that Schedule or the ancillary service specified in paragraph 1 of Part 3A of that Schedule].

(1E) . . .]

(2) There are excluded from paragraph (1) rights under any contract which is made for commercial and not investment purposes.

(3) A contract is to be regarded as made for investment purposes if it is made or traded on a recognised investment exchange, or is made otherwise than on a recognised investment exchange but is expressed to be as traded on such an exchange or on the same terms as those on which an equivalent contract would be made on such an exchange.

(4) A contract not falling within paragraph (3) is to be regarded as made for commercial purposes if under the terms of the contract delivery is to be made within seven days, unless it can be shown that there existed an understanding that (notwithstanding the express terms of the contract) delivery would not be made within seven days.

(5) The following are indications that a contract not falling within paragraph (3) or (4) is made for commercial purposes and the absence of them is an indication that it is made for investment purposes—

(a) one or more of the parties is a producer of the commodity or other property, or uses it in his business;

(b) the seller delivers or intends to deliver the property or the purchaser takes or intends to take delivery of it.

(6) It is an indication that a contract is made for commercial purposes that the prices, the lot, the delivery date or other terms are determined by the parties for the purposes of the particular contract and not by reference (or not solely by reference) to regularly published prices, to standard lots or delivery dates or to standard terms.

(7) The following are indications that a contract is made for investment purposes—

(a) it is expressed to be as traded on an investment exchange;

(b) performance of the contract is ensured by an investment exchange or a clearing house;

(c) there are arrangements for the payment or provision of margin.

(8) For the purposes of paragraph (1), a price is to be taken to be agreed on when a contract is made—

(a) notwithstanding that it is left to be determined by reference to the price at which a contract is to be entered into on a market or exchange or could be entered into at a time and place specified in the contract; or

(b) in a case where the contract is expressed to be by reference to a standard lot and quality, notwithstanding that provision is made for a variation in the price to take account of any variation in quantity or quality on delivery.

NOTES

Para (1A): inserted, together with paras (1B)–(1E), by the Financial Services and Markets Act 2000 (Regulated Activities) (Amendment No 3) Order 2006, SI 2006/3384, arts 2, 27, as from 1 April 2007 (for the purposes of enabling applications to be made for (i) a Pt IV permission, (ii) a variation of a Pt IV permission, and (iii) the Authority's approval under s 59 of the 2000 Act, in relation to an activity of the kind specified by art 25D of this Order, or in relation to an investment of the kind specified by arts 83, 84 or 85 of this Order), and as from 1 November 2007 (otherwise). Subsequently amended as follows—

Words in first pair of square brackets in sub-para (d) substituted by the Financial Services and Markets Act 2000 (Amendment) (EU Exit) Regulations 2019, SI 2019/632, regs 120, 157, as from IP completion day (as defined in the European Union (Withdrawal Agreement) Act 2020, s 39.

Words in second pair of square brackets in sub-para (d) inserted by the Financial Services and Markets Act 2000 (Regulated Activities) (Amendment) Order 2017, SI 2017/488, art 8, as from 1 April 2017 (for the purposes of (i) enabling applications to be made for a Part 4A permission, for a variation of a Part 4A permission or for an approval under FSMA 2000, s 59, or (ii) enabling such applications to be determined, in relation to any specified activity or any specified investment amended or inserted by the 2017 Order), and as from 3 January 2018 (otherwise).

Para (1B): inserted as noted to para (1A) above. Subsequently amended as follows—

Figure in square brackets in sub-para (d) substituted by SI 2017/488, art 8 (as from the same dates and for the same purposes as noted in the first note relating to the 2017 Regulations above).

Words in square brackets in sub-para (e) substituted by SI 2019/632, regs 120, 157, as from IP completion day (as defined in the European Union (Withdrawal Agreement) Act 2020, s 39.

Para (1C): inserted as noted to para (1A) above. Subsequently amended as follows—

Words in first pair of square brackets in sub-para (c) substituted by SI 2019/632, regs 120, 157, as from IP completion day (as defined in the European Union (Withdrawal Agreement) Act 2020, s 39.

Words in second pair of square brackets in sub-para (c) inserted by SI 2017/488, art 8 (as from the same dates and for the same purposes as noted in the first note relating to the 2017 Regulations above).

Para (1CA): inserted by SI 2017/488, art 8 (as from the same dates and for the same purposes as noted in the first note relating to the 2017 Regulations above). Words in square brackets substituted by SI 2019/632, regs 120, 157, as from IP completion day (as defined in the European Union (Withdrawal Agreement) Act 2020, s 39.

Para (1D): inserted as noted to para (1A) above. Subsequently amended as follows—

Words in first and second pairs of square brackets substituted by SI 2017/488, art 8 (as from the same dates and for the same purposes as noted in the first note relating to the 2017 Regulations above).

Sub-paras (a)–(d) were substituted by SI 2019/632, regs 120, 157, as from IP completion day (as defined in the European Union (Withdrawal Agreement) Act 2020, s 39).

Para (1E): originally inserted as noted to para (1A) above. Subsequently revoked by SI 2019/632, regs 120, 157, as from IP completion day (as defined in the European Union (Withdrawal Agreement) Act 2020, s 39).

[8.220]

85 Contracts for differences etc

(1) Subject to paragraph (2), rights under—

(a) a contract for differences; or

(b) any other contract the purpose or pretended purpose of which is to secure a profit or avoid a loss by reference to fluctuations in—

(i) the value or price of property of any description; or

(ii) an index or other factor designated for that purpose in the contract.

(2) There are excluded from paragraph (1)—

(a) rights under a contract if the parties intend that the profit is to be secured or the loss is to be avoided by one or more of the parties taking delivery of any property to which the contract relates;

(b) rights under a contract under which money is received by way of deposit on terms that any interest or other return to be paid on the sum deposited will be calculated by reference to fluctuations in an index or other factor;

(c) rights under any contract under which—

(i) money is received by the Director of Savings as deposits or otherwise in connection with the business of the National Savings Bank; or

(ii) money is raised under the National Loans Act 1968 under the auspices of the Director of Savings or treated as so raised by virtue of section 11(3) of the National Debt Act 1972;

(d) rights under a qualifying contract of insurance.

[(3) Subject to paragraph (4), derivative instruments for the transfer of credit risk—

(a) to which neither article 83 nor paragraph (1) applies; and

(b) to which paragraph 8 [Part 1 of Schedule 2] applies.

(4) Paragraph (3) only applies to derivatives in relation to which—

[(a) an investment firm or qualifying credit institution is providing or performing investment services and activities on a professional basis,

(b) a management company which has a Part 4A permission to do so is providing the investment service specified in paragraph 4 or 5 of Part 3 of Schedule 2 or the ancillary service specified in paragraph 1 of Part 3A of that Schedule,

(c) a market operator is providing the investment service specified in paragraph 8 or 9 of Part 3 of that Schedule,

(d) a full-scope UK AIFM which has a Part 4A permission to do so is providing the investment service specified in paragraph 1, 4 or 5 of Part 3 of that Schedule or the ancillary service specified in paragraph 1 of Part 3A of that Schedule].

[(4A) Subject to paragraph (4B), a derivative contract of a binary or other fixed outcomes nature—

(a) to which paragraph (1) does not apply;

(b) which is settled in cash; and

(c) which is a financial instrument to which paragraph 4, 5, 6, 7 or 10 of [Part 1 of Schedule 2] read with Articles 5 to 8 and 10 of the Commission Regulation ([the text of which is set out in Part 2 of Schedule 2]) applies.

(4B) Paragraph (4A) only applies to derivatives in relation to which—

[(a) an investment firm or qualifying credit institution is providing or performing investment services and activities on a professional basis,

(b) a management company which has a Part 4A permission to do so is providing the investment service specified in paragraph 4 or 5 of Part 3 of Schedule 2 or the ancillary service specified in paragraph 1 of Part 3A of that Schedule,

(c) a market operator is providing the investment service specified in paragraph 8 or 9 of Part 3 of that Schedule,

(d) a full-scope UK AIFM which has a Part 4A permission to do so is providing the investment service specified in paragraph 1, 4 or 5 of Part 3 of that Schedule or the ancillary service specified in paragraph 1 of Part 3A of that Schedule],

(e) a person is carrying on the activity specified by article 25(2).]

(5) . . .]

NOTES

Para (3): added, together with paras (4), (5), by the Financial Services and Markets Act 2000 (Regulated Activities) (Amendment No 3) Order 2006, SI 2006/3384, arts 2, 28, as from 1 April 2007 (for the purposes of enabling applications to be made for (i) a Pt IV permission, (ii) a variation of a Pt IV permission, and (iii) the Authority's approval under s 59 of the 2000 Act, in relation to an activity of the kind specified by art 25D of this Order, or in relation to an investment of the kind specified by arts 83, 84 or 85 of this Order), and as from 1 November 2007 (otherwise). Words in square brackets in sub-para (b) substituted by the Financial Services and Markets Act 2000 (Amendment) (EU Exit) Regulations 2019, SI 2019/632, regs 120, 158, as from IP completion day (as defined in the European Union (Withdrawal Agreement) Act 2020, s 39).

Para (4): added as noted to para (3) above. Sub-paras (a)–(d) substituted by SI 2019/632, regs 120, 158, as from IP completion day (as defined in the European Union (Withdrawal Agreement) Act 2020, s 39).

Para (4A): inserted, together with para (4B), by the Financial Services and Markets Act 2000 (Regulated Activities) (Amendment) Order 2017, SI 2017/488, art 9, as from 1 April 2017 (for the purposes of (i) enabling applications to be made for a Part 4A permission, for a variation of a Part 4A permission or for an approval under FSMA 2000, s 59, or (ii) enabling such applications to be determined, in relation to any specified activity or any specified investment amended or inserted by the 2017 Order), and as from 3 January 2018 (otherwise). Words in square brackets in sub-para (c) substituted by SI 2019/632, regs 120, 158, as from IP completion day (as defined in the European Union (Withdrawal Agreement) Act 2020, s 39).

Para (4B): inserted as noted to para (4A) above. Sub-paras (a)–(d) substituted by SI 2019/632, regs 120, 158, as from IP completion day (as defined in the European Union (Withdrawal Agreement) Act 2020, s 39).

Para (5): originally added as noted to para (3) above. Subsequently revoked by SI 2019/632, regs 120, 158, as from IP completion day (as defined in the European Union (Withdrawal Agreement) Act 2020, s 39).

[8.221]
86 Lloyd's syndicate capacity and syndicate membership

(1) The underwriting capacity of a Lloyd's syndicate.

(2) A person's membership (or prospective membership) of a Lloyd's syndicate.

[8.222]
87 Funeral plan contracts

Rights under a funeral plan contract.

[8.223]
88 Regulated mortgage contracts

Rights under a regulated mortgage contract.

[8.224]
[88A Regulated home reversion plans

Rights under a regulated home reversion plan.]

NOTES

Inserted, together with art 88B, by the Financial Services and Markets Act 2000 (Regulated Activities) (Amendment) (No 2) Order 2006, SI 2006/2383, arts 2, 23, as from 6 November 2006 (for the purposes of enabling applications to be made for (i) a Pt IV permission, or a variation of a Pt IV permission, in relation to activities of the kind specified by arts 25B, 25C, 53B, 53C, 63B or 63F or, so far as relevant to any such activity, art 64 of this Order; or (ii) the Authority's approval under FSMA 2000, s 59 in relation to any of those activities), and as from 6 April 2007 (otherwise).

[8.225]
[88B Regulated home purchase plans

Rights under a regulated home purchase plan.]

NOTES

Inserted as noted to art 88A at **[8.224]**.

[8.226]
[88C Regulated sale and rent back agreements

Rights under a regulated sale and rent back agreement.]

NOTES

Inserted by the Financial Services and Markets Act 2000 (Regulated Activities) (Amendment) Order 2009, SI 2009/1342, arts 2, 21, as from 1 July 2009 (other than for the purposes of enabling applications to be made for a Part IV permission, or a variation of a Part IV permission, in relation to activities of the kind specified by arts 25E, 53D or 63J or, so far as relevant to any such activity, art 64 of this Order), and as from 30 June 2010 (for those purposes).

[8.227]
[88D Credit agreement

Rights under a credit agreement.]

NOTES

Inserted, together with art 88E, by the Financial Services and Markets Act 2000 (Regulated Activities) (Amendment) (No 2) Order 2013, SI 2013/1881, arts 2, 7, as from 1 April 2014.

[8.228]
[88E Consumer hire agreement

Rights under a consumer hire agreement.]

NOTES

Inserted as note to art 88D **[8.227]**.

[8.229]
89 Rights to or interests in investments

(1) Subject to paragraphs (2) to (4), any right to or interest in anything which is specified by any other provision of this Part (other than [article 88,] [88A, 88B or 88C]).

(2) Paragraph (1) does not include interests under the trusts of an occupational pension scheme.

[(2A) Paragraph (2) does not apply where the kind of activity specified in article 53E (advising on conversion or transfer of pension benefits) is carried on by way of business in relation to the interests under the trusts of an occupational pension scheme.]

[(3) Paragraph (1) does not include any right or interest acquired as a result of entering into a funeral plan contract.]

(4) Paragraph (1) does not include anything which is specified by any other provision of this Part.

NOTES

Para (1): words in first pair of square brackets substituted by the Financial Services and Markets Act 2000 (Regulated Activities) (Amendment) (No 2) Order 2006, SI 2006/2383, arts 2, 24, as from 6 November 2006 (for the purposes of enabling applications to be made for (i) a Pt IV permission, or a variation of a Pt IV permission, in relation to activities of the kind specified by arts 25B, 25C, 53B, 53C, 63B or 63F or, so far as relevant to any such activity, art 64 of this Order; or (ii) the Authority's approval under FSMA 2000, s 59 in relation to any of those activities), and as from 6 April 2007 (otherwise). Words in second pair of square brackets substituted by the Financial Services and Markets Act 2000 (Regulated Activities) (Amendment) Order 2009, SI 2009/1342, arts 2, 22, as from 1 July 2009 (other than for the purposes of enabling applications to be made for a Part IV permission, or a variation of a Part IV permission, in relation to activities of the kind specified by arts 25E, 53D or 63J or, so far as relevant to any such activity, art 64 of this Order), and as from 30 June 2010 (for those purposes).

Para (2A): inserted by the Financial Services and Markets Act 2000 (Regulated Activities) (Amendment) (No 2) Order 2015, SI 2015/731, art 2(1), (5), as from 6 April 2015.

Para (3): substituted by the Financial Services and Markets Act 2000 (Regulated Activities) (Amendment) Order 2021, SI 2021/90, art 2(8); note that this Order comes into force (1) on 28 January 2021 (for the purposes of (a) enabling the FCA to make or approve rules and to give guidance and directions; (b) enabling applications to be made etc for: (i) a Part 4A permission under s 55A of FSMA 2000; (ii) a variation of a Part 4A permission under s 55H of that Act; and (iii) approval under Part 5 of the Act; (c) enabling the FCA to exercise any of its powers under Part 4A or Part 5 of that Act in relation to any activity which becomes a regulated activity by virtue of this Order; and (d) enabling the scheme operator to make rules and to give guidance); and (2) for all other purposes on 29 July 2022 (see art 1 of the 2021 Order, and see Part 3 of that Order for transitional provisions).

[PART 3A SPECIFIED ACTIVITIES IN RELATION TO INFORMATION

The Activities

[8.230]

89A Providing credit information services

(1) Taking any of the steps in paragraph (3) on behalf of an individual or relevant recipient of credit is a specified kind of activity.

(2) Giving advice to an individual or relevant recipient of credit in relation to the taking of any of the steps specified in paragraph (3) is a specified kind of activity.

(3) Subject to paragraph (4), the steps specified in this paragraph are steps taken with a view to—

- (a) ascertaining whether a credit information agency holds information relevant to the financial standing of an individual or relevant recipient of credit;
- (b) ascertaining the contents of such information;
- (c) securing the correction of, the omission of anything from, or the making of any other kind of modification of, such information;
- (d) securing that a credit information agency which holds such information—
  - (i) stops holding the information, or
  - (ii) does not provide it to any other person.

(4) Steps taken by a credit information agency in relation to information held by that agency are not steps specified in paragraph (3).

(5) Paragraphs (1) and (2) do not apply to an activity of the kind specified by article 36H (operating an electronic system in relation to lending).

(6) "Credit information agency" means a person who carries on by way of business an activity of the kind specified by any of the following—

- (a) article 36A (credit broking);
- (b) article 39D (debt adjusting);
- (c) article 39E (debt-counselling);
- (d) article 39F (debt-collecting);
- (e) article 39G (debt administration);
- (f) article 60B (regulated credit agreements) disregarding the effect of article 60F;
- (g) article 60N (regulated consumer hire agreements) disregarding the effect of article 60P;
- (h) article 89B (providing credit references).]

NOTES

Part 3A (arts 89A–89E) was inserted by the Financial Services and Markets Act 2000 (Regulated Activities) (Amendment) (No 2) Order 2013, SI 2013/1881, arts 2, 8(2), as from 1 April 2014.

[8.231]

[89B Providing credit references

(1) Furnishing of persons with information relevant to the financial standing of individuals or relevant recipients of credit is a specified kind of activity if the person has collected the information for that purpose.

(2) There are excluded from paragraph (1) activities carried on in the course of a business which does not primarily consist of activities of the kind specified by paragraph (1).

(3) Paragraph (1) does not apply to an activity of the kind specified by article 36H (operating an electronic system in relation to lending).]

NOTES

Inserted as noted to art 89A at **[8.230]**.

[Exclusions

[8.232]

89C Activities carried on by members of the legal profession etc

(1) There are excluded from articles 89A and 89B activities carried on by—

(a) a barrister or advocate acting in that capacity;

(b) a solicitor (within the meaning of the Solicitors Act 1974) in the course of providing advocacy services or litigation services;

(c) a solicitor (within the meaning of the Solicitors (Scotland) Act 1980) in the course of providing advocacy services or litigation services;

(d) a solicitor (within the meaning of the Solicitors (Northern Ireland) Order 1976) in the course of providing advocacy services or litigation services;

(e) a relevant person (other than a person falling within sub-paragraph (a) to (d)) in the course of providing advocacy services or litigation services.

(2) In paragraph (1)—

"advocacy services" means any services which it would be reasonable to expect a person who is exercising, or contemplating exercising, a right of audience in relation to any proceedings, or contemplated proceedings, to provide for the purpose of those proceedings or contemplated proceedings;

"litigation services" means any services which it would be reasonable to expect a person who is exercising, or contemplating exercising, a right to conduct litigation in relation to any proceedings, or contemplated proceedings, to provide for the purpose of those proceedings or contemplated proceedings;

"relevant person" means a person who, for the purposes of the Legal Services Act 2007, is an authorised person in relation to an activity which constitutes the exercise of a right of audience or the conduct of litigation (within the meaning of that Act).]

NOTES

Inserted as noted to art 89A at **[8.230]**.

Subsequently substituted by the Financial Services and Markets Act 2000 (Miscellaneous Provisions) Order 2015, SI 2015/853, art 3(1), (7), as from 24 March 2015.

[8.233]

[89D [Other exclusions]

[(1)] . . .

[(2) Article 89A is . . . subject to the exclusions in articles 72G (local authorities) and 72H (insolvency practitioners).]]

NOTES

Inserted as noted to art 89A at **[8.230]**.

Article heading substituted, para (1) numbered as such, and para (2) added, by the Financial Services and Markets Act 2000 (Regulated Activities) (Amendment) Order 2014, SI 2014/366, art 2(1), (44), (45), as from 1 April 2014.

Para (1), and the word omitted from para (2), were revoked by the Electronic Commerce and Solvency 2 (Amendment etc) (EU Exit) Regulations 2019, SI 2019/1361, reg 5(1), (3), as from IP completion day (as defined in the European Union (Withdrawal Agreement) Act 2020, s 39) (for transitional provisions, see the note in relation to art 72A of this Order *ante*).

[Supplemental

[8.234]

89E Meaning of "consumer" etc

(1) For the purposes of sections 1G, 404E and 425A of the Act (meaning of "consumer")—

(a) an individual or a relevant recipient of credit who is, may be, has been or may have been the subject of the information referred to in article 89A, and

(b) an individual or a relevant recipient of credit who is, may be, has been or may have been the subject of information furnished in the course of a person carrying on an activity of the kind specified by article 89B, [or article 64 (agreeing to carry on specified kinds of activity) in so far as that article relates to article 89B,]

is to be treated as a "consumer".

(2) For the purposes of section 328(8) of the Act (meaning of "clients")—

(a) an individual or a relevant recipient of credit who is, may be, has been or may have been the subject of the information referred to in article 89A, and

(b) an individual or a relevant recipient of credit who is, may be, has been or may have been the subject of information furnished in the course of a person carrying on an activity of the kind specified by article 89B, [or article 64 (agreeing to carry on specified kinds of activity) in so far as that article relates to article 89B,]

is to be treated as a "client".]

NOTES

Inserted as noted to art 89A at **[8.230]**.

Words in square brackets inserted by the Financial Services and Markets Act 2000 (Regulated Activities) (Amendment) Order 2014, SI 2014/366, art 2(1), (46), as from 1 April 2014.

[PART 3B CLAIMS MANAGEMENT ACTIVITIES IN GREAT BRITAIN

The activities

[8.235]

89F Specified kinds of claims management activity

(1) A claims management activity is a specified kind of activity when it is an activity specified in any of articles 89G to 89M.

(2) For the purposes of this Part—

- (a) "claimant" includes, in civil proceedings in Scotland, a pursuer;
- (b) "defendant" includes, in civil proceedings in Scotland, a defender;
- (c) "personal injury claim" means a claim for personal injury within the meaning of the Civil Procedure Rules 1998 in England and Wales and an action for damages for, or arising from, personal injuries within the meaning set out in section 8(7) of the Civil Litigation (Expenses and Group Proceedings) (Scotland) Act 2018 in Scotland;
- (d) "financial services or financial product claim" includes a claim made under section 75 of the Consumer Credit Act 1974;
- (e) "housing disrepair claim" means a claim under section 11 of the Landlord and Tenant Act 1985 or section 4 of the Defective Premises Act 1972 in England and Wales or an application in respect of the repairing standard under section 22 of the Housing (Scotland) Act 2006, or claims in relation to the disrepair of premises under a term of a tenancy agreement or lease or under the common law relating to nuisance or negligence, but does not include claims for statutory nuisance under section 82 of the Environmental Protection Act 1990;
- (f) "a claim for a specified benefit" means a claim for one of the following benefits—
  - (i) industrial injuries benefit, within the meaning given by section 94 of the Social Security Contributions and Benefits Act 1992;
  - (ii) any supplement or additional allowance, or increase of benefit or allowance to which a recipient of an industrial injuries benefit may be entitled under that Act or any other Act;
  - (iii) a benefit under a scheme referred to in paragraph 2 or 4 of Schedule 8 to that Act; or
  - (iv) a benefit under the Pneumoconiosis etc (Workers' Compensation) Act 1979.
- (g) "criminal injury claim" means a claim under the Criminal Injuries Compensation Scheme established under the Criminal Injuries Compensation Act 1995;
- (h) "employment related claim" includes a claim in relation to wages and salaries and other employment related payments and claims in relation to wrongful or unfair dismissal, redundancy, discrimination and harassment;
- (i) "investigating" means carrying out an investigation into, or commissioning the investigation of, the circumstances, merits or foundation of a claim; and
- (j) "representing" means representation in writing or orally, regardless of the tribunal, body or person before which or to whom the representation is made.

(3) A person is to be treated as carrying on a regulated claims management activity in Great Britain when the activity is carried on—

- (a) by a person who is—
  - (i) an individual who is ordinarily resident in Great Britain; or
  - (ii) a person, other than an individual, who is constituted under the law of England and Wales or Scotland; or
- (b) in respect of a claimant or potential claimant who is—
  - (i) an individual who is ordinarily resident in Great Britain; or
  - (ii) a person, other than an individual, who is constituted under the law of England and Wales or Scotland.

(4) For the purposes of this article—

- (a) a person is "ordinarily resident" in Great Britain if that person satisfies the requirements of the Statutory Residence Test as set out in Schedule 45 to the Finance Act 2013 either—
  - (i) at the time of the facts giving rise to the claim or potential claim; or
  - (ii) at the time when the regulated claims management activity is carried out in respect of that claimant or potential claimant;
- (b) the references to the "UK" in the Statutory Residence Test in Schedule 45 are to be read as if they were expressed as references to "Great Britain".]

NOTES

Part 3B (arts 89F–89W) was inserted by the Financial Services and Markets Act 2000 (Claims Management Activity) Order 2018, SI 2018/1253, arts 3, 7, as from 1 April 2019 (for provision specifying that the 2018 Order also comes into force on 29 November 2018 for the purposes of the FCA and FOS making rules and issuing guidance, and for transitional provisions in relation to carrying on a claims management activity, etc, see arts 1, 39–89 of the 2018 Order).

[8.236]

[89G Seeking out, referrals and identification of claims or potential claims

(1) Each of the following is a specified kind of activity when carried on in relation to a claim of a kind specified in paragraph (2)—

- (a) seeking out persons who may have a claim, unless that activity constitutes the communication of an invitation or inducement to engagement in claims management activity within the meaning of section 21 (restrictions on financial promotion) of the Act;
- (b) referring details of—
  - (i) a claim or potential claim; or
  - (ii) a claimant or potential claimant

  to another person (including to a person having the right to conduct litigation); and
- (c) identifying—

(i) a claim or potential claim; or
(ii) a claimant or potential claimant.

(2) The kinds of claim are—
(a) a personal injury claim;
(b) a financial services or financial product claim;
(c) a housing disrepair claim;
(d) a claim for a specified benefit;
(e) a criminal injury claim; and
(f) an employment related claim.]

NOTES

Inserted as noted to s 89E at **[8.235]**.

[8.237]

[89H Advice, investigation or representation in relation to a personal injury claim

Each of the following activities is a specified kind of activity when carried on in relation to a personal injury claim—
(a) advising a claimant or potential claimant;
(b) investigating a claim; and
(c) representing a claimant.]

NOTES

Inserted as noted to s 89E at **[8.235]**.

[8.238]

[89I Advice, investigation or representation in relation to a financial services or financial product claim

Each of the following activities is a specified kind of activity when carried on in relation to a financial services or financial product claim—
(a) advising a claimant or potential claimant;
(b) investigating a claim; and
(c) representing a claimant.]

NOTES

Inserted as noted to s 89E at **[8.235]**.

[8.239]

[89J Advice, investigation or representation in relation to a housing disrepair claim

Each of the following activities is a specified kind of activity when carried on in relation to a housing disrepair claim—
(a) advising a claimant or potential claimant;
(b) investigating a claim; and
(c) representing a claimant.]

NOTES

Inserted as noted to s 89E at **[8.235]**.

[8.240]

[89K Advice, investigation or representation in relation to a claim for a specified benefit

Each of the following activities is a specified kind of activity when carried on in relation to a claim for a specified benefit—
(a) advising a claimant or potential claimant;
(b) investigating a claim; and
(c) representing a claimant.]

NOTES

Inserted as noted to s 89E at **[8.235]**.

[8.241]

[89L Advice, investigation or representation in relation to a criminal injury claim

Each of the following activities is a specified kind of activity when carried on in relation to a criminal injury claim—
(a) advising a claimant or potential claimant;
(b) investigating a claim; and
(c) representing a claimant.]

NOTES

Inserted as noted to s 89E at **[8.235]**.

[8.242]

[89M Advice, investigation or representation in relation to an employment related claim

Each of the following activities is a specified kind of activity when carried on in relation to an employment related claim—
(a) advising a claimant or potential claimant;
(b) investigating a claim; and
(c) representing a claimant.]

NOTES

Inserted as noted to s 89E at **[8.235]**.

[Exclusions

[8.243]

89N Claims management activity conducted by legal professionals

(1) There is excluded from articles 89G to 89M any activity which is carried on in England and Wales by—

(a) a legal practitioner;

(b) a firm, organisation or body corporate that carries on the claims management activity through a legal practitioner; or

(c) an individual who carries on the claims management activity at the direction of, and under the supervision of, a legal practitioner who is—

(i) that individual's employer or fellow employee; or

(ii) a director of a company, or a member of a limited liability partnership, that provides the service and is that individual's employer.

(2) For the purposes of paragraph (1) "legal practitioner" means—

(a) a solicitor or barrister of any part of England and Wales or Northern Ireland;

(b) a Fellow of the Chartered Institute of Legal Executives;

(c) a European lawyer, as defined in the European Communities (Services of Lawyers) Order 1978 or the European Communities (Lawyer's Practice) Regulations 2000;

(d) a registered foreign lawyer, as defined in section 89(9) of the Courts and Legal Services Act 1990;

(e) any other member of a legal profession, of a jurisdiction other than England and Wales, that is recognised by the Law Society of England and Wales or the General Council of the Bar as a regulated legal profession.

(3) There is excluded from articles 89G to 89M any activity which is carried on in Scotland by—

(a) a legal practitioner;

(b) a firm, organisation or body corporate that carries on the claims management activity through or under the supervision of a legal practitioner where that firm, organisation or body corporate is—

(i) a firm of solicitors;

(ii) an incorporated practice; or

(iii) a licensed legal services provider and the activity is a legal service as defined within section 3 of the Legal Services (Scotland) Act 2010.

(4) For the purposes of paragraph (3) "legal practitioner" means—

(a) a person who is qualified to practise as a solicitor under section 4 of the Solicitors (Scotland) Act 1980;

(b) an advocate who is a member of the Faculty of Advocates;

(c) a European lawyer as defined in the European Communities (Services of Lawyers) Order 1978 or the European Communities (Lawyer's Practice) (Scotland) Regulations 2000; or

(d) a registered foreign lawyer within the meaning of section 65 of the Solicitors (Scotland) Act 1980.

(5) But an activity mentioned in paragraph (1) or (3) is only excluded from articles 89G to 89M if the legal practitioner concerned carries on the claims management activity in the ordinary course of legal practice pursuant to the professional rules to which that legal practitioner is subject.

(6) The exclusions in this article are to be read as if they were expressed as exemptions for the purposes of the following provisions of the Financial Guidance and Claims Act 2018—

(a) section 32(5)(b) (PPI claims: interim restriction on charges imposed by legal practitioners after transfer of regulation to the FCA); and

(b) section 33(11) (legal services regulators' rules: charges for claims management services).]

NOTES

Inserted as noted to s 89E at **[8.235]**.

European Communities (Services of Lawyers) Order 1978; European Communities (Lawyer's Practice) Regulations 2000: revoked by the Services of Lawyers and Lawyer's Practice (Revocation etc) (EU Exit) Regulations 2020, SI 2020/1342, as from IP completion day (as defined in the European Union (Withdrawal Agreement) Act 2020, s 39).

[8.244]

[89O Claims management activity conducted by a charity or not-for-profit agency

(1) There is excluded from articles 89G to 89M any activity carried on by a charity or a not-for-profit agency.

(2) In this article "charity" means—

(a) a charity as defined by section 1(1) of the Charities Act 2011 or the Charities and Trustee Investment (Scotland) Act 2005; or

(b) a body registered in the Scottish Charity Register.

(3) In this article "not-for-profit agency" means a body that by or under its constitution—

(a) is required to apply the whole of its net income, and any expendable capital, after payment of outgoings for charitable or public purposes; and

(b) is prohibited from distributing, directly or indirectly, any part of its net income by way of profits or its assets among any of its members.

(4) But a body is not prevented from being a not-for-profit agency for the purposes of paragraph (3) if its constitution permits—

(a) the payment, out of the body's funds, of reasonable and proper remuneration for goods or services supplied to the body by a member; or

(b) in the case of a not-for-profit body that is a charity, the payment to a member to which the member is eligible because that member is a beneficiary of the charity; or

(c) the purchase, out of the body's funds, of indemnity insurance for trustees of the body.]

NOTES

Inserted as noted to s 89E at **[8.235]**.

[8.245]

[89P Claims management activity conducted by a person appointed by a statutory or other public body

There is excluded from articles 89G to 89M any activity carried on by—

(a) any person established or appointed by virtue of an enactment;

(b) an Independent Complaints Reviewer; or

(c) an Independent Case Examiner

in the course of carrying out that individual's duties.]

NOTES

Inserted as noted to s 89E at **[8.235]**.

[8.246]

[89Q Claims management activity conducted by the Motor Insurers' Bureau

There is excluded from articles 89G to 89M any activity carried on by the Motor Insurers' Bureau in the course of carrying on its functions (being the company limited by guarantee mentioned in section 95(2) (notification of refusal of insurance on grounds of health) of the Road Traffic Act 1988).]

NOTES

Inserted as noted to s 89E at **[8.235]**.

[8.247]

[89R Claims management activity conducted by a medical defence union

There is excluded from articles 89G to 89M any activity carried on by—

(a) the Medical Protection Society Limited for its members;

(b) the Medical Defence Union Limited for its members; or

(c) the Medical and Dental Defence Union of Scotland Limited for its members.]

NOTES

Inserted as noted to s 89E at **[8.235]**.

[8.248]

[89S Claims management activity conducted an independent trade union

(1) There is excluded from articles 89G to 89M any activity carried on by an independent trade union for—

(a) a member (including a retired member or a student member) of an independent trade union;

(b) a member of the family of a member referred to in sub-paragraph (a); or

(c) a former member of the trade union to whom the trade union may, under its rules, provide claims management services, or a member of the family of such a former member.

(2) In paragraph (1), "independent trade union" has the same meaning as in the Trade Union and Labour Relations (Consolidation) Act 1992.

(3) For the purposes of paragraph (1)—

(a) subject to sub-paragraph (b), whether a person is or has been a member (including a retired member or a student member) of a trade union is to be decided in accordance with the rules of that trade union;

(b) "member" of a trade union does not include a person who, under those rules, is a member only for the purpose of pursuing a claim or claims; and

(c) whether a person is a member of the family of a member of a trade union is to be decided in accordance with the rules of that trade union.

(4) An exemption of a trade union under this article is subject to compliance by the trade union with the condition that the trade union, in carrying on a regulated claims management activity, must act in accordance with the code of practice for the provision of regulated claims management activities by trade unions issued by the Treasury.]

NOTES

Inserted as noted to s 89E at **[8.235]**.

[8.249]

[89T Claims management activity conducted by a students' union

(1) There is excluded from articles 89G to 89M any activity carried on by a students' union for a member of that students' union or a member of a constituent or affiliated association or body.

(2) In this article "students' union" has the meaning given by section 20 (meaning of "students' union") of the Education Act 1994.]

NOTES

Inserted as noted to s 89E at **[8.235]**.

[8.250]

[89U Claims management activity conducted by an insurance intermediary

There is excluded from articles 89G to 89M any regulated activity of the kind specified in article 21, 25, 39A, 53 or 64 carried on by a person who has permission to carry on that activity in relation to a contract of insurance.]

NOTES

Inserted as noted to s 89E at **[8.235]**.

[8.251]

[89V Certain providers of referrals

(1) There is excluded from article 89G the activity of referring details of a potential claim or potential claimant to another person if—

(a) the person who refers those details ("the introducer") carries on no other regulated claims management activity;

(b) the activity is incidental to the introducer's main business;

(c) the details are only referred to authorised persons, legal practitioners, or a firm, organisation or body corporate that provides the service through legal practitioners;

(d) of the claims that the introducer refers to such persons, that introducer is paid, in money or money's worth, for no more than 25 claims per calendar quarter; and

(e) the introducer, in obtaining and referring those details, has complied with the provisions of the Data Protection Act 2018, the Privacy and Electronic Communications (EC Directive) Regulations 2003, the General Data Protection Regulation (EU) of the European Parliament and of the Council 2016/679 and the Consumer Protection from Unfair Trading Regulations 2008.

(2) Paragraph (1)(e) does not apply in the case of a referral to a legal practitioner or firm, organisation or body corporate that carries on the activity through legal practitioners.

(3) In this article "legal practitioner" has the meaning given by article 89N(2) or (4)].

NOTES

Inserted as noted to s 89E at **[8.235]**.

[8.252]

[89W Services in connection with counterclaims and claims against third parties

There is excluded from articles 89G to 89M any activity carried on in circumstances where—

(a) a claim has been made by a person ("the claimant") against another person ("the defendant"); and

(b) the activity being carried on consists of the provision of a service to the defendant in connection with—

(i) the making of a counterclaim against the claimant arising out of the same set of facts as the claim referred to in sub-paragraph (a); or

(ii) the making of a claim against a third party (whether for contribution, as a subrogated claim, or otherwise) which is incidental to, or consequent on, the claim referred to in sub-paragraph (a).]

NOTES

Inserted as noted to s 89E at **[8.235]**.

90, 91 *(Arts 90, 91 (Pt IV) amended the Consumer Credit Act 1974, the Consumer Credit (Advertisements) Regulations 1989, SI 1989/1125 (revoked) and the Consumer Credit (Content of Quotations) and Consumer Credit (Advertisements) (Amendment) Regulations 1999, SI 1999/2725, (revoked) and were revoked by the Financial Services and Markets Act 2000 (Regulated Activities) (Amendment) (No 2) Order 2013, SI 2013/1881, arts 2, 9(2), (3), as from 1 April 2014.)*

[PART V UNAUTHORISED PERSONS CARRYING ON INSURANCE [DISTRIBUTION] ACTIVITIES

NOTES

Word in square brackets in the preceding heading substituted by the Insurance Distribution (Regulated Activities and Miscellaneous Amendments) Order 2018, SI 2018/546, arts 2, 7(1), (2), as from 1 October 2018.

[8.253]

92 Interpretation

In this Part—

"designated professional body" means a body which is for the time being designated by the Treasury under section 326 of the Act (designation of professional bodies);

"insurance [distribution] activity" means any regulated activity of the kind specified by article 21, 25(1) or (2), 39A or 53, or, so far as relevant to any of those articles, article 64, which is carried on in relation to a contract of insurance;

"the record" means the record maintained by [the FCA] under section 347 of the Act (public record of authorised persons etc);

"recorded insurance intermediary" has the meaning given by article 93(4);

"a relevant member", in relation to a designated professional body, means a member (within the meaning of section 325(2) of the Act) of the profession in relation to which that designated professional body is established, or a person who is controlled or managed by one or more such members.]

NOTES

Added, together with the preceding heading and arts 93–96, by the Financial Services and Markets Act 2000 (Regulated Activities) (Amendment) (No 2) Order 2003, SI 2003/1476, art 13, as from 31 October 2004 (in so far as relating to contracts of long-term care insurance), and as from 14 January 2005 (otherwise).

Word in square brackets in the definition "insurance distribution activity" (formerly "insurance mediation activity") substituted by the Insurance Distribution (Regulated Activities and Miscellaneous Amendments) Order 2018, SI 2018/546, arts 2, 7(1), (3), as from 1 October 2018.

Words in square brackets in definition "the record" substituted by the Financial Services Act 2012 (Consequential Amendments and Transitional Provisions) Order 2013, SI 2013/472, art 3, Sch 2, para 35(a), as from 1 April 2013.

[8.254]

[93 Duty to maintain a record of persons carrying on insurance [distribution] activities

(1) Subject to articles 95 and 96, [the FCA] must include in the record every person who—

(a) as a result of information obtained by virtue of its rules or by virtue of a direction given, or requirement imposed, under [section 55U(4)] of the Act (procedure for applications under [Part 4A]), appears to [the FCA] to fall within paragraph (2); or

(b) as a result of information obtained by virtue of article 94, appears to [the FCA] to fall within paragraph (3).

(2) A person falls within this paragraph if he is, or has entered into a contract by virtue of which he will be, an appointed representative who carries on any insurance [distribution] activity.

(3) A person falls within this paragraph if—

(a) he is a relevant member of a designated professional body who carries on, or is proposing to carry on, any insurance [distribution] activity; and

(b) the general prohibition does not (or will not) apply to the carrying on of those activities by virtue of section 327 of the Act (exemption from the general prohibition).

[(3A) An application for inclusion in the record made by a person who falls within paragraph (2) or (3) must be determined by the FCA before the end of the period of 3 months beginning with the date on which it received the completed application.

(3B) A notification by a designated professional body in accordance with article 94 is to be treated as an application for inclusion in the record for the purposes of paragraph (3A).]

(4) In this Part, "recorded insurance intermediary" means a person who is included in the record by virtue of paragraph (1).

(5) The record must include—

(a) in the case of any recorded insurance intermediary, its address; and

(b) in the case of a recorded insurance intermediary which is not an individual, the name of the individuals who are responsible for the management of the business carried on by the intermediary, so far as it relates to insurance [distribution] activities.]

NOTES

Added as noted to art 92 at **[8.253]**.

The word "distribution" in square brackets in the article heading and in paras (2), (3) and (5) was substituted, and paras (3A), (3B) were inserted, by the Insurance Distribution (Regulated Activities and Miscellaneous Amendments) Order 2018, SI 2018/546, arts 2, 7(1), (4), as from 1 October 2018.

The words in square brackets in para (1) were substituted by the Financial Services Act 2012 (Consequential Amendments and Transitional Provisions) Order 2013, SI 2013/472, arts 3, 4, Sch 2, para 35(a), (h), as from 1 April 2013.

[8.255]

[94 Members of designated professional bodies

(1) A designated professional body must, by notice in writing, inform [the FCA] of—

(a) the name,

(b) the address, and

(c) in the case of a relevant member which is not an individual, the name of the individuals who are responsible for the management of the business carried on by the member, so far as it relates to insurance [distribution] activities,

of any relevant member who falls within paragraph (2).

(2) A relevant member of a designated professional body falls within this paragraph if, in accordance with the rules of that body, he carries on, or proposes to carry on any insurance [distribution] activity but does not have, and does not propose to apply for, [Part 4A] permission on the basis that the general prohibition does not (or will not) apply to the carrying on of that activity by virtue of section 327 of the Act.

(3) A designated professional body must also, by notice in writing, inform [the FCA] of any change in relation to the matters specified in sub-paragraphs (a) to (c) of paragraph (1).

(4) A designated professional body must inform [the FCA] when a relevant member to whom paragraph (2) applies ceases, for whatever reason, to carry on insurance [distribution] activities.

(5) [The FCA] may give directions to a designated professional body as to the manner in which the information referred to in paragraphs (1), (3) and (4) must be provided.]

NOTES

Added as noted to art 92 at **[8.253]**.

Word "distribution" in square brackets in each place that it occurs substituted by the Insurance Distribution (Regulated Activities and Miscellaneous Amendments) Order 2018, SI 2018/546, arts 2, 7(1), (5), as from 1 October 2018.

Other words in square brackets substituted by the Financial Services Act 2012 (Consequential Amendments and Transitional Provisions) Order 2013, SI 2013/472, arts 3, 4, Sch 2, para 35(a), as from 1 April 2013.

[8.256]

[95 Exclusion from record where not fit and proper to carry on insurance [distribution] activities

(1) If it appears to [the FCA] that a person who falls within article 93(2) (appointed representatives) ("AR") is not a fit and proper person to carry on insurance [distribution] activities, it may decide not to include him in the record or, if that person is already included in the record, to remove him from the record.

[(1A) . . .]

(2) Where [the FCA] proposes to make a determination under paragraph (1), it must give AR a warning notice.

(3) If [the FCA] makes a determination under paragraph (1), it must give AR a decision notice.

(4) If [the FCA] gives AR a decision notice under paragraph (3), AR may refer the matter to the Tribunal.

(5) [The FCA] may, on the application of AR, revoke a determination under paragraph (1).

(6) If [the FCA] decides to grant the application, it must give AR written notice of its decision.

(7) If [the FCA] proposes to refuse the application, it must give AR a warning notice.

(8) If [the FCA] decides to refuse the application, it must give AR a decision notice.

(9) If [the FCA] gives AR a decision notice under paragraph (8), AR may refer the matter to the Tribunal.

(10) Sections 393 and 394 of the Act (third party rights and access to [FCA or PRA] material) apply to a warning notice given in accordance with paragraph (2) or (7) and to a decision notice given in accordance with paragraph (3) or (8).]

NOTES

Added as noted to art 92 at **[8.253]**.

Word "distribution" in square brackets in the article heading and in para (1) substituted, and para originally (1A) inserted, by the Insurance Distribution (Regulated Activities and Miscellaneous Amendments) Order 2018, SI 2018/546, arts 2, 7(1), (6), as from 1 October 2018.

Para (1A) was subsequently revoked by the Financial Services and Markets Act 2000 (Amendment) (EU Exit) Regulations 2019, SI 2019/632, regs 120, 159, as from IP completion day (as defined in the European Union (Withdrawal Agreement) Act 2020, s 39).

All other words in square brackets were substituted by the Financial Services Act 2012 (Consequential Amendments and Transitional Provisions) Order 2013, SI 2013/472, art 3, Sch 2, para 35(a), (i), as from 1 April 2013.

[8.257]

[96 Exclusion from the record where [FCA] has exercised its powers under Part XX of the Act

(1) If a person who appears to [the FCA] to fall within article 93(3) (member of a designated professional body) falls within paragraph (2) or (3), [the FCA] must not include him in the record or, if that person is already included in the record, must remove him from the record.

(2) A person falls within this paragraph if, by virtue of a direction given by [the FCA] under section 328(1) of the Act (directions in relation to the general prohibition), section 327(1) of the Act does not apply in relation to the carrying on by him of any insurance [distribution] activity.

(3) A person falls within this paragraph if [the FCA] has made an order under section 329(2) of the Act (orders in relation to the general prohibition) disapplying section 327(1) of the Act in relation to the carrying on by him of any insurance [distribution] activity.]

NOTES

Added as noted to art 92 at **[8.253]**.

Word "distribution" in square brackets in paras (2) and (3) substituted by the Insurance Distribution (Regulated Activities and Miscellaneous Amendments) Order 2018, SI 2018/546, arts 2, 7(1), (7), as from 1 October 2018.

All other words in square brackets were substituted by the Financial Services Act 2012 (Consequential Amendments and Transitional Provisions) Order 2013, SI 2013/472, art 3, Sch 2, para 35(a), (j), as from 1 April 2013.

97 *(Article 97 (Pt VI Miscellaneous) is effectively spent. It was added by the Financial Services and Markets Act 2000 (Regulated Activities) (Amendment) Order 2004, SI 2004/1610, art 3, as from 15 July 2004, and inserted the Financial Services and Markets Act 2000, s 49(2A). Part IV of the 2000 Act (ss 40–55) was substituted by a new Part 4A (ss 55A–55Z4) by the Financial Services Act 2012, as from 1 April 2012.)*

SCHEDULES

SCHEDULE 1
CONTRACTS OF INSURANCE

Article 3(1)

PART I CONTRACTS OF GENERAL INSURANCE

[8.258]

1 Accident

Contracts of insurance providing fixed pecuniary benefits or benefits in the nature of indemnity (or a combination of both) against risks of the person insured or, in the case of a contract made by virtue of section 140, 140A or 140B of the Local Government Act 1972 (or, in Scotland, section 86(1) of the Local Government (Scotland) Act 1973), a person for whose benefit the contract is made—

(a) sustaining injury as the result of an accident or of an accident of a specified class; or
(b) dying as a result of an accident or of an accident of a specified class; or
(c) becoming incapacitated in consequence of disease or of disease of a specified class,

including contracts relating to industrial injury and occupational disease but excluding contracts falling within paragraph 2 of Part I of, or paragraph IV of Part II of, this Schedule.

2 Sickness

Contracts of insurance providing fixed pecuniary benefits or benefits in the nature of indemnity (or a combination of both) against risks of loss to the persons insured attributable to sickness or infirmity but excluding contracts falling within paragraph IV of Part II of this Schedule.

3 Land vehicles

Contracts of insurance against loss of or damage to vehicles used on land, including motor vehicles but excluding railway rolling stock.

4 Railway rolling stock

Contract of insurance against loss of or damage to railway rolling stock.

5 Aircraft

Contracts of insurance upon aircraft or upon the machinery, tackle, furniture or equipment of aircraft.

6 Ships

Contracts of insurance upon vessels used on the sea or on inland water, or upon the machinery, tackle, furniture or equipment of such vessels.

7 Goods in transit

Contracts of insurance against loss of or damage to merchandise, baggage and all other goods in transit, irrespective of the form of transport.

8 Fire and natural forces

Contracts of insurance against loss of or damage to property (other than property to which paragraphs 3 to 7 relate) due to fire, explosion, storm, natural forces other than storm, nuclear energy or land subsidence.

9 Damage to property

Contracts of insurance against loss of or damage to property (other than property to which paragraphs 3 to 7 relate) due to hail or frost or any other event (such as theft) other than those mentioned in paragraph 8.

10 Motor vehicle liability

Contracts of insurance against damage arising out of or in connection with the use of motor vehicles on land, including third-party risks and carrier's liability.

11 Aircraft liability

Contracts of insurance against damage arising out of or in connection with the use of aircraft, including third-party risks and carrier's liability.

12 Liability of ships

Contracts of insurance against damage arising out of or in connection with the use of vessels on the sea or on inland water, including third party risks and carrier's liability.

13 General liability

Contracts of insurance against risks of the persons insured incurring liabilities to third parties, the risks in question not being risks to which paragraph 10, 11 or 12 relates.

14 Credit

Contracts of insurance against risks of loss to the persons insured arising from the insolvency of debtors of theirs or from the failure (otherwise than through insolvency) of debtors of theirs to pay their debts when due.

15 Suretyship

(1) Contracts of insurance against the risks of loss to the persons insured arising from their having to perform contracts of guarantee entered into by them.

(2) Fidelity bonds, performance bonds, administration bonds, bail bonds or customs bonds or similar contracts of guarantee, where these are—

(a) effected or carried out by a person not carrying on a banking business;

(b) not effected merely incidentally to some other business carried on by the person effecting them; and

(c) effected in return for the payment of one or more premiums.

16 Miscellaneous financial loss

Contracts of insurance against any of the following risks, namely—

(a) risks of loss to the persons insured attributable to interruptions of the carrying on of business carried on by them or to reduction of the scope of business so carried on;

(b) risks of loss to the persons insured attributable to their incurring unforeseen expense (other than loss such as is covered by contracts falling within paragraph 18);

(c) risks which do not fall within sub-paragraph (a) or (b) and which are not of a kind such that contracts of insurance against them fall within any other provision of this Schedule.

17 Legal expenses

Contracts of insurance against risks of loss to the persons insured attributable to their incurring legal expenses (including costs of litigation).

18 Assistance

Contracts of insurance providing either or both of the following benefits, namely—

(a) assistance (whether in cash or in kind) for persons who get into difficulties while travelling, while away from home or while away from their permanent residence; or

(b) assistance (whether in cash or in kind) for persons who get into difficulties otherwise than as mentioned in sub-paragraph (a).

PART II CONTRACTS OF LONG-TERM INSURANCE

[8.259]

I Life and annuity

Contracts of insurance on human life or contracts to pay annuities on human life, but excluding (in each case) contracts within paragraph III.

II Marriage and birth

Contract of insurance to provide a sum on marriage [or the formation of a civil partnership] or on the birth of a child, being contracts expressed to be in effect for a period of more than one year.

III Linked long term

Contracts of insurance on human life or contracts to pay annuities on human life where the benefits are wholly or partly to be determined by references to the value of, or the income from, property of any description (whether or not specified in the contracts) or by reference to fluctuations in, or in an index of, the value of property of any description (whether or not so specified).

IV Permanent health

Contracts of insurance providing specified benefits against risks of persons becoming incapacitated in consequence of sustaining injury as a result of an accident or of an accident of a specified class or of sickness or infirmity, being contracts that—

(a) are expressed to be in effect for a period of not less than five years, or until the normal retirement age for the persons concerned, or without limit of time; and

(b) either are not expressed to be terminable by the insurer, or are expressed to be so terminable only in special circumstances mentioned in the contract.

V Tontines

Tontines.

VI Capital redemption contracts

Capital redemption contracts, where effected or carried out by a person who does not carry on a banking business, and otherwise carries on a regulated activity of the kind specified by article 10(1) or (2).

VII Pension fund management

(a) Pension fund management contracts, and

(b) pension fund management contracts which are combined with contracts of insurance covering either conservation of capital or payment of a minimum interest, where effected or carried out by a person who does not carry on a banking business, and otherwise carries on a regulated activity of the kind specified by article 10(1) or (2).

VIII Collective insurance etc

Contracts of a kind referred to in [Article 2(3)(b)(v) of the Solvency 2 Directive].

IX Social insurance

Contracts of a kind referred to in [Article 2(3)(c) of the Solvency 2 Directive].

NOTES

II Marriage and birth: words in square brackets inserted by the Civil Partnership Act 2004 (Amendments to Subordinate Legislation) Order 2005, SI 2005/2114, art 2(16), Sch 16, Pt 1, para 1(1), (5), as from 5 December 2005. Note it is unclear whether these words should also be inserted after the word "Marriage" in the heading to this paragraph.

VIII Collective insurance etc: words in square brackets substituted by the Solvency 2 Regulations 2015, SI 2015/575, reg 60, Sch 2, para 11(1), (5)(a), as from 1 January 2016.

IX Social insurance: words in square brackets substituted by SI 2015/575, reg 60, Sch 2, para 11(1), (5)(b), as from 1 January 2016.

[SCHEDULE 2
[FINANCIAL INSTRUMENTS AND INVESTMENT SERVICES AND ACTIVITIES]

Article 3(1)

NOTES

Schedule heading substituted by the Markets in Financial Instruments (Amendment) (EU Exit) Regulations 2018, SI 2018/1403, reg 4(1), (2), as from IP completion day (as defined in the European Union (Withdrawal Agreement) Act 2020, s 39).

PART 1 . . .

Financial Instruments

[8.260]

1. Transferable securities;

2. Money-market instruments;

3. Units in collective investment undertakings;

4. Options, futures, swaps, forward rate agreements and any other derivative contracts relating to securities, currencies, interest rates or yields, [emission allowances] or other derivatives instruments, financial indices or financial measures which may be settled physically or in cash;

5. Options, futures, swaps, [forwards] and any other derivative contracts relating to commodities that must be settled in cash or may be settled in cash at the option of one of the parties ([other] than by reason of a default or other termination event);

6. Options, futures, swaps, and any other derivative [contract] relating to commodities that can be physically settled provided that they are traded on a [UK regulated market, a UK MTF or a UK OTF (as defined by Article 2(1)(13A), (14A) and (15A) respectively of the markets in financial instruments regulation)][, except for wholesale energy products [traded on a UK OTF] that must be physically settled];

[**7.** Option, futures, swaps, forwards and any other derivative contracts relating to commodities, that can be physically settled not otherwise mentioned in point 6 of this Section and not being for commercial purposes [or wholesale energy products traded on an EU OTF (as defined by Article 2(1)(15B) of the markets in financial instruments regulation) that must be physically settled], which have the characteristics of other derivative financial instruments;]

8. Derivative instruments for the transfer of credit risk;

9. Financial contracts for differences;

[10. Options, futures, swaps, forward rate agreements and any other derivative contracts relating to climatic variables, freight rates or inflation rates or other official economic statistics that must be settled in cash or may be settled in cash at the option of one of the parties other than by reason of default or other termination event, as well as any other derivative contracts relating to assets, rights, obligations, indices and measures not otherwise mentioned in this Section, which have the characteristics of other derivative financial instruments, having regard to whether, inter alia, they are traded on a [a UK regulated market, a UK OTF, or a UK MTF (as defined by Article 2(1)(13A), (15A) and (14A) respectively of the markets in financial instruments regulation)]];

[11. Emission allowances consisting of any units recognised for compliance with the requirements of Directive 2003/87/EC (Emissions Trading Scheme) [or allowances created under article 18 of the trading scheme order].]

NOTES

Substituted by the Financial Services and Markets Act 2000 (Regulated Activities) (Amendment No 3) Order 2006, SI 2006/3384, arts 2, 29, as from 1 April 2007 (for the purposes of enabling applications to be made for (i) a Part IV permission, (ii) a variation of a Part IV permission, and (iii) the Authority's approval under s 59 of the 2000 Act, in relation to an activity of the kind specified by art 25D of this Order, or in relation to an investment of the kind specified by arts 83, 84 or 85 of this Order), and as from 1 November 2007 (otherwise).

The Part heading was revoked by the Markets in Financial Instruments (Amendment) (EU Exit) Regulations 2018, SI 2018/1403, reg 4(1), (3)(a), as from IP completion day (as defined in the European Union (Withdrawal Agreement) Act 2020, s 39).

Para 4: words in square brackets inserted by the Financial Services and Markets Act 2000 (Regulated Activities) (Amendment) Order 2017, SI 2017/488, art 10(1), (3)(a), as from 1 April 2017 (for the purposes of (i) enabling applications to be made for a Part 4A permission, for a variation of a Part 4A permission or for an approval under FSMA 2000, s 59, or (ii) enabling such applications to be determined, in relation to any specified activity or any specified investment amended or inserted by the 2017 Order), and as from 3 January 2018 (otherwise).

Para 5: words in square brackets substituted by SI 2017/488, art 10(1), (3)(b), as from 1 April 2017 (certain purposes), and as from 3 January 2018 (otherwise) (for details, see the first note relating to the 2017 Order above).

Para 6: words "UK regulated market, a UK MTF or a UK OTF (as defined by Article 2(1)(13A), (14A) and (15A) respectively of the markets in financial instruments regulation)" and "traded on a UK OTF" in square brackets substituted by SI 2018/1403, reg 4(1), (3)(b), as from IP completion day (as defined in the European Union (Withdrawal Agreement) Act 2020, s 39). Other words in square brackets substituted by SI 2017/488, art 10(1), (3)(c), as from 1 April 2017 (certain purposes), and as from 3 January 2018 (otherwise) (for details, see the first note relating to the 2017 Order above).

Para 7: substituted by SI 2017/488, art 10(1), (3)(d), as from 1 April 2017 (certain purposes), and as from 3 January 2018 (otherwise) (for details, see the first note relating to the 2017 Order above). Words in square brackets inserted by SI 2018/1403, reg 4(1), (3)(c), as from IP completion day (as defined in the European Union (Withdrawal Agreement) Act 2020, s 39); note that reg 4(3)(c) of the 2018 Regulations was amended by the Financial Services (Miscellaneous) (Amendment) (EU Exit) Regulations 2019, SI 2019/710, reg 16, with effect from immediately before IP completion day (and the effect of the amendment has been incorporated in the text set out above).

Para 10: substituted by SI 2017/488, art 10(1), (3)(e), as from 1 April 2017 (certain purposes), and as from 3 January 2018 (otherwise) (for details, see the first note relating to the 2017 Order above). Words in square brackets substituted by SI 2018/1403, reg 4(1), (3)(d), as from IP completion day (as defined in the European Union (Withdrawal Agreement) Act 2020, s 39).

Para 11: added by SI 2017/488, art 10(1), (3)(f), as from 1 April 2017 (certain purposes), and as from 3 January 2018 (otherwise) (for details, see the first note relating to the 2017 Order above). Words in square brackets inserted by the Recognised Auction Platforms (Amendment and Miscellaneous Provisions) Regulations 2021, SI 2021/494, reg 3(7), as from 22 April 2021.

[PART 2 ARTICLES 5 TO 8, 10 AND 11 OF THE COMMISSION REGULATION

[8.261]

Article 5

Wholesale energy products that must be physically settled

(1) For the purposes of [paragraphs 6 and 7 of Part 1 of Schedule 2 to this Order], a wholesale energy product must be physically settled where all the following conditions are satisfied:

(a) it contains provisions which ensure that parties to the contract have proportionate arrangements in place to be able to make or take delivery of the underlying commodity; a balancing agreement with the Transmission System Operator in the area of electricity and gas shall be considered a proportionate arrangement where the parties to the agreement have to ensure physical delivery of electricity or gas.

(b) it establishes unconditional, unrestricted and enforceable obligations of the parties to the contract to deliver and take delivery of the underlying commodity;

(c) it does not allow either party to replace physical delivery with cash settlement;

(d) the obligations under the contract cannot be offset against obligations from other contracts between the parties concerned, without prejudice to the rights of the parties to the contract, to net their cash payment obligations.

For the purposes of point (d), operational netting in power and gas markets shall not be considered as offsetting of obligations under a contract against obligations from other contracts.

(2) Operational netting shall be understood as any nomination of quantities of power and gas to be fed into a gridwork upon being so required by the rules or requests of a Transmission System Operator as defined in Article 2(4) of Directive 2009/72/EC of the European Parliament and of the Council for an entity performing an equivalent function to a Transmission System Operator at the national level. Any nomination of quantities based on operational netting shall not be at the discretion of the parties to the contract.

(3) For the purposes of [paragraphs 6 and 7 of Part 1 of Schedule 2 to this Order], force majeure shall include any exceptional event or a set of circumstances which are outside the control of the parties to the contract, which the parties to the contract could not have reasonably foreseen or avoided by the exercise of appropriate and reasonable due diligence and which prevent one or both parties to the contract from fulfilling their contractual obligations.

(4) For the purposes of [paragraphs 6 and 7 of Part 1 of Schedule 2 to this Order] bona fide inability to settle shall include any event or set of circumstances, not qualifying as force majeure as referred to in paragraph 3, which are objectively and expressly defined in the contract terms, for one or both parties to the contract, acting in good faith, not to fulfil their contractual obligations.

(5) The existence of force majeure or bona fide inability to settle provisions shall not prevent a contract from being considered as 'physically settled' for the purposes of [paragraphs 6 and 7 of Part 1 of Schedule 2 to this Order].

(6) The existence of default clauses providing that a party is entitled to financial compensation in the case of non- or defective performance of the contract shall not prevent the contract from being considered as 'physically settled' within the meaning of [paragraphs 6 and 7 of Part 1 of Schedule 2 to this Order].

(7) The delivery methods for the contracts being considered as 'physically settled' within the meaning of [paragraphs 6 and 7 of Part 1 of Schedule 2 to this Order] shall include at least:

(a) physical delivery of the relevant commodities themselves;

(b) delivery of a document giving rights of an ownership nature to the relevant commodities or the relevant quantity of the commodities concerned;

(c) other methods of bringing about the transfer of rights of an ownership nature in relation to the relevant quantity of goods without physically delivering them including notification, scheduling or nomination to the operator of an energy supply network, that entitles the recipient to the relevant quantity of the goods.

Article 6
Energy derivative contracts relating to oil and coal and wholesale energy products

(1) For the purposes of [paragraph 6 of Part 1 of Schedule 2 to this Order], energy derivative contracts relating to oil shall be contracts with mineral oil, of any description and petroleum gases, whether in liquid or vapour form, including products, components and derivatives of oil and oil transport fuels, including those with biofuel additives, as an underlying.

(2) For the purposes of [paragraph 6 of Part 1 of Schedule 2 to this Order], energy derivative contracts relating to coal shall be contracts with coal, defined as a black or dark-brown combustible mineral substance consisting of carbonised vegetable matter, used as a fuel, as an underlying.

(3) For the purposes of [paragraphs 6 and 7 of Schedule 2 to this Order] derivative contracts that have the characteristics of wholesale energy products as defined in Article 2(4) of Regulation (EU) 1227/2011 of the European Parliament and Council shall be derivatives with electricity or natural gas as an underlying, in accordance with points (b) and (d) of Article 2(4) of that Regulation.

Article 7
Other derivative financial instruments

(1) For the purposes of [paragraph 7 of Part 1 of Schedule 2 to this Order], a contract which is not a spot contract in accordance with paragraph 2 and which is not for commercial purposes as laid down in paragraph 4 shall be considered as having the characteristics of other derivative financial instruments where it satisfies the following conditions:

(a) it meets one of the following criteria:

[(i) it is traded on a third country trading venue which is a regulated market, an MTF or an OTF (as defined by Article 2(1)(13), (14) and (15) respectively of the markets in financial instruments regulation);]

(ii) it is expressly stated to be traded on, or is subject to the rules of, [a UK regulated market, a UK MTF, a UK OTF (as defined by Article 2(1)(13A), (14A) and (15A) respectively of the markets in financial instruments regulation)] or such a third country trading venue;

(iii) it is equivalent to a contract traded on [a UK regulated market, a UK MTF, a UK OTF] or such a third country trading venue, with regards to the price, the lot, the delivery date and other contractual terms;

(b) it is standardised so that the price, the lot, the delivery date and other terms are determined principally by reference to regularly published prices, standard lots or standard delivery dates.

(2) A spot contract for the purposes of paragraph 1 shall be a contract for the sale of a commodity, asset or right, under the terms of which delivery is scheduled to be made within the longer of the following periods:

(a) 2 trading days;

(b) the period generally accepted in the market for that commodity, asset or right as the standard delivery period.

A contract shall not be considered a spot contract where, irrespective of its explicit terms, there is an understanding between the parties to the contract that delivery of the underlying is to be postponed and not to be performed within the period referred to in paragraph 2.

(3) For the purposes of [paragraph 10 of Part 1 of Schedule 2 to this Order], a derivative contract relating to an underlying referred to in that Section or in Article 8 of this Regulation shall be considered to have the characteristics of other derivative financial instruments where one of the following conditions is satisfied:

(a) it is settled in cash or may be settled in cash at the option of one or more of the parties, otherwise than by reason of a default or other termination event;

(b) it is traded on a regulated market, an MTF, an OTF . . . ;

(c) the conditions laid down in paragraph 1 are satisfied in relation to that contract.

(4) A contract shall be considered to be for commercial purposes for the purposes of [paragraph 7 of Part 1 of Schedule 2 to this Order], and as not having the characteristics of other derivative financial instruments for the purposes of [paragraphs 7 and 10 of Part 1 of Schedule 2 to this Order], where the following conditions are both met:

(a) it is entered into with or by an operator or administrator of an energy transmission grid, energy balancing mechanism or pipeline network,

(b) it is necessary to keep in balance the supplies and uses of energy at a given time, including the case when the reserve capacity contracted by an electricity transmission system operator as defined in [Article 5(8)] is being transferred from one prequalified balancing service provider to another prequalified balancing service provider with the consent of the relevant transmission system operator.

Article 8
Derivatives under [paragraph 10 of Part 1 of Schedule 2]

In addition to derivative contracts expressly referred to in [paragraph 10 of Part 1 of Schedule 2 to this Order], a derivative contract shall be subject to the provisions in [that Part] where it meets the criteria set out in [that Part] and in Article 7(3) of this Regulation and it relates to any of the following:

(a) telecommunications bandwidth;
(b) commodity storage capacity;
(c) transmission or transportation capacity relating to commodities, whether cable, pipeline or other means with the exception of transmission rights related to electricity transmission cross zonal capacities when they are, on the primary market, entered into with or by a transmission system operator or any persons acting as service providers on their behalf and in order to allocate the transmission capacity;
(d) an allowance, credit, permit, right or similar asset which is directly linked to the supply, distribution or consumption of energy derived from renewable resources, except if the contract is already with the scope of [paragraph 4 of Part 1 of Schedule 2 to this Order];
(e) a geological, environmental or other physical variable, except if the contract is relating to any [emission allowances referred to in paragraph 11 of Part 1 of Schedule 2 to this Order];
(f) any other asset or right of a fungible nature, other than a right to receive a service, that is capable of being transferred;
(g) an index or measure related to the price or value of, or volume of transactions in any asset, right, service or obligation;
(h) an index or measure based on actuarial statistics.

Article 10
Characteristics of other derivative contracts relating to currencies

(1) For the purposes of [paragraph 4 of Part 1 of Schedule 2 to this Order], other derivative contracts relating to a currency shall not be a financial instrument where the contract is one of the following:

(a) a spot contract within the meaning of paragraph 2 of this Article,
(b) a means of payment that:
  (i) must be settled physically otherwise than by reason of a default or other termination event;
  (ii) is entered into by at least a person which is not a financial counterparty within the meaning of Article 2(8) of Regulation (EU) No 648/2012 of the European Parliament and of the Council;
  (iii) is entered into in order to facilitate payment for identifiable goods, services or direct investment; and
  (iv) is not traded on a trading venue.

(2) A spot contract for the purposes of paragraph 1 shall be a contract for the exchange of one currency against another currency, under the terms of which delivery is scheduled to be made within the longer of the following periods:

(a) 2 trading days in respect of any pair of the major currencies set out in paragraph 3;
(b) for any pair of currencies where at least one currency is not a major currency, the longer of 2 trading days or the period generally accepted in the market for that currency pair as the standard delivery period;
(c) where the contract for the exchange of those currencies is used for the main purpose of the sale or purchase of a transferable security or a unit in a collective investment undertaking, the period generally accepted in the market for the settlement of that transferable security or a unit in a collective investment undertaking as the standard delivery period or 5 trading days, whichever is shorter.

A contract shall not be considered a spot contract where, irrespective of its explicit terms, there is an understanding between the parties to the contract that delivery of the currency is to be postponed and not to be performed within the period set out in the first subparagraph.

(3) The major currencies for the purposes of paragraph 2 shall only include the US dollar, Euro, Japanese yen, Pound sterling, Australian dollar, Swiss franc, Canadian dollar, Hong Kong dollar, Swedish krona, New Zealand dollar, Singapore dollar, Norwegian krone, Mexican peso, Croatian kuna, Bulgarian lev, Czech koruna, Danish krone, Hungarian forint, Polish zloty and Romanian leu.

(4) For the purposes of paragraph 2, a trading day shall mean any day of normal trading in the jurisdiction of both the currencies that are exchanged pursuant to the contract for the exchange of those currencies and in the jurisdiction of a third currency where any of the following conditions are met:

(a) the exchange of those currencies involves converting them through that third currency for the purposes of liquidity;
(b) the standard delivery period for the exchange of those currencies references the jurisdiction of that third currency.

Article 11

Money-market instruments

[(1)] Money-market instruments . . . shall include treasury bills, certificates of deposits, commercial papers and other instruments with substantively equivalent features where they have the following characteristics:

(a) they have a value that can be determined at any time;

(b) they are not derivatives;

(c) they have a maturity at issuance of 397 days or less.

[(2) For the purposes of this Article, "money market instruments" means those classes of instruments which are normally dealt with on the money market, such as treasury bills, certificates of deposit and commercial papers and excluding instruments of payment.]]

NOTES

Originally substituted as noted to Part 1 at **[8.260]**.

This Part was further substituted by the Financial Services and Markets Act 2000 (Regulated Activities) (Amendment) Order 2017, SI 2017/488, art 10(1), (4), as from 1 April 2017 (for the purposes of (i) enabling applications to be made for a Part 4A permission, for a variation of a Part 4A permission or for an approval under FSMA 2000, s 59, or (ii) enabling such applications to be determined, in relation to any specified activity or any specified investment amended or inserted by the 2017 Order), and as from 3 January 2018 (otherwise).

All amendments to this Part were made by the Markets in Financial Instruments (Amendment) (EU Exit) Regulations 2018, SI 2018/1403, reg 4(1), (4), as from IP completion day (as defined in the European Union (Withdrawal Agreement) Act 2020, s 39). Note that reg 4(4) of the 2018 Regulations was amended by the Financial Services (Miscellaneous) (Amendment) (EU Exit) Regulations 2019, SI 2019/710, reg 16, with effect from immediately before IP completion day (and the effect of the amendments has been incorporated in the text set out above).

[PART 3 SECTION A OF ANNEX I TO THE MARKETS IN FINANCIAL INSTRUMENTS DIRECTIVE

INVESTMENT SERVICES AND ACTIVITIES

[8.262]

1. Reception and transmission of orders in relation to one or more financial instruments.

2. Execution of orders on behalf of clients.

3. Dealing on own account.

4. Portfolio management.

5. Investment advice.

6. Underwriting of financial instruments and/or placing of financial instruments on a firm commitment basis.

7. Placing of financial instruments without a firm commitment basis.

8. Operation of [an MTF].]

[**9.** Operation of an OTF.]

NOTES

Substituted as noted to Part 1 at **[8.260]**.

Words in square brackets in para 8 substituted, and para 9 added, by the Financial Services and Markets Act 2000 (Regulated Activities) (Amendment) Order 2017, SI 2017/488, art 10(5), as from 1 April 2017 (for the purposes of (i) enabling applications to be made for a Part 4A permission, for a variation of a Part 4A permission or for an approval under FSMA 2000, s 59, or (ii) enabling such applications to be determined, in relation to any specified activity or any specified investment amended or inserted by the 2017 Order), and as from 3 January 2018 (otherwise).

[PART 3A ANCILLARY SERVICES

[8.263]

(1) Safekeeping and administration of financial instruments for the account of clients, including custodianship and related services such as cash or collateral management and excluding providing and maintaining securities accounts at the top-tier level ("central maintenance service") referred to in point (2) of Section A of the Annex to the Regulation (EU) No 909/2014 of the European Parliament and of the Council on improving securities settlement in the European Union and on central securities depositories.

(2) Granting credits or loans to an investor to allow the investor to carry out a transaction in one or more financial instruments, where the firm granting the credit or loan is involved in the transaction.

(3) Advice to undertakings on capital structure, industrial strategy and related matters and advice and services relating to mergers and the purchase of undertakings.

(4) Foreign exchange services where these are connected to the provision of investment services.

(5) Investment research and financial analysis or other forms of general recommendation relating to transactions in financial instruments.

(6) Services relating to underwriting.

(7) Investment services and activities included in Part 3 of this Schedule as well as ancillary services of the type included in this Part related to the underlying of the derivatives included in paragraphs 5, 6, 7 or 10 of Part 1 of this Schedule where these are connected to the provision of investment or ancillary services.]

NOTES

Commencement: IP completion day (as defined in the European Union (Withdrawal Agreement) Act 2020, s 39).

Inserted by the Markets in Financial Instruments (Amendment) (EU Exit) Regulations 2018, SI 2018/1403, reg 4(1), (5), as from IP completion day (as defined in the European Union (Withdrawal Agreement) Act 2020, s 39).

[PART 4 ARTICLE 9 OF THE COMMISSION REGULATION

[8.264]

Article 9
Investment advice

[For the purposes of the list of investment services and activities in Part 3 of this Schedule, "investment advice" means the provision of personal recommendations to a client, either upon its request or at the initiative of the investment firm, in respect of one or more transactions relating to financial instruments. For these purposes], a personal recommendation shall be considered a recommendation that is made to a person in his capacity as an investor or potential investor, or in his capacity as an agent for an investor or potential investor.

That recommendation shall be presented as suitable for that person, or shall be based on a consideration of the circumstances of that person, and shall constitute a recommendation to take one of the following sets of steps:

(a) to buy, sell, subscribe for, exchange, redeem, hold or underwrite a particular financial instrument;
(b) to exercise or not to exercise any right conferred by a particular financial instrument to buy, sell, subscribe for, exchange, or redeem a financial instrument.

A recommendation shall not be considered a personal recommendation if it is issued exclusively to the public.]

NOTES

Originally substituted as noted to Part 1 at **[8.260]**.

This Part was further substituted by the Financial Services and Markets Act 2000 (Regulated Activities) (Amendment) Order 2017, SI 2017/488, art 10(6), as from 1 April 2017 (for the purposes of (i) enabling applications to be made for a Part 4A permission, for a variation of a Part 4A permission or for an approval under FSMA 2000, s 59, or (ii) enabling such applications to be determined, in relation to any specified activity or any specified investment amended or inserted by the 2017 Order), and as from 3 January 2018 (otherwise).

Words in square brackets substituted by the Markets in Financial Instruments (Amendment) (EU Exit) Regulations 2018, SI 2018/1403, reg 4(1), (6), as from IP completion day (as defined in the European Union (Withdrawal Agreement) Act 2020, s 39).

[PART 5 INTERPRETATION

[8.265]

Any expression in this Schedule which is used in the markets in financial instruments regulation (as amended by the Markets in Financial Instruments (Amendment) (EU Exit) Regulations 2018) has the same meaning as in the Regulation.]

NOTES

Commencement: IP completion day (as defined in the European Union (Withdrawal Agreement) Act 2020, s 39).

Added by the Markets in Financial Instruments (Amendment) (EU Exit) Regulations 2018, SI 2018/1403, reg 4(1), (7), as from IP completion day (as defined in the European Union (Withdrawal Agreement) Act 2020, s 39).

[SCHEDULE 3
EXEMPTIONS FROM THE DEFINITION OF "INVESTMENT FIRM"

Article 3(1)

PART 1

[8.266]

1. The following persons are excluded from the definition of "investment firm"—

(a) the society incorporated by Lloyd's Act 1871 known by the name of Lloyd's;
(b) an authorised person with a Part 4A permission to carry on the regulated activity of—
  (i) effecting or carrying out contracts of insurance under article 10;
  (ii) insurance risk transformation under article 13A;
  (iii) managing the underwriting capacity of a Lloyd's syndicate under article 57,

  when carrying on those activities (and any other activities permitted by rules made by the FCA or the PRA under the Act);
(ba) a person which is a third country insurance or reinsurance undertaking (as defined by regulation 2(1) of the Solvency 2 Regulations 2015, as those regulations have been amended under the European Union (Withdrawal) Act 2018) where the undertaking is transferring risk to a transformer vehicle, provided that the assumption of risk by that vehicle is a specified kind of activity within Article 13A of this Order;
(c) a person ("P") providing investment services exclusively for P's parent undertakings, for P's subsidiaries or for other subsidiaries of P's parent undertakings;
(d) a person providing an investment service where that service is provided in an incidental manner in the course of a professional activity and that activity is regulated by legal or regulatory provisions or a code of ethics governing the profession which do not exclude the provision of that service;
(e) a person dealing on own account in financial instruments other than commodity derivatives or emission allowances or derivatives thereof and not providing any other investment services or performing any other investment activities in financial instruments other than commodity derivatives or emission allowances or derivatives thereof unless such persons—
  (i) are market makers;
  (ii) are members of or participants in a regulated market or an MTF, on the one hand, or have direct electronic access to a trading venue, on the other hand, except for non-financial entities who execute transactions on a trading venue which are objectively measurable as reducing risks directly relating to the commercial activity or treasury financing activity of those non-financial entities or their groups;

(iii) apply a high-frequency algorithmic trading technique; or
(iv) deal on own account when executing client orders;

(f) an operator (within the meaning of regulation 3(2) of the Greenhouse Gas Emissions Trading Scheme Regulations 2012), subject to compliance obligations under those Regulations who, when dealing in emission allowances, does not execute client orders and does not provide any investment services or perform any investment activities other than dealing on own account, provided that the operator does not apply a high-frequency algorithmic trading technique;

(g) a person providing investment services consisting exclusively in the administration of employee-participation schemes;

(h) a person ("P") providing investment services which only involve both the administration of employee-participation schemes and the provision of investment services exclusively for P's parent undertakings, for P's subsidiaries or for other subsidiaries of P's parent undertakings;

(i) the Treasury, the Bank of England and other public bodies charged with or intervening in the management of the public debt in the United Kingdom or members of the European System of Central Banks;

(j) a collective investment undertaking, pension fund or a depositary or manager of such an undertaking or fund;

(k) a person ("P")—
(i) dealing on own account, including a market maker, in commodity derivatives or emission allowances or derivatives thereof, excluding a person who deals on own account when executing client orders; or
(ii) providing investment services, other than dealing on own account, in commodity derivatives or emission allowances or derivatives thereof to the customers or suppliers of P's main business,

provided that in each case the activity in (i) or (ii), considered both individually and on an aggregate basis, is an ancillary activity to P's main business, when considered on a group basis, and where paragraph 2 applies;

(l) a person who provides investment advice in the course of providing another professional activity which is not an investment service or activity provided that the provision of such advice is not specifically remunerated;

(m) associations set up by Danish and Finnish pension funds with the sole aim of managing the assets of pension funds that are members of those associations;

(n) agenti di cambio whose activities and functions are governed by Article 201 of Italian Legislative Decree No 58 of 24 February 1998;

(o) subject to paragraph 3, transmission system operators within the meaning of Article 2(4) of Directive 2009/72/EC and Article 2(4) of Directive 2009/73/EC when carrying out their tasks under the law of the United Kingdom or part of the United Kingdom relied on by the United Kingdom immediately before IP completion day to implement Directive 2009/72/EC or 2009/73/EC, under Regulation (EC) No 714/2009, under Regulation (EC) No 715/2009 or under network codes or guidelines adopted pursuant to those Regulations, any persons acting as service providers on their behalf to carry out their task under those legislative acts or under network codes or guidelines adopted pursuant to those Regulations, and any operator or administrator of an energy balancing mechanism, pipeline network or system to keep in balance the supplies and uses of energy when carrying out such tasks;

(p) central securities depositories as defined in point (1) of Article 2(1) of Regulation (EU) 909/2014 on the European Parliament and of the Council on improving securities settlement in the European Union and on central securities depositories, except as provided for in Article 73 of that Regulation.

2. This paragraph applies if—

(a) P's main business is not—
(i) the provision of investment services;
(ii) banking activities requiring permission under Part 4A of the Act (or banking activities which would require such permission if they were carried on in the United Kingdom); or
(iii) acting as a market-maker in relation to commodity derivatives;

(b) P does not apply a high-frequency algorithmic trading technique; and

(c) P notifies the FCA under regulation 47 of the Financial Services and Markets Act 2000 (Markets in Financial Instruments) Regulations 2017 that P makes use of this exemption and reports to the FCA, upon request, the basis on which P considers that P's activity under points (i) and (ii) is ancillary to P's main business.

3. The exemption in paragraph 1(p)—

(a) only applies to the persons engaged in the activities set out in that sub-paragraph where they perform investment activities or provide investment services relating to commodity derivatives in order to carry out those activities;

(b) does not apply with regard to the operation of a secondary market, including a platform for secondary trading in financial transmission rights.

4. References in this Schedule to "regulated markets", "MTFs" and "trading venues" are to "UK regulated markets", "UK MTFs" and "UK trading venues" within the meaning of Article 2(1)(13A), (14A) and (16A) respectively of the markets in financial instruments regulation.

5. Any expression used in this Part of this Schedule which is used in the markets in financial instruments regulation (as amended by the Markets in Financial Instruments (Amendment) (EU Exit) Regulations 2018) has the same meaning as in the regulation.]

NOTES

Commencement: IP completion day (as defined in the European Union (Withdrawal Agreement) Act 2020, s 39).

Substituted by the Markets in Financial Instruments (Amendment) (EU Exit) Regulations 2018, SI 2018/1403, reg 4(1), (8), as from IP completion day (as defined in the European Union (Withdrawal Agreement) Act 2020, s 39). Note reg 4(8) of the 2018 Regulations was amended by the Financial Services (Miscellaneous) (Amendment) (EU Exit) Regulations 2019, SI 2019/710, reg 16, and by the Risk Transformation and Solvency 2 (Amendment) (EU Exit) Regulations 2019, SI 2019/1233, reg 3 (with effect from immediately before IP completion day); and the effect of the amendments has been incorporated in the text set out above.

[PART 2 PROVISION OF INVESTMENT SERVICE IN AN INCIDENTAL MANNER

[8.267]

6. For the purpose of the exemption in paragraph 1(d), an investment service shall be deemed to be provided in an incidental manner in the course of a professional activity where the following conditions are satisfied—

(a) a close and factual connection exists between the professional activity and the provision of the investment service to the same client, such that the investment service can be regarded as accessory to the main professional activity;

(b) the provision of investment services to the clients of the main professional activity does not aim to provide a systematic source of income to the person providing the professional activity; and

(c) the persons providing the professional activity do not market or otherwise promote their ability to provide investment services, except where these are disclosed to clients as being accessory to the main professional activity.]

NOTES

Commencement: IP completion day (as defined in the European Union (Withdrawal Agreement) Act 2020, s 39).

Substituted by the Markets in Financial Instruments (Amendment) (EU Exit) Regulations 2018, SI 2018/1403, reg 4(1), (8), as from IP completion day (as defined in the European Union (Withdrawal Agreement) Act 2020, s 39). Note reg 4(8) of the 2018 Regulations was amended by the Financial Services (Miscellaneous) (Amendment) (EU Exit) Regulations 2019, SI 2019/710, reg 16, and by the Risk Transformation and Solvency 2 (Amendment) (EU Exit) Regulations 2019, SI 2019/1233, reg 3 (with effect from immediately before IP completion day); and the effect of the amendments has been incorporated in the text set out above.

[SCHEDULE 4
RELEVANT TEXT OF THE INSURANCE DISTRIBUTION DIRECTIVE

Article 4

PART 1 ARTICLE 1.3

[8.268]

"This Directive shall not apply to ancillary insurance intermediaries carrying out insurance distribution activities where all the following conditions are met—

(a) the insurance is complementary to the good or service supplied by a provider, where such insurance covers—

(i) the risk of breakdown, loss of, or damage to, the good or the non-use of the service supplied by that provider; or

(ii) damage to, or loss of, baggage and other risks linked to travel booked with that provider;

(b) the amount of the premium paid for the insurance product does not exceed EUR 600 calculated on a *pro rata* annual basis;

(c) by way of derogation from point (b), where the insurance is complementary to a service referred to in point (a) and the duration of that service is equal to, or less than, three months, the amount of the premium paid per person does not exceed EUR 200."]

NOTES

Originally added by the Financial Services and Markets Act 2000 (Regulated Activities) (Amendment) (No 2) Order 2003, SI 2003/1476, art 12, as from 31 October 2004 (in so far as relating to contracts of long-term care insurance), and as from 14 January 2005 (otherwise).

Subsequently substituted by the Insurance Distribution (Regulated Activities and Miscellaneous Amendments) Order 2018, SI 2018/546, arts 2, 8, as from 1 October 2018.

[PART 2 ARTICLE 2.1(1)

[8.269]

"For the purposes of this Directive "insurance distribution" means the activities of advising on, proposing, or carrying out other work preparatory to the conclusion of contracts of insurance, of concluding such contracts, or of assisting in the administration and performance of such contracts, in particular in the event of a claim, including the provision of information concerning one or more insurance contracts in accordance with criteria selected by customers through a website or other media and the compilation of an insurance product ranking list, including price and product comparison, or a discount on the price of an insurance contract, when the customer is able to directly or indirectly conclude an insurance contract using a website or other media."]

NOTES

Originally added, and subsequently substituted, as noted to Part 1 of this Schedule at **[8.268]**.

[PART 3 ARTICLE 2.1(2)

[8.270]

"For the purposes of this Directive "reinsurance distribution" means the activities of advising on, proposing, or carrying out other work preparatory to the conclusion of contracts of reinsurance, of concluding such contracts, or of assisting in the administration and performance of such contracts, in particular in the event of a claim, including when carried out by a reinsurance undertaking without the intervention of a reinsurance intermediary."]

NOTES

Originally added, and subsequently substituted, as noted to Part 1 of this Schedule at **[8.268]**.

[PART 4 ARTICLE 2.1(4)

[8.271]

"“ancillary insurance intermediary” means any natural or legal person, other than a credit institution or an investment firm as defined in points (1) and (2) of Article 4(1) of Regulation (EU) No 575/2013 of the European Parliament and of the Council, who, for remuneration, takes up or pursues the activity of insurance distribution on an ancillary basis, provided that all the following conditions are met—

(a) the principal professional activity of that natural or legal person is other than insurance distribution;

(b) the natural or legal person only distributes certain insurance products that are complementary to a good or service;

(c) the insurance products concerned do not cover life assurance or liability risks, unless that cover complements the good or service which the intermediary provides as its principal professional activity."]

NOTES

Originally added, and subsequently substituted, as noted to Part 1 of this Schedule at **[8.268]**.

[PART 5 ARTICLE 2.2

[8.272]

"For the purposes of points (1) and (2) of paragraph 1, the following shall not be considered to constitute insurance distribution or reinsurance distribution—

(a) the provision of information on an incidental basis in the context of another professional activity where—

(i) the provider does not take any additional steps to assist in concluding or performing an insurance contract;

(ii) the purpose of that activity is not to assist the customer in concluding or performing a reinsurance contract;

(b) the management of claims of an insurance undertaking or of a reinsurance undertaking on a professional basis, and loss adjusting and expert appraisal of claims;

(c) the mere provision of data and information on potential policyholders to insurance intermediaries, reinsurance intermediaries, insurance undertakings or reinsurance undertakings where the provider does not take any additional steps to assist in the conclusion of an insurance or reinsurance contract;

(d) the mere provision of information about insurance or reinsurance products, an insurance intermediary, a reinsurance intermediary, an insurance undertaking or a reinsurance undertaking to potential policyholders where the provider does not take any additional steps to assist in the conclusion of an insurance or reinsurance contract."]

NOTES

Originally added, and subsequently substituted, as noted to Part 1 of this Schedule at **[8.268]**.

[PART 6 MODIFICATIONS OF ARTICLE 1.3, 2.1(2) AND (4) AND 2.2

[8.273]

(1) This Part has effect for the purposes of article 4(5).

(2) Article 2.1(2) of the insurance distribution directive has effect—

(a) as if "within the meaning of the Financial Services and Markets Act 2000" were inserted after "a reinsurance undertaking", and

(b) as if "within the meaning given by article 33B(4) of the Financial Services and Markets Act 2000 (Regulated Activities) Order 2001" were inserted after "a reinsurance intermediary".

(3) Article 2.1(4) of the insurance distribution directive has effect as if "within the meaning of the Financial Services and Markets Act 2000" were substituted for "as defined in points (1) and (2) of Article 4(1) of Regulation (EU) No 575/2013 of the European Parliament and of the Council".

(4) Article 2.2 of the insurance distribution directive has effect as if, as the end, there were inserted—

"In points (b), (c) and (d) "insurance undertaking" and "reinsurance undertaking" have the same meaning as in the Financial Services and Markets Act 2000."]

NOTES

Commencement: IP completion day (as defined in the European Union (Withdrawal Agreement) Act 2020, s 39).

Added by the Financial Services and Markets Act 2000 (Amendment) (EU Exit) Regulations 2019, SI 2019/632, regs 120, 160, as from IP completion day (as defined in the European Union (Withdrawal Agreement) Act 2020, s 39).

[SCHEDULE 4A

MEANING OF "BORROWER" IN RELATION TO GREEN DEAL CREDIT AGREEMENTS

Article 60LB

[8.274]

Article of this Order	*References to "borrower" are to be read as references to the—*
Article 36B	improver
Article 36H	improver
Article 36J	improver
Article 39D	current bill payer previous bill payer
Article 39E	current bill payer previous bill payer

Article of this Order	*References to "borrower" are to be read as references to the—*
Article 39M	current bill payer previous bill payer
Article 60C	improver
Article 60H	improver
Article 60L, so far as relating to definitions of "deposit" and "security"	improver
Article 60LA	improver first bill payer current bill payer previous bill payer
Article 60M	improver first bill payer current bill payer previous bill payer]

NOTES

Inserted by the Financial Services and Markets Act 2000 (Regulated Activities) (Green Deal) (Amendment) Order 2014, SI 2014/1850, arts 2, 11, as from 15 July 2014.

SCHEDULES 5, 6

(Schedule 5 (Specified Benchmarks) was originally added by the Financial Services and Markets Act 2000 (Regulated Activities) (Amendment) Order 2013, SI 2013/655, arts 4, 6, as from 2 April 2013, and was subsequently substituted by the Financial Services and Markets Act 2000 (Regulated Activities) (Amendment) Order 2015, SI 2015/369, art 3, as from 1 April 2015. It was revoked by the Financial Services and Markets Act 2000 (Benchmarks) Regulations 2018, SI 2018/135, reg 53, as from 1 May 2020 (subject to transitional provisions in Part 7 of those Regulations). Schedule 6 (Functions Included in the Activity of Managing a UCITS: Annex II to the UCITS Directive) was originally added by the Alternative Investment Fund Managers Regulations 2013, SI 2013/1773, reg 81, Sch 2, Part 1, para 1(1), (17), as from 22 July 2013. It was subsequently revoked by the Financial Services and Markets Act 2000 (Amendment) (EU Exit) Regulations 2019, SI 2019/632, regs 120, 132(5), as from IP completion day (as defined in the European Union (Withdrawal Agreement) Act 2020, s 39).)

[SCHEDULE 7
ADDITIONAL ACTIVITIES INCLUDED IN THE ACTIVITY OF MANAGING AN AIF LISTED IN PARAGRAPH 2 OF ANNEX I TO THE ALTERNATIVE INVESTMENT FUND MANAGERS DIRECTIVE

Article 51ZC

[8.275]

(a) Administration—

(i) legal and fund management accounting services;
(ii) customer inquiries;
(iii) valuation and pricing, including tax returns;
(iv) regulatory compliance monitoring;
(v) maintenance of unit-/shareholder register;
(vi) distribution of income;
(vii) unit/shares issues and redemptions;
(viii) contract settlements, including certificate dispatch;
(ix) record keeping:

(b) Marketing;

(c) Activities related to the assets of AIFs, namely services necessary to meet the fiduciary duties of the AIFM, facilities management, real estate administration activities, advice to undertakings on capital structure, industrial strategy and related matters, advice and services related to mergers and the purchase of undertakings and other services connected to the management of the AIF and the companies and other assets in which it has invested.]

NOTES

Added by the Alternative Investment Fund Managers Regulations 2013, SI 2013/1773, reg 81, Sch 2, Part 1, para 1(1), (17), as from 22 July 2013.

[SCHEDULE 8
PERSONS EXCLUDED FROM REGULATED ACTIVITY OF MANAGING AN AIF

Article 51ZF

[8.276]

Interpretation of this Schedule

1. Any expression used in this Schedule which is used in the alternative investment fund managers directive[, and not referred to in paragraph 1B,] has the same meaning as in that directive.

[1A. For the purposes of paragraph 1, in Article 4(1)(o) of the alternative investment fund managers directive (definition of "holding company") the reference to the Union is to be read as a reference to the United Kingdom.

1B. In this Schedule—

"parent undertaking" has the meaning given by section 1162 of the Companies Act 2006 (read with Schedule 7 to that Act);

"subsidiary" has the meaning given to "subsidiary undertaking" by that section (read with that Schedule)].

Persons excluded

2. A small registered UK AIFM, in respect of the AIFs managed by it by virtue of which it is entitled to be registered as a small registered UK AIFM (but not in respect of any other AIFs managed by it).

3. An AIFM in so far as it manages one or more AIFs whose only investors are—

(a) the AIFM,

(b) the parent undertakings of the AIFM,

(c) the subsidiaries of the AIFM, or

(d) other subsidiaries of those parent undertakings,

provided that none of the investors is an AIF.

[**4.** The trustees and managers of an occupational pension scheme within the meaning of section 1(1) of the Pension Schemes Act 1993.]

5. . . . the European Investment Bank, the European Investment Fund, a bilateral development bank, the World Bank, the International Monetary Fund, [or any other] supranational institution or similar international organisation, . . . in the event that such institution or organisation manages AIFs and in so far as those AIFs act in the public interest.

6. A national central bank.

7. A national, regional or local government or body or other institution which manages funds supporting social security and pension systems.

8. A holding company.

9. An employee participation scheme or employee savings scheme.

10. A securitisation special purpose entity.

11. *An AIFM, the registered office of which is not in [the United Kingdom][, that is registered in the United Kingdom in accordance with [Part 3 of the Alternative Investment Fund Managers Regulations 2013]].]*

NOTES

Added by the Alternative Investment Fund Managers Regulations 2013, SI 2013/1773, reg 81, Sch 2, Part 1, para 1(1), (17), as from 22 July 2013.

Para 1: words in square brackets inserted by the Financial Services and Markets Act 2000 (Amendment) (EU Exit) Regulations 2019, SI 2019/632, regs 120, 161(1), (2), as from IP completion day (as defined in the European Union (Withdrawal Agreement) Act 2020, s 39).

Paras 1A, 1B: inserted by SI 2019/632, regs 120, 161(1), (3), as from IP completion day (as defined in the European Union (Withdrawal Agreement) Act 2020, s 39).

Para 4: substituted by SI 2019/632, regs 120, 161(1), (4), as from IP completion day (as defined in the European Union (Withdrawal Agreement) Act 2020, s 39).

Para 5: words omitted revoked, and words in square brackets substituted, by SI 2019/632, regs 120, 161(1), (5), as from IP completion day (as defined in the European Union (Withdrawal Agreement) Act 2020, s 39).

Para 11: words in first pair of square brackets and third (inner) pair of square brackets substituted by SI 2019/632, regs 120, 161(1), (6), as from IP completion day (as defined in the European Union (Withdrawal Agreement) Act 2020, s 39). Words in second (outer) pair of square brackets inserted by SI 2013/1773, reg 81(2), (3), as from 22 July 2013 (for the purpose of the FCA and PRA making rules, giving directions and imposing requirements, and for the purpose of the FCA giving guidance), and as from a day to be appointed (otherwise). The whole paragraph is revoked by the Alternative Investment Fund Managers (Amendment) Regulations 2013, SI 2013/1797, reg 4, Sch 2, para 2, as from a day to be appointed.

FINANCIAL SERVICES AND MARKETS ACT 2000 (PROMOTION OF COLLECTIVE INVESTMENT SCHEMES) (EXEMPTIONS) ORDER 2001

(SI 2001/1060)

NOTES

Made: 19 March 2001.

Authority: Financial Services and Markets Act 2000, s 238(6), (7).

Commencement: 1 December 2001.

This Order is reproduced as amended by:

2001	Financial Services and Markets Act 2000 (Financial Promotion) (Amendment) Order 2001, SI 2001/2633.
2002	Financial Services and Markets Act 2000 (Financial Promotion and Miscellaneous Amendments) Order 2002, SI 2002/1310; Financial Services and Markets Act 2000 (Financial Promotion) (Amendment) (Electronic Commerce Directive) Order 2002, SI 2002/2157.
2003	Financial Services and Markets Act 2000 (Promotion of Collective Investment Schemes etc) (Exemptions) (Amendment) Order 2003, SI 2003/2067.
2005	Financial Services and Markets Act 2000 (Financial Promotion and Promotion of Collective Investment Schemes) (Miscellaneous Amendments) Order 2005, SI 2005/270; Financial Services and Markets Act 2000 (Promotion of Collective Investment Schemes) (Exemptions) (Amendment) Order 2005, SI 2005/1532; Civil Partnership Act 2004 (Amendments to Subordinate Legislation) Order 2005, SI 2005/2114.
2011	Companies Act 2006 (Consequential Amendments and Transitional Provisions) Order 2011, SI 2011/1265.

2013	Financial Services Act 2012 (Consequential Amendments and Transitional Provisions) Order 2013, SI 2013/472; Collective Investment in Transferable Securities (Contractual Scheme) Regulations 2013, SI 2013/1388; Alternative Investment Fund Managers Regulations 2013, SI 2013/1773.
2015	European Long-term Investment Funds Regulations 2015, SI 2015/1882.
2017	Packaged Retail and Insurance-based Investment Products Regulations 2017, SI 2017/1127.
2019	Collective Investment Schemes (Amendment etc) (EU Exit) Regulations 2019, SI 2019/325.

Transitional provisions in relation to Gibraltar-based firms and activities: see the Gibraltar (Miscellaneous Amendments) (EU Exit) Regulations 2019, SI 2019/680, reg 11 at **[12.129]**.

ARRANGEMENT OF ARTICLES

PART I
GENERAL AND INTERPRETATION

PART II
TERRITORIAL SCOPE

PART III
OTHER EXEMPTIONS

SCHEDULES

PART I GENERAL AND INTERPRETATION

[8.277]

1 Citation and commencement

(1) This Order may be cited as the Financial Services and Markets Act 2000 (Promotion of Collective Investment Schemes) (Exemptions) Order 2001.

(2) This Order comes into force on the day on which section 19 of the Act comes into force.

[8.278]

2 Interpretation: general

(1) In this Order—

"the Act" means the Financial Services and Markets Act 2000;

["authorised contractual scheme" and "authorised unit trust scheme" have the meaning given in section 237(3) of the Act;]

"close relative", in relation to a person means—

(a) his spouse [or civil partner];

(b) his children and step-children, his parents and step-parents, his brothers and sisters and his step-brothers and step-sisters; and

(c) the spouse [or civil partner] of any person within sub-paragraph (b);

"overseas scheme" means an unregulated scheme which is operated and managed in a country or territory outside the United Kingdom;

"publication" means—

(a) a newspaper, journal, magazine or other periodical publication;

(b) a web site [or similar system for the electronic display of information];

(c) any programme forming part of a service consisting of the broadcast or transmission of television or radio programmes; and

(d) any teletext service, that is to say a service consisting of television transmissions consisting of a succession of visual displays (with or without accompanying sound) capable of being selected and held for separate viewing or other use;

"qualifying contract of insurance" has the meaning given in the Regulated Activities Order;

"the Regulated Activities Order" means the Financial Services and Markets Act 2000 (Regulated Activities) Order 2001;

"relevant scheme activities" means—

(i) [any activity specified by article 51ZA, 51ZB, 51ZD or 51ZE] of the Regulated Activities Order; or

(ii) any activity specified by article 14, 21, 25, 37 or 53 of that Order when carried on in relation to units;

"solicited real time communication" has the meaning given by article 5;

"units" has the meaning given by section 237(2) of the Act;

"unregulated scheme" means a collective investment scheme which is not an authorised unit trust scheme [nor an authorised contractual scheme] nor a scheme constituted by an authorised open-ended investment company nor a recognised scheme for the purposes of Part XVII of the Act;

"unsolicited real time communication" has the meaning given by article 5.

(2) In this Order, any reference to the "scheme promotion restriction" means the restriction imposed by section 238(1) of the Act.

NOTES

Para (1): definitions "authorised contractual scheme" and "authorised unit trust scheme" substituted (for the original definition "authorised unit trust scheme"), and words in square brackets in the definition "unregulated scheme" inserted, by the Collective Investment in Transferable Securities (Contractual Scheme) Regulations 2013, SI 2013/1388, reg 10, as from 6 June 2013. Words in square brackets in definition "close relative" inserted by the Civil Partnership Act 2004 (Amendments to Subordinate Legislation) Order 2005, SI 2005/2114, art 2(16), Sch 16, Pt 1, para 2, as from 5 December 2005. Words in square brackets in definition "publication" inserted by the Financial Services and Markets Act 2000 (Financial Promotion and Miscellaneous Amendments) Order 2002, SI 2002/1310, art 3(1), (2), as from 5 June 2002. Words in square brackets in the definition "relevant scheme activities" substituted by the Alternative Investment Fund Managers Regulations 2013, SI 2013/1773, reg 81, Sch 2, Part 2, para 5(1), (2), as from 22 July 2013.

Step-children, etc: as to the meaning of this and related expressions, see the Civil Partnership Act 2004, s 246 (as applied to this Order by the Civil Partnership Act 2004 (Relationships Arising Through Civil Partnership) Order 2005, SI 2005/3137, art 3, Schedule).

[8.279]

3 Interpretation: communications

In this Order—

(a) any reference to a communication is a reference to the communication, by an authorised person in the course of business, of an invitation or inducement to participate in an unregulated scheme;

(b) any reference to a communication being made to another person is a reference to a communication being addressed, whether verbally or in legible form, to a particular person or persons (for example where it is contained in a telephone call or letter);

(c) any reference to a communication being directed at persons is a reference to a communication being addressed to persons generally (for example where it is contained in a television broadcast or web site);

(d) "communicate" includes causing a communication to be made;

(e) a "recipient" of a communication is a person to whom the communication is made or, in the case of a non-real time communication which is directed at persons generally, any person who reads or hears the communication;

[(f)–(h)) . . .]

NOTES

Paras (f)–(h) originally added by the Financial Services and Markets Act 2000 (Financial Promotion) (Amendment) (Electronic Commerce Directive) Order 2002, SI 2002/2157, arts 7, 8(1), as from 21 August 2002. Subsequently revoked by the Collective Investment Schemes (Amendment etc) (EU Exit) Regulations 2019, SI 2019/325, reg 50(1), (2), as from IP completion day (as defined in the European Union (Withdrawal Agreement) Act 2020, s 39).

[8.280]

4 Interpretation: real time communications

(1) In this Order, references to a real time communication are references to any communication made in the course of a personal visit, telephone conversation or other interactive dialogue.

(2) A non-real time communication is a communication not falling within paragraph (1).

(3) For the purposes of this Order, non-real time communications include communications made by letter or e-mail or contained in a publication.

(4) For the purposes of this Order, the factors in paragraph (5) are to be treated as indications that a communication is a non-real time communication.

(5) The factors are that—

(a) the communication is made to or directed at more than one recipient in identical terms (save for details of the recipient's identity);

(b) the communication is made or directed by way of a system which in the normal course constitutes or creates a record of the communication which is available to the recipient to refer to at a later time;

(c) the communication is made or directed by way of a system which in the normal course does not enable or require the recipient to respond immediately to it.

[8.281]

5 Interpretation: solicited and unsolicited real time communications

(1) A real time communication is solicited where it is made in the course of a personal visit, telephone call or other interactive dialogue if that call, visit or dialogue—

(a) was initiated by the recipient of the communication; or

(b) takes place in response to an express request from the recipient of the communication.

(2) A real time communication is unsolicited where it is made otherwise than as described in paragraph (1).

(3) For the purposes of paragraph (1)—

(a) a person is not to be treated as expressly requesting a call, visit or dialogue—

(i) because he omits to indicate that he does not wish to receive any or any further visits or calls or to engage in any or any further dialogue;

(ii) because he agrees to standard terms that state that such visits, calls or dialogue will take place, unless he has signified clearly that, in addition to agreeing to the terms, he is willing for them to take place;

(b) a communication is solicited only if it is clear from all the circumstances when the call, visit or dialogue is initiated or requested that during the course of the visit, call or dialogue communications will be made concerning the kind of activities or investments to which the communications in fact made relate;

(c) it is immaterial whether the express request is made before or after this Order comes into force.

(4) Where a real time communication is solicited by a recipient ("R"), it is treated as having also been solicited by any other person to whom it is made at the same time as it is made to R if that other recipient is—

(a) a close relative of R; or

(b) expected to participate in the unregulated scheme jointly with R.

5A *(Originally inserted by the Financial Services and Markets Act 2000 (Financial Promotion) (Amendment) (Electronic Commerce Directive) Order 2002, SI 2002/2157, arts 7, 8(2), as from 21 August 2002. Subsequently revoked by the Collective Investment Schemes (Amendment etc) (EU Exit) Regulations 2019, SI 2019/325, reg 50(1), (3), as from IP completion day (as defined in the European Union (Withdrawal Agreement) Act 2020, s 39).)*

[8.282]

6 Degree of prominence to be given to required indications

Where a communication must, if it is to fall within any provision of this Order, be accompanied by an indication of any matter, the indication must be presented to the recipient—

(a) in a way that can be easily understood; and

(b) in such manner as, depending on the means by which the communication is made or directed, is best calculated to bring the matter in question to the attention of the recipient and to allow him to consider it.

[8.283]

7 Combination of different exemptions

Nothing in this Order is to be construed as preventing a person from relying on more than one exemption in respect of the same communication.

PART II TERRITORIAL SCOPE

[8.284]

8 Communications to overseas recipients

(1) Subject to [paragraph (2)], the scheme promotion restriction does not apply to any communication—

(a) which is made (whether from inside or outside the United Kingdom) to a person who receives the communication outside the United Kingdom; or

(b) which is directed (whether from inside or outside the United Kingdom) only at persons outside the United Kingdom.

(2) Paragraph (1) does not apply to an unsolicited real time communication unless—

(a) it is made from a place outside the United Kingdom; and

(b) it relates to an overseas scheme.

(3) For the purposes of paragraph (1)(b)—

(a) if the conditions set out in paragraph (4)(a), (b), (c) and (d) are met, a communication directed from a place inside the United Kingdom is to be regarded as directed only at persons outside the United Kingdom;

(b) if the conditions set out in paragraph (4)(c) and (d) are met, a communication directed from a place outside the United Kingdom is to be regarded as directed only at persons outside the United Kingdom;

(c) in any other case where one or more of the conditions in paragraph (4)(a) to (e) are met, that fact shall be taken into account in determining whether the communication is to be regarded as directed only at persons outside the United Kingdom (but a communication may still be regarded as directed only at persons outside the United Kingdom even if none of the conditions in paragraph (4) is met).

(4) The conditions are that—

(a) the communication is accompanied by an indication that it is directed only at persons outside the United Kingdom;

(b) the communication is accompanied by an indication that it must not be acted upon by persons in the United Kingdom;

(c) the communication is not referred to in, or directly accessible from, any other communication which is made to a person or directed at persons in the United Kingdom by or on behalf of the same person;

(d) there are in place proper systems and procedures to prevent recipients in the United Kingdom (other than those to whom the communication might otherwise lawfully have been made or directed) acquiring from the person directing the communication, a close relative of his or a company in the same group, units in the scheme to which the communication relates;

(e) the communication is included in—

(i) a web site, newspaper, journal, magazine or periodical publication which is principally accessed in or intended for a market outside the United Kingdom;

(ii) a radio or television broadcast or teletext service transmitted principally for reception outside the United Kingdom.

(5) For the purposes of paragraph (1)(b), a communication may be treated as directed only at persons outside the United Kingdom even if—

(a) it is also directed, for the purposes of article 14(1)(b), at investment professionals falling within article 14(5) (but disregarding paragraph (6) of that article for this purpose);

(b) it is also directed, for the purposes of article 22(1)(b), at high net worth persons to whom article 22 applies (but disregarding paragraph (2)(e) of that article for this purpose).

(6) Where a communication falls within paragraph (5)—

(a) the condition in paragraph (4)(a) is to be construed as requiring an indication that the communication is directed only at persons outside the United Kingdom or persons having professional experience in matters relating to investments or high net worth persons (as the case may be);

(b) the condition in paragraph (4)(b) is to be construed as requiring an indication that the communication must not be acted upon by persons in the United Kingdom or by persons who do not have professional experience in matters relating to investments or who are not high net worth persons (as the case may be).

[(7) . . .]

NOTES

Para (1): words in square brackets substituted by the Collective Investment Schemes (Amendment etc) (EU Exit) Regulations 2019, SI 2019/325, reg 50(1), (4)(a), as from IP completion day (as defined in the European Union (Withdrawal Agreement) Act 2020, s 39).

Para (7): originally added by SI 2002/2157, arts 7, 9(b), as from 21 August 2002. Subsequently revoked by SI 2019/325, reg 50(1), (4)(b), as from IP completion day (as defined in the European Union (Withdrawal Agreement) Act 2020, s 39).

[8.285]

9 Solicited real time communications from overseas

The scheme promotion restriction does not apply to any solicited real time communication which is made from outside the United Kingdom and which relates to units in an overseas scheme.

[8.286]

10 Communications from overseas to previously overseas customers

(1) The scheme promotion restriction does not apply to a non-real time or unsolicited real time communication which—

(a) is made from outside the United Kingdom by an authorised person to a previously overseas customer of his; and

(b) relates to units in an overseas scheme.

(2) In this article—

"previously overseas customer" means a person with whom the authorised person has done business within the period of twelve months ending with the day on which the communication was made ("the earlier business") and where—

(a) at the time that the earlier business was done, the customer was neither resident in the United Kingdom nor had a place of business there; or

(b) at the time the earlier business was done, the authorised person had on a former occasion done business with the customer, being business of the same description as the business to which the communication relates, and on that former occasion the customer was neither resident in the United Kingdom nor had a place of business there.

(3) For the purposes of this article, an authorised person has done business with a customer if, in the course of his overseas business, he has—

(a) effected a transaction, or arranged for a transaction to be effected, with the customer in respect of units in an overseas scheme; or

(b) given, outside the United Kingdom, any advice on the merits of the customer buying or selling units in an overseas scheme.

10A *(Originally inserted by the Financial Services and Markets Act 2000 (Financial Promotion) (Amendment) (Electronic Commerce Directive) Order 2002, SI 2002/2157, arts 7, 10, as from 21 August 2002. Subsequently revoked by the Collective Investment Schemes (Amendment etc) (EU Exit) Regulations 2019, SI 2019/325, reg 50(1), (5), as from IP completion day (as defined in the European Union (Withdrawal Agreement) Act 2020, s 39).)*

PART III OTHER EXEMPTIONS

[8.287]

11 Follow up non-real time communications and solicited real time communications

(1) Where an authorised person makes or directs a communication ("the first communication") which is exempt from the scheme promotion restriction because, in compliance with the requirements of another provision of this Order, it is accompanied by certain indications or contains certain information, then the scheme promotion restriction does not apply to any subsequent communication which complies with the requirements of paragraph (2).

(2) The requirements of this paragraph are that the subsequent communication—

- (a) is a non-real time communication or a solicited real time communication;
- (b) is made by the same person who made the first communication;
- (c) is made to a recipient of the first communication;
- (d) relates to the same unregulated scheme as the first communication; and
- (e) is made within 12 months of the recipient receiving the first communication.

(3) A communication made or directed before this Order comes into force is to be treated as a first communication falling within paragraph (1) if it would have fallen within that paragraph had it been made or directed after this Order comes into force.

[8.288]

12 Introductions

(1) If the requirements of paragraph (2) are met, the scheme promotion restriction does not apply to any real time communication which is made with a view to or for the purposes of introducing the recipient to—

- (a) an authorised person who carries on one or more relevant scheme activities in relation to units in unregulated schemes; or
- (b) a person who is exempt, as a result of an exemption order made under section 38(1) of the Act, in relation to one or more relevant scheme activities.

(2) The requirements of this paragraph are that—

- (a) the maker of the communication ("A") is not a close relative of, nor a member of the same group as, the person to whom the introduction is, or is to be, made;
- (b) A does not carry on business in relevant scheme activities in relation to units in unregulated schemes;
- (c) A does not receive from any person other than the recipient any pecuniary reward or other advantage arising out of his making the introduction; and
- (d) it is clear in all the circumstances that the recipient, in his capacity as an investor, is not seeking and has not sought advice from A as to the merits of participating in an unregulated scheme (or, if the client has sought such advice, A has declined to give it, but has recommended that the recipient seek such advice from an authorised person specialising in that kind of investment).

[8.289]

13 Generic promotions

The scheme promotion restriction does not apply to any communication which—

- (a) does not relate to units of a particular unregulated scheme identified (directly or indirectly) in the communication; and
- (b) does not identify (directly or indirectly) any person who operates a collective investment scheme or sells units.

[8.290]

14 Investment professionals

(1) The scheme promotion restriction does not apply to any communication which—

- (a) is made only to recipients whom the person making the communication believes on reasonable grounds to be investment professionals; or
- (b) may reasonably be regarded as directed only at such recipients.

(2) For the purposes of paragraph (1)(b), if all the conditions set out in paragraph (4)(a) to (c) are met in relation to the communication, it is to be regarded as directed only at investment professionals.

(3) In any other case in which one or more of the conditions set out in paragraph (4)(a) to (c) are met, that fact shall be taken into account in determining whether the communication is directed only at investment professionals (but a communication may still be regarded as so directed even if none of the conditions in paragraph (4) is met).

(4) The conditions are that—

- (a) the communication is accompanied by an indication that it is directed at persons having professional experience of participating in unregulated schemes and that the units to which the communication relates are available only to such persons;
- (b) the communication is accompanied by an indication that persons who do not have professional experience in participating in unregulated schemes should not rely on it;
- (c) there are in place proper systems and procedures to prevent recipients other than investment professionals from acquiring from the person directing the communication, a close relative of his or a company in the same group, units in the scheme to which the communication relates.

(5) "Investment professionals" means—

- (a) an authorised person;
- (b) a person who is exempt, as a result of an exemption order made under section 38(1) of the Act, in relation to one or more relevant scheme activities;

(c) any other person—
  (i) whose ordinary activities involve him in participating in unregulated schemes for the purposes of a business carried on by him; or
  (ii) who it is reasonable to expect will so participate for the purposes of a business carried on by him;

(d) a government, local authority (whether in the United Kingdom or elsewhere) or an international organisation;

(e) a person ("A") who is a director, officer or employee of a person ("B") falling within any of sub-paragraphs (a) to (d), when the communication is made to A in that capacity and where A's responsibilities when acting in that capacity involve him in B's participation in unregulated schemes.

(6) For the purposes of paragraph (1), a communication is to be treated as made only to or directed only at investment professionals even if it also made to or directed at other persons to whom it may lawfully be communicated.

(7) In this article—

"government" means the government of the United Kingdom, the Scottish Administration, the Executive Committee of the Northern Ireland Assembly, the National Assembly for Wales and any government of any country or territory outside the United Kingdom;

"international organisation" means any body the members of which comprise—
  (a) states including the United Kingdom or another EEA State; or
  (b) bodies whose members comprise states including the United Kingdom or another EEA State.

NOTES

National Assembly for Wales: see further, in relation to the renaming of the National Assembly for Wales as the Senedd Cymru or the Welsh Parliament, the Senedd and Elections (Wales) Act 2020, s 2 (with effect from 6 May 2020). See also ss 3–9 of the 2020 Act in relation to the renaming of Acts of the National Assembly for Wales, Members of the National Assembly for Wales, etc.

[8.291]

15 One off non-real time communications and solicited real time communications

(1) The scheme promotion restriction does not apply to a one off communication which is either a non-real time communication or a solicited real time communication.

(2) If both the conditions set out in paragraph (3) are met in relation to a communication it is to be regarded as a one off communication. In any other case in which either of those conditions is met, that fact is to be taken into account in determining whether the communication is a one off communication (but a communication may still be regarded as a one off communication even if neither of the conditions in paragraph (3) is met).

(3) The conditions are that—

(a) the communication is made only to one recipient or only to one group of recipients in the expectation that they would engage in any investment activity jointly;

(b) the communication is not part of an organised marketing campaign.

[8.292]

[15A One off unsolicited real time communications

(1) The scheme promotion restriction does not apply to an unsolicited real time communication if the conditions in paragraph (2) are met.

(2) The conditions in this paragraph are that—

(a) the communication is a one off communication;

(b) the communicator believes on reasonable grounds that the recipient understands the risks associated with engaging in the investment activity to which the communication relates;

(c) at the time the communication is made, the communicator believes on reasonable grounds that the recipient would expect to be contacted by him in relation to the investment activity to which the communication relates.

(3) Paragraphs (2) and (3) of article 15 apply in determining whether a communication is a one off communication for the purposes of this article as they apply for the purposes of article 15.]

NOTES

Inserted by the Financial Services and Markets Act 2000 (Financial Promotion) (Amendment) Order 2001, SI 2001/2633, art 3, as from 1 December 2001.

[8.293]

16 Communications required or authorised by enactments

[(1)] The scheme promotion restriction does not apply to any communication which is required or authorised to be communicated by or under any enactment other than the Act.

(2) A communication which may be made because a condition imposed by regulation 49 or 50 of the Alternative Investment Fund Managers Regulations 2013 has been met, is to be treated as authorised by those Regulations for the purposes of paragraph (1) in so far as it is made to a professional investor (as defined in regulation 2(1) of those Regulations).

(3) A communication permitted by Article 2.2, 4 or 14.3 of Regulation (EU) No 345/2013 of the European Parliament and the Council of 17 April 2013 on European venture capital funds [as it had effect on the day on which the Collective Investment Schemes (Amendment etc) (EU Exit) Regulations 2019 were made], or by Article 2.2, 4 or 15.3 of Regulation (EU) No 346/2013 of the European Parliament and the Council of 17 April 2013 on European social entrepreneurship funds [as it had effect on the day on which the Collective Investment Schemes (Amendment etc) (EU Exit) Regulations 2019 were made], is to be treated as authorised by another enactment for the purposes of paragraph (1).]

[(4) A communication permitted by Article 30 or 31 of Regulation (EU) No 2015/760 of the European Parliament and of the Council of 29th April 2015 on European Long-term Investment Funds is to be treated as authorised by another enactment for the purposes of paragraph (1).]

NOTES

Para (1) numbered as such, and paras (2), (3) added, by the Alternative Investment Fund Managers Regulations 2013, SI 2013/1773, reg 81, Sch 2, Part 2, para 5(1), (3), as from 22 July 2013.

Words in square brackets in para (3) inserted by the Collective Investment Schemes (Amendment etc) (EU Exit) Regulations 2019, SI 2019/325, regs 33, 50(1), (6), as from 20 February 2019.

Para (4) was added by the European Long-term Investment Funds Regulations 2015, SI 2015/1882, reg 6, as from 3 December 2015.

[8.294]
17 Persons in the business of placing promotional material

The scheme promotion restriction does not apply to any communication which is made to a person whose business it is to place, or arrange for the placing of, promotional material provided that it is communicated so that he can place or arrange for placing it.

[8.295]
18 Existing participants in an unregulated scheme

The scheme promotion restriction does not apply to any communication which is—

(a) a non-real time communication or a solicited real time communication;
(b) communicated by the operator of an unregulated scheme; and
(c) communicated to persons whom the person making the communication believes on reasonable grounds to be persons who are entitled to units in that scheme.

[8.296]
19 Group companies

The scheme promotion restriction does not apply to any communication made by one body corporate in a group to another body corporate in the same group.

[8.297]
20 Persons in the business of disseminating information

(1) The scheme promotion restriction does not apply to any communication which is made only to recipients whom the person making the communication believes on reasonable grounds to be persons to whom paragraph (2) applies.

(2) This paragraph applies to—

(a) a person who receives the communication in the course of a business which involves the dissemination through a publication of information concerning investments;
(b) a person whilst acting in the capacity of director, officer or employee of a person falling within sub-paragraph (a) being a person whose responsibilities when acting in that capacity involve him in the business referred to in that sub-paragraph;
(c) any person to whom the communication may otherwise lawfully be made.

[8.298]
[21 Certified high net worth individuals

(1) If the requirements of paragraphs (4) and (7) are met, the scheme promotion restriction does not apply to any communication which—

(a) is a non-real time communication or a solicited real time communication;
(b) is made to an individual whom the person making the communication believes on reasonable grounds to be a certified high net worth individual;
(c) relates only to units falling within paragraph (8); and
(d) does not invite or induce the recipient to enter into an agreement under the terms of which he can incur a liability or obligation to pay or contribute more than he commits by way of investment.

(2) "Certified high net worth individual" means an individual who has signed, within the period of twelve months ending with the day on which the communication is made, a statement complying with Part I of the Schedule.

(3) The validity of a statement signed for the purposes of paragraph (2) is not affected by a defect in the form or wording of the statement, provided that the defect does not alter the statement's meaning and that the words shown in bold type in Part I of the Schedule are so shown in the statement.

(4) The requirements of this paragraph are that either the communication is accompanied by the giving of a warning in accordance with paragraphs (5) and (6) or, where because of the nature of the communication this is not reasonably practicable,—

(a) a warning in accordance with paragraph (5) is given to the recipient orally at the beginning of the communication together with an indication that he will receive the warning in legible form and that, before receipt of that warning, he should consider carefully any decision to participate in a collective investment scheme to which the communication relates; and
(b) a warning in accordance with paragraphs (5) and (6) (d) to (h) is sent to the recipient of the communication within two business days of the day on which the communication is made.

(5) The warning must be in the following terms—

"Reliance on this promotion for the purpose of buying the units to which the promotion relates may expose an individual to a significant risk of losing all of the property or other assets invested.".

But, where a warning is sent pursuant to paragraph (4)(b), for the words "this promotion" in both places where they occur there must be substituted wording which clearly identifies the promotion which is the subject of the warning.

(6) The warning must—

(a) be given at the beginning of the communication;
(b) precede any other written or pictorial matter;

(c) be in a font size consistent with the text forming the remainder of the communication;
(d) be indelible;
(e) be legible;
(f) be printed in black, bold type;
(g) be surrounded by a black border which does not interfere with the text of the warning; and
(h) not be hidden, obscured or interrupted by any other written or pictorial matter.

(7) The requirements of this paragraph are that the communication is accompanied by an indication—
(a) that it is exempt from the restriction on the promotion of unregulated schemes (in section 238 of the Act) on the grounds that the communication is made to a certified high net worth individual;
(b) of the requirements that must be met for an individual to qualify as a certified high net worth individual;
(c) that any individual who is in any doubt about the units to which the communication relates should consult an authorised person specialising in advising in participation in unregulated schemes.

(8) A unit falls within this paragraph if it is in an unregulated scheme which invests wholly or predominantly in the shares in or debentures of one or more unlisted companies.

(9) "Business day" means any day except a Saturday, a Sunday, Christmas Day, Good Friday or a day which is a bank holiday under the Banking and Financial Dealings Act 1971 in any part of the United Kingdom.

(10) "Unlisted company" has the meaning given in the Financial Services and Markets Act 2000 (Financial Promotion) Order 2001.]

NOTES

Substituted by the Financial Services and Markets Act 2000 (Financial Promotion and Promotion of Collective Investment Schemes) (Miscellaneous Amendments) Order 2005, SI 2005/270, art 3, Sch 2, para 1, as from 3 March 2005.

Financial Services and Markets Act 2000 (Financial Promotion) Order 2001: revoked and replaced by the Financial Services and Markets Act 2000 (Financial Promotion) Order 2005, SI 2005/1529. As to the meaning of "unlisted company", see art 3 of that Order.

[8.299]

22 High net worth companies, unincorporated associations etc

(1) The scheme promotion restriction does not apply to any communication which—
(a) is made only to recipients whom the person making the communication believes on reasonable grounds to be persons to whom paragraph (2) applies; or
(b) may reasonably be regarded as directed only at persons to whom paragraph (2) applies.

(2) This paragraph applies to—
[(a) any body corporate which has, or which is a member of the same group as an undertaking which has, a called-up share capital or net assets of not less than—
(i) if the body corporate has more than 20 members or is a subsidiary undertaking of an undertaking which has more than 20 members, £500,000;
(ii) otherwise, £5 million;]
(b) any unincorporated association or partnership which has net assets of not less than £5 million;
(c) the trustee of a high value trust;
(d) any person ("A") whilst acting in the capacity of director, officer or employee of a person ("B") falling within any of sub-paragraphs (a) to (c), where A's responsibilities, when acting in that capacity, involve him in B's participation in unregulated schemes;
(e) any person to whom the communication might otherwise lawfully be made.

(3) For the purposes of paragraph (1)(b)—
(a) if all the conditions set out in paragraph (4)(a) to (c) are met in relation to the communication, it is to be regarded as directed at persons to whom paragraph (2) applies;
(b) in any other case in which one or more of those conditions are met, that fact is to be taken into account in determining whether the communication is directed at persons to whom paragraph (2) applies (but a communication may still be regarded as so directed even if none of the conditions in paragraph (4) is met).

(4) The conditions are that—
(a) the communication includes an indication of the description of persons to whom it is directed and an indication of the fact that the units to which it relates are available only to such persons;
(b) the communication includes an indication that persons of any other description should not rely upon it;
(c) there are in place proper systems and procedures to prevent recipients other than persons to whom paragraph (2) applies from acquiring from the person directing the communication, a close relative of his or a company in the same group, units in the scheme to which the communication relates.

(5) In this article—

"called-up share capital" has the meaning given in [section 547 of the Companies Act 2006];

"high value trust" means a trust where the aggregate value of the cash and investments which form part of the trust's assets (before deducing the amount of its liabilities)—
(a) is £10 million or more; or
(b) has been £10 million or more at any time during the year immediately preceding the date on which communication in question was first made or directed;

"net assets" has the meaning given in [section 831 of the Companies Act 2006].

NOTES

Para (2): sub-para (a) substituted by the Financial Services and Markets Act 2000 (Financial Promotion and Miscellaneous Amendments) Order 2002, SI 2002/1310, art 3(1), (3), as from 5 June 2002.

Para (5): words in square brackets in the definitions "called-up share capital" and "net assets" substituted by the Companies Act 2006 (Consequential Amendments and Transitional Provisions) Order 2011, SI 2011/1265, art 14(1), (3), as from 12 May 2011.

[8.300]
23 Sophisticated investors

(1) "Certified sophisticated investor" means a person—

(a) who has a current certificate in writing or other legible form signed by an authorised person to the effect that he is sufficiently knowledgeable to understand the risks associated with participating in unregulated schemes; and

(b) who has signed, within the period of twelve months ending with the day on which the communication is made, a statement in the following terms—

"I make this statement so that I can receive promotions which are exempt from the restriction on promotion of unregulated schemes in the Financial Services and Markets Act 2000. The exemption relates to certified sophisticated investors and I declare that I qualify as such. I accept that the schemes to which the promotions will relate are not authorised or recognised for the purposes of that Act. I am aware that it is open to me to seek advice from an authorised person who specialises in advising on this kind of investment".

[(1A) The validity of a statement signed in accordance with paragraph (1)(b) is not affected by a defect in the wording of the statement, provided that the defect does not alter the statement's meaning.]

(2) If the requirements of paragraph (3) are met, the scheme promotion restriction does not apply to any communication which—

(a) is made to a certified sophisticated investor; and

(b) does not invite or induce the recipient to participate in an unregulated scheme operated by the person who has signed the certificate referred to in paragraph (1)(a) or to acquire units from that person.

(3) The requirements of this paragraph are that the communication is accompanied by an indication—

(a) that it is exempt from the scheme promotion restriction (in section 238 of the Financial Services and Markets Act 2000) on the communication of invitations or inducements to participate in unregulated schemes on the ground that it is made to a certified sophisticated investor;

(b) of the requirements that must be met for a person to qualify as a certified sophisticated investor;

(c) that buying the units to which the communication relates may expose the individual to a significant risk of losing all of the property invested;

(d) that any individual who is in any doubt about the investment to which the invitation or inducement relates should consult an authorised person specialising in advising on investments of the kind in question.

(4) For the purposes of paragraph (1)(a), a certificate is current if it is signed and dated not more than three years before the date on which the communication is made.

NOTES

Para (1A): inserted by the Financial Services and Markets Act 2000 (Financial Promotion and Promotion of Collective Investment Schemes) (Miscellaneous Amendments) Order 2005, SI 2005/270, art 3, Sch 2, para 2, as from 3 March 2005.

[8.301]
[23A Self-certified sophisticated investors

(1) "Self-certified sophisticated investor" means an individual who has signed, within the period of twelve months ending with the day on which the communication is made, a statement complying with Part II of the Schedule.

(2) The validity of a statement signed for the purposes of paragraph (1) is not affected by a defect in the form or wording of the statement, provided that the defect does not alter the statement's meaning and that the words shown in bold type in Part II of the Schedule are so shown in the statement.

(3) If the requirements of paragraphs (4) and (7) are met, the scheme promotion restriction does not apply to any communication which—

(a) is made to an individual whom the person making the communication believes on reasonable grounds to be a self-certified sophisticated investor;

(b) relates only to units falling within paragraph (8); and

(c) does not invite or induce the recipient to enter into an agreement under the terms of which he can incur a liability or obligation to pay or contribute more than he commits by way of investment.

(4) The requirements of this paragraph are—

(a) . . .

(b) that either the communication is accompanied by the giving of a warning in accordance with paragraphs (5) and (6) or, where because of the nature of the communication this is not reasonably practicable,—

(i) a warning in accordance with paragraph (5) is given to the recipient orally at the beginning of the communication together with an indication that he will receive the warning in legible form and that, before receipt of that warning, he should consider carefully any decision to participate in a collective investment scheme to which the communication relates; and

(ii) a warning in accordance with paragraphs (5) and (6) (d) to (h) is sent to the recipient of the communication within two business days of the day on which the communication is made.

(5) The warning must be in the following terms—

"Reliance on this promotion for the purpose of buying [the] units to which the promotion relates may expose an individual to a significant risk of losing all of the property or other assets invested.".

But, where a warning is sent pursuant to paragraph (4)(b), for the words "this promotion" in both places where they occur there must be substituted wording which clearly identifies the promotion which is the subject of the warning.

(6) The warning must—

(a) be given at the beginning of the communication;

(b) precede any other written or pictorial matter;

(c) be in a font size consistent with the text forming the remainder of the communication;
(d) be indelible;
(e) be legible;
(f) be printed in black, bold type;
(g) be surrounded by a black border which does not interfere with the text of the warning; and
(h) not be hidden, obscured or interrupted by any other written or pictorial matter.

(7) The requirements of this paragraph are that the communication is accompanied by an indication—
(a) that it is exempt from the scheme promotion restriction (in section 238 of the Act) on the communication of invitations or inducements to participate in unregulated schemes on the ground that it is made to a self-certified sophisticated investor;
(b) of the requirements that must be met for an individual to qualify as a self-certified sophisticated investor;
(c) that any individual who is in any doubt about the investment to which the invitation or inducement relates should consult an authorised person specialising in advising on investments of the kind in question.

(8) A unit falls within this paragraph if it is in an unregulated scheme which invests wholly or predominantly in the shares in or debentures of one or more an unlisted companies.

(9) "Business day" means any day except a Saturday, a Sunday, Christmas Day, Good Friday or a day which is a bank holiday under the Banking and Financial Dealings Act 1971 in any part of the United Kingdom.

(10) "Unlisted company" has the meaning given in the Financial Services and Markets Act 2000 (Financial Promotion) Order 2001.]

NOTES

Inserted by the Financial Services and Markets Act 2000 (Financial Promotion and Promotion of Collective Investment Schemes) (Miscellaneous Amendments) Order 2005, SI 2005/270, art 3, Sch 2, para 3, as from 3 March 2005.

Para (4): words omitted revoked by the Financial Services and Markets Act 2000 (Promotion of Collective Investment Schemes) (Exemptions) (Amendment) Order 2005, SI 2005/1532, art 2(1), (2)(a), (b), as from 1 July 2005.

Para (5): word in square brackets substituted by SI 2005/1532, art 2(1), (2)(c), as from 1 July 2005.

Financial Services and Markets Act 2000 (Financial Promotion) Order 2001: revoked and replaced by the Financial Services and Markets Act 2000 (Financial Promotion) Order 2005, SI 2005/1529. As to the meaning of "unlisted company", see art 3 of that Order.

[8.302]

24 Associations of high net worth or sophisticated investors

The scheme promotion restriction does not apply to any non-real time communication or solicited real time communication which—
(a) is made to an association[, or to a member of an association,] the membership of which the person making the communication believes on reasonable grounds comprises wholly or predominantly persons who are—
(i) certified high net worth individuals within the meaning of article 21;
(ii) high net worth persons falling within article 22(2)(a) to (d);
(iii) certified sophisticated investors within the meaning of article 23 [or 23A]; and
(b) does not invite or induce the recipient to enter into an agreement under the terms of which he can incur a liability or obligation to pay or contribute more than he commits by way of investment.

NOTES

Words in square brackets inserted by the Financial Services and Markets Act 2000 (Promotion of Collective Investment Schemes) (Exemptions) (Amendment) Order 2005, SI 2005/1532, art 2(1), (3), as from 1 July 2005.

[8.303]

25 Settlors, trustees and personal representatives

The scheme promotion restriction does not apply to any communication which is made—
(a) by an authorised person when acting as a settlor or grantor of a trust, a trustee or a personal representative;
(b) to a trustee of the trust, a fellow trustee or a fellow personal representative (as the case may be),

if the communication is made for the purposes of the trust or estate.

[8.304]

26 Beneficiaries of trust, will or intestacy

The scheme promotion restriction does not apply to any communication which is made—
(a) by an authorised person when acting as a settlor of a trust, trustee or personal representative to a beneficiary under the trust, will or intestacy; or
(b) by an authorised person who is a beneficiary under a trust, will or intestacy to another beneficiary under the same trust, will or intestacy,

if the communication relates to the management or distribution of that trust fund or estate.

[8.305]

27 Remedy following report by Parliamentary Commissioner for Administration

The scheme promotion restriction does not apply to any communication made or directed by a person for the purpose of enabling any injustice, stated by the Parliamentary Commissioner for Administration in a report under section 10 of the Parliamentary Commissioner Act 1967 to have occurred, to be remedied with respect to the recipient.

[8.306]

28 Persons placing promotional material in particular publications

The scheme promotion restriction does not apply to any communication received by a person who receives the publication in which the communication is contained because he has himself placed an advertisement in that publication.

[8.307]

[29 Open-ended investment companies authorised in Northern Ireland

(1) The scheme promotion restriction does not apply in relation to a scheme constituted by an authorised Northern Ireland open-ended investment company.

(2) In this article—

(a) "authorised Northern Ireland open-ended investment company" means a body incorporated by virtue of regulations made under section 1 of the Open-Ended Investment Companies Act (Northern Ireland) 2002 in respect of which an authorisation order is in force; and

(b) "authorisation order" means an order made under (or having effect as made under) any provision of those regulations which is made by virtue of section 1(2)(1) of that Act (provision corresponding to Chapter 3 of Part 17 of the Act).]

NOTES

Added by the Financial Services and Markets Act 2000 (Promotion of Collective Investment Schemes etc) (Exemptions) (Amendment) Order 2003, SI 2003/2067, art 2(1), (3), as from 5 September 2003.

30 *(Originally added by the Financial Services and Markets Act 2000 (Promotion of Collective Investment Schemes etc) (Exemptions) (Amendment) Order 2003, SI 2003/2067, art 2(1), (4), as from 13 February 2004. Subsequently revoked by the Collective Investment Schemes (Amendment etc) (EU Exit) Regulations 2019, SI 2019/325, reg 50(1), (7), as from IP completion day (as defined in the European Union (Withdrawal Agreement) Act 2020, s 39).)*

[8.308]

[31 Communications required by the PRIIPs regulation: key information document

The scheme promotion restriction does not apply to any communication required by Article 13 of Regulation (EU) No 1286/2014 of the European Parliament and of the Council of 26 November 2014 on key information documents for packaged retail and insurance-based investment products.]

NOTES

Added by the Packaged Retail and Insurance-based Investment Products Regulations 2017, SI 2017/1127, reg 12, Sch 2, para 3, as from 1 January 2018.

[SCHEDULE
STATEMENTS FOR CERTIFIED HIGH NET WORTH INDIVIDUALS AND SELF-CERTIFIED SOPHISTICATED INVESTORS

Articles 21 and 23A

PART I STATEMENT FOR CERTIFIED HIGH NET WORTH INDIVIDUALS

[8.309]

1. The statement to be signed for the purposes of article 21(2) (definition of high net worth individual) must be in the following form and contain the following content—

"STATEMENT FOR CERTIFIED HIGH NET WORTH INDIVIDUAL

I declare that I am a certified high net worth individual for the purposes of the Financial Services and Markets Act 2000 (Promotion of Collective Investment Schemes) (Exemptions) Order 2001.

I understand that this means—

(a) I can receive promotions, made by a person who is authorised [under the Financial Services and Markets Act 2000], which relate to units in unregulated collective investment schemes that invest wholly or predominantly in unlisted companies;

(b) the schemes to which the promotions will relate are not authorised or recognised for the purposes of the Financial Services and Markets Act 2000.

I am a certified high net worth individual because **at least one of the following applies**—

(a) I had, during the financial year immediately preceding the date below, an annual income to the value of £100,000 or more;

(b) I held, throughout the financial year immediately preceding the date below, net assets to the value of £250,000 or more. Net assets for these purposes do not include—

(i) the property which is my primary residence or any loan secured on that residence;

(ii) any rights of mine under a qualifying contract of insurance within the meaning of the Financial Services and Markets Act 2000 (Regulated Activities) Order 2001; or

(iii) any benefits (in the form of pensions or otherwise) which are payable on the termination of my service or on my death or retirement and to which I am (or my dependants are), or may be, entitled.

I accept that I can lose my property and other assets from making investment decisions based on financial promotions.

I am aware that it is open to me to seek advice from someone who specialises in advising on unregulated collective investment schemes.

Signature. . . . .

Date. . . . ."]

NOTES

This Schedule was added by the Financial Services and Markets Act 2000 (Financial Promotion and Promotion of Collective Investment Schemes) (Miscellaneous Amendments) Order 2005, SI 2005/270, art 3, Sch 2, para 4, as from 3 March 2005.

Words in square brackets substituted by the Financial Services Act 2012 (Consequential Amendments and Transitional Provisions) Order 2013, SI 2013/472, art 3, Sch 2, para 37(b), as from 1 April 2013.

[PART II STATEMENT FOR SELF-CERTIFIED SOPHISTICATED INVESTORS

[8.310]

2. The statement to be signed for the purposes of article 23A(1) (definition of self-certified sophisticated investor) must be in the following form and contain the following content—

"STATEMENT FOR SELF-CERTIFIED SOPHISTICATED INVESTOR

I declare that I am a self-certified sophisticated investor for the purposes of the Financial Services and Markets Act 2000 (Promotion of Collective Investment Schemes) (Exemptions) Order 2001.

I understand that this means—

(a) I can receive promotions, made by a person who is authorised [under the Financial Services and Markets Act 2000], which relate to units in unregulated collective investment schemes that invest wholly or predominantly in unlisted companies;

(b) the schemes to which the promotions will relate are not authorised or recognised for the purposes of the Financial Services and Markets Act 2000.

I am a self-certified sophisticated investor because **at least one of the following applies**—

(a) I am a member of a network or syndicate of business angels and have been so for at least the last six months prior to the date below;

(b) I have made more than one investment in an unlisted company in the two years prior to the date below;

(c) I am working, or have worked in the two years prior to the date below, in a professional capacity in the private equity sector, or in the provision of finance for small and medium enterprises;

(d) I am currently, or have been in the two years prior to the date below, a director of a company with an annual turnover of at least £1 million.

I accept that I can lose my property and other assets from making investment decisions based on financial promotions.

I am aware that it is open to me to seek advice from someone who specialises in advising on unregulated collective investment schemes.

Signature. . . . .

Date. . . . . "]

NOTES

Added as noted to Pt I at **[8.309]**.

Words in square brackets substituted by the Financial Services Act 2012 (Consequential Amendments and Transitional Provisions) Order 2013, SI 2013/472, art 3, Sch 2, para 37(b), as from 1 April 2013.

FINANCIAL SERVICES AND MARKETS ACT 2000 (COLLECTIVE INVESTMENT SCHEMES) ORDER 2001

(SI 2001/1062)

NOTES

Made: 19 March 2001.

Authority: Financial Services and Markets Act 2000, s 235(5).

Commencement: 1 December 2001.

This Order is reproduced as amended by:

2001	Financial Services and Markets Act 2000 (Miscellaneous Provisions) Order 2001, SI 2001/3650.
2005	Civil Partnership Act 2004 (Amendments to Subordinate Legislation) Order 2005, SI 2005/2114.
2006	Financial Services and Markets Act 2000 (Regulated Activities) (Amendment) Order 2006, SI 2006/1969; Financial Services and Markets Act 2000 (Regulated Activities) (Amendment No 3) Order 2006, SI 2006/3384.
2007	Financial Services and Markets Act 2000 (Collective Investment Schemes) (Amendment) Order 2007, SI 2007/800.
2008	Financial Services and Markets Act 2000 (Collective Investment Schemes) (Amendment) Order 2008, SI 2008/1641.
2010	Financial Services and Markets Act 2000 (Regulated Activities) (Amendment) Order 2010, SI 2010/86; Timeshare, Holiday Products, Resale and Exchange Contracts Regulations 2010, SI 2010/2960.
2013	Collective Investment in Transferable Securities (Contractual Scheme) Regulations 2013, SI 2013/1388; Alternative Investment Fund Managers Regulations 2013, SI 2013/1773.
2014	Co-operative and Community Benefit Societies and Credit Unions Act 2010 (Consequential Amendments) Regulations 2014, SI 2014/1815.
2015	Financial Services and Markets Act 2000 (Collective Investment Schemes) (Amendment) Order 2015, SI 2015/754; Financial Services and Markets Act 2000 (Collective Investment Schemes) (Amendment) Order 2015, SI 2015/2061.
2017	Financial Services and Markets Act 2000 (Regulated Activities) (Amendment) Order 2017, SI 2017/488; Central Securities Depositories Regulations 2017, SI 2017/1064.
2019	Collective Investment Schemes (Amendment etc) (EU Exit) Regulations 2019, SI 2019/325.
2021	Financial Services and Markets Act 2000 (Collective Investment Schemes) (Amendment) Order 2021, SI 2021/566.
2022	Financial Services and Markets Act 2000 (Regulated Activities) (Amendment) Order 2022, SI 2022/466.

Transitional provisions in relation to Gibraltar-based firms and activities: see the Gibraltar (Miscellaneous Amendments) (EU Exit) Regulations 2019, SI 2019/680, reg 11 at **[12.129]**.

[8.311]

1 Citation and commencement

This Order may be cited as the Financial Services and Markets Act 2000 (Collective Investment Schemes) Order 2001 and comes into force on the day on which section 19 of the Act comes into force.

[8.312]

2 Interpretation

In this Order—

"the Act" means the Financial Services and Markets Act 2000;

"the 1988 Act" means the Income and Corporation Taxes Act 1988;

["the 2007 Act" means the Income Tax Act 2007;]

["authorised contractual scheme" and "authorised unit trust scheme" have the meaning given in section 237(3) of the Act;]

"contract of insurance" and "contract of long term insurance" have the meaning given by article 3(1) of the Regulated Activities Order;

["feeder fund" means an authorised unit trust scheme the sole object of which is investment in units of a single authorised unit trust scheme, in units of a single authorised contractual scheme or in shares in a single open-ended investment company;]

"franchise arrangements" means arrangements under which a person earns profits or income by exploiting a right conferred by the arrangements to use a trade mark or design or other intellectual property or the good-will attached to it;

"funeral plan contract" has the meaning given by article 59 of the Regulated Activities Order;

"individual pension account" has the meaning given by regulation 4 of the Personal Pension Schemes (Restriction on Discretion to Approve) (Permitted Investments) Regulations 2001;

["long-term holiday product contract" has the meaning given by regulation 8 of the Timeshare, Holiday Products, Resale and Exchange Contracts Regulations 2010;]

["occupational pension scheme" has the meaning given by section 1 of the Pension Schemes Act 1993 but with paragraph (b) of the definition omitted;]

"the operator" has the meaning given by section 237(2) of the Act;

["personal pension scheme" means a scheme or arrangement which is not an occupational pension scheme and which is comprised in one or more instruments or agreements, having or capable of having effect so as to provide benefits to or in respect of people—

(a) on retirement,

(b) on having reached a particular age, or

(c) on termination of service in an employment;]

"personal pension unit trust" means a personal pension scheme which is an authorised unit trust scheme of a kind mentioned in Part I of Schedule 1 to the Personal Pension Schemes (Appropriate Schemes) Regulations 1997;

"recognised scheme" has the meaning given by section 237(3) of the Act;

"the Regulated Activities Order" means the Financial Services and Markets Act 2000 (Regulated Activities) Order 2001;

["timeshare contract" has the meaning given by regulation 7 of the Timeshare, Holiday Products, Resale and Exchange Contracts Regulations 2010].

NOTES

Definition "the 2007 Act" inserted by the Financial Services and Markets Act 2000 (Collective Investment Schemes) (Amendment) Order 2015, SI 2015/754, art 2(1), (2), as from 13 April 2015.

Definitions "authorised contractual scheme" and "authorised unit trust scheme" substituted (for the original definition "authorised unit trust scheme"), and definition "feeder fund" substituted, by the Collective Investment in Transferable Securities (Contractual Scheme) Regulations 2013, SI 2013/1388, reg 11(1), (2), as from 6 June 2013.

Definition "long-term holiday product contract" inserted, and definition "timeshare rights" substituted, by the Timeshare, Holiday Products, Resale and Exchange Contracts Regulations 2010, SI 2010/2960, reg 36(3), Sch 6, para 8(1), (2), as from 23 February 2011.

Original (joint) definition "occupational pension scheme" and "personal pension scheme" (omitted) revoked, and new (separate) definitions "occupational pension scheme" and "personal pension scheme" inserted, by the Financial Services and Markets Act 2000 (Regulated Activities) (Amendment) Order 2006, SI 2006/1969, art 8, as from 6 April 2007.

Personal Pension Schemes (Restriction on Discretion to Approve) (Permitted Investments) Regulations 2001 (SI 2001/117): lapsed on the repeal of the enabling authority by the Finance Act 2004, s 326, Sch 42, Pt 3.

[8.313]

3 Arrangements not amounting to a collective investment scheme

Arrangements of the kind specified by the Schedule to this Order do not amount to a collective investment scheme.

SCHEDULE
ARRANGEMENTS NOT AMOUNTING TO A COLLECTIVE INVESTMENT SCHEME

Article 3

[8.314]

1 Individual investment management arrangements

Arrangements do not amount to a collective investment scheme if—

(a) the property to which the arrangements relate (other than cash awaiting investment) consists of investments of one or more of the following kinds:

(i) an investment of the kind specified by any of articles 76 to 80 of the Regulated Activities Order;

(ii) an investment of the kind specified by article 81 of that Order (units in a collective investment scheme) so far as relating to authorised unit trust schemes, [authorised contractual schemes,] recognised schemes or shares in an open-ended investment company; or

(iii) a contract of long term insurance;

(b) each participant is entitled to a part of that property and to withdraw that part at any time; and

(c) the arrangements do not have the characteristics mentioned in section 235(3)(a) of the Act and have those mentioned in section 235(3)(b) only because the parts of the property to which different participants are entitled are not bought and sold separately except where a person becomes or ceases to be a participant.

2 Enterprise initiative schemes

(1) Arrangements do not amount to a collective investment scheme if—

(a) the property to which the arrangements relate (other than cash awaiting investment) consists of shares;

(b) the arrangements constitute a complying fund;

(c) each participant is entitled to a part of the property to which the arrangements relate and—

(i) to the extent that the property to which he is entitled comprises relevant shares of a class which are admitted to official listing in [the United Kingdom or] an EEA State or to dealings on a recognised investment exchange, he is entitled to withdraw it at any time after the end of the period of five years beginning with the date on which the shares in question were issued;

(ii) to the extent that the property to which he is entitled comprises other relevant shares, he is entitled to withdraw it at any time after the end of the period of seven years beginning with the date on which the shares in question were issued;

(iii) to the extent that the property to which he is entitled comprises shares other than relevant shares, he is entitled to withdraw it at any time after the end of the period of six months beginning with the date on which the shares in question ceased to be relevant shares; and

(iv) to the extent that the property comprises cash which the operator has agreed (conditionally or unconditionally) to apply in subscribing for shares, he is entitled to withdraw it at any time; and

(d) the arrangements would meet the conditions described in paragraph 1(c) were it not for the fact that the operator is entitled to exercise all or any of the rights conferred by shares included in the property to which the arrangements relate.

(2) In sub-paragraph (1)—

(a) "shares" means investments of the kind specified by article 76 of the Regulated Activities Order (shares etc) and shares are to be regarded as relevant shares if and so long as they are shares in respect of which neither—

(i) a claim for relief made in accordance with section 306 of the 1988 Act has been disallowed; nor

(ii) an assessment has been made pursuant to section 307 of the 1988 Act withdrawing or [reducing] relief by reason of the body corporate in which the shares are held having ceased to be a body corporate which is a qualifying company for the purposes of that Act;

(b) "complying fund" means arrangements which provide that—

(i) the operator will, so far as is practicable, make investments each of which, subject to each participant's individual circumstances, qualify for relief by virtue of Chapter III of Part VII of the 1988 Act; and

(ii) the minimum contribution to the arrangements which each participant must make is not less than £2000.

[2A Social investment schemes

(1) Arrangements do not amount to a collective investment scheme if—

(a) the property to which the arrangements relate (other than cash awaiting investment) consists of shares or debentures;

(b) the arrangements constitute a complying fund;

(c) each participant is entitled to a part of the property to which the arrangements relate and—

(i) to the extent that the property to which that participant is entitled comprises relevant shares, the participant is entitled to withdraw it at any time after the end of the period of seven years beginning with the date on which the shares in question were issued;

(ii) to the extent that the property to which that participant is entitled comprises relevant debentures, the participant is entitled to withdraw it at any time after the end of the period of seven years beginning with the date on which—

(aa) the debentures in question were issued; or

(bb) in a case where there is no such issuing, when the debentures, so far as relating to the debt owed to that participant, take effect between the debtor and the participant;

(iii) to the extent that the property to which that participant is entitled comprises shares other than relevant shares, the participant is entitled to withdraw it at any time after the end of the period of six months beginning with the date on which the shares in question ceased to be relevant shares;

(iv) to the extent that the property to which that participant is entitled comprises debentures other than relevant debentures, the participant is entitled to withdraw it at any time after the end of the period of six months beginning with the date on which the debentures in question ceased to be relevant debentures; and

(v) to the extent that the property comprises cash which the operator has agreed (conditionally or unconditionally) to invest in shares or debentures, the participant is entitled to withdraw it at any time; and

(d) the arrangements would meet the conditions described in paragraph 1(c) were it not for the fact that the operator is entitled to exercise all or any of the rights conferred by shares or debentures included in the property to which the arrangements relate.

(2) In sub-paragraph (1)—

"complying fund" means arrangements which provide that—

(a) the operator will, so far as is practicable, make investments each of which, subject to each participant's individual circumstances, qualifies for relief by virtue of Part 5B of the 2007 Act; and

(b) the minimum contribution to the arrangements which each participant must make is not less than £2,000;

"debentures" has the same meaning as in section 257L(4) of the 2007 Act (definition of qualifying debt investments), and debentures are to be regarded as relevant debentures if and so long as they are debentures in respect of which—

(a) no claim for relief made in accordance with Chapter 6 of Part 5B of the 2007 Act has been disallowed; and

(b) no assessment has been made pursuant to section 257S of the 2007 Act withdrawing or reducing relief on the ground that the requirements of Chapter 4 of Part 5B of the 2007 are not met; and

"shares" means investments of the kind specified by article 76 of the Regulated Activities Order (shares etc), and shares are to be regarded as relevant shares if and so long as they are shares in respect of which—

(a) no claim for relief made in accordance with Chapter 6 of Part 5B of the 2007 Act has been disallowed; and

(b) no assessment has been made pursuant to section 257S of the 2007 Act withdrawing or reducing relief on the ground that the requirements of Chapter 4 of Part 5B of the 2007 are not met.]

3 Pure deposit based schemes

Arrangements do not amount to a collective investment scheme if the whole amount of each participant's contribution is a deposit which is accepted by an authorised person with permission to carry on an activity of the kind specified by article 5 of the Regulated Activities Order (accepting deposits) or a person who is an exempt person in relation to such an activity.

4 Schemes not operated by way of business

Arrangements do not amount to a collective investment scheme if they are operated otherwise than by way of business.

5 Debt issues

(1) Arrangements do not amount to a collective investment scheme if they are arrangements under which the rights or interests of participants are, except as provided in sub-paragraph (2), represented by investments of one, and only one, of the following descriptions:

(a) investments of the kind specified by article 77 [or 77A] of the Regulated Activities Order [(debt instruments)] which are—

(i) issued by a single body corporate other than an open-ended investment company; or

(ii) issued by a single issuer who is not a body corporate and which are guaranteed by the government of the United Kingdom, the Scottish Administration, the Executive Committee of the Northern Ireland Assembly, the National Assembly for Wales or the government of any country or territory outside the United Kingdom;

and which are not convertible into or exchangeable for investments of any other description;

(b) investments falling within sub-paragraph (a)(i) or (ii) ("the former investments") which are convertible into or exchangeable for investments of the kind specified by article 76 of the Regulated Activities Order ("the latter investments") provided that the latter investments are issued by the same person who issued the former investments or are issued by a single other issuer;

(c) investments of the kind specified by article 78 of the Regulated Activities Order (government and public securities) which are issued by a single issuer; or

(d) investments of the kind specified by article 79 of the Regulated Activities Order (instruments giving entitlement to investments) which are issued otherwise than by an open-ended investment company and which confer rights in respect of investments, issued by the same issuer, of the kind specified by article 76 of that Order or within any of paragraphs (a) to (c).

(2) Arrangements which would otherwise not amount to a collective investment scheme by virtue of the provisions of sub-paragraph (1) are not to be regarded as amounting to such a scheme by reason only that one or more of the participants ("the counterparty") is a person—

(a) whose ordinary business involves him in carrying on activities of the kind specified by any of articles 14 (dealing in investments as principal), 21 (dealing in investments as agent), 25 (arranging deals in investments), [25D (operating a multilateral trading facility),] [25DA (operating an organised trading facility),] 37 (managing investments), 40 (safeguarding and administering investments), 45 (sending dematerialised instructions), [51ZA (managing a [UK] UCITS), 51ZB (acting as trustee or depositary of a [UK] UCITS), 51ZC (managing an AIF), 51ZD (acting as trustee or depositary of an AIF), 51ZE (establishing etc collective investment scheme)], 52 (establishing etc a stakeholder pension scheme) and 53 (advising on investments) or, so far as relevant to any of those articles, article 64 of the Regulated Activities Order (agreeing to carry on specified kinds of activities), or would do so apart from any exclusion from any of those articles made by that Order; and[

(b) whose rights or interests in the arrangements are or include rights or interests under a swap arrangement.

(3) In sub-paragraph (2), "swap arrangement" means an arrangement the purpose of which is to facilitate the making of payments to participants whether in a particular amount or currency or at a particular time or rate of interest or all or any combination of those things, being an arrangement under which the counterparty—

(a) is entitled to receive amounts, whether representing principal or interest, payable in respect of any property subject to the arrangements or sums determined by reference to such amounts; and

(b) makes payments, whether or not of the same amount or in the same currency as the amounts or sums referred to in paragraph (a), which are calculated in accordance with an agreed formula by reference to those amounts or sums.

6 Common accounts

Arrangements do not amount to a collective investment scheme if—

(a) they are arrangements under which the rights or interests of participants are rights to or interests in money held in a common account; and

(b) that money is held in the account on the understanding that an amount representing the contribution of each participant is to be applied—

(i) in making payments to him;

(ii) in satisfaction of sums owed by him; or

(iii) in the acquisition of property for him or the provision of services to him.

[6A. Electronic systems in relation to lending

(1) Arrangements do not amount to a collective investment scheme in so far as they are arrangements of a kind described in one of sub-paragraphs (2) to (6).

(2) Arrangements operated by a person specified in paragraph (a) and in one or more of the circumstances specified in paragraph (b).

(a) A person who is—

(i) an authorised person with permission to carry on an activity of the kind specified by article 36H(1) of the Regulated Activities Order (operating an electronic system in relation to lending);

(ii) an appointed representative in relation to that activity;

(iii) an exempt person in relation to that activity;

(iv) a person to whom, as a result of Part 20 of the Act, the general prohibition does not apply in relation to that activity.

(b) The circumstances are—

(i) the operating of the arrangements amounts to the carrying on of an activity of the kind specified by article 36H of the Regulated Activities Order;

(ii) the arrangements amount to the holding of money on behalf of a lender or borrower under a relevant article 36H agreement, or with a view to a lender entering in to such an arrangement;

(iii) the purpose of the arrangements is to compensate a lender when a borrower fails to pay any sum due to that lender under a relevant article 36H agreement.

(3) Arrangements forming a necessary part of the operation of arrangements of the kind specified in sub-paragraph (2).

(4) Arrangements that—

(a) are operated by a person specified in sub-paragraph (2)(a), and

(b) would consist of arrangements of the kind specified in sub-paragraphs (2) or (3) except that they relate to a non-article 36H agreement rather than an article 36H agreement.

(5) Arrangements with the purpose of winding up the operations of a person who operates or operated arrangements of the kind specified in sub-paragraphs (2) to (4).

(6) Arrangements with the purpose of continuing the provision of services to a lender and borrower in relation to a relevant article 36H agreement or non-article 36H agreement, which are entered into in connection with the winding up of the operations of a person who provides or provided those services in relation to that agreement.

(7) In this paragraph—

"article 36H agreement" has the meaning given in article 36H of the Regulated Activities Order;

"borrower" means

(a) a person who receives credit under an article 36H agreement or a person to whom the rights and duties of a borrower under an agreement have passed by assignment or operation of law, or

(b) for the purposes of sub-paragraph (4)(b), a person who receives credit under an agreement of the kind described in sub-paragraph (4)(b) or a person to whom the rights and duties of a borrower under such an agreement have passed by assignment or operation of law;

"credit" has the meaning given in article 60L of the Regulated Activities Order (interpretation of Chapter 14A etc);

"lender" means—

(a) a person providing credit under an article 36H agreement,

(b) a person who by assignment or operation of law has assumed the rights of a person who provided credit under such an agreement, or

(c) for the purposes of sub-paragraph (4)(b), a person providing credit under an agreement of the sort described in sub-paragraph (4)(b), or a person who by assignment or operation of law has assumed the rights of a person who provided credit under such an agreement;

"non-article 36H agreement" means an agreement that would be a relevant article 36H agreement but for the fact that it does not satisfy the conditions in article 36H(5) and (6) of the Regulated Activities Order;

"relevant article 36H agreement" means an article 36H agreement which has been entered into with the facilitation of a person carrying on an activity of a kind specified by article 36H(1) of the Regulated Activities Order.]

[7 Certain funds relating to leasehold property

Arrangements do not amount to a collective investment scheme if the rights or interests of the participants are rights or interests—

(a) in a fund which is a trust fund within the meaning of section 42(1) of the Landlord and Tenant Act 1987 or which would be such a trust fund if the landlord were not an exempt landlord within the meaning of section 58(1) of that Act; or

(b) in money held in a designated account by the scheme administrator under a tenancy deposit scheme within the meaning of section 212(2) of the Housing Act 2004.]

8 Certain employee share schemes

(1) Arrangements do not amount to a collective investment scheme if they are operated by a person ("A"), a member of the same group as A or a relevant trustee for the purpose of enabling or facilitating—

(a) transactions in shares in, or debentures issued by, A between, or for the benefit of, any of the persons mentioned in sub-paragraph (2); or

(b) the holding of such shares or debentures by, or for the benefit of, any such persons.

(2) The persons referred to in sub-paragraph (1) are—

(a) the bona fide employees or former employees of A or of another member of the same group; or

(b) the wives, husbands, widows, widowers, [civil partners, surviving civil partners,] or children or step-children under the age of eighteen of such employees or former employees.

(3) For the purposes of this paragraph—

(a) "shares" and "debentures" have the meaning given by article 71(6)(a) of the Regulated Activities Order:

(b) "relevant trustee" means a person who, in pursuance of the arrangements, holds shares in or debentures issued by A.

[9 Schemes entered into for commercial purposes wholly or mainly related to existing business

(1) Arrangements first entered into before 15th July 2008 do not amount to a collective investment scheme if—

(a) by virtue of paragraph 9 of the Schedule to the Financial Services and Markets Act 2000 (Collective Investment Schemes) Order 2001 as it had effect immediately before 15th July 2008 they did not then do so provided that all participants are permitted participants; or

(b) in the case of arrangements which amounted to a collective investment scheme immediately before 15th July 2008—

(i) all participants are permitted participants; and

(ii) at any time each person which is at that time a participant agrees in writing in respect of the remaining life of the arrangements that the arrangements do not amount to a collective investment scheme.

(2) Arrangements first entered into on or after 15th July 2008 do not amount to a collective investment scheme if all participants are permitted participants.

(3) The exclusion in sub-paragraph (2) shall not apply to arrangements falling within that sub-paragraph if at any time each person which is at that time a permitted participant agrees in writing in respect of the life of the arrangements that the arrangements amount to a collective investment scheme.

(4) If at any time a person which is not a permitted participant participates in arrangements then for as long as that person is a participant but not a permitted participant the exclusion in sub-paragraph (1) or, as the case may be, sub-paragraph (2) shall not apply to the arrangements.

(5) For the purposes of this paragraph—

"permitted participant" means a participant which—

(a) at the time of entering into the arrangements carries on a business which is not a specified business (the "first business") but which may be in addition to any specified business carried on by that participant at that time and—

(i) does not carry on that first business solely by virtue of being—

(a) a participant in the arrangements; or

(b) a member, partner or trust beneficiary of a body corporate, unincorporated association, partnership or trust which is itself a participant in the arrangements; and

(ii) enters into the arrangements for commercial purposes wholly or mainly related to the first business; or

(b) is a body corporate, unincorporated association, partnership, or trustee of a trust (unless that trustee is an individual) which—

(i) does not carry on a specified business; and

(ii) only has as its members, partners or trust beneficiaries persons which themselves qualify, or would qualify if they participated in the arrangements, as participants of the kind mentioned in paragraph (a) of this paragraph; and

"specified business" means the business of engaging in any regulated activity of the kind specified by any of articles 14, 21, 25, 25D, [25DA,] 37, 40, 45, 51 to 53 or, so far as relevant to any of those articles, article 64 of the Regulated Activities Order.

(6) For the purposes of this paragraph, neither the entry into arrangements by any person as a further participant nor the exit from arrangements by any participant shall in itself constitute the creation of new arrangements.

(7) An agreement made in respect of any arrangements in accordance with the provisions of sub-paragraph (1)(b)(ii) or sub-paragraph (3) is not affected by—

(a) the entry into such arrangements by any person as a further participant;

(b) the exit from such arrangements of any participant;

(c) any later agreement in writing or otherwise under which, contrary to the earlier agreement, such arrangements do or, as the case may be, do not amount to a collective investment scheme.]

10 Group schemes

Arrangements do not amount to a collective investment scheme if each of the participants is a body corporate in the same group as the operator.

11 Franchise arrangements

Franchise arrangements do not amount to a collective investment scheme.

12 Trading schemes

Arrangements do not amount to a collective investment scheme if—

(a) the purpose of the arrangements is that participants should receive, by way of reward, payments or other benefits in respect of the introduction by any person of other persons who become participants;

(b) the arrangements are such that the payments or other benefits referred to in paragraph (a) are to be wholly or mainly funded out of the contributions of other participants; and

(c) the only reason why the arrangements have either or both of the characteristics mentioned in section 235(3) of the Act is because, pending their being used to fund those payments or other benefits, contributions of participants are managed as a whole by or on behalf of the operator of the scheme.

[13 Timeshare and long-term holiday product schemes

Arrangements do not amount to a collective investment scheme if the rights or interests of the participants are rights under a timeshare contract or a long-term holiday product contract.]

14 Other schemes relating to use or enjoyment of property

Arrangements do not amount to a collective investment scheme if—

(a) the predominant purpose of the arrangements is to enable the participants to share in the use or enjoyment of property or to make its use or enjoyment available gratuitously to others; and

(b) the property to which the arrangements relate does not consist of the currency of any country or territory and does not consist of or include any investment of the kind specified by Part III of the Regulated Activities Order or which would be of such a kind apart from any exclusion made by that Part of the Order.

15 Schemes involving the issue of certificates representing investments

Arrangements do not amount to a collective investment scheme if the rights or interests of the participants are investments of the kind specified by article 80 of the Regulated Activities Order (certificates representing certain securities).

16 Clearing services

Arrangements do not amount to a collective investment scheme if their purpose is the provision of clearing services and they are operated by an authorised person, a recognised clearing house or a recognised investment exchange.

[16A Settlement services

Arrangements do not amount to a collective investment scheme if their purpose is the provision of settlement services and they are operated by an authorised person or a recognised CSD.]

17 Contracts of insurance

A contract of insurance does not amount to a collective investment scheme.

[18 Funeral plan contracts

Arrangements do not amount to a collective investment scheme if they consist of, or are made pursuant to—

(a) a funeral plan contract; or

(b) a contract which would be a funeral plan contract but for the proviso to article 59(2) of the Regulated Activities Order.]

19 Individual pension accounts

An individual pension account does not amount to a collective investment scheme.

20 Occupational and personal pension schemes

(1) An occupational pension scheme does not amount to a collective investment scheme.

(2) A personal pension scheme does not amount to a collective investment scheme.

(3) Sub-paragraph (2) does not extend to a personal pension unit trust which is constituted as a feeder fund or comprises feeder funds.

[21 Bodies corporate etc

(1) Subject to sub-paragraph (2), no body incorporated under the law of, or any part of, the United Kingdom relating to building societies or [registered societies] or registered under any such law relating to friendly societies, and no other body corporate other than an open-ended investment company, amounts to a collective investment scheme.

(2) Sub-paragraph (1) does not apply to any body incorporated as a limited liability partnership.]

NOTES

Para 1: words in square brackets in sub-para (a)(ii) inserted by the Collective Investment in Transferable Securities (Contractual Scheme) Regulations 2013, SI 2013/1388, reg 11(1), (3), as from 6 June 2013.

Para 2: words in square brackets in sub-para (1)(c)(i) inserted by the Collective Investment Schemes (Amendment etc) (EU Exit) Regulations 2019, SI 2019/325, reg 51(a), as from IP completion day (as defined in the European Union (Withdrawal

Agreement) Act 2020, s 39). Word in square brackets in sub-para (2)(a)(ii) substituted by the Financial Services and Markets Act 2000 (Collective Investment Schemes) (Amendment) Order 2015, SI 2015/754, art 2(1), (3), as from 13 April 2015.

Para 2A: inserted by SI 2015/754, art 2(1), (4), as from 13 April 2015.

Para 5: words in first pair of square brackets in sub-para (1)(a) inserted, and words in second pair of square brackets in that sub-paragraph substituted, by the Financial Services and Markets Act 2000 (Regulated Activities) (Amendment) Order 2010, SI 2010/86, art 3, as from 24 February 2010. Words in first pair of square brackets in sub-para (2)(a) inserted by the Financial Services and Markets Act 2000 (Regulated Activities) (Amendment No 3) Order 2006, SI 2006/3384, art 36(1), (2), as from 1 November 2007. Words in second pair of square brackets in sub-para (2)(a) inserted by the Financial Services and Markets Act 2000 (Regulated Activities) (Amendment) Order 2017, SI 2017/488, art 14, Schedule, para 4(a), as from 3 January 2018. Words in third (outer) pair of square brackets in sub-para (2)(a) substituted by the Alternative Investment Fund Managers Regulations 2013, SI 2013/1773, reg 81, Sch 2, Part 2, para 6, as from 22 July 2013. Word "UK" in square brackets (in both places that it occurs) inserted by SI 2019/325, reg 51(b), as from IP completion day (as defined in the European Union (Withdrawal Agreement) Act 2020, s 39).

Para 6A: originally inserted by the Financial Services and Markets Act 2000 (Collective Investment Schemes) (Amendment) Order 2015, SI 2015/2061, art 2, as from 18 January 2016. Subsequently substituted by the Financial Services and Markets Act 2000 (Collective Investment Schemes) (Amendment) Order 2021, SI 2021/566, art 2, as from 18 June 2021 (note that the 2021 Order did not provide for a title for this paragraph, and that the original one has been retained).

Para 7: substituted by the Financial Services and Markets Act 2000 (Collective Investment Schemes) (Amendment) Order 2007, SI 2007/800, art 2, as from 6 April 2007.

Para 8: words in square brackets in sub-para (2)(b) inserted by the Civil Partnership Act 2004 (Amendments to Subordinate Legislation) Order 2005, SI 2005/2114, art 2(16), Sch 16, Pt 1, para 3, as from 5 December 2005.

Para 9: substituted by the Financial Services and Markets Act 2000 (Collective Investment Schemes) (Amendment) Order 2008, SI 2008/1641, art 2, as from 15 July 2008 (note that SI 2008/1641, art 2 was amended by the Financial Services and Markets Act 2000 (Collective Investment Schemes) (Amendment) (No 2) Order 2008, SI 2008/1813, art 2, as from 14 July 2008, and the effect of the amendments has been incorporated in the text set out above). Figure "25DA," in square brackets in sub-para (5) in the definition "specified business" inserted by SI 2017/488, art 14, Schedule, para 4(b), as from 3 January 2018.

Para 13: substituted by the Timeshare, Holiday Products, Resale and Exchange Contracts Regulations 2010, SI 2010/2960, reg 36(3), Sch 6, para 8(3), as from 23 February 2011.

Para 16A: inserted by the Central Securities Depositories Regulations 2017, SI 2017/1064, reg 10, Schedule, para 24, as from 28 November 2017.

Para 18: substituted by the Financial Services and Markets Act 2000 (Regulated Activities) (Amendment) Order 2022, SI 2022/466, art 3, as from 29 July 2022.

Para 21: substituted by SI 2001/3650, art 2(1), (4), as from 1 December 2001. Words in square brackets substituted by the Co-operative and Community Benefit Societies and Credit Unions Act 2010 (Consequential Amendments) Regulations 2014, SI 2014/1815, reg 2, Schedule, para 9, as from 1 August 2014.

National Assembly for Wales: see further, in relation to the renaming of the National Assembly for Wales as the Senedd Cymru or the Welsh Parliament, the Senedd and Elections (Wales) Act 2020, s 2 (with effect from 6 May 2020). See also ss 3–9 of the 2020 Act in relation to the renaming of Acts of the National Assembly for Wales, Members of the National Assembly for Wales, etc.

Step-children, etc: as to the meaning of this and related expressions, see the Civil Partnership Act 2004, s 246 (as applied to this Order by the Civil Partnership Act 2004 (Relationships Arising Through Civil Partnership) Order 2005, SI 2005/3137, art 3, Schedule).

Ss 306, 307 of the 1988 Act; Chapter III of Part VII of the 1988 Act: repealed, except in relation to shares issued before 6 April 2007, by the Income Tax Act 2007, ss 1027, 1031, 1034(3)(c), Sch 1, Pt 3, Sch 3, Pt 2. Section 306 of the 1988 Act is now ss 202–207 of the 2007 Act; s 307 is now ss 234–239 thereof; and Chapter III of Pt VII of the 1988 Act is now Pt 5 of the 2007 Act.

FINANCIAL SERVICES AND MARKETS ACT 2000 (CARRYING ON REGULATED ACTIVITIES BY WAY OF BUSINESS) ORDER 2001

(SI 2001/1177)

NOTES

Made: 26 March 2001.

Authority: Financial Services and Markets Act 2000, ss 419, 428(3).

Commencement: 1 December 2001.

This Order is reproduced as amended by:

2003	Financial Services and Markets Act 2000 (Regulated Activities) (Amendment) (No 1) Order 2003, SI 2003/1475; Financial Services and Markets Act 2000 (Regulated Activities) (Amendment) (No 2) Order 2003, SI 2003/1476.
2005	Financial Services and Markets Act 2000 (Carrying on Regulated Activities by Way of Business) (Amendment) Order 2005, SI 2005/922.
2006	Financial Services and Markets Act 2000 (Regulated Activities) (Amendment) Order 2006, SI 2006/1969; Financial Services and Markets Act 2000 (Regulated Activities) (Amendment) (No 2) Order 2006, SI 2006/2383; Financial Services and Markets Act 2000 (Regulated Activities) (Amendment No 3) Order 2006, SI 2006/3384.
2009	Financial Services and Markets Act 2000 (Regulated Activities) (Amendment) Order 2009, SI 2009/1342.
2010	Financial Services and Markets Act 2000 (Regulated Activities) (Amendment) Order 2010, SI 2010/86.
2011	Financial Services and Markets Act 2000 (Carrying on Regulated Activities by Way of Business) (Amendment) Order 2011, SI 2011/2304.
2013	Alternative Investment Fund Managers Regulations 2013, SI 2013/1773; Financial Services and Markets Act 2000 (Regulated Activities) (Amendment) (No 2) Order 2013, SI 2013/1881.

2014	Financial Services and Markets Act 2000 (Carrying on Regulated Activities by Way of Business) (Amendment) Order 2014, SI 2014/3340.
2017	Financial Services and Markets Act 2000 (Regulated Activities) (Amendment) Order 2017, SI 2017/488.
2018	Financial Services and Markets Act 2000 (Carrying on Regulated Activities by Way of Business) (Amendment) Order 2018, SI 2018/394; Insurance Distribution (Regulated Activities and Miscellaneous Amendments) Order 2018, SI 2018/546; Financial Services and Markets Act 2000 (Regulated Activities) (Amendment) Order 2018, SI 2018/831.

ARRANGEMENT OF ARTICLES

[8.315]

1 Citation, commencement and interpretation

(1) This Order may be cited as the Financial Services and Markets Act 2000 (Carrying on Regulated Activities by Way of Business) Order 2001, and comes into force on the day on which section 19 of the Financial Services and Markets Act 2000 comes into force.

(2) In this Order—
- (a) the "Regulated Activities Order" means the Financial Services and Markets Act 2000 (Regulated Activities) Order 2001;
- (b) ["contract of insurance",] "contractually based investment", "deposit", "overseas person" and "security" have the same meaning as in that Order;
- (c) "shares" and "debentures" mean any investment of the kind specified by article 76[, 77 or 77A] of that Order;
- (d) "units in a collective investment scheme" means any investment of the kind specified by article 81 of that Order;
- (e) "warrants" means any investment of the kind specified by article 79 of that Order.

NOTES

Para (2): words in square brackets in sub-para (b) inserted by the Financial Services and Markets Act 2000 (Regulated Activities) (Amendment) (No 2) Order 2003, SI 2003/1476, art 18(1), (2), as from 31 October 2004 (in so far as relating to contracts of long-term care insurance), and as from 14 January 2005 (otherwise). Words in square brackets in sub-para (c) substituted by the Financial Services and Markets Act 2000 (Regulated Activities) (Amendment) Order 2010, SI 2010/86, art 4, Schedule, para 6, as from 24 February 2010.

FSMA 2000, s 19 came into force on 1 December 2001 (see the Financial Services and Markets Act 2000 (Commencement No 7) Order 2001, SI 2001/3538).

[8.316]

2 Deposit taking business

(1) A person who carries on an activity of the kind specified by article 5 of the Regulated Activities Order (accepting deposits) is not to be regarded as doing so by way of business if—
- (a) he does not hold himself out as accepting deposits on a day to day basis; and
- (b) any deposits which he accepts are accepted only on particular occasions, whether or not involving the issue of any securities.

(2) In determining for the purposes of paragraph (1)(b) whether deposits are accepted only on particular occasions, regard is to be had to the frequency of those occasions and to any characteristics distinguishing them from each other.

[(3) A person ("B") who carries on an activity of the kind specified by article 5(1)(b) of the Regulated Activities Order (accepting deposits) is not to be regarded as doing so by way of business if—
- (a) the activity is facilitated by a person ("A");
- (b) in facilitating the activity, A was operating an electronic system in relation to lending;
- (c) B is not a credit institution or an authorised person;
- (d) B is not carrying on the business of accepting deposits;
- (e) B does not hold themselves out as accepting deposits on a day to day basis, other than where the holding-out is facilitated by persons engaged in operating an electronic system in relation to lending.

(4) For the purposes of paragraph (3)(d), if B uses the capital of, or interest on, money received by way of deposit solely to finance other business activity carried on by B, this is to be regarded as evidence indicating that B is not carrying on the business of accepting deposits.

(5) In this article—

"article 36H agreement" has the meaning given in article 36H(4) of the Regulated Activities Order;

Part 8 Financial Services SIs

"assignment", in relation to Scotland, means assignation;

"borrower" means—

(a) a person who receives credit under an agreement that is not an article 36H agreement only because it does not satisfy the conditions in article 36H(5) and (6) of the Regulated Activities Order; or

(b) a person to whom the rights and duties of a borrower under such an agreement have passed by assignment or operation of law;

"credit institution" means an undertaking the business of which is to take deposits or other repayable funds from the public and to grant credits for its own account;

"lender" means—

(a) a person providing credit under an agreement that is not an article 36H agreement only because it does not satisfy the conditions in article 36H(5) and (6) of the Regulated Activities Order; or

(b) a person who by assignment or operation of law has assumed the rights and duties of a lender under such an agreement;

"operating an electronic system in relation to lending" means carrying on an activity—

(a) of the kind specified by article 36H of the Regulated Activities Order (operating an electronic system in relation to lending), or

(b) that would be of the kind specified by article 36H but for the fact that the activity does not concern facilitating an article 36H agreement, but concerns facilitating persons becoming the lender and borrower under an agreement that is not an article 36H agreement only because it does not satisfy the conditions in article 36H(5) and (6) of the Regulated Activities Order].

NOTES

Paras (3)–(5): added by the Financial Services and Markets Act 2000 (Carrying on Regulated Activities by Way of Business) (Amendment) Order 2018, SI 2018/394, art 2, as from 22 March 2018.

[8.317]

3 Investment business

(1) A person is not to be regarded as carrying on by way of business an activity to which [paragraph (2) applies], unless he carries on the business of engaging in one or more such activities.

(2) [This paragraph] applies to an activity of the kind specified by any of the following provisions of the Regulated Activities Order, namely—

(a) article 14 (dealing in investments as principal);

(b) article 21 (dealing in investments as agent);

(c) article 25 (arranging deals in investments), except in so far as that activity relates to an investment of the kind specified by article 86 of that Order (Lloyd's syndicate capacity and syndicate membership), or article 89 of that Order (rights and interests) so far as relevant to that article;

[(ca) article 25D (operating a multilateral trading facility);]

[(cb) article 25DA (operating an organised trading facility);]

(d) article 37 (managing investments);

(e) article 40 (safeguarding and administering investments);

(f) article 45 (sending dematerialised instructions);

[(ga) article 51ZA (managing a UCITS);

(gb) article 51ZB (acting as a trustee or depositary of a UCITS);

(gc) article 51ZC (managing an AIF);

(gd) article 51ZD (acting as a trustee or depositary of an AIF);

(ge) article 51ZE (establishing etc a collective investment scheme);]

(h) article 52 (establishing etc a . . . pension scheme);

(i) article 53 (advising on investments); and

[(j) article 64 (agreeing) so far as relevant to any of the articles mentioned in sub-paragraphs (a) to (i),

but does not apply to any insurance mediation activity].

(3) [Paragraph (1)] is without prejudice to article 4 of this Order.

[(4) A person is not to be regarded as carrying on by way of business any insurance [distribution] activity unless he takes up or pursues that activity for remuneration.

(5) In this article, "insurance [distribution] activity" means any activity of the kind specified by article 21, 25(1) or (2), 39A or 53 of the Regulated Activities Order, or, so far as relevant to any of those articles, article 64 of that Order, which is carried on in relation to a contract of insurance.]

NOTES

Paras (1), (3): words in square brackets substituted by the Financial Services and Markets Act 2000 (Regulated Activities) (Amendment) (No 2) Order 2003, SI 2003/1476, art 18(1), (3)(a), (c), as from 31 October 2004 (in so far as relating to contracts of long-term care insurance), and as from 14 January 2005 (otherwise).

Para (2) is amended as follows:

Words in first pair of square brackets and sub-para (j) (and the following words) substituted by SI 2003/1476, art 18(1), (3)(b), as from 31 October 2004 (in so far as relating to contracts of long-term care insurance), and as from 14 January 2005 (otherwise).

Sub-para (ca) inserted by the Financial Services and Markets Act 2000 (Regulated Activities) (Amendment No 3) Order 2006, SI 2006/3384, art 37, as from 1 November 2007.

Sub-para (cb) inserted by the Financial Services and Markets Act 2000 (Regulated Activities) (Amendment) Order 2017, SI 2017/488, art 14, Schedule, para 5, as from 3 January 2018.

Word omitted from sub-para (h) revoked by the Financial Services and Markets Act 2000 (Regulated Activities) (Amendment) Order 2006, SI 2006/1969, art 9(1), (2), as from 6 April 2007.

Sub-paras (ga)–(ge) substituted (for the original sub-para (g)) by the Alternative Investment Fund Managers Regulations 2013, SI 2013/1773, reg 81, Sch 2, Part 2, para 7, as from 22 July 2013.

Paras (4), (5): added by SI 2003/1476, art 18(1), (3)(d), as from 31 October 2004 (in so far as relating to contracts of long-term care insurance), and as from 14 January 2005 (otherwise). Words in square brackets substituted by the Insurance Distribution (Regulated Activities and Miscellaneous Amendments) Order 2018, SI 2018/546, art 19, as from 1 October 2018.

[8.318]

[3A Arranging and advising on regulated mortgage contracts

A person is not to be regarded as carrying on by way of business an activity of the kind specified by—

(a) article 25A of the Regulated Activities Order (arranging regulated mortgage contracts);

(b) article 53A of that Order (advising on regulated mortgage contracts); or

(c) article 64 of that Order (agreeing), so far as relevant to any of the articles mentioned in sub-paragraphs (a) and (b),

unless he carries on the business of engaging in that activity.]

NOTES

Inserted by the Financial Services and Markets Act 2000 (Regulated Activities) (Amendment) (No 1) Order 2003, SI 2003/1475, art 25, as from 31 October 2004.

[8.319]

[3B Arranging and advising on regulated home reversion plans

A person is not to be regarded as carrying on by way of business an activity specified by—

(a) article 25B of the Regulated Activities Order (arranging regulated home reversion plans);

(b) article 53B of that Order (advising on regulated home reversion plans); or

(c) article 64 of that Order (agreeing), so far as relevant to either of the articles mentioned in sub-paragraphs (a) and (b),

unless he carries on the business of engaging in that activity.]

NOTES

Inserted, together with art 3C, by the Financial Services and Markets Act 2000 (Regulated Activities) (Amendment) (No 2) Order 2006, SI 2006/2383, art 29, as from 6 April 2007.

[8.320]

[3C Arranging and advising on regulated home purchase plans

A person is not to be regarded as carrying on by way of business an activity specified by—

(a) article 25C of the Regulated Activities Order (arranging regulated home purchase plans);

(b) article 53C of that Order (advising on regulated home purchase plans); or

(c) article 64 of that Order (agreeing), so far as relevant to either of the articles mentioned in sub-paragraphs (a) and (b),

unless he carries on the business of engaging in that activity.]

NOTES

Inserted as noted to art 3B at **[8.319]**.

[8.321]

[3D Arranging and advising on regulated sale and rent back agreements

A person is not to be regarded as carrying on by way of business an activity specified by—

(a) article 25E of the Regulated Activities Order (arranging regulated sale and rent back agreements);

(b) article 53D of that Order (advising on regulated sale and rent back agreements); or

(c) article 64 of that Order (agreeing), so far as relevant to either of the articles mentioned in sub-paragraphs (a) and (b),

unless that person carries on the business of engaging in that activity.]

NOTES

Inserted by the Financial Services and Markets Act 2000 (Regulated Activities) (Amendment) Order 2009, SI 2009/1342, art 27, as from 1 July 2009 (certain purposes), and as from 30 June 2010 (otherwise).

[8.322]

[3E Debt adjusting, debt-counselling etc by not-for-profit bodies

(1) A not-for-profit body which carries on an activity of the kind specified by article 39D (debt adjusting), 39E (debt-counselling) or 89A (providing credit information services) of the Regulated Activities Order or article 64 of that Order (agreeing to carry on specified kinds of activity) so far as relevant to any of those activities is to be regarded as carrying on that activity by way of business if the activities being carried on by that body consist of, or relate to, that activity.

(2) Paragraph (1) does not apply if the body carries on that activity only on an occasional basis.

(3) It is immaterial for the purposes of paragraph (1) if the activities being carried on by the body also consist of, or relates to, other activities.

(4) In this article, a "not-for-profit body" means a body which, by virtue of its constitution or any enactment—

(a) is required (after payment of outgoings) to apply the whole of its income and any capital it expends for charitable or public purposes, and

(b) is prohibited from directly or indirectly distributing amongst its members any part of its assets (otherwise than for charitable or public purposes).]

NOTES

Inserted by the Financial Services and Markets Act 2000 (Regulated Activities) (Amendment) (No 2) Order 2013, SI 2013/1881, art 13, as from 1 April 2014.

[8.323]

4 Managing investments: occupational pension schemes

(1) A person who carries on an activity of the kind specified by article 37 of the Regulated Activities Order (managing investments), where the assets in question are held for the purposes of an occupational pension scheme, is to be regarded as carrying on that activity by way of business, except where—

(a) he is a person to whom paragraph (2) applies; or

(b) all . . . day to day decisions in the carrying on of that activity (other than decisions falling within paragraph (6)), so far as relating to relevant assets, are taken on his behalf by—

(i) an authorised person who has permission to carry on activities of the kind specified by article 37 of the Regulated Activities Order;

(ii) a person who is an exempt person in relation to activities of that kind; or

(iii) an overseas person.

(2) This paragraph applies to—

(a) any trustee of a relevant scheme who is a beneficiary or potential beneficiary under the scheme; and

(b) any other trustee of a relevant scheme who takes no . . . day to day decisions relating to the management of any relevant assets.

(3) In this article—

["occupational pension scheme" has the meaning given by section 1 of the Pension Schemes Act 1993 but with paragraph (b) of the definition omitted;]

"relevant assets" means assets of the scheme in question which are securities or contractually based investments;

"relevant scheme" means any occupational pension scheme of a kind falling within paragraph (4) or (5).

(4) A scheme falls within this paragraph if—

(a) it is constituted under an irrevocable trust;

(b) it has no more than twelve relevant members;

(c) all relevant members, other than any relevant member who is unfit to act, or is incapable of acting, as trustee of the scheme, are trustees of it; and

(d) all . . . day to day decisions relating to the management of the assets of the scheme which are relevant assets are required to be taken by all, or a majority of, relevant members who are trustees of the scheme or by a person of a kind falling within paragraph (1)(b)(i) or (ii) acting alone or jointly with all, or a majority of, such relevant members;

and for these purposes a person is a relevant member of a scheme if he is an employee or former employee by or in respect of whom contributions to the scheme are being or have been made and to or in respect of whom benefits are or may become payable under the scheme.

(5) A scheme falls within this paragraph if—

(a) it has no more than fifty members;

(b) the contributions made by or in respect of each member of the scheme are used in the acquisition of a contract of insurance on the life of that member or in the acquisition of a contract to pay an annuity on that life;

(c) the only decision of a kind described in paragraph (1)(b) which may be taken in relation to the scheme is the selection of such contracts; and

(d) each member is given the opportunity to select the contract which the contributions made by or in respect of him will be used to acquire.

(6) A decision falls within this paragraph if—

[(a) it is a decision by the trustees of an occupational pension scheme to buy, sell or subscribe for—

(i) units in a collective investment scheme;

(ii) shares or debentures (or warrants relating to such shares or debentures) issued by a body corporate having as its purpose the investment of its funds with the aim of spreading investment risk and giving its members the benefit of the results of the management of those funds by or on behalf of that body; or

(iii) rights under (or rights to or interests in) any contract of insurance;]

. . .

[(b) the decision is taken after advice has been obtained and considered from a person who falls within any of the cases in paragraph (7);]

(c), (d) . . .

[(7) The cases are where the person is—

(a) an authorised person who has permission to carry on activities of the kind specified by article 53 of the Regulated Activities Order in relation to the decision in question;

(b) an exempt person in relation to such activities;

(c) exempt from the general prohibition by virtue of section 327 of the Financial Services and Markets Act 2000; or

(d) an overseas person.]

NOTES

Paras (1), (2), (4): words omitted revoked by the Financial Services and Markets Act 2000 (Carrying on Regulated Activities by Way of Business) (Amendment) Order 2005, SI 2005/922, art 2(1), (2), as from 6 April 2005.

Para (3): definition "occupational pension scheme" substituted by the Financial Services and Markets Act 2000 (Regulated Activities) (Amendment) Order 2006, SI 2006/1969, art 9(1), (3), as from 6 April 2007.

Para (6): sub-paras (a), (b) substituted, words omitted following sub-para (a) revoked, and sub-paras (c), (d) revoked, by SI 2005/922, art 2(1), (4)–(7), as from 6 April 2005.

Para (7): substituted by SI 2005/922, art 2(1), (8), as from 6 April 2005.

[8.324]

[4A Administering a benchmark

A person who carries on an activity of the kind specified by article 63S(b) of the Regulated Activities Order (administering a benchmark) is to be regarded as carrying on that activity by way of business.]

NOTES

Inserted by the Financial Services and Markets Act 2000 (Regulated Activities) (Amendment) Order 2018, SI 2018/831, art 3, as from 11 July 2018.

5 (*Originally added, together with art 6, by the Financial Services and Markets Act 2000 (Carrying on Regulated Activities by Way of Business) (Amendment) Order 2011, SI 2011/2304, art 2, as from 16 September 2011. This article ceased to have effect on 1 January 2022, in accordance with art 6 post.*)

[8.325]

[6

(1) Article 5 ceases to have effect on [1st January 2022].

(2) Before the end of [2017], the Treasury must—
- (a) carry out a review of article 5;
- (b) set out the conclusions of the review in a report; and
- (c) publish the report.

(3) The report must in particular—
- (a) set out the objectives intended to be achieved by article 5;
- (b) assess the extent to which those objectives are achieved; and
- (c) assess whether those objectives remain appropriate and, if so, the extent to which they could be achieved with a scheme that imposes less regulation.]

NOTES

Originally added as noted to art 5 *ante*.

Words in square brackets substituted by the Financial Services and Markets Act 2000 (Carrying on Regulated Activities by Way of Business) (Amendment) Order 2014, SI 2014/3340, art 2, as from 31 December 2014.

FINANCIAL SERVICES AND MARKETS ACT 2000 (EXEMPTION) ORDER 2001

(SI 2001/1201)

NOTES

Made: 26 March 2001.

Authority: Financial Services and Markets Act 2000, ss 38, 428(3).

Commencement: 1 December 2001.

This Order is reproduced as amended by:

2001	Financial Services and Markets Act 2000 (Exemption) (Amendment) Order 2001, SI 2001/3623.
2002	Financial Services and Markets Act 2000 (Financial Promotion and Miscellaneous Amendments) Order 2002, SI 2002/1310.
2003	Financial Services and Markets Act 2000 (Exemption) (Amendment) Order 2003, SI 2003/47; Financial Services and Markets Act 2000 (Exemption) (Amendment) (No 2) Order 2003, SI 2003/1675.
2005	Financial Services and Markets Act 2000 (Exemption) (Amendment) Order 2005, SI 2005/592; Civil Partnership Act 2004 (Amendments to Subordinate Legislation) Order 2005, SI 2005/2114; Wales Tourist Board (Transfer of Functions to the National Assembly for Wales and Abolition) Order 2005, SI 2005/3225.
2006	Tourist Boards (Scotland) Act 2006; Charities and Trustee Investment (Scotland) Act 2005 (Consequential Provisions and Modifications) Order 2006, SI 2006/242; Financial Services and Markets Act 2000 (Regulated Activities) (Amendment) Order 2006, SI 2006/1969; Financial Services and Markets Act 2000 (Regulated Activities) (Amendment) (No 2) Order 2006, SI 2006/2383.
2007	Financial Services and Markets Act 2000 (Exemption) (Amendment) Order 2007, SI 2007/125; Tourist Boards (Scotland) Act 2006 (Consequential Modifications) Order 2007, SI 2007/1103; Financial Services and Markets Act 2000 (Exemption) (Amendment No 2) Order 2007, SI 2007/1821.
2008	Financial Services and Markets Act 2000 (Exemption) (Amendment) Order 2008, SI 2008/682; Housing and Regeneration Act 2008 (Consequential Provisions) (No 2) Order 2008, SI 2008/2831.
2009	Financial Services and Markets Act 2000 (Exemption) (Amendment) Order 2009, SI 2009/118; Financial Services and Markets Act 2000 (Exemption) (Amendment) Order 2009, SI 2009/264; Financial Services and Markets Act 2000 (Regulated Activities) (Amendment) Order 2009, SI 2009/1342.
2010	Financial Services and Markets Act 2000 (Regulated Activities) (Amendment) Order 2010, SI 2010/86; Housing and Regeneration Act 2008 (Consequential Provisions) (No 2) Order 2010, SI 2010/671.
2011	Financial Services and Markets Act 2000 (Exemption) (Amendment) Order 2011, SI 2011/1626; Financial Services and Markets Act 2000 (Exemption) (Amendment No 2) Order 2011, SI 2011/2716.
2012	Housing (Scotland) Act 2010 (Consequential Provisions and Modifications) Order 2012, SI 2012/700; Financial Services and Markets Act 2000 (Exemption) (Amendment) Order 2012, SI 2012/763.
2013	Financial Services Act 2012 (Consequential Amendments and Transitional Provisions) Order 2013, SI 2013/472; Alternative Investment Fund Managers Regulations 2013, SI 2013/1773; Financial Services and Markets Act 2000 (Regulated Activities) (Amendment) (No 2) Order 2013, SI 2013/1881.
2014	Financial Services and Markets Act 2000 (Regulated Activities) (Amendment) Order 2014, SI 2014/366; Fi-

	nancial Services and Markets Act 2000 (Consumer Credit) (Miscellaneous Provisions) (No 2) Order 2014, SI 2014/506.
2015	Financial Services and Markets Act 2000 (Miscellaneous Provisions) (No 2) Order 2015, SI 2015/352; Financial Services and Markets Act 2000 (Exemption) (Amendment) Order 2015, SI 2015/447; Mortgage Credit Directive Order 2015, SI 2015/910.
2016	Financial Services and Markets Act 2000 (Regulated Activities) (Amendment) Order 2016, SI 2016/392.
2017	Financial Services and Markets Act 2000 (Regulated Activities) (Amendment) Order 2017, SI 2017/488.
2018	Financial Services and Markets Act 2000 (Benchmarks) Regulations 2018, SI 2018/135.
2019	Financial Services and Markets Act 2000 (Amendment) (EU Exit) Regulations 2019, SI 2019/632; Uncertificated Securities (Amendment and EU Exit) Regulations 2019, SI 2019/679; Financial Services (Miscellaneous) (Amendment) (EU Exit) Regulations 2019, SI 2019/710.
2020	Financial Services and Markets Act 2000 (Exemption) (Amendment) Order 2020, SI 2020/322.
2021	Financial Services and Markets Act 2000 (Exemption) (Amendment) Order 2021, SI 2021/1127.
2022	Financial Services and Markets Act 2000 (Exemption) (Amendment) Order 2022, SI 2022/100; Financial Services and Markets Act 2000 (Regulated Activities) (Amendment) Order 2022, SI 2022/466.

Transitional provisions in relation to Gibraltar-based firms and activities: see the Gibraltar (Miscellaneous Amendments) (EU Exit) Regulations 2019, SI 2019/680, reg 11 at **[12.129]**.

ARRANGEMENT OF ARTICLES

SCHEDULES

[8.326]

1 Citation and commencement

This Order may be cited as the Financial Services and Markets Act 2000 (Exemption) Order 2001 and comes into force on the day on which section 19 of the Act comes into force.

NOTES

FSMA 2000, s 19 came into force on 1 December 2001 (see the Financial Services and Markets Act 2000 (Commencement No 7) Order 2001, SI 2001/3538).

[8.327]

2 Interpretation

In this Order—

"the Act" means the Financial Services and Markets Act 2000;

"charity"—

(a) in relation to Scotland, means a [body entered in the Scottish Charity Register]; and

(b) otherwise, has the meaning given by section 96(1) of the Charities Act 1993 or by section 35 of the Charities Act (Northern Ireland) 1964;

[. . .]

"deposit" has the meaning given by the Regulated Activities Order;

"industrial and provident society" has the meaning given by section 417(1) of the Act but does not include a credit union within the meaning of the Credit Unions Act 1979 or the Credit Unions (Northern Ireland) Order 1985;

["investment firm" has the meaning given by the Regulated Activities Order;]

"local authority" means—

(a) in England and Wales, a local authority within the meaning of the Local Government Act 1972, the Greater London Authority, the Common Council of the City of London or the Council of the Isles of Scilly;

(b) in Scotland, a local authority within the meaning of the Local Government (Scotland) Act 1973; and

(c) in Northern Ireland, a district council within the meaning of the Local Government Act (Northern Ireland) 1972;

["non-qualifying contract of insurance" means a contract of insurance (within the meaning of the Regulated Activities Order) which is not a qualifying contract of insurance (within the meaning of that Order);]

["qualifying credit institution" has the meaning given by article 3 of the Regulated Activities Order;]

"the Regulated Activities Order" means the Financial Services and Markets Act 2000 (Regulated Activities) Order 2001.

NOTES

Words in square brackets in definition "charity" substituted by the Charities and Trustee Investment (Scotland) Act 2005 (Consequential Provisions and Modifications) Order 2006, SI 2006/242, art 5, Schedule, Pt 2, para 11, as from 1 April 2006.

Definition "credit institution" (omitted) originally inserted by the Financial Services and Markets Act 2000 (Exemption) (Amendment) Order 2007, SI 2007/125, art 3, as from 1 November 2007. Subsequently revoked by the Financial Services (Miscellaneous) (Amendment) (EU Exit) Regulations 2019, SI 2019/710, reg 7, as from IP completion day (as defined in the European Union (Withdrawal Agreement) Act 2020, s 39).

Definition "investment firm" inserted by SI 2007/125, art 3, as from 1 November 2007.

Definition "non-qualifying contract of insurance" inserted by the Financial Services and Markets Act 2000 (Exemption) (Amendment) (No 2) Order 2003, SI 2003/1675, art 2(1), (2), as from 14 January 2005.

Definition "qualifying credit institution" inserted by SI 2019/710, reg 7, as from IP completion day (as defined in the European Union (Withdrawal Agreement) Act 2020, s 39).

Charities Act 2003: repealed and replaced by the Charities Act 2011. As to the meaning of "charity" see s 1 of the 2011 Act.

[8.328]

3 Persons exempt in respect of any regulated activity other than insurance business

Each of the persons listed in Part I of the Schedule is exempt from the general prohibition in respect of any regulated activity other than an activity of the kind specified by article 10 of the Regulated Activities Order (effecting and carrying out contracts of insurance).

[8.329]

4 Persons exempt in respect of accepting deposits

Subject to the limitations, if any, expressed in relation to him, each of the persons listed in Part II of the Schedule is exempt from the general prohibition in respect of any regulated activity of the kind specified by article 5 of the Regulated Activities Order (accepting deposits).

[8.330]

5 Persons exempt in respect of particular regulated activities

(1) Subject to the limitation, if any, expressed in relation to him, each of the persons listed in Part III of the Schedule is exempt from the general prohibition in respect of any regulated activity of the kind specified by any of the following provisions of the Regulated Activities Order, or article 64 of that Order (agreeing to carry on specified kinds of activity) so far as relevant to any such activity—

(a) article 14 (dealing in investments as principal);
(b) article 21 (dealing in investments as agent);
(c) article 25 (arranging deals in investments);
[(ca) article 25D (operating a multilateral trading facility);]
[(cb) article 25DA (operating an organised trading facility);]
(d) article 37 (managing investments);
[(da) article 39A (assisting in the administration and performance of a contract of insurance);]
(e) article 40 (safeguarding and administering investments);
(f) article 45 (sending dematerialised instructions);
[(ga) article 51ZA (managing a UCITS);
(gb) article 51ZB (acting as a trustee or depositary of a UCITS);
(gc) article 51ZC (managing an AIF);
(gd) article 51ZD (acting as a trustee or depositary of an AIF);
(ge) article 51ZE (establishing etc. a collective investment scheme);]
(h) article 52 (establishing etc a . . . pension scheme);
(i) article 53 (advising on investments).

(2) Subject to the limitation, if any, expressed in relation to him, each of the persons listed in Part IV of the Schedule is exempt from the general prohibition in respect of any regulated activity of the kind referred to in relation to him, or an activity of the kind specified by article 64 of the Regulated Activities Order so far as relevant to any such activity.

NOTES

Para (1) is amended as follows:

Sub-para (ca) inserted by the Financial Services and Markets Act 2000 (Exemption) (Amendment) Order 2007, SI 2007/125, art 4, as from 1 November 2007.

Sub-para (cb) inserted by the Financial Services and Markets Act 2000 (Regulated Activities) (Amendment) Order 2017, SI 2017/488, art 14, Schedule, para 6(1), (2), as from 3 January 2018.

Sub-para (da) inserted by the Financial Services and Markets Act 2000 (Exemption) (Amendment) (No 2) Order 2003, SI 2003/1675, art 2(1), (3), as from 14 January 2005.

Sub-paras (ga)–(ge) substituted (for the original sub-para (g)) by the Alternative Investment Fund Managers Regulations 2013, SI 2013/1773, reg 81, Sch 2, Part 2, para 8, as from 22 July 2013.

Word omitted from sub-para (h) revoked by the Financial Services and Markets Act 2000 (Regulated Activities) (Amendment) Order 2006, SI 2006/1969, art 10, as from 6 April 2007.

[8.331]

[5A Persons exempt in respect of administering a benchmark

Part 1 of the Schedule does not apply to the regulated activity specified in article 63S of the Regulated Activities Order (administering a benchmark). The persons exempt in respect of the regulated activity of administering a benchmark are those listed, or carrying out an activity listed, in Article 2(2) of Regulation EU 2016/1011 of the European Parliament and of the Council of 8 June 2016 on indices used as benchmarks in financial instruments and financial contracts or to measure the performance of investment funds and amending Directives 2008/48/EC and 2014/17/EU and Regulation (EU) No 596/2014.]

NOTES

Inserted by the Financial Services and Markets Act 2000 (Benchmarks) Regulations 2018, SI 2018/135, reg 54, as from 27 February 2018.

[8.332]

6 Transitional exemption for credit unions

A credit union, within the meaning of the Credit Unions Act 1979 . . . , is exempt from the general prohibition in respect of any regulated activity of the kind specified by article 5 of the Regulated Activities Order, but only until 1st July 2002.

NOTES

Words omitted revoked by the Financial Services and Markets Act 2000 (Exemption) (Amendment) Order 2001, SI 2001/3623, arts 2, 3, as from 1 December 2001.

SCHEDULE

Articles 3 to 5

PART I PERSONS EXEMPT IN RESPECT OF ANY REGULATED ACTIVITY OTHER THAN INSURANCE BUSINESS

[8.333]

1. The Bank of England.

2–6. . . .

7. The European Investment Bank.

8. The International Bank for Reconstruction and Development.

9. The International Finance Corporation.

10. The International Monetary Fund.

11. The African Development Bank.

12. The Asian Development Bank.

13. The Caribbean Development Bank.

14. The Inter-American Development Bank.

15. The European Bank for Reconstruction and Development.

[15A. Bank for International Settlements.]

[15B. Bank of England Asset Purchase Facility Fund Limited.]

[15C. Covid Corporate Financing Facility Limited.]

[15D. UK Infrastructure Bank Limited.]

NOTES

Paras 2–6: revoked by the Financial Services and Markets Act 2000 (Amendment) (EU Exit) Regulations 2019, SI 2019/632, reg 177(1), (2), as from IP completion day (as defined in the European Union (Withdrawal Agreement) Act 2020, s 39).

Para 15A: added by the Financial Services and Markets Act 2000 (Exemption) (Amendment) Order 2003, SI 2003/47, art 2, as from 1 March 2003.

Para 15B: added by the Financial Services and Markets Act 2000 (Exemption) (Amendment) Order 2009, SI 2009/118, art 2, as from 2 February 2009.

Para 15C: added by the Financial Services and Markets Act 2000 (Exemption) (Amendment) Order 2020, SI 2020/322, art 2, as from 23 March 2020.

Para 15D: added by the Financial Services and Markets Act 2000 (Exemption) (Amendment) Order 2021, SI 2021/1127, art 2, as from 1 November 2021.

PART II PERSONS EXEMPT IN RESPECT OF ACCEPTING DEPOSITS

[8.334]

16. A municipal bank, that is to say a company which was, immediately before the coming into force of this Order, exempted from the prohibition in section 3 of the Banking Act 1987 by virtue of section 4(1) of, and paragraph 4 of Schedule 2 to, that Act.

17. (1) Keesler Federal Credit Union, in so far as it accepts deposits from members, or dependants of members, of a visiting force of the United States of America, or from members, or dependants of members, of a civilian component of such a force.

(2) In sub-paragraph (1), "member", "dependent" and "visiting force" have the meanings given by section 12 of the Visiting Forces Act 1952 and "member of a civilian component" has the meaning given by section 10 of that Act.

18. A body of persons certified as a school bank by the National Savings Bank or by an authorised person who has permission to accept deposits.

19. . . .

20. (1) Any body which by virtue of any enactment has power to issue a precept to a local authority in England or Wales or a requisition to a local authority in Scotland, or to the expenses of which, by virtue of any enactment, a local authority in the United Kingdom is or can be required to contribute.

(2) In sub-paragraph (1), "enactment" includes an enactment comprised in, or in an instrument made under, an Act of the Scottish Parliament.

[21. The Council of Europe Development Bank.]

22. A charity, in so far as it accepts deposits—

(a) from another charity; or

(b) in respect of which no interest or premium is payable.

23. The National Children's Charities Fund in so far as—

(a) it accepts deposits in respect of which no interest or premium is payable; and

(b) the total value of the deposits made by any one person does not exceed £10,000.

24. An industrial and provident society, in so far as it accepts deposits in the form of withdrawable share capital.

[24A. . . .]

25. . . .

NOTES

Para 19: revoked by the Financial Services and Markets Act 2000 (Regulated Activities) (Amendment) Order 2014, SI 2014/366, art 8(1), (2), as from 1 April 2014.

Para 21: substituted by the Financial Services and Markets Act 2000 (Financial Promotion and Miscellaneous Amendments) Order 2002, SI 2002/1310, art 4(2), as from 5 June 2002.

Para 24A: originally inserted by the Financial Services and Markets Act 2000 (Exemption) (Amendment) Order 2001, SI 2001/3623, arts 2, 4, as from 1 December 2001. Subsequently revoked by the Financial Services and Markets Act 2000 (Exemption) (Amendment No 2) Order 2011, SI 2011/2716, art 2, as from 31 March 2012.

Para 25: revoked by the Financial Services and Markets Act 2000 (Exemption) (Amendment) Order 2015, SI 2015/447, art 2(1), (2), as from 30 March 2015.

Banking Act 1987: repealed by the Financial Services and Markets Act 2000 (Consequential Amendments and Repeals) Order 2001, SI 2001/3649, as from 1 December 2001.

PART III PERSONS EXEMPT IN RESPECT OF ANY REGULATED ACTIVITY MENTIONED IN ARTICLE 5(1)

[8.335]

26. The National Debt Commissioners.

[27. Partnerships UK.]

28. The International Development Association.

29. The English Tourist Board.

30. . . .

[31. VisitScotland.]

32. The Northern Ireland Tourist Board.

33. Scottish Enterprise.

[33A. Invest Northern Ireland.]

34. The Multilateral Investment Guarantee Agency.

[34A. The Board of the Pension Protection Fund.]

[34B. Capital for Enterprise Limited, in so far as in carrying on any regulated activity it provides services only to the Crown.]

[34C. BIS (Postal Services Act 2011) Company Limited.]

35. A person acting as an official receiver within the meaning of section 399 of the Insolvency Act 1986 or article 2 of the Insolvency (Northern Ireland) Order 1989.

36, 37. . . .

38. A person acting as a judicial factor.

39. . . .]

NOTES

Para 27: substituted by the Financial Services and Markets Act 2000 (Exemption) (Amendment) (No 2) Order 2003, SI 2003/1675, art 2(1), (4)(a), as from 13 July 2003.

Para 30: revoked by the Wales Tourist Board (Transfer of Functions to the National Assembly for Wales and Abolition) Order 2005, SI 2005/3225, art 6(2), Sch 2, Pt 2, para 4, as from 1 April 2006.

Para 31: substituted by the Tourist Boards (Scotland) Act 2006, s 4, Sch 2, Pt 2, para 10, as from 1 April 2007 (in relation to Scotland), and by the Tourist Boards (Scotland) Act 2006 (Consequential Modifications) Order 2007, SI 2007/1103, art 2, Schedule, Pt 2, para 6, as from 29 March 2007 (in relation to England and Wales).

Para 33A: inserted by the Financial Services and Markets Act 2000 (Exemption) (Amendment No 2) Order 2007, SI 2007/1821, art 2(1), (2), as from 20 July 2007.

Para 34A: inserted by the Financial Services and Markets Act 2000 (Exemption) (Amendment) Order 2005, SI 2005/592, art 2(1), as from 6 April 2005.

Para 34B: inserted by the Financial Services and Markets Act 2000 (Exemption) (Amendment) Order 2008, SI 2008/682, art 2, as from 1 April 2008.

Para 34C: inserted by the Financial Services and Markets Act 2000 (Exemption) (Amendment) Order 2012, SI 2012/763, art 2, as from 1 April 2012.

Para 36: revoked by the Financial Services and Markets Act 2000 (Exemption) (Amendment) Order 2007, SI 2007/125, art 5, as from 1 November 2007.

Para 37: revoked by the Uncertificated Securities (Amendment and EU Exit) Regulations 2019, SI 2019/679, reg 7, as from 27 March 2019 (for transitional provisions and savings see regs 11, 12 of the 2019 Regulations at **[12.125]** et seq).

Para 39: revoked by the Financial Services and Markets Act 2000 (Regulated Activities) (Amendment) Order 2014, SI 2014/366, art 8(1), (3), as from 1 April 2014.

Uncertificated Securities Regulations 1995 (SI 1995/3272): revoked and replaced by the Uncertificated Securities Regulations 2001, SI 2001/3755. As to the meaning of "Operator", see reg 3 of the 2001 Regulations.

PART IV PERSONS EXEMPT IN RESPECT OF PARTICULAR REGULATED ACTIVITIES

Enterprise schemes

[8.336]

40. (1) Any body corporate which has as its principal object (or one of its principal objects)—

(a) the promotion or encouragement of industrial or commercial activity or enterprise in the United Kingdom or in any particular area of it; or

(b) the dissemination of information concerning persons engaged in such activity or enterprise or requiring capital to become so engaged;

is exempt from the general prohibition in respect of any regulated activity of the kind specified by [articles 25, 36A, 39D, 39E and 89A of the Regulated Activities Order (arranging deals in investments, credit broking, debt adjusting, debt-counselling and providing credit information services)] so long as it does not carry on that activity for, or with the prospect of, direct or indirect pecuniary gain.

(2) For the purposes of this paragraph, such sums as may reasonably be regarded as necessary to meet the costs of carrying on the activity mentioned in sub-paragraph (1) do not constitute a pecuniary gain.

[(3) This paragraph does not apply where an investment firm or [qualifying credit institution]—

(a) provides or performs investment services and activities on a professional basis, and

(b) in doing so, but for the operation of [sub-paragraph (1)], it would be treated as carrying on an activity of a kind specified by Part 2 of the Regulated Activities Order [in breach of the general prohibition].]

Employee share schemes in electricity industry shares

41. (1) Each of the persons to whom this paragraph applies is exempt from the general prohibition in respect of any regulated activity of the kind specified by article 14, 21 or 25 of the Regulated Activities Order (dealing in investments as principal or agent or arranging deals in investments) which he carries on for the purpose of—

(a) enabling or facilitating transactions in electricity industry shares or debentures between or for the benefit of any qualifying person; or

(b) the holding of electricity industry shares or debentures by or for the benefit of any qualifying person.

(2) This paragraph applies to—

(a) The National Grid Holding plc;

(b) Electricity Association Limited;

(c) any body corporate in the same group as the person mentioned in sub-paragraph (a) or (b);

(d) any company listed in Schedule 1 to the Electricity Act 1989 (Nominated Companies) (England and Wales) Order 1990; and

(e) a person holding shares in or debentures of a body corporate as trustee in pursuance of arrangements made for either of the purposes mentioned in sub-paragraph (1) by the Secretary of State, by any of the bodies mentioned in sub-paragraphs (a) to (c) or by an electricity successor company or by some or all of them.

(3) In this paragraph—

(a) "electricity industry shares or debentures" means—

(i) any investment of the kind specified by article 76[, 77 or 77A] of the Regulated Activities Order (shares or instruments creating or acknowledging indebtedness [or alternative finance investment bond]) in or of an electricity successor company;

(ii) any investment of the kind specified by article 79 or 80 of that Order (instruments giving entitlement to investments and certificates representing certain securities), so far as relevant to the investments mentioned in sub-paragraph (i); and

(iii) any investment of the kind specified by article 89 of that Order (rights to or interests in investments) so far as relevant to the investments mentioned in sub-paragraphs (i) and (ii);

(b) "qualifying person" means—

(i) the bona fide employees or former employees of The National Grid Holding plc, Electricity Association Limited or any other body corporate in the same group as either of them; and

(ii) the wives, husbands, widows, widowers[, civil partners, surviving civil partners,] or children (including, in Northern Ireland, adopted children) or step-children under the age of eighteen of such employees or former employees;

(c) references to an electricity successor company include any body corporate that is in the same group and "electricity successor company" means a body corporate which is a successor company for the purposes of Part II of the Electricity Act 1989;

(d) "former employees" of a person ("the employer") include any person who has never been employed by the employer so long as he occupied a position in relation to some other person of such a kind that it may reasonably be assumed that he would have been a former employee of the employer had the reorganisation of the electricity industry under Part II of the Electricity Act 1989 been affected before he ceased to occupy the relevant position.

Gas industry

42. (1) Transco plc is exempt from the general prohibition in respect of any regulated activity of the kind specified by article 14, 21[, 25[, 25D or 25DA]] of the Regulated Activities Order (dealing in investments as principal or agent[, arranging deals in investments[, operating a multilateral trading facility or operating an organised trading facility]]) which it carries on—

(a) in its capacity as a gas transporter under the Transco Licence; and

(b) for the purposes of enabling or facilitating gas shippers to buy or sell an investment of the kind specified by article 84 or 85 of the Regulated Activities Order (futures or contracts for differences etc).

(2) ENMO Ltd is exempt from the general prohibition in respect of any regulated activity of the kind specified by article 14, 21[, 25[, 25D or 25DA]] of the Regulated Activities Order (dealing in investments as principal or agent[, arranging deals in investments[, operating a multilateral trading facility or operating an organised trading facility]]) which it carries on—

(a) in its capacity as the operator of the balancing market; and
(b) for the purpose of enabling or facilitating Transco plc and relevant gas shippers, for the purpose of participating in the balancing market, to buy or sell investments of the kind specified by article 84 or 85 of that Order (futures or contracts for differences etc).

(3) Transco plc and relevant gas shippers are exempt from the general prohibition in respect of any regulated activity of the kind specified by article 14 or 21 of the Regulated Activities Order (dealing in investments as principal or agent) in so far as that activity relates to an investment of the kind specified by article 84 or 85 of that Order (futures or contracts for differences etc) and is carried on for the purpose of participating in the balancing market.

(4) In this paragraph—

(a) "the balancing market" means the market to regulate the delivery and off-take of gas in Transco plc's pipeline system for the purpose of balancing the volume of gas in that system;
(b) "gas shipper" has the same meaning as in Part I of the Gas Act 1986;
(c) "relevant gas shippers" means gas shippers who have entered into a subscription agreement with ENMO Ltd for the purpose of participating in the balancing market;
(d) "Transco Licence" means the licence treated as granted to Transco plc as a gas transporter under section 7 of the Gas Act 1986;
(e) the reference to enabling or facilitating includes acting pursuant to rules governing the operation of the balancing market which apply in the event of one of the participants appearing to be unable, or likely to become unable, to meet his obligations in respect of one or more contracts entered into through the balancing market.

Trade unions and employers' associations

43. (1) A trade union or employers' association is exempt from the general prohibition in respect of any regulated activity of the kind specified by article 10 of the Regulated Activities Order (effecting and carrying out contracts of insurance) which it carries on in order to provide provident benefits or strike benefits for its members.

(2) In sub-paragraph (1), "trade union" and "employers' association" have the meanings given by section 1 and section 122(1) of the Trade Union and Labour Relations (Consolidation) Act 1992 or, in Northern Ireland, the meanings given by article 3(1) and article 4(1) of the Industrial Relations (Northern Ireland) Order 1992.

Charities

44. [(A1) A charity is exempt from the general prohibition in respect of any regulated activity of the kind specified by article 36H of the Regulated Activities Order (operating an electronic system in relation to lending) which it carries on in relation to an article 36H agreement (within the meaning given in article 36H(4) of the Regulated Activities Order) under or in connection with which the only amount payable to the lender is the amount of credit provided.]

(1) A charity is exempt from the general prohibition in respect of any regulated activity of the kind specified by [articles 51ZA to 51ZE of the Regulated Activities Order (managing or acting as trustee or depositary of a UCITS or an AIF, or establishing etc a collective investment scheme)] which it carries on in relation to a fund established under—

(a) section 22A of the Charities Act 1960;
(b) section 25 of the Charities Act 1993; or
(c) section 25 of the Charities Act (Northern Ireland) 1964.

(2) A charity is exempt from the general prohibition in respect of any regulated activity of the kind specified by [articles 51ZA to 51ZE of the Regulated Activities Order (managing or acting as trustee or depositary of a UCITS or an AIF, or establishing etc a collective investment scheme)] which it carries on in relation to a pooling scheme fund established under—

(a) section 22 of the Charities Act 1960; or
(b) section 24 of the Charities Act 1993.

(3) In sub-paragraph (2), "pooling scheme fund" means a fund established by a common investment scheme the trusts of which provide that property is not to be transferred to the fund except by or on behalf of a charity, the charity trustees (within the meaning of section 97(1) of the Charities Act 1993) of which are the trustees appointed to manage the fund.

Schemes established under the Trustee Investments Act 1961

45. A person acting in his capacity as manager or operator of a fund established under section 11 of the Trustee Investments Act 1961 is exempt from the general prohibition in respect of any regulated activity of the kind specified by [articles 51ZA to 51ZE of the Regulated Activities Order (managing or acting as trustee or depositary of a UCITS or an AIF, or establishing etc a collective investment scheme)] which he carries on in relation to that fund.

Former members of Lloyd's

46. Any person who ceased to be an underwriting member (within the meaning of Lloyd's Act 1982) of Lloyd's before 24th December 1996 is exempt from the general prohibition in respect of any regulated activity of the kind specified by article 10(2) of the Regulated Activities Order (carrying out contracts of insurance) which relates to contracts of insurance that he has underwritten at Lloyd's.

Local authorities

47. . . .

Social housing

[48. (1) A relevant housing body is exempt from the general prohibition in respect of any regulated activity of the kind specified by—

(a) article 21, 25(1) or (2), 39A or 53 of the Regulated Activities Order (dealing in investments as agent, arranging deals in investments, assisting in the administration and performance of a contract of insurance or advising on investments) which relates to a non-qualifying contract of insurance; . . .

(b) [article 25A(1)(b) and (2) of that Order (arranging a regulated mortgage contract)][;

(c) article 25B, 53B or 63B of that Order (arranging, advising on, entering into or administering a regulated home reversion plan); . . .

(d) article 25C, 53C or 63F of that Order (arranging, advising on, entering into or administering a regulated home purchase plan)[;

[(e) article 25E, 53D or 63J of that Order (arranging, advising on, entering into or administering a regulated sale and rent back agreement)]].

[(1A) A relevant housing body is exempt from the general prohibition in respect of any regulated activity of the kind specified by article 25A(1)(a) or (2A), 53A or 61 of that Order (arranging, advising on, entering into or administering a regulated mortgage contract) in so far as the contract—

[(a) was entered into before 21st March 2016; or

(b) is entered into on or after 21st March 2016 and—

(i) is of a kind to which [section 423A(3) of the Act applies];

(ii) is a bridging loan; or

(iii) is a restricted public loan in relation to which the requirements of sub-paragraph (1B) are met.]

(1B) The requirements of this sub-paragraph are that—

(a) the borrower receives timely information on the main features, risks and costs of the loan at the pre-contractual stage; and

(b) any advertising of the loan is fair, clear and not misleading.]

(2) In this paragraph, "relevant housing body" means any of the following—

(a) a registered social landlord within the meaning of Part I of the Housing Act 1996;

[(aa) a non-profit registered provider of social housing;]

(b) a registered social landlord within the meaning of [the Housing (Scotland) Act 2010];

(c) . . . ;

[(ca) the Homes and Communities Agency;]

(d) . . .

(e) the body established under article 9 of the Housing (Northern Ireland) Order 1981 known as the Northern Ireland Housing Executive;

(f) . . .

[(g) a housing association within the meaning of Part 2 of the Housing (Northern Ireland) Order 1992];]

[(h) except for the purposes of sub-paragraph (1)(a), the Scottish Ministers;

(i) except for the purposes of sub-paragraph (1)(a), the Welsh Ministers].

[(3) Except for the purposes of sub-paragraph (1)(a), "relevant housing body" also includes a wholly-owned subsidiary of a body listed in sub-paragraph (2)(a), (aa), (b), (ca), (h) or (i).

(4) In this paragraph—

"bridging loan" has the meaning given by [article 60G(9) of the Regulated Activities Order];

"borrower" means a person receiving credit;

"credit" includes a cash loan and any other form of financial accommodation;

"restricted public loan" means credit that is—

(a) offered to a particular class of borrower and not offered to the public generally;

(b) offered under an enactment with a general interest purpose; and

(c) provided on terms which are more favourable to the borrower than those prevailing on the market, because it meets one of the following conditions—

(i) it is interest free;

(ii) the rate of interest is lower than that prevailing on the market; or

(iii) the rate of interest is no higher than that prevailing on the market but the other terms on which credit is provided are more favourable to the borrower; and

"wholly-owned subsidiary" has the same meaning as in section 1159 (meaning of "subsidiary" etc) of the Companies Act 2006 and, for the purposes of this definition, a relevant housing body is to be treated as a body corporate.]

[Electricity industry

49. (1) NGC is exempt from the general prohibition in respect of any regulated activity of the kind specified by article 14, 21, 25[, 25D][, 25DA] or 53 of the Regulated Activities Order (dealing in investments as principal or agent, arranging deals in investments[, operating a multilateral trading facility][, operating an organised trading facility] or advising on investments) which it carries on in the course of—

(a) its participation in the Balancing and Settlement Arrangements as operator of the electricity transmission system in [Great Britain] under the Transmission Licence; or

(b) the acquisition by it of Balancing Services in accordance with the Electricity Act 1989 and the Transmission Licence.

(2) ELEXON Clear Limited is exempt from the general prohibition in respect of any regulated activity of the kind specified by article 14, 21[, 25[, 25D or 25DA]] of that Order which it carries on in the course of its participation in the Balancing and Settlement Arrangements as clearer for the purposes of (among other things) receiving from and paying to BSC Parties trading and reconciliation charges arising under the Balancing and Settlement Arrangements.

(3) Each BSC Party is exempt from the general prohibition in respect of any regulated activity of the kind specified by article 14, 21, 25[, 25D][, 25DA] or 53 of that Order which it carries on in the course of—

(a) its participation in the Balancing and Settlement Arrangements; or

(b) the provision by it (or, in the case of an activity of the kind specified by article 21 of that Order, its principal) of Balancing Services to NGC.

(4) ELEXON Limited is exempt from the general prohibition in respect of any regulated activity of the kind specified by article 2[, 25D or 25DA] of that Order which it carries on in the course of its participation in the Balancing and Settlement Arrangements as administrator

(5) Each BSC Agent and each Volume Notification Agent is exempt from the general prohibition in respect of any regulated activity of the kind specified by article 25[, 25D or 25DA] of that Order which it carries on in that capacity.

(6) . . .

(7) In this paragraph—

"Ancillary Services" means services which generators and suppliers of electricity and those making transfers of electricity across an Interconnector are required (as a condition of their connection to the transmission system in [Great Britain]), or have agreed, to make available to NGC for the purpose of securing the stability of the electricity transmission or any distribution system in [Great Britain] or any system linked to it by an Interconnector;

"Balancing and Settlement Arrangements" means—

(a) the Balancing Mechanism; and

(b) arrangements—

(i) for the determination and allocation to BSC Parties of the quantities of electricity that have been delivered to and taken off the electricity transmission system and any distribution system in [Great Britain]; and

(ii) which set, and provide for the determination and financial settlement of, BSC Parties' obligations arising by reference to the quantities referred to in sub-paragraph (i), including the difference between such quantities (after taking account of accepted bids and offers in the Balancing Mechanism) and the quantities of electricity contracted for sale and purchase between BSC Parties;

"Balancing Mechanism" means the arrangements pursuant to which BSC Parties may make, and NGC may accept, offers or bids to increase or decrease the quantities of electricity to be delivered to or taken off the electricity transmission system or any distribution system in [Great Britain] at any time or during any period so as to assist NGC in operating and balancing the electricity transmission system, and arrangements for the settlement of financial obligations arising from the acceptance of such offers and bids;

"Balancing Services" means—

(a) offers and bids made in the Balancing Mechanism;

(b) Ancillary Services; and

(c) other services available to NGC which assist it in operating the electricity transmission system in accordance with the Electricity Act 1989 and the Transmission Licence;

"BSC Agents" means the persons for the time being engaged by or on behalf of ELEXON Limited for the purpose of providing services to all BSC Parties, NGC, ELEXON Limited and ELEXON Clear Limited in connection with the operation of the Balancing and Settlement Arrangements;

["BSC Framework Agreement" means the agreement of that title in the form approved by the Secretary of State for the purpose of conditions of the Transmission Licence and which is dated 14 August 2000; and "conditions" for the purposes of this definition means conditions determined by the Secretary of State under powers granted by section 137(1) of the Energy Act 2004. and incorporated into existing electricity transmission licences by a scheme made by the Secretary of State pursuant to section 138 of, and Schedule 17 to, that Act;]

"BSC Parties" means those persons (other than NGC, ELEXON Limited and ELEXON Clear Limited) who have signed or acceded to (in accordance with the terms of the BSC Framework Agreement), and not withdrawn from, the BSC Framework Agreement;

"Interconnector" means the electric lines and electrical plant [and meters] used [solely] for the transfer of electricity to or from the electricity transmission system . . . in [Great Britain] into or out of [Great Britain];

"NGC" means . . . National Grid Company plc;

. . .

"the Transmission Licence" means the licence to [participate in the transmission of] electricity in [Great Britain] granted[, or treated as granted,] to NGC under section 6(1)(b) of the Electricity Act 1989; and

"Volume Notification Agents" means the persons for the time being appointed and authorised under and in accordance with the Balancing and Settlement Arrangements on behalf of BSC Parties to notify to the BSC Agent designated for that purpose pursuant to the Balancing and Settlement Arrangements quantities of electricity contracted for the sale and purchase between those BSC Parties to be taken into account for the purposes of the Balancing and Settlement Arrangements.]

[Freight Forwarders and Storage Firms

50. (1) A freight forwarder or storage firm is exempt from the general prohibition in respect of any regulated activity of the kind specified by article 21, 25, 39A or 53 of the Regulated Activities Order (dealing in investments as agent, arranging deals in investments, assisting in the administration and performance of a contract of insurance or advising on investments) in the circumstances referred to in paragraph 2.

(2) The circumstances are—

(a) where a freight forwarder ("F")—

(i) holds a policy of insurance which insures F in respect of loss of or damage to goods which F transports or of which F arranges the transportation, and

(ii) makes available to a customer rights under that policy to enable the customer to claim directly against the insurer in respect of loss or damage to those goods; or

(b) where a storage firm ("S")—

(i) holds a policy of insurance which insures S in respect of loss of or damage to goods which S stores or for which S arranges storage, and

(ii) makes available to a customer rights under that policy to enable the customer to claim directly against the insurer in respect of loss or damage to those goods.

(3) In this paragraph—

(a) "freight forwarder" means a person whose principal business is arranging or carrying out the transportation of goods;

(b) "storage firm" means a person whose principal business is storing goods or arranging storage for goods;

(c) "customer" means a person . . . who uses the service of a freight forwarder or storage firm.

Policyholder Advocates

51. (1) A person acting as a policyholder advocate is exempt from the general prohibition in respect of any regulated activity of the kind specified by article 25 or 53 of the Regulated Activities Order (arranging deals in investments or advising on investments) in so far as he carries on these activities in connection with, or for the purposes of, his role as policyholder advocate.

(2) In sub-paragraph (1), "policyholder advocate" means a person who is—

(a) appointed by an insurer ("I") to represent the interests of policyholders in negotiations with I about I's proposals to redefine the rights and interests in any surplus assets arising in I's with-profits fund; and

(b) approved or nominated by the [FCA] to carry out that role.

(3) In sub-paragraph (2), "with-profits fund" means a long-term insurance fund in which policyholders are eligible to participate in surplus assets of the fund.]

[[Official receivers]

52. (1) A person acting as—

(a) . . .

(b) an official receiver within the meaning of section 399 of the Insolvency Act 1986 or article 2 of the Insolvency (Northern Ireland) Order 1989, or

(c) a judicial factor,

is exempt from the general prohibition in respect of any regulated activity of the kind specified by any of articles 39D to 39G (activities in relation to debt) or 89A (providing credit information services) of the Regulated Activities Order.

(2), (3) . . .

[(4) A person who—

(a) acts as an official receiver within the meaning of section 399 of the Insolvency Act 1986 or article 2 of the Insolvency (Northern Ireland) Order 1989, and

(b) by virtue of that office, becomes the liquidator of a company in accordance with section 136 of the Insolvency Act 1986 or article 116 of the Insolvency (Northern Ireland) Order 1989,

is exempt from the general prohibition in respect of any regulated activity of the kind specified by article 59(1A) of the Regulated Activities Order (carrying out a funeral plan contract as provider).]

Cycle to Work

53. (1) An employer who provides or makes available to their employees a cycle or cyclist's safety equipment up to the value of £1,000 under a relevant employee benefit scheme is exempt from the general prohibition in respect of any regulated activity of the kind specified by article 60N of the Regulated Activities Order (regulated consumer hire agreements).

(2) For the purposes of this paragraph—

"cycle" has the meaning given by section 192(1) of the Road Traffic Act 1988 (general interpretation);

"relevant employee benefit scheme" means a scheme operated by an employer which is designed to allow employees to take advantage of section 244 of the Income Tax (Earnings and Pensions) Act 2003 (no liability to income tax in relation to cycles and cyclist's safety equipment) and under which cycles or cyclist's safety equipment are made available in the manner described in any guidance issued by the Secretary of State.

Tracing Agents

54. (1) A person who takes steps to ascertain the identity or location (or the means of ascertaining the identity or location) of a borrower or hirer is exempt from the general prohibition in respect of any regulated activity of the kind specified by article 39F of the Regulated Activities Order (debt-collecting) so long as the person is not the lender under the agreement concerned or the owner under the consumer hire agreement concerned and takes no other steps to procure the payment of debts due under the agreement.

(2) In this [paragraph], "borrower", "hirer" "lender" and "owner" have the meanings given by the Regulated Activities Order.]

[Persons who carry on activities for the service of certain documents

54A. (1) A person who serves, or takes steps to serve, a relevant document on a borrower or hirer is exempt from the general prohibition in respect of any regulated activity of the kind specified by article 39F of the Regulated Activities Order (debt-collecting) so long as that person—

(a) is not the lender or owner under the relevant agreement; and

(b) takes no other steps to procure the payment of the debt or any other debt due from the borrower or hirer under the relevant agreement.

(2) A person who serves, or takes steps to serve, a relevant document on a borrower or hirer is exempt from the general prohibition in respect of any regulated activity of the kind specified by article 39G of the Regulated Activities Order (debt administration) so long as that person is not the lender or owner under the relevant agreement and does not take—

(a) any other steps to exercise or enforce rights under that agreement; or

(b) any steps in the performance of any duties under that agreement.

(3) In sub-paragraph (1) "relevant document" means any document which is for service for the purposes of any legal proceedings brought, or to be brought, for the payment of a debt due under the relevant agreement.

(4) In sub-paragraph (2) "relevant document" means any document which is for service for the purposes of any legal proceedings brought, or to be brought, for the exercise or enforcement of rights under the relevant agreement.

(5) In this paragraph—

"borrower", "hirer", "lender" and "owner" have the meaning given in article 3 of the Regulated Activities Order;

"legal proceedings" includes arbitration and insolvency proceedings; and

"relevant agreement", in relation to a person who is a borrower or hirer, means—

(a) the credit agreement (within the meaning given by article 60B of the Regulated Activities Order) or article 36H agreement (within the meaning given by article 36H of that Order) under which that person is the borrower; or

(b) the consumer hire agreement (within the meaning given by article 60N of the Regulated Activities Order) under which that person is the hirer.]

[Persons exercising, or having the right to exercise, the rights of the person who provided credit under a regulated credit agreement

55. (1) A person within the description in sub-paragraph (3) ("P") is exempt from the general prohibition in respect of any activity of the kind specified by article 60B(2) of the Regulated Activities Order (regulated credit agreements) carried on in relation to a qualifying agreement provided that the conditions in sub-paragraphs (4) and (5) are satisfied in respect of the agreement.

(2) Where P is exempt from the general prohibition in respect of any activity of the kind specified by article 60B(2) of the Regulated Activities Order by virtue of sub-paragraph (1), P is also exempt from the general prohibition in respect of any activity of the kind specified by article 39E(1) (debt-counselling) or 39F(1) (debt-collecting) of the Regulated Activities Order carried on in relation to the qualifying agreement in an exempt period.

(3) P is within the description in this sub-paragraph if P—

(a) is not the original lender;

(b) does not grant, is not required to grant, and does not promise to grant credit under the qualifying agreement or any other regulated credit agreement; and

(c) does not undertake any activity of the kind specified in article 39D(1) (debt adjusting), 39E(1) or 39F(1) of the Regulated Activities Order, or which would be so specified but for article 39H(1) of that Order, except in an exempt period.

(4) The condition in this sub-paragraph is that—

(a) P has entered into a servicing arrangement in relation to the qualifying agreement; or

(b) an exempt period has not expired.

(5) The condition in this sub-paragraph is that—

(a) P has arranged for the servicer to comply with the provisions listed in sub-paragraph (6); and

(b) where P (and not the servicer acting on behalf of P) varies the qualifying agreement, P complies with the provisions listed in sub-paragraph (6).

(6) The provisions are—

(a) any provision of, or made under, the Act applicable to authorised persons that relates to the exercise of the right of the lender under a regulated credit agreement to vary terms and conditions of the agreement (including, in particular, the right to vary the rate of interest, charges, or other amount due to the lender under the agreement); and

(b) the requirements of, or made under, section 82 of the Consumer Credit Act 1974 (variation of agreements).

(7) For the purposes of this paragraph, there are excluded from articles 39E(1) and 39F(1) of the Regulated Activities Order activities carried on by P under or for the purposes of a servicing arrangement.

(8) In this paragraph—

"an exempt period" is the period of thirty days beginning on the day after the day on which a servicing arrangement came to an end;

"the original lender" means the person who provided credit under the qualifying agreement;

"a qualifying agreement" means a regulated credit agreement under which P exercises, or has the right to exercise, the rights of the original lender;

"regulated credit agreement" has the meaning given in article 60B of the Regulated Activities Order;

"the servicer" means the person with whom P enters into a servicing arrangement, where that person is an authorised person with permission to carry on an activity of the kind specified in article 39F, 39G (debt administration) or 60B of the Regulated Activities Order;

"a servicing arrangement" means an arrangement between P and the servicer for the servicer to exercise on P's behalf P's rights under a qualifying agreement other than the right to transfer, assign or otherwise dispose of those rights.

Persons exercising, or having the right to exercise, the rights of the person who provided credit under a regulated consumer hire agreement

56. (1) A person within the description in sub-paragraph (3) ("P") is exempt from the general prohibition in respect of any activity of the kind specified by article 60N(2) of the Regulated Activities Order (regulated consumer hire agreements) carried on in relation to a qualifying agreement provided that the conditions in sub-paragraphs (4) and (5) are satisfied in respect of each such agreement.

(2) Where P is exempt from the general prohibition in respect of any activity of the kind specified by article 60N(2) of the Regulated Activities Order by virtue of sub-paragraph (1), P is also exempt from the general prohibition in respect of any activity of the kind specified by article 39E(2) (debt-counselling) or 39F(2) (debt-collecting) of the Regulated Activities Order carried on in relation to the qualifying agreement in an exempt period.

(3) P is within the description in this sub-paragraph if P—

(a) is not the original owner; and

(b) does not undertake any activity of the kind specified in article 39D(2) (debt adjusting), 39E(2) or 39F(2) of the Regulated Activities Order, or which would be so specified but for article 39H(2) of that Order, except in an exempt period.

(4) The condition in this sub-paragraph is that—

(a) P has entered into a servicing arrangement in relation to the qualifying agreement; or

(b) an exempt period has not expired.

(5) The condition in this sub-paragraph is that—

(a) P has arranged for the servicer to comply with the provisions listed in sub-paragraph (6); and

(b) where P (and not the servicer acting on behalf of P) varies the qualifying agreement, P complies with the provisions listed in sub-paragraph (6).

(6) The provisions are—

(a) any provision of, or made under, the Act applicable to authorised persons that relates to the exercise of the right of the owner under a regulated consumer hire agreement to vary terms and conditions of the agreement (including, in particular, the right to vary the hire payments, other charges, or any other amount due to the owner under the agreement); and

(b) the requirements of, or made under, section 82 of the Consumer Credit Act 1974 (variation of agreements).

(7) For the purposes of this paragraph, there are excluded from articles 39E(2) and 39F(2) of the Regulated Activities Order activities carried on by P under or for the purposes of a servicing arrangement.

(8) In this paragraph—

"an exempt period" is the period of thirty days beginning on the day after the day on which a servicing arrangement came to an end;

"the original owner" means the person who entered into the qualifying agreement as owner;

"a qualifying agreement" means a regulated consumer hire agreement under which P exercises, or has the right to exercise, the rights of the original owner;

"regulated consumer hire agreement" has the meaning given in article 60N of the Regulated Activities Order;

"the servicer" means the person with whom P enters into a servicing arrangement, where that person is an authorised person with permission to carry on an activity of the kind specified in article 39F, 39G (debt administration) or 60N of the Regulated Activities Order;

"a servicing arrangement" means an arrangement between P and the servicer for the servicer to exercise on P's behalf P's rights under a qualifying agreement other than the right to transfer, assign or otherwise dispose of those rights.].

[Student Loans Company

57. (1) The Student Loans Company Limited is exempt from the general prohibition in respect of—

(a) any regulated activity of the kind specified by article 5 of the Regulated Activities Order (accepting deposits) in so far as it accepts deposits from the Secretary of State or the Scottish Ministers, in connection with, or for the purposes of, enabling eligible students to receive loans;

(b) any regulated activity of the kind specified by article 39G of the Regulated Activities Order (debt administration) in connection with, or for the purposes of, loans to eligible students.

(2) In sub-paragraph (1)(a), "eligible student" means—

(a) any person who is an eligible student pursuant to regulations made under Part 2 of the Teaching and Higher Education Act 1998;

(b) any person to whom, or in respect of whom, loans may be paid under section 73(f) of the Education (Scotland) Act 1980;

(c) any person who is an eligible student pursuant to regulations made under article 3 of the Education (Student Support) (Northern Ireland) Order 1998;

(d) any person who is in receipt of or who is eligible to receive a loan of the kind mentioned in article 3(1) of the Teaching and Higher Education Act 1998 (Commencement No 2 and Transitional Provisions) Order 1998 or article 3(1) of the Education (Student Support) (Northern Ireland) Order 1998 (Commencement and Transitional Provisions) Order (Northern Ireland) 1998.

(3) In sub-paragraph (1)(b), "eligible student" means any person who is in receipt of or who is eligible to receive a loan of the kind mentioned in article 3(1) of the Teaching and Higher Education Act 1998 (Commencement No 2 and Transitional Provisions) Order 1998 or article 3(1) of the Education (Student Support) (Northern Ireland) Order 1998 (Commencement and Transitional Provisions) Order (Northern Ireland) 1998.]

[Norges Bank

58. Norges Bank is exempt from the general prohibition in respect of any regulated activity of the kind specified by article 14, 21, 25, 37, 40 or 53, of the Regulated Activities Order (dealing in investments as principal, dealing in investments as agent, arranging deals in investments, managing investments, safeguarding and administering investments, and advising on investments).]

NOTES

Para 40: words in square brackets in sub-para (1) substituted by the Financial Services and Markets Act 2000 (Regulated Activities) (Amendment) (No 2) Order 2013, SI 2013/1881, art 14(1), (2), as from 1 April 2014. Sub-para (3) added by the Financial Services and Markets Act 2000 (Exemption) (Amendment) Order 2007, SI 2007/125, art 6(a), as from 1 November 2007. Words in first pair of square brackets in that sub-paragraph substituted by the Financial Services (Miscellaneous) (Amendment) (EU Exit) Regulations 2019, SI 2019/710, reg 7, as from IP completion day (as defined in the European Union (Withdrawal Agreement) Act 2020, s 39). Words in second pair of square brackets in that sub-paragraph substituted, and words in third pair of square brackets added, by the Financial Services and Markets Act 2000 (Exemption) (Amendment No 2) Order 2007, SI 2007/1821, art 2(1), (3), as from 1 November 2007.

Para 41: words in first pair of square brackets in sub-para (3)(a) substituted, and words in second pair of square brackets in that sub-paragraph inserted, by the Financial Services and Markets Act 2000 (Regulated Activities) (Amendment) Order 2010, SI 2010/86, art 4, Schedule, para 7, as from 24 February 2010. Words in square brackets in sub-para (3)(b)(ii) inserted by the Civil Partnership Act 2004 (Amendments to Subordinate Legislation) Order 2005, SI 2005/2114, art 2(16), Sch 16, Pt 1, para 4, as from 5 December 2005.

Para 42: words in first and fifth (outer) pairs of square brackets (ie, beginning ", 25"), and words in third and seventh (outer) pairs of square brackets (ie, beginning ", arranging deals") substituted by SI 2007/125, art 6(b), as from 1 November 2007. Other words in square brackets substituted by the Financial Services and Markets Act 2000 (Regulated Activities) (Amendment) Order 2017, SI 2017/488, art 14, Schedule, para 6(1), (3)(a), as from 3 January 2018.

Para 44: sub-para (A1) inserted by the Financial Services and Markets Act 2000 (Consumer Credit) (Miscellaneous Provisions) (No 2) Order 2014, SI 2014/506, art 2(1), (2), as from 1 April 2014. Other words in square brackets substituted by the Alternative Investment Fund Managers Regulations 2013, SI 2013/1773, reg 81, Sch 2, Pt 2, para 8(1), (3), as from 22 July 2013.

Para 45: words in square brackets substituted by SI 2013/1773, reg 81, Sch 2, Pt 2, para 8(1), (3), as from 22 July 2013.

Para 47: revoked by the Financial Services and Markets Act 2000 (Regulated Activities) (Amendment) Order 2014, SI 2014/366, art 8(1), (4)(a), as from 1 April 2014.

Para 48 was substituted by SI 2003/1675, art 2(1), (4)(c), as from 31 October 2004 (in so far as providing for an exemption in relation to any mortgage activity), and as from 14 January 2005 (otherwise); and has subsequently been amended as follows:

Word omitted from sub-para (1)(a) revoked, and sub-paras (1)(c), (d) inserted, by SI 2006/2383, art 30(b), as from 6 April 2007.

Words in square brackets in sub-para (1)(b) substituted, sub-paras (1A), (1B), (3), (4) inserted and added respectively, sub-paras (2)(d), (f) revoked, and sub-paras (2)(h), (i) added, by the Mortgage Credit Directive Order 2015, SI 2015/910, Sch 1, Pt 2, para 5, as from 21 March 2016.

Word omitted from sub-para (1)(c) revoked, and sub-para (1)(e) inserted, by the Financial Services and Markets Act 2000 (Regulated Activities) (Amendment) Order 2009, SI 2009/1342, art 28(b), as from 1 July 2009 (certain purposes), and as from 30 June 2010 (otherwise).

Sub-paras (1A)(a), (b) substituted (for the original sub-paras (1A)(a)–(c)), by the Financial Services and Markets Act 2000 (Regulated Activities) (Amendment) Order 2016, SI 2016/392, art 4, as from 21 March 2016.

Words in square brackets in sub-para (1A)(b)(i) and words in square brackets in the definition "bridging loan" in sub-para (4) substituted by the Financial Services and Markets Act 2000 (Amendment) (EU Exit) Regulations 2019, SI 2019/632, reg 177(1), (3), as from IP completion day (as defined in the European Union (Withdrawal Agreement) Act 2020, s 39).

Sub-para (2)(aa) inserted by the Housing and Regeneration Act 2008 (Consequential Provisions) (No 2) Order 2010, SI 2010/671, art 4, Sch 1, para 27, as from 1 April 2010.

Words in square brackets in sub-para (2)(b) substituted by the Housing (Scotland) Act 2010 (Consequential Provisions and Modifications) Order 2012, SI 2012/700, art 4, Schedule, Pt 2, para 12, as from 1 April 2012.

Sub-para (2)(c) revoked by the Localism Act 2011 (Regulation of Social Housing) (Consequential Provisions) Order 2012, SI 2012/641, art 2(5), as from 1 April 2012.

Sub-para (2)(ca) inserted by the Housing and Regeneration Act 2008 (Consequential Provisions) (No 2) Order 2008, SI 2008/2831, arts 3, Sch 1, para 11, as from 1 December 2008.

Sub-para (2)(f) (revoked as noted above) was originally added by the Financial Services and Markets Act 2000 (Exemption) (Amendment) Order 2005, SI 2005/592, art 2(2), as from 6 April 2005.

Sub-para (2)(g) added by the Financial Services and Markets Act 2000 (Exemption) (Amendment) Order 2011, SI 2011/1626, art 2, as from 26 July 2011.

Para 49 was added by the Financial Services and Markets Act 2000 (Exemption) (Amendment) Order 2001, SI 2001/3623, arts 2, 8, as from 1 December 2001; and has subsequently been amended as follows:

Words ", operating a multilateral trading facility" in square brackets in sub-para (1) inserted, figure ", 25D" in square brackets in sub-paras (1), (3) inserted, and words in first (outer) pair of square brackets in sub-para (2) substituted, by SI 2007/125, art 6(c)(i)–(v), as from 1 November 2007.

Words ", operating an organised trading facility" in square brackets in sub-para (1) inserted, figure ", 25DA" in square brackets in sub-paras (1), (3) inserted, and words ", 25D or 25DA" in square brackets (in each place they occur) substituted, by SI 2017/488, art 14, Schedule, para 6(1), (3)(b), as from 3 January 2018.

Other words in square brackets substituted or inserted, and words omitted revoked, by the Financial Services and Markets Act 2000 (Exemption) (Amendment) Order 2005, SI 2005/592, art 3, as from 1 April 2005.

Para 50: added, together with para 51, by SI 2007/1821, art 2(1), (4), as from 20 July 2007. Words omitted from the definition "customer" revoked by the Financial Services and Markets Act 2000 (Exemption) (Amendment) Order 2009, SI 2009/264, art 2, as from 6 April 2009.

Para 51: added as noted above. Word in square brackets substituted by the Financial Services Act 2012 (Consequential Amendments and Transitional Provisions) Order 2013, SI 2013/472, art 3, Sch 2, para 38, as from 1 April 2013.

Paras 52–54: added by SI 2013/1881, art 14(1), (4), as from 1 April 2014. Words in square brackets in the heading to para 52 substituted, and paras 52(1)(a), (2) and (3) revoked, by SI 2014/366, art 8(1), (4)(b), (c), as from 1 April 2014. Para 52(4) added by the Financial Services and Markets Act 2000 (Regulated Activities) (Amendment) Order 2022, SI 2022/466, art 4, as from 29 July 2022. Word in square brackets in sub-para 54(2) substituted by the Financial Services and Markets Act 2000 (Miscellaneous Provisions) (No 2) Order 2015, SI 2015/352, art 3(1), (2)(a), as from 18 March 2015.

Para 54A: inserted by SI 2015/352, art 3(1), (2)(b), as from 18 March 2015.

Paras 55, 56: added by SI 2014/506, art 2(1), (3), as from 1 April 2014.

Para 57: added by the Financial Services and Markets Act 2000 (Exemption) (Amendment) Order 2015, SI 2015/447, art 2(1), (3), as from 30 March 2015.

Para 58: added by the Financial Services and Markets Act 2000 (Exemption) (Amendment) Order 2022, SI 2022/100, art 2, as from 31 March 2022.

Step-children, etc: as to the meaning of this, and related expressions, see the Civil Partnership Act 2004, s 246 (as applied to this Order by the Civil Partnership Act 2004 (Relationships Arising Through Civil Partnership) Order 2005, SI 2005/3137, art 3, Schedule).

Charities Act 1960, ss 22, 22A: repealed and replaced by the Charities Act 1993, ss 24, 25 respectively (see also the note below).

Charities Act 1993: repealed and replaced by the Charities Act 2011.

FINANCIAL SERVICES AND MARKETS ACT 2000 (DESIGNATED PROFESSIONAL BODIES) ORDER 2001

(SI 2001/1226)

NOTES

Made: 27 March 2001.

Authority: Financial Services and Markets Act 2000, s 326.

Commencement: 28 March 2001.

This Order is reproduced as amended by: the Financial Services and Markets Act 2000 (Designated Professional Bodies) (Amendment) Order 2004, SI 2004/3352; the Financial Services and Markets Act 2000 (Designated Professional Bodies) (Amendment) Order 2006, SI 2006/58.

[8.337]

1 Citation, commencement and interpretation

(1) This Order may be cited as the Financial Services and Markets Act 2000 (Designated Professional Bodies) Order 2001.

(2) This Order comes into force on the day after the day on which it is made.

(3) In this Order, "the Act" means the Financial Services and Markets Act 2000.

[8.338]

2 Designated professional bodies

The following bodies are designated under section 326(1) of the Act for the purposes of Part XX of the Act—

(a) the Law Society;
(b) the Law Society of Scotland;
(c) the Law Society of Northern Ireland;
(d) the Institute of Chartered Accountants in England and Wales;
(e) the Institute of Chartered Accountants of Scotland;
(f) the Institute of Chartered Accountants in Ireland;
(g) the Association of Chartered Certified Accountants;
(h) the Institute of Actuaries;
[(i) the Council for Licensed Conveyancers][;
(j) the Royal Institution of Chartered Surveyors].

NOTES

Para (i) added by the Financial Services and Markets Act 2000 (Designated Professional Bodies) (Amendment) Order 2004, SI 2004/3352, art 2, as from 14 January 2005. Para (j) added by the Financial Services and Markets Act 2000 (Designated Professional Bodies) (Amendment) Order 2006, SI 2006/58, art 2, as from 10 February 2006.

OPEN-ENDED INVESTMENT COMPANIES REGULATIONS 2001

(SI 2001/1228)

NOTES

Made: 27 March 2001.

Authority: Financial Services and Markets Act 2000, ss 262, 428(3).

Commencement: see art 1(2).

These Regulations are reproduced as amended by:

2001	Uncertificated Securities Regulations 2001, SI 2001/3755.
2003	Collective Investment Schemes (Miscellaneous Amendments) Regulations 2003, SI 2003/2066.
2005	Open-Ended Investment Companies (Amendment) Regulations 2005, SI 2005/923; Civil Partnership Act 2004 (Amendments to Subordinate Legislation) Order 2005, SI 2005/2114.
2007	Regulatory Reform (Financial Services and Markets Act 2000) Order 2007, SI 2007/1973.
2008	Companies Act 2006 (Consequential Amendments etc) Order 2008, SI 2008/948.
2009	Open-Ended Investment Companies (Amendment) Regulations 2009, SI 2009/553.
2010	Transfer of Tribunal Functions Order 2010, SI 2010/22.

2011	Companies Act 2006 (Consequential Amendments and Transitional Provisions) Order 2011, SI 2011/1265; Undertakings for Collective Investment in Transferable Securities Regulations 2011, SI 2011/1613; Open-Ended Investment Companies (Amendment) Regulations 2011, SI 2011/3049.
2013	Financial Services Act 2012 (Consequential Amendments and Transitional Provisions) Order 2013, SI 2013/472; Alternative Investment Fund Managers Regulations 2013, SI 2013/1773.
2014	Marriage (Same Sex Couples) Act 2013 (Consequential Provisions) Order 2014, SI 2014/107; Marriage and Civil Partnership (Scotland) Act 2014 and Civil Partnership Act 2004 (Consequential Provisions and Modifications) Order 2014, SI 2014/3229.
2017	Money Laundering, Terrorist Financing and Transfer of Funds (Information on the Payer) Regulations 2017, SI 2017/692.
2018	Money Market Funds Regulations 2018, SI 2018/698.
2019	Collective Investment Schemes (Amendment etc) (EU Exit) Regulations 2019, SI 2019/325.
2020	Bearer Certificates (Collective Investment Schemes) Regulations 2020, SI 2020/1346.
2022	Dormant Assets Act 2022.

Transitional provisions in relation to Gibraltar-based firms and activities: see the Gibraltar (Miscellaneous Amendments) (EU Exit) Regulations 2019, SI 2019/680, reg 11 at **[12.129]**.

ARRANGEMENT OF REGULATIONS

PART I
GENERAL

PART II
FORMATION, SUPERVISION AND CONTROL

General

Umbrella companies

Authorisation

Names

Alterations

Ending of authorisation

Powers of intervention

PART I GENERAL

[8.339]

1 Citation, commencement and extent

(1) These Regulations may be cited as the Open-Ended Investment Companies Regulations 2001.

(2) These Regulations come into force—

(a) for the purpose of regulation 6, on the day on which sections 247 and 248 of the Act come into force for the purpose of making rules;

(b) for the purposes of regulations 7, 12, 13, 18(1) and (3), 74, 77 and 80 to 82, so far as relating to the making of applications for authorisation orders to be made on or after the day mentioned in sub-paragraph (c), on the day on which section 40 of the Act comes into force;

(c) for all remaining purposes, on the day on which section 19 of the Act comes into force.

[(3) Except as otherwise provided, these Regulations extend to the whole of the United Kingdom.]

NOTES

Para (3): substituted by the Companies Act 2006 (Consequential Amendments and Transitional Provisions) Order 2011, SI 2011/1265, art 15, Sch 2, paras 1, 2, as from 12 May 2011.

[8.340]

2 Interpretation

(1) In these Regulations, except where the context otherwise requires—

"the Act" means the Financial Services and Markets Act 2000;

"the 1986 Act" means the Insolvency Act 1986;

["the 1989 Order" means the Insolvency (Northern Ireland) Order 1989;

"the 2006 Act" means the Companies Act 2006;]

"annual general meeting" has the meaning given in regulation 37(1);

"annual report" has the meaning given in regulation 66(1)(a);

"the appropriate registrar" means—

(a) the registrar of companies for England and Wales if the company's instrument of incorporation states that its head office is to be situated in England and Wales, or that it is to be situated in Wales;

(b) the registrar of companies for Scotland if the company's instrument of incorporation states that its head office is to be situated in Scotland;

[(c) the registrar of companies for Northern Ireland if the company's instrument of incorporation states that its head office is to be situated in Northern Ireland;]

"authorisation order" means an order made by the Authority under [regulation 14(1) or regulation 14(1A)];

["the Authority" means the FCA;]

"bearer shares" has the meaning given in regulation 48;

. . .

"court", in relation to any proceedings under these Regulations involving an open-ended investment company the head office of which is situated—

(a) in England and Wales [or Northern Ireland], means the High Court; and

(b) in Scotland, means the Court of Session;

"depositary", in relation to an open-ended investment company, has the meaning given in regulation 5(1);

"the designated person" means the person designated in the company's instrument of incorporation for the purposes of paragraph 4 of Schedule 4 to these Regulations;

["electronic communication" has the meaning given in section 15(1) of the Electronic Communications Act 2000;]

"[FCA rules]" means any rules made by the Authority under regulation 6(1);

"larger denomination share" has the meaning given in regulation 45(5);

["MMF Regulation" means Regulation (EU) 2017/1131 of the European Parliament and of the Council of 14 June 2017 on money market funds;]

"officer", in relation to an open-ended investment company, includes a director or any secretary or manager;

["open-ended investment company" means—

(a) a body incorporated by virtue of regulation 3(1), or

(b) a body treated as so incorporated by virtue of—

(i) regulation 85(3)(a) (bodies incorporated under earlier British regulations), or

(ii) Schedule 3 to the Companies Act 2006 (Consequential Amendments and Transitional Provisions) Order 2011 (transitional provisions: Northern Ireland open-ended investment companies);]

. . .

"prospectus" has the meaning given in regulation 6(2);

"relevant provision" means any requirement imposed by or under the Act;

"register of shareholders" means the register kept under paragraph 1(1) of Schedule 3 to these Regulations;

"scheme property", in relation to an open-ended investment company, means the property subject to the collective investment scheme constituted by the company;

"share certificate" has the meaning given in regulation 46(1);

"smaller denomination share" has the meaning given in regulation 45(5);

["sub-fund" means a separate part of the property of an umbrella company that is pooled separately;]

"transfer documents" has the meaning given in paragraph 5(3) [and (3A)] of Schedule 4 to these Regulations;

. . .

. . .

"umbrella company" means an open-ended investment company whose instrument of incorporation provides for such pooling as is mentioned in section 235(3)(a) of the Act (collective investment schemes) in relation to separate parts of the scheme property and whose shareholders are entitled to exchange rights in one part for rights in another; and

. . .

(2) In these Regulations any reference to a shareholder of an open-ended investment company is a reference to—

(a) the person who holds the share certificate, or other documentary evidence of title relating to that share mentioned in regulation 48; and

(b) the person whose name is entered on the company's register of shareholders in relation to any share other than a bearer share.

(3) In these Regulations, unless the contrary intention appears, expressions which are also used in [the Companies Acts (as defined in section 2 of the Companies Act 2006)] have the same meaning as in [those Acts].

[(4) Any reference in these Regulations to the Collective Investment Schemes sourcebook is a reference to the Collective Investment Schemes sourcebook made under the Act by the Authority, as it has effect on IP completion day.]

NOTES

Para (1) is amended as follows:

Definition "the 1985 Act" (omitted) revoked, definitions "the 1989 Order" and "the 2006 Act" inserted, words in square brackets in definitions "the appropriate registrar" and "court" inserted, and definition "open-ended investment company" substituted, by the Companies Act 2006 (Consequential Amendments and Transitional Provisions) Order 2011, SI 2011/1265, art 15, Sch 2, paras 1, 3, as from 12 May 2011.

Words in square brackets in the definition "authorisation order" substituted, and the definition "MMF Regulation" inserted, by the Money Market Funds Regulations 2018, SI 2018/698, reg 3(1), (2), as from 21 July 2018.

Definition "the Authority" inserted, and in the definition "FCA rules" words in square brackets substituted, by the Financial Services Act 2012 (Consequential Amendments and Transitional Provisions) Order 2013, SI 2013/472, art 3, Sch 2, para 41(1)–(3), as from 1 April 2013.

Definitions "certificated form", "participating issuer", "participating security", "uncertificated form" and "uncertificated unit of a security" (omitted) revoked by the Uncertificated Securities Regulations 2001, SI 2001/3755, reg 51, Sch 7, Pt 2, para 24(a), as from 26 November 2001.

Definition "electronic communication" inserted, and words in square brackets in the definition "transfer documents" inserted, by the Open-Ended Investment Companies (Amendment) Regulations 2009, SI 2009/553, reg 2(1), (3), as from 6 March 2009.

Definition "sub-fund" inserted by the Open-Ended Investment Companies (Amendment) Regulations 2011, SI 2011/3049, reg 3(1), (2), as from 21 December 2011.

Definition "the Tribunal" (omitted) revoked by the Transfer of Tribunal Functions Order 2010, SI 2010/22, art 5(2), Sch 3, paras 16, 17, as from 6 April 2010.

Definition "the UCITS directive" (omitted) revoked by the Collective Investment Schemes (Miscellaneous Amendments) Regulations 2003, SI 2003/2066, reg 13(7)(a), as from 13 February 2004.

Para (3): words in square brackets substituted by the Companies Act 2006 (Consequential Amendments etc) Order 2008, SI 2008/948, art 3(1), Sch 1, Pt 2, para 220, as from 6 April 2008.

Para (4): added by the Collective Investment Schemes (Amendment etc) (EU Exit) Regulations 2019, SI 2019/325, reg 52(1), (2), as from IP completion day (as defined in the European Union (Withdrawal Agreement) Act 2020, s 39). Note that reg 52(2) of the 2019 Regulations was amended by the Financial Services and Economic and Monetary Policy (Consequential Amendments) (EU Exit) Regulations 2020, SI 2020/1301, reg 3, Schedule, para 18(d) as from 30 December 2020 (and the effect of the amendment has been incorporated in the text set out above).

PART II FORMATION, SUPERVISION AND CONTROL

General

[8.341]

3 Open-ended investment company

(1) If the Authority makes an authorisation order then, immediately upon the coming into effect of the order, the body to which the authorisation order relates is to be incorporated as an open-ended investment company (notwithstanding that, at the point of its incorporation by virtue of this paragraph, the body will not have any shareholders or property).

(2) The name of an open-ended investment company is the name mentioned in the authorisation order made in respect of the company or, if it changes its name in accordance with these Regulations and [FCA rules], its new name.

NOTES

Para (2): words in square brackets substituted by the Financial Services Act 2012 (Consequential Amendments and Transitional Provisions) Order 2013, SI 2013/472, art 3, Sch 2, para 41(1), (2), as from 1 April 2013.

[8.342]

4 Registration by the Authority

(1) Upon making an authorisation order under regulation 14, the Authority must forthwith register—

(a) the instrument of incorporation of the company;

(b) a statement of the address of the company's head office;

(c) a statement, with respect to each person named in the application for authorisation as director of the company, of the particulars set out in regulation 13; and

(d) a statement of the corporate name and registered or principal office of the person named in the application for authorisation as the depositary of the company.

(2) In this regulation any reference to the instrument of incorporation of a company is a reference to the instrument of incorporation supplied for the purposes of regulation 14(1)(c).

[8.343]

5 Safekeeping of scheme property by depositary

(1) Subject to paragraph (2), all the scheme property of an open-ended investment company must be entrusted for safekeeping to a person appointed for the purpose ("a depositary").

(2) Nothing in paragraph (1)—

(a) applies to any scheme property designated for the purposes of this regulation by [FCA rules];

(b) prevents a depositary from—

(i) entrusting to a third party all or some of the assets in its safekeeping; or

(ii) in a case falling within sub-paragraph (i), authorising the third party to entrust all or some of those assets to other specified persons.

(3) Schedule 1 to these Regulations makes provision with respect to depositaries of open-ended investment companies.

NOTES

Para (2): words in square brackets substituted by the Financial Services Act 2012 (Consequential Amendments and Transitional Provisions) Order 2013, SI 2013/472, art 3, Sch 2, para 41(1), (2), as from 1 April 2013.

[8.344]

6 [FCA rules]

(1) The Authority's powers to make rules under section 247 (trust scheme rules) and section 248 (scheme particulars rules) of the Act in relation to authorised unit trust schemes are, subject to the provisions of these Regulations, exercisable in relation to open-ended investment companies—

(a) for like purposes; and

(b) subject to the same conditions.

(2) In these Regulations any document which a person is required to submit and publish by virtue of rules made by the Authority under paragraph (1) for like purposes to those in section 248 of the Act is referred to as a prospectus.

NOTES

Regulation heading: substituted by the Financial Services Act 2012 (Consequential Amendments and Transitional Provisions) Order 2013, SI 2013/472, art 3, Sch 2, para 41(1), (2), as from 1 April 2013.

[8.345]

7 Modification or waiver of [FCA rules]

(1) The Authority may, on the application or with the consent of any person to whom any [FCA rules] apply, direct that all or any of the [FCA rules]—

(a) are not to apply to him as respects a particular open-ended investment company; or

(b) are to apply to him as respects such a company with such modifications as may be specified in the direction.

(2) The Authority may, on the application or with the consent of an open-ended investment company and its depositary acting jointly, direct that all or any of the [FCA rules]—

(a) are not to apply to the company; or

(b) are to apply to the company with such modifications as may be specified in the direction.

(3) [Sections 138A(3) to (7) and 138B of the Act] (modification or waiver of rules) have effect in relation to a direction under paragraph (1) as they have effect in relation to a direction under [section 138A(1)] of the Act but with the following modifications—

(a) . . .

(b) any reference to the [person] is to be read as a reference to the person mentioned in paragraph (1); and

(c) [section 138B(3)(c)] is to be read, in relation to a shareholder, as if the word "commercial" were omitted.

(4) [Sections 138A(3) to (7) and 138B of the Act] have effect in relation to a direction under paragraph (2) as they have effect in relation to a direction under [section 138A(1)] of the Act but with the following modifications—

(a) [section 138A(4)(a)] is to be read as if the words "by the . . . person" were omitted;

(b) [section 138B(3)(c) and (5)] are to be read as if the reference to the . . . person were a reference to each of the company and its depositary;

(c) [section 138B(3)(c)] is to be read, in relation to a shareholder, as if the word "commercial" were omitted; and

(d) [section 138A(7)] is to be read as if the reference to the . . . person were a reference to the company and its depositary acting jointly.

NOTES

Regulation heading, paras (1), (2): words in square brackets substituted by the Financial Services Act 2012 (Consequential Amendments and Transitional Provisions) Order 2013, SI 2013/472, art 3, Sch 2, para 41(1), (2), as from 1 April 2013.

Para (3): sub-para (a) revoked, and word in square brackets in sub-para (b) substituted, by the Regulatory Reform (Financial Services and Markets Act 2000) Order 2007, SI 2007/1973, arts 2, 12(a), (b), as from 12 July 2007. Other words in square brackets substituted by SI 2013/472, art 3, Sch 2, para 41(1), (4), as from 1 April 2013.

Para (4): words omitted revoked by SI 2007/1973, arts 2, 12(c), as from 12 July 2007. Words in square brackets substituted by SI 2013/472, art 3, Sch 2, para 41(1), (4), as from 1 April 2013.

[8.346]

8 Notices: general

Subject to the provisions of these Regulations—

(a) section 387 of the Act (warning notices) applies to a warning notice given under any provision of these Regulations in the same way as it applies to a warning notice given under any provision of the Act;

(b) section 388 of the Act (decision notices) applies to a decision notice given under any provision of these Regulations in the same way as it applies to a decision notice given under any provision of the Act;

(c) section 389 of the Act (notices of discontinuance) applies to the discontinuance of the action proposed in a warning notice or the action to which a decision notice relates given under any provision of these Regulations in the same way as it applies to a warning notice or decision notice given under any provision of the Act;

(d) section 390 of the Act (final notices) applies to a decision notice given under any provision of these Regulations in the same way as it applies to a decision notice given under any provision of the Act.

[8.347]

9 Publication

Section 391 of the Act (publication) applies to the notices mentioned in regulation 8 in the same way as it applies to any such notice given under any provision of the Act.

[8.348]

10 The Authority's procedures

Section 395 of the Act [(the FCA's and the PRA's procedures)] applies to the procedure relating to the Authority's functions in relation to supervisory notices, warning notices and decision notices given under any provision of these Regulations.

NOTES

Words in square brackets substituted by the Financial Services Act 2012 (Consequential Amendments and Transitional Provisions) Order 2013, SI 2013/472, art 3, Sch 2, para 41(1), (5), as from 1 April 2013.

11 *(Revoked by the Transfer of Tribunal Functions Order 2010, SI 2010/22, art 5(2), Sch 3, paras 16, 18, as from 6 April 2010.)*

[Umbrella companies

[8.349]

11A Segregated liability of sub-funds

(1) In the case of an umbrella company, the assets of a sub-fund belong exclusively to that sub-fund and shall not be used to discharge the liabilities of or claims against the umbrella company or any other person or body, or any other sub-fund, and shall not be available for any such purpose whether such liability or claim was incurred before, on or after the date this regulation first applies to such umbrella company.

(2) Any liability incurred on behalf of or attributable to any sub-fund of an umbrella company shall be discharged solely out of the assets of that sub-fund.

(3) Any provision, whether contained in an instrument of incorporation, agreement, contract or otherwise, shall be void to the extent that it is inconsistent with paragraph (1) or (2) and any application of, or agreement to apply, assets in contravention of either such paragraph shall be void.

(4) An umbrella company may allocate any assets or liabilities which—

(a) it receives or incurs on behalf of its sub-funds or in order to enable the operation of the sub-funds; and

(b) are not attributable to any particular sub-fund,

between its sub-funds in a manner which it considers is fair to shareholders.

(5) A sub-fund of an umbrella company is not a legal person separate from that umbrella company but the property of a sub-fund is subject to orders of the court as it would have been had the sub-fund been a separate legal person.

(6) Without prejudice to paragraphs (1) and (2) and save as provided in regulation 33C(7), an umbrella company may sue and be sued in respect of a particular sub-fund and may exercise the same rights of set-off in relation to that sub-fund as apply in respect of companies.]

NOTES

Inserted, together with the preceding heading and reg 11B, by the Open-Ended Investment Companies (Amendment) Regulations 2011, SI 2011/3049, reg 3(1), (3), as from 21 December 2011.

[8.350]

[11B Cross sub-fund investment

Notwithstanding section 658 of the Companies Act 2006 and any rule of law which prohibits or restricts a company from acquiring its own shares, an umbrella company may, for the account of any of its sub-funds, and in accordance with [FCA rules], acquire by subscription or transfer for consideration, shares of any class or classes, however described, representing other sub-funds of the same umbrella company.]

NOTES

Inserted as noted to reg 11A at **[8.349]**.

Words in square brackets substituted by the Financial Services Act 2012 (Consequential Amendments and Transitional Provisions) Order 2013, SI 2013/472, art 3, Sch 2, para 41(1), (2), as from 1 April 2013.

Authorisation

[8.351]

12 Applications for authorisation

[(A1) An application for an authorisation order in respect of a body may be made to the Authority for—

(a) an order declaring the body to be an open-ended investment company;

(b) an order declaring the body to be a money market fund.]

(1) Any application for an authorisation order . . . —

(a) must be made in such manner as the Authority may direct;

(b) must state with respect to each person proposed in the application as a director of the company the particulars set out in regulation 13;

(c) must state the corporate name and registered or principal office of the person proposed in the application as depositary of the company; and

(d) must contain or be accompanied by such other information as the Authority may reasonably require for the purpose of determining the application.

(2) At any time after receiving an application and before determining it the Authority may require the applicant to furnish additional information.

(3) Different directions may be given and different requirements imposed in relation to different applications.

(4) Any information to be furnished to the Authority under this regulation must be in such form or verified in such manner as it may specify.

(5) A person commits an offence if—

(a) for the purposes of or in connection with any application under this regulation; or

(b) in purported compliance with any requirement imposed on him by or under this regulation;

he furnishes information which he knows to be false or misleading in a material particular or recklessly furnishes information which is false or misleading in a material particular.

(6) A person guilty of an offence under paragraph (5) is liable—

(a) on conviction on indictment, to imprisonment for a term not exceeding two years or to a fine or to both;

(b) on summary conviction, to imprisonment for a term not exceeding three months or to a fine not exceeding the statutory maximum or to both.

NOTES

Para (A1) was inserted, and the words omitted from para (1) were revoked, by the Money Market Funds Regulations 2018, SI 2018/698, reg 3(1), (3), as from 21 July 2018.

[8.352]

13 Particulars of directors

(1) Subject to paragraph (2), an application for an authorisation order must contain the following particulars with respect to each person proposed as a director of the company—

(a) in the case of an individual, his present name, any former name, his usual residential address, his nationality, his business occupation (if any), particulars of any other directorships held by him or which have been held by him and his date of birth;

(b) in the case of a body corporate [or firm that is a legal person under the law by which it is governed], its corporate or firm name and the address of its registered or principal office.

(2) The application need not contain particulars of a directorship—

(a) which has not been held by a director at any time during the 5 years preceding the date on which the application is delivered to the Authority;

(b) which is held by a director in a body corporate which is dormant and, if he also held that directorship for any period during those 5 years, which was dormant for the whole of that period; or

(c) which was held by a director for any period during those 5 years in a body corporate which was dormant for the whole of that period.

(3) For the purposes of paragraph (2), a body corporate is dormant during a period in which no significant transaction occurs; and it ceases to be dormant on the occurrence of such a transaction.

(4) In paragraph (1)(a)—

(a) name means a person's Christian name (or other forename) and surname, except that in the case of a peer, or an individual usually known by a title, the title may be stated instead of his Christian name (or other forename) and surname or in addition to either or both of them;

(b) the reference to a former name does not include—
   (i) in the case of a peer, or an individual normally known by a British title, the name by which he was known previous to the adoption of or succession to the title;
   (ii) in the case of any person, a former name which was changed or disused before he attained the age of 18 years or which has been changed or disused for 20 years or more; or
   [(iii) in the case of a married person, the name by which that person was known previous to the marriage; and]

(c) the reference to directorships is a reference to directorships in any body corporate whether or not incorporated in [the United Kingdom].

(5) In paragraph (3) the reference to a significant transaction is, in relation to a company within the meaning of [section 1 of the 2006 Act], a reference to a significant accounting transaction within the meaning of [section 1169(2) [of that Act], other than a transaction to which subsection (3) of that section applies].

NOTES

Para (1): words in square brackets in sub-para (b) substituted by the Companies Act 2006 (Consequential Amendments and Transitional Provisions) Order 2011, SI 2011/1265, art 15, Sch 2, paras 1, 4(a), as from 12 May 2011.

Para (4): sub-para (b)(iii) substituted, in relation to England and Wales, by the Marriage (Same Sex Couples) Act 2013 (Consequential Provisions) Order 2014, SI 2014/107, art 2, Sch 1, para 31, as from 13 March 2014 and, in relation to Scotland, by the Marriage and Civil Partnership (Scotland) Act 2014 and Civil Partnership Act 2004 (Consequential Provisions and Modifications) Order 2014, SI 2014/3229, art 29, Sch 6, para 22, as from 14 December 2014. Words in square brackets in sub-para (c) substituted by SI 2011/1265, art 15, Sch 2, paras 1, 4(b), as from 12 May 2011.

Para (5): words in first pair of square brackets and third (inner) pair of square brackets substituted by the Companies Act 2006 (Consequential Amendments and Transitional Provisions) Order 2011, SI 2011/1265, art 15, Sch 2, paras 1, 4(c), as from 12 May 2011. Words in second (outer) pair of square brackets substituted by the Companies Act 2006 (Consequential Amendments etc) Order 2008, SI 2008/948, art 3(1), Sch 1, Pt 2, para 221, as from 6 April 2008.

[8.353]

14 Authorisation

(1) Where an application is duly made under regulation 12, the Authority may make an authorisation order in respect of an open-ended investment company if—

(a) it is satisfied that the company will, on the coming into effect of the authorisation order, comply with the requirements in regulation 15;

(b) it is satisfied that the company will, at that time, comply with the requirements of [FCA rules];

(c) it has been provided with a copy of the proposed company's instrument of incorporation and a certificate signed by a solicitor to the effect that the instrument of incorporation complies with Schedule 2 to these Regulations and with such of the requirements of [FCA rules] as relate to the contents of that instrument of incorporation; and

(d) it has received a notification under regulation 18(3) from the appropriate registrar.

[(1A) Where an application is made under regulation 12(A1)(b) the Authority may make an authorisation order in respect of a body as a money market fund if conditions A and B are met.

(a) Condition A is that the Authority is satisfied that the body will be able to comply with the requirements imposed on a money market fund under the MMF Regulation.

(b) Condition B is that—
   (i) the body is an open-ended investment company; or
   (ii) the body is the subject of an application under regulation 12(A1)(a) and the requirements in regulation 15 are met in relation to that application.]

(2) If the Authority makes an order under paragraph (1), it must give written notice of the order to the applicant.

(3) In determining whether the requirement referred to in regulation 15(5) is satisfied in respect of any proposed director of a company, the Authority may take into account—

(a) any matter relating to any person who is or will be employed by or associated with the proposed director, for the purposes of the business of the company;

(b) if the proposed director is a body corporate, any matter relating to any director or controller of the body, to any other body corporate in the same group or to any director or controller of any such other body corporate;

(c) if the proposed director is a partnership, any matter relating to any of the partners; and

(d) if the proposed director is an unincorporated association, any matter relating to any member of the governing body of the association or any officer or controller of the association.

(4) [Subject to paragraph (4A)] an application must be determined by the Authority before the end of the period of six months beginning with the date on which it receives a completed application.

[(4A) Where the application relates to an open-ended investment company which is a UCITS, it must be determined by the Authority before the end of two months beginning with the date on which it receives the application.]

(5) The Authority may determine an incomplete application if it considers it appropriate to do so and, if it does so, it must determine the application within the period of twelve months beginning with the date on which it first receives the application.

(6) The applicant may withdraw his application, by giving the Authority written notice, at any time before the Authority determines it.

(7) An authorisation order must specify the date on which it is to come into effect.

(8) Schedule 2 to these Regulations makes provision with respect to the contents, alteration and binding nature of the instrument of incorporation of an open-ended investment company.

NOTES

Words in square brackets in para (1) substituted by the Financial Services Act 2012 (Consequential Amendments and Transitional Provisions) Order 2013, SI 2013/472, art 3, Sch 2, para 41(1), (2), as from 1 April 2013.

Para (1A) was inserted by the Money Market Funds Regulations 2018, SI 2018/698, reg 3(1), (4), as from 21 July 2018.

Words in square brackets in para (4) inserted, and para (4A) inserted, by the Undertakings for Collective Investment in Transferable Securities Regulations 2011, SI 2011/1613, reg 3(1), (2), as from 1 July 2011.

[8.354]

15 Requirements for authorisation

(1) The requirements referred to in regulation 14(1)(a) [and 14(1A)(b)] are as follows.

(2) The company and its instrument of incorporation must comply with the requirements of these regulations and [FCA rules].

(3) The head office of the company must be situated [in England and Wales (or Wales), in Scotland or in Northern Ireland].

(4) The company must have at least one director.

(5) The directors of the company must be fit and proper persons to act as such.

[(6) If the company has only one director, that director must be a body corporate which [is incorporated in the UK,] is an authorised person and which has a Part 4A permission to carry on the regulated activity of managing a [UK] UCITS or, as the case may be, managing an AIF.]

(7) If the company has two or more directors, the combination of their experience and expertise must be such as is appropriate for the purposes of carrying on the business of the company.

(8) The person appointed as the depositary of the company—
- (a) must be a body corporate incorporated in the United Kingdom . . . ;
- (b) must have a place of business in the United Kingdom;
- (c) must have its affairs administered in the country in which it is incorporated;
- (d) must be an authorised person;
- (e) must have permission under [Part 4A] of the Act to act as the depositary of an open-ended investment company [that is a UCITS or, as the case may be, of an open-ended investment company that is an AIF]; and
- (f) must be independent of the company and of the persons appointed as directors of the company.

(9) The name of the company must not be undesirable or misleading.

(10) The aims of the company must be reasonably capable of being achieved.

(11) The company must meet one or both of the following requirements—
- (a) shareholders are entitled to have their shares redeemed or repurchased upon request at a price related to the net value of the scheme property and determined in accordance with the company's instrument of incorporation and [FCA rules]; or
- (b) shareholders are entitled to sell their shares on an investment exchange at a price not significantly different from that mentioned in sub-paragraph (a).

NOTES

Para (1): words in square brackets inserted by the Money Market Funds Regulations 2018, SI 2018/698, reg 3(1), (5), as from 21 July 2018.

Paras (2), (11): words in square brackets substituted by the Financial Services Act 2012 (Consequential Amendments and Transitional Provisions) Order 2013, SI 2013/472, art 3, Sch 2, para 41(1), (2), as from 1 April 2013.

Para (3): words in square brackets substituted by the Companies Act 2006 (Consequential Amendments and Transitional Provisions) Order 2011, SI 2011/1265, art 15, Sch 2, paras 1, 5, as from 12 May 2011.

Para (6) substituted by the Alternative Investment Fund Managers Regulations 2013, SI 2013/1773, reg 81, Sch 2, Part 2, para 10(1), (2)(a), as from 22 July 2013. The words in square brackets were inserted by the Collective Investment Schemes (Amendment etc) (EU Exit) Regulations 2019, SI 2019/325, reg 52(1), (3), as from IP completion day (as defined in the European Union (Withdrawal Agreement) Act 2020, s 39) (note that reg 73(3) of the 2019 Regulations provides that this amendment does not prevent an authorised open-ended investment company from having as its depositary or sole director a qualifying EEA firm, and does not apply to an authorised open-ended investment company in relation to a depositary or sole director which is a qualifying EEA firm).

Para (8): the words omitted from sub-para (a) were revoked by SI 2019/325, reg 52(1), (3), as from IP completion day (as defined in the European Union (Withdrawal Agreement) Act 2020, s 39) (for savings see the note relating to SI 2019/325 above, and note that the original words were "or another EEA State"). Words in first pair of square brackets substituted by SI 2013/472, art 4, as from 1 April 2013. Words in second pair of square brackets inserted by SI 2013/1773, reg 81, Sch 2, Part 2, para 10(1), (2)(b), as from 22 July 2013.

[8.355]

16 Representations against refusal of authorisation

(1) If the Authority proposes to refuse an application made under regulation 12, it must give the applicant a warning notice.

(2) If the Authority decides to refuse the application—
- (a) it must give the applicant a decision notice; and
- (b) the applicant may refer the matter to the [Upper Tribunal].

NOTES

Para (2): words in square brackets substituted by the Transfer of Tribunal Functions Order 2010, SI 2010/22, art 5(2), Sch 3, paras 16, 19, as from 6 April 2010.

[8.356]

17 Certificates

(1) If an open-ended investment company which complies with the conditions necessary to enable it to [be a UCITS] so requests, the Authority may issue a certificate to the effect that the company complies with those conditions.

(2) Such a certificate may be issued on the making of an authorisation order in respect of the company or at any subsequent time.

NOTES

Para (1): words in square brackets substituted by the Collective Investment Schemes (Amendment etc) (EU Exit) Regulations 2019, SI 2019/325, reg 52(1), (5), as from IP completion day (as defined in the European Union (Withdrawal Agreement) Act 2020, s 39).

Names

[8.357]

18 Registrar's approval of names

(1) Where, in respect of a proposed open-ended investment company, it appears to the Authority that the requirements of regulation 14(1)(a) to (c) are or will be met, the Authority must notify the appropriate registrar of the name by which it is proposed that the company should be incorporated.

(2) Every open-ended investment company must obtain the Authority's approval to any proposed change in the name by which the company is incorporated and the Authority must notify the appropriate registrar of the proposed name.

(3) If it appears to the appropriate registrar that the provisions of regulation 19(1) are not contravened in relation to the proposed name, he must notify the Authority to that effect.

[8.358]

19 Prohibition on certain names

(1) No open-ended investment company is to have a name that—

(a) includes any of the following words or expressions, that is to say—

(i) limited, unlimited or public limited company, or their Welsh equivalents ("cyfyngedig", "anghyfyngedig" and "cwmni cyfyngedig cyhoeddus" respectively); . . .

(ii) European Economic Interest Grouping or any equivalent set out in Schedule 3 to the European Economic Interest Grouping Regulations 1989; [or]

[(iii) UK Economic Interest Grouping;]

(b) includes an abbreviation of any of the words or expressions referred to in sub-paragraph (a); or

(c) is the same as any other name appearing in the registrar's index of company names.

(2) In determining for the purposes of paragraph (1)(c) whether one name is the same as another, there are to be disregarded—

(a) the definite article, where it is the first word of the name;

(b) the following word and expressions where they appear at the end of the name—

"company" or its Welsh equivalent ("cwmni");

"and company" or its Welsh equivalent ("a'r cwmni");

"company limited" or its Welsh equivalent ("cwmni cyfyngedig");

"limited" or its Welsh equivalent ("cyfyngedig");

"unlimited" or its Welsh equivalent ("anghyfyngedig");

"public limited company" or its Welsh equivalent ("cwmni cyfyngedig cyhoeddus");

"European Economic Interest Grouping" or any equivalent set out in Schedule 3 to the European Economic Interest Grouping Regulations 1989;

"investment company with variable capital" or its Welsh equivalent ("cwmni buddsoddi â chyfalaf newidiol");

"open-ended investment company" or its Welsh equivalent ("cwmni buddsoddiant penagored");

(c) abbreviations of any of those words or expressions where they appear at the end of the name; and

(d) type and case of letters, accents, spaces between letters and punctuation marks;

and "and" and "&" are to be taken as the same.

NOTES

Para (1): the word omitted from sub-para (a)(i) was revoked, and sub-para (a)(iii) and the preceding word were inserted, by the Collective Investment Schemes (Amendment etc) (EU Exit) Regulations 2019, SI 2019/325, reg 52(1), (6), as from IP completion day (as defined in the European Union (Withdrawal Agreement) Act 2020, s 39).

[8.359]

20 Registrar's index of company names

(1) Upon making an authorisation order in respect of an open-ended investment company or upon approving any change in the name of such a company, the Authority must notify the appropriate registrar of the name by which the company is incorporated or, as the case may be, of the company's new name.

(2) . . .

NOTES

Para (2): revoked by the Companies Act 2006 (Consequential Amendments and Transitional Provisions) Order 2011, SI 2011/1265, art 15, Sch 2, paras 1, 6, as from 12 May 2011.

Alterations

[8.360]

21 The Authority's approval for certain changes in respect of a company

(1) An open-ended investment company must give written notice to the Authority of—

(a) any proposed alteration to the company's instrument of incorporation [other than one to which regulation 22A applies];

(b) any proposed alteration to the company's prospectus which, if made, would be significant;

(c) any proposed reconstruction or amalgamation involving the company [other than a proposed merger to which Part 4 of the Undertakings for Collective Investment in Transferable Securities Regulations 2010 applies];

(d) any proposal to wind up the affairs of the company [or a sub-fund of that company] otherwise than by the court;

(e) any proposal to replace a director of the company, to appoint any additional director or to decrease the number of directors in post; and

(f) any proposal to replace the depositary of the company.

(2) Any notice given under paragraph (1)(a) must be accompanied by a certificate signed by a solicitor to the effect that the change in question will not affect the compliance of the instrument of incorporation with Schedule 2 to these Regulations and with such of the requirements of [FCA rules] as relate to the contents of that instrument.

(3) Effect must not be given to any proposal falling within paragraph (1) unless—

(a) the Authority, by written notice, has given its approval to the proposal; or

(b) one month, beginning with the date on which notice of the proposal was given, has expired without the company or the depositary having received from the Authority a warning notice under regulation 22 in respect of the proposal.

(4) No change falling within paragraph (1)(e) may be made if any of the requirements set out in regulation 15(4) to (7) and (8)(f) would not be satisfied if the change were made and no change falling within paragraph (1)(f) may be made if any of the requirements in regulation 15(8) would not be satisfied if the change were made.

NOTES

Para (1): words in square brackets in sub-para (d) inserted by the Open-Ended Investment Companies (Amendment) Regulations 2011, SI 2011/3049, reg 3(1), (4), as from 21 December 2011. Other words in square brackets inserted by the Undertakings for Collective Investment in Transferable Securities Regulations 2011, SI 2011/1613, reg 3(1), (3), as from 1 July 2011.

Para (2): words in square brackets substituted by the Financial Services Act 2012 (Consequential Amendments and Transitional Provisions) Order 2013, SI 2013/472, art 3, Sch 2, para 41(1), (2), as from 1 April 2013.

[8.361]

22 Procedure when refusing approval of proposed changes

(1) If the Authority proposes to refuse approval of a proposal to replace the depositary, or any director, of an open-ended investment company, it must give a warning notice to the company.

(2) If the Authority proposes to refuse approval of any other proposal falling within regulation 21, it must give separate warning notices to the company and its depositary.

(3) To be valid the warning notice must be received by that person before the end of one month beginning with the date on which notice of the proposal was given.

(4) If, having given a warning notice to a person, the Authority decides to refuse approval—

(a) it must give him a decision notice; and

(b) he may refer the matter to the [Upper Tribunal].

(5) If, having given a warning notice to a person, the Authority decides to approve the proposal, it must give him a [written] notice.

NOTES

Para (4): words in square brackets substituted by the Transfer of Tribunal Functions Order 2010, SI 2010/22, art 5(2), Sch 3, paras 16, 20, as from 6 April 2010.

Para (5): word in square brackets substituted by the Open-Ended Investment Companies (Amendment) Regulations 2005, SI 2005/923, reg 2(1), (2), as from 6 April 2005.

[8.362]

[22A The Authority's approval for conversion of a feeder UCITS

(1) An open-ended investment company must give written notice to the Authority of any proposal to amend its instrument of incorporation to enable it to convert into a UCITS which is not a feeder UCITS.

(2) Any notice given in respect of such a proposal must be accompanied by—

(a) a certificate signed by a solicitor to the effect that the amendment will not affect the compliance of the instrument of incorporation with Schedule 2 to these Regulations and with such of the requirements of [FCA rules] as relate to the contents of that instrument; and

(b) the specified information.

(3) Paragraph (4) applies where—

(a) the notice given under subsection (1) relates to a proposal to amend the instrument of incorporation of an open-ended investment company which is a feeder UCITS to enable it to convert into a UCITS which is not a feeder UCITS following the winding-up of its master UCITS; and

(b) the proceeds of the winding-up are to be paid to the company before the date on which it proposes to start investing in accordance with the new investment objectives and policy provided for in its amended instrument of incorporation.

(4) Where this paragraph applies, the Authority may only approve the proposal subject to the conditions set out in section 283A(5) and (6) of the Act.

(5) The Authority must, within fifteen working days from the date on which it received the notice under paragraph (1), give—

(a) written notice that it approves the proposed amendments to the instrument of incorporation, or

(b) a warning notice under regulation 22 that it proposes to refuse approval of the proposed amendments.

(6) Effect is not to be given to any proposal of which notice has been given under subsection (1) unless the Authority, by written notice, has given its approval to the proposal.

(7) If the Authority proposes to refuse approval of the proposal it must give separate warning notices to the company and to its depositary.

(8) If, having given a warning notice to a person, the Authority decides to refuse approval—

(a) it must give that person a decision notice; and

(b) that person may refer the matter to the Tribunal.

(9) In this regulation, "specified" means specified in—

[(a) rule 11.6.3R(2) of the Collective Investment Schemes sourcebook, or

(b) UCITS-related direct EU legislation as defined in section 237(3) of the Act].

NOTES

Inserted by the Undertakings for Collective Investment in Transferable Securities Regulations 2011, SI 2011/1613, reg 3(1), (4), as from 1 July 2011.

Para (2): words in square brackets substituted by the Financial Services Act 2012 (Consequential Amendments and Transitional Provisions) Order 2013, SI 2013/472, art 3, Sch 2, para 41(1), (2), as from 1 April 2013.

Para (9): sub-paras (a), (b) substituted by the Collective Investment Schemes (Amendment etc) (EU Exit) Regulations 2019, SI 2019/325, reg 52(1), (7), as from IP completion day (as defined in the European Union (Withdrawal Agreement) Act 2020, s 39).

Ending of authorisation

[8.363]

23 Ending of authorisation

(1) The Authority may revoke an authorisation order if it appears to it that—

(a) any requirement for the making of the order is no longer satisfied;

(b) the company, any of its directors or its depositary—

(i) has contravened any relevant provision; or

(ii) has, in purported compliance with any such provision, knowingly or recklessly given the Authority information which is false or misleading in a material particular;

(c) no regulated activity has been carried on in relation to the company for the previous twelve months; or

(d) it is desirable to revoke the authorisation order in order to protect the interests of shareholders or potential shareholders in the company.

(2) For the purposes of paragraph (1)(d), the Authority may take into account any matter relating to—

(a) the company or its depositary;

(b) any director or controller of the depositary;

(c) any person employed by or associated, for the purposes of the business of the company, with the company or its depositary;

(d) any director of the company;

(e) any person exercising influence over any director of the company or its depositary;

(f) any body corporate in the same group as any director of the company or its depositary;

(g) any director of any such body corporate;

(h) any person exercising influence over any such body corporate;

(i) any person who would be such a person as is mentioned in regulation 14(3)(a) to (d) were it to apply to a director as it applies to a proposed director.

(3) Before revoking any authorisation order that has come into effect, the Authority must ensure that such steps as are necessary and appropriate to secure the winding up of the company (whether by the court or otherwise) have been taken.

[8.364]

24 Procedure

(1) If the Authority proposes to make an order revoking an authorisation order ("a revoking order"), it must give separate warning notices to the company and its depositary.

(2) If, having given warning notices, the Authority decides to make a revoking order it must without delay give the company and its depositary a decision notice and either of them may refer the matter to the [Upper Tribunal].

(3) Sections 393 and 394 of the Act apply to a warning notice or a decision notice given in accordance with this regulation.

NOTES

Para (2): words in square brackets substituted by the Transfer of Tribunal Functions Order 2010, SI 2010/22, art 5(2), Sch 3, paras 16, 21, as from 6 April 2010.

Powers of intervention

[8.365]

25 Directions

(1) The Authority may give a direction under this regulation if it appears to the Authority that—

(a) one or more requirements for the making of an authorisation order are no longer satisfied;

(b) the company, any of its directors or its depositary—

(i) has contravened or is likely to contravene any relevant provision; or

(ii) has, in purported compliance with any such provision, knowingly or recklessly given the Authority information which is false or misleading in a material particular; or

[(iii) has contravened a provision of the MMF Regulation; or]

(c) it is desirable to give a direction in order to protect the interests of shareholders or potential shareholders in the company.

(2) A direction under this regulation may—

(a) require the company to cease the issue or redemption, or both the issue and redemption, of shares or any class of shares in the company;

(b) in the case of a director of the company who is the designated person, require that director to cease transfers to or from, or both to and from, his own holding of shares, or of any class of shares, in the company;

(c) in the case of an umbrella company, require that investments made in respect of one or more parts of the scheme property which are pooled separately be realised and, following the discharge of such liabilities of the company as are attributable to the relevant part or parts of the scheme property, that the resulting funds be distributed to shareholders in accordance with [FCA rules];

(d) require any director of the company to present a petition to the court to wind up the company; or

(e) require that the affairs of the company be wound up otherwise than by the court.

(3) Subject to paragraph (4), if the authorisation order is revoked, the revocation does not affect the operation of any direction under this regulation which is then in force; and a direction under this regulation may be given in relation to a company in the case of which an authorisation order has been revoked if a direction under this regulation was already in force at the time of revocation.

(4) Where a winding-up order has been made by the court, no direction under this regulation is to have effect in relation to the company concerned.

(5) For the purposes of paragraph (1)(c), the Authority may take into account any matter relating to any of the persons mentioned in regulation 23(2).

(6) If a person contravenes a direction under this regulation, [section 138D] (actions for damages) applies to the contravention as it applies to a contravention mentioned in that section.

(7) The Authority may, on its own initiative or on the application of the company or its depositary, revoke or vary a direction given under this regulation if it appears to the Authority—

(a) in the case of revocation, that it is no longer necessary for the direction to take effect or continue in force;

(b) in the case of variation, that the direction should take effect or continue in force in a different form.

NOTES

Para (1): sub-para (b)(iii) inserted by the Money Market Funds Regulations 2018, SI 2018/698, reg 3(1), (6), as from 21 July 2018.

Paras (2), (6): words in square brackets substituted by the Financial Services Act 2012 (Consequential Amendments and Transitional Provisions) Order 2013, SI 2013/472, art 3, Sch 2, para 41(1), (2), (6), as from 1 April 2013.

[8.366]

26 Applications to the court

(1) This regulation applies if the Authority could give a direction under regulation 25 in relation to an open-ended investment company.

(2) The Authority may apply to the court for an order removing the depositary or any director of the company and replacing any such person with a person or persons nominated by the Authority.

(3) The Authority may nominate a person for the purposes of paragraph (2) only if it is satisfied that, if the order were made, the requirements of paragraphs (4) to (7) or, as the case may be, of paragraph (8) of regulation 15 would be met.

(4) If it appears to the Authority that there is no person whom it may nominate for the purposes of paragraph (2), it may apply to the court for an order removing the director in question or the depositary (or both) and appointing an authorised person to wind up the company.

(5) On an application under this regulation the court may make such order as it thinks fit.

(6) The court may, on the application of the Authority, rescind any such order as is mentioned in paragraph (4) and substitute such an order as is mentioned in paragraph (2).

(7) The Authority must—

(a) give written notice of the making of an application under this section to—

(i) the company;

(ii) its depositary; and

(iii) where the application seeks the removal of any director of the company, that director; and

(b) take such steps as it considers appropriate for bringing the making of the application to the attention of the shareholders of the company.

[8.367]

27 Procedure on giving directions under regulation 25 and varying them on Authority's own initiative

(1) A direction takes effect—

(a) immediately, if the notice given under paragraph (3) states that that is the case;

(b) on such date as may be specified in the notice; or

(c) if no date is specified in the notice, when the matter to which it relates is no longer open to review.

(2) A direction may be expressed to take effect immediately (or on a specified date) only if the Authority, having regard to the ground on which it is exercising its power under regulation 25, considers that it is necessary for the direction to take effect immediately (or on that date).

(3) If the Authority proposes to give a direction under regulation 25, or gives such a direction with immediate effect, it must give separate written notices to the company and its depositary.

(4) The notice must—

(a) give details of the direction;

(b) inform the person to whom it is given of when the direction takes effect;

(c) state the Authority's reasons for giving the direction and for its determination as to when the direction takes effect;

(d) inform the person to whom it is given that he may make representations to the Authority within such period as may be specified in it (whether or not he has referred the matter to the [Upper Tribunal]); and

(e) inform him of his right to refer the matter to the [Upper Tribunal].

(5) If the direction imposes a requirement under regulation 25(2)(a) or (b), the notice must state that the requirement has effect until—

(a) a specified date; or
(b) a further direction.

(6) If the direction imposes a requirement under regulation 25(2)(d) or (e), the petition must be presented (or, as the case may be, the company must be wound up)—
(a) by a date specified in the notice; or
(b) if no date is specified, as soon as possible.

(7) The Authority may extend the period allowed under the notice for making representations.

(8) If, having considered any representations made by a person to whom the notice was given, the Authority decides—
(a) to give the direction in the way proposed, or
(b) if it has been given, not to revoke the direction,
it must give separate written notices to the company and its depositary.

(9) If, having considered any representations made by a person to whom the notice was given, the Authority decides—
(a) not to give the direction in the way proposed,
(b) to give the direction in a way other than that proposed, or
(c) to revoke a direction which has effect,
it must give separate written notices to the company and its depositary.

(10) A notice given under paragraph (8) must inform the person to whom it is given of his right to refer the matter to the [Upper Tribunal].

(11) A notice under paragraph (9)(b) must comply with paragraph (4).

(12) If a notice informs a person of his right to refer a matter to the [Upper Tribunal], it must give an indication of the procedure on such a reference.

(13) This regulation applies to the variation of a direction on the Authority's own initiative as it applies to the giving of a direction.

(14) For the purposes of paragraph (1)(c), whether a matter is open to review is to be determined in accordance with section 391(8) of the Act.

(15) Section 395 of the Act [(the FCA's and PRA's procedures)] has effect as if subsection (13) included a reference to a notice given in accordance with paragraph (3), (8) or (9)(b).

NOTES

Paras (4), (10), (12): words in square brackets substituted by the Transfer of Tribunal Functions Order 2010, SI 2010/22, art 5(2), Sch 3, paras 16, 22, as from 6 April 2010.

Para (15): words in square brackets substituted by the Financial Services Act 2012 (Consequential Amendments and Transitional Provisions) Order 2013, SI 2013/472, art 3, Sch 2, para 41(1), (7), as from 1 April 2013.

[8.368]
28 Procedure: refusal to revoke or vary direction

(1) If on an application under regulation 25(7) for a direction to be revoked or varied the Authority proposes—
(a) to vary the direction otherwise than in accordance with the application, or
(b) to refuse to revoke or vary the direction,
it must give the applicant a warning notice.

(2) If the Authority decides to refuse to revoke or vary the direction—
(a) it must give the applicant a decision notice; and
(b) the applicant may refer the matter to the [Upper Tribunal].

NOTES

Para (2): words in square brackets substituted by the Transfer of Tribunal Functions Order 2010, SI 2010/22, art 5(2), Sch 3, paras 16, 23, as from 6 April 2010.

[8.369]
29 Procedure: revocation of direction and grant of request for variation

(1) If the Authority decides on its own initiative to revoke a direction under regulation 25 it must give separate written notices of its decision to the company and its depositary.

(2) If on an application made under regulation 25(7) for a direction to be revoked or varied, the Authority decides to revoke or vary it in accordance with the application, it must give the applicant written notice of its decision.

(3) A notice under this regulation must specify the date on which the decision takes effect.

(4) The Authority may publish such information about the revocation or variation, in such way, as it considers appropriate.

[Information

29A *(Originally inserted, together with reg 29B and the preceding heading, by the Undertakings for Collective Investment in Transferable Securities Regulations 2011, SI 2011/1613, reg 3(1), (5), as from 1 July 2011. Subsequently revoked by the Collective Investment Schemes (Amendment etc) (EU Exit) Regulations 2019, SI 2019/325, reg 52(1), (8), as from IP completion day (as defined in the European Union (Withdrawal Agreement) Act 2020, s 39).)*

[8.370]
[29B Information for feeder UCITS

(1) The Authority must immediately inform any authorised open-ended investment company which is a feeder UCITS of an open-ended investment company or authorised unit trust scheme (the master UCITS) of—

(a) any failure of which the Authority becomes aware by the master UCITS to comply with a provision made [by or under any enactment] in implementation of Chapter VIII of the UCITS directive;

(b) any warning notice or decision notice given to the master UCITS in relation to a contravention of any provision made in implementation of Chapter VIII of the UCITS directive by or under any enactment or in rules of the Authority;

(c) any information reported to the Authority pursuant to rules of the Authority made to implement Article 106(1) of the UCITS directive which relates to the master UCITS, or to one or more of its directors, its operator, trustee, depository or auditor.

(2), (3) . . .

NOTES

Inserted as noted to reg 29A *ante*.

The words in square brackets in para (1) were inserted, and paras (2), (3) were revoked, by the Collective Investment Schemes (Amendment etc) (EU Exit) Regulations 2019, SI 2019/325, reg 52(1), (9), as from IP completion day (as defined in the European Union (Withdrawal Agreement) Act 2020, s 39).

Investigations

[8.371]

30 Power to investigate

(1) The Authority or the Secretary of State may appoint one or more competent persons to investigate and report on the affairs of, or of any director or depositary of, an open-ended investment company if it appears to either of them that it is in the interests of shareholders or potential shareholders of the company to do so or that the matter is of public concern.

(2) A person appointed under paragraph (1) to investigate the affairs of, or of any director or depositary of, a company may also, if he thinks it necessary for the purposes of that investigation, investigate the affairs of (or of the directors, depositary, trustee or operator of)—

(a) an open-ended investment company the directors of which include any of the directors of the company whose affairs are being investigated by virtue of that paragraph;

(b) an open-ended investment company the directors of which include any of the directors of the depositary whose affairs are being investigated by virtue of that paragraph;

(c) an open-ended investment company the depositary of which is—

(i) the same as the depositary of the company whose affairs are being investigated by virtue of that paragraph; or

(ii) the depositary whose affairs are being investigated by virtue of that paragraph;

(d) an open-ended investment company the directors of which include—

(i) the director whose affairs are being investigated by virtue of that paragraph; or

(ii) any director of a body corporate which is the director whose affairs are being investigated by virtue of that paragraph;

(e) a collective investment scheme the manager, depositary or operator of which is a director of the company whose affairs are being investigated by virtue of that paragraph;

(f) a collective investment scheme the trustee of which is—

(i) the same as the depositary of the company whose affairs are being investigated by virtue of that paragraph; or

(ii) the depositary whose affairs are being investigated by virtue of that paragraph; or

(g) a collective investment scheme the manager, depositary or operator of which is—

(i) the director whose affairs are being investigated by virtue of that paragraph; or

(ii) a director of a body corporate which is the director whose affairs are being investigated by virtue of that paragraph.

(3) If the person ("A") appointed to conduct an investigation under this regulation considers that a person ("B") is or may be able to give information which is relevant to the investigation, A may require B—

(a) to produce to A any documents in B's possession or under his control which appear to A to be relevant to that investigation;

(b) to attend before A; and

(c) otherwise to give A all such assistance in connection with the investigation which B is reasonably able to give;

and it is B's duty to comply with that requirement.

(4) Subsection (5) to (9) of section 170 of the Act (investigations: general) apply if—

(a) the Authority appoints a person under this regulation to conduct an investigation on its behalf; or

(b) the Secretary of State appoints a person under this regulation to conduct an investigation on his behalf;

as they apply in the cases mentioned in subsection (1) of that section.

(5) Section 174 of the Act (admissibility of statements made to investigators) applies to a statement made by a person in compliance with a requirement imposed on him under this regulation as it applies to a statement mentioned in that section.

(6) Subsections (2) to (4) and (6) of section 175 (information and documents: supplemental provisions) and section 177 of the Act (offences) have effect as if this regulation were contained in Part XI of the Act (information gathering and investigations).

(7) Subsections (1) to (9) of section 176 of the Act (entry of premises under warrant) apply in relation to a person appointed under paragraph (1) as if—

(a) references to an investigator were references to a person so appointed;

(b) references to an information requirement were references to a requirement imposed under this regulation by a person so appointed;

(c) the premises mentioned in section 176(3)(a) were the premises of a person whose affairs are the subject of an investigation under this regulation or of an appointed representative of such a person.

(8) No person may be required under this regulation to disclose information or produce a document in respect of which he owes an obligation of confidence by virtue of carrying on a banking business unless—

(a) the imposition of the requirement is authorised by the Authority or the Secretary of State (as the case may be) or the person to whom the obligation of confidence is owed; or

(b) the person to whom it is owed is—

(i) a director or depositary of any open-ended investment company which is under investigation; or

(ii) any other person whose own affairs are under investigation.

Winding up

[8.372]

31 Winding up by the court

(1) Where an open-ended investment company is wound up as an unregistered company under Part V of the 1986 Act [or Part 6 of the 1989 Order], the provisions of that Act [or that Order] apply for the purposes of the winding up with the following modifications.

(2) A petition for the winding up of an open-ended investment company may be presented by the depositary of the company as well as by any person authorised under [section 124 of the 1986 Act or Article 104 of the 1989 Order] (application for winding up) or [section 124A of that Act or Article 104A of that Order] (petition for winding up on grounds of public interest), as those sections [or Articles] apply by virtue of Part V of that Act [or Part 6 of that Order], to present a petition for the winding up of the company.

(3) Where a petition for the winding up of an open ended investment company is presented by a person other than the Authority—

(a) that person must serve a copy of the petition on the Authority; and

(b) the Authority is entitled to be heard on the petition.

(4) If, before the presentation of a petition for the winding up by the court of an open-ended investment company as an unregistered company under Part V of the 1986 Act [or Part 6 of the 1989 Order], the affairs of the company are being wound up otherwise than by the court—

(a) [section 129(2) of that Act or Article 109(2) of that Order] (commencement of winding up by the court) is not to apply; and

(b) any winding up of the company by the court is to be deemed to have commenced—

(i) at the time at which the Authority gave its approval to a proposal mentioned in paragraph (1)(d) of regulation 21; or

(ii) in a case falling within paragraph (3)(b) of that regulation, on the day following the end of the one-month period mentioned in that paragraph.

NOTES

Paras (1), (2), (4): words in square brackets inserted or substituted by the Companies Act 2006 (Consequential Amendments and Transitional Provisions) Order 2011, SI 2011/1265, art 15, Sch 2, paras 1, 7, as from 12 May 2011.

[8.373]

32 Dissolution on winding up by the court

(1) Section 172(8) of the 1986 Act [or Article 146(7) of the 1989 Order] (final meeting of creditors and vacation of office by liquidator), as that section applies by virtue of Part V of that Act [or Part 6 of that Order] (winding up of unregistered companies) has effect, in relation to open-ended investment companies, as if the reference to the registrar of companies was a reference to the Authority.

(2) Where, in respect of an open-ended investment company, the Authority receives—

(a) a notice given for the purposes of section 172(8) of the 1986 Act [or Article 146(7) of the 1989 Order] (as aforesaid); or

(b) a notice from the official receiver that the winding up, by the court, of the company is complete;

the Authority must, on receipt of the notice, forthwith register it and, subject to the provisions of this regulation, at the end of the period of three months beginning with the day of the registration of the notice, the company is to be dissolved.

(3) The Secretary of State may, on the application of the official receiver or any other person who appears to the Secretary of State to be interested, give a direction deferring the date at which the dissolution of the company is to take effect for such period as the Secretary of State thinks fit.

(4) An appeal to the court lies from any decision of the Secretary of State on an application for a direction under paragraph (3).

(5) Paragraph (3) does not apply to a case where the winding-up order was made by the court in Scotland, but in such a case the court may, on an application by any person appearing to the court to have an interest, order that the date at which the dissolution of the company is to take effect be deferred for such period as the court thinks fit.

(6) It is the duty of the person—

(a) on whose application a direction is given under paragraph (3);

(b) in whose favour an appeal with respect to an application for such a direction is determined; or

(c) on whose application an order is made under paragraph (5);

not later than seven days after the giving of the direction, the determination of the appeal or the making of the order, to deliver to the Authority for registration a copy of the direction or determination or, in respect of an order, a certified copy of the interlocutor.

(7) If a person without reasonable excuse fails to deliver a copy as required by paragraph (6), he is guilty of an offence.

(8) A person guilty of an offence under paragraph (7) is liable, on summary conviction—

(a) to a fine not exceeding level 1 on the standard scale; and

(b) on a second or subsequent conviction instead of the penalty set out in sub-paragraph (a), to a fine of £100 for each day on which the contravention is continued.

NOTES

Paras (1), (2): words in square brackets inserted by the Companies Act 2006 (Consequential Amendments and Transitional Provisions) Order 2011, SI 2011/1265, art 15, Sch 2, paras 1, 8, as from 12 May 2011.

[8.374]

33 Dissolution in other circumstances

(1) Where the affairs of an open-ended investment company have been wound up otherwise than by the court, the Authority must, as soon as is reasonably practicable after the winding up is complete, register that fact and, subject to the provisions of this regulation, at the end of the period of three months beginning with the day of the registration, the company is to be dissolved.

(2) The court may, on the application of the Authority or the company, make an order deferring the date at which the dissolution of the company is to take effect for such period as the court thinks fit.

(3) It is the duty of the company, on whose application an order of the court under paragraph (2) is made, to deliver to the Authority, not later than seven days after the making of the order, a copy of the order for registration.

(4) Where any company, the head office of which is situated [in England and Wales (or Wales) or in Northern Ireland], is dissolved by virtue of paragraph (1), any sum of money (including unclaimed distributions) standing to the account of the company at the date of the dissolution must on such date as is determined in accordance with [FCA rules], be paid into court.

(5) Where any company, the head office of which is situated in Scotland, is dissolved by virtue of paragraph (1), any sum of money (including unclaimed dividends and unapplied or undistributable balances) standing to the account of the company at the date of the dissolution must—

(a) on such date as is determined in accordance with [FCA rules], be lodged in an appropriate bank or institution as defined in section 73(1) of the Bankruptcy (Scotland) Act 1985 (interpretation) in the name of the Accountant of the Court; and

(b) thereafter be treated as if it were a sum of money lodged in such an account by virtue of section 193 of the 1986 Act (unclaimed dividends (Scotland)), as that section applies by virtue of Part V of that Act.

[(6) The duty to deal with a sum of money in accordance with paragraph (4) or (5) does not apply if (or to the extent that) it is transferred to an authorised reclaim fund as orphan monies attributable to a collective scheme investment by virtue of sections 8 to 10 of the Dormant Assets Act 2022 (transfer of eligible amount owing by virtue of a collective scheme investment).]

NOTES

Para (4): words in first pair of square brackets substituted by the Companies Act 2006 (Consequential Amendments and Transitional Provisions) Order 2011, SI 2011/1265, art 15, Sch 2, paras 1, 9, as from 12 May 2011. Words in second pair of square brackets substituted by the Financial Services Act 2012 (Consequential Amendments and Transitional Provisions) Order 2013, SI 2013/472, art 3, Sch 2, para 41(1), (2), as from 1 April 2013.

Para (5): words in square brackets substituted by SI 2013/472, art 3, Sch 2, para 41(1), (2), as from 1 April 2013.

Para (6): added by the Dormant Assets Act 2022, s 32(3), Sch 1, para 4, as from 6 June 2022.

[8.375]

[33A Winding up of a master UCITS

(1) Paragraphs (2) and (3) apply if a master UCITS is wound up.

(2) If the Authority considers that an open-ended investment company which is a feeder UCITS of the master UCITS may be wound up under section 221 of the 1986 Act, the Authority must present a petition to the Court for the feeder UCITS to be wound up unless one of the conditions referred to in paragraph (4) is satisfied.

(3) If paragraph (2) does not apply, the Authority must require the directors of any open ended investment company which is a feeder UCITS of the master UCITS to submit a proposal under regulation 21 to wind up the affairs of the company unless one of the conditions referred to in paragraph (4) is satisfied.

(4) The conditions set out in paragraphs (2) and (3) are—

(a) the Authority approves under section 283A of the Act the investment by the feeder UCITS of at least 85% of its assets in units of another UCITS or master UCITS; or

(b) the Authority approves under regulation 22A an amendment of the instrument of incorporation of the company which would enable it to convert into a [UK] UCITS which is not a feeder UCITS.]

NOTES

Inserted, together with reg 33B, by the Undertakings for Collective Investment in Transferable Securities Regulations 2011, SI 2011/1613, reg 3(1), (6), as from 1 July 2011.

Para (4): word in square brackets inserted by the Collective Investment Schemes (Amendment etc) (EU Exit) Regulations 2019, SI 2019/325, reg 52(1), (10), as from IP completion day (as defined in the European Union (Withdrawal Agreement) Act 2020, s 39).

[8.376]

[33B Merger or division of a master UCITS

(1) Paragraph (2) applies if a master UCITS—

(a) merges with another UCITS, or

(b) is divided into two or more UCITS.

(2) The Authority must require the directors of any open-ended investment company which is a feeder UCITS of the master UCITS to prepare a proposal to wind up the affairs of the feeder UCITS under regulation 21 unless—

(a) the Authority approves under section 283A of the Act the investment by the company of at least 85% of its assets in the units of—

(i) the master UCITS which results from the merger;

(ii) one of the UCITS resulting from the division; or
(iii) another UCITS or master UCITS; or

(b) the Authority approves under regulation 22A an amendment of the instrument of incorporation of the company which would enable it to convert into a [UK] UCITS which is not a feeder UCITS.]

NOTES

Inserted as noted to reg 33A at **[8.375]**.

Para (2): word in square brackets inserted by the Collective Investment Schemes (Amendment etc) (EU Exit) Regulations 2019, SI 2019/325, reg 52(1), (11), as from IP completion day (as defined in the European Union (Withdrawal Agreement) Act 2020, s 39).

[8.377]
[33C Winding up of sub-funds

(1) Save as provided in paragraphs (2) and (3), a sub-fund may be wound up as if it were an open-ended investment company in accordance with the provisions of regulations 31 to 33 provided that the appointment of the liquidator or any provisional liquidator and the powers and duties of the liquidator or any provisional liquidator shall be confined to the sub-fund which is being wound up and its affairs, business and property.

(2) Notwithstanding paragraph (1), sections 226 to 228 of the 1986 Act shall not apply where a sub-fund is wound up in accordance with the provisions of this regulation.

(3) The provisions of Part 5 of the 1986 Act with respect to staying, sisting or restraining actions and proceedings against a company at any time after the presentation of a petition for winding up and before the making of a winding-up order extend, in the case of a sub-fund, where the application to stay, sist or restrain is presented by a creditor, to actions and proceedings against the umbrella company of that sub-fund, or any of the other sub-funds of that umbrella company, in respect of a liability of that sub-fund.

(4) Notwithstanding regulation 11A(5), a sub-fund shall be treated as if it were a separate legal person for the purposes of winding up.

(5) For the purposes of paragraph (1), in regulations 31 to 33—

(a) a reference to an open-ended investment company is taken to be a reference to a sub-fund; and
(b) a reference to a company, save in relation to the term "unregistered company", is taken to be a reference to a sub-fund.

(6) For the purposes of paragraph (1), in the provisions of the 1986 Act to which reference is made in regulations 31 to 33—

(a) references to an unregistered company and to a company are taken to be references to a sub-fund;
(b) a reference to creditors is taken to be a reference to the creditors of a sub-fund; and
(c) a reference to members is taken to be a reference to the holders of the shares in a sub-fund.

(7) Subject to paragraph (8), regulation 11A(6) shall not apply after the appointment of a liquidator or a provisional liquidator.

(8) Where an order has been made for the winding-up of a sub-fund, no action or proceedings shall be commenced or proceeded with against the umbrella company or the sub-fund in respect of any liability of the sub-fund, except by leave of the court and subject to such terms as the court may impose.]

NOTES

Inserted by the Open-Ended Investment Companies (Amendment) Regulations 2011, SI 2011/3049, reg 3(1), (5), as from 21 December 2011.

PART III CORPORATE CODE

Organs

[8.378]
34 Directors

(1) On the coming into effect of an authorisation order in respect of an open-ended investment company, the persons proposed in the application under regulation 12 as directors of the company are deemed to be appointed as its first directors.

[(2) Subject to regulations 21 and 26, any subsequent appointment as a director of a company must be made by the company in general meeting, save that the directors of the company may appoint a person to act as director to fill any vacancy until such time as the next annual general meeting of the company takes place or, if the company does not hold annual general meetings, the directors of the company may appoint a person to act as director.]

(3) Any act of a director is valid notwithstanding—

(a) any defect that may thereafter be discovered in his appointment or qualifications; or
(b) that it is afterwards discovered that his appointment had terminated by virtue of any provision contained in [FCA rules] which required a director to retire upon attaining a specified age.

(4) The business of a company must be managed—

(a) where a company has only one director, by that director; or
(b) where a company has more than one director, by the directors but subject to any provision contained in [FCA rules] as to the allocation between the directors of responsibilities for the management of the company (including any provision there may be as to the allocation of such responsibility to one or more directors to the exclusion of others).

(5) Subject to the provisions of these Regulations, [FCA rules] and the company's instrument of incorporation, the directors of a company may exercise all the powers of the company.

NOTES

Para (2): substituted by the Open-Ended Investment Companies (Amendment) Regulations 2005, SI 2005/923, reg 2(1), (3), as from 6 April 2005.

Paras (3)–(5): words in square brackets substituted by the Financial Services Act 2012 (Consequential Amendments and Transitional Provisions) Order 2013, SI 2013/472, art 3, Sch 2, para 41(1), (2), as from 1 April 2013.

[8.379]

[34A Removal of certain directors by ordinary resolution

(1) The directors of an open-ended investment company must, on a members' requisition, forthwith proceed duly to convene an extraordinary general meeting of the company and this applies notwithstanding anything in the company's instrument of incorporation.

(2) A members' requisition is a requisition—

(a) by members of the company holding at the date of the deposit of the requisition [at least the required percentage] of such of the paid-up capital of the company as at that date carries the right of voting at general meetings of the company; and

(b) which states as the object of the meeting the removal of one or more directors appointed in accordance with regulation 34(2) and which must be signed by the requisitionists and deposited at the registered office of the company.

[(2A) The required percentage is 10% unless more than twelve months has elapsed since the end of the last general meeting—

(a) called in pursuance of a members' requisition under this regulation, or

(b) in relation to which the members of the company had (by virtue of an enactment, the company's instrument of incorporation or otherwise) rights with respect to the circulation of a resolution no less extensive than they would have had if the meeting had been called at their request,

in which case the required percentage is 5%.]

(3) A company may by ordinary resolution at an extraordinary general meeting convened in accordance with paragraph (1) remove any director or directors appointed in accordance with regulation 34(2).

(4) This regulation is not to be treated as depriving a person removed under it of compensation or damages payable to him in respect of the termination of his appointment as director or as derogating from any power to remove a director which exists apart from this regulation.]

NOTES

Inserted by the Open-Ended Investment Companies (Amendment) Regulations 2005, SI 2005/923, reg 2(1), (4), as from 6 April 2005.

Words in square brackets in para (2) substituted, and para (2A) inserted, by the Companies Act 2006 (Consequential Amendments and Transitional Provisions) Order 2011, SI 2011/1265, art 15, Sch 2, paras 1, 10, as from 12 May 2011.

[8.380]

35 Directors to have regard to interests of employees

(1) The matters to which a director of an open-ended investment company must have regard in the performance of his functions include the interests of the company's employees in general, as well as the interests of its shareholders.

(2) The duty imposed by this regulation on a director is owed by him to the company (and the company alone) and is enforceable in the same way as any other fiduciary duty owed to a company by its directors.

[8.381]

36 Inspection of directors' service contracts

(1) Every open-ended investment company must keep at an appropriate place—

(a) in the case of each director whose contract of service with the company is in writing, a copy of that contract; and

(b) in the case of each director whose contract of service with the company is not in writing, a written memorandum setting out its terms.

(2) All copies and memoranda kept by a company in accordance with paragraph (1) must be kept at the same place.

(3) The following are appropriate places for the purposes of paragraph (1)—

(a) the company's head office;

[(b) a place that is situated in the part of the United Kingdom in which the company is registered, which has been notified to the Authority as being the company's alternative inspection location.]

(4) Every copy and memorandum required by paragraph (1) to be kept must be open to the inspection of any shareholder of the company.

(5) If such an inspection is refused, the court may by order compel an immediate inspection of the copy or memorandum concerned.

[(6) Every copy and memorandum required to be kept by paragraph (1) must be made available, for inspection, by the company at the company's annual general meeting or, if the company does not hold annual general meetings, sent to any shareholder at his request within ten days of the company's receipt of such request.]

(7) Paragraph (1) applies to a variation of a director's contract of service as it applies to the contract.

NOTES

Para (3); sub-para (b) substituted (for the original sub-paras (b), (c)) by the Companies Act 2006 (Consequential Amendments and Transitional Provisions) Order 2011, SI 2011/1265, art 15, Sch 2, paras 1, 11, as from 12 May 2011.

Para (6): substituted the Open-Ended Investment Companies (Amendment) Regulations 2005, SI 2005/923, reg 2(1), (5), as from 6 April 2005.

[8.382]
37 General meetings

(1) Subject to paragraph (2) [and regulation 37A], every open-ended investment company [incorporated before 6 April 2005] must in each year hold a general meeting ("annual general meeting") in addition to any other meetings, whether general or otherwise, it may hold in that year.

(2) If a company holds its first annual general meeting within 18 months of the date on which the authorisation order made by the Authority in respect of the company comes into effect, paragraph (1) does not require the company to hold any other meeting as its annual general meeting in the year of its incorporation or in the following year.

(3) Subject to paragraph (2) [and regulation 37A], not more than 15 months may elapse between the date of one annual general meeting of a company and the date of the next.

NOTES

Paras (1), (3): words in square brackets inserted by the Open-Ended Investment Companies (Amendment) Regulations 2005, SI 2005/923, reg 2(1), (6), as from 6 April 2005.

[8.383]
[37A Election to dispense with annual general meetings

(1) The directors of an open-ended investment company may elect to dispense with the holding of an annual general meeting by giving sixty days' written notice to all the company's shareholders.

(2) An election has effect for the year in which it is made and subsequent years, but does not affect any liability already incurred by reason of default in holding an annual general meeting.]

NOTES

Inserted by the Open-Ended Investment Companies (Amendment) Regulations 2005, SI 2005/923, reg 2(1), (7), as from 6 April 2005.

[8.384]
38 Capacity of company

(1) The validity of an act done by an open-ended investment company cannot be called into question on the ground of lack of capacity by reason of anything in these Regulations, [FCA rules] or the company's instrument of incorporation.

(2) Nothing in paragraph (1) affects the duty of the directors to observe any limitation on their powers.

NOTES

Para (1): words in square brackets substituted by the Financial Services Act 2012 (Consequential Amendments and Transitional Provisions) Order 2013, SI 2013/472, art 3, Sch 2, para 41(1), (2), as from 1 April 2013.

[8.385]
39 Power of directors and general meeting to bind the company

(1) In favour of a person dealing in good faith, the following powers, that is to say—

(a) the power of the directors of an open-ended investment company (whether or not acting as a board) to bind the company, or authorise others to do so; and

(b) the power of such a company in general meeting to bind the company, or authorise others to do so;

are deemed to be free of any limitation under the company's constitution.

(2) For the purposes of this regulation—

(a) a person deals with a company if he is party to any transaction or other act to which the company is a party;

(b) subject to paragraph (4), a person is not to be regarded as acting in bad faith by reason only of his knowing that, under the company's constitution, an act is beyond any of the powers referred to in paragraph (1)(a) or (b); and

(c) subject to paragraph (4), a person is presumed to have acted in good faith unless the contrary is proved.

(3) The reference in paragraph (1) to any limitation under the company's constitution on the powers therein set out includes any limitation deriving from these Regulations, from [FCA rules] or from a resolution of the company in general meeting or of a meeting of any class of shareholders.

(4) Sub-paragraphs (b) and (c) of paragraph (2) do not apply where—

(a) by virtue of a limitation deriving from these Regulations or from [FCA rules], an act is beyond any of the powers referred to in paragraph (1)(a) or (b); and

(b) the person in question—

(i) has actual knowledge of that fact; or

(ii) has deliberately failed to make enquiries in circumstances in which a reasonable and honest person would have done so.

(5) Paragraph (1) does not affect any liability incurred by the directors or any other person by reason of the directors exceeding their powers.

NOTES

Paras (3), (4): words in square brackets substituted by the Financial Services Act 2012 (Consequential Amendments and Transitional Provisions) Order 2013, SI 2013/472, art 3, Sch 2, para 41(1), (2), as from 1 April 2013.

[8.386]
40 No duty to enquire as to capacity etc

Subject to regulation 39(4)(b)(ii), a party to a transaction with an open-ended investment company is not bound to enquire—

(a) as to whether the transaction is permitted by these Regulations, [FCA rules] or the company's instrument of incorporation; or

(b) as to any limitation on the powers referred to in regulation 39(1)(a) or (b).

NOTES

Words in square brackets substituted by the Financial Services Act 2012 (Consequential Amendments and Transitional Provisions) Order 2013, SI 2013/472, art 3, Sch 2, para 41(1), (2), as from 1 April 2013.

41 (*Revoked by the Companies Act 2006 (Consequential Amendments and Transitional Provisions) Order 2011, SI 2011/1265, art 15, Sch 2, paras 1, 12, as from 12 May 2011.*)

[8.387]

42 Restraint and ratification by shareholders

(1) A shareholder of an open-ended investment company may bring proceedings to restrain the doing of an act which but for regulation 38(1) would be beyond the company's capacity.

(2) Paragraph (1) of regulation 39 does not affect any right of a shareholder of an open-ended investment company to bring proceedings to restrain the doing of an act which is beyond any of the powers referred to in that paragraph.

(3) No proceedings may be brought under paragraph (1) in respect of an act to be done in fulfilment of a legal obligation arising from a previous act of the company; and paragraph (2) does not have the effect of enabling proceedings to be brought in respect of any such act.

(4) Any action by the directors of a company—

(a) which, but for regulation 38(1), would be beyond the company's capacity; or

(b) which is within the company's capacity but beyond the powers referred to in regulation 39(1)(a);

may only be ratified by a resolution of the company in general meeting.

(5) A resolution ratifying such action does not affect any liability incurred by the directors or any other person, relief from any such liability requiring agreement by a separate resolution of the company in general meeting.

(6) Nothing in this regulation affects any power or right conferred by or arising under [section 138D] (actions for damages) or section 380, 382 or 384 of the Act (injunctions and restitution orders).

NOTES

Words in square brackets substituted by the Financial Services Act 2012 (Consequential Amendments and Transitional Provisions) Order 2013, SI 2013/472, art 3, Sch 2, para 41(1), (8), as from 1 April 2013.

[8.388]

43 Events affecting company status

(1) Where either of the conditions mentioned in paragraph (2) is satisfied, an open-ended investment company is not entitled to rely against other persons on the happening of any of the following events—

(a) any alteration of the company's instrument of incorporation;

(b) any change among the directors of the company;

(c) as regards service of any document on the company, any change in the situation of the head office of the company; or

(d) the making of a winding-up order in respect of the company or, in circumstances in which the affairs of a company are to be wound up otherwise than by the court, the commencement of the winding up.

(2) The conditions referred to in paragraph (1) are that—

(a) the event in question had not been officially notified at the material time and is not shown by the company to have been known at that time by the other person concerned; and

(b) if the material time fell on or before the 15th day after the date of official notification (or where the 15th day was a non-business day, on or before the next day that was a business day), it is shown that the other person concerned was unavoidably prevented from knowing of the event at that time.

(3) In this regulation "official notification" means the notification in the Gazette (by virtue of regulation 78) of any document containing the information referred to in paragraph (1) above, and "officially notified" is to be construed accordingly.

[8.389]

44 Invalidity of certain transactions involving directors

(1) This regulation applies where—

(a) an open-ended investment company enters into a transaction to which the parties include a director of the company or any person who is an associate of such a director; and

(b) in connection with the transaction, the directors of the company (whether or not acting as a board) exceed any limitation on their powers under the company's constitution.

(2) The transaction is voidable at the instance of the company.

(3) Whether or not the transaction is avoided, any such party to the transaction as is mentioned in paragraph (1)(a), and any director of the company who authorised the transaction, is liable—

(a) to account to the company for any gain which he has made directly or indirectly by the transaction; and

(b) to indemnify the company for any loss or damage resulting from the transaction.

(4) Nothing in paragraphs (1) to (3) is to be construed as excluding the operation of any other enactment or rule of law by virtue of which the transaction may be called into question or any liability to the company may arise.

(5) The transaction ceases to be voidable if—

(a) restitution of any money or other asset which was the subject-matter of the transaction is no longer possible;

(b) the company is indemnified for any loss or damage resulting from the transaction;

(c) rights which are acquired, bona fide for value and without actual notice of the directors concerned having exceeded their powers, by a person who is not a party to the transaction would be affected by the avoidance; or

(d) the transaction is ratified by resolution of the company in general meeting.

(6) A person other than a director of the company is not liable under paragraph (3) if he shows that at the time the transaction was entered into he did not know that the directors concerned were exceeding their powers.

(7) This regulation does not affect the operation of regulation 39 in relation to any party to the transaction not within paragraph (1)(a); but where a transaction is voidable by virtue of this regulation and valid by virtue of that regulation in favour of such a person, the court may, on the application of that person or of the company, make such order affirming, severing or setting aside the transaction, on such terms as appear to the court to be just.

(8) For the purposes of this regulation—

(a) "associate", in relation to any person who is a director of the company, means that person's spouse, [civil partner,] child or stepchild (if under 18), employee, partner or any body corporate of which that person is a director; and if that person is a body corporate, any subsidiary undertaking or director of that body corporate (including any director or employee of such subsidiary undertaking);

(b) "transaction" includes any act; and

(c) the reference in paragraph (1)(b) to any limitation on directors' powers under the company's constitution includes any limitation deriving from these Regulations, from [FCA rules] or from a resolution of the company in general meeting or of a meeting of any class of shareholders.

NOTES

Para (8): words in square brackets in sub-para (a) inserted by the Civil Partnership Act 2004 (Amendments to Subordinate Legislation) Order 2005, SI 2005/2114, art 2(16), Sch 16, Pt 1, para 5, as from 5 December 2005. Words in square brackets in sub-para (c) substituted by the Financial Services Act 2012 (Consequential Amendments and Transitional Provisions) Order 2013, SI 2013/472, art 3, Sch 2, para 41(1), (2), as from 1 April 2013.

Stepchild, etc: as to the meaning of this and related expressions, see the Civil Partnership Act 2004, s 246 (as applied to these Regulations by the Civil Partnership Act 2004 (Relationships Arising Through Civil Partnership) Order 2005, SI 2005/3137, art 3, Schedule).

Shares

[8.390]

45 Shares

(1) An open-ended investment company may issue more than one class of shares.

(2) A shareholder may not have any interest in the scheme property of the company.

(3) The rights which attach to each share of any given class are—

(a) the right, in accordance with the instrument of incorporation, to participate in or receive profits or income arising from the acquisition, holding, management or disposal of the scheme property;

(b) the right, in accordance with the instrument of incorporation, to vote at any general meeting of the company or at any relevant class meeting; and

(c) such other rights as may be provided for, in relation to shares of that class, in the instrument of incorporation of the company.

(4) In respect of any class of shares, the rights referred to in paragraph (3) may, if the company's instrument of incorporation so provides, be expressed in two denominations; and in the case of any such class, one (the "smaller") denomination is to be such proportion of the other (the "larger") denomination as is fixed by the instrument of incorporation.

(5) In respect of any class of shares within paragraph (4), any share to which are attached rights expressed in the smaller denomination is to be known as a smaller denomination share; and any share to which are attached rights expressed in the larger denomination is to be known as a larger denomination share.

(6) In respect of any class of shares, the rights which attach to each share of that class are—

(a) except in respect of a class of shares within paragraph (4), equal to the rights that attach to each other share of that class; and

(b) in respect of a class of shares within that paragraph, equal to the rights that attach to each other share of that class of the same denomination.

(7) In respect of any class of shares within paragraph (4), the rights that attach to any smaller denomination share of that class are to be a proportion of the rights that attach to any larger denomination share of that class and that proportion is to be the same as the proportion referred to in paragraph (4).

[8.391]

46 Share certificates

(1) Subject to regulations 47 and 48, an open-ended investment company must prepare documentary evidence of title to its shares ("share certificates") as follows—

(a) in respect of any new shares issued by it;

(b) where a shareholder has transferred part only of his holding back to the company, in respect of the remainder of that holding;

(c) where a shareholder has transferred part only of his holding to the designated person, in respect of the remainder of that holding;

(d) where a company has registered a transfer of shares made to a person other than the company or a person designated as mentioned in sub-paragraph (c)—

(i) in respect of the shares transferred to the transferee; and

(ii) in respect of any shares retained by the transferor which were evidenced by any certificate sent to the company for the purposes of registering the transfer;

(e) in respect of any holding of bearer shares for which a certificate evidencing title has already been issued but where the certificate has been surrendered to the company for the purpose of being replaced by two or more certificates which between them evidence title to the shares comprising that holding; and

(f) in respect of any shares for which a certificate has already been issued but where it appears to the company that the certificate needs to be replaced as a result of having been lost, stolen or destroyed or having become damaged or worn out.

(2) A company must exercise due diligence and take all reasonable steps to ensure that certificates prepared in accordance with paragraph (1)(a) to (e) are ready for delivery as soon as reasonably practicable.

(3) Certificates need be prepared in the circumstances referred to in paragraph (1)(e) and (f) only if the company has received—

(a) a request for a new certificate;
(b) the old certificate (if there is one);
(c) such indemnity as the company may require; and
(d) such reasonable sum as the company may require in respect of the expenses incurred by it in complying with the request.

(4) Each share certificate must state—

(a) the number of shares the title to which is evidenced by the certificate;
(b) where the company has more than one class of shares, the class of shares title to which is evidenced by the certificate; and
(c) except in the case of bearer shares, the name of the holder.

(5) Where, in respect of any class of shares, the rights that attach to shares of that class are expressed in two denominations, the reference in paragraph (4)(a) (as it applies to shares of that class) to the number of shares is a reference to the total of—

$$N + n / p$$

(6) In paragraph (5)—

(a) N is the relevant number of the larger denomination shares of the class in question;
(b) n is the relevant number of the smaller denomination shares of that class; and
(c) p is the number of smaller denomination shares of that class that are equivalent to one larger denomination share of that class.

(7) Nothing in these Regulations is to be taken as preventing the total arrived at under paragraph (5) being expressed on the certificate as a single entry representing the result derived from the formula set out in that paragraph.

(8) In England and Wales [or Northern Ireland], a share certificate specifying any shares held by any person which is—

(a) under the common seal of the company; or
(b) authenticated in accordance with regulation 59;

is prima facie evidence of that person's title to the shares.

(9) In Scotland, a share certificate specifying any shares held by any person which is—

(a) under the common seal of the company; or
(b) subscribed by the company in accordance with the Requirements of Writing (Scotland) Act 1995;

is, unless the contrary is shown, sufficient evidence of that person's title to the shares.

NOTES

Para (8): words in square brackets inserted by the Companies Act 2006 (Consequential Amendments and Transitional Provisions) Order 2011, SI 2011/1265, art 15, Sch 2, paras 1, 13, as from 12 May 2011.

[8.392]

47 Exceptions from regulation 46

(1) . . .

(2) Nothing in regulation 46 requires a company to prepare share certificates in the following cases.

(3) Case 1 is any case where the company's instrument of incorporation states that share certificates will not be issued and contains provision as to other procedures for evidencing a person's entitlement to shares.

(4) Case 2 is any case where a shareholder has indicated to the company in writing that he does not wish to receive a certificate.

(5) Case 3 is any case where shares are issued or transferred to the designated person.

(6) Case 4 is any case where shares are issued or transferred to a nominee of a recognised investment exchange who is designated for the purposes of this paragraph in the rules of the investment exchange in question.

NOTES

Para (1): revoked by the Uncertificated Securities Regulations 2001, SI 2001/3755, reg 52(4), as from 26 November 2001.

[8.393]

48 Bearer shares

[(1)] An open-ended investment company [authorised before the day on which the Money Laundering, Terrorist Financing and Transfer of Funds (Information on the Payer) Regulations 2017 came into force ("the relevant date")] may, if its instrument of incorporation so provides, issue shares ("bearer shares") evidenced by a share certificate, or by any other documentary evidence of title for which provision is made in its instrument of incorporation, which indicates—

(a) that the holder of the document is entitled to the shares specified in it; and
(b) that no entry will be made on the register of shareholders identifying the holder of those shares.

[(1A) An open-ended investment company authorised before the relevant date may not issue, convert or cancel bearer shares after 1 January 2021 (irrespective of whether its instrument of incorporation purports to authorise it to do so).]

[(2) An open-ended investment company authorised on or after the relevant date may not issue any bearer shares under paragraph (1), and any provision in the instrument of incorporation of such an open-ended investment company purporting to authorise it to do so is void.

(3) Paragraph (2) does not apply to an open-ended investment company if—

(a) an application for an authorisation order was made in relation to that open-ended investment company before the relevant date; and

(b) that application was not determined until a date on or after the relevant date.]

NOTES

Para (1) numbered as such, words in square brackets in that paragraph inserted, and paras (2), (3) added, by the Money Laundering, Terrorist Financing and Transfer of Funds (Information on the Payer) Regulations 2017, SI 2017/692, reg 109, Sch 7, Pt 2, para 18, as from 26 June 2017.

Para (1A) was inserted by the Bearer Certificates (Collective Investment Schemes) Regulations 2020, SI 2020/1346, reg 3, as from 1 January 2021; for transitional provisions, see the Schedule to the 2020 Regulations at **[8.578]**.

[8.394]

49 Register of shareholders

Schedule 3 to these Regulations makes provision with respect to the register of shareholders of an open-ended investment company.

50 (*Revoked by the Companies Act 2006 (Consequential Amendments and Transitional Provisions) Order 2011, SI 2011/1265, art 15, Sch 2, paras 1, 14, as from 12 May 2011.*)

[8.395]

51 Power of court to rectify register

(1) An application to the court may be made under this regulation if—

(a) the name of any person is, without sufficient cause, entered in or omitted from the register of shareholders of an open-ended investment company;

(b) default is made as to the details contained in any entry on the register in respect of a person's holding of shares in the company; or

(c) default is made or unnecessary delay takes place in amending the register so as to reflect the fact of any person having ceased to be a shareholder.

(2) An application under this regulation may be made by the person aggrieved, by any shareholder of the company or by the company itself.

(3) The court may refuse the application or may order rectification of the register of shareholders and payment by the company of any damages sustained by any party aggrieved.

(4) On such an application the court may decide any question necessary or expedient to be decided for rectification of the register of shareholders including, in particular, any question relating to the right of a person who is a party to the application to have his name entered in or omitted from the register (whether the question arises as between shareholders and alleged shareholders or as between shareholders or alleged shareholders on the one hand and the company on the other hand).

[8.396]

52 Share transfers

Schedule 4 to these Regulations makes provision for the transfer of registered and bearer shares in an open-ended investment company.

Operation

[8.397]

53 Power incidental to carrying on business

An open-ended investment company has power to do all such things as are incidental or conducive to the carrying on of its business.

[8.398]

54 Name to appear in correspondence etc

(1) Every open-ended investment company must [disclose its name in characters that can be read with the naked eye in all letters of the company, in all other documents issued by the company in the course of business, and on its website].

(2) . . .

NOTES

Words in square brackets in para (1) substituted, and para (2) revoked, by the Companies Act 2006 (Consequential Amendments and Transitional Provisions) Order 2011, SI 2011/1265, art 15, Sch 2, paras 1, 15, as from 12 May 2011.

[8.399]

55 Particulars to appear in correspondence etc

(1) Every open-ended investment company must have the following particulars [disclosed in characters that can be read with the naked eye in all letters of the company, in all other documents issued by the company in the course of business, and on its websites]—

(a) the company's place of registration;

(b) the number with which it is registered;

(c) the address of its head office; and
(d) the fact that it is an investment company with variable capital.

(2) Where, in accordance with regulation 72, the Authority makes any change of existing registered numbers in respect of any open-ended investment company then, for a period of three years beginning with the date on which the notification of the change is sent to the company by the Authority, the requirement of paragraph (1)(b) is, notwithstanding regulation 72(4), satisfied by the use of either the old number or the new.

NOTES

Para (1): words in square brackets substituted by the Companies Act 2006 (Consequential Amendments and Transitional Provisions) Order 2011, SI 2011/1265, art 15, Sch 2, paras 1, 16, as from 12 May 2011.

[8.400]
56 Contracts: England and Wales [or Northern Ireland]

Under the law of England and Wales [or Northern Ireland] a contract may be made—
(a) by an open-ended investment company by writing under its common seal; or
(b) on behalf of such a company, by any person acting under its authority (whether expressed or implied);
and any formalities required by law in the case of a contract made by an individual also apply, unless a contrary intention appears, to a contract made by or on behalf of such a company.

NOTES

Words in square brackets inserted by the Companies Act 2006 (Consequential Amendments and Transitional Provisions) Order 2011, SI 2011/1265, art 15, Sch 2, paras 1, 17, as from 12 May 2011.

[8.401]
57 Execution of documents: England and Wales [or Northern Ireland]

(1) Under the law of England and Wales [or Northern Ireland] the following provisions have effect with respect to the execution of documents by an open-ended investment company.

(2) A document is executed by a company by the affixing of its common seal.

(3) A company need not have a common seal, however, and the following provisions of this regulation apply whether it does or not.

(4) A document that is signed by at least one director and expressed (in whatever form of words) to be executed by the company has the same effect as if executed under the common seal of the company.

(5) A document executed by a company which makes it clear on its face that it is intended by the person or persons making it to be a deed has effect, upon delivery, as a deed; and it is to be presumed, unless a contrary intention is proved, to be delivered upon its being executed.

(6) In favour of a purchaser, a document is deemed to have been duly executed by a company if it purports to be signed by at least one director or, in the case of a director which is a body corporate, it purports to be executed by that director; and, where it makes it clear on its face that it is intended by the person or persons making it to be a deed, it is deemed to have been delivered upon its being executed.

(7) In paragraph (6), "purchaser" means a purchaser in good faith for valuable consideration and includes a lessee, mortgagee or other person who for valuable consideration acquires an interest in property.

NOTES

Words in square brackets inserted by the Companies Act 2006 (Consequential Amendments and Transitional Provisions) Order 2011, SI 2011/1265, art 15, Sch 2, paras 1, 18, as from 12 May 2011.

[8.402]
58 [Execution of deeds or other documents by attorney]

(1) Under the law of England and Wales [or Northern Ireland] an open-ended investment company may, [by instrument executed as a deed], empower any person, either generally or in respect of any specified matters, as its attorney, to execute deeds on its behalf . . .

(2) A deed executed by such an attorney on behalf of the company [has effect as if executed by the company].

NOTES

All amendments to this regulation were made by the Companies Act 2006 (Consequential Amendments and Transitional Provisions) Order 2011, SI 2011/1265, art 15, Sch 2, paras 1, 19, as from 12 May 2011.

59 (*Revoked by the Companies Act 2006 (Consequential Amendments and Transitional Provisions) Order 2011, SI 2011/1265, art 15, Sch 2, paras 1, 20, as from 12 May 2011.*)

[8.403]
60 Official seal for share certificates

(1) An open-ended investment company which has a common seal may have, for use for sealing shares issued by the company and for sealing documents creating or evidencing shares so issued, an official seal which is a facsimile of its common seal with the addition on its face of the word "securities".

(2) The official seal when duly affixed to a document has the same effect as the company's common seal.

(3) . . .

NOTES

Para (3): revoked by the Companies Act 2006 (Consequential Amendments and Transitional Provisions) Order 2011, SI 2011/1265, art 15, Sch 2, paras 1, 21, as from 12 May 2011.

[8.404]

61 Personal liability for contracts and deeds

(1) A contract, which purports to be made by or on behalf of an open-ended investment company at a time before the coming into effect of an authorisation order in relation to that company, has effect (subject to any agreement to the contrary) as a contract made with the person purporting to act for the company or as agent for it, and he is accordingly personally liable under the contract.

(2) Paragraph (1) applies—

(a) to the making of a deed under the law of England and Wales [or Northern Ireland]; and

(b) to the undertaking of an obligation under the law of Scotland;

as it applies to the making of a contract.

(3) If a company enters into a transaction at any time after the authorisation order made in respect of the company has been revoked and the company fails to comply with its obligations in respect of that transaction within 21 days of being called upon to do so, the person who authorised the transaction is liable, and where the transaction was authorised by two or more persons they are jointly and severally liable, to indemnify the other party to the transaction in respect of any loss or damage suffered by him by reason of the company's failure to comply with those obligations.

NOTES

Para (2): words in square brackets inserted by the Companies Act 2006 (Consequential Amendments and Transitional Provisions) Order 2011, SI 2011/1265, art 15, Sch 2, paras 1, 22, as from 12 May 2011.

[8.405]

62 Exemptions from liability to be void

(1) This regulation applies to any provision, whether contained in the instrument of incorporation of an open-ended investment company or in any contract with the company or otherwise—

(a) which exempts any officer of the company or any person (whether or not an officer of the company) employed by the company as auditor from, or indemnifies him against, any liability which by virtue of any rule of law would otherwise attach to him in respect of any negligence, default, breach of duty or breach of trust of which he may be guilty in relation to the company; or

(b) which exempts the depositary of the company from, or indemnifies him against, any liability for any failure to exercise due care and diligence in the discharge of his functions in respect of the company.

(2) Except as provided by the following paragraph, any such provision is void.

(3) [Except in the case of the depositary of an AIF (as to which see regulations 29 to 32 of the Alternative Investment Fund Managers Regulations 2013), this regulation] does not prevent a company—

(a) from purchasing and maintaining for any such officer, auditor or depositary insurance against any such liability; or

(b) from indemnifying any such officer, auditor or depositary against any liability incurred by him—

(i) in defending any proceedings (whether civil or criminal) in which judgment is given in his favour or he is acquitted; or

(ii) in connection with any application under regulation 63 in which relief is granted to him by the court.

NOTES

Para (3): words in square brackets substituted by the Alternative Investment Fund Managers Regulations 2013, SI 2013/1773, reg 81, Sch 2, Part 2, para 10(1), (3), as from 22 July 2013.

[8.406]

63 Power of court to grant relief in certain cases

(1) This regulation applies to—

(a) any proceedings for negligence, default, breach of duty or breach of trust against an officer of an open-ended investment company or a person (whether or not an officer of the company) employed by the company as auditor; or

(b) any proceedings against the depository of such a company for failure to exercise due care and diligence in the discharge of his functions in respect of the company.

(2) If, in any proceedings to which this regulation applies, it appears to the court hearing the case—

(a) that the officer, auditor or depositary is or may be liable in respect of the cause of action in question;

(b) that, nevertheless, he has acted honestly and reasonably; and

(c) that having regard to all the circumstances of the case (including those connected with his appointment) he ought fairly to be excused from the liability sought to be enforced against him;

the court may relieve him, either wholly or partly, from his liability on such terms as it may think fit.

(3) If any such officer, auditor or depositary has reason to apprehend that any claim will or might be made against him in proceedings to which this regulation applies, he may apply to the court for relief.

(4) The court, on an application under paragraph (3), has the same power to relieve the applicant as under this regulation it would have had if it had been a court before which the relevant proceedings against the applicant had been brought.

(5) Where a case to which paragraph (2) applies is being tried by a judge with a jury, the judge, after hearing the evidence, may, if he is satisfied that the defendant or defender ought in pursuance of that paragraph to be relieved either in whole or in part from the liability sought to be enforced against him, withdraw the case in whole or in part from the jury and forthwith direct judgment to be entered for the defendant or defender on such terms as to costs or otherwise as the judge may think proper.

[8.407]
64 Punishment for fraudulent trading

(1) If any business of an open-ended investment company is carried on with intent to defraud creditors of the company or creditors of any other person, or for any fraudulent purpose, every person who was knowingly a party to the carrying on of the business in that manner is guilty of an offence and liable—

(a) on conviction on indictment, to imprisonment not exceeding a term of [ten] years or to a fine or to both;

[(b) on summary conviction—

(i) in England and Wales, to imprisonment for a term not exceeding twelve months or a fine not exceeding the statutory maximum (or both);

(ii) in Scotland or Northern Ireland, to imprisonment for a term not exceeding six months or a fine not exceeding the statutory maximum (or both).]

(2) This regulation applies whether or not the company has been, or is in the course of being, wound up (whether by the court or otherwise).

NOTES

Para (1): words in square brackets substituted by the Companies Act 2006 (Consequential Amendments and Transitional Provisions) Order 2011, SI 2011/1265, art 15, Sch 2, paras 1, 23, as from 12 May 2011.

[8.408]
65 Power to provide for employees on cessation or transfer of business

(1) The powers of an open-ended investment company include power to make the following provision for the benefit of persons employed or formerly employed by the company, that is to say, provision in connection with the cessation or the transfer to any person of the whole or part of the undertaking of the company.

(2) The power conferred by paragraph (1) is exercisable notwithstanding that its exercise is not in the best interests of the company.

(3) The power which a company may exercise by virtue of paragraph (1) may only be exercised by the company—

(a) in a case not falling within sub-paragraph (b) or (c), if sanctioned by a resolution of the company in general meeting;

(b) [subject to paragraph (4)] if so authorised by the instrument of incorporation—

(i) in the case of a company that has only one director, by a resolution of that director; and

(ii) in any other case, by such resolution of directors as is required by [FCA rules]; or

(c) if the instrument of incorporation requires the exercise of the power to be sanctioned by a resolution of the company in general meeting for which more than a simple majority of the shareholders voting is necessary, by a resolution of that majority;

and in any case after compliance with any other requirements of the instrument of incorporation applicable to the exercise of the power.

[(4) A resolution of the directors is not sufficient sanction for payments to or for the benefits of directors, former directors or shadow directors.]

NOTES

Words in first pair of square brackets in para (3) inserted, and para (4) added, by the Companies Act 2006 (Consequential Amendments and Transitional Provisions) Order 2011, SI 2011/1265, art 15, Sch 2, paras 1, 24, as from 12 May 2011. Words in square brackets in sub-para (3)(b)(ii) substituted by the Financial Services Act 2012 (Consequential Amendments and Transitional Provisions) Order 2013, SI 2013/472, art 3, Sch 2, para 41(1), (2), as from 1 April 2013.

Reports

[8.409]
66 Reports: preparation

(1) The directors of an open-ended investment company must—

(a) prepare a report ("annual report") for each annual accounting period of the company; and

(b) subject to paragraph (2), prepare a report ("half-yearly report") for each half-yearly accounting period of the company.

(2) Where a company's first annual accounting period is a period of less than 12 months, a half-yearly report need not be prepared for any part of that period.

(3) . . .

(4) Nothing in this regulation or in regulation 67 prejudices the generality of regulation 6(1).

(5) In this regulation any reference to annual and half-yearly accounting periods of a company is a reference to those periods as determined in relation to that company in accordance with [FCA rules].

NOTES

Para (3): revoked by the Companies Act 2006 (Consequential Amendments and Transitional Provisions) Order 2011, SI 2011/1265, art 15, Sch 2, paras 1, 25, as from 12 May 2011.

Para (5): words in square brackets substituted by the Financial Services Act 2012 (Consequential Amendments and Transitional Provisions) Order 2013, SI 2013/472, art 3, Sch 2, para 41(1), (2), as from 1 April 2013.

[8.410]
67 Reports: accounts

(1) The annual report of an open-ended investment company must, in respect of the annual accounting period to which it relates, contain accounts of the company.

(2) The company's auditors must make a report to the company's shareholders in respect of the accounts of the company contained in its annual report.

(3) A copy of the auditor's report must form part of the company's annual report.

[8.411]
68 Reports: voluntary revision

(1) If it appears to the directors of an open-ended investment company that any annual report of the company did not comply with the requirements of these Regulations or [FCA rules], they may prepare a revised annual report.

(2) Where copies of the previous report have been laid before the company in general meeting or delivered to the Authority, the revisions must be confined to—

(a) the correction of anything in the previous report which did not comply with the requirements of these Regulations or [FCA rules]; and

(b) the making of any necessary consequential alterations.

NOTES

Words in square brackets substituted by the Financial Services Act 2012 (Consequential Amendments and Transitional Provisions) Order 2013, SI 2013/472, art 3, Sch 2, para 41(1), (2), as from 1 April 2013.

[8.412]
69 Auditors

Schedule 5 to these Regulations makes provision with respect to the auditors of open-ended investment companies.

Mergers and divisions

[8.413]
70 Mergers and divisions

Schedule 6 to these Regulations makes provision with respect to mergers and divisions involving open-ended investment companies [other than mergers [to which Part 4 of the Undertakings for Collective Investment in Transferable Securities Regulations 2011 applies]].

NOTES

Words in first (outer) pair of square brackets inserted by the Undertakings for Collective Investment in Transferable Securities Regulations 2011, SI 2011/1613, reg 3(1), (7), as from 1 July 2011. Words in second (inner) pair of square brackets substituted by the Collective Investment Schemes (Amendment etc) (EU Exit) Regulations 2019, SI 2019/325, reg 52(1), (12), as from IP completion day (as defined in the European Union (Withdrawal Agreement) Act 2020, s 39).

PART IV THE AUTHORITY'S REGISTRATION FUNCTIONS

[8.414]
71 Register of open-ended investment companies

(1) The Authority must maintain a register of open-ended investment companies.

(2) The Authority may keep the register in any form it thinks fit provided that it is possible to inspect the information contained on it and to obtain a copy of that information (or any part of it) for inspection.

[8.415]
72 Companies' registered numbers

(1) The Authority must allocate to every open-ended investment company a number, which is to be known as the company's registered number.

(2) Companies' registered numbers must be in such form, consisting of one or more sequences of figures or letters, as the Authority may from time to time determine.

(3) The Authority may, upon adopting a new form of registered number, make such changes of existing registered numbers (including numbers allocated by the appropriate registrar) as appear to it to be necessary.

(4) A change in a company's registered number has effect from the date on which the company is notified by the Authority of the change.

[8.416]
73 Delivery of documents to the Authority

Any document which is required by these Regulations to be delivered to the Authority to be recorded on the register maintained pursuant to regulation 71 must be delivered in such form as the Authority may from time to time specify.

[8.417]
74 Keeping of company records by the Authority

(1) The information contained in a document delivered to the Authority under any provision of these Regulations may be recorded and kept by it in any form it thinks fit, provided that it is possible to inspect the information and produce a copy of it . . .

[(2) The originals of documents delivered to the Authority under any provision of these Regulations in hard copy form must be kept for three years after they are received by the Authority, after which they may be destroyed provided the information contained in them has been recorded in the register.

(2A) The Authority is under no obligation to keep the originals of documents delivered in electronic form, provided the information contained in them has been recorded in the register.]

(3) Where a company has been dissolved, the Authority may, at any time after the expiration of two years from the date of the dissolution, direct that any records in its custody relating to the company may be removed to the Public Record Office; and records in respect of which such a direction is given must be disposed of in accordance with the enactments relating to that Office and the rules made under them.

(4) Paragraph (3) does not extend to Scotland.

[(5) Paragraphs (2) and (2A) apply to documents held by the Authority when this paragraph comes into force as well as to documents subsequently received.]

NOTES

Words omitted from para (1) revoked, paras (2), (2A) substituted (for the original para (2)), and para (5) added, by the Companies Act 2006 (Consequential Amendments and Transitional Provisions) Order 2011, SI 2011/1265, art 15, Sch 2, paras 1, 26, as from 12 May 2011.

[8.418]

75 Inspection etc of records kept by the Authority

[(1) Any person may inspect the register kept by the Authority for the purposes of this Part of these Regulations, and may require a copy of any material on the register.

(1A) The Authority may specify the form and manner in which an application is to be made for inspection or a copy under paragraph (1).

(1B) Copies of documents required to be registered under regulation 4 must be provided in hard copy or electronic form, as the applicant requests.

(1C) The Authority is not obliged by paragraph (1B) to provide copies in electronic form of a document that was delivered to the Authority in hard copy form if the document was delivered to the Authority on or before 31st December 2006 and ten years or more elapsed between the date of delivery and the date of receipt of the first application for a copy.

(1D) Subject to paragraphs (1B) and (1C), the Authority may determine the form and manner in which copies are to be provided.

(1E) Copies provided under paragraph (1) in hard copy form must be certified as true copies unless the applicant dispenses with such certification.

(1F) Copies provided under paragraph (1) in electronic form must not be certified as true copies unless the applicant expressly requests such certification.]

(2) The right of inspection extends to the originals of documents delivered to the Authority [in hard copy form] only where the record kept by the Authority of the contents of the document is illegible or unavailable.

(3) [A copy provided under this regulation], on which is endorsed a certificate signed by a member of the Authority's staff authorised by it for that purpose certifying that it is an accurate record of the contents of any document delivered to the Authority under these Regulations, is in all legal proceedings admissible in evidence as of equal validity with the original document and as evidence of any fact stated therein of which direct oral evidence would be admissible.

(4) No process for compelling the production of a document kept by the Authority under these Regulations is to issue from any court except with the leave of the court; and any such process must bear on it a statement that it is issued with the leave of the court.

NOTES

Paras (1)–(1F) substituted (for the original para (1)), and words in square brackets in paras (2), (3) substituted, by the Companies Act 2006 (Consequential Amendments and Transitional Provisions) Order 2011, SI 2011/1265, art 15, Sch 2, paras 1, 27, as from 12 May 2011.

[8.419]

76 Provision by the Authority of documents [in electronic form]

Any requirement of these Regulations as to the supply by the Authority of a document may, if the Authority thinks fit, be satisfied by the communication by the Authority of the information [in electronic form].

NOTES

Words in square brackets substituted by the Companies Act 2006 (Consequential Amendments and Transitional Provisions) Order 2011, SI 2011/1265, art 15, Sch 2, paras 1, 28, as from 12 May 2011.

[8.420]

77 Documents relating to Welsh open-ended investment companies

(1) This regulation applies to any document which is delivered to the Authority under these Regulations and relates to an open-ended investment company (whether already registered or to be registered) whose instrument of incorporation states that its head office is to be situated in Wales.

(2) A document to which this regulation applies may be in Welsh but must be accompanied by a certified translation into English.

(3) The requirement for a translation imposed by paragraph (2) does not apply—

- (a) to documents of such description as may be specified in [FCA rules]; or
- (b) to documents in a form prescribed in Welsh (or partly in Welsh and partly in English) by virtue of section 26 of the Welsh Language Act 1993 (powers to prescribe Welsh forms).

(4) An open-ended investment company whose instrument of incorporation states that its head office is to be situated in Wales may deliver to the Authority a certified translation into Welsh of any document in English which relates to the company and which is or has been delivered to the Authority.

(5) In this regulation "certified translation" means a translation which is certified in the manner specified in [FCA rules] to be a correct translation.

NOTES

Paras (3), (5): words in square brackets substituted by the Financial Services Act 2012 (Consequential Amendments and Transitional Provisions) Order 2013, SI 2013/472, art 3, Sch 2, para 41(1), (2), as from 1 April 2013.

78, 79 *(Reg 78 revoked by the Open-Ended Investment Companies (Amendment) Regulations 2005, SI 2005/923, reg 2(1), (7), as from 6 April 2005. Reg 79 revoked by the Companies Act 2006 (Consequential Amendments and Transitional Provisions) Order 2011, SI 2011/1265, art 15, Sch 2, paras 1, 29, as from 12 May 2011.)*

PART V MISCELLANEOUS

[8.421]

80 Contraventions

Any of the following persons, that is to say—

(a) a person who contravenes any provision of these Regulations; and

(b) an open-ended investment company (including any director or depositary of such a company) which contravenes any provision of [FCA rules],

is to be treated as having contravened rules made under [section 137A of the Act (FCA's general rules)].

NOTES

Words in square brackets substituted by the Financial Services Act 2012 (Consequential Amendments and Transitional Provisions) Order 2013, SI 2013/472, art 3, Sch 2, para 41(1), (2), (9), as from 1 April 2013.

[8.422]

81 Offences by bodies corporate etc

Section 400 of the Act (offences by bodies corporate etc) applies to an offence under these Regulations as it applies to an offence under the Act.

[8.423]

82 Jurisdiction and procedure in respect of offences

Section 403 of the Act (jurisdiction and procedure in respect of offences) applies to offences under these Regulations as it applies to offences under the Act.

[8.424]

83 Evidence of grant of probate etc

The production to a company of any document which is by law sufficient evidence of probate of the will, or letters of administration of the estate, or confirmation as executor, of a deceased person having been granted to some person must be accepted by the company as sufficient evidence of the grant.

[8.425]

[83A Disclosure under the UCITS directive

(1) This regulation applies in relation to a disclosure made by a person who falls within paragraph (2) to comply with requirements set out in rules made by the Authority to implement Chapter VIII of the UCITS directive.

(2) The following persons fall within this paragraph—

(a) the auditor of an open-ended investment company that is a master UCITS;

(b) the depositary of an open-ended investment company that is a master UCITS;

(c) the auditor of an open-ended investment company that is a feeder UCITS;

(d) the depositary of an open-ended investment company that is a feeder UCITS; or

(e) a person acting on behalf of a person within paragraphs (a), (b), (c) or (d) above.

(3) A disclosure to which this section applies is not to be taken as a contravention of any duty to which the person making the disclosure is subject."

NOTES

Inserted by the Undertakings for Collective Investment in Transferable Securities Regulations 2011, SI 2011/1613, reg 3(1), (8), as from 1 July 2011.

[8.426]

84 Minor and consequential amendments

The provisions mentioned in Schedule 7 to these Regulations (being minor amendments and amendments consequential on the provisions of these Regulations) have effect subject to the amendments specified in that Schedule.

[8.427]

85 Revocation etc

(1) *(Revokes the Open-Ended Investment Companies (Investment Companies with Variable Capital) Regulations 1996, SI 1996/2827.)*

(2) Anything done under or in accordance with the 1996 Regulations has effect as if done under or in accordance with these Regulations.

(3) Without prejudice to the generality of paragraph (2)—

(a) a body incorporated by virtue of regulation 3(1) of the 1996 Regulations is to be treated as if it had been incorporated by virtue of regulation 3(1) of these Regulations;

(b) where an application under regulation 7 of the 1996 Regulations had not been determined by the Authority at the time when this regulation comes into force, it is to be treated as if it were an application made under regulation 12 of these Regulations;

(c) the Authority's registration functions under Part IV of these Regulations apply to any documents or records delivered to the appropriate registrar pursuant to regulation 4 of, and Schedule 1 to, the 1996 Regulations.

SCHEDULES

SCHEDULE 1
DEPOSITARIES

Regulation 5

Appointment

[8.428]

1. On the coming into effect of an authorisation order in respect of an open-ended investment company, the person named in the application under regulation 12 as depositary of the company is deemed to be appointed as its first depositary.

2. Subject to regulations 21 and 26, any subsequent appointment of the depositary of a company must be made by the directors of the company.

Retirement

3. The depositary of a company may not retire voluntarily except upon the appointment of a new depositary.

Rights

4. The depositary of a company is entitled—

(a) to receive all such notices of, and other communications relating to, any general meeting of the company as a shareholder of the company is entitled to receive;

(b) to attend any general meeting of the company;

(c) to be heard at any general meeting which it attends on any part of the business of the meeting which concerns it as depositary;

(d) to convene a general meeting of the company when it sees fit;

(e) to require from the company's officers such information and explanations as it thinks necessary for the performance of its functions as depositary; and

(f) to have access, except in so far as they concern its appointment or removal, to any reports, statements or other papers which are to be considered at any meeting held by the directors of the company (when acting in their capacity as such), at any general meeting of the company or at any meeting of holders of shares of any particular class.

Statement by depositary ceasing to hold office

5. (1) Where the depositary of a company ceases, for any reason other than by virtue of a court order made under regulation 26, to hold office, it may deposit at the head office of the company a statement of any circumstances connected with its ceasing to hold office which it considers should be brought to the attention of the shareholders or creditors of the company or, if it considers that there are no such circumstances, a statement that there are none.

(2) If the statement is of circumstances which the depositary considers should be brought to the attention of the shareholders or creditors of the company, the company must, not later than 14 days after the deposit of the statement, either—

(a) send a copy of the statement to each of the shareholders whose name appears on the register of shareholders (other than the designated person) and take such steps as [FCA rules] may require for the purpose of bringing the fact that the statement has been made to the attention of the holders of any bearer shares; or

(b) apply to the court;

and, where an application is made under sub-paragraph (b), the company must notify the depositary.

(3) Unless the depositary receives notice of an application to the court before the end of the period of 21 days beginning with the day on which it deposited the statement, it must, not later than seven days after the end of that period, send a copy of the statement to the Authority.

(4) If the court is satisfied that the depositary is using the statement to secure needless publicity for defamatory matter—

(a) it must direct that copies of the statement need not be sent out and that the steps required by [FCA rules] need not be taken; and

(b) it may further order the company's costs on the application to be paid in whole or in part by the depositary notwithstanding that the depositary is not a party to the application;

and the company must, not later than 14 days after the court's decision, take such steps in relation to a statement setting out the effect of the order as are required by sub-paragraph (2)(a) in relation to the statement deposited under sub-paragraph (1).

(5) If the court is not so satisfied, the company must, not later than 14 days after the court's decision, take the steps required by sub-paragraph (2)(a) and notify the depositary of the court's decision.

(6) The depositary must, not later than seven days after receiving such a notice, send a copy of the statement to the Authority.

(7) Where a notice of appeal is filed not later than 14 days after the court's decision, any reference to that decision in sub-paragraphs (4) and (5) is to be construed as a reference to the final determination or withdrawal of that appeal (as the case may be).

6. (1) This paragraph applies where copies of a statement have been sent to shareholders under paragraph 5.

(2) The depositary who made the statement has, notwithstanding that it has ceased to hold office, the rights conferred by paragraph 4(a) to (c) in relation to the general meeting of the company next following the date on which the copies were sent out.

(3) The reference in paragraph 4(c) to business concerning the depositary as depositary is to be construed in relation to a depositary who has ceased to hold office as a reference to business concerning it as former depositary.

NOTES

Para 5: words in square brackets substituted by the Financial Services Act 2012 (Consequential Amendments and Transitional Provisions) Order 2013, SI 2013/472, art 3, Sch 2, para 41(1), (2), as from 1 April 2013.

SCHEDULE 2
INSTRUMENT OF INCORPORATION

Regulation 14

[8.429]

1. The instrument of incorporation of an open-ended investment company must—

(a) contain the statements set out in paragraph 2; and

(b) contain provision made in accordance with paragraphs 3 and 4.

2. The statements referred to in paragraph 1(a) are—

(a) the head office of the company is situated [in England and Wales (or Wales), in Scotland or in Northern Ireland] (as the case may be);

(b) the company is an open-ended investment company with variable share capital;

[(ba) in the case of an umbrella company, the assets of a sub-fund belong exclusively to that sub-fund and shall not be used to discharge the liabilities of or claims against the umbrella company or any other person or body, or any other sub-fund, and shall not be available for any such purpose;]

(c) the shareholders are not liable for the debts of the company;

(d) the scheme property is entrusted to a depositary for safekeeping (subject to any exceptions permitted by [FCA rules]); and

(e) charges or expenses of the company may be taken out of the scheme property.

3. (1) The instrument of incorporation must contain provision as to the following matters—

(a) the object of the company;

(b) any matter relating to the procedure for the appointment, retirement and removal of any director of the company for which provision is not made in these Regulations or [FCA rules]; and

(c) the currency in which the accounts of the company are to be prepared.

(2) The provision referred to in sub-paragraph (1)(a) as to the object of an open-ended investment company must state clearly the kind of property in which the company is to invest and must state that the object of the company is to invest in property of that kind with the aim of spreading investment risk and giving its shareholders the benefit of the results of the management of that property.

4. (1) The instrument of incorporation must also contain provision as to the following matters—

(a) the name of the company;

(b) the category, as specified in [FCA rules], to which the company belongs;

(c) the maximum and minimum sizes of the company's capital;

(d) in the case of an umbrella company, the investment objectives applicable to each part of the scheme property that is pooled separately;

(e) the classes of shares that the company may issue indicating, in the case of an umbrella company, which class or classes of shares may be issued in respect of each part of the scheme property that is pooled separately;

(f) the rights attaching to shares of each class (including any provision for the expression in two denominations of such rights);

(g) if the company is to be able to issue bearer shares, a statement to that effect together with details of any limitations on the classes of the company's shares which are to include bearer shares;

(h) in the case of a company which is a participating issuer, a statement to that effect together with an indication of any class of shares in the company which is a class of participating securities;

(i) if the company is to dispense with the requirements of regulation 46, the details of any substituted procedures for evidencing title to the company's shares; and

(j) the form, custody and use of the company's common seal (if any).

(2) For the purposes of sub-paragraph (1)(c), the size at any time of a company's capital is to be taken to be the value at that time, as determined in accordance with [FCA rules], of the scheme property of the company less the liabilities of the company.

5. (1) Once an authorisation order has been made in respect of a company, no amendment may be made to the statements contained in the company's instrument of incorporation which are required by paragraph 2.

(2) Subject to sub-paragraph (1) and to any restriction imposed by [FCA rules], a company may amend any provision which is contained in its instrument of incorporation.

(3) No amendment to a provision which is contained in a company's instrument of incorporation by virtue of paragraph 3 may be made unless it has been approved by the shareholders of the company in general meeting.

6. (1) The provisions of a company's instrument of incorporation are binding on the officers and depositary of the company and on each of its shareholders; and all such persons (but no others) are to be taken to have notice of the provisions of the instrument.

(2) A person is not debarred from obtaining damages or other compensation from a company by reason only of his holding or having held shares in the company.

NOTES

Para 2: words in square brackets in sub-para (a) substituted by the Companies Act 2006 (Consequential Amendments and Transitional Provisions) Order 2011, SI 2011/1265, art 15, Sch 2, paras 1, 30, as from 12 May 2011. Sub-para (ba) inserted by the Open-Ended Investment Companies (Amendment) Regulations 2011, SI 2011/3049, reg 3(1), (6), as from 21 December 2011. Words in square brackets in sub-para (d) substituted by the Financial Services Act 2012 (Consequential Amendments and Transitional Provisions) Order 2013, SI 2013/472, art 3, Sch 2, para 41(1), (2), as from 1 April 2013.

Paras 3–5: words in square brackets substituted by SI 2013/472, art 3, Sch 2, para 41(1), (2), as from 1 April 2013.

SCHEDULE 3
REGISTER OF SHAREHOLDERS

Regulation 49

General

[8.430]

1. (1) Subject to sub-paragraph (2), every open-ended investment company must keep a register of persons who hold shares in the company.

(2) Except to the extent that the aggregate numbers of shares mentioned in paragraphs 5(1)(b) and 7 include bearer shares, nothing in this Schedule requires any entry to be made in the register in respect of bearer shares.

2. (1) . . . , the register of shareholders is prima facie evidence of any matters which are by these Regulations directed or authorised to be contained in it.

(2) . . .

3. (1) In the case of companies registered in England and Wales [or Northern Ireland], no notice of any trust, express, implied or constructive, is to be entered on the company's register or be receivable by the company.

(2) A company must exercise all due diligence and take all reasonable steps to ensure that the information contained in the register is at all times complete and up to date.

Contents

5. (1) The register of shareholders must contain an entry consisting of—

(a) the name of the designated person;
(b) a statement of the aggregate number of all shares in the company held by that person; . . .
(c) . . .

(2) In sub-paragraph (1), for the purposes of sub-paragraph (b), the designated person is to be taken as holding all shares in the company which are in issue and in respect of which no other person's name is entered on the register.

(3) The statements referred to in sub-paragraph (1)(b) and (c) must be up-dated at least once a day.

6. (1) This paragraph does not apply to any issue or transfer of shares to the designated person.

(2) Where a company issues a share to any person and the name of that person is not already entered on the register, the company must enter his name on the register.

(3) In respect of any person whose name is entered on the register in accordance with sub-paragraph (2) or paragraph 6 of Schedule 4 to these Regulations, the register must contain an entry consisting of—

(a) the address of the shareholder;
(b) the date on which the shareholder's name was entered on the register;
(c) a statement of the aggregate number of shares held by the shareholder, distinguishing each share by its number (if it has one) and, where the company has more than one class of shares, by its class; . . .
(d) . . .

7. The register of shareholders must contain a monthly statement of the aggregate number of all the bearer shares in issue except for any bearer shares in issue which, at the time when the statement is made, are held by the designated person.

8. (1) This paragraph applies where the aggregate number of shares referred to in paragraphs 5 to 7 includes any shares to which attach rights expressed in two denominations.

(2) In respect of each class of shares to which are attached rights expressed in two denominations, the number of shares of that class held by any person referred to in paragraph 5 or 6, or the number of bearer shares of that class referred to in paragraph 7, is to be taken to be the total of—

$$N+n/p$$

(3) In sub-paragraph (2)—

(a) N is the relevant number of larger denomination shares of that class;
(b) n is the relevant number of smaller denomination shares of that class; and
(c) p is the number of smaller denomination shares of that class that are equivalent to one larger denomination share of that class.

(4) Nothing in these Regulations is to be taken as preventing the total arrived at under sub-paragraph (2) being expressed on the register as a single entry representing the result derived from the formula set out in that sub-paragraph.

Location

[**9.** The register of shareholders of a company must be kept available for inspection—

(a) at its head office, or
(b) where an alternative inspection location has been notified to the Authority under regulation 36(3)(b), at that place.]

Index

10. (1) Every company must keep an index of the names of the holders of its registered shares.

(2) The index must contain, in respect of each shareholder, a sufficient indication to enable the account of that shareholder in the register to be readily found.

(3) The index must be at all times kept at the same place as the register of shareholders.

(4) Not later than 14 days after the date on which any alteration is made to the register of shareholders, the company must make any necessary alteration in the index.

Inspection

11. (1) Subject to regulation 50 and to [FCA rules], the register of shareholders and the index of names must be open to the inspection of any shareholder (including any holder of bearer shares) without charge.

(2) Any shareholder may require a copy of the entries on the register relating to him and the company must cause any copy so required by a person to be sent to him free of charge.

(3) If an inspection required under this paragraph is refused, or if a copy so required is not sent, the court may by order compel an immediate inspection of the register and index, or direct that the copy required be sent to the person requiring it.

. . .

12. . . .

NOTES

Words omitted from sub-para 2(1) and the whole of sub-para 2(2) revoked by the Uncertificated Securities Regulations 2001, SI 2001/3755, regs 51, 52(4), Sch 7, Pt 2, para 24(c), as from 26 November 2001.

Words in square brackets in sub-para 3(1) inserted, para 9 substituted, and para 12 revoked, by the Companies Act 2006 (Consequential Amendments and Transitional Provisions) Order 2011, SI 2011/1265, art 15, Sch 2, paras 1, 31, as from 12 May 2011.

Sub-paras 5(1)(c), 6(3)(d) (and the preceding words) revoked by SI 2001/3755, reg 52(4), as from 26 November 2001.

Words in square brackets in sub-para 11(1) substituted by the Financial Services Act 2012 (Consequential Amendments and Transitional Provisions) Order 2013, SI 2013/472, art 3, Sch 2, para 41(1), (2), as from 1 April 2013.

Note there was no para 4 in the original Queen's printer's copy of this Schedule.

SCHEDULE 4
SHARE TRANSFERS

Regulation 52

General

[8.431]

1. The instrument of incorporation of a company may contain provision as to share transfers in respect of any matter for which provision is not made in these Regulations or [FCA rules].

2. Where any shares are transferred to the company, the company must cancel those shares.

3. . . .

Transfer of registered shares

4. (1) Where a transfer of shares is made by the person (if any) who is designated in the company's instrument of incorporation for the purposes of this paragraph, the company may not register the transfer unless such evidence as the company may require to prove that the transfer has taken place has been delivered to the company.

(2) Where for any reason a person ceases to be designated for the purposes of this paragraph—

(a) any shares held by that person which are not disposed of on or before his ceasing to be so designated are to be deemed to be the subject of a new transfer to him which takes effect immediately after he ceases to be so designated; and

(b) the company must make such adjustments to the register as are necessary to reflect his change of circumstances.

[4A. (1) Subject to sub-paragraph (2), section 136 of the Law of Property Act 1925 (which provides for certain assignments in writing to be effectual in law) applies to an absolute assignment (not purporting to be by way of charge only) of shares by means of electronic communication with the following modifications—

(a) the reference in subsection (1) to writing under the hand of the assignor refers to an electronic communication made by the assignor or by his agent authorised in writing, and

(b) the reference in that subsection to express notice in writing refers to express notice by electronic communication to the company.

(2) Sub-paragraph (1) is of no effect in a particular case if the company refuses to register the transfer of shares which would, apart from this sub-paragraph, be made by the assignment in that case.

(3) Sub-paragraph (1) shall not affect any transfer or assignment which, apart from that sub-paragraph, would be effectual in law.

(4) This paragraph extends to England and Wales only.

4B. (1) Subject to sub-paragraph (3), section 1(2)(a)(ii) of the Requirements of Writing (Scotland) Act 1995 (which requires certain gratuitous unilateral obligations to be in writing) shall not apply (if it would otherwise do so) to any gratuitous unilateral obligation relating to shares where—

(a) the obligation is created by means of electronic communication;

(b) the electronic communication is made by the debtor in the obligation;

(c) such evidence (if any) as the company may require to prove the right of the person referred to in paragraph (b) to create the obligation is provided to it.

(2) Where section 1(2)(a)(ii) of that Act does not apply by virtue of sub-paragraph (1), the obligation shall not be considered an obligation mentioned in subsection (2)(a) of that section for the purposes of subsection (3).

(3) Sub-paragraph (1) is of no effect in a particular case if the company refuses to register the transfer of shares which would, apart from this sub-paragraph, by made by the obligation in that case.

(4) This paragraph extends to Scotland only.

4C. (1) Where a transfer of shares is made by means of electronic communication, the company must take reasonable steps to ensure that any electronic communication purporting to be made by the transferor is in fact made by the transferor.

(2) Failure to take reasonable steps shall not make the transfer void or otherwise affect its validity.]

5. (1) Except in the case of any transfer of shares referred to in paragraph 4, the company may not register any transfer unless the transfer documents relating to that transfer have been delivered to the company.

(2) No share certificate has to be delivered by virtue of sub-paragraph (1) in any case where shares are transferred by a nominee of a recognised investment exchange who is designated for the purposes of regulation 47(6) in the rules of the investment exchange in question.

(3) In these Regulations "transfer documents", in relation to any transfer of registered shares [except a transfer made by means of electronic communication], means—

(a) a stock transfer within the meaning of the Stock Transfer Act 1963 [or the Stock Transfer (Northern Ireland) Act 1963] which complies with the requirements of that Act as to the execution and contents of a stock transfer or such other instrument of transfer as is authorised by, and completed and executed in accordance with any requirements in, the company's instrument of incorporation;

(b) except in a case falling within paragraph (3) or (4) of regulation 47, a share certificate relating to the shares in question;

(c) in a case falling within paragraph (3) of regulation 47, such other evidence of title to those shares as is required by the instrument of incorporation of the company; and

(d) such other evidence (if any) as the company may require to prove the right of the transferor to transfer the shares in question.

[(3A) In these Regulations "transfer documents", in relation to any transfer of registered shares made by means of electronic communication, means—

(a) such information in such form and transmitted by such method of electronic communication as is in accordance with any requirements imposed by the company for transfers by electronic communication, or if no such requirements are imposed, evidence of the electronic communication by which the transfer is made; and

(b) such evidence (if any) as the company may require to prove the right of the transferor to transfer the shares in question.]

6. [(1)] [Subject to sub-paragraph (2),] in the case of any transfer of shares which meets the requirements of paragraph 4 or 5, the company must—

(a) register the transfer; and

(b) where the name of the transferee is not already entered on the register, enter that name on the register.

[(2) The company may refuse to register any transfer of shares made by means of electronic communication.]

7. (1) A company may, before the end of the period of 21 days commencing with the date of receipt of the transfer documents relating to any transfer of shares, refuse to register the transfer if—

(a) there exists a minimum requirement as to the number or value of shares that must be held by any shareholder of the company and the transfer would result in either the transferor or transferee holding less than the required minimum; or

(b) the transfer would result in a contravention of any provision of the company's instrument of incorporation or would produce a result inconsistent with any provision of the company's prospectus.

(2) A company must give the transferee written notice of any refusal to register a transfer of shares.

(3) Nothing in these Regulations requires a company to register a transfer or give notice to any person of a refusal to register a transfer where registering the transfer or giving the notice would result in a contravention of any provision of law (including any law that is for the time being in force in a country or territory outside the United Kingdom).

8. (1) Where, in respect of any transfer of shares, the company certifies that it has received the transfer documents referred to in paragraph 5(3)(b) or (c) (as the case may be), that certification is to be taken as a representation by the company to any person acting on the faith of the certification that there has been produced to the company such evidence as on its face shows a prima facie title to the shares in the transferor named in the instrument of transfer.

(2) For the purposes of sub-paragraph (1), a certification is made by a company if the instrument of transfer—

(a) bears the words "certificate lodged" (or words to the like effect); and

(b) is signed by a person acting under authority (whether express or implied) given by the company to issue and sign such certifications.

(3) A certification under sub-paragraph (1) is not to be taken as a representation that the transferor has any title to the shares in question.

(4) Where a person acts on the faith of a false certification by a company which is made negligently or fraudulently, the company is liable to pay to that person any damages sustained by him.

Transfer of bearer shares

9. A transfer of title to any bearer share in a company is effected by the transfer from one person to another of the instrument mentioned in regulation 48 which relates to that share.

10. Where the holder of bearer shares proposes to transfer to another person a number of shares which is less than the number specified in the instrument relating to those shares, he may only do so if he surrenders the instrument to the company and obtains a new instrument specifying the number of shares to be transferred.

Miscellaneous

11. Nothing in the preceding provisions of this Schedule prejudices any power of the company to register as shareholder any person to whom the right to any shares in the company has been transmitted by operation of law.

12. A transfer of registered shares that are held by a deceased person at the time of his death which is made by his personal representative is as valid as if the personal representative had been the holder of the shares at the time of the execution of the instrument of transfer.

13. On the death of any one of the joint holders of any shares, the survivor is to be the only person recognised by the company as having any title to or any interest in those shares.

NOTES

Para 1: words in square brackets substituted by the Financial Services Act 2012 (Consequential Amendments and Transitional Provisions) Order 2013, SI 2013/472, art 3, Sch 2, para 41(1), (2), as from 1 April 2013.

Para 3: revoked by the Uncertificated Securities Regulations 2001, SI 2001/3755, reg 52(4), as from 26 November 2001.

Paras 4A–4C: inserted by the Open-Ended Investment Companies (Amendment) Regulations 2009, SI 2009/553, reg 2(1), (4)(a), as from 6 March 2009.

Para 5: words in first pair of square brackets in sub-para (3) inserted, and sub-para (3A) inserted, by the Open-Ended Investment Companies (Amendment) Regulations 2009, SI 2009/553, reg 2(1), (4)(b), as from 6 March 2009. Words in second pair of square brackets in sub-para (3) inserted by the Companies Act 2006 (Consequential Amendments and Transitional Provisions) Order 2011, SI 2011/1265, art 15, Sch 2, paras 1, 32, as from 12 May 2011.

Para 6: sub-para (1) numbered as such, words in square brackets in that sub-paragraph inserted, and sub-para (2) added, by the Open-Ended Investment Companies (Amendment) Regulations 2009, SI 2009/553, reg 2(1), (4)(c), as from 6 March 2009.

SCHEDULE 5
AUDITORS

Regulation 69

Eligibility

[8.432]

1. No person is eligible for appointment as auditor of an open-ended investment company unless he is [eligible for appointment as a statutory auditor under Part 42 of the Companies Act 2006].

2. (1) A person is ineligible for appointment as auditor of an open-ended investment company if he is—

(a) an officer or employee of the company; or

(b) a partner or employee of such a person, or a partnership of which such a person is a partner.

(2) For the purposes of sub-paragraph (1), an auditor of a company is not to be regarded as an officer or employee of the company.

[(3) A person is also ineligible for appointment if there exists between that person, or any associate of that person, and the company a connection of any such description as may be specified by regulations made by the Secretary of State under section 1214(4) of the Companies Act 2006.

(4) In sub-paragraph (3) "associate" has the same meaning as in Part 42 of that Act (see section 1260 of that Act).

(5) The power of the Secretary of State to make regulations under section 1214(4) of that Act for the purposes of subsection (1) of that section in relation to statutory auditors is exercisable, subject to the same conditions, for the purposes of sub-paragraph (3) above in relation to auditors of open-ended investment companies.]

3. (1) No person is to act as auditor of a company if he is ineligible for appointment to the office.

(2) If during his term of office an auditor of a company becomes ineligible for appointment to the office, he must thereupon vacate office and give notice in writing to the company concerned that he has vacated it by reason of ineligibility.

(3) A person who acts as auditor of a company in contravention of sub-paragraph (1) or fails to give notice of vacating his office as required by sub-paragraph (2) is guilty of an offence and liable—

(a) on conviction on indictment, to a fine;

(b) on summary conviction, to a fine not exceeding the statutory maximum.

(4) In the case of continued contravention he is liable on a second or subsequent summary conviction (instead of the fine mentioned in sub-paragraph (3)(b)) to a fine not exceeding £100 in respect of each day on which the contravention is continued.

(5) In proceedings against a person for an offence under this paragraph it is a defence for him to show that he did not know and had no reason to believe that he was, or had become, ineligible for appointment.

Appointment

4. (1) Every company must appoint an auditor or auditors in accordance with this paragraph.

(2) [Subject to sub-paragraphs (6) and (7), a company] must, at each general meeting at which the company's annual report is laid, appoint an auditor or auditors to hold office from the conclusion of that meeting until the conclusion of the next general meeting at which an annual report is laid.

(3) [Subject to sub-paragraph (6), the first] auditors of a company may be appointed by the directors of the company at any time before the first general meeting of the company at which an annual report is laid; and auditors so appointed are to hold office until the conclusion of that meeting.

(4) Where no appointment is made under sub-paragraph (3), the first auditors of any company may be appointed by the company in general meeting.

[(5) Subject to sub-paragraph (5A), no rules made under section 340 of the Act (appointment of auditors) apply in relation to open-ended investment companies.

(5A) Rules may be made under section 340 of the Act in relation to open-ended investment companies [that are UCITS].]

[(6) On the date on which the holding of an annual general meeting is dispensed with in accordance with regulation 37A, any auditor or auditors appointed in accordance with sub-paragraph (2) or (3) ceases to hold office and the directors must forthwith re-appoint the auditor or auditors or appoint a new auditor or auditors.]

[(7) The directors of any company which does not hold annual general meetings must appoint the auditor or auditors.]

5. If, in any case, no auditors are appointed as required in paragraph 4, the Authority may appoint a person to fill the vacancy.

6. (1) The directors of a company, or the company in general meeting, may fill a casual vacancy in the office of auditor.

(2) While such a vacancy continues, any surviving or continuing auditor or auditors may continue to act.

7. (1) Sub-paragraphs (2) to (5) apply to the appointment, as auditor of a company, of a partnership constituted under the law of England and Wales or Northern Ireland, or under the law of any country or territory in which a partnership is not a legal person; and sub-paragraphs (3) to (5) apply to the appointment as such an auditor of a partnership constituted under the law of Scotland, or under the law of any country or territory in which an partnership is a legal person.

(2) The appointment is, unless the contrary intention appears, an appointment of the partnership as such and not of the partners.

(3) Where the partnership ceases, the appointment is to be treated as extending to—

(a) any partnership which succeeds to the practice of that partnership and is eligible for the appointment; and

(b) any person who succeeds to that practice having previously carried it on in partnership and is eligible for the appointment.

(4) For this purpose a partnership is to be regarded as succeeding to the practice of another partnership only if the members of the successor partnership are substantially the same as those of the former partnership; and a partnership or other person is to be regarded as succeeding to the practice of a partnership only if it or he succeeds to the whole or substantially the whole of the business of the former partnership.

(5) Where the partnership ceases and no person succeeds to the appointment under sub-paragraph (3), the appointment may with the consent of the company be treated as extending to a partnership or other person eligible for the appointment who succeeds to the business of the former partnership or to such part of it as is agreed by the company to be treated as comprising the appointment.

Rights

8. (1) The auditors of a company have a right of access at all times to the company's books, accounts and vouchers and are entitled to require from the company's officers such information and explanations as they think necessary for the performance of their duties as auditors.

(2) An officer of a company commits an offence if he knowingly or recklessly makes to the company's auditors a statement (whether written or oral) which—

(a) conveys or purports to convey any information or explanations which the auditors require, or are entitled to require, as auditors of the company; and

(b) is misleading, false or deceptive in a material particular.

(3) A person guilty of an offence under sub-paragraph (2) is liable—

(a) on conviction on indictment, to imprisonment not exceeding a term of two years or to a fine or to both;

(b) on summary conviction, to imprisonment not exceeding a term of three months or to a fine not exceeding the statutory maximum or to both.

9. (1) The auditors of a company are entitled—

(a) to receive all such notices of, and other communications relating to, any general meeting of the company as a shareholder of the company is entitled to receive;

(b) to attend any general meeting of the company; and

(c) to be heard at any general meeting which they attend on any part of the business of the meeting which concerns them as auditors.

(2) The right to attend and be heard at a meeting is exercisable in the case of a body corporate or partnership by an individual authorised by it in writing to act as its representative at the meeting.

Remuneration

10. (1) The remuneration of auditors of a company who are appointed by the company in general meeting must be fixed by the company in general meeting or in such manner as the company in general meeting may decide.

(2) The remuneration of auditors who are appointed by the directors or the Authority must, as the case may be, be fixed by the directors or the Authority (and be payable by the company even where it is fixed by the Authority).

11. (1) Subject to sub-paragraph (2), the power of the Secretary of State to make regulations under [section 494 of the Companies Act 2006] (remuneration of auditors or their associates for non-audit work) in relation to company auditors is to be exercisable in relation to auditors of open-ended investment companies—

(a) for like purposes; and

(b) subject to the same conditions.

(2) For the purposes of the exercise of the power to make regulations under [section 494 of the Companies Act 2006], as extended by sub-paragraph (1), the reference in [section 494(4)] to a note to a company's accounts is to be taken to be a reference to the annual report of an open-ended investment company.

Removal

12. (1) A company may by resolution remove an auditor from office notwithstanding anything in any agreement between it and him.

(2) Where a resolution removing an auditor is passed at a general meeting of a company, the company must, not later than 14 days after the holding of the meeting, notify the Authority of the passing of the resolution.

(3) Nothing in this paragraph is to be taken as depriving a person removed under it of compensation or damages payable to him in respect of the termination of his appointment as auditor or of any appointment terminating with that as auditor.

Rights on removal or non-reappointment

13. (1) A resolution at a general meeting of a company—

(a) removing an auditor before the expiration of his period of office; or

(b) appointing as auditor a person other than the retiring auditor;

is not effective unless notice of the intention to move it has been given to the open-ended investment company at least 28 days before the meeting at which it is moved.

(2) On receipt of notice of such an intended resolution, the company must forthwith send a copy to the person proposed to be removed or, as the case may be, to the person proposed to be appointed and to the retiring auditor.

(3) The auditor proposed to be removed or, as the case may be, the retiring auditor may make with respect to the intended resolution representations in writing to the company (not exceeding a reasonable length) and request their notification to the shareholders of the company.

(4) The company must (unless the representations are received by the company too late for it to do so)—

(a) in any notice of the resolution given to the shareholders of the company, state the fact of the representations having been made;

(b) send a copy of the representations to each of the shareholders whose name appears on the register of shareholders (other than the designated person) and to whom notice of the meeting is or has been sent;

(c) take such steps as [FCA rules] may require for the purpose of bringing the fact that the representations have been made to the attention of the holders of any bearer shares; and

(d) at the request of any holder of bearer shares, provide a copy of the representations.

(5) If a copy of any such representations is not sent out as required because they were received too late or because of the company's default or if, for either of those reasons, any steps required by sub-paragraph (4)(c) or (d) are not taken, the auditor may (without prejudice to his right to be heard orally) require that the representations be read out at the meeting.

(6) Copies of the representations need not be sent out, the steps required by sub-paragraph (4)(c) or (d) need not be taken and the representations need not be read out at the meeting if, on the application of the company or any other person claiming to be aggrieved, the court is satisfied that the rights conferred by this paragraph are being abused to secure needless publicity for defamatory matter; and the court may order the costs of the company on such an application to be paid in whole or in part by the auditor, notwithstanding that he is not a party to the application.

14. (1) An auditor who has been removed from office has, notwithstanding his removal, the rights conferred by paragraph 9 in relation to any general meeting of the company at which his term of office would otherwise have expired or at which it is proposed to fill the vacancy caused by his removal.

(2) The reference in paragraph 9 to business concerning the auditors as auditors is to be construed in relation to an auditor who has been removed from office as a reference to business concerning him as former auditor.

Resignation

15. (1) An auditor of a company may resign his office by depositing a notice in writing to that effect at the company's head office.

(2) Such a notice is not effective unless it is accompanied by the statement required by paragraph 18.

(3) An effective notice of resignation operates to bring the auditor's term of office to an end as of the date on which the notice is deposited or on such later date as may be specified in it.

(4) The company must, not later than 14 days after the deposit of a notice of resignation, send a copy of the notice to the Authority.

16. (1) This paragraph applies where a notice of resignation of an auditor is accompanied by a statement of circumstances which he considers ought to be brought to the attention of the shareholders or creditors of the company.

(2) An auditor may deposit with the notice a signed requisition that a general meeting of the company be convened forthwith for the purpose of receiving and considering such explanation of the circumstances connected with his resignation as he may wish to place before the meeting.

(3) The company must, not later than 21 days after the date of the deposit of a requisition under this paragraph, proceed to convene a meeting for a day not later than 28 days after the date on which the notice convening the meeting is given.

(4) The auditor may request the company to circulate a statement in writing (not exceeding a reasonable length) of the circumstances connected with his resignation to each of the shareholders of the company whose name appears on the register of shareholders (other than the designated person)—

(a) before the meeting convened on his requisition; or

(b) before any general meeting at which his term of office would otherwise have expired or at which it is proposed to fill the vacancy caused by his resignation;

and to take such steps as [FCA rules] may require for the purpose of bringing the fact that the statement has been made to the attention of the holders of any bearer shares.

(5) The company must (unless the statement is received by it too late for it to do so)—

(a) in any notice or advertisement of the meeting given or made to shareholders of the company, state the fact of the statement having been made;

(b) send a copy of the statement to every shareholder of the company to whom notice of the meeting is or has been sent; and

(c) at the request of any holder of bearer shares, provide a copy of the statement.

(6) If a copy of the statement is not sent out or provided as required because it was received too late or because of the company's default the auditor may (without prejudice to his right to be heard orally) require that the statement be read out at the meeting.

(7) Copies of a statement need not be sent out or provided and the statement need not be read out at the meeting if, on the application of the company or any other person claiming to be aggrieved, the court is satisfied that the rights conferred by this paragraph are being abused to secure needless publicity for defamatory matter; and the court may order the costs of the company on such an application to be paid in whole or in part by the auditor, notwithstanding that he is not a party to the application.

17. (1) An auditor who has resigned has, notwithstanding his removal, the rights conferred by paragraph 9 in relation to any such general meeting of the company as is mentioned in paragraph 16(4)(a) or (b).

(2) The reference in paragraph 9 to business concerning the auditors as auditors is to be construed in relation to an auditor who has resigned as a reference to business concerning him as former auditor.

Statement by auditor ceasing to hold office

18. (1) Where an auditor ceases for any reason to hold office, he must deposit at the head office of the company a statement of any circumstances connected with his ceasing to hold office which he considers should be brought to the attention of the shareholders or creditors of the company or, if he considers that there are no such circumstances, a statement that there are none.

(2) The statement must be deposited—

- (a) in the case of resignation, along with the notice of resignation;
- (b) in the case of failure to seek re-appointment, not less than 14 days before the end of the time allowed for next appointing auditors; and
- (c) in any other case, not later than the end of the period of 14 days beginning with the date on which he ceases to hold office.

(3) If the statement is of circumstances which the auditor considers should be brought to the attention of the shareholders or creditors of the company, the company must, not later than 14 days after the deposit of the statement, either—

- (a) send a copy of the statement to each of the shareholders whose name appears on the register of shareholders (other than the designated person) and take such steps as [FCA rules] may require for the purpose of bringing the fact that the statement has been made to the attention of the holders of any bearer shares; or
- (b) apply to the court;

and, where an application is made under sub-paragraph (b), the company must notify the auditor.

(4) Unless the auditor receives notice of an application to the court before the end of the period of 21 days beginning with the day on which he deposited the statement, he must, not later than seven days after the end of that period, send a copy of the statement to the Authority.

(5) If the court is satisfied that the auditor is using the statement to secure needless publicity for defamatory matter—

- (a) it must direct that copies of the statement need not be sent out and that the steps required by [FCA rules] need not be taken; and
- (b) it may further order the company's costs on the application to be paid in whole or in part by the auditor notwithstanding that he is not a party to the application;

and the company must, not later than 14 days after the court's decision, take such steps in relation to a statement setting out the effect of the order as are required by sub-paragraph (3)(a) in relation to the statement deposited under sub-paragraph (1).

(6) If the court is not so satisfied, the company must, not later than 14 days after the court's decision, send to each of the shareholders a copy of the auditor's statement and notify the auditor of the court's decision.

(7) The auditor must, not later than 7 days after receiving such a notice, send a copy of the statement to the Authority.

(8) Where notice of appeal is filed not later than 14 days after the court's decision, any reference to that decision in sub-paragraphs (5) and (6) is to be construed as a reference to the final determination or withdrawal of that appeal, as the case may be.

19. (1) If a person ceasing to hold office as auditor fails to comply with paragraph 18 he is guilty of an offence and liable—

- (a) on conviction on indictment, to a fine;
- (b) on summary conviction, to a fine not exceeding the statutory maximum.

(2) In proceedings for an offence under sub-paragraph (1), it is a defence for the person charged to show that he took all reasonable steps and exercised all due diligence to avoid the commission of the offence.

20. Section 249(1) of the Act (disqualification of auditor for breach of trust scheme rules) applies to a failure by an auditor to comply with a duty imposed on him by [FCA rules] as it applies to a breach of trust scheme rules.

NOTES

Para 1: words in square brackets substituted by the Companies Act 2006 (Consequential Amendments etc) Order 2008, SI 2008/948, art 3(1), Sch 1, Pt 1, para 28(1), (2), as from 6 April 2008.

Para 2: sub-paras (3)–(5) substituted (for the original sub-para (3)) by SI 2008/948, art 3(1), Sch 1, Pt 1, para 28(1), (3), as from 6 April 2008.

Para 4: words in square brackets in sub-paras (2), (3) substituted, and paras (6), (7) added, by the Open-Ended Investment Companies (Amendment) Regulations 2005, SI 2005/923, reg 2(1), (9), as from 6 April 2005. Sub-paras (5), (5A) substituted (for the original sub-para (5)) by the Undertakings for Collective Investment in Transferable Securities Regulations 2011, SI 2011/1613, reg 3(1), (9), as from 1 July 2011. Words in square brackets in sub-para (5A) substituted by the Collective Investment Schemes (Amendment etc) (EU Exit) Regulations 2019, SI 2019/325, reg 52(1), (13), as from IP completion day (as defined in the European Union (Withdrawal Agreement) Act 2020, s 39).

Para 11: words in square brackets substituted by SI 2008/948, art 3(1), Sch 1, Pt 2, para 222, as from 6 April 2008.

Paras 13, 16, 18, 20: words in square brackets substituted by the Financial Services Act 2012 (Consequential Amendments and Transitional Provisions) Order 2013, SI 2013/472, art 3, Sch 2, para 41(1), (2), as from 1 April 2013.

SCHEDULE 6
MERGERS AND DIVISIONS

Regulation 70

[8.433]

1. This Schedule applies to any reconstruction or amalgamation involving an open-ended investment company which takes the form of a scheme described in paragraph 4 [other than one to which Part 4 of the Undertakings for Collective Investment in Transferable Securities Regulations 2011 applies].

2. An open-ended investment company may apply to the court under [section 896 or 899 of the Companies Act 2006] (power of company to compromise with creditors and members) [in respect of] a scheme falling within any of sub-paragraphs (a) to (c) of paragraph 4(1) where—

(a) the scheme in question involves a compromise or arrangement with its shareholders or creditors or any class of its shareholders or creditors; and

(b) the consideration for the transfer or each of the transfers envisaged by the scheme is to be—

(i) shares in the transferee company receivable by shareholders of the transferor company; or

(ii) where there is more than one transferor company and any one or more of them is a public company, shares in the transferee company receivable by shareholders or members of the transferor companies (as the case may be);

in each case with or without any cash payment to shareholders.

3. A public company may apply to the court under [section 896 or 899 of the Companies Act 2006] [in respect of] a scheme falling within sub-paragraph (b) or (c) of paragraph 4(1) where—

(a) the scheme in question involves a compromise or arrangement with its members or creditors or any class of its members or creditors; and

(b) the consideration for the transfer or each of the transfers envisaged by the scheme is to be—

(i) shares in the transferee company receivable by members of the transferor company; or

(ii) where there is more than one transferor company and any one or more of them is an open-ended investment company, shares in the transferee company receivable by shareholders or members of the transferor companies (as the case may be),

in each case with or without any cash payment to shareholders.

4. (1) The schemes falling within this paragraph are—

(a) any scheme under which the undertaking, property and liabilities of an open-ended investment company are to be transferred to another such company, other than one formed for the purpose of, or in connection with the scheme;

(b) any scheme under which the undertaking, property and liabilities of two or more bodies corporate, each of which is either—

(i) an open-ended investment company; or

(ii) a public company,

are to be transferred to an open-ended investment company formed for the purpose of, or in connection with, the scheme;

(c) any scheme under which the undertaking, property and liabilities of an open-ended investment company or a public company are to be divided among and transferred to two or more open-ended investment companies whether or not formed for the purpose of, or in connection with, the scheme.

(2) Nothing in this Schedule is to be taken as enabling the court to sanction a scheme under which the whole or any part of the undertaking, property or liabilities of an open-ended investment company may be transferred to any person other than another such company.

[5. An application made by virtue of paragraph 2 or 3 shall be treated as one to which Part 27 of the Companies Act 2006 applies (mergers and divisions of public companies), and the provisions of that Part and Part 26 of that Act have effect accordingly, subject to paragraph 6.]

6. (1) [The provisions of the Companies Act 2006] referred to in paragraph 5 have effect with such modifications as are necessary or appropriate for the purposes of this Schedule.

(2) In particular, any reference in those provisions to [a merger by absorption, a merger by formation of a new company or a division] is to be taken to be a reference to a scheme falling within sub-paragraph (a), (b) or (c) of paragraph 4(1).

(3) Without prejudice to the generality of sub-paragraph (1), the following references in those provisions have effect as follows, unless the context otherwise requires—

(a) any reference to a scheme is to be taken to be a reference to a scheme falling within any of sub-paragraphs (a) to (c) of paragraph 4(1);

(b) any reference to a company is to be taken to be a reference to an open-ended investment company;

(c) any reference to members is to be taken to be a reference to shareholders of an open-ended investment company;

(d) any reference to the registered office of a company is to be taken to be a reference to the head office of an open-ended investment company;

(e) any reference to the . . . articles of a company is to be taken to be a reference to the instrument of incorporation of an open-ended investment company;

(f) any reference to a report under [section 593 of the 2006 Act (public company: valuation of non-cash consideration for shares)] is to be taken to be a reference to any report with respect to the valuation of any non-cash consideration given for shares in an open-ended investment company which may be required by [FCA rules];

(g) any reference to annual accounts is to be taken to be a reference to the accounts contained in the annual report of an open-ended investment company;

(h) . . .

(i) any reference to the requirements of [the Companies Act 2006] as to balance sheets forming part of a company's annual accounts is to be taken to be a reference to any requirements arising by virtue of [FCA rules] as to balance sheets drawn up for the purposes of the accounts contained in the annual report of an open-ended investment company;

(j) any reference to paid up capital is to be taken to be a reference to the share capital of an open-ended investment company.

NOTES

Para 1: words in square brackets inserted by the Undertakings for Collective Investment in Transferable Securities Regulations 2011, SI 2011/1613, reg 3(1), (10), as from 1 July 2011.

Paras 2, 3: words in square brackets substituted by the Companies Act 2006 (Consequential Amendments etc) Order 2008, SI 2008/948, art 3(1), Sch 1, Pt 2, para 223(1)–(3), as from 6 April 2008.

Para 5: substituted by SI 2008/948, art 3(1), Sch 1, Pt 2, para 223(1), (4), as from 6 April 2008.

Para 6: words omitted from sub-para (3)(e) revoked, and words in first pair of square brackets in sub-para (3)(f) substituted, by the Companies Act 2006 (Consequential Amendments and Transitional Provisions) Order 2011, SI 2011/1265, art 15, Sch 2, paras 1, 33, as from 12 May 2011. Words in second pair of square brackets in sub-para (3)(f) substituted by the Financial Services Act 2012 (Consequential Amendments and Transitional Provisions) Order 2013, SI 2013/472, art 3, Sch 2, para 41(1), (2), as from 1 April 2013. Words in first pair of square brackets in sub-para (3)(i) substituted by SI 2008/948, art 3(1), Sch 1, Pt 2, para 223(1), (5), as from 6 April 2008. Words in second pair of square brackets in sub-para (3)(i) substituted by SI 2013/472, art 3, Sch 2, para 41(1), (2), as from 1 April 2013. Other words in square brackets substituted, and other words omitted revoked, by SI 2008/948, art 3(1), Sch 1, Pt 2, para 223(1), (5), as from 6 April 2008.

SCHEDULE 7

(Sch 7 (Minor and Consequential Amendments) amends the Trustee Investments Act 1961, Sch 1, Pt III (repealed subject to savings), the Stock Transfer Act 1963, s 1, the Companies Act 1985, ss 26, 199, 209, 220, 716, 718 (repealed), the Company Directors Disqualification Act 1986, Sch 1 (this amendment is now spent), the Pension Schemes Act 1993, s 38 (repealed), the Limited Liability Partnerships Act 2000, Schedule, and the Uncertificated Securities Regulations 1995, SI 1995/3272, regs 3, 19 (revoked).)

FINANCIAL SERVICES AND MARKETS ACT 2000 (OFFICIAL LISTING OF SECURITIES) REGULATIONS 2001

(SI 2001/2956)

NOTES

Made: 22 August 2001.

Authority: Financial Services and Markets Act 2000, ss 75(3), 79(3), 103(1), 417(1), 428(3), Sch 10, para 9, Sch 11, paras 16(3), (4), 20(2).

Commencement: 1 December 2001.

These Regulations are reproduced as amended by: the Financial Services and Markets Act 2000 (Official Listing of Securities) (Amendment) Regulations 2001, SI 2001/3439; the Prospectus Regulations 2005, SI 2005/1433; the Companies Act 2006 (Consequential Amendments and Transitional Provisions) Order 2011, SI 2011/1265; the Financial Services Act 2012 (Consequential Amendments and Transitional Provisions) Order 2013, SI 2013/472.

ARRANGEMENT OF REGULATIONS

PART 1
GENERAL

PART 2
MISCELLANEOUS MATTERS PRESCRIBED FOR THE PURPOSES OF PART VI OF THE ACT

PART 3
PERSONS RESPONSIBLE FOR LISTING PARTICULARS, PROSPECTUSES AND NON-LISTING PROSPECTUSES

PART 1 GENERAL

[8.434]

1 Citation and commencement

These Regulations may be cited as the Financial Services and Markets Act 2000 (Official Listing of Securities) Regulations 2001 and come into force on the day on which section 74(1) comes into force.

NOTES

FSMA 2000, s 74(1) came into force on 1 December 2001 (see the Financial Services and Markets Act 2000 (Commencement No 7) Order 2001, SI 2001/3538).

[8.435]

2 Interpretation

(1) In these Regulations—

"the Act" means the Financial Services and Markets Act 2000;

. . .

"the Financial Promotion Order" means the Financial Services and Markets Act 2000 (Financial Promotion) Order 2001;

"issuer" has the same meaning as is given, for the purposes of section 103(1), in regulation 4 below;

"non-listing prospectus" has the meaning given in section 87(2); and

"the Regulated Activities Order" means the Financial Services and Markets Act 2000 (Regulated Activities) Order 2001.

(2) Any reference in these Regulations to a section or Schedule is, unless otherwise stated or unless the context otherwise requires, a reference to that section of or Schedule to the Act.

NOTES

Para (1): definition "competent authority" (omitted) revoked by the Financial Services Act 2012 (Consequential Amendments and Transitional Provisions) Order 2013, SI 2013/472, art 3, Sch 2, para 55(a), as from 1 April 2013.

PART 2 MISCELLANEOUS MATTERS PRESCRIBED FOR THE PURPOSES OF PART VI OF THE ACT

[8.436]

3 Bodies whose securities may not be listed

For the purposes of section 75(3) (which provides that no application for listing may be entertained in respect of securities issued by a body of a prescribed kind) there are prescribed the following kinds of body—

(a) [where the securities are securities within the meaning of the Regulated Activities Order,] a private company within the meaning of [section 4(1) of the Companies Act 2006];

(b) an old public company within the meaning of section 1 of the Companies Consolidation (Consequential Provisions) Act 1985 or article 3 of the Companies Consolidation (Consequential Provisions) (Northern Ireland) Order 1986.

NOTES

Words in first pair of square brackets in para (a) inserted by the Financial Services and Markets Act 2000 (Official Listing of Securities) (Amendment) Regulations 2001, SI 2001/3439, reg 2, as from 1 December 2001. Words in second pair of square brackets substituted by the Companies Act 2006 (Consequential Amendments and Transitional Provisions) Order 2011, SI 2011/1265, art 19(1), (2), as from 12 May 2011.

Old public companies: as to the meaning of this, see now the Companies Act 2006 (Consequential Amendments and Transitional Provisions) Order 2011, SI 2011/1265, Sch 1 at **[4.428]**. Note that the Companies Consolidation (Consequential Provisions) Act 1985 was repealed by the 2011 Order, as from 12 May 2011.

[8.437]

4 Meaning of "issuer"

(1) For the purposes of section 103(1), "issuer" has the meaning given in this regulation.

(2) In relation to certificates or other instruments falling within article 80 of the Regulated Activities Order (certificates representing certain securities), "issuer" means—

(a) . . .

(b) for all other purposes, the person who issued or is to issue the securities to which the certificates or instruments relate.

(3) In relation to any other securities, "issuer" means the person by whom the securities have been or are to be issued.

NOTES

Para (2): sub-para (a) revoked by the Prospectus Regulations 2005, SI 2005/1433, reg 2(3), Sch 3, para 3, as from 1 July 2005.

[8.438]

5 Meaning of "approved exchange"

For the purposes of paragraph 9 of Schedule 10, "approved exchange" means a recognised investment exchange approved by the Treasury for the purposes of the Public Offers of Securities Regulations 1995 (either generally or in relation to dealings in securities).

PART 3 PERSONS RESPONSIBLE FOR LISTING PARTICULARS, PROSPECTUSES AND NON-LISTING PROSPECTUSES

[8.439]

6 Responsibility for listing particulars

(1) Subject to the following provisions of this Part, for the purposes of Part VI of the Act the persons responsible for listing particulars (including supplementary listing particulars) are—

(a) the issuer of the securities to which the particulars relate;

(b) where the issuer is a body corporate, each person who is a director of that body at the time when the particulars are submitted to the [FCA];

(c) where the issuer is a body corporate, each person who has authorised himself to be named, and is named, in the particulars as a director or as having agreed to become a director of that body either immediately or at a future time;

(d) each person who accepts, and is stated in the particulars as accepting, responsibility for the particulars;

(e) each person not falling within any of the foregoing sub-paragraphs who has authorised the contents of the particulars.

(2) A person is not to be treated as responsible for any particulars by virtue of paragraph (1)(b) above if they are published without his knowledge or consent and on becoming aware of their publication he forthwith gives reasonable public notice that they were published without his knowledge or consent.

(3) When accepting responsibility for particulars under paragraph (1)(d) above or authorising their contents under paragraph (1)(e) above, a person may state that he does so only in relation to certain specified parts of the particulars, or only in certain specified respects, and in such a case he is responsible under paragraph (1)(d) or (e) above—

(a) only to the extent specified; and

(b) only if the material in question is included in (or substantially in) the form and context to which he has agreed.

(4) Nothing in this regulation is to be construed as making a person responsible for any particulars by reason of giving advice as to their contents in a professional capacity.

(5) Where by virtue of this regulation the issuer of any shares pays or is liable to pay compensation under section 90 for loss suffered in respect of shares for which a person has subscribed no account is to be taken of that liability or payment in determining any question as to the amount paid on subscription for those shares or as to the amount paid up or deemed to be paid up on them.

NOTES

Para (1): word in square brackets substituted by the Financial Services Act 2012 (Consequential Amendments and Transitional Provisions) Order 2013, SI 2013/472, art 3, Sch 2, para 55(b), as from 1 April 2013.

[8.440]

7 Securities issued in connection with takeovers and mergers

(1) This regulation applies where—

(a) listing particulars relate to securities which are to be issued in connection with—

(i) an offer by the issuer (or by a wholly-owned subsidiary of the issuer) for securities issued by another person ("A");

(ii) an agreement for the acquisition by the issuer (or by a wholly-owned subsidiary of the issuer) of securities issued by another person ("A"); or

(iii) any arrangement whereby the whole of the undertaking of another person ("A") is to become the undertaking of the issuer (or of a wholly-owned subsidiary of the issuer, or of a body corporate which will become such a subsidiary by virtue of the arrangement); and

(b) each of the specified persons is responsible by virtue of regulation 6(1)(d) above for any part ("the relevant part") of the particulars relating to A or to the securities or undertaking to which the offer, agreement or arrangement relates.

(2) In paragraph (1)(b) above the "specified persons" are—

(a) A; and

(b) where A is a body corporate—

(i) each person who is a director of A at the time when the particulars are submitted to the [FCA]; and

(ii) each other person who has authorised himself to be named, and is named, in the particulars as a director of A.

(3) Where this regulation applies, no person is to be treated as responsible for the relevant part of the particulars under regulation 6(1)(a), (b) or (c) above but without prejudice to his being responsible under regulation 6(1)(d).

(4) In this regulation—

(a) "listing particulars" includes supplementary listing particulars; and

(b) "wholly-owned subsidiary" is to be construed in accordance with [section 1159 of the Companies Act 2006] (and, in relation to an issuer which is not a body corporate, means a body corporate which would be a wholly-owned subsidiary of the issuer within the meaning of that section if the issuer were a body corporate).

NOTES

Para (2): word in square brackets substituted by the Financial Services Act 2012 (Consequential Amendments and Transitional Provisions) Order 2013, SI 2013/472, art 3, Sch 2, para 55(b), as from 1 April 2013.

Para (4): words in square brackets substituted by the Companies Act 2006 (Consequential Amendments and Transitional Provisions) Order 2011, SI 2011/1265, art 19(1), (3), as from 12 May 2011.

[8.441]

8 Successor companies under legislation relating to electricity

(1) Where—

(a) the same document contains listing particulars relating to the securities of—

- (i) two or more successor companies within the meaning of Part II of the Electricity Act 1989, or
- (ii) two or more successor companies within the meaning of Part III of the Electricity (Northern Ireland) Order 1992; and

(b) the responsibility of any person for any information included in the document ("the relevant information") is stated in the document to be confined to its inclusion as part of the particulars relating to the securities of any one of those companies,

that person is not to be treated as responsible, by virtue of regulation 6 above, for the relevant information in so far as it is stated in the document to form part of the particulars relating to the securities of any other of those companies.

(2) "Listing particulars" includes supplementary listing particulars.

[8.442]
9 Specialist securities

(1) This regulation applies where listing particulars relate to securities of a kind specified by listing rules for the purposes of section 82(1)(c), other than securities which are to be issued in the circumstances mentioned in regulation 7(1)(a) above.

(2) No person is to be treated as responsible for the particulars under regulation 6(1)(a), (b) or (c) above but without prejudice to his being responsible under regulation 6(1)(d).

(3) "Listing particulars" includes supplementary listing particulars.

10–12 (*Revoked by the Prospectus Regulations 2005, SI 2005/1433, reg 2(3), Sch 3, para 3, as from 1 July 2005.*)

FINANCIAL SERVICES AND MARKETS ACT 2000 (FINANCIAL PROMOTION) ORDER 2005

(SI 2005/1529)

NOTES

Made: 8 June 2005.

Authority: Financial Services and Markets Act 2000, ss 21(5), (6), (9), (10), 428(3), Sch 2, para 25.

Commencement: 1 July 2005.

Note: this Order revokes and re-enacts, with certain amendments, the Financial Services and Markets Act 2000 (Financial Promotion) Order 2001, SI 2001/1335 (as amended).

This Order is reproduced as amended by:

2005	Financial Services and Markets Act 2000 (Financial Promotion) (Amendment) Order 2005, SI 2005/3392.
2006	Financial Services and Markets Act 2000 (Regulated Activities) (Amendment) Order 2006, SI 2006/1969; Financial Services and Markets Act 2000 (Regulated Activities) (Amendment) (No 2) Order 2006, SI 2006/2383; Financial Services and Markets Act 2000 (Regulated Activities) (Amendment No 3) Order 2006, SI 2006/3384.
2007	Companies Act 2006 (Commencement No 2, Consequential Amendments, Transitional Provisions and Savings) Order 2007, SI 2007/1093; Financial Services and Markets Act 2000 (Financial Promotion) (Amendment No 2) Order 2007, SI 2007/2615.
2009	Financial Services and Markets Act 2000 (Regulated Activities) (Amendment) Order 2009, SI 2009/1342.
2010	Financial Services and Markets Act 2000 (Regulated Activities) (Amendment) Order 2010, SI 2010/86; Financial Services and Markets Act 2000 (Financial Promotion) (Amendment) Order 2010, SI 2010/905.
2011	Financial Services and Markets Act 2000 (Regulated Activities) (Amendment) Order 2011, SI 2011/133; Companies Act 2006 (Consequential Amendments and Transitional Provisions) Order 2011, SI 2011/1265.
2013	Financial Services Act 2012 (Consequential Amendments and Transitional Provisions) Order 2013, SI 2013/472; Financial Services Act 2012 (Consequential Amendments and Transitional Provisions) (No 3) Order 2013, SI 2013/1765; Alternative Investment Fund Managers Regulations 2013, SI 2013/1773; Financial Services and Markets Act 2000 (Regulated Activities) (Amendment) (No 2) Order 2013, SI 2013/1881.
2014	Financial Services and Markets Act 2000 (Consumer Credit) (Miscellaneous Provisions) Order 2014, SI 2014/208; Financial Services and Markets Act 2000 (Regulated Activities) (Amendment) Order 2014, SI 2014/366; Financial Services and Markets Act 2000 (Consumer Credit) (Miscellaneous Provisions) (No 2) Order 2014, SI 2014/506; Co-operative and Community Benefit Societies and Credit Unions Act 2010 (Consequential Amendments) Regulations 2014, SI 2014/1815.
2015	Financial Services and Markets Act 2000 (Miscellaneous Provisions) (No 2) Order 2015, SI 2015/352; Financial Services and Markets Act 2000 (Miscellaneous Provisions) Order 2015, SI 2015/853; Mortgage Credit Directive Order 2015, SI 2015/910; European Long-term Investment Funds Regulations 2015, SI 2015/1882.
2016	Financial Services and Markets Act 2000 (Regulated Activities) (Amendment) Order 2016, SI 2016/392.
2017	Financial Services and Markets Act 2000 (Regulated Activities) (Amendment) Order 2017, SI 2017/488; Packaged Retail and Insurance-based Investment Products Regulations 2017, SI 2017/1127.
2018	Financial Services and Markets Act 2000 (Claims Management Activity) Order 2018, SI 2018/1253.
2019	Financial Services and Markets Act 2000 (Amendment) (EU Exit) Regulations 2019, SI 2019/632; Gibraltar (Miscellaneous Amendments) (EU Exit) Regulations 2019, SI 2019/680; Financial Services and Markets Act 2000 (Prospectus) Regulations 2019, SI 2019/1043; Prospectus (Amendment etc) (EU Exit) Regulations 2019, SI 2019/1234; Electronic Commerce and Solvency 2 (Amendment etc) (EU Exit) Regulations 2019, SI 2019/1361.
2021	Financial Services and Markets Act 2000 (Regulated Activities) (Amendment) Order 2021, SI 2021/90; Recognised Auction Platforms (Amendment and Miscellaneous Provisions) Regulations 2021, SI 2021/494;

	Markets in Financial Instruments, Benchmarks and Financial Promotions (Amendment) (EU Exit) Regulations 2021, SI 2021/1074.

Transitional provisions in relation to Gibraltar-based firms and activities: see the Gibraltar (Miscellaneous Amendments) (EU Exit) Regulations 2019, SI 2019/680, reg 11 at **[12.129]**.

ARRANGEMENT OF ARTICLES

PART I
CITATION, COMMENCEMENT AND INTERPRETATION

PART II
CONTROLLED ACTIVITIES AND CONTROLLED INVESTMENTS

PART III
EXEMPTIONS: INTERPRETATION AND APPLICATION

PART IV
EXEMPT COMMUNICATIONS: ALL CONTROLLED ACTIVITIES

PART V
EXEMPT COMMUNICATIONS: DEPOSITS AND INSURANCE

PART VI
EXEMPT COMMUNICATIONS: CERTAIN CONTROLLED ACTIVITIES

PART 6A
EXEMPT COMMUNICATIONS: CONTROLLED CLAIMS MANAGEMENT ACTIVITIES

PART 7
EXEMPT COMMUNICATIONS: CONTROLLED CLAIMS MANAGEMENT ACTIVITIES

SCHEDULES

PART I CITATION, COMMENCEMENT AND INTERPRETATION

[8.443]
1 Citation and commencement

This Order may be cited as the Financial Services and Markets Act 2000 (Financial Promotion) Order 2005 and comes into force on 1st July 2005.

[8.444]
2 Interpretation: general

(1) In this Order, except where the context otherwise requires—

. . .

. . .

["the 2006 Act" means the Companies Act 2006;]

"the Act" means the Financial Services and Markets Act 2000;

"close relative" in relation to a person means—

(a) his spouse [or civil partner];

(b) his children and step-children, his parents and step-parents, his brothers and sisters and his step-brothers and step-sisters; and

(c) the spouse [or civil partner] of any person within sub-paragraph (b);

"controlled activity" has the meaning given by article 4 and Schedule 1;

["controlled claims management activity" has the meaning given in article 4(3);]

"controlled investment" has the meaning given by article 4 and Schedule 1;

"deposit" means a sum of money which is a deposit for the purposes of article 5 of the Regulated Activities Order;

["direct financial benefit" includes any commission, discount, remuneration or reduction in premium;]

"equity share capital" has the meaning given in [the 2006 Act (see section 548)];

"financial promotion restriction" has the meaning given by article 5;

"government" means the government of the United Kingdom, the Scottish Administration, the Executive Committee of the Northern Ireland Assembly, the National Assembly for Wales and any government of any country or territory outside the United Kingdom;

["information society service" is to be read in accordance with the definition of "information society services" in regulation 2 of the Electronic Commerce (EC Directive) Regulations 2002;]

"instrument" includes any record whether or not in the form of a document;

"international organisation" means any body the members of which comprise—

(a) states including the United Kingdom . . . ; or

(b) bodies whose members comprise states including the United Kingdom . . . ;

"overseas communicator" has the meaning given by article 30;

"previously overseas customer" has the meaning given by article 31;

"publication" means—

(a) a newspaper, journal, magazine or other periodical publication;

(b) a web site or similar system for the electronic display of information;

(c) any programme forming part of a service consisting of the broadcast or transmission of television or radio programmes;

(d) any teletext service, that—is to say a service consisting of television transmissions consisting of a succession of visual displays (with or without accompanying sound) capable of being selected and held for separate viewing or other use;

"qualifying contract of insurance" has the meaning given in the Regulated Activities Order;

"qualifying credit" has the meaning given by paragraph 10 of Schedule 1;

"the Regulated Activities Order" means the Financial Services and Markets Act 2000 (Regulated Activities) Order 2001;

"relevant insurance activity" has the meaning given by article 21;

"relevant investment activities" has the meaning given by article 30;

["relevant UK market" means a market that meets the criteria specified in Part A1 of Schedule 3;]

"solicited real time communication" has the meaning given by article 8;

["structured deposit" means a deposit which is fully repayable at maturity on terms under which interest or a premium will be paid or is at risk, according to a formula involving factors such as—

(a) an index or combination of indices excluding variable rate deposits whose return is directly linked to an interest rate index such as Euribor or Libor;

(b) a financial instrument or combination of financial instruments;

(c) a commodity or combination of commodities or other physical or non-physical non-fungible assets; or

(d) a foreign exchange rate or combination of foreign exchange rates;]

"units", in a collective investment scheme, has the meaning given by Part XVII of the Act;

"unsolicited real time communication" has the meaning given by article 8.

(2) References to a person engaging in investment activity are to be construed in accordance with subsection (8) of section 21 of the Act; and for these purposes, "controlled activity" and "controlled investment" in that subsection have the meaning given in this Order.

NOTES

Para (1) is amended as follows:

Definitions "the 1985 Act" and "the 1986 Order" (omitted) revoked, definition the 2006 Act" inserted, and words in square brackets in definition "equity share capital" substituted, by the Companies Act 2006 (Consequential Amendments and Transitional Provisions) Order 2011, SI 2011/1265, art 26(1), (2), as from 12 May 2011.

Definition "controlled claims management activity" inserted by the Financial Services and Markets Act 2000 (Claims Management Activity) Order 2018, SI 2018/1253, arts 8, 9, as from 1 April 2019 (for full commencement details and for transitional provisions in relation to carrying on a claims management activity, etc, see arts 1, 39–89 of the 2018 Order).

Words in square brackets in definition "close relative" inserted by the Financial Services and Markets Act 2000 (Financial Promotion) (Amendment) Order 2005, SI 2005/3392, art 2(1), (2), as from 21 December 2005.

Definition "direct financial benefit" inserted by the Financial Services and Markets Act 2000 (Financial Promotion) (Amendment) Order 2010, SI 2010/905, arts 2, 3, as from 13 April 2010.

Definition "information society service" inserted by the Electronic Commerce and Solvency 2 (Amendment etc) (EU Exit) Regulations 2019, SI 2019/1361, reg 5(1), (9), as from IP completion day (as defined in the European Union (Withdrawal Agreement) Act 2020, s 39).

Words omitted from the definition "international organisation" revoked by the Financial Services and Markets Act 2000 (Amendment) (EU Exit) Regulations 2019, SI 2019/632, regs 162(1), 163, as from IP completion day (as defined in the European Union (Withdrawal Agreement) Act 2020, s 39).

Definition "relevant UK market" inserted by the Markets in Financial Instruments, Benchmarks and Financial Promotions (Amendment) (EU Exit) Regulations 2021, SI 2021/1074, reg 2(2), as from 18 October 2021.

Definition "structured deposit" inserted by the Financial Services and Markets Act 2000 (Regulated Activities) (Amendment) Order 2017, SI 2017/488, art 14, Schedule, para 9(1), (2), as from 3 January 2018.

National Assembly for Wales: see further, in relation to the renaming of the National Assembly for Wales as the Senedd Cymru or the Welsh Parliament, the Senedd and Elections (Wales) Act 2020, s 2 (with effect from 6 May 2020). See also ss 3–9 of the 2020 Act in relation to the renaming of Acts of the National Assembly for Wales, Members of the National Assembly for Wales, etc.

"Close relative": as to the meaning of "step-children", and related expressions, see the Civil Partnership Act 2004, s 246 (as applied to this Order by the Civil Partnership Act 2004 (Relationships Arising Through Civil Partnership) Order 2005, SI 2005/3137, art 3, Schedule).

[8.445]

3 Interpretation: unlisted companies

(1) In this Order, an "unlisted company" means a body corporate the shares in which are not—

(a) listed or quoted on an investment exchange whether in the United Kingdom or elsewhere;

(b) shares in respect of which information is, with the agreement or approval of any officer of the company, published for the purpose of facilitating deals in the shares indicating prices at which persons have dealt or are willing to deal in them other than persons who, at the time the information is published, are existing members of a relevant class; or

(c) subject to a marketing arrangement which accords to the company the facilities referred to in [section 693(3)(b) of the 2006 Act].

(2) For the purpose of paragraph (1)(b), a person is to be regarded as a member of a relevant class if he was, at the relevant time—

(a) an existing member or debenture holder of the company;

(b) an existing employee of the company;

(c) a close relative of such a member or employee; or

(d) a trustee (acting in his capacity as such) of a trust, the principal beneficiary of which is a person within any of sub-paragraphs (a), (b) and (c).

(3) In this Order references to shares in and debentures of an unlisted company are references to—

(a) in the case of a body corporate which is a company within the meaning of [the 2006 Act (see section 1)], shares and debentures within the meaning of that Act [(see sections 540(1) and (4) and 738)];

(b) . . .

(c) in the case of any other body corporate, investments falling within paragraph 14[, 15 or 15A] of Schedule 1 to this Order.

NOTES

Para (1): words in square brackets substituted by the Companies Act 2006 (Consequential Amendments and Transitional Provisions) Order 2011, SI 2011/1265, art 26(1), (3)(a), as from 12 May 2011.

Para (3): words in first pair of square brackets in sub-para (a) substituted, words in second pair of square brackets in that paragraph inserted, and sub-para (b) revoked, by SI 2011/1265, art 26(1), (3)(b), as from 12 May 2011. Words in square brackets in sub-para (c) substituted by the Financial Services and Markets Act 2000 (Regulated Activities) (Amendment) Order 2010, SI 2010/86, art 4, Schedule, para 9(a)(i), as from 24 February 2010.

PART II CONTROLLED ACTIVITIES AND CONTROLLED INVESTMENTS

[8.446]

4 Definition of controlled activities[, controlled claims management activities] and controlled investments

(1) For the purposes of section 21(9) of the Act, a controlled activity is an activity which falls within any of paragraphs 1 to 11 of Schedule 1.

(2) For the purposes of section 21(10) of the Act, a controlled investment is an investment which falls within any of paragraphs 12 to 27 of Schedule 1.

[(3) For the purposes of section 21(10B) of the Act, a controlled claims management activity is an activity carried on in Great Britain of a kind specified in paragraph 11A of Schedule 1.]

NOTES

Words in square brackets in the provision heading inserted, and para (3) added, by the Financial Services and Markets Act 2000 (Claims Management Activity) Order 2018, SI 2018/1253, arts 8, 10, as from 1 April 2019 (for full commencement details and for transitional provisions in relation to carrying on a claims management activity, etc, see arts 1, 39–89 of the 2018 Order).

PART III EXEMPTIONS: INTERPRETATION AND APPLICATION

[8.447]

5 Interpretation: financial promotion restriction

In this Order, any reference to the financial promotion restriction is a reference to the restriction in section 21(1) of the Act.

[8.448]

6 Interpretation: communications

In this Order—

(a) any reference to a communication is a reference to the communication, in the course of business, of an invitation or inducement to engage in investment activity;
(b) any reference to a communication being made to another person is a reference to a communication being addressed, whether orally or in legible form, to a particular person or persons (for example where it is contained in a telephone call or letter);
(c) any reference to a communication being directed at persons is a reference to a communication being addressed to persons generally (for example where it is contained in a television broadcast or web site);
(d) "communicate" includes causing a communication to be made or directed;
(e) a "recipient" of a communication is the person to whom the communication is made or, in the case of a non-real time communication which is directed at persons generally, any person who reads or hears the communication;
(f) "electronic commerce communication" means a communication, the making of which constitutes the provision of an information society service;
(g), (h) . . .

NOTES

Paras (g) and (h) revoked by the Financial Services and Markets Act 2000 (Amendment) (EU Exit) Regulations 2019, SI 2019/632, regs 162(1), 164, as from IP completion day (as defined in the European Union (Withdrawal Agreement) Act 2020, s 39) (for transitional provisions see the note below).

Transitional provisions: the Financial Services and Markets Act 2000 (Amendment) (EU Exit) Regulations 2019, SI 2019/632, reg 162(2) provides as follows. Note (i) that "this Part" of the 2019 Regulations is regs 162–176; and (ii) the text set out below is reproduced as amended by the Financial Services and Economic and Monetary Policy (Consequential Amendments) (EU Exit) Regulations 2020, SI 2020/1301, reg 3, Schedule, para 33(u), as from 30 December 2020—

"(2) Nothing in this Part causes a communication to constitute a breach of the prohibition in subsection (1) of section 21 of the Financial Services and Markets Act 2000 (restrictions on financial promotion) if—
(a) a contract entered into before IP completion day required the communication to be made, and
(b) the communication would not have constituted a breach of the prohibition had it been made before IP completion day.".

[8.449]

7 Interpretation: real time communications

(1) In this Order, references to a real time communication are references to any communication made in the course of a personal visit, telephone conversation or other interactive dialogue.

(2) A non-real time communication is a communication not falling within paragraph (1).

(3) For the purposes of this Order, non-real time communications include communications made by letter or e-mail or contained in a publication.

(4) For the purposes of this Order, the factors in paragraph (5) are to be treated as indications that a communication is a non-real time communication.

(5) The factors are that—
(a) the communication is made to or directed at more than one recipient in identical terms (save for details of the recipient's identity);
(b) the communication is made or directed by way of a system which in the normal course constitutes or creates a record of the communication which is available to the recipient to refer to at a later time;
(c) the communication is made or directed by way of a system which in the normal course does not enable or require the recipient to respond immediately to it.

[8.450]

8 Interpretation: solicited and unsolicited real time communications

(1) A real time communication is solicited where it is made in the course of a personal visit, telephone call or other interactive dialogue if that call, visit or dialogue—

(a) was initiated by the recipient of the communication; or

(b) takes place in response to an express request from the recipient of the communication.

(2) A real time communication is unsolicited where it is made otherwise than as described in paragraph (1).

(3) For the purposes of paragraph (1)—

(a) a person is not to be treated as expressly requesting a call, visit or dialogue—

(i) because he omits to indicate that he does not wish to receive any or any further visits or calls or to engage in any or any further dialogue;

(ii) because he agrees to standard terms that state that such visits, calls or dialogue will take place, unless he has signified clearly that, in addition to agreeing to the terms, he is willing for them to take place;

(b) a communication is solicited only if it is clear from all the circumstances when the call, visit or dialogue is initiated or requested that during the course of the visit, call or dialogue communications will be made concerning the kind of controlled activities or investments [or controlled claims management activities] to which the communications in fact made relate;

(c) it is immaterial whether the express request was made before or after this article comes into force.

(4) Where a real time communication is solicited by a recipient ("R"), it is treated as having also been solicited by any other person to whom it is made at the same time as it is made to R if that other recipient is—

(a) a close relative of R; or

(b) expected to engage in any investment activity [or any claims management activity] jointly with R.

NOTES

Paras (3), (4): words in square brackets inserted by the Financial Services and Markets Act 2000 (Claims Management Activity) Order 2018, SI 2018/1253, arts 8, 11, as from 1 April 2019 (for full commencement details and for transitional provisions in relation to carrying on a claims management activity, etc, see arts 1, 39–89 of the 2018 Order).

8A *(Reg 8A (Interpretation: outgoing electronic commerce communications) was revoked by the Financial Services and Markets Act 2000 (Amendment) (EU Exit) Regulations 2019, SI 2019/632, regs 162(1), 165, as from IP completion day (as defined in the European Union (Withdrawal Agreement) Act 2020, s 39) (for transitional provisions see the note on art 6 at* **[8.448]***).)*

[8.451]

9 Degree of prominence to be given to required indications

Where a communication must, if it is to fall within any provision of this Order, be accompanied by an indication of any matter, the indication must be presented to the recipient—

(a) in a way that can be easily understood; and

(b) in such manner as, depending on the means by which the communication is made or directed, is best calculated to bring the matter in question to the attention of the recipient and to allow him to consider it.

[8.452]

10 Application to qualifying contracts of insurance

(1) Nothing in this Order exempts from the application of the financial promotion restriction a communication which invites or induces a person to enter into a qualifying contract of insurance with a person who is not—

(a) an authorised person;

(b) an exempt person who is exempt in relation to effecting or carrying out contracts of insurance of the class to which the communication relates;

(c), (d) . . .

(e) a company authorised to carry on insurance business of the class to which the communication relates in any country or territory which is listed in Schedule 2.

(2) In this article, references to a class of insurance are references to the class of insurance contract described in Schedule 1 to the Regulated Activities Order into which the effecting or carrying out of the contract to which the communication relates would fall.

NOTES

Para (1): sub-paras (c) and (d) revoked by the Financial Services and Markets Act 2000 (Amendment) (EU Exit) Regulations 2019, SI 2019/632, regs 162(1), 166, as from IP completion day (as defined in the European Union (Withdrawal Agreement) Act 2020, s 39) (for transitional provisions see the note on art 6 at **[8.448]**).

[8.453]

11 Combination of different exemptions

(1) In respect of a communication relating to—

(a) a controlled activity falling within paragraph 2 of Schedule 1 carried on in relation to a qualifying contract of insurance; or

(b) a controlled activity falling within any of paragraphs 3 to [11A] of Schedule 1,

a person may rely on the application of one or more of the exemptions in Parts IV and VI.

(2) In respect of a communication relating to—

(a) an activity falling within paragraph 1 of Schedule 1; or

(b) a relevant insurance activity,

a person may rely on one or more of the exemptions in Parts IV and V; and, where a communication relates to any such activity and also to an activity mentioned in paragraph (1)(a) or (b), a person may rely on one or more of the exemptions in Parts IV and V in respect of the former activity and on one or more of the exemptions in Parts V and VI in respect of the latter activity.

NOTES

Para (1): figure in square brackets substituted by the Financial Services and Markets Act 2000 (Claims Management Activity) Order 2018, SI 2018/1253, arts 8, 12, as from 1 April 2019 (for full commencement details and for transitional provisions in relation to carrying on a claims management activity, etc, see arts 1, 39–89 of the 2018 Order).

PART IV EXEMPT COMMUNICATIONS: ALL CONTROLLED ACTIVITIES

[8.454]

12 Communications to overseas recipients

(1) Subject to [paragraphs (2), (7) and (8)], the financial promotion restriction does not apply to any communication—

(a) which is made (whether from inside or outside the United Kingdom) to a person who receives the communication outside the United Kingdom; or

(b) which is directed (whether from inside or outside the United Kingdom) only at persons outside the United Kingdom.

(2) Paragraph (1) does not apply to an unsolicited real time communication unless—

(a) it is made from a place outside the United Kingdom; and

(b) it is made for the purposes of a business which is carried on outside the United Kingdom and which is not carried on in the United Kingdom.

(3) For the purposes of paragraph (1)(b)—

(a) if the conditions set out in paragraph (4)(a), (b), (c) and (d) are met, a communication directed from a place inside the United Kingdom is to be regarded as directed only at persons outside the United Kingdom;

(b) if the conditions set out in paragraph (4)(c) and (d) are met, a communication directed from a place outside the United Kingdom is to be regarded as directed only at persons outside the United Kingdom;

(c) in any other case where one or more of the conditions in paragraph (4)(a) to (e) are met, that fact is to be taken into account in determining whether or not a communication is to be regarded as directed only at persons outside the United Kingdom (but a communication may still be regarded as directed only at persons outside the United Kingdom even if none of the conditions in paragraph (4) is met).

(4) The conditions are that—

(a) the communication is accompanied by an indication that it is directed only at persons outside the United Kingdom;

(b) the communication is accompanied by an indication that it must not be acted upon by persons in the United Kingdom;

(c) the communication is not referred to in, or directly accessible from, any other communication made to a person or directed at persons in the United Kingdom by the person directing the communication;

(d) there are in place proper systems and procedures to prevent recipients in the United Kingdom (other than those to whom the communication might otherwise lawfully have been made by the person directing it or a member of the same group) engaging in the investment activity to which the communication relates with the person directing the communication, a close relative of his or a member of the same group;

(e) the communication is included in—

(i) a web site, newspaper, journal, magazine or periodical publication which is principally accessed in or intended for a market outside the United Kingdom;

(ii) a radio or television broadcast or teletext service transmitted principally for reception outside the United Kingdom.

(5) For the purpose of paragraph (1)(b), a communication may be treated as directed only at persons outside the United Kingdom even if—

(a) it is also directed, for the purposes of article 19(1)(b), at investment professionals falling within article 19(5) (but disregarding paragraph (6) of that article for this purpose);

(b) it is also directed, for the purposes of article 49(1)(b), at high net worth persons to whom article 49 applies (but disregarding paragraph (2)(e) of that article for this purpose) and it relates to a controlled activity to which article 49 applies;

(c) it is a communication to which article 31 applies.

(6) Where a communication falls within paragraph (5)(a) or (b)—

(a) the condition in paragraph (4)(a) is to be construed as requiring an indication that the communication is directed only at persons outside the United Kingdom or persons having professional experience in matters relating to investments or high net worth persons (as the case may be);

(b) the condition in paragraph (4)(b) is to be construed as requiring an indication that the communication must not be acted upon by persons in the United Kingdom except by persons who have professional experience in matters relating to investments or who are not high net worth persons (as the case may be);

(c) the condition in paragraph (4)(c) will not apply where the other communication referred to in that paragraph is made to a person or directed at a person in the United Kingdom to whom paragraph (5) applies.

(7) . . .

[(8) Paragraph (1) does not apply to any communication in respect of a controlled claims management activity.]

NOTES

Para (1): words in square brackets substituted by the Financial Services and Markets Act 2000 (Claims Management Activity) Order 2018, SI 2018/1253, arts 8, 13(a), as from 1 April 2019 (for full commencement details and for transitional provisions in relation to carrying on a claims management activity, etc, see arts 1, 39–89 of the 2018 Order).

Para (7): revoked by the Financial Services and Markets Act 2000 (Amendment) (EU Exit) Regulations 2019, SI 2019/632, regs 162(1), 167, as from IP completion day (as defined in the European Union (Withdrawal Agreement) Act 2020, s 39) (for transitional provisions see the note on art 6 at **[8.448]**).

Para (8): added by SI 2018/1253, arts 8, 13(b), as from 1 April 2019 (as to the full commencement details, and as to transitional provisions, see the first note relating to the 2018 Order above).

[8.455]

13 Communications from customers and potential customers

(1) The financial promotion restriction does not apply to any communication made by or on behalf of a person ("customer") to one other person ("supplier")—

(a) in order to obtain information about a controlled investment [or controlled claims management activity] available from or a controlled service provided by the supplier; . . .

(b) in order that the customer can acquire a controlled investment from that supplier or be supplied with a controlled service by that supplier[; or]

[(c) in order that the customer can be supplied with services in respect of a controlled claims management activity by that supplier].

(2) For the purposes of paragraph (1), a controlled service is a service the provision of which constitutes engaging in a controlled activity by the supplier.

NOTES

Para (1): words in square brackets in sub-para (a) inserted, word omitted from that paragraph revoked, and sub-para (c) and the preceding word added, by the Financial Services and Markets Act 2000 (Claims Management Activity) Order 2018, SI 2018/1253, arts 8, 14, as from 1 April 2019 (for full commencement details and for transitional provisions in relation to carrying on a claims management activity, etc, see arts 1, 39–89 of the 2018 Order).

[8.456]

14 Follow up non-real time communications and solicited real time communications

(1) Where a person makes or directs a communication ("the first communication") which is exempt from the financial promotion restriction because, in compliance with the requirements of another provision of this Order, it is accompanied by certain indications or contains certain information, then the financial promotion restriction does not apply to any subsequent communication which complies with the requirements of paragraph (2).

(2) The requirements of this paragraph are that the subsequent communication—

(a) is a non-real time communication or a solicited real time communication;

(b) is made by, or on behalf of, the same person who made the first communication;

(c) is made to a recipient of the first communication;

(d) relates to the same controlled activity and the same controlled investment [or relates to the same controlled claims management activity] as the first communication; and

(e) is made within 12 months of the recipient receiving the first communication.

(3) The provisions of this article only apply in the case of a person who makes or directs a communication on behalf of another where the first communication is made by that other person.

(4) Where a person makes or directs a communication on behalf of another person in reliance on the exemption contained in this article the person on whose behalf the communication was made or directed remains responsible for the content of that communication.

(5) A communication made or directed before this article comes into force is to be treated as a first communication falling within paragraph (1) if it would have fallen within that paragraph had it been made or directed after this article comes into force.

NOTES

Para (2): words in square brackets in sub-para (d) inserted by the Financial Services and Markets Act 2000 (Claims Management Activity) Order 2018, SI 2018/1253, arts 8, 15, as from 1 April 2019 (for full commencement details and for transitional provisions in relation to carrying on a claims management activity, etc, see arts 1, 39–89 of the 2018 Order).

[8.457]

15 Introductions

(1) If the requirements of paragraph (2) are met, the financial promotion restriction does not apply to any communication which is made with a view to or for the purposes of introducing the recipient to—

(a) an authorised person who carries on the controlled activity to which the communication relates; or

(b) an exempt person where the communication relates to a controlled activity which is also a regulated activity in relation to which he is an exempt person.

[(1A) But paragraph (1) does not apply to any communication made with a view to or for the purpose of an introduction to a person who carries on an activity of the kind specified by—

(a) paragraph 4B of Schedule 1;

(b) paragraph 4C of that Schedule;

(c) paragraph 11 of that Schedule, to the extent that it relates to that paragraph 4B or that paragraph 4C;

[(d) paragraph 11A of that Schedule]].

(2) The requirements of this paragraph are that—

(a) the maker of the communication ("A") is not a close relative of, nor a member of the same group as, the person to whom the introduction is, or is to be, made;

(b) A does not receive from any person other than the recipient any pecuniary reward or other advantage arising out of his making the introduction; and

(c) it is clear in all the circumstances that the recipient, in his capacity as an investor, is not seeking and has not sought advice from A as to the merits of the recipient engaging in investment activity (or, if the client has sought such advice, A has declined to give it, but has recommended that the recipient seek such advice from an authorised person).

NOTES

Para (1A): inserted by the Financial Services and Markets Act 2000 (Regulated Activities) (Amendment) Order 2014, SI 2014/366, art 10(1), (2), as from 1 April 2014. Sub-para (d) added by the Financial Services and Markets Act 2000 (Claims Management Activity) Order 2018, SI 2018/1253, arts 8, 16, as from 1 April 2019 (for full commencement details and for transitional provisions in relation to carrying on a claims management activity, etc, see arts 1, 39–89 of the 2018 Order).

[8.458]

16 Exempt persons

(1) The financial promotion restriction does not apply to any communication which—

(a) is a non-real time communication or a solicited real time communication;

(b) is made or directed by an exempt person; and

(c) is for the purposes of that exempt person's business of carrying on a controlled activity [or controlled claims management activity] which is also a regulated activity in relation to which he is an exempt person.

[(1A) The financial promotion restriction also does not apply to any communication which is—

(a) a non-real time communication or a solicited real time communication;

(b) made by a person who is an appointed representative (within the meaning of section 39(2) of the Act) and is carrying on an activity to which sections 20(1) and (1A) and 23(1A) of the Act do not apply by virtue of section 39(1D); and

(c) made for the purposes of that person's business of carrying on a controlled activity which is also a regulated activity to which sections 20(1) and (1A) and 23(1A) of the Act do not apply by virtue of section 39(1D).]

(2) The financial promotion restriction does not apply to any unsolicited real time communication made by a person ("AR") who is an appointed representative (within the meaning of section 39(2) of the Act) where—

(a) the communication is made by AR in carrying on the business—

(i) for which his principal ("P") has accepted responsibility for the purposes of section 39 of the Act; and

(ii) in relation to which AR is exempt from the general prohibition by virtue of that section [or in relation to which sections 20(1) and (1A) and 23(1A) of the Act do not apply by virtue of that section]; and

(b) the communication is one which, if it were made by P, would comply with any rules made [by the FCA under section 137R] of the Act (financial promotion rules) which are relevant to a communication of that kind.

NOTES

Para (1): words in square brackets in sub-para (c) inserted by the Financial Services and Markets Act 2000 (Claims Management Activity) Order 2018, SI 2018/1253, arts 8, 17, as from 1 April 2019 (for full commencement details and for transitional provisions in relation to carrying on a claims management activity, etc, see arts 1, 39–89 of the 2018 Order).

Para (1A): inserted by the Financial Services and Markets Act 2000 (Regulated Activities) (Amendment) Order 2014, SI 2014/366, art 10(1), (3), as from 1 April 2014.

Para (2): words in square brackets in sub-para (a) inserted by the Financial Services Act 2012 (Consequential Amendments and Transitional Provisions) (No 3) Order 2013, SI 2013/1765, art 6(1), (2), as from 1 September 2013. Words in square brackets in sub-para (b) substituted by the Financial Services Act 2012 (Consequential Amendments and Transitional Provisions) Order 2013, SI 2013/472, art 3, Sch 2, para 108(a), as from 1 April 2013.

[8.459]

17 Generic promotions

The financial promotion restriction does not apply to any communication which—

(a) does not identify (directly or indirectly) a person who provides the controlled investment to which the communication relates; . . .

(b) does not identify (directly or indirectly) any person as a person who carries on a controlled activity in relation to that investment[; and]

[(c) does not identify (directly or indirectly) any person as a person who carries on a controlled claims management activity].

NOTES

Word omitted from sub-para (a) revoked, word in square brackets in sub-para (b) inserted, and sub-para (c) added, by the Financial Services and Markets Act 2000 (Claims Management Activity) Order 2018, SI 2018/1253, arts 8, 18, as from 1 April 2019 (for full commencement details and for transitional provisions in relation to carrying on a claims management activity, etc, see arts 1, 39–89 of the 2018 Order).

[8.460]

17A Communications caused to be made or directed by unauthorised persons

(1) If a condition in paragraph (2) is met, the financial promotion restriction does not apply to a communication caused to be made or directed by an unauthorised person which is made or directed by an authorised person.

(2) The conditions in this paragraph are that—

(a) the authorised person prepared the content of the communication; or

(b) it is a real-time communication.

[8.461]

18 Mere conduits

(1) Subject to paragraph (4), the financial promotion restriction does not apply to any communication which is made or directed by a person who acts as a mere conduit for it.

(2) A person acts as a mere conduit for a communication if—

(a) he communicates it in the course of an activity carried on by him, the principal purpose of which is transmitting or receiving material provided to him by others;

(b) the content of the communication is wholly devised by another person; and

(c) the nature of the service provided by him in relation to the communication is such that he does not select, modify or otherwise exercise control over its content prior to its transmission or receipt.

(3) For the purposes of paragraph (2)(c) a person does not select, modify or otherwise exercise control over the content of a communication merely by removing or having the power to remove material—

(a) which is, or is alleged to be, illegal, defamatory or in breach of copyright;

(b) in response to a request to a body which is empowered by or under any enactment to make such a request; or

(c) when otherwise required to do so by law.

(4) Nothing in paragraph (1) prevents the application of the financial promotion restriction in so far as it relates to the person who has caused the communication to be made or directed.

(5) This article does not apply to an electronic commerce communication.

[8.462]

18A Electronic commerce communications: mere conduits, caching and hosting

The financial promotion restriction does not apply to an electronic commerce communication in circumstances where—

(a) the making of the communication constitutes the provision of an information society service of a kind falling within [regulation 17(1), 18 or 19 of the Electronic Commerce (EC Directive) Regulations 2002] ("mere conduit", "caching" and "hosting"); and

(b) [the conditions mentioned in—

(i) regulation 17(1)(a) to (c) of those Regulations (where regulation 17 is the relevant regulation),

(ii) regulation 18(b)(i) to (v) of those Regulations (where regulation 18 is the relevant regulation), or

(iii) regulation 19(a)(i) and (ii) of those Regulations (where regulation 19 is the relevant regulation),

to the extent] that they are applicable at the time of, or prior to, the making of the communication, are or have been met at that time.

NOTES

Words in square brackets substituted by the Financial Services and Markets Act 2000 (Amendment) (EU Exit) Regulations 2019, SI 2019/632, regs 162(1), 168, as from IP completion day (as defined in the European Union (Withdrawal Agreement) Act 2020, s 39) (for transitional provisions see the note on art 6 at **[8.448]**).

[8.463]

19 Investment professionals

(1) The financial promotion restriction does not apply to any communication which—

(a) is made only to recipients whom the person making the communication believes on reasonable grounds to be investment professionals; or

(b) may reasonably be regarded as directed only at such recipients.

(2) For the purposes of paragraph (1)(b), if all the conditions set out in paragraph (4)(a) to (c) are met in relation to the communication, it is to be regarded as directed only at investment professionals.

(3) In any other case in which one or more of the conditions set out in paragraph (4)(a) to (c) are met, that fact is to be taken into account in determining whether the communication is directed only at investment professionals (but a communication may still be regarded as so directed even if none of the conditions in paragraph (4) is met).

(4) The conditions are that—

(a) the communication is accompanied by an indication that it is directed at persons having professional experience in matters relating to investments and that any investment or investment activity to which it relates is available only to such persons or will be engaged in only with such persons;

(b) the communication is accompanied by an indication that persons who do not have professional experience in matters relating to investments should not rely on it;

(c) there are in place proper systems and procedures to prevent recipients other than investment professionals engaging in the investment activity to which the communication relates with the person directing the communication, a close relative of his or a member of the same group.

(5) "Investment professionals" means—

(a) an authorised person;

(b) an exempt person where the communication relates to a controlled activity which is a regulated activity in relation to which the person is exempt;

(c) any other person—

(i) whose ordinary activities involve him in carrying on the controlled activity to which the communication relates for the purpose of a business carried on by him; or

(ii) who it is reasonable to expect will carry on such activity for the purposes of a business carried on by him;

(d) a government, local authority (whether in the United Kingdom or elsewhere) or an international organisation;

(e) a person ("A") who is a director, officer or employee of a person ("B") falling within any of sub-paragraphs (a) to (d) where the communication is made to A in that capacity and where A's responsibilities when acting in that capacity involve him in the carrying on by B of controlled activities.

(6) For the purposes of paragraph (1), a communication may be treated as made only to or directed only at investment professionals even if it is also made to or directed at other persons to whom it may lawfully be communicated.

[(7) Paragraph (1) does not apply to any communication in respect of a controlled claims management activity.]

NOTES

Para (7): added by the Financial Services and Markets Act 2000 (Claims Management Activity) Order 2018, SI 2018/1253, arts 8, 19, as from 1 April 2019 (for full commencement details and for transitional provisions in relation to carrying on a claims management activity, etc, see arts 1, 39–89 of the 2018 Order).

[8.464]

20 Communications by journalists

(1) Subject to paragraph (2), the financial promotion restriction does not apply to any non-real time communication if—

(a) the content of the communication is devised by a person acting in the capacity of a journalist;
(b) the communication is contained in a qualifying publication; and
(c) in the case of a communication requiring disclosure, one of the conditions in paragraph (2) is met.

(2) The conditions in this paragraph are that—

(a) the communication is accompanied by an indication explaining the nature of the author's financial interest or that of a member of his family (as the case may be);
(b) the authors are subject to proper systems and procedures which prevent the publication of communications requiring disclosure without the explanation referred to in sub-paragraph (a); or
(c) the qualifying publication in which the communication appears falls within the remit of—
 (i) the Code of Practice issued by the Press Complaints Commission;
 (ii) the OFCOM Broadcasting Code; or
 (iii) the Producers' Guidelines issued by the British Broadcasting Corporation.

(3) For the purposes of this article, a communication requires disclosure if—

(a) an author of the communication or a member of his family is likely to obtain a financial benefit or avoid a financial loss if people act in accordance with the invitation or inducement contained in the communication;
(b) the communication relates to a controlled investment of a kind falling within paragraph (4) [or to a controlled claims management activity]; and
(c) the communication identifies directly a person who issues or provides the controlled investment [or who carries on or engages in the controlled claims management activity] to which the communication relates.

(4) A controlled investment falls within this paragraph if it is—

(a) an investment falling within paragraph 14 of Schedule 1 (shares or stock in share capital);
(b) an investment falling within paragraph 21 of that Schedule (options) to acquire or dispose of an investment falling within sub-paragraph (a);
(c) an investment falling within paragraph 22 of that Schedule (futures) being rights under a contract for the sale of an investment falling within sub-paragraph (a); or
(d) an investment falling within paragraph 23 of that Schedule (contracts for differences etc) being rights under a contract relating to, or to fluctuations in, the value or price of an investment falling within sub-paragraph (a).

(5) For the purposes of this article—

(a) the authors of the communication are the person who devises the content of the communication and the person who is responsible for deciding to include the communication in the qualifying publication;
(b) a "qualifying publication" is a publication or service of the kind mentioned in paragraph (1) or (2) of article 54 of the Regulated Activities Order and which is of the nature described in that article, and for the purposes of this article, a certificate given under paragraph (3) of article 54 of that Order and not revoked is conclusive evidence of the matters certified;
(c) the members of a person's family are his spouse [or civil partner] and any children of his under the age of 18 years.

NOTES

Para (3): words in square brackets inserted by the Financial Services and Markets Act 2000 (Claims Management Activity) Order 2018, SI 2018/1253, arts 8, 20, as from 1 April 2019 (for full commencement details and for transitional provisions in relation to carrying on a claims management activity, etc, see arts 1, 39–89 of the 2018 Order).

Para (5): words in square brackets in sub-para (c) inserted by the Financial Services and Markets Act 2000 (Financial Promotion) (Amendment) Order 2005, SI 2005/3392, art 2(1), (3), as from 21 December 2005.

[8.465]

20A Promotion broadcast by company director etc

(1) The financial promotion restriction does not apply to a communication which is communicated as part of a qualifying service by a person ("D") who is a director or employee of an undertaking ("U") where—

(a) the communication invites or induces the recipient to acquire—
 (i) a controlled investment of the kind falling within article 20(4) which is issued by U (or by an undertaking in the same group as U); or
 (ii) a controlled investment issued or provided by an authorised person in the same group as U;
(b) the communication—
 (i) comprises words which are spoken by D and not broadcast, transmitted or displayed in writing; or
 (ii) is displayed in writing only because it forms part of an interactive dialogue to which D is a party and in the course of which D is expected to respond immediately to questions put by a recipient of the communication;
(c) the communication is not part of an organised marketing campaign; and
(d) the communication is accompanied by an indication that D is a director or employee (as the case may be) of U.

(2) For the purposes of this article, a "qualifying service" is a service—

(a) which is broadcast or transmitted in the form of television or radio programmes; or
(b) displayed on a web site (or similar system for the electronic display of information) comprising regularly updated news and information,

provided that the principal purpose of the service, taken as a whole and including any advertisements and other promotional material contained in it, is neither of the purposes described in article 54(1)(a) or (b) of the Regulated Activities Order.

(3) For the purposes of paragraph (2), a certificate given under article 54(3) of the Regulated Activities Order and not revoked is conclusive evidence of the matters certified.

20B *(Reg 20B (Incoming electronic commerce communications) revoked by the Financial Services and Markets Act 2000 (Amendment) (EU Exit) Regulations 2019, SI 2019/632, regs 162(1), 169, as from IP completion day (as defined in the European Union (Withdrawal Agreement) Act 2020, s 39) (for transitional provisions see the note on art 6 at* **[8.448]***).)*

[8.466]

[20C Communications required by the PRIIPs regulation: key information document

The financial promotion restriction does not apply to any communication required by Article 13 of Regulation (EU) No 1286/2014 of the European Parliament and of the Council of 26 November 2014 on key information documents for packaged retail and insurance-based investment products."]

NOTES

Inserted by the Packaged Retail and Insurance-based Investment Products Regulations 2017, SI 2017/1127, reg 12, Sch 2, para 5, as from 1 January 2018.

PART V EXEMPT COMMUNICATIONS: DEPOSITS AND INSURANCE

[8.467]

21 Interpretation: relevant insurance activity

In this Part, a "relevant insurance activity" means a controlled activity falling within paragraph 2 of Schedule 1 carried on in relation to an investment falling within paragraph 13 of that Schedule where that investment is not a qualifying contract of insurance.

[8.468]

22 Deposits: non-real time communications

(1) If the requirements of paragraph (2) are met, the financial promotion restriction does not apply to any non-real time communication which relates to a controlled activity falling within paragraph 1 of Schedule 1 [except where that controlled activity relates to a structured deposit].

(2) The requirements of this paragraph are that the communication is accompanied by an indication—

(a) of the full name of the person with whom the investment which is the subject of the communication is to be made ("deposit-taker");

(b) of the country or territory in which a deposit-taker that is a body corporate is incorporated (described as such);

(c) if different, of the country or territory in which the deposit-taker's principal place of business is situated (described as such);

(d) whether or not the deposit-taker is regulated in respect of his deposit-taking business;

(e) if the deposit-taker is so regulated, of the name of the regulator in the deposit-taker's principal place of business, or if there is more than one such regulator, the prudential regulator;

(f) whether any transaction to which the communication relates would, if entered into by the recipient and the deposit-taker, fall within the jurisdiction of any dispute resolution scheme or deposit guarantee scheme and if so, identifying each such scheme;

(g) the necessary capital information.

(3) In this article—

"full name", in relation to a person, means the name under which that person carries on business and, if different, that person's corporate name;

"liabilities" includes provisions where such provisions have not been deducted from the value of the assets;

"necessary capital information" means—

(a) in relation to a deposit-taker which is a body corporate, either the amount of its paid up capital and reserves, described as such, or a statement that the amount of its paid up capital and reserves exceeds a particular amount (stating it);

(b) in relation to a deposit-taker which is not a body corporate, either the amount of the total assets less liabilities (described as such) or a statement that the amount of its total assets exceeds a particular amount (stating it) and that its total liabilities do not exceed a particular amount (stating it).

NOTES

Para (1): words in square brackets inserted by the Financial Services and Markets Act 2000 (Regulated Activities) (Amendment) Order 2017, SI 2017/488, art 14, Schedule, para 9(1), (3), as from 3 January 2018.

[8.469]

23 Deposits: real time communications

The financial promotion restriction does not apply to any real time communication (whether solicited or unsolicited) which relates to an activity falling within paragraph 1 of Schedule 1 [except where that controlled activity relates to a structured deposit].

NOTES

Words in square brackets inserted by the Financial Services and Markets Act 2000 (Regulated Activities) (Amendment) Order 2017, SI 2017/488, art 14, Schedule, para 9(1), (4), as from 3 January 2018.

[8.470]

24 Relevant insurance activity: non-real time communications

(1) If the requirements of paragraph (2) are met, the financial promotion restriction does not apply to any non-real time communication which relates to a relevant insurance activity.

(2) The requirements of this paragraph are that the communication is accompanied by an indication—

(a) of the full name of the person with whom the investment which is the subject of the communication is to be made ("the insurer");

(b) of the country or territory in which the insurer is incorporated (described as such);

(c) if different, of the country or territory in which the insurer's principal place of business is situated (described as such);

(d) whether or not the insurer is regulated in respect of its insurance business;

(e) if the insurer is so regulated, of the name of the regulator of the insurer in its principal place of business or, if there is more than one such regulator, the name of the prudential regulator;

(f) whether any transaction to which the communication relates would, if entered into by the recipient and the insurer, fall within the jurisdiction of any dispute resolution scheme or compensation scheme and if so, identifying each such scheme.

(3) In this article "full name", in relation to a person, means the name under which that person carries on business and, if different, that person's corporate name.

[8.471]

25 Relevant insurance activity: non-real time communications: reinsurance and large risks

(1) The financial promotion restriction does not apply to any non-real time communication which relates to a relevant insurance activity and concerns only—

(a) a contract of reinsurance; or

(b) a contract that covers large risks.

(2) "Large risks" means—

(a) risks falling within paragraph 4 (railway rolling stock), 5 (aircraft), 6 (ships), 7 (goods in transit), 11 (aircraft liability) or 12 (liability of ships) of Schedule 1 to the Regulated Activities Order;

(b) risks falling within paragraph 14 (credit) or 15 (suretyship) of that Schedule provided that the risks relate to a business carried on by the recipient;

(c) risks falling within paragraph 3 (land vehicles), 8 (fire and natural forces), 9 (damage to property), 10 (motor vehicle liability), 13 (general liability) or 16 (miscellaneous financial loss) of that Schedule provided that the risks relate to a business carried on by the recipient and that the condition specified in paragraph (3) is met in relation to that business.

(3) The condition specified in this paragraph is that at least two of the three following criteria were exceeded in the most recent financial year for which information is available prior to the making of the communication—

[(a) the aggregate of the amounts shown as assets in the balance sheet of the business was 6.2 million euros;]

(b) the net turnover (within the meaning given to "turnover" by [section 474(1) of the 2006 Act] was 12.8 million euros;

(c) the number of employees (within the meaning given by [section 465(6) of the 2006 Act] was 250;

and for a financial year which is a company's financial year but not in fact a year, the net turnover of the recipient shall be proportionately adjusted.

(4) For the purposes of paragraph (3), where the recipient is a member of a group for which consolidated accounts . . . are drawn up, the question whether the condition met in that paragraph is met is to be determined by reference to those accounts.

NOTES

Para (3): words in square brackets substituted by the Companies Act 2006 (Consequential Amendments and Transitional Provisions) Order 2011, SI 2011/1265, art 26(1), (5), as from 12 May 2011.

Para (4): words omitted revoked by the Financial Services and Markets Act 2000 (Amendment) (EU Exit) Regulations 2019, SI 2019/632, regs 162(1), 170, as from IP completion day (as defined in the European Union (Withdrawal Agreement) Act 2020, s 39) (for transitional provisions see the note on art 6 at **[8.448]**).

[8.472]

26 Relevant insurance activity: real time communication

The financial promotion restriction does not apply to any real time communication (whether solicited or unsolicited) which relates to a relevant insurance activity.

PART VI EXEMPT COMMUNICATIONS: CERTAIN CONTROLLED ACTIVITIES

[8.473]

27 Application of exemptions in this Part

Except where otherwise stated, the exemptions in this Part apply to communications which relate to—

(a) a controlled activity falling within paragraph 2 of Schedule 1 carried on in relation to a qualifying contract of insurance;

(b) controlled activities falling within any of paragraphs 3 to 11 of Schedule 1;

[(c) a controlled claims management activity.]

NOTES

Para (c) added by the Financial Services and Markets Act 2000 (Claims Management Activity) Order 2018, SI 2018/1253, arts 8, 21, as from 1 April 2019 (for full commencement details and for transitional provisions in relation to carrying on a claims management activity, etc, see arts 1, 39–89 of the 2018 Order).

[8.474]
28 One off non-real time communications and solicited real time communications

(1) The financial promotion restriction does not apply to a one off communication which is either a non-real time communication or a solicited real time communication.

(2) If all the conditions set out in paragraph (3) are met in relation to a communication it is to be regarded as a one off communication. In any other case in which one or more of those conditions are met, that fact is to be taken into account in determining whether the communication is a one off communication (but a communication may still be regarded as a one off communication even if none of the conditions in paragraph (3) is met).

(3) The conditions are that—

(a) the communication is made only to one recipient or only to one group of recipients in the expectation that they would engage in any investment activity [or controlled claims management activity] jointly;

(b) the identity of the product or service to which the communication relates has been determined having regard to the particular circumstances of the recipient;

(c) the communication is not part of an organised marketing campaign.

NOTES

Para (3): words in square brackets in sub-para (a) inserted by the Financial Services and Markets Act 2000 (Claims Management Activity) Order 2018, SI 2018/1253, arts 8, 22, as from 1 April 2019 (for full commencement details and for transitional provisions in relation to carrying on a claims management activity, etc, see arts 1, 39–89 of the 2018 Order).

[8.475]
28A One off unsolicited real time communications

(1) The financial promotion restriction does not apply to an unsolicited real time communication if the conditions in paragraph (2) are met.

(2) The conditions in this paragraph are that—

(a) the communication is a one off communication;

(b) the communicator believes on reasonable grounds that the recipient understands the risks associated with engaging in the investment activity to which the communication relates;

(c) at the time that the communication is made, the communicator believes on reasonable grounds that the recipient would expect to be contacted by him in relation to the investment activity to which the communication relates.

(3) Paragraphs (2) and (3) of article 28 apply in determining whether a communication is a one off communication for the purposes of this article as they apply for the purposes of article 28.

[(4) Paragraph (1) does not apply to any communication in respect of a controlled claims management activity.]

NOTES

Para (4): added by the Financial Services and Markets Act 2000 (Claims Management Activity) Order 2018, SI 2018/1253, arts 8, 23, as from 1 April 2019 (for full commencement details and for transitional provisions in relation to carrying on a claims management activity, etc, see arts 1, 39–89 of the 2018 Order).

[8.476]
28B Real time communications: introductions . . .

(1) If the requirements of paragraph (2) are met, the financial promotion restriction does not apply to any real time communication which—

(a) relates to a controlled activity falling within [paragraph [4B, 4C, 5A, 5B,] 10, 10A, 10B, [10BA, 10BB,] 10C, 10D, 10E, 10F, [10G, 10H, 10I, 10J or 10K]] of Schedule 1; and

(b) is made for the purpose of, or with a view to, introducing the recipient to a person ("N") who is—

(i) an authorised person who carries on the controlled activity to which the communication relates,

(ii) an appointed representative, where the controlled activity to which the communication relates is also a regulated activity in respect of which he is exempt from the general prohibition [or in relation to which sections 20(1) and (1A) and 23(1A) of the Act do not apply by virtue of section 39(1D)] [or in relation to which sections 20(1) and (1A) and 23(1A) of the Act do not apply], or

(iii) an overseas person who carries on the controlled activity to which the communication relates.

(2) The requirements of this paragraph are that the maker of the communication ("M")—

(a) does not receive any money, other than money payable to M on his own account, paid by the recipient for or in connection with any transaction which the recipient enters into with or through N as a result of the introduction; and

(b) before making the introduction, discloses to the recipient such of the information mentioned in paragraph (3) as applies to M.

(3) That information is—

(a) that M is a member of the same group as N;

(b) details of any payment which M will receive from N, by way of fee or commission, for introducing the recipient to N;

(c) an indication of any other reward or advantage received or to be received by M that arises out of his making introductions to N.

(4) In this article, "overseas person" means a person who carries on controlled activities which fall within paragraph [4B, 4C, 5A, 5B,] 10, 10A [10B, 10BA or 10BB] of Schedule 1, but who does not carry on any such activity, or offer to do so, from a permanent place of business maintained by him in the United Kingdom.

NOTES

Article heading: words omitted revoked by the Financial Services and Markets Act 2000 (Regulated Activities) (Amendment) (No 2) Order 2006, SI 2006/2383, art 35(1), (2), as from 6 April 2007.

Para (1): words in first (outer) pair of square brackets in sub-para (a) substituted by SI 2006/2383, art 35(1), (3), as from 6 April 2007. Figures "4B, 4C, 5A, 5B," and "10BA, 10BB," in second and third (inner) pairs of square brackets in sub-para (a) inserted by the Financial Services and Markets Act 2000 (Regulated Activities) (Amendment) (No 2) Order 2013, SI 2013/1881, art 17(1), (2), as from 1 April 2014. Words in fourth (inner) pair of square brackets in sub-para (a) substituted by the Financial Services and Markets Act 2000 (Regulated Activities) (Amendment) Order 2009, SI 2009/1342, art 30(1), (2), as from 1 July 2009 (certain purposes), and as from 30 June 2010 (otherwise). Words in first pair of square brackets in sub-para (b) inserted by the Financial Services and Markets Act 2000 (Regulated Activities) (Amendment) Order 2014, SI 2014/366, art 10(1), (4)(a), as from 1 April 2014. Words in second pair of square brackets in sub-para (b) inserted by the Financial Services Act 2012 (Consequential Amendments and Transitional Provisions) (No 3) Order 2013, SI 2013/1765, art 6(1), (3), as from 1 September 2013.

Para (4): words in first pair of square brackets inserted, and words in second pair of square brackets substituted, by SI 2014/366, art 10(1), (4)(a), as from 1 April 2014.

[8.477]

29 Communications required or authorised by enactments

(1) Subject to paragraph (2), the financial promotion restriction does not apply to any communication which is required or authorised by or under any enactment other than the Act.

(2) This article does not apply to a communication which relates to a controlled activity falling within paragraph [4B,] 10, 10A [, 10B, 10BA or 10BB] of Schedule 1 or within paragraph 11 in so far as it relates to that activity.

[(3) A communication which may be made because a condition imposed by regulation 49 or 50 of the Alternative Investment Fund Managers Regulations 2013 has been met, is to be treated as authorised by those Regulations for the purposes of paragraph (1) in so far as it is made to a professional investor (as defined in regulation 2(1) of those Regulations).

(4) A communication permitted by Article 2.2, 4 or 14.3 of Regulation (EU) No 345/2013 of the European Parliament and the Council of 17 April 2013 on European venture capital funds, or by Article 2.2, 4 or 15.3 of Regulation (EU) No 346/2013 of the European Parliament and the Council of 17 April 2013 on European social entrepreneurship funds, is to be treated as authorised by an enactment other than the Act for the purposes of paragraph (1).]

[(4A) The reference in paragraph (4) to Regulation (EU) 345/2013 is a reference to that instrument as it has effect at the beginning of the day on which the Financial Services and Markets Act 2000 (Amendment) (EU Exit) Regulations 2019 are made (but see regulation 2 of the European Union (Withdrawal) Act 2018 (Consequential Modifications and Repeals and Revocations) Regulations 2019, which may further update the reference).]

[(5) A communication permitted by Article 30 or 31 of Regulation (EU) No 2015/760 of the European Parliament and of the Council of 29th April 2015 on European Long-term Investment Funds is to be treated as authorised by an enactment other than the Act for the purposes of paragraph (1).]

NOTES

Para (2): figure in first pair of square brackets inserted, and words in second pair of square brackets substituted, by the Financial Services and Markets Act 2000 (Regulated Activities) (Amendment) Order 2014, SI 2014/366, art 10(1), (5), as from 1 April 2014.

Paras (3), (4): added by the Alternative Investment Fund Managers Regulations 2013, SI 2013/1773, reg 81, Sch 2, Part 2, para 19(a), as from 22 July 2013.

Para (4A): inserted by the Financial Services and Markets Act 2000 (Amendment) (EU Exit) Regulations 2019, SI 2019/632, regs 162(1), 171, as from 23 March 2019 (for transitional provisions see the note on art 6 at **[8.448]**).

Para (5): added by the European Long-term Investment Funds Regulations 2015, SI 2015/1882, reg 5, as from 3 December 2015.

[8.478]

30 Overseas communicators: solicited real time communications

(1) The financial promotion restriction does not apply to any solicited real time communication which is made by an overseas communicator from outside the United Kingdom in the course of or for the purposes of his carrying on the business of engaging in relevant investment activities outside the United Kingdom.

(2) In this article—

"overseas communicator" means a person who carries on relevant investment activities outside the United Kingdom but who does not carry on any such activity from a permanent place of business maintained by him in the United Kingdom;

"relevant investment activities" means controlled activities which fall within paragraphs 3 to 7 or 10 to 10B[, 10BA or 10BB] of Schedule 1 or, so far as relevant to any of those paragraphs, paragraph 11 of that Schedule.

[(3) Paragraph (1) does not apply to any communication in respect of a controlled claims management activity.]

NOTES

Para (2): words in square brackets in definition "relevant investment activities" inserted by the Financial Services and Markets Act 2000 (Regulated Activities) (Amendment) (No 2) Order 2013, SI 2013/1881, art 17(1), (3), as from 1 April 2014.

Para (3): added by the Financial Services and Markets Act 2000 (Claims Management Activity) Order 2018, SI 2018/1253, arts 8, 24, as from 1 April 2019 (for full commencement details and for transitional provisions in relation to carrying on a claims management activity, etc, see arts 1, 39–89 of the 2018 Order).

[8.479]

31 Overseas communicators: non-real time communications to previously overseas customers

(1) The financial promotion restriction does not apply to any non-real time communication which is communicated by an overseas communicator from outside the United Kingdom to a previously overseas customer of his.

(2) In this article a "previously overseas customer" means a person with whom the overseas communicator has done business within the period of twelve months ending with the day on which the communication was received ("the earlier business") and where—

(a) at the time that the earlier business was done, the customer was neither resident in the United Kingdom nor had a place of business there; or

(b) at the time the earlier business was done, the overseas communicator had on a former occasion done business with the customer, being business of the same description as the business to which the communication relates, and on that former occasion the customer was neither resident in the United Kingdom nor had a place of business there.

(3) For the purposes of this article, an overseas communicator has done business with a customer if, in the course of carrying on his relevant investment activities outside the United Kingdom, he has—

(a) effected a transaction, or arranged for a transaction to be effected, with the customer;

(b) provided, outside the United Kingdom; a service to the customer as described in paragraph 6 of Schedule 1 (whether or not that paragraph was in force at the time the business was done); or

(c) given, outside the United Kingdom, any advice to the customer as described in paragraph 7 of that Schedule (whether or not that paragraph was in force at the time the business was done).

[(4) Paragraph (1) does not apply to any communication in respect of a controlled claims management activity.]

NOTES

Para (4): added by the Financial Services and Markets Act 2000 (Claims Management Activity) Order 2018, SI 2018/1253, arts 8, 25, as from 1 April 2019 (for full commencement details and for transitional provisions in relation to carrying on a claims management activity, etc, see arts 1, 39–89 of the 2018 Order).

[8.480]

32 Overseas communicators: unsolicited real time communications to previously overseas customers

(1) If the requirements of paragraphs (2) and (3) are met, the financial promotion restriction does not apply to an unsolicited real time communication which is made by an overseas communicator from outside the United Kingdom to a previously overseas customer of his.

(2) The requirements of this paragraph are that the terms on which previous transactions and services had been effected or provided by the overseas communicator to the previously overseas customer were such that the customer would reasonably expect, at the time that the unsolicited real time communication is made, to be contacted by the overseas communicator in relation to the investment activity to which the communication relates.

(3) The requirements of this paragraph are that the previously overseas customer has been informed by the overseas communicator on an earlier occasion—

(a) that the protections conferred by or under the Act will not apply to any unsolicited real time communication which is made by the overseas communicator and which relates to that investment activity;

(b) that the protections conferred by or under the Act may not apply to any investment activity that may be engaged in as a result of the communication; and

(c) whether any transaction between them resulting from the communication would fall within the jurisdiction of any dispute resolution scheme or compensation scheme or, if there is no such scheme, of that fact.

[(4) Paragraph (1) does not apply to any communication in respect of a controlled claims management activity.]

NOTES

Para (4): added by the Financial Services and Markets Act 2000 (Claims Management Activity) Order 2018, SI 2018/1253, arts 8, 26, as from 1 April 2019 (for full commencement details and for transitional provisions in relation to carrying on a claims management activity, etc, see arts 1, 39–89 of the 2018 Order).

[8.481]

33 Overseas communicators: unsolicited real time communications to knowledgeable customers

(1) If the requirements of paragraphs (2), (3) and (4) are met, the financial promotion restriction does not apply to an unsolicited real time communication which is made by an overseas communicator from outside the United Kingdom in the course of his carrying on relevant investment activities outside the United Kingdom.

(2) The requirements of this paragraph are that the overseas communicator believes on reasonable grounds that the recipient is sufficiently knowledgeable to understand the risks associated with engaging in the investment activity to which the communication relates.

(3) The requirements of this paragraph are that, in relation to any particular investment activity, the recipient has been informed by the overseas communicator on an earlier occasion—

(a) that the protections conferred by or under the Act will not apply to any unsolicited real time communication which is made by him and which relates to that activity;

(b) that the protections conferred by or under the Act may not apply to any investment activity that may be engaged in as a result of the communication; and

(c) whether any transaction between them resulting from the communication would fall within the jurisdiction of any dispute resolution scheme or compensation scheme or, if there is no such scheme, of that fact.

(4) The requirements of this paragraph are that the recipient, after being given a proper opportunity to consider the information given to him in accordance with paragraph (3), has clearly signified that he understands the warnings referred to in paragraph (3)(a) and (b) and that he accepts that he will not benefit from the protections referred to.

[(5) Paragraph (1) does not apply to any communication in respect of a controlled claims management activity.]

NOTES

Para (5): added by the Financial Services and Markets Act 2000 (Claims Management Activity) Order 2018, SI 2018/1253, arts 8, 27, as from 1 April 2019 (for full commencement details and for transitional provisions in relation to carrying on a claims management activity, etc, see arts 1, 39–89 of the 2018 Order).

[8.482]

34 Governments, central banks etc

The financial promotion restriction does not apply to any communication which—
- (a) is a non-real time communication or a solicited real time communication;
- (b) is communicated by and relates only to controlled investments issued, or to be issued, by—
  - (i) any government;
  - (ii) any local authority (in the United Kingdom or elsewhere) [except for a communication which relates to a regulated credit agreement (within the meaning given in article 60B of the Regulated Activities Order (regulated credit agreements)) where entering into the agreement, or exercising or having the right to exercise rights under the agreement, constitutes the carrying on of a regulated activity of the kind specified by article 60B of the Regulated Activities Order and the exclusion in article 72G of that Order (local authorities) does not apply];
  - (iii) any international organisation;
  - (iv) the Bank of England;
  - (v) . . .
  - (vi) the central bank of any country or territory outside the United Kingdom.

NOTES

Words in square brackets in sub-para (b)(ii) inserted by the Financial Services and Markets Act 2000 (Consumer Credit) (Miscellaneous Provisions) (No 2) Order 2014, SI 2014/506, art 3(1), (2), as from 1 April 2014.

Sub-para (b)(v) revoked by the Financial Services and Markets Act 2000 (Amendment) (EU Exit) Regulations 2019, SI 2019/632, regs 162(1), 172, as from IP completion day (as defined in the European Union (Withdrawal Agreement) Act 2020, s 39) (for transitional provisions see the note on art 6 at **[8.448]**).

[8.483]

35 [Registered societies]

The financial promotion restriction does not apply to any communication which—
- (a) is a non-real time communication or a solicited real time communication;
- (b) is communicated by [a registered society]; and
- (c) relates only to an investment falling within paragraph 15 [or 15A] of Schedule 1 issued, or to be issued, by the society in question.

NOTES

Words in square brackets in the article heading and in para (b) substituted by the Co-operative and Community Benefit Societies and Credit Unions Act 2010 (Consequential Amendments) Regulations 2014, SI 2014/1815, reg 2, Schedule, para 15(1), (2), as from 1 August 2014.

Words in square brackets in para (c) inserted by the Financial Services and Markets Act 2000 (Regulated Activities) (Amendment) Order 2010, SI 2010/86, art 4, Schedule, para 9(b), as from 24 February 2010.

36 *(Reg 36 (Nationals of EEA States other than United Kingdom) revoked by the Financial Services and Markets Act 2000 (Amendment) (EU Exit) Regulations 2019, SI 2019/632, regs 162(1), 173, as from IP completion day (as defined in the European Union (Withdrawal Agreement) Act 2020, s 39) (for transitional provisions see the note on art 6 at* **[8.448]***).)*

[8.484]

37 Financial markets

(1) The financial promotion restriction does not apply to any communication—
- (a) which is a non-real time communication or a solicited real time communication;
- (b) which is communicated by a relevant market; and
- (c) to which paragraph (2) or (3) applies.

(2) This paragraph applies to a communication if—
- (a) it relates only to facilities provided by the market; and
- (b) it does not identify (directly or indirectly)—
  - (i) any particular investment issued, or to be issued, by or available from an identified person as one that may be traded or dealt in on the market; or
  - (ii) any particular person as a person through whom transactions on the market may be effected.

(3) This paragraph applies to a communication if—
- (a) it relates only to a particular investment falling within paragraph 21, 22[, 23 or 23A] of Schedule 1; and
- (b) it identifies the investment as one that may be traded or dealt in on the market.

(4) "Relevant market" means a market which—
- [(za) is a relevant UK market;]
- (a) meets the criteria specified in Part I of Schedule 3; or
- (b) is specified in, or is established under the rules of an exchange specified in, Part . . . III or IV of that Schedule.

NOTES

Words in square brackets in sub-para (3)(a) substituted, and figure omitted from sub-para (4)(b) revoked, by the Financial Services and Markets Act 2000 (Regulated Activities) (Amendment) Order 2017, SI 2017/488, art 14, Schedule, para 9(1), (5), as from 3 January 2018.

In para (4), sub-para (za) was inserted by the Markets in Financial Instruments, Benchmarks and Financial Promotions (Amendment) (EU Exit) Regulations 2021, SI 2021/1074, reg 2(3), as from 18 October 2021.

[8.485]

38 Persons in the business of placing promotional material

The financial promotion restriction does not apply to any communication which is made to a person whose business it is to place, or arrange for the placing of, promotional material provided that it is communicated so that he can place or arrange for placing it.

[8.486]

39 Joint enterprises

(1) The financial promotion restriction does not apply to any communication which is made or directed by a participator in a joint enterprise to or at another participator in the same joint enterprise in connection with, or for the purposes of, that enterprise.

(2) "Joint enterprise" means an enterprise into which two or more persons ("the participators") enter for commercial purposes related to a business or businesses (other than the business of engaging in a controlled activity [or controlled claims management activity]) carried on by them; and, where a participator is a member of a group, each other member of the group is also to be regarded as a participator in the enterprise.

(3) "Participator" includes potential participator.

NOTES

Para (2): words in square brackets inserted by the Financial Services and Markets Act 2000 (Claims Management Activity) Order 2018, SI 2018/1253, arts 8, 29, as from 1 April 2019 (for full commencement details and for transitional provisions in relation to carrying on a claims management activity, etc, see arts 1, 39–89 of the 2018 Order).

[8.487]

40 Participants in certain recognised collective investment schemes

The financial promotion restriction does not apply to any non-real time communication or solicited real time communication which is made—

(a) by a person who is the operator of a scheme recognised under section . . . 272 of the Act; and
(b) to persons in the United Kingdom who are participants in any such recognised scheme operated by the person making the communication,

and which relates only to such recognised schemes as are operated by that person or to units in such schemes.

NOTES

Words omitted from para (a) revoked by the Alternative Investment Fund Managers Regulations 2013, SI 2013/1773, reg 81, Sch 2, Part 2, para 19(b), as from 22 July 2013.

[8.488]

41 Bearer instruments: promotions required or permitted by market rules

(1) The financial promotion restriction does not apply to any communication which—

(a) is a non-real time communication or a solicited real time communication;
(b) is communicated by a body corporate ("A") that is not an open-ended investment company;
(c) is made to or may reasonably be regarded as directed at persons entitled to bearer instruments issued by A, a parent undertaking of A or a subsidiary undertaking of A; and
(d) is required or permitted by the rules of a relevant market to be communicated to holders of instruments of a class which consists of or includes the bearer instruments in question.

(2) "Bearer instrument" means any of the following investments title to which is capable of being transferred by delivery—

(a) any investment falling within paragraph 14[, 15 or 15A] of Schedule 1;
(b) any investment falling within paragraph 17 or 18 of that Schedule which confers rights in respect of an investment falling within paragraph 14[, 15 or 15A].

(3) For the purposes of this article, a bearer instrument falling within paragraph 17 or 18 of Schedule 1 is treated as issued by the person ("P") who issued the investment in respect of which the bearer instrument confers rights if it is issued by—

(a) an undertaking in the same group as P; or
(b) a person acting on behalf of, or pursuant to arrangements made with, P.

(4) "Relevant market", in relation to instruments of any particular class, means any market on which instruments of that class can be traded or dealt in and which—

[(za) is a relevant UK market;]
(a) meets the criteria specified in Part I of Schedule 3; or
(b) is specified in, or established under the rules of an exchange specified in, Part . . . III of that Schedule.

NOTES

Para (2): words in square brackets in sub-paras (a), (b) substituted by the Financial Services and Markets Act 2000 (Regulated Activities) (Amendment) Order 2010, SI 2010/86, art 4, Schedule, para 9(a)(ii), as from 24 February 2010.

Para (4): sub-para (za) inserted by the Markets in Financial Instruments, Benchmarks and Financial Promotions (Amendment) (EU Exit) Regulations 2021, SI 2021/1074, reg 2(4), as from 18 October 2021. Words omitted from sub-para (b) revoked by the Financial Services and Markets Act 2000 (Regulated Activities) (Amendment) Order 2017, SI 2017/488, art 14, Schedule, para 9(1), (6), as from 3 January 2018.

Modification: by the Uncertificated Securities (Amendment) (Eligible Debt Securities) Regulations 2003, SI 2003/1633, Sch 2, para 15, a reference to bearer instruments in the Financial Services and Markets Act 2000 (Financial Promotion) Order 2001, SI 2001/1335, arts 41(1) and 42(1) (now revoked and replaced by arts 41(1) and 42(1) of this Order) included a reference to uncertificated units of an eligible debt security the holding of which conferred, in accordance with the current terms of issue of the security, rights which corresponded to those conferred by an investment of a kind falling within para 15(1) of Sch 1 to SI 2001/1335 (now para 15(1) of Sch 1 to this Order).

[8.489]

42 Bearer instruments: promotions to existing holders

(1) The financial promotion restriction does not apply to any communication which—

(a) is a non-real time communication or a solicited real time communication;

(b) is communicated by a body corporate ("A") that is not an open-ended investment company;

(c) is made to or may reasonably be regarded as directed at persons entitled to bearer instruments issued by A, a parent undertaking of A or a subsidiary undertaking of A;

(d) relates only to instruments of a class which consists of or includes either the bearer instruments to which the communication relates or instruments in respect of which those bearer instruments confer rights; and

(e) is capable of being accepted or acted on only by persons who are entitled to instruments (whether or not bearer instruments) issued by A, a parent undertaking of A or a subsidiary undertaking of A.

(2) "Bearer instruments" has the meaning given by article 41.

(3) For the purposes of this article, an instrument falling within paragraph 17 or 18 of Schedule 1 is treated as issued by the person ("P") who issued the investment in respect of which the bearer instrument confers rights if it is issued by—

(a) an undertaking in the same group as P; or

(b) a person acting on behalf of, or pursuant to arrangements made with, P.

NOTES

Modification: see the note to art 41 at **[8.488]**.

[8.490]

43 Members and creditors of certain bodies corporate

(1) The financial promotion restriction does not apply to any non-real time communication or solicited real time communication which is communicated—

(a) by, or on behalf of, a body corporate ("A") that is not an open-ended investment company; and

(b) to persons whom the person making or directing the communication believes on reasonable grounds to be persons to whom paragraph (2) applies,

and which relates only to a relevant investment which is issued or to be issued by A, or by an undertaking ("U") in the same group as A that is not an open-ended investment company.

(2) This paragraph applies to—

(a) a creditor or member of A or of U;

(b) a person who is entitled to a relevant investment which is issued, or to be issued, by A or by U;

(c) a person who is entitled, whether conditionally or unconditionally, to become a member of A or of U but who has not yet done so;

(d) a person who is entitled, whether conditionally or unconditionally, to have transferred to him title to a relevant investment which is issued by A or by U but has not yet acquired title to the investment.

(3) "Relevant investment" means—

(a) an investment falling within paragraph 14[, 15 or 15A] of Schedule 1;

(b) an investment falling within paragraph 17 or 18 of that Schedule so far as relating to any investments within sub-paragraph (a).

(4) For the purposes of this article, an investment falling within paragraph 17 or 18 of Schedule 1 is treated as issued by the person ("P") who issued the investment in respect of which the instrument confers rights if it is issued by—

(a) an undertaking in the same group as P; or

(b) a person acting on behalf of, or pursuant to arrangements made with, P.

NOTES

Para (3): words in square brackets in sub-para (a) substituted by the Financial Services and Markets Act 2000 (Regulated Activities) (Amendment) Order 2010, SI 2010/86, art 4, Schedule, para 9(a)(iii), as from 24 February 2010.

[8.491]

44 Members and creditors of open-ended investment companies

(1) The financial promotion restriction does not apply to any communication which—

(a) is a non-real time communication or a solicited real time communication;

(b) is communicated by, or on behalf of, a body corporate ("A") that is an open-ended investment company;

(c) is communicated to persons whom the person making or directing the communication believes on reasonable grounds to be persons to whom paragraph (2) applies; and

(d) relates only to an investment falling within paragraph 15, [15A,] 17 or 19 of Schedule 1 which is issued, or to be issued, by A.

(2) This paragraph applies to—

(a) a creditor or member of A;

(b) a person who is entitled to an investment falling within paragraph 15, [15A,] 17 or 19 of Schedule 1 which is issued, or to be issued, by A;

(c) a person who is entitled, whether conditionally or unconditionally, to become a member of A but who has not yet done so;

(d) a person who is entitled, whether conditionally or unconditionally, to have transferred to him title to an investment falling within paragraph 15, [15A,] 17 or 19 of Schedule 1 which is issued by A but has not yet acquired title to the investment.

(3) For the purposes of this article, an investment falling within paragraph 17 of Schedule 1 is treated as issued by the person ("P") who issued the investment in respect of which the instrument confers rights if it is issued by—

(a) an undertaking in the same group as P; or

(b) a person acting on behalf of, or pursuant to arrangements made with, P.

NOTES

Paras (1), (2): figures in square brackets inserted by the Financial Services and Markets Act 2000 (Regulated Activities) (Amendment) Order 2010, SI 2010/86, art 4, Schedule, para 9(c), as from 24 February 2010.

[8.492]

45 Group companies

The financial promotion restriction does not apply to any communication made by one body corporate in a group to another body corporate in the same group.

[8.493]

46 Qualifying credit to bodies corporate

The financial promotion restriction does not apply to any communication which relates to a controlled activity falling within paragraph 10, 10A, [10B, 10BA or 10BB] of Schedule 1 (or within paragraph 11 so far as it relates to that activity) if the communication is—

(a) made to or directed at bodies corporate only; or

(b) accompanied by an indication that the qualifying credit to which it relates is only available to bodies corporate.

NOTES

Words in square brackets substituted by the Financial Services and Markets Act 2000 (Regulated Activities) (Amendment) (No 2) Order 2013, SI 2013/1881, art 17(1), (4), as from 1 April 2014.

[8.494]

[46A Promotions of credit etc for business purposes

(1) The financial promotion restriction does not apply to a communication which relates to a controlled activity falling within paragraph 4C of Schedule 1 and which—

(a) indicates clearly (by express words or otherwise) that a person is willing to facilitate another person ("B") becoming the borrower under a paragraph 4C agreement for the purposes of B's business, and

(b) does not indicate (by express words or otherwise) that the person is willing to facilitate B becoming the borrower under such an agreement for any other purpose.

(2) The financial promotion restriction does not apply to a communication which relates to a controlled activity falling within paragraph 10BA of Schedule 1 and which—

(a) indicates clearly (by express words or otherwise) that a person is willing to enter into a relevant credit agreement as lender for the purposes of another person's business, and

(b) does not indicate (by express words or otherwise) that the person is willing to enter into a relevant credit agreement as lender for any other purpose.

(3) The financial promotion restriction does not apply to a communication which relates to a controlled activity falling within paragraph 10BB of Schedule 1 and which—

(a) indicates clearly (by express words or otherwise) that a person is willing to enter into a regulated consumer hire agreement as owner for the purposes of another person's business, and

(b) does not indicate (by express words or otherwise) that the person is willing to enter into a regulated consumer hire agreement as owner for any other purpose.

(4) In this article—

(a) references to a "business" do not include a business carried on by—

(i) the person communicating the promotion, or

(ii) a person carrying on an activity of the kind specified by article 36A of the Regulated Activities Order (credit broking) in relation to the relevant credit agreement, paragraph 4C agreement or regulated consumer hire agreement to which the promotion relates;

(b) "paragraph 4C agreement" has the meaning given in paragraph 4C of Schedule 1;

(c) "relevant credit agreement" has the meaning given in paragraph 28 of Schedule 1.]

NOTES

Inserted by the Financial Services and Markets Act 2000 (Regulated Activities) (Amendment) (No 2) Order 2013, SI 2013/1881, art 17(1), (5), as from 1 April 2014.

[8.495]

47 Persons in the business of disseminating information

(1) The financial promotion restriction does not apply to any communication which is made only to recipients whom the person making the communication believes on reasonable grounds to be persons to whom paragraph (2) applies.

(2) This paragraph applies to—

(a) a person who receives the communication in the course of a business which involves the dissemination through a publication of information concerning controlled activities [or controlled claims management activities];

(b) a person whilst acting in the capacity of director, officer or employee of a person falling within sub-paragraph (a) being a person whose responsibilities when acting in that capacity involve him in the business referred to in that sub-paragraph;

(c) any person to whom the communication may otherwise lawfully be made.

NOTES

Para (2): words in square brackets in sub-para (a) inserted by the Financial Services and Markets Act 2000 (Claims Management Activity) Order 2018, SI 2018/1253, arts 8, 30, as from 1 April 2019 (for full commencement details and for transitional provisions in relation to carrying on a claims management activity, etc, see arts 1, 39–89 of the 2018 Order).

[8.496]

48 Certified high net worth individuals

(1) If the requirements of paragraphs (4) and (7) are met, the financial promotion restriction does not apply to any communication which—

(a) is a non-real time communication or a solicited real time communication;

(b) is made to an individual whom the person making the communication believes on reasonable grounds to be a certified high net worth individual, and

(c) relates only to one or more investments falling within paragraph (8).

(2) "Certified high net worth individual" means an individual who has signed, within the period of twelve months ending with the day on which the communication is made, a statement complying with Part I of Schedule 5.

(3) The validity of a statement signed for the purposes of paragraph (2) is not affected by a defect in the form or wording of the statement, provided that the defect does not alter the statement's meaning and that the words shown in bold type in Part I of Schedule 5 are so shown in the statement.

(4) The requirements of this paragraph are that either the communication is accompanied by the giving of a warning in accordance with paragraphs (5) and (6) or where, because of the nature of the communication, this is not reasonably practicable,—

(a) a warning in accordance with paragraph (5) is given to the recipient orally at the beginning of the communication together with an indication that he will receive the warning in legible form and that, before receipt of that warning, he should consider carefully any decision to engage in investment activity to which the communication relates; and

(b) a warning in accordance with paragraphs (5) and (6) (d) to (h) is sent to the recipient of the communication within two business days of the day on which the communication is made.

(5) The warning must be in the following terms—

"The content of this promotion has not been approved by an authorised person within the meaning of the Financial Services and Markets Act 2000. Reliance on this promotion for the purpose of engaging in any investment activity may expose an individual to a significant risk of losing all of the property or other assets invested.".

But where a warning is sent pursuant to paragraph (4)(b), for the words "this promotion" in both places where they occur there must be substituted wording which clearly identifies the promotion which is the subject of the warning.

(6) The warning must—

(a) be given at the beginning of the communication;

(b) precede any other written or pictorial matter;

(c) be in a font size consistent with the text forming the remainder of the communication;

(d) be indelible;

(e) be legible;

(f) be printed in black, bold type;

(g) be surrounded by a black border which does not interfere with the text of the warning; and

(h) not be hidden, obscured or interrupted by any other written or pictorial matter.

(7) The requirements of this paragraph are that the communication is accompanied by an indication—

(a) that it is exempt from the general restriction (in section 21 of the Act) on the communication of invitations or inducements to engage in investment activity on the ground that it is made to a certified high net worth individual;

(b) of the requirements that must be met for an individual to qualify as a certified high net worth individual; and

(c) that any individual who is in any doubt about the investment to which the communication relates should consult an authorised person specialising in advising on investments of the kind in question.

(8) An investment falls within this paragraph if—

(a) it is an investment falling within paragraph 14 of Schedule 1 being stock or shares in an unlisted company;

(b) it is an investment falling within paragraph 15 of Schedule 1 being an investment acknowledging the indebtedness of an unlisted company;

[(ba) it is an investment falling within paragraph 15A of Schedule 1 being an investment constituting an alternative finance investment bond issued by an unlisted company;]

(c) it is an investment falling within paragraph 17 or 18 of Schedule 1 conferring entitlement or rights with respect to investments falling within sub-paragraph (a) or (b);

(d) it comprises units in a collective investment scheme being a scheme which invests wholly or predominantly in investments falling within sub-paragraph (a) or (b);

(e) it is an investment falling within paragraph 21 of Schedule 1 being an option to acquire or dispose of an investment falling within sub-paragraph (a), (b) or (c);

(f) it is an investment falling within paragraph 22 of Schedule 1 being rights under a contract for the sale of an investment falling within sub-paragraph (a), (b) or (c);

(g) it is an investment falling within paragraph 23 of Schedule 1 being a contract relating to, or to fluctuations in value or price of, an investment falling within sub-paragraph (a), (b) or (c),

provided in each case that it is an investment under the terms of which the investor cannot incur a liability or obligation to pay or contribute more than he commits by way of investment.

(9) "Business day" means any day except a Saturday, a Sunday, Christmas Day, Good Friday or a day which is a bank holiday under the Banking and Financial Dealings Act 1971 in any part of the United Kingdom.

NOTES

Para (8): sub-para (ba) inserted by the Financial Services and Markets Act 2000 (Regulated Activities) (Amendment) Order 2010, SI 2010/86, art 4, Schedule, para 9(d), as from 24 February 2010.

[8.497]

49 High net worth companies, unincorporated associations etc

(1) The financial promotion restriction does not apply to any communication which—

(a) is made only to recipients whom the person making the communication believes on reasonable grounds to be persons to whom paragraph (2) applies; or

(b) may reasonably be regarded as directed only at persons to whom paragraph (2) applies.

(2) This paragraph applies to—

(a) any body corporate which has, or which is a member of the same group as an undertaking which has, a called-up share capital or net assets of not less than—

(i) if the body corporate has more than 20 members or is a subsidiary undertaking of an undertaking which has more than 20 members, £500,000;

(ii) otherwise, £5 million;

(b) any unincorporated association or partnership which has net assets of not less than £5 million;

(c) the trustee of a high value trust;

(d) any person ("A") whilst acting in the capacity of director, officer or employee of a person ("B") falling within any of sub-paragraphs (a) to (c) where A's responsibilities, when acting in that capacity, involve him in B's engaging in investment activity;

(e) any person to whom the communication may otherwise lawfully be made.

(3) For the purposes of paragraph (1)(b)—

(a) if all the conditions set out in paragraph (4)(a) to (c) are met, the communication is to be regarded as directed at persons to whom paragraph (2) applies;

(b) in any other case in which one or more of those conditions are met, that fact is to be taken into account in determining whether the communication is directed at persons to whom paragraph (2) applies (but a communication may still be regarded as so directed even if none of the conditions in paragraph (4) is met).

(4) The conditions are that—

(a) the communication includes an indication of the description of persons to whom it is directed and an indication of the fact that the controlled investment or controlled activity to which it relates is available only to such persons;

(b) the communication includes an indication that persons of any other description should not act upon it;

(c) there are in place proper systems and procedures to prevent recipients other than persons to whom paragraph (2) applies engaging in the investment activity to which the communication relates with the person directing the communication, a close relative of his or a member of the same group.

(5) "Called-up share capital" has the meaning given in [the 2006 Act (see section 547)].

(6) "High value trust" means a trust where the aggregate value of the cash and investments which form part of the trust's assets (before deducting the amount of its liabilities)—

(a) is £10 million or more; or

(b) has been £10 million or more at any time during the year immediately preceding the date on which the communication in question was first made or directed.

(7) "Net assets" has the meaning given by [section 831 of the 2006 Act].

[(8) Paragraph (1) does not apply to any communication in respect of a controlled claims management activity.]

NOTES

Paras (5), (7): words in square brackets substituted by the Companies Act 2006 (Consequential Amendments and Transitional Provisions) Order 2011, SI 2011/1265, art 26(1), (6), as from 12 May 2011.

Para (8): added by the Financial Services and Markets Act 2000 (Claims Management Activity) Order 2018, SI 2018/1253, arts 8, 31, as from 1 April 2019 (for full commencement details and for transitional provisions in relation to carrying on a claims management activity, etc, see arts 1, 39–89 of the 2018 Order).

[8.498]

50 Sophisticated investors

(1) "Certified sophisticated investor", in relation to any description of investment, means a person—

(a) who has a current certificate in writing or other legible form signed by an authorised person to the effect that he is sufficiently knowledgeable to understand the risks associated with that description of investment; and

(b) who has signed, within the period of twelve months ending with the day on which the communication is made, a statement in the following terms:

"I make this statement so that I am able to receive promotions which are exempt from the restrictions on financial promotion in the Financial Services and Markets Act 2000. The exemption relates to certified sophisticated investors and I declare that I qualify as such in relation to investments of the following kind [list them]. I accept that the contents of promotions and other material that I receive may not have been approved by an authorised person and that their content may not therefore be subject to controls which would apply if the promotion were made or approved by an authorised person. I am aware that it is open to me to seek advice from someone who specialises in advising on this kind of investment.".

(1A) The validity of a statement signed in accordance with paragraph (1)(b) is not affected by a defect in the wording of the statement, provided that the defect does not alter the statement's meaning.

(2) If the requirements of paragraph (3) are met, the financial promotion restriction does not apply to any communication which—

(a) is made to a certified sophisticated investor;

(b) does not invite or induce the recipient to engage in investment activity with the person who has signed the certificate referred to in paragraph (1)(a); and

(c) relates only to a description of investment in respect of which that investor is certified.

(3) The requirements of this paragraph are that the communication is accompanied by an indication—

(a) that it is exempt from the general restriction (in section 21 of the Act) on the communication of invitations or inducements to engage in investment activity on the ground that it is made to a certified sophisticated investor;
(b) of the requirements that must be met for a person to qualify as a certified sophisticated investor;
(c) that the content of the communication has not been approved by an authorised person and that such approval is, unless this exemption or any other exemption applies, required by section 21 of the Act;
(d) that reliance on the communication for the purpose of engaging in any investment activity may expose the individual to a significant risk of losing all of the property invested or of incurring additional liability;
(e) that any person who is in any doubt about the investment to which the communication relates should consult an authorised person specialising in advising on investments of the kind in question.

(4) For the purposes of paragraph (1)(a), a certificate is current if it is signed and dated not more than three years before the date on which the communication is made.

[8.499]

50A Self-certified sophisticated investors

(1) "Self-certified sophisticated investor" means an individual who has signed within the period of twelve months ending with the day on which the communication is made, a statement complying with Part II of Schedule 5.

(2) The validity of a statement signed for the purposes of paragraph (1) is not affected by a defect in the form or wording of the statement, provided that the defect does not alter the statement's meaning and that the words shown in bold type in Part II of Schedule 5 are so shown in the statement.

(3) If the requirements of paragraphs (4) and (7) are met, the financial promotion restriction does not apply to any communication which—
(a) is made to an individual whom the person making the communication believes on reasonable grounds to be a self-certified sophisticated investor; and
(b) relates only to one or more investments falling within paragraph (8).

(4) The requirements of this paragraph are that either the communication is accompanied by the giving of a warning in accordance with paragraphs (5) and (6) or where, because of the nature of the communication this is not reasonably practicable—
(a) a warning in accordance with paragraph (5) is given to the recipient orally at the beginning of the communication together with an indication that he will receive the warning in legible form and that, before receipt of that warning, he should consider carefully any decision to engage in investment activity to which the communication relates; and
(b) a warning in accordance with paragraphs (5) and (6) (d) to (h) is sent to the recipient of the communication within two business days of the day on which the communication is made.

(5) The warning must be in the following terms—

"The content of this promotion has not been approved by an authorised person within the meaning of the Financial Services and Markets Act 2000. Reliance on this promotion for the purpose of engaging in any investment activity may expose an individual to a significant risk of losing all of the property or other assets invested.".

But where a warning is sent pursuant to paragraph (4)(b), for the words "this promotion" in both places where they occur there must be substituted wording which clearly identifies the promotion which is the subject of the warning.

(6) The warning must—
(a) be given at the beginning of the communication;
(b) precede any other written or pictorial matter;
(c) be in a font size consistent with the text forming the remainder of the communication;
(d) be indelible;
(e) be legible;
(f) be printed in black, bold type;
(g) be surrounded by a black border which does not interfere with the text of the warning; and
(h) not be hidden, obscured or interrupted by any other written or pictorial matter.

(7) The requirements of this paragraph are that the communication is accompanied by an indication—
(a) that it is exempt from the general restriction (in section 21 of the Act) on the communication of invitations or inducements to engage in investment activity on the ground that it is made to a self-certified sophisticated investor;
(b) of the requirements that must be met for an individual to qualify as a self-certified sophisticated investor;
(c) that any individual who is in any doubt about the investment to which the communication relates should consult an authorised person specialising in advising on investments of the kind in question.

(8) An investment falls within this paragraph if—
(a) it is an investment falling within paragraph 14 of Schedule 1 being stock or shares in an unlisted company;
(b) it is an investment falling within paragraph 15 of Schedule I being an investment acknowledging the indebtedness of an unlisted company;
[(ba) it is an investment falling within paragraph 15A of Schedule 1 being an investment constituting an alternative finance investment bond issued by an unlisted company;]
(c) it is an investment falling within paragraph 17 or 18 of Schedule 1 conferring entitlement or rights with respect to investments falling within sub-paragraph (a) or (b);
(d) it comprises units in a collective investment scheme being a scheme which invests wholly or predominantly in investments falling within sub-paragraph (a) or (b);
(e) it is an investment falling within paragraph 21 of Schedule 1 being an option to acquire or dispose of an investment falling within sub-paragraph (a), (b) or (c);
(f) it is an investment falling within paragraph 22 of Schedule 1 being rights under a contract for the sale of an investment falling within sub-paragraph (a), (b) or (c);
(g) it is an investment falling within paragraph 23 of Schedule 1 being a contract relating to, or to fluctuations in value or price of, an investment falling within sub-paragraph (a), (b) or (c),

provided in each case that it is an investment under the terms of which the investor cannot incur a liability or obligation to pay or contribute more than he commits by way of investment.

(9) "Business day" means any day except a Saturday, a Sunday, Christmas Day, Good Friday or a day which is a bank holiday under the Banking and Financial Dealings Act 1971 in any part of the United Kingdom.

NOTES

Para (8): sub-para (ba) inserted by the Financial Services and Markets Act 2000 (Regulated Activities) (Amendment) Order 2010, SI 2010/86, art 4, Schedule, para 9(e), as from 24 February 2010.

[8.500]

51 Associations of high net worth or sophisticated investors

The financial promotion restriction does not apply to any non-real time communication or solicited real time communication which—

(a) is made to an association, or to a member of an association, the membership of which the person making the communication believes on reasonable grounds comprises wholly or predominantly persons who are—
   (i) certified or self-certified high net worth individuals within the meaning of article 48;
   (ii) high net worth persons falling within article 49(2)(a) to (d);
   (iii) certified or self-certified sophisticated investors within the meaning of article 50 or 50A; and
(b) relates only to an investment under the terms of which a person cannot incur a liability or obligation to pay or contribute more than he commits by way of investment.

[8.501]

52 Common interest group of a company

(1) "Common interest group", in relation to a company, means an identified group of persons who at the time the communication is made might reasonably be regarded as having an existing and common interest with each other and that company in—

(a) the affairs of the company; and
(b) what is done with the proceeds arising from any investment to which the communication relates.

(2) If the requirements of paragraphs (3) and either (4) or (5) are met, the financial promotion restriction does not apply to any communication which—

(a) is a non-real time communication or a solicited real time communication;
(b) is made only to persons who are members of a common interest group of a company, or may reasonably be regarded as directed only at such persons; and
(c) relates to investments falling within paragraph 14[, 15 or 15A] of Schedule 1 which are issued, or to be issued, by that company.

(3) The requirements of this paragraph are that the communication is accompanied by an indication—

(a) that the directors of the company (or its promoters named in the communication) have taken all reasonable care to ensure that every statement of fact or opinion included in the communication is true and not misleading given the form and context in which it appears;
(b) that the directors of the company (or its promoters named in the communication) have not limited their liability with respect to the communication; and
(c) that any person who is in any doubt about the investment to which the communication relates should consult an authorised person specialising in advising on investments of the kind in question.

(4) The requirements of this paragraph are that the communication is accompanied by an indication—

(a) that the directors of the company (or its promoters named in the communication) have taken all reasonable care to ensure that any person belonging to the common interest group (and his professional advisers) can have access, at all reasonable times, to all the information that he or they would reasonably require, and reasonably expect to find, for the purpose of making an informed assessment of the assets and liabilities, financial position, profits and losses and prospects of the company and of the rights attaching to the investments in question; and
(b) describing the means by which such information can be accessed.

(5) The requirements of this paragraph are that the communication is accompanied by an indication that any person considering subscribing for the investments in question should regard any subscription as made primarily to assist the furtherance of the company's objectives (other than any purely financial objectives) and only secondarily, if at all, as an investment.

(6) For the purposes of paragraph (2)(b)—

(a) if all the conditions set out in paragraph (7) are met, the communication is to be regarded as directed at persons who are members of the common interest group;
(b) in any other case in which one or more of those conditions are met, that fact shall be taken into account in determining whether the communication is directed at persons who are members of the common interest group (but a communication may still be regarded as directed only at such persons even if none of the conditions in paragraph (7) is met).

(7) The conditions are that—

(a) the communication is accompanied by an indication that it is directed at persons who are members of the common interest group and that any investment or activity to which it relates is available only to such persons;
(b) the communication is accompanied by an indication that it must not be acted upon by persons who are not members of the common interest group;
(c) there are in place proper systems and procedures to prevent recipients other than members of the common interest group engaging in the investment activity to which the communication relates with the person directing the communication, a close relative of his or a member of the same group.

(8) Persons are not to be regarded as having an interest of the kind described in paragraph (1) if the only reason why they would be so regarded is that—

(a) they will have such an interest if they become members or creditors of the company;
(b) they all carry on a particular trade or profession; or
(c) they are persons with whom the company has an existing business relationship, whether by being its clients, customers, contractors, suppliers or otherwise.

NOTES

Para (2): words in square brackets in sub-para (c) substituted by the Financial Services and Markets Act 2000 (Regulated Activities) (Amendment) Order 2010, SI 2010/86, art 4, Schedule, para 9(a)(iv), as from 24 February 2010.

[8.502]
53 Settlors, trustees and personal representatives

The financial promotion restriction does not apply to any communication which is made between—
(a) a person when acting as a settlor or grantor of a trust, a trustee or a personal representative; and
(b) a trustee of the trust, a fellow trustee or a fellow personal representative (as the case may be),
if the communication is made for the purposes of the trust or estate.

[8.503]
54 Beneficiaries of trust, will or intestacy

The financial promotion restriction does not apply to any communication which is made—
(a) between a person when acting as a settlor or grantor of a trust, trustee or personal representative and a beneficiary under the trust, will or intestacy; or
(b) between a beneficiary under a trust, will or intestacy and another beneficiary under the same trust, will or intestacy,
if the communication relates to the management or distribution of that trust fund or estate.

[8.504]
55 Communications by members of professions

(1) The financial promotion restriction does not apply to a real time communication (whether solicited or unsolicited) which—
(a) is made by a person ("P") who carries on a regulated activity to which the general prohibition does not apply by virtue of section 327 of the Act; and
(b) is made to a recipient who has, prior to the communication being made, engaged P to provide professional services,
where the controlled activity to which the communication relates is an excluded activity which would be undertaken by P for the purposes of, and incidental to, the provision by him of professional services to or at the request of the recipient.

(2) "Professional services" has the meaning given in section 327 of the Act.

(3) An "excluded activity" is an activity to which the general prohibition would apply but for the application of—
(a) section 327 of the Act; or
(b) article 67 of the Regulated Activities Order.

[8.505]
55A Non-real time communication by members of professions

(1) The financial promotion restriction does not apply to a non-real time communication which is—
(a) made by a person ("P") who carries on Part XX activities; and
(b) limited to what is required or permitted by paragraphs (2) and (3).

(2) The communication must be in the following terms—

> "This [firm/company] is not authorised under the Financial Services and Markets Act 2000 but we are able in certain circumstances to offer a limited range of investment [and consumer credit-related] [and claims management-related] services to clients because we are members of [relevant designated professional body]. We can provide these investment [and consumer credit-related] [and claims management-related] services if they are an incidental part of the professional services we have been engaged to provide."

(3) The communication may in addition set out the Part XX activities which P is able to offer to his clients, provided it is clear that these are the investment [and consumer credit-related] [and claims management-related] services to which the statement in paragraph (2) relates.

(4) The validity of a communication made in accordance with paragraph (2) is not affected by a defect in the wording of it provided that the defect does not alter the communication's meaning.

(5) "Part XX activities" means the regulated activities to which the general prohibition does not apply when they are carried on by P by virtue of section 327 of the Act.

NOTES

Paras (2), (3): words "and consumer credit-related" in square brackets inserted by the Financial Services and Markets Act 2000 (Regulated Activities) (Amendment) Order 2014, SI 2014/366, art 10(1), (6), as from 1 April 2014. Words "and claims management-related" in square brackets inserted by the Financial Services and Markets Act 2000 (Claims Management Activity) Order 2018, SI 2018/1253, arts 8, 32, as from 1 April 2019 (for full commencement details and for transitional provisions in relation to carrying on a claims management activity, etc, see arts 1, 39–89 of the 2018 Order). Note also that the other words in square brackets in para (2) are part of the original text and not an amendment.

[8.506]
[55B Insolvency practitioners

The financial promotion restriction does not apply to any non-real time communication or solicited real time communication by a person acting as an insolvency practitioner (within the meaning of the Regulated Activities

Order) [in the course of carrying on] an activity which would be a regulated activity but for article 72H of the Regulated Activities Order (insolvency practitioners).]

NOTES

Inserted by the Financial Services and Markets Act 2000 (Consumer Credit) (Miscellaneous Provisions) (No 2) Order 2014, SI 2014/506, art 3(1), (3), as from 1 April 2014.

Words in square brackets substituted by the Financial Services and Markets Act 2000 (Miscellaneous Provisions) Order 2015, SI 2015/853, art 4(1), (2), as from 24 March 2015.

[8.507]

56 Remedy following report by Parliamentary Commissioner for Administration

The financial promotion restriction does not apply to any communication made or directed by a person for the purpose of enabling any injustice, stated by the Parliamentary Commissioner for Administration in a report under section 10 of the Parliamentary Commissioner Act 1967 to have occurred, to be remedied with respect to the recipient.

[8.508]

57 Persons placing promotional material in particular publications

The financial promotion restriction does not apply to any communication received by a person who receives the publication in which the communication is contained because he has himself placed an advertisement in that publication.

[8.509]

58 Acquisition of interest in premises run by management companies

(1) "Management company" means a company established for the purpose of—

(a) managing the common parts or fabric of premises used for residential or business purposes; or

(b) supplying services to such premises.

(2) The financial promotion restriction does not apply to any non-real time communication or solicited real time communication if it relates to an investment falling within paragraph 14 of Schedule 1 which—

(a) is issued, or to be issued, by a management company; and

(b) is to be acquired by any person in connection with the acquisition of an interest in the premises in question.

[8.510]

59 Annual accounts and directors' report

(1) If the requirements in paragraphs (2) to (5) are met, the financial promotion restriction does not apply to any communication by a body corporate (other than an open-ended investment company) which—

(a) consists of, or is accompanied by, the whole or any part of the annual accounts of a body corporate (other than an open-ended investment company); or

(b) is accompanied by any report which is prepared and approved by the directors of such a body corporate under—

[(ai) sections 414A and 414D of the 2006 Act;] [or]

[(i) sections 415 and 419 of the 2006 Act; . . .]

(ii), (iii) . . .

(2) The requirements of this paragraph are that the communication—

(a) does not contain any invitation to persons to underwrite, subscribe for, or otherwise acquire or dispose of, a controlled investment; and

(b) does not advise persons to engage in any of the activities within sub-paragraph (a).

(3) The requirements of this paragraph are that the communication does not contain any invitation to persons to—

(a) effect any transaction with the body corporate (or with any named person) in the course of that body's (or person's) carrying on of any activity falling within any of paragraphs 3 to [11A] of Schedule 1; or

(b) make use of any services provided by that body corporate (or by any named person) in the course of carrying on such activity.

(4) The requirements of this paragraph are that the communication does not contain any inducement relating to an investment other than one issued, or to be issued, by the body corporate (or another body corporate in the same group) which falls within—

(a) paragraph 14[, 15 or 15A] of Schedule 1; or

(b) paragraph 17 or 18 of that Schedule, so far as relating to any investments within sub-paragraph (a).

(5) The requirements of this paragraph are that the communication does not contain any reference to—

(a) the price at which investments issued by the body corporate have in the past been bought or sold; or

(b) the yield on such investments,

unless it is also accompanied by an indication that past performance cannot be relied on as a guide to future performance.

(6) For the purposes of paragraph (5)(b), a reference, in relation to an investment, to earnings, dividend or nominal rate of interest payable shall not be taken to be a reference to the yield on the investment.

(7) "Annual accounts" means—

(a) accounts produced by virtue of [Part 15 of the 2006 Act] (or of that Part as applied by virtue of any other enactment);

(b) . . .

(c) a summary financial statement prepared under [section 426 of the 2006 Act];

[(d) accounts produced in accordance with Chapter 3 of Part 5 of the Overseas Companies Regulations 2009 and filed with the registrar under section 441 of the 2006 Act as applied and modified by regulation 40 of those Regulations;]

(e) . . .

NOTES

Para (1) is amended as follows:

Sub-para (b)(ai) inserted by the Financial Services and Markets Act 2000 (Miscellaneous Provisions) (No 2) Order 2015, SI 2015/352, art 4(a), as from 18 March 2015.

The word "or" in square brackets at the end of sub-para (b)(ai) was inserted, the word omitted from sub-para (b)(i) was revoked, and sub-para (iii) was revoked, by the Financial Services and Markets Act 2000 (Amendment) (EU Exit) Regulations 2019, SI 2019/632, regs 162(1), 174(1), (2), as from IP completion day (as defined in the European Union (Withdrawal Agreement) Act 2020, s 39) (note that, by virtue of para (4) of reg 174, these amendments do not apply in relation to any report for a financial year beginning before IP completion day, and for further transitional provisions see the note on art 6 at **[8.448]**).

Sub-para (b)(i) was originally substituted by the Companies Act 2006 (Consequential Amendments and Transitional Provisions) Order 2011, SI 2011/1265, art 26(1), (7)(a), as from 12 May 2011.

Sub-para (b)(ii) was revoked by SI 2011/1265, art 26(1), (7)(b), as from 12 May 2011.

Para (3): figure in square brackets in sub-para (a) substituted by the Financial Services and Markets Act 2000 (Claims Management Activity) Order 2018, SI 2018/1253, arts 8, 33, as from 1 April 2019 (for full commencement details and for transitional provisions in relation to carrying on a claims management activity, etc, see arts 1, 39–89 of the 2018 Order).

Para (4): words in square brackets in sub-para (a) substituted by the Financial Services and Markets Act 2000 (Regulated Activities) (Amendment) Order 2010, SI 2010/86, art 4, Schedule, para 9(a)(v), as from 24 February 2010.

Para (7): the words in square brackets in sub-paras (a) and (c) were substituted, sub-para (b) was revoked, and sub-para (d) was substituted, by SI 2011/1265, art 26(1), (8) as from 12 May 2011. Sub-para (e) was revoked by SI 2019/632, regs 162(1), 172(1), (3), (4), as from IP completion day (as defined in the European Union (Withdrawal Agreement) Act 2020, s 39) (note that, by virtue of para (4) of reg 174, this amendment does not apply in relation to any report for a financial year beginning before IP completion day, and for further transitional provisions see the note on art 6 at **[8.448]**).

[8.511]

60 Participation in employee share schemes

(1) The financial promotion restriction does not apply to any communication by a person ("C"), a member of the same group as C or a relevant trustee where the communication is for the purposes of an employee share scheme and relates to any of the following investments issued, or to be issued, by C—

(a) investments falling within paragraph 14[, 15 or 15A] of Schedule 1;

(b) investments falling within paragraph 17 or 18 so far as relating to any investments within sub-paragraph (a); or

(c) investments falling within paragraph 21 or 27 so far as relating to any investments within sub-paragraph (a) or (b).

(2) "Employee share scheme", in relation to any investments issued by C, means arrangements made or to be made by C or by a person in the same group as C to enable or facilitate—

(a) transactions in the investments specified in paragraphs (1)(a) or (b) between or for the benefit of—

(i) the bona fide employees or former employees of C or of another member of the same group as C;

(ii) the wives, husbands, widows, widowers[, civil partners, surviving civil partners] or children or step-children under the age of eighteen of such employees or former employees; or

(b) the holding of those investments by, or for the benefit of, such persons.

(3) "Relevant trustee" means a person who, in pursuance of an actual or proposed employee share scheme, holds as trustee or will hold as trustee investments issued by C.

NOTES

Para (1): words in square brackets in sub-para (a) substituted by the Financial Services and Markets Act 2000 (Regulated Activities) (Amendment) Order 2010, SI 2010/86, art 4, Schedule, para 9(a)(vi), as from 24 February 2010.

Para (2): words in square brackets in sub-para (a)(ii) inserted by the Financial Services and Markets Act 2000 (Financial Promotion) (Amendment) Order 2005, SI 2005/3392, art 2(1), (4), as from 21 December 2005.

Step-children, etc: as to the meaning of this, and related expressions, see the Civil Partnership Act 2004, s 246 (as applied to this Order by the Civil Partnership Act 2004 (Relationships Arising Through Civil Partnership) Order 2005, SI 2005/3137, art 3, Schedule).

[8.512]

61 Sale of goods and supply of services

(1) In this article—

"supplier" means a person whose main business is to sell goods or supply services and not to carry on controlled activities [or controlled claims management activities] falling within any of paragraphs 3 to 7[, 10BA[, 10BB and 11A]] of Schedule 1 and, where the supplier is a member of a group, also means any other member of that group;

"customer" means a person, other than an individual, to whom a supplier sells goods or supplies services, or agrees to do so, and, where the customer is a member of a group, also means any other member of that group;

"a related sale or supply" means a sale of goods or supply of services to the customer otherwise than by the supplier, but for or in connection with the same purpose as the sale or supply mentioned above.

(2) The financial promotion restriction does not apply to any non-real time communication or any solicited real time communication made by a supplier to a customer of his for the purposes of, or in connection with, the sale of goods or supply of services or a related sale or supply.

(3) But the exemption in paragraph (2) does not apply if the communication relates to—

(a) a qualifying contract of insurance or units in a collective investment scheme; . . .

(b) investments falling within paragraph 27 of Schedule 1 so far as relating to investments within paragraph (a);

[(c) a relevant credit agreement (within the meaning of paragraph 28 of Schedule 1); or

(d) a consumer hire agreement (within the meaning of paragraph 28 of Schedule 1)].

[(4) The exemption in paragraph (2) also does not apply if the communication is made by a person carrying on, or in relation to, an activity of a kind specified in paragraph 4B of Schedule 1 (credit broking).]

NOTES

The words "or controlled claims management activities" in square brackets in the definition "supplier" in para (1) were inserted, and the words ", 10BB and 11A" in square brackets in that definition were substituted, by the Financial Services and Markets Act 2000 (Claims Management Activity) Order 2018, SI 2018/1253, arts 8, 34, as from 1 April 2019 (for full commencement details and for transitional provisions in relation to carrying on a claims management activity, etc, see arts 1, 39–89 of the 2018 Order).

The words in the second pair of square brackets in the definition "supplier" in para (1) were inserted, the word omitted from sub-para (3)(a) was revoked, and sub-paras (3)(c), (d) and para (4) were inserted and added respectively, by the Financial Services and Markets Act 2000 (Regulated Activities) (Amendment) Order 2014, SI 2014/366, art 10(1), (7), as from 1 April 2014.

[8.513]

62 Sale of body corporate

(1) The financial promotion restriction does not apply to any communication by, or on behalf of, a body corporate, a partnership, a single individual or a group of connected individuals which relates to a transaction falling within paragraph (2).

(2) A transaction falls within this paragraph if—

(a) it is one to acquire or dispose of shares in a body corporate other than an open-ended investment company, or is entered into for the purposes of such an acquisition or disposal; and

(b) either—

(i) the conditions set out in paragraph (3) are met; or

(ii) those conditions are not met, but the object of the transaction may nevertheless reasonably be regarded as being the acquisition of day to day control of the affairs of the body corporate.

(3) The conditions mentioned in paragraph (2)(b) are that—

(a) the shares consist of or include 50 per cent or more of the voting shares in the body corporate; or

(b) the shares, together with any already held by the person acquiring them, consist of or include at least that percentage of such shares; and

(c) in either case, the acquisition or disposal is, or is to be, between parties each of whom is a body corporate, a partnership, a single individual or a group of connected individuals.

(4) "A group of connected individuals" means—

(a) in relation to a party disposing of shares in a body corporate, a single group of persons each of whom is—

(i) a director or manager of the body corporate;

(ii) a close relative of any such director or manager; or

(iii) a person acting as trustee for, or nominee of, any person falling within paragraph (i) or (ii); and

(b) in relation to a party acquiring shares in a body corporate, a single group of persons each of whom is—

(i) a person who is or is to be a director or manager of the body corporate;

(ii) a close relative of any such person; or

(iii) a person acting as trustee for or nominee of any person falling within paragraph (i) or (ii).

(5) "Voting shares" in relation to a body corporate, means shares carrying voting rights attributable to share capital which are exercisable in all circumstances at any general meeting of that body corporate.

[8.514]

63 Takeovers of relevant unlisted companies: interpretation

(1) In this article and in articles 64, 65 and 66, a "relevant unlisted company", in relation to a takeover offer, means a company which is an unlisted company at the time that the offer is made and which has been an unlisted company throughout the period of ten years immediately preceding the date of the offer.

(2) In this article and in articles 64, 65 and 66, references to a takeover offer for a relevant unlisted company are references to an offer which meets the requirements of Part I of Schedule 4 and which is an offer—

(a) for all the shares in, or all the shares comprised in the equity or non-equity share capital of, a relevant unlisted company (other than any shares already held by or on behalf of the person making the offer); or

(b) for all the debentures of such a company (other than debentures already held by or on behalf of the person making the offer).

(3) Shares in or debentures of an unlisted company are to be regarded as being held by or on behalf of the person making the offer if the person who holds them, or on whose behalf they are held, has agreed that an offer should not be made in respect of them.

[8.515]

64 Takeovers of relevant unlisted companies

(1) If the requirements of paragraphs (2) and (3) are met, the financial promotion restriction does not apply to any communication which is communicated in connection with a takeover offer for a relevant unlisted company.

(2) The requirements of this paragraph are that the communication is accompanied by the material listed in Part II of Schedule 4.

(3) The requirements of this paragraph are that the material listed in Part III of Schedule 4 is available at a place in the United Kingdom at all times during normal office hours for inspection free of charge.

[8.516]

65 Takeovers of relevant unlisted companies: warrants etc

The financial promotion restriction does not apply to any communication which—

(a) is communicated at the same time as, or after, a takeover offer for a relevant unlisted company is made; and

(b) relates to investments falling within paragraph 17 or 18 of Schedule 1 so far as relating to the shares in or debentures of the unlisted company which are the subject of the offer.

[8.517]

66 Takeovers of relevant unlisted companies: application forms

The financial promotion restriction does not apply to any communication made in connection with a takeover offer for a relevant unlisted company which is a form of application for—

(a) shares in or debentures of the unlisted company; or

(b) investments falling within paragraphs 17 or 18 of Schedule 1 so far as relating to the shares in or debentures of the company which are the subject of the offer.

[8.518]

67 Promotions required or permitted by market rules

(1) The financial promotion restriction does not apply to any communication which—

(a) is a non-real time communication or a solicited real time communication;

(b) relates to an investment which falls within any of paragraphs 14 to 18 of Schedule 1 and which is permitted to be traded or dealt in on a relevant market; and

(c) is required or permitted to be communicated by—

(i) the rules of the relevant market;

(ii) a body which regulates the market; or

(iii) a body which regulates offers or issues of investments to be traded on such a market.

(2) "Relevant market" means a market which—

[(za) is a relevant UK market;]

(a) meets the criteria specified in Part I of Schedule 3; or

(b) is specified in, or established under the rules of an exchange specified in, Part . . . III of that Schedule.

NOTES

Para (2): sub-para (za) inserted by the Markets in Financial Instruments, Benchmarks and Financial Promotions (Amendment) (EU Exit) Regulations 2021, SI 2021/1074, reg 2(5), as from 18 October 2021. Words omitted revoked by the Financial Services and Markets Act 2000 (Regulated Activities) (Amendment) Order 2017, SI 2017/488, art 14, Schedule, para 9(1), (7), as from 3 January 2018.

[8.519]

68 Promotions in connection with admission to certain [UK and] EEA markets

(1) The financial promotion restriction does not apply to any communication—

(a) which is a non-real time communication or a solicited real time communication;

(b) which a relevant [UK market or relevant] EEA market requires to be communicated before an investment can be admitted to trading on that market;

(c) which, if it were included in a prospectus issued in accordance with prospectus rules made under Part VI of the Act, would be required to be communicated by those rules; and

(d) which is not accompanied by any information other than information which is required or permitted to be published by the rules of that market.

(2) In this article "relevant EEA market" means any market on which investments can be traded or dealt in and which—

(a) meets the criteria specified in Part I of Schedule 3; . . .

(b) . . .

NOTES

Article heading: words in square brackets inserted by the Markets in Financial Instruments, Benchmarks and Financial Promotions (Amendment) (EU Exit) Regulations 2021, SI 2021/1074, reg 2(6)(a), as from 18 October 2021.

Para (1): words in square brackets in sub-para (b) inserted by SI 2021/1074, reg 2(6)(b), as from 18 October 2021.

Para (2): sub-para (b) and the preceding word revoked by the Financial Services and Markets Act 2000 (Regulated Activities) (Amendment) Order 2017, SI 2017/488, art 14, Schedule, para 9(1), (8), as from 3 January 2018.

[8.520]

69 Promotions of securities already admitted to certain markets

(1) In this article—

"relevant investment" means any investment falling within—

(a) paragraph 14[, 15 or 15A] of Schedule 1; or

(b) paragraph 17 or 18 of that Schedule so far as relating to any investment mentioned in sub-paragraph (a);

"relevant market" means any market on which investments can be traded and which—

[(za) is a relevant UK market;]

(a) meets the criteria specified in Part I of Schedule 3; or

(b) is specified in, or established under, the rules of an exchange specified in, Part . . . III of that Schedule.

(2) If the requirements of paragraph (3) are met, the financial promotion restriction does not apply to any communication which—

(a) is a non-real time communication or a solicited real time communication;

(b) is communicated by a body corporate ("A"), other than an open-ended investment company; and

(c) relates only to relevant investments issued, or to be issued, by A or by another body corporate in the same group,

if relevant investments issued by A or by any such body corporate are permitted to be traded on a relevant market.

(3) The requirements of this paragraph are that the communication—

(a) is not, and is not accompanied by, an invitation to engage in investment activity;

(b) is not, and is not accompanied by, an inducement relating to an investment other than one issued, or to be issued, by A (or another body corporate in the same group);

(c) is not, and is not accompanied by, an inducement relating to a relevant investment which refers to—

(i) the price at which relevant investments have been bought or sold in the past, or

(ii) the yield on such investments,

unless the inducement also contains an indication that past performance cannot be relied on as a guide to future performance.

(4) For the purposes of this article, an investment falling within paragraph 17 or 18 of Schedule 1 is treated as issued by the person ("P") who issued the investment in respect of which the investment confers rights if it is issued by—

(a) an undertaking in the same group as P; or

(b) a person acting on behalf of, or pursuant to, arrangements made with P.

(5) For the purposes of paragraph (3)(a), "engaging in investment activity" has the meaning given in section 21(8) of the Act; and for the purposes of paragraph (3)(c)(ii), a reference, in relation to an investment, to earnings, dividend or nominal rate of interest payable shall not be taken to be a reference to the yield on the investment.

NOTES

Para (1) is amended as follows:

Words in square brackets in the definition "relevant investment" substituted by the Financial Services and Markets Act 2000 (Regulated Activities) (Amendment) Order 2010, SI 2010/86, art 4, Schedule, para 9(a), as from 24 February 2010.

Sub-para (za) of the definition "relevant market" was inserted by the Markets in Financial Instruments, Benchmarks and Financial Promotions (Amendment) (EU Exit) Regulations 2021, SI 2021/1074, reg 2(7), as from 18 October 2021.

Words omitted from sub-para (b) of the definition "relevant market" revoked by the Financial Services and Markets Act 2000 (Regulated Activities) (Amendment) Order 2017, SI 2017/488, art 14, Schedule, para 9(1), (9), as from 3 January 2018.

[8.521]

70 Promotions included in listing particulars etc

(1) The financial promotion restriction does not apply to any non-real time communication which is included in—

(a) listing particulars;

(b) supplementary listing particulars;

[(c) a prospectus or supplementary prospectus approved—

(i) by the [FCA] in accordance with Part 6 of the Act; . . .

(ii) . . .

or part of such a prospectus or supplementary prospectus; or]

(d) any other document required or permitted to be published by listing rules or prospectus rules under Part VI of the Act (except an advertisement within the meaning of [the prospectus regulation]).

[(1A) The financial promotion restriction does not apply to any non-real time communication—

(a) comprising the final terms of an offer or the final offer price or amount of securities which will be offered to the public; and

(b) complying with [Articles 8(1), 8(4), 8(5), 8(10), . . . 17 and 21(2) of the prospectus regulation].]

(2) In this article "listing particulars", "listing rules", "[the prospectus regulation]" and "prospectus rules" have the meaning given by Part VI of the Act.

NOTES

Para (1) is amended as follows:

Sub-para (c) substituted by the Financial Services and Markets Act 2000 (Financial Promotion) (Amendment No 2) Order 2007, SI 2007/2615, art 2(1), (2), as from 1 October 2007.

Word in square brackets in sub-para (c)(i) substituted by the Financial Services Act 2012 (Consequential Amendments and Transitional Provisions) Order 2013, SI 2013/472, art 3, Sch 2, para 108(c), as from 1 April 2013.

Sub-para (c)(ii) and the preceding word were revoked by the Prospectus (Amendment etc) (EU Exit) Regulations 2019, SI 2019/1234, reg 26(a), as from IP completion day (as defined in the European Union (Withdrawal Agreement) Act 2020, s 39); for transitional provisions, see regs 74, 75 of the 2019 Regulations at **[12.165]** et seq.

The words in square brackets in sub-para (d) were substituted by the Financial Services and Markets Act 2000 (Prospectus) Regulations 2019, SI 2019/1043, reg 38(1)(a), (b), as from 21 July 2019 (for transitional provisions in relation to a prospectus approved by the FCA, in accordance with Part 6 of FSMA 2000, before that date, see reg 40 of the 2019 Regulations at **[8.574]**).

Para (1A): inserted by SI 2007/2615, art 2(1), (3), as from 1 October 2007. The words in square brackets were substituted by SI 2019/1043, reg 38(1)(c), as from 21 July 2019 (for transitional provisions, see the first note relating to the 2019 Regulations above). The omitted was revoked by SI 2019/1234, reg 26(b), as from IP completion day (as defined in the European Union (Withdrawal Agreement) Act 2020, s 39); for transitional provisions, see regs 74, 75 of the 2019 Regulations at **[12.165]** et seq.

Para (2): words in square brackets substituted by SI 2019/1043, reg 38(1)(d), as from 21 July 2019 (for transitional provisions, see the first note relating to the 2019 Regulations above).

[8.522]

71 Material relating to prospectus for public offer of unlisted securities

(1) The financial promotion restriction does not apply to any non-real time communication relating to a prospectus or supplementary prospectus where the only reason for considering it to be an invitation or inducement is that it does one or more of the following—

(a) it states the name and address of the person by whom the transferable securities to which the prospectus or supplementary prospectus relates are to be offered;

(b) it gives other details for contacting that person;

(c) it states the nature and the nominal value of the transferable securities to which the prospectus or supplementary prospectus relates, the number offered and the price at which they are offered;

(d) it states that a prospectus or supplementary prospectus is or will be available (and, if it is not yet available, when it is expected to be);

(e) it gives instructions for obtaining a copy of the prospectus or supplementary prospectus.

(2) In this article—

(a) "transferable securities" has the same meaning as in section 102A(3) of the Act;

(b) references to a prospectus or supplementary prospectus are references to a prospectus or supplementary prospectus which is published in accordance with prospectus rules made under Part VI of the Act.

[8.523]

72 Pension products offered by employers

(1) If the requirements of paragraph (2) are met, the financial promotion restriction does not apply to any communication which is made by an employer to an employee in relation to a group personal pension scheme or a stakeholder pension scheme.

(2) The requirements of this paragraph are that—

(a) the employer will make a contribution to the group personal pension scheme or stakeholder pension scheme to which the communication relates in the event of the employee becoming a member of the scheme and the communication contains a statement informing the employee of this;

[(b) the employer has not received, and will not receive, any direct financial benefit as a result of making the communication;]

(c) the employer notifies the employee in writing prior to the employee becoming a member of the scheme of the amount of the contribution that the employer will make to the scheme in respect of that employee [or the basis on which the contribution will be calculated]; and

(d) in the case of a non-real time communication, the communication contains, or is accompanied by, a statement informing the employee of his right to seek advice from an authorised person or an appointed representative.

(3) . . .

(4) In this article—

"group personal pension scheme" means arrangements administered on a group basis under a personal pension scheme and which are available to employees of the same employer or of employers within a group;

["personal pension scheme" means a scheme or arrangement which is not an occupational pension scheme or a stakeholder pension scheme and which is comprised in one or more instruments or agreements, having or capable of having effect so as to provide benefits to or in respect of people—

(a) on retirement,

(b) on having reached a particular age, or

(c) on termination of service in an employment.]

"stakeholder pension scheme" has the meaning given by section 1 of the Welfare Reform and Pensions Act 1999.

NOTES

Para (2): sub-para (b) substituted, and words in square brackets in sub-para (c) inserted, by the Financial Services and Markets Act 2000 (Financial Promotion) (Amendment) Order 2010, SI 2010/905, arts 2, 4(a), as from 13 April 2010.

Para (3): revoked by SI 2010/905, arts 2, 4(b), as from 13 April 2010.

Para (4): definition "personal pension scheme" substituted by the Financial Services and Markets Act 2000 (Regulated Activities) (Amendment) Order 2006, SI 2006/1969, art 12(1), (2), as from 6 April 2007.

[8.524]

[72A Pension product offers communicated to employees by third parties

(1) If the requirements of paragraph (2) are met, the financial promotion restriction does not apply to any communication which is made to an employee by or on behalf of a person ("A") in relation to a group personal pension scheme or a stakeholder pension scheme.

(2) The requirements of this paragraph are that—

(a) the employer and A have entered into a written contract specifying the terms on which the communication may be made;

(b) in the case of a communication made by a person ("B") on behalf of A, A and B have also entered into a written contract specifying the terms on which the communication may be made;

(c) the employer has not received, and will not receive, any direct financial benefit as a result of the communication being made;

(d) the employer will make a contribution to the scheme in the event of the employee becoming a member of the scheme and the communication contains a statement informing the employee of this;

(e) in the case of a non-real time communication, the communication contains, or is accompanied by, a statement informing the employee of their right to seek advice from an authorised person or an appointed representative; and

(f) the employer or A notifies the employee in writing prior to the employee becoming a member of the scheme of—

(i) the amount of the contribution that the employer will make to the scheme in respect of that employee, or the basis on which the contribution will be calculated; and

(ii) any remuneration A or B has received, or will receive, as a consequence of the employee becoming a member of the scheme, or the basis on which any such remuneration will be calculated.

(3) In this article "group personal pension scheme" and "stakeholder pension scheme" have the meaning given by article 72(4).]

NOTES

Inserted, together with arts 72B–72E, by the Financial Services and Markets Act 2000 (Financial Promotion) (Amendment) Order 2010, SI 2010/905, arts 2, 5, as from 13 April 2010.

[8.525]
[72B Insurance product offers communicated to employees by employers

(1) If the requirements of paragraph (2) are met, the financial promotion restriction does not apply to any communication which is made by an employer to an employee in relation to work-related insurance.

(2) The requirements of this paragraph are that—

(a) where the provider of the insurance is not the employer, the employer has not received, and will not receive, any direct financial benefit as a result of making the communication; and

(b) in the case of a non-real time communication, the communication contains, or is accompanied by, a statement informing the employee of their right to seek advice from an authorised person or an appointed representative.

(3) In this article "work-related insurance" includes—

(a) life assurance;

(b) long term disability insurance (also known as permanent health insurance); and

(c) accidental death, injury, critical illness, medical, dental, income protection or travel insurance.]

NOTES

Inserted as noted to art 72A at **[8.524]**.

[8.526]
[72C Insurance product offers communicated to employees by third parties

(1) If the requirements of paragraph (2) are met, the financial promotion restriction does not apply to any communication which is made to an employee by or on behalf of a person ("A") in relation to work-related insurance.

(2) The requirements of this paragraph are that—

(a) the employer and A have entered into a written contract specifying the terms on which the communication may be made;

(b) in the case of a communication made by a person ("B") on behalf of A, A and B have also entered into a written contract specifying the terms on which the communication may be made;

(c) the employer has not received, and will not receive, any direct financial benefit as a result of the communication being made;

(d) in the case of a non-real time communication, the communication contains, or is accompanied by, a statement informing the employee of their right to seek advice from an authorised person or an appointed representative; and

(e) the employer or A notifies the employee in writing prior to the employee entering into a contract for the work-related insurance of any remuneration A or B has received, or will receive, as a consequence of the employee entering into the contract, or the basis on which any such remuneration will be calculated.

(3) In this article "work-related insurance" has the meaning given by article 72B(3).]

NOTES

Inserted as noted to art 72A at **[8.524]**.

[8.527]
[72D Staff mortgage offers communicated to employees by employers

(1) If the requirements of paragraph (2) are met, the financial promotion restriction does not apply to any communication which is made by an employer to an employee in relation to a staff mortgage.

(2) The requirements of this paragraph are that—

(a) where the provider of the staff mortgage is an undertaking in the same group as the employer, the employer has not received, and will not receive, any direct financial benefit as a result of making the communication; and

(b) in the case of a non-real time communication, the communication contains or is accompanied by a statement informing the employee of their right to seek advice from an authorised person or an appointed representative.

(3) In this article, "staff mortgage" means a regulated mortgage contract between the employer, or an undertaking in the same group as the employer, as lender and the employee (alone or with another person) as borrower to defray money applied for any of the following purposes—

(a) acquiring any residential land which was intended, at the time of the acquisition, for occupation by the employee as their home;

(b) carrying out repairs or improvements to any residential land which was intended, at the time of taking out the loan, for occupation by the employee as their home; or

(c) payments in respect of a loan (whether of interest or capital).

(4) In this article, "borrower", "lender" and "regulated mortgage contract" have the meaning given by article 61(3)(a) (regulated mortgage contracts) of the Financial Services and Markets Act 2000 (Regulated Activities) Order 2001.]

NOTES

Inserted as noted to art 72A at **[8.524]**.

[8.528]
[72E Staff mortgage offers communicated to employees by third parties

(1) If the requirements of paragraph (2) are met, the financial promotion restriction does not apply to any communication which is made to an employee by or on behalf of a person ("A") in relation to a staff mortgage.

(2) The requirements of this paragraph are that—

(a) the employer and A have entered into a written contract specifying the terms on which the communication may be made;

(b) in the case of a communication made by a person ("B") on behalf of A, A and B have also entered into a written contract specifying the terms on which the communication may be made;

(c) where the provider of the staff mortgage is an undertaking in the same group as the employer, the employer has not received, and will not receive, any direct financial benefit as a result of the communication being made;

(d) in the case of a non-real time communication, the communication contains, or is accompanied by, a statement informing the employee of their right to seek advice from an authorised person or an appointed representative; and

(e) the employer or A notifies the employee in writing prior to the employee entering into the staff mortgage of any remuneration A or B has received, or will receive, as a consequence of the employee entering into the staff mortgage, or the basis on which any such remuneration will be calculated.

(3) In this article "staff mortgage" has the same meaning as in article 72D(3).]

NOTES

Inserted as noted to art 72A at **[8.524]**.

[8.529]

[72F Credit agreements offered to employees by employers

(1) The financial promotion restriction does not apply to any communication which is made to an employee by or on behalf of a person in relation to an exempt staff loan.

(2) In this article, "an exempt staff loan" means a credit agreement within the meaning of article 60B (regulated credit agreements) of the Regulated Activities Order which is—

[(a) offered by a lender to a borrower as an incident of employment with the lender, or with an undertaking in the same group as the lender; and]

(b) an exempt agreement for the purposes of Chapter 14A (regulated credit agreements) of the Regulated Activities Order by virtue of a provision of article 60G (exempt agreements: exemptions relating to the total charge for credit) of that Order other than paragraph (2) of that article.]

NOTES

Inserted by the Financial Services and Markets Act 2000 (Consumer Credit) (Miscellaneous Provisions) Order 2014, SI 2014/208, art 4, as from 1 April 2014.

Para (2): sub-para (a) substituted by the Financial Services and Markets Act 2000 (Miscellaneous Provisions) Order 2015, SI 2015/853, art 4(1), (3), as from 24 March 2015.

[8.530]

73 Advice centres

(1) If the requirements of paragraph (2) are met, the financial promotion restriction does not apply to any communication which is made by a person in the course of carrying out his duties as an adviser for, or employee of, an advice centre.

(2) The requirements of this paragraph are that the communication relates to—

(a) qualifying credit;

(b) rights under, or rights to or interests in rights under, qualifying contracts of insurance; . . .

(c) a child trust fund[;

(d) a regulated home reversion plan; . . .

(e) a regulated home purchase plan][

(f) a regulated sale and rent back agreement][; or

(g) a controlled claims management activity].

(3) In this article—

"adequate professional indemnity insurance", in relation to an advice centre, means insurance providing cover that is adequate having regard to—

(a) the claims record of the centre;

(b) the financial resources of the centre; and

(c) the right of clients of the centre to be compensated for loss arising from the negligent provision of financial advice;

"advice centre" means a body which—

(a) gives advice which is free and in respect of which the centre does not receive any fee, commission or other reward;

(b) provides debt advice as its principal financial services activity; and

(c) in the case of a body which is not part of a local authority, holds adequate professional indemnity insurance or a guarantee providing comparable cover;

"child trust fund" has the meaning given by section 1(2) of the Child Trust Funds Act 2004;

"local authority" has the meaning given in article 2 of the Financial Services and Markets Act 2000 (Exemption) Order 2001.

NOTES

Para (2): word omitted from sub-para (b) revoked, and sub-paras (d), (e) inserted, by the Financial Services and Markets Act 2000 (Regulated Activities) (Amendment) (No 2) Order 2006, SI 2006/2383, art 35(1), (4), as from 6 April 2007. Word omitted from sub-para (d) revoked, and sub-para (f) (and the preceding word) inserted, by the Financial Services and Markets Act 2000 (Regulated Activities) (Amendment) Order 2009, SI 2009/1342, art 30(1), (3), as from 1 July 2009 (certain purposes), and as from 30 June 2010 (otherwise). Word omitted from sub-para (e) revoked, and sub-para (g) (and the preceding word) inserted, by the Financial Services and Markets Act 2000 (Claims Management Activity) Order 2018, SI 2018/1253, arts 8, 35, as from 1 April 2019 (for full commencement details and for transitional provisions in relation to carrying on a claims management activity, etc, see arts 1, 39–89 of the 2018 Order).

[PART 6A EXEMPT COMMUNICATIONS: CONTROLLED CLAIMS MANAGEMENT ACTIVITIES

[8.531]
73A Application of exemptions in this Part

The exemptions in this Part apply to any communication which relates to a controlled claims management activity of a kind specified in paragraph 11A of Schedule 1.]

NOTES

Part 6A (arts 73A–73J) was inserted by the Financial Services and Markets Act 2000 (Claims Management Activity) Order 2018, SI 2018/1253, arts 8, 36, as from 1 April 2019 (for full commencement details and for transitional provisions in relation to carrying on a claims management activity, etc, see arts 1, 39–89 of the 2018 Order).

[8.532]
[73B Communications made by legal professionals

(1) The financial promotion restriction does not apply to any communication which relates to a controlled claims management activity when that communication is made in England and Wales by—

- (a) a legal practitioner;
- (b) a firm, organisation or body corporate that carries on the controlled claims management activity through a legal practitioner; or
- (c) an individual who carries on the controlled claims management activity at the direction of, and under the supervision of, a legal practitioner who is—
  - (i) that individual's employer or fellow employee; or
  - (ii) a director of a company, or a member of a limited liability partnership, that provides the service and is that individual's employer.

(2) In paragraph (1) "legal practitioner" means—

- (a) a solicitor or barrister of any part of England and Wales or Northern Ireland;
- (b) a Fellow of the Chartered Institute of Legal Executives;
- (c) a European lawyer, as defined in the European Communities (Services of Lawyers) Order 1978 or the European Communities (Lawyer's Practice) Regulations 2000;
- (d) a registered foreign lawyer, as defined in section 89(9) of the Courts and Legal Services Act 1990;
- (e) any other member of a legal profession, of a jurisdiction other than England and Wales, that is recognised by the Law Society of England and Wales or the General Council of the Bar as a regulated legal profession.

(3) The financial promotion restriction does not apply to a communication which relates to a controlled claims management activity when that communication is made in Scotland by—

- (a) a legal practitioner;
- (b) a firm, organisation or body corporate that carries on the controlled claims management activity through or under the supervision of a legal practitioner where that firm, organisation or body corporate is—
  - (i) a firm of solicitors;
  - (ii) an incorporated practice; or
  - (iii) a licensed legal services provider and the activity is a legal service as defined within section 3 of the Legal Services (Scotland) Act 2010.

(4) In paragraph (3) "legal practitioner" means—

- (a) a person who is qualified to practise as a solicitor under section 4 of the Solicitors (Scotland) Act 1980;
- (b) an advocate who is a member of the Faculty of Advocates;
- (c) a European lawyer as defined in the European Communities (Services of Lawyers) Order 1978 or the European Communities (Lawyer's Practice) (Scotland) Regulations 2000; or
- (d) a registered foreign lawyer within the meaning of section 65 of the Solicitors (Scotland) Act 1980.

(5) A communication mentioned in paragraph (1) or (3) is only excluded from the financial promotion restriction if the legal practitioner concerned carries on the controlled claims management activity in the ordinary course of legal practice pursuant to the professional rules to which that legal practitioner is subject.]

NOTES

Inserted as noted to art 73A at **[8.531]**.

[8.533]
[73C Communications made by a charity or not-for-profit agency

(1) The financial promotion restriction does not apply to any communication which relates to a controlled claims management activity when that communication is made by a charity or not-for-profit agency.

(2) In this article "charity" means—

- (a) a charity as defined by section 1(1) of the Charities Act 2011 or the Charities and Trustee Investment (Scotland) Act 2005; or
- (b) a body registered in the Scottish Charity Register.

(3) In this article "not-for-profit agency" means a body that by or under its constitution—

- (a) is required to apply the whole of its net income, and any expendable capital, after payment of outgoings for charitable or public purposes; and
- (b) is prohibited from distributing, directly or indirectly, any part of its net income by way of profits or its assets among any of its members.

(4) But a body is not prevented from being a not-for-profit agency for the purposes of paragraph (3) if its constitution permits—

- (a) the payment, out of the body's funds, of reasonable and proper remuneration for goods or services supplied to the body by a member; or
- (b) in the case of a not-for-profit body that is a charity, the payment to a member to which the member is eligible because that member is a beneficiary of the charity; or

(c) the purchase, out of the body's funds, of indemnity insurance for trustees of the body.]

NOTES

Inserted as noted to art 73A at **[8.531]**.

[8.534]

[73D Communications made by a person appointed by a statutory or other public body

The financial promotion restriction does not apply to any communication which relates to a controlled claims management activity when that communication is made by—

(a) any person established or appointed by virtue of an enactment;
(b) an Independent Complaints Reviewer; or
(c) an Independent Case Examiner

when the communication is made in the course of carrying out that individual's duties.]

NOTES

Inserted as noted to art 73A at **[8.531]**.

[8.535]

[73E Communications made by the Motor Insurers' Bureau

The financial promotion restriction does not apply to any communication which relates to a controlled claims management activity when that communication is made by the Motor Insurers' Bureau in the course of carrying its functions (being the company limited by guarantee mentioned in section 95(2) (notification of refusal of insurance on grounds of health) of the Road Traffic Act 1988).]

NOTES

Inserted as noted to art 73A at **[8.531]**.

[8.536]

[73F Communications made by a medical defence union

The financial promotion restriction does not apply to any communication which relates to a controlled claims management activity when that communication is made by—

(a) the Medical Protection Society Limited for its members;
(b) the Medical Defence Union Limited for its members; or
(c) the Medical and Dental Defence Union of Scotland Limited for its members.]

NOTES

Inserted as noted to art 73A at **[8.531]**.

[8.537]

[73G Communications made by an independent trade union

(1) The financial promotion restriction does not apply to any communication which relates to a controlled claims management activity when that communication is made by an independent trade union for—

(a) a member (including a retired member or a student member) of an independent trade union;
(b) a member of the family of a member referred to in sub-paragraph (a); or
(c) a former member of the trade union to whom the trade union may, under its rules, provide claims management services, or a member of the family of such a former member.

(2) In paragraph (1) "independent trade union" has the same meaning as in the Trade Union and Labour Relations (Consolidation) Act 1992.

(3) For the purposes of paragraph (1)—

(a) subject to sub-paragraph (b), whether a person is or has been a member (including a retired member or a student member) of a trade union is to be decided in accordance with the rules of that trade union;
(b) "member" of a trade union does not include a person who, under those rules, is a member only for the purpose of pursuing a claim or claims; and
(c) whether a person is a member of the family of a member of a trade union is to be decided in accordance with the rules of that trade union.

(4) An exemption of a trade union under this article is subject to compliance by the trade union with the condition that the trade union, in making a communication which relates to a controlled claims management activity, must act in accordance with the code of practice for the provision of regulated claims management activities by trade unions issued by the Treasury.]

NOTES

Inserted as noted to art 73A at **[8.531]**.

[8.538]

[73H Communications made by a students' union

(1) The financial promotion restriction does not apply to any communication which relates to a controlled claims management activity when that communication is made by a students' union for a member of that students' union or a member of a constituent or affiliated association or body.

(2) In this article "students' union" has the meaning given by section 20 (meaning of "students' union") of the Education Act 1994.]

NOTES

Inserted as noted to art 73A at **[8.531]**.

[8.539]
[73I Communications made by an insurance intermediary

The financial promotion restriction does not apply to any communication which relates to a controlled claims management activity when that communication is made by a person who has permission to carry out a regulated activity of the kind specified in article 21, 25, 39A, 53 or 64 of the Regulated Activities Order in relation to a contract of insurance.]

NOTES

Inserted as noted to art 73A at **[8.531]**.

[8.540]
[73J Communications made by certain providers of referrals

(1) The financial promotion restriction does not apply to any communication which relates to the controlled claims management activity falling within paragraph 11A(2) of Schedule 1 of referring the details of a potential claim or potential claimant to another person if—

(a) the person who refers those details ("the introducer") carries on no other regulated claims management service;
(b) the activity is incidental to the introducer's main business;
(c) the details are only referred to authorised persons, legal practitioners, or a firm, organisation or body corporate that provides the service through legal practitioners;
(d) of the claims that the introducer refers to such persons, that introducer is paid, in money or money's worth, for no more than 25 claims per calendar quarter; and
(e) the introducer, in obtaining and referring those details has complied with the provisions of the Data Protection Act 2018, the Privacy and Electronic Communications (EC Directive) Regulations 2003, the General Data Protection Regulation (EU) of the European Parliament and of the Council 2016/679 and the Consumer Protection from Unfair Trading Regulations 2008.

(2) Paragraph 1(e) does not apply in the case of a referral to a legal practitioner or firm, organisation or body corporate that carries on the activity through legal practitioners.

(3) In this article "legal practitioner" has the meaning given by article 73B(2) or (4).]

NOTES

Inserted as noted to art 73A at **[8.531]**.

[PART 7 REVOCATIONS]

[8.541]
74 Revocation

The Orders specified in the first column of Schedule 6 are revoked to the extent specified in the third column of that Schedule.

NOTES

The Part 7 number and title above were inserted by the Financial Services and Markets Act 2000 (Claims Management Activity) Order 2018, SI 2018/1253, arts 8, 37, as from 1 April 2019 (for full commencement details and for transitional provisions in relation to carrying on a claims management activity, etc, see arts 1, 39–89 of the 2018 Order).

SCHEDULES

SCHEDULE 1

Article 4

PART I CONTROLLED ACTIVITIES

[8.542]
1 Accepting deposits

Accepting deposits is a controlled activity if—

(a) money received by way of deposit is lent to others; or
(b) any other activity of the person accepting the deposit is financed wholly, or to a material extent, out of the capital of or interest on money received by way of deposit,

and the person accepting the deposit holds himself out as accepting deposits on a day to day basis.

2 Effecting or carrying out contracts of insurance

(1) Effecting a contract of insurance as principal is a controlled activity.

(2) Carrying out a contract of insurance as principal is a controlled activity.

(3) There is excluded from sub-paragraph (1) or (2) the effecting or carrying out of a contract of insurance of the kind described in article 12 of the Regulated Activities Order by a person who does not otherwise carry on an activity falling within those sub-paragraphs.

3 Dealing in securities and contractually based investments

(1) Buying, selling, subscribing for or underwriting securities[, structured deposits] or contractually based investments . . . as principal or agent is a controlled activity.

(2) A person does not carry on the activity in sub-paragraph (1) by accepting an instrument creating or acknowledging indebtedness in respect of any loan, credit, guarantee or other similar financial accommodation or assurance which he has made, granted or provided.

(3) The reference in sub-paragraph (2) to a person accepting an instrument includes a reference to a person becoming a party to an instrument otherwise than as a debtor or a surety.

4 Arranging deals in investments

(1) Making arrangements for another person (whether as principal or agent) to buy, sell, subscribe for or underwrite a particular investment which is—

(a) a security;

[(aa) a structured deposit;]

(b) a contractually based investment; or

(c) an investment of the kind specified by paragraph 24, or paragraph 27 so far as relevant to that paragraph,

is a controlled activity.

(2) Making arrangements with a view to a person who participates in the arrangements buying, selling, subscribing for or underwriting investments falling within sub-paragraph (1)(a), [(aa),] (b) or (c) (whether as principal or agent) is a controlled activity.

(3) A person does not carry on an activity falling within paragraph (2) merely by providing means by which one party to a transaction (or potential transaction) is able to communicate with other such parties.

[4AA Operating an organised trading facility

Operating an organised trading facility on which non-equity MiFID instruments are traded is a controlled activity.]

[4A Operating a multilateral trading facility

Operating a multilateral trading facility on which MiFID instruments are traded is a controlled activity.]

[4B Credit broking

(1) Each of the following is a controlled activity—

(a) effecting an introduction of an individual or relevant recipient of credit to a person who enters into as lender relevant credit agreements [(other than credit agreements which are exempt agreements under the relevant provisions)] by way of business;

[(b) effecting an introduction of an individual or relevant recipient of credit to a person who, by way of business, enters into as owner regulated consumer hire agreements or agreements which would be regulated consumer hire agreements but for article 60O (exempt agreements: exemptions relating to nature of agreement) or article 60Q (exempt agreements: exemptions relating to the nature of the hirer) of the Regulated Activities Order;]

(c) effecting an introduction of an individual or relevant recipient of credit to a person who carries on an activity of the kind specified in paragraph (a) or (b) by way of business;

(d) presenting or offering an agreement which would (if entered into) be a relevant credit agreement [(other than a credit agreement which is an exempt agreement under the relevant provisions)] to an individual or relevant recipient of credit;

(e) assisting an individual or relevant recipient of credit by undertaking preparatory work in respect of a relevant credit agreement [(other than a credit agreement which is an exempt agreement under the relevant provisions)];

(f) entering into a relevant credit agreement [(other than a credit agreement which is an exempt agreement under the relevant provisions)] on behalf of a lender.

[(1A) But an activity is not a controlled activity falling within sub-paragraph (1) to the extent that it is a controlled activity falling within paragraph 10A (arranging qualifying credit etc).]

[(2) For the purposes of paragraph (1)—

(a) "relevant provisions" are article 60E(5) (exempt agreements: exemptions relating to the nature of the lender) and article 60F(exempt agreements: exemptions relating to number of repayments to be made) of the Regulated Activities Order;

(b) it is immaterial whether the relevant credit agreement or the consumer hire agreement is subject to the law of a country other than the United Kingdom.]

4C Operating an electronic system in relation to lending

(1) Where the [conditions in sub-paragraphs (2), (2A) and (2C) are] satisfied, operating an electronic system which enables the operator ("A") to facilitate persons ("B" and "C") becoming the lender and borrower under a paragraph 4C agreement is a controlled activity.

(2) The condition [in this sub-paragraph] is that the system operated by A is capable of determining which agreements should be made available to each of B and C (whether in accordance with general instructions provided to A by B or C or otherwise).

[(2A) The condition in this sub-paragraph is that A, or another person ("X") acting under an arrangement with A or at A's direction, undertakes to—

(a) receive payments in respect of [either interest or capital or both] due under the agreement from C, and

(b) make payments in respect of [either interest or capital or both] due under the agreement to B.

(2B) For the purposes of sub-paragraph (2A)—

(a) an agreement by A to appoint X to perform the activities in that paragraph is to be treated as an undertaking by A within the meaning of that sub-paragraph;

(b) it is immaterial that—

(i) payments may be subject to conditions;

(ii) A, or X, may be entitled to retain a portion or the entirety of any payment received from C.

(2C) The condition in this sub-paragraph is that A, or another person ("X") acting under an arrangement with A or at A's direction, undertakes to perform, or A undertakes to appoint or direct another person to perform, either or both of the following—

(a) to take steps to procure the payment of a debt under the agreement;

(b) to exercise or enforce rights under the agreement on behalf of B.]

[(2D) Where A carries on the activity specified by sub-paragraph (1), it is a controlled activity for A to operate an electronic system where—

(a) that system enables A to facilitate a person ("B") assuming the rights of the lender under a paragraph 4C agreement by assignment or operation of law, and

(b) the conditions in sub-paragraphs (2), (2A) and (2C) are satisfied where C is the borrower under the agreement in paragraph (a).]

(3) The following are controlled activities if carried on by A in the course of, or in connection with, the carrying on by A of the activity specified by [sub-paragraph] (1) [or (2D)]—

(a) presenting or offering paragraph 4C agreements to [either B or C] with a view to B becoming the lender under the paragraph 4C agreement [or] C becoming the borrower under the paragraph 4C agreement,

(b) furnishing information relevant to the financial standing of a person ("Y") with a view to assisting in the determination as to whether another person should—

(i) enter into, as the lender, a paragraph 4C agreement with Y, or

(ii) assume the rights of the lender under a paragraph 4C agreement under which Y is the borrower,

(c) taking steps to procure the payment of a debt due under a paragraph 4C agreement,

(d) [taking steps to perform duties, or exercise or enforce] rights under a paragraph 4C agreement on behalf of the lender,

(e) [taking steps with a view to] ascertaining whether a credit information agency (within the meaning given by article 89A(6)) holds information relevant to the financial standing of an individual or relevant person,

(f) [taking steps with a view to] ascertaining the contents of such information,

(g) [taking steps with a view to] securing the correction of, the omission of anything from, or the making of any other kind of modification of, such information, . . .

(h) [taking steps with a view to] securing that a credit information agency which holds such information—

(i) stops holding the information, or

(ii) does not provide it to any other person[, or

(i) giving advice in relation to the taking of any of the steps in sub-paragraphs (e) to (h)].

[(4) A "paragraph 4C agreement" is an agreement by which one person provides another person with credit and in relation to which—

(a) the condition in sub-paragraph (4A) is satisfied, and

(b) the condition in either sub-paragraph (5) or (6) is satisfied, or was satisfied at the time the agreement was entered into.

(4A) The condition in this sub-paragraph is that A does not provide credit, assume the rights (by assignment or operation of law) of a person who provided credit, or receive credit under the agreement.]

(5) The condition in this [sub-paragraph] is that the lender is an individual or relevant person.

(6) The condition in this [sub-paragraph] is that the borrower is an individual or relevant person and—

(a) the lender provides the borrower with credit less than or equal to £25,000, or

(b) the agreement is not entered into by the borrower wholly or predominantly for the purposes of a business carried on, or intended to be carried on, by the borrower.

(7) Paragraphs (5) and (6) of article 60C of the Regulated Activities Order (exempt agreements: exemptions relating to nature of agreement) apply for the purposes of paragraph (6)(b).

(8) It is immaterial for the purposes of this paragraph whether the lender is carrying on a regulated activity.

[(9) In this paragraph—

"assignment", in relation to Scotland, means assignation;

"borrower" means a person who receives credit under a paragraph 4C agreement or a person to whom the rights and duties of a borrower under such an agreement have passed by assignment or operation of law;

"credit" has the meaning given by article 60L of the Regulated Activities Order;

"lender" means—

(a) a person providing credit under a paragraph 4C agreement, or

(b) a person who by assignment or operation of law has assumed the rights of a person who provided credit under such an agreement;

"relevant person" means—

(a) a partnership consisting of two or three persons not all of whom are bodies corporate, or

(b) an unincorporated body of persons which does not consist entirely of bodies corporate and is not a partnership].

"(10) For the purposes of the application of section 21(9) and (10) of the Act (restrictions on financial promotion) to an activity of a kind specified by this paragraph, paragraph 26D of this Schedule (relevant credit agreements), and article 4 (definition of controlled activities and controlled investments) in so far as it relates to that paragraph, [have] effect as if the reference to a relevant credit agreement in paragraph 26D includes a reference to a paragraph 4C agreement.]]

5 Managing investments

Managing assets belonging to another person, in circumstances involving the exercise of discretion, is a controlled activity if—

(a) the assets consist of or include any investment which is a security[, structured deposit] or a contractually based investment; or

(b) the arrangements for their management are such that the assets may consist of or include such investments, and either the assets have at any time since 29th April 1988 done so, or the arrangements have at any time (whether before or after that date) been held out as arrangements under which the assets would do so.

[5A Debt adjusting

(1) The following activities are, when carried on in relation to debts due under a relevant credit agreement, controlled activities—

(a) negotiating with the lender, on behalf of the borrower, terms for the discharge of a debt;
(b) taking over, in return for payments by the borrower, that person's obligation to discharge a debt;
(c) any similar activity concerned with the liquidation of a debt.

(2) The following activities are, when carried on in relation to debts due under a consumer hire agreement, controlled activities—

(a) negotiating with the owner, on behalf of the hirer, terms for the discharge of a debt;
(b) taking over, in return for payments by the hirer, that person's obligation to discharge a debt;
(c) any similar activity concerned with the liquidation of a debt.

5B Debt-counselling

(1) Advising a borrower about the liquidation of a debt due under a relevant credit agreement is a controlled activity.

(2) Advising a hirer about the liquidation of a debt due under a consumer hire agreement is a controlled activity.]

6 Safeguarding and administering investments

(1) The activity consisting of both—

(a) the safeguarding of assets belonging to another; and
(b) the administration of those assets,

or arranging for one or more other persons to carry on that activity, is a controlled activity if either the condition in paragraph (a) or (b) of sub-paragraph (2) is met.

(2) The condition is that—

(a) the assets consist of or include any investment which is a security or a contractually based investment; or
(b) the arrangements for their safeguarding and administration are such that the assets may consist of or include investments of the kind mentioned in sub-paragraph (a) and either the assets have at any time since 1st June 1997 done so, or the arrangements have at any time (whether before or after that date) been held out as ones under which such investments would be safeguarded and administered.

(3) For the purposes of this article—

(a) it is immaterial that title to the assets safeguarded and administered is held in uncertificated form;
(b) it is immaterial that the assets safeguarded and administered may be transferred to another person, subject to a commitment by the person safeguarding and administering them, or arranging for their safeguarding and administration, that they will be replaced by equivalent assets at some future date or when so requested by the person to whom they belong.

(4) For the purposes of this article, the following activities do not constitute the administration of assets—

(a) providing information as to the number of units or the value of any assets safeguarded;
(b) converting currency;
(c) receiving documents relating to an investment solely for the purpose of onward transmission to, from or at the direction of the person to whom the investment belongs.

7 Advising on investments

[(1)] Advising a person is a controlled activity if the advice is—

(a) given to the person in his capacity as an investor or potential investor, or in his capacity as agent for an investor or a potential investor; and
(b) advice on the merits of his doing any of the following (whether as principal or agent)—
 (i) buying, selling, subscribing for or underwriting a particular investment which is a security[, structured deposit] or a contractually based investment; or
 (ii) exercising any right conferred by such an investment to buy, sell, subscribe for or underwrite such an investment.

[(2) Advising a person is a controlled activity if the advice is—

(a) given to the person in that person's capacity as a lender or potential lender under a relevant paragraph 4C agreement, or in that person's capacity as an agent for a lender or potential lender under such an agreement; and
(b) advice on the merits of the person doing any of the following (whether as principal or agent)—
 (i) entering into a relevant paragraph 4C agreement as a lender or assuming the rights of a lender under such an agreement,
 (ii) providing instructions to an operator with a view to entering into a relevant paragraph 4C agreement as a lender or to assuming the rights of a lender under such an agreement by assignment or operation of law, where the instructions involve—
  (aa) accepting particular parameters for the terms of the agreement presented by an operator,
  (bb) choosing between options governing the parameters of the terms of the agreement presented by an operator, or
  (cc) specifying the parameters of the terms of the agreement by other means,
 (iii) enforcing or exercising the lender's rights under a relevant paragraph 4C agreement, or
 (iv) assigning rights under a relevant paragraph 4C agreement.

(3) In sub-paragraph (2)—

"operator" means a person carrying on a controlled activity of the kind specified by paragraph 4C(1) or (2D), and

"relevant paragraph 4C agreement" means a paragraph 4C agreement (within the meaning of that paragraph) which has been, or is to be, entered into with the facilitation of a person carrying on a controlled activity of the kind specified by paragraph 4C(1) or (2D) not in contravention of the general prohibition.

(4) For the purposes of the application of section 21(9) and (10) of the Act (restrictions on financial promotion) to an activity of a kind specified by sub-paragraph (2), paragraph 26D of this Schedule (relevant credit agreements), and article 4 (definition of controlled activities and controlled investments) in so far as it relates to that paragraph, have effect as if the reference to a relevant credit agreement in paragraph 26D includes a reference to a paragraph 4C agreement.]

8 Advising on syndicate participation at Lloyd's

Advising a person to become, or continue or cease to be, a member of a particular Lloyd's syndicate is a controlled activity.

9 Providing funeral plan contracts

(1) Entering as provider into a qualifying funeral plan contract is a controlled activity.

[(1A) Carrying out a qualifying funeral plan contract as provider is a controlled activity.]

(2) A "qualifying funeral plan contract" is a contract under which—

(a) a person ("the customer") makes one or more payments to another person ("the provider");

(b) the provider undertakes to provide, or to secure that another person provides, a funeral in the United Kingdom for the customer (or some other person who is living at the date when the contract is entered into) on his death; and

[(c) the provider is a person who carries on a regulated activity specified in article 59 of the Regulated Activities Order and includes a person who has assumed the undertaking referred to in article 59(2)(b) of that Order as a result of the novation, assignment or transfer by operation of law of an existing qualifying funeral plan contract].

10 Providing qualifying credit

(1) Providing qualifying credit is a controlled activity.

(2) "Qualifying credit" is a credit provided pursuant to an agreement under which—

(a) the lender is a person who carries on the regulated activity specified in article 61 of the Regulated Activities Order; and

(b) the obligation of the borrower to repay is secured (in whole or in part) on land.

(3) "Credit" includes a cash loan and any other form of financial accommodation.

10A Arranging qualifying credit etc

[(1)] Making arrangements—

(a) for another person to enter as borrower into an agreement for the provision of qualifying credit; or

(b) for a borrower under a regulated mortgage contract [falling within sub-paragraph (2)] to vary the terms of that contract in such a way as to vary his obligations under that contract,

is a controlled activity.

[(2) A regulated mortgage contract falls within this sub-paragraph if—

(a) the contract was entered into on or after 31st October 2004; or

(b) the contract—

(i) was entered into before 31st October 2004; and

(ii) was a regulated credit agreement immediately before 21st March 2016.

(3) In this paragraph "regulated mortgage contract" has the meaning given by article 61(3) of the Regulated Activities Order.]

10B Advising on qualifying credit etc

(1) Advising a person is a controlled activity if the advice is—

(a) given to the person in his capacity as a borrower or potential borrower; and

(b) advice on the merits of his doing any of the following—

(i) entering into an agreement for the provision of qualifying credit, or

(ii) varying the terms of a regulated mortgage contract [falling within sub-paragraph (1A)] in such a way as to vary his obligations under that contract.

[(1A) A regulated mortgage contract falls within this sub-paragraph if—

(a) the contract was entered into on or after 31st October 2004; or

(b) the contract—

(i) was entered into before 31st October 2004; and

(ii) was a regulated credit agreement immediately before 21st March 2016.]

(2) In this paragraph, "borrower" and "regulated mortgage contract" have the meaning given by article 61(3) of the Regulated Activities Order.

[10BA Providing relevant consumer credit

Entering into a relevant credit agreement[, other than an agreement under which qualifying credit within the meaning of paragraph 10 is provided,] as lender, or exercising or having the rights to exercise the rights of the lender under such an agreement, is a controlled activity.

[10BAA Advising on certain relevant consumer credit relating to land

Advising a person is a controlled activity if the advice—

(a) is given to the person in the person's capacity as a recipient of credit, or potential recipient of credit; and

(b) consists of the provision of personal recommendations to the person in respect of one or more transactions relating to a relevant credit agreement where the person intends to use the credit to acquire or retain property rights in land or in an existing or projected building, other than an agreement under which qualifying credit within the meaning of paragraph 10 is provided.]

10BB Providing consumer hire

Entering into a regulated consumer hire agreement[, or an agreement that would be such an agreement but for article 60O (exempt agreements: exemptions relating to nature of agreement) or 60Q (exempt agreements: exemptions relating to nature of hirer) of the Regulated Activities Order,] as owner or exercising or having the right to exercise the rights of the owner under such an agreement is a controlled activity.]

[10C Providing a regulated home reversion plan

Entering into a regulated home reversion plan as plan provider is a controlled activity.

10D Arranging a regulated home reversion plan

Making arrangements—

(a) for another person to enter as reversion seller or plan provider into a regulated home reversion plan; or

(b) for a reversion seller or a plan provider under a regulated home reversion plan, entered into on or after 6th April 2007 by him, to vary the terms of that plan in such a way as to vary his obligations under that plan,

is a controlled activity.

10E Advising on a regulated home reversion plan

Advising a person is a controlled activity if the advice is—

(a) given to the person in his capacity as reversion seller, potential reversion seller, plan provider or potential plan provider; and

(b) advice on the merits of his doing either of the following—

(i) entering into a regulated home reversion plan, or

(ii) varying the terms of a regulated home reversion plan, entered into on or after 6th April 2007 by him, in such a way as to vary his obligations under that plan.

10F Providing a regulated home purchase plan

Entering into a regulated home purchase plan as home purchase provider is a controlled activity.

10G Arranging a regulated home purchase plan

Making arrangements—

(a) for another person to enter as home purchaser into a regulated home purchase plan; or

(b) for a home purchaser under a regulated home purchase plan, entered into on or after 6th April 2007 by him, to vary the terms of that plan in such a way as to vary his obligations under that plan,

is a controlled activity.

10H Advising on a regulated home purchase plan

Advising a person is a controlled activity if the advice is—

(a) given to the person in his capacity as home purchaser or potential home purchaser; and

(b) advice on the merits of his doing either of the following—

(i) entering into a regulated home purchase plan, or

(ii) varying the terms of a regulated home purchase plan, entered into on or after 6th April 2007 by him, in such a way as to vary his obligations under that plan.]

[10I Providing a regulated sale and rent back agreement

Entering into a regulated sale and rent back agreement as agreement provider is a controlled activity.

10J Arranging a regulated sale and rent back agreement

Making arrangements—

(a) for another person to enter as agreement seller or agreement provider into a regulated sale and rent back agreement; or

(b) for an agreement seller or an agreement provider under a regulated sale and rent back agreement, entered into on or after 1st July 2009, to vary the terms of that plan in such a way as to vary the obligations of the agreement seller or the agreement provider under that plan,

is a controlled activity.

10K Advising on a regulated sale and rent back agreement

Advising a person ("A") is a controlled activity if the advice is—

(a) given to A in A's capacity as agreement seller, potential agreement seller, agreement provider or potential agreement provider; and

(b) advice on the merits of A doing either of the following—

(i) entering into a regulated sale and rent back agreement, or

(ii) varying the terms of a regulated sale and rent back agreement, entered into on or after 1st July 2009 by A, in such a way as to vary A's obligations under that agreement.]

11 Agreeing to carry on specified kinds of activity

Agreeing to carry on any controlled activity falling within any of paragraphs 3 to [10BB] [(other than paragraph 4A)] above is a controlled activity.

NOTES

Para 3: words in square brackets in sub-para (1) inserted by the Financial Services and Markets Act 2000 (Regulated Activities) (Amendment) Order 2017, SI 2017/488, art 14, Schedule, para 9(1), (10)(a), as from 3 January 2018. The words omitted from sub-para (1) were revoked by the Financial Services and Markets Act 2000 (Regulated Activities) (Amendment) Order 2021, SI 2021/90, art 5(2); note that this Order comes into force (1) on 28 January 2021 (for the purposes of (a) enabling the FCA to make or approve rules and to give guidance and directions; (b) enabling applications to be made etc for: (i) a Part 4A permission under s 55A of FSMA 2000; (ii) a variation of a Part 4A permission under s 55H of that Act; and (iii) approval under Part 5 of the Act; (c) enabling the FCA to exercise any of its powers under Part 4A or Part 5 of that Act in relation to any activity which becomes a regulated activity by virtue of this Order; and (d) enabling the scheme operator to make rules and to give guidance); and (2) for all other purposes on 29 July 2022 (see art 1 of the 2021 Order, and see Part 3 of that Order for transitional provisions).

Para 4: sub-para (1)(aa) inserted, and in sub-para (2) "(aa)," inserted, by SI 2017/488, art 14, Schedule, para 9(1), (10)(b), as from 3 January 2018.

Para 4A: inserted by the Financial Services and Markets Act 2000 (Regulated Activities) (Amendment No 3) Order 2006, SI 2006/3384, art 40(1), (2)(a), as from 1 November 2007.

Para 4AA: inserted by SI 2017/488, art 14, Schedule, para 9(1), (10)(c), as from 3 January 2018.

Para 4B: inserted (together with para 4C) by the Financial Services and Markets Act 2000 (Regulated Activities) (Amendment) (No 2) Order 2013, SI 2013/1881, art 17(1), (6)(a), as from 1 April 2014. Sub-para (1A) inserted by the Financial Services and Markets Act 2000 (Regulated Activities) (Amendment) Order 2014, SI 2014/366, art 10(1), (8)(a), as from 1 April 2014. All other words in square brackets substituted or inserted by the Financial Services and Markets Act 2000 (Miscellaneous Provisions) Order 2015, SI 2015/853, art 4(1), (4), as from 24 March 2015.

Para 4C inserted as noted to para 4B above, and subsequently amended as follows:

Words in square brackets in sub-para (1) substituted, words in square brackets in sub-para (2) inserted, sub-paras (2A)–(2C) inserted, word "sub-paragraph" in square brackets in sub-paras (3)–(6) substituted, and sub-para (10) added, by SI 2014/366, art 10(1), (8)(b), as from 1 April 2014.

All other words in square brackets in para (4C) were substituted or inserted, and the word omitted was revoked, by the Financial Services and Markets Act 2000 (Regulated Activities) (Amendment) Order 2016, SI 2016/392, art 6(1), (2), as from 17 March 2016.

Para 5: words in square brackets in sub-para (a) inserted by SI 2017/488, art 14, Schedule, para 9(1), (10)(d), as from 3 January 2018.

Paras 5A, 5B: inserted by SI 2013/1881, art 17(1), (6)(b), as from 1 April 2014.

Para 7: sub-para (1) numbered as such, and sub-paras (2)–(4) added, by SI 2016/392, art 6(1), (2), as from 6 April 2016. Words in square brackets in sub-para (1)(b)(i) inserted by SI 2017/488, art 14, Schedule, para 9(1), (10)(e), as from 3 January 2018.

Para 9: sub-para (1A) was inserted, and sub-para (2)(c) was substituted, by SI 2021/90, art 5(3) (as to the commencement of the 2021 Order and for transitional provisions etc, see further the first note relating to the 2021 Order above).

Para 10A: sub-para (1) numbered as such, words in square brackets in that sub-paragraph substituted, and sub-paras (2), (3) added, by SI 2016/392, art 6(1), (4), as from 21 March 2016.

Para 10B: words in square brackets in sub-para (1) substituted, and sub-para (1A) inserted, by SI 2016/392, art 6(1), (5), as from 21 March 2016.

Paras 10BA, 10BB: inserted by SI 2013/1881, art 17(1), (6)(c), as from 1 April 2014. Words in square brackets inserted by SI 2014/366, art 10(1), (8)(c), (d), as from 1 April 2014.

Para 10BAA: inserted by the Mortgage Credit Directive Order 2015, SI 2015/910, Sch 1, Pt 2, para 12(1), (2), as from 21 March 2016.

Paras 10C–10H: inserted by the Financial Services and Markets Act 2000 (Regulated Activities) (Amendment) (No 2) Order 2006, SI 2006/2383, art 35(1), (5), as from 6 April 2007.

Paras 10I–10K: inserted by the Financial Services and Markets Act 2000 (Regulated Activities) (Amendment) Order 2009, SI 2009/1342, art 30(4), as from 1 July 2009 (certain purposes), and as from 30 June 2010 (otherwise).

Para 11: figure in square brackets substituted by SI 2014/366, art 10(1), (8)(e), as from 1 April 2014. Words in square brackets inserted by SI 2006/3384, art 40(1), (2)(b), as from 1 November 2007.

Modification: by the Uncertificated Securities (Amendment) (Eligible Debt Securities) Regulations 2003, SI 2003/1633, Sch 2, para 8(2)(t), a reference in the Financial Services and Markets Act 2000 (Financial Promotion) Order 2001, SI 2001/1335, Sch 1 (revoked and replaced by Sch 1 to this Order) to an instrument creating or acknowledging indebtedness included a reference to uncertificated units of eligible debt securities.

[PART 1A CONTROLLED CLAIMS MANAGEMENT ACTIVITY

[8.543]

11A. (1) A claims management activity carried out in Great Britain is a controlled claims management activity.

(2) For the purposes of this paragraph, a claims management activity is one of the following activities:

(a) seeking out persons who may have a claim, referring details of a claim or potential claim or a claimant or potential claimant to another person (including a person having the right to conduct litigation), or identifying a claim or potential claim or a claimant or potential claimant in respect of—

   (i) a personal injury claim;
   (ii) a financial services or financial product claim;
   (iii) a housing disrepair claim;
   (iv) a claim for a specified benefit;
   (v) a criminal injury claim; or
   (vi) an employment related claim.

(b) advising a claimant or potential claimant, investigating a claim or representing a claimant in respect of a personal injury claim;

(c) advising a claimant or potential claimant, investigating a claim or representing a claimant in respect of a financial services or financial product claim;

(d) advising a claimant or potential claimant, investigating a claim or representing a claimant in respect of a housing disrepair claim;

(e) advising a claimant or potential claimant, investigating a claim or representing a claimant in respect of a claim for a specified benefit;

(f) advising a claimant or potential claimant, investigating a claim or representing a claimant in respect of a criminal injury claim; or

(g) advising a claimant or potential claimant, investigating a claim or representing a claimant in respect of an employment related claim.

(3) In this paragraph—

(a) "claimant" includes, in civil proceedings in Scotland, a pursuer;

(b) "defendant" includes, in civil proceedings in Scotland, a defender;

(c) "personal injury claim" means a claim for personal injury within the meaning of the Civil Procedure Rules 1998 in England and Wales and an action for damages for, or arising from, personal injuries within the meaning set out in section 8(7) of the Civil Litigation (Expenses and Group Proceedings) (Scotland) Act 2018 in Scotland;
(d) "financial services or financial product claim" includes a claim made under section 75 of the Consumer Credit Act 1974;
(e) "housing disrepair claim" means a claim under section 11 of the Landlord and Tenant Act 1985 or section 4 of the Defective Premises Act 1972 in England and Wales or an application in respect of the repairing standard under section 22 of the Housing (Scotland) Act 2006, or claims in relation to the disrepair of premises under a term of a tenancy agreement or lease or under the common law relating to nuisance or negligence but does not include claims for statutory nuisance under section 82 of the Environmental Protection Act 1990;
(f) "a claim for a specified benefit" means a claim for one of the following benefits—
  (i) industrial injuries benefit, within the meaning given by section 94 of the Social Security Contributions and Benefits Act 1992;
  (ii) any supplement or additional allowance, or increase of benefit or allowance to which a recipient of an industrial injuries benefit may be entitled under that Act or any other Act;
  (iii) a benefit under a scheme referred to in paragraph 2 or 4 of Schedule 8 to that Act; or
  (iv) a benefit under the Pneumoconiosis etc (Workers' Compensation) Act 1979.
(g) "criminal injury claim" means a claim under the Criminal Injuries Compensation Scheme established under the Criminal Injuries Compensation Act 1995;
(h) "employment related claim" includes a claim in relation to wages and salaries and other employment related payments and claims in relation to wrongful or unfair dismissal, redundancy, discrimination and harassment;
(i) "investigating" means carrying out an investigation into, or commissioning the investigation of, the circumstances, merits or foundation of a claim; and
(j) "representing" means representation in writing or orally, regardless of the tribunal, body or person before which or to whom the representation is made.

(4) In this paragraph, a person is to be treated as carrying on a controlled claims management activity in Great Britain when the activity is carried on—
(a) by a person who is—
  (i) an individual who is ordinarily resident in Great Britain; or
  (ii) a person, other than an individual, who is constituted under the law of England and Wales or Scotland; or
(b) in respect of a claimant or potential claimant who is—
  (i) an individual who is ordinarily resident in Great Britain; or
  (ii) a person, other than an individual, who is constituted under the law of England and Wales or Scotland.

(5) For the purposes of sub-paragraph (4) a person is "ordinarily resident" in Great Britain if that person satisfies the requirements of the Statutory Residence Test as set out in Schedule 45 to the Finance Act 2013 either—
(a) at the time of the facts giving rise to the claim or potential claim; or
(b) at the time when the controlled claims management activity is carried out in respect of that claimant or potential claimant.]

NOTES

Inserted by the Financial Services and Markets Act 2000 (Claims Management Activity) Order 2018, SI 2018/1253, arts 8, 38, as from 1 April 2019 (for full commencement details and for transitional provisions in relation to carrying on a claims management activity, etc, see arts 1, 39–89 of the 2018 Order).

PART II CONTROLLED INVESTMENTS

[8.544]

12. A deposit.

13. Rights under a contract of insurance.

14. (1) Shares or stock in the share capital of—
(a) any body corporate (wherever incorporated);
(b) any unincorporated body constituted under the law of a country or territory outside the United Kingdom.

(2) Sub-paragraph (1) includes—
(a) any shares of a class defined as deferred shares for the purposes of section 119 of the Building Societies Act 1986;
(b) any transferable shares in a body incorporated under the law of, or any part of, the United Kingdom relating to [co-operative and community benefit societies,] industrial and provident societies or credit unions . . .

(3) But subject to sub-paragraph (2) there are excluded from sub-paragraph (1) shares or stock in the share capital of—
(a) an open-ended investment company;
(b) a building society incorporated under the law of, or any part of, the United Kingdom;
(c) any body incorporated under the law of, or any part of, the United Kingdom relating to [co-operative and community benefit societies,] industrial and provident societies or credit unions;
(d) . . .

15 Instruments creating or acknowledging indebtedness

(1) Subject to sub-paragraph (2), such of the following as do not fall within [paragraph . . . 16]—
(a) debentures;
(b) debenture stock;
(c) loan stock;

(d) bonds;
(e) certificates of deposit;
(f) any other instrument creating or acknowledging a present or future indebtedness.

(2) If and to the extent that they would otherwise fall within sub-paragraph (1), there are excluded from that sub-paragraph—

(a) any instrument acknowledging or creating indebtedness for, or for money borrowed to defray, the consideration payable under a contract for the supply of goods or services;
(b) a cheque or other bill of exchange, a banker's draft or a letter of credit (but not a bill of exchange accepted by a banker);
(c) a banknote, a statement showing a balance on a current, deposit or saving account, a lease or other disposition of property, a heritable security; and
(d) a contract of insurance;
[(e) . . .].

(3) An instrument excluded from sub-paragraph (1) of paragraph 16 by paragraph 16(2)(b) is not thereby to be taken to fall within sub-paragraph (1) of this paragraph.

[15A Alternative finance investment bonds

(1) Rights under an alternative finance investment bond, to the extent that they do not fall within paragraph [15 or] 16.

(2) For the purposes of this paragraph, arrangements constitute an alternative finance investment bond if—

(a) the arrangements provide for a person ("the bond-holder") to pay a sum of money ("the capital") to another ("the bond-issuer");
(b) the arrangements identify assets, or a class of assets, which the bond-issuer will acquire for the purpose of generating income or gains directly or indirectly ("the bond assets");
(c) the arrangements specify a period at the end of which they cease to have effect ("the bond term");
(d) the bond-issuer undertakes under the arrangements—
    (i) to make a repayment in respect of the capital ("the redemption payment") to the bond-holder during or at the end of the bond term (whether or not in instalments); and
    (ii) to pay to the bond-holder other payments on one or more occasions during or at the end of the bond term ("the additional payments");
(e) the amount of the additional payments does not exceed an amount which would, at the time at which the bond is issued, be a reasonable commercial return on a loan of the capital; and
[(f) the arrangements are—
    (i) a security that is admitted to the official list in accordance with Part 6 of the Act,
    (ii) a security that is admitted to an official list in the EEA (in accordance with the provisions of Directive 2001/34/EC of the European Parliament and of the Council on the admission of securities to official stock exchange listing and on information to be published on those securities) and has been so admitted since before IP completion day,
    (iii) a security that is admitted to trading on a recognised investment exchange or a UK trading venue, or
    (iv) a security that is admitted to trading on an EU trading venue and has been so admitted since before IP completion day.]

(3) For the purposes of sub-paragraph (2)—

(a) the bond-issuer may acquire the bond assets before or after the arrangements take effect;
(b) the bond assets may be property of any kind, including rights in relation to property owned by someone other than the bond-issuer;
(c) the identification of the bond assets mentioned in sub-paragraph (2)(b) and the undertakings mentioned in sub-paragraph (2)(d) may (but need not) be described as, or accompanied by a document described as, a declaration of trust;
(d) the reference to a period in sub-paragraph (2)(c) includes any period specified to end upon the redemption of the bond by the bond-issuer;
(e) the bond-holder may (but need not) be entitled under the arrangements to terminate them, or participate in terminating them, before the end of the bond term;
(f) the amount of the additional payments may be—
    (i) fixed at the beginning of the bond term;
    (ii) determined wholly or partly by reference to the value of or income generated by the bond assets; or
    (iii) determined in some other way;
(g) if the amount of the additional payments is not fixed at the beginning of the bond term, the reference in sub-paragraph (2)(e) to the amount of the additional payments is a reference to the maximum amount of the additional payments;
(h) the amount of the redemption payment may (but need not) be subject to reduction in the event of a fall in the value of the bond assets or in the rate of income generated by them; and
(i) entitlement to the redemption payment may (but need not) be capable of being satisfied (whether or not at the option of the bond-issuer or the bond-holder) by the issue or transfer of shares or other securities.

(4) An instrument excluded from sub-paragraph (1) of paragraph 16 by sub-paragraph (2)(b) of that paragraph is not thereby taken to fall within sub-paragraph (1) of this paragraph.]

16 Government and public securities

(1) Subject to sub-paragraph (2), loan stock, bonds and other instruments—

(a) creating or acknowledging indebtedness; and
(b) issued by or on behalf of a government, local authority (whether in the United Kingdom or elsewhere) or international organisation.

(2) [Subject to sub-paragraph (3),] there are excluded from sub-paragraph (1)—

(a) so far as applicable, the instruments mentioned in paragraph 15(2)(a) to (d);

(b) any instrument creating or acknowledging indebtedness in respect of—

(i) money received by the Director of Savings as deposits or otherwise in connection with the business of the National Savings Bank;

(ii) money raised under the National Loans Act 1968 under the auspices of the Director of Savings or treated as so raised by virtue of section 11(3) of the National Debt Act 1972.

[(3) Sub-paragraph (2)(a) does not exclude an instrument which meets the requirements set out in paragraphs (a) to (e) of paragraph 15A(2).]

17 Instruments giving entitlements to investments

(1) Warrants and other instruments entitling the holder to subscribe for any investment falling within paragraph 14, 15 or 16.

(2) It is immaterial whether the investment to which the entitlement relates is in existence or identifiable.

(3) An investment falling within this paragraph shall not be regarded as falling within paragraph 21, 22 or 23.

18 Certificates representing certain securities

(1) Subject to sub-paragraph (2), certificates or other instruments which confer contractual or property rights (other than rights consisting of an investment of the kind specified by paragraph 21)—

(a) in respect of any investment of the kind specified by any of paragraphs 14 to 17 being an investment held by a person other than the person on whom the rights are conferred by the certificate or instrument; and

(b) the transfer of which may be effected without the consent of that person.

(2) There is excluded from sub-paragraph (1) any instrument which confers rights in respect of two or more investments issued by different persons, or in respect of two or more different investments of the kind specified by paragraph 16 and issued by the same person.

19 Units in a collective investment scheme

Units in a collective investment scheme.

[20 Rights under a pension scheme

(1) Rights under a stakeholder pension scheme.

(2) Rights under a personal pension scheme.

(3) "Stakeholder pension scheme" and "personal pension scheme" have the meanings given by article 72(4).]

21 Options

[(1)] Options to acquire or dispose of—

(a) a security or contractually based investment (other than one of a kind specified in this paragraph);

(b) currency of the United Kingdom or of any other country or territory;

(c) palladium, platinum, gold or silver;

(d) an option to acquire or dispose of an investment falling within this paragraph by virtue of sub-paragraph (a), (b) or (c);

[(e) subject to sub-paragraph (4), an option to acquire or dispose of an option to which [paragraph 5, 6, 7 or 10 of Part 1 of Schedule 2 (read with Articles 5, 6, 7, and 8 of the Commission Regulation) applies]].

[(2) Subject to sub-paragraph (4), options—

(a) to which sub-paragraph (1) does not apply;

(b) which relate to commodities;

(c) which may be settled physically; and

(d) either—

(i) to which paragraph 5 or 6 of [Part 1 of Schedule 2] [read with Articles 5 and 6 of the Commission Regulation)] applies, or

(ii) which in accordance with Article [7] of the Commission Regulation are to be considered as having the characteristics of other derivative financial instruments and not being for commercial purposes, and to which paragraph 7 of [Part 1 of that Schedule] applies.

(3) Subject to sub-paragraph (4), options—

(a) to which sub-paragraph (1) does not apply;

(b) which may be settled physically; and

(c) to which paragraph 10 of [Part 1 of Schedule 2] (read with [Articles 7 and 8 of] the Commission Regulation) applies.

(4) Sub-paragraphs (1)(e), (2) and (3) only apply to options in relation to which—

[(a) an investment firm or qualifying credit institution is providing or performing investment services and activities on a professional basis;

(b) a management company which has a Part 4A permission to do so is providing the investment service specified in paragraph 4 or 5 of Part 3 of Schedule 2 or the ancillary service specified in paragraph 1 of Part 3A of that Schedule;

(c) a market operator is providing the investment service specified in paragraph 8 or 9 of Part 3 of that Schedule;

(d) a full-scope UK AIFM which has a Part 4A permission to do so is providing the investment service specified in paragraph 1, 4 or 5 of Part 3 of that Schedule or the ancillary service specified in paragraph 1 of Part 3A of that Schedule].

(5) . . .]

22 Futures

(1) Subject to sub-paragraph (2), rights under a contract for the sale of a commodity or property of any other description under which delivery is to be made at a future date and at a price agreed on when the contract is made.

[(1A) Subject to sub-paragraph (1D), futures—

(a) to which sub-paragraph (1) does not apply;
(b) which relate to commodities;
(c) which may be settled physically; and
(d) to which paragraph 5 or 6 of [Part 1 of Schedule 2] [(read with Articles 5 and 6 of the Commission Regulation)] applies.

(1B) Subject to sub-paragraph (1D), futures and forwards—
(a) to which sub-paragraph (1) does not apply;
(b) which relate to commodities;
(c) which may be settled physically;
(d) which in accordance with Article [7] of the Commission Regulation are to be considered as having the characteristics of other derivative financial instruments and not being for commercial purposes; and
(e) to which paragraph 7 of [Part 1 of Schedule 2] applies.

(1C) Subject to sub-paragraph (1D), futures—
(a) to which sub-paragraph (1) does not apply;
(b) which may be settled physically; and
(c) to which paragraph 10 of [Part 1 of Schedule 2] (read with [Articles 7 and 8 of] the Commission Regulation) applies.

[(1CA) Subject to sub-paragraph (1D), any other derivative contract, relating to currencies to which paragraph 4 of [Part 1 of Schedule 2] read with Article 10 of the Commission Regulation applies.]

(1D) Sub-paragraphs (1A), (1B)[, (1C) and (1CA)] only apply to futures[, forwards or derivative contacts] in relation to which—
[(a) an investment firm or qualifying credit institution is providing or performing investment services and activities on a professional basis;
(b) a management company which has a Part 4A permission to do so is providing the investment service specified in paragraph 4 or 5 of Part 3 of Schedule 2 or the ancillary service specified in paragraph 1 of Part 3A of that Schedule;
(c) a market operator is providing the investment service specified in paragraph 8 or 9 of Part 3 of that Schedule;
(d) a full-scope UK AIFM which has a Part 4A permission to do so is providing the investment service specified in paragraph 1, 4 or 5 of Part 3 of that Schedule or the ancillary service specified in paragraph 1 of Part 3A of that Schedule].

(1E) . . .]

(2) There are excluded from sub-paragraph (1) rights under any contract which is made for commercial and not investment purposes.

(3) For the purposes of sub-paragraph (2), in considering whether a contract is to be regarded as made for investment purposes or for commercial purposes, the indicators set out in article 84 of the Regulated Activities Order shall be applied in the same way as they are applied for the purposes of that article.

23 Contracts for differences etc

(1) Subject to sub-paragraph (2), rights under—
(a) a contract for differences; or
(b) any other contract the purpose or pretended purpose of which is to secure a profit or avoid a loss by reference to fluctuations in—
(i) the value or price of property of any description;
(ii) an index or other factor designated for that purpose in the contract.

(2) There are excluded from sub-paragraph (1)—
(a) rights under a contract if the parties intend that the profit is to be secured or the loss is to be avoided by one or more of the parties taking delivery of any property to which the contract relates;
(b) rights under a contract under which money is received by way of deposit on terms that any interest or other return to be paid on the sum deposited will be calculated by reference to fluctuations in an index or other factor;
(c) rights under any contract under which—
(i) money is received by the Director of Savings as deposits or otherwise in connection with the business of the National Savings Bank; or
(ii) money is raised under the National Loans Act 1968 under the auspices of the Director of Savings or treated as so raised by virtue of section 11(3) of the National Debt Act 1972;
(d) rights under a qualifying contract of insurance.

[(3) Subject to sub-paragraph (4), derivative instruments for the transfer of credit risk—
(a) to which neither paragraph 21 nor sub-paragraph (1) applies; and
(b) to which paragraph 8 of [Part 1 of Schedule 2] applies.

(4) Sub-paragraph (3) only applies to derivatives in relation to which—
[(a) an investment firm or qualifying credit institution is providing or performing investment services and activities on a professional basis;
(b) a management company which has a Part 4A permission to do so is providing the investment service specified in paragraph 4 or 5 of Part 3 of Schedule 2 or the ancillary service specified in paragraph 1 of Part 3A of that Schedule;
(c) a market operator is providing the investment service specified in paragraph 8 or 9 of Part 3 of that Schedule;
(d) a full-scope UK AIFM which has a Part 4A permission to do so is providing the investment service specified in paragraph 1, 4 or 5 of Part 3 of that Schedule or the ancillary service specified in paragraph 1 of Part 3A of that Schedule].

[(4A) Subject to sub-paragraph (4B), a derivative contract of a binary or other fixed outcomes nature—
(a) to which sub-paragraph (1) does not apply;

(b) which is settled in cash; and

(c) which is a financial instrument to which paragraph 4, 5, 6, 7 or 10 of [Part 1 of Schedule 2] read with Articles 5 to 8 and 10 of the Commission Regulation applies.

(4B) Sub-paragraph (4A) only applies to derivatives in relation to which—

[(a) an investment firm or qualifying credit institution is providing or performing investment services and activities on a professional basis;

(b) a management company which has a Part 4A permission to do so is providing the investment service specified in paragraph 4 or 5 of Part 3 of Schedule 2 or the ancillary service specified in paragraph 1 of Part 3A of that Schedule;

(c) a market operator is providing the investment service specified in paragraph 8 or 9 of Part 3 of that Schedule;

(d) a full-scope UK AIFM which has a Part 4A permission to do so is providing the investment service specified in paragraph 1, 4 or 5 of Part 3 of that Schedule or the ancillary service specified in paragraph 1 of Part 3A of that Schedule]; or

(e) a person is carrying on the controlled activity referred to in paragraph 4(2).]

(5) . . .]

[23A Emission allowances

[(1) Subject to sub-paragraph (2)—

(a) emission allowances consisting of any units recognised for compliance (by an EEA State) with the requirements of the emission allowance trading directive; and

(b) allowances created under article 18 of the Greenhouse Gas Emissions Trading Scheme Order 2020 and transferable in accordance with that order.]

(2) Sub-paragraph (1) only applies to emission allowances in relation to which—

[(a) an investment firm or qualifying credit institution is providing or performing investment services and activities on a professional basis;

(b) a management company which has a Part 4A permission to do so is providing the investment service specified in paragraph 4 or 5 of Part 3 of Schedule 2 or the ancillary service specified in paragraph 1 of Part 3A of that Schedule;

(c) a market operator is providing the investment service specified in paragraph 8 or 9 of Part 3 of that Schedule;

(d) a full-scope UK AIFM which has a Part 4A permission to do so is providing the investment service specified in paragraph 1, 4 or 5 of Part 3 of that Schedule or the ancillary service specified in paragraph 1 of Part 3A of that Schedule].

24 Lloyd's syndicate capacity and syndicate membership

(1) The underwriting capacity of a Lloyd's syndicate.

(2) A person's membership (or prospective membership) of a Lloyd's syndicate.

25 Funeral plan contracts

Rights under a qualifying funeral plan contract.

26 Agreements for qualifying credit

Rights under an agreement for qualifying credit.

[26A Regulated home reversion plans

Rights under a regulated home reversion plan.

26B Regulated home purchase plans

Rights under a regulated home purchase plan.]

[26C Regulated sale and rent back agreement

Rights under a regulated sale and rent back agreement.]

[26D Relevant credit agreements

Rights under a relevant credit agreement

26E Consumer hire agreements

Rights under a consumer hire agreement.]

27 Rights to or interests in investments

(1) Subject to sub-paragraphs (2) and (3), any right to or interest in anything which is specified by any other provision of this Part of this Schedule (other than [paragraph 26, [26A, 26B or 26C]]).

(2) Sub-paragraph (1) does not apply to interests under the trusts of an occupational pension scheme.

(2A) Sub-paragraph (1) does not apply to any right or interest acquired as a result of entering into a funeral plan contract (and for this purpose a "funeral plan contract" is a contract of a kind described in paragraph 9(2)(a) and (b)).

(3) Sub-paragraph (1) does not apply to anything which falls within any other provision of this Part of this Schedule.

28 Interpretation

In this Schedule—

["agreement provider" has the meaning given in paragraph (3) of article 63J of the Regulated Activities Order, read with paragraphs (6) and (7) of that article;

"agreement seller" has the meaning given in article 63J(3) of the Regulated Activities Order;]

["AIFM" has the meaning given in the Regulated Activities Order;]

["borrower" has the meaning given by article 60L of the Regulated Activities Order;]

"buying" includes acquiring for valuable consideration;

["Commission Regulation" [has the meaning given in the Regulated Activities Order];]

["consumer hire agreement" has the meaning given by article 60N of the Regulated Activities Order;]

"contract of insurance" has the meaning given in the Regulated Activities Order;

"contractually based investment" means—

(a) rights under a qualifying contract of insurance;

(b) any investment of the kind specified by any of paragraphs 21, 22, 23 and 25;

(c) any investment of the kind specified by paragraph 27 so far as relevant to an investment falling within (a) or (b);

[. . .]

["EU trading venue" has the meaning given by Article 2.1.16B of the markets in financial instruments regulation;]

["hirer" has the meaning given by article 60N of the Regulated Activities Order;]

["home purchase provider" and "home purchaser" have the meanings given in article 63F(3) of the Regulated Activities Order;]

["investment firm" has the meaning given in the Regulated Activities Order;]

["investment services and activities" has the meaning given in the Regulated Activities Order;]

["lender" has the meaning given by article 60L of the Regulated Activities Order;]

["management company" has the meaning given in the Regulated Activities Order;]

["market operator" has the meaning given in the Regulated Activities Order;]

["markets in financial instruments directive" means Directive 2014/65/EU of the European Parliament and of the Council of 15 May 2014 on markets in financial instruments (recast);]

["MiFID instrument" has the meaning given in article 25D(2) of the Regulated Activities Order;]

["multilateral trading facility" has the meaning given in the Regulated Activities Order;]

["non-equity MiFID instrument" has the meaning given in article 25DA of the Regulated Activities Order;]

["occupational pension scheme" has the meaning given by section 1 of the Pension Schemes Act 1993 but with paragraph (b) of the definition omitted;]

["organised trading facility" has the meaning given in the Regulated Activities Order;]

["plan provider" has the meaning given by paragraph (3) of article 63B of the Regulated Activities Order, read with paragraphs (7) and (8) of that article;]

"property" includes currency of the United Kingdom or any other country or territory;

["qualifying credit institution" has the meaning given in the Regulated Activities Order;]

"qualifying funeral plan contract" has the meaning given by paragraph 9;

["regulated consumer hire agreement" has the meaning given by article 60N of the Regulated Activities Order;]

["regulated credit agreement" has the meaning given by article 60B of the Regulated Activities Order;]

["regulated home purchase plan" has the meaning given in article 63F(3) of the Regulated Activities Order;

"regulated home reversion plan" and "reversion seller" have the meanings given in article 63B(3) of the Regulated Activities Order;]

["regulated sale and rent back agreement" has the meaning given in article 63J(3) of the Regulated Activities Order;]

["relevant credit agreement" means a credit agreement (within the meaning given by article 60B of the Regulated Activities Order) other than—

(a) a regulated mortgage contract or a regulated home purchase plan (within the meaning of that Order); or

(b) a buy-to-let mortgage contract as defined in article 4 of the Mortgage Credit Directive Order 2015;]

["relevant recipient of credit" has the meaning given by article 60L of the Regulated Activities Order;]

"security" means a controlled investment falling within any of paragraphs 14 to 20 [or 23A] or, so far as relevant to any such investment, paragraph 27;

"selling", in relation to any investment, includes disposing of the investment for valuable consideration, and for these purposes "disposing" includes—

(a) in the case of an investment consisting of rights under a contract—

(i) surrendering, assigning or converting those rights; or

(ii) assuming the corresponding liabilities under the contract;

(b) in the case of an investment consisting of rights under other arrangements, assuming the corresponding liabilities under the arrangements; and

(c) in the case of any other investment, issuing or creating the investment or granting the rights or interests of which it consists;

"syndicate" has the meaning given in the Regulated Activities Order.

["UK trading venue" has the meaning given by Article 2.1.16 of the markets in financial instruments regulation.]

NOTES

Para 14: words in square brackets substituted by the Co-operative and Community Benefit Societies and Credit Unions Act 2010 (Consequential Amendments) Regulations 2014, SI 2014/1815, reg 2, Schedule, para 15(1), (3), as from 1 August 2014. Sub-para (3)(d) and the words omitted from sub-para (2)(b) were revoked by the Financial Services and Markets Act 2000 (Amendment) (EU Exit) Regulations 2019, SI 2019/632, regs 162(1), 176(1), (2), as from IP completion day (as defined in the European Union (Withdrawal Agreement) Act 2020, s 39) (for transitional provisions see the note on art 6 at **[8.448]**).

Para 15: words in square brackets in sub-para (1) substituted, and sub-para (2)(e) originally added, by the Financial Services and Markets Act 2000 (Regulated Activities) (Amendment) Order 2010, SI 2010/86, art 4, Schedule, para 9(f)(i), (ii), as from 24 February 2010. Words omitted from sub-para (1) revoked, and sub-para (2)(e) revoked, by the Financial Services and Markets Act 2000 (Regulated Activities) (Amendment) Order 2011, SI 2011/133, art 3(1), (2)(a), (b), as from 16 February 2011 (see also the note relating to the 2011 Order on art 77 of the Regulated Activities Order at **[8.209]**).

Para 15A: inserted by SI 2010/86, art 4, Schedule, para 9(f)(iii), as from 24 February 2010. Words in square brackets in sub-para (1) inserted by SI 2011/133, art 3(1), (2)(c), as from 16 February 2011 (see also the note relating to the 2011 Order on art 77 of the Regulated Activities Order at **[8.209]**). Sub-para (2)(f) was substituted by SI 2019/632, regs 162(1), 176(1), (3), as from IP completion day (as defined in the European Union (Withdrawal Agreement) Act 2020, s 39) (for transitional provisions see the note on art 6 at **[8.448]**).

Para 16: words in square brackets in sub-para (2) inserted, and sub-para (3) added, by SI 2010/86, art 4, Schedule, para 9(f)(iv), (v), as from 24 February 2010.

Para 20: substituted by the Financial Services and Markets Act 2000 (Regulated Activities) (Amendment) Order 2006, SI 2006/1969, art 12(1), (3), as from 6 April 2007.

Para 21 is amended as follows:

Sub-para (1) numbered as such, word omitted from sub-para (1)(c) revoked, and sub-paras (1)(e), (2)–(5) added, by the Financial Services and Markets Act 2000 (Regulated Activities) (Amendment No 3) Order 2006, SI 2006/3384, art 40(1), (3), as from 1 November 2007.

The words in the second pair of square brackets in sub-paras (2)(d)(i) and (3)(c) were inserted, and the figure "7" in sub-para (2)(d)(ii) was substituted, by SI 2017/488, art 14, Schedule, para 9(1), (10)(g), as from 3 January 2018.

The words in square brackets in sub-para (1)(e), the words in the first pair of square brackets in sub-paras (2)(d)(i) and (3)(c), and the words "Part 1 of that Schedule" in square brackets in sub-para (2)(d)(ii) were substituted, sub-paras (4)(a)–(d) were substituted, and sub-para (5) was revoked, by SI 2019/632, regs 162(1), 176(1), (4), as from IP completion day (as defined in the European Union (Withdrawal Agreement) Act 2020, s 39) (for transitional provisions see the note on art 6 at **[8.448]**).

Para 22 is amended as follows:

Sub-paras (1A)–(1E) inserted by SI 2006/3384, art 40(1), (4), as from 1 November 2007.

The words "Part 1 of Schedule 2" in square brackets in sub-paras (1A)(d), (1B)(e), (1C)(c) and (1CA) were substituted, sub-paras (1D)(a)–(d) were substituted, and sub-para (1E) was revoked, by SI 2019/632, regs 162(1), 176(1), (5), as from IP completion day (as defined in the European Union (Withdrawal Agreement) Act 2020, s 39) (for transitional provisions see the note on art 6 at **[8.448]**).

All other amendments to this paragraph were made by SI 2017/488, art 14, Schedule, para 9(1), (10)(h), as from 3 January 2018.

Para 23 is amended as follows:

Sub-paras (3), (4), (5) added by SI 2006/3384, art 40(1), (5), as from 1 November 2007.

Words in square brackets in sub-paras (3)(b) and (4A)(c) substituted, paras (a)–(d) of sub-paras (4) and (4B) substituted, and sub-para (5) revoked, by SI 2019/632, regs 162(1), 176(1), (6), as from IP completion day (as defined in the European Union (Withdrawal Agreement) Act 2020, s 39) (for transitional provisions see the note on art 6 at **[8.448]**).

Sub-paras (4A), (4B) inserted by SI 2017/488, art 14, Schedule, para 9(1), (10)(i), as from 3 January 2018.

Para 23A: inserted by SI 2017/488, art 14, Schedule, para 9(1), (10)(j), as from 3 January 2018. Sub-para (1) was substituted by the Recognised Auction Platforms (Amendment and Miscellaneous Provisions) Regulations 2021, SI 2021/494, reg 4, as from 22 April 2021. Sub-paras (2)(a)–(d) were substituted, by SI 2019/632, regs 162(1), 176(1), (7), as from IP completion day (as defined in the European Union (Withdrawal Agreement) Act 2020, s 39) (for transitional provisions see the note on art 6 at **[8.448]**).

Paras 26A, 26B: inserted by the Financial Services and Markets Act 2000 (Regulated Activities) (Amendment) (No 2) Order 2006, SI 2006/2383, art 35(1), (6)(a), as from 6 April 2007.

Para 26C: inserted by the Financial Services and Markets Act 2000 (Regulated Activities) (Amendment) Order 2009, SI 2009/1342, art 30(1), (5)(a), as from 1 July 2009 (other than for the purposes of enabling applications to be made for a Part IV permission, or a variation of a Part IV permission, in relation to activities of the kind specified by arts 25E, 53D or 63J or, so far as relevant to any such activity, art 64 of this Order), and as from 30 June 2010 (for those purposes).

Paras 26D, 26E: inserted by the Financial Services and Markets Act 2000 (Regulated Activities) (Amendment) (No 2) Order 2013, SI 2013/1881, art 17(1), (6)(d), as from 1 April 2014.

Para 27: words in first (outer) pair of square brackets substituted by SI 2006/2383, art 35(1), (6)(b), as from 6 April 2007. Words in second (inner) pair of square brackets substituted by SI 2009/1342, art 30(1), (5)(b), as from 1 July 2009 (certain purposes), and as from 30 June 2010 (otherwise) (see the first note relating to the 2009 Order above).

Para 28 is amended as follows:

Definitions "agreement provider", "agreement seller", and "regulated sale and rent back agreement" inserted by SI 2009/1342, art 30(1), (5)(c), as from 1 July 2009 (certain purposes), and as from 30 June 2010 (otherwise) (see the first note relating to the 2009 Order above).

Definitions "AIFM", "markets in financial instruments directive", non-equity MiFID instrument" and "organised trading facility" inserted, words in square brackets in the definition "Commission Regulation" substituted, and words "or 23A" in the definition "security" inserted, by SI 2017/488, art 14, Schedule, para 9(1), (10)(k), as from 3 January 2018.

Definitions "borrower", "consumer hire agreement", "hirer", "lender", "regulated consumer hire agreement", "regulated credit agreement", "relevant credit agreement", and "relevant recipient of credit" inserted, by SI 2013/1881, art 17(1), (6)(d), as from 1 April 2014.

Definition "relevant credit agreement" subsequently substituted by the Mortgage Credit Directive Order 2015, SI 2015/910, Sch 1, Pt 2, para 12(1), (3), as from 21 March 2016.

Definitions "Commission Regulation", "investment firm", "investment services and activities", "management company", "market operator", "MiFID instrument", and "multilateral trading facility" inserted by SI 2006/3384, art 40(1), (6), as from 1 November 2007.

Definition "credit institution" (omitted) originally inserted by SI 2006/3384, art 40(1), (6), as from 1 November 2007. Subsequently revoked by SI 2019/632, regs 162(1), 176(1), (8), as from IP completion day (as defined in the European Union (Withdrawal Agreement) Act 2020, s 39) (for transitional provisions see the note on art 6 at **[8.448]**).

Definitions "EU trading venue", "qualifying credit institution", and "UK trading venue" inserted by SI 2019/632, regs 162(1), 176(1), (8), as from IP completion day (as defined in the European Union (Withdrawal Agreement) Act 2020, s 39) (for transitional provisions see the note on art 6 at **[8.448]**).

Definitions "home purchase provider", "home purchaser", "plan provider", "regulated home purchase plan", "regulated home reversion plan", and "reversion seller" inserted by SI 2006/2383, art 35(1), (6)(c), as from 6 April 2007.

Definition "occupational pension scheme" substituted by SI 2006/1969, art 12(1), (4), as from 6 April 2007.

Modification: see the note to Part I of this Schedule at **[8.542]**.

SCHEDULE 2
COUNTRIES AND TERRITORIES

Article 10

[8.545]

1. The Bailiwick of Guernsey.

2. The Isle of Man.

3. The Commonwealth of Pennsylvania.

4. The State of Iowa.

5. The Bailiwick of Jersey.

SCHEDULE 3
MARKETS AND EXCHANGES

Articles 37, 41, 67, 68 and 69

[PART A1 CRITERIA FOR RELEVANT UK MARKETS

[8.546]

The criteria for a "relevant UK market" are—

(a) the head office of the market must be situated in the United Kingdom; and

(b) the market must satisfy any requirements of the law of the United Kingdom as to—

(i) the manner in which it operates;

(ii) the means by which access may be had to the facilities it provides;

(iii) the conditions to be satisfied before an investment may be traded or dealt in by means of its facilities; and

(iii) the reporting and publication of transactions effected by means of its facilities.]

NOTES

Commencement: 18 October 2021.

Inserted by the Markets in Financial Instruments, Benchmarks and Financial Promotions (Amendment) (EU Exit) Regulations 2021, SI 2021/1074, reg 2(8), as from 18 October 2021.

PART I CRITERIA FOR RELEVANT EEA [OR GIBRALTAR] MARKETS

[8.547]

The criteria are—

(a) the head office of the market must be situated in an EEA State [or in Gibraltar]; and

(b) the market must be subject to requirements in the EEA State in which its head office is situated [or (where its head office is situated in Gibraltar), in Gibraltar] as to—

(i) the manner in which it operates;

(ii) the means by which access may be had to the facilities it provides;

(iii) the conditions to be satisfied before an investment may be traded or dealt in by means of its facilities;

(iv) the reporting and publication of transactions effected by means of its facilities.

NOTES

Words in square brackets (including those in the Schedule heading) inserted by the Gibraltar (Miscellaneous Amendments) (EU Exit) Regulations 2019, SI 2019/680, reg 5, as from IP completion day (as defined in the European Union (Withdrawal Agreement) Act 2020, s 39).

[PART II

(Revoked by the Financial Services and Markets Act 2000 (Regulated Activities) (Amendment) Order 2017, SI 2017/488, art 14, Schedule, para 9(1), (11), as from 3 January 2018.)

PART III CERTAIN NON-EEA INVESTMENT EXCHANGES OPERATING RELEVANT MARKETS

[8.548]

America Stock Exchange.

Australian Stock Exchange.

Basler Effektenbourse.

Boston Stock Exchange.

Bourse de Geneve.

Buenos Aires Stock Exchange.

Canadian Venture Exchange.

Chicago Board Options Exchange.

Chicago Stock Exchange.

Effektenborsenverein Zurich.

Fukuoka Stock Exchange.

Hiroshima Stock Exchange.

Iceland Stock Exchange.

Johannesburg Stock Exchange.

Korean Stock Exchange.

Kuala Lumpur Stock Exchange.

Kyoto Stock Exchange.

Midwest Stock Exchange.

Montreal Stock Exchange.

Nagoya Stock Exchange.

NASDAQ.

National Stock Exchange.

New York Stock Exchange.

New Zealand Stock Exchange Limited.

Niigita Stock Exchange.

Osaka Stock Exchange.

Oslo Stock Exchange.

Pacific Stock Exchange.

Philadelphia Stock Exchange.

Sapporo Stock Exchange.

Singapore Stock Exchange.

Stock Exchange of Hong Kong Limited.

Stock Exchange of Thailand.

Tokyo Stock Exchange.

Toronto Stock Exchange.

PART IV OTHER RELEVANT MARKETS

[8.549]

American Commodity Exchange.

Australian Financial Futures Market.

Chicago Board of Trade.

Chicago Mercantile Exchange.

Chicago Rice and Cotton Exchange.

Commodity Exchange Inc.

Eurex US.

Eurex Zurich.

International Securities Market Association.

International Petroleum Exchange.

Kansas City Board of Trade.

London Metal Exchange.

Minneapolis Grain Exchange.

New York Board of Trade.

New York Futures Exchange.

New York Mercantile Exchange.

New Zealand Futures Exchange.

Pacific Commodity Exchange.

Philadelphia Board of Trade.

Singapore International Monetary Exchange.

Sydney Futures Exchange.

Toronto Futures Exchange.

SCHEDULE 4
TAKEOVERS OF RELEVANT UNLISTED COMPANIES

Articles 63 and 64

PART I REQUIREMENTS RELATING TO THE OFFER

[8.550]

1. The terms of the offer must be recommended by all the directors of the company other than any director who is—

(a) the person by whom, or on whose behalf, an offer is made ("offeror"); or

(b) a director of the offeror.

2. (1) This paragraph applies to an offer for debentures or for non-equity share capital.

(2) Where, at the date of the offer, shares carrying 50 per cent or less of the voting rights attributable to the equity share capital are held by or on behalf of the offeror, the offer must include or be accompanied by an offer made by the offeror for the rest of the shares comprised in the equity share capital.

3. (1) This paragraph applies to an offer for shares comprised in the equity share capital.

(2) Where, at the date of the offer, shares which carry 50 per cent or less of the categories of voting rights described in sub-paragraph (3) are held by or on behalf of the offeror, it must be a condition of the offer that sufficient shares will be acquired or agreed to be acquired by the offeror pursuant to or during the offer so as to result in shares carrying more than 50 per cent of one or both categories of relevant voting rights being held by him or on his behalf.

(3) The categories of voting rights mentioned in sub-paragraph (2) are—

(a) voting rights exercisable in general meetings of the company;

(b) voting rights attributable to the equity share capital.

4. (1) Subject to sub-paragraph (2), the offer must be open for acceptance by every recipient for the period of at least 21 days beginning with the day after the day on which the invitation or inducement in question was first communicated to recipients of the offer.

(2) Sub-paragraph (1) does not apply if the offer is totally withdrawn and all persons are released from any obligation incurred under it.

5. The acquisition of the shares or debentures to which the offer relates must not be conditional upon the recipients approving, or consenting, to any payment or other benefit being made or given to any director or former director of the company in connection with, or as compensation or consideration for—

(a) his ceasing to be a director;

(b) his ceasing to hold any office held in conjunction with any directorship; or

(c) in the case of a former director, his ceasing to hold any office which he held in conjunction with his former directorship and which he continued to hold after ceasing to be a director.

6. The consideration for the shares or debentures must be—

(a) cash; or

(b) in the case of an offeror which is a body corporate other than an open-ended investment company, either cash or shares in, or debentures of, the body corporate or any combination of such cash, shares or debentures.

PART II ACCOMPANYING MATERIAL

[8.551]

7. An indication of the identity of the offeror and, if the offer is being made on behalf of another person, the identity of that person.

8. An indication of the fact that the terms of the offer are recommended by all directors of the company other than (if that is the case) any director who is the offeror or a director of the offeror.

9. An indication to the effect that any person who is in any doubt about the invitation or inducement should consult a person authorised under the Act.

10. An indication that, except insofar as the offer may be totally withdrawn and all persons released from any obligation incurred under it, the offer is open for acceptance by every recipient for the period of at least 21 days beginning with the day after the day on which the invitation or inducement in question was first communicated to recipients of the offer.

11. An indication of the date on which the invitation or inducement was first communicated to the recipients of the offer.

12. An indication that the acquisition of the shares or debentures to which the offer relates is not conditional upon the recipients approving, or consenting, to any payment or other benefit being made or given to any director or former director of the company in connection with, or as compensation or consideration for—

(a) his ceasing to be a director;

(b) his ceasing to hold any office held in conjunction with any directorship; or

(c) in the case of a former director, his ceasing to hold any office which he held in conjunction with his former directorship and which he continued to hold after ceasing to be a director.

13. An indication of the place where additional material listed in Part III may be inspected.

14. The audited accounts of the company in respect of the latest accounting reference period for which the period for laying and delivering accounts under [the 2006 Act] has passed or, if accounts in respect of a later accounting reference period have been delivered under the relevant legislation, as shown in those accounts and not the earlier accounts.

15. Advice to the directors of the company on the financial implications of the offer which is given by a competent person who is independent of and who has no substantial financial interest in the company or the offeror, being advice which gives the opinion of that person in relation to the offer.

16. An indication by the directors of the company, acting as a board, of the following matters—

(a) whether or not there has been any material change in the financial position or prospects of the company since the end of the latest accounting reference period in respect of which audited accounts have been delivered to the relevant registrar of companies under the relevant legislation;

(b) if there has been any such change, the particulars of it;

(c) any interests, in percentage terms, which any of them have in the shares in or debentures of the company . . .

(d) any interests, in percentage terms, which any of them have in the shares in or debentures of any offeror which is a body corporate . . .

17. An indication of any material interest which any director has in any contract entered into by the offeror and in any contract entered into by any member of any group of which the offeror is a member.

18. An indication as to whether or not each director intends to accept the offer in respect of his own beneficial holdings in the company.

19. In the case of an offeror which is a body corporate and the shares in or debentures of which are to be the consideration or any part of the consideration for the offer, an indication by the directors of the offeror that the information concerning the offeror and those shares or debentures contained in the document is correct.

20. If the offeror is making the offer on behalf of another person—

(a) an indication by the offeror as to whether or not he has taken any steps to ascertain whether that person will be in a position to implement the offer;

(b) if he has taken any such steps, an indication by him as to what those steps are; and

(c) the offeror's opinion as to whether that person will be in a position to implement the offer.

21. An indication that each of the following—

(a) each of the directors of the company;

(b) the offeror; and

(c) if the offeror is a body corporate, each of the directors of the offeror;

is responsible for the information required by Part I and this Part of this Schedule insofar as it relates to themselves or their respective bodies corporate and that, to the best of their knowledge and belief (having taken all reasonable care to ensure that such is the case) the information is in accordance with the facts and that no material fact has been omitted.

22. The particulars of—

(a) all shares in or debentures of the company; and

(b) all investments falling within paragraph 17, 19 or 21 of Schedule 1 so far as relating to shares in or debentures of the company;

which are held by or on behalf of the offeror or each offeror, if there is more than one, or if none are so held an appropriate negative statement.

23. An indication as to whether or not the offer is conditional upon acceptance in respect of a minimum number of shares or debentures being received and, if the offer is so conditional, what the minimum number is.

24. Where the offer is conditional upon acceptances, an indication of the date which is the latest date on which it can become unconditional.

25. If the offer is, or has become, unconditional an indication of the fact that it will remain open until further notice and that at least 14 days' notice will be given before it is closed.

26. An indication as to whether or not, if circumstances arise in which an offeror is able compulsorily to acquire shares of any dissenting minority under [Chapter 3 of Part 28 of the Companies Act 2006 (c 46)], that offeror intends to so acquire those shares.

27. If shares or debentures are to be acquired for cash, an indication of the period within which the payment will be made.

28. (1) Subject to sub-paragraph (2), if the consideration or any part of the consideration for the shares or debentures to be acquired is shares in or debentures of an offeror—

(a) an indication of the nature and particulars of the offeror's business, its financial and trading prospects and its place of incorporation;

(b) the following information, in respect of any offeror which is a body corporate and in respect of the company, for the period of five years immediately preceding the date on which the invitation or inducement in question was first communicated to recipients of the offer—

(i) turnover,

(ii) profit on ordinary activities before and after tax,

(iii) extraordinary items,

(iv) profits and loss, and

(v) the rate per cent of any dividends paid, adjusted as appropriate to take account of relevant changes over the period and the total amount absorbed thereby.

(2) In the case of a body corporate—

(a) which was incorporated during the period of five years immediately preceding the date on which the invitation or inducement in question was first communicated to recipients of the offer; or

(b) which has, at any time during that period, been exempt from the provisions of [Part 15 of the 2006 Act] relating to the audit of accounts by virtue of [section 477 or 480] of that Act . . .

the information described in sub-paragraph (1) with respect to that body corporate need be included only in relation to the period since its incorporation or since it last ceased to be exempt from those provisions of [Part 15 of the 2006 Act].

29. Particulars of the first dividend in which any such shares or debentures will participate and of the rights attaching to them (including in the case of debentures, rights as to interest) and of any restrictions on their transfer.

30. An indication of the effect of the acceptance on the capital and income position of the holder of the shares in or debentures of the company.

31. Particulars of all material contracts (not being contracts which were entered into in the ordinary course of business) which were entered into by each of the company and the offeror during the period of two years immediately preceding the date on which the invitation or inducement in question was first communicated to recipients of the offer.

32. Particulars of the terms on which shares in or debentures of the company acquired in pursuance of the offer will be transferred and any restrictions on their transfer.

33. An indication as to whether or not it is proposed, in connection with the offer, that any payment or other benefit be made or given to any director or former director of the company in connection with, or as compensation or consideration for—

(a) his ceasing to be a director;

(b) his ceasing to hold any office held in conjunction with any directorship; or

(c) in the case of a former director, his ceasing to hold any office which he held in conjunction with his former directorship and which he continued to hold after ceasing to be a director;

and, if such payments or benefits are proposed, details of each one.

34. An indication as to whether or not there exists any agreement or arrangement between—

(a) the offeror or any person with whom the offeror has an agreement of the kind described in [section 824 of the 2006 Act]; and

(b) any director or shareholder of the company or any person who has been such a director or shareholder;

at any time during the period of twelve months immediately preceding the date on which the invitation or inducement in question was first communicated to recipients of the offer, being an agreement or arrangement which is connected with or dependent on the offer and, if there is any such agreement or arrangement, particulars of it.

35. An indication whether or not the offeror has reason to believe that there has been any material change in the financial position or prospects of the company since the end of the accounting reference period to which the accounts referred to in paragraph 14 relate, and if the offeror has reason to believe that there has been such a change, the particulars of it.

36. An indication as to whether or not there is any agreement or arrangement whereby any shares or debentures acquired by the offeror in pursuance of the offer will or may be transferred to any other person, together with the names of the parties to any such agreement or arrangement and particulars of all shares and debentures in the company held by such persons.

37. Particulars of any dealings—

(a) in the shares in or debentures of the company; and

(b) if the offeror is a body corporate, in the shares in or debentures of the offeror;

which took place during the period of twelve months immediately preceding the date on which the invitation or inducement in question was first communicated to recipients of the offer and which were entered into by every person who was a director of either the company or the offeror during that period; and, if there have been no such dealings, an indication to that effect.

38. In a case in which the offeror is a body corporate which is required to deliver accounts under [the 2006 Act], particulars of the assets and liabilities as shown in its audited accounts in respect of the latest accounting reference period for which the period for laying and delivering accounts under the relevant legislation has passed or, if accounts in respect of a later accounting reference period have been delivered under the relevant legislation, as shown in those accounts and not the earlier accounts.

39. Where valuations of assets are given in connection with the offer, the basis on which the valuation was made and the names and addresses of the persons who valued them and particulars of any relevant qualifications.

40. If any profit forecast is given in connection with the offer, an indication of the assumptions on which the forecast is based.

NOTES

The amendments to paras 14, 16, 28, 34 and 38 were made by the Companies Act 2006 (Consequential Amendments and Transitional Provisions) Order 2011, SI 2011/1265, art 26(1), (9), as from 12 May 2011.

The words in square brackets in para 26 were substituted by the Companies Act 2006 (Commencement No 2, Consequential Amendments, Transitional Provisions and Savings) Order 2007, SI 2007/1093, art 6(1), Sch 3, para 10, as from 6 April 2007.

PART III ADDITIONAL MATERIAL AVAILABLE FOR INSPECTION

[8.552]

41. The memorandum and articles of association of the company.

42. If the offeror is a body corporate, the memorandum and articles of association of the offeror or, if there is no such memorandum and articles, any instrument constituting or defining the constitution of the offeror and, in either case, if the relevant document is not written in English, a certified translation in English.

43. In the case of a company that does not fall within paragraph 45—

(a) the audited accounts of the company in respect of the last two accounting reference periods for which the laying and delivering of accounts under [the 2006 Act] has passed; and

(b) if accounts have been delivered to the relevant registrar of companies, in respect of a later accounting reference period, a copy of those accounts.

44. In the case of an offeror which is required to deliver accounts to the registrar of companies and which does not fall within paragraph 45—

(a) the audited accounts of the offeror in respect of the last two accounting reference periods for which the laying and delivering of accounts under [the 2006 Act] has passed; and

(b) if accounts have been delivered to the relevant registrar of companies in respect of a later accounting reference period, a copy of those accounts.

45. In the case of a company or an offeror—

(a) which was incorporated during the period of three years immediately preceding the date on which the invitation or inducement in question was first communicated to recipients of the offer; or

(b) which has, at any time during that period, been exempt from the provisions of [Part 15 of the 2006 Act] relating to the audit of accounts by virtue of [section 477 or 480] of that Act . . .

the information described in whichever is relevant of paragraph 43 or 44 with respect to that body corporate need be included only in relation to the period since its incorporation or since it last ceased to be exempt from those provisions of [Part 15 of the 2006 Act].

46. All existing contracts of service entered into for a period of more than one year between the company and any of its directors and, if the offeror is a body corporate, between the offeror and any of its directors.

47. Any report, letter, valuation or other document any part of which is exhibited or referred to in the information required to be made available by Part II and this Part of this Schedule.

48. If the offer document contains any statement purporting to have been made by an expert, that expert's written consent to the inclusion of that statement.

49. All material contracts (if any) of the company and of the offeror (not, in either case, being contracts which were entered into in the ordinary course of business) which were entered into during the period of two years immediately preceding the date on which the invitation or inducement in question was first communicated to recipients of the offer.

NOTES

The amendments to paras 43, 44, 45 were made by the Companies Act 2006 (Consequential Amendments and Transitional Provisions) Order 2011, SI 2011/1265, art 26(1), (10), as from 12 May 2011.

SCHEDULE 5
STATEMENTS FOR CERTIFIED HIGH NET WORTH INDIVIDUALS AND SELF-CERTIFIED SOPHISTICATED INVESTORS

Articles 48 and 50A

PART I STATEMENT FOR CERTIFIED HIGH NET WORTH INDIVIDUALS

[8.553]

1. The statement to be signed for the purposes of article 48(2) (definition of high net worth individual) must be in the following form and contain the following content—

"STATEMENT FOR CERTIFIED HIGH NET WORTH INDIVIDUAL

I declare that I am a certified high net worth individual for the purposes of the Financial Services and Markets Act 2000 (Financial Promotion) Order 2005.

(a) I can receive financial promotions that may not have been approved by a person authorised by the [Financial Conduct Authority];

(b) the content of such financial promotions may not conform to rules issued by the [Financial Conduct Authority];

(c) **by signing this statement I may lose significant rights;**

(d) I may have no right to complain to either of the following—

(i) the [Financial Conduct Authority]; or

(ii) the Financial Ombudsman Scheme;

(e) I may have no right to seek compensation from the Financial Services Compensation Scheme.

I am a certified high net worth individual because **at least one of the following applies—**

(a) I had, during the financial year immediately preceding the date below, an annual income to the value of £100,000 or more;

(b) I held, throughout the financial year immediately preceding the date below, net assets to the value of £250,000 or more. Net assets for these purposes do not include—

(i) the property which is my primary residence or any loan secured on that residence;

(ii) any rights of mine under a qualifying contract of insurance within the meaning of the Financial Services and Markets Act 2000 (Regulated Activities) Order 2001; or

(iii) any benefits (in the form of pensions or otherwise) which are payable on the termination of my service or on my death or retirement and to which I am (or my dependants are), or may be, entitled.

I accept that I can lose my property and other assets from making investment decisions based on financial promotions.

I am aware that it is open to me to seek advice from someone who specialises in advising on investments.

Signature . . . .

Date . . . ."

NOTES

Words in square brackets substituted by the Financial Services Act 2012 (Consequential Amendments and Transitional Provisions) Order 2013, SI 2013/472, art 3, Sch 2, para 108(d), as from 1 April 2013.

PART II STATEMENT FOR SELF-CERTIFIED SOPHISTICATED INVESTORS

[8.554]

2. The statement to be signed for the purposes of article 50A(1) (definition of self-certified sophisticated investor) must be in the following form and contain the following content—

"STATEMENT FOR SELF-CERTIFIED SOPHISTICATED INVESTOR

I declare that I am a self-certified sophisticated investor for the purposes of the Financial Services and Markets Act (Financial Promotion) Order 2005.

I understand that this means:

(a) I can receive financial promotions that may not have been approved by a person authorised by the [Financial Conduct Authority];

(b) the content of such financial promotions may not conform to rules issued by the [Financial Conduct Authority];

(c) **by signing this statement I may lose significant rights;**

(d) I may have no right to complain to either of the following—

(i) the [Financial Conduct Authority]; or

(ii) the Financial Ombudsman Scheme;

(e) I may have no right to seek compensation from the Financial Services Compensation Scheme.

I am a self-certified sophisticated investor because **at least one of the following applies—**

(a) I am a member of a network or syndicate of business angels and have been so for at least the last six months prior to the date below;

(b) I have made more than one investment in an unlisted company in the two years prior to the date below;

(c) I am working, or have worked in the two years prior to the date below, in a professional capacity in the private equity sector, or in the provision of finance for small and medium enterprises;

(d) I am currently, or have been in the two years prior to the date below, a director of a company with an annual turnover of at least £1 million.

I accept that I can lose my property and other assets from making investment decisions based on financial promotions.

I am aware that it is open to me to seek advice from someone who specialises in advising on investments.

Signature. . . . .

Date. . . . ."

NOTES

Words in square brackets substituted by the Financial Services Act 2012 (Consequential Amendments and Transitional Provisions) Order 2013, SI 2013/472, art 3, Sch 2, para 108(d), as from 1 April 2013.

SCHEDULE 6

(Sch 6 revokes the Financial Services and Markets Act 2000 (Financial Promotion) Order 2001 (SI 2001/1335) and various Orders and provisions that amended the 2001 Order.)

FINANCIAL SERVICES AND MARKETS ACT 2000 (CONTROLLERS) (EXEMPTION) ORDER 2009

(SI 2009/774)

NOTES

Made: 24 March 2009.

Authority: Financial Services and Markets Act 2000, ss 192(a), 428(3).

Commencement: 15 April 2009.

This Order is reproduced as amended by: the Financial Services Act 2012 (Consequential Amendments and Transitional Provisions) Order 2013, SI 2013/472; the Financial Services and Markets Act 2000 (Regulated Activities) (Amendment) (No 2) Order 2013, SI 2013/1881; the Financial Services and Markets Act 2000 (Regulated Activities) (Amendment) Order 2014, SI 2014/366; the Solvency 2 Regulations 2015, SI 2015/575; the Financial Services and Markets Act 2000 (Amendment) (EU Exit) Regulations 2019, SI 2019/632.

Transitional provisions in relation to Gibraltar-based firms and activities: see the Gibraltar (Miscellaneous Amendments) (EU Exit) Regulations 2019, SI 2019/680, reg 11 at **[12.129]**.

[8.555]

1 Citation and commencement

This Order may be cited as the Financial Services and Markets Act 2000 (Controllers) (Exemption) Order 2009 and comes into force on 15th April 2009.

[8.556]

2 Interpretation

In this Order—

"the Act" means the Financial Services and Markets Act 2000;

"authorised building society" means any UK authorised person which is a building society within the meaning of section 119 of the Building Societies Act 1986 (interpretation);

["managing agent" has the meaning given in article 3 of the Financial Services and Markets Act 2000 (Regulated Activities) Order 2001;]

"relevant friendly society" means any UK authorised person which is a friendly society to which neither subsection (2) nor subsection (3) of section 37 of the Friendly Societies Act 1992 (restriction on combinations of business) applies; and

"relevant UK authorised person" means a UK authorised person other than—

[(a) a credit institution which has permission under Part 4A of the Act to carry on the regulated activity of accepting deposits;

(b) an investment firm (as defined in section 424A of the Act);

(c) a management company (as defined in section 237(2) of the Act);]

[(d) an insurance undertaking which includes for the purposes of this Order a managing agent; or

(e) a reinsurance undertaking.]

NOTES

Definition "managing agent" inserted by the Solvency 2 Regulations 2015, SI 2015/575, reg 60, Sch 2, para 30(b), as from 1 January 2016.

The definition "relevant UK authorised person" is amended as follows:

Paras (a)–(c) substituted by the Financial Services and Markets Act 2000 (Amendment) (EU Exit) Regulations 2019, SI 2019/632, reg 185, as from IP completion day (as defined in the European Union (Withdrawal Agreement) Act 2020, s 39).

Paras (d), (e) substituted by SI 2015/575, reg 60, Sch 2, para 30(a), as from 1 January 2016.

[8.557]

3 Matters affecting calculations under this Order

For the purposes of calculations under this Order—

(a) the holding of shares or voting power by a person ("A1") includes any shares or voting power held by another ("A2") if A1 and A2 are acting in concert; and

(b) the provisions of section 184 of the Act (disregarded holdings) apply.

[8.558]

4 General exemption in respect of certain non-directive firms

(1) This article provides exemptions from the obligations in sections 178 and 191D of the Act [(notifying the regulators)] in relation to a person ("A") who decides to acquire, increase, reduce or cease to have control over a relevant UK authorised person ("B").

(2) This article does not apply where B is an authorised building society or a relevant friendly society.

(3) Where A decides to acquire or increase control over B, A is exempt from the obligation imposed by section 178 unless giving effect to the decision would result in A beginning to be in the position of holding—

(a) 20% or more of the shares in B or in a parent undertaking of B ("P");
(b) 20% or more of the voting power in B or P; or
(c) shares or voting power in B or P as a result of which A is able to exercise significant influence over the management of B.

(4) Where A decides to reduce or cease to have control over B, A is exempt from the obligation imposed by section 191D unless giving effect to the decision would result in A ceasing to be in the position of holding—

(a) 20% or more of the shares in B or in a parent undertaking of B ("P");
(b) 20% or more of the voting power in B or P; or
(c) shares or voting power in B or P as a result of which A is able to exercise significant influence over the management of B.

NOTES

Para (1): words in square brackets substituted by the Financial Services Act 2012 (Consequential Amendments and Transitional Provisions) Order 2013, SI 2013/472, art 3, Sch 2, para 166, as from 1 April 2013.

5, 6 *(Art 5 (Specific exemptions in respect of authorised building societies), and art 6 (Specific exemptions in respect of friendly societies) are outside the scope of this work.)*

[8.559]

[6A Specific exemptions in respect of consumer credit

(1) This article provides exemptions from the obligations in sections 178 and 191D of the Act in relation to a person ("A") who decides to acquire, increase, reduce or cease to have control over a UK authorised person ("B") who—

(a) carries on regulated activities which are relevant credit activities [or activities to which, by virtue of section 39(1D) of the Act, sections 20(1) and (1A) and 23(1A) of the Act do not apply when carried on by B], and
(b) does not carry on any other regulated activities.

(2) Where A decides to acquire or increase control over B, A is exempt from the obligation imposed by section 178 unless giving effect to the decision would result in A beginning to be in the position of holding—

(a) 33% or more of the shares in B or in a parent undertaking of B ("P"),
(b) 33% or more of the voting power in B or P, or
(c) shares or voting power in B or P as a result of which A is able to exercise significant influence over the management of B.

(3) Where A decides to reduce or cease to have control over B, A is exempt from the obligation imposed by section 191D unless giving effect to the decision would result in A ceasing to be in the position of holding—

(a) 33% or more of the shares in B or in a parent undertaking of B ("P"),
(b) 33% or more of the voting power in B or P, or
(c) shares or voting power in B or P as a result of which A is able to exercise significant influence over the management of B.

(4) For the purposes of this article, each of the following is a "relevant credit activity"—

(a) an activity of the kind specified by article 36A of the Regulated Activities Order (credit broking) when carried on in the case specified in paragraph (6), (7) or (8),
(b) an activity of the kind specified by article 39D of that Order (debt adjusting) when carried on—
    (i) in the case specified in paragraph (6), by a person who also carries on an activity of the kind specified by sub-paragraph (a),
    (ii) by a person [in connection with an activity of the kind specified by sub-paragraph (d) or (e) and where that person] also carries on an activity of the kind specified by sub-paragraph (d) or (e), or
    (iii) by a not-for-profit body,
(c) an activity of the kind specified by article 39E of that Order (debt-counselling) when carried on—
    (i) in the case specified in paragraph (6), by a person who also carries on an activity of the kind specified by sub-paragraph (a),
    (ii) by a person [in connection with an activity of the kind specified by sub-paragraph (d) or (e) and where that person] also carries on an activity of the kind specified by sub-paragraph (d) or (e), or
    (iii) by a not-for-profit body,
(d) an activity of the kind specified by article 60B of that Order (regulated credit agreements) if—
    (i) it is carried on by a supplier,
    (ii) no charge (by way of interest or otherwise) is payable by the borrower in connection with the provision of credit under the regulated credit agreement, and
    (iii) the regulated credit agreement is not a hire-purchase agreement or a conditional sale agreement,
(e) an activity of the kind specified by article 60N of that Order (regulated consumer hire agreements),
(f) an activity of the kind specified by article 89A of that Order (providing credit information services) where carried on by a person [in connection with an activity of the kind specified by sub-paragraph (a) to (e) and where that person] also carries on an activity of the kind specified by any of sub-paragraphs (a) to (e), or
(g) an activity of the kind specified by article 64 of that Order (agreeing to carry on specified activities) so far as relevant to any activity of the kind specified by sub-paragraphs (a) to (f).

[(4A) For the purposes of paragraph (4), any activity which the person carries on is to be disregarded if sections 20(1) and (1A) and 23(1A) of the Act do not apply to the carrying on of that activity by virtue of section 39(1D) of the Act.]

(5) [Except where the activity is carried on by a not-for-profit body,] an activity is not a relevant credit activity for the purposes of—

(a) sub-paragraphs (a) to (e) of paragraph (4), and

(b) sub-paragraph (g) of that paragraph so far at it relates to activities of the kind specified by any of those sub-paragraphs,

if it relates to an agreement under which the obligation of the borrower to repay [or the hirer to pay] is secured, or is to be secured, by a legal [or equitable] mortgage on land.

(6) The case specified in this paragraph is where a supplier (other than a domestic premises supplier) carries on the activity for the purposes of, or in connection with, the sale of goods or supply of services by the supplier to a customer (who need not be the borrower under the credit agreement or the hirer under the consumer hire agreement).

(7) The case specified in this paragraph is where the activity relates to a green deal plan.

(8) The case specified in this paragraph is where activity relates to a consumer hire agreement where the good being hired is a vehicle.

(9) For the purposes of this [article]—

"borrower" includes—

(a) any person providing a guarantee or indemnity under an agreement, and

(b) a person to whom the rights and duties of the borrower under an agreement or a person falling within sub-paragraph (a) have passed by assignment or operation of law;

"conditional sale agreement" has the meaning given by article 60L of the Regulated Activities Order;

"customer" means a person to whom a supplier sells goods or supplies services or agrees to do so;

"domestic premises supplier" means a supplier who sells goods or supplies services to customers who are individuals while physically present in the dwelling of the customer or in consequence of an agreement concluded whilst the supplier was physically present in the dwelling of the customer (though a supplier who does so on an occasional basis is not to be treated as a "domestic premises supplier");

"green deal plan" has the meaning given by section 1 of the Energy Act 2011;

"hire-purchase agreement" has the meaning given by the Regulated Activities Order;

"not-for-profit body" means a body which, by virtue of its constitution or any enactment—

(a) is required (after payment of outgoings) to apply the whole of its income and any capital it expends for charitable or public purposes, and

(b) is prohibited from directly or indirectly distributing amongst its members any part of its assets (otherwise than for charitable or public purposes);

"Regulated Activities Order" means the Financial Services and Markets Act 2000 (Regulated Activities) Order 2001;

"regulated credit agreement" has the meaning given by the Regulated Activities Order;

"supplier" means a person whose main business is to sell goods or supply services and not to carry on a regulated activity, other than an activity of the kind specified by article 60N of the Regulated Activities Order (regulated consumer hire agreements).]

NOTES

Inserted by the Financial Services and Markets Act 2000 (Regulated Activities) (Amendment) (No 2) Order 2013, SI 2013/1881, art 19, as from 1 April 2014.

All amendments to this article were made by the Financial Services and Markets Act 2000 (Regulated Activities) (Amendment) Order 2014, SI 2014/366, art 14, as from 1 April 2014.

---

7 *(Revokes the Financial Services and Markets Act 2000 (Controllers) (Exemption) Order 2001, the Financial Services and Markets Act 2000 (Controllers) (Exemption) (No 2) Order 2001, and reg 21 of the Financial Services and Markets Act 2000 (Regulated Activities) (Amendment) (No 2) Order 2003.)*

FINANCIAL SERVICES ACT 2012 (MISLEADING STATEMENTS AND IMPRESSIONS) ORDER 2013

(SI 2013/637)

NOTES

Made: 13 March 2013.

Authority: Financial Services Act 2012, ss 93(3)–(5), 115(2).

Commencement: 1 April 2013.

This Order is reproduced as amended by: the Alternative Investment Fund Managers Regulations 2013, SI 2013/1773; the Financial Services and Markets Act 2000 (Regulated Activities) (Amendment) Order 2015, SI 2015/369.

[8.560]

1 Citation, commencement and interpretation

(1) This Order may be cited as the Financial Services Act 2012 (Misleading Statements and Impressions) Order 2013 and comes into force on 1st April 2013.

(2) In this Order—

"the Act" means the Financial Services Act 2012;

"contract of insurance" has the meaning given by article 3(1) of the Regulated Activities Order;

"controlled activity" means an activity which falls within Part 1 of Schedule 1 to the Financial Promotion Order;

"controlled investment" means an investment which falls within Part 2 of Schedule 1 to the Financial Promotion Order;

"the Financial Promotion Order" means the Financial Services and Markets Act 2000 (Financial Promotion) Order 2005;

"the Regulated Activities Order" means the Financial Services and Markets Act 2000 (Regulated Activities) Order 2001.

[8.561]

2 Relevant agreements—specified kinds of activity

The following kinds of activity are specified for the purposes of section 93(3)(a) of the Act (interpretation of Part 7)—

(a) a controlled activity;

(b) an activity of the kind specified by any of the following provisions of the Regulated Activities Order—

(i) article 45 (sending dematerialised instructions),

[(ia) article 51ZA (managing a UCITS),

(ib) article 51ZB (acting as a trustee or depositary of a UCITS),

(ic) article 51ZC (managing an AIF),

(id) article 51ZD (acting as a trustee or depositary of an AIF),

(ii) article 51ZE (establishing etc. a collective investment scheme),]

(iii) article 52 (establishing etc a pension scheme), or

(iv) article 57 (managing the underwriting capacity of a Lloyd's syndicate),

(c) so far as not already specified by paragraph (a), an activity of the kind specified by any of the following provisions of the Regulated Activities Order—

(i) article 14 (dealing in investments as principal),

(ii) article 21 (dealing in investments as agent),

(iii) article 25(1) or (2) (arranging deals in investments),

(iv) article 39A (assisting in the administration and performance of a contract of insurance),

(v) article 53 (advising on investments), or

(vi) so far as relevant to any of the provisions specified by sub-paragraphs (i) to (v), article 64, so far as it relates to a contract of insurance.

NOTES

Para (2): sub-paras (b)(ia)–(id), (ii) substituted (for the original sub-para (b)(ii)) by the Alternative Investment Fund Managers Regulations 2013, SI 2013/1773, reg 81, Sch 2, Part 2, para 23, as from 22 July 2013.

[8.562]

[3 Relevant benchmarks

The benchmarks known by the following names are specified for the purposes of section 93(4) of the Act—

(a) The London Interbank Offered Rate, also known as LIBOR;

(b) ISDAFIX;

(c) Sterling Overnight Index Average, also known as SONIA;

(d) Repurchase Overnight Average, also known as RONIA;

(e) WM/Reuters London 4pm Closing Spot Rate;

(f) London Gold Fixing;

(g) LBMA Silver Price;

(h) ICE Brent Index.]

NOTES

Substituted by the Financial Services and Markets Act 2000 (Regulated Activities) (Amendment) Order 2015, SI 2015/369, art 9, as from 1 April 2015.

Note that as from 1 April 2015 ISDAFIX became ICE Swap Rate; and that from 20 March 2015, the London Gold Fixing benchmark became LBMA Gold Price.

[8.563]

4 Relevant investments

Controlled investments are specified for the purposes of section 93(5) of the Act.

BANK RECOVERY AND RESOLUTION (NO 2) ORDER 2014

(SI 2014/3348)

NOTES

Made: 18 December 2014.

Authority: Financial Services and Markets Act 2000. s 192B(4); Banking Act 2009, s 230; European Communities Act 1972, s 2(2) (see the note "Statutory Instruments made under the European Communities Act 1972" preceding paragraph **[4.1]** *ante*).

Commencement: 10 January 2015.

This Order is reproduced as amended by: the Bank Recovery and Resolution Order 2016, SI 2016/1239; the Bank Recovery and Resolution and Miscellaneous Provisions (Amendment) (EU Exit) Regulations 2018, SI 2018/1394; the Companies, Limited Liability Partnerships and Partnerships (Amendment etc) (EU Exit) Regulations 2019, SI 2019/348; the Bank Recovery and Resolution (Amendment) (EU Exit) Regulations 2020, SI 2020/1350; the Financial Services Act 2021 (Prudential Regulation of Credit Institutions and Investment Firms) (Consequential Amendments and Miscellaneous Provisions) Regulations 2021, SI 2021/1376.

This Order implements, in part, Directive 2014/59/EU of the European Parliament and of the Council of 15 May 2014 establishing a framework for the recovery and resolution of credit institutions and investment firms ("the Bank Recover and

Resolution Directive"). Most of this Order is outside the scope of this work, and only the provisions relevant to this work have been included. Omitted provisions are not annotated. Amendments made by this Order have been incorporated where relevant.

ARRANGEMENT OF ARTICLES

PART 17
MODIFIED APPLICATION OF COMPANY LAW TO BANKS ETC IN RESOLUTION

SCHEDULES

PART 17 MODIFIED APPLICATION OF COMPANY LAW TO BANKS ETC IN RESOLUTION

[8.564]
216 Interpretation of Part

(1) In this Part—

["applying the public equity support tool" means participating in the recapitalisation of an institution or an entity by providing capital to the institution or entity in exchange for Common Equity Tier 1 instruments, Additional Tier 1 instruments or Tier 2 instruments;

"Common Equity Tier 1 instruments", "Additional Tier 1 instruments" and "Tier 2 instruments" have the meanings given in section 3(1) of the Banking Act 2009;]

"the use of resolution tools, powers and mechanisms" means—

(a) the exercise by the Bank or the Treasury of a stabilisation power (within the meaning given in section 1(4) of the Banking Act 2009);

(b) the making by the Bank of a mandatory reduction instrument (within the meaning given in section 6B of that Act); or

[(c) he exercise by the Treasury of its powers under section 228 of the Banking Act 2009, subject to the requirements of the capital requirements regulation [and CRR rules], where the Treasury is applying the public equity support tool; and]

"UK-registered company" has the meaning given in section 1158 of the Companies Act 2006 (meaning of UK-registered company).

(2) . . .

(3) For the purposes of this Part a company is a company under resolution if it is a UK-registered company which is subject to the use of resolution tools, powers and mechanisms.

(4) But such a company is not a company under resolution if—

(a) it has ceased to be subject to the exercise of a stabilisation power or the application of the public equity support tool; and

(b) the results which are to be achieved by an instrument made in respect of the company under Part 1 of the Banking Act 2009 have been achieved.

NOTES

The definitions "applying the public equity support tool" and "Common Equity Tier 1 instruments" in para (1) were inserted, sub-para (c) of the definition "the use of resolution tools, powers and mechanisms" was substituted, and para (2) was revoked, by the Bank Recovery and Resolution and Miscellaneous Provisions (Amendment) (EU Exit) Regulations 2018, SI 2018/1394, reg 4, Sch 3, para 108, as from IP completion day (as defined in the European Union (Withdrawal Agreement) Act 2020, s 39).

The words "and CRR rules" in square brackets in the definition "the use of resolution tools, powers and mechanisms" were inserted by the Financial Services Act 2021 (Prudential Regulation of Credit Institutions and Investment Firms) (Consequential Amendments and Miscellaneous Provisions) Regulations 2021, SI 2021/1376, reg 19(13), as from 1 January 2022.

[8.565]
217 Shadow directorship

(1) A relevant person is not to be treated, in relation to a company under resolution, as—

(a) a shadow director for the purposes of the enactments specified in paragraph (3);

(b) a person who discharges managerial responsibilities for the purposes of those enactments (unless that person has been appointed as a director); or

(c) a director by virtue of paragraph (b) of the definition of "director" given in section 417(1) of FSMA (a person in accordance with whose directions or instructions the directors of a body corporate are accustomed to act).

(2) "Relevant persons" are—

(a) the Bank; . . .

(b) persons who are employed by, or act on behalf of, the Bank;

[(c) a resolution administrator appointed under section 62B of the Banking Act 2009; and

(d) a temporary manager appointed under section 71C of the Financial Services and Markets Act 2000].

(3) The specified enactments are—
- (a) the Companies Act 2006;
- (b) the Insolvency Act 1986;
- (c) the Company Directors Disqualification Act 1986; and
- (d) FSMA.

NOTES

Para (2): word omitted from sub-para (a) revoked, and sub-paras (c), (d) inserted, by the Bank Recovery and Resolution Order 2016, SI 2016/1239, art 41(1), (15), as from 16 December 2016.

218 (*Article 218 (Modified application of legislation on cross-border mergers) was revoked by the Companies, Limited Liability Partnerships and Partnerships (Amendment etc) (EU Exit) Regulations 2019, SI 2019/348, reg 8, Sch 3, paras 35, 36, as from IP completion day (as defined in the European Union (Withdrawal Agreement) Act 2020, s 39).*)

[8.566]

219 Modified application of the Companies Act 2006 (disapplication of [Takeover Rules])

(1) . . .

(2) Part 28 of the Companies Act 2006 (Takeovers etc) has effect as if, in section 943 (rules), after subsection (1) there were inserted—

> "[(1ZA) Rules made in accordance with paragraph 7(1) and (2) of Part 2 of Schedule 1C] must provide that they do not apply in relation to any change in interests in shares or other transaction which is effected by the use of resolution tools, powers and mechanisms (within the meaning given in article 216 of the Bank Recovery and Resolution (No 2) Order 2014).".

NOTES

The words in square brackets in the article heading were substituted, para (1) was revoked, and the words in square brackets in para (2) were substituted, by the Bank Recovery and Resolution and Miscellaneous Provisions (Amendment) (EU Exit) Regulations 2018, SI 2018/1394, reg 4, Sch 3, para 110, as from IP completion day (as defined in the European Union (Withdrawal Agreement) Act 2020, s 39).

[8.567]

220 Modified application of the Companies Act 2006 (disapplication of other [requirements])

(1)–(3) . . .

(4) . . . the Companies Act 2006 applies with the modifications set out in Schedule 4 . . .

(5) . . . the Companies Act 2006 (Commencement No 8, Transitional Provisions and Savings) Order 2008 applies as if in Schedule 2 (transitional provisions and savings) after paragraph 43 (power of directors to allot shares etc: private company with only one class of shares (s. 550)) there were inserted—

> **"43A.**
>
> Paragraph 43 does not apply in relation to an existing company or a transitional company which is a company under resolution for the purposes of Part 17 of the Bank Recovery and Resolution (No 2) Order 2014.".

(6) . . .

NOTES

The word in square brackets in the article heading was substituted, and all words omitted were revoked, by the Bank Recovery and Resolution and Miscellaneous Provisions (Amendment) (EU Exit) Regulations 2018, SI 2018/1394, reg 4, Sch 3, para 111, as from IP completion day (as defined in the European Union (Withdrawal Agreement) Act 2020, s 39).

[8.568]

[220A Modified application of the Companies Act 2006 (shareholders' rights)

(1) The provisions of the Companies Act 2006 concerning the rights of shareholders to call general meetings and to amend the articles of association of the company apply to traded companies to which Part 1 of the Banking Act 2009 applies with the following modifications.

(2) "Traded company" has the meaning given in section 360C of the Companies Act 2006.

(3) Section 21 (amendment of articles) has effect as if, after subsection (3) there were inserted—

> "(4) A traded company (within the meaning of section 360C) to which Part 1 of the Banking Act 2009 applies may also amend its articles in accordance with section 307B."

(4) Section 307A (notice required of general meeting: certain meetings of traded companies), has effect as if, at the beginning of subsection (1), there were inserted "Subject to section 307B,".

(5) Part 13 (resolutions and meetings) has effect as if after section 307A there were inserted—

> **"307B Notice required of general meeting: traded companies meeting the conditions for early intervention**
>
> (1) Where the conditions in subsections (2) and (3) are satisfied, the members of a traded company to which Part 1 of the Banking Act 2009 applies may, by a resolution passed at a general meeting by a majority of two-thirds of those voting in person or by proxy—
> - (a) require the company to call a general meeting to pass a resolution to increase the company's share capital, provided that the meeting is to be called by notice of at least 10 days;
> - (b) amend the company's articles of association to permit a general meeting to be called to consider a proposal to increase the company's share capital by notice of at least 10 days.
>
> (2) The condition in this subsection is satisfied if—

Part 8 Financial Services SIs

(a) the company has infringed, or is likely in the near future to infringe—

(i) a relevant requirement within the meaning of section 204A of the Financial Services and Markets Act 2000; or

(ii) one or more of Articles 3 to 7, 14 to 17 or 24 to 26 of Regulation (EU) No 600/2014 of 15th May 2014 of the European Parliament and of the Council on Markets in Financial Instruments; or

(b) the conditions for appointment of a temporary manager under section 71C(1) of the Financial Services and Markets Act 2000 (temporary manager) are met in relation to the company.

(3) The condition in this subsection is satisfied if an increase in the share capital of the company is necessary to prevent the conditions in section 7 of the Banking Act 2009 for the exercise of the stabilisation powers provided for in Part 1 of that Act being met in relation to the company."]

NOTES

Inserted by the Bank Recovery and Resolution Order 2016, SI 2016/1239, art 41(1), (16), as from 16 December 2016.

SCHEDULE 4
MODIFIED APPLICATION OF THE COMPANIES ACT 2006 TO BANKS ETC IN RESOLUTION

Article 220(4)

PART 1 PROVISIONS CONCERNING THE EXERCISE OF CERTAIN RIGHTS OF SHAREHOLDERS IN LISTED COMPANIES

[8.569]

1 In relation to a company under resolution, this Part modifies the application of provisions of the Companies Act 2006 which concern the exercise of certain rights of shareholders in listed companies.

2 Section 145 (effect of provisions of articles as to enjoyment or exercise of members' rights) has effect as if, in subsection (3), paragraphs (ea) and (ga) were omitted.

3 Section 153 (exercise of rights where shares held on behalf of others: members' requests) has effect as if, in subsection (1), paragraph (ba) were omitted.

4 Section 282 (ordinary resolutions) has effect as if, in subsection (4), for ", by proxy or in advance (see section 322A)" there were substituted "or by proxy".

5 Section 283 (special resolutions) has effect as if, in subsection (5), for ", by proxy or in advance (see section 322A)" there were substituted "or by proxy".

6 Section 284 (votes: general rules) has effect as if, in subsection (5), the entry for section 322A were omitted.

7 Section 303 (members' power to require directors to call general meeting) has effect as if—

(a) in subsection (2)(a) and (b) for "5%" there were substituted "the required percentage"; and

(b) after subsection (2) there were inserted—

"(3A) The required percentage is 10%, except that in the case of a private company it is 5% if more than twelve months have elapsed since the end of the last general meeting—

(a) which was called in pursuance of a requirement under this section, or

(b) in relation to which any members of the company had (by virtue of an enactment, the company's articles or otherwise) rights with respect to the circulation of a resolution no less extensive than they would have had if the meeting had been so called at their request.".

8 Section 307 (notice required of general meeting) has effect as if subsections (A1) and (A2) were omitted.

9 Part 13 (resolutions and meetings) has effect as if section 307A (notice required of general meeting: certain meetings of traded companies) were omitted.

10 Section 311 (contents of notices of meetings) has effect as if—

(a) in subsection (2) the words "In relation to a company other than a traded company," were omitted; and

(b) subsection (3) were omitted.

11 Part 13 has effect as if the following sections were omitted—

(a) section 311A (traded companies: publication of information in advance of general meeting); and

(b) section 319A (traded companies: questions at meetings).

12 Section 327 (notice required of appointment of proxy etc) has effect as if—

(a) subsection (A1) were omitted; and

(b) in subsection (1) for "The following provisions apply in the case of traded companies and other companies as regards" there were substituted "This section applies to".

13 Section 330 (notice required of termination of proxy's authority) has effect as if—

(a) subsection (A1) were omitted; and

(b) in subsection (1) for "The following provisions apply in the case of traded companies and other companies as regards" there were substituted "This section applies to".

14 Part 13 has effect as if section 333A (traded company: duty to provide electronic address for receipt of proxies etc) were omitted.

15 Section 334 (application to class meetings) has effect as if—

(a) in subsection (1) for "subsections (2) to (3)" there were substituted "subsections (2) and (3)";

(b) in subsection (2)—

(i) after paragraph (a) there were inserted "and"; and

(ii) after paragraph (b) the word "and" and paragraph (c) were omitted; and

(c) subsection (2A) were omitted.

16 Section 336 (public companies and traded companies: annual general meeting) has effect as if—

(a) subsection (1A) were omitted;
(b) in subsections (2) and (3), in each place where they appear, the words "or (1A)" were omitted; and
(c) in the heading the words "and traded companies" were omitted.

17 Section 337 (public companies and traded companies: notice of AGM) has effect as if—
(a) in subsection (1) the words "or a private company that is a traded company" were omitted;
(b) in subsection (2) the words "of a public company that is not a traded company" were omitted;
(c) subsection (3) were omitted; and
(d) in the heading the words "and traded companies" were omitted.

18 Part 13 has effect as if the following sections were omitted—
(a) section 338 (public companies: members' power to require circulation of resolutions for AGMs); and
(b) section 338A (traded companies: members' power to include other matters in business dealt with at AGM).

19 Section 341 (results of poll to be made available on website) has effect as if—
(a) in subsection (1) the words "that is not a traded company" were omitted; and
(b) subsections (1A) and (1B) were omitted.

20 Section 352 (application of provisions to class meetings) has effect as if for subsections (1) and (1A) there were substituted—

"(1) The provisions of—
(a) section 341 (results of poll to be made available on website), and
(b) sections 342 to 351 (independent report on poll),
apply (with any necessary modifications) in relation to a meeting of holders of a class of shares of a quoted company in connection with the variation of the rights attached to such shares as they apply in relation to a general meeting of the company.".

21 Section 360 (computation of periods of notice etc: clear day rule) has effect as if, in subsection (1)—
(a) the entry for section 307A(1), (4), (5) and (7)(b) were omitted
(b) after the entry for section 314(4)(d) there were inserted "and"; and
(c) the entries for sections 337(3), 338(4)(d)(i) and 338A(5) were omitted.

22 Section 360A (electronic meetings and voting) has effect as if subsections (2) and (3) were omitted.

[23 Part 13 has effect as if the following sections were omitted—
(a) section 360AA (traded companies: confirmation of receipt of electronic voting);
(b) section 360B (traded companies: requirements for participating in and voting at general meetings); and
(c) section 360BA (traded companies: right to confirmation of vote after a general meeting).]

NOTES

Para 23: substituted by the Bank Recovery and Resolution (Amendment) (EU Exit) Regulations 2020, SI 2020/1350, reg 60, as from 28 December 2020.

PART 2 PROVISIONS CONCERNING MERGERS AND DIVISIONS OF PUBLIC LIMITED LIABILITY COMPANIES

[8.570]

24 In relation to a company under resolution, Part 27 of the Companies Act 2006 (mergers and divisions of public companies) has effect as if, in section 902 (application of this Part), for subsection (3) there were substituted—

"(3) This Part does not apply where the company in respect of which the compromise or arrangement is proposed—
(a) is being wound up; or
(b) is a company under resolution for the purposes of Part 17 of the Bank Recovery and Resolution (No 2) Order 2014."

PART 3 PROVISIONS CONCERNING THE MAINTENANCE AND ALTERATION OF A COMPANY'S SHARE CAPITAL

[8.571]

25 In relation to a company under resolution, this Part modifies the application of provisions of the Companies Act 2006 made—
(a) for the co-ordination of safeguards in respect of the formation of public limited liability companies and the maintenance and alteration of their capital; or
(b) for equivalent purposes in relation to companies to which the Safeguards Directive does not apply.

26 Section 550 (power of directors to allot shares etc: private company with only one class of shares) has effect as if—
(a) the existing provision were subsection (1); and
(b) after that provision there were inserted—

"(2) In relation to a company which is a company under resolution for the purposes of Part 17 of the Bank Recovery and Resolution (No 2) Order 2014, any provision in the company's articles which prohibits the directors from exercising the power referred to in subsection (1) is to be disregarded.".

27 Section 551 (power of directors to allot shares etc: authorisation by company) has effect as if after subsection (9) there were inserted—

"(10) In relation to a company which is a company under resolution for the purposes of Part 17 of the Bank Recovery and Resolution (No 2) Order 2014—

(a) the maximum amount of shares that may be allotted under the authorisation may be exceeded where necessary for the use of resolution tools, powers and mechanisms (within the meaning given in article 216 of that Order) in relation to the company;

(b) if the maximum amount is exceeded, the statement of that amount made in the authorisation is deemed to have been increased under subsection (4) by the amount of the excess;

(c) the authorisation does not expire until it is renewed or revoked after the company has ceased to be a company under resolution; and

(d) the authorisation may not be revoked or varied while the company is a company under resolution.".

28 Part 17 (a company's share capital) has effect as if the following sections were omitted—

(a) section 561 (existing shareholders' right of pre-emption); and

(b) section 568 (exclusion of pre-emption right: articles conferring corresponding right).

29 Section 569 (disapplication of pre-emption rights: private company with only one class of shares) has effect as if it provided that a determination made under subsection (1)(b) does not have effect.

30 Section 570 (disapplication of pre-emption rights: directors acting under general authorisation) has effect as if it provided that a determination made under subsection (1)(b) does not have effect.

31 Section 571 (disapplication of pre-emption rights by special resolution) has effect as if, in subsection (1)—

(a) after paragraph (a) ", or" were omitted; and

(b) paragraph (b) were omitted.

32 Section 586 (public companies: shares must be at least one-quarter paid-up) has effect as if for subsection (2) there were substituted—

"(2) This does not apply to shares allotted—

(a) in pursuance of an employers' share scheme; or

(b) by the use of resolution tools, powers and mechanisms (within the meaning given in article 216 of the Bank Recovery and Resolution (No 2) Order 2014) in relation to a company which is a company under resolution for the purposes of Part 17 of that Order.".

33 Section 593 (public company: valuation of non-cash consideration for shares) has effect as if after subsection (2) there were inserted—

"(2A) In relation to a company which is a company under resolution for the purposes of Part 17 of the Bank Recovery and Resolution (No 2) Order 2014, subsection (1) does not prevent the allotment of shares by the use of resolution tools, powers and mechanisms (within the meaning given in article 216 of that Order), and for the purposes of the Companies Acts such a share is deemed to be fully paid up.".

34 Section 617 (alteration of share capital of limited company) has effect as if, in subsection (5), at the end there were inserted—

"(f) the alteration of the share capital of a company, which is a company under resolution for the purposes of Part 17 of the Bank Recovery and Resolution (No 2) Order 2014, by the use of resolution tools, powers and mechanisms (within the meaning given in article 216 of that Order)".

35 Section 618 (sub-division or consolidation of shares) has effect—

(a) as if subsection (3) were omitted; and

(b) where the articles of a company under resolution would otherwise exclude or restrict the exercise of any power conferred by that section, as if that section provided that the exclusion or restriction does not have effect.

36 Section 656 (public companies: duty of directors to call meeting on serious loss of capital) has effect as if at the end there were inserted—

"(7) This section does not apply to a company which is a company under resolution for the purposes of Part 17 of the Bank Recovery and Resolution (No 2) Order 2014 ("the Order").

(8) Where the net assets of such a company became half or less of its called-up share capital before the date on which the company became a company under resolution—

(a) the duty of the directors to call a general meeting of the company under subsection (1) ceases to have effect on that date;

(b) a general meeting which has been called under subsection (1) but has not yet taken place is deemed to have been cancelled on that date; and

(c) any resolution passed at such a meeting which has taken place is subject to the use of resolution tools, powers and mechanisms (within the meaning given in article 216 of the Order) in relation to the company.".

FINANCIAL SERVICES AND MARKETS ACT 2000 (PROSPECTUS) REGULATIONS 2019

(SI 2019/1043)

NOTES

Made: 24 June 2019.

Authority: European Communities Act 1972, s s(2) (see the note "Statutory Instruments made under the European Communities Act 1972" preceding paragraph **[4.1]** *ante*).

Commencement: 21 July 2019.

These Regulations are reproduced as amended by: the Prospectus (Amendment etc) (EU Exit) Regulations 2019, SI 2019/1234; the Financial Services and Markets Act 2000 (Central Counterparties, Investment Exchanges, Prospectus and Benchmarks) (Amendment) Regulations 2020, SI 2020/117.

Transitional provisions in relation to Gibraltar-based firms and activities: see the Gibraltar (Miscellaneous Amendments) (EU Exit) Regulations 2019, SI 2019/680, reg 11 at **[12.129]**.

PART 1 GENERAL

[8.572]

1 Citation, commencement and interpretation

(1) These Regulations may be cited as the Financial Services and Markets Act 2000 (Prospectus) Regulations 2019 and come into force on 21st July 2019.

(2) In these Regulations—

"FSMA" means the Financial Services and Markets Act 2000;

"the FCA" means the Financial Conduct Authority;

"the EU Prospectus Regulation" means Regulation (EU) No 2017/1129 of the European Parliament and of the Council of 14 June 2017 on the prospectus to be published when securities are offered to the public or admitted to trading on a regulated market, and repealing Directive 2003/71/EC.

NOTES

Commencement: 21 July 2019.

[8.573]

2 Designation of competent authority

The FCA is designated as the competent authority for the purposes of the EU Prospectus Regulation.

NOTES

Commencement: 21 July 2019.

2A (*Originally inserted by the Financial Services and Markets Act 2000 (Central Counterparties, Investment Exchanges, Prospectus and Benchmarks) (Amendment) Regulations 2020, SI 2020/117, reg 8, as from 28 February 2020. Subsequently revoked by the Prospectus (Amendment etc) (EU Exit) Regulations 2019, SI 2019/1234, reg 30, as from IP completion day (as defined in the European Union (Withdrawal Agreement) Act 2020, s 39). Note that SI 2019/1234, reg 30 was substituted by the Financial Services (Miscellaneous Amendments) (EU Exit) Regulations 2020, SI 2020/628, reg 17(1), (2), with effect from immediately before IP completion day.*)

PARTS 2–4

3–39 (*Regs 3–35 (Pt 2) (as amended) amend the Financial Services and Markets Act 2000 at* **[7.1]**. *Regs 36, 37 (Pt 3) contain a minor and consequential amendment to the Financial Services Act 2012, and amend the Data Protection Act 2018. Regs 38, 39 (Pt 4) amend the Financial Services and Markets Act 2000 (Financial Promotion) Order 2005, SI 2005/1529 at* **[8.443]**, *and the Financial Services and Markets Act 2000 (Qualifying Provisions) Order 2013, SI 2013/419.*)

PART 5 TRANSITIONAL PROVISIONS

[8.574]

40 Transitional Provisions

(1) This regulation applies to a prospectus ("relevant prospectus") which is approved by the FCA, in accordance with Part 6 of FSMA, before 21st July 2019.

(2) This regulation ceases to apply to a relevant prospectus on 21st July 2020 or, if earlier, the date on which, in accordance with prospectus rules, the period of validity of the prospectus expires.

(3) In relation to a relevant prospectus—

(a) FSMA continues to have effect without the amendments made by Part 2 of these Regulations;

(b) the Financial Services and Markets Act 2000 (Financial Promotion) Order 2005 and the Financial Services and Markets Act 2000 (Qualifying EU Provisions) Order 2013 continue to have effect without the amendments made by Part 4 of these Regulations; and

(c) prospectus rules continue to have effect without any amendments made in consequence of, or otherwise in connection with, Part 2 of these Regulations.

(4) In this regulation—

"prospectus" includes a supplementary prospectus (within the meaning given in section 87G of FSMA without the amendments made by Part 2 of these Regulations); and

(5) "prospectus rules" has the meaning given in section 73A of FSMA.

NOTES

Commencement: 21 July 2019.

PART 6 REVIEW

[8.575]

41 Review

(1) The Treasury must from time to time—

(a) carry out a review of these Regulations;

(b) set out the conclusions of the review in a report; and

(c) publish the report.

(2) The first report under this regulation must be published on or before 21st July 2024.

(3) Subsequent reports must be published at intervals not exceeding five years.

(4) Section 30(3) of the Small Business, Enterprise and Employment Act 2015 requires that a review carried out under this regulation must, so far as is reasonable, have regard to how the EU Prospectus Regulation is implemented in other countries which are subject to its obligations.

(5) Section 30(4) of that Act requires that a report published under this regulation must, in particular—

(a) set out the objectives intended to be achieved by these Regulations;
(b) assess the extent to which those objectives are achieved;
(c) assess whether those objectives remain appropriate; and
(d) if those objectives remain appropriate, assess the extent to which they could be achieved in another way that imposes less onerous regulatory provision.

(6) In this regulation, "regulatory provision" has the same meaning as in sections 28 to 32 of the Small Business, Enterprise and Employment Act 2015 (see section 32 of that Act).

NOTES

Commencement: 21 July 2019.

BEARER CERTIFICATES (COLLECTIVE INVESTMENT SCHEMES) REGULATIONS 2020

(SI 2020/1346)

NOTES

Made: 24 November 2020.

Authority: Financial Services and Markets Act 2000, s 262; European Communities Act 1972, s 2(2) (see the note "Statutory Instruments made under the European Communities Act 1972" preceding paragraph **[4.1]** *ante*).

Commencement: 1 January 2021.

[8.576]

1 Citation, commencement and extent

(1) These Regulations may be cited as the Bearer Certificates (Collective Investment Schemes) Regulations 2020.

(2) These Regulations come into force on 1st January 2021.

(3) These Regulations extend to the whole of the United Kingdom.

NOTES

Commencement: 1 January 2021.

2, 3 (*Reg 2 inserts the Financial Services and Markets Act 2000, s 241A at* **[7.443]**. *Reg 3 inserts the Open-Ended Investment Companies Regulations 2001, SI 2001/1228, reg 48(1A) at* **[8.393]**.)

[8.577]

4 Transitional Provision

The Schedule makes transitional provision enabling the conversion and cancellation on or before 1 January 2022 of bearer shares in open-ended investment companies and bearer units in other collective investment schemes held at the end of the day on which these Regulations take effect.

NOTES

Commencement: 1 January 2021.

SCHEDULE
TRANSITIONAL PROVISION

Regulation 4

PART 1 CONVERSION AND CANCELLATION OF EXISTING BEARER SHARES IN OPEN-ENDED INVESTMENT COMPANIES ON OR BEFORE 1 JANUARY 2022

[8.578]

1. (1) An open-ended investment company may convert or cancel bearer shares on or before 1 January 2022 in accordance with this Part.

(2) This Part applies as if it were contained in the Open-Ended Investment Companies Regulations 2001 and accordingly-

(a) words and expressions used in those Regulations have the same meaning when used in this Part; and
(b) references in this Part to particular regulations are references to those Regulations.

Meaning of "outstanding bearer share" and "the surrender year"

2. In this Part—

"outstanding bearer share" means a bearer share which has been issued by an open-ended investment company before the surrender year and has not been cancelled;

"the surrender year" means the year beginning with the end of 1 January 2021.

Right to convert bearer share to registered share

3. (1) Sub-paragraphs (2) and (3) apply where, at a time in the surrender year, the person who is the bearer of an outstanding bearer share delivers to the company—

(a) the instrument mentioned in regulation 48 relating to the share,
(b) a request for the share to be converted to a registered share, and
(c) a statement of the person's name and address.

(2) Delivery of the instrument to the company does not operate as a transfer of the share.

(3) The company must—

(a) cancel the instrument,
(b) register the person as the holder of the share, and
(c) prepare a share certificate in respect of the share as registered.

(4) Sub-paragraphs (2) and (3) do not apply in relation to outstanding bearer shares of which the designated person is the bearer (but see paragraph 4).

(5) Regulation 46(2) (expeditious preparation of certificates prepared in accordance with regulation 46(1)(a) to (e)) applies also in relation to a certificate prepared in accordance with sub-paragraph (3)(c).

Cancellation of bearer shares held by the designated person

4. Where the bearer of any outstanding bearer shares is the designated person—

(a) the designated person may not, after the start of the surrender year, transfer the shares to any person other than the company, and
(b) the designated person must, as soon after the start of the surrender year as is reasonably practicable, transfer the shares to the company (so that the shares may be cancelled in accordance with paragraph 3).

Payment of dividends and other distributions during the surrender year

5. (1) A dividend or other distribution paid in the surrender year in respect of an outstanding bearer share must be paid into the account opened by the company in accordance with sub-paragraph (3).

(2) Where a share is converted under paragraph 3, the person registered under paragraph 3(3) in respect of the share is entitled to—

(a) any amounts paid into that account in respect of the share under sub-paragraph (1), and
(b) any interest accrued on those amounts while held in that account.

(3) Where any payments are to be made under sub-paragraph (1) or paragraph 6 in respect of shares of a particular open-ended investment company, the company must open a separate bank account for the purpose of receiving the payments, and must do so before the first of any such payments is to be made.

(4) The terms of the account must be such that its balance—

(a) bears interest at an appropriate rate, and
(b) can be withdrawn during bank hours without having to give prior notice.

Cancellation of bearer shares still held at the end of the surrender year

6. (1) Where a person is the bearer of an outstanding bearer share immediately before the end of the surrender year, the company must—

(a) cancel the share with effect from the end of that year, and
(b) pay the value (if any) of the share into the account opened by the company in accordance with paragraph 5(3).

(2) The person is entitled to—

(a) any amounts paid into that account in respect of the share under sub-paragraph (1) or paragraph 5(1), and
(b) any interest accrued on those amounts while held in that account.

(3) If after the surrender year the company receives the documentary evidence of title mentioned in regulation 48 relating to the share, the company may conclusively treat the person sending the documentary evidence of title as being the person entitled to those amounts and that interest.

Notifications

7. (1) This paragraph applies to an open-ended investment company if, at the start of the surrender year, any persons other than the designated person are bearers of outstanding bearer shares issued by the company.

(2) The company must, no later than 2 months after the start of the surrender year, give a notice to those persons—

(a) of their right during the surrender year to convert their bearer shares into registered shares,
(b) of what they need to do to exercise that right,
(c) of the company's duty to retain dividends and other distributions paid in the surrender year in respect of bearer shares until the shares are converted or any proceeds of their cancellation are claimed,
(d) of the company's duty to cancel bearer shares still outstanding at the end of the surrender year, and
(e) of how any proceeds of such cancelled shares may be claimed.

(3) The notice must be given by being—

(a) published in the Gazette,
(b) communicated to each of the persons in the same way (if any) as the company normally communicates with that person for other purposes relating to the person's bearer shares in the company, and
(c) published in a prominent position on the company's website (if it has one).

(4) The company must keep the notice as published on its website in a prominent position on its website until—

(a) the first anniversary of the end of the surrender year, or
(b) if earlier, the time when—
  (i) the company no longer has any bearer shares in issue, and
  (ii) all amounts (if any) paid into the account opened by the company in accordance with paragraph 5(3) have been paid out in accordance with paragraphs 5(2) and 6(2) and (3).

(5) Sub-paragraphs (2) to (4) do not apply in relation to a company if, before it gives the notice that would be required by sub-paragraph (2), it has ceased to have any bearer shares in issue.

(6) An open-ended investment company which contravenes this paragraph commits an offence.

(7) A person guilty of an offence under sub-paragraph (6) is liable on summary conviction—

(a) in England and Wales, to a fine;

(b) in Scotland or Northern Ireland, to a fine not exceeding level 5 on the standard scale.

NOTES

Commencement: 1 January 2021.

PART 2 CONVERSION AND CANCELLATION OF EXISTING BEARER UNITS IN OTHER COLLECTIVE INVESTMENT SCHEMES ON OR BEFORE 1 JANUARY 2022

[8.579]

8. (1) The operator of a collective investment scheme which is not an open-ended investment company may convert or cancel bearer units on or before 1 January 2022 in accordance with this Part.

(2) This Part applies as if it were contained within Part 17 of the Financial Services and Markets Act 2000 ("Part 17") and accordingly-

(a) words and expressions used in Part 17 have the same meaning when used in this Part; and

(b) references in this Part to particular sections and their associated subsections are references to the relevant provisions of Part 17.

General definitions

9. In this Part—

"the Gazette" means—

(a) as respects companies registered in England and Wales, the London Gazette,

(b) as respects companies registered in Scotland, the Edinburgh Gazette, and

(c) as respects companies registered in Northern Ireland, the Belfast Gazette;

"outstanding bearer unit" means a bearer unit which has been issued by a collective investment scheme (except for collective investment schemes constituted by an open-ended investment company) before the surrender year and has not been cancelled;

"scheme" means a collective investment scheme other than one constituted by an open-ended investment company;

"the surrender year" means the year beginning with the end of 1 January 2021.

Right to convert bearer unit to registered unit

10. (1) Subparagraphs (2) and (3) apply where, at a time in the surrender year, the person who is the bearer of an outstanding bearer unit delivers to the scheme—

(a) the instrument mentioned in section 241A relating to the unit,

(b) a request for the unit to be converted to a registered unit, and

(c) a statement of the person's name and address.

(2) Delivery of the instrument to the scheme does not operate as a transfer of the unit.

(3) The operator of the scheme must—

(a) cancel the instrument,

(b) register the person as the holder of the unit, and

(c) prepare a certificate in respect of the unit as registered.

(4) Subparagraphs (2) and (3) do not apply in relation to outstanding bearer units of which the operator of the scheme is the bearer (but see paragraph 11).

(5) The operator of a scheme must exercise due diligence and take all reasonable steps to ensure that a certificate prepared in accordance with subparagraph (3)(c) is ready for delivery as soon as reasonably practicable.

Cancellation of bearer units held by the operator of the scheme

11. Where the bearer of any outstanding bearer units is the operator of the scheme—

(a) the operator may not, after the start of the surrender year, transfer the shares to any person other than the scheme, and

(b) the operator must, as soon after the start of the surrender year as is reasonably practicable, transfer the shares to the scheme (so that the shares may be cancelled in accordance with paragraph 10).

Payment of dividends and other distributions during the surrender year

12. (1) A dividend or other distribution paid in the surrender year in respect of an outstanding bearer unit must be paid by the operator into the account opened by the scheme in accordance with subparagraph (3).

(2) Where a unit is converted under paragraph 10, the person registered under paragraph 10(3) in respect of the unit is entitled to—

(a) any amounts paid into that account in respect of the unit under subparagraph (1), and

(b) any interest accrued on those amounts while held in that account.

(3) Where any payments are to be made under subparagraph (1) or paragraph 13 in respect of units of a particular scheme, the operator of the scheme must open a separate bank account for the purpose of receiving the payments, and must do so before the first of any such payments is to be made.

(4) The terms of the account must be such that its balance—

(a) bears interest at an appropriate rate, and

(b) can be withdrawn during banking hours without having to give prior notice.

Cancellation of bearer units still held at the end of the surrender year

13. (1) Where a person is the bearer of an outstanding bearer unit immediately before the end of the surrender year, the operator of the scheme must—

(a) cancel the unit with effect from the end of that year, and

(b) pay the value (if any) of the unit into the account opened by the scheme in accordance with paragraph 12(3).

(2) The person is entitled to—

(a) any amounts paid into that account in respect of the unit under subparagraph (1) or paragraph 12(1), and

(b) any interest accrued on those amounts while held in that account.

(3) If after the surrender year the scheme receives the documentary evidence of title mentioned in section 241A(3) relating to the unit, the operator of the scheme may conclusively treat the person sending the documentary evidence of title as being the person entitled to those amounts and interest.

Right to amend governing documents

14. The operator of a scheme may amend any provision which is contained in its governing documents (including any trust deed) which enables the scheme to issue bearer units.

Notifications

15. (1) This paragraph applies to the operator of a scheme if, at the start of the surrender year, any persons other than the operator of the scheme are bearers of outstanding bearer units issued by the scheme.

(2) The operator of the scheme must, no later than 2 months after the start of the surrender year, give a notice to those persons—

(a) of their right during the surrender year to convert their bearer units into registered units,

(b) of what they need to do to exercise that right,

(c) of the operator's duty to retain dividends and other distributions paid in the surrender year in respect of bearer units until the bearer units are converted or any proceeds of their cancellation are claimed,

(d) of the operator's duty to cancel bearer units still outstanding at the end of the surrender year, and

(e) of how any proceeds of such cancelled units may be claimed.

(3) The notice must be given by being—

(a) published in the Gazette,

(b) communicated to each of the persons in the same way (if any) as the scheme normally communicates with that person for other purposes relating to the person's bearer units in the company, and

(c) published in a prominent position on the scheme's website (if it has one).

(4) The operator of the scheme must keep the notice as published on its website in a prominent position on its website until—

(a) the first anniversary of the end of the surrender year, or

(b) if earlier, the time when—

(i) the scheme no longer has any bearer units in issue, and

(ii) all amounts (if any) paid into the account opened by the scheme in accordance with paragraph 12(3) have been paid out in accordance with paragraphs 12(2) and 13(2) and (3).

(5) Subparagraphs (2) to (4) do not apply in relation to the operator of a scheme if, before it gives the notice that would be required by subparagraph (2), the scheme has ceased to have any bearer units in issue.

(6) The operator of a scheme which contravenes this paragraph commits an offence.

(7) A person guilty of an offence under subparagraph (6) is liable on summary conviction—

(a) in England and Wales, to a fine;

(b) in Scotland or Northern Ireland, to a fine not exceeding level 5 on the standard scale.

NOTES

Commencement: 1 January 2021.

PART 9
MISCELLANEOUS OTHER PRIMARY LEGISLATION

PARTNERSHIP ACT 1890

(1890 c 39)

NOTES

This Act is reproduced as amended by: the Statute Law Revision Act 1908; the Mental Health Act 1959; the Decimal Currency Act 1969; the Courts Act 1971; the Trusts of Land and Appointment of Trustees Act 1996; the Statute Law (Repeals) Act 1998; the Civil Partnership Act 2004; the Companies Act 2006 (Consequential Amendments, Transitional Provisions and Savings) Order 2009, SI 2009/1941; the Partnerships (Prosecution) (Scotland) Act 2013; the Crime and Courts Act 2013.

ARRANGEMENT OF SECTIONS

Nature of Partnership

Relations of Partners to persons dealing with them

Relations of Partners to one another

Dissolution of Partnership, and its consequences

Supplemental

An Act to declare and amend the Law of Partnership

[14 August 1890]

Nature of Partnership

[9.1]

1 Definition of Partnership

(1) Partnership is the relation which subsists between persons carrying on a business in common with a view of profit.

(2) But the relation between members of any company or association which is—

[(a) registered under the Companies Act 2006, or]

(b) Formed or incorporated by or in pursuance of any other Act of Parliament or letters patent, or Royal Charter . . .

(c) . . .

is not a partnership within the meaning of this Act.

NOTES

Sub-s (2): para (a) substituted by the Companies Act 2006 (Consequential Amendments, Transitional Provisions and Savings) Order 2009, SI 2009/1941, art 2(1), Sch 1, para 2, as from 1 October 2009. Para (c) and the word immediately preceding it repealed by the Statute Law (Repeals) Act 1998, as from 19 November 1998.

[9.2]

2 Rules for determining existence of partnership

In determining whether a partnership does or does not exist, regard shall be had to the following rules—

(1) Joint tenancy, tenancy in common, joint property, common property, or part ownership does not of itself create a partnership as to anything so held or owned, whether the tenants or owners do or do not share any profits made by the use thereof.

(2) The sharing of gross returns does not of itself create a partnership, whether the persons sharing such returns have or have not a joint or common right or interest in any property from which or from the use of which the returns are derived.

(3) The receipt by a person of a share of the profits of a business is *prima facie* evidence that he is a partner in the business, but receipt of such a share, or of a payment contingent on or varying with the profits of a business, does not of itself make him a partner in the business; and in particular—

(a) The receipt by a person of a debt or other liquidated amount by instalments or otherwise out of the accruing profits of a business does not of itself make him a partner in the business or liable as such:

(b) A contract for the remuneration of a servant or agent of a person engaged in a business by a share of the profits of the business does not of itself make the servant or agent a partner in the business or liable as such:

(c) A person being the widow[, widower, surviving civil partner] or child of a deceased partner, and receiving by way of annuity a portion of the profits made in the business in which the deceased person was a partner, is not by reason only of such receipt a partner in the business or liable as such:

(d) The advance of money by way of loan to a person engaged or about to engage in any business on a contract with that person that the lender shall receive a rate of interest varying with the profits, or shall receive a share of the profits arising from carrying on the business, does not of itself make the lender a partner with the person or persons carrying on the business or liable as such. Provided that the contract is in writing, and signed by or on behalf of all the parties thereto:

(e) A person receiving by way of annuity or otherwise a portion of the profits of a business in consideration of the sale by him of the goodwill of the business is not by reason only of such receipt a partner in the business or liable as such.

NOTES

Words in square brackets inserted by the Civil Partnership Act 2004, s 261(1), Sch 27, para 2, as from 5 December 2005.

[9.3]

3 Postponement of rights of person lending or selling in consideration of share of profits in case of insolvency

In the event of any person to whom money has been advanced by way of loan upon such a contract as is mentioned in the last foregoing section, or of any buyer of a goodwill in consideration of a share of the profits of the business, being adjudged a bankrupt, entering into an arrangement to pay his creditors less than [100p] in the pound, or dying in insolvent circumstances, the lender of the loan shall not be entitled to recover anything in respect of his loan, and the seller of the goodwill shall not be entitled to recover anything in respect of the share of profits contracted for, until the claims of the other creditors of the borrower or buyer for valuable consideration in money or money's worth have been satisfied.

NOTES

Sum in square brackets substituted by virtue of the Decimal Currency Act 1969, s 10(1), as from 16 May 1969.

[9.4]

4 Meaning of firm

(1) Persons who have entered into partnership with one another are for the purposes of this Act called collectively a firm, and the name under which their business is carried on is called the firm-name.

(2) In Scotland a firm is a legal person distinct from the partners of whom it is composed, but an individual partner may be charged on a decree or diligence directed against the firm, and on payment of the debts is entitled to relief pro rata from the firm and its other members.

Relations of Partners to persons dealing with them

[9.5]

5 Power of partner to bind the firm

Every partner is an agent of the firm and his other partners for the purpose of the business of the partnership; and the acts of every partner who does any act for carrying on in the usual way business of the kind carried on by the firm of which he is a member bind the firm and his partners, unless the partner so acting has in fact no authority to act for the firm in the particular matter, and the person with whom he is dealing either knows that he has no authority, or does not know or believe him to be a partner.

[9.6]

6 Partners bound by acts on behalf of firm

An act or instrument relating to the business of the firm done or executed in the firm-name, or in any other manner showing an intention to bind the firm, by any person thereto authorised, whether a partner or not, is binding on the firm and all the partners.

Provided that this section shall not affect any general rule of law relating to the execution of deeds or negotiable instruments.

[9.7]

7 Partner using credit of firm for private purposes

Where one partner pledges the credit of the firm for a purpose apparently not connected with the firm's ordinary course of business, the firm is not bound, unless he is in fact specially authorised by the other partners; but this section does not affect any personal liability incurred by an individual partner.

[9.8]

8 Effect of notice that firm will not be bound by acts of partner

If it has been agreed between the partners that any restriction shall be placed on the power of any one or more of them to bind the firm, no act done in contravention of the agreement is binding on the firm with respect to persons having notice of the agreement.

[9.9]

9 Liability of partners

Every partner in a firm is liable jointly with the other partners, and in Scotland severally also, for all debts and obligations of the firm incurred while he is a partner; and after his death his estate is also severally liable in a due course of administration for such debts and obligations, so far as they remain unsatisfied, but subject in England or Ireland to the prior payment of his separate debts.

[9.10]

10 Liability of the firm for wrongs

Where, by any wrongful act or omission of any partner acting in the ordinary course of the business of the firm, or with the authority of his co-partners, loss or injury is caused to any person not being a partner in the firm, or any penalty is incurred, the firm is liable therefor to the same extent as the partner so acting or omitting to act.

[9.11]

11 Misapplication of money or property received for or in custody of the firm

In the following cases; namely—

(a) Where one partner acting within the scope of his apparent authority receives the money or property of a third person and misapplies it; and

(b) Where a firm in the course of its business receives money or property of a third person, and the money or property so received is misapplied by one or more of the partners while it is in the custody of the firm;

the firm is liable to make good the loss.

[9.12]

12 Liability for wrongs joint and several

Every partner is liable jointly with his co-partners and also severally for everything for which the firm while he is a partner therein becomes liable under either of the two last preceding sections.

[9.13]

13 Improper employment of trust-property for partnership purposes

If a partner, being a trustee, improperly employs trust-property in the business or on the account of the partnership, no other partner is liable for the trust property to the persons beneficially interested therein:

Provided as follows—

(1) This section shall not affect any liability incurred by any partner by reason of his having notice of a breach of trust; and

(2) Nothing in this section shall prevent trust money from being followed and recovered from the firm if still in its possession or under its control.

[9.14]

14 Persons liable by "holding out"

(1) Every one who by words spoken or written or by conduct represents himself, or who knowingly suffers himself to be represented, as a partner in a particular firm, is liable as a partner to any one who has on the faith of any such representation given credit to the firm, whether the representation has or has not been made or communicated to the person so giving credit by or with the knowledge of the apparent partner making the representation or suffering it to be made.

(2) Provided that where after a partner's death the partnership business is continued in the old firm's name, the continued use of that name or of the deceased partner's name as part thereof shall not of itself make his executors or administrators estate or effects liable for any partnership debts contracted after his death.

[9.15]
15 Admissions and representation of partners
An admission or representation made by any partner concerning the partnership affairs, and in the ordinary course of its business, is evidence against the firm.

[9.16]
16 Notice to acting partner to be notice to the firm
Notice to any partner who habitually acts in the partnership business of any matter relating to partnership affairs operates as notice to the firm, except in the case of a fraud on the firm committed by or with the consent of that partner.

[9.17]
17 Liabilities of incoming and outgoing partners
(1) A person who is admitted as a partner into an existing firm does not thereby become liable to the creditors of the firm for anything done before he became a partner.
(2) A partner who retires from a firm does not thereby cease to be liable for partnership debts or obligations incurred before his retirement.
(3) A retiring partner may be discharged from any existing liabilities, by an agreement to that effect between himself and the members of the firm as newly constituted and the creditors, and this agreement may be either expressed or inferred as a fact from the course of dealing between the creditors and the firm as newly constituted.

[9.18]
18 Revocation of continuing guaranty by change in firm
A continuing guaranty or cautionary obligation given either to a firm or to a third person in respect of the transactions of a firm is, in the absence of agreement to the contrary, revoked as to future transactions by any change in the constitution of the firm to which, or of the firm in respect of the transactions of which, the guaranty or obligation was given.

Relations of Partners to one another

[9.19]
19 Variation by consent of terms of partnership
The mutual rights and duties of partners, whether ascertained by agreement or defined by this Act, may be varied by the consent of all the partners, and such consent may be either express or inferred from a course of dealing.

[9.20]
20 Partnership property
(1) All property and rights and interests in property originally brought into the partnership stock or acquired, whether by purchase or otherwise, on account of the firm, or for the purposes and in the course of the partnership business, are called in this Act partnership property, and must be held and applied by the partners exclusively for the purposes of the partnership and in accordance with the partnership agreement.
(2) Provided that the legal estate or interest in any land, or in Scotland the title to and interest in any heritable estate, which belongs to the partnership shall devolve according to the nature and tenure thereof, and the general rules of law thereto applicable, but in trust, so far as necessary, for the persons beneficially interested in the land under this section.
(3) Where co-owners of an estate or interest in any land, or in Scotland of any heritable estate, not being itself partnership property, are partners as to profits made by the use of that land or estate, and purchase other land or estate out of the profits to be used in like manner, the land or estate so purchased belongs to them, in the absence of an agreement to the contrary, not as partners, but as co-owners for the same respective estates and interests as are held by them in the land or estate first mentioned at the date of the purchase.

[9.21]
21 Property bought with partnership money
Unless the contrary intention appears, property bought with money belonging to the firm is deemed to have been bought on account of the firm.

22 *(Repealed by the Trusts of Land and Appointment of Trustees Act 1996, s 25(2), (5), Sch 4, except in relation to any circumstances involving the personal representatives of a partner who died before 1 July 1997.)*

[9.22]
23 Procedure against partnership property for a partner's separate judgement debt
(1) . . . A writ of execution shall not issue against any partnership property except on a judgment against the firm.
(2) The High Court, or a judge thereof, . . ., [or the county court in England and Wales or a county court in Northern Ireland,] may, on the application by summons of any judgment creditor of a partner, make an order charging that partner's interest in the partnership property and profits with payment of the amount of the judgment debt and interest thereon, and may by the same or a subsequent order appoint a receiver of that partner's share of profits (whether already declared or accruing), and of any other money which may be coming to him in respect of the partnership, and direct all accounts and inquiries, and give all other orders and directions which might have been directed or given if the charge had been made in favour of the judgment creditor by the partner, or which the circumstances of the case may require.
(3) The other partner or partners shall be at liberty at any time to redeem the interest charged, or in case of a sale being directed, to purchase the same.
(4) . . .
(5) This section shall not apply to Scotland.

NOTES
Sub-s (1): words omitted repealed by the Statute Law Revision Act 1908, as from 21 December 1908.
Sub-s (2): words omitted repealed by the Courts Act 1971, s 56(4), Sch 11, Pt II, as from 1 January 1972. Words in square brackets substituted by the Crime and Courts Act 2013, s 17, Sch 9, Pt 3, para 118, as from 22 April 2014.

Sub-s (4): repealed by the Statute Law (Repeals) Act 1998, as from 19 November 1998.

[9.23]

24 Rules as to interests and duties of partners subject to special agreement

The interests of partners in the partnership property and their rights and duties in relation to the partnership shall be determined, subject to any agreement express or implied between the partners, by the following rules—

(1) All the partners are entitled to share equally in the capital and profits of the business, and must contribute equally towards the losses whether of capital or otherwise sustained by the firm.

(2) The firm must indemnify every partner in respect of payments made and personal liabilities incurred by him—

(a) In the ordinary and proper conduct of the business of the firm; or,

(b) In or about anything necessarily done for the preservation of the business or property of the firm.

(3) A partner making, for the purpose of the partnership, any actual payment or advance beyond the amount of capital which he has agreed to subscribe, is entitled to interest at the rate of five per cent per annum from the date of the payment or advance.

(4) A partner is not entitled, before the ascertainment of profits, to interest on the capital subscribed by him.

(5) Every partner may take part in the management of the partnership business.

(6) No partner shall be entitled to remuneration for acting in the partnership business.

(7) No person may be introduced as a partner without the consent of all existing partners.

(8) Any difference arising as to ordinary matters connected with the partnership business may be decided by a majority of the partners, but no change may be made in the nature of the partnership business without the consent of all existing partners.

(9) The partnership books are to be kept at the place of business of the partnership (or the principal place, if there is more than one), and every partner may, when he thinks fit, have access to and inspect and copy any of them.

[9.24]

25 Expulsion of partner

No majority of the partners can expel any partner unless a power to do so has been conferred by express agreement between the partners.

[9.25]

26 Retirement from partnership at will

(1) Where no fixed term has been agreed upon for the duration of the partnership, any partner may determine the partnership at any time on giving notice of his intention so to do to all the other partners.

(2) Where the partnership has originally been constituted by deed, a notice in writing, signed by the partner giving it, shall be sufficient for this purpose.

[9.26]

27 Where partnership for term is continued over, continuance on old terms presumed

(1) Where a partnership entered into for a fixed term is continued after the term has expired, and without any express new agreement, the rights and duties of the partners remain the same as they were at the expiration of the term, so far as is consistent with the incidents of a partnership at will.

(2) A continuance of the business by the partners or such of them as habitually acted therein during the term, without any settlement or liquidation of the partnership affairs, is presumed to be a continuance of the partnership.

[9.27]

28 Duty of partners to render accounts, etc

Partners are bound to render true accounts and full information of all things affecting the partnership to any partner or his legal representatives.

[9.28]

29 Accountability of partners for private profits

(1) Every partner must account to the firm for any benefit derived by him without the consent of the other partners from any transaction concerning the partnership, or from any use by him of the partnership property name or business connexion.

(2) This section applies also to transactions undertaken after a partnership has been dissolved by the death of a partner, and before the affairs thereof have been completely wound up, either by any surviving partner or by the representatives of the deceased partner.

[9.29]

30 Duty of partner not to compete with firm

If a partner, without the consent of the other partners, carries on any business of the same nature as and competing with that of the firm, he must account for and pay over to the firm all profits made by him in that business.

[9.30]

31 Rights of assignee of share in partnership

(1) An assignment by any partner of his share in the partnership, either absolute or by way of mortgage or redeemable charge, does not, as against the other partners, entitle the assignee, during the continuance of the partnership, to interfere in the management or administration of the partnership business or affairs, or to require any accounts of the partnership transactions, or to inspect the partnership books, but entitles the assignee only to receive the share of profits to which the assigning partner would otherwise be entitled, and the assignee must accept the account of profits agreed to by the partners.

(2) In case of a dissolution of the partnership, whether as respects all the partners or as respects the assigning partner, the assignee is entitled to receive the share of the partnership assets to which the assigning partner is entitled as between himself and the other partners, and, for the purpose of ascertaining that share, to an account as from the date of the dissolution.

[9.31]

32 Dissolution by expiration or notice

Subject to any agreement between the partners, a partnership is dissolved—

(a) If entered into for a fixed term, by the expiration of that term:

(b) If entered into for a single adventure or undertaking, by the termination of that adventure or undertaking:

(c) If entered into for an undefined time, by any partner giving notice to the other or others of his intention to dissolve the partnership.

In the last-mentioned case the partnership is dissolved as from the date mentioned in the notice as the date of dissolution, or, if no date is so mentioned, as from the date of the communication of the notice.

[9.32]

33 Dissolution by bankruptcy, death or charge

(1) Subject to any agreement between the partners, every partnership is dissolved as regards all the partners by the death or bankruptcy of any partner.

(2) A partnership may, at the option of the other partners, be dissolved if any partner suffers his share of the partnership property to be charged under this Act for his separate debt.

[9.33]

34 Dissolution by illegality of partnership

A partnership is in every case dissolved by the happening of any event which makes it unlawful for the business of the firm to be carried on or for the members of the firm to carry it on in partnership.

[9.34]

35 Dissolution by the Court

On application by a partner the Court may decree a dissolution of the partnership in any of the following cases—

(a) . . .

(b) When a partner, other than the partner suing, becomes in any other way permanently incapable of performing his part of the partnership contract;

(c) When a partner, other than the partner suing, has been guilty of such conduct as, in the opinion of the Court, regard being had to the nature of the business, is calculated to prejudicially affect the carrying on of the business;

(d) When a partner, other than the partner suing, wilfully or persistently commits a breach of the partnership agreement, or otherwise so conducts himself in matters relating to the partnership business that it is not reasonably practicable for the other partner or partners to carry on the business in partnership with him;

(e) When the business of the partnership can only be carried on at a loss;

(f) Whenever in any case circumstances have arisen which, in the opinion of the Court, render it just and equitable that the partnership be dissolved.

NOTES

Para (a) repealed by the Mental Health Act 1959, s 149(2), Sch 8, as from 1 November 1960.

[9.35]

36 Rights of persons dealing with firm against apparent members of firm

(1) Where a person deals with a firm after a change in its constitution he is entitled to treat all apparent members of the old firm as still being members of the firm until he has notice of the change.

(2) An advertisement in the London Gazette as to a firm whose principal place of business is in England or Wales, in the Edinburgh Gazette as to a firm whose principal place of business is in Scotland, and in the Dublin Gazette as to a firm whose principal place of business is in Ireland, shall be notice as to persons who had not dealings with the firm before the date of the dissolution or change so advertised.

(3) The estate of a partner who dies, or who becomes bankrupt, or of a partner who, not having been known to the person dealing with the firm to be a partner, retires from the firm, is not liable for partnership debts contracted after the date of the death, bankruptcy, or retirement respectively.

NOTES

Dublin Gazette: this should now be construed as a reference to the Belfast Gazette: see the General Adaptation of Enactments (Northern Ireland) Order 1921, SR & O 1921/1804.

[9.36]

37 Right of partners to notify dissolution

On the dissolution of a partnership or retirement of a partner any partner may publicly notify the same, and may require the other partner or partners to concur for that purpose in all necessary or proper acts, if any, which cannot be done without his or their concurrence.

[9.37]

38 Continuing authority of partners for purposes of winding up

After the dissolution of a partnership the authority of each partner to bind the firm, and the other rights and obligations of the partners, continue notwithstanding the dissolution so far as may be necessary to wind up the affairs of the partnership, and to complete transactions begun but unfinished at the time of the dissolution[, and in relation to any prosecution of the partnership by virtue of section 1 of the Partnerships (Prosecution) (Scotland) Act 2013], but not otherwise.

Provided that the firm is in no case bound by the acts of a partner who has become bankrupt; but this proviso does not affect the liability of any person who has after the bankruptcy represented himself or knowingly suffered himself to be represented as a partner of the bankrupt.

NOTES

Words in square brackets inserted by the Partnerships (Prosecution) (Scotland) Act 2013, s 6(1), (2), as from 26 April 2013.

[9.38]

39 Rights of partners as to application of partnership property

On the dissolution of a partnership every partner is entitled, as against the other partners in the firm, and all persons claiming through them in respect of their interests as partners, to have the property of the partnership applied in payment of the debts and liabilities of the firm, and to have the surplus assets after such payment applied in payment of what may be due to the partners respectively after deducting what may be due from them as partners to the firm; and for that purpose any partner or his representatives may on the termination of the partnership apply to the Court to wind up the business and affairs of the firm.

[9.39]

40 Apportionment of premium where partnership prematurely dissolved

Where one partner has paid a premium to another on entering into a partnership for a fixed term, and the partnership is dissolved before the expiration of that term otherwise than by the death of a partner, the Court may order the repayment of the premium, or of such part thereof as it thinks just, having regard to the terms of the partnership contract and to the length of time during which the partnership has continued; unless—

(a) the dissolution is, in the judgment of the Court, wholly or chiefly due to the misconduct of the partner who paid the premium; or
(b) the partnership has been dissolved by an agreement containing no provision for a return of any part of the premium.

[9.40]

41 Rights where partnership dissolved for fraud or misrepresentation

Where a partnership contract is rescinded on the ground of the fraud or misrepresentation of one of the parties thereto, the party entitled to rescind is, without prejudice to any other right, entitled—

(a) to a lien on, or right of retention of, the surplus of the partnership assets, after satisfying the partnership liabilities, for any sum of money paid by him for the purchase of a share in the partnership and for any capital contributed by him, and is
(b) to stand in the place of the creditors of the firm for any payments made by him in respect of the partnership liabilities, and
(c) to be indemnified by the person guilty of the fraud or making the representation against all the debts and liabilities of the firm.

[9.41]

42 Right of outgoing partner in certain cases to share profits made after dissolution

(1) Where any member of a firm has died or otherwise ceased to be a partner, and the surviving or continuing partners carry on the business of the firm with its capital or assets without any final settlement of accounts as between the firm and the outgoing partner or his estate, then, in the absence of any agreement to the contrary, the outgoing partner or his estate is entitled at the option of himself or his representatives to such share of the profits made since the dissolution as the Court may find to be attributable to the use of his share of the partnership assets, or to interest at the rate of five per cent per annum on the amount of his share of the partnership assets.

(2) Provided that where by the partnership contract an option is given to surviving or continuing partners to purchase the interest of a deceased or outgoing partner, and that option is duly exercised, the estate of the deceased partner, or the outgoing partner or his estate, as the case may be, is not entitled to any further or other share of profits; but if any partner assuming to act in exercise of the option does not in all material respects comply with the terms thereof, he is liable to account under the foregoing provisions of this section.

[9.42]

43 Retiring or deceased partner's share to be a debt

Subject to any agreement between the partners, the amount due from surviving or continuing partners to an outgoing partner or the representatives of a deceased partner in respect of the outgoing or deceased partner's share is a debt accruing at the date of the dissolution or death.

[9.43]

44 Rule for distribution of assets on final settlement of accounts

In settling accounts between the partners after a dissolution of partnership, the following rules shall, subject to any agreement, be observed—

(a) Losses, including losses and deficiencies of capital, shall be paid first out of profits, next out of capital, and lastly, if necessary, by the partners individually in the proportion in which they were entitled to share profits;
(b) The assets of the firm including the sums, if any, contributed by the partners to make up losses or deficiencies of capital, shall be applied in the following manner and order—
    1. In paying the debts and liabilities of the firm to persons who are not partners therein:
    2. In paying to each partner rateably what is due from the firm to him for advances as distinguished from capital:
    3. In paying to each partner rateably what is due from the firm to him in respect of capital:
    4. The ultimate residue, if any, shall be divided among the partners in the proportion in which profits are divisible.

Supplemental

[9.44]

45 Definitions of "court" and "business"

In this Act, unless the contrary intention appears,—

The expression "court" includes every court and judge having jurisdiction in the case;

The expression "business" includes every trade, occupation, or profession.

[9.45]
46 Saving for rules of equity and common law
The rules of equity and of common law applicable to partnership shall continue in force except so far as they are inconsistent with the express provisions of this Act.

[9.46]
47 Provision as to bankruptcy in Scotland
(1) In the application of this Act to Scotland the bankruptcy of a firm or of an individual shall mean sequestration under the Bankruptcy (Scotland) Acts, and also in the case of an individual the issue against him of a decree of cessio bonorum.
(2) Nothing in this Act shall alter the rules of the law of Scotland relating to the bankruptcy of a firm or of the individual partners thereof.

48, 49 *(Repealed by the Statute Law Revision Act 1908.)*

[9.47]
50 Short title
This Act may be cited as the Partnership Act 1890.

SCHEDULE

(Schedule repealed by the Statute Law Revision Act 1908.)

FORGED TRANSFERS ACT 1891

(54 & 55 Vict c 43)

NOTES

This Act is reproduced as amended by: the Forged Transfers Act 1892; the Decimal Currency Act 1969; the Stock Transfer Act 1982; the Local Government Finance (Miscellaneous Amendments and Repeal) Order 1990, SI 1990/1285; the Local Government Finance Act 1992; the Police and Magistrates' Courts Act 1994; the Local Government (Translation Amendments) (Scotland) Order 1996, SI 1996/974; the Statute Law (Repeals) Act 1998; the Fire and Rescue Services Act 2004; the Statute Law (Repeals) Act 2004; the Co-operative and Community Benefit Societies Act 2014.

An Act for preserving Purchasers of Stock from Losses by Forged Transfers

[5 August 1891]

[9.48]
1 Power to make compensation for losses from forged transfer
(1) Where a company or local authority issue or have issued shares, stock, or securities transferable by an instrument in writing [or by an exempt transfer within the meaning of the Stock Transfer Act 1982] or by an entry, in any books or register kept by or on behalf of the company or local authority, they shall have power to make compensation by a cash payment out of their funds for any loss arising from a transfer of any such shares, stock, or securities, in pursuance of a [forged instrument] or of a transfer under a forged power of attorney, [. . . and whether the person receiving such compensation, or any person through whom he claims, has or has not paid any fee or otherwise contributed to any fund out of which the compensation is paid].
[(1A) In subsection (1) above "instrument" has the same meaning as in Part I of the Forgery and Counterfeiting Act 1981.]
(2) Any company or local authority may, if they think fit, provide, either by fees not exceeding the rate of [5p] on every one hundred pounds transferred [with a minimum charge equal to that for twenty-five pounds] to be paid by the transferee upon the entry of the transfer in the books of the company or local authority, or by insurance, reservation of capital, accumulation of income, or in any other manner which they may resolve upon, a fund to meet claims for such compensation.
(3) For the purpose of providing such compensation any company may borrow on the security of their property, and any local authority may borrow with the like consent and on the like security and subject to the like conditions as to repayment by means of instalments or the provision of a sinking fund and otherwise as in the case of the securities in respect of which compensation is to be provided, but any money so borrowed by a local authority shall be repaid within a term not longer than five years. Any expenses incurred by a local authority in making compensation, or in the repayment of, or the payment of interest on, or otherwise in connexion with, any loan raised as aforesaid, shall, except so far as they may be met by such fees as aforesaid, be paid out of the [revenue] on which the security in respect of which compensation is to be made is charged.
(4) Any such company or local authority may impose such reasonable restrictions on the transfer of their shares, stock, or securities, or with respect to powers of attorney for the transfer thereof, as they may consider requisite for guarding against losses arising from forgery.
(5) Where a company or local authority compensate a person under this Act for any loss arising from forgery, the company or local authority shall, without prejudice to any other rights or remedies, have the same rights and remedies against the person liable for the loss as the person compensated would have had.

NOTES

Sub-s (1): words in first pair of square brackets inserted, and words in second pair of square brackets substituted, by the Stock Transfer Act 1982, s 3, Sch 2, para 1, as from 23 July 1985. Words in third pair of square brackets added by the Forged Transfers Act 1892, s 2, as from 27 June 1892. Words omitted repealed by the Statute Law (Repeals) Act 2004, as from 22 July 2004.

Sub-s (1A): inserted by the Stock Transfer Act 1982, s 3, Sch 2, para 1, as from 23 July 1985.

Sub-s (2): reference to "5p" substituted by virtue of the Decimal Currency Act 1969, s 10(1), as from 16 May 1969. Words in square brackets added by the Forged Transfers Act 1892, s 3, as from 27 June 1892.

Sub-s (3): word in square brackets substituted by the Local Government Finance (Miscellaneous Amendments and Repeal) Order 1990, SI 1990/1285, art 2, Schedule, Pt I, para 1, as from 19 July 1990.

[9.49]

2 Definitions

For the purposes of this Act—

The expression "company" shall mean any company incorporated by or in pursuance of any Act of Parliament, or by royal charter.

[The expression "local authority" shall mean—

[(a) a billing authority or a precepting authority, as defined in section 69 of the Local Government Finance Act 1992;

[(aa) a council constituted under section 2 of the Local Government etc (Scotland) Act 1994;]

[(ab) a fire and rescue authority in Wales constituted by a scheme under section 2 of the Fire and Rescue Services Act 2004 or a scheme to which section 4 of that Act applies;]]

(b) a levying body within the meaning of section 74 of [the Local Government Finance Act 1988]; and

(c) a body as regards which section 75 of that Act applies.]

NOTES

Definition "local authority" substituted by the Local Government Finance Act (Miscellaneous Amendments and Repeal) Order 1990, SI 1990/1285, art 2, Schedule, Pt I, para 2, as from 19 July 1990. The definition has subsequently been amended as follows—

Paras (a), (aa), (ab) substituted, for the original para (a), by the Local Government Finance Act 1992, s 117(1), Sch 13, para 1, as from 1 April 1993.

Para (aa) further substituted by the Local Government (Translation Amendments) (Scotland) Order 1996, SI 1996/974, art 2(1), Sch 1, Pt I, para 1, as from 1 April 1996.

Para (ab) further substituted by the Fire and Rescue Services Act 2004, s 53, Sch 1, para 2(1), (2), as from 1 October 2004 (in relation to England and Scotland), and as from 10 November 2004 (in relation to Wales).

Words in square brackets in para (c) substituted by the Fire and Rescue Services Act 2004, s 53, Sch 1, para 2(1), (3), as from 1 October 2004 (in relation to England and Scotland), and as from 10 November 2004 (in relation to Wales).

[9.50]

3 Application to industrial societies, etc

[(1)] This Act shall apply to any . . . friendly benefit, building . . . society incorporated by or in pursuance of any Act of Parliament[, and to any registered society,] as if the society were a company.

[(2) Registered society" means—

(a) a registered society within the meaning of the Co-operative and Community Benefit Societies Act 2014, or

(b) a society registered or deemed to be registered under the Industrial and Provident Societies Act (Northern Ireland) 1969.]

NOTES

Sub-s (1) was numbered as such, the first words omitted from that subsection were repealed, the words in square brackets in that subsection were inserted, and sub-s (2) was added, by the Co-operative and Community Benefit Societies Act 2014, s 151, Sch 4, Pt 2, para 19, as from 1 August 2014.

The second words omitted from sub-s (1) were repealed by the Statute Law (Repeals) Act 2004, as from 22 July 2004.

[9.51]

4 Application to harbour and conservancy authorities

(1) This Act shall apply to any harbour authority or conservancy authority as if the authority were a company.

(2) For the purposes of this Act the expression "harbour authority" includes all persons, being proprietors of, or entrusted with the duty or invested with the power of constructing, improving, managing, regulating, maintaining, or lighting any harbour otherwise than for profit, and not being a joint stock company.

(3) For the purposes of this Act the expression "conservancy authority" includes all persons entrusted with the duty or invested with the power of conserving, maintaining, or improving the navigation of any tidal water otherwise than for profit, and not being a joint stock company.

5 *(Repealed by the Statute Law (Repeals) Act 1998, as from 19 November 1998.)*

[9.52]

6 Short title

This Act may be cited as the Forged Transfers Act 1891.

FORGED TRANSFERS ACT 1892

(55 & 56 Vict c 36)

NOTES

This Act is reproduced as amended by: the Statute Law (Repeals) Act 2004.

An Act to remove doubts as to the meaning of the Forged Transfers Act 1891

[27 June 1892]

[9.53]
1 Short title
This Act may be cited as the Forged Transfers Act 1892 and this Act and the Forged Transfers Act 1891 may be cited together as the Forged Transfers Acts 1891 and 1892.

2, 3 *(S 2 amends the Forged Transfers Act 1891, s 1, and was repealed in part by the Statute Law (Repeals) Act 2004, as from 22 July 2004; s 3 also amends s 1 of the 1891 Act.)*

[9.54]
4 Provision where one company takes over shares, etc, of another company
Where the shares, stock, or securities of a company or local authority have by amalgamation or otherwise become the shares, stock, or securities of another company or local authority, the last-mentioned company and authority shall have the same power under the Forged Transfers Act 1891 and this Act, as the original company or authority would have had if it had continued.

LIMITED PARTNERSHIPS ACT 1907

(1907 c 24)

NOTES

This Act is reproduced as amended by: the Companies (Consolidation) Act 1908; the Perjury Act 1911; the Statute Law Revision Act 1927; the Perjury Act (Northern Ireland) 1946; the Decimal Currency Act 1969; the Finance Act 1973; the Finance (Miscellaneous Provisions) (Northern Ireland) Order 1973, SI 1973/1323; the Banking Act 1979; the Regulatory Reform (Removal of 20 Member Limit in Partnerships etc) Order 2002, SI 2002/3203; the Companies Act 2006; the Legislative Reform (Limited Partnerships) Order 2009, SI 2009/1940; the Companies Act 2006 (Consequential Amendments, Transitional Provisions and Savings) Order 2009, SI 2009/1941; the Legislative Reform (Private Fund Limited Partnerships) Order 2017, SI 2017/514; the Scottish Partnerships (Register of People with Significant Control) Regulations 2017, SI 2017/694.

ARRANGEMENT OF SECTIONS

An Act to establish Limited Partnership

[28 August 1907]

[9.55]
1 Short title
This Act may be cited for all purposes as the Limited Partnerships Act 1907.

2 *(Repealed by the Statute Law Revision Act 1927.)*

[9.56]
3 Interpretation of terms
In the construction of this Act the following words and expressions shall have the meanings respectively assigned to them in this section, unless there be something in the subject or context repugnant to such construction—

"Firm," "firm name," and "business" have the same meanings as in the Partnership Act 1890;

"General partner" shall mean any partner who is not a limited partner as defined by this Act.

["Private fund limited partnership" means a limited partnership that is designated under section 8(2) as a private fund limited partnership].

NOTES

Definition "Private fund limited partnership" inserted by the Legislative Reform (Private Fund Limited Partnerships) Order 2017, SI 2017/514, art 2(1), (3), as from 6 April 2017.

[9.57]

4 Definition and constitution of limited partnership

(1) . . . Limited partnerships may be formed in the manner and subject to the conditions by this Act provided.

(2) A limited partnership . . . must consist of one or more persons called general partners, who shall be liable for all debts and obligations of the firm, and one or more persons to be called limited partners . . .

[(2A) Each limited partner in a limited partnership that is not a private fund limited partnership shall, at the time of entering into the partnership, contribute to the partnership a sum or sums as capital or property valued at a stated amount, and shall not be liable for the debts or obligations of the firm beyond the amount so contributed.

(2B) A limited partner in a private fund limited partnership—

(a) is under no obligation to contribute any capital or property to the partnership unless otherwise agreed between the partners, and

(b) is not liable for the debts or obligations of the firm beyond the amount of the partnership property which is available to the general partners to meet such debts or obligations.]

(3) [Subject to subsection (3A), a limited partner] shall not during the continuance of the partnership, either directly or indirectly, draw out or receive back any part of his contribution, and if he does so draw out or receive back any such part shall be liable for the debts and obligations of the firm up to the amount so drawn out or received back.

[(3A) In the case of a limited partner in a private fund limited partnership—

(a) where the limited partnership was registered on or after 6th April 2017, subsection (3) does not apply;

(b) where the limited partnership was registered before 6th April 2017, subsection (3) applies only in relation to the amount of any contribution made by the limited partner when the limited partnership was not a private fund limited partnership.]

(4) A body corporate may be a limited partner.

NOTES

Sub-s (1): words omitted repealed by the Statute Law Revision Act 1927, as from 22 December 1927.

Sub-s (2): first words omitted repealed by a combination of the Banking Act 1979, ss 46(b), 51(2), Sch 7, as from 19 February 1982, the Regulatory Reform (Removal of 20 Member Limit in Partnerships etc) Order 2002, SI 2002/3203, art 3, as from 21 December 2002, and the Partnerships etc (Removal of Twenty Member Limit) (Northern Ireland) Order 2003, SI 2003/2904, arts 3(1), 4, Schedule, as from 13 January 2004. Second words omitted repealed by the Legislative Reform (Private Fund Limited Partnerships) Order 2017, SI 2017/514, art 2(1), (3)(a), as from 6 April 2017.

Sub-ss (2A), (2B), (3A): inserted by SI 2017/514, art 2(1), (3)(b), (d), as from 6 April 2017.

Sub-s (3): words in square brackets substituted by SI 2017/514, art 2(1), (3)(c), as from 6 April 2017.

Note: the Regulatory Reform (Removal of 20 Member Limit in Partnerships etc) Order 2002, SI 2002/3203 reformed the law relating to the maximum limit of 20 on the number of persons who can be members of partnerships (including limited partnerships), and of certain companies or associations. It did so by repealing CA 1985, ss 716, 717 and amending sub-s (2) above, thereby removing the maximum limits on the number of members in a partnership or limited partnership, company or association.

Modification: see the Collective Investment in Transferable Securities (Contractual Scheme) Regulations 2013, SI 2013/1388, reg 16 which, as amended by the Legislative Reform (Private Fund Limited Partnerships) Order 2017, SI 2017/514, art 5, as from 6 April 2017, provides as follows—

"16 Partnership schemes

(1) The Limited Partnerships Act 1907 has effect with the following modifications in its application to a partnership scheme in respect of which an authorisation order is made.

(2) In this regulation "authorisation order" means an order made under section 261D(1) of FSMA.

(3) Section 4 (definition and constitution of limited partnership) is to be read as if—

(a) in subsection (2)—

(i) after the words "general partners, who" there were inserted ", subject to regulations 18 and 19 of the Collective Investment in Transferable Securities (Contractual Scheme) Regulations 2013,";

(ii) . . .

[(aa) in subsection (2A) there were omitted the words "and shall not be liable for the debts or obligations of the firm beyond the amount so contributed";]

(b) after [subsection (2A)] there were inserted—

"[(2AA)] The limited partners are not liable for the debts or obligations of the firm beyond the amount of the partnership property which is available to the general partner to meet such debts or obligations.

[(2AB)] A person ("P") who ceases to be a limited partner ceases to have any liability for the debts or obligations of the firm.

[(2AC)] [Subsection (2AB)] does not prevent the debts and obligations of the firm from being taken into account, after P has ceased to be a limited partner, in determining the value of P's share in the partnership."; and

(c) subsection (3) were omitted.

(4) In section 6 (modifications of general law in case of limited partnerships)—

(a) subsection (1) is to be read as if at the end there were inserted—

"For the purposes of this subsection, the exercise of rights conferred on limited partners by rules made under section 261I of the Financial Services and Markets Act 2000 does not constitute taking part in the management of the partnership business.".

(b) in subsection (3), the reference to the general partners is to be read as a reference to the general partner and the depositary of the partnership scheme; and

(c) subsection (5) is to be read as if—

(i) the words "Subject to any agreement expressed or implied between the partners" were omitted; and

(ii) in paragraph (b), at the beginning there were inserted "Subject to any express agreement between the partners,".

(5) Section 7 (law as to private partnerships to apply where not excluded by this Act) is to be read as if after the words "Subject to the provisions of this Act" there were inserted "as modified by regulation 16 of the Collective Investment in Transferable Securities (Contractual Scheme) Regulations 2013".

(6) In section 9 (registration of changes in partnerships), [subsection (1A)] is to be read as if—

(a) [paragraphs (a)(iii) and (b)(iii)] were omitted; and

(b) the changes giving rise to a duty to send a statement to the registrar included—

(i) the making and the revocation of an authorisation order in respect of a limited partnership; and

(ii) any change in the general partner or the name of the general partner of the limited partnership.

(7) Section 10 (advertisement in Gazette of statement of general partner becoming a limited partner and of assignment of share of limited partner) does not apply.".

Modification: see the European Long-term Investment Funds Regulations 2015, SI 2015/1882, reg 9 which, as amended by the Legislative Reform (Private Fund Limited Partnerships) Order 2017, SI 2017/514, art 6, as from 6 April 2017, provides as follows (note that "ELTIF" means European Long-term Investment Fund, and that "ELTIF Regulation" means Regulation 2015/760/EU of the European Parliament and of the Council on European Long-term Investment Funds)—

"9 Modifications to the Limited Partnerships Act 1907

(1) The Limited Partnerships Act 1907 has effect with the following modifications in its application to an ELTIF marketed to retail investors under Chapter 5 of the ELTIF Regulation.

(2) Section 4 (definition and constitution of limited partnership) is to be read as if—

[(a) in subsection (2A) there were omitted the words "and shall not be liable for the debts or obligations of the firm beyond the amount so contributed";]

(b) after [subsection (2A)] there were inserted—

"[(2AA)] The limited partners [in a limited partnership that is not a private fund limited partnership] are not liable for the debts or obligations of the firm beyond the amount of the partnership property which is available to the general partner to meet such debts or obligations.

[(2AB)] A person ("P") who ceases to be a limited partner [in a limited partnership that is not a private fund limited partnership] ceases to have any liability for the debts or obligations of the firm.

[(2AC)] [Subsection (2AB)] does not prevent the debts and obligations of the firm from being taken into account, after P has ceased to be a limited partner, in determining the value of P's share in the partnership."; and

(c) [subsections (2B)(b), (3) and (3A)] were omitted.

(3) In section 6 (modifications of general law in case of limited partnerships)—

(a) subsection (1) is to be read as if at the end there were inserted the words—

"For the purposes of this subsection, the exercise of rights conferred on limited partners by the rules or instruments of incorporation of a European long-term investment fund, authorised under Regulation (EU) No 2015/760 of the European Parliament and of the Council of 29th April 2015 on European Long-term Investment Funds, does not of itself constitute taking part in the management of the partnership business.";

(b) in [subsections (3) and (3A)], the reference to "general partners" is to be read as a reference to "the general partner and the depositary of the European long-term investment fund"; . . .

[(ba) in subsection (3B) the reference to "general partner" is to be read as a reference to "general partner or depositary of the European long-term investment fund";]

(c) subsection (5) is to be read as if—

(i) the words "Subject to any agreement express or implied between the partners" were omitted; and

(ii) in [paragraphs (b) and (f)], at the beginning there were inserted the words "Subject to any express agreement between the partners,"[; and

(d) in subsection (6) after "does not apply where a" insert "limited"].

(4) Section 7 (law as to private partnerships to apply where not excluded by this Act) is to be read as if after the words "Subject to the provisions of this Act," there were inserted "as modified by regulation 9 of the European Long-term Investment Funds Regulations 2015,".

(5) In section 9 (registration of changes in partnerships), [subsection (1A)] is to be read as if—

(a) [paragraphs (a)(iii) and (b)(iii)] were omitted; and

(b) the changes giving rise to a duty to send a statement to the registrar included–

(i) the granting and the revocation of a European long-term investment fund authorisation under Article 6 of the ELTIF Regulation in respect of a limited partnership; and

(ii) any change in the general partner or the name of the general partner of a limited partnership.

(6) Section 10 (advertisement in Gazette of statement of general partner becoming a limited partner and of assignment of share of limited partner) does not apply.".

[9.58]

5 Registration of limited partnership required

Every limited partnership must be registered as such in accordance with the provisions of this Act, . . .

NOTES

Words omitted repealed by the Legislative Reform (Limited Partnerships) Order 2009, SI 2009/1940, arts 2, 8, as from 1 October 2009, in relation to limited partnerships for which registration applications are received on or after that day.

[9.59]

6 Modifications of general law in case of limited partnerships

(1) A limited partner shall not take part in the management of the partnership business, and shall not have power to bind the firm—

Provided that a limited partner may by himself or his agent at any time inspect the books of the firm and examine into the state and prospects of the partnership business, and may advise with the partners thereon.

If a limited partner takes part in the management of the partnership business he shall be liable for all debts and obligations of the firm incurred while he so takes part in the management as though he were a general partner.

[(1A) Section 6A (private fund limited partnerships: actions by limited partners) makes provision, in respect of limited partners in private fund limited partnerships, supplementing subsection (1).]

(2) A limited partnership shall not be dissolved by the death or bankruptcy of a limited partner, and the lunacy of a limited partner shall not be a ground for dissolution of the partnership by the court unless the lunatic's share cannot be otherwise ascertained and realised.

(3) In the event of the dissolution of a limited partnership[, other than a private fund limited partnership,] its affairs shall be wound up by the general partners unless the court otherwise orders.

[(3A) If a private fund limited partnership is dissolved at a time when the partnership has at least one general partner, the affairs of the partnership must be wound up by those who are general partners at that time, subject to any express or implied agreement between the partners as to the winding up of the affairs of the partnership.

(3B) If a private fund limited partnership is dissolved at a time when the partnership does not have a general partner, the affairs of the partnership must be wound up by a person who is not a limited partner, appointed by those who are limited partners at that time, subject to any express or implied agreement between them as to the winding up of the affairs of the limited partnership.

(3C) Except in the phrase "a person who is not a limited partner" in subsection (3B), references in subsections (3A) and (3B) to partners do not include a partner who is insolvent.

(3D) Subsections (3A) and (3B) have effect subject to any order of the court as to the winding up of the affairs of the partnership.]

(4) . . .

(5) Subject to any agreement expressed or implied between the partners—

(a) Any difference arising as to ordinary matters connected with the partnership business may be decided by a majority of the general partners;

(b) A limited partner may, with the consent of the general partners, assign his share in the partnership, and upon such an assignment the assignee shall become a limited partner with all the rights of the assignor;

(c) The other partners shall not be entitled to dissolve the partnership by reason of any limited partner suffering his share to be charged for his separate debt;

(d) A person may be introduced as a partner without the consent of the existing limited partners;

(e) A limited partner shall not be entitled to dissolve the partnership by notice;

[(f) A limited partner in a private fund limited partnership is not subject to the duties in—

(i) section 28 of the Partnership Act 1890(a) (duty of partners to render accounts, etc), or

(ii) section 30 of that Act (duty of partner not to compete with firm)].

[(6) Section 36(1) of the Partnership Act 1890 (rights of persons dealing with firm against apparent members of firm) does not apply where a partner in a private fund limited partnership ceases to be a member of the firm.]

NOTES

Sub-ss (1A) and (3A)–(3D) were inserted, the words in square brackets in sub-s (3) were inserted, para (f) of sub-s (5) was added, and sub-s (6) was added, by the Legislative Reform (Private Fund Limited Partnerships) Order 2017, SI 2017/514, art 2(1), (4), as from 6 April 2017.

Sub-s (4) was repealed by the Companies (Consolidation) Act 1908, s 286, Sch 6, Pt I, as from 21 December 1908.

Modifications: see the note to s 4 at **[9.57]**.

[9.60]

[6A Private fund limited partnerships: actions by limited partners

(1) A limited partner in a private fund limited partnership is not to be regarded as taking part in the management of the partnership business for the purposes of section 6(1) merely because the limited partner takes any action listed in subsection (2).

(2) The actions are—

(a) taking part in a decision about—

(i) the variation of, or waiver of a term of, the partnership agreement or associated documents;

(ii) whether the general nature of the partnership business should change;

(iii) whether a person should become or cease to be a partner;

(iv) whether the partnership should end or the term of the partnership should be extended;

(b) appointing a person to wind up the partnership pursuant to section 6(3B);

(c) enforcing an entitlement under the partnership agreement, provided that the entitlement does not involve a limited partner taking part in the management of the partnership business;

(d) entering into, or acting under, a contract with the other partners in the partnership, provided that the contract does not require, or the action under the contract does not involve, a limited partner taking part in the management of the partnership business;

(e) providing surety or acting as guarantor for the partnership;

(f) approving the accounts of the partnership;

(g) reviewing or approving a valuation of the partnership's assets;

(h) discussing the prospects of the partnership business;

(i) consulting or advising with a general partner or any person appointed to manage or advise the partnership about the affairs of the partnership or about its accounts;

(j) taking part in a decision regarding changes in the persons responsible for the day-to-day management of the partnership;

(k) acting, or authorising a representative to act, as a director, member, employee, officer or agent of, or a shareholder or partner in—

(i) a general partner in the partnership; or

(ii) another person appointed to manage or advise the partnership in relation to the affairs of the partnership,

provided that this does not involve a limited partner taking part in the management of the partnership business or authorising a representative to take any action that would involve taking part in the management of the partnership business if taken by a limited partner;

(l) appointing or nominating a person to represent the limited partner on a committee, authorising such a person to take any action in that capacity that would not involve taking part in the management of the partnership business if taken by the limited partner, or revoking such an appointment or nomination;
(m) taking part in a decision about how the partnership should exercise any right as an investor in another collective investment scheme as defined in section 8D(4) ("master fund"), provided that the partnership's exercise of the right would not cause the partnership to be liable for the debts or obligations of the master fund beyond the amount contributed, or agreed to be contributed, by the partnership to the master fund;
(n) taking part in a decision approving or authorising an action proposed to be taken by a general partner or another person appointed to manage the partnership, including in particular a proposal in relation to—
 (i) the disposal of all or part of the partnership business or the acquisition of another business by the partnership;
 (ii) the acquisition or disposal of a type of investment or a particular investment by the partnership;
 (iii) the exercise of the partnership's rights in respect of an investment;
 (iv) the participation by a limited partner in a particular investment by the partnership;
 (v) the incurring, extension, variation or discharge of debt by the partnership;
 (vi) the creation, extension, variation or discharge of any other obligation owed by the partnership.

(3) The fact that a decision that affects or relates to a private fund limited partnership involves an actual or potential conflict of interest is not of itself a reason to regard a limited partner in the partnership who takes part in the decision as taking part in the management of the partnership business for the purposes of section 6(1).
(4) Nothing in this section—
(a) limits the circumstances in which a limited partner in a private fund limited partnership is not to be regarded as taking part in the management of the partnership business; or
(b) affects the circumstances in which a limited partner in a limited partnership that is not a private fund limited partnership may, or may not, be regarded as taking part in the management of the partnership business.]

NOTES

Inserted by the Legislative Reform (Private Fund Limited Partnerships) Order 2017, SI 2017/514, art 2(1), (5), as from 6 April 2017.

[9.61]
7 Law as to private partnerships to apply where not excluded by this Act
Subject to the provisions of this Act, the Partnership Act 1890 and the rules of equity and of common law applicable to partnerships, except so far as they are inconsistent with the express provisions of the last-mentioned Act, shall apply to limited partnerships.

NOTES

Modifications: see the note to s 4 at **[9.57]**.

[9.62]
[8 Duty to register [and designate]
[(1)] The registrar shall register a limited partnership if an application is made to the registrar in accordance with section 8A.
[(2) The registrar must designate a limited partnership on the register as a private fund limited partnership if an application for such designation is made to the registrar in accordance with section 8D.]]

NOTES

Substituted by the Legislative Reform (Limited Partnerships) Order 2009, SI 2009/1940, arts 2, 4, as from 1 October 2009, in relation to limited partnerships for which registration applications are received on or after that day.
Words in square brackets in the section heading inserted, sub-s (1) numbered as such, and sub-s (2) added, by the Legislative Reform (Private Fund Limited Partnerships) Order 2017, SI 2017/514, art 2(1), (6), as from 6 April 2017.

[9.63]
[8A Application for registration
(1) An application for registration must—
(a) specify the firm name, complying with section 8B, under which the limited partnership is to be registered,
(b) contain the details listed in subsection (2) [or (3)],
(c) be signed or otherwise authenticated by or on behalf of each partner, and
(d) be made to the registrar for the part of the United Kingdom in which the principal place of business of the limited partnership is to be situated.

(2) [Except in the case of an application that is accompanied by an application for designation as a private fund limited partnership, the required] details are—
(a) the general nature of the partnership business,
(b) the name of each general partner,
(c) the name of each limited partner,
(d) the amount of the capital contribution of each limited partner (and whether the contribution is paid in cash or in another specified form),
(e) the address of the proposed principal place of business of the limited partnership, and
(f) the term (if any) for which the limited partnership is to be entered into (beginning with the date of registration).

[(3) In the case of an application that is accompanied by an application for designation as a private fund limited partnership, the required details are—
(a) the name of each general partner,
(b) the name of each limited partner, and
(c) the address of the proposed principal place of business of the limited partnership.]

[(4) An application for registration of a limited partnership whose principal place of business is to be situated in Scotland must contain a statement of initial significant control.

(5) The statement of initial significant control must—

- (a) state whether, on registration, there will be any person who will count as either a registrable person or a registrable relevant legal entity in relation to the limited partnership for the purposes of regulation 10 of the Scottish Partnerships PSC Regulations (duty to investigate and obtain information),
- (b) include the required particulars of any person identified under paragraph (a), and
- (c) if there is no person identified under paragraph (a), state that fact.

(6) It is not necessary to include under subsection (5)(b) the date on which a person becomes a registrable person or a registrable relevant legal entity in relation to the limited partnership.

(7) If the statement of initial significant control includes required particulars of a registrable person, it must also contain a statement that those particulars are included with the knowledge of that individual.

(8) In this section—

"the Scottish Partnerships PSC Regulations" means the Scottish Partnerships (Register of People with Significant Control) Regulations 2017;

"registrable person", "registrable relevant legal entity" and "required particulars" have the same meaning as in the Scottish Partnerships PSC Regulations.]]

NOTES

Inserted by the Legislative Reform (Limited Partnerships) Order 2009, SI 2009/1940, arts 2, 5, as from 1 October 2009, in relation to limited partnerships for which registration applications are received on or after that day.

The words in square brackets in sub-s (1) were added, the words in square brackets in sub-s (2) were substituted, and sub-s (3) was added, by the Legislative Reform (Private Fund Limited Partnerships) Order 2017, SI 2017/514, art 2(1), (7), as from 6 April 2017.

Sub-ss (4)–(8): added by the Scottish Partnerships (Register of People with Significant Control) Regulations 2017, SI 2017/694, reg 4, as from 24 July 2017.

[9.64]

[8B Name of limited partnership

(1) This section sets out conditions which must be satisfied by the firm name of a limited partnership as specified in the application for registration.

(2) The name must end with—

- (a) the words "limited partnership" (upper or lower case, or any combination), or
- (b) the abbreviation "LP" (upper or lower case, or any combination, with or without punctuation).

(3) But if the principal place of business of a limited partnership is to be in Wales, its firm name may end with—

- (a) the words "partneriaeth cyfyngedig" (upper or lower case, or any combination), or
- (b) the abbreviation "PC" (upper or lower case, or any combination, with or without punctuation).]

NOTES

Inserted by the Legislative Reform (Limited Partnerships) Order 2009, SI 2009/1940, arts 2, 6, as from 1 October 2009, in relation to limited partnerships for which registration applications are received on or after that day.

[9.65]

[8C Certificate of registration [and certificate of designation as a private fund limited partnership]

(1) On registering a limited partnership the registrar shall issue a certificate of registration.

(2) The certificate must be—

- (a) signed by the registrar, or
- (b) authenticated with the registrar's seal.

(3) The certificate must state—

- (a) the firm name of the limited partnership given in the application for registration,
- (b) the limited partnership's registration number,
- (c) the date of registration, and
- (d) that the limited partnership is registered as a limited partnership under this Act.

(4) The certificate is conclusive evidence that a limited partnership came into existence on the date of registration.

[(5) If a limited partnership is designated on the register as a private fund limited partnership, the registrar must issue a certificate of designation as a private fund limited partnership.

(6) The certificate must be signed by the registrar or authenticated with the registrar's seal.

(7) The certificate must state—

- (a) the firm name and registration number of the limited partnership,
- (b) the date of designation as a private fund limited partnership, and
- (c) that the limited partnership is designated as a private fund limited partnership under this Act.

(8) A certificate of designation as a private fund limited partnership is conclusive evidence that the limited partnership was designated as a private fund limited partnership on the date of designation.

(9) If a limited partnership is designated as a private fund limited partnership at the same time as it is registered, the registrar may issue a combined certificate instead of issuing separate certificates under subsections (1) and (5), and that combined certificate—

- (a) must be signed by the registrar or authenticated with the registrar's seal,
- (b) must state the particulars mentioned in subsections (3) and (7), and
- (c) is conclusive evidence that—
  - (i) a limited partnership came into existence on the date of registration, and
  - (ii) the limited partnership was designated as a private fund limited partnership on the date of registration.]]

NOTES

Inserted by the Legislative Reform (Limited Partnerships) Order 2009, SI 2009/1940, arts 2, 7, as from 1 October 2009, in relation to limited partnerships for which registration applications are received on or after that day.

The words in square brackets in the section heading were added, and sub-ss (5)–(9) were added, by the Legislative Reform (Private Fund Limited Partnerships) Order 2017, SI 2017/514, art 2(1), (8), as from 6 April 2017.

[9.66]

[8D Application for designation as a private fund limited partnership

(1) An application for designation as a private fund limited partnership may be made with an application for registration under section 8A or at any time after a limited partnership has been registered.

(2) An application for designation as a private fund limited partnership must—

(a) specify the firm name of the partnership;

(b) specify the address of the partnership's principal place of business or proposed principal place of business;

(c) in the case of an application made after the firm is registered as a limited partnership, specify the limited partnership's registration number and the date of registration;

(d) include confirmation by a general partner that the partnership meets the private fund conditions;

(e) be signed or otherwise authenticated by or on behalf of each general partner; and

(f) be made to the registrar.

(3) The private fund conditions are that the partnership—

(a) is constituted by an agreement in writing, and

(b) is a collective investment scheme.

(4) In subsection (3) "collective investment scheme" has the same meaning as in Part 17 of the Financial Services and Markets Act 2000(a) (see section 235 of that Act), ignoring any order made under section 235(5) of that Act.]

NOTES

Inserted by the Legislative Reform (Private Fund Limited Partnerships) Order 2017, SI 2017/514, art 2(1), (9), as from 6 April 2017.

[9.67]

9 Registration of changes in partnerships

[(1) If during the continuance of a limited partnership any change is made or occurs as mentioned in subsection (1A), a statement, signed by the firm, specifying the nature of the change must within seven days be sent by post or delivered to the registrar.

(1A) The changes are—

(a) in the case of any limited partnership, changes to—

(i) the firm name,

(ii) the principal place of business,

(iii) the partners or the name of any partner,

(iv) the liability of any partner by reason of the partner becoming a limited instead of a general partner or a general instead of a limited partner;

(b) in the case of a limited partnership that is not a private fund limited partnership, changes to—

(i) the general nature of the business,

(ii) the term or character of the partnership,

(iii) the sum contributed by any limited partner;

(c) in the case of a private fund limited partnership that was registered as a limited partnership before 6th April 2017, any withdrawal by a limited partner of the partner's contribution which has the effect that the amount of the partner's contribution is less than it was on the date on which the limited partnership was designated as a private fund limited partnership.]

(2) If default is made in compliance with the requirements of this section each of the general partners shall, on conviction under the Summary Jurisdiction Acts, be liable to a fine not exceeding one pound for each day during which the default continues.

NOTES

Sub-ss (1), (1A): substituted (for the original sub-s (1)) by the Legislative Reform (Private Fund Limited Partnerships) Order 2017, SI 2017/514, art 2(1), (10), as from 6 April 2017.

Modifications: see the note to s 4 at **[9.57]**.

Temporary modification: this section was modified by the Companies etc (Filing Requirements) (Temporary Modifications) Regulations 2020, SI 2020/645, reg 37. By virtue of the Corporate Insolvency and Governance Act 2020, s 39(8), the modification applied from 27 June 2020 to the end of the day on 5 April 2021 (subject to the saving provision in s 39(9) which provides that the expiry of s 39 on 5 April 2021 does not affect the continued operation of any Regulations made under that section for the purpose of determining the length of any period that began before the expiry). As modified, sub-s (1) above had effect as if for the reference to "seven days" there were substituted a reference to "42 days".

[9.68]

10 Advertisement in Gazette of statement of general partner becoming a limited partner and of assignment of share of limited partner

(1) Notice of any arrangement or transaction under which any person will cease to be a general partner in any firm [that is not a private fund limited partnership], and will become a limited partner in that firm, or under which the share of a limited partner in a firm [that is not a private fund limited partnership] will be assigned to any person, shall be forthwith advertised in the Gazette, and until notice of the arrangement or transaction is so advertised the arrangement or transaction shall, for the purposes of this Act, be deemed to be of no effect.

[(1A) Notice of any arrangement or transaction under which any person will cease to be a general partner in a private fund limited partnership shall be forthwith advertised in the Gazette.

(1B) Where a person deals with a private fund limited partnership after an arrangement or transaction of the type referred to in subsection (1A), that person is entitled to treat the person who is ceasing to be a general partner as still being a general partner of the firm until the person has notice of the arrangement or transaction.

(1C) Advertisement of a notice in accordance with subsection (1A) is notice to a person dealing with the firm for the purpose of subsection (1B).]

(2) For the purposes of this section, the expression "the Gazette" means—

In the case of a limited partnership registered in England, the London Gazette.

In the case of a limited partnership registered in Scotland, the Edinburgh Gazette.

In the case of a limited partnership registered in [Northern Ireland], the [Belfast] Gazette.

NOTES

Sub-s (1): words in square brackets inserted by the Legislative Reform (Private Fund Limited Partnerships) Order 2017, SI 2017/514, art 2(1), (11)(a), as from 6 April 2017.

Sub-ss (1A)–(1C): inserted by SI 2017/514, art 2(1), (11)(b), as from 6 April 2017.

Sub-s (2): words in square brackets substituted by the Companies Act 2006 (Consequential Amendments, Transitional Provisions and Savings) Order 2009, SI 2009/1941, art 2(1), Sch 1, para 3(1), (3), as from 1 October 2009.

Modifications: see the note to s 4 at **[9.57]**.

11, 12 *(S 11 repealed by the Finance Act 1973, s 59(7), Sch 22, Pt V, as from 1 August 1973. S 12 repealed by the Perjury Act 1911, s 17, Schedule, as from 1 January 1912.)*

[9.69]

13 Registrar to file statement and issue certificate of registration

On receiving any statement made in pursuance of this Act the registrar shall cause the same to be filed, and he shall send by post to the firm from whom such statement shall have been received a certificate of the registration thereof.

[9.70]

14 Register and index to be kept

. . . the registrar shall keep . . . a register and an index of all the limited partnerships registered as aforesaid, and of all the statements registered in relation to such partnerships.

NOTES

Words omitted repealed by the Companies Act 2006 (Consequential Amendments, Transitional Provisions and Savings) Order 2009, SI 2009/1941, art 2(1), Sch 1, para 3(1), (4), as from 1 October 2009.

[9.71]

[15 The registrar

(1) The registrar of companies is the registrar of limited partnerships.

(2) In this Act—

(a) references to the registrar in relation to the registration of a limited partnership are to the registrar to whom the application for registration is to be made (see section 8A(1)(d));

(b) references to registration in a particular part of the United Kingdom are to registration by the registrar for that part of the United Kingdom;

[(ba) references to the registrar in relation to an application for designation of a limited partnership as a private fund limited partnership made with an application for registration are to the registrar to whom the application for registration is to be made (see section 8A(1)(d));]

(c) references to the registrar in relation to any other matter relating to a limited partnership are to the registrar for the part of the United Kingdom in which the partnership is registered.]

NOTES

Substituted by the Companies Act 2006 (Consequential Amendments, Transitional Provisions and Savings) Order 2009, SI 2009/1941, art 2(1), Sch 1, para 3(1), (5), as from 1 October 2009.

Sub-s (2): para (ba) inserted by the Legislative Reform (Private Fund Limited Partnerships) Order 2017, SI 2017/514, art 2(1), (12), as from 6 April 2017.

[9.72]

16 Inspection of statements registered

(1) Any person may inspect the statements filed by the registrar . . . and any person may require a certificate [mentioned in section 8C], or a copy of or extract from any registered statement, to be certified by the registrar . . .

(2) A certificate [mentioned in section 8C] or a copy of or extract from any statement registered under this Act, if duly certified to be a true copy under the hand of the registrar . . . (whom it shall not be necessary to prove to be the registrar . . .) shall, in all legal proceedings, civil or criminal, and in all cases whatsoever be received in evidence.

NOTES

Sub-s (1): first words omitted repealed by the Companies Act 2006 (Consequential Amendments, Transitional Provisions and Savings) Order 2009, SI 2009/1941, art 2(1), Sch 1, para 3(1), (6)(a), as from 1 October 2009. Words in square brackets substituted by the Legislative Reform (Private Fund Limited Partnerships) Order 2017, SI 2017/514, art 2(1), (13)(a), as from 6 April 2017. Other words omitted repealed by the Companies Act 2006, ss 1063(7)(a), 1295, Sch 16, as from 6 April 2007.

Sub-s (2): words in square brackets substituted by SI 2017/514, art 2(1), (13)(b), as from 6 April 2017. Words omitted repealed by SI 2009/1941, art 2(1), Sch 1, para 3(1), (6)(b), as from 1 October 2009.

Fees: see the Registrar of Companies (Fees) (Limited Partnerships and Newspaper Proprietors) Regulations 2009, SI 2009/2392 at **[4.370]**.

[9.73]

17 Power to Board of Trade to make rules

The Board of Trade may make rules . . . concerning any of the following matters:—

(a) . . .

(b) The duties or additional duties to be performed by the registrar for the purposes of this Act;

(c) The performance by assistant registrars and other officers of acts by this Act required to be done by the registrar;

(d) The forms to be used for the purposes of this Act;

(e) Generally, the conduct and regulation of registration under this Act and any matters incidental thereto.

NOTES

Words omitted repealed by the Companies Act 2006, ss 1063(7)(b), 1295, Sch 16, as from 6 April 2007).

See further, the Legislative Reform (Limited Partnerships) Order 2009, SI 2009/1940, art 9, which provides that nothing in that Order (which amends s 5 of this Act, substitutes s 8, and inserts ss 8A–8C (as noted *ante*)) permits anything to be done under this section that could not otherwise have been done.

Rules: the Limited Partnerships (Forms) Rules 2009, SI 2009/2160.

STOCK TRANSFER ACT 1963

(1963 c 18)

NOTES

This Act is reproduced as amended by the following Acts: the Finance Act 1964; the Post Office Act 1969; the Stock Exchange (Completion of Bargains) Act 1976; the Building Societies Act 1986; Financial Services Act 1986; the Local Government Finance Act 1992; the Requirements of Writing (Scotland) Act 1995; the Finance Act 1999; the Fire and Rescue Services Act 2004; the Co-operative and Community Benefit Societies Act 2014.

And by the following Statutory Instruments: the Stock Transfer (Amendment of Forms) Order 1974, SI 1974/1214; the Local Government Finance (Repeals, Savings and Consequential Amendments) Order 1990, SI 1990/776; the Stock Transfer (Addition and Substitution of Forms) Order 1996, SI 1996/1571; the Open Ended Investment Companies (Investment Companies with Variable Capital) Regulations 1996, SI 1996/2827; the Open-Ended Investment Companies Regulations 2001, SI 2001, SI 2001/1228; the Financial Services and Markets Act 2000 (Consequential Amendments and Repeals) Order 2001, SI 2001/3649; the Companies Act 2006 (Consequential Amendments etc) Order 2008, SI 2008/948; the Companies Act 2006 (Consequential Amendments, Transitional Provisions and Savings) Order 2009, SI 2009/1941; the Collective Investment in Transferable Securities (Contractual Scheme) Regulations 2013, SI 2013/1388; the Risk Transformation Regulations 2017, SI 2017/1212.

Note that the Uncertificated Securities Regulations 2001, SI 2001/3755, reg 37 provides that references in any enactment or rule of law to a proper instrument of transfer or to a transfer with respect to securities, or any expression having like meaning, shall be taken to include a reference to an Operator-instruction to a participating issuer to register a transfer of title on the relevant issuer register of securities in accordance with the Operator-instruction (see **[6.73]**).

ARRANGEMENT OF SECTIONS

SCHEDULES

An Act to amend the law with respect to the transfer of securities

[10 July 1963]

[9.74]

1 Simplified transfer of securities

(1) Registered securities to which this section applies may be transferred by means of an instrument under hand in the form set out in Schedule 1 to this Act (in this Act referred to as a stock transfer), executed by the transferor only and specifying (in addition to the particulars of the consideration, of the description and number or amount of the securities, and of the person by whom the transfer is made) the full name and address of the transferee.

(2) The execution of a stock transfer need not be attested; and where such a transfer has been executed for the purpose of a stock exchange transaction, the particulars of the consideration and of the transferee may either be inserted in that transfer or, as the case may require, supplied by means of separate instruments in the form set out in Schedule 2 to this Act (in this Act referred to as brokers transfers), identifying the stock transfer and specifying the securities to which each such instrument relates and the consideration paid for those securities.

(3) Nothing in this section shall be construed as affecting the validity of any instrument which would be effective to transfer securities apart from this section; and any instrument purporting to be made in any form which was common or usual before the commencement of this Act, or in any other form authorised or required for that purpose apart from this section, shall be sufficient, whether or not it is completed in accordance with the form, if it complies with the requirements as to execution and contents which apply to a stock transfer.

(4) This section applies to fully paid up registered securities of any description, being—

(a) securities issued by any company [as defined in section 1(1) of the Companies Act 2006] except a company limited by guarantee or an unlimited company;

(b) securities issued by any body (other than a company [as so defined]) incorporated in Great Britain by or under any enactment or by Royal Charter except a building society within the meaning of the Building Societies Act [1986] or [a registered society within the meaning of the Co-operative and Community Benefit Societies Act 2014];

(c) securities issued by the Government of the United Kingdom, except stock or bonds in [the National Savings Stock Register] . . . , and except national savings certificates;

(d) securities issued by any local authority;

[(e) units of an authorised unit trust scheme[, an authorised contractual scheme] or a recognised scheme within the meaning of [Part 17 of the Financial Services and Markets Act 2000]];

[(f) shares issued by an open-ended investment company within the meaning of the Open-Ended Investment Companies Regulations 2001;]

[(g) shares issued by a protected cell company within the meaning of Part 4 of the Risk Transformation Regulations 2017].

NOTES

Sub-s (4) is amended as follows:

Words in square brackets in para (a), and words in first pair of square brackets in para (b), substituted by the Companies Act 2006 (Consequential Amendments, Transitional Provisions and Savings) Order 2009, SI 2009/1941, art 2(1), Sch 1, para 10, as from 1 October 2009.

Year "1986" in second pair of square brackets in para (b) substituted by the Building Societies Act 1986, s 120(1), Sch 18, Pt I, para 5, as from 1 January 1987.

Words in third pair of square brackets in para (b) substituted by the Co-operative and Community Benefit Societies Act 2014, s 151, Sch 4, Pt 2, para 21, as from 1 August 2014.

Words in square brackets in para (c) substituted by the Post Office Act 1969, s 108(1)(f), as from 25 July 1969. Words omitted from that paragraph repealed by the Finance Act 1964, ss 24, 26(7), Sch 8, para 10, Sch 9, as from 16 July 1964.

Para (e) substituted by the Financial Services Act 1986, s 212(2), Sch 16, para 4(a), as from 29 April 1988.

Words in first pair of square brackets in para (e) inserted by the Collective Investment in Transferable Securities (Contractual Scheme) Regulations 2013, SI 2013/1388, reg 4, as from 6 June 2013.

Words in second pair of square brackets in para (e) substituted by the Financial Services and Markets Act 2000 (Consequential Amendments and Repeals) Order 2001, SI 2001/3649, art 270, as from 1 December 2001.

Para (f) originally added by the Open-Ended Investment Companies (Investment Companies with Variable Capital) Regulations 1996, SI 1996/2827, reg 75, Sch 8, Pt I, para 2, as from 6 January 1997. Subsequently substituted by the Open-Ended Investment Companies Regulations 2001, SI 2001, SI 2001/1228, reg 84, Sch 7, Pt I, para 2, as from 1 December 2001.

Para (g) added by the Risk Transformation Regulations 2017, SI 2017/1212, reg 190, Sch 4, para 1, as from 8 December 2017.

Modifications: the Stock Transfer (Substitution of Forms) Order 1990, SI 1990/18, art 3 provides as follows—

> "Section 1(3) of the Act shall apply in relation to the form for which the form set out in the Schedule to this Order is substituted as it applies to any form which was common or usual before the commencement of the Act with the modification that for the words "which was common or usual before the commencement of this Act" there shall be substituted the words "for which the form set out in the Schedule to the Stock Transfer (Substitution of Forms) Order 1990 is substituted".".

The Stock Transfer (Substitution of Forms) Order 1990, SI 1990/18, art 4 further provides that this section shall have effect in relation to the form set out in the Schedule to that Order subject to the amendment that that form need not specify (a) particulars of the consideration or (b) the address of the transferee.

The Stock Transfer (Addition and Substitution of Forms) Order 1996, SI 1996/1571, art 3 further provides as follows—

> "(1) The form set out in Schedule 2 to this Order shall be substituted for the first form set out in Schedule 1 to the Stock Transfer Act 1963 (which is referred to in that Act as a stock transfer form).
>
> (2) Subsection (3) of section 1 of the Stock Transfer Act 1963 shall apply in relation to the form for which the form set out in Schedule 2 to this Order is substituted as it applies to any form for which the form set out in the Schedule to the Stock Transfer (Substitution of Forms) Order 1990 was substituted but with the modification mentioned in paragraph (3) below.
>
> (3) The modification referred to in paragraph (2) above is the substitution for the words "for which the form set out in the Schedule to the Stock Transfer (Substitution of Forms) Order 1990 is substituted" of the words "for which the form set out in Schedule 2 to the Stock Transfer (Addition and Substitution of Forms) Order 1996 is substituted".".

[9.75]

2 Supplementary provisions as to simplified transfer

(1) Section 1 of this Act shall have effect in relation to the transfer of any securities to which that section applies notwithstanding anything to the contrary in any enactment or instrument relating to the transfer of those securities; but nothing in that section affects—

(a) any right to refuse to register a person as the holder of any securities on any ground other than the form in which those securities purport to be transferred to him: or

(b) any enactment or rule of law regulating the execution of documents by companies or other bodies corporate, or any articles of association or other instrument regulating the execution of documents by any particular company or body corporate.

(2) Subject to the provisions of this section, any enactment or instrument relating to the transfer of securities to which section 1 of this Act applies shall, with any necessary modifications, apply in relation to an instrument of transfer authorised by that section as it applies in relation to an instrument of transfer to which it applies apart from this subsection; and without prejudice to the generality of the foregoing provision, [the references to an instrument of transfer in section 775 of the Companies Act 2006 (certification of instrument of transfer)] shall be construed as including a reference to a brokers transfer.

(3) In relation to the transfer of securities by means of a stock transfer and a brokers transfer—

(a) any reference in any enactment or instrument (including in particular [section 770(1)(a) of the Companies Act 2006 (registration of transfer)] . . .) to the delivery or lodging of an instrument (or proper instrument) of transfer shall be construed as a reference to the delivery or lodging of the stock transfer and the brokers transfer;

(b) any such reference to the date on which an instrument of transfer is delivered or lodged shall be construed as a reference to the date by which the later of those transfers to be delivered or lodged has been delivered or lodged; and

(c) subject to the foregoing provisions of this subsection, the brokers transfer (and not the stock transfer) shall be deemed to be the conveyance or transfer for the purposes of the enactments relating to stamp duty.

(4) . . .

NOTES

Sub-s (2): words in square brackets substituted by the Companies Act 2006 (Consequential Amendments etc) Order 2008, SI 2008/948, art 3(1), Sch 1, Pt 2, para 37(a), as from 6 April 2008.

Sub-s (3): words in square brackets substituted by SI 2008/948, art 3(1), Sch 1, Pt 2, para 37(b), as from 6 April 2008. Words omitted from para (a) repealed by the Finance Act 1999, s 139, Sch 20, Pt V(5), with effect in relation to instruments executed from 6 February 2000. Note that these words and para (c) were to be repealed by the Finance Act 1990, s 132, Sch 19, Pt VI, with effect from an appointed day in accordance with the Finance Act 1990, ss 107–111. The Treasury order specifying the appointed day for the purposes of the Finance Act 1990, ss 107–110 was to coincide with the start of paperless trading under the Stock Exchange's planned TAURUS system (IR press release, 20.3.1990). However, on 11 March 1993 the London Stock Exchange News Release 6/93 announced that TAURUS had been abandoned.

Sub-s (4): repealed by the Requirements of Writing (Scotland) Act 1995, s 14(2), Sch 5, as from 1 August 1995.

[9.76]

3 Additional provisions as to transfer forms

(1) References in this Act to the forms set out in Schedule 1 and Schedule 2 include references to forms substantially corresponding to those forms respectively.

(2) The Treasury may by order amend the said Schedules either by altering the forms set out therein or by substituting different forms for those forms or by the addition of forms for use as alternatives to those forms; and references in this Act to the forms set out in those Schedules (including references in this section) shall be construed accordingly.

(3) Any order under subsection (2) of this section which substitutes a different form for a form set out in Schedule 1 to this Act may direct that subsection (3) of section 1 of this Act shall apply, with any necessary modifications, in relation to the form for which that form is substituted as it applies to any form which was common or usual before the commencement of this Act.

(4) Any order of the Treasury under this section shall be made by statutory instrument, and may be varied or revoked by a subsequent order; and any statutory instrument made by virtue of this section shall be subject to annulment in pursuance of a resolution of either House of Parliament.

[(5) An order under subsection (2) of this section may—

(a) provide for forms on which some of the particulars mentioned in subsection (1) of section 1 of this Act are not required to be specified;

(b) provide for that section to have effect, in relation to such forms as are mentioned in the preceding paragraph or other forms specified in the order, subject to such amendments as are so specified (which may include an amendment of the reference in subsection (1) of that section to an instrument under hand);

(c) provide for all or any of the provisions of the order to have effect in such cases only as are specified in the order.]

NOTES

Sub-s (5): added by the Stock Exchange (Completion of Bargains) Act 1976, s 6, as from 12 February 1979.

Orders: the Stock Transfer (Amendment of Forms) Order 1974, SI 1974/1214; the Stock Transfer (Addition of Forms) Order 1979, SI 1979/277; the Stock Transfer (Substitution of Forms) Order 1990, SI 1990/18; the Stock Transfer (Addition and Substitution of Forms) Order 1996, SI 1996/1571.

[9.77]

4 Interpretation

(1) In this Act the following expressions have the meanings hereby respectively assigned to them, that is to say—

"local authority" means, in relation to England and Wales—

[[(a) a billing authority or a precepting authority as defined in section 69 of the Local Government Finance Act 1992;

[(aa) a fire and rescue authority in Wales constituted by a scheme under section 2 of the Fire and Rescue Services Act 2004 or a scheme to which section 4 of that Act applies;]]

(b) a levying body within the meaning of section 74 of [the Local Government Finance Act 1988]; and

(c) a body as regards which section 75 of that Act applies,]

and, in relation to Scotland, a county council, a town council and any statutory authority, commissioners or trustees to whom section 270 of the Local Government (Scotland) Act 1947 applies;

"registered securities" means transferable securities the holders of which are entered in a register (whether maintained in Great Britain or not);

"securities" means shares, stock, debentures, debenture stock, loan stock, bonds, units of a [collective investment scheme within the meaning of the [Financial Services and Markets Act 2000]], and other securities of any description;

"stock exchange transaction" means a sale and purchase of securities in which each of the parties is a member of a stock exchange acting in the ordinary course of his business as such or is acting through the agency of such a member;

"stock exchange" means the Stock Exchange, London, and any other stock exchange (whether in Great Britain or not) which is declared by order of the Treasury to be a recognised stock exchange for the purposes of this Act.

(2) Any order of the Treasury under this section shall be made by statutory instrument and may be varied or revoked by a subsequent order.

NOTES

The definition "local authority" in sub-s (1) is amended as follows—

Paras (a)–(c) substituted by the Local Government Finance (Repeals, Savings and Consequential Amendments) Order 1990, SI 1990/776, art 8, Sch 3, para 8, as from 1 April 1990.

Paras (a), (aa) further substituted, for para (a), by the Local Government Finance Act 1992, s 117(1), Sch 13, para 12, as from 2 November 1992.

Para (aa) further substituted by the Fire and Rescue Services Act 2004, s 53, Sch 1, para 18(1), (2), as from 1 October 2004 (in relation to England and Scotland), and as from 10 November 2004 (in relation to Wales).

Words in square brackets in para (b) substituted by the Fire and Rescue Services Act 2004, s 53, Sch 1, para 18(1), (3), as from 1 October 2004 (in relation to England and Scotland), and as from 10 November 2004 (in relation to Wales).

In definition "securities" in sub-s (1) words in first (outer) pair of square brackets substituted by the Financial Services Act 1986, s 212(2), Sch 16, para 4(b), as from 29 April 1988. Words in second (inner) pair of square brackets substituted by the Financial Services and Markets Act 2000 (Consequential Amendments and Repeals) Order 2001, SI 2001/3649, art 271, as from 1 December 2001.

Local Government (Scotland) Act 1947, s 270: repealed by the Local Government (Scotland) Act 1975, s 38, Sch 7.

Orders: the Stock Transfer (Recognised Stock Exchanges) Order 1973, SI 1973/536.

5 *((Application to Northern Ireland) outside the scope of this work.)*

[9.78]

6 Short title and commencement

(1) This Act may be cited as the Stock Transfer Act 1963.

(2) Subsection (3) of section 5 of this Act shall come into force on the passing of this Act, and the remaining provisions of this Act shall come into force on such date as the Treasury may by order made by statutory instrument direct.

NOTES

Orders: the Stock Transfer Act 1963 (Commencement) Order 1963, SI 1963/1592 (bringing provisions of this Act, other than s 5(3), into force on 26 October 1963).

SCHEDULE I

[9.79]

STOCK TRANSFER FORM Consideration Money £................................		Certificate lodged with the Registrar **(For completion by the Registrar/ Stock Exchange)**
Name of Undertaking.		
Description of Security.		
Number or amount of Shares, Stock or other security and, in figures column only, number and denomination of units, if any.	Words	Figures (units of)
Name(s) of registered holder(s) should be given in full: the address should be given where there is only one holder. If the transfer is not made by the registered holder(s) insert also the name(s) and capacity (eg, Executor(s)), of the person(s) making the transfer.	in the name(s) of	

Delete words in italics except for stock exchange transactions.	I/We hereby transfer the above security out of the name(s) aforesaid to the person(s) named below *or to the several persons named in Parts 2 of Brokers Transfer Forms relating to the above security*: Signature(s) of transferor(s) 1.. 3.. 2.. 4.. A body corporate should execute this transfer under its common seal or otherwise in accordance with applicable statutory requirements.	Stamp of Selling Broker(s) or, for transactions which are not stock exchange transactions, of Agent(s), if any, acting for the Transferor(s). Date

Full name(s), full postal address(es) (including County or, if applicable, Postal District number) of the person(s) to whom the security is transferred. Please state title, if any, or whether Mr, Mrs or Miss. Please complete in type or in Block Capitals.	

I/We request that such entries be made in the register as are necessary to give effect to this transfer.

Stamp of Buying Broker(s) (if any).	Stamp or name and address of person lodging this form (if other than the Buying Broker(s)).

Reference to the Registrar in this form means the registrar or registration agent of the undertaking, not the Registrar of Companies at Companies House.

(Endorsement for use only in stock exchange transactions)

The security represented by the transfer overleaf has been sold as follows:—

......................................*Shares/Stock*	......................................*Shares/Stock*
......................................*Shares/Stock*	......................................*Shares/Stock*
......................................*Shares/Stock*	......................................*Shares/Stock*
......................................*Shares/Stock*	......................................*Shares/Stock*
......................................*Shares/Stock*	......................................*Shares/Stock*
......................................*Shares/Stock*	......................................*Shares/Stock*

Balance (if any) due to Selling Broker(s)

Amount of Certificate(s)

Brokers Transfer Forms for above amounts certified

Stamp of certifying Stock Exchange ***Stamp of Selling Broker(s)***

Above this line for Registrar's use

TRANSFER

Counter Location Stamp	Barcode or reference RN

Above this line for completion by the depositing system-user only.

	Consideration Money	Certificate(s) lodged with Registrar (To be completed by Registrar)
Name of Undertaking.		
Description of Security.		
Please complete form in type or in block capitals.	Amount of shares or other security in words	Figures
Name(s) of registered holder(s) should be given in full: the address should be given where there is only one holder. If the transfer is not made by the registered holder(s) insert also the name(s) and capacity (eg executor(s)) of the person(s) making the transfer.	In the name(s) of	Designation (if any) Balance certificate(s) required
Please Sign Here	I/We hereby transfer the above security out of the name(s) aforesaid into the name(s) of the system-member set out below and request that the necessary entries be made in the undertaking's own register of members. Signature(s) of transferor(s) 1. 2. 3. 4. A body corporate should execute this transfer under its common seal or otherwise in accordance with applicable statutory requirements.	Stamp of depositing system-user Date
Full name(s) of the person(s) to whom the security is transferred. Such person(s) must be a system-member.		Participant ID Member Account ID
Reference to the Registrar in this form means the registrar or registration agent of the undertaking, not the Registrar of the Companies at Company House.	is delivering this transfer at the direction and on behalf of the depositing system-user whose stamp appears herein and does not in any manner or to any extent warrant or represent the validity, genuineness or correctness of the transfer instructions contained herein or the genuineness of the signature(s) of the transferor(s). The depositing system-user by delivering this transfer to authorises to deliver this transfer for registration and agrees to be deemed for all the purposes to be the person(s) actually so delivering this transfer for registration.	

NOTES

First form substituted by the Stock Transfer (Addition and Substitution of Forms) Order 1996, SI 1996/1571, art 3(1), Sch 2, as from 15 July 1996, subject to art 3(2), (3) of the 1996 Order. For the effect of art 3 see s 1(3) of this Act at **[9.74]**.

Second form added by the Stock Transfer (Addition and Substitution of Forms) Order 1996, SI 1996/1571, art 2(1), Sch 1, as from 15 July 1996, for use where units of a registered security to which s 1 of this Act applies are transferred to a system-member to be held by him as uncertificated units of that security. By art 2(2) of the 1996 Order, an instrument in that form is not required to specify the address of the transferee.

The Talisman Sold Transfer Forms which were inserted and substituted by SI 1979/277 and SI 1990/18 are not reproduced. The Talisman Bought Transfer Form which was inserted by SI 1979/277 is not reproduced.

SCHEDULE II

[9.80]

BROKERS TRANSFER FORM

		Certificate lodged with the Registrar (For completion by the Registrar/ Stock Exchange)
Consideration Money	£...............	
Part 1 [Name of Undertaking.]		
[Description of Security.]		
Number or amount of Shares, Stock or other security and, in figures column only, number and denomination of units, if any.	Words	Figures (units of)
Name(s) of registered holder(s) should be given in full: the address should be given where there is only one holder. If the transfer is not made by the registered holder(s) insert also the name(s) and capacity (eg, Executor(s)), of the person(s) making the transfer.	in the name(s) of	
	I/We confirm that the Stock Transfer Form relating to the security set out above has been lodged with the Registrar, and that the said security has been sold by me/us by a stock exchange transaction within the meaning of the Stock Transfer Act 1963. *Date and Stamp of Selling Broker(s)*	

Part 2 Full name(s), full postal address(es) (including County or, if applicable, Postal District number) of the person(s) to whom the security is transferred. Please state title, if any, or whether Mr, Mrs or Miss. Please complete in typewriting or in Block Capitals.		
	I/We confirm that the security set out in Part 1 above has been purchased by a stock exchange transaction within the meaning of the Stock Transfer Act 1963, and I/we request that such entries be made in the register as are necessary to give effect to this transfer.	
	Stamp of Buying Broker(s).	Stamp of Lodging Agent (if other than the Buying Broker(s))

NOTES

Words in square brackets substituted by the Stock Transfer (Amendment of Forms) Order 1974, SI 1974/1214, art 3(2), as from 3 August 1974.

INSOLVENCY ACT 1986

(1986 c 45)

NOTES

Commencement: this Act came into force on 29 December 1986 by virtue of s 443 and the Insolvency Act 1985 (Commencement No 5) Order 1986, SI 1986/1924.

Rules: see the Insolvency (England and Wales) Rules 2016, SI 2016/1024; see also the note for the Insolvency Rules 1986, SI 1986/1925 at **[10.1]** (which were revoked and replaced (subject to transitional provisions) by SI 2016/1024, as from 6 April 2017).

Moratoriums under Part A1 of this Act: see also Sch 4 to the Corporate Insolvency and Governance Act 2020 (Moratoriums in Great Britain: Temporary Provision) at **[9.561]**.

Restriction on winding-up petitions under this Act: see also Sch 10 to the Corporate Insolvency and Governance Act 2020 (Winding-up Petitions: Great Britain) at **[9.566]**.

Application of this Act: this Act is applied, with certain modifications, to various types of business and financial sectors, etc, *including* the following:

Limited liability partnerships: as to the application of this Act to LLPs, see the notes below:
(1) The Limited Liability Partnerships Regulations 2001, SI 2001/1090, reg 5(1) applies Parts A1, I, II, III, IV, VI and VII of the First Group of Parts, and the whole of the Third Group of Parts, to limited liability partnerships (see reg 5(1) at **[10.103]**). For general modifications of this Act in its application to LLPs see reg 5(2) of those Regulations, and for specific modifications see Sch 3 (at **[10.111]**). See also reg 5(3) of, and Sch 4 to, those Regulations (which provide that certain provisions of the First and Third Groups of Parts which are applied to LLPs by reg 5(1) do not apply to Scotland). See also the Companies (Registrar, Languages and Trading Disclosures) Regulations 2006, SI 2006/3429, reg 3(3) at **[4.3]**.
(2) As to the application of this Act in relation to LLPs in Scotland, see also the Limited Liability Partnerships (Scotland) Regulations 2001, SSI 2001/128. Regulation 4(1) of those Regulations (at **[10.92]**) applies the provisions of this Act specified in Sch 2 to those Regulations (at **[10.96]**) to Scotland, subject to the general modifications provided for by reg 4(2), and the specific modifications provided for by Sch 3 (at **[10.97]**).

Payment institutions and electronic money institutions: see the Payment and Electronic Money Institution Insolvency Regulations 2021, SI 2021/716.

Banks: as to the application of certain provisions of this Act to particular banks, see the Banking (Special Provisions) Act 2008 and the Orders made under it. As to the application of this Act to banks generally, see the Banking Act 2009 and see, in particular Part 2 of that Act (bank insolvency) and Part 3 (bank administration) and the Orders and Regulations made under those Parts. In respect of the special administration regime for investment banks, see the Investment Bank Special Administration Regulations 2011, SI 2011/245.

Insolvent partnerships: see the Insolvent Partnerships Order 1994, SI 1994/2421.

Credit institutions, investment firms and group companies: see the Credit Institutions (Reorganisation and Winding up) Regulations 2004, SI 2004/1045.

Insurers: as to the application of this Act to insurers, see the Insurers (Reorganisation and Winding Up) Regulations 2004, SI 2004/353, and the Financial Services and Markets Act 2000 (Administration Orders Relating to Insurers) Order 2010, SI 2010/3023.

Members of recognised investment exchanges and clearing houses, etc: see CA 1989, s 182 at **[5.178]** (application to certain proceedings begun before the commencement of that section in respect of insolvency proceedings regarding members of recognised investment exchanges and clearing houses and persons to whom market charges have been granted).

UK Economic Interest Groupings (UKEIGs) and EEIG establishments: as to the application of this Act to European Economic Interest Groupings, see the European Economic Interest Grouping Regulations 1989, SI 1989/638, reg 19.

Open-ended investment companies: as to the application of this Act to open-ended investment companies, see the Open-Ended Investment Companies Regulations 2001, SI 2001/1228, reg 31.

Companies incorporated outside Great Britain: the Enterprise Act 2002, s 254 provides that the Secretary of State may by order provide for a provision of this Act to apply (with or without modification) in relation to a company incorporated outside Great Britain. As of 1 August 2022, no Orders had been made under that section.

Special administration regimes: see the notes to s 8 of this Act at **[9.147]**; and, with regard to companies which hold a licence under the Electricity Act 1989, s 6(1)(b) or (c) (transmission and distribution licences for electricity) or the Gas Act 1986, s 7 (licensing of gas transporters), see the Energy Act 2004, ss 154–171, Schs 20, 21.

Housing administration orders that apply in relation to companies: see the Housing and Planning Act 2016, s 105, Sch 5; the Housing Administration (England and Wales) Rules 2018, SI 2018/719; and the Insolvency of Registered Providers of Social Housing Regulations 2018, SI 2018/728.

Further education bodies that are companies or statutory corporations: see the Technical and Further Education Act 2017. See especially Part 2 of, and Schs 3, 4 to, that Act, and Part 3 of the Further Education Bodies (Insolvency) Regulations 2019, SI 2019/138.

Stand-alone co-ownership scheme and a sub-scheme of an umbrella co-ownership scheme: see the Collective Investment in Transferable Securities (Contractual Scheme) Regulations 2013, SI 2013/1388.

Financial market infrastructure companies: see the Financial Services (Banking Reform) Act 2013, Part 6 (Special Administration for operators of certain infrastructure systems) and the Financial Market Infrastructure Administration (England and Wales) Rules 2018, SI 2018/833.

Protected cell companies: see the Risk Transformation Regulations 2017, SI 2017/1212.

Other bodies: note that the application of this Act to certain other bodies (*eg* charities, Friendly Societies and Co-operative and Community Benefit Societies) is not noted as it is considered outside the scope of this work. See also the note below.

Savings for certain insolvency rules: the Deregulation Act 2015 and Small Business, Enterprise and Employment Act 2015 (Consequential Amendments) (Savings) Regulations 2017, SI 2017/540, reg 4 (as amended) provides that this Act, insofar as it applies to proceedings under the following instruments, continues to have effect without the relevant amendments for the purposes of the application of those instruments, ie: the Railway Administration Order 2001; the Energy Act 2004; the Energy Administration Rules 2005; the PPP Administration Order Rules 2007; the Water Industry (Special Administration) Rules 2009; the Energy Act 2011; the Charitable Incorporated Organisations (Insolvency and Dissolution) Regulations 2012; the Energy Supply Company Administration Rules 2013; and the Postal Administration Rules 2013. For these purposes, "the relevant amendments" means the amendments made to this Act by (a) paragraphs 12, 13(1), 14 and 15 of Schedule 6 to, the Deregulation Act 2015; and (b) sections 122, 123, 124 and 125 of, and Schedule 9 to, the Small Business, Enterprise and Employment Act 2015. See also Part 4 of the Small Business, Enterprise and Employment Act 2015 (Consequential Amendments, Savings and Transitional Provisions) Regulations 2019, SI 2019/1058. Those Regulations provide that despite the revocation of the

Insolvency (Scotland) Rules 1986, those Rules apply as they applied immediately before they were revoked such that this Act, insofar as it applies to proceedings under the following instruments, continues to have effect without the relevant amendments for the purposes of the application of those instruments: (a) the Energy Administration (Scotland) Rules 2006; (b) the Energy Supply Company Administration (Scotland) Rules 2013; and (c) the Postal Administration (Scotland) Rules 2016. For these purposes, "the relevant amendments" means the amendments made to this Act by ss 122, 124, 126(b), and Part 1 of Schedule 9 to, the Small Business, Enterprise and Employment Act 2015.

Other Modifications, etc:

Cross-Border insolvency proceedings: British insolvency law (as defined in Article 2 of the UNCITRAL Model Law as set out in Schedule 1 to the Cross-Border Insolvency Regulations 2006, SI 2006/1030) and Part III of this Act shall apply with such modifications as the context requires for the purpose of giving effect to the provisions of the 2006 Regulations; see reg 2 of the 2006 Regulations.

Scotland: by virtue of the Scotland Act 1998, s 125, Sch 8, para 23, (i) anything directed to be done, or which may be done, to or by the registrar of companies in Scotland by virtue of any of ss 53(1), 54(3), 61(6), 62(5) (so far as relating to the giving of notice), 67(1), 69(2), 84(3), 94(3), 106(3), (5), 112(3), 130(1), 147(3), 170(2) and 172(8), shall, or (as the case may be) may, also be done to or by the Accountant in Bankruptcy, and (ii) anything directed to be done, or which may be done, to or by the registrar of companies in Scotland by virtue of any of sections 89(3), 109(1), 171(5), (6), 173(2)(a) and 192(1), shall, or (as the case may be) shall instead be done to or by the Accountant in Bankruptcy. See also the Scotland Act 1998 (Insolvency Functions) Order 2018, SI 2018/174 at which provides that specific insolvency functions relating to reserved matters under Sch 5 to the 1998 Act, that are exercised by a Minister of the Crown in or as regards Scotland, are to be exercisable by both the Scottish Ministers and a Minister of the Crown, and provides for specific insolvency functions within the devolved competence of the Scottish Ministers to be exercised by both the Scottish Ministers and a Minister of the Crown.

Miscellaneous:

Registrar of companies: as to the contracting out of certain functions of the registrar of companies in relation to Scotland conferred by or under this Act, see the Contracting Out (Functions in relation to the Registration of Companies) Order 1995, SI 1995/1013, art 4, Sch 2.

Official Receiver: as to the contracting out of functions of the Official Receiver conferred by or under this Act, see the Contracting Out (Functions of the Official Receiver) Order 1995, SI 1995/1386.

Proceeds of crime: if an order for the winding up of a company is made or it passes a resolution for its voluntary winding up, the functions of the liquidator (or any provisional liquidator) are not exercisable in relation to property deemed to be the proceeds of crime; see the Proceeds of Crime Act 2002, Pt 9 (ss 417–434).

See the Serious Crime Act 2007, ss 27, 29 in relation to the power of the Director of Public Prosecutions and the Director of the Serious Fraud Office to present a petition to the court for the winding up of a company, partnership (etc) where the company, partnership (etc) has been convicted of an offence under s 25 of that Act (offence of failing to comply with serious crime prevention order) and the Director concerned considers that it would be in the public interest for the company, partnership (etc) to be wound up. See also s 27A of the 2007 Act for similar provisions in relation to Scotland (powers of Scottish Ministers to present a petition to the court for the winding up of a company, etc).

Only those provisions of this Act relating to company law are reproduced. Provisions not reproduced are not annotated.

This Act is reproduced as amended by the following Acts:

1988	Court of Session Act 1988; Criminal Justice Act 1988.
1989	Companies Act 1989; Water Act 1989.
1990	Law Reform (Miscellaneous Provisions) (Scotland) Act 1990.
1991	Water Consolidation (Consequential Provisions) Act 1991.
1993	Bankruptcy (Scotland) Act 1993; Pension Schemes Act 1993; Railways Act 1993.
1994	Insolvency Act 1994; Insolvency (No 2) Act 1994.
1995	Criminal Procedure (Consequential Provisions) (Scotland) Act 1995; Gas Act 1995; Requirements of Writing (Scotland) Act 1995.
1996	Employment Rights Act 1996.
1998	Government of Wales Act 1998.
1999	Youth Justice and Criminal Evidence Act 1999.
2000	Abolition of Feudal Tenure etc (Scotland) Act 2000; Adults with Incapacity (Scotland) Act 2000; Insolvency Act 2000; Utilities Act 2000.
2002	Commonhold and Leasehold Reform Act 2002; Enterprise Act 2002.
2003	Communications Act 2003; Courts Act 2003.
2004	Companies (Audit, Investigations and Community Enterprise) Act 2004; Civil Partnership Act 2004.
2005	Constitutional Reform Act 2005; Mental Capacity Act 2005.
2006	Companies Act 2006.
2007	Bankruptcy and Diligence etc (Scotland) Act 2007; Tribunals, Courts and Enforcement Act 2007.
2009	Banking Act 2009.
2012	Financial Services Act 2012.
2013	Crime and Courts Act 2013; Enterprise and Regulatory Reform Act 2013; Financial Services (Banking Reform) Act 2013.
2014	Bankruptcy and Debt Advice (Scotland) Act 2014.
2015	Deregulation Act 2015; Small Business, Enterprise and Employment Act 2015; Finance (No 2) Act 2015.
2020	Corporate Insolvency and Governance Act 2020; Finance Act 2020.

This Act is reproduced as amended by the following SIs:

1986	Insolvency Proceedings (Monetary Limits) Order 1986, SI 1986/1996.
1987	Insolvency (ECSC Levy Debts) Regulations 1987, SI 1987/2093.

1989	Companies (Northern Ireland) Order 1989, SI 1989/2404; Insolvency (Northern Ireland) Order 1989, SI 1989/2405.
1991	High Court and County Courts Jurisdiction Order 1991, SI 1991/724 (as amended by SI 2014/821).
1994	Insolvent Partnerships Order 1994, SI 1994/2421.
1999	Scotland Act 1998 (Consequential Modifications) (No 2) Order 1999, SI 1999/1820.
2001	Limited Liability Partnerships (Scotland) Regulations 2001, SSI 2001/128; Limited Liability Partnerships Regulations 2001, SI 2001/1090; Financial Services and Markets Act 2000 (Consequential Amendments and Repeals) Order 2001, SI 2001/3649.
2002	Insolvency Act 1986 (Amendment) Regulations 2002, SI 2002/1037; Insolvency Act 1986 (Amendment) (No 2) Regulations 2002, SI 2002/1240; Financial Services and Markets Act 2000 (Consequential Amendments) Order 2002, SI 2002/1555; Insolvency Act 1986 (Amendment) (No 3) Regulations 2002, SI 2002/1990; Insolvent Partnerships (Amendment) (No 2) Order 2002, SI 2002/2708; Company Directors Disqualification (Northern Ireland) Order 2002, SI 2002/3150.
2003	Insolvency Act 1986 (Amendment) (Administrative Receivership and Capital Market Arrangements) Order 2003, SI 2003/1468; Insolvency Act 1986 (Amendment) (Administrative Receivership and Urban Regeneration etc) Order 2003, SI 2003/1832; Enterprise Act 2002 (Insolvency) Order 2003, SI 2003/2096.
2004	Water Industry (Scotland) Act 2002 (Consequential Modifications) Order 2004, SI 2004/1822; Enterprise Act 2002 (Insolvency) Order 2004, SI 2004/2312; European Public Limited-Liability Company Regulations 2004, SI 2004/2326.
2005	Insolvency Act 1986 (Amendment) Regulations 2005, SI 2005/879; Mental Health (Care and Treatment) (Scotland) Act 2003 (Consequential Provisions) Order 2005, SI 2005/2078; Mental Health (Care and Treatment) (Scotland) Act 2003 (Modification of Enactments) Order 2005, SSI 2005/486; Railway (Licensing of Railway Undertakings) Regulations 2005, SI 2005/3050; Civil Partnership Act 2004 (Overseas Relationships and Consequential, etc Amendments) Order 2005, SI 2005/3129.
2006	Companies (Registrar, Languages and Trading Disclosures) Regulations 2006, SI 2006/3429.
2007	Companies Act 2006 (Commencement No 3, Consequential Amendments, Transitional Provisions and Savings) Order 2007, SI 2007/2194; Companies (Cross-Border Mergers) Regulations 2007, SI 2007/2974.
2008	Companies Act 2006 (Consequential Amendments etc) Order 2008, SI 2008/948; Companies (Trading Disclosures) (Insolvency) Regulations 2008, SI 2008/1897.
2009	Building Societies (Insolvency and Special Administration) Order 2009, SI 2009/805; Legislative Reform (Insolvency) (Advertising Requirements) Order 2009, SI 2009/864; Companies Act 2006 (Consequential Amendments, Transitional Provisions and Savings) Order 2009, SI 2009/1941.
2010	Legislative Reform (Insolvency) (Miscellaneous Provisions) Order 2010, SI 2010/18; Financial Services and Markets Act 2000 (Regulated Activities) (Amendment) Order 2010, SI 2010/86; Housing and Regeneration Act 2008 (Consequential Provisions) Order 2010, SI 2010/866.
2011	Insolvency Act 1986 Amendment (Appointment of Receivers) (Scotland) Regulations 2011, SSI 2011/140; Companies Act 2006 (Consequential Amendments and Transitional Provisions) Order 2011, SI 2011/1265.
2012	Housing (Scotland) Act 2010 (Consequential Provisions and Modifications) Order 2012, SI 2012/700; Electricity and Gas (Smart Meters Licensable Activity) Order 2012, SI 2012/240.
2013	Financial Services Act 2012 (Mutual Societies) Order 2013, SI 2013/496; Companies Act 2006 (Amendment of Part 25) Regulations 2013, SI 2013/600.
2014	Banks and Building Societies (Depositor Preference and Priorities) Order 2014, SI 2014/3486.
2015	Courts Reform (Scotland) Act 2014 (Consequential Provisions) Order 2015, SSI 2015/150; Deposit Guarantee Scheme Regulations 2015, SI 2015/486; Insolvency (Protection of Essential Supplies) Order 2015, SI 2015/989.
2016	Public Services Reform (Insolvency) (Scotland) Order 2016, SSI 2016/141; Enterprise and Regulatory Reform Act 2013 (Consequential Amendments) (Bankruptcy) and the Small Business, Enterprise and Employment Act 2015 (Consequential Amendments) Regulations 2016, SI 2016/481; Bankruptcy (Scotland) Act 2016 (Consequential Provisions and Modifications) Order 2016, SI 2016/1034.
2017	Public Services Reform (Corporate Insolvency and Bankruptcy) (Scotland) Order 2017, SSI 2017/209; Insolvency (Regulation (EU) 2015/848) (Miscellaneous Amendments) (Scotland) Regulations 2017, SSI 2017/210; Insolvency Amendment (EU 2015/848) Regulations 2017, SI 2017/702.
2018	Alteration of Judicial Titles (Registrar in Bankruptcy of the High Court) Order 2018, SI 2018/130; Banks and Building Societies (Priorities on Insolvency) Order 2018, SI 2018/1244; Bank Recovery and Resolution and Miscellaneous Provisions (Amendment) (EU Exit) Regulations 2018, SI 2018/1394.
2019	Insolvency (Amendment) (EU Exit) Regulations 2019, SI 2019/146; Companies, Limited Liability Partnerships and Partnerships (Amendment etc) (EU Exit) Regulations 2019, SI 2019/348; Insolvency (EU Exit) (Scotland) (Amendment) Regulations 2019, SSI 2019/94; Railway (Licensing of Railway Undertakings) (Amendment etc) (EU Exit) Regulations 2019, SI 2019/700; Financial Services (Miscellaneous) (Amendment) (EU Exit) Regulations 2019, SI 2019/710.
2020	Insolvency Act 1986 Part A1 Moratorium (Eligibility of Private Registered Providers) Regulations 2020, SI 2020/652; Insolvency Act 1986 (Scotland) Amendment Regulations 2020, SSI 2020/338; Securities Financing Transactions, Securitisation and Miscellaneous Amendments (EU Exit) Regulations 2020, SI 2020/1385.
2021	Railway (Licensing of Railway Undertakings) (Amendment) Regulations 2021, SI 2021/1105; Financial Services Act 2021 (Prudential Regulation of Credit Institutions and Investment Firms) (Consequential Amendments and Miscellaneous Provisions) Regulations 2021, SI 2021/1376.
2022	Criminal Justice Act 2003 (Commencement No 33) and Sentencing Act 2020 (Commencement No 2) Regulations 2022, SI 2022/500

ARRANGEMENT OF SECTIONS

THE FIRST GROUP OF PARTS
COMPANY INSOLVENCY; COMPANIES WINDING UP

PART A1 MORATORIUM

CHAPTER 1
INTRODUCTORY

CHAPTER 2
OBTAINING A MORATORIUM

CHAPTER 3
LENGTH OF MORATORIUM

Initial period

Extension of moratorium

Early termination on certain grounds

Obligations to notify change in end of moratorium

CHAPTER 4
EFFECTS OF MORATORIUM

Introductory

Publicity about moratorium

Effect on creditors etc

Notification of insolvency proceedings

Restrictions on transactions

Restrictions on payments and disposal of property

Disposals of property free from charges etc

PART IV WINDING UP OF COMPANIES REGISTERED UNDER THE COMPANIES ACTS

CHAPTER I
PRELIMINARY

Introductory

Contributories

CHAPTER II
VOLUNTARY WINDING UP (INTRODUCTORY AND GENERAL)

Resolutions for, and commencement of, voluntary winding up

Consequences of resolution to wind up

Declaration of solvency

CHAPTER III
MEMBERS' VOLUNTARY WINDING UP

CHAPTER IV
CREDITORS' VOLUNTARY WINDING UP

CHAPTER V
PROVISIONS APPLYING TO BOTH KINDS OF VOLUNTARY WINDING UP

CHAPTER VI
WINDING UP BY THE COURT

Jurisdiction (England and Wales)

Jurisdiction (Scotland)

Grounds and effect of winding-up petition

Commencement of winding up

Investigation procedures

Appointment of liquidator

Liquidation committees

The liquidator's functions

General powers of court

Enforcement of, and appeal from, orders

CHAPTER VII
LIQUIDATORS

Preliminary

Liquidator's powers and duties

Removal; vacation of office

Release of liquidator

CHAPTER VIII
PROVISIONS OF GENERAL APPLICATION IN WINDING UP

Moratorium: order of priority of payment of debts

Preferential debts

Non-preferential debts

Property subject to floating charge

Special managers

Disclaimer (England and Wales only)

Execution, attachment and the Scottish equivalents

Miscellaneous matters

CHAPTER IX
DISSOLUTION OF COMPANIES AFTER WINDING UP

CHAPTER X
MALPRACTICE BEFORE AND DURING LIQUIDATION; PENALISATION OF COMPANIES AND COMPANY OFFICERS; INVESTIGATIONS AND PROSECUTIONS

Offences of fraud, deception, etc

Penalisation of directors and officers

Investigation and prosecution of malpractice

PART V WINDING UP OF UNREGISTERED COMPANIES

PART VI MISCELLANEOUS PROVISIONS APPLYING TO COMPANIES WHICH ARE INSOLVENT OR IN LIQUIDATION

Office-holders

Management by administrators, liquidators, etc

Adjustment of prior transactions (administration and liquidation)

An Act to consolidate the enactments relating to company insolvency and winding up (including the winding up of companies that are not insolvent, and of unregistered companies); enactments relating to the insolvency and bankruptcy of individuals; and other enactments bearing on those two subject matters, including the functions and qualification of insolvency practitioners, the public administration of insolvency, the penalisation and redress of malpractice and wrongdoing, and the avoidance of certain transactions at an undervalue

[25 July 1986]

THE FIRST GROUP OF PARTS
COMPANY INSOLVENCY; COMPANIES WINDING UP

[PART A1 MORATORIUM

CHAPTER 1 INTRODUCTORY

[9.81]

A1 Overview

(1) This Part contains provision that enables an eligible company, in certain circumstances, to obtain a moratorium, giving it various protections from creditors set out in this Part.
(2) In this Chapter section A2 introduces Schedule ZA1 (which defines what is meant by an "eligible" company).
(3) Chapter 2 sets out how an eligible company may obtain a moratorium.
(4) Chapter 3 sets out for how long a moratorium has effect.
(5) Chapter 4 sets out the effects of a moratorium on the company and its creditors.
(6) Chapter 5 contains provision about the monitor.
(7) Chapter 6 contains provision about challenges.
(8) Chapter 7 contains provision about certain offences.
(9) Chapter 8 contains miscellaneous and general provision, including—

(a) special provision for certain kinds of company;
(b) definitions for the purposes of this Part;
(c) provision about regulations under this Part.]

NOTES

Commencement: 26 June 2020.

Part A1 was inserted by the Corporate Insolvency and Governance Act 2020, s 1(1), as from 26 June 2020 (for transitional provisions, see s 2(2), (3) of the 2020 Act (at **[9.533]**) which provides that (without prejudice to the Interpretation Act 1978, s 16) nothing in the 2020 Act affects the operation of this Act, or any other enactment, in relation to a moratorium under Sch A1 to this Act which comes into force before the repeal of that Schedule by Sch 3 to the 2020 Act (ie, 26 June 2020)). For temporary modifications of this Part during the "relevant period", see the Corporate Insolvency and Governance Act 2020, Sch 4 at **[9.561]**. Note that "relevant period" is defined in Sch 4, para 1.

[9.82]

[A2 Eligible companies

Schedule ZA1 contains provision for determining whether a company is an eligible company for the purposes of this Part.]

NOTES

Commencement: 26 June 2020.

Inserted (subject to transitional provisions and temporary modifications) as noted to s A1 at **[9.81]**.

[CHAPTER 2 OBTAINING A MORATORIUM

[9.83]

A3 Obtaining a moratorium by filing or lodging documents at court

(1) This section applies to an eligible company that—
(a) is not subject to an outstanding winding-up petition, and
(b) is not an overseas company.

(2) The directors of the company may obtain a moratorium for the company by filing the relevant documents with the court (for the relevant documents, see section A6).

(3) For the purposes of this Chapter a company is "subject to an outstanding winding-up petition" if—
(a) a petition for the winding up of the company has been presented, and
(b) the petition has not been withdrawn or determined.]

NOTES

Commencement: 26 June 2020.

Inserted (subject to transitional provisions and temporary modifications) as noted to s A1 at **[9.81]**.

[9.84]

[A4 Obtaining a moratorium for company subject to winding-up petition

(1) This section applies to an eligible company that is subject to an outstanding winding-up petition.

(2) The directors of the company may apply to the court for a moratorium for the company.

(3) The application must be accompanied by the relevant documents (for the relevant documents, see section A6).

(4) On hearing the application the court may—
(a) make an order that the company should be subject to a moratorium, or
(b) make any other order which the court thinks appropriate.

(5) The court may make an order under subsection (4)(a) only if it is satisfied that a moratorium for the company would achieve a better result for the company's creditors as a whole than would be likely if the company were wound up (without first being subject to a moratorium).]

NOTES

Commencement: 26 June 2020.

Inserted (subject to transitional provisions and temporary modifications) as noted to s A1 at **[9.81]**.

[9.85]

[A5 Obtaining a moratorium for other overseas companies

(1) This section applies to an eligible company that—
(a) is not subject to an outstanding winding-up petition, and
(b) is an overseas company.

(2) The directors of the company may apply to the court for a moratorium for the company.

(3) The application must be accompanied by the relevant documents (for the relevant documents, see section A6).

(4) On hearing the application the court may—
(a) make an order that the company should be subject to a moratorium, or
(b) make any other order which the court thinks appropriate.]

NOTES

Commencement: 26 June 2020.

Inserted (subject to transitional provisions and temporary modifications) as noted to s A1 at **[9.81]**.

[9.86]

[A6 The relevant documents

(1) For the purposes of this Chapter, "the relevant documents" are—
(a) a notice that the directors wish to obtain a moratorium,
(b) a statement from a qualified person ("the proposed monitor") that the person—
(i) is a qualified person, and
(ii) consents to act as the monitor in relation to the proposed moratorium,

(c) a statement from the proposed monitor that the company is an eligible company,
(d) a statement from the directors that, in their view, the company is, or is likely to become, unable to pay its debts, and
(e) a statement from the proposed monitor that, in the proposed monitor's view, it is likely that a moratorium for the company would result in the rescue of the company as a going concern.

(2) Where it is proposed that more than one person should act as the monitor in relation to the proposed moratorium—
(a) each of them must make a statement under subsection (1)(b), (c) and (e), and
(b) the statement under subsection (1)(b) must specify—
(i) which functions (if any) are to be exercised by the persons acting jointly, and
(ii) which functions (if any) are to be exercised by any or all of the persons.

(3) The rules may make provision about the date on which a statement comprised in the relevant documents must be made.

(4) The Secretary of State may by regulations amend this section for the purposes of adding to the list of documents in subsection (1).

(5) Regulations under subsection (4) are subject to the affirmative resolution procedure.]

NOTES

Commencement: 26 June 2020.
Inserted (subject to transitional provisions and temporary modifications) as noted to s A1 at **[9.81]**.

[9.87]
[A7 Beginning of moratorium and appointment of monitor

(1) A moratorium for a company comes into force at the time at which—
(a) in the case of a company to which section A3 applies, the relevant documents are filed with the court under subsection (2) of that section;
(b) in the case of a company to which section A4 applies, an order is made under section A4(4)(a);
(c) in the case of a company to which section A5 applies, an order is made under section A5(4)(a).

(2) On the coming into force of a moratorium, the person or persons who made the statement mentioned in section A6(1)(b) become the monitor in relation to the moratorium.]

NOTES

Commencement: 26 June 2020.
Inserted (subject to transitional provisions and temporary modifications) as noted to s A1 at **[9.81]**.

[9.88]
[A8 Obligations to notify where moratorium comes into force

(1) As soon as reasonably practicable after a moratorium for a company comes into force, the directors must notify the monitor of that fact.

(2) As soon as reasonably practicable after receiving a notice under subsection (1), the monitor must notify the following that a moratorium for the company has come into force—
(a) the registrar of companies,
(b) every creditor of the company of whose claim the monitor is aware,
(c) in a case where the company is or has been an employer in respect of an occupational pension scheme that is not a money purchase scheme, the Pensions Regulator, and
(d) in a case where the company is an employer in respect of such a pension scheme that is an eligible scheme within the meaning given by section 126 of the Pensions Act 2004, the Board of the Pension Protection Fund.

(3) A notice under subsection (2) must specify—
(a) when the moratorium came into force, and
(b) when, subject to any alteration under or by virtue of any of the provisions mentioned in section A9(3) or (4), the moratorium will come to an end.

(4) If the directors fail to comply with subsection (1), any director who did not have a reasonable excuse for the failure commits an offence.

(5) If the monitor without reasonable excuse fails to comply with subsection (2), the monitor commits an offence.]

NOTES

Commencement: 26 June 2020.
Inserted (subject to transitional provisions and temporary modifications) as noted to s A1 at **[9.81]**.

[CHAPTER 3 LENGTH OF MORATORIUM

Initial period

[9.89]
A9 End of the moratorium

(1) A moratorium ends at the end of the initial period unless it is extended, or comes to an end sooner, under or by virtue of a provision mentioned in subsection (3) or (4).

(2) In this Chapter "the initial period", in relation to a moratorium, means the period of 20 business days beginning with the business day after the day on which the moratorium comes into force.

(3) For provision under or by virtue of which a moratorium is or may be extended, see—
section A10 (extension by directors without creditor consent);
section A11 (extension by directors with creditor consent);
section A13 (extension by court on application of directors);
section A14 (extension while proposal for CVA pending);
section A15 (extension by court in course of other proceedings).

(4) For provision under or by virtue of which the moratorium is or may be terminated, see—

section A16 (termination on entry into insolvency procedure etc);
section A38 (termination by monitor);
section A42 or A44 (termination by court).

(5) A moratorium may not be extended under a provision mentioned in subsection (3) once it has come to an end.

(6) Where the application of two or more of the provisions mentioned in subsections (3) and (4) would produce a different length of moratorium, the provision that applies last is to prevail (irrespective of whether that results in a shorter or longer moratorium).]

NOTES

Commencement: 26 June 2020.

Inserted (subject to transitional provisions and temporary modifications) as noted to s A1 at **[9.81]**.

[Extension of moratorium

[9.90]

A10 Extension by directors without creditor consent

(1) During the initial period, but after the first 15 business days of that period, the directors may extend the moratorium by filing with the court—

- (a) a notice that the directors wish to extend the moratorium,
- (b) a statement from the directors that all of the following that have fallen due have been paid or otherwise discharged—
  - (i) moratorium debts, and
  - (ii) pre-moratorium debts for which the company does not have a payment holiday during the moratorium (see section A18),
- (c) a statement from the directors that, in their view, the company is, or is likely to become, unable to pay its pre-moratorium debts, and
- (d) a statement from the monitor that, in the monitor's view, it is likely that the moratorium will result in the rescue of the company as a going concern.

(2) The rules may make provision about the date on which a statement mentioned in subsection (1) must be made.

(3) On the filing with the court of the documents mentioned in subsection (1), the moratorium is extended so that it ends at the end of the period—

- (a) beginning immediately after the initial period ends, and
- (b) ending with the 20th business day after the initial period ends.]

NOTES

Commencement: 26 June 2020.

Inserted (subject to transitional provisions and temporary modifications) as noted to s A1 at **[9.81]**.

[9.91]

[A11 Extension by directors with creditor consent

(1) At any time after the first 15 business days of the initial period the directors may, if they have obtained creditor consent, extend the moratorium by filing with the court—

- (a) a notice that the directors wish to extend the moratorium,
- (b) a statement from the directors that all of the following that have fallen due have been paid or otherwise discharged—
  - (i) moratorium debts, and
  - (ii) pre-moratorium debts for which the company does not have a payment holiday during the moratorium (see section A18),
- (c) a statement from the directors that, in their view, the company is, or is likely to become, unable to pay its pre-moratorium debts,
- (d) a statement from the monitor that, in the monitor's view, it is likely that the moratorium will result in the rescue of the company as a going concern, and
- (e) a statement from the directors that creditor consent has been obtained, and of the revised end date for which that consent was obtained.

(2) The rules may make provision about the date on which a statement mentioned in subsection (1) must be made.

(3) On the filing with the court of the documents mentioned in subsection (1), the moratorium is extended so that it ends with the revised end date mentioned in the statement under subsection (1)(e).

(4) A moratorium may be extended under this section more than once.]

NOTES

Commencement: 26 June 2020.

Inserted (subject to transitional provisions and temporary modifications) as noted to s A1 at **[9.81]**.

[9.92]

[A12 Creditor consent for the purposes of section A11

(1) References in section A11 to creditor consent are to the consent of pre-moratorium creditors to a revised end date for the moratorium.

(2) The decision as to consent is to be made using a qualifying decision procedure.

(3) The revised end date must be a date before the end of the period of one year beginning with the first day of the initial period.

(4) In this section "pre-moratorium creditor" means a creditor in respect of a pre-moratorium debt—

- (a) for which the company has a payment holiday during the moratorium (see section A18), and
- (b) which has not been paid or otherwise discharged.

(5) In determining for the purposes of subsection (4) what counts as a pre-moratorium debt for which the company has a payment holiday during the moratorium, sections A18(3) and A53(1)(b) apply as if the references to the moratorium were to the moratorium as proposed to be extended.

(6) The Secretary of State may by regulations amend this section for the purposes of changing the definition of "pre-moratorium creditor".
(7) Regulations under subsection (6) are subject to the affirmative resolution procedure.]

NOTES

Commencement: 26 June 2020.
Inserted (subject to transitional provisions and temporary modifications) as noted to s A1 at **[9.81]**.

[9.93]
[A13 Extension by court on application of directors

(1) At any time after the first 15 business days of the initial period, the directors may apply to the court for an order that the moratorium be extended.
(2) The application must be accompanied by—
(a) a statement from the directors that all of the following that have fallen due have been paid or otherwise discharged—
(i) moratorium debts, and
(ii) pre-moratorium debts for which the company does not have a payment holiday during the moratorium (see section A18),
(b) a statement from the directors that, in their view, the company is, or is likely to become, unable to pay its pre-moratorium debts,
(c) a statement from the directors as to whether pre-moratorium creditors (as defined by section A12(4) and (5)) have been consulted about the application and if not why not, and
(d) a statement from the monitor that, in the monitor's view, it is likely that the moratorium will result in the rescue of the company as a going concern.
(3) The rules may make provision about the date on which a statement mentioned in subsection (2) must be made.
(4) On hearing the application the court may—
(a) make an order that the moratorium be extended to such date as is specified in the order, or
(b) make any other order which the court thinks appropriate.
(5) In deciding whether to make an order under subsection (4)(a) the court must, in particular, consider the following—
(a) the interests of pre-moratorium creditors, as defined by section A12(4) and (5), and
(b) the likelihood that the extension of the moratorium will result in the rescue of the company as a going concern.
(6) Subsection (7) applies where—
(a) an application under this section is made, and
(b) apart from that subsection, the moratorium would end at a time before the application has been disposed of.
(7) The moratorium—
(a) does not end at the time mentioned in subsection (6)(b), and
(b) instead, ends—
(i) in a case in which the court makes an order under subsection (4)(a), in accordance with the order;
(ii) otherwise, when the application is withdrawn or disposed of.
(8) A moratorium may be extended under this section more than once.]

NOTES

Commencement: 26 June 2020.
Inserted (subject to transitional provisions and temporary modifications) as noted to s A1 at **[9.81]**.

[9.94]
[A14 Extension while proposal for CVA pending

(1) Subsection (2) applies where—
(a) at any time, the directors make a proposal under Part 1 (company voluntary arrangements), and
(b) apart from that subsection, the moratorium would end at a time before the proposal is disposed of.
(2) The moratorium—
(a) does not end at the time mentioned in subsection (1)(b), and
(b) instead, ends when the proposal is disposed of.
(3) For the purposes of this section a proposal under Part 1 is "disposed of" when any of the following takes place—
(a) the company and its creditors both decide under section 4 not to approve the voluntary arrangement contained in the proposal;
(b) the decisions taken by the company and its creditors under section 4 differ, and—
(i) the period for making an application under section 4A(3) expires and either no application has been made within that period or any application made within that period has been withdrawn, or
(ii) an application is made under section 4A(3) and that application is disposed of, or it is withdrawn after the expiry of the period for making an application under section 4A(3);
(c) the voluntary arrangement contained in the proposal takes effect under section 5;
(d) the proposal is withdrawn.]

NOTES

Commencement: 26 June 2020.
Inserted (subject to transitional provisions and temporary modifications) as noted to s A1 at **[9.81]**.

[9.95]
[A15 Extension by court in the course of other proceedings

(1) Subsection (2) applies where—
(a) an application is made under section 896 or 901C(1) of the Companies Act 2006 (arrangements and reconstructions: court order for holding of meeting) in respect of a company, and

(b) during proceedings before a court in connection with the application, a moratorium for the company is in force.

(2) The court may make an order that the moratorium be extended to such date as is specified in the order.]

NOTES

Commencement: 26 June 2020.

Inserted (subject to transitional provisions and temporary modifications) as noted to s A1 at **[9.81]**.

[Early termination on certain grounds

[9.96]

A16 Company enters into insolvency procedure etc

(1) A moratorium comes to an end at any time at which the company—

(a) enters into a compromise or arrangement (see subsection (2)), or

(b) enters into a relevant insolvency procedure (see subsection (3)).

(2) For the purposes of this section a company enters into a compromise or arrangement if an order under section 899 or 901F of the Companies Act 2006 (court sanction for compromise or arrangement) comes into effect in relation to the company.

(3) For the purposes of this section a company enters into a relevant insolvency procedure if—

(a) a voluntary arrangement takes effect under section 5 in relation to the company,

(b) the company enters administration (within the meaning of Schedule B1 (see paragraph 1(2)(b) of that Schedule)),

(c) paragraph 44 of Schedule B1 (administration: interim moratorium) begins to apply in relation to the company, or

(d) the company goes into liquidation (see section 247).]

NOTES

Commencement: 26 June 2020.

Inserted (subject to transitional provisions and temporary modifications) as noted to s A1 at **[9.81]**.

[Obligations to notify change in end of moratorium

[9.97]

A17 Obligations to notify change in end of moratorium

(1) The table imposes obligations on the directors of a company to notify the monitor where a moratorium for the company is extended or comes to an end.

	Where a moratorium is extended or comes to an end under or by virtue of the following provision	*the directors must*
1	Section A10	Notify the monitor of the extension.
2	Section A11	Notify the monitor of the extension and of the revised end date.
3	Section A13(4)	Notify the monitor of the extension and provide the monitor with the court order under section A13(4).
4	Section A13(7)(a)	Notify the monitor of the extension.
5	Section A13(7)(b)(ii)	Notify the monitor that the moratorium has come to an end and of the date that it ended.
6	Section A14(2)(a)	Notify the monitor of the extension.
7	Section A14(2)(b)	Notify the monitor that the moratorium has come to an end and of the date that it ended.
8	Section A15	Notify the monitor of the extension and provide the monitor with any court order under section A15.
9	Section A16	Notify the monitor that the moratorium has come to an end.
10	Section A42	Notify the monitor that the moratorium has come to an end and provide the monitor with the court order under section A42.
11	Section A44	Notify the monitor that the moratorium has come to an end and provide the monitor with the court order under section A44.

(2) After receiving a notice under subsection (1), other than a notice under entry 4 or 6 of the table, the monitor must notify the relevant persons of when the moratorium ended or, subject to any alteration under or by virtue of any of the provisions mentioned in section A9(3) or (4), the moratorium will come to an end.

(3) After receiving a notice under entry 4 or 6 of the table, the monitor must notify the relevant persons.

(4) If a moratorium comes to an end under section A38 (termination by monitor), the monitor must notify the company and the relevant persons of when the moratorium ended.

(5) The rules may—

(a) make further provision about the timing of a notice required to be given under this section;

(b) require a notice to be accompanied by other documents.

(6) If the directors fail to comply with subsection (1), any director who did not have a reasonable excuse for the failure commits an offence.
(7) If the monitor without reasonable excuse fails to comply with any of subsections (2) to (4), the monitor commits an offence.
(8) In this section "the relevant persons" means—
(a) the registrar of companies,
(b) every creditor of the company of whose claim the monitor is aware,
(c) in a case where the company is or has been an employer in respect of an occupational pension scheme that is not a money purchase scheme, the Pensions Regulator, and
(d) in a case where the company is an employer in respect of such a pension scheme that is an eligible scheme within the meaning given by section 126 of the Pensions Act 2004, the Board of the Pension Protection Fund.]

NOTES

Commencement: 26 June 2020.
Inserted (subject to transitional provisions and temporary modifications) as noted to s A1 at **[9.81]**.

[CHAPTER 4 EFFECTS OF MORATORIUM

Introductory

[9.98]
A18 Overview and construction of references to payment holidays
(1) This Chapter makes provision about the main effects of a moratorium for a company.
(2) The provision made by this Chapter includes restrictions on the enforcement or payment of the debts that are defined by subsection (3) as pre-moratorium debts for which a company has a payment holiday during a moratorium.
(3) In this Part a reference to pre-moratorium debts for which a company has a payment holiday during a moratorium is to its pre-moratorium debts that have fallen due before the moratorium, or that fall due during the moratorium, except in so far as they consist of amounts payable in respect of—
(a) the monitor's remuneration or expenses,
(b) goods or services supplied during the moratorium,
(c) rent in respect of a period during the moratorium,
(d) wages or salary arising under a contract of employment,
(e) redundancy payments, or
(f) debts or other liabilities arising under a contract or other instrument involving financial services.
(4) The rules may make provision as to what is, or is not, to count as the supply of goods or services for the purposes of subsection (3)(b).
(5) The Secretary of State may by regulations amend this section for the purposes of changing the list in subsection (3).
(6) Regulations under subsection (5) are subject to the affirmative resolution procedure.
(7) In this section—
"contract or other instrument involving financial services" has the meaning given by Schedule ZA2;
"monitor's remuneration or expenses" does not include remuneration in respect of anything done by a proposed monitor before the moratorium begins;
"redundancy payment" means—
(a) a redundancy payment under Part 11 of the Employment Rights Act 1996 or Part 12 of the Employment Rights (Northern Ireland) Order 1996, or
(b) a payment made to a person who agrees to the termination of their employment in circumstances where they would have been entitled to a redundancy payment under that Part if dismissed;
"wages or salary" includes—
(a) a sum payable in respect of a period of holiday (for which purpose the sum is to be treated as relating to the period by reference to which the entitlement to holiday accrued),
(b) a sum payable in respect of a period of absence through illness or other good cause,
(c) a sum payable in lieu of holiday, and
(d) a contribution to an occupational pension scheme.]

NOTES

Commencement: 26 June 2020.
Inserted (subject to transitional provisions and temporary modifications) as noted to s A1 at **[9.81]**.

[Publicity about moratorium

[9.99]
A19 Publicity about moratorium
(1) During a moratorium, the company must, in any premises—
(a) where business of the company is carried on, and
(b) to which customers of the company or suppliers of goods or services to the company have access,
display, in a prominent position so that it may easily be read by such customers or suppliers, a notice containing the required information.
(2) During a moratorium, any websites of the company must state the required information.
(3) During a moratorium, every business document issued by or on behalf of the company must state the required information.
(4) For the purposes of subsections (1), (2) and (3), "the required information" is—
(a) that a moratorium is in force in relation to the company, and
(b) the name of the monitor.
(5) If subsection (1), (2) or (3) is contravened—
(a) the company commits an offence, and

(b) any officer of the company who without reasonable excuse authorised or permitted the contravention commits an offence.

(6) In this section "business document" means—

(a) an invoice,

(b) an order for goods or services,

(c) a business letter, and

(d) an order form,

whether in hard copy, electronic or any other form.]

NOTES

Commencement: 26 June 2020.

Inserted (subject to transitional provisions and temporary modifications) as noted to s A1 at **[9.81]**.

[Effect on creditors etc

[9.100]

A20 Restrictions on insolvency proceedings etc

(1) During a moratorium—

(a) no petition may be presented for the winding up of the company, except by the directors,

(b) no resolution may be passed for the voluntary winding up of the company under section 84(1)(a),

(c) a resolution for the voluntary winding up of the company under section 84(1)(b) may be passed only if the resolution is recommended by the directors,

(d) no order may be made for the winding up of the company, except on a petition by the directors,

(e) no administration application may be made in respect of the company, except by the directors,

(f) no notice of intention to appoint an administrator of the company under paragraph 14 or 22(1) of Schedule B1 may be filed with the court,

(g) no administrator of the company may be appointed under paragraph 14 or 22(1) of Schedule B1, and

(h) no administrative receiver of the company may be appointed.

(2) Subsection (1)(a) does not apply to an excepted petition; and subsection (1)(d) does not apply to an order on an excepted petition.

(3) For these purposes, "excepted petition" means a petition under—

(a) section 124A, 124B or 124C, or

(b) section 367 of the Financial Services and Markets Act 2000 on the ground mentioned in subsection (3)(b) of that section.]

NOTES

Commencement: 26 June 2020.

Inserted (subject to transitional provisions and temporary modifications) as noted to s A1 at **[9.81]**.

[9.101]

[A21 Restrictions on enforcement and legal proceedings

(1) During a moratorium—

(a) a landlord or other person to whom rent is payable may not exercise a right of forfeiture by peaceable re-entry in relation to premises let to the company, except with the permission of the court,

(b) in Scotland, a landlord or other person to whom rent is payable may not exercise a right of irritancy in relation to premises let to the company, except with the permission of the court,

(c) no steps may be taken to enforce any security over the company's property except—

(i) steps to enforce a collateral security charge (within the meaning of the Financial Markets and Insolvency (Settlement Finality) Regulations 1999 (SI 1999/2979)),

(ii) steps to enforce security created or otherwise arising under a financial collateral arrangement (within the meaning of regulation 3 of the Financial Collateral Arrangements (No 2) Regulations 2003 (SI 2003/3226)), or

(iii) steps taken with the permission of the court,

(d) no steps may be taken to repossess goods in the company's possession under any hire-purchase agreement, except with the permission of the court, and

(e) no legal process (including legal proceedings, execution, distress or diligence) may be instituted, carried out or continued against the company or its property except—

(i) employment tribunal proceedings or any legal process arising out of such proceedings,

(ii) proceedings, not within sub-paragraph (i), involving a claim between an employer and a worker, or

(iii) a legal process instituted, carried out or continued with the permission of the court.

(2) An application may not be made for permission under subsection (1) for the purposes of enforcing a pre-moratorium debt for which the company has a payment holiday during the moratorium.

(3) An application may not be made for permission under subsection (1)(c), (d) or (e) with a view to obtaining—

(a) the crystallisation of a floating charge, or

(b) the imposition, by virtue of provision in an instrument creating a floating charge, of any restriction on the disposal of any property of the company.

(4) Permission of the court under subsection (1) may be given subject to conditions.

(5) Subsection (1)(c)(iii) is subject to section A23(1).

(6) In this section—

"agency worker" has the meaning given by section 13(2) of the Employment Relations Act 1999;

"employer"—

(a) in relation to an agency worker, has the meaning given by section 13(2) of the Employment Relations Act 1999;

(b) otherwise, has the meaning given by section 230(4) of the Employment Rights Act 1996;

"worker" means an individual who is—

(a) a worker within the meaning of section 230(3) of the Employment Rights Act 1996, or
(b) an agency worker.]

NOTES

Commencement: 26 June 2020.
Inserted (subject to transitional provisions and temporary modifications) as noted to s A1 at **[9.81]**.

[9.102]

[A22 Floating charges

(1) This section applies where there is an uncrystallised floating charge on the property of a company for which a moratorium is in force.

(2) During the moratorium, the holder of the floating charge may not give any notice which would have the effect of—

(a) causing the floating charge to crystallise, or
(b) causing the imposition, by virtue of provision in the instrument creating the charge, of any restriction on the disposal of property of the company.

(3) No other event occurring during the moratorium is to have the effect mentioned in subsection (2)(a) or (b).

(4) Subsection (5) applies where—

(a) the holder of a floating charge ("the chargee") is prevented by subsection (2) from giving a notice mentioned there during the moratorium, and
(b) under the terms of the floating charge, the time for giving such a notice ends during the moratorium or before the chargee is given notice of the end of the moratorium under section A17.

(5) The chargee may give notice later than is required under the terms of the floating charge, but only if the chargee does so as soon as is practicable after—

(a) the end of the moratorium, or
(b) if later, the day on which the chargee is notified of the end of the moratorium.

(6) Where—

(a) subsection (3) prevents an event which occurs during the moratorium from having the effect mentioned there, and
(b) the holder of the floating charge gives notice of the event to the company as soon as is practicable after—
  (i) the end of the moratorium, or
  (ii) if later, the day on which the chargee is notified of the end of the moratorium,

the event is to be treated as if it had occurred when the notice was given.

(7) This section does not apply in relation to a floating charge that is—

(a) a collateral security (as defined by section A27);
(b) a market charge (as defined by section A27);
(c) a security financial collateral arrangement (within the meaning of regulation 3 of the Financial Collateral Arrangements (No 2) Regulations 2003 (SI 2003/3226));
(d) a system-charge (as defined by section A27).]

NOTES

Commencement: 26 June 2020.
Inserted (subject to transitional provisions and temporary modifications) as noted to s A1 at **[9.81]**.

[9.103]

[A23 Enforcement of security granted during moratorium

(1) Security granted by a company during a moratorium in relation to the company may be enforced only if the monitor consented to the grant of security under section A26.

(2) See also section A21(1)(c), which restricts enforcement during a moratorium.

NOTES

Commencement: 26 June 2020.
Inserted (subject to transitional provisions and temporary modifications) as noted to s A1 at **[9.81]**.

[Notification of insolvency proceedings

[9.104]

A24 Duty of directors to notify monitor of insolvency proceedings etc

(1) The directors of a company must notify the monitor before taking any of the following steps during a moratorium—

(a) presenting a petition for the winding up of the company;
(b) making an administration application in respect of the company;
(c) appointing an administrator under paragraph 22(2) of Schedule B1.

(2) The directors of a company must notify the monitor if, during a moratorium for the company, they recommend that the company passes a resolution for voluntary winding up under section 84(1)(b).

(3) The rules may make provision about the timing of a notice required to be given under subsection (1) or (2).

(4) If the directors fail to comply with subsection (1) or (2), any director who did not have a reasonable excuse for the failure commits an offence.]

NOTES

Commencement: 26 June 2020.
Inserted (subject to transitional provisions and temporary modifications) as noted to s A1 at **[9.81]**.

[Restrictions on transactions

[9.105]

A25 Restrictions on obtaining credit

(1) During a moratorium, the company may not obtain credit to the extent of £500 or more from a person unless the person has been informed that a moratorium is in force in relation to the company.

(2) The reference to the company obtaining credit includes—

(a) the company entering into a conditional sale agreement in accordance with which goods are to be sold to the company,

(b) the company entering into any other form of hire-purchase agreement under which goods are to be bailed (in Scotland, hired) to the company, and

(c) the company being paid in advance (whether in money or otherwise) for the supply of goods or services.

(3) If a company contravenes subsection (1)—

(a) the company commits an offence, and

(b) any officer of the company who without reasonable excuse authorised or permitted the obtaining of the credit commits an offence.]

NOTES

Commencement: 26 June 2020.

Inserted (subject to transitional provisions and temporary modifications) as noted to s A1 at **[9.81]**.

[9.106]

[A26 Restrictions on grant of security etc

(1) During a moratorium, the company may grant security over its property only if the monitor consents.

(2) The monitor may give consent under subsection (1) only if the monitor thinks that the grant of security will support the rescue of the company as a going concern.

(3) In deciding whether to give consent under subsection (1), the monitor is entitled to rely on information provided by the company unless the monitor has reason to doubt its accuracy.

(4) If the company grants security over its property during the moratorium otherwise than as authorised by subsection (1)—

(a) the company commits an offence, and

(b) any officer of the company who without reasonable excuse authorised or permitted the grant of the security commits an offence.

(5) For the consequences of a company granting security over its property in contravention of subsection (1), see also section A23.

(6) The monitor may not give consent under this section if the granting of security is an offence under section A27.]

NOTES

Commencement: 26 June 2020.

Inserted (subject to transitional provisions and temporary modifications) as noted to s A1 at **[9.81]**.

[9.107]

[A27 Prohibition on entering into market contracts etc

(1) If a company enters into a transaction to which this section applies during a moratorium for the company—

(a) the company commits an offence, and

(b) any officer of the company who without reasonable excuse authorised or permitted the company to enter into the transaction commits an offence.

(2) A company enters into a transaction to which this section applies if it—

(a) enters into a market contract,

(b) enters into a financial collateral arrangement,

(c) gives a transfer order,

(d) grants a market charge or a system-charge, or

(e) provides any collateral security.

(3) Where during the moratorium a company enters into a transaction to which this section applies, nothing done by or in pursuance of the transaction is to be treated as done in contravention of any of sections A19, A21, A25, A26 and A28 to A32.

(4) In this section—

"collateral security" has the same meaning as in the Financial Markets and Insolvency (Settlement Finality) Regulations 1999 (SI 1999/2979);

"financial collateral arrangement" has the same meaning as in the Financial Collateral Arrangements (No 2) Regulations 2003 (SI 2003/3226);

"market charge" has the same meaning as in Part 7 of the Companies Act 1989;

"market contract" has the same meaning as in Part 7 of the Companies Act 1989;

"system-charge" has the meaning given by the Financial Markets and Insolvency Regulations 1996 (SI 1996/1469);

"transfer order" has the same meaning as in the Financial Markets and Insolvency (Settlement Finality) Regulations 1999.]

NOTES

Commencement: 26 June 2020.

Inserted (subject to transitional provisions and temporary modifications) as noted to s A1 at **[9.81]**.

[Restrictions on payments and disposal of property

[9.108]
A28 Restrictions on payment of certain pre-moratorium debts
(1) During a moratorium, the company may make one or more relevant payments to a person that (in total) exceed the specified maximum amount only if—
 (a) the monitor consents,
 (b) the payment is in pursuance of a court order, or
 (c) the payment is required by section A31(3) or A32(3).
(2) In subsection (1)—
 "relevant payments" means payments in respect of pre-moratorium debts for which the company has a payment holiday during the moratorium (see section A18);
 "specified maximum amount" means an amount equal to the greater of—
  (a) £5000, and
  (b) 1% of the value of the debts and other liabilities owed by the company to its unsecured creditors when the moratorium began, to the extent that the amount of such debts and liabilities can be ascertained at that time.
(3) The monitor may give consent under subsection (1)(a) only if the monitor thinks that it will support the rescue of the company as a going concern.
(4) In deciding whether to give consent under subsection (1)(a), the monitor is entitled to rely on information provided by the company unless the monitor has reason to doubt its accuracy.
(5) If the company makes a payment to which subsection (1) applies otherwise than as authorised by that subsection—
 (a) the company commits an offence, and
 (b) any officer of the company who without reasonable excuse authorised or permitted the payment commits an offence.]

NOTES
Commencement: 26 June 2020.
Inserted (subject to transitional provisions and temporary modifications) as noted to s A1 at **[9.81]**.

[9.109]
[A29 Restrictions on disposal of property
(1) During a moratorium, the company may dispose of its property only if authorised by subsection (2) or (5).
(2) In the case of property that is not subject to a security interest, the company may dispose of the property if—
 (a) the disposal is made in the ordinary way of the company's business,
 (b) the monitor consents, or
 (c) the disposal is in pursuance of a court order.
(3) The monitor may give consent under subsection (2)(b) only if the monitor thinks that it will support the rescue of the company as a going concern.
(4) In deciding whether to give consent under subsection (2)(b), the monitor is entitled to rely on information provided by the company unless the monitor has reason to doubt its accuracy.
(5) In the case of property that is subject to a security interest, the company may dispose of the property if the disposal is in accordance with—
 (a) section A31(1), or
 (b) the terms of the security.
(6) If the company disposes of its property during the moratorium otherwise than as authorised by this section—
 (a) the company commits an offence, and
 (b) any officer of the company who without reasonable excuse authorised or permitted the disposal commits an offence.]

NOTES
Commencement: 26 June 2020.
Inserted (subject to transitional provisions and temporary modifications) as noted to s A1 at **[9.81]**.

[9.110]
[A30 Restrictions on disposal of hire-purchase property
(1) During a moratorium, the company may dispose of any goods in the possession of the company under a hire-purchase agreement only if the disposal is in accordance with —
 (a) section A32(1), or
 (b) the terms of the agreement.
(2) If the company disposes of goods in the possession of the company under a hire-purchase agreement otherwise than as authorised by subsection (1)—
 (a) the company commits an offence, and
 (b) any officer of the company who without reasonable excuse authorised or permitted the disposal commits an offence.]

NOTES
Commencement: 26 June 2020.
Inserted (subject to transitional provisions and temporary modifications) as noted to s A1 at **[9.81]**.

[Disposals of property free from charges etc

[9.111]
A31 Disposal of charged property free from charge
(1) During a moratorium, the company may, with the permission of the court, dispose of property which is subject to a security interest as if it were not subject to the security interest.

(2) The court may give permission under subsection (1) only if the court thinks that it will support the rescue of the company as a going concern.

(3) Where the court gives permission under subsection (1) other than in relation to a floating charge, the company must apply the following towards discharging the sums secured—

(a) the net proceeds of disposal of the property, and

(b) any money required to be added to the net proceeds so as to produce the amount determined by the court as the net amount which would be realised on a sale of the property in the open market by a willing vendor.

(4) Where the permission relates to two or more security interests, the condition in subsection (3) requires the application of money in the order of the priorities of the security interests.

(5) Where property subject to a floating charge is disposed of under subsection (1), the holder of the floating charge has the same priority in respect of acquired property as they had in respect of the property disposed of.

(6) In subsection (5) "acquired property" means property of the company which directly or indirectly represents the property disposed of.

(7) Where the court makes an order giving permission under subsection (1), the directors must, within the period of 14 days beginning with the date of the order, send a copy of it to the registrar of companies.

(8) If the directors fail to comply with subsection (7), any director who did not have a reasonable excuse for the failure commits an offence.

(9) Where property in Scotland is disposed of under subsection (1), the company must grant to the disponee an appropriate document of transfer or conveyance of the property, and—

(a) that document, or

(b) recording, intimation or registration of that document (where recording, intimation or registration of the document is a legal requirement for completion of title to the property),

has the effect of disencumbering the property of or, as the case may be, freeing the property from, the security interest.

(10) If a company fails to comply with subsection (3) or (9)—

(a) the company commits an offence, and

(b) any officer of the company who without reasonable excuse authorised or permitted the failure commits an offence.

(11) Subsection (1) does not apply in relation to any property which is subject to a financial collateral arrangement, a market charge, a system-charge or a collateral security (as defined by section A27).]

NOTES

Commencement: 26 June 2020.

Inserted (subject to transitional provisions and temporary modifications) as noted to s A1 at **[9.81]**.

[9.112]

[A32 Disposal of hire-purchase property

(1) During a moratorium, the company may, with the permission of the court, dispose of goods which are in the possession of the company under a hire-purchase agreement as if all of the rights of the owner under the agreement were vested in the company.

(2) The court may give permission under subsection (1) only if the court thinks that it will support the rescue of the company as a going concern.

(3) Where the court gives permission under subsection (1), the company must apply the following towards discharging the sums payable under the hire-purchase agreement—

(a) the net proceeds of disposal of the goods, and

(b) any additional money required to be added to the net proceeds so as to produce the amount determined by the court as the net amount which would be realised on a sale of the goods in the open market by a willing vendor.

(4) If a company fails to comply with subsection (3)—

(a) the company commits an offence, and

(b) any officer of the company who without reasonable excuse authorised or permitted the failure commits an offence.

(5) Where the court makes an order giving permission under subsection (1), the directors must, within the period of 14 days beginning with the date of the order, send a copy of it to the registrar of companies.

(6) If the directors fail to comply with subsection (5), any director who did not have a reasonable excuse for the failure commits an offence.

(7) In Scotland, where goods in the possession of the company under a hire-purchase agreement are disposed of under subsection (1), the disposal has the effect of extinguishing, as against the disponee, all rights of the owner of the goods under the agreement.]

NOTES

Commencement: 26 June 2020.

Inserted (subject to transitional provisions and temporary modifications) as noted to s A1 at **[9.81]**.

[Effect of contravention of certain provisions of Chapter

[9.113]

A33 Contravention of certain requirements imposed under this Chapter

The fact that a company contravenes section A19 or any of sections A25 to A32 does not—

(a) make any transaction void or unenforceable, or

(b) affect the validity of any other thing.]

NOTES

Commencement: 26 June 2020.

Inserted (subject to transitional provisions and temporary modifications) as noted to s A1 at **[9.81]**.

CHAPTER 5 [THE MONITOR

[9.114]

A34 Status of monitor

The monitor in relation to a moratorium is an officer of the court.]

NOTES

Commencement: 26 June 2020.

Inserted (subject to transitional provisions and temporary modifications) as noted to s A1 at **[9.81]**.

[9.115]

[A35 Monitoring

(1) During a moratorium, the monitor must monitor the company's affairs for the purpose of forming a view as to whether it remains likely that the moratorium will result in the rescue of the company as a going concern.

(2) In forming the view mentioned in subsection (1), the monitor is entitled to rely on information provided by the company, unless the monitor has reason to doubt its accuracy.]

NOTES

Commencement: 26 June 2020.

Inserted (subject to transitional provisions and temporary modifications) as noted to s A1 at **[9.81]**.

[9.116]

[A36 Provision of information to monitor

(1) The monitor may require the directors of the company to provide any information required by the monitor for the purpose of carrying out the monitor's functions.

(2) The directors must comply with a requirement to provide information as soon as practicable.

(3) For the potential consequences of failing to comply with a requirement to provide information, see section A38.]

NOTES

Commencement: 26 June 2020.

Inserted (subject to transitional provisions and temporary modifications) as noted to s A1 at **[9.81]**.

[9.117]

[A37 Application by monitor for directions

The monitor in relation to a moratorium may apply to the court for directions about the carrying out of the monitor's functions.]

NOTES

Commencement: 26 June 2020.

Inserted (subject to transitional provisions and temporary modifications) as noted to s A1 at **[9.81]**.

[9.118]

[A38 Termination of moratorium by monitor

(1) The monitor must bring a moratorium to an end by filing a notice with the court if—

- (a) the monitor thinks that the moratorium is no longer likely to result in the rescue of the company as a going concern,
- (b) the monitor thinks that the objective of rescuing the company as a going concern has been achieved,
- (c) the monitor thinks that, by reason of a failure by the directors to comply with a requirement under section A36, the monitor is unable properly to carry out the monitor's functions, or
- (d) the monitor thinks that the company is unable to pay any of the following that have fallen due—
  - (i) moratorium debts;
  - (ii) pre-moratorium debts for which the company does not have a payment holiday during the moratorium (see section A18).

(2) The rules may provide for debts that are to be disregarded for the purposes of subsection (1)(d).

(3) On the filing with the court of a notice under subsection (1), the moratorium comes to an end.

(4) The rules may make provision about the timing of a notice required to be given under subsection (1).

(5) The Secretary of State may by regulations amend this section for the purposes of changing the circumstances in which the monitor must bring a moratorium to an end under subsection (1).

(6) Regulations under subsection (5) are subject to the affirmative resolution procedure.

(7) See also section A17 (obligations to notify change in end of moratorium).]

NOTES

Commencement: 26 June 2020.

Inserted (subject to transitional provisions and temporary modifications) as noted to s A1 at **[9.81]**.

[9.119]

[A39 Replacement of monitor or appointment of additional monitor

(1) The court may make an order authorising the appointment of a qualified person to act as the monitor in relation to a moratorium instead of, or in addition to, a person who already acts as the monitor.

(2) The court may make an order providing that a person ceases to act as the monitor in relation to a moratorium.

(3) An order under subsection (1) or (2) may be made only on an application by the directors or the monitor.

(4) The court may make an order authorising the appointment of a monitor under subsection (1) only if the person has provided the court with a statement that the person—

- (a) is a qualified person, and
- (b) consents to act as the monitor in relation to the moratorium.

(5) Where it is proposed that more than one person should act as the monitor in relation to the moratorium, the statement under subsection (4) must specify—

(a) which functions (if any) are to be exercised by the persons acting jointly, and
(b) which functions (if any) are to be exercised by any or all of the persons.

(6) The rules may make provision about the date on which the statement under subsection (4) must be made.

(7) Where the court makes an order under subsection (1) or (2) the person begins to act as the monitor, or ceases to act as the monitor, in relation to the moratorium at the time specified in, or determined in accordance with, the order ("the relevant time").

(8) As soon as reasonably practicable after the relevant time, the monitor must notify the following of the effect of the order—

(a) the registrar of companies,
(b) every creditor of the company of whose claim the monitor is aware,
(c) in a case where the company is or has been an employer in respect of an occupational pension scheme that is not a money purchase scheme, the Pensions Regulator, and
(d) in a case where the company is an employer in respect of such a pension scheme that is an eligible scheme within the meaning given by section 126 of the Pensions Act 2004, the Board of the Pension Protection Fund.

(9) If the monitor without reasonable excuse fails to comply with subsection (8), the monitor commits an offence.]

NOTES

Commencement: 26 June 2020.

Inserted (subject to transitional provisions and temporary modifications) as noted to s A1 at **[9.81]**.

[9.120]

[A40 Application of Part where two or more persons act as monitor

(1) Where two or more persons act jointly as the monitor—

(a) a reference in this Act to the monitor is a reference to those persons acting jointly;
(b) where an offence of omission is committed by the monitor, each of the persons appointed to act jointly—
  (i) commits the offence, and
  (ii) may be proceeded against and punished individually.

(2) Where persons act jointly in respect of only some of the functions of the monitor, subsection (1) applies only in relation to those functions.

(3) Where two or more persons act concurrently as the monitor a reference in this Act to the monitor is a reference to any of the persons appointed (or any combination of them).]

NOTES

Commencement: 26 June 2020.

Inserted (subject to transitional provisions and temporary modifications) as noted to s A1 at **[9.81]**.

[9.121]

[A41 Presumption of validity

An act of the monitor is valid in spite of a defect in the monitor's appointment or qualification.]

NOTES

Commencement: 26 June 2020.

Inserted (subject to transitional provisions and temporary modifications) as noted to s A1 at **[9.81]**.

[CHAPTER 6 CHALLENGES

[9.122]

A42 Challenge to monitor's actions

(1) Any of the persons specified below may apply to the court on the ground that an act, omission or decision of the monitor during a moratorium has unfairly harmed the interests of the applicant.

(2) The persons who may apply are—

(a) a creditor, director or member of the company, or
(b) any other person affected by the moratorium.

(3) An application under subsection (1) may be made during the moratorium or after it has ended.

(4) On an application under subsection (1) the court may—

(a) confirm, reverse or modify any act or decision of the monitor,
(b) give the monitor directions, or
(c) make such other order as it thinks fit (but may not, under this paragraph, order the monitor to pay any compensation).

(5) Where an application under subsection (1) relates to a failure by the monitor to bring the moratorium to an end under section A38(1), an order under subsection (4) may, in particular, bring the moratorium to an end and make such consequential provision as the court thinks fit.

(6) Where an application under subsection (1) relates to the monitor bringing a moratorium to an end under section A38(1), an order under subsection (4) may, in particular, provide that the moratorium is not to be taken into account for the purposes of paragraph 2(1)(b) of Schedule ZA1 (company not eligible for moratorium if moratorium in force within previous 12 months).

(7) In making an order under subsection (4) the court must have regard to the need to safeguard the interests of persons who have dealt with the company in good faith and for value.

(8) See also section A17 (obligations to notify change in end of moratorium).]

NOTES

Commencement: 26 June 2020.

Inserted (subject to transitional provisions and temporary modifications) as noted to s A1 at **[9.81]**.

[9.123]

[A43 Challenges to monitor remuneration in insolvency proceedings

(1) The rules may confer on an administrator or liquidator of a company the right to apply to the court on the ground that remuneration charged by the monitor in relation to a prior moratorium for the company was excessive.

(2) Rules under subsection (1) may (among other things) make provision as to—

(a) time limits;

(b) disposals available to the court;

(c) the treatment of costs (or, in Scotland, the expenses) of the application in the administration or winding up.]

NOTES

Commencement: 26 June 2020.

Inserted (subject to transitional provisions and temporary modifications) as noted to s A1 at **[9.81]**.

[9.124]

[A44 Challenge to directors' actions

(1) A creditor or member of a company may apply to the court for an order under this section on the ground that—

(a) during a moratorium, the company's affairs, business and property are being or have been managed by the directors in a manner which has unfairly harmed the interests of its creditors or members generally or of some part of its creditors or members (including at least the applicant), or

(b) any actual or proposed act or omission of the directors during a moratorium causes or would cause such harm.

(2) An application under subsection (1) may be made during the moratorium or after it has ended.

(3) On an application under subsection (1) the court may make such order as it thinks fit.

(4) An order under subsection (3) may in particular—

(a) regulate the management by the directors of the company's affairs, business and property during the remainder of the moratorium,

(b) require the directors to refrain from doing or continuing an act complained of by the applicant or to do an act which the applicant has complained they have omitted to do,

(c) require a decision of the company's creditors to be sought (using a qualifying decision procedure) on such matters as the court may direct, or

(d) bring the moratorium to an end and make such consequential provision as the court thinks fit.

(5) In making an order under subsection (3) the court must have regard to the need to safeguard the interests of persons who have dealt with the company in good faith and for value.

(6) See also section A17 (obligations to notify change in end of moratorium).]

NOTES

Commencement: 26 June 2020.

Inserted (subject to transitional provisions and temporary modifications) as noted to s A1 at **[9.81]**.

[9.125]

[A45 Challenge brought by Board of the Pension Protection Fund

(1) This section applies where—

(a) a moratorium—

(i) is in force in relation to a company that is an employer in respect of an eligible scheme, or

(ii) is or has been in force in relation to a company that has been an employer in respect of an eligible scheme at any time during the moratorium, and

(b) the trustees or managers of the scheme are a creditor of the company.

(2) The Board of the Pension Protection Fund may make any application under section A42(1) or A44(1) that could be made by the trustees or managers as a creditor.

(3) For the purposes of such an application, any reference in section A42(1) or A44(1) to the interests of the applicant is to be read as a reference to the interests of the trustees or managers as a creditor.

(4) In this section "eligible scheme" has the meaning given by section 126 of the Pensions Act 2004.]

NOTES

Commencement: 26 June 2020.

Inserted (subject to transitional provisions and temporary modifications) as noted to s A1 at **[9.81]**.

[CHAPTER 7 OFFENCES: GENERAL

[9.126]

A46 Offence of fraud etc during or in anticipation of moratorium

(1) An officer of a company commits an offence if, during a moratorium for the company or at any time within the period of 12 months ending with the day on which a moratorium for the company comes into force, the officer—

(a) does any of the things mentioned in subsection (2), or

(b) was privy to the doing by others of any of the things mentioned in subsection (2)(c), (d) and (e).

(2) Those things are—

(a) concealing any part of the company's property to the value of £500 or more, or concealing any debt due to or from the company,

(b) fraudulently removing any part of the company's property to the value of £500 or more,

(c) concealing, destroying, mutilating or falsifying any document affecting or relating to the company's property or affairs,

(d) making any false entry in any document affecting or relating to the company's property or affairs,

(e) fraudulently parting with, altering or making any omission in any document affecting or relating to the company's property or affairs, or

(f) pawning, pledging or disposing of any property of the company which has been obtained on credit and has not been paid for (unless the pawning, pledging or disposal was in the ordinary way of the company's business).

(3) It is a defence—

(a) for a person charged with an offence under subsection (1) in respect of any of the things mentioned in subsection (2)(a) or (f) to prove that the person had no intent to defraud, and

(b) for a person charged with an offence under subsection (1) in respect of any of the things mentioned in subsection (2)(c) or (d) to prove that the person had no intent to conceal the state of affairs of the company or to defeat the law.

(4) Where a person pawns, pledges or disposes of any property of a company in circumstances which amount to an offence under subsection (1), every person who takes in pawn or pledge, or otherwise receives, the property commits an offence if the person knows it to be pawned, pledged or disposed of in circumstances which—

(a) amount to an offence under subsection (1), or

(b) would, if a moratorium were obtained for the company within the period of 12 months beginning with the day on which the pawning, pledging or disposal took place, amount to an offence under subsection (1).

(5) In this section, "officer" includes a shadow director.]

NOTES

Commencement: 26 June 2020.

Inserted (subject to transitional provisions and temporary modifications) as noted to s A1 at **[9.81]**.

[9.127]

[A47 Offence of false representation etc to obtain a moratorium

(1) An officer of a company commits an offence if, for the purpose of obtaining a moratorium for the company or an extension of a moratorium for the company, the officer—

(a) makes any false representation, or

(b) fraudulently does, or omits to do, anything.

(2) Subsection (1) applies even if no moratorium or extension is obtained.

(3) In this section, "officer" includes a shadow director.]

NOTES

Commencement: 26 June 2020.

Inserted (subject to transitional provisions and temporary modifications) as noted to s A1 at **[9.81]**.

[9.128]

[A48 Prosecution of delinquent officers of company

(1) This section applies where a moratorium has been obtained for a company.

(2) If it appears to the monitor that any past or present officer of the company has committed an offence in connection with the moratorium, the monitor must forthwith—

(a) report the matter to the appropriate authority, and

(b) provide the appropriate authority with such information and give the authority such access to and facilities for inspecting and taking copies of documents (being information or documents in the possession or under the control of the monitor and relating to the matter in question) as the authority requires.

(3) In subsection (2), "the appropriate authority"—

(a) in the case of a company registered in England and Wales, means the Secretary of State,

(b) in the case of a company registered in Scotland, means the Lord Advocate, and

(c) in the case of an unregistered company means—

(i) if it has a principal place of business in England and Wales but not Scotland, the Secretary of State,

(ii) if it has a principal place of business in Scotland but not England and Wales, the Lord Advocate,

(iii) if it has a principal place of business in both England and Wales and Scotland, the Secretary of State and the Lord Advocate, and

(iv) if it does not have a principal place of business in England and Wales or Scotland, the Secretary of State.

(4) Where a matter is reported to the Secretary of State under subsection (2), the Secretary of State may, for the purpose of investigating the matter and such other matters relating to the affairs of the company as appear to the Secretary of State to require investigation, exercise any of the powers which are exercisable by inspectors appointed under section 431 or 432 of the Companies Act 1985.

(5) For the purpose of such an investigation any obligation imposed on a person by any provision of the Companies Acts to produce documents or give information to, or otherwise to assist, inspectors so appointed is to be regarded as an obligation similarly to assist the Secretary of State in the Secretary of State's investigation.

(6) Where a question is put to a person in exercise of the powers conferred by subsection (4), the person's answer may be used in evidence against them.

(7) However, in criminal proceedings in which the person is charged with an offence other than a false statement offence—

(a) no evidence relating to the answer may be adduced, and

(b) no question relating to it may be asked,

by or on behalf of the prosecution, unless evidence relating to it is adduced, or a question relating to it is asked, in the proceedings by or on behalf of the person.

(8) In subsection (7) "false statement offence" means—

(a) an offence under section 2 or 5 of the Perjury Act 1911 (false statements made on oath otherwise than in judicial proceedings or made otherwise than on oath), or

(b) an offence under section 44(1) or (2) of the Criminal Law (Consolidation) (Scotland) Act 1995 (false statements made on oath or otherwise than on oath).

(9) Where a prosecuting authority institutes criminal proceedings following any report under subsection (2), the monitor, and every officer and agent of the company past and present (other than the defendant or defender), must give the authority all assistance in connection with the prosecution which they are reasonably able to give.

(10) For this purpose—

"agent" includes any banker or solicitor of the company and any person employed by the company as auditor, whether that person is or is not an officer of the company;

"prosecuting authority" means the Director of Public Prosecutions, the Lord Advocate or the Secretary of State.

(11) The court may, on the application of the prosecuting authority, direct a person who has failed to comply with subsection (9) to comply with it.]

NOTES

Commencement: 26 June 2020.

Inserted (subject to transitional provisions and temporary modifications) as noted to s A1 at **[9.81]**.

[CHAPTER 8 MISCELLANEOUS AND GENERAL

Special rules for certain kinds of company etc

[9.129]

A49 Regulated companies: modifications to this Part

(1) For the purposes of sections A3 and A4 as they apply in relation to a regulated company, section A6(1) has effect as if the documents listed there included a reference to the written consent of the appropriate regulator to the appointment of the proposed monitor.

(2) The remaining provisions of this section apply in relation to a moratorium for a regulated company.

(3) Any notice under section A8(2), A17(2) to (4) or A39(8) must also be sent by the monitor to the appropriate regulator.

(4) The directors must give the appropriate regulator notice of any qualifying decision procedure by which a decision of the company's creditors is sought for the purposes of section A12(2) or A44(4)(c).

(5) If the directors fail to comply with subsection (4), any director who did not have a reasonable excuse for the failure commits an offence.

(6) The appropriate regulator, or a person appointed by the appropriate regulator, may in the way provided for by the rules, participate (but not vote) in any qualifying decision procedure by which a decision of the company's creditors is sought for the purposes of this Part.

(7) The appropriate regulator is entitled to be heard on any application to the court for permission under section A31(1) or A32(1) (disposal of charged property, etc).

(8) The court may make an order under section A39(1) only if the appropriate regulator has given its written consent to the appointment of the proposed monitor.

(9) The persons who may apply to the court under section A39(3), A42(1) or A44(1) include the appropriate regulator.

(10) If a person other than a regulator applies to the court under section A39(3), A42(1) or A44(1) the appropriate regulator is entitled to be heard on the application.

(11) If either regulator makes an application to the court under section A39(3), A42(1) or A44(1) in relation to a PRA-regulated company, the other regulator is entitled to be heard on the application.

(12) This section does not affect any right that the appropriate regulator has (apart from this section) as a creditor of a regulated company.

(13) In this section—

"the appropriate regulator" means—

(a) where the regulated company is a PRA-regulated company, each of the Financial Conduct Authority and the Prudential Regulation Authority, and

(b) where the regulated company is not a PRA-regulated company, the Financial Conduct Authority;

"PRA-authorised person" has the meaning given by section 2B(5) of the Financial Services and Markets Act 2000;

"PRA-regulated company" means a regulated company which—

(a) is, or has been, a PRA-authorised person,

(b) is, or has been, an appointed representative within the meaning given by section 39 of the Financial Services and Markets Act 2000, whose principal (or one of whose principals) is, or was, a PRA-authorised person, or

(c) is carrying on, or has carried on, a PRA-regulated activity (within the meaning of section 22A of that Act) in contravention of the general prohibition;

"regulated activity" has the meaning given by section 22 of the Financial Services and Markets Act 2000, taken with Schedule 2 to that Act and any order under that section;

"regulated company" means a company which—

(a) is, or has been, an authorised person within the meaning given by section 31 of the Financial Services and Markets Act 2000,

(b) is, or has been, an appointed representative within the meaning given by section 39 of that Act, or

(c) is carrying on, or has carried on, a regulated activity in contravention of the general prohibition within the meaning given by section 19 of that Act;

"regulator" means the Financial Conduct Authority or the Prudential Regulation Authority.

(14) The Secretary of State may by regulations amend this section for the purposes of changing the definition of "regulated company" in subsection (13).

(15) Regulations under subsection (14) are subject to the affirmative resolution procedure.]

NOTES

Commencement: 26 June 2020.

Inserted (subject to transitional provisions and temporary modifications) as noted to s A1 at **[9.81]**.

[9.130]

[A50 Power to modify this Part etc in relation to certain companies

(1) The Secretary of State may by regulations make provision under the law of England and Wales or Scotland—

(a) to modify this Part as it applies in relation to a company for which there is a special administration regime, or

(b) in connection with the interaction between this Part and any other insolvency procedure in relation to such a company.

(2) The Welsh Ministers may by regulations make provision under the law of England and Wales—

(a) to modify this Part as it applies in relation to a company that is a social landlord registered under Part 1 of the Housing Act 1996, or

(b) make provision in connection with the interaction between this Part and any other insolvency procedure in relation to such a company.

(3) The Scottish Ministers may by regulations make provision under the law of Scotland—

(a) to modify this Part as it applies in relation to a company that is a social landlord registered under Part 2 of the Housing (Scotland) Act 2010 (asp 17), or

(b) make provision in connection with the interaction between this Part and any other insolvency procedure in relation to such a company.

(4) The Secretary of State may, by regulations, make any provision under the law of England and Wales, Scotland or Northern Ireland that appears to the Secretary of State to be appropriate in view of provision made under subsection (1), (2) or (3).

(5) The power in subsection (1), (2), (3) or (4) may, in particular, be used to amend, repeal, revoke or otherwise modify any provision made by an enactment.

(6) Regulations under subsection (1) or (4) are subject to the affirmative resolution procedure.

(7) A statutory instrument containing regulations under subsection (2) may not be made unless a draft of the statutory instrument containing them has been laid before and approved by a resolution of Senedd Cymru.

(8) Regulations made by the Scottish Ministers under subsection (3) are subject to the affirmative procedure (see section 29 of the Interpretation and Legislative Reform (Scotland) Act 2010 (asp 10)).

(9) In this section—

"insolvency procedure" includes—

(a) in relation to subsection (1)(b), the provision made by sections 143A to 159 of the Housing and Regeneration Act 2008;

(b) in relation to subsection (2)(b), the provision made by sections 39 to 50 of the Housing Act 1996;

(c) in relation to subsection (3)(b), the provision made by Part 7 of the Housing (Scotland) Act 2010;

"ordinary administration" means the insolvency procedure provided for by Schedule B1;

"special administration regime" means provision made by an enactment for an insolvency procedure that—

(a) is similar or corresponds to ordinary administration, and

(b) provides for the administrator to have one or more special objectives instead of or in addition to the objectives of ordinary administration.]

NOTES

Commencement: 26 June 2020.

Inserted (subject to transitional provisions and temporary modifications) as noted to s A1 at **[9.81]**.

Regulations: the Insolvency (Moratorium) (Special Administration for Energy Licensees) Regulations 2020, SI 2020/943.

[9.131]

[A51 Power to make provision in connection with pension schemes

(1) The Secretary of State may by regulations provide that, in a case where—

(a) a moratorium—

(i) is in force in relation to a company that is an employer in respect of an eligible scheme, or

(ii) is or has been in force in relation to a company that has been an employer in respect of an eligible scheme at any time during the moratorium, and

(b) the trustees or managers of the scheme are a creditor of the company,

the Board of the Pension Protection Fund may exercise any of the following rights.

(2) The rights are those which are exercisable by the trustees or managers as a creditor of the company under or by virtue of—

(a) section A12, or

(b) a court order under section A44(4)(c).

(3) Regulations under subsection (1) may provide that the Board may exercise any such rights—

(a) to the exclusion of the trustees or managers of the scheme, or

(b) in addition to the exercise of those rights by the trustees or managers of the scheme.

(4) Regulations under subsection (1)—

(a) may specify conditions that must be met before the Board may exercise any such rights;

(b) may provide for any such rights to be exercisable by the Board for a specified period;

(c) may make provision in connection with any such rights ceasing to be so exercisable at the end of such a period.

(5) Regulations under subsection (1) are subject to the affirmative resolution procedure.

(6) In this section "eligible scheme" has the meaning given by section 126 of the Pensions Act 2004.]

NOTES

Commencement: 26 June 2020.

Inserted (subject to transitional provisions and temporary modifications) as noted to s A1 at **[9.81]**.

Regulations: the Pension Protection Fund (Moratorium and Arrangements and Reconstructions for Companies in Financial Difficulty) Regulations 2020, SI 2020/693; the Pension Protection Fund (Moratorium and Arrangements and Reconstructions for Companies in Financial Difficulty) (Amendment and Revocation) Regulations 2020, SI 2020/990.

[Floating charges

[9.132]

A52 Void provisions in floating charge documents

(1) A provision in an instrument creating a floating charge is void if it provides for the obtaining of a moratorium, or anything done with a view to obtaining a moratorium, to be—

(a) an event causing the floating charge to crystallise,
(b) an event causing restrictions which would not otherwise apply to be imposed on the disposal of property by the company, or
(c) a ground for the appointment of a receiver.

(2) The reference in subsection (1) to anything done with a view to obtaining a moratorium includes any preliminary decision or investigation.

(3) In subsection (1) "receiver" includes a manager and a person who is appointed both receiver and manager.

(4) Subsection (1) does not apply to a provision in an instrument creating a floating charge that is—
(a) a collateral security (as defined by section A27);
(b) a market charge (as defined by section A27);
(c) a security financial collateral arrangement (within the meaning of regulation 3 of the Financial Collateral Arrangements (No 2) Regulations 2003 (SI 2003/3226));
(d) a system-charge (as defined by section A27).]

NOTES

Commencement: 26 June 2020.
Inserted (subject to transitional provisions and temporary modifications) as noted to s A1 at **[9.81]**.

[Interpretation of this Part

[9.133]

A53 Meaning of "pre-moratorium debt" and "moratorium debt"

(1) In this Part "pre-moratorium debt", in relation to a company for which a moratorium is or has been in force, means—
(a) any debt or other liability to which the company becomes subject before the moratorium comes into force, or
(b) any debt or other liability to which the company has become or may become subject during the moratorium by reason of any obligation incurred before the moratorium comes into force,

but this is subject to subsection (3).

(2) In this Part "moratorium debt", in relation to a company for which a moratorium is or has been in force, means—
(a) any debt or other liability to which the company becomes subject during the moratorium, other than by reason of an obligation incurred before the moratorium came into force, or
(b) any debt or other liability to which the company has become or may become subject after the end of the moratorium by reason of an obligation incurred during the moratorium,

but this is subject to subsection (3).

(3) For the purposes of this Part—
(a) a liability in tort or delict is a "pre-moratorium debt" if either—
(i) the cause of action has accrued before the moratorium comes into force, or
(ii) all the elements necessary to establish the cause of action exist before the moratorium comes into force except for actionable damage;
(b) a liability in tort or delict is a "moratorium debt" if it does not fall within paragraph (a) and either—
(i) the cause of action has accrued during the moratorium, or
(ii) all the elements necessary to establish the cause of action exist before the moratorium comes to an end except for actionable damage.

(4) The Secretary of State may by regulations amend this section for the purposes of changing the definition of "pre-moratorium debt" or "moratorium debt" in this Part.

(5) Regulations under subsection (4) are subject to the affirmative resolution procedure.]

NOTES

Commencement: 26 June 2020.
Inserted (subject to transitional provisions and temporary modifications) as noted to s A1 at **[9.81]**.

[9.134]

[A54 Interpretation of this Part: general

(1) In this Part—

"company" means—
(a) a company registered under the Companies Act 2006 in England and Wales or Scotland, or
(b) an unregistered company that may be wound up under Part 5 of this Act;

"the court" means such court as is prescribed;

"eligible", in relation to a company, has the meaning given by Schedule ZA1;

"employer", in relation to a pension scheme—
(a) in sections A8(2)(c), A17(8)(c) and A39(8)(c), means an employer within the meaning of section 318(1) of the Pensions Act 2004;
(b) elsewhere in this Part, has the same meaning that it has for the purposes of Part 2 of the Pensions Act 2004 (see section 318(1) and (4) of that Act);

"enactment" includes an Act of the Scottish Parliament and an instrument made under such an Act;

"hire-purchase agreement" includes a conditional sale agreement, a chattel leasing agreement and a retention of title agreement;

"liability" means (subject to subsection (2)) a liability to pay money or money's worth, including any liability under an enactment, a liability for breach of trust, any liability in contract, tort, delict or bailment, and any liability arising out of an obligation to make restitution;

"money purchase scheme" has the meaning given by section 181(1) of the Pension Schemes Act 1993;

"the monitor", in relation to a moratorium, means the person who has the functions of the monitor in relation to the moratorium (see also section A40 for cases where two or more persons act as the monitor);

"moratorium" means a moratorium under this Part;

"moratorium debt" has the meaning given by section A53;

"occupational pension scheme" has the meaning given by section 1 of the Pension Schemes Act 1993;
"pension scheme" has the meaning given by section 1 of the Pension Schemes Act 1993;
"pre-moratorium debt" has the meaning given by section A53;
"qualified person" means a person qualified to act as an insolvency practitioner;
"unable to pay its debts"—

(a) in relation to a registered company, has the same meaning as in Part 4 (see section 123);
(b) in relation to an unregistered company, has the same meaning as in Part 5 (see sections 222 to 224).

(2) For the purposes of references in any provision of this Part to a debt or liability it is immaterial whether the debt or liability is present or future, whether it is certain or contingent, or whether its amount is fixed or liquidated, or is capable of being ascertained by fixed rules or as a matter of opinion.

(3) In this Part references to filing a document with the court are, in relation to a court in Scotland, references to lodging it in court.

(4) The Secretary of State may by regulations amend this section for the purposes of changing the definition of "qualified person" in subsection (1).

(5) Regulations under subsection (4) are subject to the affirmative resolution procedure.]

NOTES

Commencement: 26 June 2020.

Inserted (subject to transitional provisions and temporary modifications) as noted to s A1 at **[9.81]**.

[Regulations

[9.135]

A55 Regulations

(1) Regulations under this Part may make—

(a) different provision for different purposes;
(b) consequential, supplementary, incidental or transitional provision or savings.

(2) Regulations under this Part are to be made by statutory instrument, unless they are made by the Scottish Ministers.

(3) Where regulations of the Secretary of State under this Part are subject to "the affirmative resolution procedure", they may not be made unless a draft of the statutory instrument containing them has been laid before Parliament and approved by a resolution of each House of Parliament.]

NOTES

Commencement: 26 June 2020.

Inserted (subject to transitional provisions and temporary modifications) as noted to s A1 at **[9.81]**.

PART I COMPANY VOLUNTARY ARRANGEMENTS

The proposal

[9.136]

1 Those who may propose an arrangement

(1) The directors of a company [(other than one which is in administration or being wound up)] may make a proposal under this Part to the company and to its creditors for a composition in satisfaction of its debts or a scheme of arrangement of its affairs (from here on referred to, in either case, as a "voluntary arrangement").

(2) A proposal under this Part is one which provides for some person ("the nominee") to act in relation to the voluntary arrangement either as trustee or otherwise for the purpose of supervising its implementation; and the nominee must be a person who is qualified to act as an insolvency practitioner [. . . in relation to the voluntary arrangement].

(3) Such a proposal may also be made—

[(a) where the company is in administration, by the administrator,] and
(b) where the company is being wound up, by the liquidator.

[(4) In this Part "company" means—

[(a) a company registered under the Companies Act 2006 in England and Wales or Scotland;]
(b) a company incorporated in an EEA State . . . ; or
(c) a company not incorporated in an EEA State but having its centre of main interests in a member State [(other than Denmark) or in the United Kingdom].

(5) In subsection (4), in relation to a company, "centre of main interests" has the same meaning as in [Article 3 of the EU Regulation].

(6) If a company incorporated outside the United Kingdom has a principal place of business in Northern Ireland, no proposal under this Part shall be made in relation to it unless it also has a principal place of business in England and Wales or Scotland (or both in England and Wales or Scotland).]

NOTES

Sub-s (1): words in square brackets substituted by the Enterprise Act 2002, s 248(3), Sch 17, paras 9, 10(a), as from 15 September 2003 (for savings and transitional provisions, see the note to s 8 at **[9.147]**).

Sub-s (2): words in square brackets substituted by the Insolvency Act 2000, s 2, Sch 2, Pt I, paras 1, 2, as from 1 January 2003. Words omitted repealed by the Deregulation Act 2015, s 19, Sch 6, Pt 6, para 20(1), (2)(a), as from 1 October 2015.

Sub-s (3): para (a) substituted by the Enterprise Act 2002, s 248(3), Sch 17, paras 9, 10(b), as from 15 September 2003 (for savings and transitional provisions, see the note to s 8 at **[9.147]**).

Sub-ss (4)–(6): substituted (for the original sub-s (4) as added by the Insolvency Act 1986 (Amendment) (No 2) Regulations 2002, SI 2002/1240, regs 3, 4) by the Insolvency Act 1986 (Amendment) Regulations 2005, SI 2005/879, reg 2(1), (2), as from 13 April 2005, except in relation to any voluntary arrangement under this Part that took effect before that date. Sub-s (4)(a) subsequently substituted by the Companies Act 2006 (Consequential Amendments, Transitional Provisions and Savings) Order 2009, SI 2009/1941, art 2(1), Sch 1, para 71(1), (2), as from 1 October 2009 (for effect see the note to s 7A at **[9.145]**). Words omitted from sub-s (4)(b) repealed, and words in square brackets in sub-s (4)(c) substituted, by the Insolvency

(Amendment) (EU Exit) Regulations 2019, SI 2019/146, reg 2, Schedule, Pt 2, paras 16, 17, as from IP completion day (as defined in the European Union (Withdrawal Agreement) Act 2020, s 39) (for savings, see reg 4 of the 2019 Regulations at **[12.82]**).

Sub-s (5): words in square brackets substituted by the Insolvency Amendment (EU 2015/848) Regulations 2017, SI 2017/702, regs 2, 3, Schedule, Pt 1, paras 1, 2, as from 26 June 2017, except in relation to proceedings opened before that date.

Temporary restriction on initiating certain insolvency arrangements (rent debts): see the note relating to the Commercial Rent (Coronavirus) Act 2022, s 25 to the Companies Act 2006, s 896 at **[1.1035]**. The relevant provisions of the 2022 Act are at **[9.700]**.

1A *(S 1A (Moratorium) was inserted by the Insolvency Act 2000, s 1, Sch 1, paras 1, 2, as from 1 January 2003. It was repealed by the Corporate Insolvency and Governance Act 2020, s 2(1), Sch 3, paras 1, 2, as from 26 June 2020. For transitional provisions, see s 2(2), (3) of the 2020 Act (at* **[9.533]***) which provides that (without prejudice to the Interpretation Act 1978, s 16) nothing in the 2020 Act affects the operation of this Act, or any other enactment, in relation to a moratorium under Sch A1 to this Act which comes into force before the repeal of that Schedule by Sch 3 to the 2020 Act (ie, 26 June 2020).)*

[9.137]

2 Procedure where nominee is not the liquidator or administrator

(1) This section applies where the nominee under section 1 is not the liquidator or administrator of the company [. . .].

(2) The nominee shall, within 28 days (or such longer period as the court may allow) after he is given notice of the proposal for a voluntary arrangement, submit a report to the court stating—

(a) [whether, in his opinion, the proposed voluntary arrangement has a reasonable prospect of being approved and implemented,]

[(b) whether, in his opinion, the proposal should be considered by a meeting of the company and by the company's creditors, and

(c) if in his opinion it should, the date on which, and time and place at which, he proposes a meeting of the company should be held.]

(3) For the purposes of enabling the nominee to prepare his report, the person intending to make the proposal shall submit to the nominee—

(a) a document setting out the terms of the proposed voluntary arrangement, and

(b) a statement of the company's affairs containing—

(i) such particulars of its creditors and of its debts and other liabilities and of its assets as may be prescribed, and

(ii) such other information as may be prescribed.

[(4) The court may—

(a) on an application made by the person intending to make the proposal, in a case where the nominee has failed to submit the report required by this section or has died, or

(b) on an application made by that person or the nominee, in a case where it is impracticable or inappropriate for the nominee to continue to act as such,

direct that the nominee be replaced as such by another person qualified to act as an insolvency practitioner . . . in relation to the voluntary arrangement.]

NOTES

Sub-s (1): the words omitted were originally inserted by the Insolvency Act 2000, s 1, Sch 1, paras 1, 3, as from 1 January 2003; and were subsequently repealed by the Corporate Insolvency and Governance Act 2020, s 2(1), Sch 3, paras 1, 3, as from 26 June 2020 (for transitional provisions, see s 2(2), (3) of the 2020 Act (at **[9.533]**) which provides that (without prejudice to the Interpretation Act 1978, s 16) nothing in the 2020 Act affects the operation of this Act, or any other enactment, in relation to a moratorium under Sch A1 to this Act which comes into force before the repeal of that Schedule by Sch 3 to the 2020 Act (ie, 26 June 2020)).

Sub-s (2): words in first pair of square brackets inserted by the Insolvency Act 2000, s 2, Sch 2, Pt I, paras 1, 3(a), as from 1 January 2003. Paras (b), (c) substituted by the Small Business, Enterprise and Employment Act 2015, s 126, Sch 9, Pt 1, paras 1, 2, as from 6 April 2017 (in relation to England and Wales), and as from 6 April 2019 (in relation to Scotland) (for transitional and savings provisions, see the notes to s 246ZE at **[9.385]**).

Sub-s (4): substituted by the Insolvency Act 2000, s 2, Sch 2, Pt I, paras 1, 3(b), as from 1 January 2003. Words omitted repealed by the Deregulation Act 2015, s 19, Sch 6, Pt 6, para 20(1), (2)(b), as from 1 October 2015.

[9.138]

3 [Consideration of proposal]

(1) Where the nominee under section 1 is not the liquidator or administrator, and it has been reported to the court [under section 2(2) that the proposal should be considered by a meeting of the company and by the company's creditors], the person making the report shall (unless the court otherwise [directs)—

(a) summon a meeting of the company to consider the proposal for the time, date and place proposed in the report, and

(b) seek a decision from the company's creditors as to whether they approve the proposal.]

(2) Where the nominee is the liquidator or administrator, he [shall—

(a) summon a meeting of the company to consider the proposal for such time, date and place as he thinks fit, and

(b) seek a decision from the company's creditors as to whether they approve the proposal.]

[(3) A decision of the company's creditors as to whether they approve the proposal is to be made by a qualifying decision procedure.

(4) Notice of the qualifying decision procedure must be given to every creditor of the company of whose claim and address the person seeking the decision is aware.]

NOTES

Section heading: words in square brackets substituted by the Small Business, Enterprise and Employment Act 2015, s 126, Sch 9, Pt 1, paras 1, 3(1), (5), as from 6 April 2017 (in relation to England and Wales), and as from 6 April 2019 (in relation to Scotland) (for transitional and savings provisions, see the notes to s 246ZE at **[9.385]**).

Sub-ss (1), (2): words in square brackets substituted by the Small Business, Enterprise and Employment Act 2015, s 126, Sch 9, Pt 1, paras 1, 3(1)–(3), as from 6 April 2017 (in relation to England and Wales), and as from 6 April 2019 (in relation to Scotland) (for transitional and savings provisions, see the notes to s 246ZE at **[9.385]**).

Sub-ss (3), (4): substituted (for the original sub-s (3)) by the Small Business, Enterprise and Employment Act 2015, s 126, Sch 9, Pt 1, paras 1, 3(1), (4), as from 6 April 2017 (in relation to England and Wales), and as from 6 April 2019 (in relation to Scotland) (for transitional and savings provisions, see the notes to s 246ZE at **[9.385]**).

Consideration and implementation of proposal

[9.139]

4 Decisions of [the company and its creditors]

[(1) This section applies where, under section 3—

(a) a meeting of the company is summoned to consider the proposed voluntary arrangement, and

(b) the company's creditors are asked to decide whether to approve the proposed voluntary arrangement.

(1A) The company and its creditors may approve the proposed voluntary arrangement with or without modifications.]

(2) The modifications may include one conferring the functions proposed to be conferred on the nominee on another person qualified to act as an insolvency practitioner [. . . in relation to the voluntary arrangement].

But they shall not include any modification by virtue of which the proposal ceases to be a proposal such as is mentioned in section 1.

(3) [Neither the company nor its creditors may] approve any proposal or modification which affects the right of a secured creditor of the company to enforce his security, except with the concurrence of the creditor concerned.

(4) Subject as follows, [neither the company nor its creditors may] approve any proposal or modification under which—

(a) any preferential debt of the company is to be paid otherwise than in priority to such of its debts as are not preferential debts, . . .

[(aa) any ordinary preferential debt of the company is to be paid otherwise than in priority to any secondary preferential debts that it may have,]

(b) a preferential creditor of the company is to be paid an amount in respect of [an ordinary preferential debt] that bears to that debt a smaller proportion than is borne to [another ordinary] preferential debt by the amount that is to be paid in respect of that other debt[, . . .

(c) a preferential creditor of the company is to be paid an amount in respect of a secondary preferential debt that bears to that debt a smaller proportion than is borne to another secondary preferential debt by the amount that is to be paid in respect of that other debt] [or

(d) in the case of a company which is a relevant financial institution (see section 387A), any non-preferential debt is to be paid otherwise than in accordance with the rules in section 176AZA(2) or (3).]

However, . . . such a proposal or modification [may be approved] with the concurrence of the . . . creditor concerned.

[(4A) Subject to subsection (4B), where the nominee's report under section 2(2) is submitted to the court before the end of the period of 12 weeks beginning with the day after the end of any moratorium for the company under Part A1, neither the company nor its creditors may approve any proposal or modification under which the following are to be paid otherwise than in full—

(a) moratorium debts (within the meaning given by section 174A);

(b) priority pre-moratorium debts (within the meaning given by section 174A).

(4B) Subsection (4A) does not prevent the approval of such a proposal or modification with the concurrence of the creditor concerned.]

(5) Subject as above, [the meeting of the company and the qualifying decision procedure] shall be conducted in accordance with the rules.

(6) After the conclusion of [the company] meeting in accordance with the rules, the chairman of the meeting shall report the result of the meeting to the court, and, immediately after reporting to the court, shall give notice of the result of the meeting to such persons as may be prescribed.

[(6A) After the company's creditors have decided whether to approve the proposed voluntary arrangement the person who sought the decision must—

(a) report the creditors' decision to the court, and

(b) immediately after reporting to the court, give notice of the creditors' decision to such persons as may be prescribed.]

(7) References in this section to preferential debts[, ordinary preferential debts, secondary preferential debts] and preferential creditors are to be read in accordance with section 386 in Part XII of this Act.

NOTES

Section heading: words in square brackets substituted by the Small Business, Enterprise and Employment Act 2015, s 126, Sch 9, Pt 1, paras 1, 4(1), (8), as from 6 April 2017 (in relation to England and Wales), and as from 6 April 2019 (in relation to Scotland) (for transitional and savings provisions, see the notes to s 246ZE at **[9.385]**).

Sub-ss (1), (1A): substituted (for the original sub-s (1)) by the Small Business, Enterprise and Employment Act 2015, s 126, Sch 9, Pt 1, paras 1, 4(1), (2), as from 6 April 2017 (in relation to England and Wales), and as from 6 April 2019 (in relation to Scotland) (for transitional and savings provisions, see the notes to s 246ZE at **[9.385]**).

Sub-s (2): words in square brackets substituted by the Insolvency Act 2000, s 2, Sch 2, Pt I, paras 1, 4, as from 1 January 2003. Words omitted repealed by the Deregulation Act 2015, s 19, Sch 6, Pt 6, para 20(1), (2)(c), as from 1 October 2015.

Sub-s (3): words in square brackets substituted by the Small Business, Enterprise and Employment Act 2015, s 126, Sch 9, Pt 1, paras 1, 4(1), (3), as from 6 April 2017 (in relation to England and Wales), and as from 6 April 2019 (in relation to Scotland) (for transitional and savings provisions, see the notes to s 246ZE at **[9.385]**).

Sub-s (4) is amended as follows:

The words in the first pair of square brackets were substituted, the penultimate words omitted were repealed, and the words "may be approved" in square brackets were inserted, by the Small Business, Enterprise and Employment Act 2015, s 126, Sch 9, Pt 1, paras 1, 4(1), (4), as from 6 April 2017 (in relation to England and Wales), and as from 6 April 2019 (in relation to Scotland) (for transitional and savings provisions, see the notes to s 246ZE at **[9.385]**).

The word omitted from the end of para (a) was repealed, para (aa) was inserted, the words in the first and second pairs of square brackets in para (b) were substituted, and para (c) (and the preceding word) was added, by the Banks and Building Societies (Depositor Preference and Priorities) Order 2014, SI 2014/3486, arts 3, 4(1), (2), as from 1 January 2015, except in relation to any insolvency proceedings commenced before that date (see further the penultimate note below).

The word omitted from the end of para (b) was repealed, para (d) (and the preceding word) was inserted, and the final word omitted was repealed, by the Banks and Building Societies (Priorities on Insolvency) Order 2018, SI 2018/1244, arts 4, 5, as from 19 December 2018, except in relation to any insolvency proceedings commenced before that date (see further the final note below).

Sub-ss (4A), (4B): inserted by the Corporate Insolvency and Governance Act 2020, s 2(1), Sch 3, paras 1, 4, as from 26 June 2020 (for transitional provisions, see s 2(2), (3) of the 2020 Act (at **[9.533]**) which provides that (without prejudice to the Interpretation Act 1978, s 16) nothing in the 2020 Act affects the operation of this Act, or any other enactment, in relation to a moratorium under Sch A1 to this Act which comes into force before the repeal of that Schedule by Sch 3 to the 2020 Act (ie, 26 June 2020)).

Sub-ss (5), (6): words in square brackets substituted by the Small Business, Enterprise and Employment Act 2015, s 126, Sch 9, Pt 1, paras 1, 4(1), (5), (6), as from 6 April 2017 (in relation to England and Wales), and as from 6 April 2019 (in relation to Scotland) (for transitional and savings provisions, see the notes to s 246ZE at **[9.385]**).

Sub-s (6A): inserted by the Small Business, Enterprise and Employment Act 2015, s 126, Sch 9, Pt 1, paras 1, 4(1), (7), as from 6 April 2017 (in relation to England and Wales), and as from 6 April 2019 (in relation to Scotland) (for transitional and savings provisions, see the notes to s 246ZE at **[9.385]**).

Sub-s (7): words in square brackets inserted by SI 2014/3486, arts 3, 4(1), (3), as from 1 January 2015, except in relation to any insolvency proceedings commenced before that date (see further the final note below).

See also the Bank Recovery and Resolution (Amendment) (EU Exit) Regulations 2020, SI 2020/1350. Regulations 108–114 make amendments to various provisions of this Act (including this section) which come into force on 28 December 2020 and cease to have effect (in accordance with reg 1 of the 2020 Regulations) on IP completion day (as defined in the European Union (Withdrawal Agreement) Act 2020, s 39).

Note that art 3(2)(b) of the Banks and Building Societies (Depositor Preference and Priorities) Order 2014, SI 2014/3486 provides that for the purposes of the 2014 Order, insolvency proceedings commence on (i) the date of presentation of a petition for a winding-up order, bank insolvency order, building society insolvency order, bankruptcy order or award of sequestration; (ii) the date on which an application is made for an administration order, bank administration order or building society administration order; (iii) the date on which notice of appointment of an administrator is given under paragraph 18 or 29 of Schedule B1 to the Insolvency Act 1986; (iv) the date on which a proposal is made by the directors of a company for a company voluntary arrangement under Part 1 of the Insolvency Act 1986 or by an individual debtor for an individual voluntary arrangement under Part 8 of the Insolvency Act 1986; (v) the date on which a resolution for voluntary winding up is passed.

Note that art 3(2)(b) of the Banks and Building Societies (Priorities on Insolvency) Order 2018, SI 2018/1244 provides that for the purposes of the 2018 Order, insolvency proceedings commence on (i) the date of presentation of a petition for a winding-up order, bank insolvency order, special administration (bank insolvency) order, building society insolvency order, bankruptcy order or award of sequestration; (ii) the date on which an application is made for an administration order, bank administration order, investment bank special administration order, special administration (bank administration) order or building society special administration order; (iii) the date on which notice of appointment of an administrator is given under paragraph 18 or 29 of Schedule B1 to the Insolvency Act 1986; (iv) the date on which a proposal is made by the directors of a company for a company voluntary arrangement under Part 1 of the Insolvency Act 1986 or by an individual debtor for an individual voluntary arrangement under Part 8 of the Insolvency Act 1986; (v) the date on which a resolution for voluntary winding up is passed.

[9.140]

[4A Approval of arrangement

(1) This section applies to a decision, under section 4, with respect to the approval of a proposed voluntary arrangement.

(2) The decision has effect if, in accordance with the rules—

- (a) it has been taken by [the meeting of the company summoned under section 3 and by the company's creditors pursuant to that section], or
- (b) (subject to any order made under subsection [(6)]) it has been taken by the [company's creditors pursuant to] that section.

(3) If the decision taken by the [company's creditors] differs from that taken by the company meeting, a member of the company may apply to the court.

(4) An application under subsection (3) shall not be made after the end of the period of 28 days beginning with—

- (a) the day on which the decision was taken by the [company's creditors], or
- (b) where the decision of the company meeting was taken on a later day, that day.

(5) Where a member of a regulated company, [as defined by section A49(13)], applies to the court under subsection (3), the [appropriate regulator] is entitled to be heard on the application.

[(5A) "The appropriate regulator" means—

- (a) where the regulated company is a PRA-regulated company [as defined by section A49(13)], the Financial Conduct Authority and the Prudential Regulation Authority, and
- (b) in any other case, the Financial Conduct Authority.]

(6) On an application under subsection (3), the court may—

- (a) order the decision of the company meeting to have effect instead of the decision of the [company's creditors], or
- (b) make such other order as it thinks fit.]

NOTES

Inserted by the Insolvency Act 2000, s 2, Sch 2, Pt I, paras 1, 5, as from 1 January 2003.

Sub-s (2): words in square brackets in paras (a), (b) substituted by the Small Business, Enterprise and Employment Act 2015, s 126, Sch 9, Pt 1, paras 1, 5(1), (2), as from 6 April 2017 (in relation to England and Wales), and as from 6 April 2019 (in relation to Scotland) (for transitional and savings provisions, see the notes to s 246ZE at **[9.385]**). The number "(6)" in square brackets was substituted by the Corporate Insolvency and Governance Act 2020, s 2(1), Sch 3, paras 1, 5(1), (2), as from 26 June 2020 (for transitional provisions, see s 2(2), (3) of the 2020 Act (at **[9.533]**) which provides that (without prejudice to the Interpretation Act 1978, s 16) nothing in the 2020 Act affects the operation of this Act, or any other enactment, in relation to a moratorium under Sch A1 to this Act which comes into force before the repeal of that Schedule by Sch 3 to the 2020 Act (ie, 26 June 2020)).

Sub-ss (3), (4), (6): words in square brackets substituted by the Small Business, Enterprise and Employment Act 2015, s 126, Sch 9, Pt 1, paras 1, 5, as from 6 April 2017 (in relation to England and Wales), and as from 6 April 2019 (in relation to Scotland) (for transitional and savings provisions, see the notes to s 246ZE at **[9.385]**).

Words "appropriate regulator" in square brackets in sub-s (5) substituted, and sub-s (5A) inserted, by the Financial Services Act 2012, s 114(1), Sch 18, Pt 2, paras 51, 52, as from 1 April 2013. The words "as defined by section A49(13)" in square brackets in sub-ss (5) and (5A) were substituted by the Corporate Insolvency and Governance Act 2020, s 2(1), Sch 3, paras 1, 5(1), (3), (4), as from 26 June 2020 (for transitional provisions, see the first note relating to the 2020 Act above).

[9.141]

5 Effect of approval

[(1) This section applies where a decision approving a voluntary arrangement has effect under section 4A.]

(2) The . . . voluntary arrangement—

(a) takes effect as if made by the company at the [time the creditors decided to approve the voluntary arrangement], and

[(b) binds every person who in accordance with the rules—

(i) was entitled to vote [in the qualifying decision procedure by which the creditors' decision to approve the voluntary arrangement was made], or

(ii) would have been so entitled if he had had notice of it,

as if he were a party to the voluntary arrangement.]

[(2A) If—

(a) when the arrangement ceases to have effect any amount payable under the arrangement to a person bound by virtue of subsection (2)(b)(ii) has not been paid, and

(b) the arrangement did not come to an end prematurely,

the company shall at that time become liable to pay to that person the amount payable under the arrangement.]

(3) Subject as follows, if the company is being wound up or [is in administration], the court may do one or both of the following, namely—

(a) by order stay or sist all proceedings in the winding up or [provide for the appointment of the administrator to cease to have effect];

(b) give such directions with respect to the conduct of the winding up or the administration as it thinks appropriate for facilitating the implementation of the . . . voluntary arrangement.

[(3A) Where immediately before the voluntary arrangement took effect a moratorium for the company was in force under Part A1 and a petition for the winding up of the company, other than an excepted petition within the meaning of section A20, was presented before the beginning of the moratorium, the court must dismiss the petition.]

(4) The court shall not make an order under subsection (3)(a) [or dismiss a petition under subsection (3A)]—

(a) at any time before the end of the period of 28 days beginning with the first day on which each of the reports required by section 4(6) [and (6A)] has been made to the court, or

(b) at any time when an application under the next section or an appeal in respect of such an application is pending, or at any time in the period within which such an appeal may be brought.

NOTES

Sub-s (1): substituted by the Insolvency Act 2000, s 2, Sch 2, Pt I, paras 1, 6(a), as from 1 January 2003.

Sub-s (2): word omitted repealed, and para (b) substituted (together with sub-s (2A) for the original para (b)), by the Insolvency Act 2000, ss 2, 15(1), Sch 2, Pt I, paras 1, 6(b), (c), Sch 5, as from 1 January 2003. Words in square brackets in paras (a), (b)(i) substituted by the Small Business, Enterprise and Employment Act 2015, s 126, Sch 9, Pt 1, paras 1, 6(1), (2), as from 6 April 2017 (in relation to England and Wales), and as from 6 April 2019 (in relation to Scotland) (for transitional and savings provisions, see the notes to s 246ZE at **[9.385]**).

Sub-s (2A): substituted as noted above.

Sub-s (3): words in square brackets substituted by the Enterprise Act 2002, s 248(3), Sch 17, paras 9, 11, as from 15 September 2003 (for savings and transitional provisions, see the note to s 8 at **[9.147]**). Word omitted repealed by the Insolvency Act 2000, ss 2, 15(1), Sch 2, Pt I, paras 1, 6(b), Sch 5, as from 1 January 2003.

Sub-s (3A): inserted by the Corporate Insolvency and Governance Act 2020, s 2(1), Sch 3, paras 1, 6(1), (2), as from 26 June 2020 (for transitional provisions, see s 2(2), (3) of the 2020 Act (at **[9.533]**) which provides that (without prejudice to the Interpretation Act 1978, s 16) nothing in the 2020 Act affects the operation of this Act, or any other enactment, in relation to a moratorium under Sch A1 to this Act which comes into force before the repeal of that Schedule by Sch 3 to the 2020 Act (ie, 26 June 2020)).

Sub-s (4): words in first pair of square brackets inserted by the Corporate Insolvency and Governance Act 2020, s 2(1), Sch 3, paras 1, 6(1), (3), as from 26 June 2020 (for transitional provisions, see the first note relating to the 2020 Act above). Words in second pair of square brackets inserted by the Small Business, Enterprise and Employment Act 2015, s 126, Sch 9, Pt 1, paras 1, 6(1), (3), as from 6 April 2017 (in relation to England and Wales), and as from 6 April 2019 (in relation to Scotland) (for transitional and savings provisions, see the notes to s 246ZE at **[9.385]**).

[9.142]

6 Challenge of decisions

(1) Subject to this section, an application to the court may be made, by any of the persons specified below, on one or both of the following grounds, namely—

(a) that a voluntary arrangement [which has effect under section 4A] unfairly prejudices the interests of a creditor, member or contributory of the company;

(b) that there has been some material irregularity at or in relation to [the meeting of the company, or in relation to the relevant qualifying decision procedure].

[(1A) In this section—

(a) the "relevant qualifying decision procedure" means the qualifying decision procedure in which the company's creditors decide whether to approve a voluntary arrangement;

(b) references to a decision made in the relevant qualifying decision procedure include any other decision made in that qualifying decision procedure.]

(2) The persons who may apply under [subsection (1)] are—

(a) a person entitled, in accordance with the rules, to vote at [the meeting of the company or in the relevant qualifying decision procedure];

[(aa) a person who would have been entitled, in accordance with the rules, to vote [in the relevant qualifying decision procedure] if he had had notice of it]

(b) the nominee or any person who has replaced him under section 2(4) or 4(2); and

(c) if the company is being wound up or [is in administration], the liquidator or administrator.

(3) An application under this section shall not be made

[(a)] after the end of the period of 28 days beginning with the first day on which each of the reports required by section 4(6) [and (6A)] has been made to the court [or

(b) in the case of a person who was not given notice of the [relevant qualifying decision procedure], after the end of the period of 28 days beginning with the day on which he became aware that [the relevant qualifying decision procedure] had taken place,

but (subject to that) an application made by a person within subsection (2)(aa) on the ground that the voluntary arrangement prejudices his interests may be made after the arrangement has ceased to have effect, unless it came to an end prematurely.]

(4) Where on such an application the court is satisfied as to either of the grounds mentioned in subsection (1), it may do [any] of the following, namely—

(a) revoke or suspend [any decision approving the voluntary arrangement which has effect under section 4A] or, in a case falling within subsection (1)(b), any [decision taken by the meeting [of the company, or in the relevant qualifying decision procedure,] which has effect under that section];

(b) give a direction to any person for the summoning of [a further company meeting] to consider any revised proposal the person who made the original proposal may make or, in a case falling within subsection (1)(b) [and relating to the company meeting, a further company] meeting to reconsider the original proposal;

[(c) direct any person—

(i) to seek a decision from the company's creditors (using a qualifying decision procedure) as to whether they approve any revised proposal the person who made the original proposal may make, or

(ii) in a case falling within subsection (1)(b) and relating to the relevant qualifying decision procedure, to seek a decision from the company's creditors (using a qualifying decision procedure) as to whether they approve the original proposal].

(5) Where at any time after giving a direction under subsection (4)(b) [or (c) in relation to] a revised proposal the court is satisfied that the person who made the original proposal does not intend to submit a revised proposal, the court shall revoke the direction and revoke or suspend any [decision approving the voluntary arrangement which has effect under section 4A].

(6) In a case where the court, on an application under this section with respect to any meeting [or relevant qualifying decision procedure]—

(a) gives a direction under subsection (4)(b) [or (c)], or

(b) revokes or suspends an approval under subsection (4)(a) or (5),

the court may give such supplemental directions as it thinks fit and, in particular, directions with respect to things done [under the voluntary arrangement since it took effect].

(7) Except in pursuance of the preceding provisions of this section—

[(a)] [a decision taken] at a [company] meeting summoned under section 3 is not invalidated by any irregularity at or in relation to the meeting[, and

(b) a decision of the company's creditors made in the relevant qualifying decision procedure is not invalidated by any irregularity in relation to the relevant qualifying decision procedure].

[(8) In this section "in energy administration" and "objective of the energy administration" are to be construed in accordance with Schedule B1 to this Act, as applied by Part 1 of Schedule 20 to the Energy Act 2004.]

NOTES

Sub-s (1): words in square brackets in para (a) substituted by the Insolvency Act 2000, s 2, Sch 2, Pt I, paras 1, 7(1), (2), as from 1 January 2003. Words in square brackets in para (b) substituted by the Small Business, Enterprise and Employment Act 2015, s 126, Sch 9, Pt 1, paras 1, 7(1), (2), as from 6 April 2017 (in relation to England and Wales), and as from 6 April 2019 (in relation to Scotland) (for transitional and savings provisions, see the notes to s 246ZE at **[9.385]**).

Sub-s (1A): inserted by the Small Business, Enterprise and Employment Act 2015, s 126, Sch 9, Pt 1, paras 1, 7(1), (3), as from 6 April 2017 (in relation to England and Wales), and as from 6 April 2019 (in relation to Scotland) (for transitional and savings provisions, see the notes to s 246ZE at **[9.385]**).

Sub-s (2): para (aa) inserted by the Insolvency Act 2000, s 2, Sch 2, Pt I, paras 1, 7(1), (3), as from 1 January 2003. Words in square brackets in para (c) substituted by the Enterprise Act 2002, s 248(3), Sch 17, paras 9, 12, as from 15 September 2003 (for savings and transitional provisions, see the note to s 8 at **[9.147]**). Words in square brackets in paras (a), (aa) substituted by the Small Business, Enterprise and Employment Act 2015, s 126, Sch 9, Pt 1, paras 1, 7(1), (4), as from 6 April 2017 (in relation to England and Wales), and as from 6 April 2019 (in relation to Scotland) (for transitional and savings provisions, see the notes to s 246ZE at **[9.385]**).

Sub-s (3): words "and (6A)" in square brackets inserted, words "relevant qualifying decision procedure" and "the relevant qualifying decision procedure" substituted, by the Small Business, Enterprise and Employment Act 2015, s 126, Sch 9, Pt 1, paras 1, 7(1), (5), (6), as from 6 April 2017 (in relation to England and Wales), and as from 6 April 2019 (in relation to Scotland) (for transitional and savings provisions, see the notes to s 246ZE at **[9.385]**). Other words in square brackets inserted by the Insolvency Act 2000, s 2, Sch 2, Pt I, paras 1, 7(1), (4), as from 1 January 2003.

Sub-s (4): word in first pair of square brackets substituted, words in third (inner) pair of square brackets in sub-para (a) substituted, in sub-para (b) words in first and second pairs of square brackets substituted, and para (c) added, by the Small Business, Enterprise and Employment Act 2015, s 126, Sch 9, Pt 1, paras 1, 7(1), (7)–(10), as from 6 April 2017 (in relation to England and Wales), and as from 6 April 2019 (in relation to Scotland) (for transitional and savings provisions, see the notes to s 246ZE at **[9.385]**). Words in first and second (outer) pairs of square brackets in sub-para (a) substituted by the Insolvency Act 2000, s 2, Sch 2, Pt I, paras 1, 7(1), (5), as from 1 January 2003.

Sub-s (5): words in first pair of square brackets substituted by the Small Business, Enterprise and Employment Act 2015, s 126, Sch 9, Pt 1, paras 1, 7(1), (11), as from 6 April 2017 (in relation to England and Wales), and as from 6 April 2019 (in relation to Scotland) (for transitional and savings provisions, see the notes to s 246ZE at **[9.385]**). Words in second pair of square brackets substituted by the Insolvency Act 2000, s 2, Sch 2, Pt I, paras 1, 7(1), (6), as from 1 January 2003.

Sub-s (6): words in first and second pairs of square brackets inserted by the Small Business, Enterprise and Employment Act 2015, s 126, Sch 9, Pt 1, paras 1, 7(1), (12), as from 6 April 2017 (in relation to England and Wales), and as from 6 April 2019 (in relation to Scotland) (for transitional and savings provisions, see the notes to s 246ZE at **[9.385]**). Words in third pair of square brackets substituted by the Insolvency Act 2000, s 2, Sch 2, Pt I, paras 1, 7(1), (7), as from 1 January 2003.

Sub-s (7): para (a) designated as such, word "company" in square brackets inserted, and para (b) added, by the Small Business, Enterprise and Employment Act 2015, s 126, Sch 9, Pt 1, paras 1, 7(1), (13), as from 6 April 2017 (in relation to England and Wales), and as from 6 April 2019 (in relation to Scotland) (for transitional and savings provisions, see the notes to s 246ZE at **[9.385]**). Words "a decision taken" in square brackets substituted by the Insolvency Act 2000, s 2, Sch 2, Pt I, paras 1, 7(1), (8), as from 1 January 2003.

Sub-s (8): added by the Energy Act 2004, s 159(1), Sch 20, Pt 4, para 44(1), (5).

[9.143]

[6A False representations, etc

(1) If, for the purpose of obtaining the approval of the members or creditors of a company to a proposal for a voluntary arrangement, a person who is an officer of the company—

(a) makes any false representation, or

(b) fraudulently does, or omits to do, anything,

he commits an offence.

(2) Subsection (1) applies even if the proposal is not approved.

(3) For purposes of this section "officer" includes a shadow director.

(4) A person guilty of an offence under this section is liable to imprisonment or a fine, or both.]

NOTES

Inserted by the Insolvency Act 2000, s 2, Sch 2, Pt I, paras 1, 8, as from 1 January 2003.

[9.144]

7 Implementation of proposal

(1) This section applies where a voluntary arrangement [has effect under section 4A].

(2) The person who is for the time being carrying out in relation to the voluntary arrangement the functions conferred—

[(a) on the nominee by virtue of the approval [of the voluntary arrangement by the company or its creditors (or both) pursuant to] section 3] or

(b) by virtue of section 2(4) or 4(2) on a person other than the nominee,

shall be known as the supervisor of the voluntary arrangement.

(3) If any of the company's creditors or any other person is dissatisfied by any act, omission or decision of the supervisor, he may apply to the court; and on the application the court may—

(a) confirm, reverse or modify any act or decision of the supervisor,

(b) give him directions, or

(c) make such other order as it thinks fit.

(4) The supervisor—

(a) may apply to the court for directions in relation to any particular matter arising under the voluntary arrangement, and

(b) is included among the persons who may apply to the court for the winding up of the company or for an administration order to be made in relation to it.

(5) The court may, whenever—

(a) it is expedient to appoint a person to carry out the functions of the supervisor, and

(b) it is inexpedient, difficult or impracticable for an appointment to be made without the assistance of the court,

make an order appointing a person who is qualified to act as an insolvency practitioner [. . . in relation to the voluntary arrangement] either in substitution for the existing supervisor or to fill a vacancy.

(6) The power conferred by subsection (5) is exercisable so as to increase the number of persons exercising the functions of supervisor or, where there is more than one person exercising those functions, so as to replace one or more of those persons.

NOTES

Sub-s (1): words in square brackets substituted by the Insolvency Act 2000, s 2, Sch 2, Pt I, paras 1, 9(a)), as from 1 January 2003.

Sub-s (2): para (a) substituted by the Insolvency Act 2000, s 2, Sch 2, Pt I, paras 1, 9(b), as from 1 January 2003. Words in square brackets in para (a) substituted by the Small Business, Enterprise and Employment Act 2015, s 126, Sch 9, Pt 1, paras 1, 8, as from 6 April 2017 (in relation to England and Wales), and as from 6 April 2019 (in relation to Scotland) (for transitional and savings provisions, see the notes to s 246ZE at **[9.385]**).

Sub-s (5): words in square brackets substituted by the Insolvency Act 2000, s 2, Sch 2, Pt I, paras 1, 9(c), as from 1 January 2003. Words omitted repealed by the Deregulation Act 2015, s 19, Sch 6, Pt 6, para 20(1), (2)(d), as from 1 October 2015.

[9.145]

[7A Prosecution of delinquent officers of company

[(1) This section applies where the approval of a voluntary arrangement in relation to a company has taken effect under section 4A.]

(2) [If it appears to the supervisor that any past or present officer of the company has committed an offence in connection with the voluntary arrangement, the supervisor must forthwith]—

(a) report the matter to the appropriate authority, and

(b) provide the appropriate authority with such information and give the authority such access to and facilities for inspecting and taking copies of documents (being information or documents in the possession or under the control of the . . . supervisor and relating to the matter in question) as the authority requires.

In this subsection, "the appropriate authority" means—

(i) in the case of a company registered in England and Wales, the Secretary of State, and

(ii) in the case of a company registered in Scotland, the Lord Advocate.

(3) Where a report is made to the Secretary of State under subsection (2), he may, for the purpose of investigating the matter reported to him and such other matters relating to the affairs of the company as appear to him to require investigation, exercise any of the powers which are exercisable by inspectors appointed under section 431 or 432 of [the Companies Act 1985] to investigate a company's affairs.

(4) For the purpose of such an investigation any obligation imposed on a person by any provision of [the Companies Acts] to produce documents or give information to, or otherwise to assist, inspectors so appointed is to be regarded as an obligation similarly to assist the Secretary of State in his investigation.

(5) An answer given by a person to a question put to him in exercise of the powers conferred by subsection (3) may be used in evidence against him.

(6) However, in criminal proceedings in which that person is charged with an offence to which this subsection applies—

(a) no evidence relating to the answer may be adduced, and

(b) no question relating to it may be asked,

by or on behalf of the prosecution, unless evidence relating to it is adduced, or a question relating to it is asked, in the proceedings by or on behalf of that person.

(7) Subsection (6) applies to any offence other than—

(a) an offence under section 2 or 5 of the Perjury Act 1911 (false statements made on oath otherwise than in judicial proceedings or made otherwise than on oath), or

(b) an offence under section 44(1) or (2) of the Criminal Law (Consolidation) (Scotland) Act 1995 (false statements made on oath or otherwise than on oath).

(8) Where a prosecuting authority institutes criminal proceedings following any report under subsection (2), the . . . supervisor, and every officer and agent of the company past and present (other than the defendant or defender), shall give the authority all assistance in connection with the prosecution which he is reasonably able to give.

For this purpose—

"agent" includes any banker or solicitor of the company and any person employed by the company as auditor, whether that person is or is not an officer of the company,

"prosecuting authority" means the Director of Public Prosecutions, the Lord Advocate or the Secretary of State.

(9) The court may, on the application of the prosecuting authority, direct any person referred to in subsection (8) to comply with that subsection if he has failed to do so.]

NOTES

Inserted, together with s 7B, by the Insolvency Act 2000, s 2, Sch 2, Pt I, paras 1, 10, as from 1 January 2003.

Sub-s (1): substituted by the Corporate Insolvency and Governance Act 2020, s 2(1), Sch 3, paras 1, 7(1), (2), as from 26 June 2020 (for transitional provisions, see s 2(2), (3) of the 2020 Act (at **[9.533]**) which provides that (without prejudice to the Interpretation Act 1978, s 16) nothing in the 2020 Act affects the operation of this Act, or any other enactment, in relation to a moratorium under Sch A1 to this Act which comes into force before the repeal of that Schedule by Sch 3 to the 2020 Act (ie, 26 June 2020)).

Sub-s (2): words in square brackets substituted, and words omitted repealed, by the Corporate Insolvency and Governance Act 2020, s 2(1), Sch 3, paras 1, 7(1), (3), as from 26 June 2020 (for transitional provisions, see the first note relating to the 2020 Act above).

Sub-ss (3), (4): words in square brackets substituted by the Companies Act 2006 (Consequential Amendments, Transitional Provisions and Savings) Order 2009, SI 2009/1941, art 2(1), Sch 1, para 71(1), (3), as from 1 October 2009 (for effect see the note below).

Sub-s (8): words omitted repealed by the Corporate Insolvency and Governance Act 2020, s 2(1), Sch 3, paras 1, 7(1), (4), as from 26 June 2020 (for transitional provisions, see the first note relating to the 2020 Act above).

Transitional provisions: the Companies Act 2006 (Consequential Amendments, Transitional Provisions and Savings) Order 2009, SI 2009/1941, art 8 (at **[4.362]**) provides as follows—

"8 Amendments of insolvency legislation

(1) The amendments by this Order of the Insolvency Act 1986 ("the 1986 Act") and the Insolvency (Northern Ireland) Order 1989 ("the 1989 Order") apply as follows.

(2) They apply where, in a company voluntary arrangement, a moratorium comes into force in relation to a company on or after 1st October 2009.

(3) They apply where a company enters administration on or after 1st October 2009, except where—

(a) it enters administration by virtue of an administration order under paragraph 10 of Schedule B1 to the 1986 Act (or paragraph 11 of Schedule B1 to the 1989 Order) on an application made before 1st October 2009,

(b) the administration is immediately preceded by a voluntary liquidation in respect of which the resolution to wind up was passed before 1st October 2009, or

(c) the administration is immediately preceded by a liquidation on the making of a winding-up order on a petition which was presented before 1st October 2009.

(4) They apply where, in a receivership, a receiver or manager is appointed in respect of a company on or after 1st October 2009.

(5) They apply where a company goes into liquidation upon the passing on or after 1st October 2009 of a resolution to wind up.

(6) They apply where a company goes into voluntary liquidation under paragraph 83 of Schedule B1 to the 1986 Act (or paragraph 84 of Schedule B1 to the 1989 Order), except where the preceding administration—

(a) commenced before 1st October 2009, or

(b) is an administration which commenced by virtue of an administration order under paragraph 10 of Schedule B1 to the 1986 Act (or paragraph 11 of Schedule B1 to the 1989 Order) on an application which was made before

1st October 2009.

(7) They apply where a company goes into liquidation on the making of a winding-up order on a petition presented on or after 1st October 2009, except where the liquidation is immediately preceded by—

(a) an administration under paragraph 10 of Schedule B1 to the 1986 Act (or paragraph 11 of Schedule B1 to the 1989 Order) where the administration order was made on an application made before 1st October 2009,

(b) an administration in respect of which the appointment of an administrator under paragraph 14 or 22 of Schedule B1 to the 1986 Act (or paragraph 15 or 23 of Schedule B1 to the 1989 Order) took effect before 1st October 2009, or

(c) a voluntary liquidation in respect of which the resolution to wind up was passed before 1st October 2009.".

[9.146]

[7B Arrangements coming to an end prematurely

For the purposes of this Part, a voluntary arrangement the approval of which has taken effect under section 4A . . . comes to an end prematurely if, when it ceases to have effect, it has not been fully implemented in respect of all persons bound by the arrangement by virtue of section 5(2)(b)(i) . . .]

NOTES

Inserted as noted to s 7A at **[9.145]**.

Words omitted repealed by the Corporate Insolvency and Governance Act 2020, s 2(1), Sch 3, paras 1, 8, as from 26 June 2020 (for transitional provisions, see s 2(2), (3) of the 2020 Act (at **[9.533]**) which provides that (without prejudice to the Interpretation Act 1978, s 16) nothing in the 2020 Act affects the operation of this Act, or any other enactment, in relation to a moratorium under Sch A1 to this Act which comes into force before the repeal of that Schedule by Sch 3 to the 2020 Act (ie, 26 June 2020)).

[PART II ADMINISTRATION

[9.147]

8 Administration

Schedule B1 to this Act (which makes provision about the administration of companies) shall have effect.]

NOTES

This section was substituted for the original Pt II of this Act (ss 8–27) by the Enterprise Act 2002, s 248(1), as from 15 September 2003, subject to the following savings and transitional provisions:

Savings in relation to special administration regimes:

The Enterprise Act 2002, s 249(1), (2) (Special administration regimes) provides as follows (note that s 248 substituted this section for the original Part II as noted above)—

"(1) Section 248 shall have no effect in relation to—

(a) a company holding an appointment under Chapter I of Part II of the Water Industry Act 1991 (c 56) (water and sewerage undertakers),

[(aa) a qualifying [water supply licensee] within the meaning of subsection (6) of section 23 of the Water Industry Act 1991 (meaning and effect of special administration order) [or a qualifying sewerage licensee within the meaning of subsection (8) of that section],]

(b) a protected railway company within the meaning of section 59 of the Railways Act 1993 (c 43) (railway administration order) (including that section as it has effect by virtue of section 19 of the Channel Tunnel Rail Link Act 1996 (c 61) (administration)),

(c) a licence company within the meaning of section 26 of the Transport Act 2000 (c 38) (air traffic services),

(d) a public-private partnership company within the meaning of section 210 of the Greater London Authority Act 1999 (c 29) (public-private partnership agreement), or

(e) a building society within the meaning of section 119 of the Building Societies Act 1986 (c 53) (interpretation).

(2) A reference in an Act listed in subsection (1) to a provision of Part II of the Insolvency Act 1986 (or to a provision which has effect in relation to a provision of that Part of that Act) shall, in so far as it relates to a company or society listed in subsection (1), continue to have effect as if it referred to Part II as it had effect immediately before the coming into force of section 248.".

In s 249 as set out above: (i) para (aa) was inserted by the Water Act 2003, s 101(1), Sch 8, para 55(1), (3), as from 1 December 2005, and that paragraph (and para (a)) are repealed by the Flood and Water Management Act 2010, s 34, Sch 5, para 6(3), as from a day to be appointed; (ii) the words in the first pair of square brackets in para (aa) were substituted, and the words in the second pair of square brackets were inserted, by the Water Act 2014, s 56, Sch 7, paras 128, 130, as from 1 April 2017.

The original Part II of this Act (ss 8–27) as it stood without the amendment made by the Enterprise Act 2002 (ie, as it applies by virtue of s 249(1) of the 2002 Act, and art 3(2) or (3) of the Enterprise Act 2002 (Commencement No 4 and Transitional Provisions and Savings) Order 2003 (as to which, see below)) has also been amended by a variety of enactments. It is considered that these are outside the scope of this work.

Transitional provisions:

The Enterprise Act 2002 (Commencement No 4 and Transitional Provisions and Savings) Order 2003, SI 2003/2093, art 3, provides as follows (note that by virtue of art 2(1) "the first commencement date" means 15 September 2003)—

"3 Administration—transitional provisions

(1) In this article "the former administration provisions" means the law relating to administration under Part II of the Insolvency Act 1986 and section 62(2)(a) of the Criminal Justice Act 1988 without the amendments and repeals made by the provisions of the Enterprise Act 2002 mentioned in paragraph (2).

(2) In a case where a petition for an administration order has been presented before the first commencement date—

(a) section 248 and Schedules 16 and 17; and

(b) section 278(2) and Schedule 26 as respects the repeals relating to sections 212, 230(1), 231, 232, 240(1) and 245(3) of the Insolvency Act 1986, the entries in Schedule 10 to the Insolvency Act 1986 in respect of sections 12(2), 15(8), 18(5), 21(3), 22(6), 23(3), 24(7) and 27(6) of that Act and section 62(2)(a) of the Criminal Justice Act 1988,

shall have no effect.

(3) The former administration provisions shall continue to apply insofar as is necessary to give effect to—

(a) the Insolvent Partnerships Order 1994;

(b) regulation 5 of the Limited Liability Partnerships Regulations 2001; and

(c) the Financial Services and Markets Act 2000 (Administration Orders relating to Insurers) Order 2002.".

See also the note "Savings for certain insolvency rules" in the introductory notes to this Act *ante*.

The Enterprise Act 2002, Sch 17, para 1 provides that in any instrument made before s 248(1)–(3) of the 2002 Act comes into force: (a) a reference to the making of an administration order shall be treated as including a reference to the appointment of an administrator under Sch B1, para 14 or 22 to this Act (as inserted by s 248(2) of the 2002 Act), and (b) a reference to making an application for an administration order by petition shall be treated as including a reference to making an administration application under that Schedule, appointing an administrator under para 14 or 22 of that Schedule or giving notice under para 15 or 26 of that Schedule.

PART III RECEIVERSHIP

CHAPTER I RECEIVERS AND MANAGERS (ENGLAND AND WALES)

Preliminary and general provisions

[9.148]

[28 Extent of this Chapter

(1) In this Chapter "company" means a company registered under the Companies Act 2006 in England and Wales or Scotland.

(2) This Chapter does not apply to receivers appointed under Chapter 2 of this Part (Scotland).]

NOTES

Substituted by the Companies Act 2006 (Consequential Amendments, Transitional Provisions and Savings) Order 2009, SI 2009/1941, art 2(1), Sch 1, para 74(1), (2), as from 1 October 2009 (for effect see the note to s 7A at **[9.145]**).

[9.149]

29 Definitions

(1) It is hereby declared that, except where the context otherwise requires—

(a) any reference in . . . this Act to a receiver or manager of the property of a company, or to a receiver of it, includes a receiver or manager, or (as the case may be) a receiver of part only of that property and a receiver only of the income arising from the property or from part of it; and

(b) any reference in . . . this Act to the appointment of a receiver or manager under powers contained in an instrument includes an appointment made under powers which, by virtue of an enactment, are implied in and have effect as if contained in an instrument.

(2) In this Chapter "administrative receiver" means—

(a) a receiver or manager of the whole (or substantially the whole) of a company's property appointed by or on behalf of the holders of any debentures of the company secured by a charge which, as created, was a floating charge, or by such a charge and one or more other securities; or

(b) a person who would be such a receiver or manager but for the appointment of some other person as the receiver of part of the company's property.

NOTES

Sub-s (1): words omitted repealed by the Companies Act 2006 (Consequential Amendments, Transitional Provisions and Savings) Order 2009, SI 2009/1941, art 2(1), Sch 1, para 74(1), (3), as from 1 October 2009 (for effect see the note to s 7A at **[9.145]**).

[9.150]

30 Disqualification of body corporate from acting as receiver

A body corporate is not qualified for appointment as receiver of the property of a company, and any body corporate which acts as such a receiver is liable to a fine.

[9.151]

[31 Disqualification of bankrupt [or person in respect of whom a debt relief order is made]

(1) A person commits an offence if he acts as receiver or manager of the property of a company on behalf of debenture holders while—

(a) he is an undischarged bankrupt,

[(aa) a moratorium period under a debt relief order applies in relation to him,] or

(b) a bankruptcy restrictions order [or a debt relief restrictions order] is in force in respect of him.

(2) A person guilty of an offence under subsection (1) shall be liable to imprisonment, a fine or both.

(3) This section does not apply to a receiver or manager acting under an appointment made by the court.]

NOTES

Substituted by the Enterprise Act 2002, s 257(3), Sch 21, para 1, as from 1 April 2004.

Section heading: words in square brackets inserted by the Tribunals, Courts and Enforcement Act 2007, s 108(3), Sch 20, Pt 1, paras 1, 2(2), as from 6 April 2009.

Sub-s (1): para (aa) inserted, and words in square brackets in para (b) inserted, by the Tribunals, Courts and Enforcement Act 2007, s 108(3), Sch 20, Pt 1, paras 1, 2(1), as from 6 April 2009.

[9.152]

32 Power for court to appoint official receiver

Where application is made to the court to appoint a receiver on behalf of the debenture holders or other creditors of a company which is being wound up by the court, the official receiver may be appointed.

Receivers and managers appointed out of court

[9.153]

33 Time from which appointment is effective

(1) The appointment of a person as a receiver or manager of a company's property under powers contained in an instrument—

(a) is of no effect unless it is accepted by that person before the end of the business day next following that on which the instrument of appointment is received by him or on his behalf, and

(b) subject to this, is deemed to be made at the time at which the instrument of appointment is so received.

(2) This section applies to the appointment of two or more persons as joint receivers or managers of a company's property under powers contained in an instrument, subject to such modifications as may be prescribed by the rules.

[9.154]
34 Liability for invalid appointment

Where the appointment of a person as the receiver or manager of a company's property under powers contained in an instrument is discovered to be invalid (whether by virtue of the invalidity of the instrument or otherwise), the court may order the person by whom or on whose behalf the appointment was made to indemnify the person appointed against any liability which arises solely by reason of the invalidity of the appointment.

[9.155]
35 Application to court for directions

(1) A receiver or manager of the property of a company appointed under powers contained in an instrument, or the persons by whom or on whose behalf a receiver or manager has been so appointed, may apply to the court for directions in relation to any particular matter arising in connection with the performance of the functions of the receiver or manager.

(2) On such an application, the court may give such directions, or may make such order declaring the rights of persons before the court or otherwise, as it thinks just.

[9.156]
36 Court's power to fix remuneration

(1) The court may, on an application made by the liquidator of a company, by order fix the amount to be paid by way of remuneration to a person who, under powers contained in an instrument, has been appointed receiver or manager of the company's property.

(2) The court's power under subsection (1), where no previous order has been made with respect thereto under the subsection—

(a) extends to fixing the remuneration for any period before the making of the order or the application for it,

(b) is exercisable notwithstanding that the receiver or manager has died or ceased to act before the making of the order or the application, and

(c) where the receiver or manager has been paid or has retained for his remuneration for any period before the making of the order any amount in excess of that so fixed for that period, extends to requiring him or his personal representatives to account for the excess or such part of it as may be specified in the order.

But the power conferred by paragraph (c) shall not be exercised as respects any period before the making of the application for the order under this section, unless in the court's opinion there are special circumstances making it proper for the power to be exercised.

(3) The court may from time to time on an application made either by the liquidator or by the receiver or manager, vary or amend an order made under subsection (1).

[9.157]
37 Liability for contracts, etc

(1) A receiver or manager appointed under powers conferred in an instrument (other than an administrative receiver) is, to the same extent as if he had been appointed by order of the court—

(a) personally liable on any contract entered into by him in the performance of his functions (except in so far as the contract otherwise provides) and on any contract of employment adopted by him in the performance of those functions, and

(b) entitled in respect of that liability to indemnity out of the assets.

(2) For the purposes of subsection (1)(a), the receiver or manager is not to be taken to have adopted a contract of employment by reason of anything done or omitted to be done within 14 days after his appointment.

(3) Subsection (1) does not limit any right to indemnity which the receiver or manager would have apart from it, nor limit his liability on contracts entered into without authority, nor confer any right to indemnity in respect of that liability.

(4) Where at any time the receiver or manager so appointed vacates office—

(a) his remuneration and any expenses properly incurred by him, and

(b) any indemnity to which he is entitled out of the assets of the company,

shall be charged on and paid out of any property of the company which is in his custody or under his control at that time in priority to any charge or other security held by the person by or on whose behalf he was appointed.

[9.158]
38 Receivership accounts to be delivered to registrar

(1) Except in the case of an administrative receiver, every receiver or manager of a company's property who has been appointed under powers contained in an instrument shall deliver to the registrar of companies for registration the requisite accounts of his receipts and payments.

(2) The accounts shall be delivered within one month (or such longer period as the registrar may allow) after the expiration of 12 months from the date of his appointment and of every subsequent period of 6 months, and also within one month after he ceases to act as receiver or manager.

(3) The requisite accounts shall be an abstract in the prescribed form showing—

(a) receipts and payments during the relevant period of 12 or 6 months, or

(b) where the receiver or manager ceases to act, receipts and payments during the period from the end of the period of 12 or 6 months to which the last preceding abstract related (or, if no preceding abstract has been delivered under this section, from the date of his appointment) up to the date of his so ceasing, and the aggregate amount of receipts and payments during all preceding periods since his appointment.

(4) In this section "prescribed" means prescribed by regulations made by statutory instrument by the Secretary of State.

(5) A receiver or manager who makes default in complying with this section is liable to a fine and, for continued contravention, to a daily default fine.

NOTES

Regulations: the Companies and Limited Liability Partnerships (Forms, etc) Amendment Regulations 2013, SI 2013/1947.

Provisions applicable to every receivership

[9.159]

39 Notification that receiver or manager appointed

[(1) Where a receiver or manager of the property of a company has been appointed—

(a) every invoice, order for goods or services, business letter or order form (whether in hard copy, electronic or any other form) issued by or on behalf of the company or the receiver or manager or the liquidator of the company; and

(b) all the company's websites,

must contain a statement that a receiver or manager has been appointed.]

(2) If default is made in complying with this section, the company and any of the following persons, who knowingly and wilfully authorises or permits the default, namely, any officer of the company, any liquidator of the company and any receiver or manager, is liable to a fine.

NOTES

Sub-s (1): substituted by the Companies (Trading Disclosures) (Insolvency) Regulations 2008, SI 2008/1897, reg 2(1), as from 1 October 2008.

[9.160]

40 Payment of debts out of assets subject to floating charge

(1) The following applies, in the case of a company, where a receiver is appointed on behalf of the holders of any debentures of the company secured by a charge which, as created, was a floating charge.

(2) If the company is not at the time in course of being wound up, its preferential debts (within the meaning given to that expression by section 386 in Part XII) shall be paid out of the assets coming to the hands of the receiver in priority to any claims for principal or interest in respect of the debentures.

(3) Payments made under this section shall be recouped, as far as may be, out of the assets of the company available for payment of general creditors.

[9.161]

41 Enforcement of duty to make returns

(1) If a receiver or manager of a company's property—

(a) having made default in filing, delivering or making any return, account or other document, or in giving any notice, which a receiver or manager is by law required to file, deliver, make or give, fails to make good the default within 14 days after the service on him of a notice requiring him to do so, or

(b) having been appointed under powers contained in an instrument, has, after being required at any time by the liquidator of the company to do so, failed to render proper accounts of his receipts and payments and to vouch them and pay over to the liquidator the amount properly payable to him,

the court may, on an application made for the purpose, make an order directing the receiver or manager (as the case may be) to make good the default within such time as may be specified in the order.

(2) In the case of the default mentioned in subsection (1)(a), application to the court may be made by any member or creditor of the company or by the registrar of companies; and in the case of the default mentioned in subsection (1)(b), the application shall be made by the liquidator.

In either case the court's order may provide that all costs of and incidental to the application shall be borne by the receiver or manager, as the case may be.

(3) Nothing in this section prejudices the operation of any enactment imposing penalties on receivers in respect of any such default as is mentioned in subsection (1).

Administrative receivers: general

[9.162]

42 General powers

(1) The powers conferred on the administrative receiver of a company by the debentures by virtue of which he was appointed are deemed to include (except in so far as they are inconsistent with any of the provisions of those debentures) the powers specified in Schedule 1 to this Act.

(2) In the application of Schedule 1 to the administrative receiver of a company—

(a) the words "he" and "him" refer to the administrative receiver, and

(b) references to the property of the company are to the property of which he is or, but for the appointment of some other person as the receiver of part of the company's property, would be the receiver or manager.

(3) A person dealing with the administrative receiver in good faith and for value is not concerned to inquire whether the receiver is acting within his powers.

[9.163]

43 Power to dispose of charged property, etc

(1) Where, on an application by the administrative receiver, the court is satisfied that the disposal (with or without other assets) of any relevant property which is subject to a security would be likely to promote a more advantageous realisation of the company's assets than would otherwise be effected, the court may by order authorise the administrative receiver to dispose of the property as if it were not subject to the security.

(2) Subsection (1) does not apply in the case of any security held by the person by or on whose behalf the administrative receiver was appointed, or of any security to which a security so held has priority.

(3) It shall be a condition of an order under this section that—

(a) the net proceeds of the disposal, and
(b) where those proceeds are less than such amount as may be determined by the court to be the net amount which would be realised on a sale of the property in the open market by a willing vendor, such sums as may be required to make good the deficiency,

shall be applied towards discharging the sums secured by the security.

(4) Where a condition imposed in pursuance of subsection (3) relates to two or more securities, that condition shall require the net proceeds of the disposal and, where paragraph (b) of that subsection applies, the sums mentioned in that paragraph to be applied towards discharging the sums secured by those securities in the order of their priorities.

(5) [A copy] of an order under this section shall, within 14 days of the making of the order, be sent by the administrative receiver to the registrar of companies.

(6) If the administrative receiver without reasonable excuse fails to comply with subsection (5), he is liable to a fine and, for continued contravention, to a daily default fine.

(7) In this section "relevant property", in relation to the administrative receiver, means the property of which he is or, but for the appointment of some other person as the receiver of part of the company's property, would be the receiver or manager.

NOTES

Sub-s (5): words in square brackets substituted by the Companies Act 2006 (Consequential Amendments, Transitional Provisions and Savings) Order 2009, SI 2009/1941, art 2(1), Sch 1, para 74(1), (4), as from 1 October 2009 (for effect see the note to s 7A at **[9.145]**).

[9.164]

44 Agency and liability for contracts

(1) The administrative receiver of a company—
(a) is deemed to be the company's agent, unless and until the company goes into liquidation;
(b) is personally liable on any contract entered into by him in the carrying out of his functions (except in so far as the contract otherwise provides) and[, to the extent of any qualifying liability,] on any contract of employment adopted by him in the carrying out of those functions; and
(c) is entitled in respect of that liability to an indemnity out of the assets of the company.

(2) For the purposes of subsection (1)(b) the administrative receiver is not to be taken to have adopted a contract of employment by reason of anything done or omitted to be done within 14 days after his appointment.

[(2A) For the purposes of subsection (1)(b), a liability under a contract of employment is a qualifying liability if—
(a) it is a liability to pay a sum by way of wages or salary or contribution to an occupational pension scheme,
(b) it is incurred while the administrative receiver is in office, and
(c) it is in respect of services rendered wholly or partly after the adoption of the contract.

(2B) Where a sum payable in respect of a liability which is a qualifying liability for the purposes of subsection (1)(b) is payable in respect of services rendered partly before and partly after the adoption of the contract, liability under subsection (1)(b) shall only extend to so much of the sum as is payable in respect of services rendered after the adoption of the contract.

(2C) For the purposes of subsections (2A) and (2B)—
(a) wages or salary payable in respect of a period of holiday or absence from work through sickness or other good cause are deemed to be wages or (as the case may be) salary in respect of services rendered in that period, and
(b) a sum payable in lieu of holiday is deemed to be wages or (as the case may be) salary in respect of services rendered in the period by reference to which the holiday entitlement arose.

(2D) . . .]

(3) This section does not limit any right to indemnity which the administrative receiver would have apart from it, nor limit his liability on contracts entered into or adopted without authority, nor confer any right to indemnity in respect of that liability.

NOTES

The words in square brackets in sub-s (1)(b) were inserted, and sub-ss (2A)–(2D) were inserted, by the Insolvency Act 1994, s 2, in relation to contracts of employment adopted on or after 15 March 1994.

Sub-s (2D): subsequently repealed by the Deregulation Act 2015, s 19, Sch 6, Pt 7, paras 24, 26, as from 26 May 2015.

[9.165]

45 Vacation of office

(1) An administrative receiver of a company may at any time be removed from office by order of the court (but not otherwise) and may resign his office by giving notice of his resignation in the prescribed manner to such persons as may be prescribed.

(2) An administrative receiver shall vacate office if he ceases to be qualified to act as an insolvency practitioner in relation to the company.

(3) Where at any time an administrative receiver vacates office—
(a) his remuneration and any expenses properly incurred by him, and
(b) any indemnity to which he is entitled out of the assets of the company,

shall be charged on and paid out of any property of the company which is in his custody or under his control at that time in priority to any security held by the person by or on whose behalf he was appointed.

(4) Where an administrative receiver vacates office otherwise than by death, he shall, within 14 days after his vacation of office, send a notice to that effect to the registrar of companies.

(5) If an administrative receiver without reasonable excuse fails to comply with subsection (4), he is liable to a fine *and, for continued contravention, to a daily default fine*.

NOTES

Sub-s (5): the words in italics are repealed by the Companies Act 1989, ss 107, 212, Sch 16, para 3, Sch 24, as from a day to be appointed (see the note below).

Repeals made by the Companies Act 1989, Sch 24: note that s 107 of, and Sch 16 to, the 1989 Act (in Part IV of that Act) made amendments consequential on the other provisions of Part IV (Registration of company charges) and that the whole of that Part was repealed by the Companies Act 2006, as from 1 October 2009, without coming into force. Although the repeal of the words in italics still exists in Sch 24 to the 1989 Act (ie, Sch 24 was not amended accordingly), it is believed that this amendment will never be brought into force.

Administrative receivers: ascertainment and investigation of company's affairs

[9.166]

46 Information to be given by administrative receiver

(1) Where an administrative receiver is appointed, he shall—

(a) forthwith send to the company and publish in the prescribed manner a notice of his appointment, and

(b) within 28 days after his appointment, unless the court otherwise directs, send such a notice to all the creditors of the company (so far as he is aware of their addresses).

(2) This section and the next do not apply in relation to the appointment of an administrative receiver to act—

(a) with an existing administrative receiver, or

(b) in place of an administrative receiver dying or ceasing to act,

except that, where they apply to an administrative receiver who dies or ceases to act before they have been fully complied with, the references in this section and the next to the administrative receiver include (subject to the next subsection) his successor and any continuing administrative receiver.

(3) If the company is being wound up, this section and the next apply notwithstanding that the administrative receiver and the liquidator are the same person, but with any necessary modifications arising from that fact.

(4) If the administrative receiver without reasonable excuse fails to comply with this section, he is liable to a fine and, for continued contravention, to a daily default fine.

[9.167]

47 Statement of affairs to be submitted

(1) Where an administrative receiver is appointed, he shall forthwith require some or all of the persons mentioned below to make out and submit to him a statement in the prescribed form as to the affairs of the company.

(2) A statement submitted under this section shall be verified by [a statement of truth] by the persons required to submit it and shall show—

(a) particulars of the company's assets, debts and liabilities;

(b) the names and addresses of its creditors;

(c) the securities held by them respectively;

(d) the dates when the securities were respectively given; and

(e) such further or other information as may be prescribed.

(3) The persons referred to in subsection (1) are—

(a) those who are or have been officers of the company;

(b) those who have taken part in the company's formation at any time within one year before the date of the appointment of the administrative receiver;

(c) those who are in the company's employment, or have been in its employment within that year, and are in the administrative receiver's opinion capable of giving the information required;

(d) those who are or have been within that year officers of or in the employment of a company which is, or within that year was, an officer of the company.

In this subsection "employment" includes employment under a contract for services.

(4) Where any persons are required under this section to submit a statement of affairs to the administrative receiver, they shall do so (subject to the next subsection) before the end of the period of 21 days beginning with the day after that on which the prescribed notice of the requirement is given to them by the administrative receiver.

(5) The administrative receiver, if he thinks fit, may—

(a) at any time release a person from an obligation imposed on him under subsection (1) or (2), or

(b) either when giving notice under subsection (4) or subsequently, extend the period so mentioned;

and where the administrative receiver has refused to exercise a power conferred by this subsection, the court, if it thinks fit, may exercise it.

(6) If a person without reasonable excuse fails to comply with any obligation imposed under this section, he is liable to a fine and, for continued contravention, to a daily default fine.

NOTES

Sub-s (2): words in square brackets substituted by the Legislative Reform (Insolvency) (Miscellaneous Provisions) Order 2010, SI 2010/18, arts 2, 5(1), as from 6 April 2010.

[9.168]

48 Report by administrative receiver

(1) Where an administrative receiver is appointed, he shall, within 3 months (or such longer period as the court may allow) after his appointment, send to the registrar of companies, to any trustees for secured creditors of the company and (so far as he is aware of their addresses) to all such creditors[, other than opted-out creditors,] a report as to the following matters, namely—

(a) the events leading up to his appointment, so far as he is aware of them;

(b) the disposal or proposed disposal by him of any property of the company and the carrying on or proposed carrying on by him of any business of the company;

(c) the amounts of principal and interest payable to the debenture holders by whom or on whose behalf he was appointed and the amounts payable to preferential creditors; and

(d) the amount (if any) likely to be available for the payment of other creditors.

(2) The administrative receiver shall also, within 3 months (or such longer period as the court may allow) after his appointment, either—

(a) send a copy of the report (so far as he is aware of their addresses) to all unsecured creditors of the company[, other than opted-out creditors,]; or

(b) publish in the prescribed manner a notice stating an address to which unsecured creditors of the company should write for copies of the report to be sent to them free of charge,

. . .

(3) . . .

(4) Where the company has gone or goes into liquidation, the administrative receiver—

(a) shall, within 7 days after his compliance with subsection (1) or, if later, the nomination or appointment of the liquidator, send a copy of the report to the liquidator, and

(b) where he does so within the time limited for compliance with subsection (2), is not required to comply with that subsection.

(5) A report under this section shall include a summary of the statement of affairs made out and submitted to the administrative receiver under section 47 and of his comments (if any) upon it.

(6) Nothing in this section is to be taken as requiring any such report to include any information the disclosure of which would seriously prejudice the carrying out by the administrative receiver of his functions.

(7) Section 46(2) applies for the purposes of this section also.

(8) If the administrative receiver without reasonable excuse fails to comply with this section, he is liable to a fine and, for continued contravention, to a daily default fine.

NOTES

Words in square brackets in sub-ss (1), (2)(a) inserted, words omitted from sub-s (2) repealed, and sub-s (3) repealed, by the Small Business, Enterprise and Employment Act 2015, s 126, Sch 9, Pt 1, paras 1, 12, as from 6 April 2017 (in relation to England and Wales), and as from 6 April 2019 (in relation to Scotland) (for transitional and savings provisions, see the notes to s 246ZE at **[9.385]**).

[9.169]

49 Committee of creditors

(1) [Where an administrative receiver has sent or published a report as mentioned in section 48(2) the company's unsecured creditors may, in accordance with the rules], establish a committee ("the creditors' committee") to exercise the functions conferred on it by or under this Act.

(2) If such a committee is established, the committee may, on giving not less than 7 days' notice, require the administrative receiver to attend before it at any reasonable time and furnish it with such information relating to the carrying out by him of his functions as it may reasonably require.

NOTES

Sub-s (1): words in square brackets substituted by the Small Business, Enterprise and Employment Act 2015, s 126, Sch 9, Pt 1, paras 1, 13, as from 6 April 2017 (in relation to England and Wales), and as from 6 April 2019 (in relation to Scotland) (for transitional and savings provisions, see the notes to s 246ZE at **[9.385]**).

CHAPTER II RECEIVERS (SCOTLAND)

[9.170]

50 Extent of this Chapter

This Chapter extends to Scotland only.

[9.171]

51 Power to appoint receiver

(1) It is competent under the law of Scotland for the holder of a floating charge over all or any part of the property (including uncalled capital), which may from time to time be comprised in the property and undertaking of an incorporated company (whether [a company registered under the Companies Act 2006] or not)—

[(a) which the Court of Session has jurisdiction to wind up; or

(b) where paragraph (a) does not apply, in respect of which a court of a member state . . . has under the EU Regulation jurisdiction to open insolvency proceedings,

to appoint a receiver of such part of the property of the company as is subject to the charge].

(2) It is competent under the law of Scotland for the court, on the application of the holder of such a floating charge, to appoint a receiver of such part of the property of the company as is subject to the charge.

[(2ZA) . . .]

[(2A) Subsections (1) and (2) are subject to section 72A.]

(3) The following are disqualified from being appointed as receiver—

(a) a body corporate;

(b) an undischarged bankrupt; and

[(ba) a person subject to a bankruptcy restrictions order;]

(c) a firm according to the law of Scotland.

(4) A body corporate or a firm according to the law of Scotland which acts as a receiver is liable to a fine.

(5) An undischarged bankrupt [or a person subject to a bankruptcy restrictions order] who so acts is liable to imprisonment or a fine, or both.

(6) In this section, "receiver" includes joint receivers[; and

"bankruptcy restrictions order" means—

(a) a bankruptcy restrictions order made under section [155 of the Bankruptcy (Scotland) Act 2016];

(b) . . .

(c) a bankruptcy restrictions order made under paragraph 1 of Schedule 4A to this Act; or

(d) a bankruptcy restrictions undertaking entered into under paragraph 7 of that Schedule

["the EU Regulation" is [Regulation (EU) 2015/848 of the European Parliament and of the Council] on insolvency proceedings [as that Regulation has effect in the law of the European Union];

"court" is to be construed in accordance with [Article 2(6)] of the EU Regulation;

"insolvency proceedings" is to be construed in accordance with [Article 2(4)] of the EU Regulation]].

NOTES

Sub-s (1): words in first pair of square brackets substituted by the Companies Act 2006 (Consequential Amendments, Transitional Provisions and Savings) Order 2009, SI 2009/1941, art 2(1), Sch 1, para 74(1), (5), as from 1 October 2009 (for effect see the note to s 7A at **[9.145]**). Words in second pair of square brackets substituted by the Insolvency Act 1986 Amendment (Appointment of Receivers) (Scotland) Regulations 2011, SSI 2011/140, reg 2(a), as from 17 March 2011. The words omitted from para (b) were repealed by the Insolvency (EU Exit) (Scotland) (Amendment) Regulations 2019, SSI 2019/94, reg 2(1), (2)(a), as from IP completion day (as defined in the European Union (Withdrawal Agreement) Act 2020, s 39) (for savings see the note below).

Sub-s (2ZA): originally inserted by SSI 2011/140, reg 2(b), as from 17 March 2011. Subsequently repealed by the Public Services Reform (Insolvency) (Scotland) Order 2016, SSI 2016/141, art 2, as from 1 April 2016 (for transitional provisions, see art 14 of the 2016 Order which provides that where a receiver is appointed in respect of a company under this section before 1 April 2016, this section continues to have effect on and after that date as if the amendment made in art 2 had not been made.)

Sub-s (2A): inserted by the Enterprise Act 2002, s 248(3), Sch 17, paras 9, 13, as from 15 September 2003 (for savings and transitional provisions, see the note to s 8 at **[9.147]**).

Sub-ss (3), (5): words in square brackets inserted by the Bankruptcy and Diligence etc (Scotland) Act 2007, s 3(1)–(3), as from 1 April 2008.

Sub-s (6): words in first (outer) pair of square brackets inserted by the Bankruptcy and Diligence etc (Scotland) Act 2007, s 3(1), (4), as from 1 April 2008. Words in square brackets in para (a) of the definition "bankruptcy restrictions order" substituted by the Bankruptcy (Scotland) Act 2016 (Consequential Provisions and Modifications) Order 2016, SI 2016/1034, art 7(1), (3), Sch 1, para 4(1), (2), as from 30 November 2016 (except in relation to (i) a sequestration as regards which the petition is presented, or the debtor application is made before that date; or (ii) a trust deed executed before that date). Para (b) of the definition "bankruptcy restrictions order" repealed by the Bankruptcy and Debt Advice (Scotland) Act 2014, s 56(2), Sch 4, as from 1 April 2015 (for transitional provisions see the Bankruptcy and Debt Advice (Scotland) Act 2014 (Commencement No 2, Savings and Transitionals) Order 2014, SSI 2015/261). Definitions "the EU Regulation", "court", and "insolvency proceedings" inserted by SSI 2011/140, reg 2(c), as from 17 March 2011. The words in the first pair of square brackets in the definition "the EU Regulation", and the words in square brackets in the definitions "court", and "insolvency proceedings", were inserted by the Insolvency (Regulation (EU) 2015/848) (Miscellaneous Amendments) (Scotland) Regulations 2017, SSI 2017/210, reg 2, as from 26 June 2017. The words in the second pair of square brackets in the definition "the EU Regulation" were inserted by SSI 2019/94, reg 2(1), (2)(b), as from IP completion day (as defined in the European Union (Withdrawal Agreement) Act 2020, s 39) (for savings see the note below).

Savings: the Insolvency (EU Exit) (Scotland) (Amendment) Regulations 2019, SSI 2019/94, reg 9 (as amended by the Insolvency (Amendment) (EU Exit) (Scotland) Regulations 2020, SSI 2020/337, reg 2) provides for the following savings—

"(1) Nothing in these Regulations affects—

(a) . . .

(b) the saving for the existing law in regulation 9 of the Insolvency (Regulation (EU) 2015/848) (Miscellaneous Amendments) (Scotland) Regulations 2017.

(2) The amendments made by regulations 2 to 8 do not apply [in respect of any insolvency proceedings and actions falling within Article 67(3)(c) of the withdrawal agreement].

(3) . . .".

[9.172]

52 Circumstances justifying appointment

(1) A receiver may be appointed under section 51(1) by the holder of the floating charge on the occurrence of any event which, by the provisions of the instrument creating the charge, entitles the holder of the charge to make that appointment and, in so far as not otherwise provided for by the instrument, on the occurrence of any of the following events, namely—

(a) the expiry of a period of 21 days after the making of a demand for payment of the whole or any part of the principal sum secured by the charge, without payment having been made;

(b) the expiry of a period of 2 months during the whole of which interest due and payable under the charge has been in arrears;

(c) the making of an order or the passing of a resolution to wind up the company;

(d) the appointment of a receiver by virtue of any other floating charge created by the company.

(2) A receiver may be appointed by the court under section 51(2) on the occurrence of any event which, by the provisions of the instrument creating the floating charge, entitles the holder of the charge to make that appointment and, in so far as not otherwise provided for by the instrument on the occurrence of any of the following events, namely—

(a) where the court, on the application of the holder of the charge, pronounces itself satisfied that the position of the holder of the charge is likely to be prejudiced if no such appointment is made;

(b) any of the events referred to in paragraphs (a) to (c) of subsection (1).

[9.173]

53 Mode of appointment by holder of charge

(1) The appointment of a receiver by the holder of the floating charge under section 51(1) shall be by means of [an instrument subscribed in accordance with the Requirements of Writing (Scotland) Act 1995] ("the instrument of appointment"), a copy (certified in the prescribed manner to be a correct copy) whereof shall be delivered by or on behalf of the person making the appointment to the registrar of companies for registration within 7 days of its execution and shall be accompanied by a notice in the prescribed form.

(2) If any person without reasonable excuse makes default in complying with the requirements of subsection (1), he is liable to a fine *and, for continued contravention, to a daily default fine.*

(3) . . .

[(4) If the receiver is to be appointed by the holders of a series of secured debentures, the instrument of appointment may be executed on behalf of the holders of the floating charge by any person authorised by resolution of the debenture-holders to execute the instrument.]

(5) On receipt of the certified copy of the instrument of appointment in accordance with subsection (1), the registrar shall, on payment of the prescribed fee, enter the particulars of the appointment in the [register].

(6) The appointment of a person as a receiver by an instrument of appointment in accordance with subsection (1)—

(a) is of no effect unless it is accepted by that person before the end of the business day next following that on which the instrument of appointment is received by him or on his behalf, and

(b) subject to paragraph (a), is deemed to be made on the day on and at the time at which the instrument of appointment is so received, as evidence by a written docquet by that person or on his behalf;

and this subsection applies to the appointment of joint receivers subject to such modifications as may be prescribed.

(7) On the appointment of a receiver under this section, the floating charge by virtue of which he was appointed attaches to the property then subject to the charge; and such attachment has effect as if the charge was a fixed security over the property to which it has attached.

NOTES

Sub-s (1): words in square brackets substituted by the Requirements of Writing (Scotland) Act 1995, s 14(1), Sch 4, para 58(a), as from 1 August 1995.

Sub-s (2): words in italics repealed by the Companies Act 1989, ss 107, 212, Sch 16, para 3, Sch 24, as from a day to be appointed (see further the note to s 45 at **[9.165]**).

Sub-s (3): repealed by the Law Reform (Miscellaneous Provisions) (Scotland) Act 1990, s 74, Sch 8, Pt II, para 35, Sch 9, as from 1 December 1990.

Sub-s (4): substituted by the Requirements of Writing (Scotland) Act 1995, s 14(1), Sch 4, para 58(b), as from 1 August 1995.

Sub-s (5): word in square brackets substituted (for the original words "register of charges") by the Companies Act 2006 (Amendment of Part 25) Regulations 2013, SI 2013/600, reg 5, Sch 2, para 2(1), (2), as from 6 April 2013, in relation to charges created on or after that date (see further the transitional provisions note at **[1.982]**).

Regulations: the Receivers (Scotland) Regulations 1986, SI 1986/1917.

[9.174]

54 Appointment by court

(1) Application for the appointment of a receiver by the court under section 51(2) shall be by petition to the court, which shall be served on the company.

(2) On such an application, the court shall, if it thinks fit, issue an interlocutor making the appointment of the receiver.

(3) A copy (certified by the clerk of the court to be a correct copy) of the court's interlocutor making the appointment shall be delivered by or on behalf of the petitioner to the registrar of companies for registration, accompanied by a notice in the prescribed form within 7 days of the date of the interlocutor or such longer period as the court may allow.

If any person without reasonable excuse makes default in complying with the requirements of this subsection, he is liable to a fine *and, for continued contravention, to a daily default fine*.

(4) On receipt of the certified copy interlocutor in accordance with subsection (3), the registrar shall, on payment of the prescribed fee, enter the particulars of the appointment in the [register].

(5) The receiver is to be regarded as having been appointed on the date of his being appointed by the court.

(6) On the appointment of a receiver under this section, the floating charge by virtue of which he was appointed attaches to the property then subject to the charge; and such attachment has effect as if the charge were a fixed security over the property to which it has attached.

(7) In making rules of court for the purposes of this section, the Court of Session shall have regard to the need for special provision for cases which appear to the court to require to be dealt with as a matter of urgency.

NOTES

Sub-s (3): words in italics repealed by the Companies Act 1989, ss 107, 212, Sch 16, para 3, Sch 24, as from a day to be appointed (see further the note to s 45 at **[9.165]**).

Sub-s (4): word in square brackets substituted (for the original words "register of charges") by the Companies Act 2006 (Amendment of Part 25) Regulations 2013, SI 2013/600, reg 5, Sch 2, para 2(1), (2), as from 6 April 2013, in relation to charges created on or after that date (see further the transitional provisions note at **[1.982]**).

Regulations: the Receivers (Scotland) Regulations 1986, SI 1986/1917.

[9.175]

55 Powers of receiver

(1) Subject to the next subsection, a receiver has in relation to such part of the property of the company as is attached by the floating charge by virtue of which he was appointed, the powers, if any, given to him by the instrument creating that charge.

(2) In addition, the receiver has under this Chapter the powers as respects that property (in so far as these are not inconsistent with any provision contained in that instrument) which are specified in Schedule 2 to this Act.

(3) Subsections (1) and (2) apply—

(a) subject to the rights of any person who has effectually executed diligence on all or any part of the property of the company prior to the appointment of the receiver, and

(b) subject to the rights of any person who holds over all or any part of the property of the company a fixed security or floating charge having priority over, or ranking pari passu with, the floating charge by virtue of which the receiver was appointed.

(4) A person dealing with a receiver in good faith and for value is not concerned to enquire whether the receiver is acting within his powers.

[9.176]

56 Precedence among receivers

(1) Where there are two or more floating charges subsisting over all or any part of the property of the company, a receiver may be appointed under this Chapter by virtue of each such charge; but a receiver appointed by, or on the application of, the holder of a floating charge having priority of ranking over any other floating charge by virtue of which a receiver has been appointed has the powers given to a receiver by section 55 and Schedule 2 to the exclusion of any other receiver.

(2) Where two or more floating charges rank with one another equally, and two or more receivers have been appointed by virtue of such charges, the receivers so appointed are deemed to have been appointed as joint receivers.

(3) Receivers appointed, or deemed to have been appointed, as joint receivers shall act jointly unless the instrument of appointment or respective instruments of appointment otherwise provide.
(4) Subject to subsection (5) below, the powers of a receiver appointed by, or on the application of, the holder of a floating charge are suspended by, and as from the date of, the appointment of a receiver by, or on the application of, the holder of a floating charge having priority of ranking over that charge to such extent as may be necessary to enable the receiver second mentioned to exercise his powers under section 55 and Schedule 2; and any powers so suspended take effect again when the floating charge having priority of ranking ceases to attach to the property then subject to the charge, whether such cessation is by virtue of section 62(6) or otherwise.
(5) The suspension of the powers of a receiver under subsection (4) does not have the effect of requiring him to release any part of the property (including any letters or documents) of the company from his control until he receives from the receiver superseding him a valid indemnity (subject to the limit of the value of such part of the property of the company as is subject to the charge by virtue of which he was appointed) in respect of any expenses, charges and liabilities he may have incurred in the performance of his functions as receiver.
(6) The suspension of the powers of a receiver under subsection (4) does not cause the floating charge by virtue of which he was appointed to cease to attach to the property to which it attached by virtue of section 53(7) or 54(6).
(7) Nothing in this section prevents the same receiver being appointed by virtue of two or more floating charges.

[9.177]
57 Agency and liability of receiver for contracts
(1) A receiver is deemed to be the agent of the company in relation to such property of the company as is attached by the floating charge by virtue of which he was appointed.
[(1A) Without prejudice to subsection (1), a receiver is deemed to be the agent of the company in relation to any contract of employment adopted by him in the carrying out of his functions.]
(2) A receiver (including a receiver whose powers are subsequently suspended under section 56) is personally liable on any contract entered into by him in the performance of his functions, except in so far as the contract otherwise provides, and[, to the extent of any qualifying liability,] on any contract of employment adopted by him in the carrying out of those functions.
[(2A) For the purposes of subsection (2), a liability under a contract of employment is a qualifying liability if—
(a) it is a liability to pay a sum by way of wages or salary or contribution to an occupational pension scheme,
(b) it is incurred while the receiver is in office, and
(c) it is in respect of services rendered wholly or partly after the adoption of the contract.
(2B) Where a sum payable in respect of a liability which is a qualifying liability for the purposes of subsection (2) is payable in respect of services rendered partly before and partly after the adoption of the contract, liability under that subsection shall only extend to so much of the sum as is payable in respect of services rendered after the adoption of the contract.
(2C) For the purposes of subsections (2A) and (2B)—
(a) wages or salary payable in respect of a period of holiday or absence from work through sickness or other good cause are deemed to be wages or (as the case may be) salary in respect of services rendered in that period, and
(b) a sum payable in lieu of holiday is deemed to be wages or (as the case may be) salary in respect of services rendered in the period by reference to which the holiday entitlement arose.
(2D) . . .]
(3) A receiver who is personally liable by virtue of subsection (2) is entitled to be indemnified out of the property in respect of which he was appointed.
(4) Any contract entered into by or on behalf of the company prior to the appointment of a receiver continues in force (subject to its terms) notwithstanding that appointment, but the receiver does not by virtue only of his appointment incur any personal liability on any such contract.
(5) For the purposes of subsection (2), a receiver is not to be taken to have adopted a contract of employment by reason of anything done or omitted to be done within 14 days after his appointment.
(6) This section does not limit any right to indemnity which the receiver would have apart from it, nor limit his liability on contracts entered into or adopted without authority, nor confer any right to indemnity in respect of that liability.
(7) Any contract entered into by a receiver in the performance of his functions continues in force (subject to its terms) although the powers of the receiver are subsequently suspended under section 56.

NOTES

Sub-ss (1A), (2A)–(2D): inserted by the Insolvency Act 1994, s 3(1), (2), (4), (5), in relation to contracts of employment adopted on or after 15 March 1994. Sub-s (2D) subsequently repealed by the Public Services Reform (Insolvency) (Scotland) Order 2016, SSI 2016/141, art 3, as from 1 April 2016.

Sub-s (2): words in square brackets inserted by the Insolvency Act 1994, s 3(1), (3), (5), in relation to contracts of employment adopted on or after 15 March 1994.

[9.178]
58 Remuneration of receiver
(1) The remuneration to be paid to a receiver is to be determined by agreement between the receiver and the holder of the floating charge by virtue of which he was appointed.
(2) Where the remuneration to be paid to the receiver has not been determined under subsection (1), or where it has been so determined but is disputed by any of the persons mentioned in paragraphs (a) to (d) below, it may be fixed instead by the Auditor of the Court of Session on application made to him by—
(a) the receiver;
(b) the holder of any floating charge or fixed security over all or any part of the property of the company;
(c) the company; or
(d) the liquidator of the company.

(3) Where the receiver has been paid or has retained for his remuneration for any period before the remuneration has been fixed by the Auditor of the Court of Session under subsection (2) any amount in excess of the remuneration so fixed for that period, the receiver or his personal representatives shall account for the excess.

[9.179]
59 Priority of debts

(1) Where a receiver is appointed and the company is not at the time of the appointment in course of being wound up, the debts which fall under subsection (2) of this section shall be paid out of any assets coming to the hands of the receiver in priority to any claim for principal or interest by the holder of the floating charge by virtue of which the receiver was appointed.

(2) Debts falling under this subsection are preferential debts (within the meaning given by section 386 in Part XII) which, by the end of a period of 6 months after advertisement by the receiver for claims in the Edinburgh Gazette and in a newspaper circulating in the district where the company carries on business either—

- (i) have been intimated to him, or
- (ii) have become known to him.

(3) Any payments made under this section shall be recouped as far as may be out of the assets of the company available for payment of ordinary creditors.

[9.180]
60 Distribution of moneys

(1) Subject to the next section, and to the rights of any of the following categories of persons (which rights shall, except to the extent otherwise provided in any instrument, have the following order of priority), namely—

- (a) the holder of any fixed security which is over property subject to the floating charge and which ranks prior to, or pari passu with, the floating charge;
- (b) all persons who have effectually executed diligence on any part of the property of the company which is subject to the charge by virtue of which the receiver was appointed;
- (c) creditors in respect of all liabilities, charges and expenses incurred by or on behalf of the receiver;
- (d) the receiver in respect of his liabilities, expenses and remuneration, and any indemnity to which he is entitled out of the property of the company; and
- (e) the preferential creditors entitled to payment under section 59,

the receiver shall pay moneys received by him to the holder of the floating charge by virtue of which the receiver was appointed in or towards satisfaction of the debt secured by the floating charge.

(2) Any balance of moneys remaining after the provisions of subsection (1) and section 61 below have been satisfied shall be paid in accordance with their respective rights and interests to the following persons, as the case may require—

- (a) any other receiver;
- (b) the holder of a fixed security which is over property subject to the floating charge;
- (c) the company or its liquidator, as the case may be.

(3) Where any question arises as to the person entitled to a payment under this section, or where a receipt or a discharge of a security cannot be obtained in respect of any such payment, the receiver shall consign the amount of such payment in any joint stock bank of issue in Scotland in name of the Accountant of Court for behoof of the person or persons entitled thereto.

[9.181]
61 Disposal of interest in property

(1) Where the receiver sells or disposes, or is desirous of selling or disposing, of any property or interest in property of the company which is subject to the floating charge by virtue of which the receiver was appointed and which is—

- (a) subject to any security or interest of, or burden or encumbrance in favour of, a creditor the ranking of which is prior to, or pari passu with, or postponed to the floating charge, or
- (b) property or an interest in property affected or attached by effectual diligence executed by any person,

and the receiver is unable to obtain the consent of such creditor or, as the case may be, such person to such a sale or disposal, the receiver may apply to the court for authority to sell or dispose of the property or interest in property free of such security, interest, burden, encumbrance or diligence.

[(1A) For the purposes of subsection (1) above, an inhibition which takes effect after the creation of the floating charge by virtue of which the receiver was appointed is not an effectual diligence.]

[(1B) For the purposes of subsection (1) above, an arrestment is an effectual diligence only where it is executed before the floating charge, by virtue of which the receiver was appointed, attaches to the property comprised in the company's property and undertaking.]

(2) Subject to the next subsection, on such an application the court may, if it thinks fit, authorise the sale or disposal of the property or interest in question free of such security, interest, burden, encumbrance or diligence, and such authorisation may be on such terms or conditions as the court thinks fit.

(3) In the case of an application where a fixed security over the property or interest in question which ranks prior to the floating charge has not been met or provided for in full, the court shall not authorise the sale or disposal of the property or interest in question unless it is satisfied that the sale or disposal would be likely to provide a more advantageous realisation of the company's assets than would otherwise be effected.

(4) It shall be a condition of an authorisation to which subsection (3) applies that—

- (a) the net proceeds of the disposal, and
- (b) where those proceeds are less than such amount as may be determined by the court to be the net amount which would be realised on a sale of the property or interest in the open market by a willing seller, such sums as may be required to make good the deficiency,

shall be applied towards discharging the sums secured by the fixed security.

(5) Where a condition imposed in pursuance of subsection (4) relates to two or more such fixed securities, that condition shall require the net proceeds of the disposal and, where paragraph (b) of that subsection applies, the sums mentioned in that paragraph to be applied towards discharging the sums secured by those fixed securities in the order of their priorities.

(6) A copy of an authorisation under subsection (2) . . . shall, within 14 days of the granting of the authorisation, be sent by the receiver to the registrar of companies.

(7) If the receiver without reasonable excuse fails to comply with subsection (6), he is liable to a fine and, for continued contravention, to a daily default fine.

(8) Where any sale or disposal is effected in accordance with the authorisation of the court under subsection (2), the receiver shall grant to the purchaser or disponee an appropriate document of transfer or conveyance of the property or interest in question, and that document has the effect, or, where recording, intimation or registration of that document is a legal requirement for completion of title to the property or interest, then that recording, intimation or registration (as the case may be) has the effect, of—

(a) disencumbering the property or interest of the security, interest, burden or encumbrance affecting it, and

(b) freeing the property or interest from the diligence executed upon it.

(9) Nothing in this section prejudices the right of any creditor of the company to rank for his debt in the winding up of the company.

NOTES

Sub-s (1A): inserted by the Bankruptcy and Diligence etc (Scotland) Act 2007, s 155(1), (2), as from 22 April 2009.

Sub-s (1B): inserted by the Bankruptcy and Diligence etc (Scotland) Act 2007, s 226, Sch 5, para 14(1), (2), as from a day to be appointed.

Sub-s (6): words omitted repealed by the Companies Act 2006 (Consequential Amendments, Transitional Provisions and Savings) Order 2009, SI 2009/1941, art 2(1), Sch 1, para 74(1), (6), as from 1 October 2009 (for effect see the note to s 7A at **[9.145]**).

[9.182]

62 Cessation of appointment of receiver

(1) A receiver may be removed from office by the court under subsection (3) below and may resign his office by giving notice of his resignation in the prescribed manner to such persons as may be prescribed.

(2) A receiver shall vacate office if he ceases to be qualified to act as an insolvency practitioner in relation to the company.

(3) Subject to the next subsection, a receiver may, on application to the court by the holder of the floating charge by virtue of which he was appointed, be removed by the court on cause shown.

(4) Where at any time a receiver vacates office—

(a) his remuneration and any expenses properly incurred by him, and

(b) any indemnity to which he is entitled out of the property of the company,

shall be paid out of the property of the company which is subject to the floating charge and shall have priority as provided for in section 60(1).

(5) When a receiver ceases to act as such otherwise than by death he shall, and, when a receiver is removed by the court, the holder of the floating charge by virtue of which he was appointed shall, within 14 days of the cessation or removal (as the case may be) give the registrar of companies notice to that effect, and the registrar shall enter the notice in the [register].

If the receiver or the holder of the floating charge (as the case may require) makes default in complying with the requirements of this subsection, he is liable to a fine *and, for continued contravention, to a daily default fine*.

(6) If by the expiry of a period of one month following upon the removal of the receiver or his ceasing to act as such no other receiver has been appointed, the floating charge by virtue of which the receiver was appointed—

(a) thereupon ceases to attach to the property then subject to the charge, and

(b) again subsists as a floating charge;

and for the purposes of calculating the period of one month under this subsection no account shall be taken of any period during which [the company is in administration,] under Part II of this Act . . .

NOTES

Sub-s (5): word in square brackets substituted (for the original words "register of charges") by the Companies Act 2006 (Amendment of Part 25) Regulations 2013, SI 2013/600, reg 5, Sch 2, para 2(1), (2), as from 6 April 2013, in relation to charges created on or after that date (see further the transitional provisions note at **[1.982]**). Words in italics repealed by the Companies Act 1989, ss 107, 212, Sch 16, para 3, Sch 24, as from a day to be appointed (see further the note to s 45 at **[9.165]**).

Sub-s (6): words in square brackets substituted, and words omitted repealed, by the Enterprise Act 2002 (Insolvency) Order 2003, SI 2003/2096, arts 4, 6, Schedule, Pt 1, paras 8, 9, as from 15 September 2003, except in relation to any case where a petition for an administration order was presented before that date.

Regulations: the Receivers (Scotland) Regulations 1986, SI 1986/1917.

[9.183]

63 Powers of court

(1) The court on the application of—

(a) the holder of a floating charge by virtue of which a receiver was appointed, or

(b) a receiver appointed under section 51,

may give directions to the receiver in respect of any matter arising in connection with the performance by him of his functions.

(2) Where the appointment of a person as a receiver by the holder of a floating charge is discovered to be invalid (whether by virtue of the invalidity of the instrument or otherwise), the court may order the holder of the floating charge to indemnify the person appointed against any liability which arises solely by reason of the invalidity of the appointment.

[9.184]

64 Notification that receiver appointed

[(1) Where a receiver has been appointed—

(a) every invoice, order for goods or services, business letter or order form (whether in hard copy, electronic or any other form) issued by or on behalf of the company or the receiver or the liquidator of the company; and

(b) all the company's websites,

must contain a statement that a receiver has been appointed.]

(2) If default is made in complying with the requirements of this section, the company and any of the following persons who knowingly and wilfully authorises or permits the default, namely any officer of the company, any liquidator of the company and any receiver, is liable to a fine.

NOTES

Sub-s (1): substituted by the Companies (Trading Disclosures) (Insolvency) Regulations 2008, SI 2008/1897, reg 2(2), as from 1 October 2008.

[9.185]

65 Information to be given by receiver

(1) Where a receiver is appointed, he shall—

(a) forthwith send to the company and publish notice of his appointment, and

(b) within 28 days after his appointment, unless the court otherwise directs, send such notice to all the creditors of the company (so far as he is aware of their addresses).

(2) This section and the next do not apply in relation to the appointment of a receiver to act—

(a) with an existing receiver, or

(b) in place of a receiver who has died or ceased to act,

except that, where they apply to a receiver who dies or ceases to act before they have been fully complied with, the references in this section and the next to the receiver include (subject to subsection (3) of this section) his successor and any continuing receiver.

(3) If the company is being wound up, this section and the next apply notwithstanding that the receiver and the liquidator are the same person, but with any necessary modifications arising from that fact.

(4) If a person without reasonable excuse fails to comply with this section, he is liable to a fine and, for continued contravention, to a daily default fine.

NOTES

Regulations: the Receivers (Scotland) Regulations 1986, SI 1986/1917.

[9.186]

66 Company's statement of affairs

(1) Where a receiver of a company is appointed, the receiver shall forthwith require some or all of the persons mentioned in subsection (3) below to make out and submit to him a statement in the prescribed form as to the affairs of the company.

(2) A statement submitted under this section shall [contain a statutory declaration] by the persons required to submit it and shall show—

(a) particulars of the company's assets, debts and liabilities;

(b) the names and addresses of its creditors;

(c) the securities held by them respectively;

(d) the dates when the securities were respectively given; and

(e) such further or other information as may be prescribed.

(3) The persons referred to in subsection (1) are—

(a) those who are or have been officers of the company;

(b) those who have taken part in the company's formation at any time within one year before the date of the appointment of the receiver;

(c) those who are in the company's employment or have been in its employment within that year, and are in the receiver's opinion capable of giving the information required;

(d) those who are or have been within that year officers of or in the employment of a company which is, or within that year was, an officer of the company.

In this subsection "employment" includes employment under a contract for services.

(4) Where any persons are required under this section to submit a statement of affairs to the receiver they shall do so (subject to the next subsection) before the end of the period of 21 days beginning with the day after that on which the prescribed notice of the requirement is given to them by the receiver.

(5) The receiver, if he thinks fit, may—

(a) at any time release a person from an obligation imposed on him under subsection (1) or (2), or

(b) either when giving the notice mentioned in subsection (4) or subsequently extend the period so mentioned,

and where the receiver has refused to exercise a power conferred by this subsection, the court, if it thinks fit, may exercise it.

(6) If a person without reasonable excuse fails to comply with any obligation imposed under this section, he is liable to a fine and, for continued contravention to a daily default fine.

NOTES

Sub-s (2): words in square brackets substituted by the Public Services Reform (Insolvency) (Scotland) Order 2016, SSI 2016/141, art 4, as from 6 April 2019. See also the savings note below.

Savings: the Public Services Reform (Insolvency) (Scotland) Order 2016, SSI 2016/141, art 15 (as amended by the Public Services Reform (Corporate Insolvency and Bankruptcy) (Scotland) Order 2017, SSI 2017/209, and the Insolvency (EU Exit) (Scotland) (Amendment) Regulations 2019, SSI 2019/94) provides as follows (note that "the day mentioned in article 1(4)" is

6 April 2019)—

"**15** (1) Where this article applies, subject to article 1(3) the Act continues to have effect on and after the day mentioned in article 1(4) as if the amendments made by articles [4 and 8 to 10] had not been made

(2) This article applies where, in a receivership, a receiver is appointed in respect of a company under section 51 of the Act before the day mentioned in article 1(4).

(3) This article applies where a company goes into liquidation upon a resolution for voluntary winding up passed before the day mentioned in article 1(4).

(4) This article applies where—

(a) there is an application for the appointment of a provisional liquidator under section 135 of the Act; or

(b) a company goes into liquidation on the making of a winding up order,

on a winding up petition presented before the day mentioned in article 1(4).

(5) This article applies where—

(a) there is an application for the appointment of a provisional liquidator under section 135 of the Act; or

(b) a company goes into liquidation on the making of a winding up order,

on a winding up petition presented on or after the day mentioned in article 1(4) if, at the time the winding up petition is presented, the company is in liquidation upon a resolution for voluntary winding up passed before the day mentioned in article 1(4).

(6) In this article—

"resolution for voluntary winding up" includes a resolution which is deemed to occur by virtue of—

(a) paragraph 83(6)(b) of Schedule B1 of the Act (administration); . . .

(b) . . .

"winding up petition" includes an administration application under paragraph 12 of Schedule B1 to the Act which the court treats as a winding up petition under paragraph 13(1)(e) of that Schedule.".

Regulations: the Receivers (Scotland) Regulations 1986, SI 1986/1917.

[9.187]

67 Report by receiver

(1) Where a receiver is appointed under section 51, he shall within 3 months (or such longer period as the court may allow) after his appointment, send to the registrar of companies, to the holder of the floating charge by virtue of which he was appointed and to any trustees for secured creditors of the company and (so far as he is aware of their addresses) to all such creditors[, other than opted-out creditors,] a report as to the following matters, namely—

(a) the events leading up to his appointment, so far as he is aware of them;

(b) the disposal or proposed disposal by him of any property of the company and the carrying on or proposed carrying on by him of any business of the company;

(c) the amounts of principal and interest payable to the holder of the floating charge by virtue of which he was appointed and the amounts payable to preferential creditors; and

(d) the amount (if any) likely to be available for the payment of other creditors.

(2) The receiver shall also, within 3 months (or such longer period as the court may allow) after his appointment, either—

(a) send a copy of the report (so far as he is aware of their addresses) to all unsecured creditors of the company[, other than opted-out creditors], or

(b) publish in the prescribed manner a notice stating an address to which unsecured creditors of the company should write for copies of the report to be sent to them free of charge,

. . .

(3) . . .

(4) Where the company has gone or goes into liquidation, the receiver—

(a) shall, within 7 days after his compliance with subsection (1) or, if later, the nomination or appointment of the liquidator, send a copy of the report to the liquidator, and

(b) where he does so within the time limited for compliance with subsection (2), is not required to comply with that subsection.

(5) A report under this section shall include a summary of the statement of affairs made out and submitted under section 66 and of his comments (if any) on it.

(6) Nothing in this section shall be taken as requiring any such report to include any information the disclosure of which would seriously prejudice the carrying out by the receiver of his functions.

(7) Section 65(2) applies for the purposes of this section also.

(8) If a person without reasonable excuse fails to comply with this section, he is liable to a fine and, for continued contravention, to a daily default fine.

(9) In this section "secured creditor", in relation to a company, means a creditor of the company who holds in respect of his debt a security over property of the company, and "unsecured creditor" shall be construed accordingly.

NOTES

Words in square brackets in sub-ss (1), (2)(a) inserted, and words omitted from sub-s (2) and the whole of sub-s (3) repealed, by the Small Business, Enterprise and Employment Act 2015, s 126, Sch 9, Pt 1, paras 1, 14, as from 6 April 2019 (for transitional and savings provisions, see the notes to s 246ZE at **[9.385]**).

Regulations: the Receivers (Scotland) Regulations 1986, SI 1986/1917.

[9.188]

68 Committee of creditors

(1) [Where a receiver has sent or published a report as mentioned in section 67(2) the company's unsecured creditors may, in accordance with the rules], establish a committee ("the creditors' committee") to exercise the functions conferred on it by or under this Act.

(2) If such a committee is established, the committee may on giving not less than 7 days' notice require the receiver to attend before it at any reasonable time and furnish it with such information relating to the carrying out by him of his functions as it may reasonably require.

NOTES

Sub-s (1): words in square brackets substituted by the Small Business, Enterprise and Employment Act 2015, s 126, Sch 9, Pt 1, paras 1, 15, as from 6 April 2019 (for transitional and savings provisions, see the notes to s 246ZE at **[9.385]**).

[9.189]

69 Enforcement of receiver's duty to make returns, etc

(1) If any receiver—

(a) having made default in filing, delivering or making any return, account or other document, or in giving any notice, which a receiver is by law required to file, deliver, make or give, fails to make good the default within 14 days after the service on him of a notice requiring him to do so; or

(b) has, after being required at any time by the liquidator of the company so to do, failed to render proper accounts of his receipts and payments and to vouch the same and to pay over to the liquidator the amount properly payable to him,

the court may, on an application made for the purpose, make an order directing the receiver to make good the default within such time as may be specified in the order.

(2) In the case of any such default as is mentioned in subsection (1)(a), an application for the purposes of this section may be made by any member or creditor of the company or by the registrar of companies; and, in the case of any such default as is mentioned in subsection (1)(b), the application shall be made by the liquidator; and, in either case, the order may provide that all expenses of and incidental to the application shall be borne by the receiver.

(3) Nothing in this section prejudices the operation of any enactments imposing penalties on receivers in respect of any such default as is mentioned in subsection (1).

[9.190]

70 Interpretation for Chapter II

(1) In this Chapter, unless the contrary intention appears, the following expressions have the following meanings respectively assigned to them—

"company" means an incorporated company (whether or not [a company registered under the Companies Act 2006]) which the Court of Session has jurisdiction to wind up;

"fixed security", in relation to any property of a company, means any security, other than a floating charge or a charge having the nature of a floating charge, which on the winding up of the company in Scotland would be treated as an effective security over that property, and (without prejudice to that generality) includes a security over that property, being a heritable security within the meaning of the Conveyancing and Feudal Reform (Scotland) Act 1970;

"instrument of appointment" has the meaning given by section 53(1);

. . .

["prescribed fee" means the fee prescribed by regulations made under this Chapter by the Secretary of State;]

"receiver" means a receiver of such part of the property of the company as is subject to the floating charge by virtue of which he has been appointed under section 51;

["the register" has the meaning given by section 1080 of the Companies Act 2006;]

"secured debenture" means a bond, debenture, debenture stock or other security which, either itself or by reference to any other instrument, creates a floating charge over all or any part of the property of the company, but does not include a security which creates no charge other than a fixed security; and

"series of secured debentures" means two or more secured debentures created as a series by the company in such a manner that the holders thereof are entitled pari passu to the benefit of the floating charge.

(2) Where a floating charge, secured debenture or series of secured debentures has been created by the company, then, except where the context otherwise requires, any reference in this Chapter to the holder of the floating charge shall—

(a) where the floating charge, secured debenture or series of secured debentures provides for a receiver to be appointed by any person or body, be construed as a reference to that person or body;

(b) where, in the case of a series of secured debentures, no such provision has been made therein but—

(i) there are trustees acting for the debenture-holders under and in accordance with a trust deed, be construed as a reference to those trustees, and

(ii) where no such trustees are acting, be construed as a reference to—

(aa) a majority in nominal value of those present or represented by proxy and voting at a meeting of debenture-holders at which the holders of at least one-third in nominal value of the outstanding debentures of the series are present or so represented, or

(bb) where no such meeting is held, the holders of at least one-half in nominal value of the outstanding debentures of the series.

(3) Any reference in this Chapter to a floating charge, secured debenture, series of secured debentures or instrument creating a charge includes, except where the context otherwise requires, a reference to that floating charge, debenture, series of debentures or instrument as varied by any instrument.

(4) References in this Chapter to the instrument by which a floating charge was created are, in the case of a floating charge created by words in a bond or other written acknowledgement, references to the bond or, as the case may be, the other written acknowledgement.

NOTES

Sub-s (1) is amended as follows:

Words in square brackets in the definition "company" substituted by the Companies Act 2006 (Consequential Amendments, Transitional Provisions and Savings) Order 2009, SI 2009/1941, art 2(1), Sch 1, para 74(1), (7), as from 1 October 2009 (for effect see the note to s 7A at **[9.145]**).

Definition "prescribed" (omitted) repealed, and definition "prescribed fee" inserted, by the Public Services Reform (Corporate Insolvency and Bankruptcy) (Scotland) Order 2017, SSI 2017/209, art 2, as from 1 October 2017.

Definition "the register" substituted (for the original definition "register of charges") by the Companies Act 2006 (Amendment of Part 25) Regulations 2013, SI 2013/600, reg 5, Sch 2, para 2(1), (3), as from 6 April 2013, in relation to charges created on or after that date (see further the transitional provisions note at **[1.982]**). The original definition (as amended by SI 2009/1941) read as follows: "register of charges" means the register kept by the registrar of companies for the purposes of [Chapter 2 of Part 25 of the Companies Act 2006].

[9.191]

71 Prescription of forms, etc; regulations

(1) The notice referred to in section 62(5), and the notice referred to in section 65(1)(a) shall be in such form as may be prescribed.

(2) Any power conferred by this Chapter on the Secretary of State to make regulations is exercisable by statutory instrument; and a statutory instrument made in the exercise of the power so conferred to prescribe a fee is subject to annulment in pursuance of a resolution of either House of Parliament.

CHAPTER III RECEIVERS' POWERS IN GREAT BRITAIN AS A WHOLE

[9.192]

72 Cross-border operation of receivership provisions

(1) A receiver appointed under the law of either part of Great Britain in respect of the whole or any part of any property or undertaking of a company and in consequence of the company having created a charge which, as created, was a floating charge may exercise his powers in the other part of Great Britain so far as their exercise is not inconsistent with the law applicable there.

(2) In subsection (1) "receiver" includes a manager and a person who is appointed both receiver and manager.

[CHAPTER IV PROHIBITION OF APPOINTMENT OF ADMINISTRATIVE RECEIVER

[9.193]

72A Floating charge holder not to appoint administrative receiver

(1) The holder of a qualifying floating charge in respect of a company's property may not appoint an administrative receiver of the company.

(2) In Scotland, the holder of a qualifying floating charge in respect of a company's property may not appoint or apply to the court for the appointment of a receiver who on appointment would be an administrative receiver of property of the company.

(3) In subsections (1) and (2)—

"holder of a qualifying floating charge in respect of a company's property" has the same meaning as in paragraph 14 of Schedule B1 to this Act, and

"administrative receiver" has the meaning given by section 251.

(4) This section applies—

(a) to a floating charge created on or after a date appointed by the Secretary of State by order made by statutory instrument, and

(b) in spite of any provision of an agreement or instrument which purports to empower a person to appoint an administrative receiver (by whatever name).

(5) An order under subsection (4)(a) may—

(a) make provision which applies generally or only for a specified purpose;

(b) make different provision for different purposes;

(c) make transitional provision.

(6) This section is subject to the exceptions specified in [sections 72B to 72GA].]

NOTES

Chapter IV (originally ss 72B–72D, 72E–72G, 72H) was inserted by the Enterprise Act 2002, s 250(1), as from 15 September 2003.

Sub-s (6): words in square brackets substituted by the Insolvency Act 1986 (Amendment) (Administrative Receivership and Urban Regeneration etc) Order 2003, SI 2003/1832, art 2(a), as from 15 September 2003.

Orders: the Insolvency Act 1986, Section 72A (Appointed Date) Order 2003, SI 2003/2095, appointing 15 September 2003 for the purposes of sub-s (4)(a) above.

[9.194]

[72B First exception: capital market

(1) Section 72A does not prevent the appointment of an administrative receiver in pursuance of an agreement which is or forms part of a capital market arrangement if—

(a) a party incurs or, when the agreement was entered into was expected to incur, a debt of at least £50 million under the arrangement, and

(b) the arrangement involves the issue of a capital market investment.

(2) In subsection (1)—

"capital market arrangement" means an arrangement of a kind described in paragraph 1 of Schedule 2A, and

"capital market investment" means an investment of a kind described in paragraph 2 or 3 of that Schedule.]

NOTES

Inserted as noted to s 72A at **[9.193]**.

[9.195]

[72C Second exception: public-private partnership

(1) Section 72A does not prevent the appointment of an administrative receiver of a project company of a project which—

(a) is a public-private partnership project, and

(b) includes step-in rights.

(2) In this section "public-private partnership project" means a project—

(a) the resources for which are provided partly by one or more public bodies and partly by one or more private persons, or

(b) which is designed wholly or mainly for the purpose of assisting a public body to discharge a function.

(3) In this section—

"step-in rights" has the meaning given by paragraph 6 of Schedule 2A, and

"project company" has the meaning given by paragraph 7 of that Schedule.]

NOTES

Inserted as noted to s 72A at **[9.193]**.

[9.196]

[72D Third exception: utilities

(1) Section 72A does not prevent the appointment of an administrative receiver of a project company of a project which—

(a) is a utility project, and

(b) includes step-in rights.

(2) In this section—

(a) "utility project" means a project designed wholly or mainly for the purpose of a regulated business,

(b) "regulated business" means a business of a kind listed in paragraph 10 of Schedule 2A,

(c) "step-in rights" has the meaning given by paragraph 6 of that Schedule, and

(d) "project company" has the meaning given by paragraph 7 of that Schedule.]

NOTES

Inserted as noted to s 72A at **[9.193]**.

[9.197]

[72DA Exception in respect of urban regeneration projects

(1) Section 72A does not prevent the appointment of an administrative receiver of a project company of a project which—

(a) is designed wholly or mainly to develop land which at the commencement of the project is wholly or partly in a designated disadvantaged area outside Northern Ireland, and

(b) includes step-in rights.

(2) In subsection (1) "develop" means to carry out—

(a) building operations,

(b) any operation for the removal of substances or waste from land and the levelling of the surface of the land, or

(c) engineering operations in connection with the activities mentioned in paragraph (a) or (b).

(3) In this section—

"building" includes any structure or erection, and any part of a building as so defined, but does not include plant and machinery comprised in a building,

"building operations" includes—

(a) demolition of buildings,

(b) filling in of trenches,

(c) rebuilding,

(d) structural alterations of, or additions to, buildings and

(e) other operations normally undertaken by a person carrying on business as a builder,

"designated disadvantaged area" means an area designated as a disadvantaged area under section 92 of the Finance Act 2001,

"engineering operations" includes the formation and laying out of means of access to highways,

"project company" has the meaning given by paragraph 7 of Schedule 2A,

"step-in rights" has the meaning given by paragraph 6 of that Schedule,

"substance" means any natural or artificial substance whether in solid or liquid form or in the form of a gas or vapour, and

"waste" includes any waste materials, spoil, refuse or other matter deposited on land.]

NOTES

Inserted by the Insolvency Act 1986 (Amendment) (Administrative Receivership and Urban Regeneration etc) Order 2003, SI 2003/1832, art 2(b), as from 15 September 2003.

[9.198]

[72E Fourth exception: project finance

(1) Section 72A does not prevent the appointment of an administrative receiver of a project company of a project which—

(a) is a financed project, and

(b) includes step-in rights.

(2) In this section—

(a) a project is "financed" if under an agreement relating to the project a project company incurs, or when the agreement is entered into is expected to incur, a debt of at least £50 million for the purposes of carrying out the project,

(b) "project company" has the meaning given by paragraph 7 of Schedule 2A, and

(c) "step-in rights" has the meaning given by paragraph 6 of that Schedule.]

NOTES

Inserted as noted to s 72A at **[9.193]**.

[9.199]

[72F Fifth exception: financial market

Section 72A does not prevent the appointment of an administrative receiver of a company by virtue of—

(a) a market charge within the meaning of section 173 of the Companies Act 1989 (c 40),

(b) a system-charge within the meaning of the Financial Markets and Insolvency Regulations 1996 (SI 1996/1469),

(c) a collateral security charge within the meaning of the Financial Markets and Insolvency (Settlement Finality) Regulations 1999 (SI 1999/2979).]

NOTES

Inserted as noted to s 72A at **[9.193]**.

[9.200]

[72G Sixth exception: [social landlords]

Section 72A does not prevent the appointment of an administrative receiver of a company which is[—

(a) a private registered provider of social housing, or

(b)] registered as a social landlord under Part I of the Housing Act 1996 (c 52) or under [Part 2 of the Housing (Scotland) Act 2010 (asp 17)].]

NOTES

Inserted as noted to s 72A at **[9.193]**.

Words in square brackets in the section heading substituted, and words in first pair of square brackets in the text inserted, by the Housing and Regeneration Act 2008 (Consequential Provisions) Order 2010, SI 2010/866, art 5, Sch 2, para 61, as from 1 April 2010.

Words in second pair of square brackets substituted by the Housing (Scotland) Act 2010 (Consequential Provisions and Modifications) Order 2012, SI 2012/700, art 4, Schedule, Pt 1, para 3, as from 1 April 2012.

[9.201]

[72GA Exception in relation to protected railway companies etc

Section 72A does not prevent the appointment of an administrative receiver of—

(a) a company holding an appointment under Chapter I of Part II of the Water Industry Act 1991,

(b) a protected railway company within the meaning of section 59 of the Railways Act 1993 (including that section as it has effect by virtue of section 19 of the Channel Tunnel Rail Link Act 1996, or

(c) a licence company within the meaning of section 26 of the Transport Act 2000.]

NOTES

Inserted by the Insolvency Act 1986 (Amendment) (Administrative Receivership and Urban Regeneration etc) Order 2003, SI 2003/1832, art 2(c), as from 15 September 2003.

[9.202]

[72H Sections 72A to 72G: supplementary

(1) Schedule 2A (which supplements sections 72B to 72G) shall have effect.

(2) The Secretary of State may by order—

(a) insert into this Act provision creating an additional exception to section 72A(1) or (2);

(b) provide for a provision of this Act which creates an exception to section 72A(1) or (2) to cease to have effect;

(c) amend section 72A in consequence of provision made under paragraph (a) or (b);

(d) amend any of sections 72B to 72G;

(e) amend Schedule 2A.

(3) An order under subsection (2) must be made by statutory instrument.

(4) An order under subsection (2) may make—

(a) provision which applies generally or only for a specified purpose;

(b) different provision for different purposes;

(c) consequential or supplementary provision;

(d) transitional provision.

(5) An order under subsection (2)—

(a) in the case of an order under subsection (2)(e), shall be subject to annulment in pursuance of a resolution of either House of Parliament,

(b) in the case of an order under subsection (2)(d) varying the sum specified in section 72B(1)(a) or 72E(2)(a) (whether or not the order also makes consequential or transitional provision), shall be subject to annulment in pursuance of a resolution of either House of Parliament, and

(c) in the case of any other order under subsection (2)(a) to (d), may not be made unless a draft has been laid before and approved by resolution of each House of Parliament.]

NOTES

Inserted as noted to s 72A at **[9.193]**.

Orders: the Insolvency Act 1986 (Amendment) (Administrative Receivership and Capital Market Arrangements) Order 2003, SI 2003/1468; the Insolvency Act 1986 (Amendment) (Administrative Receivership and Urban Regeneration etc) Order 2003, SI 2003/1832.

PART IV WINDING UP OF COMPANIES REGISTERED UNDER THE COMPANIES ACTS

CHAPTER I PRELIMINARY

[Introductory

[9.203]

73 Scheme of this Part

(1) This Part applies to the winding up of a company registered under the Companies Act 2006 in England and Wales or Scotland.

(2) The winding up may be either—

(a) voluntary (see Chapters 2 to 5), or

(b) by the court (see Chapter 6).

(3) This Chapter and Chapters 7 to 10 relate to winding up generally, except where otherwise stated.]

NOTES

Substituted (together with the heading preceding this section) by the Companies Act 2006 (Consequential Amendments, Transitional Provisions and Savings) Order 2009, SI 2009/1941, art 2(1), Sch 1, para 75(1), (2), as from 1 October 2009 (for effect see the note to s 7A at **[9.145]**).

Contributories

[9.204]

74 Liability as contributories of present and past members

(1) When a company is wound up, every present and past member is liable to contribute to its assets to any amount sufficient for payment of its debts and liabilities, and the expenses of the winding up, and for the adjustment of the rights of the contributories among themselves.

(2) This is subject as follows—

(a) a past member is not liable to contribute if he has ceased to be a member for one year or more before the commencement of the winding up;

(b) a past member is not liable to contribute in respect of any debt or liability of the company contracted after he ceased to be a member;

(c) a past member is not liable to contribute, unless it appears to the court that the existing members are unable to satisfy the contributions required to be made by them . . . ;

(d) in the case of a company limited by shares, no contribution is required from any member exceeding the amount (if any) unpaid on the shares in respect of which he is liable as a present or past member;

(e) nothing in [the Companies Acts] or this Act invalidates any provision contained in a policy of insurance or other contract whereby the liability of individual members on the policy or contract is restricted, or whereby the funds of the company are alone made liable in respect of the policy or contract;

(f) a sum due to any member of the company (in his character of a member) by way of dividends, profits or otherwise is not deemed to be a debt of the company, payable to that member in a case of competition between himself and any other creditor not a member of the company, but any such sum may be taken into account for the purpose of the final adjustment of the rights of the contributories among themselves.

(3) In the case of a company limited by guarantee, no contribution is required from any member exceeding the amount undertaken to be contributed by him to the company's assets in the event of its being wound up; but if it is a company with a share capital, every member of it is liable (in addition to the amount so undertaken to be contributed to the assets), to contribute to the extent of any sums unpaid on shares held by him.

NOTES

Sub-s (2): words omitted from para (c) repealed, and words in square brackets in para (e) substituted, by the Companies Act 2006 (Consequential Amendments, Transitional Provisions and Savings) Order 2009, SI 2009/1941, art 2(1), Sch 1, para 75(1), (3), as from 1 October 2009 (for effect see the note to s 7A at **[9.145]**).

75 *(Repealed by the Companies Act 2006 (Consequential Amendments, Transitional Provisions and Savings) Order 2009, SI 2009/1941, art 2(1), Sch 1, para 75(1), (4), as from 1 October 2009 (for effect see the note to s 7A at* **[9.145]***). Note also that the Companies Act 2006 (Consequential Amendments, Transitional Provisions and Savings) Order 2009, SI 2009/1941, art 9 (at* **[4.363]***) provides that the repeal of this section does not affect its operation in relation to liabilities arising before 1 October 2009 or in connection with the holding of an office to which a person was appointed before that date on the understanding that their liability would be unlimited.)*

[9.205]

76 Liability of past directors and shareholders

(1) This section applies where a company is being wound up and—

(a) it has under [Chapter 5 of Part 18 of the Companies Act 2006 (acquisition by limited company of its own shares: redemption or purchase by private company out of capital)] made a payment out of capital in respect of the redemption or purchase of any of its own shares (the payment being referred to below as "the relevant payment"), and

(b) the aggregate amount of the company's assets and the amounts paid by way of contribution to its assets (apart from this section) is not sufficient for payment of its debts and liabilities, and the expenses of the winding up.

(2) If the winding up commenced within one year of the date on which the relevant payment was made, then—

(a) the person from whom the shares were redeemed or purchased, and

(b) the directors who signed the [statement] made in accordance with [section 714(1) to (3) of the Companies Act 2006] for purposes of the redemption or purchase (except a director who shows that he had reasonable grounds for forming the opinion set out in the [statement]),

are, so as to enable that insufficiency to be met, liable to contribute to the following extent to the company's assets.

(3) A person from whom any of the shares were redeemed or purchased is liable to contribute an amount not exceeding so much of the relevant payment as was made by the company in respect of his shares; and the directors are jointly and severally liable with that person to contribute that amount.

(4) A person who has contributed any amount to the assets in pursuance of this section may apply to the court for an order directing any other person jointly and severally liable in respect of that amount to pay him such amount as the court thinks just and equitable.

(5) [Section 74 does not apply] in relation to liability accruing by virtue of this section.

(6) . . .

NOTES

Sub-ss (1), (5): words in square brackets substituted by the Companies Act 2006 (Consequential Amendments, Transitional Provisions and Savings) Order 2009, SI 2009/1941, art 2(1), Sch 1, para 75(1), (5)(a), (c), as from 1 October 2009 (for effect see the note to s 7A at **[9.145]**).

Sub-s (2): words in second pair of square brackets substituted by SI 2009/1941, art 2(1), Sch 1, para 75(1), (5)(b), as from 1 October 2009 (for effect see the note to s 7A at **[9.145]**). Other words in square brackets substituted by the Companies Act 2006 (Consequential Amendments and Transitional Provisions) Order 2011, SI 2011/1265, art 6(3), as from 12 May 2011.

Sub-s (6): repealed by SI 2009/1941, art 2(1), Sch 1, para 75(1), (5)(d), as from 1 October 2009 (for effect see the note to s 7A at **[9.145]**).

[9.206]

77 Limited company formerly unlimited

(1) This section applies in the case of a company being wound up which was at some former time registered as unlimited but has [re-registered as a limited company].

(2) Notwithstanding section 74(2)(a) above, a past member of the company who was a member of it at the time of re-registration, if the winding up commences within the period of 3 years beginning with the day on which the company was re-registered, is liable to contribute to the assets of the company in respect of debts and liabilities contracted before that time.

(3) If no persons who were members of the company at that time are existing members of it, a person who at that time was a present or past member is liable to contribute as above notwithstanding that the existing members have satisfied the contributions required to be made by them . . .

This applies subject to section 74(2)(a) above and to subsection (2) of this section, but notwithstanding section 74(2)(c).

(4) Notwithstanding section 74(2)(d) and (3), there is no limit on the amount which a person who, at that time, was a past or present member of the company is liable to contribute as above.

NOTES

Words in square brackets in sub-s (1) substituted, and words omitted from sub-s (3) repealed, by the Companies Act 2006 (Consequential Amendments, Transitional Provisions and Savings) Order 2009, SI 2009/1941, art 2(1), Sch 1, para 75(1), (6), as from 1 October 2009 (for effect see the note to s 7A at **[9.145]**).

[9.207]

78 Unlimited company formerly limited

(1) This section applies in the case of a company being wound up which was at some former time registered as limited but has been re-registered as unlimited . . .

(2) A person who, at the time when the application for the company to be re-registered was lodged, was a past member of the company and did not after that again become a member of it is not liable to contribute to the assets of the company more than he would have been liable to contribute had the company not been re-registered.

NOTES

Sub-s (1): words omitted repealed by the Companies Act 2006 (Consequential Amendments, Transitional Provisions and Savings) Order 2009, SI 2009/1941, art 2(1), Sch 1, para 75(1), (7), as from 1 October 2009 (for effect see the note to s 7A at **[9.145]**).

[9.208]

79 Meaning of "contributory"

(1) In this Act . . . the expression "contributory" means every person liable to contribute to the assets of a company in the event of its being wound up, and for the purposes of all proceedings for determining, and all proceedings prior to the final determination of, the persons who are to be deemed contributories, includes any person alleged to be a contributory.

(2) The reference in subsection (1) to persons liable to contribute to the assets does not include a person so liable by virtue of a declaration by the court under section 213 (imputed responsibility for company's fraudulent trading) or section 214 (wrongful trading) in Chapter X of this Part.

(3) A reference in a company's articles to a contributory does not (unless the context requires) include a person who is a contributory only by virtue of section 76.

. . .

NOTES

Sub-ss (1), (3): words omitted repealed by the Companies Act 2006 (Consequential Amendments, Transitional Provisions and Savings) Order 2009, SI 2009/1941, art 2(1), Sch 1, para 75(1), (8), as from 1 October 2009 (for effect see the note to s 7A at **[9.145]**).

[9.209]

80 Nature of contributory's liability

The liability of a contributory creates a debt (in England and Wales in the nature of [an ordinary contract debt]) accruing due from him at the time when his liability commenced, but payable at the times when calls are made for enforcing the liability.

NOTES

Words in square brackets substituted by the Companies Act 2006 (Consequential Amendments, Transitional Provisions and Savings) Order 2009, SI 2009/1941, art 2(1), Sch 1, para 75(1), (9), as from 1 October 2009 (for savings and transitional provisions see the note to s 7A at **[9.145]** and the note below).

Saving for provisions relating to nature of liability of member or contributory: the Companies Act 2006 (Consequential Amendments, Transitional Provisions and Savings) Order 2009, SI 2009/1941, art 11 (at **[4.365]**) provides that the new provisions as to the nature of a member's or contributory's liability (ie, the Companies Act 2006, s 33(2) and, in England and Wales, s 80 of the Insolvency Act 1986 as amended by that Order) apply to liabilities arising on or after 1 October 2009, and the old provisions (ie, CA 1985, s 14(2) and s 80 of the 1986 Act as it had effect prior to that amendment) continue to apply to liabilities arising before that date. Note also that for the purposes of art 11, a liability is treated as arising when the limitation period starts to run for the purposes of the Limitation Act 1980.

[9.210]

81 Contributories in case of death of a member

(1) If a contributory dies either before or after he has been placed on the list of contributories, his personal representatives, and the heirs and legatees of heritage of his heritable estate in Scotland, are liable in a due course of administration to contribute to the assets of the company in discharge of his liability and are contributories accordingly.

(2) Where the personal representatives are placed on the list of contributories, the heirs or legatees of heritage need not be added, but they may be added as and when the court thinks fit.

(3) If in England and Wales the personal representatives make default in paying any money ordered to be paid by them, proceedings may be taken for administering the estate of the deceased contributory and for compelling payment out of it of the money due.

[9.211]

82 Effect of contributory's bankruptcy

(1) The following applies if a contributory becomes bankrupt, either before or after he has been placed on the list of contributories.

(2) His trustee in bankruptcy represents him for all purposes of the winding up, and is a contributory accordingly.

(3) The trustee may be called on to admit to proof against the bankrupt's estate, or otherwise allow to be paid out of the bankrupt's assets in due course of law, any money due from the bankrupt in respect of his liability to contribute to the company's assets.

(4) There may be proved against the bankrupt's estate the estimated value of his liability to future calls as well as calls already made.

[9.212]

83 [Companies registered but not formed under the Companies Act 2006]

(1) The following applies in the event of a company being wound up which [is registered but not formed under the Companies Act 2006].

(2) Every person is a contributory, in respect of the company's debts and liabilities contracted before registration, who is liable—

- (a) to pay, or contribute to the payment of, any debt or liability so contracted, or
- (b) to pay, or contribute to the payment of, any sum for the adjustment of the rights of the members among themselves in respect of any such debt or liability, or
- (c) to pay, or contribute to the amount of, the expenses of winding up the company, so far as relates to the debts or liabilities above-mentioned.

(3) Every contributory is liable to contribute to the assets of the company, in the course of the winding up, all sums due from him in respect of any such liability.

(4) In the event of the death, bankruptcy or insolvency of any contributory, provisions of this Act, with respect to the personal representatives, to the heirs and legatees of heritage of the heritable estate in Scotland of deceased contributories and to the trustees of bankrupt or insolvent contributories respectively, apply.

NOTES

Words in square brackets substituted by the Companies Act 2006 (Consequential Amendments, Transitional Provisions and Savings) Order 2009, SI 2009/1941, art 2(1), Sch 1, para 75(1), (10), as from 1 October 2009 (for effect see the note to s 7A at **[9.145]**).

CHAPTER II VOLUNTARY WINDING UP (INTRODUCTORY AND GENERAL)

Resolutions for, and commencement of, voluntary winding up

[9.213]

84 Circumstances in which company may be wound up voluntarily

(1) A company may be wound up voluntarily—

- (a) when the period (if any) fixed for the duration of the company by the articles expires, or the event (if any) occurs, on the occurrence of which the articles provide that the company is to be dissolved, and the company in general meeting has passed a resolution requiring it to be wound up voluntarily;
- (b) if the company resolves by special resolution that it be wound up voluntarily;
- (c) . . .

(2) In this Act the expression "a resolution for voluntary winding up" means a resolution passed under [either of the paragraphs] of subsection (1).

[(2A) Before a company passes a resolution for voluntary winding up it must give written notice of the resolution to the holder of any qualifying floating charge to which section 72A applies.

(2B) Where notice is given under subsection (2A) a resolution for voluntary winding up may be passed only—

- (a) after the end of the period of five business days beginning with the day on which the notice was given, or
- (b) if the person to whom the notice was given has consented in writing to the passing of the resolution.]

[(3) Chapter 3 of Part 3 of the Companies Act 2006 (resolutions affecting a company's constitution) applies to a resolution under paragraph (a) of subsection (1) as well as a special resolution under paragraph (b).]

[(4) This section has effect subject to section 43 of the Commonhold and Leasehold Reform Act 2002.]

NOTES

Sub-s (1): para (c) repealed by the Companies Act 2006 (Commencement No 3, Consequential Amendments, Transitional Provisions and Savings) Order 2007, SI 2007/2194, art 10(1), Sch 4, Pt 3, para 39(1), (2), Sch 5, as from 1 October 2007.

Sub-s (2): words in square brackets substituted by SI 2007/2194, art 10(1), Sch 4, Pt 3, para 39(1), (3), as from 1 October 2007.

Sub-ss (2A), (2B): inserted by the Enterprise Act 2002 (Insolvency) Order 2003, SI 2003/2096, arts 4, 6, Schedule, Pt 1, paras 8, 10, as from 15 September 2003, except in relation to any case where a petition for an administration order was presented before that date.

Sub-s (3): substituted by SI 2007/2194, art 10(1), Sch 4, Pt 3, para 39(1), (4), as from 1 October 2007.

Sub-s (4): added, in relation to England and Wales only, by the Commonhold and Leasehold Reform Act 2002, s 68, Sch 5, para 6, as from 27 September 2004.

[9.214]

85 Notice of resolution to wind up

(1) When a company has passed a resolution for voluntary winding up, it shall, within 14 days after the passing of the resolution, give notice of the resolution by advertisement in the Gazette.

(2) If default is made in complying with this section, the company and every officer of it who is in default is liable to a fine and, for continued contravention, to a daily default fine.

For purposes of this subsection the liquidator is deemed an officer of the company.

[9.215]

86 Commencement of winding up

A voluntary winding up is deemed to commence at the time of the passing of the resolution for voluntary winding up.

Consequences of resolution to wind up

[9.216]

87 Effect on business and status of company

(1) In case of a voluntary winding up, the company shall from the commencement of the winding up cease to carry on its business, except so far as may be required for its beneficial winding up.

(2) However, the corporate state and corporate powers of the company, notwithstanding anything to the contrary in its articles, continue until the company is dissolved.

[9.217]

88 Avoidance of share transfers, etc after winding-up resolution

Any transfer of shares, not being a transfer made to or with the sanction of the liquidator, and any alteration in the status of the company's members, made after the commencement of a voluntary winding up, is void.

Declaration of solvency

[9.218]

89 Statutory declaration of solvency

(1) Where it is proposed to wind up a company voluntarily, the directors (or, in the case of a company having more than two directors, the majority of them) may at a directors' meeting make a statutory declaration to the effect that they have made a full inquiry into the company's affairs and that, having done so, they have formed the opinion that the company will be able to pay its debts in full, together with interest at the official rate (as defined in section 251), within such period, not exceeding 12 months from the commencement of the winding up, as may be specified in the declaration.

(2) Such a declaration by the directors has no effect for purposes of this Act unless—

(a) it is made within the 5 weeks immediately preceding the date of the passing of the resolution for winding up, or on that date but before the passing of the resolution, and

(b) it embodies a statement of the company's assets and liabilities as at the latest practicable date before the making of the declaration.

(3) The declaration shall be delivered to the registrar of companies before the expiration of 15 days immediately following the date on which the resolution for winding up is passed.

(4) A director making a declaration under this section without having reasonable grounds for the opinion that the company will be able to pay its debts in full, together with interest at the official rate, within the period specified is liable to imprisonment or a fine, or both.

(5) If the company is wound up in pursuance of a resolution passed within 5 weeks after the making of the declaration, and its debts (together with interest at the official rate) are not paid or provided for in full within the period specified, it is to be presumed (unless the contrary is shown) that the director did not have reasonable grounds for his opinion.

(6) If a declaration required by subsection (3) to be delivered to the registrar is not so delivered within the time prescribed by that subsection, the company and every officer in default is liable to a fine and, for continued contravention, to a daily default fine.

[9.219]

90 Distinction between "members'" and "creditors'" voluntary winding up

A winding up in the case of which a directors' statutory declaration under section 89 has been made is a "members' voluntary winding up"; and a winding up in the case of which such a declaration has not been made is a "creditors' voluntary winding up".

CHAPTER III MEMBERS' VOLUNTARY WINDING UP

[9.220]

91 Appointment of liquidator

(1) In a members' voluntary winding up, the company in general meeting shall appoint one or more liquidators for the purpose of winding up the company's affairs and distributing its assets.

(2) On the appointment of a liquidator all the powers of the directors cease, except so far as the company in general meeting or the liquidator sanctions their continuance.

[9.221]

92 Power to fill vacancy in office of liquidator

(1) If a vacancy occurs by death, resignation or otherwise in the office of liquidator appointed by the company, the company in general meeting may, subject to any arrangement with its creditors, fill the vacancy.

(2) For that purpose a general meeting may be convened by any contributory or, if there were more liquidators than one, by the continuing liquidators.

(3) The meeting shall be held in manner provided by this Act or by the articles, or in such manner as may, on application by any contributory or by the continuing liquidators, be determined by the court.

NOTES

Meeting held in manner provided by this Act: it is thought that the reference in sub-s (3) above to "this Act" should originally have been a reference to the Companies Act 1985. As to general meetings, see now the Companies Act 2006, s 301 et seq.

[9.222]

[92A Progress report to company . . . . . .

(1) Subject to [section 96], [. . .], the liquidator must—

(a) for each prescribed period produce a progress report relating to the prescribed matters; and

(b) within such period commencing with the end of the period referred to in paragraph (a) as may be prescribed send a copy of the progress report to—

(i) the members of the company; and

(ii) such other persons as may be prescribed.

(2) A liquidator who fails to comply with this section is liable to a fine.]

NOTES

Inserted by the Legislative Reform (Insolvency) (Miscellaneous Provisions) Order 2010, SI 2010/18, arts 2, 6(1), as from 6 April 2010, except in respect of a company in voluntary winding up where the resolution to wind up was passed before 6 April 2010.

First words omitted from the section heading repealed by the Small Business, Enterprise and Employment Act 2015, s 136(1), (2), as from 26 May 2015.

Second words omitted from the section heading repealed by the Public Services Reform (Insolvency) (Scotland) Order 2016, SSI 2016/141, art 5(1), as from 6 April 2019 (for savings, see the note below).

Words in first pair of square brackets in sub-s (1) substituted by the Small Business, Enterprise and Employment Act 2015, s 126, Sch 9, Pt 1, paras 1, 16, as from 6 April 2017 (in relation to England and Wales), and as from 6 April 2019 (in relation to Scotland) (for transitional and savings provisions, see the notes to s 246ZE at **[9.385]**).

Words omitted from sub-s (1) originally substituted by the Small Business, Enterprise and Employment Act 2015, s 136(1), (2), as from 26 May 2015, and subsequently repealed by the Public Services Reform (Insolvency) (Scotland) Order 2016, SSI 2016/141, art 5(1), as from 6 April 2019 (for savings, see the note below).

Savings: the Public Services Reform (Insolvency) (Scotland) Order 2016, SSI 2016/141, art 16 provides as follows (note that "the day mentioned in article 1(4)" is 6 April 2019)—

"16

(1) This article applies where, before the day mentioned in article 1(4)—

(a) there is a members' or creditors' voluntary winding up continuing for more than one year;

(b) the liquidator in that winding up has an obligation under—

(i) section 93 or 105 of the Act to summon a general meeting of the company, either at the end of the first year from the commencement of the winding up, or at the end of any succeeding year; or

(ii) section 105 of the Act to summon a meeting of the creditors, either at the end of the first year from the commencement of the winding up, or at the end of any succeeding year; and

(c) that obligation has not been fulfilled or the meeting has not taken place.

(2) Where this article applies, subject to article 1(3), the Act continues to have effect on and after the day mentioned in article 1(4) as if the amendments made by articles 5, 6 and 7(2) and (3) had not been made in relation to the liquidator's obligations to—

(a) summon the particular meeting;

(b) lay before that meeting an account of the liquidator's acts and dealings, and of the conduct of the winding up, in the preceding year.".

93 (*Repealed by the Public Services Reform (Insolvency) (Scotland) Order 2016, SSI 2016/141, art 5(2), as from 6 April 2019 (for savings, see the note to s 92A at* **[9.222]**.)

[9.223]

[94 Final account prior to dissolution

(1) As soon as the company's affairs are fully wound up the liquidator must make up an account of the winding up, showing how it has been conducted and the company's property has been disposed of.

(2) The liquidator must send a copy of the account to the members of the company before the end of the period of 14 days beginning with the day on which the account is made up.

(3) The liquidator must send a copy of the account to the registrar of companies before the end of that period (but not before sending it to the members of the company).

(4) If the liquidator does not comply with subsection (2) the liquidator is liable to a fine.

(5) If the liquidator does not comply with subsection (3) the liquidator is liable to a fine and, for continued contravention, a daily default fine.]

NOTES

Substituted by the Small Business, Enterprise and Employment Act 2015, s 126, Sch 9, Pt 1, paras 1, 18, as from 6 April 2017 (in relation to England and Wales), and as from 6 April 2019 (in relation to Scotland) (for transitional and savings provisions, see the notes to s 246ZE at **[9.385]**).

[9.224]

95 Effect of company's insolvency

(1) This section applies where the liquidator is of the opinion that the company will be unable to pay its debts in full (together with interest at the official rate) within the period stated in the directors' declaration under section 89.

[(1A) The liquidator must before the end of the period of 7 days beginning with the day after the day on which the liquidator formed that opinion—

(a) make out a statement in the prescribed form as to the affairs of the company, and

(b) send it to the company's creditors.]

(2) . . .

[(2A) . . .]

(3) . . .

(4) The statement as to the affairs of the company . . . shall show—

(a) particulars of the company's assets, debts and liabilities;

(b) the names and addresses of the company's creditors;

(c) the securities held by them respectively;

(d) the dates when the securities were respectively given; and

(e) such further or other information as may be prescribed.

[(4A) The statement as to the affairs of the company shall . . . —

(a) in the case of a winding up of a company registered in England and Wales [be verified by the liquidator], by a statement of truth; and

(b) in the case of a winding up of a company registered in Scotland, [contain a statutory declaration by the liquidator].]

[(4B) The company's creditors may in accordance with the rules nominate a person to be liquidator.

(4C) The liquidator must in accordance with the rules seek such a nomination from the company's creditors.]

(5)–(7) . . .

(8) If the liquidator without reasonable excuse fails to comply with [subsections (1) to (4A)], he is liable to a fine.

NOTES

Sub-ss (1A), (4B), (4C): inserted by the Small Business, Enterprise and Employment Act 2015, s 126, Sch 9, Pt 1, paras 1, 19(1), (2), (4), as from 6 April 2017 (in relation to England and Wales), and as from 6 April 2019 (in relation to Scotland) (for transitional and savings provisions, see the notes to s 246ZE at **[9.385]**).

Sub-s (2): repealed by the Small Business, Enterprise and Employment Act 2015, s 126, Sch 9, Pt 1, paras 1, 19(1), (3), as from 6 April 2019 (for transitional and savings provisions, see the notes to s 246ZE at **[9.385]**).

Sub-s (2A): originally inserted by SI 2009/864, arts 2, 3(1)(b), 4, as from 6 April 2009, except in respect of a company in voluntary winding up where the resolution to wind up was passed before that date; and subsequently repealed by the Small Business, Enterprise and Employment Act 2015, s 126, Sch 9, Pt 1, paras 1, 19(1), (3), as from 6 April 2017 (subject to transitional and savings provisions as noted to s 246ZE at **[9.385]**).

Sub-ss (3), (5)–(7): repealed by the Small Business, Enterprise and Employment Act 2015, s 126, Sch 9, Pt 1, paras 1, 19(1), (3), as from 6 April 2017 (in relation to England and Wales), and as from 6 April 2019 (in relation to Scotland) (for transitional and savings provisions, see the notes to s 246ZE at **[9.385]**).

Sub-s (4): words omitted repealed by SI 2010/18, arts 2, 5(2)(a), as from 6 April 2010.

Sub-s (4A): inserted by SI 2010/18, arts 2, 5(2)(b), as from 6 April 2010. Words omitted repealed, words in square brackets in para (a) inserted, and words in square brackets in para (b) substituted, by the Public Services Reform (Insolvency) (Scotland) Order 2016, SSI 2016/141, art 8, as from 6 April 2019 (for savings, see the note to s 66 at **[9.186]**).

Sub-s (8): words in square brackets substituted by the Small Business, Enterprise and Employment Act 2015, s 126, Sch 9, Pt 1, paras 1, 19(1), (5), as from 6 April 2017 (in relation to England and Wales), and as from 6 April 2019 (in relation to Scotland) (for transitional and savings provisions, see the notes to s 246ZE at **[9.385]**).

[9.225]

[96 Conversion to creditors' voluntary winding up

(1) The winding up becomes a creditors' voluntary winding up as from the day on which—

(a) the company's creditors under section 95 nominate a person to be liquidator, or

(b) the procedure by which the company's creditors were to have made such a nomination concludes without a nomination having been made.

(2) As from that day this Act has effect as if the directors' declaration under section 89 had not been made.

(3) The liquidator in the creditors' voluntary winding up is to be the person nominated by the company's creditors under section 95 or, where no person has been so nominated, the existing liquidator.

(4) In the case of the creditors nominating a person other than the existing liquidator any director, member or creditor of the company may, within 7 days after the date on which the nomination was made by the creditors, apply to the court for an order either—

(a) directing that the existing liquidator is to be liquidator instead of or jointly with the person nominated by the creditors, or

(b) appointing some other person to be liquidator instead of the person nominated by the creditors.

[(4A) The court shall grant an application under subsection (4) made by the holder of a qualifying floating charge in respect of the company's property (within the meaning of paragraph 14 of Schedule B1) unless the court thinks it right to refuse the application because of the particular circumstances of the case.]

(5) The "existing liquidator" is the person who is liquidator immediately before the winding up becomes a creditors' voluntary winding up.]

NOTES

Substituted by the Small Business, Enterprise and Employment Act 2015, s 126, Sch 9, Pt 1, paras 1, 20(1), as from 6 April 2017 (in relation to England and Wales), and as from 6 April 2019 (in relation to Scotland) (for transitional and savings provisions, see the notes to s 246ZE at **[9.385]**).

Sub-s (4A): inserted by the Small Business, Enterprise and Employment Act 2015, s 126, Sch 9, Pt 1, paras 1, 20(2), as from 6 April 2017 (in relation to England and Wales), and as from 6 April 2019 (in relation to Scotland), subject to transitional and savings provisions noted to s 246ZE at **[9.385]**.

CHAPTER IV CREDITORS' VOLUNTARY WINDING UP

[9.226]

97 Application of this Chapter

(1) Subject as follows, this Chapter applies in relation to a creditors' voluntary winding up.

(2) Sections [99 and 100] do not apply where, under section 96 in Chapter III, a members' voluntary winding up has become a creditors' voluntary winding up.

NOTES

Sub-s (1): words in square brackets substituted by the Small Business, Enterprise and Employment Act 2015, s 126, Sch 9, Pt 1, paras 1, 21, as from 6 April 2017 (in relation to England and Wales), and as from 6 April 2019 (in relation to Scotland) (for transitional and savings provisions, see the notes to s 246ZE at **[9.385]**).

98 (*Repealed by the Small Business, Enterprise and Employment Act 2015, s 126, Sch 9, Pt 1, paras 1, 22, as from 6 April 2017 (in relation to England and Wales), and as from 6 April 2019 (in relation to Scotland) (for transitional and savings provisions, see the notes to s 246ZE at* **[9.385]**.)

[9.227]

99 Directors to lay statement of affairs before creditors

[(1) The directors of the company must, before the end of the period of 7 days beginning with the day after the day on which the company passes a resolution for voluntary winding up—

(a) make out a statement in the prescribed form as to the affairs of the company, and

(b) send the statement to the company's creditors.]

(2) The statement as to the affairs of the company . . . shall show—

(a) particulars of the company's assets, debts and liabilities;

(b) the names and addresses of the company's creditors;

(c) the securities held by them respectively;

(d) the dates when the securities were respectively given; and

(e) such further or other information as may be prescribed.

[(2A) The statement as to the affairs of the company shall . . . —

(a) in the case of a winding up of a company registered in England and Wales, [be verified by some or all of the directors] by a statement of truth; and

(b) in the case of a winding up of a company registered in Scotland, [contain a statutory declaration by some or all of the directors].]

[(3) If the directors without reasonable excuse fail to comply with subsection (1), (2) or (2A), they are guilty of an offence and liable to a fine.]

NOTES

Sub-s (1): substituted by the Small Business, Enterprise and Employment Act 2015, s 126, Sch 9, Pt 1, paras 1, 23(1), (2), as from 6 April 2017 (in relation to England and Wales), and as from 6 April 2019 (in relation to Scotland) (for transitional and savings provisions, see the notes to s 246ZE at **[9.385]**).

Sub-s (2): words omitted repealed by the Legislative Reform (Insolvency) (Miscellaneous Provisions) Order 2010, SI 2010/18, arts 2, 5(3)(a), as from 6 April 2010.

Sub-s (2A): inserted by SI 2010/18, arts 2, 5(3)(b), as from 6 April 2010. Words omitted repealed, words in square brackets in para (a) inserted, and words in square brackets in para (b) substituted, by the Public Services Reform (Insolvency) (Scotland) Order 2016, SSI 2016/141, art 9, as from 6 April 2019 (for savings, see the note to s 66 at **[9.186]**).

Sub-s (3): substituted by the Small Business, Enterprise and Employment Act 2015, s 126, Sch 9, Pt 1, paras 1, 23(1), (3), as from 6 April 2017 (in relation to England and Wales), and as from 6 April 2019 (in relation to Scotland) (for transitional and savings provisions, see the notes to s 246ZE at **[9.385]**).

[9.228]

100 Appointment of liquidator

[(1) The company may nominate a person to be liquidator at the company meeting at which the resolution for voluntary winding up is passed.

(1A) The company's creditors may in accordance with the rules nominate a person to be liquidator.

(1B) The directors of the company must in accordance with the rules seek such a nomination from the company's creditors.]

(2) The liquidator shall be the person nominated by the creditors or, where no person has been so nominated, the person (if any) nominated by the company.

(3) In the case of different persons being nominated, any director, member or creditor of the company may, within 7 days after the date on which the nomination was made by the creditors, apply to the court for an order either—

(a) directing that the person nominated as liquidator by the company shall be liquidator instead of or jointly with the person nominated by the creditors, or

(b) appointing some other person to be liquidator instead of the person nominated by the creditors.

[(4) The court shall grant an application under subsection (3) made by the holder of a qualifying floating charge in respect of the company's property (within the meaning of paragraph 14 of Schedule B1) unless the court thinks it right to refuse the application because of the particular circumstances of the case.]

NOTES

Sub-ss (1), (1A), (1B): substituted (for the original sub-s (1)) by the Small Business, Enterprise and Employment Act 2015, s 126, Sch 9, Pt 1, paras 1, 24, as from 6 April 2017 (in relation to England and Wales), and as from 6 April 2019 (in relation to Scotland) (for transitional and savings provisions, see the notes to s 246ZE at **[9.385]**).

Sub-s (4): added by the Enterprise Act 2002, s 248(3), Sch 17, paras 9, 14, as from a day to be appointed (for savings and transitional provisions, see the note to s 8 at **[9.147]**).

[9.229]

101 Appointment of liquidation committee

[(1) The creditors may in accordance with the rules appoint a committee ("the liquidation committee") of not more than 5 persons to exercise the functions conferred on it by or under this Act.]

(2) If such a committee is appointed, the company may, either at the meeting at which the resolution for voluntary winding up is passed or at any time subsequently in general meeting, appoint such number of persons as they think fit to act as members of the committee, not exceeding 5.

(3) However, the creditors may, if they think fit, [decide] that all or any of the persons so appointed by the company ought not to be members of the liquidation committee; and if the creditors so [decide]—

(a) [those persons] are not then, unless the court otherwise directs, qualified to act as members of the committee; and

(b) on any application to the court under this provision the court may, if it thinks fit, appoint other persons to act as such members in place of [those persons].

(4) . . .

NOTES

Sub-s (1): substituted by the Small Business, Enterprise and Employment Act 2015, s 126, Sch 9, Pt 1, paras 1, 25(1), (2), as from 6 April 2017 (in relation to England and Wales), and as from 6 April 2019 (in relation to Scotland) (for transitional and savings provisions, see the notes to s 246ZE at **[9.385]**).

Sub-s (3): words in square brackets substituted by the Small Business, Enterprise and Employment Act 2015, s 126, Sch 9, Pt 1, paras 1, 25(1), (3), as from 6 April 2017 (in relation to England and Wales), and as from 6 April 2019 (in relation to Scotland) (for transitional and savings provisions, see the notes to s 246ZE at **[9.385]**).

Sub-s (4): repealed by the Public Services Reform (Corporate Insolvency and Bankruptcy) (Scotland) Order 2017, SSI 2017/209, art 3, as from 6 April 2019.

102 *(Repealed by the Small Business, Enterprise and Employment Act 2015, s 126, Sch 9, Pt 1, paras 1, 26, as from 6 April 2017 (in relation to England and Wales), and as from 6 April 2019 (in relation to Scotland) (for transitional and savings provisions, see the notes to s 246ZE at* **[9.385]**.)

[9.230]

103 Cesser of directors' powers

On the appointment of a liquidator, all the powers of the directors cease, except so far as the liquidation committee (or, if there is no such committee, the creditors) sanction their continuance.

[9.231]

104 Vacancy in office of liquidator

If a vacancy occurs, by death, resignation or otherwise, in the office of a liquidator (other than a liquidator appointed by, or by the direction of, the court), the creditors may fill the vacancy.

[9.232]

[104A Progress report to company and creditors . . . . . .

(1) [The] liquidator must—

(a) for each prescribed period produce a progress report relating to the prescribed matters; and

(b) within such period commencing with the end of the period referred to in paragraph (a) as may be prescribed send a copy of the progress report to—

(i) the members and creditors[, other than opted-out creditors] of the company; and

(ii) such other persons as may be prescribed.

(2) A liquidator who fails to comply with this section is liable to a fine.]

NOTES

Inserted by the Legislative Reform (Insolvency) (Miscellaneous Provisions) Order 2010, SI 2010/18, arts 2, 6(3), as from 6 April 2010 (for transitional provisions see art 12(1) of the 2010 Order which provides that this section does not apply in respect of a company in voluntary winding up where the resolution to wind up was passed before 6 April 2010).

First words omitted from the section heading repealed by the Small Business, Enterprise and Employment Act 2015, s 136(1), (3), as from 26 May 2015.

Second words omitted from the section heading repealed, and word in square brackets in sub-s (1) substituted, by the Public Services Reform (Insolvency) (Scotland) Order 2016, SSI 2016/141, art 6(1), as from 6 April 2019 (for savings, see the note to s 92A at **[9.222]**).

Words in square brackets in sub-s (1)(b)(i) inserted by the Small Business, Enterprise and Employment Act 2015, s 126, Sch 9, Pt 1, paras 1, 27, as from 6 April 2017 (in relation to England and Wales), and as from 6 April 2019 (in relation to Scotland) (for transitional and savings provisions, see the notes to s 246ZE at **[9.385]**).

105 *(Repealed by the Public Services Reform (Insolvency) (Scotland) Order 2016, SSI 2016/141, art 6(2), as from 6 April 2019; for savings, see the note to s 92A at* **[9.222]**.)

[9.233]

[106 Final account prior to dissolution

(1) As soon as the company's affairs are fully wound up the liquidator must make up an account of the winding up, showing how it has been conducted and the company's property has been disposed of.

(2) The liquidator must, before the end of the period of 14 days beginning with the day on which the account is made up—

(a) send a copy of the account to the company's members,

(b) send a copy of the account to the company's creditors (other than opted-out creditors), and

(c) give the company's creditors (other than opted-out creditors) a notice explaining the effect of section 173(2)(e) and how they may object to the liquidator's release.

(3) The liquidator must during the relevant period send to the registrar of companies—

(a) a copy of the account, and

(b) a statement of whether any of the company's creditors objected to the liquidator's release.

(4) The relevant period is the period of 7 days beginning with the day after the last day of the period prescribed by the rules as the period within which the creditors may object to the liquidator's release.

[(4A), (4B) . . .]

(5) If the liquidator does not comply with subsection (2) the liquidator is liable to a fine.

(6) If the liquidator does not comply with subsection (3) the liquidator is liable to a fine and, for continued contravention, a daily default fine.]

NOTES

Substituted by the Small Business, Enterprise and Employment Act 2015, s 126, Sch 9, Pt 1, paras 1, 29, as from 6 April 2017 (in relation to England and Wales), and as from 6 April 2019 (in relation to Scotland) (for transitional and savings provisions, see the notes to s 246ZE at **[9.385]**).

Sub-ss (4A), (4B) were originally inserted by the Insolvency Amendment (EU 2015/848) Regulations 2017, SI 2017/702, regs 2, 3, Schedule, Pt 1, paras 1, 3, as from 26 June 2017, except in relation to proceedings opened before that date. As originally enacted, paragraph 3 of the Schedule to the 2017 Regulations applied to England and Wales only. However, reg 2 of the 2017 Regulations (Amendments and extent) was amended by the Small Business, Enterprise and Employment Act 2015 (Commencement No 7, Consequential, Transitional and Savings Provisions) Regulations 2019, SI 2019/816, reg 6(2) (as from 6 April 2019) so as to apply the amendment made by paragraph 3 of the Schedule to the 2017 Regulations to Scotland. Sub-ss (4A), (4B) were subsequently repealed by the Insolvency (Amendment) (EU Exit) Regulations 2019, SI 2019/146, reg 2, Schedule, Pt 2, paras 16, 18, as from IP completion day (as defined in the European Union (Withdrawal Agreement) Act 2020, s 39) (for savings, see reg 4 of the 2019 Regulations at **[12.82]**).

CHAPTER V PROVISIONS APPLYING TO BOTH KINDS OF VOLUNTARY WINDING UP

[9.234]

107 Distribution of company's property

Subject to the provisions of this Act as to preferential payments, the company's property in a voluntary winding up shall on the winding up be applied in satisfaction of the company's liabilities pari passu and, subject to that application, shall (unless the articles otherwise provide) be distributed among the members according to their rights and interests in the company.

[9.235]

108 Appointment or removal of liquidator by the court

(1) If from any cause whatever there is no liquidator acting, the court may appoint a liquidator.

(2) The court may, on cause shown, remove a liquidator and appoint another.

[9.236]

109 Notice by liquidator of his appointment

(1) The liquidator shall, within 14 days after his appointment, publish in the Gazette and deliver to the registrar of companies for registration a notice of his appointment in the form prescribed by statutory instrument made by the Secretary of State.

(2) If the liquidator fails to comply with this section, he is liable to a fine and, for continued contravention, to a daily default fine.

NOTES

Regulations: the Insolvency (Miscellaneous Amendments) Regulations 2017/1119.

[9.237]

110 Acceptance of shares, etc, as consideration for sale of company property

(1) This section applies, in the case of a company proposed to be, or being, wound up voluntarily, where the whole or part of the company's business or property is proposed to be transferred or sold

[(a)] to another company ("the transferee company"), whether or not the latter is a [company registered under the Companies Act 2006][, or

(b) to a limited liability partnership (the "transferee limited liability partnership")].

(2) With the requisite sanction, the liquidator of the company being, or proposed to be, wound up ("the transferor company") may receive, in compensation or part compensation for the transfer or [sale—

(a) in the case of the transferee company, shares, policies or other like interests in the company for distribution among the members of the transferor company, or

(b) in the case of the transferee limited liability partnership, membership in the limited liability partnership for distribution among the members of the transferor company.]

(3) The sanction requisite under subsection (2) is—

(a) in the case of a members' voluntary winding up, that of a special resolution of the company, conferring either a general authority on the liquidator or an authority in respect of any particular arrangement, and

(b) in the case of a creditors' voluntary winding up, that of either the court or the liquidation committee.

(4) Alternatively to subsection (2), the liquidator may (with that sanction) enter into any other arrangement whereby the members of the transferor [company may—

(a) in the case of the transferee company, in lieu of receiving cash, shares, policies or other like interests (or in addition thereto) participate in the profits of, or receive any other benefit from, the company, or

(b) in the case of the transferee limited liability partnership, in lieu of receiving cash, or membership (or in addition thereto) participate in some other way in the profits of, or receive any other benefit from, the limited liability partnership.]

(5) A sale or arrangement in pursuance of this section is binding on members of the transferor company.

(6) A special resolution is not invalid for purposes of this section by reason that it is passed before or concurrently with a resolution for voluntary winding up or for appointing liquidators; but, if an order is made within a year for winding up the company by the court, the special resolution is not valid unless sanctioned by the court.

NOTES

Sub-s (1): para (a) designated as such, and para (b) (and the preceding word) added by the Limited Liability Partnerships Regulations 2001, SI 2001/1090, reg 9, Sch 5, para 15(1), (2), as from 6 April 2001 (in relation to England and Wales), and by the Limited Liability Partnerships (Scotland) Regulations 2001, SSI 2001/128, reg 5, Sch 4, para 1(1), (2), as from 6 April 2001 (in relation to Scotland). Words in square brackets in para (a) substituted by the Companies Act 2006 (Consequential Amendments, Transitional Provisions and Savings) Order 2009, SI 2009/1941, art 2(1), Sch 1, para 75(1), (11), as from 1 October 2009 (for effect see the note to s 7A at **[9.145]**).

Sub-ss (2), (4): words in square brackets substituted, in relation to England and Wales, by SI 2001/1090, reg 9, Sch 5, para 15(1), (3), (4), as from 6 April 2001, and in relation to Scotland, by SSI 2001/128, reg 5, Sch 4, para 1(1), (3), (4), as from 6 April 2001.

[9.238]

111 Dissent from arrangement under s 110

(1) This section applies in the case of a voluntary winding up where, for the purposes of section 110(2) or (4), there has been passed a special resolution of the transferor company providing the sanction requisite for the liquidator under that section.

(2) If a member of the transferor company who did not vote in favour of the special resolution expresses his dissent from it in writing, addressed to the liquidator and left at the company's registered office within 7 days after the passing of the resolution, he may require the liquidator either to abstain from carrying the resolution into effect or to purchase his interest at a price to be determined by agreement or by arbitration under this section.

(3) If the liquidator elects to purchase the member's interest, the purchase money must be paid before the company is dissolved and be raised by the liquidator in such manner as may be determined by special resolution.

(4) For purposes of an arbitration under this section, the provisions of the Companies Clauses Consolidation Act 1845 or, in the case of a winding up in Scotland, the Companies Clauses Consolidation (Scotland) Act 1845 with respect to the settlement of disputes by arbitration are incorporated with this Act, and—

(a) in the construction of those provisions this Act is deemed the special Act and "the company" means the transferor company, and

(b) any appointment by the incorporated provisions directed to be made under the hand of the secretary or any two of the directors may be made in writing by the liquidator (or, if there is more than one liquidator, then any two or more of them).

[9.239]

112 Reference of questions to court

(1) The liquidator or any contributory or creditor may apply to the court to determine any question arising in the winding up of a company, or to exercise, as respects the enforcing of calls or any other matter, all or any of the powers which the court might exercise if the company were being wound up by the court.

(2) The court, if satisfied that the determination of the question or the required exercise of power will be just and beneficial, may accede wholly or partially to the application on such terms and conditions as it thinks fit, or may make such other order on the application as it thinks just.

(3) A copy of an order made by virtue of this section staying the proceedings in the winding up shall forthwith be forwarded by the company, or otherwise as may be prescribed, to the registrar of companies, who shall enter it in his records relating to the company.

[9.240]

113 Court's power to control proceedings (Scotland)

If the court, on the application of the liquidator in the winding up of a company registered in Scotland, so directs, no action or proceeding shall be proceeded with or commenced against the company except by leave of the court and subject to such terms as the court may impose.

[9.241]

114 No liquidator appointed or nominated by company

(1) This section applies where, in the case of a voluntary winding up, no liquidator has been appointed or nominated by the company.

(2) The powers of the directors shall not be exercised, except with the sanction of the court or (in the case of a creditors' voluntary winding up) so far as may be necessary to secure compliance with sections . . . 99 (statement of affairs) [and 100(1B) (nomination of liquidator by creditors)], during the period before the appointment or nomination of a liquidator of the company.

(3) Subsection (2) does not apply in relation to the powers of the directors—

(a) to dispose of perishable goods and other goods the value of which is likely to diminish if they are not immediately disposed of, and

(b) to do all such other things as may be necessary for the protection of the company's assets.

(4) If the directors of the company without reasonable excuse fail to comply with this section, they are liable to a fine.

NOTES

Sub-s (2): words omitted repealed, and words in square brackets inserted, by the Small Business, Enterprise and Employment Act 2015, s 126, Sch 9, Pt 1, paras 1, 30, as from 6 April 2017 (in relation to England and Wales), and as from 6 April 2019 (in relation to Scotland) (for transitional and savings provisions, see the notes to s 246ZE at **[9.385]**).

Part 9 Misc primary legislation

[9.242]

115 Expenses of voluntary winding up

[After the payment of any liabilities to which section 174A applies,] all expenses properly incurred in the winding up, including the remuneration of the liquidator, are payable out of the company's assets in priority to all other claims.

NOTES

Words in square brackets inserted by the Corporate Insolvency and Governance Act 2020, s 2(1), Sch 3, paras 1, 9, as from 26 June 2020 (for transitional provisions, see s 2(2), (3) of the 2020 Act (at **[9.533]**) which provides that (without prejudice to the Interpretation Act 1978, s 16) nothing in the 2020 Act affects the operation of this Act, or any other enactment, in relation to a moratorium under Sch A1 to this Act which comes into force before the repeal of that Schedule by Sch 3 to the 2020 Act (ie, 26 June 2020)).

[9.243]

116 Saving for certain rights

The voluntary winding up of a company does not bar the right of any creditor or contributory to have it wound up by the court; but in the case of an application by a contributory the court must be satisfied that the rights of the contributories will be prejudiced by a voluntary winding up.

CHAPTER VI WINDING UP BY THE COURT

Jurisdiction (England and Wales)

[9.244]

117 High Court and county court jurisdiction

(1) The High Court has jurisdiction to wind up any company registered in England and Wales.

(2) Where [in the case of a company registered in England and Wales the amount of its] share capital paid up or credited as paid up does not exceed £120,000, then (subject to this section) the county court . . . has concurrent jurisdiction with the High Court to wind up the company.

[(2A) Despite subsection (2), proceedings for the exercise of the jurisdiction to wind up a company registered in England and Wales may be commenced only in the High Court if the place which has longest been the company's registered office during the 6 months immediately preceding the presentation of the petition for winding up is in the district that is the London insolvency district for the purposes of the second Group of Parts of this Act.]

(3) The money sum for the time being specified in subsection (2) is subject to increase or reduction by order under section 416 in Part XV.

(4) . . .

(5) Every court in England and Wales having winding-up jurisdiction has for the purposes of that jurisdiction all the powers of the High Court; and every prescribed officer of the court shall perform any duties which an officer of the High Court may discharge by order of a judge of that court or otherwise in relation to winding up.

(6) . . .

[(7) . . .]

[(8) The Lord Chief Justice may nominate a judicial office holder (as defined in section 109(4) of the Constitutional Reform Act 2005) to exercise his functions under this section.]

NOTES

Sub-s (2): words in square brackets substituted, and words omitted repealed, by the Crime and Courts Act 2013, s 17, Sch 9, Pt 3, para 93(a), as from 22 April 2014.

Sub-s (2A): inserted by the High Court and County Courts Jurisdiction Order 1991, SI 1991/724, art 6F, Schedule, Pt I (as amended by SI 2014/821), as from 22 April 2014 (except in relation to proceedings commenced before that date).

Sub-ss (4), (6): repealed by the Crime and Courts Act 2013, s 17, Sch 9, Pt 3, para 93(b), as from 22 April 2014.

Sub-s (7): originally added by the Insolvency Act 1986 (Amendment) (No 2) Regulations 2002, SI 2002/1240, regs 3, 6, as from 31 May 2002. Subsequently repealed by the Insolvency (Amendment) (EU Exit) Regulations 2019, SI 2019/146, reg 2, Schedule, Pt 2, paras 16, 19, as from IP completion day (as defined in the European Union (Withdrawal Agreement) Act 2020, s 39) (for savings, see reg 4 of the 2019 Regulations at **[12.82]**).

Sub-s (8): added by the Constitutional Reform Act 2005, s 15, Sch 4, Pt 1, paras 185, 186(1), (3), as from 3 April 2006.

[9.245]

118 Proceedings taken in wrong court

(1) Nothing in section 117 invalidates a proceeding by reason of its being taken in the wrong court.

(2) The winding up of a company by the court in England and Wales, or any proceedings in the winding up, may be retained in the court in which the proceedings were commenced, although it may not be the court in which they ought to have been commenced.

[9.246]

119 Proceedings in county court; case stated for High Court

(1) If any question arises in any winding-up proceedings in a county court which all the parties to the proceedings, or which one of them and the judge of the court, desire to have determined in the first instance in the High Court, the judge shall state the facts in the form of a special case for the opinion of the High Court.

(2) Thereupon the special case and the proceedings (or such of them as may be required) shall be transmitted to the High Court for the purposes of the determination.

Jurisdiction (Scotland)

[9.247]

120 Court of Session and sheriff court jurisdiction

(1) The Court of Session has jurisdiction to wind up any company registered in Scotland.

(2) When the Court of Session is in vacation, the jurisdiction conferred on that court by this section may (subject to the provisions of this Part) be exercised by the judge acting as vacation judge . . .

(3) Where the amount of a company's share capital paid up or credited as paid up does not exceed £120,000, the sheriff court of the sheriffdom in which the company's registered office is situated has concurrent jurisdiction with the Court of Session to wind up the company; but—

(a) the Court of Session may, if it thinks expedient having regard to the amount of the company's assets to do so—
   (i) remit to a sheriff court any petition presented to the Court of Session for winding up such a company, or
   (ii) require such a petition presented to a sheriff court to be remitted to the Court of Session; and

(b) the Court of Session may require any such petition as above-mentioned presented to one sheriff court to be remitted to another sheriff court; and

(c) in a winding up in the sheriff court the sheriff may submit a stated case for the opinion of the Court of Session on any question of law arising in that winding up.

(4) For purposes of this section, the expression "registered office" means the place which has longest been the company's registered office during the 6 months immediately preceding the presentation of the petition for winding up.

(5) The money sum for the time being specified in subsection (3) is subject to increase or reduction by order under section 416 in Part XV.

[(6) . . .]

NOTES

Sub-s (2): words omitted repealed by the Court of Session Act 1988, s 52(2), Sch 2, Pt III, as from 29 September 1988.

Sub-s (6): originally added by the Insolvency Act 1986 (Amendment) (No 2) Regulations 2002, SI 2002/1240, regs 3, 7, as from 31 May 2002. Subsequently repealed by the Insolvency (Amendment) (EU Exit) Regulations 2019, SI 2019/146, reg 2, Schedule, Pt 2, paras 16, 20, as from IP completion day (as defined in the European Union (Withdrawal Agreement) Act 2020, s 39) (for savings, see reg 4 of the 2019 Regulations at **[12.82]**).

[9.248]

121 Power to remit winding up to Lord Ordinary

(1) The Court of Session may, by Act of Sederunt, make provision for the taking of proceedings in a winding up before one of the Lords Ordinary; and, where provision is so made, the Lord Ordinary has, for the purposes of the winding up, all the powers and jurisdiction of the court.

(2) However, the Lord Ordinary may report to the Inner House any matter which may arise in the course of a winding up.

Grounds and effect of winding-up petition

[9.249]

122 Circumstances in which company may be wound up by the court

(1) A company may be wound up by the court if—

(a) the company has by special resolution resolved that the company be wound up by the court,

(b) being a public company which was registered as such on its original incorporation, the company has not been issued with [a trading certificate under section 761 of the Companies Act 2006 (requirement as to minimum share capital)] and more than a year has expired since it was so registered,

(c) it is an old public company, within the meaning of [Schedule 3 to the Companies Act 2006 (Consequential Amendments, Transitional Provisions and Savings) Order 2009],

(d) the company does not commence its business within a year from its incorporation or suspends its business for a whole year,

(e) . . .

(f) the company is unable to pay its debts,

[(fa) . . .]

(g) the court is of the opinion that it is just and equitable that the company should be wound up.

(2) In Scotland, a company which the Court of Session has jurisdiction to wind up may be wound up by the Court if there is subsisting a floating charge over property comprised in the company's property and undertaking, and the court is satisfied that the security of the creditor entitled to the benefit of the floating charge is in jeopardy.

For this purpose a creditor's security is deemed to be in jeopardy if the Court is satisfied that events have occurred or are about to occur which render it unreasonable in the creditor's interests that the company should retain power to dispose of the property which is subject to the floating charge.

NOTES

Sub-s (1): words in square brackets in para (b) substituted by the Companies Act 2006 (Consequential Amendments etc) Order 2008, SI 2008/948, art 3(1), Sch 1, Pt 2, para 102, as from 6 April 2008. Words in square brackets in para (c) substituted by the Companies Act 2006 (Consequential Amendments, Transitional Provisions and Savings) Order 2009, SI 2009/1941, art 2(1), Sch 1, para 75(1), (12), as from 1 October 2009 (for effect see the note to s 7A at **[9.145]**). Para (e) repealed by the Companies Act 2006 (Consequential Amendments and Transitional Provisions) Order 2011, SI 2011/1265, art 6(4), as from 12 May 2011. Para (fa) originally inserted by the Insolvency Act 2000, s 1, Sch 1, paras 1, 6, as from 1 January 2003, and subsequently repealed by the Corporate Insolvency and Governance Act 2020, s 2(1), Sch 3, paras 1, 10, as from 26 June 2020 (for transitional provisions, see s 2(2), (3) of the 2020 Act (at **[9.533]**) which provides that (without prejudice to the Interpretation Act 1978, s 16) nothing in the 2020 Act affects the operation of this Act, or any other enactment, in relation to a moratorium under Sch A1 to this Act which comes into force before the repeal of that Schedule by Sch 3 to the 2020 Act (ie, 26 June 2020)).

Prohibition on presenting a winding-up petition solely in relation to a protected rent debt: see the note to s 124 at **[9.251]**.

Old public companies: as to the meaning of this, see also the Companies Act 2006 (Consequential Amendments and Transitional Provisions) Order 2011, SI 2011/1265, Sch 1 at **[4.428]**.

[9.250]

123 Definition of inability to pay debts

(1) A company is deemed unable to pay its debts—

(a) if a creditor (by assignment or otherwise) to whom the company is indebted in a sum exceeding £750 then due has served on the company, by leaving it at the company's registered office, a written demand (in the prescribed form) requiring the company to pay the sum so due and the company has for 3 weeks thereafter neglected to pay the sum or to secure or compound for it to the reasonable satisfaction of the creditor, or

(b) if, in England and Wales, execution or other process issued on a judgment, decree or order of any court in favour of a creditor of the company is returned unsatisfied in whole or in part, or

(c) if, in Scotland, the induciae of a charge for payment on an extract decree, or an extract registered bond, or an extract registered protest, have expired without payment being made, or

(d) if, in Northern Ireland, a certificate of unenforceability has been granted in respect of a judgment against the company, or

(e) if it is proved to the satisfaction of the court that the company is unable to pay its debts as they fall due.

(2) A company is also deemed unable to pay its debts if it is proved to the satisfaction of the court that the value of the company's assets is less than the amount of its liabilities, taking into account its contingent and prospective liabilities.

(3) The money sum for the time being specified in subsection (1)(a) is subject to increase or reduction by order under section 416 in Part XV.

[9.251]

124 Application for winding up

(1) Subject to the provisions of this section, an application to the court for the winding up of a company shall be by petition presented either by the company, or the directors, or by any creditor or creditors (including any contingent or prospective creditor or creditors), contributory or contributories . . . [or by [the designated officer for a magistrates' court] in the exercise of the power conferred by section 87A of the Magistrates' Courts Act 1980 (enforcement of fines imposed on companies)], or by all or any of those parties, together or separately.

(2) Except as mentioned below, a contributory is not entitled to present a winding-up petition unless either—

(a) the number of members is reduced below 2, or

(b) the shares in respect of which he is a contributory, or some of them, either were originally allotted to him, or have been held by him, and registered in his name, for at least 6 months during the 18 months before the commencement of the winding up, or have devolved on him through the death of a former holder.

(3) A person who is liable under section 76 to contribute to a company's assets in the event of its being wound up may petition on either of the grounds set out in section 122(1)(f) and (g), and subsection (2) above does not then apply; but unless the person is a contributory otherwise than under section 76, he may not in his character as contributory petition on any other ground.

. . .

[(3A) . . .]

(4) A winding-up petition may be presented by the Secretary of State—

(a) if the ground of the petition is that in section 122(1)(b) or (c), or

[(b) in a case falling within section 124A [or 124B] below.]

[(4AA) A winding up petition may be presented by the [Financial Conduct Authority] in a case falling within section 124C(1) or (2).]

[(4A) A winding-up petition may be presented by the Regulator of Community Interest Companies in a case falling within section 50 of the Companies (Audit, Investigations and Community Enterprise) Act 2004.]

(5) Where a company is being wound up voluntarily in England and Wales, a winding-up petition may be presented by the official receiver attached to the court as well as by any other person authorised in that behalf under the other provisions of this section; but the court shall not make a winding-up order on the petition unless it is satisfied that the voluntary winding up cannot be continued with due regard to the interests of the creditors or contributories.

NOTES

Sub-s (1): words omitted repealed by the Insolvency (Amendment) (EU Exit) Regulations 2019, SI 2019/146, reg 2, Schedule, Pt 2, paras 16, 21, as from IP completion day (as defined in the European Union (Withdrawal Agreement) Act 2020, s 39) (for savings, see reg 4 of the 2019 Regulations at **[12.82]**). Words in first (outer) pair of square brackets inserted by the Criminal Justice Act 1988, s 62(2)(b), as from 5 January 1989. Words in second (inner) pair of square brackets substituted by the Courts Act 2003, s 109(1), Sch 8, para 294, as from 1 April 2005.

Sub-s (3): words omitted repealed by the Companies Act 2006 (Consequential Amendments, Transitional Provisions and Savings) Order 2009, SI 2009/1941, art 2(1), Sch 1, para 75(1), (13), as from 1 October 2009 (for effect see the note to s 7A at **[9.145]**).

Sub-s (3A): originally inserted by the Insolvency Act 2000, s 1, Sch 1, paras 1, 7, as from 1 January 2003. Subsequently repealed by the Corporate Insolvency and Governance Act 2020, s 2(1), Sch 3, paras 1, 11, as from 26 June 2020 (for transitional provisions, see s 2(2), (3) of the 2020 Act (at **[9.533]**) which provides that (without prejudice to the Interpretation Act 1978, s 16) nothing in the 2020 Act affects the operation of this Act, or any other enactment, in relation to a moratorium under Sch A1 to this Act which comes into force before the repeal of that Schedule by Sch 3 to the 2020 Act (ie, 26 June 2020)).

Sub-s (4): para (b) substituted by CA 1989, s 60(2), as from 21 February 1990. Words in square brackets in para (b) inserted by the European Public Limited-Liability Company Regulations 2004, SI 2004/2326, reg 73(4)(a), as from 8 October 2004.

Sub-s (4AA): inserted by the European Cooperative Society Regulations 2006, SI 2006/22078, reg 33(2), as from 18 August 2006. Words in square brackets substituted by the Financial Services Act 2012 (Mutual Societies) Order 2013, SI 2013/496, art 2(c), Sch 1, para 2(a), as from 1 April 2013.

Sub-s (4A): inserted by the Companies (Audit, Investigations and Community Enterprise) Act 2004, s 50(3), as from 1 July 2005.

Restriction on winding-up petitions and orders: as to the restriction on winding-up petitions and orders during "the relevant period", see the Corporate Insolvency and Governance Act 2020, Sch 10 at **[9.566]** (as to the meaning of "the relevant period", see Sch 10, para 4).

Prohibition on presenting a winding-up petition solely in relation to a protected rent debt: see the Commercial Rent (Coronavirus) Act 2022, Sch 3, para 1 (at **[9.703]**), which provides as follows—

"(1) This paragraph applies where a landlord under a business tenancy is owed a protected rent debt and the tenant is a company.

(2) The landlord may not, during the moratorium period for the debt, present a petition for the winding up of the company under section 124 of the Insolvency Act 1986 on a ground specified—

(a) in the case of a registered company, in section 122(1)(f) of that Act, or

(b) in the case of an unregistered company, in section 221(5)(b) of that Act,

unless the landlord is owed a debt by the company which is not a protected rent debt.

(3) In this paragraph—

"the moratorium period", in relation to a protected rent debt, has the same meaning as in section 23;

"registered company" means a company registered under the Companies Act 2006 in England and Wales or Scotland;

"unregistered company" has the same meaning as in Part 5 of the Insolvency Act 1986.

(4) This paragraph, so far as relating to registered companies, applies to limited liability partnerships.".

[9.252]

[124A Petition for winding up on grounds of public interest

(1) Where it appears to the Secretary of State from—

(a) any report made or information obtained under Part XIV [(except section 448A)] of the Companies Act 1985 (company investigations, &c),

[(b) any report made by inspectors under—

(i) section 167, 168, 169 or 284 of the Financial Services and Markets Act 2000, or

(ii) where the company is an open-ended investment company (within the meaning of that Act), regulations made as a result of section 262(2)(k) of that Act;

(bb) any information or documents obtained under section 165, 171, 172, 173 or 175 of that Act,]

(c) any information obtained under section 2 of the Criminal Justice Act 1987 or section 52 of the Criminal Justice (Scotland) Act 1987 (fraud investigations), or

(d) any information obtained under section 83 of the Companies Act 1989 (powers exercisable for purpose of assisting overseas regulatory authorities),

that it is expedient in the public interest that a company should be wound up, he may present a petition for it to be wound up if the court thinks it just and equitable for it to be so.

(2) This section does not apply if the company is already being wound up by the court.]

NOTES

Inserted by CA 1989, s 60(3), as from 21 February 1990.

Sub-s (1): words in square brackets in para (a) inserted by the Companies (Audit, Investigations and Community Enterprise) Act 2004, s 25, Sch 2, Pt 3, para 27, as from 6 April 2005. Paras (b), (bb) substituted, for the original para (b), by the Financial Services and Markets Act 2000 (Consequential Amendments and Repeals) Order 2001, SI 2001/3649, art 305, as from 1 December 2001.

124B, 124C *(S 124B (as inserted by the European Public Limited-Liability Company Regulations 2004, SI 2004/2326, reg 73(3), as from 8 October 2004) and s 124C (as inserted by the European Cooperative Society Regulations 2006, SI 2006/22078, reg 33(1), as from 18 August 2006) were repealed by the Financial Services (Miscellaneous) (Amendment) (EU Exit) Regulations 2019, SI 2019/710, reg 2, as from IP completion day (as defined in the European Union (Withdrawal Agreement) Act 2020, s 39).)*

[9.253]

125 Powers of court on hearing of petition

(1) On hearing a winding-up petition the court may dismiss it, or adjourn the hearing conditionally or unconditionally, or make an interim order, or any other order that it thinks fit; but the court shall not refuse to make a winding-up order on the ground only that the company's assets have been mortgaged to an amount equal to or in excess of those assets, or that the company has no assets.

(2) If the petition is presented by members of the company as contributories on the ground that it is just and equitable that the company should be wound up, the court, if it is of opinion—

(a) that the petitioners are entitled to relief either by winding up the company or by some other means, and

(b) that in the absence of any other remedy it would be just and equitable that the company should be wound up,

shall make a winding-up order; but this does not apply if the court is also of the opinion both that some other remedy is available to the petitioners and that they are acting unreasonably in seeking to have the company wound up instead of pursuing that other remedy.

[9.254]

126 Power to stay or restrain proceedings against company

(1) At any time after the presentation of a winding-up petition, and before a winding-up order has been made, the company, or any creditor or contributory, may—

(a) where any action or proceeding against the company is pending in the High Court or Court of Appeal in England and Wales or Northern Ireland, apply to the court in which the action or proceeding is pending for a stay of proceedings therein, and

(b) where any other action or proceeding is pending against the company, apply to the court having jurisdiction to wind up the company to restrain further proceedings in the action or proceeding;

and the court to which application is so made may (as the case may be) stay, sist or restrain the proceedings accordingly on such terms as it thinks fit.

(2) In the case of [a company registered but not formed under the Companies Act 2006], where the application to stay, sist or restrain is by a creditor, this section extends to actions and proceedings against any contributory of the company.

[(3) Subsection (1) applies in relation to any action being taken in respect of the company under Part 1 of Schedule 8 to the Finance (No 2) Act 2015 (enforcement by deduction from accounts) as it applies in relation to any action or proceeding mentioned in paragraph (b) of that subsection.]

NOTES

Sub-s (2): words in square brackets substituted by the Companies Act 2006 (Consequential Amendments, Transitional Provisions and Savings) Order 2009, SI 2009/1941, art 2(1), Sch 1, para 75(1), (14), as from 1 October 2009 (for effect see the note to s 7A at **[9.145]**).

Sub-s (3): added by the Finance (No 2) Act 2015, s 51, Sch 8, Pt 2, paras 26, 27, as from 18 November 2015.

[9.255]

127 Avoidance of property dispositions, etc

[(1)] In a winding up by the court, any disposition of the company's property, and any transfer of shares, or alteration in the status of the company's members, made after the commencement of the winding up is, unless the court otherwise orders, void.

[(2) This section has no effect in respect of anything done by an administrator of a company while a winding-up petition is suspended under paragraph 40 of Schedule B1.]

[(3) This section has no effect in respect of anything done during a moratorium under Part A1, or during a period mentioned in section 5(4)(a) following the end of a moratorium, where the winding-up order was made on a petition presented before the moratorium begins, unless the petition was presented under section 367 of the Financial Services and Markets Act 2000 on the ground mentioned in section 367(3)(b) of that Act.]

NOTES

Sub-s (1) numbered as such, and sub-s (2) added, by the Enterprise Act 2002, s 248(3), Sch 17, paras 9, 15, as from 15 September 2003 (for savings and transitional provisions, see the note to s 8 at **[9.147]**).

Sub-s (3): added by the Corporate Insolvency and Governance Act 2020, s 2(1), Sch 3, paras 1, 12, as from 26 June 2020 (for transitional provisions, see s 2(2), (3) of the 2020 Act (at **[9.533]**) which provides that (without prejudice to the Interpretation Act 1978, s 16) nothing in the 2020 Act affects the operation of this Act, or any other enactment, in relation to a moratorium under Sch A1 to this Act which comes into force before the repeal of that Schedule by Sch 3 to the 2020 Act (ie, 26 June 2020)).

[9.256]

128 Avoidance of attachments, etc

(1) Where a company registered in England and Wales is being wound up by the court, any attachment, sequestration, distress or execution put in force against the estate or effects of the company after the commencement of the winding up is void.

(2) This section, so far as relates to any estate or effects of the company situated in England and Wales, applies in the case of a company registered in Scotland as it applies in the case of a company registered in England and Wales.

[(3) In subsection (1) "attachment" includes a hold notice or a deduction notice under Part 1 of Schedule 8 to the Finance (No 2) Act 2015 (enforcement by deduction from accounts) and, if subsection (1) has effect in relation to a deduction notice, it also has effect in relation to the hold notice to which the deduction notice relates (whenever the hold notice was given).]

NOTES

Sub-s (3): added by the Finance (No 2) Act 2015, s 51, Sch 8, Pt 2, paras 26, 28, as from 18 November 2015.

Commencement of winding up

[9.257]

129 Commencement of winding up by the court

(1) If, before the presentation of a petition for the winding up of a company by the court, a resolution has been passed by the company for voluntary winding up, the winding up of the company is deemed to have commenced at the time of the passing of the resolution; and unless the court, on proof of fraud or mistake, directs otherwise, all proceedings taken in the voluntary winding up are deemed to have been validly taken.

[(1A) Where the court makes a winding-up order by virtue of paragraph 13(1)(e) of Schedule B1, the winding up is deemed to commence on the making of the order.]

(2) In any other case, the winding up of a company by the court is deemed to commence at the time of the presentation of the petition for winding up.

NOTES

Sub-s (1A): inserted by the Enterprise Act 2002, s 248(3), Sch 17, paras 9, 16, as from 15 September 2003 (for savings and transitional provisions, see the note to s 8 at **[9.147]**).

[9.258]

130 Consequences of winding-up order

(1) On the making of a winding-up order, a copy of the order must forthwith be forwarded by the company (or otherwise as may be prescribed) to the registrar of companies, who shall enter it in his records relating to the company.

(2) When a winding-up order has been made or a provisional liquidator has been appointed, no action or proceeding shall be proceeded with or commenced against the company or its property, except by leave of the court and subject to such terms as the court may impose.

(3) When an order has been made for winding up a company [registered but not formed under the Companies Act 2006], no action or proceeding shall be commenced or proceeded with against the company or its property or any contributory of the company, in respect of any debt of the company, except by leave of the court, and subject to such terms as the court may impose.

[(3A) In subsections (2) and (3), the reference to an action or proceeding includes action in respect of the company under Part 1 of Schedule 8 to the Finance (No 2) Act 2015 (enforcement by deduction from accounts).]

(4) An order for winding up a company operates in favour of all the creditors and of all contributories of the company as if made on the joint petition of a creditor and of a contributory.

NOTES

Sub-s (3): words in square brackets substituted by the Companies Act 2006 (Consequential Amendments, Transitional Provisions and Savings) Order 2009, SI 2009/1941, art 2(1), Sch 1, para 75(1), (15), as from 1 October 2009 (for effect see the note to s 7A at **[9.145]**).

Sub-s (3A): inserted by the Finance (No 2) Act 2015, s 51, Sch 8, Pt 2, paras 26, 29, as from 18 November 2015.

Investigation procedures

[9.259]

131 Company's statement of affairs

(1) Where the court has made a winding-up order or appointed a provisional liquidator, the official receiver may require some or all of the persons mentioned in subsection (3) below to make out and submit to him a statement in the prescribed form as to the affairs of the company.

(2) The statement . . . shall show—

(a) particulars of the company's assets and liabilities;

(b) the names and addresses of the company's creditors;

(c) the securities held by them respectively;

(d) the dates when the securities were respectively given; and

(e) such further or other information as may be prescribed or as the official receiver may require.

[(2A) The statement shall be verified . . . —

(a) in the case of an appointment of a provisional liquidator or a winding up by the court in England and Wales, [be verified by the persons required to submit it] by a statement of truth; and

(b) in the case of an appointment of a provisional liquidator or a winding up by the court in Scotland, [contain a statutory declaration by the persons required to submit it].]

(3) The persons referred to in subsection (1) are—

(a) those who are or have been officers of the company;

(b) those who have taken part in the formation of the company at any time within one year before the relevant date;

(c) those who are in the company's employment, or have been in its employment within that year, and are in the official receiver's opinion capable of giving the information required;

(d) those who are or have been within that year officers of, or in the employment of, a company which is, or within that year was, an officer of the company.

(4) Where any persons are required under this section to submit a statement of affairs to the official receiver, they shall do so (subject to the next subsection) before the end of the period of 21 days beginning with the day after that on which the prescribed notice of the requirement is given to them by the official receiver.

(5) The official receiver, if he thinks fit, may—

(a) at any time release a person from an obligation imposed on him under subsection (1) or (2) above; or

(b) either when giving the notice mentioned in subsection (4) or subsequently, extend the period so mentioned;

and where the official receiver has refused to exercise a power conferred by this subsection, the court, if it thinks fit, may exercise it.

(6) In this section—

"employment" includes employment under a contract for services; and

"the relevant date" means—

(a) in a case where a provisional liquidator is appointed, the date of his appointment; and

(b) in a case where no such appointment is made, the date of the winding-up order.

(7) If a person without reasonable excuse fails to comply with any obligation imposed under this section, he is liable to a fine and, for continued contravention, to a daily default fine.

(8) In the application of this section to Scotland references to the official receiver are to the liquidator or, in a case where a provisional liquidator is appointed, the provisional liquidator.

NOTES

Sub-s (2): words omitted repealed by the Legislative Reform (Insolvency) (Miscellaneous Provisions) Order 2010, SI 2010/18, arts 2, 5(4)(a), as from 6 April 2010.

Sub-s (2A): inserted by SI 2010/18, arts 2, 5(4)(b), as from 6 April 2010. Words omitted repealed, words in square brackets in para (a) inserted, and words in square brackets in para (b) substituted, by the Public Services Reform (Insolvency) (Scotland) Order 2016, SSI 2016/141, art 10, as from 6 April 2019 (for savings, see the note to s 66 at **[9.186]**).

[9.260]

132 Investigation by official receiver

(1) Where a winding-up order is made by the court in England and Wales, it is the duty of the official receiver to investigate—

(a) if the company has failed, the causes of the failure; and

(b) generally, the promotion, formation, business, dealings and affairs of the company,

and to make such report (if any) to the court as he thinks fit.

(2) The report is, in any proceedings, prima facie evidence of the facts stated in it.

[9.261]

133 Public examination of officers

(1) Where a company is being wound up by the court, the official receiver or, in Scotland, the liquidator may at any time before the dissolution of the company apply to the court for the public examination of any person who—

(a) is or has been an officer of the company; or

(b) has acted as liquidator or administrator of the company or as receiver or manager or, in Scotland, receiver of its property; or

(c) not being a person falling within paragraph (a) or (b), is or has been concerned, or has taken part, in the promotion, formation or management of the company.

(2) Unless the court otherwise orders, the official receiver or, in Scotland, the liquidator shall make an application under subsection (1) if he is requested in accordance with the rules to do so by—

(a) one-half, in value, of the company's creditors; or

(b) three-quarters, in value, of the company's contributories.

(3) On an application under subsection (1), the court shall direct that a public examination of the person to whom the application relates shall be held on a day appointed by the court; and that person shall attend on that day and be publicly examined as to the promotion, formation or management of the company or as to the conduct of its business and affairs, or his conduct or dealings in relation to the company.

(4) The following may take part in the public examination of a person under this section and may question that person concerning the matters mentioned in subsection (3), namely—

(a) the official receiver;

(b) the liquidator of the company;

(c) any person who has been appointed as special manager of the company's property or business;

(d) any creditor of the company who has tendered a proof or, in Scotland, submitted a claim in the winding up;

(e) any contributory of the company.

[9.262]

134 Enforcement of s 133

(1) If a person without reasonable excuse fails at any time to attend his public examination under section 133, he is guilty of a contempt of court and liable to be punished accordingly.

(2) In a case where a person without reasonable excuse fails at any time to attend his examination under section 133 or there are reasonable grounds for believing that a person has absconded, or is about to abscond, with a view to avoiding or delaying his examination under that section, the court may cause a warrant to be issued to a constable or prescribed officer of the court—

(a) for the arrest of that person; and

(b) for the seizure of any books, papers, records, money or goods in that person's possession.

(3) In such a case the court may authorise the person arrested under the warrant to be kept in custody, and anything seized under such a warrant to be held, in accordance with the rules, until such time as the court may order.

Appointment of liquidator

[9.263]

135 Appointment and powers of provisional liquidator

(1) Subject to the provisions of this section, the court may, at any time after the presentation of a winding-up petition, appoint a liquidator provisionally.

(2) In England and Wales, the appointment of a provisional liquidator may be made at any time before the making of a winding-up order; and either the official receiver or any other fit person may be appointed.

(3) In Scotland, such an appointment may be made at any time before the first appointment of liquidators.

(4) The provisional liquidator shall carry out such functions as the court may confer on him.

(5) When a liquidator is provisionally appointed by the court, his powers may be limited by the order appointing him.

[9.264]

136 Functions of official receiver in relation to office of liquidator

(1) The following provisions of this section have effect, subject to section 140 below, on a winding-up order being made by the court in England and Wales.

(2) The official receiver, by virtue of his office, becomes the liquidator of the company and continues in office until another person becomes liquidator under the provisions of this Part.

(3) The official receiver is, by virtue of his office, the liquidator during any vacancy.

(4) At any time when he is the liquidator of the company, the official receiver may [in accordance with the rules seek nominations from] the company's creditors and contributories for the purpose of choosing a person to be liquidator of the company in place of the official receiver.

(5) It is the duty of the official receiver—

(a) as soon as practicable in the period of 12 weeks beginning with the day on which the winding-up order was made, to decide whether to exercise his power under subsection (4) . . . , and

(b) if in pursuance of paragraph (a) he decides not to exercise that power, to give notice of his decision, before the end of that period, to the court and to the company's creditors and contributories, and

(c) (whether or not he has decided to exercise that power) to exercise his power . . . under subsection (4) if he is at any time requested, in accordance with the rules, to do so by one-quarter, in value, of the company's creditors;

and accordingly, where the duty imposed by paragraph (c) arises before the official receiver has performed a duty imposed by paragraph (a) or (b), he is not required to perform the latter duty.

(6) A notice given under subsection (5)(b) to the company's creditors shall contain an explanation of the creditors' power under subsection (5)(c) to require the official receiver to [seek nominations from] the company's creditors and contributories.

NOTES

Words in square brackets in sub-ss (4), (6) substituted, and words omitted from sub-s (5)) repealed, by the Small Business, Enterprise and Employment Act 2015, s 126, Sch 9, Pt 1, paras 1, 31, as from 6 April 2017 (in relation to England and Wales), and as from 6 April 2019 (in relation to Scotland) (for transitional and savings provisions, see the notes to s 246ZE at **[9.385]**).

[9.265]

137 Appointment by Secretary of State

(1) In a winding up by the court in England and Wales the official receiver may, at any time when he is the liquidator of the company, apply to the Secretary of State for the appointment of a person as liquidator in his place.

(2) If [nominations are sought from the company's creditors and contributories] in pursuance of a decision under section 136(5)(a), but no person is chosen to be liquidator as a result . . . , it is the duty of the official receiver to decide whether to refer the need for an appointment to the Secretary of State.

(3) On an application under subsection (1), or a reference made in pursuance of a decision under subsection (2), the Secretary of State shall either make an appointment or decline to make one.

(4) Where a liquidator has been appointed by the Secretary of State under subsection (3), the liquidator shall give notice of his appointment to the company's creditors or, if the court so allows, shall advertise his appointment in accordance with the directions of the court.

(5) In that notice or advertisement the liquidator [must explain the procedure for establishing a liquidation committee under section 141].

NOTES

Words in square brackets in sub-s (2) substituted, words omitted from sub-s (2) repealed, and words in square brackets in sub-s (5) substituted, by the Small Business, Enterprise and Employment Act 2015, s 126, Sch 9, Pt 1, paras 1, 32, as from 6 April 2017 (in relation to England and Wales), and as from 6 April 2019 (in relation to Scotland) (for transitional and savings provisions, see the notes to s 246ZE at **[9.385]**).

[9.266]

138 Appointment of liquidator in Scotland

(1) Where a winding-up order is made by the court in Scotland, a liquidator shall be appointed by the court at the time when the order is made.

(2) The liquidator so appointed (here referred to as "the interim liquidator") continues in office until another person becomes liquidator in his place under this section or the next.

(3) The interim liquidator shall (subject to the next subsection) as soon as practicable in the period of 28 days beginning with the day on which the winding-up order was made or such longer period as the court may allow, [in accordance with the rules seek nominations from] the company's creditors and contributories for the purpose of choosing a person (who may be the person who is the interim liquidator) to be liquidator of the company in place of the interim liquidator.

(4) If it appears to the interim liquidator, in any case where a company is being wound up on grounds including its inability to pay its debts, that it would be inappropriate to [seek a nomination from the company's contributories under subsection (3), he may seek a nomination only from] the company's creditors for the purpose mentioned in that subsection.

(5) If [a nomination is sought from the company's creditors, or nominations are sought from the company's creditors and contributories,] in pursuance of this section but no person is appointed or nominated [as a result], the interim liquidator shall make a report to the court which shall appoint either the interim liquidator or some other person to be liquidator of the company.

(6) A person who becomes liquidator of the company in place of the interim liquidator shall, unless he is appointed by the court, forthwith notify the court of that fact.

NOTES

All words in square brackets in this section were substituted by the Small Business, Enterprise and Employment Act 2015, s 126, Sch 9, Pt 1, paras 1, 33, as from 6 April 2017 (in relation to England and Wales), and as from 6 April 2019 (in relation to Scotland) (for transitional and savings provisions, see the notes to s 246ZE at **[9.385]**).

[9.267]

139 Choice of liquidator [by] creditors and contributories

(1) This section applies where a company is being wound up by the court and [nominations are sought from the company's creditors and contributories] for the purpose of choosing a person to be liquidator of the company.

(2) The creditors and the contributories [may in accordance with the rules] nominate a person to be liquidator.

(3) The liquidator shall be the person nominated by the creditors or, where no person has been so nominated, the person (if any) nominated by the contributories.

(4) In the case of different persons being nominated, any contributory or creditor may, within 7 days after the date on which the nomination was made by the creditors, apply to the court for an order either—

- (a) appointing the person nominated as liquidator by the contributories to be a liquidator instead of, or jointly with, the person nominated by the creditors; or
- (b) appointing some other person to be liquidator instead of the person nominated by the creditors.

NOTES

All words in square brackets in this section were substituted by the Small Business, Enterprise and Employment Act 2015, s 126, Sch 9, Pt 1, paras 1, 34, as from 6 April 2017 (in relation to England and Wales), and as from 6 April 2019 (in relation to Scotland) (for transitional and savings provisions, see the notes to s 246ZE at **[9.385]**).

[9.268]

140 Appointment by the court following administration or voluntary arrangement

[(1) Where a winding-up order is made immediately upon the appointment of an administrator ceasing to have effect, the court may appoint as liquidator of the company the person whose appointment as administrator has ceased to have effect.]

(2) Where a winding-up order is made at a time when there is a supervisor of a voluntary arrangement approved in relation to the company under Part I, the court may appoint as liquidator of the company the person who is the supervisor at the time when the winding-up order is made.

(3) Where the court makes an appointment under this section, the official receiver does not become the liquidator as otherwise provided by section 136(2), and [section 136(5)(a) and (b) does not apply].

NOTES

Sub-s (1): substituted by the Enterprise Act 2002, s 248(3), Sch 17, paras 9, 17, as from 15 September 2003 (for savings and transitional provisions, see the note to s 8 at **[9.147]**).

Sub-s (3): words in square brackets substituted by the Small Business, Enterprise and Employment Act 2015, s 126, Sch 9, Pt 1, paras 1, 35, as from 6 April 2017 (in relation to England and Wales), and as from 6 April 2019 (in relation to Scotland) (for transitional and savings provisions, see the notes to s 246ZE at **[9.385]**).

Liquidation committees

[9.269]

141 Liquidation committee (England and Wales)

[(1) This section applies where a winding up order has been made by the court in England and Wales.

(2) If both the company's creditors and the company's contributories decide that a liquidation committee should be established, a liquidation committee is to be established in accordance with the rules.

(3) If only the company's creditors, or only the company's contributories, decide that a liquidation committee should be established, a liquidation committee is to be established in accordance with the rules unless the court orders otherwise.

(3A) A "liquidation committee" is a committee having such functions as are conferred on it by or under this Act.

(3B) The liquidator must seek a decision from the company's creditors and contributories as to whether a liquidation committee should be established if requested, in accordance with the rules, to do so by one-tenth in value of the company's creditors.

(3C) Subsection (3B) does not apply where the liquidator is the official receiver.]

(4) The liquidation committee is not to be able or required to carry out its functions at any time when the official receiver is liquidator; but at any such time its functions are vested in the Secretary of State except to the extent that the rules otherwise provide.

(5) Where there is for the time being no liquidation committee, and the liquidator is a person other than the official receiver, the functions of such a committee are vested in the Secretary of State except to the extent that the rules otherwise provide.

NOTES

Sub-ss (1)–(3C): substituted, for the original sub-ss (1)–(3), by the Small Business, Enterprise and Employment Act 2015, s 126, Sch 9, Pt 1, paras 1, 36, as from 6 April 2017 (in relation to England and Wales), and as from 6 April 2019 (in relation to Scotland) (for transitional and savings provisions, see the notes to s 246ZE at **[9.385]**).

[9.270]

142 Liquidation committee (Scotland)

[(1) This section applies where a winding up order has been made by the court in Scotland.

(2) If both the company's creditors and the company's contributories decide that a liquidation committee should be established, a liquidation committee is to be established in accordance with the rules.

(3) If only the company's creditors, or only the company's contributories, decide that a liquidation committee should be established, a liquidation committee is to be established in accordance with the rules unless the court orders otherwise.

[(3A) A "liquidation committee" is a committee having such functions as are conferred on it by or under this Act.]

(4) A liquidator appointed by the court other than under section 139(4)(a) must seek a decision from the company's creditors and contributories as to whether a liquidation committee should be established if requested, in accordance with the rules, to do so by one-tenth in value of the company's creditors.]

(5) Where in the case of any winding up there is for the time being no liquidation committee, the functions of such a committee are vested in the court except to the extent that the rules otherwise provide.

(6) . . .

NOTES

Sub-ss (1)–(3), (4) were substituted by the Small Business, Enterprise and Employment Act 2015, s 126, Sch 9, Pt 1, paras 1, 37, as from 6 April 2017 (in relation to England and Wales), and as from 6 April 2019 (in relation to Scotland) (for transitional and savings provisions, see the notes to s 246ZE at **[9.385]**).

Sub-s (3A) was inserted, and sub-s (6) was repealed, by the Public Services Reform (Corporate Insolvency and Bankruptcy) (Scotland) Order 2017, SSI 2017/209, art 4, as from 1 October 2017 (in so far as they enable the making of (i) rules under s 411 post, or (ii) any other subordinate legislation under this Act), and as from 6 April 2019 (otherwise).

The liquidator's functions

[9.271]

143 General functions in winding up by the court

(1) The functions of the liquidator of a company which is being wound up by the court are to secure that the assets of the company are got in, realised and distributed to the company's creditors and, if there is a surplus, to the persons entitled to it.

(2) It is the duty of the liquidator of a company which is being wound up by the court in England and Wales, if he is not the official receiver—

- (a) to furnish the official receiver with such information,
- (b) to produce to the official receiver, and permit inspection by the official receiver of, such books, papers and other records, and
- (c) to give the official receiver such other assistance,

as the official receiver may reasonably require for the purposes of carrying out his functions in relation to the winding up.

[9.272]

144 Custody of company's property

(1) When a winding-up order has been made, or where a provisional liquidator has been appointed, the liquidator or the provisional liquidator (as the case may be) shall take into his custody or under his control all the property and things in action to which the company is or appears to be entitled.

(2) In a winding up by the court in Scotland, if and so long as there is no liquidator, all the property of the company is deemed to be in the custody of the court.

[9.273]

145 Vesting of company property in liquidator

(1) When a company is being wound up by the court, the court may on the application of the liquidator by order direct that all or any part of the property of whatsoever description belonging to the company or held by trustees on its behalf shall vest in the liquidator by his official name; and thereupon the property to which the order relates vests accordingly.

(2) The liquidator may, after giving such indemnity (if any) as the court may direct, bring or defend in his official name any action or other legal proceeding which relates to that property or which it is necessary to bring or defend for the purpose of effectually winding up the company and recovering its property.

[9.274]

[146 Final account

(1) This section applies where a company is being wound up by the court and the liquidator is not the official receiver.

(2) If it appears to the liquidator that the winding up of the company is for practical purposes complete the liquidator must make up an account of the winding up, showing how it has been conducted and the company's property has been disposed of.

(3) The liquidator must—

(a) send a copy of the account to the company's creditors (other than opted-out creditors), and

(b) give the company's creditors (other than opted-out creditors) a notice explaining the effect of section 174(4)(d) and how they may object to the liquidator's release.

(4) The liquidator must during the relevant period send to the court and the registrar of companies—

(a) a copy of the account, and

(b) a statement of whether any of the company's creditors objected to the liquidator's release.

(5) The relevant period is the period of 7 days beginning with the day after the last day of the period prescribed by the rules as the period within which the creditors may object to the liquidator's release.

[(6) . . .

(7) . . .]]

NOTES

Substituted by the Small Business, Enterprise and Employment Act 2015, s 126, Sch 9, Pt 1, paras 1, 38, as from 6 April 2017 (in relation to England and Wales), and as from 6 April 2019 (in relation to Scotland) (for transitional and savings provisions, see the notes to s 246ZE at **[9.385]**).

Sub-ss (6), (7) were added by the Insolvency Amendment (EU 2015/848) Regulations 2017, SI 2017/702, regs 2, 3, Schedule, Pt 1, paras 1, 7, as from 26 June 2017, except in relation to proceedings opened before that date. As originally enacted, paragraph 7 of the Schedule to the 2017 Regulations applied to England and Wales only. However, reg 2 of the 2017 Regulations (Amendments and extent) was amended by the Small Business, Enterprise and Employment Act 2015 (Commencement No 7, Consequential, Transitional and Savings Provisions) Regulations 2019, SI 2019/816, reg 6(2) (as from 6 April 2019) so as to apply the amendment made by paragraph 7 of the Schedule to the 2017 Regulations to Scotland. Sub-ss (6), (7) were subsequently repealed by the Insolvency (Amendment) (EU Exit) Regulations 2019, SI 2019/146, reg 2, Schedule, Pt 2, paras 16, 22, as from IP completion day (as defined in the European Union (Withdrawal Agreement) Act 2020, s 39) (for savings, see reg 4 of the 2019 Regulations at **[12.82]**).

146A *(S 146A was originally inserted by the Insolvency Amendment (EU 2015/848) Regulations 2017, SI 2017/702, regs 2, 3, Schedule, Pt 1, paras 1, 8, as from 26 June 2017, except in relation to proceedings opened before that date; and repealed by the Insolvency (Amendment) (EU Exit) Regulations 2019, SI 2019/146, reg 2, Schedule, Pt 2, paras 16, 23, as from IP completion day (as defined in the European Union (Withdrawal Agreement) Act 2020, s 39) (for savings, see reg 4 of the 2019 Regulations at* **[12.82]**).)

General powers of court

[9.275]

147 Power to stay or sist winding up

(1) The court may at any time after an order for winding up, on the application either of the liquidator or the official receiver or any creditor or contributory, and on proof to the satisfaction of the court that all proceedings in the winding up ought to be stayed or sisted, make an order staying or sisting the proceedings, either altogether or for a limited time, on such terms and conditions as the court thinks fit.

(2) The court may, before making an order, require the official receiver to furnish to it a report with respect to any facts or matters which are in his opinion relevant to the application.

(3) A copy of every order made under this section shall forthwith be forwarded by the company, or otherwise as may be prescribed, to the registrar of companies, who shall enter it in his records relating to the company.

[9.276]

148 Settlement of list of contributories and application of assets

(1) As soon as may be after making a winding-up order, the court shall settle a list of contributories, with power to rectify the register of members in all cases where rectification is required . . . , and shall cause the company's assets to be collected, and applied in discharge of its liabilities.

(2) If it appears to the court that it will not be necessary to make calls on or adjust the rights of contributories, the court may dispense with the settlement of a list of contributories.

(3) In settling the list, the court shall distinguish between persons who are contributories in their own right and persons who are contributories as being representatives of or liable for the debts of others.

NOTES

Sub-s (1): words omitted repealed by the Companies Act 2006 (Consequential Amendments, Transitional Provisions and Savings) Order 2009, SI 2009/1941, art 2(1), Sch 1, para 75(1), (16), as from 1 October 2009 (for effect see the note to s 7A at **[9.145]**).

[9.277]

149 Debts due from contributory to company

(1) The court may, at any time after making a winding-up order, make an order on any contributory for the time being on the list of contributories to pay, in manner directed by the order, any money due from him (or from the estate of the person who he represents) to the company, exclusive of any money payable by him or the estate by virtue of any call . . .

(2) The court in making such an order may—

(a) in the case of an unlimited company, allow to the contributory by way of set-off any money due to him or the estate which he represents from the company on any independent dealing or contract with the company, but not any money due to him as a member of the company in respect of any dividend or profit, and

(b) in the case of a limited company, make to any director or manager whose liability is unlimited or to his estate the like allowance.

(3) In the case of any company, whether limited or unlimited, when all the creditors are paid in full (together with interest at the official rate), any money due on any account whatever to a contributory from the company may be allowed to him by way of set-off against any subsequent call.

NOTES

Sub-s (1): words omitted repealed by the Companies Act 2006 (Consequential Amendments, Transitional Provisions and Savings) Order 2009, SI 2009/1941, art 2(1), Sch 1, para 75(1), (16), as from 1 October 2009 (for effect see the note to s 7A at **[9.145]**).

[9.278]

150 Power to make calls

(1) The court may, at any time after making a winding-up order, and either before or after it has ascertained the sufficiency of the company's assets, make calls on all or any of the contributories for the time being settled on the list of the contributories to the extent of their liability, for payment of any money which the court considers necessary to satisfy the company's debts and liabilities, and the expenses of winding up, and for the adjustment of the rights of the contributories among themselves, and make an order for payment of any calls so made.

(2) In making a call the court may take into consideration the probability that some of the contributories may partly or wholly fail to pay it.

151 (*Repealed by the Deregulation Act 2015, s 19, Sch 6, Pt 3, paras 8, 9, as from 1 October 2015.*)

[9.279]

152 Order on contributory to be conclusive evidence

(1) An order made by the court on a contributory is conclusive evidence that the money (if any) thereby appearing to be due or ordered to be paid is due, but subject to any right of appeal.

(2) All other pertinent matters stated in the order are to be taken as truly stated as against all persons and in all proceedings except proceedings in Scotland against the heritable estate of a deceased contributory; and in that case the order is only prima facie evidence for the purpose of charging his heritable estate, unless his heirs or legatees of heritage were on the list of contributories at the time of the order being made.

[9.280]

153 Power to exclude creditors not proving in time

The court may fix a time or times within which creditors are to prove their debts or claims or to be excluded from the benefit of any distribution made before those debts are proved.

[9.281]

154 Adjustment of rights of contributories

The court shall adjust the rights of the contributories among themselves and distribute any surplus among the persons entitled to it.

[9.282]

155 Inspection of books by creditors, etc

(1) The court may, at any time after making a winding-up order, make such order for inspection of the company's books and papers by creditors and contributories as the court thinks just; and any books and papers in the company's possession may be inspected by creditors and contributories accordingly, but not further or otherwise.

(2) Nothing in this section excludes or restricts any statutory rights of a government department or person acting under the authority of a government department.

[(3) For the purposes of subsection (2) above, references to a government department shall be construed as including references to any part of the Scottish Administration.]

NOTES

Sub-s (3): added by the Scotland Act 1998 (Consequential Modifications) (No 2) Order 1999, SI 1999/1820, art 4, Sch 2, Pt I, para 85, as from 1 July 1999.

[9.283]

156 Payment of expenses of winding up

The court may, in the event of the assets being insufficient to satisfy the liabilities, make an order as to the payment out of the assets of the expenses incurred in the winding up in such order of priority as the court thinks just.

[9.284]

157 Attendance at company meetings (Scotland)

In the winding up by the court of a company registered in Scotland, the court has power to require the attendance of any officer of the company at any meeting of creditors or of contributories, or of a liquidation committee, for the purpose of giving information as to the trade, dealings, affairs or property of the company.

[9.285]

158 Power to arrest absconding contributory

The court, at any time either before or after making a winding-up order, on proof of probable cause for believing that a contributory is about to quit the United Kingdom or otherwise to abscond or to remove or conceal any of his property for the purpose of evading payment of calls, may cause the contributory to be arrested and his books and papers and moveable personal property to be seized and him and them to be kept safely until such time as the court may order.

[9.286]

159 Powers of court to be cumulative

Powers conferred [on the court by this Act] are in addition to, and not in restriction of, any existing powers of instituting proceedings against a contributory or debtor of the company, or the estate of any contributory or debtor, for the recovery of any call or other sums.

NOTES

Words in square brackets substituted by the Companies Act 2006 (Consequential Amendments, Transitional Provisions and Savings) Order 2009, SI 2009/1941, art 2(1), Sch 1, para 75(1), (17), as from 1 October 2009 (for effect see the note to s 7A at **[9.145]**).

[9.287]

160 Delegation of powers to liquidator (England and Wales)

(1) Provision may be made by rules for enabling or requiring all or any of the powers and duties conferred and imposed on the court in England and Wales . . . in respect of the following matters—

[(a) the seeking of decisions on any matter from creditors and contributories,]

(b) the settling of lists of contributories and the rectifying of the register of members where required, and the collection and application of the assets,

(c) the payment, delivery, conveyance, surrender or transfer of money, property, books or papers to the liquidator,

(d) the making of calls,

(e) the fixing of a time within which debts and claims must be proved,

to be exercised or performed by the liquidator as an officer of the court, and subject to the court's control.

(2) But the liquidator shall not, without the special leave of the court, rectify the register of members, and shall not make any call without either that special leave or the sanction of the liquidation committee.

NOTES

Sub-s (1): words omitted repealed by the Companies Act 2006 (Consequential Amendments, Transitional Provisions and Savings) Order 2009, SI 2009/1941, art 2(1), Sch 1, para 75(1), (18), as from 1 October 2009 (for effect see the note to s 7A at **[9.145]**). Para (a) substituted by the Small Business, Enterprise and Employment Act 2015, s 126, Sch 9, Pt 1, paras 1, 39, as from 6 April 2017 (in relation to England and Wales), and as from 6 April 2019 (in relation to Scotland) (for transitional and savings provisions, see the notes to s 246ZE at **[9.385]**).

Enforcement of, and appeal from, orders

[9.288]

161 Orders for calls on contributories (Scotland)

(1) In Scotland, where an order, interlocutor or decree has been made for winding up a company by the court, it is competent to the court, on production by the liquidators of a list certified by them of the names of the contributories liable in payment of any calls, and of the amount due by each contributory, and of the date when that amount became due, to pronounce forthwith a decree against those contributories for payment of the sums so certified to be due, with interest from that date until payment (at 5 per cent. per annum) in the same way and to the same effect as if they had severally consented to registration for execution, on a charge of 6 days, of a legal obligation to pay those calls and interest.

(2) The decree may be extracted immediately, and no suspension of it is competent, except on caution or consignation, unless with special leave of the court.

[9.289]

162 Appeals from orders in Scotland

(1) Subject to the provisions of this section and to rules of court, an appeal from any order or decision made or given in the winding up of a company by the court in Scotland under this Act lies in the same manner and subject to the same conditions as an appeal from an order or decision of the court in cases within its ordinary jurisdiction.

(2) In regard to orders or judgments pronounced by the judge acting as vacation judge . . . —

(a) none of the orders specified in Part I of Schedule 3 to this Act are subject to review, reduction, suspension or stay of execution, and

(b) every other order or judgment (except as mentioned below) may be submitted to review by the Inner House by reclaiming motion enrolled within 14 days from the date of the order or judgment.

(3) However, an order being one of those specified in Part II of that Schedule shall, from the date of the order and notwithstanding that it has been submitted to review as above, be carried out and receive effect until the Inner House have disposed of the matter.

(4) In regard to orders or judgments pronounced in Scotland by a Lord Ordinary before whom proceedings in a winding up are being taken, any such order or judgment may be submitted to review by the Inner House by reclaiming motion enrolled within 14 days from its date; but should it not be so submitted to review during session, the provisions of this section in regard to orders or judgments pronounced by the judge acting as vacation judge apply.

(5) Nothing in this section affects provisions of [the Companies Acts] or this Act in reference to decrees in Scotland for payment of calls in the winding up of companies, whether voluntary or by the court.

NOTES

Sub-s (2): words omitted repealed by the Court of Session Act 1988, s 52(2), Sch 2, Pt III, as from 29 September 1988.

Sub-s (5): words in square brackets substituted by the Companies Act 2006 (Consequential Amendments, Transitional Provisions and Savings) Order 2009, SI 2009/1941, art 2(1), Sch 1, para 75(1), (19), as from 1 October 2009 (for effect see the note to s 7A at **[9.145]**).

CHAPTER VII LIQUIDATORS

Preliminary

[9.290]

163 Style and title of liquidators

The liquidator of a company shall be described—

(a) where a person other than the official receiver is liquidator, by the style of "the liquidator" of the particular company, or

(b) where the official receiver is liquidator, by the style of "the official receiver and liquidator" of the particular company;

and in neither case shall he be described by an individual name.

[9.291]

164 Corrupt inducement affecting appointment

A person who gives, or agrees or offers to give, to any member or creditor of a company any valuable consideration with a view to securing his own appointment or nomination, or to securing or preventing the appointment or nomination of some person other than himself, as the company's liquidator is liable to a fine.

Liquidator's powers and duties

[9.292]

165 Voluntary winding up

(1) This section has effect where a company is being wound up voluntarily, but subject to section 166 below in the case of a creditors' voluntary winding up.

[(2) The liquidator may exercise any of the powers specified in Parts 1 to 3 of Schedule 4.]

(4) The liquidator may—

(a) exercise the court's power of settling a list of contributories (which list is prima facie evidence of the liability of the persons named in it to be contributories),

(b) exercise the court's power of making calls,

(c) summon general meetings of the company for the purpose of obtaining its sanction by [special resolution] or for any other purpose he may think fit.

(5) The liquidator shall pay the company's debts and adjust the rights of the contributories among themselves.

(6) Where the liquidator in exercise of the powers conferred on him by this Act disposes of any property of the company to a person who is connected with the company (within the meaning of section 249 in Part VII), he shall, if there is for the time being a liquidation committee, give notice to the committee of that exercise of his powers.

NOTES

Sub-s (2): substituted (for the original sub-ss (2), (3)) by the Small Business, Enterprise and Employment Act 2015, s 120(1), (2), as from 26 May 2015.

Sub-s (4): words in square brackets substituted by the Companies Act 2006 (Commencement No 3, Consequential Amendments, Transitional Provisions and Savings) Order 2007, SI 2007/2194, art 10(1), Sch 4, Pt 3, para 41(1), as from 1 October 2007.

[9.293]

166 Creditors' voluntary winding up

(1) This section applies where, in the case of a creditors' voluntary winding up, a liquidator has been nominated by the company.

[(1A) The exercise by the liquidator of the power specified in paragraph 6 of Schedule 4 to this Act (power to sell any of the company's property) shall not be challengeable on the ground of any prior inhibition.]

(2) The powers conferred on the liquidator by section 165 shall not be exercised, except with the sanction of the court, [before—

(a) the company's creditors under section 100 nominate a person to be liquidator, or

(b) the procedure by which the company's creditors were to have made such a nomination concludes without a nomination having been made.]

(3) Subsection (2) does not apply in relation to the power of the liquidator—

(a) to take into his custody or under his control all the property to which the company is or appears to be entitled;

(b) to dispose of perishable goods and other goods the value of which is likely to diminish if they are not immediately disposed of; and

(c) to do all such other things as may be necessary for the protection of the company's assets.

(4) . . .

(5) [If the directors fail to comply with—

(a) section 99(1), (2) or (2A), or

(b) section 100(1B),]

the liquidator shall, within 7 days of the relevant day, apply to the court for directions as to the manner in which that default is to be remedied.

(6) "The relevant day" means the day on which the liquidator was nominated by the company or the day on which he first became aware of the default, whichever is the later.

(7) If the liquidator without reasonable excuse fails to comply with this section, he is liable to a fine.

NOTES

Sub-s (1A): inserted by the Bankruptcy and Diligence etc (Scotland) Act 2007, s 155(1), (3), as from 22 April 2009.

Sub-s (2): words in square brackets substituted by the Small Business, Enterprise and Employment Act 2015, s 126, Sch 9, Pt 1, paras 1, 40(1), (2), as from 6 April 2017 (in relation to England and Wales), and as from 6 April 2019 (in relation to Scotland) (for transitional and savings provisions, see the notes to s 246ZE at **[9.385]**).

Sub-s (4): repealed by the Small Business, Enterprise and Employment Act 2015, s 126, Sch 9, Pt 1, paras 1, 40(1), (3), as from 6 April 2017 (in relation to England and Wales), and as from 6 April 2019 (in relation to Scotland) (for transitional and savings provisions, see the notes to s 246ZE at **[9.385]**).

Sub-s (5): words in square brackets substituted by the Small Business, Enterprise and Employment Act 2015, s 126, Sch 9, Pt 1, paras 1, 40(1), (4), as from 6 April 2017 (in relation to England and Wales), and as from 6 April 2019 (in relation to Scotland) (for transitional and savings provisions, see the notes to s 246ZE at **[9.385]**).

[9.294]
167 Winding up by the court

[(1) Where a company is being wound up by the court, the liquidator may exercise any of the powers specified in Parts 1 to 3 of Schedule 4.]

(2) Where the liquidator (not being the official receiver), in exercise of the powers conferred on him by this Act—

(a) disposes of any property of the company to a person who is connected with the company (within the meaning of section 249 in Part VII), or

(b) employs a solicitor to assist him in the carrying out of his functions,

he shall, if there is for the time being a liquidation committee, give notice to the committee of that exercise of his powers.

(3) The exercise by the liquidator in a winding up by the court of the powers conferred by this section is subject to the control of the court, and any creditor or contributory may apply to the court with respect to any exercise or proposed exercise of any of those powers.

NOTES

Sub-s (1): substituted by the Small Business, Enterprise and Employment Act 2015, s 120(1), (3), as from 26 May 2015.

[9.295]
168 Supplementary powers (England and Wales)

(1) This section applies in the case of a company which is being wound up by the court in England and Wales.

[(2) The liquidator may seek a decision on any matter from the company's creditors or contributories; and must seek a decision on a matter—

(a) from the company's creditors, if requested to do so by one-tenth in value of the creditors;

(b) from the company's contributories, if requested to do so by one-tenth in value of the contributories.]

(3) The liquidator may apply to the court (in the prescribed manner) for directions in relation to any particular matter arising in the winding up.

(4) Subject to the provisions of this Act, the liquidator shall use his own discretion in the management of the assets and their distribution among the creditors.

(5) If any person is aggrieved by an act or decision of the liquidator, that person may apply to the court; and the court may confirm, reverse or modify the act or decision complained of, and make such order in the case as it thinks just.

[(5A) Where at any time after a winding-up petition has been presented to the court against any person (including an insolvent partnership or other body which may be wound up under Part V of the Act as an unregistered company), whether by virtue of the provisions of the Insolvent Partnerships Order 1994 or not, the attention of the court is drawn to the fact that the person in question is a member of an insolvent partnership, the court may make an order as to the future conduct of the insolvency proceedings and any such order may apply any provisions of that Order with any necessary modifications.

(5B) Any order or directions under subsection (5A) may be made or given on the application of the official receiver, any responsible insolvency practitioner, the trustee of the partnership or any other interested person and may include provisions as to the administration of the joint estate of the partnership, and in particular how it and the separate estate of any member are to be administered.

[(5C) Where the court makes an order for the winding up of an insolvent partnership under—

(a) section 72(1)(a) of the Financial Services Act 1986;

(b) section 92(1)(a) of the Banking Act 1987; or

(c) section 367(3)(a) of the Financial Services and Markets Act 2000,

the court may make an order as to the future conduct of the winding up proceedings, and any such order may apply any provisions of the Insolvent Partnerships Order 1994 with any necessary modifications.]]

NOTES

Sub-s (2): substituted by the Small Business, Enterprise and Employment Act 2015, s 126, Sch 9, Pt 1, paras 1, 41, as from 6 April 2017 (in relation to England and Wales), and as from 6 April 2019 (in relation to Scotland) (for transitional and savings provisions, see the notes to s 246ZE at **[9.385]**).

Sub-ss (5A), (5B): added, together with sub-s (5C), by the Insolvent Partnerships Order 1994, SI 1994/2421, art 14(1), as from 1 December 1994.

Sub-s (5C): added as noted above. It was repealed by the Financial Services and Markets Act 2000 (Consequential Amendments and Repeals) Order 2001, SI 2001/3649, art 306, as from 1 December 2001, but was subsequently substituted by the Financial Services and Markets Act 2000 (Consequential Amendments) Order 2002, SI 2002/1555, art 15, as from 3 July 2002, which further provided that the repeal by SI 2001/3649 was to be treated as if it had not been made.

[9.296]
169 Supplementary powers (Scotland)

(1) . . .

(2) In a winding up by the court in Scotland, the liquidator has (subject to the rules) the same powers as a trustee on a bankrupt estate.

NOTES

Sub-s (1): repealed by the Small Business, Enterprise and Employment Act 2015, s 120(1), (4), as from 26 May 2015.

[9.297]

170 Enforcement of liquidator's duty to make returns, etc

(1) If a liquidator who has made any default—

(a) in filing, delivering or making any return, account or other document, or

(b) in giving any notice which he is by law required to file, deliver, make or give,

fails to make good the default within 14 days after the service on him of a notice requiring him to do so, the court has the following powers.

(2) On an application made by any creditor or contributory of the company, or by the registrar of companies, the court may make an order directing the liquidator to make good the default within such time as may be specified in the order.

(3) The court's order may provide that all costs of and incidental to the application shall be borne by the liquidator.

(4) Nothing in this section prejudices the operation of any enactment imposing penalties on a liquidator in respect of any such default as is mentioned above.

Removal; vacation of office

[9.298]

171 Removal, etc (voluntary winding up)

(1) This section applies with respect to the removal from office and vacation of office of the liquidator of a company which is being wound up voluntarily.

(2) Subject to the next subsection, the liquidator may be removed from office only by an order of the court or—

(a) in the case of a members' voluntary winding up, by a general meeting of the company summoned specially for that purpose, or

(b) in the case of a creditors' voluntary winding up, by a [decision of the company's creditors made by a qualifying decision procedure instigated] specially for that purpose in accordance with the rules.

[(3) Where the liquidator in a members' voluntary winding up was appointed by the court under section 108, a meeting such as is mentioned in subsection (2)(a) shall be summoned only if—

(a) the liquidator thinks fit,

(b) the court so directs, or

(c) the meeting is requested in accordance with the rules by members representing not less than one-half of the total voting rights of all the members having at the date of the request a right to vote at the meeting.

(3A) Where the liquidator in a creditors' voluntary winding up was appointed by the court under section 108, a qualifying decision procedure such as is mentioned in subsection (2)(b) is to be instigated only if—

(a) the liquidator thinks fit,

(b) the court so directs, or

(c) it is requested in accordance with the rules by not less than one-half in value of the company's creditors.]

(4) A liquidator shall vacate office if he ceases to be a person who is qualified to act as an insolvency practitioner in relation to the company.

(5) A liquidator may, in the prescribed circumstances, resign his office by giving notice of his resignation to the registrar of companies.

[(6) In the case of a members' voluntary winding up where the liquidator has produced an account of the winding up under section 94 (final account), the liquidator vacates office as soon as the liquidator has complied with section 94(3) (requirement to send final account to registrar).

(7) In the case of a creditors' voluntary winding up where the liquidator has produced an account of the winding up under section 106 (final account), the liquidator vacates office as soon as the liquidator has complied with section 106(3) (requirement to send final account etc to registrar).]

NOTES

All amendments to this section were made by the Small Business, Enterprise and Employment Act 2015, s 126, Sch 9, Pt 1, paras 1, 42, as from 6 April 2017 (in relation to England and Wales), and as from 6 April 2019 (in relation to Scotland) (for transitional and savings provisions, see the notes to s 246ZE at **[9.385]**).

[9.299]

172 Removal, etc (winding up by the court)

(1) This section applies with respect to the removal from office and vacation of office of the liquidator of a company which is being wound up by the court, or of a provisional liquidator.

(2) Subject as follows, the liquidator may be removed from office only by an order of the court or by a [decision of the company's creditors made by a qualifying decision procedure instigated] specially for that purpose in accordance with the rules; and a provisional liquidator may be removed from office only by an order of the court.

(3) Where—

(a) the official receiver is liquidator otherwise than in succession under section 136(3) to a person who held office as a result of a nomination by . . . the company's creditors or contributories, or

(b) the liquidator was appointed by the court otherwise than under section 139(4)(a) or 140(1), or was appointed by the Secretary of State,

[a qualifying decision procedure such as is mentioned in subsection (2) shall be instigated only if the liquidator thinks fit, the court so directs, or it] is requested, in accordance with the rules, by not less than one-quarter, in value, of the creditors.

(4) If appointed by the Secretary of State, the liquidator may be removed from office by a direction of the Secretary of State.

(5) A liquidator or provisional liquidator, not being the official receiver, shall vacate office if he ceases to be a person who is qualified to act as an insolvency practitioner in relation to the company.

(6) A liquidator may, in the prescribed circumstances, resign his office by giving notice of his resignation to the court.

(7) Where an order is made under section 204 (early dissolution in Scotland) for the dissolution of the company, the liquidator shall vacate office when the dissolution of the company takes effect in accordance with that section.

[(8) Where the liquidator has produced an account of the winding up under section 146 (final account), the liquidator vacates office as soon as the liquidator has complied with section 146(4) (requirement to send account etc to registrar and to court).]

[(9) Subsection (10) applies where, immediately before a liquidator gives notice to the court and the registrar under subsection (8) (or, where the liquidator gives notice to the court and the registrar on different days, immediately before the liquidator gives the first of those notices), there are EU insolvency proceedings open in respect of the company in one or more other member States.

(10) The liquidator must send to the court and the registrar, with the notice, a statement—

(a) identifying those proceedings,

(b) identifying the member State liquidator appointed in each of those proceedings, and

(c) indicating, in relation to each of those member State liquidators, whether that member State liquidator consents to the company being dissolved.]

NOTES

Sub-s (2): words in square brackets substituted by the Small Business, Enterprise and Employment Act 2015, s 126, Sch 9, Pt 1, paras 1, 43(1), (2), as from 6 April 2017 (in relation to England and Wales), and as from 6 April 2019 (in relation to Scotland) (for transitional and savings provisions, see the notes to s 246ZE at **[9.385]**).

Sub-s (3): words omitted repealed, and words in square brackets substituted, by the Small Business, Enterprise and Employment Act 2015, s 126, Sch 9, Pt 1, paras 1, 43(1), (3), as from 6 April 2017 (in relation to England and Wales), and as from 6 April 2019 (in relation to Scotland) (for transitional and savings provisions, see the notes to s 246ZE at **[9.385]**).

Sub-s (8): substituted by the Small Business, Enterprise and Employment Act 2015, s 126, Sch 9, Pt 1, paras 1, 43(1), (4), as from 6 April 2017 (in relation to England and Wales), and as from 6 April 2019 (in relation to Scotland) (for transitional and savings provisions, see the notes to s 246ZE at **[9.385]**).

Sub-ss (9), (10): added, in relation to Scotland only, by the Insolvency Amendment (EU 2015/848) Regulations 2017, SI 2017/702, regs 2, 3, Schedule, Pt 4, paras 55, 57, as from 26 June 2017, except in relation to proceedings opened before that date.

Release of liquidator

[9.300]

173 Release (voluntary winding up)

(1) This section applies with respect to the release of the liquidator of a company which is being wound up voluntarily.

(2) A person who has ceased to be a liquidator shall have his release with effect from the following time, that is to say—

[(a) in the following cases, the time at which notice is given to the registrar of companies in accordance with the rules that the person has ceased to hold office—

(i) the person has been removed from office by a general meeting of the company,

(ii) the person has been removed from office by a decision of the company's creditors and the company's creditors have not decided against his release,

(iii) the person has died;

(b) in the following cases, such time as the Secretary of State may, on the application of the person, determine—

(i) the person has been removed from office by a decision of the company's creditors and the company's creditors have decided against his release,

(ii) the person has been removed from office by the court,

(iii) the person has vacated office under section 171(4);]

(c) in the case of a person who has resigned, such time as may be prescribed;

(d) in the case of a person who has vacated office under subsection [(6)] of section 171, the time at which he vacated office;

[(e) in the case of a person who has vacated office under section 171(7)—

(i) if any of the company's creditors objected to the person's release before the end of the period for so objecting prescribed by the rules, such time as the Secretary of State may, on an application by that person, determine, and

(ii) otherwise, the time at which the person vacated office.]

[(2A) Where the person is removed from office by a decision of the company's creditors, any decision of the company's creditors as to whether the person should have his release must be made by a qualifying decision procedure.]

(3) In the application of subsection (2) to the winding up of a company registered in Scotland, the references to a determination by the Secretary of State as to the time from which a person who has ceased to be liquidator shall have his release are to be read as references to such a determination by the Accountant of Court.

(4) Where a liquidator has his release under subsection (2), he is, with effect from the time specified in that subsection, discharged from all liability both in respect of acts or omissions of his in the winding up and otherwise in relation to his conduct as liquidator.

But nothing in this section prevents the exercise, in relation to a person who has had his release under subsection (2), of the court's powers under section 212 of this Act (summary remedy against delinquent directors, liquidators, etc).

NOTES

All amendments to this section were made by the Small Business, Enterprise and Employment Act 2015, s 126, Sch 9, Pt 1, paras 1, 44, as from 6 April 2017 (in relation to England and Wales), and as from 6 April 2019 (in relation to Scotland) (for transitional and savings provisions, see the notes to s 246ZE at **[9.385]**).

[9.301]

174 Release (winding up by the court)

(1) This section applies with respect to the release of the liquidator of a company which is being wound up by the court, or of a provisional liquidator.

(2) Where the official receiver has ceased to be liquidator and a person becomes liquidator in his stead, the official receiver has his release with effect from the following time, that is to say—

(a) in a case where that person was nominated by [the company's] creditors or contributories, or was appointed by the Secretary of State, the time at which the official receiver gives notice to the court that he has been replaced;

(b) in a case where that person is appointed by the court, such time as the court may determine.

(3) If the official receiver while he is a liquidator gives notice to the Secretary of State that the winding up is for practical purposes complete, he has his release with effect from such time as the Secretary of State may determine.

(4) A person other than the official receiver who has ceased to be a liquidator has his release with effect from the following time, that is to say—

[(a) in the following cases, the time at which notice is given to the court in accordance with the rules that the person has ceased to hold office—

(i) the person has been removed from office by a decision of the company's creditors and the company's creditors have not decided against his release,

(ii) the person has died;

(b) in the following cases, such time as the Secretary of State may, on the application of the person, determine—

(i) the person has been removed from office by a decision of the company's creditors and the company's creditors have decided against his release;

(ii) the person has been removed from office by the court or the Secretary of State;

(iii) the person has vacated office under section 172(5) or (7);]

(c) in the case of a person who has resigned, such time as may be prescribed;

(d) in the case of a person who has vacated office under section 172(8)—

[(i) if any of the company's creditors objected to the person's release before the end of the period for so objecting prescribed by the rules, such time as the Secretary of State may, on an application by that person, determine, and

(ii) otherwise, the time at which the person vacated office.]

[(4ZA) Where the person is removed from office by a decision of the company's creditors, any decision of the company's creditors as to whether the person should have his release must be made by a qualifying decision procedure.]

[(4A) Where a winding-up order made by the court in England and Wales is rescinded, the person (whether the official receiver or another person) who is the liquidator of the company at the time the order is rescinded has his release with effect from such time as the court may determine.]

(5) A person who has ceased to hold office as a provisional liquidator has his release with effect from such time as the court may, on an application by him, determine.

(6) Where the official receiver or a liquidator or provisional liquidator has his release under this section, he is, with effect from the time specified in the preceding provisions of this section, discharged from all liability both in respect of acts or omissions of his in the winding up and otherwise in relation to his conduct as liquidator or provisional liquidator.

But nothing in this section prevents the exercise, in relation to a person who has had his release under this section, of the court's powers under section 212 (summary remedy against delinquent directors, liquidators, etc).

(7) In the application of this section to a case where the order for winding up has been made by the court in Scotland, the references to a determination by the Secretary of State as to the time from which a person who has ceased to be liquidator has his release are to such a determination by the Accountant of Court.

NOTES

Sub-s (4A) was inserted by the Deregulation Act 2015, s 19, Sch 6, Pt 3, paras 8, 10, as from 1 October 2015.

All the other amendments to this section were made by the Small Business, Enterprise and Employment Act 2015, s 126, Sch 9, Pt 1, paras 1, 45, as from 6 April 2017 (in relation to England and Wales), and as from 6 April 2019 (in relation to Scotland) (for transitional and savings provisions, see the notes to s 246ZE at **[9.385]**).

CHAPTER VIII PROVISIONS OF GENERAL APPLICATION IN WINDING UP

[Moratorium: order of priority of payment of debts

[9.302]

174A Moratorium debts etc: priority

(1) This section applies where proceedings for the winding up of a company are begun before the end of the period of 12 weeks beginning with the day after the end of any moratorium for the company under Part A1.

(2) In the winding up, the following are payable out of the company's assets (in the order of priority shown) in preference to all other claims—

(a) any prescribed fees or expenses of the official receiver acting in any capacity in relation to the company;

(b) moratorium debts and priority pre-moratorium debts.

(3) In subsection (2)(b) "priority pre-moratorium debt" means—

(a) any pre-moratorium debt that is payable in respect of—

(i) the monitor's remuneration or expenses,

(ii) goods or services supplied during the moratorium,

(iii) rent in respect of a period during the moratorium, or

(iv) wages or salary arising under a contract of employment, so far as relating to a period of employment before or during the moratorium,

(b) any pre-moratorium debt that—

(i) consists of a liability to make a redundancy payment, and

(ii) fell due before or during the moratorium, and

(c) any pre-moratorium debt that—

(i) arises under a contract or other instrument involving financial services,

(ii) fell due before or during the moratorium, and

(iii) is not relevant accelerated debt (see subsection (4)).

(4) For the purposes of subsection (3)(c)—

"relevant accelerated debt" means any pre-moratorium debt that fell due during the relevant period by reason of the operation of, or the exercise of rights under, an acceleration or early termination clause in a contract or other instrument involving financial services;

"the relevant period" means the period—

(a) beginning with the day on which the statement under section A6(1)(e) is made, and

(b) ending with the last day of the moratorium.

(5) The rules may make provision as to the order in which the debts mentioned in subsection (2)(b) rank among themselves in a case where the assets of the company are insufficient to meet them in full.

(6) The Secretary of State may by regulations made by statutory instrument amend this section for the purposes of changing the definition of "moratorium debt" or "priority pre-moratorium debt" in this section.

(7) Regulations under subsection (6) may make consequential, supplementary, incidental or transitional provision or savings.

(8) A statutory instrument containing regulations under subsection (6) may not be made unless a draft of the instrument has been laid before and approved by a resolution of each House of Parliament.

(9) For the purposes of this section proceedings for the winding up of a company are begun when—

(a) a winding-up petition is presented, or

(b) a resolution for voluntary winding up is passed.

(10) Any rules made under section A18(4) (meaning of supply of goods or services) apply also for the purposes of subsection (3)(a)(ii) of this section.

(11) In this section—

"acceleration or early termination clause", in relation to a contract or other instrument involving financial services, means a provision of the contract or other instrument—

(a) under which, on the happening of an event—

(i) a debt or other liability falls due earlier than it otherwise would, or

(ii) a debt or other liability is terminated and replaced by another debt or liability, or

(b) which confers on a party a right which, if exercised, will result in—

(i) a debt or other liability falling due earlier than it otherwise would, or

(ii) a debt or other liability being terminated and replaced by another debt or liability;

"contract or other instrument involving financial services" has the same meaning as it has for the purposes of section A18 (see Schedule ZA2);

"monitor's remuneration or expenses" has the meaning given by section A18;

"moratorium debt" has the meaning given by section A53;

"pre-moratorium debt" has the meaning given by section A53;

"redundancy payment" has the meaning given by section A18;

"wages or salary" has the meaning given by section A18.]

NOTES

Commencement: 26 June 2020.

Inserted, together with the preceding heading, by the Corporate Insolvency and Governance Act 2020, s 2(1), Sch 3, paras 1, 13, as from 26 June 2020 (for transitional provisions, see s 2(2), (3) of the 2020 Act (at **[9.533]**) which provides that (without prejudice to the Interpretation Act 1978, s 16) nothing in the 2020 Act affects the operation of this Act, or any other enactment, in relation to a moratorium under Sch A1 to this Act which comes into force before the repeal of that Schedule by Sch 3 to the 2020 Act (ie, 26 June 2020)).

Preferential debts

[9.303]

175 Preferential debts (general provision)

(1) In a winding up the company's preferential debts . . . shall be paid in priority to all other debts [after the payment of—

(a) any liabilities to which section 174A applies, and

(b) expenses of the winding up.]

[(1A) Ordinary preferential debts rank equally among themselves . . . and shall be paid in full, unless the assets are insufficient to meet them, in which case they abate in equal proportions.

(1B) Secondary preferential debts rank equally among themselves after the ordinary preferential debts and shall be paid in full, unless the assets are insufficient to meet them, in which case they abate in equal proportions.]

(2) Preferential debts—

(a) . . .

(b) so far as the assets of the company available for payment of general creditors are insufficient to meet them, have priority over the claims of holders of debentures secured by, or holders of, any floating charge created by the company, and shall be paid accordingly out of any property comprised in or subject to that charge.

[(3) In this section "preferential debts", "ordinary preferential debts" and "secondary preferential debts" each has the meaning given in section 386 in Part 12.]

NOTES

The words omitted from sub-ss (1) and (2) were repealed, and sub-ss (1A), (1B) and (3) were inserted and added respectively, by the Banks and Building Societies (Depositor Preference and Priorities) Order 2014, SI 2014/3486, arts 3, 5, as from 1 January 2015, except in relation to any insolvency proceedings commenced before that date (see further the note relating to this Order at **[9.139]**).

The words in square brackets in sub-s (1) were inserted, and the words omitted from sub-s (1A) were repealed, by the Corporate Insolvency and Governance Act 2020, s 2(1), Sch 3, paras 1, 14, as from 26 June 2020 (for transitional provisions, see s 2(2), (3) of the 2020 Act (at **[9.533]**) which provides that (without prejudice to the Interpretation Act 1978, s 16) nothing in the 2020 Act affects the operation of this Act, or any other enactment, in relation to a moratorium under Sch A1 to this Act which comes into force before the repeal of that Schedule by Sch 3 to the 2020 Act (ie, 26 June 2020)).

[9.304]

176 Preferential charge on goods distrained[, etc]

(1) This section applies where a company is being wound up by the court in England and Wales, and is without prejudice to section 128 (avoidance of attachments, etc).

[(2) Subsection (2A) applies where—

(a) any person (whether or not a landlord or person entitled to rent) has distrained upon the goods or effects of the company, or

(b) Her Majesty's Revenue and Customs has been paid any amount from an account of the company under Part 1 of Schedule 8 to the Finance (No 2) Act 2015 (enforcement by deduction from accounts),

in the period of 3 months ending with the date of the winding-up order.

(2A) Where this subsection applies—

(a) in a case within subsection (2)(a), the goods or effects, or the proceeds of their sale, and

(b) in a case within subsection (2)(b), the amount in question,

is charged for the benefit of the company with the preferential debts of the company to the extent that the company's property is for the time being insufficient for meeting those debts.]

(3) Where by virtue of a charge under subsection [(2A)] any person surrenders any goods or effects to a company or makes a payment to a company, that person ranks, in respect of the amount of the proceeds of sale of those goods or effects by the liquidator or (as the case may be) the amount of the payment, as a preferential creditor of the company, except as against so much of the company's property as is available for the payment of preferential creditors by virtue of the surrender or payment.

NOTES

Word in square brackets in the section heading inserted, sub-ss (2), (2A) substituted (for the original sub-s (2)), and figure in square brackets in sub-s (3) substituted, by the Finance (No 2) Act 2015, s 51, Sch 8, Pt 2, paras 26, 30, as from 18 November 2015.

[Non-preferential debts

[9.305]

176AZA Non-preferential debts of financial institutions

(1) This section applies in the winding up of a company which is a relevant financial institution.

(2) The company's ordinary non-preferential debts shall be paid in priority to its secondary non-preferential debts.

(3) The company's secondary non-preferential debts—

(a) shall be paid in priority to its tertiary non-preferential debts, and

(b) rank equally among themselves after the ordinary non-preferential debts and shall be paid in full, unless the assets are insufficient to meet them, in which case they abate in equal proportions.

(4) See section 387A for definitions relevant to this section.]

NOTES

Inserted, together with preceding heading, by the Banks and Building Societies (Priorities on Insolvency) Order 2018, SI 2018/1244, arts 4, 6, as from 19 December 2018, except in relation to any insolvency proceedings commenced before that date (see further the note relating to this Order at **[9.139]**).

See also the Bank Recovery and Resolution (Amendment) (EU Exit) Regulations 2020, SI 2020/1350. Regulations 108–114 make amendments to various provisions of this Act (including this section) which come into force on 28 December 2020 and cease to have effect (in accordance with reg 1 of the 2020 Regulations) on IP completion day (as defined in the European Union (Withdrawal Agreement) Act 2020, s 39).

[Property subject to floating charge

[9.306]

[176ZA Payment of expenses of winding up (England and Wales)

(1) The expenses of winding up in England and Wales, so far as the assets of the company available for payment of general creditors are insufficient to meet them, have priority over any claims to property comprised in or subject to any floating charge created by the company and shall be paid out of any such property accordingly.

(2) In subsection (1)—

(a) the reference to assets of the company available for payment of general creditors does not include any amount made available under section 176A(2)(a);

(b) the reference to claims to property comprised in or subject to a floating charge is to the claims of—

(i) the holders of debentures secured by, or holders of, the floating charge, and

(ii) any preferential creditors entitled to be paid out of that property in priority to them.

(3) Provision may be made by rules restricting the application of subsection (1), in such circumstances as may be prescribed, to expenses authorised or approved—

(a) by the holders of debentures secured by, or holders of, the floating charge and by any preferential creditors entitled to be paid in priority to them, or

(b) by the court.

(4) References in this section to the expenses of the winding up are to all expenses properly incurred in the winding up, including the remuneration of the liquidator.]

NOTES

Inserted by the Companies Act 2006, s 1282(1), as from 6 April 2008, subject to transitional provisions in relation to resolutions passed, notices registered, and orders passed (etc) occurring before that date (see Sch 4, Pt 1, para 43(1) to the Companies Act 2006 (Commencement No 5, Transitional Provisions and Savings) Order 2007, SI 2007/3495).

[9.307]

[176ZB Application of proceeds of office-holder claims

(1) This section applies where—

(a) there is a floating charge (whether created before or after the coming into force of this section) which relates to property of a company which—

(i) is in administration, or

(ii) has gone into liquidation; and

(b) the administrator or the liquidator (referred to in this section as "the office-holder") has—

(i) brought a claim under any provision mentioned in subsection (3), or

(ii) made an assignment (or, in Scotland, assignation) in relation to a right of action under any such provision under section 246ZD.

(2) The proceeds of the claim or assignment (or, in Scotland, assignation) are not to be treated as part of the company's net property, that is to say the amount of its property which would be available for satisfaction of claims of holders of debentures secured by, or holders of, any floating charge created by the company.

(3) The provisions are—

(a) section 213 or 246ZA (fraudulent trading);

(b) section 214 or 246ZB (wrongful trading);

(c) section 238 (transactions at an undervalue (England and Wales));

(d) section 239 (preferences (England and Wales));

(e) section 242 (gratuitous alienations (Scotland));

(f) section 243 (unfair preferences (Scotland));

(g) section 244 (extortionate credit transactions).

(4) Subsection (2) does not apply to a company if or in so far as it is disapplied by—

(a) a voluntary arrangement in respect of the company, or

(b) a compromise or arrangement agreed under Part 26 [or 26A] of the Companies Act 2006 (arrangements and reconstructions).]

NOTES

Inserted by the Small Business, Enterprise and Employment Act 2015, s 119, as from 1 October 2015, in respect of a company which enters administration or goes into liquidation on or after that date.

Sub-s (4): words in square brackets inserted by the Corporate Insolvency and Governance Act 2020, s 7, Sch 9, Pt 2, paras 5, 6(1), (2), as from 26 June 2020.

Transitional provisions: see the Deregulation Act 2015, the Small Business, Enterprise and Employment Act 2015 and the Insolvency (Amendment) Act (Northern Ireland) 2016 (Consequential Amendments and Transitional Provisions) Regulations 2017, SI 2017/400, reg 14, which provides as follows (note that "the commencement date" is 7 April 2017)—

"(1) Section 176ZB (application of proceeds of office-holder claims) does not apply in relation to any relevant proceedings commenced before the commencement date.

(2) "Relevant proceedings" means—

(a) bank insolvency under Part 2 of the 2009 Act or bank administration under Part 3 of that Act;

(b) building society insolvency under Part 2 of the 2009 Act (as applied by section 90C of the Building Societies Act 1986);

(c) building society special administration under Part 3 of the 2009 Act (as applied by section 90C of the Building Societies Act 1986);

(d) the administration of a building society under Part 2 of the 1986 Act (as applied by section 90A of the Building Societies Act 1986);

(e) special administration, special administration (bank insolvency) or special administration (bank administration) under the Investment Bank Special Administration Regulations 2011; or

(f) the administration of a relevant society (within the meaning given in article 1(2) of the Co-operative and Community Benefit Societies and Credit Unions (Arrangements, Reconstructions and Administration) Order 2014) under Part 2 of the 1986 Act as applied by article 2(2) of that Order.".

[9.308]

[176A Share of assets for unsecured creditors

(1) This section applies where a floating charge relates to property of a company—

(a) which has gone into liquidation,

(b) which is in administration,

(c) of which there is a provisional liquidator, or

(d) of which there is a receiver.

(2) The liquidator, administrator or receiver—

(a) shall make a prescribed part of the company's net property available for the satisfaction of unsecured debts, and

(b) shall not distribute that part to the proprietor of a floating charge except in so far as it exceeds the amount required for the satisfaction of unsecured debts.

(3) Subsection (2) shall not apply to a company if—

(a) the company's net property is less than the prescribed minimum, and

(b) the liquidator, administrator or receiver thinks that the cost of making a distribution to unsecured creditors would be disproportionate to the benefits.

(4) Subsection (2) shall also not apply to a company if or in so far as it is disapplied by—

(a) a voluntary arrangement in respect of the company, or

(b) a compromise or arrangement agreed under [Part 26 [or 26A] of the Companies Act 2006 (arrangements and reconstructions)].

(5) Subsection (2) shall also not apply to a company if—

(a) the liquidator, administrator or receiver applies to the court for an order under this subsection on the ground that the cost of making a distribution to unsecured creditors would be disproportionate to the benefits, and

(b) the court orders that subsection (2) shall not apply.

(6) In subsections (2) and (3) a company's net property is the amount of its property which would, but for this section, be available for satisfaction of claims of holders of debentures secured by, or holders of, any floating charge created by the company.

(7) An order under subsection (2) prescribing part of a company's net property may, in particular, provide for its calculation—

(a) as a percentage of the company's net property, or

(b) as an aggregate of different percentages of different parts of the company's net property.

(8) An order under this section—

(a) must be made by statutory instrument, and

(b) shall be subject to annulment pursuant to a resolution of either House of Parliament.

(9) In this section—

"floating charge" means a charge which is a floating charge on its creation and which is created after the first order under subsection (2)(a) comes into force, and

"prescribed" means prescribed by order by the Secretary of State.

(10) An order under this section may include transitional or incidental provision.]

NOTES

Inserted, together with the heading preceding s 176ZA, by the Enterprise Act 2002, s 252, as from 15 September 2003.

Sub-s (4): words in first (outer) pair of square brackets in para (b) substituted by the Companies Act 2006 (Consequential Amendments etc) Order 2008, SI 2008/948, art 3(1), Sch 1, Pt 2, para 103, as from 6 April 2008. Words in second (inner) pair of square brackets inserted by the Corporate Insolvency and Governance Act 2020, s 7, Sch 9, Pt 2, paras 5, 6(1), (3), as from 26 June 2020.

Orders: the Insolvency Act 1986 (Prescribed Part) Order 2003, SI 2003/2097 at **[10.118]**; the Insolvency Act 1986 (Prescribed Part) (Amendment) Order 2020, SI 2020/211.

Special managers

[9.309]

177 Power to appoint special manager

(1) Where a company has gone into liquidation or a provisional liquidator has been appointed, the court may, on an application under this section, appoint any person to be the special manager of the business or property of the company.

(2) The application may be made by the liquidator or provisional liquidator in any case where it appears to him that the nature of the business or property of the company, or the interests of the company's creditors or contributories or members generally, require the appointment of another person to manage the company's business or property.

(3) The special manager has such powers as may be entrusted to him by the court.

(4) The court's power to entrust powers to the special manager includes power to direct that any provision of this Act that has effect in relation to the provisional liquidator or liquidator of a company shall have the like effect in relation to the special manager for the purposes of the carrying out by him of any of the functions of the provisional liquidator or liquidator.

(5) The special manager shall—

(a) give such security or, in Scotland, caution as may be prescribed;

(b) prepare and keep such accounts as may be prescribed; and

(c) produce those accounts in accordance with the rules to the Secretary of State or to such other persons as may be prescribed.

Disclaimer (England and Wales only)

[9.310]

178 Power to disclaim onerous property

(1) This and the next two sections apply to a company that is being wound up in England and Wales.

(2) Subject as follows, the liquidator may, by the giving of the prescribed notice, disclaim any onerous property and may do so notwithstanding that he has taken possession of it, endeavoured to sell it, or otherwise exercised rights of ownership in relation to it.

(3) The following is onerous property for the purposes of this section—

(a) any unprofitable contract, and

(b) any other property of the company which is unsaleable or not readily saleable or is such that it may give rise to a liability to pay money or perform any other onerous act.

(4) A disclaimer under this section—

(a) operates so as to determine, as from the date of the disclaimer, the rights, interests and liabilities of the company in or in respect of the property disclaimed; but

(b) does not, except so far as is necessary for the purpose of releasing the company from any liability, affect the rights or liabilities of any other person.

(5) A notice of disclaimer shall not be given under this section in respect of any property if—

(a) a person interested in the property has applied in writing to the liquidator or one of his predecessors as liquidator requiring the liquidator or that predecessor to decide whether he will disclaim or not, and

(b) the period of 28 days beginning with the day on which that application was made, or such longer period as the court may allow, has expired without a notice of disclaimer having been given under this section in respect of that property.

(6) Any person sustaining loss or damage in consequence of the operation of a disclaimer under this section is deemed a creditor of the company to the extent of the loss or damage and accordingly may prove for the loss or damage in the winding up.

[9.311]

179 Disclaimer of leaseholds

(1) The disclaimer under section 178 of any property of a leasehold nature does not take effect unless a copy of the disclaimer has been served (so far as the liquidator is aware of their addresses) on every person claiming under the company as underlessee or mortgagee and either—

(a) no application under section 181 below is made with respect to that property before the end of the period of 14 days beginning with the day on which the last notice served under this subsection was served; or

(b) where such an application has been made, the court directs that the disclaimer shall take effect.

(2) Where the court gives a direction under subsection (1)(b) it may also, instead of or in addition to any order it makes under section 181, make such orders with respect to fixtures, tenant's improvements and other matters arising out of the lease as it thinks fit.

[9.312]

180 Land subject to rentcharge

(1) The following applies where, in consequence of the disclaimer under section 178 of any land subject to a rentcharge, that land vests by operation of law in the Crown or any other person (referred to in the next subsection as "the proprietor").

(2) The proprietor and the successors in title of the proprietor are not subject to any personal liability in respect of any sums becoming due under the rentcharge except sums becoming due after the proprietor, or some person claiming under or through the proprietor, has taken possession or control of the land or has entered into occupation of it.

[9.313]

181 Powers of court (general)

(1) This section and the next apply where the liquidator has disclaimed property under section 178.

(2) An application under this section may be made to the court by—

(a) any person who claims an interest in the disclaimed property, or

(b) any person who is under any liability in respect of the disclaimed property, not being a liability discharged by the disclaimer.

(3) Subject as follows, the court may on the application make an order, on such terms as it thinks fit, for the vesting of the disclaimed property in, or for its delivery to—

(a) a person entitled to it or a trustee for such a person, or

(b) a person subject to such a liability as is mentioned in subsection (2)(b) or a trustee for such a person.

(4) The court shall not make an order under subsection (3)(b) except where it appears to the court that it would be just to do so for the purpose of compensating the person subject to the liability in respect of the disclaimer.

(5) The effect of any order under this section shall be taken into account in assessing for the purpose of section 178(6) the extent of any loss or damage sustained by any person in consequence of the disclaimer.

(6) An order under this section vesting property in any person need not be completed by conveyance, assignment or transfer.

[9.314]

182 Powers of court (leaseholds)

(1) The court shall not make an order under section 181 vesting property of a leasehold nature in any person claiming under the company as underlessee or mortgagee except on terms making that person—

(a) subject to the same liabilities and obligations as the company was subject to under the lease at the commencement of the winding up, or

(b) if the court thinks fit, subject to the same liabilities and obligations as that person would be subject to if the lease had been assigned to him at the commencement of the winding up.

(2) For the purposes of an order under section 181 relating to only part of any property comprised in a lease, the requirements of subsection (1) apply as if the lease comprised only the property to which the order relates.

(3) Where subsection (1) applies and no person claiming under the company as underlessee or mortgagee is willing to accept an order under section 181 on the terms required by virtue of that subsection, the court may, by order under that section, vest the company's estate or interest in the property in any person who is liable (whether personally or in a representative capacity, and whether alone or jointly with the company) to perform the lessee's covenants in the lease.

The court may vest that estate and interest in such a person freed and discharged from all estates, incumbrances and interests created by the company.

(4) Where subsection (1) applies and a person claiming under the company as underlessee or mortgagee declines to accept an order under section 181, that person is excluded from all interest in the property.

Execution, attachment and the Scottish equivalents

[9.315]

183 Effect of execution or attachment (England and Wales)

(1) Where a creditor has issued execution against the goods or land of a company or has attached any debt due to it, and the company is subsequently wound up, he is not entitled to retain the benefit of the execution or attachment against the liquidator unless he has completed the execution or attachment before the commencement of the winding up.

(2) However—

(a) if a creditor has had notice of a meeting having been called at which a resolution for voluntary winding up is to be proposed, the date on which he had notice is substituted, for the purpose of subsection (1), for the date of commencement of the winding up;

(b) a person who purchases in good faith under a sale by the [enforcement officer or other officer charged with the execution of the writ] any goods of a company on which execution has been levied in all cases acquires a good title to them against the liquidator; and

(c) the rights conferred by subsection (1) on the liquidator may be set aside by the court in favour of the creditor to such extent and subject to such terms as the court thinks fit.

(3) For purposes of this Act—

(a) an execution against goods is completed by seizure and sale, or by the making of a charging order under section 1 of the Charging Orders Act 1979;

(b) an attachment of a debt is completed by receipt of the debt; and

(c) an execution against land is completed by seizure, by the appointment of a receiver, or by the making of a charging order under section 1 of the Act above-mentioned.

(4) In this section, "goods" includes all chattels personal; and ["enforcement officer" means an individual who is authorised to act as an enforcement officer under the Courts Act 2003].

[(4A) For the purposes of this section, Her Majesty's Revenue and Customs is to be regarded as having attached a debt due to a company if it has taken action under Part 1 of Schedule 8 to the Finance (No 2) Act 2015 (enforcement by deduction for accounts) as a result of which an amount standing to the credit of an account held by the company is—

(a) subject to arrangements made under paragraph 6(3) of that Schedule, or

(b) the subject of a deduction notice under paragraph 13 of that Schedule.]

(5) This section does not apply in the case of a winding up in Scotland.

NOTES

Sub-ss (2), (4): words in square brackets substituted by the Courts Act 2003, s 109(1), Sch 8, para 295, as from 15 March 2004.

Sub-s (4A): inserted by the Finance (No 2) Act 2015, s 51, Sch 8, Pt 2, paras 26, 31, as from 18 November 2015.

[9.316]

184 Duties of [officers charged with execution of writs and other processes] (England and Wales)

(1) The following applies where a company's goods are taken in execution and, before their sale or the completion of the execution (by the receipt or recovery of the full amount of the levy), notice is served on the [enforcement officer, or other officer, charged with execution of the writ or other process,] that a provisional liquidator has been appointed or that a winding-up order has been made, or that a resolution for voluntary winding up has been passed.

(2) The [enforcement officer or other officer] shall, on being so required, deliver the goods and any money seized or received in part satisfaction of the execution to the liquidator; but the costs of execution are a first charge on the goods or money so delivered, and the liquidator may sell the goods, or a sufficient part of them, for the purpose of satisfying the charge.

(3) If under an execution in respect of a judgment for a sum exceeding [£500] a company's goods are sold or money is paid in order to avoid sale, the [enforcement officer or other officer] shall deduct the costs of the execution from the proceeds of sale or the money paid and retain the balance for 14 days.

(4) If within that time notice is served on the [enforcement officer or other officer] of a petition for the winding up of the company having been presented, or of a meeting having been called at which there is to be proposed a resolution for voluntary winding up, and an order is made or a resolution passed (as the case may be), the [enforcement officer or other officer] shall pay the balance to the liquidator, who is entitled to retain it as against the execution creditor.

(5) The rights conferred by this section on the liquidator may be set aside by the court in favour of the creditor to such extent and subject to such terms as the court thinks fit.

(6) In this section, "goods" includes all chattels personal; and ["enforcement officer" means an individual who is authorised to act as an enforcement officer under the Courts Act 2003].

(7) The money sum for the time being specified in subsection (3) is subject to increase or reduction by order under section 416 in Part XV.

(8) This section does not apply in the case of a winding up in Scotland.

NOTES

Section heading, sub-ss (1), (2), (4), (6): words in square brackets substituted by the Courts Act 2003, s 109(1), Sch 8, para 296, as from 15 March 2004.

Sub-s (3): sum in first pair of square brackets substituted by the Insolvency Proceedings (Monetary Limits) Order 1986, SI 1986/1996, art 2, Schedule, Pt I, with effect from 29 December 1986. Words in second pair of square brackets substituted by the Courts Act 2003, s 109(1), Sch 8, para 296(1), (3), as from 15 March 2004.

[9.317]

185 Effect of diligence (Scotland)

(1) In the winding up of a company registered in Scotland, the following provisions of the Bankruptcy (Scotland) Act [2016]—

(a) subsections (3) to (10) of section 23A (effect of sequestration on land attachment) and section 24 (effect of sequestration on diligence generally); and

(b) subsections (6), (7), (10) and (11) of section 109 (management and realisation of estate),

apply, so far as consistent with this Act, in like manner as they apply in the sequestration of a debtor's estate, with the substitutions specified below and with any other necessary modifications.

(2) The substitutions to be made in those sections of the Act of [2016] are as follows—

(a) for references to the debtor, substitute references to the company;

(b) for references to the sequestration, substitute references to the winding up;

(c) for references to the date of sequestration, substitute references to the commencement of the winding up of the company; and

(d) for references to the . . . trustee, substitute references to the liquidator.

(3) In this section, "the commencement of the winding up of the company" means, where it is being wound up by the court, the day on which the winding-up order is made.

(4) This section, so far as relating to any estate or effects of the company situated in Scotland, applies in the case of a company registered in England and Wales as in the case of one registered in Scotland.

NOTES

Sub-s (1): words in square brackets substituted by the Bankruptcy (Scotland) Act 2016 (Consequential Provisions and Modifications) Order 2016, SI 2016/1034, art 7(1), (3), Sch 1, para 4(1), (3)(a), as from 30 November 2016 (except in relation to (i) a sequestration as regards which the petition is presented, or the debtor application is made before that date; or (ii) a trust deed executed before that date).

Sub-s (2): year "2016" in square brackets substituted by SI 2016/1034, art 7(1), (3), Sch 1, para 4(1), (3)(b), as from 30 November 2016 (see also the first note relating to the 2016 Order above). Word omitted from para (d) repealed by the Bankruptcy and Diligence etc (Scotland) Act 2007, s 226, Sch 6, Pt 1, as from 1 April 2008.

Miscellaneous matters

[9.318]

186 Rescission of contracts by the court

(1) The court may, on the application of a person who is, as against the liquidator, entitled to the benefit or subject to the burden of a contract made with the company, make an order rescinding the contract on such terms as to payment by or to either party of damages for the non-performance of the contract, or otherwise as the court thinks just.

(2) Any damages payable under the order to such a person may be proved by him as a debt in the winding up.

[9.319]

187 Power to make over assets to employees

(1) On the winding up of a company (whether by the court or voluntarily), the liquidator may, subject to the following provisions of this section, make any payment which the company has, before the commencement of the winding up, decided to make under [section 247 of the Companies Act 2006] (power to provide for employees or former employees on cessation or transfer of business).

[(2) The liquidator may, after the winding up has commenced, make any such provision as is mentioned in section 247(1) if—

(a) the company's liabilities have been fully satisfied and provision has been made for the expenses of the winding up,

(b) the exercise of the power has been sanctioned by a resolution of the company, and

(c) any requirements of the company's [articles] as to the exercise of the power conferred by section 247(1) are complied with.]

(3) Any payment which may be made by a company under this section (that is, a payment after the commencement of its winding up) may be made out of the company's assets which are available to the members on the winding up.

(4) On a winding up by the court, the exercise by the liquidator of his powers under this section is subject to the court's control, and any creditor or contributory may apply to the court with respect to any exercise or proposed exercise of the power.

(5) Subsections (1) and (2) above have effect notwithstanding anything in any rule of law or in section 107 of this Act (property of company after satisfaction of liabilities to be distributed among members).

NOTES

Sub-s (1): words in square brackets substituted by the Companies Act 2006 (Commencement No 3, Consequential Amendments, Transitional Provisions and Savings) Order 2007, SI 2007/2194, art 10(1), Sch 4, Pt 3, para 42(1), (2), as from 1 October 2007.

Sub-s (2): substituted by SI 2007/2194, art 10(1), Sch 4, Pt 3, para 42(1), (3), as from 1 October 2007. Word in square brackets substituted by the Companies Act 2006 (Consequential Amendments, Transitional Provisions and Savings) Order 2009, SI 2009/1941, art 2(1), Sch 1, para 75(1), (20), as from 1 October 2009 (for effect see the note to s 7A at **[9.145]**).

[9.320]

188 Notification that company is in liquidation

[(1) When a company is being wound up, whether by the court or voluntarily—

(a) every invoice, order for goods [or services], business letter or order form (whether in hard copy, electronic or any other form) issued by or on behalf of the company, or a liquidator of the company or a receiver or manager of the company's property, . . . and

(b) all the company's websites,

must contain a statement that the company is being wound up.]

(2) If default is made in complying with this section, the company and any of the following persons who knowingly and wilfully authorises or permits the default, namely, any officer of the company, any liquidator of the company and any receiver or manager, is liable to a fine.

NOTES

Sub-s (1): substituted by the Companies (Registrar, Languages and Trading Disclosures) Regulations 2006, SI 2006/3429, reg 7(1), as from 1 January 2007. Words in square brackets inserted, and words omitted repealed, by the Companies (Trading Disclosures) (Insolvency) Regulations 2008, SI 2008/1897, reg 5(1), as from 1 October 2008.

[9.321]

189 Interest on debts

(1) In a winding up interest is payable in accordance with this section on any debt proved in the winding up, including so much of any such debt as represents interest on the remainder.

(2) Any surplus remaining after the payment of the debts proved in a winding up shall, before being applied for any other purpose, be applied in paying interest on those debts in respect of the periods during which they have been outstanding since the company went into liquidation.

(3) All interest under this section ranks equally, whether or not the debts on which it is payable rank equally.

(4) The rate of interest payable under this section in respect of any debt ("the official rate" for the purposes of any provision of this Act in which that expression is used) is whichever is the greater of—

(a) the rate specified in section 17 of the Judgments Act 1838 on the day on which the company went into liquidation, and

(b) the rate applicable to that debt apart from the winding up.

(5) In the application of this section to Scotland—

(a) references to a debt proved in a winding up have effect as references to a claim accepted in a winding up, and

(b) the reference to section 17 of the Judgments Act 1838 has effect as a reference to the rules.

[9.322]

190 Documents exempt from stamp duty

(1) In the case of a winding up by the court, or of a creditors' voluntary winding up, the following has effect as regards exemption from duties chargeable under the enactments relating to stamp duties.

(2) If the company is registered in England and Wales, the following documents are exempt from stamp duty—

(a) every assurance relating solely to freehold or leasehold property, or to any estate, right or interest in, any real or personal property, which forms part of the company's assets and which, after the execution of the assurance, either at law or in equity, is or remains part of those assets, and

(b) every writ, order, certificate, or other instrument or writing relating solely to the property of any company which is being wound up as mentioned in subsection (1), or to any proceeding under such a winding up.

"Assurance" here includes deed, conveyance, assignment and surrender.

(3) If the company is registered in Scotland, the following documents are exempt from stamp duty—

(a) every conveyance relating solely to property which forms part of the company's assets and which, after the execution of the conveyance, is or remains the company's property for the benefit of its creditors,

(b) any article of roup or sale, submission and every other instrument and writing whatsoever relating solely to the company's property, and

(c) every deed or writing forming part of the proceedings in the winding up.

"Conveyance" here includes assignation, instrument, discharge, writing and deed.

[9.323]

191 Company's books to be evidence

Where a company is being wound up, all books and papers of the company and of the liquidators are, as between the contributories of the company, prima facie evidence of the truth of all matters purporting to be recorded in them.

[9.324]

192 Information as to pending liquidations

(1) If the winding up of a company is not concluded within one year after its commencement, the liquidator shall, at such intervals as may be prescribed, until the winding up is concluded, send to the registrar of companies a statement in the prescribed form and containing the prescribed particulars with respect to the proceedings in, and position of, the liquidation.

(2) If a liquidator fails to comply with this section, he is liable to a fine and, for continued contravention, to a daily default fine.

[9.325]

193 Unclaimed dividends (Scotland)

(1) The following applies where a company registered in Scotland has been wound up, and is about to be dissolved.

(2) The liquidator shall lodge in an appropriate bank or institution as defined in section [228(1) of the Bankruptcy (Scotland) Act 2016] (not being a bank or institution in or of which the liquidator is acting partner, manager, agent or cashier) in the name of the Accountant of Court the whole unclaimed dividends and unapplied or undistributable balances, and the deposit receipts shall be transmitted to the Accountant of Court.

(3) The provisions of section [150 of the Bankruptcy (Scotland) Act 2016] (so far as consistent with this Act and [the Companies Acts]) apply with any necessary modifications to sums lodged in a bank or institution under this section as they apply to sums deposited under section [148] of the Act first mentioned.

NOTES

Sub-s (2): words in square brackets substituted by the Bankruptcy (Scotland) Act 2016 (Consequential Provisions and Modifications) Order 2016, SI 2016/1034, art 7(1), (3), Sch 1, para 4(1), (4)(a), as from 30 November 2016 (except in relation to (i) a sequestration as regards which the petition is presented, or the debtor application is made before that date; or (ii) a trust deed executed before that date).

Sub-s (3): words in first pair of square brackets and figure in third pair of square brackets substituted by SI 2016/1034, art 7(1), (3), Sch 1, para 4(1), (4)(b), as from 30 November 2016 (see also the first note relating to the 2016 Order above). Words in second pair of square brackets substituted by the Companies Act 2006 (Consequential Amendments, Transitional Provisions and Savings) Order 2009, SI 2009/1941, art 2(1), Sch 1, para 75(1), (21), as from 1 October 2009 (for effect see the note to s 7A at **[9.145]**).

194 (*Repealed by the Small Business, Enterprise and Employment Act 2015, s 126, Sch 9, Pt 1, paras 1, 46, as from 6 April 2017 (in relation to England and Wales), and as from 6 April 2019 (in relation to Scotland) (for transitional and savings provisions, see the notes to s 246ZE at* **[9.385]**.)

[9.326]

195 [Court's powers] to ascertain wishes of creditors or contributories

(1) The court may—

(a) as to all matters relating to the winding up of a company, have regard to the wishes of the creditors or contributories (as proved to it by any sufficient evidence), and

(b) if it thinks fit, for the purpose of ascertaining those wishes, direct [qualifying decision procedures to be instigated or the deemed consent procedure to be used in accordance with any directions given by the court, and appoint a person to report the result to the court].

(2) In the case of creditors, regard shall be had to the value of each creditor's debt.

(3) In the case of contributories, regard shall be had to the number of votes conferred on each contributory . . .

NOTES

Section heading, sub-s (1): words in square brackets substituted by the Small Business, Enterprise and Employment Act 2015, s 126, Sch 9, Pt 1, paras 1, 47, as from 6 April 2017 (in relation to England and Wales), and as from 6 April 2019 (in relation to Scotland) (for transitional and savings provisions, see the notes to s 246ZE at **[9.385]**).

Sub-s (3): words omitted repealed by the Companies Act 2006 (Consequential Amendments, Transitional Provisions and Savings) Order 2009, SI 2009/1941, art 2(1), Sch 1, para 75(1), (22), as from 1 October 2009 (for effect see the note to s 7A at **[9.145]**).

[9.327]

196 Judicial notice of court documents

In all proceedings under this Part, all courts, judges and persons judicially acting, and all officers, judicial or ministerial, of any court, or employed in enforcing the process of any court shall take judicial notice—

(a) of the signature of any officer of the High Court or of [the county court] in England and Wales, or of the Court of Session or a sheriff court in Scotland, or of the High Court in Northern Ireland, and also

(b) of the official seal or stamp of the several offices of the High Court in England and Wales or Northern Ireland, or of the Court of Session, appended to or impressed on any document made, issued or signed under the provisions of this Act or [the Companies Acts], or any official copy of such a document.

NOTES

Words in square brackets in para (a) substituted by the Crime and Courts Act 2013, s 17, Sch 9, Pt 3, para 52, as from 22 April 2014.

Words in square brackets in para (b) substituted by the Companies Act 2006 (Consequential Amendments, Transitional Provisions and Savings) Order 2009, SI 2009/1941, art 2(1), Sch 1, para 75(1), (23), as from 1 October 2009 (for effect see the note to s 7A at **[9.145]**).

[9.328]

197 Commission for receiving evidence

(1) When a company is wound up in England and Wales or in Scotland, the court may refer the whole or any part of the examination of witnesses—

(a) to [the] county court in England and Wales, or

(b) to the sheriff principal for a specified sheriffdom in Scotland, or

(c) to the High Court in Northern Ireland or a specified Northern Ireland County Court,

("specified" meaning specified in the order of the winding-up court).

(2) Any person exercising jurisdiction as a judge of the court to which the reference is made (or, in Scotland, the sheriff principal to whom it is made) shall then, by virtue of this section, be a commissioner for the purpose of taking the evidence of those witnesses.

(3) The judge or sheriff principal has in the matter referred the same power of summoning and examining witnesses, of requiring the production and delivery of documents, of punishing defaults by witnesses, and of allowing costs and expenses to witnesses, as the court which made the winding-up order.

These powers are in addition to any which the judge or sheriff principal might lawfully exercise apart from this section.

(4) The examination so taken shall be returned or reported to that court which made the order in such manner as the court requests.

(5) This section extends to Northern Ireland.

NOTES

Sub-s (1): word in square brackets substituted by the Crime and Courts Act 2013, s 17, Sch 9, Pt 3, para 93(c), as from 22 April 2014.

[9.329]

198 Court order for examination of persons in Scotland

(1) The court may direct the examination in Scotland of any person for the time being in Scotland (whether a contributory of the company or not), in regard to the trade, dealings, affairs or property of any company in course of being wound up, or of any person being a contributory of the company, so far as the company may be interested by reason of his being a contributory.

(2) The order or commission to take the examination shall be directed to the sheriff principal of the sheriffdom in which the person to be examined is residing or happens to be for the time; and the sheriff principal shall summon the person to appear before him at a time and place to be specified in the summons for examination on oath as a witness or as a haver, and to produce any books or papers called for which are in his possession or power.

(3) The sheriff principal may take the examination either orally or on written interrogatories, and shall report the same in writing in the usual form to the court, and shall transmit with the report the books and papers produced, if the originals are required and specified by the order or commission, or otherwise copies or extracts authenticated by the sheriff.

(4) If a person so summoned fails to appear at the time and place specified, or refuses to be examined or to make the production required, the sheriff principal shall proceed against him as a witness or haver duly cited; and failing to appear or refusing to give evidence or make production may be proceeded against by the law of Scotland.

(5) The sheriff principal is entitled to such fees, and the witness is entitled to such allowances, as sheriffs principal when acting as commissioners under appointment from the Court of Session and as witnesses and havers are entitled to in the like cases according to the law and practice of Scotland.

(6) If any objection is stated to the sheriff principal by the witness, either on the ground of his incompetency as a witness, or as to the production required, or on any other ground, the sheriff principal may, if he thinks fit, report the objection to the court, and suspend the examination of the witness until it has been disposed of by the court.

[9.330]

199 Costs of application for leave to proceed (Scottish companies)

Where a petition or application for leave to proceed with an action or proceeding against a company which is being wound up in Scotland is unopposed and is granted by the court, the costs of the petition or application shall, unless the court otherwise directs, be added to the amount of the petitioner's or applicant's claim against the company.

[9.331]

200 Affidavits etc in United Kingdom and overseas

(1) An affidavit required to be sworn under or for the purposes of this Part may be sworn in the United Kingdom, or elsewhere in Her Majesty's dominions, before any court, judge or person lawfully authorised to take and receive affidavits, or before any of Her Majesty's consuls or vice-consuls in any place outside Her dominions.

(2) All courts, judges, justices, commissioners and persons acting judicially shall take judicial notice of the seal or stamp or signature (as the case may be) of any such court, judge, person, consul or vice-consul attached, appended or subscribed to any such affidavit, or to any other document to be used for the purposes of this Part.

CHAPTER IX DISSOLUTION OF COMPANIES AFTER WINDING UP

[9.332]

201 Dissolution (voluntary winding up)

(1) This section applies, in the case of a company wound up voluntarily, where the liquidator has sent to the registrar of companies his final account . . . under section 94 (members' voluntary) or [his final account and statement under] section 106 (creditors' voluntary).

(2) The registrar on receiving the account[, or the account and statement] [. . .] shall forthwith register [it or] them; and on the expiration of 3 months from the registration of [the account] the company is deemed to be dissolved [. . .].

[(2A) . . .

(2B) . . .]

(3) However, the court may, on the application of the liquidator or any other person who appears to the court to be interested, make an order deferring the date at which the dissolution of the company is to take effect for such time as the court thinks fit.

(4) It is the duty of the person on whose application an order of the court under this section is made within 7 days after the making of the order to deliver to the registrar [a copy] of the order for registration; and if that person fails to do so he is liable to a fine and, for continued contravention, to a daily default fine.

NOTES

Sub-s (1): words omitted repealed, and words in square brackets inserted, by the Small Business, Enterprise and Employment Act 2015, s 126, Sch 9, Pt 1, paras 1, 48(1), (2), as from 6 April 2017 (in relation to England and Wales), and as from 6 April 2019 (in relation to Scotland) (for transitional and savings provisions, see the notes to s 246ZE at **[9.385]**).

Sub-s (2) is amended as follows:

The words in the first and fourth pairs of square brackets were substituted, and the words in the third pair of square brackets were inserted, by the Small Business, Enterprise and Employment Act 2015, s 126, Sch 9, Pt 1, paras 1, 48(1), (3), as from 6 April 2017 (in relation to England and Wales), and as from 6 April 2019 (in relation to Scotland) (for transitional and savings provisions, see the notes to s 246ZE at **[9.385]**).

The words omitted were originally inserted by the Insolvency Amendment (EU 2015/848) Regulations 2017, SI 2017/702, regs 2, 3, Schedule, Pt 1, paras 1, 9(1), (2), as from 26 June 2017, except in relation to proceedings opened before that date. As originally enacted, paragraph 9 of the Schedule to the 2017 Regulations applied to England and Wales only. However, reg 2 of the 2017 Regulations (Amendments and extent) was amended by the Small Business, Enterprise and Employment Act 2015 (Commencement No 7, Consequential, Transitional and Savings Provisions) Regulations 2019, SI 2019/816, reg 6(2) (as from 6 April 2019) so as to apply the amendments made by paragraph 9(2) of the Schedule to the 2017 Regulations to Scotland. See also the final note below in relation to the application of sub-s (2) to Scotland. The words were subsequently repealed by the Insolvency (Amendment) (EU Exit) Regulations 2019, SI 2019/146, reg 2, Schedule, Pt 2, paras 16, 24(1), (2), as from IP completion day (as defined in the European Union (Withdrawal Agreement) Act 2020, s 39) (for savings, see reg 4 of the 2019 Regulations at **[12.82]**).

Sub-ss (2A), (2B): originally inserted by SI 2017/702, regs 2, 3, Schedule, Pt 1, paras 1, 9(1), (3), as from 26 June 2017, except in relation to proceedings opened before that date. As originally enacted, paragraph 9 of the Schedule to the 2017 Regulations applied to England and Wales only. However, reg 2 of the 2017 Regulations (Amendments and extent) was amended by the Small Business, Enterprise and Employment Act 2015 (Commencement No 7, Consequential, Transitional and Savings Provisions) Regulations 2019, SI 2019/816, reg 6(2) (as from 6 April 2019) so as to apply the insertion made by paragraph 9(3) of the Schedule to the 2017 Regulations to Scotland. See also the final note below in relation to the application of sub-ss (2A), (2B) to Scotland. Sub-ss (2A), (2B) were subsequently repealed by SI 2019/146, reg 2, Schedule, Pt 2, paras 16, 24(1), (3), as from IP completion day (as defined in the European Union (Withdrawal Agreement) Act 2020, s 39) (for savings, see reg 4 of the 2019 Regulations at **[12.82]**).

Sub-s (4): words in square brackets substituted by the Companies (Registrar, Languages and Trading Disclosures) Regulations 2006, SI 2006/3429, reg 3(1)(d), as from 1 January 2007.

Amendment of this section in relation to Scotland: note that sub-s (2) of this section was amended, and new sub-ss (2A) and (2B) were inserted, in relation to Scotland only, by the Insolvency Amendment (EU 2015/848) Regulations 2017, SI 2017/702, regs 2, 3, Schedule, Pt 4, para 58, as from 26 June 2017, except in relation to proceedings opened before that date, as follows—

"(1) In section 201 (dissolution (voluntary winding up)) in subsection (2)—

(a) after "the account and return" insert "and any statement under section 106(8)", and

(b) at the end insert "(except where subsection (2A) applies)".

(2) After that subsection insert—

(2A) This subsection applies where a statement sent to the registrar under section 106(8) indicates that a member State liquidator does not consent to the company being dissolved.

(2B) Where subsection (2A) applies, the company is deemed to be dissolved on the expiration of 3 months from the date (if any) recorded in the register as the date on which the registrar was notified that—

(a) all proceedings identified in the statement sent under section 106(8) were closed, or

(b) every member State liquidator appointed in those proceedings consented to the company being dissolved.".

Note that paragraph 58 of the Schedule to the 2017 Regulations was revoked by the Small Business, Enterprise and Employment Act 2015 (Commencement No 7, Consequential, Transitional and Savings Provisions) Regulations 2019, SI 2019/816, reg 6(3) (as from 6 April 2019); and note also that the Insolvency (Amendment) (EU Exit) Regulations 2019, SI 2019/146, reg 2, Schedule, Pt 7, para 136 repeals all the words inserted into this section by paragraph 58 of the Schedule to the 2017 Regulations (as from IP completion day (as defined in the European Union (Withdrawal Agreement) Act 2020, s 39)). Finally note that, Schedule, Pt 7, para 136 is itself revoked by the Insolvency (Amendment) (EU Exit) (No 2) Regulations 2019, SI 2019/1459, reg 2, Schedule, para 4 (as from the same date).

[9.333]

202 Early dissolution (England and Wales)

(1) This section applies where an order for the winding up of a company has been made by the court in England and Wales.

(2) The official receiver, if—

(a) he is the liquidator of the company, and

(b) it appears to him—

(i) that the realisable assets of the company are insufficient to cover the expenses of the winding up, and

(ii) that the affairs of the company do not require any further investigation,

may at any time apply to the registrar of companies for the early dissolution of the company.

[(2A), (2B) . . .]

(3) Before making [an application under subsection (2)], the official receiver shall give not less than 28 days' notice of his intention to do so to the company's creditors[, other than opted-out creditors,] and contributories and, if there is an administrative receiver of the company, to that receiver.

(4) With the giving of that notice the official receiver ceases (subject to any directions under the next section) to be required to perform any duties imposed on him in relation to the company, its creditors or contributories by virtue of any provision of this Act, apart from a duty to make an application under subsection (2) [. . .].

(5) On the receipt of the official receiver's application under subsection (2) [. . .] the registrar shall forthwith register it [. . .] and, at the end of the period of 3 months beginning with the day of the registration of the application, the company shall be dissolved [. . .].

[(6), (7) . . .]

[(8)] However, the Secretary of State may, on the application of the official receiver or any other person who appears to the Secretary of State to be interested, give directions under section 203 at any time before the end of [the period in subsection (5) . . .].

NOTES

Sub-ss (2A), (2B): originally inserted by the Insolvency Amendment (EU 2015/848) Regulations 2017, SI 2017/702, regs 2, 3, Schedule, Pt 1, paras 1, 10(1), (2), as from 26 June 2017, except in relation to proceedings opened before that date. Subsequently repealed by the Insolvency (Amendment) (EU Exit) Regulations 2019, SI 2019/146, reg 2, Schedule, Pt 2, paras 16, 25(1), (2), as from IP completion day (as defined in the European Union (Withdrawal Agreement) Act 2020, s 39) (for savings, see reg 4 of the 2019 Regulations at **[12.82]**).

Sub-s (3): words in first pair of square brackets substituted by SI 2017/702, regs 2, 3, Schedule, Pt 1, paras 1, 10(1), (3), as from 26 June 2017, except in relation to proceedings opened before that date. Words in second pair of square brackets inserted by the Small Business, Enterprise and Employment Act 2015, s 126, Sch 9, Pt 1, paras 1, 49, as from 6 April 2017 (in relation to England and Wales), and as from 6 April 2019 (in relation to Scotland) (for transitional and savings provisions, see the notes to s 246ZE at **[9.385]**).

Sub-s (4): words omitted originally substituted by SI 2017/702, regs 2, 3, Schedule, Pt 1, paras 1, 10(1), (4), as from 26 June 2017, except in relation to proceedings opened before that date; and subsequently repealed by SI 2019/146, reg 2, Schedule, Pt 2, paras 16, 25(1), (3), as from IP completion day (as defined in the European Union (Withdrawal Agreement) Act 2020, s 39) (for savings, see reg 4 of the 2019 Regulations at **[12.82]**).

Sub-s (5): words omitted originally inserted by SI 2017/702, regs 2, 3, Schedule, Pt 1, paras 1, 10(1), (5)(a), as from 26 June 2017, except in relation to proceedings opened before that date; and subsequently repealed by SI 2019/146, reg 2, Schedule, Pt 2, paras 16, 25(1), (4), as from IP completion day (as defined in the European Union (Withdrawal Agreement) Act 2020, s 39) (for savings, see reg 4 of the 2019 Regulations at **[12.82]**).

Sub-ss (6), (7): originally added by SI 2017/702, regs 2, 3, Schedule, Pt 1, paras 1, 10(1), (5)(b), as from 26 June 2017, except in relation to proceedings opened before that date. Subsequently repealed by SI 2019/146, reg 2, Schedule, Pt 2, paras 16, 25(1), (5), as from IP completion day (as defined in the European Union (Withdrawal Agreement) Act 2020, s 39) (for savings, see reg 4 of the 2019 Regulations at **[12.82]**).

Sub-s (8): the words originally forming the second sentence of sub-s (5) were designated as sub-s (8), and the words in square brackets were substituted, by SI 2017/702, regs 2, 3, Schedule, Pt 1, paras 1, 10(1), (6), (7), as from 26 June 2017, except in relation to proceedings opened before that date. Words omitted repealed by SI 2019/146, reg 2, Schedule, Pt 2, paras 16, 25(1), (6), as from IP completion day (as defined in the European Union (Withdrawal Agreement) Act 2020, s 39) (for savings, see reg 4 of the 2019 Regulations at **[12.82]**).

[9.334]

203 Consequence of notice under s 202

(1) Where a notice has been given under section 202(3), the official receiver or any creditor or contributory of the company, or the administrative receiver of the company (if there is one) may apply to the Secretary of State for directions under this section.

(2) The grounds on which that application may be made are—

(a) that the realisable assets of the company are sufficient to cover the expenses of the winding up;

(b) that the affairs of the company do require further investigation; or

(c) that for any other reason the early dissolution of the company is inappropriate.

(3) Directions under this section—

(a) are directions making such provision as the Secretary of State thinks fit for enabling the winding up of the company to proceed as if no notice had been given under section 202(3), and

(b) may, in the case of an application under [section 202(8)], include a direction deferring the date at which the dissolution of the company is to take effect for such period as the Secretary of State thinks fit.

(4) An appeal to the court lies from any decision of the Secretary of State on an application for directions under this section.

(5) It is the duty of the person on whose application any directions are given under this section, or in whose favour an appeal with respect to an application for such directions is determined, within 7 days after the giving of the directions or the determination of the appeal, to deliver to the registrar of companies for registration such a copy of the directions or determination as is prescribed.

(6) If a person without reasonable excuse fails to deliver a copy as required by subsection (5), he is liable to a fine and, for continued contravention, to a daily default fine.

NOTES

Sub-s (3): words in square brackets substituted by the Insolvency Amendment (EU 2015/848) Regulations 2017, SI 2017/702, regs 2, 3, Schedule, Pt 1, paras 1, 11, as from 26 June 2017, except in relation to proceedings opened before that date.

[9.335]

204 Early dissolution (Scotland)

(1) This section applies where a winding-up order has been made by the court in Scotland.

(2) If after a [liquidator has been appointed] under section 138 (appointment of liquidator in Scotland) it appears to the liquidator that the realisable assets of the company are insufficient to cover the expenses of the winding up, [the liquidator may at any time apply] to the court for an order that the company be dissolved.

(3) Where the liquidator makes that application, if the court is satisfied that the realisable assets of the company are insufficient to cover the expenses of the winding up and it appears to the court appropriate to do so, the court shall make an order that the company be dissolved in accordance with this section.

(4) A copy of the order shall within 14 days from its date be forwarded by the liquidator to the registrar of companies, who shall forthwith register it; and, at the end of the period of 3 months beginning with the day of the registration of the order, the company shall be dissolved.

[(4A)–(4E) . . .]

(5) The court may, on an application by any person who appears to the court to have an interest, order that the date at which the dissolution of the company is to take effect shall be deferred for such period as the court thinks fit.

(6) It is the duty of the person on whose application an order is made under subsection (5), within 7 days after the making of the order, to deliver to the registrar of companies such a copy of the order as is prescribed.

(7) If the liquidator without reasonable excuse fails to comply with the requirements of subsection (4), he is liable to a fine and, for continued contravention, to a daily default fine.

(8) If a person without reasonable excuse fails to deliver a copy as required by subsection (6), he is liable to a fine and, for continued contravention, to a daily default fine.

NOTES

Sub-s (2): words in first pair of square brackets substituted by the Small Business, Enterprise and Employment Act 2015, s 126, Sch 9, Pt 1, paras 1, 50, as from 6 April 2017 (in relation to England and Wales), and as from 6 April 2019 (in relation to Scotland) (for transitional and savings provisions, see the notes to s 246ZE at **[9.385]**). Words in second pair of square brackets substituted by the Public Services Reform (Insolvency) (Scotland) Order 2016, SSI 2016/141, art 11, as from 6 April 2019.

Sub-ss (4A)–(4E): originally inserted, in relation to Scotland only, by the Insolvency Amendment (EU 2015/848) Regulations 2017, SI 2017/702, regs 2, 3, Schedule, Pt 4, paras 55, 59, as from 26 June 2017, except in relation to proceedings opened before that date. Subsequently repealed by the Insolvency (Amendment) (EU Exit) Regulations 2019, SI 2019/146, reg 2, Schedule, Pt 7, paras 133, 137, as from IP completion day (as defined in the European Union (Withdrawal Agreement) Act 2020, s 39) (for savings, see reg 4 of the 2019 Regulations at **[12.82]**).

[9.336]

205 Dissolution otherwise than under ss 202–204

(1) This section applies where the registrar of companies receives—

[(a) a final account and statement sent under section 146(4) (final account);]

(b) a notice from the official receiver that the winding up of a company by the court is complete.

(2) The registrar shall, on receipt of [the final account and statement or] the notice [. . .], forthwith register [them or] it; and, subject as follows, at the end of the period of 3 months beginning with the day of the registration [of the final account or notice] . . . , the company shall be dissolved.

[(2A) . . .

(2B) . . .]

(3) The Secretary of State may, on the application of the official receiver or any other person who appears to the Secretary of State to be interested, give a direction deferring the date at which the dissolution of the company is to take effect for such period as the Secretary of State thinks fit.

(4) An appeal to the court lies from any decision of the Secretary of State on an application for a direction under subsection (3).

(5) Subsection (3) does not apply in a case where the winding-up order was made by the court in Scotland, but in such a case the court may, on an application by any person appearing to the court to have an interest, order that the date at which the dissolution of the company is to take effect shall be deferred for such period as the court thinks fit.

(6) It is the duty of the person—

(a) on whose application a direction is given under subsection (3);

(b) in whose favour an appeal with respect to an application for such a direction is determined; or

(c) on whose application an order is made under subsection (5),

within 7 days after the giving of the direction, the determination of the appeal or the making of the order, to deliver to the registrar for registration such a copy of the direction, determination or order as is prescribed.

(7) If a person without reasonable excuse fails to deliver a copy as required by subsection (6), he is liable to a fine and, for continued contravention, to a daily default fine.

NOTES

Sub-s (1): para (a) substituted by the Small Business, Enterprise and Employment Act 2015, s 126, Sch 9, Pt 1, paras 1, 51(1), (2), as from 6 April 2017 (in relation to England and Wales), and as from 6 April 2019 (in relation to Scotland) (for transitional and savings provisions, see the notes to s 246ZE at **[9.385]**).

Sub-s (2) is amended as follows:

The words in the first and third pairs of square brackets were inserted, and the second words omitted were repealed, by the Small Business, Enterprise and Employment Act 2015, s 126, Sch 9, Pt 1, paras 1, 51(1), (3), as from 6 April 2017 (in relation to England and Wales), and as from 6 April 2019 (in relation to Scotland) (for transitional and savings provisions, see the notes to s 246ZE at **[9.385]**).

The first words omitted were originally inserted, and the words in the fourth pair of square brackets were inserted, by the Insolvency Amendment (EU 2015/848) Regulations 2017, SI 2017/702, regs 2, 3, Schedule, Pt 1, paras 1, 12(1), (2), as from 26 June 2017, except in relation to proceedings opened before that date. As originally enacted, paragraph 12 of the Schedule to the 2017 Regulations applied to England and Wales only. However, reg 2 of the 2017 Regulations (Amendments and extent) was amended by the Small Business, Enterprise and Employment Act 2015 (Commencement No 7, Consequential, Transitional and Savings Provisions) Regulations 2019, SI 2019/816, reg 6(2) (as from 6 April 2019) so as to apply the amendments made by paragraph 12(2) of the Schedule to the 2017 Regulations to Scotland. See also the final note below in relation to application of sub-s (2) to Scotland. The first words omitted were subsequently repealed by the Insolvency (Amendment) (EU Exit) Regulations 2019, SI 2019/146, reg 2, Schedule, Pt 2, paras 16, 26(1), (2), as from IP completion day (as defined in the European Union (Withdrawal Agreement) Act 2020, s 39) (for savings, see reg 4 of the 2019 Regulations at **[12.82]**).

Sub-ss (2A), (2B): originally inserted by SI 2017/702, regs 2, 3, Schedule, Pt 1, paras 1, 12(1), (3), as from 26 June 2017, except in relation to proceedings opened before that date. As originally enacted, paragraph 12 of the Schedule to the 2017 Regulations applied to England and Wales only. However, reg 2 of the 2017 Regulations (Amendments and extent) was amended by the Small Business, Enterprise and Employment Act 2015 (Commencement No 7, Consequential, Transitional and Savings Provisions) Regulations 2019, SI 2019/816, reg 6(2) (as from 6 April 2019) so as to apply the insertion made by paragraph 12(3) to Scotland. See also the final note below in relation to the application of sub-ss (2A) and (2B) to Scotland. These subsections were subsequently repealed by SI 2019/146, reg 2, Schedule, Pt 2, paras 16, 26(1), (3), as from IP completion day (as defined in the European Union (Withdrawal Agreement) Act 2020, s 39) (for savings, see reg 4 of the 2019 Regulations at **[12.82]**).

Amendment of this section in relation to Scotland: note that sub-s (2) of this section was amended, and new sub-ss (2A) and (2B) were inserted, in relation to Scotland only, by the Insolvency Amendment (EU 2015/848) Regulations 2017, SI 2017/702, regs 2, 3, Schedule, Pt 4, para 60, as from 26 June 2017, except in relation to proceedings opened before that date, as follows—

"(1) In section 205 (dissolution otherwise than under sections 202 to 204) in subsection (2), for "on receipt of the notice, forthwith register it" substitute "on receipt of the notice and any statement sent under section 172(10), forthwith register it or them".

(2) After that subsection insert—

(2A) Subsection (2B) applies where a statement sent to the registrar under section 172(10) indicates that a member State liquidator does not consent to the company being dissolved.

(2B) The company is not dissolved at the end of the period mentioned in subsection (2) but is instead dissolved at the end of the period of 3 months beginning with the date (if any) recorded in the register as the date on which the registrar was notified that—

(a) all proceedings identified in the statement under section 172(10) were closed, or

(b) every member State liquidator appointed in those proceedings consented to the company being dissolved.".

Note that paragraph 60 of the Schedule to the 2017 Regulations was revoked by the Small Business, Enterprise and Employment Act 2015 (Commencement No 7, Consequential, Transitional and Savings Provisions) Regulations 2019, SI 2019/816, reg 6(3) (as from 6 April 2019); and note also that the Insolvency (Amendment) (EU Exit) Regulations 2019, SI 2019/146, reg 2, Schedule, Pt 7, para 138 amends sub-s (2) to reverse the effect of the substitution made by paragraph 60(1) of the Schedule to the 2017 Regulations, and repeal sub-ss (2A), (2B) (as from IP completion day (as defined in the European Union (Withdrawal Agreement) Act 2020, s 39)). Finally note that, Schedule, Pt 7, para 138 is itself revoked by the Insolvency (Amendment) (EU Exit) (No 2) Regulations 2019, SI 2019/1459, reg 2, Schedule, para 4 (as from the same date).

CHAPTER X MALPRACTICE BEFORE AND DURING LIQUIDATION; PENALISATION OF COMPANIES AND COMPANY OFFICERS; INVESTIGATIONS AND PROSECUTIONS

Offences of fraud, deception, etc

[9.337]

206 Fraud, etc in anticipation of winding up

(1) When a company is ordered to be wound up by the court, or passes a resolution for voluntary winding up, any person, being a past or present officer of the company, is deemed to have committed an offence if, within the 12 months immediately preceding the commencement of the winding up, he has—

(a) concealed any part of the company's property to the value of [£500] or more, or concealed any debt due to or from the company, or

(b) fraudulently removed any part of the company's property to the value of [£500] or more, or

(c) concealed, destroyed, mutilated or falsified any book or paper affecting or relating to the company's property or affairs, or

(d) made any false entry in any book or paper affecting or relating to the company's property or affairs, or

(e) fraudulently parted with, altered or made any omission in any document affecting or relating to the company's property or affairs, or

(f) pawned, pledged or disposed of any property of the company which has been obtained on credit and has not been paid for (unless the pawning, pledging or disposal was in the ordinary way of the company's business).

(2) Such a person is deemed to have committed an offence if within the period above mentioned he has been privy to the doing by others of any of the things mentioned in paragraphs (c), (d) and (e) of subsection (1); and he commits an offence if, at any time after the commencement of the winding up, he does any of the things mentioned in paragraphs (a) to (f) of that subsection, or is privy to the doing by others of any of the things mentioned in paragraphs (c) to (e) of it.

(3) For purposes of this section, "officer" includes a shadow director.

(4) It is a defence—

- (a) for a person charged under paragraph (a) or (f) of subsection (1) (or under subsection (2) in respect of the things mentioned in either of those two paragraphs) to prove that he had no intent to defraud, and
- (b) for a person charged under paragraph (c) or (d) of subsection (1) (or under subsection (2) in respect of the things mentioned in either of those two paragraphs) to prove that he had no intent to conceal the state of affairs of the company or to defeat the law.

(5) Where a person pawns, pledges or disposes of any property in circumstances which amount to an offence under subsection (1)(f), every person who takes in pawn or pledge, or otherwise receives, the property knowing it to be pawned, pledged or disposed of in such circumstances, is guilty of an offence.

(6) A person guilty of an offence under this section is liable to imprisonment or a fine, or both.

(7) The money sums specified in paragraphs (a) and (b) of subsection (1) are subject to increase or reduction by order under section 416 in Part XV.

NOTES

Sub-s (1): sums in square brackets in sub-paras (a), (b) substituted by the Insolvency Proceedings (Monetary Limits) Order 1986, SI 1986/1996, art 2(1), Schedule, Pt I, with effect from 29 December 1986.

[9.338]

207 Transactions in fraud of creditors

(1) When a company is ordered to be wound up by the court or passes a resolution for voluntary winding up, a person is deemed to have committed an offence if he, being at the time an officer of the company—

- (a) has made or caused to be made any gift or transfer of, or charge on, or has caused or connived at the levying of any execution against, the company's property, or
- (b) has concealed or removed any part of the company's property since, or within 2 months before, the date of any unsatisfied judgment or order for the payment of money obtained against the company.

(2) A person is not guilty of an offence under this section—

- (a) by reason of conduct constituting an offence under subsection (1)(a) which occurred more than 5 years before the commencement of the winding up, or
- (b) if he proves that, at the time of the conduct constituting the offence, he had no intent to defraud the company's creditors.

(3) A person guilty of an offence under this section is liable to imprisonment or a fine, or both.

[9.339]

208 Misconduct in course of winding up

(1) When a company is being wound up, whether by the court or voluntarily, any person, being a past or present officer of the company, commits an offence if he—

- (a) does not to the best of his knowledge and belief fully and truly discover to the liquidator all the company's property, and how and to whom and for what consideration and when the company disposed of any part of that property (except such part as has been disposed of in the ordinary way of the company's business), or
- (b) does not deliver up to the liquidator (or as he directs) all such part of the company's property as is in his custody or under his control, and which he is required by law to deliver up, or
- (c) does not deliver up to the liquidator (or as he directs) all books and papers in his custody or under his control belonging to the company and which he is required by law to deliver up, or
- (d) knowing or believing that a false debt has been proved by any person in the winding up, fails to inform the liquidator as soon as practicable, or
- (e) after the commencement of the winding up, prevents the production of any book or paper affecting or relating to the company's property or affairs.

(2) Such a person commits an offence if after the commencement of the winding up he attempts to account for any part of the company's property by fictitious losses or expenses; and he is deemed to have committed that offence if he has so attempted [in connection with any qualifying decision procedure or deemed consent procedure] of the company's creditors within the 12 months immediately preceding the commencement of the winding up.

(3) For purposes of this section, "officer" includes a shadow director.

(4) It is a defence—

- (a) for a person charged under paragraph (a), (b) or (c) of subsection (1) to prove that he had no intent to defraud, and
- (b) for a person charged under paragraph (e) of that subsection to prove that he had no intent to conceal the state of affairs of the company or to defeat the law.

(5) A person guilty of an offence under this section is liable to imprisonment or a fine, or both.

NOTES

Sub-s (2): words in square brackets substituted by the Small Business, Enterprise and Employment Act 2015, s 126, Sch 9, Pt 1, paras 1, 52, as from 6 April 2017 (in relation to England and Wales), and as from 6 April 2019 (in relation to Scotland) (for transitional and savings provisions, see the notes to s 246ZE at **[9.385]**).

[9.340]

209 Falsification of company's books

(1) When a company is being wound up, an officer or contributory of the company commits an offence if he destroys, mutilates, alters or falsifies any books, papers or securities, or makes or is privy to the making of any false or fraudulent entry in any register, book of account or document belonging to the company with intent to defraud or deceive any person.

(2) A person guilty of an offence under this section is liable to imprisonment or a fine, or both.

[9.341]

210 Material omissions from statement relating to company's affairs

(1) When a company is being wound up, whether by the court or voluntarily, any person, being a past or present officer of the company, commits an offence if he makes any material omission in any statement relating to the company's affairs.

(2) When a company has been ordered to be wound up by the court, or has passed a resolution for voluntary winding up, any such person is deemed to have committed that offence if, prior to the winding up, he has made any material omission in any such statement.

(3) For purposes of this section, "officer" includes a shadow director.

(4) It is a defence for a person charged under this section to prove that he had no intent to defraud.

(5) A person guilty of an offence under this section is liable to imprisonment or a fine, or both.

[9.342]

211 False representations to creditors

(1) When a company is being wound up, whether by the court or voluntarily, any person, being a past or present officer of the company—

(a) commits an offence if he makes any false representation or commits any other fraud for the purpose of obtaining the consent of the company's creditors or any of them to an agreement with reference to the company's affairs or to the winding up, and

(b) is deemed to have committed that offence if, prior to the winding up, he has made any false representation, or committed any other fraud, for that purpose.

(2) For purposes of this section, "officer" includes a shadow director.

(3) A person guilty of an offence under this section is liable to imprisonment or a fine, or both.

Penalisation of directors and officers

[9.343]

212 Summary remedy against delinquent directors, liquidators, etc

(1) This section applies if in the course of the winding up of a company it appears that a person who—

(a) is or has been an officer of the company,

(b) has acted as liquidator . . . or administrative receiver of the company, or

(c) not being a person falling within paragraph (a) or (b), is or has been concerned, or has taken part, in the promotion, formation or management of the company,

has misapplied or retained, or become accountable for, any money or other property of the company, or been guilty of any misfeasance or breach of any fiduciary or other duty in relation to the company.

(2) The reference in subsection (1) to any misfeasance or breach of any fiduciary or other duty in relation to the company includes, in the case of a person who has acted as liquidator . . . of the company, any misfeasance or breach of any fiduciary or other duty in connection with the carrying out of his functions as liquidator . . . of the company.

(3) The court may, on the application of the official receiver or the liquidator, or of any creditor or contributory, examine into the conduct of the person falling within subsection (1) and compel him—

(a) to repay, restore or account for the money or property or any part of it, with interest at such rate as the court thinks just, or

(b) to contribute such sum to the company's assets by way of compensation in respect of the misfeasance or breach of fiduciary or other duty as the court thinks just.

(4) The power to make an application under subsection (3) in relation to a person who has acted as liquidator . . . of the company is not exercisable, except with the leave of the court, after [he] has had his release.

(5) The power of a contributory to make an application under subsection (3) is not exercisable except with the leave of the court, but is exercisable notwithstanding that he will not benefit from any order the court may make on the application.

NOTES

Sub-ss (1), (2): words omitted repealed by the Enterprise Act 2002, ss 248(3), 278(2), Sch 17, paras 9, 18(a), (b), Sch 26, as from 15 September 2003 (for savings and transitional provisions, see the note to s 8 at **[9.147]**).

Sub-s (4): words omitted repealed, and word in square brackets substituted, by the Enterprise Act 2002, ss 248(3), 278(2), Sch 17, paras 9, 18(c), Sch 26, as from 15 September 2003 (for savings and transitional provisions, see the note to s 8 at **[9.147]**).

[9.344]

213 Fraudulent trading

(1) If in the course of the winding up of a company it appears that any business of the company has been carried on with intent to defraud creditors of the company or creditors of any other person, or for any fraudulent purpose, the following has effect.

(2) The court, on the application of the liquidator may declare that any persons who were knowingly parties to the carrying on of the business in the manner above-mentioned are to be liable to make such contributions (if any) to the company's assets as the court thinks proper.

[9.345]

214 Wrongful trading

(1) Subject to subsection (3) below, if in the course of the winding up of a company it appears that subsection (2) of this section applies in relation to a person who is or has been a director of the company, the court, on the application of the liquidator, may declare that that person is to be liable to make such contribution (if any) to the company's assets as the court thinks proper.

(2) This subsection applies in relation to a person if—

(a) the company has gone into insolvent liquidation,

(b) at some time before the commencement of the winding up of the company, that person knew or ought to have concluded that there was no reasonable prospect that the company would avoid going into insolvent liquidation [or entering insolvent administration], and

(c) that person was a director of the company at that time;

but the court shall not make a declaration under this section in any case where the time mentioned in paragraph (b) above was before 28th April 1986.

(3) The court shall not make a declaration under this section with respect to any person if it is satisfied that after the condition specified in subsection (2)(b) was first satisfied in relation to him that person took every step with a view to minimising the potential loss to the company's creditors as ([on the assumption that he had knowledge of the matter mentioned in subsection (2)(b)]) he ought to have taken.

(4) For the purposes of subsections (2) and (3), the facts which a director of a company ought to know or ascertain, the conclusions which he ought to reach and the steps which he ought to take are those which would be known or ascertained, or reached or taken, by a reasonably diligent person having both—

(a) the general knowledge, skill and experience that may reasonably be expected of a person carrying out the same functions as are carried out by that director in relation to the company, and

(b) the general knowledge, skill and experience that that director has.

(5) The reference in subsection (4) to the functions carried out in relation to a company by a director of the company includes any functions which he does not carry out but which have been entrusted to him.

(6) For the purposes of this section a company goes into insolvent liquidation if it goes into liquidation at a time when its assets are insufficient for the payment of its debts and other liabilities and the expenses of the winding up.

[(6A) For the purposes of this section a company enters insolvent administration if it enters administration at a time when its assets are insufficient for the payment of its debts and other liabilities and the expenses of the administration.]

(7) In this section "director" includes a shadow director.

(8) This section is without prejudice to section 213.

NOTES

Words in square brackets in sub-s (2)(b) inserted, words in square brackets in sub-s (3) substituted, and sub-s (6A) inserted, by the Small Business, Enterprise and Employment Act 2015, s 117(1), (3), as from 1 October 2015, in respect of the carrying on of any business of the company on or after that date.

Suspension of liability for wrongful trading: as to the suspension of liability for wrongful trading, see further the Corporate Insolvency and Governance Act 2020, s 12 at **[9.538]**, and the Corporate Insolvency and Governance Act 2020 (Coronavirus) (Suspension of Liability for Wrongful Trading and Extension of the Relevant Period) Regulations 2020, SI 2020/1349, reg 2 at **[10.1301]**.

[9.346]

215 Proceedings under ss 213, 214

(1) On the hearing of an application under section 213 or 214, the liquidator may himself give evidence or call witnesses.

(2) Where under either section the court makes a declaration, it may give such further directions as it thinks proper for giving effect to the declaration; and in particular, the court may—

(a) provide for the liability of any person under the declaration to be a charge on any debt or obligation due from the company to him, or on any mortgage or charge or any interest in a mortgage or charge on assets of the company held by or vested in him, or any person on his behalf, or any person claiming as assignee from or through the person liable or any person acting on his behalf, and

(b) from time to time make such further order as may be necessary for enforcing any charge imposed under this subsection.

(3) For the purposes of subsection (2), "assignee"—

(a) includes a person to whom or in whose favour, by the directions of the person made liable, the debt, obligation, mortgage or charge was created, issued or transferred or the interest created, but

(b) does not include an assignee for valuable consideration (not including consideration by way of marriage [or the formation of a civil partnership]) given in good faith and without notice of any of the matters on the ground of which the declaration is made.

(4) Where the court makes a declaration under either section in relation to a person who is a creditor of the company, it may direct that the whole or any part of any debt owed by the company to that person and any interest thereon shall rank in priority after all other debts owed by the company and after any interest on those debts.

(5) Sections 213 and 214 have effect notwithstanding that the person concerned may be criminally liable in respect of matters on the ground of which the declaration under the section is to be made.

NOTES

Sub-s (3): words in square brackets inserted by the Civil Partnership Act 2004, s 261(1), Sch 27, para 112, as from 5 December 2005.

[9.347]

216 Restriction on re-use of company names

(1) This section applies to a person where a company ("the liquidating company") has gone into insolvent liquidation on or after the appointed day and he was a director or shadow director of the company at any time in the period of 12 months ending with the day before it went into liquidation.

(2) For the purposes of this section, a name is a prohibited name in relation to such a person if—

(a) it is a name by which the liquidating company was known at any time in that period of 12 months, or

(b) it is a name which is so similar to a name falling within paragraph (a) as to suggest an association with that company.

(3) Except with leave of the court or in such circumstances as may be prescribed, a person to whom this section applies shall not at any time in the period of 5 years beginning with the day on which the liquidating company went into liquidation—

(a) be a director of any other company that is known by a prohibited name, or

(b) in any way, whether directly or indirectly, be concerned or take part in the promotion, formation or management of any such company, or

(c) in any way, whether directly or indirectly, be concerned or take part in the carrying on of a business carried on (otherwise than by a company) under a prohibited name.

(4) If a person acts in contravention of this section, he is liable to imprisonment or a fine, or both.

(5) In subsection (3) "the court" means any court having jurisdiction to wind up companies; and on an application for leave under that subsection, the Secretary of State or the official receiver may appear and call the attention of the court to any matters which seem to him to be relevant.

(6) References in this section, in relation to any time, to a name by which a company is known are to the name of the company at that time or to any name under which the company carries on business at that time.

(7) For the purposes of this section a company goes into insolvent liquidation if it goes into liquidation at a time when its assets are insufficient for the payment of its debts and other liabilities and the expenses of the winding up.

(8) In this section "company" includes a company which may be wound up under Part V of this Act.

[9.348]

217 Personal liability for debts, following contravention of s 216

(1) A person is personally responsible for all the relevant debts of a company if at any time—

(a) in contravention of section 216, he is involved in the management of the company, or

(b) as a person who is involved in the management of the company, he acts or is willing to act on instructions given (without the leave of the court) by a person whom he knows at that time to be in contravention in relation to the company of section 216.

(2) Where a person is personally responsible under this section for the relevant debts of a company, he is jointly and severally liable in respect of those debts with the company and any other person who, whether under this section or otherwise, is so liable.

(3) For the purposes of this section the relevant debts of a company are—

(a) in relation to a person who is personally responsible under paragraph (a) of subsection (1), such debts and other liabilities of the company as are incurred at a time when that person was involved in the management of the company, and

(b) in relation to a person who is personally responsible under paragraph (b) of that subsection, such debts and other liabilities of the company as are incurred at a time when that person was acting or was willing to act on instructions given as mentioned in that paragraph.

(4) For the purposes of this section, a person is involved in the management of a company if he is a director of the company or if he is concerned, whether directly or indirectly, or takes part, in the management of the company.

(5) For the purposes of this section a person who, as a person involved in the management of a company, has at any time acted on instructions given (without the leave of the court) by a person whom he knew at that time to be in contravention in relation to the company of section 216 is presumed, unless the contrary is shown, to have been willing at any time thereafter to act on any instructions given by that person.

(6) In this section "company" includes a company which may be wound up under Part V.

Investigation and prosecution of malpractice

[9.349]

218 Prosecution of delinquent officers and members of company

(1) If it appears to the court in the course of a winding up by the court that any past or present officer, or any member, of the company has been guilty of any offence in relation to the company for which he is criminally liable, the court may (either on the application of a person interested in the winding up or of its own motion) direct the liquidator to refer the matter—

[(a) in the case of a winding up in England and Wales, to the Secretary of State, and

(b) in the case of a winding up in Scotland, to the Lord Advocate.]

(2) . . .

(3) If in the case of a winding up by the court in England and Wales it appears to the liquidator, not being the official receiver, that any past or present officer of the company, or any member of it, has been guilty of an offence in relation to the company for which he is criminally liable, the liquidator shall report the matter to the official receiver.

(4) If it appears to the liquidator in the course of a voluntary winding up that any past or present officer of the company, or any member of it, has been guilty of an offence in relation to the company for which he is criminally liable, he shall [forthwith report the matter—

(a) in the case of a winding up in England and Wales, to the Secretary of State, and

(b) in the case of a winding up in Scotland, to the Lord Advocate,

and shall furnish to the Secretary of State or (as the case may be) the Lord Advocate] such information and give to him such access to and facilities for inspecting and taking copies of documents (being information or documents in the possession or under the control of the liquidator and relating to the matter in question) as [the Secretary of State or (as the case may be) the Lord Advocate] requires.

[(5) Where a report is made to the Secretary of State under subsection (4) he may, for the purpose of investigating the matter reported to him and such other matters relating to the affairs of the company as appear to him to require investigation, exercise any of the powers which are exercisable by inspectors appointed under section 431 or 432 of [the Companies Act 1985] to investigate a company's affairs.]

(6) If it appears to the court in the course of a voluntary winding up that—

(a) any past or present officer of the company, or any member of it, has been guilty as above-mentioned, and

(b) no report with respect to the matter has been made by the liquidator . . . under subsection (4),

the court may (on the application of any person interested in the winding up or of its own motion) direct the liquidator to make such a report.

On a report being made accordingly, this section has effect as though the report had been made in pursuance of subsection (4).

NOTES

Sub-ss (1), (4): words in square brackets substituted by the Insolvency Act 2000, s 10(1), (2), (4), as from 2 April 2001.

Sub-s (2): repealed by the Insolvency Act 2000, ss 10(1), (3), 15(1), Sch 5, as from 2 April 2001.

Sub-s (5): substituted by the Insolvency Act 2000, s 10(1), (5), as from 2 April 2001. Words in square brackets substituted by the Companies Act 2006 (Consequential Amendments, Transitional Provisions and Savings) Order 2009, SI 2009/1941, art 2(1), Sch 1, para 75(1), (24), as from 1 October 2009 (for effect see the note to s 7A at **[9.145]**).

Sub-s (6): words omitted repealed by the Insolvency Act 2000, ss 10(1), (6), 15(1), Sch 5, as from 2 April 2001.

[9.350]

219 Obligations arising under s 218

(1) For the purpose of an investigation by the Secretary of State [in consequence of a report made to him under section 218(4)], any obligation imposed on a person by any provision of [the Companies Act 1985] to produce documents or give information to, or otherwise to assist, inspectors appointed as mentioned in [section 218(5)] is to be regarded as an obligation similarly to assist the Secretary of State in his investigation.

(2) An answer given by a person to a question put to him in exercise of the powers conferred by section 218(5) may be used in evidence against him.

[(2A) However, in criminal proceedings in which that person is charged with an offence to which this subsection applies—

(a) no evidence relating to the answer may be adduced, and

(b) no question relating to it may be asked,

by or on behalf of the prosecution, unless evidence relating to it is adduced, or a question relating to it is asked, in the proceedings by or on behalf of that person.

(2B) Subsection (2A) applies to any offence other than—

(a) an offence under section 2 or 5 of the Perjury Act 1911 (false statements made on oath otherwise than in judicial proceedings or made otherwise than on oath), or

(b) an offence under section 44(1) or (2) of the Criminal Law (Consolidation) (Scotland) Act 1995 (false statements made on oath or otherwise than on oath).]

(3) Where criminal proceedings are instituted by [the Director of Public Prosecutions, the Lord Advocate] or the Secretary of State following any report or reference under section 218, it is the duty of the liquidator and every officer and agent of the company past and present (other than the defendant or defender) to give to [the Director of Public Prosecutions, the Lord Advocate] or the Secretary of State (as the case may be) all assistance in connection with the prosecution which he is reasonably able to give.

For this purpose "agent" includes any banker or solicitor of the company and any person employed by the company as auditor, whether that person is or is not an officer of the company.

(4) If a person fails or neglects to give assistance in the manner required by subsection (3), the court may, on the application of the [Director of Public Prosecutions, the Lord Advocate] or the Secretary of State (as the case may be) direct the person to comply with that subsection; and if the application is made with respect to a liquidator, the court may (unless it appears that the failure or neglect to comply was due to the liquidator not having in his hands sufficient assets of the company to enable him to do so) direct that the costs shall be borne by the liquidator personally.

NOTES

Sub-s (1): words in first and third pairs of square brackets substituted by the Insolvency Act 2000, s 10(1), (7), as from 2 April 2001. Words in second pair of square brackets substituted by the Companies Act 2006 (Consequential Amendments, Transitional Provisions and Savings) Order 2009, SI 2009/1941, art 2(1), Sch 1, para 75(1), (24), as from 1 October 2009 (for effect see the note to s 7A at **[9.145]**).

Sub-ss (3), (4): words in square brackets substituted by the Insolvency Act 2000, s 10(1), (7), as from 2 April 2001.

Sub-ss (2A), (2B): inserted by the Insolvency Act 2000, s 11, as from 2 April 2001.

PART V WINDING UP OF UNREGISTERED COMPANIES

[9.351]

[220 Meaning of "unregistered company"

For the purposes of this Part "unregistered company" includes any association and any company, with the exception of a company registered under the Companies Act 2006 in any part of the United Kingdom.]

NOTES

Substituted by the Companies Act 2006 (Consequential Amendments, Transitional Provisions and Savings) Order 2009, SI 2009/1941, art 2(1), Sch 1, para 76(1), (2), as from 1 October 2009 (for effect see the note to s 7A at **[9.145]**).

[9.352]

221 Winding up of unregistered companies

(1) Subject to the provisions of this Part, any unregistered company may be wound up under this Act; and all the provisions of this Act . . . winding up apply to an unregistered company with the exceptions and additions mentioned in the following subsections.

(2) If an unregistered company has a principal place of business situated in Northern Ireland, it shall not be wound up under this Part unless it has a principal place of business situated in England and Wales or Scotland, or in both England and Wales and Scotland.

(3) For the purpose of determining a court's winding-up jurisdiction, an unregistered company is deemed—

(a) to be registered in England and Wales or Scotland, according as its principal place of business is situated in England and Wales or Scotland, or

(b) if it has a principal place of business situated in both countries, to be registered in both countries;

and the principal place of business situated in that part of Great Britain in which proceedings are being instituted is, for all purposes of the winding up, deemed to be the registered office of the company.

(4) No unregistered company shall be wound up under this Act voluntarily[, except in accordance with the [EU Regulation]].

(5) The circumstances in which an unregistered company may be wound up are as follows—

(a) if the company is dissolved, or has ceased to carry on business, or is carrying on business only for the purpose of winding up its affairs;

(b) if the company is unable to pay its debts;

(c) if the court is of opinion that it is just and equitable that the company should be wound up.

(6) A petition for winding up a trustee savings bank may be presented by the Trustee Savings Banks Central Board or by a commissioner appointed under section 35 of the Trustee Savings Banks Act 1981 as well as by any person authorised under Part IV of this Act to present a petition for the winding up of a company.

On such day as the Treasury appoints by order under section 4(3) of the Trustee Savings Banks Act 1985, this subsection ceases to have effect and is hereby repealed.

(7) In Scotland, an unregistered company which the Court of Session has jurisdiction to wind up may be wound up by the court if there is subsisting a floating charge over property comprised in the company's property and undertaking, and the court is satisfied that the security of the creditor entitled to the benefit of the floating charge is in jeopardy.

For this purpose a creditor's security is deemed to be in jeopardy if the court is satisfied that events have occurred or are about to occur which render it unreasonable in the creditor's interests that the company should retain power to dispose of the property which is subject to the floating charge.

NOTES

Sub-s (1): words omitted repealed by the Companies Act 2006 (Consequential Amendments, Transitional Provisions and Savings) Order 2009, SI 2009/1941, art 2(1), Sch 1, para 76(1), (3), as from 1 October 2009 (for effect see the note to s 7A at **[9.145]**).

Sub-s (4): words in first (outer) pair of square brackets added by the Insolvency Act 1986 (Amendment) (No 2) Regulations 2002, SI 2002/1240, regs 3, 9, as from 31 May 2002. Words in second (inner) pair of square brackets substituted by the Insolvency Amendment (EU 2015/848) Regulations 2017, SI 2017/702, regs 2, 3, Schedule, Pt 1, paras 1, 13, as from 26 June 2017, except in relation to proceedings opened before that date.

Sub-s (6): the Companies Act 1985, s 666(6), from which sub-s (6) above was principally derived, was repealed by the Trustee Savings Banks Act 1985, ss 4(3), 7(3), Sch 4, as from 21 July 1986 by virtue of the Trustee Savings Banks Act 1985 (Appointed Day) (No 4) Order 1986, SI 1986/1223 (made under s 4(3) of that Act). It is thought, therefore, that, as construed in accordance with s 437, Sch 11, para 27, sub-s (6) above has ceased to have effect and is thus repealed. Note also that the Trustee Savings Banks Act 1981 was repealed by the Trustee Savings Banks Act 1985.

Prohibition on presenting a winding-up petition solely in relation to a protected rent debt: see the note to s 124 at **[9.251]**.

[9.353]

222 Inability to pay debts; unpaid creditor for £750 or more

(1) An unregistered company is deemed (for the purposes of section 221) unable to pay its debts if there is a creditor, by assignment or otherwise, to whom the company is indebted in a sum exceeding £750 then due and—

(a) the creditor has served on the company, by leaving at its principal place of business, or by delivering to the secretary or some director, manager or principal officer of the company, or by otherwise serving in such manner as the court may approve or direct, a written demand in the prescribed form requiring the company to pay the sum due, and

(b) the company has for 3 weeks after the service of the demand neglected to pay the sum or to secure or compound for it to the creditor's satisfaction.

(2) The money sum for the time being specified in subsection (1) is subject to increase or reduction by regulations under section 417 in Part XV; but no increase in the sum so specified affects any case in which the winding-up petition was presented before the coming into force of the increase.

[9.354]

223 Inability to pay debts: debt remaining unsatisfied after action brought

An unregistered company is deemed (for the purposes of section 221) unable to pay its debts if an action or other proceeding has been instituted against any member for any debt or demand due, or claimed to be due, from the company, or from him in his character of member, and—

(a) notice in writing of the institution of the action or proceeding has been served on the company by leaving it at the company's principal place of business (or by delivering it to the secretary, or some director, manager or principal officer of the company, or by otherwise serving it in such manner as the court may approve or direct), and

(b) the company has not within 3 weeks after service of the notice paid, secured or compounded for the debt or demand, or procured the action or proceeding to be stayed or sisted, or indemnified the defendant or defender to his reasonable satisfaction against the action or proceeding, and against all costs, damages and expenses to be incurred by him because of it.

[9.355]

224 Inability to pay debts: other cases

(1) An unregistered company is deemed (for purposes of section 221) unable to pay its debts—

(a) if in England and Wales execution or other process issued on a judgment, decree or order obtained in any court in favour of a creditor against the company, or any member of it as such, or any person authorised to be sued as nominal defendant on behalf of the company, is returned unsatisfied;

(b) if in Scotland the induciae of a charge for payment on an extract decree, or an extract registered bond, or an extract registered protest, have expired without payment being made;

(c) if in Northern Ireland a certificate of unenforceability has been granted in respect of any judgment, decree or order obtained as mentioned in paragraph (a);

(d) it is otherwise proved to the satisfaction of the court that the company is unable to pay its debts as they fall due.

(2) An unregistered company is also deemed unable to pay its debts if it is proved to the satisfaction of the court that the value of the company's assets is less than the amount of its liabilities, taking into account its contingent and prospective liabilities.

[9.356]

225 [Company incorporated outside Great Britain] may be wound up though dissolved

[(1)] Where a company incorporated outside Great Britain which has been carrying on business in Great Britain ceases to carry on business in Great Britain, it may be wound up as an unregistered company under this Act, notwithstanding that it has been dissolved or otherwise ceased to exist as a company under or by virtue of the laws of the country under which it was incorporated.

[(2) . . .]

NOTES

Section heading: words in square brackets substituted by the Companies Act 2006 (Consequential Amendments, Transitional Provisions and Savings) Order 2009, SI 2009/1941, art 2(1), Sch 1, para 76(1), (4), as from 1 October 2009 (for effect see the note to s 7A at **[9.145]**).

Sub-s (1) numbered as such, and sub-s (2) originally added, by the Insolvency Act 1986 (Amendment) (No 2) Regulations 2002, SI 2002/1240, regs 3, 10, as from 31 May 2002. Sub-s (2) was subsequently repealed by the Insolvency (Amendment) (EU Exit) Regulations 2019, SI 2019/146, reg 2, Schedule, Pt 2, paras 16, 27, as from IP completion day (as defined in the European Union (Withdrawal Agreement) Act 2020, s 39) (for savings, see reg 4 of the 2019 Regulations at **[12.82]**).

[9.357]

226 Contributories in winding up of unregistered company

(1) In the event of an unregistered company being wound up, every person is deemed a contributory who is liable to pay or contribute to the payment of any debt or liability of the company, or to pay or contribute to the payment of any sum for the adjustment of the rights of members among themselves, or to pay or contribute to the payment of the expenses of winding up the company.

(2) Every contributory is liable to contribute to the company's assets all sums due from him in respect of any such liability as is mentioned above.

(3) In the case of an unregistered company engaged in or formed for working mines within the stannaries, a past member is not liable to contribute to the assets if he has ceased to be a member for 2 years or more either before the mine ceased to be worked or before the date of the winding-up order.

(4) . . .

NOTES

Sub-s (4): repealed by the Companies Act 2006 (Consequential Amendments, Transitional Provisions and Savings) Order 2009, SI 2009/1941, art 2(1), Sch 1, para 76(1), (5), as from 1 October 2009 (for effect see the note to s 7A at **[9.145]**).

[9.358]

227 Power of court to stay, sist or restrain proceedings

The provisions of this Part with respect to staying, sisting or restraining actions and proceedings against a company at any time after the presentation of a petition for winding up and before the making of a winding-up order extend, in the case of an unregistered company, where the application to stay, sist or restrain is presented by a creditor, to actions and proceedings against any contributory of the company.

[9.359]

228 Actions stayed on winding-up order

Where an order has been made for winding up an unregistered company, no action or proceeding shall be proceeded with or commenced against any contributory of the company in respect of any debt of the company, except by leave of the court, and subject to such terms as the court may impose.

[9.360]

229 Provisions of this Part to be cumulative

(1) The provisions of this Part with respect to unregistered companies are in addition to and not in restriction of any provisions in Part IV with respect to winding up companies by the court; and the court or liquidator may exercise any powers or do any act in the case of unregistered companies which might be exercised or done by it or him in winding up [companies registered under the Companies Act 2006 in England and Wales or Scotland].

(2) . . .

NOTES

Words in square brackets in sub-s (1) substituted, and sub-s (2) repealed, by the Companies Act 2006 (Consequential Amendments, Transitional Provisions and Savings) Order 2009, SI 2009/1941, art 2(1), Sch 1, para 76(1), (6), as from 1 October 2009 (for effect see the note to s 7A at **[9.145]**).

PART VI MISCELLANEOUS PROVISIONS APPLYING TO COMPANIES WHICH ARE INSOLVENT OR IN LIQUIDATION

Office-holders

[9.361]

230 Holders of office to be qualified insolvency practitioners

(1) . . .

(2) Where an administrative receiver of a company is appointed, he must be a person who is so qualified.

(3) Where a company goes into liquidation, the liquidator must be a person who is so qualified.

(4) Where a provisional liquidator is appointed, he must be a person who is so qualified.

(5) Subsections (3) and (4) are without prejudice to any enactment under which the official receiver is to be, or may be, liquidator or provisional liquidator.

NOTES

Sub-s (1): repealed by the Enterprise Act 2002, ss 248(3), 287(2), Sch 17, paras 9, 19, Sch 26, as from 15 September 2003 (for savings and transitional provisions, see the note to s 8 at **[9.147]**).

[9.362]

231 Appointment to office of two or more persons

(1) This section applies if an appointment or nomination of any person to the office of . . . administrative receiver, liquidator or provisional liquidator—

(a) relates to more than one person, or

(b) has the effect that the office is to be held by more than one person.

(2) The appointment or nomination shall declare whether any act required or authorised under any enactment to be done by the . . . administrative receiver, liquidator or provisional liquidator is to be done by all or any one or more of the persons for the time being holding the office in question.

NOTES

Sub-ss (1), (2): words omitted repealed by the Enterprise Act 2002, ss 248(3), 287(2), Sch 17, paras 9, 20, Sch 26, as from 15 September 2003 (for savings and transitional provisions, see the note to s 8 at **[9.147]**).

[9.363]

232 Validity of office-holder's acts

The acts of an individual as . . . administrative receiver, liquidator or provisional liquidator of a company are valid notwithstanding any defect in his appointment, nomination or qualifications.

NOTES

Word omitted repealed by the Enterprise Act 2002, ss 248(3), 287(2), Sch 17, paras 9, 21, Sch 26, as from 15 September 2003 (for savings and transitional provisions, see the note to s 8 at **[9.147]**).

Management by administrators, liquidators, etc

[9.364]

233 Supplies of gas, water, electricity, etc

(1) This section applies in the case of a company where—

[(a) the company enters administration,]

(b) an administrative receiver is appointed, or

[(ba) . . .]

(c) a voluntary arrangement [approved under Part I], has taken effect, or

(d) the company goes into liquidation, or

(e) a provisional liquidator is appointed;

and "the office-holder" means the administrator, the administrative receiver, [. . .] the supervisor of the voluntary arrangement, the liquidator or the provisional liquidator, as the case may be.

(2) If a request is made by or with the concurrence of the office-holder for the giving, after the effective date, of any of the supplies mentioned in the next subsection, the supplier—

(a) may make it a condition of the giving of the supply that the office-holder personally guarantees the payment of any charges in respect of the supply, but

(b) shall not make it a condition of the giving of the supply, or do anything which has the effect of making it a condition of the giving of the supply, that any outstanding charges in respect of a supply given to the company before the effective date are paid.

(3) The supplies referred to in subsection (2) are—

[(a) a supply of gas by a gas supplier within the meaning of Part I of the Gas Act 1986;]

[(aa) a supply of gas by a person within paragraph 1 of Schedule 2A to the Gas Act 1986 (supply by landlords etc);]

[(b) a supply of electricity by an electricity supplier within the meaning of Part I of the Electricity Act 1989;]

[(ba) a supply of electricity by a class of person within Class A (small suppliers) or Class B (resale) of Schedule 4 to the Electricity (Class Exemptions from the Requirement for a Licence) Order 2001 (SI 2001/3270);]

(c) a supply of water by [a water undertaker] or, in Scotland, [Scottish Water],

[(ca) a supply of water by a water supply licensee within the meaning of the Water Industry Act 1991;

(cb) a supply of water by a water services provider within the meaning of the Water Services etc (Scotland) Act 2005;

(cc) a supply of water by a person who has an interest in the premises to which the supply is given;]

[(d) a supply of communications services by a provider of a public electronic communications service];

[(e) a supply of communications services by a person who carries on a business which includes giving such supplies;

(f) a supply of goods or services mentioned in subsection (3A) by a person who carries on a business which includes giving such supplies, where the supply is for the purpose of enabling or facilitating anything to be done by electronic means].

[(3A) The goods and services referred to in subsection (3)(f) are—

(a) point of sale terminals;

(b) computer hardware and software;

(c) information, advice and technical assistance in connection with the use of information technology;

(d) data storage and processing;

(e) website hosting.]

(4) "The effective date" for the purposes of this section is whichever is applicable of the following dates—

[(a) the date on which the company entered administration,]

(b) the date on which the administrative receiver was appointed (or, if he was appointed in succession to another administrative receiver, the date on which the first of his predecessors was appointed), [(ba) . . .]

(c) the date on which the voluntary arrangement [took effect],

(d) the date on which the company went into liquidation,

(e) the date on which the provisional liquidator was appointed.

(5) The following applies to expressions used in subsection (3)—

(a)–(c) . . .

[(d) "communications services" do not include electronic communications services to the extent that they are used to broadcast or otherwise transmit programme services (within the meaning of the Communications Act 2003).]

NOTES

Sub-s (1) is amended as follows:

Para (a) substituted by the Enterprise Act 2002, s 248(3), Sch 17, paras 9, 22(a), as from 15 September 2003 (for savings and transitional provisions, see the note to s 8 at **[9.147]**).

Para (ba) and the final words omitted were originally inserted by the Insolvency Act 2000, s 1, Sch 1, paras 1, 8(1), (2), as from 1 January 2003. They were subsequently repealed by the Corporate Insolvency and Governance Act 2020, s 2(1), Sch 3, paras 1, 15(1), (2), as from 26 June 2020 (for transitional provisions, see s 2(2), (3) of the 2020 Act (at **[9.533]**) which provides that (without prejudice to the Interpretation Act 1978, s 16) nothing in the 2020 Act affects the operation of this Act, or any other enactment, in relation to a moratorium under Sch A1 to this Act which comes into force before the repeal of that Schedule by Sch 3 to the 2020 Act (ie, 26 June 2020)).

The words in square brackets in para (c) were substituted by the Insolvency Act 2000, s 1, Sch 1, paras 1, 8(1), (2), as from 1 January 2003.

Sub-s (3) is amended as follows:

Para (a) substituted by the Gas Act 1995, s 16(1), Sch 4, para 14(1), as from 1 March 1996.

Paras (aa), (ba), (ca)–(cc), (e), (f) inserted by the Insolvency (Protection of Essential Supplies) Order 2015, SI 2015/989, art 2(1), (2), (4), as from 1 October 2015.

Para (b) substituted by the Utilities Act 2000, s 108, Sch 6, para 47(1), (2)(a), as from 1 October 2001.

Words in first pair of square brackets in para (c) substituted by the Water Act 1989, s 190(1), Sch 25, para 78(1), as from 1 September 1989.

Words in second pair of square brackets in para (c) substituted by the Water Industry (Scotland) Act 2002 (Consequential Modifications) Order 2004, SI 2004/1822, art 2, Schedule, Pt 1, para 14(a), as from 14 July 2004.

Para (d) substituted by the Communications Act 2003, s 406, Sch 17, para 82(1), (2)(a), as from 25 July 2003 (certain purposes), and as from 29 December 2003 (otherwise).

Sub-s (3A): inserted by SI 2015/989, art 2(1), (3), as from 1 October 2015.

Sub-s (4): para (a) substituted by the Enterprise Act 2002, s 248(3), Sch 17, paras 9, 22(b), as from 15 September 2003 (for savings and transitional provisions, see the note to s 8 at **[9.147]**). Para (ba) was originally inserted, and the words in square brackets in para (c) were substituted, by the Insolvency Act 2000, s 1, Sch 1, paras 1, 8(1), (3), as from 1 January 2003. Para (ba) was subsequently repealed by the Corporate Insolvency and Governance Act 2020, s 2(1), Sch 3, paras 1, 15(1), (3), as from 26 June 2020 (for transitional provisions, see the first note relating to the 2020 Act above).

Sub-s (5): para (a) repealed by the Gas Act 1995, ss 16(1), 17(5), Sch 4, para 14(2), Sch 6, as from 1 March 1996. Para (b) repealed by the Utilities Act 2000, s 108, Sch 6, para 47(1), (2)(b), Sch 8, as from 1 October 2001. Para (c) repealed by SI 2004/1822, art 2, Schedule, Pt 1, para 14(b), as from 14 July 2004. Para (d) substituted by the Communications Act 2003, s 406, Sch 17, para 82(1), (2)(b), as from 25 July 2003 (certain purposes), and as from 29 December 2003 (otherwise).

See further the Enterprise and Regulatory Reform Act 2013, s 92(1) which provides that the Secretary of State may by order amend this section so as to add to the supplies mentioned in sub-s (3) above any of the following (a) a supply of gas, electricity, water or communication services by a specified description of person; (b) a supply of a specified description of goods or services by a specified description of person where the supply is for the purpose of enabling or facilitating anything to be done by electronic means. See also s 93 of the 2013 Act which provides that the Secretary of State may by order make provision for insolvency-related terms of a contract for the supply of essential goods or services to a company to cease to have effect where (a) the company enters administration or a voluntary arrangement under Part I of this Act takes effect in relation to it, and (b) any conditions specified in the order are met. A contract for the supply of essential goods or services for these purposes is a contract for a supply mentioned in sub-s (3) above. See also s 95 of that Act with regard to supplementary matters relating to orders under s 93. Note that the Insolvency (Protection of Essential Supplies) Order 2015, SI 2015/989 (which amends this section as noted above) was made under the powers conferred by those sections of the 2013 Act.

[9.365]

[233A Further protection of essential supplies

(1) An insolvency-related term of a contract for the supply of essential goods or services to a company ceases to have effect if—

(a) the company enters administration, or

(b) a voluntary arrangement approved under Part 1 takes effect in relation to the company.

(2) An insolvency-related term of a contract does not cease to have effect by virtue of subsection (1) to the extent that—

(a) it provides for the contract or the supply to terminate, or any other thing to take place, because the company becomes subject to an insolvency procedure other than administration or a voluntary arrangement;

(b) it entitles a supplier to terminate the contract or the supply, or do any other thing, because the company becomes subject to an insolvency procedure other than administration or a voluntary arrangement; or

(c) it entitles a supplier to terminate the contract or the supply because of an event that occurs, or may occur, after the company enters administration or the voluntary arrangement takes effect.

(3) Where an insolvency-related term of a contract ceases to have effect under this section the supplier may—

(a) terminate the contract, if the condition in subsection (4) is met;

(b) terminate the supply, if the condition in subsection (5) is met.

(4) The condition in this subsection is that—

(a) the insolvency office-holder consents to the termination of the contract,

(b) the court grants permission for the termination of the contract, or

(c) any charges in respect of the supply that are incurred after the company entered administration or the voluntary arrangement took effect are not paid within the period of 28 days beginning with the day on which payment is due.

The court may grant permission under paragraph (b) only if satisfied that the continuation of the contract would cause the supplier hardship.

(5) The condition in this subsection is that—

(a) the supplier gives written notice to the insolvency office-holder that the supply will be terminated unless the office-holder personally guarantees the payment of any charges in respect of the continuation of the supply after the company entered administration or the voluntary arrangement took effect, and

(b) the insolvency office-holder does not give that guarantee within the period of 14 days beginning with the day the notice is received.

(6) For the purposes of securing that the interests of suppliers are protected, where—

(a) an insolvency-related term of a contract (the "original term") ceases to have effect by virtue of subsection (1), and

(b) the company subsequently enters administration, or a voluntary arrangement subsequently has effect in relation to it,

the contract is treated for the purposes of subsections (1) to (5) as if, immediately before the subsequent administration is entered into or the subsequent voluntary arrangement takes effect, it included an insolvency-related term identical to the original term.

(7) A contract for the supply of essential goods or services is a contract for a supply mentioned in section 233(3).

(8) An insolvency-related term of a contract for the supply of essential goods or services to a company is a provision of the contract under which—

(a) the contract or the supply would terminate, or any other thing would take place, because the company enters administration or the voluntary arrangement takes effect,

(b) the supplier would be entitled to terminate the contract or the supply, or to do any other thing, because the company enters administration or the voluntary arrangement takes effect, or

(c) the supplier would be entitled to terminate the contract or the supply because of an event that occurred before the company enters administration or the voluntary arrangement takes effect.

(9) In this section "insolvency office-holder" means—

(a) in a case where a company enters administration, the administrator;

(b) in a case where a voluntary arrangement under Part 1 takes effect in relation to a company, the supervisor of the voluntary arrangement.

(10) Subsection (1) does not have effect in relation to a contract entered into before 1st October 2015.]

NOTES

Inserted by the Insolvency (Protection of Essential Supplies) Order 2015, SI 2015/989, art 4, as from 1 October 2015.

[9.366]

[233B Protection of supplies of goods and services

(1) This section applies where a company becomes subject to a relevant insolvency procedure.

(2) A company becomes subject to a relevant insolvency procedure for the purposes of this section where—

(a) a moratorium under Part A1 comes into force for the company,

(b) the company enters administration,

(c) an administrative receiver of the company is appointed (otherwise than in succession to another administrative receiver),

(d) a voluntary arrangement approved under Part 1 takes effect in relation to the company,

(e) the company goes into liquidation,

(f) a provisional liquidator of the company is appointed (otherwise than in succession to another provisional liquidator), or

(g) a court order is made under section 901C(1) of the Companies Act 2006 in relation to the company (order summoning meeting relating to compromise or arrangement).

(3) A provision of a contract for the supply of goods or services to the company ceases to have effect when the company becomes subject to the relevant insolvency procedure if and to the extent that, under the provision—

(a) the contract or the supply would terminate, or any other thing would take place, because the company becomes subject to the relevant insolvency procedure, or

(b) the supplier would be entitled to terminate the contract or the supply, or to do any other thing, because the company becomes subject to the relevant insolvency procedure.

(4) Where—

(a) under a provision of a contract for the supply of goods or services to the company the supplier is entitled to terminate the contract or the supply because of an event occurring before the start of the insolvency period, and

(b) the entitlement arises before the start of that period,

the entitlement may not be exercised during that period.

(5) Where a provision of a contract ceases to have effect under subsection (3) or an entitlement under a provision of a contract is not exercisable under subsection (4), the supplier may terminate the contract if—

(a) in a case where the company has become subject to a relevant insolvency procedure as specified in subsection (2)(b), (c), (e) or (f), the office-holder consents to the termination of the contract,

(b) in any other case, the company consents to the termination of the contract, or

(c) the court is satisfied that the continuation of the contract would cause the supplier hardship and grants permission for the termination of the contract.

(6) Where a provision of a contract ceases to have effect under subsection (3) and the company becomes subject to a further relevant insolvency procedure, the supplier may terminate the contract in accordance with subsection (5)(a) to (c).

(7) The supplier shall not make it a condition of any supply of goods and services after the time when the company becomes subject to the relevant insolvency procedure, or do anything which has the effect of making it a condition of such a supply, that any outstanding charges in respect of a supply made to the company before that time are paid.

(8) In this section "the insolvency period", in relation to a relevant insolvency procedure, means the period beginning when the company becomes subject to the relevant insolvency procedure and ending—

(a) in the case of a moratorium under Part A1, when the moratorium comes to an end,

(b) in the case of the company entering administration, when the appointment of the administrator ceases to have effect under—

(i) paragraphs 76 to 84 of Schedule B1, or

(ii) an order under section 901F of the Companies Act 2006,

(c) in the case of the appointment of an administrative receiver of the company, when the receiver or any successor to the receiver ceases to hold office without a successor being appointed,

(d) in the case of a voluntary arrangement approved under Part 1 taking effect in relation to the company, when the arrangement ceases to have effect,

(e) in the case of the company going into liquidation, when—

(i) the liquidator complies with section 94(2), 106(2) or 146(3) (duties relating to final account), or

(ii) the appointment of the liquidator ceases to have effect under an order under section 901F of the Companies Act 2006,

(f) in the case of the appointment of a provisional liquidator for the company, when the provisional liquidator or any successor to the provisional liquidator ceases to hold office without a successor being appointed, and

(g) in the case of the making of a court order under section 901C(1) of the Companies Act 2006 in relation to the company, when—

(i) an order made by the court under section 901F of that Act takes effect, or

(ii) the court decides not to make such an order.

(9) In this section "office-holder", in relation to a company which has entered into an insolvency procedure as specified in subsection (2)(b), (c), (e) or (f), means the administrator, administrative receiver, liquidator or provisional liquidator respectively.

(10) Schedule 4ZZA provides for exclusions from the operation of this section.]

NOTES

Commencement: 26 June 2020.

Inserted, together with s 233C, by the Corporate Insolvency and Governance Act 2020, s 14(1), as from 26 June 2020.

See also Sch 4ZZA to this Act (at **[9.481]** et seq) which provides for exclusions from the operation of section; and note also that the amendments made by s 14 of the 2020 Act have effect in relation to a company which becomes subject to a relevant insolvency procedure on or after the day on which that section comes into force (ie, 26 June 2020) (but in respect of contracts entered into before, as well as those entered into on or after, that day). Section 14 of the 2020 Act is at **[9.539]**.

Temporary exclusion for small suppliers: this section does not apply in relation to a contract for the supply of goods or services to a company where: (a) the company becomes subject to a relevant insolvency procedure during the relevant period; and (b) the supplier is a small entity at the time the company becomes subject to the procedure. See the Corporate Insolvency and Governance Act 2020, s 15 at **[9.540]**; and see subsection (2) of that section for the meaning of "relevant period".

[9.367]

[233C Powers to amend section 233B and Schedule 4ZZA

(1) The Secretary of State may by regulations omit any of paragraphs (a) to (g) of section 233B(2) (relevant insolvency procedures).

(2) The Secretary of State may by regulations amend Schedule 4ZZA so as to—

(a) remove or amend any exclusion from section 233B for the time being specified there, or

(b) add further exclusions from section 233B.

(3) In subsection (2), references to exclusions from section 233B are to circumstances in which section 233B, or any provision of that section, does not apply.

(4) The circumstances referred to in subsection (3) may be framed by reference to kinds of company, supplier, contract, goods or services or in any other way.

(5) Regulations under this section may make—

(a) different provision for different purposes;

(b) consequential provision;

(c) transitional and supplementary provision.

(6) Regulations under this section made by virtue of subsection (5) may in particular make provision amending this Act or any other enactment whenever passed or made (including, if paragraph 1(1) or (2) of Schedule 4ZZA is omitted, provision omitting section 233A or 233 respectively).

(7) Regulations under subsection (1) may not omit section 233B(2)(c) unless the Secretary of State has first consulted the Scottish Ministers.

(8) In this section "enactment" includes an Act of the Scottish Parliament and an instrument made under such an Act.

(9) Regulations under this section are to be made by statutory instrument.

(10) A statutory instrument containing regulations under this section may not be made unless a draft of the instrument has been laid before and approved by a resolution of each House of Parliament.]

NOTES

Commencement: 26 June 2020.

Inserted as noted to s 233B at **[9.366]**.

[9.368]

234 Getting in the company's property

(1) This section applies in the case of a company where—

[(a) the company enters administration,] or

(b) an administrative receiver is appointed, or

(c) the company goes into liquidation, or
(d) a provisional liquidator is appointed;

and "the office-holder" means the administrator, the administrative receiver, the liquidator or the provisional liquidator, as the case may be.

(2) Where any person has in his possession or control any property, books, papers or records to which the company appears to be entitled, the court may require that person forthwith (or within such period as the court may direct) to pay, deliver convey, surrender or transfer the property, books, papers or records to the office-holder.

(3) Where the office-holder—

(a) seizes or disposes of any property which is not property of the company, and
(b) at the time of seizure or disposal believes, and has reasonable grounds for believing, that he is entitled (whether in pursuance of an order of the court or otherwise) to seize or dispose of that property,

the next subsection has effect.

(4) In that case the office-holder—

(a) is not liable to any person in respect of any loss or damage resulting from the seizure or disposal except in so far as that loss or damage is caused by the office-holder's own negligence, and
(b) has a lien on the property, or the proceeds of its sale, for such expenses as were incurred in connection with the seizure or disposal.

NOTES

Sub-s (1): para (a) substituted by the Enterprise Act 2002, s 248(3), Sch 17, paras 9, 23, as from 15 September 2003 (for savings and transitional provisions, see the note to s 8 at **[9.147]**).

[9.369]

235 Duty to co-operate with office-holder

(1) This section applies as does section 234; and it also applies, in the case of a company in respect of which a winding-up order has been made by the court in England and Wales, as if references to the office-holder included the official receiver, whether or not he is the liquidator.

(2) Each of the persons mentioned in the next subsection shall—

(a) give to the office-holder such information concerning the company and its promotion, formation, business, dealings, affairs or property as the office-holder may at any time after the effective date reasonably require, and
(b) attend on the office-holder at such times as the latter may reasonably require.

(3) The persons referred to above are—

(a) those who are or have at any time been officers of the company,
(b) those who have taken part in the formation of the company at any time within one year before the effective date,
(c) those who are in the employment of the company, or have been in its employment (including employment under a contract for services) within that year, and are in the office-holder's opinion capable of giving information which he requires,
(d) those who are, or have within that year been, officers of, or in the employment (including employment under a contract for services) of, another company which is, or within that year was, an officer of the company in question, and
(e) in the case of a company being wound up by the court, any person who has acted as administrator, administrative receiver or liquidator of the company.

(4) For the purposes of subsections (2) and (3), "the effective date" is whichever is applicable of the following dates—

[(a) the date on which the company entered administration,]
(b) the date on which the administrative receiver was appointed or, if he was appointed in succession to another administrative receiver, the date on which the first of his predecessors was appointed,
(c) the date on which the provisional liquidator was appointed, and
(d) the date on which the company went into liquidation.

(5) If a person without reasonable excuse fails to comply with any obligation imposed by this section, he is liable to a fine and, for continued contravention, to a daily default fine.

NOTES

Sub-s (4): para (a) substituted by the Enterprise Act 2002, s 248(3), Sch 17, paras 9, 24, as from 15 September 2003 (for savings and transitional provisions, see the note to s 8 at **[9.147]**).

[9.370]

236 Inquiry into company's dealings, etc

(1) This section applies as does section 234; and it also applies in the case of a company in respect of which a winding-up order has been made by the court in England and Wales as if references to the office-holder included the official receiver, whether or not he is the liquidator.

(2) The court may, on the application of the office-holder, summon to appear before it—

(a) any officer of the company,
(b) any person known or suspected to have in his possession any property of the company or supposed to be indebted to the company, or
(c) any person whom the court thinks capable of giving information concerning the promotion, formation, business, dealings, affairs or property of the company.

(3) The court may require any such person as is mentioned in subsection (2)(a) to (c) to submit [to the court] an account of his dealings with the company or to produce any books, papers or other records in his possession or under his control relating to the company or the matters mentioned in paragraph (c) of the subsection.

[(3A) An account submitted to the court under subsection (3) must be contained in—

(a) a witness statement verified by a statement of truth (in England and Wales), and

(b) an affidavit (in Scotland).]

(4) The following applies in a case where—

(a) a person without reasonable excuse fails to appear before the court when he is summoned to do so under this section, or

(b) there are reasonable grounds for believing that a person has absconded, or is about to abscond, with a view to avoiding his appearance before the court under this section.

(5) The court may, for the purpose of bringing that person and anything in his possession before the court, cause a warrant to be issued to a constable or prescribed officer of the court—

(a) for the arrest of that person, and

(b) for the seizure of any books, papers, records, money or goods in that person's possession.

(6) The court may authorise a person arrested under such a warrant to be kept in custody, and anything seized under such a warrant to be held, in accordance with the rules, until that person is brought before the court under the warrant or until such other time as the court may order.

NOTES

Sub-s (3): words in square brackets substituted by the Legislative Reform (Insolvency) (Miscellaneous Provisions) Order 2010, SI 2010/18, arts 2, 5(6)(a), as from 6 April 2010.

Sub-s (3A): inserted by SI 2010/18, arts 2, 5(6)(b), as from 6 April 2010.

[9.371]

237 Court's enforcement powers under s 236

(1) If it appears to the court, on consideration of any evidence obtained under section 236 or this section, that any person has in his possession any property of the company, the court may, on the application of the office-holder, order that person to deliver the whole or any part of the property to the officer-holder at such time, in such manner and on such terms as the court thinks fit.

(2) If it appears to the court, on consideration of any evidence so obtained, that any person is indebted to the company, the court may, on the application of the office-holder, order that person to pay to the office-holder, at such time and in such manner as the court may direct, the whole or any part of the amount due, whether in full discharge of the debt or otherwise, as the court thinks fit.

(3) The court may, if it thinks fit, order that any person who if within the jurisdiction of the court would be liable to be summoned to appear before it under section 236 or this section shall be examined in any part of the United Kingdom where he may for the time being be, or in a place outside the United Kingdom.

(4) Any person who appears or is brought before the court under section 236 or this section may be examined on oath, either orally or (except in Scotland) by interrogatories, concerning the company or the matters mentioned in section 236(2)(c).

Adjustment of prior transactions (administration and liquidation)

[9.372]

238 Transactions at an undervalue (England and Wales)

(1) This section applies in the case of a company where—

[(a) the company enters administration,] or

(b) the company goes into liquidation;

and "the office-holder" means the administrator or the liquidator, as the case may be.

(2) Where the company has at a relevant time (defined in section 240) entered into a transaction with any person at an undervalue, the office-holder may apply to the court for an order under this section.

(3) Subject as follows, the court shall, on such an application, make such order as it thinks fit for restoring the position to what it would have been if the company had not entered into that transaction.

(4) For the purposes of this section and section 241, a company enters into a transaction with a person at an undervalue if—

(a) the company makes a gift to that person or otherwise enters into a transaction with that person on terms that provide for the company to receive no consideration, or

(b) the company enters into a transaction with that person for a consideration the value of which, in money or money's worth, is significantly less than the value, in money or money's worth, of the consideration provided by the company.

(5) The court shall not make an order under this section in respect of a transaction at an undervalue if it is satisfied—

(a) that the company which entered into the transaction did so in good faith and for the purpose of carrying on its business, and

(b) that at the time it did so there were reasonable grounds for believing that the transaction would benefit the company.

NOTES

Sub-s (1): para (a) substituted by the Enterprise Act 2002, s 248(3), Sch 17, paras 9, 25, as from 15 September 2003 (for savings and transitional provisions, see the note to s 8 at **[9.147]**).

[9.373]

239 Preferences (England and Wales)

(1) This section applies as does section 238.

(2) Where the company has at a relevant time (defined in the next section) given a preference to any person, the office-holder may apply to the court for an order under this section.

(3) Subject as follows, the court shall, on such an application, make such order as it thinks fit for restoring the position to what it would have been if the company had not given that preference.

(4) For the purposes of this section and section 241, a company gives a preference to a person if—

(a) that person is one of the company's creditors or a surety or guarantor for any of the company's debts or other liabilities, and

(b) the company does anything or suffers anything to be done which (in either case) has the effect of putting that person into a position which, in the event of the company going into insolvent liquidation, will be better than the position he would have been in if that thing had not been done.

(5) The court shall not make an order under this section in respect of a preference given to any person unless the company which gave the preference was influenced in deciding to give it by a desire to produce in relation to that person the effect mentioned in subsection (4)(b).

(6) A company which has given a preference to a person connected with the company (otherwise than by reason only of being its employee) at the time the preference was given is presumed, unless the contrary is shown, to have been influenced in deciding to give it by such a desire as is mentioned in subsection (5).

(7) The fact that something has been done in pursuance of the order of a court does not, without more, prevent the doing or suffering of that thing from constituting the giving of a preference.

[9.374]

240 "Relevant time" under ss 238, 239

(1) Subject to the next subsection, the time at which a company enters into a transaction at an undervalue or gives a preference is a relevant time if the transaction is entered into, or the preference given—

(a) in the case of a transaction at an undervalue or of a preference which is given to a person who is connected with the company (otherwise than by reason only of being its employee), at a time in the period of 2 years ending with the onset of insolvency (which expression is defined below),

(b) in the case of a preference which is not such a transaction and is not so given, at a time in the period of 6 months ending with the onset of insolvency, . . .

[(c) in either case, at a time between the making of an administration application in respect of the company and the making of an administration order on that application, and

(d) in either case, at a time between the filing with the court of a copy of notice of intention to appoint an administrator under paragraph 14 or 22 of Schedule B1 and the making of an appointment under that paragraph.]

(2) Where a company enters into a transaction at an undervalue or gives a preference at a time mentioned in subsection (1)(a) or (b), that time is not a relevant time for the purposes of section 238 or 239 unless the company—

(a) is at that time unable to pay its debts within the meaning of section 123 in Chapter VI of Part IV, or

(b) becomes unable to pay its debts within the meaning of that section in consequence of the transaction or preference;

but the requirements of this subsection are presumed to be satisfied, unless the contrary is shown, in relation to any transaction at an undervalue which is entered into by a company with a person who is connected with the company.

(3) For the purposes of subsection (1), the onset of insolvency is—

[(a) in a case where section 238 or 239 applies by reason of an administrator of a company being appointed by administration order, the date on which the administration application is made,

(b) in a case where section 238 or 239 applies by reason of an administrator of a company being appointed under paragraph 14 or 22 of Schedule B1 following filing with the court of a copy of a notice of intention to appoint under that paragraph, the date on which the copy of the notice is filed,

(c) in a case where section 238 or 239 applies by reason of an administrator of a company being appointed otherwise than as mentioned in paragraph (a) or (b), the date on which the appointment takes effect,

(d) in a case where section 238 or 239 applies by reason of a company going into liquidation . . . at the time when the appointment of an administrator ceases to have effect, the date on which the company entered administration (or, if relevant, the date on which the application for the administration order was made or a copy of the notice of intention to appoint was filed), and

(e) in a case where section 238 or 239 applies by reason of a company going into liquidation at any other time, the date of the commencement of the winding up.]

NOTES

Sub-s (1): word omitted from para (b) repealed, and paras (c), (d) substituted (for the original para (c)), by the Enterprise Act 2002, ss 248(3), 278(2), Sch 17, paras 9, 26(1)–(3), Sch 26, as from 15 September 2003 (for savings and transitional provisions, see the note to s 8 at **[9.147]**).

Sub-s (3): paras (a)–(e) substituted (for paras (a), (aa), (b)), by the Enterprise Act 2002, s 248(3), Sch 17, paras 9, 26(1), (4), as from 15 September 2003 (for savings and transitional provisions, see the note to s 8 at **[9.147]**). The original para (aa) was inserted by the Insolvency Act 1986 (Amendment) (No 2) Regulations 2002, SI 2002/1240, regs 3, 11, as from 31 May 2002. Words omitted from para (d) repealed by the Insolvency (Amendment) (EU Exit) Regulations 2019, SI 2019/146, reg 2, Schedule, Pt 2, paras 16, 28, as from IP completion day (as defined in the European Union (Withdrawal Agreement) Act 2020, s 39) (for savings, see reg 4 of the 2019 Regulations at **[12.82]**).

[9.375]

241 Orders under ss 238, 239

(1) Without prejudice to the generality of sections 238(3) and 239(3), an order under either of those sections with respect to a transaction or preference entered into or given by a company may (subject to the next subsection)—

(a) require any property transferred as part of the transaction, or in connection with the giving of the preference, to be vested in the company,

(b) require any property to be so vested if it represents in any person's hands the application either of the proceeds of sale of property so transferred or of money so transferred,

(c) release or discharge (in whole or in part) any security given by the company,

(d) require any person to pay, in respect of benefits received by him from the company, such sums to the office-holder as the court may direct,

(e) provide for any surety or guarantor whose obligations to any person were released or discharged (in whole or in part) under the transaction, or by the giving of the preference, to be under such new or revived obligations to that person as the court thinks appropriate,

(f) provide for security to be provided for the discharge of any obligation imposed by or arising under the order, for such an obligation to be charged on any property and for the security or charge to have the same priority as a security or charge released or discharged (in whole or in part) under the transaction or by the giving of the preference, and

(g) provide for the extent to which any person whose property is vested by the order in the company, or on whom obligations are imposed by the order, is to be able to prove in the winding up of the company for debts or other liabilities which arose from, or were released or discharged (in whole or in part) under or by, the transaction or the giving of the preference.

(2) An order under section 238 or 239 may affect the property of, or impose any obligation on, any person whether or not he is the person with whom the company in question entered into the transaction or (as the case may be) the person to whom the preference was given; but such an order—

(a) shall not prejudice any interest in property which was acquired from a person other than the company and was acquired [in good faith and for value], or prejudice any interest deriving from such an interest, and

(b) shall not require a person who received a benefit from the transaction or preference [in good faith and for value] to pay a sum to the office-holder, except where that person was a party to the transaction or the payment is to be in respect of a preference given to that person at a time when he was a creditor of the company.

[(2A) Where a person has acquired an interest in property from a person other than the company in question, or has received a benefit from the transaction or preference, and at the time of that acquisition or receipt—

(a) he had notice of the relevant surrounding circumstances and of the relevant proceedings, or

(b) he was connected with, or was an associate of, either the company in question or the person with whom that company entered into the transaction or to whom that company gave the preference,

then, unless the contrary is shown, it shall be presumed for the purposes of paragraph (a) or (as the case may be) paragraph (b) of subsection (2) that the interest was acquired or the benefit was received otherwise than in good faith.]

[(3) For the purposes of subsection (2A)(a), the relevant surrounding circumstances are (as the case may require)—

(a) the fact that the company in question entered into the transaction at an undervalue; or

(b) the circumstances which amounted to the giving of the preference by the company in question;

and subsections (3A) to (3C) have effect to determine whether, for those purposes, a person has notice of the relevant proceedings.

[(3A) Where section 238 or 239 applies by reason of a company's entering administration, a person has notice of the relevant proceedings if he has notice that—

(a) an administration application has been made,

(b) an administration order has been made,

(c) a copy of a notice of intention to appoint an administrator under paragraph 14 or 22 of Schedule B1 has been filed, or

(d) notice of the appointment of an administrator has been filed under paragraph 18 or 29 of that Schedule.]

[(3B) Where section 238 or 239 applies by reason of a company's going into liquidation at the time when the appointment of an administrator of the company ceases to have effect, a person has notice of the relevant proceedings if he has notice that—

(a) an administration application has been made,

(b) an administration order has been made,

(c) a copy of a notice of intention to appoint an administrator under paragraph 14 or 22 of Schedule B1 has been filed,

(d) notice of the appointment of an administrator has been filed under paragraph 18 or 29 of that Schedule, or

(e) the company has gone into liquidation.]

(3C) In a case where section 238 or 239 applies by reason of the company in question going into liquidation at any other time, a person has notice of the relevant proceedings if he has notice—

(a) where the company goes into liquidation on the making of a winding-up order, of the fact that the petition on which the winding-up order is made has been presented or of the fact that the company has gone into liquidation;

(b) in any other case, of the fact that the company has gone into liquidation.]

(4) The provisions of sections 238 to 241 apply without prejudice to the availability of any other remedy, even in relation to a transaction or preference which the company had no power to enter into or give.

NOTES

Sub-s (2): words in square brackets in paras (a), (b) substituted by the Insolvency (No 2) Act 1994, s 1(1), in relation to interests acquired and benefits received after 26 July 1994.

Sub-s (2A): inserted by the Insolvency (No 2) Act 1994, s 1(2), in relation to interests acquired and benefits received after 26 July 1994.

Sub-ss (3), (3C): substituted together with sub-ss (3A), (3B), for the original sub-s (3), by the Insolvency (No 2) Act 1994, s 1(3), in relation to interests acquired and benefits received after 26 July 1994.

Sub-ss (3A), (3B): substituted as noted above; further substituted by the Enterprise Act 2002, s 248(3), Sch 17, paras 9, 27, as from 15 September 2003 (for savings and transitional provisions, see the note to s 8 at **[9.147]**).

[9.376]

242 Gratuitous alienations (Scotland)

(1) Where this subsection applies and—

(a) the winding up of a company has commenced, an alienation by the company is challengeable by—

(i) any creditor who is a creditor by virtue of a debt incurred on or before the date of such commencement, or

(ii) the liquidator;

(b) [a company enters administration], an alienation by the company is challengeable by the administrator.

(2) Subsection (1) applies where—

(a) by the alienation, whether before or after 1st April 1986 (the coming into force of section 75 of the Bankruptcy (Scotland) Act 1985), any part of the company's property is transferred or any claim or right of the company is discharged or renounced, and

(b) the alienation takes place on a relevant day.

(3) For the purposes of subsection (2)(b), the day on which an alienation takes place is the day on which it becomes completely effectual; and in that subsection "relevant day" means, if the alienation has the effect of favouring—

(a) a person who is an associate (within the meaning of the Bankruptcy (Scotland) Act [2016]) of the company, a day not earlier than 5 years before the date on which—

(i) the winding up of the company commences, or

(ii) as the case may be, [the company enters administration]; or

(b) any other person, a day not earlier than 2 years before that date.

(4) On a challenge being brought under subsection (1), the court shall grant decree of reduction or for such restoration of property to the company's assets or other redress as may be appropriate; but the court shall not grant such a decree if the person seeking to uphold the alienation establishes—

(a) that immediately, or at any other time, after the alienation the company's assets were greater than its liabilities, or

(b) that the alienation was made for adequate consideration, or

(c) that the alienation—

(i) was a birthday, Christmas or other conventional gift, or

(ii) was a gift made, for a charitable purpose, to a person who is not an associate of the company,

which, having regard to all the circumstances, it was reasonable for the company to make:

Provided that this subsection is without prejudice to any right or interest acquired in good faith and for value from or through the transferee in the alienation.

(5) In subsection (4) above, "charitable purpose" means any charitable, benevolent or philanthropic purpose, whether or not it is charitable within the meaning of any rule of law.

(6) For the purposes of the foregoing provisions of this section, an alienation in implementation of a prior obligation is deemed to be one for which there was no consideration or no adequate consideration to the extent that the prior obligation was undertaken for no consideration or no adequate consideration.

(7) A liquidator and an administrator have the same right as a creditor has under any rule of law to challenge an alienation of a company made for no consideration or no adequate consideration.

(8) This section applies to Scotland only.

NOTES

Sub-s (1): words in square brackets substituted by the Enterprise Act 2002, s 248(3), Sch 17, paras 9, 28, as from 15 September 2003 (for savings and transitional provisions, see the note to s 8 at **[9.147]**).

Sub-s (3): year "2016" in square brackets substituted by the Bankruptcy (Scotland) Act 2016 (Consequential Provisions and Modifications) Order 2016, SI 2016/1034, art 7(1), (3), Sch 1, para 4(1), (5), as from 30 November 2016 (except in relation to (i) a sequestration as regards which the petition is presented, or the debtor application is made before that date; or (ii) a trust deed executed before that date); other words in square brackets substituted by the Enterprise Act 2002, s 248(3), Sch 17, paras 9, 28, as from 15 September 2003 (for savings and transitional provisions, see the note to s 8 at **[9.147]**).

[9.377]

243 Unfair preferences (Scotland)

(1) Subject to subsection (2) below, subsection (4) below applies to a transaction entered into by a company, whether before or after 1st April 1986, which has the effect of creating a preference in favour of a creditor to the prejudice of the general body of creditors, being a preference created not earlier than 6 months before the commencement of the winding up of the company or [the company enters administration].

(2) Subsection (4) below does not apply to any of the following transactions—

(a) a transaction in the ordinary course of trade or business;

(b) a payment in cash for a debt which when it was paid had become payable, unless the transaction was collusive with the purpose of prejudicing the general body of creditors;

(c) a transaction whereby the parties to it undertake reciprocal obligations (whether the performance by the parties of their respective obligations occurs at the same time or at different times) unless the transaction was collusive as aforesaid;

(d) the granting of a mandate by a company authorising an arrestee to pay over the arrested funds or part thereof to the arrester where—

(i) there has been a decree for payment or a warrant for summary diligence, and

(ii) the decree or warrant has been preceded by an arrestment on the dependence of the action or followed by an arrestment in execution.

(3) For the purposes of subsection (1) above, the day on which a preference was created is the day on which the preference became completely effectual.

(4) A transaction to which this subsection applies is challengeable by—

(a) in the case of a winding up—

(i) any creditor who is a creditor by virtue of a debt incurred on or before the date of commencement of the winding up, or

(ii) the liquidator; and

(b) [where the company has entered administration], the administrator.

(5) On a challenge being brought under subsection (4) above, the court, if satisfied that the transaction challenged is a transaction to which this section applies, shall grant decree of reduction or for such restoration of property to the company's assets or other redress as may be appropriate:

Provided that this subsection is without prejudice to any right or interest acquired in good faith and for value from or through the creditor in whose favour the preference was created.

(6) A liquidator and an administrator have the same right as a creditor has under any rule of law to challenge a preference created by a debtor.

(7) This section applies to Scotland only.

NOTES

Sub-ss (1), (4): words in square brackets substituted by the Enterprise Act 2002, s 248(3), Sch 17, paras 9, 29, as from 15 September 2003 (for savings and transitional provisions, see the note to s 8 at **[9.147]**).

[9.378]

244 Extortionate credit transactions

(1) This section applies as does section 238, and where the company is, or has been, a party to a transaction for, or involving, the provision of credit to the company.

(2) The court may, on the application of the office-holder, make an order with respect to the transaction if the transaction is or was extortionate and was entered into in the period of 3 years ending with [the day on which the company entered administration or went into liquidation].

(3) For the purposes of this section a transaction is extortionate if, having regard to the risk accepted by the person providing the credit—

(a) the terms of it are or were such as to require grossly exorbitant payments to be made (whether unconditionally or in certain contingencies) in respect of the provision of the credit, or

(b) it otherwise grossly contravened ordinary principles of fair dealing;

and it shall be presumed, unless the contrary is proved, that a transaction with respect to which an application is made under this section is or, as the case may be, was extortionate.

(4) An order under this section with respect to any transaction may contain such one or more of the following as the court thinks fit, that is to say—

(a) provision setting aside the whole or part of any obligation created by the transaction,

(b) provision otherwise varying the terms of the transaction or varying the terms on which any security for the purposes of the transaction is held,

(c) provision requiring any person who is or was a party to the transaction to pay to the office-holder any sums paid to that person, by virtue of the transaction, by the company,

(d) provision requiring any person to surrender to the office-holder any property held by him as security for the purposes of the transaction,

(e) provision directing accounts to be taken between any persons.

(5) The powers conferred by this section are exercisable in relation to any transaction concurrently with any powers exercisable in relation to that transaction as a transaction at an undervalue or under section 242 (gratuitous alienations in Scotland).

NOTES

Sub-s (2): words in square brackets substituted by the Enterprise Act 2002, s 248(3), Sch 17, paras 9, 30, as from 15 September 2003 (for savings and transitional provisions, see the note to s 8 at **[9.147]**).

[9.379]

245 Avoidance of certain floating charges

(1) This section applies as does section 238, but applies to Scotland as well as to England and Wales.

(2) Subject as follows, a floating charge on the company's undertaking or property created at a relevant time is invalid except to the extent of the aggregate of—

(a) the value of so much of the consideration for the creation of the charge as consists of money paid, or goods or services supplied, to the company at the same time as, or after, the creation of the charge,

(b) the value of so much of that consideration as consists of the discharge or reduction, at the same time as, or after, the creation of the charge, of any debt of the company, and

(c) the amount of such interest (if any) as is payable on the amount falling within paragraph (a) or (b) in pursuance of any agreement under which the money was so paid, the goods or services were so supplied or the debt was so discharged or reduced.

(3) Subject to the next subsection, the time at which a floating charge is created by a company is a relevant time for the purposes of this section if the charge is created—

(a) in the case of a charge which is created in favour of a person who is connected with the company, at a time in the period of 2 years ending with the onset of insolvency,

(b) in the case of a charge which is created in favour of any other person, at a time in the period of 12 months ending with the onset of insolvency, . . .

[(c) in either case, at a time between the making of an administration application in respect of the company and the making of an administration order on that application, or

(d) in either case, at a time between the filing with the court of a copy of notice of intention to appoint an administrator under paragraph 14 or 22 of Schedule B1 and the making of an appointment under that paragraph.]

(4) Where a company creates a floating charge at a time mentioned in subsection (3)(b) and the person in favour of whom the charge is created is not connected with the company, that time is not a relevant time for the purposes of this section unless the company—

(a) is at that time unable to pay its debts within the meaning of section 123 in Chapter VI of Part IV, or

(b) becomes unable to pay its debts within the meaning of that section in consequence of the transaction under which the charge is created.

(5) For the purposes of subsection (3), the onset of insolvency is—

[(a) in a case where this section applies by reason of an administrator of a company being appointed by administration order, the date on which the administration application is made,

(b) in a case where this section applies by reason of an administrator of a company being appointed under paragraph 14 or 22 of Schedule B1 following filing with the court of a copy of notice of intention to appoint under that paragraph, the date on which the copy of the notice is filed,

(c) in a case where this section applies by reason of an administrator of a company being appointed otherwise than as mentioned in paragraph (a) or (b), the date on which the appointment takes effect, and

(d) in a case where this section applies by reason of a company going into liquidation, the date of the commencement of the winding up.]

(6) For the purposes of subsection (2)(a) the value of any goods or services supplied by way of consideration for a floating charge is the amount in money which at the time they were supplied could reasonably have been expected to be obtained for supplying the goods or services in the ordinary course of business and on the same terms (apart from the consideration) as those on which they were supplied to the company.

NOTES

Sub-s (3): word omitted from para (b) repealed, and paras (c), (d) substituted (for the original para (c)), by the Enterprise Act 2002, ss 248(3), 278(2), Sch 17, paras 9, 31(1)–(3), Sch 26, as from 15 September 2003 (for savings and transitional provisions, see the note to s 8 at **[9.147]**).

Sub-s (5): paras (a)–(d) substituted (for the original paras (a), (b)) by the Enterprise Act 2002, s 248(3), Sch 17, paras 9, 31(1), (4), as from 15 September 2003 (for savings and transitional provisions, see the note to s 8 at **[9.147]**).

[9.380]

246 Unenforceability of liens on books, etc

(1) This section applies in the case of a company where—

[(a) the company enters administration,] or

(b) the company goes into liquidation, or

(c) a provisional liquidator is appointed;

and "the office-holder" means the administrator, the liquidator or the provisional liquidator, as the case may be.

(2) Subject as follows, a lien or other right to retain possession of any of the books, papers or other records of the company is unenforceable to the extent that its enforcement would deny possession of any books, papers or other records to the office-holder.

(3) This does not apply to a lien on documents which give a title to property and are held as such.

NOTES

Sub-s (1): para (a) substituted by the Enterprise Act 2002, s 248(3), Sch 17, paras 9, 32, as from 15 September 2003 (for savings and transitional provisions, see the note to s 8 at **[9.147]**).

[Administration: penalisation of directors etc

[9.381]

246ZA Fraudulent trading: administration

(1) If while a company is in administration it appears that any business of the company has been carried on with intent to defraud creditors of the company or creditors of any other person, or for any fraudulent purpose, the following has effect.

(2) The court, on the application of the administrator, may declare that any persons who were knowingly parties to the carrying on of the business in the manner mentioned in subsection (1) are to be liable to make such contributions (if any) to the company's assets as the court thinks proper.]

NOTES

Inserted, together with the preceding heading and ss 246ZB, 246ZC, by the Small Business, Enterprise and Employment Act 2015, s 117(1), (2), as from 1 October 2015, in respect of the carrying on of any business of the company on or after that date.

Transitional provisions: for transitional provisions in relation to bank administration and the administration of a building society (etc), see the Deregulation Act 2015, the Small Business, Enterprise and Employment Act 2015 and the Insolvency (Amendment) Act (Northern Ireland) 2016 (Consequential Amendments and Transitional Provisions) Regulations 2017, SI 2017/400, reg 15.

[9.382]

[246ZB Wrongful trading: administration

(1) Subject to subsection (3), if while a company is in administration it appears that subsection (2) applies in relation to a person who is or has been a director of the company, the court, on the application of the administrator, may declare that that person is to be liable to make such contribution (if any) to the company's assets as the court thinks proper.

(2) This subsection applies in relation to a person if—

(a) the company has entered insolvent administration,

(b) at some time before the company entered administration, that person knew or ought to have concluded that there was no reasonable prospect that the company would avoid entering insolvent administration or going into insolvent liquidation, and

(c) the person was a director of the company at that time.

(3) The court must not make a declaration under this section with respect to any person if it is satisfied that, after the condition specified in subsection (2)(b) was first satisfied in relation to the person, the person took every step with a view to minimising the potential loss to the company's creditors as (on the assumption that the person had knowledge of the matter mentioned in subsection (2)(b)) the person ought to have taken.

(4) For the purposes of subsections (2) and (3), the facts which a director of a company ought to know or ascertain, the conclusions which the director ought to reach and the steps which the director ought to take are those which would be known or ascertained, or reached or taken, by a reasonably diligent person having both—

(a) the general knowledge, skill and experience that may reasonably be expected of a person carrying out the same functions as are carried out by that director in relation to the company, and

(b) the general knowledge, skill and experience that that director has.

(5) The reference in subsection (4) to the functions carried out in relation to a company by a director of the company includes any functions which the director does not carry out but which have been entrusted to the director.

(6) For the purposes of this section—

(a) a company enters insolvent administration if it enters administration at a time when its assets are insufficient for the payment of its debts and other liabilities and the expenses of the administration;

(b) a company goes into insolvent liquidation if it goes into liquidation at a time when its assets are insufficient for the payment of its debts and other liabilities and the expenses of the winding up.

(7) In this section "director" includes shadow director.

(8) This section is without prejudice to section 246ZA.]

NOTES

Inserted as noted to s 246ZA at **[9.381]**.

Suspension of liability for wrongful trading: as to the suspension of liability for wrongful trading, see further the Corporate Insolvency and Governance Act 2020, s 12 at **[9.538]**, and the Corporate Insolvency and Governance Act 2020 (Coronavirus) (Suspension of Liability for Wrongful Trading and Extension of the Relevant Period) Regulations 2020, SI 2020/1349, reg 2 at **[10.1301]**.

[9.383]

[246ZC Proceedings under section 246ZA or 246ZB

Section 215 applies for the purposes of an application under section 246ZA or 246ZB as it applies for the purposes of an application under section 213 but as if the reference in subsection (1) of section 215 to the liquidator was a reference to the administrator.]

NOTES

Inserted as noted to s 246ZA at **[9.381]**.

[Power to assign certain causes of action

[9.384]

[246ZD Power to assign

(1) This section applies in the case of a company where—

(a) the company enters administration, or

(b) the company goes into liquidation;

and "the office-holder" means the administrator or the liquidator, as the case may be.

(2) The office-holder may assign a right of action (including the proceeds of an action) arising under [or by virtue of] any of the following—

[(za) section A43 (challenges to monitor remuneration in subsequent insolvency proceedings);]

(a) section 213 or 246ZA (fraudulent trading);

(b) section 214 or 246ZB (wrongful trading);

(c) section 238 (transactions at an undervalue (England and Wales));

(d) section 239 (preferences (England and Wales));

(e) section 242 (gratuitous alienations (Scotland));

(f) section 243 (unfair preferences (Scotland));

(g) section 244 (extortionate credit transactions).]

NOTES

Inserted by the Small Business, Enterprise and Employment Act 2015, s 118, as from 1 October 2015, in respect of a company which enters administration or goes into liquidation on or after that date.

Sub-s (2): words in first pair of square brackets, and para (za), inserted by the Corporate Insolvency and Governance Act 2020, s 2(1), Sch 3, paras 1, 16, as from 26 June 2020 (for transitional provisions, see s 2(2), (3) of the 2020 Act (at **[9.533]**) which provides that (without prejudice to the Interpretation Act 1978, s 16) nothing in the 2020 Act affects the operation of this Act, or any other enactment, in relation to a moratorium under Sch A1 to this Act which comes into force before the repeal of that Schedule by Sch 3 to the 2020 Act (ie, 26 June 2020)).

Transitional provisions: for transitional provisions in relation to bank administration and the administration of a building society (etc), see the Deregulation Act 2015, the Small Business, Enterprise and Employment Act 2015 and the Insolvency (Amendment) Act (Northern Ireland) 2016 (Consequential Amendments and Transitional Provisions) Regulations 2017, SI 2017/400, reg 16.

[Decisions by creditors and contributories

[9.385]

246ZE Decisions by creditors and contributories: general

(1) This section applies where, for the purposes of this Group of Parts, a person ("P") seeks a decision about any matter from a company's creditors or contributories.

(2) The decision may be made by any qualifying decision procedure P thinks fit, except that it may not be made by a creditors' meeting or (as the case may be) a contributories' meeting unless subsection (3) applies.

(3) This subsection applies if at least the minimum number of creditors or (as the case may be) contributories make a request to P in writing that the decision be made by a creditors' meeting or (as the case may be) a contributories' meeting.

(4) If subsection (3) applies P must summon a creditors' meeting or (as the case may be) a contributories' meeting.

(5) Subsection (2) is subject to any provision of this Act, the rules or any other legislation, or any order of the court—

(a) requiring a decision to be made, or prohibiting a decision from being made, by a particular qualifying decision procedure (other than a creditors' meeting or a contributories' meeting);

(b) permitting or requiring a decision to be made by a creditors' meeting or a contributories' meeting.

(6) Section 246ZF provides that in certain cases the deemed consent procedure may be used instead of a qualifying decision procedure.

(7) For the purposes of subsection (3) the "minimum number" of creditors or contributories is any of the following—

(a) 10% in value of the creditors or contributories;

(b) 10% in number of the creditors or contributories;

(c) 10 creditors or contributories.

(8) The references in subsection (7) to creditors are to creditors of any class, even where a decision is sought only from creditors of a particular class.

(9) In this section references to a meeting are to a meeting where the creditors or (as the case may be) contributories are invited to be present together at the same place (whether or not it is possible to attend the meeting without being present at that place).

(10) Except as provided by subsection (8), references in this section to creditors include creditors of a particular class.

(11) In this Group of Parts "qualifying decision procedure" means a procedure prescribed or authorised under paragraph 8A of Schedule 8.]

NOTES

Inserted, together with the preceding heading and ss 246ZF, 246ZG, by the Small Business, Enterprise and Employment Act 2015, s 122(1), (2), as from 26 May 2015 (for the purposes of enabling the exercise of any power to make provision by regulations, rules or order made by statutory instrument or to prepare and issue guidance), as from 6 April 2017 (in relation to England and Wales and subject to transitional and savings provisions in SI 2016/1020 as noted below), and as from 6 April 2019 (in relation to Scotland and subject to transitional and savings provisions in SI 2019/816 as noted below).

Transitional and savings provisions (England and Wales): the Small Business, Enterprise and Employment Act 2015 (Commencement No 6 and Transitional and Savings Provisions) Regulations 2016, SI 2016/1020, reg 5 (as amended by the Small Business, Enterprise and Employment Act 2015 (Commencement No 6 and Transitional and Savings Provisions) Regulations 2016 (Amendment) Regulations 2017, SI 2017/363) provides as follows—

"5 Transitional and saving provision

(1) This regulation applies where on or after 6th April 2017—

(a) a creditors' or contributories' meeting is to be held as a result of a notice issued before that date in relation to a meeting for which provision is made by the Insolvency Rules 1986 or the 1986 Act;

(b) a meeting is to be held as a result of a requisition by a creditor or contributory made before that date;

(c) a meeting is to be held as a result of a statement made under paragraph 52(1)(b) of Schedule B1 to the 1986 Act and a request made before that date which obliges the administrator to summon an initial creditors' meeting;

(d) a . . . meeting is required by [sections 93 or 105] of the 1986 Act in the winding up of a company where the resolution to wind up was passed before 6th April 2010; or

(e) a meeting is to be held under section 94, 106, 146 or 331 of the 1986 Act as a result of—

(i) a final report to creditors sent under rule 4.49D of the Insolvency Rules 1986 (final report to creditors in liquidation),

(ii) a final report to creditors and bankrupt sent under rule 6.78B of the Insolvency Rules 1986 (final report to creditors and bankrupt), or

(iii) a meeting being called under section 94 of the 1986 Act (final meeting prior to dissolution).

(2) Where such a meeting is to be held, the 1986 Act applies without the amendments made by—

(a) section 122 of the 2015 Act;

(b) section 123 of the 2015 Act; and

(c) section 126 and Schedule 9 to the 2015 Act, insofar as those amendments relate to the abolition of requirements to hold meetings.".

Transitional and savings provisions (Scotland): the Small Business, Enterprise and Employment Act 2015 (Commencement No 7, Consequential, Transitional and Savings Provisions) Regulations 2019, SI 2019/816, reg 5 provides as follows—

"5 Savings in respect of meetings taking place on or after 6th April 2019

(1) This regulation applies where on or after 6th April 2019—

(a) a creditors' or contributories' meeting is to be held as a result of a notice issued before that date in relation to a meeting for which provision is made by the Insolvency (Scotland) Rules 1986 or the 1986 Act;

(b) a meeting is to be held as a result of a requisition by a creditor or contributory made before that date;

(c) an initial creditors' meeting is to be held as a result of an invitation issued before that date under paragraph 51(1) of Schedule B1 of the 1986 Act or a request made before that date under paragraph 52(2) of that Schedule; or

(d) a meeting is to be held as a result of a meeting being called under section 94, 106 or 146 of the 1986 Act.

(2) Where such a meeting is to be held, the 1986 Act applies without the amendments made by—

(a) section 122 of the 2015 Act; and

(b) section 126 and Part 1 of Schedule 9 to the 2015 Act, insofar as those amendments relate to the abolition of requirements to hold meetings.".

Note that the Insolvency Rules 1986, SI 1986/1925 were revoked and replaced (subject to transitional provisions) by the Insolvency (England and Wales) Rules 2016, SI 2016/1024, as from 6 April 2017.

[9.386]

[246ZF Deemed consent procedure

(1) The deemed consent procedure may be used instead of a qualifying decision procedure where a company's creditors or contributories are to make a decision about any matter, unless—

(a) a decision about the matter is required by virtue of this Act, the rules, or any other legislation to be made by a qualifying decision procedure, or

(b) the court orders that a decision about the matter is to be made by a qualifying decision procedure.

(2) If the rules provide for a company's creditors or contributories to make a decision about the remuneration of any person, they must provide that the decision is to be made by a qualifying decision procedure.

(3) The deemed consent procedure is that the relevant creditors (other than opted-out creditors) or (as the case may be) the relevant contributories are given notice of—

(a) the matter about which they are to make a decision,

(b) the decision that the person giving the notice proposes should be made (the "proposed decision"),

(c) the effect of subsections (4) and (5), and

(d) the procedure for objecting to the proposed decision.

(4) If less than the appropriate number of relevant creditors or (as the case may be) relevant contributories object to the proposed decision in accordance with the procedure set out in the notice, the creditors or (as the case may be) the contributories are to be treated as having made the proposed decision.

(5) Otherwise—

(a) the creditors or (as the case may be) the contributories are to be treated as not having made a decision about the matter in question, and

(b) if a decision about that matter is again sought from the creditors or (as the case may be) the contributories, it must be sought using a qualifying decision procedure.

(6) For the purposes of subsection (4) the "appropriate number" of relevant creditors or relevant contributories is 10% in value of those creditors or contributories.

(7) "Relevant creditors" means the creditors who, if the decision were to be made by a qualifying decision procedure, would be entitled to vote in the procedure.

(8) "Relevant contributories" means the contributories who, if the decision were to be made by a qualifying decision procedure, would be entitled to vote in the procedure.

(9) In this section references to creditors include creditors of a particular class.

(10) The rules may make further provision about the deemed consent procedure.]

NOTES

Inserted as noted to s 246ZE at **[9.385]**.

[9.387]

[246ZG Power to amend sections 246ZE and 246ZF

(1) The Secretary of State may by regulations amend section 246ZE so as to change the definition of—

(a) the minimum number of creditors;

(b) the minimum number of contributories.

(2) The Secretary of State may by regulations amend section 246ZF so as to change the definition of—

(a) the appropriate number of relevant creditors;

(b) the appropriate number of relevant contributories.

(3) Regulations under this section may define the minimum number or the appropriate number by reference to any one or more of—

(a) a proportion in value,

(b) a proportion in number,

(c) an absolute number,

and the definition may include alternative, cumulative or relative requirements.

(4) Regulations under subsection (1) may define the minimum number of creditors or contributories by reference to all creditors or contributories, or by reference to creditors or contributories of a particular description.

(5) Regulations under this section may make provision that will result in section 246ZE or 246ZF having different definitions for different cases, including—

(a) for creditors and for contributories,

(b) for different kinds of decisions.

(6) Regulations under this section may make transitional provision.

(7) The power of the Secretary of State to make regulations under this section is exercisable by statutory instrument.

(8) A statutory instrument containing regulations under this section may not be made unless a draft of the instrument has been laid before, and approved by a resolution of, each House of Parliament.]

NOTES

Inserted as noted to s 246ZE at **[9.385]**.

[Remote attendance at meetings

[9.388]

246A Remote attendance at meetings

(1) Subject to subsection (2), this section [applies to any meeting of the members of a company summoned by the office-holder under this Act or the rules, other than a meeting of the members of the company in a members' voluntary winding up.]

(2) . . .

(3) Where the person summoning a meeting ("the convener") considers it appropriate, the meeting may be conducted and held in such a way that persons who are not present together at the same place may attend it.

(4) Where a meeting is conducted and held in the manner referred to in subsection (3), a person attends the meeting if that person is able to exercise any rights which that person may have to speak and vote at the meeting.

(5) For the purposes of this section—

(a) a person is able to exercise the right to speak at a meeting when that person is in a position to communicate to all those attending the meeting, during the meeting, any information or opinions which that person has on the business of the meeting; and

(b) a person is able to exercise the right to vote at a meeting when—

(i) that person is able to vote, during the meeting, on resolutions put to the vote at the meeting, and

(ii) that person's vote can be taken into account in determining whether or not such resolutions are passed at the same time as the votes of all the other persons attending the meeting.

(6) The convener of a meeting which is to be conducted and held in the manner referred to in subsection (3) shall make whatever arrangements the convener considers appropriate to—

(a) enable those attending the meeting to exercise their rights to speak or vote, and

(b) ensure the identification of those attending the meeting and the security of any electronic means used to enable attendance.

(7) Where in the reasonable opinion of the convener—

(a) a meeting will be attended by persons who will not be present together at the same place, and

(b) it is unnecessary or inexpedient to specify a place for the meeting,

any requirement under this Act or the rules to specify a place for the meeting may be satisfied by specifying the arrangements the convener proposes to enable persons to exercise their rights to speak or vote.

(8) In making the arrangements referred to in subsection (6) and in forming the opinion referred to in subsection (7)(b), the convener must have regard to the legitimate interests of the [members] and others attending the meeting in the efficient despatch of the business of the meeting.

(9) If—

(a) the notice of a meeting does not specify a place for the meeting,

(b) the convener is requested in accordance with the rules to specify a place for the meeting, and

(c) that request is [made] by members representing not less than ten percent of the total voting rights of all the members having at the date of the request a right to vote at the meeting,

it shall be the duty of the convener to specify a place for the meeting.

(10) In this section, "the office-holder", in relation to a company, means—

[(za) the monitor in relation to a moratorium under Part A1,]

(a) its liquidator, provisional liquidator, administrator, [receiver (appointed under section 51)] or administrative receiver, or

(b) where a voluntary arrangement in relation to the company is proposed or has taken effect under Part 1, the nominee or the supervisor of the voluntary arrangement.]

NOTES

Inserted, together with the preceding heading and s 246B, by the Legislative Reform (Insolvency) (Miscellaneous Provisions) Order 2010, SI 2010/18, arts 2, 3(1), as from 6 April 2010.

Sub-ss (1), (8), (9): words in square brackets substituted by the Small Business, Enterprise and Employment Act 2015, s 126, Sch 9, Pt 1, paras 1, 54, as from 6 April 2017 (in relation to England and Wales), and as from 6 April 2019 (in relation to Scotland) (for transitional and savings provisions, see the notes to s 246ZE at **[9.385]**).

Sub-s (2): repealed by the Public Services Reform (Corporate Insolvency and Bankruptcy) (Scotland) Order 2017, SSI 2017/209, art 5(a), as from 6 April 2019.

Sub-s (10): para (za) inserted by the Corporate Insolvency and Governance Act 2020, s 2(1), Sch 3, paras 1, 17, as from 26 June 2020 (for transitional provisions, see s 2(2), (3) of the 2020 Act (at **[9.533]**) which provides that (without prejudice to the Interpretation Act 1978, s 16) nothing in the 2020 Act affects the operation of this Act, or any other enactment, in relation to a moratorium under Sch A1 to this Act which comes into force before the repeal of that Schedule by Sch 3 to the 2020 Act (ie, 26 June 2020)). Words in square brackets in para (a) inserted by SSI 2017/209, art 5(b), as from 6 April 2019.

[[Giving of notices etc by office-holders]

NOTES

The preceding heading was substituted by the Small Business, Enterprise and Employment Act 2015, s 124(1), (2), as from 6 April 2017 (in relation to England and Wales), and as from 6 April 2019 (in relation to Scotland) (for transitional and savings provisions, see the notes to s 246ZE at **[9.385]**).

[9.389]

246B Use of websites

(1) Subject to subsection (2), where any provision of this Act or the rules requires the office-holder to give, deliver, furnish or send a notice or other document or information to any person, that requirement is satisfied by making the notice, document or information available on a website—

(a) in accordance with the rules, and

(b) in such circumstances as may be prescribed.

(2) . . .

(3) In this section, "the office-holder" means—

[(za) the monitor in relation to a moratorium under Part A1,]

(a) the liquidator, provisional liquidator, administrator, [receiver (appointed under section 51),] or administrative receiver of a company, or

(b) where a voluntary arrangement in relation to a company is proposed or has taken effect under Part 1, the nominee or the supervisor of the voluntary arrangement.]

NOTES

Inserted as noted to s 246A at **[9.388]**.

Sub-s (2) repealed, and words in square brackets in sub-s (3) inserted, by the Public Services Reform (Insolvency) (Scotland) Order 2016, SSI 2016/141, art 12, as from 6 April 2019.

Sub-s (3)(za) was inserted by the Corporate Insolvency and Governance Act 2020, s 2(1), Sch 3, paras 1, 18, as from 26 June 2020 (for transitional provisions, see s 2(2), (3) of the 2020 Act (at **[9.533]**) which provides that (without prejudice to the Interpretation Act 1978, s 16) nothing in the 2020 Act affects the operation of this Act, or any other enactment, in relation to a moratorium under Sch A1 to this Act which comes into force before the repeal of that Schedule by Sch 3 to the 2020 Act (ie, 26 June 2020)).

[9.390]

[246C Creditors' ability to opt out of receiving certain notices

(1) Any provision of the rules which requires an office-holder of a company to give a notice to creditors of the company does not apply, in circumstances prescribed by the rules, in relation to opted-out creditors.

(2) Subsection (1)—

(a) does not apply in relation to a notice of a distribution or proposed distribution to creditors;

(b) is subject to any order of the court requiring a notice to be given to all creditors (or all creditors of a particular category).

(3) Except as provided by the rules, a creditor may participate and vote in a qualifying decision procedure or a deemed consent procedure even though, by virtue of being an opted-out creditor, the creditor does not receive notice of it.

(4) In this section—

"give" includes deliver, furnish or send;

"notice" includes any document or information in any other form;

"office-holder", in relation to a company, means—

(a) a liquidator, provisional liquidator, administrator or administrative receiver of the company,

(b) a receiver appointed under section 51 in relation to any property of the company, or

(c) the supervisor of a voluntary arrangement which has taken effect under Part 1 in relation to the company.]

NOTES

Inserted by the Small Business, Enterprise and Employment Act 2015, s 124(1), (3), as from 6 April 2017 (in relation to England and Wales), and as from 6 April 2019 (in relation to Scotland) (for transitional and savings provisions, see the notes to s 246ZE at **[9.385]**).

PART VII INTERPRETATION FOR FIRST GROUP OF PARTS

[9.391]

247 "Insolvency" and "go into liquidation"

(1) In this Group of Parts, except in so far as the context otherwise requires, "insolvency", in relation to a company, includes [the coming into force of a moratorium for the company under Part A1] the approval of a voluntary arrangement under Part I, [or the appointment of an administrator or administrative receiver].

(2) For the purposes of any provision in this Group of Parts, a company goes into liquidation if it passes a resolution for voluntary winding up or an order for its winding up is made by the court at a time when it has not already gone into liquidation by passing such a resolution.

[(3) The reference to a resolution for voluntary winding up in subsection (2) includes a reference to a resolution which is deemed to occur by virtue of—

(a) paragraph 83(6)(b) of Schedule B1 . . .

(b) . . .]

NOTES

Sub-s (1): words in first pair of square brackets inserted by the Corporate Insolvency and Governance Act 2020, s 2(1), Sch 3, paras 1, 19, as from 26 June 2020 (for transitional provisions, see s 2(2), (3) of the 2020 Act (at **[9.533]**) which provides that (without prejudice to the Interpretation Act 1978, s 16) nothing in the 2020 Act affects the operation of this Act, or any other enactment, in relation to a moratorium under Sch A1 to this Act which comes into force before the repeal of that Schedule by Sch 3 to the 2020 Act (ie, 26 June 2020)). Words in second pair of square brackets substituted by the Enterprise Act 2002, s 248(3), Sch 17, paras 9, 33(1), (2), as from 15 September 2003 (for savings and transitional provisions, see the note to s 8 at **[9.147]**).

Sub-s (3): originally added by the Insolvency Act 1986 (Amendment) (No 2) Regulations 2002, SI 2002/1240, regs 3, 12, as from 31 May 2002. Subsequently substituted by the Enterprise Act 2002, s 248(3), Sch 17, paras 9, 33(1), (3), as from 15 September 2003 (for savings and transitional provisions, see the note to s 8 at **[9.147]**). Para (b) and the word immediately preceding it were repealed by the Insolvency (Amendment) (EU Exit) Regulations 2019, SI 2019/146, reg 2, Schedule, Pt 2, paras 16, 29, as from IP completion day (as defined in the European Union (Withdrawal Agreement) Act 2020, s 39) (for savings, see reg 4 of the 2019 Regulations at **[12.82]**).

[9.392]

248 "Secured creditor", etc

In this Group of Parts, except in so far as the context otherwise requires—

(a) "secured creditor", in relation to a company, means a creditor of the company who holds in respect of his debt a security over property of the company, and "unsecured creditor" is to be read accordingly; and

(b) "security" means—

(i) in relation to England and Wales, any mortgage, charge, lien or other security, and

(ii) in relation to Scotland, any security (whether heritable or moveable), any floating charge and any right of lien or preference and any right of retention (other than a right of compensation or set off).

[9.393]

[248A "Opted-out creditor"

(1) For the purposes of this Group of Parts "opted-out creditor", in relation to an office-holder of a company, means a person who—

(a) is a creditor of the company, and

(b) in accordance with the rules has elected (or is deemed to have elected) to be (and not to cease to be) an opted-out creditor in relation to the office-holder.

(2) In this section, "office-holder", in relation to a company, means—

(a) a liquidator, provisional liquidator, administrator or administrative receiver of the company,

(b) a receiver appointed under section 51 in relation to any property of the company, or

(c) the supervisor of a voluntary arrangement which has taken effect under Part 1 in relation to the company.]

NOTES

Inserted by the Small Business, Enterprise and Employment Act 2015, s 124(1), (4), as from 6 April 2017 (in relation to England and Wales), and as from 6 April 2019 (in relation to Scotland) (for transitional and savings provisions, see the notes to s 246ZE at **[9.385]**).

[9.394]

249 "Connected" with a company

For the purposes of any provision in this Group of Parts, a person is connected with a company if—

(a) he is a director or shadow director of the company or an associate of such a director or shadow director, or

(b) he is an associate of the company;

and "associate" has the meaning given by section 435 in Part XVIII of this Act.

[9.395]

250 "Member" of a company

For the purposes of any provision in this Group of Parts, a person who is not a member of a company but to whom shares in the company have been transferred, or transmitted by operation of law, is to be regarded as a member of the company, and references to a member or members are to be read accordingly.

[9.396]

251 Expressions used generally

In this Group of Parts, except in so far as the context otherwise requires—

"administrative receiver" means—

(a) an administrative receiver as defined by section 29(2) in Chapter I of Part III, or

(b) a receiver appointed under section 51 in Chapter II of that Part in a case where the whole (or substantially the whole) of the company's property is attached by the floating charge;

["agent" does not include a person's counsel acting as such;]

["books and papers" and "books or papers" includes accounts, deeds, writing and documents;]

"business day" means any day other than a Saturday, a Sunday, Christmas Day, Good Friday or a day which is a bank holiday in any part of Great Britain;

"chattel leasing agreement" means an agreement for the bailment or, in Scotland, the hiring of goods which is capable of subsisting for more than 3 months;

"contributory" has the meaning given by section 79;

["the court", in relation to a company, means a court having jurisdiction to wind up the company;]

["deemed consent procedure" means the deemed consent procedure provided for by section 246ZF;]

"director" includes any person occupying the position of director, by whatever name called;

["document" includes summons, notice, order and other legal process, and registers;]

[. . .]

"floating charge" means a charge which, as created, was a floating charge and includes a floating charge within section 462 of the Companies Act (Scottish floating charges);

["the Gazette" means—

(a) as respects companies registered in England and Wales, the London Gazette;

(b) as respects companies registered in Scotland, the Edinburgh Gazette;]

. . .

[. . .]

["officer", in relation to a body corporate, includes a director, manager or secretary;]

"the official rate", in relation to interest, means the rate payable under section 189(4);

"prescribed" means prescribed by the rules;

["qualifying decision procedure" has the meaning given by section 246ZE(11);]

"receiver", in the expression "receiver or manager", does not include a receiver appointed under section 51 in Chapter II of Part III;

"retention of title agreement" means an agreement for the sale of goods to a company, being an agreement—

(a) which does not constitute a charge on the goods, but

(b) under which, if the seller is not paid and the company is wound up, the seller will have priority over all other creditors of the company as respects the goods or any property representing the goods;

"the rules" means rules under section 411 in Part XV; and

"shadow director", in relation to a company, means a person in accordance with whose directions or instructions the directors of the company are accustomed to act[, but so that a person is not deemed a shadow director by reason only that the directors act—

(a) on advice given by that person in a professional capacity;

(b) in accordance with instructions, a direction, guidance or advice given by that person in the exercise of a function conferred by or under an enactment (within the meaning given by section 1293 of the Companies Act 2006);

(c) in accordance with guidance or advice given by that person in that person's capacity as a Minister of the Crown (within the meaning of the Ministers of the Crown Act 1975)].

[. . .]

NOTES

Definitions "deemed consent procedure" and "qualifying decision procedure" inserted by the Small Business, Enterprise and Employment Act 2015, s 122(1), (4), as from 6 April 2017 (in relation to England and Wales), and as from 6 April 2019 (in relation to Scotland) (for transitional and savings provisions, see the notes to s 246ZE at **[9.385]**).

Definitions "EU insolvency proceedings" and "member State liquidator" (omitted) originally inserted by the Insolvency Amendment (EU 2015/848) Regulations 2017, SI 2017/702, regs 2, 3, Schedule, Pt 1, paras 1, 17, as from 26 June 2017, except in relation to proceedings opened before that date, and subsequently repealed by the Insolvency (Amendment) (EU Exit) Regulations 2019, SI 2019/146, reg 2, Schedule, Pt 2, paras 16, 30, as from IP completion day (as defined in the European Union (Withdrawal Agreement) Act 2020, s 39) (for savings, see reg 4 of the 2019 Regulations at **[12.82]**).

All other definitions in square brackets inserted, and the definition "office copy" (omitted) repealed, by the Companies Act 2006 (Consequential Amendments, Transitional Provisions and Savings) Order 2009, SI 2009/1941, art 2(1), Sch 1, para 77(1)–(3), as from 1 October 2009 (for effect see the note to s 7A at **[9.145]**).

Words in square brackets in the definition "shadow director" substituted by the Small Business, Enterprise and Employment Act 2015, s 90(1), as from 26 May 2015.

The final words omitted were originally substituted by the Companies Act 2006 (Commencement No 3, Consequential Amendments, Transitional Provisions and Savings) Order 2007, SI 2007/2194, art 10(1), Sch 4, Pt 3, para 43, as from 1 October 2007, and were subsequently repealed by SI 2009/1941, art 2(1), Sch 1, para 77(1), (4), as from 1 October 2009 (for effect see the note to s 7A at **[9.145]**).

251A–385 *(The Second Group of Parts (Pts VIIA–XI) concerns individual insolvency and bankruptcy and is outside the scope of this work.)*

THE THIRD GROUP OF PARTS
MISCELLANEOUS MATTERS BEARING ON BOTH COMPANY AND INDIVIDUAL INSOLVENCY; GENERAL INTERPRETATION; FINAL PROVISIONS

PART XII PREFERENTIAL [AND NON-PREFERENTIAL] DEBTS IN COMPANY AND INDIVIDUAL INSOLVENCY

NOTES

The words in square brackets in the Part heading were inserted by the Banks and Building Societies (Priorities on Insolvency) Order 2018, SI 2018/1244, arts 4, 10, as from 19 December 2018, except in relation to any insolvency proceedings commenced before that date (see further the note relating to this Order at **[9.139]**).

[9.397]

386 Categories of preferential debts

(1) A reference in this Act to the preferential debts of a company or an individual is to the debts listed in Schedule 6 to this Act [(contributions to occupational pension schemes; remuneration, &c. of employees; levies on coal and steel production)][; debts owed to the Financial Services Compensation Scheme][; deposits covered by Financial Services Compensation Scheme][; other deposits][; certain HMRC debts]; and references to preferential creditors are to be read accordingly.

[(1A) A reference in this Act to the "ordinary preferential debts" of a company or an individual is to the preferential debts listed in any of paragraphs 8 to 15B of Schedule 6 to this Act.

(1B) A reference in this Act to the "secondary preferential debts" of a company or an individual is to the preferential debts listed in paragraph 15BA[, 15BB or 15D] of Schedule 6 to this Act.]

(2) In [Schedule 6] "the debtor" means the company or the individual concerned.

(3) Schedule 6 is to be read with [Schedule 4 to the Pension Schemes Act 1993] (occupational pension scheme contributions).

NOTES

Sub-s (1): words in first pair of square brackets substituted by the Enterprise Act 2002, s 251(3), as from 15 September 2003 (note that art 4 of the Enterprise Act 2002 (Commencement No 4 and Transitional Provisions and Savings) Order 2003, SI 2003/2093 (as amended) contains detailed transitional provisions in relation to the abolition of preferential status for Crown debts. Broadly speaking, preferential status will continue to apply in those cases which were started before 15 September 2003). Words in second pair of square brackets inserted by the Deposit Guarantee Scheme Regulations 2015, SI 2015/486, reg 14(1), (2), as from 26 March 2015. Words in third pair of square brackets inserted by the Financial Services (Banking Reform) Act 2013, s 13(2), as from 31 December 2014. Words in fourth pair of square brackets inserted by the Banks and Building Societies (Depositor Preference and Priorities) Order 2014, SI 2014/3486, arts 3, 8(1), (2), as from 1 January 2015, except in relation to any insolvency proceedings commenced before that date (see further the note relating to this Order at **[9.139]**). Words in fifth pair of square brackets inserted by the Finance Act 2020, s 98(1)(a) (this amendment applies in relation to any case where the relevant date is on or after 1 December 2020).

Sub-ss (1A), (1B): inserted by SI 2014/3486, arts 3, 8(1), (3), as from 1 January 2015, except in relation to any insolvency proceedings commenced before that date (see further the note relating to this Order at **[9.139]**). Words in square brackets in sub-s (1B) substituted by the Finance Act 2020, s 98(1)(b) (this amendment applies in relation to any case where the relevant date is on or after 1 December 2020).

Sub-s (2): words in square brackets substituted by SI 2014/3486, arts 3, 8(1), (4), as from 1 January 2015, except in relation to any insolvency proceedings commenced before that date (see further the note relating to this Order at **[9.139]**).

Sub-s (3): words in square brackets substituted by the Pension Schemes Act 1993, s 190, Sch 8, para 8, as from 7 February 1994.

[9.398]

387 "The relevant date"

(1) This section explains references in Schedule 6 to the relevant date (being the date which determines the existence and amount of a preferential debt).

(2) For the purposes of section 4 in Part I ([consideration of] company voluntary arrangement), the relevant date in relation to a company which is not being wound up is—

[(a) if the company is in administration, the date on which it entered administration, and

(b) if the company is not in administration, the date on which the voluntary arrangement takes effect.]

[(2A) . . .]

(3) In relation to a company which is being wound up, the following applies—

(a) if the winding up is by the court, and the winding-up order was made immediately upon the discharge of an administration order, the relevant date is [the date on which the company entered administration];

[(aa) . . .

(ab) . . .

(b) if the case does not fall within paragraph (a) [. . .] and the company—

(i) is being wound up by the court, and

(ii) had not commenced to be wound up voluntarily before the date of the making of the winding-up order,

the relevant date is the date of the appointment (or first appointment) of a provisional liquidator or, if no such appointment has been made, the date of the winding-up order;

[(ba) if the case does not fall within paragraph (a) . . . or (b) and the company is being wound up following administration pursuant to paragraph 83 of Schedule B1, the relevant date is the date on which the company entered administration;]

(c) if the case does not fall within [paragraph (a) . . . , (b) or (ba)], the relevant date is the date of the passing of the resolution for the winding up of the company.

[(3A) In relation to a company which is in administration (and to which no other provision of this section applies) the relevant date is the date on which the company enters administration.]

(4) In relation to a company in receivership (where section 40 or, as the case may be, section 59 applies), the relevant date is—

(a) in England and Wales, the date of the appointment of the receiver by debenture-holders, and

(b) in Scotland, the date of the appointment of the receiver under section 53(6) or (as the case may be) 54(5).

(5) For the purposes of section 258 in Part VIII (individual voluntary arrangements), the relevant date is, in relation to a debtor who is not an undischarged bankrupt

[(a) where an interim order has been made under section 252 with respect to his proposal, the date of that order, and

(b) in any other case, the date on which the voluntary arrangement takes effect.]

(6) In relation to a bankrupt, the following applies—

(a) where at the time the bankruptcy order was made there was an interim receiver appointed under section 286, the relevant date is the date on which the interim receiver was first appointed after [the making of the bankruptcy application or (as the case may be)] the presentation of the bankruptcy petition;

(b) otherwise, the relevant date is the date of the making of the bankruptcy order.

NOTES

Sub-s (2): words in first pair of square brackets substituted by the Small Business, Enterprise and Employment Act 2015, s 126, Sch 9, Pt 1, paras 1, 55, as from 6 April 2017 (in relation to England and Wales), and as from 6 April 2019 (in relation to Scotland) (for transitional and savings provisions, see the notes to s 246ZE at **[9.385]**). Paras (a), (b) substituted by the Enterprise Act 2002, s 248(3), Sch 17, paras 9, 34(1), (2), as from 15 September 2003 (for savings and transitional provisions, see the note to s 8 at **[9.147]**).

Sub-s (2A): originally inserted by the Insolvency Act 2000, s 1, Sch 1, paras 1, 9, as from 1 January 2003. Subsequently repealed by the Corporate Insolvency and Governance Act 2020, s 2(1), Sch 3, paras 1, 20, as from 26 June 2020 (for transitional provisions, see s 2(2), (3) of the 2020 Act (at **[9.533]**) which provides that (without prejudice to the Interpretation Act 1978, s 16) nothing in the 2020 Act affects the operation of this Act, or any other enactment, in relation to a moratorium under Sch A1 to this Act which comes into force before the repeal of that Schedule by Sch 3 to the 2020 Act (ie, 26 June 2020)).

Sub-s (3): paras (aa), (ab) and the words omitted from para (b) were originally inserted by the Insolvency Act 1986 (Amendment) (No 2) Regulations 2002, SI 2002/1240, regs 3, 16, as from 31 May 2002. Words in square brackets in paras (a), (aa), (ab), (c) substituted, and para (ba) inserted, by the Enterprise Act 2002, s 248(3), Sch 17, paras 9, 34(1), (3), as from 15 September 2003 (for savings and transitional provisions, see the note to s 8 at **[9.147]**). Paras (aa), (ab) and the words omitted from paras (b), (ba), (c) were repealed by the Insolvency (Amendment) (EU Exit) Regulations 2019, SI 2019/146, reg 2, Schedule, Pt 2, paras 16, 35, as from IP completion day (as defined in the European Union (Withdrawal Agreement) Act 2020, s 39) (for savings, see reg 4 of the 2019 Regulations at **[12.82]**).

Sub-s (3A): inserted by the Enterprise Act 2002, s 248(3), Sch 17, paras 9, 34(1), (4), as from 15 September 2003 (for savings and transitional provisions, see the note to s 8 at **[9.147]**).

Sub-s (5): words in square brackets substituted by the Insolvency Act 2000, s 3, Sch 3, paras 1, 15, as from 1 January 2003.

Sub-s (6): words in square brackets inserted by the Enterprise and Regulatory Reform Act 2013, s 71(3), Sch 19, paras 1, 56, as from 6 April 2016, except in respect of a petition for a bankruptcy order presented to the court by a debtor before that date.

[9.399]

[387A Financial institutions and their non-preferential debts

(1) In this Act "relevant financial institution" means any of the following—

(a) a credit institution,

(b) an investment firm,

(c) a financial holding company,

(d) a mixed financial holding company,

[(da) an investment holding company,]

[(e) a financial institution which is—

(i) a subsidiary of an entity referred to in paragraphs (a) to (da), and

(ii) covered by the supervision of that entity on a consolidated basis by the Financial Conduct Authority in accordance with Part 9C rules or by the Prudential Regulation Authority in accordance with Regulation (EU) No 575/2013 of the European Parliament and of the Council of 26 June 2013 on prudential requirements for credit institutions and investment firms or CRR rules, or,]

(f) a mixed-activity holding company.

(2) The definitions in Article 4 of Regulation (EU) No 575/2013 apply for the purposes of subsection (1)[, except for the definitions of "consolidated basis" and "consolidated situation"].

[(2A) For the purposes of subsection (1)—

"on a consolidated basis" means on the basis of the consolidated situation;

"consolidated situation" means the situation that results from an entity being treated, for the purposes of Part 9C rules, Regulation (EU) 575/2013 or CRR rules (as appropriate), as if that entity and one or more other entities formed a single entity;

"CRR rules" has the meaning given in section 144A of the Financial Services and Markets Act 2000;

"Part 9C rules" has the meaning given in section 143F of the Financial Services and Markets Act 2000.]

(3) In this Act, in relation to a relevant financial institution—

(a) "ordinary non-preferential debts" means non-preferential debts which are neither secondary non-preferential debts nor tertiary non-preferential debts;

(b) "secondary non-preferential debts" means non-preferential debts issued under an instrument where—

(i) the original contractual maturity of the instrument is of at least one year,

(ii) the instrument is not a derivative and contains no embedded derivative, and

(iii) the relevant contractual documentation and where applicable the prospectus related to the issue of the debts explain the priority of the debts under this Act, and

(c) "tertiary non-preferential debts" means all subordinated debts, including (but not limited to) debts under Common Equity Tier 1 instruments, Additional Tier 1 instruments and Tier 2 instruments (all within the meaning of Part 1 of the Banking Act 2009).

(4) In subsection (3)(b), "derivative" has the same meaning as in Article 2(5) of Regulation (EU) No 648/2012.

(5) For the purposes of subsection (3)(b)(ii) an instrument does not contain an embedded derivative merely because—

(a) it provides for a variable interest rate derived from a broadly used reference rate, or

(b) it is not denominated in the domestic currency of the person issuing the debt (provided that the principal, repayment and interest are denominated in the same currency).]

NOTES

Inserted by the Banks and Building Societies (Priorities on Insolvency) Order 2018, SI 2018/1244, arts 4, 11, as from 19 December 2018, except in relation to any insolvency proceedings commenced before that date (see further the note relating to this Order at **[9.139]**).

Para (da) of sub-s (1) was inserted, para (e) of that subsection was substituted, the words in square brackets in sub-s (2) were inserted, and sub-s (2A) was inserted, by the Financial Services Act 2021 (Prudential Regulation of Credit Institutions and Investment Firms) (Consequential Amendments and Miscellaneous Provisions) Regulations 2021, SI 2021/1376, reg 2, as from 1 January 2022.

See also the Bank Recovery and Resolution (Amendment) (EU Exit) Regulations 2020, SI 2020/1350. Regulations 108–114 make amendments to various provisions of this Act (including this section) which come into force on 28 December 2020 and cease to have effect (in accordance with reg 1 of the 2020 Regulations) on IP completion day (as defined in the European Union (Withdrawal Agreement) Act 2020, s 39).

PART XIII INSOLVENCY PRACTITIONERS AND THEIR QUALIFICATION

Restrictions on unqualified persons acting as liquidator, trustee in bankruptcy, etc

[9.400]

388 Meaning of "act as insolvency practitioner"

(1) A person acts as an insolvency practitioner in relation to a company by acting—

(a) as its liquidator, provisional liquidator, administrator[, administrative receiver or monitor], or

[(b) where a voluntary arrangement in relation to the company is proposed or approved under Part I, as nominee or supervisor].

(2) A person acts as an insolvency practitioner in relation to an individual by acting—

(a) as his trustee in bankruptcy or interim receiver of his property or as [trustee (or interim trustee)] in the sequestration of his estate; or

(b) as trustee under a deed which is a deed of arrangement made for the benefit of his creditors or, in Scotland, a trust deed for his creditors; or

[(c) where a voluntary arrangement in relation to the individual is proposed or approved under Part VIII, as nominee or supervisor]

(d) in the case of a deceased individual to the administration of whose estate this section applies by virtue of an order under section 421 (application of provisions of this Act to insolvent estates of deceased persons), as administrator of that estate.

[(2A) A person acts as an insolvency practitioner in relation to an insolvent partnership by acting—

(a) as its liquidator, provisional liquidator or administrator, or

(b) as trustee of the partnership under article 11 of the Insolvent Partnerships Order 1994, or

[(c) where a voluntary arrangement in relation to the insolvent partnership is proposed or approved under Part I of the Act, as nominee or supervisor].]

[(2B) In relation to a voluntary arrangement proposed under Part I or VIII, a person acts as nominee if he performs any of the functions conferred on nominees under the Part in question.]

(3) References in this section to an individual include, except in so far as the context otherwise requires, references . . . to any debtor within the meaning of the Bankruptcy (Scotland) Act [2016].

(4) In this section—

"administrative receiver" has the meaning given by section 251 in Part VII;

["company" means—

(a) a company registered under the Companies Act 2006 in England and Wales or Scotland, or

(b) a company that may be wound up under Part 5 of this Act (unregistered companies);]

["monitor" has the same meaning as in Part A1 (moratorium);]

["sequestration" means sequestration under the Bankruptcy (Scotland) Act 2016].

[(5) Nothing in this section applies to anything done by—

(a) the official receiver; or

(b) the Accountant in Bankruptcy (within the meaning of the Bankruptcy (Scotland) Act [2016]).]

[(6) . . .]

NOTES

Sub-s (1): words in square brackets in para (a) substituted by the Corporate Insolvency and Governance Act 2020, s 2(1), Sch 3, paras 1, 21(1), (2), as from 26 June 2020 (for transitional provisions, see s 2(2), (3) of the 2020 Act (at **[9.533]**) which provides that (without prejudice to the Interpretation Act 1978, s 16) nothing in the 2020 Act affects the operation of this Act, or any other enactment, in relation to a moratorium under Sch A1 to this Act which comes into force before the repeal of that Schedule by Sch 3 to the 2020 Act (ie, 26 June 2020)). Para (b) substituted by the Insolvency Act 2000, s 4(1), (2)(a), as from 1 January 2003.

Sub-s (2): words in square brackets in para (a) substituted by the Bankruptcy (Scotland) Act 2016 (Consequential Provisions and Modifications) Order 2016, SI 2016/1034, art 7(1), (3), Sch 1, para 4(1), (6)(a), as from 30 November 2016 (except in relation to (i) a sequestration as regards which the petition is presented, or the debtor application is made before that date; or (ii) a trust deed executed before that date). Para (c) substituted by the Insolvency Act 2000, s 4(1), (2)(b), as from 1 January 2003.

Sub-s (2A): inserted by the Insolvent Partnerships Order 1994, SI 1994/2421, art 15(1), as from 1 December 1994. Para (c) substituted by the Insolvent Partnerships (Amendment) (No 2) Order 2002, SI 2002/2708, art 3, as from 1 January 2003.

Sub-s (2B): inserted by the Insolvency Act 2000, s 4(1), (2)(c), as from 1 January 2003.

Sub-s (3): words omitted repealed by SI 1994/2421, art 15(2), as from 1 December 1994. Year "2016" in square brackets substituted by SI 2016/1034, art 7(1), (3), Sch 1, para 4(1), (6)(b), as from 30 November 2016 (see also the first note relating to the 2016 Order above).

Sub-s (4): definition "company" substituted by the Companies Act 2006 (Consequential Amendments, Transitional Provisions and Savings) Order 2009, SI 2009/1941, art 2(1), Sch 1, para 78(1), (2), as from 1 October 2009 (for effect see the note to s 7A at **[9.145]**). Definition "monitor" inserted by the Corporate Insolvency and Governance Act 2020, s 2(1), Sch 3, paras 1, 21(1), (3), as from 26 June 2020 (for transitional provisions, see the first note relating to the 2020 Act above). Definition "sequestration" substituted (for the original definitions "interim trustee" and "permanent trustee") by SI 2016/1034, art 7(1), (3), Sch 1, para 4(1), (6)(c), as from 30 November 2016 (see also the first note relating to the 2016 Order above).

Sub-s (5): substituted by the Bankruptcy (Scotland) Act 1993, s 11(1), as from 1 April 1993. Year "2016" in square brackets substituted by SI 2016/1034, art 7(1), (3), Sch 1, para 4(1), (6)(d), as from 30 November 2016 (see also the first note relating to the 2016 Order above).

Sub-s (6): originally added by the Insolvency Act 1986 (Amendment) (No 2) Regulations 2002, SI 2002/1240, regs 3, 17, as from 31 May 2002. Words in square brackets substituted by the Insolvency Amendment (EU 2015/848) Regulations 2017, SI 2017/702, regs 2, 3, Schedule, Pt 1, paras 1, 23, as from 26 June 2017, except in relation to proceedings opened before that date. This subsection was subsequently repealed by the Insolvency (Amendment) (EU Exit) Regulations 2019, SI 2019/146, reg 2, Schedule, Pt 2, paras 16, 36, as from IP completion day (as defined in the European Union (Withdrawal Agreement) Act 2020, s 39) (for savings, see reg 4 of the 2019 Regulations at **[12.82]**).

[9.401]
389 Acting without qualification an offence
(1) A person who acts as an insolvency practitioner in relation to a company or an individual at a time when he is not qualified to do so is liable to imprisonment or a fine, or to both.
[(1A) . . .]
(2) This section does not apply to the official receiver [or the Accountant in Bankruptcy (within the meaning of the Bankruptcy (Scotland) Act [2016])].

NOTES
Sub-s (1A): originally inserted by the Insolvency Act 2000, s 4(1), (3), as from 1 January 2003. Subsequently repealed by the Deregulation Act 2015, s 19, Sch 6, Pt 6, paras 17, 18, as from 1 October 2015.

Sub-s (2): words in first pair of square brackets added by the Bankruptcy (Scotland) Act 1993, s 11(2), as from 1 April 1993. The year "2016" in square brackets was substituted by the Bankruptcy (Scotland) Act 2016 (Consequential Provisions and Modifications) Order 2016, SI 2016/1034, art 7(1), (3), Sch 1, para 4(1), (7), as from 30 November 2016 (except in relation to (i) a sequestration as regards which the petition is presented, or the debtor application is made before that date; or (ii) a trust deed executed before that date).

389A (*Originally inserted by the Insolvency Act 2000, s 4(1), (4), as from 1 January 2003, and repealed by the Deregulation Act 2015, s 19, Sch 6, Pt 6, paras 17, 19, as from 1 October 2015.*)

[9.402]
[389B Official receiver as nominee or supervisor
(1) The official receiver is authorised to act as nominee or supervisor in relation to a voluntary arrangement approved under Part VIII provided that the debtor is an undischarged bankrupt when the arrangement is proposed.
(2) The Secretary of State may by order repeal the proviso in subsection (1).
(3) An order under subsection (2)—
(a) must be made by statutory instrument, and
(b) shall be subject to annulment in pursuance of a resolution of either House of Parliament.]

NOTES
Inserted, in relation to England and Wales only, by the Enterprise Act 2002, s 264(1), Sch 22, para 3, as from 1 April 2004.

The requisite qualification, and the means of obtaining it

[9.403]
390 Persons not qualified to act as insolvency practitioners
(1) A person who is not an individual is not qualified to act as an insolvency practitioner.
[(2) A person is not qualified to act as an insolvency practitioner at any time unless at that time the person is appropriately authorised under section 390A.]
(3) A person is not qualified to act as an insolvency practitioner in relation to another person at any time unless—
(a) there is in force at that time security or, in Scotland, caution for the proper performance of his functions, and
(b) that security or caution meets the prescribed requirements with respect to his so acting in relation to that other person.
(4) A person is not qualified to act as an insolvency practitioner at any time if at that time—
(a) he has been [made] bankrupt [under this Act or the Insolvency (Northern Ireland) Order 1989] or sequestration of his estate has been awarded and (in either case) he has not been discharged,
[(aa) a moratorium period under a debt relief order [under this Act or the Insolvency (Northern Ireland) Order 1989] applies in relation of him,]
[(b) he is subject to a disqualification order made or a disqualification undertaking accepted under the Company Directors Disqualification Act 1986 or the Company Directors Disqualification (Northern Ireland) Order 2002,]
(c) he is a patient within the meaning of . . . [section 329(1) of the Mental Health (Care and Treatment) (Scotland) Act 2003] [or has had a guardian appointed to him under the Adults with Incapacity (Scotland) Act 2000 (asp 4)][, or
(d) he lacks capacity (within the meaning of the Mental Capacity Act 2005) to act as an insolvency practitioner].
[(5) A person is not qualified to act as an insolvency practitioner while there is in force in respect of that person—
(a) a bankruptcy restrictions order under this Act, the Bankruptcy (Scotland) Act 1985 [or the Bankruptcy (Scotland) Act 2016] or the Insolvency (Northern Ireland) Order 1989, or
(b) a debt relief restrictions order under this Act or that Order.]

NOTES

Sub-s (2): substituted by the Deregulation Act 2015, s 17(1), (2), as from 1 October 2015.

Sub-s (4) is amended as follows:

Word in first pair of square brackets in para (a) substituted by the Enterprise and Regulatory Reform Act 2013, s 71(3), Sch 19, paras 1, 58, as from 6 April 2016, except in respect of a petition for a bankruptcy order presented to the court by a debtor before that date.

Words in second pair of square brackets in para (a) and words in square brackets in para (aa) inserted by the Small Business, Enterprise and Employment Act 2015, s 115(a), as from 1 October 2015, in relation to an individual in respect of whom a bankruptcy restrictions order or a debt relief restrictions order is made or granted on or after that date.

Para (aa) inserted by the Tribunals, Courts and Enforcement Act 2007, s 108(3), Sch 20, Pt 1, paras 1, 5(1), (2), as from 6 April 2009.

Para (b) substituted by the Companies Act 2006 (Consequential Amendments, Transitional Provisions and Savings) Order 2009, SI 2009/1941, art 2(1), Sch 1, para 78(1), (4), as from 1 October 2009 (for effect see the note to s 7A at **[9.145]**).

Words in first pair of square brackets in para (c) substituted, in relation to Scotland, by the Mental Health (Care and Treatment) (Scotland) Act 2003 (Modification of Enactments) Order 2005, SSI 2005/486, art 2, Sch 1, para 18(1), (3), as from 27 September 2005, and, in relation to England and Wales, by the Mental Health (Care and Treatment) (Scotland) Act 2003 (Consequential Provisions) Order 2005, SI 2005/2078, art 15, Sch 1, para 3(1), (3), as from 5 October 2005.

Words in second pair of square brackets in para (c) added by the Adults with Incapacity (Scotland) Act 2000, s 88(2), Sch 5, para 18, as from 1 April 2002.

Para (d) and the word immediately preceding it inserted by the Mental Capacity Act 2005, s 67(1), (2), Sch 6, para 31(1), (3), Sch 7, as from 1 October 2007.

Sub-s (5): substituted by the Small Business, Enterprise and Employment Act 2015, s 115(b), as from 1 October 2015, in relation to an individual in respect of whom a bankruptcy restrictions order or a debt relief restrictions order is made or granted on or after that date. Words in square brackets inserted by the Bankruptcy (Scotland) Act 2016 (Consequential Provisions and Modifications) Order 2016, SI 2016/1034, art 7(1), (3), Sch 1, para 4(1), (8), as from 30 November 2016 (except in relation to (i) a sequestration as regards which the petition is presented, or the debtor application is made before that date; or (ii) a trust deed executed before that date).

Regulations: the Insolvency Practitioners Regulations 2005, SI 2005/524; the Provision of Services (Insolvency Practitioners) Regulations 2009, SI 2009/3081.

[9.404]

[390A Authorisation

(1) In this Part—

"partial authorisation" means authorisation to act as an insolvency practitioner—

(a) only in relation to companies, or

(b) only in relation to individuals;

"full authorisation" means authorisation to act as an insolvency practitioner in relation to companies, individuals and insolvent partnerships;

"partially authorised" and "fully authorised" are to be construed accordingly.

(2) A person is fully authorised under this section to act as an insolvency practitioner—

(a) by virtue of being a member of a professional body recognised under section 391(1) and being permitted to act as an insolvency practitioner for all purposes by or under the rules of that body, or

(b) by holding an authorisation granted by the Department of Enterprise, Trade and Investment in Northern Ireland under Article 352 of the Insolvency (Northern Ireland) Order 1989.

(3) A person is partially authorised under this section to act as an insolvency practitioner—

(a) by virtue of being a member of a professional body recognised under section 391(1) and being permitted to act as an insolvency practitioner in relation only to companies or only to individuals by or under the rules of that body, or

(b) by virtue of being a member of a professional body recognised under section 391(2) and being permitted to act as an insolvency practitioner by or under the rules of that body.]

NOTES

Inserted, together with s 390B, by Deregulation Act 2015, s 17(1), (3), as from 1 October 2015.

[9.405]

[390B Partial authorisation: acting in relation to partnerships

(1) A person who is partially authorised to act as an insolvency practitioner in relation to companies may nonetheless not accept an appointment to act in relation to a company if at the time of the appointment the person is aware that the company—

(a) is or was a member of a partnership, and

(b) has outstanding liabilities in relation to the partnership.

(2) A person who is partially authorised to act as an insolvency practitioner in relation to individuals may nonetheless not accept an appointment to act in relation to an individual if at the time of the appointment the person is aware that the individual—

(a) is or was a member of a partnership other than a Scottish partnership, and

(b) has outstanding liabilities in relation to the partnership.

(3) Subject to subsection (9), a person who is partially authorised to act as an insolvency practitioner in relation to companies may nonetheless not continue to act in relation to a company if the person becomes aware that the company—

(a) is or was a member of a partnership, and

(b) has outstanding liabilities in relation to the partnership,

unless the person is granted permission to continue to act by the court.

(4) Subject to subsection (9), a person who is partially authorised to act as an insolvency practitioner in relation to individuals may nonetheless not continue to act in relation to an individual if the person becomes aware that the individual—

(a) is or was a member of a partnership other than a Scottish partnership, and
(b) has outstanding liabilities in relation to the partnership,

unless the person is granted permission to continue to act by the court.

(5) The court may grant a person permission to continue to act for the purposes of subsection (3) or (4) if it is satisfied that the person is competent to do so.

(6) A person who is partially authorised and becomes aware as mentioned in subsection (3) or (4) may alternatively apply to the court for an order (a "replacement order") appointing in his or her place a person who is fully authorised to act as an insolvency practitioner in relation to the company or (as the case may be) the individual.

(7) A person may apply to the court for permission to continue to act or for a replacement order under—

(a) where acting in relation to a company, this section or, if it applies, section 168(5B) (member of insolvent partnership: England and Wales);
(b) where acting in relation to an individual, this section or, if it applies, section 303(2C) (member of insolvent partnership: England and Wales).

(8) A person who acts as an insolvency practitioner in contravention of any of subsections (1) to (4) is guilty of an offence under section 389 (acting without qualification).

(9) A person does not contravene subsection (3) or (4) by continuing to act as an insolvency practitioner during the permitted period if, within the period of 7 business days beginning with the day after the day on which the person becomes aware as mentioned in the subsection, the person—

(a) applies to the court for permission to continue to act, or
(b) applies to the court for a replacement order.

(10) For the purposes of subsection (9)—

"business day" means any day other than a Saturday, a Sunday, Christmas Day, Good Friday or a day which is a bank holiday in any part of Great Britain;

"permitted period" means the period beginning with the day on which the person became aware as mentioned in subsection (3) or (4) and ending on the earlier of—

(a) the expiry of the period of 6 weeks beginning with the day on which the person applies to the court as mentioned in subsection (9)(a) or (b), and
(b) the day on which the court disposes of the application (by granting or refusing it);

"replacement order" has the meaning given by subsection (6).]

NOTES

Inserted as noted to s 390A at **[9.404]**.

[9.406]

[391 Recognised professional bodies

(1) The Secretary of State may by order, if satisfied that a body meets the requirements of subsection (4), declare the body to be a recognised professional body which is capable of providing its insolvency specialist members with full authorisation or partial authorisation.

(2) The Secretary of State may by order, if satisfied that a body meets the requirements of subsection (4), declare the body to be a recognised professional body which is capable of providing its insolvency specialist members with partial authorisation only of the kind specified in the order (as to which, see section 390A(1)).

(3) Section 391A makes provision about the making by a body of an application to the Secretary of State for an order under this section.

(4) The requirements are that—

(a) the body regulates (or is going to regulate) the practice of a profession,
(b) the body has rules which it is going to maintain and enforce for securing that its insolvency specialist members—
   (i) are fit and proper persons to act as insolvency practitioners, and
   (ii) meet acceptable requirements as to education and practical training and experience, and
(c) the body's rules and practices for or in connection with authorising persons to act as insolvency practitioners, and its rules and practices for or in connection with regulating persons acting as such, are designed to ensure that the regulatory objectives are met (as to which, see section 391C).

(5) An order of the Secretary of State under this section has effect from such date as is specified in the order.

(6) An order under this section may be revoked by an order under section 391L or 391N (and see section 415A(1)(b)).

(7) In this Part—

(a) references to members of a recognised professional body are to persons who, whether members of that body or not, are subject to its rules in the practice of the profession in question;
(b) references to insolvency specialist members of a professional body are to members who are permitted by or under the rules of the body to act as insolvency practitioners.

(8) A reference in this Part to a recognised professional body is to a body recognised under this section (and see sections 391L(6) and 391N(5)).]

NOTES

Substituted, together with s 391A for the original s 391, by the Small Business, Enterprise and Employment Act 2015, s 137(1), as from 1 October 2015 (and immediately after the Deregulation Act 2015, s 17 comes into force (see further the note below)).

This section was also substituted by the Deregulation Act 2015, s 17(1), (4). The Deregulation Act 2015 (Commencement No 3 and Transitional and Saving Provisions) Order 2015, SI 2015/1732 brought s 17 into force on 1 October 2015. See, however, the Small Business, Enterprise and Employment Act 2015 (Commencement No 2 and Transitional Provisions) Regulations 2015, SI 2015/1689, reg 3 which provides that the Small Business, Enterprise and Employment Act 2015, s 137 comes into force immediately after the coming into force of the Deregulation Act 2015, s 17.

Orders: the Insolvency Practitioners (Recognised Professional Bodies) Order 1986, SI 1986/1764 recognising the following bodies for the purposes of this section: the Insolvency Practitioners Association; the Institute of Chartered Accountants in England and Wales; the Institute of Chartered Accountants in Ireland; the Institute of Chartered Accountants of Scotland. Note that the Law Society and the Law Society of Scotland were removed from the list of recognised bodies by the Insolvency Practitioners (Recognised Professional Bodies) (Revocation of Recognition) Order 2016, SI 2016/403 (as from 5 April 2016), and the Insolvency Practitioners (Recognised Professional Bodies) (Revocation of Recognition) Order 2015, SI 2015/2067 (as from 18 January 2016) respectively. Note also that the Chartered Association of Certified Accountants was removed from this list by the Insolvency Practitioners (Recognised Professional Bodies) (Revocation of Recognition) Order 2021, SI 2021/110 (as from 1 March 2021).

Note that the Small Business, Enterprise and Employment Act 2015, s 137(2) provides that an Order made under sub-ss (1) or (2) before 1 October 2015 is, on that date, to be treated as if it were made under sub-ss (1) or (2) as substituted by s 137(1) of the 2015 Act.

[9.407]

[391A Application for recognition as recognised professional body

(1) An application for an order under section 391(1) or (2) must—

(a) be made to the Secretary of State in such form and manner as the Secretary of State may require,

(b) be accompanied by such information as the Secretary of State may require, and

(c) be supplemented by such additional information as the Secretary of State may require at any time between receiving the application and determining it.

(2) The requirements which may be imposed under subsection (1) may differ as between different applications.

(3) The Secretary of State may require information provided under this section to be in such form, and verified in such manner, as the Secretary of State may specify.

(4) An application for an order under section 391(1) or (2) must be accompanied by—

(a) a copy of the applicant's rules,

(b) a copy of the applicant's policies and practices, and

(c) a copy of any guidance issued by the applicant in writing.

(5) The reference in subsection (4)(c) to guidance issued by the applicant is a reference to guidance or recommendations which are—

(a) issued or made by it which will apply to its insolvency specialist members or to persons seeking to become such members,

(b) relevant for the purposes of this Part, and

(c) intended to have continuing effect,

including guidance or recommendations relating to the admission or expulsion of members.

(6) The Secretary of State may refuse an application for an order under section 391(1) or (2) if the Secretary of State considers that recognition of the body concerned is unnecessary having regard to the existence of one or more other bodies which have been or are likely to be recognised under section 391.

(7) Subsection (8) applies where the Secretary of State refuses an application for an order under section 391(1) or (2); and it applies regardless of whether the application is refused on the ground mentioned in subsection (6), because the Secretary of State is not satisfied as mentioned in section 391(1) or (2) or because a fee has not been paid (see section 415A(1)(b)).

(8) The Secretary of State must give the applicant a written notice of the Secretary of State's decision; and the notice must set out the reasons for refusing the application.]

NOTES

Substituted as noted to s 391 at **[9.406]**.

[Regulatory objectives

[9.408]

391B Application of regulatory objectives

(1) In discharging regulatory functions, a recognised professional body must, so far as is reasonably practicable, act in a way—

(a) which is compatible with the regulatory objectives, and

(b) which the body considers most appropriate for the purpose of meeting those objectives.

(2) In discharging functions under this Part, the Secretary of State must have regard to the regulatory objectives.]

NOTES

Inserted, together with the preceding heading and s 391C, by the Small Business, Enterprise and Employment Act 2015, s 138(1), as from 1 October 2015.

[9.409]

391C Meaning of "regulatory functions" and "regulatory objectives"

(1) This section has effect for the purposes of this Part.

(2) "Regulatory functions", in relation to a recognised professional body, means any functions the body has—

(a) under or in relation to its arrangements for or in connection with—

(i) authorising persons to act as insolvency practitioners, or

(ii) regulating persons acting as insolvency practitioners, or

(b) in connection with the making or alteration of those arrangements.

(3) "Regulatory objectives" means the objectives of—

(a) having a system of regulating persons acting as insolvency practitioners that—

(i) secures fair treatment for persons affected by their acts and omissions,

(ii) reflects the regulatory principles, and

(iii) ensures consistent outcomes,

(b) encouraging an independent and competitive insolvency-practitioner profession whose members—

(i) provide high quality services at a cost to the recipient which is fair and reasonable,

(ii) act transparently and with integrity, and

(iii) consider the interests of all creditors in any particular case,

(c) promoting the maximisation of the value of returns to creditors and promptness in making those returns, and

(d) protecting and promoting the public interest.

(4) In subsection (3)(a), "regulatory principles" means—

(a) the principles that regulatory activities should be transparent, accountable, proportionate, consistent and targeted only at cases in which action is needed, and

(b) any other principle appearing to the body concerned (in the case of the duty under section 391B(1)), or to the Secretary of State (in the case of the duty under section 391B(2)), to lead to best regulatory practice.]

NOTES

Inserted as noted to s 391B at **[9.408]**.

[Oversight of recognised professional bodies

[9.410]

391D Directions

(1) This section applies if the Secretary of State is satisfied that an act or omission of a recognised professional body (or a series of such acts or omissions) in discharging one or more of its regulatory functions has had, or is likely to have, an adverse impact on the achievement of one or more of the regulatory objectives.

(2) The Secretary of State may, if in all the circumstances of the case satisfied that it is appropriate to do so, direct the body to take such steps as the Secretary of State considers will counter the adverse impact, mitigate its effect or prevent its occurrence or recurrence.

(3) A direction under this section may require a recognised professional body—

(a) to take only such steps as it has power to take under its regulatory arrangements;

(b) to take steps with a view to the modification of any part of its regulatory arrangements.

(4) A direction under this section may require a recognised professional body—

(a) to take steps with a view to the institution of, or otherwise in respect of, specific regulatory proceedings;

(b) to take steps in respect of all, or a specified class of, such proceedings.

(5) For the purposes of this section, a direction to take steps includes a direction which requires a recognised professional body to refrain from taking a particular course of action.

(6) In this section "regulatory arrangements", in relation to a recognised professional body, means the arrangements that the body has for or in connection with—

(a) authorising persons to act as insolvency practitioners, or

(b) regulating persons acting as insolvency practitioners.]

NOTES

Inserted, together with the preceding heading and ss 391D–391K, by the Small Business, Enterprise and Employment Act 2015, s 139(1), as from 1 October 2015.

[9.411]

[391E Directions: procedure

(1) Before giving a recognised professional body a direction under section 391D, the Secretary of State must give the body a notice accompanied by a draft of the proposed direction.

(2) The notice under subsection (1) must—

(a) state that the Secretary of State proposes to give the body a direction in the form of the accompanying draft,

(b) specify why the Secretary of State has reached the conclusions mentioned in section 391D(1) and (2), and

(c) specify a period within which the body may make written representations with respect to the proposal.

(3) The period specified under subsection (2)(c)—

(a) must begin with the date on which the notice is given to the body, and

(b) must not be less than 28 days.

(4) On the expiry of that period, the Secretary of State must decide whether to give the body the proposed direction.

(5) The Secretary of State must give notice of that decision to the body.

(6) Where the Secretary of State decides to give the proposed direction, the notice under subsection (5) must—

(a) contain the direction,

(b) state the time at which the direction is to take effect, and

(c) specify the Secretary of State's reasons for the decision to give the direction.

(7) Where the Secretary of State decides to give the proposed direction, the Secretary of State must publish the notice under subsection (5); but this subsection does not apply to a direction to take any step with a view to the institution of, or otherwise in respect of, regulatory proceedings against an individual.

(8) The Secretary of State may revoke a direction under section 391D; and, where doing so, the Secretary of State—

(a) must give the body to which the direction was given notice of the revocation, and

(b) must publish the notice and, if the notice under subsection (5) was published under subsection (7), must do so (if possible) in the same manner as that in which that notice was published.]

NOTES

Inserted as noted to s 391D at **[9.410]**.

[9.412]

[391F Financial penalty

(1) This section applies if the Secretary of State is satisfied—

(a) that a recognised professional body has failed to comply with a requirement to which this section applies, and

(b) that, in all the circumstances of the case, it is appropriate to impose a financial penalty on the body.

(2) This section applies to a requirement imposed on the recognised professional body—

(a) by a direction given under section 391D, or

(b) by a provision of this Act or of subordinate legislation under this Act.

(3) The Secretary of State may impose a financial penalty, in respect of the failure, of such amount as the Secretary of State considers appropriate.

(4) In deciding what amount is appropriate, the Secretary of State—

(a) must have regard to the nature of the requirement which has not been complied with, and
(b) must not take into account the Secretary of State's costs in discharging functions under this Part.

(5) A financial penalty under this section is payable to the Secretary of State; and sums received by the Secretary of State in respect of a financial penalty under this section (including by way of interest) are to be paid into the Consolidated Fund.

(6) In sections 391G to 391I, "penalty" means a financial penalty under this section.]

NOTES

Inserted as noted to s 391D at **[9.410]**.

[9.413]

[391G Financial penalty: procedure

(1) Before imposing a penalty on a recognised professional body, the Secretary of State must give notice to the body—

(a) stating that the Secretary of State proposes to impose a penalty and the amount of the proposed penalty,
(b) specifying the requirement in question,
(c) stating why the Secretary of State is satisfied as mentioned in section 391F(1), and
(d) specifying a period within which the body may make written representations with respect to the proposal.

(2) The period specified under subsection (1)(d)—

(a) must begin with the date on which the notice is given to the body, and
(b) must not be less than 28 days.

(3) On the expiry of that period, the Secretary of State must decide—

(a) whether to impose a penalty, and
(b) whether the penalty should be the amount stated in the notice or a reduced amount.

(4) The Secretary of State must give notice of the decision to the body.

(5) Where the Secretary of State decides to impose a penalty, the notice under subsection (4) must—

(a) state that the Secretary of State has imposed a penalty on the body and its amount,
(b) specify the requirement in question and state—
 (i) why it appears to the Secretary of State that the requirement has not been complied with, or
 (ii) where, by that time, the requirement has been complied with, why it appeared to the Secretary of State when giving the notice under subsection (1) that the requirement had not been complied with, and
(c) specify a time by which the penalty is required to be paid.

(6) The time specified under subsection (5)(c) must be at least three months after the date on which the notice under subsection (4) is given to the body.

(7) Where the Secretary of State decides to impose a penalty, the Secretary of State must publish the notice under subsection (4).

(8) The Secretary of State may rescind or reduce a penalty imposed on a recognised professional body; and, where doing so, the Secretary of State—

(a) must give the body notice that the penalty has been rescinded or reduced to the amount stated in the notice, and
(b) must publish the notice; and it must (if possible) be published in the same manner as that in which the notice under subsection (4) was published.]

NOTES

Inserted as noted to s 391D at **[9.410]**.

[9.414]

[391H Appeal against financial penalty

(1) A recognised professional body on which a penalty is imposed may appeal to the court on one or more of the appeal grounds.

(2) The appeal grounds are—

(a) that the imposition of the penalty was not within the Secretary of State's power under section 391F;
(b) that the requirement in respect of which the penalty was imposed had been complied with before the notice under section 391G(1) was given;
(c) that the requirements of section 391G have not been complied with in relation to the imposition of the penalty and the interests of the body have been substantially prejudiced as a result;
(d) that the amount of the penalty is unreasonable;
(e) that it was unreasonable of the Secretary of State to require the penalty imposed to be paid by the time specified in the notice under section 391G(5)(c).

(3) An appeal under this section must be made within the period of three months beginning with the day on which the notice under section 391G(4) in respect of the penalty is given to the body.

(4) On an appeal under this section the court may—

(a) quash the penalty,
(b) substitute a penalty of such lesser amount as the court considers appropriate, or
(c) in the case of the appeal ground in subsection (2)(e), substitute for the time imposed by the Secretary of State a different time.

(5) Where the court substitutes a penalty of a lesser amount, it may require the payment of interest on the substituted penalty from such time, and at such rate, as it considers just and equitable.

(6) Where the court substitutes a later time for the time specified in the notice under section 391G(5)(c), it may require the payment of interest on the penalty from the substituted time at such rate as it considers just and equitable.

(7) Where the court dismisses the appeal, it may require the payment of interest on the penalty from the time specified in the notice under section 391G(5)(c) at such rate as it considers just and equitable.

(8) In this section, "the court" means the High Court or, in Scotland, the Court of Session.]

NOTES

Inserted as noted to s 391D at **[9.410]**.

[9.415]

[391I Recovery of financial penalties

(1) If the whole or part of a penalty is not paid by the time by which it is required to be paid, the unpaid balance from time to time carries interest at the rate for the time being specified in section 17 of the Judgments Act 1838 (but this is subject to any requirement imposed by the court under section 391H(5), (6) or (7)).

(2) If an appeal is made under section 391H in relation to a penalty, the penalty is not required to be paid until the appeal has been determined or withdrawn.

(3) Subsection (4) applies where the whole or part of a penalty has not been paid by the time it is required to be paid and—

- (a) no appeal relating to the penalty has been made under section 391H during the period within which an appeal may be made under that section, or
- (b) an appeal has been made under that section and determined or withdrawn.

(4) The Secretary of State may recover from the recognised professional body in question, as a debt due to the Secretary of State, any of the penalty and any interest which has not been paid.]

NOTES

Inserted as noted to s 391D at **[9.410]**.

[9.416]

[391J Reprimand

(1) This section applies if the Secretary of State is satisfied that an act or omission of a recognised professional body (or a series of such acts or omissions) in discharging one or more of its regulatory functions has had, or is likely to have, an adverse impact on the achievement of one or more of the regulatory objectives.

(2) The Secretary of State may, if in all the circumstances of the case satisfied that it is appropriate to do so, publish a statement reprimanding the body for the act or omission (or series of acts or omissions).]

NOTES

Inserted as noted to s 391D at **[9.410]**.

[9.417]

[391K Reprimand: procedure

(1) If the Secretary of State proposes to publish a statement under section 391J in respect of a recognised professional body, it must give the body a notice—

- (a) stating that the Secretary of State proposes to publish such a statement and setting out the terms of the proposed statement,
- (b) specifying the acts or omissions to which the proposed statement relates, and
- (c) specifying a period within which the body may make written representations with respect to the proposal.

(2) The period specified under subsection (1)(c)—

- (a) must begin with the date on which the notice is given to the body, and
- (b) must not be less than 28 days.

(3) On the expiry of that period, the Secretary of State must decide whether to publish the statement.

(4) The Secretary of State may vary the proposed statement; but before doing so, the Secretary of State must give the body notice—

- (a) setting out the proposed variation and the reasons for it, and
- (b) specifying a period within which the body may make written representations with respect to the proposed variation.

(5) The period specified under subsection (4)(b)—

- (a) must begin with the date on which the notice is given to the body, and
- (b) must not be less than 28 days.

(6) On the expiry of that period, the Secretary of State must decide whether to publish the statement as varied.]

NOTES

Inserted as noted to s 391D at **[9.410]**.

[Revocation etc of recognition

[9.418]

391L Revocation of recognition at instigation of Secretary of State

(1) An order under section 391(1) or (2) in relation to a recognised professional body may be revoked by the Secretary of State by order if the Secretary of State is satisfied that—

- (a) an act or omission of the body (or a series of such acts or omissions) in discharging one or more of its regulatory functions has had, or is likely to have, an adverse impact on the achievement of one or more of the regulatory objectives, and
- (b) it is appropriate in all the circumstances of the case to revoke the body's recognition under section 391.

(2) If the condition set out in subsection (3) is met, an order under section 391(1) in relation to a recognised professional body may be revoked by the Secretary of State by an order which also declares the body concerned to be a recognised professional body which is capable of providing its insolvency specialist members with partial authorisation only of the kind specified in the order (see section 390A(1)).

(3) The condition is that the Secretary of State is satisfied—

- (a) as mentioned in subsection (1)(a), and

(b) that it is appropriate in all the circumstances of the case for the body to be declared to be a recognised professional body which is capable of providing its insolvency specialist members with partial authorisation only of the kind specified in the order.

(4) In this Part—

(a) an order under subsection (1) is referred to as a "revocation order";

(b) an order under subsection (2) is referred to as a "partial revocation order".

(5) A revocation order or partial revocation order—

(a) has effect from such date as is specified in the order, and

(b) may make provision for members of the body in question to continue to be treated as fully or partially authorised (as the case may be) to act as insolvency practitioners for a specified period after the order takes effect.

(6) A partial revocation order has effect as if it were an order made under section 391(2).]

NOTES

Inserted, together with the preceding heading and ss 391M, 391N, by the Small Business, Enterprise and Employment Act 2015, s 140(1), as from 1 October 2015.

[9.419]

[391M Orders under section 391L: procedure

(1) Before making a revocation order or partial revocation order in relation to a recognised professional body, the Secretary of State must give notice to the body—

(a) stating that the Secretary of State proposes to make the order and the terms of the proposed order,

(b) specifying the Secretary of State's reasons for proposing to make the order, and

(c) specifying a period within which the body, members of the body or other persons likely to be affected by the proposal may make written representations with respect to it.

(2) Where the Secretary of State gives a notice under subsection (1), the Secretary of State must publish the notice on the same day.

(3) The period specified under subsection (1)(c)—

(a) must begin with the date on which the notice is given to the body, and

(b) must not be less than 28 days.

(4) On the expiry of that period, the Secretary of State must decide whether to make the revocation order or (as the case may be) partial revocation order in relation to the body.

(5) The Secretary of State must give notice of the decision to the body.

(6) Where the Secretary of State decides to make the order, the notice under subsection (5) must specify—

(a) when the order is to take effect, and

(b) the Secretary of State's reasons for making the order.

(7) A notice under subsection (5) must be published; and it must (if possible) be published in the same manner as that in which the notice under subsection (1) was published.]

NOTES

Inserted as noted to s 391L at **[9.418]**.

[9.420]

[391N Revocation of recognition at request of body

(1) An order under section 391(1) or (2) in relation to a recognised professional body may be revoked by the Secretary of State by order if—

(a) the body has requested that an order be made under this subsection, and

(b) the Secretary of State is satisfied that it is appropriate in all the circumstances of the case to revoke the body's recognition under section 391.

(2) An order under section 391(1) in relation to a recognised professional body may be revoked by the Secretary of State by an order which also declares the body concerned to be a recognised professional body which is capable of providing its insolvency specialist members with partial authorisation only of the kind specified in the order (see section 390A(1)) if—

(a) the body has requested that an order be made under this subsection, and

(b) the Secretary of State is satisfied that it is appropriate in all the circumstances of the case for the body to be declared to be a recognised professional body which is capable of providing its insolvency specialist members with partial authorisation only of the kind specified in the order.

(3) Where the Secretary of State decides to make an order under this section the Secretary of State must publish a notice specifying—

(a) when the order is to take effect, and

(b) the Secretary of State's reasons for making the order.

(4) An order under this section—

(a) has effect from such date as is specified in the order, and

(b) may make provision for members of the body in question to continue to be treated as fully or partially authorised (as the case may be) to act as insolvency practitioners for a specified period after the order takes effect.

(5) An order under subsection (2) has effect as if it were an order made under section 391(2).]

NOTES

Inserted as noted to s 391L at **[9.418]**.

Orders: the Insolvency Practitioners (Recognised Professional Bodies) (Revocation of Recognition) Order 2015, SI 2015/2067; the Insolvency Practitioners (Recognised Professional Bodies) (Revocation of Recognition) Order 2016, SI 2016/403; the Insolvency Practitioners (Recognised Professional Bodies) (Revocation of Recognition) Order 2021, SI 2021/110 (see further the notes to s 391 *ante*).

[Court sanction of insolvency practitioners in public interest cases

[9.421]

391O Direct sanctions orders

(1) For the purposes of this Part a "direct sanctions order" is an order made by the court against a person who is acting as an insolvency practitioner which—

(a) declares that the person is no longer authorised (whether fully or partially) to act as an insolvency practitioner;

(b) declares that the person is no longer fully authorised to act as an insolvency practitioner but remains partially authorised to act as such either in relation to companies or individuals, as specified in the order;

(c) declares that the person's authorisation to act as an insolvency practitioner is suspended for the period specified in the order or until such time as the requirements so specified are complied with;

(d) requires the person to comply with such other requirements as may be specified in the order while acting as an insolvency practitioner;

(e) requires the person to make such contribution as may be specified in the order to one or more creditors of a company, individual or insolvent partnership in relation to which the person is acting or has acted as an insolvency practitioner.

(2) Where the court makes a direct sanctions order, the relevant recognised professional body must take all necessary steps to give effect to the order.

(3) A direct sanctions order must not be made against a person whose authorisation to act as an insolvency practitioner was granted by the Department of Enterprise, Trade and Investment in Northern Ireland (see section 390A(2)(b)).

(4) A direct sanctions order must not specify a contribution as mentioned in subsection (1)(e) which is more than the remuneration that the person has received or will receive in respect of acting as an insolvency practitioner in the case.

(5) In this section and section 391P—

"the court" means the High Court or, in Scotland, the Court of Session;

"relevant recognised professional body", in relation to a person who is acting as an insolvency practitioner, means the recognised professional body by virtue of which the person is authorised so to act.]

NOTES

Inserted, together with the preceding heading and ss 391P–391R, by the Small Business, Enterprise and Employment Act 2015, s 141, as from 1 October 2015. Note that ss 391O–391R apply in respect of conduct of an individual acting as an insolvency practitioner where that conduct occurs on or after 1 October 2015 notwithstanding the date of the individual's authorisation to act as an insolvency or appointment as office holder in a particular insolvency.

[9.422]

[391P Application for, and power to make, direct sanctions order

(1) The Secretary of State may apply to the court for a direct sanctions order to be made against a person if it appears to the Secretary of State that it would be in the public interest for the order to be made.

(2) The Secretary of State must send a copy of the application to the relevant recognised professional body.

(3) The court may make a direct sanctions order against a person where, on an application under this section, the court is satisfied that condition 1 and at least one of conditions 2, 3, 4 and 5 are met in relation to the person.

(4) The conditions are set out in section 391Q.

(5) In deciding whether to make a direct sanctions order against a person the court must have regard to the extent to which—

(a) the relevant recognised professional body has taken action against the person in respect of the failure mentioned in condition 1, and

(b) that action is sufficient to address the failure.]

NOTES

Inserted as noted to s 391O at **[9.421]**.

[9.423]

[391Q Direct sanctions order: conditions

(1) Condition 1 is that the person, in acting as an insolvency practitioner or in connection with any appointment as such, has failed to comply with—

(a) a requirement imposed by the rules of the relevant recognised professional body;

(b) any standards, or code of ethics, for the insolvency-practitioner profession adopted from time to time by the relevant recognised professional body.

(2) Condition 2 is that the person—

(a) is not a fit and proper person to act as an insolvency practitioner;

(b) is a fit and proper person to act as an insolvency practitioner only in relation to companies, but the person's authorisation is not so limited; or

(c) is a fit and proper person to act as an insolvency practitioner only in relation to individuals, but the person's authorisation is not so limited.

(3) Condition 3 is that it is appropriate for the person's authorisation to act as an insolvency practitioner to be suspended for a period or until one or more requirements are complied with.

(4) Condition 4 is that it is appropriate to impose other restrictions on the person acting as an insolvency practitioner.

(5) Condition 5 is that loss has been suffered as a result of the failure mentioned in condition 1 by one or more creditors of a company, individual or insolvent partnership in relation to which the person is acting or has acted as an insolvency practitioner.

(6) In this section "relevant recognised professional body" has the same meaning as in section 391O.]

NOTES

Inserted as noted to s 391O at **[9.421]**.

[9.424]

[391R Direct sanctions direction instead of order

(1) The Secretary of State may give a direction (a "direct sanctions direction") in relation to a person acting as an insolvency practitioner to the relevant recognised professional body (instead of applying, or continuing with an application, for a direct sanctions order against the person) if the Secretary of State is satisfied that—

(a) condition 1 and at least one of conditions 2, 3, 4 and 5 are met in relation to the person (see section 391Q), and

(b) it is in the public interest for the direction to be given.

(2) But the Secretary of State may not give a direct sanctions direction in relation to a person without that person's consent.

(3) A direct sanctions direction may require the relevant recognised professional body to take all necessary steps to secure that—

(a) the person is no longer authorised (whether fully or partially) to act as an insolvency practitioner;

(b) the person is no longer fully authorised to act as an insolvency practitioner but remains partially authorised to act as such either in relation to companies or individuals, as specified in the direction;

(c) the person's authorisation to act as an insolvency practitioner is suspended for the period specified in the direction or until such time as the requirements so specified are complied with;

(d) the person must comply with such other requirements as may be specified in the direction while acting as an insolvency practitioner;

(e) the person makes such contribution as may be specified in the direction to one or more creditors of a company, individual or insolvent partnership in relation to which the person is acting or has acted as an insolvency practitioner.

(4) A direct sanctions direction must not be given in relation to a person whose authorisation to act as an insolvency practitioner was granted by the Department of Enterprise, Trade and Investment in Northern Ireland (see section 390A(2)(b)).

(5) A direct sanctions direction must not specify a contribution as mentioned in subsection (3)(e) which is more than the remuneration that the person has received or will receive in respect of acting as an insolvency practitioner in the case.

(6) In this section "relevant recognised professional body" has the same meaning as in section 391O.]

NOTES

Inserted as noted to s 391O at **[9.421]**.

[General

[9.425]

391S Power for Secretary of State to obtain information

(1) A person mentioned in subsection (2) must give the Secretary of State such information as the Secretary of State may by notice in writing require for the exercise of the Secretary of State's functions under this Part.

(2) Those persons are—

(a) a recognised professional body;

(b) any individual who is or has been authorised under section 390A to act as an insolvency practitioner;

(c) any person who is connected to such an individual.

(3) A person is connected to an individual who is or has been authorised to act as an insolvency practitioner if, at any time during the authorisation—

(a) the person was an employee of the individual;

(b) the person acted on behalf of the individual in any other way;

(c) the person employed the individual;

(d) the person was a fellow employee of the individual's employer;

(e) in a case where the individual was employed by a firm, partnership or company, the person was a member of the firm or partnership or (as the case may be) a director of the company.

(4) In imposing a requirement under subsection (1) the Secretary of State may specify—

(a) the time period within which the information in question is to be given, and

(b) the manner in which it is to be verified.]

NOTES

Inserted, together with the preceding heading, by the Small Business, Enterprise and Employment Act 2015, s 142, as from 1 October 2015.

[9.426]

[391T Compliance orders

(1) If at any time it appears to the Secretary of State that—

(a) a recognised professional body has failed to comply with a requirement imposed on it by or by virtue of this Part, or

(b) any other person has failed to comply with a requirement imposed on the person by virtue of section 391S, the Secretary of State may make an application to the court.

(2) If, on an application under this section, the court decides that the body or other person has failed to comply with the requirement in question, it may order the body or person to take such steps as the court considers will secure that the requirement is complied with.

(3) In this section, "the court" means the High Court or, in Scotland, the Court of Session.]

NOTES

Inserted by the Small Business, Enterprise and Employment Act 2015, s 143, as from 1 October 2015.

392–398 (*Repealed by the Deregulation Act 2015, s 19, Sch 6, Pt 6, paras 17, 21, as from 1 October 2015.*)

PART XIV PUBLIC ADMINISTRATION (ENGLAND AND WALES)

[Adjudicators

[9.427]

398A Appointment etc of adjudicators and assistants

(1) The Secretary of State may appoint persons to the office of adjudicator.

(2) A person appointed under subsection (1)—

(a) is to be paid out of money provided by Parliament such salary as the Secretary of State may direct,

(b) holds office on such other terms and conditions as the Secretary of State may direct, and

(c) may be removed from office by a direction of the Secretary of State.

(3) A person who is authorised to act as an official receiver may not be appointed under subsection (1).

(4) The Secretary of State may appoint officers of the Secretary of State's department to assist adjudicators in the carrying out of their functions."]

NOTES

Inserted, together with the preceding heading, by the Enterprise and Regulatory Reform Act 2013, s 71(1), as from 6 April 2016.

Official Receivers

[9.428]

399 Appointment, etc of official receivers

(1) For the purposes of this Act the official receiver, in relation to any bankruptcy[, winding up[, individual voluntary arrangement, debt relief order or application for such an order]], is any person who by virtue of the following provisions of this section or section 401 below is authorised to act as the official receiver in relation to that bankruptcy[, winding up[, individual voluntary arrangement, debt relief order or application for such an order]].

(2) The Secretary of State may (subject to the approval of the Treasury as to numbers) appoint persons to the office of official receiver, and a person appointed to that office (whether under this section or section 70 of the Bankruptcy Act 1914)—

(a) shall be paid out of money provided by Parliament such salary as the Secretary of State may with the concurrence of the Treasury direct,

(b) shall hold office on such other terms and conditions as the Secretary of State may with the concurrence of the Treasury direct, and

(c) may be removed from office by a direction of the Secretary of State.

(3) Where a person holds the office of official receiver, the Secretary of State shall from time to time attach him either to the High Court or to [the county court].

(4) Subject to any directions under subsection (6) below, an official receiver attached to a particular court is the person authorised to act as the official receiver in relation to every bankruptcy[, winding up[, individual voluntary arrangement, debt relief order or application for such an order]] falling within the jurisdiction of that court.

(5) The Secretary of State shall ensure that there is, at all times, at least one official receiver attached to the High Court and at least one attached to [the county court]; but he may attach the same official receiver to [both] courts.

(6) The Secretary of State may give directions with respect to the disposal of the business of official receivers, and such directions may, in particular—

(a) authorise an official receiver attached to one court to act as the official receiver in relation to any case or description of cases falling within the jurisdiction of [the other] court;

(b) provide, where there is more than one official receiver authorised to act as the official receiver in relation to cases falling within the jurisdiction of any court, for the distribution of their business between or among themselves.

(7) A person who at the coming into force of section 222 of the Insolvency Act 1985 (replaced by this section) is an official receiver attached to a court shall continue in office after the coming into force of that section as an official receiver attached to that court under this section.

NOTES

Sub-s (1): words in first and third (outer) pairs of square brackets substituted by the Enterprise Act 2002, s 269, Sch 23, paras 1, 14, as from 1 April 2004. Words in second and fourth (inner) pairs of square brackets substituted by the Tribunals, Courts and Enforcement Act 2007, s 108(3), Sch 20, Pt 1, paras 1, 7, as from 6 April 2009.

Sub-ss (3), (5), (6): words in square brackets substituted by the Crime and Courts Act 2013, s 17, Sch 9, Pt 3, para 93(h)–(j), as from 22 April 2014.

Sub-s (4): words in first (outer) pair of square brackets substituted by the Enterprise Act 2002, s 269, Sch 23, paras 1, 14, as from 1 April 2004. Words in second (inner) pair of square brackets substituted by the Tribunals, Courts and Enforcement Act 2007, s 108(3), Sch 20, Pt 1, paras 1, 7, as from 6 April 2009.

[9.429]

400 Functions and status of official receivers

(1) In addition to any functions conferred on him by this Act, a person holding the office of official receiver shall carry out such other functions as may from time to time be conferred on him by the Secretary of State.

(2) In the exercise of the functions of his office a person holding the office of official receiver shall act under the general directions of the Secretary of State and shall also be an officer of the court in relation to which he exercises those functions.

(3) Any property vested in his official capacity in a person holding the office of official receiver shall, on his dying, ceasing to hold office or being otherwise succeeded in relation to the bankruptcy or winding up in question by another official receiver, vest in his successor without any conveyance, assignment or transfer.

[9.430]

401 Deputy official receivers and staff

(1) The Secretary of State may, if he thinks it expedient to do so in order to facilitate the disposal of the business of the official receiver attached to any court, appoint an officer of his department to act as deputy to that official receiver.

(2) Subject to any directions given by the Secretary of State under section 399 or 400, a person appointed to act as deputy to an official receiver has, on such conditions and for such period as may be specified in the terms of his appointment, the same status and functions as the official receiver to whom he is appointed deputy.

Accordingly, references in this Act (except section 399(1) to (5)) to an official receiver include a person appointed to act as his deputy.

(3) An appointment made under subsection (1) may be terminated at any time by the Secretary of State.

(4) The Secretary of State may, subject to the approval of the Treasury as to numbers and remuneration and as to the other terms and conditions of the appointments, appoint officers of his department to assist official receivers in the carrying out of their functions.

The Official Petitioner

[9.431]

402 Official Petitioner

(1) There continues to be an officer known as the Official Petitioner for the purpose of discharging, in relation to cases in which a criminal bankruptcy order is made, the functions assigned to him by or under this Act; and the Director of Public Prosecutions continues, by virtue of his office, to be the Official Petitioner.

(2) The functions of the Official Petitioner include the following—

- *(a) to consider whether, in a case in which a criminal bankruptcy order is made, it is in the public interest that he should himself present a petition under section 264(1)(d) of this Act;*
- *(b) to present such a petition in any case where he determines that it is in the public interest for him to do so;*
- *(c) to make payments, in such cases as he may determine, towards expenses incurred by other persons in connection with proceedings in pursuance of such a petition; and*
- *(d) to exercise, so far as he considers it in the public interest to do so, any of the powers conferred on him by or under this Act.*

(3) Any functions of the Official Petitioner may be discharged on his behalf by any person acting with his authority.

(4) Neither the Official Petitioner nor any person acting with his authority is liable to any action or proceeding in respect of anything done or omitted to be done in the discharge, or purported discharge, of the functions of the Official Petitioner.

(5) In this section "criminal bankruptcy order" means an order under section 39(1) of the Powers of Criminal Courts Act 1973.

NOTES

Repealed by the Criminal Justice Act 1988, s 170(2), Sch 16, as from a day to be appointed.

Insolvency Service finance, accounting and investment

[9.432]

403 Insolvency Services Account

(1) All money received by the Secretary of State in respect of proceedings under this Act as it applies to England and Wales shall be paid into the Insolvency Services Account kept by the Secretary of State with the Bank of England; and all payments out of money standing to the credit of the Secretary of State in that account shall be made by the Bank of England in such manner as he may direct.

(2) Whenever the cash balance standing to the credit of the Insolvency Services Account is in excess of the amount which in the opinion of the Secretary of State is required for the time being to answer demands in respect of bankrupts' estates or companies' estates, the Secretary of State shall—

- (a) notify the excess to the National Debt Commissioners, and
- (b) pay into the Insolvency Services Investment Account ("the Investment Account") kept by the Commissioners with the Bank of England the whole or any part of the excess as the Commissioners may require for investment in accordance with the following provisions of this Part.

(3) Whenever any part of the money so invested is, in the opinion of the Secretary of State, required to answer any demand in respect of bankrupt's estates or companies' estates, he shall notify to the National Debt Commissioners the amount so required and the Commissioners—

- (a) shall thereupon repay to the Secretary of State such sum as may be required to the credit of the Insolvency Services Account, and
- (b) for that purpose may direct the sale of such part of the securities in which the money has been invested as may be necessary.

[9.433]

404 Investment Account

Any money standing to the credit of the Investment Account (including any money received by the National Debt Commissioners by way of interest on or proceeds of any investment under this section) may be invested by the Commissioners, in accordance with such directions as may be given by the Treasury, in any manner for the time being specified in Part II of Schedule 1 to the Trustee Investments Act 1961.

405 *(Repealed by the Enterprise Act 2002, ss 272(1), 278(2), Sch 26, as from 1 April 2004.)*

[9.434]

406 [Interest on money received by liquidators or trustees in bankruptcy and invested]

Where under rules made by virtue of paragraph 16 of Schedule 8 to this Act (investment of money received by company liquidators) [or paragraph 21 of Schedule 9 to this Act (investment of money received by trustee in bankruptcy) a company or a bankrupt's estate] has become entitled to any sum by way of interest, the Secretary of State shall certify that sum and the amount of tax payable on it to the National Debt Commissioners; and the Commissioners shall pay, out of the Investment Account—

(a) into the Insolvency Services Account, the sum so certified less the amount of tax so certified, and

(b) to the Commissioners of Inland Revenue, the amount of tax so certified.

NOTES

Words in square brackets substituted by the Insolvency Act 2000, s 13(2), as from 2 April 2001.

Commissioners of Inland Revenue: a reference to the Commissioners of Inland Revenue is now to be taken as a reference to the Commissioners for Her Majesty's Revenue and Customs; see the Commissioners for Revenue and Customs Act 2005, s 50(1), (7).

[9.435]

407 Unclaimed dividends and undistributed balances

(1) The Secretary of State shall from time to time pay into the Consolidated Fund out of the Insolvency Services Account so much of the sums standing to the credit of that Account as represents—

(a) dividends which were declared before such date as the Treasury may from time to time determine and have not been claimed, and

(b) balances ascertained before that date which are too small to be divided among the persons entitled to them.

(2) For the purposes of this section the sums standing to the credit of the Insolvency Services Account are deemed to include any sums paid out of that Account and represented by any sums or securities standing to the credit of the Investment Account.

(3) The Secretary of State may require the National Debt Commissioners to pay out of the Investment Account into the Insolvency Services Account the whole or part of any sum which he is required to pay out of that account under subsection (1); and the Commissioners may direct the sale of such securities standing to the credit of the Investment Account as may be necessary for that purpose.

[9.436]

[408 Adjustment of balances

(1) The Treasury may direct the payment out of the Consolidated Fund of sums into—

(a) the Insolvency Services Account;

(b) the Investment Account.

(2) The Treasury shall certify to the House of Commons the reason for any payment under subsection (1).

(3) The Secretary of State may pay sums out of the Insolvency Services Account into the Consolidated Fund.

(4) The National Debt Commissioners may pay sums out of the Investment Account into the Consolidated Fund.]

NOTES

Substituted by the Enterprise Act 2002, s 272(2), as from 1 April 2004.

[9.437]

409 Annual financial statement and audit

(1) The National Debt Commissioners shall for each year ending on 31st March prepare a statement of the sums credited and debited to the Investment Account in such form and manner as the Treasury may direct and shall transmit it to the Comptroller and Auditor General before the end of November next following the year.

(2) The Secretary of State shall for each year ending 31st March prepare a statement of the sums received or paid by him under section 403 above in such form and manner as the Treasury may direct and shall transmit each statement to the Comptroller and Auditor General before the end of November next following the year.

(3) Every such statement shall include such additional information as the Treasury may direct.

(4) The Comptroller and Auditor General shall examine, certify and report on every such statement and shall lay copies of it, and of his report, before Parliament.

Supplementary

[9.438]

410 Extent of this Part

This Part of this Act extends to England and Wales only.

PART XV SUBORDINATE LEGISLATION

General insolvency rules

[9.439]

411 Company insolvency rules

(1) Rules may be made—

(a) in relation to England and Wales, by the Lord Chancellor with the concurrence of the Secretary of State [and, in the case of rules that affect court procedure, with the concurrence of the Lord Chief Justice], or

(b) in relation to Scotland, by the Secretary of State,

for the purpose of giving effect to [Parts A1] to VII of this Act [or the [EU Regulation]].

[(1A) Rules may also be made for the purpose of giving effect to Part 2 of the Banking Act 2009 (bank insolvency orders); and rules for that purpose shall be made—

(a) in relation to England and Wales, by the Lord Chancellor with the concurrence of—

(i) the Treasury, and

(ii) in the case of rules that affect court procedure, the Lord Chief Justice, or

(b) in relation to Scotland, by the Treasury.]

[(1B) Rules may also be made for the purpose of giving effect to Part 3 of the Banking Act 2009 (bank administration); and rules for that purpose shall be made—

(a) in relation to England and Wales, by the Lord Chancellor with the concurrence of—

(i) the Treasury, and

(ii) in the case of rules that affect court procedure, the Lord Chief Justice, or

(b) in relation to Scotland, by the Treasury.]

(2) Without prejudice to the generality of subsection (1), [(1A)] [or (1B)] or to any provision of those Parts by virtue of which rules under this section may be made with respect to any matter, rules under this section may contain—

(a) any such provision as is specified in Schedule 8 to this Act or corresponds to provision contained immediately before the coming into force of section 106 of the Insolvency Act 1985 in rules made, or having effect as if made, under section 663(1) or (2) of [the Companies Act 1985] (old winding-up rules), and

(b) such incidental, supplemental and transitional provisions as may appear to the Lord Chancellor or, as the case may be, the Secretary of State [or the Treasury] necessary or expedient.

[(2A) For the purposes of subsection (2), a reference in Schedule 8 to this Act to doing anything under or for the purposes of a provision of this Act includes a reference to doing anything under or for the purposes of the [EU Regulation] (in so far as the provision of this Act relates to a matter to which the [EU Regulation] applies).

(2B) Rules under this section for the purpose of giving effect to the [EU Regulation] may not create [a new relevant offence].]

[(2C) For the purposes of subsection (2), a reference in Schedule 8 to this Act to doing anything under or for the purposes of a provision of this Act includes a reference to doing anything under or for the purposes of Part 2 of the Banking Act 2009.]

[(2D) For the purposes of subsection (2), a reference in Schedule 8 to this Act to doing anything under or for the purposes of a provision of this Act includes a reference to doing anything under or for the purposes of Part 3 of the Banking Act 2009.]

(3) In Schedule 8 to this Act "liquidator" includes a provisional liquidator [or bank liquidator] [or administrator]; and references above in this section to [Parts A1] to VII of this Act [or Part 2 [or 3] of the Banking Act 2009] are to be read as including [the Companies Acts] so far as relating to, and to matters connected with or arising out of, the insolvency or winding up of companies.

[(3A) In this section references to Part 2 or 3 of the Banking Act 2009 include references to those Parts as applied to building societies (see section 90C of the Building Societies Act 1986).]

(4) Rules under this section shall be made by statutory instrument subject to annulment in pursuance of a resolution of either House of Parliament.

(5) Regulations made by the Secretary of State [or the Treasury] under a power conferred by rules under this section shall be made by statutory instrument and, after being made, shall be laid before each House of Parliament.

(6) Nothing in this section prejudices any power to make rules of court.

[(7) The Lord Chief Justice may nominate a judicial office holder (as defined in section 109(4) of the Constitutional Reform Act 2005) to exercise his functions under this section.]

NOTES

Sub-s (1) is amended as follows:

Words in square brackets in para (a) inserted by the Constitutional Reform Act 2005, s 15, Sch 4, Pt 1, paras 185, 188(1), (2), as from 3 April 2006.

Words "Parts A1" in square brackets substituted by the Corporate Insolvency and Governance Act 2020, s 2(1), Sch 3, paras 1, 22(1), (2), as from 26 June 2020 (for transitional provisions, see s 2(2), (3) of the 2020 Act (at **[9.533]**) which provides that (without prejudice to the Interpretation Act 1978, s 16) nothing in the 2020 Act affects the operation of this Act, or any other enactment, in relation to a moratorium under Sch A1 to this Act which comes into force before the repeal of that Schedule by Sch 3 to the 2020 Act (ie, 26 June 2020)).

Words in third (outer) pair of square brackets inserted by the Insolvency Act 1986 (Amendment) Regulations 2002, SI 2002/1037, regs 2, 3(1), as from 3 May 2002.

Words in fourth (inner) pair of square brackets substituted by the Insolvency Amendment (EU 2015/848) Regulations 2017, SI 2017/702, regs 2, 3, Schedule, Pt 1, paras 1, 24, as from 26 June 2017, except in relation to proceedings opened before that date.

Sub-ss (1A), (1B), (2C), (2D): inserted by the Banking Act 2009, ss 125(1), (2), (4), 160(1), (2), (4), as from 17 February 2009 (in so far as conferring or relating to any power to make subordinate legislation), and as from 21 February 2009 (otherwise).

Sub-s (2): words in square brackets in the introductory wording and in para (b) inserted by the Banking Act 2009, ss 125(1), (3), (6), 160(1), (3), as from 17 February 2009 (in so far as conferring or relating to any power to make subordinate legislation), and as from 21 February 2009 (otherwise). Words in square brackets in para (a) substituted by the Companies Act 2006 (Consequential Amendments, Transitional Provisions and Savings) Order 2009, SI 2009/1941, art 2(1), Sch 1, para 79, as from 1 October 2009 (for effect see the note to s 7A at **[9.145]**).

Sub-ss (2A), (2B): inserted by SI 2002/1037, regs 2, 3(2), as from 3 May 2002. Words "EU Regulation" in square brackets in both subsections substituted by SI 2017/702, regs 2, 3, Schedule, Pt 1, paras 1, 24, as from 26 June 2017, except in relation to proceedings opened before that date. Words "a new relevant offence" in square brackets in sub-s (2B) substituted by the Insolvency (Amendment) (EU Exit) Regulations 2019, SI 2019/146, reg 2, Schedule, Pt 2, paras 16, 37, as from IP completion day (as defined in the European Union (Withdrawal Agreement) Act 2020, s 39) (for savings, see reg 4 of the 2019 Regulations at **[12.82]**).

Sub-s (3) is amended as follows:

Words "Parts A1" in square brackets substituted by the Corporate Insolvency and Governance Act 2020, s 2(1), Sch 3, paras 1, 22(1), (3), as from 26 June 2020 (for transitional provisions, see the first note relating to the 2020 Act above).

Words in the final pair of square brackets substituted by the Companies Act 2006 (Commencement No 3, Consequential Amendments, Transitional Provisions and Savings) Order 2007, SI 2007/2194, art 10(1), Sch 4, Pt 3, para 44, as from 1 October 2007.

All other words in square brackets were inserted by the Banking Act 2009, ss 125(1), (5). 160(1), (5), as from 21 February 2009.

Sub-s (3A): inserted by the Building Societies (Insolvency and Special Administration) Order 2009, SI 2009/805, art 13, as from 30 March 2009.

Sub-s (5): words in square brackets inserted by the Banking Act 2009, ss 125(1), (3), (6), 160(1), (3), as from 17 February 2009 (in so far as conferring or relating to any power to make subordinate legislation), and as from 21 February 2009 (otherwise).

Sub-s (7): added by the Constitutional Reform Act 2005, s 15, Sch 4, Pt 1, paras 185, 188(1), (3), as from 3 April 2006.

See further, the Scotland Act 1998 (Insolvency Functions) Order 2018, SI 2018/174. The 2018 Order provides that specific insolvency functions which relate to reserved matters under Schedule 5 to the Scotland Act 1998, that are exercised by a Minister of the Crown in or as regards Scotland, are to be exercisable by both the Scottish Ministers and a Minister of the Crown. The specific insolvency functions to which the Order applies are the making of winding up rules for Scotland in relation to companies under sub-ss (1)(b) and (2) above, and the making of winding up rules for Scotland which apply to incorporated friendly societies under those subsections (as applied by the Friendly Societies Act 1992,Sch 10, para 69).

Rules: many sets of Rules have been made under this section, many of them outside the scope of this work. The most relevant ones are the following: the Insolvency (Scotland) Rules 1986, SI 1986/1915 (revoked subject to savings and transitional provisions and savings as from 6 April 2019); the Insolvency Rules 1986, SI 1986/1925 at **[10.1]** (revoked subject to transitional provisions and savings as from 6 April 2017); the Insolvent Companies (Disqualification of Unfit Directors) Proceedings Rules 1987, SI 1987/2023 at **[10.2]**; the Insurers (Winding Up) Rules 2001, SI 2001/3635; the Insurers (Winding Up) (Scotland) Rules 2001, SI 2001/4040; the Bank Administration (Scotland) Rules 2009, SI 2009/350; the Bank Insolvency (Scotland) Rules 2009, SI 2009/351; the Bank Insolvency (England and Wales) Rules 2009, SI 2009/356; the Bank Administration (England and Wales) Rules 2009, SI 2009/357; the Companies (Unfair Prejudice Applications) Proceedings Rules 2009, SI 2009/2469 at **[10.420]**; the Investment Bank Special Administration (England and Wales) Rules 2011, SI 2011/1301; the Investment Bank Special Administration (Scotland) Rules 2011, SI 2011/2262; the Insolvent Companies (Reports on Conduct of Directors) (England and Wales) Rules 2016, SI 2016/180 at **[10.432]**; the Insolvent Companies (Reports on Conduct of Directors) (Scotland) Rules 2016, SI 2016/185 at **[10.442]**; the Insolvency (England and Wales) Rules 2016, SI 2016/1024 at **[10.474]**; the Financial Market Infrastructure Administration (England and Wales) Rules 2018, SI 2018/833; the Insolvency (Scotland) (Company Voluntary Arrangements and Administration) Rules 2018, SI 2018/1082; the Insolvency (Scotland) (Receivership and Winding up) Rules 2018, SSI 2018/347; the Payment and Electronic Money Institution Insolvency (England and Wales) Rules 2021, SI 2021/1178.

Regulations: the Insolvency Regulations 1994, SI 1994/2507 at **[10.34]**.

412 (*Section 412 (Individual insolvency rules: England and Wales) is outside the scope of this work.*)

[9.440]

413 Insolvency Rules Committee

(1) The committee established under section 10 of the Insolvency Act 1976 (advisory committee on bankruptcy and winding-up rules) continues to exist for the purpose of being consulted under this section.

(2) The Lord Chancellor shall consult the committee before making any rules under section 411 or 412 [other than rules which contain a statement that the only provision made by the rules is provision applying rules made under section 411, with or without modifications, for the purposes of provision made by [any of sections 23 to 26 of the Water Industry Act 1991 or Schedule 3 to that Act]] [or by any of sections 59 to 65 of, or Schedule 6 or 7 to, the Railways Act 1993].

(3) Subject to the next subsection, the committee shall consist of—

(a) a judge of the High Court attached to the Chancery Division;
(b) a circuit judge;
(c) [an insolvency and companies court judge];
[(d) a district judge;]
(e) a practising barrister;
(f) a practising solicitor; and
(g) a practising accountant;

and the appointment of any person as a member of the committee shall be made [in accordance with subsection (3A) or (3B)].

[(3A) The Lord Chief Justice must appoint the persons referred to in paragraphs (a) to (d) of subsection (3), after consulting the Lord Chancellor.

(3B) The Lord Chancellor must appoint the persons referred to in paragraphs (e) to (g) of subsection (3), after consulting the Lord Chief Justice.]

(4) The Lord Chancellor may appoint as additional members of the committee any persons appearing to him to have qualifications or experience that would be of value to the committee in considering any matter with which it is concerned.

[(5) The Lord Chief Justice may nominate a judicial office holder (as defined in section 109(4) of the Constitutional Reform Act 2005) to exercise his functions under this section.]

NOTES

Sub-s (2): words in first (outer) pair of square brackets substituted by the Water Act 1989, s 190(1), Sch 25, para 78(2), as from 1 September 1989. Words in second (inner) pair of square brackets substituted by the Water Consolidation (Consequential Provisions) Act 1991, s 2(1), Sch 1, para 46, as from 1 December 1991. Words in third pair of square brackets added by the Railways Act 1993, s 152, Sch 12, para 25, as from 1 April 1994.

Sub-s (3): words in square brackets in para (c) substituted by the Alteration of Judicial Titles (Registrar in Bankruptcy of the High Court) Order 2018, SI 2018/130, art 2, Schedule, para 7(b), as from 26 February 2018. Para (d) substituted by the Crime and Courts Act 2013, s 17, Sch 9, Pt 3, para 93(k), as from 22 April 2014. Other words in square brackets substituted by the Constitutional Reform Act 2005, s 15, Sch 4, Pt 1, paras 185, 190(1), (2), as from 3 April 2006.

Sub-ss (3A), (3B), (5): inserted and added respectively by the Constitutional Reform Act 2005, s 15, Sch 4, Pt 1, paras 185, 190(1), (3), (4), as from 3 April 2006.

Fees orders

[9.441]

414 Fees orders (company insolvency proceedings)

(1) There shall be paid in respect of—

(a) proceedings under any of [Parts A1] to VII of this Act, and

(b) the performance by the official receiver or the Secretary of State of functions under those Parts,

such fees as the competent authority may with the sanction of the Treasury by order direct.

(2) That authority is—

(a) in relation to England and Wales, the Lord Chancellor, and

(b) in relation to Scotland, the Secretary of State.

(3) The Treasury may by order direct by whom and in what manner the fees are to be collected and accounted for.

(4) The Lord Chancellor may, with the sanction of the Treasury, by order provide for sums to be deposited, by such persons, in such manner and in such circumstances as may be specified in the order, by way of security for fees payable by virtue of this section.

(5) An order under this section may contain such incidental, supplemental and transitional provisions as may appear to the Lord Chancellor, the Secretary of State or (as the case may be) the Treasury necessary or expedient.

(6) An order under this section shall be made by statutory instrument and, after being made, shall be laid before each House of Parliament.

(7) Fees payable by virtue of this section shall be paid into the Consolidated Fund.

(8) References in subsection (1) to [Parts A1] to VII of this Act are to be read as including [the Companies Acts] so far as relating to, and to matters connected with or arising out of, the insolvency or winding up of companies.

[(8A) This section applies in relation to Part 2 of the Banking Act 2009 (bank insolvency) as in relation to Parts I to VII of this Act.]

[(8B) This section applies in relation to Part 3 of the Banking Act 2009 (bank administration) as in relation to Parts I to VII of this Act.]

[(8C) In subsections (8A) and (8B) the reference to Parts 2 and 3 of the Banking Act 2009 include references to those Parts as applied to building societies (see section 90C of the Building Societies Act 1986).]

(9) Nothing in this section prejudices any power to make rules of court; and the application of this section to Scotland is without prejudice to section 2 of the Courts of Law Fees (Scotland) Act 1895.

NOTES

Sub-s (1): words "Parts A1" in square brackets substituted by the Corporate Insolvency and Governance Act 2020, s 2(1), Sch 3, paras 1, 23(1), (2), as from 26 June 2020 (for transitional provisions, see s 2(2), (3) of the 2020 Act (at **[9.533]**) which provides that (without prejudice to the Interpretation Act 1978, s 16) nothing in the 2020 Act affects the operation of this Act, or any other enactment, in relation to a moratorium under Sch A1 to this Act which comes into force before the repeal of that Schedule by Sch 3 to the 2020 Act (ie, 26 June 2020)).

Sub-s (8): words "Parts A1" in square brackets substituted by the Corporate Insolvency and Governance Act 2020, s 2(1), Sch 3, paras 1, 23(1), (3), as from 26 June 2020 (for transitional provisions, see the first note relating to the 2020 Act above). Words in second pair of square brackets substituted by the Companies Act 2006 (Commencement No 3, Consequential Amendments, Transitional Provisions and Savings) Order 2007, SI 2007/2194, art 10(1), Sch 4, Pt 3, para 44, as from 1 October 2007.

Sub-ss (8A), (8B): inserted by the Banking Act 2009, ss 126, 161, as from 17 February 2009 (in so far as conferring or relating to any power to make subordinate legislation), and as from 21 February 2009 (otherwise).

Sub-s (8C): inserted by the Building Societies (Insolvency and Special Administration) Order 2009, SI 2009/805, art 14, as from 30 March 2009.

Sub-s (9): repealed, in relation to Scotland, by the Courts Reform (Scotland) Act 2014 (Consequential Provisions) Order 2015, SSI 2015/150, art 2, Schedule, Pt 1, para 4, as from 1 April 2015.

Orders: the main Orders made under this section are the following: the Civil Proceedings Fees Order 2008, SI 2008/1053; the Insolvency Proceedings (Fees) Order 2016, SI 2016/692 at **[10.457]**; the Disqualified Directors Compensation Orders (Fees) (England and Wales) Order 2016, SI 2016/1047; the Disqualified Directors Compensation Orders (Fees) (Scotland) Order 2016, SI 2016/1048.

415 *(Section 415 (Fees orders (individual insolvency proceedings: England and Wales) is outside the scope of this work.)*

[9.442]

[415A Fees orders (general)

[(A1) The Secretary of State—

(a) may by order require a person or body to pay a fee in connection with the grant or maintenance of a designation of that person or body as a competent authority under section 251U, and

(b) may refuse to grant, or may withdraw, any such designation where a fee is not paid.]

(1) The Secretary of State—

(a) may by order require a body to pay a fee in connection with the grant or maintenance of recognition of the body under section 391 [or (2)], and

(b) may refuse recognition, or revoke an order of recognition under section 391(1) by a further order, where a fee is not paid.

[(1A) Fees under subsection (1) may vary according to whether the body is recognised under section 391(1) (body providing full and partial authorisation) or under section 391(2) (body providing partial authorisation).]

[(1B) In setting under subsection (1) the amount of a fee in connection with maintenance of recognition, the matters to which the Secretary of State may have regard include, in particular, the costs of the Secretary of State in connection with any functions under sections 391D, 391E, 391J, 391K and 391N.]

(2) . . .

(3) The Secretary of State may by order require the payment of fees in respect of—

(a) the operation of the Insolvency Services Account;

(b) payments into and out of that Account.

(4) The following provisions of section 414 apply to fees under this section as they apply to fees under that section—

(a) subsection (3) (manner of payment),

(b) subsection (5) (additional provision),

(c) subsection (6) (statutory instrument),

(d) subsection (7) (payment into Consolidated Fund), and

(e) subsection (9) (saving for rules of court).

[(5) Section 391M applies for the purposes of an order under subsection (1)(b) as it applies for the purposes of a revocation order made under section 391L.]]

NOTES

Inserted by the Enterprise Act 2002, s 270(1), as from 18 December 2003, subject to s 270(2) of that Act which provides that an Order made under this section may relate to the maintenance of recognition or authorisation granted before that date.

Sub-s (A1): inserted by the Tribunals, Courts and Enforcement Act 2007, s 108(3), Sch 20, Pt 1, paras 1, 10, as from 24 February 2009 (for the purpose of making orders), and as from 6 April 2009 (otherwise).

Sub-s (1): words in square brackets inserted by the Deregulation Act 2015, s 17(1), (5)(a), as from 1 October 2015.

Sub-s (1A): inserted by the Deregulation Act 2015, s 17(1), (5)(b), as from 1 October 2015.

Sub-ss (1B), (5): inserted and added respectively by the Small Business, Enterprise and Employment Act 2015, ss 139(2), 140(2), as from 1 October 2015.

Sub-s (2): repealed by the Deregulation Act 2015, s 19, Sch 6, Pt 6, para 22(1), (5), as from 1 October 2015.

Orders: the main Order made under this section is the Insolvency Practitioners and Insolvency Services Account (Fees) Order 2003, SI 2003/3363.

Specification, increase and reduction of money sums relevant in the operation of this Act

[9.443]

[415B Monetary limits (company moratorium)

(1) The Secretary of State may by regulations increase or reduce any of the money sums for the time being specified in the following provisions of Part A1—

(a) section A25(1) (maximum amount of credit which company may obtain without disclosing moratorium);
(b) section A28(2) (maximum amount for certain payments without obtaining monitor consent etc);
(c) section A46(2) (minimum value of company property concealed or fraudulently removed, affecting criminal liability of company's officer).

(2) Regulations under this section may contain such transitional provisions as may appear to the Secretary of State necessary or expedient.

(3) Regulations under this section are to be made by statutory instrument subject to annulment in pursuance of a resolution of either House of Parliament.]

NOTES

Commencement: 26 June 2020.

Inserted by the Corporate Insolvency and Governance Act 2020, s 2(1), Sch 3, paras 1, 24, as from 26 June 2020 (for transitional provisions, see s 2(2), (3) of the 2020 Act (at **[9.533]**) which provides that (without prejudice to the Interpretation Act 1978, s 16) nothing in the 2020 Act affects the operation of this Act, or any other enactment, in relation to a moratorium under Sch A1 to this Act which comes into force before the repeal of that Schedule by Sch 3 to the 2020 Act (ie, 26 June 2020)).

[9.444]

416 Monetary limits (companies winding up)

(1) The Secretary of State may by order in a statutory instrument increase or reduce any of the money sums for the time being specified in the following provisions in the first Group of Parts—

section 117(2) (amount of company's share capital determining whether county court has jurisdiction to wind it up);
section 120(3) (the equivalent as respects sheriff court jurisdiction in Scotland);
section 123(1)(a) (minimum debt for service of demand on company by unpaid creditor);
section 184(3) (minimum value of judgment, affecting sheriff's duties on levying execution);
section 206(1)(a) and (b) (minimum value of company property concealed or fraudulently removed, affecting criminal liability of company's officer).

(2) An order under this section may contain such transitional provisions as may appear to the Secretary of State necessary or expedient.

(3) No order under this section increasing or reducing any of the money sums for the time being specified in section 117(2), 120(3) or 123(1)(a) shall be made unless a draft of the order has been laid before and approved by a resolution of each House of Parliament.

(4) A statutory instrument containing an order under this section, other than an order to which subsection (3) applies, is subject to annulment in pursuance of a resolution of either House of Parliament.

NOTES

Orders: the Insolvency Proceedings (Monetary Limits) Order 1986, SI 1986/1996 (increasing the sums specified in ss 184(3), 206(1)(a), (b)).

[9.445]

417 Money sum in s 222

The Secretary of State may by regulations in a statutory instrument increase or reduce the money sum for the time being specified in section 222(1) (minimum debt for service of demand on unregistered company by unpaid creditor); but such regulations shall not be made unless a draft of the statutory instrument containing them has been approved by resolution of each House of Parliament.

417A, 418 *(Section 417A (Money sums (company moratorium)) was originally inserted by the Insolvency Act 2000, s 1, Sch 1, paras 1, 10, as from 1 January 2003. Subsequently repealed by the Corporate Insolvency and Governance Act 2020, s 2(1), Sch 3, paras 1, 25, as from 26 June 2020. For transitional provisions, see s 2(2), (3) of the 2020 Act (at* **[9.533]***) which provides that (without prejudice to the Interpretation Act 1978, s 16) nothing in the 2020 Act affects the operation of this Act, or any other enactment, in relation to a moratorium under Sch A1 to this Act which comes into force before the repeal of that Schedule by Sch 3 to the 2020 Act (ie, 26 June 2020). Section 418 (Monetary limits – bankruptcy) is outside the scope of this work.)*

Insolvency practice

[9.446]

419 Regulations for purposes of Part XIII

(1) The Secretary of State may make regulations for the purpose of giving effect to Part XIII of this Act; and "prescribed" in that Part means prescribed by regulations made by the Secretary of State.

(2) Without prejudice to the generality of subsection (1) or to any provision of that Part by virtue of which regulations may be made with respect to any matter, regulations under this section may contain—

(a) provision as to the matters to be taken into account in determining whether a person is a fit and proper person to act as an insolvency practitioner;

(b) provision prohibiting a person from so acting in prescribed cases, being cases in which a conflict of interest will or may arise;

(c) provision imposing requirements with respect to—

 (i) the preparation and keeping by a person who acts as an insolvency practitioner of prescribed books, accounts and other records, and

 (ii) the production of those books, accounts and records to prescribed persons;

(d) provision conferring power on prescribed persons—

 (i) to require any person who acts or has acted as an insolvency practitioner to answer any inquiry in relation to a case in which he is so acting or has so acted, and

 (ii) to apply to a court to examine such a person or any other person on oath concerning such a case;

(e) provision making non-compliance with any of the regulations a criminal offence; and

(f) such incidental, supplemental and transitional provisions as may appear to the Secretary of State necessary or expedient.

(3) Any power conferred by Part XIII or this Part to make regulations, rules or orders is exercisable by statutory instrument subject to annulment by resolution of either House of Parliament.

(4) Any rule or regulation under Part XIII or this Part may make different provision with respect to different cases or descriptions of cases, including different provision for different areas.

[(5) In making regulations under this section, the Secretary of State must have regard to the regulatory objectives (as defined by section 391C(3)).]

NOTES

Sub-s (5): added by the Small Business, Enterprise and Employment Act 2015, s 138(2), as from 1 October 2015.

Regulations: the Insolvency Practitioners (Recognised Professional Bodies) Order 1986, SI 1986/1764; the Insolvency Practitioners Regulations 2005, SI 2005/524; the Provision of Services (Insolvency Practitioners) Regulations 2009, SI 2009/3081; the Insolvency Practitioners (Amendment) Regulations 2015, SI 2015/391; the Insolvency Practitioners (Recognised Professional Bodies) (Revocation of Recognition) Order 2021, SI 2021/110.

Other order making powers

[9.447]

420 Insolvent partnerships

(1) The Lord Chancellor may, by order made with the concurrence of the Secretary of State [and the Lord Chief Justice], provide that such provisions of this Act as may be specified in the order shall apply in relation to insolvent partnerships with such modifications as may be so specified.

[(1A) An order under this section may make provision in relation to the [EU Regulation].

(1B) But provision made by virtue of this section in relation to the [EU Regulation] may not create [a new relevant offence].]

(2) An order under this section may make different provision for different cases and may contain such incidental, supplemental and transitional provisions as may appear to the Lord Chancellor [and the Lord Chief Justice] necessary or expedient.

(3) An order under this section shall be made by statutory instrument subject to annulment in pursuance of a resolution of either House of Parliament.

[(4) The Lord Chief Justice may nominate a judicial office holder (as defined in section 109(4) of the Constitutional Reform Act 2005) to exercise his functions under this section.]

NOTES

Sub-ss (1), (2): words in square brackets inserted by the Constitutional Reform Act 2005, s 15(1), Sch 4, Pt 1, paras 185, 191(1)–(3), as from 3 April 2006.

Sub-ss (1A), (1B): inserted by the Insolvency Act 1986 (Amendment) Regulations 2002, SI 2002/1037, regs 2, 3(5), as from 3 May 2002. Words "EU Regulation" in square brackets in both subsections substituted by the Insolvency Amendment (EU 2015/848) Regulations 2017, SI 2017/702, regs 2, 3, Schedule, Pt 1, paras 1, 26, as from 26 June 2017, except in relation to proceedings opened before that date. Words "a new relevant offence" in square brackets in sub-s (1B) substituted by the Insolvency (Amendment) (EU Exit) Regulations 2019, SI 2019/146, reg 2, Schedule, Pt 2, paras 16, 39, as from IP completion day (as defined in the European Union (Withdrawal Agreement) Act 2020, s 39) (for savings, see reg 4 of the 2019 Regulations at **[12.82]**).

Sub-s (4): added by the Constitutional Reform Act 2005, s 15(1), Sch 4, Pt 1, paras 185, 191(1), (4), as from 3 April 2006.

Orders: the main Order under this section is the Insolvent Partnerships Order 1994, SI 1994/2421.

421, 421A (*Section 421 (Insolvent estates of deceased persons) and s 421A (Insolvent estates – joint tenancies) are outside the scope of this work.*)

[9.448]

422 [Formerly authorised banks]

[(1) The Secretary of State may by order made with the concurrence of the Treasury and after consultation with the [Financial Conduct Authority and the Prudential Regulation Authority] provide that specified provisions in the first Group of Parts shall apply with specified modifications in relation to any person who—

(a) has a liability in respect of a deposit which he accepted in accordance with the Banking Act 1979 (c 37) or 1987 (c 22), but
(b) does not have permission under [Part 4A] of the Financial Services and Markets Act 2000 (c 8) (regulated activities) to accept deposits.

(1A) Subsection (1)(b) shall be construed in accordance with—
(a) section 22 of the Financial Services and Markets Act 2000 (classes of regulated activity and categories of investment),
(b) any relevant order under that section, and
(c) Schedule 2 to that Act (regulated activities).]

[(1A) . . .]

(2) An order under this section may make different provision for different cases and may contain such incidental, supplemental and transitional provisions as may appear to the Secretary of State necessary or expedient.

(3) An order under this section shall be made by statutory instrument subject to annulment in pursuance of a resolution of either House of Parliament.

NOTES

Section heading: substituted by the Financial Services and Markets Act 2000 (Consequential Amendments) Order 2002, SI 2002/1555, art 16(1), (2), as from 3 July 2002.

Sub-s (1): substituted, together with first sub-s (1A), for the original sub-s (1), by the Enterprise Act 2002, s 248(3), Sch 17, paras 9, 35, as from 15 September 2003 (for savings and transitional provisions, see the note to s 8 at **[9.147]**). Words in square brackets substituted by the Financial Services Act 2012, s 114(1), Sch 18, Pt 2, paras 51, 53, as from 1 April 2013.

First sub-s (1A): substituted as noted to sub-s (1) above.

Second sub-s (1A): originally inserted by SI 2002/1555, art 16(1), (4), as from 3 July 2002. Subsequently repealed by the Enterprise Act 2002 (Insolvency) Order 2003, SI 2003/2096, arts 4, 6, Schedule, Pt 1, paras 8, 11, as from 15 September 2003, except in relation to any case where a petition for an administration order was presented before that date.

Banking Act 1987: repealed by SI 2001/3649, art 3(1)(d), as from 1 December 2001.

Orders: the Banks (Former Authorised Institutions) (Insolvency) Order 2006, SI 2006/3107.

[9.449]
[422A Meaning of "relevant offence"

In this Part "relevant offence" means a criminal offence punishable with imprisonment for more than two years or punishable on summary conviction with imprisonment for more than three months or with a fine of more than level 5 on the standard scale (if not calculated on a daily basis) or with a fine of more than £100 a day.]

NOTES

Commencement: IP completion day (as defined in the European Union (Withdrawal Agreement) Act 2020, s 39).

Inserted by the Insolvency (Amendment) (EU Exit) Regulations 2019, SI 2019/146, reg 2, Schedule, Pt 2, paras 16, 41, as from IP completion day (as defined in the European Union (Withdrawal Agreement) Act 2020, s 39) (for savings, see reg 4 of the 2019 Regulations at **[12.82]**).

PART XVI PROVISIONS AGAINST DEBT AVOIDANCE (ENGLAND AND WALES ONLY)

[9.450]
423 Transactions defrauding creditors

(1) This section relates to transactions entered into at an undervalue; and a person enters into such a transaction with another person if—
(a) he makes a gift to the other person or he otherwise enters into a transaction with the other on terms that provide for him to receive no consideration;
(b) he enters into a transaction with the other in consideration of marriage [or the formation of a civil partnership]; or
(c) he enters into a transaction with the other for a consideration the value of which, in money or money's worth, is significantly less than the value, in money or money's worth, of the consideration provided by himself.

(2) Where a person has entered into such a transaction, the court may, if satisfied under the next subsection, make such order as it thinks fit for—
(a) restoring the position to what it would have been if the transaction had not been entered into, and
(b) protecting the interests of persons who are victims of the transaction.

(3) In the case of a person entering into such a transaction, an order shall only be made if the court is satisfied that it was entered into by him for the purpose—
(a) of putting assets beyond the reach of a person who is making, or may at some time make, a claim against him, or
(b) of otherwise prejudicing the interests of such a person in relation to the claim which he is making or may make.

(4) In this section "the court" means the High Court or—
(a) if the person entering into the transaction is an individual, any other court which would have jurisdiction in relation to a bankruptcy petition relating to him;
(b) if that person is a body capable of being wound up under Part IV or V of this Act, any other court having jurisdiction to wind it up.

(5) In relation to a transaction at an undervalue, references here and below to a victim of the transaction are to a person who is, or is capable of being, prejudiced by it; and in the following two sections the person entering into the transaction is referred to as "the debtor".

NOTES

Sub-s (1): words in square brackets inserted by the Civil Partnership Act 2004, s 261(1), Sch 27, para 121, as from 5 December 2005.

[9.451]

424 Those who may apply for an order under s 423

(1) An application for an order under section 423 shall not be made in relation to a transaction except—

(a) in a case where the debtor has been [made] bankrupt or is a body corporate which is being wound up or [is in administration], by the official receiver, by the trustee of the bankrupt's estate or the liquidator or administrator of the body corporate or (with the leave of the court) by a victim of the transaction;

(b) in a case where a victim of the transaction is bound by a voluntary arrangement approved under Part I or Part VIII of this Act, by the supervisor of the voluntary arrangement or by any person who (whether or not so bound) is such a victim; or

(c) in any other case, by a victim of the transaction.

(2) An application made under any of the paragraphs of subsection (1) is to be treated as made on behalf of every victim of the transaction.

NOTES

Sub-s (1): word in first pair of square brackets in para (a) substituted by the Enterprise and Regulatory Reform Act 2013, s 71(3), Sch 19, paras 1, 61, as from 6 April 2016, except in respect of a petition for a bankruptcy order presented to the court by a debtor before that date. Words in second pair of square brackets in para (a) substituted by the Enterprise Act 2002, s 248(3), Sch 17, paras 9, 36, as from 15 September 2003 (for savings and transitional provisions, see the note to s 8 at **[9.147]**).

[9.452]

425 Provision which may be made by order under s 423

(1) Without prejudice to the generality of section 423, an order made under that section with respect to a transaction may (subject as follows)—

(a) require any property transferred as part of the transaction to be vested in any person, either absolutely or for the benefit of all the persons on whose behalf the application for the order is treated as made;

(b) require any property to be so vested if it represents, in any person's hands, the application either of the proceeds of sale of property so transferred or of money so transferred;

(c) release or discharge (in whole or in part) any security given by the debtor;

(d) require any person to pay to any other person in respect of benefits received from the debtor such sums as the court may direct;

(e) provide for any surety or guarantor whose obligations to any person were released or discharged (in whole or in part) under the transaction to be under such new or revived obligations as the court thinks appropriate;

(f) provide for security to be provided for the discharge of any obligation imposed by or arising under the order, for such an obligation to be charged on any property and for such security or charge to have the same priority as a security or charge released or discharged (in whole or in part) under the transaction.

(2) An order under section 423 may affect the property of, or impose any obligation on, any person whether or not he is the person with whom the debtor entered into the transaction; but such an order—

(a) shall not prejudice any interest in property which was acquired from a person other than the debtor and was acquired in good faith, for value and without notice of the relevant circumstances, or prejudice any interest deriving from such an interest, and

(b) shall not require a person who received a benefit from the transaction in good faith, for value and without notice of the relevant circumstances to pay any sum unless he was a party to the transaction.

(3) For the purposes of this section the relevant circumstances in relation to a transaction are the circumstances by virtue of which an order under section 423 may be made in respect of the transaction.

(4) In this section "security" means any mortgage, charge, lien or other security.

PART XVII MISCELLANEOUS AND GENERAL

426–429 (*These sections concern various matters such as cooperation between courts exercising jurisdiction in relation to insolvency, and disqualification from Parliament, and are outside the scope of this work.*)

[9.453]

430 Provision introducing Schedule of punishments

(1) Schedule 10 to this Act has effect with respect to the way in which offences under this Act are punishable on conviction.

(2) In relation to an offence under a provision of this Act specified in the first column of the Schedule (the general nature of the offence being described in the second column), the third column shows whether the offence is punishable on conviction on indictment, or on summary conviction, or either in the one way or the other.

(3) The fourth column of the Schedule shows, in relation to an offence, the maximum punishment by way of fine or imprisonment under this Act which may be imposed on a person convicted of the offence in the way specified in relation to it in the third column (that is to say, on indictment or summarily), a reference to a period of years or months being to a term of imprisonment of that duration.

(4) The fifth column shows (in relation to an offence for which there is an entry in that column) that a person convicted of the offence after continued contravention is liable to a daily default fine; that is to say, he is liable on a second or subsequent conviction of the offence to the fine specified in that column for each day on which the contravention is continued (instead of the penalty specified for the offence in the fourth column of the Schedule).

[(4A) In relation to an offence committed before [2 May 2022], a reference in Schedule 10 to 12 months on summary conviction in England and Wales is to be read as a reference to 6 months.]

(5) For the purpose of any enactment in this Act whereby an officer of a company who is in default is liable to a fine or penalty, the expression "officer who is in default" means any officer of the company who knowingly and wilfully authorises or permits the default, refusal or contravention mentioned in the enactment.

NOTES

Sub-s (4A): inserted by the Corporate Insolvency and Governance Act 2020, s 2(1), Sch 3, paras 1, 26, as from 26 June 2020 (for transitional provisions, see s 2(2), (3) of the 2020 Act (at **[9.533]**) which provides that (without prejudice to the Interpretation Act 1978, s 16) nothing in the 2020 Act affects the operation of this Act, or any other enactment, in relation to a moratorium under Sch A1 to this Act which comes into force before the repeal of that Schedule by Sch 3 to the 2020 Act (ie, 26 June 2020)). Words in square brackets substituted by the Criminal Justice Act 2003 (Commencement No 33) and Sentencing Act 2020 (Commencement No 2) Regulations 2022, SI 2022/500, reg 5, Schedule, Pt 1, as from 28 April 2022.

[9.454]

431 Summary proceedings

(1) Summary proceedings for any offence under any of [Parts A1] to VII of this Act may (without prejudice to any jurisdiction exercisable apart from this subsection) be taken against a body corporate at any place at which the body has a place of business, and against any other person at any place at which he is for the time being.

(2) Notwithstanding anything in section 127(1) of the Magistrates' Courts Act 1980, an information relating to such an offence which is triable by a magistrates' court in England and Wales may be so tried if it is laid at any time within 3 years after the commission of the offence and within 12 months after the date on which evidence sufficient in the opinion of the Director of Public Prosecutions or the Secretary of State (as the case may be) to justify the proceedings comes to his knowledge.

(3) Summary proceedings in Scotland for such an offence shall not be commenced after the expiration of 3 years from the commission of the offence.

Subject to this (and notwithstanding anything in [section 136 of the Criminal Procedure (Scotland) Act 1995]), such proceedings may (in Scotland) be commenced at any time within 12 months after the date on which evidence sufficient in the Lord Advocate's opinion to justify the proceedings came to his knowledge or, where such evidence was reported to him by the Secretary of State, within 12 months after the date on which it came to the knowledge of the latter; and subsection (3) of that section applies for the purpose of this subsection as it applies for the purpose of that section.

(4) For purposes of this section, a certificate of the Director of Public Prosecutions, the Lord Advocate or the Secretary of State (as the case may be) as to the date on which such evidence as is referred to above came to his knowledge is conclusive evidence.

NOTES

Sub-s (1): words in square brackets substituted by the Corporate Insolvency and Governance Act 2020, s 2(1), Sch 3, paras 1, 27, as from 26 June 2020 (for transitional provisions, see s 2(2), (3) of the 2020 Act (at **[9.533]**) which provides that (without prejudice to the Interpretation Act 1978, s 16) nothing in the 2020 Act affects the operation of this Act, or any other enactment, in relation to a moratorium under Sch A1 to this Act which comes into force before the repeal of that Schedule by Sch 3 to the 2020 Act (ie, 26 June 2020)).

Sub-s (3): words in square brackets substituted by the Criminal Procedure (Consequential Provisions) (Scotland) Act 1995, s 5, Sch 4, para 61, as from 1 April 1996.

[9.455]

432 Offences by bodies corporate

(1) This section applies to offences under this Act other than those excepted by subsection (4).

(2) Where a body corporate is guilty of an offence to which this section applies and the offence is proved to have been committed with the consent or connivance of, or to be attributable to any neglect on the part of, any director, manager, secretary or other similar officer of the body corporate or any person who was purporting to act in any such capacity he, as well as the body corporate, is guilty of the offence and liable to be proceeded against and punished accordingly.

(3) Where the affairs of a body corporate are managed by its members, subsection (2) applies in relation to the acts and defaults of a member in connection with his functions of management as if he were a director of the body corporate.

(4) The offences excepted from this section are those under sections [A19(5), A25(3), A26(4), A27(1), A28(5), A29(6), A30(2), A31(10), A32(4),] 30, 39, 51, 53, 54, 62, 64, 66, 85, 89, 164, 188, 201, 206, 207, 208, 209, 210 and 211 [. . .].

NOTES

Sub-s (4): the section numbers in the first pair of square brackets were inserted, and the words omitted were repealed, by the Corporate Insolvency and Governance Act 2020, s 2(1), Sch 3, paras 1, 28, as from 26 June 2020 (for transitional provisions, see s 2(2), (3) of the 2020 Act (at **[9.533]**) which provides that (without prejudice to the Interpretation Act 1978, s 16) nothing in the 2020 Act affects the operation of this Act, or any other enactment, in relation to a moratorium under Sch A1 to this Act which comes into force before the repeal of that Schedule by Sch 3 to the 2020 Act (ie, 26 June 2020)). The omitted words were originally added by the Insolvency Act 2000, s 1, Sch 1, paras 1, 11, as from 1 January 2003.

[9.456]

433 Admissibility in evidence of statements of affairs, etc

[(1)] In any proceedings (whether or not under this Act)—

(a) a statement of affairs prepared for the purposes of any provision of this Act which is derived from the Insolvency Act 1985,

[(aa) a statement made in pursuance of a requirement imposed by or under Part 2 of the Banking Act 2009 (bank insolvency),]

[(ab) a statement made in pursuance of a requirement imposed by or under Part 3 of that Act (bank administration),] and

(b) any other statement made in pursuance of a requirement imposed by or under any such provision or by or under rules made under this Act,

may be used in evidence against any person making or concurring in making the statement.

[(2) However, in criminal proceedings in which any such person is charged with an offence to which this subsection applies—

(a) no evidence relating to the statement may be adduced, and

(b) no question relating to it may be asked,

by or on behalf of the prosecution, unless evidence relating to it is adduced, or a question relating to it is asked, in the proceedings by or on behalf of that person.

(3) Subsection (2) applies to any offence other than—

(a) an offence under section 22(6), 47(6), 48(8), 66(6), 67(8), 95(8), . . . [99(3)], 131(7), 192(2), 208(1)(a) or (d) or (2), 210, 235(5), 353(1), 354(1)(b) or (3) or 356(1) or (2)(a) or (b) or paragraph 4(3)(a) of Schedule 7;

(b) an offence which is—

(i) created by rules made under this Act, and

(ii) designated for the purposes of this subsection by such rules or by regulations made by the Secretary of State;

(c) an offence which is—

(i) created by regulations made under any such rules, and

(ii) designated for the purposes of this subsection by such regulations;

(d) an offence under section 1, 2 or 5 of the Perjury Act 1911 (false statements made on oath or made otherwise than on oath); or

(e) an offence under section 44(1) or (2) of the Criminal Law (Consolidation) (Scotland) Act 1995 (false statements made on oath or otherwise than on oath).

(4) Regulations under subsection (3)(b)(ii) shall be made by statutory instrument and, after being made, shall be laid before each House of Parliament.]

NOTES

Sub-s (1): numbered as such by the Youth Justice and Criminal Evidence Act 1999, s 59, Sch 3, para 7, as from 14 April 2000 (in relation to England and Wales), and 1 January 2001 (in relation to Scotland). Paras (aa), (ab) inserted by the Banking Act 2009, ss 128, 162, as from 21 February 2009.

Sub-s (2): added, together with sub-ss (3) and (4), by the Youth Justice and Criminal Evidence Act 1999, s 59, Sch 3, para 7, as from 14 April 2000 (in relation to England and Wales), and 1 January 2001 (in relation to Scotland).

Sub-s (3): added as noted above. Figure omitted repealed, and figure in square brackets substituted, by the Small Business, Enterprise and Employment Act 2015, s 126, Sch 9, Pt 1, paras 1, 56, as from 6 April 2017 (in relation to England and Wales), and as from 6 April 2019 (in relation to Scotland) (for transitional and savings provisions, see the notes to s 246ZE at **[9.385]**).

Sub-s (4): added as noted above.

[9.457]

434 Crown application

For the avoidance of doubt it is hereby declared that provisions of this Act which derive from the Insolvency Act 1985 [and Part A1] [and sections 233A and 233B and Schedule 4ZZA] bind the Crown so far as affecting or relating to the following matters, namely—

(a) remedies against, or against the property of, companies or individuals;

(b) priorities of debts;

(c) transactions at an undervalue or preferences;

(d) voluntary arrangements approved under Part I or Part VIII, and

(e) discharge from bankruptcy.

NOTES

Words in square first pair of brackets inserted by the Corporate Insolvency and Governance Act 2020, s 2(1), Sch 3, paras 1, 29, as from 26 June 2020 (for transitional provisions, see s 2(2), (3) of the 2020 Act (at **[9.533]**) which provides that (without prejudice to the Interpretation Act 1978, s 16) nothing in the 2020 Act affects the operation of this Act, or any other enactment, in relation to a moratorium under Sch A1 to this Act which comes into force before the repeal of that Schedule by Sch 3 to the 2020 Act (ie, 26 June 2020)).

Words in square second pair of brackets inserted by the Corporate Insolvency and Governance Act 2020, s 14(2), as from 26 June 2020. Note that the amendments made by this s 14 of the 2020 Act have effect in relation to a company which becomes subject to a relevant insolvency procedure on or after the day on which that section comes into force (ie, 26 June 2020) (but in respect of contracts entered into before, as well as those entered into on or after, that day). See also the note to s 233B of this Act at **[9.366]**.

[PART 17A SUPPLEMENTARY PROVISIONS

[9.458]

434A Introductory

The provisions of this Part have effect for the purposes of—

(a) the First Group of Parts, and

(b) sections 411, 413, 414, 416 and 417 in Part 15.]

NOTES

Inserted, together with the preceding heading and ss 434B, 434C, by the Companies Act 2006 (Consequential Amendments etc) Order 2008, SI 2008/948, art 3(1), Sch 1, Pt 2, para 105, as from 6 April 2008.

[9.459]

[434B Representation of corporations [in decision procedures and] at meetings

(1) If a corporation is a creditor or debenture-holder, it may by resolution of its directors or other governing body authorise a person or persons to act as its representative or representatives—

[(a) in a qualifying decision procedure, held in pursuance of this Act or of rules made under it, by which a decision is sought from the creditors of a company, or]

(b) at any meeting of a company held in pursuance of the provisions contained in a debenture or trust deed.

(2) Where the corporation authorises only one person, that person is entitled to exercise the same powers on behalf of the corporation as the corporation could exercise if it were an individual creditor or debenture-holder.

(3) Where the corporation authorises more than one person, any one of them is entitled to exercise the same powers on behalf of the corporation as the corporation could exercise if it were an individual creditor or debenture-holder.

(4) Where the corporation authorises more than one person and more than one of them purport to exercise a power under subsection (3)—

(a) if they purport to exercise the power in the same way, the power is treated as exercised in that way;

(b) if they do not purport to exercise the power in the same way, the power is treated as not exercised.]

NOTES

Inserted as noted to s 434A at **[9.458]**.

The words in square brackets in the section heading were inserted, and sub-s (1)(a) was substituted, by the Small Business, Enterprise and Employment Act 2015, s 126, Sch 9, Pt 1, paras 1, 57, as from 6 April 2017 (in relation to England and Wales), and as from 6 April 2019 (in relation to Scotland) (for transitional and savings provisions, see the notes to s 246ZE at **[9.385]**).

[9.460]

[434C Legal professional privilege

In proceedings against a person for an offence under this Act nothing in this Act is to be taken to require any person to disclose any information that he is entitled to refuse to disclose on grounds of legal professional privilege (in Scotland, confidentiality of communications).]

NOTES

Inserted as noted to s 434A at **[9.458]**.

[9.461]

434D Enforcement of company's filing obligations

(1) This section applies where a company has made default in complying with any obligation under this Act—

(a) to deliver a document to the registrar, or

(b) to give notice to the registrar of any matter.

(2) The registrar, or any member or creditor of the company, may give notice to the company requiring it to comply with the obligation.

(3) If the company fails to make good the default within 14 days after service of the notice, the registrar, or any member or creditor of the company, may apply to the court for an order directing the company, and any specified officer of it, to make good the default within a specified time.

(4) The court's order may provide that all costs (in Scotland, expenses) of or incidental to the application are to be borne by the company or by any officers of it responsible for the default.

(5) This section does not affect the operation of any enactment imposing penalties on a company or its officers in respect of any such default.]

NOTES

Inserted, together with s 434E, by the Companies Act 2006 (Consequential Amendments, Transitional Provisions and Savings) Order 2009, SI 2009/1941, art 2(1), Sch 1, para 81, as from 1 October 2009 (for effect see the note to s 7A at **[9.145]**).

[9.462]

[434E Application of filing obligations to overseas companies

The provisions of this Act requiring documents to be forwarded or delivered to, or filed with, the registrar of companies apply in relation to an overseas company that is required to register particulars under section 1046 of the Companies Act 2006 as they apply in relation to a company registered under that Act in England and Wales or Scotland.]

NOTES

Inserted as noted to s 434D at **[9.461]**.

PART XVIII INTERPRETATION

[9.463]

435 Meaning of "associate"

(1) For the purposes of this Act any question whether a person is an associate of another person is to be determined in accordance with the following provisions of this section (any provision that a person is an associate of another person being taken to mean that they are associates of each other).

[(2) A person is an associate of an individual if that person is—

(a) the individual's husband or wife or civil partner,

(b) a relative of—

(i) the individual, or

(ii) the individual's husband or wife or civil partner, or

(c) the husband or wife or civil partner of a relative of—

(i) the individual, or

(ii) the individual's husband or wife or civil partner.]

(3) A person is an associate of any person with whom he is in partnership, and of the husband or wife [or civil partner] or a relative of any individual with whom he is in partnership; and a Scottish firm is an associate of any person who is a member of the firm.

(4) A person is an associate of any person whom he employs or by whom he is employed.

(5) A person in his capacity as trustee of a trust other than—

(a) a trust arising under any of the second Group of Parts or the Bankruptcy (Scotland) Act [2016], or

(b) a pension scheme or an employees' share scheme . . . ,

is an associate of another person if the beneficiaries of the trust include, or the terms of the trust confer a power that may be exercised for the benefit of, that other person or an associate of that other person.

(6) A company is an associate of another company—

(a) if the same person has control of both, or a person has control of one and persons who are his associates, or he and persons who are his associates, have control of the other, or

(b) if a group of two or more persons has control of each company, and the groups either consist of the same persons or could be regarded as consisting of the same persons by treating (in one or more cases) a member of either group as replaced by a person of whom he is an associate.

(7) A company is an associate of another person if that person has control of it or if that person and persons who are his associates together have control of it.

(8) For the purposes of this section a person is a relative of an individual if he is that individual's brother, sister, uncle, aunt, nephew, niece, lineal ancestor or lineal descendant, treating—

(a) any relationship of the half blood as a relationship of the whole blood and the stepchild or adopted child of any person as his child, and

(b) an illegitimate child as the legitimate child of his mother and reputed father;

and references in this section to a husband or wife include a former husband or wife and a reputed husband or wife [and references to a civil partner include a former civil partner] [and a reputed civil partner].

(9) For the purposes of this section any director or other officer of a company is to be treated as employed by that company.

(10) For the purposes of this section a person is to be taken as having control of a company if—

(a) the directors of the company or of another company which has control of it (or any of them) are accustomed to act in accordance with his directions or instructions, or

(b) he is entitled to exercise, or control the exercise of, one third or more of the voting power at any general meeting of the company or of another company which has control of it;

and where two or more persons together satisfy either of the above conditions, they are to be taken as having control of the company.

(11) In this section "company" includes any body corporate (whether incorporated in Great Britain or elsewhere); and references to directors and other officers of a company and to voting power at any general meeting of a company have effect with any necessary modifications.

NOTES

Sub-s (2): substituted by the Civil Partnership Act 2004, s 261(1), Sch 27, para 122(1), (2), as from 5 December 2005.

Sub-s (3): words in square brackets inserted by the Civil Partnership Act 2004, s 261(1), Sch 27, para 122(1), (3), as from 5 December 2005.

Sub-s (5): year "2016" in square brackets substituted by the Bankruptcy (Scotland) Act 2016 (Consequential Provisions and Modifications) Order 2016, SI 2016/1034, art 7(1), (3), Sch 1, para 4(1), (10), as from 30 November 2016 (except in relation to (i) a sequestration as regards which the petition is presented, or the debtor application is made before that date; or (ii) a trust deed executed before that date). Words omitted repealed by the Companies Act 2006 (Consequential Amendments, Transitional Provisions and Savings) Order 2009, SI 2009/1941, art 2(1), Sch 1, para 82(1), (2), as from 1 October 2009 (for effect see the note to s 7A at **[9.145]**).

Sub-s (8): words in first pair of square brackets inserted by the Civil Partnership Act 2004, s 261(1), Sch 27, para 122(1), (4), as from 5 December 2005. Words in second pair of square brackets inserted by the Civil Partnership Act 2004 (Overseas Relationships and Consequential, etc Amendments) Order 2005, SI 2005/3129, art 4(4), Sch 4, para 8, as from 5 December 2005.

Stepchild: this includes relationships arising through civil partnerships; see the Civil Partnership Act 2004, ss 246, 247, Sch 21.

[9.464]

436 Expressions used generally

[(1)] In this Act, except in so far as the context otherwise requires (and subject to Parts VII and XI)—

"the appointed day" means the day on which this Act comes into force under section 443;

"associate" has the meaning given by section 435;

["body corporate" includes a body incorporated outside Great Britain, but does not include—

(a) a corporation sole, or

(b) a partnership that, whether or not a legal person, is not regarded as a body corporate under the law by which it is governed;]

"business" includes a trade or profession;

. . .

["the Companies Acts" means the Companies Acts (as defined in section 2 of the Companies Act 2006) as they have effect in Great Britain;]

"conditional sale agreement" and "hire-purchase agreement" have the same meanings as in the Consumer Credit Act 1974;

["distress" includes use of the procedure in Schedule 12 to the Tribunals, Courts and Enforcement Act 2007, and references to levying distress, seizing goods and related expressions shall be construed accordingly;]

[. . .]

["EEA State" means a state that is a Contracting Party to the Agreement on the European Economic Area signed at Oporto on 2nd May 1992 as adjusted by the Protocol signed at Brussels on 17th March 1993;]

["the EU Regulation" means Regulation (EU) 2015/848 of the European Parliament and of the Council of 20 May 2015 on insolvency proceedings [as it forms part of domestic law on and after exit day];]

["employees' share scheme" means a scheme for encouraging or facilitating the holding of shares in or debentures of a company by or for the benefit of—

(a) the bona fide employees or former employees of—

(i) the company,

(ii) any subsidiary of the company, or

(iii) the company's holding company or any subsidiary of the company's holding company, or

(b) the spouses, civil partners, surviving spouses, surviving civil partners, or minor children or step-children of such employees or former employees.]

"modifications" includes additions, alterations and omissions and cognate expressions shall be construed accordingly;

"property" includes money, goods, things in action, land and every description of property wherever situated and also obligations and every description of interest, whether present or future or vested or contingent, arising out of, or incidental to, property;

"records" includes computer records and other non-documentary records;

"subordinate legislation" has the same meaning as in the Interpretation Act 1978; and

"transaction" includes a gift, agreement or arrangement, and references to entering into a transaction shall be construed accordingly.

[(2) The following expressions have the same meaning in this Act as in the Companies Acts—

"articles", in relation to a company (see section 18 of the Companies Act 2006);

"debenture" (see section 738 of that Act);

"holding company" (see sections 1159 and 1160 of, and Schedule 6 to, that Act);

"the Joint Stock Companies Acts" (see section 1171 of that Act);

"overseas company" (see section 1044 of that Act);

"paid up" (see section 583 of that Act);

"private company" and "public company" (see section 4 of that Act);

"registrar of companies" (see section 1060 of that Act);

"share" (see section 540 of that Act);

"subsidiary" (see sections 1159 and 1160 of, and Schedule 6 to, that Act).]

NOTES

Sub-s (1) numbered as such, definitions "body corporate" and "employees' share scheme" inserted, definition "the Companies Act" (omitted) repealed, and sub-s (2) added, by the Companies Act 2006 (Consequential Amendments, Transitional Provisions and Savings) Order 2009, SI 2009/1941, art 2(1), Sch 1, para 82(1), (3), as from 1 October 2009 (for effect see the note to s 7A at **[9.145]**).

Definition "distress" inserted by the Tribunals, Courts and Enforcement Act 2007, s 62(3), Sch 13, para 85, as from 6 April 2014.

Definition "the EC Regulation" (omitted) originally inserted by the Insolvency Act 1986 (Amendment) Regulations 2002, SI 2002/1037, regs 2, 4, as from 3 May 2002; and subsequently repealed by the Insolvency Amendment (EU 2015/848) Regulations 2017, SI 2017/702, regs 2, 3, Schedule, Pt 1, paras 1, 28(a), as from 26 June 2017, except in relation to proceedings opened before that date.

Definition "EEA State" inserted by the Insolvency Act 1986 (Amendment) Regulations 2005, SI 2005/879, reg 2(1), (3), as from 13 April 2005, except in relation to any voluntary arrangement under Part I, or the appointment of an administrator under Part II, that took effect before that date.

Definition "the EU Regulation" inserted by SI 2017/702, regs 2, 3, Schedule, Pt 1, paras 1, 28(b), as from 26 June 2017, except in relation to proceedings opened before that date. Words in square brackets in that definition inserted by the Insolvency (Amendment) (EU Exit) Regulations 2019, SI 2019/146, reg 2, Schedule, Pt 2, paras 16, 42, as from IP completion day (as defined in the European Union (Withdrawal Agreement) Act 2020, s 39) (for savings, see reg 4 of the 2019 Regulations at **[12.82]**).

436A *(Inserted by the Insolvency Act 1986 (Amendment) (No 2) Regulations 2002, SI 2002/1240, regs 3, 18, as from 31 May 2002, and repealed by the Insolvency (Amendment) (EU Exit) Regulations 2019, SI 2019/146, reg 2, Schedule, Pt 2, paras 16, 43, as from IP completion day (as defined in the European Union (Withdrawal Agreement) Act 2020, s 39) (for savings, see reg 4 of the 2019 Regulations at* **[12.82]**).)

[9.465]

[436B References to things in writing

(1) A reference in this Act to a thing in writing includes that thing in electronic form.

(2) Subsection (1) does not apply to the following provisions—

(a) section 53 (mode of appointment by holder of charge),

(b) . . .

(c) section 70(4) (reference to instrument creating a charge),

(d) section 111(2) (dissent from arrangement under s 110),

(e) . . .

(f) section 123(1) (definition of inability to pay debts),

(g) section 198(3) (duties of sheriff principal as regards examination),

(h) section 222(1) (inability to pay debts: unpaid creditor for £750 or more), and

(i) section 223 (inability to pay debts: debt remaining unsatisfied after action brought).]

NOTES

Inserted by the Legislative Reform (Insolvency) (Miscellaneous Provisions) Order 2010, SI 2010/18, arts 2, 4(1), as from 6 April 2010.

Sub-s (2): paras (b), (e) repealed by the Public Services Reform (Insolvency) (Scotland) Order 2016, SSI 2016/141, art 13, as from 6 April 2019.

PART XIX FINAL PROVISIONS

437–439 *(Introduce Schs 11–13 (transitional provisions; repeals; and consequential amendments) (all omitted).)*

[9.466]

440 Extent (Scotland)

(1) Subject to the next subsection, provisions of this Act contained in the first Group of Parts extend to Scotland except where otherwise stated.

(2) The following provisions of this Act do not extend to Scotland—

(a) In the first Group of Parts—

section 43;

sections 238 to 241; and

section 246;
(b) the second Group of Parts;
(c) in the third Group of Parts—
sections 399 to 402,
sections 412, 413, 415, [415A(3),] 418, 420 and 421,
sections 423 to 425, and
section 429(1) and (2); and
(d) in the Schedules—
Parts II and III of Schedule 11; and
Schedules 12 and 14 so far as they repeal or amend enactments which extend to England and Wales only.

NOTES

Sub-s (2): figure in square brackets inserted by the Enterprise Act 2002, s 270(4), as from 18 December 2003. For the words in italics there are substituted the words "section 429(1) to (2A)" by the Tribunals, Courts and Enforcement Act 2007, s 106, Sch 16, para 4, as from a day to be appointed (except in relation to any case in which an administration order was made, or an application for such an order was made, before the day on which s 106 comes into force).

441 (*Section 441 (Extent – Northern Ireland) is outside the scope of this work.*)

[9.467]
442 Extent (other territories)

Her Majesty may, by Order in Council, direct that such of the provisions of this Act as are specified in the Order, being provisions formerly contained in the Insolvency Act 1985, shall extend to any of the Channel Islands or any colony with such modifications as may be so specified.

NOTES

Orders: the Insolvency Act 1986 (Guernsey) Order 1989, SI 1989/2409.

[9.468]
443 Commencement

This Act comes into force on the day appointed under section 236(2) of the Insolvency Act 1985 for the coming into force of Part III of that Act (individual insolvency and bankruptcy), immediately after that Part of that Act comes into force for England and Wales.

NOTES

See the note "Commencement" at the beginning of this Act.

[9.469]
444 Citation

This Act may be cited as the Insolvency Act 1986.

SCHEDULES

[SCHEDULE ZA1
MORATORIUM: ELIGIBLE COMPANIES

Section A2

Eligible companies

[9.470]

1. A company is "eligible" for the purposes of this Part unless it is excluded from being eligible by any of the following—
paragraph 2 (current or recent insolvency procedure);
[paragraph 2A (private registered providers of social housing);]
[paragraph 2B (a registered social landlord under Part 2 of the Housing (Scotland) Act 2010);]
paragraph 3 (insurance companies);
paragraph 4 (banks);
paragraph 5 (electronic money institutions);
paragraph 6 (investment banks and investment firms);
paragraph 7 (market contracts, market charges, etc);
paragraph 8 (participants in designated systems);
paragraph 9 (payment institutions);
paragraph 10 (operators of payment systems, infrastructure providers etc);
paragraph 11 (recognised investment exchanges, clearing houses and CSDs);
paragraph 12 (securitisation companies);
paragraph 13 (parties to capital market arrangements);
paragraph 15 (public-private partnership project companies);
paragraph 18 (certain overseas companies).

Companies subject to, or recently subject to, moratorium or an insolvency procedure

2. (1) A company is excluded from being eligible if—
(a) on the filing date, a moratorium for the company is in force, or
(b) at any time during the period of 12 months ending with the filing date, a moratorium for the company was in force (but see section A42(6) for power of the court to modify the effect of this paragraph).

(2) A company is excluded from being eligible if—
(a) on the filing date, the company is subject to an insolvency procedure, or

(b) at any time during the period of 12 months ending with the filing date, the company was subject to an insolvency procedure within sub-paragraph (3)(a) or (b).

(3) For the purposes of sub-paragraph (2), a company is subject to an insolvency procedure at any time if at that time—

(a) a voluntary arrangement has effect in relation to the company,
(b) the company is in administration,
(c) paragraph 44 of Schedule B1 applies in relation to the company (administration: interim moratorium),
(d) there is an administrative receiver of the company,
(e) there is a provisional liquidator of the company,
(f) the company is being wound up, or
(g) a relevant petition for the winding up of the company has been presented and has not been withdrawn or determined.

(4) In sub-paragraph (3)(g) "relevant petition" means a petition under—

(a) section 124A (winding up on grounds of public interest),
(b) section 124B (winding up of SE), or
(c) section 124C (winding up of SCE).

[Private registered providers of social housing

2A. A company is excluded from being eligible if it is a private registered provider of social housing.]

[Registered social landlord under Part 2 of the Housing (Scotland) Act 2010

2B. A company is excluded from being eligible if it is a registered social landlord under Part 2 of the Housing (Scotland) Act 2010.]

Insurance companies

3. (1) A company is excluded from being eligible if—

(a) it carries on the regulated activity of effecting or carrying out contracts of insurance, and
(b) it is not an exempt person in relation to that activity.

(2) In this paragraph—

"exempt person", in relation to a regulated activity, has the meaning given by section 417 of the Financial Services and Markets Act 2000;

"regulated activity" has the meaning given by section 22 of that Act, taken with Schedule 2 to that Act and any order under that section.

Banks

4. (1) A company is excluded from being eligible if—

(a) it has permission under Part 4A of the Financial Services and Markets Act 2000 to carry on the regulated activity of accepting deposits,
(b) it is a banking group company within the meaning of Part 1 of the Banking Act 2009 (see section 81D of that Act), or
(c) it has a liability in respect of a deposit which it accepted in accordance with the Banking Act 1979 or the Banking Act 1987.

(2) In sub-paragraph (1)(a) "regulated activity" has the meaning given by section 22 of the Financial Services and Markets Act 2000, taken with Schedule 2 to that Act and any order under that section.

Electronic money institutions

5. A company is excluded from being eligible if it is an electronic money institution within the meaning of the Electronic Money Regulations 2011 (SI 2011/99) (see regulation 2 of those Regulations).

Investment banks and investment firms

6. (1) A company is excluded from being eligible if it is an investment bank or an investment firm.

(2) In this paragraph—

"investment bank" means a company that has permission under Part 4A of the Financial Services and Markets Act 2000 to carry on the regulated activity of—

(a) safeguarding and administering investments,
(b) managing an AIF or a UCITS,
(c) acting as trustee or depositary of an AIF or a UCITS,
(d) dealing in investments as principal, or
(e) dealing in investments as agent,

but does not include a company that has permission to arrange for one or more others to carry on the activity mentioned in paragraph (a) if it does not otherwise have permission to carry on any of the activities mentioned in paragraphs (a) to (e);

"investment firm" has the same meaning as in the Banking Act 2009 (see section 258A of that Act), disregarding any order made under section 258A(2)(b) of that Act;

"regulated activity" has the meaning given by section 22 of the Financial Services and Markets Act 2000, taken with Schedule 2 to that Act and any order under that section.

Companies that are party to market contracts or subject to market charges, etc

7. (1) A company is excluded from being eligible if it is a party to a market contract for the purposes of Part 7 of the Companies Act 1989 (see section 155 of that Act).

(2) A company is excluded from being eligible if any of its property is subject to a market charge for the purposes of Part 7 of the Companies Act 1989 (see section 173 of that Act).

(3) A company is excluded from being eligible if any of its property is subject to a charge that is a system-charge, within the meaning of the Financial Markets and Insolvency Regulations 1996 (SI 1996/1469) (see regulation 2 of those Regulations).

Participants in designated systems

8. A company is excluded from being eligible if—

(a) it is a participant in a designated system, within the meaning of the Financial Markets and Insolvency (Settlement Finality) Regulations 1999 (SI 1999/2979) (see regulation 2 of those Regulations), or

(b) any of its property is subject to a collateral security charge within the meaning of those Regulations (see regulation 2 of those Regulations).

Payment institutions

9. A company is excluded from being eligible if it is an authorised payment institution, a small payment institution or a registered account information service provider within the meaning of the Payment Services Regulations 2017 (SI 2017/752) (see regulation 2 of those Regulations).

Operators of payment systems, infrastructure providers etc

10. A company is excluded from being eligible if—

(a) it is the operator of a payment system or an infrastructure provider within the meaning of Part 5 of the Financial Services (Banking Reform) Act 2013 (see section 42 of that Act), or

(b) it is an infrastructure company, within the meaning of Part 6 of that Act (see section 112 of that Act).

Recognised investment exchanges, clearing houses and CSDs

11. A company is excluded from being eligible if it is a recognised investment exchange, a recognised clearing house or a recognised CSD within the meaning of the Financial Services and Markets Act 2000 (see section 285 of that Act).

Securitisation companies

12. A company is excluded from being eligible if it is a securitisation company within the meaning of the Taxation of Securitisation Companies Regulations 2006 (SI 2006/3296) (see regulation 4 of those Regulations).

Parties to capital market arrangements

13. (1) A company is excluded from being eligible if, on the filing date—

(a) it is a party to an agreement which is or forms part of a capital market arrangement (see sub-paragraph (2)),

(b) a party has incurred, or when the agreement was entered into was expected to incur, a debt of at least £10 million under the arrangement (at any time during the life of the capital market arrangement), and

(c) the arrangement involves the issue of a capital market investment (see paragraph 14).

(2) For the purposes of this paragraph, an arrangement is a "capital market arrangement" if any of the following applies—

(a) it involves a grant of security to a person holding it as trustee for a person who holds a capital market investment issued by a party to the arrangement;

(b) at least one party guarantees the performance of obligations of another party;

(c) at least one party provides security in respect of the performance of obligations of another party;

(d) the arrangement involves an investment of a kind described in articles 83 to 85 of the Financial Services and Markets Act 2000 (Regulated Activities) Order 2001 (SI 2001/544) (options, futures and contracts for differences).

(3) For the purposes of sub-paragraph (2)—

(a) a reference to holding a security as trustee includes a reference to holding it as nominee or agent,

(b) a reference to holding for a person who holds a capital market investment includes a reference to holding for a number of persons at least one of whom holds a capital market investment, and

(c) a reference to holding a capital market investment is to holding a legal or beneficial interest in it.

(4) For the purposes of sub-paragraph (1)(b), where a debt is denominated wholly or partly in a foreign currency, the sterling equivalent is to be calculated as at the time when the arrangement is entered into.

14. (1) For the purposes of paragraph 13 an investment is a "capital market investment" if condition A or B is met.

(2) Condition A is that the investment—

(a) is within article 77 or 77A of the Financial Services and Markets Act 2000 (Regulated Activities) Order 2001 (SI 2001/544) (debt instruments), and

(b) is rated, listed or traded or designed to be rated, listed or traded.

(3) In sub-paragraph (2)—

"listed" means admitted to the official list within the meaning given by section 103(1) of the Financial Services and Markets Act 2000 (interpretation);

"rated" means rated for the purposes of investment by an internationally recognised rating agency;

"traded" means admitted to trading on a market established under the rules of a recognised investment exchange or on a foreign market.

(4) In sub-paragraph (3)—

"foreign market" has the same meaning as "relevant market" in article 67(2) of the Financial Services and Markets Act 2000 (Financial Promotion) Order 2005 (SI 2005/1529) (foreign markets);

"recognised investment exchange" has the meaning given by section 285 of the Financial Services and Markets Act 2000 (recognised investment exchange).

(5) Condition B is that the investment consists of a bond or commercial paper issued to one or more of the following—

(a) an investment professional within the meaning of article 19(5) of the Financial Services and Markets Act 2000 (Financial Promotion) Order 2005 (SI 2005/1529);

(b) a person who, when the agreement mentioned in paragraph 13(1) is entered into, is a certified high net worth individual in relation to a communication within the meaning of article 48(2) of that Order;
(c) a person to whom article 49(2) of that Order applies (high net worth company, etc);
(d) a person who, when the agreement mentioned in paragraph 13(1) is entered into, is a certified sophisticated investor in relation to a communication within the meaning of article 50(1) of that Order;
(e) a person in a State other than the United Kingdom who under the law of that State is not prohibited from investing in bonds or commercial paper.

(6) For the purposes of sub-paragraph (5)—
(a) in applying article 19(5) of the Financial Services and Markets Act 2000 (Financial Promotion) Order 2005—
(i) in article 19(5)(b), ignore the words after "exempt person",
(ii) in article 19(5)(c)(i), for the words from "the controlled activity" to the end substitute "a controlled activity", and
(iii) in article 19(5)(e), ignore the words from "where the communication" to the end;
(b) in applying article 49(2) of that Order, ignore article 49(2)(e);
(c) "bond" means—
(i) a bond that is within article 77(1) of the Financial Services and Markets Act 2000 (Regulated Activities) Order 2001, or
(ii) an alternative finance investment bond within the meaning of article 77A of that Order;
(d) "commercial paper" has the meaning given by article 9(3) of that Order.

Public-private partnership project companies

15. (1) A company is excluded from being eligible if, on the filing date, it is a project company of a project which—
(a) is a public-private partnership project (see paragraph 16), and
(b) includes step-in rights (see paragraph 17).

(2) For the purposes of this paragraph a company is a "project company" of a project if any of the following applies—
(a) it holds property for the purpose of the project;
(b) it has sole or principal responsibility under an agreement for carrying out all or part of the project;
(c) it is one of a number of companies which together carry out the project;
(d) it has the purpose of supplying finance to enable the project to be carried out;
(e) it is the holding company of a company within any of paragraphs (a) to (d).

(3) But a company is not a "project company" of a project if—
(a) it performs a function within sub-paragraph (2)(a) to (d) or is within sub-paragraph (2)(e), but
(b) it also performs a function which is not—
(i) within sub-paragraph (2)(a) to (d),
(ii) related to a function within sub-paragraph (2)(a) to (d), or
(iii) related to the project.

(4) For the purposes of this paragraph a company carries out all or part of a project whether or not it acts wholly or partly through agents.

16. (1) For the purposes of paragraph 15 "public-private partnership project" means a project—
(a) the resources for which are provided partly by one or more public bodies and partly by one or more private persons, or
(b) which is designed wholly or mainly for the purpose of assisting a public body to discharge a function.

(2) In sub-paragraph (1) "public body" means—
(a) a body which exercises public functions,
(b) a body specified for the purposes of this paragraph by the Secretary of State, or
(c) a body within a class specified for the purposes of this paragraph by the Secretary of State.

(3) In sub-paragraph (1)(a) "resources" includes—
(a) funds (including payment for the provision of services or facilities);
(b) assets;
(c) professional skill;
(d) the grant of a concession or franchise;
(e) any other commercial resource.

(4) A specification under sub-paragraph (2) may be—
(a) general, or
(b) for the purpose of the application of paragraph 15 to a specified case.

17. (1) For the purposes of paragraph 15 a project has "step-in rights" if a person who provides finance in connection with the project has a conditional entitlement under an agreement to—
(a) assume sole or principal responsibility under an agreement for carrying out all or part of the project, or
(b) make arrangements for carrying out all or part of the project.

(2) In sub-paragraph (1) a reference to the provision of finance includes a reference to the provision of an indemnity.

Overseas companies with corresponding functions

18. A company is excluded from being eligible if its registered office or head office is outside the United Kingdom and—
(a) its functions correspond to those of a company mentioned in any of the previous paragraphs of this Schedule apart from [paragraphs 2 and 2A] and, if it were a company registered under the Companies Act 2006 in England and Wales or Scotland, it would be excluded from being eligible by that paragraph, or

(b) it has entered into a transaction or done anything else that, if done in England and Wales or Scotland by a company registered under the Companies Act 2006 in England and Wales or Scotland, would result in the company being excluded by any of the previous paragraphs of this Schedule apart from [paragraphs 2 and 2A].

Interpretation of Schedule

19. (1) This paragraph applies for the purposes of this Schedule.

(2) "Agreement" includes any agreement or undertaking effected by—

(a) contract,

(b) deed, or

(c) any other instrument intended to have effect in accordance with the law of England and Wales, Scotland or another jurisdiction.

(3) "The filing date" means the date on which documents are filed with the court under section A3, A4 or A5.

(4) "Party" to an arrangement includes a party to an agreement which—

(a) forms part of the arrangement,

(b) provides for the raising of finance as part of the arrangement, or

(c) is necessary for the purposes of implementing the arrangement.

Powers to amend Schedule

20. (1) The Secretary of State may by regulations amend this Schedule, apart from paragraph 2, so as to alter the circumstances in which a company is "eligible" for the purposes of this Part.

(2) Regulations under this paragraph are subject to the affirmative resolution procedure.

21. (1) The Welsh Ministers may by regulations amend this Schedule—

(a) so as to provide that a social landlord registered under Part 1 of the Housing Act 1996 is excluded from being "eligible" for the purposes of this Part;

(b) so as to reverse the effect of any provision made under paragraph (a).

(2) Regulations under this paragraph extend to England and Wales only.

(3) A statutory instrument containing regulations under this paragraph may not be made unless a draft of the statutory instrument containing them has been laid before and approved by a resolution of Senedd Cymru.

22. (1) The Scottish Ministers may by regulations amend this Schedule—

(a) so as to provide that a social landlord registered under Part 2 of the Housing (Scotland) Act 2010 (asp 17) is excluded from being "eligible" for the purposes of this Part;

(b) so as to reverse the effect of any provision made under paragraph (a).

(2) Regulations under this paragraph extend to Scotland only.

(3) Regulations under this paragraph are subject to the affirmative procedure (see section 29 of the Interpretation and Legislative Reform (Scotland) Act 2010 (asp 10)).]

NOTES

Commencement: 26 June 2020.

Inserted by the Corporate Insolvency and Governance Act 2020, s 1(2), Sch 1, as from 26 June 2020 (for transitional provisions, see s 2(2), (3) of the 2020 Act (at **[9.533]**) which provides that (without prejudice to the Interpretation Act 1978, s 16) nothing in the 2020 Act affects the operation of this Act, or any other enactment, in relation to a moratorium under Sch A1 to this Act which comes into force before the repeal of that Schedule by Sch 3 to the 2020 Act (ie, 26 June 2020)). For temporary modifications, see the Corporate Insolvency and Governance Act 2020, Sch 4 at **[9.561]**.

The words in the first pair of square brackets in para 1 were inserted, para 2A was inserted, and the words in square brackets in para 18 were substituted, by the Insolvency Act 1986 Part A1 Moratorium (Eligibility of Private Registered Providers) Regulations 2020, SI 2020/652, reg 2, as from 29 June 2020.

The words in the second pair of square brackets in para 1 were inserted, and para 2B was inserted, by the Insolvency Act 1986 (Scotland) Amendment Regulations 2020, SSI 2020/338, reg 2, as from 29 October 2020.

Regulations: the Insolvency Act 1986 (Scotland) Amendment Regulations 2020, SSI 2020/338.

[SCHEDULE ZA2
MORATORIUM: CONTRACT OR OTHER INSTRUMENT INVOLVING FINANCIAL SERVICES

Section A18

Introductory

[9.471]

1. For the purposes of section A18 "contract or other instrument involving financial services" means a contract or other instrument to which any of the following paragraphs applies.

Financial contracts

2. (1) This paragraph applies to a financial contract.

(2) "Financial contract" means—

(a) a contract for the provision of financial services consisting of—

(i) lending (including the factoring and financing of commercial transactions),

(ii) financial leasing, or

(iii) providing guarantees or commitments;

(b) a securities contract, including—

(i) a contract for the purchase, sale or loan of a security, group or index of securities;

(ii) an option on a security or group or index of securities;

(iii) a repurchase or reverse repurchase transaction on any such security, group or index;

(c) a commodities contract, including—

(i) a contract for the purchase, sale or loan of a commodity or group or index of commodities for future delivery;
(ii) an option on a commodity or group or index of commodities;
(iii) a repurchase or reverse repurchase transaction on any such commodity, group or index;

(d) a futures or forwards contract, including a contract (other than a commodities contract) for the purchase, sale or transfer of a commodity or property of any other description, service, right or interest for a specified price at a future date;

(e) a swap agreement, including—
(i) a swap or option relating to interest rates, spot or other foreign exchange agreements, currency, an equity index or equity, a debt index or debt, commodity indexes or commodities, weather, emissions or inflation;
(ii) a total return, credit spread or credit swap;
(iii) any agreement or transaction that is similar to an agreement that is referred to in sub-paragraph (i) or (ii) and is the subject of recurrent dealing in the swaps or derivatives markets;

(f) an inter-bank borrowing agreement where the term of the borrowing is three months or less;

(g) a master agreement for any of the contracts or agreements referred to in paragraphs (a) to (f).

(3) For the purposes of this paragraph "commodities" includes—
(a) units recognised for compliance with the requirements of EU Directive 2003/87/EC establishing a scheme for greenhouse gas emission allowance trading,
(b) allowances under paragraph 5 of Schedule 2 to the Climate Change Act 2008 relating to a trading scheme dealt with under Part 1 of that Schedule (schemes limiting activities relating to emissions of greenhouse gas), and
(c) renewables obligation certificates issued—
(i) by the Gas and Electricity Markets Authority under an order made under section 32B of the Electricity Act 1989, or
(ii) by the Northern Ireland Authority for Utility Regulation under the Energy (Northern Ireland) Order 2003 (SI 2003/419 (NI 6)) and pursuant to an order made under Articles 52 to 55F of that Order.

Securities financing transactions

3. (1) This paragraph applies to—
(a) a securities financing transaction, and
(b) a master agreement for securities financing transactions.

(2) "Securities financing transaction" has the meaning given by Article 3(11) of Regulation (EU) 2015/2365 on the transparency of securities financing transactions.

(3) But for the purposes of that Article as it applies for the purposes of this paragraph, references to "commodities" in that Regulation are to be taken as including the units, allowances and certificates referred to in paragraph 2(3)(a), (b) and (c).

Derivatives

4. (1) This paragraph applies to—
(a) a derivative, and
(b) a master agreement for derivatives.

(2) "Derivative" has the meaning given by Article 2(5) of Regulation (EU) No 648/2012.

Spot contracts

5. (1) This paragraph applies to—
(a) a spot contract, and
(b) a master agreement for spot contracts.

(2) "Spot contract" has the meaning given by Article 7(2) or 10(2) of Commission Delegated Regulation of 25.4.2016 supplementing Directive 2014/65/EU of the European Parliament and of the Council as regards organisational requirements and operating conditions for investment firms and defined terms for the purposes of that Directive.

Capital market investments

6. (1) This paragraph applies to an agreement which is, or forms part of, an arrangement involving the issue of a capital market investment.

(2) "Capital market investment" has the meaning given by paragraph 14 of Schedule ZA1.

Contracts forming part of a public-private partnership

7. This paragraph applies to a contract forming part of a public-private partnership project within the meaning given by paragraph 16 of Schedule ZA1.

Market contracts

8. This paragraph applies to a market contract within the meaning of Part 7 of the Companies Act 1989 (see section 155 of that Act).

Qualifying collateral arrangements and qualifying property transfers

9. This paragraph applies to qualifying collateral arrangements and qualifying property transfers within the meaning of Part 7 of the Companies Act 1989 (see section 155A of that Act).

Contracts secured by certain charges or arrangements

10. This paragraph applies to a contract where any obligation under the contract is—
(a) secured by a market charge within the meaning of Part 7 of the Companies Act 1989 (see section 173 of that Act),

(b) secured by a system-charge within the meaning of the Financial Markets and Insolvency Regulations 1996 (SI 1996/1469) (see regulation 2 of those Regulations), or

(c) secured or otherwise covered by a financial collateral arrangement within the meaning of the Financial Collateral Arrangements (No 2) Regulations 2003 (SI 2003/3226) (see regulation 3 of those Regulations).

Default arrangements and transfer orders

11. This paragraph applies to a contract which is included in default arrangements, or a transfer order, within the meaning of the Financial Markets and Insolvency (Settlement Finality) Regulations 1999 (SI 1999/2979) (see regulation 2 of those Regulations).

Card-based payment transactions

12. This paragraph applies to a contract to accept and process card-based payment transactions within the meaning given by Regulation (EU) 2015/751 of the European Parliament and of the Council of 29th April 2015 on interchange fees for card-based payment transactions.

Power to amend Schedule

13. (1) The Secretary of State may by regulations amend this Schedule so as to change the meaning of "contract or other instrument involving financial services" for the purposes of section A18.

(2) Regulations under this paragraph are subject to the affirmative resolution procedure.]

NOTES

Commencement: 26 June 2020.

Inserted by the Corporate Insolvency and Governance Act 2020, s 1(3), Sch 2, as from 26 June 2020.

SCHEDULE A1

(Schedule A1 (Moratorium Where Directors Propose Voluntary Arrangement) was originally inserted by the Insolvency Act 2000, s 1, Sch 1, paras 1, 4, as from 1 January 2003. It was subsequently repealed by the Corporate Insolvency and Governance Act 2020, s 2(1), Sch 3, paras 1, 30, as from 26 June 2020 (for transitional provisions, see s 2(2), (3) of the 2020 Act (at **[9.533]***) which provides that (without prejudice to the Interpretation Act 1978, s 16) nothing in the 2020 Act affects the operation of this Act, or any other enactment, in relation to a moratorium under this Schedule which comes into force before its repeal by Sch 3 to the 2020 Act (ie, 26 June 2020)).)*

[SCHEDULE B1
ADMINISTRATION

Section 8

[9.472]

Arrangement of Schedule

NATURE OF ADMINISTRATION

Administration

1. (1) For the purposes of this Act "administrator" of a company means a person appointed under this Schedule to manage the company's affairs, business and property.

(2) For the purposes of this Act—

(a) a company is "in administration" while the appointment of an administrator of the company has effect,

(b) a company "enters administration" when the appointment of an administrator takes effect,

(c) a company ceases to be in administration when the appointment of an administrator of the company ceases to have effect in accordance with this Schedule, and

(d) a company does not cease to be in administration merely because an administrator vacates office (by reason of resignation, death or otherwise) or is removed from office.

2. A person may be appointed as administrator of a company—

(a) by administration order of the court under paragraph 10,

(b) by the holder of a floating charge under paragraph 14, or

(c) by the company or its directors under paragraph 22.

Purpose of administration

3. (1) The administrator of a company must perform his functions with the objective of—

(a) rescuing the company as a going concern, or

(b) achieving a better result for the company's creditors as a whole than would be likely if the company were wound up (without first being in administration), or

(c) realising property in order to make a distribution to one or more secured or preferential creditors.

(2) Subject to sub-paragraph (4), the administrator of a company must perform his functions in the interests of the company's creditors as a whole.

(3) The administrator must perform his functions with the objective specified in sub-paragraph (1)(a) unless he thinks either—

(a) that it is not reasonably practicable to achieve that objective, or

(b) that the objective specified in sub-paragraph (1)(b) would achieve a better result for the company's creditors as a whole.

(4) The administrator may perform his functions with the objective specified in sub-paragraph (1)(c) only if—

(a) he thinks that it is not reasonably practicable to achieve either of the objectives specified in sub-paragraph (1)(a) and (b), and

(b) he does not unnecessarily harm the interests of the creditors of the company as a whole.

4. The administrator of a company must perform his functions as quickly and efficiently as is reasonably practicable.

Status of administrator

5. An administrator is an officer of the court (whether or not he is appointed by the court).

General restrictions

6. A person may be appointed as administrator of a company only if he is qualified to act as an insolvency practitioner in relation to the company.

7. A person may not be appointed as administrator of a company which is in administration (subject to the provisions of paragraphs 90 to 97 and 100 to 103 about replacement and additional administrators).

8. (1) A person may not be appointed as administrator of a company which is in liquidation by virtue of—

(a) a resolution for voluntary winding up, or

(b) a winding-up order.

(2) Sub-paragraph (1)(a) is subject to paragraph 38.

(3) Sub-paragraph (1)(b) is subject to paragraphs 37 and 38.

9. (1) A person may not be appointed as administrator of a company which—

(a) has a liability in respect of a deposit which it accepted in accordance with the Banking Act 1979 (c 37) or 1987 (c 22), but

(b) is not an authorised deposit taker.

(2) A person may not be appointed as administrator of a company which effects or carries out contracts of insurance.

(3) But sub-paragraph (2) does not apply to a company which—

(a) is exempt from the general prohibition in relation to effecting or carrying out contracts of insurance, or

(b) is an authorised deposit taker effecting or carrying out contracts of insurance in the course of a banking business.

(4) In this paragraph—

"authorised deposit taker" means a person with permission under Part IV of the Financial Services and Markets Act 2000 (c 8) to accept deposits, and

"the general prohibition" has the meaning given by section 19 of that Act.

(5) This paragraph shall be construed in accordance with—

(a) section 22 of the Financial Services and Markets Act 2000 (classes of regulated activity and categories of investment),

(b) any relevant order under that section, and

(c) Schedule 2 to that Act (regulated activities).

APPOINTMENT OF ADMINISTRATOR BY COURT

Administration order

10. An administration order is an order appointing a person as the administrator of a company.

Conditions for making order

11. The court may make an administration order in relation to a company only if satisfied—

(a) that the company is or is likely to become unable to pay its debts, and

(b) that the administration order is reasonably likely to achieve the purpose of administration.

Administration application

12. (1) An application to the court for an administration order in respect of a company (an "administration application") may be made only by—

(a) the company,

(b) the directors of the company,

(c) one or more creditors of the company,

(d) the [designated officer] for a magistrates' court in the exercise of the power conferred by section 87A of the Magistrates' Courts Act 1980 (c 43) (fine imposed on company), or

(e) a combination of persons listed in paragraphs (a) to (d).

(2) As soon as is reasonably practicable after the making of an administration application the applicant shall notify—

(a) any person who has appointed an administrative receiver of the company,
(b) any person who is or may be entitled to appoint an administrative receiver of the company,
(c) any person who is or may be entitled to appoint an administrator of the company under paragraph 14, and
(d) such other persons as may be prescribed.

(3) An administration application may not be withdrawn without the permission of the court.

(4) In sub-paragraph (1) "creditor" includes a contingent creditor and a prospective creditor.

[(5) Sub-paragraph (1) is without prejudice to section 7(4)(b).]

Powers of court

13. (1) On hearing an administration application the court may—
(a) make the administration order sought;
(b) dismiss the application;
(c) adjourn the hearing conditionally or unconditionally;
(d) make an interim order;
(e) treat the application as a winding-up petition and make any order which the court could make under section 125;
(f) make any other order which the court thinks appropriate.

(2) An appointment of an administrator by administration order takes effect—
(a) at a time appointed by the order, or
(b) where no time is appointed by the order, when the order is made.

(3) An interim order under sub-paragraph (1)(d) may, in particular—
(a) restrict the exercise of a power of the directors or the company;
(b) make provision conferring a discretion on the court or on a person qualified to act as an insolvency practitioner in relation to the company.

(4) This paragraph is subject to paragraph 39.

APPOINTMENT OF ADMINISTRATOR BY HOLDER OF FLOATING CHARGE

Power to appoint

14. (1) The holder of a qualifying floating charge in respect of a company's property may appoint an administrator of the company.

(2) For the purposes of sub-paragraph (1) a floating charge qualifies if created by an instrument which—
(a) states that this paragraph applies to the floating charge,
(b) purports to empower the holder of the floating charge to appoint an administrator of the company,
(c) purports to empower the holder of the floating charge to make an appointment which would be the appointment of an administrative receiver within the meaning given by section 29(2), or
(d) purports to empower the holder of a floating charge in Scotland to appoint a receiver who on appointment would be an administrative receiver.

(3) For the purposes of sub-paragraph (1) a person is the holder of a qualifying floating charge in respect of a company's property if he holds one or more debentures of the company secured—
(a) by a qualifying floating charge which relates to the whole or substantially the whole of the company's property,
(b) by a number of qualifying floating charges which together relate to the whole or substantially the whole of the company's property, or
(c) by charges and other forms of security which together relate to the whole or substantially the whole of the company's property and at least one of which is a qualifying floating charge.

Restrictions on power to appoint

15. (1) A person may not appoint an administrator under paragraph 14 unless—
(a) he has given at least two business days' written notice to the holder of any prior floating charge which satisfies paragraph 14(2), or
(b) the holder of any prior floating charge which satisfies paragraph 14(2) has consented in writing to the making of the appointment.

(2) One floating charge is prior to another for the purposes of this paragraph if—
(a) it was created first, or
(b) it is to be treated as having priority in accordance with an agreement to which the holder of each floating charge was party.

(3) Sub-paragraph (2) shall have effect in relation to Scotland as if the following were substituted for paragraph (a)—

"(a) it has priority of ranking in accordance with section 464(4)(b) of the Companies Act 1985 (c 6),

16. An administrator may not be appointed under paragraph 14 while a floating charge on which the appointment relies is not enforceable.

17. An administrator of a company may not be appointed under paragraph 14 if—
(a) a provisional liquidator of the company has been appointed under section 135, or
(b) an administrative receiver of the company is in office.

Notice of appointment

18. (1) A person who appoints an administrator of a company under paragraph 14 shall file with the court—
(a) a notice of appointment, and
(b) such other documents as may be prescribed.

(2) The notice of appointment must include a statutory declaration by or on behalf of the person who makes the appointment—

(a) that the person is the holder of a qualifying floating charge in respect of the company's property,
(b) that each floating charge relied on in making the appointment is (or was) enforceable on the date of the appointment, and
(c) that the appointment is in accordance with this Schedule.

(3) The notice of appointment must identify the administrator and must be accompanied by a statement by the administrator—
(a) that he consents to the appointment,
(b) that in his opinion the purpose of administration is reasonably likely to be achieved, and
(c) giving such other information and opinions as may be prescribed.

(4) For the purpose of a statement under sub-paragraph (3) an administrator may rely on information supplied by directors of the company (unless he has reason to doubt its accuracy).

(5) The notice of appointment and any document accompanying it must be in the prescribed form.

(6) A statutory declaration under sub-paragraph (2) must be made during the prescribed period.

(7) A person commits an offence if in a statutory declaration under sub-paragraph (2) he makes a statement—
(a) which is false, and
(b) which he does not reasonably believe to be true.

Commencement of appointment

19. The appointment of an administrator under paragraph 14 takes effect when the requirements of paragraph 18 are satisfied.

20. A person who appoints an administrator under paragraph 14—
(a) shall notify the administrator and such other persons as may be prescribed as soon as is reasonably practicable after the requirements of paragraph 18 are satisfied, and
(b) commits an offence if he fails without reasonable excuse to comply with paragraph (a).

Invalid appointment: indemnity

21. (1) This paragraph applies where—
(a) a person purports to appoint an administrator under paragraph 14, and
(b) the appointment is discovered to be invalid.

(2) The court may order the person who purported to make the appointment to indemnify the person appointed against liability which arises solely by reason of the appointment's invalidity.

APPOINTMENT OF ADMINISTRATOR BY COMPANY OR DIRECTORS

Power to appoint

22. (1) A company may appoint an administrator.

(2) The directors of a company may appoint an administrator.

Restrictions on power to appoint

23. (1) This paragraph applies where an administrator of a company is appointed—
(a) under paragraph 22, or
(b) on an administration application made by the company or its directors.

(2) An administrator of the company may not be appointed under paragraph 22 during the period of 12 months beginning with the date on which the appointment referred to in sub-paragraph (1) ceases to have effect.

24. . . .

25. An administrator of a company may not be appointed under paragraph 22 if—
(a) a petition for the winding up of the company has been presented and is not yet disposed of,
(b) an administration application has been made and is not yet disposed of, or
(c) an administrative receiver of the company is in office.

[25A. (1) Paragraph 25(a) does not prevent the appointment of an administrator of a company if the petition for the winding up of the company was presented after the person proposing to make the appointment filed the notice of intention to appoint with the court under paragraph 27.

(2) But sub-paragraph (1) does not apply if the petition was presented under a provision mentioned in paragraph 42(4).]

Notice of intention to appoint

26. (1) A person who proposes to make an appointment under paragraph 22 shall give at least five business days' written notice to—
(a) any person who is or may be entitled to appoint an administrative receiver of the company, and
(b) any person who is or may be entitled to appoint an administrator of the company under paragraph 14.

(2) A person who [gives notice of intention to appoint under sub-paragraph (1)] shall also give such notice as may be prescribed to such other persons as may be prescribed.

(3) A notice under this paragraph must—
(a) identify the proposed administrator, and
(b) be in the prescribed form.

27. (1) A person who gives notice of intention to appoint under paragraph 26 shall file with the court as soon as is reasonably practicable a copy of—
(a) the notice, and
(b) any document accompanying it.

(2) The copy filed under sub-paragraph (1) must be accompanied by a statutory declaration made by or on behalf of the person who proposes to make the appointment—

(a) that the company is or is likely to become unable to pay its debts,

(b) that the company is not in liquidation, and

(c) that, so far as the person making the statement is able to ascertain, the appointment is not prevented by paragraphs 23 to 25, and

(d) to such additional effect, and giving such information, as may be prescribed.

(3) A statutory declaration under sub-paragraph (2) must—

(a) be in the prescribed form, and

(b) be made during the prescribed period.

(4) A person commits an offence if in a statutory declaration under sub-paragraph (2) he makes a statement—

(a) which is false, and

(b) which he does not reasonably believe to be true.

28. (1) An appointment may not be made under paragraph 22 unless the person who makes the appointment has complied with any requirement of paragraphs 26 and 27 and—

(a) the period of notice specified in paragraph 26(1) has expired, or

(b) each person to whom notice has been given under paragraph 26(1) has consented in writing to the making of the appointment.

(2) An appointment may not be made under paragraph 22 after the period of ten business days beginning with the date on which the notice of intention to appoint is filed under paragraph 27(1).

Notice of appointment

29. (1) A person who appoints an administrator of a company under paragraph 22 shall file with the court—

(a) a notice of appointment, and

(b) such other documents as may be prescribed.

(2) The notice of appointment must include a statutory declaration by or on behalf of the person who makes the appointment—

(a) that the person is entitled to make an appointment under paragraph 22,

(b) that the appointment is in accordance with this Schedule, and

(c) that, so far as the person making the statement is able to ascertain, the statements made and information given in the statutory declaration filed with the notice of intention to appoint remain accurate.

(3) The notice of appointment must identify the administrator and must be accompanied by a statement by the administrator—

(a) that he consents to the appointment,

(b) that in his opinion the purpose of administration is reasonably likely to be achieved, and

(c) giving such other information and opinions as may be prescribed.

(4) For the purpose of a statement under sub-paragraph (3) an administrator may rely on information supplied by directors of the company (unless he has reason to doubt its accuracy).

(5) The notice of appointment and any document accompanying it must be in the prescribed form.

(6) A statutory declaration under sub-paragraph (2) must be made during the prescribed period.

(7) A person commits an offence if in a statutory declaration under sub-paragraph (2) he makes a statement—

(a) which is false, and

(b) which he does not reasonably believe to be true.

30. In a case in which no person is entitled to notice of intention to appoint under paragraph 26(1) (and paragraph 28 therefore does not apply)—

(a) the statutory declaration accompanying the notice of appointment must include the statements and information required under paragraph 27(2), and

(b) paragraph 29(2)(c) shall not apply.

Commencement of appointment

31. The appointment of an administrator under paragraph 22 takes effect when the requirements of paragraph 29 are satisfied.

32. A person who appoints an administrator under paragraph 22—

(a) shall notify the administrator and such other persons as may be prescribed as soon as is reasonably practicable after the requirements of paragraph 29 are satisfied, and

(b) commits an offence if he fails without reasonable excuse to comply with paragraph (a).

33. If before the requirements of paragraph 29 are satisfied the company enters administration by virtue of an administration order or an appointment under paragraph 14—

(a) the appointment under paragraph 22 shall not take effect, and

(b) paragraph 32 shall not apply.

Invalid appointment: indemnity

34. (1) This paragraph applies where—

(a) a person purports to appoint an administrator under paragraph 22, and

(b) the appointment is discovered to be invalid.

(2) The court may order the person who purported to make the appointment to indemnify the person appointed against liability which arises solely by reason of the appointment's invalidity.

ADMINISTRATION APPLICATION—SPECIAL CASES

Application by holder of floating charge

35. (1) This paragraph applies where an administration application in respect of a company—

(a) is made by the holder of a qualifying floating charge in respect of the company's property, and

(b) includes a statement that the application is made in reliance on this paragraph.

(2) The court may make an administration order—

(a) whether or not satisfied that the company is or is likely to become unable to pay its debts, but

(b) only if satisfied that the applicant could appoint an administrator under paragraph 14.

Intervention by holder of floating charge

36. (1) This paragraph applies where—

(a) an administration application in respect of a company is made by a person who is not the holder of a qualifying floating charge in respect of the company's property, and

(b) the holder of a qualifying floating charge in respect of the company's property applies to the court to have a specified person appointed as administrator (and not the person specified by the administration applicant).

(2) The court shall grant an application under sub-paragraph (1)(b) unless the court thinks it right to refuse the application because of the particular circumstances of the case.

Application where company in liquidation

37. (1) This paragraph applies where the holder of a qualifying floating charge in respect of a company's property could appoint an administrator under paragraph 14 but for paragraph 8(1)(b).

(2) The holder of the qualifying floating charge may make an administration application.

(3) If the court makes an administration order on hearing an application made by virtue of sub-paragraph (2)—

(a) the court shall discharge the winding-up order,

(b) the court shall make provision for such matters as may be prescribed,

(c) the court may make other consequential provision,

(d) the court shall specify which of the powers under this Schedule are to be exercisable by the administrator, and

(e) this Schedule shall have effect with such modifications as the court may specify.

38. (1) The liquidator of a company may make an administration application.

(2) If the court makes an administration order on hearing an application made by virtue of sub-paragraph (1)—

(a) the court shall discharge any winding-up order in respect of the company,

(b) the court shall make provision for such matters as may be prescribed,

(c) the court may make other consequential provision,

(d) the court shall specify which of the powers under this Schedule are to be exercisable by the administrator, and

(e) this Schedule shall have effect with such modifications as the court may specify.

Effect of administrative receivership

39. (1) Where there is an administrative receiver of a company the court must dismiss an administration application in respect of the company unless—

(a) the person by or on behalf of whom the receiver was appointed consents to the making of the administration order,

(b) the court thinks that the security by virtue of which the receiver was appointed would be liable to be released or discharged under sections 238 to 240 (transaction at undervalue and preference) if an administration order were made,

(c) the court thinks that the security by virtue of which the receiver was appointed would be avoided under section 245 (avoidance of floating charge) if an administration order were made, or

(d) the court thinks that the security by virtue of which the receiver was appointed would be challengeable under section 242 (gratuitous alienations) or 243 (unfair preferences) or under any rule of law in Scotland.

(2) Sub-paragraph (1) applies whether the administrative receiver is appointed before or after the making of the administration application.

EFFECT OF ADMINISTRATION

Dismissal of pending winding-up petition

40. (1) A petition for the winding up of a company—

(a) shall be dismissed on the making of an administration order in respect of the company, and

(b) shall be suspended while the company is in administration following an appointment under paragraph 14.

(2) Sub-paragraph (1)(b) does not apply to a petition presented under—

(a) section 124A (public interest),

[(aa) section 124B (SEs),] or

(b) section 367 of the Financial Services and Markets Act 2000 (c 8) (petition by [Financial Conduct Authority or Prudential Regulation Authority]).

(3) Where an administrator becomes aware that a petition was presented under a provision referred to in sub-paragraph (2) before his appointment, he shall apply to the court for directions under paragraph 63.

Dismissal of administrative or other receiver

41. (1) When an administration order takes effect in respect of a company any administrative receiver of the company shall vacate office.

(2) Where a company is in administration, any receiver of part of the company's property shall vacate office if the administrator requires him to.

(3) Where an administrative receiver or receiver vacates office under sub-paragraph (1) or (2)—

(a) his remuneration shall be charged on and paid out of any property of the company which was in his custody or under his control immediately before he vacated office, and

(b) he need not take any further steps under section 40 or 59.

(4) In the application of sub-paragraph (3)(a)—

(a) "remuneration" includes expenses properly incurred and any indemnity to which the administrative receiver or receiver is entitled out of the assets of the company,

(b) the charge imposed takes priority over security held by the person by whom or on whose behalf the administrative receiver or receiver was appointed, and

(c) the provision for payment is subject to paragraph 43.

Moratorium on insolvency proceedings

42. (1) This paragraph applies to a company in administration.

(2) No resolution may be passed for the winding up of the company.

(3) No order may be made for the winding up of the company.

(4) Sub-paragraph (3) does not apply to an order made on a petition presented under—

(a) section 124A (public interest),

[(aa) section 124B (SEs),] or

(b) section 367 of the Financial Services and Markets Act 2000 (c 8) (petition by [Financial Conduct Authority or Prudential Regulation Authority]).

(5) If a petition presented under a provision referred to in sub-paragraph (4) comes to the attention of the administrator, he shall apply to the court for directions under paragraph 63.

Moratorium on other legal process

43. (1) This paragraph applies to a company in administration.

(2) No step may be taken to enforce security over the company's property except—

(a) with the consent of the administrator, or

(b) with the permission of the court.

(3) No step may be taken to repossess goods in the company's possession under a hire-purchase agreement except—

(a) with the consent of the administrator, or

(b) with the permission of the court.

(4) A landlord may not exercise a right of forfeiture by peaceable re-entry in relation to premises let to the company except—

(a) with the consent of the administrator, or

(b) with the permission of the court.

(5) In Scotland, a landlord may not exercise a right of irritancy in relation to premises let to the company except—

(a) with the consent of the administrator, or

(b) with the permission of the court.

(6) No legal process (including legal proceedings, execution, distress and diligence) may be instituted or continued against the company or property of the company except—

(a) with the consent of the administrator, or

(b) with the permission of the court.

[(6A) An administrative receiver of the company may not be appointed.]

(7) Where the court gives permission for a transaction under this paragraph it may impose a condition on or a requirement in connection with the transaction.

(8) In this paragraph "landlord" includes a person to whom rent is payable.

Interim moratorium

44. (1) This paragraph applies where an administration application in respect of a company has been made and—

(a) the application has not yet been granted or dismissed, or

(b) the application has been granted but the administration order has not yet taken effect.

(2) This paragraph also applies from the time when a copy of notice of intention to appoint an administrator under paragraph 14 is filed with the court until—

(a) the appointment of the administrator takes effect, or

(b) the period of five business days beginning with the date of filing expires without an administrator having been appointed.

(3) Sub-paragraph (2) has effect in relation to a notice of intention to appoint only if it is in the prescribed form.

(4) This paragraph also applies from the time when a copy of notice of intention to appoint an administrator is filed with the court under paragraph 27(1) until—

(a) the appointment of the administrator takes effect, or

(b) the period specified in paragraph 28(2) expires without an administrator having been appointed.

(5) The provisions of paragraphs 42 and 43 shall apply (ignoring any reference to the consent of the administrator).

(6) If there is an administrative receiver of the company when the administration application is made, the provisions of paragraphs 42 and 43 shall not begin to apply by virtue of this paragraph until the person by or on behalf of whom the receiver was appointed consents to the making of the administration order.

(7) This paragraph does not prevent or require the permission of the court for—

(a) the presentation of a petition for the winding up of the company under a provision mentioned in paragraph 42(4),

(b) the appointment of an administrator under paragraph 14,

(c) the appointment of an administrative receiver of the company, or

(d) the carrying out by an administrative receiver (whenever appointed) of his functions.

Publicity

[45. (1) While a company is in administration, every business document issued by or on behalf of the company or the administrator, and all the company's websites, must state—

(a) the name of the administrator, and
(b) that the affairs, business and property of the company are being managed by the administrator.

(2) Any of the following persons commits an offence if without reasonable excuse the person authorises or permits a contravention of sub-paragraph (1)—

(a) the administrator,
(b) an officer of the company, and
(c) the company.

(3) In sub-paragraph (1) "business document" means—

(a) an invoice,
(b) an order for goods or services,
(c) a business letter, and
(d) an order form,

whether in hard copy, electronic or any other form.]

PROCESS OF ADMINISTRATION

Announcement of administrator's appointment

46. (1) This paragraph applies where a person becomes the administrator of a company.

(2) As soon as is reasonably practicable the administrator shall—

(a) send a notice of his appointment to the company, and
(b) publish a notice of his appointment in the prescribed manner.

(3) As soon as is reasonably practicable the administrator shall—

(a) obtain a list of the company's creditors, and
(b) send a notice of his appointment to each creditor of whose claim and address he is aware.

(4) The administrator shall send a notice of his appointment to the registrar of companies before the end of the period of 7 days beginning with the date specified in sub-paragraph (6).

(5) The administrator shall send a notice of his appointment to such persons as may be prescribed before the end of the prescribed period beginning with the date specified in sub-paragraph (6).

(6) The date for the purpose of sub-paragraphs (4) and (5) is—

(a) in the case of an administrator appointed by administration order, the date of the order,
(b) in the case of an administrator appointed under paragraph 14, the date on which he receives notice under paragraph 20, and
(c) in the case of an administrator appointed under paragraph 22, the date on which he receives notice under paragraph 32.

(7) The court may direct that sub-paragraph (3)(b) or (5)—

(a) shall not apply, or
(b) shall apply with the substitution of a different period.

(8) A notice under this paragraph must—

(a) contain the prescribed information, and
(b) be in the prescribed form.

(9) An administrator commits an offence if he fails without reasonable excuse to comply with a requirement of this paragraph.

Statement of company's affairs

47. (1) As soon as is reasonably practicable after appointment the administrator of a company shall by notice in the prescribed form require one or more relevant persons to provide the administrator with a statement of the affairs of the company.

(2) The statement must—

(a) be verified by a statement of truth in accordance with Civil Procedure Rules,
(b) be in the prescribed form,
(c) give particulars of the company's property, debts and liabilities,
(d) give the names and addresses of the company's creditors,
(e) specify the security held by each creditor,
(f) give the date on which each security was granted, and
(g) contain such other information as may be prescribed.

(3) In sub-paragraph (1) "relevant person" means—

(a) a person who is or has been an officer of the company,
(b) a person who took part in the formation of the company during the period of one year ending with the date on which the company enters administration,
(c) a person employed by the company during that period, and
(d) a person who is or has been during that period an officer or employee of a company which is or has been during that year an officer of the company.

(4) For the purpose of sub-paragraph (3) a reference to employment is a reference to employment through a contract of employment or a contract for services.

(5) In Scotland, a statement of affairs under sub-paragraph (1) must be a statutory declaration made in accordance with the Statutory Declarations Act 1835 (c 62) (and sub-paragraph (2)(a) shall not apply).

48. (1) A person required to submit a statement of affairs must do so before the end of the period of 11 days beginning with the day on which he receives notice of the requirement.

(2) The administrator may—

(a) revoke a requirement under paragraph 47(1), or

(b) extend the period specified in sub-paragraph (1) (whether before or after expiry).

(3) If the administrator refuses a request to act under sub-paragraph (2)—

(a) the person whose request is refused may apply to the court, and

(b) the court may take action of a kind specified in sub-paragraph (2).

(4) A person commits an offence if he fails without reasonable excuse to comply with a requirement under paragraph 47(1).

Administrator's proposals

49. (1) The administrator of a company shall make a statement setting out proposals for achieving the purpose of administration.

(2) A statement under sub-paragraph (1) must, in particular—

(a) deal with such matters as may be prescribed, and

(b) where applicable, explain why the administrator thinks that the objective mentioned in paragraph 3(1)(a) or (b) cannot be achieved.

(3) Proposals under this paragraph may include—

(a) a proposal for a voluntary arrangement under Part I of this Act (although this paragraph is without prejudice to section 4(3));

(b) a proposal for a compromise or arrangement to be sanctioned under [Part 26 [or 26A] of the Companies Act 2006 (arrangements and reconstructions)].

(4) The administrator shall send a copy of the statement of his proposals—

(a) to the registrar of companies,

(b) to every creditor of the company[, other than an opted-out creditor,] of whose claim and address he is aware, and

(c) to every member of the company of whose address he is aware.

(5) The administrator shall comply with sub-paragraph (4)—

(a) as soon as is reasonably practicable after the company enters administration, and

(b) in any event, before the end of the period of eight weeks beginning with the day on which the company enters administration.

(6) The administrator shall be taken to comply with sub-paragraph (4)(c) if he publishes in the prescribed manner a notice undertaking to provide a copy of the statement of proposals free of charge to any member of the company who applies in writing to a specified address.

(7) An administrator commits an offence if he fails without reasonable excuse to comply with sub-paragraph (5).

(8) A period specified in this paragraph may be varied in accordance with paragraph 107.

. . .

50. . . .

[Consideration of administrator's proposals by creditors]

51. [(1) The administrator must seek a decision from the company's creditors as to whether they approve the proposals set out in the statement made under paragraph 49(1).

(2) The initial decision date for that decision must be within the period of 10 weeks beginning with the day on which the company enters administration.

(3) The "initial decision date" for that decision—

(a) if the decision is initially sought using the deemed consent procedure, is the date on which a decision will be made if the creditors by that procedure approve the proposals, and

(b) if the decision is initially sought using a qualifying decision procedure, is the date on or before which a decision will be made if it is made by that qualifying decision procedure (assuming that date does not change after the procedure is instigated).]

(4) A period specified in this paragraph may be varied in accordance with paragraph 107.

(5) An administrator commits an offence if he fails without reasonable excuse to comply with a requirement of this paragraph.

52. (1) Paragraph 51(1) shall not apply where the statement of proposals states that the administrator thinks—

(a) that the company has sufficient property to enable each creditor of the company to be paid in full,

(b) that the company has insufficient property to enable a distribution to be made to unsecured creditors other than by virtue of section 176A(2)(a), or

(c) that neither of the objectives specified in paragraph 3(1)(a) and (b) can be achieved.

(2) But the administrator shall [seek a decision from the company's creditors as to whether they approve the proposals set out in the statement made under paragraph 49(1) if requested to do so]—

(a) by creditors of the company whose debts amount to at least 10% of the total debts of the company,

(b) in the prescribed manner, and

(c) in the prescribed period.

[(3) Where a decision is sought by virtue of sub-paragraph (2) the initial decision date (as defined in paragraph 51(3)) must be within the prescribed period.]

(4) The period prescribed under sub-paragraph (3) may be varied in accordance with paragraph 107.

[Creditors' decision]

53. [(1) The company's creditors may approve the administrator's proposals—

(a) without modification, or

(b) with modification to which the administrator consents.]

(2) [The] administrator shall as soon as is reasonably practicable report any decision taken [by the company's creditors] to—

(a) the court,

(b) the registrar of companies, and

(c) such other persons as may be prescribed.

(3) An administrator commits an offence if he fails without reasonable excuse to comply with sub-paragraph (2).

Revision of administrator's proposals

54. (1) This paragraph applies where—

(a) an administrator's proposals have been approved (with or without modification) [by the company's creditors],

(b) the administrator proposes a revision to the proposals, and

(c) the administrator thinks that the proposed revision is substantial.

(2) The administrator shall—

(a) . . .

(b) send a statement in the prescribed form of the proposed revision . . . to each creditor [who is not an opted-out creditor],

(c) send a copy of the statement, within the prescribed period, to each member of the company of whose address he is aware, and

[(d) seek a decision from the company's creditors as to whether they approve the proposed revision.]

(3) The administrator shall be taken to have complied with sub-paragraph (2)(c) if he publishes a notice undertaking to provide a copy of the statement free of charge to any member of the company who applies in writing to a specified address.

(4) A notice under sub-paragraph (3) must be published—

(a) in the prescribed manner, and

(b) within the prescribed period.

[(5) The company's creditors may approve the proposed revision—

(a) without modification, or

(b) with modification to which the administrator consents.]

(6) [The] administrator shall as soon as is reasonably practicable report any decision taken [by the company's creditors] to—

(a) the court,

(b) the registrar of companies, and

(c) such other persons as may be prescribed.

(7) An administrator commits an offence if he fails without reasonable excuse to comply with sub-paragraph (6).

Failure to obtain approval of administrator's proposals

55. [(1) This paragraph applies where an administrator—

(a) reports to the court under paragraph 53 that a company's creditors have failed to approve the administrator's proposals, or

(b) reports to the court under paragraph 54 that a company's creditors have failed to approve a revision of the administrator's proposals.]

(2) The court may—

(a) provide that the appointment of an administrator shall cease to have effect from a specified time;

(b) adjourn the hearing conditionally or unconditionally;

(c) make an interim order;

(d) make an order on a petition for winding up suspended by virtue of paragraph 40(1)(b);

(e) make any other order (including an order making consequential provision) that the court thinks appropriate.

Further creditors' [decisions]

56. (1) The administrator of a company shall [seek a decision from the company's creditors on a matter] if—

(a) it is requested in the prescribed manner by creditors of the company whose debts amount to at least 10% of the total debts of the company, or

(b) he is directed by the court to [do so].

(2) An administrator commits an offence if he fails without reasonable excuse to [seek a decision from the company's creditors on a matter] as required by this paragraph.

Creditors' committee

57. (1) [The company's creditors may, in accordance with the rules,] establish a creditors' committee.

(2) A creditors' committee shall carry out functions conferred on it by or under this Act.

(3) A creditors' committee may require the administrator—

(a) to attend on the committee at any reasonable time of which he is given at least seven days' notice, and

(b) to provide the committee with information about the exercise of his functions.

. . .

58. . . .

FUNCTIONS OF ADMINISTRATOR

General powers

59. (1) The administrator of a company may do anything necessary or expedient for the management of the affairs, business and property of the company.

(2) A provision of this Schedule which expressly permits the administrator to do a specified thing is without prejudice to the generality of sub-paragraph (1).

(3) A person who deals with the administrator of a company in good faith and for value need not inquire whether the administrator is acting within his powers.

60. [(1)] The administrator of a company has the powers specified in Schedule 1 to this Act.

[(2) But the power to sell, hire out or otherwise dispose of property is subject to any regulations that may be made under paragraph 60A.]

[60A. (1) The Secretary of State may by regulations make provision for—

(a) prohibiting, or

(b) imposing requirements or conditions in relation to,

the disposal, hiring out or sale of property of a company by the administrator to a connected person in circumstances specified in the regulations.

(2) Regulations under this paragraph may in particular require the approval of, or provide for the imposition of requirements or conditions by—

(a) creditors of the company,

(b) the court, or

(c) a person of a description specified in the regulations.

(3) In sub-paragraph (1), "connected person", in relation to a company, means—

(a) a relevant person in relation to the company, or

(b) a company connected with the company.

(4) For the purposes of sub-paragraph (3)—

(a) "relevant person", in relation to a company, means—

  (i) a director or other officer, or shadow director, of the company;

  (ii) a non-employee associate of such a person;

  (iii) a non-employee associate of the company;

(b) a company is connected with another if any relevant person of one is or has been a relevant person of the other.

(5) In sub-paragraph (4), "non-employee associate" of a person means a person who is an associate of that person otherwise than by virtue of employing or being employed by that person.

(6) Subsection (10) of section 435 (extended definition of company) applies for the purposes of sub-paragraphs (3) to (5) as it applies for the purposes of that section.

(7) Regulations under this paragraph may—

(a) make different provision for different purposes;

(b) make incidental, consequential, supplemental and transitional provision.

(8) Regulations under this paragraph are to be made by statutory instrument.

(9) Regulations under this paragraph may not be made unless a draft of the statutory instrument containing the regulations has been laid before Parliament and approved by a resolution of each House of Parliament.

[(10) This paragraph expires at the end of June 2021 unless the power conferred by it is exercised before then.]]

61. The administrator of a company—

(a) may remove a director of the company, and

(b) may appoint a director of the company (whether or not to fill a vacancy).

62. The administrator of a company [may—

(a) call a meeting of members of the company;

(b) seek a decision on any matter from the company's creditors.]

63. The administrator of a company may apply to the court for directions in connection with his functions.

64. (1) A company in administration or an officer of a company in administration may not exercise a management power without the consent of the administrator.

(2) For the purpose of sub-paragraph (1)—

(a) "management power" means a power which could be exercised so as to interfere with the exercise of the administrator's powers,

(b) it is immaterial whether the power is conferred by an enactment or an instrument, and

(c) consent may be general or specific.

Distribution

[64A. (1) This paragraph applies where a company enters administration before the end of the period of 12 weeks beginning with the day after the end of any moratorium for the company under Part A1.

(2) The administrator must make a distribution to the creditors of the company in respect of—

(a) moratorium debts (within the meaning given by section 174A), and

(b) priority pre-moratorium debts (within the meaning given by section 174A).

(3) A sum payable under sub-paragraph (2) is to be paid in priority to—

(a) any security to which paragraph 70 applies or paragraph 115(1) applies;

(b) any sums payable under paragraph 99.

(4) The administrator must realise any property necessary to comply with sub-paragraph (2).

(5) The rules may make provision as to the order in which the moratorium and priority pre-moratorium debts rank among themselves for the purposes of this paragraph in a case where the assets of the company are insufficient to meet them in full.]

65. [(1) If the assets of a company are sufficient to meet any debts or other liabilities payable under paragraph 64A in full, the administrator of the company may make a distribution to any other creditor of the company.]

(2) [Sections 175 and 176AZA] shall apply in relation to a distribution under this paragraph as [they apply] in relation to a winding up.

(3) A payment may not be made by way of distribution under this paragraph to a creditor of the company who is neither secured nor preferential [unless—

(a) the distribution is made by virtue of section 176A(2)(a), or

(b)] the court gives permission.

66. [If the debts and other liabilities payable under paragraph 64A have been met, the administrator of a company] may make a payment otherwise than in accordance with paragraph 65 or paragraph 13 of Schedule 1 if he thinks it likely to assist achievement of the purpose of administration.

General duties

67. The administrator of a company shall on his appointment take custody or control of all the property to which he thinks the company is entitled.

68. (1) Subject to sub-paragraph (2), the administrator of a company shall manage its affairs, business and property in accordance with—

(a) any proposals approved under paragraph 53,

(b) any revision of those proposals which is made by him and which he does not consider substantial, and

(c) any revision of those proposals approved under paragraph 54.

(2) If the court gives directions to the administrator of a company in connection with any aspect of his management of the company's affairs, business or property, the administrator shall comply with the directions.

(3) The court may give directions under sub-paragraph (2) only if—

(a) no proposals have been approved under paragraph 53,

(b) the directions are consistent with any proposals or revision approved under paragraph 53 or 54,

(c) the court thinks the directions are required in order to reflect a change in circumstances since the approval of proposals or a revision under paragraph 53 or 54, or

(d) the court thinks the directions are desirable because of a misunderstanding about proposals or a revision approved under paragraph 53 or 54.

Administrator as agent of company

69. In exercising his functions under this Schedule the administrator of a company acts as its agent.

Charged property: floating charge

70. (1) The administrator of a company may dispose of or take action relating to property which is subject to a floating charge as if it were not subject to the charge.

(2) Where property is disposed of in reliance on sub-paragraph (1) the holder of the floating charge shall have the same priority in respect of acquired property as he had in respect of the property disposed of.

(3) In sub-paragraph (2) "acquired property" means property of the company which directly or indirectly represents the property disposed of.

Charged property: non-floating charge

71. (1) The court may by order enable the administrator of a company to dispose of property which is subject to a security (other than a floating charge) as if it were not subject to the security.

(2) An order under sub-paragraph (1) may be made only—

(a) on the application of the administrator, and

(b) where the court thinks that disposal of the property would be likely to promote the purpose of administration in respect of the company.

(3) An order under this paragraph is subject to the condition that there be applied towards discharging the sums secured by the security—

(a) the net proceeds of disposal of the property, and

(b) any additional money required to be added to the net proceeds so as to produce the amount determined by the court as the net amount which would be realised on a sale of the property at market value.

(4) If an order under this paragraph relates to more than one security, application of money under sub-paragraph (3) shall be in the order of the priorities of the securities.

(5) An administrator who makes a successful application for an order under this paragraph shall send a copy of the order to the registrar of companies before the end of the period of 14 days starting with the date of the order.

(6) An administrator commits an offence if he fails to comply with sub-paragraph (5) without reasonable excuse.

Hire-purchase property

72. (1) The court may by order enable the administrator of a company to dispose of goods which are in the possession of the company under a hire-purchase agreement as if all the rights of the owner under the agreement were vested in the company.

(2) An order under sub-paragraph (1) may be made only—

(a) on the application of the administrator, and

(b) where the court thinks that disposal of the goods would be likely to promote the purpose of administration in respect of the company.

(3) An order under this paragraph is subject to the condition that there be applied towards discharging the sums payable under the hire-purchase agreement—

(a) the net proceeds of disposal of the goods, and

(b) any additional money required to be added to the net proceeds so as to produce the amount determined by the court as the net amount which would be realised on a sale of the goods at market value.

(4) An administrator who makes a successful application for an order under this paragraph shall send a copy of the order to the registrar of companies before the end of the period of 14 days starting with the date of the order.

(5) An administrator commits an offence if he fails without reasonable excuse to comply with sub-paragraph (4).

Protection for [priority] creditor

73. (1) An administrator's statement of proposals under paragraph 49 may not include any action which—

(a) affects the right of a secured creditor of the company to enforce his security,

(b) would result in a preferential debt of the company being paid otherwise than in priority to its non-preferential debts, . . .

[(bb) would result in an ordinary preferential debt of the company being paid otherwise than in priority to any secondary preferential debts that it may have,]

(c) would result in one preferential creditor of the company being paid a smaller proportion of [an ordinary preferential debt] than another[, . . .

(d) would result in one preferential creditor of the company being paid a smaller proportion of a secondary preferential debt than another], [or

(e) if the company is a relevant financial institution (see section 387A), would result in any non-preferential debt being paid otherwise than in accordance with the rules in section 176AZA(2) or (3).]

(2) Sub-paragraph (1) does not apply to—

(a) action to which the relevant creditor consents,

(b) a proposal for a voluntary arrangement under Part I of this Act (although this sub-paragraph is without prejudice to section 4(3)), . . .

(c) a proposal for a compromise or arrangement to be sanctioned under [Part 26 [or 26A] of the Companies Act 2006 (arrangements and reconstructions)]; [. . .

(d) . . .]

(3) The reference to a statement of proposals in sub-paragraph (1) includes a reference to a statement as revised or modified.

Challenge to administrator's conduct of company

74. (1) A creditor or member of a company in administration may apply to the court claiming that—

(a) the administrator is acting or has acted so as unfairly to harm the interests of the applicant (whether alone or in common with some or all other members or creditors), or

(b) the administrator proposes to act in a way which would unfairly harm the interests of the applicant (whether alone or in common with some or all other members or creditors).

(2) A creditor or member of a company in administration may apply to the court claiming that the administrator is not performing his functions as quickly or as efficiently as is reasonably practicable.

(3) The court may—

(a) grant relief;

(b) dismiss the application;

(c) adjourn the hearing conditionally or unconditionally;

(d) make an interim order;

(e) make any other order it thinks appropriate.

(4) In particular, an order under this paragraph may—

(a) regulate the administrator's exercise of his functions;

(b) require the administrator to do or not do a specified thing;

[(c) require a decision of the company's creditors to be sought on a matter;]

(d) provide for the appointment of an administrator to cease to have effect;

(e) make consequential provision.

(5) An order may be made on a claim under sub-paragraph (1) whether or not the action complained of—

(a) is within the administrator's powers under this Schedule;

(b) was taken in reliance on an order under paragraph 71 or 72.

(6) An order may not be made under this paragraph if it would impede or prevent the implementation of—

(a) a voluntary arrangement approved under Part I,

(b) a compromise or arrangement sanctioned under [Part 26 [or 26A] of the Companies Act 2006 (arrangements and reconstructions)], . . .

[(ba) . . .]

(c) proposals or a revision approved under paragraph 53 or 54 more than 28 days before the day on which the application for the order under this paragraph is made.

Misfeasance

75. (1) The court may examine the conduct of a person who—

(a) is or purports to be the administrator of a company, or

(b) has been or has purported to be the administrator of a company.

(2) An examination under this paragraph may be held only on the application of—

(a) the official receiver,

(b) the administrator of the company,

(c) the liquidator of the company,

(d) a creditor of the company, or

(e) a contributory of the company.

(3) An application under sub-paragraph (2) must allege that the administrator—

(a) has misapplied or retained money or other property of the company,
(b) has become accountable for money or other property of the company,
(c) has breached a fiduciary or other duty in relation to the company, or
(d) has been guilty of misfeasance.

(4) On an examination under this paragraph into a person's conduct the court may order him—

(a) to repay, restore or account for money or property;
(b) to pay interest;
(c) to contribute a sum to the company's property by way of compensation for breach of duty or misfeasance.

(5) In sub-paragraph (3) "administrator" includes a person who purports or has purported to be a company's administrator.

(6) An application under sub-paragraph (2) may be made in respect of an administrator who has been discharged under paragraph 98 only with the permission of the court.

ENDING ADMINISTRATION

Automatic end of administration

76. (1) The appointment of an administrator shall cease to have effect at the end of the period of one year beginning with the date on which it takes effect.

(2) But—

(a) on the application of an administrator the court may by order extend his term of office for a specified period, and
(b) an administrator's term of office may be extended for a specified period not exceeding [one year] by consent.

77. (1) An order of the court under paragraph 76—

(a) may be made in respect of an administrator whose term of office has already been extended by order or by consent, but
(b) may not be made after the expiry of the administrator's term of office.

(2) Where an order is made under paragraph 76 the administrator shall as soon as is reasonably practicable notify the registrar of companies.

(3) An administrator who fails without reasonable excuse to comply with sub-paragraph (2) commits an offence.

78. (1) In paragraph 76(2)(b) "consent" means consent of—

(a) each secured creditor of the company, and
[(b) if the company has unsecured debts, the unsecured creditors of the company.]

(2) But where the administrator has made a statement under paragraph 52(1)(b) "consent" means—

(a) consent of each secured creditor of the company, or
(b) if the administrator thinks that a distribution may be made to preferential creditors, consent of—
    (i) each secured creditor of the company, and
    [(ii) the preferential creditors of the company.]

[(2A) Whether the company's unsecured creditors or preferential creditors consent is to be determined by the administrator seeking a decision from those creditors as to whether they consent.]

(3) . . .

(4) An administrator's term of office—

(a) may be extended by consent only once,
(b) may not be extended by consent after extension by order of the court, and
(c) may not be extended by consent after expiry.

(5) Where an administrator's term of office is extended by consent he shall as soon as is reasonably practicable—

(a) file notice of the extension with the court, and
(b) notify the registrar of companies.

(6) An administrator who fails without reasonable excuse to comply with sub-paragraph (5) commits an offence.

Court ending administration on application of administrator

79. (1) On the application of the administrator of a company the court may provide for the appointment of an administrator of the company to cease to have effect from a specified time.

(2) The administrator of a company shall make an application under this paragraph if—

(a) he thinks the purpose of administration cannot be achieved in relation to the company,
(b) he thinks the company should not have entered administration, or
(c) [the company's creditors decide that he must] make an application under this paragraph.

(3) The administrator of a company shall make an application under this paragraph if—

(a) the administration is pursuant to an administration order, and
(b) the administrator thinks that the purpose of administration has been sufficiently achieved in relation to the company.

(4) On an application under this paragraph the court may—

(a) adjourn the hearing conditionally or unconditionally;
(b) dismiss the application;
(c) make an interim order;
(d) make any order it thinks appropriate (whether in addition to, in consequence of or instead of the order applied for).

Termination of administration where objective achieved

80. (1) This paragraph applies where an administrator of a company is appointed under paragraph 14 or 22.

(2) If the administrator thinks that the purpose of administration has been sufficiently achieved in relation to the company he may file a notice in the prescribed form—

(a) with the court, and

(b) with the registrar of companies.

(3) The administrator's appointment shall cease to have effect when the requirements of sub-paragraph (2) are satisfied.

(4) Where the administrator files a notice he shall within the prescribed period send a copy to every creditor of the company[, other than an opted-out creditor,] of whose claim and address he is aware.

(5) The rules may provide that the administrator is taken to have complied with sub-paragraph (4) if before the end of the prescribed period he publishes in the prescribed manner a notice undertaking to provide a copy of the notice under sub-paragraph (2) to any creditor of the company who applies in writing to a specified address.

(6) An administrator who fails without reasonable excuse to comply with sub-paragraph (4) commits an offence.

Court ending administration on application of creditor

81. (1) On the application of a creditor of a company the court may provide for the appointment of an administrator of the company to cease to have effect at a specified time.

(2) An application under this paragraph must allege an improper motive—

(a) in the case of an administrator appointed by administration order, on the part of the applicant for the order, or

(b) in any other case, on the part of the person who appointed the administrator.

(3) On an application under this paragraph the court may—

(a) adjourn the hearing conditionally or unconditionally;

(b) dismiss the application;

(c) make an interim order;

(d) make any order it thinks appropriate (whether in addition to, in consequence of or instead of the order applied for).

Public interest winding-up

82. (1) This paragraph applies where a winding-up order is made for the winding up of a company in administration on a petition presented under—

(a) section 124A (public interest),

[(aa) section 124B (SEs),] or

(b) section 367 of the Financial Services and Markets Act 2000 (c 8) (petition by [Financial Conduct Authority or Prudential Regulation Authority]).

(2) This paragraph also applies where a provisional liquidator of a company in administration is appointed following the presentation of a petition under any of the provisions listed in sub-paragraph (1).

(3) The court shall order—

(a) that the appointment of the administrator shall cease to have effect, or

(b) that the appointment of the administrator shall continue to have effect.

(4) If the court makes an order under sub-paragraph (3)(b) it may also—

(a) specify which of the powers under this Schedule are to be exercisable by the administrator, and

(b) order that this Schedule shall have effect in relation to the administrator with specified modifications.

Moving from administration to creditors' voluntary liquidation

83. (1) This paragraph applies in England and Wales where the administrator of a company thinks—

(a) that the total amount which each secured creditor of the company is likely to receive has been paid to him or set aside for him, and

(b) that a distribution will be made to unsecured creditors of the company (if there are any [which is not a distribution by virtue of section 176A(2)(a)]).

(2) This paragraph applies in Scotland where the administrator of a company thinks—

(a) that each secured creditor of the company will receive payment in respect of his debt, and

(b) that a distribution will be made to unsecured creditors (if there are any [which is not a distribution by virtue of section 176A(2)(a)]).

(3) The administrator may send to the registrar of companies a notice that this paragraph applies.

(4) On receipt of a notice under sub-paragraph (3) the registrar shall register it.

(5) If an administrator sends a notice under sub-paragraph (3) he shall as soon as is reasonably practicable—

(a) file a copy of the notice with the court, and

(b) send a copy of the notice to each creditor[, other than an opted-out creditor,] of whose claim and address he is aware.

(6) On the registration of a notice under sub-paragraph (3)—

(a) the appointment of an administrator in respect of the company shall cease to have effect, and

(b) the company shall be wound up as if a resolution for voluntary winding up under section 84 were passed on the day on which the notice is registered.

(7) The liquidator for the purposes of the winding up shall be—

(a) a person nominated by the creditors of the company in the prescribed manner and within the prescribed period, or

(b) if no person is nominated under paragraph (a), the administrator.

(8) In the application of Part IV to a winding up by virtue of this paragraph—

(a) section 85 shall not apply,

(b) section 86 shall apply as if the reference to the time of the passing of the resolution for voluntary winding up were a reference to the beginning of the date of registration of the notice under sub-paragraph (3),
(c) section 89 does not apply,
(d) sections . . . 99 and 100 shall not apply,
(e) section 129 shall apply as if the reference to the time of the passing of the resolution for voluntary winding up were a reference to the beginning of the date of registration of the notice under sub-paragraph (3), and
(f) any creditors' committee which is in existence immediately before the company ceases to be in administration shall continue in existence after that time as if appointed as a liquidation committee under section 101.

Moving from administration to dissolution

84. (1) If the administrator of a company thinks that the company has no property which might permit a distribution to its creditors, he shall send a notice to that effect to the registrar of companies.

[(1A), (1B) . . .]

(2) The court may on the application of the administrator of a company disapply sub-paragraph (1) in respect of the company.

(3) On receipt of a notice under sub-paragraph (1) [. . .] the registrar shall register it [. . .].

(4) On the registration of a notice in respect of a company under sub-paragraph (1) the appointment of an administrator of the company shall cease to have effect.

(5) If an administrator sends a notice under sub-paragraph (1) he shall as soon as is reasonably practicable—
(a) file a copy of the notice with the court, and
(b) send a copy of the notice to each creditor[, other than an opted-out creditor,] of whose claim and address he is aware.

(6) At the end of the period of three months beginning with the date of registration of a notice in respect of a company under sub-paragraph (1) the company is deemed to be dissolved [. . .].

[(6A), (6B) . . .]

(7) On an application in respect of a company by the administrator or another interested person the court may—
(a) extend the period specified in sub-paragraph (6) [. . .],
(b) suspend that period, or
(c) disapply sub-paragraph (6) [. . .].

(8) Where an order is made under sub-paragraph (7) in respect of a company the administrator shall as soon as is reasonably practicable notify the registrar of companies.

(9) An administrator commits an offence if he fails without reasonable excuse to comply with sub-paragraph (5).

Discharge of administration order where administration ends

85. (1) This paragraph applies where—
(a) the court makes an order under this Schedule providing for the appointment of an administrator of a company to cease to have effect, and
(b) the administrator was appointed by administration order.

(2) The court shall discharge the administration order.

Notice to Companies Registrar where administration ends

86. (1) This paragraph applies where the court makes an order under this Schedule providing for the appointment of an administrator to cease to have effect.

(2) The administrator shall send a copy of the order to the registrar of companies within the period of 14 days beginning with the date of the order.

(3) An administrator who fails without reasonable excuse to comply with sub-paragraph (2) commits an offence.

REPLACING ADMINISTRATOR

Resignation of administrator

87. (1) An administrator may resign only in prescribed circumstances.

(2) Where an administrator may resign he may do so only—
(a) in the case of an administrator appointed by administration order, by notice in writing to the court,
(b) in the case of an administrator appointed under paragraph 14, by notice in writing to the [holder of the floating charge by virtue of which the appointment was made],
(c) in the case of an administrator appointed under paragraph 22(1), by notice in writing to the company, or
(d) in the case of an administrator appointed under paragraph 22(2), by notice in writing to the directors of the company.

Removal of administrator from office

88. The court may by order remove an administrator from office.

Administrator ceasing to be qualified

89. (1) The administrator of a company shall vacate office if he ceases to be qualified to act as an insolvency practitioner in relation to the company.

(2) Where an administrator vacates office by virtue of sub-paragraph (1) he shall give notice in writing—
(a) in the case of an administrator appointed by administration order, to the court,
(b) in the case of an administrator appointed under paragraph 14, to the [holder of the floating charge by virtue of which the appointment was made],
(c) in the case of an administrator appointed under paragraph 22(1), to the company, or
(d) in the case of an administrator appointed under paragraph 22(2), to the directors of the company.

(3) An administrator who fails without reasonable excuse to comply with sub-paragraph (2) commits an offence.

Supplying vacancy in office of administrator

90. Paragraphs 91 to 95 apply where an administrator—

(a) dies,
(b) resigns,
(c) is removed from office under paragraph 88, or
(d) vacates office under paragraph 89.

91. (1) Where the administrator was appointed by administration order, the court may replace the administrator on an application under this sub-paragraph made by—

(a) a creditors' committee of the company,
(b) the company,
(c) the directors of the company,
(d) one or more creditors of the company, or
(e) where more than one person was appointed to act jointly or concurrently as the administrator, any of those persons who remains in office.

(2) But an application may be made in reliance on sub-paragraph (1)(b) to (d) only where—

(a) there is no creditors' committee of the company,
(b) the court is satisfied that the creditors' committee or a remaining administrator is not taking reasonable steps to make a replacement, or
(c) the court is satisfied that for another reason it is right for the application to be made.

92. Where the administrator was appointed under paragraph 14 the holder of the floating charge by virtue of which the appointment was made may replace the administrator.

93. (1) Where the administrator was appointed under paragraph 22(1) by the company it may replace the administrator.

(2) A replacement under this paragraph may be made only—

(a) with the consent of each person who is the holder of a qualifying floating charge in respect of the company's property, or
(b) where consent is withheld, with the permission of the court.

94. (1) Where the administrator was appointed under paragraph 22(2) the directors of the company may replace the administrator.

(2) A replacement under this paragraph may be made only—

(a) with the consent of each person who is the holder of a qualifying floating charge in respect of the company's property, or
(b) where consent is withheld, with the permission of the court.

95. The court may replace an administrator on the application of a person listed in paragraph 91(1) if the court—

(a) is satisfied that a person who is entitled to replace the administrator under any of paragraphs 92 to 94 is not taking reasonable steps to make a replacement, or
(b) that for another reason it is right for the court to make the replacement.

Substitution of administrator: competing floating charge-holder

96. (1) This paragraph applies where an administrator of a company is appointed under paragraph 14 by the holder of a qualifying floating charge in respect of the company's property.

(2) The holder of a prior qualifying floating charge in respect of the company's property may apply to the court for the administrator to be replaced by an administrator nominated by the holder of the prior floating charge.

(3) One floating charge is prior to another for the purposes of this paragraph if—

(a) it was created first, or
(b) it is to be treated as having priority in accordance with an agreement to which the holder of each floating charge was party.

(4) Sub-paragraph (3) shall have effect in relation to Scotland as if the following were substituted for paragraph (a)—

"(a) it has priority of ranking in accordance with section 464(4)(b) of the Companies Act 1985 (c 6),

Substitution of administrator appointed by company or directors: creditors' [decision]

97. (1) This paragraph applies where—

(a) an administrator of a company is appointed by a company or directors under paragraph 22, and
(b) there is no holder of a qualifying floating charge in respect of the company's property.

[(2) The administrator may be replaced by a decision of the creditors made by a qualifying decision procedure.

(3) The decision has effect only if, before the decision is made, the new administrator has consented to act in writing.]

Vacation of office: discharge from liability

98. (1) Where a person ceases to be the administrator of a company (whether because he vacates office by reason of resignation, death or otherwise, because he is removed from office or because his appointment ceases to have effect) he is discharged from liability in respect of any action of his as administrator.

(2) The discharge provided by sub-paragraph (1) takes effect—

(a) in the case of an administrator who dies, on the filing with the court of notice of his death,
(b) in the case of an administrator appointed under paragraph 14 or 22 [who has not made a statement under paragraph 52(1)(b)], at a time appointed by resolution of the creditors' committee or, if there is no committee, by [decision] of the creditors,

[(ba) in the case of an administrator appointed under paragraph 14 or 22 who has made a statement under paragraph 52(1)(b), at a time decided by the relevant creditors,] or
(c) in any case, at a time specified by the court.

(3) [For the purposes of sub-paragraph (2)(ba), the "relevant creditors" of a company are—]
(a) each secured creditor of the company, or
(b) if the administrator has made a distribution to preferential creditors or thinks that a distribution may be made to preferential creditors—
(i) each secured creditor of the company, and
[(ii) the preferential creditors of the company.]

[(3A) In a case where the administrator is removed from office, a decision of the creditors for the purposes of sub-paragraph (2)(b), or of the preferential creditors for the purposes of sub-paragraph (2)(ba), must be made by a qualifying decision procedure.]

(4) Discharge—
(a) applies to liability accrued before the discharge takes effect, and
(b) does not prevent the exercise of the court's powers under paragraph 75.

Vacation of office: charges and liabilities

99. (1) This paragraph applies where a person ceases to be the administrator of a company (whether because he vacates office by reason of resignation, death or otherwise, because he is removed from office or because his appointment ceases to have effect).

(2) In this paragraph—
"the former administrator" means the person referred to in sub-paragraph (1), and
"cessation" means the time when he ceases to be the company's administrator.

(3) The former administrator's remuneration and expenses shall be—
(a) charged on and payable out of property of which he had custody or control immediately before cessation, and
(b) payable in priority to any security to which paragraph 70 applies.

(4) A sum payable in respect of a debt or liability arising out of a contract entered into by the former administrator or a predecessor before cessation shall be—
(a) charged on and payable out of property of which the former administrator had custody or control immediately before cessation, and
(b) payable in priority to any charge arising under sub-paragraph (3).

(5) Sub-paragraph (4) shall apply to a liability arising under a contract of employment which was adopted by the former administrator or a predecessor before cessation; and for that purpose—
(a) action taken within the period of 14 days after an administrator's appointment shall not be taken to amount or contribute to the adoption of a contract,
(b) no account shall be taken of a liability which arises, or in so far as it arises, by reference to anything which is done or which occurs before the adoption of the contract of employment, and
(c) no account shall be taken of a liability to make a payment other than wages or salary.

(6) In sub-paragraph (5)(c) "wages or salary" includes—
(a) a sum payable in respect of a period of holiday (for which purpose the sum shall be treated as relating to the period by reference to which the entitlement to holiday accrued),
(b) a sum payable in respect of a period of absence through illness or other good cause,
(c) a sum payable in lieu of holiday,
(d) . . . and
(e) a contribution to an occupational pension scheme.

GENERAL

Joint and concurrent administrators

100. (1) In this Schedule—
(a) a reference to the appointment of an administrator of a company includes a reference to the appointment of a number of persons to act jointly or concurrently as the administrator of a company, and
(b) a reference to the appointment of a person as administrator of a company includes a reference to the appointment of a person as one of a number of persons to act jointly or concurrently as the administrator of a company.

(2) The appointment of a number of persons to act as administrator of a company must specify—
(a) which functions (if any) are to be exercised by the persons appointed acting jointly, and
(b) which functions (if any) are to be exercised by any or all of the persons appointed.

101. (1) This paragraph applies where two or more persons are appointed to act jointly as the administrator of a company.

(2) A reference to the administrator of the company is a reference to those persons acting jointly.

(3) But a reference to the administrator of a company in paragraphs 87 to 99 of this Schedule is a reference to any or all of the persons appointed to act jointly.

(4) Where an offence of omission is committed by the administrator, each of the persons appointed to act jointly—
(a) commits the offence, and
(b) may be proceeded against and punished individually.

(5) The reference in paragraph 45(1)(a) to the name of the administrator is a reference to the name of each of the persons appointed to act jointly.

(6) Where persons are appointed to act jointly in respect of only some of the functions of the administrator of a company, this paragraph applies only in relation to those functions.

102. (1) This paragraph applies where two or more persons are appointed to act concurrently as the administrator of a company.

(2) A reference to the administrator of a company in this Schedule is a reference to any of the persons appointed (or any combination of them).

103. (1) Where a company is in administration, a person may be appointed to act as administrator jointly or concurrently with the person or persons acting as the administrator of the company.

(2) Where a company entered administration by administration order, an appointment under sub-paragraph (1) must be made by the court on the application of—

(a) a person or group listed in paragraph 12(1)(a) to (e), or
(b) the person or persons acting as the administrator of the company.

(3) Where a company entered administration by virtue of an appointment under paragraph 14, an appointment under sub-paragraph (1) must be made by—

(a) the holder of the floating charge by virtue of which the appointment was made, or
(b) the court on the application of the person or persons acting as the administrator of the company.

(4) Where a company entered administration by virtue of an appointment under paragraph 22(1), an appointment under sub-paragraph (1) above must be made either by the court on the application of the person or persons acting as the administrator of the company or—

(a) by the company, and
(b) with the consent of each person who is the holder of a qualifying floating charge in respect of the company's property or, where consent is withheld, with the permission of the court.

(5) Where a company entered administration by virtue of an appointment under paragraph 22(2), an appointment under sub-paragraph (1) must be made either by the court on the application of the person or persons acting as the administrator of the company or—

(a) by the directors of the company, and
(b) with the consent of each person who is the holder of a qualifying floating charge in respect of the company's property or, where consent is withheld, with the permission of the court.

(6) An appointment under sub-paragraph (1) may be made only with the consent of the person or persons acting as the administrator of the company.

Presumption of validity

104. An act of the administrator of a company is valid in spite of a defect in his appointment or qualification.

Majority decision of directors

105. A reference in this Schedule to something done by the directors of a company includes a reference to the same thing done by a majority of the directors of a company.

Penalties

106. (1) A person who is guilty of an offence under this Schedule is liable to a fine (in accordance with section 430 and Schedule 10).

(2) A person who is guilty of an offence under any of the following paragraphs of this Schedule is liable to a daily default fine (in accordance with section 430 and Schedule 10)—

(a) paragraph 20,
(b) paragraph 32,
(c) paragraph 46,
(d) paragraph 48,
(e) paragraph 49,
(f) paragraph 51,
(g) paragraph 53,
(h) paragraph 54,
(i) paragraph 56,
(j) paragraph 71,
(k) paragraph 72,
(l) paragraph 77,
(m) paragraph 78,
(n) paragraph 80,
(o) paragraph 84,
(p) paragraph 86, and
(q) paragraph 89.

Extension of time limit

107. (1) Where a provision of this Schedule provides that a period may be varied in accordance with this paragraph, the period may be varied in respect of a company—

(a) by the court, and
(b) on the application of the administrator.

(2) A time period may be extended in respect of a company under this paragraph—

(a) more than once, and
(b) after expiry.

108. (1) A period specified in paragraph 49(5) . . . or 51(2) may be varied in respect of a company by the administrator with consent.

(2) In sub-paragraph (1) "consent" means consent of—

(a) each secured creditor of the company, and
[(b) if the company has unsecured debts, the unsecured creditors of the company.]

(3) But where the administrator has made a statement under paragraph 52(1)(b) "consent" means—

(a) consent of each secured creditor of the company, or

(b) if the administrator thinks that a distribution may be made to preferential creditors, consent of—

(i) each secured creditor of the company, and

[(ii) the preferential creditors of the company.]

[(3A) Whether the company's unsecured creditors or preferential creditors consent is to be determined by the administrator seeking a decision from those creditors as to whether they consent.]

(4) . . .

(5) The power to extend under sub-paragraph (1)—

(a) may be exercised in respect of a period only once,

(b) may not be used to extend a period by more than 28 days,

(c) may not be used to extend a period which has been extended by the court, and

(d) may not be used to extend a period after expiry.

109. Where a period is extended under paragraph 107 or 108, a reference to the period shall be taken as a reference to the period as extended.

Amendment of provision about time

110. (1) The Secretary of State may by order amend a provision of this Schedule which—

(a) requires anything to be done within a specified period of time,

(b) prevents anything from being done after a specified time, or

(c) requires a specified minimum period of notice to be given.

(2) An order under this paragraph—

(a) must be made by statutory instrument, and

(b) shall be subject to annulment in pursuance of a resolution of either House of Parliament.

Interpretation

111. (1) In this Schedule—

"administrative receiver" has the meaning given by section 251,

"administrator" has the meaning given by paragraph 1 and, where the context requires, includes a reference to a former administrator,

. . .

. . .

. . .

"enters administration" has the meaning given by paragraph 1,

"floating charge" means a charge which is a floating charge on its creation,

"in administration" has the meaning given by paragraph 1,

"hire-purchase agreement" includes a conditional sale agreement, a chattel leasing agreement and a retention of title agreement,

"holder of a qualifying floating charge" in respect of a company's property has the meaning given by paragraph 14,

"market value" means the amount which would be realised on a sale of property in the open market by a willing vendor,

"the purpose of administration" means an objective specified in paragraph 3, and

"unable to pay its debts" has the meaning given by section 123.

[(1A) In this Schedule, "company" means—

[(a) a company registered under the Companies Act 2006 in England and Wales or Scotland,]

(b) a company incorporated in an EEA State . . . , or

(c) a company not incorporated in an EEA State but having its centre of main interests in a member State [(other than Denmark) or in the United Kingdom].

(1B) In sub-paragraph (1A), in relation to a company, "centre of main interests" has the same meaning as in [Article 3 of the EU Regulation].]

(2) . . .

(3) In this Schedule a reference to action includes a reference to inaction.

[Non-UK companies

111A. A company incorporated outside the United Kingdom that has a principal place of business in Northern Ireland may not enter administration under this Schedule unless it also has a principal place of business in England and Wales or Scotland (or both in England and Wales and in Scotland).]

Scotland

112. In the application of this Schedule to Scotland—

(a) a reference to filing with the court is a reference to lodging in court, and

(b) a reference to a charge is a reference to a right in security.

113. Where property in Scotland is disposed of under paragraph 70 or 71, the administrator shall grant to the disponee an appropriate document of transfer or conveyance of the property, and—

(a) that document, or

(b) recording, intimation or registration of that document (where recording, intimation or registration of the document is a legal requirement for completion of title to the property),

has the effect of disencumbering the property of or, as the case may be, freeing the property from, the security.

114. In Scotland, where goods in the possession of a company under a hire-purchase agreement are disposed of under paragraph 72, the disposal has the effect of extinguishing as against the disponee all rights of the owner of the goods under the agreement.

115. (1) In Scotland, the administrator of a company may make, in or towards the satisfaction of the debt secured by the floating charge, a payment to the holder of a floating charge which has attached to the property subject to the charge.

[(1A) In Scotland, sub-paragraph (1B) applies in connection with the giving by the court of permission as provided for in paragraph 65(3)(b).

(1B) On the giving by the court of such permission, any floating charge granted by the company shall, unless it has already so attached, attach to the property which is subject to the charge.]

(2) In Scotland, where the administrator thinks that the company has insufficient property to enable a distribution to be made to unsecured creditors other than by virtue of section 176A(2)(a), he may file a notice to that effect with the registrar of companies.

(3) On delivery of the notice to the registrar of companies, any floating charge granted by the company shall, unless it has already so attached, attach to the property which is subject to the charge . . .

[(4) Attachment of a floating charge under sub-paragraph (1B) or (3) has effect as if the charge is a fixed security over the property to which it has attached.]

116. In Scotland, the administrator in making any payment in accordance with paragraph 115 shall make such payment subject to the rights of any of the following categories of persons (which rights shall, except to the extent provided in any instrument, have the following order of priority)—

(a) the holder of any fixed security which is over property subject to the floating charge and which ranks prior to, or pari passu with, the floating charge,
(b) creditors in respect of all liabilities and expenses incurred by or on behalf of the administrator,
(c) the administrator in respect of his liabilities, expenses and remuneration and any indemnity to which he is entitled out of the property of the company,
(d) the preferential creditors entitled to payment in accordance with paragraph 65,
(e) the holder of the floating charge in accordance with the priority of that charge in relation to any other floating charge which has attached, and
(f) the holder of a fixed security, other than one referred to in paragraph (a), which is over property subject to the floating charge.]

NOTES

Inserted by the Enterprise Act 2002, s 248(2), Sch 16, as from 15 September 2003 (for savings and transitional provisions, see the note to s 8 at **[9.147]**).

Para 12: words in square brackets in sub-para (1)(d) substituted by the Courts Act 2003, s 109(1), Sch 8, para 299, as from 1 April 2005. Sub-para (5) added by the Enterprise Act 2002 (Insolvency) Order 2003, SI 2003/2096, arts 2(1), (2), 6, as from 15 September 2003, except in relation to any case where a petition for an administration order was presented before that date.

Para 24: repealed by the Corporate Insolvency and Governance Act 2020, s 2(1), Sch 3, paras 1, 31(1), (2), as from 26 June 2020 (for transitional provisions, see s 2(2), (3) of the 2020 Act (at **[9.533]**) which provides that (without prejudice to the Interpretation Act 1978, s 16) nothing in the 2020 Act affects the operation of this Act, or any other enactment, in relation to a moratorium under Sch A1 to this Act which comes into force before the repeal of that Schedule by Sch 3 to the 2020 Act (ie, 26 June 2020)).

Para 25A: inserted by the Deregulation Act 2015, s 19, Sch 6, Pt 2, paras 4, 5, as from 26 May 2015.

Para 26: words in square brackets substituted by the Deregulation Act 2015, s 19, Sch 6, Pt 2, paras 4, 6, as from 1 October 2015.

Para 40: sub-para (2)(aa) inserted by the European Public Limited-Liability Company Regulations 2004, SI 2004/2326, reg 73(4)(c), as from 8 October 2004. Words in square brackets in sub-para (2)(b) substituted by the Financial Services Act 2012, s 114(1), Sch 18, Pt 2, paras 51, 55(1), (2), as from 1 April 2013.

Para 42: sub-para (4)(aa) inserted by SI 2004/2326, reg 73(4)(c), as from 8 October 2004. Words in square brackets in sub-para (4)(b) substituted by the Financial Services Act 2012, s 114(1), Sch 18, Pt 2, paras 51, 55(1), (3), as from 1 April 2013.

Para 43: sub-para (6A) inserted by SI 2003/2096, art 2(1), (3) as from 15 September 2003, except in relation to any case where a petition for an administration order was presented before that date.

Para 45: substituted by the Companies (Trading Disclosures) (Insolvency) Regulations 2008, SI 2008/1897, reg 4(1), as from 1 October 2008.

Para 49: words in first (outer) pair of square brackets in sub-para (3)(b) substituted by the Companies Act 2006 (Consequential Amendments etc) Order 2008, SI 2008/948, art 3(1), Sch 1, Pt 2, para 100(a), as from 6 April 2008. Words in second (inner) pair of square brackets in sub-para (3)(b) inserted by the Corporate Insolvency and Governance Act 2020, s 7, Sch 9, Pt 2, paras 5, 7(1), (2), as from 26 June 2020. Words in square brackets in sub-para (4)(b) inserted by the Small Business, Enterprise and Employment Act 2015, s 126, Sch 9, Pt 1, paras 1, 10(1), (2), as from 6 April 2017 (in relation to England and Wales), and as from 6 April 2019 (in relation to Scotland) (for transitional and savings provisions, see the notes to s 246ZE at **[9.385]**).

Para 50: repealed by the Small Business, Enterprise and Employment Act 2015, s 126, Sch 9, Pt 1, paras 1, 10(1), (3), as from 6 April 2017 (in relation to England and Wales), and as from 6 April 2019 (in relation to Scotland) (for transitional and savings provisions, see the notes to s 246ZE at **[9.385]**).

Para 51: the heading preceding this paragraph was substituted, and sub-paras (1)–(3) were substituted, by the Small Business, Enterprise and Employment Act 2015, s 126, Sch 9, Pt 1, paras 1, 10(1), (4), (5), as from 6 April 2017 (in relation to England and Wales), and as from 6 April 2019 (in relation to Scotland) (for transitional and savings provisions, see the notes to s 246ZE at **[9.385]**).

Para 52: words in square brackets in sub-para (2) substituted, and sub-para (3) substituted, by the Small Business, Enterprise and Employment Act 2015, s 126, Sch 9, Pt 1, paras 1, 10(1), (6), (7), as from 6 April 2017 (in relation to England and Wales), and as from 6 April 2019 (in relation to Scotland) (for transitional and savings provisions, see the notes to s 246ZE at **[9.385]**).

Para 53: all amendments to this paragraph were made by the Small Business, Enterprise and Employment Act 2015, s 126, Sch 9, Pt 1, paras 1, 10(1), (8)–(10), as from 6 April 2017 (in relation to England and Wales), and as from 6 April 2019 (in relation to Scotland) (for transitional and savings provisions, see the notes to s 246ZE at **[9.385]**).

Para 54: all amendments to this paragraph were made by the Small Business, Enterprise and Employment Act 2015, s 126, Sch 9, Pt 1, paras 1, 10(1), (11)–(16), as from 6 April 2017 (in relation to England and Wales), and as from 6 April 2019 (in relation to Scotland) (for transitional and savings provisions, see the notes to s 246ZE at **[9.385]**).

Para 55: sub-para (1) substituted by the Small Business, Enterprise and Employment Act 2015, s 126, Sch 9, Pt 1, paras 1, 10(1), (17), as from 6 April 2017 (in relation to England and Wales), and as from 6 April 2019 (in relation to Scotland) (for transitional and savings provisions, see the notes to s 246ZE at **[9.385]**).

Para 56: all words in square brackets were substituted by the Small Business, Enterprise and Employment Act 2015, s 126, Sch 9, Pt 1, paras 1, 10(1), (18)–(20), as from 6 April 2017 (in relation to England and Wales), and as from 6 April 2019 (in relation to Scotland) (for transitional and savings provisions, see the notes to s 246ZE at **[9.385]**).

Para 57: words in square brackets in sub-para (1) substituted by the Small Business, Enterprise and Employment Act 2015, s 126, Sch 9, Pt 1, paras 1, 10(1), (21), as from 6 April 2017 (in relation to England and Wales), and as from 6 April 2019 (in relation to Scotland) (for transitional and savings provisions, see the notes to s 246ZE at **[9.385]**).

Para 58: repealed by the Small Business, Enterprise and Employment Act 2015, s 126, Sch 9, Pt 1, paras 1, 10(1), (22), as from 6 April 2017 (in relation to England and Wales), and as from 6 April 2019 (in relation to Scotland) (for transitional and savings provisions, see the notes to s 246ZE at **[9.385]**).

Para 60: sub-para (1) numbered as such, and sub-para (2) added, by the Small Business, Enterprise and Employment Act 2015, s 129(1)–(3), as from 26 May 2015.

Para 60A: originally inserted by the Small Business, Enterprise and Employment Act 2015, s 129(1), (4), as from 26 May 2015. Note that as originally enacted, this paragraph expired on 26 May 2020 by virtue of the original sub-para (10) which provided: "This paragraph expires at the end of the period of 5 years beginning with the day on which it comes into force unless the power conferred by it is exercised during that period". See, however, the Corporate Insolvency and Governance Act 2020, s 8 (at **[9.536]**) which provides: "Paragraph 60A of Schedule B1 to the Insolvency Act 1986 (which expired in May 2020) is revived". Note also that s 8 of the 2020 Act substituted sub-para (10) of para 60A and, by virtue of that substitution, para 60A was due to expire at the end of June 2021 unless the power conferred by it was exercised before then. The power to make Regulations was exercised – see the Administration (Restrictions on Disposal etc to Connected Persons) Regulations 2021, SI 2021/427 (made under para 60A(1), (2) and (7)) at **[10.1306]**) and, therefore, this paragraph did not expire on 30 June 2021.

Para 62: words in square brackets substituted by the Small Business, Enterprise and Employment Act 2015, s 126, Sch 9, Pt 1, paras 1, 10(1), (23), as from 6 April 2017 (in relation to England and Wales), and as from 6 April 2019 (in relation to Scotland) (for transitional and savings provisions, see the notes to s 246ZE at **[9.385]**).

Para 64A: inserted by the Corporate Insolvency and Governance Act 2020, s 2(1), Sch 3, paras 1, 31(1), (3), as from 26 June 2020 (for transitional provisions, see the note relating to the 2020 Act to para 24 above).

Para 65 is amended as follows:

Sub-para (1) substituted by the Corporate Insolvency and Governance Act 2020, s 2(1), Sch 3, paras 1, 31(1), (4), as from 26 June 2020 (for transitional provisions, see the note relating to the 2020 Act to para 24 above).

The words in square brackets in sub-para (2) were substituted by the Banks and Building Societies (Priorities on Insolvency) Order 2018, SI 2018/1244, arts 4, 13(1), (2), as from 19 December 2018, except in relation to any insolvency proceedings commenced before that date (see further the note relating to this Order at **[9.139]**).

The words in square brackets in sub-para (3) were substituted by the Small Business, Enterprise and Employment Act 2015, s 128(1), (2), as from 26 May 2015.

Para 66: words in square brackets substituted by the Corporate Insolvency and Governance Act 2020, s 2(1), Sch 3, paras 1, 31(1), (5), as from 26 June 2020 (for transitional provisions, see the note relating to the 2020 Act to para 24 above).

Para 73 is amended as follows:

The word in square brackets in the heading was substituted, the word "or" at end of sub-para (1)(c) was repealed, and sub-para (1)(d) (and the preceding word) was inserted, by the Banks and Building Societies (Priorities on Insolvency) Order 2018, SI 2018/1244, arts 4, 13(1), (3), as from 19 December 2018, except in relation to any insolvency proceedings commenced before that date (see further the note relating to this Order at **[9.139]**).

The word omitted from sub-para (1)(b) was repealed, sub-para (1)(bb) was inserted, the words in square brackets in sub-para (1)(c) were substituted, and sub-para (1)(d) (and the preceding word) was added, by the Banks and Building Societies (Depositor Preference and Priorities) Order 2014, SI 2014/3486, arts 3, 10, as from 1 January 2015, except in relation to any insolvency proceedings commenced before that date (see further the note relating to this Order at **[9.139]**).

The word omitted from sub-para (2)(b) was repealed, and sub-para (2)(d) (and the preceding word) was added, by the Companies (Cross-Border Mergers) Regulations 2007, SI 2007/2974, reg 65(1)–(3), as from 15 December 2007.

The words in the first (outer) pair of square brackets in sub-para (2)(c) were substituted by SI 2008/948, art 3(1), Sch 1, Pt 2, para 100(a), as from 6 April 2008.

The words in the second (inner) pair of square brackets in sub-para (2)(c) were inserted by the Corporate Insolvency and Governance Act 2020, s 7, Sch 9, Pt 2, paras 5, 7(1), (3), as from 26 June 2020.

Sub-para (2)(d) and the word immediately preceding it were repealed by the Companies, Limited Liability Partnerships and Partnerships (Amendment etc) (EU Exit) Regulations 2019, SI 2019/348, reg 8, Sch 3, para 1, as from IP completion day (as defined in the European Union (Withdrawal Agreement) Act 2020, s 39).

Para 74: sub-para (4)(c) was substituted by the Small Business, Enterprise and Employment Act 2015, s 126, Sch 9, Pt 1, paras 1, 10(1), (24), as from 6 April 2017 (in relation to England and Wales), and as from 6 April 2019 (in relation to Scotland) (for transitional and savings provisions, see the notes to s 246ZE at **[9.385]**). Word omitted from sub-para (6)(b) repealed, and sub-para (6)(ba) added, by SI 2007/2974, reg 65(1), (4), (5), as from 15 December 2007. Words in first (outer) pair of square brackets in sub-para (6)(b) substituted by SI 2008/948, art 3(1), Sch 1, Pt 2, 100(b), as from 6 April 2008. Words in the second (inner) pair of square brackets in sub-para (6)(b) inserted by the Corporate Insolvency and Governance Act 2020, s 7, Sch 9, Pt 2, paras 5, 7(1), (4), as from 26 June 2020. Sub-para (6)(ba) was repealed by SI 2019/348, reg 8, Sch 3, para 1, as from IP completion day (as defined in the European Union (Withdrawal Agreement) Act 2020, s 39).

Para 76: words in square brackets in sub-para (2) substituted by the Small Business, Enterprise and Employment Act 2015, s 127, as from 26 May 2015.

Para 78: all amendments to this paragraph were made by the Small Business, Enterprise and Employment Act 2015, s 126, Sch 9, Pt 1, paras 1, 10(1), (25)–(28), as from 6 April 2017 (in relation to England and Wales), and as from 6 April 2019 (in relation to Scotland) (for transitional and savings provisions, see the notes to s 246ZE at **[9.385]**).

Para 79: words in square brackets in sub-para (2)(c) substituted by the Small Business, Enterprise and Employment Act 2015, s 126, Sch 9, Pt 1, paras 1, 10(1), (29), as from 6 April 2017 (in relation to England and Wales), and as from 6 April 2019 (in relation to Scotland) (for transitional and savings provisions, see the notes to s 246ZE at **[9.385]**).

Para 80: words in square brackets in sub-para (4) inserted by the Small Business, Enterprise and Employment Act 2015, s 126, Sch 9, Pt 1, paras 1, 10(1), (30), as from 6 April 2017 (in relation to England and Wales), and as from 6 April 2019 (in relation to Scotland) (for transitional and savings provisions, see the notes to s 246ZE at **[9.385]**).

Para 82: sub-para (1)(aa) inserted by SI 2004/2326, reg 73(4)(c), as from 8 October 2004. Words in square brackets in sub-para (1)(b) substituted by the Financial Services Act 2012, s 114(1), Sch 18, Pt 2, paras 51, 55(1), (4), as from 1 April 2013.

Para 83: words in square brackets in sub-paras (1)(b) and (2)(b) inserted by the Small Business, Enterprise and Employment Act 2015, s 128(1), (3), as from 26 May 2015. Words in square brackets in sub-para (5)(b) inserted, and figure omitted from sub-para (8)(d) repealed, by s 126 of, and Sch 9, Pt 1, paras 1, 10(1), (31), (32) to, the 2015 Act, as from 6 April 2017 (in relation to England and Wales), and as from 6 April 2019 (in relation to Scotland) (for transitional and savings provisions, see the notes to s 246ZE at **[9.385]**).

Para 84: sub-paras (1A), (1B), (6A), (6B) and the words omitted from sub-paras (3), (6), (7) were originally inserted by the Insolvency Amendment (EU 2015/848) Regulations 2017, SI 2017/702, regs 2, 3, Schedule, Pt 1, paras 1, 30, as from 26 June 2017, except in relation to proceedings opened before that date. These sub-paragraphs and words were subsequently repealed by the Insolvency (Amendment) (EU Exit) Regulations 2019, SI 2019/146, reg 2, Schedule, Pt 2, paras 16, 44(a), as from IP completion day (as defined in the European Union (Withdrawal Agreement) Act 2020, s 39) (for savings, see reg 4 of the 2019 Regulations at **[12.82]**). Words in square brackets in sub-para (5)(b) inserted by the Small Business, Enterprise and Employment Act 2015, s 126, Sch 9, Pt 1, paras 1, 10(1), (33), as from 6 April 2017 (in relation to England and Wales), and as from 6 April 2019 (in relation to Scotland) (for transitional and savings provisions, see the notes to s 246ZE at **[9.385]**).

Paras 87, 89: words in square brackets in sub-para (2)(b) substituted by SI 2003/2096, arts 2(1), (4), (5), 6, as from 15 September 2003, except in relation to any case where a petition for an administration order was presented before that date.

Para 97: word in square brackets in the preceding heading substituted, and sub-paras (2), (3) substituted, by the Small Business, Enterprise and Employment Act 2015, s 126, Sch 9, Pt 1, paras 1, 10(1), (34), (35), as from 6 April 2017 (in relation to England and Wales), and as from 6 April 2019 (in relation to Scotland) (for transitional and savings provisions, see the notes to s 246ZE at **[9.385]**).

Para 98 is amended as follows:

Words in first pair of square brackets in sub-para (2)(b) inserted, sub-para (2)(ba) inserted, and words in square brackets in sub-para (3) substituted, by the Deregulation Act 2015, s 19, Sch 6, Pt 2, paras 4, 7, as from 1 October 2015.

Words in second pair of square brackets in sub-para (2)(b) substituted, sub-para (3)(b)(ii) substituted, and sub-para (3A) inserted, by the Small Business, Enterprise and Employment Act 2015, s 126, Sch 9, Pt 1, paras 1, 10(1), (36)–(38), as from 6 April 2017 (in relation to England and Wales), and as from 6 April 2019 (in relation to Scotland) (for transitional and savings provisions, see the notes to s 246ZE at **[9.385]**).

Para 99: words omitted from sub-para (6)(d) repealed by the Deregulation Act 2015, s 19, Sch 6, Pt 7, paras 24, 27, as from 26 May 2015.

Para 108: all amendments to this paragraph were made by the Small Business, Enterprise and Employment Act 2015, s 126, Sch 9, Pt 1, paras 1, 10(1), (39)–(43), as from 6 April 2017 (in relation to England and Wales), and as from 6 April 2019 (in relation to Scotland) (for transitional and savings provisions, see the notes to s 246ZE at **[9.385]**).

Para 111 is amended as follows:

Definition "Company" omitted from sub-para (1) repealed, and sub-paras (1A), (1B) inserted, by the Insolvency Act 1986 (Amendment) Regulations 2005, SI 2005/879, reg 2(1), (4)(a), (b), as from 13 April 2005, except in relation to the appointment of an administrator that took effect before that date.

Definitions "correspondence" and "creditors' meeting" omitted from sub-para (1) repealed by the Small Business, Enterprise and Employment Act 2015, s 126, Sch 9, Pt 1, paras 1, 10(1), (44), as from 6 April 2017 (in relation to England and Wales), and as from 6 April 2019 (in relation to Scotland) (for transitional and savings provisions, see the notes to s 246ZE at **[9.385]**).

Sub-para (1A)(a) substituted by the Companies Act 2006 (Consequential Amendments, Transitional Provisions and Savings) Order 2009, SI 2009/1941, art 2(1), Sch 1, para 72, as from 1 October 2009 (for effect see the note to s 7A at **[9.145]**).

The words omitted from sub-para (1A)(b) were repealed, and the words in square brackets in sub-para (1A)(c) were substituted, by the Insolvency (Amendment) (EU Exit) Regulations 2019, SI 2019/146, reg 2, Schedule, Pt 2, paras 16, 44(b), as from IP completion day (as defined in the European Union (Withdrawal Agreement) Act 2020, s 39) (for savings, see reg 4 of the 2019 Regulations at **[12.82]**).

Words in square brackets in sub-para (1B) substituted by the Insolvency Amendment (EU 2015/848) Regulations 2017, SI 2017/702, regs 2, 3, Schedule, Pt 1, paras 1, 31, as from 26 June 2017, except in relation to proceedings opened before that date.

Sub-para (2) repealed by the Legislative Reform (Insolvency) (Miscellaneous Provisions) Order 2010, SI 2010/18, arts 2, 4(2), as from 6 April 2010. Note that this paragraph is effectively replaced by a new s 436B of this Act which was also added by the 2010 Order as from 6 April 2010. That section provides that a reference in this Act to a thing in writing includes that thing in electronic form (except in certain specified sections).

Para 111A: inserted by SI 2005/879, reg 2(1), (4)(c), as from 13 April 2005, except in relation to the appointment of an administrator that took effect before that date.

Para 115: sub-paras (1A), (1B) inserted, words omitted from sub-para (3) repealed, and sub-para (4) added, by the Small Business, Enterprise and Employment Act 2015, s 130, as from 26 May 2015.

See also the Bank Recovery and Resolution (Amendment) (EU Exit) Regulations 2020, SI 2020/1350. Regulations 108–114 make amendments to various provisions of this Act (including this Schedule) which come into force on 28 December 2020 and cease to have effect (in accordance with reg 1 of the 2020 Regulations) on IP completion day (as defined in the European Union (Withdrawal Agreement) Act 2020, s 39).

Regulations: the Administration (Restrictions on Disposal etc to Connected Persons) Regulations 2021, SI 2021/427 (made under para 60A(1), (2) and (7)) at **[10.1306]**.

SCHEDULE 1
POWERS OF ADMINISTRATOR OR ADMINISTRATIVE RECEIVER

Sections 14, 42

[9.473]

1. Power to take possession of, collect and get in the property of the company and, for that purpose, to take such proceedings as may seem to him expedient.

2. Power to sell or otherwise dispose of the property of the company by public auction or private contract or, in Scotland, to sell, . . . hire out or otherwise dispose of the property of the company by public roup or private bargain.

3. Power to raise or borrow money and grant security therefor over the property of the company.

4. Power to appoint a solicitor or accountant or other professionally qualified person to assist him in the performance of his functions.

5. Power to bring or defend any action or other legal proceedings in the name and on behalf of the company.

6. Power to refer to arbitration any question affecting the company.

7. Power to effect and maintain insurances in respect of the business and property of the company.

8. Power to use the company's seal.

9. Power to do all acts and to execute in the name and on behalf of the company any deed, receipt or other document.

10. Power to draw, accept, make and endorse any bill of exchange or promissory note in the name and on behalf of the company.

11. Power to appoint any agent to do any business which he is unable to do himself or which can more conveniently be done by an agent and power to employ and dismiss employees.

12. Power to do all such things (including the carrying out of works) as may be necessary for the realisation of the property of the company.

13. Power to make any payment which is necessary or incidental to the performance of his functions.

14. Power to carry on the business of the company.

15. Power to establish subsidiaries of the company.

16. Power to transfer to subsidiaries of the company the whole or any part of the business and property of the company.

17. Power to grant or accept a surrender of a lease or tenancy of any of the property of the company, and to take a lease or tenancy of any property required or convenient for the business of the company.

18. Power to make any arrangement or compromise on behalf of the company.

19. Power to call up any uncalled capital of the company.

20. Power to rank and claim in the bankruptcy, insolvency, sequestration or liquidation of any person indebted to the company and to receive dividends, and to accede to trust deeds for the creditors of any such person.

21. Power to present or defend a petition for the winding up of the company.

22. Power to change the situation of the company's registered office.

23. Power to do all other things incidental to the exercise of the foregoing powers.

NOTES

Para 2: word omitted repealed by the Abolition of Feudal Tenure etc (Scotland) Act 2000, s 76(2), Sch 13, Pt I, as from 28 November 2004.

SCHEDULE 2
POWERS OF A SCOTTISH RECEIVER (ADDITIONAL TO THOSE CONFERRED ON HIM BY THE INSTRUMENT OF CHARGE)

Section 55

[9.474]

1. Power to take possession of, collect and get in the property from the company or a liquidator thereof or any other person, and for that purpose, to take such proceedings as may seem to him expedient.

2. Power to sell, . . . hire out or otherwise dispose of the property by public roup or private bargain and with or without advertisement.

3. Power to raise or borrow money and grant security therefor over the property.

4. Power to appoint a solicitor or accountant or other professionally qualified person to assist him in the performance of his functions.

5. Power to bring or defend any action or other legal proceedings in the name and on behalf of the company.

6. Power to refer to arbitration all questions affecting the company.

7. Power to effect and maintain insurances in respect of the business and property of the company.

8. Power to use the company's seal.

9. Power to do all acts and to execute in the name and on behalf of the company any deed, receipt or other document.

10. Power to draw, accept, make and endorse any bill of exchange or promissory note in the name and on behalf of the company.

11. Power to appoint any agent to do any business which he is unable to do himself or which can more conveniently be done by an agent, and power to employ and dismiss employees.

12. Power to do all such things (including the carrying out of works), as may be necessary for the realisation of the property.

13. Power to make any payment which is necessary or incidental to the performance of his functions.

14. Power to carry on the business of the company or any part of it.

15. Power to grant or accept a surrender of a lease or tenancy of any of the property, and to take a lease or tenancy of any property required or convenient for the business of the company.

16. Power to make any arrangement or compromise on behalf of the company.

17. Power to call up any uncalled capital of the company.

18. Power to establish subsidiaries of the company.

19. Power to transfer to subsidiaries of the company the business of the company or any part of it and any of the property.

20. Power to rank and claim in the bankruptcy, insolvency, sequestration or liquidation of any person or company indebted to the company and to receive dividends, and to accede to trust deeds for creditors of any such person.

21. Power to present or defend a petition for the winding up of the company.

22. Power to change the situation of the company's registered office.

23. Power to do all other things incidental to the exercise of the powers mentioned in section 55(1) of this Act or above in this Schedule.

NOTES

Para 2: word omitted repealed by the Abolition of Feudal Tenure etc (Scotland) Act 2000, s 76(2), Sch 13, Pt I, as from 28 November 2004.

[SCHEDULE 2A
EXCEPTIONS TO PROHIBITION ON APPOINTMENT OF ADMINISTRATIVE RECEIVER: SUPPLEMENTARY PROVISIONS

Section 72H

Capital market arrangement

[9.475]

1. (1) For the purposes of section 72B an arrangement is a capital market arrangement if—

(a) it involves a grant of security to a person holding it as trustee for a person who holds a capital market investment issued by a party to the arrangement, or

[(aa) it involves a grant of security to—

(i) a party to the arrangement who issues a capital market investment, or

(ii) a person who holds the security as trustee for a party to the arrangement in connection with the issue of a capital market investment, or

(ab) it involves a grant of security to a person who holds the security as trustee for a party to the arrangement who agrees to provide finance to another party, or]

(b) at least one party guarantees the performance of obligations of another party, or

(c) at least one party provides security in respect of the performance of obligations of another party, or

(d) the arrangement involves an investment of a kind described in articles 83 to 85 of the Financial Services and Markets Act 2000 (Regulated Activities) Order 2001 (SI 2001/544) (options, futures and contracts for differences).

(2) For the purposes of sub-paragraph (1)—

(a) a reference to holding as trustee includes a reference to holding as nominee or agent,

(b) a reference to holding for a person who holds a capital market investment includes a reference to holding for a number of persons at least one of whom holds a capital market investment, and

(c) a person holds a capital market investment if he has a legal or beneficial interest in it[; and

(d) the reference to the provision of finance includes the provision of an indemnity].

(3) In section 72B(1) and this paragraph "party" to an arrangement includes a party to an agreement which—

(a) forms part of the arrangement,

(b) provides for the raising of finance as part of the arrangement, or

(c) is necessary for the purposes of implementing the arrangement.

Capital market investment

2. (1) For the purposes of section 72B an investment is a capital market investment if it—

(a) is within article 77 [or 77A] of the Financial Services and Markets Act 2000 (Regulated Activities) Order 2001 (SI 2001/544) (debt instruments), and

(b) is rated, listed or traded or designed to be rated, listed or traded.

(2) In sub-paragraph (1)—

"rated" means rated for the purposes of investment by an internationally recognised rating agency,

"listed" means admitted to the official list within the meaning given by section 103(1) of the Financial Services and Markets Act 2000 (c 8) (interpretation), and

"traded" means admitted to trading on a market established under the rules of a recognised investment exchange or on a foreign market.

(3) In sub-paragraph (2)—

"recognised investment exchange" has the meaning given by section 285 of the Financial Services and Markets Act 2000 (recognised investment exchange), and

"foreign market" has the same meaning as "relevant market" in article 67(2) of the Financial Services and Markets Act 2000 (Financial Promotion) Order 2001 (SI 2001/1335) (foreign markets).

3. (1) An investment is also a capital market investment for the purposes of section 72B if it consists of a bond or commercial paper issued to one or more of the following—

(a) an investment professional within the meaning of article 19(5) of the Financial Services and Markets Act 2000 (Financial Promotion) Order 2001,

(b) a person who is, when the agreement mentioned in section 72B(1) is entered into, a certified high net worth individual in relation to a communication within the meaning of article 48(2) of that order,

(c) a person to whom article 49(2) of that order applies (high net worth company, &c),

(d) a person who is, when the agreement mentioned in section 72B(1) is entered into, a certified sophisticated investor in relation to a communication within the meaning of article 50(1) of that order, and

(e) a person in a State other than the United Kingdom who under the law of that State is not prohibited from investing in bonds or commercial paper.

(2) In sub-paragraph (1)—

"bond" shall be construed in accordance with article 77 of the Financial Services and Markets Act 2000 (Regulated Activities) Order 2001 (SI 2001/544)[, and includes any instrument falling within article 77A of that Order], and

"commercial paper" has the meaning given by article 9(3) of that order.

(3) For the purposes of sub-paragraph (1)—

(a) in applying article 19(5) of the Financial Promotion Order for the purposes of sub-paragraph (1)(a)—

(i) in article 19(5)(b), ignore the words after "exempt person",

(ii) in article 19(5)(c)(i), for the words from "the controlled activity" to the end substitute "a controlled activity", and

(iii) in article 19(5)(e) ignore the words from "where the communication" to the end, and

(b) in applying article 49(2) of that order for the purposes of sub-paragraph (1)(c), ignore article 49(2)(e).

"Agreement"

4. For the purposes of sections 72B and 72E and this Schedule "agreement" includes an agreement or undertaking effected by—

(a) contract,

(b) deed, or

(c) any other instrument intended to have effect in accordance with the law of England and Wales, Scotland or another jurisdiction.

Debt

5. The debt of at least £50 million referred to in section 72B(1)(a) or 72E(2)(a)—

(a) may be incurred at any time during the life of the capital market arrangement or financed project, and

(b) may be expressed wholly or partly in foreign currency (in which case the sterling equivalent shall be calculated as at the time when the arrangement is entered into or the project begins).

Step-in rights

6. (1) For the purposes of sections 72C to 72E a project has "step-in rights" if a person who provides finance in connection with the project has a conditional entitlement under an agreement to—

(a) assume sole or principal responsibility under an agreement for carrying out all or part of the project, or

(b) make arrangements for carrying out all or part of the project.

(2) In sub-paragraph (1) a reference to the provision of finance includes a reference to the provision of an indemnity.

Project company

7. (1) For the purposes of sections 72C to 72E a company is a "project company" of a project if—

(a) it holds property for the purpose of the project,

(b) it has sole or principal responsibility under an agreement for carrying out all or part of the project,

(c) it is one of a number of companies which together carry out the project,

(d) it has the purpose of supplying finance to enable the project to be carried out, or

(e) it is the holding company of a company within any of paragraphs (a) to (d).

(2) But a company is not a "project company" of a project if—

(a) it performs a function within sub-paragraph (1)(a) to (d) or is within sub-paragraph (1)(e), but

(b) it also performs a function which is not—

(i) within sub-paragraph (1)(a) to (d),

(ii) related to a function within sub-paragraph (1)(a) to (d), or

(iii) related to the project.

(3) For the purposes of this paragraph a company carries out all or part of a project whether or not it acts wholly or partly through agents.

"Resources"

8. In section 72C "resources" includes—

(a) funds (including payment for the provision of services or facilities),

(b) assets,

(c) professional skill,

(d) the grant of a concession or franchise, and

(e) any other commercial resource.

"Public body"

9. (1) In section 72C "public body" means—

(a) a body which exercises public functions,

(b) a body specified for the purposes of this paragraph by the Secretary of State, and

(c) a body within a class specified for the purposes of this paragraph by the Secretary of State.

(2) A specification under sub-paragraph (1) may be—

(a) general, or

(b) for the purpose of the application of section 72C to a specified case.

Regulated business

10. (1) For the purposes of section 72D a business is regulated if it is carried on—

(a) . . .

(b) in reliance on a licence under section 7[, 7A or 7B] of the Gas Act 1986 (c 44) (transport and supply of gas),

(c) in reliance on a licence granted by virtue of section 41C of that Act (power to prescribe additional licensable activity),

(d) in reliance on a licence under section 6 of the Electricity Act 1989 (c 29) (supply of electricity),

(e) by a water undertaker,

(f) by a sewerage undertaker,
(g) by a universal service provider within the meaning [of Part 3 of the Postal Services Act 2011],
[(h) by a Post Office company within the meaning of Part 1 of that Act,]
(i) . . .
(j) in reliance on a licence under section 8 of the Railways Act 1993 (c 43) (railway services),
(k) in reliance on a licence exemption under section 7 of that Act (subject to sub-paragraph (2) below),
(l) by the operator of a system of transport which is deemed to be a railway for a purpose of Part I of that Act by virtue of section 81(2) of that Act (tramways, &c), . . .
(m) by the operator of a vehicle carried on flanged wheels along a system within paragraph (l); [or
[(n) in reliance on a railway undertaking licence granted pursuant to the Railway (Licensing of Railway Undertakings) Regulations 2005 [or a relevant European licence].]

(2) Sub-paragraph (1)(k) does not apply to the operator of a railway asset on a railway unless on some part of the railway there is a permitted line speed exceeding 40 kilometres per hour.

[(2A) For the purposes of section 72D a business is also regulated to the extent that it consists in the provision of a public electronic communications network or a public electronic communications service.]

[(2B) . . .]

[(3) In sub-paragraph (1)(n) "relevant European licence" has the meaning given by section 6(2) of the Railways Act 1993.]

"Person"

11. A reference to a person in this Schedule includes a reference to a partnership or another unincorporated group of persons.]

NOTES

Inserted by the Enterprise Act 2002, s 250(2), Sch 18, as from 15 September 2003.

Para 1: sub-paras (1)(aa), (ab), (2)(d) (and the word immediately preceding it) inserted by the Insolvency Act 1986 (Amendment) (Administrative Receivership and Capital Market Arrangements) Order 2003, SI 2003/1468, arts 2, 3, as from 15 September 2003.

Paras 2, 3: words in square brackets inserted by the Financial Services and Markets Act 2000 (Regulated Activities) (Amendment) Order 2010, SI 2010/86, art 4, Schedule, para 2, as from 24 February 2010.

Para 10 is amended as follows:

Sub-para (1)(a) repealed, and sub-para (2A) inserted, by the Communications Act 2003, s 406, Sch 17, para 82(1), (4), Sch 19, as from 25 July 2003 (certain purposes), and as from 29 December 2003 (otherwise).

Words in square brackets in sub-para (1)(b) substituted by the Electricity and Gas (Smart Meters Licensable Activity) Order 2012, SI 2012/2400, art 29, as from 19 September 2012.

Words in square brackets in sub-para (1)(g) substituted, sub-para (1)(h) substituted, and sub-para (1)(i) repealed, by the Postal Services Act 2011, s 91(1), (2), Sch 12, Pt 3, paras 124, 126, as from 1 October 2011.

Word omitted from sub-para (1)(l) repealed, and sub-para (1)(n) (and the word immediately preceding it) and sub-para (2B) inserted, by the Railway (Licensing of Railway Undertakings) Regulations 2005, SI 2005/3050, as from 28 November 2005.

Sub-para (1)(n) substituted, and sub-para (2B) repealed, by the Railway (Licensing of Railway Undertakings) (Amendment etc) (EU Exit) Regulations 2019, SI 2019/700, reg 21, as from IP completion day (as defined in the European Union (Withdrawal Agreement) Act 2020, s 39).

Words in square brackets in sub-para (1)(n) inserted, and sub-para (3) added, by the Railway (Licensing of Railway Undertakings) (Amendment) Regulations 2021, SI 2021/1105, reg 9, as from 31 January 2020 (at 11pm).

Modification: a reference to commercial paper in this Schedule includes a reference to uncertificated units of an eligible debt security where the issue of the units corresponds, in accordance with the current terms of issue of the security, to the issue of commercial paper within the meaning of the Financial Services and Markets Act 2000 (Regulated Activities) Order 2001, SI 2001/544, art 9(3); see the Uncertificated Securities (Amendment) (Eligible Debt Securities) Regulations 2003, SI 2003/1633, reg 15, Sch 2, para 7.

Financial Services and Markets Act 2000 (Financial Promotion) Order 2001, SI 2001/1335: revoked and replaced by the Financial Services and Markets Act 2000 (Financial Promotion) Order 2005, SI 2005/1529.

SCHEDULE 3
ORDERS IN COURSE OF WINDING UP PRONOUNCED IN VACATION (SCOTLAND)

Section 162

PART I ORDERS WHICH ARE TO BE FINAL

[9.476]

Orders under section 153, as to the time for proving debts and claims.

Orders under section 195 as to meetings for ascertaining wishes of creditors or contributories.

Orders under section 198, as to the examination of witnesses in regard to the property or affairs of a company.

PART II ORDERS WHICH ARE TO TAKE EFFECT UNTIL MATTER DISPOSED OF BY INNER HOUSE

[9.477]

Orders under section 126(1), 130(2) or (3), 147, 227 or 228, restraining or permitting the commencement or the continuance of legal proceedings.

Orders under section 135(5), limiting the powers of provisional liquidators.

Orders under section 108, appointing a liquidator to fill a vacancy.

. . .

Orders under section 158, as to the arrest and detention of an absconding contributory and his property.

NOTES

Words omitted repealed by the Small Business, Enterprise and Employment Act 2015, s 120(1), (5), as from 26 May 2015.

SCHEDULE 4
POWERS OF LIQUIDATOR IN A WINDING UP

Sections 165, 167

PART I . . .

[9.478]

1. Power to pay any class of creditors in full.

2. Power to make any compromise or arrangement with creditors or persons claiming to be creditors, or having or alleging themselves to have any claim (present or future, certain or contingent, ascertained or sounding only in damages) against the company, or whereby the company may be rendered liable.

3. [. . .] power to compromise, on such terms as may be agreed—

(a) all calls and liabilities to calls, all debts and liabilities capable of resulting in debts, and all claims (present or future, certain or contingent, ascertained or sounding only in damages) subsisting or supposed to subsist between the company and a contributory or alleged contributory or other debtor or person apprehending liability to the company, and

(b) all questions in any way relating to or affecting the assets or the winding up of the company,

and take any security for the discharge of any such call, debt, liability or claim and give a complete discharge in respect of it.

[3A. Power to bring legal proceedings under section 213, 214, 238, 239, 242, 243 or 423.]

NOTES

Part heading: repealed by the Small Business, Enterprise and Employment Act 2015, s 121(1), (6)(c), as from 26 May 2015.

Para 3: words omitted originally inserted by the Legislative Reform (Insolvency) (Miscellaneous Provisions) Order 2010, SI 2010/18, arts 2, 10(1), as from 6 April 2010; and subsequently repealed by the Small Business, Enterprise and Employment Act 2015, s 121(1), (6)(a), as from 26 May 2015.

Para 3A: added by the Enterprise Act 2002, s 253, as from 15 September 2003, except in relation to any proceedings of a kind mentioned in that paragraph which were commenced prior to that date.

PART II . . .

[9.479]

4. Power to bring or defend any action or other legal proceeding in the name and on behalf of the company.

5. Power to carry on the business of the company so far as may be necessary for its beneficial winding up.

NOTES

Part heading: repealed by the Small Business, Enterprise and Employment Act 2015, s 121(1), (6)(c), as from 26 May 2015.

PART III . . .

[9.480]

6. Power to sell any of the company's property by public auction or private contract with power to transfer the whole of it to any person or to sell the same in parcels.

[6A. . . .]

7. Power to do all acts and execute, in the name and on behalf of the company, all deeds, receipts and other documents and for that purpose to use, when necessary, the company's seal.

8. Power to prove, rank and claim in the bankruptcy, insolvency or sequestration of any contributory for any balance against his estate, and to receive dividends in the bankruptcy, insolvency or sequestration in respect of that balance, as a separate debt due from the bankrupt or insolvent, and rateably with the other separate creditors.

9. Power to draw, accept, make and indorse any bill of exchange or promissory note in the name and on behalf of the company, with the same effect with respect to the company's liability as if the bill or note had been drawn, accepted, made or indorsed by or on behalf of the company in the course of its business.

10. Power to raise on the security of the assets of the company any money requisite.

11. Power to take out in his official name letters of administration to any deceased contributory, and to do in his official name any other act necessary for obtaining payment of any money due from a contributory or his estate which cannot conveniently be done in the name of the company.

In all such cases the money due is deemed, for the purpose of enabling the liquidator to take out the letters of administration or recover the money, to be due to the liquidator himself.

12. Power to appoint an agent to do any business which the liquidator is unable to do himself.

13. Power to do all such other things as may be necessary for winding up the company's affairs and distributing its assets.

NOTES

Part heading: repealed by the Small Business, Enterprise and Employment Act 2015, s 121(1), (6)(c), as from 26 May 2015.

Para 6A: originally inserted by the Legislative Reform (Insolvency) (Miscellaneous Provisions) Order 2010, SI 2010/18, arts 2, 10(2), as from 6 April 2010; and subsequently repealed by the Small Business, Enterprise and Employment Act 2015, s 121(1), (6)(b), as from 26 May 2015.

[SCHEDULE 4ZZA
PROTECTION OF SUPPLIES UNDER SECTION 233B: EXCLUSIONS

Section 233B

PART 1 ESSENTIAL SUPPLIES

Essential supplies

[9.481]

1. (1) Section 233B(3) and (4) do not apply in relation to provision of a contract if—

(a) the company becomes subject to a relevant insolvency procedure as specified in section 233B(2)(b) or (d), and

(b) the provision of the contract ceases to have effect under section 233A(1).

(2) Section 233B(7) does not apply in relation to a supply to the company if—

(a) the company becomes subject to a relevant insolvency procedure as specified in section 233B(2)(b) to (f), and

(b) the supply is a supply mentioned in section 233(3).

NOTES

Commencement: 26 June 2020.

This Schedule was inserted by the Corporate Insolvency and Governance Act 2020, s 14(3), Sch 12, Pt 1, para 1, as from 26 June 2020. See also s 14(4) of the 2020 Act which provides that the amendments made by Sch 12 to the 2020 Act have effect in relation to a company which becomes subject to a relevant insolvency procedure on or after 26 June 2020, but in respect of contracts entered into before, as well as those entered into on or after, that day.

PART 2 PERSONS INVOLVED IN FINANCIAL SERVICES

Introductory

[9.482]

2. Section 233B does not apply in relation to a contract for the supply of goods or services to a company ("the company") where any of paragraphs 3 to 11 applies.

Insurers

3. (1) This paragraph applies where either the company or the supplier—

(a) carries on the regulated activity of effecting or carrying out contracts of insurance, and

(b) is not an exempt person in relation to that activity.

(2) In this paragraph—

"exempt person", in relation to a regulated activity, has the meaning given by section 417 of the Financial Services and Markets Act 2000;

"regulated activity" has the meaning given by section 22 of that Act, taken with Schedule 2 to that Act and any order under that section.

Banks

4. (1) This paragraph applies where either the company or the supplier—

(a) has permission under Part 4A of the Financial Services and Markets Act 2000 to carry on the regulated activity of accepting deposits,

(b) is a banking group company within the meaning of Part 1 of the Banking Act 2009 (see section 81D of that Act), or

(c) has a liability in respect of a deposit which it accepted in accordance with the Banking Act 1979 or the Banking Act 1987.

(2) In sub-paragraph (1)(a) "regulated activity" has the meaning given by section 22 of the Financial Services and Markets Act 2000 2000, taken with Schedule 2 to that Act and any order under that section.

Electronic money institutions

5. This paragraph applies where either the company or the supplier is an electronic money institution within the meaning of the Electronic Money Regulations 2011 (SI 2011/99) (see regulation 2 of those Regulations).

Investment banks and investment firms

6. (1) This paragraph applies where either the company or the supplier is an investment bank or an investment firm.

(2) In this paragraph—

"investment bank" means a company or other entity that has permission under Part 4A of the Financial Services and Markets Act 2000 to carry on the regulated activity of—

(a) safeguarding and administering investments,

(b) managing an AIF or a UCITS,

(c) acting as trustee or depositary of an AIF or a UCITS,

(d) dealing in investments as principal, or

(e) dealing in investments as agent;

"investment firm" has the same meaning as in the Banking Act 2009 (see section 258A of that Act), disregarding any order made under section 258A(2)(b) of that Act;

"regulated activity" has the meaning given by section 22 of the Financial Services and Markets Act 2000, taken with Schedule 2 to that Act and any order under that section.

Payment institutions

7. This paragraph applies where either the company or the supplier is an authorised payment institution, a small payment institution or a registered account information service provider within the meaning of the Payment Services Regulations 2017 (SI 2017/752) (see regulation 2 of those Regulations).

Operators of payment systems, infrastructure providers etc

8. This paragraph applies where either the company or the supplier is—

(a) the operator of a payment system or an infrastructure provider within the meaning of Part 5 of the Financial Services (Banking Reform) Act 2013 (see section 42 of that Act), or
(b) an infrastructure company within the meaning of Part 6 of that Act (see section 112 of that Act).

Recognised investment exchanges etc

9. This paragraph applies where either the company or the supplier is a recognised investment exchange, a recognised clearing house or a recognised CSD within the meaning of the Financial Services and Markets Act 2000 (see section 285 of that Act).

Securitisation companies

10. This paragraph applies where either the company or the supplier is a securitisation company within the meaning of the Taxation of Securitisation Companies Regulations 2006 (SI 2006/3296) (see regulation 4 of those Regulations).

Overseas activities

11. This paragraph applies where either the company or the supplier does or has done anything outside the United Kingdom which, if done in the United Kingdom, would cause any of the preceding paragraphs of this Part of this Schedule to apply.

NOTES

Commencement: 26 June 2020.
Inserted as note to Part 1 of this Schedule at **[9.481]**.

PART 3 CONTRACTS INVOLVING FINANCIAL SERVICES

Introductory

[9.483]
12. To the extent that anything to which any of paragraphs 13 to 18 applies is a contract for the supply of goods or services, section 233B does not apply in relation to it.

Financial contracts

13. (1) This paragraph applies to a financial contract.
(2) "Financial contract" means—
(a) a contract for the provision of financial services consisting of—
(i) lending (including the factoring and financing of commercial transactions),
(ii) financial leasing, or
(iii) providing guarantees or commitments;
(b) a securities contract, including—
(i) a contract for the purchase, sale or loan of a security or group or index of securities;
(ii) an option on a security or group or index of securities;
(iii) a repurchase or reverse repurchase transaction on any such security, group or index;
(c) a commodities contract, including—
(i) a contract for the purchase, sale or loan of a commodity or group or index of commodities for future delivery;
(ii) an option on a commodity or group or index of commodities;
(iii) a repurchase or reverse repurchase transaction on any such commodity, group or index;
(d) a futures or forwards contract, including a contract (other than a commodities contract) for the purchase, sale or transfer of a commodity or property of any other description, service, right or interest for a specified price at a future date;
(e) a swap agreement, including—
(i) a swap or option relating to interest rates, spot or other foreign exchange agreements, currency, an equity index or equity, a debt index or debt, commodity indexes or commodities, weather, emissions or inflation;
(ii) a total return, credit spread or credit swap;
(iii) any agreement or transaction similar to an agreement that is referred to in sub-paragraph (i) or (ii) and is the subject of recurrent dealing in the swaps or derivatives markets;
(f) an inter-bank borrowing agreement where the term of the borrowing is three months or less;
(g) a master agreement for any of the contracts or agreements referred to in paragraphs (a) to (f).
(3) For the purposes of this paragraph "commodities" includes—
(a) units recognised for compliance with the requirements of EU Directive 2003/87/EC establishing a scheme for greenhouse gas emission allowance trading,
(b) allowances under paragraph 5 of Schedule 2 to the Climate Change Act 2008 relating to a trading scheme dealt with under Part 1 of that Schedule (schemes limiting activities relating to emissions of greenhouse gas), and
(c) renewables obligation certificates issued—
(i) by the Gas and Electricity Markets Authority under an order made under section 32B of the Electricity Act 1989, or
(ii) by the Northern Ireland Authority for Utility Regulation under the Energy (Northern Ireland) Order 2003 (SI 2003/419 (NI 6)) and pursuant to an order made under Articles 52 to 55F of that Order.

Securities financing transactions

14. (1) This paragraph applies to—
(a) a securities financing transaction, and
(b) a master agreement for securities financing transactions.
(2) "Securities financing transaction" has the meaning given by Article 3(11) of Regulation (EU) 2015/2365 on the transparency of securities financing transactions.

(3) But for the purposes of that Article as it applies for the purposes of this paragraph, references to "commodities" in that Regulation are to be taken as including the units, allowances and certificates referred to in paragraph 13(3)(a) to (c).

Derivatives

15. (1) This paragraph applies to—

(a) a derivative, and
(b) a master agreement for derivatives.

(2) "Derivative" has the meaning given by Article 2(5) of Regulation (EU) No 648/2012.

Spot contracts

16. (1) This paragraph applies to—

(a) a spot contract, and
(b) a master agreement for spot contracts.

(2) "Spot contract" has the meaning given by Article 7(2) or 10(2) of Commission Delegated Regulation of 25.4.2016 supplementing Directive 2014/65/EU of the European Parliament and of the Council as regards organisational requirements and operating conditions for investment firms and defined terms for the purposes of that Directive.

Capital market investments

17. (1) This paragraph applies to an agreement which is, or forms part of, an arrangement involving the issue of a capital market investment.

(2) "Capital market investment" has the meaning given by paragraph 14 of Schedule ZA1.

Contracts forming part of a public-private partnership

18. This paragraph applies to a contract forming part of a public-private partnership project within the meaning given by paragraph 16 of Schedule ZA1.

NOTES

Commencement: 26 June 2020.

Inserted as note to Part 1 of this Schedule at **[9.481]**.

PART 4 OTHER EXCLUSIONS

Financial markets and insolvency

[9.484]

19. Nothing in section 233B affects the operation of—

(a) Part 7 of the Companies Act 1989 (financial markets and insolvency),
(b) the Financial Markets and Insolvency Regulations 1996 (SI 1996/1469),
(c) the Financial Markets and Insolvency (Settlement Finality) Regulations 1999 (SI 1999/2979), or
(d) the Financial Collateral Arrangements (No 2) Regulations 2003 (SI 2003/3226).

Set-off and netting

20. Nothing in section 233B affects any set-off or netting arrangements (within the meanings given by section 48(1)(c) and (d) of the Banking Act 2009).

Aircraft equipment

21. Nothing in section 233B affects the International Interests in Aircraft Equipment (Cape Town Convention) Regulations 2015 (SI 2015/912).]

NOTES

Commencement: 26 June 2020.

Inserted as note to Part 1 of this Schedule at **[9.481]**.

SCHEDULES 4ZA, 4ZB, 4A, 5

(*Sch 4ZA (Conditions for Making a Debt Relief Order), Sch 4ZB (Debt Relief Restrictions Orders and Undertakings), Sch 4A (Bankruptcy Restrictions Order and Undertaking), Sch 5 (Powers of Trustee in Bankruptcy) are outside the scope of this work.*)

SCHEDULE 6
THE CATEGORIES OF PREFERENTIAL DEBTS

Section 386

[9.485]

1–7. . . .

Category 4: Contributions to occupational pension schemes, etc

8. Any sum which is owed by the debtor and is a sum to which [Schedule 4 to the Pension Schemes Act 1993] applies (contributions to occupational pension schemes and state scheme premiums).

Category 5: Remuneration, etc, of employees

9. So much of any amount which—

(a) is owed by the debtor to a person who is or has been an employee of the debtor, and
(b) is payable by way of remuneration in respect of the whole or any part of the period of 4 months next before the relevant date,

as does not exceed so much as may be prescribed by order made by the Secretary of State.

10. An amount owed by way of accrued holiday remuneration, in respect of any period of employment before the relevant date, to a person whose employment by the debtor has been terminated, whether before, on or after that date.

11. So much of any sum owed in respect of money advanced for the purpose as has been applied for the payment of a debt which, if it had not been paid, would have been a debt falling within paragraph 9 or 10.

12. So much of any amount which—
- (a) is ordered (whether before or after the relevant date) to be paid by the debtor under the Reserve Forces (Safeguard of Employment) Act 1985, and
- (b) is so ordered in respect of a default made by the debtor before that date in the discharge of his obligations under that Act,

as does not exceed such amount as may be prescribed by order made by the Secretary of State.

Interpretation for Category 5

13. (1) For the purposes of paragraphs 9 to 12, a sum is payable by the debtor to a person by way of remuneration in respect of any period if—
- (a) it is paid as wages or salary (whether payable for time or for piece work or earned wholly or partly by way of commission) in respect of services rendered to the debtor in that period, or
- (b) it is an amount falling within the following sub-paragraph and is payable by the debtor in respect of that period.

[(2) An amount falls within this sub-paragraph if it is—
- (a) a guarantee payment under Part III of the Employment Rights Act 1996 (employee without work to do);
- (b) any payment for time off under section 53 (time off to look for work or arrange training) or section 56 (time off for ante-natal care) of that Act or under section 169 of the Trade Union and Labour Relations (Consolidation) Act 1992 (time off for carrying out trade union duties etc);
- (c) remuneration on suspension on medical grounds, or on maternity grounds, under Part VII of the Employment Rights Act 1996; or
- (d) remuneration under a protective award under section 189 of the Trade Union and Labour Relations (Consolidation) Act 1992 (redundancy dismissal with compensation).]

14. (1) This paragraph relates to a case in which a person's employment has been terminated by or in consequence of his employer going into liquidation or being [made] bankrupt or (his employer being a company not in liquidation) by or in consequence of—
- (a) a receiver being appointed as mentioned in section 40 of this Act (debenture-holders secured by floating charge), or
- (b) the appointment of a receiver under section 53(6) or 54(5) of this Act (Scottish company with property subject to floating charge), or
- (c) the taking of possession by debenture-holders (so secured), as mentioned in [section 754 of the Companies Act 2006].

(2) For the purposes of paragraphs 9 to 12, holiday remuneration is deemed to have accrued to that person in respect of any period of employment if, by virtue of his contract of employment or of any enactment that remuneration would have accrued in respect of that period if his employment had continued until he became entitled to be allowed the holiday.

(3) The reference in sub-paragraph (2) to any enactment includes an order or direction made under an enactment.

15. Without prejudice to paragraphs 13 and 14—
- (a) any remuneration payable by the debtor to a person in respect of a period of holiday or of absence from work through sickness or other good cause is deemed to be wages or (as the case may be) salary in respect of services rendered to the debtor in that period, . . .
- (b) . . .

[Category 6: Levies on coal and steel production

15A. Any sums due at the relevant date from the debtor in respect of:
- (a) the levies on the production of coal and steel referred to in Articles 49 and 50 of the ECSC Treaty, or
- (b) any surcharge for delay provided for in Article 50(3) of that Treaty and Article 6 of Decision 3/52 of the High Authority of the Coal and Steel Community.]

[Category 6A: Debts owed to the Financial Services Compensation Scheme

15AA. Any debt owed by the debtor to the scheme manager of the Financial Services Compensation Scheme under section 215(2A) of the Financial Services and Markets Act 2000.]

[Category 7: Deposits covered by Financial Services Compensation Scheme

15B. So much of any amount owed at the relevant date by the debtor in respect of an eligible deposit as does not exceed the compensation that would be payable in respect of the deposit under the Financial Services Compensation Scheme to the person or persons to whom the amount is owed.

[Category 8: Other deposits

[15BA. So much of any amount owed at the relevant date by the debtor to one or more eligible persons in respect of an eligible deposit as exceeds any compensation that would be payable in respect of the deposit under the Financial Services Compensation Scheme to that person or those persons.

15BB. An amount owed at the relevant date by the debtor to one or more eligible persons in respect of a deposit that—
- (a) was made through a [non-UK] branch of a credit institution authorised by the competent authority of [the United Kingdom], and
- (b) would have been an eligible deposit if it had been made through [a UK] branch of that credit institution.]

Interpretation for [Categories 6A, 7 and 8]

15C. (A1) In paragraph 15AA "the scheme manager" has the meaning given in section 212(1) of the Financial Services and Markets Act 2000.]

(1) In [paragraphs 15B to 15BB] "eligible deposit" means a deposit in respect of which the person, or any of the persons, to whom it is owed would be eligible for compensation under the Financial Services Compensation Scheme.

(2) For [the purposes of those paragraphs and this paragraph] a "deposit" means rights of the kind described in—

(a) paragraph 22 of Schedule 2 to the Financial Services and Markets Act 2000 (deposits), or

(b) section 1(2)(b) of the Dormant Bank and Building Society Accounts Act 2008 (balances transferred under that Act to authorised reclaim fund).

[(3) In paragraphs 15BA and 15BB, "eligible person" means—

(a) an individual, or

[(b) any micro, small and medium-sized enterprise, as defined with regard to the annual turnover criterion referred to in Article 2(1) of the Annex to Commission recommendation 2003/361/EC.]

(4) In paragraph 15BB—

(a) "credit institution" has the meaning given in Article 4.1(1) of the capital requirements regulation;

[(b) "non-UK branch" means a branch, as defined in Article 4.1(17) of the capital requirements regulation, which is established outside the United Kingdom;

(c) "UK branch" means a branch, as so defined, which is established in the United Kingdom,]

and for this purpose "the capital requirements regulation" means Regulation (EU) No 575/2013 of the European Parliament and of the Council of 26th June 2013 on prudential requirements for credit institutions and investment firms and amending Regulation (EU) No 648/2012[, as it [forms part of retained EU law]].]]

[Category 9: Certain HMRC debts

15D. (1) Any amount owed at the relevant date by the debtor to the Commissioners in respect of—

(a) value added tax, or

(b) a relevant deduction.

(2) In sub-paragraph (1), the reference to "any amount" is subject to any regulations under section 99(1) of the Finance Act 2020.

(3) For the purposes of sub-paragraph (1)(b) a deduction is "relevant" if—

(a) the debtor is required, by virtue of an enactment, to make the deduction from a payment made to another person and to pay an amount to the Commissioners on account of the deduction,

(b) the payment to the Commissioners is credited against any liabilities of the other person, and

(c) the deduction is of a kind specified in regulations under section 99(3) of the Finance Act 2020.

(4) In this paragraph "the Commissioners" means the Commissioners for Her Majesty's Revenue and Customs.]

Orders

16. An order under paragraph 9 or 12—

(a) may contain such transitional provisions as may appear to the Secretary of State necessary or expedient;

(b) shall be made by statutory instrument subject to annulment in pursuance of a resolution of either House of Parliament.

NOTES

Paras 1–7: repealed by the Enterprise Act 2002, ss 251(1), 278(2), Sch 26, as from 15 September 2003. Note that art 4 of the Enterprise Act 2002 (Commencement No 4 and Transitional Provisions and Savings) Order 2003, SI 2003/2093 (as amended) contains detailed transitional provisions in relation to the abolition of preferential status for Crown debts. Broadly speaking, preferential status will continue to apply in those cases which were started before 15 September 2003.

Para 8: words in square brackets substituted by the Pension Schemes Act 1993, s 190, Sch 8, para 18, as from 7 February 1994.

Para 13: sub-para (2) substituted by the Employment Rights Act 1996, s 240, Sch 1, para 29, as from 22 August 1996.

Para 14: word in first pair of square brackets substituted (for the original word "adjudged"), in relation to England and Wales, by the Enterprise and Regulatory Reform Act 2013, s 71(3), Sch 19, paras 1, 64, as from 6 April 2016, except in respect of a petition for a bankruptcy order presented to the court by a debtor before that date. Words in square brackets in sub-para (1)(c) substituted by the Companies Act 2006 (Consequential Amendments etc) Order 2008, SI 2008/948, art 3(1), Sch 1, Pt 2, para 104, as from 6 April 2008.

Para 15: sub-para (b) (and the preceding word) repealed by the Deregulation Act 2015, s 19, Sch 6, Pt 7, paras 24, 28, as from 26 May 2015.

Para 15A: inserted by the Insolvency (ECSC Levy Debts) Regulations 1987, SI 1987/2093, reg 2(1), (3), as from 1 January 1988.

Para 15AA: inserted by the Deposit Guarantee Scheme Regulations 2015, SI 2015/486, reg 14(1), (3)(a), as from 26 March 2015.

Para 15B: inserted, together with para 15C, by the Financial Services (Banking Reform) Act 2013, s 13(1), as from 31 December 2014.

Paras 15BA, 15BB: inserted by the Banks and Building Societies (Depositor Preference and Priorities) Order 2014, SI 2014/3486, arts 3, 11(1), (2), as from 1 January 2015, except in relation to any insolvency proceedings commenced before that date (see further the note relating to this Order at **[9.139]**). Words in square brackets in para 15BB substituted by the Bank Recovery and Resolution and Miscellaneous Provisions (Amendment) (EU Exit) Regulations 2018, SI 2018/1394, reg 3, Sch 2, paras 1, 2, as from IP completion day (as defined in the European Union (Withdrawal Agreement) Act 2020, s 39).

Para 15C was inserted as noted above, and is amended as follows:

The words in square brackets in the heading preceding para 15C were substituted, and sub-para (A1) was inserted, by SI 2015/486, reg 14(1), (3)(b), (c), as from 26 March 2015.

The words in square brackets in sub-paras (1), (2) were substituted, and sub-paras (3), (4) were added, by SI 2014/3486, arts 3, 11(1), (3), (4), as from 1 January 2015, except in relation to any insolvency proceedings commenced before that date (see further the note relating to this Order at **[9.139]**).

Sub-paras (3)(b), (4)(b), (c) were substituted by SI 2018/1394, reg 3, Sch 2, paras 1, 3(a), (b), as from IP completion day (as defined in the European Union (Withdrawal Agreement) Act 2020, s 39).

In the final words of sub-para (4), the words in the first (outer) pair of square brackets were inserted by SI 2018/1394, reg 3, Sch 2, paras 1, 3(c), as from 21 December 2018; and the words in the second (inner) pair of square brackets were substituted by the Securities Financing Transactions, Securitisation and Miscellaneous Amendments (EU Exit) Regulations 2020, SI 2020/1385, reg 37, with effect from immediately before IP completion day (as defined in the European Union (Withdrawal Agreement) Act 2020, s 39).

Para 15D: inserted by the Finance Act 2020, s 98(2) (this amendment does not apply in relation to any case where the relevant date is before 1 December 2020). See also the note "Priority on Insolvency (HMRC Debts)" below.

Priority on insolvency (HMRC debts): see the Insolvency Act 1986 (HMRC Debts: Priority on Insolvency) Regulations 2020, SI 2020/983 at **[10.1298]**.

Orders: the Insolvency Proceedings (Monetary Limits) Order 1986, SI 1986/1996 prescribing £800 for the purposes of paras 9, 12 above (see art 4).

SCHEDULE 7

(Sch 7 (Insolvency Practitioners Tribunal) repealed by the Deregulation Act 2015, s 19, Sch 6, Pt 6, paras 17, 21, as from 1 October 2015.)

SCHEDULE 8
PROVISIONS CAPABLE OF INCLUSION IN COMPANY INSOLVENCY RULES

Section 411

Courts

[9.486]

1. Provision for supplementing, in relation to the insolvency or winding up of companies, any provision made by or under section 117 of this Act (jurisdiction in relation to winding up).

2. [(1)] Provision for regulating the practice and procedure of any court exercising jurisdiction for the purposes of [Parts A1] to VII of this Act or [the Companies Acts] so far as relating to, and to matters connected with or arising out of, the insolvency or winding up of companies, being any provision that could be made by rules of court.

[(2) Rules made by virtue of this paragraph about the consequence of failure to comply with practice or procedure may, in particular, include provision about the termination of administration.]

Notices, etc

3. Provision requiring notice of any proceedings in connection with or arising out of the insolvency or winding up of a company to be given or published in the manner prescribed by the rules.

4. Provision with respect to the form, manner of serving, contents and proof of any petition, application, order, notice, statement or other document required to be presented, made, given, published or prepared under any enactment or subordinate legislation relating to, or to matters connected with or arising out of, the insolvency or winding up of companies.

5. Provision specifying the persons to whom any notice is to be given.

[5A. Provision for enabling a creditor of a company to elect to be, or to cease to be, an opted-out creditor in relation to an office-holder of the company (within the meaning of section 248A), including, in particular, provision—

(a) for requiring an office-holder to provide information to creditors about how they may elect to be, or cease to be, opted-out creditors;

(b) for deeming an election to be, or cease to be, an opted-out creditor in relation to a particular office-holder of a company to be such an election also in relation to any other office-holder of the company.]

Registration of voluntary arrangements

6. Provision for the registration of voluntary arrangements approved under Part I of this Act, including provision for the keeping and inspection of a register.

Provisional liquidator

7. Provision as to the manner in which a provisional liquidator appointed under section 135 is to carry out his functions.

Conduct of insolvency

8. Provision with respect to the certification of any person as, and as to the proof that a person is [the monitor in relation to a moratorium under Part A1 or], the liquidator, administrator or administrative receiver of a company.

[8A. (1) Provision about the making of decisions by creditors and contributories, including provision—

(a) prescribing particular procedures by which creditors and contributories may make decisions;

(b) authorising the use of other procedures for creditors and contributories to make decisions, if those procedures comply with prescribed requirements.

(2) Provision under sub-paragraph (1) may in particular include provision about—

(a) how creditors and contributories may request that a creditors' meeting or a contributories' meeting be held,

(b) the rights of creditors, contributories and others to be given notice of, and participate in, procedures,

(c) creditors' and contributories' rights to vote in procedures,

(d) the period within which any right to participate or vote is to be exercised,

(e) the proportion of creditors or contributories that must vote for a proposal for it to be approved,

(f) how the value of any debt or contribution should be determined,

(g) the time at which decisions taken by a procedure are to be treated as having been made.]

9. The following provision with respect to meetings of a company's creditors, contributories or members—

(a) provision as to the manner of summoning a meeting (including provision as to how any power to require a meeting is to be exercised, provision as to the manner of determining the value of any debt or contribution for the purposes of any such power and provision making the exercise of any such power subject to the deposit of a sum sufficient to cover the expenses likely to be incurred in summoning and holding a meeting);
(b) provision specifying the time and place at which a meeting may be held and the period of notice required for a meeting;
(c) provision as to the procedure to be followed at a meeting (including the manner in which decisions may be reached by a meeting and the manner in which the value of any vote at a meeting is to be determined);
(d) provision for requiring a person who is or has been an officer of the company to attend a meeting;
(e) provision creating, in the prescribed circumstances, a presumption that a meeting has been duly summoned and held;
(f) provision as to the manner of proving the decisions of a meeting.

[9A. Provision about how a company's creditors may nominate a person to be liquidator, including in the case of a voluntary winding up provision conferring functions on the directors of the company.]

10. (1) Provision as to the [establishment,] functions, membership and proceedings of a committee [provided for by] [section 49, 68, 101, 141 or 142 of, or paragraph 57 of Schedule B1 to, this Act].

(2) The following provision with respect to the establishment of a committee under section 101, 141 or 142 of this Act, that is to say—
(a) provision for resolving differences between . . . the company's creditors and . . . its contributories or members;
(b) provision authorising the establishment of the committee without [seeking a decision from] contributories in a case where a company is being wound up on grounds including its inability to pay its debts; and
(c) provision modifying the requirements of this Act with respect to the establishment of the committee in a case where a winding-up order has been made immediately upon the discharge of an administration order.

11. Provision as to the manner in which any requirement that may be imposed on a person under any of Parts I to VII of this Act by the official receiver, the liquidator, administrator or administrative receiver of a company or a special manager appointed under section 177 is to be so imposed.

12. Provision as to the debts that may be proved in a winding up, as to the manner and conditions of proving a debt and as to the manner and expenses of establishing the value of any debt or security.

13. Provision with respect to the manner of the distribution of the property of a company that is being wound up, including provision with respect to unclaimed funds and dividends.

[13A. Provision for a creditor who has not proved a small debt to be treated as having done so for purposes relating to the distribution of a company's property (and for provisions of, or contained in legislation made under, this Act to apply accordingly).]

14. Provision which, with or without modifications, applies in relation to the winding up of companies any enactment contained in Parts VIII to XI of this Act or in the Bankruptcy (Scotland) Act [2016].

[14A. Provision about the application of section 176A of this Act which may include, in particular—
(a) provision enabling a receiver to institute winding up proceedings;
(b) provision requiring a receiver to institute winding up proceedings.]

[Administration

14B. Provision which—
(a) applies in relation to administration, with or without modifications, a provision of Parts IV to VII of this Act, or
(b) serves a purpose in relation to administration similar to a purpose that may be served by the rules in relation to winding up by virtue of a provision of this Schedule.]

Financial provisions

15. Provision as to the amount, or manner of determining the amount, payable to the liquidator, administrator or administrative receiver of a company or a special manager appointed under section 177, by way of remuneration for the carrying out of functions in connection with or arising out of the insolvency or winding up of a company.

16. Provision with respect to the manner in which moneys received by the liquidator of a company in the course of carrying out his functions as such are to be invested or otherwise handled and with respect to the payment of interest on sums which, in pursuance of rules made by virtue of this paragraph, have been paid into the Insolvency Services Account.

[16A. Provision enabling the Secretary of State to set the rate of interest paid on sums which have been paid into the Insolvency Services Account.]

17. Provision as to the fees, costs, charges and other expenses that may be treated as the expenses of a winding up.

18. Provision as to the fees, costs, charges and other expenses that may be treated as properly incurred by the administrator or administrative receiver of a company.

19. Provision as to the fees, costs, charges and other expenses that may be incurred for any of the purposes of Part I of this Act or in the administration of any voluntary arrangement approved under that Part.

Information and records

20. Provision requiring registrars and other officers of courts having jurisdiction in England and Wales in relation to, or to matters connected with or arising out of, the insolvency or winding up of companies—
(a) to keep books and other records with respect to the exercise of that jurisdiction, and
(b) to make returns to the Secretary of State of the business of those courts.

21. Provision requiring a creditor, member or contributory, or such a committee as is mentioned in paragraph 10 above, to be supplied (on payment in prescribed cases of the prescribed fee) with such information and with copies of such documents as may be prescribed.

22. Provision as to the manner in which public examinations under sections 133 and 134 of this Act and proceedings under sections 236 and 237 are to be conducted, as to the circumstances in which records of such examinations or proceedings are to be made available to prescribed persons and as to the costs of such examinations and proceedings.

23. Provision imposing requirements with respect to—

(a) the preparation and keeping by the liquidator, administrator or administrative receiver of a company, or by the supervisor of a voluntary arrangement approved under Part I of this Act, of prescribed books, accounts and other records;

(b) the production of those books, accounts and records for inspection by prescribed persons;

(c) the auditing of accounts kept by the liquidator, administrator or administrative receiver of a company, or the supervisor of such a voluntary arrangement; and

(d) the issue by the administrator or administrative receiver of a company of such a certificate as is mentioned in section 22(3)(b) of the Value Added Tax Act 1983 (refund of tax in cases of bad debts) and the supply of copies of the certificate to creditors of the company.

24. Provision requiring the person who is the supervisor of a voluntary arrangement approved under Part I, when it appears to him that the voluntary arrangement has been fully implemented and that nothing remains to be done by him under the arrangement—

(a) to give notice of that fact to persons bound by the voluntary arrangement, and

(b) to report to those persons on the carrying out of the functions conferred on the supervisor of the arrangement.

25. Provision as to the manner in which the liquidator of a company is to act in relation to the books, papers and other records of the company, including provision authorising their disposal.

26. Provision imposing requirements in connection with the carrying out of functions under section [7A] of the Company Directors Disqualification Act 1986 (including, in particular, requirements with respect to the making of periodic returns).

General

27. Provision conferring power on the Secretary of State [or the Treasury] to make regulations with respect to so much of any matter that may be provided for in the rules as relates to the carrying out of the functions of the liquidator, administrator or administrative receiver of a company.

28. Provision conferring a discretion on the court.

29. Provision conferring power on the court to make orders for the purpose of securing compliance with obligations imposed by or under [section 47, 66, 131, 143(2) or 235 of, or paragraph 47 of Schedule B1 to, this Act] or section 7(4) of the Company Directors Disqualification Act 1986.

30. Provision making non-compliance with any of the rules a criminal offence.

31. Provision making different provision for different cases or descriptions of cases, including different provisions for different areas.

NOTES

Para 2: sub-para (1) numbered as such, and sub-para (2) added, by the Enterprise Act 2002, s 248(3), Sch 17, paras 9, 38(1), (2), as from 15 September 2003 (for savings and transitional provisions, see the note to s 8 at **[9.147]**). Words in first pair of square brackets in sub-para (1) substituted by the Corporate Insolvency and Governance Act 2020, s 2(1), Sch 3, paras 1, 32(1), (2), as from 26 June 2020 (for transitional provisions, see s 2(2), (3) of the 2020 Act (at **[9.533]**) which provides that (without prejudice to the Interpretation Act 1978, s 16) nothing in the 2020 Act affects the operation of this Act, or any other enactment, in relation to a moratorium under Sch A1 to this Act which comes into force before the repeal of that Schedule by Sch 3 to the 2020 Act (ie, 26 June 2020)). Words in second pair of square brackets in sub-para (1) substituted by the Companies Act 2006 (Commencement No 3, Consequential Amendments, Transitional Provisions and Savings) Order 2007, SI 2007/2194, art 10(1), (2), Sch 4, Pt 3, para 44, as from 1 October 2007.

Paras 5A, 8A, 9A: inserted by the Small Business, Enterprise and Employment Act 2015, ss 122(1), (3), 124(1), (5), 126, Sch 9, Pt 1, paras 1, 58, as from 6 April 2017 (in relation to England and Wales), and as from 6 April 2019 (in relation to Scotland) (for transitional and savings provisions, see the notes to s 246ZE at **[9.385]**).

Para 8: words in square brackets inserted by the Corporate Insolvency and Governance Act 2020, s 2(1), Sch 3, paras 1, 32(1), (3), as from 26 June 2020 (for transitional provisions, see the first note relating to the 2020 Act above).

Para 10: the words in the third pair of square brackets in sub-para (1) were substituted by the Enterprise Act 2002, s 248(3), Sch 17, paras 9, 38(1), (3), as from 15 September 2003 (for savings and transitional provisions, see the note to s 8 at **[9.147]**). All other amendments to this paragraph were made by the Small Business, Enterprise and Employment Act 2015, s 126, Sch 9, Pt 1, paras 1, 59, as from 6 April 2017 (in relation to England and Wales), and as from 6 April 2019 (in relation to Scotland) (for transitional and savings provisions, see the notes to s 246ZE at **[9.385]**).

Para 13A: inserted by the Small Business, Enterprise and Employment Act 2015, s 131, as from 26 May 2015.

Para 14: year "2016" in square brackets substituted by the Bankruptcy (Scotland) Act 2016 (Consequential Provisions and Modifications) Order 2016, SI 2016/1034, art 7(1), (3), Sch 1, para 4(1), (11), as from 30 November 2016 (except in relation to (i) a sequestration as regards which the petition is presented, or the debtor application is made before that date; or (ii) a trust deed executed before that date).

Paras 14A, 14B: inserted by the Enterprise Act 2002, s 248(3), Sch 17, paras 9, 38(1), (4), (5), as from 15 September 2003 (for savings and transitional provisions, see the note to s 8 at **[9.147]**).

Paras 16A: inserted by the Enterprise Act 2002, s 271(1), as from 18 December 2003.

Para 26: figure in square brackets substituted by the Enterprise and Regulatory Reform Act 2013 (Consequential Amendments) (Bankruptcy) and the Small Business, Enterprise and Employment Act 2015 (Consequential Amendments) Regulations 2016, SI 2016/481, reg 3, as from 6 April 2016.

Para 27: words in square brackets inserted by the Banking Act 2009, s 125(7), as from 17 February 2009.

Para 29: words in square brackets substituted by the Enterprise Act 2002, s 248(3), Sch 17, paras 9, 38(1), (6), as from 15 September 2003 (for savings and transitional provisions, see the note to s 8 at **[9.147]**).

Note that the Small Business, Enterprise and Employment Act 2015, ss 122, 124, 126 and Sch 9 also come into force on 26 May 2015 for the purposes of enabling the exercise of any power to make provision by regulations, rules or order made by statutory instrument or to prepare and issue guidance).

Regulations: the main Regulations made under this Schedule are the Insolvency Regulations 1994, SI 1994/2507 at **[10.34]**.

SCHEDULES 9–14

(Sch 9 (Provisions Capable of Inclusion in Individual Insolvency Rules) is outside the scope of this work. Sch 10 (Punishment of Offences Under this Act) was included in previous editions of this Handbook but is now omitted due to constraints on space in this work. Sch 11 (Transitional Provisions and Savings) is largely considered to be spent and is otherwise outside the scope of this work. Sch 12 contains repeals only. Sch 13 (Consequential Amendments of Companies Act 1985) is now spent. Sch 14 contains consequential amendments.)

COMPANY AND BUSINESS NAMES (CHAMBER OF COMMERCE, ETC) ACT 1999

(1999 c 19)

NOTES

This Act is reproduced as amended by: the Companies Act 2006 (Consequential Amendments, Transitional Provisions and Savings) Order 2009, SI 2009/1941.

An Act to make provision concerning the approval of company or business names containing the expression "chamber of commerce" or any related expression; and for connected purposes

[27 July 1999]

[9.487]

1 Approval to be required for company or business names including the expression "chamber of commerce"

It is the duty of the Secretary of State to secure that the expression "chamber of commerce" and its Welsh equivalent ("siambr fasnach") is specified—

(a) in regulations under [section 55 of the Companies Act 2006 (company names requiring approval of Secretary of State)], and

(b) in regulations under [section 1194 of that Act (business names requiring approval of Secretary of State)],

as an expression for the registration of which as or as part of a company's name, or for the use of which as or as part of a business name, the approval of the Secretary of State is required.

NOTES

Words in square brackets substituted by the Companies Act 2006 (Consequential Amendments, Transitional Provisions and Savings) Order 2009, SI 2009/1941, art 2(1), Sch 1, para 176(1), (2), as from 1 October 2009.

[9.488]

2 Approval of certain company names

(1) Before determining under [section 55 of the Companies Act 2006] whether to approve the registration of a company under a name which includes—

(a) the expression "chamber of commerce" or "siambr fasnach", or

(b) any other expression for the time being specified in regulations under [that section] which begins with the words "chamber of" or "chambers of" (or the Welsh equivalents),

the Secretary of State must consult at least one relevant representative body.

(2) The Secretary of State may publish guidance with respect to factors which may be taken into account in determining whether to approve the registration of a name to which this section applies.

NOTES

Sub-s (1): words in square brackets substituted by the Companies Act 2006 (Consequential Amendments, Transitional Provisions and Savings) Order 2009, SI 2009/1941, art 2(1), Sch 1, para 176(1), (3), as from 1 October 2009.

[9.489]

3 Approval of certain business names

(1) Before determining under [section 1194 of the Companies Act 2006] whether to approve the carrying on of a business under a name which includes—

(a) the expression "chamber of commerce" or "siambr fasnach", or

(b) any other expression for the time being specified in regulations under [that section] which begins with the words "chamber of" or "chambers of" (or the Welsh equivalents),

the Secretary of State must consult at least one relevant representative body.

(2) The Secretary of State may publish guidance with respect to factors which may be taken into account in determining whether to approve the use of a business name to which this section applies.

NOTES

Sub-s (1): words in square brackets substituted by the Companies Act 2006 (Consequential Amendments, Transitional Provisions and Savings) Order 2009, SI 2009/1941, art 2(1), Sch 1, para 176(1), (4), as from 1 October 2009.

[9.490]

4 Relevant representative bodies

(1) The relevant representative bodies for the purposes of this Act are—

(a) British Chambers of Commerce;
(b) the body known as Scottish Chambers of Commerce.

(2) The Secretary of State may by order amend subsection (1) by adding to or deleting from it the name of any body (whether corporate or unincorporated).

(3) The power to make an order under this section is exercisable by statutory instrument which shall be liable to annulment in pursuance of a resolution of either House of Parliament.

[9.491]

5 Citation, commencement and extent

(1) This Act may be cited as the Company and Business Names (Chamber of Commerce, Etc) Act 1999.

(2) This Act shall come into force on such day as the Secretary of State may by order made by statutory instrument appoint.

(3) This Act does not extend to Northern Ireland.

NOTES

Orders: the Company and Business Names (Chamber of Commerce, etc) Act 1999 (Commencement) Order 2001, SI 2001/258 (bringing this Act into force on 10 May 2001).

LIMITED LIABILITY PARTNERSHIPS ACT 2000

(2000 c 12)

NOTES

This Act is reproduced as amended by: the Open-Ended Investment Companies Regulations 2001, SI 2001/1228; the Limited Liability Partnerships (Particulars of Usual Residential Address) (Confidentiality Orders) Regulations 2002, SI 2002/915; the Companies (Audit, Investigations and Community Enterprise) Act 2004; the Companies Act 2006; the Income Tax Act 2007; the Limited Liability Partnerships (Application of Companies Act 2006) Regulations 2009, SI 2009/1804; the Corporation Tax Act 2010; the Limited Liability Partnerships (Register of People with Significant Control) Regulations 2016, SI 2016/340; the Bankruptcy (Scotland) Act 2016 (Consequential Provisions and Modifications) Order 2016, SI 2016/1034; the Corporate Insolvency and Governance Act 2020.

Application of the Banking Act 2009: s 132 of the Banking Act 2009 provides that the Lord Chancellor may, by order made with the concurrence of the Secretary of State and the Lord Chief Justice, modify provisions of Part 2 of the 2009 Act (bank insolvency) in their application to partnerships. See also s 163 of the 2009 Act which makes the same provision with regard to the application of Part 3 of that Act (bank administration). Similar provision is made with regard to Scottish partnerships by ss 133 and 164 respectively.

ARRANGEMENT OF SECTIONS

An Act to make provision for limited liability partnerships

[20 July 2000]

Introductory

[9.492]

1 Limited liability partnerships

(1) There shall be a new form of legal entity to be known as a limited liability partnership.

(2) A limited liability partnership is a body corporate (with legal personality separate from that of its members) which is formed by being incorporated under this Act; and—

(a) in the following provisions of this Act (except in the phrase "oversea limited liability partnership"), and

(b) in any other enactment (except where provision is made to the contrary or the context otherwise requires),

references to a limited liability partnership are to such a body corporate.

(3) A limited liability partnership has unlimited capacity.

(4) The members of a limited liability partnership have such liability to contribute to its assets in the event of its being wound up as is provided for by virtue of this Act.

(5) Accordingly, except as far as otherwise provided by this Act or any other enactment, the law relating to partnerships does not apply to a limited liability partnership.

(6) The Schedule (which makes provision about the names and registered offices of limited liability partnerships) has effect.

Incorporation

[9.493]

2 Incorporation document etc

(1) For a limited liability partnership to be incorporated—

(a) two or more persons associated for carrying on a lawful business with a view to profit must have subscribed their names to an incorporation document,

[(b) the incorporation document or a copy of it must have been delivered to the registrar, and]

(c) there must have been so delivered a statement . . . made by either a solicitor engaged in the formation of the limited liability partnership or anyone who subscribed his name to the incorporation document, that the requirement imposed by paragraph (a) has been complied with.

(2) The incorporation document must—

(a) . . .

(b) state the name of the limited liability partnership,

(c) state whether the registered office of the limited liability partnership is to be situated in England and Wales, in Wales[, in Scotland or in Northern Ireland],

(d) state the address of that registered office,

[(e) give the required particulars of each of the persons who are to be members of the limited liability partnership on incorporation, . . .]

(f) either specify which of those persons are to be designated members or state that every person who from time to time is a member of the limited liability partnership is a designated member[; and].

[(g) include a statement of initial significant control].

[(2ZA) The required particulars mentioned in subsection (2)(e) are the particulars required to be stated in the LLP's register of members and register of members' residential addresses.]

[(2A), (2B) . . .]

(3) If a person makes a false statement under subsection (1)(c) which he—

(a) knows to be false, or

(b) does not believe to be true,

he commits an offence.

(4) A person guilty of an offence under subsection (3) is liable—

(a) on summary conviction, to imprisonment for a period not exceeding six months or a fine not exceeding the statutory maximum, or to both, or

(b) on conviction on indictment, to imprisonment for a period not exceeding two years or a fine, or to both.

NOTES

Sub-s (1): words omitted from para (c) repealed, and para (b) substituted, by the Limited Liability Partnerships (Application of Companies Act 2006) Regulations 2009, SI 2009/1804, reg 85, Sch 3, Pt 1, para 1(1)–(3), as from 1 October 2009.

Sub-s (2): para (a) repealed, words in square brackets in para (c) substituted, and para (e) substituted, by SI 2009/1804, reg 85, Sch 3, Pt 1, para 1(1), (4), as from 1 October 2009. The word omitted from para (e) was repealed, the word in square brackets in para (f) was inserted, and para (g) was added, by the Limited Liability Partnerships (Register of People with Significant Control) Regulations 2016, SI 2016/340, reg 5, Sch 3, para 1, as from 30 June 2016.

Sub-s (2ZA): inserted by SI 2009/1804, reg 85, Sch 3, Pt 1, para 1(1), (5), as from 1 October 2009.

Sub-ss (2A), (2B): originally inserted by the Limited Liability Partnerships (Particulars of Usual Residential Address) (Confidentiality Orders) Regulations 2002, SI 2002/915, reg 16, Sch 2, para 1, as from 2 April 2002. Subsequently repealed by SI 2009/1804, reg 85, Sch 3, Pt 1, para 1(1), (6), as from 1 October 2009.

[9.494]

3 Incorporation by registration

[(1) The registrar, if satisfied that the requirements of section 2 are complied with, shall—

(a) register the documents delivered under that section, and

(b) give a certificate that the limited liability partnership is incorporated.

(1A) The certificate must state—

(a) the name and registered number of the limited liability partnership,

(b) the date of its incorporation, and

(c) whether the limited liability partnership's registered office is situated in England and Wales (or in Wales), in Scotland or in Northern Ireland.]

(2) The registrar may accept the statement delivered under paragraph (c) of subsection (1) of section 2 as sufficient evidence that the requirement imposed by paragraph (a) of that subsection has been complied with.
(3) The certificate shall either be signed by the registrar or be authenticated by his official seal.
(4) The certificate is conclusive evidence that the requirements of section 2 are complied with and that the limited liability partnership is incorporated by the name specified in the incorporation document.

NOTES

Sub-ss (1), (1A): substituted (for the original sub-s (1)) by the Limited Liability Partnerships (Application of Companies Act 2006) Regulations 2009, SI 2009/1804, reg 85, Sch 3, Pt 1, para 2, as from 1 October 2009.

Membership

[9.495]
4 Members

(1) On the incorporation of a limited liability partnership its members are the persons who subscribed their names to the incorporation document (other than any who have died or been dissolved).
(2) Any other person may become a member of a limited liability partnership by and in accordance with an agreement with the existing members.
(3) A person may cease to be a member of a limited liability partnership (as well as by death or dissolution) in accordance with an agreement with the other members or, in the absence of agreement with the other members as to cessation of membership, by giving reasonable notice to the other members.
(4) A member of a limited liability partnership shall not be regarded for any purpose as employed by the limited liability partnership unless, if he and the other members were partners in a partnership, he would be regarded for that purpose as employed by the partnership.

[9.496]
[4A Minimum membership for carrying on business

(1) This section applies where a limited liability partnership carries on business without having at least two members, and does so for more than 6 months.
(2) A person who, for the whole or any part of the period that it so carries on business after those 6 months—
  (a) is a member of the limited liability partnership, and
  (b) knows that it is carrying on business with only one member,
is liable (jointly and severally with the limited liability partnership) for the payment of the limited liability partnership's debts contracted during the period or, as the case may be, that part of it.]

NOTES

Inserted by the Limited Liability Partnerships (Application of Companies Act 2006) Regulations 2009, SI 2009/1804, reg 85, Sch 3, Pt 1, para 3, as from 1 October 2009.

[9.497]
5 Relationship of members etc

(1) Except as far as otherwise provided by this Act or any other enactment, the mutual rights and duties of the members of a limited liability partnership, and the mutual rights and duties of a limited liability partnership and its members, shall be governed—
  (a) by agreement between the members, or between the limited liability partnership and its members, or
  (b) in the absence of agreement as to any matter, by any provision made in relation to that matter by regulations under section 15(c).
(2) An agreement made before the incorporation of a limited liability partnership between the persons who subscribe their names to the incorporation document may impose obligations on the limited liability partnership (to take effect at any time after its incorporation).

[9.498]
6 Members as agents

(1) Every member of a limited liability partnership is the agent of the limited liability partnership.
(2) But a limited liability partnership is not bound by anything done by a member in dealing with a person if—
  (a) the member in fact has no authority to act for the limited liability partnership by doing that thing, and
  (b) the person knows that he has no authority or does not know or believe him to be a member of the limited liability partnership.
(3) Where a person has ceased to be a member of a limited liability partnership, the former member is to be regarded (in relation to any person dealing with the limited liability partnership) as still being a member of the limited liability partnership unless—
  (a) the person has notice that the former member has ceased to be a member of the limited liability partnership, or
  (b) notice that the former member has ceased to be a member of the limited liability partnership has been delivered to the registrar.
(4) Where a member of a limited liability partnership is liable to any person (other than another member of the limited liability partnership) as a result of a wrongful act or omission of his in the course of the business of the limited liability partnership or with its authority, the limited liability partnership is liable to the same extent as the member.

[9.499]
7 Ex-members

(1) This section applies where a member of a limited liability partnership has either ceased to be a member or—
  (a) has died,
  (b) has become bankrupt or had his estate sequestrated or has been wound up,
  (c) has granted a trust deed for the benefit of his creditors, or
  (d) has assigned the whole or any part of his share in the limited liability partnership (absolutely or by way of charge or security).

(2) In such an event the former member or—

(a) his personal representative,

(b) his trustee in bankruptcy[, the trustee or interim trustee in the sequestration, under the Bankruptcy (Scotland) Act 2016, of the former member's estate or the former member's] liquidator,

(c) his trustee under the trust deed for the benefit of his creditors, or

(d) his assignee,

may not interfere in the management or administration of any business or affairs of the limited liability partnership.

(3) But subsection (2) does not affect any right to receive an amount from the limited liability partnership in that event.

NOTES

Sub-s (2): words in square brackets substituted by the Bankruptcy (Scotland) Act 2016 (Consequential Provisions and Modifications) Order 2016, SI 2016/1034, art 7(1), (3), Sch 1, para 22, as from 30 November 2016 (except in relation to (i) a sequestration as regards which the petition is presented, or the debtor application is made before that date; or (ii) a trust deed executed before that date).

[9.500]

8 Designated members

(1) If the incorporation document specifies who are to be designated members—

(a) they are designated members on incorporation, and

(b) any member may become a designated member by and in accordance with an agreement with the other members,

and a member may cease to be a designated member in accordance with an agreement with the other members.

(2) But if there would otherwise be no designated members, or only one, every member is a designated member.

(3) If the incorporation document states that every person who from time to time is a member of the limited liability partnership is a designated member, every member is a designated member.

(4) A limited liability partnership may at any time deliver to the registrar—

(a) notice that specified members are to be designated members, or

(b) notice that every person who from time to time is a member of the limited liability partnership is a designated member,

and, once it is delivered, subsection (1) (apart from paragraph (a)) and subsection (2), or subsection (3), shall have effect as if that were stated in the incorporation document.

(5) . . .

(6) A person ceases to be a designated member if he ceases to be a member.

NOTES

Sub-s (5): repealed by the Limited Liability Partnerships (Application of Companies Act 2006) Regulations 2009, SI 2009/1804, reg 85, Sch 3, Pt 1, para 4, as from 1 October 2009.

[9.501]

9 Registration of membership changes

(1) A limited liability partnership must ensure that—

(a) where a person becomes or ceases to be a member or designated member, notice is delivered to the registrar within fourteen days, and

(b) where there is any change in the [particulars contained in its register of members or its register of members' residential addresses], notice is delivered to the registrar within [14 days].

(2) Where all the members from time to time of a limited liability partnership are designated members, subsection (1)(a) does not require notice that a person has become or ceased to be a designated member as well as a member.

[(3) A notice delivered under subsection (1) that relates to a person becoming a member or designated member must contain—

(a) a statement that the member or designated member consents to acting in that capacity, and

(b) in the case of a person becoming a member, a statement of the particulars of the new member that are required to be included in the limited liability partnership's register of members and its register of residential addresses.]

[(3ZA) Where—

(a) a limited liability partnership gives notice of a change of a member's service address as stated in its register of members, and

(b) the notice is not accompanied by notice of any resulting change in the particulars contained in its register of members' residential addresses,

the notice must be accompanied by a statement that no such change is required.]

[(3A), (3B) . . .]

(4) If a limited liability partnership fails to comply with [this section], the partnership and every designated member commits an offence.

(5) But it is a defence for a designated member charged with an offence under subsection (4) to prove that he took all reasonable steps for securing that [this section] was complied with.

(6) A person guilty of an offence under subsection (4) is liable on summary conviction to a fine not exceeding level 5 on the standard scale.

NOTES

Sub-ss (1), (4), (5): words in square brackets substituted by the Limited Liability Partnerships (Application of Companies Act 2006) Regulations 2009, SI 2009/1804, reg 85, Sch 3, Pt 1, para 5(1), (2), (6), as from 1 October 2009.

Sub-s (3): substituted by SI 2009/1804, reg 85, Sch 3, Pt 1, para 5(1), (3), as from 1 October 2009.

Sub-s (3ZA): inserted by SI 2009/1804, reg 85, Sch 3, Pt 1, para 5(1), (4), as from 1 October 2009.

Sub-ss (3A), (3B): originally inserted by the Limited Liability Partnerships (Particulars of Usual Residential Address) (Confidentiality Orders) Regulations 2002, SI 2002/915, reg 16, Sch 2, para 1, as from 2 April 2002. Subsequently repealed by SI 2009/1804, reg 85, Sch 3, Pt 1, para 5(1), (5), as from 1 October 2009.

Temporary modification: this section was modified by the Companies etc (Filing Requirements) (Temporary Modifications) Regulations 2020, SI 2020/645, reg 39. By virtue of the Corporate Insolvency and Governance Act 2020, s 39(8), the modification applied from 27 June 2020 to the end of the day on 5 April 2021 (subject to the saving provision in s 39(9) which provides that the expiry of s 39 on 5 April 2021 does not affect the continued operation of any Regulations made under that section for the purpose of determining the length of any period that began before the expiry). As modified, sub-s (1) above had effect as if for the references to "fourteen days" and "14 days" there were substituted references to "42 days".

Taxation

10, 11 *(S 10 amends the Income and Corporation Taxes Act 1988 and the Taxation of Chargeable Gains Act 1992; s 11 amends the Inheritance Tax Act 1984.)*

[9.502]
12 Stamp duty

(1) Stamp duty shall not be chargeable on an instrument by which property is conveyed or transferred by a person to a limited liability partnership in connection with its incorporation within the period of one year beginning with the date of incorporation if the following two conditions are satisfied.

(2) The first condition is that at the relevant time the person—
- (a) is a partner in a partnership comprised of all the persons who are or are to be members of the limited liability partnership (and no-one else), or
- (b) holds the property conveyed or transferred as nominee or bare trustee for one or more of the partners in such a partnership.

(3) The second condition is that—
- (a) the proportions of the property conveyed or transferred to which the persons mentioned in subsection (2)(a) are entitled immediately after the conveyance or transfer are the same as those to which they were entitled at the relevant time, or
- (b) none of the differences in those proportions has arisen as part of a scheme or arrangement of which the main purpose, or one of the main purposes, is avoidance of liability to any duty or tax.

(4) For the purposes of subsection (2) a person holds property as bare trustee for a partner if the partner has the exclusive right (subject only to satisfying any outstanding charge, lien or other right of the trustee to resort to the property for payment of duty, taxes, costs or other outgoings) to direct how the property shall be dealt with.

(5) In this section "the relevant time" means—
- (a) if the person who conveyed or transferred the property to the limited liability partnership acquired the property after its incorporation, immediately after he acquired the property, and
- (b) in any other case, immediately before its incorporation.

(6) An instrument in respect of which stamp duty is not chargeable by virtue of subsection (1) shall not be taken to be duly stamped unless—
- (a) it has, in accordance with section 12 of the Stamp Act 1891, been stamped with a particular stamp denoting that it is not chargeable with any duty or that it is duly stamped, or
- (b) it is stamped with the duty to which it would be liable apart from that subsection.

13 *(Amends the Social Security Contributions and Benefits Act 1992, and the Social Security Contributions and Benefits (Northern Ireland) Act 1992.)*

Regulations

[9.503]
14 Insolvency and winding up

(1) Regulations shall make provision about the insolvency and winding up of limited liability partnerships by applying or incorporating, with such modifications as appear appropriate[—
- (a) in relation to a limited liability partnership registered in Great Britain, [Parts A1] to 4, 6 and 7 of the Insolvency Act 1986;
- (b) in relation to a limited liability partnership registered in Northern Ireland, [Parts 1A] to 5 and 7 of the Insolvency (Northern Ireland) Order 1989, and so much of Part 1 of that Order as applies for the purposes of those Parts.]

(2) Regulations may make other provision about the insolvency and winding up of limited liability partnerships, and provision about the insolvency and winding up of oversea limited liability partnerships, by—
- (a) applying or incorporating, with such modifications as appear appropriate, any law relating to the insolvency or winding up of companies or other corporations which would not otherwise have effect in relation to them, or
- (b) providing for any law relating to the insolvency or winding up of companies or other corporations which would otherwise have effect in relation to them not to apply to them or to apply to them with such modifications as appear appropriate.

(3) In this Act "oversea limited liability partnership" means a body incorporated or otherwise established outside [the United Kingdom] and having such connection with [the United Kingdom], and such other features, as regulations may prescribe.

NOTES

Sub-s (1): words in first (outer) pair of square brackets substituted by the Limited Liability Partnerships (Application of Companies Act 2006) Regulations 2009, SI 2009/1804, reg 85, Sch 3, Pt 1, para 6, as from 9 July 2009 (for the purpose of enabling the exercise of powers to make regulations or orders by statutory instrument), and as from 1 October 2009 (otherwise). Words in square brackets in para (a) substituted by the Corporate Insolvency and Governance Act 2020, s 2(1), Sch 3, para 36, as from 26 June 2020 (for transitional provisions, see s 2(2), (3) of the 2020 Act (at **[9.533]**) which provides that (without prejudice to the Interpretation Act 1978, s 16) nothing in the 2020 Act affects the operation of the Insolvency Act 1986, or any other enactment, in relation to a moratorium under Sch A1 to the 1986 Act which comes into force before the repeal of that Schedule by Sch 3 to the 2020 Act (ie, 26 June 2020)). Words in square brackets in para (b) substituted by the Corporate

Insolvency and Governance Act 2020, s 5(1), Sch 3, para 31, as from 26 June 2020 (for transitional provisions, see s 5(2), (3) of the 2020 Act which provides that (without prejudice to the Interpretation Act 1978, s 16) nothing in the 2020 Act affects the operation of the Insolvency (Northern Ireland) Order 1989, or any other enactment, in relation to a moratorium under Sch A1 to the 1989 Order which comes into force before the repeal of that Schedule by Sch 7 to the 2020 Act (ie, 26 June 2020)).

Sub-s (3): words in square brackets substituted by SI 2009/1804, reg 85, Sch 3, Pt 1, para 6, as from 9 July 2009 (for the purpose of enabling the exercise of powers to make regulations or orders by statutory instrument), and as from 1 October 2009 (otherwise).

See further, the Scotland Act 1998 (Insolvency Functions) Order 2018, SI 2018/174. The 2018 Order provides that specific insolvency functions which relate to reserved matters under Schedule 5 to the Scotland Act 1998, that are exercised by a Minister of the Crown in or as regards Scotland, are to be exercisable by both the Scottish Ministers and a Minister of the Crown. The specific insolvency functions to which the Order applies are the making of Regulations for Scotland under sub-s (2)(a) above, and ss16 17(1), (2) and (3) of this Act, for the purpose of applying winding up rules made under the Insolvency Act 1986, s 411(1)(b) and (2), in relation to winding up of limited liability partnerships and oversea limited liability partnerships.

Regulations: the Limited Liability Partnerships (Scotland) Regulations 2001, SSI 2001/128 at **[10.89]**; the Limited Liability Partnerships Regulations 2001, SI 2001/1090 at **[10.99]**; the Limited Liability Partnerships (Amendment) Regulations 2005, SI 2005/1989; the Enterprise and Regulatory Reform Act 2013 (Consequential Amendments) (Bankruptcy) and the Small Business, Enterprise and Employment Act 2015 (Consequential Amendments) Regulations 2016, SI 2016/481; the Insolvency (Miscellaneous Amendments) Regulations 2017, SI 2017/1119; the Limited Liability Partnerships (Amendment etc) Regulations 2021, SI 2021/60 at **[10.1303]**.

[9.504]

15 Application of company law etc

Regulations may make provision about limited liability partnerships and oversea limited liability partnerships (not being provision about insolvency or winding up) by—

(a) applying or incorporating, with such modifications as appear appropriate, any law relating to companies or other corporations which would not otherwise have effect in relation to them,

(b) providing for any law relating to companies or other corporations which would otherwise have effect in relation to them not to apply to them or to apply to them with such modifications as appear appropriate, or

(c) applying or incorporating, with such modifications as appear appropriate, any law relating to partnerships.

NOTES

Regulations: the Limited Liability Partnerships (Scotland) Regulations 2001, SSI 2001/128 at **[10.89]**; the Limited Liability Partnerships Regulations 2001, SI 2001/1090 at **[10.99]**; the Limited Liability Partnerships (Amendment) Regulations 2005, SI 2005/1989; the Companies (Registrar, Languages and Trading Disclosures) Regulations 2006, SI 2006/3429 at **[4.1]**; the Limited Liability Partnerships (Amendment) Regulations 2007, SI 2007/2073; the Companies (Late Filing Penalties) and Limited Liability Partnerships (Filing Periods and Late Filing Penalties) Regulations 2008, SI 2008/497 at **[4.125]**; the Limited Liability Partnerships (Accounts and Audit) (Application of Companies Act 2006) Regulations 2008, SI 2008/1911 at **[10.223]**; the Small Limited Liability Partnerships (Accounts) Regulations 2008, SI 2008/1912 at **[10.288]**; the Large and Medium-sized Limited Liability Partnerships (Accounts) Regulations 2008, SI 2008/1913 at **[10.302]**; the Limited Liability Partnerships (Application of Companies Act 2006) Regulations 2009, SI 2009/1804 at **[10.319]**; the Limited Liability Partnerships (Amendment) Regulations 2009, SI 2009/1833; the Companies Act 2006 and Limited Liability Partnerships (Transitional Provisions and Savings) (Amendment) Regulations 2009, SI 2009/2476 at **[4.424]**; the Limited Liability Partnerships (Amendment) (No 2) Regulations 2009, SI 2009/2995; the Companies and Limited Liability Partnerships (Accounts and Audit Exemptions and Change of Accounting Framework) Regulations 2012, SI 2012/2301; the Limited Liability Partnerships (Application of Companies Act 2006) (Amendment) Regulations 2013, SI 2013/618; the Companies and Partnerships (Accounts and Audit) Regulations 2013, SI 2013/2005; the Reports on Payments to Governments Regulations 2014, SI 2014/3209; the Companies and Limited Liability Partnerships (Filing Requirements) Regulations 2015, SI 2015/1695; the Limited Liability Partnerships (Register of People with Significant Control) Regulations 2016, SI 2016/340 at **[10.452]**; the Companies (Address of Registered Office) Regulations 2016, SI 2016/423 at **[4.621]**; the Limited Liability Partnerships, Partnerships and Groups (Accounts and Audit) Regulations 2016, SI 2016/575; the Companies and Limited Liability Partnerships (Filing Requirements) Regulations 2016, SI 2016/599 at **[4.640]**; the Limited Liability Partnerships (Reporting on Payment Practices and Performance) Regulations 2017, SI 2017/425 at **[10.1181]**; the Statutory Auditors Regulations 2017, SI 2017/1164 at **[4.671]**; the Companies (Disclosure of Address) (Amendment) Regulations 2018, SI 2018/528; the Companies (Directors' Report) and Limited Liability Partnerships (Energy and Carbon Report) Regulations 2018, SI 2018/1155; the Statutory Auditors and Third Country Auditors (Amendment) (EU Exit) Regulations 2019, SI 2019/177 at **[12.83]**; the Statutory Auditors, Third Country Auditors and International Accounting Standards (Amendment) (EU Exit) Regulations 2019, SI 2019/1392; the Statutory Auditors and Third Country Auditors (Amendment) (EU Exit) Regulations 2020, SI 2020/108 at **[12.171]**; the Limited Liability Partnerships (Amendment etc) Regulations 2021, SI 2021/60 at **[10.1303]**; the European Grouping of Territorial Cooperation and Limited Liability Partnerships etc (Revocations and Amendments) (EU Exit) Regulations 2021, SI 2021/153; the Limited Liability Partnerships (Climate-related Financial Disclosure) Regulations 2022, SI 2022/46.

[9.505]

16 Consequential amendments

(1) Regulations may make in any enactment such amendments or repeals as appear appropriate in consequence of this Act or regulations made under it.

(2) The regulations may, in particular, make amendments and repeals affecting companies or other corporations or partnerships.

NOTES

See further the Corporate Insolvency and Governance Act 2020, Sch 3, para 37, which provides that the provision that may be made under sub-s (1) above includes provision in consequence of the amendment made by Sch 3, para 38 to that Act. Sch 3, para 38 amends the Limited Liability Partnerships Regulations 2001, SI 2001/1090, reg 5 at **[10.103]**.

See further, as to the making of Regulations with regard to Scotland, the note to s 14 at **[9.503]**.

Regulations: the Limited Liability Partnerships (Scotland) Regulations 2001, SSI 2001/128 at **[10.89]**; the Limited Liability Partnerships Regulations 2001, SI 2001/1090 at **[10.99]**.

[9.506]

17 General

(1) In this Act "regulations" means regulations made by the Secretary of State by statutory instrument.

(2) Regulations under this Act may in particular—

(a) make provisions for dealing with non-compliance with any of the regulations (including the creation of criminal offences),

(b) impose fees (which shall be paid into the Consolidated Fund), and

(c) provide for the exercise of functions by persons prescribed by the regulations.

(3) Regulations under this Act may—

(a) contain any appropriate consequential, incidental, supplementary or transitional provisions or savings, and

(b) make different provision for different purposes.

(4) No regulations to which this subsection applies shall be made unless a draft of the statutory instrument containing the regulations (whether or not together with other provisions) has been laid before, and approved by a resolution of, each House of Parliament.

(5) Subsection (4) applies to—

(a) regulations under section 14(2) not consisting entirely of the application or incorporation (with or without modifications) of provisions contained in or made under the Insolvency Act 1986 [or the Insolvency (Northern Ireland) Order 1989],

[(b) regulations under section 15 not consisting entirely of the application or incorporation (with or without modifications) of provisions contained in or made under the following provisions of the Companies Act 2006 (c 46)—

Part 4 (a company's capacity and related matters);
Part 5 (a company's name);
Part 6 (a company's registered office);
Chapters 1 and 8 of Part 10 (register of directors);
Part 15 (accounts and reports);
Part 16 (audit);
Part 19 (debentures);
Part 21 (certification and transfer of securities);
Part 24 (a company's annual return);
Part 25 (company charges);
Part 26 (arrangements and reconstructions[: general]);
[Part 26A (arrangements and reconstructions: companies in financial difficulty);]
Part 29 (fraudulent trading);
Part 30 (protection of members against unfair prejudice);
Part 31 (dissolution and restoration to the register);
Part 35 (the registrar of companies);
Part 36 (offences under the Companies Acts);
Part 37 (supplementary provisions);
Part 38 (interpretation).]

(c) regulations under section 14 or 15 making provision about oversea limited liability partnerships, and

(d) regulations under section 16.

(6) A statutory instrument containing regulations under this Act shall (unless a draft of it has been approved by a resolution of each House of Parliament) be subject to annulment in pursuance of a resolution of either House of Parliament.

NOTES

Sub-s (5): words in square brackets in para (a) inserted, and para (b) substituted, by the Limited Liability Partnerships (Application of Companies Act 2006) Regulations 2009, SI 2009/1804, reg 85, Sch 3, Pt 1, para 7, as from 9 July 2009 (for the purpose of enabling the exercise of powers to make regulations or orders by statutory instrument), and as from 1 October 2009 (otherwise). Words in square brackets in the entry relating to Part 26 in para (b) inserted, and entry relating to Part 26A inserted, by the Corporate Insolvency and Governance Act 2020, s 7, Sch 9, Pt 2, para 21, as from 26 June 2020.

See further, as to the making of Regulations with regard to Scotland, the note to s 14 at **[9.503]**.

Supplementary

[9.507]

18 Interpretation

In this Act—

. . .

"business" includes every trade, profession and occupation,

"designated member" shall be construed in accordance with section 8,

"enactment" includes subordinate legislation (within the meaning of the Interpretation Act 1978),

"incorporation document" shall be construed in accordance with section 2,

"limited liability partnership" has the meaning given by section 1(2),

"member" shall be construed in accordance with section 4,

"modifications" includes additions and omissions,

"name", in relation to a member of a limited liability partnership, means—

(a) if an individual, his forename and surname (or, in the case of a peer or other person usually known by a title, his title instead of or in addition to either or both his forename and surname), and

(b) if a corporation or Scottish firm, its corporate or firm name,

"oversea limited liability partnership" has the meaning given by section 14(3),

["the registrar" means—

(a) if the registered office of the limited liability partnership is, or is to be, in England and Wales (or Wales), the registrar of companies for England and Wales,

(b) if the registered office of the limited liability partnership is, or is to be, in Scotland, the registrar of companies for Scotland, and

(c) if the registered office of the limited liability partnership is, or is to be, in Northern Ireland, the registrar of companies for Northern Ireland;]

"regulations" has the meaning given by section 17(1).

NOTES

Definition "address" (omitted) repealed, and definition "the registrar" substituted, by the Limited Liability Partnerships (Application of Companies Act 2006) Regulations 2009, SI 2009/1804, reg 85, Sch 3, Pt 1, para 8, as from 1 October 2009.

As to the meaning of "the registrar" and "the register", and as to the construction of references to registration in a particular part of the United Kingdom, see also the Limited Liability Partnerships (Application of Companies Act 2006) Regulations 2009, SI 2009/1804, reg 85, Sch 3, Pt 2, para 12 at **[10.419]**.

[9.508]

19 Commencement, extent and short title

(1) The preceding provisions of this Act shall come into force on such day as the Secretary of State may by order made by statutory instrument appoint; and different days may be appointed for different purposes.

(2) The Secretary of State may by order made by statutory instrument make any transitional provisions and savings which appear appropriate in connection with the coming into force of any provision of this Act.

(3) For the purposes of the Scotland Act 1998 this Act shall be taken to be a pre-commencement enactment within the meaning of that Act.

[(4) This Act extends to the whole of the United Kingdom.]

(5) This Act may be cited as the Limited Liability Partnerships Act 2000.

NOTES

Sub-s (4): substituted by the Limited Liability Partnerships (Application of Companies Act 2006) Regulations 2009, SI 2009/1804, reg 85, Sch 3, Pt 1, para 9, as from 1 October 2009.

Orders: the Limited Liability Partnerships Act 2000 (Commencement) Order 2000, SI 2000/3316 (bringing this Act (with the exception of this section which came into force on Royal assent) into force on 6 April 2001).

SCHEDULE
NAMES AND REGISTERED OFFICES

Section 1

PART I NAMES

[9.509]

1. . . .

Name to indicate status

2. (1) The name of a limited liability partnership must end with—

(a) the expression "limited liability partnership", or

(b) the abbreviation "llp" or "LLP".

(2) But if the incorporation document for a limited liability partnership states that the registered office is to be situated in Wales, its name must end with—

(a) one of the expressions "limited liability partnership" and "partneriaeth atebolrwydd cyfyngedig", or

(b) one of the abbreviations "llp", "LLP", "pac" and "PAC".

3. . . .

Change of name

4. (1) A limited liability partnership may change its name at any time.

[(2) The name of a limited liability partnership may also be changed—

(a) on the determination of a new name by a company names adjudicator under section 73 of the Companies Act 2006 (C 46) as applied to limited liability partnerships (powers of adjudicator on upholding objection to name);

(b) on the determination of a new name by the court under section 74 of the Companies Act 2006 as so applied (appeal against decision of company names adjudicator);

(c) under section 1033 as so applied (name on restoration to the register).]

Notification of change of name

5. (1) Where a limited liability partnership changes its name it shall deliver notice of the change to the registrar.

(2) . . .

(3) Where the registrar receives [notice of a change of name] he shall (unless the new name is one by which a limited liability partnership may not be registered)—

[(a) enter the new name on the register in place of the former name, and]

(b) issue a certificate of the change of name.

(4) The change of name has effect from the date on which the certificate is issued.

Effect of change of name

6. A change of name by a limited liability partnership does not—

(a) affect any of its rights or duties,

(b) render defective any legal proceedings by or against it,

and any legal proceedings that might have been commenced or continued against it by its former name may be commenced or continued against it by its new name.

Improper use of "limited liability partnership" etc

7. (1) If any person carries on a business under a name or title which includes as the last words—

(a) the expression "limited liability partnership" or "partneriaeth atebolrwydd cyfyngedig", or

(b) any contraction or imitation of either of those expressions,

that person, unless a limited liability partnership or oversea limited liability partnership, commits an offence.

(2) A person guilty of an offence under sub-paragraph (1) is liable on summary conviction to a fine not exceeding level 3 on the standard scale.

8. . . .

NOTES

Para 1: repealed by the Companies Act 2006, s 1295, Sch 16, as from 1 October 2009.

Para 3: repealed by the Limited Liability Partnerships (Application of Companies Act 2006) Regulations 2009, SI 2009/1804, reg 85, Sch 3, Pt 1, para 10(1), (2), as from 1 October 2009.

Para 4: sub-para (2) substituted (for the original sub-paras (2)–(9)) by SI 2009/1804, reg 85, Sch 3, Pt 1, para 10(1), (3), as from 1 October 2009.

Para 5: sub-para (2) repealed, and words in square brackets substituted, by SI 2009/1804, reg 85, Sch 3, Pt 1, para 10(1), (4), as from 1 October 2009.

Para 8: repealed by SI 2009/1804, reg 85, Sch 3, Pt 1, para 10(1), (5), as from 1 October 2009.

(Schedule, Pt II repealed by the Limited Liability Partnerships (Application of Companies Act 2006) Regulations 2009, SI 2009/1804, reg 85, Sch 3, Pt 1, para 10(1), (6), as from 1 October 2009.)

FINANCIAL SERVICES (BANKING REFORM) ACT 2013

(2013 c 33)

An Act to make further provision about banking and other financial services, including provision about the Financial Services Compensation Scheme; to make provision for the amounts owed in respect of certain deposits to be treated as a preferential debt on insolvency; to make further provision about payment systems and securities settlement systems; to make provision about the accounts of the Bank of England and its wholly owned subsidiaries; to make provision in relation to persons providing claims management services; and for connected purposes

[18 December 2013]

NOTES

Only those provisions of this Act relevant to company law are reproduced. Provisions not reproduced are not annotated. By virtue of s 147 (Extent) the sections reproduced below apply to the whole of the UK.

This Act is reproduced as amended by: the Bank of England and Financial Services Act 2016; the Criminal Justice Act 2003 (Commencement No 33) and Sentencing Act 2020 (Commencement No 2) Regulations 2022, SI 2022/500.

PART 4 CONDUCT OF PERSONS WORKING IN FINANCIAL SERVICES SECTOR

18–35 *(Ss 18–33 contain various amendments to Part V of the Financial Services and Markets Act 2000 (Performance of Regulated Activities) at* **[7.115]** *et seq. S 34 contains a consequential amendment to s 347 of the 2000 Act; s 35 introduces Sch 3 to this Act (Consequential amendments relating to this Part).)*

Offence

[9.510]

36 Offence relating to a decision causing a financial institution to fail

(1) A person ("S") commits an offence if—

(a) at a time when S is a senior manager in relation to a financial institution ("F"), S—

  (i) takes, or agrees to the taking of, a decision by or on behalf of F as to the way in which the business of a group institution is to be carried on, or

  (ii) fails to take steps that S could take to prevent such a decision being taken,

(b) at the time of the decision, S is aware of a risk that the implementation of the decision may cause the failure of the group institution,

(c) in all the circumstances, S's conduct in relation to the taking of the decision falls far below what could reasonably be expected of a person in S's position, and

(d) the implementation of the decision causes the failure of the group institution.

(2) A "group institution", in relation to a financial institution ("F"), means F or any other financial institution that is a member of F's group for the purpose of FSMA 2000 (see section 421 of that Act).

(3) Subsections (1) and (2) are to be read with the interpretative provisions in section 37.

(4) A person guilty of an offence under this section is liable—

(a) on summary conviction—

  (i) in England and Wales, to imprisonment for a term not exceeding 12 months (or 6 months, if the offence was committed before [2 May 2022]) or a fine, or both;

  (ii) in Scotland, to imprisonment for a term not exceeding 12 months or a fine not exceeding the statutory maximum, or both;

  (iii) in Northern Ireland, to imprisonment for a term not exceeding 6 months or a fine not exceeding the statutory maximum, or both;

(b) on conviction on indictment, to imprisonment for a term not exceeding 7 years or a fine, or both.

NOTES

Sub-s (4): words in square brackets substituted by the Criminal Justice Act 2003 (Commencement No 33) and Sentencing Act 2020 (Commencement No 2) Regulations 2022, SI 2022/500, reg 5, Schedule, Pt 1, as from 28 April 2022.

[9.511]

37 Section 36: interpretation

(1) This section has effect for the interpretation of section 36.

(2) "Financial institution" means a UK institution which—

(a) meets condition A or B, and

(b) is not an insurer or a credit union.

(3) Condition A is that it has permission under Part 4A of FSMA 2000 to carry on the regulated activity of accepting deposits.

(4) Condition B is that—

(a) it is for the purposes of FSMA 2000 an investment firm (see section 424A of that Act),

(b) it has permission under Part 4A of that Act to carry on the regulated activity of dealing in investments as principal, and

(c) when carried on by it, that activity is a PRA-regulated activity.

(5) In subsection (2)—

(a) "UK institution" means an institution which is incorporated in, or formed under the law of any part of, the United Kingdom;

(b) "insurer" means an institution which is authorised under FSMA 2000 to carry on the regulated activity of effecting or carrying out contracts of insurance as principal;

(c) "credit union" means a credit union as defined by section 31 of the Credit Unions Act 1979 or a credit union as defined by Article 2(2) of the Credit Unions (Northern Ireland) Order 1985.

(6) Subsections (3), (4) and (5)(b) are to be read in accordance with sections 22 and 22A of FSMA 2000, taken with Schedule 2 to that Act and any order under section 22.

(7) A person is a "senior manager" in relation to a financial institution if, under an arrangement entered into by the institution, or by a contractor of the institution, in relation to the carrying on by the institution of a regulated activity, the person performs a senior management function.

[(8) "Senior management function" means—

(a) a function of a description specified in rules made by the FCA under section 59(3)(a) or (b) of FSMA 2000 which is designated as a senior management function by the FCA under section 59(6A) of that Act;

(b) a function of a description specified in rules made by the PRA under section 59(3)(a) of that Act.]

(9) A financial institution ("F") is to be regarded as failing where—

(a) F enters insolvency,

(b) any of the stabilisation options in Part 1 of the Banking Act 2009 is achieved in relation to F, or

(c) F is taken for the purposes of the Financial Services Compensation Scheme to be unable, or likely to be unable, to satisfy claims against F.

(10) In subsection (9)(a) "insolvency" includes—

(a) bankruptcy,

(b) liquidation,

(c) bank insolvency,

[(ca) building society insolvency,

(cb) investment bank insolvency,]

(d) administration,

(e) bank administration,

[(ea) building society special administration,]

(f) receivership,

(g) a composition between F and F's creditors, and

(h) a scheme of arrangement of F's affairs.

[(11) For the purposes of subsection (10)—

"bank administration" has the same meaning as in the Banking Act 2009 (see section 136 of that Act);

"bank insolvency" has the same meaning as in that Act (see section 90 of that Act);

"building society insolvency" and "building society special administration" have the same meaning as in the Building Societies Act 1986 (see section 119 of that Act);

"investment bank insolvency" means any procedure established by regulations under section 233 of the Banking Act 2009.]

NOTES

Sub-s (8) was substituted by the Bank of England and Financial Services Act 2016, s 21, Sch 4, paras 1, 22(1), (6). Note that s 21 and Sch 4 come into force as follows: (i) 13 September 2018 (for the purpose of making rules, giving directions, imposing requirements and making statements of policy by the appropriate regulator for insurers); (ii) 10 December 2018 (for all other purposes for insurers (except in relation to Sch 4, para 11)), and 10 December 2019 (Sch 4, para 11 for insurers); (iii) 18 July 2019 (for the purpose of the making of rules, the giving of directions, the imposition of requirements and the issuing of statements of policy by the FCA for remaining purposes); (iv) 9 August 2019 (for remaining purposes in relation to authorised persons who are not solo-regulated firms); (v) 9 December 2019 (for remaining purposes in relation to solo-regulated firms other than benchmark firms (except as provided for by (vii) below)); (vi) 7 December 2020 (for remaining purposes in relation to benchmark firms (except as provided for by (viii) below)); (vii) 31 March 2021 (in relation to the employee certification provisions for remaining purposes in relation to solo-regulated firms other than benchmark firms); (viii) 7 December 2021 (in relation to the employee certification provisions for remaining purposes in relation to benchmark firms). For transitional provisions in connection with (i)–(iii) above, see the Bank of England and Financial Services Act 2016 (Commencement No 5 and Transitional Provisions) Regulations 2018, SI 2018/990; and for transitional provisions in connection with the other commencement dates, see the Bank of England and Financial Services Act 2016 (Commencement No 6 and Transitional Provisions) Regulations 2019, SI 2019/1136.

Paras (ca), (cb), (ea) of sub-s (10) were inserted, and sub-s (11) was added, by the Bank of England and Financial Services Act 2016, s 26, as from 6 July 2016.

[9.512]

38 Institution of proceedings

(1) In this section "an offence" means an offence under section 36.

(2) Proceedings for an offence may be instituted in England and Wales only—

(a) by the FCA, the PRA or the Secretary of State, or

(b) by or with the consent of the Director of Public Prosecutions.

(3) Proceedings for an offence may be instituted in Northern Ireland only—

(a) by the FCA, the PRA or the Secretary of State, or

(b) by or with the consent of the Director of Public Prosecutions for Northern Ireland.

(4) In exercising its power to institute proceedings for an offence, the FCA or the PRA must comply with any conditions or restrictions imposed in writing by the Treasury.

(5) Conditions or restrictions may be imposed under subsection (4) in relation to—

(a) proceedings generally, or

(b) such proceedings, or categories of proceedings, as the Treasury may direct.

SMALL BUSINESS, ENTERPRISE AND EMPLOYMENT ACT 2015

(2015 c 26)

An Act to make provision about improved access to finance for businesses and individuals; to make provision about regulatory provisions relating to business and certain voluntary and community bodies; to make provision about the exercise of procurement functions by certain public authorities; to make provision for the creation of a Pubs Code and Adjudicator for the regulation of dealings by pub-owning businesses with their tied pub tenants; to make provision about the regulation of the provision of childcare; to make provision about information relating to the evaluation of education; to make provision about the regulation of companies; to make provision about company filing requirements; to make provision about the disqualification from appointments relating to companies; to make provision about insolvency; to make provision about the law relating to employment; and for connected purposes

[26 March 2015]

NOTES

Most of this Act deals with matters not related to company law and is outside the scope of this work. The relevant substantive provisions are reproduced below; provisions not reproduced are not annotated. Many provisions of this Act contain amendments to other legislation in the Handbook: Part 7 (Companies – Transparency), Part 8 (Company Filing Requirements), Part 9 (Directors' Disqualification etc), and Part 10 (Insolvency) contain substantial amendments to the Companies Act 2006, the Company Directors Disqualification Act 1986, and the Insolvency Act 1986. Where relevant, these amendments have been incorporated in the appropriate place.

ARRANGEMENT OF SECTIONS

PART 1 ACCESS TO FINANCE

Business Payment Practices

[9.513]

3 Companies: duty to publish report on payment practices and performance

(1) The Secretary of State may by regulations impose a requirement, on such descriptions of companies as may be prescribed, to publish, at such intervals and in such manner as may be prescribed, prescribed information about—

(a) the company's payment practices and policies relating to relevant contracts of a prescribed description, and
(b) the company's performance by reference to those practices and policies.

(2) For the purposes of this section—

"company" has the meaning given by section 1(1) of the Companies Act 2006 (but see subsection (3));
a contract is a "relevant contract" if—

(a) it is a contract for goods, services or intangible assets (including intellectual property), and
(b) the parties to the contract have entered into it in connection with the carrying on of a business;

"prescribed" means prescribed by the regulations.

(3) The regulations may not impose a requirement on a company in relation to any time during which—

(a) it qualifies as a micro-entity for the purposes of section 384A of the Companies Act 2006,
(b) the small companies regime under that Act applies to it (see section 381 of that Act), or
(c) it qualifies as medium-sized for the purposes of section 465 or 466 of that Act.

(4) "The company's payment practices and policies" has such meaning as may be prescribed and the information which may be prescribed may, in particular, include information—

(a) about the standard payment terms of the company and whether these are part of any code of conduct or code of ethics of the company,
(b) about payment terms of the company which are not standard,
(c) about the processing and payment of invoices,
(d) by reference to such codes of conduct or standards as may be prescribed and as are applicable to companies generally or to companies of a prescribed description,
(e) about disputes relating to the payment of invoices, including any dispute resolution mechanism that the company uses,
(f) about payments owed or paid by the company due to late payment of invoices, whether in respect of interest or otherwise.

(5) The regulations may require that information published in accordance with the regulations must be approved or signed by such description of person as may be prescribed.

(6) The regulations may require such of the information required to be published as may be prescribed to be given, in such form as may be prescribed, to prescribed persons.

(7) The regulations may make provision for a prescribed breach by a prescribed description of person of a requirement imposed by the regulations to be an offence punishable on summary conviction—

(a) in England and Wales, by a fine;
(b) in Scotland or Northern Ireland, by a fine not exceeding level 5 on the standard scale.

(8) Before making regulations under this section the Secretary of State must consult such persons as the Secretary of State considers appropriate.

(9) Regulations under this section are subject to affirmative resolution procedure.

NOTES

Regulations: the Reporting on Payment Practices and Performance Regulations 2017, SI 2017/395 at **[10.1169]**.

PART 2 REGULATORY REFORM

Streamlined Company Registration

[9.514]

15 Target for streamlined company registration

(1) The Secretary of State must secure that, by no later than 31 May 2017, a system for streamlined company registration is in place.

(2) For the purposes of this section and section 16, a system for streamlined company registration is a system which enables all of the registration information to be delivered by or on behalf of a person who wishes to form a company after 31 May 2017—

(a) on a single occasion to a single recipient, and

(b) by electronic means.

(3) "Registration information" means—

(a) the documents which must be delivered to the registrar under section 9 of the Companies Act 2006 (registration documents) in respect of the formation of a company;

(b) the documents or other information which must or may be delivered to Her Majesty's Revenue and Customs in respect of registration of a company for purposes connected with VAT, corporation tax and PAYE.

(4) In this section—

"company", "electronic means" and "the registrar" have the same meanings as in the Companies Acts (see sections 1(1), 1168(4) and 1060 of the Companies Act 2006 respectively);

"VAT" means value added tax charged in accordance with the Value Added Tax Act 1994.

[9.515]

16 Streamlined company registration: duty to report on progress

(1) The Secretary of State must prepare a report before the end of each reporting period about the progress that has been made during that period towards putting in place a system for streamlined company registration.

(2) The following are reporting periods—

(a) the period beginning with the day on which this section comes into force and ending on 31 March 2016;

(b) the subsequent period of 12 months ending on 31 March 2017.

(3) The first report must set out the steps which the Secretary of State expects will be taken during the next reporting period towards putting the system in place.

(4) Both reports must include the Secretary of State's assessment as to when the system for streamlined company registration will be in place.

(5) The second report must include an assessment of what steps, if any, the Secretary of State expects to take to put in place a system for the streamlining of other information delivery processes relating to businesses.

(6) The Secretary of State must—

(a) publish each report, and

(b) lay each report before Parliament.

Definitions of Small and Micro Business

[9.516]

33 Definitions of small and micro business

(1) This section applies where any subordinate legislation made by a Minister of the Crown (the "underlying provision")—

(a) uses the term "small business" or "micro business", and

(b) defines that term by reference to this section.

(2) In the underlying provision "small business" means an undertaking other than a micro business (see subsection (3)) which meets the following conditions ("the small business size conditions")—

(a) it has a headcount of staff of less than 50, and

(b) it has—

(i) a turnover, or

(ii) a balance sheet total,

of an amount less than or equal to the small business threshold.

(3) In the underlying provision "micro business" means an undertaking which meets the following conditions ("the micro business size conditions")—

(a) it has a headcount of staff of less than 10, and

(b) it has—

(i) a turnover, or

(ii) a balance sheet total,

of an amount less than or equal to the micro business threshold.

(4) The Secretary of State may by regulations (referred to as "the small and micro business regulations") make further provision about the meanings of "small business" and "micro business".

(5) This section and the small and micro business regulations are to be read subject to any modifications made by the underlying provision in any particular case.

(6) In this section—

"balance sheet total", "headcount of staff", "micro business threshold", "small business threshold" and "turnover" have such meanings as may be prescribed by the small and micro business regulations;

"Minister of the Crown" has the same meaning as in the Ministers of the Crown Act 1975;

"subordinate legislation" has the same meaning as in the Interpretation Act 1978 (see section 21 of that Act);

"undertaking" means—

(a) a person carrying on one or more businesses;

(b) a voluntary or community body within the meaning given by section 27;

(c) a body which is formed or recognised under the law of a country or territory outside the United Kingdom and which is equivalent in nature to a body falling within the definition of voluntary or community body.

(7) The small and micro business regulations are subject to negative resolution procedure.

NOTES

Commencement: 26 May 2015 (sub-ss (4), (6), (7)); to be appointed (otherwise).

[9.517]

34 Small and micro business regulations: further provision

(1) The small and micro business regulations may make provision—

(a) about the calculation of the headcount of staff, turnover and balance sheet total of an undertaking, including provision about the period ("assessment period") in respect of which they are to be calculated;

(b) for the headcount of staff, turnover and balance sheet total, or a proportion of such, of any undertaking which satisfies such conditions as may be prescribed in relation to another undertaking (the "principal undertaking") to be treated as part of the principal undertaking's headcount of staff, turnover and balance sheet total.

(2) Conditions which may be prescribed under subsection (1)(b) include, in particular, conditions relating to—

(a) the extent of ownership (whether direct or indirect) of one undertaking by one or more other undertakings;

(b) the degree of control exercised (whether directly or indirectly) by one or more undertakings over another.

(3) The small and micro business regulations may make provision about—

(a) the assessment period or periods in respect of which an undertaking must meet the small business size conditions or the micro business size conditions in order to be a small business or (as the case may be) micro business;

(b) the circumstances in which an undertaking which has been established for less than a complete assessment period is to be regarded as meeting the small business size conditions or the micro business size conditions.

(4) Provision made by virtue of subsection (3) may, in particular, provide that—

(a) an undertaking is a small business or a micro business if it meets the relevant size conditions in respect of each of its two most recent assessment periods;

(b) where there has been only one complete assessment period since an undertaking was established, the undertaking is a small business or a micro business if it meets the relevant size conditions in respect of that period;

(c) an undertaking which is a small business or a micro business does not cease to be such unless it fails to meet the relevant size conditions in respect of two consecutive assessment periods.

(5) The small and micro business regulations may make provision for one undertaking ("undertaking A") which satisfies such conditions as may be prescribed in relation to another undertaking ("undertaking B"), to be treated as being undertaking B (whether or not undertaking B is still in existence) for such purposes as may be prescribed.

(6) Conditions which may be prescribed under subsection (5) include, in particular, conditions relating to—

(a) the transfer of a business from undertaking B to undertaking A;

(b) the carrying on by undertaking A of a business on undertaking B ceasing to carry on the activities, or most of the activities, of which the business consists in consequence of arrangements involving both undertakings;

(c) the existence of some other connection between undertaking A and undertaking B.

(7) The purposes which may be prescribed under subsection (5) include, in particular—

(a) determining the date on which undertaking A was established (and so the number of assessment periods there have been since it was established);

(b) determining which periods are assessment periods in respect of undertaking A;

(c) calculating the headcount of staff, turnover and balance sheet total of undertaking A.

(8) The small and micro business regulations may provide that an undertaking of such description as may be prescribed is not a small business or a micro business even if it falls within the relevant definition.

(9) In this section—

"micro business size conditions", "small business size conditions" and "undertaking" have the same meanings as in section 33;

"prescribed" means prescribed in the small and micro business regulations.

PART 7 COMPANIES: TRANSPARENCY

Register of People with Significant Control

[9.518]

82 Review of provisions about PSC registers

(1) The Secretary of State must before the end of the review period—

(a) carry out a review of Part 21A of the Companies Act 2006 (inserted by Schedule 3 to this Act) and of other provisions of the Companies Act 2006 inserted by this Act that relate to that Part, and

(b) prepare and publish a report setting out the conclusions of the review.

(2) The report must in particular—

(a) set out the objectives intended to be achieved by the provisions of the Companies Act 2006 mentioned in subsection (1)(a),

(b) assess the extent to which those objectives have been achieved, and

(c) assess whether those objectives remain appropriate and, if so, the extent to which they could be achieved in another way that imposed less regulation.

(3) The Secretary of State must lay the report before Parliament.

(4) The "review period" is the period of 3 years beginning with the day on which section 92 (duty to deliver confirmation statement instead of annual return) comes into force.

Abolition of Share Warrants to Bearer

[9.519]

84 Abolition of share warrants to bearer

(1), (2) (*Amends the Companies Act 2006, s 779 at* **[1.864]**.)

(3) Schedule 4—

(a) makes provision for arrangements by which share warrants issued before this section comes into force are to be converted into registered shares or cancelled, and

(b) makes amendments consequential on that provision.

[9.520]

85 Amendment of company's articles to reflect abolition of share warrants

(1) This section applies in the case of a company limited by shares if, immediately before the day on which section 84 comes into force, the company's articles contain provision authorising the company to issue share warrants ("the offending provision").

(2) The company may amend its articles for the purpose of removing the offending provision—

(a) without having passed a special resolution as required by section 21 of the Companies Act 2006;

(b) without complying with any provision for entrenchment which is relevant to the offending provision (see section 22 of that Act).

(3) Section 26 of the Companies Act 2006 sets out the duty of a company to send the registrar a copy of its articles where they have been amended.

(4) Expressions defined for the purposes of the Companies Act 2006 have the same meaning in this section as in that Act.

[9.521]

86 Review of section 84

(1) The Secretary of State must, as soon as reasonably practicable after the end of the period of 5 years beginning with the day on which section 84 comes into force—

(a) carry out a review of section 84, and

(b) prepare and publish a report setting out the conclusions of the review.

(2) The report must in particular—

(a) set out the objectives intended to be achieved by the section, and

(b) assess the extent to which those objectives have been achieved.

(3) The Secretary of State must lay the report before Parliament.

Corporate Directors

[9.522]

88 Review of section 87

(1) The Secretary of State must, before the end of each review period—

(a) carry out a review of section 87, and

(b) prepare and publish a report setting out the conclusions of the review.

(2) The report must in particular—

(a) set out the objectives intended to be achieved by the section,

(b) assess the extent to which those objectives have been achieved, and

(c) assess whether those objectives remain appropriate and, if so, the extent to which they could be achieved in another way which imposed less regulation.

(3) The Secretary of State must lay the report before Parliament.

(4) Each of the following is a review period for the purposes of this section—

(a) the period of 5 years beginning with the day on which section 87 comes into force (whether wholly or partly), and

(b) each successive period of 5 years.

NOTES

Commencement: to be appointed.

Note that s 87 (Requirement for all company directors to be natural persons) amends the Companies Act 2006. In particular, it inserts ss 156A–156C of that Act at **[1.170]** et seq.

Shadow Directors

[9.523]

89 Application of directors' general duties to shadow directors

(1) (*Amends the Companies Act 2006, s 170 at* **[1.193]**.)

(2) The Secretary of State may by regulations make provision about the application of the general duties of directors to shadow directors.

(3) The regulations may, in particular, make provision—

(a) for prescribed general duties of directors to apply to shadow directors with such adaptations as may be prescribed;

(b) for prescribed general duties of directors not to apply to shadow directors.

(4) In this section—

"director" and "shadow director" have the same meanings as in the Companies Act 2006;

"general duties of directors" means the duties specified in sections 171 to 177 of that Act;

"prescribed" means prescribed in regulations.

(5) Regulations under this section are subject to affirmative resolution procedure.

PART 10 INSOLVENCY

Power to Establish Single Regulator of Insolvency Practitioners

[9.524]

144 Power to establish single regulator of insolvency practitioners

(1) The Secretary of State may by regulations designate a body for the purposes of—

(a) authorising persons to act as insolvency practitioners, and

(b) regulating persons acting as such.

(2) The designated body may be either—

(a) a body corporate established by the regulations, or

(b) a body (whether a body corporate or an unincorporated association) already in existence when the regulations are made (an "existing body").

(3) The regulations may, in particular, confer the following functions on the designated body—

(a) establishing criteria for determining whether a person is a fit and proper person to act as an insolvency practitioner;

(b) establishing the requirements as to education, practical training and experience which a person must meet in order to act as an insolvency practitioner;

(c) establishing and maintaining a system for providing full authorisation or partial authorisation to persons who meet those criteria and requirements;

(d) imposing technical standards for persons so authorised and enforcing compliance with those standards;

(e) imposing professional and ethical standards for persons so authorised and enforcing compliance with those standards;

(f) monitoring the performance and conduct of persons so authorised;

(g) investigating complaints made against, and other matters concerning the performance or conduct of, persons so authorised.

(4) The regulations may require the designated body, in discharging regulatory functions, so far as is reasonably practicable, to act in a way—

(a) which is compatible with the regulatory objectives, and

(b) which the body considers most appropriate for the purpose of meeting those objectives.

(5) Provision made under subsection (3)(d) or (3)(e) for the enforcement of the standards concerned may include provision enabling the designated body to impose a financial penalty on a person who is or has been authorised to act as an insolvency practitioner.

(6) The regulations may, in particular, include provision for the purpose of treating a person authorised to act as an insolvency practitioner by virtue of being a member of a professional body recognised under section 391 of the Insolvency Act 1986 immediately before the regulations come into force as authorised to act as an insolvency practitioner by the body designated by the regulations after that time.

(7) Expressions used in this section which are defined for the purposes of Part 13 of the Insolvency Act 1986 have the same meaning in this section as in that Part.

(8) Section 145 makes further provision about regulations under this section which designate an existing body.

(9) Schedule 11 makes supplementary provision in relation to the designation of a body by regulations under this section.

[9.525]

145 Regulations under section 144: designation of existing body

(1) The Secretary of State may make regulations under section 144 designating an existing body only if it appears to the Secretary of State that—

(a) the body is able and willing to exercise the functions that would be conferred by the regulations, and

(b) the body has arrangements in place relating to the exercise of those functions which are such as to be likely to ensure that the conditions in subsection (2) are met.

(2) The conditions are—

(a) that the functions in question will be exercised effectively, and

(b) where the regulations are to contain any requirements or other provisions prescribed under subsection (3), that those functions will be exercised in accordance with any such requirements or provisions.

(3) Regulations which designate an existing body may contain such requirements or other provisions relating to the exercise of the functions by the designated body as appear to the Secretary of State to be appropriate.

[9.526]

146 Regulations under section 144: timing and supplementary

(1) Section 144 and, accordingly, section 145 and subsections (3) and (4) below expire at the end of the relevant period unless the power conferred by subsection (1) of section 144 is exercised before the end of that period.

(2) The "relevant period" is the period of 7 years beginning with the day on which section 144 comes into force.

(3) Regulations under section 144 are subject to affirmative resolution procedure.

(4) If a draft of a statutory instrument containing regulations under section 144 would, apart from this subsection, be treated for the purposes of the Standing Orders of either House of Parliament as a hybrid instrument, it is to proceed in that House as if it were not a hybrid instrument.

PART 12 GENERAL

[9.527]

163 Extent

(1) Subject to subsections (2) to (4), this Act extends to England and Wales, Scotland and Northern Ireland.

(2) Any amendment, repeal or revocation made by this Act has the same extent as the enactment amended, repealed or revoked, except the amendments made by sections 113 and 114, which extend as mentioned in subsection (1).

(3) Part 4 extends to England and Wales only.

(4) In Part 10, sections 144 to 146 and Schedule 11 extend to England and Wales and Scotland only.

[9.528]
164 Commencement

(1) The provisions of this Act come into force on such day as a Minister of the Crown may by regulations appoint, subject to subsections (2) to (5).

(2) The following provisions of this Act come into force on the day this Act is passed—

(a)–(d) . . .

(e) this Part 2.

(3) The following provisions of this Act come into force at the end of the period of two months beginning with the day on which this Act is passed—

(a) in Part 1—

(i) . . .

(ii) section 3 (companies: duty to publish report on payment practices),

(iii)–(v) . . .

(b) in Part 2—

(i) sections 15 and 16 (streamlined company registration),

(ii), (iii) . . .

(c)–(f) . . .

(g) in Part 7—

(i) section 83 (amendment of section 813 of the Companies Act 2006),

(ii) sections 84 to 86 and Schedule 4 (abolition of share warrants to bearer), and

(iii) sections 89 to 91 (shadow directors);

(h) in Part 8—

(i) section 95 (recording of optional information on register),

(ii) section 99 (address of company registered office);

(i) in Part 10—

(i) sections 120 and 121 (removing requirements to seek sanction),

(ii) sections 127 to 130 (administration),

(iii) sections 131 and 132 (small debts),

(iv) sections 134 and 135 (voluntary arrangements), and

(v) section 136 (voluntary winding-up: progress reports);

(j) . . .

(4)–(6) . . .

NOTES

Note: the text not reproduced relates to the commencement of provisions not relevant to this work.

Regulations: the Small Business, Enterprise and Employment Act 2015 (Commencement No 1) Regulations 2015, SI 2015/1329; the Small Business, Enterprise and Employment Act 2015 (Commencement No 2 and Transitional Provisions) Regulations 2015, SI 2015/1689; the Small Business, Enterprise and Employment Act 2015 (Commencement No 1) (Wales) Regulations 2015, SI 2015/1710; the Small Business, Enterprise and Employment Act 2015 (Commencement No 3) Regulations 2015, SI 2015/2029; the Small Business, Enterprise and Employment Act 2015 (Commencement No 4, Transitional and Savings Provisions) Regulations 2016, SI 2016/321; the Small Business, Enterprise and Employment Act 2015 (Commencement No 5 and Saving Provision) Regulations 2016, SI 2016/532; the Small Business, Enterprise and Employment Act 2015 (Commencement No 6 and Transitional and Savings Provisions) Regulations 2016, SI 2016/1020; the Small Business, Enterprise and Employment Act 2015 (Commencement No 7, Consequential, Transitional and Savings Provisions) Regulations 2019, SI 2019/816 (see further the note at **[9.385]**).

[9.529]
165 Short title

This Act may be cited as the Small Business, Enterprise and Employment Act 2015.

SCHEDULES

SCHEDULE 4
ABOLITION OF SHARE WARRANTS TO BEARER

Section 84

PART 1 ARRANGEMENTS FOR CONVERSION AND CANCELLATION OF EXISTING SHARE WARRANTS

Right of surrender during surrender period

[9.530]

1. (1) This paragraph applies in relation to a company which has issued a share warrant which has not been surrendered for cancellation before the day on which section 84 comes into force (the "commencement date").

(2) During the period of 9 months beginning with the commencement date (the "surrender period") the bearer of the share warrant has a right of surrender in relation to the warrant.

(3) For the purposes of this Schedule, if the bearer of a share warrant has a right of surrender in relation to the warrant, the bearer is entitled on surrendering the warrant for cancellation—

(a) to have the bearer's name entered as a member in the register of members of the company concerned, or

(b) where an election is in force under section 128B of the Companies Act 2006 (option to keep membership information on central register) in respect of the company, to have the bearer's name and other particulars delivered to the registrar, and the document containing that information registered by the registrar and the date recorded, as if the information were information required to be delivered under section 128E of that Act.

(4) A company must, as soon as reasonably practicable and in any event before the end of the period of 2 months beginning with the day on which a share warrant is surrendered for cancellation pursuant to a right of surrender, complete and have ready for delivery the certificates of the shares specified in the warrant.

(5) If a company fails to comply with sub-paragraph (4) an offence is committed by every officer of the company who is in default.

2. (1) A company must, as soon as reasonably practicable and in any event before the end of the period of 1 month beginning with the commencement date, give notice to the bearer of a share warrant issued by the company of—

(a) the bearer's right of surrender,

(b) the consequences of not exercising that right before the end of the period of 7 months beginning with the commencement date (see paragraph 3),

(c) the fact that the right will cease to be exercisable at the end of the surrender period, and

(d) the consequences of not exercising the right before the end of that period (see in particular paragraphs 5, 6 and 9 to 12).

(2) If a company fails to comply with this paragraph an offence is committed by every officer of the company who is in default.

Consequences of failure to surrender during first 7 months of surrender period

3. (1) This paragraph applies in relation to a share warrant of a company which has not been surrendered by the bearer for cancellation before the end of the period of 7 months beginning with the commencement date.

(2) Any transfer of, or agreement to transfer, the share warrant made after the end of that period is void.

(3) With effect from the end of that period, all rights which are attached to the shares specified in the warrant are suspended (including any voting rights and any right to receive a dividend or other distribution).

(4) The company must pay into a separate bank account that complies with sub-paragraph (5) any dividend or other distribution which the bearer of the share warrant would, but for the suspension, have been entitled to receive.

(5) A bank account complies with this sub-paragraph if the balance of the account—

(a) bears interest at an appropriate rate, and

(b) can be withdrawn by such notice (if any) as is appropriate.

(6) If the share warrant is subsequently surrendered in accordance with this Schedule—

(a) the suspension ceases to have effect on surrender, and

(b) the suspension period amount must be paid to the bearer by the company.

(7) The "suspension period amount", in relation to a share warrant, is—

(a) the aggregate amount of any dividends or other distributions which the bearer of the warrant would, but for the suspension, have been entitled to receive, plus

(b) any interest accrued on that amount.

Second notice of right to surrender

4. (1) A company must, before the end of the period of 8 months beginning with the commencement date, give further notice to the bearer of a share warrant of the company of—

(a) the bearer's right of surrender,

(b) the consequences of not having exercised the right of surrender before the end of the period of 7 months beginning with the commencement date (see paragraph 3), and

(c) the matters referred to in paragraph 2(1)(c) and (d).

(2) If a company fails to comply with this paragraph an offence is committed by every officer of the company who is in default.

Expiry of right to surrender and applications for cancellation of outstanding share warrants

5. (1) This paragraph applies in relation to a company which has issued a share warrant which has not been surrendered for cancellation before the end of the surrender period.

(2) The company must, as soon as reasonably practicable and in any event before the end of the period of 3 months beginning with the day after the end of the surrender period, apply to the court for an order (referred to in this Schedule as a "cancellation order") cancelling with effect from the date of the order—

(a) the share warrant, and

(b) the shares specified in it.

(3) The company must give notice to the bearer of the share warrant of the fact that an application has been made under this paragraph before the end of the period of 14 days beginning with the day on which it is made; and the notice must include a copy of the application.

(4) If a company fails to comply with sub-paragraph (2) or (3) an offence is committed by every officer of the company who is in default.

(5) A company must, on making an application for a cancellation order, immediately give notice to the registrar.

(6) If a company fails to comply with sub-paragraph (5) an offence is committed by—

(a) the company, and

(b) every officer of the company who is in default.

Cancellation orders and suspended cancellation orders

6. (1) The court must make a cancellation order in respect of a share warrant if, on an application under paragraph 5, it is satisfied that—

(a) the company has given notice to the bearer of the share warrant as required by paragraphs 2 and 4, or

(b) the bearer had actual notice by other means of the matters mentioned in paragraph 2(1).

(2) If, on such an application, the court is not so satisfied, it must instead make a suspended cancellation order in respect of the share warrant.

(3) A "suspended cancellation order" is an order—

(a) requiring the company to give notice to the bearer of the share warrant containing the information set out in sub-paragraph (4) before the end of the period of 5 working days beginning with the day the order is made,

(b) providing that the bearer of the share warrant has a right of surrender during the period of 2 months beginning with the day the order is made (referred to in this Schedule as "the grace period"), and

(c) if the share warrant is not so surrendered, cancelling it and the shares specified in it with effect from the end of the grace period.

(4) A notice required to be given by a suspended cancellation order must—

(a) inform the bearer of the share warrant of the fact that the bearer has a right of surrender during the grace period,

(b) inform the bearer of the consequences of not having exercised that right before the end of the period of 7 months beginning with the commencement date (see paragraph 3), and

(c) explain that the share warrant will be cancelled with effect from the end of the grace period if it is not surrendered before then.

(5) Where a share warrant is cancelled by an order under this paragraph, the company concerned must, as soon as reasonably practicable—

(a) enter the cancellation date in its register of members, or

(b) where an election is in force under section 128B of the Companies Act 2006 (option to keep membership information on central register) in respect of the company, deliver that information to the registrar as if it were information required to be delivered under section 128E of that Act.

(6) In this Schedule "the cancellation date", in relation to a share warrant, means the day its cancellation by a cancellation order or suspended cancellation order takes effect.

Registration of reduction of share capital

7. (1) This paragraph applies in relation to a company if a share warrant of the company and the shares specified in it are cancelled by a cancellation order or a suspended cancellation order.

(2) The company must, before the end of the period of 15 days beginning with the cancellation date, deliver to the registrar—

(a) a copy of the order,

(b) in the case of a suspended cancellation order, a statement confirming that the share warrant and the shares specified in it have been cancelled by the order with effect from the cancellation date, and

(c) a statement of capital.

(3) The statement of capital must state with respect to the company's share capital as reduced by the cancellation of the share warrant and the shares specified in it—

(a) the total number of shares of the company,

(b) the aggregate nominal value of those shares,

(c) the aggregate amount (if any) unpaid on those shares (whether on account of their nominal value or by way of premium), and

(d) for each class of shares—

(i) such particulars of the rights attached to the shares as are prescribed by the Secretary of State under section 644(2)(c)(i) of the Companies Act 2006,

(ii) the total number of shares of that class, and

(iii) the aggregate nominal value of shares of that class.

(4) If the company fails to comply with this paragraph an offence is committed by—

(a) the company, and

(b) every officer of the company who is in default.

(5) In the case of a public company, a statement of capital delivered under this paragraph is to be treated as a document subject to the Directive disclosure requirements for the purposes of the Companies Act 2006 (see section 1078 of that Act).

Reduction of share capital below authorised minimum in case of public company

8. (1) This paragraph applies where the court makes a cancellation order or a suspended cancellation order in relation to a public company and—

(a) in the case of a cancellation order, the order has the effect of bringing the nominal value of its allotted share capital below the authorised minimum, or

(b) in the case of a suspended cancellation order, the order may have that effect from the end of the grace period.

(2) The registrar must not register the cancellation order or (as the case may be) the suspended cancellation order if it has that effect from the end of the grace period unless—

(a) the court so directs in the order concerned, or

(b) the company is first re-registered as a private company.

(3) The expedited procedure for re-registration provided by section 651 of the Companies Act 2006 applies for the purposes of this paragraph as it applies for the purposes of section 650 of that Act.

(4) Where the court makes an order under section 651 of that Act in connection with a suspended cancellation order, the order under section 651 must be conditional on the suspended cancellation order having the effect mentioned in sub-paragraph (1)(b) from the end of the grace period.

Payment into court in connection with cancellation

9. (1) Where a share warrant is cancelled by a cancellation order or suspended cancellation order, the company concerned must, before the end of the period of 14 days beginning with the cancellation date, make a payment into court of an amount equal to—

(a) the aggregate nominal value of the shares specified in the warrant and the whole of any premium paid on them, plus

(b) the suspension period amount.

(2) If a company fails to comply with sub-paragraph (1) an offence is committed by every officer of the company who is in default.

10. (1) A person who, at the end of the period of 7 months beginning with the commencement date, was the bearer of a share warrant which has been cancelled by a cancellation order or a suspended cancellation order may apply to the court for the sum paid into court under paragraph 9(1) in respect of the shares specified in the warrant to be paid to that person.

(2) Such an application may only be made during the period—

(a) beginning with the day which is 6 months after the cancellation date, and

(b) ending with the day which is 3 years after the cancellation date.

(3) The court may grant an application under sub-paragraph (1) only if it is satisfied that there are exceptional circumstances justifying the failure of the bearer of the share warrant to exercise the right of surrender—

(a) in the case of a warrant cancelled by a cancellation order, before the end of the surrender period, or

(b) in the case of a warrant cancelled by a suspended cancellation order, before the end of the grace period.

11. (1) This paragraph applies in relation to a company in respect of which a cancellation order or suspended cancellation order has been made if any of the following is appointed in relation to the company after the cancellation date—

(a) an administrator;

(b) an administrative receiver;

(c) a liquidator;

and that person is referred to in this paragraph as the "office-holder".

(2) The office-holder may apply to the court for the sum paid into court under paragraph 9(1)(a) to be paid to the office-holder by way of a contribution to the company's assets.

(3) Such an application may only be made during the period—

(a) beginning with the cancellation date, and

(b) ending with the day which is 3 years after that date.

12. (1) Anything left of a sum paid into court under paragraph 9(1) immediately after the end of the period mentioned in paragraph 11(3) must be paid into the Consolidated Fund.

(2) Sub-paragraph (1) does not apply to any amount in respect of which an application under paragraph 10(1) or 11(2) has been made but not yet determined before the end of that period unless and until the application is dismissed and either—

(a) the period for bringing an appeal against the dismissal has expired, or

(b) in a case where an appeal is brought before the end of that period, the appeal is dismissed, abandoned or otherwise ceases to have effect.

Company with outstanding share warrants: prohibition on striking off

13. (1) An application under section 1003 of the Companies Act 2006 (application for voluntary striking off) on behalf of a company must not be made at a time when there is a share warrant issued by the company.

(2) It is an offence for a person to make an application in contravention of this section.

(3) In proceedings for such an offence it is a defence for the accused to prove that the accused did not know, and could not reasonably have known, of the existence of the share warrant.

Notices

14. (1) A notice required by virtue of any provision of this Schedule to be given to the bearer of a share warrant must be—

(a) published in the Gazette,

(b) communicated to that person in the same way (if any) as the company concerned normally communicates with that person for other purposes relating to the shares specified in the warrant, and

(c) made available in a prominent position on the company's website (if it has one) during the period mentioned in sub-paragraph (2) (and see sub-paragraph (3)).

(2) That period is the period beginning with the day on which the notice is published in the Gazette and ending with—

(a) in the case of a notice required by paragraph 2, the day on which a notice required by paragraph 4 is made available on the company's website;

(b) in the case of a notice required by paragraph 4, the day on which a notice required by paragraph 5(3) is made available on the company's website;

(c) in the case of a notice required by paragraph 5(3), the day on which the court makes a cancellation order or (as the case may be) suspended cancellation order in respect of the share warrant;

(d) in the case of a notice required by virtue of paragraph 6(3)(a), the end of the grace period.

(3) Nothing in this paragraph requires a notice to be made available on the company's website after the day on which the last of the share warrants issued by the company to be surrendered is surrendered.

(4) Sections 1143 to 1148 of the Companies Act 2006 (company communications provisions) apply for the purposes of this Part of this Schedule as they apply for the purposes of the Companies Acts.

Company filings: language requirements

15. Sections 1103, 1104 and 1107 of the Companies Act 2006 (language requirements) apply to all documents required to be delivered to the registrar under this Part of this Schedule.

Application of sections 1112 and 1113 of the Companies Act 2006

16. Sections 1112 (general false statement offence) and 1113 (enforcement of company's filing obligations) of the Companies Act 2006 apply for the purposes of this Part of this Schedule as they apply for the purposes of the Companies Acts.

Offences

17. For the purposes of any offence under this Part of this Schedule a shadow director is treated as an officer of the company.

18. (1) A person guilty of an offence under paragraph 1(5) of this Schedule is liable on summary conviction to a fine not exceeding level 3 on the standard scale and, for continued contravention, a daily default fine not exceeding one-tenth of level 3 on the standard scale.

(2) A person guilty of an offence under any other provision of this Schedule is liable—

(a) on conviction on indictment, to a fine;

(b) on summary conviction—

(i) in England and Wales, to a fine;

(ii) in Scotland or Northern Ireland, to a fine not exceeding the statutory maximum.

19. The following sections of the Companies Act 2006 apply for the purposes of this Part of this Schedule as they apply for the purposes of the Companies Acts—

(a) sections 1121 and 1122 (liability of officer in default);

(b) section 1125 (meaning of "daily default fine");

(c) sections 1127 and 1128 (general provision about summary proceedings);

(d) section 1129 (legal professional privilege);

(e) section 1132 (production and inspection of documents).

Interpretation

20. (1) In this Part of this Schedule—

"cancellation date" has the meaning given by paragraph 6(6);

"cancellation order" has the meaning given by paragraph 5(2);

"commencement date" has the meaning given by paragraph 1(1);

"Companies Acts" has the same meaning as in the Companies Act 2006 (see section 2 of that Act);

"grace period" has the meaning given by paragraph 6(3)(b);

"surrender period" has the meaning given by paragraph 1(2);

"suspended cancellation order" has the meaning given by paragraph 6(3);

"suspension period amount" has the meaning given by paragraph 3(7);

"right of surrender" has the meaning given by paragraph 1(3).

(2) Expressions defined for the purposes of the Companies Acts have the same meaning in this Part of this Schedule as in those Acts.

Transitory provision

21. (1) Until section 94 (option to keep information on central register) comes into force, this Schedule has effect as if, in each of paragraphs 1(3) and 6(5), paragraph (b) (and the "or" preceding it) were omitted.

(2) Until section 97 (contents of statements of capital) comes into force, paragraph 7(3) of this Schedule has effect as if—

(a) paragraph (c) were omitted, and

(b) after paragraph (d) there were inserted ", and

(e) the amount paid up and the amount (if any) unpaid on each share (whether on account of the nominal value of the share or by way of premium)."

PART 2

(*(Part 2 contains consequential amendments to the Companies Act 2006.*)

SCHEDULE 11
SINGLE REGULATOR OF INSOLVENCY PRACTITIONERS: SUPPLEMENTARY PROVISION

Section 144

Operation of this Schedule

[9.531]

1. (1) This Schedule has effect in relation to regulations under section 144 designating a body (referred to in this Schedule as "the Regulations") as follows—

(a) paragraphs 2 to 13 have effect where the Regulations establish the body;

(b) paragraphs 6, 7 and 9 to 13 have effect where the Regulations designate an existing body (see section 144(2)(b));

(c) paragraph 14 also has effect where the Regulations designate an existing body that is an unincorporated association.

(2) Provision made in the Regulations by virtue of paragraph 6 or 12, where that paragraph has effect as mentioned in sub-paragraph (1)(b), may only apply in relation to—

(a) things done by or in relation to the body in or in connection with the exercise of functions conferred on it by the Regulations, and

(b) functions of the body which are functions so conferred.

Name, members and chair

2. (1) The Regulations must prescribe the name by which the body is to be known.

(2) The Regulations must provide that the members of the body must be appointed by the Secretary of State after such consultation as the Secretary of State thinks appropriate.

(3) The Regulations must provide that the Secretary of State must appoint one of the members as the chair of the body.

(4) The Regulations may include provision about—

(a) the terms on which the members of the body hold and vacate office;

(b) the terms on which the person appointed as the chair holds and vacates that office.

Remuneration etc

3. (1) The Regulations must provide that the body must pay to its chair and members such remuneration and allowances in respect of expenses properly incurred by them in the exercise of their functions as the Secretary of State may determine.

(2) The Regulations must provide that, as regards any member (including the chair) in whose case the Secretary of State so determines, the body must pay or make provision for the payment of—

(a) such pension, allowance or gratuity to or in respect of that person on retirement or death as the Secretary of State may determine, or

(b) such contributions or other payment towards the provision of such a pension, allowance or gratuity as the Secretary of State may determine.

(3) The Regulations must provide that where—

(a) a person ceases to be a member of the body otherwise than on the expiry of the term of office, and

(b) it appears to the Secretary of State that there are special circumstances which make it right for that person to be compensated,

the body must make a payment to the person by way of compensation of such amount as the Secretary of State may determine.

Staff

4. The Regulations must provide that—

(a) the body may appoint such persons to be its employees as the body considers appropriate, and

(b) the employees are to be appointed on such terms and conditions as the body may determine.

Proceedings

5. (1) The Regulations may make provision about the proceedings of the body.

(2) The Regulations may, in particular—

(a) authorise the body to exercise any function by means of committees consisting wholly or partly of members of the body;

(b) provide that the validity of proceedings of the body, or of any such committee, is not affected by any vacancy among the members or any defect in the appointment of a member.

Fees

6. (1) The Regulations may make provision—

(a) about the setting and charging of fees by the body in connection with the exercise of its functions;

(b) for the retention by the body of any such fees payable to it;

(c) about the application by the body of such fees.

(2) The Regulations may, in particular, make provision—

(a) for the body to be able to set such fees as appear to it to be sufficient to defray the expenses of the body exercising its functions, taking one year with another;

(b) for the setting of fees by the body to be subject to the approval of the Secretary of State.

(3) The expenses referred to in sub-paragraph (2)(a) include any expenses incurred by the body on such staff, accommodation, services and other facilities as appear to it to be necessary or expedient for the proper exercise of its functions.

Consultation

7. The Regulations may make provision as to the circumstances and manner in which the body must consult others before exercising any function conferred on it by the Regulations.

Training and other services

8. (1) The Regulations may make provision authorising the body to provide training or other services to any person.

(2) The Regulations may make provision authorising the body—

(a) to charge for the provision of any such training or other services, and

(b) to calculate any such charge on the basis that it considers to be the appropriate commercial basis.

Report and accounts

9. (1) The Regulations must require the body, at least once in each 12 month period, to report to the Secretary of State on—

(a) the exercise of the functions conferred on it by the Regulations, and

(b) such other matters as may be prescribed in the Regulations.

(2) The Regulations must require the Secretary of State to lay before Parliament a copy of each report received under this paragraph.

(3) Unless section 394 of the Companies Act 2006 applies to the body (duty on every company to prepare individual accounts), the Regulations must provide that the Secretary of State may give directions to the body with respect to the preparation of its accounts.

(4) Unless the body falls within sub-paragraph (5), the Regulations must provide that the Secretary of State may give directions to the body with respect to the audit of its accounts.

(5) The body falls within this sub-paragraph if it is a company whose accounts—

(a) are required to be audited in accordance with Part 16 of the Companies Act 2006 (see section 475 of that Act), or

(b) are exempt from the requirements of that Part under section 482 of that Act (non-profit making companies subject to public sector audit).

(6) The Regulations may provide that, whether or not section 394 of the Companies Act 2006 applies to the body, the Secretary of State may direct that any provisions of that Act specified in the directions are to apply to the body with or without modifications.

Funding

10. The Regulations may provide that the Secretary of State may make grants to the body.

Financial penalties

11. (1) This paragraph applies where the Regulations include provision enabling the body to impose a financial penalty on a person who is, or has been, authorised to act as an insolvency practitioner (see section 144(5)).

(2) The Regulations—

(a) must include provision about how the body is to determine the amount of a penalty, and

(b) may, in particular, prescribe a minimum or maximum amount.

(3) The Regulations must provide that, unless the Secretary of State (with the consent of the Treasury) otherwise directs, income from penalties imposed by the body is to be paid into the Consolidated Fund.

(4) The Regulations may also, in particular—

(a) include provision for a penalty imposed by the body to be enforced as a debt;

(b) prescribe conditions that must be met before any action to enforce a penalty may be taken.

Status etc

12. The Regulations must provide that—

(a) the body is not to be regarded as acting on behalf of the Crown, and

(b) its members, officers and employees are not to be regarded as Crown servants.

Transfer schemes

13. (1) This paragraph applies if the Regulations make provision designating a body (whether one established by the Regulations or one already in existence) in place of a body designated by earlier regulations under section 144; and those bodies are referred to as the "new body" and the "former body" respectively.

(2) The Regulations may make provision authorising the Secretary of State to make a scheme (a "transfer scheme") for the transfer of property, rights and liabilities from the former body to the new body.

(3) The Regulations may provide that a transfer scheme may include provision—

(a) about the transfer of property, rights and liabilities that could not otherwise be transferred;

(b) about the transfer of property acquired, and rights and liabilities arising, after the making of the scheme.

(4) The Regulations may provide that a transfer scheme may make consequential, supplementary, incidental or transitional provision and may in particular—

(a) create rights, or impose liabilities, in relation to property or rights transferred;

(b) make provision about the continuing effect of things done by the former body in respect of anything transferred;

(c) make provision about the continuation of things (including legal proceedings) in the process of being done by, on behalf of or in relation to the former body in respect of anything transferred;

(d) make provision for references to the former body in an instrument or other document in respect of anything transferred to be treated as references to the new body;

(e) make provision for the shared ownership or use of property;

(f) if the TUPE regulations do not apply to in relation to the transfer, make provision which is the same or similar.

(5) The Regulations must provide that, where the former body is an existing body, a transfer scheme may only make provision in relation to—

(a) things done by or in relation to the former body in or in connection with the exercise of functions conferred on it by previous regulations under section 144, and

(b) functions of the body which are functions so conferred.

(6) In sub-paragraph (4)(f), "TUPE regulations" means the Transfer of Undertakings (Protection of Employment) Regulations 2006 (SI 2006/246).

(7) In this paragraph—

(a) references to rights and liabilities include rights and liabilities relating to a contract of employment;

(b) references to the transfer of property include the grant of a lease.

Additional provision where body is unincorporated association

14. (1) This paragraph applies where the body is an unincorporated association.

(2) The Regulations must provide that any relevant proceedings may be brought by or against the body in the name of any body corporate whose constitution provides for the establishment of the body.

(3) In sub-paragraph (2) "relevant proceedings" means proceedings brought in or in connection with the exercise of any function conferred on the body by the Regulations.

MODERN SLAVERY ACT 2015

(2015 c 30)

NOTES

Only s 54 of this Act is relevant to company law, and the omitted provisions of this Act are not annotated. By virtue of s 60 of this Act, s 54 applies to the whole of the United Kingdom. Section 54 came into force on 29 October 2015, but does not have effect in respect of a financial year ending before 31 March 2016 (see the Modern Slavery Act 2015 (Commencement No 3 and Transitional Provision) Regulations 2015, SI 2015/1816).

This Act is reproduced as amended by: the Human Trafficking and Exploitation (Scotland) Act 2015 (Consequential Provisions and Modifications) Order 2016, SI 2016/1031.

An Act to make provision about slavery, servitude and forced or compulsory labour and about human trafficking, including provision for the protection of victims; to make provision for an Independent Anti-slavery Commissioner; and for connected purposes

[26 March 2015]

PART 6 TRANSPARENCY IN SUPPLY CHAINS ETC

[9.532]

54 Transparency in supply chains etc

(1) A commercial organisation within subsection (2) must prepare a slavery and human trafficking statement for each financial year of the organisation.

(2) A commercial organisation is within this subsection if it—

(a) supplies goods or services, and

(b) has a total turnover of not less than an amount prescribed by regulations made by the Secretary of State.

(3) For the purposes of subsection (2)(b), an organisation's total turnover is to be determined in accordance with regulations made by the Secretary of State.

(4) A slavery and human trafficking statement for a financial year is—

(a) a statement of the steps the organisation has taken during the financial year to ensure that slavery and human trafficking is not taking place—

(i) in any of its supply chains, and

(ii) in any part of its own business, or

(b) a statement that the organisation has taken no such steps.

(5) An organisation's slavery and human trafficking statement may include information about—

(a) the organisation's structure, its business and its supply chains;

(b) its policies in relation to slavery and human trafficking;

(c) its due diligence processes in relation to slavery and human trafficking in its business and supply chains;

(d) the parts of its business and supply chains where there is a risk of slavery and human trafficking taking place, and the steps it has taken to assess and manage that risk;

(e) its effectiveness in ensuring that slavery and human trafficking is not taking place in its business or supply chains, measured against such performance indicators as it considers appropriate;

(f) the training about slavery and human trafficking available to its staff.

(6) A slavery and human trafficking statement—

(a) if the organisation is a body corporate other than a limited liability partnership, must be approved by the board of directors (or equivalent management body) and signed by a director (or equivalent);

(b) if the organisation is a limited liability partnership, must be approved by the members and signed by a designated member;

(c) if the organisation is a limited partnership registered under the Limited Partnerships Act 1907, must be signed by a general partner;

(d) if the organisation is any other kind of partnership, must be signed by a partner.

(7) If the organisation has a website, it must—

(a) publish the slavery and human trafficking statement on that website, and

(b) include a link to the slavery and human trafficking statement in a prominent place on that website's homepage.

(8) If the organisation does not have a website, it must provide a copy of the slavery and human trafficking statement to anyone who makes a written request for one, and must do so before the end of the period of 30 days beginning with the day on which the request is received.

(9) The Secretary of State—

(a) may issue guidance about the duties imposed on commercial organisations by this section;

(b) must publish any such guidance in a way the Secretary of State considers appropriate.

(10) The guidance may in particular include further provision about the kind of information which may be included in a slavery and human trafficking statement.

(11) The duties imposed on commercial organisations by this section are enforceable by the Secretary of State bringing civil proceedings in the High Court for an injunction or, in Scotland, for specific performance of a statutory duty under section 45 of the Court of Session Act 1988.

(12) For the purposes of this section—

"commercial organisation" means—

(a) a body corporate (wherever incorporated) which carries on a business, or part of a business, in any part of the United Kingdom, or

(b) a partnership (wherever formed) which carries on a business, or part of a business, in any part of the United Kingdom,

and for this purpose "business" includes a trade or profession;

"partnership" means—

(a) a partnership within the Partnership Act 1890,

(b) a limited partnership registered under the Limited Partnerships Act 1907, or

(c) a firm, or an entity of a similar character, formed under the law of a country outside the United Kingdom;

"slavery and human trafficking" means—

(a) conduct which constitutes an offence under any of the following—

(i) section 1, 2 or 4 of this Act,

(ii) section 1, 2 or 4 of the Human Trafficking and Exploitation (Criminal Justice and Support for Victims) Act (Northern Ireland) 2015 (c 2 (NI)) (equivalent offences in Northern Ireland),

[(iii) section 1 or 4 of the Human Trafficking and Exploitation (Scotland) Act 2015 (asp 12) (equivalent offences in Scotland), or]

(b) conduct which would constitute an offence in a part of the United Kingdom under any of those provisions if the conduct took place in that part of the United Kingdom.

NOTES

Sub-s (12): in the definition "slavery and human trafficking", sub-para (a)(iii) was substituted (for the original sub-paras (a)(iii)–(v)) by the Human Trafficking and Exploitation (Scotland) Act 2015 (Consequential Provisions and Modifications) Order 2016, SI 2016/1031, art 3, Schedule, para 3(1), (5), as from 17 December 2016.

Guidance issued under sub-s (9) above: see Transparency in Supply Chains etc – A practical guide (2015).

Regulations: the Modern Slavery Act 2015 (Transparency in Supply Chains) Regulations 2015, SI 2015/1833 at **[10.428]**.

CORPORATE INSOLVENCY AND GOVERNANCE ACT 2020

(2020 c 12)

NOTES

This Act is reproduced as amended by: the Corporate Insolvency and Governance Act 2020 (Coronavirus) (Extension of the Relevant Period) Regulations 2020, SI 2020/1031; the Corporate Insolvency and Governance Act 2020 (Coronavirus) (Suspension of Liability for Wrongful Trading and Extension of the Relevant Period) Regulations 2020, SI 2020/1349; the Corporate Insolvency and Governance Act 2020 (Coronavirus) (Extension of the Relevant Period) (No 2) Regulations 2020, SI 2020/1483; the Corporate Insolvency and Governance Act 2020 (Meetings of Scottish Charitable Incorporated Organisations) (Coronavirus) (No 2) Regulations 2020, SSI 2020/421; the Corporate Insolvency and Governance Act 2020 (Coronavirus) (Extension of the Relevant Period) Regulations 2021, SI 2021/375; the Corporate Insolvency and Governance Act 2020 (Coronavirus) (Change of Expiry Date) Regulations 2021, SI 2021/441; the Corporate Insolvency and Governance Act 2020 (Coronavirus) (Amendment of Schedule 10) (No 2) Regulations 2021, SI 2021/1091.

An Act to make provision about companies and other entities in financial difficulty; and to make temporary changes to the law relating to the governance and regulation of companies and other entities

[25 June 2020]

ARRANGEMENT OF SECTIONS

Moratorium

1 (*Inserts the Insolvency Act 1986, Part A1 at* **[9.81]**.)

[9.533]

2 Moratoriums in Great Britain: further amendments and transition

(1) Schedule 3 contains consequential and other amendments to do with moratoriums under new Part A1 of the Insolvency Act 1986.

(2) Nothing in this Act affects the operation of the Insolvency Act 1986, or any other enactment, in relation to a moratorium under Schedule A1 to that Act which comes into force before the repeal of that Schedule by Schedule 3 to this Act.

(3) Subsection (2) is without prejudice to the operation of section 16 of the Interpretation Act 1978 (general savings).

NOTES

Commencement: 26 June 2020.

[9.534]

3 Moratoriums in Great Britain: temporary modifications

Schedule 4 makes temporary modifications to Part A1 of the Insolvency Act 1986 (moratorium) and other temporary provision in connection with that Part.

NOTES

Commencement: 26 June 2020.

4–6 (*Ss 4–6 (Moratoriums in Northern Ireland, etc) are outside the scope of this work.*)

Arrangements and reconstructions for companies in financial difficulty

[9.535]

7 Arrangements and reconstructions for companies in financial difficulty

Schedule 9 contains provision about arrangements and reconstructions for companies in financial difficulty.

NOTES

Commencement: 26 June 2020.

Administration: sales to connected persons

[9.536]

8 Administration in Great Britain: sales to connected persons

(1) Paragraph 60A of Schedule B1 to the Insolvency Act 1986 (which expired in May 2020) is revived.

(2) (*Substitutes the Insolvency Act 1986, Sch B1, para 60A(10) at* **[9.472]**.)

NOTES

Commencement: 26 June 2020.

Note that the Sch B1, para 60A(10) substituted by sub-s (2) above provides that para 60A will expire at the end of June 2021 (unless the power conferred by it is exercised before then). See also the Administration (Restrictions on Disposal etc to Connected Persons) Regulations 2021, SI 2021/427 (made under para 60A(1), (2) and (7)) at **[10.1306]**).

9 *(S 9 (Administration in Northern Ireland: sales to connected persons) is outside the scope of this work.)*

Winding-up petitions

[9.537]

10 Winding-up petitions: Great Britain

Schedule 10 contains temporary provision in relation to winding-up petitions in Great Britain.

NOTES

Commencement: 26 June 2020.

11 *(S 11 (Winding-up petitions: Northern Ireland) is outside the scope of this work.)*

Wrongful trading

[9.538]

12 Suspension of liability for wrongful trading: Great Britain

(1) In determining for the purposes of section 214 or 246ZB of the Insolvency Act 1986 (liability of director for wrongful trading) the contribution (if any) to a company's assets that it is proper for a person to make, the court is to assume that the person is not responsible for any worsening of the financial position of the company or its creditors that occurs during the relevant period.

(2) In this section the "relevant period" is the period which—

- (a) begins with 1 March 2020, and
- (b) ends with 30 September 2020.

(3) Subsection (1) does not apply if at any time during the relevant period the company concerned is excluded from being eligible by any of the paragraphs of Schedule ZA1 to the Insolvency Act 1986 listed in subsection (4), as they apply for the purposes of this subsection (see subsection (5)).

(4) The paragraphs of Schedule ZA1 to the Insolvency Act 1986 are—

- (a) paragraph 3 (insurance companies),
- (b) paragraph 4 (banks),
- (c) paragraph 5 (electronic money institutions),
- (d) paragraph 6 (investment banks and investment firms),
- (e) paragraph 9 (payment institutions),
- (f) paragraph 10 (operators of payment systems etc),
- (g) paragraph 11 (recognised investment exchanges, clearing houses etc),
- (h) paragraph 12 (securitisation companies),
- (i) paragraph 13 (parties to capital market arrangements),
- (j) paragraph 15 (public-private partnership project companies), and
- (k) paragraph 18 (certain overseas companies).

(5) In their application for the purposes of subsection (3)—

- (a) each of paragraphs 13 and 15 of Schedule ZA1 to the Insolvency Act 1986 has effect as if in sub-paragraph (1)—
  - (i) the words ", on the filing date" were omitted, and
  - (ii) paragraph (b) were omitted, and
- (b) paragraph 18 of that Schedule has effect as if for "paragraph 2", in both places, there were substituted "paragraphs 2, 7 and 8".

(6) Subsection (1) also does not apply if at any time during the relevant period the company concerned—

- (a) has permission under Part 4A of the Financial Services and Markets Act 2000 to carry on a regulated activity, and
- (b) is not subject to a requirement imposed under that Act to refrain from holding money for clients.

(7) This section has effect—

- (a) in so far as it relates to section 214 of the Insolvency Act 1986, as if it were contained in Part 4 of that Act, and
- (b) in so far as it relates to section 246ZB of the Insolvency Act 1986, as if it were contained in Part 6 of that Act.

(8) But this section does not have effect in relation to the following bodies (which are bodies to which provisions contained in Parts 4 and 6 of the Insolvency Act 1986 apply)—

- (a) a society that is registered within the meaning of the Friendly Societies Act 1974 and that at any time during the relevant period carries on the regulated activity of effecting or carrying out contracts of insurance;
- (b) a building society within the meaning of the Building Societies Act 1986;
- (c) a society that is incorporated under the Friendly Societies Act 1992;
- (d) a registered society within the meaning of the Co-operative and Community Benefit Societies Act 2014 that is registered under that Act as a credit union;
- (e) a registered society within the meaning of the Co-operative and Community Benefit Societies Act 2014 that at any time during the relevant period carries on the regulated activity of effecting or carrying out contracts of insurance.

(9) In this section "regulated activity" has the meaning given by section 22 of the Financial Services and Markets Act 2000, taken with Schedule 2 to that Act and any order under that section.

NOTES

Commencement: 26 June 2020.

13 *(S 13 (Suspension of liability for wrongful trading: Northern Ireland) is outside the scope of this work.)*

Termination clauses in supply contracts

[9.539]

14 Protection of supplies of goods and services: Great Britain

(1), (2) (*Inserts the Insolvency Act 1986, ss 233B, 233C at* **[9.366]**, **[9.367]**, *and amends s 434 of that Act.*)

(3) Schedule 12—

(a) inserts a new Schedule into the Insolvency Act 1986 which provides for exclusions from the operation of section 233B of that Act, and

(b) contains consequential amendments.

(4) The amendments made by this section and Schedule 12 have effect in relation to a company which becomes subject to a relevant insolvency procedure on or after the day on which this section comes into force (but in respect of contracts entered into before, as well as those entered into on or after, that day).

NOTES

Commencement: 26 June 2020.

[9.540]

15 Temporary exclusion for small suppliers: Great Britain

(1) Section 233B of the Insolvency Act 1986 does not apply in relation to a contract for the supply of goods or services to a company where—

(a) the company becomes subject to a relevant insolvency procedure during the relevant period, and

(b) the supplier is a small entity at the time the company becomes subject to the procedure.

(2) In subsection (1)(a) "relevant period" means the period which—

(a) begins with the day on which this section comes into force, and

(b) ends with [30 June 2021].

(3) For the purposes of subsection (1)(b), whether the supplier is a "small entity" at the time the company becomes subject to a relevant insolvency procedure (the "relevant time") is to be determined under subsections (4) to (10).

(4) Where the supplier is not in its first financial year at the relevant time, the supplier is a small entity at the relevant time if at least two of the following conditions were met in relation to its most recent financial year—

Condition 1: the supplier's turnover was not more than £10.2 million;

Condition 2: the supplier's balance sheet total was not more than £5.1 million;

Condition 3: the number of the supplier's employees was not more than 50.

(5) For the purposes of Condition 1 in subsection (4), if the supplier's most recent financial year was not 12 months, the maximum figure for turnover must be proportionately adjusted.

(6) For the purposes of Condition 2 in subsection (4), the supplier's balance sheet total means the aggregate of the amounts shown as assets in the supplier's balance sheet.

(7) For the purposes of Condition 3 in subsection (4), the number of the supplier's employees means the average number of persons employed by the supplier in its most recent financial year, determined as follows—

(a) find for each month in that financial year the number of persons employed under contracts of service by the supplier in that month (whether throughout the month or not),

(b) add together the monthly totals, and

(c) divide by the number of months in the financial year.

(8) In subsections (4) to (7) the supplier's "most recent financial year" is the financial year of the supplier which, at the relevant time, has ended most recently.

(9) Where the supplier is in its first financial year at the relevant time, the supplier is a small entity at the relevant time if at least two of the following conditions are met—

Condition 1: the supplier's average turnover for each complete month in the supplier's first financial year is not more than £850,000;

Condition 2: the aggregate of amounts which would be shown in a balance sheet of the supplier drawn up at the relevant time is not more than £5.1 million;

Condition 3: the average number of persons employed by the supplier in the supplier's first financial year (determined as specified in subsection (7)) is not more than 50.

(10) In this section—

"entity" means—

(a) a company,

(b) a limited liability partnership,

(c) any other association or body of persons, whether or not incorporated, and

(d) an individual carrying on a trade or business;

"relevant insolvency procedure" has the same meaning as in section 233B of the Insolvency Act 1986.

(11) This section has effect as if it were included in Part 6 of the Insolvency Act 1986.

NOTES

Commencement: 26 June 2020.

Sub-s (2): words in square brackets substituted by the Corporate Insolvency and Governance Act 2020 (Coronavirus) (Extension of the Relevant Period) Regulations 2021, SI 2021/375, reg 3(2), as from 26 March 2021.

16–19 (*Apply to Northern Ireland only and are outside the scope of this work.*)

Power to amend corporate insolvency or governance legislation: Great Britain

[9.541]

20 Regulations to amend legislation: Great Britain

(1) The Secretary of State may by regulations amend, or modify the effect of, corporate insolvency or governance legislation so as to—

(a) change the conditions that must be met before a corporate insolvency or restructuring procedure applies to entities of any description (whether by adding, varying or removing any condition),

(b) change the way in which a corporate insolvency or restructuring procedure applies in relation to entities of any description, or

(c) change or disapply any duty of a person with corporate responsibility or the liability of such a person to any sanction.

(2) Regulations under this section may—

(a) make different provision for different purposes;

(b) make provision binding the Crown.

(3) Regulations under this section must be made in accordance with sections 21 to 26.

NOTES

Commencement: 26 June 2020.

Regulations: the Corporate Insolvency and Governance Act 2020 (Coronavirus) (Suspension of Liability for Wrongful Trading and Extension of the Relevant Period) Regulations 2020, SI 2020/1349 at **[10.1300]**; the Corporate Insolvency and Governance Act 2020 (Coronavirus) (Extension of the Relevant Period) Regulations 2021, SI 2021/375; the Corporate Insolvency and Governance Act 2020 (Coronavirus) (Amendment of Schedule 10) (No 2) Regulations 2021, SI 2021/1091.

[9.542]

21 Purposes

(1) The Secretary of State may only make regulations under section 20(1)(a) or (b) if satisfied that the regulations are expedient for any of the following purposes—

(a) reducing, or assisting in the reduction of, the number of entities entering into corporate insolvency or restructuring procedures for reasons relating to the effects of coronavirus on businesses or on the economy of the United Kingdom;

(b) mitigating or otherwise dealing with the effect on corporate insolvency or restructuring procedures of any increase or potential increase in the number of entities entering into those procedures for the reasons referred to in paragraph (a);

(c) mitigating difficulties that corporate insolvency or restructuring procedures might impose on a business in view of—

(i) any worsening of the financial position of the business in consequence of, or for reasons relating to, coronavirus,

(ii) constraints on people's ability to work, or to be in proximity to each other, as a result of coronavirus, or

(iii) measures for public health taken in response to coronavirus.

(2) The Secretary of State may only make regulations under section 20(1)(c) if satisfied that the regulations are expedient for the purpose of securing that the duties of persons with corporate responsibility, or the liability of those persons to any sanction, take due account of the effects of coronavirus on businesses or on the economy of the United Kingdom.

NOTES

Commencement: 26 June 2020.

[9.543]

22 Restrictions

(1) Before making regulations under section 20 the Secretary of State must consider the effect of the regulations on persons likely to be affected by them (for example, debtors, creditors or employees).

(2) The Secretary of State may only make regulations under section 20 if satisfied—

(a) that the need for the provision made by the regulations is urgent,

(b) that the provision made by the regulations is proportionate to the purpose for which it is made,

(c) that it is not practicable without legislation to bring about the result intended to be brought about by that provision, and

(d) if the Secretary of State could make the same provision in other subordinate legislation, that doing so would risk not achieving the purpose for which the regulations are made (because of possible delay or for any other reason).

(3) Regulations under section 20—

(a) may not create a criminal offence or civil penalty (but may modify the circumstances in which a person is guilty of an existing offence or liable for an existing civil penalty);

(b) may not make provision so as to impose or increase a fee.

(4) Regulations under section 20 may not make provision that could be made by an Act of the Scottish Parliament unless the Secretary of State has first consulted the Scottish Ministers.

NOTES

Commencement: 26 June 2020.

[9.544]

23 Time-limited effect

(1) Regulations under section 20 must be framed so that any provision made by them—

(a) has effect only for a period not exceeding six months, or

(b) applies only in relation to circumstances occurring in a period not exceeding six months.

(2) This does not prevent further regulations under section 20 from—

(a) making the same provision for, or applying in relation to, subsequent periods (not exceeding six months at a time);

(b) extending (by up to six months) the period for or in relation to which earlier regulations under that section apply.

(3) The Secretary of State must keep regulations under section 20 under review during the period for which they have effect or in relation to which they apply.

(4) If on such a review the Secretary of State is satisfied that that period—

(a) is longer than expedient for the purpose for which the regulations were made, or

(b) has ceased to be proportionate to that purpose,

the Secretary of State must by regulations under this subsection revoke or amend the regulations as appropriate.

(5) Regulations under subsection (4) may contain transitional provision or savings.

NOTES

Commencement: 26 June 2020.

[9.545]

24 Expiry

(1) The Secretary of State may not make regulations under section 20 after [29 April 2022].

(2) Where regulations under section 20 are in force on the date specified in subsection (1), that subsection does not—

(a) affect the continued operation of the regulations, or

(b) prevent the making of further regulations under section 20 on one or more occasions, where those further regulations make the same provision for, or applying in relation to, subsequent periods (not exceeding six months at a time).

(3) The Secretary of State may by regulations substitute a later date for the date for the time being specified in subsection (1).

(4) The power in subsection (3)—

(a) may not be exercised so as to substitute a date which is—

(i) after the period of one year beginning with the date for the time being specified in subsection (1), or

(ii) after the period of two years beginning with the date on which this Act is passed, but

(b) may be exercised more than once.

NOTES

Commencement: 26 June 2020.

Sub-s (1): words in square brackets substituted by the Corporate Insolvency and Governance Act 2020 (Coronavirus) (Change of Expiry Date) Regulations 2021, SI 2021/441, reg 2, as from 1 April 2021.

Regulations: the Corporate Insolvency and Governance Act 2020 (Coronavirus) (Change of Expiry Date) Regulations 2021, SI 2021/441 (which amend sub-s (1) above).

[9.546]

25 Consequential provision etc

(1) The Secretary of State may by regulations make consequential, incidental or supplementary provision, or transitional provision or savings, in connection with provision made by regulations under section 20.

(2) Regulations under this section may—

(a) make provision by amending or modifying the effect of any enactment (including this Act);

(b) make different provision for different purposes;

(c) make provision binding the Crown.

NOTES

Commencement: 26 June 2020.

Regulations: the Corporate Insolvency and Governance Act 2020 (Coronavirus) (Amendment of Schedule 10) (No 2) Regulations 2021, SI 2021/1091.

[9.547]

26 Procedure for regulations

(1) Regulations under sections 20 to 25 are to be made by statutory instrument.

(2) A statutory instrument containing—

(a) regulations made under section 20, other than one to which subsection (6)(a) applies, or

(b) regulations made under section 25 which make provision by amending an Act or an Act of the Scottish Parliament,

must be laid before Parliament as soon as reasonably practicable after being made.

(3) Regulations contained in a statutory instrument laid before Parliament by virtue of subsection (2) cease to have effect at the end of the period of 40 days beginning with the day on which the instrument is made, unless during that period the instrument is approved by a resolution of each House of Parliament.

(4) In calculating the period of 40 days, no account is to be taken of any time during which—

(a) Parliament is dissolved or prorogued, or

(b) both Houses of Parliament are adjourned for more than 4 days.

(5) Where regulations cease to have effect as a result of subsection (3) that does not—

(a) affect anything previously done under or by virtue of the regulations, or

(b) prevent the making of new regulations.

(6) A statutory instrument containing—

(a) regulations under section 20 which merely revoke other regulations under that section (with or without transitional provision), or

(b) regulations under section 23(4),

is subject to annulment in pursuance of a resolution of either House of Parliament.

(7) Regulations under section 24(3) may not be made unless a draft of the statutory instrument containing them has been laid before, and approved by a resolution of, each House of Parliament.

(8) A statutory instrument containing regulations under section 25 which do not make provision by amending an Act or an Act of the Scottish Parliament is subject to annulment in pursuance of a resolution of either House of Parliament (unless the regulations were contained in a statutory instrument laid before Parliament by virtue of subsection (2)).

NOTES

Commencement: 26 June 2020.

[9.548]
27 Interpretation
(1) In sections 20 to 26 and this section—
"coronavirus" means severe acute respiratory syndrome coronavirus 2 (SARS-CoV-2);
"corporate insolvency or governance legislation" means—
(a) the Insolvency Act 1986, except so far as relating to the insolvency or bankruptcy of individuals,
(b) Part 26A of the Companies Act 2006 (arrangements and reconstructions for companies in financial difficulty),
(c) the Company Directors Disqualification Act 1986,
(d) this Act,
(e) any subordinate legislation made under the enactments specified in paragraphs (a) to (d),
(f) the Cross-Border Insolvency Regulations 2006 (SI 2006/1030), and
(g) after IP completion day, Regulation (EU) 2015/848 on insolvency proceedings;
"corporate insolvency or restructuring procedure" means—
(a) a moratorium under Part A1 of the Insolvency Act 1986;
(b) a company voluntary arrangement under Part 1 of that Act (including a moratorium under section 1A of that Act in a case where such a moratorium applies after the coming into force of paragraph 30 of Schedule 3);
(c) administration under Part 2 of that Act;
(d) receivership to which Part 3 of that Act applies;
(e) winding up under Part 4 or 5 of that Act;
(f) the procedure provided for by Part 26A of the Companies Act 2006;
"enactment" includes an Act of the Scottish Parliament and an instrument made under such an Act;
"person with corporate responsibility" means—
(a) in relation to a company, a director, manager, secretary or other officer of the body,
(b) in relation to a partnership or limited liability partnership, a partner or member, and
(c) in relation to any other entity, a person with responsibility for managing the entity;
"subordinate legislation" has the meaning given by section 21(1) of the Interpretation Act 1978.
(2) References to an enactment in subsection (1) include in particular that enactment as applied by any other enactment, with or without modifications, to partnerships, limited liability partnerships or other entities.

NOTES
Commencement: 26 June 2020.

28–36 *(Ss 28–36 (Power to amend corporate insolvency or governance legislation: Northern Ireland) are outside the scope of this work.)*

Meetings and filings

[9.549]
37 Meetings of companies and other bodies
Schedule 14 makes provision about meetings of companies and other bodies.

NOTES
Commencement: 26 June 2020.

[9.550]
38 Temporary extension of period for public company to file accounts
(1) This section applies where (but for this section) the period allowed for the directors of a public company to comply with their obligation under section 441 of the Companies Act 2006 to deliver accounts and reports for a financial year to the registrar would end—
(a) after 25 March 2020, and
(b) before the relevant day.
(2) The period allowed for the directors to comply with that obligation is to be taken to be (and always to have been) a period that ends with the relevant day.
(3) The relevant day is whichever is the earlier of—
(a) 30 September 2020, and
(b) the last day of the period of 12 months immediately following the end of the relevant accounting reference period.
(4) Expressions used in this section and section 442 of the Companies Act 2006 (period allowed for filing accounts) have the same meaning in this section as in that section.

NOTES
Commencement: 26 June 2020.

[9.551]
39 Temporary power to extend periods for providing information to registrar
(1) The Secretary of State may by regulations provide that any provision listed in section 40 is to have effect as if for a reference in the provision to a period of days or months ("the existing period") there were substituted a reference to such longer period ("the substituted period") as is specified in the regulations.
(2) The substituted period must not exceed—
(a) 42 days, in a case where the existing period is 21 days or fewer, and
(b) 12 months, in a case where the existing period is 3, 6 or 9 months.
(3) The power conferred by this section may not be exercised in relation to a reference to a period of 12 months.
(4) Regulations under this section may make—
(a) different provision for different purposes;

(b) consequential, incidental or supplementary provision (including provision modifying an enactment);
(c) transitional provision or savings.

(5) In subsection (4) "enactment" includes an Act of the Scottish Parliament and an instrument made under such an Act.

(6) Regulations under this section are to be made by statutory instrument.

(7) A statutory instrument containing regulations under this section is subject to annulment in pursuance of a resolution of either House of Parliament.

(8) This section expires at the end of the day on 5 April 2021.

(9) The expiry of this section does not affect the continued operation of any regulations made under this section for the purpose of determining the length of any period that begins before the expiry.

NOTES

Commencement: 26 June 2020.

This section expired at the end of the day on 5 April 2021, in accordance with sub-s (8) above.

Regulations: the Companies etc (Filing Requirements) (Temporary Modifications) Regulations 2020, SI 2020/645 at **[4.681]**.

[9.552]

40 Section 39: the listed provisions

The provisions referred to in section 39(1) are—

(a) section 9 of the Limited Partnerships Act 1907 (registration of changes to a limited partnership);
(b) section 466 of the Companies Act 1985 (registration of alteration to a floating charge);
(c) section 9 of the Limited Liability Partnerships Act 2000 (notice of membership changes);
(d) regulation 80C of the European Public Limited-Liability Company Regulations 2004 (SI 2004/2326) (notice of change in members of the supervisory organ);
(e) the following sections of the Companies Act 2006—
section 87 (notice of change of address of registered office);
section 114 (notice of place where register of members is kept);
section 162 (notice of place where register of directors is kept);
section 167 (notice of change in directors etc);
section 275 (notice of place where register of secretaries is kept);
section 276 (notice of change in secretaries etc);
section 442 (period allowed for filing accounts);
section 790M (register of people with significant control);
section 790N (notice of place where PSC register is kept);
section 790VA (notice of change to the PSC register);
section 853A(1) (confirmation statements);
section 859A (registration of charge);
section 859B (registration of charge contained in debentures);
section 859Q (notice of place where copies of instruments creating charges are kept);
(f) the following provisions of the Scottish Partnerships (Register of People with Significant Control) Regulations 2017 (SI 2017/694)—
regulation 7 (notice of change to the registration information);
regulation 8 (notice of ceasing to be a Scottish qualifying partnership);
the provisions of Part 5 (duties to deliver information);
regulation 35 (confirmation statements).

NOTES

Commencement: 26 June 2020.

Powers to change periods

[9.553]

41 Power to change duration of temporary provisions: Great Britain

(1) The Secretary of State may by regulations made by statutory instrument amend a relevant provision so as to—
(a) curtail the period for the time being specified in that provision, or
(b) prolong that period by up to six months if the Secretary of State considers it reasonable to do so to mitigate an effect of coronavirus.

(2) In this section—
"coronavirus" means severe acute respiratory syndrome coronavirus 2 (SARS-CoV-2);
"relevant provision" means—
(a) section 12(2),
(b) section 15(2),
(c) paragraph 1 of Schedule 4, or
(d) . . .

(3) A statutory instrument containing regulations made under subsection (1)(a) is subject to annulment in pursuance of a resolution of either House of Parliament.

(4) A statutory instrument containing regulations made under subsection (1)(b) must be laid before Parliament as soon as reasonably practicable after being made.

(5) Subsection (4) does not apply if a draft of the statutory instrument has been laid before and approved by a resolution of each House of Parliament.

(6) Regulations contained in a statutory instrument laid before Parliament by virtue of subsection (4) cease to have effect at the end of the period of 40 days beginning with the day on which the instrument is made, unless during that period the instrument is approved by a resolution of each House of Parliament.

(7) In calculating the period of 40 days, no account is to be taken of any time during which—

(a) Parliament is dissolved or prorogued, or
(b) both Houses of Parliament are adjourned for more than 4 days.

(8) Where regulations relating to any relevant provision cease to have effect as a result of subsection (6), the period specified in the relevant provision ends—
(a) at the time it would have ended under the relevant provision if the regulations had not been made, or
(b) if later, at the end of the period of 40 days mentioned in subsection (6).

(9) Where regulations cease to have effect as a result of subsection (6) that does not prevent the making of new regulations.

(10) Regulations under this section may make—
(a) different provision for the purposes of different relevant provisions;
(b) consequential, transitional or transitory provision or savings.

NOTES

Commencement: 26 June 2020.

Sub-s (2): para (d) of the definition "relevant provision" was repealed by the Corporate Insolvency and Governance Act 2020 (Coronavirus) (Amendment of Schedule 10) (No 2) Regulations 2021, SI 2021/1091, reg 4, as from 1 October 2021.

Regulations: the Corporate Insolvency and Governance Act 2020 (Coronavirus) (Extension of the Relevant Period) Regulations 2020, SI 2020/1031; the Corporate Insolvency and Governance Act 2020 (Coronavirus) (Extension of the Relevant Period) (No 2) Regulations 2020, SI 2020/1483; the Corporate Insolvency and Governance Act 2020 (Coronavirus) (Extension of the Relevant Period) Regulations 2021, SI 2021/375; the Corporate Insolvency and Governance Act 2020 (Coronavirus) (Extension of the Relevant Period) (No 2) Regulations 2021, SI 2021/718.

42 (*S 42 (Power to change duration of temporary provisions: Northern Ireland) is outside the scope of this work.*)

Implementation of insolvency measures

[9.554]

43 Modified procedure for regulations of the Secretary of State

(1) During the period of six months beginning with the day on which this section comes into force, any relevant provision that may be made by the Secretary of State by regulations that are subject to the affirmative resolution procedure may be made by regulations that are subject to the made affirmative procedure.

(2) In subsection (1) "relevant provision" means—
(a) provision under section A50(1) or (4) of the Insolvency Act 1986 (power to modify moratorium provisions in relation to certain companies);
(b) provision under section A51(1) of the Insolvency Act 1986 (moratorium: power to make provision in connection with pension schemes);
(c) provision under paragraph 20 of Schedule ZA1 to the Insolvency Act 1986 to exclude private registered providers of social housing from being eligible companies for the purposes of Part A1 of that Act;
(d) provision under section 14 or 16 of the Limited Liability Partnerships Act 2000 (insolvency etc and power to make consequential amendments) to the extent that the provision is made in connection with the application of Part A1 of the Insolvency Act 1986 to limited liability partnerships that are registered providers of social housing;
(e) provision under section 245 of the Charities Act 2011 (insolvency etc of charitable incorporated organisations etc) to the extent that the provision applies, or is otherwise made in connection with, the new insolvency measures.

(3) During the period of six months beginning with the day on which this section comes into force, the consultation duty in section 348(4) of the Charities Act 2011 does not apply in relation to regulations under section 245 of that Act to the extent that they contain provision which applies, or is otherwise made in connection with, the new insolvency measures.

(4) In subsections (2) and (3) "the new insolvency measures" means the provision made by—
(a) sections 1 to 3 and Schedules 1 to 4 (moratorium);
(b) sections 14 and 15 and Schedule 12 (termination clauses in supply contracts).

(5) For the purposes of this section —
(a) "regulations that are subject to the affirmative resolution procedure" means regulations that may not be made unless a draft of the statutory instrument containing them has been laid before and approved by a resolution of each House of Parliament;
(b) "regulations that are subject to the made affirmative procedure" means regulations that—
 (i) are contained in a statutory instrument that must be laid before Parliament as soon as reasonably practicable after being made, and
 (ii) cease to have effect at the end of the period of 40 days beginning with the day on which the instrument is made, unless during that period the instrument is approved by a resolution of each House of Parliament.

(6) In calculating the period of 40 days mentioned in subsection (5)(b)(ii), no account is to be taken of any time during which—
(a) Parliament is dissolved or prorogued, or
(b) both Houses of Parliament are adjourned for more than 4 days.

(7) Where by virtue of this section the Secretary of State makes regulations that are subject to the made affirmative procedure and the regulations cease to have effect because they are not approved within the period mentioned in subsection (5)(b)(ii), the fact that the regulations cease to have effect does not—
(a) affect anything previously done under or by virtue of the regulations, or
(b) prevent the making of new regulations.

NOTES

Commencement: 26 June 2020.

Regulations: the Pension Protection Fund (Moratorium and Arrangements and Reconstructions for Companies in Financial Difficulty) Regulations 2020, SI 2020/693; the Pension Protection Fund (Moratorium and Arrangements and Reconstructions for Companies in Financial Difficulty) (Amendment and Revocation) Regulations 2020, SI 2020/990.

[9.555]

44 Modified procedure for regulations of the Welsh Ministers

(1) During the period of six months beginning with the day on which this section comes into force, any relevant provision that may be made by the Welsh Ministers by regulations that are subject to the affirmative resolution procedure may be made by regulations that are subject to the made affirmative procedure.

(2) In subsection (1) "relevant provision" means—

(a) provision under section A50(2) of the Insolvency Act 1986 (power to modify moratorium provisions in relation to certain companies);

(b) provision under paragraph 21 of Schedule ZA1 to the Insolvency Act 1986 (exclusion of registered social landlords from eligibility under Part A1 of that Act);

(c) provision under section 247A of the Charities Act 2011 (regulations about moratoriums for charitable incorporated organisations that are registered social landlords).

(3) During the period of six months beginning with the day on which this section comes into force, the consultation duty in section 247A(6) of the Charities Act 2011 does not apply in relation to regulations under section 247A of that Act.

(4) For the purposes of this section —

(a) "regulations that are subject to the affirmative resolution procedure" means regulations that may not be made unless a draft of the statutory instrument containing them has been laid before and approved by a resolution of Senedd Cymru;

(b) "regulations that are subject to the made affirmative procedure" means regulations that—

(i) are contained in a statutory instrument that must be laid before Senedd Cymru as soon as reasonably practicable after being made, and

(ii) cease to have effect at the end of the period of 40 days beginning with the day on which the instrument is made, unless during that period the instrument is approved by a resolution of Senedd Cymru.

(5) In calculating the period of 40 days mentioned in subsection (4)(b)(ii), no account is to be taken of any time during which Senedd Cymru is—

(a) dissolved, or

(b) in recess for more than 4 days.

(6) Where by virtue of this section the Welsh Ministers make regulations that are subject to the made affirmative procedure and the regulations cease to have effect because they are not approved within the period mentioned in subsection (4)(b)(ii), the fact that the regulations cease to have effect does not—

(a) affect anything previously done under or by virtue of the regulations, or

(b) prevent the making of new regulations.

NOTES

Commencement: 26 June 2020.

[9.556]

45 Modified procedure for regulations of the Scottish Ministers

(1) During the period of six months beginning with the day on which this section comes into force, any relevant provision that may be made by the Scottish Ministers by regulations that are subject to the affirmative procedure (see section 29 of the Interpretation and Legislative Reform (Scotland) Act 2010 (asp 10)) may be made by regulations that are subject to the made affirmative procedure.

(2) In subsection (1) "relevant provision" means—

(a) provision under section A50(3) of the Insolvency Act 1986 (power to modify moratorium provisions in relation to certain companies);

(b) provision under paragraph 22 of Schedule ZA1 to the Insolvency Act 1986 (exclusion of registered social landlords from eligibility under Part A1 of that Act).

(3) For the purposes of this section "regulations that are subject to the made affirmative procedure" means regulations that—

(a) must be laid before the Scottish Parliament as soon as reasonably practicable after being made, and

(b) cease to have effect at the end of the period of 40 days beginning with the day on which the regulations are made, unless during that period the regulations are approved by a resolution of the Scottish Parliament.

(4) In calculating the period of 40 days mentioned in subsection (3)(b), no account is to be taken of any time during which the Scottish Parliament is—

(a) dissolved, or

(b) in recess for more than 4 days.

(5) Where by virtue of this section the Scottish Ministers make regulations that are subject to the made affirmative procedure and the regulations cease to have effect because they are not approved within the period mentioned in subsection (3)(b), the fact that the regulations cease to have effect does not—

(a) affect anything previously done under or by virtue of the regulations, or

(b) prevent the making of new regulations.

(6) Section 30 of the Interpretation and Legislative Reform (Scotland) Act 2010 does not apply in relation to regulations that are subject to the made affirmative procedure by virtue of this section.

NOTES

Commencement: 26 June 2020.

46 *(S 46 (Modified procedure for regulations of Northern Ireland departments) is outside the scope of this work.)*

General

[9.557]

47 Power to make consequential provision

(1) The Secretary of State or the Treasury may by regulations make provision that is consequential on this Act.

(2) The power in subsection (1) may, in particular, be used to amend, repeal, revoke or otherwise modify any provision of this Act or any provision made by or under primary legislation passed or made—

(a) before this Act, or

(b) later in the same session of Parliament as this Act.

(3) But the power to amend or repeal any provision made by this Act may not be used after the period of 3 years beginning with the day on which it is passed.

(4) Regulations under this section—

(a) may make different provision for different purposes;

(b) may include transitional or transitory provision or savings.

(5) Regulations under this section are to be made by statutory instrument.

(6) A statutory instrument containing regulations under this section that amend or repeal provision made by primary legislation (whether alone or with other provision) may not be made unless a draft of the instrument has been laid before and approved by a resolution of each House of Parliament.

(7) Any other statutory instrument containing regulations under this section is subject to annulment in pursuance of a resolution of either House of Parliament.

(8) In this section "primary legislation" means—

(a) an Act,

(b) an Act or Measure of Senedd Cymru,

(c) an Act of the Scottish Parliament, or

(d) Northern Ireland legislation.

NOTES

Commencement: 26 June 2020.

Orders: the Co-operative and Community Benefit Societies and Credit Unions (Arrangements, Reconstructions and Administration) (Amendment) and Consequential Amendments Order 2020, SI 2020/744.

[9.558]

48 Extent

(1) An amendment, repeal or revocation made by this Act has the same extent within the United Kingdom as the provision amended, repealed or revoked.

(2) The following provisions extend to England and Wales and Scotland only—

(a) section 3 and Parts 1 and 2 of Schedule 4;

(b) section 10 and Schedule 10;

(c) section 12;

(d) section 15;

(e) sections 20 to 24;

(f) section 41.

(3) The following provisions extend to England and Wales only—

(a) section 44;

(b) Part 3 of Schedule 4.

(4) The following provisions extend to Scotland only—

(a) section 45;

(b) Part 4 of Schedule 4.

(5) The following provisions extend to Northern Ireland only—

(a) section 6 and Schedule 8;

(b) section 11 and Schedule 11;

(c) section 13;

(d) section 19;

(e) sections 28 to 36;

(f) section 42.

(6) Subject to the above, this Act extends to England and Wales, Scotland and Northern Ireland.

NOTES

Commencement: 26 June 2020.

[9.559]

49 Commencement

(1) This Act comes into force on the day after that on which it is passed, subject to subsection (2).

(2) Paragraph 51 of Schedule 3 comes into force on such day as the Secretary of State may by regulations appoint.

(3) Different days may be appointed for different purposes.

(4) The Secretary of State may by regulations make transitional or saving provision in connection with the coming into force of any provision of this Act.

(5) The power to make regulations under subsection (4) includes power to make different provision for different purposes.

(6) Regulations under this section are to be made by statutory instrument.

NOTES

Commencement: 26 June 2020.

Orders: the Co-operative and Community Benefit Societies and Credit Unions (Arrangements, Reconstructions and Administration) (Amendment) and Consequential Amendments Order 2020, SI 2020/744. Article 3 of which brings Sch 3, para 51 to this Act into force on 18 July 2020.

[9.560]

50 Short title

This Act may be cited as the Corporate Insolvency and Governance Act 2020.

NOTES

Commencement: 26 June 2020.

SCHEDULES

SCHEDULE 1
MORATORIUMS IN GREAT BRITAIN: ELIGIBLE COMPANIES

(*Inserts the Insolvency Act 1986, Sch ZA1 at* **[9.470]**.)

SCHEDULE 2
MORATORIUMS IN GREAT BRITAIN: CONTRACTS INVOLVING FINANCIAL SERVICES

(*Inserts the Insolvency Act 1986, Sch ZA2 at* **[9.471]**.)

SCHEDULE 3
MORATORIUMS IN GREAT BRITAIN: FURTHER AMENDMENTS

(*This Schedule contains further amendments to the Insolvency Act 1986 relating to moratoriums in Great Britain. It also contains consequential amendments to various Acts and statutory instruments which, in so far as relevant to this work, have been incorporated at the appropriate place.*)

SCHEDULE 4
MORATORIUMS IN GREAT BRITAIN: TEMPORARY PROVISION

NOTES

Application of this Schedule to LLPs: see the Limited Liability Partnerships (Amendment etc) Regulations 2021, SI 2021/60, reg 6 at **[10.1305]** which provides as follows:

"Schedule 4 to the 2020 Act (moratoriums in Great Britain: temporary provision) applies to limited liability partnerships registered in Great Britain, except where the context otherwise requires, with the following modifications—

(a) references to a company include references to a limited liability partnership;
(b) references to a director of a company include references to a designated member of a limited liability partnership;
(c) such further modifications as the context requires for the purpose of giving effect to that Schedule as applied by these Regulations.".

Section 3

PART 1 "RELEVANT PERIOD" AND POWERS TO TURN OFF TEMPORARY PROVISION

"Relevant period"

[9.561]

1. In this Schedule "relevant period" means the period which—

(a) begins with the day on which this Schedule comes into force, and
(b) ends with [30 September 2021].

Power to turn off particular provisions of Part 2 of this Schedule early

2. (1) The Secretary of State may by regulations made by statutory instrument provide for any provision made by Part 2 of this Schedule to cease to have effect before the end of the relevant period.

(2) The regulations may include transitional provision or savings.

(3) A statutory instrument containing regulations under sub-paragraph (1) is subject to annulment in pursuance of a resolution of either House of Parliament.

Power to turn off provisions of Parts 3 and 4 of this Schedule early etc

3. Rules under section 411 of the Insolvency Act 1986 may provide for any provision made by paragraphs 13 to 51 or 53 to 90 to cease to have effect before the end of the relevant period.

4. Rules under section 411 of the Insolvency Act 1986 may make transitional provision or savings in connection with any provision made by paragraphs 13 to 51 or 53 to 90 ceasing to have effect (whether by virtue of paragraph 3 or 12).

NOTES

Commencement: 26 June 2020.

Para 1: words in square brackets in sub-para (b) substituted by the Corporate Insolvency and Governance Act 2020 (Coronavirus) (Extension of the Relevant Period) Regulations 2021, SI 2021/375, reg 3(3), as from 26 March 2021.

Application of this Schedule to LLPs: see the note following the title of this Schedule *ante*.

Regulations: the Corporate Insolvency and Governance Act 2020 (Coronavirus) (Early Termination of Certain Temporary Provisions) Regulations 2020, SI 2020/1033.

PART 2 MODIFICATIONS TO PRIMARY LEGISLATION

[9.562]

5. . . .

Relaxation of conditions for obtaining moratorium etc

6. (1) For the purposes of obtaining a moratorium under section A3 of the Insolvency Act 1986 during the relevant period—

(a) section A3 of that Act has effect as if subsection (1)(a) were omitted;

(b) . . .

(c) Schedule ZA1 to that Act has effect as if paragraph 2(1)(b) and (2)(b) were omitted.

(2) During the relevant period, only an overseas company may obtain a moratorium under section A4 of the Insolvency Act 1986.

7. In relation to an application for a moratorium made under section A4 or A5 of the Insolvency Act 1986 during the relevant period—

(a) . . .

(b) Schedule ZA1 to that Act has effect as if paragraph 2(1)(b) and (2)(b) were omitted.

8–11. . . .

NOTES

Commencement: 26 June 2020.

Paras 5, 6(1)(b), 7(a) and 8–11 were repealed by the Corporate Insolvency and Governance Act 2020 (Coronavirus) (Early Termination of Certain Temporary Provisions) Regulations 2020, SI 2020/1033, reg 2, as from 1 October 2020, subject to the following savings in reg 3 of those Regulations—

"Regulation 2 does not apply in relation to a moratorium if—

(a) that moratorium has come into force, or

(b) in the case of a moratorium for a company to which either section A4 or A5 of the Insolvency Act 1986 applies, the application for a moratorium under section A4, or, as the case may be, section A5, has been made to the court,

before 1st October 2020.".

Application of this Schedule to LLPs: see the note following the title of this Schedule *ante*.

PART 3 TEMPORARY RULES: ENGLAND AND WALES

Introductory

[9.563]

12. Paragraphs 13 to 51 cease to have effect at the end of the relevant period, subject to paragraph 3.

Definition of "the court"

13. Section A54(1) of the Insolvency Act 1986 has effect as if for the definition of "the court" there were substituted—

""the court", in relation to a company, means a court having jurisdiction to wind up the company;".

Content of documents relating to the obtaining or extending of a moratorium: general

14. A notice or statement under section A6(1), A8(2), A10(1), A11(1) or A13(2) of the Insolvency Act 1986 must state—

(a) the provision under which it is given or made,

(b) the nature of the notice or statement,

(c) the date of the notice or statement, and

(d) the identification details for the company to which it relates.

Authentication of documents relating to obtaining or extending moratorium: general

15. (1) A notice or statement under section A6(1), A10(1), A11(1) or A13(2) of the Insolvency Act 1986 must be authenticated by or on behalf of the person giving the notice or making the statement.

(2) A notice under section A8(2)(a) of the Insolvency Act 1986 must be authenticated by the monitor.

(3) Rule 1.5 of the England and Wales Insolvency Rules applies for the purposes of authentication under this paragraph.

Notice that directors wish to obtain a moratorium

16. A notice under section A6(1)(a) of the Insolvency Act 1986 must state—

(a) the company's address for service, and

(b) the court (and where applicable, the division or district registry of that court) or hearing centre in which the documents are to be filed under section A3 or the application under section A4 or A5 is to be made.

Proposed monitor's statement and consent to act

17. (1) A statement under section A6(1)(b) of the Insolvency Act 1986 must be headed "Proposed monitor's statement and consent to act" and must contain the following—

(a) a certificate that the proposed monitor is qualified to act as an insolvency practitioner in relation to the company,

(b) the proposed monitor's IP number,

(c) the name of the relevant recognised professional body which is the source of the proposed monitor's authorisation to act in relation to the company, and

(d) a statement that the proposed monitor consents to act as monitor in relation to the company.

(2) In this paragraph "IP number" means the number assigned to an office-holder as an insolvency practitioner by the Secretary of State.

Timing of statements for obtaining moratorium

18. Each statement under section A6(1)(b) to (e) of the Insolvency Act 1986 must be made within the period of 5 days ending with the day on which the documents under section A6(1)(a) to (e) are filed with the court (or, if the documents are filed on different days, the last of those days).

Notice by monitor where moratorium comes into force

19. A notice under section A8(2) of the Insolvency Act 1986 must—

(a) state that it is given by the monitor acting in that capacity, and
(b) state the name and contact details of the monitor.

Notice that directors wish to extend a moratorium

20. A notice under section A10(1)(a) or A11(1)(a) of the Insolvency Act 1986 must state—

(a) the company's address for service, and
(b) the court (and where applicable, the division or district registry of that court) or hearing centre in which the notice is to be filed.

Extension under section A10 or A11 of the Insolvency Act 1986: notices and statements

21. A statement by the monitor under section A10(1)(d) or A11(1)(d) of the Insolvency Act 1986 must contain contact details of the monitor.

Timing of statements for extension under section A10 or A11

22. Each statement under section A10(1)(b) to (d) or A11(1)(b) to (e) of the Insolvency Act 1986 must be made within the period of 3 days ending with the day on which the documents under section A10(1)(a) to (d) or A11(1)(a) to (e) are filed with the court (or, if the documents are filed on different days, the last of those days).

Obtaining creditor consent: qualifying decision procedure

23. (1) The following apply, so far as relevant, for the purposes of a decision to consent to a revised end date for a moratorium under section A12 of the Insolvency Act 1986—

(a) Part 15 of the England and Wales Insolvency Rules (decision making), apart from rule 15.8(3)(f) and (g);
(b) Part 16 of the England and Wales Insolvency Rules (proxies), apart from rule 16.7.

(2) In its application by virtue of sub-paragraph (1), Part 15 has effect subject to the modifications set out in paragraphs 24 to 28.

24. Rule 15.11 of the England and Wales Insolvency Rules (notice of decision procedures etc) has effect as if, before the first entry in the table, there were inserted—

"moratorium	decision of pre-moratorium creditors under section A12 of the Act	the pre-moratorium creditors	5 days"

25. Rule 15.28 of the England and Wales Insolvency Rules (creditors' voting rights) has effect as if, before paragraph (1), there were inserted—

"(A1) A pre-moratorium creditor is entitled to vote in a decision procedure under section A12 of the Act only if—

(a) the creditor has delivered to the convener a proof of the debt claimed in accordance with paragraph (3) including any calculation for the purposes of rule 15.31 or 15.32, and
(b) the proof was received by the convener—
  (i) not later than the decision date, or in the case of a meeting, 4pm on the business day before the meeting, or
  (ii) in the case of a meeting, later than the time given in sub-paragraph (i) where the chair is content to accept the proof, and
(c) the proof has been admitted for the purposes of entitlement to vote."

26. Rule 15.31 of the England and Wales Insolvency Rules (calculation of voting rights) has effect as if—

(a) before paragraph (1) there were inserted—

"(A1) In relation to a decision to consent to a revised end date for a moratorium under section A12 of the Act votes are calculated according to the amount of each creditor's claim at the decision date.";

(b) after paragraph (2) there were inserted—

"(2A) But in relation to a decision to consent to a revised end date for a moratorium under section A12 of the Act, a debt of an unliquidated or unascertained amount is to be valued at £1 for the purposes of voting unless the convener or chair or an appointed person decides to put a higher value on it.";

(c) in paragraph (6), after sub-paragraph (b) there were inserted—

"(c) where the decision relates to whether to consent to a revised end date for a moratorium under section A12 of the Act."

27. Rule 15.32 of the England and Wales Insolvency Rules (calculation of voting rights: special cases) has effect as if, before paragraph (1), there were inserted—

"(A1) In relation to a decision to consent to a revised end date for a moratorium under section A12 of the Act, a pre-moratorium creditor under a hire-purchase agreement is entitled to vote in respect of the amount of the debt due and payable by the company at the decision date.

(B1) In calculating the amount of any debt for the purpose of paragraph (A1), no account is to be taken of any amount attributable to the exercise of any right under the relevant agreement so far as the right has become exercisable solely by virtue of a moratorium for the company coming into force."

28. Rule 15.34 of the England and Wales Insolvency Rules (requisite majorities) has effect as if, before paragraph (1), there were inserted—

"(A1) Subject to paragraph (B1), a decision to consent to a revised end date for a moratorium under section A12 of the Act is made if, of those voting—

(a) a majority (in value) of the pre-moratorium creditors who are secured creditors vote in favour of the proposed decision, and

(b) a majority (in value) of the pre-moratorium creditors who are unsecured creditors vote in favour of the proposed decision.

(B1) But a decision to consent to a revised end date for a moratorium under section A12 of the Act is not made if, of those voting either—

(a) a majority of the pre-moratorium creditors who are unconnected secured creditors vote against the proposed end date, or

(b) a majority of the pre-moratorium creditors who are unconnected unsecured creditors vote against the proposed end date.

(C1) For the purposes of paragraph (B1)—

(a) a creditor is unconnected unless the convener or chair decides that the creditor is connected, and

(b) the total value of the unconnected creditors is the total value of those unconnected creditors whose claims have been admitted for voting."

Content of application to the court for extension of moratorium

29. (1) An application by the directors of a company for the extension of a moratorium under section A13 of the Insolvency Act 1986 must state—

(a) that it is made under that section,
(b) the length of the extension sought,
(c) identification details for the company to which the application relates,
(d) the company's address for service, and
(e) the court (and where applicable, the division or district registry of that court) or hearing centre in which the application is made.

(2) The application must be authenticated by or on behalf of the directors.

(3) Rule 1.5 of the England and Wales Insolvency Rules applies for the purposes of authentication under sub-paragraph (2).

Timing of statements accompanying application to court for extension of moratorium

30. A statement under section A13(2) must be made within the period of 3 days ending with the day on which the application under that section is made.

Notices about change in end of moratorium

31. (1) A notice under section A17(1) of the Insolvency Act 1986 must be given within the period of 5 days beginning with the day on which the duty to give the notice arises.

(2) The notice must state—

(a) the name of the company to which it relates, and
(b) the provision by virtue of which the moratorium was extended or came to an end.

32. (1) A notice under section A17(2) or (3) of the Insolvency Act 1986 must be given within the period of 5 days beginning with the day on which the duty to give the notice arises.

(2) The notice must state—

(a) the provision under which it is given,
(b) the nature of the notice,
(c) the date of the notice,
(d) that it is given by the monitor acting in that capacity,
(e) the name and contact details of the monitor, and
(f) the identification details for the company to which it relates.

(3) A notice under section A17(2) or (3) of the Insolvency Act 1986 that is given to the registrar of companies must be authenticated by or on behalf of the monitor.

(4) Rule 1.5 of the England and Wales Insolvency Rules applies for the purposes of authentication under sub-paragraph (3).

33. Where a moratorium comes to an end under section A16 of the Insolvency Act 1986 because the company has entered into a relevant insolvency procedure within the meaning of that section, the notices under section A17(1) and (2) must state—

(a) the date on which the company entered into the relevant insolvency procedure, and
(b) the name and contact details of the supervisor of the voluntary arrangement, the administrator or the liquidator.

34. (1) A notice under section A17(4) of the Insolvency Act 1986 must be given within the period of 3 business days beginning with the day on which the notice under section A38(1) of that Act is filed with the court.

(2) The notice under section A17(4) of that Act must be accompanied by the notice that the monitor has filed with the court under section A38(1) of that Act.

Notification by directors of insolvency proceedings etc

35. (1) A notice under section A24(1) of the Insolvency Act 1986 must be given before the period of 3 days ending with the day on which the step mentioned there is taken.

(2) A notice under section A24(2) of the Insolvency Act 1986 must be given within the period of 3 days beginning with the day on which the duty to give the notice arises.

Notice of termination of moratorium

36. (1) A notice under section A38(1) of the Insolvency Act 1986 must be filed with the court as soon as practicable after the duty in that subsection arises.

(2) The notice must state—

(a) the provision under which it is given,

(b) the nature of the notice,

(c) the date of the notice,

(d) the name and contact details of the monitor,

(e) the identification details for the company to which it relates,

(f) the grounds on which the moratorium is being terminated,

(g) the monitor's reasons for concluding that those grounds are made out,

(h) the date on which the monitor concluded that those grounds were made out, and

(i) the court (and where applicable, the division or district registry of that court) or hearing centre in which the notice is to be filed.

(3) The notice must be authenticated by or on behalf of the monitor.

(4) Rule 1.5 of the England and Wales Insolvency Rules applies for the purposes of authentication under sub-paragraph (3).

Termination of moratorium under section A38(1)(d) of the Insolvency Act 1986

37. For the purposes of deciding whether to bring a moratorium to an end under section A38(1)(d) of the Insolvency Act 1986 the monitor must disregard—

(a) any debts that the monitor has reasonable grounds for thinking are likely to be paid within 5 days of the decision, and

(b) any debts in respect of which the creditor has agreed to defer payment until a time that is later than the decision.

Replacement of monitor or additional monitor: statement and consent to act

38. (1) A statement under section A39(4) of the Insolvency Act 1986 must be headed "Proposed monitor's statement and consent to act" and must contain the following—

(a) a certificate that the proposed monitor is qualified to act as an insolvency practitioner in relation to the company,

(b) the proposed monitor's IP number,

(c) the name of the relevant recognised professional body which is the source of the proposed monitor's authorisation to act in relation to the company, and

(d) a statement that the proposed monitor consents to act as monitor in relation to the company.

(2) The statement must be made within the period of 5 days ending with the day on which it is filed with the court.

(3) In this paragraph "IP number" means the number assigned to an office-holder as an insolvency practitioner by the Secretary of State.

Replacement of monitor or additional monitor: notification

39. (1) A notice under section A39(8) of the Insolvency Act 1986 must state—

(a) the provision under which it is given,

(b) the nature of the notice,

(c) the date of the notice,

(d) the identification details for the company to which it relates,

(e) that it is given by the monitor acting in that capacity, and

(f) the name and contact details of the monitor.

(2) The notice must be authenticated by the monitor.

(3) Rule 1.5 of the England and Wales Insolvency Rules applies for the purposes of authentication under this paragraph.

Challenge to monitor's remuneration

40. (1) An administrator or liquidator of a company may apply to the court on the ground that remuneration charged by the monitor in relation to a prior moratorium for the company under Part A1 of the Insolvency Act 1986 was excessive.

(2) An application under this paragraph may not be made after the end of the period of 2 years beginning with the day after the moratorium ends.

(3) On an application under this paragraph the court may—

(a) dismiss the application,

(b) order the monitor to repay some or all of the remuneration, or

(c) make such other order as it thinks fit.

(4) The costs of an application under this paragraph are, unless the court orders otherwise, to be paid as an expense of the administration or liquidation.

Challenge to directors' actions: qualifying decision procedure

41. Where the court makes an order by virtue of section A44(4)(c) of the Insolvency Act 1986 requiring a decision of a company's creditors, the following provisions of the England and Wales Insolvency Rules apply for the purposes of that decision to the extent set out in the court's order and subject to any modifications set out in the court's order—

(a) Part 15 (decision making);
(b) Part 16 (proxies).

Priority of moratorium debts etc in subsequent winding up

42. (1) Where section 174A of the Insolvency Act 1986 applies, the moratorium debts and pre-moratorium debts mentioned in subsection (2)(b) of that section are payable in the following order of priority—

(a) amounts payable in respect of goods or services supplied during the moratorium under a contract where, but for section 233B(3) or (4) of that Act, the supplier would not have had to make that supply;
(b) wages or salary arising under a contract of employment;
(c) other debts or other liabilities apart from the monitor's remuneration or expenses;
(d) the monitor's remuneration or expenses.

(2) In this paragraph "wages or salary" has the same meaning as in section A18 of the Insolvency Act 1986.

Priority of moratorium debts etc in subsequent administration

43. (1) Where paragraph 64A(1) of Schedule B1 to the Insolvency Act 1986 applies, the moratorium debts and pre-moratorium debts mentioned in paragraph 64A(2) of that Schedule are payable in the following order of priority—

(a) amounts payable in respect of goods or services supplied during the moratorium under a contract where, but for section 233B(3) or (4) of that Act, the supplier would not have had to make that supply;
(b) wages or salary arising under a contract of employment;
(c) other debts or other liabilities apart from the monitor's remuneration or expenses;
(d) the monitor's remuneration or expenses.

(2) In this paragraph "wages or salary" has the same meaning as in section A18 of the Insolvency Act 1986.

Prescribed format of documents

44. Rule 1.4 of the England and Wales Insolvency Rules (requirement for writing and form of documents) applies for the purposes of Part A1 of the Insolvency Act 1986.

45. (1) The following provisions of the England and Wales Insolvency Rules apply, so far as relevant, to any requirement imposed by a provision of this Part of this Schedule—

rule 1.8 (prescribed format of documents), and
rule 1.9(1) (variations from prescribed contents).

(2) In their application by virtue of sub-paragraph (1), a reference in rule 1.8 or 1.9(1) to the requirements of a rule is to be read as a reference to the requirements of the provision of this Part of this Schedule.

Delivery of documents

46. The following provisions of Chapter 9 of Part 1 of the England and Wales Insolvency Rules apply for the purposes of proceedings under Part A1 of the Insolvency Act 1986 as if rule 1.36(1) included a reference to such proceedings—

rule 1.36(2) (delivery to registrar of companies);
rule 1.40 (delivery of documents to authorised recipients);
rule 1.41 (delivery of documents to joint office-holders);
rule 1.42 (postal delivery of documents);
rule 1.43 (delivery by document exchange);
rule 1.44 (personal delivery of documents);
rule 1.45 (electronic delivery of documents).

Applications to court

47. (1) The provisions of the England and Wales Insolvency Rules specified in the Table apply, so far as relevant, for the purposes of proceedings under—

(a) Part A1 of the Insolvency Act 1986;
(b) this Part of this Schedule.

(2) In their application by virtue of sub-paragraph (1), the provisions listed in the Table have effect with—

(a) the modification set out in sub-paragraph (3),
(b) the modifications specified in the Table, and
(c) any other necessary modifications.

(3) The modification is that any reference to Part 1 of the Insolvency Act 1986 includes a reference to Part A1 of that Act and this Part of this Schedule.

(4) This is the Table referred to in sub-paragraphs (1) and (2)—

Insolvency Rules	*Topic*	*Modifications*
Rule 1.35	Standard contents and authentication of applications	
Rules 12.1 and 12.2	Court rules and practice to apply etc	
Rule 12.3 and Schedule 6	Commencement of proceedings	
Rules 12.7 to 12.11 and 12.13	Making applications to court: general	Rule 12.9 has effect as if, in relation to a regulated company (within the meaning of section A49 of the Insolvency Act 1986), it also required the application to be served

Insolvency Rules	*Topic*	*Modifications*
		on the appropriate regulator (within the meaning of that section).
Rules 12.27 to 12.29	Obtaining information and evidence	Rule 12.29(3) has effect as if it included a reference to the monitor in relation to a moratorium.
Rules 12.30, 12.31, 12.33 and 12.35 to 12.38	Transfer of proceedings	(a) Rule 12.36(2) has effect as if the list of office-holders included the monitor in relation to a moratorium.
		(b) Rule 12.37(2) and (3) have effect as if the list of provisions included section A39 of the Insolvency Act 1986.
Rules 12.39 and 12.40	The court file	
Rules 12.41, 12.42(5), 12.47, 12.48 and 12.50	Costs	Rule 12.48(2) has effect as if it required the applicant to serve a sealed copy of the application on the monitor and the company to which the moratorium relates.
Rule 12.51	Enforcement of court orders	
Rules 12.58, 12.59 and 12.61 and Schedule 10	Appeals	
Rules 12.63 to 12.65	Court orders, formal defects and shorthand writers	
Schedule 4, paragraphs 1, 4, 5 and 6		These paragraphs of Schedule 4 apply only for the purposes of the rules applied by this Table.

Identification details for a company

48. (1) Where a provision of this Part of this Schedule requires a document to contain identification details for a company that is registered under the Companies Act 2006 in England and Wales, the following information must be given—

(a) the company's registered name;

(b) its registered number;

(2) Where a provision of this Part of this Schedule requires a document to contain identification details for a company that has registered particulars under section 1046(1) of the Companies Act 2006 (registered overseas companies), the following information must be given—

(a) the name registered by the company under section 1047 of that Act,

(b) the number under which it is registered, and

(c) the country or territory in which it is incorporated.

(3) Where a provision of this Part of this Schedule requires a document to contain identification details for an unregistered company that does not come within sub-paragraph (2) the following information must be given—

(a) the company's name, and

(b) the postal address of any principal place of business.

Contact details of a monitor or other office-holder

49. Where a provision of this Part of this Schedule requires a document to contain contact details of a monitor or other office-holder, the following information must be given—

(a) a postal address for the monitor or office-holder, and

(b) either an email address, or a telephone number, through which the monitor may be contacted.

"The England and Wales Insolvency Rules"

50. In this Part of this Schedule "the England and Wales Insolvency Rules" means the Insolvency (England and Wales) Rules 2016.

Interpretation: general

51. Expressions used in this Part of this Schedule are to be construed as if this Part of this Schedule were contained in Part A1 of the Insolvency Act 1986.

NOTES

Commencement: 26 June 2020.

Application of this Schedule to LLPs: see the note following the title of this Schedule *ante*.

PART 4 TEMPORARY RULES: SCOTLAND

Introductory

[9.564]

52. Paragraphs 53 to 90 cease to have effect at the end of the relevant period, subject to paragraph 3.

Definition of "the court"

53. Section A54(1) of the Insolvency Act 1986 has effect as if for the definition of "the court" there were substituted—

""the court", in relation to a company, means a court having jurisdiction to wind up the company;".

Content of documents relating to the obtaining or extending of a moratorium: general

54. A notice or statement under section A6(1), A8(2), A10(1), A11(1) or A13(2) of the Insolvency Act 1986 must state—

(a) the provision under which it is given or made,
(b) the nature of the notice or statement,
(c) the date of the notice or statement, and
(d) the identification details for the company to which it relates.

Authentication of documents relating to obtaining or extending moratorium: general

55. (1) A notice or statement under section A6(1), A10(1), A11(1) or A13(2) of the Insolvency Act 1986 must be authenticated by or on behalf of the person giving the notice or making the statement.

(2) A notice under section A8(2)(a) of the Insolvency Act 1986 must be authenticated by the monitor.

(3) Rule 1.6 of the Scottish Insolvency Rules applies for the purposes of authentication under this paragraph.

Notice that directors wish to obtain a moratorium

56. A notice under section A6(1)(a) of the Insolvency Act 1986 must state—

(a) the company's address for service, and
(b) the court in which the documents are to be lodged under section A3 or the application under section A4 or A5 is to be made.

Proposed monitor's statement and consent to act

57. (1) A statement under section A6(1)(b) of the Insolvency Act 1986 must be headed "Proposed monitor's statement and consent to act" and must contain the following—

(a) a certificate that the proposed monitor is qualified to act as an insolvency practitioner in relation to the company,
(b) the proposed monitor's IP number,
(c) the name of the relevant recognised professional body which is the source of the proposed monitor's authorisation to act in relation to the company, and
(d) a statement that the proposed monitor consents to act as monitor in relation to the company.

(2) In this paragraph "IP number" means the number assigned to an office-holder as an insolvency practitioner by the Secretary of State.

Timing of statements for obtaining moratorium

58. Each statement under section A6(1)(b) to (e) of the Insolvency Act 1986 must be made within the period of 5 days ending with the day on which the documents under section A6(1)(a) to (e) are lodged in the court (or, if the documents are lodged on different days, the last of those days).

Notice by monitor where moratorium comes into force

59. A notice under section A8(2) of the Insolvency Act 1986 must—

(a) state that it is given by the monitor acting in that capacity, and
(b) state the name and contact details of the monitor.

Notice that directors wish to extend a moratorium

60. A notice under section A10(1)(a) or A11(1)(a) of the Insolvency Act 1986 must state—

(a) the company's address for service,
(b) the court in which the notice is to be lodged.

Extension under section A10 or A11 of the Insolvency Act 1986: notices and statements

61. A statement by the monitor under section A10(1)(d) or A11(1)(d) of the Insolvency Act 1986 must contain contact details of the monitor.

Timing of statements for extension under section A10 or A11

62. Each statement under section A10(1)(b) to (d) or A11(1)(b) to (e) of the Insolvency Act 1986 must be made within the period of 3 days ending with the day on which the documents under section A10(1)(a) to (d) or A11(1)(a) to (e) are lodged in the court (or, if the documents are lodged on different days, the last of those days).

Obtaining creditor consent: qualifying decision procedure

63. (1) The following apply, so far as relevant, for the purposes of a decision to consent to a revised end date for a moratorium under section A12 of the Insolvency Act 1986—

(a) Part 5 of the Scottish Insolvency Rules (decision making), apart from rule 5.8(3)(f) and (g);
(b) Part 6 of the Scottish Insolvency Rules (proxies), apart from rule 6.7.

(2) In its application by virtue of sub-paragraph (1), Part 5 has effect subject to the modifications set out in paragraphs 64 to 68.

64. Rule 5.11 of the Scottish Insolvency Rules (notice of decision procedures etc) has effect as if, before the first entry in the table, there were inserted—

"moratorium	decision of pre-moratorium creditors under section A12 of the Act	the pre-moratorium creditors	5 days"

65. Rule 5.26 of the Scottish Insolvency Rules (creditors' voting rights) has effect as if, before paragraph (1), there were inserted—

"(A1) A pre-moratorium creditor is entitled to vote in a decision procedure under section A12 of the Act only if—

(a) the creditor has delivered to the convener a statement of claim and documentary evidence of debt, including any calculation for the purposes of rule 5.28 or 5.29,

(b) the statement of claim and documentary evidence of debt were received by the convener not later than the decision date, or in the case of a meeting, at or before the meeting, and

(c) the statement of claim and documentary evidence of debt has been admitted for the purposes of entitlement to vote."

66. Rule 5.28 of the Scottish Insolvency Rules (calculation of voting rights) has effect as if—

(a) before paragraph (1) there were inserted—

"(A1) In relation to a decision to consent to a revised end date for a moratorium under section A12 of the Act votes are calculated according to the amount of each creditor's claim at the decision date.";

(b) after paragraph (2) there were inserted—

"(2A) But in relation to a decision to consent to a revised end date for a moratorium under section A12 of the Act, a debt of an unliquidated or unascertained amount is to be valued at £1 for the purposes of voting unless the convener or chair or an appointed person decides to put a higher value on it.";

(c) in paragraph (6), after sub-paragraph (b) there were inserted—

"(c) where the decision relates to whether to consent to a revised end date for a moratorium under section A12 of the Act."

67. Rule 5.29 of the Scottish Insolvency Rules (calculation of voting rights: hire-purchase agreements) has effect as if, before paragraph (1), there were inserted—

"(A1) In relation to a decision to consent to a revised end date for a moratorium under section A12 of the Act, a pre-moratorium creditor under a hire-purchase agreement is entitled to vote in respect of the amount of the debt due and payable by the company at the decision date.

(B1) In calculating the amount of any debt for the purpose of paragraph (A1), no account is to be taken of any amount attributable to the exercise of any right under the relevant agreement so far as the right has become exercisable solely by virtue of a moratorium for the company coming into force."

68. Rule 5.31 of the Scottish Insolvency Rules (requisite majorities) has effect as if, before paragraph (1), there were inserted—

"(A1) Subject to paragraph (B1), a decision to consent to a revised end date for a moratorium under section A12 of the Act is made if, of those voting—

(a) a majority (in value) of the pre-moratorium creditors who are secured creditors vote in favour of the proposed decision, and

(b) a majority (in value) of the pre-moratorium creditors who are unsecured creditors vote in favour of the proposed decision.

(B1) But a decision to consent to a revised end date for a moratorium under section A12 of the Act is not made if, of those voting either—

(a) a majority of the pre-moratorium creditors who are unconnected secured creditors vote against the proposed end date, or

(b) a majority of the pre-moratorium creditors who are unconnected unsecured creditors vote against the proposed end date.

(C1) For the purposes of paragraph (B1)—

(a) a creditor is unconnected unless the convener or chair decides that the creditor is connected, and

(b) the total value of the unconnected creditors is the total value of those unconnected creditors whose claims have been admitted for voting."

Content of application to the court for extension of moratorium

69. (1) An application by the directors of a company for the extension of a moratorium under section A13 of the Insolvency Act 1986 must state—

(a) that it is made under that section,
(b) the length of the extension sought,
(c) identification details for the company to which the application relates,
(d) the company's address for service, and
(e) the court in which the application is made.

(2) The application must be authenticated by or on behalf of the directors.

(3) Rule 1.6 of the Scottish Insolvency Rules applies for the purposes of authentication under sub-paragraph (2).

Timing of statements accompanying application to court for extension of moratorium

70. A statement under section A13(2) must be made within the period of 3 days ending with the day on which the application under that section is made.

Notices about change in end of moratorium

71. (1) A notice under section A17(1) of the Insolvency Act 1986 must be given within the period of 5 days beginning with the day on which the duty to give the notice arises.

(2) The notice must state—

(a) the name of the company to which it relates, and
(b) the provision by virtue of which the moratorium was extended or came to an end.

72. (1) A notice under section A17(2) or (3) of the Insolvency Act 1986 must be given within the period of 5 days beginning with the day on which the duty to give the notice arises.

(2) The notice must state—

(a) the provision under which it is given,
(b) the nature of the notice,
(c) the date of the notice,
(d) that it is given by the monitor acting in that capacity,
(e) the name and contact details of the monitor, and
(f) the identification details for the company to which it relates.

(3) A notice under section A17(2) or (3) of the Insolvency Act 1986 that is given to the registrar of companies must be authenticated by or on behalf of the monitor.

(4) Rule 1.6 of the Scottish Insolvency Rules applies for the purposes of authentication under sub-paragraph (3).

73. Where a moratorium comes to an end under section A16 of the Insolvency Act 1986 because the company has entered into a relevant insolvency procedure within the meaning of that section, the notices under section A17(1) and (2) must state—

(a) the date on which the company entered into the relevant insolvency procedure, and
(b) the name and contact details of the supervisor of the voluntary arrangement, the administrator or the liquidator.

74. (1) A notice under section A17(4) of the Insolvency Act 1986 must be given within the period of 3 business days beginning with the day on which the notice under section A38(1) is lodged in the court.

(2) The notice under section A17(4) of that Act must be accompanied by the notice that the monitor has lodged in the court under section A38(1) of that Act.

Notification by directors of insolvency proceedings etc

75. (1) A notice under section A24(1) of the Insolvency Act 1986 must be given before the period of 3 days ending with the day on which the step mentioned there is taken.

(2) A notice under section A24(2) of the Insolvency Act 1986 must be given within the period of 3 days beginning with the day on which the duty to give the notice arises.

Notice of termination of moratorium

76. (1) A notice under section A38(1) of the Insolvency Act 1986 must be lodged in the court as soon as practicable after the duty in that subsection arises.

(2) The notice must state—

(a) the provision under which it is given,
(b) the nature of the notice,
(c) the date of the notice,
(d) the name and contact details of the monitor,
(e) the identification details for the company to which it relates,
(f) the grounds on which the moratorium is being terminated,
(g) the monitor's reasons for concluding that those grounds are made out,
(h) the date on which the monitor concluded that those grounds were made out, and
(i) the court in which the notice is to be lodged.

(3) The notice must be authenticated by or on behalf of the monitor.

(4) Rule 1.6 of the Scottish Insolvency Rules applies for the purposes of authentication under sub-paragraph (3).

Termination of moratorium under section A38(1)(d) of the Insolvency Act 1986

77. For the purposes of deciding whether to bring a moratorium to an end under section A38(1)(d) of the Insolvency Act 1986 the monitor must disregard—

(a) any debts that the monitor has reasonable grounds for thinking are likely to be paid within 5 days of the decision, and
(b) any debts in respect of which the creditor has agreed to defer payment until a time that is later than the decision.

Replacement of monitor or additional monitor: statement and consent to act

78. (1) A statement under section A39(4) of the Insolvency Act 1986 must be headed "Proposed monitor's statement and consent to act" and must contain the following—

(a) a certificate that the proposed monitor is qualified to act as an insolvency practitioner in relation to the company,
(b) the proposed monitor's IP number,
(c) the name of the relevant recognised professional body which is the source of the proposed monitor's authorisation to act in relation to the company, and
(d) a statement that the proposed monitor consents to act as monitor in relation to the company.

(2) The statement must be made within the period of 5 days ending with the day on which it is lodged in the court.

(3) In this paragraph "IP number" means the number assigned to an office-holder as an insolvency practitioner by the Secretary of State.

Replacement of monitor or additional monitor: notification

79. (1) A notice under section A39(8) of the Insolvency Act 1986 must state—

(a) the provision under which it is given,
(b) the nature of the notice,
(c) the date of the notice,
(d) the identification details for the company to which it relates,
(e) that it is given by the monitor acting in that capacity, and
(f) the name and contact details of the monitor.

(2) The notice must be authenticated by the monitor.

(3) Rule 1.6 of the Scottish Insolvency Rules applies for the purposes of authentication under sub-paragraph (2).

Challenge to monitor's remuneration

80. (1) An administrator or liquidator of a company may apply to the court on the ground that remuneration charged by the monitor in relation to a prior moratorium for the company under Part A1 of the Insolvency Act 1986 was excessive.

(2) An application under this paragraph may not be made after the end of the period of 2 years beginning with the day after the moratorium ends.

(3) On an application under this paragraph the court may—

- (a) dismiss the application,
- (b) order the monitor to repay some or all of the remuneration, or
- (c) make such other order as it thinks fit.

(4) The expenses of an application under this paragraph are, unless the court orders otherwise, to be paid as an expense of the administration or liquidation.

Challenge to directors' actions: qualifying decision procedure

81. Where the court makes an order by virtue of section A44(4)(c) of the Insolvency Act 1986 requiring a decision of a company's creditors, the following provisions of the Scottish Insolvency Rules apply for the purposes of that decision to the extent set out in the court's order and subject to any modifications set out in the court's order—

- (a) Part 5 (decision making);
- (b) Part 6 (proxies).

Priority of moratorium debts etc in subsequent winding up

82. (1) Where section 174A of the Insolvency Act 1986 applies, the moratorium debts and pre-moratorium debts mentioned in subsection (2)(b) of that section are payable in the following order of priority—

- (a) amounts payable in respect of goods or services supplied during the moratorium under a contract where, but for section 233B(3) or (4) of that Act, the supplier would not have had to make that supply;
- (b) wages or salary arising under a contract of employment;
- (c) other debts or other liabilities apart from the monitor's remuneration or expenses;
- (d) the monitor's remuneration or expenses.

(2) In this paragraph "wages or salary" has the same meaning as in section A18 of the Insolvency Act 1986.

Priority of moratorium debts etc in subsequent administration

83. (1) Where paragraph 64A(1) of Schedule B1 to the Insolvency Act 1986 applies, the moratorium debts and pre-moratorium debts mentioned in paragraph 64A(2) of that Schedule are payable in the following order of priority—

- (a) amounts payable in respect of goods or services supplied during the moratorium under a contract where, but for section 233B(3) or (4) of that Act, the supplier would not have had to make that supply;
- (b) wages or salary arising under a contract of employment;
- (c) other debts or other liabilities apart from the monitor's remuneration or expenses;
- (d) the monitor's remuneration or expenses.

(2) In this paragraph "wages or salary" has the same meaning as in section A18 of the Insolvency Act 1986.

Prescribed format of documents

84. Rule 1.5 of the Scottish Insolvency Rules (requirement for writing and form of documents) applies for the purposes of Part A1 of the Insolvency Act 1986.

85. (1) The following provisions of the Scottish Insolvency Rules apply, so far as relevant, to any requirement imposed by a provision of this Part of this Schedule—

rule 1.9 (prescribed format of documents), and
rule 1.10 (variations from prescribed contents).

(2) In their application by virtue of sub-paragraph (1), a reference in rule 1.9 or 1.10 to the requirements of a rule is to be read as a reference to the requirements of the provision of this Part of this Schedule.

Delivery of documents

86. The following provisions of Chapter 9 of Part 1 of the Scottish Insolvency Rules apply for the purposes of proceedings under Part A1 of the Insolvency Act 1986 as if rule 1.32(1) included a reference to such proceedings—

rule 1.32(2) to (3) (delivery to registrar of companies);
rule 1.36 (delivery of documents to authorised recipients);
rule 1.37 (delivery of documents to joint office-holders);
rule 1.38 (postal delivery of documents);
rule 1.39 (delivery by document exchange);
rule 1.40 (personal delivery of documents);
rule 1.41 (electronic delivery of documents).

Identification details for a company

87. (1) Where a provision of this Part of this Schedule requires a document to contain identification details for a company that is registered under the Companies Act 2006 in Scotland, the following information must be given—

- (a) the company's registered name;
- (b) its registered number;

(2) Where a provision of this Part of this Schedule requires a document to contain identification details for a company that has registered particulars under section 1046(1) of the Companies Act 2006 (registered overseas companies), the following information must be given—

- (a) the name registered by the company under section 1047 of that Act,
- (b) the number under which it is registered, and

(c) the country or territory in which it is incorporated.

(3) Where a provision of this Part of this Schedule requires a document to contain identification details for an unregistered company that does not come within sub-paragraph (2) the following information must be given—

(a) the company's name, and

(b) the postal address of any principal place of business.

Contact details of a monitor or other office-holder

88. Where a provision of this Part of this Schedule requires a document to contain contact details of a monitor or other office-holder, the following information must be given—

(a) a postal address for the monitor or office-holder, and

(b) either an email address, or a telephone number, through which the monitor may be contacted.

"The Scottish Insolvency Rules"

89. In this Part of this Schedule "the Scottish Insolvency Rules" means the Insolvency (Scotland) (Company Voluntary Arrangements and Administration) Rules 2018 (SI 2018/1082).

Interpretation: general

90. Expressions used in this Part of this Schedule are to be construed as if this Part of this Schedule were contained in Part A1 of the Insolvency Act 1986.

NOTES

Commencement: 26 June 2020.

Application of this Schedule to LLPs: see the note following the title of this Schedule *ante*.

PART 5 ENTITIES OTHER THAN COMPANIES

[9.565]

91. Regulations under section 14(1) of the Limited Liability Partnership Act 2000 may make provision applying or incorporating provision made by or under this Schedule, with such modifications as appear appropriate, in relation to a limited liability partnership registered in Great Britain.

92. An order or regulations under section 118(1)(a), (3B) or (3C) of the Co-operative and Community Benefit Societies Act 2014 may provide for provision made by or under this Schedule to apply (with or without modifications) in relation to registered societies (or to registered societies of the kind mentioned there).

NOTES

Commencement: 26 June 2020.

Application of this Schedule to LLPs: see the note following the title of this Schedule *ante*.

Regulations: the Co-operative and Community Benefit Societies and Credit Unions (Arrangements, Reconstructions and Administration) (Amendment) and Consequential Amendments Order 2020, SI 2020/744; the Limited Liability Partnerships (Amendment etc) Regulations 2021, SI 2021/60 at **[10.1303]**.

SCHEDULES 5–8

(*Schedules 5–8 concern moratoriums in Northern Ireland and are outside the scope of this work.*)

SCHEDULE 9
ARRANGEMENTS AND RECONSTRUCTIONS FOR COMPANIES IN FINANCIAL DIFFICULTY

(*Sch 9, Pt 1 inserts the Companies Act 2006, Part 26A (ss 901A–901L) at* **[1.1042]** *et seq. Sch 9, Pt 2 contains consequential amendments to various Acts and statutory instruments which, in so far as relevant to this work, have been incorporated at the appropriate place.*)

[SCHEDULE 10
RESTRICTION ON WINDING-UP PETITIONS: GREAT BRITAIN

Section 10

Restriction on winding-up petitions

[9.566]

1. (1) During the relevant period a creditor may not present a petition for the winding up of a company under section 124 of the 1986 Act on the ground specified—

(a) in the case of a registered company, in section 122(1)(f) of that Act, or

(b) in the case of an unregistered company, in section 221(5)(b) of that Act,

unless conditions A to D are met (subject to sub-paragraphs (9) to (11)).

(2) Condition A is that the creditor is owed a debt by the company—

(a) whose amount is liquidated,

(b) which has fallen due for payment, and

(c) which is not an excluded debt.

(3) Condition B is that the creditor has delivered written notice to the company in accordance with sub-paragraphs (4) to (6).

(4) Notice under sub-paragraph (3) must contain the following—

(a) identification details for the company,

(b) the name and address of the creditor,

(c) the amount of the debt and the way in which it arises,

(d) the date of the notice,

(e) a statement that the creditor is seeking the company's proposals for the payment of the debt, and

(f) a statement that if no proposal to the creditor's satisfaction is made within the period of 21 days beginning with the date on which the notice is delivered, the creditor intends to present a petition to the court for the winding-up of the company.

(5) Notice under sub-paragraph (3) must be delivered—

(a) to the company's registered office, or

(b) in accordance with sub-paragraph (6) if—

(i) for any reason it is not practicable to deliver the notice to the company's registered office,

(ii) the company has no registered office, or

(iii) the company is an unregistered company.

(6) Where this sub-paragraph applies the notice may be delivered to—

(a) the company's last known principal place of business, or

(b) the secretary, or a director, manager or (in relation to an unregistered company) principal officer of the company.

(7) Condition C is that at end of the period of 21 days beginning with the day on which condition B was met the company has not made a proposal for the payment of the debt that is to the creditor's satisfaction.

(8) Condition D is that—

(a) where the petition is presented by one creditor, the sum of the debts (or the debt, if there is only one) owed by the company to that creditor in respect of which conditions A to C are met is £10,000 or more;

(b) where the petition is presented by more than one creditor, the sum of the debts owed by the company to the creditors in respect of which conditions A to C are met is £10,000 or more.

(9) A creditor may at any time apply to the court for an order that, in respect of a specified debt—

(a) conditions B and C shall not apply, or

(b) condition C shall apply as if the reference to the period of 21 days were to such shorter period as the court may direct.

(10) Where an order is made under sub-paragraph (9)(a), the references in sub-paragraph (8) to conditions A to C are to be read as references to condition A.

(11) If the court makes an order under sub-paragraph (9)(b) it may—

(a) give such directions as to delivery of the written notice referred to in condition B as it thinks fit, or

(b) direct that sub-paragraphs (4) to (6) shall apply in respect of the delivery of that notice subject to such modifications it thinks fit.

Modification of Insolvency Rules and Rules of Court

2. (1) This paragraph applies in relation to a petition which is presented in England and Wales by a creditor under section 124 of the 1986 Act during the relevant period.

(2) Rule 7.5(1) of the Insolvency Rules has effect as if it also required the petition to contain a statement—

(a) that the requirements in paragraph 1 of this Schedule are met, and

(b) that no proposals for the payment of the debt have been made, or a summary of the reasons why the proposals are not to the creditor's satisfaction (as the case may be).

3. (1) This paragraph applies in relation to a petition which is presented in Scotland by a creditor under section 124 of the 1986 Act during the relevant period.

(2) Rules of Court in Scotland have effect as if they required the petition to contain an averment—

(a) that the requirements in paragraph 1 of this Schedule are met, and

(b) that no proposals for the payment of the debt have been made, or a summary of the reasons why the proposals are not to the creditor's satisfaction (as the case may be).

Interpretation

4. (1) In this Schedule "relevant period" means the period which—

(a) begins with 1 October 2021, and

(b) ends with 31 March 2022.

(2) For the purposes of this Schedule, references to a petition presented by a creditor—

(a) do not include a petition presented by one or more creditors together with one or more other persons, but

(b) subject to that, do include a petition presented by more than one creditor, in which case the conditions specified in paragraph 1(2) to (7) must be met in relation to each creditor presenting the petition.

(3) For the purposes of this Schedule—

"the 1986 Act" means the Insolvency Act 1986;

"coronavirus" means severe acute respiratory syndrome coronavirus 2 (SARS-Cov-2);

"excluded debt" means a debt in respect of rent, or any sum or other payment that a tenant is liable to pay, under—

(a) in England and Wales, a relevant business tenancy; or

(b) in Scotland, a lease as defined in section 7(1) of the Law Reform (Miscellaneous Provisions) (Scotland) Act 1985,

and which is unpaid by reason of a financial effect of coronavirus;

"Insolvency Rules" means the Insolvency (England and Wales) Rules 2016 (SI 2016/1024);

"registered company" means a company registered under the Companies Act 2006 in England and Wales or Scotland;

"relevant business tenancy" means—

(a) a tenancy to which Part 2 of the Landlord and Tenant Act 1954 applies, or

(b) a tenancy to which that Part of that Act would apply if any relevant occupier were the tenant;

"relevant occupier" in relation to a tenancy, means a person, other than the tenant, who lawfully occupies premises which are, or form part of, the property comprised in the tenancy; and

"unregistered company" has the meaning given in Part 5 of the 1986 Act.

General

5. (1) The provisions of this Schedule, so far as relating to registered companies, have effect as if they were included in Part 4 of the 1986 Act.

(2) Sub-paragraph (1) does not apply in relation to paragraphs 2 and 3 (modification of insolvency rules).]

NOTES

This Schedule was substituted by the Corporate Insolvency and Governance Act 2020 (Coronavirus) (Amendment of Schedule 10) (No 2) Regulations 2021, SI 2021/1091, reg 3, as from 1 October 2021. See para 4 above which defines the "relevant period" for the purposes of this Schedule.

SCHEDULE 11

(Sch 11 concerns winding-up petitions in Northern Ireland and is outside the scope of this work.)

SCHEDULE 12
PROTECTION OF SUPPLIES OF GOODS AND SERVICES: GREAT BRITAIN

(Sch 12, Pt 1 inserts the Insolvency Act 1986, Sch 4ZZA at **[9.481]**. *Sch 12, Pt 2 contains consequential amendments which, in so far as relevant to this work, have been incorporated at the appropriate place.)*

SCHEDULE 13

(Sch 13 (Protection of Supplies of Goods and Services: Northern Ireland) is outside the scope of this work.)

SCHEDULE 14
MEETINGS OF COMPANIES AND OTHER BODIES

Section 37

Meaning of "qualifying body"

[9.567]

1. In this Schedule "qualifying body" means—
- (a) a registered society within the meaning of the Co-operative and Community Benefit Societies Act (Northern Ireland) 1969 (c 24 (NI)),
- (b) a credit union within the meaning of the Credit Unions (Northern Ireland) Order 1985 (SI 1985/1205 (NI 12)),
- (c) a building society within the meaning of the Building Societies Act 1986,
- (d) a society that is registered within the meaning of the Friendly Societies Act 1974 or incorporated under the Friendly Societies Act 1992,
- (e) a registered branch within the meaning of the Friendly Societies Act 1992,
- (f) a Scottish charitable incorporated organisation within the meaning of Chapter 7 of Part 1 of the Charities and Trustee Investment (Scotland) Act 2005 (asp 10),
- (g) a company within the meaning of section 1(1) of the Companies Act 2006,
- (h) a charitable incorporated organisation within the meaning of Part 11 of the Charities Act 2011, and
- (i) a registered society within the meaning of the Co-operative and Community Benefit Societies Act 2014.

Meaning of "relevant period"

2. (1) In this Schedule the "relevant period" means the period which—
- (a) begins with 26 March 2020, and
- (b) ends with [30 March 2021].

(2) The appropriate national authority may by regulations substitute for the date for the time being specified in sub-paragraph (1)(b)—
- (a) an earlier date, or
- (b) a later date that is not more than three months after the date for the time being so specified and is not later than 5 April 2021.

(3) Regulations under sub-paragraph (2) may make consequential or transitional provision or savings.

(4) In sub-paragraph (2) "the appropriate national authority" means—
- (a) in relation to a qualifying body within paragraph 1(c), (d), (e), (g), (h), or (i), the Secretary of State,
- (b) in relation to a qualifying body within paragraph 1(f), the Scottish Ministers, and
- (c) in relation to a qualifying body within paragraph 1(a) or (b), the Department for the Economy in Northern Ireland.

Meetings of qualifying bodies held during the relevant period

3. (1) This paragraph applies to a meeting within sub-paragraph (2) that is held during the relevant period.

(2) A meeting is within this sub-paragraph if it is—
- (a) a general meeting of a qualifying body,
- (b) a meeting of any class of members of a qualifying body, or
- (c) a meeting of delegates appointed by members of a qualifying body.

(3) The meeting need not be held at any particular place.

(4) The meeting may be held, and any votes may be permitted to be cast, by electronic means or any other means.

(5) The meeting may be held without any number of those participating in the meeting being together at the same place.

(6) A member of the qualifying body does not have a right—

(a) to attend the meeting in person,

(b) to participate in the meeting other than by voting, or

(c) to vote by particular means.

(7) The provisions of any enactment relating to meetings within sub-paragraph (2) have effect subject to this paragraph.

(8) The provisions of the constitution or rules of the qualifying body have effect subject to this paragraph.

Meetings of qualifying bodies held during the relevant period: power to make further provision

4. (1) The appropriate national authority may by regulations make provision for the purposes of, or in connection with, paragraph 3.

(2) The appropriate national authority may by regulations make provision about the means by which, the form in which, and the period within which, any notice or other document relating to a meeting to which paragraph 3 applies or is expected to apply may be given or made available.

(3) Regulations under this paragraph may—

(a) disapply or modify provisions of an enactment relating to meetings within paragraph 3(2);

(b) disapply or modify provisions of the constitution or rules of a qualifying body;

(c) make different provision for different purposes;

(d) make consequential, incidental or supplementary provision (including provision disapplying or modifying a provision of an enactment);

(e) make transitional provision or savings.

(4) In this paragraph "the appropriate national authority" means—

(a) in relation to qualifying bodies within paragraph 1(g) or (h), the Secretary of State,

(b) in relation to qualifying bodies within paragraph 1(c), (d), (e) or (i), the Treasury,

(c) in relation to qualifying bodies within paragraph 1(f), the Scottish Ministers, and

(d) in relation to qualifying bodies within paragraph 1(a) or (b), the Department for the Economy in Northern Ireland.

Extension of period for qualifying body to hold annual general meeting

5. (1) This paragraph applies where by reason of any provision a qualifying body is or was under a duty to hold a general meeting as its annual general meeting during a period ("the due period") that ends during the relevant period.

(2) The provision is to be read as if it imposes (and had always imposed) a duty on the qualifying body to hold a general meeting as its annual general meeting during the period that begins with the due period and ends with the relevant period (but this is subject to regulations under paragraph 6).

(3) If by reason of regulations made under paragraph 2 the relevant period is a period that ends after 30 September 2020 this paragraph has effect as if the relevant period were a period that ends with 30 September 2020.

(4) In this paragraph a reference to "any provision" is a reference to any provision of an enactment or of the constitution or rules of the qualifying body.

(5) In the application of this paragraph in relation to a public company, the references to a duty to hold a general meeting as its annual general meeting are to be read as including a reference to a duty to hold an accounts meeting.

Power to extend period for qualifying body to hold annual general meeting

6. (1) The appropriate national authority may by regulations provide for any provision that would (but for the regulations) have the effect mentioned in sub-paragraph (2) to be read as if instead it had (and always had had) the effect mentioned in sub-paragraph (3).

(2) The effect is that of imposing on a qualifying body a duty to hold a general meeting as its annual general meeting during a period ("the overlapping period") that overlaps to any extent with the relevant period.

(3) The effect is that of imposing on the qualifying body a duty to hold a general meeting as its annual general meeting during a period that—

(a) begins with the overlapping period, and

(b) ends with such period immediately following the end of the overlapping period as is specified in the regulations.

(4) A period specified in regulations for the purposes of sub-paragraph (3)(b) must not exceed 8 months.

(5) Regulations under this paragraph may—

(a) make different provision for different purposes;

(b) make consequential, incidental or supplementary provision (including provision disapplying or modifying a provision of an enactment);

(c) make transitional provision or savings.

(6) In sub-paragraph (1) the reference to "any provision" is a reference to any provision of an enactment or of the constitution or rules of a qualifying body.

(7) In this paragraph "the appropriate national authority" has the same meaning as in paragraph 4.

(8) In the application of this paragraph in relation to a public company, the references to a duty to hold a general meeting as its annual general meeting are to be read as including a reference to a duty to hold an accounts meeting.

Regulations made by the Secretary of State or the Treasury

7. (1) Regulations made by the Secretary of State or the Treasury under this Schedule are to be made by statutory instrument.

(2) A statutory instrument containing regulations made by the Secretary of State under paragraph 2(2)(a) of this Schedule is subject to annulment in pursuance of a resolution of either House of Parliament.

(3) A statutory instrument containing regulations made by the Secretary of State under paragraph 2(2)(b) of this Schedule or containing regulations made by the Secretary of State or the Treasury under paragraph 4 or 6 of this Schedule must be laid before Parliament as soon as reasonably practicable after being made.

(4) Sub-paragraph (3) does not apply if a draft of the statutory instrument has been laid before and approved by a resolution of each House of Parliament.

(5) Regulations contained in a statutory instrument laid before Parliament by virtue of sub-paragraph (3) cease to have effect at the end of the period of 40 days beginning with the day on which the instrument is made, unless during that period the instrument is approved by a resolution of each House of Parliament.

(6) In calculating the period of 40 days, no account is to be taken of any time during which—

(a) Parliament is dissolved or prorogued, or

(b) both Houses of Parliament are adjourned for more than 4 days.

(7) Where regulations cease to have effect as a result of sub-paragraph (5) that does not—

(a) affect anything previously done under or by virtue of the regulations, or

(b) prevent the making of new regulations.

Regulations made by the Scottish Ministers

8. (1) Regulations made by the Scottish Ministers under paragraph 2(2)(a) of this Schedule are subject to the negative procedure (see section 28 of the Interpretation and Legislative Reform (Scotland) Act 2010 (asp 10)).

(2) Regulations made by the Scottish Ministers under paragraph 2(2)(b), 4 or 6 of this Schedule must be laid before the Scottish Parliament as soon as reasonably practicable after being made.

(3) Sub-paragraph (2) does not apply if the regulations have been subject to the affirmative procedure (see section 29 of the Interpretation and Legislative Reform (Scotland) Act 2010).

(4) Regulations laid before the Scottish Parliament by virtue of sub-paragraph (2) cease to have effect at the end of the period of 40 days beginning with the day on which they are made, unless during that period the regulations are approved by a resolution of the Scottish Parliament.

(5) In calculating the period of 40 days, no account is to be taken of any time during which the Scottish Parliament is—

(a) dissolved, or

(b) in recess for more than 4 days.

(6) Where regulations cease to have effect as a result of sub-paragraph (4) that does not—

(a) affect anything previously done under or by virtue of the regulations, or

(b) prevent the making of new regulations.

(7) Section 30 of the Interpretation and Legislative Reform (Scotland) Act 2010 does not apply in relation to regulations to which sub-paragraph (2) applies.

Regulations made by the Department for the Economy in Northern Ireland

9. (1) Regulations made by the Department for the Economy in Northern Ireland under paragraph 2(2)(a) of this Schedule are subject to negative resolution within the meaning of section 41(6) of the Interpretation Act (Northern Ireland) 1954 (c 33 (NI)).

(2) Regulations made by the Department for the Economy in Northern Ireland under paragraph 2(2)(b), 4 or 6 of this Schedule must be laid before the Assembly as soon as reasonably practicable after being made.

(3) Sub-paragraph (2) does not apply if a draft of the regulations has been laid before, and approved by a resolution of, the Assembly.

(4) Section 41(3) of the Interpretation Act (Northern Ireland) 1954 applies for the purposes of sub-paragraph (3) in relation to the laying of a draft as it applies in relation to the laying of a statutory document under an enactment.

(5) Regulations laid before the Assembly by virtue of sub-paragraph (2) cease to have effect at the end of the period of 40 days beginning with the day on which the regulations are made, unless during that period the regulations are approved by a resolution of the Assembly.

(6) In calculating the period of 40 days, no account is to be taken of any time during which the Assembly is—

(a) dissolved,

(b) in recess for more than 4 days, or

(c) adjourned for more than 6 days.

(7) Where regulations cease to have effect as a result of sub-paragraph (5) that does not—

(a) affect anything previously done under or by virtue of the regulations, or

(b) prevent the making of new regulations.

(8) A power of the Department for the Economy in Northern Ireland to make regulations under this Schedule is exercisable by statutory rule for the purposes of the Statutory Rules (Northern Ireland) Order 1979 (SI 1979/1573 (NI 12)).

(9) In this paragraph "the Assembly" means the Northern Ireland Assembly.

Other interpretation

10. In this Schedule—

"accounts meeting" means a general meeting of a public company at which the company's annual accounts and reports (within the meaning given by section 471 of the Companies Act 2006) are laid;

"constitution", in relation to a company, is to be construed in accordance with section 17 of the Companies Act 2006;

"enactment" includes an Act of the Scottish Parliament and an instrument made under such an Act;

"public company" has the meaning given by section 4(2) of the Companies Act 2006.

NOTES

Commencement: 26 June 2020.

Para 2: words in square brackets in sub-para (1)(b) substituted by the Corporate Insolvency and Governance Act 2020 (Coronavirus) (Suspension of Liability for Wrongful Trading and Extension of the Relevant Period) Regulations 2020, SI 2020/1349, reg 3(1), as from 26 November 2020. Note that the amendment made by SI 2020/1349 only has effect in relation to the bodies that fall within sub-paragraphs (c)–(e) and (g)–(i) of the definition of "qualifying body" in para 1 above. In relation to the other bodies, the original date of 30 September 2020 was not amended. See, also, the Corporate Insolvency and Governance Act 2020 (Meetings of Scottish Charitable Incorporated Organisations) (Coronavirus) (No 2) Regulations 2020, SSI 2020/421, reg 2, which substitutes the date of 30 March 2021 in relation to a Scottish charitable incorporated organisation within the meaning of Chapter 7 of Part 1 of the Charities and Trustee Investment (Scotland) Act 2005. Amendments in relation to sub-paragraphs (a) and (b) of the definition of "qualifying body" in para 1 relate to Northern Ireland and are not noted.

Regulations: the Corporate Insolvency and Governance Act 2020 (Meetings of Scottish Charitable Incorporated Organisations) (Coronavirus) Regulations 2020, SSI 2020/284; the Corporate Insolvency and Governance Act 2020 (Coronavirus) (Extension of the Relevant Period) Regulations 2020, SI 2020/1031; the Corporate Insolvency and Governance Act 2020 (Coronavirus) (Suspension of Liability for Wrongful Trading and Extension of the Relevant Period) Regulations 2020, SI 2020/1349 at **[10.1300]**; the Corporate Insolvency and Governance Act 2020 (Meetings of Scottish Charitable Incorporated Organisations) (Coronavirus) (No 2) Regulations 2020, SSI 2020/421 (all made under paragraph 2(2)(b)).

NATIONAL SECURITY AND INVESTMENT ACT 2021

(2021 c 25)

NOTES

This Act is reproduced as amended by: the Criminal Justice Act 2003 (Commencement No 33) and Sentencing Act 2020 (Commencement No 2) Regulations 2022, SI 2022/500.

An Act to make provision for the making of orders in connection with national security risks arising from the acquisition of control over certain types of entities and assets; and for connected purposes

[29 April 2021]

ARRANGEMENT OF SECTIONS

PART 2
REMEDIES

Assessment period

PART 1 CALL-IN FOR NATIONAL SECURITY

CHAPTER 1 CALL-IN POWER

[9.568]

1 Call-in notice for national security purposes

(1) The Secretary of State may give a notice if the Secretary of State reasonably suspects that—

(a) a trigger event has taken place in relation to a qualifying entity or qualifying asset, and the event has given rise to or may give rise to a risk to national security, or

(b) arrangements are in progress or contemplation which, if carried into effect, will result in a trigger event taking place in relation to a qualifying entity or qualifying asset, and the event may give rise to a risk to national security.

(2) For the purposes of this Act, in considering whether a trigger event has taken place, or whether arrangements are in progress or contemplation which, if carried into effect, will result in a trigger event taking place, the effect of section 13(1) (notifiable acquisitions that are void) must be disregarded.

(3) A notice under subsection (1) is referred to in this Act as a call-in notice.

(4) If the Secretary of State decides to give a call-in notice, the notice must be given to—

(a) the acquirer,

(b) if the trigger event relates to a qualifying entity, the entity, and

(c) such other persons as the Secretary of State considers appropriate.

(5) The call-in notice must include a description of the trigger event to which it relates and state the names of the persons to whom the notice is given.

(6) The Secretary of State may not give a call-in notice unless a statement has been published (and not withdrawn) for the purposes of section 3.

(7) The Secretary of State must have regard to that statement before giving a call-in notice.

(8) But nothing in the statement limits the power to give a call-in notice.

NOTES

Commencement: 4 January 2022.

[9.569]

2 Further provision about call-in notices

(1) No more than one call-in notice may be given in relation to each trigger event.

(2) Subject to subsections (3) and (4), a call-in notice given on the grounds mentioned in section 1(1)(a)—

(a) may not be given after the end of the period of 6 months beginning with the day on which the Secretary of State became aware of the trigger event, and

(b) may not be given after the end of the period of 5 years beginning with the day on which the trigger event took place.

(3) Subsection (2)(b) does not apply where the trigger event is one in relation to which section 13(1) has effect.

(4) In relation to a trigger event taking place during the period beginning with 12 November 2020 and ending with the day before commencement day, a call-in notice given on the grounds mentioned in section 1(1)(a)—

(a) if the Secretary of State became aware of the trigger event before commencement day, may not be given after the end of the period of 6 months beginning with commencement day,

(b) if the Secretary of State became aware of the trigger event on or after commencement day—

(i) may not be given after the end of the period of 6 months beginning with the day on which the Secretary of State became aware of the trigger event, and

(ii) may not be given after the end of the period of 5 years beginning with commencement day.

(5) In this section "commencement day" means the day on which this section comes into force.

(6) This section is subject to section 22 (and see section 62).

NOTES

Commencement: 4 January 2022.

[9.570]

3 Statement about exercise of call-in power

(1) The Secretary of State may publish a statement for the purposes of this section if the requirements set out in section 4(1) are satisfied.

(2) The statement is a statement prepared by the Secretary of State that sets out how the Secretary of State expects to exercise the power to give a call-in notice.

(3) The statement may include, in particular—

(a) details of sectors of the economy in relation to which the Secretary of State considers that trigger events are more likely to give rise to a risk to national security,

(b) details of the trigger events, qualifying entities and qualifying assets in relation to which the Secretary of State expects to exercise the power to give a call-in notice, and

(c) details of factors that the Secretary of State expects to take into account when deciding whether or not to exercise the power.

(4) The Secretary of State must review a statement published under this section at least once every 5 years.

(5) A statement published under this section may be amended or replaced by a subsequent statement, and this section and section 4 apply in relation to any amended or replacement statement as in relation to the original statement.

(6) Nothing in a statement published under this section affects the power of the Secretary of State to make notifiable acquisition regulations (see section 6).

NOTES

Commencement: 1 July 2021.

[9.571]

4 Consultation and parliamentary procedure

(1) Before the Secretary of State may publish a statement for the purposes of section 3 the Secretary of State must—

(a) carry out such consultation as the Secretary of State thinks appropriate in relation to a draft of the statement,

(b) make any changes to the draft that appear to the Secretary of State to be necessary in view of the responses to the consultation, and

(c) lay the statement before Parliament.

(2) Either House of Parliament may at any time before the expiry of the 40-day period resolve not to approve the statement.

(3) If either House of Parliament resolves not to approve the statement under subsection (2), the Secretary of State must withdraw the statement.

(4) Any such resolution under subsection (2) does not affect the validity of a call-in notice given following the publication of the statement prior to its withdrawal, and does not affect the publication of a new statement.

(5) "The 40-day period" is the period of 40 days beginning with the day on which the statement is laid before Parliament (or, if it is not laid before each House of Parliament on the same day, the later of the days on which it is laid).

(6) When calculating the 40-day period, ignore any period during which Parliament is dissolved or prorogued or during which both Houses are adjourned for more than 4 days.

(7) The requirements in subsection (1)(a) and (b) may be met by consultation carried out before this section comes into force.

NOTES

Commencement: 1 July 2021.

CHAPTER 2 INTERPRETATION

[9.572]

5 Meaning of "trigger event" and "acquirer"

(1) For the purposes of this Act, a "trigger event" takes place when—

(a) a person gains control of a qualifying entity, as set out in section 8, or

(b) a person gains control of a qualifying asset, as set out in section 9.

(2) In this Act "acquirer" means the person who gains the control referred to in subsection (1) (or in relation to a trigger event that has not yet taken place, would gain that control).

NOTES

Commencement: 4 January 2022.

[9.573]

6 Notifiable acquisitions

(1) The Secretary of State may make regulations for the purposes of this section ("notifiable acquisition regulations").

(2) A notifiable acquisition takes place when a person gains control, by virtue of one or more of the cases described in subsection (2), (5) or (6) of section 8, of a qualifying entity of a specified description.

(3) But a notifiable acquisition does not take place if complying with the requirement to give a mandatory notice under section 14(1) would be impossible for the person within subsection (2).

(4) A description of qualifying entity that is specified must include provision that the entity carries on activities in the United Kingdom which are of a specified description (whether or not it also carries on other activities).

(5) Notifiable acquisition regulations may—

(a) amend this section in relation to the circumstances in which a notifiable acquisition takes place or does not take place,

(b) make provision for exemptions by reference to the characteristics of the person within subsection (2),

(c) make consequential amendments of other provisions of this Act.

(6) Notifiable acquisition regulations may by virtue of subsection (5)(a) include, in particular, provision about the circumstances in which the gaining of control of a qualifying asset of a specified description is a notifiable acquisition.

(7) A description specified under subsection (6) may only include qualifying assets within section 7(6) if it includes provision that any such asset is used in connection with activities carried on in the United Kingdom which are of a specified description (whether or not it is also used in connection with other activities).

(8) In this section "specified" means specified in notifiable acquisition regulations.

NOTES

Commencement: 29 April 2021 (sub-s (1)); 1 July 2021 (otherwise).

Regulations: the National Security and Investment Act 2021 (Notifiable Acquisition) (Specification of Qualifying Entities) Regulations 2021, SI 2021/1264 at **[10.1324]**.

[9.574]

7 Qualifying entities and assets

(1) This section defines "qualifying entity" and "qualifying asset" for the purposes of this Act.

(2) A "qualifying entity" is (subject to subsection (3)) any entity, whether or not a legal person, that is not an individual, and includes a company, a limited liability partnership, any other body corporate, a partnership, an unincorporated association and a trust.

(3) An entity which is formed or recognised under the law of a country or territory outside the United Kingdom is a "qualifying entity" only if it—

(a) carries on activities in the United Kingdom, or

(b) supplies goods or services to persons in the United Kingdom.

(4) A "qualifying asset" is (subject to subsection (6)) an asset of any of the following types—

(a) land,

(b) tangible (or, in Scotland, corporeal) moveable property,

(c) ideas, information or techniques which have industrial, commercial or other economic value.

(5) Examples of assets within subsection (4)(c) include—

(a) trade secrets,

(b) databases,

(c) source code,

(d) algorithms,

(e) formulae,

(f) designs,

(g) plans, drawings and specifications,

(h) software.

(6) Land or moveable property situated outside the United Kingdom or the territorial sea, or any asset within subsection (4)(c), is a "qualifying asset" only if it is used in connection with—

(a) activities carried on in the United Kingdom, or

(b) the supply of goods or services to persons in the United Kingdom.

NOTES

Commencement: 4 January 2022.

[9.575]

8 Control of entities

(1) For the purposes of this Act, a person gains control of a qualifying entity if the person acquires a right or interest in, or in relation to, the entity and as a result one or more of the cases described in this section arises.

(2) The first case is where the percentage of the shares that the person holds in the entity increases—

(a) from 25% or less to more than 25%,

(b) from 50% or less to more than 50%, or

(c) from less than 75% to 75% or more.

(3) In subsection (2), the reference to holding a percentage of shares is—

(a) in the case of an entity that has a share capital, to holding shares comprised in the issued share capital of the entity of a nominal value (in aggregate) of that percentage of the share capital,

(b) in the case of an entity that does not have a share capital, to holding a right to a share of that percentage of the capital or profits of the entity,

(c) in the case of a limited liability partnership, to holding a right to a share of that percentage of any surplus assets of the partnership on a winding up.

(4) For the purposes of subsection (3)(c), to the extent that rights to share in any surplus assets of the limited liability partnership on a winding up are not expressly provided for, each member of the partnership is to be treated as holding the right to an equal share of such assets.

(5) The second case is where the percentage of the voting rights that the person holds in the entity increases—

(a) from 25% or less to more than 25%,

(b) from 50% or less to more than 50%, or

(c) from less than 75% to 75% or more.

(6) The third case is where the acquisition is of voting rights in the entity that (whether alone or together with other voting rights held by the person) enable the person to secure or prevent the passage of any class of resolution governing the affairs of the entity.

(7) In subsections (5) and (6), a reference to the voting rights in an entity is—

(a) in the case of an entity that has a share capital, to the rights conferred on shareholders in respect of their shares to vote at general meetings of the entity on all or substantially all matters,

(b) in the case of an entity that does not have a share capital, to the rights conferred on members to vote at general meetings of the entity on all or substantially all matters,

and, in the case of an entity that does not have general meetings at which matters are decided by such votes, includes any rights in relation to the entity that are of the equivalent effect.

(8) The fourth case is (subject to subsection (9)) where the acquisition, whether alone or together with other interests or rights held by the person, enables the person materially to influence the policy of the entity.

(9) Subsection (8) does not include a case where the person already holds any interest or right that enables the person materially to influence the policy of the entity.

NOTES

Commencement: 4 January 2022.

[9.576]

9 Control of assets

(1) For the purposes of this Act, a person gains control of a qualifying asset if the person acquires a right or interest in, or in relation to, the asset and as a result the person is able—

(a) to use the asset, or use it to a greater extent than prior to the acquisition, or

(b) to direct or control how the asset is used, or direct or control how it is used to a greater extent than prior to the acquisition.

This is subject to section 11.

(2) In this section, references to the use of an asset include references to its exploitation, alteration, manipulation, disposal or destruction.

NOTES

Commencement: 4 January 2022.

[9.577]

10 Holding and acquiring interests and rights: supplementary

(1) Schedule 1 provides for particular cases in which a person is to be treated for the purposes of this Act as holding an interest or right.

(2) A person is to be treated for the purposes of this Act as acquiring an interest or right (to the extent that the person would not otherwise be regarded as doing so) where—

(a) the interest or right becomes treated as held by the person by virtue of Schedule 1, or

(b) the person is already treated as holding the interest or right by virtue of that Schedule and something occurs in relation to the interest or right which would be regarded as its acquisition by the person (including by virtue of paragraph (a)) if the person was not already treated as holding it.

NOTES

Commencement: 4 January 2022.

[9.578]

11 Exceptions relating to control of assets

(1) For the purposes of this Act a person is not to be regarded as gaining control of a qualifying asset by reason of an acquisition made by an individual for purposes that are wholly or mainly outside the individual's trade, business or craft.

(2) Subsection (1) does not apply in relation to an asset that—

(a) is land, or

(b) falls within any of the following (as it has effect from time to time)—

(i) the Schedule to the Export of Radioactive Sources (Control) Order 2006 (SI 2006/1846),

(ii) article 4A of, or Schedule 2 or 3 to, the Export Control Order 2008 (SI 2008/3231),

(iii) Annex I or IV to Council Regulation (EC) No 428/2009 of 5 May 2009,

(iv) Annex I to Regulation (EU) No 258/2012 of the European Parliament and of the Council of 14 March 2012,

(v) Annex II or III to Regulation (EU) 2019/125 of the European Parliament and of the Council of 1 January 2019.

(3) The Secretary of State may by regulations—

(a) amend subsection (2) so as to add, vary or remove any asset or description of asset,

(b) prescribe other circumstances, or descriptions of circumstances, in which a person is not to be regarded for the purposes of this Act as gaining control of a qualifying asset.

NOTES

Commencement: 29 April 2021 (sub-s (3)); 4 January 2022 (otherwise).

[9.579]

12 Trigger events: supplementary

(1) If a trigger event takes place over a period of more than one day, or if it is unclear when during a period of more than one day the event has taken place, it is treated for the purposes of this Act as taking place on the last day of the period.

(2) Subsections (3) and (4) apply if a person enters into an agreement or arrangement that enables the person (contingently or not) to do something in the future that would result in a trigger event taking place.

(3) For the purposes of this Act, entering into the agreement or arrangement does not necessarily establish that arrangements are in progress or contemplation which, if carried into effect, would result in a trigger event taking place.

(4) The question of whether such arrangements are in progress or contemplation (at the time of entry into the agreement or arrangement or subsequently) is to be determined by reference to all the circumstances, including how likely it is in practice that person will do the thing that would result in a trigger event taking place.

NOTES

Commencement: 4 January 2022.

CHAPTER 3 APPROVAL OF NOTIFIABLE ACQUISITION

[9.580]

13 Approval of notifiable acquisition

(1) A notifiable acquisition that is completed without the approval of the Secretary of State is void.

(2) The Secretary of State may approve a notifiable acquisition by—

(a) giving a notification under section 14(8)(b)(ii),

(b) making a final order under section 26, subject to subsection (3),

(c) giving a final notification under section 26.

(3) A notifiable acquisition, in relation to which a final order has been made, that is completed otherwise than in accordance with the final order, is void.

NOTES

Commencement: 4 January 2022.

CHAPTER 4 PROCEDURE

Procedure in respect of notifiable acquisition

[9.581]

14 Mandatory notification procedure

(1) Subject to subsection (2), a person must give notice to the Secretary of State before the person, pursuant to a notifiable acquisition, gains control in circumstances falling within section 6(2).

(2) Subsection (1) does not apply if the Secretary of State has already given a call-in notice, which has not been revoked, in relation to the proposed notifiable acquisition.

(3) A notice under subsection (1) is referred to in this Act as a mandatory notice.

(4) The Secretary of State may by regulations prescribe the form and content of a mandatory notice.

(5) As soon as reasonably practicable after receiving a mandatory notice, the Secretary of State must decide whether to reject or accept the notice.

(6) The Secretary of State may reject the mandatory notice on one or more of the following grounds—

(a) it does not meet the requirements of this section,

(b) it does not meet the requirements prescribed by the regulations,

(c) it does not contain sufficient information to allow the Secretary of State to decide whether to give a call-in notice in relation to the proposed notifiable acquisition.

(7) If the mandatory notice is rejected, the Secretary of State must, as soon as practicable, provide reasons in writing for that decision to the person who gave the notice.

(8) If the mandatory notice is accepted, the Secretary of State must—

(a) as soon as practicable, notify each relevant person, and

(b) before the end of the review period—

(i) give a call-in notice in relation to the proposed notifiable acquisition, or

(ii) notify each relevant person that no further action will be taken under this Act in relation to the proposed notifiable acquisition.

(9) The "review period" is the period of 30 working days beginning with the day on which the notification under subsection (8)(a) is given to the person who gave the mandatory notice.

(10) In this section "relevant person" means the person who gave the mandatory notice and such other persons as the Secretary of State considers appropriate.

NOTES

Commencement: 29 April 2021 (sub-s (4)); 4 January 2022 (otherwise).

Regulations: the National Security and Investment Act 2021 (Prescribed Form and Content of Notices and Validation Applications) Regulations 2021, SI 2021/1272 at **[10.1352]**; the National Security and Investment Act 2021 (Prescribed Form and Content of Notices and Validation Applications) (Amendment) Regulations 2022, SI 2022/398.

[9.582]

15 Requirement to consider retrospective validation without application

(1) This section and section 16 apply to a notifiable acquisition that is completed without the approval of the Secretary of State and, accordingly, is void (see section 13(1)).

(2) The Secretary of State must, before the end of the period of 6 months beginning with the day on which the Secretary of State becomes aware of the notifiable acquisition—

(a) give a call-in notice in relation to the acquisition, or

(b) give a validation notice in relation to the acquisition to each relevant person and notify those persons that no further action will be taken under this Act in relation to the acquisition.

(3) The effect of a validation notice given under this section or section 16 or 17, is that the notifiable acquisition to which it relates is to be treated as having been completed with the approval of the Secretary of State (and, accordingly, is not void).

(4) In this section "relevant person" means—

(a) the person who was required to give a mandatory notice to the Secretary of State in relation to the acquisition (see section 14(1)), and

(b) such other persons as the Secretary of State considers appropriate.

NOTES

Commencement: 4 January 2022.

[9.583]

16 Application for retrospective validation of notifiable acquisition

(1) Any person materially affected by the fact that a notifiable acquisition to which this section applies (see section 15(1)) is void, may apply to the Secretary of State for a validation notice in relation to the acquisition.

(2) An application under subsection (1) is referred to in this Act as a validation application.

(3) The Secretary of State may by regulations prescribe the form and content of a validation application.

(4) Subject to subsection (8), as soon as reasonably practicable after receiving a validation application, the Secretary of State must decide whether to reject or accept the application.

(5) The Secretary of State may reject the application on one or more of the following grounds—

(a) it does not meet the requirements of this section,

(b) it does not meet the requirements prescribed by the regulations,

(c) it does not contain sufficient information to allow the Secretary of State to decide whether to give a call-in notice in relation to the acquisition.

(6) If the application is rejected, the Secretary of State must, as soon as practicable, provide reasons in writing for that decision to the person who made the application.

(7) If the application is accepted, the Secretary of State must—

(a) as soon as practicable, notify each relevant person, and

(b) before the end of the review period—

(i) give a call-in notice in relation to the acquisition, or

(ii) give a validation notice in relation to the acquisition to each relevant person and notify those persons that no further action will be taken under this Act in relation to the acquisition.

(8) The Secretary of State is not required to consider a validation application in relation to an acquisition if, in the opinion of the Secretary of State, there has been no material change in circumstances since a previous validation application in relation to the acquisition was made.

(9) In this section—

"relevant person" means the person who made the validation application and such other persons as the Secretary of State considers appropriate;

the "review period" is the period of 30 working days beginning with the day on which the notification under subsection (7)(a) is given to the person who made the validation application.

NOTES

Commencement: 29 April 2021 (sub-s (3)); 4 January 2022 (otherwise).

Regulations: the National Security and Investment Act 2021 (Prescribed Form and Content of Notices and Validation Applications) Regulations 2021, SI 2021/1272 at **[10.1352]**; the National Security and Investment Act 2021 (Prescribed Form and Content of Notices and Validation Applications) (Amendment) Regulations 2022, SI 2022/398.

[9.584]

17 Retrospective validation of notifiable acquisition following call-in

(1) This section applies where the Secretary of State has given a call-in notice pursuant to—

(a) subsection (2)(a) of section 15, or

(b) subsection (7)(b)(i) of section 16,

(and, accordingly, the trigger event to which the call-in notice relates is, or includes, a notifiable acquisition to which those sections apply.)

(2) If the Secretary of State gives a final notification in relation to the call-in notice, the Secretary of State must also give a validation notice in relation to the acquisition.

(3) A validation notice under this section must be given to—

(a) each person to whom the final notification is given,

(b) the person (if any) who made an application in relation to the acquisition under section 16, and

(c) such other persons as the Secretary of State considers appropriate.

(4) Subsection (5) applies if the Secretary of State makes a final order in relation to the call-in notice.

(5) So much of the notifiable acquisition as would, had it been completed after the making of the final order, have been completed in accordance with the order is to be treated as having been completed with the approval of the Secretary of State (and, accordingly, is not void).

NOTES

Commencement: 4 January 2022.

Voluntary notification of trigger event

[9.585]

18 Voluntary notification procedure

(1) This section does not apply in relation to—

(a) arrangements which would result in a notifiable acquisition,

(b) a trigger event that is, or includes, a notifiable acquisition.

(2) A seller, acquirer or the qualifying entity concerned may give a notice to the Secretary of State stating that —

(a) a trigger event has taken place in relation to a qualifying entity or a qualifying asset, or

(b) arrangements are in progress or contemplation which, if carried into effect, will result in a trigger event taking place in relation to a qualifying entity or a qualifying asset.

(3) A notice under subsection (2) is referred to in this Act as a voluntary notice.

(4) The Secretary of State may by regulations prescribe the form and content of a voluntary notice.

(5) As soon as reasonably practicable after receiving the voluntary notice, the Secretary of State must decide whether to reject or accept the notice.

(6) The Secretary of State may reject the voluntary notice on one or more of the following grounds—

(a) it does not meet the requirements of this section,

(b) it does not meet the requirements prescribed by the regulations,

(c) it does not contain sufficient information to allow the Secretary of State to decide whether to give a call-in notice,

(d) there is no reasonable prospect of being able to give a call-in notice due to the operation of the time-limits in subsection (2) or (4) of section 2.

(7) If the voluntary notice is rejected, the Secretary of State must, as soon as practicable, provide reasons in writing for that decision to each relevant person.

(8) If the voluntary notice is accepted, the Secretary of State must—

(a) as soon as practicable, notify each relevant person, and

(b) before the end of the review period—

(i) give a call-in notice in relation to the trigger event, or

(ii) notify each relevant person that no further action will be taken under this Act in relation to the trigger event.

(9) The "review period" is the period of 30 working days beginning with the day on which the notification under subsection (8)(a) is given to the person who gave the voluntary notice; but this does not affect the operation of the time-limits in subsections (2) and (4) of section 2.

(10) In this section—

"relevant person" means the person who gave the voluntary notice and such other persons as the Secretary of State considers appropriate,

"seller", in relation to a trigger event, means a person who has ceded control of the qualifying entity or a qualifying asset (or in relation to a trigger event that has not yet taken place, would cede that control).

NOTES

Commencement: 29 April 2021 (sub-s (4)); 4 January 2022 (otherwise).

Regulations: the National Security and Investment Act 2021 (Prescribed Form and Content of Notices and Validation Applications) Regulations 2021, SI 2021/1272 at **[10.1352]**; the National Security and Investment Act 2021 (Prescribed Form and Content of Notices and Validation Applications) (Amendment) Regulations 2022, SI 2022/398.

Information, etc

[9.586]

19 Power to require information

(1) The Secretary of State may give a notice to a person (subject to section 21) to require the person to provide any information in relation to the exercise of the Secretary of State's functions under this Act which—

(a) is specified or described in the notice, or falls within a category of information specified or described in the notice, and

(b) is within that person's possession or power.

(2) The Secretary of State is not to require the provision of information under this section except where the requirement to provide information is proportionate to the use to which the information is to be put in the carrying out of the Secretary of State's functions under this Act.

(3) A notice under subsection (1) is referred to in this Act as an information notice.

(4) An information notice may—

(a) specify the manner in which the information is to be provided,

(b) specify a time limit for—

(i) providing the information,

(ii) notifying the Secretary of State that the information is not in the person's possession or power, or

(c) require the person to provide any information within their possession or power which would enable the Secretary of State to find the information required by the notice.

(5) An information notice must—

(a) specify the purpose for which the notice is given, and

(b) state the possible consequences of not complying with the notice.

(6) A person is not required under this section to provide any information which that person could not be compelled to provide in evidence in civil proceedings before the court.

(7) A reference in this section to the provision of information includes a reference to the provision of a legible and intelligible copy of information recorded otherwise than in legible form.

(8) A person to whom information is provided under this section may copy the information.

(9) In this section "the court" means—

(a) in relation to England and Wales or Northern Ireland, the High Court,

(b) in relation to Scotland, the Court of Session, and

(c) in relation to a person outside the United Kingdom, the High Court of England and Wales.

NOTES

Commencement: 4 January 2022.

[9.587]

20 Attendance of witnesses

(1) The Secretary of State may give a notice to a person (subject to section 21) to require the person—

(a) to attend at a time and place specified in the notice, and

(b) to give evidence to the Secretary of State in relation to the exercise of the Secretary of State's functions under this Act.

(2) The Secretary of State is not to require the giving of evidence under this section except where the requirement to give evidence is proportionate to the use to which the evidence is to be put in the carrying out of the Secretary of State's functions under this Act.

(3) A notice under subsection (1) is referred to in this Act as an attendance notice.

(4) An attendance notice must—

(a) specify the purpose for which the notice is given, and

(b) state the possible consequences of not complying with the notice.

(5) A person is not required under this section to give any evidence which that person could not be compelled to give in civil proceedings before the court.

(6) A person is not required, in compliance with an attendance notice, to go more than 10 miles from their place of residence unless necessary travelling expenses are paid or offered to that person.
(7) In this section "the court" means—
(a) in relation to evidence given in England and Wales or Northern Ireland, the High Court,
(b) in relation to evidence given in Scotland, the Court of Session, and
(c) in relation to evidence given outside the United Kingdom, the High Court of England and Wales.

NOTES
Commencement: 4 January 2022.

[9.588]
21 Information notices and attendance notices: persons outside the UK
(1) The Secretary of State may give an information notice or an attendance notice to a person outside the United Kingdom only if the person falls within subsection (2), (3) or (4) of this section.
(2) A person falls within this subsection if the person is—
(a) a United Kingdom national,
(b) an individual ordinarily resident in the United Kingdom,
(c) a body incorporated or constituted under the law of any part of the United Kingdom, or
(d) carrying on business in the United Kingdom.
(3) A person falls within this subsection if—
(a) a trigger event has taken place in relation to a qualifying entity which is formed or recognised under the law of any part of the United Kingdom, or
(b) arrangements are in progress or contemplation which, if carried into effect, will result in a trigger event taking place in relation to a qualifying entity of that description,
and the person is the acquirer.
(4) A person falls within this subsection if—
(a) a trigger event has taken place in relation to a qualifying asset which —
(i) is within section 7(4)(a) or (b) and is situated in the United Kingdom or the territorial sea, or
(ii) is within section 7(4)(c) and is used in connection with activities carried on in the United Kingdom, or
(b) arrangements are in progress or contemplation which, if carried into effect, will result in a trigger event taking place in relation to a qualifying asset within paragraph (a),
and the person is the acquirer.

NOTES
Commencement: 4 January 2022.

[9.589]
22 False or misleading information
(1) This section applies where false or misleading information is provided to the Secretary of State—
(a) in a mandatory notice,
(b) in a validation application,
(c) in a voluntary notice,
(d) in response to an information notice, or
(e) in response to an attendance notice.
(2) Where a decision made by the Secretary of State under this Act is materially affected by the false or misleading information, the Secretary of State may reconsider the decision and may affirm, vary or revoke it.
(3) Where a decision is varied or revoked under this section, the Secretary of State must give notice to that effect to such persons as the Secretary of State considers appropriate.
(4) If a revoked decision was—
(a) a decision to give a call-in notice,
(b) a decision to make or revoke a final order, or
(c) a decision to give a final notification,
the Secretary of State may give a further call-in notice and section 2(1) does not apply.
(5) Where a decision is revoked under this section, the time limits in section 2(2) and (4) do not apply to the case concerned, but a call-in notice (or a further call-in notice) may not be given after the end of the period of 6 months beginning with the day on which the information was discovered to be false or misleading.

NOTES
Commencement: 4 January 2022.

PART 2 REMEDIES

Assessment period

[9.590]
23 Meaning of "assessment period"
(1) This section defines "assessment period" in relation to a call-in notice.
(2) The assessment period begins with the day on which the call-in notice is given to the acquirer.
(3) In this section—
(a) "the initial period" is the period of 30 working days beginning with the day mentioned in subsection (2),
(b) "the additional period" is the period of 45 working days beginning with the first working day after the day on which the initial period ends,
(c) a "voluntary period" is such period of working days, beginning with the first working day after the day on which the additional period (or the previous voluntary period) ends, as may be agreed in writing between the Secretary of State and the acquirer.

(4) The assessment period ends at the end of the initial period unless, before the end of the initial period, the Secretary of State gives an additional period notice to each person to whom the call-in notice was given (see subsection (8)).

(5) If an additional period notice is given, the assessment period ends at the end of the additional period unless, before the end of the additional period, a voluntary period is agreed.

(6) If a voluntary period is agreed, the assessment period ends at the end of the voluntary period, or at the end of any further voluntary period which is agreed.

(7) The Secretary of State must give notice of any voluntary period, or further voluntary period to each person to whom the call-in notice was given.

(8) An "additional period notice" is a notice which the Secretary of State may give if the Secretary of State—

- (a) reasonably believes that—
  - (i) a trigger event has taken place or that arrangements are in progress or contemplation which, if carried into effect, will result in a trigger event, and
  - (ii) a risk to national security has arisen from the trigger event or would arise from the trigger event if carried into effect, and
- (b) reasonably considers that the additional period is required to assess the trigger event further.

(9) A voluntary period or further voluntary period may be agreed by the Secretary of State only if the Secretary of State—

- (a) is satisfied, on the balance of probabilities, that—
  - (i) a trigger event has taken place or that arrangements are in progress or contemplation which, if carried into effect, will result in a trigger event, and
  - (ii) a risk to national security has arisen from the trigger event or would arise from the trigger event if carried into effect, and
- (b) reasonably considers that the period is required to consider whether to make a final order or what provision a final order should contain.

NOTES

Commencement: 4 January 2022.

[9.591]

24 Effect of information notice and attendance notice

(1) This section applies if an information notice or an attendance notice is given at any time during the assessment period in relation to a call-in notice.

(2) As soon as practicable after giving the information notice or attendance notice, the Secretary of State must notify each relevant person of—

- (a) the fact that an information notice or attendance notice has been given, and
- (b) the time limit specified in the notice for complying with the requirements of the notice.

(3) As soon as practicable after—

- (a) the Secretary of State is satisfied that the requirements of the information notice or the attendance notice have been complied with, or
- (b) (if earlier) the time specified in the information notice or the attendance notice for complying with those requirements has passed,

the Secretary of State must notify each relevant person confirming that fact.

(4) Any day falling within the period beginning with the day on which the notice under subsection (2) is given and ending with the day on which a notice under subsection (3) is given does not count for the purposes of calculating the initial, additional or voluntary period under section 23.

(5) In this section "relevant person" means each person to whom the call-in notice was given.

NOTES

Commencement: 4 January 2022.

Interim and final orders

[9.592]

25 Interim orders

(1) The Secretary of State may, during the assessment period in relation to a call-in notice, make an order if the Secretary of State reasonably considers that the provisions of the order are necessary and proportionate for the purpose of preventing or reversing pre-emptive action, or mitigating its effects.

(2) In subsection (1), "pre-emptive action" means action which might prejudice the exercise of the Secretary of State's functions under this Act in relation to the call-in notice.

(3) An order under subsection (1) is referred to in this Act as an "interim order".

(4) An interim order may include—

- (a) provision requiring a person, or description of person, to do, or not to do, particular things,
- (b) provision for the appointment of a person to conduct or supervise the conduct of activities on such terms and with such powers as may be specified or described in the order,
- (c) provision requiring a person, or description of person, not to disclose the contents of the order except to the extent permitted by the order,
- (d) consequential, supplementary or incidental provision.

(5) Provision made by or under an interim order may extend to a person's conduct outside the United Kingdom or the territorial sea only if the person is—

- (a) a United Kingdom national,
- (b) an individual ordinarily resident in the United Kingdom,
- (c) a body incorporated or constituted under the law of any part of the United Kingdom, or
- (d) carrying on business in the United Kingdom.

(6) An interim order comes into force at such time as is determined by or under the order.

(7) An interim order ceases to have effect at the earliest of—

(a) the giving of a final notification or the coming into force of a final order in relation to the call-in notice,

(b) such time as is determined by or under the order,

(c) such time as it is revoked.

NOTES

Commencement: 4 January 2022.

[9.593]

26 Final orders and final notifications

(1) The Secretary of State must, before the end of the assessment period in relation to a call-in notice—

(a) make a final order, or

(b) give a final notification to each person to whom the call-in notice was given.

(2) In this section—

(a) a "final notification" is a notification that no further action in relation to the call-in notice is to be taken under this Act,

(b) a "final order" is an order under subsection (3).

(3) The Secretary of State may, during the assessment period, make a final order if the Secretary of State—

(a) is satisfied, on the balance of probabilities, that—

(i) a trigger event has taken place or that arrangements are in progress or contemplation which, if carried into effect, will result in a trigger event, and

(ii) a risk to national security has arisen from the trigger event or would arise from the trigger event if carried into effect, and

(b) reasonably considers that the provisions of the order are necessary and proportionate for the purpose of preventing, remedying or mitigating the risk.

(4) Before making a final order the Secretary of State must consider any representations made to the Secretary of State.

(5) A final order may include—

(a) provision requiring a person, or description of person, to do, or not to do, particular things,

(b) provision for the appointment of a person to conduct or supervise the conduct of activities on such terms and with such powers as may be specified or described in the order,

(c) provision requiring a person, or description of person, not to disclose the contents of the order except to the extent permitted by the order,

(d) consequential, supplementary or incidental provision.

(6) Provision made by or under a final order may extend to a person's conduct outside the United Kingdom or the territorial sea only if the person is—

(a) a United Kingdom national,

(b) an individual ordinarily resident in the United Kingdom,

(c) a body incorporated or constituted under the law of any part of the United Kingdom, or

(d) carrying on business in the United Kingdom.

(7) A final order comes into force at such time as is determined by or under the order.

(8) A final order ceases to have effect at such time as is determined by or under the order, unless it is revoked before that time.

NOTES

Commencement: 4 January 2022.

[9.594]

27 Review, variation and revocation of orders

(1) This section applies in relation to an interim order and a final order.

(2) The Secretary of State must keep each order under review and may vary or revoke it.

(3) If a person required to comply with an order requests that the Secretary of State vary or revoke it, the Secretary of State must consider the request as soon as practicable after receiving it.

(4) But the Secretary of State is not required to consider such a request in relation to a final order if, in the opinion of the Secretary of State, there has been no material change of circumstances—

(a) since the order was made or last varied, or

(b) in the case of a request from a person who has made a previous request in relation to the order, since the previous request was made.

NOTES

Commencement: 4 January 2022.

[9.595]

28 Orders: supplementary

(1) This section applies in relation to an interim order and a final order.

(2) As soon as practicable after making or varying an order, the Secretary of State must serve the order, or the order as varied, on—

(a) each person who is required to comply with the order,

(b) each person to whom the call-in notice was given, and

(c) such other persons as the Secretary of State considers appropriate.

(3) As soon as practicable after varying an order, the Secretary of State must give notice to any person who was previously required to comply with the order but is no longer required to comply with it.

(4) Subject to subsection (5), each order (including each order as varied) or explanatory material accompanying the order must—

(a) state the date on which the order or any variation comes into force or how that date is to be determined,

(b) state each person, or description of person, who is required to comply with the order,
(c) describe the trigger event and entity or asset concerned,
(d) state the reasons for making or varying the order,
(e) state the possible consequences of not complying with the order,
(f) provide information about—
 (i) how to apply to the Secretary of State for an order to be varied or revoked, and
 (ii) the procedure for judicial review or, in Scotland, an application to the supervisory jurisdiction of the Court of Session.

(5) The Secretary of State may exclude from the copy of an order served on any person within subsection (2), or from any explanatory material accompanying the order, anything the disclosure of which the Secretary of State considers—
(a) would be likely to prejudice the commercial interests of any person, or
(b) would be contrary to the interests of national security.

(6) As soon as practicable after revoking an order, the Secretary of State must give notice to the persons mentioned in subsection (2) that the order has been revoked.

NOTES

Commencement: 4 January 2022.

[9.596]

29 Publication of notice of final order

(1) Subject to subsection (3), the Secretary of State must publish, in such manner as the Secretary of State considers appropriate, notice of the fact that—
(a) a final order has been made,
(b) a final order has been varied or revoked.

(2) The notice under subsection (1) must be published as soon as practicable and must—
(a) state the date on which the order, variation or revocation comes into force, or how that date is to be determined,
(b) state each person, and each description of person, who is required to comply with the order,
(c) describe the trigger event and entity or asset concerned,
(d) include a summary of the order, variation or revocation, its effect and the reasons for it,
(e) include any other information that the Secretary of State considers it appropriate to include.

(3) The Secretary of State may exclude from the notice under subsection (1) anything the publication of which the Secretary of State considers—
(a) would be likely to prejudice the commercial interests of any person, or
(b) would be contrary to the interests of national security.

NOTES

Commencement: 4 January 2022.

Financial assistance

[9.597]

30 Financial assistance

(1) The Secretary of State may, with the consent of the Treasury, give financial assistance to or in respect of an entity in consequence of the making of a final order.

(2) "Financial assistance" means loans, guarantees or indemnities, or any other kind of financial assistance (actual or contingent).

(3) If during any relevant period the amount given under this section totals £100 million or more, the Secretary of State must as soon as practicable lay a report of the amount before the House of Commons.

(4) If during a relevant period in which a report has been laid under subsection (3) any further amount is given under this section, the Secretary of State must as soon as practicable lay a report of the amount before the House of Commons.

(5) "Relevant period" means—
(a) the period beginning with the day on which this section comes into force and ending with the following 31 March, and
(b) each subsequent period of 12 months.

NOTES

Commencement: 4 January 2022.

CMA functions

[9.598]

31 Interaction with CMA functions under Part 3 of Enterprise Act 2002

(1) This section applies at any time when a final order is in force, or a final notification has been given, in relation to a trigger event which involves, or would involve, two or more enterprises ceasing to be distinct enterprises for the purposes of Part 3 of the Enterprise Act 2002 ("the 2002 Act").

(2) The Secretary of State may direct the Competition and Markets Authority ("the CMA") to do, or not to do, anything under Part 3 of the 2002 Act in relation to the trigger event if the Secretary of State reasonably considers that the direction is necessary and proportionate for the purpose of preventing, remedying or mitigating a risk to national security.

(3) Before giving a direction under this section, the Secretary of State must consult the CMA and such other persons as the Secretary of State considers appropriate.

(4) The Secretary of State must publish a direction given under this section in such manner as the Secretary of State considers appropriate.

(5) The duty of the CMA to comply with a direction given under this section applies regardless of any other duty imposed on the CMA.

NOTES

Commencement: 4 January 2022.

PART 3 ENFORCEMENT AND APPEALS

Offences

[9.599]

32 Offence of completing notifiable acquisition without approval

(1) A person who, pursuant to a notifiable acquisition, gains control in circumstances falling within section 6(2) commits an offence if, without reasonable excuse, that person completes the notifiable acquisition without the approval of the Secretary of State in one of the ways mentioned in section 13(2).

(2) Subsection (1) applies even if a call-in notice or a validation notice has been given in relation to the notifiable acquisition.

(3) An offence is committed under this section notwithstanding the effect of section 13(1).

NOTES

Commencement: 4 January 2022.

[9.600]

33 Offence of failing to comply with order

(1) A person commits an offence if, without reasonable excuse, the person fails to comply with a requirement to which the person is subject under or by virtue of an interim order or a final order.

(2) Where a person is convicted of an offence under this section, the court may make an order requiring that person, within such period as may be specified by the order, to comply with a requirement to which the person is subject under or by virtue of an interim order or a final order.

NOTES

Commencement: 4 January 2022.

[9.601]

34 Offences: information and attendance of witnesses

(1) A person commits an offence if—

(a) the person fails, without reasonable excuse, to comply with a requirement of an information notice or an attendance notice, or

(b) the person intentionally or recklessly alters, suppresses or destroys or causes or permits the alteration, suppression or destruction of any information the person has been required by an information notice to provide.

(2) A person commits an offence if the person intentionally obstructs or delays the making of a copy of information provided in response to an information notice.

(3) A person commits an offence if—

(a) the person supplies any information to the Secretary of State (including by way of giving evidence pursuant to an attendance notice) in connection with a function of the Secretary of State under this Act,

(b) the information is false or misleading in a material respect, and

(c) the person knows that, or is reckless as to whether, it is false or misleading in a material respect.

(4) A person commits an offence if—

(a) the person supplies any information to another person (other than the Secretary of State),

(b) the person supplying the information knows that the information is to be used for the purpose of supplying information to the Secretary of State in connection with a function of the Secretary of State under this Act,

(c) the information is false or misleading in a material respect, and

(d) the person supplying the information knows that, or is reckless as to whether, it is false or misleading in a material respect.

(5) Where a person is convicted of an offence under subsection (1) or (2), the court may make an order requiring that person, within such period as may be specified by the order—

(a) to comply with a requirement in an information notice,

(b) to comply with a requirement in an attendance notice, or

(c) to permit the making of a copy of information.

(6) Any reference in subsection (1) to destroying information includes a reference to destroying the means of reproducing information recorded otherwise than in legible form.

NOTES

Commencement: 4 January 2022.

[9.602]

35 Offences in relation to sharing information

(1) It is an offence for a person to use or disclose information in contravention of section 54 or 55(1).

(2) It is a defence for a person charged with an offence under this section to prove that the person reasonably believed that—

(a) the use or disclosure was lawful, or

(b) the information had already and lawfully been made available to the public.

NOTES

Commencement: 4 January 2022.

[9.603]

36 Offences by bodies corporate etc

(1) If an offence under this Act is committed by a body—

(a) with the consent or connivance of an officer of the body, or

(b) due to any neglect on the part of such an officer,

the officer, as well as the body, is guilty of the offence and liable to be proceeded against and punished accordingly.

(2) In this section—

"body" means a body corporate, a partnership or an unincorporated association other than a partnership,

"officer of a body"—

(a) in relation to a body corporate, means a director, member of the committee of management, chief executive, manager, secretary or other similar officer of the body, or a person purporting to act in any such capacity,

(b) in relation to a partnership, means a partner or person purporting to act as a partner,

(c) in relation to an unincorporated association other than a partnership, means a person who is concerned in the management or control of the body or purports to act in the capacity of a person so concerned.

(3) In subsection (2) "director" includes—

(a) a person occupying in relation to a body corporate the position of a director (by whatever name called),

(b) a person in accordance with whose directions or instructions (not being advice given in a professional capacity) the directors of that body are accustomed to act, and

(c) a person who has an interest or right in, or in relation to, the body corporate that (whether alone or together with other interests or rights held by the person) enables the person materially to influence the policy of the body corporate.

(4) If the affairs of a body corporate are managed by its members, subsection (1) applies in relation to the acts and defaults of a member in connection with the member's functions of management as if the member were a director of the body.

(5) The Secretary of State may by regulations provide for the modification of any provision of this section in its application to a body corporate or unincorporated association formed or recognised under the law of a country or territory outside the United Kingdom.

NOTES

Commencement: 29 April 2021 (sub-s (5)); 4 January 2022 (otherwise).

Prosecution and penalties

[9.604]

37 Prosecution

Proceedings for an offence under this Act may be instituted—

(a) in England and Wales, only by the Director of Public Prosecutions, and

(b) in Northern Ireland, only by the Director of Public Prosecutions for Northern Ireland.

NOTES

Commencement: 4 January 2022.

[9.605]

38 Proceedings against partnerships etc

(1) Proceedings for an offence under this Act may be brought—

(a) where the offence is alleged to have been committed by a partnership, against the partnership in the firm name,

(b) where the offence is alleged to have been committed by an unincorporated association other than a partnership, against the association in its own name.

(2) Rules of court relating to the service of documents have effect in relation to such proceedings as if the partnership or unincorporated association were a body corporate.

(3) For the purposes of such proceedings the following provisions apply as they apply in relation to a body corporate—

(a) section 33 of the Criminal Justice Act 1925 and Schedule 3 to the Magistrates' Courts Act 1980,

(b) section 18 of the Criminal Justice Act (Northern Ireland) 1945 (c 15 (NI)) and Schedule 4 to the Magistrates' Court (Northern Ireland) Order 1981 (SI 1981/1675 (NI 26)).

(4) A fine imposed on a partnership on its conviction for an offence is to be paid out of the partnership assets.

(5) A fine imposed on an unincorporated association other than a partnership on its conviction for an offence is to be paid out of the funds of the association.

NOTES

Commencement: 4 January 2022.

[9.606]

39 Offences: penalties

(1) A person who commits an offence under section 32 (completing notifiable acquisition without approval) or 33 (failing to comply with interim or final order) is liable—

(a) on summary conviction in England and Wales, to imprisonment for a term not exceeding 12 months, or a fine (or both),

(b) on summary conviction in Scotland, to imprisonment for a term not exceeding 12 months, or a fine not exceeding the statutory maximum (or both),

(c) on summary conviction in Northern Ireland, to imprisonment for a term not exceeding 6 months, or a fine not exceeding the statutory maximum (or both),

(d) on conviction on indictment, to imprisonment for a term not exceeding 5 years, or a fine (or both).

(2) A person who commits an offence under section 34 (offences in relation to supplying information and attendance of witnesses) or 35 (offences in relation to sharing information) is liable—

(a) on summary conviction in England and Wales, to imprisonment for a term not exceeding 12 months, or a fine (or both),

(b) on summary conviction in Scotland, to imprisonment for a term not exceeding 12 months, or a fine not exceeding the statutory maximum (or both),

(c) on summary conviction in Northern Ireland, to imprisonment for a term not exceeding 6 months, or a fine not exceeding the statutory maximum (or both),

(d) on conviction on indictment, to imprisonment for a term not exceeding 2 years, or a fine (or both).

(3) In relation to an offence committed before [2 May 2022], the references in subsections (1)(a) and (2)(a) to 12 months are to be read as references to 6 months.

NOTES

Commencement: 4 January 2022.

Sub-s (3): words in square brackets substituted by the Criminal Justice Act 2003 (Commencement No 33) and Sentencing Act 2020 (Commencement No 2) Regulations 2022, SI 2022/500, reg 5, Schedule, Pt 1, as from 28 April 2022.

Civil sanctions

[9.607]

40 Power to impose monetary penalties

(1) Subject to section 43(1), the Secretary of State may give a notice imposing a monetary penalty on a person if the Secretary of State is satisfied, beyond reasonable doubt, that the person has committed an offence under—

(a) section 32 (completing notifiable acquisition without approval),

(b) section 33 (failing to comply with interim or final order), or

(c) section 34 (offences in relation to supplying information and attendance of witnesses),

(including where the person is liable to be proceeded against by virtue of section 36).

(2) A notice under this section is referred to in this Act as a penalty notice.

(3) In this Act "monetary penalty" means a requirement to pay to the Secretary of State a penalty of an amount determined by the Secretary of State.

(4) For an offence under section 33 or 34(1)(a), a monetary penalty may be—

(a) a fixed amount ("a fixed penalty"),

(b) an amount calculated by reference to a daily rate ("a daily rate penalty"), or

(c) a combination of a fixed penalty and a daily rate penalty.

(5) For an offence under section 32 or for any other offence under section 34, the monetary penalty may be a fixed penalty only.

(6) The amount of the monetary penalty is to be such amount as the Secretary of State considers appropriate but it may not exceed the permitted maximum, as set out in section 41.

(7) When determining a monetary penalty under this section, the Secretary of State must have regard, in particular, to—

(a) the seriousness of the offence,

(b) the desirability of deterring both the person on whom the penalty is imposed and others from committing the offence to which the penalty relates,

(c) the possibility, and desirability, of rectifying any failure to which the offence relates,

(d) any steps taken by the person on whom the penalty is imposed towards rectifying any failure to which the offence relates, and

(e) the ability of the person on whom the penalty is imposed to pay the penalty.

(8) A penalty notice must include information as to—

(a) the grounds for imposing the monetary penalty,

(b) whether the penalty is a fixed penalty, a daily rate penalty or a combination of both and how it is calculated,

(c) in the case of a fixed penalty, the amount of the penalty,

(d) in the case of a daily rate penalty, the amount of the daily rate, the day on which the amount first starts to accumulate and the day on which, or the circumstances in which, it ceases to accumulate,

(e) how the amount of the penalty was determined,

(f) how payment may be made,

(g) the period within which payment is to be made (which must be at least 28 days),

(h) rights of appeal,

(i) the consequences of non-payment.

(9) For the purposes of a daily rate penalty—

(a) the first day on which the amount may start to accumulate is the day after the day on which the penalty notice is given,

(b) unless the Secretary of State determines an earlier date, the daily rate ceases to accumulate at the beginning of the earliest of—

(i) the day on which the requirement to comply to which the offence relates is satisfied,

(ii) the day on which that requirement no longer applies.

(10) A monetary penalty imposed under this section is to be paid out of—

(a) the partnership assets where imposed on a partnership, and

(b) the funds of the association where imposed on an unincorporated association other than a partnership.

NOTES

Commencement: 4 January 2022.

[9.608]

41 Permitted maximum penalties

(1) The following are the permitted maximum fixed penalties for an offence under section 32 or 33—

(a) if the offence is committed by a business, the higher of 5% of the total value of the turnover of the business (both in and outside the United Kingdom and including any business owned or controlled by the business) and £10 million,

(b) if the offence is committed otherwise than by a business, £10 million.

(2) The following are the permitted maximum amounts per day for a daily rate penalty for an offence under section 33—

(a) if the offence is committed by a business, the higher of 0.1% of the total turnover of the business (both in and outside the United Kingdom and including any business owned or controlled by the business) and £200,000,

(b) if the offence is committed otherwise than by a business, £200,000.

(3) The permitted maximum fixed penalty for an offence under section 34(1)(a) is £30,000.

(4) The permitted maximum amount per day for a daily rate penalty for an offence under section 34(1)(a) is £15,000.

(5) The permitted maximum fixed penalty for an offence under section 34(1)(b) is £30,000.

(6) The permitted maximum fixed penalty for an offence under section 34(2) is £30,000.

(7) The permitted maximum fixed penalty for an offence under section 34(3) or (4) is £30,000.

(8) The Secretary of State may by regulations—

(a) provide that a person of a description specified in the regulations is or is not a business for the purposes of this section,

(b) make provision for determining when a business is to be treated as controlled by another business for the purposes of this section,

(c) make provision for determining the turnover (both in and outside the United Kingdom) of a business for the purposes of this section,

(d) amend subsection (1) or (2) so as to alter the percentage for the time being specified there,

(e) amend any of subsections (1) to (7) by substituting a different sum for any sum for the time being specified there.

(9) The regulations may in particular—

(a) include by virtue of subsection (8)(c) provision as to the amounts which are, or which are not, to be treated as comprising the turnover of a business, or provision as to the date or dates by reference to which the turnover of a business is to be determined,

(b) make provision for the Secretary of State to determine matters of a description specified in the regulations (including the matters mentioned in paragraph (a)).

NOTES

Commencement: 29 April 2021 (sub-s (8)); 1 July 2021 (sub-s (9)); 4 January 2022 (otherwise).

Regulations: the National Security and Investment Act 2021 (Monetary Penalties) (Turnover of a Business) Regulations 2021, SI 2021/1262 at **[10.1319]**.

[9.609]

42 Review, variation and revocation of monetary penalties

(1) The Secretary of State must keep a monetary penalty imposed by a penalty notice under review and may vary or revoke the penalty notice as the Secretary of State considers appropriate.

(2) If a penalty is revoked under this section, the Secretary of State must, as soon as practicable, give a notice to the person upon whom the penalty was imposed.

(3) If a penalty, or the period within which a penalty is to be paid, is varied under this section, the Secretary of State must, as soon as practicable, give a notice to the person on whom the penalty was imposed which—

(a) states the variation and the reasons for the variation,

(b) includes information about rights of appeal and consequences of non-payment.

(4) A notice under subsection (3) is referred to in this Act as a penalty variation notice.

NOTES

Commencement: 4 January 2022.

[9.610]

43 Monetary penalties: criminal proceedings and convictions

(1) A penalty notice may not be given to a person in respect of an offence if—

(a) criminal proceedings have been instituted but not concluded in respect of the offence, or

(b) the person has been convicted of the offence.

(2) Where a person has paid, or is required to pay, a monetary penalty under a penalty notice, no criminal proceedings may be instituted against the person in respect of the offence to which the notice relates.

NOTES

Commencement: 4 January 2022.

[9.611]

44 Recovering penalties

(1) Subsections (2) to (8) apply if all or part of a monetary penalty imposed by a penalty notice is unpaid by the time it is required to be paid.

(2) The unpaid balance carries interest from time to time at the rate for the time being specified in section 17 of the Judgments Act 1838.

(3) Where the Secretary of State considers it appropriate to do so, the Secretary of State may require so much of the penalty as has not already been paid to be paid immediately.

(4) The Secretary of State may recover any of the penalty and any interest that has not been paid if—

(a) no appeal relating to the penalty has been brought under section 50 during the period within which such an appeal may be brought, or

(b) an appeal has been determined or withdrawn.

(5) In England and Wales, and in Northern Ireland, the penalty is recoverable as if it were payable under an order of the High Court.

(6) In Scotland, the penalty may be enforced in the same manner as an extract registered decree arbitral bearing a warrant for execution issued by the sheriff court of any sheriffdom in Scotland.

(7) Where action is taken under this section for the recovery of a sum payable under a penalty notice, the penalty is—

(a) in relation to England and Wales, to be treated for the purposes of section 98 of the Courts Act 2003 (register of judgments and orders etc) as if it were a judgment entered in the High Court, and

(b) in relation to Northern Ireland, to be treated for the purposes of Article 116 of the Judgments Enforcement (Northern Ireland) Order 1981 (SI 1981/226 (NI 6)) (register of judgments) as if it were a judgment in respect of which an application has been accepted under Article 22 or 23(1) of that Order.

(8) Any sums received by the Secretary of State by way of a monetary penalty, or interest in respect of such a penalty, under this Act must be paid into the Consolidated Fund.

NOTES

Commencement: 4 January 2022.

[9.612]

45 Monetary penalties: cost recovery

(1) The Secretary of State may give a notice to a person requiring the person to pay to the Secretary of State the costs incurred by the Secretary of State in relation to the imposition of a monetary penalty on that person under section 40.

(2) A notice under subsection (1) is referred to in this Act as a cost recovery notice.

(3) The reference to "costs" in subsection (1) includes, in particular—

(a) investigation costs,

(b) administration costs,

(c) costs of obtaining expert advice (including legal advice).

(4) A cost recovery notice must specify the amount to be paid and include information as to—

(a) the grounds for giving the notice,

(b) how payment may be made,

(c) the period within which payment is to be made (which must be at least 28 days),

(d) rights of appeal,

(e) the consequences of non-payment.

(5) A person required to pay an amount to the Secretary of State under this section may require the Secretary of State to give a detailed breakdown of that amount.

(6) Costs imposed under this section are to be paid out of—

(a) the partnership assets where imposed on a partnership, and

(b) the funds of the association where imposed on an unincorporated association other than a partnership.

NOTES

Commencement: 4 January 2022.

[9.613]

46 Review, variation and revocation of cost recovery notice

(1) The Secretary of State must keep a cost recovery notice under review and may vary or revoke it as the Secretary of State considers appropriate.

(2) If a cost recovery notice is revoked under this section, the Secretary of State must, as soon as practicable, give a notice to the person to whom the cost recovery notice was given.

(3) If the costs, or the period within which the costs are to be paid, is varied under this section, the Secretary of State must, as soon as practicable, give a notice to the person to whom the cost recovery notice was given which—

(a) states the variation and the reasons for the variation,

(b) includes information about rights of appeal and consequences of non-payment.

(4) A notice under subsection (3) is referred to in this Act as a cost variation notice.

NOTES

Commencement: 4 January 2022.

[9.614]

47 Enforcement of cost recovery notice

(1) Subsections (2) to (8) apply if some or all of the costs payable under a cost recovery notice are unpaid by the time when they are required to be paid.

(2) The unpaid balance carries interest from time to time at the rate for the time being specified in section 17 of the Judgments Act 1838.

(3) Where the Secretary of State considers it appropriate to do so, the Secretary of State may require so much of the costs as have not already been paid to be paid immediately.

(4) The Secretary of State may recover from the person any of the costs and any interest as has not been paid if—

(a) no appeal relating to the costs has been brought under section 51 during the period within which such an appeal may be brought, or

(b) an appeal has been determined or withdrawn.

(5) In England and Wales, and in Northern Ireland, the costs are recoverable as if they were payable under an order of the High Court.

(6) In Scotland, the costs may be enforced in the same manner as an extract registered decree arbitral bearing a warrant for execution issued by the sheriff court of any sheriffdom in Scotland.

(7) Where action is taken under this section for the recovery of a sum payable under a cost recovery notice, the costs are—

(a) in relation to England and Wales, to be treated for the purposes of section 98 of the Courts Act 2003 (register of judgments and orders etc) as if they were a judgment entered in the High Court, and

(b) in relation to Northern Ireland, to be treated for the purposes of Article 116 of the Judgments Enforcement (Northern Ireland) Order 1981 (SI 1981/226 (NI 6)) (register of judgments) as if they were a judgment in respect of which an application has been accepted under Article 22 or 23(1) of that Order.

(8) Any sums received by the Secretary of State by way of costs, or interest in respect of such costs, under this Act must be paid into the Consolidated Fund.

NOTES

Commencement: 4 January 2022.

Civil proceedings

[9.615]

48 Enforcement through civil proceedings

(1) A person's duty to comply with a requirement to which the person is subject under or by virtue of an information notice, an attendance notice, an interim order or a final order is enforceable by civil proceedings by the Secretary of State for an injunction, or for specific performance of a statutory duty under section 45 of the Court of Session Act 1988, or for any other appropriate relief or remedy.

(2) Subsection (1) applies whether or not the person is in the United Kingdom.

NOTES

Commencement: 4 January 2022.

Judicial review and appeals

[9.616]

49 Procedure for judicial review of certain decisions

(1) This section applies to a claim for judicial review of a relevant decision.

(2) A "relevant decision" means—

(a) a decision or action under or by virtue of any of the following provisions, but not including any such decision or action that is directly related to a Part 3 function of the Secretary of State—

(i) section 19,

(ii) section 20,

(iii) section 21,

(iv) section 54(1) and (2)(a),

(v) section 54(6) to (8), insofar as the decision or action is related to the disclosure of information under section 54(2)(a),

(vi) section 55(1) and (3), insofar as the decision or action is related to the disclosure of information under section 54(2)(a),

(vii) section 56,

(viii) section 57, other than a decision or action related to the disclosure of information under section 54(2)(b) to (f) or (3),

(b) a decision or action under or by virtue of section 54(9), insofar as the decision or action is related to a decision or action falling within paragraph (a)(iv) or (v),

(c) a decision or action under or by virtue of—

(i) any provision of Part 1 of this Act not mentioned in paragraph (a),

(ii) Part 2 of this Act,

(iii) section 53, or

(iv) section 62,

and "action" includes a failure to act.

(3) A "Part 3 function" means a function under or by virtue of this Part of this Act.

(4) The court may entertain proceedings for a claim to which this section applies only if the claim form is filed before the end of the period of 28 days beginning with the day after the day on which the grounds to make the claim first arose, unless the court considers that exceptional circumstances apply.

(5) In the application of this section to Scotland—

(a) subsection (1) has effect with the substitution of "an application to the supervisory jurisdiction of the court in respect" for "a claim for judicial review",

(b) subsection (4) has effect with the substitution of—

(i) "an application" for "a claim",

(ii) "application is made" for "claim form is filed",

(iii) "the application" for "the claim".

(6) In the application of this section to Northern Ireland—

(a) subsection (1) has effect with the substitution of "an application" for "a claim",

(b) subsection (4) has effect with the substitution of—

(i) "an application" for "a claim",

(ii) "application for leave to apply for judicial review" for "claim form is filed",

(iii) "the application" for "the claim".

(7) In this section "the court" means—

(a) the High Court in England and Wales,

(b) the Court of Session in Scotland, and

(c) the High Court in Northern Ireland.

NOTES

Commencement: 4 January 2022.

[9.617]

50 Appeals against monetary penalties

(1) A person who is given a penalty notice or a variation notice may appeal to the court.

(2) A person may not appeal under this section after the end of the period of 28 days beginning with the day after the day on which the notice is given to the person.

(3) On an appeal against a penalty notice the court may—

(a) confirm or quash the decision to impose the monetary penalty,

(b) confirm or reduce the amount of the penalty,

(c) confirm or vary the period within which all or part of the penalty is to be paid.

(4) On an appeal against a variation notice the court may confirm, vary or quash the variation but may not increase the amount of the monetary penalty.

(5) In this section "the court" means—

(a) the High Court in England and Wales,

(b) the Court of Session in Scotland, and

(c) the High Court in Northern Ireland.

(6) Where an appeal is brought under this section, the monetary penalty is not payable until the appeal is determined or withdrawn, unless the court orders otherwise.

NOTES

Commencement: 4 January 2022.

[9.618]

51 Appeals against costs

(1) A person given a cost recovery notice or a cost variation notice may appeal to the court.

(2) A person may not appeal under this section after the end of the period of 28 days beginning with the day after the day on which the notice is given to the person.

(3) On an appeal against a cost recovery notice the court may—

(a) confirm or quash the decision to impose costs,

(b) confirm or reduce the amount payable,

(c) confirm or vary the period within which payment is to be made.

(4) On an appeal against a cost variation notice the court may confirm, vary or quash the variation but may not increase the amount payable.

(5) In this section "the court" means—

(a) the High Court in England and Wales,

(b) the Court of Session in Scotland, and

(c) the High Court in Northern Ireland.

(6) Where an appeal is brought under this section, the costs are not payable until the appeal is determined or withdrawn, unless the court orders otherwise.

NOTES

Commencement: 4 January 2022.

Territorial application

[9.619]

52 Extra-territorial application and jurisdiction to try offences

(1) Sections 32, 33, 34 and 35 apply—

(a) whether the offence is committed in the United Kingdom or elsewhere,

(b) if the offence is committed by an individual, whatever the nationality of the individual committing the offence,

(c) if the offence is committed otherwise than by an individual, regardless of whether the body corporate or unincorporated association is formed or recognised under the law of a country or territory outside the United Kingdom.

(2) Where an offence under this Part is committed outside the United Kingdom—

(a) proceedings for the offence may be taken at any place in the United Kingdom, and

(b) the offence may for all incidental purposes be treated as having been committed at any such place.

(3) In the application of subsection (2) to Scotland, any such proceedings against a person may be taken—

(a) in any sheriff court district in which the person is apprehended or is in custody, or

(b) in such sheriff court district as the Lord Advocate may determine.

(4) In subsection (3) "sheriff court district" is to be read in accordance with the Criminal Procedure (Scotland) Act 1995 (see section 307(1) of that Act).

NOTES

Commencement: 4 January 2022.

PART 4 MISCELLANEOUS

Administrative requirements

[9.620]

53 Procedure for service, etc

(1) The Secretary of State may by regulations make provision for the procedure which must be followed when a provision of or made under this Act requires or allows a notice, order, notification or document of any kind to be given or served.

(2) The regulations may, in particular, make provision—

(a) as to the manner in which a document must be given or served,

(b) as to the address to which a document must be sent,

(c) requiring, or allowing, a document to be sent electronically,

(d) for treating a document as having been given, received or served on a date or at a time determined in accordance with the regulations,

(e) as to what must, or may, be done if a sender or an intended recipient is not an individual,

(f) as to what must, or may, be done if a person is treated by virtue of Schedule 1 as holding an interest or right for the purposes of this Act,

(g) as to what must, or may, be done if a sender or an intended recipient is outside the United Kingdom.

(3) Section 7 of the Interpretation Act 1978 (service of notice by post) has effect in relation to provisions made under this Act subject to any provision made by regulations under this section.

NOTES

Commencement: 29 April 2021 (sub-s (1)); 1 July 2021 (otherwise).

Regulations: the National Security and Investment Act 2021 (Procedure for Service) Regulations 2021, SI 2021/1267 at **[10.1345]**.

Information gateways

[9.621]

54 Disclosure of information

(1) A public authority may disclose information to the Secretary of State for the purpose of facilitating the exercise by the Secretary of State of functions under this Act.

(2) The Secretary of State may disclose information received under this Act to a public authority or an overseas public authority—

(a) for the purpose of facilitating the exercise by the Secretary of State of functions under this Act,

(b) for the prevention or detection of crime,

(c) for the purposes of a criminal investigation,

(d) for the purposes of criminal proceedings,

(e) for the purposes of civil proceedings under this Act, or

(f) for the purpose of protecting national security.

(3) The Secretary of State may also disclose such information to an overseas public authority for the purpose of the exercise of corresponding functions of overseas public authorities.

(4) A person who receives information under subsection (2) or (3) may not—

(a) use the information for a purpose other than the purpose for which it was disclosed, or

(b) further disclose the information,

except with the consent of the Secretary of State (which may be general or specific).

(5) Subsection (4) does not apply to information to which section 55 applies (information received from HMRC).

(6) In deciding whether to disclose information under this section, the Secretary of State must consider whether the disclosure would prejudice, to an unreasonable degree, the commercial interests of any person concerned.

(7) In deciding whether to disclose information to an overseas public authority under this section, the Secretary of State must have regard, in particular, to the following considerations—

(a) whether the law of the country or territory to whose authority the disclosure would be made provides protection against self-incrimination in criminal proceedings which corresponds to the protection provided in any part of the United Kingdom, and

(b) whether the matter in respect of which the disclosure is sought is sufficiently serious to justify making the disclosure.

(8) Except as provided by section 57, the disclosure of information under this section does not breach—

(a) any obligation of confidence owed by the person making the disclosure, or

(b) any other restriction on the disclosure of information (however imposed).

(9) In this section—

"overseas public authority" means a person in any country or territory outside the United Kingdom which appears to the Secretary of State to exercise functions of a public nature which—

(a) correspond to the functions of the Secretary of State under this Act, or

(b) relate to any of the purposes mentioned in paragraphs (b) to (f) of subsection (2),

"public authority" has the same meaning as in section 6 of the Human Rights Act 1998.

NOTES

Commencement: 4 January 2022.

[9.622]

55 Disclosure of information held by HMRC

(1) A person who receives information disclosed under section 54 by Her Majesty's Revenue and Customs (or anyone acting on their behalf) may not—

(a) use the information for a purpose other than the purpose mentioned in section 54(1), or

(b) further disclose the information,

except with the consent of the Commissioners for Her Majesty's Revenue and Customs (which may be general or specific).

(2) If a person discloses information in contravention of subsection (1)(b) which relates to a person whose identity—

(a) is specified in the disclosure, or

(b) can be deduced from it,

section 19 of the Commissioners for Revenue and Customs Act 2005 (offence of wrongful disclosure) applies in relation to that disclosure as it applies in relation to a disclosure of information in contravention of section 20(9) of that Act (and, accordingly, section 35 of this Act does not apply to that disclosure).

(3) Except as provided by section 57, the disclosure of information under this section does not breach—

(a) any obligation of confidence owed by the person disclosing the information, or

(b) any other restriction on the disclosure of information (however imposed).

NOTES

Commencement: 4 January 2022.

CMA information

[9.623]

56 Duty of CMA to provide information and assistance

The Competition and Markets Authority must give the Secretary of State—

(a) such information in its possession as the Secretary of State may by direction reasonably require to enable the Secretary of State to exercise functions under this Act,

(b) any other assistance which the Secretary of State may by direction reasonably require for the purpose of facilitating the exercise by the Secretary of State of functions under this Act and which it is within the power of the Authority to give.

NOTES

Commencement: 4 January 2022.

Data protection

[9.624]

57 Data protection

(1) This section applies to a duty or power to disclose or use information where the duty or power is imposed or conferred by or under any provision of Parts 1 to 4 of this Act.

(2) A duty or power to which this section applies does not operate to require or authorise the disclosure or use of information if the disclosure or use—

(a) would contravene the data protection legislation (but the duty or power is to be taken into account in determining whether the disclosure or use would contravene that legislation), or

(b) is prohibited by any of Parts 1 to 7 of, or Chapter 1 of Part 9 of, the Investigatory Powers Act 2016.

(3) In this section "data protection legislation" has the same meaning as in the Data Protection Act 2018 (see section 3 of that Act).

NOTES

Commencement: 4 January 2022.

58, 59 *(S 58 introduces Sch 2 to this Act (Minor and consequential amendments and revocations). S 59 amends the Enterprise Act 2002, s 243.)*

Defamation

[9.625]

60 Defamation

For the purposes of the law relating to defamation, absolute privilege attaches to any notice or direction given, or decision, report or order made, by the Secretary of State or the Competition and Markets Authority in the exercise of functions under or by virtue of this Act.

NOTES

Commencement: 4 January 2022.

Annual report

[9.626]

61 Annual report

(1) The Secretary of State must, in relation to each relevant period—

(a) prepare a report in accordance with this section, and

(b) lay a copy of it before each House of Parliament as soon as is practicable after the end of that period.

(2) Each report must provide details of—

(a) the expenditure incurred by the Secretary of State in giving, or in connection with giving, financial assistance falling within section 30,

(b) the amount of the actual or contingent liabilities of the Secretary of State at the end of the relevant period in respect of such financial assistance,

(c) the number of mandatory notices accepted,

(d) the number of mandatory notices rejected,

(e) the average number of working days—

(i) from receipt of a mandatory notice to notification of a decision to accept that notice, and

(ii) from receipt of a mandatory notice to giving written reasons for a decision to reject that notice,

(f) the sectors of the economy in relation to which mandatory notices were given,

(g) the number of voluntary notices accepted,

(h) the number of voluntary notices rejected,

(i) the average number of working days—

(i) from receipt of a voluntary notice to notification of a decision to accept that notice, and

(ii) from receipt of a voluntary notice to giving written reasons for a decision to reject that notice,

(j) the sectors of the economy in relation to which voluntary notices were given,

(k) the number of call-in notices given,

(l) the sectors of the economy in relation to which call-in notices were given,

(m) the number of final notifications given,

(n) the number of final orders made,

(o) the number of final orders varied,

(p) the number of final orders revoked.

(3) "Relevant period" means—

(a) the period beginning with the day on which this section comes into force and ending with the following 31 March, and

(b) each subsequent period of 12 months.

NOTES

Commencement: 4 January 2022.

PART 5 FINAL PROVISIONS

[9.627]

62 Transitional and saving provision in relation to the Enterprise Act 2002

(1) Nothing in this Act has effect in relation to anything that took place before 12 November 2020.

(2) Subsections (3) and (4) apply in relation to events which constitute a trigger event described in section 2(4), unless any action has been taken under this Act in relation to the events.

(3) If, disregarding the effect of any amendment made by this Act to the Enterprise Act 2002, the Secretary of State could, in relation to the events—

(a) give an intervention notice under section 42(2) of that Act,

(b) give a special intervention notice under section 59(2) of that Act, or

(c) give a European intervention notice under section 67(2) of that Act,

the Secretary of State may give the notice on or after the day on which this section comes into force.

(4) If any such notice is given in relation to events to which this section applies—

(a) before the day on which this section comes into force, or

(b) by virtue of subsection (3), on or after the day on which this section comes into force,

nothing in this Act has effect in relation to the events (and, accordingly, the Enterprise Act 2002 continues to have effect in relation to the events, disregarding the effect of any amendment made by this Act to that Act.)

(5) Regulations under section 66(4)(b) may make further provision for the purposes of this section.

NOTES

Commencement: 29 April 2021.

[9.628]

63 Regulations under this Act

(1) This section applies to regulations under this Act other than regulations under section 66 (commencement regulations).

(2) Regulations are to be made by statutory instrument.

(3) Regulations may contain consequential, transitional, transitory or saving provision.

(4) Subject to subsection (5), a statutory instrument containing regulations is subject to annulment in pursuance of a resolution of either House of Parliament.

(5) A statutory instrument containing (whether alone or with other provision) regulations under any of the following may not be made unless a draft of it has been laid before Parliament and approved by a resolution of each House—

(a) section 6(1),

(b) section 11(3),

(c) section 41(8).

NOTES

Commencement: 29 April 2021.

[9.629]

64 Financial provision

Any expenditure incurred by the Secretary of State under or by virtue of this Act is to be paid out of money provided by Parliament.

NOTES

Commencement: 29 April 2021.

[9.630]

65 Interpretation

In this Act—

"acquirer" has the meaning given by section 5(2),

"assessment period" has the meaning given in section 23,

"attendance notice" means a notice given under section 20(1),

"business" includes—

(a) a professional practice,

(b) an undertaking which is carried on for gain or reward,

(c) an undertaking in the course of which goods or services are supplied otherwise than free of charge, and

references to a person carrying on business include references to a person carrying on business in partnership with one or more other persons,

"call-in notice" means a notice given under section 1(1),

"cost recovery notice" means a notice given under section 45(1),

"cost variation notice" means a notice given under section 46(3),

"final notification" has the meaning given by section 26(2),

"final order" means an order made under section 26(3),

"information notice" means a notice given under section 19(1),

"interim order" means an order made under section 25(1),

"mandatory notice" means a notice given under section 14(1),

"monetary penalty" has the meaning given by section 40(3),

"notifiable acquisition" has the meaning given by section 6(2) (and see subsection (3) of that section),

"notifiable acquisition regulations" means regulations made under section 6(1),

"penalty notice" means a notice given under section 40(1),
"penalty variation notice" means a notice given under section 42(3),
"qualifying asset" has the meaning given by section 7(4),
"qualifying entity" has the meaning given by section 7(2),
"the territorial sea" means the territorial sea adjacent to the United Kingdom,
"trigger event" has the meaning given by section 5(1) and includes, where the context requires, a trigger event that has not yet taken place,
"United Kingdom national" means an individual who is—
(a) a British citizen, a British overseas territories citizen, a British National (Overseas) or a British Overseas citizen,
(b) a person who under the British Nationality Act 1981 is a British subject, or
(c) a British protected person within the meaning of that Act,
"validation application" has the meaning given by section 16(2),
"validation notice" means a notice given under section 15(2)(b), 16(7)(b)(ii) or 17(2) (and see section 15(3)),
"voluntary notice" means a notice given under section 18(2),
"working day", in relation to a part of the United Kingdom, means a day other than—
(a) a Saturday or Sunday, or
(b) a day which is a bank holiday under the Banking and Financial Dealings Act 1971 in that or any other part of the United Kingdom.

NOTES

Commencement: 29 April 2021.

[9.631]

66 Short title, commencement and extent

(1) This Act may be cited as the National Security and Investment Act 2021.

(2) This Part of this Act and the following provisions of this Act (which contain powers to make regulations) come into force on the day on which this Act is passed—
(a) section 6(1),
(b) section 11(3),
(c) section 14(4),
(d) section 16(3),
(e) section 18(4),
(f) section 36(5),
(g) section 41(8),
(h) section 53(1).

(3) The rest of this Act comes into force on such day as the Secretary of State may by regulations made by statutory instrument appoint.

(4) Regulations under subsection (3) may—
(a) appoint different days for different purposes;
(b) make transitional, transitory or saving provision.

(5) This Act extends to England and Wales, Scotland and Northern Ireland, except that the amendment or repeal of any enactment has the same extent as the enactment amended or repealed.

NOTES

Commencement: 29 April 2021.

Regulations: the National Security and Investment Act 2021 (Commencement No 1 and Transitional Provision) Regulations 2021, SI 2021/788; the National Security and Investment Act 2021 (Commencement No 2 and Transitional and Saving Provision) Regulations 2021, SI 2021/1465 (see the note below).

Transitional Provisions etc: the National Security and Investment Act 2021 (Commencement No 2 and Transitional and Saving Provision) Regulations 2021, SI 2021/1465 brings this Act into force on 4 January 2022 in so far as not already in force, and contains the following transitional provisions: (a) Regulation 4 provides that this Act does not apply to a proposed merger where the Secretary of State has given an intervention notice under sections 42(2), 59(2) or 67(2) of the Enterprise Act 2002 in relation to the proposed merger before 4 January 2022 citing national security as the public interest consideration and that the provisions of the 2002 Act continue to apply; (b) Regulation 5 provides that where, immediately before 4 January 2022, the Competition and Markets Authority has made a reference under ss 22 or 33 of the 2002 Act or is considering whether to make a such a reference and the initial period as defined in s 34ZA of the 2002 Act has commenced, the provisions of the 2002 Act shall apply as if unamended by this Act.

SCHEDULES

SCHEDULE 1
TRIGGER EVENTS: HOLDING OF INTERESTS AND RIGHTS

Section 10

[9.632]

Joint interests

1. If two or more persons each hold an interest or right jointly, each of them is treated as holding that interest or right.

Joint arrangements

2. (1) If interests or rights held by a person and interests or rights held by another person are the subject of a joint arrangement between those persons, each of them is treated as holding the combined interests or rights of both of them.

(2) A "joint arrangement" is an arrangement between the holders of interests or rights that they will exercise all or substantially all the rights conferred by their respective interests, or their respective rights, jointly in a way that is pre-determined by the arrangement.

Indirect holdings

3. (1) An interest or right held indirectly by a person is to be treated as held by the person.

(2) A person holds an interest or right "indirectly" if the person has a majority stake in an entity and that entity—

- (a) holds the interest or right, or
- (b) is part of a chain of entities—
  - (i) each of which (other than the last) has a majority stake in the entity immediately below it in the chain, and
  - (ii) the last of which holds the interest or right.

(3) For these purposes, A has a "majority stake" in B if—

- (a) A holds a majority of voting rights in B,
- (b) A is a member of B and has the right to appoint or remove a majority of the board of directors of B,
- (c) A is a member of B and controls alone, pursuant to an agreement with other shareholders or members, a majority of the voting rights in B, or
- (d) A has the right to exercise, or actually exercises, dominant influence or control over B.

(4) In the application of this paragraph to the right to appoint or remove a majority of the board of directors, an entity is to be treated as having the right to appoint a director if—

- (a) a person's appointment as director follows necessarily from that person's appointment as director of the entity, or
- (b) the directorship is held by the entity itself.

(5) In this paragraph—

- (a) the reference to the right to appoint or remove a majority of the board of directors of an entity is to the right to appoint or remove directors holding a majority of the voting rights at meetings of the board on all or substantially all matters,
- (b) the reference to the board of directors, in the case of an entity that does not have such a board, is to be read as a reference to the equivalent management body of that entity,
- (c) references to "voting rights" are to be read in accordance with section 8(7).

Interests held by nominees

4. An interest held by a person as nominee for another is to be treated as held by the other (and not by the nominee).

Rights treated as held by person who controls their exercise

5. (1) Where a person controls a right, the right is to be treated as held by that person (and not by the person who in fact holds the right, unless that person also controls it).

(2) A person "controls" a right if, by virtue of any arrangement between that person and others, the right is exercisable only—

- (a) by that person,
- (b) in accordance with that person's directions or instructions, or
- (c) with that person's consent or concurrence.

Rights exercisable only in certain circumstances etc

6. (1) Rights that are exercisable by a person only in certain circumstances are to be treated as held by the person only—

- (a) when the circumstances have arisen, and for so long as they continue to obtain, or
- (b) when the circumstances are within the control of the person.

(2) But rights that are exercisable by an administrator or by creditors while an entity is in relevant insolvency proceedings are not to be regarded as held by the administrator or creditors even while the entity is in those proceedings.

(3) "Relevant insolvency proceedings" means—

- (a) administration within the meaning of the Insolvency Act 1986,
- (b) administration within the meaning of the Insolvency (Northern Ireland) Order 1989 (SI 1989/2405 (NI 19)), or
- (c) proceedings under the insolvency law of another country or territory during which an entity's assets and affairs are subject to the control or supervision of a third party or creditor.

(4) Rights that are normally exercisable but are temporarily incapable of exercise are not for that reason to be treated as not being held.

Rights attached to shares held by way of security

7. Rights attached to shares held by way of security provided by a person are to be treated as held by that person—

- (a) where apart from the right to exercise them for the purpose of preserving the value of the security, or of realising it, the rights are exercisable only in accordance with that person's instructions, and
- (b) where the shares are held in connection with the granting of loans as part of normal business activities and apart from the right to exercise them for the purpose of preserving the value of the security, or of realising it, the rights are exercisable only in that person's interests.

Connected persons

8. Two or more persons who are connected with each other (within the meaning given by paragraph 9 or 10) are each to be treated as holding the combined interests or rights of both or all of them.

9. (1) Two or more undertakings are connected if they are group undertakings in respect of each other.

(2) In sub-paragraph (1), "undertaking" and "group undertaking" have the same meanings as in the Companies Act 2006 (see section 1161 of that Act).

10. (1) An individual, A, is connected with another individual, B, if—

(a) A is B's spouse, civil partner or cohabitee,
(b) A is a relative of B,
(c) A is the spouse, civil partner or cohabitee of a relative of B,
(d) A is a relative of B's spouse, civil partner or cohabitee, or
(e) A is the spouse, civil partner or cohabitee of a relative of B's spouse, civil partner or cohabitee.

(2) For the purposes of sub-paragraph (1)—

(a) two persons who are living together as if they were a married couple or civil partners are cohabitees,
(b) references to a spouse, civil partner or cohabitee include a former spouse, civil partner or cohabitee, and
(c) "relative" means a brother, sister, uncle, aunt, nephew, niece, lineal ancestor or descendant (the stepchild of any person, or anyone adopted by a person, whether legally or otherwise, as their child, being regarded as a relative or taken into account to trace a relationship in the same way as that person's child).

Common purpose

11. (1) Two or more persons who share a common purpose in relation to an asset or entity are each to be treated as holding the combined interests or rights of both or all of them.

(2) The cases in which persons share a common purpose in relation to an entity include (but are not limited to) cases in which the persons co-ordinate their influence on the activities, operations, governance or strategy of the entity.

(3) The cases in which persons share a common purpose in relation to an asset include (but are not limited to) cases in which the persons co-ordinate their influence on the way in which the asset is used, and section 9(2) applies for the purposes of this sub-paragraph.

Arrangements

12. (1) In this Schedule "arrangement" includes—

(a) any scheme, agreement or understanding, whether or not it is legally enforceable, and
(b) any convention, custom or practice of any kind.

(2) But something does not count as an arrangement unless there is at least some degree of stability about it (whether by its nature or terms, the time it has been in existence or otherwise).

NOTES

Commencement: 4 January 2022.

SCHEDULE 2

(Sch 2 (minor and consequential amendments and revocations) amends the Enterprise Act 2002, and revokes the following: the Enterprise Act 2002 (Share of Supply Test) (Amendment) Order 2018 (SI 2018/578); the Enterprise Act 2002 (Turnover Test) (Amendment) Order 2018 (SI 2018/593); the Enterprise Act 2002 (Share of Supply) (Amendment) Order 2020 (SI 2020/748); and the Enterprise Act 2002 (Turnover Test) (Amendment) Order 2020 (SI 2020/763).)

RATING (CORONAVIRUS) AND DIRECTORS DISQUALIFICATION (DISSOLVED COMPANIES) ACT 2021 (NOTE)

(2021 c 34)

[9.633]

NOTES

Section 1 of this Act (Determinations in respect of certain non-domestic rating lists) is outside the scope of this work.

Section 2 (Unfit directors of dissolved companies: Great Britain) amends the Company Directors Disqualification Act 1986 at **[5.76]** et seq. Subsection (1) of this section introduces the amendments made by sub-ss (2)–(13) (ie, amendments to ss 6, 7, 8ZA, 8ZB, 15A, 22A–22C and 22E–22H of the 1986 Act, which have been incorporated at the appropriate place). Subsection (14) provides that the amendments made by sub-ss (2)–(13) have effect in relation to conduct of directors of companies occurring, and in relation to companies dissolved, at any time before, as well as after, the passing of this Act (ie, 15 December 2021).

Section 3 (Unfit directors of dissolved companies: Northern Ireland) makes the equivalent amendments to Northern Ireland legislation (the Company Directors Disqualification (Northern Ireland) Order 2002) and is outside the scope of this work.

Section 4 provides for extent, commencement and short title. In so far as relevant to this work, note that the amendments made to the Company Directors Disqualification Act 1986 apply to England and Wales and to Scotland. Note also that s 2 of the Act comes into force on 15 December 2021 for the purposes of the exercise by the Secretary of State or the official receiver of powers under s 7(4) of the 1986 Act, and on 15 February 2022 for all other purposes.

ECONOMIC CRIME (TRANSPARENCY AND ENFORCEMENT) ACT 2022

(2022 c 10)

NOTES

Only Part 1 of this Act (Registration of Overseas Entities), and Part 4 (General provisions) are relevant this work. Part 2 (Unexplained Wealth Orders) and Part 3 (Sanctions) have not been included; the omitted provisions have not been annotated.

This Act is reproduced as amended by: the Money Laundering and Terrorist Financing (Amendment) (No 2) Regulations 2022, SI 2022/860.

ARRANGEMENT OF SECTIONS

PART 1
REGISTRATION OF OVERSEAS ENTITIES

An Act to set up a register of overseas entities and their beneficial owners and require overseas entities who own land to register in certain circumstances; to make provision about unexplained wealth orders; and to make provision about sanctions

[15 March 2022]

PART 1 REGISTRATION OF OVERSEAS ENTITIES

Introduction

[9.634]

1 Overview

This Part—

(a) sets up a register of overseas entities, which will include information about their beneficial owners (sections 3 to 32), and
(b) makes provision that, broadly speaking, is designed to compel overseas entities to register if they own land (sections 33 and 34).

NOTES

Commencement: 1 August 2022 (see further the note below).

Note that the Economic Crime (Transparency and Enforcement) Act 2022 (Commencement No 3) Regulations 2022, SI 2022/876 brings into force ss 1–6, 12–32, and 39–44 of this Act on 1 August 2022, except in so far as those sections relate to ss 7–11 of this Act.

[9.635]

2 Definition of "overseas entity" etc

(1) In this Part "overseas entity" means a legal entity that is governed by the law of a country or territory outside the United Kingdom.

(2) In this Part "legal entity" means a body corporate, partnership or other entity that (in each case) is a legal person under the law by which it is governed.

NOTES

Commencement: 1 August 2022 (see further the note to s 1 at **[9.634]**).

The register and registration

[9.636]

3 Register of overseas entities

(1) The registrar of companies for England and Wales ("the registrar") must keep a register of overseas entities in accordance with this Part.

(2) The register is to consist of—

(a) a list of registered overseas entities,

(b) documents delivered to the registrar under this Part or regulations made under it, or otherwise in connection with the register, and

(c) any other information required to be included in the register by this Part or regulations made under it.

(3) The list of registered overseas entities must contain the name of each overseas entity that—

(a) has made an application for registration in accordance with the requirements of this Part (see section 4), and

(b) has not been removed from the list under section 10.

NOTES

Commencement: 1 August 2022 (see further the note to s 1 at **[9.634]**).

[9.637]

4 Application for registration

(1) An application by an overseas entity for registration must be delivered to the registrar and contain—

(a) the statement and information listed in row 1, 2 or 3 of the table, and, where applicable, the statement and information mentioned in subsection (3),

(b) a statement that the entity has complied with section 12 (duty to take steps to identify registrable beneficial owners etc),

(c) anything required by regulations under section 16 (verification of registrable beneficial owners and managing officers) to be delivered to the registrar, and

(d) the name and contact details of an individual who may be contacted about the application.

(2) This is the table—

	Statement	*Information*
1	A statement: (a) that the entity has identified one or more registrable beneficial owners and that it has no reasonable cause to believe there are others, and (b) that the entity is able to provide the required information about each registrable beneficial owner it has identified.	(1) The required information about the entity. (2) The required information about each registrable beneficial owner that the entity has identified.
2	A statement that the entity has no reasonable cause to believe that it has any registrable beneficial owners.	(1) The required information about the entity. (2) The required information about each managing officer of the entity.
3	A statement: (a) that the entity has reasonable cause to believe that there is at least one registrable beneficial owner that it has not identified, (b) that the entity is not able to provide the required information about one or more of the registrable beneficial owners it has identified, or (c) that paragraphs (a) and (b) both apply.	(1) The required information about the entity. (2) The required information about each managing officer of the entity. (3) The required information about each registrable beneficial owner that the entity has identified or so much of that information as it has been able to obtain.

(3) Where an application includes information that a registrable beneficial owner is a trustee (see paragraphs 3(1)(f) and 5(1)(h) of Schedule 1), the application must also include—

(a) the required information about the trust or so much of that information as the overseas entity has been able to obtain, and

(b) a statement as to whether the entity has any reasonable cause to believe that there is required information about the trust that it has not been able to obtain.

(4) For the required information, see Schedule 1.

(5) For the meaning of "registrable beneficial owner", see Schedule 2.

(6) The Secretary of State may by regulations specify additional statements or information that must be included in an application under this section.

(7) Regulations under subsection (6) are subject to the negative resolution procedure.

NOTES

Commencement: 1 August 2022 (see further the note to s 1 at **[9.634]**).

[9.638]

5 Registration and allocation of overseas entity ID

(1) On the registration of an overseas entity under this Part, the registrar must—

(a) record the date of registration in the register,

(b) allocate an overseas entity ID to the entity, and

(c) record the overseas entity ID in the register.

(2) Overseas entity IDs are to be in such form, consisting of one or more sequences of figures or letters, as the registrar may determine.

(3) The registrar may adopt a new form of overseas entity ID and make such changes to existing overseas entity IDs as appear necessary.

(4) A change of an overseas entity ID has effect from the date on which the overseas entity is notified by the registrar of the change.

NOTES

Commencement: 1 August 2022 (see further the note to s 1 at **[9.634]**).

[9.639]

6 Notice of registration

(1) On the registration of an overseas entity under this Part, the registrar must notify the overseas entity that it has been registered.

(2) The notice must state—

(a) the date of registration, and

(b) the overseas entity ID allocated to the entity.

(3) The notice must also contain information about—

(a) the updating duty under section 7 and the consequences of failing to comply with it;

(b) applying under section 9 for removal from the list of registered overseas entities.

NOTES

Commencement: 1 August 2022 (see further the note to s 1 at **[9.634]**).

Updating

[9.640]

7 Updating duty

(1) A registered overseas entity must, within the period of 14 days after each update period, deliver to the registrar—

(a) the statement and information listed in row 1, 2 or 3 of the table in section 4(2), and, where applicable, the statement and information mentioned in subsection (3),

(b) the statement in row 1 of the table set out in subsection (2) or the statement and information listed in row 2 of that table, and, where applicable, the statement and information mentioned in subsection (4),

(c) a statement that the entity has complied with section 12 (duty to take steps to identify registrable beneficial owners etc),

(d) anything required by regulations under section 16 (verification of registrable beneficial owners and managing officers) to be delivered to the registrar, and

(e) the name and contact details of an individual who may be contacted about the statements and information.

(2) This is the table referred to in subsection (1)(b)—

	Statement	*Information*
1	A statement that the entity has no reasonable cause to believe that anyone has become or ceased to be a registrable beneficial owner during the update period.	
2	A statement that the entity has reasonable cause to believe that at least one person has become or ceased to be a registrable beneficial owner during the update period.	(1) The required information about each person who has become or ceased to be a registrable beneficial owner during the update period, or so much of that information as the entity has been able to obtain. (2) The date on which each of them became or ceased to be a registrable beneficial owner, if the entity has been able to obtain that information.

(3) Where information provided under subsection (1)(a) includes information that a registrable beneficial owner is a trustee (see paragraphs 3(1)(f) and 5(1)(h) of Schedule 1), the overseas entity is also required by subsection (1)(a) to provide—

(a) the required information about the trust or so much of that information as the overseas entity has been able to obtain, and

(b) a statement as to whether the entity has any reasonable cause to believe that there is required information about the trust that it has not been able to obtain.

(4) Where information provided under subsection (1)(b) includes information that a person who became or ceased to be a registrable beneficial owner was a trustee (see paragraphs 3(1)(f) and 5(1)(h) of Schedule 1), the overseas entity is also required by subsection (1)(b) to provide—

(a) the required information about the trust or so much of that information as the overseas entity has been able to obtain, and

(b) a statement as to whether the entity has any reasonable cause to believe that there is required information about the trust that it has not been able to obtain.

(5) For the required information, see Schedule 1.

(6) The information required by subsection (1)(a), and any statements required by subsection (1)(a) or (b), must relate to the state of affairs as at the end of the update period.

(7) Any information required by subsection (1)(b) as a result of a person having become or ceased to be a registrable beneficial owner must relate to the time when the person became or ceased to be a registrable beneficial owner.

(8) A requirement in subsection (1) to provide information may be met (in whole or in part) by confirming information previously provided.

(9) For the purposes of this section, each of the following is an update period—

(a) the period of 12 months beginning with the date of the overseas entity's registration;

(b) each period of 12 months beginning with the day after the end of the previous update period.

(10) But a registered overseas entity may shorten an update period by—

(a) notifying the registrar of the shortened update period, and

(b) delivering the statements and information required by subsection (1) within the period of 14 days after that shortened update period.

(11) The Secretary of State may by regulations amend this section for the purpose of changing the meaning of update period in this section.

(12) Regulations under this section are subject to the affirmative resolution procedure.

NOTES

Commencement: to be appointed.

[9.641]

8 Failure to comply with updating duty

(1) If a registered overseas entity fails to comply with the duty under section 7 an offence is committed by—

(a) the entity, and

(b) every officer of the entity who is in default.

(2) A person guilty of an offence under subsection (1) is liable on summary conviction—

(a) in England and Wales to a fine and, for continued contravention, a daily default fine not exceeding the greater of £2,500 and one half of level 4 on the standard scale;

(b) in Scotland or Northern Ireland, to a fine not exceeding level 5 on the standard scale and, for continued contravention, a daily default fine not exceeding one half of level 5 on the standard scale.

(3) The contravention continues until such time as the registered overseas entity has delivered the statements and information required by section 7(1).

(4) In the case of continued contravention, an offence is also committed by every officer of the registered overseas entity who did not commit an offence under subsection (1) in relation to the initial contravention but who is in default in relation to the continued contravention.

(5) A person guilty of an offence under subsection (4) is liable on summary conviction—

(a) in England and Wales, to a fine not exceeding the greater of £2,500 and one half of level 4 on the standard scale for each day on which the contravention continues and the person is in default;

(b) in Scotland or Northern Ireland, to a fine not exceeding one half of level 5 on the standard scale for each day on which the contravention continues and the person is in default.

NOTES

Commencement: to be appointed.

Removal

[9.642]

9 Application for removal

(1) An application by a registered overseas entity for removal from the list of registered overseas entities must be delivered to the registrar and contain—

(a) a statement confirming that the entity is not registered as the proprietor of a relevant interest in land,

(b) the statement and information listed in row 1, 2 or 3 of the table in section 4(2), and, where applicable, the statement and information mentioned in subsection (3),

(c) the statement in row 1 of the table set out in subsection (2) or the statement and information listed in row 2 of that table, and, where applicable, the statement and information mentioned in subsection (4),

(d) a statement that the entity has complied with section 12 (duty to take steps to identify registrable beneficial owners etc),

(e) anything required by regulations under section 16 (verification of registrable beneficial owners and managing officers) to be delivered to the registrar, and

(f) the name and contact details of an individual who may be contacted about the application.

(2) This is the table referred to in subsection (1)(c)—

	Statement	*Information*
1	A statement that the entity has no reasonable cause to believe that anyone has become or ceased to be a registrable beneficial owner during the relevant period.	
2	A statement that the entity has reasonable cause to believe that at least one person has become or ceased to be a registrable beneficial owner during the relevant period.	(1) The required information about each person who has become or ceased to be a registrable beneficial owner during the relevant period, or so much of that information as the entity has been able to obtain. (2) The date on which each of them became or ceased to be a registrable beneficial owner, if the entity has been able to obtain that information.

(3) Where information provided under subsection (1)(b) includes information that a registrable beneficial owner is a trustee (see paragraphs 3(1)(f) and 5(1)(h) of Schedule 1), the overseas entity is also required by subsection (1)(b) to provide—

(a) the required information about the trust or so much of that information as the overseas entity has been able to obtain, and

(b) a statement as to whether the entity has any reasonable cause to believe that there is required information about the trust that it has not been able to obtain.

(4) Where information provided under subsection (1)(c) includes information that a person who became or ceased to be a registrable beneficial owner was a trustee (see paragraphs 3(1)(f) and 5(1)(h) of Schedule 1), the overseas entity is also required by subsection (1)(c) to provide—

(a) the required information about the trust or so much of that information as the overseas entity has been able to obtain, and

(b) a statement as to whether the entity has any reasonable cause to believe that there is required information about the trust that it has not been able to obtain.

(5) For the required information, see Schedule 1.

(6) For the purposes of subsection (2) "the relevant period" means the period—

(a) beginning with the date of the overseas entity's registration or (if later) the end of its last update period, and

(b) ending with the date of the application for removal.

(7) The information required by subsection (1)(b), and any statements required by subsection (1)(b) or (c), must relate to the state of affairs as at the time of the application for removal.

(8) Any information required by subsection (1)(c) as a result of a person having become or ceased to be a registrable beneficial owner must relate to the time when the person became or ceased to be a registrable beneficial owner.

(9) The requirement in subsection (1) to provide information may be met (in whole or in part) by confirming information previously provided.

(10) For the purposes of this section and section 10 an overseas entity is registered as the proprietor of a relevant interest in land if—

(a) the entity—

(i) is registered in the register of title kept under the Land Registration Act 2002 as the proprietor of a qualifying estate within the meaning of Schedule 4A to that Act, and

(ii) became so registered in pursuance of an application made on or after 1 January 1999,

(b) the entity—

(i) is entered, on or after 8 December 2014, as proprietor in the proprietorship section of the title sheet for a plot of land that is registered in the Land Register of Scotland,

(ii) in relation to a lease that was recorded in the General Register of Sasines or registered in the Land Register of Scotland before that date is, by virtue of an assignation of the lease registered in the Land Register of Scotland on or after that date, the tenant under the lease, or

(iii) is the tenant under a lease that was registered in the Land Register of Scotland on or after that date, or

(c) the entity—

(i) is registered in the register kept under the Land Registration Act (Northern Ireland) 1970 (c 18 (NI)) as the owner of a qualifying estate within the meaning of Schedule 8A to that Act, and

(ii) became so registered on or after the day on which that Schedule came into force.

(11) In subsection (10)(b), "lease", "plot of land" and "proprietor" have the meanings given by section 113(1) of the Land Registration etc (Scotland) Act 2012 (asp 5).

(12) For the purposes of subsection (10)(b)(i)—

(a) the reference to an overseas entity's being entered as proprietor in the proprietorship section of a title sheet is a reference to the name of the entity being so entered, and

(b) the date on which an overseas entity is entered as proprietor in the proprietorship section of a title sheet is, where the entry is made by virtue of an application for registration, the date of registration as determined under section 37 of the Land Registration etc (Scotland) Act 2012 (date and time of registration).

NOTES

Commencement: 5 September 2022 (sub-ss (9)–(12)); to be appointed (otherwise).

[9.643]

10 Processing of application under section 9

(1) On receipt of an application by a registered overseas entity under section 9, the registrar must check whether the overseas entity is registered as the proprietor of a relevant interest in land (see subsection (10) of that section).

(2) If the overseas entity is not registered as the proprietor of a relevant interest in land, the registrar must remove it from the list of registered overseas entities.

(3) If the overseas entity is registered as the proprietor of a relevant interest in land, the registrar must refuse the application.

(4) The registrar must send the overseas entity a notice stating—

(a) whether the application for removal has been successful, and

(b) if it has been successful, the date of removal from the list of registered overseas entities.

(5) Where an overseas entity is removed from the list of registered overseas entities, the registrar must record the date of removal in the register.

NOTES

Commencement: to be appointed.

[9.644]

11 Transfer of documents to Public Record Office

Where an overseas entity has been removed from the list of registered overseas entities for at least two years, the registrar may transfer any records relating to that entity to the Public Record Office.

NOTES

Commencement: to be appointed.

Obtaining, updating and verifying information

[9.645]

12 Identifying registrable beneficial owners

(1) An overseas entity must comply with this section before—

(a) making an application under section 4 for registration;

(b) complying with the updating duty under section 7;

(c) making an application under section 9 for removal.

(2) The overseas entity must take reasonable steps—

(a) to identify any registrable beneficial owners in relation to the entity, and

(b) if it identifies any, to obtain, for the purposes of the application under section 4 or 9 or for the purposes of complying with the updating duty under section 7—

(i) the required information about each registrable beneficial owner, and

(ii) in respect of any registrable beneficial owner who is a trustee, the required information about the trust.

(3) The steps that an overseas entity must take include giving an information notice under this section to any person that it knows, or has reasonable cause to believe, is a registrable beneficial owner in relation to the entity.

(4) An information notice under this section is a notice requiring the person to whom it is given—

(a) to state whether or not the person is a registrable beneficial owner in relation to the overseas entity,

(b) if the person is a registrable beneficial owner, to confirm or correct any of the required information about the person that is specified in the notice and to supply any of the required information that the notice states the overseas entity does not already have, and

(c) if the person is a registrable beneficial owner by virtue of being a trustee, to confirm or correct any of the required information about the trust that is specified in the notice and to supply any of the required information about the trust that the notice states the overseas entity does not already have.

(5) An information notice under this section must require the person to whom it is given to comply with the notice within the period of one month beginning with the day on which it is given.

NOTES

Commencement: 1 August 2022 (see further the note to s 1 at **[9.634]**).

[9.646]

13 Additional powers to obtain information

(1) An overseas entity may give a person an information notice under this section if it knows or has reasonable cause to believe that the person knows the identity of—

(a) a person who is a registrable beneficial owner in relation to the overseas entity,

(b) any legal entity not falling within paragraph (a) that is a beneficial owner in relation to the overseas entity, or

(c) a person likely to have knowledge of the identity of a person within paragraph (a) or (b).

(2) An information notice under this section is a notice requiring the addressee—

(a) to state whether or not the addressee knows the identity of a person within paragraph (a), (b) or (c) of subsection (1), and

(b) if so—

(i) to supply any information that the addressee has that might help the overseas entity to identify that person, and

(ii) to state whether that information is being supplied with the knowledge of the person to whom it relates.

(3) An information notice under this section must require the person to whom it is given to comply with the notice within the period of one month beginning with the day on which it is given.

(4) A person given a notice under subsection (1) is not required by that notice to disclose any information in respect of which a claim to legal professional privilege or, in Scotland, confidentiality of communications, could be maintained in legal proceedings.

(5) In this section a reference to knowing the identity of a person includes knowing information from which that person can be identified.

NOTES

Commencement: 1 August 2022 (see further the note to s 1 at **[9.634]**).

[9.647]

14 Sections 12 and 13: supplementary

(1) The Secretary of State may by regulations make further provision about the giving of notices under section 12 or 13, including provision about the form and content of any such notices and the manner in which they must be given.

(2) Regulations under subsection (1) are subject to the negative resolution procedure.

NOTES

Commencement: 1 August 2022 (see further the note to s 1 at **[9.634]**).

[9.648]

15 Failure to comply with notice under section 12 or 13

(1) A person who, without reasonable excuse, fails to comply with a notice under section 12 or 13 commits an offence.

(2) A person who is given a notice under section 12 or 13 commits an offence if, in purported compliance with the notice, the person—

(a) makes a statement that the person knows to be false in a material particular, or

(b) recklessly makes a statement that is false in a material particular.

(3) Where an offence under subsection (1) or (2) is committed by a legal entity, the offence is also committed by every officer of the entity who is in default.

(4) A person does not commit an offence under subsection (1), or under subsection (3) as it applies in relation to subsection (1), if the person proves that the requirement to give information was frivolous or vexatious.

(5) A person guilty of an offence under this section is liable—

(a) on summary conviction in England and Wales, to imprisonment for the maximum summary term for either-way offences or a fine (or both);

(b) on summary conviction in Scotland, to imprisonment for a term not exceeding 12 months or a fine not exceeding the statutory maximum (or both);

(c) on summary conviction in Northern Ireland, to imprisonment for a term not exceeding 6 months or a fine not exceeding the statutory maximum (or both);

(d) on conviction on indictment, to imprisonment for a term not exceeding two years or a fine (or both).

(6) In subsection (5)(a) "the maximum summary term for either-way offences" means—

(a) in relation to an offence committed before the time when paragraph 24(2) of Schedule 22 to the Sentencing Act 2020 comes into force, 6 months;

(b) in relation to an offence committed after that time, 12 months.

NOTES

Commencement: 1 August 2022 (see further the note to s 1 at **[9.634]**).

[9.649]

16 Verification of registrable beneficial owners and managing officers

(1) The Secretary of State must by regulations make provision requiring the verification of information before an overseas entity—

(a) makes an application under section 4 for registration;

(b) complies with the updating duty under section 7;

(c) makes an application under section 9 for removal.

(2) Regulations under this section may, among other things, make provision—

(a) about the information that must be verified;

(b) about the person by whom the information must be verified;

(c) requiring a statement, evidence or other information to be delivered to the registrar for the purposes of sections 4(1)(c), 7(1)(d) and 9(1)(e).

(3) The first regulations under this section must be made so as to come into force before any applications may be made under section 4(1).

(4) Regulations under this section are subject to the negative resolution procedure.

NOTES

Commencement: 1 August 2022 (see further the note to s 1 at **[9.634]**).

Regulations: the Register of Overseas Entities (Verification and Provision of Information) Regulations 2022, SI 2022/725 at **[10.1363]**.

Exemptions

[9.650]

17 Power to modify application process etc in certain cases

(1) The Secretary of State may by regulations modify the application requirements or the update requirements in relation to overseas entities of a description specified in the regulations.

(2) The regulations may modify the application or update requirements in relation to a description of overseas entity only if the Secretary of State considers that the modifications are appropriate in light of the information that is publicly available otherwise than by virtue of this Part.

(3) Regulations under subsection (1) may make such modifications to this Part as are consequential on those regulations.

(4) Regulations under subsection (1) are subject to the negative resolution procedure.

(5) In this section—

"the application requirements" means the requirements as to the contents of applications under section 4 or 9;

"the update requirements" means the requirements as to the material that must be delivered to the registrar under section 7.

NOTES

Commencement: 1 August 2022 (see further the note to s 1 at **[9.634]**).

[9.651]

18 Exemptions

(1) The Secretary of State may, by giving written notice to a person, exempt the person under this section if satisfied that to do so is necessary—

(a) in the interests of national security;

(b) for the purposes of preventing or detecting serious crime.

(2) The effect of an exemption is that—

(a) overseas entities are not required to take steps or give notices under section 12 in relation to the exempt person,

(b) the exempt person is not required to comply with any notice given by an overseas entity under section 12 or 13 if the exempt person brings the existence of the exemption to the attention of the entity,

(c) a notice given by an overseas entity under section 13 does not require any other person to supply information about the exempt person, and

(d) the exempt person does not count as a registrable beneficial owner in relation to any overseas entity for the purposes of this Part.

(3) For the purposes of subsection (1)(b)—

(a) "crime" means conduct which—

(i) constitutes a criminal offence, or

(ii) is, or corresponds to, any conduct which, if it all took place in any one part of the United Kingdom, would constitute a criminal offence, and

(b) crime is "serious" if—

(i) the offence which is or would be constituted by the conduct is an offence for which the maximum sentence (in any part of the United Kingdom) is imprisonment for 3 years or more, or

(ii) the conduct involves the use of violence, results in substantial financial gain or is conduct by a large number of persons in pursuit of a common purpose.

NOTES

Commencement: 1 August 2022 (see further the note to s 1 at **[9.634]**).

Language requirement

[9.652]

19 Documents to be in English

Documents delivered to the registrar under this Part, or under regulations made under it, must be drawn up and delivered in English.

NOTES

Commencement: 1 August 2022 (see further the note to s 1 at **[9.634]**).

Annotation of the register

[9.653]

20 Annotation of the register

(1) The registrar must place a note in the register recording—

(a) the date on which a document is delivered to the registrar under this Part or regulations made under it, or otherwise in connection with the register;

(b) if a document is replaced (whether or not material derived from it is removed), the fact that it has been replaced and the date of delivery of the replacement;

(c) if material is removed—

(i) what was removed (giving a general description of its contents),

(ii) under what power, and

(iii) the date on which that was done.

(2) The Secretary of State may by regulations make provision—

(a) authorising or requiring the registrar to annotate the register in such other circumstances as may be specified in the regulations, and

(b) as to the contents of any such annotation.

(3) No annotation is required in the case of a document that by virtue of section 1072(2) of the Companies Act 2006 (documents not meeting requirements for proper delivery) is treated as not having been delivered.

(4) A note may be removed if it no longer serves any useful purpose.

(5) Any duty or power of the registrar with respect to annotation of the register is subject to the court's power under section 31 (powers of court on ordering removal of material from the register) to direct—

(a) that a note be removed from the register, or

(b) that no note may be made of the removal of material that is the subject of the court's order.

(6) Regulations under this section are subject to the negative resolution procedure.

NOTES

Commencement: 1 August 2022 (see further the note to s 1 at **[9.634]**).

See also the note to s 42 at **[9.676]** *post*.

Inspection of the register and protection of information

[9.654]

21 Inspection and copies of register

(1) Any person may—

(a) inspect the register (but see the exceptions in section 22);

(b) require a copy of any material on the register that is available for inspection.

(2) The registrar may specify the form and manner in which an application is to be made for inspection or a copy.

(3) The registrar may determine the form and manner in which copies are to be provided.

(4) Section 1091 of the Companies Act 2006 (certification of copies), and any regulations made under it, apply in relation to copies provided under this section as they apply in relation to the copies provided as mentioned in that section.

NOTES

Commencement: 1 August 2022 (see further the note to s 1 at **[9.634]**).

[9.655]

22 Material unavailable for inspection

(1) The following material must not be made available by the registrar for public inspection—

(a) any date of birth or residential address information protected under subsection (2),

(b) the name or contact details of an individual delivered to the registrar under section 4(1)(d) (application for registration), 7(1)(e) (updating duty) or 9(1)(f) (application for removal),

(c) any required information about a trust delivered to the registrar by virtue of section 4(3), 7(3) or (4) or 9(3) or (4) (required information about trusts),

(d) information that, by virtue of regulations under section 25 (power to protect other information), the registrar must omit from the material on the register that is available for inspection,

(e) any application or other document delivered to the registrar under section 29 (application for rectification of register),
(f) any court order under section 30 (rectification of the register under court order) that the court has directed under section 31 is not to be made available for public inspection, and
(g) any email address, identification code or password deriving from a document delivered for the purpose of authorising or facilitating electronic filing procedures or providing information by telephone.

(2) Date of birth information or residential address information is "protected" if—
(a) it relates to a registrable beneficial owner or managing officer in relation to an overseas entity,
(b) it is contained in a document delivered to the registrar in which date of birth information or residential address information is required to be stated,
(c) in the case of a document having more than one part, it is contained in a part of the document in which date of birth information or residential address information is required to be stated, and
(d) it is not information about a trust delivered to the registrar by virtue of section 4(3), 7(3) or (4) or 9(3) or (4).

(3) In this section—
"date of birth information" means information as to the day of the month on which an individual was born (but not the month or year);
"residential address information" means—
(a) information as to the usual residential address of an individual, or
(b) information that the service address of an individual is the individual's usual residential address.

(4) Nothing in this section obliges the registrar to check documents other than those mentioned in subsection (2)(b), or parts of documents other than those mentioned in subsection (2)(c), to ensure the absence of date of birth information or residential address information.

NOTES

Commencement: 1 August 2022 (see further the note to s 1 at **[9.634]**).

[9.656]

23 Disclosure of information about trusts

(1) This section applies to information delivered to the registrar by virtue of section 4(3), 7(3) or (4) or 9(3) or (4) (required information about trusts).

(2) The registrar may not disclose the information unless—
(a) the same information is made available by the registrar for public inspection otherwise than by virtue of being delivered to the registrar by virtue of a provision mentioned in subsection (1), or
(b) the disclosure is permitted by subsection (3).

(3) The registrar may disclose the information to—
(a) the Commissioners for Her Majesty's Revenue and Customs, or
(b) any other person who—
(i) has functions of a public nature, and
(ii) is specified for the purposes of this section by regulations made by the Secretary of State.

(4) Regulations under this section are subject to the negative resolution procedure.

NOTES

Commencement: 1 August 2022 (see further the note to s 1 at **[9.634]**).

[9.657]

24 Disclosure of protected information

(1) The registrar must not disclose protected date of birth information or protected residential address information about a person unless—
(a) the same information about the person (whether in the same or a different capacity) is made available by the registrar for public inspection as a result of being contained in another description of document in relation to which no restriction under section 22 applies, or
(b) disclosure is permitted by subsection (2).

(2) The registrar may disclose protected date of birth information or residential address information to any person who—
(a) has functions of a public nature, and
(b) is specified for the purposes of this section by regulations made by the Secretary of State.

(3) The Secretary of State may by regulations make provision—
(a) specifying conditions for the disclosure of protected date of birth information or residential address information in accordance with this section, and
(b) providing for the charging of fees.

(4) This section does not apply to protected date of birth information, or protected residential address information, about a person in their capacity as a registrable beneficial owner or managing officer if an application under regulations made under section 25 has been granted in respect of that information and has not been revoked.

(5) In this section—
"date of birth information" has the meaning given by section 22(3);
"protected" has the meaning given by section 22(2);
"residential address information" has the meaning given by section 22(3).

(6) Regulations under this section are subject to the negative resolution procedure.

NOTES

Commencement: 1 August 2022 (see further the note to s 1 at **[9.634]**).

[9.658]

25 Power to protect other information

(1) The Secretary of State may by regulations make provision requiring the registrar, on application—

(a) to make information relating to a relevant individual unavailable for public inspection, and
(b) to refrain from disclosing that information or to refrain from doing so except in specified circumstances.

(2) In this section "relevant individual" means an individual who is or used to be—
(a) a registrable beneficial owner in relation to an overseas entity, or
(b) a managing officer of an overseas entity.

(3) Regulations under this section may make provision as to—
(a) who may make an application,
(b) the grounds on which an application may be made,
(c) the information to be included in and documents to accompany an application,
(d) how an application is to be determined,
(e) the recording of restrictions in the register,
(f) the duration of and procedures for revoking the restrictions on disclosure, and
(g) the charging of fees by the registrar for disclosing information where the regulations permit disclosure, by way of exception, in specified circumstances.

(4) The provision that may be made under subsection (3)(d) or (f) includes provision—
(a) conferring a discretion on the registrar;
(b) providing for a question to be referred to a person other than the registrar for the purposes of determining the application or revoking the restrictions.

(5) Regulations under this section may impose a duty on the registrar to publish, in relation to such periods as may be specified—
(a) details of how many applications have been made under the regulations and how many of them have been allowed, and
(b) such other details in connection with applications under the regulations as may be specified in the regulations.

(6) Regulations under this section are subject to the affirmative resolution procedure.

(7) Nothing in this section or in regulations made under it affects the disclosure of information about a person in any capacity other than that mentioned in subsection (2).

NOTES

Commencement: 1 August 2022 (see further the note to s 1 at **[9.634]**).

Regulations: the Register of Overseas Entities (Delivery, Protection and Trust Services) Regulations 2022, SI 2022/870 at **[10.1376]**.

[9.659]

26 Data protection

(1) Nothing in section 21, 23 or 24 authorises or requires a disclosure of information which, although made in accordance with that section, would contravene the data protection legislation.

(2) In this section "the data protection legislation" has the same meaning as in the Data Protection Act 2018 (see section 3 of that Act).

NOTES

Commencement: 1 August 2022 (see further the note to s 1 at **[9.634]**).

Correction or removal of material on the register

[9.660]

27 Resolving inconsistencies in the register

(1) Where it appears to the registrar that the information contained in a document delivered to the registrar is inconsistent with other information on the register, the registrar may give notice to the overseas entity to which the document relates—
(a) stating in what respects the information contained in it appears to be inconsistent with other information on the register, and
(b) requiring the overseas entity to take steps to resolve the inconsistency.

(2) The notice must—
(a) state the date on which it is issued, and
(b) require the delivery to the registrar, within 14 days after that date, of such replacement or additional documents as may be required to resolve the inconsistency.

(3) If the necessary documents are not delivered within the period specified, an offence is committed by—
(a) the overseas entity, and
(b) every officer of the overseas entity who is in default.

(4) A person guilty of an offence under subsection (3) is liable on summary conviction—
(a) in England and Wales, to a fine and, for continued contravention, a daily default fine not exceeding the greater of £2,500 and one half of level 4 on the standard scale;
(b) in Scotland or Northern Ireland, to a fine not exceeding level 5 on the standard scale and, for continued contravention, a daily default fine not exceeding one half of level 5 on the standard scale.

NOTES

Commencement: 1 August 2022 (see further the note to s 1 at **[9.634]**).

[9.661]

28 Administrative removal of material from register

(1) The registrar may remove from the register—
(a) anything that there was power, but no duty, to include;
(b) anything listed in section 22(1) (material unavailable for public inspection), if it no longer appears to the registrar reasonably necessary for the purposes for which it was delivered to the registrar.

(2) The power in subsection (1)(a) is exercisable, in particular, so as to remove—
(a) unnecessary material within the meaning of section 1074 of the Companies Act 2006,

(b) material derived from a document that has been replaced under section 1076 of that Act (replacement of document not meeting requirements for proper delivery), or

(c) material derived from a document that has been replaced under section 27.

(3) On or before removing any material under subsection (1)(a) (otherwise than at the request of the overseas entity) the registrar must give notice—

(a) to the person by whom the material was delivered (if the identity, and name and address of that person are known), or

(b) to the overseas entity to which the material relates (if notice cannot be given under paragraph (a) and the identity of that overseas entity is known).

(4) The notice must—

(a) state what material the registrar proposes to remove, or has removed, and on what grounds, and

(b) state the date on which it is issued.

NOTES

Commencement: 1 August 2022 (see further the note to s 1 at **[9.634]**).

See also the note to s 42 at **[9.676]** *post*.

[9.662]

29 Application to rectify register

(1) The Secretary of State may by regulations make provision requiring the registrar, on application, to remove from the register material of a description specified in the regulations that—

(a) derives from anything invalid or ineffective or that was done without the authority of the overseas entity, or

(b) is factually inaccurate, or is derived from something that is factually inaccurate, or forged.

(2) The regulations may make provision as to—

(a) who may make an application,

(b) the information to be included in and documents to accompany an application,

(c) the notice to be given of an application and of its outcome,

(d) a period in which objections to an application may be made, and

(e) how an application is to be determined.

(3) An application must—

(a) specify what is to be removed from the register and indicate where on the register it is, and

(b) be accompanied by a statement that the material specified in the application complies with this section and the regulations.

(4) If no objections are made to the application, the registrar may accept the statement as sufficient evidence that the material specified in the application should be removed from the register.

(5) Regulations under this section are subject to the affirmative resolution procedure.

NOTES

Commencement: 1 August 2022 (see further the note to s 1 at **[9.634]**).

[9.663]

[29A

(1) This section applies where—

(a) a material discrepancy in information relating to any registrable beneficial owner is reported to the registrar(e) under regulation 30A(2) or (2B) of the Money Laundering, Terrorist Financing and Transfer of Funds (Information on the Payer) Regulations 2017 (requirement to report discrepancies in information about beneficial ownership), and

(b) the registrar determines, having investigated under regulation 30A(5) of those Regulations, that there is a material discrepancy

(2) The registrar may remove material from the register if doing so is necessary to resolve the discrepancy.]

NOTES

Commencement:1 April 2023.

Inserted by the Money Laundering and Terrorist Financing (Amendment) (No 2) Regulations 2022, SI 2022/860, reg 17, as from 1 April 2023.

[9.664]

30 Court order to rectify register

(1) The registrar must remove from the register any material—

(a) that derives from anything that the court has declared to be invalid or ineffective, or to have been done without the authority of the overseas entity, or

(b) that a court declares to be factually inaccurate, or to be derived from something that is factually inaccurate, or forged,

and that the court directs should be removed from the register.

(2) The court order must specify what is to be removed from the register and indicate where on the register it is.

(3) A copy of the court's order must be sent to the registrar for registration.

NOTES

Commencement: 1 August 2022 (see further the note to s 1 at **[9.634]**).

See also the note to s 42 at **[9.676]** *post*.

[9.665]

31 Court powers on ordering removal of material from the register

(1) Where the court makes an order for the removal of anything from the register under section 30, it may give directions under this section.

(2) It may direct that any note on the register that is related to the material that is the subject of the court's order is to be removed from the register.

(3) It may direct that its order is not to be available for public inspection as part of the register.

(4) It may direct—

(a) that no note is to be made on the register as a result of its order, or

(b) that any such note is to be restricted to such matters as may be specified by the court in the direction.

(5) The court must not give any direction under this section unless it is satisfied—

(a) that—

(i) the presence on the register of the note or, as the case may be, of an unrestricted note, or

(ii) the availability for public inspection of the court's order,

may cause damage to the overseas entity, and

(b) that the overseas entity's interest in non-disclosure outweighs any interest of other persons in disclosure.

(6) In this section "note" means a note placed in the register under section 20 or regulations made under it.

NOTES

Commencement: 1 August 2022 (see further the note to s 1 at **[9.634]**).

False statements

[9.666]

32 General false statement offence

(1) It is an offence for a person, without reasonable excuse, to—

(a) deliver or cause to be delivered to the registrar for the purposes of this Part any document that is misleading, false or deceptive in a material particular, or

(b) make to the registrar, for the purposes of this Part, any statement that is misleading, false or deceptive in a material particular.

(2) An offence under this section is aggravated if, when the document or statement is delivered, the person knows that it is misleading, false or deceptive in a material particular.

(3) A person guilty of an offence under this section, other than an aggravated offence, is liable—

(a) on summary conviction in England and Wales, to a fine;

(b) on summary conviction in Scotland, to a fine not exceeding level 5 on the standard scale;

(c) on summary conviction in Northern Ireland, to a fine not exceeding level 5 on the standard scale.

(4) A person guilty of an aggravated offence under this section is liable—

(a) on summary conviction in England and Wales, to imprisonment for the maximum summary term for either-way offences or a fine (or both);

(b) on summary conviction in Scotland, to imprisonment for a term not exceeding 12 months or a fine not exceeding the statutory maximum (or both);

(c) on summary conviction in Northern Ireland, to imprisonment for a term not exceeding 6 months or a fine not exceeding the statutory maximum (or both);

(d) on conviction on indictment, to imprisonment for a term not exceeding two years or a fine (or both).

(5) In subsection (4)(a) "the maximum summary term for either-way offences" means—

(a) in relation to an offence committed before the time when paragraph 24(2) of Schedule 22 to the Sentencing Act 2020 comes into force, 6 months;

(b) in relation to an offence committed after that time, 12 months.

NOTES

Commencement: 1 August 2022 (see further the note to s 1 at **[9.634]**).

Land ownership and transactions

[9.667]

33 Land ownership and transactions

(1) Schedule 3 contains amendments about—

(a) the ownership of registered land in England and Wales by overseas entities, and

(b) land transactions in England and Wales involving overseas entities.

(2) Schedule 4—

(a) makes similar provision for Scotland, and

(b) confers a related power to make further or alternative provision (see Part 3 of the Schedule).

(3) Schedule 5 makes similar provision for Northern Ireland.

(4) The Secretary of State may by regulations amend Schedule 8A to the Land Registration Act (Northern Ireland) 1970 (inserted by Schedule 5 to this Act) to make provision similar or corresponding to the provision made by paragraphs 3(2)(e), 4(2)(e) and 5 of Schedule 4A to the Land Registration Act 2002 (inserted by Schedule 3 to this Act) (including the provision to make subordinate legislation).

(5) The provision which may be made by regulations under subsection (4) by virtue of section 67(3) includes provision amending other provisions of the Land Registration (Northern Ireland) Act 1970.

(6) The Secretary of State must consult the Department of Finance in Northern Ireland before making regulations under subsection (4).

(7) Regulations under subsection (4) are subject to the affirmative resolution procedure.

NOTES

Commencement: 5 September 2022.

[9.668]

34 Power to require overseas entity to register if it owns certain land

(1) The Secretary of State may by notice require an overseas entity to apply for registration in the register of overseas entities within the period of 6 months beginning with the date of the notice if at the time the notice is given—

(a) the entity is registered as the proprietor of a relevant interest in land within the meaning given by section 9(10), and
(b) the entity is not registered as an overseas entity, has not made an application for registration that is pending and is not an exempt overseas entity.

(2) A notice under subsection (1) lapses if, before the end of the period mentioned there, the overseas entity—
(a) ceases to be registered as the proprietor of a relevant interest in land within the meaning given by section 9(10), or
(b) becomes an exempt overseas entity.

(3) If an overseas entity fails to comply with a notice under subsection (1), an offence is committed by—
(a) the entity, and
(b) every officer of the entity who is in default.

(4) A person guilty of an offence under subsection (3) is liable—
(a) on summary conviction in England and Wales, to imprisonment for the maximum summary term for either-way offences or a fine (or both);
(b) on summary conviction in Scotland, to imprisonment for a term not exceeding 12 months or a fine not exceeding the statutory maximum (or both);
(c) on summary conviction in Northern Ireland, to imprisonment for a term not exceeding 6 months or a fine not exceeding the statutory maximum (or both);
(d) on conviction on indictment, to imprisonment for a term not exceeding two years or a fine (or both).

(5) In subsection (4)(a) "the maximum summary term for either-way offences" means—
(a) in relation to an offence committed before the time when paragraph 24(2) of Schedule 22 to the Sentencing Act 2020 comes into force, 6 months;
(b) in relation to an offence committed after that time, 12 months.

(6) In this section "exempt overseas entity" means an overseas entity of such description as may be specified in regulations made by the Secretary of State for the purposes of this section.

(7) Regulations under subsection (6) are subject to the affirmative resolution procedure.

NOTES

Commencement: 5 September 2022.

Supplementary provision about offences

[9.669]

35 Liability of officers in default

(1) Sections 1121 to 1123 of the Companies Act 2006 (liability of officers in default: interpretation etc) apply for the purposes of any provision made by this Part as they apply for the purposes of provisions of the Companies Acts.

(2) In those sections as applied, a reference to an officer includes a person in accordance with whose directions or instructions the board of directors or equivalent management body of a legal entity are accustomed to act.

(3) A person is not to be regarded as falling within subsection (2) by reason only that the board of directors or equivalent management body acts on advice given by the person in a professional capacity.

NOTES

Commencement: 1 August 2022 (see further the note to s 1 at **[9.634]**).

[9.670]

36 Meaning of "daily default fine"

Section 1125 of the Companies Act 2006 (meaning of "daily default fine") applies for purpose of any provision made by this Part as it applies for the purposes of provisions of the Companies Acts.

NOTES

Commencement: 1 August 2022 (see further the note to s 1 at **[9.634]**).

[9.671]

37 Consent required for prosecutions

Proceedings for an offence under this Part—
(a) may not be brought in England and Wales except by or with the consent of the Secretary of State or the Director of Public Prosecutions;
(b) may not be brought in Northern Ireland except by or with the consent of the Secretary of State or the Director of Public Prosecutions for Northern Ireland.

NOTES

Commencement: 1 August 2022 (see further the note to s 1 at **[9.634]**).

[9.672]

38 Further provision about proceedings

The following provisions of the Companies Act 2006 apply in relation to offences under this Part as they apply in relation to offences under the Companies Acts—
(a) section 1128 (summary proceedings: time limits);
(b) section 1130 (proceedings against unincorporated bodies).

NOTES

Commencement: 1 August 2022 (see further the note to s 1 at **[9.634]**).

Financial penalties

[9.673]

39 Financial penalties

(1) The Secretary of State may by regulations make provision conferring power on the registrar to impose a financial penalty on a person if satisfied, beyond reasonable doubt, that the person has engaged in conduct amounting to an offence under this Part.

(2) The regulations may include provision—

(a) about the procedure to be followed in imposing penalties;
(b) about the amount of penalties;
(c) for the imposition of interest or additional penalties for late payment;
(d) conferring rights of appeal against penalties;
(e) about the enforcement of penalties.

(3) The provision that may be made about enforcement includes—

(a) in relation to England and Wales or Northern Ireland, provision for unpaid amounts to be secured by a charge on an interest in land (including provision about the priority of any such charge), and
(b) in relation to Scotland, provision for penalties to be enforced in the same manner as an extract registered decree arbitral bearing a warrant for execution issued by the sheriff court of any sheriffdom in Scotland.

(4) The regulations must provide that—

(a) no financial penalty may be imposed under the regulations on a person in respect of conduct amounting to an offence if the person has been convicted of that offence in respect of that conduct, and
(b) no proceedings may be brought or continued against a person in respect of conduct amounting to an offence if the person has been given a financial penalty under the regulations in respect of that conduct.

(5) Amounts recovered by the registrar under the regulations are to be paid into the Consolidated Fund.

(6) The provision which may be made by regulations under this section by virtue of section 67(3) includes provision amending provision made by or under any of the following, whenever passed or made—

(a) an Act;
(b) an Act of the Scottish Parliament;
(c) Northern Ireland legislation.

(7) Regulations under this section are subject to the affirmative resolution procedure.

(8) In this section "conduct" means an act or omission.

NOTES

Commencement: 1 August 2022 (see further the note to s 1 at **[9.634]**).

Sharing of information by HMRC

[9.674]

40 Sharing of information by HMRC

(1) The Commissioners for Her Majesty's Revenue and Customs may disclose information to the Secretary of State or the registrar for the purpose of the taking of action in connection with an offence under this Part.

(2) For the purposes of this section, the taking of action in connection with an offence under this Part includes any of the following—

(a) investigating whether an offence has been committed;
(b) prosecuting an offence;
(c) imposing financial penalties for conduct amounting to an offence.

(3) A person who receives information as a result of this section—

(a) may not use the information other than for the purpose of the taking of action in connection with an offence under this Part;
(b) may not further disclose the information unless the disclosure is necessary for the taking of action in connection with an offence under this Part.

(4) It is an offence for a person to disclose, in contravention of subsection (3)(b), any revenue and customs information relating to a person whose identity—

(a) is specified in the disclosure, or
(b) can be deduced from it.

(5) It is a defence for a person charged with an offence under subsection (4) to prove that the person reasonably believed—

(a) that the disclosure was lawful, or
(b) that the information had already lawfully been made available to the public.

(6) Subsections (4) to (7) of section 19 of the Commissioners for Revenue and Customs Act 2005 apply to an offence under subsection (4) as they apply to an offence under that section.

(7) In this section "revenue and customs information relating to a person" has the same meaning as in section 19 of the Commissioners for Revenue and Customs Act 2005 (see section 19(2) of that Act).

NOTES

Commencement: 1 August 2022 (see further the note to s 1 at **[9.634]**).

Transitional provision

[9.675]

41 Applications in the transitional period: information about land transactions

(1) This section applies where an overseas entity makes an application under section 4 for registration before the end of the transitional period.

(2) If the entity has not made any relevant dispositions of land during the period—

(a) beginning with 28 February 2022, and
(b) ending with the making of the application,

the application must include a statement to that effect.

(3) If the entity has made any relevant dispositions of land during the period mentioned in subsection (2), the application must include—

(a) the required information about each relevant disposition of land made during that period (see subsection (5)),

(b) in relation to each such disposition, the statements and information mentioned in paragraphs (a), (b) and (c) of section 4(1) expressed by reference to the state of affairs immediately before the making of the disposition, and

(c) a statement that all of the information required by paragraphs (a) and (b) of this subsection has been included in the application.

(4) In this section "relevant disposition of land", in relation to an overseas entity, means—

(a) a registrable disposition of a qualifying estate within section 27(2)(a), (b)(i) or (f) of the Land Registration Act 2002 other than—

(i) a disposition made in pursuance of a statutory obligation or court order, or occurring by operation of law, or

(ii) a disposition made by a specified insolvency practitioner in specified circumstances (within the meaning of paragraph 3(3) of Schedule 4A to the Land Registration Act 2002, as inserted by Schedule 3 to this Act);

(b) the delivery by the entity of a qualifying registrable deed granted by it where the entity's interest in respect of which the deed was granted was registered in the Land Register of Scotland on or after 8 December 2014, unless the deed was granted—

(i) in pursuance of a statutory obligation or court order, or

(ii) by a specified insolvency practitioner in specified circumstances (within the meaning of paragraph 2(5) of schedule 1A of the Land Registration etc (Scotland) Act 2012, as inserted by Schedule 4 to this Act).

(5) The required information about a relevant disposition of land is—

(a) where the relevant disposition of land is within subsection (4)(a)—

(i) the date of disposition, and

(ii) the registered title number of the qualifying estate;

(b) where the relevant disposition of land is within subsection (4)(b)—

(i) the date of delivery of the deed, and

(ii) the title number of the title sheet in which the entity's interest is entered.

(6) In subsection (4)(a) "qualifying estate" means—

(a) a freehold estate in land, or

(b) a leasehold estate in land granted for a term of more than seven years from the date of grant,

of which the overseas entity became a registered proprietor in pursuance of an application made on or after 1 January 1999.

(7) In subsection (6) "registered proprietor" in relation to an estate means the person entered as proprietor of the estate in the register of title kept by the Chief Land Registrar.

(8) In subsection (4)(b) "qualifying registrable deed" means a registrable deed (within the meaning of the Land Registration etc (Scotland) Act 2012) which is—

(a) a disposition,

(b) a standard security,

(c) a lease (including a sub-lease), or

(d) an assignation of a lease (including a sub-lease).

(9) For the purposes of subsection (4)(b), a qualifying registrable deed is to be treated, as at the date of delivery, as having been granted even if at that time it has been executed by the overseas entity only.

(10) In this section "the transitional period" means the period of 6 months beginning with the day on which section 3(1) comes fully into force.

NOTES

Commencement: 1 August 2022 (see further the note to s 1 at **[9.634]**).

[9.676]

42 Requirement for certain unregistered overseas entities to provide information

(1) An overseas entity, and every officer of the entity who is in default, commits an offence if—

(a) at any time during the period beginning with 28 February 2022 and ending with the end of the transitional period, the entity has made a relevant disposition of land,

(b) at the end of the transitional period the entity—

(i) is not registered as an overseas entity,

(ii) has not made an application for registration as an overseas entity that is pending, and

(iii) is not an exempt overseas entity, and

(c) the entity has not, after making the relevant disposition of land and before the end of the transitional period, delivered to the registrar—

(i) statements and information of the kind mentioned in paragraphs (a), (b), (c) and (d) of section 4(1), expressed by reference to the state of affairs immediately before the making of the relevant disposition of land, and

(ii) the required information about the relevant disposition of land (within the meaning of section 41(5)).

(2) A person guilty of an offence under subsection (1) is liable on summary conviction—

(a) in England and Wales to a fine and, for continued contravention, a daily default fine not exceeding the greater of £2,500 and one half of level 4 on the standard scale;

(b) in Scotland or Northern Ireland, to a fine not exceeding level 5 on the standard scale and, for continued contravention, a daily default fine not exceeding one half of level 5 on the standard scale.

(3) The contravention continues until such time as the overseas entity has delivered the statements and information mentioned in subsection (1)(c).

(4) In the case of continued contravention, an offence is also committed by every officer of the overseas entity who did not commit an offence under subsection (1) in relation to the initial contravention but who is in default in relation to the continued contravention.

(5) A person guilty of an offence under subsection (4) is liable on summary conviction—

(a) in England and Wales, to a fine not exceeding the greater of £2,500 and one half of level 4 on the standard scale for each day on which the contravention continues and the person is in default;

(b) in Scotland or Northern Ireland, to a fine not exceeding one half of level 5 on the standard scale for each day on which the contravention continues and the person is in default.

(6) In this section—

"exempt overseas entity" means an entity of a description specified in regulations under section 34(6);

"relevant disposition of land" has the meaning given by section 41(4);

"transitional period" has the meaning given by section 41(10).

NOTES

Commencement: 1 August 2022 (see further the note to s 1 at **[9.634]**).

Information under sub-s (1)(c): see further the Register of Overseas Entities (Verification and Provision of Information) Regulations 2022, SI 2022/725, regs 9–13 at **[10.1371]** et seq. Regulation 9 makes provision about the provision of s 42(1)(c) information; reg 10 relates to the publication of such information; regs 11–13 modify ss 20, 28 and 30 of this Act in relation to such information.

[9.677]

43 Section 42: supplementary

(1) Section 12 has effect as if—

(a) subsection (1) included a reference to an overseas entity being under a duty to comply with that section before delivering statements and information under section 42(1)(c)(i);

(b) subsection (2) included a reference to obtaining information for the purposes of section 42(1)(c)(i).

(2) The Secretary of State may by regulations make further provision in connection with—

(a) the provision of information under section 42(1)(c),

(b) the verification of that information, or

(c) the processing of that information by the registrar,

including provision modifying any provision made by or under this Part or applying any provision made by or under this Part with modifications.

(3) Regulations under this section are subject to the negative resolution procedure.

NOTES

Commencement: 1 August 2022 (see further the note to s 1 at **[9.634]**).

Regulations: the Register of Overseas Entities (Verification and Provision of Information) Regulations 2022, SI 2022/725 at **[10.1363]**.

Interpretation

[9.678]

44 Interpretation

(1) In this Part—

"beneficial owner", in relation to an overseas entity, has the meaning given by Part 2 of Schedule 2;

"the court" has the same meaning as in the Companies Acts (see section 1156 of the Companies Act 2006);

"document" means information in any recorded form;

"government or public authority" means—

(a) a corporation sole;

(b) a government or government department of a country or territory or a part of a country or territory;

(c) an international organisation whose members include two or more countries or territories (or their governments);

(d) a local authority or local government body in the United Kingdom or elsewhere;

(e) any other public authority in the United Kingdom or elsewhere;

"legal entity" has the meaning given by section 2;

"managing officer", in relation to an overseas entity, includes a director, manager or secretary;

"overseas entity" has the meaning given by section 2;

"register" means the register kept under section 3;

"registered": an overseas entity is registered if its name appears in the list of registered overseas entities kept in accordance with section 3(3);

"registrable beneficial owner", in relation to an overseas entity, has the meaning given by Schedule 2;

"the registrar" has the meaning given by section 3(1).

(2) A reference in section 12 or 13 to a person who is a registrable beneficial owner of an overseas entity includes, in connection with the obtaining of information required by section 7(1)(b), 9(1)(c), 41(3)(b) or 42(1)(c)(i), a reference to a person who has ceased to be a registrable beneficial owner.

(3) A reference in this Part to a trust includes arrangements, under the law of a country or territory outside the United Kingdom, that are of a similar character to a trust, and any related expressions are to be read accordingly.

(4) The Secretary of State may by regulations make provision specifying descriptions of arrangements that are, or are not, to be treated as being of a similar character to a trust for the purposes of subsection (3).

(5) Regulations under subsection (4) are subject to the negative resolution procedure.

NOTES

Commencement: 1 August 2022 (see further the note to s 1 at **[9.634]**).

PART 4 GENERAL

[9.679]

67 Regulations

(1) A power to make regulations under this Act is exercisable by statutory instrument.

(2) Regulations under this Act may make different provision for different purposes.

(3) Regulations under this Act may—

(a) include supplementary, incidental and consequential provision;

(b) make transitional provision and savings.

(4) Where regulations under this Act are subject to "the affirmative resolution procedure", the regulations may not be made unless a draft of the statutory instrument containing them has been laid before and approved by a resolution of each House of Parliament.

(5) Where regulations under this Act are subject to "the negative resolution procedure", the statutory instrument containing the regulations is subject to annulment in pursuance of a resolution of either House of Parliament.

(6) Any provision that may be made by regulations under this Act subject to the negative resolution procedure may be made by regulations subject to the affirmative resolution procedure.

(7) This section does not apply to regulations under section 69.

NOTES

Commencement: 15 March 2022.

[9.680]

68 Extent

(1) Except as mentioned in subsections (2) to (4), this Act extends to—

(a) England and Wales,

(b) Scotland, and

(c) Northern Ireland.

(2) In Part 1—

(a) section 33(1) and Schedule 3 extend to England and Wales only;

(b) section 33(2) and Parts 1 and 2 of Schedule 4 extend to Scotland only;

(c) section 33(3) to (7) and Schedule 5 extend to Northern Ireland only.

(3) In Part 2, section 51 extends to England and Wales only.

(4) The amendments made by the rest of Part 2 and by Part 3 have the same extent as the provisions amended.

NOTES

Commencement: 15 March 2022.

[9.681]

69 Commencement

(1) Parts 1 and 2 come into force on such day as the Secretary of State may by regulations appoint.

(2) Chapter 1 of Part 3 comes into force on such day as the Treasury may by regulations appoint.

(3) Chapter 2 of Part 3 and this Part come into force on the day on which this Act is passed.

(4) The Secretary of State may by regulations make transitional or saving provision in connection with the coming into force of any provision of Parts 1 and 2 or this Part.

(5) The Secretary of State or the Treasury may by regulations make transitional or saving provision in connection with the coming into force of any provision of Part 3.

(6) Regulations under this section may make different provision for different purposes.

(7) A power to make regulations under this section is exercisable by statutory instrument.

NOTES

Commencement: 15 March 2022.

Regulations: the Economic Crime (Transparency and Enforcement) Act 2022 (Commencement No 1) Regulations 2022, SI 2022/519; the Economic Crime (Transparency and Enforcement) Act 2022 (Commencement No 2 and Saving Provision) Regulations 2022, SI 2022/638; the Economic Crime (Transparency and Enforcement) Act 2022 (Commencement No 3) Regulations 2022, SI 2022/876.

[9.682]

70 Short title

This Act may be cited as the Economic Crime (Transparency and Enforcement) Act 2022.

NOTES

Commencement: 15 March 2022.

SCHEDULES

SCHEDULE 1
APPLICATIONS: REQUIRED INFORMATION

Sections 4, 7 and 9

PART 1 INTRODUCTION

[9.683]

1. This Schedule sets out the required information for the purposes of sections 4, 7 and 9.

NOTES

Commencement: 1 August 2022 (see further the note to s 1 at **[9.634]**).

Note that, as of 1 August 2022, sections 7 and 9 of this Act had not been brought into force.

PART 2 OVERSEAS ENTITIES

[9.684]

2. (1) The required information about an overseas entity is—

(a) name;
(b) country of incorporation or formation;
(c) registered or principal office;
(d) a service address;
(e) an email address;
(f) the legal form of the entity and the law by which it is governed;
(g) any public register in which it is entered and, if applicable, its registration number in that register.

(2) In sub-paragraph (1)(g) "public register" means a register kept by a government or public authority in the country in which the overseas entity was incorporated or formed.

NOTES

Commencement: 1 August 2022 (see further the note to s 1 at **[9.634]**).

Note that, as of 1 August 2022, sections 7 and 9 of this Act had not been brought into force.

PART 3 REGISTRABLE BENEFICIAL OWNERS

Individuals

[9.685]

3. (1) Where a registrable beneficial owner is an individual, the required information about the owner is—

(a) name, date of birth and nationality;
(b) usual residential address;
(c) a service address;
(d) the date on which the individual became a registrable beneficial owner in relation to the overseas entity;
(e) which of the conditions in paragraph 6 of Schedule 2 is met in relation to the registrable beneficial owner and a statement as to why that condition is met;
(f) whether the individual meets that condition by virtue of being a trustee;
(g) whether the individual is a designated person (within the meaning of section 9(2) of the Sanctions and Anti-Money Laundering Act 2018), where that information is publicly available.

(2) For the purposes of sub-paragraph (1)(a), "name" means a person's first name (or other forename) and surname, except that in the case of—

(a) a peer, or
(b) an individual usually known by a title,

the title may be stated instead of the person's first name (or other forename) and surname or in addition to either or both of them.

Governments and public authorities

4. Where a registrable beneficial owner is a government or public authority, the required information about the owner is—

(a) name;
(b) principal office;
(c) a service address;
(d) its legal form and the law by which it is governed;
(e) the date on which the entity became a registrable beneficial owner in relation to the overseas entity;
(f) which of the conditions in paragraph 6 of Schedule 2 is met in relation to the registrable beneficial owner and a statement as to why that condition is met;
(g) whether the entity is a designated person (within the meaning of section 9(2) of the Sanctions and Anti-Money Laundering Act 2018), where that information is publicly available.

Other legal entities

5. (1) Where the registrable beneficial owner is a legal entity other than a government or public authority, the required information about the owner is—

(a) name;
(b) registered or principal office;
(c) a service address;
(d) the legal form of the entity and the law by which it is governed;
(e) any public register in which it is entered and, if applicable, its registration number in that register;
(f) the date on which the entity became a registrable beneficial owner in relation to the overseas entity;
(g) which of the conditions in paragraph 6 of Schedule 2 is met in relation to the registrable beneficial owner and a statement as to why that condition is met;
(h) whether the entity meets that condition by virtue of being a trustee;
(i) whether the entity is a designated person (within the meaning of section 9(2) of the Sanctions and Anti-Money Laundering Act 2018), where that information is publicly available.

(2) In sub-paragraph (1)(e) "public register" has the meaning given by paragraph 2(2).

NOTES

Commencement: 1 August 2022 (see further the note to s 1 at **[9.634]**).

Note that, as of 1 August 2022, sections 7 and 9 of this Act had not been brought into force.

PART 4 MANAGING OFFICERS

Individuals

[9.686]

6. (1) Where a managing officer is an individual, the required information about the officer is—

(a) name, date of birth and nationality;
(b) any former name (unless sub-paragraph (2) applies);
(c) usual residential address;
(d) a service address (which may be stated as the entity's registered or principal office);
(e) business occupation (if any);
(f) a description of the officer's roles and responsibilities in relation to the entity.

(2) This sub-paragraph applies in the following cases—

(a) in the case of a peer or an individual normally known by a British title, where the name is one by which the person was known previous to the adoption of or succession to the title;
(b) in the case of any person, where the former name—
 (i) was changed or disused before the person attained the age of 16 years, or
 (ii) has been changed or disused for 20 years or more.

(3) In sub-paragraph (1)(a), "name" has the meaning given by paragraph 3(2).

(4) For the purposes of sub-paragraph (1)(b), "former name" means a name by which the individual was formerly known for business purposes.
Where a person is or was formerly known by more than one such name, each of them must be stated.

Persons other than individuals

7. (1) Where a managing officer is not an individual, the required information about the officer is—

(a) name;
(b) registered or principal office;
(c) a service address;
(d) the legal form of the entity and the law by which it is governed;
(e) any public register in which it is entered and, if applicable, its registration number in that register;
(f) a description of the officer's roles and responsibilities in relation to the entity;
(g) the name and contact details of an individual who may be contacted about the managing officer.

(2) In sub-paragraph (1)(e) "public register" has the meaning given by paragraph 2(2).

(3) In sub-paragraph (1)(g), "name" has the meaning given by paragraph 3(2).

NOTES

Commencement: 1 August 2022 (see further the note to s 1 at **[9.634]**).
Note that, as of 1 August 2022, sections 7 and 9 of this Act had not been brought into force.

PART 5 TRUSTS

[9.687]

8. (1) The required information about a trust is—

(a) the name of the trust or, if it does not have a name, a description by which it may be identified;
(b) the date on which the trust was created;
(c) in relation to each person who has at any time been a registrable beneficial owner in relation to the overseas entity by virtue of being a trustee of the trust—
 (i) the person's name,
 (ii) the date on which the person became a registrable beneficial owner in that capacity, and
 (iii) if relevant, the date on which the person ceased to be a registrable beneficial owner in that capacity;
(d) in relation to each beneficiary under the trust, the information that would be required under paragraph 3(1)(a) to (c) or 5(1)(a) to (e) if the beneficiary were a registrable beneficial owner in relation to the overseas entity;
(e) in relation to each settlor or grantor, the information that would be required under paragraph 3(1)(a) to (c) or 5(1)(a) to (e) if the settlor or grantor were a registrable beneficial owner in relation to the overseas entity;
(f) in relation to any interested person (see sub-paragraph (3))—
 (i) the information that would be required under paragraph 3(1)(a) to (c) or 5(1)(a) to (e) if the interested person were a registrable beneficial owner in relation to the overseas entity, and
 (ii) the date on which the person became an interested person.

(2) In sub-paragraph (1)(c), "name", in relation to an individual, has the meaning given by paragraph 3(2).

(3) In sub-paragraph (1)(f), "interested person", in relation to a trust, means any person who, under the terms of the trust, has rights in respect of—

(a) the appointment or removal of trustees, or
(b) the exercise by the trustees of their functions.

NOTES

Commencement: 1 August 2022 (see further the note to s 1 at **[9.634]**).
Note that, as of 1 August 2022, sections 7 and 9 of this Act had not been brought into force.

PART 6 POWERS TO MAKE FURTHER PROVISION UNDER THIS SCHEDULE

[9.688]

9. (1) The Secretary of State may by regulations make further provision about the information required by paragraphs 2 to 8.

(2) Regulations under this paragraph are subject to the negative resolution procedure.

10. (1) The Secretary of State may by regulations amend this Schedule so as to add to or remove from any list of information in this Schedule.

(2) Regulations under this paragraph are subject to the affirmative resolution procedure.

NOTES

Commencement: 1 August 2022 (see further the note to s 1 at **[9.634]**).

Note that, as of 1 August 2022, sections 7 and 9 of this Act had not been brought into force.

SCHEDULE 2
REGISTRABLE BENEFICIAL OWNERS

Section 4

PART 1 MEANING OF "REGISTRABLE BENEFICIAL OWNER"

Introduction

[9.689]

1. (1) This Part defines "registrable beneficial owner" for the purposes of this Part of this Act.

(2) A registrable beneficial owner may be—

(a) an individual (see paragraph 2),

(b) a legal entity (see paragraph 3), or

(c) a government or public authority (see paragraph 4).

Registrable beneficial owners: individuals

2. An individual is a "registrable beneficial owner" in relation to an overseas entity if the individual—

(a) is a beneficial owner of the overseas entity (see Part 2), and

(b) is not exempt from being registered (see Part 4).

Registrable beneficial owners: legal entities

3. A legal entity other than a government or public authority is a "registrable beneficial owner" in relation to an overseas entity if it—

(a) is a beneficial owner of the overseas entity (see Part 2),

(b) is subject to its own disclosure requirements (see Part 3), and

(c) is not exempt from being registered (see Part 4).

Registrable beneficial owners: government or public authority

4. A government or public authority is a "registrable beneficial owner" in relation to an overseas entity in all cases where it is a beneficial owner of the entity (see Part 2).

NOTES

Commencement: 1 August 2022 (see further the note to s 1 at **[9.634]**).

PART 2 MEANING OF "BENEFICIAL OWNER"

Introduction

[9.690]

5. This Part defines "beneficial owner" for the purposes of this Part of this Act.

Beneficial owners

6. A person ("X") is a "beneficial owner" of an overseas entity or other legal entity ("Y") if one or more of the following conditions are met.

Ownership of shares

Condition 1 is that X holds, directly or indirectly, more than 25% of the shares in Y.

Voting rights

Condition 2 is that X holds, directly or indirectly, more than 25% of the voting rights in Y.

Right to appoint or remove directors

Condition 3 is that X holds the right, directly or indirectly, to appoint or remove a majority of the board of directors of Y.

Significant influence or control

Condition 4 is that X has the right to exercise, or actually exercises, significant influence or control over Y.

Trusts, partnerships, etc

Condition 5 is that—

(a) the trustees of a trust, or the members of a partnership, unincorporated association or other entity, that is not a legal person under the law by which it is governed meet any of the conditions specified above (in their capacity as such) in relation to Y, and

(b) X has the right to exercise, or actually exercises, significant influence or control over the activities of that trust or entity.

NOTES

Commencement: 1 August 2022 (see further the note to s 1 at **[9.634]**).

PART 3 MEANING OF "SUBJECT TO ITS OWN DISCLOSURE REQUIREMENTS"

[9.691]

7. (1) For the purposes of this Schedule a legal entity is "subject to its own disclosure requirements" if—

(a) Part 21A of the Companies Act 2006 applies to it (whether by virtue of section 790B of that Act or another enactment that extends the application of that Part),

(b) it is a company to which section 790C(7)(b) of that Act applies (companies with voting shares traded on UK or EU regulated markets),

(c) it is of a description specified in regulations under section 790B(1)(b) or 790C(7)(d) of that Act (or under either of those sections as extended),

(d) it is an eligible Scottish partnership within the meaning of regulation 3 of the Scottish Partnerships (Register of People with Significant Control) Regulations 2017 (SI 2017/694),

(e) it is registered in the register of overseas entities under this Part of this Act, or

(f) it is of a description specified by the Secretary of State in regulations under this paragraph.

(2) Regulations under sub-paragraph (1)(f) are subject to the affirmative resolution procedure.

NOTES

Commencement: 1 August 2022 (see further the note to s 1 at **[9.634]**).

Regulations: the Register of Overseas Entities (Delivery, Protection and Trust Services) Regulations 2022, SI 2022/870 at **[10.1376]**.

PART 4 BENEFICIAL OWNERS EXEMPT FROM REGISTRATION

"Exempt from being registered"

[9.692]

8. For the purposes of paragraphs 2(b) and 3(c) a person who is a beneficial owner of an overseas entity is "exempt from being registered" if—

(a) the person does not hold any interest in the overseas entity other than through one or more legal entities (see paragraph 9),

(b) the person is a beneficial owner of every legal entity through which the person holds such an interest (see paragraph 9),

(c) as respects any shares or right in the overseas entity which the person holds indirectly as described in paragraph 9(3)(b)(i), the legal entity through which the shares or right are held is a beneficial owner of the overseas entity and is subject to its own disclosure requirements, and

(d) as respects any shares or right in the overseas entity which the person holds indirectly as described in paragraph 9(3)(b)(ii), at least one of the legal entities in the chain is a beneficial owner of the overseas entity and is subject to its own disclosure requirements.

Holding an interest in an overseas entity etc

9. (1) This paragraph specifies the circumstances in which, for the purposes of paragraph 8—

(a) a person ("V") is to be regarded as holding an interest in an overseas entity ("entity W");

(b) an interest held by V in entity W is to be regarded as held through a legal entity.

(2) V holds an interest in entity W if—

(a) V holds, directly or indirectly, shares in entity W,

(b) V holds, directly or indirectly, voting rights in entity W,

(c) V holds, directly or indirectly, the right to appoint or remove any member of the board of directors of entity W,

(d) V has the right to exercise, or actually exercises, significant influence or control over entity W, or

(e) the following conditions are both satisfied—

(i) the trustees of a trust, or the members of a partnership, unincorporated association or other entity, that is not a legal person under the law by which it is governed hold an interest in entity W in a way mentioned in any of paragraphs (a) to (d);

(ii) V has the right to exercise, or actually exercises, significant influence or control over the activities of that trust or entity.

(3) Where V—

(a) holds an interest in entity W by virtue of indirectly holding shares or a right, and

(b) does so by virtue of having a majority stake (see paragraph 18) in—

(i) a legal entity ("L") which holds the shares or right directly, or

(ii) a legal entity that is part of a chain of legal entities such as is described in paragraph 18(1)(b) or (2)(b) that includes L,

V holds the interest in entity W through L and, where relevant, through each other legal entity in the chain.

NOTES

Commencement: 1 August 2022 (see further the note to s 1 at **[9.634]**).

PART 5 SUPPLEMENTARY PROVISION ABOUT INTERPRETATION OF SCHEDULE

Introduction

[9.693]

10. This Part sets out further rules for the interpretation of this Schedule.

Joint interests

11. If two or more persons hold a share or right jointly, each of them is treated for the purposes of this Schedule as holding that share or right.

Joint arrangements

12. (1) If shares or rights held by a person and shares or rights held by another person are the subject of a joint arrangement between those persons, each of them is treated for the purposes of this Schedule as holding the combined shares or rights of both of them.

(2) A "joint arrangement" is an arrangement between the holders of shares (or rights) that they will exercise all or substantially all the rights conferred by their respective shares (or rights) jointly in a way that is pre-determined by the arrangement.

(3) "Arrangement" includes—

(a) any scheme, agreement or understanding, whether or not it is legally enforceable, and
(b) any convention, custom or practice of any kind.

(4) But something does not count as an arrangement unless there is at least some degree of stability about it (whether by its nature or terms, or the time it has been in existence, or otherwise).

Calculating shareholdings

13. (1) In relation to a legal entity that has a share capital, a reference to holding "more than 25% of the shares" in that entity is a reference to holding shares comprised in the issued share capital of that entity of a nominal value exceeding (in aggregate) 25% of that share capital.

(2) In relation to a legal entity that does not have a share capital—
(a) a reference to holding shares in that entity is a reference to holding a right to share in the capital or, as the case may be, profits of that entity;
(b) a reference to holding "more than 25% of the shares" in that entity is a reference to holding a right or rights to share in more than 25% of the capital or, as the case may be, profits of that entity.

Voting rights

14. (1) A reference to the voting rights in a legal entity is to the rights conferred on shareholders in respect of their shares (or, in the case of an entity not having a share capital, on members) to vote at general meetings of the entity on all or substantially all matters.

(2) In relation to a legal entity that does not have general meetings at which matters are decided by the exercise of voting rights—
(a) a reference to exercising voting rights in the entity is to be read as a reference to exercising rights in relation to the entity that are equivalent to those of a person entitled to exercise voting rights in a company registered under the Companies Act 2006;
(b) a reference to exercising more than 25% of the voting rights in the entity is to be read as a reference to exercising the right under the constitution of the entity to block changes to the overall policy of the entity or to the terms of its constitution.

15. In applying this Schedule, the voting rights in a legal entity are to be reduced by any rights held by the entity itself.

Rights to appoint or remove members of the board

16. A reference to the right to appoint or remove a majority of the board of directors of a legal entity is a reference to the right to appoint or remove directors holding a majority of the voting rights at meetings of the board on all or substantially all matters.

17. References to a board of directors, in the case of an entity that does not have such a board, are to be read as references to the equivalent management body of that entity.

Shares or rights held "indirectly"

18. (1) A person holds a share "indirectly" if the person has a majority stake in a legal entity and that entity—
(a) holds the share in question, or
(b) is part of a chain of legal entities—
(i) each of which (other than the last) has a majority stake in the entity immediately below it in the chain, and
(ii) the last of which holds the share.

(2) A person holds a right "indirectly" if the person has a majority stake in a legal entity and that entity—
(a) holds that right, or
(b) is part of a chain of legal entities—
(i) each of which (other than the last) has a majority stake in the entity immediately below it in the chain, and
(ii) the last of which holds that right.

(3) For these purposes, A has a "majority stake" in B if—
(a) A holds a majority of the voting rights in B,
(b) A is a member of B and has the right to appoint or remove a majority of the board of directors of B,
(c) A is a member of B and controls alone, or pursuant to an agreement with other shareholders or members, a majority of the voting rights in B, or
(d) A has the right to exercise, or actually exercises, dominant influence or control over B.

(4) In the application of this paragraph to the right to appoint or remove a majority of the board of directors, a legal entity is to be treated as having the right to appoint a director if—
(a) a person's appointment as director follows necessarily from that person's appointment as director of the legal entity, or
(b) the directorship is held by the legal entity itself.

Shares held by nominees

19. A share held by a person as nominee for another is to be treated for the purposes of this Schedule as held by the other (and not by the nominee).

Rights treated as held by a person who controls their exercise

20. (1) Where a person controls a right, the right is to be treated for the purposes of this Schedule as held by that person (and not by the person who in fact holds the right, unless that person also controls it).

(2) A person "controls" a right if, by virtue of any arrangement between that person and others, the right is exercisable only—
(a) by that person,
(b) in accordance with that person's directions or instructions, or

(c) with that person's consent or concurrence.

(3) "Arrangement" has the meaning given in paragraph 12(3) and (4).

Rights exercisable only in certain circumstances etc

21. (1) Rights that are exercisable only in certain circumstances are to be taken into account only—

(a) when the circumstances have arisen, and for so long as they continue to obtain, or

(b) when the circumstances are within the control of the person having the rights.

(2) But rights that are exercisable by an administrator or by creditors while a legal entity is in relevant insolvency proceedings are not to be taken into account even while the entity is in those proceedings.

(3) "Relevant insolvency proceedings" means—

(a) administration within the meaning of the Insolvency Act 1986,

(b) administration within the meaning of the Insolvency (Northern Ireland) Order 1989 (SI 1989/2405 (NI 19)), or

(c) proceedings under the insolvency law of a country or territory outside the United Kingdom during which an entity's assets and affairs are subject to the control or supervision of a third party or creditor.

(4) Rights that are normally exercisable but are temporarily incapable of exercise are to continue to be taken into account.

Rights attached to shares held by way of security

22. Rights attached to shares held by way of security provided by a person are to be treated for the purposes of this Schedule as held by that person—

(a) where apart from the right to exercise them for the purpose of preserving the value of the security, or of realising it, the rights are exercisable only in accordance with that person's instructions, and

(b) where the shares are held in connection with the granting of loans as part of normal business activities and apart from the right to exercise them for the purpose of preserving the value of the security, or of realising it, the rights are exercisable only in that person's interests.

Limited partnerships

23. (1) A person does not meet Condition 1, 2 or 3 of paragraph 6 in relation to an overseas entity by virtue only of being a limited partner.

(2) A person does not meet Condition 1, 2 or 3 of paragraph 6 in relation to an overseas entity by virtue only of, directly or indirectly—

(a) holding shares, or

(b) holding a right,

in or in relation to a limited partner.

(3) Sub-paragraphs (1) and (2) do not apply for the purposes of determining whether the requirement set out in Condition 5(a) of paragraph 6 is met.

(4) In this paragraph "limited partner" means—

(a) a limited partner in a limited partnership registered under the Limited Partnerships Act 1907 (other than one who takes part in the management of the partnership business), or

(b) a foreign limited partner.

(5) In this paragraph "foreign limited partner" means an individual who—

(a) participates in arrangements established under the law of a country or territory outside the United Kingdom, and

(b) has the characteristics prescribed by regulations made by the Secretary of State.

(6) Regulations under this paragraph may, among other things, prescribe characteristics by reference to—

(a) the nature of arrangements;

(b) the nature of an individual's participation in the arrangements.

(7) Regulations under this paragraph are subject to the affirmative resolution procedure.

Meaning of "director"

24. In this Schedule "director" includes any person occupying the position of director, by whatever name called.

NOTES

Commencement: 1 August 2022 (see further the note to s 1 at **[9.634]**).

PART 6 POWER TO AMEND THRESHOLDS ETC

[9.694]

25. (1) The Secretary of State may by regulations amend this Schedule for a permitted purpose.

(2) The permitted purposes are—

(a) to replace any or all references in this Schedule to a percentage figure with references to some other (larger or smaller) percentage figure;

(b) to change or supplement the conditions in paragraph 6 so as to include circumstances (for example, circumstances involving more complex structures) that give individuals a level of control over entity Y broadly similar to the level of control given by the other conditions in that paragraph;

(c) in consequence of any provision made by virtue of paragraph (b), to change or supplement paragraph 9 so that the circumstances specified in that paragraph in which a person is to be regarded as holding an interest in an overseas entity correspond to any of the conditions in paragraph 6, or would do so but for the extent of the interest.

(3) Regulations under this paragraph are subject to the affirmative resolution procedure.

NOTES

Commencement: 1 August 2022 (see further the note to s 1 at **[9.634]**).

SCHEDULE 3
LAND OWNERSHIP AND TRANSACTIONS: ENGLAND AND WALES

Section 33(1)

PART 1 AMENDMENTS TO LAND REGISTRATION ACT 2002

[9.695]

1. The Land Registration Act 2002 is amended as follows.

2. After section 85 insert—

"Overseas entities

85A Overseas entities

Schedule 4A is about the ownership of registered land by overseas entities and about registrable dispositions made by them."

3. After Schedule 4 insert—

"SCHEDULE 4A
OVERSEAS ENTITIES

Section 85A

Meaning of "qualifying estate"

1. In this Schedule "qualifying estate" means—

(a) a freehold estate in land, or
(b) a leasehold estate in land granted for a term of more than seven years from the date of grant.

Registration

2. No application may be made to register an overseas entity as the proprietor of a qualifying estate unless, at the time of the application, the entity—

(a) is a registered overseas entity, or
(b) is an exempt overseas entity.

Restrictions on disposal

3. (1) The registrar must enter a restriction in the register in relation to a qualifying estate if satisfied that—

(a) an overseas entity is registered as the proprietor of the estate, and
(b) the entity became registered as the proprietor in pursuance of an application made on or after 1 January 1999.

(2) The restriction must prohibit the registration of any disposition within section 27(2)(a), (b)(i) or (f) unless—

(a) the entity is a registered overseas entity, or is an exempt overseas entity, at the time of the disposition,
(b) the disposition is made in pursuance of a statutory obligation or court order, or occurs by operation of law,
(c) the disposition is made in pursuance of a contract made before the restriction is entered in the register,
(d) the disposition is made in the exercise of a power of sale or leasing conferred on the proprietor of a registered charge or a receiver appointed by such a proprietor,
(e) the Secretary of State gives consent under paragraph 5 to the registration of the disposition, or
(f) the disposition is made by a specified insolvency practitioner in specified circumstances.

(3) In sub-paragraph (2), in paragraph (f)—

"specified circumstances" means circumstances specified in regulations made by the Secretary of State for the purposes of that paragraph;

"specified insolvency practitioner" means an insolvency practitioner of a description specified in regulations made by the Secretary of State for the purposes of that paragraph.

Registrable dispositions by overseas entity entitled to be registered (but not registered)

4. (1) This paragraph applies where—

(a) an overseas entity is entitled to be registered as the proprietor of a qualifying estate,
(b) the overseas entity became entitled to be registered as the proprietor of that estate on or after the day on which this paragraph comes into force, and
(c) the entity makes a registrable disposition within section 27(2)(a), (b)(i) or (f).

(2) The disposition must not be registered unless—

(a) the entity is a registered overseas entity, or is an exempt overseas entity, at the time of the disposition,
(b) the disposition is made in pursuance of a statutory obligation or court order, or occurs by operation of law,
(c) the disposition is made in pursuance of a contract made before the overseas entity became entitled to be registered,
(d) the disposition is made in the exercise of a power of sale or leasing conferred on the proprietor of a registered charge or a receiver appointed by such a proprietor,
(e) the Secretary of State gives consent under paragraph 5 to the registration of the disposition, or

(f) the disposition is made by a specified insolvency practitioner in specified circumstances.

(3) In sub-paragraph (2)(f) "specified circumstances" and "specified insolvency practitioner" have the meanings given by paragraph 3(3).

Consent to registration of dispositions that cannot otherwise be registered

5. (1) The Secretary of State may consent to the registration of a disposition that would otherwise be prohibited by a restriction entered under paragraph 3, or by paragraph 4, if satisfied—

(a) that at the time of the disposition the person to whom it was made did not know, and could not reasonably have been expected to know, of the prohibition, and

(b) that in all the circumstances it would be unjust for the disposition not to be registered.

(2) The Secretary of State may by regulations make provision in connection with applications for consent, and the giving of consent, under sub-paragraph (1).

(3) The regulations may, for example, make provision about—

(a) who may apply;

(b) evidence;

(c) time limits.

Making dispositions that cannot be registered

6. (1) An overseas entity must not make a registrable disposition of a qualifying estate if, disregarding the possibility of consent under paragraph 5, the registration of the disposition is prohibited by—

(a) a restriction entered under paragraph 3, or

(b) paragraph 4.

(2) If an overseas entity breaches sub-paragraph (1) an offence is committed by—

(a) the entity, and

(b) every officer of the entity who is in default.

(3) Nothing in this paragraph affects the validity of a disposition made in breach of sub-paragraph (1).

(4) Sections 1121 to 1123 of the Companies Act 2006 (liability of officers in default: interpretation etc) apply for the purposes of this paragraph as they apply for the purposes of provisions of the Companies Acts.

(5) In those sections as applied, a reference to an officer includes a person in accordance with whose directions or instructions the board of directors or equivalent management body of an overseas entity are accustomed to act.

(6) A person is not to be regarded as falling within sub-paragraph (5) by reason only that the board of directors or equivalent management body acts on advice given by the person in a professional capacity.

(7) A person guilty of an offence under this paragraph is liable—

(a) on summary conviction, to imprisonment for a term not exceeding the maximum summary term for either-way offences or a fine (or both);

(b) on conviction on indictment, to imprisonment for a term not exceeding 5 years or a fine (or both).

(8) In sub-paragraph (7)(a) "the maximum summary term for either-way offences" means—

(a) in relation to an offence committed before the time when paragraph 24(2) of Schedule 22 to the Sentencing Act 2020 comes into force, 6 months;

(b) in relation to an offence committed after that time, 12 months.

(9) Proceedings for an offence under this may only be brought by or with the consent the Secretary of State or the Director of Public Prosecutions.

Interpretation etc

7. In this Schedule—

"exempt overseas entity" means an overseas entity of a description specified in regulations under section 34(6) of the Economic Crime (Transparency and Enforcement) Act 2022;

"overseas entity" has the meaning given by section 2 of the Economic Crime (Transparency and Enforcement) Act 2022;

"qualifying estate" has the meaning given by paragraph 1;

"register of overseas entities" means the register kept under section 3 of the Economic Crime (Transparency and Enforcement) Act 2022;

"registered overseas entity" means an overseas entity that is registered in the register of overseas entities (but see paragraph 8).

8. (1) For the purpose of this Schedule, an overseas entity that fails to comply with the duty in section 7 of the Economic Crime (Transparency and Enforcement) Act 2022 (updating duty) is not to be treated as being a "registered overseas entity" until it remedies the failure.

(2) For the purpose of sub-paragraph (1), an overseas entity "remedies" the failure when it delivers the statements and information mentioned in section 7(1)(a), (b) and (c) of the 2022 Act."

4. In section 128 (regulations), in subsection (4)—

(a) omit the "or" at the end of paragraph (b);

(b) at the end of paragraph (d) insert ", or

(e) regulations under paragraph 3(3) or 5(2) of Schedule 4A."

NOTES

Commencement: 5 September 2022.

PART 2 TRANSITION: QUALIFYING ESTATES REGISTERED PRE-COMMENCEMENT

Duty of proprietor to register as an overseas entity within transitional period

[9.696]

5. (1) An overseas entity, and every officer of the entity who is in default, commits an offence if—

(a) at the end of the transitional period, the entity—

(i) is the registered proprietor of a qualifying estate, but

(ii) the entity is not registered as an overseas entity, has not made an application for registration as an overseas entity that is pending and is not an exempt overseas entity, and

(b) the entity became the registered proprietor of that qualifying estate in pursuance of an application made on or after 1 January 1999 but before the commencement date.

(2) A person guilty of an offence under this paragraph is liable—

(a) on summary conviction, to imprisonment for a term not exceeding the maximum summary term for either-way offences or a fine (or both);

(b) on conviction on indictment, to imprisonment for a term not exceeding 2 years or a fine (or both).

(3) In sub-paragraph (2)(a) "the maximum summary term for either-way offences" means—

(a) in relation to an offence committed before the time when paragraph 24(2) of Schedule 22 to the Sentencing Act 2020 comes into force, 6 months;

(b) in relation to an offence committed after that time, 12 months.

(4) In this paragraph "exempt overseas entity" means an overseas entity of a description specified in regulations under section 34(6).

(5) Nothing in this paragraph limits the power to give a notice under section 34 at any time.

Registrar's duty to enter restriction in relation to qualifying estate

6. (1) This paragraph applies where the Chief Land Registrar is satisfied that—

(a) an overseas entity is the registered proprietor of a qualifying estate, and

(b) the entity became the registered proprietor of that estate in pursuance of an application made before the commencement date.

(2) The Chief Land Registrar must comply with the duty to enter a restriction under paragraph 3 of Schedule 4A to the Land Registration Act 2002 (inserted by Part 1 of this Schedule) in relation to the estate as soon as reasonably practicable and in any event before the end of the transitional period.

(3) But the restriction does not take effect until the end of the transitional period.

Interpretation

7. In this Part of this Schedule—

"the commencement date" means the day on which section 3(1) comes fully into force;

"registered proprietor", in relation to a qualifying estate, means the person entered as proprietor of the estate in the register of title kept by the Chief Land Registrar;

"qualifying estate" has the meaning given by paragraph 1 of Schedule 4A to the Land Registration Act 2002;

"the transitional period" has the meaning given by section 41(10).

NOTES

Commencement: 5 September 2022.

SCHEDULE 4
LAND OWNERSHIP AND TRANSACTIONS: SCOTLAND

Section 33(2)

PART 1 AMENDMENTS

Conveyancing (Scotland) Act 1924

[9.697]

1. (1) Section 4A of the Conveyancing (Scotland) Act 1924 (completion of title by registration of notice of title in Land Register of Scotland) is amended as follows.

(2) The existing text becomes subsection (1).

(3) After that subsection insert—

"(2) Subsection (1) is subject to paragraphs 3 and 4 of schedule 1A to the Land Registration etc (Scotland) Act 2012."

Land Registration etc (Scotland) Act 2012 (asp 5)

2. The Land Registration etc (Scotland) Act 2012 is amended as follows.

3. In section 21 (application for registration of deed)—

(a) in subsection (4), after "45(5)" insert "and paragraphs 1 to 5 of schedule 1A", and

(b) after that subsection insert—

"(5) Schedule 1A makes provision about certain land transactions involving overseas entities."

4. In section 27 (application for voluntary registration), after subsection (4) insert—

"(4A) Subsection (3) is subject to paragraph 6 of schedule 1A."

5. In section 46 (the title of which becomes "Meaning of "disposition" in certain provisions")—

(a) after "48" insert "and schedule 1A", and

(b) after "sections" insert "or that schedule".

6. The italic heading before section 112 becomes "Offences".

7. After section 112 insert—

"112A Offence by overseas entity

(1) An overseas entity must not deliver to a person a qualifying registrable deed granted by the overseas entity if (disregarding the possibility of consent under paragraph 7(2) of schedule 1A) by virtue of paragraph 2 of schedule 1A the Keeper would be required to reject an application under section 21 for registration of the deed.

(2) A qualifying registrable deed is to be treated as having been granted for the purposes of subsection (1) even if at the time when it is delivered it has been executed by the overseas entity only.

(3) If an overseas entity breaches subsection (1), an offence is committed by—

(a) the entity, and

(b) every officer of the entity who is in default.

(4) Nothing in this section affects the validity of a qualifying registrable deed delivered in breach of subsection (1).

(5) A person guilty of an offence under subsection (3) is liable—

(a) on summary conviction, to imprisonment for a term not exceeding 12 months or a fine not exceeding the statutory maximum (or both);

(b) on conviction on indictment, to imprisonment for a term not exceeding 5 years or a fine (or both).

(6) Sections 1121 to 1123 of the Companies Act 2006 (liability of officers in default: interpretation etc) apply for the purposes of this section as they apply for the purposes of provisions of the Companies Acts.

(7) In those sections as applied, a reference to an officer includes a person in accordance with whose directions or instructions the board of directors or equivalent management body of an overseas entity are accustomed to act.

(8) A person is not to be regarded as falling within subsection (7) by reason only that the board of directors or equivalent management body acts on advice given by the person in a professional capacity.

(9) In this section—

"overseas entity" has the meaning given by section 2 of the Economic Crime (Transparency and Enforcement) Act 2022;

"qualifying registrable deed" means a registrable deed which is—

(a) a disposition;

(b) a standard security;

(c) a lease;

(d) an assignation of a lease."

8. In section 116(2) (orders and regulations subject to the negative procedure)—

(a) for "sections", in the first place it occurs, substitute "provisions", and

(b) after paragraph (h) insert—

"(i) paragraph 2(5) or 7(5) of schedule 1A."

9. After schedule 1 insert—

"SCHEDULE 1A
LAND TRANSACTIONS: OVERSEAS ENTITIES

Section 21

Cases where Keeper must reject application under section 21

1. (1) This paragraph applies where—

(a) a person applies under section 21 for registration of a qualifying registrable deed, and

(b) if the application is accepted by the Keeper—

(i) the name of an overseas entity would be entered as proprietor in the proprietorship section of the title sheet of a registered plot of land, or

(ii) an overseas entity would be the tenant under a registered lease.

(2) The Keeper must reject the application unless the overseas entity is—

(a) a registered overseas entity, or

(b) an exempt overseas entity.

(3) Sub-paragraph (2) does not apply where—

(a) the application is made by a person other than the overseas entity referred to in sub-paragraph (1)(b)(i), and

(b) the deed in respect of which the application is made is a lease or an assignation of a lease the subjects of which consist of or form part of an unregistered plot of land of which that overseas entity is the proprietor.

2. (1) This paragraph applies where—

(a) a person applies under section 21 for registration of a qualifying registrable deed or a registrable deed which is a standard security,

(b) the granter of the deed is an overseas entity whose interest is registered, having been so registered on or after 8 December 2014, and

(c) as at the date of delivery of the deed, the entity was not a registered overseas entity or an exempt overseas entity.

(2) The Keeper must reject the application unless one of the following conditions is met—

(a) the application is made—

(i) in pursuance of a statutory obligation or court order, or

(ii) in respect of a transfer of ownership or other event that occurs by operation of law,

(b) the application is made in pursuance of a contract entered into before the later of the dates mentioned in sub-paragraph (3);

(c) the application is made in pursuance of the exercise of a power of sale or lease by the creditor in a standard security that was registered on or after 8 December 2014;

(d) the application is made in pursuance of the exercise of a right conferred on a body by relevant legislation to buy land or the interest of a tenant under a lease;

(e) the Scottish Ministers give consent under paragraph 7(2) to the registration of the deed;

(f) the deed is granted by a specified insolvency practitioner in specified circumstances.

(3) The dates are—

(a) the date on which the granter's interest was registered;

(b) the commencement date.

(4) In sub-paragraph (2)(d), "relevant legislation" means Part 2, 3 or 3A of the Land Reform (Scotland) Act 2003 or Part 5 of the Land Reform (Scotland) Act 2016 (being provisions which confer on certain community bodies etc the right to buy certain types of land or the interest of a tenant under a lease of certain types of land).

(5) In sub-paragraph (2), in paragraph (f)—

"specified circumstances" means circumstances specified in regulations made by the Scottish Ministers for the purposes of that paragraph;

"specified insolvency practitioner" means an insolvency practitioner of a description specified in regulations made by the Scottish Ministers for the purposes of that paragraph.

Cases where Keeper must reject application to register notice of title

3. (1) This paragraph applies where—

(a) by virtue of section 4A of the Conveyancing (Scotland) Act 1924, a person makes an application under section 21 for registration of a notice of title completing title in respect of a qualifying registrable deed, and

(b) if the application is accepted by the Keeper—

(i) the name of an overseas entity would be entered as proprietor in the proprietorship section of the title sheet of a registered plot of land, or

(ii) an overseas entity would be the tenant under a registered lease.

(2) The Keeper must reject the application unless the overseas entity is—

(a) a registered overseas entity, or

(b) an exempt overseas entity.

(3) Sub-paragraph (2) does not apply where—

(a) the application is made by a person other than the overseas entity referred to in sub-paragraph (1)(b)(i), and

(b) the deed in respect of which title is being completed is a lease or an assignation of a lease the subjects of which consist of or form part of an unregistered plot of land of which that overseas entity is the proprietor.

4. (1) This paragraph applies where—

(a) by virtue of section 4A of the Conveyancing (Scotland) Act 1924, a person makes an application under section 21 for registration of a notice of title completing title in respect of—

(i) a qualifying registrable deed, or

(ii) a registrable deed which is a standard security,

(b) the granter of the deed is an overseas entity whose interest is registered, having been so registered on or after 8 December 2014, and

(c) as at the date on which the application for registration of the notice of title was made, the entity was not a registered overseas entity or an exempt overseas entity.

(2) The Keeper must reject the application unless one of the following conditions is met—

(a) the application is made—

(i) in pursuance of a statutory obligation or court order, or

(ii) in respect of a transfer of ownership or other event that occurs by operation of law,

(b) the application is made in pursuance of a contract entered into before the later of the dates mentioned in sub-paragraph (3);

(c) the application is made in pursuance of the exercise of a power of sale or lease by the creditor in a standard security that was registered on or after 8 December 2014;

(d) the application is made in pursuance of the exercise of a right conferred on a body by relevant legislation to buy land or the interest of a tenant under a lease;

(e) the Scottish Ministers give consent under paragraph 7(4) to the registration of the notice of title;

(f) the deed in respect of which title is being completed is granted by a specified insolvency practitioner in specified circumstances.

(3) The dates are—

(a) the date on which the granter's interest was registered;

(b) the commencement date.

(4) In sub-paragraph (2)(d), "relevant legislation" means Part 2, 3 or 3A of the Land Reform (Scotland) Act 2003 or Part 5 of the Land Reform (Scotland) Act 2016 (being provisions which confer on certain community bodies etc the right to buy certain types of land or the interest of a tenant under a lease of certain types of land).

(5) In sub-paragraph (2)(f) "specified circumstances" and "specified insolvency practitioner" have the meanings given by paragraph 2(5).

Case where Keeper must reject prescriptive application

5. (1) This paragraph applies where—

(a) an application under section 21 is received by the Keeper by virtue of section 43(1) or (5), and

(b) if the application is accepted by the Keeper—

(i) the name of an overseas entity would be entered as proprietor in the proprietorship section of the title sheet of a registered plot of land, and

(ii) that entry would be marked as provisional under section 44(1).

(2) The Keeper must reject the application unless the overseas entity is—

(a) a registered overseas entity, or
(b) an exempt overseas entity.

Case where Keeper must reject voluntary application

6. (1) This paragraph applies where—
(a) an application is made under section 27, and
(b) if the application is accepted by the Keeper, the name of an overseas entity would be entered as proprietor in the proprietorship section of the title sheet of a registered plot of land.
(2) The Keeper must reject the application unless the overseas entity is—
(a) a registered overseas entity, or
(b) an exempt overseas entity.

Consent to registration of certain deeds that cannot otherwise be registered

7. (1) Sub-paragraph (2) applies where the Keeper would be required by paragraph 2(2) to reject an application for registration of a qualifying registrable deed or a registrable deed which is a standard security.
(2) The Scottish Ministers may consent to registration of the deed if satisfied—
(a) that at the time of delivery of the deed the person in whose favour it was granted did not know, and could not reasonably have been expected to know, of the duty imposed on the Keeper by paragraph 2(2), and
(b) that in all the circumstances it would be unjust for the deed not to be registered.
(3) Sub-paragraph (4) applies where the Keeper would be required by paragraph 4(2) to reject an application for registration of a notice of title in respect of a qualifying registrable deed or a registrable deed which is a standard security.
(4) The Scottish Ministers may consent to registration of the notice of title if satisfied—
(a) that at the time of delivery of the qualifying registrable deed or (as the case may be) registrable deed which is a standard security the person in whose favour the deed was granted did not know, and could not reasonably have been expected to know, of the duty imposed on the Keeper by paragraph 4(2), and
(b) that in all the circumstances it would be unjust for the notice of title not to be registered.
(5) The Scottish Ministers may by regulations make provision in connection with applications for consent, and the giving of consent, under sub-paragraphs (2) and (4).
(6) The regulations may, for example, make provision about—
(a) who may apply;
(b) evidence;
(c) time limits.

Partially executed deeds

8. For the purposes of paragraphs 2(1)(c) and 7(2)(a) and (4)(a), a qualifying registrable deed or registrable deed which is a standard security is to be treated, as at the date of delivery of the deed, as having been granted even if at that time it has been executed by the overseas entity only.

Interpretation

9. (1) In this schedule—
"the commencement date" means the day on which Part 1 of Schedule 4 to the Economic Crime (Transparency and Enforcement) Act 2022 comes into force;
"exempt overseas entity" means an overseas entity of a description specified in regulations under section 34(6) of the Economic Crime (Transparency and Enforcement) Act 2022;
"overseas entity" has the meaning given by section 2 of the Economic Crime (Transparency and Enforcement) Act 2022;
"qualifying registrable deed" means a registrable deed which is—
(a) a disposition;
(b) a lease;
(c) an assignation of a lease;
"register of overseas entities" means the register kept under section 3 of the Economic Crime (Transparency and Enforcement) Act 2022;
"registered overseas entity" means an overseas entity that is registered in the register of overseas entities (but see sub-paragraphs (2) and (3)).
(2) For the purposes of this Schedule, an overseas entity that fails to comply with the duty in section 7 of the Economic Crime (Transparency and Enforcement) Act 2022 (updating duty) is not to be treated as being a "registered overseas entity" until it remedies the failure.
(3) For the purpose of sub-paragraph (2), an overseas entity "remedies" the failure when it delivers the statements and information mentioned in section 7(1)(a), (b) and (c) of the 2022 Act."

NOTES

Commencement: 5 September 2022.

PART 2 TRANSITION: DEEDS REGISTERED PRE-COMMENCEMENT

Duty to register as an overseas entity within transitional period

[9.698]

10. (1) This paragraph applies where—
(a) an overseas entity is entered as proprietor in the proprietorship section of the title sheet for a plot of land that is registered in the Land Register of Scotland, having been so entered during the pre-commencement period,

(b) in relation to a lease that was recorded in the General Register of Sasines or registered in the Land Register of Scotland before 8 December 2014, an overseas entity is, by virtue of an assignation of the lease registered in the Land Register of Scotland during the pre-commencement period, the tenant under the lease, or

(c) an overseas entity is the tenant under a lease that was registered in the Land Register of Scotland during the pre-commencement period.

(2) An overseas entity, and every officer of the entity who is in default, commits an offence if—

(a) on the expiry of the transitional period, the paragraph of sub-paragraph (1) that applied in relation to the overseas entity immediately before the beginning of the transitional period continues to apply in relation to the overseas entity, and

(b) the entity is not registered as an overseas entity, has not made an application for registration as an overseas entity that is pending and is not an exempt overseas entity.

(3) A person guilty of an offence under this paragraph is liable—

(a) on summary conviction, to imprisonment for a term not exceeding 12 months or a fine not exceeding the statutory maximum (or both);

(b) on conviction on indictment, to imprisonment for a term not exceeding 2 years or a fine (or both).

(4) Nothing in this paragraph limits the power to give a notice under section 34 at any time.

Disapplication of certain provisions during transitional period

11. (1) This paragraph applies where—

(a) an overseas entity is entered as proprietor in the proprietorship section of the title sheet for a plot of land that is registered in the Land Register of Scotland, having been so entered during the pre-commencement period,

(b) in relation to a lease that was recorded in the General Register of Sasines or registered in the Land Register of Scotland before 8 December 2014, an overseas entity is, by virtue of an assignation of the lease registered in the Land Register of Scotland during the pre-commencement period, the tenant under the lease, or

(c) an overseas entity is the tenant under a lease that was registered in the Land Register of Scotland during the pre-commencement period.

(2) During any part of the transitional period in which the paragraph of sub-paragraph (1) that applied in relation to the overseas entity during the pre-commencement period continues to apply in relation to the overseas entity, the Land Registration etc (Scotland) Act 2012 (asp 5) ("the 2012 Act") applies subject to the following modifications.

(3) Section 112A of the 2012 Act does not apply in relation to the entity or an officer of the entity as regards the plot of land or, as the case may be, lease.

(4) Paragraphs 2 and 4 of schedule 1A to the 2012 Act do not apply in relation to the entity as regards the plot of land or, as the case may be, lease.

Interpretation

12. In this Part of this Schedule—

"the commencement date" means the day on which section 3(1) comes fully into force;

"exempt overseas entity" means an overseas entity of a description specified in regulations under section 34(6);

"lease" has the meaning given by section 113(1) of the Land Registration etc (Scotland) Act 2012;

"plot of land" has the meaning given by section 113(1) of the Land Registration etc (Scotland) Act 2012;

"pre-commencement period" means the period beginning with 8 December 2014 and ending immediately before the commencement date;

"proprietor" has the meaning given by section 113(1) of the Land Registration etc (Scotland) Act 2012;

"transitional period" has the meaning given by section 41(10).

13. For the purposes of paragraphs 10(1)(a) and 11(1)(a)—

(a) references to an overseas entity's being entered as proprietor in the proprietorship section of a title sheet are references to the name of the entity being so entered, and

(b) the date on which an overseas entity was entered as proprietor in the proprietorship section of a title sheet is, where the entry was made by virtue of an application for registration, the date of registration as determined under section 37 of the Land Registration etc (Scotland) Act 2012 (date and time of registration).

NOTES

Commencement: 5 September 2022.

PART 3 POWER TO MAKE FURTHER PROVISION

[9.699]

14. (1) The Secretary of State may by regulations make further or alternative provision for the purpose of requiring or encouraging an overseas entity that owns or holds a right or interest in or over land in Scotland, or enters into land transactions in Scotland, to register as an overseas entity.

(2) No regulations may be made under this paragraph after the end of the transitional period (within the meaning given by section 41(10)).

(3) Regulations under this paragraph may amend, repeal or revoke provision made by this Schedule, or any provision made by or under any other Act or Act of the Scottish Parliament, made—

(a) before this Act, or

(b) later in the same session of Parliament as this Act.

(4) The provision which may be made by regulations under this paragraph by virtue of section 67(3) includes (in addition to provision of the kind mentioned in sub-paragraph (3)) provision amending any other provision of this Part of this Act.

(5) The Secretary of State must consult the Scottish Ministers before making regulations under this paragraph that contain provision that would be within the legislative competence of the Scottish Parliament if contained in an Act of that Parliament.

(6) Regulations under this paragraph are subject to the affirmative resolution procedure.

NOTES

Commencement: 5 September 2022.

COMMERCIAL RENT (CORONAVIRUS) ACT 2022

(2022 c 12)

An Act to make provision enabling relief from payment of certain rent debts under business tenancies adversely affected by coronavirus to be available through arbitration; and for connected purposes

[24 March 2022]

NOTES

Most of this Act is outside the scope of this work, and the omitted provisions are not annotated. Section 31 provides that Parts 1–3 of this Act extend to England and Wales only, subject to certain exceptions, including that paragraph 1 of Schedule 3 (and s 27 in so far as relating to that paragraph) also apply to Scotland. The commencement of this Act is also provided by s 31, and commencement dates are noted on the individual provisions below.

The main effect of this Act (for the purposes of this Handbook) is to prevent applications for certain arrangements and insolvency proceedings in respect of certain debts. See ss 896 and 901C of the Companies Act 2006 at **[1.1035]** and **[1.1044]**, and ss 1, 122(1)(f), 124, and 221(5)(b) of the Insolvency Act 1986 at **[9.136]**, **[9.249]**, **[9.251]**, and **[9.352]**. See also s 25(4) and Sch 3, para 1(4) below as regards the application of this Act to LLPs.

PART 1 INTRODUCTORY PROVISIONS

[9.700]

1 Overview

(1) This Act enables the matter of relief from payment of protected rent debts due from the tenant to the landlord under a business tenancy to be resolved by arbitration (if not resolved by agreement).

(2) In this Act—

- (a) sections 2 to 6 define for the purposes of this Act the terms "protected rent debt", "the matter of relief from payment" and other key terms used in this Act;
- (b) Part 2 provides for statutory arbitration between the landlord and the tenant under a business tenancy in relation to the matter of relief from payment of a protected rent debt;
- (c) Part 3 provides for temporary restrictions on the availability of certain remedies and insolvency arrangements that would otherwise be available in relation to a protected rent debt.

(3) Nothing in this Act is to be taken as—

- (a) affecting the capacity of the parties to a business tenancy to resolve by agreement, at any time, the matter of relief from payment of a protected rent debt (or any other matter relating to the tenancy), or
- (b) preventing an agreement resolving the matter of relief from payment of a protected rent debt from having effect or being enforced.

NOTES

Commencement: 24 March 2022.

PART 3 MORATORIUM ON CERTAIN REMEDIES AND INSOLVENCY ARRANGEMENTS

[9.701]

25 Temporary restriction on initiating certain insolvency arrangements

(1) This section applies where the matter of relief from payment of a protected rent debt has been referred to arbitration.

(2) During the relevant period—

- (a) no proposal for a company voluntary arrangement under section 1 of the Insolvency Act 1986 which relates to the whole or part of the debt may be made,
- (b) no proposal for an individual voluntary arrangement under section 256A of that Act, or an application for an interim order under section 253 of that Act, which relates to the whole or part of the debt may be made, and
- (c) no application for a compromise or arrangement under section 896 or 901C of the Companies Act 2006 (court orders for holding of meetings) which relates to the whole or part of the debt may be made.

(3) In this section "the relevant period" means the period beginning with the day on which an arbitrator is appointed and ending with—

- (a) where the arbitrator makes an award in accordance with section 14, the day which is 12 months after the day on which that award is made,
- (b) where the arbitrator makes an award dismissing a reference under section 13(2) or (3), the day on which that award is made,
- (c) where an award made in accordance with section 14 is set aside on appeal, the day on which that decision is made, or
- (d) where the arbitration proceedings are abandoned or withdrawn by the parties, the day of that abandonment or withdrawal.

(4) This section, so far as relating to a company voluntary arrangement and a compromise or arrangement under section 899 or 901F of the Companies Act 2006, applies to limited liability partnerships (as well as to companies).

NOTES

Commencement: 24 March 2022.

[9.702]

27 Temporary restriction on winding-up petitions and petitions for bankruptcy orders

Schedule 3 contains temporary provision in relation to winding up petitions and petitions for bankruptcy orders.

NOTES

Commencement: 24 March 2022 (except in so far as relating to Sch 3, para 1 *post*); 1 April 2022 (otherwise).

SCHEDULES

SCHEDULE 3
WINDING-UP AND BANKRUPTCY PETITIONS

Section 27

Prohibition on presenting a winding-up petition solely in relation to a protected rent debt

[9.703]

1. (1) This paragraph applies where a landlord under a business tenancy is owed a protected rent debt and the tenant is a company.

(2) The landlord may not, during the moratorium period for the debt, present a petition for the winding up of the company under section 124 of the Insolvency Act 1986 on a ground specified—

(a) in the case of a registered company, in section 122(1)(f) of that Act, or

(b) in the case of an unregistered company, in section 221(5)(b) of that Act,

unless the landlord is owed a debt by the company which is not a protected rent debt.

(3) In this paragraph—

"the moratorium period", in relation to a protected rent debt, has the same meaning as in section 23;

"registered company" means a company registered under the Companies Act 2006 in England and Wales or Scotland;

"unregistered company" has the same meaning as in Part 5 of the Insolvency Act 1986.

(4) This paragraph, so far as relating to registered companies, applies to limited liability partnerships.

Prohibition on presenting a bankruptcy order petition in relation to a protected rent debt

2, 3. *(Para 2 (Prohibition on presenting a bankruptcy order petition in relation to a protected rent debt), and para 3 (Bankruptcy orders made before the day on which this Act is passed) are outside the scope of this work.)*

Interpretation

4. (1) In this Schedule—

"interim receiver" means a person appointed under section 286 of the Insolvency Act 1986;

"special manager" means a person appointed under section 370 of that Act;

"trustee" means the trustee of a bankrupt's estate.

(2) In this Schedule, references to the "tenant" include—

(a) a person who has guaranteed the obligations of the tenant under a business tenancy,

(b) a person other than the tenant who is liable on an indemnity basis for the payment of rent under a business tenancy, and

(c) a former tenant who is liable for the payment of rent under a business tenancy.

NOTES

Commencement: 24 March 2022 (except in so far as relating to para 1 above); 1 April 2022 (para 1).

PART 10
MISCELLANEOUS OTHER STATUTORY INSTRUMENTS

INSOLVENCY RULES 1986 (NOTE)

(SI 1986/1925)

[10.1]

NOTES

Revocation of these Rules and transitional provisions: these Rules were revoked by the Insolvency (England and Wales) Rules 2016, SI 2016/1024, r 2, Sch 1, as from 6 April 2017. Schedule 2 to the 2016 Rules (at **[10.1162]**) provides for various transitional and savings provisions in relation to the revocation of these Rules including the following relating to applications already before the court (note that "the commencement date" is 6 April 2017; and that para 14 below is reproduced as amended as noted at **[10.1162]** *post*):

14.—(1) [Subject to paragraph (1A), where] an application to court is filed or a petition is presented under the Act or under the 1986 Rules before the commencement date and the court remains seised of that application or petition on the commencement date, the 1986 rules continue to apply to that application or petition.

[(1A) Where the 1986 Rules apply by virtue of paragraph (1) they are to apply as though—

(a) in rules 7.47(2)(a)(ii), (b)(iii) and (c) and 13.2(3A)(a) for "a Registrar in Bankruptcy of the High Court" there were substituted "an Insolvency and Companies Court Judge", and

(b) in rule 7.47(5), for the words "Registrar in Bankruptcy of the High Court" both times they appear there were substituted "Insolvency and Companies Court Judge.]

(2) For the purpose of paragraph (1), the court is no longer seised of an application when—

(a) it makes an order having the effect of determining of the application; or

(b) in relation to a petition for bankruptcy or winding up when—

(i) the court makes a bankruptcy order or a winding up order,

(ii) the court dismisses the petition, or

(iii) the petition is withdrawn.

(3) Any application to the court to review, rescind[, vary] or appeal an order made under paragraph [14(2)] is to be made in accordance with Part 12 of these Rules.

Savings provision (special insolvency regimes): the Insolvency (England and Wales) Rules 2016 (Consequential Amendments and Savings) Rules 2017, SI 2017/369, r 3 (as amended by the Insolvency (Miscellaneous Amendments) Regulations 2017, SI 2017/1119, as from 8 December 2017) provides as follows:

"The Insolvency Rules 1986, as they had effect immediately before 6th April 2017, insofar as they apply to proceedings under the following instruments, continue to have effect for the purposes of the application of—

(a) the Railway Administration Order 2001;

(b) . . .

(c) the Energy Act 2004;

(d) the Energy Administration Rules 2005;

(e) the PPP Administration Order Rules 2007;

(f) the Water Industry (Special Administration) Rules 2009;

(g) the Energy Act 2011;

(h) the Charitable Incorporated Organisations (Insolvency and Dissolution) Regulations 2012;

(i) the Energy Supply Company Administration Rules 2013; and

(j) the Postal Administration Rules 2013.".

See also the Small Business, Enterprise and Employment Act 2015 (Consequential Amendments, Savings and Transitional Provisions) Regulations 2018, SI 2018/208, regs 24, 25, which provide as follows:

"24 Savings in relation to special insolvency rules

(1) Despite the revocation of the Insolvency Rules 1986, those Rules apply as they applied before they were revoked for the purposes of the application of—

(a) the Bank Insolvency (England and Wales) Rules 2009;

(b) the Bank Administration (England and Wales) Rules 2009;

(c) the Building Society Special Administration (England and Wales) Rules 2010; and

(d) the Building Society Insolvency (England and Wales) Rules 2010.

(2) Despite the revocation of the Insolvency Rules, Rule 12A.30 of, and Schedule 4 to, the Insolvency Rules 1986 (forms for use in insolvency proceedings) apply as they applied before they were revoked for the purpose of prescribing forms for the statement of affairs required to be delivered and for any statement of concurrence required to be submitted under rule 54 of the Investment Bank Special Administration (England and Wales) Rules 2011 (verification and filing).

25 Savings in relation to insolvency proceedings

(1) Despite the revocation of the Insolvency Rules, those Rules apply as they applied before they were revoked for the purposes of—

(a) a proposal to a society and its creditors for a voluntary arrangement within the meaning given in section 1 of the Insolvency Act 1986 as applied in relation to a relevant society by article 2(1) of the 2014 Order;

(b) the administration of a society under Part 2 of the Insolvency Act 1986 as applied by article 2(2) of the 2014 Order; and

(c) proceedings instituted in England and Wales for the winding up of a relevant scheme (within the meaning given in regulation 17(1)(a) of the Collective Investment in Transferable Securities (Contractual Scheme) Regulations 2013).

(2) In this regulation—

"the 2014 Order" means the Co-operative and Community Benefit Societies and Credit Unions (Arrangements, Reconstructions and Administration) Order 2014; and

"society" means a relevant society within the meaning given in article 1(2) of the 2014 Order which the courts in England and Wales have jurisdiction to wind up.

The relevant parts of the Insolvency Rules 1986, as they stood at 1 July 2016, were included in the 30th edition of this Handbook. However, they have not been included in this edition due to space considerations, and it is recommended that users of the Handbook retain the 2016 edition for reference.

Provisions of the 1986 Rules that were amended between 1 July 2016 and 6 April 2017 (the date of their revocation) are set out below, together with notes relating to those provisions.

THE THIRD GROUP OF PARTS

PART 7
COURT PROCEDURE AND PRACTICE

CHAPTER 8 APPEALS IN INSOLVENCY PROCEEDINGS

7.47 Appeals and reviews of court orders [in corporate insolvency]

(1) Every court having jurisdiction [for the purposes of Parts 1 to 4 of the Act and Parts 1 to 4 of the Rules,] may review, rescind or vary any order made by it in the exercise of that jurisdiction.

[(2) Appeals in civil matters in proceedings under Parts 1 to 4 of the Act and Parts 1 to 4 of the Rules lie as follows—

[(a) where the decision appealed against is made by a district judge sitting in the county court hearing centre specified in the first column of the table in Schedule 2D—

(i) to a High Court Judge sitting in a district registry; or

(ii) to a Registrar in Bankruptcy of the High Court,

as specified in the corresponding entry in the second column of the table;

(b) to a High Court Judge where the decision appealed against is made by—

(i) a Circuit Judge sitting in the county court;

(ii) a Master;

(iii) a Registrar in Bankruptcy of the High Court, if that decision is made at first instance; or

(iv) a district judge sitting in a district registry;

(c) to the Civil Division of the Court of Appeal where the decision appealed against is made by a Registrar in Bankruptcy of the High Court, if that decision is an appeal from a decision made by a District Judge; and

(d) to the Civil Division of the Court of Appeal where the decision appealed against is made by a High Court Judge.]]

(3) [The county court] is not, in the exercise of its jurisdiction [for the purposes of Parts 1 to 4 of the Act and Parts 1 to 4 of the Rules], subject to be restrained by the order of any other court, and no appeal lies from its decision in the exercise of that jurisdiction except as provided by this Rule.

(4) Any application for the rescission of a winding-up order shall be made within [5 business] days after the date on which the order was made.

[(5) In this rule—

"Circuit Judge sitting in the county court" means a judge sitting pursuant to section 5(1)(a) of the County Courts Act 1984;

"Civil Division of the Court of Appeal" means the division of the Court of Appeal established by section 3(1) of the Senior Courts Act 1981;

"Chancery Division of the High Court" means the division of the High Court established by section 5(1)(a) of the Senior Courts Act 1981;

"county court" means the court established by section A1 of the County Courts Act 1984;

"district judge" means a person appointed a district judge under section 6(1) of the County Courts Act 1984;

"district judge sitting in a district registry" means a district judge sitting in an assigned district registry as a district judge of the High Court under section 100 of the Senior Courts Act 1981;

"district registry" means a district registry of the High Court under section 99 of the Senior Courts Act 1981;

"High Court Judge" means a judge listed in section 4(1) of the Senior Courts Act 1981;

"Master" means a person appointed to the office of Master, Chancery Division under section 89(1) of the Senior Courts Act 1981;

"Registrar in Bankruptcy of the High Court" means a person appointed to the office of Registrar in Bankruptcy of the High Court under section 89(1) of the Senior Courts Act 1981;

and for the purposes of each definition a person appointed to act as a deputy for any person holding that office is included.]

NOTES

Rule heading: words in square brackets substituted by the Insolvency (Amendment) Rules 2010, SI 2010/686, r 2, Sch 1, para 466(1), (2).

Para (1): words in square brackets substituted by SI 2010/686, r 2, Sch 1, para 466(1), (3).

Para (2): substituted by SI 2010/686, r 2, Sch 1, para 466(1), (4). Sub-paras (a)–(d) substituted (for the original sub-paras (a), (b)) by the Insolvency (Amendment) (No 2) Rules 2016, SI 2016/903, rr 2, 3, 6, as from 3 October 2016, except where a person has filed a notice of appeal or applied for permission to appeal before that date.

Para (3): words in first pair of square brackets substituted by the Insolvency (Commencement of Proceedings) and Insolvency Rules 1986 (Amendment) Rules 2014, SI 2014/817, r 4, Sch 2, para 16; words in second pair of square brackets substituted by SI 2010/686, r 2, Sch 1, para 466(1), (5).

Para (4): words in square brackets substituted by SI 2010/686, r 2, Sch 1, para 466(1), (6).

Para (5): added by SI 2016/903, rr 2, 4, 6, as from 3 October 2016, except where a person has filed a notice of appeal or applied for permission to appeal before that date.

PART 13
INTERPRETATION AND APPLICATION

13.13 Expressions used generally

(1) . . .

(2) "The Department" means [the Department for Business, Energy and Industrial Strategy].

[(2A)]–(19) . . .

NOTES

Paras (1), (2A)–(19): see the 30th edition of this Handbook.

Para (2): words in square brackets substituted by the Secretaries of State for Business, Energy and Industrial Strategy, for International Trade and for Exiting the European Union and the Transfer of Functions (Education and Skills) Order 2016, SI 2016/992, art 14, Schedule, para 15, as from 9 November 2016.

[SCHEDULE 2D

DESTINATION OF APPEALS FROM DECISIONS OF DISTRICT JUDGES IN INSOLVENCY MATTERS

County Court Hearing Centre	*Destination of Appeal*
Aberystwyth	Cardiff District Registry
Aylesbury	Registrar in Bankruptcy
Banbury	Birmingham District Registry
Barnsley	Leeds District Registry
Barnstaple	Bristol District Registry
Barrow-in-Furness	Liverpool District Registry or Manchester District Registry
Bath	Bristol District Registry
Bedford	Birmingham District Registry
Birkenhead	Liverpool District Registry or Manchester District Registry
Birmingham	Birmingham District Registry
Blackburn	Liverpool District Registry or Manchester District Registry
Blackpool	Liverpool District Registry or Manchester District Registry
Blackwood	Cardiff District Registry
Bolton	Liverpool District Registry or Manchester District Registry
Boston	Birmingham District Registry
Bournemouth and Poole	Registrar in Bankruptcy
Bradford	Leeds District Registry
Bridgend	Cardiff District Registry
Brighton	Registrar in Bankruptcy
Bristol	Bristol District Registry
Burnley	Liverpool District Registry or Manchester District Registry
Bury	Liverpool District Registry or Manchester District Registry
Bury St Edmunds	Registrar in Bankruptcy
Caernarfon	Cardiff District Registry
Cambridge	Registrar in Bankruptcy
Canterbury	Registrar in Bankruptcy
Cardiff	Cardiff District Registry
Carlisle	Liverpool District Registry or Manchester District Registry
Caernarfon	Cardiff District Registry
County Court at Central London	Registrar in Bankruptcy
Chelmsford	Registrar in Bankruptcy
Chester	Liverpool District Registry or Manchester District Registry
Chesterfield	Leeds District Registry
Colchester	Registrar in Bankruptcy
Coventry	Birmingham District Registry
Crewe	Liverpool District Registry or Manchester District Registry
Croydon	Registrar in Bankruptcy
Darlington	Newcastle District Registry
Derby	Birmingham District Registry
Doncaster	Leeds District Registry
Dudley	Birmingham District Registry
Durham	Leeds District Registry or Newcastle District Registry
Eastbourne	Registrar in Bankruptcy
Exeter	Bristol District Registry
Gloucester and Cheltenham	Bristol District Registry
Great Grimsby	Leeds District Registry
Guildford	Registrar in Bankruptcy
Halifax	Leeds District Registry
Harrogate	Leeds District Registry
Hastings	Registrar in Bankruptcy
Haverfordwest	Cardiff District Registry

County Court Hearing Centre	*Destination of Appeal*
Hereford	Bristol District Registry
Hertford	Registrar in Bankruptcy
Huddersfield	Leeds District Registry
Ipswich	Registrar in Bankruptcy
Kendal	Liverpool District Registry or Manchester District Registry
Kings Lynn	Registrar in Bankruptcy
Kingston-upon-Hull	Leeds District Registry
Kingston-upon-Thames	Registrar in Bankruptcy
Lancaster	Liverpool District Registry or Manchester District Registry
Leeds	Leeds District Registry
Leicester	Birmingham District Registry
Lincoln	Leeds District Registry or Birmingham District Registry
Liverpool	Liverpool District Registry or Manchester District Registry
Llangefni	Cardiff District Registry
Luton	Registrar in Bankruptcy
Maidstone	Registrar in Bankruptcy
Manchester	Manchester District Registry
Merthyr Tydfil	Cardiff District Registry
Middlesbrough	Newcastle District Registry
Milton Keynes	Birmingham District Registry
Newcastle upon Tyne	Newcastle District Registry
Newport (Gwent)	Cardiff District Registry
Newport (Isle of Wight)	Registrar in Bankruptcy
Northampton	Birmingham District Registry
Norwich	Registrar in Bankruptcy
Nottingham	Birmingham District Registry
Oldham	Liverpool District Registry or Manchester District Registry
Oxford	Registrar in Bankruptcy
Peterborough	Registrar in Bankruptcy
Plymouth	Bristol District Registry
Pontypridd	Cardiff District Registry
Portsmouth	Registrar in Bankruptcy
Port Talbot Justice Centre	Cardiff District Registry
Preston	Liverpool District Registry or Manchester District Registry
Reading	Registrar in Bankruptcy
Rhyl	Cardiff District Registry
Romford	Registrar in Bankruptcy
Salisbury	Registrar in Bankruptcy
Scarborough	Leeds District Registry
Scunthorpe	Leeds District Registry
Sheffield	Leeds District Registry
Slough	Registrar in Bankruptcy
Southampton	Registrar in Bankruptcy
Southend-on-Sea	Registrar in Bankruptcy
Stafford	Birmingham District Registry
St Albans	Registrar in Bankruptcy
Stockport	Liverpool District Registry or Manchester District Registry
Stoke-on-Trent	Manchester District Registry
Sunderland	Newcastle District Registry
Swansea	Cardiff District Registry
Swindon	Bristol District Registry
Tameside	Liverpool District Registry or Manchester District Registry
Taunton	Bristol District Registry
Telford	Birmingham District Registry
Torquay & Newton Abbot	Bristol District Registry
Truro	Bristol District Registry

County Court Hearing Centre	*Destination of Appeal*
Tunbridge Wells	Registrar in Bankruptcy
Wakefield	Leeds District Registry
Walsall	Birmingham District Registry
Warrington	Liverpool District Registry or Manchester District Registry
Warwick	Birmingham District Registry
Welshpool & Newton	Cardiff District Registry
West Cumbria	Liverpool District Registry or Manchester District Registry
Wigan	Liverpool District Registry or Manchester District Registry
Winchester	Registrar in Bankruptcy
Wolverhampton	Birmingham District Registry
Worcester	Birmingham District Registry
Wrexham	Cardiff District Registry
Yeovil	Bristol District Registry
York	Leeds District Registry]

NOTES

Inserted by the Insolvency (Amendment) (No 2) Rules 2016, SI 2016/903, rr 2, 5, 6, Schedule, except where a person has filed a notice of appeal or applied for permission to appeal before 3 October 2016.

Note: this Schedule is reproduced as per the Queen's printer's copy of the 2016 Rules, and includes two entries for Caernarfon.

INSOLVENT COMPANIES (DISQUALIFICATION OF UNFIT DIRECTORS) PROCEEDINGS RULES 1987

(SI 1987/2023)

NOTES

Made: 25 November 1987.

Authority: Insolvency Act 1986, s 411; Company Directors Disqualification Act 1986, s 21.

Commencement: 11 January 1988.

These Rules are reproduced as amended by: the Insolvent Companies (Disqualification of Unfit Directors) Proceedings (Amendment) Rules 1999, SI 1999/1023; the Insolvent Companies (Disqualification of Unfit Directors) Proceedings (Amendment) Rules 2001, SI 2001/765; the Insolvent Companies (Disqualification of Unfit Directors) Proceedings (Amendment) Rules 2003, SI 2003/1367; the Insolvent Companies (Disqualification of Unfit Directors) Proceedings (Amendment) Rules 2007, SI 2007/1906; the Enterprise and Regulatory Reform Act 2013 (Competition) (Consequential, Transitional and Saving Provisions) (No 2) Order 2014, SI 2014/549; the Deregulation Act 2015 (Insolvency) (Consequential Amendments and Transitional and Savings Provisions) Order 2015, SI 2015/1641; the Small Business, Enterprise and Employment Act 2015 (Consequential Amendments) (Insolvency and Company Directors Disqualification) Regulations 2015, SI 2015/1651; the Insolvency (England and Wales) Rules 2016 (Consequential Amendments and Savings) Rules 2017, SI 2017/369.

Application of these Rules to Limited Liability Partnerships: see the Limited Liability Partnerships Regulations 2001, SI 2001/1090, reg 10, Sch 6, Pt III.

ARRANGEMENT OF RULES

[10.2]

1 Citation, commencement and interpretation

(1) These Rules may be cited as the Insolvent Companies (Disqualification of Unfit Directors) Proceedings Rules 1987 and shall come into force on 11th January 1988.

[(2) In these Rules—

(a) "the Companies Act" means the Companies Act 1985,

(b) "the Company Directors Disqualification Act" means the Company Directors Disqualification Act 1986,

(c) "CPR" followed by a Part or rule by number means that Part or rule with that number in the Civil Procedure Rules 1998,
(d) "practice direction" means a direction as to the practice and procedure of any court within the scope of the Civil Procedure Rules,
[(e) "registrar" has the same meaning as in rule 1.2(2) of the Insolvency (England and Wales) Rules 2016, and]
(f) "file in court" means deliver to the court for filing.]

[(3) These Rules apply to an application made under the Company Directors Disqualification Act on or after 6th August 2007—
(a) for leave to commence proceedings for a disqualification order after the end of the period mentioned in section 7(2) of that Act;
(b) to enforce any duty arising under section 7(4) of that Act;
(c) for a disqualification order where made—
(i) by the Secretary of State or the official receiver under section 7(1) of that Act (disqualification of unfit directors of insolvent companies);
(ii) [by the Secretary of State under section 5A (disqualification for certain convictions abroad), 8 (disqualification of director on finding of unfitness), 8ZB (Application for order under section 8ZA) or 8ZD (order disqualifying person instructing unfit director: other cases) of that Act;] or
(iii) by the [Competition and Markets Authority] or a specified regulator under section 9A of that Act (competition disqualification order);
(d) under section 8A of that Act (variation etc of disqualification undertaking); or—
(e) for leave to act under—
(i) section 1A(1) or 9B(4) of that Act (and section 17 of that Act as it applies for the purposes of either of those sections); or
(ii) sections 1 and 17 as they apply for the purposes of section [5A,] 6, 7(1), 8, [8ZA, 8ZC, 8ZD, 8ZE,] 9A or 10 of that Act.]

NOTES

Para (2): substituted by the Insolvent Companies (Disqualification of Unfit Directors) Proceedings (Amendment) Rules 1999, SI 1999/1023, r 3, Schedule, para 2, as from 26 April 1999. Sub-para (e) substituted by the Insolvency (England and Wales) Rules 2016 (Consequential Amendments and Savings) Rules 2017, SI 2017/369, r 2(2), Sch 2, para 3(1), (2), as from 6 April 2017.

Para (3): substituted by the Insolvent Companies (Disqualification of Unfit Directors) Proceedings (Amendment) Rules 2007, SI 2007/1906, rr 1(3), 2, as from 6 August 2007, except in relation to any application made in accordance with these Rules before that date. Words in square brackets in sub-para (c)(ii) substituted, and figures in square brackets in sub-para (e) inserted, by the Small Business, Enterprise and Employment Act 2015 (Consequential Amendments) (Insolvency and Company Directors Disqualification) Regulations 2015, SI 2015/1651, reg 2(1)–(3), as from 1 October 2015. Words in square brackets in sub-para (c)(iii) substituted by the Enterprise and Regulatory Reform Act 2013 (Competition) (Consequential, Transitional and Saving Provisions) (No 2) Order 2014, SI 2014/549, art 2, Schedule, Pt 2, para 24, as from 1 April 2014.

[10.3]

[2 Form and conduct of applications

(1) The Civil Procedure Rules 1998, and any relevant practice direction, apply in respect of any application to which these Rules apply, except where these Rules make provision to inconsistent effect.

[(2) Subject to paragraph (5), an application shall be made either—
(a) by claim form as provided by the relevant practice direction and the claimant must use the CPR Part 8 (alternative procedure for claims) procedure, or
(b) by application notice as provided for by the relevant practice direction.]

(3) CPR rule 8.1(3) (power of the court to order the claim to continue as if the claimant had not used the Part 8 procedure), CPR rule 8.2 (contents of the claim form) and CPR rule 8.7 (Part 20 claims) do not apply.

[(4) Rule 12.59 (appeals and reviews of court orders in corporate insolvency) and rule 12.62 (procedure on appeal) of the Insolvency (England and Wales) Rules 2016 apply.]

[(5) [The Insolvency (England and Wales) Rules 2016] shall apply to an application to enforce any duty arising under section 7(4) of the Company Directors Disqualification Act . . .]

NOTES

Substituted by the Insolvent Companies (Disqualification of Unfit Directors) Proceedings (Amendment) Rules 1999, SI 1999/1023, r 3, Schedule, para 3, as from 26 April 1999.

Para (2): substituted by the Insolvent Companies (Disqualification of Unfit Directors) Proceedings (Amendment) Rules 2007, SI 2007/1906, rr 1(3), 3(1), (2), as from 6 August 2007, except in relation to any application made in accordance with these Rules before that date.

Para (4): substituted by the Insolvency (England and Wales) Rules 2016 (Consequential Amendments and Savings) Rules 2017, SI 2017/369, r 2(2), Sch 2, para 3(1), (3)(a), as from 6 April 2017.

Para (5): added by SI 2007/1906, rr 1(3), 3(1), (3), as from 6 August 2007, except in relation to any application made in accordance with these Rules before that date. Words in square brackets substituted by SI 2017/369, r 2(2), Sch 2, para 3(1), (3)(b), as from 6 April 2017. Words omitted revoked by the Deregulation Act 2015 (Insolvency) (Consequential Amendments and Transitional and Savings Provisions) Order 2015, SI 2015/1641, art 6, Sch 3, para 2, as from 1 October 2015.

[10.4]

[2A Application of Rules 3 to 8

Rules 3 to 8 only apply to the types of application referred to in Rule 1(3)(c).]

NOTES

Inserted by the Insolvent Companies (Disqualification of Unfit Directors) Proceedings (Amendment) Rules 2007, SI 2007/1906, rr 1(3), 4, as from 6 August 2007, except in relation to any application made in accordance with these Rules before that date.

[10.5]

3 The case against the [defendant]

(1) There shall, at the time when the [claim form] is issued, be filed in court evidence in support of the application for a disqualification order; and copies of the evidence shall be served with the [claim form] on the [defendant].

(2) The evidence shall be by one or more affidavits, except where the [claimant] is the official receiver, in which case it may be in the form of a written report (with or without affidavits by other persons) which shall be treated as if it had been verified by affidavit by him and shall be prima facie evidence of any matter contained in it.

(3) There shall in the affidavit or affidavits or (as the case may be) the official receiver's report be included a statement of the matters by reference to which the [defendant] is alleged to be unfit to be concerned in the management of a company.

NOTES

Words in square brackets substituted by the Insolvent Companies (Disqualification of Unfit Directors) Proceedings (Amendment) Rules 1999, SI 1999/1023, r 3, Schedule, para 1, as from 26 April 1999.

[10.6]

4 Endorsement on [claim form]

There shall on the [claim form] be endorsed information to the [defendant] as follows—

- (a) that the application is made in accordance with these Rules;
- (b) that, in accordance with the relevant enactments, the court has power to impose disqualifications as follows—
  - (i) where the application is under section 7 [or 8ZB] of the Company Directors Disqualification Act, for a period of not less than 2, and up to 15, years; and
  - (ii) where the application is [under section [5A,] 8[, 8ZD,] or 9A of that Act], for a period of up to 15 years;
- (c) that the application for a disqualification order may, in accordance with these Rules, be heard and determined summarily, without further or other notice to the [defendant], and that, if it is so heard and determined, the court may impose disqualification for a period of up to 5 years;
- (d) that if at the hearing of the application the court, on the evidence then before it, is minded to impose, in the [defendant]'s case, disqualification for any period longer than 5 years, it will not make a disqualification order on that occasion but will adjourn the application to be heard (with further evidence, if any) at a later date to be notified; and
- (e) that any evidence which the [defendant] wishes to be taken into consideration by the court must be filed in court in accordance with the time limits imposed under Rule 6 (the provisions of which shall be set out on the [claim form]).

NOTES

Words in first (outer) pair of square brackets in sub-para (b)(ii) substituted by the Insolvent Companies (Disqualification of Unfit Directors) Proceedings (Amendment) Rules 2003, SI 2003/1367, r 3, Schedule, para 2, as from 20 June 2003. Words in square brackets in sub-para (b)(i) and figures in second and third (inner) pairs of square brackets in sub-para (b)(ii) inserted, by the Small Business, Enterprise and Employment Act 2015 (Consequential Amendments) (Insolvency and Company Directors Disqualification) Regulations 2015, SI 2015/1651, reg 2(1), (4), (5), as from 1 October 2015. Other words in square brackets substituted by the Insolvent Companies (Disqualification of Unfit Directors) Proceedings (Amendment) Rules 1999, SI 1999/1023, r 3, Schedule, para 1, as from 26 April 1999.

[10.7]

5 Service and acknowledgement

(1) The [claim form] shall be served on the [defendant] by sending it by first class post to his last known address; and the date of service shall, unless the contrary is shown, be deemed to be the 7th day next following that on which the [claim form] was posted.

(2) Where any process or order of the court or other document is required under proceedings subject to these Rules to be served on any person who is not in England and Wales, the court may order service on him of that process or order or other document to be effected within such time and in such manner as it thinks fit, and may also require such proof of service as it thinks fit.

[(3) The claim form served on the defendant shall be accompanied by an acknowledgment of service as provided for by practice direction and CPR rule 8.3(2) (dealing with the contents of an acknowledgment of service) does not apply.]

(4) The . . . acknowledgement of service shall state that the [defendant] should indicate—

- (a) whether he contests the application on the grounds that, in the case of any particular company—
  - (i) he was not a director or shadow director of the company at a time when conduct of his, or of other persons, in relation to that company is in question, or
  - (ii) his conduct as director or shadow director of that company was not as alleged in support of the application for a disqualification order,
- (b) whether, in the case of any conduct of his, he disputes the allegation that such conduct makes him unfit to be concerned in the management of a company, and
- (c) whether he, while not resisting the application for a disqualification order, intends to adduce mitigating factors with a view to justifying only a short period of disqualification.

NOTES

Para (1): words in square brackets substituted by the Insolvent Companies (Disqualification of Unfit Directors) Proceedings (Amendment) Rules 1999, SI 1999/1023, r 3, Schedule, para 1, as from 26 April 1999.

Para (3): substituted by SI 1999/1023, r 3, Schedule, para 4(1), as from 26 April 1999.

Para (4): words omitted revoked, and word in square brackets substituted, by SI 1999/1023, r 3, Schedule, paras 1, 4(2), as from 26 April 1999.

[10.8]

6 Evidence

(1) The [defendant] shall, within 28 days from the date of service of the [claim form], file in court any affidavit evidence in opposition to the application he wishes the court to take into consideration and shall forthwith serve upon the [claimant] a copy of such evidence.

(2) The [claimant] shall, within 14 days from receiving the copy of the [defendant]'s evidence, file in court any further evidence in reply he wishes the court to take into consideration and shall forthwith serve a copy of that evidence upon the [defendant].

[(3) CPR rules 8.5 (filing and serving written evidence) and 8.6(1) (requirements where written evidence is to be relied on) do not apply.]

NOTES

Paras (1), (2): words in square brackets substituted by the Insolvent Companies (Disqualification of Unfit Directors) Proceedings (Amendment) Rules 1999, SI 1999/1023, r 3, Schedule, para 1, as from 26 April 1999.

Para (3): added by SI 1999/1023, r 3, Schedule, para 5, as from 26 April 1999.

[10.9]

7 The hearing of the application

[(1) When the claim form is issued, the court will fix a date for the first hearing of the claim which shall not be less than 8 weeks from the date of issue of the claim form.]

(2) The hearing shall in the first instance be before the registrar in open court.

(3) The registrar shall either determine the case on the date fixed or adjourn it.

(4) The registrar shall adjourn the case for further consideration if—

(a) he forms the provisional opinion that a disqualification order ought to be made, and that a period of disqualification longer than 5 years is appropriate, or

(b) he is of opinion that questions of law or fact arise which are not suitable for summary determination.

(5) If the registrar adjourns the case for further consideration he shall—

(a) direct whether the case is to be heard by a registrar or, if he thinks it appropriate, by the judge, for determination by him;

(b) state the reasons for the adjournment; and

(c) give directions as to the following matters—

(i) the manner in which and the time within which notice of the adjournment and the reasons for it are to be given to the [defendant],

(ii) the filing in court and the service of further evidence (if any) by the parties,

(iii) such other matters as the registrar thinks necessary or expedient with a view to an expeditious disposal of the application, and

(iv) the time and place of the adjourned hearing.

(6) Where a case is adjourned other than to the judge, it may be heard by the registrar who originally dealt with the case or by another registrar.

NOTES

Para (1): substituted by the Insolvent Companies (Disqualification of Unfit Directors) Proceedings (Amendment) Rules 1999, SI 1999/1023, r 3, Schedule, para 6, as from 26 April 1999.

Para (5): word in square brackets in sub-para (c) substituted by SI 1999/1023, r 3, Schedule, para 1, as from 26 April 1999.

[10.10]

8 Making and setting aside of disqualification order

(1) The court may make a disqualification order against the [defendant], whether or not the latter appears, and whether or not he has completed and returned the acknowledgement of service of the [claim form], or filed evidence in accordance with Rule 6.

(2) Any disqualification order made in the absence of the [defendant] may be set aside or varied by the court on such terms as it thinks just.

NOTES

Words in square brackets substituted by the Insolvent Companies (Disqualification of Unfit Directors) Proceedings (Amendment) Rules 1999, SI 1999/1023, r 3, Schedule, para 1, as from 26 April 1999.

9 (*Revoked by the Insolvent Companies (Disqualification of Unfit Directors) Proceedings (Amendment) Rules 2001, SI 2001/765, as from 2 April 2001.*)

[10.11]

10 Right of audience

Official receivers and deputy official receivers have right of audience in any proceedings to which these Rules apply, whether the application is made by the Secretary of State or by the official receiver at his direction, and whether made in the High Court or a county court.

[10.12]

11 Revocation and saving

(1) (*Revokes the Insolvent Companies (Disqualification of Unfit Directors) Proceedings Rules 1986, SI 1986/612.*)

(2) Notwithstanding paragraph (1) the former Rules shall continue to apply and have effect in relation to any application described in paragraph 3(a) or (b) of Rule 1 of these Rules made before the date on which these Rules come into force.

EUROPEAN ECONOMIC INTEREST GROUPING REGULATIONS 1989

(SI 1989/638)

NOTES

Made: 10 April 1989.

Authority: European Communities Act 1972, s 2 (see the note "Statutory Instruments made under the European Communities Act 1972" preceding paragraph **[4.1]** *ante*).

Commencement: 1 July 1989.

These Regulations are reproduced as amended by: the Deregulation and Contracting Out Act 1994; the Constitutional Reform Act 2005; the Companies Act 2006 (Consequential Amendments etc) Order 2008, SI 2008/948; the European Economic Interest Grouping (Amendment) Regulations 2009, SI 2009/2399; the European Economic Interest Grouping and European Public Limited-Liability Company (Amendment) Regulations 2014, SI 2014/2382; the Company, Limited Liability Partnership and Business (Names and Trading Disclosures) Regulations 2015, SI 2015/17; the Companies and Limited Liability Partnerships (Filing Requirements) Regulations 2015, SI 2015/1695; the European Economic Interest Grouping (Amendment) (EU Exit) Regulations 2018, SI 2018/1299.

References to "the European Community", "Community", etc: see the Treaty of Lisbon (Changes in Terminology) Order 2011, SI 2011/1043, which provides that (as from 22 April 2011) "EU" should be substituted for the word "Community" (subject to certain exceptions) in references to "Community treaties", "Community instrument", "Community obligation", "Community law", "Community legislation", etc.

Registrar of Companies: as to the contracting out of certain functions of the registrar of companies conferred by or under these regulations, see the Contracting Out (Functions in relation to the Registration of Companies) Order 1995, SI 1995/1013.

Fees: as to fees, see the note for the European Economic Interest Grouping (Fees) Regulations 2004, SI 2004/2643, and the Registrar of Companies (Fees) (European Economic Interest Grouping and European Public Limited-Liability Company) Regulations 2012, SI 2012/1908 at **[4.470]**.

ARRANGEMENT OF REGULATIONS

PART I GENERAL

PART II PROVISIONS RELATING TO ARTICLES 1–38 OF THE EC REGULATION

PART III REGISTRATION ETC (ARTICLE 39 OF THE EC REGULATION)

PART IV SUPPLEMENTAL PROVISIONS

SCHEDULES

PART I GENERAL

[10.13]

1 Citation, commencement and extent

These Regulations, which extend to [the whole of the United Kingdom], may be cited as the European Economic Interest Grouping Regulations 1989 and shall come into force on 1st July 1989.

NOTES

Words in square brackets substituted by the European Economic Interest Grouping (Amendment) Regulations 2009, SI 2009/2399, regs 3, 4, as from 1 October 2009.

[10.14]

2 Interpretation

(1) In these Regulations—

"the 1985 Act" means the Companies Act 1985;

["the 2006 Act" means the Companies Act 2006;]

["the Companies Acts" has the meaning given by section 2 of [the 2006 Act];]

"the contract" means the contract for the formation of [a UKEIG or an EEIG, as the case may be];

"the EC Regulation" means Council Regulation (EEC) No 2137/85 [on the European Economic Interest Grouping (EEIG)];

["EEIG" means a European Economic Interest Grouping, being a grouping—

(a) formed in pursuance of Article 1 of Council Regulation (EEC) No 2137/85 of 25 July 1985 on the European Economic Interest Grouping (EEIG) as it applies in the European Union and as amended from time to time; and

(b) registered in a Member State;]

["EEIG establishment" means an establishment of an EEIG where the establishment is registered in the United Kingdom;]

["officer", in relation to a UKEIG or an EEIG, includes a manager, or any other person provided for in the contract as an organ of the UKEIG or the EEIG, as the case may be;]

["the registrar" has the same meaning as in the Companies Acts (see section 1060 of the 2006 Act);]

["UKEIG" means a UK Economic Interest Grouping;]

and other expressions used in these Regulations and defined [for the purposes of the Companies Acts] or in relation to insolvency and winding up by the Insolvency Act 1986 [or, as regards Northern Ireland, by the Insolvency (Northern Ireland) Order 1989] have the meanings assigned to them by those provisions as if any reference to a company in any such definition were a reference to [a UKEIG or an EEIG, as the case may be].

[(2) . . .]

(3) In these Regulations, "certified translation" means a translation certified to be a correct translation—

(a) if the translation was made in the United Kingdom, by

(i) a notary public in any part of the United Kingdom;

(ii) a solicitor (if the translation was made in Scotland), a solicitor of the Supreme Court of Judicature of England and Wales (if it was made in England or Wales), or a [solicitor of the Court of Judicature of Northern Ireland] (if it was made in Northern Ireland); or

(iii) a person certified by a person mentioned above to be known to him to be competent to translate the document into English; or

(b) if the translation was made outside the United Kingdom, by—

(i) a notary public;

(ii) a person authorised in the place where the translation was made to administer an oath;

(iii) any of the British officials mentioned in section 6 of the Commissioners for Oaths Act 1889;

(iv) a person certified by a person mentioned in sub-paragraph (i), (ii) or (iii) of this paragraph to be known to him to be competent to translate the document into English.

NOTES

Para (1) is amended as follows:

Definition "the Companies Acts" inserted, and words "for the purposes of the Companies Acts" in square brackets substituted, by the Companies Act 2006 (Consequential Amendments etc) Order 2008, SI 2008/948, art 3(1), Sch 1, Pt 2, para 161, as from 6 April 2008.

Definition "the 2006 Act" inserted, words in square brackets in the definition "the Companies Acts" substituted, definition "the registrar" substituted, and words in final pair of square brackets inserted, by the European Economic Interest Grouping (Amendment) Regulations 2009, SI 2009/2399, regs 3, 5(1), (2), as from 1 October 2009.

Words in square brackets in the definitions "the contract" and "the EC Regulation" substituted by the European Economic Interest Grouping (Amendment) (EU Exit) Regulations 2018, SI 2018/1299, regs 2, 3(a), (b), as from IP completion day (as defined in the European Union (Withdrawal Agreement) Act 2020, s 39).

Definitions "EEIG" and "officer" substituted by SI 2018/1299, regs 2, 3(c), (e), as from IP completion day (as defined in the European Union (Withdrawal Agreement) Act 2020, s 39).

Definitions "EEIG establishment" and "UKEIG" inserted by SI 2018/1299, regs 2, 3(d), (f), as from IP completion day (as defined in the European Union (Withdrawal Agreement) Act 2020, s 39).

Words "a UKEIG or an EEIG, as the case may be" in final pair of square brackets substituted by SI 2018/1299, regs 2, 3(g), as from IP completion day (as defined in the European Union (Withdrawal Agreement) Act 2020, s 39).

Para (2): revoked by the European Economic Interest Grouping and European Public Limited-Liability Company (Amendment) Regulations 2014, SI 2014/2382, regs 2, 3, as from 1 October 2014; it had previously been substituted by SI 2009/2399, regs 3, 5(1), (3), as from 1 October 2009.

Para (3): words in square brackets substituted by the Constitutional Reform Act 2005, s 59, Sch 11, Pt 2, para 5, as from 1 October 2009.

PART II PROVISIONS RELATING TO ARTICLES 1–38 OF THE EC REGULATION

3, 4 (*Revoked by the European Economic Interest Grouping (Amendment) (EU Exit) Regulations 2018, SI 2018/1299, regs 2, 4, as from IP completion day (as defined in the European Union (Withdrawal Agreement) Act 2020, s 39).)*

[10.15]

5 Managers (Article 19(2) of the EC Regulation)

(1) A manager of [a UKEIG] may be a legal person other than a natural person, on condition that it designates one or more natural persons to represent it and notice of particulars of each such person is sent to the registrar . . . as though he were a manager.

(2) Any natural person designated under paragraph (1) above shall be subject to the same liabilities as if he himself were a manager.

[(3) Where a notice is required to be delivered to the registrar under article 7(d) of the EC Regulation, the notice must contain—

(a) in the case of an individual, the particulars specified in section 163 of the 2006 Act,

(b) in the case of a body corporate, or a firm that is a legal person under the law by which it is governed, the particulars specified in section 164 of the 2006 Act, and section 163 of that Act in respect of the person authorised to represent the manager, and

(c) [a statement that the person appointed has consented to act as a manager of the [UKEIG]].]

(3A) Subsections (2) to (4) of section 163 of the 2006 Act apply for the purposes of paragraph [(3)] above as they apply for the purposes of that section.

(3B) For the purposes of paragraph [(3)] above, a person's service address may be stated to be "The [UKEIG's] official address"]

[(3C) A notice required to be delivered to the registrar under article 7(d) of the EC Regulation must state the date of the manager's appointment.

(3D) Notice of any changes to the particulars of a manager delivered under paragraph (3) must be delivered to the registrar stating the manager's name registered prior to the change and the date on which the change took place.

(3E) Notice of the termination of any manager's appointment required to be delivered to the registrar under article 7(d) of the EC Regulation must state the manager's name and the date on which the termination took place.

(3F) Regulation 13 shall have effect for the purpose of the delivery of the notices required to be delivered to the registrar under this regulation.]

(4) . . .

NOTES

Para (1): words in square brackets substituted by the European Economic Interest Grouping (Amendment) (EU Exit) Regulations 2018, SI 2018/1299, regs 2, 5(a), as from IP completion day (as defined in the European Union (Withdrawal Agreement) Act 2020, s 39). Words omitted revoked by the European Economic Interest Grouping and European Public Limited-Liability Company (Amendment) Regulations 2014, SI 2014/2382, regs 2, 5(1), (2), as from 1 October 2014.

Paras (3)–(3B) were substituted (for the original para (3)) by SI 2009/2399, regs 3, 8(1), (3), as from 1 October 2009, and have subsequently been amended as follows:

Para (3) was further substituted, and the figures in square brackets in paras (3A), (3B) were substituted, by SI 2014/2382, regs 2, 5(1), (3)–(5), as from 1 October 2014.

The words in the first (outer) pair of square brackets in sub-para (3)(c) were substituted by the Companies and Limited Liability Partnerships (Filing Requirements) Regulations 2015, SI 2015/1695, reg 8(1), (2), as from 10 October 2015 (note that this amendment does not apply in respect of a statement or notice received by the registrar before 10 October 2015).

The word "UKEIG" in sub-para (3)(c) was substituted by SI 2018/1299, regs 2, 5(b), as from IP completion day (as defined in the European Union (Withdrawal Agreement) Act 2020, s 39).

The word in square brackets in para (3B) was substituted by SI 2018/1299, regs 2, 5(c), as from IP completion day (as defined in the European Union (Withdrawal Agreement) Act 2020, s 39).

Paras (3C)–(3F): inserted by SI 2014/2382, regs 2, 5(1), (6), as from 1 October 2014. For transitional provisions in relation to para (3D), see the Companies, Limited Liability Partnerships and Partnerships (Amendment etc) (EU Exit) Regulations 2019, SI 2019/348, Sch 4, para 2 **[12.105]**.

Para (4): revoked by SI 2009/2399, regs 3, 8(1), (4), as from 1 October 2009.

[10.16]

6 Cessation of membership (Article 28(1) of the EC Regulation)

For the purposes of national law on liquidation, winding up, insolvency or cessation of payments, a member of [a UKEIG] registered under these Regulations shall cease to be a member if—

(a) in the case of an individual—

(i) a bankruptcy order has been made against him in England and Wales [or Northern Ireland]; or

(ii) sequestration of his estate has been awarded by the court in Scotland under the Bankruptcy (Scotland) Act 1985;

(b) in the case of a partnership—

(i) a winding up order has been made against the partnership in England and Wales [or Northern Ireland];

[(ii) a bankruptcy order has been made against each of the partnership's members in England and Wales on a bankruptcy petition presented under Article 11(1) of the Insolvent Partnerships Order 1994;

(iia) a bankruptcy order has been made against each of the partnership's members in Northern Ireland on a bankruptcy petition presented under Article 11(1) of the Insolvent Partnerships Order (Northern Ireland) 1995; or]

(iii) sequestration of the estate of the partnership has been awarded by the court in Scotland under the Bankruptcy (Scotland) Act 1985;

(c) in the case of a company, the company goes into liquidation in [the United Kingdom]; or

(d) in the case of any legal person or partnership, it is otherwise wound up or otherwise ceases to exist after the conclusion of winding up or insolvency.

NOTES

Words in first pair of square brackets substituted by the European Economic Interest Grouping (Amendment) (EU Exit) Regulations 2018, SI 2018/1299, regs 2, 6, as from IP completion day (as defined in the European Union (Withdrawal Agreement) Act 2020, s 39).

Words in second and third pairs of square brackets inserted, and other words in square brackets substituted, by the European Economic Interest Grouping (Amendment) Regulations 2009, SI 2009/2399, regs 3, 9, as from 1 October 2009.

[10.17]

7 Competent authority ([Article] 32(1) . . . of the EC Regulation)

[(1) The competent authority for the purposes of making an application to the court under Article 32(1) of the EC Regulation (winding up of [UKEIG] in certain circumstances) shall be—

(a) in the case of [a UKEIG] whose official address is in Northern Ireland, the Department of Enterprise, Trade and Investment in Northern Ireland;

(b) in any other case, the Secretary of State.]

(2) The court may, on an application by [the appropriate authority], order the winding up of [a UKEIG], if [the UKEIG] acts contrary to the public interest and it is expedient in the public interest that [the UKEIG] should be wound up and the court is of the opinion that it is just and equitable for it to be so.

[(2A) In paragraph (2) above "the appropriate authority" means—

(a) in the case of [a UKEIG] whose official address is in Great Britain, the Secretary of State;

(b) in the case of [a UKEIG] whose official address is in Northern Ireland, the Department of Enterprise, Trade and Investment in Northern Ireland.]

(3) The court, on an application by [the appropriate authority], [may prohibit any activity carried on in the United Kingdom by a UKEIG] where such an activity is in contravention of the public interest there.

[(4) In paragraph (3) above "the appropriate authority" means—

(a) in the case of any activity carried on in Great Britain, the Secretary of State;

(b) in the case of any activity carried on in Northern Ireland, the Department of Enterprise, Trade and Investment in Northern Ireland.]

NOTES

Regulation heading: word in square brackets substituted, and words omitted revoked, by the European Economic Interest Grouping (Amendment) (EU Exit) Regulations 2018, SI 2018/1299, regs 2, 7(a), as from IP completion day (as defined in the European Union (Withdrawal Agreement) Act 2020, s 39).

Para (1): substituted by the European Economic Interest Grouping (Amendment) Regulations 2009, SI 2009/2399, regs 3, 10(1), (2), as from 1 October 2009. Words in square brackets substituted by SI 2018/1299, regs 2, 7(b), as from IP completion day (as defined in the European Union (Withdrawal Agreement) Act 2020, s 39).

Para (2): words in first pair of square brackets substituted by SI 2009/2399, regs 3, 10(1), (3)(a), as from 1 October 2009. All other words in square brackets were substituted by SI 2018/1299, regs 2, 7(c), as from IP completion day (as defined in the European Union (Withdrawal Agreement) Act 2020, s 39).

Para (2A): inserted by SI 2009/2399, regs 3, 10(1), (4), as from 1 October 2009. Words in square brackets substituted by SI 2018/1299, regs 2, 7(d), as from IP completion day (as defined in the European Union (Withdrawal Agreement) Act 2020, s 39).

Para (3): words in first pair of square brackets substituted by SI 2009/2399, regs 3, 10(1), (5)(a), as from 1 October 2009. Words in second pair of square brackets substituted by SI 2018/1299, regs 2, 7(e), as from IP completion day (as defined in the European Union (Withdrawal Agreement) Act 2020, s 39).

Para (4): added by SI 2009/2399, regs 3, 10(1), (6), as from 1 October 2009.

[10.18]

8 Winding up and conclusion of liquidation (Articles 35 and 36 of the EC Regulation)

(1) Where [a UKEIG] is wound up as an unregistered company under Part V of the Insolvency Act 1986, the provisions of Part V shall apply in relation to [the UKEIG] as if any reference in that Act . . . to a director or past director of a company included a reference to a manager of [the UKEIG] and any other person who has or has had control or management of the [UKEIG's] business and with the modification that in section 221(1) after the words "all the provisions" there shall be added the words "of Council Regulation (EEC) No 2137/85 and".

[(1A) Where [a UKEIG] is wound up as an unregistered company under Part 6 of the Insolvency (Northern Ireland) Order 1989, the provisions of Part 6 shall apply in relation to [the UKEIG] as if—

(a) any reference in that Order to a director or past director of a company included a reference to a manager of [the UKEIG] and any other person who has or has had control or management of the [UKEIG's] business; and

(b) in Article 185(1) after "all the provisions" there were inserted "of Council Regulation (EEC) No 2137/85 and".]

(2) At the end of the period of three months beginning with the day of receipt by the registrar of a notice of the conclusion of the liquidation of [a UKEIG], [the UKEIG] shall be dissolved.

NOTES

The words "a UKEIG", "the UKEIG" and "UKEIG's", in each place that they appear, were substituted by the European Economic Interest Grouping (Amendment) (EU Exit) Regulations 2018, SI 2018/1299, regs 2, 8, as from IP completion day (as defined in the European Union (Withdrawal Agreement) Act 2020, s 39). This regulation has also been amended as follows:

Para (1): words omitted revoked by the Companies Act 2006 (Consequential Amendments etc) Order 2008, SI 2008/948, art 3(1), Sch 1, Pt 2, para 162, as from 6 April 2008.

Para (1A): inserted by the European Economic Interest Grouping (Amendment) Regulations 2009, SI 2009/2399, regs 3, 11, as from 1 October 2009.

PART III REGISTRATION ETC (ARTICLE 39 OF THE EC REGULATION)

[10.19]

[9 Amendment of the register on conversion and issue of certificate of conversion

(1) The registrar must, within the period beginning with IP completion day and ending at the end of the day after the day on which IP completion day falls, amend the name of a grouping which is converted from an EEIG to a UKEIG under Article 1 of the EC Regulation to reflect that conversion on the register.

(2) But the registrar is not required to amend the name of a grouping for the purposes of paragraph (1) in documents and particulars relating to that grouping and filed with the registrar before IP completion day.

(3) The registrar must issue a certificate to the UKEIG (a "certificate of conversion") to confirm that the UKEIG has converted, on IP completion day, pursuant to Article 1 of the EC Regulation.

(4) The certificate of conversion must be—

(a) signed by the registrar or authenticated by the registrar's official seal; and

(b) issued to the UKEIG within the period of 21 days beginning with IP completion day.

(5) Any communication or notice may be addressed to a UKEIG at its official address as notified to the registrar or in the case of any change of that address at any new official address notified to the registrar.

(6) Where, before IP completion day, a transfer proposal in relation to a grouping has been drawn up, filed and published under Article 14, paragraphs (1) to (4) do not apply in relation to that grouping, until such time as the registrar is satisfied that the transfer did not take effect before IP completion day.

(7) Paragraph (8) applies in relation to an EEIG—

(a) which immediately before IP completion day is registered in a Member State pursuant to a transfer of its official address from the United Kingdom to that Member State in accordance with Article 14; but

(b) whose registration in the United Kingdom has not been terminated before IP completion day.

(8) The registrar must delete the registration of an EEIG to which this paragraph applies as soon as reasonably practicable.

(9) In this regulation, "Article 14" means Article 14 of Council Regulation (EEC) No 2137/85 of 25 July 1985 on the European Economic Interest Grouping (EEIG) as it applied in the European Union immediately before IP completion day.]

NOTES

Commencement: IP completion day (as defined in the European Union (Withdrawal Agreement) Act 2020, s 39).

Substituted by the European Economic Interest Grouping (Amendment) (EU Exit) Regulations 2018, SI 2018/1299, regs 2, 9, as from IP completion day (as defined in the European Union (Withdrawal Agreement) Act 2020, s 39).

Note that the 2018 Regulations were amended by the Companies and Statutory Auditors etc (Consequential Amendments) (EU Exit) Regulations 2020, SI 2020/523, reg 7, with effect from immediately before IP completion day; and that the effect of the amendment has been incorporated into the text above.

[10.20]

10 Prohibition on registration of certain names

[(A1) This regulation applies for the purposes of registering—

(a) a new name under regulation 11; or

(b) an EEIG establishment under regulation 12.]

[(1) [A UKEIG or an EEIG establishment] shall not be registered in the United Kingdom . . . by a name which includes—

(a) any of the words or abbreviations specified in inverted commas in paragraph 1 of Schedule 2 to the [Company, Limited Liability Partnership and Business (Names and Trading Disclosures) Regulations 2015];

(b) any word or abbreviation specified as similar to a word or abbreviation falling within sub-paragraph (a) above, within the meaning of paragraph 2 of that Schedule;

[(c) in the case of a UKEIG, any of the expressions or abbreviations specified in inverted commas in sub-paragraphs (a) to (j) and (l) to (y) of paragraph 3 of that Schedule;]

[(ca) in the case of an EEIG establishment, any of the expressions or abbreviations specified in inverted commas in sub-paragraphs (a) to (y) of paragraph 3 of that Schedule;]

(d) any expression or abbreviation specified as similar to an expression or abbreviation falling within sub-paragraph [(c) or sub-paragraph (ca), as the case may be], within the meaning of paragraph 4 of that Schedule.

(1A) The provisions specified in paragraph (1B) below apply to [UKEIGs and EEIG establishments] registered or in the process of being registered under these Regulations, as if they were companies formed and registered under the 2006 Act or in the process of being registered under the 2006 Act.

(1B) The provisions are—

(a) section 53 of the 2006 Act (prohibited names);

(b) section 54 of that Act (names suggesting connection with government or public authority);

(c) section 55 of that Act (other sensitive words or expressions);

(d) section 56 of that Act (duty to seek comments of government department or other specified body) and any regulations made by virtue of that section;

(e) section 57(3) of that Act (permitted characters etc);

(f) section 66(1) of that Act (name not to be the same as another in the index) and any regulations made under that section.

(1C) The provisions specified in paragraph (1B) above have effect with the following modifications—

(a) any reference to the 2006 Act is to be read as including a reference to these Regulations;

(b) the reference in section 56(4)(a) to a director or secretary of the company is to be read as a reference to a manager of the [UKEIG or the EEIG establishment];

(c) any requirement imposed by regulations under section 66 to disregard the words "["UK Economic Interest Grouping", "European Economic Interest Grouping" or the abbreviations "UKEIG" or] "EEIG" where those words or that abbreviation appears in a name—
   (i) is to apply wherever in the name those words or that abbreviation appears; and
   (ii) is to be taken to include a requirement to disregard the authorised equivalents of those words or that abbreviation in official languages of the Economic Community other than English.

(2) Schedule 3 to these Regulations sets out the authorised equivalents referred to in paragraph (1C)(c)(ii) above.]

NOTES

Para (A1): inserted by the European Economic Interest Grouping (Amendment) (EU Exit) Regulations 2018, SI 2018/1299, regs 2, 10(a), as from IP completion day (as defined in the European Union (Withdrawal Agreement) Act 2020, s 39).

Para (1): substituted (together with paras (1A)–(1C), (2)) for the original paras (1), (2) by SI 2009/2399, regs 3, 13, as from 1 October 2009; and is further amended as follows:

The words in the first pair of square brackets were substituted, the words omitted were revoked, sub-para (c) was substituted, sub-para (ca) was inserted, and the words in square brackets in sub-para (d) were substituted by SI 2018/1299, regs 2, 10(b), as from IP completion day (as defined in the European Union (Withdrawal Agreement) Act 2020, s 39).

The words in square brackets in sub-para (a) were substituted by the Company, Limited Liability Partnership and Business (Names and Trading Disclosures) Regulations 2015, SI 2015/17, reg 30, Sch 6, para 2, as from 31 January 2015.

Para (1A): substituted as noted above. Words in square brackets substituted by SI 2018/1299, regs 2, 10(c), as from IP completion day (as defined in the European Union (Withdrawal Agreement) Act 2020, s 39).

Paras (1B), (2): substituted as noted above.

Para (1C): substituted as noted above. Words in square brackets in sub-paras (b), (c) substituted by SI 2018/1299, regs 2, 10(d), as from IP completion day (as defined in the European Union (Withdrawal Agreement) Act 2020, s 39).

References to the European Community and related expressions: see the note "References to "the European Community", "Community", etc" in the introductory notes to these Regulations.

[10.21]

11 Change of name

(1) . . .

[(1A) Sections 67(1) and 68 of the 2006 Act (power to direct change of name in case of similarity to existing name) apply to [UKEIGs and EEIG] establishments, registered under these Regulations, as if they were companies formed and registered under the 2006 Act.

(1B) In the application of section 68 of the 2006 Act to [UKEIGs and EEIG] establishments—
(a) subsection (5) is to be read as if—
   (i) the reference in paragraph (b) to an officer of the company were a reference to an officer of the [UKEIG or the EEIG], within the meaning of these Regulations; and
   (ii) the second sentence were omitted;
(b) subsection (6) is to be read as if the reference to a daily default fine were omitted.]

[(2) Paragraphs (2A) and (2B) below apply where the registrar receives notice of a change of [name for a UKEIG or an EEIG establishment].

(2A) If the registrar is satisfied—
(a) that the new name complies with the requirements of regulation 10(1) and the provisions applied by regulation 10(1A) above, and
(b) that any requirements applying under or by virtue of these Regulations with respect to a change of name are complied with,

the registrar shall enter the new name on the register in place of the former name.

(2B) On the registration of the new name, the registrar shall issue a certificate of registration altered to meet the circumstances of the case.

(3) A change of [name for a UKEIG or an EEIG establishment] has effect from the date on which the new certificate of registration is issued.

(4) The change does not affect any rights or obligations of the [UKEIG or the EEIG establishment] or render defective any legal proceedings by or against it.

(5) Any legal proceedings that might have been continued or commenced against it by its former name may be continued or commenced against it by its new name.]

NOTES

Para (1) was revoked, paras (1A), (1B) were inserted, and paras (2A)–(5) were substituted (for the original paras (2), (3)), by the European Economic Interest Grouping (Amendment) Regulations 2009, SI 2009/2399, regs 3, 14, as from 1 October 2009.

Para (1A): inserted as noted above. Words in square brackets substituted by the European Economic Interest Grouping (Amendment) (EU Exit) Regulations 2018, SI 2018/1299, regs 2, 11(a), as from IP completion day (as defined in the European Union (Withdrawal Agreement) Act 2020, s 39).

Para (1B): inserted as noted above. Words in square brackets substituted by SI 2018/1299, regs 2, 11(b), as from IP completion day (as defined in the European Union (Withdrawal Agreement) Act 2020, s 39).

Paras (2), (3): substituted as noted above. Words in square brackets substituted by SI 2018/1299, regs 2, 11(c), as from IP completion day (as defined in the European Union (Withdrawal Agreement) Act 2020, s 39).

Para (4): substituted as noted above. Words in square brackets substituted by SI 2018/1299, regs 2, 11(d), as from IP completion day (as defined in the European Union (Withdrawal Agreement) Act 2020, s 39).

[10.22]

12 Registration of establishment of EEIG whose official address is outside the United Kingdom

(1) The registrar for the purposes of registration under this regulation of an EEIG establishment situated in [the United Kingdom] where the EEIG's official address is outside the United Kingdom shall be the registrar within the meaning of [the Companies Acts].

(2) For the purposes of registration under paragraph (1) above there shall be delivered, within one month of the establishment becoming so situated at any place in [the United Kingdom], to the registrar at the registration office in England and Wales[, Scotland or Northern Ireland], according to where the establishment is situated, a certified copy of the contract together with—

(a) a certified translation into English of the contract and other documents and particulars to be filed with it under article 10 of the EC Regulation if the contract and other documents and particulars, or any part thereof, are not in English; . . .

[(b) an application for registration containing the following particulars—

(i) a statement of the names and particulars set out in [the first paragraph of Article 5 and in Article] 10 of the EC Regulation;

(ii) the name of the Member State in which the official address of the EEIG is situated; and

(iii) the address of the EEIG's establishment being registered in the United Kingdom; and]

[(c) a statement that all the requirements of these Regulations and of the EC Regulation as to registration have been complied with.]

[(2A) An application under paragraph (2)(b) may also contain a statement under regulation 12A(2).]

(3) Paragraph (2) above shall not apply where an establishment is already registered in [the United Kingdom] under paragraph (1) above.

(4) The registrar shall not register an EEIG establishment under this regulation unless he is satisfied that all the requirements of these Regulations and of the EC Regulation [as to registration have been complied with but the registrar may accept a statement under paragraph (2)(c)] as sufficient evidence of compliance.

(5) Subject to paragraph (4) above, the registrar shall retain the copy of the contract, and any certified translation, delivered to him under paragraph (2) above and register the EEIG establishment.

(6) Any communication or notice may be addressed to an EEIG where its official address is outside the United Kingdom at any of its establishments in [the United Kingdom].

(7) . . .

(8) If an EEIG fails to comply with any provision of paragraph (2) above, the EEIG, and any officer of it who intentionally authorises or permits the default, is guilty of an offence and liable on summary conviction to a fine not exceeding level 3 on the standard scale and if the failure to comply with any such provision continues after conviction, the EEIG and any such officer shall be guilty of a further offence of failure to comply with that provision and shall be liable to be proceeded against and punished accordingly.

[(9) For the purposes of carrying out the obligation at paragraph (2)(b)(i), the first paragraph of Article 5 of the EC Regulation must be read as if references in that paragraph to "the grouping" or "a grouping" were references to "the EEIG" or "an EEIG".]

NOTES

The word omitted from sub-para (2)(a) was revoked, sub-para (2)(b) was substituted, sub-para (2)(c) and para (2A) were inserted, and the words in square brackets in para (4) were substituted, by the European Economic Interest Grouping and European Public Limited-Liability Company (Amendment) Regulations 2014, SI 2014/2382, regs 2, 7, as from 1 October 2014.

The words in square brackets in sub-para (2)(b)(i) were substituted, para (7) was revoked, and para (9) was added, by the European Economic Interest Grouping (Amendment) (EU Exit) Regulations 2018, SI 2018/1299, regs 2, 12, as from IP completion day (as defined in the European Union (Withdrawal Agreement) Act 2020, s 39).

All other words in square brackets in this regulation were substituted by the European Economic Interest Grouping (Amendment) Regulations 2009, SI 2009/2399, regs 3, 15, as from 1 October 2009.

[10.23]

[12A Registration under alternative name

(1) This regulation applies to an EEIG—

(a) whose official address is outside the United Kingdom, and

(b) which has an establishment that is registered or is in the process of being registered under regulation 12 above.

[(2) The EEIG may at any time deliver to the registrar a statement specifying a name, other than its grouping name, under which it proposes to carry on business in the United Kingdom.

(3) A statement under paragraph (2) must contain the following particulars—

(a) the EEIG's registered number and name;

(b) the Member State in which the EEIG's official address is situated;

(c) the proposed name; and

(d) in cases where a duty arises under section 56 of the 2006 Act (as it applies in accordance with regulation 10) to seek comments of a specified government department or other body regarding the proposed name, a statement that such a request has been made and a copy of any response received.

(3A) An EEIG that has delivered a statement under paragraph (2) may at any time deliver to the registrar a further statement specifying a name, other than its grouping name, under which it proposes to carry on business in the United Kingdom.

(3B) The statement under paragraph (3A) must contain the particulars specified in sub-paragraphs (a) to (d) of paragraph (3).]

(4) The alternative name for the time being registered under this regulation is treated for all purposes of the law applying in the United Kingdom as the EEIG's grouping name.

(5) This does not—

(a) affect the references in this regulation to the EEIG's grouping name,

(b) affect any rights or obligations of the EEIG, or

(c) render defective any legal proceedings by or against the EEIG.

(6) Any legal proceedings that might have been continued or commenced against the EEIG by its grouping name, or any name previously registered under this regulation, may be continued or commenced against it by its name for the time being so registered.

(7) Any reference in this regulation to the "grouping name" of an EEIG is a reference to the name of the EEIG referred to in the contract for its formation.]

NOTES

Inserted by the European Economic Interest Grouping (Amendment) Regulations 2009, SI 2009/2399, regs 3, 16, as from 1 October 2009.

Paras (2)–(3B): substituted (for the original paras (2), (3)) by the European Economic Interest Grouping and European Public Limited-Liability Company (Amendment) Regulations 2014, SI 2014/2382, regs 2, 8, as from 1 October 2014.

[10.24]

[13 Delivery of documents

(1) This regulation applies to the documents and particulars which are—

(a) referred to in paragraphs (a) to (j) of article 7 of the EC Regulation, and

(b) are required to be filed . . . in accordance with these Regulations.

(2) The documents and particulars referred to in paragraph (1) must be delivered to the registrar—

(a) in the case of [a UKEIG], within 15 days of the event to which the document in question relates;

(b) in the case of an EEIG . . . , within 30 days of such event.

(3) The following must be delivered to the registrar with any documents and particulars under paragraph (1)—

[(a) particulars of the UKEIG's or the EEIG's registered number and name, and, in the case of an EEIG, the Member State in which its official address is situated,]

(b) a translation into English of any documents and particulars being delivered, or any part of those documents and particulars that are not in English, certified as an accurate translation.

(4) Where a notice is filed in accordance with article 7(b) of the EC Regulation—

(a) the notice must contain particulars of the address at which the establishment has been set up or closed, and

(b) where[, in the case of the closure of an EEIG establishment,] the EEIG will have more than one address in the UK, the notice may contain particulars of an address in the United Kingdom at which the EEIG wishes to receive correspondence.

(5) If [a UKEIG or] an EEIG fails to comply with any provision of this regulation, [the UKEIG or] the EEIG, and any officer of [the UKEIG or] the EEIG who intentionally authorises or permits the default, is guilty of an offence and liable on summary conviction to a fine not exceeding level 3 on the standard scale and if the failure to comply with any such provision continues after conviction, [the UKEIG or] the EEIG and any such officer shall be guilty of a further offence of failure to comply with that provision and shall be liable to be proceeded against and punished accordingly.]

NOTES

Substituted by the European Economic Interest Grouping and European Public Limited-Liability Company (Amendment) Regulations 2014, SI 2014/2382, regs 2, 9, as from 1 October 2014.

The words omitted from sub-paras (1)(b), (2)(b) were revoked, the words in square brackets in sub-paras (2)(a), (4)(b) were substituted, sub-para (3)(a) was substituted, and the words in square brackets in para (5) were inserted, by the European Economic Interest Grouping (Amendment) (EU Exit) Regulations 2018, SI 2018/1299, regs 2, 13, as from IP completion day (as defined in the European Union (Withdrawal Agreement) Act 2020, s 39).

[10.25]

14 Inspection of documents

Any person may—

(a) inspect any document or particulars kept by the registrar under these Regulations or a copy thereof; and

(b) require the registrar to deliver or send by post to him a copy or extract of any such document or particulars or any part thereof.

[10.26]

[15 Publication of documents in the Gazette

The registrar must cause to be published in the Gazette—

(a) any amendments (stated in full) to the particulars which must be included in the contract for the formation of a grouping pursuant to the first paragraph of Article 5 of the EC Regulation and which are filed with the registrar;

(b) notice (stated in full) of the termination of a grouping's registration;

(c) in the case of those documents and particulars referred to in Article 7(b) to (j) of the EC Regulation, a notice stating the name of the UKEIG or the EEIG, the description of the documents or particulars and the date of receipt.]

NOTES

Commencement: IP completion day (as defined in the European Union (Withdrawal Agreement) Act 2020, s 39).

Substituted by the European Economic Interest Grouping (Amendment) (EU Exit) Regulations 2018, SI 2018/1299, regs 2, 14, as from IP completion day (as defined in the European Union (Withdrawal Agreement) Act 2020, s 39).

[10.27]

16 [UKEIG and EEIG establishment] identification

(1) If [a UKEIG or an EEIG] fails to comply with article 25 of the EC Regulation it is guilty of an offence and liable on summary conviction to a fine not exceeding level 3 on the standard scale.

(2) If an officer of [a UKEIG or an EEIG] or a person on its behalf issues or authorises the issue of any letter, order form or similar document not complying with the requirements of article 25 of the EC Regulation, he is guilty of an offence and liable on summary conviction to a fine not exceeding level 3 on the standard scale.

NOTES

All words in square brackets were substituted by the European Economic Interest Grouping (Amendment) (EU Exit) Regulations 2018, SI 2018/1299, regs 2, 15, as from IP completion day (as defined in the European Union (Withdrawal Agreement) Act 2020, s 39).

PART IV SUPPLEMENTAL PROVISIONS

17 *(Revoked by the European Economic Interest Grouping (Amendment) Regulations 2009, SI 2009/2399, regs 3, 18, as from 1 October 2009.)*

[10.28]

[18 Application of provisions of the Companies Acts

(1) The provisions of the Companies Acts specified in Schedule 4 to these Regulations apply to [UKEIGs and EEIG establishments] registered or in the process of being registered under these Regulations, as if they were companies formed and registered or in the process of being registered under [the 2006 Act].

(2) The provisions applied have effect with the following adaptations—

(a) any reference to the 1985 Act[, the 2006 Act] or the Companies Acts includes a reference to these Regulations;

(b) any reference to a registered office includes a reference to an official address;

[(ba) any reference to the register is to be read as a reference to the [Groupings] register;

(bb) any reference to an officer of a company is to be read as a reference to an officer of [a UKEIG or an EEIG], within the meaning of these Regulations;]

(c) any reference to a daily default fine shall be omitted.

(3) The provisions applied also have effect subject to any limitations mentioned in relation to those provisions in that Schedule.]

[(4) In this regulation "the [Groupings] register" means—

(a) the documents and particulars required to be kept by the registrar under these Regulations; and

(b) the records falling within section 1080(1) of the 2006 Act which relate to [UKEIGs or EEIG establishments].

(5) This regulation does not affect the application of provisions of the Companies Acts to [UKEIGs or EEIG establishments] otherwise than by virtue of this regulation.]

NOTES

Substituted by the Companies Act 2006 (Consequential Amendments etc) Order 2008, SI 2008/948, art 3(1), Sch 1, Pt 2, para 163, as from 6 April 2008.

Para (1): words in first pair of square brackets substituted by the European Economic Interest Grouping (Amendment) (EU Exit) Regulations 2018, SI 2018/1299, regs 2, 16(a), as from IP completion day (as defined in the European Union (Withdrawal Agreement) Act 2020, s 39). Words in second pair of square brackets substituted by the European Economic Interest Grouping (Amendment) Regulations 2009, SI 2009/2399, regs 3, 19(1), (2), as from 1 October 2009.

Para (2): words in square brackets in sub-para (a) inserted by SI 2009/2399, regs 3, 19(1), (3), as from 1 October 2009. Words in square brackets in sub-paras (ba), (bb) substituted by SI 2018/1299, regs 2, 16(b), as from IP completion day (as defined in the European Union (Withdrawal Agreement) Act 2020, s 39).

Para (4): added by SI 2009/2399, regs 3, 19(1), (43), as from 1 October 2009. Words in square brackets substituted by SI 2018/1299, regs 2, 16(c), as from IP completion day (as defined in the European Union (Withdrawal Agreement) Act 2020, s 39).

Para (5): added by SI 2009/2399, regs 3, 19(1), (43), as from 1 October 2009. Words in square brackets substituted by SI 2018/1299, regs 2, 16(d), as from IP completion day (as defined in the European Union (Withdrawal Agreement) Act 2020, s 39).

[10.29]

19 [Application of insolvency legislation]

(1) Part III of the Insolvency Act 1986 shall apply to [UKEIGs and EEIG establishments] registered under these Regulations [in England and Wales or Scotland], as if they were companies registered under [the 2006 Act].

[(1A) Part 4 of the Insolvency (Northern Ireland) Order 1989 shall apply to [UKEIGs and EEIG establishments] registered under these Regulations in Northern Ireland, as if they were companies registered under the 2006 Act.]

(2) Section 120 of the Insolvency Act 1986 shall apply to [a UKEIG and an EEIG establishment] registered under these Regulations in Scotland, as if it were a company registered in Scotland the paid-up or credited as paid-up share capital of which did not exceed £120,000 and as if in that section any reference to the Company's registered office were a reference to the official address of [the UKEIG or the EEIG].

NOTES

Regulation heading: substituted by the European Economic Interest Grouping (Amendment) Regulations 2009, SI 2009/2399, regs 3, 20(1), (4), as from 1 October 2009.

Para (1): words in first pair of square brackets substituted by the European Economic Interest Grouping (Amendment) (EU Exit) Regulations 2018, SI 2018/1299, regs 2, 19(a), as from IP completion day (as defined in the European Union (Withdrawal Agreement) Act 2020, s 39). Words in second pair of square brackets inserted, and words in third pair of square brackets substituted, by SI 2009/2399, regs 3, 20(1), (2), as from 1 October 2009.

Para (1A): inserted by SI 2009/2399, regs 3, 20(1), (3), as from 1 October 2009. Words in square brackets substituted by SI 2018/1299, regs 2, 19(a), as from IP completion day (as defined in the European Union (Withdrawal Agreement) Act 2020, s 39).

Para (2): words in square brackets substituted by SI 2018/1299, regs 2, 17(b), as from IP completion day (as defined in the European Union (Withdrawal Agreement) Act 2020, s 39).

[10.30]

20 [Application of legislation relating to disqualification of directors]

[(1)] Where [a UKEIG or an EEIG establishment] is wound up as an unregistered company under Part V of the Insolvency Act 1986, the provisions of sections 1, 2, [4 to 7, 8, 9, 10, 11], 12(2), 15 to 17, 20 and 22 of, and Schedule 1 to, the Company Directors Disqualification Act 1986 shall apply in relation to [the UKEIG or the EEIG establishment] as if any reference to a director or past director of a company included a reference to a manager of [the UKEIG or the EEIG establishment] and any other person who has or has had control or management of [the UKEIG's or the EEIG establishment's] business and [the UKEIG or the EEIG establishment] were a company as defined by section 22(2)(b) of that Act.

[(2) Where [a UKEIG or an EEIG establishment] is wound up as an unregistered company under Part 6 of the Insolvency (Northern Ireland) Order 1989 the provisions of Articles 2(2) to (6), 3, 5, 7 to 11, 13, 14, 15, 16(2), 19 to 21 and 23 of, and Schedule 1 to, the Company Directors Disqualification (Northern Ireland) Order 2002 shall apply in relation to [the UKEIG or the EEIG establishment] as if—

(a) any reference to a director or past director of a company included a reference to a manager of [the UKEIG or the EEIG establishment] and any other person who has or has had control or management of [the UKEIG's or the EEIG establishment's] business; and

(b) [the UKEIG or the EEIG establishment] were a company as defined by Article 2(2) of that Order.]

NOTES

The words "a UKEIG or an EEIG establishment", "the UKEIG or the EEIG establishment", and "the UKEIG's or the EEIG establishment's" (in each place they occur), were substituted by the European Economic Interest Grouping (Amendment) (EU Exit) Regulations 2018, SI 2018/1299, regs 2, 18, as from IP completion day (as defined in the European Union (Withdrawal Agreement) Act 2020, s 39). This regulation has also been amended as follows:

Regulation heading: substituted by the European Economic Interest Grouping (Amendment) Regulations 2009, SI 2009/2399, regs 3, 21(1), (5), as from 1 October 2009.

Para (1): numbered as such, and words "4 to 7, 8, 9, 10, 11" in square brackets substituted, by SI 2009/2399, regs 3, 21(1)–(3), as from 1 October 2009.

Para (2): added by SI 2009/2399, regs 3, 21(1), (4), as from 1 October 2009.

21 *(Revoked by the European Economic Interest Grouping (Amendment) (EU Exit) Regulations 2018, SI 2018/1299, regs 2, 19, as from IP completion day (as defined in the European Union (Withdrawal Agreement) Act 2020, s 39).)*

SCHEDULES

SCHEDULES 1, 2

(Sch 1 was revoked by the European Economic Interest Grouping (Amendment) (EU Exit) Regulations 2018, SI 2018/1299, regs 2, 20, as from IP completion day (as defined in the European Union (Withdrawal Agreement) Act 2020, s 39). Sch 2 was revoked by the European Economic Interest Grouping and European Public Limited-Liability Company (Amendment) Regulations 2014, SI 2014/2382, regs 2, 10, as from 1 October 2014.)

SCHEDULE 3
AUTHORISED EQUIVALENTS IN . . . COMMUNITY OFFICIAL LANGUAGES OF "EUROPEAN ECONOMIC INTEREST GROUPING" AND "EEIG"

Regulation 10(2)

[10.31]

DANISH:	Europaeiske Økonomiske Firmagruppe (EØFG)
DUTCH:	Europese Economische Samenwerkingsverbanden (EESV)
FRENCH:	Groupement Européen d'intérêt économique (GEIE)
GERMAN:	Europäische Wirtschaftliche Interessenvereinigung (EWIV)
GREEK:	Ευρωπαικος ομιλος οικονομικου σκοπου (ΕΟΟΣ) (written phonetically in letters of the Latin alphabet as "Evropaikos omilos economicou skopou (EOOS)")
IRISH:	Grupail Eorpach um Leas Eacnamaioch (GELE)
ITALIAN:	Gruppo Europeo di Interesse Economico (GEIE)
PORTUGUESE:	Agrupamento Europeu de Interesse Econômico (AEIE)
SPANISH:	Agrupación Europea de Interés Económico (AEIE)

NOTES

Schedule heading: word omitted revoked by the European Economic Interest Grouping (Amendment) (EU Exit) Regulations 2018, SI 2018/1299, regs 2, 21, as from IP completion day (as defined in the European Union (Withdrawal Agreement) Act 2020, s 39).

References to the European Community and related expressions: see the note "References to "the European Community", "Community", etc" in the introductory notes to these Regulations.

SCHEDULE 4
PROVISIONS OF [COMPANIES ACTS] APPLYING TO [UKEIGS AND EEIG ESTABLISHMENTS]

Regulation 18

[PART 1 PROVISIONS OF COMPANIES ACT 1985]

[10.32]

1–4. . . .

5. [section 432(1), (2) and (2A)].

6. section 434 so far as it refers to inspectors appointed under section 432 as applied by regulation 18 above and this Schedule.

7. section 436 so far as it refers to inspectors appointed under section 432, and to section 434, as applied by regulation 18 above and this Schedule.

8. sections [437 and 439].

9. section 441 so far as it applies to inspectors appointed under section 432 as applied by regulation 18 above and this Schedule.

10. [sections 447 and 447A] . . .

11. sections 448 to 452.

12. . . .

13. Part XVIII relating to floating charges and receivers (Scotland).

14–24. . . .

NOTES

The words in the first pair of square brackets in the Schedule heading were substituted, the Part 1 heading was inserted, and paras 12, 24 were revoked, by the Companies Act 2006 (Consequential Amendments etc) Order 2008, SI 2008/948, art 3(1), Sch 1, Pt 2, para 164(1)–(4), as from 6 April 2008.

The words in the second pair of square brackets in the Schedule heading were substituted by the European Economic Interest Grouping (Amendment) (EU Exit) Regulations 2018, SI 2018/1299, regs 2, 22(a), as from IP completion day (as defined in the European Union (Withdrawal Agreement) Act 2020, s 39).

All other amendments were made by the European Economic Interest Grouping (Amendment) Regulations 2009, SI 2009/2399, regs 3, 23(1), (2), as from 1 October 2009.

[PART 2 PROVISIONS OF COMPANIES ACT 2006

[10.33]

[25. Section 75 (provision of misleading information etc), as if the second sentence of subsection (5) were omitted.

26. Part 25 (company charges).

27. Section 993 (offence of fraudulent trading).

28. Section 1066(2) to (4) (registered numbers).

29. Section 1081 (annotation of the register), as if—

(a) after subsection (1) there were inserted—

"(1A) Where it appears to the registrar that material on the register is misleading or confusing, the registrar may place a note in the register containing such information as appears to the registrar to be necessary to remedy, as far as possible, the misleading or confusing nature of the material.", and

(b) subsection (5) were omitted.

30. Section 1082 (allocation of unique identifiers), as if—

(a) the reference in subsection (1)(a) to a director of a company were a reference to a manager of [a UKEIG or an EEIG], and

(b) paragraphs (b) and (c) of subsection (1) were omitted.

31. Section 1084 (records relating to companies that have been dissolved etc), as if subsection (4) were omitted.

32. In section 1087 (material not available for public inspection)—

[(a) subsection (1)(a), (d) and (da), and]

(b) subsections (2) and (3), so far as relating to material falling within paragraph (a) or (d) of subsection (1).

[32A. (1) Sections 1087A and 1087B, as if a reference to a director of a company were a reference to a manager of [a UKEIG or an EEIG].

(2) For the purposes of subparagraph (1), section 243 will apply in so far as necessary for the application of section 1087B(3).]

33. Section 1089(1) (form of application for inspection or copy), as if—

(a) the reference to inspection under section 1085 were a reference to inspection under regulation 14(a) above, and

(b) the reference to a copy under section 1086 were a reference to a copy or extract under regulation 14(b) above.

34. Section 1090(4) (power to determine form and manner in which copies to be provided), as if—

(a) for "the preceding provisions of this section" there were substituted "[Part 3 of the European Economic Interest Grouping Regulations 1989]", and

(b) the reference to copies being provided were a reference to copies or extracts being provided under regulation 14(b) above.

35. Section 1091 (certification of copies as accurate), as if—

(a) any reference in that section to copies were a reference to copies or extracts,
(b) any reference to section 1086 were a reference to regulation 14(b) above,
(c) subsections (2) and (4) were omitted, and
(d) in subsection (5) the words preceding "copies" were omitted.

36. Section 1094 (administrative removal of material from the register), as if—
(a) the reference in subsection (2) to section 1093 were omitted, and
(b) in subsection (3)(a), sub-paragraphs (iii) to (vii) were omitted.

37. Section 1112 (general false statement offence).

38. Section 1117 (registrar's rules), so far as relating to sections 1066(2), 1089(1) and 1090(4).

39. The following provisions of Part 36 (offences), so far as relating to offences under sections applied by these Regulations—
(a) section 1121 (liability of officer in default), as if subsection (2) were omitted;
(b) section 1122 (liability of company as officer in default), as if the words ""officer" and" in subsection (3) were omitted;
(c) sections 1126 to 1130 (consents for prosecutions, venue and time limit for summary proceedings, privilege and unincorporated bodies);
(d) section 1132 (production and inspection of documents where offence suspected), as if the reference in subsection (3)(b) to the secretary of the company were omitted;
(e) section 1133 (provisions not to apply to offences committed before commencement).

40. Sections 1139 to 1141 (service addresses), as if the reference in section 1140(2)(a) to a director or secretary of a company were a reference to a manager of [a UKEIG or an EEIG].]]

NOTES

This Part was added by the Companies Act 2006 (Consequential Amendments etc) Order 2008, SI 2008/948, art 3(1), Sch 1, Pt 2, para 164(1), (5), as from 6 April 2008.

The original paras 1, 2 were substituted by new paras 25–40 by the European Economic Interest Grouping (Amendment) Regulations 2009, SI 2009/2399, regs 3, 23(1), (3), as from 1 October 2009. These paragraphs have subsequently been amended as follows:

Para 30: words in square brackets substituted by the European Economic Interest Grouping (Amendment) (EU Exit) Regulations 2018, SI 2018/1299, regs 2, 22(b), as from IP completion day (as defined in the European Union (Withdrawal Agreement) Act 2020, s 39).

Para 32: sub-para (a) substituted by the Companies and Limited Liability Partnerships (Filing Requirements) Regulations 2015, SI 2015/1695, reg 8(1), (3), as from 10 October 2015.

Para 32A: inserted by SI 2015/1695, reg 8(1), (4), as from 10 October 2015. Words in square brackets substituted by SI 2018/1299, regs 2, 22(b), as from IP completion day (as defined in the European Union (Withdrawal Agreement) Act 2020, s 39).

Para 34: words in square brackets substituted by SI 2018/1299, regs 2, 22(c), as from IP completion day (as defined in the European Union (Withdrawal Agreement) Act 2020, s 39).

Para 40: words in square brackets substituted by SI 2018/1299, regs 2, 22(d), as from IP completion day (as defined in the European Union (Withdrawal Agreement) Act 2020, s 39).

INSOLVENCY REGULATIONS 1994

(SI 1994/2507)

NOTES

Made: 26 September 1994.

Authority: Insolvency Rules 1986, SI 1986/1925, r 12.1 (revoked); Insolvency Act 1986, ss 411, 412, Sch 8, para 27, Sch 9, para 30.

Commencement: 24 October 1994.

These Regulations are reproduced as amended by: the Insolvency (Amendment) Regulations 2000, SI 2000/485; the Financial Services and Markets Act 2000 (Consequential Amendments and Repeals) Order 2001, SI 2001/3649; the Insolvency (Amendment) Regulations 2004, SI 2004/472; the Insolvency (Amendment) Regulations 2005, SI 2005/512; the Secretaries of State for Children, Schools and Families, for Innovation, Universities and Skills and for Business, Enterprise and Regulatory Reform Order 2007, SI 2007/3224; the Insolvency (Amendment) Regulations 2008, SI 2008/670; the Insolvency (Amendment) Regulations 2009, SI 2009/482; the Secretary of State for Business, Innovation and Skills Order 2009, SI 2009/2748; the Insolvency (Amendment) Regulations 2011, SI 2011/2203; the Secretaries of State for Business, Energy and Industrial Strategy, for International Trade and for Exiting the European Union and the Transfer of Functions (Education and Skills) Order 2016, SI 2016/992; the Insolvency (England and Wales) Rules 2016 (Consequential Amendments and Savings) Rules 2017, SI 2017/369; the Insolvency (England and Wales) and Insolvency (Scotland) (Miscellaneous and Consequential Amendments) Rules 2017, SI 2017/1115.

Application of these Regulations to Limited Liability Partnerships: see the Limited Liability Partnerships Regulations 2001, SI 2001/1090, reg 10, Sch 6, Pt II.

Official Receiver: provision for the contracting out of the functions of the Official Receiver under these Regulations is made by the Contracting Out (Functions of the Official Receiver) Order 1995, SI 1995/1386.

Note: Part 3 of these Regulations (Bankruptcy) has been omitted as outside the scope of this work.

ARRANGEMENT OF REGULATIONS

PART 1
GENERAL

PART 1 GENERAL

[10.34]

1 Citation and commencement

These Regulations may be cited as the Insolvency Regulations 1994 and shall come into force on 24th October 1994.

[10.35]

2 Revocations

Subject to regulation 37 below, the Regulations listed in Schedule 1 to these Regulations are hereby revoked.

[10.36]

3 Interpretation and application

(1) In these Regulations, except where the context otherwise requires—

["bank" means—

(a) a person who has permission under Part 4 of the Financial Services and Markets Act 2000 to accept deposits, or

(b) an EEA firm of the kind mentioned in paragraph 5(b) of Schedule 3 to that Act, which has permission under paragraph 15 of that Schedule (as a result of qualifying for authorisation under paragraph 12(1) of that Schedule) to accept deposits;]

"bankrupt" means the bankrupt or his estate;

"company" means the company which is being wound up;

"creditors' committee" means any committee established under section 301;

["electronic transfer" means transmission by any electronic means;]

"liquidation committee" means, in the case of a winding up by the court, any committee established under section 141 and, in the case of a creditors' voluntary winding up, any committee established under section 101;

"liquidator" includes, in the case of a company being wound up by the court, the official receiver when so acting;

"local bank" means any bank in, or in the neighbourhood of, the insolvency district, or the district in respect of which the court has winding-up jurisdiction, in which the proceedings are taken, or in the locality in which any business of the company or, as the case may be, the bankrupt is carried on;

"local bank account" means, in the case of a winding up by the court, a current account opened with a local bank under regulation 6(2) below and, in the case of a bankruptcy, a current account opened with a local bank under regulation 21(1) below;

"payment instrument" means a cheque or payable order;

"the Rules" means [the Insolvency (England and Wales) Rules 2016]; and

"trustee", subject to regulation 19(2) below, means trustee of a bankrupt's estate including the official receiver when so acting;

and other expressions used in these Regulations and defined by the Rules have the meanings which they bear in the Rules.

(2) A Rule referred to in these Regulations by number means the Rule so numbered in the Rules.

(3) Any application to be made to the Secretary of State or to the Department or anything required to be sent to the Secretary of State or to the Department under these Regulations shall be addressed to [the Department for Business, Energy and Industrial Strategy], The Insolvency Service, PO Box 3690, Birmingham B2 4UY.

(4) Where a regulation makes provision for the use of a form obtainable from the Department, the Department may provide different forms for different cases arising under that regulation.

(5) Subject to regulation 37 below, these Regulations [(except for regulations 3A and 36A)] apply—

(a) to winding-up proceedings commenced on or after 29th December 1986; and

(b) to bankruptcy proceedings where the bankruptcy petition is or was presented on or after that day.

[(6) Regulation 3A applies in any case where a company entered into administration on or after 15th September 2003 other than a case where the company entered into administration by virtue of a petition presented before that date.

(7) Regulation 36A applies in any case where an insolvency practitioner is appointed on or after 1st April 2005.]

NOTES

Para (1): definition "bank" substituted by the Financial Services and Markets Act 2000 (Consequential Amendments and Repeals) Order 2001, SI 2001/3649, art 471, as from 1 December 2001. Definition "electronic transfer" inserted by the Insolvency (Amendment) Regulations 2000, SI 2000/485, reg 3, Schedule, para 1, as from 31 March 2000. Words in square brackets in the definition "the Rules" substituted by the Insolvency (England and Wales) Rules 2016 (Consequential Amendments and Savings) Rules 2017, SI 2017/369, r 2(2), Sch 2, para 4(1), (2), as from 6 April 2017.

Para (3): words in square brackets substituted by the Secretaries of State for Business, Energy and Industrial Strategy, for International Trade and for Exiting the European Union and the Transfer of Functions (Education and Skills) Order 2016, SI 2016/992, art 14, Schedule, Pt 2, para 19, as from 9 November 2016.

Para (5): words in square brackets inserted by the Insolvency (Amendment) Regulations 2005, SI 2005/512, regs 4, 5(1), (2), as from 1 April 2005.

Paras (6), (7): added by SI 2005/512, regs 4, 5(1), (3), as from 1 April 2005.

[PART 1A ADMINISTRATION

[10.37]

3A Disposal of company's records and provision of information to the Secretary of State

(1) The person who was the last administrator of a company which has been dissolved may, at any time after the expiration of a period of one year from the date of dissolution, destroy or otherwise dispose of the books, papers and other records of the company.

(2) An administrator or former administrator shall within 14 days of a request by the Secretary of State give the Secretary of State particulars of any money in his hands or under his control representing unclaimed or undistributed assets of the company or dividends or other sums due to any person as a member or former member of the company.]

NOTES

Inserted, together with the preceding heading, by the Insolvency (Amendment) Regulations 2005, SI 2005/512, regs 4, 6, as from 1 April 2005.

[10.38]

[3B Payment of unclaimed dividends or other money

(1) This regulation applies to monies which—

(a) are held by the former administrator of a dissolved company, and
(b) represent either or both of the following—
(i) unclaimed dividends due to creditors, or
(ii) sums held by the company in trust in respect of dividends or other sums due to any person as a member or former member of the company.

(2) Any monies to which this regulation applies may be paid into the Insolvency Services Account.

(3) Where under this regulation the former administrator pays any sums into the Insolvency Services Account, he shall at the same time give notice to the Secretary of State of—
(a) the name of the company,
(b) the name and address of the person to whom the dividend or other sum is payable,
(c) the amount of the dividend or other sum, and
(d) the date on which it was paid.

(4) Where a dividend or other sum is paid to a person by way of a payment instrument, any payment into the Insolvency Services Account in respect of that dividend or sum pursuant to paragraph (2) may not be made earlier than on or after the expiry of 6 months from the date of the payment instrument.]

NOTES

Inserted by the Insolvency (Amendment) Regulations 2008, SI 2008/670, reg 3(1), (2), as from 6 April 2008.

[PART 1B ADMINISTRATIVE RECEIVERSHIP

[10.39]

3C Payment of unclaimed dividends or other money

(1) This regulation applies to monies which—
(a) are held by the former administrative receiver of a dissolved company, and
(b) represent either or both of the following—
(i) unclaimed dividends due to creditors, or
(ii) sums held by the company in trust in respect of dividends or other sums due to any person as a member or former member of the company.

(2) Any monies to which this regulation applies may be paid into the Insolvency Services Account.

(3) Where under this regulation the former administrative receiver pays any sums into the Insolvency Services Account, he shall at the same time give notice to the Secretary of State of—
(a) the name of the company,
(b) the name and address of the person to whom the dividend or other sum is payable,
(c) the amount of the dividend or other sum, and
(d) the date on which it was paid.

(4) Where a dividend or other sum is paid to a person by way of a payment instrument, any payment in respect of that dividend or sum into the Insolvency Services Account pursuant to paragraph (2) may not be made earlier than on or after the expiry of 6 months from the date of the payment instrument.]

NOTES

Inserted, together with the preceding heading, by the Insolvency (Amendment) Regulations 2008, SI 2008/670, reg 3(1), (2), as from 6 April 2008.

Note that in the Queen's Printer's copy of the 2008 Regulations there are two paragraphs numbered as paragraph (3). In the above text, the second of these has been changed to paragraph (4).

PART 2 WINDING UP

[10.40]

4 Introductory

This Part of these Regulations relates to—
(a) voluntary winding up and
(b) winding up by the court
of companies which the courts in England and Wales have jurisdiction to wind up.

PAYMENT INTO AND OUT OF THE INSOLVENCY SERVICES ACCOUNT

[10.41]

5 Payments into the Insolvency Services Account

(1) In the case of a winding up by the court, subject to regulation 6 below, the liquidator shall pay all money received by him in the course of carrying out his functions as such without any deduction into the Insolvency Services Account kept by the Secretary of State with the Bank of England to the credit of the company once every 14 days or forthwith if £5,000 or more has been received.

[(2) . . .]

[(3) Every payment of money into the Insolvency Services Account under this regulation shall be—
(a) made through the Bank Giro system; or
(b) sent direct to the Bank of England, Threadneedle Street, London EC2R 8AH by cheque drawn in favour of the "Insolvency Services Account" and crossed "A/c payee only" "Bank of England"; or
(c) made by electronic transfer,
and the liquidator shall on request be given by the Department a receipt for the money so paid.]

(4) Every payment of money [made under sub-paragraph (a) or (b) of paragraph (3) above] shall be accompanied by a form obtainable from the Department for that purpose or by a form that is substantially similar.

[Every payment of money made under sub-paragraph (c) of paragraph (3) above shall specify the name of the liquidator making the payment and the name of the company to whose credit such payment is made.]

Part 10 Miscellaneous other SIs

(5) Where in a voluntary winding up a liquidator pays any unclaimed dividend into the Insolvency Services Account, he shall at the same time give notice to the Secretary of State, on a form obtainable from the Department or on one that is substantially similar, of the name and address of the person to whom the dividend is payable and the amount of the dividend.

NOTES

Para (2): revoked by the Insolvency (Amendment) Regulations 2011, SI 2011/2203, reg 3, Schedule, para 1, as from 1 October 2011. The paragraph was previously substituted by the Insolvency (Amendment) Regulations 2004, SI 2004/472, reg 2, Schedule, para 1, as from 1 April 2004.

Para (3): substituted by the Insolvency (Amendment) Regulations 2000, SI 2000/485, reg 3, Schedule, para 2, as from 31 March 2000.

Para (4): words in first pair of square brackets substituted, and words in second pair of square brackets added, by SI 2000/485, reg 3, Schedule, para 3, as from 31 March 2000.

[10.42]

6 Local bank account and handling of funds not belonging to the company

(1) This regulation does not apply in the case of a voluntary winding up.

(2) Where the liquidator intends to exercise his power to carry on the business of the company, he may apply to the Secretary of State for authorisation to open a local bank account, and the Secretary of State may authorise him to make his payments into and out of a specified bank, subject to a limit, instead of into and out of the Insolvency Services Account if satisfied that an administrative advantage will be derived from having such an account.

(3) Money received by the liquidator relating to the purpose for which the account was opened may be paid into the local bank account to the credit of the company to which the account relates.

(4) Where the liquidator opens a local bank account pursuant to an authorisation granted under paragraph (2) above, he shall open and maintain the account in the name of the company.

(5) Where money which is not an asset of the company is provided to the liquidator for a specific purpose, it shall be clearly identifiable in a separate account.

(6) The liquidator shall keep proper records, including documentary evidence of all money paid into and out of every local bank account opened and maintained under this regulation.

(7) The liquidator shall pay without deduction any surplus over any limit imposed by an authorisation granted under paragraph (2) above into the Insolvency Services Account in accordance with regulation 5 above as that regulation applies in the case of a winding up by the court.

(8) As soon as the liquidator ceases to carry on the business of the company or vacates office or an authorisation given in pursuance of an application under paragraph (2) above is withdrawn, he shall close the account and pay any balance into the Insolvency Services Account in accordance with regulation 5 above as that regulation applies in the case of a winding up by the court.

[10.43]

7 Payment of disbursements etc out of the Insolvency Services Account

[(A1) Paragraphs (1) [and (2)] of this regulation are subject to paragraph (3A).]

(1) In the case of a winding up by the court, on application to the Department, the liquidator shall be repaid all necessary disbursements made by him, and expenses properly incurred by him, in the course of his administration to the date of his vacation of office out of any money standing to the credit of the company in the Insolvency Services Account.

(2) In the case of a winding up by the court, the liquidator shall on application to the Department obtain payment instruments to the order of the payee for sums which become payable on account of the company for delivery by the liquidator to the persons to whom the payments are to be made.

(3) . . .

[(3A) In respect of an application made by the liquidator under [paragraph (1) or (2)] above, the Secretary of State, if requested to do so by the liquidator, may, at his discretion,

(a) make the payment which is the subject of the application to the liquidator by electronic transfer; or
(b) as an alternative to the issue of payment instruments, make payment by electronic transfer to the persons to whom the liquidator would otherwise deliver payment instruments.]

(4) Any application under this regulation shall be made by the liquidator on a form obtainable from the Department for the purpose or on a form that is substantially similar.

(5) In the case of a winding up by the court, on the liquidator vacating office, he shall be repaid by any succeeding liquidator out of any funds available for the purpose any necessary disbursements made by him and any expenses properly incurred by him but not repaid before he vacates office.

NOTES

Para (A1): inserted by the Insolvency (Amendment) Regulations 2000, SI 2000/485, reg 3, Schedule, para 4, as from 31 March 2000. Words in square brackets substituted by the Insolvency (Amendment) Regulations 2011, SI 2011/2203, reg 3, Schedule, para 2, as from 1 October 2011.

Para (3): revoked by SI 2011/2203, reg 3, Schedule, para 3, as from 1 October 2011.

Para (3A): inserted by SI 2000/485, reg 3, Schedule, para 5, as from 31 March 2000. Words in square brackets substituted by SI 2011/2203, reg 3, Schedule, para 4, as from 1 October 2011.

DIVIDENDS TO CREDITORS AND RETURNS OF CAPITAL TO CONTRIBUTORIES OF A COMPANY

[10.44]

8 Payment

[(A1) Paragraphs (1) [and (2)] of this regulation are subject to paragraph (3A).]

(1) In the case of a winding up by the court, the liquidator shall pay every dividend by payment instruments which shall be prepared by the Department on the application of the liquidator and transmitted to him for distribution amongst the creditors.

(2) In the case of a winding up by the court, the liquidator shall pay every return of capital to contributories by payment instruments which shall be prepared by the Department on application.

(3) . . .

[(3A) In respect of an application made by the liquidator under [paragraph (1) or (2)] above, the Secretary of State, if requested to do so by the liquidator, may, at his discretion,

(a) as an alternative to the issue of payment instruments, make payment by electronic transfer to the persons to whom the liquidator would otherwise deliver payment instruments; or

(b) make the payment which is the subject of the application to the liquidator by electronic transfer.]

(4) Any application under this regulation for a payment instrument [or payment by electronic transfer] shall be made by the liquidator on a form obtainable from the Department for the purpose or on a form which is substantially similar.

(5) In the case of a winding up by the court, the liquidator shall enter the total amount of every dividend and of every return to contributories that he desires to pay under this regulation in the records to be kept under regulation 10 below in one sum.

(6) On the liquidator vacating office, he shall send to the Department any valid unclaimed or undelivered payment instruments for dividends or returns to contributories after endorsing them with the word "cancelled".

NOTES

Para (A1): inserted by the Insolvency (Amendment) Regulations 2000, SI 2000/485, reg 3, Schedule, para 6, as from 31 March 2000. Words in square brackets substituted by the Insolvency (Amendment) Regulations 2011, SI 2011/2203, reg 3, Schedule, para 5, as from 1 October 2011.

Para (3): revoked by SI 2011/2203, reg 3, Schedule, para 6, as from 1 October 2011.

Para (3A): inserted by SI 2000/485, reg 3, Schedule, para 7, as from 31 March 2000. Words in square brackets substituted by SI 2011/2203, reg 3, Schedule, para 7, as from 1 October 2011.

Para (4): words in square brackets inserted by SI 2000/485, reg 3, Schedule, para 8, as from 31 March 2000.

INVESTMENT OR OTHERWISE HANDLING OF FUNDS IN WINDING UP OF COMPANIES AND PAYMENT OF INTEREST

[10.45]

9

(1) When the cash balance standing to the credit of the company in the account in respect of that company kept by the Secretary of State is in excess of the amount which, in the opinion of the liquidator, is required for the immediate purposes of the winding up and should be invested, he may request the Secretary of State to invest the amount not so required in Government securities, to be placed to the credit of that account for the company's benefit.

(2) When any of the money so invested is, in the opinion of the liquidator, required for the immediate purposes of the winding up, he may request the Secretary of State to raise such sum as may be required by the sale of such of those securities as may be necessary.

(3) In cases where investments have been made at the request of the liquidator in pursuance of paragraph (1) above and additional sums to the amounts so invested, including money received under paragraph (7) below, are paid into the Insolvency Services Account to the credit of the company, a request shall be made to the Secretary of State by the liquidator if it is desired that these additional sums should be invested.

(4) Any request relating to the investment in, or sale of, as the case may be, Treasury Bills made under paragraphs (1), (2) or (3) above shall be made on a form obtainable from the Department or on one that is substantially similar and any request relating to the purchase or sale, as the case may be, of any other type of Government security made under the provisions of those paragraphs shall be made in writing.

(5) Any request made under paragraphs (1), (2) or (3) above shall be sufficient authority to the Secretary of State for the investment or sale as the case may be.

[(6) Subject to paragraphs (6A) and (6B), at any time after 1st April 2004 whenever there are any monies standing to the credit of the company in the Insolvency Services Account the company shall be entitled to interest on those monies at the rate of 4.25 per cent per annum.

(6A) Interest shall cease to accrue pursuant to paragraph (6) from the date of receipt by the Secretary of State of a notice in writing from the liquidator that in the opinion of the liquidator it is necessary or expedient in order to facilitate the conclusion of the winding up that interest should cease to accrue but interest shall start to accrue again pursuant to paragraph (6) where the liquidator gives a further notice in writing to the Secretary of State requesting that interest should start to accrue again.

(6B) The Secretary of State may by notice published in the London Gazette vary the rate of interest prescribed by paragraph (6) and such variation shall have effect from the day after the date of publication of the notice in the London Gazette or such later date as may be specified in the notice.]

(7) All money received in respect of investments and interest earned under this regulation shall be paid into the Insolvency Services Account to the credit of the company.

(8) . . .

NOTES

Paras (6), (6A), (6B): substituted (for the original para (6)) by the Insolvency (Amendment) Regulations 2004, SI 2004/472, reg 2, Schedule, para 2, as from 1 April 2004.

Para (8): revoked by the Insolvency (Amendment) Regulations 2011, SI 2011/2203, reg 3, Schedule, para 8, as from 1 October 2011.

Treasury bills: a reference to a Treasury bill in this regulation includes a reference to uncertificated units of eligible Treasury bills; see the Uncertificated Securities (Amendment) (Eligible Debt Securities) Regulations 2003, SI 2003/1633, reg 15, Sch 2, para 2(h).

RECORDS TO BE MAINTAINED BY LIQUIDATORS AND THE PROVISION OF INFORMATION

[10.46]

10 Financial records

(1) This regulation does not apply in the case of a members' voluntary winding up.

(2) The liquidator shall prepare and keep—

(a) separate financial records in respect of each company; and

(b) such other financial records as are required to explain the receipts and payments entered in the records described in sub-paragraph (a) above or regulation 12(2) below, including an explanation of the source of any receipts and the destination of any payments;

and shall, subject to regulation 12(2) below as to trading accounts, from day to day enter in those records all the receipts and payments . . . made by him.

(3) In the case of a winding up by the court, the liquidator shall obtain and keep bank statements relating to any local bank account in the name of the company.

(4) The liquidator shall submit financial records to the liquidation committee when required for inspection.

(5) In the case of a winding up by the court, if the liquidation committee is not satisfied with the contents of the financial records submitted under paragraph (4) above it may so inform the Secretary of State, giving the reasons for its dissatisfaction, and the Secretary of State may take such action as he thinks fit.

NOTES

Para (2): words omitted revoked by the Insolvency (Amendment) Regulations 2011, SI 2011/2203, reg 3, Schedule, para 9, as from 1 October 2011.

[10.47]

11 Provision of information by liquidator

(1) In the case of a winding up by the court, the liquidator shall, within 14 days of the receipt of a request for a statement of his receipts and payments as liquidator from any creditor, contributory or director of the company, supply free of charge to the person making the request, a statement of his receipts and payments as liquidator during the period of one year ending on the most recent anniversary of his becoming liquidator which preceded the request.

(2) In the case of a voluntary winding up, the liquidator shall, on request from any creditor, contributory or director of the company for a copy of a statement for any period, including future periods, sent to the registrar of companies under section 192, send such copy free of charge to the person making the request and the copy of the statement shall be sent within 14 days of the liquidator sending the statement to the registrar or the receipt of the request whichever is the later.

[10.48]

12 Liquidator carrying on business

(1) This regulation does not apply in the case of a members' voluntary winding up.

(2) Where the liquidator carries on any business of the company, he shall—

(a) keep a separate and distinct account of the trading, including, where appropriate, in the case of a winding up by the court, particulars of all local bank account transactions; and

(b) incorporate in the financial records required to be kept under regulation 10 above the total weekly amounts of the receipts and payments made by him in relation to the account kept under sub-paragraph (a) above.

[10.49]

13 Retention and delivery of records

(1) All records kept by the liquidator under regulations 10 and 12(2) and any such records received by him from a predecessor in that office shall be retained by him for a period of 6 years following—

(a) his vacation of office, or

(b) in the case of the official receiver, his release as liquidator under section 174,

unless he delivers them to another liquidator who succeeds him in office.

(2) Where the liquidator is succeeded in office by another liquidator, the records referred to in paragraph (1) above shall be delivered to that successor forthwith, unless, in the case of a winding up by the court, the winding up is for practical purposes complete and the successor is the official receiver, in which case the records are only to be delivered to the official receiver if the latter so requests.

[10.50]

14 Provision of accounts by liquidator and audit of accounts

(1) The liquidator shall, if required by the Secretary of State at any time, send to the Secretary of State an account in relation to the company of the liquidator's receipts and payments covering such period as the Secretary of State may direct and such account shall, if so required by the Secretary of State, be certified by the liquidator.

(2) Where the liquidator in a winding up by the court vacates office prior to [sending the final account to creditors] under section 146, he shall within 14 days of vacating office send to the Secretary of State an account of his receipts and payments as liquidator for any period not covered by an account previously so sent by him or if no such account has been sent, an account of his receipts and payments in respect of the whole period of his office.

(3) In the case of a winding up by the court, where—

(a) a final general meeting of creditors has been held pursuant to section 146, or

(b) a final general meeting is deemed to have been held by virtue of [rules 7.69 and 7.70],

the liquidator shall send to the Secretary of State, in case (a), within 14 days of the holding of the final general meeting of creditors and, in case (b), within 14 days of his report to the court pursuant to [rules 7.69 and 7.70], an account of his receipts and payments as liquidator which are not covered by any previous account so sent by him, or if no such account has been sent an account of his receipts and payments in respect of the whole period of his office.

(4) In the case of a winding up by the court, where a statement of affairs has been submitted under the Act, any account sent under this regulation shall be accompanied by a summary of that statement of affairs and shall show the amount of any assets realised and explain the reasons for any non-realisation of any assets not realised.

(5) In the case of a winding up by the court, where a statement of affairs has not been submitted under the Act, any account sent under this regulation shall be accompanied by a summary of all known assets and their estimated values and shall show the amounts actually realised and explain the reasons for any non-realisation of any assets not realised.

(6) Any account sent to the Secretary of State shall, if he so requires, be audited, but whether or not the Secretary of State requires the account to be audited, the liquidator shall send to the Secretary of State on demand any documents (including vouchers and bank statements) and any information relating to the account.

NOTES

Para (2): words in square brackets substituted by the Insolvency (England and Wales) and Insolvency (Scotland) (Miscellaneous and Consequential Amendments) Rules 2017, SI 2017/1115, rr 15, 16(1), (2), as from 8 December 2017.

Para (3): substituted by SI 2017/1115, rr 15, 16(1), (3), as from 8 December 2017.

[10.51]

15 Production and inspection of records

(1) The liquidator shall produce on demand to the Secretary of State, and allow him to inspect, any accounts, books and other records kept by him (including any passed to him by a predecessor in office), and this duty to produce and allow inspection shall extend—

(a) to producing and allowing inspection at the premises of the liquidator; and

(b) to producing and allowing inspection of any financial records of the kind described in regulation 10(2)(b) above prepared by the liquidator (or any predecessor in office of his) before 24th October 1994 and kept by the liquidator;

and any such demand may—

(i) require the liquidator to produce any such accounts, books or other records to the Secretary of State, and allow him to inspect them—

(a) at the same time as any account is sent to the Secretary of State under regulation 14 above; or

(b) at any time after such account is sent to the Secretary of State;

whether or not the Secretary of State requires the account to be audited; or

(ii) where it is made for the purpose of ascertaining whether the provisions of these Regulations relating to the handling of money received by the liquidator in the course of carrying out his functions have been or are likely to be complied with, be made at any time, whether or not an account has been sent or should have been sent to the Secretary of State under regulation 14 above and whether or not the Secretary of State has required any account to be audited.

(2) The liquidator shall allow the Secretary of State on demand to remove and take copies of any accounts, books and other records kept by the liquidator (including any passed to him by a predecessor in office), whether or not they are kept at the premises of the liquidator.

[10.52]

16 Disposal of company's books, papers and other records

(1) The liquidator in a winding up by the court, on the authorisation of the official receiver, during his tenure of office or on vacating office, or the official receiver while acting as liquidator, may at any time sell, destroy or otherwise dispose of the books, papers and other records of the company.

(2) In the case of a voluntary winding up, the person who was the last liquidator of a company which has been dissolved may, at any time after the expiration of a period of one year from the date of dissolution, destroy or otherwise dispose of the books, papers and other records of the company.

[10.53]

17 Voluntary liquidator to provide information to Secretary of State

(1) In the case of a voluntary winding up, a liquidator or former liquidator, . . . shall, within 14 days of a request by the Secretary of State, give the Secretary of State particulars of any money in his hands or under his control representing unclaimed or undistributed assets of the company or dividends or other sums due to any person as a member or former member of the company . . .

(2) . . .

NOTES

First words omitted from para (1) revoked by the Insolvency (England and Wales) Rules 2016 (Consequential Amendments and Savings) Rules 2017, SI 2017/369, r 2(2), Sch 2, para 4(1), (4), as from 6 April 2017.

Second words omitted from para (1) revoked, and para (2) revoked, by the Insolvency (Amendment) Regulations 2011, SI 2011/2203, reg 3, Schedule, paras 10, 11, as from 1 October 2011.

[10.54]
[18 Payment of unclaimed dividends or other money

(1) This regulation applies to monies which—
- (a) are held by the former liquidator of a dissolved company, and
- (b) represent either or both of the following—
  - (i) unclaimed dividends due to creditors, or
  - (ii) sums held by the company in trust in respect of dividends or other sums due to any person as a member or former member of the company.

(2) Monies to which this regulation applies—
- (a) may in the case of a voluntary winding up,
- (b) must in the case of a winding up by the court,

be paid into the Insolvency Services Account.

(3) Where the former liquidator pays any sums into the Insolvency Services Account pursuant to paragraph (2), he shall at the same time give notice to the Secretary of State of—
- (a) the name of the company,
- (b) the name and address of the person to whom the dividend or other sum is payable,
- (c) the amount of the dividend, and
- (d) the date on which it was paid.

(4) Where a dividend or other sum is paid to a person by way of a payment instrument, any payment into the Insolvency Services Account in respect of that dividend or sum pursuant to paragraph (2) may not be made earlier than on or after the expiry of 6 months from the date of the payment instrument.]

NOTES

Substituted by the Insolvency (Amendment) Regulations 2008, SI 2008/670, reg 2(1), (3), as from 6 April 2008.

19–31 *(Regs 19–31 (Part 3: Bankruptcy) outside the scope of this work.)*

PART 4 CLAIMING MONEY PAID INTO THE INSOLVENCY SERVICES ACCOUNT

[10.55]
32

(1) Any person claiming to be entitled to any money paid into the Insolvency Services Account may apply to the Secretary of State for payment and shall provide such evidence of his claim as the Secretary of State may require.

(2) Any person dissatisfied with the decision of the Secretary of State in respect of his claim made under this regulation may appeal to the court.

PART 5 REMUNERATION OF OFFICIAL RECEIVER

33, 34 (*Revoked by the Insolvency (Amendment) Regulations 2004, SI 2004/472, reg 2, Schedule, para 4, as from 1 April 2004.*)

[10.56]
[35 Official receiver's general remuneration while acting as interim receiver, provisional liquidator, liquidator or trustee

(1) The official receiver shall be entitled to remuneration calculated in accordance with the applicable hourly rates set out in paragraph (2) for services provided by him (or any of his officers) in relation to—
- (a) a distribution made by him when acting as liquidator or trustee to creditors (including preferential or secured creditors or both such classes of creditor);
- (b) the realisation of assets on behalf of the holder of a fixed or floating charge or both types of those charges;
- (c) the supervision of a special manager;
- (d) the performance by him of any functions where he acts as provisional liquidator; or
- (e) the performance by him of any functions where he acts as an interim receiver.

(2) The applicable hourly rates referred to in paragraph (1) are—
- (a) in relation to the official receiver of the London insolvency district, those set out in Table 2 in Schedule 2; and
- (b) in relation to any other official receiver, those set out in Table 3 in Schedule 2.]

NOTES

Substituted by the Insolvency (Amendment) Regulations 2005, SI 2005/512, regs 3, 4, 7, as from 1 April 2005. Note that this substitution only applies in relation to services provided by the official receiver (or any of his officers) in relation to (a) a company in respect of which a winding-up order is made on or after that date; (b) a bankruptcy where the bankruptcy order is made on or after that date; or (c) his appointment as an interim receiver or provisional liquidator where he is appointed on or after that date.

36 (*Revoked by the Insolvency (Amendment) Regulations 2004, SI 2004/472, reg 2, Schedule, para 4, as from 1 April 2004.*)

[PART 5A INFORMATION ABOUT TIME SPENT ON A CASE TO BE PROVIDED BY INSOLVENCY PRACTITIONER TO CREDITORS ETC

[10.57]
36A

(1) Subject as set out in this regulation, in respect of any case in which he acts, an insolvency practitioner shall on request in writing made by any person mentioned in paragraph (2), supply free of charge to that person a statement of the kind described in paragraph (3).

(2) The persons referred to in paragraph (1) are—

(a) any creditor in the case;
(b) where the case relates to a company, any director or contributory of that company; and
(c) where the case relates to an individual, that individual.

(3) The statement referred to in paragraph (1) shall comprise in relation to the period beginning with the date of the insolvency practitioner's appointment and ending with the relevant date the following details—

(a) the total number of hours spent on the case by the insolvency practitioner and any staff assigned to the case during that period;
(b) for each grade of individual so engaged, the average hourly rate at which any work carried out by individuals in that grade is charged; and
(c) the number of hours spent by each grade of staff during that period.

(4) In relation to paragraph (3) the "relevant date" means the date next before the date of the making of the request on which the insolvency practitioner has completed any period in office which is a multiple of six months or, where the insolvency practitioner has vacated office, the date that he vacated office.

(5) Where an insolvency practitioner has vacated office, an obligation to provide information under this regulation shall only arise in relation to a request that is made within 2 years of the date he vacates office.

(6) Any statement required to be provided to any person under this regulation shall be supplied within 28 days of the date of the receipt of the request by the insolvency practitioner.

(7) In this regulation the expression "insolvency practitioner" shall be construed in accordance with section 388 of the Insolvency Act 1986.]

NOTES

Inserted, together with the preceding heading, by the Insolvency (Amendment) Regulations 2005, SI 2005/512, regs 4, 8, as from 1 April 2005.

PART 6 TRANSITIONAL AND SAVING PROVISIONS

[10.58]
37

The Regulations shall have effect subject to the transitional and saving provisions set out in Schedule 3 to these Regulations.

SCHEDULES

SCHEDULE 1

(Revokes the Insolvency Regulations 1986, SI 1986/1994, and the amending SI 1987/1959, SI 1988/1739, and SI 1991/380.)

SCHEDULE 2

Regulations 33 to 36

[10.59]

. . .

[TABLE 2—LONDON RATES

Grade according to the Insolvency Service grading structure/Status of Official	Total hourly rate £
D2/Official Receiver	75
C2/Deputy or Assistant Official Receiver	63
C1/Senior Examiner	58
L3/Examiner	46
L2/Examiner	42
B2/Administrator	46
L1/Examiner	40
B1/Administrator	46
A2/Administrator	40
A1/Administrator	35]

[TABLE 3—PROVINCIAL RATES

Grade according to the Insolvency Service grading structure /Status of Official	Total hourly rate £
D2/Official Receiver	69
C2/Deputy or Assistant Official Receiver	58
C1/Senior Examiner	52
L3/Examiner	46
L2 Examiner	40

Grade according to the Insolvency Service grading structure /Status of Official	Total hourly rate £
B2/Administrator	43
L1/Examiner	38
B1/Administrator	42
A2/Administrator	36
A1/Administrator	31]

NOTES

Table 1: revoked by the Insolvency (Amendment) Regulations 2004, SI 2004/472, reg 2, Schedule, para 6, as from 1 April 2004.

Tables 2, 3: substituted by the Insolvency (Amendment) Regulations 2009, SI 2009/482, reg 2, as from 6 April 2009.

SCHEDULE 3

Regulation 37

[10.60]

1 Interpretation

In this Schedule the expression "the former Regulations" means the Insolvency Regulations 1986 as amended by the Insolvency (Amendment) Regulations 1987, the Insolvency (Amendment) Regulations 1988 and the Insolvency (Amendment) Regulations 1991.

2 Requests pursuant to regulation 13(1) of the former Regulations

Any request made pursuant to regulation 13(1) of the former Regulations which has not been complied with prior to 24th October 1994 shall be treated, in the case of a company that is being wound up by the court, as a request made pursuant to regulation 11(1) of these Regulations and, in the case of a bankruptcy, as a request made pursuant to regulation 25 of these Regulations and in each case the request shall be treated as if it had been made on 24th October 1994.

3 Things done under the provisions of the former Regulations

So far as anything done under, or for the purposes of, any provision of the former Regulations could have been done under, or for the purposes of, the corresponding provision of these Regulations, it is not invalidated by the revocation of that provision but has effect as if done under, or for the purposes of, the corresponding provision.

4 Time periods

Where any period of time specified in a provision of the former Regulations is current immediately before 24th October 1994, these Regulations have effect as if the corresponding provision of these Regulations had been in force when the period began to run; and (without prejudice to the foregoing) any period of time so specified and current is deemed for the purposes of these Regulations—

(a) to run from the date or event from which it was running immediately before 24th October 1994, and

(b) to expire whenever it would have expired if these Regulations had not been made;

and any rights, obligations, requirements, powers or duties dependent on the beginning, duration or end of such period as above-mentioned shall be under these Regulations as they were or would have been under the former Regulations.

5 References to other provisions

Where in any provision of these Regulations there is reference to another provision of these Regulations, and the first-mentioned provision operates, or is capable of operating, in relation to things done or omitted, or events occurring or not occurring, in the past (including in particular past acts of compliance with the former Regulations), the reference to that other provision is to be read as including a reference to the corresponding provision of the former Regulations.

6 Provisions of Schedule to be without prejudice to the operation of sections 16 and 17 of the Interpretation Act 1978

The provisions of this Schedule are to be without prejudice to the operation of sections 16 and 17 of the Interpretation Act 1978 (saving from, and effect of, repeals) as they are applied by section 23 of that Act.

7 Meaning of "corresponding provision"

(1) A provision in the former Regulations, except regulation 13(1) of those Regulations, is to be regarded as the corresponding provision of a provision in these Regulations notwithstanding any modifications made to the provision as it appears in these Regulations.

(2) Without prejudice to the generality of the term "corresponding provision" the following table shall, subject to sub-paragraph (3) below, have effect in the interpretation of that expression with a provision of these Regulations listed in the left hand column being regarded as the corresponding provision of a provision of the former Regulations listed opposite it in the right hand column and that latter provision being regarded as the corresponding provision of the first-mentioned provision—

TABLE

Provision in these Regulations	Provision in the former Regulations
5(1), 5(3), 5(4)	4
5(2), 5(3), 5(4)	24
6	6
7(1), 7(2), 7(4), 7(5)	5

Provision in these Regulations	Provision in the former Regulations
7(3), 7(4)	25
8(1), 8(2), 8(4), 8(5), 8(6)	15
8(3), 8(4)	25
9	18, 34
10	9, 27
11(2)	31
12	10, 28
13	10A, 28A
15	12A, 30A
16(1)	14
16(2)	32
17	35
18	16, 33
20	4
21	6
22	5
23	15
24	9
26	10
27	10A
29	12A
30	14
31	16A
32	17, 33
33, Table 1 in Schedule 2	19
35, Tables 2 and 3 in Schedule 2	20
36, Table 1 in Schedule 2	22

(3) Where a provision of the former Regulations is expressed in the Table in sub-paragraph (2) above to be the corresponding provision of a provision in these Regulations and the provision in the former Regulations was capable of applying to other proceedings in addition to those to which the provision in these Regulations is capable of applying, the provision in the former Regulations shall be construed as the corresponding provision of the provision in these Regulations only to the extent that they are both capable of applying to the same type of proceedings.

FINANCIAL MARKETS AND INSOLVENCY (SETTLEMENT FINALITY) REGULATIONS 1999

(SI 1999/2979)

NOTES

Made: 2 November 1999.

Authority: European Communities Act 1972, s 2(2) (see the note "Statutory Instruments made under the European Communities Act 1972" preceding paragraph **[4.1]** *ante*).

Commencement: 11 December 1999.

These Regulations are reproduced as amended by: the Banking Consolidation Directive (Consequential Amendments) Regulations 2000, SI 2000/2952; the Civil Jurisdiction and Judgments Order 2001, SI 2001/3929; the Electronic Money (Miscellaneous Amendments) Regulations 2002, SI 2002/765; the Financial Services and Markets Act 2000 (Consequential Amendments) Order 2002, SI 2002/1555; the Enterprise Act 2002 (Insolvency) Order 2003, SI 2003/2096; the Financial Markets and Insolvency (Settlement Finality) (Amendment) Regulations 2006, SI 2006/50; the Capital Requirements Regulations 2006, SI 2006/3221; the Financial Services (EEA State) Regulations 2007, SI 2007/108; the Financial Services and Markets Act 2000 (Markets in Financial Instruments) Regulations 2007, SI 2007/126; the Financial Markets and Insolvency (Settlement Finality) (Amendment) Regulations 2007, SI 2007/832; the Civil Jurisdiction and Judgments Regulations 2007, SI 2007/1655; the Financial Markets and Insolvency (Settlement Finality) (Amendment) Regulations 2009, SI 2009/1972; the Financial Markets and Insolvency (Settlement Finality and Financial Collateral Arrangements) (Amendment) Regulations 2010, SI 2010/2993; the Electronic Money Regulations 2011, SI 2011/99; the Financial Services Act 2012 (Consequential Amendments and Transitional Provisions) Order 2013, SI 2013/472; the Financial Services and Markets Act 2000 (Over the Counter Derivatives, Central Counterparties and Trade Repositories) Regulations 2013, SI 2013/504; the Capital Requirements Regulations 2013, SI 2013/3115; the Civil Jurisdiction and Judgments (Amendment) Regulations 2014, SI 2014/2947; the Bank Recovery and Resolution (No 2) Order 2014, SI 2014/3348; the Financial Markets and Insolvency (Settlement Finality) (Amendment) Regulations 2015, SI 2015/347; the Financial Services and Markets (Disclosure of Information to the European Securities and Markets Authority etc and Other Provisions) Regulations 2016, SI 2016/1095; the Bank of England and Financial Services (Consequential Amendments) Regulations 2017, SI 2017/80; the Financial Services and Markets Act 2000 (Markets in Financial Instruments) Regulations 2017, SI 2017/701; the Central Securities Depositories

Regulations 2017, SI 2017/1064; the Payment Systems and Services and Electronic Money (Miscellaneous Amendments) Regulations 2017, SI 2017/1173; the Financial Markets and Insolvency (Amendment and Transitional Provision) (EU Exit) Regulations 2019, SI 2019/341; the Financial Services and Markets (Insolvency) (Amendment of Miscellaneous Enactments) Regulations 2019, SI 2019/755; the Co-operative and Community Benefit Societies and Credit Unions (Arrangements, Reconstructions and Administration) (Amendment) and Consequential Amendments Order 2020, SI 2020/744; the Corporate Insolvency and Governance Act 2020; the Bank Recovery and Resolution (Amendment) (EU Exit) Regulations 2020, SI 2020/1350.

ARRANGEMENT OF REGULATIONS

PART I GENERAL

PART II DESIGNATED SYSTEMS

PART III TRANSFER ORDERS EFFECTED THROUGH A DESIGNATED SYSTEM AND COLLATERAL SECURITY

SCHEDULES

PART I GENERAL

[10.61]

1 Citation, commencement and extent

(1) These Regulations may be cited as the Financial Markets and Insolvency (Settlement Finality) Regulations 1999 and shall come into force on 11th December 1999.

(2) . . .

NOTES

Para (2): revoked by the Financial Markets and Insolvency (Settlement Finality) (Amendment) Regulations 2006, SI 2006/50, reg 2(1), (2), as from 2 February 2006. Para (2) previously provided that these Regulations do not extend to Northern Ireland.

[10.62]

2 Interpretation

(1) In these Regulations—

["the 2000 Act" means the Financial Services and Markets Act 2000;]

["administration" and "administrator" shall be interpreted in accordance with the modifications made by the enactments mentioned in paragraph (5)]

["business day" shall cover both day and night-time settlements and shall encompass all events happening during the business cycle of a system;]

["central bank" means—

(a) the Bank of England; or

(b) any central bank (or other monetary authority) of a country or territory outside the United Kingdom that is a central bank (or other monetary authority) of an EEA state (including the European Central Bank) or a member of the Bank for International Settlements (including the Bank for International Settlements), as may be notified by the Bank of England to the Treasury from time to time;]

"central counterparty" means a body corporate or unincorporated association interposed between the institutions in a . . . system and which acts as the exclusive counterparty of those institutions with regard to transfer orders;

"charge" means any form of security, including a mortgage and, in Scotland, a heritable security;

"clearing house" means a body corporate or unincorporated association which is responsible for the calculation of the net positions of institutions and any central counterparty or settlement agent in a . . . system;

"collateral security" means any realisable assets provided under a charge or a repurchase or similar agreement, or otherwise (including [credit claims and] money provided under a charge)—

(a) for the purpose of securing rights and obligations potentially arising in connection with a . . . system ("collateral security in connection with participation in a . . . "); or

(b) to a central bank for the purpose of securing rights and obligations in connection with its operations in carrying out its functions as a central bank ("collateral security in connection with the functions of a central bank");

"collateral security charge" means, where collateral security consists of realisable assets (including money) provided under a charge, that charge;

["credit claims" means pecuniary claims arising out of an agreement whereby a credit institution grants credit in the form of a loan;]

["credit institution" means a body corporate or unincorporated association whose head office is in the United Kingdom and whose business is to take deposits or other repayable funds from the public and to grant credits for its own account;]

"creditors' voluntary winding-up resolution" means a resolution for voluntary winding up (within the meaning of the Insolvency Act 1986 [or the Insolvency (Northern Ireland) Order 1989]) where the winding up is a creditors' winding up (within the meaning of that Act [or that Order]);

"default arrangements" means the arrangements put in place by a designated system [or by a system which is an interoperable system in relation to that system] to limit systemic and other types of risk which arise in the event of a participant [or a system operator of an interoperable system] appearing to be unable, or likely to become unable, to meet its obligations in respect of a transfer order, including, for example, any default rules within the meaning of Part VII [or Part V] or any other arrangements for—

(a) netting,

(b) the closing out of open positions, . . .

(c) the application or transfer of collateral security; [or]

[(d) the transfer of assets or positions on the default of a participant in the system;]

"defaulter" means a person in respect of whom action has been taken by a designated system under its default arrangements;

["designated system" means—

(a) a system which is declared by a designation order for the time being in force to be a designated system for the purposes of these Regulations; or

(b) a system which has temporary designation in accordance with Part 4 of the Financial Markets and Insolvency (Amendment and Transitional Provision) (EU Exit) Regulations 2019;]

["designating authority" means—

(a) in the case of a system which is, or the operator of which is, a recognised investment exchange for the purposes of the 2000 Act, the FCA;

(b) in any other case, the Bank of England;]

"designation order" has the meaning given by regulation 4;

["EEA State" has the meaning given by Schedule 1 to the Interpretation Act 1978;]

[. . .]

"guidance", in relation to a designated system, means guidance issued or any recommendation made by it which is intended to have continuing effect and is issued in writing or other legible form to all or any class of its participants or users or persons seeking to participate in the system or to use its facilities and which would, if it were a rule, come within the definition of a rule;

["the FCA" means the Financial Conduct Authority;]

["indirect participant" means an institution, central counterparty, settlement agent, clearing house or system operator—

(a) which has a contractual relationship with a participant in a designated system that enables the indirect participant to effect transfer orders through that system, and

(b) the identity of which is known to the system operator;]

["insolvency proceedings" means any collective measure provided for in the law applicable within the United Kingdom or any part of the United Kingdom, or a third country, either to wind up the participant or to reorganise it, where such measure involves the suspending of, or imposing limitations on, transfers or payments;]

"institution" means—

(a) a credit institution;

[(aa) an electronic money institution within the meaning of regulation 2(1) of the Electronic Money Regulations 2011;]

[(ab) an authorised payment institution or small payment institution as defined in regulation 2(1) of the Payment Services Regulations 2017 . . . ;]

[(b) an investment firm as defined in Article 2.1A of Regulation (EU) No 600/2014 of the European Parliament and of the Council of 15 May 2014 on markets in financial instruments and amending Regulation (EU) No 648/2012;]

(c) a public authority or publicly guaranteed undertaking;

[(d) any undertaking whose head office, registered office or place of residence is outside the United Kingdom and whose functions correspond to those of a credit institution, an electronic money institution, an authorised payment institution, a small payment institution, or an investment firm as defined in sub-paragraphs (a), (aa), (ab), and (b) respectively above; or]

(e) any undertaking which is treated by the designating authority as an institution in accordance with regulation 8(1),

which participates in a . . . system and which is responsible for discharging the financial obligations arising from transfer orders which are effected through the system;

["interoperable system" in relation to a system ("the first system"), means a second system whose system operator has entered into an arrangement with the system operator of the first system that involves cross-system execution of transfer orders;]

"netting" means the conversion into one net claim or obligation of different claims or obligations between participants resulting from the issue and receipt of transfer orders between them, whether on a bilateral or multilateral basis and whether through the interposition of a clearing house, central counterparty or settlement agent or otherwise;

["Part V" means Part V of the Companies (No 2) (Northern Ireland) Order 1990;]

"Part VII" means Part VII of the Companies Act 1989;

"participant" means—

(a) an institution,

[(aa) a system operator;]

(b) a body corporate or unincorporated association which carries out any combination of the functions of a central counterparty, a settlement agent or a clearing house, with respect to a system, or

(c) an indirect participant which is treated as a participant, or is a member of a class of indirect participants which are treated as participants, in accordance with regulation 9;

["the PRA" means the Prudential Regulation Authority;]

"protected trust deed" and "trust deed" shall be construed in accordance with section 73(1) of the Bankruptcy (Scotland) Act 1985 (interpretation);

"relevant office-holder" means—

(a) the official receiver;

(b) any person acting in relation to a company as its liquidator, provisional liquidator, or administrator;

(c) any person acting in relation to an individual (or, in Scotland, any debtor within the meaning of the Bankruptcy (Scotland) Act 1985) as his trustee in bankruptcy or interim receiver of his property or as permanent or interim trustee in the sequestration of his estate or as his trustee under a protected trust deed; . . .

(d) any person acting as administrator of an insolvent estate of a deceased person;

and in sub-paragraph (b), "company" means any company, society, association, partnership or other body which may be wound up under the Insolvency Act 1986 [or the Insolvency (Northern Ireland) Order 1989]; [or]

[(e) any person appointed pursuant to insolvency proceedings of a country or territory outside the United Kingdom;]

"rules", in relation to a designated system, means rules or conditions governing the system with respect to the matters dealt with in these Regulations;

["securities" means (except for the purposes of the definition of "charge") any instruments referred to in Part 1 of Schedule 2 to the Financial Services and Markets Act 2000 (Regulated Activities) Order 2001;]

"settlement account" means an account at a central bank, a settlement agent or a central counterparty used to hold funds or securities (or both) and to settle transactions between participants in a . . . system

"settlement agent" means a body corporate or unincorporated association providing settlement accounts to the institutions and any central counterparty in a . . . system for the settlement of transfer orders within the system and, as the case may be, for extending credit to such institutions and any such central counterparty for settlement purposes;

["system operator" means the entity or entities legally responsible for the operation of a system. A system operator may also act as a settlement agent, central counterparty or clearing house;]

"the Settlement Finality Directive" means Directive 98/26/EC of the European Parliament and of the Council of 19th May 1998 on settlement finality in payment and securities settlement systems[, as last amended by Regulation (EU) No 909/2014 of the European Parliament and of the Council of 23rd July 2014 on improving securities settlement in the European Union and on central securities depositories];

["system" means a formal arrangement—

(a) between two or more participants, without counting a settlement agent, a central counterparty, a clearing house or an indirect participant, with common rules and standardised arrangements for the clearing, whether or not through a central counterparty, or execution of transfer orders between the participants; and

(b) governed by the law of a country or territory chosen by the participants; the participants may, however, only choose the law of a country or territory in which at least one of them has its head office;]

["third country" means a country or territory other than the United Kingdom;]

"transfer order" means—

(a) an instruction by a participant to place at the disposal of a recipient an amount of money by means of a book entry on the accounts of a credit institution, a central bank[, a central counterparty] or a settlement agent, or an instruction which results in the assumption or discharge of a payment obligation as defined by the rules of a designated system ("a payment transfer order"); or

(b) an instruction by a participant to transfer the title to, or interest in, securities by means of a book entry on a register, or otherwise ("a securities transfer order");

["winding-up" means—

(a) winding up by the court or creditors' voluntary winding up within the meaning of the Insolvency Act 1986 or the Insolvency (Northern Ireland) Order 1989 (but does not include members' voluntary winding up within the meaning of that Act or that Order);

(b) sequestration of a Scottish partnership under the Bankruptcy (Scotland) Act 1985;

(c) . . .

[and shall be interpreted in accordance with the modifications made by the enactments mentioned in paragraph (5); and "liquidator" shall be construed accordingly.]

(2) In these Regulations—

[(za) references to the Bank of England do not include the Bank acting in its capacity as the Prudential Regulation Authority;]

[(a) references to the law of insolvency—

(i) include references to every provision made by or under the Bankruptcy (Scotland) Act 1985, Part 10 of the Building Societies Act 1986, the Insolvency Act 1986, the Insolvency (Northern Ireland) Order 1989 and in relation to a building society references to insolvency law or to any provision of the Insolvency Act 1986 or the Insolvency (Northern Ireland) Order 1989 are to that law or provision as modified by the Building Societies Act 1986;

(ii) shall also be interpreted in accordance with the modifications made by the enactments mentioned in paragraph (5);]

(b) in relation to Scotland, references to—

(i) sequestration include references to the administration by a judicial factor of the insolvent estate of a deceased person,

(ii) an interim or permanent trustee include references to a judicial factor on the insolvent estate of a deceased person, and

(iii) "set off" include compensation.

[(2A) For the purposes of these regulations, references to insolvency proceedings do not include crisis prevention measures or crisis management measures taken in relation to an undertaking . . . unless—

(a) express provision is made in [the rules of the system in which the undertaking is a participant] that crisis prevention measures or crisis management measures taken in relation to the undertaking are to be treated as insolvency proceedings; and

(b) the substantive obligations provided for in the [rules] containing that provision (including payment and delivery obligations and provision of collateral) are no longer being performed.

(2B) For the purposes of paragraph (2A)—

(a) "crisis prevention measure" and "crisis management measure" have the meaning given in section 48Z of the Banking Act 2009; and

(b) . . .]

(3) . . .

(4) References in these Regulations to things done, or required to be done, by or in relation to a designated system shall, in the case of a designated system which is neither a body corporate nor an unincorporated association, be treated as references to things done, or required to be done, by or in relation to the operator of that system.

[(5) The enactments referred to in the definitions of "administration", "administrator", "liquidator" and "winding up" in paragraph (1), and in paragraph (2)(a)(ii), are—

(a) article 3 of, and the Schedule to, the Banking Act 2009 (Parts 2 and 3 Consequential Amendments) Order 2009;

(b) article 18 of, and paragraphs (1)(a), (2) and (3) of Schedule 2 to, the Building Societies (Insolvency and Special Administration) Order 2009;

(c) regulation 27 of, and Schedule 6 to, the Investment Bank Special Administration Regulations 2011;

[(d) section 121 of, and Schedule 6 to, the Financial Services (Banking Reform) Act 2013].]

[(6) For the purposes of these Regulations—

(a) a reference to a system governed by the law of the United Kingdom is a reference to a system of which the governing law is the law of England and Wales, Northern Ireland, or Scotland;

(b) a reference to a system being designated in Gibraltar means designated under a Gibraltar law corresponding to these Regulations;

(c) a participant is regarded as established in the United Kingdom if its head office, registered office or place of residence is in the United Kingdom or if it has a branch in the United Kingdom (within the meaning of section 1046(3) of the Companies Act 2006).

(7) For the purposes of sub-paragraph (b) of the definition of "central bank", the designating authority must publish on its website a list of central banks.]

NOTES

Para (1) is amended as follows:

Definition "the 2000 Act" substituted (for the original definition "the 1986 Act") by the Financial Services and Markets Act 2000 (Consequential Amendments) Order 2002, SI 2002/1555, art 39(1), (2)(a), as from 3 July 2002.

Definitions "administration" and "administrator" inserted by the Financial Services and Markets Act 2000 (Over the Counter Derivatives, Central Counterparties and Trade Repositories) Regulations 2013, SI 2013/504, reg 32(1), (2)(a)(i), as from 1 April 2013.

Definitions "business day", "credit claims", "interoperable system", and "system operator" inserted, and words omitted from the definitions "central counterparty", "clearing house", "settlement account", and "settlement agent" revoked, by the Financial Markets and Insolvency (Settlement Finality and Financial Collateral Arrangements) (Amendment) Regulations 2010, SI 2010/2993, reg 2(1), (2)(a)–(c), (k), (l), as from 6 April 2011.

Definitions "central bank", "credit institution", "designated system", "securities" substituted by the Financial Markets and Insolvency (Amendment and Transitional Provision) (EU Exit) Regulations 2019, SI 2019/341, regs 4, 5(1), (2)(a)–(c), (f), as from IP completion day (as defined in the European Union (Withdrawal Agreement) Act 2020, s 39).

In the definition "collateral security", words in square brackets inserted, and words omitted revoked, by SI 2010/2993, reg 2(1), (2)(d), as from 6 April 2011.

Words in square brackets in the definition "creditors' voluntary winding up resolution" inserted, and definition "Part V" inserted, by SI 2006/50, reg 2(1), (3)(a), (c), as from 2 February 2006.

In the definition "default arrangements" words "or Part V" in square brackets inserted by the Financial Markets and Insolvency (Settlement Finality) (Amendment) Regulations 2006, SI 2006/50, reg 2(1), (3)(b), as from 2 February 2006. Word omitted from para (b) revoked, and para (d) (and the word preceding it) added, by SI 2013/504, reg 32(1), (2)(a)(ii), as from 1 April 2013. Other words in square brackets inserted by SI 2010/2993, reg 2(1), (2)(f), as from 6 April 2011.

Definition "designating authority" substituted, and definitions "the FCA" and "the PRA" inserted, by the Financial Services Act 2012 (Consequential Amendments and Transitional Provisions) Order 2013, SI 2013/472, art 3, Sch 2, para 27(a), as from 1 April 2013.

Definition "EEA State" substituted by the Financial Services (EEA State) Regulations 2007, SI 2007/108, reg 5, as from 13 February 2007.

Definition "ESMA" (omitted) originally inserted by the Financial Services and Markets (Disclosure of Information to the European Securities and Markets Authority etc and Other Provisions) Regulations 2016, SI 2016/1095, reg 2(1), (2), as from 8 December 2016; and subsequently revoked by SI 2019/341, regs 4, 5(1), (2)(d), as from IP completion day (as defined in the European Union (Withdrawal Agreement) Act 2020, s 39).

Definitions "indirect participant" and "winding-up" substituted by SI 2010/2993, reg 2(1), (2)(g), (o), as from 6 April 2011.

Definition "insolvency proceedings" inserted by SI 2019/341, regs 4, 5(1), (2)(g), as from IP completion day (as defined in the European Union (Withdrawal Agreement) Act 2020, s 39).

The definition "institution" has been amended as follows:

Sub-para (aa) was inserted by SI 2010/2993, reg 2(1), (2)(h)(i), as from 6 April 2011; and subsequently substituted by SI 2019/341, regs 4, 5(1), (2)(e)(i), as from IP completion day (as defined in the European Union (Withdrawal Agreement) Act 2020, s 39).

Sub-para (ab) was inserted by the Payment Systems and Services and Electronic Money (Miscellaneous Amendments) Regulations 2017, SI 2017/1173, reg 2, as from 13 January 2018. The words omitted were revoked by SI 2019/341, regs 4, 5(1), (2)(e)(ii), as from IP completion day (as defined in the European Union (Withdrawal Agreement) Act 2020, s 39).

Sub-paras (b), (d) were substituted by SI 2019/341, regs 4, 5(1), (2)(e)(iii), (iv), as from IP completion day (as defined in the European Union (Withdrawal Agreement) Act 2020, s 39).

Word omitted from the final sentence revoked by SI 2010/2993, reg 2(1), (2)(h)(ii), as from 6 April 2011.

Sub-para (aa) of the definition "participant" was inserted by SI 2010/2993, reg 2(1), (2)(i), as from 6 April 2011.

Words "or the Insolvency (Northern Ireland) Order 1989" in square brackets in the definition "relevant office-holder" inserted by SI 2006/50, reg 2(1), (3)(d), as from 2 February 2006. Other words in square brackets inserted, and word omitted revoked, by SI 2010/2993, reg 2(1), (2)(j), as from 6 April 2011.

Words in square brackets in the definition "the Settlement Finality Directive" substituted by the Financial Markets and Insolvency (Settlement Finality) (Amendment) Regulations 2015, SI 2015/347, reg 2(1), (2), as from 18 March 2015.

Definition "system" inserted by SI 2019/341, regs 4, 5(1), (2)(g), as from IP completion day (as defined in the European Union (Withdrawal Agreement) Act 2020, s 39).

Definition "third country" inserted by SI 2019/341, regs 4, 5(1), (2)(g), as from IP completion day (as defined in the European Union (Withdrawal Agreement) Act 2020, s 39).

Words in square brackets in the definition "transfer order" inserted by SI 2010/2993, reg 2(1), (2)(n), as from 6 April 2011.

Words omitted from the definition "winding-up" revoked, and words in square brackets inserted, by SI 2013/504, reg 32(1), (2)(a)(iii), as from 1 April 2013.

Para (2): sub-para (za) inserted by the Bank of England and Financial Services (Consequential Amendments) Regulations 2017, SI 2017/80, reg 2, Schedule, Pt 2, para 23, as from 1 March 2017. Sub-para (a) substituted by SI 2013/504, reg 32(1), (2)(b), as from 1 April 2013.

Paras (2A), (2B): inserted by the Bank Recovery and Resolution (No 2) Order 2014, SI 2014/3348, art 226, Sch 3, Pt 3, para 7, as from 10 January 2015. The words omitted from para (2A) were revoked, the words in square brackets in para (2A) were substituted, and sub-para (2B)(b) was revoked, by SI 2019/341, regs 4, 5(1), (3), (4), as from IP completion day (as defined in the European Union (Withdrawal Agreement) Act 2020, s 39). Note that SI 2019/341, reg 5(3) was amended by the Financial Services (Miscellaneous) (Amendment) (EU Exit) Regulations 2019, SI 2019/710, reg 20 (this amendment came into force immediately before IP completion day and the effect of it has been incorporated).

Para (3): revoked by SI 2019/341, regs 4, 5(1), (5), as from IP completion day (as defined in the European Union (Withdrawal Agreement) Act 2020, s 39).

Para (5): added by SI 2013/504, reg 32(1), (2)(c), as from 1 April 2013. Sub-para (d) added by SI 2019/341, regs 4, 5(1), (6), as from IP completion day (as defined in the European Union (Withdrawal Agreement) Act 2020, s 39).

Paras (6), (7): added by SI 2019/341, regs 4, 5(1), (7), (8), as from IP completion day (as defined in the European Union (Withdrawal Agreement) Act 2020, s 39).

PART II DESIGNATED SYSTEMS

NOTES

Transitional provisions in connection with exiting the European Union: see the Financial Markets and Insolvency (Amendment and Transitional Provision) (EU Exit) Regulations 2019, SI 2019/341 at **[12.90]** et seq. Part 4 of those Regulations establishes a temporary designation regime. It applies to a system ("S") and a body corporate or unincorporated body of persons ("P") that is the operator of S, where: (a) immediately before IP completion day, S is specified as a system and P is specified as the system operator in relation to S, by an EEA state (other than the UK), to be included within the scope of the Settlement Finality Directive in accordance with Article 10 of that Directive; and (b) P intends S to have temporary designation and has so notified the designating authority in accordance with the Regulations. Part 5 of the 2019 Regulations further provides that nothing in those Regulations affects any designation order, or any other decision of a designating authority, made under these Regulations in relation to a designated system, which order or decision is in force immediately before IP completion day.

Other transitional provisions: (i) nothing in the Financial Markets and Insolvency (Settlement Finality and Financial Collateral Arrangements) (Amendment) Regulations 2010, SI 2010/2993 (which amend these Regulations) affects any designation order in force under these Regulations in relation to a designated system, and no system operator shall be required to apply for an amended designation order in consequence only of the 2010 Regulations (see reg 3 of the 2010 Regulations); (ii) nothing in the Financial Services and Markets Act 2000 (Over the Counter Derivatives, Central Counterparties and Trade Repositories) Regulations 2013, SI 2013/504 (which amend these Regulations) affects any designation order in force under these Regulations in relation to a designated system, and no system operator shall be required to apply for an amended designation order in consequence only of the 2013 Regulations (see reg 55 of the 2013 Regulations); (iii) nothing in the Central Securities Depositories Regulations 2017, SI 2017/1064 (which amend these Regulations) affects any designation order under these Regulations in relation to a designated system in force at 28 November 2017, and no system operator shall be required to apply for a new or amended designation order in consequence only of the 2017 Regulations (see reg 9 of the 2017 Regulations).

[10.63]

3 Application for designation

(1) Any body corporate or unincorporated association may apply to the designating authority for an order declaring it, or any system of which it is the operator, to be a designated system for the purposes of these Regulations.

(2) Any such application—

(a) shall be made in such manner as the designating authority may direct; and

(b) shall be accompanied by such information as the designating authority may reasonably require for the purpose of determining the application.

(3) At any time after receiving an application and before determining it, the designating authority may require the applicant to furnish additional information.

(4) The directions and requirements given or imposed under paragraphs (2) and (3) may differ as between different applications.

(5) Any information to be furnished to the designating authority under this regulation shall be in such form or verified in such manner as it may specify.

(6) Every application shall be accompanied by copies of the rules of the system to which the application relates and any guidance relating to that system.

[10.64]

4 Grant and refusal of designation

(1) Where—

(a) an application has been duly made under regulation 3;

(b) the applicant has paid any fee charged by virtue of regulation 5(1); and

(c) the designating authority is satisfied that the requirements of the Schedule are satisfied with respect to the system to which the application relates;

the designating authority may make an order (a "designation order") declaring the system to be a designated system [and identifying the system operator of that system] for the purposes of these Regulations.

(2) In determining whether to make a designation order, the designating authority shall have regard to systemic risks.

(3) Where an application has been made to the [FCA] under regulation 3 in relation to a system through which both securities transfer orders and payment transfer orders are effected, the Authority shall consult the Bank of England before deciding whether to make a designation order.

(4) A designation order shall state the date on which it takes effect.

(5) Where the designating authority refuses an application for a designation order it shall give the applicant a written notice to that effect stating the reasons for the refusal.

[(6) . . .]

NOTES

Para (1): words in square brackets inserted by the Financial Markets and Insolvency (Settlement Finality and Financial Collateral Arrangements) (Amendment) Regulations 2010, SI 2010/2993, reg 2(1), (3), as from 6 April 2011.

Para (3): word in square brackets substituted by the Financial Services Act 2012 (Consequential Amendments and Transitional Provisions) Order 2013, SI 2013/472, art 3, Sch 2, para 27(b), as from 1 April 2013.

Para (6): originally added by the Financial Markets and Insolvency (Settlement Finality) (Amendment) Regulations 2015, SI 2015/347, reg 2(1), (3), as from 18 March 2015. Subsequently revoked by the Financial Markets and Insolvency (Amendment and Transitional Provision) (EU Exit) Regulations 2019, SI 2019/341, regs 4, 6(1), as from IP completion day (as defined in the European Union (Withdrawal Agreement) Act 2020, s 39).

[10.65]

5 Fees

(1) The designating authority may charge a fee to an applicant for a designation order.

(2) The designating authority may charge [the system operator of] a designated system a periodical fee.

(3) Fees chargeable by the designating authority under this regulation shall not exceed an amount which reasonably represents the amount of costs incurred or likely to be incurred—

(a) in the case of a fee charged to an applicant for a designation order, in determining whether the designation order should be made; and

(b) in the case of a periodical fee, in satisfying itself that the designated [system and its system operator continue] to meet the requirements of the Schedule and [are complying] with any obligations to which [they are subject] by virtue of these Regulations.

NOTES

Para (2): words in square brackets inserted by the Financial Markets and Insolvency (Settlement Finality and Financial Collateral Arrangements) (Amendment) Regulations 2010, SI 2010/2993, reg 2(1), (4)(a), as from 6 April 2011.

Para (3): words in square brackets substituted by SI 2010/2993, reg 2(1), (4)(b), as from 6 April 2011.

[10.66]

6 Certain bodies deemed to satisfy requirements for designation

[(1) Subject to paragraph (2), a recognised body . . . , a third country central counterparty . . . and a third country CSD shall be deemed to satisfy the requirements in paragraphs 2 and 3 of the Schedule.]

(2) Paragraph (1) does not apply to overseas investment exchanges or overseas clearing houses within the meaning of [the 2000 Act].

[(3) . . . "third country central counterparty" . . . and "third country CSD" have the meanings given by section 285 of the 2000 Act.

(4) "recognised body" has the meaning given by section 313 of the 2000 Act.]

NOTES

Para (1): substituted by the Central Securities Depositories Regulations 2017, SI 2017/1064, reg 10, Schedule, para 22(1), (2)(a), as from 28 November 2017. Words omitted revoked by the Financial Markets and Insolvency (Amendment and Transitional Provision) (EU Exit) Regulations 2019, SI 2019/341, regs 4, 6(2), as from IP completion day (as defined in the European Union (Withdrawal Agreement) Act 2020, s 39).

Para (2): words in square brackets substituted by the Financial Markets and Insolvency (Settlement Finality) (Amendment) Regulations 2009, SI 2009/1972, regs 2, 3, as from 1 October 2009.

Paras (3), (4): substituted (for para (3) as originally added by SI 2013/504, reg 32) by SI 2017/1064, reg 10, Schedule, para 22(1), (2)(b), as from 28 November 2017. Words omitted from para (3) revoked by SI 2019/341, regs 4, 6(2), as from IP completion day (as defined in the European Union (Withdrawal Agreement) Act 2020, s 39).

[10.67]

7 Revocation of designation

(1) A designation order may be revoked by a further order made by the designating authority if at any time it appears to the designating authority—

- (a) that any requirement of the Schedule is not satisfied in the case of the system to which the designation order relates; or
- (b) that the system [or the system operator of that system] has failed to comply with any obligation to which [they are subject] by virtue of these Regulations.

(2) [[Subsections (1) to (6)] of section 298 of the 2000 Act] shall apply in relation to the revocation of a designation order under paragraph (1) as they apply in relation to the revocation of a recognition order under [section 297(2) of that Act]; and in those subsections as they so apply—

- [(a) any reference to a recognised body shall be taken to be a reference to a designated system;
- (b) any reference to members of a recognised body shall be taken to be a reference to participants in a designated system;
- [(ba) any reference to the appropriate regulator shall be taken to be a reference to the designating authority;]
- (c) . . .
- [(d) subsection (4) has effect as if the period for making representations specified in the notice must be at least three months.]]

[(3) An order revoking a designation order—

- (a) shall state the date on which it takes effect, being no earlier than three months after the day on which the revocation order is made; and
- (b) may contain such transitional provisions as the designating authority thinks necessary or expedient.

(4) A designation order may be revoked at the request or with the consent of the [system operator of the] designated system, and any such revocation shall not be subject to the restriction imposed by paragraph (3)(a), or to the requirements imposed by subsections (1) to (6) of section 298 of the 2000 Act.]

NOTES

Para (1): words in first pair of square brackets inserted, and words in second pair of square brackets substituted, by the Financial Markets and Insolvency (Settlement Finality and Financial Collateral Arrangements) (Amendment) Regulations 2010, SI 2010/2993, reg 2(1), (5), as from 6 April 2011.

Para (2) is amended as follows:

Words "Subsections (1) to (6)" in square brackets substituted, sub-para (ba) inserted, and sub-para (d) substituted, by the Central Securities Depositories Regulations 2017, SI 2017/1064, reg 10, Schedule, para 22(1), (3), as from 28 November 2017.

Sub-para (c) revoked by the Financial Services Act 2012 (Consequential Amendments and Transitional Provisions) Order 2013, SI 2013/472, art 3, Sch 2, para 27(c), as from 1 April 2013.

Other words in square brackets substituted by the Financial Services and Markets Act 2000 (Consequential Amendments) Order 2002, SI 2002/1555, art 39(1), (4), as from 3 July 2002.

Paras (3), (4): added by SI 2002/1555, art 39(1), (5), as from 3 July 2002. Words in square brackets in para (4) inserted by SI 2010/2993, reg 2(1), (6), as from 6 April 2011.

[10.68]

8 Undertakings treated as institutions

(1) A designating authority may treat as an institution any undertaking which participates in a designated system and which is responsible for discharging financial obligations arising from transfer orders effected through that system, provided that—

- (a) the designating authority considers such treatment to be required on grounds of systemic risk, and

(b) the designated system is one in which at least three institutions (other than any undertaking treated as an institution by virtue of this paragraph) participate . . .

(2) Where a designating authority decides to treat an undertaking as an institution in accordance with paragraph (1), it shall give written notice of that decision to the designated system in which the undertaking is to be treated as a participant [and to the system operator of that system].

NOTES

Para (1): words omitted revoked by the Financial Markets and Insolvency (Amendment and Transitional Provision) (EU Exit) Regulations 2019, SI 2019/341, regs 4, 6(3), as from IP completion day (as defined in the European Union (Withdrawal Agreement) Act 2020, s 39).

Para (2): words in square brackets added by the Financial Markets and Insolvency (Settlement Finality and Financial Collateral Arrangements) (Amendment) Regulations 2010, SI 2010/2993, reg 2(1), (7), as from 6 April 2011.

[10.69]

9 Indirect participants treated as participants

(1) A designating authority may treat—

(a) an indirect participant as a participant in a designated system, or

(b) a class of indirect participants as participants in a designated system,

where it considers this to be required on grounds of systemic risk, and shall give written notice of any decision to that effect to the designated system [and to the system operator of that system].

[(2) Where a designating authority, in accordance with paragraph (1), treats an indirect participant as a participant in a designated system, the liability of the participant through which that indirect participant passes transfer orders to the designated system is not affected.]

NOTES

Words in square brackets in para (1) added, and para (2) added, by the Financial Markets and Insolvency (Settlement Finality and Financial Collateral Arrangements) (Amendment) Regulations 2010, SI 2010/2993, reg 2(1), (8), as from 6 April 2011.

[10.70]

10 Provision of information by designated systems

[(1) The system operator of a designated system [governed by the law of the United Kingdom] shall, when that system is declared to be a designated system, provide to the designating authority in writing a list of the participants (including the indirect participants) in the designated system and shall give written notice to the designating authority of any amendment to the list within seven days of such amendment.]

[(1A) The system operator of a designated system governed by the law of a third country must, when that system is declared to be a designated system—

(a) provide to the designating authority in writing a list of any participants in the designated system that are established in the United Kingdom (including any indirect participants in the designated system that are established in the United Kingdom); and

(b) give written notice to the designating authority of any amendment to that list within 7 days of such amendment.]

(2) The designating authority may, in writing, require [the system operator of a designated system] to furnish to it such other information relating to that designated system as it reasonably requires for the exercise of its functions under these Regulations, within such time, in such form, at such intervals and verified in such manner as the designating authority may specify.

(3) When [the system operator of a designated system] amends, revokes or adds to its rules or its guidance, it shall within fourteen days give written notice to the designating authority of the amendment, revocation or addition.

(4) [The system operator of a designated system] [governed by the law of the United Kingdom] shall give the designating authority at least [three months'] written notice of any proposal to amend, revoke or add to its default arrangements.

[(4A) The designating authority may, if it considers it appropriate, agree a shorter period of notice.]

[(4B) When the system operator of a designated system governed by the law of a third country amends, revokes or adds to its default arrangements, it must within 7 days give written notice to the designating authority of the amendment, revocation or addition.]

(5) Nothing in this regulation shall require [the system operator of a designated system] [governed by the law of the United Kingdom] to give any notice or furnish any information to [the FCA or the Bank of England where the notice or information has already been given or furnished to the FCA or the Bank of England (as the case may be)] pursuant to any requirement imposed by or under [section 293 of the 2000 Act] (notification requirements) or any other enactment.

NOTES

Para (1) substituted, words in square brackets in paras (2), (3) substituted, words in first pair of square brackets in para (4) substituted, and words in first and fourth pairs of square brackets in para (5) substituted, by the Financial Markets and Insolvency (Settlement Finality and Financial Collateral Arrangements) (Amendment) Regulations 2010, SI 2010/2993, reg 2(1), (9), as from 6 April 2011.

The words in square brackets in para (1), the whole of paras (1A) and (4B), and the words in the second pair of square brackets in paras (4) and (5), were inserted by the Financial Markets and Insolvency (Amendment and Transitional Provision) (EU Exit) Regulations 2019, SI 2019/341, regs 4, 6(4), as from IP completion day (as defined in the European Union (Withdrawal Agreement) Act 2020, s 39).

Words in third pair of square brackets in para (4) substituted, and para (4A) inserted, by the Financial Services and Markets Act 2000 (Over the Counter Derivatives, Central Counterparties and Trade Repositories) Regulations 2013, SI 2013/504, reg 32(1), (4), as from 1 April 2013.

Words in third pair of square brackets in para (5) substituted by the Financial Services Act 2012 (Consequential Amendments and Transitional Provisions) Order 2013, SI 2013/472, art 3, Sch 2, para 27(d), as from 1 April 2013.

[10.71]

11 Exemption from liability in damages

(1) Neither the designating authority nor any person who is, or is acting as, a member, officer or member of staff of the designating authority shall be liable in damages for anything done or omitted in the discharge, or purported discharge, of the designating authority's functions under these Regulations.

(2) Paragraph (1) does not apply—

(a) if the act or omission is shown to have been in bad faith; or

(b) so as to prevent an award of damages made in respect of an act or omission on the ground that the act or omission was unlawful as a result of section 6(1) of the Human Rights Act 1998 (acts of public authorities).

[10.72]

12 Publication of information and advice

A designating authority may publish information or give advice, or arrange for the publication of information or the giving of advice, in such form and manner as it considers appropriate with respect to any matter dealt with in these Regulations.

PART III TRANSFER ORDERS EFFECTED THROUGH A DESIGNATED SYSTEM AND COLLATERAL SECURITY

[10.73]

13 Modifications of the law of insolvency

(1) The general law of insolvency has effect in relation to—

(a) transfer orders effected through a designated system and action taken under the rules of a designated system with respect to such orders; and

(b) collateral security,

subject to the provisions of this Part.

(2) Those provisions apply in relation to—

[(a) insolvency proceedings in respect of a participant in a designated system, or of a participant in a system which is an interoperable system in relation to that designated system;]

[(b) insolvency proceedings in respect of a provider of collateral security, in so far as the proceedings affect the rights of the collateral-taker; and]

[(c) insolvency proceedings in respect of a system operator of a designated system or of a system which is an interoperable system in relation to that designated system;]

but not in relation to any other insolvency proceedings, notwithstanding that rights or liabilities arising from transfer orders or collateral security fall to be dealt with in the proceedings.

(3) Subject to regulation 21, nothing in this Part shall have the effect of disapplying Part VII [or Part V].

[(4) References in this Part to "insolvency proceedings" [include winding up and administration.]

(a), (b) . . .]

NOTES

Para (2): sub-para (a) substituted, and sub-para (c) added, by the Financial Markets and Insolvency (Settlement Finality and Financial Collateral Arrangements) (Amendment) Regulations 2010, SI 2010/2993, reg 2(1), (10)(a), (c), as from 6 April 2011. Sub-para (b) substituted by the Financial Markets and Insolvency (Amendment and Transitional Provision) (EU Exit) Regulations 2019, SI 2019/341, regs 4, 7, as from IP completion day (as defined in the European Union (Withdrawal Agreement) Act 2020, s 39).

Para (3): words in square brackets added by the Financial Markets and Insolvency (Settlement Finality) (Amendment) Regulations 2006, SI 2006/50, reg 2(1), (5), as from 2 February 2006.

Para (4): added by SI 2010/2993, reg 2(1), (10)(d), as from 6 April 2011. Words in square brackets substituted, and sub-paras (a), (b) revoked, by the Financial Services and Markets Act 2000 (Over the Counter Derivatives, Central Counterparties and Trade Repositories) Regulations 2013, SI 2013/504, reg 32(1), (5), as from 1 April 2013.

[10.74]

14 Proceedings of designated system take precedence over insolvency proceedings

(1) None of the following shall be regarded as to any extent invalid at law on the ground of inconsistency with the law relating to the distribution of the assets of a person on bankruptcy, winding up, [administration,] sequestration or under a protected trust deed, or in the administration of an insolvent estate [or with the law relating to other insolvency proceedings of a country or territory outside the United Kingdom]—

(a) a transfer order;

(b) the default arrangements of a designated system;

(c) the rules of a designated system as to the settlement of transfer orders not dealt with under its default arrangements;

(d) a contract for the purpose of realising collateral security in connection with participation in a designated system [or in a system which is an interoperable system in relation to that designated system] otherwise than pursuant to its default arrangements; or

(e) a contract for the purpose of realising collateral security in connection with the functions of a central bank.

(2) The powers of a relevant office-holder in his capacity as such, and the powers of the court under the Insolvency Act 1986[, the Insolvency (Northern Ireland) Order 1989] or the Bankruptcy (Scotland) Act 1985, shall not be exercised in such a way as to prevent or interfere with—

(a) the settlement in accordance with the rules of a designated system of a transfer order not dealt with under its default arrangements;

(b) any action taken under [the default arrangements of a designated system];

(c) any action taken to realise collateral security in connection with participation in a designated system [or in a system which is an interoperable system in relation to that designated system] otherwise than pursuant to its default arrangements; or

(d) any action taken to realise collateral security in connection with the functions of a central bank.

. . .

(3) Nothing in the following provisions of this Part shall be construed as affecting the generality of the above provisions.

(4) A debt or other liability arising out of a transfer order which is the subject of action taken under default arrangements may not be proved in a winding up[, bankruptcy, or administration], or in Scotland claimed in a winding up, sequestration or under a protected trust deed, until the completion of the action taken under default arrangements.

A debt or other liability which by virtue of this paragraph may not be proved or claimed shall not be taken into account for the purposes of any set-off until the completion of the action taken under default arrangements.

(5) Paragraph (1) has the effect that the following provisions (which relate to preferential debts and the payment of expenses etc) apply subject to paragraph (6), namely—

(a) in the case of collateral security provided by a company (within the meaning of section [section 1 of the Companies Act 2006) or by a building society (within the meaning of section 119 of the Building Societies Act 1986)])—

[(i) sections [174A] 175, 176ZA and 176A of, and [paragraphs 64A and 65(2)] of Schedule B1 to, the Insolvency Act 1986 or Articles [148A,] 149, 150ZA, and 150A of, and [paragraphs 65A and 66(2)] of Schedule B1 to, the Insolvency (Northern Ireland) Order 1989;

(ii) [rules 6.42(2)(b) and 7.38(3) of the Insolvency (England and Wales) Rules 2016], Rules 4.033(3) and 4.228(2)(b) of the Insolvency Rules (Northern Ireland) 1991 and [rule 5.9(4) of the Insolvency (Scotland) (Receivership and Winding up) Rules 2018];]

[(iii) section 40 (or in Scotland, section 59 and 60(1)(e)) of the Insolvency Act 1986, paragraph 99(3) of Schedule B1 to that Act and section 19(4) of that Act as that section has effect by virtue of section 249(1) of the Enterprise Act 2002;

[(iv) paragraph 100(3) of Schedule B1 to the Insolvency (Northern Ireland) Order 1989, Article 31(4) of that Order, as it has effect by virtue of Article 4(1) of the Insolvency (Northern Ireland) Order 2005, and Article 50 of the Insolvency (Northern Ireland) Order 1989; and]

(v) section 754 of the Companies Act 2006 [(including that section as applied or modified by any enactment made under the Banking Act 2009)]; and]

(b) in the case of collateral security provided by an individual, section 328(1) and (2) of the Insolvency Act 1986[or, in Northern Ireland, Article 300(1) and (2) of the Insolvency (Northern Ireland) Order 1989] or, in Scotland, in the case of collateral security provided by an individual or a partnership, section 51 of the Bankruptcy (Scotland) Act 1985 and any like provision or rule of law affecting a protected trust deed.

(6) The claim of a participant[, system operator] or central bank to collateral security shall be paid in priority to—

(a) the expenses of the winding up mentioned in sections 115 and 156 of the Insolvency Act 1986 [or Articles 100 and 134 of the Insolvency (Northern Ireland) Order 1989], the expenses of the bankruptcy within the meaning of that Act [or that Order] or, as the case may be, the remuneration and expenses of the administrator mentioned in [paragraph 99(3) of Schedule B1 to that Act] [and in section 19(4) of that Act as that section has effect by virtue of section 249(1) of the Enterprise Act 2002] [or in paragraph 100(3) to Schedule B1 to that Order] [and Article 31(4) of that Order, as that Article has effect by virtue of Article 4(1) of the Insolvency (Northern Ireland) Order 2005], and

(b) the preferential debts of the company or the individual (as the case may be) within the meaning given by section 386 of that Act [or Article 346 of that Order], [and

(c) the debts or liabilities arising or incurred under contracts mentioned in—

(i) paragraph 99(4) of Schedule B1 to the Insolvency Act 1986 and section 19(5) of that Act, as that section has effect by virtue of section 249(1) of the Enterprise Act 2002, or

(ii) paragraph 100(4) of Schedule B1 to, the Insolvency (Northern Ireland) Order 1989 and Article 31(5) of that Order as that article has effect by virtue of Article 4(1) of the Insolvency (Northern Ireland) Order 2005,]

unless the terms on which the collateral security was provided expressly provide that such expenses, remuneration or preferential debts are to have priority.

(7) As respects Scotland—

(a) the reference in paragraph (6)(a) to the expenses of bankruptcy shall be taken to be a reference to the matters mentioned in paragraphs (a) to (d) of section 51(1) of the Bankruptcy (Scotland) Act 1985, or any like provision or rule of law affecting a protected trust deed; and

(b) the reference in paragraph (6)(b) to the preferential debts of the individual shall be taken to be a reference to the preferred debts of the debtor within the meaning of the Bankruptcy (Scotland) Act 1985, or any like definition applying with respect to a protected trust deed by virtue of any provision or rule of law affecting it.

NOTES

Para (1): word in first pair of square brackets inserted by the Financial Markets and Insolvency (Settlement Finality) (Amendment) Regulations 2009, SI 2009/1972, regs 2, 4(a), as from 1 October 2009. Other words in square brackets inserted by the Financial Markets and Insolvency (Settlement Finality and Financial Collateral Arrangements) (Amendment) Regulations 2010, SI 2010/2993, reg 2(1), (11)(a), (b), as from 6 April 2011.

Para (2): words in first pair of square brackets inserted by the Financial Markets and Insolvency (Settlement Finality) (Amendment) Regulations 2006, SI 2006/50, reg 2(1), (6)(a), as from 2 February 2006. Words in square brackets in sub-para (b) substituted, and words in square brackets in sub-para (c) inserted, by SI 2010/2993, reg 2(1), (11)(c), (d), as from 6 April 2011. Words omitted revoked by SI 2009/1972, regs 2, 4(b), as from 1 October 2009.

Para (4): words in square brackets substituted by SI 2009/1972, regs 2, 4(c), as from 1 October 2009.

Para (5) is amended as follows:

Except as noted below, all words in square brackets were substituted by SI 2009/1972, regs 2, 4(d), as from 1 October 2009.

The words and figures in square brackets in sub-para (a)(i) were substituted by the Co-operative and Community Benefit Societies and Credit Unions (Arrangements, Reconstructions and Administration) (Amendment) and Consequential Amendments Order 2020, SI 2020/744, art 14, as from 18 July 2020.

The words in square brackets in sub-para (a)(ii) were substituted by the Financial Services and Markets (Insolvency) (Amendment of Miscellaneous Enactments) Regulations 2019, SI 2019/755, reg 2(1), (2), as from 23 April 2019.

Sub-para (a)(iv) was substituted, and the words in square brackets in sub-para (a)(v) were inserted, by SI 2010/2993, reg 2(1), (11)(e), (f), as from 6 April 2011.

The words in square brackets in sub-para (b) were inserted by SI 2006/50, reg 2(1), (6), as from 2 February 2006.

Para (6) is amended as follows:

Words in first pair of square brackets inserted by SI 2010/2993, reg 2(1), (11)(g), as from 6 April 2011.

In sub-para (a), words "or Articles 100 and 134 of the Insolvency (Northern Ireland) Order 1989" and "or that Order" in square brackets inserted by SI 2006/50, reg 2(1), (6)(f), as from 2 February 2006.

In sub-para (a), words "paragraph 99(3) of Schedule B1 to that Act" in square brackets substituted by the Enterprise Act 2002 (Insolvency) Order 2003, SI 2003/2096, art 5, Schedule, Pt 2, paras 74, 75(b), as from 15 September 2003, except in relation to any case where a petition for an administration order was presented before that date.

In sub-para (a), words "and in section 19(4) of that Act as that section has effect by virtue of section 249(1) of the Enterprise Act 2002" in square brackets inserted by SI 2009/1972, regs 2, 4(e)(i)(aa), as from 1 October 2009.

In sub-para (a), words "or in paragraph 100(3) to Schedule B1 to that Order" in square brackets substituted by the Financial Markets and Insolvency (Settlement Finality) (Amendment) Regulations 2007, SI 2007/832, reg 2(1), (3), as from 6 April 2007.

In sub-para (a), words "and Article 31(4) of that Order, as that Article has effect by virtue of Article 4(1) of the Insolvency (Northern Ireland) Order 2005" in square brackets inserted by SI 2009/1972, regs 2, 4(e)(i)(bb), as from 1 October 2009.

In sub-para (b), words "or Article 346 of that Order" in square brackets inserted by SI 2006/50, reg 2(1), (6)(g), as from 2 February 2006.

Sub-para (c) and the word "and" immediately preceding it inserted by SI 2009/1972, regs 2, 4(e)(ii), as from 1 October 2009.

[10.75]

15 Net sum payable on completion of action taken under default arrangements

(1) The following provisions apply with respect to any sum which is owed on completion of action taken under default arrangements [of a designated system] by or to a defaulter but do not apply to any sum which (or to the extent that it) arises from a transfer order which is also a market contract within the meaning of Part VII [or Part V], in which case sections 162 and 163 of the Companies Act 1989 [or Articles 85 and 86 of the Companies (No 2) (Northern Ireland) Order 1990] apply subject to the modification made by regulation 21.

(2) If, in England and Wales [or Northern Ireland], a bankruptcy[, winding-up or administration] order has been made or a creditors' voluntary winding-up resolution has been passed, the debt—

- (a) is provable in the bankruptcy[, winding-up or administration] or, as the case may be, is payable to the relevant office-holder; and
- (b) shall be taken into account, where appropriate, under section 323 of the Insolvency Act 1986 [or Article 296 of the Insolvency (Northern Ireland) Order 1989] [or [rule 14.24 of the Insolvency (England and Wales) Rules 2016] or Rule 2.086 of the Insolvency Rules (Northern Ireland) 1991] (mutual dealings and set-off) or the corresponding provision applicable in the case of winding up [or administration];

in the same way as a debt due before the commencement of bankruptcy, the date on which the body corporate goes into liquidation (within the meaning of section 247 of the Insolvency Act 1986 [or Article 6 of the Insolvency (Northern Ireland) Order 1989]) or [enters into administration (within the meaning of paragraph 1 of Schedule B1 to the Insolvency Act 1986 or paragraph 2 of Schedule B1 to the Insolvency (Northern Ireland) Order 1989) or], in the case of a partnership, the date of the winding-up order.

(3) If, in Scotland, an award of sequestration or a winding-up order has been made, or a creditors' voluntary winding-up resolution has been passed, or a trust deed has been granted and it has become a protected trust deed, the debt—

- (a) may be claimed in the sequestration or winding up or under the protected trust deed or, as the case may be, is payable to the relevant office-holder; and
- (b) shall be taken into account for the purposes of any rule of law relating to set-off applicable in sequestration, winding up or in respect of a protected trust deed;

in the same way as a debt due before the date of sequestration (within the meaning of section 73(1) of the Bankruptcy (Scotland) Act 1985) or the commencement of the winding up (within the meaning of section 129 of the Insolvency Act 1986) or the grant of the trust deed.

[(4) A reference in this regulation to "administration order" shall include—

- (a) the appointment of an administrator under paragraph 14 or 22 of Schedule B1 to the Insolvency Act 1986 or under paragraph 15 or 23 of Schedule B1 to the Insolvency (Northern Ireland) Order 1989;
- (b) the making of an order under section 8 of that Act as it has effect by virtue of section 249(1) of the Enterprise Act 2002; and
- (c) the making of an order under Article 21 of that Order as it has effect by virtue of Article 4(1) of the Insolvency (Northern Ireland) Order 2005;

and "administration" shall be construed accordingly.]

NOTES

Para (1): words in first pair of square brackets inserted by the Financial Markets and Insolvency (Settlement Finality and Financial Collateral Arrangements) (Amendment) Regulations 2010, SI 2010/2993, reg 2(1), (12), as from 6 April 2011. Other words in square brackets inserted by the Financial Markets and Insolvency (Settlement Finality) (Amendment) Regulations 2006, SI 2006/50, reg 2(1), (7)(a), as from 2 February 2006.

Para (2): words "or Northern Ireland," "or Article 296 of the Insolvency (Northern Ireland) Order 1989", and "or Article 6 of the Insolvency (Northern Ireland) Order 1989" inserted by SI 2006/50, reg 2(1), (7)(b), as from 2 February 2006. Words "rule 14.24 of the Insolvency (England and Wales) Rules 2016" in square brackets substituted by the Financial Services and Markets (Insolvency) (Amendment of Miscellaneous Enactments) Regulations 2019, SI 2019/755, reg 2(1), (3), as from 23 April 2019. All other words in square brackets were either inserted or substituted by the Financial Markets and Insolvency (Settlement Finality) (Amendment) Regulations 2009, SI 2009/1972, regs 2, 5(a), as from 1 October 2009.

Para (4): added by SI 2009/1972, regs 2, 5(c), as from 1 October 2009.

[10.76]

16 Disclaimer of property, rescission of contracts, &c

(1) Sections 178, 186, 315 and 345 of the Insolvency Act 1986 [or Articles 152, 157, 288 and 318 of the Insolvency (Northern Ireland) Order 1989] (power to disclaim onerous property and court's power to order rescission of contracts, &c) do not apply in relation to—

(a) a transfer order; or

(b) a contract for the purpose of realising collateral security.

In the application of this paragraph in Scotland, the reference to sections 178, 315 and 345 shall be construed as a reference to any rule of law having the like effect as those sections.

(2) In Scotland, a permanent trustee on the sequestrated estate of a defaulter or a liquidator or a trustee under a protected trust deed granted by a defaulter is bound by any transfer order given by that defaulter and by any such contract as is mentioned in paragraph (1)(b) notwithstanding section 42 of the Bankruptcy (Scotland) Act 1985 or any rule of law having the like effect applying in liquidations or any like provision or rule of law affecting the protected trust deed.

(3) [Sections 88, 127, 245 and 284 of the Insolvency Act 1986], [Articles 74, 107, 207 and 257 of the Insolvency (Northern Ireland) Order 1989] (avoidance of property dispositions effected after commencement of winding up or presentation of bankruptcy petition), section 32(8) of the Bankruptcy (Scotland) Act 1985 (effect of dealing with debtor relating to estate vested in permanent trustee) and any like provision or rule of law affecting a protected trust deed, do not apply to—

(a) a transfer order, or any disposition of property in pursuance of such an order;

(b) the provision of collateral security;

(c) a contract for the purpose of realising collateral security or any disposition of property in pursuance of such a contract; or

(d) any disposition of property in accordance with the rules of a designated system as to the application of collateral security.

NOTES

Para (1): words in square brackets inserted by the Financial Markets and Insolvency (Settlement Finality) (Amendment) Regulations 2006, SI 2006/50, reg 2(1), (8), as from 2 February 2006.

Para (3): words in square brackets substituted by the Financial Markets and Insolvency (Settlement Finality) (Amendment) Regulations 2009, SI 2009/1972, regs 2, 6, as from 1 October 2009.

[10.77]

17 Adjustment of prior transactions

(1) No order shall be made in relation to a transaction to which this regulation applies under—

(a) section 238 or 339 of the Insolvency Act 1986 [or Article 202 or 312 of the Insolvency (Northern Ireland) Order 1989] (transactions at an undervalue);

(b) section 239 or 340 of that Act [or Article 203 or 313 of that Order] (preferences); or

(c) section 423 of that Act [or Article 367 of that Order] (transactions defrauding creditors).

(2) As respects Scotland, no decree shall be granted in relation to any such transaction—

(a) under section 34 or 36 of the Bankruptcy (Scotland) Act 1985 or section 242 or 243 of the Insolvency Act 1986 (gratuitous alienations and unfair preferences); or

(b) at common law on grounds of gratuitous alienations or fraudulent preferences.

(3) This regulation applies to—

(a) a transfer order, or any disposition of property in pursuance of such an order;

(b) the provision of collateral security;

(c) a contract for the purpose of realising collateral security or any disposition of property in pursuance of such a contract; or

(d) any disposition of property in accordance with the rules of a designated system as to the application of collateral security.

NOTES

Para (1): words in square brackets inserted by the Financial Markets and Insolvency (Settlement Finality) (Amendment) Regulations 2006, SI 2006/50, reg 2(1), (9), as from 2 February 2006.

Collateral security charges

[10.78]

18 Modifications of the law of insolvency

The general law of insolvency has effect in relation to a collateral security charge and the action taken to enforce such a charge, subject to the provisions of regulation 19.

[10.79]

19 Administration orders, &c

(1) The following provisions of [Schedule B1 to] the Insolvency Act 1986 (which relate to administration orders and administrators) do not apply in relation to a collateral security charge—

[(a) paragraph 43(2) including that provision as applied by paragraph 44; and

(b) paragraphs 70, 71 and 72 of that Schedule,]

and [paragraph 41(2) of that Schedule] (receiver to vacate office when so required by administrator) does not apply to a receiver appointed under such a charge.

[(1ZA) The following provisions of the Insolvency Act 1986 (which relate to administration orders and administrators), as they have effect by virtue of section 249(1) of the Enterprise Act 2002, do not apply in relation to a collateral security charge—

(a) sections 10(1)(b) and 11(3)(c) (restriction on enforcement of security while petition for administration order pending or order in force); and

(b) sections 15(1) and (2) (power of administrator to deal with charged property);

and section 11(2) (receiver to vacate office when so required by administrator) does not apply to a receiver appointed under such a charge.]

[(1A) The following provisions of [Schedule B1 to] the Insolvency (Northern Ireland) Order 1989 (which relate to administration orders and administrators) do not apply in relation to a collateral security charge—

[(a) paragraph 44(2), including that provision as applied by paragraph 45 (restrictions on enforcement of security where company in administration or where administration application has been made); and

(b) paragraphs 71, 72 and 73 (charged and hire purchase property);]

and [paragraph 42(2)] (receiver to vacate office when so required by administrator) does not apply to a receiver appointed under such a charge.]

[(1B) The following provisions of the Insolvency (Northern Ireland) Order 1989 (administration), as they have effect by virtue of Article 4(1) of the Insolvency (Northern Ireland) Order 2005, do not apply in relation to a collateral security charge—

(a) Article 23(1)(b) and Article 24(3)(c) (restriction on enforcement of security while petition for administration order pending or order in force); and

(b) Article 28(1) and (2) (power of administrator to deal with charged property);

and Article 24(2) of that Order (receiver to vacate office at request of administrator) shall not apply to a receiver appointed under such a charge.]

(2) However, where a collateral security charge falls to be enforced after an administration order has been made or a petition for an administration order has been presented, and there exists another charge over some or all of the same property ranking in priority to or *pari passu* with the collateral security charge, on the application of any person interested, the court may order that there shall be taken after enforcement of the collateral security charge such steps as the court may direct for the purpose of ensuring that the chargee under the other charge is not prejudiced by the enforcement of the collateral security charge.

[(2A) A reference in paragraph (2) to "an administration order" shall include the appointment of an administrator under paragraph 14 or 22 of Schedule B1 to the Insolvency Act 1986 [or under paragraph 15 or 23 of Schedule B1 to the Insolvency (Northern Ireland) Order 1989].]

(3) Sections 127 and 284 of the Insolvency Act 1986 [or Articles 107 and 257 of the Insolvency (Northern Ireland) Order 1989] (avoidance of property dispositions effected after commencement of winding up or presentation of bankruptcy petition), section 32(8) of the Bankruptcy (Scotland) Act 1985 (effect of dealing with debtor relating to estate vested in permanent trustee) and any like provision or rule of law affecting a protected trust deed, do not apply to a disposition of property as a result of which the property becomes subject to a collateral security charge or any transactions pursuant to which that disposition is made.

[(4) . . .]

NOTES

Para (1): words in first pair of square brackets inserted, words in third pair of square brackets substituted, and sub-paras (a), (b) substituted, by the Enterprise Act 2002 (Insolvency) Order 2003, SI 2003/2096, arts 5, 6, Schedule, Pt 2, paras 74, 76(a), as from 15 September 2003, except in relation to any case where a petition for an administration order was presented before that date.

Paras (1ZA), (1B): inserted by the Financial Markets and Insolvency (Settlement Finality) (Amendment) Regulations 2009, SI 2009/1972, regs 2, 7, as from 1 October 2009.

Para (1A): inserted by the Financial Markets and Insolvency (Settlement Finality) (Amendment) Regulations 2006, SI 2006/50, reg 2(1), (10)(a), as from 2 February 2006. Words in square brackets substituted by the Financial Markets and Insolvency (Settlement Finality) (Amendment) Regulations 2007, SI 2007/832, reg 2(1), (4), as from 6 April 2007.

Para (2A): inserted by SI 2003/2096, arts 5, 6, Schedule, Pt 2, paras 74, 76(b), as from 15 September 2003, except in relation to any case where a petition for an administration order was presented before that date. Words in square brackets inserted by SI 2007/832, reg 2(1), (5), as from 6 April 2007.

Para (3): words in square brackets inserted by SI 2006/50, reg 2(1), (10)(b), as from 2 February 2006.

Para (4): originally added by SI 2009/1972, regs 2, 7, as from 1 October 2009. Subsequently revoked by the Corporate Insolvency and Governance Act 2020, s 2(1), Sch 3, para 35, as from 26 June 2020 (for transitional provisions, see s 2(2), (3) of the 2020 Act (at **[9.533]**) which provides that (without prejudice to the Interpretation Act 1978, s 16) nothing in the 2020 Act affects the operation of the Insolvency Act 1986, or any other enactment, in relation to a moratorium under Sch A1 to the 1986 Act which comes into force before the repeal of that Schedule by Sch 3 to the 2020 Act (ie, 26 June 2020)).

General

[10.80]

20 Transfer order entered into designated system following insolvency

(1) This Part does not apply in relation to any transfer order given by a participant which is entered into a designated system after—

(a) a court has made an order of a type referred to in regulation 22 [in respect of—

(i) that participant;

(ii) a participant in a system which is an interoperable system in relation to the designated system; or

(iii) a system operator which is not a participant in the designated system, or]

[(aa) the appointment of an administrator under paragraph 14 or paragraph 22 of Schedule B1 to the Insolvency Act 1986 has taken effect;]

(b) that participant[, a participant in a system which is an interoperable system in relation to the designated system or a system operator of that designated system] has passed a creditors' voluntary winding-up resolution, or

(c) a trust deed granted by that participant[, a participant in a system which is an interoperable system in relation to the designated system or a system operator of that designated system] has become a protected trust deed,

unless the [conditions mentioned in either paragraph (2) or paragraph (4)] are satisfied.

(2) [The conditions referred to in this paragraph] are that—

(a) the transfer order is carried out on the [same business day of the designated system] that the event specified in paragraph (1)(a), [(aa),] (b) or (c) occurs, and

(b) [the system operator] can show that it did not have notice of that event at [the time the transfer order became irrevocable].

(3) For the purposes of paragraph (2)(b), [the relevant system operator] shall be taken to have notice of an event specified in paragraph (1)(a), [(aa),] (b) or (c) if it deliberately failed to make enquiries as to that matter in circumstances in which a reasonable and honest person would have done so.

[(4) The conditions referred to in this paragraph are that—

(a) a recognised central counterparty . . . or third country central counterparty is the system operator;

(b) a clearing member of that central counterparty has defaulted; and

(c) the transfer order has been entered into the system pursuant to the provisions of the default rules of the central counterparty that provide for the transfer of the positions or assets of a clearing member on its default.

(5) In paragraph (4)—

(a) "recognised central counterparty" . . . and "third country central counterparty" have the meanings given by section 285 of the 2000 Act; and

(b) "clearing member" has the meaning given by section 190(1) of the Companies Act 1989.]

NOTES

The words "conditions mentioned in either paragraph (2) or paragraph (4)" in square brackets in para (1) and "The conditions referred to in this paragraph" in square brackets in para (2) were substituted, and paras (4), (5) were added, by the Financial Services and Markets Act 2000 (Over the Counter Derivatives, Central Counterparties and Trade Repositories) Regulations 2013, SI 2013/504, reg 32(1), (6), as from 1 April 2013.

Sub-para (1)(aa) and the references to "(aa)," in sub-para (2)(a) and para (3) were inserted, and the words omitted from sub-paras (4)(a) and (5)(a) were revoked, by the Financial Markets and Insolvency (Amendment and Transitional Provision) (EU Exit) Regulations 2019, SI 2019/341, regs 4, 8(1), as from IP completion day (as defined in the European Union (Withdrawal Agreement) Act 2020, s 39).

All other words in square brackets in this regulation were substituted or inserted by the Financial Markets and Insolvency (Settlement Finality and Financial Collateral Arrangements) (Amendment) Regulations 2010, SI 2010/2993, reg 2(1), (13), as from 6 April 2011.

[10.81]

21 Disapplication of certain provisions of Part VII [and Part V]

(1) The provisions of the Companies Act 1989 [or the Companies (No 2) (Northern Ireland) Order 1990] mentioned in paragraph (2) do not apply in relation to—

(a) a market contract which is also a transfer order effected through a designated system; or

(b) a market charge which is also a collateral security charge.

(2) The provisions referred to in paragraph (1) are as follows—

(a) section 163(4) to (6) [and Article 86(3) to (5)] (net sum payable on completion of default proceedings);

(b) section 164(4) to (6) [and Article 87(3) to (5)] (disclaimer of property, rescission of contracts, &c); and

(c) section 175(5) and (6) [and Article 97(5) and (6)] (administration orders, &c).

NOTES

Words in square brackets inserted by the Financial Markets and Insolvency (Settlement Finality) (Amendment) Regulations 2006, SI 2006/50, reg 2(1), (11), as from 2 February 2006.

[10.82]

22 Notification of insolvency order or passing of resolution for creditors' voluntary winding up

(1) Upon the making of an order for bankruptcy, sequestration, administration or winding up in respect of a participant in a designated system, the court shall forthwith notify both [the system operator of that designated system] and the designating authority that such an order has been made.

(2) Following receipt of—

(a) such notification from the court, or

(b) notification from a participant of the passing of a creditors' voluntary winding-up resolution or of a trust deed becoming a protected trust deed, [or the appointment of an administrator taking effect] pursuant to paragraph 5(4) of the Schedule,

the designating authority shall forthwith inform the Treasury [. . .] of the notification.

[(3) . . .]

NOTES

Para (1): words in square brackets substituted by the Financial Markets and Insolvency (Settlement Finality and Financial Collateral Arrangements) (Amendment) Regulations 2010, SI 2010/2993, reg 2(1), (14), as from 6 April 2011.

Para (2): the words omitted were originally inserted by the Financial Services and Markets (Disclosure of Information to the European Securities and Markets Authority etc and Other Provisions) Regulations 2016, SI 2016/1095, reg 2(1), (4)(a), as from 8 December 2016. These words were revoked, and the words in the first pair of square brackets were inserted, by the Financial Markets and Insolvency (Amendment and Transitional Provision) (EU Exit) Regulations 2019, SI 2019/341, regs 4, 8(2)(a), as from IP completion day (as defined in the European Union (Withdrawal Agreement) Act 2020, s 39).

Para (3): originally added by SI 2016/1095, reg 2(1), (4)(b), as from 8 December 2016. Subsequently revoked by SI 2019/341, regs 4, 8(2)(b), as from IP completion day (as defined in the European Union (Withdrawal Agreement) Act 2020, s 39).

[10.83]

23 Applicable law relating to securities held as collateral security

Where—

(a) securities (including rights in securities) are provided as collateral security to a participant [or a system operator, in each case in a system designated for the purposes of these Regulations or designated in Gibraltar, or a central bank (including any nominee, agent or third party acting on behalf of the participant, the system operator or the central bank), and]

(b) a register, account or centralised deposit system . . . legally records the entitlement of that person to the collateral security,

[the rights of that person as a holder of collateral security in relation to those securities are governed by the domestic law of the country or territory or, where appropriate, the law of the part of the country or territory, where the register, account, or centralised deposit system is maintained].

NOTES

Words in square brackets substituted, and words omitted revoked, by the Financial Markets and Insolvency (Amendment and Transitional Provision) (EU Exit) Regulations 2019, SI 2019/341, regs 4, 8(3), as from IP completion day (as defined in the European Union (Withdrawal Agreement) Act 2020, s 39).

[10.84]

24 Applicable law where insolvency proceedings are brought

Where insolvency proceedings are brought in any jurisdiction against a person who participates, or has participated, in a system designated for the purposes of [these Regulations or designated in Gibraltar], any question relating to the rights and obligations arising from, or in connection with, that participation and falling to be determined by a court in England and Wales[, the High Court in Northern Ireland] or in Scotland shall (subject to regulation 23) be determined in accordance with the law governing that system.

NOTES

Words in first pair of square brackets substituted by the Financial Markets and Insolvency (Amendment and Transitional Provision) (EU Exit) Regulations 2019, SI 2019/341, regs 4, 8(4), as from IP completion day (as defined in the European Union (Withdrawal Agreement) Act 2020, s 39). Note that reg 8(4) of the 2019 Regulations also provides that for the word "participants" there should be substituted the word "participates" – however, the word "participants" does not appear in this regulation.

Words in second pair of square brackets inserted by the Financial Markets and Insolvency (Settlement Finality) (Amendment) Regulations 2006, SI 2006/50, reg 2(1), (12), as from 2 February 2006.

[10.85]

25 Insolvency proceedings in other jurisdictions

(1) The references to insolvency law in section 426 of the Insolvency Act 1986 (co-operation between courts exercising jurisdiction in relation to insolvency) include, in relation to a part of the United Kingdom, this Part and, in relation to a relevant country or territory within the meaning of that section, so much of the law of that country or territory as corresponds to this Part.

(2) A court shall not, in pursuance of that section or any other enactment or rule of law, recognise or give effect to—

(a) any order of a court exercising jurisdiction in relation to insolvency law in a country or territory outside the United Kingdom, or

(b) any act of a person appointed in such a country or territory to discharge any functions under insolvency law, in so far as the making of the order or the doing of the act would be prohibited in the case of a court in England and Wales or Scotland[, the High Court in Northern Ireland] or a relevant office-holder by this Part.

(3) Paragraph (2) does not affect the recognition or enforcement of a judgment required to be recognised or enforced under or by virtue of the Civil Jurisdiction and Judgments Act 1982 . . .

NOTES

Para (2): words in square brackets inserted by the Financial Markets and Insolvency (Settlement Finality) (Amendment) Regulations 2006, SI 2006/50, reg 2(1), (13), as from 2 February 2006.

Para (3): words omitted revoked by the Financial Markets and Insolvency (Amendment and Transitional Provision) (EU Exit) Regulations 2019, SI 2019/341, regs 4, 8(5), as from IP completion day (as defined in the European Union (Withdrawal Agreement) Act 2020, s 39).

[10.86]

26 [Systems designated in Gibraltar]

(1) Where an equivalent overseas order or equivalent overseas security is subject to the insolvency law of England and Wales or Scotland [or Northern Ireland], this Part shall apply—

(a) in relation to the equivalent overseas order as it applies in relation to a transfer order; and

(b) in relation to the equivalent overseas security as it applies in relation to collateral security . . .

(2) In paragraph (1)—

[(a) "equivalent overseas order" means an order having the like effect as a transfer order which is effected through a system designated in Gibraltar and which is governed by the law of Gibraltar; and]

[(b) "equivalent overseas security" means any realisable assets provided under a charge or a repurchase or similar agreement, or otherwise (including credit claims and money provided under a charge)—

(i) for the purpose of securing rights and obligations potentially arising in connection with such a system, . . .

(ii) . . .]

NOTES

The regulation heading and sub-para (2)(a) were substituted, and sub-para (2)(b)(ii) and the preceding word were revoked, by the Financial Markets and Insolvency (Amendment and Transitional Provision) (EU Exit) Regulations 2019, SI 2019/341, regs 4, 8(6), as from IP completion day (as defined in the European Union (Withdrawal Agreement) Act 2020, s 39).

Words "or Northern Ireland" in square brackets in para (1) inserted, by the Financial Markets and Insolvency (Settlement Finality) (Amendment) Regulations 2006, SI 2006/50, reg 2(1), (14)(b), as from 2 February 2006.

Words omitted from sub-para (1)(b) revoked, and sub-para (2)(b) substituted, by the Financial Markets and Insolvency (Settlement Finality and Financial Collateral Arrangements) (Amendment) Regulations 2010, SI 2010/2993, reg 2(1), (16), as from 6 April 2011.

[10.87]

[27 Applicable law for orders made and collateral provided before IP completion day

(1) After IP completion day the provisions of these Regulations as they were in force immediately before IP completion day continue to apply to—

- (a) transfer orders entered into a designated system and collateral security provided, prior to IP completion day;
- (b) equivalent overseas orders entered, prior to IP completion day, into a system designated for the purposes of the Settlement Finality Directive in an EEA state or designated in Gibraltar; and
- (c) equivalent overseas security provided prior to IP completion day.

(2) Expressions used in sub-paragraphs (a) to (c) above have the meanings given to them in these Regulations as they were in force immediately before IP completion day.]

NOTES

Commencement: IP completion day (as defined in the European Union (Withdrawal Agreement) Act 2020, s 39).

Inserted by the Financial Markets and Insolvency (Amendment and Transitional Provision) (EU Exit) Regulations 2019, SI 2019/341, regs 4, 9, as from IP completion day (as defined in the European Union (Withdrawal Agreement) Act 2020, s 39). Note that reg 9 of the 2019 Regulations was amended by the Financial Services (Miscellaneous) (Amendment) (EU Exit) Regulations 2019, SI 2019/710, reg 20 (with effect from immediately before IP completion day), and by the Financial Services and Economic and Monetary Policy (Consequential Amendments) (EU Exit) Regulations 2020, SI 2020/1301, reg 3, Schedule, para 23(a) (as from 30 December 2020); and the effect of the amendments has been incorporated in the text set out above.

SCHEDULE
REQUIREMENTS FOR DESIGNATION OF SYSTEM

Regulation 4(1)

[10.88]

1 Establishment, participation and governing law

(1) . . .

(2) There must be not less than three institutions participating in the system, unless otherwise determined by the designating authority in any case where—

- (a) there are two institutions participating in a system; and
- (b) the designating authority considers that designation is required on the grounds of systemic risk.

(3) The system must be a system through which transfer orders are effected.

(4) Where orders relating to financial instruments other than securities are effected through the system—

- (a) the system must primarily be a system through which securities transfer orders are effected; and
- (b) the designating authority must consider that designation is required on grounds of systemic risk.

[(5) An arrangement entered into between interoperable systems shall not constitute a system.]

2 Arrangements and resources

The system must have adequate arrangements and resources for the effective monitoring and enforcement of compliance with its rules or, as respects monitoring, arrangements providing for that function to be performed on its behalf (and without affecting its responsibility) by another body or person who is able and willing to perform it.

3 Financial resources

The [system operator] must have financial resources sufficient for the proper performance of its functions as a *system*.

4 Co-operation with other authorities

[The system operator] must be able and willing to co-operate, by the sharing of information and otherwise, with—

- (a) the [FCA],
- (b) the Bank of England,
- [(ba) the PRA,]
- (c) any relevant office-holder, and
- (d) any authority, body or person having responsibility for any matter arising out of, or connected with, the default of a participant.

5 Specific provision in the rules

(1) The rules of the system must—

- (a) specify the point at which a transfer order takes effect as having been entered into the system,
- (b) specify the point after which a transfer order may not be revoked by a participant or any other party, and
- (c) prohibit the revocation by a participant or any other party of a transfer order from the point specified in accordance with paragraph (b).

[(1A) Where the system has one or more interoperable systems, the rules required under paragraph (1)(a) and (b) shall, as far as possible, be co-ordinated with the rules of those interoperable systems.

(1B) The rules of the system which are referred to in paragraph (1)(a) and (b) shall not be affected by any rules of that system's interoperable systems in the absence of express provision in the rules of the system and all of those interoperable systems.]

(2) The rules of [a system governed by the law of the United Kingdom] must require each institution [whose head office is in the United Kingdom] which participates in the system to provide upon payment of a reasonable charge the information mentioned in sub-paragraph (3) to any person who requests it, save where the request is frivolous or vexatious. The rules must require the information to be provided within fourteen days of the request being made.

(3) The information referred to in sub-paragraph (2) is as follows—

(a) details of the systems which are designated for the purposes of [these Regulations] in which the institution participates, and

(b) information about the main rules governing the functioning of those systems.

(4) The rules of [a system governed by the law of the United Kingdom] must require each participant [established in the United Kingdom] upon—

(a) the passing of a creditors' voluntary winding up resolution, . . .

(b) a trust deed granted by him becoming a protected trust deed, [or]

[(c) the appointment of an administrator under paragraph 14 or paragraph 22 of Schedule B1 to the Insolvency Act 1986 taking effect,]

[to notify forthwith both the system and the designating authority that such a resolution has been passed, that such a trust deed has become a protected trust deed or, as the case may be, that such appointment has taken effect].

6 Default arrangements

The system must have default arrangements which are appropriate for that system in all the circumstances.

NOTES

Para 1: sub-para (1) was revoked by the Financial Markets and Insolvency (Amendment and Transitional Provision) (EU Exit) Regulations 2019, SI 2019/341, regs 4, 10(a), as from IP completion day (as defined in the European Union (Withdrawal Agreement) Act 2020, s 39). Sub-para (5) added by the Financial Markets and Insolvency (Settlement Finality and Financial Collateral Arrangements) (Amendment) Regulations 2010, SI 2010/2993, reg 2(1), (17)(a), as from 6 April 2011.

Para 3: words in square brackets substituted by SI 2010/2993, reg 2(1), (17)(b), as from 6 April 2011.

Para 4: words in first pair of square brackets substituted by SI 2010/2993, reg 2(1), (17)(c), as from 6 April 2011. Word in square brackets in sub-para (a) substituted, and sub-para (ba) inserted, by the Financial Services Act 2012 (Consequential Amendments and Transitional Provisions) Order 2013, SI 2013/472, art 3, Sch 2, para 27(e), as from 1 April 2013.

Para 5: sub-paras (1A), (1B) inserted by SI 2010/2993, reg 2(1), (17)(d), as from 6 April 2011. The words in the first and second pairs of square brackets in sub-paras (2) and (4) were substituted and inserted respectively, the words in square brackets in sub-para (3)(a) were substituted, the word omitted from sub-para (4)(a) was revoked, sub-para (4)(c) and the preceding word was inserted, and the final words in square brackets in sub-para (4) were substituted, by SI 2019/341, regs 4, 10(b)–(d), as from IP completion day (as defined in the European Union (Withdrawal Agreement) Act 2020, s 39); note that reg 10 of the 2019 Regulations was amended by the Financial Services (Miscellaneous) (Amendment) (EU Exit) Regulations 2019, SI 2019/710, reg 20, with effect from immediately before IP completion day (and the effect of the amendments has been incorporated in the text set out above).

LIMITED LIABILITY PARTNERSHIPS (SCOTLAND) REGULATIONS 2001

(SSI 2001/128)

NOTES

Made: 28 March 2001.

Authority: Limited Liability Partnerships Act 2000, ss 14(1), (2), 15, 16, 17(1), (3).

Commencement: 6 April 2001.

These Regulations are reproduced as amended by: the Limited Liability Partnerships (Scotland) Amendment Regulations 2009, SSI 2009/310; the Insolvency (Protection of Essential Supplies) Order 2015, SI 2015/989; the Public Services Reform (Insolvency) (Scotland) Order 2016, SSI 2016/141; the Insolvency (Miscellaneous Amendments) Regulations 2017, SI 2017/1119; the Corporate Insolvency and Governance Act 2020.

ARRANGEMENT OF REGULATIONS

PART I CITATION, COMMENCEMENT EXTENT AND INTERPRETATION

[10.89]

1 Citation, commencement and extent

(1) These Regulations may be cited as the Limited Liability Partnerships (Scotland) Regulations 2001 and shall come into force on 6th April 2001.

(2) These Regulations extend to Scotland only.

[10.90]

2 Interpretation

In these Regulations—

"the 1985 Act" means the Companies Act 1985;

"the 1986 Act" means the Insolvency Act 1986;

"limited liability partnership agreement", in relation to a limited liability partnership, means any agreement, express or implied, made between the members of the limited liability partnership or between the limited liability partnership and the members of the limited liability partnership which determines the mutual rights and duties of the members, and their rights and duties in relation to the limited liability partnership;

"the principal Act" means the Limited Liability Partnerships Act 2000; and

"shadow member", in relation to a limited liability partnership, means a person in accordance with whose directions or instructions the members of the limited liability partnership are accustomed to act (but so that a person is not deemed a shadow member by reason only that the members of the limited liability partnership act on advice given by that person in a professional capacity).

NOTES

General note as to interpretation: as to the meaning of "the registrar" and "the register", and as to the construction of references to registration in a particular part of the United Kingdom, in any enactment relating to LLPs, see the Limited Liability Partnerships (Application of Companies Act 2006) Regulations 2009, SI 2009/1804, Sch 3, Pt 2, para 12 at **[10.419]**.

PART II COMPANIES ACT

[10.91]

3 Application of the 1985 Act to limited liability partnerships

The provisions of the 1985 Act specified in the first column of Schedule 1 to these Regulations shall apply to limited liability partnerships, with the following modifications—

(a) references to a company shall include references to a limited liability partnership;
(b) references to the Companies Acts shall include references to the principal Act and any regulations made thereunder;
(c) references to the 1986 Act shall include references to that Act as it applies to limited liability partnerships by virtue of Part III of these Regulations;
(d) references in a provision of the 1985 Act to other provisions of that Act shall include references to those other provisions as they apply to limited liability partnerships by virtue of these Regulations; and
(e) the modifications, if any, specified in the second column of Schedule 1 of the provision specified opposite them in the first column.

PART III WINDING UP AND INSOLVENCY

[10.92]

4 Application of the 1986 Act to limited liability partnerships

(1) Subject to paragraph (2), the provisions of the 1986 Act listed in Schedule 2 shall apply in relation to limited liability partnerships as they apply in relation to companies.

(2) The provisions of the 1986 Act referred to in paragraph (1) shall so apply, with the following modifications—

(a) references to a company shall include references to a limited liability partnership;
(b) references to a director or to an officer of a company shall include references to a member of a limited liability partnership;
(c) references to a shadow director shall include references to a shadow member;
(d) references to the 1985 Act, the Company Directors Disqualification Act 1986, the Companies Act 1989 or to any provisions of those Acts or to any provisions of the 1986 Act shall include references to those Acts or provisions as they apply to limited liability partnerships by virtue of the principal Act or these Regulations; and
(e) the modifications set out in Schedule 3 to these Regulations.

PART IV MISCELLANEOUS

[10.93]

5 General and consequential amendments

The enactments referred to in Schedule 4 shall have effect subject to the amendments specified in that Schedule.

[10.94]

6 Application of subordinate legislation

(1) The Insolvency (Scotland) Rules 1986 shall apply to limited liability partnerships with such modifications as the context requires for the purpose of giving effect to the provisions of the Insolvency Act 1986 which are applied by these Regulations.

(2) In the case of any conflict between any provision of the subordinate legislation applied by paragraph (1) and any provision of these Regulations, the latter shall prevail.

SCHEDULES

SCHEDULE 1
MODIFICATIONS TO PROVISIONS OF THE 1985 ACT

Regulation 3

[10.95]

Formalities of Carrying on Business	
36B (execution of documents by companies)	
Floating charges and Receivers (Scotland)	
462 (power of incorporated company to create floating charge)	In subsection (1), for the words "an incorporated company (whether a company within the meaning of this Act or not)," substitute "a limited liability partnership", and the words "(including uncalled capital)" are omitted.
463 (effect of floating charge on winding up)	
466 (alteration of floating charges)	
Subsections (1), (2), (3) and (6)	
486 (interpretation for Part XVIII generally)	For the definition of "company" substitute ""company" means a limited liability partnership;"
487 (extent of Part XVIII)	

NOTES

Note that s 36B of the Companies Act 1985 was repealed by the Companies Act 2006, s 1295, Sch 16, as from 1 October 2009.

SCHEDULE 2
PROVISIONS OF THE 1986 ACT

Regulation 4(1)

[10.96]

The relevant provisions of the 1986 Act are as follows:

Sections 50 to 52;

Section 53(1) and (2), to the extent that those subsections do not relate to the requirement for a copy of the instrument and notice being delivered to the registrar of companies;

Section 53(4), (6) and (7);

Section 54(1), (2), (3) (to the extent that that subsection does not relate to the requirement for a copy of the interlocutor to be delivered to the registrar of companies), and subsections (5), (6) and (7);

Sections 55 to 58;

Section 60, other than subsection (1);

Section 61, including subsections (6) and (7) to the extent that those subsections do not relate to anything to be done or which may be sent to the registrar of companies;

Section 62, including subsection (5) to the extent that that subsection does not relate to anything to be done or which may be sent to the registrar of companies;

Sections 63 to 66;

Section 67, including subsections (1) and (8) to the extent that those subsections do not relate to anything to be sent to the registrar of companies;

Section 68;

Section 69, including subsections (1) and (2) to the extent that those subsections do not relate to anything to be done or which may be done by the registrar of companies;

Sections 70 and 71;

Subsection 84(3) to the extent that it does not concern the copy of the resolution being forwarded to the registrar of companies within 15 days;

Sections 91 to [92A];

Section 94, including subsections (3) and (4) to the extent that those subsections do not relate to the liquidator being required to send to the registrar of companies a copy of the account and a return of the final meeting;

Section 95;

Section 97;

Sections 100 to 102;

Sections 104 to [104A];

Section 106, including subsections [(3) to (7)] to the extent that those subsections do not relate to the liquidator being required to send to the registrar of companies a copy of the account of winding up and a return of the final meeting/quorum [or a statement about a member State liquidator];

Sections 109 to 111;

Section 112, including subsection (3) to the extent that that subsection does not relate to the liquidator being required to send to the registrar of companies a copy of the order made by the court;

Sections 113 to 115;

Sections 126 to 128;

Section 130(1) to the extent that that subsection does not relate to a copy of the order being forwarded by the court to the registrar of companies;

Section 131;

Sections 133 to 135;

Sections 138 to 140;

Sections 142 to 146;

Section 147, including subsection (3) to the extent that that subsection does not relate to a copy of the order being forwarded by the company to the registrar of companies;

Section 162 to the extent that the section concerns the matters set out in Section C 2 of Schedule 5 to the Scotland Act 1998 as being exceptions to the reservation of insolvency;

Sections 163 to 167;

Section 169;

Section 170, including subsection (2) to the extent that that subsection does not relate to an application being made by the registrar to make good the default;

Section 171;

Section 172, including [subsections (8) to (10) to the extent that those subsections do] not relate to the liquidator being required to give notice to the registrar of companies [or a statement about a member State liquidator];

Sections 173 and 174;

Section 177;

Sections 185 to 189;

Sections 191 to 194;

Section 196;

Section 199;

Section 200;

Sections 206 to 215;

Section 218 subsections (1), (2), (4) and (6);

Sections 231 to 232 to the extent that the sections apply to administrative receivers, liquidators and provisional liquidators;

Section 233 to the extent that that section applies in the case of the appointment of an administrative receiver, of a voluntary arrangement taking effect, of a company going into liquidation or where a provisional liquidator is appointed;

[Section 233A to the extent that that section applies in the case of a voluntary arrangement taking effect]

[Section 233B to the extent that that section applies in the case of the appointment of an administrative receiver.]

Section 234 to the extent that that section applies to situations other than those where an administration [has been entered into];

Section 235 to the extent that that section applies to situations other than those where an administration [has been entered into];

Sections 236 to 237 to the extent that those sections apply to situations other than [administrations entered into] and winding up;

Sections 242 to 243;

Section 244 to the extent that that section applies in circumstances other than a company which [has entered into administration];

Section 245;

Section 251;

Section 416(1) and (4) to the extent that those subsections apply to section 206(1)(a) and (b) in connection with the offence provision relating to the winding up of a limited liability partnership;

Section 430;

Section 436;

Schedule 2;

Schedule 3;

Schedule 4;

Schedule 8 to the extent that that Schedule does not apply to voluntary arrangements or administrations within the meaning of Parts I and II of the 1986 Act;

Schedule 10 to the extent that it refers to any of the sections referred to above.

NOTES

Figures "92A" and "104A" substituted by the Public Services Reform (Insolvency) (Scotland) Order 2016, SSI 2016/141, art 7(2)(a), as from 6 April 2019 (for savings, see the note to the Insolvency Act 1986, s 92A at **[9.222]**).

In the entries relating to sections 106 and 172, the words in the first pair of square brackets were substituted, and the words in the second pair of square brackets were inserted, by the Insolvency (Miscellaneous Amendments) Regulations 2017, SI 2017/1119, reg 2, Sch 1, Pt 3, para 57, as from 8 December 2017.

Entry relating to section 233A inserted by the Insolvency (Protection of Essential Supplies) Order 2015, SI 2015/989, art 6, Schedule, para 3, as from 1 October 2015.

Entry relating to section 233B inserted by the Corporate Insolvency and Governance Act 2020, s 14(3), Sch 12, Pt 2, para 7, as from 26 June 2020. See also s 14(4) of the 2020 Act which provides that the amendments made by Sch 12 to the 2020 Act have effect in relation to a company which becomes subject to a relevant insolvency procedure on or after 26 June 2020, but in respect of contracts entered into before, as well as those entered into on or after, that day.

All other words in square brackets were substituted by the Limited Liability Partnerships (Scotland) Amendment Regulations 2009, SSI 2009/310, reg 3, Sch 1, as from 1 October 2009.

SCHEDULE 3
MODIFICATIONS TO PROVISIONS OF THE 1986 ACT

Regulation 4(2)

[10.97]

Provisions	**Modifications**
Section 84 (circumstances in which company may be wound up voluntarily)	
Subsection (3)	For subsection (3) substitute the following—
	"(3) Within 15 days after a limited liability partnership has determined

Provisions	Modifications
	that it be wound up there shall be forwarded to the registrar of companies either a printed copy or a copy in some other form approved by the registrar of the determination."
	After subsection (3) insert a new subsection—
Subsection [(3A)]	"[(3A)] If a limited liability partnership fails to comply with this regulation the limited liability partnership and every designated member of it who is in default is liable on summary conviction to a fine not exceeding level 3 on the standard scale."
Section 91 (appointment of liquidator)	
Subsection (1)	Delete "in general meeting".
Subsection (2)	For subsection (2) substitute the following—
	"(2) On the appointment of a liquidator the powers of the members of the limited liability partnership shall cease except to the extent that a meeting of the members of the limited liability partnership summoned for the purpose or the liquidator sanctions their continuance."
	After subsection (2) insert—
	"(3) Subsections (3) and (4) of section 92 shall apply for the purposes of this section as they apply for the purposes of that section."
Section 92 (power to fill vacancy in office of liquidator)	
Subsection (1)	For "the company in general meeting" substitute "a meeting of the members of the limited liability partnership summoned for the purpose".
Subsection (2)	For "a general meeting" substitute "a meeting of the members of the limited liability partnership".
Subsection (3)	In subsection (3), for "articles" substitute "limited liability partnership agreement".
new subsection (4)	Add a new subsection (4) as follows—
	"(4) The quorum required for a meeting of the members of the limited liability partnership shall be any quorum required by the limited liability partnership agreement for meetings of the members of the limited liability partnership and if no requirement for a quorum has been agreed upon the quorum shall be 2 members."
. . .	
Section 94 (final meeting prior to dissolution)	
subsection (1)	For "a general meeting of the company" substitute "a meeting of the members of the limited liability partnership".
new subsection (5A)	Add a new subsection (5A) as follows—
	"(5A) Subsections (3) and (4) of section 92 shall apply for the purposes of this section as they apply for the purposes of that section."
subsection (6)	For "a general meeting of the company" substitute "a meeting of the members of the limited liability partnership".
Section 95 (effect of company's insolvency)	
subsection (1)	For "directors'" substitute "designated members'".
subsection (7)	For subsection (7) substitute the following—
	"(7) In this section 'the relevant period' means the period of 6 months immediately preceding the date on which the limited liability partnership determined that it be wound up voluntarily."
Section 100 (appointment of liquidator)	
subsection (1)	For "The creditors and the company at their respective meetings mentioned in section 98" substitute "The creditors at their meeting mentioned in section 98 and the limited liability partnership".
subsection (3)	Delete "director,".
Section 101 (appointment of liquidation committee)	
subsection (2)	For subsection (2) substitute the following—
	"(2) If such a committee is appointed, the limited liability partnership may, when it determines that it be wound up voluntarily or at any time thereafter, appoint such number of persons as they think fit to act as members of the committee, not exceeding 5."
. . .	
Section 106 (final meeting prior to dissolution)	
subsection (1)	For "a general meeting of the company" substitute "a meeting of the members of the limited liability partnership".
new subsection (5A)	After subsection (5) insert a new subsection (5A) as follows—

Provisions	**Modifications**
	"(5A) Subsections (3) and (4) of section 92 shall apply for the purposes of this section as they apply for the purposes of that section."
subsection (6)	For "a general meeting of the company" substitute "a meeting of the members of the limited liability partnership".
Sections 110 (acceptance of shares, etc, as consideration for sale of company property)	
	For the existing section substitute the following: "(1) This section applies, in the case of a limited liability partnership proposed to be, or being, wound up voluntarily, where the whole or part of the limited liability partnership's business or property is proposed to be transferred or sold to another company whether or not it is a company within the meaning of the Companies Act ("the transferee company") or to a limited liability partnership ("the transferee limited liability partnership"). (2) With the requisite sanction, the liquidator of the limited liability partnership being, or proposed to be, wound up ("the transferor limited liability partnership") may receive, in compensation or part compensation for the transfer or sale, shares, policies or other like interests in the transferee company or the transferee limited liability partnership for distribution among the members of the transferor limited liability partnership. (3) The sanction required under subsection (2) is— (a) in the case of a members' voluntary winding up, that of a determination of the limited liability partnership at a meeting of the members of the limited liability partnership conferring either a general authority on the liquidator or an authority in respect of any particular arrangement, (subsections (3) and (4) of section 92 to apply for this purpose as they apply for the purposes of that section), and (b) in the case of a creditor's voluntary winding up, that of either court or the liquidation committee. (4) Alternatively to subsection (2), the liquidator may (with the sanction) enter into any other arrangement whereby the members of the transferor limited liability partnership may, in lieu of receiving cash, shares, policies or other like interests (or in addition thereto), participate in the profits, or receive any other benefit from the transferee company or the transferee limited liability partnership. (5) A sale or arrangement in pursuance of this section is binding on members of the transferor limited liability partnership. (6) A determination by the limited liability partnership is not invalid for the purposes of this section by reason that it is made before or concurrently with a determination by the limited liability partnership that it be wound up voluntarily or for appointing liquidators; but, if an order is made within a year for winding up the limited liability partnership by the court, the determination by the limited liability partnership is not valid unless sanctioned by the court."
Section 111 (dissent from arrangement under section 110)	
subsections (1)–(3)	For subsections (1)–(3) substitute the following— "(1) This section applies in the case of a voluntary winding up where, for the purposes of section 110(2) or (4), a determination of the limited liability partnership has provided the sanction requisite for the liquidator under that section. (2) If a member of the transferor limited liability partnership who did not vote in favour of providing the sanction required for the liquidator under section 110 expresses his dissent from it in writing addressed to the liquidator and left at the registered office of the limited liability partnership within 7 days after the date on which that sanction was given, he may require the liquidator either to abstain from carrying the arrangement so sanctioned into effect or to purchase his interest at a price to be determined by agreement or arbitration under this section. (3) If the liquidator elects to purchase the member's interest, the purchase money must be paid before the limited liability partnership is dissolved and be raised by the liquidator in such manner as may be determined by the limited liability partnership."
subsection (4)	Omit subsection (4).
Section 126 (power to stay or restrain proceedings against company)	
subsection (2)	Delete subsection (2).
Section 127 (avoidance of property dispositions, etc)	
	For "any transfer of shares" substitute "any transfer by a member of the limited liability partnership of his interest in the property of the limited

Provisions	Modifications
	liability partnership".
Section 165 (voluntary winding up)	
subsection (2)	In paragraph (a) for "an extraordinary resolution of the company" substitute "a determination by a meeting of the members of the limited liability partnership".
subsection (4)	For paragraph (c) substitute the following—
	"(c) summon meetings of the members of the limited liability partnership for the purpose of obtaining their sanction or for any other purpose he may think fit."
new subsection (4A)	Insert a new subsection (4A) as follows—
	"(4A) Subsections (3) and (4) of section 92 shall apply for the purposes of this section as they apply for the purposes of that section."
Section 166 (creditors' voluntary winding up)	
subsection (5)	In paragraph (b) for "directors" substitute "designated members".
Section 171 (removal, etc (voluntary winding up))	
subsection (2)	For paragraph (a) substitute the following—
	"(a) in the case of a members' voluntary winding up, by a meeting of the members of the limited liability partnership summoned specially for that purpose, or".
subsection (6)	In paragraph (a) for "final meeting of the company" substitute "final meeting of the members of the limited liability partnership" and in paragraph (b) for "final meetings of the company" substitute "final meetings of the members of the limited liability partnership".
new subsection (7)	Insert a new subsection (7) as follows—
	"(7) Subsections (3) and (4) of section 92 apply for the purposes of this section as they apply for the purposes of that section."
Section 173 (release (voluntary winding up))	
subsection (2)	In paragraph (a) for "a general meeting of the company" substitute "a meeting of the members of the limited liability partnership".
Section 187 (power to make over assets to employees)	
	Delete section 187
Section 194 (resolutions passed at adjourned meetings)	
	After "contributories" insert "or of the members of a limited liability partnership".
Section 206 (fraud, etc in anticipation of winding up)	
subsection (1)	For "passes a resolution for voluntary winding up" substitute "makes a determination that it be wound up voluntarily".
Section 207 (transactions in fraud of creditors)	
subsection (1)	For "passes a resolution for voluntary winding up" substitute "makes a determination that it be wound up voluntarily".
Section 210 (material omissions from statement relating to company's affairs)	
subsection (2)	For "passed a resolution for voluntary winding up" substitute "made a determination that it be wound up voluntarily".
Section 214 (wrongful trading)	
subsection (2)	Delete from "but the court shall not" to the end of the subsection.
After section 214	Insert the following new section 214A
	"214A Adjustment of withdrawals
	(1) This section has effect in relation to a person who is or has been a member of a limited liability partnership where, in the course of the winding up of that limited liability partnership, it appears that subsection (2) of this section applies in relation to that person.
	(2) This subsection applies in relation to a person if—
	(a) within the period of two years ending with the commencement of the winding up, he was a member of the limited liability partnership who withdrew property of the limited liability partnership, whether in the form of a share of profits, salary, repayment of or payment of interest on a loan to the limited liability partnership or any other withdrawal of property, and
	(b) it is proved by the liquidator to the satisfaction of the court that at the time of the withdrawal he knew or had reasonable grounds for believing that the limited liability partnership—
	(i) was at the time of the withdrawal unable to pay its debts within

Provisions	Modifications
	the meaning of section 123 of the Act, or (ii) would become so unable to pay its debts after the assets of the limited liability partnership had been depleted by that withdrawal taken together with all other withdrawals (if any) made by any members contemporaneously with that withdrawal or in contemplation when that withdrawal was made. (3) Where this section has effect in relation to any person the court, on the application of the liquidator, may declare that that person is to be liable to make such contribution (if any) to the limited liability partnership's assets as the court thinks proper. (4) The court shall not make a declaration in relation to any person the amount of which exceeds the aggregate of the amounts or values of all the withdrawals referred to in subsection (2) made by that person within the period of 2 years referred to in that subsection. (5) The court shall not make a declaration under this section with respect to any person unless that person knew or ought to have concluded that after each withdrawal referred to in subsection (2) there was no reasonable prospect that the limited liability partnership would avoid going into insolvent liquidation. (6) For the purposes of subsection (5) the facts which a member ought to know or ascertain, the conclusions which he ought to reach and the steps which he ought to have taken are those which would be known or ascertained, or reached or taken, by a reasonably diligent person having both: (a) the general knowledge, skill and experience that may reasonably be expected of a person carrying out the same functions as are carried out by that member in relation to the limited liability partnership, and (b) the general knowledge, skill and experience that that member has. (7) For the purposes of this section a limited liability partnership goes into insolvent liquidation if it goes into liquidation at a time when its assets are insufficient for the payment of its debts and other liabilities and the expenses of the winding up. (8) In this section "member" includes a shadow member. (9) This section is without prejudice to section 214."
Section 215 (proceedings under ss 213, 214)	
subsection (1)	Omit the word "or" between the words "213" and "214" and insert after "214" "or 214A".
subsection (2)	For "either section" substitute "any of those sections".
subsection (4)	For "either section" substitute "any of those sections".
subsection (5)	For "Sections 213 and 214" substitute "Sections 213, 214 or 214A".
Section 218 (prosecution of delinquent officers and members of company)	
subsection (1)	For "officer, or any member, of the company" substitute "member of the limited liability partnership"
subsections (4) and (6)	For "officer of the company, or any member of it," substitute "officer or member of the limited liability partnership".
. . .	
Section 251 (expressions used generally)	
	Delete the word "and" appearing after the definition of "the rules" and insert the word "and" after the definition of "shadow director". After the definition of "shadow director" insert the following— ""shadow member", in relation to a limited liability partnership, means a person in accordance with whose directions or instructions the members of the limited liability partnership are accustomed to act (but so that a person is not deemed a shadow member by reason only that the members of the limited liability partnership act on advice given by him in a professional capacity);"
Section 416 (monetary limits (companies winding up))	
subsection (1)	In subsection (1), omit the words "section 117(2) (amount of company's share capital determining whether county court has jurisdiction to wind it up);" and the words "section 120(3) (the equivalent as respects sheriff court jurisdiction in Scotland);".
Section 436 (expressions used generally)	
	The following expressions and definitions shall be added to the section— "designated member" has the same meaning as it has in the Limited Liability Partnerships Act 2000;

Provisions	Modifications
	"limited liability partnership" means a limited liability partnership formed and registered under the Limited Liability Partnership Act 2000; "limited liability partnership agreement", in relation to a limited liability partnership, means any agreement, express or implied, made between the members of the limited liability partnership or between the limited liability partnership and the members of the limited liability partnership which determines the mutual rights and duties of the members, and their rights and duties in relation to the limited liability partnership.
Schedule 2	
Paragraph 17	For paragraph 17 substitute the following— "**17.** Power to enforce any rights the limited liability partnership has against the members under the terms of the limited liability partnership agreement"
Schedule 10	
Section 93(3)	In the entry relating to section 93(3) for "general meeting of the company" substitute "meeting of members of the limited liability partnership".
Section 105(3)	In the entry relating to section 105(3) for "company general meeting" substitute "meeting of the members of the limited liability partnership".
Section 106(6)	In the entry relating to section 106(6) for "company" substitute "the members of the limited liability partnership"

NOTES

Figures in square brackets in the entry relating to section 84 substituted, and entry relating to section 233 (omitted) revoked, by the Limited Liability Partnerships (Scotland) Amendment Regulations 2009, SSI 2009/310, reg 4, Sch 2, as from 1 October 2009.

Entries relating to ss 93 and 105 (omitted) revoked by the Public Services Reform (Insolvency) (Scotland) Order 2016, SSI 2016/141, art 7(2)(b), as from 6 April 2019 (for savings, see the note to the Insolvency Act 1986, s 92A at **[9.222]**).

SCHEDULE 4
GENERAL AND CONSEQUENTIAL AMENDMENTS IN OTHER LEGISLATION

Regulation 5

[10.98]
1–5. (*Amend the Insolvency Act 1986, s 110 at* **[9.237]**, *the Criminal Procedure (Scotland) Act 1995, ss 70, 141, 143, and the Requirements of Writing (Scotland) Act 1995, s 7, Schs 1, 2.*)

Culpable officer provision

6. (1) A culpable officer provision applies in the case of a limited liability partnership as if the reference in the provision to a director (or a person purporting to act as a director) were a reference to a member (or a person purporting to act as a member) of the limited liability partnership.

(2) A culpable officer provision is a devolved provision in any Act or subordinate legislation (within the meaning of the Interpretation Act 1978 or the Scotland Act 1998 (Transitory and Transitional Provisions) (Publication and Interpretation etc of Acts of the Scottish Parliament) Order 1999) to the effect that where—
(a) a body corporate is guilty of a particular offence, and
(b) the offence is proved to have been committed with the consent or connivance of, or to be attributable to the neglect on the part of, (among others) a director of the body corporate,

he (as well as the body corporate) is guilty of the offence.

(3) In this paragraph "devolved provision" means any provision that would be within devolved competence for the purposes of section 101 of the Scotland Act 1998.

LIMITED LIABILITY PARTNERSHIPS REGULATIONS 2001

(SI 2001/1090)

NOTES

Made: 19 March 2001.
Authority: Limited Liability Partnerships Act 2000, ss 14–17.
Commencement: 6 April 2001.

These Regulations are reproduced as amended by: the Financial Services and Markets Act 2000 (Consequential Amendments) Order 2004, SI 2004/355; the Limited Liability Partnerships (Amendment) Regulations 2005, SI 2005/1989; the Civil Partnership Act 2004 (Amendments to Subordinate Legislation) Order 2005, SI 2005/2114; the Companies Act 1985 (Operating and Financial Review) (Repeal) Regulations 2005, SI 2005/3442; the Companies Act 1985 (Small Companies' Accounts and Audit) Regulations 2006, SI 2006/2782; the Limited Liability Partnerships (Amendment) Regulations 2007, SI 2007/2073; the Markets in Financial Instruments Directive (Consequential Amendments) Regulations 2007, SI 2007/2932; the Companies (Late Filing Penalties) and Limited Liability Partnerships (Filing Periods and Late Filing Penalties) Regulations 2008, SI 2008/497; the Limited Liability Partnerships (Accounts and Audit) (Application of Companies Act 2006) Regulations 2008, SI 2008/1911; the Limited Liability Partnerships (Application of Companies Act 2006) Regulations 2009, SI 2009/1804; the Companies Act 2006 (Consequential Amendments, Transitional Provisions and Savings) Order 2009, SI 2009/1941; the Insolvency (Protection of Essential Supplies) Order 2015, SI 2015/989; the Deregulation Act 2015

(Insolvency) (Consequential Amendments and Transitional and Savings Provisions) Order 2015, SI 2015/1641; the Public Services Reform (Insolvency) (Scotland) Order 2016, SSI 2016/141; the Enterprise and Regulatory Reform Act 2013 (Consequential Amendments) (Bankruptcy) and the Small Business, Enterprise and Employment Act 2015 (Consequential Amendments) Regulations 2016, SI 2016/481; the Insolvency (Miscellaneous Amendments) Regulations 2017, SI 2017/1119; the Corporate Insolvency and Governance Act 2020; the Limited Liability Partnerships (Amendment etc) Regulations 2020, SI 2021/60.

Contractual rights of third parties: the Contracts (Rights of Third Parties) Act 1999, s 1, confers no rights on a third party in the case of any incorporation document of a limited liability partnership, or any agreement (express or implied) between the members of a limited liability partnership, or between a limited liability partnership and its members, that determines the mutual rights and duties of the members and their rights and duties in relation to the limited liability partnership; see s 6(2A) of the 1999 Act (as inserted by Sch 5, para 20 to these Regulations, and as subsequently amended).

Savings for the Companies Act 1985 as applied by these Regulations: nothing in any of the following Orders affects any provision of the Companies Act 1985 as applied by these Regulations; ie, the Companies Act 2006 (Commencement No 1, Transitional Provisions and Savings) Order 2006 (SI 2006/3428), the Companies Act 2006 (Commencement No 2, Consequential Amendments, Transitional Provisions and Savings) Order 2007 (SI 2007/1093), the Companies Act 2006 (Commencement No 3, Consequential Amendments, Transitional Provisions and Savings) Order 2007 (SI 2007/2194), the Companies Act 2006 (Commencement No 5, Transitional Provisions and Savings) Order 2007 (SI 2007/3495), the Companies Act 2006 (Commencement No 6, Saving and Commencement Nos 3 and 5 (Amendment)) Order 2008 (SI 2008/674), the Companies Act 2006 (Commencement No 7, Transitional Provisions and Savings) Order 2008 (SI 2008/1886), and the Companies Act 2006 (Consequential Amendments etc) Order 2008 (SI 2008/948); see art 8 of the fist commencement Order, art 11 of the second commencement Order, art 12 of the third commencement Order, art 12 of the fifth commencement Order, art 6 of the sixth commencement Order, art 7 of the seventh commencement Order, and art 11 of SI 2008/948 (at **[4.146]**). See also the Limited Liability Partnerships (Application of Companies Act 2006) Regulations 2009, SI 2009/1804 at **[10.319]** which applies various provisions of the Companies Act 2006 to LLPs and revokes (as from 1 October 2009) most of Sch 2, Pt I to these Regulations (as noted *post*). Schedule 1 to the 2009 Regulations (at **[10.409]** et seq) provides for detailed transitional provisions and savings in relation to the application of the 2006 Act to LLPs and the revocation of these Regulations in so far as they apply provisions of the 1985 Act to LLPs.

ARRANGEMENT OF REGULATIONS

PART I CITATION, COMMENCEMENT AND INTERPRETATION

[10.99]

1 Citation and commencement

These Regulations may be cited as the Limited Liability Partnerships Regulations 2001 and shall come into force on 6th April 2001.

[10.100]

2 Interpretation

In these Regulations—

"the 1985 Act" means the Companies Act 1985;

"the 1986 Act" means the Insolvency Act 1986;

"the 2000 Act" means the Financial Services and Markets Act 2000;

"devolved", in relation to the provisions of the 1986 Act, means the provisions of the 1986 Act which are listed in Schedule 4 and, in their application to Scotland, concern wholly or partly, matters which are set out in Section C 2 of Schedule 5 to the Scotland Act 1998 as being exceptions to the reservations made in that Act in the field of insolvency;

"limited liability partnership agreement", in relation to a limited liability partnership, means any agreement express or implied between the members of the limited liability partnership or between the limited liability partnership and the members of the limited liability partnership which determines the mutual rights and duties of the members, and their rights and duties in relation to the limited liability partnership;

"the principal Act" means the Limited Liability Partnerships Act 2000; and

"shadow member", in relation to limited liability partnerships, means a person in accordance with whose directions or instructions the members of the limited liability partnership are accustomed to act (but so that a person is not deemed a shadow member by reason only that the members of the limited partnership act on advice given by him in a professional capacity).

NOTES

General note as to interpretation: as to the meaning of "the registrar" and "the register", and as to the construction of references to registration in a particular part of the United Kingdom, in any enactment relating to LLPs, see the Limited Liability Partnerships (Application of Companies Act 2006) Regulations 2009, SI 2009/1804, Sch 3, Pt 2, para 12 at **[10.419]**.

[10.101]

[2A Application of provisions

(1) The provisions of these Regulations applying—

(a) the Company Directors Disqualification Act 1986, or

(b) provisions of the Insolvency Act 1986,

have effect only in relation to limited liability partnerships registered in Great Britain.

(2) The other provisions of these Regulations have effect in relation to limited liability partnerships registered in any part of the United Kingdom.]

NOTES

Inserted by the Limited Liability Partnerships (Application of Companies Act 2006) Regulations 2009, SI 2009/1804, reg 85, Sch 3, Pt 2, para 13(1), (2), as from 1 October 2009.

PART II ACCOUNTS AND AUDIT

3 *Reg 3 (Application of the accounts and audit provisions of the 1985 Act to limited liability partnerships) was revoked by the Limited Liability Partnerships (Accounts and Audit) (Application of Companies Act 2006) Regulations 2008, SI 2008/1911, reg 58(1)(a), as from 1 October 2008, except in relation to accounts for, and otherwise as regards, financial years beginning before that date (see reg 58(3) at* **[10.286]***).)*

PART III COMPANIES ACT 1985 AND COMPANY DIRECTORS DISQUALIFICATION ACT 1986

[10.102]

4 Application of [certain provisions] of the 1985 Act and of the provisions of the Company Directors Disqualification Act 1986 to limited liability partnerships

(1) The provisions of the 1985 Act specified in the first column of Part I of Schedule 2 to these Regulations shall apply to limited liability partnerships, except where the context otherwise requires, with the following modifications—

(a) references to a company shall include references to a limited liability partnership;

(b) . . .

(c) references to the Insolvency Act 1986 shall include references to that Act as it applies to limited liability partnerships by virtue of Part IV of these Regulations;

[(d) references in a provision of the 1985 Act to—

(i) other provisions of that Act, or

(ii) provisions of the Companies Act 2006,

shall include references to those provisions as they apply to limited liability partnerships.]

(e), (f) . . .

(g) references to a director of a company or to an officer of a company shall include references to a member of a limited liability partnership;

(h) the modifications, if any, specified in the second column of Part I of Schedule 2 opposite the provision specified in the first column; and

(i) such further modifications as the context requires for the purpose of giving effect to that legislation as applied by these Regulations.

(2) The provisions of the Company Director Disqualification Act 1986 shall apply to limited liability partnerships, except where the context otherwise requires, with the following modifications—

(a) references to a company shall include references to a limited liability partnership;

(b) references to the Companies Acts shall include references to the principal Act and regulations made thereunder and references to the companies legislation shall include references to the principal Act, regulations made thereunder and to any enactment applied by regulations to limited liability partnerships;

(d) references to the Insolvency Act 1986 shall include references to that Act as it applies to limited liability partnerships by virtue of Part IV of these Regulations;

(e) . . .

(f) references to a shadow director shall include references to a shadow member;

(g) references to a director of a company or to an officer of a company shall include references to a member of a limited liability partnership;

(h) the modifications, if any, specified in the second column of Part II of Schedule 2 opposite the provision specified in the first column; and

(i) such further modifications as the context requires for the purpose of giving effect to that legislation as applied by these Regulations.

NOTES

Regulation heading: words in square brackets substituted by the Limited Liability Partnerships (Application of Companies Act 2006) Regulations 2009, SI 2009/1804, reg 85, Sch 3, Pt 2, para 13(1), (3)(a), as from 1 October 2009.

Para (1): sub-paras (b), (e), (f) revoked, and sub-para (d) substituted, by SI 2009/1804, reg 85, Sch 3, Pt 2, para 13(1), (3)(b), as from 1 October 2009.

Para (2): sub-para (e) revoked by the Companies Act 2006 (Consequential Amendments, Transitional Provisions and Savings) Order 2009, SI 2009/1941, art 2(1), Sch 1, para 192(1), (2), as from 1 October 2009.

PART IV WINDING UP AND INSOLVENCY

[10.103]

5 Application of the 1986 Act to limited liability partnerships

(1) Subject to paragraphs (2) and (3), the following provisions of the 1986 Act, shall apply to limited liability partnerships—

(a) Parts [A1,] I, II, III, IV, VI and VII of the First Group of Parts (company insolvency; companies winding up),

(b) the Third Group of Parts (miscellaneous matters bearing on both company and individual insolvency; general interpretation; final provisions).

(2) The provisions of the 1986 Act referred to in paragraph (1) shall apply to limited liability partnerships, except where the context otherwise requires, with the following modifications—

(a) references to a company shall include references to a limited liability partnership;

(b) references to a director or to an officer of a company shall include references to a member of a limited liability partnership;

(c) references to a shadow director shall include references to a shadow member;

(d) references to [the Companies Acts], the Company Directors Disqualification Act 1986, the Companies Act 1989 or to any provisions of those Acts or to any provisions of the 1986 Act shall include references to those Acts or provisions as they apply to limited liability partnerships by virtue of the principal Act;

(e) references . . . to the articles of association of a company shall include references to the limited liability partnership agreement of a limited liability partnership;

(f) the modifications set out in Schedule 3 to these Regulations; and

(g) such further modifications as the context requires for the purpose of giving effect to that legislation as applied by these Regulations.

(3) In the application of this regulation to Scotland, the provisions of the 1986 Act referred to in paragraph (1) shall not include the provisions listed in Schedule 4 to the extent specified in that Schedule.

NOTES

Para (1): reference to "A1," in square brackets inserted by the Corporate Insolvency and Governance Act 2020, s 2(1), Sch 3, para 38, as from 26 June 2020 (for transitional provisions, see s 2(2), (3) of the 2020 Act (at **[9.533]**) which provides that (without prejudice to the Interpretation Act 1978, s 16) nothing in the 2020 Act affects the operation of the Insolvency Act 1986, or any other enactment, in relation to a moratorium under Sch A1 to the 1986 Act which comes into force before the repeal of that Schedule by Sch 3 to the 2020 Act (ie, 26 June 2020)).

Para (2): words in square brackets in sub-para (d) substituted, and words omitted from sub-para (e) revoked, by the Companies Act 2006 (Consequential Amendments, Transitional Provisions and Savings) Order 2009, SI 2009/1941, art 2(1), Sch 1, para 192(1), (3), as from 1 October 2009.

Temporary restriction on initiating certain insolvency arrangements (rent debts): see the note relating to the Commercial Rent (Coronavirus) Act 2022, s 25 to the Companies Act 2006, s 896 at **[1.1035]**.

Prohibition on presenting a winding-up petition solely in relation to a protected rent debt: see the note to the Insolvency Act 1986, s 124 at **[9.251]**.

PART V FINANCIAL SERVICES AND MARKETS

[10.104]

6 Application of provisions contained in Parts XV and XXIV of the 2000 Act to limited liability partnerships

(1) Subject to paragraph (2), sections 215(3), (4) and (6), 356, 359(1) to (4), 361 to 365, 367, 370 and 371 of the 2000 Act shall apply to limited liability partnerships.

(2) The provisions of the 2000 Act referred to in paragraph (1) shall apply to limited liability partnerships, except where the context otherwise requires, with the following modifications—

(a) references to a company shall include references to a limited liability partnership;

(b) references to body shall include references to a limited liability partnership; and

(c) references to the 1985 Act, the 1986 Act or to any of the provisions of those Acts shall include references to those Acts or provisions as they apply to limited liability partnerships by virtue of the principal Act.

PART VI DEFAULT PROVISION

[10.105]

7 Default provision for limited liability partnerships

The mutual rights and duties of the members and the mutual rights and duties of the limited liability partnership and the members shall be determined, subject to the provisions of the general law and to the terms of any limited liability partnership agreement, by the following rules:

(1) All the members of a limited liability partnership are entitled to share equally in the capital and profits of the limited liability partnership.

(2) The limited liability partnership must indemnify each member in respect of payments made and personal liabilities incurred by him—

- (a) in the ordinary and proper conduct of the business of the limited liability partnership; or
- (b) in or about anything necessarily done for the preservation of the business or property of the limited liability partnership.

(3) Every member may take part in the management of the limited liability partnership.

(4) No member shall be entitled to remuneration for acting in the business or management of the limited liability partnership.

(5) No person may be introduced as a member or voluntarily assign an interest in a limited liability partnership without the consent of all existing members.

(6) Any difference arising as to ordinary matters connected with the business of the limited liability partnership may be decided by a majority of the members, but no change may be made in the nature of the business of the limited liability partnership without the consent of all the members.

(7) The books and records of the limited liability partnership are to be made available for inspection at the registered office of the limited liability partnership or at such other place as the members think fit and every member of the limited liability partnership may when he thinks fit have access to and inspect and copy any of them.

(8) Each member shall render true accounts and full information of all things affecting the limited liability partnership to any member or his legal representatives.

(9) If a member, without the consent of the limited liability partnership, carries on any business of the same nature as and competing with the limited liability partnership, he must account for and pay over to the limited liability partnership all profits made by him in that business.

(10) Every member must account to the limited liability partnership for any benefit derived by him without the consent of the limited liability partnership from any transaction concerning the limited liability partnership, or from any use by him of the property of the limited liability partnership, name or business connection.

[10.106]

8 Expulsion

No majority of the members can expel any member unless a power to do so has been conferred by express agreement between the members.

PART VII MISCELLANEOUS

[10.107]

9 General and consequential amendments

(1) Subject to paragraph (2), the enactments mentioned in Schedule 5 shall have effect subject to the amendments specified in that Schedule.

(2) In the application of this regulation to Scotland—

- (a) paragraph 15 of Schedule 5 which amends section 110 of the 1986 Act shall not extend to Scotland; and
- (b) paragraph 22 of Schedule 5 which applies to limited liability partnerships the culpable officer provisions in existing primary legislation shall not extend to Scotland insofar as it relates to matters which have not been reserved by Schedule 5 to the Scotland Act 1998.

[10.108]

10 Application of subordinate legislation

(1) The subordinate legislation specified in Schedule 6 shall apply as from time to time in force to limited liability partnerships and—

- (a) in the case of the subordinate legislation listed in Part I of that Schedule with such modifications as the context requires for the purpose of giving effect to the provisions of the Companies Act 1985 which are applied by these Regulations;
- (b) in the case of the subordinate legislation listed in Part II of that Schedule with such modifications as the context requires for the purpose of giving effect to the provisions of the Insolvency Act 1986 which are applied by these Regulations; and
- (c) in the case of the subordinate legislation listed in Part III of that Schedule with such modifications as the context requires for the purpose of giving effect to the provisions of . . . the Company Directors Disqualification Act 1986 which are applied by these Regulations.

(2) In the case of any conflict between any provision of the subordinate legislation applied by paragraph (1) and any provision of these Regulations, the latter shall prevail.

NOTES

Para (1): words omitted from sub-para (c) revoked by the Limited Liability Partnerships (Application of Companies Act 2006) Regulations 2009, SI 2009/1804, reg 85, Sch 3, Pt 2, para 13(1), (4), as from 1 October 2009.

SCHEDULES

SCHEDULE 1

(Sch 1 (Modifications to Provisions of Part VII of the 1985 Act Applied by these Regulations) was revoked by the Limited Liability Partnerships (Accounts and Audit) (Application of Companies Act 2006) Regulations 2008, SI 2008/1911, reg 58(1)(a), as from 1 October 2008, except in relation to accounts for, and otherwise as regards, financial years beginning before that date (see reg 58(3) at **[10.286]***).)*

SCHEDULE 2

PART I MODIFICATIONS TO PROVISIONS OF THE 1985 ACT APPLIED TO LIMITED LIABILITY PARTNERSHIPS

Regulation 4

[10.109]

Provisions	**Modification**
. . .	
Investigation of companies and their affairs: Requisition of documents	
431 (investigation of a company on its own application or that of its members)	For subsection (2) substitute the following—
	"(2) The appointment may be made on the application of the limited liability partnership or on the application of not less than one-fifth in number of those who appear from notifications made to the registrar of companies to be currently members of the limited liability partnership."
432 (other company investigations)	
subsection (4)	For the words "but to whom shares in the company have been transferred or transmitted by operation of law" substitute "but to whom a member's share in the limited liability partnership has been transferred or transmitted by operation of law."
433 (inspectors' powers during investigation)	
434 (production of documents and evidence to inspectors)	
436 (obstruction of inspectors treated as contempt of court)	
437 (inspectors' reports)	
. . .	
439 (expenses of investigating a company's affairs)	
subsection (5)	Omit paragraph (b) together with the word "or" at the end of paragraph (a).
441 (inspectors' report to be evidence)	
[446A (general powers to give directions)	
446B (direction to terminate investigation)	
446C (resignation and revocation of appointment)	
446D (appointment of replacement inspectors)	
446E (obtaining information from former inspectors etc)]	
447 (Secretary of State's power to require production of documents)	
[447A (information provided: evidence)]	
448 (entry and search of premises)	
[448A (protection in relation to certain disclosures: information provided to Secretary of State)]	
449 (provision for security of information obtained)	
450 (punishment for destroying, mutilating etc company documents)	[Omit subsection (1A).]
451 (punishment for furnishing false information)	
451A (disclosure of information by Secretary of State or inspector)	[In subsection (1), for the words "sections 434 to 446E" substitute "sections 434 to 441 and 446E"]
	Omit subsection (5).
452 (privileged information)	[In subsection (1), for the words "In subsection (1), for the words "sections 431 to 446E" substitute "sections 431 to 441 and 446E"]

Provisions	Modification
	In subsection (1A), for the words "sections 434, 443 or 446" substitute "section 434".
[453A (power to enter and remain on premises)	In subsection (7), for the words "section 431, 432 or 442" substitute "section 431 or 432.
453B (power to enter and remain on premises: procedural)	
453C (failure to comply with certain requirements)]	
. . .	
Floating charges and Receivers (Scotland)	
464 (ranking of floating charges)	In subsection (1), for the words "section 462" substitute "the law of Scotland".
466 (alteration of floating charges)	Omit subsections (1), (2), (3) and (6).
486 (interpretation for Part XVIII generally)	For the current definition of "company" substitute ""company" means a limited liability partnership;" Omit the definition of "Register of Sasines".
487 (extent of Part XVIII)	
. . .	
[Schedule 15C (Security of information obtained: specified persons)	
Schedule 15D (Security of information obtained: specified disclosures)]	
. . .	

NOTES

Entries relating to ss 384, 385, 387, 388, 388A, 389A, 390, 390A, 390B, 391, 391A, 392, 392A, 394, 394A and 742 revoked by the Limited Liability Partnerships (Accounts and Audit) (Application of Companies Act 2006) Regulations 2008, SI 2008/1911, reg 58(1)(b), as from 1 October 2008.

All the other entries in this Schedule (except those relating to Part XIV (Investigation of companies and their affairs: Requisition of documents) (but including s 438) and Part XVIII (Floating charges and Receivers (Scotland))) were revoked by the Limited Liability Partnerships (Application of Companies Act 2006) Regulations 2009, SI 2009/1804, reg 85, Sch 3, Pt 2, para 13(5)(a), (b), as from 1 October 2009 (note that Sch 3, Pt 2, para 13(5)(a) was amended by the Limited Liability Partnerships (Amendment) Regulations 2009, SI 2009/1833, reg 33, as from the same date in order to correct a drafting error in the original Regulations). Note also that the revocation of the entry relating to s 438 does not affect proceedings brought under that section (as applied to LLPs) before 1 October 2009.

Entries relating to ss 446A–446E inserted by SI 2009/1804, reg 85, Sch 3, Pt 2, para 13(5)(c), as from 1 October 2009.

Entries relating to ss 447A, 448A, 453A–453C, Schs 15C, 15D inserted by the Limited Liability Partnerships (Amendment) Regulations 2007, SI 2007/2073, regs 2, 3, as from 1 October 2007.

Words in square brackets in entry relating to s 450 substituted, and words omitted from entry relating to s 460 revoked, by the Financial Services and Markets Act 2000 (Consequential Amendments) Order 2004, SI 2004/355, art 9, as from 4 March 2004.

Words in square brackets in entry relating to ss 451A, 452(1) substituted by SI 2009/1804, reg 85, Sch 3, Pt 2, para 13(5)(d), as from 1 October 2009.

PART II MODIFICATIONS TO THE COMPANY DIRECTORS DISQUALIFICATION ACT 1986

[10.110]

Part II of Schedule I	*After paragraph 8 insert—* *"8A The extent of the member's and shadow members' responsibility for events leading to a member or shadow member, whether himself or some other member or shadow member, being declared by the court to be liable to make a contribution to the assets of the limited liability partnership under section 214A of the Insolvency Act 1986."*

NOTES

Revoked, in relation to England and Wales, by the Insolvency (Miscellaneous Amendments) Regulations 2017, SI 2017/1119, reg 2, Sch 1, Pt 2, paras 4, 5, as from 8 December 2017.

SCHEDULE 3
MODIFICATIONS TO THE 1986 ACT

Regulation 5

[10.111]

Provisions	Modifications
[Section A3 (obtaining a moratorium by filing or lodging documents at court)	
subsection (1)	Omit paragraph (b) and the "and" preceding it.

Provisions	**Modifications**
subsection (2)	For "directors" substitute "designated members".
Section A4 (obtaining a moratorium for company subject to winding-up petition)	
subsection (2)	For "directors" substitute "designated members".
Section A5 (obtaining a moratorium for other overseas companies)	Omit.
Section A6 (the relevant documents)	
subsection (1)	In paragraph (a) for "directors wish" substitute "limited liability partnership wishes". In paragraph (d) for "directors" substitute "designated members".
Section A7 (beginning of moratorium and appointment of monitor)	
subsection (1)	Omit paragraph (c).
Section A8 (obligations to notify where moratorium comes into force)	
subsection (1)	For "directors" substitute "designated members".
subsection (4)	For "directors" substitute "designated members", and for "director" substitute "designated member".
Section A10 (extension by directors without creditor consent)	
subsection (1)	In the words before paragraph (a) for "directors" substitute "designated members". In paragraph (a) for "directors wish" substitute "limited liability partnership wishes". In paragraph (b) for "directors" substitute "designated members". In paragraph (c) for "directors" substitute "designated members".
Section A11 (extension by directors with creditor consent)	
subsection (1)	In the words before paragraph (a) for "directors" substitute "designated members". In paragraph (a) for "directors wish" substitute "limited liability partnership wishes". In paragraph (b) for "directors" substitute "designated members". In paragraph (c) for "directors" substitute "designated members". In paragraph (e) for "directors" substitute "designated members".
Section A13 (extension by court on application of directors)	
subsection (1)	For "directors" substitute "designated members".
subsection (2)	In paragraph (a) for "directors" substitute "designated members". In paragraph (b) for "directors" substitute "designated members". In paragraph (c) for "directors" substitute "designated members".
Section A14 (extension while proposal for CVA pending)	
subsection (1)	In paragraph (a) for "directors make" substitute "limited liability partnership makes".
subsection (3)	In paragraph (a) for "company and its creditors both" substitute "creditors of the limited liability partnership". Omit paragraph (b).
Section A17 (obligations to notify change in end of moratorium)	
subsection (1)	For "directors of a company" substitute "designated members of a limited liability partnership". In the table, for the heading of the third column substitute "the designated members must".
subsection (6)	For "directors" substitute "designated members", and for "director" substitute "designated member".
Section A20 (restrictions on insolvency proceedings etc)	
subsection (1)	In paragraph (a) for "directors" substitute "limited liability partnership". Omit paragraphs (b) and (c). In paragraph (d) for "directors" substitute "limited liability partnership". In paragraph (e) for "directors" substitute "limited liability partner-

Provisions	Modifications
	ship". In paragraph (f) omit "or 22(1)". In paragraph (g) omit "or 22(1)".
Section A24 (duty of directors to notify monitor of insolvency proceedings etc)	
subsection (1)	For "directors of a company must notify the monitor before taking" substitute "designated members of a limited liability partnership must notify the monitor before the limited liability partnership takes". In paragraph (c) substitute "22" for "22(2)".
subsection (2)	Omit.
subsection (3)	Omit "or (2)".
subsection (4)	For subsection (4) substitute— "(4) If the designated members fail to comply with subsection (1), any designated member who did not have a reasonable excuse for the failure commits an offence."
Section A31 (disposal of charged property free from charge)	
subsection (7)	For "directors" substitute "designated members".
subsection (8)	For "directors" substitute "designated members", and for "director" substitute "designated member".
Section A32 (disposal of hire-purchase property)	
subsection (5)	For "directors" substitute "designated members".
subsection (6)	For "directors" substitute "designated members", and for "director" substitute "designated member".
Section A36 (provision of information to monitor)	
subsection (1)	For "directors" substitute "designated members".
subsection (2)	For "directors" substitute "designated members".
Section A38 (termination of moratorium by monitor)	
subsection (1)	In paragraph (c) for "directors" substitute "designated members".
Section A39 (replacement of monitor or appointment of additional monitor)	
subsection (3)	For "directors" substitute "designated members".
Section A42 (challenge to monitor's actions)	
subsection (2)	In paragraph (a) omit ", director".
Section A44 (challenge to directors' actions)	
subsection (1)	In the text before paragraph (a) omit "or member". In paragraph (a), omit "or members" in both places where it appears.
Section A48 (prosecution of delinquent officers of company)	
subsection (3)	Omit paragraph (c) and the "and" preceding it.
Section A49 (regulated companies: modifications to this Part)	
subsection (4)	For "directors" substitute "designated members".
subsection (5)	For "directors" substitute "designated members", and for "director" substitute "designated member".]
Section 1 (those who may propose an arrangement)	
subsection (1)	For "The directors of a company" substitute "A limited liability partnership" and delete "to the company and".
subsection (3)	At the end add "but where a proposal is so made it must also be made to the limited liability partnership".
[*Section 1A (moratorium)*	
subsection (1)	*For "the directors of an eligible company intend" substitute "an eligible limited liability partnership intends".* *For "they" substitute "it".*]

The following modifications to sections 2 to 7 apply where a proposal under section 1 has been made by the limited liability partnership.

Provisions	**Modifications**
Section 2 (procedure where the nominee is not the liquidator or administrator)	
[*subsection (1)*	[*For "the directors do" substitute "the limited liability partnership does".*
[subsection (2)	In paragraph (b) omit "a meeting of the company and by". Omit paragraph (c).]
subsection (3)	For "the person intending to make the proposal" substitute "the designated members of the limited liability partnership".
subsection (4)	[In paragraph (a)] for "the person intending to make the proposal" substitute "the designated members of the limited liability partnership". [In paragraph (b) for "that person" substitute "those designated members".]
Section 3 (summoning of meetings)	
[subsection (1)	For subsection (1) substitute— "(1) Where the nominee under section 1 is not the liquidator or administrator, and it has been reported to the court under section 2(2) that the proposal should be considered by the creditors of the limited liability partnership, the person making the report shall (unless the court otherwise directs) seek a decision from the creditors of the limited liability partnership as to whether they approve the proposal.".
subsection (2)	Omit paragraph (a).]
Section 4 (decisions of meetings)	
[subsection (1)	Omit paragraph (a).]
[subsection (1A)	For "The company and its creditors" substitute "The creditors of the limited liability partnership".
subsection (3)	For "Neither the company nor its creditors" substitute "The creditors of the limited liability partnership may not".
subsection (4)	For "Neither the company nor its creditors" substitute "The creditors of the limited liability partnership may not".]
[subsection (4A)	For "neither the company nor its creditors may" substitute "the creditors of the limited liability partnership may not".]
[subsection (5)	Omit "the meeting of the company and".]
[new subsection (5A)	Insert a new subsection (5A) as follows— "(5A) If modifications to the proposal are proposed by creditors, the nominee under section 1(2) must, before the date on which the creditors are to be asked whether to approve the proposed voluntary arrangement, ascertain from the limited liability partnership whether or not it agrees to the proposed modifications; and if at that date the limited liability partnership has failed to respond to a proposed modification, it shall be presumed not to have agreed to it."]
[subsection (6)	Omit.]
[subsection (6A)	In paragraph (a) after "creditors' decision" insert "(including, where modifications to the proposal were proposed, the response of the limited liability partnership)". In paragraph (b) after "be prescribed" insert "and to the limited liability partnership".
[Section 4A (approval of arrangement)	
[subsection (2)	In paragraph (a) for "meeting of the company summoned under section 3 and by the company's creditors pursuant to that section, or", substitute "the creditors of the limited liability partnership pursuant to section 3"; Omit paragraph (b).]
subsection (3)	Omit.
subsection (4)	Omit.
subsection (5)	Omit.
[subsection (5A)	Omit.]
subsection (6)	Omit.]
Section 5 (effect of approval)	
. . .	. . .
[subsection (4)	In paragraph (a) for "each of the reports required by section 4(6) and (6A)" substitute "the report required by section 4(6A)".]

Provisions	Modifications
Section 6 (challenge of decisions)	
[subsection (1)	In paragraph (b) omit "the meeting of the company, or in relation to".
subsection (2)	In paragraph (a) omit "at the meeting of the company or". After paragraph (aa) insert a new paragraph as follows— "(ab) any member of the limited liability partnership; and". Omit the word "and" at the end of paragraph (b). Omit paragraph (c).]
subsection (3)	In paragraph (a) for "each for the reports required by section 4(6) and (6A)" substitute "the report required by section 4(6A)".
subsection (4)	For subsection (4) substitute the following— "(4) Where on such an application the court is satisfied as to either of the grounds mentioned in subsection (1), it may do either of the following, namely— (a) revoke or suspend any decision approving the voluntary arrangement which has effect under section 4A or, in a case falling within subsection (1)(b) any decision taken in the relevant qualifying decision procedure which has effect under that section; (b) direct any person— (i) to seek a decision from the creditors of the limited liability partnership, using a qualifying decision procedure, as to whether they approve any revised proposal the person who made the original proposal may make; or (ii) in a case falling within subsection (1)(b) and relating to the relevant qualifying decision procedure, to seek a decision from the creditors of the limited liability partnership, using a qualifying decision procedure, as to whether they approve the original proposal."
subsection (5)	Omit "or (c)".]
[subsection (7)	Omit paragraph (a).]
[Section 6A (false representations, etc)	
subsection (1)	Omit "members or".]
Section 7 (implementation of proposal)	
. . .	. . .
[subsection (2)	In paragraph (a) for "company or its creditors (or both)" substitute "creditors of the limited liability partnership".]

The following modifications to sections 2 and 3 apply where a proposal under section 1 has been made, where [the limited liability partnership is in administration], by the administrator or, where the limited liability partnership is being wound up, by the liquidator.

Provisions	Modifications
Section 2	
[subsection (2)	In paragraph (b) for "the company" substitute "members of the limited liability partnership".]
Section 3 (summoning of meetings)	
[subsection (2)	In paragraph (a) for "the company" substitute "members of the limited liability partnership".]
. . .	. . .
. . .	. . .
. . .	. . .
. . .	. . .
. . .	. . .
. . .	. . .
. . .	. . .
Section 74 (liability as contributories of present and past members)	For section 74 there shall be substituted the following— "74. When a limited liability partnership is wound up every present and past member of the limited liability partnership who has agreed with the other members or with the limited liability partnership that he will, in circumstances which have arisen, be liable to contribute to the assets of the limited liability partnership in the event that the limited liability partnership goes into liquidation is liable, to the extent that he has so agreed, to contribute to its assets to any amount sufficient for payment of its debts and liabili-

Provisions	Modifications
	ties, and the expenses of the winding up, and for the adjustment of the rights of the contributories among themselves. However, a past member shall only be liable if the obligation arising from such agreement survived his ceasing to be a member of the limited liability partnership."
Section 75 to 78	Delete sections 75 to 78.
Section 79 (meaning of "contributory")	
subsection (1)	In subsection (1) for "every person" substitute "(a) every present member of the limited liability partnership and (b) every past member of the limited liability partnership".
subsection (2)	After "section 214 (wrongful trading)" insert "or 214A (adjustment of withdrawals)".
subsection (3)	Delete subsection (3).
Section 83 (companies registered under Companies Act, Part XXII, Chapter II)	Delete section 83.
Section 84 (circumstances in which company may be wound up voluntarily)	
subsection (1)	For subsection (1) substitute the following— "(1) A limited liability partnership may be wound up voluntarily when it determines that it is to be wound up voluntarily."
subsection (2)	Omit subsection (2).
[subsection (2A)	For "company passes a resolution for voluntary winding up" substitute "limited liability partnership determines that it is to be wound up voluntarily" and for "resolution" where it appears for the second time substitute "determination".
subsection (2B)	For "resolution for voluntary winding up may be passed only" substitute "determination to wind up voluntarily may only be made" and in sub-paragraph (b), for "passing of the resolution" substitute "making of the determination".]
subsection (3)	For subsection (3) substitute the following— "(3) Within 15 days after a limited liability partnership has determined that it be wound up there shall be forwarded to the registrar of companies either a printed copy or else a copy in some other form approved by the registrar of the determination."
subsection [(5)]	After subsection [(4)] insert a new subsection [(5)]— "[(5)] If a limited liability partnership fails to comply with this regulation the limited liability partnership and every designated member of it who is in default is liable on summary conviction to a fine not exceeding level 3 on the standard scale."
Section 85 (notice of resolution to wind up)	
subsection (1)	For subsection (1) substitute the following— "(1) When a limited liability partnership has determined that it shall be wound up voluntarily, it shall within 14 days after the making of the determination give notice of the determination by advertisement in the Gazette."
Section 86 (commencement of winding up)	Substitute the following new section— "86. A voluntary winding up is deemed to commence at the time when the limited liability partnership determines that it be wound up voluntarily.".
Section 87 (effect on business and status of company)	
subsection (2)	In subsection (2), for "articles" substitute "limited liability partnership agreement".
Section 88 (avoidance of share transfers, etc after winding-up resolution)	For "shares" substitute "the interest of any member in the property of the limited liability partnership".
Section 89 (statutory declaration of solvency)	For "director(s)" wherever it appears in section 89 substitute "designated member(s)";

Provisions	Modifications
subsection (2)	For paragraph (a) substitute the following— "(a) it is made within the 5 weeks immediately preceding the date when the limited liability partnership determined that it be wound up voluntarily or on that date but before the making of the determination, and".
subsection (3)	For "the resolution for winding up is passed" substitute "the limited liability partnership determined that it be wound up voluntarily".
subsection (5)	For "in pursuance of a resolution passed" substitute "voluntarily".
Section 90 (distinction between "members" and "creditors" voluntary winding up)	For "directors'" substitute "designated members'".
Section 91 (appointment of liquidator)	
subsection (1)	Delete "in general meeting".
subsection (2)	For the existing wording substitute— "(2) On the appointment of a liquidator the powers of the members of the limited liability partnership shall cease except to the extent that a meeting of the members of the limited liability partnership summoned for the purpose or the liquidator sanctions their continuance." After subsection (2) insert— "(3) Subsections (3) and (4) of section 92 shall apply for the purposes of this section as they apply for the purposes of that section."
Section 92 (power to fill vacancy in office of liquidator)	
subsection (1)	For "the company in general meeting" substitute "a meeting of the members of the limited liability partnership summoned for the purpose".
subsection (2)	For "a general meeting" substitute "a meeting of the members of the limited liability partnership".
subsection (3)	In subsection (3), for "articles" substitute "limited liability partnership agreement".
new subsection (4)	Add a new subsection (4) as follows— "(4) The quorum required for a meeting of the members of the limited liability partnership shall be any quorum required by the limited liability partnership agreement for meetings of the members of the limited liability partnership and if no requirement for a quorum has been agreed upon the quorum shall be 2 members."
. . .	
. . .	. . .
Section 95 (effect of company's insolvency)	
subsection (1)	For "directors'" substitute "designated members'".
. . .	
Section 96 (conversion to creditors' voluntary winding up)	
[subsection (2)	For "directors" substitute "designated members".]
. . .	
. . .	. . .
Section 99 (directors to lay statement of affairs before creditors)	
[subsection (1)	For "directors of the company" substitute "designated members".
subsection (2A)	For "directors" substitute "designated members".
subsection (3)	For "directors" substitute "designated members".]
Section 100 (appointment of liquidator)	
[subsection (1)	For subsection (1) substitute the following— "(1) The members of the limited liability partnership may nominate a person to be liquidator at the meeting at which the resolution for voluntary winding up is passed."
[subsection (1B)	For "directors of the company" substitute "designated members".]
subsection (3)	Delete "director,".
Section 101 (appointment of liquidation	

Provisions	**Modifications**
committee)	
subsection (2)	For subsection (2) substitute the following— "(2) If such a committee is appointed, the limited liability partnership may, when it determines that it be wound up voluntarily or at any time thereafter, appoint such number of persons as they think fit to act as members of the committee, not exceeding 5."
. . .	
. . .	. . .
Section 110 (acceptance of shares, etc, as consideration for sale of company property)	For the existing section substitute the following— "(1) This section applies, in the case of a limited liability partnership proposed to be, or being, wound up voluntarily, where the whole or part of the limited liability partnership's business or property is proposed to be transferred or sold to another company whether or not it is a company within the meaning of the Companies Act ("the transferee company") or to a limited liability partnership ("the transferee limited liability partnership"). (2) With the requisite sanction, the liquidator of the limited liability partnership being, or proposed to be, wound up ("the transferor limited liability partnership") may receive, in compensation or part compensation for the transfer or sale, shares, policies or other like interests in the transferee company or the transferee limited liability partnership for distribution among the members of the transferor limited liability partnership. (3) The sanction required under subsection (2) is— (a) in the case of a members' voluntary winding up, that of a determination of the limited liability partnership at a meeting of the members of the limited liability partnership conferring either a general authority on the liquidator or an authority in respect of any particular arrangement, (subsections (3) and (4) of section 92 to apply for this purpose as they apply for the purposes of that section), and (b) in the case of a creditor's voluntary winding up, that of either court or the liquidation committee. (4) Alternatively to subsection (2), the liquidator may (with the sanction) enter into any other arrangement whereby the members of the transferor limited liability partnership may, in lieu of receiving cash, shares, policies or other like interests (or in addition thereto), participate in the profits, or receive any other benefit from the transferee company or the transferee limited liability partnership. (5) A sale or arrangement in pursuance of this section is binding on members of the transferor limited liability partnership. (6) A determination by the limited liability partnership is not invalid for the purposes of this section by reason that it is made before or concurrently with a determination by the limited liability partnership that it be wound up voluntarily or for appointing liquidators; but, if an order is made within a year for winding up the limited liability partnership by the court, the determination by the limited liability partnership is not valid unless sanctioned by the court."
Section 111 (dissent from arrangement under section 110)	
subsections (1)–(3)	For subsections (1)–(3) substitute the following— "(1) This section applies in the case of a voluntary winding up where, for the purposes of section 110(2) or (4), a determination of the limited liability partnership has provided the sanction requisite for the liquidator under that section. (2) If a member of the transferor limited liability partnership who did not vote in favour of providing the sanction required for the liquidator under section 110 expresses his dissent from it in writing addressed to the liquidator and left at the registered office of the limited liability partnership within 7 days after the date on which that sanction was given, he may require the liquidator either to abstain from carrying the arrangement so sanctioned into effect or to purchase his interest at a price to be determined by agreement or arbitration under this section.

Provisions	Modifications
	(3) If the liquidator elects to purchase the member's interest, the purchase money must be paid before the limited liability partnership is dissolved and be raised by the liquidator in such manner as may be determined by the limited liability partnership."
subsection (4)	Omit subsection (4).
Section 117 (high court and county court jurisdiction)	
subsection (2)	Delete "Where the amount of a company's share capital paid up or credited as paid up does not exceed £120,000, then (subject to this section)".
subsection (3)	Delete subsection (3).
Section 120 (court of session and sheriff court jurisdiction)	
subsection (3)	Delete "Where the amount of a company's share capital paid up or credited as paid up does not exceed £120,000,".
subsection (5)	Delete subsection (5).
Section 122 (circumstances in which company may be wound up by the court)	
subsection (1)	For subsection (1) substitute the following— "(1) A limited liability partnership may be wound up by the court if— (a) the limited liability partnership has determined that the limited liability partnership be wound up by the court, (b) the limited liability partnership does not commence its business within a year from its incorporation or suspends its business for a whole year, (c) the number of members is reduced below two, (d) the limited liability partnership is unable to pay its debts . . . [*(da) at the time at which a moratorium for the limited liability partnership under section 1A comes to an end, no voluntary arrangement approved under Part I has effect in relation to the limited liability partnership,*] (e) the court is of the opinion that it is just and equitable that the limited liability partnership should be wound up."
Section 124 (application for winding up)	
subsections (2), (3) and (4)(a)	Delete these subsections.
[*subsection (3A)*	*For "122(1)(fa)" substitute "122(1)(da)".*]
Section 124A (petition for winding-up on grounds of public interest)	
subsection (1)	[Omit paragraphs (b) and (bb).]
Section 126 (power to stay or restrain proceedings against company)	
subsection (2)	Delete subsection (2).
Section 127 (avoidance of property dispositions, etc)	
[subsection (1)]	For "any transfer of shares" substitute "any transfer by a member of the limited liability partnership of his interest in the property of the limited liability partnership".
Section 129 (commencement of winding up by the court)	
subsection (1)	For "a resolution has been passed by the company" substitute "a determination has been made" and for "at the time of the passing of the resolution" substitute "at the time of that determination".
Section 130 (consequences of winding-up order)	
subsection (3)	Delete subsection (3).
Section 148 (settlement of list of contributories and application of assets)	
subsection (1)	Delete ", with power to rectify the register of members in all cases where rectification is required in pursuance of the Companies Act or this Act,".

Provisions	Modifications
Section 149 (debts due from contributory to company)	
subsection (1)	Delete "the Companies Act or".
subsection (2)	Delete subsection (2).
subsection (3)	Delete ", whether limited or unlimited,".
Section 160 (delegation of powers to liquidator (England and Wales))	
subsection (1)	In subsection (1)(b) delete "and the rectifying of the register of members".
subsection (2)	For subsection (2) substitute the following—
	"(2) But the liquidator shall not make any call without the special leave of the court or the sanction of the liquidation committee."
Section 165 (voluntary winding up)	
. . .	. . .
subsection (4)	For paragraph (c) substitute the following—
	"(c) summon meetings of the members of the limited liability partnership for the purpose of obtaining their sanction or for any other purpose he may think fit."
new subsection (4A)	Insert a new subsection (4A) as follows—
	"(4A) Subsections (3) and (4) of section 92 shall apply for the purposes of this section as they apply for the purposes of that section."
Section 166 (creditors' voluntary winding up)	
[subsection (5)	For "directors" substitute "designated members".]
Section 171 (removal, etc (voluntary winding up))	
subsection (2)	For paragraph (a) substitute the following—
	"(a) in the case of a members' voluntary winding up, by a meeting of the members of the limited liability partnership summoned specially for that purpose, or".
[new subsection (8)	Insert a new subsection (8) as follows—
	"(8) subsections (3) and (4) of section 92 are to apply for the purposes of this section as they apply for the purposes of that section."]
Section 173 (release (voluntary winding up))	
[subsection (2)	In paragraph (a)(i) for "a general meeting of the company" substitute "a meeting of the members of the limited liability partnership".]
[Section 174A (moratorium debts etc: priority)	
subsection (9)	For paragraph (b) substitute—
	"(b) the limited liability partnership determines that it is to be wound up voluntarily.".]
Section 183 (effect of execution or attachment (England and Wales))	
subsection (2)	Delete paragraph (a).
Section 184 (duties of sheriff (England and Wales))	
subsection (1)	For "a resolution for voluntary winding up has been passed" substitute "the limited liability partnership has determined that it be wound up voluntarily".
subsection (4)	Delete "or of a meeting having been called at which there is to be proposed a resolution for voluntary winding up," and "or a resolution is passed (as the case may be)".
Section 187 (power to make over assets to employees)	
	Delete section 187.
. . .	. . .
Section 195 (meetings to ascertain wishes of creditors or contributories)	
subsection (3)	Delete "the Companies Act or".
Section 206 (fraud, etc in anticipation of winding up)	

Provisions	Modifications
subsection (1)	For "passes a resolution for voluntary winding up" substitute "makes a determination that it be wound up voluntarily".
Section 207 (transactions in fraud of creditors)	
subsection (1)	For "passes a resolution for voluntary winding up" substitute "makes a determination that it be wound up voluntarily".
Section 210 (material omissions from statement relating to company's affairs)	
subsection (2)	For "passed a resolution for voluntary winding up" substitute "made a determination that it be wound up voluntarily".
Section 214 (wrongful trading)	
subsection (2)	Delete from "but the court shall not" to the end of the subsection.
After section 214	Insert the following new section 214A— "**214A Adjustment of withdrawals** (1) This section has effect in relation to a person who is or has been a member of a limited liability partnership where, in the course of the winding up of that limited liability partnership, it appears that subsection (2) of this section applies in relation to that person. (2) This subsection applies in relation to a person if— (a) within the period of two years ending with the commencement of the winding up, he was a member of the limited liability partnership who withdrew property of the limited liability partnership, whether in the form of a share of profits, salary, repayment of or payment of interest on a loan to the limited liability partnership or any other withdrawal of property, and (b) it is proved by the liquidator to the satisfaction of the court that at the time of the withdrawal he knew or had reasonable ground for believing that the limited liability partnership— (i) was at the time of the withdrawal unable to pay its debts within the meaning of section 123, or (ii) would become so unable to pay its debts after the assets of the limited liability partnership had been depleted by that withdrawal taken together with all other withdrawals (if any) made by any members contemporaneously with that withdrawal or in contemplation when that withdrawal was made. (3) Where this section has effect in relation to any person the court, on the application of the liquidator, may declare that that person is to be liable to make such contribution (if any) to the limited liability partnership's assets as the court thinks proper. (4) The court shall not make a declaration in relation to any person the amount of which exceeds the aggregate of the amounts or values of all the withdrawals referred to in subsection (2) made by that person within the period of two years referred to in that subsection. (5) The court shall not make a declaration under this section with respect to any person unless that person knew or ought to have concluded that after each withdrawal referred to in subsection (2) there was no reasonable prospect that the limited liability partnership would avoid going into insolvent liquidation. (6) For the purposes of subsection (5) the facts which a member ought to know or ascertain and the conclusions which he ought to reach are those which would be known, ascertained, or reached by a reasonably diligent person having both: (a) the general knowledge, skill and experience that may reasonably be expected of a person carrying out the same functions as are carried out by that member in relation to the limited liability partnership, and (b) the general knowledge, skill and experience that that member has. (7) For the purposes of this section a limited liability partnership goes into insolvent liquidation if it goes into liquidation at a time when its assets are insufficient for the payment of its debts and other liabilities and the expenses of the winding up. (8) In this section "member" includes a shadow member.

Provisions	Modifications
	(9) This section is without prejudice to section 214."
Section 215 (proceedings under ss 213, 214)	
subsection (1)	Omit the word "or" between the words "213" and "214" and insert after "214" "or 214A".
subsection (2)	For "either section" substitute "any of those sections".
subsection (4)	For "either section" substitute "any of those sections".
subsection (5)	For "Sections 213 and 214" substitute "Sections 213, 214 or 214A".
Section 218 (prosecution of delinquent officers and members of company)	
subsection (1)	For "officer, or any member, of the company" substitute "member of the limited liability partnership".
subsections (3), (4) and (6)	For "officer of the company, or any member of it," substitute "officer or member of the limited liability partnership".
. . .	. . .
Section 247 ("insolvency" and "go into liquidation")	
subsection (2)	For "passes a resolution for voluntary winding up" substitute "makes a determination that it be wound up voluntarily" and for "passing such a resolution" substitute "making such a determination".
[subsection (3)	For "resolution for voluntary winding up" substitute "determination to wind up voluntarily".]
Section 249 ("connected with a company")	For the existing words substitute— "For the purposes of any provision in this Group of Parts, a person is connected with a company (including a limited liability partnership) if— (a) he is a director or shadow director of a company or an associate of such a director or shadow director (including a member or a shadow member of a limited liability partnership or an associate of such a member or shadow member); or (b) he is an associate of the company or of the limited liability partnership."
Section 250 ("member" of a company)	Delete section 250.
Section 251 (expressions used generally)	Delete the word "and" appearing after the definition of "the rules" and insert the word "and" after the definition of "shadow director". After the definition of "shadow director" insert the following— ""shadow member", in relation to a limited liability partnership, means a person in accordance with whose directions or instructions the members of the limited liability partnership are accustomed to act (but so that a person is not deemed a shadow member by reason only that the members of the limited liability partnership act on advice given by him in a professional capacity);".
Section 386 (categories of preferential debts)	
subsection (1)	In subsection (1), omit the words "or an individual".
subsection (2)	In subsection (2), omit the words "or the individual".
Section 387 ("the relevant date")	
subsection (3)	[In paragraph (ab) for "passed a resolution for voluntary winding up" substitute "made a determination that it be wound up voluntarily".] In paragraph (c) for "passing of the resolution for the winding up of the company" substitute "making of the determination by the limited liability partnership that it be wound up voluntarily".
subsection (5)	Omit subsection (5).
subsection (6)	Omit subsection (6).
Section 388 (meaning of "act as insolvency practitioner")	
subsection (2)	Omit subsection (2).

Provisions	Modifications
subsection (3)	Omit subsection (3).
subsection (4)	Delete ""company" means a company within the meaning given by section 735(1) of the Companies Act or a company which may be wound up under Part V of this Act (unregistered companies);" and delete ""interim trustee" and "permanent trustee" mean the same as the Bankruptcy (Scotland) Act 1985".
Section 389 (acting without qualification an offence)	
subsection (1)	Omit the words "or an individual".
. . .	. . .
Section 402 (official petitioner)	Delete section 402.
Section 412 (individual insolvency rules (England and Wales))	Delete section 412.
Section 415 (Fees orders (individual insolvency proceedings in England and Wales))	Delete section 415.
Section 416 (monetary limits (companies winding up))	
subsection (1)	In subsection (1), omit the words "section 117(2) (amount of company's share capital determining whether county court has jurisdiction to wind it up);" and the words "section 120(3) (the equivalent as respects sheriff court jurisdiction in Scotland);".
subsection (3)	In subsection (3), omit the words "117(2), 120(3) or".
Section 418 (monetary limits (bankruptcy))	Delete section 418.
Section 420 (insolvent partnerships)	Delete section 420.
Section 421 (insolvent estates of deceased persons)	Delete section 421.
Section 422 (recognised banks, etc)	Delete section 422.
[Section 426A (disqualification from Parliament (England and Wales))	Omit.
Section 426B (devolution)	Omit.
Section 426C (irrelevance of privilege)	Omit.]
Section 427 (parliamentary disqualification)	Delete section 427.
Section 429 (disabilities on revocation or administration order against an individual)	Delete section 429.
Section 432 (offences by bodies corporate)	
subsection (2)	Delete "secretary or".
Section 435 (meaning of "associate")	
new subsection (3A)	Insert a new subsection (3A) as follows— "(3A) A member of a limited liability partnership is an associate of that limited liability partnership and of every other member of that limited liability partnership and of the husband or wife [or civil partner] or relative of every other member of that limited liability partnership.".
subsection (11)	For subsection (11) there shall be substituted— "(11) In this section "company" includes any body corporate (whether incorporated in Great Britain or elsewhere); and references to directors and other officers of a company and to voting power at any general meeting of a company have effect with any necessary modifications.".
Section 436 (expressions used generally)	The following expressions and definitions shall be added to the section— ""designated member" has the same meaning as it has in the Limited Liability Partnerships Act 2000; "limited liability partnership" means a limited liability partnership formed and registered under the Limited Liability Partnerships Act 2000; "limited liability partnership agreement", in relation to a limited

Provisions	Modifications
	liability partnership, means any agreement, express or implied, made between the members of the limited liability partnership or between the limited liability partnership and the members of the limited liability partnership which determines the mutual rights and duties of the members, and their rights and duties in relation to the limited liability partnership.".
Section 437 (transitional provisions, and savings)	Delete section 437.
Section 440 (extent (Scotland))	
subsection (2)	In subsection (2), omit paragraph (b).
Section 441 (extent (Northern Ireland))	
	Delete section 441.
Section 442 (extent (other territories))	
	Delete section 442.
[***Schedule A1***	
Paragraph 6	
sub-paragraph (1)	*For "directors of a company wish" substitute "limited liability partnership wishes".*
	For "they" substitute "the designated members of the limited liability partnership".
[sub-paragraph (2)	*For "directors" substitute "designated members of the limited liability partnership".*
	In sub-paragraph (c) for "company and by the company's creditors" substitute "creditors of the limited liability partnership".]
Paragraph 7	
[sub-paragraph (1)	*For "directors of a company" substitute "designated members of the limited liability partnership".*
	In sub-paragraph (e)(iii) for "company and by the company's creditors" substitute "creditors of the limited liability partnership".]
Paragraph 8	
[sub-paragraph (2)(a)	*Omit.*
sub-paragraph (3A)	*Omit.*
sub-paragraph (4)(a)	*Omit.*
sub-paragraph (6)(c)(i)	*Omit.*]
Paragraph 9	
sub-paragraph (1)	*For "directors" substitute "designated members of the limited liability partnership".*
sub-paragraph (2)	*For "directors" substitute "designated members of the limited liability partnership".*
Paragraph 12	
sub-paragraph (1)(b)	*Omit.*
sub-paragraph (1)(c)	*For "resolution may be passed" substitute "determination that it may be wound up may be made".*
sub-paragraph (2)	*For "transfer of shares" substitute "any transfer by a member of the limited liability partnership of his interest in the property of the limited liability partnership".*
Paragraph 20	
sub-paragraph (8)	*For "directors" substitute "designated members of the limited liability partnership".*
sub-paragraph (9)	*For "directors" substitute "designated members of the limited liability partnership".*
Paragraph 24	
sub-paragraph (2)	*For "directors" substitute "designated members of the limited liability partnership".*
Paragraph 25	
sub-paragraph (2)(c)	*For "directors" substitute "designated members of the limited liability partnership".*
Paragraph 26	
sub-paragraph (1)	*Omit ", director".*
Paragraph 29	

Provisions	Modifications
[sub-paragraph (1)(a)	*Omit.]*
Paragraph 30	
[sub-paragraph (1)	*Omit "the company meeting summoned under paragraph 29 and". For "that paragraph" substitute "paragraph 29".*
new sub-paragraph (1A)	*"If modifications to the proposal are proposed by creditors, the nominee must, before the date on which the creditors are to be asked whether to approve the proposed voluntary arrangement, ascertain from the limited liability partnership whether or not it agrees to the proposed modifications; and if at that date the limited liability partnership has failed to respond to a proposed modification, it shall be presumed not to have agreed to it.".]*
[sub-paragraph (2)	*Omit.]*
. . .	. . .
[sub-paragraph (3)	*Omit.]*
Paragraph 31	
[sub-paragraph (1)(a)	*Omit.*
sub-paragraph (1A)	*For "The company and its creditors" substitute "The creditors of the limited liability partnership".*
sub-paragraph (4)	*For "Neither the company nor its creditors may" substitute "The creditors of the limited liability partnership may not".*
sub-paragraph (5)	*For "neither the company nor its creditors may" substitute "the creditors of the limited liability partnership may not".*
sub-paragraph (7)	*For sub-paragraph (7) substitute the following—* *"(7) The designated members of the limited liability partnership may, before the beginning of the relevant period, give notice to the nominee of any modifications of the proposal for which the designated members intend to seek the approval of the creditors.".*
sub-paragraph (7A)(a)	*Omit.]*
Paragraph 32	
[sub-paragraph (1)	*Omit.*
sub-paragraph (3)	*Omit "the meeting of the company or (as the case may be) inform".*
sub-paragraph (4)	*For sub-paragraph (4) substitute—* *"(4) Where, in accordance with sub-paragraph (3)(b) the nominee informs the creditors of the limited liability partnership, of the expected cost of his intended actions, the creditors by a qualifying decision procedure shall decide whether or not to approve that expected cost.".*
sub-paragraph (6)	*For "A meeting of the company may resolve, and the creditors by a qualifying decision procedure may decide," substitute "The creditors by a qualifying decision procedure may decide".]*
[Paragraph 35	
sub-paragraph (1)	*Omit "a meeting of the company resolves, or".*
sub-paragraph (1A)	*Omit "meeting may resolve, and the".* *Omit "by the meeting or (as the case may be)".*
sub-paragraph (2)	*Omit.]*
Paragraph 36	
sub-paragraph (2)	*For sub-paragraph (2) substitute—* *"(2) The decision has effect if, in accordance with the rules, it has been taken by the creditors' meeting summoned under paragraph 29.".*
sub-paragraph (3)	*Omit.*
sub-paragraph (4)	*Omit.*
sub-paragraph (5)	*Omit.*
. . .	. . .
Paragraph 38	
[sub-paragraph (1)(b)	*Omit "at or in relation to the meeting of the company summoned under paragraph 29, or".*
sub-paragraph (2)(a)	*Omit "at the meeting of the company or".*
sub-paragraph (3)(a)	*For "30(3) and (4)" substitute "30(4)".*
sub-paragraph (4)(a)(ii)	*Omit "by the meeting of the company, or".*

Provisions	Modifications
sub-paragraph (4)(b)	*Omit.*
sub-paragraph (5)	*Omit "(b)(i) or".*
sub-paragraph (6)	*For "(4)(b) or (c)" substitute "(4)(c)".*
sub-paragraph (7)(a)	*Omit "(b) or".*]
. . .	. . .
Schedule B1	
Paragraph 2	
sub-paragraph (c)	For "company or its directors" substitute "limited liability partnership".
Paragraph 8	
sub-paragraph (1)(a)	For "resolution for voluntary winding up" substitute "determination to wind up voluntarily".
Paragraph 9	Omit.
Paragraph 12	
sub-paragraph (1)(b)	Omit.
Paragraph 22	For sub-paragraph (1) substitute— "(1) A limited liability partnership may appoint an administrator.". Omit sub-paragraph (2).
Paragraph 23	
sub-paragraph (1)(b)	Omit "or its directors".
Paragraph 42	
sub-paragraph (2)	For "resolution may be passed for the winding up of" substitute "determination to wind up voluntarily may be made by".
[Paragraph 60A	
sub-paragraph (3)(b)	For "a company connected with the company." substitute "a company or limited liability partnership connected with the limited liability partnership.".]
Paragraph 61	For paragraph 61 substitute—" "61. The administrator has power to prevent any person from taking part in the management of the business of the limited liability partnership and to appoint any person to be a manager of that business.".
Paragraph 62	At the end add the following— "Subsections (3) and (4) of section 92 shall apply for the purposes of this paragraph as they apply for the purposes of that section.".
Paragraph 83	
sub-paragraph (6)(b)	For "resolution for voluntary winding up" substitute "determination to wind up voluntarily".
sub-paragraph (8)(b)	For "passing of the resolution for voluntary winding up" substitute "determination to wind up voluntarily".
sub-paragraph (8)(e)	For "passing of the resolution for voluntary winding up" substitute "determination to wind up voluntarily".
Paragraph 87	
sub-paragraph (2)(b)	Insert at the end "or".
sub-paragraph (2)(c)	Omit ", or".
sub-paragraph (2)(d)	Omit the words from "(d)" to "company".
Paragraph 89	
sub-paragraph (2)(b)	Insert at the end "or".
sub-paragraph (2)(c)	Omit ", or".
sub-paragraph (2)(d)	Omit the words from "(d)" to "company".
Paragraph 91	
sub-paragraph (1)(c)	Omit.
Paragraph 94	Omit.
Paragraph 95	For "to 94" substitute "and 93".
Paragraph 97	
sub-paragraph (1)(a)	Omit "or directors".
Paragraph 103	
sub-paragraph (5)	Omit.

Provisions	Modifications
Paragraph 105	Omit.]
Schedule 1	
Paragraph 19	For paragraph 19 substitute the following—
	"19. Power to enforce any rights the limited liability partnership has against the members under the terms of the limited liability partnership agreement."
Schedule 10	
Section A8(4)	For "Directors" substitute "Designated members".
Section A17(6)	For "Directors" substitute "Designated members".
Section A24(4)	For "Directors" substitute "Designated members".
Section A31(8)	For "Directors" substitute "Designated members".
Section A32(6)	For "Directors" substitute "Designated members".
Section A49(5)	For "Directors" substitute "Designated members".]
[Section 6A(1)	In the entry relating to section 6A omit "members' or".]
Section 85(2)	In the entry relating to section 85(2) for "resolution for voluntary winding up" substitute "making of determination for voluntary winding up".
Section 89(4)	In the entry relating to section 89(4) for "Director" substitute "Designated member".
Section 93(3)	In the entry relating to section 93(3) for "general meeting of the company" substitute "meeting of members of the limited liability partnership".
Section 99(3)	In the entries relating to section 99(3) for "director" and "directors" where they appear substitute "designated member" or "designated members" as appropriate.
Section 105(3)	In the entry relating to section 105(3) for "company general meeting" substitute "meeting of the members of the limited liability partnership".
. . .	. . .
Sections 353(1) to 362	Delete the entries relating to sections 353(1) to 362 inclusive.
Section 429(5)	Delete the entry relating to section 429(5).
[*Schedule A1, paragraph 9(2)*	*For "Directors" substitute "Designated Members".*
Schedule A1, paragraph 20(9)	*For "Directors" substitute "Designated Members".*
Schedule B1, paragraph 27(4)	Omit "or directors".
Schedule B1, paragraph 29(7)	Omit "or directors".
Schedule B1, paragraph 32	Omit "or directors".]

NOTES

Entries relating to sections A3–A49 inserted by the Limited Liability Partnerships (Amendment etc) Regulations 2021, SI 2021/60, reg 3, Sch 1, paras 1, 2, as from 16 February 2021. See also reg 3(2) of the 2021 Regulations (at **[10.1304]**) which provides that nothing in those Regulations affects the operation of the Insolvency Act 1986, or any other enactment, in relation to a moratorium under Sch A1 to that Act which comes into force before the repeal of that Schedule by Sch 3 to the Corporate Insolvency and Governance Act 2020 (ie, 26 June 2020). Note also that this amendment is identical to an earlier amendment made by the Limited Liability Partnerships (Amendment etc) Regulations 2020, SI 2020/643 which applied from 26 June 2020 (the 2020 Regulations were revoked by the 2021 Regulations as from 16 February 2021).

Entries relating to sections 1A, 4A, 6A, 389A, 426A–426C inserted by the Limited Liability Partnerships (Amendment) Regulations 2005, SI 2005/1989, reg 3, Sch 2, paras 1, 2, 3(b), (e), 12, 13, as from 1 October 2005, except in relation to a case where a petition for an administration order has been presented before that date; and subsequently amended as follows:

Entry relating to section 1A revoked by SI 2021/60, reg 3, Sch 1, paras 1, 3, as from 16 February 2021 (for transitional provisions, etc, see the note relating to sections A3–A49 above).

Entry relating to s 389A (omitted) revoked by the Deregulation Act 2015 (Insolvency) (Consequential Amendments and Transitional and Savings Provisions) Order 2015, SI 2015/1641, art 4, Sch 1, para 3(1), (2), as from 1 October 2015.

The following amendments relate to the entries for ss 2–7 following the heading "The following modifications to sections 2 to 7 apply where a proposal under section 1 has been made by the limited liability partnership":

(i) In the entry relating to section 2, the entry for sub-s (2) was substituted by the Insolvency (Miscellaneous Amendments) Regulations 2017, SI 2017/1119, reg 2, Sch 1, Pt 2, paras 6, 7, as from 8 December 2017 (note that Sch 1, Pt 2 to the 2017 Regulations applies to England and Wales only, and this entry, as it had effect before the amendments made by the 2017 Regulations, is set out below). Other words in square brackets inserted by SI 2005/1989, reg 3, Sch 2, paras 1, 3(a), as from 1 October 2005, except in relation to a case where a petition for an administration order has been presented before that date. The entry relating to sub-s (1) was revoked by SI 2021/60, reg 3, Sch 1, paras 1, 4(a), as from 16 February 2021 (for transitional provisions, etc, see the note relating to sections A3–A49 above).

(ii) Entries relating to sub-ss (1) and (2) of section 3 substituted by SI 2017/1119, reg 2, Sch 1, Pt 2, paras 6, 8, as from 8 December 2017 (note that Sch 1, Pt 2 to the 2017 Regulations applies to England and Wales only, and these entries, as they had effect before the amendments made by the 2017 Regulations, are set out below).

(iii) Entries relating to sub-ss (1), (5), (5A), (6) of section 4 substituted, and entries relating to sub-ss (1A), (3), (4), (6A) inserted, by SI 2017/1119, reg 2, Sch 1, Pt 2, paras 6, 9–14, as from 8 December 2017 (note that Sch 1, Pt 2 to the 2017

Regulations applies to England and Wales only, and these entries, as they had effect before the amendments made by the 2017 Regulations, are set out below). The entry relating to sub-s (4A) was inserted by SI 2021/60, reg 3, Sch 1, paras 1, 4(b), as from 16 February 2021 (for transitional provisions, etc, see the note relating to sections A3–A49 above).

(iv) Entry relating to sub-s (2) of section 4A substituted, and entry relating to sub-s (5A) inserted, by SI 2017/1119, reg 2, Sch 1, Pt 2, paras 6, 15, 16, as from 8 December 2017 (note that Sch 1, Pt 2 to the 2017 Regulations applies to England and Wales only, and this entry, as it had effect before the amendments made by the 2017 Regulations, is set out below).

(v) Entry relating to sub-s (4) of section 5 substituted, by SI 2017/1119, reg 2, Sch 1, Pt 2, paras 6, 17, as from 8 December 2017 (note that Sch 1, Pt 2 to the 2017 Regulations applies to England and Wales only, and this entry, as it had effect before the amendments made by the 2017 Regulations, is set out below). Words omitted from entry relating to section 5 revoked by SI 2005/1989, reg 3, Sch 2, paras 1, 3(c), as from 1 October 2005, except in relation to a case where a petition for an administration order has been presented before that date.

(vi) Entries relating to sub-ss (1)–(5) of section 6 substituted, and entry relating to sub-s (7) inserted, by SI 2017/1119, reg 2, Sch 1, Pt 2, paras 6, 18, 19, as from 8 December 2017 (note that Sch 1, Pt 2 to the 2017 Regulations applies to England and Wales only, and these entries, as they had effect before the amendments made by the 2017 Regulations, are set out below).

(vii) Entry relating to sub-s (1) of section 7 revoked, and entry relating to sub-s (2) originally inserted, by SI 2005/1989, reg 3, Sch 2, paras 1, 3(f), as from 1 October 2005, except in relation to a case where a petition for an administration order has been presented before that date. Entry relating to sub-s (2) subsequently substituted by SI 2017/1119, reg 2, Sch 1, Pt 2, paras 6, 20, as from 8 December 2017 (note that Sch 1, Pt 2 to the 2017 Regulations applies to England and Wales only, and this entry, as it had effect before the amendments made by the 2017 Regulations, is set out below).

In the paragraph following the entry for section 7, the words in square brackets were substituted by SI 2005/1989, reg 3, Sch 2, paras 1, 3(g), as from 1 October 2005, except in relation to a case where a petition for an administration order has been presented before that date.

The following amendments relate to the entries for ss 2, 3 following the heading "The following modifications to sections 2 and 3 apply where a proposal under section 1 has been made, where the limited liability partnership is in administration, by the administrator or, where the limited liability partnership is being wound up, by the liquidator" (as amended as noted above):

(i) Entry relating to sub-s (2) of section 2 substituted by SI 2017/1119, reg 2, Sch 1, Pt 2, paras 6, 21(1), (2), as from 8 December 2017 (note that Sch 1, Pt 2 to the 2017 Regulations applies to England and Wales only, and this entry, as it had effect before the amendments made by the 2017 Regulations, is set out below).

(ii) Entry relating to sub-s (2) of section 3 substituted by SI 2017/1119, reg 2, Sch 1, Pt 2, paras 6, 21(1), (3), as from 8 December 2017 (note that Sch 1, Pt 2 to the 2017 Regulations applies to England and Wales only, and this entry, as it had effect before the amendments made by the 2017 Regulations, is set out below).

Entries relating to sections 8, 9, 10, 11, 13, 14 revoked by SI 2005/1989, reg 3, Sch 2, paras 1, 4, as from 1 October 2005, except in relation to a case where a petition for an administration order has been presented before that date.

Entries relating to sections 73, 94, 98, 194 revoked by SI 2017/1119, reg 2, Sch 1, Pt 2, paras 6, 22, 23, 27, 36, as from 8 December 2017 (note that Sch 1, Pt 2 to the 2017 Regulations applies to England and Wales only, and these entries, as they had effect before the amendments made by the 2017 Regulations, are set out below).

Entries relating to sub-s (2A), (2B) of section 84 inserted, and in the entry relating to sub-s (5) the figures in square brackets were substituted, by SI 2005/1989, reg 3, Sch 2, paras 1, 5, as from 1 October 2005, except in relation to a case where a petition for an administration order has been presented before that date.

Entries relating to sections 93 and 105 revoked by the Public Services Reform (Insolvency) (Scotland) Order 2016, SSI 2016/141, art 7(3)(a), as from 6 April 2019 (for savings, see the note to the Insolvency Act 1986, s 92A at **[9.222]**).

Entry relating to sub-s (7) of section 95 revoked by SI 2017/1119, reg 2, Sch 1, Pt 2, paras 6, 24, as from 8 December 2017 (note that Sch 1, Pt 2 to the 2017 Regulations applies to England and Wales only, and this entry, as it had effect before the amendments made by the 2017 Regulations, is set out below).

Entry relating to sub-s (2) of section 96 substituted, and words omitted revoked, by SI 2017/1119, reg 2, Sch 1, Pt 2, paras 6, 25, 26, as from 8 December 2017 (note that Sch 1, Pt 2 to the 2017 Regulations applies to England and Wales only, and this entry, as it had effect before the amendments made by the 2017 Regulations, is set out below).

Entries relating to sub-ss (1), (2A), (3) of section 99 substituted by SI 2017/1119, reg 2, Sch 1, Pt 2, paras 6, 28, as from 8 December 2017 (note that Sch 1, Pt 2 to the 2017 Regulations applies to England and Wales only, and these entries, as they had effect before the amendments made by the 2017 Regulations, are set out below).

Entry relating to sub-s (1) of section 100 substituted, and entry relating to sub-s (1B) inserted, by SI 2017/1119, reg 2, Sch 1, Pt 2, paras 6, 29, 30, as from 8 December 2017 (note that Sch 1, Pt 2 to the 2017 Regulations applies to England and Wales only, and this entry, as it had effect before the amendments made by the 2017 Regulations, is set out below).

Entry relating to section 106: revoked by SI 2017/1119, reg 2, Sch 1, Pt 2, paras 6, 31, as from 8 December 2017 (note that Sch 1, Pt 2 to the 2017 Regulations applies to England and Wales only, and this entry, as it had effect before the amendments made by the 2017 Regulations, is set out below). Note that para 31 provides that the entry relating to "subsection (1) of section 106 (including the heading)" should be omitted. On a strict interpretation of this wording, that would leave the entries for sub-ss (5A) and (6) of section 106 in the table (without a heading above them). BEIS have subsequently confirmed that the intention was to omit the entire entry.

Words in square brackets in entry relating to section 122 inserted by SI 2005/1989, reg 3, Sch 2, paras 1, 6, as from 1 October 2005, except in relation to a case where a petition for an administration order has been presented before that date. The entry relating to para (da) of sub-s (1) was revoked by SI 2021/60, reg 3, Sch 1, paras 1, 5, as from 16 February 2021 (for transitional provisions, etc, see the note relating to sections A3–A49 above).

Words in square brackets in entry relating to section 124 inserted by SI 2005/1989, reg 3, Sch 2, paras 1, 7, as from 1 October 2005, except in relation to a case where a petition for an administration order has been presented before that date. The entry relating to sub-s (3A) was revoked by SI 2021/60, reg 3, Sch 1, paras 1, 6, as from 16 February 2021 (for transitional provisions, etc, see the note relating to sections A3–A49 above).

Words in square brackets in entries relating to sections 127, 247, 387 inserted by SI 2005/1989, reg 3, Sch 2, paras 1, 8, 10, 11, as from 1 October 2005, except in relation to a case where a petition for an administration order has been presented before that date.

In entry relating to section 124A, words in square brackets substituted by the Financial Services and Markets Act 2000 (Consequential Amendments) Order 2004, SI 2004/355, art 10(1), (3), as from 4 March 2004.

Entry relating to sub-s (2) of section 165 revoked by SI 2017/1119, reg 2, Sch 1, Pt 2, paras 6, 32, as from 8 December 2017 (note that Sch 1, Pt 2 to the 2017 Regulations applies to England and Wales only, and this entry, as it had effect before the amendments made by the 2017 Regulations, is set out below).

Entry relating to sub-s (5) of section 166 substituted by SI 2017/1119, reg 2, Sch 1, Pt 2, paras 6, 33, as from 8 December 2017 (note that Sch 1, Pt 2 to the 2017 Regulations applies to England and Wales only, and this entry, as it had effect before the amendments made by the 2017 Regulations, is set out below).

Entry relating to sub-s (8) of section 171 substituted by SI 2017/1119, reg 2, Sch 1, Pt 2, paras 6, 34, as from 8 December 2017 (note that Sch 1, Pt 2 to the 2017 Regulations applies to England and Wales only, and this entry, as it had effect before the amendments made by the 2017 Regulations, is set out below).

Entry relating to sub-s (2) of section 173 substituted by SI 2017/1119, reg 2, Sch 1, Pt 2, paras 6, 35, as from 8 December 2017 (note that Sch 1, Pt 2 to the 2017 Regulations applies to England and Wales only, and this entry, as it had effect before the amendments made by the 2017 Regulations, is set out below).

The entry relating to section 174A was inserted by SI 2021/60, reg 3, Sch 1, paras 1, 7, as from 16 February 2021 (for transitional provisions, etc, see the note relating to sections A3–A49 above).

Entry relating to section 233 revoked by SI 2005/1989, reg 3, Sch 2, paras 1, 9, as from 1 October 2005, except in relation to a case where a petition for an administration order has been presented before that date.

In entry relating to section 435, words in square brackets inserted by the Civil Partnership Act 2004 (Amendments to Subordinate Legislation) Order 2005, SI 2005/2114, art 2(18), Sch 18, Pt 1, para 3, as from 5 December 2005.

Entries relating to Sch A1 and Sch B1 inserted by SI 2005/1989, reg 3, Sch 2, paras 1, 14, as from 1 October 2005, except in relation to a case where a petition for an administration order has been presented before that date. All amendments in the entries relating to Sch A1 and Sch B1 were made by SI 2017/1119, reg 2, Sch 1, Pt 2, paras 6, 37–53, as from 8 December 2017 (note that Sch 1, Pt 2 to the 2017 Regulations applies to England and Wales only, and the relevant entries, as they had effect before the amendments made by the 2017 Regulations, are set out below). The entire entry relating to Sch 1A was revoked by SI 2021/60, reg 3, Sch 1, paras 1, 8, as from 16 February 2021 (for transitional provisions, etc, see the note relating to sections A3–A49 above).

The entry relating to Sch 10 is amended as follows:

The entries relating to sections A8(4), A17(6), A24(4), A31(8), A32(6), A49(5) were inserted, and both entries relating to Sch A1 (in italics) were revoked, by SI 2021/60, reg 3, Sch 1, paras 1, 9, as from 16 February 2021 (for transitional provisions, etc, see the note relating to sections A3–A49 above).

Other entries in square brackets inserted by SI 2005/1989, reg 3, Sch 2, paras 1, 15, as from 1 October 2005, except in relation to a case where a petition for an administration order has been presented before that date.

Entry omitted revoked by SI 2017/1119, reg 2, Sch 1, Pt 2, paras 6, 54, as from 8 December 2017 (note that Sch 1, Pt 2 to the 2017 Regulations applies to England and Wales only, and this entry, as it had effect before the amendments made by the 2017 Regulations, is set out below).

Transitional provisions and savings: see further Sch 7 *post*.

Note: as noted above, the Insolvency (Miscellaneous Amendments) Regulations 2017, SI 2017/1119, Sch 1, Pt 2 applies to England and Wales only. The entries amended by those Regulations (as they had effect before those amendments were made) read as follows—

Provisions	Modifications
The following modifications to sections 2 to 7 apply where a proposal under section 1 has been made by the limited liability partnership.	
Section 2 (procedure where the nominee is not the liquidator or administrator)	***Editorial note: as to the subsequent amendment of this entry, see the equivalent note relating to it above***
[subsection (1)	[For "the directors do" substitute "the limited liability partnership does".
subsection (2)	In paragraph [(aa)] for "meetings of the company and of it creditors" substitute "a meeting of the creditors of the limited liability partnership";
	In paragraph (b) for the first "meetings" substitute "a meeting" and for the second "meetings" substitute "meeting".
subsection (3)	For "the person intending to make the proposal" substitute "the designated members of the limited liability partnership".
subsection (4)	[In paragraph (a)] for "the person intending to make the proposal" substitute "the designated members of the limited liability partnership". [In paragraph (b) for "that person" substitute "those designated members".]
Section 3 (summoning of meetings)	
subsection (1)	For "such meetings as are mentioned in section 2(2)" substitute "a meeting of creditors" and for "those meetings" substitute "that meeting".
subsection (2)	Delete subsection (2).
Section 4 (decisions of meetings)	***Editorial note: as to the subsequent amendment of this entry, see the equivalent note relating to it above***
subsection (1)	For "meetings" substitute "meeting".
subsection (5)	For "each of the meetings" substitute "the meeting".
new subsection (5A)	Insert a new subsection (5A) as follows—
	"(5A) If modifications to the proposal are proposed at the meeting the chairman of the meeting shall, before the conclusion of the meeting, ascertain from the limited liability partnership whether or not it accepts the proposed modifications; and if at that conclusion the limited liability partnership has failed to respond to a proposed modification it shall be presumed not to have agreed to it."
subsection (6)	For "either" substitute "the"; after "the result of the meeting", in the first place where it occurs, insert "(including, where modifications to the proposal were proposed at the meeting, the response to those proposed modifications made by the limited liability partnership)"; and at the end add "and to the limited liability partnership".

Provisions	**Modifications**
[Section 4A (approval of arrangement)	
subsection (2)	Omit "—(a)".
	For "both meetings" substitute "the meeting".
	Omit the words from ", or" to "that section".
subsection (3)	Omit.
subsection (4)	Omit.
subsection (5)	Omit.
subsection (6)	Omit.]
Section 5 (effect of approval)	
. . .	. . .
subsection (4)	For "each of the reports" substitute "the report".
Section 6 (challenge of decisions)	
subsection (1)	For . . . "either of the meetings" substitute "the meeting".
subsection (2)	For "either of the meetings" substitute "the meeting" and after paragraph [(aa)] add a new paragraph [(ab) as follows—
	"(ab)] any member of the limited liability partnership; and".
	Omit the word "and" at the end of paragraph (b) and omit paragraph (c).
subsection (3)	For "each of the reports" substitute "the report".
subsection (4)	For subsection (4) substitute the following—
	"(4) Where on such an application the court is satisfied as to either of the grounds mentioned in subsection (1), it may do one or both of the following, namely—
	(a) revoke or suspend [any decision approving the voluntary arrangement which has effect under section 4A];
	(b) give a direction to any person for the summoning of a further meeting to consider any revised proposal the limited liability partnership may make or, in a case falling within subsection (1)(b), a further meeting to consider the original proposal.".
subsection (5)	For . . . "meetings" substitute "a meeting", for . . . and for "person who made the original proposal" substitute "limited liability partnership".
Section 7 (implementation of proposal)	
. . .	. . .
[subsection (2)	In paragraph (a) omit "one or both of" and for "meetings" substitute "meeting".]

The following modifications to sections 2 and 3 apply where a proposal under section 1 has been made, where [the limited liability partnership is in administration], by the administrator or, where the limited liability partnership is being wound up, by the liquidator.

Section 2 (procedure where the nominee is not the liquidator or administrator)	
subsection (2)	In paragraph (a) for "meetings of the company" substitute "meetings of the members of the limited liability partnership".
Section 3 (summoning of meetings)	
subsection (2)	For "meetings of the company" substitute "a meeting of the members of the limited liability partnership".
Section 73 (alternative modes of winding up)	
subsection (1)	Delete ", within the meaning given to that expression by section 735 of the Companies Act,".
Section 94 (final meeting prior to dissolution)	
subsection (1)	For "a general meeting of the company" substitute "a meeting of the members of the limited liability partnership".
new subsection (5A)	Add a new subsection (5A) as follows
	"(5A) Subsections (3) and (4) of section 92 shall apply for the purposes of this section as they apply for the purposes of that section."
subsection (6)	For "a general meeting of the company" substitute "a meeting of the members of the limited liability partnership".
Section 95 (effect of company's insolvency)	
subsection (1)	For "directors'" substitute "designated members'".
subsection (7)	For subsection (7) substitute the following—
	"(7) In this section "the relevant period" means the period of 6 months immediately preceding the date on which the limited li-

Part 10 Miscellaneous other SIs

Provisions		Modifications
		ability partnership determined that it be wound up voluntarily."
Section 96 (conversion to creditors' voluntary winding up)		
	paragraph (a)	For "directors'" substitute "designated members'".
	paragraph (b)	Substitute a new paragraph (b) as follows— "(b) the creditors' meeting was the meeting mentioned in section 98 in the next Chapter;".
Section 98 (meeting of creditors)		
	subsection (1)	For paragraph (a) substitute the following— "(a) cause a meeting of its creditors to be summoned for a day not later than the 14th day after the day on which the limited liability partnership determines that it be wound up voluntarily;".
	subsection (5)	For "were sent the notices summoning the company meeting at which it was resolved that the company be wound up voluntarily" substitute "the limited liability partnership determined that it be wound up voluntarily".
Section 99 (directors to lay statement of affairs before creditors)		
	subsection (1)	For "the directors of the company" substitute "the designated members" and for "the director so appointed" substitute "the designated member so appointed".
	subsection (2)	For "directors" substitute "designated members".
	subsection (3)	For "directors" substitute "designated members" and for "director" substitute "designated member".
Section 100 (appointment of liquidator)		
	subsection (1)	For "The creditors and the company at their respective meetings mentioned in section 98" substitute "The creditors at their meeting mentioned in section 98 and the limited liability partnership".
	subsection (3)	Delete "director,".
Section 106 (final meeting prior to dissolution)		
	subsection (1)	For "a general meeting of the company" substitute "a meeting of the members of the limited liability partnership".
	new subsection (5A)	After subsection (5) insert a new subsection (5A) as follows— "(5A) Subsections (3) and (4) of section 92 shall apply for the purposes of this section as they apply for the purposes of that section."
	subsection (6)	For "a general meeting of the company" substitute "a meeting of the members of the limited liability partnership".
Section 165 (voluntary winding up)		
	subsection (2)	In paragraph (a) for "an extraordinary resolution of the company" substitute "a determination by a meeting of the members of the limited liability partnership".
	subsection (4)	For paragraph (c) substitute the following— "(c) summon meetings of the members of the limited liability partnership for the purpose of obtaining their sanction or for any other purpose he may think fit."
	new subsection (4A)	Insert a new subsection (4A) as follows— "(4A) Subsections (3) and (4) of section 92 shall apply for the purposes of this section as they apply for the purposes of that section."
Section 166 (creditors' voluntary winding up)		
	subsection (5)	In paragraph (b) for "directors" substitute "designated members".
Section 171 (removal, etc (voluntary winding up))		
	subsection (2)	For paragraph (a) substitute the following— "(a) in the case of a members' voluntary winding up, by a meeting of the members of the limited liability partnership summoned specially for that purpose, or".
	subsection (6)	In paragraph (a) for "final meeting of the company" substitute "final meeting of the members of the limited liability partnership" and in paragraph (b) for "final meetings of the company" substitute "final meetings of the members of the limited liability partnership".
	new subsection (7)	Insert a new subsection (7) as follows— "(7) Subsections (3) and (4) of section 92 are to apply for the purposes of this section as they apply for the purposes of that section."
Section 173 (release (voluntary winding up))		
	subsection (2)	In paragraph (a) for "a general meeting of the company" substitute

Provisions	Modifications
	"a meeting of the members of the limited liability partnership".
Section 194 (resolutions passed at adjourned meetings)	
	After "contributories" insert "or of the members of a limited liability partnership".
[Schedule A1	***Editorial note: as to the subsequent revocation of this entry, see the equivalent note relating to it above***
Paragraph 6	
sub-paragraph (1)	For "directors of a company wish" substitute "limited liability partnership wishes".
	For "they" substitute "the designated members of the limited liability partnership".
sub-paragraph (2)	For "directors" substitute "the designated members of the limited liability partnership".
	In sub-paragraph (c), for "meetings of the company and" substitute "a meeting of".
Paragraph 7	
sub-paragraph (1)	For "directors of a company" substitute "designated members of the limited liability partnership".
	In sub-paragraph (e)(iii), for "meetings of the company and" substitute "a meeting of".
Paragraph 8	
sub-paragraph (2)	For "meetings" substitute "meeting".
	For "are" substitute "is".
	Omit the words in parenthesis.
sub-paragraph (3)	For "either of those meetings" substitute "the meeting".
	For "those meetings were" substitute "that meeting was".
	Omit the words in parenthesis.
sub-paragraph (4)	For "either" substitute "the".
sub-paragraph (6)(c)	For "one or both of the meetings" substitute "the meeting".
Paragraph 29	
sub-paragraph (1)	For "meetings of the company and its creditors" substitute "a meeting of the creditors of the limited liability partnership".
Paragraph 30	
sub-paragraph (1)	For "meetings" substitute "meeting".
new sub-paragraph (2A)	Insert new sub-paragraph (2A) as follows—
	"(2A) If modifications to the proposal are proposed at the meeting the chairman of the meeting shall, before the conclusion of the meeting, ascertain from the limited liability partnership whether or not it accepts the proposed modifications; and if at that conclusion the limited liability partnership has failed to respond to a proposed modification it shall be presumed not to have agreed to it.".
sub-paragraph (3)	For "either" substitute "the".
	After "the result of the meeting" in the first place where it occurs insert "(including, where modifications to the proposal were proposed at the meeting, the response to those proposed modifications made by the limited liability partnership)".
	At the end add "and to the limited liability partnership".
Paragraph 31	
sub-paragraph (1)	For "meetings" substitute "meeting".
sub-paragraph (7)	For "directors of the company" substitute "designated members of the limited liability partnership".
	For "meetings (or either of them)" substitute "meeting".
	For "directors" substitute "limited liability partnership".
	For "those meetings" substitute "that meeting".
Paragraph 32	
sub-paragraph (2)	For sub-paragraphs (a) and (b) substitute "with the day on which the meeting summoned under paragraph 29 is first held.".
Paragraph 37	
sub-paragraph (5)	For "each of the reports of the meetings" substitute "the report of the meeting".
Paragraph 38	

Provisions	Modifications
sub-paragraph (1)(a)	For "one or both of the meetings" substitute "the meeting".
sub-paragraph (1)(b)	For "either of those meetings" substitute "the meeting".
sub-paragraph (2)(a)	For "either of the meetings" substitute "the meeting".
	After sub-paragraph (2)(a) insert new (aa) as follows—
	"(aa) any member of the limited liability partnership;".
sub-paragraph (2)(b)	Omit "creditors'".
sub-paragraph (3)(a)	For "each of the reports" substitute "the report".
sub-paragraph (3)(b)	Omit "creditors'".
sub-paragraph (4)(a)(ii)	Omit "in question".
sub-paragraph (4)(b)(i)	For "further meetings" substitute "a further meeting" and for "directors" substitute "limited liability partnership".
sub-paragraph (4)(b)(ii)	Omit "company or (as the case may be) creditors'".
sub-paragraph (5)	For "directors do" substitute "limited liability partnerships does".
Paragraph 39	
sub-paragraph (1)	For "one or both of the meetings" substitute "the meeting".
Schedule 10	
Section 106(6)	In the entry relating to section 106(6) for "final meeting of the company" substitute "final meeting of the members of the limited liability partnership".

SCHEDULE 4

Regulation 5(3)

[10.112]

The provisions listed in this Schedule are not applied to Scotland to the extent specified below—

Sections 50 to 52;
Section 53(1) and (2), to the extent that those subsections do not relate to the requirement for a copy of the instrument and notice being forwarded to the registrar of companies;
Section 53(4) (6) and (7);
Section 54(1), (2), (3) (to the extent that that subsection does not relate to the requirement for a copy of the interlocutor to be sent to the registrar of companies), and subsections (5), (6) and (7);
Sections 55 to 58;
Section 60, other than subsection (1);
Section 61, including subsections (6) and (7) to the extent that those subsections do not relate to anything to be done or which may be done to or by the registrar of companies;
Section 62, including subsection (5) to the extent that that subsection does not relate to anything to be done or which may be done to or by the registrar of companies;
Sections 63 to 66;
Section 67, including subsections (1) and (8) to the extent that those subsections do not relate to anything to be done or which may be done to the registrar of companies;
Section 68;
Section 69, including subsections (1) and (2) to the extent that those subsections do not relate to anything to be done or which may be done by the registrar of companies;
Sections 70 and 71;
Subsection 84(3), to the extent that it does not concern the copy of the resolution being forwarded to the registrar of companies within 15 days;
Sections 91 to [92A];
Section 94, including subsections (3) and (4) to the extent that those subsections do not relate to the liquidator being required to send to the registrar of companies a copy of the account and a return of the final meeting;
Section 95;
Section 97;
Sections 100 to 102;
Sections 104 to [104A];
Section 106, including subsections [(3) to (7)] to the extent that those subsections do not relate to the liquidator being required to send to the registrar of companies a copy of the account of winding up and a return of the final meeting/quorum [or a statement about a member State liquidator];
Sections 109 to 111;
Section 112, including subsection (3) to the extent that that subsection does not relate to the liquidator being required to send to the registrar a copy of the order made by the court;
Sections 113 to 115;
Sections 126 to 128;
Section 130(1) to the extent that that subsection does not relate to a copy of the order being forwarded by the court to the registrar;
Section 131;
Sections 133 to 135;
Sections 138 to 140;
Sections 142 to 146;

Section 147, including subsection (3) to the extent that that subsection does not relate to a copy of the order being forwarded by the company to the registrar;
Section 162 to the extent that that section concerns the matters set out in Section C.2 of Schedule 5 to the Scotland Act 1998 as being exceptions to the insolvency reservation;
Sections 163 to 167;
Section 169;
Section 170, including subsection (2) to the extent that that subsection does not relate to an application being made by the registrar to make good the default;
Section 171;
Section 172, including [subsections (8) to (10) to the extent that those subsections do] not relate to the liquidator being required to give notice to the registrar [or a statement about a member State liquidator];
Sections 173 and 174;
Section 177;
Sections 185 to 189;
Sections 191 to 194;
Section 196 to the extent that that section applies to the specified devolved functions of Part IV of the Insolvency Act 1986;
Section 199;
Section 200 to the extent that it applies to the specified devolved functions of Part IV of the First Group of Parts of the 1986 Act;
Sections 206 to 215;
Section 218 subsections (1), (2), (4) and (6);
Section 231 to 232 to the extent that the sections apply to administrative receivers, liquidators and provisional liquidators;
Section 233, to the extent that that section applies in the case of the appointment of an administrative receiver, of a voluntary arrangement taking effect, of a company going into liquidation or where a provisional liquidator is appointed;
[Section 233A to the extent that that section applies in the case of a voluntary arrangement taking effect]
[Section 233B to the extent that that section applies in the case of the appointment of an administrative receiver.]
Section 234 to the extent that that section applies to situations other than those where an administration order applies;
Section 235 to the extent that that section applies to situations other than those where an administration order applies;
Sections 236 to 237 to the extent that those sections apply to situations other than administration orders and winding up;
Sections 242 to 243;
Section 244 to the extent that that section applies in circumstances other than a company which is subject to an administration order;
Section 245;
Section 251, to the extent that that section contains definitions which apply only to devolved matters;
Section 416(1) and (4), to the extent that those subsections apply to section 206(1)(a) and (b) in connection with the offence provision relating to the winding up of a limited liability partnership;
Schedule 2;
Schedule 3;
Schedule 4;
Schedule 8, to the extent that that Schedule does not apply to voluntary arrangements or administrations within the meaning of Parts I and II of the 1986 Act.
In addition, Schedule 10, which concerns punishment of offences under the Insolvency Act 1986, lists various sections of the Insolvency Act 1986 which create an offence. The following sections, which are listed in Schedule 10, are devolved in their application to Scotland:
Section 51(4);
Section 51(5);
Sections 53(2) to 62(5) to the extent that those subsections relate to matters other than delivery to the registrar of companies;
Section 64(2);
Section 65(4);
Section 66(6);
Section 67(8) to the extent that that subsection relates to matters other than delivery to the registrar of companies;
Section 93(3);
Section 94(4) to the extent that that subsection relates to matters other than delivery to the registrar of companies;
Section 94(6);
Section 95(8);
Section 105(3);
Section 106(4) to the extent that that subsection relates to matters other than delivery to the registrar of companies;
Section 106(6);
Section 109(2);
Section 114(4);
Section 131(7);
Section 164;

Section 166(7);
Section 188(2);
Section 192(2);
Sections 206 to 211; and
Section 235(5) to the extent that it relates to matters other than administration orders.

NOTES

Figures "92A" and "104A" substituted by the Public Services Reform (Insolvency) (Scotland) Order 2016, SSI 2016/141, art 7(3)(b), as from 6 April 2019 (for savings, see the note to the Insolvency Act 1986, s 92A at **[9.222]**).

In the entries relating to sections 106 and 172, the words in the first pair of square brackets were substituted, and the words in the final pair of square brackets were inserted, by the Insolvency (Miscellaneous Amendments) Regulations 2017, SI 2017/1119, reg 2, Sch 1, Pt 3, para 56, as from 8 December 2017.

Entry relating to section 233A inserted by the Insolvency (Protection of Essential Supplies) Order 2015, SI 2015/989, art 6, Schedule, para 2, as from 1 October 2015.

Entry relating to section 233B inserted by the Corporate Insolvency and Governance Act 2020, s 14(3), Sch 12, Pt 2, para 6, as from 26 June 2020. See also s 14(4) of the 2020 Act which provides that the amendments made by Sch 12 to the 2020 Act have effect in relation to a company which becomes subject to a relevant insolvency procedure on or after 26 June 2020, but in respect of contracts entered into before, as well as those entered into on or after, that day.

SCHEDULE 5
GENERAL AND CONSEQUENTIAL AMENDMENTS IN OTHER LEGISLATION

Regulation 9

[10.113]

1–21. (*In so far as these paragraphs have not been revoked, they contain amendments which, in so far as relevant to this work, are incorporated at the appropriate place.*)

Culpable officer provisions

22. (1) A culpable officer provision applies in the case of a limited liability partnership as if the reference in the provision to a director (or a person purporting to act as a director) were a reference to a member (or a person purporting to act as a member) of the limited liability partnership.

(2) A culpable officer provision is a provision in any Act or subordinate legislation (within the meaning of the Interpretation Act 1978) to the effect that where—

(a) a body corporate is guilty of a particular offence, and
(b) the offence is proved to have been committed with the consent or connivance of, or to be attributable to the neglect on the part of, (among others) a director of the body corporate,

he (as well as the body corporate) is guilty of the offence.

SCHEDULE 6
APPLICATION OF SUBORDINATE LEGISLATION

Regulation 10

PART I REGULATIONS MADE UNDER THE 1985 ACT

[10.114]

1–6. . . .

[**7.** The Companies Act 1985 (Power to Enter and Remain on Premises: Procedural) Regulations 2005.]

NOTES

Paras 1–3, 6: revoked by the Limited Liability Partnerships (Accounts and Audit) (Application of Companies Act 2006) Regulations 2008, SI 2008/1911, reg 58(1)(c), as from 1 October 2008, except in relation to accounts for, and otherwise as regards, financial years beginning before that date (see reg 58(3) at **[10.286]**).

Paras 4, 5: revoked by the Limited Liability Partnerships (Application of Companies Act 2006) Regulations 2009, SI 2009/1804, reg 85, Sch 3, Pt 2, para 13(7)(a), as from 1 October 2009.

Para 7: added by the Limited Liability Partnerships (Amendment) Regulations 2007, SI 2007/2073, reg 4, as from 1 October 2007.

PART II REGULATIONS MADE UNDER THE 1986 ACT

[10.115]

1. Insolvency Practitioners Regulations 1990

2. The Insolvency Practitioners (Recognised Professional Bodies) Order 1986

3. The [Insolvency (England and Wales) Rules 2016] and the Insolvency (Scotland) Rules 1986 (except in so far as they relate to the exceptions to the reserved matters specified in section C2 of Part II of Schedule 5 to the Scotland Act 1998)

4. The Insolvency Fees Order 1986

5. The Co-operation of Insolvency Courts (Designation of Relevant Countries and Territories) Order 1986

6. The Co-operation of Insolvency Courts (Designation of Relevant Countries and Territories) Order 1996

7. The Co-operation of Insolvency Courts (Designation of Relevant Country) Order 1998

8. Insolvency Proceedings (Monetary Limits) Order 1986

9. . . .

10. Insolvency Regulations 1994

11. Insolvency (Amendment) Regulations 2000.

NOTES

Para 3: words in square brackets substituted by the Insolvency (Miscellaneous Amendments) Regulations 2017, SI 2017/1119, reg 2, Sch 1, Pt 1, para 1, as from 8 December 2017.

Para 9: revoked by the Deregulation Act 2015 (Insolvency) (Consequential Amendments and Transitional and Savings Provisions) Order 2015, SI , art 4, Sch 1, para 3(1), (2), as from 1 October 2015.

Insolvency Practitioners Regulations 1990, SI 1990/439: revoked and replaced by the Insolvency Practitioners Regulations 2005, SI 2005/524.

Insolvency (Scotland) Rules 1986: the 1986 Rules were revoked in their entirety (as from 6 April 2019, and subject to savings and transitional provisions) by a combination of the Insolvency (Scotland) (Company Voluntary Arrangements and Administration) Rules 2018, SI 2018/1082, and the Insolvency (Scotland) (Receivership and Winding up) Rules 2018, SSI 2018/347.

Insolvency Fees Order 1986, SI 1986/2030: revoked and replaced by the Insolvency Proceedings (Fees) Order 2004, SI 2004/593. The 2004 Order was revoked (subject to savings) and replaced by the Insolvency Proceedings (Fees) Order 2016, SI 2016/692, as from 21 July 2016.

Co-operation of Insolvency Courts (Designation of Relevant Countries and Territories) Order 1996: it is assumed that this refers to the Co-operation of Insolvency Courts (Designation of Relevant Countries) Order 1996, SI 1996/253.

PART III REGULATIONS MADE UNDER OTHER LEGISLATION

[10.116]

1. . . .

2. The Companies (Disqualification Orders) Regulations 1986

3. The Insolvent Companies (Disqualification of Unfit Directors) Proceedings Rules 1987

4. The Contracting Out (Functions of the Official Receiver) Order 1995

5. The Uncertificated Securities Regulations 1995

6. [The Insolvent Companies (Reports on Conduct of Directors) (England and Wales) Rules 2016]

7. [The Insolvent Companies (Reports on Conduct of Directors) (Scotland) Rules 2016].

NOTES

Para 1: revoked by the Limited Liability Partnerships (Application of Companies Act 2006) Regulations 2009, SI 2009/1804, reg 85, Sch 3, Pt 2, para 13(7)(b), as from 1 October 2009.

Paras 6, 7: words in square brackets substituted by the Enterprise and Regulatory Reform Act 2013 (Consequential Amendments) (Bankruptcy) and the Small Business, Enterprise and Employment Act 2015 (Consequential Amendments) Regulations 2016, SI 2016/481, reg 4, as from 6 April 2016.

The Companies (Disqualification Orders) Regulations 1986, SI 1986/2067 were revoked and replaced by the Companies (Disqualification Orders) Regulations 2001, SI 2001/967. The 2001 Regulations were themselves revoked and replaced by the Companies (Disqualification Orders) Regulations 2009, SI 2009/2471.

The Uncertificated Securities Regulations 1995, SI 1995/3272 were revoked and replaced by the Uncertificated Securities Regulations 2001, SI 2001/3755.

[SCHEDULE 7
TRANSITIONAL AND SAVINGS PROVISIONS

[10.117]

1 Interpretation

In this Schedule—

"the 1986 Act" means the Insolvency Act 1986, as applied to limited liability partnerships;

"the 1986 Rules" means the Insolvency Rules 1986 as they had effect immediately before the 6th April 2017 in their application to limited liability partnerships;

"the 2016 Rules" means the Insolvency (England and Wales) Rules 2016, as applied to limited liability partnerships; and

"the commencement date" means the date this Schedule comes into force.

2 Amendments to the 2016 Rules made by the Insolvency Amendment (EU 2015/848) Regulations 2017 do not apply where proceedings opened before commencement date

(1) The amendments made by the Insolvency Amendment (EU 2015/848) Regulations 2017 to the 2016 Rules do not apply where proceedings in relation to a limited liability partnership opened before the commencement date.

(2) The time at which proceedings are opened is to be determined for the purpose of this paragraph in accordance with Article 2(8) of Regulation (EU) 2015/848 of the European Parliament and of the Council of 20th May 2015.

3 Requirement for office-holder to provide information to creditors on opting out

(1) Rule 1.39 of the 2016 Rules (which requires an office-holder to inform a creditor in the first communication that the creditor may elect to opt out of receiving further documents relating to the proceedings) does not apply to an office-holder in relation to a limited liability partnership who delivers the first communication before the commencement date.

(2) However, if such an office-holder informs a creditor in a communication that the creditor may elect to opt out as mentioned in sub-paragraph (1), the communication must contain the information required by rule 1.39(2) of the 2016 Rules.

4 Electronic communication

(1) Where proceedings in relation to a limited liability partnership commence before the commencement date, Rule 1.45(4) of the 2016 Rules does not apply.

(2) For the purposes of this paragraph proceedings "commence" on—

(a) the delivery of a proposal for a voluntary arrangement to the intended nominee;

(b) the appointment of an administrator under paragraph 14 or 22 of Schedule B1 to the 1986 Act;
(c) the making of an administration order;
(d) the appointment of an administrative receiver;
(e) the passing or deemed passing of a resolution to wind up a limited liability partnership; or
(f) the making of a winding-up order.

5 Statements of affairs

(1) Where proceedings in relation to a limited liability partnership commence before the commencement date and a person is required to provide a statement of affairs, the provisions of the 2016 Rules relating to statements of affairs in administration, administrative receivership and winding up do not apply and the following rules in the 1986 Rules continue to apply—
(a) rules 2.28 to 2.32 (administration);
(b) rules 3.3 to 3.8 (administrative receivership); and
(c) rules 4.32 to 4.42 (winding up).

(2) For the purposes of this paragraph proceedings "commence" on—
(a) the appointment of an administrator under paragraph 14 or 22 of Schedule B1;
(b) the making of an administration order;
(c) the appointment of an administrative receiver
(d) the passing or deemed passing of a resolution to wind up a limited liability partnership; or
(e) the making of a winding-up order.

6 Savings in respect of meetings taking place on or after the commencement date and resolutions by correspondence

(1) This paragraph applies where in relation to a limited liability partnership on or after the commencement date—
(a) a creditors' or contributories' meeting is to be held as a result of a notice issued before that date in relation to a meeting for which provision is made by the 1986 Rules or the 1986 Act;
(b) a meeting is to be held as a result of a requisition by a creditor or contributory made before that date;
(c) a meeting is to be held as a result of a statement made under paragraph 52(1)(b) of Schedule B1 to the 1986 Act and a request is made before that date which obliges the administrator to summon an initial creditors' meeting; or
(d) a meeting is required by sections 93 or 105 of the 1986 Act in the winding up of a limited liability partnership where the resolution to wind up was passed before 6th April 2010.

(2) Where a meeting referred to in sub-paragraph (1)(a) to (d) is held in relation to a limited liability partnership, Part 15 of the 2016 Rules does not apply and the provisions of the 1986 Rules relating to the following continue to apply—
(a) the requirement to hold the meeting;
(b) notice and advertisement of the meeting;
(c) governance of the meeting;
(d) recording and taking minutes of the meeting;
(e) the report or return of the meeting;
(f) membership and formalities of establishment of liquidation and creditors' committees where a resolution to form the committee is passed at the meeting;
(g) the office-holder's resignation or removal at the meeting;
(h) the office-holder's release;
(i) fixing the office-holder's remuneration;
(j) hand-over of assets to a supervisor of a voluntary arrangement where the proposal is approved at the meeting;
(k) the notice of the appointment of a supervisor of a voluntary arrangement where the appointment is made at the meeting;
(l) claims that remuneration is or that other expenses are excessive; and
(m) complaints about exclusion at the meeting.

(3) Where in relation to a limited liability partnership, before the commencement date, the office-holder seeks to obtain the passing of a resolution by correspondence under rule 2.48, 4.63A or 6.88A of the 1986 Rules—
(a) the relevant provisions of the 2016 Rules do not apply;
(b) the provisions of the 1986 Rules relating to resolutions by correspondence continue to apply; and
(c) the provisions of the 1986 Rules referred to in sub-paragraph (2) of this paragraph apply in relation to any meeting that those provisions require the office-holder to summon.

(4) However, any application to the court in respect of a meeting or vote to which this paragraph applies is to be made in accordance with Part 12 of the 2016 Rules.

7 Savings in respect of final meetings taking place on or after the commencement date

(1) This paragraph applies where—
(a) before the commencement date—
 (i) a final report to creditors is sent under rule 4.49D of the 1986 Rules (final report to creditors in liquidation),
 (ii) a final report to creditors and bankrupt is sent under rule 6.78B of the 1986 Rules (final report to creditors and bankrupt), or
 (iii) a meeting is called under sections 94, 106, 146 or 331 of the 1986 Act (final meeting); and
(b) a meeting under section 94, 106, 146 or 331 of the 1986 Act is held on or after the commencement date.

(2) Where this paragraph applies, Part 15 of the 2016 Rules does not apply and the provisions of the 1986 Rules relating to the following continue to apply—
(a) the requirement to hold the meeting;
(b) notice and advertisement of the meeting;
(c) governance of the meeting;

(d) recording and taking minutes of the meeting;
(e) the form and content of the final report;
(f) the office-holder's resignation or removal;
(g) the office-holder's release;
(h) fixing the office-holder's remuneration;
(i) requests for further information from creditors;
(j) claims that remuneration is or other expenses are excessive; and
(k) complaints about exclusion at the meeting.

(3) However, any application to the court in respect of such a meeting is to be made in accordance with Part 12 of the 2016 Rules.

8 Progress reports and statements to the registrar of companies

(1) Where in relation to a limited liability partnership an obligation to prepare a progress report arises but is not fulfilled before the commencement date the following provisions of the 1986 Rules continue to apply—

(a) rule 2.47 (reports to creditors in administration); and
(b) rules 4.49B and 4.49C (progress reports—winding up).

(2) Where before the commencement date, a notice under paragraph 83(3) of Schedule B1 to the 1986 Act is sent to the registrar of companies, rule 2.117A(1) of the 1986 Rules continues to apply.

(3) The provisions of the 2016 Rules relating to progress reporting do not apply in the case of the winding up of a limited liability partnership, where the winding-up order was made on a petition presented before 6th April 2010.

(4) Where the voluntary winding up of a limited liability partnership commenced before 6th April 2010, rule 4.223-CVL of the 1986 Rules as it had effect immediately before that date in its application to limited liability partnerships, continues to apply

(5) Where, in relation to a limited liability partnership, before the commencement date an office-holder ceases to act, or an administrator sends a progress report to creditors in support of a request for their consent to an extension of the administration, resulting in a change in reporting period under rule 2.47(3A), 2.47(3B), 4.49B(5), 4.49C(3), or 6.78A(4) of the 1986 Rules, the period for which reports must be made is the period for which reports were required to be made under the 1986 Rules immediately before the commencement date.

9 Foreign currency

(1) Where, in relation to a limited liability partnership, before the commencement date an amount stated in a foreign currency on an application, claim or proof of debt is converted into sterling by the office-holder under rules 2.86, 4.91, 5A.3 or 6.111 of the 1986 Rules, the office-holder and any successor to the office-holder must continue to use the same exchange rate for subsequent conversions of that currency into sterling for the purpose of distributing any assets of the limited liability partnership.

(2) However when, in relation to a limited liability partnership, an office-holder, convener, appointed person or chair uses an exchange rate to convert an application, claim or proof in a foreign currency into sterling solely for voting purposes before the commencement date, sub-paragraph (1) does not prevent the office-holder from using an alternative rate for subsequent conversions.

10 CVA moratoria

Where, before the commencement date, the designated members of a limited liability partnership submit to the nominee the document, statement and information required under paragraph 6(1) of Schedule A1 to the 1986 Act, the provisions of the 1986 Rules relating to moratoria continue to apply to the proposed voluntary arrangement.

11 Priority of expenses of voluntary arrangements

Rule 4.21A of the 1986 Rules (expenses of voluntary arrangement) continues to apply in relation to a limited liability partnership where a winding up petition is presented before the commencement date.

12 General powers of liquidator

Rule 4.184 of the 1986 Rules (general powers of liquidator) continues to apply in relation to a limited liability partnership as regards a person dealing in good faith and for value with a liquidator and in respect of the power of the court or the liquidation committee to ratify anything done by the liquidator without permission before the commencement date.

13 Applications before the court

(1) Where, in relation to a limited liability partnership, an application to court is filed or a petition for winding up is presented under the 1986 Act or under the 1986 Rules before the commencement date and the court remains seised of that application or petition on the commencement date, the 1986 Rules continue to apply to that application or petition.

(2) For the purpose of sub-paragraph (1), the court is no longer seised of an application or petition for winding up when—

(a) in relation to an application, it makes an order having the effect of determining of the application; or
(b) in relation to a petition for winding up—
  (i) the court makes a winding up order,
  (ii) the court dismisses the petition, or
  (iii) the petition is withdrawn.

14 Forms

A form contained in Schedule 4 to the 1986 Rules may be used in relation to a limited liability partnership on or after the commencement date if—

(a) the form is used to provide a statement of affairs in proceedings where pursuant to paragraph 5 of this Schedule the provisions of the 1986 Rules set out in that paragraph continue to apply;
(b) the form relates to a meeting held under the 1986 Rules as described in paragraph 6(1) of this Schedule;

(c) the form is required because before the commencement date, the office-holder seeks to obtain the passing of a resolution by correspondence; or
(d) the form relates to any application to the court or petition for winding up presented before the commencement date.

15 Administrations commenced before 15th September 2003

The 1986 Rules continue to apply to administrations of limited liability partnerships where the petition for an administration order was presented before 15th September 2003.

16 Set-off in insolvency proceedings commenced before 1st April 2005

Where before 1st April 2005 a limited liability partnership entered administration or went into liquidation, the office-holder calculating any set-off must apply the 1986 Rules as they had effect in their application to limited liability partnerships immediately before 1st April 2005.

17 Calculating the value of future debts in insolvency proceedings commenced before 1st April 2005

Where before 1st April 2005 a limited liability partnership entered administration or went into liquidation the office-holder calculating the value of a future debt for the purpose of dividend (and no other purpose) must apply the 1986 Rules as they had effect in their application to limited liability partnerships immediately before 1st April 2005.

18 Insolvency practitioner fees and expenses estimates

(1) Rules 18.4(1)(e), 18.16(4) to (10), and 18.30 of the 2016 Rules do not apply in relation to limited liability partnerships where before 1st October 2015—
(a) the appointment of an administrator took effect;
(b) a liquidator was nominated under section 100(2), or 139(3) of the 1986 Act;
(c) a liquidator was appointed under section 139(4) or 140 of the 1986 Act;
(d) a person was directed by the court or appointed to be a liquidator under section 100(3) of the 1986 Act; or
(e) a liquidator was nominated or the administrator became the liquidator under paragraph 83(7) of Schedule B1 to the 1986 Act.

(2) Rule 18.20(4) and (5) of the 2016 Rules do not apply in relation to a limited liability partnership where an administrator was appointed before 1st October 2015 and—
(a) the limited liability partnership is wound up under paragraph 83 of Schedule B1 to the 1986 Act on or after the commencement date and the administrator becomes the liquidator; or
(b) a winding-up order is made upon the appointment of an administrator ceasing to have effect on or after the commencement date and the court under section 140(1) of the 1986 Act appoints as liquidator the person whose appointment as administrator has ceased to have effect.

19 Transitional provision for limited liability partnerships entering administration before 6th April 2010 and moving to voluntary liquidation between 6th April 2010 and commencement (inclusive of those dates)

Where—
(a) a limited liability partnership went into administration before 6th April 2010, and
(b) the limited liability partnership goes into voluntary liquidation under paragraph 83 of Schedule B1 between 6th April 2010 and commencement (inclusive of those dates),

the 1986 Rules as amended by the Insolvency (Amendment) Rules 2010 apply to the extent necessary to give effect to section 104A of the Act notwithstanding that by virtue of paragraph 1(6)(a) or (b) of Schedule 4 to the Insolvency (Amendment) Rules 2010 those amendments to the Insolvency Rules 1986 would otherwise not apply.]

NOTES

Added by the Insolvency (Miscellaneous Amendments) Regulations 2017, SI 2017/1119, reg 2, Sch 1, Pt 2, paras 6, 55, as from 8 December 2017.

INSOLVENCY ACT 1986 (PRESCRIBED PART) ORDER 2003

(SI 2003/2097)

NOTES

Made: 8 August 2003.
Authority: Insolvency Act 1986, s 176A.
Commencement: 15 September 2003.
This Order is reproduced as amended by: the Insolvency Act 1986 (Prescribed Part) (Amendment) Order 2020, SI 2020/211.

[10.118]

1 Citation, commencement and Interpretation

(1) This Order may be cited as the Insolvency Act 1986 (Prescribed Part) Order 2003 and shall come into force on 15th September 2003.

(2) In this order "the 1986 Act" means the Insolvency Act 1986.

[10.119]

2 Minimum value of the company's net property

For the purposes of section 176A(3)(a) of the 1986 Act the minimum value of the company's net property is £10,000.

[10.120]

3 Calculation of prescribed part

(1) The prescribed part of the company's net property to be made available for the satisfaction of unsecured debts of the company pursuant to section 176A of the 1986 Act shall be calculated as follows—

(a) where the company's net property does not exceed £10,000 in value, 50% of that property;

(b) subject to paragraph (2), where the company's net property exceeds £10,000 in value the sum of—

(i) 50% of the first £10,000 in value; and

(ii) 20% of that part of the company's net property which exceeds £10,000 in value.

(2) The value of the prescribed part of the company's net property to be made available for the satisfaction of unsecured debts of the company pursuant to section 176A shall not exceed [£800,000].

NOTES

Para (2): sum in square brackets substituted by the Insolvency Act 1986 (Prescribed Part) (Amendment) Order 2020, SI 2020/211, art 2, as from 6 April 2020. That article further provides that the substitution does not apply where the company's net property is available to be distributed to the holder of a relevant floating charge. For these purposes, a relevant floating charge is one (a) created before 6 April 2020; and (b) in respect of which no floating charge over any of the company's assets created on or after that date ranks equally or in priority. The previous sum was £600,000.

FINANCIAL COLLATERAL ARRANGEMENTS (NO 2) REGULATIONS 2003

(SI 2003/3226)

NOTES

Made: 10 December 2003.

Authority: European Communities Act 1972, s 2 (see the note "Statutory Instruments made under the European Communities Act 1972" preceding paragraph **[4.1]** *ante*).

Commencement: 11 December 2003 (reg 2); 26 December 2003 (otherwise).

Application of these Regulations: see further, the Financial Services Act 2021, s 41(1), (2) at **[7.757]**. It provides that the Financial Collateral Arrangements (No 2) Regulations 2003 as originally made, and all amendments made to these Regulations, have effect, and are to be treated as having had effect, despite any lack of power to make the Regulations and amendments. Accordingly, the validity of anything done under, or in reliance on, these Regulations (whether as originally made or as amended) is to be treated as unaffected by any such lack of power.

These Regulations are reproduced as amended by: the Financial Collateral Arrangements (No 2) Regulations 2003 (Amendment) Regulations 2009, SI 2009/2462; the Financial Markets and Insolvency (Settlement Finality and Financial Collateral Arrangements) (Amendment) Regulations 2010, SI 2010/2993; the Companies Act 2006 (Amendment of Part 25) Regulations 2013, SI 2013/600; the Capital Requirements Regulations 2013, SI 2013/3115; the Bank Recovery and Resolution (No 2) Order 2014, SI 2014/3348; the Small Business, Enterprise and Employment Act 2015 (Consequential Amendments, Savings and Transitional Provisions) Regulations 2018, SI 2018/208; the Financial Markets and Insolvency (Amendment and Transitional Provision) (EU Exit) Regulations 2019, SI 2019/341; the Financial Services and Markets (Insolvency) (Amendment of Miscellaneous Enactments) Regulations 2019, SI 2019/755; the Small Business, Enterprise and Employment Act 2015 (Consequential Amendments, Savings and Transitional Provisions) Regulations 2019, SI 2019/1058; the Corporate Insolvency and Governance Act 2020; the Co-operative and Community Benefit Societies and Credit Unions (Arrangements, Reconstructions and Administration) (Amendment) and Consequential Amendments Order 2020, SI 2020/744.

ARRANGEMENT OF REGULATIONS

PART I
GENERAL

PART 2
MODIFICATION OF LAW REQUIRING FORMALITIES

PART 3
MODIFICATION OF INSOLVENCY LAW

PART 1 GENERAL

[10.121]

1 Citation and commencement

(1) These Regulations may be cited as the Financial Collateral Arrangements (No 2) Regulations 2003.

(2) Regulation 2 shall come into force on 11th December 2003 and all other Regulations thereof shall come into force on 26th December 2003.

2 (*Revokes the Financial Collateral Arrangements Regulations 2003, SI 2003/3112.*)

[10.122]

3 Interpretation

[(1)] In these Regulations—

"book entry securities collateral" means financial collateral subject to a financial collateral arrangement which consists of financial instruments, title to which is evidenced by entries in a register or account maintained by or on behalf of an intermediary;

"cash" means money in any currency, credited to an account, or a similar claim for repayment of money and includes money market deposits and sums due or payable to, or received between the parties in connection with the operation of a financial collateral arrangement or a close-out netting provision;

"close-out netting provision" means a term of a financial collateral arrangement, or of an arrangement of which a financial collateral arrangement forms part, or any legislative provision under which on the occurrence of an enforcement event, whether through the operation of netting or set-off or otherwise—

(a) the obligations of the parties are accelerated to become immediately due and expressed as an obligation to pay an amount representing the original obligation's estimated current value or replacement cost, or are terminated and replaced by an obligation to pay such an amount; or

(b) an account is taken of what is due from each party to the other in respect of such obligations and a net sum equal to the balance of the account is payable by the party from whom the larger amount is due to the other party;

["credit claims" means pecuniary claims which arise out of an agreement whereby a credit institution, as defined in Article 4(1)(1) of Regulation (EU) 575/2013 of the European Parliament and of the Council of 26 June 2013, and including the institutions listed in Article 2(5)(2) to (23) of Directive 2013/36/EU of the European Parliament and of the Council of 26 June 2013, grants credit in the form of a loan;]

. . .

"equivalent financial collateral" means—

(a) in relation to cash, a payment of the same amount and in the same currency;

(b) in relation to financial instruments, financial instruments of the same issuer or debtor, forming part of the same issue or class and of the same nominal amount, currency and description or, where the financial collateral arrangement provides for the transfer of other assets following the occurrence of any event relating to or affecting any financial instruments provided as financial collateral, those other assets;

and includes the original financial collateral provided under the arrangement;

"financial collateral arrangement" means a title transfer financial collateral arrangement or a security financial collateral arrangement, whether or not these are covered by a master agreement or general terms and conditions;

"financial collateral" means either [cash, financial instruments or credit claims];

"financial instruments" means—

(a) shares in companies and other securities equivalent to shares in companies;

(b) bonds and other forms of instruments giving rise to or acknowledging indebtedness if these are tradeable on the capital market; and

(c) any other securities which are normally dealt in and which give the right to acquire any such shares, bonds, instruments or other securities by subscription, purchase or exchange or which give rise to a cash settlement (excluding instruments of payment);

and includes units of a collective investment scheme within the meaning of the Financial Services and

Markets Act 2000, eligible debt securities within the meaning of the Uncertificated Securities Regulations 2001, money market instruments, claims relating to or rights in or in respect of any of the financial instruments included in this definition and any rights, privileges or benefits attached to or arising from any such financial instruments;

"intermediary" means a person that maintains registers or accounts to which financial instruments may be credited or debited, for others or both for others and for its own account but does not include—

(a) a person who acts as a registrar or transfer agent for the issuer of financial instruments; or

(b) a person who maintains registers or accounts in the capacity of operator of a system for the holding and transfer of financial instruments on records of the issuer or other records which constitute the primary record of entitlement to financial instruments as against the issuer;

"non-natural person" means any corporate body, unincorporated firm, partnership or body with legal personality except an individual, including any such entity constituted under the law of a country or territory outside the United Kingdom or any such entity constituted under international law;

[. . .]

"relevant account" means, in relation to book entry securities collateral which is subject to a financial collateral arrangement, the register or account, which may be maintained by the collateral-taker, in which entries are made, by which that book entry securities collateral is transferred or designated so as to be in the possession or under the control of the collateral-taker or a person acting on its behalf;

"relevant financial obligations" means the obligations which are secured or otherwise covered by a financial collateral arrangement, and such obligations may consist of or include—

(a) present or future, actual or contingent or prospective obligations (including such obligations arising under a master agreement or similar arrangement);

(b) obligations owed to the collateral-taker by a person other than the collateral-provider;

(c) obligations of a specified class or kind arising from time to time;

"reorganisation measures" means—

(a) administration within the meaning of the Insolvency Act 1986 or the Insolvency (Northern Ireland) Order 1989;

(b) a company voluntary arrangement within the meaning of that Act or that Order;

(c) administration of a partnership within the meaning of that Act or that Order or, in the case of a Scottish partnership, [a protected trust deed within the meaning of] the Bankruptcy (Scotland) Act 1985;

(d) a partnership voluntary arrangement within the meaning of the Insolvency Act 1986 or the Insolvency (Northern Ireland) Order 1989 or, in the case of a Scottish partnership, [a protected trust deed within the meaning of] the Bankruptcy (Scotland) Act 1985; and

(e) the making of an interim order on an administration application;

"security financial collateral arrangement" means an agreement or arrangement, evidenced in writing, where—

(a) the purpose of the agreement or arrangement is to secure the relevant financial obligations owed to the collateral-taker;

(b) the collateral-provider creates or there arises a security interest in financial collateral to secure those obligations;

(c) the financial collateral is delivered, transferred, held, registered or otherwise designated so as to be in the possession or under the control of the collateral-taker or a person acting on its behalf; any right of the collateral-provider to substitute [financial collateral of the same or greater value] or withdraw excess financial collateral [or to collect the proceeds of credit claims until further notice] shall not prevent the financial collateral being in the possession or under the control of the collateral-taker; and

(d) the collateral-provider and the collateral-taker are both non-natural persons;

"security interest" means any legal or equitable interest or any right in security, other than a title transfer financial collateral arrangement, created or otherwise arising by way of security including—

(a) a pledge;

(b) a mortgage;

(c) a fixed charge;

(d) a charge created as a floating charge where the financial collateral charged is delivered, transferred, held, registered or otherwise designated so as to be in the possession or under the control of the collateral-taker or a person acting on its behalf; any right of the collateral-provider to substitute [financial collateral of the same or greater value] or withdraw excess financial collateral [or to collect the proceeds of credit claims until further notice] shall not prevent the financial collateral being in the possession or under the control of the collateral-taker; or

(e) a lien;

"title transfer financial collateral arrangement" means an agreement or arrangement, including a repurchase agreement, evidenced in writing, where—

(a) the purpose of the agreement or arrangement is to secure or otherwise cover the relevant financial obligations owed to the collateral-taker;

(b) the collateral-provider transfers legal and beneficial ownership in financial collateral to a collateral-taker on terms that when the relevant financial obligations are discharged the collateral-taker must transfer legal and beneficial ownership of equivalent financial collateral to the collateral-provider; and

(c) the collateral-provider and the collateral-taker are both non-natural persons;

["winding-up proceedings" means—

(a) winding up by the court or voluntary winding up within the meaning of the Insolvency Act 1986 or the Insolvency (Northern Ireland) Order 1989;

(b) sequestration of a Scottish partnership under the Bankruptcy (Scotland) Act 1985;

(c) bank insolvency within the meaning of the Banking Act 2009.]

[(1A) For the purpose of these Regulations—

(a) "enforcement event" means an event of default, or (subject to sub-paragraph (b)) any similar event as agreed between the parties, on the occurrence of which, under the terms of a financial collateral agreement or by operation of law, the collateral taker is entitled to realise or appropriate financial collateral or a close-out netting provision comes into effect;

(b) a crisis management measure or crisis prevention measure taken in relation to an entity . . . shall not be considered to be an enforcement event pursuant to an agreement between the parties if the substantive obligations provided for in that agreement (including payment and delivery obligations and provision of collateral) continue to be performed; and

(c) for the purposes of sub-paragraph (b) "crisis prevention measure" and "crisis management measure" have the meaning given in section 48Z of the Banking Act 2009.]

[(2) For the purposes of these Regulations "possession" of financial collateral in the form of cash or financial instruments includes the case where financial collateral has been credited to an account in the name of the collateral-taker or a person acting on his behalf (whether or not the collateral-taker, or person acting on his behalf, has credited the financial collateral to an account in the name of the collateral-provider on his, or that person's, books) provided that any rights the collateral-provider may have in relation to that financial collateral are limited to the right to substitute financial collateral of the same or greater value or to withdraw excess financial collateral.]

NOTES

Para (1): was numbered as such by the Financial Markets and Insolvency (Settlement Finality and Financial Collateral Arrangements) (Amendment) Regulations 2010, SI 2010/2993, reg 4(1), (2)(a), as from 6 April 2011, and is amended as follows—

Definition "credit claims" originally inserted by SI 2010/2993, reg 4(1), (2)(b)(i), as from 6 April 2011. Subsequently substituted by the Capital Requirements Regulations 2013, SI 2013/3115, reg 46(1), Sch 2, Pt 3, para 61, as from 1 January 2014.

Definition "enforcement event" (omitted) revoked by the Bank Recovery and Resolution (No 2) Order 2014, SI 2014/3348, art 226, Sch 3, Pt 3, para 9(1), (2)(a), as from 10 January 2015.

Definition "recovery and resolution directive" (omitted) originally inserted by SI 2014/3348, art 226, Sch 3, Pt 3, para 9(1), (2)(a), as from 10 January 2015. Subsequently revoked by the Financial Markets and Insolvency (Amendment and Transitional Provision) (EU Exit) Regulations 2019, SI 2019/341, reg 12(1), (2)(a), as from IP completion day (as defined in the European Union (Withdrawal Agreement) Act 2020, s 39).

Words in square brackets in the definition "financial collateral" substituted by SI 2010/2993, reg 4(1), (2)(b)(ii), as from 6 April 2011.

Words in square brackets in the definition "reorganisation measures" inserted by SI 2010/2993, reg 4(1), (2)(b)(iii), as from 6 April 2011.

In the definitions "security financial collateral arrangement" and "security interest" the words "financial collateral of the same or greater value" were substituted, and the other words in square brackets were inserted, by SI 2010/2993, reg 4(1), (2)(b)(iv), as from 6 April 2011.

Definition "winding up proceedings" substituted by SI 2010/2993, reg 4(1), (2)(b)(v), as from 6 April 2011.

Para (1A): inserted by SI 2014/3348, art 226, Sch 3, Pt 3, para 9(1), (2)(b), as from 10 January 2015. Words omitted from sub-para (b) revoked by SI 2019/341, reg 12(1), (2)(b), as from IP completion day (as defined in the European Union (Withdrawal Agreement) Act 2020, s 39).

Para (2): added by SI 2010/2993, reg 4(1), (2)(c), as from 6 April 2011.

PART 2 MODIFICATION OF LAW REQUIRING FORMALITIES

[10.123]

4 Certain legislation requiring formalities not to apply to financial collateral arrangements

(1) Section 4 of the Statute of Frauds 1677 (no action on a third party's promise unless in writing and signed) shall not apply (if it would otherwise do so) in relation to a financial collateral arrangement.

(2) Section 53(1)(c) of the Law of Property Act 1925 (disposition of equitable interest to be in writing and signed) shall not apply (if it would otherwise do so) in relation to a financial collateral arrangement.

(3) Section 136 of the Law of Property Act 1925 (legal assignments of things in action) shall not apply (if it would otherwise do so) in relation to a financial collateral arrangement, to the extent that the section requires an assignment to be signed by the assignor or a person authorised on its behalf, in order to be effectual in law.

(4) [[Sections 859A] (charges created by a company) and [859H] (consequence of failure to register charges created by a company) of the Companies Act 2006] shall not apply [(if they would otherwise do so)] in relation to a security financial collateral arrangement or any charge created or otherwise arising under a security financial collateral arrangement [or, in Scotland, to relation to any charge created or arising under a financial collateral arrangement].

(5) Section 4 of the Industrial and Provident Societies Act 1967 (filing of information relating to charges) shall not apply (if it would otherwise do so) in relation to a . . . financial collateral arrangement or any charge created or otherwise arising under a . . . financial collateral arrangement.

NOTES

Para (4): words in first (outer) pair of square brackets and words in fourth pair of square brackets substituted by the Financial Collateral Arrangements (No 2) Regulations 2003 (Amendment) Regulations 2009, SI 2009/2462, reg 2(1), (2), as from 1 October 2009. Words in second (inner) pair of square brackets and number in third (inner) pair of square brackets substituted (for the original words "Sections 860" and the original number "874" respectively), by the Companies Act 2006 (Amendment of Part 25) Regulations 2013, SI 2013/600, reg 5, Sch 2, para 4(1), (2), as from 6 April 2013, in relation to charges created on or after that date. Words in final pair of square brackets inserted by the Financial Markets and Insolvency (Settlement Finality and Financial Collateral Arrangements) (Amendment) Regulations 2010, SI 2010/2993, reg 4(1), (3)(a), as from 6 April 2011.

Para (5): words omitted revoked by SI 2010/2993, reg 4(1), (3)(b), as from 6 April 2011.

Industrial and Provident Societies Act 1967: repealed by the Co-operative and Community Benefit Societies Act 2014.

[10.124]

5 Certain legislation affecting Scottish companies not to apply to financial collateral arrangements

[Sections 878 (charges created by a company) and 889 (charges void unless registered) of the Companies Act 2006] shall not apply [(if they would otherwise do so)] in relation to a . . . financial collateral arrangement or any charge created or otherwise arising under a . . . financial collateral arrangement.

NOTES

Revoked by the Companies Act 2006 (Amendment of Part 25) Regulations 2013, SI 2013/600, reg 5, Sch 2, para 4(1), (3), as from 6 April 2013, in relation to charges created on or after that date.

Words in square brackets substituted by the Financial Collateral Arrangements (No 2) Regulations 2003 (Amendment) Regulations 2009, SI 2009/2462, reg 2(1), (3), as from 1 October 2009.

Words omitted revoked by the Financial Markets and Insolvency (Settlement Finality and Financial Collateral Arrangements) (Amendment) Regulations 2010, SI 2010/2993, reg 4(1), (4), as from 6 April 2011.

[10.125]

6 No additional formalities required for creation of a right in security over book entry securities collateral in Scotland

(1) Where under the law of Scotland an act is required as a condition for transferring, creating or enforcing a right in security over any book entry securities collateral, that requirement shall not apply (if it would otherwise do so).

(2) For the purposes of paragraph (1) an "act"—

(a) is any act other than an entry on a register or account maintained by or on behalf of an intermediary which evidences title to the book entry securities collateral;

(b) includes the entering of the collateral-taker's name in a company's register of members.

[10.126]

[6A Certain legislation affecting overseas companies not to apply to financial collateral arrangements

Any provision about registration of charges made by regulations under section 1052 of the Companies Act 2006 (overseas companies) does not apply (if it would otherwise do so) in relation to a security financial collateral arrangement or any charge created or otherwise arising under a security financial collateral arrangement [or, in Scotland, to any charge created or arising under a financial collateral arrangement].]

NOTES

Inserted by the Financial Collateral Arrangements (No 2) Regulations 2003 (Amendment) Regulations 2009, SI 2009/2462, reg 2(1), (4), as from 1 October 2009.

Words in square brackets added by the Financial Markets and Insolvency (Settlement Finality and Financial Collateral Arrangements) (Amendment) Regulations 2010, SI 2010/2993, reg 4(1), (8), as from 6 April 2011.

7 *(Revoked by the Financial Collateral Arrangements (No 2) Regulations 2003 (Amendment) Regulations 2009, SI 2009/2462, reg 2(1), (5), as from 1 October 2009.)*

PART 3 MODIFICATION OF INSOLVENCY LAW

[10.127]

8 Certain legislation restricting enforcement of security not to apply to financial collateral arrangements

(1) The following provisions of Schedule B1 to the Insolvency Act 1986 (administration) shall not apply to any security interest created or otherwise arising under a financial collateral arrangement—

(a) paragraph 43(2) (restriction on enforcement of security or repossession of goods) including that provision as applied by paragraph 44 (interim moratorium); . . .

[(aa) paragraph 65(2) (distribution);]

(b) paragraphs 70 and 71 (power of administrator to deal with charged property); [and]

[(c) paragraph 99(3) and (4) (administrator's remuneration, expenses and liabilities)].

(2) Paragraph 41(2) of Schedule B1 to the Insolvency Act 1986 (receiver to vacate office when so required by administrator) shall not apply to a receiver appointed under a charge created or otherwise arising under a financial collateral arrangement.

(3) The following provisions of the Insolvency Act 1986 (administration) shall not apply in relation to any security interest created or otherwise arising under a financial collateral arrangement—

(a) sections 10(1)(b) and 11(3)(c) (restriction on enforcement of security while petition for administration order pending or order in force); and

(b) section 15(1) and 15(2) (power of administrator to deal with charged property); [and]

[(c) section 19(4) and 19(5) (administrator's remuneration, expenses and liabilities)].

(4) Section 11(2) of the Insolvency Act 1986 (receiver to vacate office when so required by administrator) shall not apply to a receiver appointed under a charge created or otherwise arising under a financial collateral arrangement.

(5) . . .

NOTES

Para (1): word omitted from sub-para (a) revoked, word in square brackets in sub-para (b) inserted, and sub-paras (aa), (c) inserted, by the Financial Markets and Insolvency (Settlement Finality and Financial Collateral Arrangements) (Amendment) Regulations 2010, SI 2010/2993, reg 4(1), (6)(a)–(d), as from 6 April 2011.

Para (3): sub-para (c) and the word immediately preceding it inserted by SI 2010/2993, reg 4(1), (6)(e), as from 6 April 2011.

Para (5): revoked by the Corporate Insolvency and Governance Act 2020, s 2(1), Sch 3, para 40, as from 26 June 2020 (for transitional provisions, see ss 2(2), (3) of the 2020 Act which provides that (without prejudice to the Interpretation Act 1978, s 16) nothing in the 2020 Act affects the operation of the Insolvency Act 1986, or any other enactment, in relation to a moratorium under Sch A1 to the 1986 Act which comes into force before the repeal of that Schedule by Sch 3 to the 2020 Act (ie, 26 June 2020)).

[10.128]

9 Certain Northern Ireland legislation restricting enforcement of security not to apply to financial collateral arrangements

(1) The following provisions of the Insolvency (Northern Ireland) Order 1989 (administration) shall not apply to any security interest created or otherwise arising under a financial collateral arrangement—

(a) Article 23(1)(b) and Article 24(3)(c) (restriction on enforcement of security while petition for administration order pending or order in force); . . .

(b) Article 28(1) and (2) (power of administrator to deal with charged property).

[(c) Article 31(4) and (5) (administrator's remuneration, expenses and liabilities); and

(d) Paragraphs 44(2), 45 (restriction on enforcement of security), 66(2) (distribution), 71, 72 (power of administrator to deal with charged property), 100(3) and (4) (administrator's remuneration, expenses and liabilities) of Schedule B1 to the Order].

(2) Article 24(2) of that Order (receiver to vacate office at request of administrator) shall not apply to a receiver appointed under a charge created or otherwise arising under a financial collateral arrangement.

NOTES

Para (1): word omitted from sub-para (a) revoked, and sub-paras (c), (d) added, by the Financial Markets and Insolvency (Settlement Finality and Financial Collateral Arrangements) (Amendment) Regulations 2010, SI 2010/2993, reg 4(1), (7), as from 6 April 2011.

[10.129]

10 Certain insolvency legislation on avoidance of contracts and floating charges not to apply to financial collateral arrangements

(1) In relation to winding-up proceedings of a collateral-taker or collateral-provider, section 127 of the Insolvency Act 1986 (avoidance of property dispositions, etc) shall not apply (if it would otherwise do so)—

(a) to any property or security interest subject to a disposition or created or otherwise arising under a financial collateral arrangement; or

(b) to prevent a close-out netting provision taking effect in accordance with its terms.

(2) Section 88 of the Insolvency Act 1986 (avoidance of share transfers, etc after winding-up resolution) shall not apply (if it would otherwise do so) to any transfer of shares under a financial collateral arrangement.

[(2A) Sections 40 (or in Scotland, sections 59, 60(1)(e)) and 175 of the Insolvency Act 1986 (preferential debts) shall not apply to any debt which is secured by a charge created or otherwise arising under a financial collateral arrangement.

[(2AA) Section 174A of the Insolvency Act 1986 (moratorium debts etc priority) shall not apply (if it otherwise would do so) to any charge created or otherwise arising under a financial collateral arrangement.

(2B) Section 176ZA of the Insolvency Act 1986 (expenses of winding up) shall not apply in relation to any claim to any property which is subject to a disposition or created or otherwise arising under a financial collateral arrangement.]

(3) Section 176A of the Insolvency Act 1986 (share of assets for unsecured creditors) shall not apply (if it would otherwise do so) to any charge created or otherwise arising under a financial collateral arrangement.

(4) Section 178 of the Insolvency Act 1986 (power to disclaim onerous property) or, in Scotland, any rule of law having the same effect as that section, shall not apply where the collateral-provider or collateral-taker under the arrangement is [subject to winding-up proceedings], to any financial collateral arrangement.

(5) Section 245 of the Insolvency Act 1986 (avoidance of certain floating charges) shall not apply (if it would otherwise do so) to any charge created or otherwise arising under a security financial collateral arrangement.

[(5A) Paragraph 64A of Schedule B1 to the Insolvency Act 1986 shall not apply (if it otherwise would do so) to any charge created or otherwise arising under a financial collateral arrangement.]

(6) [Section 754 of the Companies Act 2006 (priorities where debentures secured by floating charge)] [(including that section as applied or modified by any enactment made under the Banking Act 2009)] shall not apply (if it would otherwise do so) to any charge created or otherwise arising under a financial collateral arrangement.

NOTES

Paras (2A), (2B): inserted by the Financial Markets and Insolvency (Settlement Finality and Financial Collateral Arrangements) (Amendment) Regulations 2010, SI 2010/2993, reg 4(1), (8)(a), as from 6 April 2011.

Paras (2AA), (5A): inserted by the Co-operative and Community Benefit Societies and Credit Unions (Arrangements, Reconstructions and Administration) (Amendment) and Consequential Amendments Order 2020, SI 2020/744, art 15(1), (2), as from 18 July 2020.

Para (4): words in square brackets substituted by SI 2010/2993, reg 4(1), (8)(b), as from 6 April 2011.

Para (6): words in first pair of square brackets substituted by the Financial Collateral Arrangements (No 2) Regulations 2003 (Amendment) Regulations 2009, SI 2009/2462, reg 2(1), (6), as from 1 October 2009. Words in second pair of square brackets inserted by SI 2010/2993, reg 4(1), (8)(c), as from 6 April 2011.

[10.130]

11 Certain Northern Ireland insolvency legislation on avoidance of contracts and floating charges not to apply to financial collateral arrangements

(1) In relation to winding-up proceedings of a collateral-provider or collateral-taker, Article 107 of the Insolvency (Northern Ireland) Order 1989 (avoidance of property dispositions effected after commencement of winding up) shall not apply (if it would otherwise do so)—

(a) to any property or security interest subject to a disposition or created or otherwise arising under a financial collateral arrangement; or

(b) to prevent a close-out netting provision taking effect in accordance with its terms.

[(1A) Article 50 of that Order (payment of debts out of assets subject to floating charge) shall not apply (if it would otherwise do so), to any charge created or otherwise arising under a financial collateral arrangement.]

(2) Article 74 of that Order (avoidance of share transfers, etc after winding-up resolution) shall not apply (if it would otherwise do so) to any transfer of shares under a financial collateral arrangement.

[(2A) [Articles 148A (moratorium debts etc priority) and 149 (preferential debts) of that Order] and 150ZA (expenses of winding up) shall not apply (if they would otherwise do so) to any charge created or otherwise arising under a financial collateral arrangement.]

(3) Article 152 of that Order (power to disclaim onerous property) shall not apply where the collateral-provider or collateral-taker under the arrangement is being wound-up, to any financial collateral arrangement.

(4) Article 207 of that Order (avoidance of certain floating charges) shall not apply (if it would otherwise do so) to any charge created or otherwise arising under a security financial collateral arrangement.

(5) . . .

NOTES

Paras (1A), (2A): inserted by the Financial Markets and Insolvency (Settlement Finality and Financial Collateral Arrangements) (Amendment) Regulations 2010, SI 2010/2993, reg 4(1), (9), as from 6 April 2011. Words in square brackets in para (2A) substituted by the Co-operative and Community Benefit Societies and Credit Unions (Arrangements, Reconstructions and Administration) (Amendment) and Consequential Amendments Order 2020, SI 2020/744, art 15(1), (3), as from 18 July 2020.

Para (5): revoked by the Financial Collateral Arrangements (No 2) Regulations 2003 (Amendment) Regulations 2009, SI 2009/2462, reg 2(1), (7), as from 1 October 2009.

[10.131]

12 Close-out netting provisions to take effect in accordance with their terms

(1) A close-out netting provision shall, subject to paragraph (2), take effect in accordance with its terms notwithstanding that the collateral-provider or collateral-taker under the arrangement is subject to winding-up proceedings or reorganisation measures.

(2) Paragraph (1) shall not apply if at the time that a party to a financial collateral arrangement entered into such an arrangement or that the relevant financial obligations came into existence—

(a) that party was aware or should have been aware that winding up proceedings or re-organisation measures had commenced in relation to the other party;

[(aa) in Scotland, that party had notice that [a statement as to the affairs of the other party had been sent to the other party's creditors under section 99(1) of that Act] . . . ;

(ab) in England and Wales, that party had notice that a statement as to the affairs of the other party had been sent to the other party's creditors under section 99(1) of that Act(c);

(ac) that party had notice that a meeting of creditors of the other party had been summoned under Article 84 of the Insolvency (Northern Ireland) Order 1989;]

(b) that party had notice . . . that a petition for the winding-up of [or, in Scotland, a petition for winding-up proceedings in relation to] the other party was pending;

(c) that party had notice that an application for an administration order was pending or that any person had given notice of an intention to appoint an administrator; or

(d) that party had notice that an application for an administration order was pending or that any person had given notice of an intention to appoint an administrator and liquidation of the other party to the financial collateral arrangement was immediately preceded by an administration of that party.

(3) For the purposes of paragraph (2)—

(a) winding-up proceedings commence on the making of a winding-up order [or, in the case of a Scottish partnership, the award of sequestration] by the court; and

(b) reorganisation measures commence on the appointment of an administrator, whether by a court or otherwise [or, in the case of a Scottish partnership, when a protected trust deed is entered into].

[(4) The following provisions of the Insolvency (England and Wales) Rules 2016, or, in Scotland, any rule of law with the same or similar effect to the effect of these Rules, do not apply to a close-out netting provision unless paragraph (2)(a) applies—

(a) in rule 14.24 (administration: mutual dealings and set-off), in paragraph (6), in the definition of "mutual dealings", paragraphs (a) and (d); and

(b) in rule 14.25 (winding up: mutual dealings and set-off), in paragraph (6), in the definition of "mutual dealings", paragraph (c).

(4A) Rules 2.086(2)(a) and (d) and 4.096(2)(c) of the Insolvency Rules (Northern Ireland) 1991 (mutual credits and set off) do not apply to a close-out netting provision unless paragraph (2)(a) applies.]

[(5) Nothing in this regulation prevents the Bank of England imposing a restriction on the effect of a close out netting provision in the exercise of its powers under Part 1 of the Banking Act 2009.]

NOTES

Para (2): sub-para (aa)–(ac) were inserted, and the words omitted from sub-para (b) were revoked, by the Small Business, Enterprise and Employment Act 2015 (Consequential Amendments, Savings and Transitional Provisions) Regulations 2018, SI 2018/208, reg 8, as from 13 March 2018 (for transitional provisions, see the note relating to the 2018 Regulations below). The words in square brackets in sub-para (aa) were inserted, and the words omitted from that sub-paragraph were revoked, by the Small Business, Enterprise and Employment Act 2015 (Consequential Amendments, Savings and Transitional Provisions) Regulations 2019, SI 2019/1058, reg 5, as from 23 July 2019 (for transitional provisions see the note relating to the 2019 Regulations below).

Paras (4), (4A): substituted (for the original para (4)) by the Financial Services and Markets (Insolvency) (Amendment of Miscellaneous Enactments) Regulations 2019, SI 2019/755, reg 3(1), (2), as from 23 April 2019.

Para (5): added by the Bank Recovery and Resolution (No 2) Order 2014, SI 2014/3348, art 226, Sch 3, Pt 3, para 9(1), (3), as from 10 January 2015.

All other words in square brackets in this regulation were inserted by the Financial Markets and Insolvency (Settlement Finality and Financial Collateral Arrangements) (Amendment) Regulations 2010, SI 2010/2993, reg 4(1), (10), as from 6 April 2011.

Transitional provisions: the Small Business, Enterprise and Employment Act 2015 (Consequential Amendments, Savings and Transitional Provisions) Regulations 2018, SI 2018/208, regs 16, 19 provide as follows—

"16 Interpretation of Part 4

In this Part—

"the 1986 Act" means the Insolvency Act 1986;

"the 2000 Act" means the Financial Services and Markets Act 2000;

"the 2009 Act" means the Banking Act 2009; and

"relevant meeting" means a meeting of creditors which is to be held on or after the date on which Parts 2 and 3 of these Regulations come into force, and was—

(a) called, summoned or otherwise required before 6th April 2017 under a provision of the 1986 Act or the Insolvency Rules 1986;

(b) requisitioned by a creditor before 6th April 2017 under a provision of the 1986 Act or the Insolvency Rules 1986; or

(c) called or summoned under section 106, 146 or 331 of the 1986 Act as a result of—

(i) a final report to creditors sent before 6th April 2017 under rule 4.49D of the Insolvency Rules 1986 (final report to creditors in liquidation);

(ii) a final report to creditors and bankrupt sent before that date under rule 6.78B of those Rules (final report to creditors and bankrupt).

19 Transitional provision for regulation 8

(1) Paragraph (2) applies where a relevant meeting is to be held in winding up proceedings or in relation to reorganisation measures commenced in England and Wales in respect of the collateral-provider or collateral-taker under—

(a) a financial collateral arrangement; or

(b) an arrangement of which a financial collateral arrangement forms part.

(2) Regulation 12 of the Financial Collateral Arrangements (No 2) Regulations 2003 applies in relation to the meeting without the amendments made by regulation 8.

(3) In this regulation—

(a) the reference to the commencement of winding up proceedings or reorganisation measures is to be construed in accordance with regulation 12(3) of those Regulations;

(b) "financial collateral arrangement" has the same meaning as in those Regulations;

(c) "reorganisation measures" means—

(i) administration under Schedule B1 to the 1986 Act;

(ii) administration of a partnership under Schedule B1 to the 1986 Act (as applied to insolvent partnerships under section 420 of that Act);

(iii) a proposal for a company voluntary arrangement under Part 1 of the 1986 Act (company voluntary arrangements);

(iv) a proposal for a partnership voluntary arrangement under Part 1 of the 1986 Act (as applied to insolvent partnerships under section 420 of that Act); or

(v) the making of an interim order on an administration application (within the meaning given in paragraph 12 of Schedule B1 to the 1986 Act, including that paragraph as applied to insolvent partnerships); and

(d) "winding up proceedings" means—

(i) voluntary winding up or winding up by the court under Part 4 of the 1986 Act; or

(ii) bank insolvency under Part 2 of the 2009 Act.".

Transitional provisions: the Small Business, Enterprise and Employment Act 2015 (Consequential Amendments, Savings and Transitional Provisions) Regulations 2019, SI 2019/1058, reg 10 provides as follows—

"10 Transitional provision for regulation 5

(1) Paragraph (2) applies where a relevant meeting is to be held in winding up proceedings or in relation to reorganisation measures commenced in Scotland in respect of the collateral-provider or collateral-taker under—

(a) a financial collateral arrangement; or

(b) an arrangement of which a financial collateral arrangement forms part.

(2) Regulation 12 of the Financial Collateral Arrangements (No 2) Regulations 2003 applies in relation to the meeting without the amendments made by regulation 5.

(3) In this regulation—

(a) the reference to the commencement of winding up proceedings or reorganisation measures is to be construed in accordance with regulation 12(3) of those Regulations;

(b) "financial collateral arrangement" has the same meaning as in those Regulations;

(c) "reorganisation measures" means—

(i) administration under Schedule B1 to the 1986 Act;

(ii) a proposal for a company voluntary arrangement under Part 1 of the 1986 Act (company voluntary arrangements); or

(iii) the making of an interim order on an administration application (within the meaning given in paragraph 12 of Schedule B1 to the 1986 Act).

(d) "winding up proceedings" means—

(i) voluntary winding up or winding up by the court under Part 4 of the 1986 Act; or

(ii) bank insolvency under Part 2 of the 2009 Act.".

Note that the Insolvency Rules 1986, SI 1986/1925 were revoked and replaced (subject to transitional provisions) by the Insolvency (England and Wales) Rules 2016, SI 2016/1024, as from 6 April 2017.

[10.132]

13 Financial collateral arrangements to be enforceable where collateral-taker not aware of commencement of winding-up proceedings or reorganisation measures

(1) Where any of the events specified in paragraph (2) occur on the day of, but after the moment of commencement of, winding-up proceedings or reorganisation measures those events, arrangements and obligations shall be legally enforceable and binding on third parties if the collateral-taker can show that he was not aware, nor should have been aware, of the commencement of such proceedings or measures.

(2) The events referred to in paragraph (1) are—

(a) a financial collateral arrangement coming into existence;

(b) a relevant financial obligation secured by a financial collateral arrangement coming into existence; or

(c) the delivery, transfer, holding, registering or other designation of financial collateral so as to be in the possession or under the control of the collateral-taker.

(3) For the purposes of paragraph (1)—

(a) the commencement of winding-up proceedings means the making of a winding-up order [or, in the case of a Scottish partnership, the award of sequestration] by the court; and

(b) commencement of reorganisation measures means the appointment of an administrator, whether by a court or otherwise [or, in the case of a Scottish partnership, the date of registration of a protected trust deed].

NOTES

Para (3): words in square brackets inserted by the Financial Markets and Insolvency (Settlement Finality and Financial Collateral Arrangements) (Amendment) Regulations 2010, SI 2010/2993, reg 4(1), (11), as from 6 April 2011.

[10.133]

14 Modification of the [Insolvency (England and Wales) Rules 2016] and the Insolvency Rules (Northern Ireland) 1991

Where the collateral-provider or the collateral-taker under a financial collateral arrangement goes into liquidation or administration and the arrangement or a close out netting provision provides for, or the mechanism provided under the arrangement permits, either—

(a) the debt owed by the party in liquidation or administration under the arrangement, to be assessed or paid in a currency other than sterling; or

(b) the debt to be converted into sterling at a rate other than the official exchange rate prevailing on the date when that party went into liquidation or administration;

then [rule 14.21 of the Insolvency (England and Wales) Rules 2016 (debts in foreign currency)], or rule 4.097 of the Insolvency Rules (Northern Ireland) 1991 (liquidation, debt in foreign currency), as appropriate, shall not apply unless the arrangement provides for an unreasonable exchange rate or the collateral-taker uses the mechanism provided under the arrangement to impose an unreasonable exchange rate in which case the appropriate rule shall apply.

NOTES

Words in square brackets substituted by the Financial Services and Markets (Insolvency) (Amendment of Miscellaneous Enactments) Regulations 2019, SI 2019/755, reg 3(1), (3), as from 23 April 2019.

[10.134]

15 Modification of the [Insolvency (Scotland) (Receivership and Winding up) Rules 2018 and the Insolvency (Scotland) (Company Voluntary Arrangements and Administration) Rules 2018]

Where the collateral-provider or the collateral-taker under a financial collateral arrangement goes into liquidation [or administration] or, in the case of a partnership, sequestration and the arrangement provides for, or the mechanism provided under the arrangement permits, either—

(a) the debt owed by the party in liquidation or sequestration under the arrangement, to be assessed or paid in a currency other than sterling; or

(b) the debt to be converted into sterling at a rate other than the official exchange rate prevailing on the date when that party went into liquidation or sequestration;

then [rule 7.25 of the Insolvency (Scotland) (Receivership and Winding up) Rules 2018 and rule 3.114 of the Insolvency (Scotland) Company Voluntary Arrangements and Administration Rules 2018], as appropriate, shall not apply unless the arrangement provides for an unreasonable exchange rate or the collateral-taker uses the mechanism provided under the arrangement to impose an unreasonable exchange rate in which case the appropriate rule shall apply.

NOTES

Words in square brackets in the regulation heading and in para (b) substituted by the Financial Services and Markets (Insolvency) (Amendment of Miscellaneous Enactments) Regulations 2019, SI 2019/755, reg 3(1), (4), as from 23 April 2019.

Words "or administration" in square brackets substituted by the Financial Markets and Insolvency (Settlement Finality and Financial Collateral Arrangements) (Amendment) Regulations 2010, SI 2010/2993, reg 4(1), (12), as from 6 April 2011.

[10.135]

[15A Insolvency proceedings in other jurisdictions

(1) The references to insolvency law in section 426 of the Insolvency Act 1986 (co-operation between courts exercising jurisdiction in relation to insolvency) include, in relation to a part of the United Kingdom, this Part of these Regulations and, in relation to a relevant country or territory within the meaning of that section, so much of the law of that country or territory as corresponds to this Part.

(2) A court shall not, in pursuance of that section or any other enactment or rule of law, recognise or give effect to—

(a) any order of a court exercising jurisdiction in relation to insolvency law in a country or territory outside the United Kingdom, or

(b) any act of a person appointed in such a country or territory to discharge any functions under insolvency law,

Part 10 Miscellaneous other SIs

in so far as the making of the order or the doing of the act would be prohibited by this Part in the case of a court in England and Wales or Scotland, the High Court in Northern Ireland or a relevant office holder.

(3) Paragraph (2) does not affect the recognition of a judgment required to be recognised or enforced under or by virtue of the Civil Jurisdiction and Judgments Act 1982 . . .]

NOTES

Inserted by the Financial Markets and Insolvency (Settlement Finality and Financial Collateral Arrangements) (Amendment) Regulations 2010, SI 2010/2993, reg 4(1), (13), as from 6 April 2011.

Para (3): words omitted revoked by the Financial Markets and Insolvency (Amendment and Transitional Provision) (EU Exit) Regulations 2019, SI 2019/341, reg 12(1), (3), as from IP completion day (as defined in the European Union (Withdrawal Agreement) Act 2020, s 39).

PART 4 RIGHT OF USE AND APPROPRIATION

[10.136]

16 Right of use under a security financial collateral arrangement

(1) If a security financial collateral arrangement provides for the collateral-taker to use and dispose of any financial collateral provided under the arrangement, as if it were the owner of it, the collateral-taker may do so in accordance with the terms of the arrangement.

(2) If a collateral-taker exercises such a right of use, it is obliged to replace the original financial collateral by transferring equivalent financial collateral on or before the due date for the performance of the relevant financial obligations covered by the arrangement or, if the arrangement so provides, it may set off the value of the equivalent financial collateral against or apply it in discharge of the relevant financial obligations in accordance with the terms of the arrangement.

(3) The equivalent financial collateral which is transferred in discharge of an obligation as described in paragraph (2), shall be subject to the same terms of the security financial collateral arrangement as the original financial collateral was subject to and shall be treated as having been provided under the security financial collateral arrangement at the same time as the original financial collateral was first provided.

[(3A) In Scotland, paragraphs (1) and (3) apply to title transfer financial collateral arrangements as they apply to security financial collateral arrangements.]

(4) If a collateral-taker has an outstanding obligation to replace the original financial collateral with equivalent financial collateral when an enforcement event occurs, that obligation may be the subject of a close-out netting provision.

[(5) This regulation does not apply in relation to credit claims.]

NOTES

Paras (3A), (5): inserted and added respectively by the Financial Markets and Insolvency (Settlement Finality and Financial Collateral Arrangements) (Amendment) Regulations 2010, SI 2010/2993, reg 4(1), (14), as from 6 April 2011.

[10.137]

[17 Appropriation of financial collateral under a security financial collateral arrangement

(1) Where a security interest is created or arises under a security financial collateral arrangement on terms that include a power for the collateral-taker to appropriate the financial collateral, the collateral-taker may exercise that power in accordance with the terms of the security financial collateral arrangement, without any order for foreclosure from the courts (and whether or not the remedy of foreclosure would be available).

(2) Upon the exercise by the collateral-taker of the power to appropriate the financial collateral, the equity of redemption of the collateral-provider shall be extinguished and all legal and beneficial interest of the collateral-provider in the financial collateral shall vest in the collateral taker.]

NOTES

Substituted by the Financial Markets and Insolvency (Settlement Finality and Financial Collateral Arrangements) (Amendment) Regulations 2010, SI 2010/2993, reg 4(1), (15), as from 6 April 2011.

[10.138]

18 Duty to value collateral and account for any difference in value on appropriation

(1) Where a collateral-taker exercises a power contained in a security financial collateral arrangement to appropriate the financial collateral the collateral-taker must value the financial collateral in accordance with the terms of the arrangement and in any event in a commercially reasonable manner.

(2) Where a collateral-taker exercises such a power and the value of the financial collateral appropriated differs from the amount of the relevant financial obligations, then as the case may be, either—

- (a) the collateral-taker must account to the collateral-provider for the amount by which the value of the financial collateral exceeds the relevant financial obligations; or
- (b) the collateral-provider will remain liable to the collateral-taker for any amount whereby the value of the financial collateral is less than the relevant financial obligations.

[10.139]

[18A Restrictions on enforcement of financial collateral arrangements, etc

(1) Nothing in regulations 16 and 17 prevents the Bank of England imposing a restriction—

- (a) on the enforcement of financial collateral arrangements, or
- (b) on the effect of a security financial collateral arrangement, close out netting provision or set-off arrangement,

in the exercise of its powers under Part 1 of the Banking Act 2009.

(2) For the purpose of paragraph (1) "set-off arrangement" [means an arrangement under which two or more debts, claims or obligations can be set off against each other].]

NOTES

Inserted by the Bank Recovery and Resolution (No 2) Order 2014, SI 2014/3348, art 226, Sch 3, Pt 3, para 9(1), (4), as from 10 January 2015.

Para (2): words in square brackets substituted by the Financial Markets and Insolvency (Amendment and Transitional Provision) (EU Exit) Regulations 2019, SI 2019/341, reg 12(1), (4), as from IP completion day (as defined in the European Union (Withdrawal Agreement) Act 2020, s 39).

PART 5 CONFLICT OF LAWS

[10.140]

19 Standard test regarding the applicable law to book entry securities financial collateral arrangements

(1) This regulation applies to financial collateral arrangements where book entry securities collateral is used as collateral under the arrangement and are held through one or more intermediaries.

(2) Any question relating to the matters specified in paragraph (4) of this regulation which arises in relation to book entry securities collateral which is provided under a financial collateral arrangement shall be governed by the domestic law of the country[, or territory, or where appropriate, the law of the part of the country or territory,] in which the relevant account is maintained.

(3) For the purposes of paragraph (2) "domestic law" excludes any rule under which, in deciding the relevant question, reference should be made to the law of another country [or territory].

(4) The matters referred to in paragraph (2) are—

(a) the legal nature and proprietary effects of book entry securities collateral;

(b) the requirements for perfecting a financial collateral arrangement relating to book entry securities collateral and the transfer or passing of control or possession of book entry securities collateral under such an arrangement;

(c) the requirements for rendering a financial collateral arrangement which relates to book entry securities collateral effective against third parties;

(d) whether a person's title to or interest in such book entry securities collateral is overridden by or subordinated to a competing title or interest; and

(e) the steps required for the realisation of book entry securities collateral following the occurrence of any enforcement event.

NOTES

Paras (2), (3): words in square brackets inserted by the Financial Markets and Insolvency (Amendment and Transitional Provision) (EU Exit) Regulations 2019, SI 2019/341, reg 12(1), (5), as from IP completion day (as defined in the European Union (Withdrawal Agreement) Act 2020, s 39).

INSOLVENCY PRACTITIONERS REGULATIONS 2005

(SI 2005/524)

NOTES

Made: 8 March 2005.

Authority: IA 1986, ss 390, 392, 393, 419.

Commencement: 1 April 2005.

These Regulations are reproduced as amended by: the Secretaries of State for Children, Schools and Families, for Innovation, Universities and Skills and for Business, Enterprise and Regulatory Reform Order 2007, SI 2007/3224; the Secretary of State for Business, Innovation and Skills Order 2009, SI 2009/2748; the Provision of Services (Insolvency Practitioners) Regulations 2009, SI 2009/3081; the Insolvency Practitioners (Amendment) Regulations 2015, SI 2015/391; the Deregulation Act 2015 (Insolvency) (Consequential Amendments and Transitional and Savings Provisions) Order 2015, SI ; the Provision of Services (Amendment etc) (EU Exit) Regulations 2018, SI 2018/1329; the Insolvency (Scotland) Rules 2018 (Miscellaneous Amendments) Rules 2019, SI 2019/1059; the Corporate Insolvency and Governance Act 2020.

ARRANGEMENT OF REGULATIONS

PART 1
INTRODUCTORY

PART 3
THE REQUIREMENTS FOR SECURITY AND CAUTION FOR THE PROPER PERFORMANCE OF THE FUNCTIONS OF AN INSOLVENCY PRACTITIONER ETC

PART 4
RECORDS TO BE MAINTAINED BY INSOLVENCY PRACTITIONERS—INSPECTION OF RECORDS

SCHEDULES

PART 1 INTRODUCTORY

[10.141]
1 Citation and commencement.
These Regulations may be cited as the Insolvency Practitioners Regulations 2005 and shall come into force on 1st April 2005.

[10.142]
2 Interpretation: general
(1) In these Regulations—
"the Act" means the Insolvency Act 1986;
"commencement date" means the date on which these Regulations come into force;
"initial capacity" shall be construed in accordance with regulation 3;
"insolvency practitioner" means [a person who is authorised to act as an insolvency practitioner under section 390A of the Act];
"insolvent" means a person in respect of whom an insolvency practitioner is acting;
"interim trustee", "permanent trustee" and "trust deed for creditors" have the same meanings as in the Bankruptcy (Scotland) Act 1985;
"subsequent capacity" shall be construed in accordance with regulation 3.

(2) In these Regulations a reference to the date of release or discharge of an insolvency practitioner includes—
[(za) where the insolvency practitioner acts as the monitor in relation to a moratorium under Part A1 of the Act, whichever is the earlier of the date on which—
(i) the moratorium comes to an end, or
(ii) the insolvency practitioner otherwise ceases to act as the monitor in relation to the moratorium;]
(a) where the insolvency practitioner acts as nominee in relation to proposals for a voluntary arrangement under Part I or VIII of the Act, whichever is the earlier of the date on which—
(i) the proposals are rejected by creditors;
(ii) he is replaced as nominee by another insolvency practitioner; or
(iii) the arrangement takes effect without his becoming supervisor in relation to it; and
(b) where an insolvency practitioner acts as supervisor of a voluntary arrangement, whichever is the earlier of the date on which—
(i) the arrangement is completed or terminated; or
(ii) the insolvency practitioner otherwise ceases to act as supervisor in relation to the arrangement.

NOTES
Para (1): words in square brackets in definition "insolvency practitioner" substituted by the Deregulation Act 2015 (Insolvency) (Consequential Amendments and Transitional and Savings Provisions) Order 2015, SI 2015/1641, art 4, Sch 1, para 5(1), (2), as from 1 October 2015.
Para (2): sub-para (za) inserted by the Corporate Insolvency and Governance Act 2020, s 2(1), Sch 3, para 41, as from 26 June 2020 (for transitional provisions, see s 2(2), (3) of the 2020 Act (at **[9.533]**) which provides that (without prejudice to the Interpretation Act 1978, s 16) nothing in the 2020 Act affects the operation of the Insolvency Act 1986, or any other enactment, in relation to a moratorium under Sch A1 to the 1986 Act which comes into force before the repeal of that Schedule by Sch 3 to the 2020 Act (ie, 26 June 2020)).

[10.143]
3 Interpretation—meaning of initial and subsequent capacity
(1) In these Regulations an insolvency practitioner holds office in relation to an insolvent in a "subsequent capacity" where he holds office in relation to that insolvent in one of the capacities referred to in paragraph (3) and immediately prior to his holding office in that capacity, he held office in relation to that insolvent in another of the capacities referred to in that paragraph.

(2) The first office held by the insolvency practitioner in the circumstances referred to in paragraph (1) is referred to in these Regulations as the "initial capacity".

(3) The capacities referred to in paragraph (1) are, nominee in relation to proposals for a voluntary arrangement under Part I of the Act, supervisor of a voluntary arrangement under Part I of the Act, administrator, provisional liquidator, liquidator, nominee in relation to proposals for a voluntary arrangement under Part VIII of the Act, supervisor of a voluntary arrangement under Part VIII of the Act, trustee, interim trustee and permanent trustee.

[10.144]
4 Revocations and transitional and saving provisions
(1) Subject to paragraphs (2), (3) and (4), the Regulations listed in Schedule 1 are revoked.

(2) . . .

(3) Parts I, III and IV of the Insolvency Practitioners Regulations 1990 shall continue to apply in relation to any case in respect of which an insolvency practitioner is appointed—
(a) before the commencement date; or
(b) in a subsequent capacity and he was appointed in an initial capacity in that case before the commencement date.

(4) Only regulations 16 and 17 of these Regulations shall apply in relation to the cases mentioned in paragraph (3).

NOTES

Para (2): revoked by the Deregulation Act 2015 (Insolvency) (Consequential Amendments and Transitional and Savings Provisions) Order 2015, SI 2015/1641, art 4, Sch 1, para 5(1), (3), as from 1 October 2015.

PART 2

5–11 (*Regs 5–9, 11 were revoked by the Deregulation Act 2015 (Insolvency) (Consequential Amendments and Transitional and Savings Provisions) Order 2015, SI 2015/1641, art 4, Sch 1, para 5(1), (4), as from 1 October 2015. Reg 10 was revoked by the Provision of Services (Insolvency Practitioners) Regulations 2009, SI 2009/3081, regs 4, 5, Schedule, para 5, as from 28 December 2009, except in relation to an application for authorisation to act as an insolvency practitioner under the Insolvency Act 1986, s 393 made or granted before that date.*)

PART 3 THE REQUIREMENTS FOR SECURITY AND CAUTION FOR THE PROPER PERFORMANCE OF THE FUNCTIONS OF AN INSOLVENCY PRACTITIONER ETC

[10.145]
12

(1) Schedule 2 shall have effect in respect of the requirements prescribed for the purposes of section 390(3)(b) in relation to security or caution for the proper performance of the functions of an insolvency practitioner and for related matters.

(2) Where two or more persons are appointed jointly to act as insolvency practitioners in relation to any person, the provisions of this regulation shall apply to each of them individually.

[(3) Where, in accordance with sections 390(2) and 390A(2)(b) of the Act a person is qualified to act as an insolvency practitioner by virtue of an authorisation granted by the Department of Enterprise, Trade and Investment for Northern Ireland under Article 352 of the Insolvency (Northern Ireland) Order 1989, this Part applies in relation to that person as if that authorisation had been granted pursuant to section 393 of the Act immediately before 1st October 2015.]

NOTES

Para (3): originally added by the Provision of Services (Insolvency Practitioners) Regulations 2009, SI 2009/3081, regs 4, 5, Schedule, para 7, as from 28 December 2009 (except in relation to an application for authorisation to act as an insolvency practitioner under the Insolvency Act 1986, s 393 made or granted before that date). Subsequently substituted by the Deregulation Act 2015 (Insolvency) (Consequential Amendments and Transitional and Savings Provisions) Order 2015, SI 2015/1641, art 4, Sch 1, para 5(1), (6), as from 1 October 2015.

PART 4 RECORDS TO BE MAINTAINED BY INSOLVENCY PRACTITIONERS—INSPECTION OF RECORDS

[10.146]
13 Records to be maintained by insolvency practitioners

[(1) In respect of each case in which an insolvency practitioner acts, the insolvency practitioner shall maintain records containing information sufficient to show and explain—

(a) the administration of that case by the insolvency practitioner and the insolvency practitioner's staff; and
(b) any decisions made by the insolvency practitioner which materially affect that case.]

(2) Where at any time the records referred to in paragraph (1) do not contain all the information referred to in [paragraph (1)], the insolvency practitioner shall forthwith make such changes to the records as are necessary to ensure that the records contains all such information.

(3), (4) . . .

(5) Any records created in relation to a case pursuant to this regulation shall be preserved by the insolvency practitioner until whichever is the later of—

(a) the sixth anniversary of the date of the grant to the insolvency practitioner of his release or discharge in that case; or
(b) the sixth anniversary of the date on which any security or caution maintained in that case expires or otherwise ceases to have effect.

NOTES

Para (1): substituted by the Insolvency Practitioners (Amendment) Regulations 2015, SI 2015/391, reg 3(1), as from 1 October 2015.

Para (2): words in square brackets substituted by SI 2015/391, reg 3(2), as from 1 October 2015.

Paras (3), (4): revoked by SI 2015/391, reg 3(3), as from 1 October 2015.

14 (*Revoked by the Deregulation Act 2015 (Insolvency) (Consequential Amendments and Transitional and Savings Provisions) Order 2015, SI 2015/1641, art 4, Sch 1, para 5(1), (7), as from 1 October 2015.*)

[10.147]
15 Inspection of records

(1) Any records maintained by an insolvency practitioner pursuant to this Part shall on the giving of reasonable notice be made available by him for inspection by—

(a) any professional body recognised under section 391 of the Act of which he is a member and the rules of membership of which entitle him to act as an insolvency practitioner;
(b) . . .
(c) the Secretary of State.

(2) Any person who is entitled to inspect any record pursuant to paragraph (1) shall also be entitled to take a copy of those records.

NOTES

Para (1): sub-para (b) revoked by the Deregulation Act 2015 (Insolvency) (Consequential Amendments and Transitional and Savings Provisions) Order 2015, SI 2015/1641, art 4, Sch 1, para 5(1), (8), as from 1 October 2015.

16 (*Revoked by the Deregulation Act 2015 (Insolvency) (Consequential Amendments and Transitional and Savings Provisions) Order 2015, SI 2015/1641, art 4, Sch 1, para 5(1), (9), as from 1 October 2015.*)

[10.148]

17 Inspection of records in administration and administrative receiverships

On the giving of reasonable notice to the insolvency practitioner, the Secretary of State shall be entitled to inspect and take copies of any records in the possession or control of that insolvency practitioner which—

(a) were required to be created by or under any provision of the Act (or any provision made under the Act); and

(b) relate to an administration or an administrative receivership.

SCHEDULES

SCHEDULE 1

(*Sch 1 revokes the Insolvency Practitioners Regulations 1990, SI 1990/439, and the amending SI 1993/221, SI 2002/2710, SI 2002/2748, and SI 2004/373.*)

SCHEDULE 2
REQUIREMENTS FOR SECURITY OR CAUTION AND RELATED MATTERS

Regulation 12

PART 1 INTERPRETATION

[10.149]

1 Interpretation

In this Schedule—

"cover schedule" means the schedule referred to in paragraph 3(2)(c);

"the insolvent" means the individual or company in relation to which an insolvency practitioner is acting;

"general penalty sum" shall be construed in accordance with paragraph 3(2)(b);

"insolvent's assets" means all assets comprised in the insolvent's estate together with any monies provided by a third party for the payment of the insolvent's debts or the costs and expenses of administering the insolvent's estate;

["professional liability insurance" means insurance taken out by the insolvency practitioner in respect of potential liabilities to the insolvent and third parties arising out of acting as an insolvency practitioner;]

"specific penalty sum" shall be construed in accordance with paragraph 3(2)(a).

NOTES

Definition "professional liability insurance" inserted by the Provision of Services (Insolvency Practitioners) Regulations 2009, SI 2009/3081, regs 4, 5, Schedule, para 8(1), (2), as from 28 December 2009 (except in relation to an application for authorisation to act as an insolvency practitioner under the Insolvency Act 1986, s 393 made or granted before that date).

PART 2 REQUIREMENTS RELATING TO SECURITY AND CAUTION

[10.150]

2 Requirements in respect of security or caution

The requirements in respect of security or caution for the proper performance of the duties of insolvency practitioners prescribed for the purposes of section 390(3)(b) shall be as set out in this Part.

[2A Requirement for bond . . .

Where an insolvency practitioner is appointed to act in respect of an insolvent there must be in force—

(a) a bond in a form approved by the Secretary of State which complies with paragraph 3; . . .

(b) . . .]

[3 Terms of the bond

(1) The bond must—

(a) be in writing or in electronic form;

(b) contain provision whereby a surety or cautioner undertakes to be jointly and severally liable for losses in relation to the insolvent caused by—

(i) the fraud or dishonesty of the insolvency practitioner whether acting alone or in collusion with one or more persons; or

(ii) the fraud or dishonesty of any person committed with the connivance of the insolvency practitioner; and

(c) otherwise conform to the requirements of this paragraph and paragraphs 4 to 8.]

(2) The terms of the bond shall provide—

(a) for the payment, in respect of each case where the insolvency practitioner acts, of claims in respect of liabilities for losses of the kind mentioned in sub-paragraph (1) up to an aggregate maximum sum in respect of that case ("the specific penalty sum") calculated in accordance with the provisions of this Schedule;

(b) in the event that any amounts payable under (a) are insufficient to meet all claims arising out of any case, for a further sum of £250,000 ("the general penalty sum") out of which any such claims are to be met;

(c) for a schedule containing the name of the insolvent and the value of the insolvent's assets to be submitted to the surety or cautioner within such period as may be specified in the bond;

(d) that where at any time before the insolvency practitioner obtains his release or discharge in respect of his acting in relation to an insolvent, he forms the opinion that the value of that insolvent's assets is greater than the current specific penalty sum, a revised specific penalty sum shall be applicable on the submission within such time as may be specified in the bond of a cover schedule containing a revised value of the insolvent's assets;

(e) for the payment of losses of the kind mentioned in sub-paragraph (1), whether they arise during the period in which the insolvency practitioner holds office in the capacity in which he was initially appointed or a subsequent period where he holds office in a subsequent capacity;

(3) The terms of the bond may provide—

(a) that total claims in respect of the acts of the insolvency practitioner under all bonds relating to him are to be limited to a maximum aggregate sum (which shall not be less than £25,000,000); and

(b) for a time limit within which claims must be made.

4. Subject to paragraphs 5, 6 and 7, the amount of the specific penalty in respect of a case in which the insolvency practitioner acts, shall equal at least the value of the insolvent's assets as estimated by the insolvency practitioner as at the date of his appointment but ignoring the value of any assets—

(a) charged to a third party to the extent of any amount which would be payable to that third party; or

(b) held on trust by the insolvent to the extent that any beneficial interest in those assets does not belong to the insolvent.

5. In a case where an insolvency practitioner acts as a nominee or supervisor of a voluntary arrangement under Part I or Part VIII of the Act, the amount of the specific penalty shall be equal to at least the value of those assets subject to the terms of the arrangement (whether or not those assets are in his possession) including, where under the terms of the arrangement the debtor or a third party is to make payments, the aggregate of any payments to be made.

6. Where the value of the insolvent's assets is less than £5,000, the specific penalty sum shall be £5,000.

7. Where the value of the insolvent's assets is more than £5,000,000 the specific penalty sum shall be £5,000,000.

8. In estimating the value of an insolvent's assets, unless he has reason to doubt their accuracy, the insolvency practitioner may rely upon—

(a) any statement of affairs produced in relation to that insolvent pursuant to any provision of the Act; and

(b) in the case of a sequestration—

(i) the debtor's list of assets and liabilities under section 19 of the Bankruptcy (Scotland) Act 1985;

(ii) the preliminary statement under that Act; or

(iii) the final statement of the debtor's affairs by the interim trustee under section 23 of the Bankruptcy (Scotland) Act 1985.

[8A–8E. . . .]

NOTES

Para 2A and paras 8A–8E were inserted and added respectively, and the paragraph title of para 3 and sub-para (1) of that paragraph were substituted, by the Provision of Services (Insolvency Practitioners) Regulations 2009, SI 2009/3081, regs 4, 5, Schedule, para 8(1)–(5), as from 28 December 2009 (except in relation to an application for authorisation to act as an insolvency practitioner under the Insolvency Act 1986, s 393 made or granted before that date).

The words omitted from para 2A were revoked, and paras 8A–8E were revoked, by the Provision of Services (Amendment etc) (EU Exit) Regulations 2018, SI 2018/1329, reg 23(1)–(4), as from IP completion day (as defined in the European Union (Withdrawal Agreement) Act 2020, s 39).

PART 3 RECORDS RELATING TO BONDING AND CONNECTED MATTERS

[10.151]

9 Record of specific penalty sums to be maintained by insolvency practitioner

(1) An insolvency practitioner shall maintain a record of all specific penalty sums that are applicable in relation to any case where he is acting and such record shall contain the name of each person to whom the specific penalty sum relates and the amount of each penalty sum that is in force.

(2) Any record maintained by an insolvency practitioner pursuant to this paragraph shall, on the giving of reasonable notice, be made available for inspection by—

(a) any professional body recognised under section 391 of the Act of which he is or was a member and the rules of membership of which entitle or entitled him to act as an insolvency practitioner;

(b) . . .

(c) the Secretary of State.

[(3), (4) . . .]

10 Retention of bond by recognised professional body or competent authority

[(1) [The bond referred to in paragraph 3] or a copy must] be sent by the insolvency practitioner to—

(a) any professional body recognised under section 391 of the Act of which he is a member and the rules of membership of which entitle him to act as an insolvency practitioner; . . .

(b) . . .

[(2) . . .

(3) [The bond referred to in paragraph 3] or a copy of it may be sent electronically.]

11 Inspection and retention requirements relating to cover schedule—England and Wales

(1) This regulation applies to an insolvency practitioner appointed in insolvency proceedings under the Act to act—

(a) in relation to a company which the courts in England and Wales have jurisdiction to wind up; or

(b) in respect of an individual.

(2) The insolvency practitioner shall retain a copy of the cover schedule submitted by him in respect of his acting in relation to the company or, as the case may be, individual until the second anniversary of the date on which he is granted his release or discharge in relation to that company or, as the case may be, that individual.

(3) The copy of a schedule kept by an insolvency practitioner in pursuance of sub-paragraph (2) shall be produced by him on demand for inspection by—

(a) any creditor of the person to whom the schedule relates;
(b) where the schedule relates to an insolvent who is an individual, that individual;
(c) where the schedule relates to an insolvent which is a company, any contributory or director or other officer of the company; and
(d) the Secretary of State.

[(4), (5) . . .]

12 Inspection and retention requirements relating to the cover schedule—Scotland

[(1) Where an insolvency practitioner is appointed to act in relation to a company which is in administration, or for which there is a proposal for a company voluntary arrangement, the practitioner shall retain in the sederunt book kept under rule 1.54 of the Insolvency (Scotland) (Company Voluntary Arrangements and Administration) Rules 2018 (sederunt book), the principal copy of any cover schedule containing entries in relation to the insolvency practitioner so acting.

(1A) Where an insolvency practitioner is appointed to act in relation to a company which is subject to proceedings for winding up, the practitioner shall retain in the sederunt book kept under rule 1.54 of the Insolvency (Scotland) (Receivership and Winding Up) Rules 2018 (sederunt book) the principal copy of any cover schedule containing entries in relation to the insolvency practitioner so acting.]

(2) Where an insolvency practitioner is appointed to act as interim trustee or permanent trustee or as a trustee under a trust deed for creditors, he shall retain in the sederunt book kept for those proceedings, the principal copy of any cover schedule containing entries in relation to his so acting.

13 Requirements to submit cover schedule to authorising body

(1) Every insolvency practitioner shall submit to his authorising body not later than 20 days after the end of each month during which he holds office in a case—

(a) the information submitted to a surety or cautioner in any cover schedule related to that month;
(b) where no cover schedule is submitted in relation to the month, a statement either that there are no relevant particulars to be supplied or, as the case may be, that it is not practicable to supply particulars in relation to any appointments taken in that month; and
(c) a statement identifying any case in respect of which he has been granted his release or discharge.

(2) In this regulation "authorising body" means in relation to an insolvency practitioner—

(a) any professional body recognised under section 391 of the Act of which he is a member and the rules of membership of which entitle him to act as an insolvency practitioner; . . .
(b) . . .

NOTES

Sub-paras 9(2)(b), 10(1)(b) and 13(2)(b) (and the word preceding sub-paras 10(1)(b) and 13(2)(b)) were revoked by the Deregulation Act 2015 (Insolvency) (Consequential Amendments and Transitional and Savings Provisions) Order 2015, SI 2015/1641, art 4, Sch 1, para 5(1), (10)–(12), as from 1 October 2015.

Sub-paras 9(3), (4), 10(2), (3), 11(4), (5) were added, and the words in the first (outer) pair of square brackets in para 10 were substituted, by the Provision of Services (Insolvency Practitioners) Regulations 2009, SI 2009/3081, regs 4, 5, Schedule, para 8(1), (6)–(8), as from 28 December 2009 (except in relation to an application for authorisation to act as an insolvency practitioner under the Insolvency Act 1986, s 393 made or granted before that date).

Sub-paras 9(3), (4), 10(2), 11(4), (5) were revoked, and the words in second (inner) and third pairs of square brackets in para 10 were substituted, by the Provision of Services (Amendment etc) (EU Exit) Regulations 2018, SI 2018/1329, reg 23(1), (5)–(7), as from IP completion day (as defined in the European Union (Withdrawal Agreement) Act 2020, s 39).

Sub-paras 12(1), (1A) substituted (for the original sub-para 12(1)) by the Insolvency (Scotland) Rules 2018 (Miscellaneous Amendments) Rules 2019, SI 2019/1059, r 4, as from 23 July 2019.

SCHEDULE 3

(Sch 3 (Records to be Maintained—Minimum Requirements) revoked by the Insolvency Practitioners (Amendment) Regulations 2015, SI 2015/391, reg 7, as from 1 October 2015.)

TRANSFER OF UNDERTAKINGS (PROTECTION OF EMPLOYMENT) REGULATIONS 2006

(SI 2006/246)

NOTES

Made: 6 February 2006.

Authority: European Communities Act 1972, s 2(2); Employment Relations Act 1999, s 38 (see the note "Statutory Instruments made under the European Communities Act 1972" preceding paragraph **[4.1]** *ante*).

Commencement: 6 April 2006.

These Regulations are reproduced as amended by: the Transfer of Undertakings (Protection of Employment) (Amendment) Regulations 2009, SI 2009/592; the Agency Workers Regulations 2010, SI 2010/93; the Collective Redundancies and Transfer of Undertakings (Protection of Employment) (Amendment) Regulations 2014, SI 2014/16; the Enterprise and Regulatory Reform Act 2013 (Consequential Amendments) (Employment) Order 2014, SI 2014/386.

Application and modification: these Regulations (and the Transfer of Undertakings (Protection of Employment) Regulations 1981, SI 1981/1794 which they replaced) are (or were) applied and modified by a variety of other enactments for the purposes of specific transfer schemes made thereunder. These are generally outside the scope of this work.

ARRANGEMENT OF REGULATIONS

[10.152]

1 Citation, commencement and extent

(1) These Regulations may be cited as the Transfer of Undertakings (Protection of Employment) Regulations 2006.

(2) These Regulations shall come into force on 6 April 2006.

(3) These Regulations shall extend to Northern Ireland, except where otherwise provided.

[10.153]

2 Interpretation

(1) In these Regulations—

"assigned" means assigned other than on a temporary basis;

"collective agreement", "collective bargaining" and "trade union" have the same meanings respectively as in the 1992 Act;

"contract of employment" means any agreement between an employee and his employer determining the terms and conditions of his employment;

references to "contractor" in regulation 3 shall include a sub-contractor;

"employee" means any individual who works for another person whether under a contract of service or apprenticeship or otherwise but does not include anyone who provides services under a contract for services and references to a person's employer shall be construed accordingly;

"insolvency practitioner" has the meaning given to the expression by Part XIII of the Insolvency Act 1986;

references to "organised grouping of employees" shall include a single employee;

"recognised" has the meaning given to the expression by section 178(3) of the 1992 Act;

"relevant transfer" means a transfer or a service provision change to which these Regulations apply in accordance with regulation 3 and "transferor" and "transferee" shall be construed accordingly and in the case of a service provision change falling within regulation 3(1)(b), "the transferor" means the person who carried out the activities prior to the service provision change and "the transferee" means the person who carries out the activities as a result of the service provision change;

"the 1992 Act" means the Trade Union and Labour Relations (Consolidation) Act 1992;

"the 1996 Act" means the Employment Rights Act 1996;

"the 1996 Tribunals Act" means the Employment Tribunals Act 1996;

"the 1981 Regulations" means the Transfer of Undertakings (Protection of Employment) Regulations 1981.

(2) For the purposes of these Regulations the representative of a trade union recognised by an employer is an official or other person authorised to carry on collective bargaining with that employer by that trade union.

(3) In the application of these Regulations to Northern Ireland the Regulations shall have effect as set out in Schedule 1.

[10.154]

3 A relevant transfer

(1) These Regulations apply to—

(a) a transfer of an undertaking, business or part of an undertaking or business situated immediately before the transfer in the United Kingdom to another person where there is a transfer of an economic entity which retains its identity;

(b) a service provision change, that is a situation in which—

(i) activities cease to be carried out by a person ("a client") on his own behalf and are carried out instead by another person on the client's behalf ("a contractor");

(ii) activities cease to be carried out by a contractor on a client's behalf (whether or not those activities had previously been carried out by the client on his own behalf) and are carried out instead by another person ("a subsequent contractor") on the client's behalf; or

(iii) activities cease to be carried out by a contractor or a subsequent contractor on a client's behalf (whether or not those activities had previously been carried out by the client on his own behalf) and are carried out instead by the client on his own behalf,

and in which the conditions set out in paragraph (3) are satisfied.

(2) In this regulation "economic entity" means an organised grouping of resources which has the objective of pursuing an economic activity, whether or not that activity is central or ancillary.

[(2A) References in paragraph (1)(b) to activities being carried out instead by another person (including the client) are to activities which are fundamentally the same as the activities carried out by the person who has ceased to carry them out.]

(3) The conditions referred to in paragraph (1)(b) are that—

(a) immediately before the service provision change—

(i) there is an organised grouping of employees situated in Great Britain which has as its principal purpose the carrying out of the activities concerned on behalf of the client;

(ii) the client intends that the activities will, following the service provision change, be carried out by the transferee other than in connection with a single specific event or task of short-term duration; and

(b) the activities concerned do not consist wholly or mainly of the supply of goods for the client's use.

(4) Subject to paragraph (1), these Regulations apply to—

(a) public and private undertakings engaged in economic activities whether or not they are operating for gain;

(b) a transfer or service provision change howsoever effected notwithstanding—

(i) that the transfer of an undertaking, business or part of an undertaking or business is governed or effected by the law of a country or territory outside the United Kingdom or that the service provision change is governed or effected by the law of a country or territory outside Great Britain;

(ii) that the employment of persons employed in the undertaking, business or part transferred or, in the case of a service provision change, persons employed in the organised grouping of employees, is governed by any such law;

(c) a transfer of an undertaking, business or part of an undertaking or business (which may also be a service provision change) where persons employed in the undertaking, business or part transferred ordinarily work outside the United Kingdom.

(5) An administrative reorganisation of public administrative authorities or the transfer of administrative functions between public administrative authorities is not a relevant transfer.

(6) A relevant transfer—

(a) may be effected by a series of two or more transactions; and

(b) may take place whether or not any property is transferred to the transferee by the transferor.

(7) Where, in consequence (whether directly or indirectly) of the transfer of an undertaking, business or part of an undertaking or business which was situated immediately before the transfer in the United Kingdom, a ship within the meaning of the Merchant Shipping Act 1995 registered in the United Kingdom ceases to be so registered, these Regulations shall not affect the right conferred by section 29 of that Act (right of seamen to be discharged when ship ceases to be registered in the United Kingdom) on a seaman employed in the ship.

NOTES

Para (2A): inserted by the Collective Redundancies and Transfer of Undertakings (Protection of Employment) (Amendment) Regulations 2014, SI 2014/16, regs 4, 5, in relation to a TUPE transfer which takes place on or after 31 January 2014. Note that for these purposes a "TUPE transfer" means (a) a relevant transfer under these Regulations, or (b) anything else regarded, by virtue of an enactment, as a relevant transfer for the purposes of these Regulations (see reg 2 of the 2014 Regulations).

[10.155]

4 Effect of relevant transfer on contracts of employment

(1) Except where objection is made under paragraph (7), a relevant transfer shall not operate so as to terminate the contract of employment of any person employed by the transferor and assigned to the organised grouping of resources or employees that is subject to the relevant transfer, which would otherwise be terminated by the transfer, but any such contract shall have effect after the transfer as if originally made between the person so employed and the transferee.

(2) Without prejudice to paragraph (1), but subject to paragraph (6), and regulations 8 and 15(9), on the completion of a relevant transfer—

(a) all the transferor's rights, powers, duties and liabilities under or in connection with any such contract shall be transferred by virtue of this regulation to the transferee; and

(b) any act or omission before the transfer is completed, of or in relation to the transferor in respect of that contract or a person assigned to that organised grouping of resources or employees, shall be deemed to have been an act or omission of or in relation to the transferee.

(3) Any reference in paragraph (1) to a person employed by the transferor and assigned to the organised grouping of resources or employees that is subject to a relevant transfer, is a reference to a person so employed immediately before the transfer, or who would have been so employed if he had not been dismissed in the circumstances described in regulation 7(1), including, where the transfer is effected by a series of two or more transactions, a person so employed and assigned or who would have been so employed and assigned immediately before any of those transactions.

[(4) Subject to regulation 9, any purported variation of a contract of employment that is, or will be, transferred by paragraph (1), is void if the sole or principal reason for the variation is the transfer.

(5) Paragraph (4) does not prevent a variation of the contract of employment if—

(a) the sole or principal reason for the variation is an economic, technical, or organisational reason entailing changes in the workforce, provided that the employer and employee agree that variation; or

(b) the terms of that contract permit the employer to make such a variation.

(5A) In paragraph (5), the expression "changes in the workforce" includes a change to the place where employees are employed by the employer to carry on the business of the employer or to carry out work of a particular kind for the employer (and the reference to such a place has the same meaning as in section 139 of the 1996 Act).

(5B) Paragraph (4) does not apply in respect of a variation of the contract of employment in so far as it varies a term or condition incorporated from a collective agreement, provided that—

(a) the variation of the contract takes effect on a date more than one year after the date of the transfer; and

(b) following that variation, the rights and obligations in the employee's contract, when considered together, are no less favourable to the employee than those which applied immediately before the variation.

(5C) Paragraphs (5) and (5B) do not affect any rule of law as to whether a contract of employment is effectively varied.]

(6) Paragraph (2) shall not transfer or otherwise affect the liability of any person to be prosecuted for, convicted of and sentenced for any offence.

(7) Paragraphs (1) and (2) shall not operate to transfer the contract of employment and the rights, powers, duties and liabilities under or in connection with it of an employee who informs the transferor or the transferee that he objects to becoming employed by the transferee.

(8) Subject to paragraphs (9) and (11), where an employee so objects, the relevant transfer shall operate so as to terminate his contract of employment with the transferor but he shall not be treated, for any purpose, as having been dismissed by the transferor.

(9) Subject to regulation 9, where a relevant transfer involves or would involve a substantial change in working conditions to the material detriment of a person whose contract of employment is or would be transferred under paragraph (1), such an employee may treat the contract of employment as having been terminated, and the employee shall be treated for any purpose as having been dismissed by the employer.

(10) No damages shall be payable by an employer as a result of a dismissal falling within paragraph (9) in respect of any failure by the employer to pay wages to an employee in respect of a notice period which the employee has failed to work.

(11) Paragraphs (1), (7), (8) and (9) are without prejudice to any right of an employee arising apart from these Regulations to terminate his contract of employment without notice in acceptance of a repudiatory breach of contract by his employer.

NOTES

Paras (4)–(5C): substituted (for the original paras (4), (5)) by the Collective Redundancies and Transfer of Undertakings (Protection of Employment) (Amendment) Regulations 2014, SI 2014/16, regs 4, 6, in relation to any purported variation of a contract of employment that is transferred by a TUPE transfer if (a) the TUPE transfer takes place on or after 31 January 2014, and (b) that purported variation is agreed on or after 31 January 2014, or, in a case where the variation is not agreed, it starts to have effect on or after that date (as to the meaning of "TUPE transfer", see reg 3 *ante*).

[10.156]

[4A Effect of relevant transfer on contracts of employment which incorporate provisions of collective agreements

(1) Where a contract of employment, which is transferred by regulation 4(1), incorporates provisions of collective agreements as may be agreed from time to time, regulation 4(2) does not transfer any rights, powers, duties and liabilities in relation to any provision of a collective agreement if the following conditions are met—

(a) the provision of the collective agreement is agreed after the date of the transfer; and

(b) the transferee is not a participant in the collective bargaining for that provision.

(2) For the purposes of regulation 4(1), the contract of employment has effect after the transfer as if it does not incorporate provisions of a collective agreement which meet the conditions in paragraph (1).]

NOTES

Inserted by the Collective Redundancies and Transfer of Undertakings (Protection of Employment) (Amendment) Regulations 2014, SI 2014/16, regs 4, 7, in relation to a TUPE transfer which takes place on or after 31 January 2014 (as to the meaning of "TUPE transfer", see reg 3 *ante*).

[10.157]

5 Effect of relevant transfer on collective agreements

Where at the time of a relevant transfer there exists a collective agreement made by or on behalf of the transferor with a trade union recognised by the transferor in respect of any employee whose contract of employment is preserved by regulation 4(1) above, then—

(a) without prejudice to sections 179 and 180 of the 1992 Act (collective agreements presumed to be unenforceable in specified circumstances) that agreement, in its application in relation to the employee, shall, after the transfer, have effect as if made by or on behalf of the transferee with that trade union, and accordingly anything done under or in connection with it, in its application in relation to the employee, by or in relation to the transferor before the transfer, shall, after the transfer, be deemed to have been done by or in relation to the transferee; and

(b) any order made in respect of that agreement, in its application in relation to the employee, shall, after the transfer, have effect as if the transferee were a party to the agreement.

[10.158]

6 Effect of relevant transfer on trade union recognition

(1) This regulation applies where after a relevant transfer the transferred organised grouping of resources or employees maintains an identity distinct from the remainder of the transferee's undertaking.

(2) Where before such a transfer an independent trade union is recognised to any extent by the transferor in respect of employees of any description who in consequence of the transfer become employees of the transferee, then, after the transfer—

(a) the trade union shall be deemed to have been recognised by the transferee to the same extent in respect of employees of that description so employed; and

(b) any agreement for recognition may be varied or rescinded accordingly.

[10.159]

7 Dismissal of employee because of relevant transfer

[(1) Where either before or after a relevant transfer, any employee of the transferor or transferee is dismissed, that employee is to be treated for the purposes of Part 10 of the 1996 Act (unfair dismissal) as unfairly dismissed if the sole or principal reason for the dismissal is the transfer.

(2) This paragraph applies where the sole or principal reason for the dismissal is an economic, technical or organisational reason entailing changes in the workforce of either the transferor or the transferee before or after a relevant transfer.

(3) Where paragraph (2) applies—

(a) paragraph (1) does not apply;

(b) without prejudice to the application of section 98(4) of the 1996 Act (test of fair dismissal), for the purposes of sections 98(1) and 135 of that Act (reason for dismissal)—

(i) the dismissal is regarded as having been for redundancy where section 98(2)(c) of that Act applies; or

(ii) in any other case, the dismissal is regarded as having been for a substantial reason of a kind such as to justify the dismissal of an employee holding the position which that employee held.

(3A) In paragraph (2), the expression "changes in the workforce" includes a change to the place where employees are employed by the employer to carry on the business of the employer or to carry out work of a particular kind for the employer (and the reference to such a place has the same meaning as in section 139 of the 1996 Act).]

(4) The provisions of this regulation apply irrespective of whether the employee in question is assigned to the organised grouping of resources or employees that is, or will be, transferred.

(5) Paragraph (1) shall not apply in relation to the dismissal of any employee which was required by reason of the application of section 5 of the Aliens Restriction (Amendment) Act 1919 to his employment.

(6) Paragraph (1) shall not apply in relation to a dismissal of an employee if the application of section 94 of the 1996 Act to the dismissal of the employee is excluded by or under any provision of the 1996 Act, the 1996 Tribunals Act or the 1992 Act.

NOTES

Paras (1)–(3A): substituted (for the original paras (1)–(3)) by the Collective Redundancies and Transfer of Undertakings (Protection of Employment) (Amendment) Regulations 2014, SI 2014/16, regs 4, 8, in relation to any case where (a) the TUPE transfer takes place on or after 31 January 2014, and (b) the date when any notice of termination is given by an employer or an employee in respect of any dismissal is 31 January 2014 or later, or, in a case where no notice is given, the date on which the termination takes effect is 31 January 2014 or later (as to the meaning of "TUPE transfer", see reg 3 *ante*).

[10.160]

8 Insolvency

(1) If at the time of a relevant transfer the transferor is subject to relevant insolvency proceedings paragraphs (2) to (6) apply.

(2) In this regulation "relevant employee" means an employee of the transferor—

(a) whose contract of employment transfers to the transferee by virtue of the operation of these Regulations; or

(b) whose employment with the transferor is terminated before the time of the relevant transfer in the circumstances described in regulation 7(1).

(3) The relevant statutory scheme specified in paragraph (4)(b) (including that sub-paragraph as applied by paragraph 5 of Schedule 1) shall apply in the case of a relevant employee irrespective of the fact that the qualifying requirement that the employee's employment has been terminated is not met and for those purposes the date of the transfer shall be treated as the date of the termination and the transferor shall be treated as the employer.

(4) In this regulation the "relevant statutory schemes" are—

(a) Chapter VI of Part XI of the 1996 Act;

(b) Part XII of the 1996 Act.

(5) Regulation 4 shall not operate to transfer liability for the sums payable to the relevant employee under the relevant statutory schemes.

(6) In this regulation "relevant insolvency proceedings" means insolvency proceedings which have been opened in relation to the transferor not with a view to the liquidation of the assets of the transferor and which are under the supervision of an insolvency practitioner.

(7) Regulations 4 and 7 do not apply to any relevant transfer where the transferor is the subject of bankruptcy proceedings or any analogous insolvency proceedings which have been instituted with a view to the liquidation of the assets of the transferor and are under the supervision of an insolvency practitioner.

[10.161]

9 Variations of contract where transferors are subject to relevant insolvency proceedings

(1) If at the time of a relevant transfer the transferor is subject to relevant insolvency proceedings these Regulations shall not prevent the transferor or transferee (or an insolvency practitioner) and appropriate representatives of assigned employees agreeing to permitted variations.

(2) For the purposes of this regulation "appropriate representatives" are—

(a) if the employees are of a description in respect of which an independent trade union is recognised by their employer, representatives of the trade union; or

(b) in any other case, whichever of the following employee representatives the employer chooses—

(i) employee representatives appointed or elected by the assigned employees (whether they make the appointment or election alone or with others) otherwise than for the purposes of this regulation, who (having regard to the purposes for, and the method by which they were appointed or elected) have authority from those employees to agree permitted variations to contracts of employment on their behalf;

(ii) employee representatives elected by assigned employees (whether they make the appointment or election alone or with others) for these particular purposes, in an election satisfying requirements identical to those contained in regulation 14 except those in regulation 14(1)(d).

(3) An individual may be an appropriate representative for the purposes of both this regulation and regulation 13 provided that where the representative is not a trade union representative he is either elected by or has authority from assigned employees (within the meaning of this regulation) and affected employees (as described in regulation 13(1)).

(4) (*Amends the Trade Union and Labour Relations (Consolidation) Act 1992, s 168.*)

(5) Where assigned employees are represented by non-trade union representatives—

(a) the agreement recording a permitted variation must be in writing and signed by each of the representatives who have made it or, where that is not reasonably practicable, by a duly authorised agent of that representative; and

(b) the employer must, before the agreement is made available for signature, provide all employees to whom it is intended to apply on the date on which it is to come into effect with copies of the text of the agreement and such guidance as those employees might reasonably require in order to understand it fully.

(6) A permitted variation shall take effect as a term or condition of the assigned employee's contract of employment in place, where relevant, of any term or condition which it varies.

(7) In this regulation—

"assigned employees" means those employees assigned to the organised grouping of resources or employees that is the subject of a relevant transfer;

"permitted variation" is a variation to the contract of employment of an assigned employee where—

[(a) the sole or principal reason for the variation is the transfer and not a reason referred to in regulation 4(5)(a); and]

(b) it is designed to safeguard employment opportunities by ensuring the survival of the undertaking, business or part of the undertaking or business that is the subject of the relevant transfer;

"relevant insolvency proceedings" has the meaning given to the expression by regulation 8(6).

NOTES

Para (7): para (a) of the definition "permitted variation" was substituted by the Collective Redundancies and Transfer of Undertakings (Protection of Employment) (Amendment) Regulations 2014, SI 2014/16, regs 4, 9, in relation to any case where (a) the TUPE transfer takes place on or after 31 January 2014, and (b) the permitted variation is agreed on or after 31 January 2014 (as to the meaning of "TUPE transfer", see reg 3 *ante*).

[10.162]

10 Pensions

(1) Regulations 4 and 5 shall not apply—

(a) to so much of a contract of employment or collective agreement as relates to an occupational pension scheme within the meaning of the Pension Schemes Act 1993; or

(b) to any rights, powers, duties or liabilities under or in connection with any such contract or subsisting by virtue of any such agreement and relating to such a scheme or otherwise arising in connection with that person's employment and relating to such a scheme.

(2) For the purposes of paragraphs (1) and (3), any provisions of an occupational pension scheme which do not relate to benefits for old age, invalidity or survivors shall not be treated as being part of the scheme.

(3) An employee whose contract of employment is transferred in the circumstances described in regulation 4(1) shall not be entitled to bring a claim against the transferor for—

(a) breach of contract; or

(b) constructive unfair dismissal under section 95(1)(c) of the 1996 Act,

arising out of a loss or reduction in his rights under an occupational pension scheme in consequence of the transfer, save insofar as the alleged breach of contract or dismissal (as the case may be) occurred prior to the date on which these Regulations took effect.

[10.163]

11 Notification of Employee Liability Information

(1) The transferor shall notify to the transferee the employee liability information of any person employed by him who is assigned to the organised grouping of resources or employees that is the subject of a relevant transfer—

(a) in writing; or

(b) by making it available to him in a readily accessible form.

(2) In this regulation and in regulation 12 "employee liability information" means—

(a) the identity and age of the employee;

(b) those particulars of employment that an employer is obliged to give to an employee pursuant to section 1 of the 1996 Act;

(c) information of any—

(i) disciplinary procedure taken against an employee;

(ii) grievance procedure taken by an employee,

within the previous two years, in circumstances where [a Code of Practice issued under Part IV of the Trade Union and Labour Relations Act 1992 which relates exclusively or primarily to the resolution of disputes applies];

(d) information of any court or tribunal case, claim or action—

(i) brought by an employee against the transferor, within the previous two years;

(ii) that the transferor has reasonable grounds to believe that an employee may bring against the transferee, arising out of the employee's employment with the transferor; and

(e) information of any collective agreement which will have effect after the transfer, in its application in relation to the employee, pursuant to regulation 5(a).

(3) Employee liability information shall contain information as at a specified date not more than fourteen days before the date on which the information is notified to the transferee.

(4) The duty to provide employee liability information in paragraph (1) shall include a duty to provide employee liability information of any person who would have been employed by the transferor and assigned to the organised grouping of resources or employees that is the subject of a relevant transfer immediately before the transfer if he had not been dismissed in the circumstances described in regulation 7(1), including, where the transfer is effected by a series of two or more transactions, a person so employed and assigned or who would have been so employed and assigned immediately before any of those transactions.

(5) Following notification of the employee liability information in accordance with this regulation, the transferor shall notify the transferee in writing of any change in the employee liability information.

(6) A notification under this regulation shall be given not less than [28 days] before the relevant transfer or, if special circumstances make this not reasonably practicable, as soon as reasonably practicable thereafter.

(7) A notification under this regulation may be given—

(a) in more than one instalment;

(b) indirectly, through a third party.

NOTES

Para (2): words in square brackets substituted by the Transfer of Undertakings (Protection of Employment) (Amendment) Regulations 2009, SI 2009/592, reg 2(1), (2), as from 6 April 2009.

Para (6): words in square brackets substituted by the Collective Redundancies and Transfer of Undertakings (Protection of Employment) (Amendment) Regulations 2014, SI 2014/16, regs 4, 10, in relation to a TUPE transfer which takes place on or after 1 May 2014 (as to the meaning of "TUPE transfer", see reg 3 *ante*).

[10.164]

12 Remedy for failure to notify employee liability information

(1) On or after a relevant transfer, the transferee may present a complaint to an employment tribunal that the transferor has failed to comply with any provision of regulation 11.

(2) An employment tribunal shall not consider a complaint under this regulation unless it is presented—

(a) before the end of the period of three months beginning with the date of the relevant transfer;

(b) within such further period as the tribunal considers reasonable in a case where it is satisfied that it was not reasonably practicable for the complaint to be presented before the end of that period of three months.

[(2A) Regulation 16A (extension of time limits to facilitate conciliation before institution of proceedings) applies for the purposes of paragraph (2).]

(3) Where an employment tribunal finds a complaint under paragraph (1) well-founded, the tribunal—

(a) shall make a declaration to that effect; and

(b) may make an award of compensation to be paid by the transferor to the transferee.

(4) The amount of the compensation shall be such as the tribunal considers just and equitable in all the circumstances, subject to paragraph (5), having particular regard to—

(a) any loss sustained by the transferee which is attributable to the matters complained of; and

(b) the terms of any contract between the transferor and the transferee relating to the transfer under which the transferor may be liable to pay any sum to the transferee in respect of a failure to notify the transferee of employee liability information.

(5) Subject to paragraph (6), the amount of compensation awarded under paragraph (3) shall be not less than £500 per employee in respect of whom the transferor has failed to comply with a provision of regulation 11, unless the tribunal considers it just and equitable, in all the circumstances, to award a lesser sum.

(6) In ascertaining the loss referred to in paragraph (4)(a) the tribunal shall apply the same rule concerning the duty of a person to mitigate his loss as applies to any damages recoverable under the common law of England and Wales, Northern Ireland or Scotland, as applicable.

(7) [Sections 18A to 18C] of the 1996 Tribunals Act (conciliation) shall apply to the right conferred by this regulation and to proceedings under this regulation as it applies to the rights conferred by that Act and the employment tribunal proceedings mentioned in that Act.

NOTES

Para (2A): inserted by the Enterprise and Regulatory Reform Act 2013 (Consequential Amendments) (Employment) (No 2) Order 2014, SI 2014/853, arts 2(1), (2), 3, as from 20 April 2014, with effect in any case where the worker concerned complies with the requirement in the Employment Tribunals Act 1996, s 18A(1), on or after that date.

Para (7): words in square brackets substituted by the Enterprise and Regulatory Reform Act 2013 (Consequential Amendments) (Employment) Order 2014, SI 2014/386, art 2, Schedule, paras 36, 37, as from 6 April 2014.

[10.165]

13 Duty to inform and consult representatives

(1) In this regulation and regulations [13A], 14 and 15 references to affected employees, in relation to a relevant transfer, are to any employees of the transferor or the transferee (whether or not assigned to the organised grouping of resources or employees that is the subject of a relevant transfer) who may be affected by the transfer or may be affected by measures taken in connection with it; and references to the employer shall be construed accordingly.

(2) Long enough before a relevant transfer to enable the employer of any affected employees to consult the appropriate representatives of any affected employees, the employer shall inform those representatives of—

(a) the fact that the transfer is to take place, the date or proposed date of the transfer and the reasons for it;

(b) the legal, economic and social implications of the transfer for any affected employees;

(c) the measures which he envisages he will, in connection with the transfer, take in relation to any affected employees or, if he envisages that no measures will be so taken, that fact; and

(d) if the employer is the transferor, the measures, in connection with the transfer, which he envisages the transferee will take in relation to any affected employees who will become employees of the transferee after the transfer by virtue of regulation 4 or, if he envisages that no measures will be so taken, that fact.

[(2A) Where information is to be supplied under paragraph (2) by an employer—

(a) this must include suitable information relating to the use of agency workers (if any) by that employer; and

(b) "suitable information relating to the use of agency workers" means—

(i) the number of agency workers working temporarily for and under the supervision and direction of the employer;

(ii) the parts of the employer's undertaking in which those agency workers are working; and

(iii) the type of work those agency workers are carrying out.]

(3) For the purposes of this regulation the appropriate representatives of any affected employees are—

(a) if the employees are of a description in respect of which an independent trade union is recognised by their employer, representatives of the trade union; or

(b) in any other case, whichever of the following employee representatives the employer chooses—

(i) employee representatives appointed or elected by the affected employees otherwise than for the purposes of this regulation, who (having regard to the purposes for, and the method by which they were appointed or elected) have authority from those employees to receive information and to be consulted about the transfer on their behalf;

(ii) employee representatives elected by any affected employees, for the purposes of this regulation, in an election satisfying the requirements of regulation 14(1).

(4) The transferee shall give the transferor such information at such a time as will enable the transferor to perform the duty imposed on him by virtue of paragraph (2)(d).

(5) The information which is to be given to the appropriate representatives shall be given to each of them by being delivered to them, or sent by post to an address notified by them to the employer, or (in the case of representatives of a trade union) sent by post to the trade union at the address of its head or main office.

(6) An employer of an affected employee who envisages that he will take measures in relation to an affected employee, in connection with the relevant transfer, shall consult the appropriate representatives of that employee with a view to seeking their agreement to the intended measures.

(7) In the course of those consultations the employer shall—

(a) consider any representations made by the appropriate representatives; and

(b) reply to those representations and, if he rejects any of those representations, state his reasons.

(8) The employer shall allow the appropriate representatives access to any affected employees and shall afford to those representatives such accommodation and other facilities as may be appropriate.

(9) If in any case there are special circumstances which render it not reasonably practicable for an employer to perform a duty imposed on him by any of paragraphs (2) to (7), he shall take all such steps towards performing that duty as are reasonably practicable in the circumstances.

(10) Where—

(a) the employer has invited any of the affected employee to elect employee representatives; and

(b) the invitation was issued long enough before the time when the employer is required to give information under paragraph (2) to allow them to elect representatives by that time,

the employer shall be treated as complying with the requirements of this regulation in relation to those employees if he complies with those requirements as soon as is reasonably practicable after the election of the representatives.

(11) If, after the employer has invited any affected employees to elect representatives, they fail to do so within a reasonable time, he shall give to any affected employees the information set out in paragraph (2).

(12) The duties imposed on an employer by this regulation shall apply irrespective of whether the decision resulting in the relevant transfer is taken by the employer or a person controlling the employer.

NOTES

Para (1): figure in square brackets inserted by the Collective Redundancies and Transfer of Undertakings (Protection of Employment) (Amendment) Regulations 2014, SI 2014/16, regs 4, 11(1), (5), in relation to a TUPE transfer which takes place on or after 31 July 2014 (as to the meaning of "TUPE transfer", see reg 3 *ante*).

Para (2A): inserted by the Agency Workers Regulations 2010, SI 2010/93, reg 25, Sch 2, Pt 2, pars 28, 29, as from 1 October 2011.

[10.166]

[13A Micro-business's duty to inform and consult where no appropriate representatives

(1) This regulation applies if, at the time when the employer is required to give information under regulation 13(2)—

(a) the employer employs fewer than 10 employees;

(b) there are no appropriate representatives within the meaning of regulation 13(3); and

(c) the employer has not invited any of the affected employees to elect employee representatives.

(2) The employer may comply with regulation 13 by performing any duty which relates to appropriate representatives as if each of the affected employees were an appropriate representative.]

NOTES

Inserted by the Collective Redundancies and Transfer of Undertakings (Protection of Employment) (Amendment) Regulations 2014, SI 2014/16, regs 4, 11(2), (5), in relation to a TUPE transfer which takes place on or after 31 July 2014 (as to the meaning of "TUPE transfer", see reg 3 *ante*).

[10.167]

14 Election of employee representatives

(1) The requirements for the election of employee representatives under regulation 13(3) are that—

(a) the employer shall make such arrangements as are reasonably practicable to ensure that the election is fair;

(b) the employer shall determine the number of representatives to be elected so that there are sufficient representatives to represent the interests of all affected employees having regard to the number and classes of those employees;

(c) the employer shall determine whether the affected employees should be represented either by representatives of all the affected employees or by representatives of particular classes of those employees;

(d) before the election the employer shall determine the term of office as employee representatives so that it is of sufficient length to enable information to be given and consultations under regulation 13 to be completed;

(e) the candidates for election as employee representatives are affected employees on the date of the election;

(f) no affected employee is unreasonably excluded from standing for election;

(g) all affected employees on the date of the election are entitled to vote for employee representatives;

(h) the employees entitled to vote may vote for as many candidates as there are representatives to be elected to represent them or, if there are to be representatives for particular classes of employees, may vote for as many candidates as there are representatives to be elected to represent their particular class of employee;

(i) the election is conducted so as to secure that—

(i) so far as is reasonably practicable, those voting do so in secret; and

(ii) the votes given at the election are accurately counted.

(2) Where, after an election of employee representatives satisfying the requirements of paragraph (1) has been held, one of those elected ceases to act as an employee representative and as a result any affected employees are no longer represented, those employees shall elect another representative by an election satisfying the requirements of paragraph (1)(a), (e), (f) and (i).

[10.168]

15 Failure to inform or consult

(1) Where an employer has failed to comply with a requirement of regulation 13 or regulation 14, a complaint may be presented to an employment tribunal on that ground—

(a) in the case of a failure relating to the election of employee representatives, by any of his employees who are affected employees;

(b) in the case of any other failure relating to employee representatives, by any of the employee representatives to whom the failure related;

(c) in the case of failure relating to representatives of a trade union, by the trade union; and

(d) in any other case, by any of his employees who are affected employees.

(2) If on a complaint under paragraph (1) a question arises whether or not it was reasonably practicable for an employer to perform a particular duty or as to what steps he took towards performing it, it shall be for him to show—

(a) that there were special circumstances which rendered it not reasonably practicable for him to perform the duty; and

(b) that he took all such steps towards its performance as were reasonably practicable in those circumstances.

(3) If on a complaint under paragraph (1) a question arises as to whether or not an employee representative was an appropriate representative for the purposes of regulation 13, it shall be for the employer to show that the employee representative had the necessary authority to represent the affected employees [except where the question is whether or not regulation 13A applied].

[(3A) If on a complaint under paragraph (1), a question arises as to whether or not regulation 13A applied, it is for the employer to show that the conditions in sub-paragraphs (a) and (b) of regulation 13A(1) applied at the time referred to in regulation 13A(1).]

(4) On a complaint under paragraph (1)(a) it shall be for the employer to show that the requirements in regulation 14 have been satisfied.

(5) On a complaint against a transferor that he had failed to perform the duty imposed upon him by virtue of regulation 13(2)(d) or, so far as relating thereto, regulation 13(9), he may not show that it was not reasonably practicable for him to perform the duty in question for the reason that the transferee had failed to give him the requisite information at the requisite time in accordance with regulation 13(4) unless he gives the transferee notice of his intention to show that fact; and the giving of the notice shall make the transferee a party to the proceedings.

(6) In relation to any complaint under paragraph (1), a failure on the part of a person controlling (directly or indirectly) the employer to provide information to the employer shall not constitute special circumstances rendering it not reasonably practicable for the employer to comply with such a requirement.

(7) Where the tribunal finds a complaint against a transferee under paragraph (1) well-founded it shall make a declaration to that effect and may order the transferee to pay appropriate compensation to such descriptions of affected employees as may be specified in the award.

(8) Where the tribunal finds a complaint against a transferor under paragraph (1) well-founded it shall make a declaration to that effect and may—

- (a) order the transferor, subject to paragraph (9), to pay appropriate compensation to such descriptions of affected employees as may be specified in the award; or
- (b) if the complaint is that the transferor did not perform the duty mentioned in paragraph (5) and the transferor (after giving due notice) shows the facts so mentioned, order the transferee to pay appropriate compensation to such descriptions of affected employees as may be specified in the award.

(9) The transferee shall be jointly and severally liable with the transferor in respect of compensation payable under sub-paragraph (8)(a) or paragraph (11).

(10) An employee may present a complaint to an employment tribunal on the ground that he is an employee of a description to which an order under paragraph (7) or (8) relates and that—

- (a) in respect of an order under paragraph (7), the transferee has failed, wholly or in part, to pay him compensation in pursuance of the order;
- (b) in respect of an order under paragraph (8), the transferor or transferee, as applicable, has failed, wholly or in part, to pay him compensation in pursuance of the order.

(11) Where the tribunal finds a complaint under paragraph (10) well-founded it shall order the transferor or transferee as applicable to pay the complainant the amount of compensation which it finds is due to him.

(12) An employment tribunal shall not consider a complaint under paragraph (1) or (10) unless it is presented to the tribunal before the end of the period of three months beginning with—

- (a) in respect of a complaint under paragraph (1), the date on which the relevant transfer is completed; or
- (b) in respect of a complaint under paragraph (10), the date of the tribunal's order under paragraph (7) or (8),

or within such further period as the tribunal considers reasonable in a case where it is satisfied that it was not reasonably practicable for the complaint to be presented before the end of the period of three months.

[(13) Regulation 16A (extension of time limits to facilitate conciliation before institution of proceedings) applies for the purposes of paragraph (12).]

NOTES

Words in square brackets in para (3) inserted, and para (3A) inserted, by the Collective Redundancies and Transfer of Undertakings (Protection of Employment) (Amendment) Regulations 2014, SI 2014/16, regs 4, 11(3)–(5), in relation to a TUPE transfer which takes place on or after 31 July 2014 (as to the meaning of "TUPE transfer", see reg 3 *ante*).

Para (13) was added by the Enterprise and Regulatory Reform Act 2013 (Consequential Amendments) (Employment) (No 2) Order 2014, SI 2014/853, arts 2(1), (3), 3, as from 20 April 2014, with effect in any case where the worker concerned complies with the requirement in the Employment Tribunals Act 1996, s 18A(1), on or after that date.

[10.169]

16 Failure to inform or consult: supplemental

(1) Section 205(1) of the 1996 Act (complaint to be sole remedy for breach of relevant rights) and [sections 18A to 18C] of the 1996 Tribunals Act (conciliation) shall apply to the rights conferred by regulation 15 and to proceedings under this regulation as they apply to the rights conferred by those Acts and the employment tribunal proceedings mentioned in those Acts.

(2) An appeal shall lie and shall lie only to the Employment Appeal Tribunal on a question of law arising from any decision of, or arising in any proceedings before, an employment tribunal under or by virtue of these Regulations; and section 11(1) of the Tribunals and Inquiries Act 1992 (appeals from certain tribunals to the High Court) shall not apply in relation to any such proceedings.

(3) "Appropriate compensation" in regulation 15 means such sum not exceeding thirteen weeks' pay for the employee in question as the tribunal considers just and equitable having regard to the seriousness of the failure of the employer to comply with his duty.

(4) Sections 220 to 228 of the 1996 Act shall apply for calculating the amount of a week's pay for any employee for the purposes of paragraph (3) and, for the purposes of that calculation, the calculation date shall be—

(a) in the case of an employee who is dismissed by reason of redundancy (within the meaning of sections 139 and 155 of the 1996 Act) the date which is the calculation date for the purposes of any entitlement of his to a redundancy payment (within the meaning of those sections) or which would be that calculation date if he were so entitled;

(b) in the case of an employee who is dismissed for any other reason, the effective date of termination (within the meaning of sections 95(1) and (2) and 97 of the 1996 Act) of his contract of employment;

(c) in any other case, the date of the relevant transfer.

NOTES

Para (1): words in square brackets substituted by the Enterprise and Regulatory Reform Act 2013 (Consequential Amendments) (Employment) Order 2014, SI 2014/386, art 2, Schedule, paras 36, 38, as from 6 April 2014.

[10.170]

[16A Extension of time limit to facilitate conciliation before institution of proceedings

(1) This regulation applies where these Regulations provide for it to apply for the purposes of a provision in these Regulations ("a relevant provision").

(2) In this regulation—

(a) Day A is the day on which the worker concerned complies with the requirement in subsection (1) of section 18A of the Employment Tribunals Act 1996 (requirement to contact ACAS before instituting proceedings) in relation to the matter in respect of which the proceedings are brought, and

(b) Day B is the day on which the worker concerned receives or, if earlier, is treated as receiving (by virtue of regulations made under subsection (11) of that section) the certificate issued under subsection (4) of that section.

(3) In working out when the time limit set by a relevant provision expires the period beginning with the day after Day A and ending with Day B is not to be counted.

(4) If the time limit set by a relevant provision would (if not extended by this paragraph) expire during the period beginning with Day A and ending one month after Day B, the time limit expires instead at the end of that period.

(5) Where an employment tribunal has power under these Regulations to extend the time limit set by a relevant provision, the power is exercisable in relation to that time limit as extended by this regulation.]

NOTES

Inserted by the Enterprise and Regulatory Reform Act 2013 (Consequential Amendments) (Employment) (No 2) Order 2014, SI 2014/853, arts 2(1), (4), 3, as from 20 April 2014, with effect in any case where the worker concerned complies with the requirement in the Employment Tribunals Act 1996, s 18A(1), on or after that date.

[10.171]

17 Employers' Liability Compulsory Insurance

(1) Paragraph (2) applies where—

(a) by virtue of section 3(1)(a) or (b) of the Employers' Liability (Compulsory Insurance) Act 1969 ("the 1969 Act"), the transferor is not required by that Act to effect any insurance; or

(b) by virtue of section 3(1)(c) of the 1969 Act, the transferor is exempted from the requirement of that Act to effect insurance.

(2) Where this paragraph applies, on completion of a relevant transfer the transferor and the transferee shall be jointly and severally liable in respect of any liability referred to in section 1(1) of the 1969 Act, in so far as such liability relates to the employee's employment with the transferor.

[10.172]

18 Restriction on contracting out

Section 203 of the 1996 Act (restrictions on contracting out) shall apply in relation to these Regulations as if they were contained in that Act, save for that section shall not apply in so far as these Regulations provide for an agreement (whether a contract of employment or not) to exclude or limit the operation of these Regulations.

19 (*Amends the Employment Rights Act 1996, s 104.*)

[10.173]

20 Repeals, revocations and amendments

(1) Subject to regulation 21, the 1981 Regulations are revoked.

(2) Section 33 of, and paragraph 4 of Schedule 9 to, the Trade Union Reform and Employment Rights Act 1993 are repealed.

(3) Schedule 2 (consequential amendments) shall have effect.

[10.174]

21 Transitional provisions and savings

(1) These Regulations shall apply in relation to—

(a) a relevant transfer that takes place on or after 6 April 2006;

(b) a transfer or service provision change, not falling within sub-paragraph (a), that takes place on or after 6 April 2006 and is regarded by virtue of any enactment as a relevant transfer.

(2) The 1981 Regulations shall continue to apply in relation to—

(a) a relevant transfer (within the meaning of the 1981 Regulations) that took place before 6 April 2006;

(b) a transfer, not falling within sub-paragraph (a), that took place before 6 April 2006 and is regarded by virtue of any enactment as a relevant transfer (within the meaning of the 1981 Regulations).

(3) In respect of a relevant transfer that takes place on or after 6 April 2006, any action taken by a transferor or transferee to discharge a duty that applied to them under regulation 10 or 10A of the 1981 Regulations shall be deemed to satisfy the corresponding obligation imposed by regulations 13 and 14 of these Regulations, insofar as that action would have discharged those obligations had the action taken place on or after 6 April 2006.

(4) The duty on a transferor to provide a transferee with employee liability information shall not apply in the case of a relevant transfer that takes place on or before 19 April 2006.

(5) Regulations 13, 14, 15 and 16 shall not apply in the case of a service provision change that is not also a transfer of an undertaking, business or part of an undertaking or business that takes place on or before 4 May 2006.

(6) The repeal of paragraph 4 of Schedule 9 to the Trade Union Reform and Employment Rights Act 1993 does not affect the continued operation of that paragraph so far as it remains capable of having effect.

SCHEDULES 1 AND 2

(Sch 1 (Application of the Regulations to Northern Ireland), Sch 2 (Consequential Amendments) outside the scope of this work.)

CROSS-BORDER INSOLVENCY REGULATIONS 2006

(SI 2006/1030)

NOTES

Made: 3 April 2006.

Authority: Insolvency Act 2000, s 14.

Commencement: 4 April 2006.

These Regulations are reproduced as amended by: the Third Parties (Rights against Insurers) Act 2010; the Companies Act 2006 (Consequential Amendments, Transitional Provisions and Savings) Order 2009, SI 2009/1941; the Financial Services Act 2012 (Consequential Amendments and Transitional Provisions) Order 2013, SI 2013/472; the Insolvency (England and Wales) Rules 2016 (Consequential Amendments and Savings) Rules 2017, SI 2017/369; the Water Act 2014 (Consequential Amendments etc) Order 2017, SI 2017/506; the Insolvency Amendment (EU 2015/848) Regulations 2017, SI 2017/702; the Insolvency (England and Wales) and Insolvency (Scotland) (Miscellaneous and Consequential Amendments) Rules 2017, SI 2017/1115; the Insolvency (Miscellaneous Amendments) Regulations 2017, SI 2017/1119; the Alteration of Judicial Titles (Registrar in Bankruptcy of the High Court) Order 2018, SI 2018/130; the Insolvency (Amendment) (EU Exit) Regulations 2019, SI 2019/146.

ARRANGEMENT OF REGULATIONS

SCHEDULES

[10.175]

1 Citation, commencement and interpretation

(1) These Regulations may be cited as the Cross-Border Insolvency Regulations 2006 and shall come into force on the day after the day on which they are made.

(2) In these Regulations "the UNCITRAL Model Law" means the Model Law on cross-border insolvency as adopted by the United Nations Commission on International Trade Law on 30th May 1997.

[(3) In these Regulations "overseas company" has the meaning given by section 1044 of the Companies Act 2006 and "establishment", in relation to such a company, has the same meaning as in the Overseas Companies Regulations 2009.]

NOTES

Para (3): added by the Companies Act 2006 (Consequential Amendments, Transitional Provisions and Savings) Order 2009, SI 2009/1941, art 2(1), Sch 1, para 264(1), (2), as from 1 October 2009.

[10.176]

2 UNCITRAL Model Law to have force of law

(1) The UNCITRAL Model Law shall have the force of law in Great Britain in the form set out in Schedule 1 to these Regulations (which contains the UNCITRAL Model Law with certain modifications to adapt it for application in Great Britain).

(2) Without prejudice to any practice of the courts as to the matters which may be considered apart from this paragraph, the following documents may be considered in ascertaining the meaning or effect of any provision of the UNCITRAL Model Law as set out in Schedule 1 to these Regulations—

(a) the UNCITRAL Model Law;

(b) any documents of the United Nations Commission on International Trade Law and its working group relating to the preparation of the UNCITRAL Model Law; and

(c) the Guide to Enactment of the UNCITRAL Model Law (UNCITRAL document A/CN 9/442) prepared at the request of the United Nations Commission on International Trade Law made in May 1997.

[10.177]

3 Modification of British insolvency law

(1) British insolvency law (as defined in article 2 of the UNCITRAL Model Law as set out in Schedule 1 to these Regulations) and Part 3 of the Insolvency Act 1986 shall apply with such modifications as the context requires for the purpose of giving effect to the provisions of these Regulations.

(2) In the case of any conflict between any provision of British insolvency law or of Part 3 of the Insolvency Act 1986 and the provisions of these Regulations, the latter shall prevail.

[10.178]

4 Procedural matters in England and Wales

Schedule 2 to these Regulations (which makes provision about procedural matters in England and Wales in connection with the application of the UNCITRAL Model Law as set out in Schedule 1 to these Regulations) shall have effect.

[10.179]

5 Procedural matters in Scotland

Schedule 3 to these Regulations (which makes provision about procedural matters in Scotland in connection with the application of the UNCITRAL Model Law as set out in Schedule 1 to these Regulations) shall have effect.

[10.180]

6 Notices delivered to the registrar of companies

Schedule 4 to these Regulations (which makes provision about notices delivered to the registrar of companies under these Regulations) shall have effect.

[10.181]

7 Co-operation between courts exercising jurisdiction in relation to cross-border insolvency

(1) An order made by a court in either part of Great Britain in the exercise of jurisdiction in relation to the subject matter of these Regulations shall be enforced in the other part of Great Britain as if it were made by a court exercising the corresponding jurisdiction in that other part.

(2) However, nothing in paragraph (1) requires a court in either part of Great Britain to enforce, in relation to property situated in that part, any order made by a court in the other part of Great Britain.

(3) The courts having jurisdiction in relation to the subject matter of these Regulations in either part of Great Britain shall assist the courts having the corresponding jurisdiction in the other part of Great Britain.

[10.182]

8 Disapplication of section 388 of the Insolvency Act 1986

Nothing in section 388 of the Insolvency Act 1986 applies to anything done by a foreign representative—

(a) under or by virtue of these Regulations;

(b) in relation to relief granted or cooperation or coordination provided under these Regulations.

SCHEDULES

SCHEDULE 1
UNCITRAL MODEL LAW ON CROSS-BORDER INSOLVENCY

Regulation 2(1)

CHAPTER I GENERAL PROVISIONS

Article 1
Scope of Application

[10.183]

1. This Law applies where—
- (a) assistance is sought in Great Britain by a foreign court or a foreign representative in connection with a foreign proceeding; or
- (b) assistance is sought in a foreign State in connection with a proceeding under British insolvency law; or
- (c) a foreign proceeding and a proceeding under British insolvency law in respect of the same debtor are taking place concurrently; or
- (d) creditors or other interested persons in a foreign State have an interest in requesting the commencement of, or participating in, a proceeding under British insolvency law.

2. This Law does not apply to a proceeding concerning—
- (a) a company holding an appointment under Chapter 1 of Part 2 of the Water Industry Act 1991 (water and sewage undertakers) or a qualifying [water supply licensee] within the meaning of section 23(6) of that Act (meaning and effect of special administration order);
- (b) Scottish Water established under section 20 of the Water Industry (Scotland) Act 2002 (Scottish Water);
- (c) a protected railway company within the meaning of section 59 of the Railways Act 1993 (railway administration order) (including that section as it has effect by virtue of section 19 of the Channel Tunnel Rail Link Act 1996 (administration));
- (d) a licence company within the meaning of section 26 of the Transport Act 2000 (air traffic services);
- (e) a public private partnership company within the meaning of section 210 of the Greater London Authority Act 1999 (public-private partnership agreement);
- (f) a protected energy company within the meaning of section 154(5) of the Energy Act 2004 (energy administration orders);
- (g) a building society within the meaning of section 119 of the Building Societies Act 1986 (interpretation);
- (h) a UK credit institution or an EEA credit institution or any branch of either such institution as those expressions are defined by regulation 2 of the Credit Institutions (Reorganisation and Winding Up) Regulations 2004 (interpretation);
- (i) a third country credit institution within the meaning of regulation 36 of the Credit Institutions (Reorganisation and Winding Up) Regulations 2004 (interpretation of this Part);
- (j) a person who has permission under or by virtue of Parts 4 or 19 of the Financial Services and Markets Act 2000 to effect or carry out contracts of insurance;
- (k) an EEA insurer within the meaning of regulation 2 of the Insurers (Reorganisation and Winding Up) Regulations 2004 (interpretation);
- (l) a person (other than one included in paragraph 2(j)) pursuing the activity of reinsurance who has received authorisation for that activity from a competent authority within an EEA State; or
- (m) any of the Concessionaires within the meaning of section 1 of the Channel Tunnel Act 1987.

3. In paragraph 2 of this article—
- (a) in sub-paragraph (j) the reference to "contracts of insurance" must be construed in accordance with—
  - (i) section 22 of the Financial Services and Markets Act 2000 (classes of regulated activity and categories of investment);
  - (ii) any relevant order under that section; and
  - (iii) Schedule 2 to that Act (regulated activities);
- (b) in sub-paragraph (1) "EEA State" means a State . . . which is a contracting party to the agreement on the European Economic Area signed at Oporto on 2 May 1992.

4. The court shall not grant any relief, or modify any relief already granted, or provide any co-operation or coordination, under or by virtue of any of the provisions of this Law if and to the extent that such relief or modified relief or cooperation or coordination would—
- (a) be prohibited under or by virtue of—
  - (i) Part 7 of the Companies Act 1989;
  - (ii) Part 3 of the Financial Markets and Insolvency (Settlement Finality) Regulations 1999; or
  - (iii) Part 3 of the Financial Collateral Arrangements (No 2) Regulations 2003;

  in the case of a proceeding under British insolvency law; or
- (b) interfere with or be inconsistent with any rights of a collateral taker under Part 4 of the Financial Collateral Arrangements (No 2) Regulations 2003 which could be exercised in the case of such a proceeding.

5. Where a foreign proceeding regarding a debtor who is an insured in accordance with the provisions of the [Third Parties (Rights against Insurers) Act 2010] is recognised under this Law, any stay and suspension referred to in article 20(1) and any relief granted by the court under article 19 or 21 shall not apply to or affect—
- (a) any transfer of rights of the debtor under that Act; or
- (b) any claim, action, cause or proceeding by a third party against an insurer under or in respect of rights of the debtor transferred under that Act.

6. Any suspension under this Law of the right to transfer, encumber or otherwise dispose of any of the debtor's assets—

(a) is subject to section 26 of the Land Registration Act 2002 where owner's powers are exercised in relation to a registered estate or registered charge;
(b) is subject to section 52 of the Land Registration Act 2002, where the powers referred to in that section are exercised by the proprietor of a registered charge; and
(c) in any other case, shall not bind a purchaser of a legal estate in good faith for money or money's worth unless the purchaser has express notice of the suspension.

7. In paragraph 6—
(a) "owner's powers" means the powers described in section 23 of the Land Registration Act 2002 and "registered charge" and "registered estate" have the same meaning as in section 132(1) of that Act; and
(b) "legal estate" and "purchaser" have the same meaning as in section 17 of the Land Charges Act 1972.

Article 2
Definitions

For the purposes of this Law—
(a) "British insolvency law" means—
(i) in relation to England and Wales, provision extending to England and Wales and made by or under [the EU Insolvency Regulation,] the Insolvency Act 1986 (with the exception of Part 3 of that Act) or by or under that [Regulation or] Act as extended or applied by or under any other enactment (excluding these Regulations); and
(ii) in relation to Scotland, provision extending to Scotland and made by or under [the EU Insolvency Regulation,] the Insolvency Act 1986 (with the exception of Part 3 of that Act), the Bankruptcy (Scotland) Act 1985 or by or under [that Regulation or] those Acts as extended or applied by or under any other enactment (excluding these Regulations);
(b) "British insolvency officeholder" means—
(i) the official receiver within the meaning of section 399 of the Insolvency Act 1986 when acting as liquidator, provisional liquidator, trustee, interim receiver or nominee or supervisor of a voluntary arrangement;
(ii) a person acting as an insolvency practitioner within the meaning of section 388 of that Act but shall not include a person acting as an administrative receiver; and
(iii) the Accountant in Bankruptcy within the meaning of section 1 of the Bankruptcy (Scotland) Act 1985 when acting as interim or permanent trustee;
(c) "the court" except as otherwise provided in articles 14(4) and 23(6)(b), means in relation to any matter the court which in accordance with the provisions of article 4 of this Law has jurisdiction in relation to that matter;
[(d) "the EU Insolvency Regulation" means Regulation (EU) 2015/848 of the European Parliament and of the Council of 20 May 2015 [as that Regulation forms part of domestic law on and after exit day];]
(e) "establishment" means any place of operations where the debtor carries out a non-transitory economic activity with human means and assets or services;
(f) "foreign court" means a judicial or other authority competent to control or supervise a foreign proceeding;
(g) "foreign main proceeding" means a foreign proceeding taking place in the State where the debtor has the centre of its main interests;
(h) "foreign non-main proceeding" means a foreign proceeding, other than a foreign main proceeding, taking place in a State where the debtor has an establishment within the meaning of sub-paragraph (e) of this article;
(i) "foreign proceeding" means a collective judicial or administrative proceeding in a foreign State, including an interim proceeding, pursuant to a law relating to insolvency in which proceeding the assets and affairs of the debtor are subject to control or supervision by a foreign court, for the purpose of reorganisation or liquidation;
(j) "foreign representative" means a person or body, including one appointed on an interim basis, authorised in a foreign proceeding to administer the reorganisation or the liquidation of the debtor's assets or affairs or to act as a representative of the foreign proceeding;
(k) "hire-purchase agreement" includes a conditional sale agreement, a chattel leasing agreement and a retention of title agreement;
(l) "section 426 request" means a request for assistance in accordance with section 426 of the Insolvency Act 1986 made to a court in any part of the United Kingdom;
(m) "secured creditor" in relation to a debtor, means a creditor of the debtor who holds in respect of his debt a security over property of the debtor;
(n) "security" means—
(i) in relation to England and Wales, any mortgage, charge, lien or other security; and
(ii) in relation to Scotland, any security (whether heritable or moveable), any floating charge and any right of lien or preference and any right of retention (other than a right of compensation or set off);
(o) in the application of Articles 20 and 23 to Scotland, "an individual" means any debtor within the meaning of the Bankruptcy (Scotland) Act 1985;
(p) in the application of this Law to Scotland, references howsoever expressed to—
(i) "filing" an application or claim are to be construed as references to lodging an application or submitting a claim respectively;
(ii) "relief" and "standing" are to be construed as references to "remedy" and "title and interest" respectively; and
(iii) a "stay" are to be construed as references to restraint, except in relation to continuation of actions or proceedings when they shall be construed as a reference to sist; and
(q) references to the law of Great Britain include a reference to the law of either part of Great Britain (including its rules of private international law).

Article 3

. . .

Article 4

Competent Court

1. The functions referred to in this Law relating to recognition of foreign proceedings and cooperation with foreign courts shall be performed by the High Court and assigned to the Chancery Division, as regards England and Wales and the Court of Session as regards Scotland.

2. Subject to paragraph 1 of this article, the court in either part of Great Britain shall have jurisdiction in relation to the functions referred to in that paragraph if—

(a) the debtor has—

(i) a place of business; or

(ii) in the case of an individual, a place of residence; or

(iii) assets,

situated in that part of Great Britain; or

(b) the court in that part of Great Britain considers for any other reason that it is the appropriate forum to consider the question or provide the assistance requested.

3. In considering whether it is the appropriate forum to hear an application for recognition of a foreign proceeding in relation to a debtor, the court shall take into account the location of any court in which a proceeding under British insolvency law is taking place in relation to the debtor and the likely location of any future proceedings under British insolvency law in relation to the debtor.

Article 5

Authorisation of British Insolvency Officeholders to Act in a Foreign State

A British insolvency officeholder is authorised to act in a foreign State on behalf of a proceeding under British insolvency law, as permitted by the applicable foreign law.

Article 6

Public Policy Exception

Nothing in this Law prevents the court from refusing to take an action governed by this Law if the action would be manifestly contrary to the public policy of Great Britain or any part of it.

Article 7

Additional Assistance under other Laws

Nothing in this Law limits the power of a court or a British insolvency officeholder to provide additional assistance to a foreign representative under other laws of Great Britain.

Article 8

Interpretation

In the interpretation of this Law, regard is to be had to its international origin and to the need to promote uniformity in its application and the observance of good faith.

CHAPTER II ACCESS OF FOREIGN REPRESENTATIVES AND CREDITORS TO COURTS IN GREAT BRITAIN

Article 9

Right of Direct Access

A foreign representative is entitled to apply directly to a court in Great Britain.

Article 10

Limited Jurisdiction

The sole fact that an application pursuant to this Law is made to a court in Great Britain by a foreign representative does not subject the foreign representative or the foreign assets and affairs of the debtor to the jurisdiction of the courts of Great Britain or any part of it for any purpose other than the application.

Article 11

Application by a Foreign Representative to Commence a Proceeding under British Insolvency Law

A foreign representative appointed in a foreign main proceeding or foreign non-main proceeding is entitled to apply to commence a proceeding under British insolvency law if the conditions for commencing such a proceeding are otherwise met.

Article 12

Participation of a Foreign Representative in a Proceeding under British Insolvency Law

Upon recognition of a foreign proceeding, the foreign representative is entitled to participate in a proceeding regarding the debtor under British insolvency law.

Article 13

Access of Foreign Creditors to a Proceeding under British Insolvency Law

1. Subject to paragraph 2 of this article, foreign creditors have the same rights regarding the commencement of, and participation in, a proceeding under British insolvency law as creditors in Great Britain.

2. Paragraph 1 of this article does not affect the ranking of claims in a proceeding under British insolvency law, except that the claim of a foreign creditor shall not be given a lower priority than that of general unsecured claims solely because the holder of such a claim is a foreign creditor.

3. A claim may not be challenged solely on the grounds that it is a claim by a foreign tax or social security authority but such a claim may be challenged—

(a) on the ground that it is in whole or in part a penalty, or

(b) on any other ground that a claim might be rejected in a proceeding under British insolvency law.

Article 14

Notification to Foreign Creditors of a Proceeding under British Insolvency Law

1. Whenever under British insolvency law notification is to be given to creditors in Great Britain, such notification shall also be given to the known creditors that do not have addresses in Great Britain. The court may order that appropriate steps be taken with a view to notifying any creditor whose address is not yet known.

2. Such notification shall be made to the foreign creditors individually, unless—

(a) the court considers that under the circumstances some other form of notification would be more appropriate; or

(b) the notification to creditors in Great Britain is to be by advertisement only, in which case the notification to the known foreign creditors may be by advertisement in such foreign newspapers as the British insolvency officeholder considers most appropriate for ensuring that the content of the notification comes to the notice of the known foreign creditors.

3. When notification of a right to file a claim is to be given to foreign creditors, the notification shall—

(a) indicate a reasonable time period for filing claims and specify the place for their filing;

(b) indicate whether secured creditors need to file their secured claims; and

(c) contain any other information required to be included in such a notification to creditors pursuant to the law of Great Britain and the orders of the court.

4. In this article "the court" means the court which has jurisdiction in relation to the particular proceeding under British insolvency law under which notification is to be given to creditors.

CHAPTER III RECOGNITION OF A FOREIGN PROCEEDING AND RELIEF

Article 15

Application for Recognition of a Foreign Proceeding

1. A foreign representative may apply to the court for recognition of the foreign proceeding in which the foreign representative has been appointed.

2. An application for recognition shall be accompanied by—

(a) a certified copy of the decision commencing the foreign proceeding and appointing the foreign representative; or

(b) a certificate from the foreign court affirming the existence of the foreign proceeding and of the appointment of the foreign representative; or

(c) in the absence of evidence referred to in sub-paragraphs (a) and (b), any other evidence acceptable to the court of the existence of the foreign proceeding and of the appointment of the foreign representative.

3. An application for recognition shall also be accompanied by a statement identifying all foreign proceedings, proceedings under British insolvency law and section 426 requests in respect of the debtor that are known to the foreign representative.

4. The foreign representative shall provide the court with a translation into English of documents supplied in support of the application for recognition.

Article 16

Presumptions Concerning Recognition

1. If the decision or certificate referred to in paragraph 2 of article 15 indicates that the foreign proceeding is a proceeding within the meaning of sub-paragraph (i) of article 2 and that the foreign representative is a person or body within the meaning of sub-paragraph (j) of article 2, the court is entitled to so presume.

2. The court is entitled to presume that documents submitted in support of the application for recognition are authentic, whether or not they have been legalised.

[2A. Where the EU Insolvency Regulation applies the centre of the debtor's main interests is to be determined in accordance with that Regulation.]

[**3.** Subject to paragraph 2A, in the absence of proof to the contrary, the debtor's registered office, or habitual residence in the case of an individual, is presumed to be the centre of the debtor's main interests.]

Article 17

Decision to Recognise a Foreign Proceeding

1. Subject to article 6, a foreign proceeding shall be recognised if—

(a) it is a foreign proceeding within the meaning of sub-paragraph (i) of article 2;

(b) the foreign representative applying for recognition is a person or body within the meaning of sub-paragraph (j) of article 2;

(c) the application meets the requirements of paragraphs 2 and 3 of article 15; and

(d) the application has been submitted to the court referred to in article 4.

2. The foreign proceeding shall be recognised—

(a) as a foreign main proceeding if it is taking place in the State where the debtor has the centre of its main interests; or

(b) as a foreign non-main proceeding if the debtor has an establishment within the meaning of sub-paragraph (e) of article 2 in the foreign State.

3. An application for recognition of a foreign proceeding shall be decided upon at the earliest possible time.

4. The provisions of articles 15 to 16, this article and article 18 do not prevent modification or termination of recognition if it is shown that the grounds for granting it were fully or partially lacking or have fully or partially ceased to exist and in such a case, the court may, on the application of the foreign representative or a person affected by recognition, or of its own motion, modify or terminate recognition, either altogether or for a limited time, on such terms and conditions as the court thinks fit.

Article 18

Subsequent Information

From the time of filing the application for recognition of the foreign proceeding, the foreign representative shall inform the court promptly of—

(a) any substantial change in the status of the recognised foreign proceeding or the status of the foreign representative's appointment; and

(b) any other foreign proceeding, proceeding under British insolvency law or section 426 request regarding the same debtor that becomes known to the foreign representative.

Article 19

Relief that may be Granted upon Application for Recognition of a Foreign Proceeding

1. From the time of filing an application for recognition until the application is decided upon, the court may, at the request of the foreign representative, where relief is urgently needed to protect the assets of the debtor or the interests of the creditors, grant relief of a provisional nature, including—

(a) staying execution against the debtor's assets;

(b) entrusting the administration or realisation of all or part of the debtor's assets located in Great Britain to the foreign representative or another person designated by the court, in order to protect and preserve the value of assets that, by their nature or because of other circumstances, are perishable, susceptible to devaluation or otherwise in jeopardy; and

(c) any relief mentioned in paragraph 1 (c), (d) or (g) of article 21.

2. Unless extended under paragraph 1(f) of article 21, the relief granted under this article terminates when the application for recognition is decided upon.

3. The court may refuse to grant relief under this article if such relief would interfere with the administration of a foreign main proceeding.

Article 20

Effects of Recognition of a Foreign Main Proceeding

1. Upon recognition of a foreign proceeding that is a foreign main proceeding, subject to paragraph 2 of this article—

(a) commencement or continuation of individual actions or individual proceedings concerning the debtor's assets, rights, obligations or liabilities is stayed;

(b) execution against the debtor's assets is stayed; and

(c) the right to transfer, encumber or otherwise dispose of any assets of the debtor is suspended.

2. The stay and suspension referred to in paragraph 1 of this article shall be—

(a) the same in scope and effect as if the debtor, in the case of an individual, had been adjudged bankrupt under the Insolvency Act 1986 or had his estate sequestrated under the Bankruptcy (Scotland) Act 1985, or, in the case of a debtor other than an individual, had been made the subject of a winding-up order under the Insolvency Act 1986; and

(b) subject to the same powers of the court and the same prohibitions, limitations, exceptions and conditions as would apply under the law of Great Britain in such a case,

and the provisions of paragraph 1 of this article shall be interpreted accordingly.

3. Without prejudice to paragraph 2 of this article, the stay and suspension referred to in paragraph 1 of this article, in particular, does not affect any right—

(a) to take any steps to enforce security over the debtor's property;
(b) to take any steps to repossess goods in the debtor's possession under a hire-purchase agreement;
(c) exercisable under or by virtue of or in connection with the provisions referred to in article 1(4); or
(d) of a creditor to set off its claim against a claim of the debtor,

being a right which would have been exercisable if the debtor, in the case of an individual, had been adjudged bankrupt under the Insolvency Act 1986 or had his estate sequestrated under the Bankruptcy (Scotland) Act 1985, or, in the case of a debtor other than an individual, had been made the subject of a winding-up order under the Insolvency Act 1986.

4. Paragraph 1(a) of this article does not affect the right to—
(a) commence individual actions or proceedings to the extent necessary to preserve a claim against the debtor; or
(b) commence or continue any criminal proceedings or any action or proceedings by a person or body having regulatory, supervisory or investigative functions of a public nature, being an action or proceedings brought in the exercise of those functions.

5. Paragraph 1 of this article does not affect the right to request or otherwise initiate the commencement of a proceeding under British insolvency law or the right to file claims in such a proceeding.

6. In addition to and without prejudice to any powers of the court under or by virtue of paragraph 2 of this article, the court may, on the application of the foreign representative or a person affected by the stay and suspension referred to in paragraph 1 of this article, or of its own motion, modify or terminate such stay and suspension or any part of it, either altogether or for a limited time, on such terms and conditions as the court thinks fit.

Article 21

Relief that may be Granted upon Recognition of a Foreign Proceeding

1. Upon recognition of a foreign proceeding, whether main or non-main, where necessary to protect the assets of the debtor or the interests of the creditors, the court may, at the request of the foreign representative, grant any appropriate relief, including—
(a) staying the commencement or continuation of individual actions or individual proceedings concerning the debtor's assets, rights, obligations or liabilities, to the extent they have not been stayed under paragraph 1(a) of article 20;
(b) staying execution against the debtor's assets to the extent it has not been stayed under paragraph 1(b) of article 20;
(c) suspending the right to transfer, encumber or otherwise dispose of any assets of the debtor to the extent this right has not been suspended under paragraph 1(c) of article 20;
(d) providing for the examination of witnesses, the taking of evidence or the delivery of information concerning the debtor's assets, affairs, rights, obligations or liabilities;
(e) entrusting the administration or realisation of all or part of the debtor's assets located in Great Britain to the foreign representative or another person designated by the court;
(f) extending relief granted under paragraph 1 of article 19; and
(g) granting any additional relief that may be available to a British insolvency officeholder under the law of Great Britain, including any relief provided under paragraph 43 of Schedule B1 to the Insolvency Act 1986.

2. Upon recognition of a foreign proceeding, whether main or non-main, the court may, at the request of the foreign representative, entrust the distribution of all or part of the debtor's assets located in Great Britain to the foreign representative or another person designated by the court, provided that the court is satisfied that the interests of creditors in Great Britain are adequately protected.

3. In granting relief under this article to a representative of a foreign non-main proceeding, the court must be satisfied that the relief relates to assets that, under the law of Great Britain, should be administered in the foreign non-main proceeding or concerns information required in that proceeding.

4. No stay under paragraph 1(a) of this article shall affect the right to commence or continue any criminal proceedings or any action or proceedings by a person or body having regulatory, supervisory or investigative functions of a public nature, being an action or proceedings brought in the exercise of those functions.

Article 22

Protection of Creditors and other Interested Persons

1. In granting or denying relief under article 19 or 21, or in modifying or terminating relief under paragraph 3 of this article or paragraph 6 of article 20, the court must be satisfied that the interests of the creditors (including any secured creditors or parties to hire-purchase agreements) and other interested persons, including if appropriate the debtor, are adequately protected.

2. The court may subject relief granted under article 19 or 21 to conditions it considers appropriate, including the provision by the foreign representative of security or caution for the proper performance of his functions.

3. The court may, at the request of the foreign representative or a person affected by relief granted under article 19 or 21, or of its own motion, modify or terminate such relief.

Article 23

Actions to Avoid Acts Detrimental to Creditors

1. Subject to paragraphs 6 and 9 of this article, upon recognition of a foreign proceeding, the foreign representative has standing to make an application to the court for an order under or in connection with sections 238, 239, 242, 243, 244, 245, 339, 340, 342A, 343, and 423 of the Insolvency Act 1986 and sections 34, 35, 36, 36A and 61 of the Bankruptcy (Scotland) Act 1985.

2. Where the foreign representative makes such an application ("an article 23 application"), the sections referred to in paragraph 1 of this article and sections 240, 241, 341, 342, 342B to 342F, 424 and 425 of the Insolvency Act 1986 and sections 36B and 36C of the Bankruptcy (Scotland) Act 1985 shall apply—

(a) whether or not the debtor, in the case of an individual, has been adjudged bankrupt or had his estate sequestrated, or, in the case of a debtor other than an individual, is being wound up or is in administration, under British insolvency law; and

(b) with the modifications set out in paragraph 3 of this article.

3. The modifications referred to in paragraph 2 of this article are as follows—

(a) for the purposes of sections 241(2A)(a) and 342(2A)(a) of the Insolvency Act 1986, a person has notice of the relevant proceedings if he has notice of the opening of the relevant foreign proceeding;

(b) for the purposes of sections 240(1) and 245(3) of that Act, the onset of insolvency shall be the date of the opening of the relevant foreign proceeding;

(c) the periods referred to in sections 244(2), 341(1)(a) to (c) and 343(2) of that Act shall be periods ending with the date of the opening of the relevant foreign proceeding;

(d) for the purposes of sections 242(3)(a), (3)(b) and 243(1) of that Act, the date on which the winding up of the company commences or it enters administration shall be the date of the opening of the relevant foreign proceeding; and

(e) for the purposes of sections 34(3)(a), (3)(b), 35(1)(c), 36(1)(a) and (1)(b) and 61(2) of the Bankruptcy (Scotland) Act 1985, the date of sequestration or granting of the trust deed shall be the date of the opening of the relevant foreign proceeding.

4. For the purposes of paragraph 3 of this article, the date of the opening of the foreign proceeding shall be determined in accordance with the law of the State in which the foreign proceeding is taking place, including any rule of law by virtue of which the foreign proceeding is deemed to have opened at an earlier time.

5. When the foreign proceeding is a foreign non-main proceeding, the court must be satisfied that the article 23 application relates to assets that, under the law of Great Britain, should be administered in the foreign non-main proceeding.

6. At any time when a proceeding under British insolvency law is taking place regarding the debtor—

(a) the foreign representative shall not make an article 23 application except with the permission of—

(i) in the case of a proceeding under British insolvency law taking place in England and Wales, the High Court; or

(ii) in the case of a proceeding under British insolvency law taking place in Scotland, the Court of Session; and

(b) references to "the court" in paragraphs 1, 5 and 7 of this article are references to the court in which that proceeding is taking place.

7. On making an order on an article 23 application, the court may give such directions regarding the distribution of any proceeds of the claim by the foreign representative, as it thinks fit to ensure that the interests of creditors in Great Britain are adequately protected.

8. Nothing in this article affects the right of a British insolvency officeholder to make an application under or in connection with any of the provisions referred to in paragraph 1 of this article.

9. Nothing in paragraph 1 of this article shall apply in respect of any preference given, floating charge created, alienation, assignment or relevant contributions (within the meaning of section 342A(5) of the Insolvency Act 1986) made or other transaction entered into before the date on which this Law comes into force.

Article 24

Intervention by a Foreign Representative in Proceedings in Great Britain

Upon recognition of a foreign proceeding, the foreign representative may, provided the requirements of the law of Great Britain are met, intervene in any proceedings in which the debtor is a party.

CHAPTER IV COOPERATION WITH FOREIGN COURTS AND FOREIGN REPRESENTATIVES

Article 25

Cooperation and Direct Communication between a Court of Great Britain and Foreign Courts or Foreign Representatives

1. In matters referred to in paragraph 1 of article 1, the court may cooperate to the maximum extent possible with foreign courts or foreign representatives, either directly or through a British insolvency officeholder.

2. The court is entitled to communicate directly with, or to request information or assistance directly from, foreign courts or foreign representatives.

Article 26

Cooperation and Direct Communication between the British Insolvency Officeholder and Foreign Courts or Foreign Representatives

1. In matters referred to in paragraph 1 of article 1, a British insolvency officeholder shall to the extent consistent with his other duties under the law of Great Britain, in the exercise of his functions and subject to the supervision of the court, cooperate to the maximum extent possible with foreign courts or foreign representatives.

2. The British insolvency officeholder is entitled, in the exercise of his functions and subject to the supervision of the court, to communicate directly with foreign courts or foreign representatives.

Article 27

Forms of Cooperation

Cooperation referred to in articles 25 and 26 may be implemented by any appropriate means, including—

(a) appointment of a person to act at the direction of the court;
(b) communication of information by any means considered appropriate by the court;
(c) coordination of the administration and supervision of the debtor's assets and affairs;
(d) approval or implementation by courts of agreements concerning the coordination of proceedings;
(e) coordination of concurrent proceedings regarding the same debtor.

CHAPTER V CONCURRENT PROCEEDINGS

Article 28

Commencement of a Proceeding Under British Insolvency Law after Recognition of a Foreign Main Proceeding

After recognition of a foreign main proceeding, the effects of a proceeding under British insolvency law in relation to the same debtor shall, insofar as the assets of that debtor are concerned, be restricted to assets that are located in Great Britain and, to the extent necessary to implement cooperation and coordination under articles 25, 26 and 27, to other assets of the debtor that, under the law of Great Britain, should be administered in that proceeding.

Article 29

Coordination of a Proceeding Under British Insolvency Law and a Foreign Proceeding

Where a foreign proceeding and a proceeding under British insolvency law are taking place concurrently regarding the same debtor, the court may seek cooperation and coordination under articles 25, 26 and 27, and the following shall apply—

(a) when the proceeding in Great Britain is taking place at the time the application for recognition of the foreign proceeding is filed—
   (i) any relief granted under article 19 or 21 must be consistent with the proceeding in Great Britain; and
   (ii) if the foreign proceeding is recognised in Great Britain as a foreign main proceeding, article 20 does not apply;
(b) when the proceeding in Great Britain commences after the filing of the application for recognition of the foreign proceeding—
   (i) any relief in effect under article 19 or 21 shall be reviewed by the court and shall be modified or terminated if inconsistent with the proceeding in Great Britain;
   (ii) if the foreign proceeding is a foreign main proceeding, the stay and suspension referred to in paragraph 1 of article 20 shall be modified or terminated pursuant to paragraph 6 of article 20, if inconsistent with the proceeding in Great Britain; and
   (iii) any proceedings brought by the foreign representative by virtue of paragraph 1 of article 23 before the proceeding in Great Britain commenced shall be reviewed by the court and the court may give such directions as it thinks fit regarding the continuance of those proceedings; and
(c) in granting, extending or modifying relief granted to a representative of a foreign non-main proceeding, the court must be satisfied that the relief relates to assets that, under the law of Great Britain, should be administered in the foreign non-main proceeding or concerns information required in that proceeding.

Article 30

Coordination of more than one Foreign Proceeding

In matters referred to in paragraph 1 of article 1, in respect of more than one foreign proceeding regarding the same debtor, the court may seek cooperation and coordination under articles 25, 26 and 27, and the following shall apply—

(a) any relief granted under article 19 or 21 to a representative of a foreign non-main proceeding after recognition of a foreign main proceeding must be consistent with the foreign main proceeding;
(b) if a foreign main proceeding is recognised after the filing of an application for recognition of a foreign non-main proceeding, any relief in effect under article 19 or 21 shall be reviewed by the court and shall be modified or terminated if inconsistent with the foreign main proceeding; and
(c) if, after recognition of a foreign non-main proceeding, another foreign non-main proceeding is recognised, the court shall grant, modify or terminate relief for the purpose of facilitating coordination of the proceedings.

Article 31

Presumption of Insolvency Based on Recognition of a Foreign Main Proceeding

In the absence of evidence to the contrary, recognition of a foreign main proceeding is, for the purpose of commencing a proceeding under British insolvency law, proof that the debtor is unable to pay its debts or, in relation to Scotland, is apparently insolvent within the meaning given to those expressions under British insolvency law.

Article 32

Rule of Payment in Concurrent Proceedings

Without prejudice to secured claims or rights in rem, a creditor who has received part payment in respect of its claim in a proceeding pursuant to a law relating to insolvency in a foreign State may not receive a payment for the same claim in a proceeding under British insolvency law regarding the same debtor, so long as the payment to the other creditors of the same class is proportionately less than the payment the creditor has already received.

NOTES

Article 1: words in square brackets in para 2 substituted by the Water Act 2014 (Consequential Amendments etc) Order 2017, SI 2017/506, art 24, as from 31 March 2017. Words omitted from para 3(b) revoked by the Insolvency (Amendment) (EU Exit) Regulations 2019, SI 2019/146, reg 2, Schedule, Pt 6, paras 112–114, as from IP completion day (as defined in the European Union (Withdrawal Agreement) Act 2020, s 39) (for savings, see reg 4 of the 2019 Regulations at **[12.82]**). Words in square brackets in para 5 substituted by the Third Parties (Rights against Insurers) Act 2010, s 20, Sch 2, para 5, as from 1 August 2016.

Article 2: words in square brackets in paras (a), (d) inserted by SI 2019/146, reg 2, Schedule, Pt 6, paras 112, 113, 115, as from IP completion day (as defined in the European Union (Withdrawal Agreement) Act 2020, s 39) (for savings, see reg 4 of the 2019 Regulations at **[12.82]**). Para (d) substituted by the Insolvency Amendment (EU 2015/848) Regulations 2017, SI 2017/702, regs 2, 3, Schedule, Pt 6, para 94(1), (2), as from 26 June 2017, except in relation to proceedings opened before that date.

Article 3: revoked by SI 2019/146, reg 2, Schedule, Pt 6, paras 112, 113, 116, as from IP completion day (as defined in the European Union (Withdrawal Agreement) Act 2020, s 39) (for savings, see reg 4 of the 2019 Regulations at **[12.82]**).

Article 16: para 2A inserted, and para 3 substituted, by SI 2019/146, reg 2, Schedule, Pt 6, paras 112, 113, 117, as from IP completion day (as defined in the European Union (Withdrawal Agreement) Act 2020, s 39) (for savings, see reg 4 of the 2019 Regulations at **[12.82]**).

SCHEDULE 2
PROCEDURAL MATTERS IN ENGLAND AND WALES

Regulation 4

PART 1 INTRODUCTORY PROVISIONS

[10.184]

1 Interpretation

(1) In this Schedule—

"the 1986 Act" means the Insolvency Act 1986;

"article 21 relief application" means an application to the court by a foreign representative under article 21(1) or (2) of the Model Law for relief;

"business day" means any day other than a Saturday, a Sunday, Christmas Day, Good Friday or a day which is a bank holiday in England and Wales under or by virtue of the Banking and Financial Dealings Act 1971;

"CPR" means the Civil Procedure Rules 1998 and "CPR" followed by a Part or rule by number means the Part or rule with that number in those Rules;

"enforcement officer" means an individual who is authorised to act as an enforcement officer under the Courts Act 2003;

"file in court" and "file with the court" means deliver to the court for filing;

"the Gazette" means the London Gazette;

"interim relief application" means an application to the court by a foreign representative under article 19 of the Model Law for interim relief;

. . .

. . .

"the Model Law" means the UNCITRAL Model Law as set out in Schedule 1 to these Regulations;

"modification or termination order" means an order by the court pursuant to its powers under the Model Law modifying or terminating recognition of a foreign proceeding, the stay and suspension referred to in article 20(1) or any part of it or any relief granted under article 19 or 21 of the Model Law;

"originating application" means an application to the court which is not an application in pending proceedings before the court;

"ordinary application" means any application to the court other than an originating application;

"practice direction" means a direction as to the practice and procedure of any court within the scope of the CPR;

"recognition application" means an application to the court by a foreign representative in accordance with article 15 of the Model Law for an order recognising the foreign proceeding in which he has been appointed;

"recognition order" means an order by the court recognising a proceeding the subject of a recognition application as a foreign main proceeding or foreign non-main proceeding, as appropriate;

["relevant company" means a company that is—

(a) registered under the Companies Act 2006,

(b) subject to a requirement imposed by regulations under section 1043 of that Act 2006 (unregistered UK companies) to deliver any documents to the registrar of companies, or

(c) subject to a requirement imposed by regulations under section 1046 of that Act (overseas companies) to deliver any documents to the registrar of companies;]

"review application" means an application to the court for a modification or termination order;

"the Rules" means the [Insolvency (England and Wales) Rules 2016] and "Rule" followed by a number means the rule with that number in those Rules;

. . .

. . .

(2) Expressions defined in the Model Law have the same meaning when used in this Schedule.

(3) In proceedings under these Regulations, "Registrar" means—

(a) [an Insolvency and Companies Court Judge]; and

(b) where the proceedings are in a district registry, the district judge.

(4) References to the "venue" for any proceedings or attendance before the court, are to the time, date and place for the proceedings or attendance.

(5) References in this Schedule to ex parte hearings shall be construed as references to hearings without notice being served on any other party, and references to applications made ex parte as references to applications made without notice being served on any other party; and other references which include the expression "ex parte" shall be similarly construed.

[(6) References in this Schedule to a debtor who is of interest to the Financial Conduct Authority are references to a debtor who—

(a) is, or has been, an authorised person within the meaning of the Financial Services and Markets Act 2000;

(b) is, or has been, an appointed representative within the meaning of section 39 of the Financial Services and Markets Act 2000; or

(c) is carrying on, or has carried on, a regulated activity in contravention of the general prohibition.

(6A) References in this Schedule to a debtor who is of interest to the Prudential Regulation Authority are references to a debtor who—

(a) is, or has been, a PRA-authorised person within the meaning of the Financial Services and Markets Act 2000; or

(b) is carrying on, or has carried on, a PRA-regulated activity within the meaning of the Financial Services and Markets Act 2000 in contravention of the general prohibition.]

(7) In [sub-paragraphs (6) and (6A)] "the general prohibition" has the meaning given by section 19 of the Financial Services and Markets Act 2000 and the reference to a "regulated activity" must be construed in accordance with—

(a) section 22 of that Act (classes of regulated activity and categories of investment);

(b) any relevant order under that section; and

(c) Schedule 2 to that Act (regulated activities).

(8) References in this Schedule to a numbered form are to the form that bears that number in Schedule 5.

NOTES

Para 1 is amended as follows:

Definitions "main proceedings", "member State liquidator", "secondary proceedings" and "territorial proceedings" (all omitted) revoked by the Insolvency (Amendment) (EU Exit) Regulations 2019, SI 2019/146, reg 2, Schedule, Pt 6, paras 112, 118, 119, as from IP completion day (as defined in the European Union (Withdrawal Agreement) Act 2020, s 39) (for savings, see reg 4 of the 2019 Regulations at **[12.82]**).

Definition "relevant company" substituted by the Companies Act 2006 (Consequential Amendments, Transitional Provisions and Savings) Order 2009, SI 2009/1941, art 2(1), Sch 1, para 264(1), (3)(a), as from 1 October 2009.

Words in square brackets in the definition "the Rules" substituted by the Insolvency (England and Wales) and Insolvency (Scotland) (Miscellaneous and Consequential Amendments) Rules 2017, SI 2017/1115, rr 20, 21, as from 8 December 2017.

Words in square brackets in sub-para (3)(a) substituted by the Alteration of Judicial Titles (Registrar in Bankruptcy of the High Court) Order 2018, SI 2018/130, art 2, Schedule, para 12(d), as from 26 February 2018.

Sub-paras (6), (6A) substituted (for the original sub-para (6)), and words in square brackets in sub-para (7) substituted, by the Financial Services Act 2012 (Consequential Amendments and Transitional Provisions) Order 2013, SI 2013/472, art 3, Sch 2, para 116(a)(i), as from 1 April 2013.

PART 2 APPLICATIONS TO COURT FOR RECOGNITION OF FOREIGN PROCEEDINGS

[10.185]

2 Affidavit in support of recognition application

A recognition application shall be in Form ML1 and shall be supported by an affidavit sworn by the foreign representative complying with paragraph 4.

3 Form and content of application

The application shall state the following matters—

(a) the name of the applicant and his address for service within England and Wales;

(b) the name of the debtor in respect of which the foreign proceeding is taking place;

(c) the name or names in which the debtor carries on business in the country where the foreign proceeding is taking place and in this country, if other than the name given under sub-paragraph (b);

(d) the principal or last known place of business of the debtor in Great Britain (if any) and, in the case of an individual, his usual or last known place of residence in Great Britain (if any);

(e) any registered number allocated to the debtor under [the Companies Act 2006];

(f) brief particulars of the foreign proceeding in respect of which recognition is applied for, including the country in which it is taking place and the nature of the proceeding;

(g) that the foreign proceeding is a proceeding within the meaning of article 2(i) of the Model Law;

(h) that the applicant is a foreign representative within the meaning of article 2(j) of the Model Law;

(i) the address of the debtor's centre of main interests and, if different, the address of its registered office or habitual residence, as appropriate; and

(j) if the debtor does not have its centre of main interests in the country where the foreign proceeding is taking place, whether the debtor has an establishment within the meaning of article 2(e) of the Model Law in that country, and if so, its address.

4 Contents of affidavit in support

(1) There shall be attached to the application an affidavit in support which shall contain or have exhibited to it—

(a) the evidence and statement required under article 15(2) and (3) respectively of the Model Law;

(b) any other evidence which in the opinion of the applicant will assist the court in deciding whether the proceeding the subject of the application is a foreign proceeding within the meaning of article 2(i) of the Model Law and whether the applicant is a foreign representative within the meaning of article 2(j) of the Model Law;

(c) evidence that the debtor has its centre of main interests or an establishment, as the case may be, within the country where the foreign proceeding is taking place; and

(d) any other matters which in the opinion of the applicant will assist the court in deciding whether to make a recognition order.

(2) . . .

(3) The affidavit shall also have exhibited to it the translations required under article 15(4) of the Model Law and a translation in English of any other document exhibited to the affidavit which is in a language other than English.

(4) All translations referred to in sub-paragraph (3) must be certified by the translator as a correct translation.

5 The hearing and powers of court

(1) On hearing a recognition application the court may in addition to its powers under the Model Law to make a recognition order—

(a) dismiss the application;
(b) adjourn the hearing conditionally or unconditionally;
(c) make any other order which the court thinks appropriate.

(2) If the court makes a recognition order, it shall be in Form ML2.

6 Notification of subsequent information

(1) The foreign representative shall set out any subsequent information required to be given to the court under article 18 of the Model Law in a statement which he shall attach to Form ML3 and file with the court.

(2) The statement shall include—

(a) details of the information required to be given under article 18 of the Model Law . . .
(b) . . .

(3) The foreign representative shall send a copy of the Form ML3 and attached statement filed with the court to the following—

(a) the debtor; and
(b) those persons referred to in paragraph 26(3).

NOTES

Para 3: words in square brackets in sub-para (e) substituted by the Companies Act 2006 (Consequential Amendments, Transitional Provisions and Savings) Order 2009, SI 2009/1941, art 2(1), Sch 1, para 264(1), (3)(b), as from 1 October 2009.

Para 4: sub-para (2) revoked by the Insolvency (Amendment) (EU Exit) Regulations 2019, SI 2019/146, reg 2, Schedule, Pt 6, paras 112, 118, 120, as from IP completion day (as defined in the European Union (Withdrawal Agreement) Act 2020, s 39) (for savings, see reg 4 of the 2019 Regulations at **[12.82]**).

Para 6: sub-para (2)(b) and the preceding word revoked by SI 2019/146, reg 2, Schedule, Pt 6, paras 112, 118, 121, as from IP completion day (as defined in the European Union (Withdrawal Agreement) Act 2020, s 39) (for savings, see reg 4 of the 2019 Regulations at **[12.82]**).

PART 3 APPLICATIONS FOR RELIEF UNDER THE MODEL LAW

[10.186]

7 Application for interim relief—affidavit in support

(1) An interim relief application must be supported by an affidavit sworn by the foreign representative stating—

(a) the grounds on which it is proposed that the interim relief applied for should be granted;
(b) details of any proceeding under British insolvency law taking place in relation to the debtor;
(c) whether, to the foreign representative's knowledge, an administrative receiver or receiver or manager of the debtor's property is acting in relation to the debtor;
(d) an estimate of the value of the assets of the debtor in England and Wales in respect of which relief is applied for;
(e) whether, to the best of the knowledge and belief of the foreign representative, the interests of the debtor's creditors (including any secured creditors or parties to hire-purchase agreements) and any other interested parties, including if appropriate the debtor, will be adequately protected;
(f) whether, to the best of the foreign representative's knowledge and belief, the grant of any of the relief applied for would interfere with the administration of a foreign main proceeding; and
(g) all other matters that in the opinion of the foreign representative will assist the court in deciding whether or not it is appropriate to grant the relief applied for.

8 Service of interim relief application not required

Unless the court otherwise directs, it shall not be necessary to serve the interim relief application on, or give notice of it to, any person.

9 The hearing and powers of court

On hearing an interim relief application the court may in addition to its powers under the Model Law to make an order granting interim relief under article 19 of the Model Law—

(a) dismiss the application;
(b) adjourn the hearing conditionally or unconditionally;
(c) make any other order which the court thinks appropriate.

10 Application for relief under article 21 of the Model Law—affidavit in support

An article 21 relief application must be supported by an affidavit sworn by the foreign representative stating—

(a) the grounds on which it is proposed that the relief applied for should be granted;
(b) an estimate of the value of the assets of the debtor in England and Wales in respect of which relief is applied for;
(c) in the case of an application by a foreign representative who is or believes that he is a representative of a foreign non-main proceeding, the reasons why the applicant believes that the relief relates to assets that, under the law of Great Britain, should be administered in the foreign non-main proceeding or concerns information required in that proceeding;

(d) whether, to the best of the knowledge and belief of the foreign representative, the interests of the debtor's creditors (including any secured creditors or parties to hire-purchase agreements) and any other interested parties, including if appropriate the debtor, will be adequately protected; and

(e) all other matters that in the opinion of the foreign representative will assist the court in deciding whether or not it is appropriate to grant the relief applied for.

11 The hearing and powers of court

On hearing an article 21 relief application the court may in addition to its powers under the Model Law to make an order granting relief under article 21 of the Model Law—

(a) dismiss the application;

(b) adjourn the hearing conditionally or unconditionally;

(c) make any other order which the court thinks appropriate.

PART 4 REPLACEMENT OF FOREIGN REPRESENTATIVE

[10.187]

12 Application for confirmation of status of replacement foreign representative

(1) This paragraph applies where following the making of a recognition order the foreign representative dies or for any other reason ceases to be the foreign representative in the foreign proceeding in relation to the debtor.

(2) In this paragraph "the former foreign representative" shall mean the foreign representative referred to in sub-paragraph (1).

(3) If a person has succeeded the former foreign representative or is otherwise holding office as foreign representative in the foreign proceeding in relation to the debtor, that person may apply to the court for an order confirming his status as replacement foreign representative for the purpose of proceedings under these Regulations.

13 Contents of application and affidavit in support

(1) An application under paragraph 12(3) shall in addition to the matters required to be stated by paragraph 19(2) state the following matters—

(a) the name of the replacement foreign representative and his address for service within England and Wales;

(b) details of the circumstances in which the former foreign representative ceased to be foreign representative in the foreign proceeding in relation to the debtor (including the date on which he ceased to be the foreign representative);

(c) details of his own appointment as replacement foreign representative in the foreign proceeding (including the date of that appointment).

(2) The application shall be accompanied by an affidavit in support sworn by the applicant which shall contain or have attached to it—

(a) a certificate from the foreign court affirming—

(i) the cessation of the appointment of the former foreign representative as foreign representative; and

(ii) the appointment of the applicant as the foreign representative in the foreign proceeding; or

(b) in the absence of such a certificate, any other evidence acceptable to the court of the matters referred to in paragraph (a); and

(c) a translation in English of any document exhibited to the affidavit which is in a language other than English.

(3) All translations referred to in paragraph (c) must be certified by the translator as a correct translation.

14 The hearing and powers of court

(1) On hearing an application under paragraph 12(3) the court may—

(a) make an order confirming the status of the replacement foreign representative as foreign representative for the purpose of proceedings under these Regulations;

(b) dismiss the application;

(c) adjourn the hearing conditionally or unconditionally;

(d) make an interim order;

(e) make any other order which the court thinks appropriate, including in particular an order making such provision as the court thinks fit with respect to matters arising in connection with the replacement of the foreign representative.

(2) If the court dismisses the application, it may also if it thinks fit make an order terminating recognition of the foreign proceeding and—

(a) such an order may include such provision as the court thinks fit with respect to matters arising in connection with the termination; and

(b) paragraph 15 shall not apply to such an order.

PART 5 REVIEWS OF COURT ORDERS

[10.188]

15 Reviews of court orders—where court makes order of its own motion

(1) The court shall not of its own motion make a modification or termination order unless the foreign representative and the debtor have either—

(a) had an opportunity of being heard on the question; or

(b) consented in writing to such an order.

(2) Where the foreign representative or the debtor desires to be heard on the question of such an order, the court shall give all relevant parties notice of a venue at which the question will be considered and may give directions as to the issues on which it requires evidence.

(3) For the purposes of sub-paragraph (2), all relevant parties means the foreign representative, the debtor and any other person who appears to the court to have an interest justifying his being given notice of the hearing.

(4) If the court makes a modification or termination order, the order may include such provision as the court thinks fit with respect to matters arising in connection with the modification or termination.

16 Review application—affidavit in support

A review application must be supported by an affidavit sworn by the applicant stating—

(a) the grounds on which it is proposed that the relief applied for should be granted;

(b) whether, to the best of the knowledge and belief of the applicant, the interests of the debtor's creditors (including any secured creditors or parties to hire-purchase agreements) and any other interested parties, including if appropriate the debtor, will be adequately protected; and

(c) all other matters that in the opinion of the applicant will assist the court in deciding whether or not it is appropriate to grant the relief applied for.

17 Hearing of review application and powers of the court

On hearing a review application, the court may in addition to its powers under the Model Law to make a modification or termination order—

(a) dismiss the application;

(b) adjourn the hearing conditionally or unconditionally;

(c) make an interim order;

(c) make any other order which the court thinks appropriate, including an order making such provision as the court thinks fit with respect to matters arising in connection with the modification or termination.

PART 6 COURT PROCEDURE AND PRACTICE WITH REGARD TO PRINCIPAL APPLICATIONS AND ORDERS

[10.189]

18 Preliminary and interpretation

(1) This Part applies to—

(a) any of the following applications made to the court under these Regulations—

(i) a recognition application;

(ii) an article 21 relief application;

(iii) an application under paragraph 12(3) for an order confirming the status of a replacement foreign representative;

(iv) a review application; and

(b) any of the following orders made by the court under these Regulations—

(i) a recognition order;

(ii) an order granting interim relief under article 19 of the Model Law;

(iii) an order granting relief under article 21 of the Model Law;

(iv) an order confirming the status of a replacement foreign representative; and

(v) a modification or termination order.

19 Form and contents of application

(1) Subject to sub-paragraph (4) every application to which this Part applies shall be an ordinary application and shall be in Form ML5.

(2) Each application shall be in writing and shall state—

(a) the names of the parties;

(b) the nature of the relief or order applied for or the directions sought from the court;

(c) the names and addresses of the persons (if any) on whom it is intended to serve the application;

(d) the names and addresses of all those persons on whom these Regulations require the application to be served (so far as known to the applicant); and

(e) the applicant's address for service.

(3) The application must be signed by the applicant if he is acting in person, or, when he is not so acting, by or on behalf of his solicitor.

(4) This paragraph does not apply to a recognition application.

20 Filing of application

(1) The application (and all supporting documents) shall be filed with the court, with a sufficient number of copies for service and use as provided by paragraph 21(2).

(2) Each of the copies filed shall have applied to it the seal of the court and be issued to the applicant; and on each copy there shall be endorsed the date and time of filing.

(3) The court shall fix a venue for the hearing of the application and this also shall be endorsed on each copy of the application issued under sub-paragraph (2).

21 Service of the application

(1) In sub-paragraph (2), references to the application are to a sealed copy of the application issued by the court together with any affidavit in support of it and any documents exhibited to the affidavit.

(2) Unless the court otherwise directs, the application shall be served on the following persons, unless they are the applicant—

(a) on the foreign representative;

(b) on the debtor;

(c) if a British insolvency officeholder is acting in relation to the debtor, on him;

(d) if any person has been appointed an administrative receiver of the debtor or, to the knowledge of the foreign representative, as a receiver or manager of the property of the debtor in England and Wales, on him;

(e) . . .

(f) if to the knowledge of the foreign representative a foreign representative has been appointed in any other foreign proceeding regarding the debtor, on him;

(g) if there is pending in England and Wales a petition for the winding up or bankruptcy of the debtor, on the petitioner;

(h) on any person who to the knowledge of the foreign representative is or may be entitled to appoint an administrator of the debtor under paragraph 14 of Schedule B1 to the 1986 Act (appointment of administrator by holder of qualifying floating charge); . . .

[(i) if the debtor is a debtor who is of interest to the Financial Conduct Authority, on that Authority; and

(j) if the debtor is a debtor who is of interest to the Prudential Regulation Authority, on that Authority].

22 Manner in which service to be effected

(1) Service of the application in accordance with paragraph 21(2) shall be effected by the applicant, or his solicitor, or by a person instructed by him or his solicitor, not less than 5 business days before the date fixed for the hearing.

(2) Service shall be effected by delivering the documents to a person's proper address or in such other manner as the court may direct.

(3) A person's proper address is any which he has previously notified as his address for service within England and Wales; but if he has not notified any such address or if for any reason service at such address is not practicable, service may be effected as follows—

(a) (subject to sub-paragraph (4)) in the case of a company incorporated in England and Wales, by delivery to its registered office;

(b) in the case of any other person, by delivery to his usual or last known address or principal place of business in Great Britain.

(4) If delivery to a company's registered office is not practicable, service may be effected by delivery to its last known principal place of business in Great Britain.

(5) Delivery of documents to any place or address may be made by leaving them there or sending them by first class post in accordance with the provisions of paragraphs 70 and 75(1).

23 Proof of service

(1) Service of the application shall be verified by an affidavit of service in Form ML6, specifying the date on which, and the manner in which, service was effected.

(2) The affidavit of service, with a sealed copy of the application exhibited to it, shall be filed with the court as soon as reasonably practicable after service, and in any event not less than 1 business day before the hearing of the application.

24 In case of urgency

Where the case is one of urgency, the court may (without prejudice to its general power to extend or abridge time limits)—

(a) hear the application immediately, either with or without notice to, or the attendance of, other parties; or

(b) authorise a shorter period of service than that provided for by paragraph 22(1),

and any such application may be heard on terms providing for the filing or service of documents, or the carrying out of other formalities, as the court thinks fit.

25 The hearing

(1) At the hearing of the application, the applicant and any of the following persons (not being the applicant) may appear or be represented—

(a) the foreign representative;

(b) the debtor and, in the case of any debtor other than an individual, any one or more directors or other officers of the debtor, including—

  [(i) where applicable, any person specified in particulars registered under section 1046 of the Companies Act 2006 (overseas companies) as authorised to represent the debtor;]

  (ii) in the case of a debtor which is a partnership, any person who is an officer of the partnership within the meaning of article 2 of the Insolvent Partnerships Order 1994;

(c) if a British insolvency officeholder is acting in relation to the debtor, that person;

(d) if any person has been appointed an administrative receiver of the debtor or as a receiver or manager of the property of the debtor in England and Wales, that person;

(e) . . .

(f) if a foreign representative has been appointed in any other foreign proceeding regarding the debtor, that person;

(g) any person who has presented a petition for the winding up or bankruptcy of the debtor in England and Wales;

(h) any person who is or may be entitled to appoint an administrator of the debtor under paragraph 14 of Schedule B1 to the 1986 Act (appointment of administrator by holder of qualifying floating charge);

[(i) if the debtor is a debtor who is of interest to the Financial Conduct Authority, that Authority;

(ia) if the debtor is a debtor who is of interest to the Prudential Regulation Authority, that Authority; and]

(j) with the permission of the court, any other person who appears to have an interest justifying his appearance.

26 Notification and advertisement of order

(1) If the court makes any of the orders referred to in paragraph 18(1)(b), it shall as soon as reasonably practicable send two sealed copies of the order to the foreign representative.

(2) The foreign representative shall send a sealed copy of the order as soon as reasonably practicable to the debtor.

(3) The foreign representative shall, as soon as reasonably practicable after the date of the order give notice of the making of the order—

(a) if a British insolvency officeholder is acting in relation to the debtor, to him;

(b) if any person has been appointed an administrative receiver of the debtor or, to the knowledge of the foreign representative, as a receiver or manager of the property of the debtor, to him;

(c) . . .

(d) if to his knowledge a foreign representative has been appointed in any other foreign proceeding regarding the debtor, that person;

(e) if there is pending in England and Wales a petition for the winding up or bankruptcy of the debtor, to the petitioner;

(f) to any person who to his knowledge is or may be entitled to appoint an administrator of the debtor under paragraph 14 of Schedule B1 to the 1986 Act (appointment of administrator by holder of qualifying floating charge);

[(g) if the debtor is a debtor who is of interest to the Financial Conduct Authority, to that Authority;

(ga) if the debtor is a debtor who is of interest to the Prudential Regulation Authority, to that Authority;]

(h) to such other persons as the court may direct.

(4) In the case of an order recognising a foreign proceeding in relation to the debtor as a foreign main proceeding, or an order under article 19 or 21 of the Model Law staying execution, distress or other legal process against the debtor's assets, the foreign representative shall also, as soon as reasonably practicable after the date of the order give notice of the making of the order—

(a) to any enforcement officer or other officer who to his knowledge is charged with an execution or other legal process against the debtor or its property; and

(b) to any person who to his knowledge is distraining against the debtor or its property.

(5) In the application of sub-paragraphs (3) and (4) the references to property shall be taken as references to property situated within England and Wales.

(6) Where the debtor is a relevant company, the foreign representative shall send notice of the making of the order to the registrar of companies before the end of the period of 5 business days beginning with the date of the order. The notice to the registrar of companies shall be in Form ML7.

(7) The foreign representative shall advertise the making of the following orders once in the Gazette and once in such newspaper as he thinks most appropriate for ensuring that the making of the order comes to the notice of the debtor's creditors—

(a) a recognition order;

(b) an order confirming the status of a replacement foreign representative; and

(c) a modification or termination order which modifies or terminates recognition of a foreign proceeding,

and the advertisement shall be in Form ML8.

27 Adjournment of hearing; directions

(1) This paragraph applies in any case where the court exercises its power to adjourn the hearing of the application.

(2) The court may at any time give such directions as it thinks fit as to—

(a) service or notice of the application on or to any person, whether in connection with the venue of a resumed hearing or for any other purpose;

(b) the procedure on the application;

(c) the manner in which any evidence is to be adduced at a resumed hearing and in particular as to—

(i) the taking of evidence wholly or in part by affidavit or orally;

(ii) the cross-examination on the hearing in court or in chambers, of any deponents to affidavits;

(d) the matters to be dealt with in evidence.

NOTES

Paras 21(2)(e), 25(1)(e), 26(3)(c) revoked by the Insolvency (Amendment) (EU Exit) Regulations 2019, SI 2019/146, reg 2, Schedule, Pt 6, paras 112, 118, 122–124, as from IP completion day (as defined in the European Union (Withdrawal Agreement) Act 2020, s 39) (for savings, see reg 4 of the 2019 Regulations at **[12.82]**).

The word omitted from sub-para 21(2)(h) was revoked, sub-paras 21(2)(i), (j) were substituted (for the original sub-para 21(2)(i)), sub-paras 25(1)(i), (ia) were substituted (for the original sub-para 25(1)(i)), and sub-paras 26(3)(g), (ga) were substituted (for the original sub-para 26(3)(g)), by the Financial Services Act 2012 (Consequential Amendments and Transitional Provisions) Order 2013, SI 2013/472, art 3, Sch 2, para 116(a)(ii), (iii), as from 1 April 2013.

Sub-para 25(1)(b)(i) was substituted by the Companies Act 2006 (Consequential Amendments, Transitional Provisions and Savings) Order 2009, SI 2009/1941, art 2(1), Sch 1, para 264(1), (3)(c), as from 1 October 2009.

PART 7 APPLICATIONS TO THE CHIEF LAND REGISTRAR

[10.190]

28 Applications to Chief Land Registrar following court orders

(1) Where the court makes any order in proceedings under these Regulations which is capable of giving rise to an application or applications under the Land Registration Act 2002, the foreign representative shall, as soon as reasonably practicable after the making of the order or at the appropriate time, make the appropriate application or applications to the Chief Land Registrar.

(2) In sub-paragraph (1) an appropriate application is—

(a) in any case where—

(i) a recognition order in respect of a foreign main proceeding or an order suspending the right to transfer, encumber or otherwise dispose of any assets of the debtor is made, and

(ii) the debtor is the registered proprietor of a registered estate or registered charge and holds it for his sole benefit,

an application under section 43 of the Land Registration Act 2002 for a restriction of the kind referred to in sub-paragraph (3) to be entered in the relevant registered title; and

(b) in any other case, an application under the Land Registration Act 2002 for such an entry in the register as shall be necessary to reflect the effect of the court order under these Regulations.

Part 10 Miscellaneous other SIs

(3) The restriction referred to in sub-paragraph (2)(a) is a restriction to the effect that no disposition of the registered estate or registered charge (as appropriate) by the registered proprietor of that estate or charge is to be completed by registration within the meaning of section 27 of the Land Registration Act 2002 except under a further order of the court.

PART 8 MISFEASANCE

[10.191]

29 Misfeasance by foreign representative

(1) The court may examine the conduct of a person who—
- (a) is or purports to be the foreign representative in relation to a debtor; or
- (b) has been or has purported to be the foreign representative in relation to a debtor.

(2) An examination under this paragraph may be held only on the application of—
- (a) a British insolvency officeholder acting in relation to the debtor;
- (b) a creditor of the debtor; or
- (c) with the permission of the court, any other person who appears to have an interest justifying an application.

(3) An application under sub-paragraph (2) must allege that the foreign representative—
- (a) has misapplied or retained money or other property of the debtor;
- (b) has become accountable for money or other property of the debtor;
- (c) has breached a fiduciary or other duty in relation to the debtor; or
- (d) has been guilty of misfeasance.

(4) On an examination under this paragraph into a person's conduct the court may order him—
- (a) to repay, restore or account for money or property;
- (b) to pay interest;
- (c) to contribute a sum to the debtor's property by way of compensation for breach of duty or misfeasance.

(4) In sub-paragraph (3) "foreign representative" includes a person who purports or has purported to be a foreign representative in relation to a debtor.

PART 9 GENERAL PROVISION AS TO COURT PROCEDURE AND PRACTICE

[10.192]

30 Principal court rules and practice to apply with modifications

(1) The CPR and the practice and procedure of the High Court (including any practice direction) shall apply to proceedings under these Regulations in the High Court with such modifications as may be necessary for the purpose of giving effect to the provisions of these Regulations and in the case of any conflict between any provision of the CPR and the provisions of these Regulations, the latter shall prevail.

(2) All proceedings under these Regulations shall be allocated to the multi-track for which CPR Part 29 (the multi-track) makes provision, and accordingly those provisions of the CPR which provide for allocation questionnaires and track allocation shall not apply.

31 Applications other than the principal applications—preliminary

Paragraphs 32 to 37 of this Part apply to any application made to the court under these Regulations, except any of the applications referred to in paragraph 18(1)(a).

32 Form and contents of application

(1) Every application shall be in the form appropriate to the application concerned. Forms ML4 and ML5 shall be used for an originating application and an ordinary application respectively under these Regulations.

(2) Each application shall be in writing and shall state—
- (a) the names of the parties;
- (b) the nature of the relief or order applied for or the directions sought from the court;
- (c) the names and addresses of the persons (if any) on whom it is intended to serve the application or that no person is intended to be served;
- (d) where these Regulations require that notice of the application is to be given to specified persons, the names and addresses of all those persons (so far as known to the applicant); and
- (e) the applicant's address for service.

(3) An originating application shall set out the grounds on which the applicant claims to be entitled to the relief or order sought.

(4) The application must be signed by the applicant if he is acting in person or, when he is not so acting, by or on behalf of his solicitor.

33 Filing and service of application

(1) The application shall be filed in court, accompanied by one copy and a number of additional copies equal to the number of persons who are to be served with the application.

(2) Subject as follows in this paragraph and in paragraph 34, or unless the court otherwise orders, upon the presentation of the documents mentioned in sub-paragraph (1), the court shall fix a venue for the application to be heard.

(3) Unless the court otherwise directs, the applicant shall serve a sealed copy of the application, endorsed with the venue of the hearing, on the respondent named in the application (or on each respondent if more than one).

(4) The court may give any of the following directions—
- (a) that the application be served upon persons other than those specified by the relevant provision of these Regulations;
- (b) that the giving of notice to any person may be dispensed with;
- (c) that notice be given in some way other than that specified in sub-paragraph (3).

(5) Subject to sub-paragraph (6), the application must be served at least 10 business days before the date fixed for the hearing.

(6) Where the case is one of urgency, the court may (without prejudice to its general power to extend or abridge time limits)—

(a) hear the application immediately, either with or without notice to, or the attendance of, other parties; or

(b) authorise a shorter period of service than that provided for by sub-paragraph (5);

and any such application may be heard on terms providing for the filing or service of documents, or the carrying out of other formalities, as the court thinks fit.

34 Other hearings *ex parte*

(1) Where the relevant provisions of these Regulations do not require service of the application on, or notice of it to be given to, any person, the court may hear the application *ex parte*.

(2) Where the application is properly made *ex parte*, the court may hear it forthwith, without fixing a venue as required by paragraph 33(2).

(3) Alternatively, the court may fix a venue for the application to be heard, in which case paragraph 33 applies (so far as relevant).

35 Use of affidavit evidence

(1) In any proceedings evidence may be given by affidavit unless the court otherwise directs; but the court may, on the application of any party, order the attendance for cross-examination of the person making the affidavit.

(2) Where, after such an order has been made, the person in question does not attend, his affidavit shall not be used in evidence without the permission of the court.

36 Filing and service of affidavits

(1) Unless the court otherwise allows—

(a) if the applicant intends to rely at the first hearing on affidavit evidence, he shall file the affidavit or affidavits (if more than one) in court and serve a copy or copies on the respondent, not less than 10 business days before the date fixed for the hearing; and

(b) where a respondent to an application intends to oppose it and to rely for that purpose on affidavit evidence, he shall file the affidavit or affidavits (if more than one) in court and serve a copy or copies on the applicant, not less than 5 business days before the date fixed for the hearing.

(2) Any affidavit may be sworn by the applicant or by the respondent or by some other person possessing direct knowledge of the subject matter of the application.

37 Adjournment of hearings; directions

The court may adjourn the hearing of an application on such terms (if any) as it thinks fit and in the case of such an adjournment paragraph 27(2) shall apply.

38 Transfer of proceedings within the High Court

(1) The High Court may, having regard to the criteria in CPR rule 30.3(2), order proceedings in the Royal Courts of Justice or a district registry, or any part of such proceedings (such as an application made in the proceedings), to be transferred—

(a) from the Royal Courts of Justice to a district registry; or

(b) from a district registry to the Royal Courts of Justice or to another district registry.

(2) The High Court may order proceedings before a district registry for the detailed assessment of costs to be transferred to another district registry if it is satisfied that the proceedings could be more conveniently or fairly taken in that other district registry.

(3) An application for an order under sub-paragraph (1) or (2) must, if the claim is proceeding in a district registry, be made to that registry.

(4) A transfer of proceedings under this paragraph may be ordered—

(a) by the court of its own motion; or

(b) on the application of a person appearing to the court to have an interest in the proceedings.

(5) Where the court orders proceedings to be transferred, the court from which they are to be transferred must give notice of the transfer to all the parties.

(6) An order made before the transfer of the proceedings shall not be affected by the order to transfer.

39 Transfer of proceedings—actions to avoid acts detrimental to creditors

(1) If—

(a) in accordance with article 23(6) of the Model Law, the court grants a foreign representative permission to make an application in accordance with paragraph 1 of that article; and

(b) the relevant proceedings under British insolvency law taking place regarding the debtor are taking place in the county court,

the court may also order those proceedings to be transferred to the High Court.

(2) Where the court makes an order transferring proceedings under sub-paragraph (1)—

(a) it shall send sealed copies of the order to the county court from which the proceedings are to be transferred, and to the official receivers attached to that court and the High Court respectively; and

(b) the county court shall send the file of the proceedings to the High Court.

(3) Following compliance with this paragraph, if the official receiver attached to the court to which the proceedings are transferred is not already, by virtue of directions given by the Secretary of State under section 399(6)(a) of the 1986 Act, the official receiver in relation to those proceedings, he becomes, in relation to those proceedings, the official receiver in place of the official receiver attached to the other court concerned.

40 Shorthand writers

(1) The judge may in writing nominate one or more persons to be official shorthand writers to the court.

(2) The court may, at any time in the course of proceedings under these Regulations, appoint a shorthand writer to take down the evidence of a person examined in pursuance of a court order under article 19 or 21 of the Model Law.

(3) The remuneration of a shorthand writer appointed in proceedings under these Regulations shall be paid by the party at whose instance the appointment was made or otherwise as the court may direct.

(4) Any question arising as to the rates of remuneration payable under this paragraph shall be determined by the court in its discretion.

41 Enforcement procedures

In any proceedings under these Regulations, orders of the court may be enforced in the same manner as a judgment to the same effect.

42 Title of proceedings

(1) Every proceeding under these Regulations shall, with any necessary additions, be intituled "IN THE MATTER OF . . . (naming the debtor to which the proceedings relate) AND IN THE MATTER OF THE CROSS-BORDER INSOLVENCY REGULATIONS 2006".

(2) Sub-paragraph (1) shall not apply in respect of any form prescribed under these Regulations.

43 Court records

The court shall keep records of all proceedings under these Regulations, and shall cause to be entered in the records the taking of any step in the proceedings, and such decisions of the court in relation thereto, as the court thinks fit.

44 Inspection of records

(1) Subject as follows, the court's records of proceedings under these Regulations shall be open to inspection by any person.

(2) If in the case of a person applying to inspect the records the Registrar is not satisfied as to the propriety of the purpose for which inspection is required, he may refuse to allow it. That person may then apply forthwith and *ex parte* to the judge, who may refuse the inspection or allow it on such terms as he thinks fit.

(3) The decision of the judge under sub-paragraph (2) is final.

45 File of court proceedings

(1) In respect of all proceedings under these Regulations, the court shall open and maintain a file for each case; and (subject to directions of the Registrar) all documents relating to such proceedings shall be placed on the relevant file.

(2) No proceedings under these Regulations shall be filed in the Central Office of the High Court.

46 Right to inspect the file

(1) In the case of any proceedings under these Regulations, the following have the right, at all reasonable times, to inspect the court's file of the proceedings—

(a) the Secretary of State;

(b) the person who is the foreign representative in relation to the proceedings;

(c) if a foreign representative has been appointed in any other foreign proceeding regarding the debtor to which the proceedings under these Regulations relate, that person;

(d) if a British insolvency officeholder is acting in relation to the debtor to which the proceedings under these Regulations relate, that person;

(e) any person stating himself in writing to be a creditor of the debtor to which the proceedings under these Regulations relate;

(f) . . .

(g) the debtor to which the proceedings under these Regulations relate, or, if that debtor is a company, corporation or partnership, every person who is, or at any time has been—

 (i) a director or officer of the debtor;

 (ii) a member of the debtor; or

 [(iii) where applicable, any person specified in particulars registered under section 1046 of the Companies Act 2006 (overseas companies) as authorised to represent the debtor;]

(2) The right of inspection conferred as above on any person may be exercised on his behalf by a person properly authorised by him.

(3) Any person may, by leave of the court, inspect the file.

(4) The right of inspection conferred by this paragraph is not exercisable in the case of documents, or parts of documents, as to which the court directs (either generally or specially) that they are not to be made open to inspection without the court's permission.

An application for a direction of the court under this sub-paragraph may be made by the foreign representative or by any party appearing to the court to have an interest.

(5) If, for the purpose of powers conferred by the 1986 Act or the Rules, the Secretary of State or the official receiver wishes to inspect the file of any proceedings under these Regulations, and requests the transmission of the file, the court shall comply with such request (unless the file is for the time being in use for the court's purposes).

(6) Paragraph 44(2) and (3) apply in respect of the court's file of any proceedings under these Regulations as they apply in respect of court records.

(7) Where these Regulations confer a right for any person to inspect documents on the court's file of proceedings, the right includes that of taking copies of those documents on payment of the fee chargeable under any order made under section 92 of the Courts Act 2003.

47 Copies of court orders

(1) In any proceedings under these Regulations, any person who under paragraph 46 has a right to inspect documents on the court file also has the right to require the foreign representative in relation to those proceedings to furnish him with a copy of any court order in the proceedings.

(2) Sub-paragraph (1) does not apply if a copy of the court order has been served on that person or notice of the making of the order has been given to that person under other provisions of these Regulations.

48 Filing of Gazette notices and advertisements

(1) In any court in which proceedings under these Regulations are pending, an officer of the court shall file a copy of every issue of the Gazette which contains an advertisement relating to those proceedings.

(2) Where there appears in a newspaper an advertisement relating to proceedings under these Regulations pending in any court, the person inserting the advertisement shall file a copy of it in that court.

The copy of the advertisement shall be accompanied by, or have endorsed on it, such particulars as are necessary to identify the proceedings and the date of the advertisement's appearance.

(3) An officer of any court in which proceedings under these Regulations are pending shall from time to time file a memorandum giving the dates of, and other particulars relating to, any notice published in the Gazette, and any newspaper advertisements, which relate to proceedings so pending.

The officer's memorandum is prima facie evidence that any notice or advertisement mentioned in it was duly inserted in the issue of the newspaper or the Gazette which is specified in the memorandum.

49 Persons incapable of managing their affairs—introductory

(1) Paragraphs 50 to 52 apply where in proceedings under these Regulations it appears to the court that a person affected by the proceedings is one who is incapable of managing and administering his property and affairs either—
- (a) by reason of mental disorder within the meaning of the Mental Health Act 1983; or
- (b) due to physical affliction or disability.

(2) The person concerned is referred to as "the incapacitated person".

50 Appointment of another person to act

(1) The court may appoint such person as it thinks fit to appear for, represent or act for the incapacitated person.

(2) The appointment may be made either generally or for the purpose of any particular application or proceeding, or for the exercise of particular rights or powers which the incapacitated person might have exercised but for his incapacity.

(3) The court may make the appointment either of its own motion or on application by—
- (a) a person who has been appointed by a court in the United Kingdom or elsewhere to manage the affairs of, or to represent, the incapacitated person; or
- (b) any relative or friend of the incapacitated person who appears to the court to be a proper person to make the application; or
- (c) in any case where the incapacitated person is the debtor, the foreign representative.

(4) Application under sub-paragraph (3) may be made *ex parte*; but the court may require such notice of the application as it thinks necessary to be given to the person alleged to be incapacitated, or any other person, and may adjourn the hearing of the application to enable the notice to be given.

51 Affidavit in support of application

An application under paragraph 50(3) shall be supported by an affidavit of a registered medical practitioner as to the mental or physical condition of the incapacitated person.

52 Service of notices following appointment

Any notice served on, or sent to, a person appointed under paragraph 50 has the same effect as if it had been served on, or given to, the incapacitated person.

53 Rights of audience

Rights of audience in proceedings under these Regulations are the same as obtain in proceedings under British insolvency law.

54 Right of attendance

(1) Subject as follows, in proceedings under these Regulations, any person stating himself in writing, in records kept by the court for that purpose, to be a creditor of the debtor to which the proceedings relate, is entitled at his own cost, to attend in court or in chambers at any stage of the proceedings.

(2) Attendance may be by the person himself, or his solicitor.

(3) A person so entitled may request the court in writing to give him notice of any step in the proceedings; and, subject to his paying the costs involved and keeping the court informed as to his address, the court shall comply with the request.

(4) If the court is satisfied that the exercise by a person of his rights under this paragraph has given rise to costs for the estate of the debtor which would not otherwise have been incurred and ought not, in the circumstances, to fall on that estate, it may direct that the costs be paid by the person concerned, to an amount specified.

The rights of that person under this paragraph shall be in abeyance so long as those costs are not paid.

(5) The court may appoint one or more persons to represent the creditors of the debtor to have the rights conferred by this paragraph, instead of the rights being exercised by any or all of them individually.

If two or more persons are appointed under this paragraph to represent the same interest, they must (if at all) instruct the same solicitor.

55 Right of attendance for member State liquidator

For the purposes of paragraph 54(1), a member State liquidator appointed in relation to a debtor subject to proceedings under these Regulations shall be deemed to be a creditor.

56 British insolvency officeholder's solicitor

Where in any proceedings the attendance of the British insolvency officeholder's solicitor is required, whether in court or in chambers, the British insolvency officeholder himself need not attend, unless directed by the court.

57 Formal defects

No proceedings under these Regulations shall be invalidated by any formal defect or by any irregularity, unless the court before which objection is made considers that substantial injustice has been caused by the defect or irregularity, and that the injustice cannot be remedied by any order of the court.

58 Restriction on concurrent proceedings and remedies

Where in proceedings under these Regulations the court makes an order staying any action, execution or other legal process against the property of a debtor, service of the order may be effected by sending a sealed copy of the order to whatever is the address for service of the claimant or other party having the carriage of the proceedings to be stayed.

59 Affidavits

(1) Where in proceedings under these Regulations, an affidavit is made by any British insolvency officeholder acting in relation to the debtor, he shall state the capacity in which he makes it, the position which he holds and the address at which he works.

(2) Any officer of the court duly authorised in that behalf, may take affidavits and declarations.

(3) Subject to sub-paragraph (4), where these Regulations provide for the use of an affidavit, a witness statement verified by a statement of truth may be used as an alternative.

(4) Sub-paragraph (3) does not apply to paragraphs 4 (affidavit in support of recognition application), 7 (affidavit in support of interim relief application), 10 (affidavit in support of article 21 relief application), 13 (affidavit in support of application regarding status of replacement foreign representative) and 16 (affidavit in support of review application).

60 Security in court

(1) Where security has to be given to the court (otherwise than in relation to costs), it may be given by guarantee, bond or the payment of money into court.

(2) A person proposing to give a bond as security shall give notice to the party in whose favour the security is required, and to the court, naming those who are to be sureties to the bond.

(3) The court shall forthwith give notice to the parties concerned of a venue for the execution of the bond and the making of any objection to the sureties.

(4) The sureties shall make an affidavit of their sufficiency (unless dispensed with by the party in whose favour the security is required) and shall, if required by the court, attend the court to be cross-examined.

61 Further information and disclosure

(1) Any party to proceedings under these Regulations may apply to the court for an order—

- (a) that any other party—
  - (i) clarify any matter which is in dispute in the proceedings; or
  - (ii) give additional information in relation to any such matter,

  in accordance with CPR Part 18 (further information); or
- (b) to obtain disclosure from any other party in accordance with CPR Part 31 (disclosure and inspection of documents).

(2) An application under this paragraph may be made without notice being served on any other party.

62 Office copies of documents

(1) Any person who has under these Regulations the right to inspect the court file of proceedings may require the court to provide him with an office copy of any document from the file.

(2) A person's right under this paragraph may be exercised on his behalf by his solicitor.

(3) An office copy provided by the court under this paragraph shall be in such form as the Registrar thinks appropriate, and shall bear the court's seal.

63 "The court"

(1) Anything to be done in proceedings under these Regulations by, to or before the court may be done by, to or before a judge of the High Court or a Registrar.

(2) Where these Regulations require or permit the court to perform an act of a formal or administrative character, that act may be performed by a court officer.

NOTES

Para 46: sub-para (1)(f) revoked by the Insolvency (Amendment) (EU Exit) Regulations 2019, SI 2019/146, reg 2, Schedule, Pt 6, paras 112, 118, 125, as from IP completion day (as defined in the European Union (Withdrawal Agreement) Act 2020, s 39) (for savings, see reg 4 of the 2019 Regulations at **[12.82]**). Sub-para (1)(g)(iii) substituted by the Companies Act 2006 (Consequential Amendments, Transitional Provisions and Savings) Order 2009, SI 2009/1941, art 2(1), Sch 1, para 264(1), (3)(d), as from 1 October 2009.

PART 10 COSTS AND DETAILED ASSESSMENT

[10.193]

64 Requirement to assess costs by the detailed procedure

In any proceedings before the court, the court may order costs to be decided by detailed assessment.

65 Costs of officers charged with execution of writs or other process

(1) Where by virtue of article 20 of the Model Law or a court order under article 19 or 21 of the Model Law an enforcement officer, or other officer, charged with execution of the writ or other process—

(a) is required to deliver up goods or money; or

(b) has deducted costs from the proceeds of an execution or money paid to him,

the foreign representative may require in writing that the amount of the enforcement officer's or other officer's bill of costs be decided by detailed assessment.

(2) Where such a requirement is made, if the enforcement officer or other officer does not commence detailed assessment proceedings within 3 months of the requirement under sub-paragraph (1), or within such further time as the court, on application, may permit, any claim by the enforcement officer or other officer in respect of his costs is forfeited by such failure to commence proceedings.

(3) Where, in the case of a deduction of costs by the enforcement officer or other officer, any amount deducted is disallowed at the conclusion of the detailed assessment proceedings, the enforcement officer or other officer shall forthwith pay a sum equal to that disallowed to the foreign representative for the benefit of the debtor.

66 Final costs certificate

(1) A final costs certificate of the costs officer is final and conclusive as to all matters which have not been objected to in the manner provided for under the rules of the court.

(2) Where it is proved to the satisfaction of a costs officer that a final costs certificate has been lost or destroyed, he may issue a duplicate.

PART 11 APPEALS IN PROCEEDINGS UNDER THESE REGULATIONS

[10.194]

67 Appeals from court orders

(1) An appeal from a decision of a Registrar of the High Court in proceedings under these Regulations lies to a single judge of the High Court; and an appeal from a decision of that judge on such an appeal lies, with the permission of the Court of Appeal, to the Court of Appeal.

(2) An appeal from a decision of a judge of the High Court in proceedings under these Regulations which is not a decision on an appeal made to him under sub-paragraph (1) lies, with the permission of that judge or the Court of Appeal, to the Court of Appeal.

68 Procedure on appeals

(1) Subject as follows, CPR Part 52 (appeals to the Court of Appeal) and its practice direction apply to appeals in proceedings under these Regulations.

(2) The provisions of Part 4 of the practice direction on Insolvency Proceedings supporting CPR Part 49 relating to first appeals (as defined in that Part) apply in relation to any appeal to a single judge of the High Court under paragraph 67, with any necessary modifications.

(3) In proceedings under these Regulations, the procedure under CPR Part 52 is by ordinary application and not by appeal notice.

PART 12 GENERAL

[10.195]

69 Notices

(1) All notices required or authorised by or under these Regulations to be given must be in writing, unless it is otherwise provided, or the court allows the notice to be given in some other way.

(2) Where in proceedings under these Regulations a notice is required to be sent or given by any person, the sending or giving of it may be proved by means of a certificate by that person that he posted the notice, or instructed another person (naming him) to do so.

(3) A certificate under this paragraph may be endorsed on a copy or specimen of the notice to which it relates.

70 "Give notice" etc

(1) A reference in these Regulations to giving notice, or to delivering, sending or serving any document, means that the notice or document may be sent by post.

(2) Subject to paragraph 75, any form of post may be used.

(3) Personal service of a document is permissible in all cases.

(4) Notice of the venue fixed for an application may be given by service of the sealed copy of the application under paragraph 33(3).

71 Notice, etc to solicitors

Where in proceedings under these Regulations a notice or other document is required or authorised to be given to a person, it may, if he has indicated that his solicitor is authorised to accept service on his behalf, be given instead to the solicitor.

72 Notice to joint British insolvency officeholders

Where two or more persons are acting jointly as the British insolvency officeholder in proceedings under British insolvency law, delivery of a document to one of them is to be treated as delivery to them all.

73 Forms for use in proceedings under these Regulations

(1) The forms contained in Schedule 5 to these Regulations shall be used in, and in connection with, proceedings under these Regulations.

(2) The forms shall be used with such variations, if any, as the circumstances may require.

Part 10 Miscellaneous other SIs

74 Time limits

(1) The provisions of CPR Rule 2.8 (time) apply, as regards computation of time, to anything required or authorised to be done by these Regulations.

(2) The provisions of CPR rule 3.1(2)(a) (the court's general powers of management) apply so as to enable the court to extend or shorten the time for compliance with anything required or authorised to be done by these Regulations.

75 Service by post

(1) For a document to be properly served by post, it must be contained in an envelope addressed to the person on whom service is to be effected, and pre-paid for first class post.

(2) A document to be served by post may be sent to the last known address of the person to be served.

(3) Where first class post is used, the document is treated as served on the second business day after the date of posting, unless the contrary is shown.

(4) The date of posting is presumed, unless the contrary is shown, to be the date shown in the post-mark on the envelope in which the document is contained.

76 General provisions as to service and notice

Subject to paragraphs 22, 75 and 77, CPR Part 6 (service of documents) applies as regards any matter relating to the service of documents and the giving of notice in proceedings under these Regulations.

77 Service outside the jurisdiction

(1) Sections III and IV of CPR Part 6 (service out of the jurisdiction and service of process of foreign court) do not apply in proceedings under these Regulations.

(2) Where for the purposes of proceedings under these Regulations any process or order of the court, or other document, is required to be served on a person who is not in England and Wales, the court may order service to be effected within such time, on such person, at such place and in such manner as it thinks fit, and may also require such proof of service as it thinks fit.

(3) An application under this paragraph shall be supported by an affidavit stating—

(a) the grounds on which the application is made; and

(b) in what place or country the person to be served is, or probably may be found.

78 False claim of status as creditor

(1) Rule 12.18 (false claim of status as creditor, etc) shall apply with any necessary modifications in any case where a person falsely claims the status of a creditor of a debtor, with the intention of obtaining a sight of documents whether on the court's file or in the hands of the foreign representative or other person, which he has not under these Regulations any right to inspect.

(2) Rule 21.21 and Schedule 5 of the Rules shall apply to an offence under Rule 12.18 as applied by sub-paragraph (1) as they apply to an offence under Rule 12.18.

79 The Gazette

(1) A copy of the Gazette containing any notice required by these Regulations to be gazetted is evidence of any fact stated in the notice.

(2) In the case of an order of the court notice of which is required by these Regulations to be gazetted, a copy of the Gazette containing the notice may in any proceedings be produced as conclusive evidence that the order was made on the date specified in the notice.

SCHEDULE 3
PROCEDURAL MATTERS IN SCOTLAND

Regulation 5

PART 1 INTERPRETATION

[10.196]

1 Interpretation

(1) In this Schedule—

"the 1986 Act" means the Insolvency Act 1986;

"article 21 remedy application" means an application to the court by a foreign representative under article 21(1) or (2) of the Model Law for remedy;

"business day" means any day other than a Saturday, a Sunday, Christmas Day, Good Friday or a day which is a bank holiday in Scotland under or by virtue of the Banking and Financial Dealings Act 1971;

"the Gazette" means the Edinburgh Gazette;

. . .

. . .

"the Model Law" means the UNCITRAL Model Law as set out in Schedule 1 to these Regulations;

"modification or termination order" means an order by the court pursuant to its powers under the Model Law modifying or terminating recognition of a foreign proceeding, the sist, restraint or suspension referred to in article 20(1) or any part of it or any remedy granted under article 19 or 21 of the Model Law;

"recognition application" means an application to the court by a foreign representative in accordance with article 15 of the Model Law for an order recognising the foreign proceeding in which he has been appointed;

"recognition order" means an order by the court recognising a proceeding the subject of a recognition application as a foreign main proceeding or foreign non-main proceeding, as appropriate;

["relevant company" means a company that is—

(a) registered under the Companies Act 2006,

(b) subject to a requirement imposed by regulations under section 1043 of that Act (unregistered UK companies) to deliver any documents to the registrar of companies, or

(c) subject to a requirement imposed by regulations under section 1046 of that Act (overseas companies) to deliver any documents to the registrar of companies;]

"review application" means an application to the court for a modification or termination order.

(2) Expressions defined in the Model Law have the same meaning when used in this Schedule.

[(3) References in this Schedule to a debtor who is of interest to the Financial Conduct Authority are references to a debtor who—

(a) is, or has been, an authorised person within the meaning of the Financial Services and Markets Act 2000;

(b) is, or has been, an appointed representative within the meaning of section 39 of the Financial Services and Markets Act 2000; or

(c) is carrying on, or has carried on, a regulated activity in contravention of the general prohibition.

(3A) References in this Schedule to a debtor who is of interest to the Prudential Regulation Authority are references to a debtor who—

(a) is, or has been, a PRA-authorised person within the meaning of the Financial Services and Markets Act 2000; or

(b) is carrying on, or has carried on, a PRA-regulated activity within the meaning of the Financial Services and Markets Act 2000 in contravention of the general prohibition.]

(4) In [sub-paragraphs (3) and (3A)] "the general prohibition" has the meaning given by section 19 of the Financial Services and Markets Act 2000 and the reference to a "regulated activity" must be construed in accordance with—

(a) section 22 of that Act (classes of regulated activity and categories of investment);

(b) any relevant order under that section; and

(c) Schedule 2 to that Act (regulated activities).

(5) References in this Schedule to a numbered form are to the form that bears that number in Schedule 5.

NOTES

Sub-para (1) is amended as follows:

Definitions "main proceedings" and "member state liquidator" (omitted) revoked by the Insolvency (Amendment) (EU Exit) Regulations 2019, SI 2019/146, reg 2, Schedule, Pt 6, paras 112, 126, 127, as from IP completion day (as defined in the European Union (Withdrawal Agreement) Act 2020, s 39) (for savings, see reg 4 of the 2019 Regulations at **[12.82]**).

Definition "relevant company" substituted by the Companies Act 2006 (Consequential Amendments, Transitional Provisions and Savings) Order 2009, SI 2009/1941, art 2(1), Sch 1, para 264(1), (4)(a), as from 1 October 2009.

Sub-paras (3), (3A) were substituted (for the original sub-para (3)), and the words in square brackets in sub-para (4) were substituted, by the Financial Services Act 2012 (Consequential Amendments and Transitional Provisions) Order 2013, SI 2013/472, art 3, Sch 2, para 116(b)(i), as from 1 April 2013.

PART 2 THE FOREIGN REPRESENTATIVE

[10.197]

2 Application for confirmation of status of replacement foreign representative

(1) This paragraph applies where following the making of a recognition order the foreign representative dies or for any other reason ceases to be the foreign representative in the foreign proceedings in relation to the debtor.

(2) In this paragraph "the former foreign representative" means the foreign representative referred to in sub-paragraph (1).

(3) If a person has succeeded the former foreign representative or is otherwise holding office as foreign representative in the foreign proceeding in relation to the debtor, that person may apply to the court for an order confirming his status as replacement foreign representative for the purpose of proceedings under these Regulations.

(4) If the court dismisses an application under sub-paragraph (3) then it may also, if it thinks fit, make an order terminating recognition of the foreign proceeding and—

(a) such an order may include such provision as the court thinks fit with respect to matters arising in connection with the termination; and

(b) paragraph 5 shall not apply to such an order.

3 Misfeasance by a foreign representative

(1) The court may examine the conduct of a person who—

(a) is or purports to be the foreign representative in relation to a debtor, or

(b) has been or has purported to be the foreign representative in relation to a debtor.

(2) An examination under this paragraph may be held only on the application of—

(a) a British insolvency officeholder acting in relation to the debtor,

(b) a creditor of the debtor, or

(c) with the permission of the court, any other person who appears to have an interest justifying an application.

(3) An application under sub-paragraph (2) must allege that the foreign representative—

(a) has misapplied or retained money or other property of the debtor,

(b) has become accountable for money or other property of the debtor,

(c) has breached a fiduciary duty or other duty in relation to the debtor, or

(d) has been guilty of misfeasance.

(4) On an examination under this paragraph into a person's conduct the court may order him—

(a) to repay, restore or account for money or property;

(b) to pay interest;

(c) to contribute a sum to the debtor's property by way of compensation for breach of duty or misfeasance.

(5) In sub-paragraph (3), "foreign representative" includes a person who purports or has purported to be a foreign representative in relation to a debtor.

PART 3 COURT PROCEDURE AND PRACTICE

[10.198]

4 Preliminary and interpretation

(1) This Part applies to—

(a) any of the following applications made to the court under these Regulations—

(i) a recognition application;

(ii) an article 21 remedy application;

(iii) an application under paragraph 2(3) for an order confirming the status of a replacement foreign representative;

(iv) a review application; and

(b) any of the following orders made by the court under these Regulations—

(i) a recognition order;

(ii) an order granting interim remedy under article 19 of the Model Law;

(iii) an order granting remedy under article 21 of the Model Law;

(iv) an order confirming the status of a replacement foreign representative; or

(v) a modification or termination order.

5 Reviews of court orders—where court makes order of its own motion

(1) The court shall not of its own motion make a modification or termination order unless the foreign representative and the debtor have either—

(a) had an opportunity of being heard on the question, or

(b) consented in writing to such an order.

(2) If the court makes a modification or termination order, the order may include such provision as the court thinks fit with respect to matters arising in connection with the modification or termination.

6 The hearing

(1) At the hearing of the application, the applicant and any of the following persons (not being the applicant) may appear or be represented—

(a) the foreign representative;

(b) the debtor and, in the case of any debtor other than an individual, any one or more directors or other officers of the debtor, including—

[(i) where applicable, any person specified in particulars registered under section 1046 of the Companies Act 2006 (overseas companies) as authorised to represent the debtor;]

(ii) in the case of a debtor which is a partnership, any person who is a member of the partnership;

(c) if a British insolvency officeholder is acting in relation to the debtor, that person;

(d) if any person has been appointed an administrative receiver of the debtor or as a receiver or manager of the property of the debtor, that person;

(e) . . .

(f) if a foreign representative has been appointed in any other foreign proceeding regarding the debtor, that person;

(g) any person who has presented a petition for the winding up or sequestration of the debtor in Scotland;

(h) any person who is or may be entitled to appoint an administrator of the debtor under paragraph 14 of Schedule B1 to the 1986 Act (appointment of administrator by holder of qualifying floating charge);

[(i) if the debtor is a debtor who is of interest to the Financial Conduct Authority, that Authority;

(ia) if the debtor is a debtor who is of interest to the Prudential Regulation Authority, that Authority; and]

(j) with the permission of the court, any other person who appears to have an interest justifying his appearance.

7 Notification and advertisement of order

(1) This paragraph applies where the court makes any of the orders referred to in paragraph 4(1)(b).

(2) The foreign representative shall send a certified copy of the interlocutor as soon as reasonably practicable to the debtor.

(3) The foreign representative shall, as soon as reasonably practicable after the date of the order, give notice of the making of the order—

(a) if a British insolvency officeholder is acting in relation to the debtor, to him;

(b) if any person has been appointed an administrative receiver of the debtor or, to the knowledge of the foreign representative, as a receiver or manager of the property of the debtor, to him;

(c) . . .

(d) if to his knowledge a foreign representative has been appointed in any other foreign proceeding regarding the debtor, that person;

(e) if there is pending in Scotland a petition for the winding up or sequestration of the debtor, to the petitioner;

(f) to any person who to his knowledge is or may be entitled to appoint an administrator of the debtor under paragraph 14 of Schedule B1 to the 1986 Act (appointment of administrator by holder of qualifying floating charge);

[(g) if the debtor is a debtor who is of interest to the Financial Conduct Authority, to that Authority;

(ga) if the debtor is a debtor who is of interest to the Prudential Regulation Authority, to that Authority; and]

(h) to such persons as the court may direct.

(4) Where the debtor is a relevant company, the foreign representative shall send notice of the making of the order to the registrar of companies before the end of the period of 5 business days beginning with the date of the order. The notice to the registrar of companies shall be in Form ML7.

(5) The foreign representative shall advertise the making of the following orders once in the Gazette and once in such newspaper as he thinks most appropriate for ensuring that the making of the order comes to the notice of the debtor's creditors—

(a) a recognition order,

(b) an order confirming the status of a replacement foreign representative, and

(c) a modification or termination order which modifies or terminates recognition of a foreign proceeding,

and the advertisement shall be in Form ML8.

8 Registration of court order

(1) Where the court makes a recognition order in respect of a foreign main proceeding or an order suspending the right to transfer, encumber or otherwise dispose of any assets of the debtor being heritable property, the clerk of the court shall send forthwith a certified copy of the order to the keeper of the register of inhibitions and adjudications for recording in that register.

(2) Recording under sub-paragraph (1) or (3) shall have the effect as from the date of the order of an inhibition and of a citation in an adjudication of the debtor's heritable estate at the instance of the foreign representative.

(3) Where the court makes a modification or termination order, the clerk of the court shall send forthwith a certified copy of the order to the keeper of the register of inhibitions and adjudications for recording in that register.

(4) The effect mentioned in sub-paragraph (2) shall expire—

(a) on the recording of a modification or termination order under sub-paragraph (3); or

(b) subject to sub-paragraph (5), if the effect has not expired by virtue of paragraph (a), at the end of the period of 3 years beginning with the date of the order.

(5) The foreign representative may, if recognition of the foreign proceeding has not been modified or terminated by the court pursuant to its powers under the Model Law, before the end of the period of 3 years mentioned in sub-paragraph (4)(b), send a memorandum in a form prescribed by the Court of Session by act of sederunt to the keeper of the register of inhibitions and adjudications for recording in that register, and such recording shall renew the effect mentioned in sub-paragraph (2); and thereafter the said effect shall continue to be preserved only if such memorandum is so recorded before the expiry of every subsequent period of 3 years.

9 Right to inspect court process

(1) In the case of any proceedings under these Regulations, the following have the right, at all reasonable times, to inspect the court process of the proceedings—

(a) the Secretary of State;

(b) the person who is the foreign representative in relation to the proceedings;

(c) if a foreign representative has been appointed in any other foreign proceeding regarding the debtor, that person;

(d) if a British insolvency officeholder is acting in relation to the debtor, that person;

(e) any person stating himself in writing to be a creditor of the debtor to which the proceedings under these Regulations relate;

(f) . . .

(g) the debtor to which the proceedings under these Regulations relate, or, if that debtor is a company, corporation or partnership, every person who is, or at any time has been—

(i) a director or officer of the debtor,

(ii) a member of the debtor, or

[(iii) where applicable, any person specified in particulars registered under section 1046 of the Companies Act 2006 (overseas companies) as authorised to represent the debtor;]

(2) The right of inspection conferred as above on any person may be exercised on his behalf by a person properly authorised by him.

10 Copies of court orders

(1) In any proceedings under these Regulations, any person who under paragraph 9 has a right to inspect documents in the court process also has the right to require the foreign representative in relation to those proceedings to furnish him with a copy of any court order in the proceedings.

(2) Sub-paragraph (1) does not apply if a copy of the court order has been served on that person or notice of the making of the order has been given to that person under other provisions of these Regulations.

11 Transfer of proceedings—actions to avoid acts detrimental to creditors

If, in accordance with article 23(6) of the Model Law, the court grants a foreign representative permission to make an application in accordance with paragraph (1) of that article, it may also order the relevant proceedings under British insolvency law taking place regarding the debtor to be transferred to the Court of Session if those proceedings are taking place in Scotland and are not already in that court.

NOTES

Para 6(1)(b)(i) was substituted by the Companies Act 2006 (Consequential Amendments, Transitional Provisions and Savings) Order 2009, SI 2009/1941, art 2(1), Sch 1, para 264(1), (4)(b), as from 1 October 2009.

Paras 6(1)(e), 7(3)(c) and 9(1)(f) were revoked by the Insolvency (Amendment) (EU Exit) Regulations 2019, SI 2019/146, reg 2, Schedule, Pt 6, paras 112, 126, 128–130, as from IP completion day (as defined in the European Union (Withdrawal Agreement) Act 2020, s 39) (for savings, see reg 4 of the 2019 Regulations at **[12.82]**).

Paras 6(1)(i) and (ia) were substituted (for the original para 6(1)(i)), and paras 7(3)(g) and (ga) were substituted (for the original para 7(3)(g)), by the Financial Services Act 2012 (Consequential Amendments and Transitional Provisions) Order 2013, SI 2013/472, art 3, Sch 2, para 116(b)(ii), (iii), as from 1 April 2013.

Para 9(1)(g)(iii) was substituted by SI 2009/1941, art 2(1), Sch 1, para 264(1), (4)(c), as from 1 October 2009.

PART 4 GENERAL

NOTES

It is assumed that this Part should be Part 4 but it was numbered as a second Part 3 in the original Queen's Printer's copy.

[10.199]

12 Giving of notices, etc

(1) All notices required or authorised by or under these Regulations to be given, sent or delivered must be in writing, unless it is otherwise provided, or the court allows the notice to be sent or given in some other way.

(2) Any reference in these Regulations to giving, sending or delivering a notice or any such document means, without prejudice to any other way and unless it is otherwise provided, that the notice or document may be sent by post, and that, subject to paragraph 13, any form of post may be used. Personal service of the notice or document is permissible in all cases.

(3) Where under these Regulations a notice or other document is required or authorised to be given, sent or delivered by a person ("the sender") to another ("the recipient"), it may be given, sent or delivered by any person duly authorised by the sender to do so to any person duly authorised by the recipient to receive or accept it.

(4) Where two or more persons are acting jointly as the British insolvency officeholder in proceedings under British insolvency law, the giving, sending or delivering of a notice or document to one of them is to be treated as the giving, sending or delivering of a notice or document to each or all.

13 Sending by post

(1) For a document to be properly sent by post, it must be contained in an envelope addressed to the person to whom it is to be sent, and pre-paid for either first or second class post.

(2) Any document to be sent by post may be sent to the last known address of the person to whom the document is to be sent.

(3) Where first class post is used, the document is to be deemed to be received on the second business day after the date of posting, unless the contrary is shown.

(4) Where second class post is used, the document is to be deemed to be received on the fourth business day after the date of posting, unless the contrary is shown.

14 Certificate of giving notice, etc

(1) Where in any proceedings under these Regulations a notice or document is required to be given, sent or delivered by any person, the date of giving, sending or delivery of it may be proved by means of a certificate by that person that he gave, posted or otherwise sent or delivered the notice or document on the date stated in the certificate, or that he instructed another person (naming him) to do so.

(2) A certificate under this paragraph may be endorsed on a copy of the notice to which it relates.

(3) A certificate purporting to be signed by or on behalf of the person mentioned in sub-paragraph (1) shall be deemed, unless the contrary is shown, to be sufficient evidence of the matters stated therein.

15 Forms for use in proceedings under these Regulations

(1) Forms ML7 and ML8 contained in Schedule 5 to these Regulations shall be used in, and in connection with, proceedings under these Regulations.

(2) The forms shall be used with such variations, if any, as the circumstances may require.

SCHEDULE 4
NOTICES DELIVERED TO THE REGISTRAR OF COMPANIES

Regulation 6

[10.200]

1 Interpretation

(1) In this Schedule—

. . .

"electronic communication" means the same as in the Electronic Communications Act 2000;

"Model Law notice" means a notice delivered to the registrar of companies under paragraph 26(6) of Schedule 2 or paragraph 7(4) of Schedule 3.

(2) Expressions defined in the Model Law or Schedule 2 or 3, as appropriate, have the same meaning when used in this Schedule.

(3) References in this Schedule to delivering a notice include sending, forwarding, producing or giving it.

2 Functions of the registrar of companies

(1) Where a Model Law notice is delivered to the registrar of companies in respect of a relevant company, the registrar shall enter a note in the register relating to that company.

(2) The note referred to in sub-paragraph (1) shall contain the following particulars, in each case as stated in the notice delivered to the registrar—

(a) brief details of the court order made;

(b) the date of the court order; and

(c) the name and address for service of the person who is the foreign representative in relation to the company.

3. . . .

4 Delivery to registrar of notices

(1) Electronic communications may be used for the delivery of any Model Law notice, provided that such delivery is in such form and manner as is directed by the registrar.

(2) Where the Model Law notice is required to be signed, it shall instead be authenticated in such manner as is directed by the registrar.

(3) If a Model Law notice is delivered to the registrar which does not comply with the requirements of these Regulations, he may serve on the person by whom the notice was delivered (or, if there are two or more such persons, on any of them) a notice (a non-compliance notice) indicating the respect in which the Model Law notice does not comply.

(4) Where the registrar serves a non-compliance notice, then, unless a replacement Model Law notice—

(a) is delivered to him within 14 days after the service of the non-compliance notice, and

(b) complies with the requirements of these Regulations or is not rejected by him for failure to comply with those requirements,

the original Model Law notice shall be deemed not to have been delivered to him.

5 Enforcement of foreign representative's duty to give notice to registrar

(1) If a foreign representative, having made default in complying with paragraph 26(6) of Schedule 2 or paragraph 7(4) of Schedule 3 fails to make good the default within 14 days after the service of a notice on the foreign representative requiring him to do so, the court may, on an application made to it by any creditor, member, director or other officer of the debtor or by the registrar of companies, make an order directing the foreign representative to make good the default within such time as may be specified in the order.

(2) The court's order may provide that all costs of and incidental to the application shall be borne by the foreign representative.

6 Rectification of the register under court order

(1) The registrar shall remove from the register any note, or part of a note—

(a) that relates to or is derived from a court order that the court has declared to be invalid or ineffective, or

(b) that the court declares to be factually inaccurate or derived from something that is factually inaccurate or forged,

and that the court directs should be removed from the register.

(2) The court order must specify what is to be removed from the register and indicate where on the register it is and the registrar shall carry out his duty under sub-paragraph (1) within a reasonable time of receipt by him of the relevant court order.

NOTES

Para 1: definition "the 1985 Act" (omitted) revoked by the Companies Act 2006 (Consequential Amendments, Transitional Provisions and Savings) Order 2009, SI 2009/1941, art 2(1), Sch 1, para 264(1), (5)(a), as from 1 October 2009.

Para 3: revoked by SI 2009/1941, art 2(1), Sch 1, para 264(1), (5)(b), as from 1 October 2009.

SCHEDULE 5
FORMS

[10.201]

NOTES

This Schedule sets out the forms prescribed for use in connection with proceedings under these Regulations. The forms are not reproduced here but details are given in the table below. The forms have been amended as noted below.

Form No	Description	Prescribed by
ML1	Recognition application	Sch 2, para 2. Amended by SI 2009/1941
ML2	Recognition order	Sch 2, para 5(2)
ML3	Statement of subsequent information	Sch 2, para 6
ML4	Originating application	Sch 2, para 32
ML5	Affidavit of service of application under the Cross-Border Insolvency Regulations 2006Ordinary application	Sch 2, paras 19, 32
ML6	Affidavit of service of application under the Cross-Border Insolvency Regulations 2006	Sch 2, para 23. Amended by SI 2013/472, and SI 2019/146
ML7	Notice to registrar of companies of order under the Cross-Border Insolvency Regulations 2006	Sch 2, para 26(6) Sch 3, para 7(4). Amended by SI 2009/1941
ML8	Notification of order under the Cross-Border Insolvency Regulations 2006 (for newspaper and London or Edinburgh Gazette)	Sch 2, para 26(7) Sch 3, para 7(5)

PARTNERSHIPS (ACCOUNTS) REGULATIONS 2008

(SI 2008/569)

NOTES

Made: 26 February 2008.

Authority: European Communities Act 1972, s 2(2), Companies Act 2006, ss 1210(1)(h), 1292(2) (see the note "Statutory Instruments made under the European Communities Act 1972" preceding paragraph **[4.1]** *ante*).

Commencement: 6 April 2008.

For a summary of all Orders and Regulations made under the Companies Act 2006, see Appendix 4 at **[A4]**.

These Regulations are reproduced as amended by: the Companies and Partnerships (Accounts and Audit) Regulations 2013, SI 2013/2005; the Companies, Partnerships and Groups (Accounts and Reports) Regulations 2015, SI 2015/980; the

Limited Liability Partnerships, Partnerships and Groups (Accounts and Audit) Regulations 2016, SI 2016/575; the Statutory Auditors and Third Country Auditors Regulations 2016, SI 2016/649; the Accounts and Reports (Amendment) (EU Exit) Regulations 2019, SI 2019/145.

ARRANGEMENT OF REGULATIONS

PART 1 INTRODUCTION

[10.202]

1 Citation, commencement and application

(1) These Regulations may be cited as the Partnerships (Accounts) Regulations 2008.

(2) These Regulations come into force on 6th April 2008 and apply in relation to—

(a) qualifying partnerships' financial years beginning on or after that date, and
(b) auditors appointed in respect of those financial years.

[10.203]

2 Interpretation

(1) In these Regulations—

[. . .]

"the accounts", in relation to a qualifying partnership, means the annual accounts [and reports] . . . required by regulation 4,

"dealt with on a consolidated basis" means dealt with by the method of full consolidation, the method of proportional consolidation or the equity method of accounting,

"financial year", in relation to a qualifying partnership, means any period of not more than 18 months in respect of which a profit and loss account of the partnership is required to be made up by or in accordance with its constitution or, failing any such requirement, each period of 12 months beginning with 1st April,

. . .

"general partner" has the same meaning as in the Limited Partnerships Act 1907,

"the Large and Medium-sized Companies Accounts Regulations" means the Large and Medium-sized Companies and Groups (Accounts and Reports) Regulations 2008,

"limited company" means a company limited by shares or limited by guarantee,

"limited partnership" means a partnership formed in accordance with the Limited Partnerships Act 1907,

"qualifying partnership" has the meaning given by regulation 3, "the Small Companies Accounts Regulations" means the Small Companies and Groups (Accounts and Directors' Report) Regulations 2008,

and except as otherwise provided in these Regulations, words and expressions used in the Companies Act 2006 have the same meaning in these Regulations as they have in that Act.

(2) . . .

NOTES

Para (1) is amended as follows:

Definition "the Accounting Directive" (omitted) originally inserted, and definitions "the Fourth Directive" and "the Seventh Directive" (omitted) revoked, by the Companies, Partnerships and Groups (Accounts and Reports) Regulations 2015, SI 2015/980, reg 42(1), (2), as from 6 April 2015, in relation to (a) financial years beginning on or after 1 January 2016, and (b) a financial year of a company beginning on or after 1 January 2015, but before 1 January 2016, if the directors of the company so decide (subject to transitional provisions, etc, in regs 2, 3 of the 2015 Regulations at **[4.549]** et seq).

Definition "the Accounting Directive" subsequently revoked by the Accounts and Reports (Amendment) (EU Exit) Regulations 2019, SI 2019/145, reg 6, Sch 3, paras 6, 7, as from IP completion day (as defined in the European Union (Withdrawal Agreement) Act 2020, s 39).

Words in square brackets in the definition "the accounts" substituted, and words omitted revoked, by the Companies and Partnerships (Accounts and Audit) Regulations 2013, SI 2013/2005, reg 4(1), (2)(a), in relation to a financial year of a qualifying partnership beginning on or after 1 October 2013 and auditors appointed in respect of that financial year.

Para (2): revoked by SI 2013/2005, reg 4(1), (2)(b), in relation to a financial year of a qualifying partnership beginning on or after 1 October 2013 and auditors appointed in respect of that financial year.

[10.204]

[3 Qualifying partnerships

(1) A "qualifying partnership" is a partnership formed under the law of any part of the United Kingdom each of whose members or, in the case of a limited partnership, each of whose general partners is—

(a) a limited company;
(b) an unlimited company each of whose members is a limited company;
(c) a Scottish partnership which is not a limited partnership, each of whose members is a limited company; or
(d) a Scottish partnership which is a limited partnership, each of whose general partners is a limited company.

(2) Each reference in paragraph (1) to a limited company includes a reference to any comparable undertaking incorporated in a country or territory outside the United Kingdom.

(3) The reference in paragraph (1)(b) to an unlimited company includes a reference to any comparable undertaking incorporated in a country or territory outside the United Kingdom.

(4) The reference in paragraph (1)(c) to a Scottish partnership which is not a limited partnership includes a reference to any undertaking comparable to such a Scottish partnership incorporated in or formed under the law of a country or territory outside the United Kingdom.

(5) The reference in paragraph (1)(d) to a Scottish partnership which is a limited partnership includes a reference to any undertaking comparable to such a Scottish partnership incorporated in or formed under the law of a country or territory outside the United Kingdom; and in relation to such an undertaking the reference in that paragraph to the general partners is to be construed as a reference to the members of the undertaking comparable to general partners.

(6) The requirements of these Regulations apply without regard to any change in the members (or in the members of any member) of a qualifying partnership which does not result in it ceasing to be a qualifying partnership.]

NOTES

Substituted, together with reg 3A (for the original reg 3) by the Companies and Partnerships (Accounts and Audit) Regulations 2013, SI 2013/2005, reg 4(1), (3), in relation to a financial year of a qualifying partnership beginning on or after 1 October 2013 and auditors appointed in respect of that financial year.

[10.205]

[3A References to members of a qualifying partnership

(1) The references in regulations 4 to 15 to the members, or any member, of a qualifying partnership are to be construed as follows.

(2) Where the qualifying partnership is not a limited partnership its members are, for the purposes of those regulations—

(a) its members (irrespective of their place of incorporation or the law under which they were formed);
(b) where any of its members is an unlimited company, the limited companies which are the members of that unlimited company;
(c) where any of its members is a Scottish partnership which is not a limited partnership, the limited companies which are the members of that Scottish partnership; and
(d) where any of its members is a Scottish partnership which is a limited partnership, the limited companies which are the general partners of that Scottish limited partnership.

(3) Where the qualifying partnership is a limited partnership its members are, for the purposes of those regulations—

(a) its general partners (irrespective of their place of incorporation or the law under which they were formed);
(b) where any of its general partners is an unlimited company, the limited companies which are the members of that unlimited company;
(c) where any of its general partners is a Scottish partnership which is not a limited partnership, the limited companies which are the members of that Scottish partnership; and
(d) where any of its general partners is a Scottish partnership which is a limited partnership, the limited companies which are the general partners of that Scottish limited partnership.

(4) Each reference in paragraphs (2) and (3) to a limited company includes a reference to any comparable undertaking incorporated in a country or territory outside the United Kingdom.

(5) The references in paragraphs (2)(b) and (3)(b) to an unlimited company include references to any comparable undertaking incorporated in a country or territory outside the United Kingdom.

(6) The references in paragraphs (2)(c) and (3)(c) to a Scottish partnership which is not a limited partnership include references to any undertaking comparable to such a Scottish partnership incorporated in or formed under the law of a country or territory outside the United Kingdom.

(7) The references in paragraphs (2)(d) and (3)(d) to a Scottish partnership which is a limited partnership include references to any undertaking comparable to such a Scottish partnership incorporated in or formed under the law of a country or territory outside the United Kingdom; and in relation to such an undertaking the references in those paragraphs to the general partners are to be construed as references to the members of the undertaking comparable to general partners.]

NOTES

Substituted as noted to reg 3 at **[10.204]**.

PART 2 PARTNERSHIP ACCOUNTS

[10.206]

4 Preparation of accounts of qualifying partnerships

(1) Subject to regulation 7, the persons who are members of a qualifying partnership at the end of any financial year of the partnership must, in respect of that year—

(a) prepare the like annual accounts and [reports], and

(b) cause to be prepared such an auditor's report,

as would be required, if the partnership were a company, under Part 15 (accounts and reports) and Chapter 1 of Part 16 (requirement for audited accounts) of the Companies Act 2006, and under the Small Companies Accounts Regulations or the Large and Medium-sized Companies Accounts Regulations (as the case may be).

(2) Regulations 4 to 6 of the Companies (Disclosure of Auditor Remuneration and Liability Limitation Agreements) Regulations 2008 apply in relation to the accounts required by this regulation as they apply in relation to the annual accounts of a company or group.

(3) The accounts required by this regulation must—

(a) be prepared within the period of 9 months beginning immediately after the end of the partnership's financial year, and

(b) state that they are prepared under this regulation.

(4) Part 1 of the Schedule to these Regulations sets out certain modifications and adaptations for the purposes of this regulation.

NOTES

Para (1): word in square brackets substituted by the Companies and Partnerships (Accounts and Audit) Regulations 2013, SI 2013/2005, reg 4(1), (4), in relation to a financial year of a qualifying partnership beginning on or after 1 October 2013 and auditors appointed in respect of that financial year.

[10.207]

5 Delivery of accounts of qualifying partnerships to registrar etc

(1) Subject to regulation 7, each limited company which is a member of a qualifying partnership at the end of any financial year of the partnership must append to the copy of its accounts and reports which is next delivered to the registrar in accordance with section 441(1) of the Companies Act 2006 (duty to file accounts and reports with the registrar) a copy of the accounts of the partnership prepared for that year under regulation 4.

(2) Subject to regulation 7, a limited company which is a member of a qualifying partnership must supply to any person upon request—

(a) the name of each member of the partnership which is to deliver, or has delivered, a copy of the latest accounts of the partnership to the registrar under paragraph (1), . . .

(b) . . .

NOTES

Para (2): sub-para (b) and the preceding word revoked by the Accounts and Reports (Amendment) (EU Exit) Regulations 2019, SI 2019/145, reg 6, Sch 3, paras 6, 8, as from IP completion day (as defined in the European Union (Withdrawal Agreement) Act 2020, s 39).

[10.208]

6 Publication of accounts of qualifying partnerships at head office

[(1) [Subject to regulation 7,] this regulation applies where none of the members of a qualifying partnership is a limited company.

(2) . . .]

(3) The members of the qualifying partnership—

[(a) must make the latest accounts available for inspection by any person, without charge and during business hours as follows—

(i) where a qualifying partnership has a principal place of business in the United Kingdom, at that principal place of business;

(ii) where the qualifying partnership has no principal place of business in the United Kingdom, but at least one of its members has a principal place of business or a head office in the United Kingdom, at a member's principal place of business or head office in the United Kingdom nominated by the members of the qualifying partnership for the purposes of this regulation;

(iii) where the qualifying partnership has no principal place of business in the United Kingdom and none of its members has a principal place of business or a head office in the United Kingdom, at an address in the United Kingdom nominated by the members of a qualifying partnership, and]

(b) if any document comprised in those accounts is in a language other than English, must annex to that document a translation of it into English, certified as an accurate translation—

(i) if the translation was made in the United Kingdom, by—

(aa) a notary public in any part of the United Kingdom;

(bb) a solicitor (if the translation was made in Scotland), a solicitor of the Supreme Court of Judicature of England and Wales (if it was made in England or Wales), or a solicitor of the Supreme Court of Judicature of Northern Ireland (if it was made in Northern Ireland); or

(cc) a person certified by a person mentioned above to be known to be competent to translate the document into English; or

(ii) if the translation was made outside the United Kingdom, by—

(aa) a notary public;

(bb) a person authorised in the place where the translation was made to administer an oath;

(cc) any of the British officials mentioned in section 6 of the Commissioners for Oaths Act 1889;

(dd) a person certified by a person mentioned above to be known to be competent to translate the document into English.

(4) A member of the qualifying partnership must supply to any person upon request—

(a) a copy of the accounts required by paragraph (3)(a) to be made available for inspection, and

(b) a copy of any translation required by paragraph (3)(b) to be annexed to any document comprised in those accounts,

at a price not exceeding the administrative cost of making the copy.

NOTES

Paras (1), (2): substituted by the Companies and Partnerships (Accounts and Audit) Regulations 2013, SI 2013/2005, reg 4(1), (5)(a), in relation to a financial year of a qualifying partnership beginning on or after 1 October 2013 and auditors appointed in respect of that financial year. The words in square brackets in para (1) were inserted, and para (2) was revoked, by the Accounts and Reports (Amendment) (EU Exit) Regulations 2019, SI 2019/145, reg 6, Sch 3, paras 6, 9, as from IP completion day (as defined in the European Union (Withdrawal Agreement) Act 2020, s 39).

Para (3): sub-para (a) substituted by SI 2013/2005, reg 4(1), (5)(b), in relation to a financial year of a qualifying partnership beginning on or after 1 October 2013 and auditors appointed in respect of that financial year.

[10.209]

7 Exemption from regulations 4 to 6 where accounts consolidated

(1) The members of a qualifying partnership are exempt from the requirements of regulations 4 to 6 if the partnership is dealt with on a consolidated basis in group accounts prepared by—

(a) a member of the partnership which is established under the law of [any part of the United Kingdom], or

(b) a parent undertaking of such a member which parent undertaking is so established,

and (in either case) the conditions mentioned in paragraph (2) are complied with.

(2) The conditions are—

[(a) that the group accounts are prepared and audited, if the undertaking is a company, in accordance with the requirements of the Companies Act 2006, or, if the undertaking is not a company, the legal requirements which apply to the preparation and audit of consolidated accounts for that undertaking, and]

(b) the notes to those accounts disclose that advantage has been taken of the exemption conferred by this regulation.

(3) Where advantage is taken of the exemption conferred by this regulation, any member of the qualifying partnership which is a limited company must disclose on request the name of at least one member or parent undertaking in whose group accounts the partnership has been or is to be dealt with on a consolidated basis.

NOTES

Para (1): words in square brackets in sub-para (a) substituted by the Accounts and Reports (Amendment) (EU Exit) Regulations 2019, SI 2019/145, reg 6, Sch 3, paras 6, 10(a), as from IP completion day (as defined in the European Union (Withdrawal Agreement) Act 2020, s 39).

Para (2): sub-para (a) substituted by SI 2019/145, reg 6, Sch 3, paras 6, 10(b), as from IP completion day (as defined in the European Union (Withdrawal Agreement) Act 2020, s 39).

PART 3 AUDITORS

[10.210]

8 Appointment of auditor

An auditor may be appointed for the purposes of regulation 4(1)(b) only by the members of a qualifying partnership.

[10.211]

9 Functions of auditor

(1) The following provisions of the Companies Act 2006 apply to the auditor of a qualifying partnership as they apply to an auditor of a company—

(a) section 495 (auditor's report on company's annual accounts);

[(aa) section 496 (auditor's report on strategic report and director's report);]

(b) section 498 (duties of auditor);

(c) section 499 (auditor's general right to information).

(2) The auditor of a qualifying partnership must supply the members of the qualifying partnership with such information as is necessary to enable any disclosure required by regulation 4(2) to be made.

NOTES

Para (1): sub-para (aa) inserted by the Statutory Auditors and Third Country Auditors Regulations 2016, SI 2016/649, reg 14, as from 17 June 2016.

[10.212]

10 Signature of auditor's report

Sections 503 to 506 of the Companies Act 2006 (signature of auditor's report) apply in relation to the auditor's report required by regulation 4(1)(b), subject to—

(a) any necessary modifications to take account of the fact that the qualifying partnership is unincorporated, and

(b) the modification set out in Part 2 of the Schedule to these Regulations.

[10.213]

11 Removal of auditors on improper grounds

(1) Where the auditor of a qualifying partnership is removed from office an application may be made to the High Court under this regulation.

(2) The persons who may make such an application are—

(a) any member of the qualifying partnership who was also a member at the time of the removal, and

(b) the Secretary of State.

(3) If the court is satisfied that the removal was—

(a) on grounds of divergence of opinion on accounting treatments or audit procedures, or

(b) on any other improper grounds,

it may make such order as it thinks fit for giving relief in respect of the removal.

(4) The court may, in particular—

(a) declare that any decision of the qualifying partnership removing an auditor, or appointing a new auditor in his place, is void;

(b) require the members of the qualifying partnership to re-appoint the dismissed auditor;

(c) give directions as to the conduct of the qualifying partnership's affairs in the future.

(5) In the application of this regulation to a qualifying partnership formed under the law of Scotland or Northern Ireland, references to the High Court are to be read as references to the Court of Session or, as the case may be, the High Court in Northern Ireland.

[10.214]

12 Duty of auditor to notify supervisory body

(1) Where an auditor of a qualifying partnership ceases to hold office before the end of his term of office, he must notify the supervisory body of which he is a member.

(2) The notice must—

(a) inform the supervisory body that he has ceased to hold office, and

(b) be accompanied by a statement of any circumstances connected with his ceasing to hold office.

(3) The auditor must notify the supervisory body not more than 14 days after the date on which he ceases to hold office.

(4) In this regulation and regulation 13, "supervisory body" has the same meaning as in Part 42 of the Companies Act 2006 (statutory auditors) (see section 1217).

[10.215]

13 Duty of members of qualifying partnership to notify supervisory body

(1) Where an auditor of a qualifying partnership ceases to hold office before the end of his term of office, the members of the partnership must notify the supervisory body of which the auditor is a member.

(2) The notice must—

(a) inform the supervisory body that the auditor has ceased to hold office, and

(b) be accompanied by a statement by the body of the reasons for his ceasing to hold office.

(3) The members of the qualifying partnership must notify the supervisory body not more than 14 days after the date on which the auditor ceases to hold office.

[10.216]

14 Statutory auditors

For the purposes of section 1210(1)(h) of the Companies Act 2006 (meaning of "statutory auditor")—

(a) a qualifying partnership is a prescribed person, and

(b) regulation 4(1)(b) is a prescribed enactment,

and accordingly a person appointed as auditor of a qualifying partnership for the purposes of regulation 4(1)(b) is a statutory auditor.

PART 4 OFFENCES

[10.217]

15 Penalties for non-compliance by members of qualifying partnership

(1) If, in respect of a financial year of a qualifying partnership, the requirements of paragraph (1) of regulation 4 are not complied with within the period referred to in paragraph (3) of that regulation, every person who was a member of the partnership or a director of such a member at the end of that year is liable on summary conviction to a fine not exceeding level 5 on the standard scale.

(2) If the accounts of a qualifying partnership—

(a) a copy of which is delivered to the registrar under regulation 5, or

(b) which are made available for inspection under regulation 6,

do not comply with the requirements of regulation 4(1), every person who, at the time when the copy was so delivered or (as the case may be) the accounts were first made available for inspection, was a member of the partnership or a director of such a member is liable on summary conviction to a fine not exceeding level 5 on the standard scale.

(3) If a member of a qualifying partnership fails to comply with regulation 5, 6, 7(3) or 13, that member and any director of that member is liable on summary conviction to a fine not exceeding level 5 on the standard scale.

(4) In proceedings for an offence under this section it is a defence for the person charged to show that he took all reasonable steps and exercised all due diligence to avoid the commission of the offence.

(5) The following provisions of the Companies Act 2006, namely—

(a) sections 1127 and 1128 (summary proceedings: venue and time limit for proceedings), and

(b) section 1130 (proceedings against unincorporated bodies),

apply to an offence under this regulation.

[10.218]

16 Penalties for non-compliance by auditors of qualifying partnerships

(1) If a person ceasing to hold office as auditor fails to comply with regulation 12, an offence is committed by—

(a) that person, and

(b) if that person is a firm, every officer of the firm who is in default.

(2) In proceedings for an offence under this section it is a defence for the person charged to show that he took all reasonable steps and exercised all due diligence to avoid the commission of the offence.

(3) A person guilty of an offence under this regulation is liable—

(a) on conviction on indictment, to a fine, and

(b) on summary conviction, to a fine not exceeding the statutory maximum.

(4) The following provisions of the Companies Act 2006, namely—

(a) sections 1121 to 1123 (liability of officer in default),

(b) sections 1127 and 1128 (summary proceedings: venue and time limit for proceedings), and

(c) section 1130 (proceedings against unincorporated bodies),

apply to an offence under this regulation.

PART 5 FINAL PROVISIONS

17 (*Amends the Small Companies and Groups (Accounts and Directors' Report) Regulations 2008, SI 2008/409, Sch 2, Pt 1, (now revoked) and Sch 6, Pt 2 at* **[4.55]**, *and the Large and Medium-sized Companies and Groups (Accounts and Reports) Regulations 2008, SI 2008/410, Sch 4, Pt 1 at* **[4.86]**.)

[10.219]

18 Revocation and transitional provisions etc

(1) The Partnerships and Unlimited Companies (Accounts) Regulations 1993 and the Partnerships and Unlimited Companies (Accounts) Regulations (Northern Ireland) 1994 are revoked.

(2) The regulations specified in paragraph (1) continue to apply to any financial year of a qualifying partnership beginning before 6th April 2008.

[10.220]

[19 Review

(1) The Secretary of State must from time to time—

(a) carry out a review of regulations 4(1) and 9(1) and Part 1 of the Schedule,

(b) set out the conclusions of the review in a report, and

(c) publish the report.

(2) The report must, in particular—

(a) set out the objectives intended to be achieved by those provisions,

(b) assess the extent to which those objectives are achieved,

(c) assess whether those objectives remain appropriate, and

(d) if those objectives remain appropriate, assess the extent to which they could be achieved in another way which involves less onerous regulatory provision.

(3) In carrying out the review, the Secretary of State must have regard to how the provisions of Directive 2013/34/EU of 26 June 2013 on the annual financial statements etc of certain types of undertakings are implemented in other Member States.

(4) The first report under this regulation must be published before the end of the period of 5 years beginning with the date on which the Limited Liability Partnerships, Partnerships and Groups (Accounts and Audit) Regulations 2016 come into force.

(5) Subsequent reports under this regulation must be published at intervals not exceeding 5 years.

(6) In this regulation, "regulatory provision" has the meaning given by section 32(4) of the Small Business, Enterprise and Employment Act 2015.]

NOTES

Inserted by the Limited Liability Partnerships, Partnerships and Groups (Accounts and Audit) Regulations 2016, SI 2016/575, reg 64, as from 17 May 2016.

SCHEDULE

Regulations 4(4) and 10(b)

PART 1 MODIFICATIONS AND ADAPTATIONS FOR PURPOSES OF REGULATION 4

[10.221]

1. (1) Accounts prepared under regulation 4 of these Regulations must comply with the requirements of Part 15 and Chapter 1 of Part 16 of the Companies Act 2006, and with the Small Companies Accounts Regulations or the Large and Medium-sized Companies Accounts Regulations (as the case may be) subject to—

(a) the provisions of section 1161(2) and (3) of that Act (how to construe "shares" and other expressions appropriate to companies),

(b) the omission of the provisions of the Small Companies Accounts Regulations mentioned in paragraph 2(1) below,

(c) the omission of the provisions of the Large and Medium-sized Companies Accounts Regulations mentioned in paragraph 2(2) below, and

(d) any necessary modifications to take account of the fact that partnerships are unincorporated.

(2) For the purposes of the provisions of Part 15 and Chapter 1 of Part 16 of the Companies Act 2006 and of the Small Companies Accounts Regulations and the Large and Medium-sized Companies Accounts Regulations as applied to the accounts and report so prepared, these Regulations are to be regarded as part of the requirements of that Act and those regulations.

2. (1) The provisions of the Small Companies Accounts Regulations referred to in paragraph 1(1)(b) are—

(a) in Part 1 of Schedule 1—

(i) in paragraph 3(2), the words from "used" to the end, and

(ii) paragraph 6,

(b) in Part 2 of Schedule 1, paragraph 21,

[(c) in Part 3 of Schedule 1, paragraph 49,]

(d), (e) . . .

(f) Schedule 5, and

(g) in Part 1 of Schedule 6, paragraphs 13(3) and (4), 14 and 15, and in Part 2 of that Schedule, paragraph 36.

(2) The provisions of the Large and Medium-sized Companies Accounts Regulations referred to in paragraph 1(1)(c) are—

(a) in Part 1 of Schedule 1—

(i) in paragraph 3(2), the words from "used" to the end, and

(ii) paragraph 6,

(b) in Part 2 of Schedule 1, paragraph 21,

(c) in Part 3 of Schedule 1, paragraphs 45, 50, 52, 53, 54, 64(2), 66 and 67,

(d) in Part 1 of Schedule 4, paragraph 9, and in Part 2 paragraph 12,

(e) in Schedule 5, paragraphs 2, 4 and 5,

(f) in Part 1 of Schedule 6 to those Regulations, paragraphs 13(3) and (4), 14 and 15, and

(g) Schedule 7 to those Regulations except paragraph 7.

(3) Sub-paragraphs (1) and (2) are not to be construed as affecting the requirement to give a true and fair view under sections 393, 396 and 404 of the Companies Act 2006.

NOTES

Para 2: sub-para (1)(c) substituted, and sub-paras (1)(d) and (e) revoked, by the Companies, Partnerships and Groups (Accounts and Reports) Regulations 2015, SI 2015/980, reg 42(1), (5), as from 6 April 2015, in relation to (a) financial years beginning on or after 1 January 2016, and (b) a financial year of a company beginning on or after 1 January 2015, but before 1 January 2016, if the directors of the company so decide (subject to transitional provisions, etc, in regs 2, 3 of the 2015 Regulations at **[4.549]** et seq).

PART 2 MODIFICATION FOR PURPOSES OF REGULATION 10

[10.222]

3. In section 506(1)(b) of the Companies Act 2006 the reference to the copy of the report delivered to the registrar under Chapter 10 of Part 15 (filing of accounts and reports) is treated as a reference to the copy of the accounts required to be delivered to the registrar under regulation 5(1).

LIMITED LIABILITY PARTNERSHIPS (ACCOUNTS AND AUDIT) (APPLICATION OF COMPANIES ACT 2006) REGULATIONS 2008

(SI 2008/1911)

NOTES

Made: 17 July 2008.

Authority: Limited Liability Partnerships Act 2000, ss 15, 17; Companies Act 2006, ss 1210(1)(h), 1292(2).

Commencement: 1 October 2008.

For a summary of all Orders and Regulations made under the Companies Act 2006, see Appendix 4 at **[A4]**.

These Regulations are reproduced as amended by: the Financial Services and Markets Act 2000 (Regulated Activities) (Amendment) Order 2009, SI 2009/1342; the Limited Liability Partnerships (Application of Companies Act 2006) Regulations 2009, SI 2009/1804; the Electronic Money Regulations 2011, SI 2011/99; the Supervision of Accounts and Reports (Prescribed Body) and Companies (Defective Accounts and Directors' Reports) (Authorised Person) Order 2012, SI 2012/1439; the Statutory Auditors (Amendment of Companies Act 2006 and Delegation of Functions etc) Order 2012, SI 2012/1741; the Companies and Limited Liability Partnerships (Accounts and Audit Exemptions and Change of Accounting Framework) Regulations 2012, SI 2012/2301; the Financial Services Act 2012 (Consequential Amendments and Transitional Provisions) Order 2013, SI 2013/472; the Companies and Partnerships (Accounts and Audit) Regulations 2013, SI 2013/2005; the Co-operative and Community Benefit Societies and Credit Unions Act 2010 (Consequential Amendments) Regulations 2014, SI 2014/1815; the Limited Liability Partnerships, Partnerships and Groups (Accounts and Audit) Regulations 2016, SI 2016/575; the Bank of England and Financial Services (Consequential Amendments) Regulations 2017, SI 2017/80; the Statutory Auditors Regulations 2017, SI 2017/1164; the Occupational Pension Schemes (Master Trusts) Regulations 2018, SI 2018/1030; the Companies (Directors' Report) and Limited Liability Partnerships (Energy and Carbon Report) Regulations 2018, SI 2018/1155; the Accounts and Reports (Amendment) (EU Exit) Regulations 2019, SI 2019/145; the Statutory Auditors and Third Country Auditors (Amendment) (EU Exit) Regulations 2019, SI 2019/177; the Companies, Limited Liability Partnerships and Partnerships (Amendment etc) (EU Exit) Regulations 2019, SI 2019/348; the International Accounting Standards and European Public Limited-Liability Company (Amendment etc) (EU Exit) Regulations 2019, SI 2019/685; the European Grouping of Territorial Cooperation and Limited Liability Partnerships etc (Revocations and Amendments) (EU Exit) Regulations 2021, SI 2021/153; the Supervision of Accounts and Reports (Prescribed Body) and Companies (Defective Accounts and Reports) (Authorised Person) Order 2021, SI 2021/465; the Limited Liability Partnerships (Climate-related Financial Disclosure) Regulations 2022, SI 2022/46.

ARRANGEMENT OF REGULATIONS

PART 1 GENERAL INTRODUCTORY PROVISIONS

[10.223]

1 Citation and commencement

These Regulations may be cited as the Limited Liability Partnerships (Accounts and Audit) (Application of Companies Act 2006) Regulations 2008 and come into force on 1st October 2008.

[10.224]

2 Application

(1) Subject to paragraphs (2) to (11), these Regulations apply to accounts for financial years beginning on or after 1st October 2008.

(2) Any question whether—

(a) for the purposes of section 382, 383, 384(3) or 467(3) of the Companies Act 2006, as applied to limited liability partnerships by regulations 5 and 26, a limited liability partnership or group qualified as small in a financial year beginning before 1st October 2008, or

(b) for the purposes of section 465 or 466 of that Act, as applied to limited liability partnerships by regulation 26, a limited liability partnership or group qualified as medium-sized in any such financial year,

is to be determined by reference to the corresponding provisions of the Companies Act 1985 or the Companies (Northern Ireland) Order 1986 as applied to limited liability partnerships by the Limited Liability Partnerships Regulations 2001 or the Limited Liability Partnerships Regulations (Northern Ireland) 2004.

(3) Sections 485 to 488 of the Companies Act 2006, as applied to limited liability partnerships by regulation 36, apply in relation to appointments of auditors for financial years beginning on or after 1st October 2008.

(4) Sections 492, 494 and 499 to 501 of the Companies Act 2006, as applied to limited liability partnerships by regulations 37, 38 and 40, apply to auditors appointed for financial years beginning on or after 1st October 2008.

(5) Section 502 of the Companies Act 2006, as applied to limited liability partnerships by regulation 40, applies to auditors appointed on or after 1st October 2008.

(6) Sections 495, 498 and 503 to 509 of the Companies Act 2006, as applied to limited liability partnerships by regulations 39 to 42, apply to auditors' reports on accounts for financial years beginning on or after 1st October 2008.

(7) Sections 510 to 513 of the Companies Act 2006, as applied to limited liability partnerships by regulations 43 and 44, apply where notice of the proposed removal is given to the auditor on or after 1st October 2008.

(8) Section 515 of the Companies Act 2006, as applied to limited liability partnerships by regulation 45, applies to appointments of auditors for financial years beginning on or after 1st October 2008.

(9) Sections 516 to 518 of the Companies Act 2006, as applied to limited liability partnerships by regulation 45, apply to resignations occurring on or after 1st October 2008.

(10) Sections 519 to 525 of the Companies Act 2006, as applied to limited liability partnerships by regulation 46, apply where the auditor ceases to hold office on or after 1st October 2008.

(11) Section 526 of the Companies Act 2006, as applied to limited liability partnerships by regulation 46, applies where the vacancy occurs on or after 1st October 2008.

[10.225]

3 Interpretation

(1) In these Regulations—

"1985 Act" means the Companies Act 1985,

"1986 Order" means the Companies (Northern Ireland) Order 1986, and

"LLP" means a limited liability partnership [registered under the Limited Liability Partnerships Act 2000].

(2) In these Regulations, unless the context otherwise requires—

(a) any reference to a numbered Part, section or Schedule is to the Part, section or Schedule so numbered in the Companies Act 2006,

(b) references in provisions applied to LLPs to other provisions of the Companies Act 2006 are to those provisions as applied to LLPs by these Regulations, and

(c) references in provisions applied to LLPs to provisions of the Insolvency Act 1986 or the Insolvency (Northern Ireland) Order 1989 are to those provisions as applied to LLPs by the Limited Liability Partnerships Regulations 2001 or the Limited Liability Partnerships Regulations (Northern Ireland) 2004.

NOTES

Para (1): words in square brackets substituted by the Limited Liability Partnerships (Application of Companies Act 2006) Regulations 2009, SI 2009/1804, reg 85, Sch 3, Pt 2, para 15(1), (2), as from 1 October 2009.

General note as to interpretation: as to the meaning of "the registrar" and "the register", and as to the construction of references to registration in a particular part of the United Kingdom, in any enactment relating to LLPs, see the Limited Liability Partnerships (Application of Companies Act 2006) Regulations 2009, SI 2009/1804, Sch 3, Pt 2, para 12 at **[10.419]**.

[10.226]

4 Scheme of Part 15 as applied to LLPs

Section 380 applies to LLPs, modified so that it reads as follows—

"380 Scheme of this Part

(1) The requirements of this Part as to accounts[, auditor's reports and energy and carbon reports] apply in relation to each financial year of an LLP.

(2) In certain respects different provisions apply to different kinds of LLP.

(3), (4) . . ."

NOTES

In s 380(1) as set out above, the words in square brackets were substituted by the Companies (Directors' Report) and Limited Liability Partnerships (Energy and Carbon Report) Regulations 2018, SI 2018/1155, regs 8, 9, as from 1 April 2019, in respect of financial years beginning on or after that date.

In s 380 as set out above, sub-ss (3), (4) were revoked by the Limited Liability Partnerships, Partnerships and Groups (Accounts and Audit) Regulations 2016, SI 2016/575, regs 3, 4, as from 17 May 2016, in relation to (a) financial years beginning on or after 1 January 2016; and (b) a financial year of an LLP beginning on or after 1 January 2015, but before 1 January 2016, if (i) the members of the LLP so decide, and (ii) a copy of the LLP's accounts for that financial year has not been delivered to the registrar in accordance with ss 444, 445 or 446 of the Companies Act 2006 as applied to LLPs by the Limited Liability Partnerships (Accounts and Audit) (Application of Companies Act 2006) Regulations before 17 May 2016. As to the commencement of this amendment, see further reg 2(3)–(5) of the 2016 Regulations, which provide as follows—

"(3) But where—

(a) by virtue of paragraph (2)(b), the amendments made by Parts 2 to 4 of these Regulations have effect in relation to a financial year beginning on or after 1st January 2015, but before 1st January 2016, and

(b) as a result the LLP qualifies as a small LLP in relation to that year,

the LLP is not exempt from the requirements of the Act as applied to LLPs by the 2008 Regulations relating to the audit of annual accounts for that year if the LLP would not have been so exempt had the amendments not had effect in relation to that year.

(4) In determining whether an LLP or group qualifies as small or medium-sized under section 382(2), 383(3), 465(2) or 466(3) of the Act as applied to LLPs by the 2008 Regulations (qualification in relation to subsequent financial year by reference to circumstances in preceding financial years) in relation to a financial year in relation to which the amendments made by Parts 2 to 4 of these Regulations have effect, the LLP or group is to be treated as having qualified as small or medium-sized (as the case may be) in any previous year in which it would have so qualified if amendments to the same effect as the amendments made by Parts 2 to 4 of these Regulations had had effect in relation to that previous year.

(5) Notwithstanding paragraph (2), the members of an LLP cannot take advantage of section 410(2) of the Act as applied to LLPs by the 2008 Regulations (information about related undertakings: alternative compliance) in relation to annual accounts of the LLP approved, pursuant to section 414 of the Act as applied to LLPs by the 2008 Regulations, on or after 1st July 2016.".

PART 2 LLPS QUALIFYING AS SMALL

[10.227]

5 LLPs subject to the small LLPs regime

Sections 381 to 384 apply to LLPs, modified so that they read as follows—

"381 LLPs subject to the small LLPs regime

The small LLPs regime applies to an LLP for a financial year in relation to which the LLP—

(a) qualifies as small (see sections 382 and 383), and

(b) is not excluded from the regime (see section 384).

382 LLPs qualifying as small: general

(1) An LLP qualifies as small in relation to its first financial year if the qualifying conditions are met in that year.

[(1A) Subject to subsection (2), an LLP qualifies as small in relation to a subsequent financial year if the qualifying conditions are met in that year.]

[(2) In relation to a subsequent financial year, where on its balance sheet date an LLP meets or ceases to meet the qualifying conditions, that affects its qualification as a small LLP only if it occurs in two consecutive financial years.]

(3) The qualifying conditions are met by an LLP in a year in which it satisfies two or more of the following requirements—

1. Turnover	[Not more than £10.2 million]
2. Balance sheet total	[Not more than £5.1 million]
3. Number of employees	Not more than 50

(4) For a period that is an LLP's financial year but not in fact a year the maximum figures for turnover must be proportionately adjusted.

(5) The balance sheet total means the aggregate of the amounts shown as assets in the LLP's balance sheet.

(6) The number of employees means the average number of persons employed by the LLP in the year, determined as follows—

(a) find for each month in the financial year the number of persons employed under contracts of service by the LLP in that month (whether throughout the month or not),

(b) add together the monthly totals, and

(c) divide by the number of months in the financial year.

(7) This section is subject to section 383 (LLPs qualifying as small: parent LLPs).

383 LLPs qualifying as small: parent LLPs

(1) A parent LLP qualifies as a small LLP in relation to a financial year only if the group headed by it qualifies as a small group.

(2) A group qualifies as small in relation to the parent LLP's first financial year if the qualifying conditions are met in that year.

[(2A) Subject to subsection (3), a group qualifies as small in relation to a subsequent financial year of the parent LLP if the qualifying conditions are met in that year.]

[(3) In relation to a subsequent financial year of the parent LLP, where on the parent LLP's balance sheet date the group meets or ceases to meet the qualifying conditions, that affects the group's qualification as a small group only if it occurs in two consecutive financial years.]

(4) The qualifying conditions are met by a group in a year in which it satisfies two or more of the following requirements—

1. Aggregate turnover	[Not more than £10.2 million net (or £12.2 million gross)]
2. Aggregate balance sheet total	[Not more than £5.1 million net (or £6.1 million gross)]

3. Aggregate number of employees Not more than 50

(5) The aggregate figures are ascertained by aggregating the relevant figures determined in accordance with section 382 for each member of the group.

(6) In relation to the aggregate figures for turnover and balance sheet total—

"net" means after any set-offs and other adjustments made to eliminate group transactions—

(a) in the case of non-IAS accounts in accordance with Part 1 of Schedule 4 to the Small Limited Liability Partnerships (Accounts) Regulations 2008 (SI 2008/1912) or Schedule 3 to the Large and Medium-sized Limited Liability Partnerships (Accounts) Regulations 2008 (SI 2008/1913),

(b) in the case of IAS accounts, in accordance with [UK-adopted international accounting standards]; and

"gross" means without those set-offs and other adjustments.

An LLP may satisfy any relevant requirement on the basis of either the net or the gross figure.

(7) The figures for each subsidiary undertaking shall be those included in its individual accounts for the relevant financial year, that is—

(a) if its financial year ends with that of the parent LLP, that financial year, and

(b) if not, its financial year ending last before the end of the financial year of the parent LLP.

If those figures cannot be obtained without disproportionate expense or undue delay, the latest available figures shall be taken.

384 LLPs excluded from the small LLPs regime

(1) The small LLPs regime does not apply to an LLP that . . . was at any time within the financial year to which the accounts relate—

[(a) a traded LLP,]

(b) an LLP that—

(i) is an authorised insurance company, a banking LLP, an e-money issuer, a MiFID investment firm or a UCITS management company, . . .

(ii) carries on insurance market activity, or

[(iii) is a scheme funder of a Master Trust scheme within the meanings given by section 39(1) of the Pension Schemes Act 2017 (interpretation of Part 1), or]

(c) a member of an ineligible group.

(2) A group is ineligible if any of its members is—

[(a) a traded company,]

(b) a body corporate (other than a company) whose shares are admitted to trading on a [UK regulated market],

(c) a person (other than a small company or small LLP) who has permission under Part 4 of the Financial Services and Markets Act 2000 (c 8) to carry on a regulated activity,

[(ca) an e-money issuer,]

(d) a small company or small LLP that is an authorised insurance company, a banking company or banking LLP, . . . a MiFID investment firm or a UCITS management company, . . .

(e) a person who carries on insurance market activity, [or]

[(f) a a scheme funder of a Master Trust scheme within the meanings given by section 39(1) of the Pension Schemes Act 2017 (interpretation of Part 1)].

(3) A company or LLP is a small company or small LLP for the purposes of subsection (2) if it qualified as small in relation to its last financial year ending on or before the end of the financial year to which the accounts relate."

NOTES

In s 382 as set out above, sub-s (1A) was inserted, sub-s (2) was substituted, and in sub-s (3) the words in square brackets in items 1 and 2 of the Table were substituted, by the Limited Liability Partnerships, Partnerships and Groups (Accounts and Audit) Regulations 2016, SI 2016/575, regs 3, 5(1), (2), as from 17 May 2016, in relation to (a) financial years beginning on or after 1 January 2016; and (b) a financial year of an LLP beginning on or after 1 January 2015, but before 1 January 2016, if (i) the members of the LLP so decide, and (ii) a copy of the LLP's accounts for that financial year has not been delivered to the registrar in accordance with ss 444, 445 or 446 of the Companies Act 2006 as applied to LLPs by the Limited Liability Partnerships (Accounts and Audit) (Application of Companies Act 2006) Regulations before 17 May 2016 (see further the note at **[10.226]**).

In s 383 as set out above, sub-s (2A) was inserted, sub-s (3) was substituted, and in sub-s (4) the words in square brackets in items 1 and 2 of the Table were substituted, by SI 2016/575, regs 3, 5(1), (3), as from 17 May 2016, in relation to (a) financial years beginning on or after 1 January 2016; and (b) a financial year of an LLP beginning on or after 1 January 2015, but before 1 January 2016, if (i) the members of the LLP so decide, and (ii) a copy of the LLP's accounts for that financial year has not been delivered to the registrar in accordance with ss 444, 445 or 446 of the Companies Act 2006 as applied to LLPs by the Limited Liability Partnerships (Accounts and Audit) (Application of Companies Act 2006) Regulations before 17 May 2016 (see further the note at **[10.226]**). Words in square brackets in sub-s (6) substituted by the International Accounting Standards and European Public Limited-Liability Company (Amendment etc) (EU Exit) Regulations 2019, SI 2019/685, reg 19, Sch 1, Pt 2, para 58(1), (2), in relation to accounts for financial years beginning on or after IP completion day (as defined in the European Union (Withdrawal Agreement) Act 2020, s 39) (note also that in relation to accounts for financial years which begin before but end on or after IP completion day, the enactments amended by Parts 1–3 of Sch 1 to the 2019 Regulations have effect as if the UK were a member State until the end of the financial year in question).

s 384 as set out above is amended as follows:

The first words omitted from sub-s (1) were revoked and sub-ss (1)(a), (2)(a) were substituted by SI 2016/575, regs 3, 5(1), (4), as from 17 May 2016, in relation to (a) financial years beginning on or after 1 January 2016; and (b) a financial year of an LLP beginning on or after 1 January 2015, but before 1 January 2016, if (i) the members of the LLP so decide, and (ii) a copy of the LLP's accounts for that financial year has not been delivered to the registrar in accordance with ss 444, 445 or 446 of the Companies Act 2006 as applied to LLPs by the Limited Liability Partnerships (Accounts and Audit) (Application of Companies Act 2006) Regulations before 17 May 2016 (see further the note at **[10.226]**). In sub-s (1), the word omitted from the end of sub-para (b)(i) was revoked, and sub-para (b)(iii) was inserted, by the Occupational Pension Schemes (Master Trusts) Regulations 2018, SI 2018/1030, reg 31(1), (2)(a), as from 1 October 2018.

Words in square brackets in sub-s (2)(b) substituted by the Accounts and Reports (Amendment) (EU Exit) Regulations 2019, SI 2019/145, reg 6, Sch 3, paras 11, 12, in relation to financial years beginning on or after IP completion day (as defined in the European Union (Withdrawal Agreement) Act 2020, s 39) (for transitional provisions see reg 7 of the 2019 Regulations at **[12.79]**).

In sub-s (2), para (ca) was inserted, and the first words omitted from para (d) were revoked, by the Companies and Partnerships (Accounts and Audit) Regulations 2013, SI 2013/2005, reg 3(1), (2), in relation to a financial year of an LLP beginning on or after 1 October 2013.

In sub-s (2), the word omitted from the end of para (d) was revoked, the word in square brackets in para (e) was inserted, and para (f) was added, by SI 2018/1030, reg 31(1), (2)(b), as from 1 October 2018.

[10.228]

[5A LLPs qualifying as micro-entities

Sections 384A and 384B apply to LLPs, modified so that they read as follows—

"384A 384A LLPs qualifying as micro-entities

(1) An LLP qualifies as a micro-entity in relation to its first financial year if the qualifying conditions are met in that year.

(2) Subject to subsection (3), an LLP qualifies as a micro-entity in relation to a subsequent financial year if the qualifying conditions are met in that year.

(3) In relation to a subsequent financial year, where on its balance sheet date an LLP meets or ceases to meet the qualifying conditions, that affects its qualification as a micro-entity only if it occurs in two consecutive financial years.

(4) The qualifying conditions are met by an LLP in a year in which it satisfies two or more of the following requirements—

1 Turnover	Not more than £632,000
2 Balance sheet total	Not more than £316,000
3 Number of employees	Not more than 10

(5) For a period that is an LLP's financial year but not in fact a year the maximum figure for turnover must be proportionately adjusted.

(6) The balance sheet total means the aggregate of the amounts shown as assets in the LLP's balance sheet.

(7) The number of employees means the average number of persons employed by the LLP in the year, determined as follows—

(a) find for each month in the financial year the number of persons employed under contracts of service by the LLP in that month (whether throughout the month or not),

(b) add together the monthly totals, and

(c) divide by the number of months in the financial year.

(8) In the case of an LLP which is a parent LLP, the LLP qualifies as a micro-entity in relation to a financial year only if—

(a) the LLP qualifies as a micro-entity in relation to that year, as determined by subsections (1) to (7), and

(b) the group headed by the LLP qualifies as a small group, as determined by section 383(2) to (7).

384B LLPs excluded from being treated as micro-entities

(1) The micro-entity provisions do not apply in relation to an LLP's accounts for a particular financial year if the LLP . . . at any time within that year—

(a) [was] an LLP excluded from the small LLPs regime by virtue of section 384,

(b) [would have been] an investment undertaking as defined in Article 2(14) of Directive 2013/34/EU of 26 June 2013 on the annual financial statements etc of certain types of undertakings [were the United Kingdom a member State],

(c) [would have been] a financial holding undertaking as defined in Article 2(15) of that Directive [were the United Kingdom a member State],

[(d) a credit institution within the meaning given by Article 4(1)(1) of Regulation (EU) No 575/2013 of the European Parliament and of the Council, [which is a CRR firm within the meaning of Article 4(1)(2A) of that Regulation,]] or

(e) [would have been] an insurance undertaking as defined in Article 2(1) of Council Directive 91/674/EEC of 19 December 1991 on the annual accounts and consolidated accounts of insurance undertakings [were the United Kingdom a member State].

(2) The micro-entity provisions also do not apply in relation to an LLP's accounts for a financial year if—

(a) the LLP is a parent LLP which prepares group accounts for that year as permitted by section [399(4)], or

(b) the LLP is not a parent LLP but its accounts are included in consolidated group accounts for that year."]

NOTES

Inserted by the Limited Liability Partnerships, Partnerships and Groups (Accounts and Audit) Regulations 2016, SI 2016/575, regs 3, 6, as from 17 May 2016, in relation to (a) financial years beginning on or after 1 January 2016; and (b) a financial year of an LLP beginning on or after 1 January 2015, but before 1 January 2016, if (i) the members of the LLP so decide, and (ii) a copy of the LLP's accounts for that financial year has not been delivered to the registrar in accordance with ss 444, 445 or 446 of the Companies Act 2006 as applied to LLPs by the Limited Liability Partnerships (Accounts and Audit) (Application of Companies Act 2006) Regulations before 17 May 2016 (see further the note at **[10.226]**).

Section 384B as set out above is amended as follows:

The word omitted from sub-s (1) was revoked, the words in square brackets in paras (a)–(c) and (e) of sub-s (1) were inserted, and the words in square brackets in para (d) of sub-s (1) were substituted, by the Accounts and Reports (Amendment) (EU Exit) Regulations 2019, SI 2019/145, reg 6, Sch 3, paras 11, 13, in relation to financial years beginning on or after IP completion day (as defined in the European Union (Withdrawal Agreement) Act 2020, s 39) (for transitional provisions see reg 7 of the 2019 Regulations at **[12.79]**).

In sub-s (1), para (d) was substituted by SI 2019/145, reg 4, Sch 1, para 3, as from 6 February 2019.

In sub-s (2)(a), the figure in square brackets was substituted by the Statutory Auditors Regulations 2017, SI 2017/1164, reg 5, Sch 3, paras 1, 2, as from 1 January 2018, in relation to financial years of companies beginning on or after 1 January 2017 (as to the application of the 2017 Regulations, see **[4.671]** et seq).

PART 3 ACCOUNTING RECORDS

[10.229]

6 LLP's accounting records

Sections 386 to 389 apply to LLPs, modified so that they read as follows—

"386 Duty to keep accounting records

(1) Every LLP must keep adequate accounting records.

(2) Adequate accounting records means records that are sufficient—

(a) to show and explain the LLP's transactions,

(b) to disclose with reasonable accuracy, at any time, the financial position of the LLP at that time, and

(c) to enable the members of the LLP to ensure that any accounts required to be prepared comply with the requirements of this Act.

(3) Accounting records must, in particular, contain—

(a) entries from day to day of all sums of money received and expended by the LLP and the matters in respect of which the receipt and expenditure takes place, and

(b) a record of the assets and liabilities of the LLP.

(4) If the LLP's business involves dealing in goods, the accounting records must contain—

(a) statements of stock held by the LLP at the end of each financial year of the LLP,

(b) all statements of stocktakings from which any statement of stock as is mentioned in paragraph (a) has been or is to be prepared, and

(c) except in the case of goods sold by way of ordinary retail trade, statements of all goods sold and purchased, showing the goods and the buyers and sellers in sufficient detail to enable all these to be identified.

(5) A parent LLP that has a subsidiary undertaking in relation to which the above requirements do not apply must take reasonable steps to secure that the undertaking keeps such accounting records as to enable the members of the parent LLP to ensure that any accounts required to be prepared under this Part comply with the requirements of this Act.

387 Duty to keep accounting records: offence

(1) If an LLP fails to comply with any provision of section 386 (duty to keep accounting records), an offence is committed by every member of the LLP who is in default.

(2) It is a defence for a person charged with such an offence to show that he acted honestly and that in the circumstances in which the LLP's business was carried on the default was excusable.

(3) A person guilty of an offence under this section is liable—

(a) on conviction on indictment, to imprisonment for a term not exceeding two years or a fine (or both);

(b) on summary conviction—

(i) in England and Wales [or Scotland], to imprisonment for a term not exceeding twelve months or to a fine not exceeding the statutory maximum (or both);

(ii) in . . . Northern Ireland, to imprisonment for a term not exceeding six months, or to a fine not exceeding the statutory maximum (or both).

388 Where and for how long records to be kept

(1) An LLP's accounting records—

(a) must be kept at its registered office or such other place as the members think fit, and

(b) must at all times be open to inspection by the members of the LLP.

(2) If accounting records are kept at a place outside the United Kingdom, accounts and returns with respect to the business dealt with in the accounting records so kept must be sent to, and kept at, a place in the United Kingdom, and must at all times be open to such inspection.

(3) The accounts and returns to be sent to the United Kingdom must be such as to—

(a) disclose with reasonable accuracy the financial position of the business in question at intervals of not more than six months, and

(b) enable the members of the LLP to ensure that the accounts required to be prepared under this Part comply with the requirements of this Act.

(4) Accounting records that an LLP is required by section 386 to keep must be preserved by it for three years from the date on which they are made.

(5) Subsection (4) is subject to any provision contained in rules made under section 411 of the Insolvency Act 1986 (c.45) (company insolvency rules) or Article 359 of the Insolvency (Northern Ireland) Order 1989 (SI 1989/2405 (NI 19)).

389 Where and for how long records to be kept: offences

(1) If an LLP fails to comply with any provision of subsections (1) to (3) of section 388 (requirements as to keeping of accounting records), an offence is committed by every member of the LLP who is in default.

(2) It is a defence for a person charged with such an offence to show that he acted honestly and that in the circumstances in which the LLP's business was carried on the default was excusable.

(3) A member of an LLP commits an offence if he—

(a) fails to take all reasonable steps for securing compliance by the LLP with subsection (4) of that section (period for which records to be preserved), or

(b) intentionally causes any default by the LLP under that subsection.

(4) A person guilty of an offence under this section is liable—

(a) on conviction on indictment, to imprisonment for a term not exceeding two years or a fine (or both);

(b) on summary conviction—

(i) in England and Wales [or Scotland], to imprisonment for a term not exceeding twelve months or to a fine not exceeding the statutory maximum (or both);

(ii) in . . . Northern Ireland, to imprisonment for a term not exceeding six months, or to a fine not exceeding the statutory maximum (or both)."

NOTES

In ss 387(3)(b) and 389(4)(b) as set out above, the words in square brackets were inserted, and the words omitted were revoked, by the Limited Liability Partnerships (Application of Companies Act 2006) Regulations 2009, SI 2009/1804, reg 85, Sch 3, Pt 2, para 16, as from 1 October 2009.

PART 4 FINANCIAL YEARS

[10.230]

7 An LLP's financial year

(1) Sections 390 to 392 apply to LLPs, modified so that they read as follows—

"390 An LLP's financial year

(1) An LLP's financial year is determined as follows.

(2) Its first financial year—

(a) begins with the first day of its first accounting reference period, and

(b) ends with the last day of that period or such other date, not more than seven days before or after the end of that period, as the members of the LLP may determine.

(3) Subsequent financial years—

(a) begin with the day immediately following the end of the LLP's previous financial year, and

(b) end with the last day of its next accounting reference period or such other date, not more than seven days before or after the end of that period, as the members of the LLP may determine.

(4) In relation to an undertaking that is not an LLP, references in this Act to its financial year are to any period in respect of which a profit and loss account of the undertaking is required to be made up (by its constitution or by the law under which it is established), whether that period is a year or not.

(5) The members of a parent LLP must secure that, except where in their opinion there are good reasons against it, the financial year of each of its subsidiary undertakings coincides with the LLP's own financial year.

391 Accounting reference periods and accounting reference date

(1) An LLP's accounting reference periods are determined according to its accounting reference date in each calendar year.

(2) The accounting reference date of an LLP is the last day of the month in which the anniversary of its incorporation falls.

(3) An LLP's first accounting reference period is the period of more than six months, but not more than 18 months, beginning with the date of its incorporation and ending with its accounting reference date.

(4) Its subsequent accounting reference periods are successive periods of twelve months beginning immediately after the end of the previous accounting reference period and ending with its accounting reference date.

(5) This section has effect subject to the provisions of section 392 (alteration of accounting reference date).

392 Alteration of accounting reference date

(1) An LLP may by notice given to the registrar specify a new accounting reference date having effect in relation to—

(a) the LLP's current accounting reference period and subsequent periods, or

(b) the LLP's previous accounting reference period and subsequent periods.

An LLP's "previous accounting reference period" means the one immediately preceding its current accounting reference period.

(2) The notice must state whether the current or previous accounting reference period—

(a) is to be shortened, so as to come to an end on the first occasion on which the new accounting reference date falls or fell after the beginning of the period, or

(b) is to be extended, so as to come to an end on the second occasion on which that date falls or fell after the beginning of the period.

(3) A notice extending an LLP's current or previous accounting reference period is not effective if given less than five years after the end of an earlier accounting reference period of the LLP that was extended under this section.

This does not apply—

(a) to a notice given by an LLP that is a subsidiary undertaking or parent undertaking of another [UK] undertaking if the new accounting reference date coincides with that of the other [UK] undertaking or, where that undertaking is not a company or an LLP, with the last day of its financial year, or

(b) where the LLP is in administration under Part 2 of the Insolvency Act 1986 (c.45) or Part 3 of the Insolvency (Northern Ireland) Order 1989 (SI 1989/2405 (NI 19)), or

(c) where the Secretary of State directs that it should not apply, which he may do with respect to a notice that has been given or that may be given.

(4) A notice under this section may not be given in respect of a previous accounting reference period if the period for filing the accounts and auditor's report for the financial year determined by reference to that accounting reference period has already expired.

(5) An accounting reference period may not be extended so as to exceed 18 months and a notice under this section is ineffective if the current or previous accounting reference period as extended in accordance with the notice would exceed that limit.

This does not apply where the LLP is in administration under Part 2 of the Insolvency Act 1986 (c.45) or Part 3 of the Insolvency (Northern Ireland) Order 1989 (SI 1989/2405 (NI 19)).

(6) In this section "[UK undertaking]" means an undertaking established under the law of any part of the United Kingdom . . . "

(2) Until section 1068(1) comes fully into force, the notice referred to in section 392 (notice of alteration of accounting reference date) as applied to LLPs by paragraph (1) must be given in the form prescribed for the purposes of—

(a) section 225(1) of the 1985 Act as applied to LLPs by regulation 3 of, and Schedule 1 to, the Limited Liability Partnerships Regulations 2001, or

(b) Article 233(1) of the 1986 Order as applied to LLPs by regulation 3 of, and Schedule 1 to, the Limited Liability Partnerships Regulations (Northern Ireland) 2004.

NOTES

In s 392 as set out above, the words in square brackets in sub-ss (3), (6) were substituted, and the words omitted from sub-s (6) were revoked, by the Accounts and Reports (Amendment) (EU Exit) Regulations 2019, SI 2019/145, reg 6, Sch 3, paras 11, 14, as from IP completion day (as defined in the European Union (Withdrawal Agreement) Act 2020, s 39).

PART 5 ANNUAL ACCOUNTS

[10.231]

8 Annual accounts to give true and fair view

Section 393 applies to LLPs, modified so that it reads as follows—

"393 Accounts to give true and fair view

(1) The members of an LLP must not approve accounts for the purposes of this Chapter unless they are satisfied that they give a true and fair view of the assets, liabilities, financial position and profit or loss—

(a) in the case of the LLP's individual accounts, of the LLP;

(b) in the case of the LLP's group accounts, of the undertakings included in the consolidation as a whole, so far as concerns members of the LLP.

[(1A) Subsection (1B) applies to the members of an LLP which qualifies as a micro-entity in relation to a financial year (see sections 384A and 384B) in their consideration of whether the non-IAS individual accounts of the LLP for that year give a true and fair view as required by subsection (1)(a).

(1B) Where the accounts contain an item of information additional to the micro-entity minimum accounting items, the members must have regard to any provision of an accounting standard which relates to that item.]

(2) The auditor of an LLP in carrying out his functions under this Act in relation to the LLP's annual accounts must have regard to the members' duty under subsection (1)."

NOTES

In s 393 as set out above, sub-ss (1A), (1B) were inserted by the Limited Liability Partnerships, Partnerships and Groups (Accounts and Audit) Regulations 2016, SI 2016/575, regs 3, 7, as from 17 May 2016, in relation to (a) financial years beginning on or after 1 January 2016; and (b) a financial year of an LLP beginning on or after 1 January 2015, but before 1 January 2016, if (i) the members of the LLP so decide, and (ii) a copy of the LLP's accounts for that financial year has not been delivered to the registrar in accordance with ss 444, 445 or 446 of the Companies Act 2006 as applied to LLPs by the Limited Liability Partnerships (Accounts and Audit) (Application of Companies Act 2006) Regulations before 17 May 2016 (see further the note at **[10.226]**).

[10.232]

9 Individual accounts

Sections 394 to 397 apply to LLPs, modified so that they read as follows—

"394 Duty to prepare individual accounts

The members of every LLP must prepare accounts for the LLP for each of its financial years [unless the LLP is exempt from that requirement under section 394A].

Those accounts are referred to as the LLP's "individual accounts".

[394A Individual accounts: exemption for dormant subsidiaries

(1) An LLP is exempt from the requirement to prepare individual accounts in a financial year if—

(a) it is itself a subsidiary undertaking,

(b) it has been dormant throughout the whole of that year, and

(c) its parent undertaking is established under the law of [any part of the United Kingdom].

(2) Exemption is conditional upon compliance with all of the following conditions—

(a) all members of the LLP must agree to the exemption in respect of the financial year in question,

(b) the parent undertaking must give a guarantee under section 394C in respect of that year,

(c) the LLP must be included in the consolidated accounts drawn up for that year or to an earlier date in that year by the parent undertaking in accordance with—

[(i) if the undertaking is a company, the requirements of this Part of this Act, or, if the undertaking is not a company, the legal requirements which apply to the drawing up of consolidated accounts for that undertaking, or]
(ii) [UK-adopted international accounting standards],
(d) the parent undertaking must disclose in the notes to the consolidated accounts that the LLP is exempt from the requirement to prepare individual accounts by virtue of this section,
(e) the designated members of the LLP must deliver to the registrar, within the period for filing the LLP's account and auditor's report for that year—
(i) a written notice of the agreement referred to in subsection (2)(a),
(ii) the statement referred to in section 394C(1),
(iii) a copy of the consolidated accounts referred to in subsection (2)(c),
(iv) a copy of the auditor's report on those accounts, and
(v) a copy of the consolidated annual report drawn up by the parent undertaking.

394B LLPs excluded from the dormant subsidiaries exemption

An LLP is not entitled to the exemption conferred by section 394A (dormant subsidiaries) if it was at any time within the financial year in question—
[(za) a traded LLP,]
(a) an LLP that—
(i) is an authorised insurance company, a banking LLP, an e-money issuer, a MiFID investment firm or a UCITS management company, or
(ii) carries on insurance market activity, or
(b) an employers' association as defined in section 122 of the Trade Union and Labour Relations (Consolidation) Act 1992 (c 52) or Article 4 of the Industrial Relations (Northern Ireland) Order 1992 (SI 1992/807) (NI 5).

394C Dormant subsidiaries exemption: parent undertaking declaration of guarantee

(1) A guarantee is given by a parent undertaking under this section when the designated members of the subsidiary LLP deliver to the registrar a statement by the parent undertaking that it guarantees the subsidiary LLP under this section.
(2) The statement under subsection (1) must be authenticated by the parent undertaking and must specify—
(a) the name of the parent undertaking,
[(b) the registered number of the parent undertaking (if any),]
(c) . . .
(d) the name and registered number of the subsidiary LLP in respect of which the guarantee is being given,
(e) the date of the statement, and
(f) the financial year to which the guarantee relates.
(3) A guarantee given under this section has the effect that—
(a) the parent undertaking guarantees all outstanding liabilities to which the subsidiary LLP is subject at the end of the financial year to which the guarantee relates, until they are satisfied in full, and
(b) the guarantee is enforceable against the parent undertaking by any person to whom the subsidiary LLP is liable in respect of those liabilities.]

395 Individual accounts: applicable accounting framework

(1) An LLP's individual accounts may be prepared—
(a) in accordance with section 396 ("non-IAS individual accounts"), or
(b) in accordance with [UK-adopted international accounting standards] ("IAS individual accounts").

This is subject to the following provisions of this section and to section 407 (consistency of financial reporting within group).

(2) After the first financial year in which the members of an LLP prepare IAS individual accounts ("the first IAS year"), all subsequent individual accounts of the LLP must be prepared in accordance with [UK-adopted international accounting standards] unless there is a relevant change of circumstance. [This is subject to subsection (3A)].
(3) There is a relevant change of circumstance if, at any time during or after the first IAS year—
(a) the LLP becomes a subsidiary undertaking of another undertaking that does not prepare IAS individual accounts,
(b) the LLP ceases to be a subsidiary undertaking,
(c) the LLP ceases to be an LLP with securities admitted to trading on a [UK regulated market], or
(d) a parent undertaking of the LLP ceases to be an undertaking with securities admitted to trading on a [UK regulated market].

[(3A) After a financial year in which the members of an LLP prepare IAS individual accounts, the members may change to preparing non-IAS individual accounts for a reason other than a relevant change of circumstance provided they have not changed to non-IAS individual accounts in the period of five years preceding the first day of that financial year.
(3B) In calculating the five year period for the purpose of subsection (3A), no account should be taken of a change due to a relevant change of circumstance.]
(4) If, having changed to preparing non-IAS individual accounts . . . , the members again prepare IAS individual accounts for the LLP, subsections (2) and (3) apply again as if the first financial year for which such accounts are again prepared were the first IAS year.

396 Non-IAS individual accounts

[(A1) Non-IAS individual accounts must state—

(a) the part of the United Kingdom in which the LLP is registered,

(b) the LLP's registered number,

(c) the address of the LLP's registered office, and

(d) where appropriate, the fact that the LLP is being wound up.]

(1) Non-IAS individual accounts must comprise—

(a) a balance sheet as at the last day of the financial year, and

(b) a profit and loss account.

(2) The accounts must—

(a) in the case of the balance sheet, give a true and fair view of the state of affairs of the LLP as at the end of the financial year, and

(b) in the case of the profit and loss account, give a true and fair view of the profit or loss of the LLP for the financial year.

[(2A) In the case of the individual accounts of an LLP which qualifies as a micro-entity in relation to the financial year (see sections 384A and 384B), the micro-entity minimum accounting items included in the LLP's accounts for the year are presumed to give the true and fair view required by subsection (2).]

(3) The accounts must comply with the provisions of—

(a) regulation 3 of the Small Limited Liability Partnerships (Accounts) Regulations 2008 (non-IAS individual accounts of LLP subject to the small LLPs regime) (SI 2008/1912), or

(b) regulations 3 and 4 of the Large and Medium-sized Limited Liability Partnerships (Accounts) Regulations 2008 (non-IAS individual accounts of large and medium-sized LLPs) (SI 2008/1913),

as to the form and content of the balance sheet and profit and loss account, and additional information to be provided by way of notes to the accounts.

(4) If compliance with the regulations specified in subsection (3), and any other provision made by or under this Act as to the matters to be included in an LLP's individual accounts or in notes to those accounts, would not be sufficient to give a true and fair view, the necessary additional information must be given in the accounts or in a note to them.

(5) If in special circumstances compliance with any of those provisions is inconsistent with the requirement to give a true and fair view, the members must depart from that provision to the extent necessary to give a true and fair view.

Particulars of any such departure, the reasons for it and its effect must be given in a note to the accounts.

[(6) Subsections (4) and (5) do not apply in relation to the micro-entity minimum accounting items included in the individual accounts of an LLP for a financial year in relation to which the LLP qualifies as a micro-entity.]

[397 IAS individual accounts

(1) IAS individual accounts must state—

(a) the part of the United Kingdom in which the LLP is registered,

(b) the LLP's registered number,

(c) the address of the LLP's registered office, and

(d) where appropriate, the fact that the LLP is being wound up.

(2) The notes to the accounts must state that the accounts have been prepared in accordance with [UK-adopted international accounting standards].]".

NOTES

In s 394 as set out above, the words "unless the LLP is exempt from that requirement under section 394A" in square brackets were inserted by the Companies and Limited Liability Partnerships (Accounts and Audit Exemptions and Change of Accounting Framework) Regulations 2012, SI 2012/2301, reg 20(1), (5)(a), as from 1 October 2012 (in relation to accounts for financial years ending on or after that date).

Ss 394A–394C as set out above were inserted by SI 2012/2301, reg 20(1), (5)(b), as from 1 October 2012 (in relation to accounts for financial years ending on or after that date). These sections have subsequently been amended as follows:

The words in square brackets in sub-s (1)(c) of s 394A and sub-s (2)(c)(i) of that section were substituted by the Accounts and Reports (Amendment) (EU Exit) Regulations 2019, SI 2019/145, reg 6, Sch 3, paras 11, 15(a), in relation to financial years beginning on or after IP completion day (as defined in the European Union (Withdrawal Agreement) Act 2020, s 39) (for transitional provisions see reg 7 of the 2019 Regulations at **[12.79]**).

Words in square brackets in s 394A(2)(c)(ii) substituted by the International Accounting Standards and European Public Limited-Liability Company (Amendment etc) (EU Exit) Regulations 2019, SI 2019/685, reg 19, Sch 1, Pt 2, para 58(1), (3)(a), in relation to accounts for financial years beginning on or after IP completion day (as defined in the European Union (Withdrawal Agreement) Act 2020, s 39) (note also that in relation to accounts for financial years which begin before but end on or after IP completion day, the enactments amended by Parts 1–3 of Sch 1 to the 2019 Regulations have effect as if the UK were a member State until the end of the financial year in question).

Para (za) of s 394B was inserted by SI 2016/575, regs 3(1), 8(1), (3), as from 17 May 2016, in relation to (a) financial years beginning on or after 1 January 2016; and (b) a financial year of an LLP beginning on or after 1 January 2015, but before 1 January 2016, if (i) the members of the LLP so decide, and (ii) a copy of the LLP's accounts for that financial year has not been delivered to the registrar in accordance with ss 444, 445 or 446 of the Companies Act 2006 as applied to LLPs by the Limited Liability Partnerships (Accounts and Audit) (Application of Companies Act 2006) Regulations before 17 May 2016 (see further the note at **[10.226]**).

Sub-s (2)(b) of s 394C was substituted, and sub-s (2)(c) of that section was revoked, by SI 2019/145, reg 6, Sch 3, paras 11, 15(b), in relation to financial years beginning on or after IP completion day (as defined in the European Union (Withdrawal Agreement) Act 2020, s 39) (for transitional provisions see reg 7 of the 2019 Regulations at **[12.79]**).

Section 395 as set out above has been amended as follows:

The words "UK-adopted international accounting standards" in square brackets in sub-ss (1)(b) and (2) were substituted by SI 2019/685, reg 19, Sch 1, Pt 2, para 58(1), (3)(b), in relation to accounts for financial years beginning on or after IP completion day (as defined in the European Union (Withdrawal Agreement) Act 2020, s 39) (note also that in relation to accounts for financial years which begin before but end on or after IP completion day, the enactments amended by Parts 1–3 of Sch 1 to the 2019 Regulations have effect as if the UK were a member State until the end of the financial year in question – and see further the transitional provisions note below).

The words "This is subject to subsection (3A)" in square brackets in sub-s (2) were inserted by SI 2012/2301, reg 20(1), (8)(a), as from 1 October 2012 (in relation to accounts for financial years ending on or after that date).

Words in square brackets in sub-s (3)(c), (d) substituted by SI 2019/145, reg 6, Sch 3, paras 11, 15(c), in relation to financial years beginning on or after IP completion day (as defined in the European Union (Withdrawal Agreement) Act 2020, s 39) (for transitional provisions see reg 7 of the 2019 Regulations at **[12.79]**).

Sub-ss (3A), (3B) were inserted by SI 2012/2301, reg 20(1), (8)(b), as from 1 October 2012 (in relation to accounts for financial years ending on or after that date).

The words omitted from sub-s (4) were revoked by SI 2012/2301, reg 20(1), (8)(c), as from 1 October 2012 (in relation to accounts for financial years ending on or after that date).

In s 396 as set out above, sub-ss (1A) and (2A) were inserted, and sub-s (6) was added, by SI 2016/575, regs 3(1), 8(1), (4) (as to the commencement of the 2016 Regulations, see the first note relating to them above).

Section 397 as set out above was substituted by SI 2016/575, regs 3(1), 8(1), (5) (as to the commencement of the 2016 Regulations, see the first note relating to them above). Words in square brackets in sub-s (2) substituted by SI 2019/685, reg 19, Sch 1, Pt 2, para 58(1), (3)(c), in relation to accounts for financial years beginning on or after IP completion day (as defined in the European Union (Withdrawal Agreement) Act 2020, s 39) (note also that in relation to accounts for financial years which begin before but end on or after IP completion day, the enactments amended by Parts 1–3 of Sch 1 to the 2019 Regulations have effect as if the UK were a member State until the end of the financial year in question).

Transitional provisions: the International Accounting Standards and European Public Limited-Liability Company (Amendment etc) (EU Exit) Regulations 2019, SI 2019/685, Sch 1, Pt 4, para 65 provides as follows:

"65.

(1) Where an LLP's individual accounts are prepared in accordance with the pre-commencement version of section 395(1)(b) of the Companies Act 2006 as applied to LLPs, the accounts are to continue to be treated as "IAS individual accounts" for the purposes of that Act as applied to LLPs.

(2) Where, in the last financial year of an LLP to begin before IP completion day, the LLP's individual accounts are prepared in accordance with the pre-commencement version of section 395(1)(b) of that Act as applied to LLPs, section 395(3) and (4) of that Act as applied to LLPs have effect in relation to the LLP as if the references to the first IAS year were to that financial year.

(3) Where the group accounts of an LLP are prepared in accordance with the pre-commencement version of section 403(1)(b) of the Companies Act 2006 as applied to LLPs, the accounts are to continue to be treated as "IAS group accounts" for the purposes of that Act as applied to LLPs.

(4) Where, in the last financial year of an LLP to begin before IP completion day, the group accounts of the LLP are prepared in accordance with the pre-commencement version of section 403(1)(b) of that Act as applied to LLPs, section 403(2) and (3) of that Act as applied to LLPs have effect in relation to the LLP as if the reference to the first IAS year were to that financial year.

(5) In this paragraph—

(a) "LLP" means a limited liability partnership registered under the Limited Liability Partnerships Act 2000;

(b) references to a provision of the Companies Act 2006 "as applied to LLPs" means to that provision as applied to LLPs by regulation 9 of the Limited Liability Partnerships (Accounts and Audit) (Application of Companies Act 2006) Regulations 2008;

(c) references to the "pre-commencement version" of a provision of the Companies Act 2006 as applied to LLPs are to that provision as applied to LLPs, as it had effect before IP completion day in relation to a financial year of an LLP that began before IP completion day.".

Note that SI 2019/685, Sch 1, Pt 4, para 65 as set out above was amended by the Companies and Statutory Auditors etc (Consequential Amendments) (EU Exit) Regulations 2020, SI 2020/523, reg 25, with effect from immediately before IP completion day; and that the amendments have been incorporated.

[10.233]

10 Group accounts

Sections 398 to 408 apply to LLPs, modified so that they read as follows—

398

. . .

399 Duty to prepare group accounts

(1) . . .

(2) If at the end of a financial year [an LLP] is a parent LLP the members, as well as preparing individual accounts for the year, must prepare group accounts for the year unless the LLP is exempt from that requirement.

[(2A) An LLP is exempt from the requirement to prepare group accounts if—

(a) at the end of the financial year, the LLP is subject to the small LLPs regime, and

(b) is not a member of a group which, at any time during the financial year, has an undertaking falling within subsection (2B) as a member.

(2B) An undertaking falls within this subsection if—

(a) it is established under the law of [any part of the United Kingdom],

(b) it has to prepare accounts in accordance with [the requirements of this Part of this Act], and

[(c) it—

(i) is an undertaking whose transferable securities are admitted to trading on a UK regulated market,

(ii) is a credit institution within the meaning given by Article 4(1)(1) of Regulation (EU) No 575/2013 of the European Parliament and of the Council, which is a CRR firm within the meaning of Article 4(1)(2A) of that Regulation, or

(iii) would be an insurance undertaking within the meaning given by Article 2(1) of Council Directive 91/674/EEC of the European Parliament and of the Council on the annual accounts of insurance undertakings were the United Kingdom a member State.]

(3) There are exemptions under—

(a) section 400 (LLP included in [UK] accounts of larger group),

(b) section 401 (LLP included in [non-UK] accounts of larger group), and

(c) section 402 (LLP none of whose subsidiary undertakings need be included in the consolidation).

(4) An LLP . . . which is exempt from the requirement to prepare group accounts, may do so.

400 Exemption for LLP included in [UK] group accounts of larger group

(1) An LLP is exempt from the requirement to prepare group accounts if it is itself a subsidiary undertaking and its immediate parent undertaking is established under the law of [any part of the United Kingdom], in the following cases—

(a) where the LLP is a wholly-owned subsidiary of that parent undertaking;

[(b) where that parent undertaking holds 90% or more of the shares in the LLP and the remaining members have approved the exemption;

(c) where that parent undertaking holds more than 50% (but less than 90%) of the shares in the LLP and notice requesting the preparation of group accounts has not been served on the LLP by the members holding in aggregate at least 5% of the shares in the LLP.

Such notice must be served at least six months before the end of the financial year to which it relates.]

(2) Exemption is conditional upon compliance with all of the following conditions—

(a) the LLP must be included in consolidated accounts for a larger group drawn up to the same date, or to an earlier date in the same financial year, by a parent undertaking established under the law of [any part of the United Kingdom];

(b) those accounts must be drawn up and audited, and that parent undertaking's annual report must be drawn up . . . —

[(i) if the undertaking is a company, in accordance with the requirements of this Part of this Act, or, if the undertaking is not a company, the legal requirements which apply to the drawing up of consolidated accounts for that undertaking, or]

(ii) in accordance with [UK-adopted international accounting standards];

(c) the LLP must disclose in [the notes to] its individual accounts that it is exempt from the obligation to prepare and deliver group accounts;

(d) the LLP must state in its individual accounts the name of the parent undertaking that draws up the group accounts referred to above and—

[(i) the address of the undertaking's registered office . . . or]

(ii) if it is unincorporated, the address of its principal place of business;

(e) the LLP must deliver to the registrar, within the period for filing its accounts and auditor's report for the financial year in question, copies of those group accounts, together with the auditor's report on them;

(f) any requirement of Part 35 of this Act as to the delivery to the registrar of a certified translation into English must be met in relation to any document comprised in the accounts and reports delivered in accordance with paragraph (e).

(3) For the purposes of subsection (1)(b) [and (c)] shares held by a wholly-owned subsidiary of the parent undertaking, or held on behalf of the parent undertaking or a wholly-owned subsidiary, shall be attributed to the parent undertaking.

(4) The exemption does not apply to an LLP [which is a traded LLP].

(5) . . .

401 Exemption for LLP included in [non-UK] group accounts of larger group

(1) An LLP is exempt from the requirement to prepare group accounts if it is itself a subsidiary undertaking and its parent undertaking is not established under the law of [any part of the United Kingdom], in the following cases—

(a) where the LLP is a wholly-owned subsidiary of that parent undertaking;

[(b) where that parent undertaking holds 90% or more of the shares in the LLP and the remaining members have approved the exemption;

(c) where that parent undertaking holds more than 50% (but less than 90%) of the shares in the LLP and notice requesting the preparation of group accounts has not been served on the LLP by the members holding in aggregate at least 5% of the shares in the LLP.

Such notice must be served at least six months before the end of the financial year to which it relates.]

(2) Exemption is conditional upon compliance with all of the following conditions—

(a) the LLP and all of its subsidiary undertakings must be included in consolidated accounts for a larger group drawn up to the same date, or to an earlier date in the same financial year, by a parent undertaking;

[(b) those accounts must be drawn up—

(i) . . .

(ii) in a manner equivalent to consolidated accounts [drawn up in accordance with the requirements of this Part of this Act],

(iii) in accordance with [UK-adopted international accounting standards] adopted pursuant to the IAS Regulation, or

(iv) in accordance with accounting standards which are equivalent to such international accounting standards, as determined pursuant to Commission Regulation (EC) No 1569/2007 of 21 December 2007 establishing a mechanism for the determination of

Part 10 Miscellaneous other SIs

equivalence of accounting standards applied by third country issuers of securities pursuant to Directives 2003/71/EC and 2004/109/EC of the European Parliament and of the Council;]

(c) the group accounts must be audited by one or more persons authorised to audit accounts under the law under which the parent undertaking which draws them up is established;

(d) the LLP must disclose in its individual accounts that it is exempt from the obligation to prepare and deliver group accounts;

(e) the LLP must state in its individual accounts the name of the parent undertaking which draws up the group accounts referred to above and—

[(i) the address of the undertaking's registered office (whether in or outside the United Kingdom), or]

(ii) if it is unincorporated, the address of its principal place of business;

(f) the LLP must deliver to the registrar, within the period for filing its accounts and auditor's report for the financial year in question, copies of the group accounts, together with the auditor's report on them;

(g) any requirement of Part 35 of this Act as to the delivery to the registrar of a certified translation into English must be met in relation to any document comprised in the accounts and reports delivered in accordance with paragraph (f).

(3) For the purposes of subsection (1)(b) [and (c)] shares held by a wholly-owned subsidiary of the parent undertaking, or held on behalf of the parent undertaking or a wholly-owned subsidiary, shall be attributed to the parent undertaking.

(4) The exemption does not apply to an LLP [which is a traded LLP].

(5) . . .

402 Exemption if no subsidiary undertakings need be included in the consolidation

A parent LLP is exempt from the requirement to prepare group accounts if under section 405 all of its subsidiary undertakings could be excluded from consolidation in non-IAS group accounts.

403 Group accounts: applicable accounting framework

(1) The group accounts of a parent LLP may be prepared—

(a) in accordance with section 404 ("non-IAS group accounts"), or

(b) in accordance with [UK-adopted international accounting standards] ("IAS group accounts").

This is subject to the following provisions of this section.

(2) After the first financial year in which the members of a parent LLP prepare IAS group accounts ("the first IAS year"), all subsequent group accounts of the LLP must be prepared in accordance with [UK-adopted international accounting standards] unless there is a relevant change of circumstance. [This is subject to subsection (3A).]

(3) There is a relevant change of circumstance if, at any time during or after the first IAS year—

(a) the LLP becomes a subsidiary undertaking of another undertaking that does not prepare IAS group accounts,

(b) the LLP ceases to be an LLP with securities admitted to trading on a [UK regulated market], or

(c) a parent undertaking of the LLP ceases to be an undertaking with securities admitted to trading on a [UK regulated market].

[(3A) After a financial year in which the members of a parent LLP prepare IAS group accounts, the members may change to preparing non-IAS group accounts for a reason other than a relevant change of circumstance provided they have not changed to non-IAS group accounts in the period of five years preceding the first day of that financial year.

(3B) In calculating the five year period for the purpose of subsection (3A), no account should be taken of a change due to a relevant change of circumstance.]

(4) If, having changed to preparing non-IAS group accounts . . . , the members again prepare IAS group accounts for the LLP, subsections (2) and (3) apply again as if the first financial year for which such accounts are again prepared were the first IAS year.

404 Non-IAS group accounts

[(A1) Non-IAS group accounts must state, in respect of the parent LLP—

(a) the part of the United Kingdom in which the LLP is registered,

(b) the LLP's registered number,

(c) the address of the LLP's registered office, and

(d) where appropriate, the fact that the LLP is being wound up.]

(1) Non-IAS group accounts must comprise—

(a) a consolidated balance sheet dealing with the state of affairs of the parent LLP and its subsidiary undertakings, and

(b) a consolidated profit and loss account dealing with the profit or loss of the parent LLP and its subsidiary undertakings.

(2) The accounts must give a true and fair view of the state of affairs as at the end of the financial year, and the profit or loss for the financial year, of the undertakings included in the consolidation as a whole, so far as concerns members of the LLP.

(3) The accounts must comply with the provisions of—

(a) regulation 6 of the Small Limited Liability Partnerships (Accounts) Regulations 2008 (non-IAS group accounts of small parent LLP opting to prepare group accounts) (SI 2008/1912), or

(b) regulation 6 of the Large and Medium-sized Limited Liability Partnerships (Accounts) Regulations 2008 (non-IAS group accounts of large and medium-sized parent LLPs) (SI 2008/1913), as to the form and content of the consolidated balance sheet and consolidated profit and loss account, and additional information to be provided by way of notes to the accounts.

(4) If compliance with the regulations specified in subsection (3), and any other provision made by or under this Act as to the matters to be included in an LLP's group accounts or in notes to those accounts, would not be sufficient to give a true and fair view, the necessary additional information must be given in the accounts or in a note to them.

(5) If in special circumstances compliance with any of those provisions is inconsistent with the requirement to give a true and fair view, the members must depart from that provision to the extent necessary to give a true and fair view.

Particulars of any such departure, the reasons for it and its effect must be given in a note to the accounts.

405 Non-IAS group accounts: subsidiary undertakings included in the consolidation

(1) Where a parent LLP prepares non-IAS group accounts, all the subsidiary undertakings of the LLP must be included in the consolidation, subject to the following exceptions.

(2) A subsidiary undertaking may be excluded from consolidation if its inclusion is not material for the purpose of giving a true and fair view (but two or more undertakings may be excluded only if they are not material taken together).

(3) A subsidiary undertaking may be excluded from consolidation where—
- (a) severe long-term restrictions substantially hinder the exercise of the rights of the parent LLP over the assets or management of that undertaking, or
- (b) [extremely rare circumstances mean that] the information necessary for the preparation of group accounts cannot be obtained without disproportionate expense or undue delay, or
- (c) the interest of the parent LLP is held exclusively with a view to subsequent resale.

(4) The reference in subsection (3)(a) to the rights of the parent LLP and the reference in subsection (3)(c) to the interest of the parent LLP are, respectively, to rights and interests held by or attributed to the LLP for the purposes of the definition of "parent undertaking" (see section 1162) in the absence of which it would not be the parent LLP.

[406 IAS group accounts

(1) IAS group accounts must state—
- (a) the part of the United Kingdom in which the LLP is registered,
- (b) the LLP's registered number,
- (c) the address of the LLP's registered office, and
- (d) where appropriate, the fact that the LLP is being wound up.

(2) The notes to the accounts must state that the accounts have been prepared in accordance with [UK-adopted international accounting standards].]

407 Consistency of financial reporting within group

(1) The members of a parent LLP must secure that the individual accounts of—
- (a) the parent LLP, and
- (b) each of its subsidiary undertakings,

are all prepared using the same financial reporting framework, except to the extent that in their opinion there are good reasons for not doing so.

(2) Subsection (1) does not apply if the members do not prepare group accounts for the parent LLP.

(3) Subsection (1) only applies to accounts of subsidiary undertakings that are required to be prepared under this Part.

(4) Subsection (1)(a) does not apply where the members of a parent LLP prepare IAS group accounts and IAS individual accounts.

408 Individual profit and loss account where group accounts prepared

(1) This section applies where—
- (a) an LLP prepares group accounts in accordance with this Act, and
- [(b) the LLP's individual balance sheet shows the LLP's profit and loss for the financial year determined in accordance with this Act.]

(2) . . .

(3) The LLP's individual profit and loss account must be approved in accordance with section 414(1) (approval by members) but may be omitted from the LLP's annual accounts for the purposes of the other provisions of this Act.

(4) The exemption conferred by this section is conditional upon its being disclosed in the LLP's annual accounts that the exemption applies."

NOTES

Section 398 as originally set out above was revoked by the Statutory Auditors Regulations 2017, SI 2017/1164, reg 5, Sch 3, paras 1, 3(a), as from 1 January 2018, in relation to financial years of companies beginning on or after 1 January 2017 (as to the application of the 2017 Regulations, see **[4.671]** et seq).

Section 399 as set out above has been amended as follows:

Sub-s (1) was revoked by SI 2017/1164, reg 5, Sch 3, paras 1, 3(b)(i), as from 1 January 2018, in relation to financial years of companies beginning on or after 1 January 2017 (as to the application of the 2017 Regulations, see **[4.671]** et seq).

In sub-s (2), the words "an LLP" in square brackets were substituted by SI 2017/1164, reg 5, Sch 3, paras 1, 3(b)(ii), as from 1 January 2018, in relation to financial years of companies beginning on or after 1 January 2017 (as to the application of the 2017 Regulations, see **[4.671]** et seq).

Sub-ss (2A), (2B) were inserted by SI 2017/1164, reg 5, Sch 3, paras 1, 3(b)(iii), as from 1 January 2018, in relation to financial years of companies beginning on or after 1 January 2017 (as to the application of the 2017 Regulations, see **[4.671]** et seq).

Sub-s (2B)(c) and the words in square brackets in sub-s (2B)(a), (b) and sub-s (3)(a), (b) were substituted by the Accounts and Reports (Amendment) (EU Exit) Regulations 2019, SI 2019/145, reg 6, Sch 3, paras 11, 16(a), in relation to financial years beginning on or after IP completion day (as defined in the European Union (Withdrawal Agreement) Act 2020, s 39) (for transitional provisions see reg 7 of the 2019 Regulations at **[12.79]**).

Section 400 as set out above has been amended as follows:

The word "UK" in the section heading and the words in the first pair of square brackets in sub-s (1) were substituted by SI 2019/145, reg 6, Sch 3, paras 11, 16(b)(i), (ii), in relation to financial years beginning on or after IP completion day (as defined in the European Union (Withdrawal Agreement) Act 2020, s 39) (for transitional provisions see reg 7 of the 2019 Regulations at **[12.79]**).

Sub-s (1)(b), (c) were substituted (for the original sub-s (1)(b)) by SI 2016/575, regs 3(1), 9(1), (2)(a), as from 17 May 2016, in relation to (a) financial years beginning on or after 1 January 2016; and (b) a financial year of an LLP beginning on or after 1 January 2015, but before 1 January 2016, if (i) the members of the LLP so decide, and (ii) a copy of the LLP's accounts for that financial year has not been delivered to the registrar in accordance with ss 444, 445 or 446 of the Companies Act 2006 as applied to LLPs by the Limited Liability Partnerships (Accounts and Audit) (Application of Companies Act 2006) Regulations before 17 May 2016 (see further the note at **[10.226]**).

Words in square brackets in sub-s (2)(a) substituted, and words omitted from sub-s (2)(b) revoked, by SI 2019/145, reg 6, Sch 3, paras 11, 16(b)(iii)(aa), (bb), in relation to financial years beginning on or after IP completion day (as defined in the European Union (Withdrawal Agreement) Act 2020, s 39) (for transitional provisions see reg 7 of the 2019 Regulations at **[12.79]**).

Sub-s (2)(b)(i) substituted by SI 2019/145, reg 6, Sch 3, paras 11, 16(b)(iii)(cc), in relation to financial years beginning on or after IP completion day (as defined in the European Union (Withdrawal Agreement) Act 2020, s 39) (for transitional provisions see reg 7 of the 2019 Regulations at **[12.79]**).

Words in square brackets in sub-s (2)(b)(ii) substituted by the International Accounting Standards and European Public Limited-Liability Company (Amendment etc) (EU Exit) Regulations 2019, SI 2019/685, reg 19, Sch 1, Pt 2, para 58(1), (4)(a), in relation to accounts for financial years beginning on or after IP completion day (as defined in the European Union (Withdrawal Agreement) Act 2020, s 39) (note also that in relation to accounts for financial years which begin before but end on or after IP completion day, the enactments amended by Parts 1–3 of Sch 1 to the 2019 Regulations have effect as if the UK were a member State until the end of the financial year in question).

In sub-s (2)(c), the words "the notes to" in square brackets were inserted by SI 2016/575, regs 3(1), 9(1), (2)(c) (as to the commencement of the 2016 Regulations, see the first note relating to them above).

Sub-s (2)(d)(i) was substituted by SI 2016/575, regs 3(1), 9(1), (2)(d) (as to the commencement of the 2016 Regulations, see the first note relating to them above).

The words omitted from sub-s (2)(d)(i) were revoked by SI 2019/145, reg 6, Sch 3, paras 11, 16(b)(iii)(dd), in relation to financial years beginning on or after IP completion day (as defined in the European Union (Withdrawal Agreement) Act 2020, s 39) (for transitional provisions see reg 7 of the 2019 Regulations at **[12.79]**).

In sub-s (3), the words "and (c)" in square brackets were inserted by SI 2016/575, regs 3(1), 9(1), (2)(e) (as to the commencement of the 2016 Regulations, see the first note relating to them above).

In sub-s (4), the words "which is a traded LLP" in square brackets were substituted by SI 2016/575, regs 3(1), 9(1), (2)(f) (as to the commencement of the 2016 Regulations, see the first note relating to them above).

Sub-s (5) was revoked by SI 2016/575, regs 3(1), 9(1), (2)(g) (as to the commencement of the 2016 Regulations, see the first note relating to them above).

Section 401 as set out above has been amended as follows:

Words in square brackets in the section heading and words in first pair of square brackets in sub-s (1) substituted by SI 2019/145, reg 6, Sch 3, paras 11, 16(c)(i), (ii), in relation to financial years beginning on or after IP completion day (as defined in the European Union (Withdrawal Agreement) Act 2020, s 39) (for transitional provisions see reg 7 of the 2019 Regulations at **[12.79]**).

Sub-s (1)(b), (c) were substituted (for the original sub-s (1)(b)) by SI 2016/575, regs 3(1), 9(1), (3)(a) (as to the commencement of the 2016 Regulations, see the first note relating to them above).

Sub-s (2)(b) was substituted by SI 2016/575, regs 3(1), 9(1), (3)(b) (as to the commencement of the 2016 Regulations, see the first note relating to them above).

Sub-s (2)(b)(i) was revoked, and the words in square brackets in sub-s (2)(b)(ii) were substituted, by SI 2019/145, reg 6, Sch 3, paras 11, 16(c)(iii), in relation to financial years beginning on or after IP completion day (as defined in the European Union (Withdrawal Agreement) Act 2020, s 39) (for transitional provisions see reg 7 of the 2019 Regulations at **[12.79]**).

Words in square brackets in sub-s (2)(b)(iii) substituted by SI 2019/685, reg 19, Sch 1, Pt 2, para 58(1), (4)(b), in relation to accounts for financial years beginning on or after IP completion day (as defined in the European Union (Withdrawal Agreement) Act 2020, s 39) (note also that in relation to accounts for financial years which begin before but end on or after IP completion day, the enactments amended by Parts 1–3 of Sch 1 to the 2019 Regulations have effect as if the UK were a member State until the end of the financial year in question).

Sub-s (2)(e)(i) was substituted by SI 2016/575, regs 3(1), 9(1), (3)(c) (as to the commencement of the 2016 Regulations, see the first note relating to them above).

In sub-s (3), the words "and (c)" in square brackets were inserted by SI 2016/575, regs 3(1), 9(1), (3)(d) (as to the commencement of the 2016 Regulations, see the first note relating to them above).

In sub-s (4), the words "which is a traded LLP" in square brackets were substituted by SI 2016/575, regs 3(1), 9(1), (3)(e) (as to the commencement of the 2016 Regulations, see the first note relating to them above).

Sub-s (5) was revoked by SI 2016/575, regs 3(1), 9(1), (3)(f) (as to the commencement of the 2016 Regulations, see the first note relating to them above).

Section 403 as set out above has been amended as follows:

The words "UK-adopted international accounting standards" in square brackets in sub-s (1)(b) and (2) were substituted by SI 2019/685, reg 19, Sch 1, Pt 2, para 58(1), (4)(c), in relation to accounts for financial years beginning on or after IP completion day (as defined in the European Union (Withdrawal Agreement) Act 2020, s 39) (note also that in relation to accounts for financial years which begin before but end on or after IP completion day, the enactments amended by Parts 1–3 of Sch 1 to the 2019 Regulations have effect as if the UK were a member State until the end of the financial year in question – and see further the transitional provisions note to reg 9 at **[10.232]**).

In sub-s (2), the words "This is subject to subsection (3A)" in square brackets were inserted by SI 2012/2301, reg 20(1), (9)(a), as from 1 October 2012 (in relation to accounts for financial years ending on or after that date).

The words in square brackets in sub-s (3)(b) and (c) were substituted by SI 2019/145, reg 6, Sch 3, paras 11, 16(d), in relation to financial years beginning on or after IP completion day (as defined in the European Union (Withdrawal Agreement) Act 2020, s 39) (for transitional provisions see reg 7 of the 2019 Regulations at **[12.79]**).

Sub-ss (3A), (3B) were inserted by SI 2012/2301, reg 20(1), (9)(b), as from 1 October 2012 (in relation to accounts for financial years ending on or after that date).

The words omitted from sub-s (4) were revoked by SI 2012/2301, reg 20(1), (9)(c), as from 1 October 2012 (in relation to accounts for financial years ending on or after that date).

Section 404 as set out above has been amended as follows:

Sub-s (A1) was inserted by SI 2016/575, regs 3(1), 9(1), (4) (as to the commencement of the 2016 Regulations, see the first note relating to them above).

Section 405 as set out above has been amended as follows:

In sub-s (3)(b), the words "extremely rare circumstances mean that" in square brackets were inserted by SI 2016/575, regs 3(1), 9(1), (5) (as to the commencement of the 2016 Regulations, see the first note relating to them above).

Section 406 as set out above was substituted by SI 2016/575, regs 3(1), 9(1), (6) (as to the commencement of the 2016 Regulations, see the first note relating to them above). The words in square brackets in sub-s (2) were substituted by SI 2019/685, reg 19, Sch 1, Pt 2, para 58(1), (4)(c), in relation to accounts for financial years beginning on or after IP completion day (as defined in the European Union (Withdrawal Agreement) Act 2020, s 39) (note also that in relation to accounts for financial years which begin before but end on or after IP completion day, the enactments amended by Parts 1–3 of Sch 1 to the 2019 Regulations have effect as if the UK were a member State until the end of the financial year in question).

Section 408 as set out above has been amended as follows:

Sub-s (1)(b) was substituted, and sub-s (2) was revoked, by SI 2016/575, regs 3(1), 9(1), (7) (as to the commencement of the 2016 Regulations, see the first note relating to them above).

[10.234]

11 Information to be given in notes to accounts

[Sections 409, 410A and 411 apply to LLPs], modified so that they read as follows—

"409 Information about related undertakings

(1) The notes to the LLP's annual accounts must contain the information about related undertakings required by—

(a) regulations 4 and 7 of the Small Limited Liability Partnerships (Accounts) Regulations 2008 (information about related undertakings: non-IAS or IAS individual or group accounts) (SI 2008/1912), or

(b) regulation 5 of the Large and Medium-sized Limited Liability Partnerships (Accounts) Regulations 2008 (information about related undertakings: non-IAS or IAS individual or group accounts) (SI 2008/1913).

(2) That information need not be disclosed with respect to an undertaking that—

(a) is established under the law of a country outside the United Kingdom, or

(b) carries on business outside the United Kingdom,

if the following conditions are met.

(4) The conditions are—

(a) that in the opinion of the members of the LLP the disclosure would be seriously prejudicial to the business of—

(i) that undertaking,

(ii) the LLP,

(iii) any of the LLP's subsidiary undertakings, or

(iv) any other undertaking which is included in the consolidation;

(b) that the Secretary of State agrees that the information need not be disclosed.

(5) Where advantage is taken of any such exemption, that fact must be stated in a note to the LLP's annual accounts.

410

. . .

410A Information about off-balance sheet arrangements

[(1) If in any financial year—

(a) an LLP is or has been party to arrangements that are not reflected in its balance sheet, and

(b) at the balance sheet date the risks or benefits arising from those arrangements are material,

the information required by this section must be given in the notes to the LLP's annual accounts.]

(2) The information required is—

(a) the nature and business purpose of the arrangements, and

(b) the financial impact of the arrangements on the LLP.

(3) The information need only be given to the extent necessary for enabling the financial position of the LLP to be assessed.

[(4) If the LLP is subject to the small LLPs regime in relation to the financial year (see section 381), it need not comply with subsection (2)(b).]

(5) This section applies in relation to group accounts as if the undertakings included in the consolidation were a single LLP.

411 Information about employee numbers and costs

[(1) The notes to an LLP's annual accounts must disclose the average number of persons employed by the LLP in the financial year.

(1A) In the case of an LLP not subject to the small LLPs regime, the notes to the LLP's accounts must also disclose the average number of persons within each category of persons so employed.]

(2) The categories by reference to which the number required to be disclosed by [subsection (1A)] is to be determined must be such as the members may select having regard to the manner in which the LLP's activities are organised.

(3) The average number required by [subsection (1) or (1A)] is determined by dividing the relevant annual number by the number of months in the financial year.

(4) The relevant annual number is determined by ascertaining for each month in the financial year—

(a) for the purposes of [subsection (1)], the number of persons employed under contracts of service by the LLP in that month (whether throughout the month or not);

(b) for the purposes of [subsection (1A)], the number of persons in the category in question of persons so employed;

and adding together all the monthly numbers.

[(5) Except in the case of an LLP subject to the small LLPs regime, the notes to the LLP's annual accounts or the profit and loss account must disclose, with reference to all persons employed by the LLP during the financial year, the total staff costs of the LLP relating to the financial year broken down between—

(a) wages and salaries paid or payable in respect of that year to those persons,

(b) social security costs incurred by the LLP on their behalf, and

(c) other pension costs so incurred.]

(6) In subsection (5)—

"pension costs" includes any costs incurred by the LLP in respect of—

(a) any pension scheme established for the purpose of providing pensions for persons currently or formerly employed by the LLP,

(b) any sums set aside for the future payment of pensions directly by the LLP to current or former employees, and

(c) any pensions paid directly to such persons without having first been set aside;

"social security costs" means any contributions by the LLP to any state social security or pension scheme, fund or arrangement.

(7) This section applies in relation to group accounts as if the undertakings included in the consolidation were a single LLP."

NOTES

All amendments to this regulation (which are noted below) were made by the Limited Liability Partnerships, Partnerships and Groups (Accounts and Audit) Regulations 2016, SI 2016/575, regs 3, 10, as from 17 May 2016, in relation to (a) financial years beginning on or after 1 January 2016; and (b) a financial year of an LLP beginning on or after 1 January 2015, but before 1 January 2016, if (i) the members of the LLP so decide, and (ii) a copy of the LLP's accounts for that financial year has not been delivered to the registrar in accordance with ss 444, 445 or 446 of the Companies Act 2006 as applied to LLPs by the Limited Liability Partnerships (Accounts and Audit) (Application of Companies Act 2006) Regulations before 17 May 2016 (see further the note at **[10.226]**).

The first words in square brackets were substituted.

S 410 as set out above was revoked.

In s 410A as set out above, sub-ss (1), (4) were substituted.

In s 411 as set out above, sub-ss (1), (1A) were substituted (for the original sub-s (1)).

In s 411 as set out above, the words in square brackets in sub-ss (2), (3), (4)(a), (b) were substituted.

In s 411 as set out above, sub-s (5) was substituted.

[10.235]

12 Approval and signing of accounts

Section 414 applies to LLPs, modified so that it reads as follows—

"414 Approval and signing of accounts

(1) An LLP's annual accounts must be approved by the members, and signed on behalf of all the members by a designated member.

(2) The signature must be on the LLP's balance sheet.

[(3) If the accounts are prepared in accordance with the small LLPs regime, the balance sheet must contain, in a prominent position above the signature—

(a) in the case of individual accounts prepared in accordance with the micro-entity provisions, a statement to that effect,

(b) in the case of accounts not prepared as mentioned in paragraph (a), a statement to the effect that the accounts have been prepared in accordance with the provisions applicable to LLPs subject to the small LLPs regime.]

(4) If annual accounts are approved that do not comply with the requirements of this Act, every member of the LLP who—

(a) knew that they did not comply, or was reckless as to whether they complied, and

(b) failed to take reasonable steps to secure compliance with those requirements or, as the case may be, to prevent the accounts from being approved,

commits an offence.

(5) A person guilty of an offence under this section is liable—

(a) on conviction on indictment, to a fine;

(b) on summary conviction, to a fine not exceeding the statutory maximum."

NOTES

In s 414 as set out above, sub-s (3) was substituted by the Limited Liability Partnerships, Partnerships and Groups (Accounts and Audit) Regulations 2016, SI 2016/575, regs 3, 11, as from 17 May 2016, in relation to (a) financial years beginning on or after 1 January 2016; and (b) a financial year of an LLP beginning on or after 1 January 2015, but before 1 January 2016, if (i) the members of the LLP so decide, and (ii) a copy of the LLP's accounts for that financial year has not been delivered to the registrar in accordance with ss 444, 445 or 446 of the Companies Act 2006 as applied to LLPs by the Limited Liability Partnerships (Accounts and Audit) (Application of Companies Act 2006) Regulations before 17 May 2016 (see further the note at **[10.226]**).

[10.236]

[12A Strategic report

Sections 414A, 414C and 414D apply to LLPs, modified so that they read as follows—

"414A Duty to prepare strategic report

(1) The members of an LLP which is—

(a) a traded LLP, or

(b) a banking LLP,

must prepare a strategic report for each financial year of the LLP.

(2) For a financial year in which—

(a) the LLP is a parent LLP, and

(b) the members of the LLP prepare group accounts,

the strategic report must be a consolidated report (a "group strategic report") relating to the undertakings included in the consolidation.

(3) A group strategic report may, where appropriate, give greater emphasis to the matters that are significant to the undertakings included in the consolidation, taken as a whole.

(4) In the case of failure to comply with the requirement to prepare a strategic report, an offence is committed by every person who—

(a) was a member of the LLP immediately before the end of the period for filing accounts and reports for the financial year in question, and

(b) failed to take all reasonable steps for securing compliance with that requirement.

(5) A person guilty of an offence under this section is liable—

(a) on conviction on indictment, to a fine;

(b) on summary conviction, to a fine not exceeding the statutory maximum.

414C Contents of strategic report

[(1) The strategic report of a traded LLP and of a banking LLP—

(a) must contain a fair review of the LLP's business and a description of the principal risks and uncertainties facing the LLP; and

(b) where subsection (1A) applies, must in addition to the information described in paragraph (a), contain climate-related financial disclosures.

(1A) This subsection applies to any traded LLP or banking LLP which, in the relevant year to which the strategic report relates, either—

(a) has more than 500 employees; or

(b) is a parent LLP and the aggregate number of employees for a group headed by the LLP is more than 500.

(1B) For the purposes of subsection (1A), the number of employees of an LLP or of a group headed by an LLP means the average number of persons employed by the LLP or the group headed by the LLP in the year, determined as follows—

(a) find for each month in the financial year the number of persons employed under contracts of service by the LLP or the group headed by the LLP in that month (whether throughout the month or not);

(b) add together the monthly totals; and

(c) divide by the number of months in the financial year.]

(2) The review required is a balanced and comprehensive analysis of—

(a) the development and performance of the LLP's business during the financial year, and

(b) the position of the LLP's business at the end of that year,

consistent with the size and complexity of the business.

(3) The review must, to the extent necessary for an understanding of the development, performance or position of the LLP's business, include—

(a) analysis using financial key performance indicators, and

(b) where appropriate, analysis using other key performance indicators, including information relating to environmental matters and employee matters.

(4) In subsection (3), "key performance indicators" means factors by reference to which the development, performance or position of the LLP's business can be measured effectively.

[(4A) In this section and section 416A, "climate-related financial disclosures" means—

(a) a description of the LLP's governance arrangements in relation to assessing and managing climate-related risks and opportunities;

(b) a description of how the LLP identifies, assesses, and manages climate-related risks and opportunities;

(c) a description of how processes for identifying, assessing, and managing climate-related risks are integrated into the LLP's overall risk management process;

(d) a description of—

(i) the principal climate-related risks and opportunities arising in connection with the LLP's operations, and

(ii) the time periods by reference to which those risks and opportunities are assessed;

(e) a description of the actual and potential impacts of the principal climate-related risks and opportunities on the LLP's business model and strategy;

(f) an analysis of the resilience of the LLP's business model and strategy, taking into consideration different climate-related scenarios;

(g) a description of the targets used by the LLP to manage climate-related risks and to realise climate-related opportunities and of performance against those targets; and

(h) a description of the key performance indicators used to assess progress against targets used to manage climate-related risks and realise climate-related opportunities and of the calculations on which those key performance indicators are based.

(4B) Where the members of an LLP reasonably believe that, having regard to the nature of the LLP's business, and the manner in which it is carried on, the whole or a part of a climate-related financial disclosure required by subsection (4A)(e), (f), (g) or (h) is not necessary for an understanding of the LLP's business, the members may omit the whole or (as the case requires) the relevant part of that climate-related financial disclosure.

(4C) Where the members omit the whole or part of a climate-related financial disclosure in reliance on subsection (4B) the strategic report must provide a clear and reasoned explanation of the members' reasonable belief mentioned in that subsection.

(4D) The Secretary of State may issue guidance on the climate-related financial disclosures, which are described in subsection (4A), and otherwise in connection with the requirements of this section.]

(5) The report must, where appropriate, include references to, and additional explanations of, amounts included in the LLP's annual accounts.

(6) In relation to a group strategic report this section has effect as if the references to the LLP were references to the undertakings included in the consolidation.

(7) Nothing in this section requires the disclosure of information about impending developments or matters in the course of negotiation if the disclosure would, in the opinion of the members, be seriously prejudicial to the interests of the LLP.

414D Approval and signing of strategic report

(1) The strategic report must be approved by the members and signed on behalf of all the members by a designated member.

(2) If a strategic report is approved that does not comply with the requirements of this Act, every member who—

- (a) knew that it did not comply, or was reckless as to whether it complied, and
- (b) failed to take reasonable steps to secure compliance with those requirements or, as the case may be, to prevent the report from being approved,

commits an offence.

(3) A person guilty of an offence under this section is liable—

- (a) on conviction on indictment, to a fine;
- (b) on summary conviction, to a fine not exceeding the statutory maximum."]

NOTES

Inserted by the Statutory Auditors Regulations 2017, SI 2017/1164, reg 5, Sch 3, paras 1, 4, in relation to financial years of companies beginning on or after 17 June 2016 (as to the application of the 2017 Regulations, see **[4.671]** et seq).

Section 414C as set out above, is amended as follows:

Sub-ss (1)–(1B) were substituted (for the original sub-s (1)) by the Limited Liability Partnerships (Climate-related Financial Disclosure) Regulations 2022, SI 2022/46, reg 2(2), as from 6 April 2022, in respect of any financial year of a limited liability partnership which commences on or after that date. The original sub-s (1) read as follows—

"(1) The strategic report must contain—

(a) a fair review of the LLP's business, and
(b) a description of the principal risks and uncertainties facing the LLP.".

Sub-ss (4A)–(4D) were inserted by SI 2022/46, reg 2(2), as from 6 April 2022, in respect of any financial year of a limited liability partnership which commences on or after that date.

Guidance under section 414C(4D): the Department for Business, Energy & Industrial Strategy issued the relevant guidance on 23 February 2022. The guidance (*Mandatory climate-related financial disclosures by publicly quoted companies, large private companies and LLPs – Non-binding guidance*) aims to help in-scope companies and limited liability partnerships understand how to meet new mandatory climate-related financial disclosure requirements under the Companies (Strategic Report) (Climate-related Financial Disclosure) Regulations 2022, and the Limited Liability Partnerships (Climate-related Financial Disclosure) Regulations 2022. The Regulations apply to reporting for financial years starting on or after 6 April 2022. See www.gov.uk/government/publications/climate-related-financial-disclosures-for-companies-and-limited-liability-partnerships-llps.

[PART 5A ENERGY AND CARBON REPORT

[10.237]
12B. Energy and carbon report

Sections 415, 415A, 416 and 419 apply to LLPs, modified so that they read as follows—

"415 Duty to prepare energy and carbon report

(1) Unless the LLP is exempted under section 415A(1) or (4), and subject to subsection (4), the members of an LLP must prepare an energy and carbon report for each financial year of the LLP.

(2) For a financial year in which—

- (a) the LLP is a parent LLP, and
- (b) the members of the LLP prepare group accounts,

the energy and carbon report must be a consolidated report ("a group energy and carbon report") relating to the undertakings included in the consolidation.

(3) A group energy and carbon report may, where appropriate, give greater emphasis to the matters that are significant to the undertakings included in the consolidation, taken as a whole.

(4) Subsection (1) does not apply if—

- (a) the LLP is a subsidiary undertaking at the end of the financial year;
- (b) the LLP is included in the group report of a parent undertaking;
- (c) the group report is prepared for a financial year of the parent undertaking that ends at the same time as, or before the end of, the LLP's financial year; and—

(i) if the group report is a group energy and carbon report, it complies with Part 7A of Schedule 7 to the Large and Medium-sized Companies and Groups (Accounts and Reports) Regulations 2008 as applied and modified by regulation 12B of the Limited Liability Partnerships (Accounts and Audit) (Application of Companies Act 2006) Regulations 2008 other than in reliance on paragraph 20D(7)(b); or

(ii) if the group report is a group directors' report—

(aa) of a quoted company, it complies with Part 7 of Schedule 7 to the Large and Medium-sized Companies and Groups (Accounts and Reports) Regulations 2008 other than in reliance on paragraph 15(5)(b); or

(bb) of an unquoted company it complies with Part 7A of Schedule 7 to those Regulations other than in reliance on paragraph 20D(7)(b).

(5) For the purpose of subsection (4)—

"group directors' report" means a report prepared in accordance with section 415(2);

"quoted company" and "unquoted company" have the meanings given in section 385.

(6) In the case of failure to comply with the requirement to prepare an energy and carbon report, an offence is committed by every person who—

(a) was a member of the LLP immediately before the end of the period for filing accounts and reports for the financial year in question; and

(b) failed to take all reasonable steps for securing compliance with that requirement.

(7) A person guilty of an offence under this section is liable—

(a) on conviction on indictment, to a fine;

(b) on summary conviction—

(i) in England and Wales, to a fine;

(ii) in Scotland or Northern Ireland, to a fine not exceeding the statutory maximum.

415A Exemption to duty to prepare energy and carbon report

(1) Unless the LLP is a parent LLP, an LLP is exempted under this subsection—

(a) in relation to its first financial year if the qualifying conditions in subsection (2) are met in that year;

(b) in relation to a subsequent financial year—

(i) if the qualifying conditions are met in that year and were also met in relation to the preceding financial year;

(ii) if—

(aa) the qualifying conditions are met in that year, and

(bb) the LLP was exempted in relation to the preceding financial year; or

(iii) if—

(aa) the qualifying conditions were met in the preceding financial year, and

(bb) the LLP was exempted in relation to the preceding financial year.

(2) The qualifying conditions referred to in subsection (1) are met by an LLP in a year in which it satisfies two or more of the following requirements—

1. Turnover	not more than £36 million
2. Balance sheet total	not more than £18 million
3. Number of employees	not more than 250

(3) For the purposes of subsection (2)—

(a) for a period that is an LLP's financial year but not in fact a year the figure for turnover must be proportionately adjusted;

(b) the balance sheet total means the aggregate of the amounts shown as assets in the LLP's balance sheet;

(c) the number of employees means the average number of persons employed by the LLP in the year, determined as follows—

(i) find for each month in the financial year the number of persons employed under contracts of service by the LLP in that month (whether throughout the month or not),

(ii) add together the monthly totals, and

(iii) divide by the number of months in the financial year.

(4) A parent LLP is exempted under this subsection—

(a) in relation to the parent LLP's first financial year if the qualifying conditions in subsection (5) are met in that year by the group headed by it;

(b) in relation to a subsequent financial year of the parent LLP—

(i) if the qualifying conditions are met in that year and the preceding financial year by the group headed by the parent LLP;

(ii) if—

(aa) the qualifying conditions are met in that year by the group, and

(bb) the parent LLP was exempted in relation to the preceding financial year; or

(iii) if—

(aa) the qualifying conditions were met in the preceding financial year by the group, and

(bb) the parent LLP was exempted in relation to the preceding financial year.

(5) The qualifying conditions referred to in subsection (4) are met by a group in a year in which it satisfies two or more of the following requirements—

1. Aggregate turnover	not more than £36 million net (or £43.2 million gross)

Part 10 Miscellaneous other SIs

2. Aggregate balance sheet total	not more than £18 million net (or £21.6 million gross)
3. Aggregate number of employees	not more than 250

(6) For the purposes of subsection (5), the aggregate figures are to be ascertained by aggregating the relevant figures determined in accordance with subsections (1) to (3) for each member of the group.

(7) In relation to the aggregate figures for turnover and balance sheet total—

(a) "net" means after any set-offs and other adjustments made to eliminate group transactions—

(i) in the case of non-IAS accounts, in accordance with Schedule 3 to the Large and Medium-sized Limited Liability Partnerships (Accounts) Regulations 2008;

(ii) in the case of IAS accounts, in accordance with international accounting standards; and

(b) "gross" means without those set-offs and other adjustments.

(8) An LLP may satisfy any requirements in subsection (5) on the basis of either the net or the gross figure.

(9) For the purposes of subsection (5)—

(a) the figures for each subsidiary undertaking must be those included in its individual accounts for the relevant financial year, that is—

(i) if its financial year ends with that of the parent LLP, that financial year, and

(ii) if not, its financial year ending last before the end of the financial year of the parent LLP; or

(b) if those figures cannot be obtained without disproportionate expense or undue delay, the latest available figures may be taken.

416 Contents of energy and carbon report

(1) The energy and carbon report for a financial year must state—

(a) the names of the persons who, at any time during the financial year, were members of the LLP; and

(b) the name of the designated member signing the report in accordance with section 419.

(2) Regulation 10(1) and Part 7A of Schedule 7 to the Large and Medium-sized Companies and Groups (Accounts and Reports) Regulations 2008 apply to LLPs with the following modifications—

(a) in regulation 10(1)—

(i) for "directors of a company", substitute "members of an LLP";

(ii) for "directors' report", substitute "energy and carbon report";

(iii) for "Schedule 7", substitute "Part 7A of Schedule 7";

(b) in Part 7A—

(i) in the heading, omit "by unquoted companies";

(ii) for paragraph 20A(1), substitute "This Part of this Schedule applies to the energy and carbon report for a financial year.";

(iii) omit paragraphs 20A(2) and (3), 20B and 20C;

(iv) in paragraphs 20D, 20E(1) and 20E(3), for each reference to "company" except on the third and fourth occasion it appears in paragraph 20E(1) and where it appears in paragraphs 20E(3)(a) and (b), substitute "LLP";

(v) in paragraphs 20D and 20G, for each reference to "company's", substitute "LLP's";

(vi) in paragraphs 20D, 20F, 20G, 20H, 20I and 20J, for each reference to "directors' report", substitute "energy and carbon report";

(vii) in paragraph 20D(7)(b), for the reference to "directors", substitute "members";

(viii) in paragraph 20E(1), for the reference to "group directors' report", substitute "group energy and carbon report";

(ix) in paragraphs 20E(2) and (3)(a) and 20K, for each reference to "Part 7 of this Schedule", substitute "Part 7 of Schedule 7 to the Large and Medium-sized Companies and Groups (Accounts and Reports) Regulations 2008";

(x) in paragraph 20E(3)(b), for the reference to "this Part of this Schedule", substitute "Part 7A of Schedule 7 to the Large and Medium-sized Companies and Groups (Accounts and Reports) Regulations 2008";

(xi) for paragraph 20E(4), substitute "For the purpose of this paragraph, "quoted company" and "unquoted company" have the meanings given in section 385.".

[416A Climate-related financial disclosures in the energy and carbon report

(1) The energy and carbon report of a large LLP for a financial year must set out climate-related financial disclosures.

(2) A "large LLP" means—

(a) an LLP which is not a traded LLP nor a banking LLP;

(b) where in the relevant financial year—

(i) the LLP is not a parent LLP, an LLP which has more than 500 employees and an annual turnover of more than £500 million;

(ii) the LLP is a parent LLP, the aggregate number of employees for a group headed by that LLP is more than 500 and the group headed by it has an annual turnover of more £500 million.

(3) For the purposes of subsection (2), the number of employees of an LLP or of a group headed by an LLP means the average number of persons employed by the LLP or the group headed by the LLP in the year, determined as follows—

(a) find for each month in the financial year the number of persons employed under contracts of service by the LLP or the group headed by the LLP in that month (whether throughout the month or not);

(b) add together the monthly totals; and

(c) divide by the number of months in the financial year.

(4) For a period that is an LLP's financial year but not in fact a year the figure of £500 million for annual turnover given by subsection (2) must be proportionately adjusted.

(5) If the LLP's energy and carbon report is a group energy and carbon report, the figures for each subsidiary undertaking must be those included in its individual accounts for the relevant financial year, that is—

(a) if its financial year ends with that of the parent LLP, that financial year; and

(b) if not, its financial year ending last before the end of the financial year of the parent LLP.

(6) If the figures referred to in paragraph (5) cannot be obtained without disproportionate expense or undue delay, the latest available figures must be taken.

(7) In this section, "climate-related financial disclosures" has the same meaning as set out in section 414C(4A).

(8) Where the members of an LLP reasonably believe that, having regard to the nature of the LLP's business, and the manner in which it is carried on, the whole or a part of a climate-related financial disclosure described in subsection 414C(4A)(e), (f), (g) or (h) is not necessary for an understanding of the LLP's business, the members may omit the whole or (as the case requires) the relevant part of that climate-related financial disclosure.

(9) Where the members omit the whole or part of a climate-related financial disclosure in reliance on subsection (8) the strategic report must provide a clear and reasoned explanation of the members' reasonable belief mentioned in that subsection.

(10) The Secretary of State may issue guidance on the climate-related financial disclosures, which are required by subsection (1), and otherwise in connection with the requirements of this section.]

419 Approval and signing of energy and carbon report

(1) The energy and carbon report must be approved by the members and signed on behalf of all the members by a designated member.

(2) If an energy and carbon report is approved that does not comply with the requirements of this Act, every member who—

(a) knew that it did not comply, or was reckless as to whether it complied, and

(b) failed to take reasonable steps to secure compliance with those requirements or, as the case may be, to prevent the report from being approved,

commits an offence.

(3) A person guilty of an offence under this section is liable—

(a) on conviction on indictment, to a fine;

(b) on summary conviction—

(i) in England and Wales, to a fine;

(ii) in Scotland or Northern Ireland, to a fine not exceeding the statutory maximum.]

NOTES

Part 5A (reg 12B only) was inserted by the Companies (Directors' Report) and Limited Liability Partnerships (Energy and Carbon Report) Regulations 2018, SI 2018/1155, regs 8, 10, as from 1 April 2019, in respect of financial years beginning on or after that date.

Section 416A as set out above, was inserted by the Limited Liability Partnerships (Climate-related Financial Disclosure) Regulations 2022, SI 2022/46, reg 4, as from 6 April 2022, in respect of any financial year of a limited liability partnership which commences on or after that date.

PART 6 PUBLICATION OF [ACCOUNTS AND REPORTS]

NOTES

Words in square brackets in the preceding heading substituted (for the original words "accounts, auditor's report and energy and carbon report") by the European Grouping of Territorial Cooperation and Limited Liability Partnerships etc (Revocations and Amendments) (EU Exit) Regulations 2021, SI 2021/153, reg 5, as from 8 March 2021, in relation to financial years beginning on or after 6 April 2021.

[10.238]

13 Publication of [annual accounts and reports]

Section 423 applies to LLPs, modified so that it reads as follows—

"423 Duty to circulate copies of [annual accounts and reports]

(1) Every LLP must send a copy of its [annual accounts and reports] for each financial year to—

(a) every member of the LLP, and

(b) every holder of the LLP's debentures,

not later than the end of the period for filing accounts[, the strategic report (if any)] [, the auditor's report on them and the energy and carbon report], or, if earlier, the date on which it actually delivers its accounts[, the strategic report (if any)] and the auditor's report on those accounts [and that strategic report] [and the energy and carbon report (if any)] to the registrar.

(2) Copies need not be sent to a person for whom the LLP does not have a current address.

(3) An LLP has a "current address" for a person if—

(a) an address has been notified to the LLP by the person as one at which documents may be sent to him, and

(b) the LLP has no reason to believe that documents sent to him at that address will not reach him.

(4) Where copies are sent out over a period of days, references in this Act to the day on which copies are sent out shall be read as references to the last day of that period."

NOTES

The words in square brackets in the regulation heading were substituted (for the original words "accounts, auditor's report and energy and carbon report") by the European Grouping of Territorial Cooperation and Limited Liability Partnerships etc (Revocations and Amendments) (EU Exit) Regulations 2021, SI 2021/153, reg 6(2), as from 8 March 2021, in relation to financial years beginning on or after 6 April 2021.

Section 423 as set out above is amended as follows:

The words in square brackets in the heading were substituted (for the original words "accounts, auditor's report and energy and carbon report") by the European Grouping of Territorial Cooperation and Limited Liability Partnerships etc (Revocations and Amendments) (EU Exit) Regulations 2021, SI 2021/153, reg 6(3), as from 8 March 2021, in relation to financial years beginning on or after 6 April 2021.

The words in the first pair of square brackets in para (1) were substituted (for the original words "annual accounts and auditor's report and energy and carbon report (if any)") by SI 2021/153, reg 6(3), as from 8 March 2021, in relation to financial years beginning on or after 6 April 2021.

The words ", the strategic report (if any)" and "and that strategic report" square brackets in para (1) were inserted by SI 2021/153, reg 6(3), as from 8 March 2021, in relation to financial years beginning on or after 6 April 2021.

The other words in square brackets in para (1) were inserted, by the Companies (Directors' Report) and Limited Liability Partnerships (Energy and Carbon Report) Regulations 2018, SI 2018/1155, regs 8, 12(3), as from 1 April 2019, in respect of financial years beginning on or after that date.

[10.239]

14 Default in sending out copies of [accounts and reports]

Section 425 applies to LLPs, modified so that it reads as follows—

"425 Default in sending out copies of [accounts and reports]: offences

(1) If default is made in complying with section 423, an offence is committed by—

(a) the LLP, and

(b) every member of the LLP who is in default.

(2) A person guilty of an offence under this section is liable—

(a) on conviction on indictment, to a fine;

(b) on summary conviction, to a fine not exceeding the statutory maximum."

NOTES

The words in square brackets in the regulation heading were substituted (for the original words "accounts, auditor's report and energy and carbon report") by the European Grouping of Territorial Cooperation and Limited Liability Partnerships etc (Revocations and Amendments) (EU Exit) Regulations 2021, SI 2021/153, reg 7(2), as from 8 March 2021, in relation to financial years beginning on or after 6 April 2021.

The words in square brackets in the heading to section 425 as set out above were substituted (for the original words "accounts, auditor's report and energy and carbon report") by SI 2021/153, reg 7(3), as from 8 March 2021, in relation to financial years beginning on or after 6 April 2021.

[10.240]

15 Right of member or debenture holder to copies of [accounts and reports]

Section 431 applies to LLPs, modified so that it reads as follows—

"431 Right of member or debenture holder to copies of [accounts and reports]

(1) A member of, or holder of debentures of, an LLP is entitled to be provided, on demand and without charge, with a copy of—

(a) the LLP's last annual accounts, . . .

[(aa) the last strategic report (if any),]

(b) the auditor's report on those accounts [(including the statement (where applicable) on that strategic report)][, and]

[(c) the last energy and carbon report (if any)].

(2) The entitlement under this section is to a single copy of those documents, but that is in addition to any copy to which a person may be entitled under section 423.

(3) If a demand made under this section is not complied with within seven days of receipt by the LLP, an offence is committed by—

(a) the LLP, and

(b) every member of the LLP who is in default.

(4) A person guilty of an offence under this section is liable on summary conviction to a fine not exceeding level 3 on the standard scale and, for continued contravention, a daily default fine not exceeding one-tenth of level 3 on the standard scale."

NOTES

The words in square brackets in the regulation heading were substituted (for the original words "accounts, auditor's report and energy and carbon report") by the European Grouping of Territorial Cooperation and Limited Liability Partnerships etc (Revocations and Amendments) (EU Exit) Regulations 2021, SI 2021/153, reg 8(2), as from 8 March 2021, in relation to financial years beginning on or after 6 April 2021.

Section 431 as set out above is amended as follows:

The words in square brackets in the heading were substituted (for the original words "accounts, auditor's report and energy and carbon report") by SI 2021/153, reg 8(3), as from 8 March 2021, in relation to financial years beginning on or after 6 April 2021.

Para (aa) of sub-s (1), and the words "(including the statement (where applicable) on that strategic report)" in square brackets in para (b), were inserted by SI 2021/153, reg 8(3), as from 8 March 2021, in relation to financial years beginning on or after 6 April 2021.

The word omitted from sub-s (1)(a) was revoked, and sub-s (1)(c) and the preceding word were inserted, by the Companies (Directors' Report) and Limited Liability Partnerships (Energy and Carbon Report) Regulations 2018, SI 2018/1155, regs 8, 14(1), (3), as from 1 April 2019, in respect of financial years beginning on or after that date.

[10.241]

16 Requirements in connection with publication of [accounts and reports]

Sections 433 to 436 apply to LLPs, modified so that they read as follows—

"433 Name of signatory to be stated in published copies of [accounts and reports]

(1) Every copy of the LLP's balance sheet[, strategic report] [and energy and carbon report] that is published by or on behalf of the LLP must state the name of the person who signed it on behalf of the members of the LLP.

(2) If a copy is published without the required statement of the signatory's name, an offence is committed by—

(a) the LLP, and

(b) every member of the LLP who is in default.

(3) A person guilty of an offence under this section is liable on summary conviction to a fine not exceeding level 3 on the standard scale.

434 Requirements in connection with publication of statutory accounts

(1) If an LLP publishes any of its statutory accounts, they must be accompanied by the auditor's report on those accounts (unless the LLP is exempt from audit and the members have taken advantage of that exemption).

(2) An LLP that prepares statutory group accounts for a financial year must not publish its statutory individual accounts for that year without also publishing with them its statutory group accounts.

(3) An LLP's "statutory accounts" are its accounts for a financial year as required to be delivered to the registrar under section 441.

(4) If an LLP contravenes any provision of this section, an offence is committed by—

(a) the LLP, and

(b) every member of the LLP who is in default.

(5) A person guilty of an offence under this section is liable on summary conviction to a fine not exceeding level 3 on the standard scale.

435 Requirements in connection with publication of non-statutory accounts

(1) If an LLP publishes non-statutory accounts, it must publish with them a statement indicating—

(a) that they are not the LLP's statutory accounts,

(b) whether statutory accounts dealing with any financial year with which the non-statutory accounts purport to deal have been delivered to the registrar, and

(c) whether an auditor's report has been made on the LLP's statutory accounts for any such financial year, and if so whether the report—

(i) was qualified or unqualified, or included a reference to any matters to which the auditor drew attention by way of emphasis without qualifying the report, or

(ii) contained a statement under section 498(2) (accounting records or returns inadequate or accounts not agreeing with records and returns), or section 498(3) (failure to obtain necessary information and explanations).

(2) The LLP must not publish with non-statutory accounts the auditor's report on the LLP's statutory accounts.

(3) References in this section to the publication by an LLP of "non-statutory accounts" are to the publication of—

(a) any balance sheet or profit and loss account relating to, or purporting to deal with, a financial year of the LLP, or

(b) an account in any form purporting to be a balance sheet or profit and loss account for a group headed by the LLP relating to, or purporting to deal with, a financial year of the LLP,

otherwise than as part of the LLP's statutory accounts.

(4) In subsection (3)(b) "a group headed by the LLP" means a group consisting of the LLP and any other undertaking (regardless of whether it is a subsidiary undertaking of the LLP) other than a parent undertaking of the LLP.

(5) If an LLP contravenes any provision of this section, an offence is committed by—

(a) the LLP, and

(b) every member of the LLP who is in default.

(6) A person guilty of an offence under this section is liable on summary conviction to a fine not exceeding level 3 on the standard scale.

436 Meaning of "publication" in relation to [accounts and reports]

(1) This section has effect for the purposes of—

- section 433 (name of signatory to be stated in published copies of [accounts and reports]),
- section 434 (requirements in connection with publication of statutory accounts), and
- section 435 (requirements in connection with publication of non-statutory accounts).

(2) For the purposes of those sections an LLP is regarded as publishing a document if it publishes, issues or circulates it or otherwise makes it available for public inspection in a manner calculated to invite members of the public generally, or any class of members of the public, to read it."

NOTES

The words in square brackets in the regulation heading were substituted (for the original words "accounts, auditor's report and energy and carbon report") by the European Grouping of Territorial Cooperation and Limited Liability Partnerships etc

(Revocations and Amendments) (EU Exit) Regulations 2021, SI 2021/153, reg 9(2), as from 8 March 2021, in relation to financial years beginning on or after 6 April 2021.

Section 433 as set out above is amended as follows:

The words in square brackets in the heading were substituted (for the original words "accounts and energy and carbon report") by SI 2021/153, reg 9(3), as from 8 March 2021, in relation to financial years beginning on or after 6 April 2021.

The words ", strategic report" in square brackets in sub-s (1) were inserted by SI 2021/153, reg 9(3), as from 8 March 2021, in relation to financial years beginning on or after 6 April 2021.

The words "and energy and carbon report" in square brackets in sub-s (1) were inserted by the Companies (Directors' Report) and Limited Liability Partnerships (Energy and Carbon Report) Regulations 2018, SI 2018/1155, regs 8, 15(1), (3), as from 1 April 2019, in respect of financial years beginning on or after that date.

Section 436 as set out above is amended as follows:

The words in square brackets in the heading were substituted (for the original words "accounts, auditor's report and energy and carbon report") by SI 2021/153, reg 9(4), as from 8 March 2021, in relation to financial years beginning on or after 6 April 2021.

The words in square brackets in sub-s (1) were substituted (for the original words "accounts and energy and carbon report") by SI 2021/153, reg 9(4), as from 8 March 2021, in relation to financial years beginning on or after 6 April 2021.

PART 7 FILING OF [ACCOUNTS AND REPORTS]

NOTES

Words in square brackets in the preceding heading substituted (for the original words "accounts, auditor's report and energy and carbon report") by the European Grouping of Territorial Cooperation and Limited Liability Partnerships etc (Revocations and Amendments) (EU Exit) Regulations 2021, SI 2021/153, reg 10, as from 8 March 2021, in relation to financial years beginning on or after 6 April 2021.

[10.242]

17 Duty to file accounts and reports

(1) Sections 441 to 444 apply to LLPs, modified so that they read as follow—

"[441 [Duty to file accounts and reports with the registrar]

(1) The designated members of an LLP must deliver to the registrar for each financial year the [accounts, auditor's report, strategic report and energy and carbon report] required by—

section 444 (filing obligations of LLPs subject to small LLPs regime),

section 445 (filing obligations of medium-sized LLPs), or

section 446 (filing obligations of large LLPs).

(2) This is subject to section 448A (dormant subsidiary LLPs exempt from obligation to file accounts).]

442 Period allowed for filing accounts [and reports]

(1) This section specifies the period allowed for the designated members of an LLP to comply with their obligation under section 441 to deliver accounts[the auditor's report[, strategic report] and the energy and carbon report] for a financial year to the registrar.

This is referred to in this Act as the "period for filing" those accounts and [those reports].

(2) The period is nine months after the end of the relevant accounting reference period.

This is subject to the following provisions of this section.

(3) If the relevant accounting reference period is the LLP's first and is a period of more than twelve months, the period is—

(a) nine months from the first anniversary of the incorporation of the LLP, or

(b) three months after the end of the accounting reference period,

whichever last expires.

(4) If the relevant accounting reference period is treated as shortened by virtue of a notice given by the LLP under section 392 (alteration of accounting reference date), the period is—

(a) that applicable in accordance with the above provisions, or

(b) three months from the date of the notice under that section,

whichever last expires.

(5) [Subject to subsection (5A), if] for any special reason the Secretary of State thinks fit he may, on an application made before the expiry of the period otherwise allowed, by notice in writing to an LLP extend that period by such further period as may be specified in the notice.

[(5A) Any such extension must not have the effect of extending the period for filing to more than twelve months after the end of the relevant accounting reference period.]

(6) In this section "the relevant accounting reference period" means the accounting reference period by reference to which the financial year for the accounts in question was determined.

443 Calculation of period allowed

(1) This section applies for the purposes of calculating the period for filing an LLP's accounts[, auditor's report[, strategic report] and energy and carbon report] which is expressed as a specified number of months from a specified date or after the end of a specified previous period.

(2) Subject to the following provisions, the period ends with the date in the appropriate month corresponding to the specified date or the last day of the specified previous period.

(3) If the specified date, or the last day of the specified previous period, is the last day of a month, the period ends with the last day of the appropriate month (whether or not that is the corresponding date).

(4) If—

(a) the specified date, or the last day of the specified previous period, is not the last day of a month but is the 29th or 30th, and

(b) the appropriate month is February,

the period ends with the last day of February.

(5) "The appropriate month" means the month that is the specified number of months after the month in which the specified date, or the end of the specified previous period, falls.

444 Filing obligations of LLPs subject to small LLPs regime

(1) The designated members of an LLP subject to the small LLPs regime—

(a) must deliver to the registrar for each financial year a copy of [the balance sheet] drawn up as at the last day of that year, and

(b) may also deliver to the registrar a copy of the LLP's profit and loss account for that year.

(2) [Where the designated members deliver to the registrar a copy of the LLP's profit and loss account under subsection (1)(b), the] designated members must also deliver to the registrar a copy of the auditor's report on the accounts that they deliver.

This does not apply if the LLP is exempt from audit and the members have taken advantage of that exemption.

[(2A) Where the balance sheet or profit and loss account is abridged pursuant to paragraph 1A of Schedule 1 to the Small Limited Liability Partnerships (Accounts) Regulations 2008 (SI 2008/1912), the designated members must also deliver to the registrar a statement by the LLP that all the members of the LLP have consented to the abridgement.]

(3) The copies of accounts and auditors' reports delivered to the registrar must be copies of the LLP's annual accounts and auditor's report . . .

. . .

(4) . . .

(5) Where the designated members of an LLP subject to the small LLPs regime . . . do not deliver to the registrar a copy of the LLP's profit and loss account, the copy of the balance sheet delivered to the registrar must contain in a prominent position a statement that the LLP's annual accounts have been delivered in accordance with the provisions applicable to LLPs subject to the small LLPs regime.

[(5A) Subject to subsection (5C), where the designated members of an LLP subject to the small LLPs regime do not deliver to the registrar a copy of the LLP's profit and loss account—

(a) the copy of the balance sheet delivered to the registrar must disclose that fact, and

(b) unless the LLP is exempt from audit and the members have taken advantage of that exemption, the notes to the balance sheet delivered must satisfy the requirements in subsection (5B).

(5B) Those requirements are that the notes to the balance sheet must—

(a) state whether the auditor's report was qualified or unqualified,

(b) where that report was qualified, disclose the basis of the qualification (reproducing any statement under section 498(2)(a) or (b) or (3), if applicable),

(c) where that report was unqualified, include a reference to any matters to which the auditor drew attention by way of emphasis, and

(d) state—

(i) the name of the auditor and (where the auditor is a firm) the name of the person who signed the auditor's report as senior statutory auditor, or

(ii) if the conditions in section 506 (circumstances in which names may be omitted) are met, that a determination has been made and notified to the Secretary of State in accordance with that section.

(5C) Subsection (5A) does not apply in relation to an LLP if—

(a) the LLP qualifies as a micro-entity (see sections 384A and 384B) in relation to a financial year, and

(b) the LLP's accounts are prepared for that year in accordance with any of the micro-entity provisions.]

(6) The copy of the balance sheet delivered to the registrar under this section must state the name of the person who signed it on behalf of the members.

(7) The copy of the auditor's report delivered to the registrar under this section must—

(a) state the name of the auditor and (where the auditor is a firm) the name of the person who signed it as senior statutory auditor, or

(b) if the conditions in section 506 (circumstances in which names may be omitted) are met, state that a determination has been made and notified to the Secretary of State in accordance with that section.

[(8) If more than one person is appointed as auditor, the references in subsections (5B)(d)(i) and (7)(a) to the name of the auditor are to be read as references to the names of all the auditors.]

(2) Until section 1068 comes fully into force, for subsections (6) and (7) of section 444 as applied to LLPs by paragraph (1) substitute—

"(6) The copy of the balance sheet delivered to the registrar under this section must—

(a) state the name of the person who signed it on behalf of the members under section 414, and

(b) be signed on behalf of the members by a designated member.

(7) The copy of the auditor's report delivered to the registrar under this section must—

(a) state the name of the auditor and (where the auditor is a firm) the name of the person who signed it as senior statutory auditor, and

(b) be signed by the auditor or (where the auditor is a firm) in the name of the firm by a person authorised to sign on its behalf,

or, if the conditions in section 506 (circumstances in which names may be omitted) are met, state that a determination has been made and notified to the Secretary of State in accordance with that section."

NOTES

Section 441 as set out above is amended as follows:

The whole section 441 was substituted by the Companies and Limited Liability Partnerships (Accounts and Audit Exemptions and Change of Accounting Framework) Regulations 2012, SI 2012/2301, regs 2, 20(1), (6), as from 1 October 2012 (in relation to accounts for financial years ending on or after that date).

The heading was inserted by the European Grouping of Territorial Cooperation and Limited Liability Partnerships etc (Revocations and Amendments) (EU Exit) Regulations 2021, SI 2021/153, reg 11(2), as from 8 March 2021, in relation to financial years beginning on or after 6 April 2021.

The words in square brackets in sub-s (1) were substituted (for the original words "accounts and auditor's report and energy and carbon report") by SI 2021/153, reg 11(2), as from 8 March 2021, in relation to financial years beginning on or after 6 April 2021.

Section 442 as set out above is amended as follows:

The words in square brackets in the heading were inserted by the Companies (Directors' Report) and Limited Liability Partnerships (Energy and Carbon Report) Regulations 2018, SI 2018/1155, regs 8, 17(3), as from 1 April 2019, in respect of financial years beginning on or after that date.

The words in the first (outer) pair of square brackets in sub-s (1) were substituted by SI 2018/1155, regs 8, 17(3), as from 1 April 2019, in respect of financial years beginning on or after that date.

The words in the second (inner) pair of square brackets in sub-s (1) were inserted by SI 2021/153, reg 11(3), as from 8 March 2021, in relation to financial years beginning on or after 6 April 2021.

The words in square brackets in sub-s (5) were substituted, and sub-s (5A) was inserted, by the Limited Liability Partnerships, Partnerships and Groups (Accounts and Audit) Regulations 2016, SI 2016/575, regs 3, 12(2), as from 17 May 2016, in relation to (a) financial years beginning on or after 1 January 2016; and (b) a financial year of an LLP beginning on or after 1 January 2015, but before 1 January 2016, if (i) the members of the LLP so decide, and (ii) a copy of the LLP's accounts for that financial year has not been delivered to the registrar in accordance with ss 444, 445 or 446 of the Companies Act 2006 as applied to LLPs by the Limited Liability Partnerships (Accounts and Audit) (Application of Companies Act 2006) Regulations before 17 May 2016 (see further the note at **[10.226]**).

Section 443 as set out above is amended as follows:

The words in the first (outer) pair of square brackets in sub-s (1) were substituted by SI 2018/1155, regs 8, 17(4), as from 1 April 2019, in respect of financial years beginning on or after that date.

The words in the second (inner) pair of square brackets in sub-s (1) were inserted by SI 2021/153, reg 11(4), as from 8 March 2021, in relation to financial years beginning on or after 6 April 2021.

Section 444 as set out above is amended as follows:

The words in square brackets in sub-ss (1)(a) and (2) were substituted, sub-ss (2A), (5A)–(5C) were inserted, the words omitted from sub-ss (3) and (5) were revoked, and sub-s (4) was revoked, by SI 2016/575, regs 3, 12(3), as from 17 May 2016, in relation to (a) financial years beginning on or after 1 January 2016; and (b) a financial year of an LLP beginning on or after 1 January 2015, but before 1 January 2016, if (i) the members of the LLP so decide, and (ii) a copy of the LLP's accounts for that financial year has not been delivered to the registrar in accordance with ss 444, 445 or 446 of the Companies Act 2006 as applied to LLPs by the Limited Liability Partnerships (Accounts and Audit) (Application of Companies Act 2006) Regulations before 17 May 2016 (see further the note at **[10.226]**).

Sub-s (8) was added by the Statutory Auditors Regulations 2017, SI 2017/1164, reg 5, Sch 3, paras 1, 5, in relation to financial years of companies beginning on or after 17 June 2016 (as to the application of the 2017 Regulations, see **[4.671]** et seq).

Temporary modification: this regulation was modified by the Companies etc (Filing Requirements) (Temporary Modifications) Regulations 2020, SI 2020/645, reg 12. By virtue of the Corporate Insolvency and Governance Act 2020, s 39(8), the modification applied from 27 June 2020 to the end of the day on 5 April 2021 (subject to the saving provision in s 39(9) which provides that the expiry of s 39 on 5 April 2021 does not affect the continued operation of any Regulations made under that section for the purpose of determining the length of any period that began before the expiry). As modified, section 442, as it applies to limited liability partnerships, by virtue of this regulation 17, had effect as if for each reference to "nine months" there were substituted a reference to "twelve months".

[10.243]
18 Filing obligations of medium-sized LLPs

(1) Section 445 applies to LLPs, modified so that it reads as follows—

> **"445 Filing obligations of medium-sized LLPs**
>
> (1) The designated members of an LLP that qualifies as a medium-sized LLP in relation to a financial year (see sections 465 to 467) must deliver a copy of the LLP's annual accounts to the registrar.
>
> (2) They must also deliver to the registrar a copy of the auditor's report on those accounts.
>
> [This does not apply if the LLP is exempt from audit and the members have taken advantage of that exemption.]
>
> (3), (4) . . .
>
> (5) The copy of the balance sheet delivered to the registrar under this section must state the name of the person who signed it on behalf of the members.
>
> (6) The copy of the auditor's report delivered to the registrar under this section must—
>
> (a) state the name of the auditor and (where the auditor is a firm) the name of the person who signed it as senior statutory auditor, or
>
> (b) if the conditions in section 506 (circumstances in which names may be omitted) are met, state that a determination has been made and notified to the Secretary of State in accordance with that section.
>
> [(6A) If more than one person is appointed as auditor, the reference in subsection (6)(a) to the name of the auditor is to be read as a reference to the names of all the auditors.]
>
> (7) This section does not apply to LLPs within section 444 (filing obligations of LLPs subject to the small LLPs regime)."

(2) Until section 1068 comes fully into force, for subsections (5) and (6) of section 445 as applied to LLPs by paragraph (1) substitute—

> "(5) The copy of the balance sheet delivered to the registrar under this section must—
>
> (a) state the name of the person who signed it on behalf of the members under section 414, and

(b) be signed on behalf of the members by a designated member.

(6) The copy of the auditor's report delivered to the registrar under this section must—

(a) state the name of the auditor and (where the auditor is a firm) the name of the person who signed it as senior statutory auditor, and

(b) be signed by the auditor or (where the auditor is a firm) in the name of the firm by a person authorised to sign on its behalf,

or, if the conditions in section 506 (circumstances in which names may be omitted) are met, state that a determination has been made and notified to the Secretary of State in accordance with that section."

NOTES

In s 445 as set out above, the words in square brackets in sub-s (2) were added, and sub-ss (3), (4) were revoked, by the Limited Liability Partnerships, Partnerships and Groups (Accounts and Audit) Regulations 2016, SI 2016/575, regs 3, 13, as from 17 May 2016, in relation to (a) financial years beginning on or after 1 January 2016; and (b) a financial year of an LLP beginning on or after 1 January 2015, but before 1 January 2016, if (i) the members of the LLP so decide, and (ii) a copy of the LLP's accounts for that financial year has not been delivered to the registrar in accordance with ss 444, 445 or 446 of the Companies Act 2006 as applied to LLPs by the Limited Liability Partnerships (Accounts and Audit) (Application of Companies Act 2006) Regulations before 17 May 2016 (see further the note at **[10.226]**).

In s 445 as set out above, sub-s (6A) was inserted by the Statutory Auditors Regulations 2017, SI 2017/1164, reg 5, Sch 3, paras 1, 6, in relation to financial years of companies beginning on or after 17 June 2016 (as to the application of the 2017 Regulations, see **[4.671]** et seq).

[10.244]

19 Filing obligations of large LLPs

(1) Section 446 applies to LLPs, modified so as to read as follows—

"446 Filing obligations of large LLPs

(1) The designated members of an LLP that does not qualify as small or medium-sized must deliver to the registrar for each financial year of the LLP a copy of the LLP's annual accounts.

(2) The designated members must also deliver to the registrar a copy of the auditor's report on those accounts.

[This does not apply if the LLP is exempt from audit and the members have taken advantage of that exemption.]

[(2A) The designated members must also deliver to the registrar a copy of the energy and carbon report for each financial year of the LLP, unless the members of the LLP are, by virtue of sections 415(4) or 415A, not under a duty to prepare an energy and carbon report.]

[(2B) The designated members must also deliver to the registrar a copy of the strategic report for each financial year of the LLP if the members of the LLP are under a duty to prepare a strategic report by virtue of section 414A.]

(3) The copy of the balance sheet delivered to the registrar under this section must state the name of the person who signed it on behalf of the members.

(4) The copy of the auditor's report delivered to the registrar under this section must—

(a) state the name of the auditor and (where the auditor is a firm) the name of the person who signed it as senior statutory auditor, or

(b) if the conditions in section 506 (circumstances in which names may be omitted) are met, state that a determination has been made and notified to the Secretary of State in accordance with that section.

[(4A) If more than one person is appointed as auditor, the reference in subsection (4)(a) to the name of the auditor is to be read as a reference to the names of all the auditors.]

(5) This section does not apply to LLPs within—

(a) section 444 (filing obligations of LLPs subject to the small LLPs regime), or

(b) section 445 (filing obligations of medium-sized LLPs)."

(2) Until section 1068 comes fully into force, for subsections (3) and (4) of section 446 as applied to LLPs by paragraph (1) substitute—

"(3) The copy of the balance sheet delivered to the registrar under this section must—

(a) state the name of the person who signed it on behalf of the members under section 414, and

(b) be signed on behalf of the members by a designated member.

(4) The copy of the auditor's report delivered to the registrar under this section must—

(a) state the name of the auditor and (where the auditor is a firm) the name of the person who signed it as senior statutory auditor, and

(b) be signed by the auditor or (where the auditor is a firm) in the name of the firm by a person authorised to sign on its behalf,

or, if the conditions in section 506 (circumstances in which names may be omitted) are met, state that a determination has been made and notified to the Secretary of State in accordance with that section."

NOTES

In s 446 as set out above, the words in square brackets in sub-s (2) were added by the Limited Liability Partnerships, Partnerships and Groups (Accounts and Audit) Regulations 2016, SI 2016/575, regs 3, 14, as from 17 May 2016, in relation to (a) financial years beginning on or after 1 January 2016; and (b) a financial year of an LLP beginning on or after 1 January 2015, but before 1 January 2016, if (i) the members of the LLP so decide, and (ii) a copy of the LLP's accounts for that financial year has not been delivered to the registrar in accordance with ss 444, 445 or 446 of the Companies Act 2006 as applied to LLPs by the Limited Liability Partnerships (Accounts and Audit) (Application of Companies Act 2006) Regulations before 17 May 2016 (see further the note at **[10.226]**).

In s 446 as set out above, sub-s (2A) was inserted by the Companies (Directors' Report) and Limited Liability Partnerships (Energy and Carbon Report) Regulations 2018, SI 2018/1155, regs 8, 18, as from 1 April 2019, in respect of financial years beginning on or after that date.

In s 446 as set out above, sub-s (2B) was inserted by the European Grouping of Territorial Cooperation and Limited Liability Partnerships etc (Revocations and Amendments) (EU Exit) Regulations 2021, SI 2021/153, reg 12, as from 8 March 2021, in relation to financial years beginning on or after 6 April 2021.

In s 446 as set out above, sub-s (4A) was inserted by the Statutory Auditors Regulations 2017, SI 2017/1164, reg 5, Sch 3, paras 1, 7, in relation to financial years of companies beginning on or after 17 June 2016 (as to the application of the 2017 Regulations, see **[4.671]** et seq).

[10.245]

[19A Exemption for dormant subsidiary LLPs

Section 448A applies to LLPs, modified so as to read as follows—

"448A Dormant subsidiary LLPs exempt from obligation to file accounts

(1) The designated members of an LLP are not required to deliver a copy of the LLP's individual accounts to the registrar in respect of a financial year if—

(a) the LLP is a subsidiary undertaking,

(b) it has been dormant throughout the whole of that year, and

(c) its parent undertaking is established under laws of [any part of the United Kingdom].

(2) Exemption is conditional upon compliance with all of the following conditions—

(a) all members of the LLP must agree to the exemption in respect of the financial year in question,

(b) the parent undertaking must give a guarantee under section 448C in respect of that year,

(c) the LLP must be included in the consolidated accounts drawn up for that year or to an earlier date in that year by the parent undertaking in accordance with—

[(i) if the undertaking is a company, the requirements of this Part of this Act, or, if the undertaking is not a company, the legal requirements which apply to the drawing up of consolidated accounts for that undertaking, or]

(ii) international accounting standards,

(d) the parent undertaking must disclose in the notes to the consolidated accounts that the designated members of the LLP are exempt from the requirement to deliver a copy of the LLP's individual accounts to the registrar by virtue of this section,

(e) the designated members of the LLP must deliver to the registrar, within the period for filing the LLP's accounts and auditor's report for that year—

(i) a written notice of the agreement referred to in subsection (2)(a),

(ii) the statement referred to in section 448C(1),

(iii) a copy of the consolidated accounts referred to in subsection 2(c),

(iv) a copy of the auditor's report on those accounts, and

(v) a copy of the consolidated annual report drawn up by the parent undertaking.

448B LLPs excluded from the dormant subsidiaries exemption

The designated members of an LLP are not entitled to the exemption conferred by section 448A (dormant subsidiaries) if the LLP was at any time within the financial year in question—

[(za) a traded LLP,]

(a) an LLP that—

(i) is an authorised insurance company, a banking LLP, an e-money issuer, a MiFID investment firm or a UCITS management company, or

(ii) carries on insurance market activity, or

(b) an employers' association as defined in section 122 of the Trade Union and Labour Relations (Consolidation) Act 1992 (c 52) or Article 4 of the Industrial Relations (Northern Ireland) Order 1992 (SI 1992/807) (NI 5).

448C Dormant subsidiaries exemption: parent undertaking declaration of guarantee

(1) A guarantee is given by a parent undertaking under this section when the designated members of the subsidiary LLP deliver to the registrar a statement by the parent undertaking that it guarantees the subsidiary LLP under this section.

(2) The statement under subsection (1) must be authenticated by the parent undertaking and must specify—

(a) the name of the parent undertaking,

[(b) the registered number of the parent undertaking (if any),]

(c) . . .

(d) the name and registered number of the subsidiary LLP in respect of which the guarantee is being given,

(e) the date of the statement, and

(f) the financial year to which the guarantee relates.

(3) A guarantee given under this section has the effect that—

(a) the parent undertaking guarantees all outstanding liabilities to which the subsidiary LLP is subject at the end of the financial year to which the guarantee relates, until they are satisfied in full, and

(b) the guarantee is enforceable against the parent undertaking by any person to whom the subsidiary LLP is liable in respect of those liabilities.]

NOTES

Inserted by the Companies and Limited Liability Partnerships (Accounts and Audit Exemptions and Change of Accounting Framework) Regulations 2012, SI 2012/2301, regs 2, 20(1), (7), as from 1 October 2012 (in relation to accounts for financial years ending on or after that date).

Section 448A as set out above is amended as follows:

Sub-s (2)(c)(i) and the words in square brackets in sub-s (1)(c) were substituted by the Accounts and Reports (Amendment) (EU Exit) Regulations 2019, SI 2019/145, reg 6, Sch 3, paras 11, 17(a), in relation to financial years beginning on or after IP completion day (as defined in the European Union (Withdrawal Agreement) Act 2020, s 39) (for transitional provisions see reg 7 of the 2019 Regulations at **[12.79]**).

In s 448B as set out above, para (za) was inserted by the Limited Liability Partnerships, Partnerships and Groups (Accounts and Audit) Regulations 2016, SI 2016/575, regs 3, 15(3), as from 17 May 2016, in relation to (a) financial years beginning on or after 1 January 2016; and (b) a financial year of an LLP beginning on or after 1 January 2015, but before 1 January 2016, if (i) the members of the LLP so decide, and (ii) a copy of the LLP's accounts for that financial year has not been delivered to the registrar in accordance with ss 444, 445 or 446 of the Companies Act 2006 as applied to LLPs by the Limited Liability Partnerships (Accounts and Audit) (Application of Companies Act 2006) Regulations before 17 May 2016 (see further the note at **[10.226]**).

In s 448C as set out above, sub-s (2)(b) was substituted, and sub-s (2)(c) was revoked, by SI 2019/145, reg 6, Sch 3, paras 11, 17(b), in relation to financial years beginning on or after IP completion day (as defined in the European Union (Withdrawal Agreement) Act 2020, s 39) (for transitional provisions see reg 7 of the 2019 Regulations at **[12.79]**).

20, 21 *(Revoked by the Limited Liability Partnerships, Partnerships and Groups (Accounts and Audit) Regulations 2016, SI 2016/575, regs 3, 16, as from 17 May 2016, in relation to (a) financial years beginning on or after 1 January 2016; and (b) a financial year of an LLP beginning on or after 1 January 2015, but before 1 January 2016, if (i) the members of the LLP so decide, and (ii) a copy of the LLP's accounts for that financial year has not been delivered to the registrar in accordance with ss 444, 445 or 446 of the Companies Act 2006 as applied to LLPs by the Limited Liability Partnerships (Accounts and Audit) (Application of Companies Act 2006) Regulations before 17 May 2016 (see further the note at* **[10.226]**.*)*

[10.246]

22 Failure to file [accounts and reports]

(1) Sections 451 to 453 apply to LLPs, modified so that they read as follow—

"451 Default in filing [accounts and reports]: offences

(1) If the requirements of [section 441 (duty to file accounts and reports with the registrar)] are not complied with in relation to an LLP's [accounts and reports for a financial year] [before the end of the period for filing those accounts and reports], every person who immediately before the end of that period was a designated member of the LLP commits an offence.

(2) It is a defence for a person charged with such an offence to prove that he took all reasonable steps for securing that those requirements would be complied with before the end of that period.

(3) It is not a defence to prove that the documents in question were not in fact prepared as required by this Part.

(4) A person guilty of an offence under this section is liable on summary conviction to a fine not exceeding level 5 on the standard scale and, for continued contravention, a daily default fine not exceeding one-tenth of level 5 on the standard scale.

452 Default in filing [accounts and reports]: court order

(1) If—

(a) the requirements of [section 441 (duty to file accounts and reports with the registrar)] are not complied with in relation to an LLP's [accounts and reports for a financial year] [before the end of the period for filing those accounts and reports], and

(b) the designated members of the LLP fail to make good the default within 14 days after the service of a notice on them requiring compliance,

the court may, on the application of any member or creditor of the LLP or of the registrar, make an order directing the designated members (or any of them) to make good the default within such time as may be specified in the order.

(2) The court's order may provide that all costs (in Scotland, expenses) of and incidental to the application are to be borne by the members.

453 Civil penalty for failure to file accounts [strategic report,][, auditor's report and energy and carbon report]

(1) Where the requirements of section 441 are not complied with in relation to an LLP's [accounts and reports for a financial year] [before the end of the period for filing those accounts and reports], the LLP is liable to a civil penalty.

This is in addition to any liability of the designated members under section 451.

(2) Regulations 1(3) and 4(2) and (3) of the Companies (Late Filing Penalties) and Limited Liability Partnerships (Filing Periods and Late Filing Penalties) Regulations 2008 (SI 2008/497) apply to LLPs with the following modifications—

(a) references to a company or private company include references to an LLP;

(b) references to 6th April 2008 are to be read as references to 1st October 2008; and

(c) the second column of the table in regulation 4(2) (penalties for public companies) is omitted.

(3) The penalty may be recovered by the registrar and is to be paid into the Consolidated Fund.

(4) It is not a defence in proceedings under this section to prove that the documents in question were not in fact prepared as required by this Part."

(2) *(Amends the Companies (Late Filing Penalties) and Limited Liability Partnerships (Filing Periods and Late Filing Penalties) Regulations 2008, SI 2008/497, reg 6 at* **[4.128]**.*)*

NOTES

The words in square brackets in the regulation heading were substituted (for the original words "accounts, auditor's report and energy and carbon report") by the European Grouping of Territorial Cooperation and Limited Liability Partnerships etc

Part 10 Miscellaneous other SIs

(Revocations and Amendments) (EU Exit) Regulations 2021, SI 2021/153, reg 13(2), as from 8 March 2021, in relation to financial years beginning on or after 6 April 2021.

Section 451 as set out above is amended as follows:

The words in square brackets in the heading were substituted (for the original words "accounts, auditor's report and energy and carbon report") by SI 2021/153, reg 13(3), as from 8 March 2021, in relation to financial years beginning on or after 6 April 2021.

The words in the first pair of square brackets in sub-s (1) were substituted (for the original words "section 441 (duty to file accounts and auditor's report)") by SI 2021/153, reg 13(3), as from 8 March 2021, in relation to financial years beginning on or after 6 April 2021.

The words in the second pair of square brackets in sub-s (1) were substituted (for the original words "accounts for a financial year, the auditor's report on those accounts and the energy and carbon report") by SI 2021/153, reg 13(3), as from 8 March 2021, in relation to financial years beginning on or after 6 April 2021.

The final words in square brackets in sub-s (1) were substituted by virtue of the Companies (Directors' Report) and Limited Liability Partnerships (Energy and Carbon Report) Regulations 2018, SI 2018/1155, regs 8, 19(3), as from 1 April 2019, in respect of financial years beginning on or after that date.

Section 452 as set out above is amended as follows:

The words in square brackets in the heading were substituted (for the original words "accounts, auditor's report and energy and carbon report") by SI 2021/153, reg 13(4), as from 8 March 2021, in relation to financial years beginning on or after 6 April 2021.

The words in the first pair of square brackets in sub-s (1) were substituted (for the original words "section 441 (duty to file accounts and auditor's report and energy and carbon report)") by SI 2021/153, reg 13(4), as from 8 March 2021, in relation to financial years beginning on or after 6 April 2021.

The words in the second pair of square brackets in sub-s (1) were substituted (for the original words "accounts for a financial year, the auditor's report on those accounts and the energy and carbon report") by SI 2021/153, reg 13(4), as from 8 March 2021, in relation to financial years beginning on or after 6 April 2021.

The final words in square brackets in sub-s (1) were substituted by virtue of SI 2018/1155, regs 8, 19(4), as from 1 April 2019, in respect of financial years beginning on or after that date.

Section 453 as set out above is amended as follows:

The words in the first pair of square brackets in the heading were inserted by SI 2021/153, reg 13(5), as from 8 March 2021, in relation to financial years beginning on or after 6 April 2021.

The words in the second pair of square brackets in the heading were substituted by SI 2018/1155, regs 8, 19(5), as from 1 April 2019, in respect of financial years beginning on or after that date.

The words in the first pair of square brackets in sub-s (1) were substituted (for the original words "accounts for a financial year, the auditor's report on those accounts and the energy and carbon report") by SI 2021/153, reg 13(5), as from 8 March 2021, in relation to financial years beginning on or after 6 April 2021.

The words in the second pair of square brackets in sub-s (1) were substituted by virtue of SI 2018/1155, regs 8, 19(5), as from 1 April 2019, in respect of financial years beginning on or after that date.

PART 8 REVISION OF DEFECTIVE [ACCOUNTS AND REPORTS]

NOTES

The words in square brackets in the preceding heading were substituted (for the original words "accounts or energy and carbon report") by the European Grouping of Territorial Cooperation and Limited Liability Partnerships etc (Revocations and Amendments) (EU Exit) Regulations 2021, SI 2021/153, reg 14, as from 8 March 2021, in relation to financial years beginning on or after 6 April 2021.

[10.247]

23 Revision of defective accounts[, strategic report] [or energy and carbon report]

Sections 454 to 456 apply to LLPs, modified so that they read as follows—

"454 [Voluntary revision of accounts etc]

[(1) If it appears to the members of an LLP that the LLP's annual accounts[, the LLP's strategic report] or the LLP's energy and carbon report did not comply with the requirements of this Act, they may prepare revised accounts[, a revised strategic report] or a revised energy and carbon report.]

(2) Where copies of the previous accounts[, strategic report] [or energy and carbon report] have been sent out to members or delivered to the registrar, the revisions must be confined to—

(a) the correction of those respects in which the previous accounts[, strategic report] [or energy and carbon report] did not comply with the requirements of this Act, and

(b) the making of any necessary consequential alterations.

(3) The Companies (Revision of Defective Accounts and Reports) Regulations 2008 (SI 2008/373) apply for the purposes of this section with the following modifications—

(a) references to a company include references to an LLP; . . .

(b) references to a director or to an officer of a company include references to a member of an LLP;

[(c) references to a directors' report include references to an energy and carbon report;

(d) references to a revised directors' report include references to revised energy and carbon report except for the purposes of regulation 7;

(e) references to the date on which the original directors' report was approved by the board of directors include references to the date on which the original energy and carbon report was approved by the members of an LLP;

(f) references to the date on which a revised directors' report is approved by the board of directors include references to the date on which a revised energy and carbon report is approved by the members of an LLP; and

(g) the reference in regulation 5 to section 419(3) and (4) includes a reference to section 419(2) and (3) as applied and modified by regulation 12B].

455 Secretary of State's notice in respect of accounts[, strategic report] [or energy and carbon report]

(1) This section applies where copies of an LLP's annual accounts[, strategic report] [or energy and carbon report] have been delivered to the registrar, and it appears to the Secretary of State that there is, or may be, a question whether the accounts [or report] comply with the requirements of this Act.

(2) The Secretary of State may give notice to the members of the LLP indicating the respects in which it appears that such a question arises or may arise.

(3) The notice must specify a period of not less than one month for the members to give an explanation of the accounts[, strategic report] [or energy and carbon report] or prepare revised accounts[, a revised strategic report] [or a revised energy and carbon report].

(4) If at the end of the specified period, or such longer period as the Secretary of State may allow, it appears to the Secretary of State that the members have not—

(a) given a satisfactory explanation of the accounts [or [reports]], or

(b) revised the accounts [or [reports]] so as to comply with the requirements of this Act,

the Secretary of State may apply to the court.

(5) The provisions of this section apply equally to revised annual accounts[, revised strategic reports] [and revised energy and carbon reports], in which case they have effect as if the references to revised accounts [or reports] were references to further revised accounts [or reports].

456 Application to court in respect of defective accounts[, strategic report] [or energy and carbon report]

(1) An application may be made to the court—

(a) by the Secretary of State, after having complied with section 455, or

(b) [the Financial Reporting Council Limited]

for a declaration (in Scotland, a declarator) that the annual accounts of an LLP do not comply, [a strategic report does not comply][, or an energy and carbon report does not comply,] with the requirements of this Act and for an order requiring the members of the LLP to prepare revised accounts [or a revised report].

(2) Notice of the application, together with a general statement of the matters at issue in the proceedings, shall be given by the applicant to the registrar for registration.

(3) If the court orders the preparation of revised accounts, it may give directions as to—

(a) the auditing of the accounts, . . .

[(aa) the revision of any [strategic report or] energy and carbon report, and]

(b) the taking of steps by the members to bring the making of the order to the notice of persons likely to rely on the previous accounts,

and such other matters as the court thinks fit.

[(3A) If the court orders the preparation of a [revised strategic report or] revised energy and carbon report, it may give directions as to—

(a) the taking of steps by the members to bring the making of the order to the notice of persons likely to rely on the previous report, and

(b) such other matters as the court thinks fit.]

(4) If the court finds that the accounts [or report] did not comply with the requirements of this Act it may order that all or part of—

(a) the costs (in Scotland, expenses) of and incidental to the application, and

(b) any reasonable expenses incurred by the LLP in connection with or in consequence of the preparation of revised accounts [or a revised report],

are to be borne by such of the members as were party to the approval of the defective accounts [or report].

For this purpose every member of the LLP at the time of the approval of the accounts [or report] shall be taken to have been a party to the approval unless he shows that he took all reasonable steps to prevent that approval.

(5) Where the court makes an order under subsection (4) it shall have regard to whether the members party to the approval of the defective accounts [or report] knew or ought to have known that the accounts [or report] did not comply with the requirements of this Act, and it may exclude one or more members from the order or order the payment of different amounts by different members.

(6) On the conclusion of proceedings on an application under this section, the applicant must send to the registrar for registration a copy of the court order or, as the case may be, give notice to the registrar that the application has failed or been withdrawn.

(7) The provisions of this section apply equally to revised annual accounts[, revised strategic reports] [and revised energy and carbon reports], in which case they have effect as if the references to revised accounts [or reports] were references to further revised accounts [or reports]."

NOTES

The words in the first pair of square brackets in the regulation heading were inserted by the European Grouping of Territorial Cooperation and Limited Liability Partnerships etc (Revocations and Amendments) (EU Exit) Regulations 2021, SI 2021/153, reg 15(2), as from 8 March 2021, in relation to financial years beginning on or after 6 April 2021. The words in the second pair of square brackets were inserted by the Companies (Directors' Report) and Limited Liability Partnerships (Energy and Carbon Report) Regulations 2018, SI 2018/1155, regs 8, 21(1), (2), as from 1 April 2019, in respect of financial years beginning on or after that date.

Section 454 as set out above is amended as follows:

The heading was inserted by SI 2021/153, reg 15(3), as from 8 March 2021, in relation to financial years beginning on or after 6 April 2021.

The words ", the LLP's strategic report" and ", a revised strategic report" in square brackets in sub-s (1) were inserted by SI 2021/153, reg 15(3), as from 8 March 2021, in relation to financial years beginning on or after 6 April 2021.

The words ", strategic report" in square brackets (in both places that they occur in sub-s (2)) were inserted by SI 2021/153, reg 15(3), as from 8 March 2021, in relation to financial years beginning on or after 6 April 2021.

All other amendments to s 454 as set out above were made by the Companies (Directors' Report) and Limited Liability Partnerships (Energy and Carbon Report) Regulations 2018, SI 2018/1155, regs 8, 21(3), as from 1 April 2019, in respect of financial years beginning on or after that date.

Section 455 as set out above is amended as follows:

The words ", strategic report" in square brackets in the heading and in sub-ss (1) and (3) were inserted, the words ", a revised strategic report" in square brackets in sub-s (3) were inserted, the words ", revised strategic reports" in square brackets in sub-s (5) were inserted, and the word "reports" in square brackets (in both places that it occurs in sub-s (4)) was substituted (for the original word "report"), by SI 2021/153, reg 15(4), as from 8 March 2021, in relation to financial years beginning on or after 6 April 2021.

All other words in square brackets in s 455 as set out above were inserted by SI 2018/1155, regs 8, 21 (4), as from 1 April 2019, in respect of financial years beginning on or after that date.

Section 456 as set out above is amended as follows:

The words ", strategic report" in the heading, "a strategic report does not comply" in sub-s (1), "strategic report or" in sub-s (3)(aa), "revised strategic report or" in sub-s (3A), and ", revised strategic reports" in sub-s (7), were inserted by SI 2021/153, reg 15(5), as from 8 March 2021, in relation to financial years beginning on or after 6 April 2021.

The words "the Financial Reporting Council Limited" in square brackets in sub-s (1)(b) were substituted by the Supervision of Accounts and Reports (Prescribed Body) and Companies (Defective Accounts and Reports) (Authorised Person) Order 2021, SI 2021/465, art 6(2), as from 6 May 2021 (see art 9 of the 2021 Order for transitional provisions in relation to the continuity of functions, etc at **[4.727]**).

All other amendments to s 456 as set out above were made by SI 2018/1155, regs 8, 21(1), (5), as from 1 April 2019, in respect of financial years beginning on or after that date.

[10.248]

24 Disclosure of information

Sections 458 to 461 apply to LLPs, modified so that they read as follows—

"458 Disclosure of information by tax authorities

(1) The Commissioners for Her Majesty's Revenue and Customs may disclose information to [the Financial Reporting Council Limited] for the purpose of facilitating—

(a) the taking of steps by [the Financial Reporting Council Limited] to discover whether there are grounds for an application to the court under section 456 (application in respect of [defective accounts, strategic report or energy and carbon report] etc), or

(b) a decision by [the Financial Reporting Council Limited] whether to make such an application.

(2) This section applies despite any statutory or other restriction on the disclosure of information.

Provided that, in the case of personal data within the meaning of the Data Protection Act 1998 (c.29), information is not to be disclosed in contravention of that Act.

(3) Information disclosed to [the Financial Reporting Council Limited] under this section—

(a) may not be used except in or in connection with—

(i) taking steps to discover whether there are grounds for an application to the court under section 456, or

(ii) deciding whether or not to make such an application,

or in, or in connection with, proceedings on such an application; and

(b) must not be further disclosed except—

(i) to the person to whom the information relates, or

(ii) in, or in connection with, proceedings on any such application to the court.

(4) A person who contravenes subsection (3) commits an offence unless—

(a) he did not know, and had no reason to suspect, that the information had been disclosed under this section, or

(b) he took all reasonable steps and exercised all due diligence to avoid the commission of the offence.

(5) A person guilty of an offence under subsection (4) is liable—

(a) on conviction on indictment, to imprisonment for a term not exceeding two years or a fine (or both);

(b) on summary conviction—

(i) in England and Wales [or Scotland], to imprisonment for a term not exceeding twelve months or to a fine not exceeding the statutory maximum (or both);

(ii) in . . . Northern Ireland, to imprisonment for a term not exceeding six months, or to a fine not exceeding the statutory maximum (or both).

(6) Where an offence under this section is committed by a body corporate, every officer of the body who is in default also commits the offence.

For this purpose—

(a) any person who purports to act as director, manager or secretary of the body is treated as an officer of the body, and

(b) if the body is a company, any shadow director is treated as an officer of the company.

459 Power of [the Financial Reporting Council Limited] to require documents, information and explanations

(1) This section applies where it appears to [the Financial Reporting Council Limited] that there is, or may be, a question whether an LLP's annual accounts[, strategic report] [or energy and carbon report] comply with the requirements of this Act.

(2) [the Financial Reporting Council Limited] may require any of the persons mentioned in subsection (3) to produce any document, or to provide him with any information or explanations, that he may reasonably require for the purpose of—

(a) discovering whether there are grounds for an application to the court under section 456, or

(b) deciding whether to make such an application.

(3) Those persons are—

(a) the LLP;

(b) any member, employee, or auditor of the LLP;

(c) any persons who fell within paragraph (b) at a time to which the document or information required by [the Financial Reporting Council Limited] relates.

(4) If a person fails to comply with such a requirement, [the Financial Reporting Council Limited] may apply to the court.

(5) If it appears to the court that the person has failed to comply with a requirement under subsection (2), it may order the person to take such steps as it directs for securing that the documents are produced or the information or explanations are provided.

(6) A statement made by a person in response to a requirement under subsection (2) or an order under subsection (5) may not be used in evidence against him in any criminal proceedings.

(7) Nothing in this section compels any person to disclose documents or information in respect of which a claim to legal professional privilege (in Scotland, to confidentiality of communications) could be maintained in legal proceedings.

(8) In this section "document" includes information recorded in any form.

460 Restrictions on disclosure of information obtained under compulsory powers

(1) This section applies to information (in whatever form) obtained in pursuance of a requirement or order under section 459 (power of [Financial Reporting Council Limited] to require documents etc) that relates to the private affairs of an individual or to any particular business.

(2) No such information may, during the lifetime of that individual or so long as that business continues to be carried on, be disclosed without the consent of that individual or the person for the time being carrying on that business.

(3) This does not apply—

(a) to disclosure permitted by section 461 (permitted disclosure of information obtained under compulsory powers), or

(b) to the disclosure of information that is or has been available to the public from another source.

(4) A person who discloses information in contravention of this section commits an offence, unless—

(a) he did not know, and had no reason to suspect, that the information had been disclosed under section 459, or

(b) he took all reasonable steps and exercised all due diligence to avoid the commission of the offence.

(5) A person guilty of an offence under this section is liable—

(a) on conviction on indictment, to imprisonment for a term not exceeding two years or a fine (or both);

(b) on summary conviction—

(i) in England and Wales [or Scotland], to imprisonment for a term not exceeding twelve months or to a fine not exceeding the statutory maximum (or both);

(ii) in . . . Northern Ireland, to imprisonment for a term not exceeding six months, or to a fine not exceeding the statutory maximum (or both).

(6) Where an offence under this section is committed by a body corporate, every officer of the body who is in default also commits the offence.

For this purpose—

(a) any person who purports to act as director, manager or secretary of the body is treated as an officer of the body, and

(b) if the body is a company, any shadow director is treated as an officer of the company.

461 Permitted disclosure of information obtained under compulsory powers

(1) The prohibition in section 460 of the disclosure of information obtained in pursuance of a requirement or order under section 459 (power of [Financial Reporting Council Limited] to require documents etc) that relates to the private affairs of an individual or to any particular business has effect subject to the following exceptions.

(2) It does not apply to the disclosure of information for the purpose of facilitating the carrying out by [the Financial Reporting Council Limited] of its functions under section 456.

(3) It does not apply to disclosure to—

(a) the Secretary of State,

(b) the Department of Enterprise, Trade and Investment for Northern Ireland,

(c) the Treasury,

(d) the Bank of England,

[(e) Financial Conduct Authority,

(ea) Prudential Regulation Authority, or]

(f) the Commissioners for Her Majesty's Revenue and Customs.

(4) It does not apply to disclosure—

[(a) for the purpose of assisting the Financial Reporting Council Limited to exercise it functions under Part 42 of this Act;]

[(aa) for the purpose of assisting the competent authority to exercise its functions under the Statutory Auditors and Third Country Auditors Regulations 2016 and under the Audit Regulation;]

(b) with a view to the institution of, or otherwise for the purposes of, disciplinary proceedings relating to the performance by an accountant or auditor of his professional duties;

(c) for the purpose of enabling or assisting the Secretary of State or the Treasury to exercise any of their functions under any of the following—

(i) the Companies Acts,

(ii) Part 5 of the Criminal Justice Act 1993 (c.36) (insider dealing),

Part 10 Miscellaneous other SIs

(iii) the Insolvency Act 1986 (c.45) or the Insolvency (Northern Ireland) Order 1989 (SI 1989/2405 (NI 19)),
(iv) the Company Directors Disqualification Act 1986 (c.46) or the Company Directors Disqualification (Northern Ireland) Order 2002 (SI 2002/3150 (NI 4)),
(v) the Financial Services and Markets Act 2000 (c.8);

(d) for the purpose of enabling or assisting the Department of Enterprise, Trade and Investment for Northern Ireland to exercise any powers conferred on it by the enactments relating to companies, directors' disqualification or insolvency;

[(e) for the purpose of enabling or assisting the Bank of England to exercise its functions when acting otherwise than in its capacity as the Prudential Regulation Authority;]

(f) for the purpose of enabling or assisting the Commissioners for Her Majesty's Revenue and Customs to exercise their functions;

(g) for the purpose of enabling or assisting the [Financial Conduct Authority or the Prudential Regulation Authority] to exercise its functions under any of the following—
(i) the legislation relating to friendly societies . . .
[(ia) the legislation relating to a society, other than a society registered as a credit union, which is—
(aa) a registered society within the meaning given by section 1(1) of the Co-operative and Community Benefit Societies Act 2014, or
(ab) a society registered or deemed to be registered under the Industrial and Provident Societies Act (Northern Ireland) 1969,]
(ii) the Building Societies Act 1986 (c.53),
(iii) Part 7 of the Companies Act 1989 (c.40),
(iv) the Financial Services and Markets Act 2000; or

(h) in pursuance of any [retained] [EU] obligation.

(5) It does not apply to disclosure to a body exercising functions of a public nature under legislation in any country or territory outside the United Kingdom that appear to [the Financial Reporting Council Limited] to be similar to its functions under section 456 for the purpose of enabling or assisting that body to exercise those functions.

(6) In determining whether to disclose information to a body in accordance with subsection (5), [the Financial Reporting Council Limited] must have regard to the following considerations—

(a) whether the use which the body is likely to make of the information is sufficiently important to justify making the disclosure;

(b) whether the body has adequate arrangements to prevent the information from being used or further disclosed other than—
(i) for the purposes of carrying out the functions mentioned in that subsection, or
(ii) for other purposes substantially similar to those for which information disclosed to [the Financial Reporting Council Limited] could be used or further disclosed.

(7) Nothing in this section authorises the making of a disclosure in contravention of the Data Protection Act 1998 (c.29)."

NOTES

Section 458 as set out above is amended as follows:

The words "the Financial Reporting Council Limited" in square brackets (in every place that they occur) were substituted by the Supervision of Accounts and Reports (Prescribed Body) and Companies (Defective Accounts and Reports) (Authorised Person) Order 2021, SI 2021/465, art 6(3), as from 6 May 2021 (see art 9 of the 2021 Order for transitional provisions in relation to the continuity of functions, etc at **[4.727]**).

The words "defective accounts, strategic report or energy and carbon report" in square brackets in sub-s (1)(a) were substituted (for the original words "defective accounts") by the European Grouping of Territorial Cooperation and Limited Liability Partnerships etc (Revocations and Amendments) (EU Exit) Regulations 2021, SI 2021/153, reg 16(2), as from 8 March 2021, in relation to financial years beginning on or after 6 April 2021.

The words in square brackets in sub-s (5)(b) were inserted, and the words omitted were revoked, by the Limited Liability Partnerships (Application of Companies Act 2006) Regulations 2009, SI 2009/1804, reg 85, Sch 3, Pt 2, para 16, as from 1 October 2009.

Section 459 as set out above is amended as follows:

The words "the Financial Reporting Council Limited" in square brackets (in every place that they occur) were substituted by SI 2021/465, art 6(3), as from 6 May 2021 (see art 9 of the 2021 Order for transitional provisions in relation to the continuity of functions, etc at **[4.727]**).

The words ", strategic report" in square brackets in sub-s (1) were inserted by SI 2021/153, reg 16(3), as from 8 March 2021, in relation to financial years beginning on or after 6 April 2021.

The words "or energy and carbon report" in square brackets in sub-s (1) were inserted by the Companies (Directors' Report) and Limited Liability Partnerships (Energy and Carbon Report) Regulations 2018, SI 2018/1155, regs 8, 22, as from 1 April 2019, in respect of financial years beginning on or after that date.

Section 460 as set out above is amended as follows:

The words "Financial Reporting Council Limited" in square brackets were substituted by SI 2021/465, art 6(3), as from 6 May 2021 (see art 9 of the 2021 Order for transitional provisions in relation to the continuity of functions, etc at **[4.727]**).

The words in square brackets in sub-s (5)(b) were inserted, and the words omitted were revoked, by SI 2009/1804, reg 85, Sch 3, Pt 2, para 16, as from 1 October 2009.

Section 461 as set out above is amended as follows:

The words "Financial Reporting Council Limited" and "the Financial Reporting Council Limited" in square brackets (in every place that they occur) were substituted by SI 2021/465, art 6(3), as from 6 May 2021 (see art 9 of the 2021 Order for transitional provisions in relation to the continuity of functions, etc at **[4.727]**).

Sub-s (3)(e), (ea) were substituted (for the original sub-s (3)(e)), and the words in square brackets in sub-s (4)(g) were substituted, by the Financial Services Act 2012 (Consequential Amendments and Transitional Provisions) Order 2013, SI 2013/472, art 3, Sch 2, para 143(a), as from 1 April 2013.

Sub-s (4)(a) was substituted by the Statutory Auditors (Amendment of Companies Act 2006 and Delegation of Functions etc) Order 2012, SI 2012/1741, art 3, Schedule, Pt 1, para 2, as from 2 July 2012.

Sub-s (4)(aa) was inserted by the Statutory Auditors Regulations 2017, SI 2017/1164, reg 5, Sch 3, paras 1, 8, in relation to financial years of companies beginning on or after 17 June 2016 (as to the application of the 2017 Regulations, see **[4.671]** et seq).

Sub-s (4)(e) was substituted by the Bank of England and Financial Services (Consequential Amendments) Regulations 2017, SI 2017/80, reg 2, Schedule, Pt 2, para 28, as from 1 March 2017.

The words omitted from sub-s (4)(g)(i) were revoked, and sub-s (4)(g)(ia) was inserted, by the Co-operative and Community Benefit Societies and Credit Unions Act 2010 (Consequential Amendments) Regulations 2014, SI 2014/1815, reg 2, Schedule, para 22, as from 1 August 2014.

In sub-s (4)(h), the word "retained" in square brackets was inserted by the Accounts and Reports (Amendment) (EU Exit) Regulations 2019, SI 2019/145, reg 6, Sch 3, paras 11, 18, as from IP completion day (as defined in the European Union (Withdrawal Agreement) Act 2020, s 39).

In sub-s (4)(h), the word "EU" in square brackets was substituted by virtue of the Treaty of Lisbon (Changes in Terminology) Order 2011, SI 2011/1043, art 6(1)(e), as from 22 April 2011.

Modification: unless the context otherwise requires, references to the Data Protection Act 1998 have effect as references to the Data Protection Act 2018 or, as the case may be, the data protection legislation. See the Data Protection Act 2018, Sch 19, Pt 3.

PART 9 ACCOUNTS: SUPPLEMENTARY PROVISIONS [AND REPORTS]

NOTES

Words in square brackets in the preceding heading inserted by the Companies (Directors' Report) and Limited Liability Partnerships (Energy and Carbon Report) Regulations 2018, SI 2018/1155, regs 8, 23, as from 1 April 2019, in respect of financial years beginning on or after that date.

[10.249]

[24A

Section 463 applies to LLPs, modified so that it reads as follows—

"463 Liability for false or misleading statements in strategic report [or energy and carbon report]

(1) A member of an LLP is liable to compensate the LLP for any loss suffered by it as a result of—

(a) any untrue or misleading statement in a strategic report [or energy and carbon report], or

(b) the omission from a strategic report [or energy and carbon report] of anything required to be included in it.

(2) The member is so liable only if—

(a) the member knew the statement to be untrue or misleading or was reckless as to whether it was untrue or misleading, or

(b) the member knew the omission to be dishonest concealment of a material fact.

(3) No person shall be subject to any liability to a person other than the LLP resulting from reliance, by that person or another, on information in a report to which this section applies.

(4) The reference in subsection (3) to a person being subject to a liability includes a reference to another person being entitled as against him to be granted any civil remedy or to rescind or repudiate an agreement.

(5) This section does not affect—

(a) liability for a civil penalty, or

(b) liability for a criminal offence."]

NOTES

Inserted by the Statutory Auditors Regulations 2017, SI 2017/1164, reg 5, Sch 3, paras 1, 9, in relation to financial years of companies beginning on or after 17 June 2016 (as to the application of the 2017 Regulations, see **[4.671]** et seq).

In s 463 as set out above, the words in square brackets in the heading and in sub-s (1) were inserted by the Companies (Directors' Report) and Limited Liability Partnerships (Energy and Carbon Report) Regulations 2018, SI 2018/1155, regs 8, 24, as from 1 April 2019, in respect of financial years beginning on or after that date.

[10.250]

[25 Accounting standards

Section 464 applies to LLPs, modified so that it reads as follows—

"464 Accounting standards

(1) In this Part "accounting standards" means statements of standard accounting practice issued by the Financial Reporting Council Limited.

(2) References in this Part to accounting standards applicable to an LLP's annual accounts are to such standards as are, in accordance with their terms, relevant to the LLP's circumstances and to the accounts.".]

NOTES

Substituted by the Statutory Auditors (Amendment of Companies Act 2006 and Delegation of Functions etc) Order 2012, SI 2012/1741, art 3, Schedule, Pt 2, para 8, as from 2 July 2012.

[10.251]

26 Medium-sized LLPs

Sections 465 to 467 apply to LLPs, modified so that they read as follows—

"465 LLPs qualifying as medium-sized: general

(1) An LLP qualifies as medium-sized in relation to its first financial year if the qualifying conditions are met in that year.

(2) An LLP qualifies as medium-sized in relation to a subsequent financial year—

(a) if the qualifying conditions are met in that year and the preceding financial year;

(b) if the qualifying conditions are met in that year and the LLP qualified as medium-sized in relation to the preceding financial year;

(c) if the qualifying conditions were met in the preceding financial year and the LLP qualified as medium-sized in relation to that year.

(3) The qualifying conditions are met by an LLP in a year in which it satisfies two or more of the following requirements—

1. Turnover	[Not more than £36 million]
2. Balance sheet total	[Not more than £18 million]
3. Number of employees	Not more than 250

(4) For a period that is an LLP's financial year but not in fact a year the maximum figures for turnover must be proportionately adjusted.

(5) The balance sheet total means the aggregate of the amounts shown as assets in the LLP's balance sheet.

(6) The number of employees means the average number of persons employed by the LLP in the year, determined as follows—

(a) find for each month in the financial year the number of persons employed under contracts of service by the LLP in that month (whether throughout the month or not),

(b) add together the monthly totals, and

(c) divide by the number of months in the financial year.

(7) This section is subject to section 466 (LLPs qualifying as medium-sized: parent LLPs).

466 LLPs qualifying as medium-sized: parent LLPs

(1) A parent LLP qualifies as a medium-sized LLP in relation to a financial year only if the group headed by it qualifies as a medium-sized group.

(2) A group qualifies as medium-sized in relation to the parent LLP's first financial year if the qualifying conditions are met in that year.

(3) A group qualifies as medium-sized in relation to a subsequent financial year of the parent LLP—

(a) if the qualifying conditions are met in that year and the preceding financial year;

(b) if the qualifying conditions are met in that year and the group qualified as medium-sized in relation to the preceding financial year;

(c) if the qualifying conditions were met in the preceding financial year and the group qualified as medium-sized in relation to that year.

(4) The qualifying conditions are met by a group in a year in which it satisfies two or more of the following requirements—

1. Aggregate turnover	[Not more than £36 million net (or £43.2 million gross)]
2. Aggregate balance sheet total	[Not more than £18 million net (or £21.6 million gross)]
3. Aggregate number of employees	Not more than 250

(5) The aggregate figures are ascertained by aggregating the relevant figures determined in accordance with section 465 for each member of the group.

(6) In relation to the aggregate figures for turnover and balance sheet total—

"net" means after any set-offs and other adjustments made to eliminate group transactions—

(a) in the case of non-IAS accounts, in accordance with Schedule 3 to the Large and Medium-sized Limited Liability Partnerships (Accounts) Regulations 2008 (SI 2008/1913),

(b) in the case of IAS accounts, in accordance with [UK-adopted international accounting standards]; and

"gross" means without those set-offs and other adjustments.

An LLP may satisfy any relevant requirement on the basis of either the net or the gross figure.

(7) The figures for each subsidiary undertaking shall be those included in its individual accounts for the relevant financial year, that is—

(a) if its financial year ends with that of the parent LLP, that financial year, and

(b) if not, its financial year ending last before the end of the financial year of the parent LLP.

If those figures cannot be obtained without disproportionate expense or undue delay, the latest available figures shall be taken.

467 LLPs excluded from being treated as medium-sized

(1) An LLP is not entitled to take advantage of any of the provisions of this Part relating to LLPs qualifying as medium-sized if it was at any time within the financial year in question—

[(a) a traded LLP,]

(b) an LLP that—

(i) has permission under Part 4 of the Financial Services and Markets Act 2000 (c.8) to carry on a regulated activity, . . .

(ii) carries on insurance market activity,

[(iii) is a scheme funder of a Master Trust scheme within the meanings given by section 39(1) of the Pension Schemes Act 2017 (interpretation of Part 1),]

[(ba) an e-money issuer,] or

(c) a member of an ineligible group.

(2) A group is ineligible if any of its members is—

[(a) a traded company,]

(b) a body corporate (other than a company) whose shares are admitted to trading on a [UK] regulated market,

(c) a person (other than a small company or small LLP) who has permission under Part 4 of the Financial Services and Markets Act 2000 to carry on a regulated activity,

[(ca) an e-money issuer,]

(d) a small company or small LLP that is an authorised insurance company, a banking company or banking LLP, . . . a MiFID investment firm or a UCITS management company . . .

(e) a person who carries on insurance market activity, [or]

[(f) a scheme funder of a Master Trust scheme within the meanings given by section 39(1) of the Pension Schemes Act 2017 (interpretation of Part 1)].

(3) An LLP is a small LLP for the purposes of subsection (2) if it qualified as small in relation to its last financial year ending on or before the end of the financial year in question."

NOTES

In s 465 as set out above, in sub-s (3) the words in square brackets in items 1 and 2 of the Table were substituted by the Limited Liability Partnerships, Partnerships and Groups (Accounts and Audit) Regulations 2016, SI 2016/575, regs 3, 17(1), (2), as from 17 May 2016, in relation to (a) financial years beginning on or after 1 January 2016; and (b) a financial year of an LLP beginning on or after 1 January 2015, but before 1 January 2016, if (i) the members of the LLP so decide, and (ii) a copy of the LLP's accounts for that financial year has not been delivered to the registrar in accordance with ss 444, 445 or 446 of the Companies Act 2006 as applied to LLPs by the Limited Liability Partnerships (Accounts and Audit) (Application of Companies Act 2006) Regulations before 17 May 2016 (see further the note at **[10.226]**).

In s 466 as set out above, in sub-s (4) the words in square brackets in items 1 and 2 of the Table were substituted by SI 2016/575, regs 3, 17(1), (3), as from 17 May 2016, in relation to (a) financial years beginning on or after 1 January 2016; and (b) a financial year of an LLP beginning on or after 1 January 2015, but before 1 January 2016, if (i) the members of the LLP so decide, and (ii) a copy of the LLP's accounts for that financial year has not been delivered to the registrar in accordance with ss 444, 445 or 446 of the Companies Act 2006 as applied to LLPs by the Limited Liability Partnerships (Accounts and Audit) (Application of Companies Act 2006) Regulations before 17 May 2016 (see further the note at **[10.226]**). The words in square brackets in sub-s (6) were substituted by the International Accounting Standards and European Public Limited-Liability Company (Amendment etc) (EU Exit) Regulations 2019, SI 2019/685, reg 19, Sch 1, Pt 2, para 58(1), (5), in relation to accounts for financial years beginning on or after IP completion day (as defined in the European Union (Withdrawal Agreement) Act 2020, s 39) (note also that in relation to accounts for financial years which begin before but end on or after IP completion day, the enactments amended by Parts 1–3 of Sch 1 to the 2019 Regulations have effect as if the UK were a member State until the end of the financial year in question).

Section 467 as set out above is amended as follows:

Sub-ss (1)(ba), (2)(ca) were inserted, and the first words omitted from sub-s (2)(d) were revoked, by the Companies and Partnerships (Accounts and Audit) Regulations 2013, SI 2013/2005, reg 3(1), (3), in relation to a financial year of an LLP beginning on or after 1 October 2013.

Sub-ss (1)(a), (2)(a) were substituted by SI 2016/575, regs 3, 17(1), (4), as from 17 May 2016, in relation to (a) financial years beginning on or after 1 January 2016; and (b) a financial year of an LLP beginning on or after 1 January 2015, but before 1 January 2016, if (i) the members of the LLP so decide, and (ii) a copy of the LLP's accounts for that financial year has not been delivered to the registrar in accordance with ss 444, 445 or 446 of the Companies Act 2006 as applied to LLPs by the Limited Liability Partnerships (Accounts and Audit) (Application of Companies Act 2006) Regulations before 17 May 2016 (see further the note at **[10.226]**).

In sub-s (1), the word omitted from sub-para (i) was revoked, and sub-para (iii) was inserted, and in sub-s (2) the word omitted from the end of para (d) was revoked, the word in square brackets in para (e) was inserted, and para (f) was added, by the Occupational Pension Schemes (Master Trusts) Regulations 2018, SI 2018/1030, reg 31(1), (3), as from 1 October 2018.

In sub-s (2)(b) the word "UK" in square brackets was inserted by the Accounts and Reports (Amendment) (EU Exit) Regulations 2019, SI 2019/145, reg 6, Sch 3, paras 11, 19, in relation to financial years beginning on or after IP completion day (as defined in the European Union (Withdrawal Agreement) Act 2020, s 39) (for transitional provisions see reg 7 of the 2019 Regulations at **[12.79]**).

[10.252]

27 General power to make further provision about accounts

Section 468 applies to LLPs, modified so that it reads as follows—

"468 General power to make further provision about accounts

(1) The Secretary of State may make provision by regulations about—

(a) the accounts that LLPs are required to prepare;

(b) the categories of LLPs required to prepare accounts of any description;

(c) the form and content of the accounts that LLPs are required to prepare;

(d) the obligations of LLPs and others as regards—

(i) the approval of accounts,

(ii) the sending of accounts to members and others,

(iii) the delivery of copies of accounts to the registrar, and

(iv) the publication of accounts.

(2) The regulations may amend this Part by adding, altering or repealing provisions.

(3) But they must not amend (other than consequentially)—

(a) section 393 (accounts to give true and fair view), or

(b) the provisions of Chapter 11 (revision of defective accounts and reports).

(4) The regulations may create criminal offences in cases corresponding to those in which an offence is created by an existing provision of this Part.

The maximum penalty for any such offence may not be greater than is provided in relation to an offence under the existing provision.

(5) The regulations may provide for civil penalties in circumstances corresponding to those within section 453(1) (civil penalty for failure to file accounts and reports).

The provisions of section 453(3) and (4) apply in relation to any such penalty."

[10.253]

28 Other supplementary provisions

Section 469 applies to LLPs, modified so that it reads as follows—

"469 Preparation and filing of accounts in euros

(1) The amounts set out in the annual accounts of an LLP may also be shown in the same accounts translated into euros.

(2) When complying with section 441 (duty to file accounts and auditor's report), the designated members of an LLP may deliver to the registrar an additional copy of the LLP's annual accounts in which the amounts have been translated into euros.

(3) In both cases—

(a) the amounts must have been translated at the exchange rate prevailing on the date to which the balance sheet is made up, and

(b) that rate must be disclosed in the notes to the accounts.

[(3A) Subsection (3)(b) does not apply to the non-IAS individual accounts of an LLP for a financial year in which the LLP qualifies as a micro-entity (see sections 384A and 384B).]

(4) For the purposes of sections 434 and 435 (requirements in connection with published accounts) any additional copy of the LLP's annual accounts delivered to the registrar under subsection (2) above shall be treated as statutory accounts of the LLP.

In the case of such a copy, references in those sections to the auditor's report on the LLP's annual accounts shall be read as references to the auditor's report on the annual accounts of which it is a copy."

NOTES

In s 469 as set out above, sub-s (3A) was inserted by the Limited Liability Partnerships, Partnerships and Groups (Accounts and Audit) Regulations 2016, SI 2016/575, regs 3, 18, as from 17 May 2016, in relation to (a) financial years beginning on or after 1 January 2016; and (b) a financial year of an LLP beginning on or after 1 January 2015, but before 1 January 2016, if (i) the members of the LLP so decide, and (ii) a copy of the LLP's accounts for that financial year has not been delivered to the registrar in accordance with ss 444, 445 or 446 of the Companies Act 2006 as applied to LLPs by the Limited Liability Partnerships (Accounts and Audit) (Application of Companies Act 2006) Regulations before 17 May 2016 (see further the note at **[10.226]**).

[10.254]

29 Meaning of "annual accounts"

Section 471 applies to LLPs, modified so that it reads as follows—

"471 Meaning of "annual accounts" and related expressions

(1) In this Part an LLP's "annual accounts", in relation to a financial year, means—

[(a) any individual accounts prepared by the LLP for that year (see section 394), and]

(b) any group accounts prepared by the LLP for that year (see [section] 399).

This is subject to section 408 (option to omit individual profit and loss account from annual accounts where information [given in notes to the individual balance sheet]).

[(2) In this Part an LLP's "annual accounts and reports" for a financial year are—

(a) its annual accounts,

(b) the strategic report (if any),

(c) the energy and carbon report (if any),

(d) the auditor's report on those accounts and the strategic report (where this is covered by the auditor's report), unless the LLP is exempt from audit.]

NOTES

Section 471 as set out above is amended as follows:

Sub-s (1)(a) was substituted by the Companies and Limited Liability Partnerships (Accounts and Audit Exemptions and Change of Accounting Framework) Regulations 2012, SI 2012/2301, regs 2, 20(2), as from 1 October 2012 (in relation to accounts for financial years ending on or after that date).

The word in square brackets in sub-s (1)(b) was substituted by the Statutory Auditors Regulations 2017, SI 2017/1164, reg 5, Sch 3, paras 1, 10, as from 1 January 2018, in relation to financial years of companies beginning on or after 1 January 2017 (as to the application of the 2017 Regulations, see **[4.671]** et seq).

The words in the final pair of square brackets in sub-s (1) were substituted by the Limited Liability Partnerships, Partnerships and Groups (Accounts and Audit) Regulations 2016, SI 2016/575, regs 3, 19, as from 17 May 2016, in relation to (a) financial years beginning on or after 1 January 2016; and (b) a financial year of an LLP beginning on or after 1 January 2015, but before 1 January 2016, if (i) the members of the LLP so decide, and (ii) a copy of the LLP's accounts for that financial year has not been delivered to the registrar in accordance with ss 444, 445 or 446 of the Companies Act 2006 as applied to LLPs by the Limited Liability Partnerships (Accounts and Audit) (Application of Companies Act 2006) Regulations before 17 May 2016 (see further the note at **[10.226]**).

Sub-s (2) was substituted by the European Grouping of Territorial Cooperation and Limited Liability Partnerships etc (Revocations and Amendments) (EU Exit) Regulations 2021, SI 2021/153, reg 17, as from 8 March 2021, in relation to financial years beginning on or after 6 April 2021. The original text read as follows—

"(2) In this Part an LLP's "annual accounts and auditor's report" for a financial year are—

(a) its annual accounts,

(b) the auditor's report on those accounts (unless the LLP is exempt from audit).".

[10.255]

30 Notes to the accounts

Section 472 applies to LLPs, modified so that it reads as follows—

"472 Notes to the accounts

(1) . . .

[(1A) In the case of an LLP which qualifies as a micro-entity in relation to a financial year (see sections 384A and 384B), the notes to the accounts for that year required by regulation 5A of, and paragraph 55 of Part 3 of Schedule 1 to, the Small Limited Liability Partnerships (Accounts) Regulations 2008 (SI 2008/1912) must be included at the foot of the balance sheet.]

(2) References in this Part to an LLP's annual accounts, or to a balance sheet or profit and loss account, include notes to the accounts giving information which is required by any provision of this Act or [UK-adopted international accounting standards], and required or allowed by any such provision to be given in a note to LLP accounts."

NOTES

Section 472 as set out above is amended as follows:

Sub-s (1) was revoked, and sub-s (1A) was inserted, by the Limited Liability Partnerships, Partnerships and Groups (Accounts and Audit) Regulations 2016, SI 2016/575, regs 3, 20, as from 17 May 2016, in relation to (a) financial years beginning on or after 1 January 2016; and (b) a financial year of an LLP beginning on or after 1 January 2015, but before 1 January 2016, if (i) the members of the LLP so decide, and (ii) a copy of the LLP's accounts for that financial year has not been delivered to the registrar in accordance with ss 444, 445 or 446 of the Companies Act 2006 as applied to LLPs by the Limited Liability Partnerships (Accounts and Audit) (Application of Companies Act 2006) Regulations before 17 May 2016 (see further the note at **[10.226]**).

The words in square brackets in sub-s (2) were substituted by the International Accounting Standards and European Public Limited-Liability Company (Amendment etc) (EU Exit) Regulations 2019, SI 2019/685, reg 19, Sch 1, Pt 2, para 58(1), (6), in relation to accounts for financial years beginning on or after IP completion day (as defined in the European Union (Withdrawal Agreement) Act 2020, s 39) (note also that in relation to accounts for financial years which begin before but end on or after IP completion day, the enactments amended by Parts 1–3 of Sch 1 to the 2019 Regulations have effect as if the UK were a member State until the end of the financial year in question).

[10.256]

31 Parliamentary procedure for regulations under section 468

Section 473 applies to LLPs, modified so that it reads as follows—

"473 Parliamentary procedure for regulations under section 468

(1) This section applies to regulations under section 468 (general power to make further provision about accounts).

(2) Any such regulations may make consequential amendments or repeals in other provisions of this Act, or in other enactments.

(3) Regulations that—

(a) restrict the classes of LLP which have the benefit of any exemption, exception or special provision,

(b) require additional matter to be included in a document of any class, or

(c) otherwise render the requirements of this Part more onerous,

are subject to affirmative resolution procedure.

(4) Otherwise, the regulations are subject to negative resolution procedure."

[10.257]

32 Minor definitions

Section 474 applies to LLPs, modified so that it reads as follows—

"474 Minor definitions

(1) In this Part—

"authorised insurance company" means a person (whether incorporated or not) who has permission under Part 4 of the Financial Services and Markets Act 2000 (c.8) to effect or carry out contracts of insurance, but does not include a friendly society within the meaning of the Friendly Societies Act 1992 (c.40);

"banking company" means a person who has permission under Part 4 of the Financial Services and Markets Act 2000 to accept deposits, other than—

(a) a person who is not a company, and

(b) a person who has such permission only for the purpose of carrying on another regulated activity in accordance with permission under that Part;

"banking LLP" means an LLP which has permission under Part 4 of the Financial Services and Markets Act 2000 to accept deposits (but does not include such an LLP which has permission to accept deposits only for the purpose of carrying on another regulated activity in accordance with that permission);

[. . .]

"e-money issuer" means a person [who is registered as an authorised electronic money institution or a small electronic money institution within the meaning of the Electronic Money Regulations 2011 or] who has permission under Part 4 of the Financial Services and Markets Act 2000 to carry on the activity of issuing electronic money within the meaning of article 9B of the Financial Services and Markets Act 2000 (Regulated Activities) Order 2001 (SI 2001/544);

. . .

"group" means a parent undertaking and its subsidiary undertakings;

. . .

"included in the consolidation", in relation to group accounts, or "included in consolidated group accounts", means that the undertaking is included in the accounts by the method of full (and not proportional) consolidation, and references to an undertaking excluded from consolidation shall be construed accordingly;

"insurance company" means—

(a) an authorised insurance company, or

(b) any other person (whether incorporated or not) who—

(i) carries on insurance market activity (within the meaning of section 316(3) of the Financial Services and Markets Act 2000), or

(ii) may effect or carry out contracts of insurance under which the benefits provided by that person are exclusively or primarily benefits in kind in the event of accident to or breakdown of a vehicle,

but does not include a friendly society within the meaning of the Friendly Societies Act 1992;

"international accounting standards" means the international accounting standards, within the meaning of [Article 2 of Regulation (EC) No 1606/2002 of the European Parliament and of the Council of 19 July 2002 on the application of international accounting standards];

"LLP" means a limited liability partnership [registered under the Limited Liability Partnerships Act 2000];

["micro-entity minimum accounting item" means an item of information required by this Part or by the Small Limited Liability Partnerships (Accounts) Regulations 2008 (SI 2008/1912) to be contained in the non-IAS individual accounts of an LLP for a financial year in relation to which it qualifies as a micro-entity (see sections 384A and 384B);]

["micro-entity provisions" means any provisions of this Part, Part 16 or the Small Limited Liability Partnerships (Accounts) Regulations 2008 (SI 2008/1912) relating specifically to the individual accounts of an LLP which qualifies as a micro-entity;]

"MiFID investment firm" means an investment firm within the meaning of Article 4.1.1 of Directive 2004/39/EC of the European Parliament and of the Council of 21 April 2004 on markets in financial instruments other than—

(a) an LLP [which is exempted from the definition of "investment firm" by Schedule 3 to the Financial Services and Markets Act 2000 (Regulated Activities) Order 2001,]

(b) an LLP which is an exempt investment firm within the meaning of regulation 4A(3) of the Financial Services and Markets Act 2000 (Markets in Financial Instruments) Regulations 2007 (SI 2007/126), and

(c) any other LLP which fulfils all the requirements set out in regulation 4C(3) of those Regulations;

"profit and loss account", in relation to an LLP that prepares IAS accounts, includes an income statement or other equivalent financial statement required to be prepared by [UK-adopted international accounting standards];

["qualified", in relation to an auditor's report, means that the report does not state the auditor's unqualified opinion that the accounts have been properly prepared in accordance with this Act;]

"regulated activity" has the meaning given in section 22 of the Financial Services and Markets Act 2000, except that it does not include activities of the kind specified in any of the following provisions of the Financial Services and Markets Act 2000 (Regulated Activities) Order 2001 (SI 2001/544)—

(a) article 25A (arranging regulated mortgage contracts),

(b) article 25B (arranging regulated home reversion plans),

(c) article 25C (arranging regulated home purchase plans),

[(ca) article 25E (arranging regulated sale and rent back agreements),]

(d) article 39A (assisting administration and performance of a contract of insurance),

(e) article 53A (advising on regulated mortgage contracts),

(f) article 53B (advising on regulated home reversion plans),

(g) article 53C (advising on regulated home purchase plans),

[(ga) article 53D (advising on regulated sale and rent back agreements),]

(h) article 21 (dealing as agent), article 25 (arranging deals in investments) or article 53 (advising on investments) where the activity concerns relevant investments that are not contractually based investments (within the meaning of article 3 of that Order), or

(i) article 64 (agreeing to carry on a regulated activity of the kind mentioned in paragraphs (a) to (h));

["traded company" means a company any of whose transferable securities are admitted to trading on a [UK regulated market];]

["traded LLP" means an LLP any of whose transferable securities are admitted to trading on a [UK regulated market];]

"turnover", in relation to an LLP, means the amounts derived from the provision of goods and services . . . , after deduction of—

(a) trade discounts,

(b) value added tax, and

(c) any other taxes based on the amounts so derived;

["UCITS management company" has the meaning given by the Glossary to the Handbook made by the Financial Conduct Authority under the Financial Services and Markets Act 2000;]

"wholly-owned subsidiary" has the meaning given in section 1159(2) of this Act;

["UK-adopted international accounting standards" means the international accounting standards which are adopted for use within the United Kingdom by virtue of the International Accounting Standards and European Public Limited-Liability Company (Amendment etc) (EU Exit) Regulations 2019].

(2) In subsection (1)—

(a) the definitions of "banking company" and "banking LLP", and

(b) references in the definition of "insurance company" to contracts of insurance and to the effecting or carrying out of such contracts,

must be read with—

(i) section 22 of the Financial Services and Markets Act 2000,

(ii) the Financial Services and Markets Act 2000 (Regulated Activities) Order 2001 (SI 2001/544), and

(iii) Schedule 2 to that Act."

NOTES

Section 474(1) as set out above is amended as follows:

The definition "Conduct Committee" (omitted) was originally inserted by the Supervision of Accounts and Reports (Prescribed Body) and Companies (Defective Accounts and Directors' Reports) (Authorised Person) Order 2012, SI 2012/1439, art 8(1), (4)(a), as from 2 July 2012. It was subsequently revoked by the Supervision of Accounts and Reports (Prescribed Body) and Companies (Defective Accounts and Reports) (Authorised Person) Order 2021, SI 2021/465, art 6(4), as from 6 May 2021 (see art 9 of the 2021 Order for transitional provisions in relation to the continuity of functions, etc at **[4.727]**).

In the definition "e-money issuer", the words in square brackets were inserted by the Electronic Money Regulations 2011, SI 2011/99, reg 79, Sch 4, Pt 2, para 20, as from 30 April 2011.

Definition "Financial Reporting Review Panel" (omitted) revoked by SI 2012/1439, art 8(1), (4)(b), as from 2 July 2012.

The definition "IAS Regulation" (omitted) was revoked, the words in square brackets in the definitions "international accounting standards" and "profit and loss account" were substituted, and the definition "UK-adopted international accounting standards" was inserted, by the International Accounting Standards and European Public Limited-Liability Company (Amendment etc) (EU Exit) Regulations 2019, SI 2019/685, reg 19, Sch 1, Pt 2, para 58(1), (7), in relation to accounts for financial years beginning on or after IP completion day (as defined in the European Union (Withdrawal Agreement) Act 2020, s 39) (note also that in relation to accounts for financial years which begin before but end on or after IP completion day, the enactments amended by Parts 1–3 of Sch 1 to the 2019 Regulations have effect as if the UK were a member State until the end of the financial year in question).

In the definition "LLP" the words "registered under the Limited Liability Partnerships Act 2000" in square brackets were substituted by the Limited Liability Partnerships (Application of Companies Act 2006) Regulations 2009, SI 2009/1804, reg 85, Sch 3, Pt 2, para 15(3), as from 1 October 2009.

Definition "micro-entity minimum accounting item" inserted by the Limited Liability Partnerships, Partnerships and Groups (Accounts and Audit) Regulations 2016, SI 2016/575, regs 3(1), 21(1), (2)(a), as from 17 May 2016, in relation to (a) financial years beginning on or after 1 January 2016; and (b) a financial year of an LLP beginning on or after 1 January 2015, but before 1 January 2016, if (i) the members of the LLP so decide, and (ii) a copy of the LLP's accounts for that financial year has not been delivered to the registrar in accordance with ss 444, 445 or 446 of the Companies Act 2006 as applied to LLPs by the Limited Liability Partnerships (Accounts and Audit) (Application of Companies Act 2006) Regulations before 17 May 2016 (see further the note at **[10.226]**).

Definition "micro-entity provisions" inserted by SI 2016/575, regs 3(1), 21(1), (2)(a) (as to the commencement of the 2016 Regulations, see the first note relating to them above).

Words in square brackets in para (a) of the definition "MiFID investment firm" substituted by the Accounts and Reports (Amendment) (EU Exit) Regulations 2019, SI 2019/145, reg 6, Sch 3, paras 11, 20(a)(ii), in relation to financial years beginning on or after IP completion day (as defined in the European Union (Withdrawal Agreement) Act 2020, s 39) (for transitional provisions see reg 7 of the 2019 Regulations at **[12.79]**). Note that SI 2019/145, reg 6, Sch 3, para 20(a)(i) provides that in the opening words of this definition, for the words "Article 4.1.1 of Directive 2014/65/EU" there is substituted "Article 2.1A of Regulation (EU) No 600/2014". However, the words "Article 4.1.1 of Directive 2014/65/EU" do not appear in this definition. Note also that in the definition "MiFID investment firm" in s 474 of the Companies Act 2006 itself, the words "Directive 2014/65/EU of the European Parliament and of the Council of 15 May 2014" were substituted for the original words "Article 4.1.1 of Directive 2004/39/EC of the European Parliament and of the Council of 21 April 2004" by the Financial Services and Markets Act 2000 (Markets in Financial Instruments) Regulations 2017, SI 2017/701, reg 50(2), Sch 4, para 9(1), (2)(a). However, no such amendment was made to the definition as set out in this regulation.

Definition "qualified" inserted by SI 2016/575, regs 3(1), 21(1), (2)(a) (as to the commencement of the 2016 Regulations, see the first note relating to them above).

In the definition "regulated activity", paras (ca) and (ga) were inserted by the Financial Services and Markets Act 2000 (Regulated Activities) (Amendment) Order 2009, SI 2009/1342, art 31, as from 1 July 2009 (certain purposes), and as from 30 June 2010 (otherwise).

Definition "traded company" inserted by SI 2016/575, regs 3(1), 21(1), (2)(a) (as to the commencement of the 2016 Regulations, see the first note relating to them above). Words in square brackets in that definition substituted by SI 2019/145, reg 6, Sch 3, paras 11, 20(b), in relation to financial years beginning on or after IP completion day (as defined in the European Union (Withdrawal Agreement) Act 2020, s 39) (for transitional provisions see reg 7 of the 2019 Regulations at **[12.79]**).

Definition "traded LLP" inserted by SI 2016/575, regs 3(1), 21(1), (2)(a) (as to the commencement of the 2016 Regulations, see the first note relating to them above). The words in square brackets were substituted (for the original words "regulated market") by the Limited Liability Partnerships (Climate-related Financial Disclosure) Regulations 2022, SI 2022/46, reg 3, as from 6 April 2022, in respect of any financial year of a limited liability partnership which commences on or after that date.

Words omitted from the definition "turnover" revoked by SI 2016/575, regs 3(1), 21(1), (2)(b) (as to the commencement of the 2016 Regulations, see the first note relating to them above).

Definition "UCITS management company" substituted by the Financial Services Act 2012 (Consequential Amendments and Transitional Provisions) Order 2013, SI 2013/472, art 3, Sch 2, para 143(b)), as from 1 April 2013.

PART 10 AUDIT REQUIREMENT

[10.258]

33 Requirement for audited accounts

Section 475 applies to LLPs, modified so that it reads as follows—

"475 Requirement for audited accounts

(1) An LLP's annual accounts for a financial year must be audited in accordance with this Part unless the LLP is exempt from audit under—

(a) section 477 (small LLPs),

[(aa) section 479A (subsidiary LLPs)], or

(b) section 480 (dormant LLPs).

(2) An LLP is not entitled to any such exemption unless its balance sheet contains a statement by the members to that effect.

(3) An LLP is not entitled to exemption under any of the provisions mentioned in subsection (1)(a) unless its balance sheet contains a statement by the members to the effect that the members acknowledge their responsibilities for complying with the requirements of this Act with respect to accounting records and the preparation of accounts.

(4) The statement required by subsection (2) or (3) must appear on the balance sheet above the signature required by section 414."

NOTES

In s 475(1) as set out above, para (aa) was inserted by the Companies and Limited Liability Partnerships (Accounts and Audit Exemptions and Change of Accounting Framework) Regulations 2012, SI 2012/2301, regs 2, 20(1), (2), as from 1 October 2012 (in relation to accounts for financial years ending on or after that date).

[10.259]

34 Exemption from audit: small LLPs

Sections 477 to 479 apply to LLPs, modified so that they read as follows—

"477 Small LLPs: conditions for exemption from audit

(1) An LLP that [qualifies as a small LLP in relation to] a financial year is exempt from the requirements of this Act relating to the audit of accounts for that year.

(2), (3) . . .

(4) For the purposes of this section—

(a) whether an LLP qualifies as a small LLP shall be determined in accordance with section 382(1) to (6), . . .

(b) . . .

(5) This section has effect subject to—

- section 475(2) and (3) (requirements as to statements to be contained in balance sheet),
- section 478 (LLPs excluded from small LLPs exemption), and
- section 479 (availability of small LLPs exemption in case of group LLP).

478 LLPs excluded from small LLPs exemption

An LLP is not entitled to the exemption conferred by section 477 (small LLPs) if it was at any time within the financial year in question—

(a) an LLP whose securities are admitted to trading on a [UK regulated market],

(b) an LLP that—

(i) is an authorised insurance company, a banking LLP, an e-money issuer, a MiFID investment firm or a UCITS management company, . . .

(ii) carries on insurance market activity, or

[(iii) is a scheme funder of a Master Trust scheme within the meanings given by section 39(1) of the Pension Schemes Act 2017 (interpretation of Part 1), or]

(c) an employers' association as defined in section 122 of the Trade Union and Labour Relations (Consolidation) Act 1992 (c.52) or Article 4 of the Industrial Relations (Northern Ireland) Order 1992 (SI 1992/807 (NI 5)).

479 Availability of small LLPs exemption in case of group LLP

(1) An LLP is not entitled to the exemption conferred by section 477 (small LLPs) in respect of a financial year during any part of which it was a group LLP unless—

[(a) the group—

(i) qualifies as a small group in relation to that financial year, and

(ii) was not at any time in that year an ineligible group, or]

(b) subsection (3) applies.

(2) . . .

(3) An LLP is not excluded by subsection (1) if, throughout the whole of the period or periods during the financial year when it was a group LLP, it was both a subsidiary undertaking and dormant.

(4) In this section—

(a) "group LLP" means an LLP that is a parent LLP or a subsidiary undertaking, and

(b) "the group", in relation to a group LLP, means that LLP together with all its associated undertakings.

For this purpose undertakings are associated if one is a subsidiary undertaking of the other or both are subsidiary undertakings of a third undertaking.

(5) For the purposes of this section—

(a) whether a group qualifies as small shall be determined in accordance with section 383 (LLPs qualifying as small: parent LLPs);

(b) "ineligible group" has the meaning given by section 384(2) and (3);

(c)–(e) . . .

(6) The provisions mentioned in subsection (5) apply for the purposes of this section as if all the bodies corporate in the group were LLPs or companies."

NOTES

In s 477 as set out above, the words in square brackets were substituted, and sub-ss (2), (3), (4)(b) (and the word preceding sub-s (4)(b)) were revoked, by the Companies and Limited Liability Partnerships (Accounts and Audit Exemptions and Change of Accounting Framework) Regulations 2012, SI 2012/2301, regs 2, 20(1), (3)(a), as from 1 October 2012 (in relation to accounts for financial years ending on or after that date).

In s 478 as set out above, the words in square brackets in para (a) were substituted by the Statutory Auditors and Third Country Auditors (Amendment) (EU Exit) Regulations 2019, SI 2019/177, regs 49, 50(a), as from IP completion day (as defined in the European Union (Withdrawal Agreement) Act 2020, s 39) (for transitional provisions, see Sch 4 to the 2019 Regulations at **[12.88]**).

In s 478 as set out above, the word omitted from sub-para (b)(i) was revoked, and sub-para (b)(iii) was inserted, by the Occupational Pension Schemes (Master Trusts) Regulations 2018, SI 2018/1030, reg 31(1), (4), as from 1 October 2018.

In s 479 as set out above, sub-s (1)(a) was substituted, and sub-ss (2), (5)(a)–(c) were revoked, by SI 2012/2301, regs 2, 20(1), (3)(b), as from 1 October 2012 (in relation to accounts for financial years ending on or after that date).

[10.260]

[34A Exemption from audit: qualifying subsidiaries

Sections 479A, 479B and 479C apply to LLPs, modified so that they read as follows—

"479A Subsidiary LLPs: conditions for exemption from audit

(1) An LLP is exempt from the requirements of this Act relating to the audit of individual accounts for a financial year if—

(a) it is itself a subsidiary undertaking, and

(b) its parent undertaking is established under the law of [any part of the United Kingdom].

(2) Exemption is conditional upon compliance with all of the following conditions—

(a) all members of the LLP must agree to the exemption in respect of the financial year in question,

(b) the parent undertaking must give a guarantee under section 479C in respect of that year,

(c) the LLP must be included in the consolidated accounts drawn up for that year or to an earlier date in that year by the parent undertaking in accordance with—

[(i) if the undertaking is a company, the requirements of Part 15 of this Act, or, if the undertaking is not a company, the legal requirements which apply to the drawing up of consolidated accounts for that undertaking, or]

(ii) [UK-adopted international accounting standards (within the meaning given by section 474(1))],

(d) the parent undertaking must disclose in the notes to the consolidated accounts that the LLP is exempt from the requirements of this Act relating to the audit of individual accounts by virtue of this section,

(e) the designated members of the LLP must deliver to the registrar on or before the date that they file the LLP's accounts for that year—

(i) a written notice of the agreement referred to in subsection (2)(a),

(ii) the statement referred to in section 479C(1),

(iii) a copy of the consolidated accounts referred to in subsection 2(c),

(iv) a copy of the consolidated annual report drawn up by the parent undertaking, and

(v) a copy of the auditor's report on those accounts.

(3) This section has effect subject to—

section 475(2) and (3) (requirements as to statements contained in balance sheet).

479B LLPs excluded from the subsidiary LLPs audit exemption

An LLP is not entitled to the exemption conferred by section 479A (subsidiary LLPs) if it was at any time within the financial year in question—

[(za) a traded LLP as defined in section 474(1),]

(a) an LLP that—

(i) is an authorised insurance company, a banking LLP, an e-money issuer, a MiFID investment firm or a UCITS management company, . . .

(ii) carries on insurance market activity, or

[(iii) is a scheme funder of a Master Trust scheme within the meanings given by section 39(1) of the Pension Schemes Act 2017 (interpretation of Part 1), or]

(b) an employers' association as defined in section 122 of the Trade Union and Labour Relations (Consolidation) Act 1992 (c 52) or Article 4 of the Industrial Relations (Northern Ireland) Order 1992 (SI 1992/807) (NI 5).

479C Parent undertaking declaration of guarantee of subsidiary's liabilities

(1) A guarantee is given by a parent undertaking under this section when the designated members of the subsidiary LLP deliver to the registrar a statement by the parent undertaking that it guarantees the subsidiary LLP under this section.

(2) The statement under subsection (1) must be authenticated by the parent undertaking and must specify—

(a) the name of the parent undertaking,

[(b) the registered number (if any) of the parent undertaking,]

(c) . . .

(d) the name and registered number of the subsidiary LLP in respect of which the guarantee is being given,

(e) the date of the statement, and

(f) the financial year to which the guarantee relates.

(3) A guarantee given under this section has the effect that—

(a) the parent undertaking guarantees all outstanding liabilities to which the subsidiary LLP is subject at the end of the financial year to which the guarantee relates, until they are satisfied in full, and

(b) the guarantee is enforceable against the parent undertaking by any person to whom the subsidiary LLP is liable in respect of those liabilities.".]

Part 10 Miscellaneous other SIs

NOTES

Inserted by the Companies and Limited Liability Partnerships (Accounts and Audit Exemptions and Change of Accounting Framework) Regulations 2012, SI 2012/2301, regs 2, 20(1), (4), as from 1 October 2012 (in relation to accounts for financial years ending on or after that date).

Section 479A as set out above, is amended as follows:

The words in square brackets in sub-s (1)(b) were substituted, and sub-s (2)(c)(i) was substituted, by the Statutory Auditors and Third Country Auditors (Amendment) (EU Exit) Regulations 2019, SI 2019/177, regs 49, 50(b), as from IP completion day (as defined in the European Union (Withdrawal Agreement) Act 2020, s 39) (for transitional provisions, see Sch 4 to the 2019 Regulations at **[12.88]**).

Note that SI 2019/177, reg 50(b) was substituted by the Statutory Auditors, Third Country Auditors and International Accounting Standards (Amendment) (EU Exit) Regulations 2019, SI 2019/1392, regs 2, 7, with effect from immediately before IP completion day, and that the effect of that amendment has been incorporated in the text set out above.

The words in square brackets in sub-s (2)(c)(ii) were substituted by the International Accounting Standards and European Public Limited-Liability Company (Amendment etc) (EU Exit) Regulations 2019, SI 2019/685, reg 19, Sch 1, Pt 2, para 58(1), (8), in relation to accounts for financial years beginning on or after IP completion day (as defined in the European Union (Withdrawal Agreement) Act 2020, s 39) (note also that in relation to accounts for financial years which begin before but end on or after IP completion day, the enactments amended by Parts 1–3 of Sch 1 to the 2019 Regulations have effect as if the UK were a member State until the end of the financial year in question).

Section 479B as set out above, is amended as follows:

Para (za) inserted by SI 2016/575, regs 3, 22(1), (3) (as to the commencement of this amendment, see the first note relating to the 2016 Regulations above).

The word omitted from sub-para (a)(i) was revoked, and sub-para (a)(iii) was inserted, by the Occupational Pension Schemes (Master Trusts) Regulations 2018, SI 2018/1030, reg 31(1), (5), as from 1 October 2018.

Section 479C as set out above, is amended as follows:

Sub-s (2)(b) was substituted, and sub-s (2)(c) was revoked, by the Statutory Auditors and Third Country Auditors (Amendment) (EU Exit) Regulations 2019, SI 2019/177, regs 49, 50(c), as from IP completion day (as defined in the European Union (Withdrawal Agreement) Act 2020, s 39) (for transitional provisions, see Sch 4 to the 2019 Regulations at **[12.88]**). Note that SI 2019/177, reg 50(c) was inserted by virtue of the Statutory Auditors, Third Country Auditors and International Accounting Standards (Amendment) (EU Exit) Regulations 2019, SI 2019/1392, regs 2, 7, with effect from immediately before IP completion day.

[10.261]

35 Exemption from audit: dormant LLPs

Sections 480 and 481 apply to LLPs, modified so that they read as follows—

"480 Dormant LLPS: conditions for exemption from audit

(1) An LLP is exempt from the requirements of this Act relating to the audit of accounts in respect of a financial year if—

(a) it has been dormant since its formation, or

(b) it has been dormant since the end of the previous financial year and the following conditions are met.

(2) The conditions are that the LLP—

(a) as regards its individual accounts for the financial year in question—

(i) is entitled to prepare accounts in accordance with the small LLPs regime (see sections 381 to 384), or

(ii) would be so entitled but for having been a member of an ineligible group, and

(b) is not required to prepare group accounts for that year.

(3) This section has effect subject to—

- section 475(2) and (3) (requirements as to statements to be contained in balance sheet), and
- section 481 (LLPs excluded from dormant LLPs exemption).

481 LLPs excluded from dormant LLPs exemption

An LLP is not entitled to the exemption conferred by section 480 (dormant LLPs) if it was at any time within the financial year in question an LLP that—

[(za) is a traded LLP as defined in section 474(1),]

(a) is an authorised insurance company, a banking LLP, an e-money issuer, a MiFID investment firm or a UCITS management company, or

(b) carries on insurance market activity."

NOTES

In s 481 as set out above, para (za) was inserted by the Limited Liability Partnerships, Partnerships and Groups (Accounts and Audit) Regulations 2016, SI 2016/575, regs 3, 23, as from 17 May 2016, in relation to (a) financial years beginning on or after 1 January 2016; and (b) a financial year of an LLP beginning on or after 1 January 2015, but before 1 January 2016, if (i) the members of the LLP so decide, and (ii) a copy of the LLP's accounts for that financial year has not been delivered to the registrar in accordance with ss 444, 445 or 446 of the Companies Act 2006 as applied to LLPs by the Limited Liability Partnerships (Accounts and Audit) (Application of Companies Act 2006) Regulations before 17 May 2016 (see further the note at **[10.226]**).

PART 11 APPOINTMENT OF AUDITORS

[10.262]

36 Appointment of auditors

Sections 485 to 488 apply to LLPs, modified so that they read as follows—

"485 Appointment of auditors: general

(1) An auditor or auditors of an LLP must be appointed for each financial year of the LLP, unless the designated members reasonably determine otherwise on the ground that audited accounts are unlikely to be required.

(2) For each financial year for which an auditor or auditors is or are to be appointed (other than the LLP's first financial year), the appointment must be made before the end of the period of 28 days beginning with—

- (a) the end of the time allowed for sending out copies of the LLP's [annual accounts and reports] for the previous financial year (see section 423), or
- (b) if earlier, the day on which copies of the LLP's [annual accounts and reports] for the previous financial year are sent out under section 423.

This is the "period for appointing auditors".

(3) The designated members may appoint an auditor or auditors—

- (a) at any time before the LLP's first period for appointing auditors,
- (b) following a period during which the LLP (being exempt from audit) did not have any auditor, at any time before the LLP's next period for appointing auditors, or
- (c) to fill a casual vacancy in the office of auditor.

(4) The members may appoint an auditor or auditors—

- (a) during a period for appointing auditors,
- (b) if the LLP should have appointed an auditor or auditors during a period for appointing auditors but failed to do so, or
- (c) where the designated members had power to appoint under subsection (3) but have failed to make an appointment.

(5) An auditor or auditors of an LLP may only be appointed—

- (a) in accordance with this section, or
- (b) in accordance with section 486 [or section 486A] (default power of Secretary of State).

This is without prejudice to any deemed re-appointment under section 487.

[485A Appointment of auditors: additional requirements for public interest entities with audit committees

(1) This section applies to the appointment under section 485(4) of an auditor or auditors of an LLP—

- (a) which is also a public interest entity; and
- (b) which has an audit committee.

(2) But it does not apply to the appointment of an Auditor General as auditor or one of the auditors of the LLP.

(3) Before an appointment to which this section applies is made—

- (a) the audit committee of the LLP must make a recommendation to the designated members in connection with the appointment, and
- (b) the designated members must propose an auditor or auditors for appointment.

(4) Before the audit committee makes a recommendation or the designated members make a proposal under subsection (3), the committee must carry out a selection procedure in accordance with Article 16(3) of the Audit Regulation.

(5) The audit committee must in its recommendation—

- (a) identify its first and second choice candidates for appointment, drawn from those auditors who have participated in a selection procedure under subsection (4),
- (b) give reasons for the choices so identified,
- (c) state that—
  - (i) the recommendation is free from influence by a third party, and
  - (ii) no contractual term of the kind mentioned in Article 16(6) of the Audit Regulation has been imposed on the LLP.

(6) The designated members must include in their proposal—

- (a) the recommendation made by the audit committee in connection with the appointment, and
- (b) if the proposal of the designated members departs from the preference of the audit committee——
  - (i) a recommendation for a candidate or candidates for appointment drawn from those auditors who have participated in a selection procedure under subsection (4), and
  - (ii) the reasons for not following the audit committee's recommendation.

(7) Where the audit committee recommends re-appointment of the LLP's existing auditor or auditors, and the designated members are in agreement, subsections (4) and (5)(a) and (b) do not apply.

485B Appointment of auditors: additional requirements for public interest entities without audit committees

(1) This section applies to the appointment under section 485(4) of an auditor or auditors of an LLP—

- (a) which is also a public interest entity; and
- (b) which does not have an audit committee.

(2) But it does not apply to the appointment of an Auditor General as auditor or one of the auditors of the LLP.

(3) Before an appointment to which this section applies is made the designated members must propose an auditor or auditors for appointment.

(4) Before the designated members make a proposal under subsection (3), they must carry out a selection procedure in accordance with Article 16(3) of the Audit Regulation, from which their proposed auditor or auditors must be drawn.

(5) Subsection (4) does not apply in relation to a proposal to re-appoint the LLP's existing auditor or auditors.

485C Restriction on appointment of auditor of LLP which is a public interest entity

(1) A person who has been, or will have been, auditor of an LLP which is a public interest entity for every financial year comprised in the maximum engagement period (see section 494ZA) may not be appointed as auditor of the LLP for any financial year which begins within the period of 4 years beginning with the day after the last day of the last financial year of the maximum engagement period.

(2) A person who is a member of the same network as the auditor mentioned in subsection (1) may not be appointed as auditor of the LLP for any financial year which begins within the period of 4 years mentioned in that subsection.

(3) This section does not apply in relation to an Auditor General.]

486 Appointment of auditor: default power of Secretary of State

(1) If an LLP fails to appoint an auditor or auditors in accordance with section 485, the Secretary of State may appoint one or more persons to fill the vacancy.

(2) Where subsection (2) of that section applies and the LLP fails to make the necessary appointment before the end of the period for appointing auditors, the LLP must within one week of the end of that period give notice to the Secretary of State of his power having become exercisable.

(3) If an LLP fails to give the notice required by this section, an offence is committed by—

(a) the LLP, and

(b) every designated member who is in default.

(4) A person guilty of an offence under this section is liable on summary conviction to a fine not exceeding level 3 on the standard scale and, for continued contravention, a daily default fine not exceeding one-tenth of level 3 on the standard scale.

[486A Defective appointments: default power of Secretary of State

(1) If—

(a) an LLP appoints, or purports to appoint, an auditor or auditors, and

(b) the appointment or purported appointment is made in breach of section 485A, 485B or 485C (requirements applying to appointment of auditors by public interest entities),

the Secretary of State may appoint another auditor or auditors in place of the auditor or auditors referred to in paragraph (a).

(2) The breach of section 485A, 485B or 485C does not invalidate any report made under Chapter 3 of this Part by the auditor or auditors on the LLP's annual reports or accounts before the auditor or auditors are replaced under subsection (1) of this section.

(3) But where the breach in question is a breach of section 485C, sections 1248 and 1249 (Secretary of State's power to require second audit for companies) apply as if—

(a) the LLP was a company;

(b) the auditor was not an appropriate person, or the auditors were not appropriate persons, for the period during which the audit was conducted.

(4) Within one week of becoming aware of the breach of section 485A, 485B or 485C, the LLP must give notice to the Secretary of State that the power under subsection (1) of this section has become exercisable.

(5) If the LLP fails to give the notice required by subsection (4), an offence is committed by—

(a) the LLP, and

(b) every member of the LLP who is in default.

(6) A person guilty of an offence under this section is liable on summary conviction to a fine not exceeding level 3 on the standard scale and, for continued contravention, a daily default fine not exceeding one-tenth of level 3 on the standard scale.]

487 Term of office of auditors

(1) An auditor or auditors of an LLP hold office in accordance with the terms of their appointment, subject to the requirements that—

(a) they do not take office until any previous auditor or auditors cease to hold office, and

(b) they cease to hold office at the end of the next period for appointing auditors unless re-appointed.

(2) Where no auditor has been appointed by the end of the next period for appointing auditors, any auditor in office immediately before that time is deemed to be re-appointed at that time, unless—

(a) the LLP agreement requires actual re-appointment, or

(b) the deemed re-appointment is prevented by the members under section 488, or

(c) the members have determined that he should not be re-appointed, or

(d) the designated members have determined that no auditor or auditors should be appointed for the financial year in question[, or

(e) the auditor's appointment would be in breach of section 485C.]

(3) This is without prejudice to the provisions of this Part as to removal and resignation of auditors.

(4) No account shall be taken of any loss of the opportunity of deemed reappointment under this section in ascertaining the amount of any compensation or damages payable to an auditor on his ceasing to hold office for any reason.

488 Prevention by members of deemed re-appointment of auditor

(1) An auditor of an LLP is not deemed to be re-appointed under section 487(2) if the LLP has received notices under this section from members representing at least the requisite percentage of the total voting rights in the LLP that the auditor should not be re-appointed.

(2) The "requisite percentage" is 5%, or such lower percentage as is specified for this purpose in the LLP agreement.

(3) A notice under this section—

(a) may be in hard copy or electronic form,

(b) must be authenticated by the person or persons giving it, and

(c) must be received by the LLP before the end of the accounting reference period immediately preceding the time when the deemed reappointment would have effect."

NOTES

In s 485(2) as set out above, the words "annual accounts and reports" in square brackets were substituted (for the original words "annual accounts and auditor's report") by the European Grouping of Territorial Cooperation and Limited Liability Partnerships etc (Revocations and Amendments) (EU Exit) Regulations 2021, SI 2021/153, reg 18, as from 8 March 2021, in relation to financial years beginning on or after 6 April 2021.

All other words in square brackets in this regulation were inserted by the Statutory Auditors Regulations 2017, SI 2017/1164, reg 5, Sch 3, paras 1, 11, in relation to financial years of companies beginning on or after 17 June 2016 (as to the application of the 2017 Regulations, see **[4.671]** et seq).

[10.263]

37 Fixing of auditor remuneration

Section 492 applies to LLPs, modified so that it reads as follows—

"492 Fixing of auditor's remuneration

(1) The remuneration of an auditor appointed by the LLP must be fixed by the designated members or in such manner as the members of the LLP may determine.

(2) The remuneration of an auditor appointed by the Secretary of State must be fixed by the Secretary of State.

(3) For the purposes of this section "remuneration" includes sums paid in respect of expenses.

(4) This section applies in relation to benefits in kind as to payments of money."

[10.264]

38 Disclosure of auditor remuneration

Section 494 applies to LLPs, modified so that it reads as follows—

"494 Disclosure of services provided by auditor or associates and related remuneration

Parts 1 and 2 of the Companies (Disclosure of Auditor Remuneration and Liability Limitation Agreements) Regulations 2008 (SI 2008/489) apply to LLPs with the following modifications—

(a) in regulation 3(1), omit the definition of "principal terms";

(b) references to 6th April 2008 are to be read as references to 1st October 2008;

(c) references to a company include references to an LLP; and

(d) except in paragraph 3 of Schedule 1, references to a director or to an officer of a company include references to a member of an LLP."

[10.265]

[38A The maximum engagement period

Section 494ZA applies to LLPs, modified so that it reads as follows—

"494ZA

(1) Where a person is auditor of an LLP for consecutive financial years, the maximum engagement period of the person as auditor of the LLP—

(a) begins with the first of those years (see the appropriate entry in the first column of the following Table), and

(b) ends with the financial year specified in the corresponding entry in the second column of the Table:

First financial year of the maximum engagement period	***Last financial year of the maximum engagement period***
A financial year of the LLP beginning before 17 June 1994.	The last financial year of the LLP to begin before 17 June 2020.
A financial year of the LLP beginning— (a) on or after 17 June 1994, and (b) before 17 June 2003.	The last financial year of the LLP to begin before 17 June 2023.
A financial year of the LLP beginning— (a) on or after 17 June 2003, and (b) before 17 June 2016.	*No qualifying selection procedure* Where neither the first financial year of the maximum engagement period nor any subsequent financial year is one for which the auditor has been appointed following the carrying out of a qualifying selection procedure, the later of— (a) the last financial year of the LLP to begin before 17 June 2016, and (b) the last financial year of the LLP to begin within the period of 10 years beginning with the first day of the first financial year of the maximum engagement period. *No qualifying selection procedure within 10 years* Where the last day of the last financial year of the LLP to begin within the period of 10 years beginning with the first day of the last financial year of the LLP for which the auditor was appointed following a qualifying selection procedure is before 17 June 2016— (a) the last financial year of the LLP to begin before 17 June 2016, unless

Part 10 Miscellaneous other SIs

First financial year of the maximum engagement period	*Last financial year of the maximum engagement period*
	(b) the auditor is appointed following a qualifying selection procedure for the first financial year of the LLP to begin on or after 17 June 2016, in which case it is the last financial year of the LLP to begin within the period of 20 years beginning with the first day of the first financial year of the maximum engagement period. *Qualifying selection procedure within 10 years* In any other case, the earlier of— (a) the last financial year of the LLP to begin within the period of 10 years beginning with the first day of the last financial year of the LLP for which the auditor was appointed following a qualifying selection procedure, and (b) the last financial year of the LLP to begin within the period of 20 years beginning with the first day of the first financial year of the maximum engagement period.
A financial year of the LLP beginning on or after 17 June 2016.	The earlier of— (a) the last financial year of the LLP to begin within the period of 10 years beginning with the first day of the last financial year of the LLP for which the auditor was appointed following a qualifying selection procedure, and (b) the last financial year of the LLP to begin within the period of 20 years beginning with the first day of the first financial year of the maximum engagement period.

(2) Where the first financial year of the maximum engagement period begins on or after 17 June 2003, the maximum engagement period may be extended by a period of no more than 2 years with the approval of the competent authority.

(3) Such approval may be given by the competent authority only if it is satisfied that exceptional circumstances exist.

(4) Where the competent authority gives its approval as mentioned in subsection (2)—

(a) the second column of the Table in subsection (1) has effect with the necessary modifications, and

(b) the first appointment to be made after the end of the period as so extended must be made following a qualifying selection procedure.

(5) In this section "qualifying selection procedure" means—

(a) in the case of an appointment for a financial year beginning on or after 17 June 2016 made after the Statutory Auditors and Third Country Auditors Regulations 2017 come into force—

(i) if the LLP has an audit committee, a selection procedure that complies with the requirements of section 485A(4) and (5)(a) and (b), and

(ii) if the LLP does not have an audit committee, a selection procedure that complies with the requirements of [section 485B(4)];

(b) in any other case, a selection procedure that substantially meets the requirements of Article 16(2) to (5) of the Audit Regulation [as it had effect immediately before IP completion day], having regard to the circumstances at the time (including whether the LLP had an audit committee)."]

NOTES

Inserted by the Statutory Auditors Regulations 2017, SI 2017/1164, reg 5, Sch 3, paras 1, 12, in relation to financial years of companies beginning on or after 17 June 2016 (as to the application of the 2017 Regulations, see **[4.671]** et seq).

In s 494ZA as set out above, the words in square brackets in sub-s (5)(a)(ii) were substituted, and the words in square brackets in sub-s (5)(b) were inserted, by the Statutory Auditors and Third Country Auditors (Amendment) (EU Exit) Regulations 2019, SI 2019/177, regs 49, 51(a), as from IP completion day (as defined in the European Union (Withdrawal Agreement) Act 2020, s 39) (for transitional provisions, see Sch 4 to the 2019 Regulations at **[12.88]**). Note that reg 51 of the 2019 Regulations was amended by the Companies and Statutory Auditors etc (Consequential Amendments) (EU Exit) Regulations 2020, SI 2020/523, reg 15(a)(i), with effect from immediately before IP completion day; and that the effect of the amendment has been incorporated in the text above.

[10.266]

[38B Interpretation

Section 494A applies to LLPs, modified so that it reads as follows—

"494A Interpretation

In this Chapter—

["audit committee" means a body which performs—

(a) the functions referred to in—

(i) rule 7.1.3 of the Disclosure Guidance and Transparency Rules sourcebook made by the Financial Conduct Authority (audit committees and their functions) under the Financial Services and Markets Act 2000, or

(ii) rule 2.4 of the Audit Committee Part of the Rulebook made by the Prudential Regulation Authority under that Act,

as they have effect on IP completion day, or

(b) equivalent functions.]

"Audit Directive" means Directive 2006/43/EC of the European Parliament and of the Council on statutory audits of annual accounts and consolidated accounts, amending Council Directives 78/660/EEC and 83/349/EEC and repealing Council Directive 84/253/EEC;

"Auditor General" means—

(a) the Comptroller and Auditor General,
(b) the Auditor General for Scotland,
(c) the Auditor General for Wales, or
(d) the Comptroller and Auditor General for Northern Ireland;

"issuer" has the same meaning as in Part 6 of the Financial Services and Markets Act 2000 (see section 102A(6));

"network" means an association of persons other than a firm co-operating in audit work by way of—

(a) profit-sharing;
(b) cost sharing;
(c) common ownership, control or management;
(d) common quality control policies and procedures;
(e) common business strategy; or
(f) use of a common name;

"public interest entity" means—

(a) an issuer whose transferable securities are admitted to trading on a [UK regulated market];
(b) a credit institution within the meaning given by Article 4(1)(1) of Regulation (EU) No 575/2013 of the European Parliament and of the Council, [which is a CRR firm within the meaning of Article 4(1)(2A) of that Regulation];

. . .

. . ."]

NOTES

Inserted by the Statutory Auditors Regulations 2017, SI 2017/1164, reg 5, Sch 3, paras 1, 12, in relation to financial years of companies beginning on or after 17 June 2016 (as to the application of the 2017 Regulations, see **[4.671]** et seq).

In s 494A as set out above, the definition "audit committee" was substituted, the words in square brackets in paras (a) and (b) of the definition "public interest entity" were substituted, and the definitions "regulated market" and "transferable securities" (omitted) were revoked, by the Statutory Auditors and Third Country Auditors (Amendment) (EU Exit) Regulations 2019, SI 2019/177, regs 49, 51(b), as from IP completion day (as defined in the European Union (Withdrawal Agreement) Act 2020, s 39) (for transitional provisions, see Sch 4 to the 2019 Regulations at **[12.88]**). Note that reg 51 of the 2019 Regulations was amended by the Companies and Statutory Auditors etc (Consequential Amendments) (EU Exit) Regulations 2020, SI 2020/523, reg 15(a)(ii), with effect from immediately before IP completion day; and that the effect of the amendment has been incorporated in the text above.

PART 12 FUNCTIONS OF AUDITOR

[10.267]

39 Auditor's report

[Sections 495 and 496 apply to LLPs, modified so that they read] as follows—

"495 Auditor's report on LLP's annual accounts

(1) An LLP's auditor must make a report to the LLP's members on all annual accounts of the LLP of which copies are, during his tenure of office to be sent out to members under section 423.

[(2) The auditor's report must include—

(a) the identity of the LLP whose annual accounts are the subject of the audit,
(b) a description of the annual accounts that are the subject of the audit (including the period covered by those accounts),
(c) a description of the financial reporting framework that has been applied in the preparation of those accounts, and
(d) a description of the scope of the audit identifying the auditing standards in accordance with which the audit was conducted.]

(3) The report must state clearly whether, in the auditor's opinion, the annual accounts—

(a) give a true and fair view—
(i) in the case of an individual balance sheet, of the state of affairs of the LLP as at the end of the financial year,
(ii) in the case of an individual profit and loss account, of the profit or loss of the LLP for the financial year,
(iii) in the case of group accounts, of the state of affairs as at the end of the financial year and of the profit or loss for the financial year of the undertakings included in the consolidation as a whole, so far as concerns members of the LLP;
(b) have been properly prepared in accordance with the relevant financial reporting framework; and
(c) have been prepared in accordance with the requirements of this Act.

Expressions used in this subsection [or subsection (3A)] that are defined for the purposes of Part 15 (see [sections 464, 471 and 474]) have the same meaning as in that Part.

[(3A) Subsection (3B) applies to the auditors of an LLP which qualifies as a micro-entity in relation to a financial year (see sections 384A and 384B) in their consideration of whether the non-IAS individual accounts of the LLP for that year give a true and fair view as mentioned in subsection (3)(a).

(3B) Where the accounts contain an item of information additional to the micro-entity minimum accounting items, the auditors must have regard to any provision of an accounting standard which relates to that item.]

[(4) The auditor's report—

(a) must be either unqualified or qualified,

(b) must include a reference to any matters to which the auditor wishes to draw attention by way of emphasis without qualifying the report,

(c) must include a statement on any material uncertainty relating to events or conditions that may cast significant doubt about the LLP's ability to continue to adopt the going concern basis of accounting, and

(d) must identify the auditor's place of establishment.

(5) Where more than one person is appointed as an auditor—

(a) all the persons appointed must jointly make a report under this section and the report must include a statement as to whether all the persons appointed agree on the matters contained in the report, and

(b) if all the persons appointed cannot agree on the matters contained in the report, the report must include the opinions of each person appointed and give reasons for the disagreement.]

[496 Auditor's report on strategic report

(1) In his report on the LLP's annual accounts, the auditor must—

(a) state whether, in his opinion, based on the work undertaken in the course of the audit—

(i) the information given in the strategic report (if any) for the financial year for which the accounts are prepared is consistent with those accounts, and

(ii) any such strategic report have been prepared in accordance with applicable legal requirements,

(b) state whether, in the light of the knowledge and understanding of the LLP and its environment obtained in the course of the audit, he has identified material misstatements in the strategic report (if any), and

(c) if applicable, give an indication of the nature of each of the misstatements referred to in paragraph (b).

(2) Where more than one person is appointed as auditor, the report must include a statement as to whether all the persons appointed agree on the statements and indications given under subsection (1) and, if they cannot agree on those statements and indications, the report must include the opinions of each person appointed and give reasons for the disagreement.]

NOTES

The words in the first pair of square brackets were substituted by the Statutory Auditors Regulations 2017, SI 2017/1164, reg 5, Sch 3, paras 1, 13(a), in relation to financial years of companies beginning on or after 17 June 2016 (as to the application of the 2017 Regulations, see **[4.671]** et seq).

In s 495 as set out above, sub-ss (2) and (4) were substituted by SI 2017/1164, reg 5, Sch 3, paras 1, 13(b), in relation to financial years of companies beginning on or after 17 June 2016 (as to the application of the 2017 Regulations, see **[4.671]** et seq).

In s 495 as set out above, in sub-s (3) the words in the first pair of square brackets were inserted, and the words in the second pair of square brackets were substituted, and sub-ss (3A), (3B) were inserted, by the Limited Liability Partnerships, Partnerships and Groups (Accounts and Audit) Regulations 2016, SI 2016/575, regs 3, 24, as from 17 May 2016, in relation to (a) financial years beginning on or after 1 January 2016; and (b) a financial year of an LLP beginning on or after 1 January 2015, but before 1 January 2016, if (i) the members of the LLP so decide, and (ii) a copy of the LLP's accounts for that financial year has not been delivered to the registrar in accordance with ss 444, 445 or 446 of the Companies Act 2006 as applied to LLPs by the Limited Liability Partnerships (Accounts and Audit) (Application of Companies Act 2006) Regulations before 17 May 2016 (see further the note at **[10.226]**).

Section 496 as set out above was inserted by SI 2017/1164, reg 5, Sch 3, paras 1, 13(c), in relation to financial years of companies beginning on or after 17 June 2016 (as to the application of the 2017 Regulations, see **[4.671]** et seq).

Audit of LLPs connected with local authorities in England and Wales: see the Local Democracy, Economic Development and Construction Act 2009, s 44 in relation to the application of sub-ss (2)–(4) of this section (as applied to LLPs) and ss 498–501 of the 2006 Act (as applied to LLPs) where a person is appointed under the Local Democracy, Economic Development and Construction Act 2009, Pt 2, Chapter 3 (audit of entities connected with local authorities). Note that as of 1 August 2022, s 44 of the 2009 Act had not been brought into force.

[10.268]

40 Duties and rights of auditors

Sections 498 to 502 apply to LLPs, modified so that they read as follows—

"498 Duties of auditor

(1) An LLP's auditor, in preparing his report, must carry out such investigations as will enable him to form an opinion as to—

(a) whether adequate accounting records have been kept by the LLP and returns adequate for their audit have been received from branches not visited by him, and

(b) whether the LLP's individual accounts are in agreement with the accounting records and returns.

(2) If the auditor is of the opinion—

(a) that adequate accounting records have not been kept, or that returns adequate for their audit have not been received from branches not visited by him, or

(b) that the LLP's individual accounts are not in agreement with the accounting records and returns,

the auditor shall state that fact in his report.

(3) If the auditor fails to obtain all the information and explanations which, to the best of his knowledge and belief, are necessary for the purposes of his audit, he shall state that fact in his report.

(4) If the members of the LLP have prepared accounts in accordance with the small LLPs regime and in the auditor's opinion they were not entitled so to do, the auditor shall state that fact in his report.

[(5) Where more than one person is appointed as auditor, the report must include a statement as to whether all the persons appointed agree on the statements given under subsections (2) to (5) and, if they cannot agree on those statements, the report must include the opinions of each person appointed and give reasons for the disagreement.]

499 Auditor's general right to information

(1) An auditor of an LLP—

(a) has a right of access at all times to the LLP's books, accounts and vouchers (in whatever form they are held), and

(b) may require any of the following persons to provide him with such information or explanations as he thinks necessary for the performance of his duties as auditor.

(2) Those persons are—

(a) any member or employee of the LLP;

(b) any person holding or accountable for any of the LLP's books, accounts or vouchers;

(c) any subsidiary undertaking of the LLP which is a body corporate incorporated in the United Kingdom;

(d) any officer, employee or auditor of any such subsidiary undertaking or any person holding or accountable for any books, accounts or vouchers of any such subsidiary undertaking;

(e) any person who fell within any of paragraphs (a) to (d) at a time to which the information or explanations required by the auditor relates or relate.

(3) A statement made by a person in response to a requirement under this section may not be used in evidence against him in criminal proceedings except proceedings for an offence under section 501.

(4) Nothing in this section compels a person to disclose information in respect of which a claim to legal professional privilege (in Scotland, to confidentiality of communications) could be maintained in legal proceedings.

500 Auditor's right to information from overseas subsidiaries

(1) Where a parent LLP has a subsidiary undertaking that is not a body corporate incorporated in the United Kingdom, the auditor of the parent LLP may require it to obtain from any of the following persons such information or explanations as he may reasonably require for the purposes of his duties as auditor.

(2) Those persons are—

(a) the undertaking;

(b) any officer, employee or auditor of the undertaking;

(c) any person holding or accountable for any of the undertaking's books, accounts or vouchers;

(d) any person who fell within paragraph (b) or (c) at a time to which the information or explanations relates or relate.

(3) If so required, the parent LLP must take all such steps as are reasonably open to it to obtain the information or explanations from the person concerned.

(4) A statement made by a person in response to a requirement under this section may not be used in evidence against him in criminal proceedings except proceedings for an offence under section 501.

(5) Nothing in this section compels a person to disclose information in respect of which a claim to legal professional privilege (in Scotland, to confidentiality of communications) could be maintained in legal proceedings.

501 Auditor's right to information: offences

(1) A person commits an offence who knowingly or recklessly makes to an auditor of an LLP a statement (oral or written) that—

(a) conveys or purports to convey any information or explanations which the auditor requires, or is entitled to require, under section 499, and

(b) is misleading, false or deceptive in a material particular.

(2) A person guilty of an offence under subsection (1) is liable—

(a) on conviction on indictment, to imprisonment for a term not exceeding two years or a fine (or both);

(b) on summary conviction—

(i) in England and Wales [or Scotland], to imprisonment for a term not exceeding twelve months or to a fine not exceeding the statutory maximum (or both);

(ii) in . . . Northern Ireland, to imprisonment for a term not exceeding six months or to a fine not exceeding the statutory maximum (or both).

(3) A person who fails to comply with a requirement under section 499 without delay commits an offence unless it was not reasonably practicable for him to provide the required information or explanations.

(4) If a parent LLP fails to comply with section 500, an offence is committed by—

(a) the LLP, and

(b) every member of the LLP who is in default.

(5) A person guilty of an offence under subsection (3) or (4) is liable on summary conviction to a fine not exceeding level 3 on the standard scale.

(6) Nothing in this section affects any right of an auditor to apply for an injunction (in Scotland, an interdict or an order for specific performance) to enforce any of his rights under section 499 or 500.

502 Auditor's rights in relation to meetings

(1) An LLP's auditor is entitled—

(a) to receive all notices of, and other communications relating to, any meeting which a member of the LLP is entitled to receive, where any part of the business of the meeting concerns them as auditors,

(b) to attend any meeting of the LLP where any part of the business of the meeting concerns them as auditors, and

(c) to be heard at any meeting which he attends on any part of the business of the meeting which concerns him as auditor.

(2) Where the auditor is a firm, the right to attend or be heard at a meeting is exercisable by an individual authorised by the firm in writing to act as its representative at the meeting."

NOTES

In s 498 as set out above, sub-s (5) was inserted by the Statutory Auditors Regulations 2017, SI 2017/1164, reg 5, Sch 3, paras 1, 14, in relation to financial years of companies beginning on or after 17 June 2016 (as to the application of the 2017 Regulations, see **[4.671]** et seq).

In s 501(2)(b) as set out above, the words in square brackets were inserted, and the words omitted were revoked, by the Limited Liability Partnerships (Application of Companies Act 2006) Regulations 2009, SI 2009/1804, reg 85, Sch 3, Pt 2, para 16, as from 1 October 2009.

Audit of LLPs connected with local authorities in England and Wales: see the note at **[10.267]**.

[10.269]
41 Signature of auditor's report

Sections 503 to 506 apply to LLPs, modified so that they read as follows—

"503 Signature of auditor's report

(1) The auditor's report must state the name of the auditor and be signed and dated.

(2) Where the auditor is an individual, the report must be signed by him.

(3) Where the auditor is a firm, the report must be signed by the senior statutory auditor in his own name, for and on behalf of the auditor.

[(4) Where more than one person is appointed as auditor, the report must be signed by all those appointed.]

504 Senior statutory auditor

(1) The senior statutory auditor means the individual identified by the firm as senior statutory auditor in relation to the audit in accordance with—

(a) . . .

(b) . . . any relevant guidance issued by—

(i) the Secretary of State, or

[(ii) the Financial Reporting Council Limited.]

(2) The person identified as senior statutory auditor must be eligible for appointment as auditor of the LLP in question (see Chapter 2 of Part 42 of this Act).

(3) The senior statutory auditor is not, by reason of being named or identified as senior statutory auditor or by reason of his having signed the auditor's report, subject to any civil liability to which he would not otherwise be subject.

(4) An order appointing a body for the purpose of subsection (1)(b)(ii) is subject to negative resolution procedure.

505 Names to be stated in published copies of auditor's report

(1) Every copy of the auditor's report that is published by or on behalf of the LLP must—

(a) state the name of the auditor and (where the auditor is a firm) the name of the person who signed it as senior statutory auditor, or

(b) if the conditions in section 506 (circumstances in which names may be omitted) are met, state that a determination has been made and notified to the Secretary of State in accordance with that section.

[(1A) If more than one person is appointed as auditor, the reference in subsection (1)(a) to the name of the auditor is to be read as a reference to the names of all the auditors.]

(2) For the purposes of this section an LLP is regarded as publishing the report if it publishes, issues or circulates it or otherwise makes it available for public inspection in a manner calculated to invite members of the public generally, or any class of members of the public, to read it.

(3) If a copy of the auditor's report is published without the statement required by this section, an offence is committed by—

(a) the LLP, and

(b) every designated member of the LLP who is in default.

(4) A person guilty of an offence under this section is liable on summary conviction to a fine not exceeding level 3 on the standard scale.

506 Circumstances in which names may be omitted

(1) [An auditor's] name and, where the auditor is a firm, the name of the person who signed the report as senior statutory auditor, may be omitted from—

(a) published copies of the report, and

(b) the copy of the report delivered to the registrar under Chapter 10 of Part 15 (filing of accounts and reports),

if the following conditions are met.

(2) The conditions are that the LLP—

(a) considering on reasonable grounds that statement of the name would create or be likely to create a serious risk that the auditor or senior statutory auditor, or any other person, would be subject to violence or intimidation, has determined that the name should not be stated, and

(b) has given notice of the determination to the Secretary of State, stating—

(i) the name and registered number of the LLP,

(ii) the financial year of the LLP to which the report relates, and

(iii) the name of the auditor and (where the auditor is a firm) the name of the person who signed the report as senior statutory auditor."

NOTES

All words in square brackets in this regulation were inserted or substituted by the Statutory Auditors Regulations 2017, SI 2017/1164, reg 5, Sch 3, paras 1, 15, in relation to financial years of companies beginning on or after 17 June 2016 (as to the application of the 2017 Regulations, see **[4.671]** et seq).

In s 504 as set out above, sub-s (1)(a) and the words omitted from sub-s (1)(b) were revoked, by the Statutory Auditors and Third Country Auditors (Amendment) (EU Exit) Regulations 2019, SI 2019/177, regs 49, 52, as from IP completion day (as defined in the European Union (Withdrawal Agreement) Act 2020, s 39) (for transitional provisions, see Sch 4 to the 2019 Regulations at **[12.88]**).

[10.270]

42 Offences in connection with auditor's report

Sections 507 to 509 apply to LLPs, modified so that they read as follows—

"507 Offences in connection with auditor's report

(1) A person to whom this section applies commits an offence if he knowingly or recklessly causes a report under section 495 (auditor's report on LLP's annual accounts) to include any matter that is misleading, false or deceptive in a material particular.

(2) A person to whom this section applies commits an offence if he knowingly or recklessly causes such a report to omit a statement required by—

(a) section 498(2)(b) (statement that LLP's accounts do not agree with accounting records and returns),

(b) section 498(3) (statement that necessary information and explanations not obtained), or

(c) section 498(4) (statement that members wrongly prepared accounts in accordance with the small LLPs regime).

(3) This section applies to—

(a) where the auditor is an individual, that individual and any employee or agent of his who is eligible for appointment as auditor of the LLP;

(b) where the auditor is a firm, any director, member, employee or agent of the firm who is eligible for appointment as auditor of the LLP.

(4) A person guilty of an offence under this section is liable—

(a) on conviction on indictment, to a fine;

(b) on summary conviction, to a fine not exceeding the statutory maximum.

508 Guidance for regulatory and prosecuting authorities: England, Wales and Northern Ireland

(1) The Secretary of State may issue guidance for the purpose of helping relevant regulatory and prosecuting authorities to determine how they should carry out their functions in cases where behaviour occurs that—

(a) appears to involve the commission of an offence under section 507 (offences in connection with auditor's report), and

(b) has been, is being or may be investigated pursuant to arrangements—

(i) under paragraph 15 of Schedule 10 (investigation of complaints against auditors and supervisory bodies), or

(ii) of a kind mentioned in paragraph 24 of that Schedule (independent investigation for disciplinary purposes of public interest cases).

(2) The Secretary of State must obtain the consent of the Attorney General before issuing any such guidance.

(3) In this section "relevant regulatory and prosecuting authorities" means—

(a) supervisory bodies within the meaning of Part 42 of this Act,

(b) bodies to which the Secretary of State may make grants under section 16(1) of the Companies (Audit, Investigations and Community Enterprise) Act 2004 (c.27) (bodies concerned with accounting standards etc),

(c) the Director of the Serious Fraud Office,

(d) the Director of Public Prosecutions or the Director of Public Prosecutions for Northern Ireland, and

(e) the Secretary of State.

(4) This section does not apply to Scotland.

509 Guidance for regulatory authorities: Scotland

(1) The Lord Advocate may issue guidance for the purpose of helping relevant regulatory authorities to determine how they should carry out their functions in cases where behaviour occurs that—

(a) appears to involve the commission of an offence under section 507 (offences in connection with auditor's report), and

(b) has been, is being or may be investigated pursuant to arrangements—

(i) under paragraph 15 of Schedule 10 (investigation of complaints against auditors and supervisory bodies), or

(ii) of a kind mentioned in paragraph 24 of that Schedule (independent investigation for disciplinary purposes of public interest cases).

(2) The Lord Advocate must consult the Secretary of State before issuing any such guidance.

(3) In this section "relevant regulatory authorities" means—

(a) supervisory bodies within the meaning of Part 42 of this Act,

(b) bodies to which the Secretary of State may make grants under section 16(1) of the Companies (Audit, Investigations and Community Enterprise) Act 2004 (c.27) (bodies concerned with accounting standards etc), and

(c) the Secretary of State.

(4) This section applies only to Scotland."

PART 13 REMOVAL, RESIGNATION, ETC OF AUDITORS

[10.271]

43 Removal, resignation, etc of auditors

(1) Sections 510 to 512 apply to LLPs, modified so that they read as follows—

"510 Removal of auditor

(1) The members of an LLP may remove an auditor from office at any time.

(2) Nothing in this section is to be taken as depriving the person removed of compensation or damages payable to him in respect of the termination—

(a) of his appointment as auditor, or

(b) of any appointment terminating with that as auditor.

[(3) An auditor may not be removed from office before the expiration of his term of office except—

(a) by resolution under this section, or

(b) in accordance with section 511A.]

511 Notice of removal of auditor

(1) No determination to remove an auditor before the expiration of his term of office may be made under section 510 unless the LLP has given 7 days' prior notice to any auditor whom it is proposed to remove

(2) The auditor proposed to be removed may make with respect to the proposal representations in writing to the LLP (not exceeding a reasonable length) and request their notification to members of the LLP.

(3) The LLP must upon receipt send a copy of the representations to every member.

(4) Copies of the representations need not be sent out if, on the application either of the LLP or of any other person claiming to be aggrieved, the court is satisfied that the auditor is using the provisions of this section to secure needless publicity for defamatory matter.

The court may order the LLP's costs (in Scotland, expenses) on the application to be paid in whole or in part by the auditor, notwithstanding that he is not a party to the application.

[511A Public interest LLP: application to court to remove auditor from office

(1) This section applies only to a public interest LLP.

(2) The competent authority may apply to the court for an order removing an auditor of an LLP from office if the authority considers that there are proper grounds for removing the auditor from office.

(3) The members of an LLP may apply to the court for an order removing an auditor of the LLP from office if the applicant or applicants consider that there are proper grounds for removing the auditor from office.

(4) If the court is satisfied, on hearing an application under subsection (2), that there are proper grounds for removing the auditor from office, it may make an order removing the auditor from office.

(5) If the court is satisfied, on hearing an application under subsection (3), that—

(a) the applicants represent in total not less than 5% of the voting rights of all the members having a right to vote at a general meeting of the LLP, and

(b) there are proper grounds for removing the auditor from office,

the court may make an order removing the auditor from office.

(6) For the purposes of this section, divergence of opinions on accounting treatments or audit procedures are not to be taken to be proper grounds for removing an auditor from office.]

512

. . .

(2) Until section 1068(1) comes into force, the notice referred to in section 512(1) as applied to LLPs by paragraph (1) must be in the form prescribed for the purposes of section 391(2) of the 1985 Act or Article 399(2) of the 1986 Order as applied to LLPs.

NOTES

Section 510(3) as set out above was substituted, s 511A as set out above was inserted, and s 512 as originally set out above was revoked, by the Statutory Auditors Regulations 2017, SI 2017/1164, reg 5, Sch 3, paras 1, 16, in relation to financial years of companies beginning on or after 17 June 2016 (as to the application of the 2017 Regulations, see **[4.671]** et seq).

[10.272]

44 Rights of auditor removed from office

(1) Section 513 applies to LLPs, modified so that it reads as follows—

"513 Rights of auditor who has been removed from office

(1) An auditor who has been removed [by the members under section 510 or by order of the court under section 511A] has, notwithstanding his removal, the rights conferred by section 502(1) in relation to any meeting of the LLP—

(a) at which his term of office would otherwise have expired, or

(b) at which it is proposed to fill the vacancy caused by his removal.

(2) In such a case the references in that section to matters concerning the auditor as auditor shall be construed as references to matters concerning him as a former auditor."

(2) In section 513 (applied to LLPs by paragraph (1)) as it applies in relation to an auditor appointed before 1st October 2008, the reference to rights under section 502(1) shall be read as a reference to rights under section 390(1) of the 1985 Act or Article 398(1) of the 1986 Order as applied to LLPs.

NOTES

In s 513(1) as set out above, the words in square brackets were inserted by the Statutory Auditors Regulations 2017, SI 2017/1164, reg 5, Sch 3, paras 1, 17, in relation to financial years of companies beginning on or after 17 June 2016 (as to the application of the 2017 Regulations, see **[4.671]** et seq).

[10.273]

45 Rights of auditor not re-appointed

(1) Sections 515 to 518 apply to LLPs, modified so that they read as follows—

"515 Failure to re-appoint auditor: rights of auditor who is not re-appointed

[(1) If an LLP wishes to appoint a person as auditor in place of a person who is an auditor of the LLP and who is to cease to hold office at the end of a period for appointing auditors (the "outgoing auditor"), the LLP must give the outgoing auditor seven days' notice; no person may be appointed as auditor in the absence of such notice.

But notice is not required under this subsection if the auditor is to cease to hold office by virtue of section 510, 511A or 516.

(2) The outgoing auditor may, in response to receipt of a notice given under subsection (1), make representations in writing to the LLP (not exceeding a reasonable length) and request their notification to members of the LLP.]

(3) The LLP must upon receipt send a copy of the representations to every member.

(4) Copies of the representations need not be sent out if, on the application either of the LLP or of any other person claiming to be aggrieved, the court is satisfied that the auditor is using the provisions of this section to secure needless publicity for defamatory matter.

The court may order the LLP's costs (in Scotland, expenses) on the application to be paid in whole or in part by the auditor, notwithstanding that he is not a party to the application.

516 Resignation of auditor

(1) An auditor of an LLP may resign his office by [sending a notice to that effect to the LLP].

(2) [Where the LLP is a public interest LLP, the] notice is not effective unless it is accompanied by the statement required by section 519.

(3) An effective notice of resignation operates to bring the auditor's term of office to an end as of the date on which the notice is [received] or on such later date as may be specified in it.

517

. . .

518 Rights of resigning auditor

[(1) This section applies where an auditor's (A's) notice of resignation is accompanied by a statement under section 519 except where—

(a) the LLP is a non-public interest LLP, and

(b) the statement includes a statement to the effect that A considers that none of the reasons for A's ceasing to hold office, and no matters (if any) connected with A's ceasing to hold office, need to be brought to the attention of members or creditors of the LLP (as required by section 519(2E)).]

(2) He may [send] with the notice [an authenticated] requisition calling on the designated members of the LLP forthwith duly to convene a meeting of the members of the LLP for the purpose of receiving and considering such explanation of the [reasons for, and matters connected with,] his resignation as he may wish to place before the meeting.

(3) He may request the LLP to circulate to its members before the meeting convened on his requisition, a statement in writing (not exceeding a reasonable length) of the [reasons for, and matters connected with,] his resignation.

(4) The LLP must (unless the statement is received too late for it to comply)—

(a) in any notice of the meeting given to members of the LLP, state the fact of the statement having been made, and

(b) send a copy of the statement to every member of the LLP to whom notice of the meeting is or has been sent.

(5) The designated members must within 21 days from the date [on which the LLP receives] a requisition under this section proceed duly to convene a meeting for a day not more than 28 days after the date on which the notice convening the meeting is given.

(6) If default is made in complying with subsection (5), every designated member who failed to take all reasonable steps to secure that a meeting was convened commits an offence.

(7) A person guilty of an offence under this section is liable—

(a) on conviction on indictment, to a fine;

(b) on summary conviction to a fine not exceeding the statutory maximum.

(8) If a copy of the statement mentioned above is not sent out as required because received too late or because of the LLP's default, the auditor may (without prejudice to his right to be heard orally) require that the statement be read out at the meeting.

(9) Copies of a statement need not be sent out and the statement need not be read out at the meeting if, on the application either of the LLP or of any other person who claims to be aggrieved, the court is satisfied that the auditor is using the provisions of this section to secure needless publicity for defamatory matter.

The court may order the LLP's costs (in Scotland, expenses) on such an application to be paid in whole or in part by the auditor, notwithstanding that he is not a party to the application.

(10) An auditor who has resigned has, notwithstanding his resignation, the rights conferred by section 502(1) in relation to any such meeting of the LLP as is mentioned in subsection (3).

In such a case the references in that section to matters concerning the auditor as auditor shall be construed as references to matters concerning him as a former auditor."

(2) In section 518 (applied to LLPs by paragraph (1)) as it applies in relation to an auditor appointed before 1st October 2008, the reference to rights under section 502(1) shall be read as a reference to rights under section 390(1) of the 1985 Act or Article 398(1) of the 1986 Order as applied to LLPs.

NOTES

In s 515 as set out above, sub-ss (1) and (2) were substituted, all words in square brackets in s 516 as set out above were substituted, s 517 as originally set out above was revoked, and all words in square brackets in s 518 as set out above were substituted, by the Statutory Auditors Regulations 2017, SI 2017/1164, reg 5, Sch 3, paras 1, 18, in relation to financial years of companies beginning on or after 17 June 2016 (as to the application of the 2017 Regulations, see **[4.671]** et seq).

[10.274]

46 Auditor statements

Sections 519 to 526 apply to LLPs, modified so that they read as follows—

"519 Statement by auditor to be [sent to] LLP

[(1) An auditor of a public interest LLP who is ceasing to hold office (at any time and for any reason) must send to the LLP a statement of the reasons for doing so.

(2) An auditor ("A") of a non-public interest LLP who is ceasing to hold office must send to the LLP a statement of the reasons for doing so unless A satisfies the first or second condition.

(2A) The first condition is that A is ceasing to hold office at the end of a period for appointing auditors.

(2B) The second condition is that—

(a) A's reasons for ceasing to hold office are all exempt reasons (as to which see section 519A(3)), and

(b) there are no matters connected with A's ceasing to hold office that A considers need to be brought to the attention of members or creditors of the LLP.

(2C) A statement under this section must include—

(a) the auditor's name and address;

(b) the number allocated to the auditor on being entered in the register of auditors kept under section 1239;

(c) the LLP's name and registered number.

(2D) Where there are matters connected with an auditor's ceasing to hold office that the auditor considers need to be brought to the attention of members or creditors of the LLP, the statement under this section must include details of those matters.

(2E) Where—

(a) an auditor ("A") of a non-public interest LLP is required by subsection (2) to send a statement, and

(b) A considers that none of the reasons for A's ceasing to hold office, and no matters (if any) connected with A's ceasing to hold office, need to be brought to the attention of members or creditors of the LLP,

A's statement under this section must include a statement to that effect.]

(3) [A statement under this section] must be [sent]—

(a) in the case of resignation, along with the notice of resignation;

(b) in the case of failure to seek re-appointment, not less than 14 days before the end of the time allowed for next appointing an auditor;

(c) in any other case, not later than the end of the period of 14 days beginning with the date on which he ceases to hold office.

(4) A person ceasing to hold office as auditor who fails to comply with this section commits an offence.

(5) In proceedings for such an offence it is a defence for the person charged to show that he took all reasonable steps and exercised all due diligence to avoid the commission of the offence.

(6) A person guilty of an offence under this section is liable—

(a) on conviction on indictment, to a fine;

(b) on summary conviction, to a fine not exceeding the statutory maximum.

(7) Where an offence under this section is committed by a body corporate, every officer of the body who is in default also commits the offence.

For this purpose—

(a) any person who acts as director, manager or secretary of the body is treated as an officer of the body, and

(b) if the body is a company, any shadow director is treated as an officer of the company.

[519A Meaning of "public interest LLP", "non-public interest LLP" and "exempt reasons"

(1) In this Chapter—

"public interest LLP" means an LLP—

(a) an issuer whose transferable securities are admitted to trading on a [UK regulated market]; or

(b) a credit institution within the meaning given by Article 4(1)(1) of Regulation (EU) No 575/2013 of the European Parliament and of the Council, [which is a CRR firm within the meaning of Article 4(1)(2A) of the same Regulation];

"non-public interest LLP" means an LLP that is not a public interest LLP.

(2) For the purposes of the definition of "public interest LLP"—

"issuer" has the same meaning as in Part 6 of the Financial Services and Markets Act 2000 (see section 102A(6));

. . .

. . .

(3) In the application of this Chapter to an auditor ("A") of an LLP ceasing to hold office, the following are "exempt reasons"—

(a) A is no longer to carry out statutory audit work within the meaning of Part 42 (see section 1210(1));

(b) the LLP is, or is to become, exempt from audit under section 477, 479A or 480, and intends to include in its balance sheet a statement of the type described in section 475(2);

(c) the LLP is a subsidiary undertaking of a parent undertaking that is incorporated in the United Kingdom and—

(i) the parent undertaking prepares group accounts, and

(ii) A is being replaced as auditor of the LLP by the auditor who is conducting, or is to conduct, an audit of the group accounts;

(d) the LLP is being wound up under Part 4 of the Insolvency Act 1986 or Part 5 of the Insolvency (Northern Ireland) Order 1989 (SI 1989/2405 (NI 19)), whether voluntarily or by the court, or a petition under Part 4 of that Act or Part 5 of that Order (as applied to LLPs) for the winding up of the LLP has been presented and not finally dealt with or withdrawn.

In this paragraph the references—

(i) to Part 4 of the Insolvency Act 1986 are to that Part as applied to LLPs by the Limited Liability Partnerships Regulations 2001 (SI 2001/1090), and

(ii) to Part 5 of the Insolvency (Northern Ireland) Order 1989 are to that Part as applied to LLPs by the Limited Liability Partnerships Regulations (Northern Ireland) 2004 (SR (NI) 2004 No 307).

(4) But the reason described in subsection (3)(c) is only an exempt reason if the auditor who is conducting, or is to conduct, an audit of the group accounts is also conducting, or is also to conduct, the audit (if any) of the accounts of each of the subsidiary undertakings (of the parent undertaking) that is incorporated in the United Kingdom and included in the consolidation.]

520 LLP's duties in relation to statement

[(1) This section applies where an LLP receives from an auditor ("A") who is ceasing to hold office a statement under section 519 except where—

(a) the LLP is a non-public interest LLP, and

(b) the statement includes a statement to the effect that A considers that none of the reasons for A's ceasing to hold office, and no matters (if any) connected with A's ceasing to hold office, need to be brought to the attention of members or creditors of the LLP (as required by section 519(2E)).]

(2) [Where this section applies, the] LLP must within 14 days of the [receipt] of the statement either—

(a) send a copy of it to every person who under section 423 is entitled to be sent copies of the accounts, or

(b) apply to the court.

(3) If it applies to the court, the LLP must notify the auditor of the application.

(4) If the court is satisfied that the auditor is using the provisions of section 519 to secure needless publicity for defamatory matter—

(a) it shall direct that copies of the statement need not be sent out, and

(b) it may further order the LLP's costs (in Scotland, expenses) on the application to be paid in whole or in part by the auditor, even if he is not a party to the application.

The LLP must within 14 days of the court's decision send to the persons mentioned in subsection (2)(a) a statement setting out the effect of the order.

(5) If no such direction is made the LLP must send copies of the statement to the persons mentioned in subsection (2)(a) within 14 days of the court's decision or, as the case may be, of the discontinuance of the proceedings.

(6) In the event of default in complying with this section an offence is committed by every designated member of the LLP who is in default.

(7) In proceedings for such an offence it is a defence for the person charged to show that he took all reasonable steps and exercised all due diligence to avoid the commission of the offence.

(8) A person guilty of an offence under this section is liable—

(a) on conviction on indictment, to a fine;

(b) on summary conviction, to a fine not exceeding the statutory maximum.

521 Copy of statement to be sent to registrar

[(A1) This section applies where an auditor ("A") of an LLP sends a statement to the LLP under section 519 except where—

(a) the LLP is a non-public interest LLP, and

(b) the statement includes a statement to the effect that A considers that none of the reasons for A's ceasing to hold office, and no matters (if any) connected with A's ceasing to hold office, need to be brought to the attention of members or creditors of the LLP (as required by section 519(2E)).]

(1) [Where this section applies, unless] within 21 days beginning with the day on which he [sent] the statement under section 519 the auditor receives notice of an application to the court under section 520, he must within a further seven days send a copy of the statement to the registrar.

(2) If an application to the court is made under section 520 and the auditor subsequently receives notice under subsection (5) of that section, he must within seven days of receiving the notice send a copy of the statement to the registrar.

(3) An auditor who fails to comply with subsection (1) or (2) commits an offence.

(4) In proceedings for such an offence it is a defence for the person charged to show that he took all reasonable steps and exercised all due diligence to avoid the commission of the offence.

(5) A person guilty of an offence under this section is liable—

(a) on conviction on indictment, to a fine;

(b) on summary conviction, to a fine not exceeding the statutory maximum.

(6) Where an offence under this section is committed by a body corporate, every officer of the body who is in default also commits the offence.

For this purpose—

(a) any person who acts as director, manager or secretary of the body is treated as an officer of the body, and

(b) if the body is a company, any shadow director is treated as an officer of the company.

522 Duty of auditor to [send statement to] appropriate audit authority

[(1) Where an auditor of an LLP sends a statement under section 519, the auditor must at the same time send a copy of the statement to the appropriate audit authority.]

(5) A person ceasing to hold office as auditor who fails to comply with this section commits an offence.

(6) If that person is a firm an offence is committed by—

(a) the firm, and

(b) every officer of the firm who is in default.

(7) In proceedings for an offence under this section it is a defence for the person charged to show that he took all reasonable steps and exercised all due diligence to avoid the commission of the offence.

(8) A person guilty of an offence under this section is liable—

(a) on conviction on indictment, to a fine;

(b) on summary conviction, to a fine not exceeding the statutory maximum.

523 Duty of LLP to notify appropriate audit authority

[(1) This section applies if an auditor is ceasing to hold office at any time other than at the end of a period for appointing auditors.

(1A) But this section does not apply if the LLP reasonably believes that the only reasons for the auditor's ceasing to hold office are exempt reasons (as to which see section 519A(3)).

(2) Where this section applies, the LLP must give notice to the appropriate audit authority that the auditor is ceasing to hold office.

(2A) The notice is to take the form of a statement by the LLP of what the LLP believes to be the reasons for the auditor's ceasing to hold office and must include the information listed in section 519(2C).

This is subject to subsection (2C).

(2B) Subsection (2C) applies where—

(a) the LLP receives a statement from the auditor under section 519,

(b) the statement is sent at the time required by section 519(3), and

(c) the LLP agrees with the contents of the statement.

(2C) Where this subsection applies, the notice may instead take the form of a copy of the statement endorsed by the LLP to the effect that it agrees with the contents of the statement.

(3) A notice under this section must be given within the period of 28 days beginning with the day on which the auditor ceases to hold office.]

(4) If an LLP fails to comply with this section, an offence is committed by—

(a) the LLP, and

(b) every designated member of the LLP who is in default.

(5) In proceedings for such an offence it is a defence for the person charged to show that he took all reasonable steps and exercised all due diligence to avoid the commission of the offence.

(6) A person guilty of an offence under this section is liable—

(a) on conviction on indictment, to a fine;

(b) on summary conviction, to a fine not exceeding the statutory maximum.

524 [Provision of information] to accounting authorities

[(1) Where the appropriate audit authority receives a statement under section 522 or a notice under section 523, the authority may forward to the accounting authorities—

(a) a copy of the statement or notice, and

(b) any other information the authority has received from the auditor or the LLP concerned in connection with the auditor's ceasing to hold office.]

(2) The accounting authorities are—

(a) the Secretary of State, and

(b) [the Financial Reporting Council Limited].

(3) If either of the accounting authorities is also the appropriate audit authority it is only necessary to comply with this section as regards any other accounting authority.

(4) If the court has made an order under section 520(4) directing that copies of the statement need not be sent out by the LLP, sections 460 and 461 (restriction on further disclosure) apply in relation to the copies sent to the accounting authorities as they apply to information obtained under section 459 (power to require documents etc).

525 Meaning of "appropriate audit authority" . . .

(1) In sections 522, 523 and 524 "appropriate audit authority" means—

[(a) [in relation to an auditor of a public interest LLP (other than an Auditor General)], the Financial Reporting Council Limited;]

(b) [in relation to an auditor of a non-public interest LLP (other than an Auditor General)], the relevant supervisory body;

(c) [in relation to] an Auditor General, the Independent Supervisor.

"Supervisory body" and "Independent Supervisor" have the same meaning as in Part 42 (statutory auditors) (see sections 1217 and 1228).

(2), (3) . . .

526 Effect of casual vacancies

If an auditor ceases to hold office for any reason, any surviving or continuing auditor or auditors may continue to act."

NOTES

In s 519A as set out above, the words in square brackets in sub-s (1)(a) and (b) were substituted, and the definitions "regulated market" and "transferable securities" omitted from sub-s (2) were revoked, by the Statutory Auditors and Third Country Auditors (Amendment) (EU Exit) Regulations 2019, SI 2019/177, regs 49, 53, as from IP completion day (as defined in the European Union (Withdrawal Agreement) Act 2020, s 39) (for transitional provisions, see Sch 4 to the 2019 Regulations at **[12.88]**).

In s 524 as set out above, the words in square brackets in sub-s (2) were substituted by the Supervision of Accounts and Reports (Prescribed Body) and Companies (Defective Accounts and Reports) (Authorised Person) Order 2021, SI 2021/465, art 6(5), as from 6 May 2021 (see art 9 of the 2021 Order for transitional provisions in relation to the continuity of functions, etc at **[4.727]**).

Section 525(1)(a) as set out above was substituted by the Statutory Auditors (Amendment of Companies Act 2006 and Delegation of Functions etc) Order 2012, SI 2012/1741, art 3, Schedule, Pt 1, para 3, as from 2 July 2012.

All other amendments to this regulation were made by the Statutory Auditors Regulations 2017, SI 2017/1164, reg 5, Sch 3, paras 1, 19, in relation to financial years of companies beginning on or after 17 June 2016 (as to the application of the 2017 Regulations, see **[4.671]** et seq).

PART 14 LLP AUDIT: SUPPLEMENTARY PROVISIONS

[10.275]

47 Minor definitions

Section 539 applies to LLPs, modified so that it reads as follows—

"539 Minor definitions

In this Part—

"e-money issuer" means a person [who is registered as an authorised electronic money institution or a small electronic money institution within the meaning of the Electronic Money Regulations 2011 or] who has permission under Part 4 of the Financial Services and Markets Act 2000 (c 8) to carry on the activity of issuing electronic money within the meaning of article 9B of the Financial Services and Markets Act 2000 (Regulated Activities) Order 2001 (SI 2001/544);

"LLP agreement" means any agreement express or implied between the members of the LLP or between the LLP and the members of the LLP which determines the mutual rights and duties of the members, and their rights and duties in relation to the LLP;

["MiFID investment firm" means an investment firm within the meaning of Article 2(1A) of Regulation (EU) No 600/2014 of the European Parliament and of the Council of 15 May 2014 on markets in financial instruments and amending Regulation (EU) No 648/2012, other than—

(a) an LLP which is exempted from the definition of "investment firm" by Schedule 3 to the Financial Services and Markets Act 2000 (Regulated Activities) Order 2001 (SI 2001/544),

(b) an LLP which is an exempt investment firm as defined by regulation 8 (meaning of exemption of investment firm in Chapter 1) of the Financial Services and Markets Act 2000 (Markets in Financial Instruments) Regulations 2017 (SI 2017/701), and

(c) any other LLP which fulfils all the requirements set out in regulation 6(3) of those Regulations;]

"qualified", in relation to an auditor's report (or a statement contained in an auditor's report), means that the report or statement does not state the auditor's unqualified opinion that the accounts have been properly prepared in accordance with this Act or, in the case of an undertaking not required to prepare accounts in accordance with this Act, under any corresponding legislation under which it is required to prepare accounts;

"turnover", in relation to an LLP, means the amounts derived from the provision of goods and services falling within the LLP's ordinary activities, after deduction of—

(a) trade discounts,

(b) value added tax, and

(c) any other taxes based on the amounts so derived;

["UCITS management company" has the meaning given by the Glossary to the Handbook made by the Financial Conduct Authority under the Financial Services and Markets Act 2000].

NOTES

Section 539 as set out above is amended as follows:

Words in square brackets in the definition "e-money issuer" inserted by the Electronic Money Regulations 2011, SI 2011/99, reg 79, Sch 4, Pt 2, para 20, as from 30 April 2011.

The definition "MiFID investment firm" was substituted by the Statutory Auditors and Third Country Auditors (Amendment) (EU Exit) Regulations 2019, SI 2019/177, regs 49, 54, as from IP completion day (as defined in the European Union (Withdrawal Agreement) Act 2020, s 39) (for transitional provisions, see Sch 4 to the 2019 Regulations at **[12.88]**).

The definition "UCITS management company" was substituted by the Financial Services Act 2012 (Consequential Amendments and Transitional Provisions) Order 2013, SI 2013/472, art 3, Sch 2, para 143(c), as from 1 April 2013.

PART 15 STATUTORY AUDITORS

[10.276]

48 Extension of Part 42

For the purposes of section 1210(1)(h) (meaning of "statutory auditor")—

(a) an LLP is a prescribed person, and

(b) Part 16 of the Companies Act 2006 as applied to LLPs is a prescribed enactment,

(and accordingly a person appointed as auditor of an LLP under Part 16 of that Act as applied to LLPs by these Regulations is a statutory auditor).

PART 16 OFFENCES

[10.277]

49 Liability of member in default

Sections 1121 and 1122 apply to LLPs [for the purposes of these Regulations], modified so that they read as follows—

"1121 Liability of member in default

(1) This section has effect for the purposes of any provision of the Companies Acts to the effect that, in the event of contravention of an enactment in relation to an LLP, an offence is committed by every member or, as the case may be, every designated member of the LLP who is in default.

(2) A member or designated member is "in default" for the purposes of the provision if he authorises or permits, participates in, or fails to take all reasonable steps to prevent, the contravention.

1122 Liability of company as member in default

(1) Where a company is a member or designated member of an LLP, it does not commit an offence as a member or designated member in default unless one of its officers is in default.

(2) Where any such offence is committed by a company the officer in question also commits the offence and is liable to be proceeded against and punished accordingly.

(3) In this section—

(a) officer" includes any director, manager or secretary, and

(b) an officer is "in default" for the purposes of the provision if he authorises or permits, participates in, or fails to take all reasonable steps to prevent, the contravention."

NOTES

Words in square brackets inserted by the Limited Liability Partnerships (Application of Companies Act 2006) Regulations 2009, SI 2009/1804, reg 85, Sch 3, Pt 2, para 15(4), as from 1 October 2009.

[10.278]

50 General provisions

Sections 1125 to 1132 apply to LLPs [for the purposes of these Regulations], modified so that they read as follows—

"1125 Meaning of "daily default fine

(1) This section defines what is meant in the Companies Acts where it is provided that a person guilty of an offence is liable on summary conviction to a fine not exceeding a specified amount "and, for continued contravention, a daily default fine" not exceeding a specified amount.

(2) This means that the person is liable on a second or subsequent summary conviction of the offence to a fine not exceeding the latter amount for each day on which the contravention is continued (instead of being liable to a fine not exceeding the former amount).

1126 Consents required for certain prosecutions

(1) This section applies to proceedings for an offence under section 458 or 460 of this Act.

(2) No such proceedings are to be brought in England and Wales except by or with the consent of the Secretary of State or the Director of Public Prosecutions.

(3) No such proceedings are to be brought in Northern Ireland except by or with the consent of the Secretary of State or the Director of Public Prosecutions for Northern Ireland.

1127 Summary proceedings: venue

(1) Summary proceedings for any offence under the Companies Acts may be taken—

(a) against a body corporate, at any place at which the body has a place of business, and

(b) against any other person, at any place at which he is for the time being.

(2) This is without prejudice to any jurisdiction exercisable apart from this section.

1128 Summary proceedings: time limit for proceedings

(1) An information relating to an offence under the Companies Acts that is triable by a magistrates' court in England and Wales may be so tried if it is laid—

(a) at any time within three years after the commission of the offence, and

(b) within twelve months after the date on which evidence sufficient in the opinion of the Director of Public Prosecutions or the Secretary of State (as the case may be) to justify the proceedings comes to his knowledge.

(2) Summary proceedings in Scotland for an offence under the Companies Acts—

(a) must not be commenced after the expiration of three years from the commission of the offence;

(b) subject to that, may be commenced at any time—

(i) within twelve months after the date on which evidence sufficient in the Lord Advocate's opinion to justify the proceedings came to his knowledge, or

(ii) where such evidence was reported to him by the Secretary of State, within twelve months after the date on which it came to the knowledge of the latter.

Section 136(3) of the Criminal Procedure (Scotland) Act 1995 (c.46) (date when proceedings deemed to be commenced) applies for the purposes of this subsection as for the purposes of that section.

(3) A magistrates' court in Northern Ireland has jurisdiction to hear and determine a complaint charging the commission of a summary offence under the Companies Acts provided that the complaint is made—

(a) within three years from the time when the offence was committed, and

(b) within twelve months from the date on which evidence sufficient in the opinion of the Director of Public Prosecutions for Northern Ireland or the Secretary of State (as the case may be) to justify the proceedings comes to his knowledge.

(4) For the purposes of this section a certificate of the Director of Public Prosecutions, the Lord Advocate, the Director of Public Prosecutions for Northern Ireland or the Secretary of State (as the case may be) as to the date on which such evidence as is referred to above came to his notice is conclusive evidence.

1129 Legal professional privilege

In proceedings against a person for an offence under the Companies Acts, nothing in those Acts is to be taken to require any person to disclose any information that he is entitled to refuse to disclose on grounds of legal professional privilege (in Scotland, confidentiality of communications).

1130 Proceedings against unincorporated bodies

(1) Proceedings for an offence under the Companies Acts alleged to have been committed by an unincorporated body must be brought in the name of the body (and not in that of any of its members).

(2) For the purposes of such proceedings—

(a) any rules of court relating to the service of documents have effect as if the body were a body corporate, and

(b) the following provisions apply as they apply in relation to a body corporate—

(i) in England and Wales, section 33 of the Criminal Justice Act 1925 (c.86) and Schedule 3 to the Magistrates' Courts Act 1980 (c.43),

(ii) in Scotland, sections 70 and 143 of the Criminal Procedure (Scotland) Act 1995 (c.46),

(iii) in Northern Ireland, section 18 of the Criminal Justice Act (Northern Ireland) 1945 (c.15 (NI)) and Article 166 of and Schedule 4 to the Magistrates' Courts (Northern Ireland) Order 1981 (SI 1981/1675 (NI 26)).

(3) A fine imposed on an unincorporated body on its conviction of an offence under the Companies Acts must be paid out of the funds of the body.

1131 Imprisonment on summary conviction in England and Wales: transitory provision

(1) This section applies to any provision of the Companies Acts that provides that a person guilty of an offence is liable on summary conviction in England and Wales to imprisonment for a term not exceeding twelve months.

(2) In relation to an offence committed before the commencement of section 154(1) of the Criminal Justice Act 2003 (c.44), for "twelve months" substitute "six months".

1132 Production and inspection of documents where offence suspected

(1) An application under this section may be made—

(a) in England and Wales, to a judge of the High Court by the Director of Public Prosecutions, the Secretary of State or a chief officer of police;

(b) in Scotland, to one of the Lords Commissioners of Justiciary by the Lord Advocate;

(c) in Northern Ireland, to the High Court by the Director of Public Prosecutions for Northern Ireland, the Department of Enterprise, Trade and Investment or a chief superintendent of the Police Service of Northern Ireland.

(2) If on an application under this section there is shown to be reasonable cause to believe—

(a) that any person has, while a member of an LLP, committed an offence in connection with the management of the LLP's affairs, and

(b) that evidence of the commission of the offence is to be found in any documents in the possession or control of the LLP, an order under this section may be made.

(3) The order may—

(a) authorise any person named in it to inspect the documents in question, or any of them, for the purpose of investigating and obtaining evidence of the offence, or

(b) require such member of the LLP as may be named in the order, to produce the documents (or any of them) to a person named in the order at a place so named.

(4) This section applies also in relation to documents in the possession or control of a person carrying on the business of banking, so far as they relate to the LLP's affairs, as it applies to documents in the possession or control of the LLP, except that no such order as is referred to in subsection (3)(b) may be made by virtue of this subsection."

The decision under this section of a judge of the High Court, any of the Lords Commissioners of Justiciary or the High Court is not appealable.

In this section "document" includes information recorded in any form.

NOTES

Words in square brackets inserted by the Limited Liability Partnerships (Application of Companies Act 2006) Regulations 2009, SI 2009/1804, reg 85, Sch 3, Pt 2, para 15(4), as from 1 October 2009.

PART 17 LLPS: SUPPLEMENTARY AND INTERPRETATION

[10.279]

51 Courts and legal proceedings

Section 1157 applies to LLPs [for the purposes of these Regulations], modified so that it reads as follows—

"1157 Power of court to grant relief in certain cases

(1) If in proceedings for negligence, default, breach of duty or breach of trust against—

(a) a member of an LLP, or
(b) a person employed by an LLP as auditor,

it appears to the court hearing the case that the member or person is or may be liable but that he acted honestly and reasonably, and that having regard to all the circumstances of the case (including those connected with his appointment) he ought fairly to be excused, the court may relieve him, either wholly or in part, from his liability on such terms as it thinks fit.

(2) If any such member or person has reason to apprehend that a claim will or might be made against him in respect of negligence, default, breach of duty or breach of trust—

(a) he may apply to the court for relief, and
(b) the court has the same power to relieve him as it would have had if it had been a court before which proceedings against him for negligence, default, breach of duty or breach of trust had been brought.

(3) Where a case to which subsection (1) applies is being tried by a judge with a jury, the judge, after hearing the evidence, may, if he is satisfied that the defendant (in Scotland, the defender) ought in pursuance of that subsection to be relieved either in whole or in part from the liability sought to be enforced against him, withdraw the case from the jury and forthwith direct judgment to be entered for the defendant (in Scotland, grant decree of absolvitor) on such terms as to costs (in Scotland, expenses) or otherwise as the judge may think proper."

NOTES

Words in square brackets inserted by the Limited Liability Partnerships (Application of Companies Act 2006) Regulations 2009, SI 2009/1804, reg 85, Sch 3, Pt 2, para 15(4), as from 1 October 2009.

[10.280]

52 Meaning of "undertaking" and related expressions

Sections 1161 and 1162 and Schedule 7 apply to LLPs, modified so that they read as follows—

"1161 Meaning of "undertaking" and related expressions

(1) In this Act "undertaking" means—

(a) a body corporate or partnership, or
(b) an unincorporated association carrying on a trade or business, with or without a view to profit.

(2) In this Act references to shares—

(a) in relation to an undertaking with capital but no share capital, are to rights to share in the capital of the undertaking; and
(b) in relation to an undertaking without capital, are to interests—
    (i) conferring any right to share in the profits or liability to contribute to the losses of the undertaking, or
    (ii) giving rise to an obligation to contribute to the debts or expenses of the undertaking in the event of a winding up.

(3) Other expressions appropriate to companies shall be construed, in relation to an undertaking which is not a company, as references to the corresponding persons, officers, documents or organs, as the case may be, appropriate to undertakings of that description.

This is subject to provision in any specific context providing for the translation of such expressions.

(4) References in this Act to "fellow subsidiary undertakings" are to undertakings which are subsidiary undertakings of the same parent undertaking but are not parent undertakings or subsidiary undertakings of each other.

(5) In this Act "group undertaking", in relation to an undertaking, means an undertaking which is—

(a) a parent undertaking or subsidiary undertaking of that undertaking, or
(b) a subsidiary undertaking of any parent undertaking of that undertaking.

1162 Parent and subsidiary undertakings

(1) This section (together with Schedule 7) defines "parent undertaking" and "subsidiary undertaking" for the purposes of this Act.

(2) An undertaking is a parent undertaking in relation to another undertaking, a subsidiary undertaking, if—

(a) it holds a majority of the voting rights in the undertaking, or
(b) it is a member of the undertaking and has the right to appoint or remove a majority of its board of directors, or
(c) it has the right to exercise a dominant influence over the undertaking—
    (i) by virtue of provisions contained in the undertaking's articles or in an LLP Agreement, or
    (ii) by virtue of a control contract, or
(d) it is a member of the undertaking and controls alone, pursuant to an agreement with other shareholders or members, a majority of the voting rights in the undertaking.

(3) For the purposes of subsection (2) an undertaking shall be treated as a member of another undertaking—

(a) if any of its subsidiary undertakings is a member of that undertaking, or
(b) if any shares in that other undertaking are held by a person acting on behalf of the undertaking or any of its subsidiary undertakings.

(4) An undertaking is also a parent undertaking in relation to another undertaking, a subsidiary undertaking, if—

(a) it has the power to exercise, or actually exercises, dominant influence or control over it, or
(b) it and the subsidiary undertaking are managed on a unified basis.

(5) A parent undertaking shall be treated as the parent undertaking of undertakings in relation to which any of its subsidiary undertakings are, or are to be treated as, parent undertakings; and references to its subsidiary undertakings shall be construed accordingly.

(6) Schedule 7 contains provisions explaining expressions used in this section and otherwise supplementing this section.

(7) In this section and that Schedule references to shares, in relation to an undertaking, are to allotted shares."

"SCHEDULE 7
PARENT AND SUBSIDIARY UNDERTAKINGS: SUPPLEMENTARY PROVISIONS

Introduction

1.

The provisions of this Schedule explain expressions used in section 1162 (parent and subsidiary undertakings) and otherwise supplement that section.

Voting rights in an undertaking

2.

(1) In section 1162(2)(a) and (d) the references to the voting rights in an undertaking are to the rights conferred on shareholders in respect of their shares or, in the case of an undertaking not having a share capital, on members, to vote at general meetings of the undertaking on all, or substantially all, matters.

(2) In relation to an undertaking which does not have general meetings at which matters are decided by the exercise of voting rights the references to holding a majority of the voting rights in the undertaking are to be construed as references to having the right under the constitution of the undertaking to direct the overall policy of the undertaking or to alter the terms of its constitution.

Right to appoint or remove a majority of members or directors

3.

(1) In section 1162(2)(b) the reference to the right to appoint or remove a majority of the board of directors is to the right to appoint or remove directors holding a majority of the voting rights at meetings of the board on all, or substantially all, matters.

(2) An undertaking shall be treated as having the right to appoint to a directorship if—

- (a) a person's appointment to it follows necessarily from his appointment as director of the undertaking, or
- (b) the directorship is held by the undertaking itself.

(3) A right to appoint or remove which is exercisable only with the consent or concurrence of another person shall be left out of account unless no other person has a right to appoint or, as the case may be, remove in relation to that directorship.

(4) (4) In relation to an undertaking the business of which is managed by the members, references to the board of directors or directors are to be construed as references to members.

Right to exercise dominant influence

4.

(1) For the purposes of section 1162(2)(c) an undertaking shall not be regarded as having the right to exercise a dominant influence over another undertaking unless it has a right to give directions with respect to the operating and financial policies of that other undertaking which its directors are obliged to comply with whether or not they are for the benefit of that other undertaking.

(2) A "control contract" means a contract in writing conferring such a right which—

- (a) is of a kind authorised by the articles of the undertaking or by the LLP agreement of the LLP in relation to which the right is exercisable, and
- (b) is permitted by the law under which that undertaking is established.

(3) In relation to an undertaking the business of which is managed by the members, references to directors are to be construed as references to members.

(4) This paragraph shall not be read as affecting the construction of section 1162(4)(a).

Rights exercisable only in certain circumstances or temporarily incapable of exercise

5.

(1) Rights which are exercisable only in certain circumstances shall be taken into account only—

- (a) when the circumstances have arisen, and for so long as they continue to obtain, or
- (b) when the circumstances are within the control of the person having the rights.

(2) Rights which are normally exercisable but are temporarily incapable of exercise shall continue to be taken into account.

Rights held by one person on behalf of another

6.

Rights held by a person in a fiduciary capacity shall be treated as not held by him.

7.

(1) Rights held by a person as nominee for another shall be treated as held by the other.

(2) Rights shall be regarded as held as nominee for another if they are exercisable only on his instructions or with his consent or concurrence.

Rights attached to shares held by way of security

8.

Rights attached to shares held by way of security shall be treated as held by the person providing the security—

(a) where apart from the right to exercise them for the purpose of preserving the value of the security, or of realising it, the rights are exercisable only in accordance with his instructions, and

(b) where the shares are held in connection with the granting of loans as part of normal business activities and apart from the right to exercise them for the purpose of preserving the value of the security, or of realising it, the rights are exercisable only in his interests.

Rights attributed to parent undertaking

9.

(1) Rights shall be treated as held by a parent undertaking if they are held by any of its subsidiary undertakings.

(2) Nothing in paragraph 7 or 8 shall be construed as requiring rights held by a parent undertaking to be treated as held by any of its subsidiary undertakings.

(3) For the purposes of paragraph 8 rights shall be treated as being exercisable in accordance with the instructions or in the interests of an undertaking if they are exercisable in accordance with the instructions of or, as the case may be, in the interests of any group undertaking.

Disregard of certain rights

10.

The voting rights in an undertaking shall be reduced by any rights held by the undertaking itself.

Supplementary

11.

References in any provision of paragraphs 6 to 10 to rights held by a person include rights falling to be treated as held by him by virtue of any other provision of those paragraphs but not rights which by virtue of any such provision are to be treated as not held by him."

[10.281]

53 Meaning of "dormant"

Section 1169 applies to LLPs, modified so that it reads as follows—

"1169 Dormant LLPs

(1) For the purposes of this Act an LLP is "dormant" during any period in which it has no significant accounting transaction.

(2) A "significant accounting transaction" means a transaction that is required by section 386 to be entered in the LLP's accounting records.

(3) In determining whether or when an LLP is dormant, there shall be disregarded any transaction consisting of the payment of—

(a) a fee to the registrar on a change of the LLP's name,

(b) a penalty under section 453 (penalty for failure to file accounts), or

(c) a fee to the registrar for the registration of an annual return."

[10.282]

54 Requirements of this Act

Section 1172 applies to LLPs [for the purposes of these Regulations], modified so that it reads as follows—

"1172 References to requirements of this Act

References in the provisions of this Act applied to LLPs to the requirements of this Act include the requirements of regulations and orders made under it."

NOTES

Words in square brackets inserted by the Limited Liability Partnerships (Application of Companies Act 2006) Regulations 2009, SI 2009/1804, reg 85, Sch 3, Pt 2, para 15(4), as from 1 October 2009.

[10.283]

55 Minor definitions

Section 1173 applies to LLPs [for the purposes of these Regulations], modified so that it reads as follows—

"1173 Minor definitions: general

(1) In this Act—

["the Audit Regulation" means Regulation 537/2014 of the European Parliament and of the Council on specific requirements regarding statutory audit of public interest entities;]

"body corporate" includes a body incorporated outside the United Kingdom, but does not include—

(a) a corporation sole, or

(b) a partnership that, whether or not a legal person, is not regarded as a body corporate under the law by which it is governed;

["the competent authority" means the Financial Reporting Council Limited]

. . .

["EU regulated market" has the meaning given in Article 2.1.13B of Regulation (EU) No 600/2014 of the European Parliament and of the Council of 15 May 2014 and amending Regulation (EU) No 648/2012;]

["firm" means any entity, whether or not a legal person, that is not an individual and includes a body corporate, a corporation sole and a partnership or other unincorporated association;]

"parent LLP" means an LLP that is a parent undertaking (see section 1162 and Schedule 7);

"regulated activity" has the meaning given by section 22 of the Financial Services and Markets Act 2000 (c.8);

["regulated market" has the meaning given in Article 2.1.13 of Regulation (EU) No 600/2014 of the European Parliament and of the Council of 15 May 2014 and amending Regulation (EU) No 648/2012;]

["transferable securities" has the meaning given by Article 2.1.24 of Regulation (EU) No 600/2014 of the European Parliament and of the Council of 15 May 2014 and amending Regulation (EU) No 648/2012;]

["UK regulated market" has the meaning given in Article 2.1.13A of Regulation (EU) No 600/2014 of the European Parliament and of the Council of 15 May 2014 and amending Regulation (EU) No 648/2012].

(2) . . .

NOTES

First words in square brackets inserted by the Limited Liability Partnerships (Application of Companies Act 2006) Regulations 2009, SI 2009/1804, reg 85, Sch 3, Pt 2, para 15(4), as from 1 October 2009.

Section 1173(1) as set out above is amended as follows:

Definitions "the Audit Regulation" and "the competent authority" inserted by the Statutory Auditors Regulations 2017, SI 2017/1164, reg 5, Sch 3, paras 1, 20, as from 1 January 2018 (as to the application of the 2017 Regulations, see **[4.671]** et seq).

Definition "EEA undertaking" (omitted) revoked by the Accounts and Reports (Amendment) (EU Exit) Regulations 2019, SI 2019/145, reg 6, Sch 3, paras 11, 21(a)(i), in relation to financial years beginning on or after IP completion day (as defined in the European Union (Withdrawal Agreement) Act 2020, s 39) (for transitional provisions see reg 7 of the 2019 Regulations at **[12.79]**).

Definitions "EU regulated market" and "UK regulated market" inserted by SI 2019/145, reg 6, Sch 3, paras 11, 21(a)(iii), (iv), in relation to financial years beginning on or after IP completion day (as defined in the European Union (Withdrawal Agreement) Act 2020, s 39) (for transitional provisions see reg 7 of the 2019 Regulations at **[12.79]**).

Definition "firm" inserted by SI 2009/1804, reg 85, Sch 3, Pt 2, para 15(5), as from 1 October 2009.

Definition "regulated market" substituted by SI 2019/145, reg 6, Sch 3, paras 11, 21(a)(ii), in relation to financial years beginning on or after IP completion day (as defined in the European Union (Withdrawal Agreement) Act 2020, s 39) (for transitional provisions see reg 7 of the 2019 Regulations at **[12.79]**).

Definition "transferable securities" originally inserted by the Limited Liability Partnerships, Partnerships and Groups (Accounts and Audit) Regulations 2016, SI 2016/575, regs 3, 25, as from 17 May 2016. Subsequently substituted by the Companies, Limited Liability Partnerships and Partnerships (Amendment etc) (EU Exit) Regulations 2019, SI 2019/348, reg 8, Sch 3, paras 18, 19(a), as from IP completion day (as defined in the European Union (Withdrawal Agreement) Act 2020, s 39).

Section 1173(2) as set out above was revoked by SI 2019/145, reg 6, Sch 3, paras 11, 21(b), in relation to financial years beginning on or after IP completion day (as defined in the European Union (Withdrawal Agreement) Act 2020, s 39) (for transitional provisions see reg 7 of the 2019 Regulations at **[12.79]**). It was also subsequently revoked by SI 2019/348, reg 8, Sch 3, paras 18, 19(b), as from IP completion day (as defined in the European Union (Withdrawal Agreement) Act 2020, s 39).

[10.284]

56 Regulations

Sections 1288 to 1290 apply to LLPs [for the purposes of these Regulations], modified so that they read as follows—

"1288 Regulations: statutory instrument

Except as otherwise provided, regulations under this Act shall be made by statutory instrument.

1289 Regulations: negative resolution procedure

Where regulations under this Act are subject to "negative resolution procedure" the statutory instrument containing the regulations or order shall be subject to annulment in pursuance of a resolution of either House of Parliament.

1290 Regulations: affirmative resolution procedure

Where regulations under this Act are subject to "affirmative resolution procedure" the regulations must not be made unless a draft of the statutory instrument containing them has been laid before Parliament and approved by a resolution of each House of Parliament."

NOTES

Words in square brackets inserted by the Limited Liability Partnerships (Application of Companies Act 2006) Regulations 2009, SI 2009/1804, reg 85, Sch 3, Pt 2, para 15(4), as from 1 October 2009.

[10.285]

57

Section 1292 applies to LLPs [for the purposes of these Regulations], modified so that it reads as follows—

"1292 Regulations and orders: supplementary

(1) Regulations under this Act may—

(a) make different provision for different cases or circumstances,

(b) include supplementary, incidental and consequential provision, and

(c) make transitional provision and savings.

(2) Any provision that may be made by regulations under this Act subject to negative resolution procedure may be made by regulations subject to affirmative resolution procedure."

NOTES

Words in square brackets inserted by the Limited Liability Partnerships (Application of Companies Act 2006) Regulations 2009, SI 2009/1804, reg 85, Sch 3, Pt 2, para 15(4), as from 1 October 2009.

PART 18 FINAL PROVISIONS

[10.286]

58 Revocation and transitional provisions

(1) Subject to paragraphs (3) to (11), the following provisions of the Limited Liability Partnerships Regulations 2001 are revoked—

(a) regulation 3 and Schedule 1,

(b) in Schedule 2, the entries relating to sections 384, 385, 387, 388, 388A, 389A, 390, 390A, 390B, 391, 391A, 392, 392A, 394, 394A and 742, and

(c) entries 1, 2, 3 and 6 in Part I of Schedule 6.

(2) Subject to paragraphs (3) to (11), the following provisions of the Limited Liability Partnerships Regulations (Northern Ireland) 2004 are revoked—

(a) regulation 3 and Schedule 1,

(b) in Schedule 2, the entries relating to Articles 10, 392, 393, 395, 396, 396A, 397A, 398, 398A, 398B, 399, 399A, 400, 400A, 401A and 401B, and

(c) entries 1, 2, 3 and 6 in Part I of Schedule 5.

(3) The provisions specified in paragraphs (1)(a) and (c) and (2)(a) and (c), and the entries specified in paragraphs (1)(b) and (2)(b) relating to section 742 of the 1985 Act or Article 10 of the 1986 Order, continue to apply to accounts for, and otherwise as regards, financial years beginning before 1st October 2008.

(4) The entries specified in paragraphs (1)(b) and (2)(b) relating to sections 384, 385, 387, 388 and 388A of the 1985 Act or Articles 392, 393, 395, 396 and 396A of the 1986 Order continue to apply in relation to appointments of auditors for financial years beginning before 1st October 2008, and section 388(2) of the 1985 Act or Article 396(2) of the 1986 Order as applied to LLPs continues to apply where the vacancy occurs before that date.

(5) The entries specified in paragraphs (1)(b) and (2)(b) relating to section 389A of the 1985 Act or Article 397A of the 1986 Order continue to apply as regards financial years beginning before 1st October 2008.

(6) The entries specified in paragraphs (1)(b) and (2)(b) relating to section 390 of the 1985 Act or Article 398 of the 1986 Order continue to apply to auditors appointed before 1st October 2008.

(7) The entries specified in paragraphs (1)(b) and (2)(b) relating to sections 390A and 390B of the 1985 Act or Articles 398A and 398B of the 1986 Order continue to apply to auditors appointed for financial years beginning before 1st October 2008.

(8) The entries specified in paragraphs (1)(b) and (2)(b) relating to sections 391 and 391A of the 1985 Act or Articles 399 and 399A of the 1986 Order continue to apply as respects removal of auditors where notice is given to the auditor before 1st October 2008.

(9) The entries specified in paragraphs (1)(b) and (2)(b) relating to section 391A of the 1985 Act or Article 399A of the 1986 Order continue to apply as regards failure to re-appoint an auditor to appointments for financial years beginning before 1st October 2008.

(10) The entries specified in paragraphs (1)(b) and (2)(b) relating to sections 392 and 392A of the 1985 Act or Articles 400 and 400A of the 1986 Order continue to apply to resignations occurring before 1st October 2008.

(11) The entries specified in paragraphs (1)(b) and (2)(b) relating to sections 394 and 394A of the 1985 Act or Articles 401A and 401B of the 1986 Order continue to apply where the auditor ceases to hold office before 1st October 2008.

[10.287]

[59 Review

(1) The Secretary of State must from time to time—

[(a) carry out a review, respectively, of the regulatory provision contained in these Regulations to which amendments have been made by—

(i) Part 2 of the Limited Liability Partnerships, Partnerships and Groups (Accounts and Audit) Regulations 2016 ("the 2016 Regulations"),

(ii) Schedule 3 to the Statutory Auditors Regulations 2017, and

(iii) Part 3 of the Companies (Directors' Report) and Limited Liability Partnerships (Energy and Carbon Report) Regulations 2018 ("the 2018 Regulations"),]

(b) set out the conclusions of [each review] in a [separate] report, and

(c) publish the report.

[(1A) . . .]

(2) [Section 30(4) of the Small Business, Enterprise and Employment Act 2015 requires that a report published under this regulation] must, in particular—

(a) set out the objectives intended to be achieved by those provisions,

(b) assess the extent to which those objectives are achieved,

(c) assess whether those objectives remain appropriate, and

(d) if those objectives remain appropriate, assess the extent to which they could be achieved in another way which involves less onerous regulatory provision.

[(3) The first report under—

(a) paragraph (1)(a)(i) and (ii) must be published before the end of the period of 5 years beginning with the date on which the 2016 Regulations come into force;

(b) paragraph (1)(a)(iii) must be published before the end of the period of 5 years beginning with the date on which the 2018 Regulations come into force.]

(4) Subsequent reports under this regulation must be published at intervals not exceeding 5 years.

(5) In this regulation, "regulatory provision" has the [same meaning as in sections 28 to 32] of the Small Business, Enterprise and Employment Act 2015 [(see section 32 of that Act)].]

NOTES

Added by the Limited Liability Partnerships, Partnerships and Groups (Accounts and Audit) Regulations 2016, SI 2016/575, regs 3, 26, as from 17 May 2016.

Sub-para (1)(a) substituted, para (1A) originally inserted, words in square brackets in para (2) substituted, words in first pair of square brackets in para (5) substituted, and words in second pair of square brackets in that paragraph inserted, by the Statutory Auditors Regulations 2017, SI 2017/1164, reg 5, Sch 3, paras 1, 21, as from 1 January 2018 (as to the application of the 2017 Regulations, see **[4.671]** et seq).

Sub-para (1)(a) was further substituted by the Companies (Directors' Report) and Limited Liability Partnerships (Energy and Carbon Report) Regulations 2018, SI 2018/1155, regs 8, 25(1), (2), as from 1 April 2019.

The words in the first pair of square brackets in sub-para (1)(b) were substituted, and the word in the second pair of square brackets was inserted, by SI 2018/1155, regs 8, 25(1), (3), as from 1 April 2019.

Para (1A) was revoked by the Accounts and Reports (Amendment) (EU Exit) Regulations 2019, SI 2019/145, reg 6, Sch 3, paras 11, 22, as from IP completion day (as defined in the European Union (Withdrawal Agreement) Act 2020, s 39), and by the Statutory Auditors and Third Country Auditors (Amendment) (EU Exit) Regulations 2019, SI 2019/177, regs 49, 55, as from IP completion day (as defined in the European Union (Withdrawal Agreement) Act 2020, s 39) (for transitional provisions, see Sch 4 to the 2019 Regulations at **[12.88]**).

Para (3) was substituted by SI 2018/1155, regs 8, 25(1), (4), as from 1 April 2019.

SMALL LIMITED LIABILITY PARTNERSHIPS (ACCOUNTS) REGULATIONS 2008

(SI 2008/1912)

NOTES

Made: 17 July 2008.

Authority: Limited Liability Partnerships Act 2000, ss 15, 17.

Commencement: 1 October 2008.

These Regulations are reproduced as amended by: the Limited Liability Partnerships, Partnerships and Groups (Accounts and Audit) Regulations 2016, SI 2016/575; the International Accounting Standards and European Public Limited-Liability Company (Amendment etc) (EU Exit) Regulations 2019, SI 2019/685.

ARRANGEMENT OF REGULATIONS

PART 1 INTRODUCTION

[10.288]

1 Citation and interpretation

(1) These Regulations may be cited as the Small Limited Liability Partnerships (Accounts) Regulations 2008.

(2) In these Regulations—

"the 2006 Act" means the Companies Act 2006;

["LLP" means a limited liability partnership registered under the Limited Liability Partnerships Act 2000;]

"the Small Companies Accounts Regulations" means the Small Companies and Groups (Accounts and Directors' Report) Regulations 2008.

(3) Any reference in these Regulations to a numbered Part or section of the 2006 Act is a reference to that Part or section as applied to LLPs by the Limited Liability Partnerships (Accounts and Audit) (Application of Companies Act 2006) Regulations 2008.

NOTES

Para (2): definition "LLP" substituted by the Limited Liability Partnerships, Partnerships and Groups (Accounts and Audit) Regulations 2016, SI 2016/575, regs 27, 28, as from 17 May 2016, in relation to (a) financial years beginning on or after 1 January 2016; and (b) a financial year of an LLP beginning on or after 1 January 2015, but before 1 January 2016, if (i) the members of the LLP so decide, and (ii) a copy of the LLP's accounts for that financial year has not been delivered to the registrar in accordance with ss 444, 445 or 446 of the Companies Act 2006 as applied to LLPs by the Limited Liability Partnerships (Accounts and Audit) (Application of Companies Act 2006) Regulations before 17 May 2016 (see further the note at **[10.226]**).

General note as to interpretation: as to the meaning of "the registrar" and "the register", and as to the construction of references to registration in a particular part of the United Kingdom, in any enactment relating to LLPs, see the Limited Liability Partnerships (Application of Companies Act 2006) Regulations 2009, SI 2009/1804, Sch 3, Pt 2, para 12 at **[10.419]**.

[10.289]

2 Commencement and application

(1) These Regulations come into force on 1st October 2008.

(2) They apply in relation to financial years beginning on or after 1st October 2008.

(3) They apply to LLPs which are subject to the small LLPs regime under Part 15 of the 2006 Act (see section 381 of that Act) provisions of the Small Companies Accounts Regulations, with modifications.

PART 2 FORM AND CONTENT OF INDIVIDUAL ACCOUNTS

[10.290]

3 Non-IAS individual accounts

(1) Regulation 3 of the Small Companies Accounts Regulations applies to LLPs, modified so that it reads as follows—

> **"3 Non-IAS individual accounts**
>
> (1) [Subject to the following provisions of this regulation and regulation 5A,] non-IAS individual accounts under section 396 of the 2006 Act (non-IAS individual accounts) must comply with the provisions of Schedule 1 to the Small Limited Liability Partnerships (Accounts) Regulations 2008 as to the form and content of the balance sheet and profit and loss account, and additional information to be provided by way of notes to the accounts.
>
> [(1A) Sections C (alternative accounting rules) and D (fair value accounting) in Part 2 of Schedule 1 to these Regulations do not apply to an LLP which qualifies as a micro-entity in relation to a financial year (see sections 384A and 384B of the 2006 Act) and whose accounts for that year are prepared in accordance with the exemption permitted by—
>
> (a) regulation 5A, or
>
> (b) paragraph 1(1A) of Section A in Part 1 of Schedule 1 to these Regulations.]
>
> (2) . . .
>
> (3) Accounts are treated as having complied with any provision of Schedule 1 to the Small Limited Liability Partnerships (Accounts) Regulations 2008 if they comply instead with the corresponding provision of Schedule 1 to the Large and Medium-sized Limited Liability Partnerships (Accounts) Regulations 2008.".

(2) The provisions of Schedule 1 to the Small Companies Accounts Regulations apply to LLPs, modified so that they are the provisions set out in Schedule 1 to these Regulations.

NOTES

Para (1): in reg 3 as set out above, the words in square brackets in para (1) were inserted, para (1A) was inserted and para (2) was revoked, by the Limited Liability Partnerships, Partnerships and Groups (Accounts and Audit) Regulations 2016, SI 2016/575, regs 27, 29, as from 17 May 2016, in relation to (a) financial years beginning on or after 1 January 2016; and (b) a financial year of an LLP beginning on or after 1 January 2015, but before 1 January 2016, if (i) the members of the LLP so decide, and (ii) a copy of the LLP's accounts for that financial year has not been delivered to the registrar in accordance with ss 444, 445 or 446 of the Companies Act 2006 as applied to LLPs by the Limited Liability Partnerships (Accounts and Audit) (Application of Companies Act 2006) Regulations before 17 May 2016 (see further the note at **[10.226]**).

4, 5 *(Revoked by the Limited Liability Partnerships, Partnerships and Groups (Accounts and Audit) Regulations 2016, SI 2016/575, regs 27, 30, 31, as from 17 May 2016, in relation to (a) financial years beginning on or after 1 January 2016; and (b) a financial year of an LLP beginning on or after 1 January 2015, but before 1 January 2016, if (i) the members of the LLP so decide, and (ii) a copy of the LLP's accounts for that financial year has not been delivered to the registrar in accordance with ss 444, 445 or 446 of the Companies Act 2006 as applied to LLPs by the Limited Liability Partnerships (Accounts and Audit) (Application of Companies Act 2006) Regulations before 17 May 2016 (see further the note at***[10.226]***).)*

[10.291]

[5A Non-IAS individual accounts: micro-entities—notes to the accounts

Regulation 5A of the Small Companies Accounts Regulations applies to LLPs, modified so that it reads as follows—

> **"5A Non-IAS individual accounts: micro-entities—notes to the accounts**
> Nothing in Schedule 1 to these Regulations requires the non-IAS individual accounts of an LLP for a financial year in which the LLP qualifies as a micro-entity (see sections 384A and 384B of the 2006 Act) to contain any information by way of notes to the accounts, except that the LLP is required to disclose by way of notes to the accounts the information required by paragraph 55 in Part 3 of Schedule 1."]

NOTES

Inserted by the Limited Liability Partnerships, Partnerships and Groups (Accounts and Audit) Regulations 2016, SI 2016/575, regs 27, 32, as from 17 May 2016, in relation to (a) financial years beginning on or after 1 January 2016; and (b) a financial year of an LLP beginning on or after 1 January 2015, but before 1 January 2016, if (i) the members of the LLP so decide, and (ii) a copy of the LLP's accounts for that financial year has not been delivered to the registrar in accordance with ss 444, 445 or 446 of the Companies Act 2006 as applied to LLPs by the Limited Liability Partnerships (Accounts and Audit) (Application of Companies Act 2006) Regulations before 17 May 2016 (see further the note at **[10.226]**).

PART 3 FORM AND CONTENT OF GROUP ACCOUNTS

[10.292]

6 Non-IAS group accounts

(1) Regulation 8 of the Small Companies Accounts Regulations applies to LLPs, modified so that it reads as follows—

> **"8 Non-IAS group accounts**
> (1) Where the members of a parent LLP which—
> (a) is subject to the small LLPs regime, and
> (b) has prepared non-IAS individual accounts in accordance with regulation 3,
>
> prepare non-IAS group accounts under section 398 of the 2006 Act (option to prepare group accounts), those accounts must comply with the provisions of . . . Schedule 4 to the Small Limited Liability Partnerships (Accounts) Regulations 2008 as to the form and content of the consolidated balance sheet and consolidated profit and loss account, and additional information to be provided by way of notes to the accounts.
> (2) Accounts are treated as having complied with any provision of . . . Schedule 4 to the Small Limited Liability Partnerships (Accounts) Regulations 2008 if they comply instead with the corresponding provision of Schedule 3 to the Large and Medium-sized Limited Liability Partnerships (Accounts) Regulations 2008.".

(2) The provisions of Part 1 of Schedule 6 to the Small Companies Accounts Regulations apply to LLPs, modified so that they are the provisions set out in Part 1 of Schedule 4 to these Regulations.

NOTES

Para (1): in reg 8 as set out above, the words omitted were revoked by the Limited Liability Partnerships, Partnerships and Groups (Accounts and Audit) Regulations 2016, SI 2016/575, regs 27, 33, as from 17 May 2016, in relation to (a) financial years beginning on or after 1 January 2016; and (b) a financial year of an LLP beginning on or after 1 January 2015, but before 1 January 2016, if (i) the members of the LLP so decide, and (ii) a copy of the LLP's accounts for that financial year has not been delivered to the registrar in accordance with ss 444, 445 or 446 of the Companies Act 2006 as applied to LLPs by the Limited Liability Partnerships (Accounts and Audit) (Application of Companies Act 2006) Regulations before 17 May 2016 (see further the note at **[10.226]**).

[10.293]

7 Information about related undertakings (Non-IAS or IAS group accounts)

(1) Regulation 10 of the Small Companies Accounts Regulations applies to LLPs, modified so that it reads as follows—

> **"10 Information about related undertakings (Non-IAS or IAS group accounts)**
> (1) Non-IAS or IAS group accounts must comply with the provisions of Part 2 of Schedule 4 to the Small Limited Liability Partnerships (Accounts) Regulations 2008 as to information about related undertakings to be given in notes to the LLP's accounts.
> (2) Information otherwise required to be given by Part 2 of Schedule 4 to the Small Limited Liability Partnerships (Accounts) Regulations 2008 need not be disclosed with respect to an undertaking that—
> (a) is established under the law of a country outside the United Kingdom, or
> (b) carries on business outside the United Kingdom,
>
> if the conditions specified in section 409(4) of the 2006 Act are met (see section 409(5) of the 2006 Act for disclosure required where advantage taken of this exemption).".

(2) The provisions of Part 2 of Schedule 6 to the Small Companies Accounts Regulations apply to LLPs, modified so that they are the provisions set out in Part 2 of Schedule 4 to these Regulations.

PART 4 INTERPRETATION

[10.294]

8 General interpretation

(1) Regulation 13 of the Small Companies Accounts Regulations applies to LLPs, modified so that it reads as follows—

> **"13 General interpretation**
> Schedule 5 to the Small Limited Liability Partnerships (Accounts) Regulations 2008 contains general definitions for the purposes of these Regulations.".

(2) The provisions of Schedule 8 to the Small Companies Accounts Regulations apply to LLPs, modified so that they are the provisions set out in Schedule 5 to these Regulations.

[PART 5 REVIEW

[10.295]

9 Review

(1) The Secretary of State must from time to time—

(a) carry out a review of the provisions of these Regulations to which amendments have been made by Part 3 of the Limited Liability Partnerships, Partnerships and Groups (Accounts and Audit) Regulations 2016 ("the 2016 Regulations"),

(b) set out the conclusions of the review in a report, and

(c) publish the report.

(2) The report must, in particular—

(a) set out the objectives intended to be achieved by those provisions,

(b) assess the extent to which those objectives are achieved,

(c) assess whether those objectives remain appropriate, and

(d) if those objectives remain appropriate, assess the extent to which they could be achieved in another way which involves less onerous regulatory provision.

(3) The first report under this regulation must be published before the end of the period of 5 years beginning with the date on which the 2016 Regulations come into force.

(4) Subsequent reports under this regulation must be published at intervals not exceeding 5 years.

(5) In this regulation, "regulatory provision" has the meaning given by section 32(4) of the Small Business, Enterprise and Employment Act 2015.]

NOTES

Added, together with preceding Part heading, by the Limited Liability Partnerships, Partnerships and Groups (Accounts and Audit) Regulations 2016, SI 2016/575, regs 27, 46, as from 17 May 2016.

SCHEDULES

SCHEDULE 1
NON-IAS INDIVIDUAL ACCOUNTS

Regulation 3

PART 1 GENERAL RULES AND FORMATS

SECTION A GENERAL RULES

[10.296]

1. (1) Subject to the following provisions of this Schedule—

(a) every balance sheet of an LLP must show the items listed in either of the balance sheet formats in Section B of this Part, and

(b) every profit and loss account must show the items listed in either of the profit and loss account formats in Section B.

[(1A) But, subject to the following provisions of this Schedule, in relation to an LLP which qualifies as a micro-entity in relation to a financial year (see sections 384A and 384B of the 2006 Act)—

(a) the only items which must be shown on the LLP's balance sheet for that year are those listed in either of the balance sheet formats in Section C of this Part, and

(b) the only items which must be shown on the LLP's profit and loss account for that year are those listed in the profit and loss account format in Section C.]

(2) References in this Schedule to the items listed in any of the formats in Section B [and Section C] are to those items read together with any of the notes following the formats which apply to those items.

(3) [Subject to paragraph 1A,] the items must be shown in the order and under the headings and sub-headings given in the particular format used, but—

(a) the notes to the formats may permit alternative positions for any particular items, and

(b) the heading or sub-heading for any item does not have to be distinguished by any letter or number assigned to that item in the format used.

[1A. (1) Where appropriate to the circumstances of an LLP's business, the members of the LLP may, with reference to one of the formats in Section B, draw up an abridged balance sheet showing only those items in that format preceded by letters and roman numerals, provided that—

(a) in the case of format 1, note (3) of the notes to the formats is complied with,

(b) in the case of format 2, notes (3) and (8) of those notes are complied with,

(c) all of the members of the LLP have consented to the drawing up of the abridged balance sheet.

(2) Where appropriate to the circumstances of an LLP's business, the members of the LLP may, with reference to one of the formats in Section B, draw up an abridged profit and loss account, combining under one item called "Gross profit or loss"—

(a) items 1, 2, 3 and 6 in the case of format 1, and

(b) items 1 to 5 in the case of format 2,

provided that, in either case, all of the members of the LLP have consented to the drawing up of the abridged profit and loss account.

(3) Such consent as is referred to in sub-paragraphs (1) and (2) may only be given as regards the preparation of, as appropriate, the balance sheet or profit and loss account in respect of the preceding financial year.

1B. (1) The members of the LLP may adapt one of the balance sheet formats in Section B so to distinguish between current and non-current items in a different way, provided that—

(a) the information given is at least equivalent to that which would have been required by the use of such format had it not been thus adapted, and

(b) the presentation of those items is in accordance with generally accepted accounting principles or practice.

(2) The members of the LLP may, otherwise than pursuant to paragraph 1A(2), adapt one of the profit and loss account formats in Section B, provided that—

(a) the information given is at least equivalent to that which would have been required by the use of such format had it not been thus adapted, and

(b) the presentation is in accordance with generally accepted accounting principles or practice.

1C. So far as is practicable, the following provisions of this Section apply to the balance sheet or profit and loss account of an LLP notwithstanding any such abridgment or adaptation pursuant to paragraph 1A or 1B.]

2. (1) Where in accordance with [paragraph 1(1)] an LLP's balance sheet or profit and loss account for any financial year has been prepared by reference to one of the formats in Section B, the members of the LLP must use the same format in preparing non-IAS individual accounts for subsequent financial years, unless in their opinion there are special reasons for a change.

(2) Particulars of any such change must be given in a note to the accounts in which the new format is first used, and the reasons for the change must be explained.

[2A. Where in accordance with paragraph 1(1A) an LLP's balance sheet or profit and loss account for any financial year has been prepared by reference to one of the formats in Section C, the members of the LLP must use the same format in preparing non-IAS individual accounts for subsequent financial years, unless in their opinion there are special reasons for a change.]

3. (1) Any item required to be shown in an LLP's balance sheet or profit and loss account may be shown in greater detail than required by the particular format used.

(2) The balance sheet or profit and loss account may include an item representing or covering the amount of any asset or liability, income or expenditure not otherwise covered by any of the items listed in the format used, save that none of the following may be treated as assets in any balance sheet—

(a) preliminary expenses,

(b) expenses of, and commission on, any issue of debentures,

(c) costs of research.

4. (1) Where the special nature of the LLP's business requires it, the members of the LLP must adapt the arrangement, headings and sub-headings otherwise required in respect of items given an Arabic number in the balance sheet or profit and loss account format used.

(2) The members may combine items to which Arabic numbers are given in any of the formats set out in Section B if—

(a) their individual amounts are not material to assessing the state of affairs or profit or loss of the LLP for the financial year in question, or

(b) the combination facilitates that assessment.

(3) Where sub-paragraph (2)(b) applies, the individual amounts of any items which have been combined must be disclosed in a note to the accounts.

5. (1) Subject to sub-paragraph (2), the members must not include a heading or sub-heading corresponding to an item in the balance sheet or profit and loss account format used if there is no amount to be shown for that item for the financial year to which the balance sheet or profit and loss account relates.

(2) Where an amount can be shown for the item in question for the immediately preceding financial year that amount must be shown under the heading or sub-heading required by the format for that item.

6. Every profit and loss account [other than one prepared by reference to the format in Section C] must show the amount of an LLP's profit or loss . . . before taxation.

7. (1) For every item shown in the balance sheet or profit and loss account the corresponding amount for the immediately preceding financial year must also be shown.

(2) Where that corresponding amount is not comparable with the amount to be shown for the item in question in respect of the financial year to which the balance sheet or profit and loss account relates, the former amount may be adjusted, and particulars of the non-comparability and of any adjustment must be disclosed in a note to the accounts.

8. Amounts in respect of items representing assets or income may not be set off against amounts in respect of items representing liabilities or expenditure (as the case may be), or vice versa.

9. The members of the LLP must, in determining how amounts are presented within items in the profit and loss account and balance sheet, have regard to the substance of the reported transaction or arrangement, in accordance with generally accepted accounting principles or practice.

[9A. Where an asset or liability relates to more than one item in the balance sheet, the relationship of such asset or liability to the relevant items must be disclosed either under those items or in the notes to the accounts.]

SECTION B [THE REQUIRED FORMATS FOR THE ACCOUNTS OF LLPS OTHER THAN MICRO-ENTITIES]

Balance sheet formats

Format 1

A. Fixed assets

I. Intangible assets

1. Goodwill [(1)]
2. Other intangible assets [(2)]

II. Tangible assets
1. Land and buildings
2. Plant and machinery etc.

III. Investments
1. Shares in group undertakings and participating interests
2. Loans to group undertakings and undertakings in which the LLP has a participating interest
3. Other investments other than loans
4. Other investments

B. Current assets

I. Stocks
1. Stocks
2. Payments on account

II. Debtors [(3)]
1. Trade debtors
2. Amounts owed by group undertakings and undertakings in which the LLP has a participating interest
3. Other debtors

III. Investments
1. Shares in group undertakings
2. Other investments

IV. Cash at bank and in hand

C. Prepayments and accrued income [(4)]

D. Creditors: amounts falling due within one year
1. Bank loans and overdrafts
2. Trade creditors
3. Amounts owed to group undertakings and undertakings in which the LLP has a participating interest
4. Other creditors [(5)]

E. Net current assets (liabilities) [(6)]

F. Total assets less current liabilities

G. Creditors: amounts falling due after more than one year
1. Bank loans and overdrafts
2. Trade creditors
3. Amounts owed to group undertakings and undertakings in which the LLP has a participating interest
4. Other creditors [(5)]

H. Provisions for liabilities

I. Accruals and deferred income [(5)]

J. Loans and other debts due to members [(7)]

K. Members' other interests

I. Members' capital

II. Revaluation reserve

III. Other reserves

Balance sheet formats

Format 2

ASSETS

A. Fixed assets

I. Intangible assets
1. Goodwill [(1)]
2. Other intangible assets [(2)]

II. Tangible assets
1. Land and buildings
2. Plant and machinery etc.

III. Investments
1. Shares in group undertakings and participating interests
2. Loans to group undertakings and undertakings in which the LLP has a participating interest
3. Other investments other than loans
4. Other investments

B. Current assets

I. Stocks
1. Stocks
2. Payments on account

II. Debtors [(3)]
1. Trade debtors
2. Amounts owed by group undertakings and undertakings in which the LLP has a participating interest
3. Other debtors

III. Investments

1. Shares in group undertakings
2. Other investments

IV. Cash at bank and in hand

C. Prepayments and accrued income [(4)]

[CAPITAL, RESERVES AND LIABILITIES]

A. Loans and other debts due to members [(7)]

B. Members' other interests

I. Members' capital [(7)]
II. Revaluation reserve
III. Other reserves

C. Provisions for liabilities

D. Creditors [(8)]

1. Bank loans and overdrafts
2. Trade creditors
3. Amounts owed to group undertakings and undertakings in which the LLP has a participating interest
4. Other creditors [(5)]

E. Accruals and deferred income [(5)]

Notes on the balance sheet formats

(1) Goodwill

(Formats 1 and 2, item A.I.1.)

Amounts representing goodwill must only be included to the extent that the goodwill was acquired for valuable consideration.

(2) Other intangible assets

(Formats 1 and 2, item A.I.2.)

Amounts in respect of concessions, patents, licences, trade marks and similar rights and assets must only be included in an LLP's balance sheet under this item if either—

(a) the assets were acquired for valuable consideration and are not required to be shown under goodwill, or
(b) the assets in question were created by the LLP itself.

(3) Debtors

(Formats 1 and 2, items B.II.1 to 3.)

The amount falling due after more than one year must be shown separately for each item included under debtors [and, in the case of format 2, the aggregate amount falling due after more than one year must also be shown].

(4) Prepayments and accrued income

(Formats 1 and 2, item C.)

This item may alternatively be included under item B.II.3 in Format 1 or 2.

(5) Other creditors

(Format 1, items D.4, G.4 and I and Format 2, items D.4 and E.)

There must be shown separately—

(a) the amount of any convertible loans, and
(b) the amount for creditors in respect of taxation and social security.

Payments received on account of orders must be included in so far as they are not shown as deductions from stocks.

In Format 1, accruals and deferred income may be shown under item I or included under item D.4 or G.4, or both (as the case may require). In Format 2, accruals and deferred income may be shown under item E or within item D.4 under Liabilities.

(6) Net current assets (liabilities)

(Format 1, item E.)

In determining the amount to be shown under this item any prepayments and accrued income must be taken into account wherever shown.

(7) Loans and other debts due to members

(Format 1, item J and Format 2, Liabilities item A)

The following amounts must be shown separately under this item—

(a) the aggregate amount of money advanced to the LLP by the members by way of loan,
(b) the aggregate amount of money owed to members by the LLP in respect of profits,
(c) any other amounts.

(8) Creditors

(Format 2, Liabilities items D.1 to 4.)

Amounts falling due within one year and after one year must be shown separately for each of these items and for the aggregate of all of these items . . .

Part 10 Miscellaneous other SIs

Profit and loss account formats

Format 1
(see note (12) below)

1. Turnover
2. Cost of sales [(9)]
3. Gross profit or loss
4. Distribution costs [(9)]
5. Administrative expenses [(9)]
6. Other operating income
7. Income from shares in group undertakings
8. Income from participating interests
9. Income from other fixed asset investments [(10)]
10. Other interest receivable and similar income [(10)]
11. Amounts written off investments
12. Interest payable and similar [expenses] [(11)]
13. Tax on profit or loss . . .
14. Profit or loss . . . after taxation

15–18. . . .

19. Other taxes not shown under the above items
20. Profit or loss for the financial year before members' remuneration and profit shares

Profit and loss account formats

Format 2

1. Turnover
2. Change in stocks of finished goods and in work in progress
3. Own work capitalised
4. Other operating income
5.
   (a) Raw materials and consumables
   (b) Other external charges
6. Staff costs
   (a) wages and salaries
   (b) social security costs
   (c) other pension costs
7.
   (a) Depreciation and other amounts written off tangible and intangible fixed assets
   [(b) Amounts written off current assets, to the extent that they exceed write-offs which are normal in the undertaking concerned]
8. Other operating [expenses]
9. Income from shares in group undertakings
10. Income from participating interests
11. Income from other fixed asset investments [(10)]
12. Other interest receivable and similar income [(10)]
13. Amounts written off investments
14. Interest payable and similar [expenses][(11)]
15. Tax on profit or loss . . .
16. Profit or loss . . . after taxation

17–20. . . .

21. Other taxes not shown under the above items
22. Profit or loss for the financial year before members' remuneration and profit shares

Notes on the profit and loss account formats

(9) Cost of sales: distribution costs: administrative expenses

(Format 1, items 2, 4 and 5.)

These items must be stated after taking into account any necessary provisions for depreciation or diminution in value of assets.

(10) Income from other fixed asset investments: other interest receivable and similar income

(Format 1, items 9 and 10; Format 2, items 11 and 12.)

Income and interest derived from group undertakings must be shown separately from income and interest derived from other sources. Interest receivable from members must not be included under this item.

(11) Interest payable and similar [expenses]

(Format 1, item 12; Format 2, item 14.)

The amount payable to group undertakings must be shown separately. Interest payable to members must not be included under this item.

(12) . . .

[SECTION C THE REQUIRED FORMATS FOR THE ACCOUNTS OF MICRO-ENTITIES

Balance Sheet Formats

Format 1

A Fixed assets

B Current assets

C Prepayments and accrued income

D Creditors: amounts falling due within one year

E Net current assets (liabilities)

F Total assets less current liabilities

G Creditors: amounts falling due after more than one year

H Provisions for liabilities

I Accruals and deferred income

J Loans and other debts due to members

K Members' other interests

Format 2

ASSETS

A Fixed assets

B Current Assets

C Prepayments and accrued income

CAPITAL, RESERVES AND LIABILITIES

A Loans and other debts due to members

B Members' other interests

C Provisions for liabilities

D Creditors (1)

E Accruals and deferred income

Notes on the balance sheet formats

(1) Creditors

(Format 2, item D under Capital, Reserves and Liabilities)

Aggregate amounts falling due within one year and after one year must be shown separately.

Profit and loss account format

A Turnover

B Other income

C Cost of raw materials and consumables

D Staff costs

E Depreciation and other amounts written off assets

F Other charges

G Tax

H Profit or loss for the financial year before members' remuneration and profit shares.]

NOTES

All the amendments to Part 1 of this Schedule, as noted below, were made by the Limited Liability Partnerships, Partnerships and Groups (Accounts and Audit) Regulations 2016, SI 2016/575, regs 27, 34–36, as from 17 May 2016, in relation to (a) financial years beginning on or after 1 January 2016; and (b) a financial year of an LLP beginning on or after 1 January 2015, but before 1 January 2016, if (i) the members of the LLP so decide, and (ii) a copy of the LLP's accounts for that financial year has not been delivered to the registrar in accordance with ss 444, 445 or 446 of the Companies Act 2006 as applied to LLPs by the Limited Liability Partnerships (Accounts and Audit) (Application of Companies Act 2006) Regulations before 17 May 2016 (see further the note at **[10.226]**).

Section A is amended as follows:

in para 1, sub-para (1A) and the words in square brackets in sub-paras (2), (3) were inserted;

paras 1A–1C, 2A, 9A were inserted;

the words in square brackets in para 2 were substituted; and

in para 6, the words in square brackets were inserted and the words omitted were revoked.

Section B is amended as follows:

the words in square brackets in the Section heading were substituted;

in balance sheet Format 2, the words in square brackets in the heading were substituted;

in the notes on the balance sheet formats, the words in square brackets in note (3) were substituted, and the words omitted from note (8) were revoked;

in profit and loss account Format 1, the word in square brackets in item 12 was substituted, the words omitted from items 13 and 14 were revoked, and items 15–18 were revoked;

in profit and loss account Format 2, item 7(b) was substituted, the word in square brackets in items 8, 14 was substituted, the words omitted from items 15 and 16 were revoked, and items 17–20 were revoked;

in the notes on the profit and loss account formats the word in square brackets in the title to note (11) was substituted and note (12) was revoked.

Section C was inserted.

PART 2 ACCOUNTING PRINCIPLES AND RULES

SECTION A ACCOUNTING PRINCIPLES

Preliminary

[10.297]

10. (1) The amounts to be included in respect of all items shown in an LLP's accounts must be determined in accordance with the principles set out in this Section.

(2) But if it appears to the members of the LLP that there are special reasons for departing from any of those principles in preparing the LLP's accounts in respect of any financial year they may do so, in which case particulars of the departure, the reasons for it and its effect must be given in a note to the accounts.

Accounting principles

11. The LLP is presumed to be carrying on business as a going concern.

12. Accounting policies [and measurement bases] must be applied consistently within the same accounts and from one financial year to the next.

13. The amount of any item must be determined on a prudent basis, and in particular—

(a) only profits realised at the balance sheet date must be included in the profit and loss account, . . .

(b) all liabilities which have arisen in respect of the financial year to which the accounts relate or a previous financial year must be taken into account, including those which only become apparent between the balance sheet date and the date on which it is signed on behalf of the members in accordance with section 414 of the 2006 Act (approval and signing of accounts),

[(c) all provisions for diminution of value must be recognised, whether the result of the financial year is a profit or a loss,

(d) at the balance sheet date, a provision must represent the best estimate of the expenses likely to be incurred or, in the case of a liability, of the amount required to meet that liability, and

(e) provisions must not be used to adjust the values of assets.]

14. All income and charges relating to the financial year to which the accounts relate must be taken into account, without regard to the date of receipt or payment.

15. In determining the aggregate amount of any item, the amount of each individual asset or liability that falls to be taken into account must be determined separately.

[15A. The opening balance sheet for each financial year must correspond to the closing balance sheet for the preceding financial year.]

SECTION B HISTORICAL COST ACCOUNTING RULES

Preliminary

16. Subject to Sections C and D of this Part of this Schedule, the amounts to be included in respect of all items shown in an LLP's accounts must be determined in accordance with the rules set out in this Section.

Fixed assets

General rules

17. (1) The amount to be included in respect of any fixed asset must be its purchase price or production cost.

(2) This is subject to any provision for depreciation or diminution in value made in accordance with paragraphs 18 to 20.

Rules for depreciation and diminution in value

18. In the case of any fixed asset which has a limited useful economic life, the amount of—

(a) its purchase price or production cost, or

(b) where it is estimated that any such asset will have a residual value at the end of the period of its useful economic life, its purchase price or production cost less that estimated residual value,

must be reduced by provisions for depreciation calculated to write off that amount systematically over the period of the asset's useful economic life.

19. (1) Where a fixed asset investment of a description falling to be included under item A.III of either of the balance sheet formats set out in [Section B of] Part 1 of this Schedule has diminished in value, provisions for diminution in value may be made in respect of it and the amount to be included in respect of it may be reduced accordingly.

(2) Provisions for diminution in value must be made in respect of any fixed asset which has diminished in value if the reduction in its value is expected to be permanent (whether its useful economic life is limited or not), and the amount to be included in respect of it must be reduced accordingly.

[(3) Provisions made under sub-paragraph (1) or (2) must be charged to the profit and loss account and disclosed separately in a note to the accounts if not shown separately in the profit and loss account.]

20. (1) Where the reasons for which any provision was made in accordance with paragraph 19 have ceased to apply to any extent, that provision must be written back to the extent that it is no longer necessary.

[(1A) But provision made in accordance with paragraph 19(2) in respect of goodwill must not be written back to any extent.]

[(2) Any amounts written back under sub-paragraph (1) must be recognised in the profit and loss account and disclosed separately in a note to the accounts if not shown separately in the profit and loss account.]

[Intangible assets

21. (1) Where this is in accordance with generally accepted accounting principles or practice, development costs may be included in "other intangible assets" under "fixed assets" in the balance sheet formats set out in Section B of Part 1 of this Schedule.

(2) If any amount is included in an LLP's balance sheet in respect of development costs, the note on accounting policies (see paragraph 44 of this Schedule) must include the following information—

(a) the period over which the amount of those costs originally capitalised is being or is to be written off, and

(b) the reasons for capitalising the development costs in question.

22. (1) Intangible assets must be written off over the useful economic life of the intangible asset.

(2) Where in exceptional cases the useful life of intangible assets cannot be reliably estimated, such assets must be written off over a period chosen by the members of the LLP.

(3) The period referred to in sub-paragraph (2) must not exceed ten years.

(4) There must be disclosed in a note to the accounts the period referred to in sub-paragraph (2) and the reasons for choosing that period.]

Current assets

23. Subject to paragraph 24, the amount to be included in respect of any current asset must be its purchase price or production cost.

24. (1) If the net realisable value of any current asset is lower than its purchase price or production cost, the amount to be included in respect of that asset must be the net realisable value.

(2) Where the reasons for which any provision for diminution in value was made in accordance with sub-paragraph (1) have ceased to apply to any extent, that provision must be written back to the extent that it is no longer necessary.

Miscellaneous and supplementary provisions

Excess of money owed over value received as an asset item

25. (1) Where the amount repayable on any debt owed by an LLP is greater than the value of the consideration received in the transaction giving rise to the debt, the amount of the difference may be treated as an asset.

(2) Where any such amount is so treated—

(a) it must be written off by reasonable amounts each year and must be completely written off before repayment of the debt, and

(b) if the current amount is not shown as a separate item in the LLP's balance sheet, it must be disclosed in a note to the accounts.

Assets included at a fixed amount

26. [(1) Subject to sub-paragraph (2), the following may be included at a fixed quantity and value in the balance sheet formats set out in Section B of Part 1 of this Schedule—

(a) assets which fall to be included amongst the fixed assets of an LLP under the item "intangible assets", and

(b) raw materials and consumables within the item "stocks".]

(2) Sub-paragraph (1) applies to assets of a kind which are constantly being replaced where—

(a) their overall value is not material to assessing the LLP's state of affairs, and

(b) their quantity, value and composition are not subject to material variation.

Determination of purchase price or production cost

27. (1) The purchase price of an asset is to be determined by adding to the actual price paid any expenses incidental to its acquisition [and then subtracting any incidental reductions in the cost of acquisition].

(2) The production cost of an asset is to be determined by adding to the purchase price of the raw materials and consumables used the amount of the costs incurred by the LLP which are directly attributable to the production of that asset.

(3) In addition, there may be included in the production cost of an asset—

(a) a reasonable proportion of the costs incurred by the LLP which are only indirectly attributable to the production of that asset, but only to the extent that they relate to the period of production, and

(b) interest on capital borrowed to finance the production of that asset, to the extent that it accrues in respect of the period of production,

provided, however, in a case within paragraph (b), that the inclusion of the interest in determining the cost of that asset and the amount of the interest so included is disclosed in a note to the accounts.

(4) In the case of current assets distribution costs may not be included in production costs.

28. (1) The purchase price or production cost of—

(a) any assets which[, by virtue of regulation 3(1) and Section B of Part 1 of this Schedule,] fall to be included under any item shown in an LLP's balance sheet under the general item "stocks", and

(b) any assets which are fungible assets (including investments),

may be determined by the application of any of the methods mentioned in sub-paragraph (2) in relation to any such assets of the same class, provided that the method chosen is one which appears to the members to be appropriate in the circumstances of the LLP.

(2) Those methods are—

(a) the method known as "first in, first out" (FIFO),

(b) the method known as "last in, first out" (LIFO),

(c) a weighted average price, and

(d) any other method [reflecting generally accepted best practice].

(3) For the purposes of this paragraph, assets of any description must be regarded as fungible if assets of that description are substantially indistinguishable one from another.

Substitution of original stated amount where price or cost unknown

29. (1) This paragraph applies where—

(a) there is no record of the purchase price or production cost of any asset of an LLP or of any price, expenses or costs relevant for determining its purchase price or production cost in accordance with paragraph 27, or

(b) any such record cannot be obtained without unreasonable expense or delay.

(2) In such a case, the purchase price or production cost of the asset must be taken, for the purposes of paragraphs 17 to 24, to be the value ascribed to it in the earliest available record of its value made on or after its acquisition or production by the LLP.

[Equity method in respect of participating interests

29A. Participating interests may be accounted for using the equity method.]

SECTION C ALTERNATIVE ACCOUNTING RULES

Preliminary

30. (1) The rules set out in Section B are referred to below in this Schedule as the historical cost accounting rules.

(2) Those rules, with the omission of paragraphs 16, 22 and 26 to 29, are referred to below in this Part of this Schedule as the depreciation rules; and references below in this Schedule to the historical cost accounting rules do not include the depreciation rules as they apply by virtue of paragraph 33.

31. Subject to paragraphs 33 to 35, the amounts to be included in respect of assets of any description mentioned in paragraph 32 may be determined on any basis so mentioned.

Alternative accounting rules

32. (1) Intangible fixed assets, other than goodwill, may be included at their current cost.

(2) Tangible fixed assets may be included at a market value determined as at the date of their last valuation or at their current cost.

(3) Investments of any description falling to be included under item A.III of either of the balance sheet formats set out Part 1 of this Schedule may be included either—

(a) at a market value determined as at the date of their last valuation, or

(b) at a value determined on any basis which appears to the members to be appropriate in the circumstances of the LLP.

But in the latter case particulars of the method of valuation adopted and of the reasons for adopting it must be disclosed in a note to the accounts.

(4), (5) . . .

Application of the depreciation rules

33. (1) Where the value of any asset of an LLP is determined on any basis mentioned in paragraph 32, that value must be, or (as the case may require) be the starting point for determining, the amount to be included in respect of that asset in the LLP's accounts, instead of its purchase price or production cost or any value previously so determined for that asset.

The depreciation rules apply accordingly in relation to any such asset with the substitution for any reference to its purchase price or production cost of a reference to the value most recently determined for that asset on any basis mentioned in paragraph 32.

(2) The amount of any provision for depreciation required in the case of any fixed asset by paragraphs 18 to 20 as they apply by virtue of sub-paragraph (1) is referred to below in this paragraph as the adjusted amount, and the amount of any provision which would be required by any of those paragraphs in the case of that asset according to the historical cost accounting rules is referred to as the historical cost amount.

(3) Where sub-paragraph (1) applies in the case of any fixed asset the amount of any provision for depreciation in respect of that asset—

(a) included in any item shown in the profit and loss account in respect of amounts written off assets of the description in question, or

(b) taken into account in stating any item so shown which is required by note (9) of the notes on the profit and loss account formats set out in Part 1 of this Schedule to be stated after taking into account any necessary provision for depreciation or diminution in value of assets included under it,

may be the historical cost amount instead of the adjusted amount, provided that the amount of any difference between the two is shown separately in the profit and loss account or in a note to the accounts.

Additional information to be provided in case of departure from historical cost accounting rules

34. (1) This paragraph applies where the amounts to be included in respect of assets covered by any items shown in an LLP's accounts have been determined on any basis mentioned in paragraph 32.

(2) The items affected and the basis of valuation adopted in determining the amounts of the assets in question in the case of each such item must be disclosed in [the note on accounting policies (see paragraph 44 of this Schedule)].

[(3) In the case of each balance sheet item affected, the comparable amounts determined according to the historical cost accounting rules must be shown in a note to the accounts.]

(4) In sub-paragraph (3), references in relation to any item to the comparable amounts determined as there mentioned are references to—

(a) the aggregate amount which would be required to be shown in respect of that item if the amounts to be included in respect of all the assets covered by that item were determined according to the historical cost accounting rules, and

(b) the aggregate amount of the cumulative provisions for depreciation or diminution in value which would be permitted or required in determining those amounts according to those rules.

Revaluation reserve

35. (1) With respect to any determination of the value of an asset of an LLP on any basis mentioned in paragraph 32, the amount of any profit or loss arising from that determination (after allowing, where appropriate, for any provisions for depreciation or diminution in value made otherwise than by reference to the value so determined and any adjustments of any such provisions made in the light of that determination) must be credited or (as the case may be) debited to a separate reserve ("the revaluation reserve").

(2) The amount of the revaluation reserve [under "Members' other interests"] must be shown in the LLP's balance sheet under a separate sub-heading in the position given for the item "revaluation reserve" in Format 1 or 2 of the balance sheet formats set out in Part 1 of this Schedule . . .

(3) The treatment for taxation purposes of amounts credited or debited to the revaluation reserve must be disclosed in a note to the accounts.

SECTION D FAIR VALUE ACCOUNTING

Inclusion of financial instruments at fair value

36. (1) Subject to sub-paragraphs (2) to (5), financial instruments (including derivatives) may be included at fair value.

(2) Sub-paragraph (1) does not apply to financial instruments that constitute liabilities unless—

(a) they are held as part of a trading portfolio,
(b) they are derivatives, or
(c) they are financial instruments falling within sub-paragraph (4).

(3) Unless they are financial instruments falling within sub-paragraph (4), sub-paragraph (1) does not apply to—

(a) financial instruments (other than derivatives) held to maturity,
(b) loans and receivables originated by the LLP and not held for trading purposes,
(c) interests in subsidiary undertakings, associated undertakings and joint ventures,
(d) equity instruments issued by the LLP,
(e) contracts for contingent consideration in a business combination, or
(f) other financial instruments with such special characteristics that the instruments, according to generally accepted accounting principles or practice, should be accounted for differently from other financial instruments.

[(4) Financial instruments which under [UK-adopted international accounting standards] may be included in accounts at fair value, may be so included, provided that the disclosures required by such accounting standards are made.]

(5) If the fair value of a financial instrument cannot be determined reliably in accordance with paragraph 37, sub-paragraph (1) does not apply to that financial instrument.

(6) In this paragraph—

"associated undertaking" has the meaning given by paragraph 19 of Schedule 4 to these Regulations;
"joint venture" has the meaning given by paragraph 18 of that Schedule.

Determination of fair value

37. (1) The fair value of a financial instrument is its value determined in accordance with this paragraph.

(2) If a reliable market can readily be identified for the financial instrument, its fair value is to be determined by reference to its market value.

(3) If a reliable market cannot readily be identified for the financial instrument but can be identified for its components or for a similar instrument, its fair value is determined by reference to the market value of its components or of the similar instrument.

(4) If neither sub-paragraph (2) nor (3) applies, the fair value of the financial instrument is a value resulting from generally accepted valuation models and techniques.

(5) Any valuation models and techniques used for the purposes of sub-paragraph (4) must ensure a reasonable approximation of the market value.

Hedged items

38. An LLP may include any assets and liabilities, or identified portions of such assets or liabilities, that qualify as hedged items under a fair value hedge accounting system at the amount required under that system.

[Other assets that may be included at fair value

39. (1) This paragraph applies to—

(a) stocks,
(b) investment property, and
(c) living animals and plants.

(2) Stocks, investment property, and living animals and plants may be included at fair value, provided that, as the case may be, all such stocks, investment property, and living animals and plants are so included where their fair value can reliably be determined.

(3) In this paragraph "fair value" means fair value determined in accordance with generally accepted accounting principles or practice.]

Accounting for changes in value

40. (1) This paragraph applies where a financial instrument is valued in accordance with paragraph 36 or 38 or an asset is valued in accordance with paragraph 39.

(2) Notwithstanding paragraph 13 in this Part of this Schedule, and subject to sub-paragraphs (3) and (4), a change in the value of the financial instrument or of the investment property or living animal or plant must be included in the profit and loss account.

(3) Where—

(a) the financial instrument accounted for is a hedging instrument under a hedge accounting system that allows some or all of the change in value not to be shown in the profit and loss account, or

(b) the change in value relates to an exchange difference arising on a monetary item that forms part of an LLP's net investment in a foreign entity,

the amount of the change in value must be credited to or (as the case may be) debited from a separate reserve ("the fair value reserve").

(4) Where the instrument accounted for—

(a) is an available for sale financial asset, and

(b) is not a derivative,

the change in value may be credited to or (as the case may be) debited from the fair value reserve.

The fair value reserve

41. (1) The fair value reserve must be adjusted to the extent that the amounts shown in it are no longer necessary for the purposes of paragraph 40(3) or (4).

(2) . . .

NOTES

The words in square brackets in para 36(4) were substituted by the International Accounting Standards and European Public Limited-Liability Company (Amendment etc) (EU Exit) Regulations 2019, SI 2019/685, reg 19, Sch 1, Pt 2, para 59(a), in relation to accounts for financial years beginning on or after IP completion day (as defined in the European Union (Withdrawal Agreement) Act 2020, s 39) (note also that in relation to accounts for financial years which begin before but end on or after IP completion day, the enactments amended by Parts 1–3 of Sch 1 to the 2019 Regulations have effect as if the UK were a member State until the end of the financial year in question).

All other amendments to Part 2 of this Schedule, as noted below, were made by the Limited Liability Partnerships, Partnerships and Groups (Accounts and Audit) Regulations 2016, SI 2016/575, regs 27, 37–40, as from 17 May 2016, in relation to (a) financial years beginning on or after 1 January 2016; and (b) a financial year of an LLP beginning on or after 1 January 2015, but before 1 January 2016, if (i) the members of the LLP so decide, and (ii) a copy of the LLP's accounts for that financial year has not been delivered to the registrar in accordance with ss 444, 445 or 446 of the Companies Act 2006 as applied to LLPs by the Limited Liability Partnerships (Accounts and Audit) (Application of Companies Act 2006) Regulations before 17 May 2016 (see further the note at **[10.226]**).

The words in square brackets in para 12 were inserted, in para 13 the word omitted from sub-para (a) was revoked, sub-paras (c)–(e) were inserted, and para 15A was inserted.

In para 19, the words in square brackets sub-para (1) were inserted, and sub-para (3) was substituted.

In para 20, sub-para (1A) was inserted, and sub-para (2) was substituted.

Paras 21, 22 were substituted.

In para 26, sub-para (1) was substituted.

In para 27, the words in square brackets in sub-para (1) were inserted.

In para 28, the words in square brackets in sub-para (1)(a) were inserted, and the words in square brackets in sub-para (2)(d) were substituted.

Para 29A was inserted.

In para 32, sub-paras (4), (5) were revoked.

In para 34, the words in square brackets in sub-para (2) were substituted, and sub-para (3) was substituted.

In para 35, the words in square brackets in sub-para (2) were inserted, and the words omitted were revoked.

In para 36, sub-para (4) was substituted.

Para 39 was substituted.

In para 41, sub-para (2) was revoked.

PART 3 NOTES TO THE ACCOUNTS

[Preliminary

[10.298]

42. (1) Any information required in the case of an LLP by the following provisions of this Part of this Schedule must be given by way of a note to the accounts.

(2) These notes must be presented in the order in which, where relevant, the items to which they relate are presented in the balance sheet and in the profit and loss account.]

Reserves

43. . . .

Disclosure of accounting policies

44. The accounting policies adopted by the LLP in determining the amounts to be included in respect of items shown in the balance sheet and in determining the profit or loss of the LLP must be stated (including such policies with respect to the depreciation and diminution in value of assets).

Information supplementing the balance sheet

45. Paragraphs [47 to 55] require information which either supplements the information given with respect to any particular items shown in the balance sheet or is otherwise relevant to assessing the LLP's state of affairs in the light of the information so given.

Loans and other debts due to members

46. . . .

Fixed assets

47. (1) In respect of each item which is or would but for paragraph 4(2)(b) be shown under the general item "fixed assets" in the LLP's balance sheet the following information must be given—

(a) the appropriate amounts in respect of that item as at the date of the beginning of the financial year and as at the balance sheet date respectively,

(b) the effect on any amount shown in the balance sheet in respect of that item of—

(i) any revision of the amount in respect of any assets included under that item made during that year on any basis mentioned in paragraph 32,

(ii) acquisitions during that year of any assets,

(iii) disposals during that year of any assets, and

(iv) any transfers of assets of the LLP to and from that item during that year.

(2) The reference in sub-paragraph (1)(a) to the appropriate amounts in respect of any item as at any date there mentioned is a reference to amounts representing the aggregate amounts determined, as at that date, in respect of assets falling to be included under that item on either of the following bases, that is to say—

(a) on the basis of purchase price or production cost (determined in accordance with paragraphs 27 and 28), or

(b) on any basis mentioned in paragraph 32,

(leaving out of account in either case any provisions for depreciation or diminution in value).

(3) In respect of each item within sub-paragraph (1) there must also be stated—

(a) the cumulative amount of provisions for depreciation or diminution in value of assets included under that item as at each date mentioned in sub-paragraph (1)(a),

(b) the amount of any such provisions made in respect of the financial year,

(c) the amount of any adjustments made in respect of any such provisions during that year in consequence of the disposal of any assets, and

(d) the amount of any other adjustments made in respect of any such provisions during that year.

48. Where any fixed assets of the LLP (other than listed investments) are included under any item shown in the LLP's balance sheet at an amount determined on any basis mentioned in paragraph 32, the following information must be given—

(a) the years (so far as they are known to the members) in which the assets were severally valued and the several values, and

(b) in the case of assets that have been valued during the financial year, the names of the persons who valued them or particulars of their qualifications for doing so and (whichever is stated) the bases of valuation used by them.

Investments

49. . . .

[Information about fair value of assets and liabilities

50. (1) This paragraph applies where financial instruments or other assets have been valued in accordance with, as appropriate, paragraph 36, 38 or 39.

(2) There must be stated—

(a) the significant assumptions underlying the valuation models and techniques used to determine the fair values,

(b) for each category of financial instrument or other asset, the fair value of the assets in that category and the changes in value—

(i) included directly in the profit and loss account, or

(ii) credited to or (as the case may be) debited from the fair value reserve,

in respect of those assets, and

(c) for each class of derivatives, the extent and nature of the instruments, including significant terms and conditions that may affect the amount, timing and certainty of future cash flows.

(3) Where any amount is transferred to or from the fair value reserve during the financial year, there must be stated in tabular form—

(a) the amount of the reserve as at the date of the beginning of the financial year and as at the balance sheet date respectively, and

(b) the amount transferred to or from the reserve during that year.]

51. . . .

Information where investment property and living animals and plants included at fair value

52. . . .

[Information about revalued fixed assets

53. (1) This paragraph applies where fixed assets are measured at revalued amounts.

(2) Where this paragraph applies, the following information must be given in tabular form—

(a) movements in the revaluation reserve in the financial year, with an explanation of the tax treatment of items therein, and

(b) the carrying amount in the balance sheet that would have been recognised had the fixed assets not been revalued.]

Details of indebtedness

54. (1) For the aggregate of all items shown under "creditors" in the LLP's balance sheet there must be stated the aggregate of the following amounts—

(a) the amount of any debts included under "creditors" which are payable or repayable otherwise than by instalments and fall due for payment or repayment after the end of the period of five years beginning with the day next following the end of the financial year, and

(b) in the case of any debts so included which are payable or repayable by instalments, the amount of any instalments which fall due for payment after the end of that period.

(2) In respect of each item shown under "creditors" in the LLP's balance sheet there must be stated the aggregate amount of any debts included under that item in respect of which any security has been given by the LLP [with an indication of the nature and form of any such security].

(3) References above in this paragraph to an item shown under "creditors" in the LLP's balance sheet include references, where amounts falling due to creditors within one year and after more than one year are distinguished in the balance sheet—

(a) in a case within sub-paragraph (1), to an item shown under the latter of those categories,

(b) in a case within sub-paragraph (2), to an item shown under either of those categories.

References to items shown under "creditors" include references to items which would but for paragraph 4(2)(b) be shown under that heading.

[Guarantees and other financial commitments

55. (1) The total amount of any financial commitments, guarantees and contingencies that are not included in the balance sheet must be stated.

(2) An indication of the nature and form of any valuable security given by the LLP in respect of commitments, guarantees and contingencies within sub-paragraph (1) must be given.

(3) The total amount of any commitments within sub-paragraph (1) concerning pensions must be separately disclosed.

(4) The total amount of any commitments within sub-paragraph (1) which are undertaken on behalf of or for the benefit of—

(a) any parent undertaking, fellow subsidiary undertaking or any subsidiary undertaking of the LLP, or

(b) any undertaking in which the LLP has a participating interest,

must be separately stated and those within paragraph (a) must also be stated separately from those within paragraph (b).]

Miscellaneous matters

56. . . .

Information supplementing the profit and loss account

57. . . .

Particulars of turnover

58. . . .

Miscellaneous matters

59. (1) Where any amount relating to any preceding financial year is included in any item in the profit and loss account, the effect must be stated.

[(2) The amount and nature of any individual items of income or expenditure of exceptional size or incidence must be stated.]

Sums denominated in foreign currencies

60. . . .

Dormant LLPs acting as agents

61. . . .

[Post balance sheet events

62. The nature and financial effect of material events arising after the balance sheet date which are not reflected in the profit and loss account or balance sheet must be stated.

Parent undertaking information

63. Where the LLP is a subsidiary undertaking, the following information must be given in respect of the parent undertaking of the smallest group of undertakings for which group accounts are drawn up of which the LLP is a member—

(a) the name of the parent undertaking which draws up the group accounts,

(b) the address of the undertaking's registered office (whether in or outside the United Kingdom), or

(c) if it is incorporated, the address of its principal place of business.

Related party transactions

64. (1) Particulars may be given of transactions which the LLP has entered into with related parties, and must be given if such transactions are material and have not been concluded under normal market conditions with—

(a) members of the LLP that are related parties; and
(b) undertakings in which the LLP itself has a participating interest.

(2) Particulars of the transactions required to be disclosed under sub-paragraph (1) must include—
(a) the amount of such transactions,
(b) the nature of the related party relationship, and
(c) other information about the transactions necessary for an understanding of the financial position of the LLP.

(3) Information about individual transactions may be aggregated according to their nature, except where separate information is necessary for an understanding of the effects of the related party transactions on the financial position of the LLP.

(4) Particulars need not be given of transactions entered into between two or more members of a group, provided that any subsidiary undertaking which is a party to the transaction is wholly-owned by such a member.

(5) In this paragraph "related party" has the same meaning as in [UK-adopted international accounting standards].]

NOTES

Words in square brackets in para 64(5) substituted by the International Accounting Standards and European Public Limited-Liability Company (Amendment etc) (EU Exit) Regulations 2019, SI 2019/685, reg 19, Sch 1, Pt 2, para 59(b), in relation to accounts for financial years beginning on or after IP completion day (as defined in the European Union (Withdrawal Agreement) Act 2020, s 39) (note also that in relation to accounts for financial years which begin before but end on or after IP completion day, the enactments amended by Parts 1–3 of Sch 1 to the 2019 Regulations have effect as if the UK were a member State until the end of the financial year in question).

All other amendments to Part 3 of this Schedule, as noted below, were made by the Limited Liability Partnerships, Partnerships and Groups (Accounts and Audit) Regulations 2016, SI 2016/575, regs 27, 41, as from 17 May 2016, in relation to (a) financial years beginning on or after 1 January 2016; and (b) a financial year of an LLP beginning on or after 1 January 2015, but before 1 January 2016, if (i) the members of the LLP so decide, and (ii) a copy of the LLP's accounts for that financial year has not been delivered to the registrar in accordance with ss 444, 445 or 446 of the Companies Act 2006 as applied to LLPs by the Limited Liability Partnerships (Accounts and Audit) (Application of Companies Act 2006) Regulations before 17 May 2016 (see further the note at **[10.226]**).

Paras 42, 50, 53, 55 were substituted.
Paras 43, 46, 49, 51, 52, 56–58, 60, 61 were revoked.
In paras 45, 54, the words in square brackets were substituted.
In para 59, sub-para (2) was substituted (for the original sub-paras (2), (3)).
Paras 62, 63, 64 were inserted.

SCHEDULES 2, 3

(Sch 2 (Information about Related Undertakings where LLP not Preparing Group Accounts (Non-IAS or IAS Individual Accounts)), and Sch 3 (Non-IAS Abbreviated Accounts for Delivery to Registrar of Companies) were revoked by the Limited Liability Partnerships, Partnerships and Groups (Accounts and Audit) Regulations 2016, SI 2016/575, regs 27, 42, as from 17 May 2016, in relation to (a) financial years beginning on or after 1 January 2016; and (b) a financial year of an LLP beginning on or after 1 January 2015, but before 1 January 2016, if (i) the members of the LLP so decide, and (ii) a copy of the LLP's accounts for that financial year has not been delivered to the registrar in accordance with ss 444, 445 or 446 of the Companies Act 2006 as applied to LLPs by the Limited Liability Partnerships (Accounts and Audit) (Application of Companies Act 2006) Regulations before 17 May 2016 (see further the note at **[10.226]***).)*

SCHEDULE 4
GROUP ACCOUNTS

Regulations 6 and 7

PART 1 FORM AND CONTENT OF NON-IAS GROUP ACCOUNTS

General rules

[10.299]

1. (1) Subject to [the following provisions of this Schedule], group accounts must comply so far as practicable with the provisions of Schedule 1 to these Regulations (non-IAS individual accounts) as if the undertakings included in the consolidation ("the group") were a single LLP.

[(1A) Paragraph 1A of Schedule 1 to these Regulations does not apply to group accounts.]

(2) For item A.III in each balance sheet format set out in [Section B of Part 1 of] that Schedule substitute—

"A.III. Investments
1. Shares in group undertakings
2. Interests in associated undertakings
3. Other participating interests
4. Loans to group undertakings and undertakings in which a participating interest is held
5. Other investments other than loans
6. Others".

(3) In the profit and loss account formats [in Section B of Part 1 of that Schedule] replace the items headed "Income from participating interests", that is—
(a) in Format 1, item 8, and
(b) in Format 2, item 10,
by two items: "Income from interests in associated undertakings" and "Income from other participating interests".

Part 10 Miscellaneous other SIs

2. (1) The consolidated balance sheet and profit and loss account must incorporate in full the information contained in the individual accounts of the undertakings included in the consolidation, subject to the adjustments authorised or required by the following provisions of this Schedule and to such other adjustments (if any) as may be appropriate in accordance with generally accepted accounting principles or practice.

[(1A) Group accounts must be drawn up as at the same date as the accounts of the parent LLP.]

(2) If the financial year of a subsidiary undertaking included in the consolidation does not end with that of the parent LLP, the group accounts must be made up—

(a) from the accounts of the subsidiary undertaking for its financial year last ending before the end of the parent LLP's financial year, provided that year ended no more than three months before that of the parent LLP, or

(b) from interim accounts prepared by the subsidiary undertaking as at the end of the parent LLP's financial year.

3. (1) Where assets and liabilities to be included in the group accounts have been valued or otherwise determined by undertakings according to accounting rules differing from those used for the group accounts, the values or amounts must be adjusted so as to accord with the rules used for the group accounts.

(2) If it appears to the members of the parent LLP that there are special reasons for departing from sub-paragraph (1) they may do so, but particulars of any such departure, the reasons for it and its effect must be given in a note to the accounts.

(3) The adjustments referred to in this paragraph need not be made if they are not material for the purpose of giving a true and fair view.

4. Any differences of accounting rules as between a parent LLP's individual accounts for a financial year and its group accounts must be disclosed in a note to the latter accounts and the reasons for the difference given.

5. Amounts that in the particular context of any provision of this Schedule are not material may be disregarded for the purposes of that provision.

Elimination of group transactions

6. (1) Debts and claims between undertakings included in the consolidation, and income and expenditure relating to transactions between such undertakings, must be eliminated in preparing the group accounts.

(2) Where profits and losses resulting from transactions between undertakings included in the consolidation are included in the book value of assets, they must be eliminated in preparing the group accounts.

(3) The elimination required by sub-paragraph (2) may be effected in proportion to the group's interest in the shares of the undertakings.

(4) Sub-paragraphs (1) and (2) need not be complied with if the amounts concerned are not material for the purpose of giving a true and fair view.

Acquisition and merger accounting

7. (1) The following provisions apply where an undertaking becomes a subsidiary undertaking of the parent LLP.

(2) That event is referred to in those provisions as an "acquisition", and references to the "undertaking acquired" are to be construed accordingly.

8. An acquisition must be accounted for by the acquisition method of accounting unless the conditions for accounting for it as a merger are met and the merger method of accounting is adopted.

9. (1) The acquisition method of accounting is as follows.

(2) The identifiable assets and liabilities of the undertaking acquired must be included in the consolidated balance sheet at their fair values as at the date of acquisition.

(3) The income and expenditure of the undertaking acquired must be brought into the group accounts only as from the date of the acquisition.

(4) There must be set off against the acquisition cost of the interest in the shares of the undertaking held by the parent LLP and its subsidiary undertakings the interest of the parent LLP and its subsidiary undertakings in the adjusted capital and reserves of the undertaking acquired.

(5) The resulting amount if positive must be treated as goodwill, and if negative as a negative consolidation difference.

[(6) Negative goodwill may be transferred to the consolidated profit and loss account where such a treatment is in accordance with the principles and rules of Part 2 of Schedule 1 to these Regulations.]

10. The conditions for accounting for an acquisition as a merger are that adoption of the merger method of accounting accords with generally accepted accounting principles or practice.

11. (1) Where an LLP adopts the merger method of accounting, it must comply with this paragraph, and with generally accepted accounting principles or practice.

(2) The assets and liabilities of the undertaking acquired must be brought into the group accounts at the figures at which they stand in the undertaking's accounts, subject to any adjustment authorised or required by this Schedule.

(3) The income and expenditure of the undertaking acquired must be included in the group accounts for the entire financial year, including the period before the acquisition.

(4) The group accounts must show corresponding amounts relating to the previous financial year as if the undertaking acquired had been included in the consolidation throughout that year.

12. (1) Where a group is acquired, paragraphs 9 to 11 apply with the following adaptations.

(2) References to shares of the undertaking acquired are to be construed as references to shares of the parent undertaking of the group.

(3) Other references to the undertaking acquired are to be construed as references to the group; and references to the assets and liabilities, income and expenditure and capital and reserves of the undertaking acquired must be construed as references to the assets and liabilities, income and expenditure and capital and reserves of the group after making the set-offs and other adjustments required by this Schedule in the case of group accounts.

13. (1) The following information with respect to acquisitions taking place in the financial year must be given in a note to the accounts.

(2) There must be stated—

(a) the name of the undertaking acquired or, where a group was acquired, the name of the parent undertaking of that group, and

(b) whether the acquisition has been accounted for by the acquisition or the merger method of accounting;

and in relation to an acquisition which significantly affects the figures shown in the group accounts, the following further information must be given.

(3) The composition and fair value of the consideration for the acquisition given by the parent LLP and its subsidiary undertakings must be stated.

(4) Where the acquisition method of accounting has been adopted, the book values immediately prior to the acquisition, and the fair values at the date of acquisition, of each class of assets and liabilities of the undertaking or group acquired must be stated in tabular form, including a statement of the amount of any goodwill or negative consolidation difference arising on the acquisition, together with an explanation of any significant adjustments made.

(5) In ascertaining for the purposes of sub-paragraph (4) the profit or loss of a group, the book values and fair values of assets and liabilities of a group or the amount of the assets and liabilities of a group, the set-offs and other adjustments required by this Schedule in the case of group accounts must be made.

14. (1) There must also be stated in a note to the accounts the cumulative amount of goodwill resulting from acquisitions in that and earlier financial years which has been written off otherwise than in the consolidated profit and loss account for that or any earlier financial year.

(2) That figure must be shown net of any goodwill attributable to subsidiary undertakings or businesses disposed of prior to the balance sheet date.

15. Where during the financial year there has been a disposal of an undertaking or group which significantly affects the figures shown in the group accounts, there must be stated in a note to the accounts—

(a) the name of that undertaking or, as the case may be, of the parent undertaking of that group, and

(b) the extent to which the profit or loss shown in the group accounts is attributable to profit or loss of that undertaking or group.

16. The information required by paragraph 13, 14 or 15 need not be disclosed with respect to an undertaking which—

(a) is established under the law of a country outside the United Kingdom, or

(b) carries on business outside the United Kingdom,

if in the opinion of the members of the parent LLP the disclosure would be seriously prejudicial to the business of that undertaking or to the business of the parent LLP or any of its subsidiary undertakings and the Secretary of State agrees that the information should not be disclosed.

[16A. Where an acquisition has taken place in the financial year and the merger method of accounting has been adopted, the notes to the accounts must also disclose the names and the addresses of the registered offices of the undertakings concerned (whether in or outside the United Kingdom).]

[Non-controlling interests

17. (1) The formats set out in Section B of Part 1 of Schedule 1 to these Regulations have effect in relation to group accounts with the following additions.

(2) In the Balance Sheet Formats there must be shown, as a separate item and under the heading "non-controlling interests", the amount of capital and reserves attributable to shares in subsidiary undertakings included in the consolidation held by or on behalf of persons other than the parent LLP and its subsidiary undertakings.

(3) In the Profit and Loss Account Formats there must be shown, as a separate item and under the heading "non-controlling interests", the amount of any profit or loss attributable to shares in subsidiary undertakings included in the consolidation held by or on behalf of persons other than the parent LLP and its subsidiary undertakings.

(4) For the purposes of paragraph 4 of Schedule 1 (power to adapt or combine items)—

(a) the additional item required by sub-paragraph (2) above is treated as one to which a letter is assigned, and

(b) the additional item required by sub-paragraph (3) above is treated as one to which an Arabic number is assigned.]

Joint ventures

18. (1) Where an undertaking included in the consolidation manages another undertaking jointly with one or more undertakings not included in the consolidation, that other undertaking ("the joint venture") may, if it is not—

(a) a body corporate, or

(b) a subsidiary undertaking of the parent LLP,

be dealt with in the group accounts by the method of proportional consolidation.

(2) The provisions of this Schedule relating to the preparation of consolidated accounts [and sections 402 and 405 of the 2006 Act] apply, with any necessary modifications, to proportional consolidation under this paragraph.

[(3) In addition to the disclosure of the average number of employees employed during the financial year (see section 411(7) of the 2006 Act), there must be a separate disclosure in the notes to the accounts of the average number of employees employed by undertakings that are proportionately consolidated.]

Part 10 Miscellaneous other SIs

Associated undertakings

19. (1) An "associated undertaking" means an undertaking in which an undertaking included in the consolidation has a participating interest and over whose operating and financial policy it exercises a significant influence, and which is not—

(a) a subsidiary undertaking of the parent LLP, or

(b) a joint venture dealt with in accordance with paragraph 18.

(2) Where an undertaking holds 20% or more of the voting rights in another undertaking, it is presumed to exercise such an influence over it unless the contrary is shown.

(3) The voting rights in an undertaking means the rights conferred on shareholders in respect of their shares or, in the case of an undertaking not having a share capital, on members, to vote at general meetings of the undertaking on all, or substantially all, matters.

(4) The provisions of paragraphs 5 to 11 of Schedule 7 to the 2006 Act (parent and subsidiary undertakings: rights to be taken into account and attribution of rights) apply in determining for the purposes of this paragraph whether an undertaking holds 20% or more of the voting rights in another undertaking.

20. (1) The interest of an undertaking in an associated undertaking, and the amount of profit or loss attributable to such an interest, must be shown by the equity method of accounting (including dealing with any goodwill arising in accordance with paragraphs 17 to 20 and 22 of Schedule 1 to these Regulations).

(2) Where the associated undertaking is itself a parent undertaking, the net assets and profits or losses to be taken into account are those of the parent and its subsidiary undertakings (after making any consolidation adjustments).

(3) The equity method of accounting need not be applied if the amounts in question are not material for the purpose of giving a true and fair view.

[Deferred tax balances

20A. Deferred tax balances must be recognised on consolidation where it is probable that a charge to tax will arise within the foreseeable future for one of the undertakings included in the consolidation.

Related party transactions

20B. Paragraph 64 of Schedule 1 to these Regulations applies to transactions which the parent LLP, or other undertakings included in the consolidation, have entered into with related parties, unless they are intra-group transactions.]

NOTES

All amendments to Part 1 of this Schedule, as noted below, were made by the Limited Liability Partnerships, Partnerships and Groups (Accounts and Audit) Regulations 2016, SI 2016/575, regs 27, 43, as from 17 May 2016, in relation to (a) financial years beginning on or after 1 January 2016; and (b) a financial year of an LLP beginning on or after 1 January 2015, but before 1 January 2016, if (i) the members of the LLP so decide, and (ii) a copy of the LLP's accounts for that financial year has not been delivered to the registrar in accordance with ss 444, 445 or 446 of the Companies Act 2006 as applied to LLPs by the Limited Liability Partnerships (Accounts and Audit) (Application of Companies Act 2006) Regulations before 17 May 2016 (see further the note at **[10.226]**).

In para 1, the words in square brackets in sub-para (1) were substituted, para (1A) was inserted, and the words in square brackets in sub-paras (2), (3) were inserted.

In para 2, sub-para (1A) was inserted.

In para 9, sub-para (6) was added.

Paras 16A, 20A, 20B were inserted.

Para 17 was substituted.

In para 18, the words in square brackets in sub-para (2) were inserted and sub-para (3) was added.

PART 2 INFORMATION ABOUT RELATED UNDERTAKINGS WHERE LLP PREPARING GROUP ACCOUNTS (NON-IAS OR IAS GROUP ACCOUNTS)

Introduction and interpretation

[10.300]

21. In this Part of this Schedule "the group" means the group consisting of the parent LLP and its subsidiary undertakings.

Subsidiary undertakings

22. (1) The following information must be given with respect to the undertakings that are subsidiary undertakings of the parent LLP at the end of the financial year.

(2) The name of each undertaking must be stated.

(3) There must be stated—

[(a) the address of the undertaking's registered office (whether in or outside the United Kingdom),]

(b) if it is unincorporated, the address of its principal place of business.

(4) It must also be stated whether the subsidiary undertaking is included in the consolidation and, if it is not, the reasons for excluding it from consolidation must be given.

(5) It must be stated with respect to each subsidiary undertaking by virtue of which of the conditions specified in section 1162(2) or (4) of the 2006 Act it is a subsidiary undertaking of its immediate parent undertaking.

That information need not be given if the relevant condition is that specified in subsection (2)(a) of that section (holding of a majority of the voting rights) and the immediate parent undertaking holds the same proportion of the shares in the undertaking as it holds voting rights.

Holdings in subsidiary undertakings

23. (1) The following information must be given with respect to the shares of a subsidiary undertaking held—

(a) by the parent LLP, and

(b) by the group,

and the information under paragraphs (a) and (b) must (if different) be shown separately.

(2) There must be stated—

(a) the identity of each class of shares held, and

(b) the proportion of the nominal value of the shares of that class represented by those shares.

Financial information about subsidiary undertakings not included in the consolidation

24. (1) There must be shown with respect to each subsidiary undertaking not included in the consolidation—

(a) the aggregate amount of its capital and reserves as at the end of its relevant financial year, and

(b) its profit or loss for that year.

(2) That information need not be given if the group's investment in the undertaking is included in the accounts by way of the equity method of valuation or if—

(a) the undertaking is not required by any provision of the 2006 Act to deliver a copy of its balance sheet for its relevant financial year and does not otherwise publish that balance sheet in the United Kingdom or elsewhere, and

(b) the holding of the group is less than 50% of the nominal value of the shares in the undertaking.

(3) Information otherwise required by this paragraph need not be given if it is not material.

(4) For the purposes of this paragraph the "relevant financial year" of a subsidiary undertaking is—

(a) if its financial year ends with that of the LLP, that year, and

(b) if not, its financial year ending last before the end of the LLP's financial year.

Joint ventures

25. (1) The following information must be given where an undertaking is dealt with in the consolidated accounts by the method of proportional consolidation in accordance with paragraph 18 of this Schedule (joint ventures)—

(a) the name of the undertaking,

[(b) the address of the undertaking's registered office (whether in or outside the United Kingdom),]

(c) the factors on which joint management of the undertaking is based, and

(d) the proportion of the capital of the undertaking held by [or on behalf of] undertakings included in the consolidation.

(2) Where the financial year of the undertaking did not end with that of the LLP, there must be stated the date on which a financial year of the undertaking last ended before that date.

Associated undertakings

26. (1) The following information must be given where an undertaking included in the consolidation has an interest in an associated undertaking.

(2) The name of the associated undertaking must be stated.

(3) There must be stated—

[(a) the address of the undertaking's registered office (whether in or outside the United Kingdom),]

(b) if it is unincorporated, the address of its principal place of business.

(4) The following information must be given with respect to the shares of the undertaking held—

(a) by the parent LLP, and

(b) by the group,

and the information under paragraphs (a) and (b) must be shown separately.

(5) There must be stated—

(a) the identity of each class of shares held, and

(b) the proportion of the nominal value of the shares of that class represented by those shares.

(6) In this paragraph "associated undertaking" has the meaning given by paragraph 19 of this Schedule; and the information required by this paragraph must be given notwithstanding that paragraph 20(3) of this Schedule (materiality) applies in relation to the accounts themselves.

Other significant holdings of parent LLP or group

27. (1) The information required by paragraphs 28 and 29 must be given where at the end of the financial year the parent LLP has a significant holding in an undertaking which is not one of its subsidiary undertakings and does not fall within paragraph 25 (joint ventures) or paragraph 26 (associated undertakings).

(2) A holding is significant for this purpose if—

(a) it amounts to 20% or more of the nominal value of any class of shares in the undertaking, or

(b) the amount of the holding (as stated or included in the LLP's individual accounts) exceeds 20% of the amount of its assets (as so stated).

28. (1) The name of the undertaking must be stated.

(2) There must be stated—

[(a) the address of the undertaking's registered office (whether in or outside the United Kingdom),]

(b) if it is unincorporated, the address of its principal place of business.

(3) The following information must be given with respect to the shares of the undertaking held by the parent LLP.

(4) There must be stated—

(a) the identity of each class of shares held, and

(b) the proportion of the nominal value of the shares of that class represented by those shares.

29. (1) There must also be stated—

(a) the aggregate amount of the capital and reserves of the undertaking as at the end of its relevant financial year, and

(b) its profit or loss for that year.

(2) That information need not be given in respect of an undertaking if—

(a) the undertaking is not required by any provision of the 2006 Act to deliver a copy of its balance sheet for its relevant financial year and does not otherwise publish that balance sheet in the United Kingdom or elsewhere, and

(b) the LLP's holding is less than 50% of the nominal value of the shares in the undertaking.

(3) Information otherwise required by this paragraph need not be given if it is not material.

(4) For the purposes of this paragraph the "relevant financial year" of an undertaking is—

(a) if its financial year ends with that of the LLP, that year, and

(b) if not, its financial year ending last before the end of the LLP's financial year.

30. (1) The information required by paragraphs 31 and 32 must be given where at the end of the financial year the group has a significant holding in an undertaking which is not a subsidiary undertaking of the parent LLP and does not fall within paragraph 25 (joint ventures) or paragraph 26 (associated undertakings).

(2) A holding is significant for this purpose if—

(a) it amounts to 20% or more of the nominal value of any class of shares in the undertaking, or

(b) the amount of the holding (as stated or included in the group accounts) exceeds 20% of the amount of the group's assets (as so stated).

31. (1) The name of the undertaking must be stated.

(2) There must be stated—

[(a) the address of the undertaking's registered office (whether in or outside the United Kingdom),]

(b) if it is unincorporated, the address of its principal place of business.

(3) The following information must be given with respect to the shares of the undertaking held by the group.

(4) There must be stated—

(a) the identity of each class of shares held, and

(b) the proportion of the nominal value of the shares of that class represented by those shares.

32. (1) There must also be stated—

(a) the aggregate amount of the capital and reserves of the undertaking as at the end of its relevant financial year, and

(b) its profit or loss for that year.

(2) That information need not be given if—

(a) the undertaking is not required by any provision of the 2006 Act to deliver a copy of its balance sheet for its relevant financial year and does not otherwise publish that balance sheet in the United Kingdom or elsewhere, and

(b) the holding of the group is less than 50% of the nominal value of the shares in the undertaking.

(3) Information otherwise required by this paragraph need not be given if it is not material.

(4) For the purposes of this paragraph the "relevant financial year" of an outside undertaking is—

(a) if its financial year ends with that of the parent LLP, that year, and

(b) if not, its financial year ending last before the end of the parent LLP's financial year.

Parent undertaking drawing up accounts for larger group

33. (1) Where the parent LLP is itself a subsidiary undertaking, the following information must be given with respect to that parent undertaking of the LLP which heads—

(a) the largest group of undertakings for which group accounts are drawn up and of which that LLP is a member, and

(b) the smallest such group of undertakings.

(2) The name of the parent undertaking must be stated.

(3) There must be stated—

(a) if the undertaking is incorporated outside the United Kingdom, the country in which it is incorporated,

(b) if it is unincorporated, the address of its principal place of business.

(4) If copies of the group accounts referred to in sub-paragraph (1) are available to the public, there must also be stated the addresses from which copies of the accounts can be obtained.

Identification of ultimate parent

34. (1) Where the parent LLP is itself a subsidiary undertaking, the following information must be given with respect to the body corporate (if any) regarded by the members as being that LLP's ultimate parent.

(2) The name of that body corporate must be stated.

(3) If that body corporate is incorporated outside the United Kingdom, the country in which it is incorporated must be stated (if known to the members).

Construction of references to shares held by parent LLP or group

35. (1) References in this Part of this Schedule to shares held by the parent LLP or the group are to be construed as follows.

(2) For the purposes of paragraphs 23, 26(4) and (5) and 27 to 29 (information about holdings in subsidiary and other undertakings)—

(a) there must be attributed to the parent LLP shares held on its behalf by any person; but

(b) there must be treated as not held by the parent LLP shares held on behalf of a person other than the LLP.

(3) References to shares held by the group are to any shares held by or on behalf of the parent LLP or any of its subsidiary undertakings; but any shares held on behalf of a person other than the parent LLP or any of its subsidiary undertakings are not to be treated as held by the group.

(4) Shares held by way of security must be treated as held by the person providing the security—

(a) where apart from the right to exercise them for the purpose of preserving the value of the security, or of realising it, the rights attached to the shares are exercisable only in accordance with his instructions, and
(b) where the shares are held in connection with the granting of loans as part of normal business activities and apart from the right to exercise them for the purpose of preserving the value of the security, or of realising it, the rights attached to the shares are exercisable only in his interests.

NOTES

Paras 22(3)(a), 26(3)(a), 28(2)(a) and 31(2)(a) were substituted by the Limited Liability Partnerships, Partnerships and Groups (Accounts and Audit) Regulations 2016, SI 2016/575, regs 27, 44, as from 17 May 2016, in relation to (a) financial years beginning on or after 1 January 2016; and (b) a financial year of an LLP beginning on or after 1 January 2015, but before 1 January 2016, if (i) the members of the LLP so decide, and (ii) a copy of the LLP's accounts for that financial year has not been delivered to the registrar in accordance with ss 444, 445 or 446 of the Companies Act 2006 as applied to LLPs by the Limited Liability Partnerships (Accounts and Audit) (Application of Companies Act 2006) Regulations before 17 May 2016 (see further the note at **[10.226]**).

SCHEDULE 5
GENERAL INTERPRETATION

Regulation 8

Financial instruments

[10.301]

1. References to "derivatives" include commodity-based contracts that give either contracting party the right to settle in cash or in some other financial instrument, except where such contracts—

(a) were entered into for the purpose of, and continue to meet, the LLP's expected purchase, sale or usage requirements,
(b) were designated for such purpose at their inception, and
(c) are expected to be settled by delivery of the commodity.

2. [(1) The expressions listed in sub-paragraph (2) have the same meaning as they have in Directive 2013/34/EU of 26 June 2013 on the annual financial statements etc of certain types of undertakings.]

(2) Those expressions are "available for sale financial asset", "business combination", "commodity-based contracts", "derivative", "equity instrument", "exchange difference", "fair value hedge accounting system", "financial fixed asset", "financial instrument", "foreign entity", "hedge accounting", "hedge accounting system", "hedged items", "hedging instrument", "held for trading purposes", "held to maturity", "monetary item", "receivables", "reliable market" and "trading portfolio".

Fixed and current assets

3. "Fixed assets" means assets of an LLP which are intended for use on a continuing basis in the LLP's activities, and "current assets" means assets not intended for such use.

Historical cost accounting rules

4. References to the historical cost accounting rules are to be read in accordance with paragraph 30 of Schedule 1 to these Regulations.

Listed investments

5. (1) "Listed investment" means an investment as respects which there has been granted a listing on—

(a) a recognised investment exchange other than an overseas investment exchange, or
(b) a stock exchange of repute outside the United Kingdom.

(2) "Recognised investment exchange" and "overseas investment exchange" have the meaning given in Part 18 of the Financial Services and Markets Act 2000.

Loans

6. A loan is treated as falling due for repayment, and an instalment of a loan is treated as falling due for payment, on the earliest date on which the lender could require repayment or (as the case may be) payment, if he exercised all options and rights available to him.

Materiality

7. Amounts which in the particular context of any provision of Schedule 1 to these Regulations are not material may be disregarded for the purposes of that provision.

Participating interests

8. (1) A "participating interest" means an interest held by an undertaking in the shares of another undertaking which it holds on a long-term basis for the purpose of securing a contribution to its activities by the exercise of control or influence arising from or related to that interest.

(2) A holding of 20% or more of the shares of the undertaking is to be presumed to be a participating interest unless the contrary is shown.

(3) The reference in sub-paragraph (1) to an interest in shares includes—

(a) an interest which is convertible into an interest in shares, and
(b) an option to acquire shares or any such interest,

and an interest or option falls within paragraph (a) or (b) notwithstanding that the shares to which it relates are, until the conversion or the exercise of the option, unissued.

(4) For the purposes of this paragraph an interest held on behalf of an undertaking is to be treated as held by it.

(5) In the balance sheet and profit and loss formats set out in [Section B of] Part 1 of Schedule 1 . . . to these Regulations, "participating interest" does not include an interest in a group undertaking.

(6) For the purpose of this paragraph as it applies in relation to the expression "participating interest"—

(a) in those formats as they apply in relation to group accounts, and

(b) in paragraph 19 of Schedule 4 (group accounts: undertakings to be accounted for as associated undertakings), the references in sub-paragraphs (1) to (4) to the interest held by, and the purposes and activities of, the undertaking concerned are to be construed as references to the interest held by, and the purposes and activities of, the group (within the meaning of paragraph 1 of that Schedule).

Provisions

9. (1) References to provisions for depreciation or diminution in value of assets are to any amount written off by way of providing for depreciation or diminution in value of assets.

(2) Any reference in the profit and loss account formats set out in Part 1 of Schedule 1 to these Regulations to the depreciation of, or amounts written off, assets of any description is to any provision for depreciation or diminution in value of assets of that description.

10. References to provisions for liabilities are to any amount retained as reasonably necessary for the purpose of providing for any liability the nature of which is clearly defined and which is either likely to be incurred, or certain to be incurred but uncertain as to amount or as to the date on which it will arise.

Purchase price

11. "Purchase price", in relation to an asset of an LLP or any raw materials or consumables used in the production of such an asset, includes any consideration (whether in cash or otherwise) given by the LLP in respect of that asset or those materials or consumables, as the case may be.

Staff costs

12. (1) "Social security costs" means any contributions by the LLP to any state social security or pension scheme, fund or arrangement.

(2) "Pension costs" includes—

(a) any costs incurred by the LLP in respect of any pension scheme established for the purpose of providing pensions for persons currently or formerly employed by the LLP,

(b) any sums set aside for the future payment of pensions directly by the LLP to current or former employees, and

(c) any pensions paid directly to such persons without having first been set aside.

(3) Any amount stated in respect of the item "social security costs" or in respect of the item "wages and salaries" in [the profit and loss account Format 2 in Section B of Part 1 of Schedule 1] must be determined by reference to payments made or costs incurred in respect of all persons employed by the LLP during the financial year under contracts of service.

NOTES

Para 2(1) was substituted, the words in square brackets in para 8(5) were inserted, the words omitted from that paragraph were revoked, and the words in square brackets in para 12(3) were substituted, by the Limited Liability Partnerships, Partnerships and Groups (Accounts and Audit) Regulations 2016, SI 2016/575, regs 27, 45, as from 17 May 2016, in relation to (a) financial years beginning on or after 1 January 2016; and (b) a financial year of an LLP beginning on or after 1 January 2015, but before 1 January 2016, if (i) the members of the LLP so decide, and (ii) a copy of the LLP's accounts for that financial year has not been delivered to the registrar in accordance with ss 444, 445 or 446 of the Companies Act 2006 as applied to LLPs by the Limited Liability Partnerships (Accounts and Audit) (Application of Companies Act 2006) Regulations before 17 May 2016 (see further the note at **[10.226]**).

LARGE AND MEDIUM-SIZED LIMITED LIABILITY PARTNERSHIPS (ACCOUNTS) REGULATIONS 2008

(SI 2008/1913)

NOTES

Made: 17 July 2008.

Authority: Limited Liability Partnerships Act 2000, ss 15, 17.

Commencement: 1 October 2008.

These Regulations are reproduced as amended by: the Limited Liability Partnerships, Partnerships and Groups (Accounts and Audit) Regulations 2016, SI 2016/575; the International Accounting Standards and European Public Limited-Liability Company (Amendment etc) (EU Exit) Regulations 2019, SI 2019/685.

ARRANGEMENT OF REGULATIONS

PART 1
INTRODUCTION

PART 2
FORM AND CONTENT OF ACCOUNTS

PART 1 INTRODUCTION

[10.302]

1 Citation and interpretation

(1) These Regulations may be cited as the Large and Medium-sized Limited Liability Partnerships (Accounts) Regulations 2008.

(2) In these Regulations—

"the 2006 Act" means the Companies Act 2006;

"the Large and Medium-sized Companies Accounts Regulations" means the Large and Medium-sized Companies and Groups (Accounts and Reports) Regulations 2008;

["LLP" means a limited liability partnership registered under the Limited Liability Partnerships Act 2000.]

(3) Any reference in these Regulations to a numbered Part or section of the 2006 Act is a reference to that Part or section as applied to LLPs by the Limited Liability Partnerships (Accounts and Audit) (Application of Companies Act 2006) Regulations 2008.

NOTES

Para (2): definition "LLP" substituted by the Limited Liability Partnerships, Partnerships and Groups (Accounts and Audit) Regulations 2016, SI 2016/575, regs 47, 48, as from 17 May 2016, in relation to (a) financial years beginning on or after 1 January 2016; and (b) a financial year of an LLP beginning on or after 1 January 2015, but before 1 January 2016, if (i) the members of the LLP so decide, and (ii) a copy of the LLP's accounts for that financial year has not been delivered to the registrar in accordance with ss 444, 445 or 446 of the Companies Act 2006 as applied to LLPs by the Limited Liability Partnerships (Accounts and Audit) (Application of Companies Act 2006) Regulations before 17 May 2016 (see further the note at **[10.226]**).

General note as to interpretation: as to the meaning of "the registrar" and "the register", and as to the construction of references to registration in a particular part of the United Kingdom, in any enactment relating to LLPs, see the Limited Liability Partnerships (Application of Companies Act 2006) Regulations 2009, SI 2009/1804, Sch 3, Pt 2, para 12 at **[10.419]**.

[10.303]

2 Commencement and application

(1) These Regulations come into force on 1st October 2008.

(2) They apply in relation to financial years beginning on or after 1st October 2008.

(3) They apply to LLPs, with modifications, provisions of the Large and Medium-sized Companies Accounts Regulations.

(4) They do not apply to LLPs which are subject to the small LLPs regime under Part 15 of the 2006 Act.

PART 2 FORM AND CONTENT OF ACCOUNTS

[10.304]

3 Non-IAS individual accounts

(1) Regulation 3 of the Large and Medium-sized Companies Accounts Regulations applies to LLPs, modified so that it reads as follows—

> **"3 Non-IAS individual accounts**
>
> (1) Subject to regulation 4, non-IAS individual accounts under section 396 of the 2006 Act (non-IAS individual accounts) must comply with the provisions of Schedule 1 to the Large and Medium-sized Limited Liability Partnerships (Accounts) Regulations 2008 as to the form and content of the balance sheet and profit and loss account, and additional information to be provided by way of notes to the accounts.
>
> (2) The profit and loss account of an LLP that falls within section 408 of the 2006 Act (individual profit and loss account where group accounts prepared) need not contain the information specified in paragraphs 62 to 67 of Schedule 1 to the Large and Medium-sized Limited Liability Partnerships (Accounts) Regulations 2008 (information supplementing the profit and loss account).".

(2) The provisions of Schedule 1 to the Large and Medium-sized Companies Accounts Regulations apply to LLPs, modified so that they are the provisions set out in Schedule 1 to these Regulations.

[10.305]

4 Medium-sized LLPs: exemptions for non-IAS individual accounts

Regulation 4 of the Large and Medium-sized Companies Accounts Regulations applies to LLPs, modified so that it reads as follows—

"4 Medium-sized LLPs: exemptions for non-IAS individual accounts

(1) This regulation applies to an LLP—

(a) which qualifies as medium-sized in relation to a financial year under section 465 of the 2006 Act, and

(b) the members of which are preparing non-IAS individual accounts under section 396 of that Act for that year.

[(2A) The individual accounts for the year need not comply with paragraph 45 (disclosure with respect to compliance with accounting standards) of Schedule 1 to these Regulations.

(2B) Paragraph 70 (related party transactions) applies with the modification that only particulars of transactions which have not been concluded under normal market conditions with the following must be disclosed—

(a) members of the LLP that are related parties; and

(b) undertakings in which the LLP itself has a participating interest.]

(3) . . .

NOTES

In reg 4 as set out above, paras (2A), (2B) were substituted (for the original para (2)), and para (3) was revoked by the Limited Liability Partnerships, Partnerships and Groups (Accounts and Audit) Regulations 2016, SI 2016/575, regs 47, 49, as from 17 May 2016, in relation to (a) financial years beginning on or after 1 January 2016; and (b) a financial year of an LLP beginning on or after 1 January 2015, but before 1 January 2016, if (i) the members of the LLP so decide, and (ii) a copy of the LLP's accounts for that financial year has not been delivered to the registrar in accordance with ss 444, 445 or 446 of the Companies Act 2006 as applied to LLPs by the Limited Liability Partnerships (Accounts and Audit) (Application of Companies Act 2006) Regulations before 17 May 2016 (see further the note at **[10.226]**).

[10.306]

5 Information about related undertakings (non-IAS or IAS individual or group accounts)

(1) Regulation 7 of the Large and Medium-sized Companies Accounts Regulations applies to LLPs, modified so that it reads as follows—

"7 Information about related undertakings (non-IAS or IAS individual or group accounts

(1) Non-IAS or IAS individual or group accounts must comply with the provisions of Schedule 2 to the Large and Medium-sized Limited Liability Partnerships (Accounts) Regulations 2008 as to information about related undertakings to be given in notes to the LLP's accounts.

(2) In Schedule 2 to the Large and Medium-sized Limited Liability Partnerships (Accounts) Regulations 2008—

- Part 1 contains provisions applying to all LLPs
- Part 2 contains provisions applying only to LLPs not required to prepare group accounts
- Part 3 contains provisions applying only to LLPs required to prepare group accounts.

(3) Information otherwise required to be given by Schedule 2 need not be disclosed with respect to an undertaking that—

(a) is established under the law of a country outside the United Kingdom, or

(b) carries on business outside the United Kingdom,

if the conditions specified in section 409(4) of the 2006 Act are met (see section 409(5) of the 2006 Act for disclosure required where advantage taken of this exemption).".

(2) The provisions of Schedule 4 to the Large and Medium-sized Companies Accounts Regulations apply to LLPs, modified so that they are the provisions set out in Schedule 2 to these Regulations.

[10.307]

6 Non-IAS group accounts

(1) Regulation 9 of the Large and Medium-sized Companies Accounts Regulations applies to LLPs, modified so that it reads as follows—

"9 Non-IAS group accounts

Where the members of a parent LLP prepare non-IAS group accounts under section 403 of the 2006 Act (group accounts: applicable accounting framework), those accounts must comply with the provisions of Schedule 3 to the Large and Medium-sized Limited Liability Partnerships (Accounts) Regulations 2008 as to the form and content of the consolidated balance sheet and consolidated profit and loss account, and additional information to be provided by way of notes to the accounts.".

(2) The provisions of Part 1 of Schedule 6 to the Large and Medium-sized Companies Accounts Regulations apply to LLPs, modified so that they are the provisions set out in Schedule 3 to these Regulations.

PART 3 INTERPRETATION

[10.308]

7 General interpretation

(1) Regulation 13 of the Large and Medium-sized Companies Accounts Regulations applies to LLPs, modified so that it reads as follows—

"13 General interpretation

Schedule 4 to the Large and Medium-sized Limited Liability Partnerships (Accounts) Regulations 2008 contains general definitions for the purposes of these Regulations as applied to LLPs.".

(2) The provisions of Schedule 10 to the Large and Medium-sized Companies Accounts Regulations apply to LLPs, modified so that they are the provisions set out in Schedule 4 to these Regulations.

[PART 4 REVIEW

[10.309]

8 Review

(1) The Secretary of State must from time to time—
- (a) carry out a review of the provisions of these Regulations to which amendments have been made by Part 4 of the Limited Liability Partnerships, Partnerships and Groups (Accounts and Audit) Regulations 2016 ("the 2016 Regulations"),
- (b) set out the conclusions of the review in a report, and
- (c) publish the report.

(2) The report must, in particular—
- (a) set out the objectives intended to be achieved by those provisions,
- (b) assess the extent to which those objectives are achieved,
- (c) assess whether those objectives remain appropriate, and
- (d) if those objectives remain appropriate, assess the extent to which they could be achieved in another way which involves less onerous regulatory provision.

(3) The first report under this regulation must be published before the end of the period of 5 years beginning with the date on which the 2016 Regulations come into force.

(4) Subsequent reports under this regulation must be published at intervals not exceeding 5 years.

(5) In this regulation, "regulatory provision" has the meaning given by section 32(4) of the Small Business, Enterprise and Employment Act 2015.]

NOTES

Added, together with preceding Part heading, by the Limited Liability Partnerships, Partnerships and Groups (Accounts and Audit) Regulations 2016, SI 2016/575, regs 47, 62, as from 17 May 2016.

Part 10 Miscellaneous other SIs

SCHEDULES

SCHEDULE 1
NON-IAS INDIVIDUAL ACCOUNTS

Regulation 3

PART 1 GENERAL RULES AND FORMATS

SECTION A GENERAL RULES

[10.310]

1. (1) Subject to the following provisions of this Schedule—
- (a) every balance sheet of an LLP must show the items listed in either of the balance sheet formats in Section B of this Part, and
- (b) every profit and loss account must show the items listed in either of the profit and loss account formats in Section B.

(2) References in this Schedule to the items listed in any of the formats in Section B are to those items read together with any of the notes following the formats which apply to those items.

(3) [Subject to paragraph 1A,] the items must be shown in the order and under the headings and sub-headings given in the particular format used, but—
- (a) the notes to the formats may permit alternative positions for any particular items, and
- (b) the heading or sub-heading for any item does not have to be distinguished by any letter or number assigned to that item in the format used.

[1A. (1) The members of the LLP may adapt one of the balance sheet formats in Section B so as to distinguish between current and non-current items in a different way, provided that—
- (a) the information given is at least equivalent to that which would have been required by the use of such format had it not been thus adapted, and
- (b) the presentation of those items is in accordance with generally accepted accounting principles or practice.

(2) The members of the LLP may adapt one of the profit and loss account formats in Section B, provided that—
- (a) the information given is at least equivalent to that which would have been required by the use of such format had it not been thus adapted, and
- (b) the presentation is in accordance with generally accepted accounting principles or practice.

(3) So far as is practicable, the following provisions of this Section apply to the balance sheet or profit or loss account of an LLP notwithstanding any such adaptation pursuant to this paragraph.]

2. (1) Where in accordance with paragraph 1 an LLP's balance sheet or profit and loss account for any financial year has been prepared by reference to one of the formats in Section B, the members of the LLP must use the same format in preparing non-IAS individual accounts for subsequent financial years, unless in their opinion there are special reasons for a change.

(2) Particulars of any such change must be given in a note to the accounts in which the new format is first used, and the reasons for the change must be explained.

3. (1) Any item required to be shown in an LLP's balance sheet or profit and loss account may be shown in greater detail than required by the particular format used.

(2) The balance sheet or profit and loss account may include an item representing or covering the amount of any asset or liability, income or expenditure not otherwise covered by any of the items listed in the format used, save that none of the following may be treated as assets in any balance sheet—

(a) preliminary expenses,

(b) expenses of, and commission on, any issue of debentures, and

(c) costs of research.

4. (1) Where the special nature of the LLP's business requires it, the members of the LLP must adapt the arrangement, headings and sub-headings otherwise required in respect of items given an Arabic number in the balance sheet or profit and loss account format used.

(2) The members may combine items to which Arabic numbers are given in any of the formats in Section B if—

(a) their individual amounts are not material to assessing the state of affairs or profit or loss of the LLP for the financial year in question, or

(b) the combination facilitates that assessment.

(3) Where sub-paragraph (2)(b) applies, the individual amounts of any items which have been combined must be disclosed in a note to the accounts.

5. (1) Subject to sub-paragraph (2), the members must not include a heading or sub-heading corresponding to an item in the balance sheet or profit and loss account format used if there is no amount to be shown for that item for the financial year to which the balance sheet or profit and loss account relates.

(2) Where an amount can be shown for the item in question for the immediately preceding financial year that amount must be shown under the heading or sub-heading required by the format for that item.

6. Every profit and loss account must show the amount of an LLP's profit or loss . . . before taxation.

7. (1) For every item shown in the balance sheet or profit and loss account the corresponding amount for the immediately preceding financial year must also be shown.

(2) Where that corresponding amount is not comparable with the amount to be shown for the item in question in respect of the financial year to which the balance sheet or profit and loss account relates, the former amount may be adjusted, and particulars of the non-comparability and of any adjustment must be disclosed in a note to the accounts.

8. Amounts in respect of items representing assets or income may not be set off against amounts in respect of items representing liabilities or expenditure (as the case may be), or vice versa.

9. The members of the LLP must, in determining how amounts are presented within items in the profit and loss account and balance sheet, have regard to the substance of the reported transaction or arrangement, in accordance with generally accepted accounting principles or practice.

[9A. Where an asset or liability relates to more than one item in the balance sheet, the relationship of such asset or liability to the relevant items must be disclosed either under those items or in the notes to the accounts.]

SECTION B THE REQUIRED FORMATS FOR ACCOUNTS

Balance sheet formats

Format 1

A. Fixed assets

I. Intangible assets

1. Development costs
2. Concessions, patents, licences, trade marks and similar rights and assets[(1)]
3. Goodwill[(2)]
4. Payments on account

II. Tangible assets

1. Land and buildings
2. Plant and machinery
3. Fixtures, fittings, tools and equipment
4. Payments on account and assets in course of construction

III. Investments

1. Shares in group undertakings
2. Loans to group undertakings
3. Participating interests
4. Loans to undertakings in which the LLP has a participating interest
5. Other investments other than loans
6. Other loans

B. Current assets

I. Stocks

1. Raw materials and consumables
2. Work in progress
3. Finished goods and goods for resale
4. Payments on account

II. Debtors[(3)]

1. Trade debtors
2. Amounts owed by group undertakings
3. Amounts owed by undertakings in which the LLP has a participating interest

4. Other debtors
5. Prepayments and accrued income[(4)]

III. Investments
1. Shares in group undertakings
2. Other investments

IV. Cash at bank and in hand

C. Prepayments and accrued income[(4)]

D. Creditors: amounts falling due within one year
1. Debenture loans[(5)]
2. Bank loans and overdrafts
3. Payments received on account[(6)]
4. Trade creditors
5. Bills of exchange payable
6. Amounts owed to group undertakings
7. Amounts owed to undertakings in which the LLP has a participating interest
8. Other creditors including taxation and social security[(7)]
9. Accruals and deferred income[(8)]

E. Net current assets (liabilities)[(9)]

F. Total assets less current liabilities

G. Creditors: amounts falling due after more than one year
1. Debenture loans[(5)]
2. Bank loans and overdrafts
3. Payments received on account[(6)]
4. Trade creditors
5. Bills of exchange payable
6. Amounts owed to group undertakings
7. Amounts owed to undertakings in which the LLP has a participating interest
8. Other creditors including taxation and social security[(7)]
9. Accruals and deferred income[(8)]

H. Provisions for liabilities
1. Pensions and similar obligations
2. Taxation, including deferred taxation
3. Other provisions

I. Accruals and deferred income[(8)]

J. Loans and other debts due to members[(10)]

K. Members' other interests

I. Members' capital

II. Revaluation reserve

III. Other reserves[, including the fair value reserve]

Balance sheet formats

Format 2

ASSETS

A. Fixed assets

I. Intangible assets
1. Development costs
2. Concessions, patents, licences, trade marks and similar rights and assets[(1)]
3. Goodwill[(2)]
4. Payments on account

II. Tangible assets
1. Land and buildings
2. Plant and machinery
3. Fixtures, fittings, tools and equipment
4. Payments on account and assets in course of construction

III. Investments
1. Shares in group undertakings
2. Loans to group undertakings
3. Participating interests
4. Loans to undertakings in which the LLP has a participating interest
5. Other investments other than loans
6. Other loans

B. Current assets

I. Stocks
1. Raw materials and consumables
2. Work in progress
3. Finished goods and goods for resale
4. Payments on account

II. Debtors[3]
1. Trade debtors
2. Amounts owed by group undertakings
3. Amounts owed by undertakings in which the LLP has a participating interest
4. Other debtors
5. Prepayments and accrued income[4]

III. Investments
1. Shares in group undertakings
2. Other investments

IV. Cash at bank and in hand

C. Prepayments and accrued income[4]

[CAPITAL, RESERVES AND LIABILITIES]

A. Loans and other debts due to members[10]

B. Members' other interests
I. Members' capital
II. Revaluation reserve
III. Other reserves[, including the fair value reserve]

C. Provisions for liabilities
1. Pensions and similar obligations
2. Taxation, including deferred taxation
3. Other provisions

D. Creditors[11]
1. Debenture loans[5]
2. Bank loans and overdrafts
3. Payments received on account[6]
4. Trade creditors
5. Bills of exchange payable
6. Amounts owed to group undertakings
7. Amounts owed to undertakings in which the LLP has a participating interest
8. Other creditors including taxation and social security[7]
9. Accruals and deferred income[8]

E. Accruals and deferred income[8]

Notes on the balance sheet formats

(1) Concessions, patents, licences, trade marks and similar rights and assets

(Formats 1 and 2, item A.I.2.)

Amounts in respect of assets are only to be included in an LLP's balance sheet under this item if either—

(a) the assets were acquired for valuable consideration and are not required to be shown under goodwill, or

(b) the assets in question were created by the LLP itself.

(2) Goodwill

(Formats 1 and 2, item A.I.3.)

Amounts representing goodwill are only to be included to the extent that the goodwill was acquired for valuable consideration.

(3) Debtors

(Formats 1 and 2, items B.II.1 to 5.)

The amount falling due after more than one year must be shown separately for each item included under debtors.

(4) Prepayments and accrued income

(Formats 1 and 2, items B.II.5 and C.)

This item may be shown in either of the two positions given in Formats 1 and 2.

(5) Debenture loans

(Format 1, items D.1 and G.1 and Format 2, item D.1.)

The amount of any convertible loans must be shown separately.

(6) Payments received on account

(Format 1, items D.3 and G.3 and Format 2, item D.3.)

Payments received on account of orders must be shown for each of these items in so far as they are not shown as deductions from stocks.

(7) Other creditors including taxation and social security

(Format 1, items D.8 and G.8 and Format 2, item D.8.)

The amount for creditors in respect of taxation and social security must be shown separately from the amount for other creditors.

(8) Accruals and deferred income

(Format 1, items D.9, G.9 and I and Format 2, items D.9 and E.)

The two positions given for this item in Format 1 at D.9 and G.9 are an alternative to the position at I, but if the item is not shown in a position corresponding to that at I it may be shown in either or both of the other two positions (as the case may require).

The two positions given for this item in Format 2 are alternatives.

(9) Net current assets (liabilities)

(Format 1, item E.)

In determining the amount to be shown for this item any amounts shown under "prepayments and accrued income" must be taken into account wherever shown.

(10) Loans and other debts due to members

(Format 1, item J and Format 2, Liabilities item A.)

The following amounts must be shown separately under this item—

(a) the aggregate amount of money advanced to the LLP by the members by way of loan,
(b) the aggregate amount of money owed to members by the LLP in respect of profits,
(c) any other amounts.

(11) Creditors

(Format 2, items D.1 to 9.)

Amounts falling due within one year and after one year must be shown separately for each of these items and for the aggregate of all of these items.

Profit and loss account formats

Format 1
(see note (15) below)

1. Turnover
2. Cost of sales[(12)]
3. Gross profit or loss
4. Distribution costs[(12)]
5. Administrative expenses[(12)]
6. Other operating income
7. Income from shares in group undertakings
8. Income from participating interests
9. Income from other fixed asset investments[(13)]
10. Other interest receivable and similar income[(13)]
11. Amounts written off investments
12. Interest payable and similar [expenses][(14)]
13. Tax on profit or loss . . .
14. Profit or loss . . . after taxation

15–18. . . .

19. Other taxes not shown under the above items
20. Profit or loss for the financial year before members' remuneration and profit shares

Profit and loss account formats

Format 2

1. Turnover
2. Change in stocks of finished goods and in work in progress
3. Own work capitalised
4. Other operating income
5.
   (a) Raw materials and consumables
   (b) Other external [expenses]
6. Staff costs
   (a) wages and salaries
   (b) social security costs
   (c) other pension costs
7.
   (a) Depreciation and other amounts written off tangible and intangible fixed assets
   [(b) Amounts written off current assets, to the extent that they exceed write-offs which are normal in the undertaking concerned]
8. Other operating [expenses]
9. Income from shares in group undertakings
10. Income from participating interests
11. Income from other fixed asset investments[(13)]

12. Other interest receivable and similar income[(13)]

13. Amounts written off investments

14. Interest payable and similar [expenses][(14)]

15. Tax on profit or loss . . .

16. Profit or loss . . . after taxation

17–20.

21. Other taxes not shown under the above items

22. Profit or loss for the financial year before members' remuneration and profit shares

Notes on the profit and loss account formats

(12) Cost of sales: distribution costs: administrative expenses

(Format 1, items 2, 4 and 5.)

These items must be stated after taking into account any necessary provisions for depreciation or diminution in value of assets.

(13) Income from other fixed asset investments: other interest receivable and similar income

(Format 1, items 9 and 10; Format 2, items 11 and 12.)

Income and interest derived from group undertakings must be shown separately from income and interest derived from other sources. Interest receivable from members must not be included under this item.

(14) Interest payable and similar [expenses]

(Format 1, item 12; Format 2, item 14.)

The amount payable to group undertakings must be shown separately. Interest payable to members must not be included under this item.

(15) Format 1

The amount of any provisions for depreciation and diminution in value of tangible and intangible fixed assets falling to be shown under item 7(a) in Format 2 must be disclosed in a note to the accounts in any case where the profit and loss account is prepared using Format 1.

NOTES

All amendments to Part 1 of this Schedule, as noted below, were made by the Limited Liability Partnerships, Partnerships and Groups (Accounts and Audit) Regulations 2016, SI 2016/575, regs 47, 50, 51, as from 17 May 2016, in relation to (a) financial years beginning on or after 1 January 2016; and (b) a financial year of an LLP beginning on or after 1 January 2015, but before 1 January 2016, if (i) the members of the LLP so decide, and (ii) a copy of the LLP's accounts for that financial year has not been delivered to the registrar in accordance with ss 444, 445 or 446 of the Companies Act 2006 as applied to LLPs by the Limited Liability Partnerships (Accounts and Audit) (Application of Companies Act 2006) Regulations before 17 May 2016 (see further the note at **[10.226]**).

Section A is amended as follows:
in para 1(3), the words in square brackets were inserted;
paras 1A, 9A were inserted; and
in para 6, the words omitted were revoked.
Section B is amended as follows:
in balance sheet Format 1, the words in square brackets in item K III were inserted;
in balance sheet Format 2, the words "CAPITAL, RESERVES AND LIABILITIES" in square brackets were substituted, and the words in square brackets in item B III were inserted;
in profit and loss account Format 1, the word in square brackets in item 12 was substituted, the words omitted from items 13 and 14 were revoked, and items 15–18 were revoked;
in profit and loss account Format 2, the words in square brackets in items 5(b) 8, 14 were substituted, item 7(b) was substituted, the words omitted from items 15 and 16 were revoked, and items 17–20 were revoked;
in the notes on the profit and loss account formats the word in square brackets in the title to note (14) was substituted.

PART 2 ACCOUNTING PRINCIPLES AND RULES

SECTION A ACCOUNTING PRINCIPLES

Preliminary

[10.311]

10. (1) The amounts to be included in respect of all items shown in an LLP's accounts must be determined in accordance with the principles set out in this Section.

(2) But if it appears to the LLP's members that there are special reasons for departing from any of those principles in preparing the LLP's accounts in respect of any financial year they may do so, in which case particulars of the departure, the reasons for it and its effect must be given in a note to the accounts.

Accounting principles

11. The LLP is presumed to be carrying on business as a going concern.

12. Accounting policies [and measurement bases] must be applied consistently within the same accounts and from one financial year to the next.

13. The amount of any item must be determined on a prudent basis, and in particular—

(a) only profits realised at the balance sheet date are to be included in the profit and loss account, . . .

(b) all liabilities which have arisen in respect of the financial year to which the accounts relate or a previous financial year must be taken into account, including those which only become apparent between the balance sheet date and the date on which it is signed on behalf of the members in accordance with section 414 of the 2006 Act (approval and signing of accounts);

[(c) all provisions for diminution of value must be recognised, whether the result of the financial year is a profit or a loss,

(d) at the balance sheet date, a provision must represent the best estimate of the expenses likely to be incurred or, in the case of a liability, of the amount required to meet that liability, and

(e) provisions must not be used to adjust the value of assets.]

14. All income and charges relating to the financial year to which the accounts relate must be taken into account, without regard to the date of receipt or payment.

15. In determining the aggregate amount of any item, the amount of each individual asset or liability that falls to be taken into account must be determined separately.

[15A. The opening balance sheet for each financial year must correspond to the closing balance sheet for the preceding financial year.]

SECTION B HISTORICAL COST ACCOUNTING RULES

Preliminary

16. Subject to Sections C and D of this Part of this Schedule, the amounts to be included in respect of all items shown in an LLP's accounts must be determined in accordance with the rules set out in this Section.

Fixed assets

General rules

17. (1) The amount to be included in respect of any fixed asset must be its purchase price or production cost.

(2) This is subject to any provision for depreciation or diminution in value made in accordance with paragraphs 18 to 20.

Rules for depreciation and diminution in value

18. In the case of any fixed asset which has a limited useful economic life, the amount of—

(a) its purchase price or production cost, or

(b) where it is estimated that any such asset will have a residual value at the end of the period of its useful economic life, its purchase price or production cost less that estimated residual value,

must be reduced by provisions for depreciation calculated to write off that amount systematically over the period of the asset's useful economic life.

19. (1) Where a fixed asset investment falling to be included under item A.III of either of the balance sheet formats set out in Part 1 of this Schedule has diminished in value, provisions for diminution in value may be made in respect of it and the amount to be included in respect of it may be reduced accordingly.

(2) Provisions for diminution in value must be made in respect of any fixed asset which has diminished in value if the reduction in its value is expected to be permanent (whether its useful economic life is limited or not), and the amount to be included in respect of it must be reduced accordingly.

[(3) Provisions made under sub-paragraph (1) or (2) must be charged to the profit and loss account and disclosed separately in a note to the accounts if not shown separately in the profit and loss account.]

20. (1) Where the reasons for which any provision was made in accordance with paragraph 19 have ceased to apply to any extent, that provision must be written back to the extent that it is no longer necessary.

[(1A) But provision made in accordance with paragraph 19(2) in respect of goodwill must not be written back to any extent.]

[(2) Any amounts written back under sub-paragraph (1) must be recognised in the profit and loss account and disclosed separately in a note to the accounts if not shown separately in the profit and loss account.]

[Intangible Assets

21. (1) Where this is in accordance with generally accepted accounting principles or practice, development costs may be included in "other intangible assets" under "fixed assets" in the balance sheet formats set out in Section B of Part 1 of this Schedule.

(2) If any amount is included in an LLP's balance sheet in respect of development costs, the note on accounting policies (see paragraph 44 of this Schedule) must include the following information—

(a) the period over which the amount of those costs originally capitalised is being or is to be written off, and

(b) the reasons for capitalising the development costs in question.

22. (1) Intangible assets must be written off over the useful economic life of the intangible asset.

(2) Where in exceptional cases the useful life of intangible assets cannot be reliably estimated, such assets must be written off over a period chosen by the members of the LLP.

(3) The period referred to in sub-paragraph (2) must not exceed ten years.

(4) There must be disclosed in a note to the accounts the period referred to in sub-paragraph (2) and the reasons for choosing that period.]

Current assets

23. Subject to paragraph 24, the amount to be included in respect of any current asset must be its purchase price or production cost.

24. (1) If the net realisable value of any current asset is lower than its purchase price or production cost, the amount to be included in respect of that asset must be the net realisable value.

(2) Where the reasons for which any provision for diminution in value was made in accordance with sub-paragraph (1) have ceased to apply to any extent, that provision must be written back to the extent that it is no longer necessary.

Miscellaneous and supplementary provisions

Excess of money owed over value received as an asset item

25. (1) Where the amount repayable on any debt owed by an LLP is greater than the value of the consideration received in the transaction giving rise to the debt, the amount of the difference may be treated as an asset.

(2) Where any such amount is so treated—

(a) it must be written off by reasonable amounts each year and must be completely written off before repayment of the debt, and

(b) if the current amount is not shown as a separate item in the LLP's balance sheet, it must be disclosed in a note to the accounts.

Assets included at a fixed amount

26. (1) Subject to sub-paragraph (2), assets which fall to be included—

(a) amongst the fixed assets of an LLP under the item "tangible assets", or

(b) amongst the current assets of an LLP under the item "raw materials and consumables",

may be included at a fixed quantity and value.

(2) Sub-paragraph (1) applies to assets of a kind which are constantly being replaced where—

(a) their overall value is not material to assessing the LLP's state of affairs, and

(b) their quantity, value and composition are not subject to material variation.

Determination of purchase price or production cost

27. (1) The purchase price of an asset is to be determined by adding to the actual price paid any expenses incidental to its acquisition [and then subtracting any incidental reductions in the cost of acquisition].

(2) The production cost of an asset is to be determined by adding to the purchase price of the raw materials and consumables used the amount of the costs incurred by the LLP which are directly attributable to the production of that asset.

(3) In addition, there may be included in the production cost of an asset—

(a) a reasonable proportion of the costs incurred by the LLP which are only indirectly attributable to the production of that asset, but only to the extent that they relate to the period of production, and

(b) interest on capital borrowed to finance the production of that asset, to the extent that it accrues in respect of the period of production,

provided, however, in a case within paragraph (b), that the inclusion of the interest in determining the cost of that asset and the amount of the interest so included is disclosed in a note to the accounts.

(4) In the case of current assets distribution costs may not be included in production costs.

28. (1) The purchase price or production cost of—

(a) any assets which fall to be included under any item shown in an LLP's balance sheet under the general item "stocks", and

(b) any assets which are fungible assets (including investments),

may be determined by the application of any of the methods mentioned in sub-paragraph (2) in relation to any such assets of the same class, provided that the method chosen is one which appears to the members to be appropriate in the circumstances of the LLP.

(2) Those methods are—

(a) the method known as "first in, first out" (FIFO),

(b) the method known as "last in, first out" (LIFO),

(c) a weighted average price, and

(d) any other method [reflecting generally accepted best practice].

(3) Where in the case of any LLP—

(a) the purchase price or production cost of assets falling to be included under any item shown in the LLP's balance sheet has been determined by the application of any method permitted by this paragraph, and

(b) the amount shown in respect of that item differs materially from the relevant alternative amount given below in this paragraph,

the amount of that difference must be disclosed in a note to the accounts.

(4) Subject to sub-paragraph (5), for the purposes of sub-paragraph (3)(b), the relevant alternative amount, in relation to any item shown in an LLP's balance sheet, is the amount which would have been shown in respect of that item if assets of any class included under that item at an amount determined by any method permitted by this paragraph had instead been included at their replacement cost as at the balance sheet date.

(5) The relevant alternative amount may be determined by reference to the most recent actual purchase price or production cost before the balance sheet date of assets of any class included under the item in question instead of by reference to their replacement cost as at that date, but only if the former appears to the members of the LLP to constitute the more appropriate standard of comparison in the case of assets of that class.

(6) "Fungible assets" means assets of any description which are substantially indistinguishable one from another.

Substitution of original stated amount where price or cost unknown

29. (1) This paragraph applies where—

(a) there is no record of the purchase price or production cost of any asset of an LLP or of any price, expenses or costs relevant for determining its purchase price or production cost in accordance with paragraph 27, or

(b) any such record cannot be obtained without unreasonable expense or delay.

(2) In such a case, the purchase price or production cost of the asset must be taken, for the purposes of paragraphs 17 to 24, to be the value ascribed to it in the earliest available record of its value made on or after its acquisition or production by the LLP.

[Equity method in respect of participating interests

29A. Participating interests may be accounted for using the equity method.]

SECTION C ALTERNATIVE ACCOUNTING RULES

Preliminary

30. (1) The rules set out in Section B are referred to below in this Schedule as the historical cost accounting rules.

(2) Those rules, with the omission of paragraphs 16, 22 and 26 to 29, are referred to below in this Part of this Schedule as the depreciation rules; and references below in this Schedule to the historical cost accounting rules do not include the depreciation rules as they apply by virtue of paragraph 33.

31. Subject to paragraphs 33 to 35, the amounts to be included in respect of assets of any description mentioned in paragraph 32 may be determined on any basis so mentioned.

Alternative accounting rules

32. (1) Intangible fixed assets, other than goodwill, may be included at their current cost.

(2) Tangible fixed assets may be included at a market value determined as at the date of their last valuation or at their current cost.

(3) Investments of any description falling to be included under item A III of either of the balance sheet formats set out in Part 1 of this Schedule may be included either—

(a) at a market value determined as at the date of their last valuation, or

(b) at a value determined on any basis which appears to the members to be appropriate in the circumstances of the LLP.

But in the latter case particulars of the method of valuation adopted and of the reasons for adopting it must be disclosed in a note to the accounts.

(4), (5) . . .

Application of the depreciation rules

33. (1) Where the value of any asset of an LLP is determined on any basis mentioned in paragraph 32, that value must be, or (as the case may require) be the starting point for determining, the amount to be included in respect of that asset in the LLP's accounts, instead of its purchase price or production cost or any value previously so determined for that asset.

The depreciation rules apply accordingly in relation to any such asset with the substitution for any reference to its purchase price or production cost of a reference to the value most recently determined for that asset on any basis mentioned in paragraph 32.

(2) The amount of any provision for depreciation required in the case of any fixed asset by paragraphs 18 to 20 as they apply by virtue of sub-paragraph (1) is referred to below in this paragraph as the adjusted amount, and the amount of any provision which would be required by any of those paragraphs in the case of that asset according to the historical cost accounting rules is referred to as the historical cost amount.

(3) Where sub-paragraph (1) applies in the case of any fixed asset the amount of any provision for depreciation in respect of that asset—

(a) included in any item shown in the profit and loss account in respect of amounts written off assets of the description in question, or

(b) taken into account in stating any item so shown which is required by note (12) of the notes on the profit and loss account formats set out in Part 1 of this Schedule to be stated after taking into account any necessary provision for depreciation or diminution in value of assets included under it,

may be the historical cost amount instead of the adjusted amount, provided that the amount of any difference between the two is shown separately in the profit and loss account or in a note to the accounts.

Additional information to be provided in case of departure from historical cost accounting rules

34. (1) This paragraph applies where the amounts to be included in respect of assets covered by any items shown in an LLP's accounts have been determined on any basis mentioned in paragraph 32.

(2) The items affected and the basis of valuation adopted in determining the amounts of the assets in question in the case of each such item must be disclosed in [the note on accounting policies (see paragraph 44 of this Schedule)].

[(3) In the case of each balance sheet item affected, the comparable amounts determined according to the historical cost accounting rules must be shown in a note to the accounts.]

(4) In sub-paragraph (3), references in relation to any item to the comparable amounts determined as there mentioned are references to—

(a) the aggregate amount which would be required to be shown in respect of that item if the amounts to be included in respect of all the assets covered by that item were determined according to the historical cost accounting rules, and

(b) the aggregate amount of the cumulative provisions for depreciation or diminution in value which would be permitted or required in determining those amounts according to those rules.

Revaluation reserve

35. (1) With respect to any determination of the value of an asset of an LLP on any basis mentioned in paragraph 32, the amount of any profit or loss arising from that determination (after allowing, where appropriate, for any provisions for depreciation or diminution in value made otherwise than by reference to the value so determined and any adjustments of any such provisions made in the light of that determination) must be credited or (as the case may be) debited to a separate reserve ("the revaluation reserve").

(2) The amount of the revaluation reserve [under "Members' other interests"] must be shown in the LLP's balance sheet under a separate sub-heading in the position given for the item "revaluation reserve" in Format 1 or 2 of the balance sheet formats set out in Part 1 of this Schedule . . .

(3) The treatment for taxation purposes of amounts credited or debited to the revaluation reserve must be disclosed in a note to the accounts.

SECTION D FAIR VALUE ACCOUNTING

Inclusion of financial instruments at fair value

36. (1) Subject to sub-paragraphs (2) to (5), financial instruments (including derivatives) may be included at fair value.

(2) Sub-paragraph (1) does not apply to financial instruments that constitute liabilities unless—
- (a) they are held as part of a trading portfolio,
- (b) they are derivatives, or
- (c) they are financial instruments falling within sub-paragraph (4).

(3) Unless they are financial instruments falling within sub-paragraph (4), sub-paragraph (1) does not apply to—
- (a) financial instruments (other than derivatives) held to maturity,
- (b) loans and receivables originated by the LLP and not held for trading purposes,
- (c) interests in subsidiary undertakings, associated undertakings and joint ventures,
- (d) equity instruments issued by the LLP,
- (e) contracts for contingent consideration in a business combination, or
- (f) other financial instruments with such special characteristics that the instruments, according to generally accepted accounting principles or practice, should be accounted for differently from other financial instruments.

[(4) Financial instruments which under [UK-adopted international accounting standards] may be included in accounts at fair value, may be so included, provided that the disclosures required by such accounting standards are made.]

(5) If the fair value of a financial instrument cannot be determined reliably in accordance with paragraph 37, sub-paragraph (1) does not apply to that financial instrument.

(6) In this paragraph—

"associated undertaking" has the meaning given by paragraph 19 of Schedule 3 to these Regulations;

"joint venture" has the meaning given by paragraph 18 of that Schedule.

Determination of fair value

37. (1) The fair value of a financial instrument is its value determined in accordance with this paragraph.

(2) If a reliable market can readily be identified for the financial instrument, its fair value is determined by reference to its market value.

(3) If a reliable market cannot readily be identified for the financial instrument but can be identified for its components or for a similar instrument, its fair value is determined by reference to the market value of its components or of the similar instrument.

(4) If neither sub-paragraph (2) nor (3) applies, the fair value of the financial instrument is a value resulting from generally accepted valuation models and techniques.

(5) Any valuation models and techniques used for the purposes of sub-paragraph (4) must ensure a reasonable approximation of the market value.

Hedged items

38. An LLP may include any assets and liabilities, or identified portions of such assets or liabilities, that qualify as hedged items under a fair value hedge accounting system at the amount required under that system.

Other assets that may be included at fair value

[39. (1) This paragraph applies to—
- (a) stocks,
- (b) investment property, and
- (c) living animals and plants.

(2) Stocks, investment property, and living animals and plants may be included at fair value, provided that, as the case may be, all such stocks, investment property, and living animals and plants are so included where their fair value can reliably be determined.

(3) In this paragraph, "fair value" means fair value determined in accordance with generally accepted accounting principles or practice.]

Accounting for changes in value

40. (1) This paragraph applies where a financial instrument is valued in accordance with paragraph 36 or 38 or an asset is valued in accordance with paragraph 39.

(2) Notwithstanding paragraph 13 in this Part of this Schedule, and subject to sub-paragraphs (3) and (4), a change in the value of the financial instrument or of the investment property or living animal or plant must be included in the profit and loss account.

(3) Where—

(a) the financial instrument accounted for is a hedging instrument under a hedge accounting system that allows some or all of the change in value not to be shown in the profit and loss account, or

(b) the change in value relates to an exchange difference arising on a monetary item that forms part of an LLP's net investment in a foreign entity,

the amount of the change in value must be credited to or (as the case may be) debited from a separate reserve ("the fair value reserve").

(4) Where the instrument accounted for—

(a) is an available for sale financial asset, and

(b) is not a derivative,

the change in value may be credited to or (as the case may be) debited from the fair value reserve.

The fair value reserve

41. (1) The fair value reserve must be adjusted to the extent that the amounts shown in it are no longer necessary for the purposes of paragraph 40(3) or (4).

(2) The treatment for taxation purposes of amounts credited or debited to the fair value reserve must be disclosed in a note to the accounts.

NOTES

Words in square brackets in para 36(4) substituted by the International Accounting Standards and European Public Limited-Liability Company (Amendment etc) (EU Exit) Regulations 2019, SI 2019/685, reg 19, Sch 1, Pt 2, para 60(a), in relation to accounts for financial years beginning on or after IP completion day (as defined in the European Union (Withdrawal Agreement) Act 2020, s 39) (note also that in relation to accounts for financial years which begin before but end on or after IP completion day, the enactments amended by Parts 1–3 of Sch 1 to the 2019 Regulations have effect as if the UK were a member State until the end of the financial year in question).

All other amendments to Part 2 of this Schedule noted below were made by the Limited Liability Partnerships, Partnerships and Groups (Accounts and Audit) Regulations 2016, SI 2016/575, regs 47, 52–55, as from 17 May 2016, in relation to (a) financial years beginning on or after 1 January 2016; and (b) a financial year of an LLP beginning on or after 1 January 2015, but before 1 January 2016, if (i) the members of the LLP so decide, and (ii) a copy of the LLP's accounts for that financial year has not been delivered to the registrar in accordance with ss 444, 445 or 446 of the Companies Act 2006 as applied to LLPs by the Limited Liability Partnerships (Accounts and Audit) (Application of Companies Act 2006) Regulations before 17 May 2016 (see further the note at **[10.226]**).

In para 12, the words in square brackets were inserted, in para 13, the word omitted from sub-para (a) was revoked and sub-paras (c)–(e) were inserted, and para 15A was inserted.

Para 19(3) was substituted.

In para 20, sub-para (1A) was inserted, and sub-para (2) was substituted.

Paras 21, 22 were substituted.

In para 27 the words in square brackets were inserted.

In para 28(2)(d), the words in square brackets were substituted.

Para 29A was inserted.

In para 32, sub-paras (4), (5) were revoked.

In para 34, the words in square brackets in sub-para (2) were substituted, and sub-para (3) was substituted.

In para 35(2), the words in square brackets were inserted, and the words omitted were revoked.

Para 36(4) was substituted.

Para 39 was substituted.

PART 3 NOTES TO THE ACCOUNTS

Preliminary

[10.312]

[42. (1) Any information required in the case of an LLP by the following provisions of this Part of this Schedule must be given by way of a note to the accounts.

(2) These notes must be presented in the order in which, where relevant, the items to which they relate are presented in the balance sheet and in the profit and loss account.]

General

Reserves

43. Any amount set aside or proposed to be set aside to, or withdrawn or proposed to be withdrawn from, reserves must be stated.

Disclosure of accounting policies

44. The accounting policies adopted by the LLP in determining the amounts to be included in respect of items shown in the balance sheet and in determining the profit or loss of the LLP must be stated (including such policies with respect to the depreciation and diminution in value of assets).

45. It must be stated whether the accounts have been prepared in accordance with applicable accounting standards and particulars of any material departure from those standards and the reasons for it must be given (see regulation 4 for exemption for medium-sized LLPs).

Information supplementing the balance sheet

46. Paragraphs 47 to 61 require information which either supplements the information given with respect to any particular items shown in the balance sheet or is otherwise relevant to assessing the LLP's state of affairs in the light of the information so given.

Loans and other debts due to members

47. The following information must be given—

Part 10 Miscellaneous other SIs

(a) the aggregate amount of loans and other debts due to members as at the date of the beginning of the financial year,
(b) the aggregate amounts contributed by members during the financial year,
(c) the aggregate amounts transferred to or from the profit and loss account during that year,
(d) the aggregate amounts withdrawn by members or applied on behalf of members during that year,
(e) the aggregate amount of loans and other debts due to members as at the balance sheet date, and
(f) the aggregate amount of loans and other debts due to members that fall due after one year.

Debentures

48. (1) If the LLP has issued any debentures during the financial year to which the accounts relate, the following information must be given—
(a) the classes of debentures issued, and
(b) as respects each class of debentures, the amount issued and the consideration received by the LLP for the issue.

(2) Where any of the LLP's debentures are held by a nominee of or trustee for the LLP, the nominal amount of the debentures and the amount at which they are stated in the accounting records kept by the LLP in accordance with section 386 of the 2006 Act (duty to keep accounting records) must be stated.

Fixed assets

49. (1) In respect of each item which is or would but for paragraph 4(2)(b) be shown under the general item "fixed assets" in the LLP's balance sheet the following information must be given—
(a) the appropriate amounts in respect of that item as at the date of the beginning of the financial year and as at the balance sheet date respectively,
(b) the effect on any amount shown in the balance sheet in respect of that item of—
(i) any revision of the amount in respect of any assets included under that item made during that year on any basis mentioned in paragraph 32,
(ii) acquisitions during that year of any assets,
(iii) disposals during that year of any assets, and
(iv) any transfers of assets of the LLP to and from that item during that year.

(2) The reference in sub-paragraph (1)(a) to the appropriate amounts in respect of any item as at any date there mentioned is a reference to amounts representing the aggregate amounts determined, as at that date, in respect of assets falling to be included under that item on either of the following bases, that is to say—
(a) on the basis of purchase price or production cost (determined in accordance with paragraphs 27 and 28), or
(b) on any basis mentioned in paragraph 32,
(leaving out of account in either case any provisions for depreciation or diminution in value).

(3) In respect of each item within sub-paragraph (1) there must also be stated—
(a) the cumulative amount of provisions for depreciation or diminution in value of assets included under that item as at each date mentioned in sub-paragraph (1)(a),
(b) the amount of any such provisions made in respect of the financial year,
(c) the amount of any adjustments made in respect of any such provisions during that year in consequence of the disposal of any assets, and
(d) the amount of any other adjustments made in respect of any such provisions during that year.

50. Where any fixed assets of the LLP (other than listed investments) are included under any item shown in the LLP's balance sheet at an amount determined on any basis mentioned in paragraph 32, the following information must be given—
(a) the years (so far as they are known to the members) in which the assets were severally valued and the several values, and
(b) in the case of assets that have been valued during the financial year, the names of the persons who valued them or particulars of their qualifications for doing so and (whichever is stated) the bases of valuation used by them.

51. (1) In relation to any amount which is or would but for paragraph 4(2)(b) be shown in respect of the item "land and buildings" in the LLP's balance sheet there must be stated—
(a) how much of that amount is ascribable to land of freehold tenure and how much to land of leasehold tenure, and
(b) how much of the amount ascribable to land of leasehold tenure is ascribable to land held on long lease and how much to land held on short lease.

(2) In this paragraph—
(a) "long lease" means a lease in the case of which the portion of the term for which it was granted remaining unexpired at the end of the financial year is not less than 50 years,
(b) "short lease" means a lease which is not a long lease, and
(c) "lease" includes an agreement for a lease.

(3) In the application of this regulation to Scotland, "land of freehold tenure" means land in respect of which the LLP is the owner; "land of leasehold tenure" means land of which the company is the tenant under a lease.

Investments

52. (1) In respect of the amount of each item which is or would but for paragraph 4(2)(b) be shown in the LLP's balance sheet under the general item "investments" (whether as fixed assets or as current assets) there must be stated how much of that amount is ascribable to listed investments.

(2) Where the amount of any listed investments is stated for any item in accordance with sub-paragraph (1), the following amounts must also be stated—
(a) the aggregate market value of those investments where it differs from the amount so stated, and

(b) both the market value and the stock exchange value of any investments of which the former value is, for the purposes of the accounts, taken as being higher than the latter.

Information about fair value of assets and liabilities

[**53** (1) This paragraph applies where financial instruments or other assets have been valued in accordance with, as appropriate, paragraph 36, 38, or 39.

(2) There must be stated—

(a) the significant assumptions underlying the valuation models and techniques used to determine the fair value of the instruments or other assets,

(b) for each category of financial instrument or other asset, the fair value of the assets in that category and the changes in value—

(i) included directly in the profit and loss account, or

(ii) credited to or (as the case may be) debited from the fair value reserve,

in respect of those assets, and

(c) for each class of derivatives, the extent and nature of the instruments, including significant terms and conditions that may affect the amount, timing and certainty of future cash flows.

(3) Where any amount is transferred to or from the fair value reserve during the financial year, there must be stated in tabular form—

(a) the amount of the reserve as at the date of the beginning of the financial year and as at the balance sheet date respectively,

(b) the amount transferred to or from the reserve during the year, and

(c) the source and application respectively of the amounts so transferred.]

54. Where the LLP has derivatives that it has not included at fair value, there must be stated for each class of such derivatives—

(a) the fair value of the derivatives in that class, if such a value can be determined in accordance with paragraph 37, and

(b) the extent and nature of the derivatives.

55. (1) This paragraph applies if—

(a) the LLP has financial fixed assets that could be included at fair value by virtue of paragraph 36,

(b) the amount at which those items are included under any item in the LLP's accounts is in excess of their fair value, and

(c) the LLP has not made provision for diminution in value of those assets in accordance with paragraph 19(1) of this Schedule.

(2) There must be stated—

(a) the amount at which either the individual assets or appropriate groupings of those individual assets are included in the LLP's accounts,

(b) the fair value of those assets or groupings, and

(c) the reasons for not making a provision for diminution in value of those assets, including the nature of the evidence that provides the basis for the belief that the amount at which they are stated in the accounts will be recovered.

Information where investment property and living animals and plants included at fair value

56. (1) This paragraph applies where the amounts to be included in an LLP's accounts in respect of [stocks,] investment property or living animals and plants have been determined in accordance with paragraph 39.

(2) The balance sheet items affected and the basis of valuation adopted in determining the amounts of the assets in question in the case of each such item must be disclosed in a note to the accounts.

(3) In the case of investment property, for each balance sheet item affected there must be shown, either separately in the balance sheet or in a note to the accounts—

(a) the comparable amounts determined according to the historical cost accounting rules, or

(b) the differences between those amounts and the corresponding amounts actually shown in the balance sheet in respect of that item.

(4) In sub-paragraph (3), references in relation to any item to the comparable amounts determined in accordance with that sub-paragraph are to—

(a) the aggregate amount which would be required to be shown in respect of that item if the amounts to be included in respect of all the assets covered by that item were determined according to the historical cost accounting rules, and

(b) the aggregate amount of the cumulative provisions for depreciation or diminution in value which would be permitted or required in determining those amounts according to those rules.

Reserves and provisions

57. (1) This paragraph applies where any amount is transferred—

(a) to or from any reserves, or

(b) to any provision for liabilities, or

(c) from any provision for liabilities otherwise than for the purpose for which the provision was established,

and the reserves or provisions are or would but for paragraph 4(2)(b) be shown as separate items in the LLP's balance sheet.

(2) The following information must be given in respect of the aggregate of reserves or provisions included in the same item [in tabular form]—

(a) the amount of the reserves or provisions as at the date of the beginning of the financial year and as at the balance sheet date respectively,

(b) any amounts transferred to or from the reserves or provisions during that year, and

(c) the source and application respectively of any amounts so transferred.

(3) Particulars must be given of each provision included in the item "other provisions" in the LLP's balance sheet in any case where the amount of that provision is material.

Provision for taxation

58. The amount of any provision for deferred taxation must be stated separately from the amount of any provision for other taxation.

Details of indebtedness

59. (1) For the aggregate of all items shown under "creditors" in the LLP's balance sheet there must be stated the aggregate of the following amounts—

(a) the amount of any debts included under "creditors" which are payable or repayable otherwise than by instalments and fall due for payment or repayment after the end of the period of five years beginning with the day next following the end of the financial year, and

(b) in the case of any debts so included which are payable or repayable by instalments, the amount of any instalments which fall due for payment after the end of that period.

(2) Subject to sub-paragraph (3), in relation to each debt falling to be taken into account under sub-paragraph (1), the terms of payment or repayment and the rate of any interest payable on the debt must be stated.

(3) If the number of debts is such that, in the opinion of the members, compliance with sub-paragraph (2) would result in a statement of excessive length, it is sufficient to give a general indication of the terms of payment or repayment and the rates of any interest payable on the debts.

(4) In respect of each item shown under "creditors" in the LLP's balance sheet there must be stated—

(a) the aggregate amount of any debts included under that item in respect of which any security has been given by the LLP, and

(b) an indication of the nature [and form] of the securities so given.

(5) References above in this paragraph to an item shown under "creditors" in the LLP's balance sheet include references, where amounts falling due to creditors within one year and after more than one year are distinguished in the balance sheet—

(a) in a case within sub-paragraph (1), to an item shown under the latter of those categories, and

(b) in a case within sub-paragraph (4), to an item shown under either of those categories.

References to items shown under "creditors" include references to items which would but for paragraph 4(2)(b) be shown under that heading.

Guarantees and other financial commitments

[60. (1) Particulars must be given of any charge on the assets of the LLP to secure the liabilities of any other person including the amount secured.

(2) Particulars and the total amount of any financial commitments, guarantees and contingencies that are not included in the balance sheet must be disclosed.

(3) An indication of the nature and form of any valuable security given by the LLP in respect of commitments, guarantees and contingencies within sub-paragraph (2) must be given.

(4) The total amount of any commitments within sub-paragraph (2) concerning pensions must be separately disclosed.

(5) Particulars must be given of pension commitments which are included in the balance sheet.

(6) Where any commitment within sub-paragraph (4) or (5) relates wholly or partly to pensions payable to past members of the LLP separate particulars must be given of that commitment.

(7) The total amount of any commitments, guarantees and contingencies within sub-paragraph (2) which are undertaken on behalf of or for the benefit of—

(a) any parent undertaking or fellow subsidiary undertaking of the LLP,

(b) any subsidiary undertaking of the LLP, or

(c) any undertaking in which the LLP has a participating interest,

must be separately stated and those within each of paragraphs (a), (b) and (c) must also be stated separately from those within any other of those paragraphs.]

Miscellaneous matters

61. Particulars must be given of any case where the purchase price or production cost of any asset is for the first time determined under paragraph 29.

Information supplementing the profit and loss account

62. Paragraphs 63 to 67 require information which either supplements the information given with respect to any particular items shown in the profit and loss account or otherwise provides particulars of income or expenditure of the LLP or of circumstances affecting the items shown in the profit and loss account (see regulation 3 for exemption for LLP falling within section 408 of the 2006 Act (individual profit and loss account where group accounts prepared)).

Separate statement of certain items of income and expenditure

63. (1) Subject to sub-paragraph (2), there must be stated the amount of the interest on or any similar charges in respect of bank loans and overdrafts, and loans of any other kind made to the LLP.

(2) Sub-paragraph (1) does not apply to interest or charges on loans to the LLP from group undertakings, but, with that exception, it applies to interest or charges on all loans, whether made on the security of debentures or not.

Particulars of tax

64. (1) Particulars must be given of any special circumstances which affect liability in respect of taxation of profits, income or capital gains for the financial year or liability in respect of taxation of profits, income or capital gains for succeeding financial years.

(2) The following amounts must be stated—

(a) the amount of the charge for United Kingdom corporation tax,

(b) if that amount would have been greater but for relief from double taxation, the amount which it would have been but for such relief,

(c) the amount of the charge for United Kingdom income tax, and

(d) the amount of the charge for taxation imposed outside the United Kingdom of profits, income and (so far as charged to revenue) capital gains.

[These amounts must be stated separately in respect of each of the amounts which is or would but for paragraph 4(2)(b) be shown under the item "tax on profit or loss" in the profit and loss account.]

Particulars of turnover

65. (1) If in the course of the financial year the LLP has carried on business of two or more classes that, in the opinion of the members, differ substantially from each other, the amount of the turnover attributable to each class must be stated and the class described (see regulation 4(3)(b) for exemption for medium-sized LLP in accounts delivered to registrar).

(2) If in the course of the financial year the LLP has supplied markets that, in the opinion of the members, differ substantially from each other, the amount of the turnover attributable to each such market must also be stated.

In this paragraph "market" means a market delimited by geographical bounds.

(3) In analysing for the purposes of this paragraph the source (in terms of business or in terms of market) of turnover, the members of the LLP must have regard to the manner in which the LLP's activities are organised.

(4) For the purposes of this paragraph—

(a) classes of business which, in the opinion of the members, do not differ substantially from each other must be treated as one class, and

(b) markets which, in the opinion of the members, do not differ substantially from each other must be treated as one market,

and any amounts properly attributable to one class of business or (as the case may be) to one market which are not material may be included in the amount stated in respect of another.

(5) Where in the opinion of the members the disclosure of any information required by this paragraph would be seriously prejudicial to the interests of the LLP, that information need not be disclosed, but the fact that any such information has not been disclosed must be stated.

Particulars of members

66. (1) Particulars must be given of the average number of members of the LLP in the financial year, which number is to be determined by dividing the relevant annual number by the number of months in the financial year.

(2) The relevant annual number is to be determined by ascertaining for each month in the financial year the number of members of the LLP for all or part of that month, and adding together all the monthly numbers.

(3) Where the amount of the profit of the LLP for the financial year before members' remuneration and profit shares exceeds £200,000, there must be disclosed the amount of profit (including remuneration) which is attributable to the member with the largest entitlement to profit (including remuneration).

(4) For the purpose of determining the amount to be disclosed under sub-paragraph (3), "remuneration" includes any emoluments specified in paragraph 1(1)(a), (c) or (d) of Schedule 5 to the Large and Medium-sized Companies and Groups (Accounts and Reports) Regulations 2008(12) receivable from—

(a) the LLP,

(b) the LLP's subsidiary undertakings, and

(c) any other person.

Miscellaneous matters

67. (1) Where any amount relating to any preceding financial year is included in any item in the profit and loss account, the effect must be stated.

[(2) The amount, nature and effect of any individual items of income or expenditure which are of exceptional size or incidence must be stated.]

Sums denominated in foreign currencies

68. Where any sums originally denominated in foreign currencies have been brought into account under any items shown in the balance sheet format or profit and loss account formats, the basis on which those sums have been translated into sterling (or the currency in which the accounts are drawn up) must be stated.

Dormant LLPs acting as agents

69. Where the members of an LLP take advantage of the exemption conferred by section 480 of the 2006 Act (dormant LLPs: exemption from audit), and the LLP has during the financial year in question acted as an agent for any person, the fact that it has so acted must be stated.

Related party transactions

70. (1) Particulars may be given of transactions which the LLP has entered into with related parties, and must be given if such transactions are material and have not been concluded under normal market conditions (see [regulation 4(2B) for a modification] for medium-sized LLPs).

(2) The particulars of transactions required to be disclosed by sub-paragraph (1) must include—

(a) the amount of such transactions,
(b) the nature of the related party relationship, and
(c) other information about the transactions necessary for an understanding of the financial position of the LLP.

(3) Information about individual transactions may be aggregated according to their nature, except where separate information is necessary for an understanding of the effects of related party transactions on the financial position of the LLP.

(4) Particulars need not be given of transactions entered into between two or more members of a group, provided that any subsidiary undertaking which is a party to the transaction is wholly-owned by such a member.

(5) In this paragraph, "related party" has the same meaning as in [UK-adopted international accounting standards].

[Post balance sheet events

70A. The nature and financial effect of material events arising after the balance sheet date which are not reflected in the profit and loss account or balance sheet must be stated.

Appropriations

70B. Particulars must be given of the proposed appropriation of profit or treatment of loss or, where applicable, particulars of the actual appropriation of the profits or treatment of the losses.]

NOTES

Words in square brackets in para 70(5) substituted by the International Accounting Standards and European Public Limited-Liability Company (Amendment etc) (EU Exit) Regulations 2019, SI 2019/685, reg 19, Sch 1, Pt 2, para 60(b), in relation to accounts for financial years beginning on or after IP completion day (as defined in the European Union (Withdrawal Agreement) Act 2020, s 39) (note also that in relation to accounts for financial years which begin before but end on or after IP completion day, the enactments amended by Parts 1–3 of Sch 1 to the 2019 Regulations have effect as if the UK were a member State until the end of the financial year in question).

All other amendments to Part 3 of this Schedule, as noted below, were made by the Limited Liability Partnerships, Partnerships and Groups (Accounts and Audit) Regulations 2016, SI 2016/575, regs 47, 56, as from 17 May 2016, in relation to (a) financial years beginning on or after 1 January 2016; and (b) a financial year of an LLP beginning on or after 1 January 2015, but before 1 January 2016, if (i) the members of the LLP so decide, and (ii) a copy of the LLP's accounts for that financial year has not been delivered to the registrar in accordance with ss 444, 445 or 446 of the Companies Act 2006 as applied to LLPs by the Limited Liability Partnerships (Accounts and Audit) (Application of Companies Act 2006) Regulations before 17 May 2016 (see further the note at **[10.226]**).

Paras 42, 53, 60 were substituted.

In paras 56(1), 57(2), 59(4), the words in square brackets were inserted.

In para 64(2), the words in square brackets were substituted.

in para 67, sub-para (2) substituted (for the original sub-paras (2), (3)).

In para 70(1), the words in square brackets were substituted.

Paras 70A, 70B were inserted.

PART 4

(Revoked by the Limited Liability Partnerships, Partnerships and Groups (Accounts and Audit) Regulations 2016, SI 2016/575, regs 47, 57, as from 17 May 2016, in relation to (a) financial years beginning on or after 1 January 2016; and (b) a financial year of an LLP beginning on or after 1 January 2015, but before 1 January 2016, if (i) the members of the LLP so decide, and (ii) a copy of the LLP's accounts for that financial year has not been delivered to the registrar in accordance with ss 444, 445 or 446 of the Companies Act 2006 as applied to LLPs by the Limited Liability Partnerships (Accounts and Audit) (Application of Companies Act 2006) Regulations before 17 May 2016 (see further the note at **[10.226]***)).*

SCHEDULE 2
INFORMATION ON RELATED UNDERTAKINGS REQUIRED WHETHER PREPARING NON-IAS OR IAS ACCOUNTS

Regulation 5

PART 1 PROVISIONS APPLYING TO ALL LLPS

Subsidiary undertakings

[10.313]

1. (1) The following information must be given where at the end of the financial year the LLP has subsidiary undertakings.

(2) The name of each subsidiary undertaking must be stated.

(3) There must be stated with respect to each subsidiary undertaking—
[(a) the address of the undertaking's registered office (whether in or outside the United Kingdom),]
(b) if it is unincorporated, the address of its principal place of business.

Financial information about subsidiary undertakings

2. (1) There must be disclosed with respect to each subsidiary undertaking not included in consolidated accounts by the LLP—
(a) the aggregate amount of its capital and reserves as at the end of its relevant financial year, and
(b) its profit or loss for that year.

(2) That information need not be given if the LLP is exempt by virtue of section 400 or 401 of the 2006 Act from the requirement to prepare group accounts (parent LLP included in accounts of larger group).

(3) That information need not be given if the LLP's investment in the subsidiary undertaking is included in the LLP's accounts by way of the equity method of valuation.

(4) That information need not be given if—

(a) the subsidiary undertaking is not required by any provision of the 2006 Act to deliver a copy of its balance sheet for its relevant financial year and does not otherwise publish that balance sheet in the United Kingdom or elsewhere, and

(b) the LLP's holding is less than 50% of the nominal value of the shares in the undertaking.

(5) Information otherwise required by this paragraph need not be given if it is not material.

(6) For the purposes of this paragraph the "relevant financial year" of a subsidiary undertaking is—

(a) if its financial year ends with that of the LLP, that year, and

(b) if not, its financial year ending last before the end of the LLP's financial year.

Significant holdings in undertakings other than subsidiary undertakings

3. (1) The information required by paragraphs 4 and 5 must be given where at the end of the financial year the LLP has a significant holding in an undertaking which is not a subsidiary undertaking of the LLP, and which does not fall within paragraph 16 (joint ventures) or 17 (associated undertakings).

(2) A holding is significant for this purpose if—

(a) it amounts to 20% or more of the nominal value of any class of shares in the undertaking, or

(b) the amount of the holding (as stated or included in the LLP's individual accounts) exceeds one-fifth of the amount (as so stated) of the LLP's assets.

4. (1) The name of the undertaking must be stated.

(2) There must be stated—

[(a) the address of the undertaking's registered office (whether in or outside the United Kingdom),]

(b) if it is unincorporated, the address of its principal place of business.

(3) There must also be stated—

(a) the identity of each class of shares in the undertaking held by the LLP, and

(b) the proportion of the nominal value of the shares of that class represented by those shares.

5. (1) Subject to paragraph 12, there must also be stated—

(a) the aggregate amount of the capital and reserves of the undertaking as at the end of its relevant financial year, and

(b) its profit or loss for that year.

(2) That information need not be given in respect of an undertaking if—

(a) the undertaking is not required by any provision of the 2006 Act to deliver a copy of its balance sheet for its relevant financial year and does not otherwise publish that balance sheet in the United Kingdom or elsewhere, and

(b) the LLP's holding is less than 50% of the nominal value of the shares in the undertaking.

(3) Information otherwise required by this paragraph need not be given if it is not material.

(4) For the purposes of this paragraph the "relevant financial year" of an undertaking is—

(a) if its financial year ends with that of the LLP, that year, and

(b) if not, its financial year ending last before the end of the LLP's financial year.

Parent undertaking drawing up accounts for larger group

6. (1) Where the LLP is a subsidiary undertaking, the following information must be given with respect to the parent undertaking of—

(a) the largest group of undertakings for which group accounts are drawn up and of which the LLP is a member, and

(b) the smallest such group of undertakings.

(2) The name of the parent undertaking must be stated.

(3) There must be stated—

[(a) the address of the undertaking's registered office (whether in or outside the United Kingdom),]

(b) if it is unincorporated, the address of its principal place of business.

(4) If copies of the group accounts referred to in sub-paragraph (1) are available to the public, there must also be stated the addresses from which copies of the accounts can be obtained.

Identification of ultimate parent

7. (1) Where the LLP is a subsidiary undertaking, the following information must be given with respect to the body corporate (if any) regarded by the members as being the LLP's ultimate parent.

(2) The name of that body corporate must be stated.

(3) If that body corporate is incorporated outside the United Kingdom, the country in which it is incorporated must be stated (if known to the members).

NOTES

Paras 1(3)(a), 4(2)(a) and 6(3)(a) were substituted by the Limited Liability Partnerships, Partnerships and Groups (Accounts and Audit) Regulations 2016, SI 2016/575, regs 47, 58, as from 17 May 2016, in relation to (a) financial years beginning on or after 1 January 2016; and (b) a financial year of an LLP beginning on or after 1 January 2015, but before 1 January 2016, if (i) the members of the LLP so decide, and (ii) a copy of the LLP's accounts for that financial year has not been delivered to the registrar in accordance with ss 444, 445 or 446 of the Companies Act 2006 as applied to LLPs by the Limited Liability Partnerships (Accounts and Audit) (Application of Companies Act 2006) Regulations before 17 May 2016 (see further the note at **[10.226]**).

PART 2 LLP NOT REQUIRED TO PREPARE GROUP ACCOUNTS

Reason for not preparing group accounts

[10.314]

8. (1) The reason why the LLP is not required to prepare group accounts must be stated.

(2) If the reason is that all the subsidiary undertakings of the LLP fall within the exclusions provided for in section 405 of the 2006 Act (non-IAS group accounts: subsidiary undertakings included in the consolidation), it must be stated with respect to each subsidiary undertaking which of those exclusions applies.

Holdings in subsidiary undertakings

9. (1) There must be stated in relation to shares of each class held by the LLP in a subsidiary undertaking—

(a) the identity of the class, and

(b) the proportion of the nominal value of the shares of that class represented by those shares.

(2) The shares held by or on behalf of the LLP itself must be distinguished from those attributed to the LLP which are held by or on behalf of a subsidiary undertaking.

Financial years of subsidiary undertakings

10. Where—

(a) disclosure is made under paragraph 2(1) with respect to a subsidiary undertaking, and

(b) that undertaking's financial year does not end with that of the LLP,

there must be stated in relation to that undertaking the date on which its last financial year ended (last before the end of the LLP's financial year).

Exemption from giving information about significant holdings in non-subsidiary undertakings

11. The information otherwise required by paragraph 3 (significant holdings in undertakings other than subsidiary undertaking) need not be given if—

(a) the LLP is exempt by virtue of section 400 or 401 of the 2006 Act from the requirement to prepare group accounts (parent LLP included in accounts of larger group), and

(b) the investment of the LLP in all undertakings in which it has such a holding as is mentioned in sub-paragraph (1) is shown, in aggregate, in the notes to the accounts by way of the equity method of valuation.

Construction of references to shares held by LLP

12. (1) References in Parts 1 and 2 of this Schedule to shares held by an LLP are to be construed as follows.

(2) For the purposes of paragraphs 2, 9 and 10 (information about subsidiary undertakings)—

(a) there must be attributed to the LLP any shares held by a subsidiary undertaking, or by a person acting on behalf of the LLP or a subsidiary undertaking; but

(b) there must be treated as not held by the LLP any shares held on behalf of a person other than the LLP or a subsidiary undertaking.

(3) For the purposes of paragraphs 3 to 5 (information about undertakings other than subsidiary undertakings)—

(a) there must be attributed to the LLP shares held on its behalf by any person; but

(b) there must be treated as not held by an LLP shares held on behalf of a person other than the LLP.

(4) For the purposes of any of those provisions, shares held by way of security must be treated as held by the person providing the security—

(a) where apart from the right to exercise them for the purpose of preserving the value of the security, or of realising it, the rights attached to the shares are exercisable only in accordance with that person's instructions, and

(b) where the shares are held in connection with the granting of loans as part of normal business activities and apart from the right to exercise them for the purpose of preserving the value of the security, or of realising it, the rights attached to the shares are exercisable only in that person's interests.

PART 3 LLP REQUIRED TO PREPARE GROUP ACCOUNTS

Introductory

[10.315]

13. In this Part of this Schedule "the group" means the group consisting of the parent LLP and its subsidiary undertakings.

Subsidiary undertakings

14. (1) In addition to the information required by paragraph 2, the following information must also be given with respect to the undertakings which are subsidiary undertakings of the parent LLP at the end of the financial year.

(2) It must be stated whether the subsidiary undertaking is included in the consolidation and, if it is not, the reasons for excluding it from consolidation must be given.

(3) It must be stated with respect to each subsidiary undertaking by virtue of which of the conditions specified in section 1162(2) or (4) of the 2006 Act it is a subsidiary undertaking of its immediate parent undertaking.

That information need not be given if the relevant condition is that specified in subsection (2)(a) of that section (holding of a majority of the voting rights) and the immediate parent undertaking holds the same proportion of the shares in the undertaking as it holds voting rights.

Holdings in subsidiary undertakings

15. (1) The following information must be given with respect to the shares of a subsidiary undertaking held—

(a) by the parent LLP, and

(b) by the group,

and the information under paragraphs (a) and (b) must (if different) be shown separately.

(2) There must be stated—

(a) the identity of each class of shares held, and

(b) the proportion of the nominal value of the shares of that class represented by those shares.

Joint ventures

16. (1) The following information must be given where an undertaking is dealt with in the consolidated accounts by the method of proportional consolidation in accordance with paragraph 18 of Schedule 3 to these Regulations (joint ventures)—

(a) the name of the undertaking,

[(b) the address of the undertaking's registered office (whether in or outside the United Kingdom),]

(c) the factors on which joint management of the undertaking is based, and

(d) the proportion of the capital of the undertaking held by undertakings included in the consolidation.

(2) Where the financial year of the undertaking did not end with that of the LLP, there must be stated the date on which a financial year of the undertaking last ended before that date.

Associated undertakings

17. (1) The following information must be given where an undertaking included in the consolidation has an interest in an associated undertaking.

(2) The name of the associated undertaking must be stated.

(3) There must be stated—

(a) if the undertaking is incorporated outside the United Kingdom, the country in which it is incorporated,

[(b) the address of the undertaking's registered office (whether in or outside the United Kingdom).]

(4) The following information must be given with respect to the shares of the undertaking held—

(a) by the parent LLP, and

(b) by the group,

and the information under paragraphs (a) and (b) must be shown separately.

(5) There must be stated—

(a) the identity of each class of shares held, and

(b) the proportion of the nominal value of the shares of that class represented by those shares.

(6) In this paragraph "associated undertaking" has the meaning given by paragraph 19 of Schedule 3 to these Regulations; and the information required by this paragraph must be given notwithstanding that paragraph 21(3) of that Schedule (materiality) applies in relation to the accounts themselves.

Requirement to give information about other significant holdings of parent LLP or group

18. (1) The information required by paragraphs 4 and 5 must also be given where at the end of the financial year the group has a significant holding in an undertaking which is not a subsidiary undertaking of the parent LLP and does not fall within paragraph 16 (joint ventures) or 17 (associated undertakings), as though the references to the LLP in those paragraphs were a reference to the group.

(2) A holding is significant for this purpose if—

(a) it amounts to 20% or more of the nominal value of any class of shares in the undertaking, or

(b) the amount of the holding (as stated or included in the group accounts) exceeds one-fifth of the amount of the group's assets (as so stated).

(3) For the purposes of those paragraphs as applied to a group the "relevant financial year" of an outside undertaking is—

(a) if its financial year ends with that of the parent LLP, that year, and

(b) if not, its financial year ending last before the end of the parent LLP's financial year.

Construction of references to shares held by parent LLP or group

19. (1) References in Parts 1 and 3 of this Schedule to shares held by that parent LLP or group are to be construed as follows.

(2) For the purposes of paragraphs 3 to 5, 15 and 17(4) and (5) (information about holdings in subsidiary and other undertakings)—

(a) there must be attributed to the parent LLP shares held on its behalf by any person; but

(b) there must be treated as not held by the parent LLP shares held on behalf of a person other than the LLP.

(3) References to shares held by the group are to any shares held by or on behalf of the parent LLP or any of its subsidiary undertakings; but any shares held on behalf of a person other than the parent LLP or any of its subsidiary undertakings are not to be treated as held by the group.

(4) Shares held by way of security must be treated as held by the person providing the security—

(a) where apart from the right to exercise them for the purpose of preserving the value of the security, or of realising it, the rights attached to the shares are exercisable only in accordance with his instructions, and

(b) where the shares are held in connection with the granting of loans as part of normal business activities and apart from the right to exercise them for the purpose of preserving the value of the security, or of realising it, the rights attached to the shares are exercisable only in his interests.

NOTES

Paras 16(1)(b) and 17(3)(b) were substituted by the Limited Liability Partnerships, Partnerships and Groups (Accounts and Audit) Regulations 2016, SI 2016/575, regs 47, 59, as from 17 May 2016, in relation to (a) financial years beginning on or after 1 January 2016; and (b) a financial year of an LLP beginning on or after 1 January 2015, but before 1 January 2016, if (i) the members of the LLP so decide, and (ii) a copy of the LLP's accounts for that financial year has not been delivered to the registrar in accordance with ss 444, 445 or 446 of the Companies Act 2006 as applied to LLPs by the Limited Liability

Partnerships (Accounts and Audit) (Application of Companies Act 2006) Regulations before 17 May 2016 (see further the note at **[10.226]**).

SCHEDULE 3
NON-IAS GROUP ACCOUNTS

Regulation 6

General rules

[10.316]

1. Group accounts must comply so far as practicable with the provisions of Schedule 1 to these Regulations as if the undertakings included in the consolidation ("the group") were a single LLP.

2. (1) The consolidated balance sheet and profit and loss account must incorporate in full the information contained in the individual accounts of the undertakings included in the consolidation, subject to the adjustments authorised or required by the following provisions of this Schedule and to such other adjustments (if any) as may be appropriate in accordance with generally accepted accounting principles or practice.

[(1A) Group accounts must be drawn up as at the same date as the accounts of the parent LLP.]

(2) If the financial year of a subsidiary undertaking included in the consolidation does not end with that of the parent LLP, the group accounts must be made up—

- (a) from the accounts of the subsidiary undertaking for its financial year last ending before the end of the parent LLP's financial year, provided that year ended no more than three months before that of the parent LLP, or
- (b) from interim accounts prepared by the subsidiary undertaking as at the end of the parent LLP's financial year.

3. (1) Where assets and liabilities to be included in the group accounts have been valued or otherwise determined by undertakings according to accounting rules differing from those used for the group accounts, the values or amounts must be adjusted so as to accord with the rules used for the group accounts.

(2) If it appears to the members of the parent LLP that there are special reasons for departing from sub-paragraph (1) they may do so, but particulars of any such departure, the reasons for it and its effect must be given in a note to the accounts.

(3) The adjustments referred to in this paragraph need not be made if they are not material for the purpose of giving a true and fair view.

4. Any differences of accounting rules as between a parent LLP's individual accounts for a financial year and its group accounts must be disclosed in a note to the latter accounts and the reasons for the difference given.

5. Amounts that in the particular context of any provision of this Schedule are not material may be disregarded for the purposes of that provision.

Elimination of group transactions

6. (1) Debts and claims between undertakings included in the consolidation, and income and expenditure relating to transactions between such undertakings, must be eliminated in preparing the group accounts.

(2) Where profits and losses resulting from transactions between undertakings included in the consolidation are included in the book value of assets, they must be eliminated in preparing the group accounts.

(3) The elimination required by sub-paragraph (2) may be effected in proportion to the group's interest in the shares of the undertakings.

(4) Sub-paragraphs (1) and (2) need not be complied with if the amounts concerned are not material for the purpose of giving a true and fair view.

Acquisition and merger accounting

7. (1) The following provisions apply where an undertaking becomes a subsidiary undertaking of the parent LLP.

(2) That event is referred to in those provisions as an "acquisition", and references to the "undertaking acquired" are to be construed accordingly.

8. An acquisition must be accounted for by the acquisition method of accounting unless the conditions for accounting for it as a merger are met and the merger method of accounting is adopted.

9. (1) The acquisition method of accounting is as follows.

(2) The identifiable assets and liabilities of the undertaking acquired must be included in the consolidated balance sheet at their fair values as at the date of acquisition.

(3) The income and expenditure of the undertaking acquired must be brought into the group accounts only as from the date of the acquisition.

(4) There must be set off against the acquisition cost of the interest in the shares of the undertaking held by the parent LLP and its subsidiary undertakings the interest of the parent LLP and its subsidiary undertakings in the adjusted capital and reserves of the undertaking acquired.

(5) The resulting amount if positive must be treated as goodwill, and if negative as a negative consolidation difference.

[(6) Negative goodwill may be transferred to the consolidated profit and loss account where such a treatment is in accordance with the principles and rules of Part 2 of Schedule 1 to these Regulations.]

10. The conditions for accounting for an acquisition as a merger are that adoption of the merger method of accounting accords with generally accepted accounting principles or practice.

11. (1) Where an LLP adopts the merger method of accounting it must comply with this paragraph, and with generally accepted accounting principles or practice.

(2) The assets and liabilities of the undertaking acquired must be brought into the group accounts at the figures at which they stand in the undertaking's accounts, subject to any adjustment authorised or required by this Schedule.

(3) The income and expenditure of the undertaking acquired must be included in the group accounts for the entire financial year, including the period before the acquisition.

(4) The group accounts must show corresponding amounts relating to the previous financial year as if the undertaking acquired had been included in the consolidation throughout that year.

12. (1) Where a group is acquired, paragraphs 9 to 11 apply with the following adaptations.

(2) References to shares of the undertaking acquired are to be construed as references to shares of the parent undertaking of the group.

(3) Other references to the undertaking acquired are to be construed as references to the group; and references to the assets and liabilities, income and expenditure and capital and reserves of the undertaking acquired must be construed as references to the assets and liabilities, income and expenditure and capital and reserves of the group after making the set-offs and other adjustments required by this Schedule in the case of group accounts.

13. (1) The following information with respect to acquisitions taking place in the financial year must be given in a note to the accounts.

(2) There must be stated—

(a) the name of the undertaking acquired or, where a group was acquired, the name of the parent undertaking of that group, and

(b) whether the acquisition has been accounted for by the acquisition or the merger method of accounting;

and in relation to an acquisition which significantly affects the figures shown in the group accounts, the following further information must be given.

(3) The composition and fair value of the consideration for the acquisition given by the parent LLP and its subsidiary undertakings must be stated.

(4) Where the acquisition method of accounting has been adopted, the book values immediately prior to the acquisition, and the fair values at the date of acquisition, of each class of assets and liabilities of the undertaking or group acquired must be stated in tabular form, including a statement of the amount of any goodwill or negative consolidation difference arising on the acquisition, together with an explanation of any significant adjustments made.

(5) In ascertaining for the purposes of sub-paragraph (4) the profit or loss of a group, the book values and fair values of assets and liabilities of a group or the amount of the assets and liabilities of a group, the set-offs and other adjustments required by this Schedule in the case of group accounts must be made.

14. (1) There must also be stated in a note to the accounts the cumulative amount of goodwill resulting from acquisitions in that and earlier financial years which has been written off otherwise than in the consolidated profit and loss account for that or any earlier financial year.

(2) That figure must be shown net of any goodwill attributable to subsidiary undertakings or businesses disposed of prior to the balance sheet date.

15. Where during the financial year there has been a disposal of an undertaking or group which significantly affects the figure shown in the group accounts, there must be stated in a note to the accounts—

(a) the name of that undertaking or, as the case may be, of the parent undertaking of that group, and

(b) the extent to which the profit or loss shown in the group accounts is attributable to profit or loss of that undertaking or group.

16. The information required by paragraph 13, 14 or 15 need not be disclosed with respect to an undertaking which—

(a) is established under the law of a country outside the United Kingdom, or

(b) carries on business outside the United Kingdom,

if in the opinion of the members of the parent LLP the disclosure would be seriously prejudicial to the business of that undertaking or to the business of the parent LLP or any of its subsidiary undertakings and the Secretary of State agrees that the information should not be disclosed.

[16A. Where an acquisition has taken place in the financial year and the merger method of accounting has been adopted, the notes to the accounts must also disclose the names and the addresses of the registered offices of the undertakings concerned (whether in or outside the United Kingdom).]

[Non-controlling interests

17. (1) The formats set out in Schedule 1 to these Regulations have effect in relation to group accounts with the following additions.

(2) In the balance sheet formats there must be shown, as a separate item and under the heading "non-controlling interests", the amount of capital and reserves attributable to shares in subsidiary undertakings included in the consolidation held by or on behalf of persons other than the parent LLP and its subsidiary undertakings.

(3) In the profit and loss account formats there must be shown, as a separate item and under the heading "non-controlling interests", the amount of any profit or loss attributable to shares in subsidiary undertakings included in the consolidation held by or on behalf of persons other than the parent LLP and its subsidiary undertakings.

(4) For the purpose of paragraph 4(1) and (2) of Schedule 1 (power to adapt or combine items)—

(a) the additional item required by sub-paragraph (2) above is treated as one to which a letter is assigned, and

(b) the additional item required by sub-paragraph (3) above is treated as one to which an Arabic number is assigned.]

Joint ventures

18. (1) Where an undertaking included in the consolidation manages another undertaking jointly with one or more undertakings not included in the consolidation, that other undertaking ("the joint venture") may, if it is not—

Part 10 Miscellaneous other SIs

(a) a body corporate, or
(b) a subsidiary undertaking of the parent LLP,

be dealt with in the group accounts by the method of proportional consolidation.

(2) The provisions of this Schedule relating to the preparation of consolidated accounts [and sections 402 and 405 of the 2006 Act] apply, with any necessary modifications, to proportional consolidation under this paragraph.

[(3) In addition to the disclosure of the average number of employees employed during the financial year (see section 411(7) of the 2006 Act), there must be a separate disclosure in the notes to the accounts of the average number of employees employed by undertakings that are proportionately consolidated.]

Associated undertakings

19. (1) An "associated undertaking" means an undertaking in which an undertaking included in the consolidation has a participating interest and over whose operating and financial policy it exercises a significant influence, and which is not—

(a) a subsidiary undertaking of the parent LLP, or
(b) a joint venture dealt with in accordance with paragraph 18.

(2) Where an undertaking holds 20% or more of the voting rights in another undertaking, it is presumed to exercise such an influence over it unless the contrary is shown.

(3) The voting rights in an undertaking means the rights conferred on shareholders in respect of their shares or, in the case of an undertaking not having a share capital, on members, to vote at general meetings of the undertaking on all, or substantially all, matters.

(4) The provisions of paragraphs 5 to 11 of Schedule 7 to the 2006 Act (parent and subsidiary undertakings: rights to be taken into account and attribution of rights) apply in determining for the purposes of this paragraph whether an undertaking holds 20% or more of the voting rights in another undertaking.

20. (1) The formats set out in Schedule 1 to these Regulations have effect in relation to group accounts with the following modifications.

(2) In the balance sheet formats replace the items headed "Participating interests", that is—

(a) in format 1, item A.III.3, and
(b) in format 2, item A.III.3 under the heading "ASSETS",

by two items: "Interests in associated undertakings" and "Other participating interests".

(3) In the profit and loss account formats replace the items headed "Income from participating interests", that is—

(a) in format 1, item 8, and
(b) in format 2, item 10,

by two items: "Income from interests in associated undertakings" and "Income from other participating interests".

21. (1) The interest of an undertaking in an associated undertaking, and the amount of profit or loss attributable to such an interest, must be shown by the equity method of accounting (including dealing with any goodwill arising in accordance with paragraphs 17 to 20 and 22 of Schedule 1 to these Regulations).

(2) Where the associated undertaking is itself a parent undertaking, the net assets and profits or losses to be taken into account are those of the parent and its subsidiary undertakings (after making any consolidation adjustments).

(3) The equity method of accounting need not be applied if the amounts in question are not material for the purpose of giving a true and fair view.

Related party transactions

22. Paragraph 70 of Schedule 1 to these Regulations applies to transactions which the parent LLP, or other undertakings included in the consolidation, have entered into with related parties, unless they are intra group transactions.

[Deferred tax balances

22A. Deferred tax balances must be recognised on consolidation where it is probable that a charge to tax will arise within the foreseeable future for one of the undertakings included in the consolidation.]

NOTES

Paras 2(1A), 9(6), 16A and 18(3) were inserted, para 17 was substituted, the words in square brackets in para 18(2) were inserted, and para 22A was added, by the Limited Liability Partnerships, Partnerships and Groups (Accounts and Audit) Regulations 2016, SI 2016/575, regs 47, 60, as from 17 May 2016, in relation to (a) financial years beginning on or after 1 January 2016; and (b) a financial year of an LLP beginning on or after 1 January 2015, but before 1 January 2016, if (i) the members of the LLP so decide, and (ii) a copy of the LLP's accounts for that financial year has not been delivered to the registrar in accordance with ss 444, 445 or 446 of the Companies Act 2006 as applied to LLPs by the Limited Liability Partnerships (Accounts and Audit) (Application of Companies Act 2006) Regulations before 17 May 2016 (see further the note at **[10.226]**).

SCHEDULE 4
GENERAL INTERPRETATION

Regulation 7

Financial instruments

[10.317]

1. References to "derivatives" include commodity-based contracts that give either contracting party the right to settle in cash or in some other financial instrument, except where such contracts—

(a) were entered into for the purpose of, and continue to meet, the LLP's expected purchase, sale or usage requirements,
(b) were designated for such purpose at their inception, and

(c) are expected to be settled by delivery of the commodity.

2. (1) The expressions listed in sub-paragraph (2) have the same meaning as they have in [Directive 2013/34/EU of 26 June 2013 on the annual financial statements etc of certain types of undertakings and Council Directive 91/674/EEC of 19 December 1991 on the annual accounts and consolidated accounts of insurance undertakings.]

(2) Those expressions are "available for sale financial asset", "business combination", "commodity-based contracts", "derivative", "equity instrument", "exchange difference", "fair value hedge accounting system", "financial fixed asset", "financial instrument", "foreign entity", "hedge accounting", "hedge accounting system", "hedged items", "hedging instrument", "held for trading purposes", "held to maturity", "monetary item", "receivables", "reliable market" and "trading portfolio".

Fixed and current assets

3. "Fixed assets" means assets of an LLP which are intended for use on a continuing basis in the LLP's activities, and "current assets" means assets not intended for such use.

Historical cost accounting rules

4. References to the historical cost accounting rules are to be read in accordance with paragraph 30 of Schedule 1 to these Regulations.

Listed investments

5. (1) "Listed investment" means an investment as respects which there has been granted a listing on—

(a) a recognised investment exchange other than an overseas investment exchange, or

(b) a stock exchange of repute outside the United Kingdom.

(2) "Recognised investment exchange" and "overseas investment exchange" have the meaning given in Part 18 of the Financial Services and Markets Act 2000(14).

Loans

6. A loan or advance (including a liability comprising a loan or advance) is treated as falling due for repayment, and an instalment of a loan or advance is treated as falling due for payment, on the earliest date on which the lender could require repayment or (as the case may be) payment, if he exercised all options and rights available to him.

Materiality

7. Amounts which in the particular context of any provision of Schedule 1 to these Regulations are not material may be disregarded for the purposes of that provision.

Participating interests

8. (1) A "participating interest" means an interest held by an undertaking in the shares of another undertaking which it holds on a long-term basis for the purpose of securing a contribution to its activities by the exercise of control or influence arising from or related to that interest.

(2) A holding of 20% or more of the shares of the undertaking is to be presumed to be a participating interest unless the contrary is shown.

(3) The reference in sub-paragraph (1) to an interest in shares includes—

(a) an interest which is convertible into an interest in shares, and

(b) an option to acquire shares or any such interest,

and an interest or option falls within paragraph (a) or (b) notwithstanding that the shares to which it relates are, until the conversion or the exercise of the option, unissued.

(4) For the purposes of this paragraph an interest held on behalf of an undertaking is to be treated as held by it.

(5) In the balance sheet and profit and loss formats set out in Schedule 1 to these Regulations, "participating interest" does not include an interest in a group undertaking.

(6) For the purpose of this paragraph as it applies in relation to the expression "participating interest"—

(a) in those formats as they apply in relation to group accounts, and

(b) in paragraph 19 of Schedule 3 (group accounts: undertakings to be accounted for as associated undertakings),

the references in sub-paragraphs (1) to (4) to the interest held by, and the purposes and activities of, the undertaking concerned are to be construed as references to the interest held by, and the purposes and activities of, the group (within the meaning of paragraph 1 of that Schedule).

Provisions

9. (1) References to provisions for depreciation or diminution in value of assets are to any amount written off by way of providing for depreciation or diminution in value of assets.

(2) Any reference in the profit and loss account formats set out in Schedule 1 to these Regulations to the depreciation of, or amounts written off, assets of any description is to any provision for depreciation or diminution in value of assets of that description.

10. References to provisions for liabilities are to any amount retained as reasonably necessary for the purpose of providing for any liability the nature of which is clearly defined and which is either likely to be incurred, or certain to be incurred but uncertain as to amount or as to the date on which it will arise.

Purchase price

11. "Purchase price", in relation to an asset of an LLP or any raw materials or consumables used in the production of such an asset, includes any consideration (whether in cash or otherwise) given by the LLP in respect of that asset or those materials or consumables, as the case may be.

Staff costs

12. (1) "Social security costs" means any contributions by the LLP to any state social security or pension scheme, fund or arrangement.

(2) "Pension costs" includes—

(a) any costs incurred by the LLP in respect of any pension scheme established for the purpose of providing pensions for persons currently or formerly employed by the LLP,

(b) any sums set aside for the future payment of pensions directly by the LLP to current or former employees, and

(c) any pensions paid directly to such persons without having first been set aside.

(3) Any amount stated in respect of the item "social security costs" or in respect of the item "wages and salaries" in the LLP's profit and loss account must be determined by reference to payments made or costs incurred in respect of all persons employed by the LLP during the financial year under contracts of service.

NOTES

The words in square brackets in para 2(1) were substituted by the Limited Liability Partnerships, Partnerships and Groups (Accounts and Audit) Regulations 2016, SI 2016/575, regs 47, 61, as from 17 May 2016, in relation to (a) financial years beginning on or after 1 January 2016; and (b) a financial year of an LLP beginning on or after 1 January 2015, but before 1 January 2016, if (i) the members of the LLP so decide, and (ii) a copy of the LLP's accounts for that financial year has not been delivered to the registrar in accordance with ss 444, 445 or 446 of the Companies Act 2006 as applied to LLPs by the Limited Liability Partnerships (Accounts and Audit) (Application of Companies Act 2006) Regulations before 17 May 2016 (see further the note at **[10.226]**).

COMPANIES (SHAREHOLDERS' RIGHTS) REGULATIONS 2009 (NOTE)

(SI 2009/1632)

[10.318]

NOTES

These Regulations were made on 2 July 2009 under the powers conferred by the European Communities Act 1972, s 2(2) (see the note "Statutory Instruments made under the European Communities Act 1972" preceding paragraph **[4.1]** *ante*). They came into force on 3 August 2009 and apply in relation to meetings of which notice is given, or first given, on or after that date (see reg 1). These Regulations implement Directive 2007/36/EC of the European Parliament and of the Council on the exercise of certain rights of shareholders in listed companies (at **[11.118]**) so far as it is not already given effect in UK law. Except in one respect (reg 22), they do so by amendment of Part 13 (Resolutions and Meetings) of the Companies Act 2006 at **[1.316]** et seq.

Part 2 of these Regulations (Amendments of General application) provides as follows. Regulation 2 enables Article 10 of the Directive (proxy voting) and Article 13(4) (split votes by nominee shareholders) to be implemented by clarifying the relationship between the general voting rules in ss 282–284 of the 2006 Act and the rules about nominee shareholders, proxies, split votes and corporate representatives in ss 152, 285, 322, 322A and 323. Regulation 3 implements Article 10(1) (shareholders' rights are the same whether exercised in person or by proxy) and Article 10(5) (proxies for more than one shareholder may split their votes) by replacing the existing s 285 with two new sections, ie, ss 285 and 285A. Regulation 4 implements Article 6(2) (minimum stake to require a meeting to be called must not exceed 5%) by providing a single percentage, 5%, of the members of any type of company who may require the directors to call a general meeting. Regulation 5 implements Article 12 (voting by correspondence) by providing for votes to be cast in advance. Regulation 6 implements Article 13(4) (split votes by nominee shareholders) by enabling corporate representatives to vote in different ways from one another in respect of different blocks of shares. Regulation 7 implements Article 10(4) (proxies to vote in accordance with instructions). Regulation 8 implements Article 8 (participation in general meetings by electronic means) by preventing anything in Part 13 of CA 2006 from being an obstacle to meetings being held electronically. Regulation 9 implements Article 5(1) (period of notice for general meetings) by amending ss 307 and 360 and inserting a new s 307A. The changes from existing s 307 are that annual general meetings of private companies with traded shares require 21 days' notice, and that other general meetings of companies (public and private) with traded shares also require 21 days' notice unless electronic voting is available and a resolution reducing the period to not less than 14 days was passed at the previous AGM or at a general meeting held since then.

Part 3 of these Regulations (Amendments relating to Traded Companies) provides as follows. Regulations 10 and 11 implement Article 5(3), (4) (contents of notices of, and website publication of advance information about, general meetings of companies with traded shares). Regulation 12 implements Article 9 (right to ask questions at general meetings). Regulation 13 implements Article 11 (formalities for proxy holder appointment and notification). Regulation 14 makes consequential provision in respect of class meetings. Regulation 15 requires private companies with traded shares to hold AGMs. This implements the obligation to apply the provisions of the Directive about annual general meetings to such companies which arises from the scope of the Directive provided for in Article 1(1). Regulation 16 implements Article 5(3)(b)(i) (notice of rights under Article 6) in respect of annual general meetings by providing for notice to be given of the right to require a company with traded shares to circulate a resolution to be moved at its AGM or to include something on the AGM agenda. Regulation 17 implements Article 6(1)(a), (2), (3) (right to put items other than resolutions on the agenda of a general meeting) in respect of annual general meetings. Regulation 18 implements Article 6(4) (revised agenda to be circulated when right to put items other than resolutions on the agenda of a general meeting exercised) in respect of annual general meetings and ensures that there is no obstacle to enjoyment of Article 6 rights by placing on the company the cost of circulating resolutions for the annual general meeting of a company with traded shares. Regulation 19 implements Article 14 (determination of voting results and publication on website). Regulation 20 implements Article 7 (requirements for participation and voting at general meetings). Regulation 21 defines a company with traded voting shares as a "traded company", if the shares are admitted to trading by or with consent of the company. Regulation 22 implements Article 4 (equal treatment of shareholders) by excluding traded companies from the operation of the provision in the amended Companies Act 2006 (Commencement No 3, Consequential Amendments, Transitional Provisions and Savings) Order 2007 (SI 2007/2194) preserving articles in force before 1 October 2007 which provide for the chairman of a company general meeting to have a casting vote. Regulation 23 makes transitional provisions in connection with the new s 307A of the 2006 Act.

LIMITED LIABILITY PARTNERSHIPS (APPLICATION OF COMPANIES ACT 2006) REGULATIONS 2009

(SI 2009/1804)

NOTES

Made: 8 July 2009.

Authority: Limited Liability Partnerships Act 2000, ss 15, 17; Companies Act 2006, ss 1101, 1292, 1294, 1296.

Commencement: 9 July 2009 (regs 8, 64, 77, 80, 81, Sch 3, paras 6, 7 for the purpose of enabling the exercise of powers to make regulations or orders by statutory instrument); 1 October 2009 (otherwise).

For a summary of all Orders and Regulations made under the Companies Act 2006, see Appendix 4 at **[A4]**.

These Regulations are reproduced as amended by: the Limited Liability Partnerships (Amendment) Regulations 2009, SI 2009/1833; the Companies Act 2006 and Limited Liability Partnerships (Transitional Provisions and Savings) (Amendment) Regulations 2009, SI 2009/2476; the Limited Liability Partnerships (Amendment) (No 2) Regulations 2009, SI 2009/2995; the Companies and Limited Liability Partnerships (Accounts and Audit Exemptions and Change of Accounting Framework) Regulations 2012, SI 2012/2301; the Financial Services Act 2012 (Consequential Amendments and Transitional Provisions) Order 2013, SI 2013/472; the Limited Liability Partnerships (Application of Companies Act 2006) (Amendment) Regulations 2013, SI 2013/618; the Companies (Striking Off) (Electronic Communications) Order 2014, SI 2014/1602; the Reports on Payments to Governments Regulations 2014, SI 2014/3209; the Company, Limited Liability Partnership and Business (Names and Trading Disclosures) Regulations 2015, SI 2015/17; the Legal Aid, Sentencing and Punishment of Offenders Act 2012 (Fines on Summary Conviction) Regulations 2015, SI 2015/664; the Companies and Limited Liability Partnerships (Filing Requirements) Regulations 2015, SI 2015/1695; the Limited Liability Partnerships (Register of People with Significant Control) Regulations 2016, SI 2016/340; the Companies (Address of Registered Office) Regulations 2016, SI 2016/423; the Companies and Limited Liability Partnerships (Filing Requirements) Regulations 2016, SI 2016/599; the Information about People with Significant Control (Amendment) Regulations 2017, SI 2017/693; the Scottish Partnerships (Register of People with Significant Control) Regulations 2017, SI 2017/694; the Central Securities Depositories Regulations 2017, SI 2017/1064; the Companies (Disclosure of Address) (Amendment) Regulations 2018, SI 2018/528; the Companies, Limited Liability Partnerships and Partnerships (Amendment etc) (EU Exit) Regulations 2019, SI 2019/348; the Money Laundering and Terrorist Financing (Amendment) Regulations 2019, SI 2019/1511; the Limited Liability Partnerships (Amendment etc) Regulations 2021, SI 2021/60.

ARRANGEMENT OF REGULATIONS

PART 1
GENERAL INTRODUCTORY PROVISIONS

PART 1A
INCORPORATION

PART 2
FORMALITIES OF DOING BUSINESS

PART 3
AN LLP'S NAME

CHAPTER 1 GENERAL REQUIREMENTS

CHAPTER 2 SIMILARITY TO OTHER NAMES

CHAPTER 3 OTHER POWERS OF THE SECRETARY OF STATE

CHAPTER 4 TRADING DISCLOSURES

PART 4
AN LLP'S REGISTERED OFFICE

PART 5
AN LLP'S MEMBERS

CHAPTER 1 REGISTER OF MEMBERS

CHAPTER 1A OPTION TO KEEP INFORMATION ON THE CENTRAL REGISTER

CHAPTER 2 MEMBERS' RESIDENTIAL ADDRESSES: PROTECTION FROM DISCLOSURE

PART 6
DEBENTURES

PART 7
CERTIFICATION AND TRANSFER OF DEBENTURES

PART 8
ANNUAL CONFIRMATION BY LLP OF ACCURACY OF INFORMATION ON REGISTER

PART 8A
AN LLPS REGISTER OF PEOPLE WITH SIGNIFICANT CONTROL

PART 9
LLP CHARGES

PART 10
ARRANGEMENTS, RECONSTRUCTIONS AND CROSS-BORDER MERGERS

PART 11
FRAUDULENT TRADING

PART 12
PROTECTION OF MEMBERS AGAINST UNFAIR PREJUDICE

PART 13
DISSOLUTION AND RESTORATION TO THE REGISTER

CHAPTER 1 STRIKING OFF

CHAPTER 2 PROPERTY OF DISSOLVED LLP

CHAPTER 3 RESTORATION TO THE REGISTER

PART 14
OVERSEAS LLPS

PART 15
THE REGISTRAR OF COMPANIES

PART 16
OFFENCES

PART 17
SUPPLEMENTARY PROVISIONS AND INTERPRETATION

PART 18
TRANSITIONAL AND CONSEQUENTIAL PROVISIONS

SCHEDULES

PART 1 GENERAL INTRODUCTORY PROVISIONS

[10.319]

1 Citation

These Regulations may be cited as the Limited Liability Partnerships (Application of Companies Act 2006) Regulations 2009.

[10.320]

2 Commencement

(1) The provisions of these Regulations come into force as follows.

(2) Regulations 8, 64, 77, 80 and 81 of, and paragraphs 6 and 7 of Schedule 3 to, these Regulations come into force on the day after the Regulations are made for the purpose of enabling the exercise of powers to make regulations or orders by statutory instrument.

(3) Otherwise, the Regulations come into force on 1st October 2009.

[10.321]

3 Interpretation

(1) In these Regulations "LLP" means a limited liability partnership registered under the Limited Liability Partnerships Act 2000.

(2) In these Regulations, unless the context otherwise requires—

(a) any reference to a numbered Part, section or Schedule is to the Part, section or Schedule so numbered in the Companies Act 2006;

(b) references in provisions applied to LLPs—

(i) to provisions of the Companies Act 2006, or

(ii) to provisions of instruments made under that Act,

are to those provisions as applied to LLPs by these Regulations or by the Limited Liability Partnerships (Accounts and Audit) (Application of Companies Act 2006) Regulations 2008;

(c) references in provisions applied to LLPs to provisions of the Insolvency Act 1986 or the Insolvency (Northern Ireland) Order 1989 are to those provisions as applied to LLPs by the Limited Liability Partnerships Regulations 2001 or the Limited Liability Partnerships Regulations (Northern Ireland) 2004;

[(d) references in provisions applied to LLPs to provisions of the Register of People with Significant Control Regulations 2016 are to those provisions as applied to LLPs by the Limited Liability Partnerships (Register of People with Significant Control) Regulations 2016.]

NOTES

Para (2): sub-para (d) added by the Limited Liability Partnerships (Register of People with Significant Control) Regulations 2016, SI 2016/340, reg , Sch 3, para 2, as from 6 April 2016.

[PART 1A INCORPORATION

[10.322]

3A Statement of initial significant control

Section 12A applies to LLPs, modified so that it reads as follows—

"12A Statement of initial significant control

(1) The statement of initial significant control required to be included in the incorporation document delivered to the registrar must—

(a) state whether, on incorporation, there will be anyone who will count for the purposes of section 790M (register of people with significant control over an LLP) as either a registrable person or a registrable relevant legal entity in relation to the LLP,

(b) include the required particulars of anyone who will count as such, and

(c) include any other matters that on incorporation will be required (or, in the absence of an election under section 790X, would be required) to be entered in the LLP's PSC register by virtue of section 790M.

(2) It is not necessary to include under subsection (1)(b) the date on which someone becomes a registrable person or a registrable relevant legal entity in relation to the LLP.

(3) If the statement includes required particulars of an individual, it must also contain a statement that those particulars are included with the knowledge of that individual.

(4) "Registrable person", "registrable relevant legal entity" and "required particulars" have the meanings given in sections 790C and 790K."]

NOTES

Part 1A (reg 3A only) was Inserted by the Limited Liability Partnerships (Register of People with Significant Control) Regulations 2016, SI 2016/340, reg 5, Sch 3, para 3, as from 30 June 2016.

PART 2 FORMALITIES OF DOING BUSINESS

[10.323]

4 Formalities of doing business under the law of England and Wales or Northern Ireland

Sections 43 to 47 apply to LLPs, modified so that they read as follows—

"43 LLP contracts

(1) Under the law of England and Wales or Northern Ireland a contract may be made—

(a) by an LLP, by writing under its common seal, or

(b) on behalf of an LLP, by a person acting under its authority, express or implied.

(2) This is without prejudice to section 6 of the Limited Liability Partnerships Act 2000 (c 12) (members as agents).

(3) Any formalities required by law in the case of a contract made by an individual also apply, unless a contrary intention appears, to a contract made by or on behalf of an LLP.

44 Execution of documents

(1) Under the law of England and Wales or Northern Ireland a document is executed by an LLP—

(a) by the affixing of its common seal, or

(b) by signature in accordance with the following provisions.

(2) A document is validly executed by an LLP if it is signed on behalf of the LLP—

(a) by two members, or

(b) by a member of the LLP in the presence of a witness who attests the signature.

(3) A document signed in accordance with subsection (2) and expressed, in whatever words, to be executed by the LLP has the same effect as if executed under the common seal of the LLP.

(4) In favour of a purchaser a document is deemed to have been duly executed by an LLP if it purports to be signed in accordance with subsection (2).

A "purchaser" means a purchaser in good faith for valuable consideration and includes a lessee, mortgagee or other person who for valuable consideration acquires an interest in property.

(5) Where a document is to be signed by a person on behalf of more than one LLP, or on behalf of an LLP and a company, it is not duly signed by that person for the purposes of this section unless he signs it separately in each capacity.

(6) References in this section to a document being (or purporting to be) signed by a member are to be read, in a case where that member is a firm, as references to its being (or purporting to be) signed by an individual authorised by the firm to sign on its behalf.

(7) This section applies to a document that is (or purports to be) executed by an LLP in the name of or on behalf of another person whether or not that person is also an LLP.

45 Common seal

(1) An LLP may have a common seal, but need not have one.

(2) An LLP which has a common seal shall have its name engraved in legible characters on the seal.

(3) If an LLP fails to comply with subsection (2) an offence is committed by—

(a) the LLP, and

(b) every member of the LLP who is in default.

(4) A member of an LLP, or a person acting on behalf of an LLP, commits an offence if he uses, or authorises the use of, a seal purporting to be a seal of the LLP on which its name is not engraved as required by subsection (2).

(5) A person guilty of an offence under this section is liable on summary conviction to a fine not exceeding level 3 on the standard scale.

(6) This section does not form part of the law of Scotland.

46 Execution of deeds

(1) A document is validly executed by an LLP as a deed for the purposes of section 1(2)(b) of the Law of Property (Miscellaneous Provisions) Act 1989 (c 34) and for the purposes of the law of Northern Ireland if, and only if—

(a) it is duly executed by the LLP, and

(b) it is delivered as a deed.

(2) For the purposes of subsection (1)(b) a document is presumed to be delivered upon its being executed, unless a contrary intention is proved.

47 Execution of deeds or other documents by attorney

(1) Under the law of England and Wales or Northern Ireland an LLP may, by instrument executed as a deed, empower a person, either generally or in respect of specified matters, as its attorney to execute deeds or other documents on its behalf.

(2) A deed or other document so executed, whether in the United Kingdom or elsewhere, has effect as if executed by the LLP.".

[10.324]

5 Formalities of doing business under the law of Scotland

Section 48 applies to LLPs, modified so that it reads as follows—

"48 Execution of documents by LLPs: Scotland

(1) The following provisions form part of the law of Scotland only.

(2) Notwithstanding the provisions of any enactment, an LLP need not have a common seal.

(3) For the purposes of any enactment—

(a) providing for a document to be executed by an LLP by affixing its common seal, or

(b) referring (in whatever terms) to a document so executed,

a document signed or subscribed by or on behalf of the LLP in accordance with the provisions of the Requirements of Writing (Scotland) Act 1995 (c 7) has effect as if so executed.".

[10.325]

6 Official seal for use abroad

Section 49 applies to LLPs, modified so that it reads as follows—

"49 Official seal for use abroad

(1) An LLP that has a common seal may have an official seal for use outside the United Kingdom.

(2) The official seal must be a facsimile of the LLP's common seal, with the addition on its face of the place or places where it is to be used.

(3) The official seal when duly affixed to a document has the same effect as the LLP's common seal. This subsection does not extend to Scotland.

(4) An LLP having an official seal for use outside the United Kingdom may—

(a) by writing under its common seal, or

(b) as respects Scotland, by writing subscribed in accordance with the Requirements of Writing (Scotland) Act 1995,

authorise any person appointed for the purpose to affix the official seal to any deed or other document to which the LLP is party.

(5) As between the LLP and a person dealing with such an agent, the agent's authority continues—

(a) during the period mentioned in the instrument conferring the authority, or

(b) if no period is mentioned, until notice of the revocation or termination of the agent's authority has been given to the person dealing with him.

(6) The person affixing the official seal must certify in writing on the deed or other document to which the seal is affixed the date on which, and place at which, it is affixed.".

[10.326]

7 Other matters

Sections 51 and 52 apply to LLPs, modified so that they read as follows—

"51 Pre-incorporation contracts, deeds and obligations

(1) A contract that purports to be made by or on behalf of an LLP at a time when the LLP has not been formed has effect, subject to any agreement to the contrary, as one made with the person purporting to act for the LLP or as agent for it, and he is personally liable on the contract accordingly.

(2) Subsection (1) applies—

(a) to the making of a deed under the law of England and Wales or Northern Ireland, and

(b) to the undertaking of an obligation under the law of Scotland,

as it applies to the making of a contract.

52 Bills of exchange and promissory notes

A bill of exchange or promissory note is deemed to have been made, accepted or endorsed on behalf of an LLP if made, accepted or endorsed in the name of, or by or on behalf or on account of, the LLP by a person acting under its authority.".

PART 3 AN LLP'S NAME

CHAPTER 1 GENERAL REQUIREMENTS

[10.327]

8 Prohibited names and sensitive words and expressions

Sections 53 to 56 apply to LLPs, modified so that they read as follows—

"53 Prohibited names

An LLP must not be registered under the Limited Liability Partnerships Act 2000 (c 12) by a name if, in the opinion of the Secretary of State—

(a) its use by the LLP would constitute an offence, or

(b) it is offensive.

54 Names suggesting connection with government or public authority

(1) The approval of the Secretary of State is required for an LLP to be registered under the Limited Liability Partnerships Act 2000 (c 12) by a name that would be likely to give the impression that the LLP is connected with—

(a) Her Majesty's Government, any part of the Scottish Administration[, the Welsh Assembly Government] or Her Majesty's Government in Northern Ireland,

(b) a local authority, or

(c) any public authority specified for the purposes of this section by regulations made by the Secretary of State.

(2) For the purposes of this section—

"local authority" means—

(a) a local authority within the meaning of the Local Government Act 1972 (c 70), the Common Council of the City of London or the Council of the Isles of Scilly,

(b) a council constituted under section 2 of the Local Government etc (Scotland) Act 1994 (c 39), or

(c) a district council in Northern Ireland;

"public authority" includes any person or body having functions of a public nature.

(3) Regulations under this section are subject to affirmative resolution procedure.

55 Other sensitive words or expressions

(1) The approval of the Secretary of State is required for an LLP to be registered under the Limited Liability Partnerships Act 2000 (c 12) by a name that includes a word or expression for the time being specified in regulations made by the Secretary of State under this section.

(2) Regulations under this section are subject to approval after being made.

56 Duty to seek comments of government department or other specified body

(1) The Secretary of State may by regulations under—

(a) section 54 (name suggesting connection with government or public authority), or

(b) section 55 (other sensitive words or expressions),

require that, in connection with an application for the approval of the Secretary of State under that section, the applicant must seek the view of a specified Government department or other body.

(2) Where such a requirement applies, the applicant must request the specified department or other body (in writing) to indicate whether (and if so why) it has any objections to the proposed name.

(3) Where a request under this section is made in connection with an application for the registration of an LLP under the Limited Liability Partnerships Act 2000 (c 12), the application must—

(a) include a statement that a request under this section has been made, and

(b) be accompanied by a copy of any response received.

(4) Where a request under this section is made in connection with a change in an LLP's name, the notice of the change sent to the registrar must—

(a) include a statement by a designated member of the LLP that a request under this section has been made, and

(b) be accompanied by a copy of any response received.

(5) In this section "specified" means specified in the regulations.".

NOTES

Words in square brackets in s 54(1)(a) as set out above inserted by the Limited Liability Partnerships (Amendment) (No 2) Regulations 2009, SI 2009/2995, reg 2, as from 14 December 2009.

See further, in relation to the renaming of the Welsh Assembly Government as the Welsh Government, the Wales Act 2014, s 4(4)(a). See also, in relation to the renaming of the National Assembly for Wales as the Senedd Cymru or the Welsh Parliament, the Senedd and Elections (Wales) Act 2020, s 2 (with effect from 6 May 2020).

[10.328]

9 Permitted characters etc

Section 57 applies to LLPs, modified so that it reads as follows—

["57 Permitted characters etc

(1) The provisions of the Company, Limited Liability Partnership and Business (Names and Trading Disclosures) Regulations 2015 relating to the characters, signs or symbols and punctuation that may be used in a registered name apply to LLPs.

(2) Those provisions are—

(a) regulation 2 and Schedule 1, and

(b) any other provisions of those Regulations having effect for the purpose of those provisions.

(3) In those provisions as they apply to LLPs—

(a) for "company" substitute "LLP", and

(b) for "the Act" substitute "the Limited Liability Partnerships Act 2000".

(4) An LLP may not be registered under the Limited Liability Partnerships Act 2000 by a name that consists of or includes anything that is not permitted in accordance with the provisions applied by this section.".]

NOTES

Section 57 as set out above was substituted the Company, Limited Liability Partnership and Business (Names and Trading Disclosures) Regulations 2015, SI 2015/17, reg 11, Sch 5, paras 1, 2, as from 31 January 2015.

[10.329]

10 Inappropriate use of indications of company type or legal form

Section 65 applies to LLPs, modified so that it reads as follows—

["65 Inappropriate use of indications of company type or legal form

(1) The provisions of the Company, Limited Liability Partnership and Business (Names and Trading Disclosures) Regulations 2015 relating to inappropriate use of indications of company type or legal form apply to LLPs.

(2) Those provisions are—

(a) regulation 4 and Schedule 2, and

(b) any other provisions of those Regulations having effect for the purpose of those provisions.

(3) As applied to LLPs regulation 4 is modified so as to read as follows—

"4 Inappropriate indication of legal form: generally applicable provisions

(1) An LLP must not be registered under the Limited Liability Partnerships Act 2000 by a name that includes in any part of the name—

(a) an expression or abbreviation specified in inverted commas in paragraph 3(a) to (o) or (r) to (y) in Schedule 2 (other than the abbreviation "LLP" or "PAC" (with or without full stops) at the end of its name), or

(b) an expression or abbreviation specified as similar.

(2) An LLP must not be registered under the Limited Liability Partnerships Act 2000 by a name that includes, immediately before the expression "LIMITED LIABILITY PARTNERSHIP" OR "PARTNERIAETH ATEBOLRWYDD CYFYNGEDIG" or the abbreviations "LLP" or "PAC", an abbreviation specified in inverted commas in paragraph 3(y) of that Schedule (or any abbreviation specified as similar)".".]

NOTES

Section 65 as set out above was substituted the Company, Limited Liability Partnership and Business (Names and Trading Disclosures) Regulations 2015, SI 2015/17, reg 11, Sch 5, paras 1, 3, as from 31 January 2015.

CHAPTER 2 SIMILARITY TO OTHER NAMES

[10.330]

11 Similarity to other name on registrar's index

Sections 66 to 68 apply to LLPs, modified so that they read as follows—

["66 Name not to be the same as another in the index

(1) An LLP must not be registered under the Limited Liability Partnerships Act 2000 by a name that is the same as another name appearing in the registrar's index of company names.

(2) The provisions of the Company, Limited Liability Partnership and Business (Names and Trading Disclosures) Regulations 2015 supplementing this section apply to LLPs.

(3) Those provisions are—

(a) regulation 7 and Schedule 3 (matters that are to be disregarded and words, expressions, signs and symbols that are to be regarded as the same),

(b) regulation 8 (consent to registration of a name which is the same as another in the registrar's index of company names), and

(c) any other provisions of those Regulations having effect for the purpose of those provisions.

(4) In regulation 8 as applied to LLPs—

(a) for "a company" or "the company" substitute "an LLP" or "the LLP",

(b) for "Company Y" substitute "LLP Y", and

(c) in paragraph (1), for "the Act" substitute "the Limited Liability Partnerships Act 2000".."]

67 Power to direct change of name in case of similarity to existing name

The Secretary of State may direct an LLP to change its name if it has been registered in a name that is the same as or, in the opinion of the Secretary of State, too like—

(a) a name appearing at the time of the registration in the registrar's index of company names, or

(b) a name that should have appeared in that index at that time.

68 Direction to change names: supplementary provisions

(1) The following provisions have effect in relation to a direction under section 67 (power to direct change of name in case of similarity to existing name).

(2) Any such direction—

(a) must be given within twelve months of the LLP's registration by the name in question, and

(b) must specify the period within which the LLP is to change its name.

(3) The Secretary of State may by a further direction extend that period.

Any such direction must be given before the end of the period for the time being specified.

(4) A direction under section 67 or this section must be in writing.

(5) If an LLP fails to comply with the direction, an offence is committed by—

(a) the LLP, and

(b) every designated member of the LLP who is in default.

(6) A person guilty of an offence under this section is liable on summary conviction to a fine not exceeding level 3 on the standard scale and, for continued contravention, a daily default fine not exceeding one-tenth of level 3 on the standard scale.".

NOTES

Section 66 as set out above was substituted the Company, Limited Liability Partnership and Business (Names and Trading Disclosures) Regulations 2015, SI 2015/17, reg 11, Sch 5, paras 1, 4, as from 31 January 2015.

[10.331]

12 Similarity to other name in which person has goodwill

Sections 69 to 74 apply to LLPs, modified so that they read as follows—

"69 Objection to LLP's registered name

(1) A person ("the applicant") may object to an LLP's registered name on the ground—

(a) that it is the same as a name associated with the applicant in which he has goodwill, or

(b) that it is sufficiently similar to such a name that its use in the United Kingdom would be likely to mislead by suggesting a connection between the LLP and the applicant.

(2) The objection must be made by application to a company names adjudicator (see section 70).

(3) The LLP concerned shall be the primary respondent to the application.

Any of its members may be joined as respondents.

(4) If the ground specified in subsection (1)(a) or (b) is established, it is for the respondents to show—

(a) that the name was registered before the commencement of the activities on which the applicant relies to show goodwill; or

(b) that the LLP—

(i) is operating under the name, or

(ii) is proposing to do so and has incurred substantial start-up costs in preparation, or

(iii) was formerly operating under the name and is now dormant; or

(c) that the name was registered in the ordinary course of an LLP formation business and the LLP is available for sale to the applicant on the standard terms of that business; or

(d) that the name was adopted in good faith; or

(e) that the interests of the applicant are not adversely affected to any significant extent.

If none of those is shown, the objection shall be upheld.

(5) If the facts mentioned in subsection (4)(a), (b) or (c) are established, the objection shall nevertheless be upheld if the applicant shows that the main purpose of the respondents (or any of them) in registering the name was to obtain money (or other consideration) from the applicant or prevent him from registering the name.

(6) If the objection is not upheld under subsection (4) or (5), it shall be dismissed.

(7) In this section "goodwill" includes reputation of any description.

70 Company names adjudicators

(1) The Secretary of State shall appoint persons to be company names adjudicators.

(2) The persons appointed must have such legal or other experience as, in the Secretary of State's opinion, makes them suitable for appointment.

(3) An adjudicator—

- (a) holds office in accordance with the terms of his appointment,
- (b) is eligible for re-appointment when his term of office ends,
- (c) may resign at any time by notice in writing given to the Secretary of State, and
- (d) may be dismissed by the Secretary of State on the ground of incapacity or misconduct.

(4) One of the adjudicators shall be appointed Chief Adjudicator.

He shall perform such functions as the Secretary of State may assign to him.

(5) The other adjudicators shall undertake such duties as the Chief Adjudicator may determine.

(6) The Secretary of State may—

- (a) appoint staff for the adjudicators;
- (b) pay remuneration and expenses to the adjudicators and their staff;
- (c) defray other costs arising in relation to the performance by the adjudicators of their functions;
- (d) compensate persons for ceasing to be adjudicators.

71 Procedural rules

(1) The Company Names Adjudicator Rules 2008 (SI 2008/1738) apply to LLPs.

(2) As they apply to LLPs, omit—

- (a) in rule 3(6) (persons joined as respondent), the reference to a director of the primary respondent;
- (b) rule 13(2) (registered office treated as address for service).

72 Decision of adjudicator to be made available to public

(1) A company names adjudicator must, within 90 days of determining an application under section 69, make his decision and his reasons for it available to the public.

(2) He may do so by means of a website or by such other means as appear to him to be appropriate.

73 Order requiring name to be changed

(1) If an application under section 69 is upheld, the adjudicator shall make an order—

- (a) requiring the respondent LLP to change its name to one that is not an offending name, and
- (b) requiring all the respondents—
  - (i) to take all such steps as are within their power to make, or facilitate the making, of that change, and
  - (ii) not to cause or permit any steps to be taken calculated to result in another LLP being registered with a name that is an offending name.

(2) An "offending name" means a name that, by reason of its similarity to the name associated with the applicant in which he claims goodwill, would be likely—

- (a) to be the subject of a direction under section 67 (power of Secretary of State to direct change of name), or
- (b) to give rise to a further application under section 69.

(3) The order must specify a date by which the respondent LLP's name is to be changed and may be enforced—

- (a) in England and Wales or Northern Ireland, in the same way as an order of the High Court;
- (b) in Scotland, in the same way as a decree of the Court of Session.

(4) If the respondent LLP's name is not changed in accordance with the order by the specified date, the adjudicator may determine a new name for the LLP.

(5) If the adjudicator determines a new name for the respondent LLP he must give notice of his determination—

- (a) to the applicant,
- (b) to the respondents, and
- (c) to the registrar.

(6) For the purposes of this section an LLP's name is changed when the change takes effect in accordance with paragraph 5(4) in Part 1 of the Schedule to the Limited Liability Partnerships Act 2000 (c 12) (on the issue of the certificate of the change of name).

74 Appeal from adjudicator's decision

(1) An appeal lies to the court from any decision of a company names adjudicator to uphold or dismiss an application under section 69.

(2) Notice of appeal against a decision upholding an application must be given before the date specified in the adjudicator's order by which the respondent LLP's name is to be changed.

(3) If notice of appeal is given against a decision upholding an application, the effect of the adjudicator's order is suspended.

(4) If on appeal the court—

- (a) affirms the decision of the adjudicator to uphold the application, or
- (b) reverses the decision of the adjudicator to dismiss the application,

the court may (as the case may require) specify the date by which the adjudicator's order is to be complied with, remit the matter to the adjudicator or make any order or determination that the adjudicator might have made.

(5) If the court determines a new name for the LLP it must give notice of the determination—

- (a) to the parties to the appeal, and

(b) to the registrar.".

CHAPTER 3 OTHER POWERS OF THE SECRETARY OF STATE

[10.332]

13 Provision of misleading information etc

Sections 75 and 76 apply to LLPs, modified so that they read as follows—

"75 Provision of misleading information etc

(1) If it appears to the Secretary of State—

(a) that misleading information has been given for the purposes of an LLP's registration by a particular name, or

(b) that an undertaking or assurance has been given for that purpose and has not been fulfilled,

the Secretary of State may direct the LLP to change its name.

(2) Any such direction—

(a) must be given within five years of the LLP's registration by that name, and

(b) must specify the period within which the LLP is to change its name.

(3) The Secretary of State may by a further direction extend the period within which the LLP is to change its name.

Any such direction must be given before the end of the period for the time being specified.

(4) A direction under this section must be in writing.

(5) If an LLP fails to comply with a direction under this section, an offence is committed by—

(a) the LLP, and

(b) every designated member of the LLP who is in default.

(6) A person guilty of an offence under this section is liable on summary conviction to a fine not exceeding level 3 on the standard scale and, for continued contravention, a daily default fine not exceeding one-tenth of level 3 on the standard scale.

76 Misleading indication of activities

(1) If in the opinion of the Secretary of State the name by which an LLP is registered gives so misleading an indication of the nature of its activities as to be likely to cause harm to the public, the Secretary of State may direct the LLP to change its name.

(2) The direction must be in writing.

(3) The direction must be complied with within a period of six weeks from the date of the direction or such longer period as the Secretary of State may think fit to allow.

This does not apply if an application is duly made to the court under the following provisions.

(4) The LLP may apply to the court to set the direction aside.

The application must be made within the period of three weeks from the date of the direction.

(5) The court may set the direction aside or confirm it.

If the direction is confirmed, the court shall specify the period within which the direction is to be complied with.

(6) If an LLP fails to comply with a direction under this section, an offence is committed by—

(a) the LLP, and

(b) every designated member of the LLP who is in default.

(7) A person guilty of an offence under this section is liable on summary conviction to a fine not exceeding level 3 on the standard scale and, for continued contravention, a daily default fine not exceeding one-tenth of level 3 on the standard scale.".

CHAPTER 4 TRADING DISCLOSURES

Requirement to disclose LLP name etc

[10.333]

14

Sections 82 and 83 apply to LLPs, modified so that they read as follows—

["82 Requirements to disclose LLP name etc

(1) The provisions of the Company, Limited Liability Partnership and Business (Names and Trading Disclosures) Regulations 2015 relating to Trading Disclosures apply to LLPs.

(2) As they apply to LLPs—

(a) read references to a company as references to an LLP;

(b) read references to a director as references to a member of an LLP;

(c) read references to an officer of a company as references to a designated member of an LLP;

(d) in regulation 25 (further particulars to appear in business letters, order forms and websites), for paragraphs (2)(d) to (f) and (3) substitute—

"(d) in the case of an LLP whose name ends with the abbreviation "llp", "LLP", "pac" or "PAC", the fact that it is an LLP or a partneriaeth atebolrwydd cyfyngedig.";

(e) in regulation 26 (disclosure of names of members)—

(i) at the beginning of paragraph (1) insert "Subject to paragraph (3)," and

(ii) after paragraph (2) insert—

"(3) Paragraph (1) does not apply in relation to any document issued by an LLP with more than 20 members which maintains at its principal place of business a list of the names of all the members if the document states in legible characters the address of the principal place of business of the LLP and that the list of the members' names is open to inspection at that place.

(4) Where an LLP maintains a list of the members' names for the purposes of paragraph (3), any person may inspect the list during office hours.";

(f) omit regulation 28(3) (offences: shadow directors).

83 Civil consequences of failure to make required disclosure

(1) This section applies to any legal proceedings brought by an LLP to which section 82 applies (requirement to disclose LLP name etc) to enforce a right arising out of a contract made in the course of a business in respect of which the LLP was, at the time the contract was made, in breach of the Company, Limited Liability Partnership and Business (Names and Trading Disclosures) Regulations 2015.

(2) The proceedings shall be dismissed if the defendant (in Scotland, the defender) to the proceedings shows—

(a) that he has a claim against the claimant (pursuer) arising out of the contract that he has been unable to pursue by reason of the latter's breach of the regulations, or

(b) that he has suffered some financial loss in connection with the contract by reason of the claimant's (pursuer's) breach of the regulations,

unless the court before which the proceedings are brought is satisfied that it is just and equitable to permit the proceedings to continue.

(3) This section does not affect the right of any person to enforce such rights as he may have against another person in any proceedings brought by that person.".]

NOTES

Sections 82, 83 as set out above were substituted the Company, Limited Liability Partnership and Business (Names and Trading Disclosures) Regulations 2015, SI 2015/17, reg 11, Sch 5, paras 1, 5, as from 31 January 2015.

[10.334]
15

Section 85 applies to LLPs, modified so that it reads as follows—

["85 Minor variation in form of name to be left out of account

(1) For the purposes of this Chapter, in considering an LLP's name no account is to be taken of—

(a) whether upper or lower case characters (or a combination of the two) are used,

(b) whether diacritical marks or punctuation are present or absent,

provided there is no real likelihood of names differing only in those respects being taken to be different names.

(2) This does not affect the operation of provisions of the Company, Limited Liability Partnership and Business (Names and Trading Disclosures) Regulations 2015 permitting only specified characters or punctuation.".]

NOTES

Section 85 as set out above was substituted the Company, Limited Liability Partnership and Business (Names and Trading Disclosures) Regulations 2015, SI 2015/17, reg 11, Sch 5, paras 1, 6, as from 31 January 2015.

PART 4 AN LLP'S REGISTERED OFFICE

[10.335]
16 General

Sections 86 and 87 apply to LLPs, modified so that they read as follows—

"86 An LLP's registered office

(1) An LLP must at all times have a registered office situated in England and Wales (or in Wales), in Scotland or in Northern Ireland, to which all communications and notices may be addressed.

(2) On the incorporation of an LLP the situation of its registered office shall be that stated in the incorporation document.

87 Change of address of registered office

(1) An LLP may change the address of its registered office by giving notice to the registrar.

(2) The change takes effect upon the notice being registered by the registrar, but until the end of the period of 14 days beginning with the date on which it is registered a person may validly serve any document on the LLP at the address previously registered.

(3) For the purposes of any duty of an LLP—

(a) to keep available for inspection at its registered office any register, index or other document, or

(b) to mention the address of its registered office in any document,

an LLP that has given notice to the registrar of a change in the address of its registered office may act on the change as from such date, not more than 14 days after the notice is given, as it may determine.

(4) Where an LLP unavoidably ceases to perform at its registered office any such duty as is mentioned in subsection (3)(a) in circumstances in which it was not practicable to give prior notice to the registrar of a change in the address of its registered office, but—

(a) resumes performance of that duty at other premises as soon as practicable, and

(b) gives notice accordingly to the registrar of a change in the situation of its registered office within 14 days of doing so,

it is not to be treated as having failed to comply with that duty.".

[10.336]
17 Welsh LLPs

Section 88 applies to LLPs, modified so that it reads as follows—

"88 Welsh LLPs

(1) In this Act a "Welsh LLP" means an LLP as to which it is stated in the register that its registered office is to be situated in Wales.

(2) An LLP—

(a) whose registered office is in Wales, and

(b) as to which it is stated in the register that its registered office is to be situated in England and Wales,

may determine that the register be amended so that it states that the LLP's registered office is to be situated in Wales.

(3) An LLP—

(a) whose registered office is in Wales, and

(b) as to which it is stated in the register that its registered office is to be situated in Wales,

may determine that the register be amended so that it states that the LLP's registered office is to be situated in England and Wales.

(4) Where an LLP makes a determination under this section it must give notice to the registrar, who shall—

(a) amend the register accordingly, and

(b) issue a new certificate of incorporation altered to meet the circumstances of the case.".

PART 5 AN LLP'S MEMBERS

CHAPTER 1 REGISTER OF MEMBERS

[10.337]

[17A Alternative method of record-keeping

Section 161A applies to LLPs, modified so that it reads as follows—

"161A Alternative method of record-keeping

Sections 162 to 165 must be read with Chapter 1A (which allows for an alternative method of record-keeping in the case of LLPs).".]

NOTES

Inserted by the Companies and Limited Liability Partnerships (Filing Requirements) Regulations 2016, SI 2016/599, reg 3, Sch 1, paras 1, 2, as from 30 June 2016.

[10.338]

18 Requirements for register of members

Sections 162 to 165 apply to LLPs, modified so that they read as follows—

"162 Register of members

(1) Every LLP must keep a register of its members.

(2) The register must contain the required particulars (see sections 163 and 164) of each person who is a member of the LLP.

(3) The register must be kept available for inspection—

(a) at the LLP's registered office, or

(b) at a place specified in Part 2 of the Companies (Company Records) Regulations 2008 (SI 2008/3006).

(4) The LLP must give notice to the registrar—

(a) of the place at which the register is kept available for inspection, and

(b) of any change in that place,

unless it has at all times been kept at the LLP's registered office.

(5) The register must be open to the inspection—

(a) of any member of the LLP without charge, and

(b) of any other person on payment of the fee prescribed by regulation 2(a) of the Companies (Fees for Inspection of Company Records) Regulations 2008 (SI 2008/3007).

(6) If default is made in complying with subsection (1), (2) or (3) or if default is made for 14 days in complying with subsection (4), or if an inspection required under subsection (5) is refused, an offence is committed by—

(a) the LLP, and

(b) every designated member of the LLP who is in default.

(7) A person guilty of an offence under this section is liable on summary conviction to a fine not exceeding level 5 on the standard scale and, for continued contravention, a daily default fine not exceeding [one-tenth of the greater of £5,000 or level 4 on the standard scale].

(8) In the case of a refusal of inspection of the register, the court may by order compel an immediate inspection of it.

163 Particulars of members to be registered: individuals

(1) An LLP's register of members must contain the following particulars in the case of an individual—

(a) name and any former name;

(b) a service address;

(c) the country or state (or part of the United Kingdom) in which he is usually resident;

(d) date of birth;

(e) whether he is a designated member.

(2) For the purposes of this section "name" means a person's Christian name (or other forename) and surname, except that in the case of—

(a) a peer, or

(b) an individual usually known by a title,

the title may be stated instead of his Christian name (or other forename) and surname or in addition to either or both of them.

(3) For the purposes of this section a "former name" means a name by which the individual was formerly known for business purposes.

Where a person is or was formerly known by more than one such name, each of them must be stated.

(4) It is not necessary for the register to contain particulars of a former name in the following cases—

(a) in the case of a peer or an individual normally known by a British title, where the name is one by which the person was known previous to the adoption of or succession to the title;

(b) in the case of any person, where the former name—

(i) was changed or disused before the person attained the age of 16 years, or

(ii) has been changed or disused for 20 years or more.

(5) A person's service address may be stated to be "The LLP's registered office".

164 Particulars of members to be registered: corporate members and firms

An LLP's register of members must contain the following particulars in the case of a body corporate, or a firm that is a legal person under the law by which it is governed—

(a) corporate or firm name;

(b) registered or principal office;

[(c) in the case of a limited company that is a UK-registered company, the registered number;]

(d) in any other case, particulars of—

(i) the legal form of the company or firm and the law by which it is governed, and

(ii) if applicable, the register in which it is entered (including details of the state) and its registration number in that register;

(e) whether it is a designated member.

165 Register of members' residential addresses

(1) Every LLP must keep a register of members' residential addresses.

(2) The register must state the usual residential address of each of the LLP's members.

(3) If a member's usual residential address is the same as his service address (as stated in the LLP's register of members), the register of members' residential addresses need only contain an entry to that effect.

This does not apply if his service address is stated to be "The LLP's registered office".

(4) If default is made in complying with this section, an offence is committed by—

(a) the LLP, and

(b) every designated member of the LLP who is in default.

(5) A person guilty of an offence under this section is liable on summary conviction to a fine not exceeding level 5 on the standard scale and, for continued contravention, a daily default fine not exceeding one-tenth of level 5 on the standard scale.

(6) This section applies only to members who are individuals, not where the member is a body corporate or a firm that is a legal person under the law by which it is governed.".

NOTES

Words in square brackets in s 162(7) as set out above substituted (for the original words "one-tenth of level 5 on the standard scale") by the Legal Aid, Sentencing and Punishment of Offenders Act 2012 (Fines on Summary Conviction) Regulations 2015, SI 2015/664, regs 3, 5, Sch 3, Pt 1, para 14(1), (2), as from 12 March 2015, in relation to England and Wales only (except in relation to (a) fines for offences committed before 12 March 2015, (b) the operation of restrictions on fines that may be imposed on a person aged under 18, or (c) fines that may be imposed on a person convicted by a magistrates' court who is to be sentenced as if convicted on indictment).

Para (c) of s 164 as set out above was substituted by the Companies, Limited Liability Partnerships and Partnerships (Amendment etc) (EU Exit) Regulations 2019, SI 2019/348, reg 8, Sch 3, paras 22, 23, as from IP completion day (as defined in the European Union (Withdrawal Agreement) Act 2020, s 39) (for transitional provisions see Sch 4, para 2 to the 2019 Regulations at **[12.105]**).

[CHAPTER 1A OPTION TO KEEP INFORMATION ON THE CENTRAL REGISTER

[10.339]

[18A

Sections 167A to 167E apply to LLPs, modified so that they read as follows—

"167A Right to make an election

(1) An election may be made under this section in respect of a register of members or a register of members' residential addresses (or both).

(2) The election may be made—

(a) by the proposed members of a proposed LLP, or

(b) by the LLP itself once it is formed and registered under the Limited Liability Partnerships Act 2000.

(3) The election is made by giving notice of election to the registrar.

(4) If the notice is given by proposed members of a proposed LLP, it must be given when the documents required to be delivered under section 2 of the Limited Liability Partnerships Act 2000 are delivered to the registrar.

167B Effective date of election

(1) An election made under section 167A takes effect when the notice of election is registered by the registrar.

(2) The election remains in force until a notice of withdrawal sent by the LLP under section 167E is registered by the registrar.

167C Effect of election on obligations under sections 162 and 165

(1) In the period during which an election under section 167A is in force, with respect to an LLP, the obligations set out in sections 162 and 165(1) do not apply to that LLP.

167D Duty to notify registrar of changes

(1) The duty under subsection (2) applies during the period when an election under section 167A is in force.

(2) The LLP must deliver to the registrar—

(a) any information of which the LLP would during that period have been obliged to give notice under section 9 of the Limited Liability Partnerships Act 2000, had the election not been in force, and

(b) any statement that would have been required to accompany such a notice.

(3) The information (and any accompanying statement) must be delivered as soon as reasonably practicable after the LLP becomes aware of the information and, in any event, no later than the time by which the LLP would have been required under section 9 of the Limited Liability Partnerships Act 2000 to give notice of the information.

(4) If default is made in complying with this section, an offence is committed by—

(a) the LLP, and

(b) every designated member of the LLP who is in default.

(5) A person guilty of an offence under this section is liable on summary conviction—

(a) in England and Wales, to a fine and, for continued contravention, a daily default fine not exceeding the greater of £500 and one-tenth of level 4 on the standard scale;

(b) in Scotland and Northern Ireland, to a fine not exceeding level 5 on the standard scale and, for continued contravention, a daily default fine not exceeding one-tenth of level 5 on the standard scale.

167E Withdrawing the election

(1) An LLP may withdraw an election made by or in respect of it under section 167A.

(2) Withdrawal is achieved by giving notice of withdrawal to the registrar.

(3) The withdrawal takes effect when the notice is registered by the registrar.

(4) The effect of withdrawal is that the LLP's obligation under section 162 or (as the case may be) section 165 to keep and maintain a register of the relevant kind apply from then on with respect to the period going forward.

(5) The reference in subsection (4) to a register "of the relevant kind" is to a register (whether a register of members or a register of members' usual residential addresses) of the kind in respect of which the election was made.

(6) This means that, when the withdrawal takes effect—

(a) the LLP must enter in that register all the information that is required to be contained in that register in respect of matters that are current as at that time, but

(b) the LLP is not required to enter in its register information relating to the period when the election was in force that is no longer current."]

NOTES

Inserted, together with the preceding heading, by the Companies and Limited Liability Partnerships (Filing Requirements) Regulations 2016, SI 2016/599, reg 3, Sch 1, paras 1, 3, as from 30 June 2016.

CHAPTER 2 MEMBERS' RESIDENTIAL ADDRESSES: PROTECTION FROM DISCLOSURE

[10.340]

19 Members' residential addresses: protection from disclosure

Sections 240 to 246 apply to LLPs, modified so that they read as follows—

"240 Protected information

(1) This Chapter makes provision for protecting, in the case of an LLP member who is an individual—

(a) information as to his usual residential address;

(b) the information that his service address is his usual residential address.

(2) That information is referred to in this Chapter as "protected information".

(3) Information does not cease to be protected information on the individual ceasing to be a member of the LLP.

References in this Chapter to a member include, to that extent, a former member.

241 Protected information: restriction on use or disclosure by LLP

(1) An LLP must not use or disclose protected information about any of its members, except—

(a) for communicating with the member concerned,

(b) in order to comply with any requirement of this Act or of the Limited Liability Partnerships Act 2000 (c 12) as to particulars to be sent to the registrar, or

(c) in accordance with section 244 (disclosure under court order).

(2) Subsection (1) does not prohibit any use or disclosure of protected information with the consent of the member concerned.

242 Protected information: restriction on use or disclosure by registrar

(1) The registrar must omit protected information from the material on the register that is available for inspection where—

(a) it is contained in a document delivered to him in which such information is required to be stated, and

(b) in the case of a document having more than one part, it is contained in a part of the document in which such information is required to be stated.

(2) The registrar is not obliged—

(a) to check other documents or (as the case may be) other parts of the document to ensure the absence of protected information, or

(b) to omit from the material that is available for public inspection anything registered before 1st October 2009.

(3) The registrar must not use or disclose protected information except—

(a) as permitted by section 243 (permitted use or disclosure by registrar), or

(b) in accordance with section 244 (disclosure under court order).

243 Permitted use or disclosure by the registrar

(1) The registrar may use protected information for communicating with the member in question.

(2) The registrar may disclose protected information—

(a) to a public authority specified for the purposes of this section, or

(b) to a credit reference agency.

(3) The provisions of the Companies (Disclosure of Address) Regulations 2009 (SI 2009/214) relating to disclosure of protected information under this section apply to LLPs.

(4) The provisions are—

(a) Part 2 (disclosure of protected information),

(b) Part 4 (matters relating to applications), so far as relating to disclosure under this section, and

(c) any other provisions of the Regulations having effect for the purposes of those provisions.

(5) As those provisions apply to LLPs—

(a) references to provisions of the Companies Act 1985 (c 6), the Insolvency Act 1986 (c 45), the Companies (Northern Ireland) Order 1986 (SI 1986/1032 (NI 6)) or the Insolvency (Northern Ireland) Order 1989 (SI 1989/2405 (NI 9)) are to those provisions as applied to LLPs by the Limited Liability Partnerships Regulations 2001 (SI 2001/1090) or the Limited Liability Partnerships Regulations (Northern Ireland) 2004 (SR (NI) 2004 No 307);

(b) read references to a company or proposed company as references to an LLP or proposed LLP;

(c) read references to a director as references to a member of an LLP;

(d) read references to a subscriber to a memorandum of association as references to a proposed member of a proposed LLP;

(e) in regulation 1(2), for the definition of "former name" substitute—

""former name" means a name by which an individual was formerly known and which has been notified to the registrar under section 2 or 9 of the Limited Liability Partnerships Act 2000;".

[(f) in regulation 5(2)(a), for the words after "will be subjected to violence or intimidation as a result of the activities of at least one of" substitute—

"(i) the companies of which he is, or proposes to become, a director;

(ii) the companies of which he was a director;

(iii) the overseas companies of which he is or has been a director, secretary or permanent representative;

(iv) the limited liability partnerships of which he is or has been a member;

(v) the limited liability partnerships of which he proposes to become a member;

(vi) the companies of which he is, or proposes to become a registrable person under Part 21A of the Act;

(vii) the companies of which he used to be a registrable person under Part 21A of the Act;

(viii) the limited liability partnerships of which that individual is, or proposes to become a registrable person under Part 21A of the Act as applied to limited liability partnerships by Part 8 of these Regulations; and

(ix) the limited liability partnerships of which that individual used to be a registrable person under Part 21A of the Act as applied to limited liability partnerships by Part 8 of these Regulations."]

(6) In this section—

"credit reference agency" means a person carrying on a business comprising the furnishing of information relevant to the financial standing of individuals, being information collected by the agency for that purpose; and

"public authority" includes any person or body having functions of a public nature.

244 Disclosure under court order

(1) The court may make an order for the disclosure of protected information by the LLP or by the registrar if—

(a) there is evidence that service of documents at a service address other than the member's usual residential address is not effective to bring them to the notice of the member, or

(b) it is necessary or expedient for the information to be provided in connection with the enforcement of an order or decree of the court,

and the court is otherwise satisfied that it is appropriate to make the order.

(2) An order for disclosure by the registrar is to be made only if the LLP—

(a) does not have the member's usual residential address, or

(b) has been dissolved.

(3) The order may be made on the application of a liquidator, creditor or member of the LLP, or any other person appearing to the court to have a sufficient interest.

(4) The order must specify the persons to whom, and purposes for which, disclosure is authorised.

245 Circumstances in which registrar may put address on the public record

(1) The registrar may put a member's usual residential address on the public record if—

(a) communications sent by the registrar to the member and requiring a response within a specified period remain unanswered, or

(b) there is evidence that service of documents at a service address provided in place of the member's usual residential address is not effective to bring them to the notice of the member.

(2) The registrar must give notice of the proposal—

(a) to the member, and

(b) to every LLP of which the registrar has been notified that the individual is a member.

(3) The notice must—

(a) state the grounds on which it is proposed to put the member's usual residential address on the public record, and

(b) specify a period within which representations may be made before that is done.

(4) It must be sent to the member at his usual residential address, unless it appears to the registrar that service at that address may be ineffective to bring it to the individual's notice, in which case it may be sent to any service address provided in place of that address.

(5) The registrar must take account of any representations received within the specified period.

(6) What is meant by putting the address on the public record is explained in section 246.

246 Putting the address on the public record

(1) The registrar, on deciding in accordance with section 245 that a member's usual residential address is to be put on the public record, shall proceed as if notice of a change of registered particulars had been given—

(a) stating that address as the member's service address, and

(b) stating that the member's usual residential address is the same as his service address.

(2) The registrar must give notice of having done so—

(a) to the member, and

(b) to the LLP.

(3) On receipt of the notice the LLP must—

(a) enter the member's usual residential address in its register of members as his service address, and

(b) state in its register of members' residential addresses that his usual residential address is the same as his service address.

[(3A) But—

(a) subsection (3)(a) does not apply if an election under section 167A is in force in respect of the LLP's register of members, and

(b) subsection (3)(b) does not apply if an election under section 167A is in force in respect of the LLP's register of members' residential addresses.]

(4) If the LLP has been notified by the member in question of a more recent address as his usual residential address, it must—

(a) enter that address in its register of members as the member's service address, and

(b) give notice to the registrar as on a change of registered particulars.

[(4A) If an election under section 167A is in force in respect of the LLP's register of members, the LLP must, in place of doing the things mentioned in subsection (4)(a) and (b), deliver the particulars to the registrar in accordance with section 167D.]

(5) If an LLP fails to comply with subsection (3)[, (4) or (4A)], an offence is committed by—

(a) the LLP, and

(b) every designated member of the LLP who is in default.

(6) A person guilty of an offence under subsection (5) is liable on summary conviction to a fine not exceeding level 5 on the standard scale and, for continued contravention, a daily default fine not exceeding [one-tenth of the greater of £5,000 or level 4 on the standard scale].

(7) A member whose usual residential address has been put on the public record by the registrar under this section may not register a service address other than his usual residential address for a period of five years from the date of the registrar's decision.".

NOTES

Words in square brackets in s 243 as set out above inserted by the Limited Liability Partnerships (Register of People with Significant Control) Regulations 2016, SI 2016/340, reg 5, Sch 3, para 4, as from 6 April 2016.

In s 246 as set out above, sub-ss (3A), (4A) were inserted, and the words in square brackets in sub-s (5) were substituted, by the Companies and Limited Liability Partnerships (Filing Requirements) Regulations 2016, SI 2016/599, reg 3, Sch 1, paras 1, 4, as from 30 June 2016.

Words in square brackets in s 246(6) as set out above substituted (for the original words "one-tenth of level 5 on the standard scale") by the Legal Aid, Sentencing and Punishment of Offenders Act 2012 (Fines on Summary Conviction) Regulations 2015, SI 2015/664, regs 3, 5, Sch 3, Pt 1, para 14(1), (3), as from 12 March 2015, in relation to England and Wales only (except in relation to (a) fines for offences committed before 12 March 2015, (b) the operation of restrictions on fines that may be imposed on a person aged under 18, or (c) fines that may be imposed on a person convicted by a magistrates' court who is to be sentenced as if convicted on indictment).

PART 6 DEBENTURES

[10.341]

20 General provisions

Sections 738 to 742 apply to LLPs, modified so that they read as follows—

"738 Meaning of "debenture"

In this Act "debenture" includes debenture stock, bonds and any other securities of an LLP, whether or not constituting a charge on the assets of the LLP.

739 Perpetual debentures

(1) A condition contained in debentures, or in a deed for securing debentures, is not invalid by reason only that the debentures are made—

(a) irredeemable, or

(b) redeemable only—

(i) on the happening of a contingency (however remote), or

(ii) on the expiration of a period (however long),

any rule of equity to the contrary notwithstanding.

(2) Subsection (1) applies to debentures whenever issued and to deeds whenever executed.

740 Enforcement of contract to subscribe for debentures

A contract with an LLP to take up and pay for debentures of the LLP may be enforced by an order for specific performance.

741 Registration of allotment of debentures

(1) An LLP must register an allotment of debentures as soon as practicable and in any event within two months after the date of the allotment.

(2) If an LLP fails to comply with this section, an offence is committed by—

(a) the LLP, and

(b) every member of the LLP who is in default.

(3) A person guilty of an offence under this section is liable on summary conviction to a fine not exceeding level 3 on the standard scale and, for continued contravention, a daily default fine not exceeding one-tenth of level 3 on the standard scale.

(4) For the duties of the LLP as to the issue of the debentures, or certificates of debenture stock, see Part 21 (certification and transfer of securities).

742 Debentures to bearer (Scotland)

Notwithstanding anything in the statute of the Scots Parliament of 1696, chapter 25, debentures to bearer issued in Scotland are valid and binding according to their terms.".

[10.342]

21 Register of debenture holders

Sections 743 to 748 apply to LLPs, modified so that they read as follows—

"743 Register of debenture holders

(1) Any register of debenture holders of an LLP that is kept by the LLP must be kept available for inspection—

(a) at the LLP's registered office, or

(b) at a place specified in Part 2 of the Companies (Company Records) Regulations 2008 (SI 2008/3006).

(2) An LLP must give notice to the registrar of the place where any such register is kept available for inspection and of any change in that place.

(3) No such notice is required if the register has, at all times since it came into existence, been kept available for inspection at the LLP's registered office.

(4) If an LLP makes default for 14 days in complying with subsection (2), an offence is committed by—

(a) the LLP, and

(b) every member of the LLP who is in default.

(5) A person guilty of an offence under this section is liable on summary conviction to a fine not exceeding level 3 on the standard scale and, for continued contravention, a daily default fine not exceeding one-tenth of level 3 on the standard scale.

(6) References in this section to a register of debenture holders include a duplicate—

(a) of a register of debenture holders that is kept outside the United Kingdom, or

(b) of any part of such a register.

744 Register of debenture holders: right to inspect and require copy

(1) Every register of debenture holders of an LLP must, except when duly closed, be open to the inspection—

(a) of the registered holder of any such debentures, or any member of the LLP, without charge, and

(b) of any other person on payment of the fee prescribed by regulation 2 of the Companies (Fees for Inspection and Copying of Company Records) (No 2) Regulations 2007 (SI 2007/3535).

(2) Any person may require a copy of the register, or any part of it, on payment of the fee prescribed by regulation 3 of the Companies (Fees for Inspection and Copying of Company Records) (No 2) Regulations 2007 (SI 2007/3535).

(3) A person seeking to exercise either of the rights conferred by this section must make a request to the LLP to that effect.

(4) The request must contain the following information—

(a) in the case of an individual, his name and address;

(b) in the case of an organisation, the name and address of an individual responsible for making the request on behalf of the organisation;

(c) the purpose for which the information is to be used; and

(d) whether the information will be disclosed to any other person, and if so—

(i) where that person is an individual, his name and address,

(ii) where that person is an organisation, the name and address of an individual responsible for receiving the information on its behalf, and

(iii) the purpose for which the information is to be used by that person.

(5) For the purposes of this section a register is "duly closed" if it is closed in accordance with provision contained—

(a) in the debentures,

(b) in the case of debenture stock in the stock certificates, or

(c) in the trust deed or other document securing the debentures or debenture stock.

The total period for which a register is closed in any year must not exceed 30 days.

(6) References in this section to a register of debenture holders include a duplicate—

(a) of a register of debenture holders that is kept outside the United Kingdom, or

(b) of any part of such a register.

745 Register of debenture holders: response to request for inspection or copy

(1) Where an LLP receives a request under section 744 (register of debenture holders: right to inspect and require copy), it must within five working days either—

(a) comply with the request, or

(b) apply to the court.

(2) If it applies to the court it must notify the person making the request.

(3) If on an application under this section the court is satisfied that the inspection or copy is not sought for a proper purpose—

(a) it shall direct the LLP not to comply with the request, and

(b) it may further order that the LLP's costs (in Scotland, expenses) on the application be paid in whole or in part by the person who made the request, even if he is not a party to the application.

(4) If the court makes such a direction and it appears to the court that the LLP is or may be subject to other requests made for a similar purpose (whether made by the same person or different persons), it may direct that the LLP is not to comply with any such request.

The order must contain such provision as appears to the court appropriate to identify the requests to which it applies.

(5) If on an application under this section the court does not direct the LLP not to comply with the request, the LLP must comply with the request immediately upon the court giving its decision or, as the case may be, the proceedings being discontinued.

746 Register of debenture holders: refusal of inspection or default in providing copy

(1) If an inspection required under section 744 (register of debenture holders: right to inspect and require copy) is refused or default is made in providing a copy required under that section, otherwise than in accordance with an order of the court, an offence is committed by—

(a) the LLP, and

(b) every member of the LLP who is in default.

(2) A person guilty of an offence under this section is liable on summary conviction to a fine not exceeding level 3 on the standard scale and, for continued contravention, a daily default fine not exceeding one-tenth of level 3 on the standard scale.

(3) In the case of any such refusal or default the court may by order compel an immediate inspection or, as the case may be, direct that the copy required be sent to the person requesting it.

747 Register of debenture holders: offences in connection with request for or disclosure of information

(1) It is an offence for a person knowingly or recklessly to make in a request under section 744 (register of debenture holders: right to inspect and require copy) a statement that is misleading, false or deceptive in a material particular.

(2) It is an offence for a person in possession of information obtained by exercise of either of the rights conferred by that section—

(a) to do anything that results in the information being disclosed to another person, or

(b) to fail to do anything with the result that the information is disclosed to another person,

knowing, or having reason to suspect, that person may use the information for a purpose that is not a proper purpose.

(3) A person guilty of an offence under this section is liable—

(a) on conviction on indictment, to imprisonment for a term not exceeding two years or a fine (or both);

(b) on summary conviction—

(i) in England and Wales or Scotland, to imprisonment for a term not exceeding twelve months or to a fine not exceeding the statutory maximum (or both);

(ii) in Northern Ireland, to imprisonment for a term not exceeding six months, or to a fine not exceeding the statutory maximum (or both).

748 Time limit for claims arising from entry in register

(1) Liability incurred by an LLP—

(a) from the making or deletion of an entry in the register of debenture holders, or

(b) from a failure to make or delete any such entry,

is not enforceable more than ten years after the date on which the entry was made or deleted or, as the case may be, the failure first occurred.

(2) This is without prejudice to any lesser period of limitation (and, in Scotland, to any rule that the obligation giving rise to the liability prescribes before the expiry of that period).".

Supplementary provisions

[10.343]
22

Sections 749 and 750 apply to LLPs, modified so that they read as follows—

"749 Right of debenture holder to copy of deed

(1) Any holder of debentures of an LLP is entitled, on request and on payment of the fee prescribed by regulation 4 of the Companies (Fees for Inspection and Copying of Company Records) (No 2) Regulations 2007 (SI 2007/3535), to be provided with a copy of any trust deed for securing the debentures.

(2) If default is made in complying with this section, an offence is committed by every member of the LLP who is in default.

(3) A person guilty of an offence under this section is liable on summary conviction to a fine not exceeding level 3 on the standard scale and, for continued contravention, a daily default fine not exceeding one-tenth of level 3 on the standard scale.

(4) In the case of any such default the court may direct that the copy required be sent to the person requiring it.

750 Liability of trustees of debentures

(1) Any provision contained in—

(a) a trust deed for securing an issue of debentures, or

(b) any contract with the holders of debentures secured by a trust deed,

is void in so far as it would have the effect of exempting a trustee of the deed from, or indemnifying him against, liability for breach of trust where he fails to show the degree of care and diligence required of him as trustee, having regard to the provisions of the trust deed conferring on him any powers, authorities or discretions.

(2) Subsection (1) does not invalidate—

(a) a release otherwise validly given in respect of anything done or omitted to be done by a trustee before the giving of the release;

(b) any provision enabling such a release to be given—

(i) on being agreed to by a majority of not less than 75% in value of the debenture holders present and voting in person or, where proxies are permitted, by proxy at a meeting summoned for the purpose, and

(ii) either with respect to specific acts or omissions or on the trustee dying or ceasing to act.".

[10.344]

23

Sections 752 to 754 apply to LLPs, modified so that they read as follows—

"752 Power to re-issue redeemed debentures

(1) Where an LLP has redeemed debentures previously issued, then unless—

(a) provision to the contrary (express or implied) is contained in any contract made by the LLP, or

(b) the LLP has, by making a determination to that effect or by some other act, manifested its intention that the debentures shall be cancelled,

the LLP may re-issue the debentures, either by re-issuing the same debentures or by issuing new debentures in their place.

This subsection is deemed always to have had effect.

(2) On a re-issue of redeemed debentures the person entitled to the debentures has (and is deemed always to have had) the same priorities as if the debentures had never been redeemed.

(3) The re-issue of a debenture or the issue of another debenture in its place under this section is treated as the issue of a new debenture for the purposes of stamp duty.

It is not so treated for the purposes of any provision limiting the amount or number of debentures to be issued.

(4) A person lending money on the security of a debenture re-issued under this section which appears to be duly stamped may give the debenture in evidence in any proceedings for enforcing his security without payment of the stamp duty or any penalty in respect of it, unless he had notice (or, but for his negligence, might have discovered) that the debenture was not duly stamped.

In that case the LLP is liable to pay the proper stamp duty and penalty.

753 Deposit of debentures to secure advances

Where an LLP has deposited any of its debentures to secure advances from time to time on current account or otherwise, the debentures are not treated as redeemed by reason only of the LLP's account having ceased to be in debit while the debentures remained so deposited.

754 Priorities where debentures secured by floating charge

(1) This section applies where debentures of an LLP registered in England and Wales or Northern Ireland are secured by a charge that, as created, was a floating charge.

(2) If possession is taken, by or on behalf of the holders of the debentures, of any property comprised in or subject to the charge, and the LLP is not at that time in the course of being wound up, the LLP's preferential debts shall be paid out of assets coming to the hands of the persons taking possession in priority to any claims for principal or interest in respect of the debentures.

(3) "Preferential debts" means the categories of debts listed in Schedule 6 to the Insolvency Act 1986 (c 45) or Schedule 4 to the Insolvency (Northern Ireland) Order 1989 (SI 1989/2405 (NI 19)).

For the purposes of those Schedules "the relevant date" is the date of possession being taken as mentioned in subsection (2).

(4) Payments under this section shall be recouped, as far as may be, out of the assets of the LLP available for payment of general creditors.".

PART 7 CERTIFICATION AND TRANSFER OF DEBENTURES

[10.345]
24 Issue of certificates etc on allotment
Section 769 applies to LLPs, modified so that it reads as follows—

"769 Duty of LLP as to issue of certificates etc on allotment
(1) An LLP must, within two months after the allotment of any of its debentures or debenture stock, complete and have ready for delivery—
(a) the debentures allotted, or
(b) the certificates of the debenture stock allotted.
(2) Subsection (1) does not apply—
(a) if the conditions of issue of the debentures or debenture stock provide otherwise, or
(b) in the case of allotment to a financial institution (see section 778).
(3) If default is made in complying with subsection (1) an offence is committed by every member of the LLP who is in default.
(4) A person guilty of an offence under subsection (3) is liable on summary conviction to a fine not exceeding level 3 on the standard scale and, for continued contravention, a daily default fine not exceeding one-tenth of level 3 on the standard scale.".

[10.346]
25 Transfer of debentures
Sections 770 and 771 apply to LLPs, modified so that they read as follows—

"770 Registration of transfer
(1) An LLP may not register a transfer of debentures of the LLP unless—
(a) a proper instrument of transfer has been delivered to it, or
(b) the transfer is an exempt transfer within the Stock Transfer Act 1982 (c 41).
(2) Subsection (1) does not affect any power of the LLP to register as debenture holder a person to whom the right to any debentures of the LLP has been transmitted by operation of law.

771 Procedure on transfer being lodged
(1) When a transfer of debentures of an LLP has been lodged with the LLP, the LLP must either—
(a) register the transfer, or
(b) give the transferee notice of refusal to register the transfer, together with its reasons for the refusal,
as soon as practicable and in any event within two months after the date on which the transfer is lodged with it.
(2) If the LLP refuses to register the transfer, it must provide the transferee with such further information about the reasons for the refusal as the transferee may reasonably request.
This does not include copies of minutes of meetings of members.
(3) If an LLP fails to comply with this section, an offence is committed by—
(a) the LLP, and
(b) every member of the LLP who is in default.
(4) A person guilty of an offence under this section is liable on summary conviction to a fine not exceeding level 3 on the standard scale and, for continued contravention, a daily default fine not exceeding one-tenth of level 3 on the standard scale.
(5) This section does not apply in relation to the transmission of debentures by operation of law.".

[10.347]
26 Other matters
Sections 774 and 775 apply to LLPs, modified so that they read as follows—

"774 Evidence of grant of probate etc
The production to an LLP of any document that is by law sufficient evidence of the grant of—
(a) probate of the will of a deceased person,
(b) letters of administration of the estate of a deceased person, or
(c) confirmation as executor of a deceased person,
shall be accepted by the LLP as sufficient evidence of the grant.

775 Certification of instrument of transfer
(1) The certification by an LLP of an instrument of transfer of any debentures of the LLP is to be taken as a representation by the LLP to any person acting on the faith of the certification that there have been produced to the LLP such documents as on their face show a prima facie title to the debentures in the transferor named in the instrument.
(2) The certification is not to be taken as a representation that the transferor has any title to the debentures.
(3) Where a person acts on the faith of a false certification by an LLP made negligently, the LLP is under the same liability to him as if the certification had been made fraudulently.
(4) For the purposes of this section—
(a) an instrument of transfer is certificated if it bears the words "certificate lodged" (or words to the like effect);
(b) the certification of an instrument of transfer is made by an LLP if—
(i) the person issuing the instrument is a person authorised to issue certificated instruments of transfer on the LLP's behalf, and

(ii) the certification is signed by a person authorised to certificate transfers on the LLP's behalf or by a member or employee of the LLP or by an officer or employee of a body corporate so authorised;

(c) a certification is treated as signed by a person if—

(i) it purports to be authenticated by his signature or initials (whether handwritten or not), and

(ii) it is not shown that the signature or initials was or were placed there neither by himself nor by a person authorised to use the signature or initials for the purpose of certificating transfers on the LLP's behalf.".

[10.348]

27 Issue of certificates etc on transfer

Section 776 applies to LLPs, modified so that it reads as follows—

"776 Duty of LLP as to issue of certificates etc on transfer

(1) An LLP must, within two months after the date on which a transfer of any of its debentures or debenture stock is lodged with the LLP, complete and have ready for delivery—

(a) the debentures transferred, or

(b) the certificates of the debenture stock transferred.

(2) For this purpose a "transfer" means—

(a) a transfer duly stamped and otherwise valid, or

(b) an exempt transfer within the Stock Transfer Act 1982 (c 41),

but does not include a transfer that the LLP is for any reason entitled to refuse to register and does not register.

(3) Subsection (1) does not apply—

(a) if the conditions of issue of the debentures or debenture stock provide otherwise, or

(b) in the case of a transfer to a financial institution (see section 778).

(4) If default is made in complying with subsection (1) an offence is committed by every member of the LLP who is in default.

(5) A person guilty of an offence under this section is liable on summary conviction to a fine not exceeding level 3 on the standard scale and, for continued contravention, a daily default fine not exceeding one-tenth of level 3 on the standard scale.".

[10.349]

28 Issue of certificates etc on allotment or transfer to financial institution

Section 778 applies to LLPs, modified so that it reads as follows—

"778 Issue of certificates etc: allotment or transfer to financial institution

(1) An LLP—

(a) of which debentures are allotted to a financial institution,

(b) of which debenture stock is allotted to a financial institution, or

(c) with which a transfer for transferring debentures or debenture stock to a financial institution is lodged,

is not required in consequence of that allotment or transfer to comply with section 769(1) or 776(1) (duty of LLP as to issue of certificates etc).

(2) A "financial institution" means—

(a) a recognised clearing house [or a recognised CSD] acting in relation to a recognised investment exchange, or

(b) a nominee of—

(i) a recognised clearing house [or a recognised CSD] acting in that way, or

(ii) a recognised investment exchange,

designated for the purposes of this section in the rules of the recognised investment exchange in question.

(3) Expressions used in subsection (2) have the same meaning as in Part 18 of the Financial Services and Markets Act 2000 (c 8).".

NOTES

In s 778 as set out above, the words in square brackets in sub-s (2) were inserted by the Central Securities Depositories Regulations 2017, SI 2017/1064, reg 10, Schedule, para 33, as from 28 November 2017.

[10.350]

29 Supplementary provisions

Section 782 is applied to LLPs, modified so that it reads as follows—

"782 Issue of certificates etc: court order to make good default

(1) If an LLP on which a notice has been served requiring it to make good any default in complying with—

(a) section 769(1) (duty of LLP as to issue of certificates etc on allotment), or

(b) section 776(1) (duty of LLP as to issue of certificates etc on transfer),

fails to make good the default within ten days after service of the notice, the person entitled to have the certificates or the debentures delivered to him may apply to the court.

(2) The court may on such an application make an order directing the LLP and any member of it to make good the default within such time as may be specified in the order.

(3) The order may provide that all costs (in Scotland, expenses) of and incidental to the application are to be borne by the LLP or by a member of it responsible for the default.".

[PART 8 ANNUAL CONFIRMATION BY LLP OF ACCURACY OF INFORMATION ON REGISTER

[10.351]
30

Sections 853A and 853B apply to LLPs, modified so that they read as follows—

"853A Duty to deliver confirmation statements

(1) Every LLP must, before the end of the period of 14 days after the end of each review period, deliver to the registrar—

(a) such information as is necessary to ensure that the LLP is able to make the statement referred to in paragraph (b), and

(b) a statement ("a confirmation statement") confirming that all information required to be delivered by the LLP to the registrar in relation to the confirmation period concerned under [any duty to notify a relevant event (see section 853B)] either—

(i) has been delivered, or

(ii) is being delivered at the same time as the confirmation statement.

(2) . . .

(3) In this Part "confirmation period"—

(a) in relation to an LLP's first confirmation statement, means the period beginning with the day of the LLP's incorporation and ending with the date specified in the statement ("confirmation date");

(b) in relation to any other confirmation statement of the LLP, means the period beginning with the day after the confirmation date of the last such statement and ending with the confirmation date of the confirmation statement concerned.

(4) The confirmation date of a confirmation statement must be no later than the last day of the review period concerned.

(5) For the purposes of this Part, each of the following is a review period—

(a) the period of 12 months beginning with the day of the LLP's incorporation,

(b) each period of 12 months beginning with the day after the end of the previous review period.

(6) But where an LLP delivers a confirmation statement with a confirmation date which is earlier than the last day of the review period concerned, the next review period is the period of 12 months beginning with the day after the confirmation date.

(7) For the purpose of making a confirmation statement, an LLP is entitled to assume that any information has been properly delivered to the registrar if it has been delivered within the period of 5 days ending with the date on which the statement is delivered.

(8) But subsection (7) does not apply in a case where the LLP has received notice from the registrar that such information has not been properly delivered.

853B Duty to notify a relevant event

The following duties are duties to notify a relevant event—

(a) the duty to give notice of a change in the address of the LLP's registered office under section 87;

(b) in the case of an LLP in respect of which an election is in force under section 167A (election to keep the register of members or the register of members' residential addresses (or both) on the central register), the duty to deliver anything as mentioned in section 167D;

[(ba) in the case of an LLP to which Part 21A (information about people with significant control) applies, and in respect of which an election is not in force under section 790X (election to keep information in PSC register on central register), the duty to give notice of a change as mentioned in section 790VA (notification to the registrar of changes to the LLP's PSC register);]

(c) in the case of an LLP in respect of which an election is in force under section 790X (election to keep information in PSC register on central register), the duty to deliver anything as mentioned in section 790ZA;

(d) the duty to give notice of a change under section 9 (registration of membership changes) of the Limited Liability Partnerships Act 2000 (in the absence of an election under section 167A); and

(e) in the case of an LLP which, in accordance with regulations under section 1136 (where certain LLP records to be kept available for inspection), keeps any LLP records at a place other than its registered office, any duty under the regulations to give notice of a change of address of that place.".]

NOTES

Part 8 (regs 30, 31, 31ZA) was substituted for the original Part 8 (regs 30, 31) by the Companies and Limited Liability Partnerships (Filing Requirements) Regulations 2016, SI 2016/599, reg 3, Sch 1, paras 1, 5, as from 30 June 2016. For transitional provisions see reg 3 of the 2016 Regulations at **[4.642]**.

In s 853A as set out above, the words in square brackets in sub-s (1) were substituted, and sub-s (2) was revoked, by the Information about People with Significant Control (Amendment) Regulations 2017, SI 2017/693, regs 20, 21, (1), (2), as from 26 June 2017 (for transitional arrangements, see Schedule, Pt 2 to the 2017 Regulations at **[10.1196]**).

In s 853B as set out above, para (ba) was inserted by SI 2017/693, regs 20, 21, (1), (3), as from 26 June 2017 (for transitional arrangements, see Schedule, Pt 2 to the 2017 Regulations at **[10.1196]**).

31 (*Revoked by the Information about People with Significant Control (Amendment) Regulations 2017, SI 2017/693, regs 20, 22, as from 26 June 2017 (for transitional arrangements, see Schedule, Pt 2 to the 2017 Regulations at* **[10.1196]**).)

[10.352]
[31ZA

Section 853L applies to LLPs, modified so that it reads as follows—

"853L Failure to deliver confirmation statement

(1) If an LLP fails to deliver a confirmation statement before the end of the period of 14 days after the end of a review period an offence is committed by—

(a) the LLP, and

(b) every designated member of the LLP.

(2) A person guilty of an offence under subsection (1) is liable on summary conviction—

(a) in England and Wales to a fine, and, for continued contravention, a daily default fine not exceeding the greater of £500 and one-tenth of level 4 on the standard scale;

(b) in Scotland or Northern Ireland, to a fine not exceeding level 5 on the standard scale and, for continued contravention, a daily default fine not exceeding one-tenth of level 5 on the standard scale.

(3) The contravention continues until such time as a confirmation statement specifying a confirmation date no later than the last day of the review period concerned is delivered by the LLP to the registrar.

(4) It is a defence for a designated member charged with an offence under subsection (1)(b) to prove that the person took all reasonable steps to avoid the commission or continuation of the offence.

(5) In the case of continued contravention, an offence is also committed by a designated member who did not commit an offence under subsection (1) in relation to the initial contravention but who is in default in relation to the continued contravention.

(6) A person guilty of an offence under subsection (5) is liable on summary conviction—

(a) in England and Wales to a fine not exceeding the greater of £500 and one-tenth of level 4 on the standard scale for each day on which the contravention continues and the person is in default;

(b) in Scotland or Northern Ireland, to a fine not exceeding level 5 on the standard scale for each day on which the contravention continues and the person is in default."]

NOTES

Substituted as noted to reg 30 at **[10.351]**.

Note that the number of this regulation was originally 31A, but was corrected by a correction slip published on 29 June 2016.

[PART 8A AN LLP'S REGISTER OF PEOPLE WITH SIGNIFICANT CONTROL

[10.353]

31A Overview

Section 790A applies to LLPs, modified so that it reads as follows—

"790A Overview

This Part is arranged as follows—

(a) Section 790C explains some key terms, including what it means to have "significant control" over an LLP;

(b) Sections 790D to 790K impose duties on LLPs to gather information, and on others to supply information, to enable LLPs to keep the register required by the remainder of this Part;

(c) Section 790M to 790V require LLPs to keep a register, referred to as a register of people with significant control over the LLP, and to make the register available to the public;

(d) Sections 790W to 790ZD give LLPs the option of using an alternative method of record-keeping; and

(e) Sections 790ZF and 790ZG make provision for excluding certain material from the information available to the public."]

NOTES

Part 8A was inserted by the Limited Liability Partnerships (Register of People with Significant Control) Regulations 2016, SI 2016/340, reg 3, Sch 1.

[10.354]

[31B Key terms

(1) Section 790C applies to LLPs with the following modifications.

(2) Read references to a company as references to an LLP.

(3) Subsection (7) is modified so that it reads as follows—

"(7) A legal entity is "subject to its own disclosure requirements" if—

(a) this Part applies to it (whether by virtue of the Limited Liability Partnerships (Application of Companies Act 2006) Regulations 2009 or otherwise),

[(aa) it is an eligible Scottish partnership within the meaning of regulation 3(2) of the Scottish Partnerships (Register of People with Significant Control) Regulations 2017,]

(b) [it has voting shares admitted to trading on a [UK regulated market or an EU regulated market]],

(c) it is a company or other legal entity which has voting shares admitted to trading—

(i) . . .

(ii) on a market listed in Schedule 1 to the PSC Regulations.".

(4) Omit subsection (11).

(5) In subsection (12), omit "and to any modifications prescribed by regulations under this subsection".

(6) After subsection (12), insert—

"(12A) Sections 790M(2) to [(6A) and (10)] of the Act are to be read and have effect as if a person within subsection (12) were an individual.

(12B) "PSC Regulations" means the Register of People with Significant Control Regulations 2016.

(12C) "Voting shares" means shares . . . carrying voting rights.

(12D) For the purposes of subsection (12C), "voting rights" means rights to vote at general meetings of the company or legal entity in question, including rights that arise only in certain circumstances, and in relation to a legal entity that does not have general meetings at which matters are decided by the exercise of voting rights, a reference to voting rights is to be read as a reference to rights in relation to the entity that are equivalent to those of a person entitled to exercise voting rights in a company.

[(12E) "EU regulated market", "Regulated market" and "UK regulated market" have the same meanings as in section 1173 of the Companies Act 2006.]

(7) Omit subsections (13) and (14).]

NOTES

Inserted as noted to reg 31A at **[10.353]**.

In s 790C(7) as set out above, para (aa) was inserted by the Scottish Partnerships (Register of People with Significant Control) Regulations 2017, SI 2017/694, reg 79, as from 26 June 2017, subject to transitional provisions in reg 80 of the 2017 Regulations at **[10.1276]**.

The words in square brackets in s 790C(7)(b) as set out above were substituted, and s 790C(12E) as set out above was substituted, by the Companies, Limited Liability Partnerships and Partnerships (Amendment etc) (EU Exit) Regulations 2019, SI 2019/348, reg 8, Sch 3, paras 22, 24, as from IP completion day (as defined in the European Union (Withdrawal Agreement) Act 2020, s 39).

All other amendments to this regulation were made by the Information about People with Significant Control (Amendment) Regulations 2017, SI 2017/693, regs 23, 24, as from 26 June 2017 (for transitional arrangements, see Schedule, Pt 2 to the 2017 Regulations at **[10.1196]**).

[10.355]

[31C Information gathering

(1) Sections 790D to 790J apply to LLPs.

(2) As those provisions apply to LLPs—

(a) read references to a company as references to an LLP;

(b) omit "to which this Part applies" where it occurs;

(c) read references to an officer as references to a designated member;

(d) read section 790D as if subsections (9) and (10) were omitted; and

(e) read section 790E(7) as if for "Subsections (8) to (10) of section 790D applies" there were substituted "Section 790D(8) applies".]

NOTES

Inserted as noted to reg 31A at **[10.353]**.

[10.356]

[31D Required particulars

Section 790K applies to LLPs, modified so that it reads as follows—

"790K Required particulars

(1) The "required particulars" of an individual who is a registrable person are—

(a) name,

(b) a service address,

(c) the country or state (or part of the United Kingdom) in which the individual is usually resident,

(d) nationality,

(e) date of birth,

(f) usual residential address,

(g) the date on which the individual became a registrable person in relation to the LLP in question,

(h) the nature of his or her control over that LLP (see Schedule 1A of this Act and regulation 7 of, and Schedule 2 to, the PSC Regulations), and

(i) if, in relation to that LLP, restrictions on using or disclosing any of the individual's PSC particulars (within the meaning of section 790ZG(2)) are in force under Part 7 of the PSC Regulations, that fact.

(2) In the case of a person in relation to which this Part has effect by virtue of section 790C(12) as if the person were an individual, the "required particulars" are—

(a) name,

(b) principal office,

(c) the legal form of the person and the law by which it is governed,

(d) the date on which it became a registrable person in relation to the LLP in question, and

(e) the nature of its control over the LLP (see Schedule 1A and regulation 7 of, and Schedule 2 to, the PSC Regulations).

(3) The "required particulars" of a registrable relevant legal entity are—

(a) corporate or firm name,

(b) registered or principal office,

(c) the legal form of the entity and the law by which it is governed,

(d) if applicable, the register of companies in which it is entered (including details of the state) and its registration number in that register,

(e) the date on which it became a registrable relevant legal entity in relation to the LLP in question, and

(f) the nature of its control over that LLP (see Schedule 1A and regulation 7 of, and Schedule 2 to, the PSC Regulations).

(4) Section 163(2) (particulars of members to be registered: individuals) applies for the purposes of subsection (1)."]

NOTES

Inserted as noted to reg 31A at **[10.353]**.

[10.357]

[31E Register of people with significant control

(1) Section 790M (1) to [(6A)] applies to LLPs, modified so that it reads as follows—

"790M Duty to keep register

(1) An LLP must keep a register of people with significant control over the LLP.

(2) The required particulars of any individual with significant control over the LLP who is "registrable" in relation to the LLP must be entered in the register [before the end of the period of 14 days beginning with the day after all the required particulars of that individual are first confirmed].

(3) The LLP must not enter any of the individual's particulars in the register until they have all been confirmed.

(4) Particulars of any individual with significant control over the LLP who is "non-registrable" in relation to the LLP must not be entered in the register.

[(5) The required particulars of any entity that is a registrable relevant legal entity in relation to the LLP must be entered in the register before the end of the period of 14 days beginning with the day after the LLP first has all the required particulars of that entity].

(6) If the LLP becomes aware of a relevant change (within the meaning of section 790E) with respect to a registrable person . . . whose particulars are stated in the register[, the LLP must enter in the register—

(a) the changes to the required particulars resulting from the relevant change, and

(b) the date on which the relevant change occurred,

before the end of the period of 14 days beginning with the day after all of those changes and that date are first confirmed.]

[(6A) If the LLP becomes aware of a relevant change (within the meaning of section 790E) with respect to a registrable relevant legal entity whose particulars are stated in the register, the LLP must enter in the register—

(a) the changes to the required particulars resulting from the relevant change, and

(b) the date on which the relevant change occurred,

before the end of the period of 14 days beginning with the day after the LLP first has details of all of those changes and that date.]

[(1A) Section 790M(7A) applies to LLPs, modified so that it reads as follows—

"(7A) If an LLP is required by the PSC Regulations to note an additional matter in its PSC register, the LLP must note the additional matter before the end of the period of 14 days beginning with the day after the requirement arises."]

(2) Section 790M(9) to (14) applies to LLPs, modified so that it reads as follows—

"(9) A person's required particulars, [a change to such particulars and the date of any relevant change with respect to a person], are considered for the purposes of this section to have been "confirmed" if—

(a) the person supplied or confirmed them to the LLP (whether voluntarily, pursuant to a duty imposed by this Part or otherwise),

(b) another person did so but with that person's knowledge, or

(c) they were included in a statement of initial significant control delivered to the registrar under section 12A by the persons who subscribed their names to the incorporation document in relation to the LLP.

(10) In the case of someone who was a registrable person or a registrable relevant legal entity in relation to the LLP on its incorporation—

(a) the date to be entered in the register as the date on which the individual became a registrable person, or the entity became a registrable relevant legal entity, is to be the date of incorporation, and

(b) in the case of a registrable person, that particular is deemed to have been "confirmed".

(11) For the purposes of this section—

(a) if a person's usual residential address is the same as his or her service address, the entry for him or her in the register may state that fact instead of repeating the address (but this does not apply in a case where the service address is stated to be "The LLP's registered office");

(b) see section 790J (exemptions) for cases where a person does not count as a registrable person or a registrable relevant legal entity.

(12) If an LLP makes default in complying with this section, an offence is committed by—

(a) the LLP, and

(b) every designated member of the LLP who is in default.

(13) A person guilty of an offence under this section is liable on summary conviction to a fine not exceeding level 3 on the standard scale and, for continued contravention, a daily default fine not exceeding one-tenth of level 3 on the standard scale.

(14) An LLP is not by virtue of anything done for the purposes of this section affected with notice of, or put upon inquiry as to, the rights of any person in relation to any shares or rights in or with respect to the LLP."]

NOTES

Inserted as noted to reg 31A at **[10.353]**.

All amendments to this regulation were made by the Information about People with Significant Control (Amendment) Regulations 2017, SI 2017/693, regs 23, 25, as from 26 June 2017 (for transitional arrangements, see Schedule, Pt 2 to the 2017 Regulations at **[10.1196]**).

[10.358]

[31F Inspection and copies of the register

Sections 790N and 790O apply to LLPs, modified so that they read as follows—

"790N Register to be kept available for inspection

(1) An LLP's PSC register must be kept available for inspection—

(a) at its registered office, or

(b) at a place specified in Part 2 of the Companies (Company Records) Regulations 2008 (SI 2008/3006).

(2) An LLP must give notice to the registrar of the place where its PSC register is kept available for inspection and of any change in that place.

(3) No such notice is required if the register has, at all times since it came into existence, been kept available for inspection at the LLP's registered office.

(4) If an LLP makes default for 14 days in complying with subsection (2), an offence is committed by—

(a) the LLP, and

(b) every designated member of the LLP who is in default.

(5) A person guilty of an offence under this section is liable on summary conviction to a fine not exceeding level 3 on the standard scale and, for continued contravention, a daily default fine not exceeding one-tenth of level 3 on the standard scale.

790O Rights to inspect and require copies

(1) An LLP's PSC register must be open to the inspection of any person without charge.

(2) Any person may require a copy of an LLP's PSC register, or any part of it, on payment of the fee prescribed by regulation 6 of the PSC Regulations.

(3) A person seeking to exercise either of the rights conferred by this section must make a request to the LLP to that effect.

(4) The request must contain the following information—

(a) in the case of an individual, his or her name and address,

(b) in the case of an organisation, the name and address of an individual responsible for making the request on behalf of the organisation, and

(c) the purpose for which the information is to be used."]

NOTES

Inserted as noted to reg 31A at **[10.353]**.

[10.359]

[31G Supplementary provision regarding requests to inspect and copies of PSC register

(1) Sections 790P to 790S apply to LLPs.

(2) As those provisions apply to LLPs—

(a) read references to a company as references to an LLP;

(b) read references to an officer as references to a designated member.]

NOTES

Inserted as noted to reg 31A at **[10.353]**.

[10.360]

[31H Protected information

Section 790T applies to LLPs, modified so that it reads as follows—

"790T Protected information

Section 790N and subsections (1) and (2) of section 790O are subject to—

(a) section 790ZF (protection of information as to usual residential address), and

(b) Part 7 of the PSC Regulations."]

NOTES

Inserted as noted to reg 31A at **[10.353]**.

[10.361]

[31I Removal of entries from the register

Section 790U applies to LLPs, with the references to a company read as references to an LLP.]

NOTES

Inserted as noted to reg 31A at **[10.353]**.

[10.362]

[31J Power of court to rectify an LLP's PSC register

Section 790V applies to LLPs, modified so that it reads as follows—

"790V Power of court to rectify register

(1) If—

(a) the name of any person is, without sufficient cause, entered in or omitted from an LLP's PSC register as a registrable person or registrable relevant legal entity, or

(b) default is made or unnecessary delay takes place in entering on the PSC register the fact that a person has ceased to be a registrable person or registrable relevant legal entity,

the person aggrieved or any other interested party may apply to the court for rectification of the register.

(2) The court may either refuse the application or may order rectification of the register and payment by the LLP of any damages sustained by any party aggrieved.

(3) On such an application, the court may—

(a) decide any question as to whether the name of any person who is a party to the application should or should not be entered in or omitted from the register, and

(b) more generally, decide any question necessary or expedient to be decided for rectification of the register.

(4) In the case of an LLP required by this Act to send information stated in its PSC register to the registrar, the court, when making an order for rectification of the register, must by its order direct notice of the rectification to be given to the registrar.

(5) The reference in this section to "any other interested party" is to—

(a) any member of the LLP, and

(b) any other person who is a registrable person or a registrable relevant legal entity in relation to the LLP."]

NOTES

Inserted as noted to reg 31A at **[10.353]**.

[10.363]

[31JA Notification of changes to the registrar

(1) Section 790VA applies to LLPs, modified so that it reads as follows—

"790VA Notification of changes to the registrar

(1) Subsection (2) applies where an LLP—

(a) enters required particulars in its PSC register,

(b) alters required particulars in its PSC register, or

(c) notes in its PSC register an additional matter that is required to be noted by the PSC Regulations.

(2) The LLP must give notice to the registrar of the change made to its PSC register, and the date on which the change was made, before the end of the period of 14 days beginning with the day after it makes the change.

(3) If default is made in complying with this section, an offence is committed by—

(a) the LLP, and

(b) every designated member of the LLP who is in default.

(4) A person guilty of an offence under this section is liable on summary conviction to a fine not exceeding level 3 on the standard scale and, for continued contravention, a daily default fine not exceeding one-tenth of level 3 on the standard scale."]

NOTES

Inserted by the Information about People with Significant Control (Amendment) Regulations 2017, SI 2017/693, regs 23, 26, as from 26 June 2017 (for transitional arrangements, see Schedule, Pt 2 to the 2017 Regulations at **[10.1196]**).

[10.364]

[31K Alternative method of record keeping

(1) Sections 790W to 790ZD apply to LLPs modified so that those sections read as follows—

"790W Introductory

(1) This Chapter sets out rules allowing LLPs to keep information on the register kept by the registrar instead of entering it in their PSC register.

(2) The register kept by the registrar (see section 1080) is referred to in this Chapter as "the central register".

(3) Chapter 3 must be read with this Chapter.

(4) Nothing in this Chapter affects the duties imposed by Chapter 2.

(5) Where an election under section 790X is in force in respect of an LLP, references in Chapter 2 to the LLP's PSC register are to be read as references to the central register.

790X Right to make an election

(1) An election may be made under this section—

(a) by the subscribers wishing to form an LLP under the Limited Liability Partnerships Act 2000, or

(b) by the LLP itself once it is formed and registered.

(2) The election is of no effect unless—

(a) notice of the intention to make the election was given to each eligible person at least 14 days before the day on which the election was made, and

(b) no objection was received by the subscribers or, as the case may be, the LLP from any eligible person within that notice period.

(3) A person is an "eligible person" if—

(a) in a case of an election by the subscribers wishing to form an LLP, the person's particulars would, but for the election, be required to be entered in the LLP's PSC register on its incorporation, and

(b) in the case of an election by the LLP itself—

(i) the person is a registrable person or a registrable relevant legal entity in relation to the LLP, and

(ii) the person's particulars are stated in the LLP's PSC register.

(4) An election under this section is made by giving notice of election to the registrar.

(5) If the notice is given by the subscribers wishing to form an LLP—

(a) it must be given when the documents required to be delivered under section 2 of the Limited Liability Partnerships Act 2000 are delivered to the registrar, and

(b) it must be accompanied by a statement confirming that no objection was received as mentioned in subsection (2).

(6) If the notice is given by the LLP, it must be accompanied by—

(a) a statement confirming that no objection was received as mentioned in subsection (2), and

(b) a statement containing all the information that is required to be contained in the LLP's PSC register as at the date of the notice in respect of matters that are current as at that date.

(7) The LLP must where necessary update the statement sent under subsection (6)(b) to ensure that the final version delivered to the registrar contains all the information that is required to be contained in the LLP's PSC register as at the time immediately before the election takes effect (see section 790Y) in respect of matters that are current as at that time.

(8) The obligation in subsection (7) to update the statement includes an obligation to rectify it (where necessary) in consequence of the LLP's PSC register being rectified (whether before or after the election takes effect).

(9) If default is made in complying with subsection (7), an offence is committed by—

(a) the LLP, and

(b) every designated member of the LLP who is in default.

(10) A person guilty of an offence under this section is liable on summary conviction to a fine not exceeding level 3 on the standard scale and, for continued contravention, a daily default fine not exceeding one-tenth of level 3 on the standard scale.

(11) A reference in this Chapter to matters that are current as at a given date or time is a reference to—

(a) persons who are a registrable person or registrable relevant legal entity in relation to the LLP as at that date or time and whose particulars are required to be contained in the LLP's PSC register as at that date or time, and

(b) any other matters that are current as at that date or time.

790Y Effective date of election

(1) An election made under section 790X takes effect when the notice of election is registered by the registrar.

(2) The election remains in force until a notice of withdrawal sent by the LLP under section 790ZD is registered by the registrar.

790Z Effect of election on obligations under Chapter 3

(1) The effect of an election under section 790X on an LLP's obligations under Chapter 3 is as follows.

(2) The LLP's obligation to maintain a PSC register does not apply with respect to the period when the election is in force.

(3) This means that, during that period—

(a) the LLP must continue to keep a PSC register in accordance with Chapter 3 (a "historic" register) containing all the information that was required to be stated in that register as at the time immediately before the election took effect, but

(b) the LLP does not have to update that register to reflect any changes that occur after that time.

(4) The provisions of Chapter 3 (including the rights to inspect or require copies of the PSC register) continue to apply to the historic register during the period when the election is in force.

(5) The LLP must place a note in its historic register—

(a) stating that an election under section 790X is in force,

(b) recording when that election took effect, and

(c) indicating that up-to-date information about people with significant control over the LLP is available for public inspection on the central register.

(6) Subsections (12) and (13) of section 790M apply if an LLP makes default in complying with subsection (5) as they apply if an LLP makes default in complying with that section.

(7) The obligations under this section with respect to a historic register do not apply in a case where the election was made by subscribers wishing to form an LLP.

790ZA Duty to notify registrar of changes

(1) The duty under subsection (2) applies during the period when an election under section 790X is in force.

(2) The LLP must deliver to the registrar any information that the LLP would during that period have been obliged under Chapter 3 to enter in its PSC register, had the election not been in force.

(3) The information must be delivered as soon as reasonably practicable after the LLP becomes aware of it and, in any event, no later than the time by which the LLP would have been required to enter the information in its PSC register.

(4) If default is made in complying with this section, an offence is committed by—

(a) the LLP, and

(b) every designated member of the LLP who is in default.

(5) A person guilty of an offence under this section is liable on summary conviction to a fine not exceeding level 3 on the standard scale and, for continued contravention, a daily default fine not exceeding one-tenth of level 3 on the standard scale.

790ZB Information as to state of central register

(1) When a person inspects or requests a copy of material on the central register relating to an LLP in respect of which an election under section 790X is in force, the person may ask the LLP to confirm that all information that the LLP is required to deliver to the registrar under this Chapter has been delivered.

(2) If an LLP fails to respond to a request under subsection (1), an offence is committed by—

(a) the LLP, and

(b) every designated member of the LLP who is in default.

(3) A person guilty of an offence under this section is liable on summary conviction to a fine not exceeding level 3 on the standard scale.

790ZC Power of court to order an LLP to remedy default or delay

(1) This section applies if—

(a) the name of a person is without sufficient cause included in, or omitted from, information that an LLP delivers to the registrar under this Chapter concerning persons who are a registrable person or a registrable relevant legal entity in relation to the LLP, or

(b) default is made or unnecessary delay takes place in informing the registrar under this Chapter that a person—

(i) has become a registrable person or a registrable relevant legal entity in relation to the LLP, or

(ii) has ceased to be a registrable person or a registrable relevant legal entity in relation to it.

(2) The person aggrieved, or any other interested party, may apply to the court for an order requiring the LLP to deliver to the registrar the information (or statements) necessary to rectify the position.

(3) The court may either refuse the application or may make the order and order the LLP to pay any damages sustained by any party aggrieved.

(4) On such an application the court may decide—

(a) any question as to whether the name of any person who is a party to the application should or should not be included in or omitted from information delivered to the registrar under this Chapter about persons who are a registrable person or a registrable relevant legal entity in relation to the LLP, and

(b) any question necessary or expedient to be decided for rectifying the position.

(5) Nothing in this section affects a person's rights under section 1095 or 1096 (rectification of register on application to registrar or under court order).

(6) The reference in this section to "any other interested party" is to—

(a) any member of the LLP, and

(b) any other person who is a registrable person or a registrable relevant legal entity in relation to the LLP.

790ZD Withdrawing the election

(1) An LLP may withdraw an election made by or in respect of it under section 790X.

(2) Withdrawal is achieved by giving notice of withdrawal to the registrar.

(3) The withdrawal takes effect when the notice is registered by the registrar.

(4) The effect of withdrawal is that the LLP's obligation to maintain a PSC register applies from then on with respect to the period going forward.

(5) This means that, when the withdrawal takes effect—

(a) the LLP must enter in its PSC register all the information that is required to be contained in that register in respect of matters that are current as at that time,

(b) the LLP must also retain in its register all the information that it was required under section 790Z(3)(a) to keep in a historic register while the election was in force, but

(c) the LLP is not required to enter in its register information relating to the period when the election was in force that is no longer current.

(6) The LLP must place a note in its PSC register—

(a) stating that the election under section 790X has been withdrawn,

(b) recording when that withdrawal took effect, and

(c) indicating that information about people with significant control over the LLP relating to the period when the election was in force that is no longer current is available for public inspection on the central register.

(7) Subsections (12) and (13) of section 790M apply if an LLP makes default in complying with subsection (6) as they apply if a LLP makes default in complying with that section.".]

NOTES

Inserted as noted to reg 31A at **[10.353]**.

[10.365]

[31L Protection from disclosure

(1) Sections 790ZF and 790ZG(2) apply to LLPs.

(2) As those sections apply to LLPs—

(a) read references to a company as references to an LLP;

(b) read references to a director as a reference to a member of an LLP; and

(c) subsection 790ZF(3) applies to LLPs modified so that it reads as follows—

"(3) Subsection (1) does not apply to information relating to a person if an application under Part 7 of the PSC Regulations has been granted with respect to that information and has not been revoked."]

NOTES

Inserted as noted to reg 31A at **[10.353]**.

[10.366]

[31M Schedule 1A

Paragraphs 1 to 24 of Schedule 1A apply to LLPs, modified so that they read as follows

"SCHEDULE 1A

REFERENCES TO PEOPLE WITH SIGNIFICANT CONTROL OVER AN LLP

Section 790C(3)

PART 1 THE SPECIFIED CONDITIONS

1 Introduction

This Part of this Schedule specifies the conditions at least one of which must be met by an individual ("X") in relation to an LLP ("LLP Y") in order for the individual to be a person with "significant control" over LLP Y.

2 Right to share in surplus assets on a winding up

(1) The first condition is that X holds, directly or indirectly, the right to share in more than 25% of any surplus assets of LLP Y on a winding up.

(2) For the purpose of sub-paragraph (1), to the extent that the holding of a right to share in any surplus assets of LLP Y on a winding up is not expressly provided for, each member of the LLP shall be treated as holding the right to an equal share in any surplus assets on a winding up.

3 Ownership of voting rights

The second condition is that X holds, directly or indirectly, more than 25% of the rights to vote on those matters which are to be decided upon by a vote of the members of LLP Y.

4 Ownership of right to appoint or remove the persons entitled to manage the LLP

(1) The third condition is that X holds, directly or indirectly, the right to appoint or remove the majority of the persons who are entitled to take part in the management of LLP Y.

(2) For the purposes of sub-paragraph (1), the right to appoint or remove a majority of the persons who are entitled to take part in the management of LLP Y includes the right to appoint or remove those persons who hold a majority of the voting rights at meetings of the management body of LLP Y.

5 Significant influence or control

The fourth condition is that X has the right to exercise, or actually exercises, significant influence or control over LLP Y.

6 Trusts, partnerships etc

The fifth condition is that—

(a) the trustees of a trust or the members of a firm that, under the law by which it is governed, is not a legal person meet any of the other specified conditions (in their capacity as such) in relation to LLP Y, or would do so if they were individuals, and

(b) X has the right to exercise, or actually exercises, significant influence or control over the activities of that trust or firm.

PART 2 HOLDING AN INTEREST IN AN LLP, ETC

7 Introduction

This Part of this Schedule specifies the circumstances in which, for the purposes of section 790C(4) or (8)—

(a) a person ("V") is to be regarded as holding an interest in an LLP ("LLP W");

(b) an interest held by V in LLP W is to be regarded as held through a legal entity.

8 Holding an interest

(1) V holds an interest in LLP W if—

(a) V holds, directly or indirectly, the right to share in any surplus assets of LLP W on a winding up;

(b) V holds, directly or indirectly, voting rights in LLP W;

(c) V holds, directly or indirectly, the right to appoint or remove any of the persons entitled to take part in the management of LLP W;

(d) V has the right to exercise, or actually exercises, significant influence or control over LLP W; or

(e) sub-paragraph (2) is satisfied.

(2) This sub-paragraph is satisfied where—

(a) the trustees of a trust or the members of a firm that, under the law by which it is governed, is not a legal person hold an interest in LLP W in a way mentioned in sub-paragraph (1)(a) to (d), and

(b) V has the right to exercise, or actually exercises, significant influence or control over the activities of that trust or firm.

9 Interests held through a legal entity

(1) This paragraph applies where V—

(a) holds an interest in LLP W by virtue of indirectly holding a right, and

(b) does so by virtue of having a majority stake (see paragraph 13) in—

(i) a legal entity ("L") which holds the right directly, or

(ii) a legal entity that is part of a chain of legal entities such as is described in paragraph 13(1)(b) that includes L.

(2) Where this paragraph applies, V holds the interest in LLP W—

(a) through L, and

(b) through each other legal entity in the chain mentioned in sub-paragraph (1)(b)(ii).

PART 3 SUPPLEMENTARY PROVISION

10 Introduction

This Part sets out rules for the interpretation of this Schedule subject to the fact that paragraph 21(1) does not apply to the interpretation of paragraph 2 of Part 1.

11 Joint interests

If two or more persons each hold a share or right jointly, each of them is treated for the purposes of this Schedule as holding that share or right.

12 Joint arrangements

(1) If shares or rights held by a person and shares or rights held by another person are the subject of a joint arrangement between those persons, each of them is treated for the purposes of this Schedule as holding the combined shares or rights of both of them.

(2) A "joint arrangement" is an arrangement between the holders of shares (or rights) that they will exercise all or substantially all the rights conferred by their respective shares (or rights) jointly in a way that is pre-determined by the arrangement.

(3) "Arrangement" has the meaning given by paragraph 20.

13 Shares or rights held "indirectly"

(1) A person holds a right "indirectly" if the person has a majority stake in a legal entity and that entity—

- (a) holds that right, or
- (b) is part of a chain of legal entities—
  - (i) each of which (other than the last) has a majority stake in the entity immediately below it in the chain, and
  - (ii) the last of which holds that right.

(2) For these purposes, A has a "majority stake" in B if—

- (a) A holds a majority of the voting rights in B,
- (b) A is a member of B and has the right to appoint or remove a majority of the board of directors of B,
- (c) A is a member of B and controls alone, pursuant to an agreement with other shareholders or members, a majority of the voting rights in B, or
- (d) A has the right to exercise, or actually exercises, dominant influence or control over B.

(3) In the application of this paragraph to the right to appoint or remove a majority of the board of directors, a legal entity is to be treated as having the right to appoint a director if—

- (a) a person's appointment as director follows necessarily from that person's appointment as director of the legal entity, or
- (b) the directorship is held by the legal entity itself.

14.

(1) For the purposes of paragraph 13, a reference to the voting rights in a legal entity is to the rights conferred on shareholders in respect of their shares (or, in the case of an entity not having a share capital, on members) to vote at general meetings of the entity on all or substantially all matters.

(2) In relation to a legal entity that does not have general meetings at which matters are decided by the exercise of voting rights a reference to exercising voting rights in the entity is to be read as a reference to exercising rights in relation to the entity that are equivalent to those of a person entitled to exercise voting rights in a company.

15.

In applying paragraph 13, the voting rights in a legal entity are to be reduced by any rights held by the entity itself.

16.

A reference in paragraph 13 to the right to appoint or remove a majority of the board of directors of a legal entity is to the right to appoint or remove directors holding a majority of the voting rights at meetings of the board on all or substantially all matters.

17.

References in paragraph 13 to a board of directors, in the case of an entity that does not have such a board, are to be read as references to the equivalent management body of that entity.

18 Shares and rights held by nominees

A share or right held by a person as nominee for another is to be treated for the purposes of this Schedule as held by the other (and not by the nominee).

19 Rights treated as held by person who controls their exercise

(1) Where a person controls a right, the right is to be treated for the purposes of this Schedule as held by that person (and not by the person who in fact holds the right, unless that person also controls it).

(2) A person "controls" a right if, by virtue of any arrangement between that person and others, the right is exercisable only—

- (a) by that person,
- (b) in accordance with that person's directions or instructions, or
- (c) with that person's consent or concurrence.

20.

(1) "Arrangement" includes—

- (a) any scheme, agreement or understanding, whether or not it is legally enforceable, and
- (b) any convention, custom or practice of any kind.

(2) But something does not count as an arrangement unless there is at least some degree of stability about it (whether by its nature or terms, the time it has been in existence or otherwise).

21 Rights exercisable only in certain circumstances etc

(1) Rights that are exercisable only in certain circumstances are to be taken into account only—

(a) when the circumstances have arisen, and for so long as they continue to obtain, or

(b) when the circumstances are within the control of the person having the rights.

(2) But rights that are exercisable by an administrator or by creditors while a legal entity is in relevant insolvency proceedings are not to be taken into account even while the entity is in those proceedings.

(3) "Relevant insolvency proceedings" means—

(a) administration within the meaning of the Insolvency Act 1986,

(b) administration within the meaning of the Insolvency (Northern Ireland) Order 1989 (SI 1989/2405 (NI 19)), or

(c) proceedings under the insolvency law of another country or territory during which an entity's assets and affairs are subject to the control or supervision of a third party or creditor.

(4) Rights that are normally exercisable but are temporarily incapable of exercise are to continue to be taken into account.

22 Rights attached to shares held by way of security

Rights attached to shares held by way of security provided by a person are to be treated for the purposes of this Schedule as held by that person—

(a) where apart from the right to exercise them for the purpose of preserving the value of the security, or of realising it, the rights are exercisable only in accordance with that person's instructions, and

(b) where the shares are held in connection with the granting of loans as part of normal business activities and apart from the right to exercise them for the purpose of preserving the value of the security, or of realising it, the rights are exercisable only in that person's interests.

23 Significant influence or control

(1) (1)The Secretary of State must issue guidance about the meaning of "significant influence or control" for the purposes of this Schedule.

(2) Regard must be had to that guidance in interpreting references in this Schedule to "significant influence or control".

(3) Before issuing guidance under this paragraph the Secretary of State must lay a draft of it before Parliament.

(4) If, within the 40-day period, either House of Parliament resolves not to approve the draft guidance, the Secretary of State must take no further steps in relation to it.

(5) If no such resolution is made within that period, the Secretary of State must issue and publish the guidance in the form of the draft.

(6) Sub-paragraph (4) does not prevent a new draft of proposed guidance from being laid before Parliament.

(7) In this section "the 40-day period", in relation to draft guidance, means the period of 40 days beginning with the day on which the draft is laid before Parliament (or, if it is not laid before each House on the same day, the later of the days on which it is laid).

(8) In calculating the 40-day period, no account is to be taken of any period during which—

(a) Parliament is dissolved or prorogued, or

(b) both Houses are adjourned for more than 4 days.

(9) The Secretary of State may revise guidance issued under this paragraph, and a reference in this paragraph to guidance includes a reference to revised guidance.

24 Limited partnerships

(1) An individual does not meet the specified condition in paragraphs 2, 3, 4, 5 or 6 in relation to an LLP by virtue only of being a limited partner.

(2) An individual does not meet the specified condition in paragraphs 2, 3, 4, 5 or 6 in relation to an LLP by virtue only of, directly or indirectly—

(a) holding shares, or

(b) holding a right,

in or in relation to a limited partner which (in its capacity as such) would meet the condition if it were an individual.

(3) Sub-paragraphs (1) and (2) do not apply for the purposes of determining whether the requirement set out in paragraph (a) of the specified condition in paragraph 6 is met.

(4) In this paragraph "limited partner" means—

(a) a limited partner in a limited partnership registered under the Limited Partnerships Act 1907 (other than one who takes part in the management of the partnership business), or

(b) a foreign limited partner.

(5) In this paragraph "foreign limited partner" means an individual who—

(a) participates in arrangements established under the law of a country or territory outside the United Kingdom, and

(b) has the characteristics prescribed by regulation 8 of the PSC Regulations."]

NOTES

Inserted as noted to reg 31A at **[10.353]**.

[10.367]

[31N Schedule 1B

Schedule 1B to the Act applies to LLPs, but with the omission of paragraph (6) and with the other paragraphs modified so that they read as follows—

"SCHEDULE 1B
ENFORCEMENT OF DISCLOSURE REQUIREMENTS

Section 790I

1 Right to issue restrictions notice

(1) This paragraph applies if—

(a) a notice under section 790D or 790E is served by an LLP on a person who has a relevant interest in the LLP, and

(b) the person fails to comply with that notice within the time specified in it.

(2) The LLP may give the person a notice under this paragraph (a "warning notice") informing the person that it is proposing to issue the person with a notice (a "restrictions notice") with respect to the relevant interest.

(3) The LLP may issue the restrictions notice if, by the end of the period of one month beginning with the date on which the warning notice was given—

(a) the person has not complied with the notice served under section 790D or 790E, and

(b) the LLP has not been provided with a valid reason sufficient to justify the person's failure to comply with the notice served under that section.

(4) A restrictions notice is issued on a person by sending the notice to the person.

(5) The effect of a restrictions notice is set out in paragraph 3.

(6) In deciding whether to issue a restrictions notice, the LLP must have regard to the effect of the notice on the rights of third parties in respect of the relevant interest.

2 Relevant interests

(1) For the purposes of this Schedule, a person has a relevant interest in an LLP if the person—

(a) holds any interest in the LLP;

(b) holds any rights to vote on those matters which are to be decided upon by a vote of the members of the LLP; or

(c) holds the right to appoint or remove any person entitled to manage the LLP.

(2) References to "the relevant interest" are to the right in question.

(3) Part 3 of Schedule 1A applies for the interpretation of sub-paragraph (1) save that, where the relevant interest is by virtue of paragraphs 13 or 18 of that Schedule treated for the purposes of that Schedule as held by a person other than the person who in fact holds the interest, both the holder and the other person are to be regarded for the purposes of this Schedule as having the relevant interest.

3 Effect of restrictions notice

(1) The effect of a restrictions notice issued under paragraph 1 with respect to a relevant interest is as follows—

(a) any transfer of the interest is void,

(b) no rights are exercisable in respect of the interest,

(c) except in a liquidation, no payment may be made of sums due from the LLP in respect of the interest, whether in respect of capital or otherwise.

(2) An agreement to transfer an interest that is subject to the restriction in sub-paragraph (1)(a) is void.

(3) Sub-paragraph (2) does not apply to an agreement to transfer the interest on the making of an order under paragraph 8 made by virtue of sub-paragraph (3)(b) of that paragraph (removal of restrictions in case of court-approved transfer).

(4) An agreement to transfer any associated right (otherwise than in a liquidation) is void.

(5) Sub-paragraph (4) does not apply to an agreement to transfer any such right on the making of an order under paragraph 8 made by virtue of sub-paragraph (3)(b) of that paragraph (removal of restrictions in case of court-approved transfer).

(6) An "associated right", in relation to a relevant interest, is a right to receive payment of any sums due from the LLP in respect of the relevant interest.

(7) The provisions of this section are subject to any directions given under paragraph 4.

4 Protection of third party rights

(1) The court may give a direction under this paragraph if, on application by any person aggrieved, the court is satisfied that a restrictions notice issued by the LLP under paragraph 1 unfairly affects the rights of third parties in respect of the relevant interest.

(2) The direction is given for the purpose of protecting those third party rights.

(3) The direction is a direction that certain acts will not constitute a breach of the restrictions placed on the relevant interest by the restrictions notice.

(4) An order containing a direction under this paragraph—

(a) must specify the acts that will not constitute a breach of the restrictions, and

(b) may confine the direction to cases where those acts are done by persons, or for purposes, described in the order.

(5) The direction may be given subject to such terms as the court thinks fit.

5 Breach of restrictions

(1) A person commits an offence if the person does anything listed in sub-paragraph (2) knowing that the interest is subject to restrictions.

(2) The things are—

(a) exercising or purporting to exercise any right to dispose of a relevant interest,

(b) exercising or purporting to exercise any right to dispose of any right to be issued with a relevant interest, or

(c) voting in respect of a relevant interest (whether as holder of the interest or as proxy) or appointing a proxy to vote in respect of a relevant interest.

(3) A person who has a relevant interest that the person knows to be subject to restrictions commits an offence if the person—

(a) knows a person to be entitled (apart from the restrictions) to vote in respect of the interest, whether as holder or as proxy,

(b) does not know the person to be aware of the fact that the interest is subject to restrictions, and

(c) fails to notify the person of that fact.

(4) A person commits an offence if the person—

(a) either has a relevant interest that the person knows to be subject to restrictions or is entitled to an associated right, and

(b) enters in that capacity into an agreement that is void by virtue of paragraph 3(2) or (4).

(5) References in this Schedule to an interest being "subject to restrictions" are to an interest being subject to restrictions by virtue of a restrictions notice under paragraph 1.

6.

[Omitted.]

7.

(1) A person guilty of an offence under paragraph 5 is liable—

(a) on conviction on indictment, to a fine;

(b) on summary conviction—

(i) in England and Wales, to a fine,

(ii) in Scotland or Northern Ireland, to a fine not exceeding the statutory maximum.

(2) The provisions of those paragraphs are subject to any direction given under paragraph 4 or 8.

8 Relaxation of restrictions

(1) An application may be made to the court for an order directing that the relevant interest cease to be subject to restrictions.

(2) An application for an order under this paragraph may be made by the LLP in question or by any person aggrieved.

(3) The court must not make an order under this paragraph unless—

(a) it is satisfied that the information required by the notice served under section 790D or 790E has been disclosed to the LLP and no unfair advantage has accrued to any person as a result of the earlier failure to make that disclosure, or

(b) the relevant interest is to be transferred for valuable consideration and the court approves the transfer.

(4) An order under this paragraph made by virtue of sub-paragraph (3)(b) may continue, in whole or in part, the restrictions mentioned in paragraph 3(1)(c) so far as they relate to a right acquired or offer made before the transfer.

(5) Where any restrictions continue in force under sub-paragraph (4)—

(a) an application may be made under this paragraph for an order directing that the relevant interest cease to be subject to those restrictions, and

(b) sub-paragraph (3) does not apply in relation to the making of such an order.

9 Orders for sale

(1) The court may order that the relevant interest subject to restrictions be sold subject to the court's approval as to the sale.

(2) An application for an order under sub-paragraph (1) may only be made by the LLP in question.

(3) If the court makes an order under this paragraph, it may make such further order relating to the sale or transfer of the interest as it thinks fit.

(4) An application for an order under sub-paragraph (3) may be made—

(a) by the LLP in question,

(b) by the person appointed by or in pursuance of the order to effect the sale, or

(c) by any person with an interest in the relevant interest.

(5) On making an order under sub-paragraph (1) or (3), the court may order that the applicant's costs (in Scotland, expenses) be paid out of the proceeds of sale.

10.

(1) If a relevant interest is sold in pursuance of an order under paragraph 9, the proceeds of the sale, less the costs of the sale, must be paid into court for the benefit of those who are beneficially interested in the relevant interest.

(2) A person who is beneficially interested in the relevant interest may apply to the court for the whole or part of those proceeds to be paid to that person.

(3) On such an application, the court must order the payment to the applicant of—

(a) the whole of the proceeds of sale together with any interest on the proceeds, or

(b) if another person was also beneficially interested in the relevant interest at the time of the sale, such proportion of the proceeds (and any interest) as the value of the applicant's interest bears to the total value of the relevant interest.

(4) If the court has ordered under paragraph 9 that the costs (in Scotland, expenses) of an applicant under that paragraph are to be paid out of the proceeds of sale, the applicant is entitled to payment of those costs (or expenses) out of the proceeds before any person receives any part of the proceeds under this paragraph.

11 LLP's power to withdraw restrictions notice

An LLP that issues a person with a restrictions notice under paragraph 1 must by notice withdraw the restrictions notice if—

(a) it is satisfied that there is a valid reason sufficient to justify the person's failure to comply with the notice served under section 790D or 790E,
(b) the notice served under section 790D or 790E is complied with, or
(c) it discovers that the rights of a third party in respect of the relevant interest are being unfairly affected by the restrictions notice.

12 Supplementary provision

In issuing and withdrawing restriction notices, LLPs must follow the procedures prescribed by Part 5 of the PSC Regulations.

13 Offences for failing to comply with notices

(1) A person to whom a notice under section 790D or 790E is addressed commits an offence if the person—
(a) fails to comply with the notice, or
(b) in purported compliance with the notice—
(i) makes a statement that the person knows to be false in a material particular, or
(ii) recklessly makes a statement that is false in a material particular.

(2) Where the person is a legal entity, an offence is also committed by every officer of the entity who is in default.

(3) A person does not commit an offence under sub-paragraph (1)(a) (or sub-paragraph (2) as it applies in relation to that sub-paragraph) if the person proves that the requirement to give information was frivolous or vexatious.

(4) A person guilty of an offence under this paragraph is liable—
(a) on conviction on indictment, to imprisonment for a term not exceeding two years or a fine (or both);
(b) on summary conviction—
(i) in England and Wales, to imprisonment for a term not exceeding twelve months or to a fine (or both);
(ii) in Scotland, to imprisonment for a term not exceeding twelve months or to a fine not exceeding the statutory maximum (or both);
(iii) in Northern Ireland, to imprisonment for a term not exceeding six months or to a fine not exceeding the statutory maximum (or both).

14 Offences for failing to provide information

(1) A person commits an offence if the person—
(a) fails to comply with a duty under section 790G or 790H, or
(b) in purported compliance with such a duty—
(i) makes a statement that the person knows to be false in a material particular, or
(ii) recklessly makes a statement that is false in a material particular.

(2) Where the person is a legal entity, an offence is also committed by every officer of the entity who is in default.

(3) A person guilty of an offence under this paragraph is liable—
(a) on conviction on indictment, to imprisonment for a term not exceeding two years or a fine (or both);
(b) on summary conviction—
(i) in England and Wales, to imprisonment for a term not exceeding twelve months or to a fine (or both);
(ii) in Scotland, to imprisonment for a term not exceeding twelve months or to a fine not exceeding the statutory maximum (or both);
(iii) in Northern Ireland, to imprisonment for a term not exceeding six months or to a fine not exceeding the statutory maximum (or both)."]

NOTES

Inserted as noted to reg 31A at **[10.353]**.

[PART 9 LLP CHARGES

[10.368]
32 Registration of charges

Sections 859A to 859Q apply to LLPs, modified so that they read as follows—

"859A Charges created by an LLP

(1) Subject to subsection (6), this section applies where an LLP creates a charge.

(2) The registrar must register the charge if, before the end of the period allowed for delivery, the LLP or any person interested in the charge delivers to the registrar for registration a section 859D statement of particulars.

(3) Where the charge is created or evidenced by an instrument, the registrar is required to register it only if a certified copy of the instrument is delivered to the registrar with the statement of particulars.

(4) "The period allowed for delivery" is 21 days beginning with the day after the date of creation of the charge (see section 859E), unless an order allowing an extended period is made under section 859F(3).

(5) Where an order is made under section 859F(3) a copy of the order must be delivered to the registrar with the statement of particulars.

(6) This section does not apply to—
(a) a charge in favour of a landlord on a cash deposit given as a security in connection with the lease of land;
(b) a charge created by a member of Lloyd's (within the meaning of the Lloyd's Act 1982) to secure its obligations in connection with its underwriting business at Lloyd's;
(c) a charge excluded from the application of this section by or under any other Act.

Part 10 Miscellaneous other SIs

(7) In this Part—

"cash" includes foreign currency,

"charge" includes—

(a) a mortgage;

(b) a standard security, assignation in security, and any other right in security constituted under the law of Scotland, including any heritable security, but not including a pledge, and

"LLP" means an LLP registered in England and Wales or in Northern Ireland or in Scotland.

859B Charge in series of debentures

(1) This section applies where—

(a) an LLP creates a series of debentures containing a charge, or giving a charge by reference to another instrument, and

(b) debenture holders of that series are entitled to the benefit of the charge pari passu.

(2) The registrar must register the charge if, before the end of the period allowed for delivery, the LLP or any person interested in the charge delivers to the registrar for registration, a section 859D statement of particulars which also contains the following—

(a) either—

(i) the name of each of the trustees for the debenture holders, or

(ii) where there are more than four such persons, the names of any four persons listed in the charge instrument as trustees for the debenture holders, and a statement that there are other such persons;

(b) the dates of the determinations of the LLP authorising the issue of the series;

(c) the date of the covering instrument (if any) by which the series is created or defined.

(3) Where the charge is created or evidenced by an instrument, the registrar is required to register it only if a certified copy of the instrument is delivered to the registrar with the statement of particulars.

(4) Where the charge is not created or evidenced by an instrument, the registrar is required to register it only if a certified copy of one of the debentures in the series is delivered to the registrar with the statement of particulars.

(5) For the purposes of this section a statement of particulars is taken to be a section 859D statement of particulars even if it does not contain the names of the debenture holders.

(6) "The period allowed for delivery" is—

(a) if there is a deed containing the charge, 21 days beginning with the day after the date on which the deed is executed;

(b) if there is no deed containing the charge, 21 days beginning with the day after the date on which the first debenture of the series is executed

(7) Where an order is made under section 859F(3) a copy of the order must be delivered to the registrar with the statement of particulars.

(8) In this section "deed" means—

(a) a deed governed by the law of England and Wales or Northern Ireland, or

(b) an instrument governed by a law other than the law of England and Wales or Northern Ireland which requires delivery under that law in order to take effect.

859C Charges existing on property or undertaking acquired

(1) This section applies where an LLP acquires property or undertaking which is subject to a charge of a kind which would, if it had been created by the LLP after the acquisition of the property or undertaking, have been capable of being registered under section 859A.

(2) The registrar must register the charge if the LLP or any person interested in the charge delivers to the registrar for registration a section 859D statement of particulars.

(3) Where the charge is created or evidenced by an instrument, the registrar is required to register it only if a certified copy of the instrument is delivered to the registrar with the statement of particulars.

859D Particulars to be delivered to registrar

(1) A statement of particulars relating to a charge created by an LLP is a "section 859D statement of particulars" if it contains the following particulars—

(a) the registered name and number of the LLP;

(b) the date of creation of the charge and (if the charge is one to which section 859C applies) the date of acquisition of the property or undertaking concerned;

(c) where the charge is created or evidenced by an instrument, the particulars listed in subsection (2);

(d) where the charge is not created or evidenced by an instrument, the particulars listed in subsection (3).

(2) The particulars referred to in subsection (1)(c) are—

(a) any of the following—

(i) the name of each of the persons in whose favour the charge has been created or of the security agents or trustees holding the charge for the benefit of one or more persons; or,

(ii) where there are more than four such persons, security agents or trustees, the names of any four such persons, security agents or trustees listed in the charge instrument, and a statement that there are other such persons, security agents or trustees;

(b) whether the instrument is expressed to contain a floating charge and, if so, whether it is expressed to cover all the property and undertaking of the LLP;

(c) whether any of the terms of the charge prohibit or restrict the LLP from creating further security that will rank equally with or ahead of the charge;

(d) whether (and if so, a short description of) any land, ship, aircraft or intellectual property, that is registered or required to be registered in the United Kingdom, is subject to a charge (which is not a floating charge) or fixed security included in the instrument;

(e) whether the instrument includes a charge (which is not a floating charge) or fixed security over—
 (i) any tangible or corporeal property, or
 (ii) any intangible or incorporeal property,
 not described in paragraph (d).

(3) The particulars referred to in subsection (1)(d) are—
 (a) a statement that there is no instrument creating or evidencing the charge;
 (b) the names of each of the persons in whose favour the charge has been created or the names of any security agents or trustees holding the charge for the benefit of one or more persons;
 (c) the nature of the charge;
 (d) a short description of the property or undertaking charged;
 (e) the obligations secured by the charge.

(4) In this section "fixed security" has the meaning given in section 486(1) of the Companies Act 1985.

(5) In this section "intellectual property" includes—
 (a) any patent, trade mark, registered design, copyright or design right;
 (b) any licence under or in respect of any such right.

859E Date of creation of charge

(1) For the purposes of this Part, a charge of the type described in column 1 of the Table below is taken to be created on the date given in relation to it in column 2 of that Table.

1 Type of charge	*2 When charge created*
Standard security	The date of its recording in the Register of Sasines or its registration in the Land Register of Scotland
Charge other than a standard security, where created or evidenced by an instrument	Where the instrument is a deed that has been executed and has immediate effect on execution and delivery, the date of delivery
	Where the instrument is a deed that has been executed and held in escrow, the date of delivery into escrow
	Where the instrument is a deed that has been executed and held as undelivered, the date of delivery
	Where the instrument is not a deed and has immediate effect on execution, the date of execution
	Where the instrument is not a deed and does not have immediate effect on execution, the date on which the instrument takes effect
Charge other than a standard security, where not created or evidenced by an instrument	The date on which the charge comes into effect.

(2) Where a charge is created or evidenced by an instrument made between two or more parties, references in the Table in subsection (1) to execution are to execution by all the parties to the instrument whose execution is essential for the instrument to take effect as a charge.

(3) This section applies for the purposes of this Chapter even if further forms, notices, registrations or other actions or proceedings are necessary to make the charge valid or effectual for any other purposes.

(4) For the purposes of this Chapter, the registrar is entitled without further enquiry to accept a charge as created on the date given as the date of creation of the charge in a section 859D statement of particulars.

(5) In this section "deed" means—
 (a) a deed governed by the law of England and Wales or Northern Ireland, or
 (b) an instrument governed by a law other than the law of England and Wales or Northern Ireland which requires delivery under that law in order to take effect.

(6) References in this section to delivery, in relation to a deed, include delivery as a deed where required.

859F Extension of period allowed for delivery

(1) Subsection (3) applies if the court is satisfied that—
 (a) neither the LLP nor any other person interested in the charge has delivered to the registrar the documents required under section 859A or (as the case may be) 859B before the end of the period allowed for delivery under the section concerned, and
 (b) the requirement in subsection (2) is met.

(2) The requirement is—
 (a) that the failure to deliver those documents—
  (i) was accidental or due to inadvertence or to some other sufficient cause, or
  (ii) is not of a nature to prejudice the position of creditors of the LLP, or
 (b) that on other grounds it is just and equitable to grant relief.

(3) The court may, on the application of the LLP or a person interested, and on such terms and conditions as seem to the court just and expedient, order that the period allowed for delivery be extended.

859G Personal information etc in certified copies

(1) The following are not required to be included in a certified copy of an instrument or debenture delivered to the registrar for the purposes of any provision of this Chapter—

Part 10 Miscellaneous other SIs

(a) personal information relating to an individual (other than the name of an individual);
(b) the number or other identifier of a bank or securities account of an LLP or individual;
(c) a signature.

(2) The registrar is entitled without further enquiry, to accept the certified copy of an instrument whether or not any of the information in subsection (1) is contained within the instrument.

Consequence of non-delivery

859H Consequence of failure to deliver charges

(1) This section applies if—
(a) an LLP creates a charge to which section 859A or 859B applies, and
(b) the documents required by section 859A or (as the case may be) 859B are not delivered to the registrar by the LLP or another person interested in the charge before the end of the relevant period allowed for delivery.

(2) "The relevant period allowed for delivery" is—
(a) the period allowed for delivery under the section in question, or
(b) if an order under section 859F(3) has been made, the period allowed by the order.

(3) Where this section applies, the charge is void (so far as any security on the LLP's property or undertaking is conferred by it) against—
(a) a liquidator of the LLP,
(b) an administrator of the LLP, and
(c) a creditor of the LLP.

(4) Subsection (3) is without prejudice to any contract or obligation for repayment of the money secured by the charge; and when a charge becomes void under this section, the money secured by it immediately becomes payable.

The register

859I Entries on the register

(1) This section applies where a charge is registered in accordance with a provision of this Chapter.

(2) The registrar must—
(a) allocate to the charge a unique reference code and place a note in the register recording that reference code; and
(b) include in the register any documents delivered under section 859A(3) or (5), 859B(3), (4) or (7) or 859C(3).

(3) The registrar must give a certificate of the registration of the charge to the person who delivered to the registrar a section 859D statement of particulars relating to the charge.

(4) The certificate must state—
(a) the registered name and number of the LLP in respect of which the charge was registered; and
(b) the unique reference code allocated to the charge.

(5) The certificate must be signed by the registrar or authenticated by the registrar's official seal.

(6) In the case of registration under section 859A or 859B, the certificate is conclusive evidence that the documents required by the section concerned were delivered to the registrar before the end of the relevant period allowed for delivery.

(7) "The relevant period allowed for delivery" is—
(a) the period allowed for delivery under the section in question, or
(b) if an order under section 859F(3) has been made, the period allowed by the order.

859J LLP holding property or undertaking as trustee

(1) Where an LLP is acting as trustee of property or an undertaking which is the subject of a charge delivered for registration under this Chapter, the LLP or any person interested in the charge may deliver to the registrar a statement to that effect.

(2) A statement delivered after the delivery for registration of the charge must include—
(a) the registered name and number of the LLP; and
(b) the unique reference code allocated to the charge.

859K Registration of enforcement of security

(1) Subsection (2) applies where a person—
(a) obtains an order for the appointment of a receiver or manager of an LLP's property or undertaking, or
(b) appoints such a receiver or manager under powers contained in an instrument.

(2) The person must, within 7 days of the order or of the appointment under those powers—
(a) give notice to the registrar of that fact, and
(b) if the order was obtained, or the appointment made, by virtue of a registered charge held by the person give the registrar a notice containing—
(i) in the case of a charge created before 6th April 2013, the information specified in subsection (4);
(ii) in the case of a charge created on or after 6th April 2013, the unique reference code allocated to the charge.

(3) Where a person appointed receiver or manager of an LLP's property or undertaking under powers contained in an instrument ceases to act as such a receiver or manager, the person must, on so ceasing—
(a) give notice to the registrar of that fact, and—
(b) give the registrar a notice containing—
(i) in the case of a charge created before 6th April 2013, the information specified in subsection (4), or

(ii) in the case of a charge created on or after 6th April 2013, the unique reference code allocated to the charge.

(4) The information referred to in subsections (2)(b)(i) and (3)(b)(i) is—

(a) the date of the creation of the charge;

(b) a description of the instrument (if any) creating or evidencing the charge;

(c) short particulars of the property or undertaking charged.

(5) The registrar must include in the register—

(a) a fact of which notice is given under subsection (2)(a), and

(c) a fact of which notice is given under subsection (3)(a).

(6) A person who makes default in complying with the requirements of subsections (2) or (3) of this section commits an offence.

(7) A person guilty of an offence under this section is liable on summary conviction to a fine not exceeding level 3 on the standard scale and, for continued contravention, a daily default fine not exceeding one-tenth of level 3 on the standard scale.

(8) This section applies only to a receiver or manager appointed—

(a) by a court in England and Wales or Northern Ireland, or

(b) under an instrument governed by the law of England and Wales or Northern Ireland.

(9) This section does not apply to a receiver appointed under Chapter 2 of Part 3 of the Insolvency Act 1986 (receivers (Scotland)).

859L Entries of satisfaction and release

(1) Subsection (5) applies if the statement set out in subsection (2) and the particulars set out in subsection (4) are delivered to the registrar with respect to a registered charge.

(2) The statement referred to in subsection (1) is a statement to the effect that—

(a) the debt for which the charge was given has been paid or satisfied in whole or in part, or

(b) all or part of the property or undertaking charged—

(i) has been released from the charge, or

(ii) has ceased to form part of the LLP's property or undertaking.

(3) Where a statement within subsection (2)(b) relates to part only of the property or undertaking charged, the statement must include a short description of that part.

(4) The particulars referred to in subsection (1) are—

(a) the name and address of the person delivering the statement and an indication of their interest in the charge;

(b) the registered name and number of the LLP that—

(i) created the charge (in a case within section 859A or 859B), or

(ii) acquired the property or undertaking subject to the charge (in a case within section 859C);

(c) in respect of a charge created before 6th April 2013—

(i) the date of creation of the charge;

(ii) a description of the instrument (if any) by which the charge is created or evidenced;

(iii) short particulars of the property or undertaking charged;

(d) in respect of a charge created on or after 6th April 2013, the unique reference code allocated to the charge.

(5) The registrar may include in the register—

(a) a statement of satisfaction in whole or in part, or

(b) a statement of the fact that all or part of the property or undertaking has been released from the charge or has ceased to form part of the LLP's property or undertaking (as the case may be).

859M Rectification of register

(1) Subsection (3) applies if the court is satisfied that—

(a) there has been an omission or mis-statement in any statement or notice delivered to the registrar in accordance with this Chapter, and

(b) the requirement in subsection (2) is met.

(2) The requirement is that the court is satisfied—

(a) that the omission or mis-statement—

(i) was accidental or due to inadvertence or to some other sufficient cause, or

(ii) is not of a nature to prejudice the position of creditors of the LLP, or

(b) that on other grounds it is just and equitable to grant relief.

(3) The court may, on the application of the LLP or a person interested, and on such terms and conditions as seem to the court just and expedient, order that the omission or mis-statement be rectified.

(4) A copy of the court's order must be sent by the applicant to the registrar for registration.

859N Replacement of instrument or debenture

(1) Subsection (2) applies if the court is satisfied that—

(a) a copy of an instrument or debenture delivered to the registrar under this Chapter contains material which could have been omitted under section 859G;

(b) the wrong instrument or debenture was delivered to the registrar; or

(c) the copy was defective.

(2) The court may, on the application of the LLP or a person interested, and on such terms and conditions as seem to the court just and expedient, order that the copy of the instrument or debenture be removed from the register and replaced.

(3) (3)A copy of the court's order must be sent by the applicant to the registrar for registration.

859O Notification of addition or amendment of charge

(1) This section applies where, after the creation of a charge, the charge is amended by adding or amending a term that—

(a) prohibits or restricts the creation of any fixed security or any other charge having priority over, or ranking pari passu with, the charge; or

(b) varies, or otherwise regulates the order of, the ranking of the charge in relation to any fixed security or any other charge.

(2) Either the LLP that created the charge or the person taking the benefit of the charge (or another charge referred to in subsection (1)(b)) may deliver to the registrar for registration—

(a) a certified copy of the instrument effecting the amendment, variation or regulation, and

(b) a statement of the particulars set out in subsection (3).

(3) The particulars to be included in the statement are—

(a) the registered name and number of the LLP;

(b) in the case of a charge created before 6th April 2013—

(i) the date of creation of the charge;

(ii) a description of the instrument (if any) by which the charge was created or evidenced;

(iii) short particulars of the property or undertaking charged as set out when the charge was registered;

(c) in the case of a charge created on or after 6th April 2013, (where allocated) the unique reference code allocated to the charge.

(4) Subsections (1) to (3) do not affect the continued application of section 466 of the Companies Act 1985.

(5) In this section "fixed security" has the meaning given in section 486(1) of the Companies Act 1985.

LLPs' records and registers

859P LLPs to keep copies of instruments creating and amending charges

(1) An LLP must keep available for inspection a copy of every—

(a) instrument creating a charge capable of registration under this Chapter, and

(b) instrument effecting any variation or amendment of such a charge.

(2) In the case of a charge contained in a series of uniform debentures, a copy of one of the debentures of the series is sufficient for the purposes of subsection (1)(a).

(3) If the particulars referred to in section 859D(1) or the particulars of the property or undertaking charged are not contained in the instrument creating the charge, but are instead contained in other documents which are referred to in or otherwise incorporated into the instrument, then the LLP must also keep available for inspection a copy of those other documents.

(4) It is sufficient for the purposes of subsection (1)(a) if the LLP keeps a copy of the instrument in the form delivered to the registrar under section 859A(3), 859B(3) or (4) or 859C(3).

(5) Where a translation has been delivered to the registrar in accordance with section 1105, the LLP must keep available for inspection a copy of the translation.

859Q Instruments creating charges to be available for inspection

(1) This section applies to documents required to be kept available for inspection under section 859P (copies of instruments creating and amending charges).

(2) The documents must be kept available for inspection—

(a) at the LLP's registered office, or

(b) at a place specified in Part 2 of the Companies (Company Records) Regulations 2008 (SI 2008/3006).

(3) The LLP must give notice to the registrar—

(a) of the place at which the documents are kept available for inspection, and

(b) of any change in that place,

unless they have at all times been kept at the LLP's registered office.

(4) The documents must be open to the inspection—

(a) of any creditor or member of the LLP without charge, and

(b) of any other person on payment of the fee prescribed by regulation (2)(c) of the Companies (Fees for Inspection of Company Records) Regulations 2008 (SI 2008/3007).

(5) If default is made for 14 days in complying with subsection (3) or an inspection required under subsection (4) is refused, an offence is committed by—

(a) the LLP, and

(b) every member of the LLP who is in default.

(6) A person guilty of an offence under this section is liable on summary conviction to a fine not exceeding level 3 on the standard scale and, for continued contravention, a daily default fine not exceeding one-tenth of level 3 on the standard scale.

(7) If an inspection required under subsection (4) is refused the court may by order compel an immediate inspection.

(8) Where the LLP and a person wishing to carry out an inspection under subsection (4) agree, the inspection may be carried out by electronic means.]

NOTES

Part 9 (reg 32 only) was substituted for the original Part 9 (regs 32–44) by the Limited Liability Partnerships (Application of Companies Act 2006) (Amendment) Regulations 2013, SI 2013/618, reg 2, Schedule, as from 6 April 2013, subject to transitional provisions as noted below.

Transitional provisions: the Limited Liability Partnerships (Application of Companies Act 2006) (Amendment) Regulations 2013, SI 2013/618, reg 8 provides as follows—

"8 Transitional provisions

(1) Subject to paragraph (3) the provisions set out in the Schedule apply to charges created on or after 6th April 2013.

(2) Subject to paragraph (3), the provisions of Part 9 of the principal Regulations as they stood immediately before 6th April 2013 continue to apply to charges created before 6th April 2013.

(3) Sections 859K, 859L and 859O of the Companies Act 2006 also apply to charges created before 6th April 2013.

(4) The amendments made by regulations 3 to 7 of these Regulations apply to charges created on or after 6th April 2013.".

This Part originally read as follows—

"PART 9
LLP CHARGES

CHAPTER 1
LLPS REGISTERED IN ENGLAND AND WALES OR IN NORTHERN IRELAND

32 Requirement to register LLP charges

Sections 860 to 862 apply to LLPs, modified so that they read as follows—

"860 Charges created by an LLP

(1) An LLP that creates a charge to which this section applies must deliver the required particulars of the charge, together with the instrument (if any) by which the charge is created or evidenced, to the registrar for registration before the end of the period allowed for registration.

(2) The required particulars are those prescribed by regulation 2 of the Companies (Particulars of Company Charges) Regulations 2008 (SI 2008/2996).

(3) Registration of a charge to which this section applies may instead be effected on the application of a person interested in it.

(4) Where registration is effected on the application of some person other than the LLP, that person is entitled to recover from the LLP the amount of any fees properly paid by him to the registrar on registration.

(5) If an LLP fails to comply with subsection (1), an offence is committed by—

(a) the LLP, and

(b) every member of it who is in default.

(6) A person guilty of an offence under this section is liable—

(a) on conviction on indictment, to a fine;

(b) on summary conviction, to a fine not exceeding the statutory maximum.

(7) Subsection (5) does not apply if registration of the charge has been effected on the application of some other person.

(8) This section applies to the following charges—

(a) a charge on land or any interest in land, other than a charge for any rent or other periodical sum issuing out of land,

(b) a charge created or evidenced by an instrument which, if executed by an individual, would require registration as a bill of sale,

(c) a charge for the purposes of securing any issue of debentures,

(d) a charge on book debts of the LLP,

(e) a floating charge on the LLP's property or undertaking,

(f) a charge on a ship or aircraft, or any share in a ship,

(g) a charge on goodwill or on any intellectual property.

861 Charges which have to be registered: supplementary

(1) The holding of debentures entitling the holder to a charge on land is not, for the purposes of section 860(8)(a), an interest in the land.

(2) It is immaterial for the purposes of this Chapter where land subject to a charge is situated.

(3) The deposit by way of security of a negotiable instrument given to secure the payment of book debts is not, for the purposes of section 860(8)(d), a charge on those book debts.

(4) For the purposes of section 860(8)(g), "intellectual property" means—

(a) any patent, trade mark, registered design, copyright or design right;

(b) any licence under or in respect of any such right.

(5) In this Chapter—

"charge" includes mortgage, and

"LLP" means an LLP registered in England and Wales or in Northern Ireland.

862 Charges existing on property acquired

(1) This section applies where an LLP acquires property which is subject to a charge of a kind which would, if it had been created by the LLP after the acquisition of the property, have been required to be registered under this Chapter.

(2) The LLP must deliver the required particulars of the charge, together with a certified copy of the instrument (if any) by which the charge is created or evidenced, to the registrar for registration.

(3) The required particulars are those prescribed by regulation 4 of the Companies (Particulars of Company Charges) Regulations 2008 (SI 2008/2996).

(4) Subsection (2) must be complied with before the end of the period allowed for registration.

(5) If default is made in complying with this section, an offence is committed by—

(a) the LLP, and

(b) every member of it who is in default.

(6) A person guilty of an offence under this section is liable—

(a) on conviction on indictment, to a fine;

(b) on summary conviction, to a fine not exceeding the statutory maximum.".

33 Special rules about debentures

Sections 863 to 865 apply to LLPs, modified so that they read as follows—

"863 Charge in series of debentures

(1) Where a series of debentures containing, or giving by reference to another instrument, any charge to the benefit of which debenture holders of that series are entitled *pari passu* is created by an LLP, it is for the purposes of section 860(1) sufficient if the required particulars, together with the deed containing the charge (or, if there is no such deed, one of the debentures of the series), are delivered to the registrar before the end of the period allowed for registration.

(2) The following are the required particulars—

(a) the total amount secured by the whole series, and

Part 10 Miscellaneous other SIs

(b) the dates of the determinations of the LLP authorising the issue of the series and the date of the covering deed (if any) by which the series is created or defined, and

(c) a general description of the property charged, and

(d) the names of the trustees (if any) for the debenture holders.

(3) Particulars of the date and amount of each issue of debentures of a series of the kind mentioned in subsection (1) must be sent to the registrar for entry in the register of charges.

(4) Failure to comply with subsection (3) does not affect the validity of the debentures issued.

(5) Subsections (3) to (7) of section 860 apply for the purposes of this section as they apply for the purposes of that section, but as if references to the registration of a charge were references to the registration of a series of debentures.

864 Additional registration requirement for commission etc in relation to debentures

(1) Where any commission, allowance or discount has been paid or made either directly or indirectly by an LLP to a person in consideration of his—

(a) subscribing or agreeing to subscribe, whether absolutely or conditionally, for debentures in an LLP, or

(b) procuring or agreeing to procure subscriptions, whether absolute or conditional, for such debentures,

the particulars required to be sent for registration under section 860 shall include particulars as to the amount or rate per cent. of the commission, discount or allowance so paid or made.

(2) The deposit of debentures as security for a debt of the LLP is not, for the purposes of this section, treated as the issue of debentures at a discount.

(3) Failure to comply with this section does not affect the validity of the debentures issued.

865 Endorsement of certificate on debentures

(1) The LLP shall cause a copy of every certificate of registration given under section 869 to be endorsed on every debenture or certificate of debenture stock which is issued by the LLP, and the payment of which is secured by the charge so registered.

(2) But this does not require an LLP to cause a certificate of registration of any charge so given to be endorsed on any debenture or certificate of debenture stock issued by the LLP before the charge was created.

(3) If a person knowingly and wilfully authorises or permits the delivery of a debenture or certificate of debenture stock which under this section is required to have endorsed on it a copy of a certificate of registration, without the copy being so endorsed upon it, he commits an offence.

(4) A person guilty of an offence under this section is liable on summary conviction to a fine not exceeding level 3 on the standard scale.".

34 Charges in other jurisdictions

Sections 866 and 867 apply to LLPs, modified so that they read as follows—

"866 Charges created in, or over property in, jurisdictions outside the United Kingdom

(1) Where a charge is created outside the United Kingdom comprising property situated outside the United Kingdom, the delivery to the registrar of a verified copy of the instrument by which the charge is created or evidenced has the same effect for the purposes of this Chapter as the delivery of the instrument itself.

(2) Where a charge is created in the United Kingdom but comprises property outside the United Kingdom, the instrument creating or purporting to create the charge may be sent for registration under section 860 even if further proceedings may be necessary to make the charge valid or effectual according to the law of the country in which the property is situated.

867 Charges created in, or over property in, another United Kingdom jurisdiction

(1) Subsection (2) applies where—

(a) a charge comprises property situated in a part of the United Kingdom other than the part in which the LLP is registered, and

(b) registration in that other part is necessary to make the charge valid or effectual under the law of that part of the United Kingdom.

(2) The delivery to the registrar of a verified copy of the instrument by which the charge is created or evidenced, together with a certificate stating that the charge was presented for registration in that other part of the United Kingdom on the date on which it was so presented has, for the purposes of this Chapter, the same effect as the delivery of the instrument itself.".

35 Orders charging land: Northern Ireland

Section 868 applies to LLPs, modified so that it reads as follows—

"868 Northern Ireland: registration of certain charges etc affecting land

(1) Where a charge imposed by an order under Article 46 of the 1981 Order or notice of such a charge is registered in the Land Registry against registered land or any estate in registered land of an LLP, the Registrar of Titles shall as soon as may be cause two copies of the order made under Article 46 of that Order or of any notice under Article 48 of that Order to be delivered to the registrar.

(2) Where a charge imposed by an order under Article 46 of the 1981 Order is registered in the Registry of Deeds against any unregistered land or estate in land of an LLP, the Registrar of Deeds shall as soon as may be cause two copies of the order to be delivered to the registrar.

(3) On delivery of copies under this section, the registrar shall—

(a) register one of them in accordance with section 869, and

(b) not later than 7 days from that date of delivery, cause the other copy together with a certificate of registration under section 869(5) to be sent to the LLP against which judgment was given.

(4) Where a charge to which subsection (1) or (2) applies is vacated, the Registrar of Titles or, as the case may be, the Registrar of Deeds shall cause a certified copy of the certificate of satisfaction lodged under Article 132(1) of the 1981 Order to be delivered to the registrar for entry of a memorandum of satisfaction in accordance with section 872.

(5) In this section—

"the 1981 Order" means the Judgments Enforcement (Northern Ireland) Order 1981 (SI 1981/226 (NI 6));

"the Registrar of Deeds" means the registrar appointed under the Registration of Deeds Act (Northern Ireland) 1970 (c 25);

"Registry of Deeds" has the same meaning as in the Registration of Deeds Acts;

"Registration of Deeds Acts" means the Registration of Deeds Act (Northern Ireland) 1970 and every statutory provision for the time being in force amending that Act or otherwise relating to the registry of deeds, or the registration of deeds, orders or other instruments or documents in such registry;

"the Land Registry" and "the Registrar of Titles" are to be construed in accordance with section 1 of the Land Registration Act (Northern Ireland) 1970 (c 18);

"registered land" and "unregistered land" have the same meaning as in Part 3 of the Land Registration Act (Northern Ireland) 1970.".

36 The register of charges

Sections 869 to 873 apply to LLPs, modified so that they read as follows—

"869 Register of charges to be kept by registrar

(1) The registrar shall keep, with respect to each LLP, a register of all the charges requiring registration under this Chapter.

(2) In the case of a charge to the benefit of which holders of a series of debentures are entitled, the registrar shall enter in the register the required particulars specified in section 863(2).

(3) In the case of a charge imposed by the Enforcement of Judgments Office under Article 46 of the Judgments Enforcement (Northern Ireland) Order 1981, the registrar shall enter in the register the date on which the charge became effective.

(4) In the case of any other charge, the registrar shall enter in the register the following particulars—

(a) if it is a charge created by an LLP, the date of its creation and, if it is a charge which was existing on property acquired by the LLP, the date of the acquisition,

(b) the amount secured by the charge,

(c) short particulars of the property charged, and

(d) the persons entitled to the charge.

(5) The registrar shall give a certificate of the registration of any charge registered in pursuance of this Chapter, stating the amount secured by the charge.

(6) The certificate—

(a) shall be signed by the registrar or authenticated by the registrar's official seal, and

(b) is conclusive evidence that the requirements of this Chapter as to registration have been satisfied.

(7) The register kept in pursuance of this section shall be open to inspection by any person.

870 The period allowed for registration

(1) The period allowed for registration of a charge created by an LLP is—

(a) 21 days beginning with the day after the day on which the charge is created, or

(b) if the charge is created outside the United Kingdom, 21 days beginning with the day after the day on which the instrument by which the charge is created or evidenced (or a copy of it) could, in due course of post (and if despatched with due diligence) have been received in the United Kingdom.

(2) The period allowed for registration of a charge to which property acquired by an LLP is subject is—

(a) 21 days beginning with the day after the day on which the acquisition is completed, or

(b) if the property is situated and the charge was created outside the United Kingdom, 21 days beginning with the day after the day on which the instrument by which the charge is created or evidenced (or a copy of it) could, in due course of post (and if despatched with due diligence) have been received in the United Kingdom.

(3) The period allowed for registration of particulars of a series of debentures as a result of section 863 is—

(a) if there is a deed containing the charge mentioned in section 863(1), 21 days beginning with the day after the day on which that deed is executed, or

(b) if there is no such deed, 21 days beginning with the day after the day on which the first debenture of the series is executed.

871 Registration of enforcement of security

(1) If a person obtains an order for the appointment of a receiver or manager of an LLP's property, or appoints such a receiver or manager under powers contained in an instrument, he shall within 7 days of the order or of the appointment under those powers, give notice of the fact to the registrar.

(2) Where a person appointed receiver or manager of an LLP's property under powers contained in an instrument ceases to act as such receiver or manager, he shall, on so ceasing, give the registrar notice to that effect.

(3) The registrar must enter a fact of which he is given notice under this section in the register of charges.

(4) A person who makes default in complying with the requirements of this section commits an offence.

(5) A person guilty of an offence under this section is liable on summary conviction to a fine not exceeding level 3 on the standard scale and, for continued contravention, a daily default fine not exceeding one-tenth of level 3 on the standard scale.

872 Entries of satisfaction and release

(1) Subsection (2) applies if a statement is delivered to the registrar verifying with respect to a registered charge—

(a) that the debt for which the charge was given has been paid or satisfied in whole or in part, or

(b) that part of the property or undertaking charged has been released from the charge or has ceased to form part of the LLP's property or undertaking.

(2) The registrar may enter on the register a memorandum of satisfaction in whole or in part, or of the fact part of the property or undertaking has been released from the charge or has ceased to form part of the LLP's property or undertaking (as the case may be).

(3) Where the registrar enters a memorandum of satisfaction in whole, the registrar shall if required send the LLP a copy of it.

873 Rectification of register of charges

(1) Subsection (2) applies if the court is satisfied—

(a) that the failure to register a charge before the end of the period allowed for registration, or the omission or mis-statement of any particular with respect to any such charge or in a memorandum of satisfaction—

(i) was accidental or due to inadvertence or to some other sufficient cause, or

(ii) is not of a nature to prejudice the position of creditors of the LLP, or

(b) that on other grounds it is just and equitable to grant relief.

(2) The court may, on the application of the LLP or a person interested, and on such terms and conditions as seem to the court just and expedient, order that the period allowed for registration shall be extended or, as the case may be, that the omission or mis-statement shall be rectified.".

37 Avoidance of certain charges

Section 874 applies to LLPs, modified so that it reads as follows—

"874 Consequence of failure to register charges created by an LLP

(1) If an LLP creates a charge to which section 860 applies, the charge is void (so far as any security on the LLP's property or undertaking is conferred by it) against—

(a) a liquidator of the LLP,

(b) an administrator of the LLP, and

(c) a creditor of the LLP,

unless that section is complied with.

(2) Subsection (1) is subject to the provisions of this Chapter.

(3) Subsection (1) is without prejudice to any contract or obligation for repayment of the money secured by the charge; and when a charge becomes void under this section, the money secured by it immediately becomes payable.".

38 LLPs' records and registers

Sections 875 to 877 apply to LLPs, modified so that they read as follows—

"875 LLPs to keep copies of instruments creating charges

(1) An LLP must keep available for inspection a copy of every instrument creating a charge requiring registration under this Chapter, including any document delivered to the LLP under section 868(3)(b) (Northern Ireland: orders imposing charges affecting land).

(2) In the case of a series of uniform debentures, a copy of one of the debentures of the series is sufficient.

876 LLP's register of charges

(1) Every LLP shall keep available for inspection a register of charges and enter in it—

(a) all charges specifically affecting property of the LLP, and

(b) all floating charges on the whole or part of the LLP's property or undertaking.

(2) The entry shall in each case give a short description of the property charged, the amount of the charge and, except in the cases of securities to bearer, the names of the persons entitled to it.

(3) If a member of the LLP knowingly and wilfully authorises or permits the omission of an entry required to be made in pursuance of this section, he commits an offence.

(4) A person guilty of an offence under this section is liable—

(a) on conviction on indictment, to a fine;

(b) on summary conviction, to a fine not exceeding the statutory maximum.

877 Instruments creating charges and register of charges to be available for inspection

(1) This section applies to—

(a) documents required to be kept available for inspection under section 875 (copies of instruments creating charges), and

(b) an LLP's register of charges kept in pursuance of section 876.

(2) The documents and register must be kept available for inspection—

(a) at the LLP's registered office, or

(b) at a place specified in Part 2 of the Companies (Company Records) Regulations 2008 (SI 2008/3006).

(3) The LLP must give notice to the registrar—

(a) of the place at which the documents and register are kept available for inspection, and

(b) of any change in that place,

unless they have at all times been kept at the LLP's registered office.

(4) The documents and register shall be open to the inspection—

(a) of any creditor or member of the LLP without charge, and

(b) of any other person on payment of the fee prescribed by regulation 2(c) of the Companies (Fees for Inspection of Company Records) Regulations 2008 (SI 2008/3007).

(5) If default is made for 14 days in complying with subsection (3) or an inspection required under subsection (4) is refused, an offence is committed by—

(a) the LLP, and

(b) every member of the LLP who is in default.

(6) A person guilty of an offence under this section is liable on summary conviction to a fine not exceeding level 3 on the standard scale and, for continued contravention, a daily default fine not exceeding one-tenth of level 3 on the standard scale.

(7) If an inspection required under subsection (4) is refused the court may by order compel an immediate inspection.".

CHAPTER 2
LLPS REGISTERED IN SCOTLAND

39 Charges requiring registration

Sections 878 to 881 apply to LLPs, modified so that they read as follows—

"878 Charges created by an LLP

(1) An LLP that creates a charge to which this section applies must deliver the required particulars of the charge, together with a copy certified as a correct copy of the instrument (if any) by which the charge is created or evidenced, to the registrar for registration before the end of the period allowed for registration.

(2) The required particulars are those prescribed by regulation 3 of the Companies (Particulars of Company Charges) Regulations 2008 (SI 2008/2996).

(3) Registration of a charge to which this section applies may instead be effected on the application of a person interested in it.

(4) Where registration is effected on the application of some person other than the LLP, that person is entitled to recover from the LLP the amount of any fees properly paid by him to the registrar on the registration.

(5) If an LLP fails to comply with subsection (1), an offence is committed by—

(a) the LLP, and
(b) every member of the LLP who is in default.

(6) A person guilty of an offence under this section is liable—
(a) on conviction on indictment, to a fine;
(b) on summary conviction, to a fine not exceeding the statutory maximum.

(7) Subsection (5) does not apply if registration of the charge has been effected on the application of some other person.

(8) This section applies to the following charges—
(a) a charge on land or any interest in such land, other than a charge for any rent or other periodical sum payable in respect of the land,
(b) a security over incorporeal moveable property of any of the following categories—
(i) goodwill,
(ii) a patent or a licence under a patent,
(iii) a trade mark,
(iv) a copyright or a licence under a copyright,
(v) a registered design or a licence in respect of such a design,
(vi) a design right or a licence under a design right, and
(vii) the book debts (whether book debts of the LLP or assigned to it),
(c) a security over a ship or aircraft or any share in a ship,
(d) a floating charge.

879 Charges which have to be registered: supplementary

(1) A charge on land, for the purposes of section 878(8)(a), includes a charge created by a heritable security within the meaning of section 9(8) of the Conveyancing and Feudal Reform (Scotland) Act 1970 (c 35).

(2) The holding of debentures entitling the holder to a charge on land is not, for the purposes of section 878(8)(a), deemed to be an interest in land.

(3) It is immaterial for the purposes of this Chapter where land subject to a charge is situated.

(4) The deposit by way of security of a negotiable instrument given to secure the payment of book debts is not, for the purposes of section 878(8)(b)(vii), to be treated as a charge on those book debts.

(5) References in this Chapter to the date of the creation of a charge are—
(a) in the case of a floating charge, the date on which the instrument creating the floating charge was executed by the LLP creating the charge, and
(b) in any other case, the date on which the right of the person entitled to the benefit of the charge was constituted as a real right.

(6) In this Chapter "LLP" means an LLP registered in Scotland.

880 Duty to register charges existing on property acquired

(1) Subsection (2) applies where an LLP acquires any property which is subject to a charge of any kind as would, if it had been created by the LLP after the acquisition of the property, have been required to be registered under this Chapter.

(2) The LLP must deliver the required particulars of the charge, together with a copy (certified to be a correct copy) of the instrument (if any) by which the charge was created or is evidenced, to the registrar for registration before the end of the period allowed for registration.

(3) The required particulars are those prescribed by regulation 4 of the Companies (Particulars of Company Charges) Regulations 2008 (SI 2008/2996).

(4) If default is made in complying with this section, an offence is committed by—
(a) the LLP, and
(b) every member of it who is in default.

(5) A person guilty of an offence under this section is liable—
(a) on conviction on indictment, to a fine;
(b) on summary conviction, to a fine not exceeding the statutory maximum.

881 Charge by way of ex facie absolute disposition, etc

(1) For the avoidance of doubt, it is hereby declared that, in the case of a charge created by way of an ex facie absolute disposition or assignation qualified by a back letter or other agreement, or by a standard security qualified by an agreement, compliance with section 878(1) does not of itself render the charge unavailable as security for indebtedness incurred after the date of compliance.

(2) Where the amount secured by a charge so created is purported to be increased by a further back letter or agreement, a further charge is held to have been created by the ex facie absolute disposition or assignation or (as the case may be) by the standard security, as qualified by the further back letter or agreement.

(3) In that case, the provisions of this Chapter apply to the further charge as if—
(a) references in this Chapter (other than in this section) to a charge were references to the further charge, and
(b) references to the date of the creation of a charge were references to the date on which the further back letter or agreement was executed.".

40 Special rules about debentures

Sections 882 and 883 apply to LLPs, modified so that they read as follows—

"882 Charge in series of debentures

(1) Where a series of debentures containing, or giving by reference to any other instrument, any charge to the benefit of which the debenture-holders of that series are entitled *pari passu*, is created by an LLP, it is sufficient for purposes of section 878 if the required particulars, together with a copy of the deed containing the charge (or, if there is no such deed, of one of the debentures of the series) are delivered to the registrar before the end of the period allowed for registration.

(2) The following are the required particulars—
(a) the total amount secured by the whole series,
(b) the dates of the determinations of the LLP authorising the issue of the series and the date of the covering deed (if any) by which the security is created or defined,
(c) a general description of the property charged,
(d) the names of the trustees (if any) for the debenture-holders, and

(e) in the case of a floating charge, a statement of any provisions of the charge and of any instrument relating to it which prohibit or restrict or regulate the power of the LLP to grant further securities ranking in priority to, or *pari passu* with, the floating charge, or which vary or otherwise regulate the order of ranking of the floating charge in relation to subsisting securities.

(3) Where more than one issue is made of debentures in the series, particulars of the date and amount of each issue of debentures of the series must be sent to the registrar for entry in the register of charges.

(4) Failure to comply with subsection (3) does not affect the validity of any of those debentures.

(5) Subsections (3) to (7) of section 878 apply for the purposes of this section as they apply for the purposes of that section but as if for the reference to the registration of the charge there was substituted a reference to the registration of the series of debentures.

883 Additional registration requirement for commission etc in relation to debentures

(1) Where any commission, allowance or discount has been paid or made either directly or indirectly by an LLP to a person in consideration of his—

(a) subscribing or agreeing to subscribe, whether absolutely or conditionally, for debentures in an LLP, or

(b) procuring or agreeing to procure subscriptions, whether absolute or conditional, for such debentures,

the particulars required to be sent for registration under section 878 shall include particulars as to the amount or rate per cent. of the commission, discount or allowance so paid or made.

(2) The deposit of debentures as security for a debt of the LLP is not, for the purposes of this section, treated as the issue of debentures at a discount.

(3) Failure to comply with this section does not affect the validity of the debentures issued.".

41 Charges on property outside the United Kingdom

Section 884 applies to LLPs, modified so that it reads as follows—

"884 Charges on property outside United Kingdom

Where a charge is created in the United Kingdom but comprises property outside the United Kingdom, the copy of the instrument creating or purporting to create the charge may be sent for registration under section 878 even if further proceedings may be necessary to make the charge valid or effectual according to the law of the country in which the property is situated.".

42 The register of charges

Sections 885 to 888 apply to LLPs, modified so that they read as follows—

"885 Register of charges to be kept by registrar

(1) The registrar shall keep, with respect to each LLP, a register of all the charges requiring registration under this Chapter.

(2) In the case of a charge to the benefit of which holders of a series of debentures are entitled, the registrar shall enter in the register the required particulars specified in section 882(2).

(3) In the case of any other charge, the registrar shall enter in the register the following particulars—

(a) if it is a charge created by an LLP, the date of its creation and, if it is a charge which was existing on property acquired by the LLP, the date of the acquisition,

(b) the amount secured by the charge,

(c) short particulars of the property charged,

(d) the persons entitled to the charge, and

(e) in the case of a floating charge, a statement of any of the provisions of the charge and of any instrument relating to it which prohibit or restrict or regulate the LLP's power to grant further securities ranking in priority to, or *pari passu* with, the floating charge, or which vary or otherwise regulate the order of ranking of the floating charge in relation to subsisting securities.

(4) The registrar shall give a certificate of the registration of any charge registered in pursuance of this Chapter, stating—

(a) the name of the LLP and the person first-named in the charge among those entitled to the benefit of the charge (or, in the case of a series of debentures, the name of the holder of the first such debenture issued), and

(b) the amount secured by the charge.

(5) The certificate—

(a) shall be signed by the registrar or authenticated by the registrar's official seal, and

(b) is conclusive evidence that the requirements of this Chapter as to registration have been satisfied.

(6) The register kept in pursuance of this section shall be open to inspection by any person.

886 The period allowed for registration

(1) The period allowed for registration of a charge created by an LLP is—

(a) 21 days beginning with the day after the day on which the charge is created, or

(b) if the charge is created outside the United Kingdom, 21 days beginning with the day after the day on which a copy of the instrument by which the charge is created or evidenced could, in due course of post (and if despatched with due diligence) have been received in the United Kingdom.

(2) The period allowed for registration of a charge to which property acquired by an LLP is subject is—

(a) 21 days beginning with the day after the day on which the transaction is settled, or

(b) if the property is situated and the charge was created outside the United Kingdom, 21 days beginning with the day after the day on which a copy of the instrument by which the charge is created or evidenced could, in due course of post (and if despatched with due diligence) have been received in the United Kingdom.

(3) The period allowed for registration of particulars of a series of debentures as a result of section 882 is—

(a) if there is a deed containing the charge mentioned in section 882(1), 21 days beginning with the day after the day on which that deed is executed, or

(b) if there is no such deed, 21 days beginning with the day after the day on which the first debenture of the series is executed.

887 Entries of satisfaction and relief

(1) Subsection (2) applies if a statement is delivered to the registrar verifying with respect to any registered charge—

(a) that the debt for which the charge was given has been paid or satisfied in whole or in part, or

(b) that part of the property charged has been released from the charge or has ceased to form part of the LLP's property.

(2) If the charge is a floating charge, the statement must be accompanied by either—

(a) a statement by the creditor entitled to the benefit of the charge, or a person authorised by him for the purpose, verifying that the statement mentioned in subsection (1) is correct, or

(b) a direction obtained from the court, on the ground that the statement by the creditor mentioned in paragraph (a) could not be readily obtained, dispensing with the need for that statement.

(3) The registrar may enter on the register a memorandum of satisfaction (in whole or in part) regarding the fact contained in the statement mentioned in subsection (1).

(4) Where the registrar enters a memorandum of satisfaction in whole, he shall, if required, furnish the LLP with a copy of the memorandum.

(5) Nothing in this section requires the LLP to submit particulars with respect to the entry in the register of a memorandum of satisfaction where the LLP, having created a floating charge over all or any part of its property, disposes of part of the property subject to the floating charge.

888 Rectification of register of charges

(1) Subsection (2) applies if the court is satisfied—

(a) that the failure to register a charge before the end of the period allowed for registration, or the omission or mis-statement of any particular with respect to any such charge or in a memorandum of satisfaction—

(i) was accidental or due to inadvertence or to some other sufficient cause, or

(ii) is not of a nature to prejudice the position of creditors of the LLP, or

(b) that on other grounds it is just and equitable to grant relief.

(2) The court may, on the application of the LLP or a person interested, and on such terms and conditions as seem to the court just and expedient, order that the period allowed for registration shall be extended or, as the case may be, that the omission or mis-statement shall be rectified.".

43 Avoidance of certain charges

Section 889 applies to LLPs, modified so that it reads as follows—

"889 Charges void unless registered

(1) If an LLP creates a charge to which section 878 applies, the charge is void (so far as any security on the LLP's property or any part of it is conferred by the charge) against—

(a) the liquidator of the LLP,

(b) an administrator of the LLP, and

(c) any creditor of the LLP,

unless that section is complied with.

(2) Subsection (1) is without prejudice to any contract or obligation for repayment of the money secured by the charge; and when a charge becomes void under this section the money secured by it immediately becomes payable.".

44 LLPs' records and registers

Sections 890 to 892 apply to LLPs, modified so that they read as follows—

"890 Copies of instruments creating charges to be kept by LLP

(1) Every LLP shall cause a copy of every instrument creating a charge requiring registration under this Chapter to be kept available for inspection.

(2) In the case of a series of uniform debentures, a copy of one debenture of the series is sufficient.

891 LLP's register of charges

(1) Every LLP shall keep available for inspection a register of charges and enter in it all charges specifically affecting property of the LLP, and all floating charges on any property of the LLP.

(2) There shall be given in each case a short description of the property charged, the amount of the charge and, except in the case of securities to bearer, the names of the persons entitled to it.

(3) If a member of the LLP knowingly and wilfully authorises or permits the omission of an entry required to be made in pursuance of this section, he commits an offence.

(4) A person guilty of an offence under this section is liable—

(a) on conviction on indictment, to a fine;

(b) on summary conviction, to a fine not exceeding the statutory maximum.

892 Instruments creating charges and register of charges to be available for inspection

(1) This section applies to—

(a) documents required to be kept available for inspection under section 890 (copies of instruments creating charges), and

(b) an LLP's register of charges kept in pursuance of section 891.

(2) The documents and register must be kept available for inspection—

(a) at the LLP's registered office, or

(b) at a place specified in Part 2 of the Companies (Company Records) Regulations 2008 (SI 2008/3006).

(3) The LLP must give notice to the registrar—

(a) of the place at which the documents and register are kept available for inspection, and

(b) of any change in that place,

unless they have at all times been kept at the LLP's registered office.

(4) The documents and register shall be open to the inspection—

(a) of any creditor or member of the LLP without charge, and

(b) of any other person on payment of the fee prescribed by regulation 2(d) of the Companies (Fees for Inspection of Company Records) Regulations (SI 2008/3007).

(5) If default is made for 14 days in complying with subsection (3) or an inspection required under subsection (4) is refused, an offence is committed by—

(a) the LLP, and

(b) every member of the LLP who is in default.

(6) A person guilty of an offence under this section is liable on summary conviction to a fine not exceeding level 3 on the standard scale and, for continued contravention, a daily default fine not exceeding one-tenth of level 3 on the standard scale.

(7) If an inspection required under subsection (4) is refused the court may by order compel an immediate inspection.".

PART 10 ARRANGEMENTS, RECONSTRUCTIONS AND CROSS-BORDER MERGERS

[10.369]

45 Arrangements and reconstructions[: general]

(1) Sections 895 to 900 apply to LLPs, modified so that they read as follows—

"895 Application of this Part

The provisions of this Part apply where a compromise or arrangement is proposed between an LLP and—

(a) its creditors, or any class of them, or

(b) its members, or any class of them.

896 Court order for holding of meeting

(1) The court may, on an application under this section, order a meeting of the creditors or class of creditors, or of the members of the LLP or class of members (as the case may be), to be summoned in such manner as the court directs.

(2) An application under this section may be made by—

(a) the LLP,

(b) any creditor or member of the LLP,

(c) if the LLP is being wound up, the liquidator, or

(d) if the LLP is in administration, the administrator.

[(4) This section is subject to section 899A (moratorium debts, etc).]

897 Statement to be circulated or made available

(1) Where a meeting is summoned under section 896—

(a) every notice summoning the meeting that is sent to a creditor or member must be accompanied by a statement complying with this section, and

(b) every notice summoning the meeting that is given by advertisement must either—

(i) include such a statement, or

(ii) state where and how creditors or members entitled to attend the meeting may obtain copies of such a statement.

(2) The statement must—

(a) explain the effect of the compromise or arrangement, and

(b) in particular, state—

(i) any material interests of the members of the LLP (whether as members or as creditors of the LLP or otherwise), and

(ii) the effect on those interests of the compromise or arrangement, in so far as it is different from the effect on the like interests of other persons.

(3) Where the compromise or arrangement affects the rights of debenture holders of the LLP, the statement must give the like explanation as respects the trustees of any deed for securing the issue of the debentures as it is required to give as respects the LLP's members.

(4) Where a notice given by advertisement states that copies of an explanatory statement can be obtained by creditors or members entitled to attend the meeting, every such creditor or member is entitled, on making application in the manner indicated by the notice, to be provided by the LLP with a copy of the statement free of charge.

(5) If an LLP makes default in complying with any requirement of this section, an offence is committed by—

(a) the LLP, and

(b) every member of the LLP who is in default.

This is subject to subsection (7) below.

(6) For this purpose the following are treated as members of the LLP—

(a) a liquidator or administrator of the LLP, and

(b) a trustee of a deed for securing the issue of debentures of the LLP.

(7) A person is not guilty of an offence under this section if he shows that the default was due to the refusal of a member or trustee for debenture holders to supply the necessary particulars of his interests.

(8) A person guilty of an offence under this section is liable—

(a) on conviction on indictment, to a fine;

(b) on summary conviction, to a fine not exceeding the statutory maximum.

898 Duty of members and trustees to provide information

(1) It is the duty of—

(a) any member of the LLP, and

(b) any trustee for its debenture holders,

to give notice to the LLP of such matters relating to himself as may be necessary for the purposes of section 897 (explanatory statement to be circulated or made available).

(2) Any person who makes default in complying with this section commits an offence.

(3) A person guilty of an offence under this section is liable on summary conviction to a fine not exceeding level 3 on the standard scale.

899 Court sanction for compromise or arrangement

(1) If a majority in number representing 75% in value of the creditors or class of creditors or members or class of members (as the case may be), present and voting either in person or by proxy at the meeting summoned under section 896, agree a compromise or arrangement, the court may, on an application under this section, sanction the compromise or arrangement.

[(1A) Subsection (1) is subject to section 899A (moratorium debts, etc).]

(2) An application under this section may be made by—

(a) the LLP,

(b) any creditor or member of the LLP,

(c) if the LLP is being wound up, the liquidator, or

(d) if the LLP is in administration, the administrator.

(3) A compromise or agreement sanctioned by the court is binding on—

(a) all creditors or the class of creditors or on the members or class of members (as the case may be), and

(b) the LLP or, in the case of an LLP in the course of being wound up, the liquidator and contributories of the LLP.

(4) The court's order has no effect until a copy of it has been delivered to the registrar.

[899A Moratorium debts, etc

(1) This section applies where—

(a) an application under section 896 in respect of a compromise or arrangement is made before the end of the period of 12 weeks beginning with the day after the end of any moratorium for the LLP under Part A1 of the Insolvency Act 1986 or Part 1A of the Insolvency (Northern Ireland) Order 1989 (SI 1989/2405 (NI 19)), and

(b) the creditors with whom the compromise or arrangement is proposed include any relevant creditors (see subsection (2)).

(2) In this section "relevant creditor" means—

(a) a creditor in respect of a moratorium debt, or

(b) a creditor in respect of a priority pre-moratorium debt.

(3) The relevant creditors may not participate in the meeting summoned under section 896.

(4) For the purposes of section 897 (statement to be circulated or made available)—

(a) the requirement in section 897(1)(a) is to be read as including a requirement to send each relevant creditor a statement complying with section 897;

(b) any reference to creditors entitled to attend the meeting summoned under section 896 includes a reference to relevant creditors.

(5) The court may not sanction the compromise or arrangement under section 899 if it includes provision in respect of any relevant creditor who has not agreed to it.

(6) In this section—

"moratorium debt"—

(a) in the case of a moratorium under Part A1 of the Insolvency Act 1986, has the same meaning as in section 174A of that Act;

(b) in the case of a moratorium under Part 1A of the Insolvency (Northern Ireland) Order 1989, has the same meaning as in Article 148A of that Order;

"priority pre-moratorium debt"—

(a) in the case of a moratorium under Part A1 of the Insolvency Act 1986, has the same meaning as in section 174A of that Act;

(b) in the case of a moratorium under Part 1A of the Insolvency (Northern Ireland) Order 1989, has the same meaning as in Article 148A of that Order.]

900 Powers of court to facilitate reconstruction or amalgamation

(1) This section applies where application is made to the court under section 899 to sanction a compromise or arrangement and it is shown that—

(a) the compromise or arrangement is proposed for the purposes of, or in connection with, a scheme for the reconstruction of any LLP or LLPs, or the amalgamation of any two or more relevant bodies corporate (where one or more of them is an LLP), and

(b) under the scheme the whole or any part of the undertaking or the property of any LLP concerned in the scheme ("a transferor LLP") is to be transferred to another relevant body corporate ("the transferee body corporate").

(2) The court may, either by the order sanctioning the compromise or arrangement or by a subsequent order, make provision for all or any of the following matters—

(a) the transfer to the transferee body corporate of the whole or any part of the undertaking and of the property or liabilities of any transferor LLP;

(b) the allotting or appropriation by the transferee body corporate of any shares, debentures, policies or other like interests in that body corporate which under the compromise or arrangement are to be allotted or appropriated by that body corporate to or for any person;

(c) the continuation by or against the transferee body corporate of any legal proceedings pending by or against any transferor LLP;

(d) the dissolution, without winding up, of any transferor LLP;

(e) the provision to be made for any persons who, within such time and in such manner as the court directs, dissent from the compromise or arrangement;

(f) such incidental, consequential and supplemental matters as are necessary to secure that the reconstruction or amalgamation is fully and effectively carried out.

(3) If an order under this section provides for the transfer of property or liabilities—

(a) the property is by virtue of the order transferred to, and vests in, the transferee body corporate, and

(b) the liabilities are, by virtue of the order, transferred to and become liabilities of that body corporate.

(4) The property (if the order so directs) vests freed from any charge that is by virtue of the compromise or arrangement to cease to have effect.

(5) In this section—

"relevant body corporate" means an LLP or a company;

"property" includes property, rights and powers of every description; and "liabilities" includes duties.

(6) Every body corporate in relation to which an order is made under this section must cause a copy of the order to be delivered to the registrar within seven days after its making.

(7) If default is made in complying with subsection (6) an offence is committed by—

(a) the LLP, and every member of the LLP who is in default, and

(b) the company, and every officer of the company who is in default.

(8) A person guilty of an offence under subsection (7) is liable on summary conviction to a fine not exceeding level 3 on the standard scale and, for continued contravention, a daily default fine not exceeding one-tenth of level 3 on the standard scale.".

(2) Section 323 of the Companies Act 2006 (representation of corporations at meetings) applies to a meeting of creditors of the LLP under section 896 . . . of that Act.

NOTES

The words in square brackets in the regulation heading, and the entries relating to s 896(4), 899(1A) and 899A in para (1), were inserted, and the words omitted from para (2) were revoked, by the Limited Liability Partnerships (Amendment etc) Regulations 2021, SI 2021/60, reg 5, Sch 3, paras 1, 2, as from 16 February 2021. Note that this amendment is identical to an earlier amendment made by the Limited Liability Partnerships (Amendment etc) Regulations 2020, SI 2020/643 which applied from 26 June 2020 (the 2020 Regulations were revoked by the 2021 Regulations as from 16 February 2021). Note also, with regard to the entry relating to s 896 that, although the Companies Act 2006, s 896 does contain a sub-s (3), this entry has not been amended to include that subsection.

Temporary restriction on initiating certain insolvency arrangements (rent debts): see the note relating to the Commercial Rent (Coronavirus) Act 2022, s 25 to the Companies Act 2006, s 896 at **[1.1035]**.

[10.370]

[45A Arrangements and reconstructions: LLPs in financial difficulty

Sections 901A to 901J apply to LLPs, modified so that they read as follows—

"901A Application of this Part

(1) The provisions of this Part apply where conditions A and B are met in relation to an LLP.

(2) Condition A is that the LLP has encountered, or is likely to encounter, financial difficulties that are affecting, or will or may affect, its ability to carry on business as a going concern.

(3) Condition B is that—

(a) a compromise or arrangement is proposed between the LLP and—

(i) its creditors, or any class of them, or

(ii) its members, or any class of them, and

(b) the purpose of the compromise or arrangement is to eliminate, reduce or prevent, or mitigate the effect of, any of the financial difficulties mentioned in subsection (2).

901B Power to exclude LLPs providing financial services, etc

(1) The Secretary of State may by regulations provide that this Part does not apply—

(a) where the LLP in respect of which a compromise or arrangement is proposed is an authorised person, or an authorised person of a specified description;

(b) where—

(i) a compromise or arrangement is proposed between an LLP, or an LLP of a specified description, and any creditors of the LLP, and

(ii) those creditors consist of or include creditors of a specified description.

(2) In this section—

"authorised person" has the same meaning as in the Financial Services and Markets Act 2000 (see section 31 of that Act);

"specified" means specified in the regulations.

(3) Regulations under this section are subject to affirmative resolution procedure.

901C Court order for holding of meeting

(1) The court may, on an application under this subsection, order a meeting of the creditors or class of creditors, or of the members of the LLP or class of members (as the case may be), to be summoned in such manner as the court directs.

(2) An application under subsection (1) may be made by—

(a) the LLP,

(b) any creditor or member of the LLP,

(c) if the LLP is being wound up, the liquidator, or

(d) if the LLP is in administration, the administrator.

(3) Every creditor or member of the LLP whose rights are affected by the compromise or arrangement must be permitted to participate in a meeting ordered to be summoned under subsection (1).

(4) But subsection (3) does not apply in relation to a class of creditors or members of the LLP if, on an application under this subsection, the court is satisfied that none of the members of that class has a genuine economic interest in the LLP.

(5) An application under subsection (4) is to be made by the person who made the application under subsection (1) in respect of the compromise or arrangement.

(6) If a corporation (whether or not a company under the meaning of this Act) is a creditor, it may by resolution of its directors or other governing body authorise a person or persons to act as its representative or representatives at any meeting ordered to be summoned under subsection (1).

(7) A person authorised by a corporation is entitled to exercise (on behalf of the corporation) the same powers as the corporation could exercise if it were an individual creditor.

(8) Where a corporation authorises more than one person, subsection (7) is subject to subsections (9) and (10).

(9) On a vote on a resolution on a show of hands at a meeting ordered to be summoned under subsection (1), each authorised person has the same voting rights as the corporation would be entitled to.

(10) Where subsection (9) does not apply and more than one authorised person purport to exercise a power under subsection (7) in respect of the same shares—

- (a) if they purport to exercise the power in the same way as each other, the power is treated as exercised in that way;
- (b) if they do not purport to exercise the power in the same way as each other, the power is treated as not exercised.

(11) This section is subject to section 901H (moratorium debts, etc).

901D Statement to be circulated or made available

(1) Where a meeting is summoned under section 901C—

- (a) every notice summoning the meeting that is sent to a creditor or member must be accompanied by a statement complying with this section, and
- (b) every notice summoning the meeting that is given by advertisement must either—
  - (i) include such a statement, or
  - (ii) state where and how creditors or members entitled to attend the meeting may obtain copies of such a statement.

(2) The statement must—

- (a) explain the effect of the compromise or arrangement, and
- (b) in particular, state—
  - (i) any material interests of the members of the LLP (whether as members or as creditors of the LLP or otherwise), and
  - (ii) the effect on those interests of the compromise or arrangement, in so far as it is different from the effect on the like interests of other persons.

(3) Where the compromise or arrangement affects the rights of debenture holders of the LLP, the statement must give the like explanation as respects the trustees of any deed for securing the issue of the debentures as it is required to give as respects the LLP's members.

(4) Where a notice given by advertisement states that copies of an explanatory statement can be obtained by creditors or members entitled to attend the meeting, every such creditor or member is entitled, on making application in the manner indicated by the notice, to be provided by the LLP with a copy of the statement free of charge.

(5) If an LLP makes default in complying with any requirement of this section, an offence is committed by—

- (a) the LLP, and
- (b) every member of the LLP who is in default.

This is subject to subsection (7).

(6) For this purpose the following are treated as members of the LLP—

- (a) a liquidator or administrator of the LLP, and
- (b) a trustee of a deed for securing the issue of debentures of the LLP.

(7) A person is not guilty of an offence under this section if the person shows that the default was due to the refusal of a member or trustee for debenture holders to supply the necessary particulars of the member's or (as the case may be) the trustee's interests.

(8) A person guilty of an offence under this section is liable—

- (a) on conviction on indictment, to a fine;
- (b) on summary conviction in England and Wales, to a fine;
- (c) on summary conviction in Scotland or Northern Ireland, to a fine not exceeding the statutory maximum.

901E Duty of members and trustees to provide information

(1) It is the duty of—

- (a) any member of the LLP, and
- (b) any trustee for its debenture holders,

to give notice to the LLP of such matters relating to that member or trustee as may be necessary for the purposes of section 901D (explanatory statement to be circulated or made available).

(2) Any person who makes default in complying with this section commits an offence.

(3) A person guilty of an offence under this section is liable on summary conviction to a fine not exceeding level 3 on the standard scale.

901F Court sanction for compromise or arrangement

(1) If a number representing 75% in value of the creditors or class of creditors or members or class of members (as the case may be), present and voting either in person or by proxy at the meeting summoned under section 901C, agree a compromise or arrangement, the court may, on an application under this section, sanction the compromise or arrangement.

(2) Subsection (1) is subject to—

- (a) section 901G (sanction for compromise or arrangement where one or more classes dissent), and
- (b) section 901H (moratorium debts, etc).

(3) An application under this section may be made by—

- (a) the LLP,
- (b) any creditor or member of the LLP,
- (c) if the LLP is being wound up, the liquidator, or
- (d) if the LLP is in administration, the administrator.

(4) Where the court makes an order under this section in relation to an LLP that is in administration or is being wound up, the court may by the order—

- (a) provide for the appointment of the administrator or liquidator to cease to have effect;

Part 10 Miscellaneous other SIs

(b) stay or sist all proceedings in the administration or the winding up;
(c) impose any requirements with respect to the conduct of the administration or the winding up which the court thinks appropriate for facilitating the compromise or arrangement.

(5) A compromise or arrangement sanctioned by the court is binding—
(a) on all creditors or the class of creditors or on the members or class of members (as the case may be), and
(b) on the LLP or, in the case of an LLP in the course of being wound up, the liquidator and contributories of the LLP.

(6) The court's order has no effect until a copy of it has been delivered to the registrar.

901G Sanction for compromise or arrangement where one or more classes dissent

(1) This section applies if the compromise or arrangement is not agreed by a number representing at least 75% in value of a class of creditors or (as the case may be) of members of the LLP ("the dissenting class"), present and voting either in person or by proxy at the meeting summoned under section 901C.

(2) If conditions A and B are met, the fact that the dissenting class has not agreed the compromise or arrangement does not prevent the court from sanctioning it under section 901F.

(3) Condition A is that the court is satisfied that, if the compromise or arrangement were to be sanctioned under section 901F, none of the members of the dissenting class would be any worse off than they would be in the event of the relevant alternative (see subsection (4)).

(4) For the purposes of this section "the relevant alternative" is whatever the court considers would be most likely to occur in relation to the LLP if the compromise or arrangement were not sanctioned under section 901F.

(5) Condition B is that the compromise or arrangement has been agreed by a number representing 75% in value of a class of creditors or (as the case may be) of members, present and voting either in person or by proxy at the meeting summoned under section 901C, who would receive a payment, or have a genuine economic interest in the LLP, in the event of the relevant alternative.

(6) The Secretary of State may by regulations amend this section for the purpose of—
(a) adding to the conditions that must be met for the purposes of this section;
(b) removing or varying any of those conditions.

(7) Regulations under subsection (6) are subject to affirmative resolution procedure.

901H Moratorium debts, etc

(1) This section applies where—
(a) an application under section 901C(1) in respect of a compromise or arrangement is made before the end of the period of 12 weeks beginning with the day after the end of any moratorium for the LLP under Part A1 of the Insolvency Act 1986 or Part 1A of the Insolvency (Northern Ireland) Order 1989 (SI 1989/2405 (NI 19)), and
(b) the creditors with whom the compromise or arrangement is proposed include any relevant creditors (see subsection (2)).

(2) In this section "relevant creditor" means—
(a) a creditor in respect of a moratorium debt, or
(b) a creditor in respect of a priority pre-moratorium debt.

(3) The relevant creditors may not participate in the meeting summoned under section 901C.

(4) For the purposes of section 901D (statement to be circulated or made available)—
(a) the requirement in section 901D(1)(a) is to be read as including a requirement to send each relevant creditor a statement complying with section 901D;
(b) any reference to creditors entitled to attend the meeting summoned under section 901C includes a reference to relevant creditors.

(5) The court may not sanction the compromise or arrangement under section 901F if it includes provision in respect of any relevant creditor who has not agreed to it.

(6) In this section—

"moratorium debt"—
(a) in the case of a moratorium under Part A1 of the Insolvency Act 1986, has the same meaning as in section 174A of that Act;
(b) in the case of a moratorium under Part 1A of the Insolvency (Northern Ireland) Order 1989, has the same meaning as in Article 148A of that Order;

"priority pre-moratorium debt"—
(a) in the case of a moratorium under Part A1 of the Insolvency Act 1986, has the same meaning as in section 174A of that Act;
(b) in the case of a moratorium under Part 1A of the Insolvency (Northern Ireland) Order 1989, has the same meaning as in Article 148A of that Order.

901I Pension schemes

(1) In a case where the LLP in respect of which a compromise or arrangement is proposed is or has been an employer in respect of an occupational pension scheme that is not a money purchase scheme, any notice or other document required to be sent to a creditor of the LLP must also be sent to the Pensions Regulator.

(2) In a case where the LLP in respect of which a compromise or arrangement is proposed is an employer in respect of an eligible scheme, any notice or other document required to be sent to a creditor of the LLP must also be sent to the Board of the Pension Protection Fund ("the Board").

(3) The Secretary of State may by regulations provide that, in a case where—
(a) the LLP in respect of which a compromise or arrangement is proposed is an employer in respect of an eligible scheme, and
(b) the trustees or managers of the scheme are a creditor of the LLP,

the Board may exercise any rights, or any rights of a specified description, that are exercisable under this Part by the trustees or managers as a creditor of the LLP.

(4) Regulations under this section may provide that the Board may exercise any such rights—

(a) to the exclusion of the trustees or managers of the scheme, or

(b) in addition to the exercise of those rights by the trustees or managers of the scheme.

(5) Regulations under this section—

(a) may specify conditions that must be met before the Board may exercise any such rights;

(b) may provide for any such rights to be exercisable by the Board for a specified period;

(c) may make provision in connection with any such rights ceasing to be so exercisable at the end of such a period.

(6) Regulations under this section are subject to affirmative resolution procedure (but see subsection (7)).

(7) During the period of six months beginning with the day on which this section comes into force, regulations under this section are subject to approval after being made (and subsection (6) does not apply).

(8) For the purposes of subsection (7), section 1291 has effect as if any reference in that section to a period of 28 days were to a period of 40 days.

(9) In this section—

"eligible scheme" means any pension scheme that is an eligible scheme for the purposes of section 126 of the Pensions Act 2004 or Article 110 of the Pensions (Northern Ireland) Order 2005 (SI 2005/255 (NI 1));

"employer"—

(a) in subsection (1), means an employer within the meaning of section 318(1) of the Pensions Act 2004 or Article 2(2) of the Pensions (Northern Ireland) Order 2005;

(b) in subsections (2) and (3)—

(i) in the case of a pension scheme that is an eligible scheme for the purposes of section 126 of the Pensions Act 2004, has the same meaning as it has for the purposes of Part 2 of that Act (see section 318(1) and (4) of that Act);

(ii) in the case of a pension scheme that is an eligible scheme for the purposes of Article 110 of the Pensions (Northern Ireland) Order 2005, has the same meaning as it has for the purposes of Part 3 of that Order (see Article 2(2) and (5) of that Order);

"money purchase scheme" means a pension scheme that is a money purchase scheme for the purposes of the Pension Schemes Act 1993 (see section 181(1) of that Act) or the Pension Schemes (Northern Ireland) Act 1993 (see section 176(1) of that Act);

"occupational pension scheme" and "pension scheme" have the meaning given by section 1 of the Pension Schemes Act 1993;

"specified" means specified in regulations under this section.

901J Powers of court to facilitate reconstruction or amalgamation

(1) This section applies where application is made to the court under section 901F to sanction a compromise or arrangement and it is shown that—

(a) the compromise or arrangement is proposed in connection with a scheme for the reconstruction of any LLP or LLPs, or the amalgamation of any two or more relevant bodies corporate (where one or more of them is an LLP), and

(b) under the scheme the whole or any part of the undertaking or the property of any LLP concerned in the scheme (a "transferor LLP") is to be transferred to another relevant body corporate ("the transferee body corporate").

(2) The court may, either by the order sanctioning the compromise or arrangement or by a subsequent order, make provision for all or any of the following matters—

(a) the transfer to the transferee body corporate of the whole or any part of the undertaking and of the property or liabilities of any transferor LLP;

(b) the allotting or appropriation by the transferee body corporate of any shares, debentures, policies or other like interests in that body corporate which under the compromise or arrangement are to be allotted or appropriated by that body corporate to or for any person;

(c) the continuation by or against the transferee body corporate of any legal proceedings pending by or against any transferor LLP;

(d) the dissolution, without winding up, of any transferor LLP;

(e) the provision to be made for any persons who, within such time and in such manner as the court directs, dissent from the compromise or arrangement;

(f) such incidental, consequential and supplemental matters as are necessary to secure that the reconstruction or amalgamation is fully and effectively carried out.

(3) If an order under this section provides for the transfer of property or liabilities—

(a) the property is by virtue of the order transferred to, and vests in, the transferee body corporate, and

(b) the liabilities are, by virtue of the order, transferred to and become liabilities of that body corporate.

(4) The property (if the order so directs) vests freed from any charge that is by virtue of the compromise or arrangement to cease to have effect.

(5) In this section—

"relevant body corporate" means an LLP or a company;

"property" includes property, rights and powers of every description; and

"liabilities" includes duties.

(6) Every body corporate in relation to which an order is made under this section must cause a copy of the order to be delivered to the registrar within seven days after its making.

(7) If default is made in complying with subsection (6) an offence is committed by—

(a) the LLP, and every member of the LLP who is in default, and

(b) the company, and every officer of the company who is in default.

(8) A person guilty of an offence under subsection (7) is liable on summary conviction to a fine not exceeding level 3 on the standard scale and, for continued contravention, a daily default fine not exceeding one-tenth of level 3 on the standard scale."]

NOTES

Commencement: 16 February 2021.

Inserted by the Limited Liability Partnerships (Amendment etc) Regulations 2021, SI 2021/60, reg 5, Sch 3, paras 1, 3, as from 16 February 2021 (see also the note below).

Temporary restriction on initiating certain insolvency arrangements (rent debts): see the note relating to the Commercial Rent (Coronavirus) Act 2022, s 25 to the Companies Act 2006, s 896 at **[1.1035]**.

Note that the Limited Liability Partnerships (Amendment etc) Regulations 2020, SI 2020/643 previously inserted a reg 45A, as from 26 June 2020. The 2021 Regulations replicate the provisions of the 2020 Regulations, with minor modifications (see the explanatory note to the 2021 Regulations at www.legislation.gov.uk/uksi/2021/60/pdfs/uksiem_20210060_en.pdf). Note also that the 2020 Regulations were revoked by the 2021 Regulations as from 16 February 2021.

46 (*Reg 46 (Cross-border mergers) revoked by the Companies, Limited Liability Partnerships and Partnerships (Amendment etc) (EU Exit) Regulations 2019, SI 2019/348, reg 8, Sch 3, paras 22, 25, as from IP completion day (as defined in the European Union (Withdrawal Agreement) Act 2020, s 39).*)

PART 11 FRAUDULENT TRADING

[10.371]

47 Offence of fraudulent trading

Section 993 applies to LLPs, modified so that it reads as follows—

"993 Offence of fraudulent trading

(1) If any business of an LLP is carried on with intent to defraud creditors of the LLP or creditors of any other person, or for any fraudulent purpose, every person who is knowingly a party to the carrying on of the business in that manner commits an offence.

(2) This applies whether or not the LLP has been, or is in the course of being, wound up.

(3) A person guilty of an offence under this section is liable—

(a) on conviction on indictment, to imprisonment for a term not exceeding ten years or a fine (or both);

(b) on summary conviction—

(i) in England and Wales or Scotland, to imprisonment for a term not exceeding twelve months or a fine not exceeding the statutory maximum (or both);

(ii) in Northern Ireland, to imprisonment for a term not exceeding six months or a fine not exceeding the statutory maximum (or both).".

PART 12 PROTECTION OF MEMBERS AGAINST UNFAIR PREJUDICE

[10.372]

48 Main provisions

Sections 994 to 996 apply to LLPs, modified so that they read as follows—

"994 Petition by LLP member

(1) A member of an LLP may apply to the court by petition for an order under this Part on the ground—

(a) that the LLP's affairs are being or have been conducted in a manner that is unfairly prejudicial to the interests of members generally or of some part of its members (including at least himself), or

(b) that an actual or proposed act or omission of the LLP (including an act or omission on its behalf) is or would be so prejudicial.

(2) For the purposes of subsection (1)(a), a removal of the LLP's auditor from office—

(a) on grounds of divergence of opinions on accounting treatments or audit procedures, or

(b) on any other improper grounds,

shall be treated as being unfairly prejudicial to the interests of some part of the LLP's members.

(3) The members of an LLP may by unanimous agreement exclude the right contained in subsection (1) either indefinitely or for such period as is specified in the agreement. The agreement must be recorded in writing.

995 Petition by Secretary of State

(1) This section applies to an LLP in respect of which—

(a) the Secretary of State has received a report under section 437 of the Companies Act 1985 (c 6) (inspector's report);

(b) the Secretary of State has exercised his powers under section 447 or 448 of that Act (powers to require documents and information or to enter and search premises);

(c) [the Secretary of State, the Bank of England, the Financial Conduct Authority or the Prudential Regulation Authority] has exercised his or its powers under Part 11 of the Financial Services and Markets Act 2000 (c 8) (information gathering and investigations); or

(d) the Secretary of State has received a report from an investigator [appointed by the Secretary of State, the Bank of England, the Financial Conduct Authority or the Prudential Regulation Authority] under that Part.

(2) If it appears to the Secretary of State that in the case of such an LLP—

(a) the LLP's affairs are being or have been conducted in a manner that is unfairly prejudicial to the interests of members generally or of some part of its members, or

(b) an actual or proposed act or omission of the LLP (including an act or omission on its behalf) is or would be so prejudicial,

he may apply to the court by petition for an order under this Part.

(3) The Secretary of State may do this in addition to, or instead of, presenting a petition for the winding up of the LLP.

996 Powers of the court under this Part

(1) If the court is satisfied that a petition under this Part is well founded, it may make such order as it thinks fit for giving relief in respect of the matters complained of.

(2) Without prejudice to the generality of subsection (1), the court's order may—

(a) regulate the conduct of the LLP's affairs in the future;

(b) require the LLP—

(i) to refrain from doing or continuing an act complained of, or

(ii) to do an act that the petitioner has complained it has omitted to do;

(c) authorise civil proceedings to be brought in the name and on behalf of the LLP by such person or persons and on such terms as the court may direct;

(d) require the LLP or the members of the LLP not to make any, or any specified, alterations in the LLP agreement without the leave of the court;

(e) provide for the purchase of the rights and interests of any members in the LLP by other members or by the LLP itself.".

NOTES

Words in square brackets in s 995(1)(c), (d) as set out above substituted by the Financial Services Act 2012 (Consequential Amendments and Transitional Provisions) Order 2013, SI 2013/472, art 3, Sch 2, para 174, as from 1 April 2013.

[10.373]

49 Supplementary provision

Section 997 applies to LLPs as follows—

"997 Application of general rule-making powers

The power to make rules under section 411 of the Insolvency Act 1986 (c 45) or Article 359 of the Insolvency (Northern Ireland) Order 1989 (SI 1989/2405 (NI 19)), so far as relating to a winding-up petition, applies for the purposes of a petition under this Part.".

PART 13 DISSOLUTION AND RESTORATION TO THE REGISTER

CHAPTER 1 STRIKING OFF

[10.374]

50 Registrar's power to strike off defunct LLP

Sections 1000 to 1002 apply to LLPs, modified so that they read as follows—

"1000 Power to strike off LLP not carrying on business or in operation

(1) If the registrar has reasonable cause to believe that an LLP is not carrying on business or in operation, the registrar may send to the LLP [a communication] inquiring whether the LLP is carrying on business or in operation.

(2) If the registrar does not within [14 days of sending] [the communication] receive any answer to it, the registrar must within 14 days after the expiration of [that period] send to the LLP [a second communication referring to the first communication], and stating—

(a) that no answer to it has been received, and

(b) that if an answer is not received to the second [communication] within [14 days] from its date, a notice will be published in the Gazette with a view to striking the LLP's name off the register.

(3) If the registrar—

(a) receives an answer to the effect that the LLP is not carrying on business or in operation, or

(b) does not within [14 days] after sending the second [communication] receive any answer,

the registrar may publish in the Gazette, and send to the LLP . . . , a notice that at the expiration of [2 months] from the date of the notice the name of the LLP mentioned in it will, unless cause is shown to the contrary, be struck off the register and the LLP will be dissolved.

(4) At the expiration of the time mentioned in the notice the registrar may, unless cause to the contrary is previously shown by the LLP, strike its name off the register.

(5) The registrar must publish notice in the Gazette of the LLP's name having been struck off the register.

(6) On the publication of the notice in the Gazette the LLP is dissolved.

(7) However—

(a) the liability (if any) of every member of the LLP continues and may be enforced as if the LLP had not been dissolved, and

(b) nothing in this section affects the power of the court to wind up an LLP the name of which has been struck off the register.

1001 Duty to act in case of LLP being wound up

(1) If, in a case where an LLP is being wound up—

(a) the registrar has reasonable cause to believe—

(i) that no liquidator is acting, or

(ii) that the affairs of the LLP are fully wound up, and

(b) the returns required to be made by the liquidator have not been made for a period of six consecutive months,

the registrar must publish in the Gazette and send to the LLP or the liquidator (if any) a notice that at the expiration of [2 months] from the date of the notice the name of the LLP mentioned in it will, unless cause is shown to the contrary, be struck off the register and the LLP will be dissolved.

(2) At the expiration of the time mentioned in the notice the registrar may, unless cause to the contrary is previously shown by the LLP, strike its name off the register.

(3) The registrar must publish notice in the Gazette of the LLP's name having been struck off the register.

(4) On the publication of the notice in the Gazette the LLP is dissolved.

(5) However—

(a) the liability (if any) of every member of the LLP continues and may be enforced as if the LLP had not been dissolved, and

(b) nothing in this section affects the power of the court to wind up an LLP the name of which has been struck off the register.

1002 Supplementary provisions as to service of [communication] or notice

[(1) If the registrar is not able to send a communication or notice under section 1000 or 1001 to an LLP, the communication may be sent to a member of the LLP at an address for that member that has been notified to the registrar by the LLP.]

(2) If there is no member of the LLP whose name and address are known to the registrar, the [communication] or notice may be sent to each of the persons who subscribed the incorporation document (if their addresses are known to the registrar).

[(3) A notice to be sent to a liquidator under section 1001 may be sent to the address of the liquidator's last known place of business or to an address specified by the liquidator to the registrar for the purpose of receiving notices, or notices of that kind.

[(4) In this section "address" includes a number or address used for the purposes of sending or receiving documents or information by electronic means.

(5) For the purposes of subsection (4) a document or information is sent or received by electronic means if it is—

(a) sent initially and received at its destination by means of electronic equipment for the processing (which expression includes digital compression) or storage of data, and

(b) entirely transmitted, conveyed and received by wire, by radio, by optical means or by other electromagnetic means.

References to electronic means have a corresponding meaning.]".

NOTES

In s 1000 as set out above, the words in square brackets were substituted by the Companies and Limited Liability Partnerships (Filing Requirements) Regulations 2015, SI 2015/1695, regs 4, 5(1), (2), as from 10 October 2015. Note that these amendments do not apply in cases where the communication mentioned in s 1000(1) above has already been sent before 10 October 2015.

The other words in square brackets in s 1000 as set out above were substituted, and the words omitted from sub-s (3) were revoked, by the Companies (Striking Off) (Electronic Communications) Order 2014, SI 2014/1602, art 3(1), (2), as from 11 July 2014.

In s 1001 as set out above, the words in square brackets were substituted by SI 2015/1695, regs 4, 5(1), (3), as from 10 October 2015. Note that this amendment does not apply in cases where the notice mentioned in s 1001(1) above has already been published in the Gazette before 10 October 2015.

In s 1002 as set out above, the words in square brackets in the section heading and in sub-s (2) were substituted, sub-ss (1) and (3) were substituted, and sub-ss (4), (5) were added, by SI 2014/1602, art 3(1), (3), as from 11 July 2014.

[10.375]

51 Voluntary striking off

Sections 1003 to 1011 apply to LLPs, modified so that they read as follows—

"1003 Striking off on application by LLP

(1) The registrar of companies may strike the LLP's name off the register on application by—

(a) a majority of the members of an LLP, or

(b) if there are only two such members, by both of them, or

(c) if there is only one remaining member of an LLP, by that member.

(2) The application must contain a declaration by the member or members making the application that neither section 1004 nor 1005 prevents the application from being made.

(3) The registrar may not strike an LLP off under this section until after the expiration of [2 months] from the publication by the registrar in the Gazette of a notice—

(a) stating that the registrar may exercise the power under this section in relation to the LLP, and

(b) inviting any person to show cause why that should not be done.

(4) The registrar must publish notice in the Gazette of the LLP's name having been struck off.

(5) On the publication of the notice in the Gazette the LLP is dissolved.

(6) However—

(a) the liability (if any) of every member of the LLP continues and may be enforced as if the LLP had not been dissolved, and

(b) nothing in this section affects the power of the court to wind up an LLP the name of which has been struck off the register.

1004 Circumstances in which application not to be made: activities of LLP

(1) An application under section 1003 (application for voluntary striking off) on behalf of an LLP must not be made if, at any time in the previous three months, the LLP has—

(a) changed its name,

(b) traded or otherwise carried on business,

(c) made a disposal for value of property or rights that, immediately before ceasing to trade or otherwise carry on business, it held for the purpose of disposal for gain in the normal course of trading or otherwise carrying on business, or

(d) engaged in any other activity, except one which is—
(i) necessary or expedient for the purpose of making an application under that section, or deciding whether to do so,
(ii) necessary or expedient for the purpose of concluding the affairs of the LLP, or
(iii) necessary or expedient for the purpose of complying with any statutory requirement.

(2) For the purposes of this section, an LLP is not to be treated as trading or otherwise carrying on business by virtue only of the fact that it makes a payment in respect of a liability incurred in the course of trading or otherwise carrying on business.

(3) It is an offence for a person to make an application in contravention of this section.

(4) In proceedings for such an offence it is a defence for the accused to prove that he did not know, and could not reasonably have known, of the existence of the facts that led to the contravention.

(5) A person guilty of an offence under this section is liable—
(a) on conviction on indictment, to a fine;
(b) on summary conviction, to a fine not exceeding the statutory maximum.

1005 Circumstances in which application not to be made: proceedings pending

(1) An application under section 1003 (application for voluntary striking off) on behalf of an LLP must not be made at a time when—
(a) an application to the court under Part 26 [or 26A] has been made on behalf of the LLP for the sanctioning of a compromise or arrangement and the matter has not been finally concluded;
(b) a voluntary arrangement in relation to the LLP has been proposed under Part 1 of the Insolvency Act 1986 (c 45) or Part 2 of the Insolvency (Northern Ireland) Order 1989 (SI 1989/2405 (NI 19)) and the matter has not been finally concluded;
(c) the LLP is in administration under Part 2 of that Act or Part 3 of that Order;
(d) paragraph 44 of Schedule B1 to that Act or paragraph 45 of Schedule B1 to that Order applies (interim moratorium on proceedings where application to the court for an administration order has been made or notice of intention to appoint administrator has been filed);
(e) the LLP is being wound up under Part 4 of that Act or Part 5 of that Order, whether voluntarily or by the court, or a petition under that Part for winding up of the LLP by the court has been presented and not finally dealt with or withdrawn;
(f) there is a receiver or manager of the LLP's property;
(g) the LLP's estate is being administered by a judicial factor.

(2) For the purposes of subsection (1)(a), the matter is finally concluded if—
(a) the application has been withdrawn,
(b) the application has been finally dealt with without a compromise or arrangement being sanctioned by the court, or
(c) a compromise or arrangement has been sanctioned by the court and has, together with anything required to be done under any provision made in relation to the matter by order of the court, been fully carried out.

(3) For the purposes of subsection (1)(b), the matter is finally concluded if—
(a) no meeting is to be summoned under section 3 of the Insolvency Act 1986 (c 45) or Article 16 of the Insolvency (Northern Ireland) Order 1989,
(b) the meeting summoned under that section or Article fails to approve the arrangement with no, or the same, modifications,
(c) an arrangement approved by a meeting summoned under that section, or in consequence of a direction under section 6(4)(b) of that Act or Article 19(4)(b) of that Order, has been fully implemented, or
(d) the court makes an order under section 6(5) of that Act or Article 19(5) of that Order revoking approval given at a previous meeting and, if the court gives any directions under section 6(6) of that Act or Article 19(6) of that Order, the LLP has done whatever it is required to do under those directions.

(4) It is an offence for a person to make an application in contravention of this section.

(5) In proceedings for such an offence it is a defence for the accused to prove that he did not know, and could not reasonably have known, of the existence of the facts that led to the contravention.

(6) A person guilty of an offence under this section is liable—
(a) on conviction on indictment, to a fine;
(b) on summary conviction, to a fine not exceeding the statutory maximum.

1006 Copy of application to be given to members, employees etc

(1) A person who makes an application under section 1003 (application for voluntary striking off) on behalf of an LLP must secure that, within seven days from the day on which the application is made, a copy of it is given to every person who at any time on that day is—
(a) a member of the LLP,
(b) an employee of the LLP,
(c) a creditor of the LLP, or
(d) a manager or trustee of any pension fund established for the benefit of employees of the LLP.

(2) Subsection (1) does not require a copy of the application to be given to a member who is a party to the application.

(3) The duty imposed by this section ceases to apply if the application is withdrawn before the end of the period for giving the copy application.

(4) A person who fails to perform the duty imposed on him by this section commits an offence. If he does so with the intention of concealing the making of the application from the person concerned, he commits an aggravated offence.

(5) In proceedings for an offence under this section it is a defence for the accused to prove that he took all reasonable steps to perform the duty.

(6) A person guilty of an offence under this section (other than an aggravated offence) is liable—

(a) on conviction on indictment, to a fine;

(b) on summary conviction, to a fine not exceeding the statutory maximum.

(7) A person guilty of an aggravated offence under this section is liable—

(a) on conviction on indictment, to imprisonment for a term not exceeding seven years or a fine (or both);

(b) on summary conviction—

(i) in England and Wales or Scotland, to imprisonment for a term not exceeding twelve months or to a fine not exceeding the statutory maximum (or both);

(ii) in Northern Ireland, to imprisonment for a term not exceeding six months, or to a fine not exceeding the statutory maximum (or both).

1007 Copy of application to be given to new members, employees, etc

(1) This section applies in relation to any time after the day on which an LLP makes an application under section 1003 (application for voluntary striking off) and before the day on which the application is finally dealt with or withdrawn.

(2) A person who is a member of the LLP at the end of a day on which a person (other than himself) becomes—

(a) a member of the LLP,

(b) an employee of the LLP,

(c) a creditor of the LLP, or

(d) a manager or trustee of any pension fund established for the benefit of employees of the LLP,

must secure that a copy of the application is given to that person within seven days from that day.

(3) The duty imposed by this section ceases to apply if the application is finally dealt with or withdrawn before the end of the period for giving the copy application.

(4) A person who fails to perform the duty imposed on him by this section commits an offence.

If he does so with the intention of concealing the making of the application from the person concerned, he commits an aggravated offence.

(5) In proceedings for an offence under this section it is a defence for the accused to prove—

(a) that at the time of the failure he was not aware of the fact that the LLP had made an application under section 1003, or

(b) that he took all reasonable steps to perform the duty.

(6) A person guilty of an offence under this section (other than an aggravated offence) is liable—

(a) on conviction on indictment, to a fine;

(b) on summary conviction, to a fine not exceeding the statutory maximum.

(7) A person guilty of an aggravated offence under this section is liable—

(a) on conviction on indictment, to imprisonment for a term not exceeding seven years or a fine (or both);

(b) on summary conviction—

(i) in England and Wales or Scotland, to imprisonment for a term not exceeding twelve months or to a fine not exceeding the statutory maximum (or both);

(ii) in Northern Ireland, to imprisonment for a term not exceeding six months, or to a fine not exceeding the statutory maximum (or both).

1008 Copy of application: provisions as to service of documents

(1) The following provisions have effect for the purposes of—

section 1006 (copy of application to be given to members, employees, etc), and

section 1007 (copy of application to be given to new members, employees, etc).

(2) A document is treated as given to a person if it is—

(a) delivered to him, or

(b) left at his proper address, or

(c) sent by post to him at that address.

(3) For the purposes of subsection (2) and section 7 of the Interpretation Act 1978 (c 30) (service of documents by post) as it applies in relation to that subsection, the proper address of a person is—

(a) in the case of a firm incorporated or formed in the United Kingdom, its registered or principal office;

(b) in the case of a firm incorporated or formed outside the United Kingdom—

(i) if it has a place of business in the United Kingdom, its principal office in the United Kingdom, or

(ii) if it does not have a place of business in the United Kingdom, its registered or principal office;

(c) in the case of an individual, his last known address.

(4) In the case of a creditor of the LLP a document is treated as given to him if it is left or sent by post to him—

(a) at the place of business of his with which the LLP has had dealings by virtue of which he is a creditor of the LLP, or

(b) if there is more than one such place of business, at each of them.

1009 Circumstances in which application to be withdrawn

(1) This section applies where, at any time on or after the day on which an LLP makes an application under section 1003 (application for voluntary striking off) and before the day on which the application is finally dealt with or withdrawn—

(a) the LLP—

(i) changes its name,

(ii) trades or otherwise carries on business,

(iii) makes a disposal for value of any property or rights other than those which it was necessary or expedient for it to hold for the purpose of making, or proceeding with, an application under that section, or

(iv) engages in any activity, except one to which subsection (4) applies;

(b) an application is made to the court under Part 26 [or 26A] on behalf of the LLP for the sanctioning of a compromise or arrangement;

(c) a voluntary arrangement in relation to the LLP is proposed under Part 1 of the Insolvency Act 1986 (c 45) or Part 2 of the Insolvency (Northern Ireland) Order 1989 (SI 1989/2405 (NI 19));

(d) an application to the court for an administration order in respect of the LLP is made under paragraph 12 of Schedule B1 to that Act or paragraph 13 of Schedule B1 to that Order;

(e) an administrator is appointed in respect of the LLP under paragraph 14 or 22 of Schedule B1 to that Act or paragraph 15 or 23 of Schedule B1 to that Order, or a copy of notice of intention to appoint an administrator of the LLP under any of those provisions is filed with the court;

(f) there arise any of the circumstances in which, under section 84(1) of that Act or Article 70 of that Order, the LLP may be voluntarily wound up;

(g) a petition is presented for the winding up of the LLP by the court under Part 4 of that Act or Part 5 of that Order;

(h) a receiver or manager of the LLP's property is appointed; or

(i) a judicial factor is appointed to administer the LLP's estate.

(2) A person who, at the end of a day on which any of the events mentioned in subsection (1) occurs, is a member of the LLP must secure that the LLP's application is withdrawn forthwith.

(3) For the purposes of subsection (1)(a), an LLP is not treated as trading or otherwise carrying on business by virtue only of the fact that it makes a payment in respect of a liability incurred in the course of trading or otherwise carrying on business.

(4) The excepted activities referred to in subsection (1)(a)(iv) are any activity necessary or expedient for the purposes of—

(a) making, or proceeding with, an application under section 1003 (application for voluntary striking off),

(b) concluding affairs of the LLP that are outstanding because of what has been necessary or expedient for the purpose of making, or proceeding with, such an application, or

(c) complying with any statutory requirement.

(5) A person who fails to perform the duty imposed on him by this section commits an offence.

(6) In proceedings for an offence under this section it is a defence for the accused to prove—

(a) that at the time of the failure he was not aware of the fact that the LLP had made an application under section 1003, or

(b) that he took all reasonable steps to perform the duty.

(7) A person guilty of an offence under this section is liable—

(a) on conviction on indictment, to a fine;

(b) on summary conviction, to a fine not exceeding the statutory maximum.

1010 Withdrawal of application

An application under section 1003 is withdrawn by notice to the registrar.

1011 Meaning of "creditor"

In this Chapter "creditor" includes a contingent or prospective creditor.".

NOTES

In s 1003 as set out above, the words in square brackets were substituted by the Companies and Limited Liability Partnerships (Filing Requirements) Regulations 2015, SI 2015/1695, regs 4, 5(1), (4), as from 10 October 2015. Note that this amendment does not apply in cases where the application under s 1003(3) above has already been made before 10 October 2015.

In ss 1005 and 1009 as set out above, the words "or 26A" in square brackets were inserted by the Limited Liability Partnerships (Amendment etc) Regulations 2021, SI 2021/60, reg 5, Sch 3, paras 1, 4, as 16 February 2021. Note that this amendment is identical to an earlier amendment made by the Limited Liability Partnerships (Amendment etc) Regulations 2020, SI 2020/643 which applied from 26 June 2020 (the 2020 Regulations were revoked by the 2021 Regulations as from 16 February 2021).

CHAPTER 2 PROPERTY OF DISSOLVED LLP

[10.376]

52 Property of dissolved LLP vesting as bona vacantia

Sections 1012 to 1014 apply to LLPs, modified so that they read as follows—

"1012 Property of dissolved LLP to be bona vacantia

(1) When an LLP is dissolved, all property and rights whatsoever vested in or held on trust for the LLP immediately before its dissolution (including leasehold property, but not including property held by the LLP on trust for another person) are deemed to be *bona vacantia* and—

(a) accordingly belong to the Crown, or to the Duchy of Lancaster or to the Duke of Cornwall for the time being (as the case may be), and

(b) vest and may be dealt with in the same manner as other *bona vacantia* accruing to the Crown, to the Duchy of Lancaster or to the Duke of Cornwall.

(2) Subsection (1) has effect subject to the possible restoration of the LLP to the register under Chapter 3 (see section 1034).

1013 Crown disclaimer of property vesting as bona vacantia

(1) Where property vests in the Crown under section 1012, the Crown's title to it under that section may be disclaimed by a notice signed by the Crown representative, that is to say the Treasury Solicitor, or, in relation to property in Scotland, the Queen's and Lord Treasurer's Remembrancer.

(2) The right to execute a notice of disclaimer under this section may be waived by or on behalf of the Crown either expressly or by taking possession.

(3) A notice of disclaimer must be executed within three years after—

(a) the date on which the fact that the property may have vested in the Crown under section 1012 first comes to the notice of the Crown representative, or

(b) if ownership of the property is not established at that date, the end of the period reasonably necessary for the Crown representative to establish the ownership of the property.

(4) If an application in writing is made to the Crown representative by a person interested in the property requiring him to decide whether he will or will not disclaim, any notice of disclaimer must be executed within twelve months after the making of the application or such further period as may be allowed by the court.

(5) A notice of disclaimer under this section is of no effect if it is shown to have been executed after the end of the period specified by subsection (3) or (4).

(6) A notice of disclaimer under this section must be delivered to the registrar and retained and registered by him.

(7) Copies of it must be published in the Gazette and sent to any persons who have given the Crown representative notice that they claim to be interested in the property.

(8) This section applies to property vested in the Duchy of Lancaster or the Duke of Cornwall under section 1012 as if for references to the Crown and the Crown representative there were respectively substituted references to the Duchy of Lancaster and to the Solicitor to that Duchy, or to the Duke of Cornwall and to the Solicitor to the Duchy of Cornwall, as the case may be.

1014 Effect of Crown disclaimer

(1) Where notice of disclaimer is executed under section 1013 as respects any property, that property is deemed not to have vested in the Crown under section 1012.

(2) The following sections contain provisions as to the effect of the Crown disclaimer—

sections 1015 to 1019 apply in relation to property in England and Wales or Northern Ireland;

sections 1020 to 1022 apply in relation to property in Scotland.".

[10.377]

53 Effect of Crown disclaimer: England and Wales and Northern Ireland

Sections 1015 to 1019 apply to LLPs, modified so that they read as follows—

"1015 General effect of disclaimer

(1) The Crown's disclaimer operates so as to terminate, as from the date of the disclaimer, the rights, interests and liabilities of the LLP in or in respect of the property disclaimed.

(2) It does not, except so far as is necessary for the purpose of releasing the LLP from any liability, affect the rights or liabilities of any other person.

1016 Disclaimer of leaseholds

(1) The disclaimer of any property of a leasehold character does not take effect unless a copy of the disclaimer has been served (so far as the Crown representative is aware of their addresses) on every person claiming under the LLP as underlessee or mortgagee, and either—

(a) no application under section 1017 (power of court to make vesting order) is made with respect to that property before the end of the period of 14 days beginning with the day on which the last notice under this paragraph was served, or

(b) where such an application has been made, the court directs that the disclaimer shall take effect.

(2) Where the court gives a direction under subsection (1)(b) it may also, instead of or in addition to any order it makes under section 1017, make such order as it thinks fit with respect to fixtures, tenant's improvements and other matters arising out of the lease.

(3) In this section the "Crown representative" means—

(a) in relation to property vested in the Duchy of Lancaster, the Solicitor to that Duchy;

(b) in relation to property vested in the Duke of Cornwall, the Solicitor to the Duchy of Cornwall;

(c) in relation to property in Scotland, the Queen's and Lord Treasurer's Remembrancer;

(d) in relation to other property, the Treasury Solicitor.

1017 Power of court to make vesting order

(1) The court may on application by a person who—

(a) claims an interest in the disclaimed property, or

(b) is under a liability in respect of the disclaimed property that is not discharged by the disclaimer,

make an order under this section in respect of the property.

(2) An order under this section is an order for the vesting of the disclaimed property in, or its delivery to—

(a) a person entitled to it (or a trustee for such a person), or

(b) a person subject to such a liability as is mentioned in subsection (1)(b) (or a trustee for such a person).

(3) An order under subsection (2)(b) may only be made where it appears to the court that it would be just to do so for the purpose of compensating the person subject to the liability in respect of the disclaimer.

(4) An order under this section may be made on such terms as the court thinks fit.

(5) On a vesting order being made under this section, the property comprised in it vests in the person named in that behalf in the order without conveyance, assignment or transfer.

1018 Protection of persons holding under a lease

(1) The court must not make an order under section 1017 vesting property of a leasehold nature in a person claiming under the LLP as underlessee or mortgagee except on terms making that person—

(a) subject to the same liabilities and obligations as those to which the LLP was subject under the lease, or

(b) if the court thinks fit, subject to the same liabilities and obligations as if the lease had been assigned to him.

(2) Where the order relates to only part of the property comprised in the lease, subsection (1) applies as if the lease had comprised only the property comprised in the vesting order.

(3) A person claiming under the LLP as underlessee or mortgagee who declines to accept a vesting order on such terms is excluded from all interest in the property.

(4) If there is no person claiming under the LLP who is willing to accept an order on such terms, the court has power to vest the LLP's estate and interest in the property in any person who is liable (whether personally or in a representative character, and whether alone or jointly with the LLP) to perform the lessee's covenants in the lease.

(5) The court may vest that estate and interest in such a person freed and discharged from all estates, incumbrances and interests created by the LLP.

1019 Land subject to rentcharge

Where in consequence of the disclaimer land that is subject to rentcharge vests in any person, neither he nor his successors in title are subject to any personal liability in respect of sums becoming due under the rentcharge, except sums becoming due after he, or some person claiming under or through him, has taken possession or control of the land or has entered into occupation of it.".

[10.378]

54 Effect of Crown disclaimer: Scotland

Sections 1020 to 1022 apply to LLPs, modified so that they read as follows—

"1020 General effect of disclaimer

(1) The Crown's disclaimer operates to determine, as from the date of the disclaimer, the rights, interests and liabilities of the LLP, and the property of the LLP, in or in respect of the property disclaimed.

(2) It does not (except so far as is necessary for the purpose of releasing the LLP and its property from liability) affect the rights or liabilities of any other person.

1021 Power of court to make vesting order

(1) The court may—

(a) on application by a person who either claims an interest in disclaimed property or is under a liability not discharged by this Act in respect of disclaimed property, and

(b) on hearing such persons as it thinks fit,

make an order for the vesting of the property in or its delivery to any persons entitled to it, or to whom it may seem just that the property should be delivered by way of compensation for such liability, or a trustee for him.

(2) The order may be made on such terms as the court thinks fit.

(3) On a vesting order being made under this section, the property comprised in it vests accordingly in the person named in that behalf in the order, without conveyance or assignation for that purpose.

1022 Protection of persons holding under a lease

(1) Where the property disclaimed is held under a lease the court must not make a vesting order in favour of a person claiming under the LLP, whether—

(a) as sub-lessee, or

(b) as creditor in a duly registered or (as the case may be) recorded heritable security over a lease,

except on the following terms.

(2) The person must by the order be made subject—

(a) to the same liabilities and obligations as those to which the LLP was subject under the lease in respect of the property, or

(b) if the court thinks fit, only to the same liabilities and obligations as if the lease had been assigned to him.

In either event (if the case so requires) the liabilities and obligations must be as if the lease had comprised only the property comprised in the vesting order.

(3) A sub-lessee or creditor declining to accept a vesting order on such terms is excluded from all interest in and security over the property.

(4) If there is no person claiming under the LLP who is willing to accept an order on such terms, the court has power to vest the LLP's estate and interest in the property in any person liable (either personally or in a representative character, and either alone or jointly with the LLP) to perform the lessee's obligations under the lease.

(5) The court may vest that estate and interest in such a person freed and discharged from all interests, rights and obligations created by the LLP in the lease or in relation to the lease.

(6) For the purposes of this section a heritable security—

(a) is duly recorded if it is recorded in the Register of Sasines, and

(b) is duly registered if registered in accordance with the Land Registration (Scotland) Act 1979 (c 33).".

[10.379]

55 Supplementary provisions

Section 1023 applies to LLPs, modified so that it reads as follows—

"1023 Liability for rentcharge on LLP's land after dissolution

(1) This section applies where on the dissolution of an LLP land in England and Wales or Northern Ireland that is subject to a rentcharge vests by operation of law in the Crown or any other person ("the proprietor").

(2) Neither the proprietor nor his successors in title are subject to any personal liability in respect of sums becoming due under the rentcharge, except sums becoming due after the proprietor, or some person claiming under or through him, has taken possession or control of the land or has entered into occupation of it.".

CHAPTER 3 RESTORATION TO THE REGISTER

[10.380]

56 Administrative restoration to the register

Sections 1024 to 1028 apply to LLPs, modified so that they read as follows—

"1024 Application for administrative restoration to the register

(1) An application may be made to the registrar to restore to the register an LLP that has been struck off the register under section 1000 or 1001 (power of registrar to strike off defunct LLP).

(2) An application under this section may be made whether or not the LLP has in consequence been dissolved.

(3) An application under this section may only be made by a former member of the LLP.

(4) An application under this section may not be made after the end of the period of six years from the date of the dissolution of the LLP.

For this purpose an application is made when it is received by the registrar.

1025 Requirements for administrative restoration

(1) On an application under section 1024 the registrar shall restore the LLP to the register if, and only if, the following conditions are met.

(2) The first condition is that the LLP was carrying on business or in operation at the time of its striking off.

(3) The second condition is that, if any property or right previously vested in or held on trust for the LLP has vested as *bona vacantia*, the Crown representative has signified to the registrar in writing consent to the LLP's restoration to the register.

(4) It is the applicant's responsibility to obtain that consent and to pay any costs (in Scotland, expenses) of the Crown representative—

- (a) in dealing with the property during the period of dissolution, or
- (b) in connection with the proceedings on the application,

that may be demanded as a condition of giving consent.

(5) The third condition is that the applicant has—

- (a) delivered to the registrar such documents relating to the LLP as are necessary to bring up to date the records kept by the registrar, and
- (b) paid any penalties under section 453 or corresponding earlier provisions (civil penalty for failure to deliver accounts) that were outstanding at the date of dissolution or striking off.

(6) The fourth condition is that the applicant has sent notice of the application under section 1024 to all those who were members of the LLP at the time of its striking off.

(7) In this section the "Crown representative" means—

- (a) in relation to property vested in the Duchy of Lancaster, the Solicitor to that Duchy;
- (b) in relation to property vested in the Duke of Cornwall, the Solicitor to the Duchy of Cornwall;
- (c) in relation to property in Scotland, the Queen's and Lord Treasurer's Remembrancer;
- (d) in relation to other property, the Treasury Solicitor.

1026 Application to be accompanied by statement of compliance

(1) An application under section 1024 (application for administrative restoration to the register) must be accompanied by a statement of compliance.

(2) The statement of compliance required is a statement—

- (a) that the person making the application has standing to apply (see subsection (3) of that section), and
- (b) that the requirements for administrative restoration (see section 1025) are met.

(3) The registrar may accept the statement of compliance as sufficient evidence of those matters.

1027 Registrar's decision on application for administrative restoration

(1) The registrar must give notice to the applicant of the decision on an application under section 1024 (application for administrative restoration to the register).

(2) If the decision is that the LLP should be restored to the register, the restoration takes effect as from the date that notice is sent.

(3) In the case of such a decision, the registrar must—

- (a) enter on the register a note of the date as from which the LLP's restoration to the register takes effect, and
- (b) cause notice of the restoration to be published in the Gazette.

(4) The notice under subsection (3)(b) must state—

- (a) the name of the LLP or, if the LLP is restored to the register under a different name (see section 1033), that name and its former name,
- (b) the LLP's registered number, and
- (c) the date as from which the restoration of the LLP to the register takes effect.

1028 Effect of administrative restoration

(1) The general effect of administrative restoration to the register is that the LLP is deemed to have continued in existence as if it had not been dissolved or struck off the register.

(2) The LLP is not liable to a penalty under section 453 or any corresponding earlier provision (civil penalty for failure to deliver accounts) for a financial year in relation to which the period for filing accounts and reports ended—

(a) after the date of dissolution or striking off, and

(b) before the restoration of the LLP to the register.

(3) The court may give such directions and make such provision as seems just for placing the LLP and all other persons in the same position (as nearly as may be) as if the LLP had not been dissolved or struck off the register.

(4) An application to the court for such directions or provision may be made any time within three years after the date of restoration of the LLP to the register.".

[10.381]

57 Restoration to the register by the court

Sections 1029 to 1032 apply to LLPs, modified so that they read as follows—

"1029 Application to court for restoration to the register

(1) An application may be made to the court to restore to the register an LLP—

(a) that has been dissolved under Chapter 9 of Part 4 of the Insolvency Act 1986 (c 45) or Chapter 9 of Part 5 of the Insolvency (Northern Ireland) Order 1989 (SI 1989/2405 (NI 19)) (dissolution of LLP after winding up),

(b) that is deemed to have been dissolved under paragraph 84(6) of Schedule B1 to that Act or paragraph 85(6) of Schedule B1 to that Order (dissolution of LLP following administration), or

(c) that has been struck off the register—

(i) under section 1000 or 1001 (power of registrar to strike off defunct LLP), or

(ii) under section 1003 (voluntary striking off),

whether or not the LLP has in consequence been dissolved.

(2) An application under this section may be made by—

(a) the Secretary of State,

(b) any person having an interest in land in which the LLP had a superior or derivative interest,

(c) any person having an interest in land or other property—

(i) that was subject to rights vested in the LLP, or

(ii) that was benefited by obligations owed by the LLP,

(d) any person who but for the LLP's dissolution would have been in a contractual relationship with it,

(e) any person with a potential legal claim against the LLP,

(f) any manager or trustee of a pension fund established for the benefit of employees of the LLP,

(g) any former member of the LLP (or the personal representatives of such a person),

(h) any person who was a creditor of the LLP at the time of its striking off or dissolution,

(i) any former liquidator of the LLP,

or by any other person appearing to the court to have an interest in the matter.

1030 When application to the court may be made

(1) An application to the court for restoration of an LLP to the register may be made at any time for the purpose of bringing proceedings against the LLP for damages for personal injury.

(2) No order shall be made on such an application if it appears to the court that the proceedings would fail by virtue of any enactment as to the time within which proceedings must be brought.

(3) In making that decision the court must have regard to its power under section 1032(3) (power to give consequential directions etc) to direct that the period between the dissolution (or striking off) of the LLP and the making of the order is not to count for the purposes of any such enactment.

(4) In any other case an application to the court for restoration of an LLP to the register may not be made after the end of the period of six years from the date of the dissolution of the LLP, subject as follows.

(5) In a case where—

(a) the LLP has been struck off the register under section 1000 or 1001 (power of registrar to strike off defunct LLP),

(b) an application to the registrar has been made under section 1024 (application for administrative restoration to the register) within the time allowed for making such an application, and

(c) the registrar has refused the application,

an application to the court under this section may be made within 28 days of notice of the registrar's decision being issued by the registrar, even if the period of six years mentioned in subsection (4) above has expired.

(6) For the purposes of this section—

(a) "personal injury" includes any disease and any impairment of a person's physical or mental condition; and

(b) references to damages for personal injury include—

(i) any sum claimed by virtue of section 1(2)(c) of the Law Reform (Miscellaneous Provisions) Act 1934 (c 41) or section 14(2)(c) of the Law Reform (Miscellaneous Provisions) Act (Northern Ireland) 1937 (1937 C 9 (NI)) (funeral expenses), and

(ii) damages under the Fatal Accidents Act 1976 (c 30), the Damages (Scotland) Act 1976 (c 13) or the Fatal Accidents (Northern Ireland) Order 1977 (SI 1977/1251 (NI 18)).

1031 Decision on application for restoration by the court

(1) On an application under section 1029 the court may order the restoration of the LLP to the register—

(a) if the LLP was struck off the register under section 1000 or 1001 (power of registrar to strike off defunct LLPs) and the LLP was, at the time of the striking off, carrying on business or in operation;
(b) if the LLP was struck off the register under section 1003 (voluntary striking off) and any of the requirements of sections 1004 to 1009 was not complied with;
(c) if in any other case the court considers it just to do so.

(2) If the court orders restoration of the LLP to the register, the restoration takes effect on a copy of the court's order being delivered to the registrar.
(3) The registrar must cause to be published in the Gazette notice of the restoration of the LLP to the register.
(4) The notice must state—
(a) the name of the LLP or, if the LLP is restored to the register under a different name (see section 1033), that name and its former name,
(b) the LLP's registered number, and
(c) the date on which the restoration took effect.

1032 Effect of court order for restoration to the register
(1) The general effect of an order by the court for restoration to the register is that the LLP is deemed to have continued in existence as if it had not been dissolved or struck off the register.
(2) The LLP is not liable to a penalty under section 453 or any corresponding earlier provision (civil penalty for failure to deliver accounts) for a financial year in relation to which the period for filing accounts and reports ended—
(a) after the date of dissolution or striking off, and
(b) before the restoration of the LLP to the register.
(3) The court may give such directions and make such provision as seems just for placing the LLP and all other persons in the same position (as nearly as may be) as if the LLP had not been dissolved or struck off the register.
(4) The court may also give directions as to—
(a) the delivery to the registrar of such documents relating to the LLP as are necessary to bring up to date the records kept by the registrar,
(b) the payment of the costs (in Scotland, expenses) of the registrar in connection with the proceedings for the restoration of the LLP to the register,
(c) where any property or right previously vested in or held on trust for the LLP has vested as *bona vacantia*, the payment of the costs (in Scotland, expenses) of the Crown representative—
(i) in dealing with the property during the period of dissolution, or
(ii) in connection with the proceedings on the application.
(5) In this section the "Crown representative" means—
(a) in relation to property vested in the Duchy of Lancaster, the Solicitor to that Duchy;
(b) in relation to property vested in the Duke of Cornwall, the Solicitor to the Duchy of Cornwall;
(c) in relation to property in Scotland, the Queen's and Lord Treasurer's Remembrancer;
(d) in relation to other property, the Treasury Solicitor.".

[10.382]
58 Supplementary provisions
Sections 1033 and 1034 apply to LLPs, modified so that they read as follows—

"1033 LLP's name on restoration
(1) An LLP is restored to the register with the name it had before it was dissolved or struck off the register, subject to the following provisions.
(2) If at the date of restoration the LLP could not be registered under its former name without contravening section 66 (name not to be the same as another in the registrar's index of names), it must be restored to the register—
(a) under another name specified—
(i) in the case of administrative restoration, in the application to the registrar, or
(ii) in the case of restoration under a court order, in the court's order, or
(b) as if its registered number was also its name.

References to an LLP's being registered in a name, and to registration in that context, shall be read as including the LLP's being restored to the register.
(3) If an LLP is restored to the register under a name specified in the application to the registrar, the provisions of—
paragraph 5 of the Schedule to the Limited Liability Partnerships Act 2000 (c 12) (change of name: registration and issue of certificate of change of name), and
paragraph 6 of that Schedule (change of name: effect),
apply as if the application to the registrar were notice of a change of name.
(4) If an LLP is restored to the register under a name specified in the court's order, the provisions of—
paragraph 5 of the Schedule to the Limited Liability Partnerships Act 2000 (c 12) (change of name: registration and issue of certificate of change of name), and
paragraph 6 of that Schedule (change of name: effect),
apply as if the copy of the court order delivered to the registrar were notice of a change a name.
(5) If the LLP is restored to the register as if its registered number was also its name—
(a) the LLP must change its name within 14 days after the date of the restoration,
(b) the change may be made by determination of the members,
(c) the LLP must give notice to the registrar of the change, and
(d) paragraphs 5 and 6 of the Schedule to the Limited Liability Partnerships Act 2000 (c 12) apply as regards the registration and effect of the change.

(6) If the LLP fails to comply with subsection (5)(a) or (c) an offence is committed by—
- (a) the LLP, and
- (b) every designated member of the LLP who is in default.

(7) A person guilty of an offence under subsection (6) is liable on summary conviction to a fine not exceeding level 5 on the standard scale and, for continued contravention, a daily default fine not exceeding [one-tenth of the greater of £5,000 or level 4 on the standard scale].

1034 Effect of restoration to the register where property has vested as bona vacantia

(1) The person in whom any property or right is vested by section 1012 (property of dissolved LLP to be *bona vacantia*) may dispose of, or of an interest in, that property or right despite the fact that the LLP may be restored to the register under this Chapter.

(2) If the LLP is restored to the register—
- (a) the restoration does not affect the disposition (but without prejudice to its effect in relation to any other property or right previously vested in or held on trust for the LLP), and
- (b) the Crown or, as the case may be, the Duke of Cornwall shall pay to the LLP an amount equal to—
  - (i) the amount of any consideration received for the property or right or, as the case may be, the interest in it, or
  - (ii) the value of any such consideration at the time of the disposition,

  or, if no consideration was received an amount equal to the value of the property, right or interest disposed of, as at the date of the disposition.

(3) There may be deducted from the amount payable under subsection (2)(b) the reasonable costs of the Crown representative in connection with the disposition (to the extent that they have not been paid as a condition of administrative restoration or pursuant to a court order for restoration).

(4) Where a liability accrues under subsection (2) in respect of any property or right which before the restoration of the LLP to the register had accrued as *bona vacantia* to the Duchy of Lancaster, the Attorney General of that Duchy shall represent Her Majesty in any proceedings arising in connection with that liability.

(5) Where a liability accrues under subsection (2) in respect of any property or right which before the restoration of the LLP to the register had accrued as *bona vacantia* to the Duchy of Cornwall, such persons as the Duke of Cornwall (or other possessor for the time being of the Duchy) may appoint shall represent the Duke (or other possessor) in any proceedings arising out of that liability.

(6) In this section the "Crown representative" means—
- (a) in relation to property vested in the Duchy of Lancaster, the Solicitor to that Duchy;
- (b) in relation to property vested in the Duke of Cornwall, the Solicitor to the Duchy of Cornwall;
- (c) in relation to property in Scotland, the Queen's and Lord Treasurer's Remembrancer;
- (d) in relation to other property, the Treasury Solicitor.".

NOTES

Words in square brackets in s 1033(7) as set out above substituted (for the original words "one-tenth of level 5 on the standard scale") by the Legal Aid, Sentencing and Punishment of Offenders Act 2012 (Fines on Summary Conviction) Regulations 2015, SI 2015/664, regs 3, 5, Sch 3, Pt 1, para 14(1), (5), as from 12 March 2015, in relation to England and Wales only (except in relation to (a) fines for offences committed before 12 March 2015, (b) the operation of restrictions on fines that may be imposed on a person aged under 18, or (c) fines that may be imposed on a person convicted by a magistrates' court who is to be sentenced as if convicted on indictment).

PART 14 OVERSEAS LLPS

[10.383]

59 Trading disclosures

Section 1051 applies to LLPs, modified so that it reads as follows—

"1051 Trading disclosures

(1) The following provisions of Part 7 of the Overseas Companies Regulations 2009 (SI 2009/1801) (trading disclosures) apply to LLPs—
- (a) regulation 58(2);
- (b) regulation 59;
- (c) regulations 61 and 62;
- (d) regulation 66;
- (e) regulation 67(1) and (2).

(2) As those provisions apply to LLPs—
- (a) for references to an overseas company substitute references to an overseas LLP;
- (b) for references to an officer of a company substitute references to a member of an LLP;
- (c) for regulation 61(1) substitute—
  "(1) Every overseas LLP must display the name of the LLP and the country in which it is incorporated or otherwise established at every location where it carries on business in the United Kingdom.";
- (d) for the introductory words to regulation 62 substitute—
  "Every overseas LLP must state the LLP's name and the country in which it is incorporated on all—".

(3) For the purposes of paragraph (2)(a) above, "overseas LLP" means a body incorporated or otherwise established outside the United Kingdom whose name under its law of incorporation or establishment includes (or when translated into English includes) the words "limited liability partnership" or the abbreviation "llp" or "LLP".".

PART 15 THE REGISTRAR OF COMPANIES

[10.384]

60 Provisions of general application

(1) The application to LLPs by the following regulations of certain provisions of Part 35 of the Companies Act 2006 is without prejudice to the application in relation to LLPs of the provisions of that Part that are of general application.

(2) Those provisions are—

sections 1060(1) and (2) and 1061 to 1063 (the registrar),
sections 1068 to 1071 (delivery of documents to the registrar),
sections 1072 to 1076 (requirements for proper delivery),
sections 1080(1), (4) and (5) and 1092 (keeping and production of records),
section 1083 (preservation of original documents),
sections 1108 to 1110 (language requirements: transliteration),
sections 1111 and 1114 to 1119 (supplementary provisions).

[10.385]

61 Certificates of incorporation

Sections 1064 and 1065 apply to LLPs, modified so that they read as follows—

"1064 Public notice of issue of certificate of incorporation

(1) The registrar must cause to be published—

(a) in the Gazette, or

(b) in accordance with section 1116 (alternative means of giving public notice),

notice of the issue by the registrar of any certificate of incorporation of an LLP.

(2) The notice must state the name and registered number of the LLP and the date of issue of the certificate.

(3) This section applies to a certificate issued under—

(a) paragraph 5 of the Schedule to the Limited Liability Partnerships Act 2000 (c 12) (change of name: registration and issue of certificate of change of name), or

(b) section 88(4) of this Act (Welsh LLPs),

as well as to the certificate issued on an LLP's formation.

1065 Right to certificate of incorporation

Any person may require the registrar to provide him with a copy of any certificate of incorporation of an LLP, signed by the registrar or authenticated by the registrar's seal.".

[10.386]

62 Registered numbers

Section 1066 applies to LLPs, modified so that it reads as follows—

"1066 LLP's registered numbers

(1) The registrar shall allocate to every LLP a number, which shall be known as the LLP's registered number.

(2) LLPs' registered numbers shall be in such form, consisting of one or more sequences of figures or letters, as the registrar may determine.

(3) The registrar may on adopting a new form of registered number make such changes of existing registered numbers as appear necessary.

(4) A change of an LLP's registered number has effect from the date on which the LLP is notified by the registrar of the change.

(5) For a period of three years beginning with that date any requirement to disclose the LLP's registered number imposed by section 82 or section 1051 (trading disclosures) is satisfied by the use of either the old number or the new.".

[10.387]

63 Public notice of receipt of certain documents

Sections 1077 to 1079 apply to LLPs, modified so that they read as follows—

"1077 Public notice of receipt of certain documents

(1) The registrar must cause to be published—

(a) in the Gazette, or

(b) in accordance with section 1116 (alternative means of giving public notice),

notice of the receipt by the registrar of any document specified in section 1078.

(2) The notice must state the name and registered number of the LLP, the description of document and the date of receipt.

(3) The registrar is not required to cause notice of the receipt of a document to be published before the date of incorporation of the LLP to which the document relates.

1078 The section 1077 documents

The following documents are specified for the purposes of section 1077—

Constitutional documents

1. The LLP's incorporation document.
2. Any notice delivered under section 8(4) of the Limited Liability Partnerships Act 2000 (c 12).
3. Any notice of the change of the LLP's name.

Members

1. Notification of any change in the membership of the LLP.
2. Notification of any change in the particulars of members required to be delivered to the registrar.

Accounts and [confirmation statements]

1. All documents required to be delivered to the registrar under section 441 (annual accounts).
[1A. All documents delivered to the registrar under sections 394A(2)(e), 448A(2)(e) and 479A(2)(e) (qualifying subsidiaries: conditions for exemptions from the audit, preparation and filing of individual accounts).]
2. [The LLP's confirmation statement].
[Reports
1. Any report or consolidated report on payments to governments required to be delivered to the registrar by regulation 14 of the Reports on Payments to Governments Regulations 2014.
2. Any information on payments to governments which is contained in a report or consolidated report prepared in accordance with equivalent reporting requirements (within the meaning of the Reports on Payments to Governments Regulations 2014) and is required to be delivered to the registrar by regulation 15 of those Regulations.]
Registered office
Notification of any change of the LLP's registered office.
Winding up
1. Copy of any winding-up order in respect of the LLP.
2. Notice of the appointment of liquidators.
3. Order for the dissolution of an LLP on a winding up.
4. Return by a liquidator of the final meeting of an LLP on a winding up.

1079 Effect of failure to give public notice

(1) An LLP is not entitled to rely against other persons on the happening of any event to which this section applies unless—
(a) the event has been officially notified at the material time, or
(b) the LLP shows that the person concerned knew of the event at the material time.
(2) The events to which this section applies are—
(a) (as regards service of any document on the LLP) a change of the LLP's registered office,
(b) the making of a winding-up order in respect of the LLP, or
(c) the appointment of a liquidator in a voluntary winding up of the LLP.
(3) If the material time falls—
(a) on or before the 15th day after the date of official notification, or
(b) where the 15th day was not a working day, on or before the next day that was,
the LLP is not entitled to rely on the happening of the event as against a person who shows that he was unavoidably prevented from knowing of the event at that time.
(4) "Official notification" means—
(a) in relation to anything stated in a document specified in section 1078, notification of that document in accordance with section 1077;
(b) in relation to the appointment of a liquidator in a voluntary winding up, notification of that event in accordance with section 109 of the Insolvency Act 1986 (c 45) or Article 95 of the Insolvency (Northern Ireland) Order 1989 (SI 1989/2405 (NI 19)).".

NOTES

In s 1078 as set out above, the words "confirmation statements" and "The LLP's confirmation statement" in square brackets were substituted by the Companies and Limited Liability Partnerships (Filing Requirements) Regulations 2016, SI 2016/599, reg 3, Sch 1, paras 1, 6, as from 30 June 2016.

Para 1A of the entry relating to "Accounts and returns" in s 1078 as set out above was inserted by the Companies and Limited Liability Partnerships (Accounts and Audit Exemptions and Change of Accounting Framework) Regulations 2012, SI 2012/2301, regs 2, 22(1), (2), as from 1 October 2012 (in relation to accounts for financial years ending on or after that date).

The entry relating to "Reports" in s 1078 as set out above was inserted by the Reports on Payments to Governments Regulations 2014, SI 2014/3209, reg 20(1), as from 1 December 2014, in relation to a financial year of an undertaking beginning on or after 1 January 2015 (note that this amendment does not apply in relation to a financial year beginning before 1 January 2016 of an undertaking that is a subsidiary undertaking and whose parent undertaking is required to prepare consolidated group accounts in a member State other than the UK).

[10.388]

64 The register

Sections 1081 and 1082 apply to LLPs, modified so that they read as follows—

"1081 Annotation of the register

(1) The registrar must place a note in the register recording—
(a) the date on which a document is delivered to the registrar;
(b) if a document is corrected under section 1075, the nature and date of the correction;
(c) if a document is replaced (whether or not material derived from it is removed), the fact that it has been replaced and the date of delivery of the replacement;
(d) if material is removed—
(i) what was removed (giving a general description of its contents),
(ii) under what power, and
(iii) the date on which that was done;
[(e) if a document is rectified under section 859M, the nature and date of rectification;
(f) if a document is replaced under section 859N, the fact that it has been replaced and the date of delivery of the replacement.]
(2) Regulation 3 of the Registrar of Companies and Applications for Striking Off Regulations 2009 (SI 2009/1803) applies to LLPs as regards—
(a) other circumstances in which the registrar is required or authorised to annotate the register, and
(b) the contents of any such annotation.

Part 10 Miscellaneous other SIs

(3) No annotation is required in the case of a document that by virtue of section 1072(2) (documents not meeting requirements for proper delivery) is treated as not having been delivered.

(4) A note may be removed if it no longer serves any useful purpose.

(5) Any duty or power of the registrar with respect to annotation of the register is subject to the court's power under section 1097 (powers of court on ordering removal of material from the register) to direct—

(a) that a note be removed from the register, or

(b) that no note shall be made of the removal of material that is the subject of the court's order.

(6) Notes placed in the register in accordance with subsection (1), or in pursuance of the provision referred to in subsection (2), are part of the register for all purposes of the Companies Acts and the Limited Liability Partnerships Act 2000.

1082 Allocation of unique identifiers

(1) The Secretary of State may make provision for the use, in connection with the register, of reference numbers ("unique identifiers") to identify each person who is a member of an LLP.

(2) The regulations may—

(a) provide that a unique identifier may be in such form, consisting of one or more sequences of letters or numbers, as the registrar may from time to time determine;

(b) make provision for the allocation of unique identifiers by the registrar;

(c) require there to be included, in any specified description of documents delivered to the registrar, as well as a statement of the person's name—

(i) a statement of the person's unique identifier, or

(ii) a statement that the person has not been allocated a unique identifier;

(d) enable the registrar to take steps where a person appears to have more than one unique identifier to discontinue the use of all but one of them.

(3) The regulations may contain provision for the application of the scheme in relation to persons appointed, and documents registered, before the commencement of this Act.

(4) The regulations may make different provision for different descriptions of person and different descriptions of document.

(5) Regulations under this section are subject to affirmative resolution procedure.".

NOTES

In s 1081 as set out above, sub-s (1)(e) and (f) were added by the Limited Liability Partnerships (Application of Companies Act 2006) (Amendment) Regulations 2013, SI 2013/618, reg 3, as from 6 April 2013, in relation to charges created on or after that date (see the transitional provisions note at **[10.368]**).

[10.389]

65 Records relating to dissolved LLPs

Section 1084 applies to LLPs, modified so that it reads as follows—

"1084 Records relating to LLPs that have been dissolved

(1) This section applies where an LLP is dissolved.

(2) At any time after two years from the date on which it appears to the registrar that the LLP has been dissolved, the registrar may direct that records relating to the LLP may be removed to the Public Record Office or, as the case may be, the Public Record Office of Northern Ireland.

(3) Records in respect of which such a direction is given shall be disposed of under the enactments relating to that Office and the rules made under them.

[(3A) This section has effect subject to section 1087ZA (required particulars available for public inspection for limited period).]

(4) This section does not extend to Scotland.".

NOTES

In s 1084 as set out above, sub-s (3A) wad inserted by the Money Laundering and Terrorist Financing (Amendment) Regulations 2019, SI 2019/1511, reg 17(1), (2), as from 10 January 2020.

[10.390]

66 Inspection etc of the register

Sections 1085 to 1091 apply to LLPs, modified so that they read as follows—

"1085 Inspection of the register

(1) Any person may inspect the register.

(2) The right of inspection extends to the originals of documents delivered to the registrar in hard copy form if, and only if, the record kept by the registrar of the contents of the document is illegible or unavailable.

The period for which such originals are to be kept is limited by section 1083(1).

(3) This section has effect subject to section 1087 (material not available for public inspection) [and section 1087ZA (required particulars available for public inspection for limited period)].

1086 Right to copy of material not on the register

(1) Any person may require a copy of any material on the register.

(2) The fee for any such copy of material derived from a document specified for the purposes of section 1077, whether in hard copy or electronic form, must not exceed the administrative cost of providing it.

(3) This section has effect subject to section 1087 (material not available for public inspection) [and section 1087ZA (required particulars available for public inspection for limited period)].

1087 Material not available for public inspection

(1) The following material must not be made available by the registrar for public inspection—

(a) the contents of any document sent to the registrar containing views expressed pursuant to section 56 (comments on proposal by LLP to use certain words or expressions in LLP name);
(b) protected information within section 242(1) (members' residential addresses: restriction on disclosure by registrar);
(c) representations received by the registrar in response to a notice under section 245(2) (notice of proposal to put member's usual residential address on the public record);
[(ca) information to which sections 240 to 244 are applied by section 790ZF(1) (residential addresses of people with significant control over the LLP);
(cb) information that, by virtue of regulations under section 790ZG, the registrar must omit from the material on the register that is available for public inspection;]
(d) any application to the registrar under section 1024 (application for administrative restoration to the register) that has not yet been determined or was not successful;
(e) any document received by the registrar in connection with the giving or withdrawal of consent under section 1075 (informal correction of documents);
[(ea) information falling within section 1087A(1) (information about a person's date of birth);]
(f) any application or other document delivered to the registrar under section 1088 (application to make address unavailable for public inspection) and any address in respect of which such an application is successful;
(g) any application or other document delivered to the registrar under section 1095 (application for rectification of register);
(h) any court order under section 1096 (rectification of the register under court order) that the court has directed under section 1097 (powers of court on ordering removal of material from the register) is not to be made available for public inspection;
[(ha) any application or document delivered to the registrar under section 1097A (rectification of LLP registered office) other than an order or direction of the court;]
(i) the contents of—
(i) any instrument creating or evidencing a charge, or
(ii) any certified or verified copy of an instrument creating or evidencing a charge,
delivered to the registrar under Part 25 (LLP charges);
(j) any e-mail address, identification code or password deriving from a document delivered for the purpose of authorising or facilitating electronic filing procedures or providing information by telephone;
(k) any other material excluded from public inspection by or under any other enactment.

(2) A restriction applying by reference to material deriving from a particular description of document does not affect the availability for public inspection of the same information contained in material derived from another description of document in relation to which no such restriction applies.

(3) Material to which this section applies need not be retained by the registrar for longer than appears to the registrar reasonably necessary for the purposes for which the material was delivered to the registrar.

[1087ZA Required particulars available for public inspection for limited period

(1) This section applies where—
(a) a notice is given to the registrar by an LLP under section 790VA (notification of changes to the registrar), or
(b) a document is delivered to the registrar by an LLP under section 790ZA (duty to notify registrar of changes).

(2) The notice or document, and any record of the information contained in the notice or document, must not be made available by the registrar for public inspection after the expiration of ten years beginning with the date on which the LLP is dissolved.

(3) The power in section 1084(2) (power of registrar to direct that records of an LLP that has been dissolved may be removed to the Public Record Office etc) may not be exercised in relation to the notice or document, or any record of the information contained in the notice or document, before the expiration of ten years beginning with the date on which the LLP is dissolved.

(4) Subsection (2) does not affect the availability for public inspection of the same information contained in material derived from another description of document in relation to which no such restriction applies.]

[1087A Information about a person's date of birth

(1) Information falls within this subsection at any time ("the relevant time") if—
(a) it is DOB information,
(b) it is contained in a document delivered to the registrar that is protected at the relevant time as regards that information,
(c) the document is one in which such information is required to be stated, and
(d) if the document has more than one part, the part in which the information is contained is a part in which such information is required to be stated.

(2) "DOB information" is information as to the day of the month (but not the month or year) on which a relevant person was born.

[(3) A "relevant person" is an individual—
(a) who is an LLP member, or
(b) whose particulars are stated in an LLP's PSC register as a registrable person in relation to that LLP (see Part 21A).

(4) A document delivered to the registrar is "protected" at any time unless—
(a) it is an election period document,
(b) subsection (7) applies to it at the time, or
(c) it was registered before this section comes into force.

(5) As regards DOB information about a relevant person in his or her capacity as a member of the LLP, each of the following is an "election period document"—

(a) a statement of the proposed members of the proposed LLP delivered under section 2 of the Limited Liability Partnerships Act 2000 in circumstances where the proposed members gave notice of election under section 167A (election to keep information on central register) in respect of the LLP's register of members when the statement was delivered;

(b) a document delivered by the LLP under section 167D (duty to notify register of changes while election in force).

(6) As regards DOB information about a relevant person in his or her capacity as someone whose particulars are stated in the LLP's PSC register, each of the following is an "election period document"—

(a) a statement of initial significant control delivered under section 2 of the Limited Liability Partnerships Act 2000 in circumstances where the subscribers wishing to form an LLP gave notice of an election under section 790X in respect of an LLP when the statement was delivered;

(b) a document containing a statement or updated statement delivered by the LLP under section 790X(6)(b) or (7) (statement accompanying notice of election made after incorporation);

(c) a document delivered by the LLP under section 790ZA (duty to notify registrar of changes while election in force).

(7) This subsection applies to a document if—

(a) the DOB information relates to the relevant person in his or her capacity as a member of the LLP,

(b) an election under section 167A is or has previously been in force in respect of the LLP's register of members,

(c) the document was delivered to the registrar at some point before that election took effect,

(d) the relevant person was a member of the LLP when that election took effect, and

(e) the document was either—

(i) a statement of proposed members delivered under section 2 of the Limited Liability Partnerships Act 2000 (Incorporation document etc) naming the relevant person as someone who was to be a member of the LLP, or

(ii) notice given under section 9 of that Act (registration of membership changes) of the relevant person having become a member of the LLP.

(8) Information about a person does not cease to fall within subsection (1) when he or she ceases to be a relevant person and, to that extent, references in this section to a relevant person include someone who used to be a relevant person.

(9) Nothing in subsection (1) obliges the registrar to check other documents or (as the case may be) other parts of the document to ensure the absence of DOB information.]

1087B Disclosure of DOB information

(1) The registrar must not disclose restricted DOB information unless—

(a) the same information about the relevant person (whether in the same or a different capacity) is made available by the registrar for public inspection as a result of being contained in another description of document in relation to which no restriction under section 1087 applies (see subsection (2) of that section), or

(b) disclosure of the information by the registrar is permitted by subsection (2) or another provision of this Act.

(2) The registrar may disclose restricted DOB information—

(a) to a public authority specified for the purposes of this subsection by regulations made by the Secretary of State, or

(b) to a credit reference agency.

(3)

(a) The provisions of The Companies (Disclosure of Date of Birth Information) Regulations 2015 (SI 2015/1694) apply to LLPs.

(b) As those provisions apply to LLPs—

(i) read references to protected information as references to restricted DOB information.

(ii) references to provisions of the Companies Act 1985 (c 6), the Insolvency Act 1986 (c 45), the Companies (Northern Ireland) Order 1986 (SI 1986/1032 (N.I.6)) or the Insolvency (Northern Ireland) Order 1989 (SI 1989/2405 (N.I.9)) are to those provisions as applied to LLPs by the Limited Liability Partnerships Regulations 2001 (SI 2001/1090) or the Limited Liability Partnerships Regulations (Northern Ireland) 2004 (SR (NI) 2004 No 307);

(iii) read references to a company as references to an LLP or proposed LLP;

(iv) read references to a director as references to a member of an LLP.

[(4) This section does not apply to restricted DOB information about a relevant person in his or her capacity as someone whose particulars are stated in the LLP's PSC register if an application under regulations made under section 790ZG (regulations for protecting PSC particulars) has been granted with respect to that information and not been revoked.

(5) "Restricted DOB information" means information falling within section 1087A(1).]]

1088 Application to registrar to make address unavailable for public inspection

(1) The provisions of the Companies (Disclosure of Address) Regulations 2009 (SI 2009/214) relating to applications to make an address unavailable for inspection under this section apply to LLPs.

(2) The provisions are—

(a) Part 3 (disclosure of protected information),

(b) Part 4 (matters relating to applications), so far as relating to applications to make an address unavailable for inspection under this section, and

(c) any other provisions of the Regulations having effect for the purposes of those provisions.

(3) As those provisions apply to LLPs—

(a) references in the regulations to provisions of the Companies Act 1985 (c 6) or the Companies (Northern Ireland) Order 1986 (SI 1986/1032 (NI 6)) are to those provisions as applied to LLPs by the Limited Liability Partnerships Regulations 2001 (SI 2001/1090) or the Limited Liability Partnerships Regulations (Northern Ireland) 2004 (SR (NI) 2004 No 307);

(b) read references to a company as references to an LLP;

(c) read references to a director as references to a member of an LLP;

(d) omit all references to secretaries or permanent representatives;

(e) in regulation 1(2) for the definition of "former name" substitute—

""former name" means a name by which the individual was formerly known and which has been notified to the registrar under section 2 or 9 of the Limited Liability Partnerships Act 2000;";

[(f) in regulation 9, for paragraph (1) substitute—

"(1) Where an individual's usual residential address is on the register, that individual may make a section 1088 application in respect of that address, where that address was placed on the register in the individual's capacity as—

(a) a proposed member or member under—

(i) section 2 (incorporation document etc) or 9 (registration of membership changes) of the Limited Liability Partnerships Act 2000,

(ii) section 2 (incorporation document etc) or 9 (registration of membership changes) of the Limited Liability Partnerships Act (Northern Ireland) 2002,

(iii) section 288 (register of directors and secretaries) or 363 (duty to deliver annual returns) of the 1985 Act,

(iv) article 296 (register of directors and secretaries) or 371 (duty to deliver annual returns) of the 1986 Order,

(v) section 855 (contents of annual return) or 167D (duty to notify registrar of changes);

(b) a registrable person under—

(i) section 2 of the Limited Liability Partnerships Act 2000 (incorporation document etc),

(ii) any obligation in Part 21A (information about people with significant control)."].

(g) omit regulation 10.

1089 Form of application for inspection or copy

The registrar may specify the form and manner in which application is to be made for—

(a) inspection under section 1085, or

(b) a copy under section 1086.

1090 Form and manner in which copies to be provided

The registrar may determine the form and manner in which copies are to be provided.

1091 Certification of copies as accurate

(1) Copies provided under section 1086 in hard copy form must be certified as true copies unless the applicant dispenses with such certification.

(2) Copies so provided in electronic form must not be certified as true copies unless the applicant expressly requests such certification.

(3) A copy provided under section 1086, certified by the registrar (whose official position it is unnecessary to prove) to be an accurate record of the contents of the original document, is in all legal proceedings admissible in evidence—

(a) as of equal validity with the original document, and

(b) as evidence (in Scotland, sufficient evidence) of any fact stated in the original document of which direct oral evidence would be admissible.

(4) Regulation 2 of the Companies (Registrar, Languages and Trading Disclosures) Regulations 2006 (SI 2006/3429) (certification of electronic copies by registrar) applies where the copy is provided in electronic form.

(5) Copies provided by the registrar may, instead of being certified in writing to be an accurate record, be sealed with the registrar's official seal.".

NOTES

In ss 1085 and 1086 as set out above, the words in square brackets in sub-s (3) were inserted by the Money Laundering and Terrorist Financing (Amendment) Regulations 2019, SI 2019/1511, reg 17(1), (3)(a), (b), as from 10 January 2020.

In s 1087 as set out above, sub-s (1)(ca), (cb) were inserted by the Limited Liability Partnerships (Register of People with Significant Control) Regulations 2016, SI 2016/340, reg 5, Sch 3, para 5, as from 6 April 2016.

In s 1087 as set out above, sub-s (1)(ea) was inserted by the Companies and Limited Liability Partnerships (Filing Requirements) Regulations 2015, SI 2015/1695, regs 4, 6(1), (2), as from 10 October 2015.

In s 1087 as set out above, sub-s (1)(ha) was inserted by the Companies (Address of Registered Office) Regulations 2016, SI 2016/423, regs 19, 20, as from 6 April 2016.

In s 1087 as set out above, sub-s (1)(i) was revoked by the Limited Liability Partnerships (Application of Companies Act 2006) (Amendment) Regulations 2013, SI 2013/618, reg 4, as from 6 April 2013, in relation to charges created on or after that date (see the transitional provisions note at **[10.368]**).

S 1087ZA as set out above was inserted by SI 2019/1511, reg 17(1), (3)(c), as from 10 January 2020.

Ss 1087A, 1087B as set out above were inserted by SI 2015/1695, regs 4, 6(1), (3), as from 10 October 2015.

In s 1087A as set out above, sub-ss (3)–(9) were substituted (for the original sub-ss (3)–(6)), and in s 1087B as set out above, sub-ss (4), (5) were substituted (for the original sub-s (4)), by the Companies and Limited Liability Partnerships (Filing Requirements) Regulations 2016, SI 2016/599, reg 3, Sch 1, paras 1, 7, as from 30 June 2016.

In s 1088 as set out above, sub-s (3)(f) was substituted by the Companies (Disclosure of Address) (Amendment) Regulations 2018, SI 2018/528, reg 7, as from 26 April 2018 (note that reg 8 of the 2018 Regulations provides that if a section 1088 application was received by the registrar before that date, the application must be dealt with by the registrar in accordance with these Regulations as they applied before that date).

[10.391]

67 Correction or removal of material on the register

Sections 1093 to 1098 apply to LLPs, modified so that they read as follows—

"1093 Registrar's notice to resolve inconsistency on the register

(1) Where it appears to the registrar that the information contained in a document delivered to the registrar is inconsistent with other information on the register, the registrar may give notice to the LLP to which the document relates—

(a) stating in what respects the information contained in it appears to be inconsistent with other information on the register, and

(b) requiring the LLP to take steps to resolve the inconsistency.

(2) The notice must—

(a) state the date on which it is issued, and

(b) require the delivery to the registrar, within 14 days after that date, of such replacement or additional documents as may be required to resolve the inconsistency.

(3) If the necessary documents are not delivered within the period specified, an offence is committed by—

(a) the LLP, and

(b) every member of the LLP who is in default.

(4) A person guilty of an offence under subsection (3) is liable on summary conviction to a fine not exceeding level 5 on the standard scale and, for continued contravention, a daily default fine not exceeding [one-tenth of the greater of £5,000 or level 4 on the standard scale].

1094 Administrative removal of material from the register

(1) The registrar may remove from the register anything that there was power, but no duty, to include.

(2) This power is exercisable, in particular, so as to remove—

(a) unnecessary material within the meaning of section 1074, and

(b) material derived from a document that has been replaced under—

section 1076 (replacement of document not meeting requirements for proper delivery), or
section 1093 (notice to remedy inconsistency on the register).

(3) This section does not authorise the removal from the register of—

(a) anything whose registration has had legal consequences in relation to the LLP as regards—

(i) its formation,
(ii) a change of name,
(iii) a change of registered office,
(iv) a change in the situation of a registered office,
(v) the registration of a charge, or
(vi) its dissolution;

(b) an address that is a person's registered address for the purposes of section 1140 (service of documents on members and others).

(4) On or before removing any material under this section (otherwise than at the request of the LLP) the registrar must give notice—

(a) to the person by whom the material was delivered (if the identity, and name and address of that person are known), or

(b) to the LLP to which the material relates (if notice cannot be given under paragraph (a) and the identity of that LLP is known).

(5) The notice must—

(a) state what material the registrar proposes to remove, or has removed, and on what grounds, and

(b) state the date on which it is issued.

1095 Rectification of register on application to registrar

(1) The provisions of the Registrar of Companies and Applications for Striking Off Regulations 2009 (SI 2009/1803) requiring the registrar, on application, to remove from the register material that—

(a) derives from anything invalid or ineffective or that was done without authority, or

(b) is factually inaccurate, or is derived from something that is factually inaccurate or forged,

apply to LLPs.

(2) Those provisions are—

(a) regulations 4 and 5, and

(b) any other provisions of the regulations having effect for the purposes of those provisions.

(2A) In those provisions as they apply to LLPs—

(a) for "company" substitute "LLP", and for "relevant company form" substitute "relevant LLP form";

(b) omit all references to overseas companies and overseas company forms;

(c) omit all references to secretaries;

(d) in regulation 4—

(i) for paragraph (3) substitute—

"(3) A "relevant LLP form" is—

(a) a standard form required for giving notice under section 87 of the Companies Act 2006 (change of address of registered office) or section 9 of the Limited Liability Partnerships Act 2000 (c 12) (changes relating to members); or

(b) so much of a standard form required for delivering an application under section 2 of the Limited Liability Partnerships Act 2000 (incorporation document etc) as is required for the statement of those who are to be members of the LLP referred to in section 2(2)(e).",
(ii) omit paragraphs (4) and (6),
(iii) in paragraph (7) omit "or (6)", and
(iv) in paragraph (8)(a), for "(2), (3), (4) or (5)" substitute "(2) or (3)";
(e) in regulation 5—
(i) in paragraph (1)(b), omit "or (6)",
(ii) in paragraphs (2)(b) and (3)(b), for "director or secretary of the company" substitute "designated member of the LLP",
(iii) omit paragraphs (4) to (7) and (16),
(iv) in paragraphs (8), (11), (12) and (14)(c), for "(2), (3), (4) or (5)" substitute "(2) or (3)"; and
(v) omit paragraph (8)(b) and (c).

(3) An application must—
(a) specify what is to be removed from the register and indicate where on the register it is, and
(b) be accompanied by a statement that the material specified in the application complies with this section and the regulations.

(4) If no objections are made to the application, the registrar may accept the statement as sufficient evidence that the material specified in the application should be removed from the register.

(5) Where anything is removed from the register under this section the registration of which had legal consequences as mentioned in section 1094(3), any person appearing to the court to have a sufficient interest may apply to the court for such consequential orders as appear just with respect to the legal effect (if any) to be accorded to the material by virtue of its having appeared on the register.

[1095A Rectification of register to resolve a discrepancy

(1) This section applies where—
(a) a discrepancy in information relating to an LLP is reported to the registrar under regulation 30A(2) of the Money Laundering, Terrorist Financing and Transfer of Funds (Information on the Payer) Regulations 2017 (requirement to report discrepancies in information about beneficial ownership), and
(b) the registrar determines, having investigated the discrepancy under regulation 30A(5) of those Regulations, that there is a discrepancy.

(2) The registrar may remove material from the register if doing so is necessary to resolve the discrepancy.]

1096 Rectification of the register under court order

(1) The registrar shall remove from the register any material—
(a) that derives from anything that the court has declared to be invalid or ineffective, or to have been done without the authority of the LLP, or
(b) that a court declares to be factually inaccurate, or to be derived from something that is factually inaccurate, or forged,

and that the court directs should be removed from the register.

(2) The court order must specify what is to be removed from the register and indicate where on the register it is.

(3) The court must not make an order for the removal from the register of anything the registration of which had legal consequences as mentioned in section 1094(3) unless satisfied—
(a) that the presence of the material on the register has caused, or may cause, damage to the LLP, and
(b) that the LLP's interest in removing the material outweighs any interest of other persons in the material continuing to appear on the register.

(4) Where in such a case the court does make an order for removal, it may make such consequential orders as appear just with respect to the legal effect (if any) to be accorded to the material by virtue of its having appeared on the register.

(5) A copy of the court's order must be sent to the registrar for registration.

(6) This section does not apply where the court has other, specific, powers to deal with the matter, for example under—
(a) the provisions of Part 15 relating to the revision of defective accounts, or
(b) section [859M (rectification of register)].

1097 Powers of court on ordering removal of material from the register

(1) Where the court makes an order for the removal of anything from the register under section 1096 (rectification of the register), it may give directions under this section.

(2) It may direct that any note on the register that is related to the material that is the subject of the court's order shall be removed from the register.

(3) It may direct that its order shall not be available for public inspection as part of the register.

(4) It may direct—
(a) that no note shall be made on the register as a result of its order, or
(b) that any such note shall be restricted to such matters as may be specified by the court.

(5) The court shall not give any direction under this section unless it is satisfied—
(a) that—
(i) the presence on the register of the note or, as the case may be, of an unrestricted note, or
(ii) the availability for public inspection of the court's order,
may cause damage to the LLP, and
(b) that the LLP's interest in non-disclosure outweighs any interest of other persons in disclosure.

[1097A Rectification of register relating to LLP registered office

(1) The provisions of the Companies (Address of Registered Office) Regulations 2016 (SI 2016/423) requiring the registrar, on application, to change the address of a company's registered office if the registrar is satisfied that the company is not authorised to use the address, apply to LLPs.

(2) Those provisions are—

(a) regulations 1 to 18; and

(b) the Schedule.

(3) In those provisions as they apply to LLPs—

(a) for "company" substitute "LLP";

(b) for "a company" substitute "an LLP";

(c) for "director" substitute "member";

(d) omit the references to "or secretary", "or register of secretaries" and "or section 276";

(e) all references to "the Act" include references to the Act as applied with modifications to LLPs;

(f) all references to the "2015 Regulations" include references to the 2015 Regulations as applied with modifications to LLPs;

(g) in regulation 5, omit paragraph (b)(iv);

(h) for regulation 11 substitute—

"11 Effect of change of address

Where the registrar changes the address of an LLP's registered office under section 1097A(6) of the Act or these Regulations, the following duties of the LLP under the Act are suspended for a period of 28 days beginning on the day the address was changed—

(a) the duty to make LLP records available for inspection including—

(i) register of members (section 162);

(ii) accounting records (section 388);

(iii) register of debenture holders (section 743); and

(iv) instruments creating charges (section 859Q);

(b) the duty to display an LLP's registered name at the LLP's registered office under regulation 21(1)(a) of the 2015 Regulations;

(c) the duty to state information about the LLP's registered office in descriptions of document or communication specified under regulation 25(1) of the 2015 Regulations;

(d) the duty to provide information about an LLP's registered office on request to those persons the LLP deals with in the course of business under regulation 27(1)(a) of the 2015 Regulations."; and

(i) in regulation 16, for "section 1097A(6)" substitute "section 1097A(5)".

(4) The applicant and the LLP must provide such information as the registrar may require for the purposes of determining such an application.

(5) The applicant or the LLP may appeal the outcome of an application under this section to the court.

(6) On an appeal, the court must direct the registrar to register such address as the registered office of the LLP as the court considers appropriate in all the circumstances of the case.]

1098 Public notice of removal of certain material from the register

(1) The registrar must cause to be published—

(a) in the Gazette, or

(b) in accordance with section 1116 (alternative means of giving public notice),

notice of the removal from the register of any document specified in section 1078 or of any material derived from such a document.

(2) The notice must state the name and registered number of the LLP, the description of document and the date of receipt.".

NOTES

Words in square brackets in s 1093(4) as set out above substituted (for the original words "one-tenth of level 5 on the standard scale") by the Legal Aid, Sentencing and Punishment of Offenders Act 2012 (Fines on Summary Conviction) Regulations 2015, SI 2015/664, regs 3, 5, Sch 3, Pt 1, para 14(1), (6), as from 12 March 2015, in relation to England and Wales only (except in relation to (a) fines for offences committed before 12 March 2015, (b) the operation of restrictions on fines that may be imposed on a person aged under 18, or (c) fines that may be imposed on a person convicted by a magistrates' court who is to be sentenced as if convicted on indictment).

S 1095A as set out above was inserted by the Money Laundering and Terrorist Financing (Amendment) Regulations 2019, SI 2019/1511, reg 17(1), (4), as from 10 January 2020.

In s 1096 as set out above, the words in square brackets in sub-s (6)(b) were substituted (for the original words "873 and 888 (rectification of the register of charges)") by the Limited Liability Partnerships (Application of Companies Act 2006) (Amendment) Regulations 2013, SI 2013/618, reg 5, as from 6 April 2013, in relation to charges created on or after that date (see the transitional provisions note at **[10.368]**).

S 1097A as set out above was inserted by the Companies (Address of Registered Office) Regulations 2016, SI 2016/423, regs 19, 21, as from 6 April 2016.

[10.392]

68 Language requirements: translation

Sections 1103 to 1107 apply to LLPs, modified so that they read as follows—

"1103 Documents to be drawn up and delivered in English

(1) The general rule is that all documents required to be delivered to the registrar must be drawn up and delivered in English.

(2) This is subject to—

section 1104 (documents relating to Welsh LLPs) and

section 1105 (documents that may be drawn up and delivered in other languages).

1104 Documents relating to Welsh LLPs

(1) Documents relating to a Welsh LLP may be drawn up and delivered to the registrar in Welsh.

(2) On delivery to the registrar any such document must be accompanied by a certified translation into English, unless they are—

(a) annual accounts and auditors' reports required to be delivered to the registrar under Part 15,

(b) revised accounts, and any auditor's report on such revised accounts, required to be delivered to the registrar by the Companies (Revision of Defective Accounts and Reports) Regulations 2008 (SI 2008/373), or

(c) in a form prescribed in Welsh (or partly in Welsh and partly in English) by virtue of section 26 of the Welsh Language Act 1993 (c 38);

[(d) documents to be delivered to the registrar under sections 394A(2)(e), 448A(2)(e) and 479A(2)(e) (qualifying subsidiaries: conditions for exemptions from the audit, preparation and filing of individual accounts)].

(3) Where a document is properly delivered to the registrar in Welsh without a certified translation into English, the registrar must obtain such a translation if the document is to be available for public inspection.

The translation is treated as if delivered to the registrar in accordance with the same provision as the original.

(4) A Welsh LLP may deliver to the registrar a certified translation into Welsh of any document in English that relates to the LLP and is or has been delivered to the registrar.

(5) Section 1105 (which requires certified translations into English of documents delivered to the registrar in another language) does not apply to a document relating to a Welsh LLP that is drawn up and delivered in Welsh.

1105 Documents that may be drawn up and delivered in other languages

(1) Documents to which this section applies may be drawn up and delivered to the registrar in a language other than English, but when delivered to the registrar they must be accompanied by a certified translation into English.

(2) This section applies to—

(a) documents required to be delivered under section 400(2)(e) or section 401(2)(f) (LLP included in accounts of larger group: required to deliver copy of group accounts);

(b) [certified copies] delivered under Part 25 (LLP charges);

(c) any order made by a competent court in the United Kingdom or elsewhere;

[(d) copies of the consolidated accounts, the auditor's report and the consolidated annual report to be delivered to the registrar under sections 394A(2)(e), 448A(2)(e) and 479A(2)(e) (qualifying subsidiaries: conditions for exemption from the audit, preparation and filing of individual accounts)].

1106 Voluntary filing of translations

(1) An LLP may deliver to the registrar one or more certified translations of any document relating to the LLP that is or has been delivered to the registrar.

(2) The facility described in subsection (1) is available in relation to—

(a) all the official languages of the European Union, and

(b) all the documents specified by section 1078.

(3) The power of the registrar to impose requirements as to the form and manner of delivery includes power to impose requirements as to the identification of the original document and the delivery of the translation in a form and manner enabling it to be associated with the original.

(4) This section does not apply where the original document was delivered to the registrar before this section came into force.

1107 Certified translations

(1) In this Part a "certified translation" means a translation certified to be a correct translation.

(2) In the case of any discrepancy between the original language version of a document and a certified translation—

(a) the LLP may not rely on the translation as against a third party, but

(b) a third party may rely on the translation unless the LLP shows that the third party had knowledge of the original.

(3) A "third party" means a person other than the LLP or the registrar.".

NOTES

In ss 1104, 1105 as set out above, sub-s (2)(d) was inserted by the Companies and Limited Liability Partnerships (Accounts and Audit Exemptions and Change of Accounting Framework) Regulations 2012, SI 2012/2301, regs 2, 22(1), (3), as from 1 October 2012 (in relation to accounts for financial years ending on or after that date).

In s 1105 as set out above, the words in square brackets in sub-s (2)(b) were substituted (for the original words "instruments or copy instruments required to be") by the Limited Liability Partnerships (Application of Companies Act 2006) (Amendment) Regulations 2013, SI 2013/618, reg 6, as from 6 April 2013, in relation to charges created on or after that date (see the transitional provisions note at **[10.368]**).

[10.393]

69 Supplementary provisions

Sections 1112 and 1113 apply to LLPs, modified so that they read as follows—

"1112 General false statement offence

(1) It is an offence for a person knowingly or recklessly—

(a) to deliver or cause to be delivered to the registrar, for any purpose of this Act or the Limited Liability Partnerships Act 2000 (c 12), a document, or

(b) to make to the registrar, for any such purpose, a statement,

that is misleading, false or deceptive in a material particular.

(2) A person guilty of an offence under this section is liable—

(a) on conviction on indictment, to imprisonment for a term not exceeding two years or a fine (or both);

(b) on summary conviction—

(i) in England and Wales or Scotland, to imprisonment for a term not exceeding twelve months or to a fine not exceeding the statutory maximum (or both);

(ii) in Northern Ireland, to imprisonment for a term not exceeding six months, or to a fine not exceeding the statutory maximum (or both).

1113 Enforcement of LLP's filing obligations

(1) This section applies where an LLP has made default in complying with any obligation under this Act or the Limited Liability Partnerships Act 2000 (c 12)—

(a) to deliver a document to the registrar, or

(b) to give notice to the registrar of any matter.

(2) The registrar, or any member or creditor of the LLP, may give notice to the LLP requiring it to comply with the obligation.

(3) If the LLP fails to make good the default within 14 days after service of the notice, the registrar, or any member or creditor of the LLP, may apply to the court for an order directing the LLP, and any specified member of it, to make good the default within a specified time.

(4) The court's order may provide that all costs (in Scotland, expenses) of or incidental to the application are to be borne by the LLP or by any members of it responsible for the default.

(5) This section does not affect the operation of any enactment making it an offence, or imposing a civil penalty, for the default.".

PART 16 OFFENCES

[10.394]

70 Liability of member in default

Sections 1121 and 1122 apply to LLPs for the purposes of these Regulations, modified so that they read as follows—

"1121 Liability of member in default

(1) This section has effect for the purposes of any provision of the Companies Acts to the effect that, in the event of contravention of an enactment in relation to an LLP, an offence is committed by every member or, as the case may be, every designated member of the LLP who is in default.

(2) A member or designated member is "in default" for the purposes of the provision if he authorises or permits, participates in, or fails to take all reasonable steps to prevent, the contravention.

1122 Liability of company or LLP as member in default

(1) Where a company or an LLP is a member or designated member of an LLP, it does not commit an offence as a member or designated member in default unless (in the case of a company) one of its officers is in default, or (in the case of a member LLP) one of its members is in default.

(2) Where any such offence is committed by a company or LLP the officer or member in question also commits the offence and is liable to be proceeded against and punished accordingly.

(3) In this section an officer or member is "in default" for the purposes of the provision if he authorises or permits, participates in, or fails to take all reasonable steps to prevent, the contravention.".

[10.395]

71 Daily default fine

Section 1125 applies to LLPs for the purposes of these Regulations as follows—

"1125 Meaning of "daily default fine"

(1) This section defines what is meant in the Companies Acts where it is provided that a person guilty of an offence is liable on summary conviction to a fine not exceeding a specified amount "and, for continued contravention, a daily default fine" not exceeding a specified amount.

(2) This means that the person is liable on a second or subsequent summary conviction of the offence to a fine not exceeding the latter amount for each day on which the contravention is continued (instead of being liable to a fine not exceeding the former amount).".

[10.396]

72 Consents for certain prosecutions

Section 1126 applies to LLPs, modified so that it reads as follows—

"1126 Consents required for certain prosecutions

(1) This section applies to proceedings for an offence under section 448, 449, 450, 451 or 453A of the Companies Act 1985 [or under section 1112 of this Act], as applied to LLPs.

(2) No such proceedings are to be brought in England and Wales except by or with the consent of the Secretary of State or the Director of Public Prosecutions.

(3) No such proceedings are to be brought in Northern Ireland except by or with the consent of the Secretary of State or the Director of Public Prosecutions for Northern Ireland.".

NOTES

Words in square brackets in s 1126(1) as set out above inserted by the Limited Liability Partnerships (Register of People with Significant Control) Regulations 2016, SI 2016/340, reg 5, Sch 3, para 6, as from 6 April 2016.

[10.397]

73 General provisions

Sections 1127 to 1133 apply to LLPs for the purposes of these Regulations, modified so that they read as follows—

"1127 Summary proceedings: venue

(1) Summary proceedings for any offence under the Companies Acts may be taken—

(a) against a body corporate, at any place at which the body has a place of business, and

(b) against any other person, at any place at which he is for the time being.

(2) This is without prejudice to any jurisdiction exercisable apart from this section.

1128 Summary proceedings: time limit for proceedings

(1) An information relating to an offence under the Companies Acts that is triable by a magistrates' court in England and Wales may be so tried if it is laid—

(a) at any time within three years after the commission of the offence, and

(b) within twelve months after the date on which evidence sufficient in the opinion of the Director of Public Prosecutions or the Secretary of State (as the case may be) to justify the proceedings comes to his knowledge.

(2) Summary proceedings in Scotland for an offence under the Companies Acts—

(a) must not be commenced after the expiration of three years from the commission of the offence;

(b) subject to that, may be commenced at any time—

(i) within twelve months after the date on which evidence sufficient in the Lord Advocate's opinion to justify the proceedings came to his knowledge, or

(ii) where such evidence was reported to him by the Secretary of State, within twelve months after the date on which it came to the knowledge of the latter.

Section 136(3) of the Criminal Procedure (Scotland) Act 1995 (c 46) (date when proceedings deemed to be commenced) applies for the purposes of this subsection as for the purposes of that section.

(3) A magistrates' court in Northern Ireland has jurisdiction to hear and determine a complaint charging the commission of a summary offence under the Companies Acts provided that the complaint is made—

(a) within three years from the time when the offence was committed, and

(b) within twelve months from the date on which evidence sufficient in the opinion of the Director of Public Prosecutions for Northern Ireland or the Secretary of State (as the case may be) to justify the proceedings comes to his knowledge.

(4) For the purposes of this section a certificate of the Director of Public Prosecutions, the Lord Advocate, the Director of Public Prosecutions for Northern Ireland or the Secretary of State (as the case may be) as to the date on which such evidence as is referred to above came to his notice is conclusive evidence.

1129 Legal professional privilege

In proceedings against a person for an offence under the Companies Acts, nothing in those Acts is to be taken to require any person to disclose any information that he is entitled to refuse to disclose on grounds of legal professional privilege (in Scotland, confidentiality of communications).

1130 Proceedings against unincorporated bodies

(1) Proceedings for an offence under the Companies Acts alleged to have been committed by an unincorporated body must be brought in the name of the body (and not in that of any of its members).

(2) For the purposes of such proceedings—

(a) any rules of court relating to the service of documents have effect as if the body were a body corporate, and

(b) the following provisions apply as they apply in relation to a body corporate—

(i) in England and Wales, section 33 of the Criminal Justice Act 1925 (c 86) and Schedule 3 to the Magistrates' Courts Act 1980 (c 43),

(ii) in Scotland, sections 70 and 143 of the Criminal Procedure (Scotland) Act 1995 (c 46),

(iii) in Northern Ireland, section 18 of the Criminal Justice Act (Northern Ireland) 1945 (c 15 (NI)) and Article 166 of and Schedule 4 to the Magistrates' Courts (Northern Ireland) Order 1981 (SI 1981/1675 (NI 26)).

(3) A fine imposed on an unincorporated body on its conviction of an offence under the Companies Acts must be paid out of the funds of the body.

1131 Imprisonment on summary conviction in England and Wales: transitory provision

(1) This section applies to any provision of the Companies Acts that provides that a person guilty of an offence is liable on summary conviction in England and Wales to imprisonment for a term not exceeding twelve months.

(2) In relation to an offence committed before the commencement of section 154(1) of the Criminal Justice Act 2003 (c 44), for "twelve months" substitute "six months".

1132 Production and inspection of documents where offence suspected

(1) An application under this section may be made—

(a) in England and Wales, to a judge of the High Court by the Director of Public Prosecutions, the Secretary of State or a chief officer of police;

(b) in Scotland, to one of the Lords Commissioners of Justiciary by the Lord Advocate;

(c) in Northern Ireland, to the High Court by the Director of Public Prosecutions for Northern Ireland, the Department of Enterprise, Trade and Investment or a chief superintendent of the Police Service of Northern Ireland.

(2) If on an application under this section there is shown to be reasonable cause to believe—

(a) that any person has, while a member of an LLP, committed an offence in connection with the management of the LLP's affairs, and

(b) that evidence of the commission of the offence is to be found in any documents in the possession or control of the LLP,

an order under this section may be made.

(3) The order may—

(a) authorise any person named in it to inspect the documents in question, or any of them, for the purpose of investigating and obtaining evidence of the offence, or

(b) require such member of the LLP as may be named in the order, to produce the documents (or any of them) to a person named in the order at a place so named.

(4) This section applies also in relation to documents in the possession or control of a person carrying on the business of banking, so far as they relate to the LLP's affairs, as it applies to documents in the possession or control of the LLP, except that no such order as is referred to in subsection (3)(b) may be made by virtue of this subsection.

(5) The decision under this section of a judge of the High Court, any of the Lords Commissioners of Justiciary or the High Court is not appealable.

(6) In this section "document" includes information recorded in any form.

1133 Transitional provision

The provisions of this Part except section 1132 do not apply to offences committed before 1st October 2009.".

PART 17 SUPPLEMENTARY PROVISIONS AND INTERPRETATION

[10.398]

74 LLP records

Sections 1134 to 1138 apply to LLPs, modified so that they read as follows—

"1134 Meaning of "LLP records"

In this Part "LLP records" means—

(a) any register, index, accounting records, agreement, memorandum, minutes or other document required by this Act to be kept by an LLP, and

(b) any register kept by an LLP of its debenture holders.

1135 Form of LLP records

(1) LLP records—

(a) may be kept in hard copy or electronic form, and

(b) may be arranged in such manner as the members of the LLP think fit,

provided the information in question is adequately recorded for future reference.

(2) Where the records are kept in electronic form, they must be capable of being reproduced in hard copy form.

(3) If an LLP fails to comply with this section, an offence is committed by every member of the LLP who is in default.

(4) A person guilty of an offence under this section is liable on summary conviction to a fine not exceeding level 3 on the standard scale and, for continued contravention, a daily default fine not exceeding one-tenth of level 3 on the standard scale.

1136 Where certain LLP records to be kept available for inspection

(1) The provisions of the Companies (Company Records) Regulations 2008 (SI 2008/3006) relating to places other than the registered office at which records required to be kept available for inspection under a relevant provision may be so kept in compliance with that provision apply to LLPs.

(2) The "relevant provisions" are—

section 162 (register of members);

section 743 (register of debenture holders);

[section 790M (register of people with significant control over an LLP);

section 790Z (historic PSC register);]

[section 859Q (instruments creating charges)].

(3) The provisions applied by subsection (1) are—

(a) regulation 3, and

(b) any other provision of the regulations having effect for the purposes of that provision.

(4) In the application of those provisions to LLPs for "company" substitute "LLP".

1137 Inspection of records and provision of copies

(1) The provisions of the Companies (Company Records) Regulations 2008 (SI 2008/3006) as to the obligations of an LLP that is required by any provision of this Act or of the Limited Liability Partnerships Act 2000 (c 12)—

(a) to keep available for inspection any LLP records, or

(b) to provide copies of any LLP records,

apply to LLPs.

(2) Those provisions are—

(a) Part 3 (inspection of records),

(b) Part 4 (provision of copies of records), and

(c) any other provision of the regulations having effect for the purposes of those provisions.

(3) As those provisions apply to LLPs—

(a) for "a company" or "the company" substitute "an LLP" or "the LLP";

(b) for "company record" substitute "LLP record";

(c) in regulation 4 (inspection: private company)—

(i) for the reference in paragraph (1) to a private company substitute a reference to an LLP,

(ii) for sub-paragraph (b) substitute—

"(b) that person gives the LLP at least 10 working days' notice of the specified day.";

(d) omit paragraphs (2) and (3); and

(e) omit regulation 5 (inspection: public company).

(4) An LLP that fails to comply with the regulations is treated as having refused inspection or, as the case may be, having failed to provide a copy.

(5) Nothing in any provision of this Act or in the regulations shall be read as preventing an LLP—

(a) from affording more extensive facilities than are required by the regulations, or

(b) where a fee may be charged, from charging a lesser fee than that prescribed or none at all.

1138 Duty to take precautions against falsification

(1) Where LLP records are kept otherwise than in bound books, adequate precautions must be taken—

(a) to guard against falsification, and

(b) to facilitate the discovery of falsification.

(2) If an LLP fails to comply with this section, an offence is committed by every member of the LLP who is in default.

(3) A person guilty of an offence under this section is liable on summary conviction to a fine not exceeding level 3 on the standard scale and, for continued contravention, a daily default fine not exceeding one-tenth of level 3 on the standard scale.".

NOTES

In s 1136 as set out above, the words in the first pair of square brackets in sub-s (2) were substituted by the Limited Liability Partnerships (Register of People with Significant Control) Regulations 2016, SI 2016/340, reg 5, Sch 3, para 7, as from 6 April 2016.

In s 1136 as set out above, the words in the second pair of square brackets in sub-s (2) were substituted (for the original words "section 877 (instruments creating charges and register of charges: England and Wales); section 892 (instruments creating charges and register of charges: Scotland)") by the Limited Liability Partnerships (Application of Companies Act 2006) (Amendment) Regulations 2013, SI 2013/618, reg 7, as from 6 April 2013, in relation to charges created on or after that date (see the transitional provisions note at **[10.368]**).

[10.399]

75 Service addresses

Sections 1139 to 1142 apply to LLPs, modified so that they read as follows—

"1139 Service of documents on LLP

(1) A document may be served on an LLP by leaving it at, or sending it by post to, the LLP's registered office.

(2) Where an LLP registered in Scotland or Northern Ireland carries on business in England and Wales, the process of any court in England and Wales may be served on the LLP by leaving it at, or sending it by post to, the LLP's principal place of business in England and Wales, addressed to the manager or a designated member in England and Wales of the LLP.

Where process is served on an LLP under this subsection, the person issuing out the process must send a copy of it by post to the LLP's registered office.

1140 Service of documents on members and others

(1) A document may be served on—

(a) a member of an LLP, or

(b) a person appointed in relation to an LLP as a judicial factor (in Scotland),

by leaving it at, or sending it by post to, the member's or factor's registered address.

(2) This section applies whatever the purpose of the document in question.

(3) For the purposes of this section a person's "registered address" means any address for the time being shown as a current address in relation to that person in the part of the register available for public inspection.

(4) If notice of a change of that address is given to the registrar, a person may validly serve a document at the address previously registered until the end of the period of 14 days beginning with the date on which notice of the change is registered.

(5) Service may not be effected by virtue of this section at an address if notice has been registered of the cessation of the membership or (as the case may be) termination of the appointment in relation to which the address was registered and the address is not a registered address of the person concerned in relation to any other appointment.

(6) Nothing in this section shall be read as affecting any enactment or rule of law under which permission is required for service out of the jurisdiction.

1141 Service addresses

(1) In this Act a "service address", in relation to a person, means an address at which documents may be effectively served on that person.

(2) The service address must be a place where—

(a) the service of documents can be effected by physical delivery; and

(b) the delivery of documents is capable of being recorded by the obtaining of an acknowledgment of delivery.

1142 Requirement to give service address

Any obligation under this Act to give a person's address is, unless otherwise expressly provided, to give a service address for that person.".

[10.400]
76 Notice of appointment of judicial factor

Sections 1154 and 1155 apply to LLPs, modified so that they read as follows—

"1154 Duty to notify registrar of appointment of judicial factor

(1) Notice must be given to the registrar of the appointment in relation to an LLP of a judicial factor (in Scotland).

(2) The notice must be given by the judicial factor.

(3) The notice must specify an address at which service of documents (including legal process) may be effected on the judicial factor.

Notice of a change in the address for service may be given to the registrar by the judicial factor.

(4) Where notice has been given under this section of the appointment of a judicial factor, notice must also be given to the registrar by the judicial factor of the termination of the appointment.

1155 Offence of failure to give notice

(1) If a judicial factor fails to give notice of his appointment in accordance with section 1154 within the period of 14 days after the appointment he commits an offence.

(2) A person guilty of an offence under this section is liable on summary conviction to a fine not exceeding level 5 on the standard scale and, for continued contravention, a daily default fine not exceeding one-tenth of level 5 on the standard scale.".

[10.401]
77 Courts and legal proceedings

Sections 1156 and 1157 apply to LLPs for the purposes of these Regulations, modified so that they read as follows—

"1156 Meaning of "the court"

(1) Except as otherwise provided, in this Act "the court" means—

(a) in England and Wales, the High Court or (subject to subsection (3)) a county court;
(b) in Scotland, the Court of Session or the sheriff court;
(c) in Northern Ireland, the High Court.

(2) The provisions of the Companies Acts conferring jurisdiction on "the court" as defined above have effect subject to any enactment or rule of law relating to the allocation of jurisdiction or distribution of business between courts in any part of the United Kingdom.

(3) The Lord Chancellor may, with the concurrence of the Lord Chief Justice, by order—

(a) exclude a county court from having jurisdiction under this Act, and
(b) for the purposes of that jurisdiction attach that court's district, or any part of it, to another county court.

(4) The Lord Chief Justice may nominate a judicial office holder (as defined in section 109(4) of the Constitutional Reform Act 2005 (c 4)) to exercise his functions under subsection (3).

1157 Power of court to grant relief in certain cases

(1) If in proceedings for negligence, default, breach of duty or breach of trust against—

(a) a member of an LLP, or
(b) a person employed by an LLP as auditor,

it appears to the court hearing the case that the member or person is or may be liable but that he acted honestly and reasonably, and that having regard to all the circumstances of the case (including those connected with his appointment) he ought fairly to be excused, the court may relieve him, either wholly or in part, from his liability on such terms as it thinks fit.

(2) If any such member or person has reason to apprehend that a claim will or might be made against him in respect of negligence, default, breach of duty or breach of trust—

(a) he may apply to the court for relief, and
(b) the court has the same power to relieve him as it would have had if it had been a court before which proceedings against him for negligence, default, breach of duty or breach of trust had been brought.

(3) Where a case to which subsection (1) applies is being tried by a judge with a jury, the judge, after hearing the evidence, may, if he is satisfied that the defendant (in Scotland, the defender) ought in pursuance of that subsection to be relieved either in whole or in part from the liability sought to be enforced against him, withdraw the case from the jury and forthwith direct judgment to be entered for the defendant (in Scotland, grant decree of absolvitor) on such terms as to costs (in Scotland, expenses) or otherwise as the judge may think proper.".

[10.402]
78 Requirements of this Act

Section 1172 applies to LLPs for the purposes of these Regulations, modified so that it reads as follows—

"1172 References to requirements of this Act

References in the provisions of this Act applied to LLPs to the requirements of this Act include the requirements of regulations and orders made under it.".

[10.403]
79 Minor definitions

Section 1173 applies to LLPs for the purposes of these Regulations, modified so that it reads as follows—

"1173 Minor definitions: general

(1) In this Act—

"body corporate" and "corporation" include a body incorporated outside the United Kingdom, but do not include—
(a) a corporation sole, or
(b) a partnership that, whether or not a legal person, is not regarded as a body corporate under the law by which it is governed;

"the Companies Acts" is to be construed in accordance with section 2;

"firm" means any entity, whether or not a legal person, that is not an individual and includes a body corporate, a corporation sole and a partnership or other unincorporated association;

"the Gazette" means—
(a) as respects LLPs registered in England and Wales, the London Gazette,
(b) as respects LLPs registered in Scotland, the Edinburgh Gazette, and
(c) as respects LLPs registered in Northern Ireland, the Belfast Gazette;

"LLP" means a limited liability partnership registered under the Limited Liability Partnerships Act 2000 (c 12);

"LLP agreement" means any agreement, express or implied, between the members of the LLP or between the LLP and the members of the LLP which determines the mutual rights and duties of the members, and their rights and duties in relation to the LLP;

"officer", in relation to a body corporate, includes a director, manager or secretary;

"working day", in relation to an LLP, means a day that is not a Saturday or Sunday, Christmas Day, Good Friday or any day that is a bank holiday under the Banking and Financial Dealings Act 1971 (c 80) in the part of the United Kingdom where the LLP is registered.

(2) In this Act, unless the context otherwise requires, "enactment" includes—
(a) an enactment contained in subordinate legislation within the meaning of the Interpretation Act 1978 (c 30),
(b) an enactment contained in, or in an instrument made under, an Act of the Scottish Parliament, and
(c) an enactment contained in, or in an instrument made under, Northern Ireland legislation within the meaning of the Interpretation Act 1978.".

Regulations and orders

[10.404]
80
Sections 1288 to 1290 apply to LLPs for the purposes of these Regulations, modified so that they read as follows—

"1288 Regulations and orders: statutory instrument
Except as otherwise provided, regulations and orders under this Act shall be made by statutory instrument.

1289 Regulations: negative resolution procedure
Where regulations under this Act are subject to "negative resolution procedure" the statutory instrument containing the regulations shall be subject to annulment in pursuance of a resolution of either House of Parliament.

1290 Regulations: affirmative resolution procedure
Where regulations under this Act are subject to "affirmative resolution procedure" the regulations must not be made unless a draft of the statutory instrument containing them has been laid before Parliament and approved by a resolution of each House of Parliament.".

[10.405]
81
Section 1292 applies to LLPs for the purposes of these Regulations, modified so that it reads as follows—

"1292 Regulations and orders: supplementary
(1) Regulations or orders under this Act may—
(a) make different provision for different cases or circumstances,
(b) include supplementary, incidental and consequential provision, and
(c) make transitional provision and savings.

(2) Any provision that may be made by regulations under this Act may be made by order; and any provision that may be made by order under this Act may be made by regulations.

(3) Any provision that may be made by regulations or order under this Act for which no Parliamentary procedure is prescribed may be made by regulations subject to negative or affirmative resolution procedure.

(4) Any provision that may be made by regulations under this Act subject to negative resolution procedure may be made by regulations subject to affirmative resolution procedure.".

[10.406]
82 Continuity of the law
Section 1297 applies to LLPs, modified so that it reads as follows—

"1297 Continuity of the law
(1) This section applies where any provision of this Act applied to LLPs re-enacts (with or without modification) an enactment repealed by this Act which was applied to LLPs.

(2) The repeal and re-enactment does not affect the continuity of the law.

(3) Anything done (including subordinate legislation made and applied to LLPs), or having effect as if done, under or for the purposes of the repealed provision as applied to LLPs that could have been done under or for the purposes of the corresponding provision of this Act as applied to LLPs, if in force or effective immediately before the commencement of that corresponding provision, has effect thereafter as if done under or for the purposes of that corresponding provision.

(4) Any reference (express or implied) in this Act or any other enactment, instrument or document to a provision of this Act as applied to LLPs shall be construed (so far as the context permits) as including, as respects times, circumstances or purposes in relation to which the corresponding repealed provision had effect, a reference to that corresponding provision.

(5) Any reference (express or implied) in any enactment, instrument or document to a repealed provision which was applied to LLPs shall be construed (so far as the context permits), as respects times, circumstances and purposes in relation to which the corresponding provision of this Act applied to LLPs has effect, as being or (according to the context) including a reference to the corresponding provision of this Act.

(6) This section has effect subject to any specific transitional provision or saving contained in this Act as applied to LLPs.

(7) References in this section to this Act as applied to LLPs include subordinate legislation made under this Act as so applied.

(8) In this section "subordinate legislation" has the same meaning as in the Interpretation Act 1978 (c 30).".

PART 18 TRANSITIONAL AND CONSEQUENTIAL PROVISIONS

[10.407]
83 Transitional provisions: application of provisions of Companies Act 2006

Schedule 1 to these Regulations contains transitional and savings provisions in connection with the application to LLPs of provisions of the Companies Act 2006.

84 *(Reg 84 (Transitional provisions: Northern Ireland LLPs) outside the scope of this work.)*

[10.408]
85 Consequential amendments and revocations

Schedule 3 to these Regulations contains consequential amendments and revocations.

SCHEDULES

SCHEDULE 1
TRANSITIONAL PROVISIONS: APPLICATION OF PROVISIONS OF COMPANIES ACT 2006

Regulation 83

PART 1 INTRODUCTORY

[10.409]
1 Introduction

(1) This Schedule contains transitional provisions and savings in connection with the coming into force of the provisions of these Regulations applying provisions of the Companies Act 2006 to LLPs.

(2) In this Schedule—
"the 1985 Act" means the Companies Act 1985, and
"the 1986 Order" means the Companies (Northern Ireland) Order 1986.

(3) References in this Schedule to an LLP in relation to times before 1st October 2009 include a limited liability partnership registered under the Limited Liability Partnerships Act (Northern Ireland) 2002.

(4) References in this Schedule to an LLP registered immediately before 1st October 2009 include a limited liability partnership registered under that Act on an application made before, but not determined before, that date (see paragraph 2 of Schedule 2 below).

PART 2 FORMALITIES OF DOING BUSINESS

[10.410]
2 Execution of deeds etc

(1) Section 47 of the Companies Act 2006 (execution of deeds or other documents by attorney), as applied to LLPs by regulation 4, applies where the instrument empowering a person to act as an LLP's attorney is executed on or after 1st October 2009.

(2) Section 38 of the 1985 Act or Article 48 of the 1986 Order, as applied to LLPs, continues to have effect where the power to act as an LLP's attorney was conferred before that date (including in relation to instruments executed by the attorney on behalf of the LLP on or after that date).

PART 3 AN LLP'S NAME

An LLP's name

[10.411]
3. (1) The following provisions of the Companies Act 2006, as applied to LLPs by regulations 8 to 11, do not affect the continued registration of an LLP by a name by which it was duly registered immediately before 1st October 2009.

(2) The provisions are—
(a) section 54 (name suggesting connection with government or public authority);
(b) section 55 (other sensitive words or expressions);
(c) section 57 (permitted characters etc);

(d) section 65 (inappropriate use of indications of company type or legal form);

(e) section 66 (name not to be the same as another in registrar's index).

4. Sections 54 to 56 of the Companies Act 2006 (sensitive words and expressions), as applied to LLPs by regulation 8, apply to applications for approval received by the Secretary of State on or after 1st October 2009.

PART 4 AN LLP'S MEMBERS

Particulars to be registered

[10.412]

5. (1) The duty of an LLP to keep a register of members under section 162 of the Companies Act 2006 (register of members), as applied to LLPs by regulation 18, has effect on and after 1st October 2009.

(2) In the case of an LLP that was registered immediately before 1st October 2009—

(a) the address of a member notified under—

(i) section 2(2)(e) or 9(1)(b) of the Limited Liability Partnerships Act 2000, or

(ii) Article 2(2)(e) or 9(1)(b) of the Limited Liability Partnerships Act (Northern Ireland) 2002,

is to be treated, on and after 1st October 2009, as a service address, and

(b) any entry in the LLP's register of members stating that address is treated as complying with the obligation in section 163(1)(b) of the Companies Act 2006, as applied to LLPs by regulation 18, to state a service address.

(3) The operation of this paragraph does not give rise to any obligation to notify the registrar under section 9(1)(b) of the Limited Liability Partnerships Act 2000.

Register of members' residential addresses

6. (1) The duty of an LLP to keep a register of members' residential addresses under section 165 of the Companies Act 2006 (register of residential addresses), as applied to LLPs by regulation 18, has effect on and after 1st October 2009.

(2) The entry on that register of information does not give rise to any duty to notify the registrar under section 9 of the Limited Liability Partnerships Act 2000 (registration of membership changes).

Members: entries on the register of companies

7. (1) The registrar may make such entries in the register as appear to be appropriate having regard to paragraphs 5 and 6 above and the information appearing on the register immediately before 1st October 2009 or notified to the registrar in pursuance of an obligation arising before that date.

(2) In particular, the registrar may record an address falling within paragraph 5 as a service address.

(3) Any notification of a change of an address of a member occurring before 1st October 2009 that is received by the registrar on or after that date is treated as being or including notification of a change of service address.

Members' residential addresses: protection from disclosure

8. Where a member's usual residential address appears as a service address—

(a) in the LLP's register of members by virtue of paragraph 5 above, or

(b) in the register of LLPs by virtue of paragraph 7,

that address is not protected information for the purposes of sections 240 to 246 of the Companies Act 2006, as applied to LLPs by regulation 19.

9. (1) Section 242(1) of the Companies Act 2006 (duty of registrar to omit protected information from material available for inspection), as applied to LLPs by regulation 19, does not apply—

(a) to material delivered to the registrar before 1st October 2009, or

(b) to material delivered to the registrar on or after 1st October 2009 by virtue of paragraph 7(3) (notification of change occurring before that date).

(2) Sub-paragraph (1) above has effect subject to paragraph 11 below (which provides for the continued protection of information formerly protected by a confidentiality order).

10. In determining under section 245(1) of the Companies Act 2006, as applied to LLPs by regulation 19, whether to put a member's usual residential address on the public record, the registrar may take into account only—

(a) communications sent by the registrar on or after 1st October 2009, and

(b) evidence as to the effectiveness of service coming to the registrar's attention on or after that date.

Continuation of protection afforded by confidentiality orders under the 1985 Act

11. (1) A member in relation to whom a confidentiality order under section 723B of the 1985 Act, as applied to LLPs, was in force immediately before 1st October 2009 is treated on and after that date as if—

(a) the member had made an application under section 1088 of the Companies Act 2006 (application to make address unavailable for public inspection), as applied to LLPs, in respect of any address that immediately before that date was contained in "confidential records" as defined in section 723D(3) of the 1985 Act, and

(b) that application had been determined by the registrar in the member's favour.

(2) The provisions of Parts 1, 3 and 4 of the Companies (Disclosure of Address) Regulations 2009 relating to decisions of the registrar in favour of an applicant (in particular, as to the duration and revocation of such a decision) apply accordingly.

(3) As those regulations apply in accordance with this paragraph any reference to an offence under section 1112 of the Companies Act 2006 (false statement) as applied to LLPs by regulation 69 shall be read as a reference to an offence under the Limited Liability Partnerships (Particulars of Usual Residential Address) (Confidentiality Orders) Regulations 2002 in relation to the application for the confidentiality order.

12. (1) A member in relation to whom a confidentiality order under section 723B of the 1985 Act as applied to LLPs was in force immediately before 1st October 2009 is treated on and after that date as if—

(a) the member had made an application under section 243(5) of the Companies Act 2006 (application to prevent disclosure of protected information by registrar to credit reference agency), as applied to LLPs by regulation 19, and

(b) that application had been determined by the registrar in the member's favour.

(2) The provisions of Parts 1, 2 and 4 of the Companies (Disclosure of Address) Regulations 2009 relating to decisions of the registrar in favour of an applicant (in particular, as to the duration and revocation of such a decision) apply accordingly.

(3) As those regulations apply in accordance with this paragraph any reference to an offence under section 1112 (false statement) as applied to LLPs by regulation 69 shall be read as a reference to an offence under the Limited Liability Partnerships (Particulars of Usual Residential Address) (Confidentiality Orders) Regulations 2002 in relation to the application for the confidentiality order.

13. Where a confidentiality order under section 723B of the 1985 Act as applied to LLPs was in force immediately before 1st October 2009 in relation to a member, section 162(5) and (8) of the Companies Act 2006 as applied to LLPs by regulation 18 do not apply in relation to the part of the LLP's register containing particulars of the usual residential address of the individual that before that date were protected from disclosure.

Effect of pending application for confidentiality order

14. (1) The Limited Liability Partnerships (Particulars of Usual Residential Address) (Confidentiality Orders) Regulations 2002 continue to apply in relation to an application for a confidentiality order made before 1st October 2009.

(2) Paragraphs 11 to 13 above (continuity of protection afforded by confidentiality orders) apply to a person in respect of whom such an application has been made, and has not been determined or withdrawn, as to a person in relation to whom a confidentiality order was in force immediately before that date.

(3) If the application is dismissed or withdrawn, those paragraphs cease to apply.

(4) If the application is successful those paragraphs continue to apply as in the case of an individual in relation to whom a confidentiality order was in force immediately before 1st October 2009.

PART 5 AN LLP'S ANNUAL RETURN

[10.413]

15 Annual returns

(1) Sections 854, 855, 855A and 858 of the Companies Act 2006 (annual returns), as applied to LLPs by regulations 30 and 31, apply to annual returns made up to a date on or after 1st October 2009.

(2) Sections 363 and 364 of the 1985 Act or Articles 371 and 372 of the 1986 Order, as applied to LLPs, continue to apply to annual returns made up to a date before 1st October 2009.

(3) Any reference in the Companies Act 2006 (as applied to LLPs) to an LLP's last return, or to a return delivered in accordance with Part 24 of that Act, shall be read as including (so far as necessary to ensure the continuity of the law) a return made up to a date before 1st October 2009 or delivered in accordance with the 1985 Act or the 1986 Order (as applied to LLPs).

PART 6 LLP CHARGES

LLP charges

[10.414]

16. (1) Sections 860 and 878 of the Companies Act 2006 (charges created by LLP), as applied to LLPs by regulations 32 and 39, apply to charges created on or after 1st October 2009.

(2) The corresponding provisions of the 1985 Act or 1986 Order, as applied to LLPs, continue to apply to charges created before that date.

17. (1) Sections 862 and 880 of the Companies Act 2006 (charges existing on property acquired), as applied to LLPs by regulations 32 and 39, apply to property acquired on or after 1st October 2009.

(2) Sections 400 and 416 of the 1985 Act or Article 407 of the 1986 Order, as applied to LLPs, continue to apply to property acquired before that date.

18. (1) Sections 863 and 882 of the Companies Act 2006 (charge in series of debentures), as applied to LLPs by regulations 33 and 40, apply where the first debenture of the series is executed on or after 1st October 2009.

(2) The corresponding provisions of the 1985 Act or the 1986 Order, as applied to LLPs, continue to apply where the first debenture of the series is executed before that date.

19. (1) Section 868 of the Companies Act 2006 (Northern Ireland: registration of certain charges etc affecting land), as applied to LLPs by regulation 35, applies where the date of registration of the charge in the Land Registry is on or after 1st October 2009.

(2) Article 408 of the 1986 Order, as applied to LLPs, continues to apply where the date of registration of the charge in the Land Registry is before that date.

20. (1) Section 871 of the Companies Act 2006 (notice to registrar of appointment of receiver or manager etc), as applied to LLPs by regulation 36, applies where the order or appointment is made, or the receiver or manager ceases to act, on or after 1st October 2009.

(2) Section 405 of the 1985 Act or Article 413 of the 1986 Order, as applied to LLPs, continues to apply where the order or appointment is made, or the receiver or manager ceases to act, before that date.

21. (1) Sections 872 and 887 of the Companies Act 2006 (entries of satisfaction and release), as applied to LLPs by regulations 36 and 42, apply to statements delivered to the registrar on or after 1st October 2009.

(2) Section 403 or 419 of the 1985 Act or Article 411 of the 1986 Order, as applied to LLPs, continues to apply where the relevant statutory declaration, statement or application and statutory declaration or statement is received by the registrar before that date.

PART 7 DISSOLUTION AND RESTORATION TO THE REGISTER

[Property of dissolved LLP

[10.415]

22. (1) Sections 1012 to 1023 of the Companies Act 2006 (property of dissolved LLP), as applied to LLPs by regulations 52 to 55, apply in relation to the property of an LLP dissolved on or after 1st October 2009.

(2) Subject to paragraph 22A, the corresponding provisions of the 1985 Act or 1986 Order, as applied to LLPs, continue to apply in relation to the property of an LLP dissolved before that date.

22A. (1) Section 1013 of the Companies Act 2006 (Crown disclaimer of property vesting as bona vacantia), as applied to LLPs by regulation 52, applies in relation to property of an LLP dissolved before 1st October 2009 if at that date—

(a) no period has begun to run in relation to the property under section 656(3)(a) or (b) of the 1985 Act or Article 607(3)(a) or (b) of the 1986 Order (period within which notice of disclaimer must be executed), as applied to LLPs, and

(b) the right to disclaim has not ceased to be exercisable in relation to the property by virtue of section 656(2) of the 1985 Act or Article 607(2) of the 1986 Order (waiver of right to disclaim), as applied to LLPs.

(2) In section 1013, as applied to LLPs and as it applies by virtue of this paragraph, the references to property vesting under section 1012 (as applied to LLPs by regulation 52) shall be read as references to its vesting under section 654 of the 1985 Act or Article 605 of the 1986 Order as applied to LLPs.

(3) Where section 1013 (as applied to LLPs by regulation 52) applies by virtue of this paragraph—

(a) the other provisions of sections 1012 to 1022 of the Companies Act 2006 (as applied to LLPs by regulations 52 to 54) apply accordingly, and

(b) the corresponding provisions of the 1985 Act or 1986 Order (as applied to LLPs) do not apply.]

Saving for applications to court made before 1st October 2009

23. The repeal of the following provisions, as applied to LLPs—

(a) section 651 of the 1985 Act or Article 602 of the 1986 Order (power of court to declare dissolution of LLP void), or

(b) section 653 of the 1985 Act or Article 604 of the 1986 Order (objection to striking off by person aggrieved),

does not affect an application made under that section or Article before 1st October 2009.

Application to court for restoration to the register

24. Sections 1029 to 1032 of the Companies Act 2006 (restoration to register by the court), as applied to LLPs by regulation 57, apply whether the LLP was dissolved or struck off the register before, on or after 1st October 2009.

25. (1) The following provisions apply where the LLP was dissolved or struck off the register before 1st October 2009.

(2) In section 1029 (application to court for restoration to register), as applied to LLPs, the references in subsection (1) to enactments under which an LLP may have been dissolved or struck off include corresponding earlier enactments as applied to LLPs (and for this purpose sections 1000 and 1003 of the Companies Act 2006 are regarded as corresponding to sections 652 and 652A of the 1985 Act and Articles 603 and 603A of the 1986 Order).

(3) No application under section 1029 as applied to LLPs may be made if an application in respect of the same dissolution or striking off has been made under section 653 of the 1985 Act or Article 604 of the 1986 Order (objection to striking off by person aggrieved) as applied to LLPs, and has not been withdrawn.

(4) Section 1030(4) (general time limit of six years) as applied to LLPs does not enable an application to be made in respect of an LLP dissolved before 1st October 2007, subject to sub-paragraphs (5) and (6).

(5) If the LLP was struck off under section 652 or 652A of the 1985 Act or Article 603 or 603A of the 1986 Order as applied to LLPs, section 1030(4) as applied to LLPs does not prevent an application being made at any time before—

(a) 1st October 2015 (that is, six years after commencement), or

(b) the expiration of the period of 20 years from publication in the Gazette of notice under the relevant section or Article,

whichever occurs first.

(6) Section 1030(5) (extension of period for application where application for administrative restoration refused), as applied to LLPs, applies in relation to the time limit under sub-paragraph (5) above as in relation to the time limit in section 1030(4).

Effect of restoration to the register where property has vested as bona vacantia

26. (1) Section 1034 of the Companies Act 2006 (effect of restoration to the register where property has vested as *bona vacantia*), as applied to LLPs by regulation 58, applies whenever the LLP was dissolved.

(2) The following provisions apply where the LLP was dissolved before 1st October 2009.

(3) The reference in section 1034(1) to section 1012 (property of dissolved LLP to be *bona vacantia*) shall be read as a reference to section 654 of the 1985 Act or Article 605 of the 1986 Order as applied to LLPs.

(4) No deduction is to be made under section 1034(3) (deduction of reasonable costs of Crown representative from amount payable to LLP) as applied to LLPs from consideration realised before 1st October 2009.

NOTES

Paras 22, 22A: substituted, for the original para 22, by the Companies Act 2006 and Limited Liability Partnerships (Transitional Provisions and Savings) (Amendment) Regulations 2009, SI 2009/2476, reg 3, as from 1 October 2009.

PART 8 THE REGISTRAR OF COMPANIES

[10.416]

27 Provisions of general application

The general provisions of Part 35 of the Companies Act 2006 mentioned in regulation 60 apply to LLPs subject to relevant transitional provisions and savings in Schedule 2 to the Companies Act 2006 (Commencement No 8, Transitional Provisions and Savings) Order 2008 and in the Schedule to the Companies Act 2006 (Part 35) (Consequential Amendments, Transitional Provisions and Savings) Order 2009.

28 Certificates of incorporation

Sections 1064 and 1065 of the Companies Act 2006 (certificates of incorporation), as applied to LLPs by regulation 61, apply to certificates of incorporation whenever issued.

29 Annotation of the register

(1) Section 1081 of the Companies Act 2006 (annotation of the register), as applied to LLPs by regulation 64, applies in relation to—

(a) documents delivered to the registrar on or after 1st October 2009 other than those delivered in pursuance of an obligation arising before that date, and

(b) certificates issued by the registrar on or after 1st October 2009 other than those issued in response to a document delivered to the registrar before that date or in pursuance of an obligation arising before that date,

and in relation to the content of, and material derived from, such documents and certificates.

(2) The provisions applicable before 1st October 2009 (and the registrar's former practice with respect to annotation of the register) continue to apply in relation to—

(a) documents delivered to the registrar before that date, or in pursuance of an obligation arising before that date, and

(b) certificates issued by the registrar before that date or in response to a document delivered to the registrar before that date or in pursuance of an obligation arising before that date,

and in relation to the content of, and material derived from, such documents and certificates.

30 Registrar's notice to resolve inconsistency on the register

(1) Section 1093 of the Companies Act 2006 (registrar's notice to resolve inconsistency on the register), as applied to LLPs by regulation 67, applies where—

(a) a document is delivered to the registrar on or after 1st October 2009 otherwise than in pursuance of an obligation arising before that date, and

(b) it appears to the registrar that the information contained in the document is inconsistent with other information on the register.

(2) The provisions applicable before 1st October 2009 (and the registrar's former practice with respect to inconsistencies on the register) continue to apply in relation to documents delivered to the registrar before that date or in pursuance of an obligation arising before that date.

31 Removal of material from the register

(1) This paragraph applies to—

(a) sections 1094 to 1097 of the Companies Act 2006 (removal of material from the register), as applied to LLPs by regulation 67, and

(b) section 1098 of that Act (public notice of removal of certain material from the register), as so applied.

(2) Those provisions apply in relation to—

(a) documents delivered to the registrar on or after 1st October 2009 other than those delivered in pursuance of an obligation arising before that date, and

(b) certificates issued by the registrar on or after 1st October 2009, other than those issued in response to a document delivered to the registrar before that date or in pursuance of an obligation arising before that date,

and in relation to the content of, and material derived from, such documents and certificates.

(3) The provisions applicable before 1st October 2009 (and the registrar's former practice with respect to removal of material from the register) continue to apply in relation to—

(a) documents delivered to the registrar before that date, or in pursuance of an obligation arising before that date, and

(b) certificates issued by the registrar before that date or in response to a document delivered to the registrar before that date or in pursuance of an obligation arising before that date,

and in relation to the content of, and material derived from, such documents or certificates.

32 General false statement offence

Section 1112 of the Companies Act 2006 (general false statement offence), as applied to LLPs by regulation 69, applies to all documents delivered, and statements made, on or after 1st October 2009.

33 Provision and authentication by registrar of documents sent by electronic means

The repeal of section 710A of the 1985 Act or Article 659A of the 1986 Order (provision and authentication by registrar of documents in non-legible form) does not affect the application of those provisions as applied to LLPs on or after 1st October 2009 in relation to saved provisions of that Act or Order as applied to LLPs.

PART 9 SUPPLEMENTARY

[10.417]

34 Forms

(1) Any saving in these Regulations for the effect of a provision of the 1985 Act or the 1986 Order, as applied to LLPs, requiring the use of a prescribed form extends to the form and the power under which it is prescribed.

(2) Any saving in these Regulations for the effect of a provision of the 1985 Act or the 1986 Order requiring a document to be delivered to the registrar extends to section 707B of the 1985 Act or Article 656B of the 1986 Order (delivery to the registrar using electronic communications) so far as relating to the provision in question and the delivery of documents under it.

35 Offences

Any saving in—

(a) this Schedule, or

(b) the Limited Liability Partnerships (Accounts and Audit) (Application of Companies Act 2006) Regulations 2008,

for the effect of a provision of the 1985 Act or the 1986 Order as applied to LLPs that creates an offence extends to the entry relating to that provision in Schedule 24 to that Act or Schedule 23 to that Order (punishment of offences) as applied to LLPs.

36 Fees

(1) The repeal of section 708 of the 1985 Act or Article 657 of the 1986 Order, as applied to LLPs, shall not prevent the registrar from continuing to charge fees under that section or Article, as applied to LLPs, of which notice had before the repeal been given to those to whom the services in question have been, are being or are to be provided (including notice by publication of a list of fees in respect of services provided to any person who seeks their provisions).

(2) Any regulations under section 708 of the 1985 Act or Article 657 of the 1986 Order as applied to LLPs (fees payable to registrar) that are in force immediately before 1st October 2009 have effect on or after that date as if made under section 1063 of the Companies Act 2006.

SCHEDULE 2

(Sch 2 (Transitional Provisions: Northern Ireland LLPs) outside the scope of this work.)

SCHEDULE 3
CONSEQUENTIAL AMENDMENTS AND REVOCATIONS

Regulation 85

PART 1 CONSEQUENTIAL AMENDMENTS OF THE LIMITED LIABILITY PARTNERSHIPS ACT 2000

[10.418]

1–10. *(Amend the Limited Liability Partnerships Act 2000, ss 2, 3, 8, 9, 14, 17–19, Schedule, and add s 4A (see the 2000 Act at* **[9.492]** *et seq).)*

11 Saving

The amendments made by this Part of this Schedule do not affect an obligation arising before 1st October 2009 to deliver a document to the registrar.

PART 2 OTHER CONSEQUENTIAL AMENDMENTS AND REVOCATIONS

[10.419]

12 General

(1) In any enactment relating to LLPs—

(a) "the registrar" has the meaning given by section 18 of the Limited Liability Partnerships Act 2000,

(b) "the register" means the records kept by the registrar relating to LLPs, and

(c) references to registration in a particular part of the United Kingdom are to registration by the registrar for that part of the United Kingdom.

(2) In sub-paragraph (1) "enactment" includes—

(a) an enactment contained in subordinate legislation within the meaning of the Interpretation Act 1978,

(b) an enactment contained in, or in an instrument made under, an Act of the Scottish Parliament,

(c) an enactment contained in, or in an instrument made under, Northern Ireland legislation, and

(d) an enactment contained in, or in an instrument made under, a Measure or Act of the National Assembly for Wales.

13–17. *(Para 13 amends the Limited Liability Partnerships Regulations 2001, SI 2001/1090, regs 4, 10, Sch 2, Pt I, Sch 5, Sch 6, Pts I, III, and inserts reg 2A (see the 2001 Regulations at* **[10.99]** *et seq); para 14 amends the Limited Liability Partnerships Regulations (Northern Ireland) 2004, SR 2004/307 (outside the scope of this work); paras 15, 16 amend the Limited Liability Partnerships (Accounts and Audit) (Application of Companies Act 2006) Regulations 2008, SI 2008/1911, regs 3, 6, 24, 32, 40, 49–51, 54–57 (see the 2008 Regulations at* **[10.223]** *et seq); para 17 revokes the Limited Liability Partnerships (No 2) Regulations 2002, SI 2002/913, and the Limited Liability Partnerships (Particulars of Usual Residential Address) (Confidentiality Orders) Regulations 2002, SI 2002/915.)*

NOTES

National Assembly for Wales: see further, in relation to the renaming of the National Assembly for Wales as the Senedd Cymru or the Welsh Parliament, the Senedd and Elections (Wales) Act 2020, s 2 (with effect from 6 May 2020). See also ss 3–9 of the 2020 Act in relation to the renaming of Acts of the National Assembly for Wales, Members of the National Assembly for Wales, etc.

Note that para 13(5) of this Schedule (amendment of Sch 2, Pt I to the Limited Liability Partnerships Regulations 2001, SI 2001/1090) was amended by the Limited Liability Partnerships (Amendment) Regulations 2009, SI 2009/1833 to correct a drafting error.

COMPANIES (UNFAIR PREJUDICE APPLICATIONS) PROCEEDINGS RULES 2009

(SI 2009/2469)

NOTES

Made: 8 September 2009.
Authority: Insolvency Act 1986, s 411.
Commencement: 1 October 2009.

ARRANGEMENT OF RULES

SCHEDULES

[10.420]

1 Citation, commencement, interpretation and revocation

(1) These Rules may be cited as the Companies (Unfair Prejudice Applications) Proceedings Rules 2009 and come into force on 1st October 2009.

(2) In these Rules "the Act" means the Companies Act 2006.

(3) The Companies (Unfair Prejudice Applications) Proceedings Rules 1986 ("the 1986 Rules") are hereby revoked.

[10.421]

2 Preliminary

(1) These Rules apply in relation to petitions presented to the court under Part 30 of the Act (protection of company's members against unfair prejudice) by a member of a company under section 994(1), by a person treated as a member under section 994(2) or by the Secretary of State under section 995.

(2) Except so far as inconsistent with the Act and these Rules, the Civil Procedure Rules 1998 apply to proceedings under Part 30 of the Act with any necessary modifications.

[10.422]

3 Presentation of petition

(1) The petition shall be in the form set out in the Schedule to these Rules, with such variations, if any, as the circumstances may require.

(2) The petition shall specify the grounds on which it is presented and the nature of the relief which is sought by the petitioner, and shall be delivered to the court for filing with sufficient copies for service under Rule 4.

(3) The court shall fix a hearing for a day ("the return day") on which, unless the court otherwise directs, the petitioner and any respondent (including the company) shall attend before the registrar or District Judge for directions to be given in relation to the procedure on the petition.

(4) On fixing the return day, the court shall return to the petitioner sealed copies of the petition for service, each endorsed with the return day and the time of hearing.

[10.423]

4 Service of petition

(1) The petitioner shall, at least 14 days before the return day, serve a sealed copy of the petition on the company.

(2) In the case of a petition based upon section 994 of the Act, the petitioner shall also, at least 14 days before the return day, serve a sealed copy of the petition on every respondent named in the petition.

[10.424]

5 Return of petition

On the return day, or at any time after it, the court shall give such directions as it thinks appropriate with respect to the following matters—

(a) service of the petition on any person, whether in connection with the time, date and place of a further hearing, or for any other purpose;
(b) whether points of claim and defence are to be delivered;
(c) whether, and if so by what means, the petition is to be advertised;

(d) the manner in which any evidence is to be adduced at any hearing before the judge and in particular (but without prejudice to the generality of the above) as to—
  (i) the taking of evidence wholly or in part by witness statement or orally;
  (ii) the cross-examination of any persons making a witness statement;
  (iii) the matters to be dealt with in evidence;

(e) any other matter affecting the procedure on the petition or in connection with the hearing and disposal of the petition; and

(f) such orders, if any, including a stay for any period, as the court thinks fit, with a view to mediation or other alternative dispute resolution.

[10.425]
6 Advertisement of the order

If the court considers that the order should be advertised, it shall give directions as to the manner and time of advertisement.

[10.426]
7 Transitional provision

These Rules shall not apply, and the provisions of the 1986 Rules shall continue to apply, to any petition presented to the court under Part XVII of the Companies Act 1985 before 1st October 2009.

SCHEDULE

Rule 3

[10.427]

Petition on Ground that Members Unfairly Prejudiced

(a) Insert title of court	To (a) . . . .
(b) Insert full name(s) and address(es) of petitioner(s)	The petition of (b) . . . .
(c) Insert full name and registered no of company subject to petition	1. (c) . . . . ("the company") was incorporated on
(d) Insert date of incorporation	(d) . . . . under the Companies Act . . . .
(e) Insert address of registered office	2. The registered office of the company is at (e) . . . .
(f) Insert amount of nominal capital and how it is divided	3. The nominal capital of the company is (f) £ . . . . divided into . .shares of £ . .each. The amount of the capital paid up or credited as paid up is (g) £ . . . .
(g) Insert amount of capital paid up or credited as paid up	The petitioner is the holder of . . . . . . .shares of £ . . . . . . .each
	4. The principal business which is carried on by the company is: . . . .
(h) Set out the grounds on which the petition is presented	5. (h) . . . .
Delete as applicable	In these circumstances your petitioner submits that the affairs of the company are being conducted in a manner which is unfairly prejudicial to the interests of [some part of the members (including your petitioner)]/[your petitioner]. or
Delete as applicable	[The act or omission]/[the proposed act or omission referred to in part 5 above [is]/[would be] unfairly prejudicial to the interests of [some part of the members (including your petitioner)]/[your petitioner].
(i) Set out the nature of the relief sought	The petitioner therefore prays as follows: (i) . . . . or that such other order may be made as the court thinks fit.
Insert the name or names of the intended respondents	It is intended to serve this petition on . . . .

Endorsement to be completed by the court

This petition having been presented to the court on. . . . .
all parties should attend before [The Registrar]/[District Judge] on

(Date) . . . . at
(Time). . . . . hours
(Place) . . . .

for directions to be given.

The solicitor(s) for the petitioner is/are:—

Name. . . . .
Address . . . .
. . . .

Telephone No: . . . .

Reference . . . .

[Whose Agents are:— . . . .

Name. . . . .
Address . . . .
. . . .

MODERN SLAVERY ACT 2015 (TRANSPARENCY IN SUPPLY CHAINS) REGULATIONS 2015

(SI 2015/1833)

NOTES

Made: 28 October 2015.
Authority: Modern Slavery Act 2015, s 54(2)(b), (3).
Commencement: 29 October 2015.

[10.428]

1 Citation, commencement and interpretation

(1) These Regulations may be cited as the Modern Slavery Act 2015 (Transparency in Supply Chains) Regulations 2015 and come into force on the day after the day on which they are made.

(2) In these Regulations—

(a) "the 2015 Act" means the Modern Slavery Act 2015;
(b) "subsidiary undertaking" has the meaning given by section 1162 of the Companies Act 2006.

[10.429]

2 Prescribed amount of total turnover

The amount of total turnover prescribed for the purposes of section 54(2)(b) of the 2015 Act is £36 million.

[10.430]

3 Determination of total turnover

(1) For the purposes of section 54(2)(b) of the 2015 Act the total turnover of a commercial organisation is—

(a) the turnover of that organisation; and
(b) the turnover of any of its subsidiary undertakings.

(2) In paragraph (1), "turnover" means the amount derived from the provision of goods and services falling within the ordinary activities of the commercial organisation or subsidiary undertaking, after deduction of—

(a) trade discounts;
(b) value added tax; and
(c) any other taxes based on the amounts so derived.

[10.431]

4 Review

(1) The Secretary of State must from time to time—

(a) carry out a review of these Regulations;
(b) set out the conclusions of the review in a report; and
(c) publish the report.

(2) The report must in particular—

(a) set out the objectives intended to be achieved by these Regulations;
(b) assess the extent to which those objectives are achieved; and
(c) assess whether those objectives remain appropriate and, if so, the extent to which they could be achieved with a system that imposes less regulation.

(3) The first report under this regulation must be published before the end of the period of five years beginning with the day on which these Regulations come into force.

(4) Reports under this regulation are afterwards to be published at intervals not exceeding five years.

INSOLVENT COMPANIES (REPORTS ON CONDUCT OF DIRECTORS) (ENGLAND AND WALES) RULES 2016

(SI 2016/180)

NOTES

Made: 11 February 2016.
Authority: Insolvency Act 1986, s 411(1)(a); Company Directors Disqualification Act 1986, s 21(2).
Commencement: 6 April 2016.

ARRANGEMENT OF RULES

[10.432]
1 Citation, extent, commencement and interpretation

(1) These Rules may be cited as the Insolvent Companies (Reports on Conduct of Directors) (England and Wales) Rules 2016, and extend to England and Wales only.

(2) These Rules come into force on 6th April 2016.

(3) In these Rules—

"by electronic means" means sent initially and received at its destination by means of electronic equipment for the processing (which expression includes digital compression) or storage of data, and entirely transmitted, conveyed and received by wire, by radio, by optical means or by other electromagnetic means;

"the Act" means the Company Directors Disqualification Act 1986;

"the former Rules" means the Insolvent Companies (Reports on Conduct of Directors) Rules 1996; and

"the portal" means a digital service provided by the Secretary of State for the functions of both the sending and acknowledgement of receipt, by electronic means, of reports, applications, information and notifications in accordance with these Rules.

[10.433]
2 Revocations

Subject to rule 10, the following are revoked—

(a) the former Rules;
(b) the Insolvent Companies (Reports on Conduct of Directors) (Amendment) Rules 2001; and
(c) the Enterprise Act 2002 (Insolvency) Order 2003, paragraphs 68 to 70 of the Schedule.

[10.434]
3 Enforcement of section 7(4) of the Act

(1) This rule applies where, for the purpose of determining whether to exercise any function under section 7 of the Act (disqualification orders under section 6: applications and acceptance of undertakings), the Secretary of State or the official receiver requires or has required a person to—

(a) furnish the Secretary of State or (as the case may be) the official receiver with information under section 7(4)(a), or
(b) produce and permit inspection of books, papers and other records in accordance with section 7(4)(b).

(2) On the application of the Secretary of State or (as the case may be) the official receiver, the court may make an order directing compliance within such period as may be specified.

(3) The court's order may provide that all costs of and incidental to the application are to be borne by the person to whom the order is directed.

[10.435]
4 Conduct reports required to be sent under section 7A(4) of the Act

(1) This rule is subject to rule 7.

(2) A conduct report required to be sent under section 7A(4) of the Act must be sent by the office-holder to the Secretary of State by electronic means via the portal.

(3) The Secretary of State must as soon as reasonably practicable acknowledge receipt, by electronic means via the portal, of a conduct report sent in accordance with this rule.

[10.436]
5 Applications for a longer period under section 7A(4)(b) of the Act

(1) This rule is subject to rule 7.

(2) This rule applies where the particular circumstances of a case may require a period longer than that provided for by section 7A(4)(a) of the Act for the sending of a conduct report to the Secretary of State.

(3) The office-holder may apply to the Secretary of State for a longer period in which to send the report.

(4) The application must be sent by electronic means via the portal before the expiry of the period specified in section 7A(4)(a) of the Act.

(5) The application must explain the particular circumstances for the making of the application.

(6) The Secretary of State must as soon as reasonably practicable acknowledge receipt, by electronic means via the portal, of an application sent in accordance with this rule.

(7) The Secretary of State must, as soon as is reasonably practicable, notify the office-holder, by electronic means via the portal,—

(a) of the outcome of the application; and

(b) if the application is successful, of the longer period considered appropriate in the particular circumstances for the sending of the report to the Secretary of State under section 7A(4)(b) of the Act.

[10.437]

6 New information required to be sent under section 7A(5) of the Act

(1) This rule is subject to rule 7.

(2) New information required to be sent under section 7A(5) of the Act must be sent by the office-holder to the Secretary of State by electronic means via the portal.

(3) The Secretary of State must as soon as reasonably practicable acknowledge receipt, by electronic means via the portal, of new information sent in accordance with this rule.

[10.438]

7 Unavailability of the portal

(1) The Secretary of State—

(a) may at any time when the portal is unable to carry out one or more of its functions, and

(b) must, where the portal has been unable to carry out one or more of its functions for a period of 7 business days,

provide alternative means for complying with a requirement under rules 4, 5 or 6.

(2) The Secretary of State must give notice to office-holders specifying the means provided for the purposes of paragraph (1) and the period of time for which those means are made available.

(3) The Secretary of State may by notice vary the means provided under paragraph (1) or the period of time for which those means are made available.

(4) A notice under paragraph (3) must give office-holders at least 1 business day's notice before any variation takes effect.

(5) The time within which an office-holder must comply with rules 4, 5 or 6 does not include any day the whole or part of which forms part of a suspension period.

(6) For the purpose of paragraph (5) a suspension period is a period of time during which—

(a) the portal is unable to receive reports, applications or information;

(b) no notice under paragraph (2) or (3) is in force; and

(c) the office-holder has attempted to and been prevented from sending a report, application or information at least once during that period on the basis of sub-paragraph (a).

(7) In this rule, "business day" means any day other than a Saturday, a Sunday, Christmas Day, Good Friday or a day which is a bank holiday in any part of Great Britain.

[10.439]

8 Enforcement of rules 4 to 6

(1) An office-holder who without reasonable excuse fails to comply with any of the obligations imposed by section 7A(4) or 7A(5) of the Act is guilty of an offence and—

(a) on summary conviction of the offence, is liable to a fine not exceeding level 3 on the standard scale, and

(b) for continued contravention, is liable to a daily default fine; that is to say, the office-holder is liable on a second or subsequent summary conviction of the offence to a fine not exceeding one-tenth of level 3 on the standard scale for each day on which the contravention is continued (instead of the penalty specified in sub-paragraph (a)).

(2) Section 431 of the Insolvency Act 1986 (summary proceedings), as it applies to England and Wales, has effect in relation to an offence under this rule as to offences under Parts 1 to 7 of that Act.

[10.440]

9 Review

(1) The Secretary of State must from time to time—

(a) carry out a review of these Rules,

(b) set out the conclusions of the review in a report, and

(c) publish the report.

(2) The report must in particular—

(a) set out the objectives intended to be achieved by the regulatory system established by these Rules,

(b) assess the extent to which those objectives are achieved, and

(c) assess whether those objectives remain appropriate and, if so, the extent to which they could be achieved with a system that imposes less regulation.

(3) The first report under this rule must be published before the end of the period of 5 years beginning on 6th April 2016.

(4) Reports under this rule are afterwards to be published at intervals not exceeding 5 years.

[10.441]

10 Transitional and savings provisions

(1) Rule 6 of the former Rules continues to apply when a period referred to in rule 6(2) of the former Rules has not expired by 6th April 2016.

(2) Until 6th October 2016 rules 3 to 5 of the former Rules continue to apply as if the former Rules had not been revoked when the relevant date for the purposes of rule 4 of the former Rules occurred before 6th April 2016.

(3) Until 6th October 2016 the forms contained in the Schedule to the former Rules must be used for the purpose of complying with rules 3 to 5 of the former Rules.

INSOLVENT COMPANIES (REPORTS ON CONDUCT OF DIRECTORS) (SCOTLAND) RULES 2016

(SI 2016/185)

NOTES

Made: 7 February 2016.

Authority: Insolvency Act 1986, s 411(1)(b); Company Directors Disqualification Act 1986, s 21(2).

Commencement: 6 April 2016.

ARRANGEMENT OF RULES

[10.442]

1 Citation, extent commencement and interpretation

(1) These Rules may be cited as the Insolvent Companies (Reports on Conduct of Directors) (Scotland) Rules 2016, and extend to Scotland only.

(2) These Rules come into force on 6th April 2016.

(3) In these Rules—

"by electronic means" means sent initially and received at its destination by means of electronic equipment for the processing (which expression includes digital compression) or storage of data, and entirely transmitted, conveyed and received by wire, by radio, by optical means or by other electromagnetic means;

"the Act" means the Company Directors Disqualification Act 1986;

"the former Rules" means the Insolvent Companies (Reports on Conduct of Directors) (Scotland) Rules 1996; and

"the portal" means a digital service provided by the Secretary of State for the functions of both the sending and acknowledgement of receipt, by electronic means, of reports, applications, information and notifications in accordance with these Rules.

[10.443]

2 Revocation

Subject to rule 10 the following are revoked—

(a) the former Rules,

(b) the Insolvent Companies (Reports on Conduct of Directors) (Scotland) (Amendment) Rules 2001.

[10.444]

3 Enforcement of section 7(4) of the Act

(1) This rule applies where, for the purpose of determining whether to exercise any function under section 7 of the Act (disqualification orders under section 6: applications and acceptance of undertakings), the Secretary of State requires or has required a person to—

(a) furnish the Secretary of State with information under section 7(4)(a), or

(b) produce and permit inspection of books, papers and other records in accordance with section 7(4)(b).

(2) On the application of the Secretary of State the court may make an order directing compliance within such period as may be specified.

(3) The court's order may provide that all expenses of and incidental to the application are to be borne by the person to whom the order is directed.

[10.445]

4 Conduct reports required to be sent under section 7A(4) of the Act

(1) This rule is subject to rule 7.

(2) A conduct report required to be sent under section 7A(4) of the Act must be sent by the office-holder to the Secretary of State by electronic means via the portal.

(3) The Secretary of State must as soon as reasonably practicable acknowledge receipt, by electronic means via the portal, of a conduct report sent in accordance with this rule.

[10.446]

5 Applications for a longer period under section 7A(4)(b) of the Act

(1) This rule is subject to rule 7.

(2) This rule applies where the particular circumstances of a case may require a period longer than that provided for by section 7A(4)(a) of the Act for the sending of a conduct report to the Secretary of State.

(3) The office-holder may apply to the Secretary of State for a longer period in which to send the report.

(4) The application must be sent by electronic means via the portal before the expiry of the period specified in section 7A(4)(a) of the Act.

(5) The application must explain the particular circumstances for the making of the application.

(6) The Secretary of State must as soon as reasonably practicable acknowledge receipt, by electronic means via the portal, of an application sent in accordance with this rule.

(7) The Secretary of State must, as soon as is reasonably practicable, notify the office-holder, by electronic means via the portal,—

(a) of the outcome of the application; and

(b) if the application is successful, of the longer period considered appropriate in the particular circumstances for the sending of the report to the Secretary of State under section 7A(4)(b) of the Act.

[10.447]

6 New information required to be sent under section 7A(5) of the Act

(1) This rule is subject to rule 7.

(2) New information required to be sent under section 7A(5) of the Act must be sent by the office-holder to the Secretary of State by electronic means via the portal.

(3) The Secretary of State must as soon as reasonably practicable acknowledge receipt, by electronic means via the portal, of new information sent in accordance with this rule.

[10.448]

7 Unavailability of the portal

(1) The Secretary of State—

(a) may at any time when the portal is unable to carry out one or more of its functions, and

(b) must, where the portal has been unable to carry out one or more of its functions for a period of 7 business days,

provide alternative means for complying with a requirement under rules 4, 5 or 6.

(2) The Secretary of State must give notice to office-holders specifying the means provided for the purposes of paragraph (1) and the period of time for which those means are made available.

(3) The Secretary of State may by notice vary the means provided under paragraph (1) or the period of time for which those means are made available.

(4) A notice under paragraph (3) must give office-holders at least 1 business day's notice before any variation takes effect.

(5) The time within which an office-holder must comply with rules 4, 5 or 6 does not include any day the whole or part of which forms part of a suspension period.

(6) For the purpose of paragraph (5) a suspension period is a period of time during which—

(a) the portal is unable to receive reports, applications or information;

(b) no notice under paragraph (2) or (3) is in force; and

(c) the office-holder has attempted to and been prevented from sending a report, application or information at least once during that period on the basis of sub-paragraph (a).

(7) In this rule "business day" means any day other than a Saturday, a Sunday, Christmas Day, Good Friday or a day which is a bank holiday in any part of Great Britain.

[10.449]

8 Enforcement of rules 4 to 6

(1) An office-holder who without reasonable excuse fails to comply with any of the obligations imposed by section 7A(4) or 7A(5) of the Act is guilty of an offence and—

(a) on summary conviction of the offence, is liable to a fine not exceeding level 3 on the standard scale, and

(b) for continued contravention, is liable to a daily default fine; that is to say, the office-holder is liable on a second or subsequent summary conviction of the offence to a fine not exceeding one-tenth of level 3 on the standard scale for each day on which the contravention is continued (instead of the penalty specified in sub-paragraph (a)).

(2) Section 431 of the Insolvency Act 1986 (summary proceedings), as it applies to Scotland, has effect in relation to an offence under this rule as to offences under Parts 1 to 7 of that Act.

[10.450]
9 Review

(1) The Secretary of State must from time to time—

(a) carry out a review of these Rules,
(b) set out the conclusions of the review in a report, and
(c) publish the report.

(2) The report must in particular—

(a) set out the objectives intended to be achieved by the regulatory system established by these Rules,
(b) assess the extent to which those objectives are achieved, and
(c) assess whether those objectives remain appropriate and, if so, the extent to which they could be achieved with a system that imposes less regulation.

(3) The first report under this rule must be published before the end of the period of 5 years beginning on 6th April 2016.

(4) Reports under this rule are afterwards to be published at intervals not exceeding 5 years.

[10.451]
10 Transitional and savings provisions

(1) Rule 6 of the former Rules continues to apply when a period referred to in rule 6(2) of the former Rules has not expired by 6th April 2016.

(2) Until 6th October 2016 rules 3 to 5 of the former Rules continue to apply as if the former Rules had not been revoked when the relevant date for the purposes of rule 4 of the former Rules occurred before 6th April 2016.

(3) Until 6th October 2016 the forms contained in the Schedule to the former Rules must be used for the purpose of complying with rules 3 to 5 of the former Rules.

LIMITED LIABILITY PARTNERSHIPS (REGISTER OF PEOPLE WITH SIGNIFICANT CONTROL) REGULATIONS 2016

(SI 2016/340)

NOTES

Made: 15 March 2016.

Authority: Limited Liability Partnerships Act 2000, ss 15, 17(1)–(3).

Commencement: 6 April 2016 (certain purposes); 30 June 2016 (otherwise) (see reg 1 *post*).

These Regulations are reproduced as amended by: the Information about People with Significant Control (Amendment) Regulations 2017, SI 2017/693.

[10.452]

1 Citation and commencement

(1) These Regulations may be cited as the Limited Liability Partnerships (Register of People with Significant Control) Regulations 2016.

(2) The following provisions come into force on 30th June 2016—

- (a) Section 790M(9)(c) as set out in paragraph 31E of Part 8A of the Limited Liability Partnerships (Application of Companies Act 2006) Regulations 2009 as inserted by Schedule 1 to these Regulations;
- (b) Sections 790W to 790ZD as set out in paragraph 31K of Part 8A of those Regulations as inserted by Schedule 1 to these Regulations; and
- (c) Paragraphs 1 and 3 of Schedule 3 to these Regulations.

(3) The remainder of these Regulations come into force on 6th April 2016.

[10.453]

2 Interpretation

In these Regulations—

"LLP" means a limited liability partnership incorporated under the Limited Liability Partnerships Act 2000;

"principal Regulations" means the Limited Liability Partnerships (Application of Companies Act 2006) Regulations 2009; and

"PSC Regulations" means the Register of People with Significant Control Regulations 2016.

3 (*Reg 3 introduces Sch 1 to these Regulations which inserts the Limited Liability Partnerships (Application of Companies Act 2006) Regulations 2009, SI 2009/1804, Part 8A at* **[10.353]**.)

[10.454]

4 Application of the PSC Regulations

The PSC Regulations apply to LLPs in accordance with the principal Regulations and Schedule 2 to these Regulations.

5 (*Reg 5 introduces Sch 3 to these Regulations (Consequential and Supplementary Amendments).*)

[10.455]

6 Review

(1) The Secretary of State must from time to time—

- (a) carry out a review of these Regulations;
- (b) set out the conclusions of the review in a report; and
- (c) publish the report.

(2) The report must in particular—

- (a) set out the objectives intended to be achieved by the regulatory system established by these Regulations;
- (b) assess the extent to which those objectives have been achieved; and
- (c) assess whether those objectives remain appropriate and, if so, the extent to which they could be achieved in another way that imposed less regulation.

(3) The first report under this regulation must be published within the period in which the Secretary of State is required to publish a report under section 82 of the Small Business, Enterprise and Employment Act 2015.

(4) Reports under this regulation are afterwards to be published at intervals not exceeding five years.

SCHEDULES

SCHEDULE 1
APPLICATION OF PART 21A COMPANIES ACT 2006

(*Inserts the Limited Liability Partnerships (Application of Companies Act 2006) Regulations 2009, SI 2009/1804, Part 8A at* **[10.353]**.)

SCHEDULE 2
APPLICATION OF THE PSC REGULATIONS

Regulation 4

GENERAL INTRODUCTORY PROVISIONS

[10.456]

1. Regulation 2 of the PSC Regulations applies to LLPs, modified so that it reads as follows—

"2 Interpretation

In these Regulations—

"the Act" means the Companies Act 2006;

"the 2009 Regulations" means the Companies (Disclosure of Address) Regulations 2009;

["credit institution" has the same meaning as in regulation 10(1) of the Money Laundering, Terrorist Financing and Transfer of Funds (Information on the Payer) Regulations 2017;]

["financial institution" has the same meaning as in regulation 10(2) of the Money Laundering, Terrorist Financing and Transfer of Funds (Information on the Payer) Regulations 2017;]

"former name" means a name by which an individual was formerly known for business purposes;

"LLP" means a limited liability partnership incorporated under the Limited Liability Partnerships Act 2000;

"LLP voting rights" means the right to vote on those matters which are to be decided upon by a vote of the members of the LLP;

"name" means a person's forename and surname, except that in the case of—

(a) a peer; or

(b) an individual usually known by a title,

the title may be stated instead of that person's forename and surname or in addition to either or both of them;

"personal representative" means the executor or administrator for the time being of a deceased person;

"principal Regulations" means the Limited Liability Partnerships (Application of Companies Act 2006) Regulations 2009

"PSC Regulations" means the Register of People with Significant Control Regulations 2016;

"relevant body" means—

(a) a police force within the meaning of section 101(1) of the Police Act 1996;

(b) the Police Service of Northern Ireland; and

(c) the Police Service of Scotland;

"section 243 decision" means a determination under the 2009 Regulations (including those regulations as applied by the principal Regulations) which is a section 243 decision within the meaning of those Regulations;

"secured information" means the required particulars (other than the particular required by section 790K(1)(i) of the Act) of a registrable person in relation to an LLP;

"specified public authorities" has the meaning given in regulation 22(1);

"voting rights" means rights to vote at general meetings of the company or legal entity in question, including rights that arise only in certain circumstances, and in relation to a legal entity that does not have general meetings at which matters are decided by the exercise of voting rights, a reference to voting rights is to be read as a reference to rights in relation to the entity that are equivalent to those of a person entitled to exercise voting rights in a company;

"voting shares" means shares or equivalent interests carrying voting rights; and

"withdrawal notice" has the meaning given in regulation 21.".

2. Regulation 6, in Part 2 of the PSC Regulations, applies to LLPs modified so that it reads as follows—

"6 Fee for a copy of an LLP's PSC register

(1) The fee prescribed for the purpose of section 790O(2) of the Act is £12.

(2) That fee applies to any single request for a copy of an LLP's PSC register, or any part of it, regardless of how many parts are required to be copied.".

3. Regulations 7 to 47, in Parts 3 to 8 of the PSC Regulations, apply to LLPs modified so that they read as follows—

"PART 3

NATURE OF CONTROL AND FOREIGN LIMITED PARTNERS

7 Particulars required as to nature of control

The particulars required by sections 790K(1)(h), 790K(2)(e) and 790K(3)(f) of the Act (particulars as to nature of control over the LLP) are—

(a) where the person meets the first specified condition, the statement listed in Part 1 of Schedule 2 which is applicable to that person;

(b) where the person meets the second specified condition, the statement listed in Part 2 of Schedule 2 which is applicable to that person;

(c) where the person meets the third specified condition, the statement listed in Part 3 of Schedule 2;

(d) where the person meets the fourth specified condition and does not meet the first, second or third specified condition, the statement listed in Part 4 of Schedule 2;

(e) where the person meets the fifth specified condition in connection with a trust, every statement listed in Part 5 of Schedule 2 which is applicable to that person;

(f) where the person meets the fifth specified condition in connection with a firm, every statement listed in Part 6 of Schedule 2 which is applicable to that person.

8 Characteristics of a foreign limited partner

(1) The characteristics prescribed for the purposes of paragraph 25(5)(b) of Schedule 1A to the Act are that the individual—

(a) participates in a foreign limited partnership as a limited liability participant; or

(b) directly or indirectly, holds shares or a right in or in relation to a legal entity which participates in a foreign limited partnership as a limited liability participant.

(2) In this regulation—

(a) a "foreign limited partnership" is an arrangement which—

(i) is established under the law of a country or territory outside the United Kingdom;

(ii) consists of at least one person who has unlimited liability for the debts and obligations of the arrangement; and

(iii) consists of at least one person who has no, or limited, liability for the debts and obligations of the arrangement for so long as that person does not take part in the management of the arrangement's business; and

(b) a "limited liability participant" is a person who—

(i) has no, or limited, liability for the debts and obligations of the foreign limited partnership for so long as that person does not take part in the management of the foreign limited partnership's business; and

(ii) does not take part in the management of the foreign limited partnership's business.

PART 4
ADDITIONAL MATTERS

9 Additional matters to be noted in a PSC register

(1) The additional matters required to be noted in an LLP's PSC register under section 790M(7) of the Act are the matters required to be noted by regulations 10 to 17.

(2) Where any additional matter noted in an LLP's PSC register in accordance with regulation 10, 11, 12 or 13 ceases to be true, the LLP must note in its PSC register—

(a) that the additional matter has ceased to be true; and

(b) the date on which the additional matter ceased to be true.

10 Additional matters where there is no registrable person or registrable relevant legal entity

(1) This regulation applies where an LLP knows or has reasonable cause to believe that there is no registrable person or registrable relevant legal entity in relation to the LLP.

(2) The LLP must note in its PSC register that it knows or has reasonable cause to believe that there is no registrable person or registrable relevant legal entity in relation to the LLP.

11 Additional matters where there is an unidentified registrable person

(1) This regulation applies where an LLP—

(a) knows or has reasonable cause to believe that there is a registrable person in relation to the LLP; and

(b) has not been able to identify the registrable person.

(2) The LLP must—

(a) note in its PSC register that it knows or has reasonable cause to believe that there is a registrable person in relation to the LLP but it has not identified the registrable person; and

(b) make a separate note in its PSC register in respect of each registrable person which the LLP has been unable to identify.

12 Additional matters where an identified registrable person's particulars are not confirmed

(1) This regulation applies where—

(a) an LLP has identified a registrable person in relation to the LLP; and

(b) all the required particulars of that person have not been confirmed for the purposes of section 790M of the Act.

(2) The LLP must—

(a) note in its PSC register that it has identified a registrable person in relation to the LLP but all the required particulars of that person have not been confirmed; and

(b) make a separate note in its PSC register in respect of each registrable person which the LLP has been unable to identify.

13 Additional matters where an LLP's investigations are ongoing

(1) This regulation applies where an LLP—

(a) is not required to place a note in its PSC register by regulation 10, 11 or 12;

(b) has not entered, and is not required to enter, the required particulars of any registrable person or registrable relevant legal entity in its PSC register; and

(c) has not yet completed taking reasonable steps to find out if there is anyone who is a registrable person or a registrable relevant legal entity in relation to the LLP under section 790D of the Act.

(2) The LLP must note in its PSC register that it has not yet completed taking reasonable steps to find out if there is anyone who is a registrable person or a registrable relevant legal entity in relation to the LLP.

14 Additional matters where there is a failure to comply with a notice given under section 790D of the Act

(1) This regulation applies where—

(a) an LLP has given a notice under section 790D of the Act; and

(b) the addressee of the notice has failed to comply with the notice within the time specified in it.

(2) The LLP must—

(a) note in its PSC register that it has given a notice under section 790D of the Act which has not been complied with; and

(b) make a separate note in its PSC register in respect of each notice under section 790D which has not been complied with.

15 Additional matters where there is a failure to comply with a notice given under section 790E of the Act

(1) This regulation applies where—

(a) an LLP has given a notice under section 790E of the Act; and

(b) the addressee of the notice has failed to comply with the notice within the time specified in it.

(2) The LLP must note in the entry in its PSC register for the addressee that the addressee has failed to comply with a notice given by the LLP under section 790E of the Act.

16 Additional matters where a notice given under section 790D or section 790E of the Act is complied with after the time specified in the notice

(1) This regulation applies where—

(a) a note has been placed in an LLP's register under regulation 14 or 15; and

(b) the addressee of the notice to which the note relates has complied with the notice after the time specified in the notice.

(2) The LLP must note in its PSC register—

(a) that the notice has been complied with after the time specified in the notice; and

(b) the date on which the notice was complied with.

17 Additional matters where an LLP has issued a restrictions notice

(1) This regulation applies where an LLP has issued a restrictions notice under paragraph 1 of Schedule 1B to the Act.

(2) The LLP must—

(a) note in its PSC register that it has issued a restrictions notice under paragraph 1 of Schedule 1B to the Act; and

(b) make a separate note in its PSC register in respect of each registrable person which the LLP has been unable to identify.

(3) Where the LLP withdraws the restrictions notice under paragraph 11 of Schedule 1B to the Act, the LLP must note in its PSC register—

(a) that it has withdrawn the restrictions notice by giving a withdrawal notice; and

(b) the date specified in the withdrawal notice as the date on which the withdrawal notice was given.

(4) Where a court makes an order under paragraph 8 of Schedule 1B to the Act directing that a relevant interest in the LLP cease to be subject to restrictions, the LLP must note in its PSC register—

(a) that the court has made an order under paragraph 8 of Schedule 1B to the Act directing that a relevant interest in the LLP cease to be subject to restrictions; and

(b) the date on which that order takes effect.

PART 5

WARNING AND RESTRICTIONS NOTICES

18 Content of warning notice

A warning notice given under paragraph 1 of Schedule 1B to the Act must—

(a) specify the date on which the warning notice is given;

(b) be accompanied by a copy of the notice given under section 790D or 790E of the Act to which the warning notice relates;

(c) identify the addressee's relevant interest in the LLP;

(d) state that the LLP will consider reasons provided to it as to why the addressee failed to comply with the notice given under section 790D or 790E of the Act;

(e) explain the effect of a restrictions notice; and

(f) state that, by virtue of a restrictions notice, certain acts or failures to act may constitute an offence.

19 Content of restrictions notice

A restrictions notice issued under paragraph 1 of Schedule 1B to the Act must—

(a) specify the date on which the restrictions notice is issued;

(b) be accompanied by a copy of the warning notice which preceded the restrictions notice;

(c) identify the addressee's relevant interest in the LLP;

(d) explain the effect of the restrictions notice;

(e) state that, by virtue of the restrictions notice, certain acts or failures to act may constitute an offence; and

(f) state that an aggrieved person may apply to the court for an order directing that the relevant interest cease to be subject to restrictions.

20 Failure to comply with section 790D or 790E notice: valid reason

An LLP must take into account any incapacity of the addressee of a notice given under section 790D or 790E of the Act in deciding what counts as a "valid reason" sufficient to justify the addressee's failure to comply with the notice.

21 Withdrawal of restrictions notice

Where an LLP is required to withdraw a restrictions notice under paragraph 11 of Schedule 1B to the Act by notice (a "withdrawal notice"), the withdrawal notice must—

(a) be given before the end of the period of 14 days beginning with the day on which the LLP became required to withdraw the restrictions notice under that paragraph;

(b) specify the date on which the withdrawal notice is given;

(c) identify the addressee's relevant interest in the LLP; and

(d) state that the relevant interest is no longer subject to restrictions.

PART 6
THE PROTECTION OF USUAL RESIDENTIAL ADDRESS INFORMATION

22 Permitted disclosure of usual residential address information by the registrar to specified public authorities

(1) The public authorities listed in Schedule 3 to the PSC Regulations ("specified public authorities") are specified for the purposes of section 243 of the Act (as applied by section 790ZF of the Act).

(2) The conditions specified for the disclosure of information within section 790ZF(2) of the Act by the registrar to specified public authorities in accordance with section 243 of the Act (as applied by section 790ZF of the Act) are listed in Part 1 of Schedule 4 to the PSC Regulations.

23 Permitted disclosure of usual residential address information by the registrar to credit reference agencies

(1) The conditions specified for the disclosure of information within section 790ZF(2) of the Act by the registrar to a credit reference agency in accordance with section 243 of the Act (as applied by section 790ZF of the Act) are listed in Part 2 of Schedule 4 of the PSC Regulations.

(2) The registrar may rely on a statement delivered to the registrar by a credit reference agency under Schedule 4 of the PSC Regulations as sufficient evidence of the matters stated in it.

24 Circumstances where the registrar must refrain from disclosure of usual residential address information

(1) The registrar must not disclose information within section 790ZF(2) of the Act to a credit reference agency if in relation to that information an application has been made under regulation 25, 26 or 27—

(a) which has not yet been determined by the registrar and has not been withdrawn under regulation 29;

(b) which has been determined by the registrar in favour of the applicant (but see paragraph (2);

(c) which was unsuccessful and the period for applying for permission to appeal in regulation 30(3) has not passed;

(d) which was unsuccessful and an appeal to the court in respect of that application under regulation 30 has not been determined by the court; or

(e) which was unsuccessful and the applicant has successfully appealed the determination.

(2) Paragraph (1)(b) does not apply where the determination has ceased to have effect under regulation 31.

(3) For the purposes of this regulation, an application is made when it has been registered by the registrar.

25 Application by an individual requiring the registrar to refrain from disclosing that individual's usual residential address information to a credit reference agency

(1) An individual who is, or proposes to become, a registrable person in relation to an LLP may make an application to the registrar requiring the registrar to refrain from disclosing to a credit reference agency information within section 790ZF(2) relating to that individual.

(2) The grounds on which an application may be made are that—

(a) the applicant reasonably believes that there is a serious risk that the applicant, or a person who lives with the applicant, will be subjected to violence or intimidation as a result of the activities of at least one of—

(i) the companies in relation to which the applicant is, or proposes to become, a registrable person;

(ii) the companies in relation to which the applicant used to be a registrable person;

(iii) the LLPs in relation to which the applicant is, or proposes to become, a registrable person;

(iv) the LLPs in relation to which the applicant used to be a registrable person;

(v) the LLPs in relation to which the applicant is or proposes to become a member;

(vi) the LLPs in relation to which the applicant used to be a member;

(vii) the companies in relation to which the applicant is, or proposes to become, a director;

(viii) the companies in relation to which the applicant used to be a director; or

(ix) the overseas companies of which the applicant is or used to be a director, secretary or permanent representative; or

(b) a section 243 decision has been made in respect of the applicant which has not ceased to have effect.

(3) The application must contain—

(a) a statement of the grounds on which the application is made;

(b) the name and any former name of the applicant;

(c) the date of birth of the applicant;

(d) the usual residential address of the applicant;

(e) the email address of the applicant, if any;

(f) the name and registered number of each LLP in relation to which the applicant is, or proposes to become, a registrable person;

(g) where the grounds of the application are those described in paragraphs (2)(a)(ii) to (ix), the names and registered numbers of the companies, limited liability partnerships and overseas companies whose activities are relevant to the application; and

(h) where the grounds of the application are those described in paragraph (2)(b), the name and registered number of the company in relation to which the section 243 decision was made, unless the section 243 decision relates to a proposed company which was never incorporated.

(4) Where the grounds of the application are those described in paragraph (2)(a), the application must be accompanied by evidence which supports the applicant's statement of the grounds on which the application is made.

(5) The registrar must determine the application and, within 7 days beginning with the date that the determination is made, send to the applicant notice of the determination.

(6) Where the application is unsuccessful, the notice under paragraph (5) must inform the applicant of the applicant's right to apply for permission to appeal against the determination within 28 days beginning with the date of the notice.

26 Application by an LLP requiring the registrar to refrain from disclosing an individual's usual residential address information to a credit reference agency

(1) An LLP ("the applicant") may make an application to the registrar requiring the registrar to refrain from disclosing to a credit reference agency information within section 790ZF(2) of the Act relating to an individual ("R") who is, or proposes to become, a registrable person in relation to the LLP.

(2) An LLP may only make an application under paragraph (1) where R has given consent for the LLP to make the application on R's behalf.

(3) The grounds on which an application may be made are that—

(a) the applicant reasonably believes that there is a serious risk that R, or a person who lives with R, will be subjected to violence or intimidation as a result of the applicant's activities; or

(b) a section 243 decision has been made in respect of R which has not ceased to have effect.

(4) Where the grounds of the application are those described in paragraph (3)(b), the application must only relate to one individual who is, or proposes to become, a registrable person in relation to the LLP.

(5) The application must contain—

(a) a statement of the grounds on which the application is made;

(b) confirmation that R consents to the making of the application;

(c) the name and registered number of the applicant;

(d) the address of the registered office of the applicant;

(e) the email address of the applicant, if any;

(f) the name and any former name of R;

(g) the date of birth of R;

(h) the usual residential address of R;

(i) the email address of R, if any;

(j) where R is a registrable person in relation to another LLP or company, the name and registered number of that LLP or company; and

(k) where the grounds of the application are those described in paragraph (3)(b), the name and registered number of the company in relation to which the section 243 decision was made, unless the decision relates to a proposed company which was never incorporated.

(6) Where the grounds of the application are those described in paragraph (3)(a), the application must be accompanied by evidence which supports the applicant's statement of the grounds on which the application is made.

(7) The registrar must determine the application and, within 7 days beginning with the date that the determination is made, send to the applicant notice of the determination.

(8) Where the application is unsuccessful, the notice under paragraph (7) must inform the applicant of the applicant's right to apply for permission to appeal against the determination within 28 days beginning with the date of the notice.

27 Application by a proposed member of a proposed LLP requiring the registrar to refrain from disclosing an individual's usual residential address information to a credit reference agency

(1) A proposed member of a proposed LLP ("the applicant") may make an application to the registrar requiring the registrar to refrain from disclosing to a credit reference agency information within section 790ZF(2) relating to an individual ("R") who proposes to become, on or after the formation of the proposed LLP, a registrable person in relation to the LLP.

(2) A proposed member of a proposed LLP may only make an application under paragraph (1) where R has given consent for the proposed member to make the application on R's behalf.

(3) The grounds on which an application may be made are that—

(a) the applicant reasonably believes that there is a serious risk that R, or a person who lives with R, will be subjected to violence or intimidation as a result of the proposed activities of the proposed LLP; or

(b) a section 243 decision has been made in respect of R which has not ceased to have effect.

(4) Where the grounds of the application are those described in paragraph 3(b), the application must only relate to one individual who proposes to become a registrable person in relation to the proposed LLP.

(5) The application must contain—

(a) a statement of the grounds on which the application is made;

(b) confirmation that R consents to the making of the application;

(c) the name and any former name of the applicant;

(d) the usual residential address of the applicant;

(e) the email address of the applicant, if any;

(f) the name of the proposed LLP to which the memorandum relates;

(g) the name and any former name of R;

(h) the date of birth of R;

(i) the usual residential address of R;

(j) the email address of R, if any;

(k) where R is a registrable person in relation to another LLP or company, the name and registered number of that LLP or company; and

(l) where the grounds of the application are those described in paragraph (3)(b), the name and registered number of the LLP in relation to which the section 243 decision was made, unless the section 243 decision relates to a proposed company which was never incorporated.

(6) Where the grounds of the application are those described in paragraph (3)(a), the application must be accompanied by evidence which supports the applicant's statement of the grounds on which the application is made.

(7) The registrar must determine the application and, within 7 days beginning with the date that the determination is made, send to the applicant notice of the determination.

(8) Where the application is unsuccessful, the notice under paragraph (7) must inform the applicant of the applicant's right to apply for permission to appeal against the determination within 28 days beginning with the date of the notice.

28 Matters relating to an application made under regulation 25, 26 or 27

(1) For the purpose of determining an application made under regulation 25, 26 or 27 the registrar may—

- (a) direct that additional information or evidence should be delivered to the registrar;
- (b) refer any question relating to an assessment of the nature or extent of any risk of violence or intimidation to a relevant body or to any other person the registrar considers may be able to assist in making the assessment; and
- (c) accept any answer to a question referred under paragraph (1)(b) as providing sufficient evidence of the nature or extent of any risk.

(2) The registrar must not make available for public inspection—

- (a) any application made under regulation 25, 26 or 27;
- (b) any documents provided in support of that application;
- (c) any notice provided under regulation 29 (notice of withdrawal of application);
- (d) any notice provided under regulation 30(4) (notice of an appeal);
- (e) any notice provided under regulation 31 (notice that determination no longer wanted); or
- (f) any representations delivered under regulation 32 (representations as to why determination should not be revoked).

(3) A person who makes an application under regulation 25, 26 or 27 must inform the registrar in writing without delay upon becoming aware of any change to any information or evidence provided to the registrar in connection with the application.

29 Withdrawal of an application made under regulation 25, 26 or 27

If a person in relation to whom an application has been made under regulation 25, 26 or 27 that has not yet been determined notifies the registrar in writing that the person no longer wishes the registrar to determine the application, the registrar is not required to determine the application under regulation 25(5), 26(7) or 27(7) (as the case may be).

30 Appealing against a determination made under regulation 25, 26 or 27

(1) Subject to paragraph (2), an applicant who has received notice under regulation 25(5), 26(7) or 27(7) that the applicant's application has been unsuccessful may appeal to the High Court or, in Scotland, the Court of Session on the grounds that the determination—

- (a) is unlawful;
- (b) is irrational or unreasonable; or
- (c) has been made on the basis of a procedural impropriety or otherwise contravenes the rules of natural justice.

(2) No appeal may be brought unless the permission of the court has been obtained.

(3) No application for such permission may be made after 28 days beginning with the date of the notice under regulation 25(5), 26(7), or 27(7) unless the court is satisfied that there was good reason for the failure of the applicant to seek permission before the end of that period.

(4) An applicant who seeks permission to appeal must serve written notice of the application on the registrar within 7 days beginning with the date on which the application for permission was issued.

(5) The court determining an appeal may—

- (a) dismiss the appeal; or
- (b) quash the determination.

(6) Where the court quashes a determination it may refer the matter to the registrar with a direction to reconsider it and make a determination in accordance with the findings of the court.

31 Duration of a determination made under regulation 25, 26 or 27

A determination made under regulation 25(5), 26(7) or 27(7) that an application is successful continues to have effect until—

- (a) either—
  - (i) the person to whom the determination relates; or
  - (ii) that person's personal representative,

  notifies the registrar in writing that he or she wishes the determination to cease to have effect; or
- (b) the registrar revokes the determination under regulation 32.

32 Revocation of a determination made under regulation 25, 26 or 27

(1) The registrar may revoke a determination made under regulation 25(5), 26(7) or 27(7) that an application is successful if—

- (a) the applicant in relation to the determination or (if different) any person to whom the application relates has been found guilty of an offence under section 1112 of the Act (general false statement offence) in respect of purported compliance with any provision of this Part;
- (b) the registrar has sent a notice in accordance with paragraph (2) to the applicant in relation to the determination and (if different) the person to whom the determination relates; and
- (c) the period of 28 days beginning with the date of that notice has expired.

(2) The notice mentioned in paragraph (1)(b) must inform the addressee—

- (a) of the registrar's intention to revoke the determination;

(b) that the addressee may, within 28 days beginning with the date of the notice, deliver representations in writing to the registrar as to why the registrar should not revoke the determination; and

(c) that if the registrar receives such representations within that period, the registrar will have regard to the representations in deciding whether to revoke the determination.

(3) If within the period specified in paragraph (2)(b) the addressee of the notice delivers representations in writing to the registrar as to why the registrar should not revoke the determination, the registrar must have regard to the representations in deciding whether to revoke the determination.

(4) The registrar must send notice of the registrar's decision as to whether to revoke a determination to the applicant in relation to the determination and (if different) the person to whom the determination relates within 7 days beginning with the date of the decision.

PART 7
PROTECTION OF SECURED INFORMATION

33 Circumstances where the registrar must omit secured information from material on the register available for public inspection

(1) The registrar must omit secured information from the material on the register that is available for public inspection if—

(a) in relation to that information an application has been made under regulation 36, 37 or 38—

(i) which has not yet been determined by the registrar and has not been withdrawn under regulation 40;

(ii) which has been determined by the registrar in favour of the applicant (but see paragraph (4));

(iii) which was unsuccessful and a period of 42 days beginning with the date of the notice sent under regulation 36(5), 37(5) or 38(5) has not passed;

(iv) which was unsuccessful and an appeal to the court in respect of that application under regulation 41 has not been determined by the court; or

(v) which was unsuccessful and the applicant has successfully appealed the determination; and

(b) that information is contained in a document delivered to the registrar in which such information is required to be stated and, in the case of a document having more than one part, the information is contained in a part of the document in which such information is required to be stated.

(2) The registrar is not obliged to check documents, other than those described in paragraph (1)(b), to ensure the absence of secured information in relation to which an application under regulation 36, 37 or 38 has been made.

(3) If the secured information in relation to which an application under regulation 36, 37 or 38 is made is available for public inspection on the register at the time that the application is made, the registrar must comply with paragraph (1) as soon as reasonably practicable.

(4) Paragraph (1)(a)(ii) does not apply where the determination has ceased to have effect under regulation 43.

(5) For the purposes of this regulation an application under regulation 36, 37 or 38 is made when it has been registered by the registrar.

34 Circumstances where the registrar must not use or disclose secured information

(1) Subject to paragraph (3), the registrar must not use or disclose secured information if in relation to that information an application has been made under regulation 36, 37 or 38—

(a) which has not yet been determined by the registrar and has not been withdrawn under regulation 40;

(b) which has been determined by the registrar in favour of the applicant (but see paragraph (2));

(c) which was unsuccessful and a period of 42 days beginning with the date of the notice sent under regulation 36(5), 37(5) or 38(5) has not passed;

(d) which was unsuccessful and an appeal to the court in respect of that application under regulation 41 has not been determined by the court; or

(e) which was unsuccessful and the applicant has successfully appealed the determination.

(2) Paragraph (1)(b) does not apply where the determination has ceased to have effect under regulation 43.

(3) Where the prohibition in paragraph (1) applies in relation to secured information, the registrar may—

(a) use or disclose that secured information for communicating with the person to whom the application under regulation 36, 37 or 38 relates and, if different, the applicant; . . .

(b) disclose the secured information to a specified public authority where the conditions specified in Part 1 of Schedule 4 are satisfied[; and

(c) disclose such of the secured information as is specified in paragraph (3A) to a credit institution or a financial institution which satisfies the conditions specified in Part 2A of Schedule 4].

[(3A) The information specified for disclosure under paragraph (3)(c) is—

(a) name,

(b) a service address,

(c) the country or state (or part of the United Kingdom) in which the individual is usually resident,

(d) nationality,

(e) month and year of birth,

(f) the date on which the individual became a registrable person in relation to the company in question, and

(g) the nature of his or her control over that company (see Schedule 1A to the Act and regulation 7 of, and Schedule 2 to, these Regulations).

(3B) The registrar may rely on a statement delivered to the registrar by a credit institution or a financial institution under Part 2A of Schedule 4 as sufficient evidence of the matters stated in it.]

(4) For the purposes of this regulation an application under regulation 36, 37 or 38 is made when it has been registered by the registrar.

35 Fee payable for the disclosure by the registrar of secured information

(1) On the disclosure of secured information under regulation 34(3)(b) the specified public authority to which the information is disclosed must pay a fee to the registrar for the disclosure of that information.

(2) The fee payable under paragraph (1) is—

(a) where the request for secured information by the specified public authority is made by reference to an individual, £5.00 per individual specified in the request; or

(b) where the request for secured information by the specified public authority is made by reference to an LLP, £5.00 per LLP specified in the request.

[35A Fee payable for the disclosure by the registrar of information to a credit institution or a financial institution

(1) On the disclosure of information under regulation 34(3)(c) the credit institution or the financial institution to which the information is disclosed must pay a fee to the registrar for the disclosure of the information.

(2) The fee payable under paragraph (1) is—

(a) where the request for information is made by reference to an individual, £5.00 per individual specified in the request; or

(b) where the request for information is made by reference to a company, £5.00 per company specified in the request.]

36 Application by an individual requiring the registrar to refrain from using or disclosing that individual's secured information

(1) An individual may make an application to the registrar requiring the registrar to refrain from using or disclosing secured information relating to that individual if that individual—

(a) is a registrable person in relation to an LLP;

(b) proposes to become a registrable person in relation to an LLP; or

(c) used to be a registrable person in relation to an LLP.

(2) The grounds on which an application may be made are that the applicant reasonably believes that if that secured information is disclosed by the registrar—

(a) the activities of that LLP; or

(b) one or more characteristics or personal attributes of the applicant when associated with that LLP,

will put the applicant or a person living with the applicant at serious risk of being subjected to violence or intimidation.

(3) The application must—

(a) contain—

(i) a statement of the grounds on which the application is made;

(ii) the name and any former name of the applicant;

(iii) the date of birth of the applicant;

(iv) the usual residential address of the applicant;

(v) the email address of the applicant, if any;

(vi) the name and registered number of the LLP in relation to which the applicant is, proposes to become, or used to be a registrable person; and

(vii) if relevant, a statement that in relation to the applicant an application has also been made under regulation 25, 26 or 27 or a determination has been made in relation to an application under regulation 25(5), 26(7) or 27(7) in favour of the applicant; and

(b) be accompanied by evidence which supports the applicant's statement of the grounds on which the application is made.

(4) Where an individual who is or used to be a registrable person in relation to an LLP sends an application under paragraph (1) to the registrar in relation to that LLP, that individual must inform the LLP of that fact as soon as reasonably practicable.

(5) The registrar must determine the application and, within 7 days beginning with the date that the determination is made, send to the applicant notice of the determination.

(6) Where the application is unsuccessful, the notice under paragraph (5) must inform the applicant of the applicant's right to apply for permission to appeal against the determination within 28 days beginning with the date of the notice.

37 Application by an LLP requiring the registrar to refrain from using or disclosing an individual's secured information

(1) An LLP ("the applicant") may make an application to the registrar requiring the registrar to refrain from using or disclosing secured information relating to an individual ("S") who—

(a) is a registrable person;

(b) proposes to become a registrable person; or

(c) used to be a registrable person,

in relation to that LLP.

(2) An LLP may only make an application under paragraph (1) where S has given consent for the LLP to make the application on S's behalf.

(3) The grounds on which an application may be made are that the applicant reasonably believes that if the secured information is disclosed by the registrar—

(a) the activities of the applicant; or

(b) one or more characteristics or personal attributes of S when associated with the applicant,

will put S or a person living with S at serious risk of being subjected to violence or intimidation.

(4) The application must—

(a) contain—

(i) a statement of the grounds on which the application is made;

(ii) confirmation that S consents to the making of the application;

(iii) the name and registered number of the applicant;

(iv) the address of the registered office of the applicant;

(v) the email address of the applicant, if any;

(vi) the name and any former name of S;

(vii) the date of birth of S;

(viii) the usual residential address of S; and

(ix) the email address of S, if any; and

(b) be accompanied by evidence which supports the applicant's statement of the grounds on which the application is made.

(5) The registrar must determine the application and, within 7 days beginning with the date that the determination is made, send to the applicant notice of the determination.

(6) Where the application is unsuccessful the notice under paragraph (5) must inform the applicant of the applicant's right to apply for permission to appeal against the determination within 28 days beginning with the date of the notice.

38 Application by a proposed member of a proposed LLP requiring the registrar to refrain from using or disclosing an individual's secured information

(1) A proposed member of a proposed LLP ("the applicant") may make an application to the registrar requiring the registrar to refrain from using or disclosing secured information relating to an individual ("S") who proposes to become, on or after the formation of proposed the LLP, a registrable person in relation to the proposed LLP.

(2) A proposed member of a proposed LLP may only make an application under paragraph (1) where S has given consent for the proposed member to make the application on S's behalf.

(3) The grounds on which an application may be made are that the applicant reasonably believes that if the secured information is disclosed by the registrar—

(a) the proposed activities of the proposed LLP; or

(b) one or more characteristics or personal attributes of S when associated with the proposed LLP,

will put S or a person living with S at serious risk of being subjected to violence or intimidation.

(4) The application must—

(a) contain—

(i) a statement of the grounds on which the application is made;

(ii) confirmation that S consents to the making of the application;

(iii) the name and any former name of the applicant;

(iv) the usual residential address of the applicant;

(v) the email address of the applicant, if any;

(vi) the name of the proposed LLP;

(vii) the name and any former name of S;

(viii) the date of birth of S;

(ix) the usual residential address of S; and

(x) the email address of S, if any; and

(b) be accompanied by evidence which supports the applicant's statement of the grounds on which the application is made.

(5) The registrar must determine the application and, within 7 days beginning with the date that the determination is made, send to the applicant notice of the determination.

(6) Where the application is unsuccessful, the notice under paragraph (5) must inform the applicant of the applicant's right to apply for permission to appeal against the determination within 28 days beginning with the date of the notice.

39 Matters relating to an application made under regulation 36, 37 or 38

(1) For the purpose of determining an application made under regulation 36, 37 or 38 the registrar may—

(a) direct that additional information or evidence should be delivered to the registrar;

(b) refer any question relating to an assessment of the nature or extent of any risk of violence or intimidation to a relevant body or to any other person the registrar considers may be able to assist in making that assessment; and

(c) accept any answer to a question referred under paragraph (1)(b) as providing sufficient evidence of the nature or extent of any risk.

(2) The registrar must not make available for public inspection—

(a) any application made under regulation 36, 37 or 38;

(b) any documents provided in support of that application;

(c) any notice provided under regulation 40 (notice of withdrawal of application);

(d) any notice provided under regulation 41 (notice of an appeal);

(e) any notice provided under regulation 43 (notice that determination no longer wanted);

(f) any notice provided under regulation 44 (representations as to why determination should not be revoked); or

(g) any notice provided under regulation 46 (notice that a person is no longer a registrable person).

(3) A person who makes an application under regulation 36, 37 or 38 must inform the registrar in writing without delay upon becoming aware of any change to any information or evidence provided to the registrar in connection with the application.

(4) For the purposes of this regulation an application under regulation 36, 37 or 38 is made when it has been registered by the registrar.

40 Withdrawal of an application made under regulation 36, 37 or 38

(1) If a person in relation to whom an application has been made under regulation 36, 37 or 38 that has not yet been determined notifies the registrar in writing that the person no longer wishes the registrar to determine the application, the registrar is not required to determine the application under regulation 36(5), 37(5) or 38(5) (as the case may be).

(2) Where a person in relation to whom an application under regulation 36 or 37 has been made sends a notice to the registrar under paragraph (1), that person must notify the LLP to which the application related of this fact as soon as reasonably practicable.

(3) Where a person in relation to whom an application under regulation 38 has been made sends a notice to the registrar under paragraph (1), that person must notify the proposed member of the proposed LLP who made the application and, if incorporated, the LLP to which the application related of this fact as soon as reasonably practicable.

(4) For the purposes of this regulation an application under regulation 36, 37 or 38 is made when it has been registered by the registrar.

41 Appealing against an unsuccessful application made under regulation 36, 37 or 38

(1) Subject to paragraph (2), an applicant who has received notice under regulation 36(5), 37(5) or 38(5) that the applicant's application has been unsuccessful may appeal to the High Court or, in Scotland, the Court of Session on the grounds that the determination—

(a) is unlawful;

(b) is irrational or unreasonable; or

(c) has been made on the basis of a procedural impropriety or otherwise contravenes the rules of natural justice.

(2) No appeal may be brought unless the permission of the court has been obtained.

(3) No application for such permission may be made after 28 days beginning with the date of the notice under regulation 36(5), 37(5) or 38(5) unless the court is satisfied that there was good reason for the failure of the applicant to seek permission before the end of that period.

(4) An applicant who seeks permission to appeal must serve written notice of the application on the registrar within 7 days beginning with the date on which the application for permission was issued.

(5) The court determining an appeal may—

(a) dismiss the appeal; or

(b) quash the determination.

(6) Where the court quashes a determination it may refer the matter to the registrar with a direction to reconsider it and make a determination in accordance with the findings of the court.

42 Unsuccessful determination made under regulation 36, 37 or 38

(1) This regulation applies where the registrar has made a determination in respect of an application made under regulation 36, 37 or 38 that is not in favour of the applicant.

(2) The registrar must make secured information on the register to which the application under regulation 36, 37 or 38 relates available for public inspection on the register—

(a) where notice of an application for permission to appeal has not been served on the registrar in accordance with regulation 41(4), at the end of the period of 42 days beginning with the date of the notice given under regulation 36(5), 37(5) or 38(5); or

(b) where notice of an application for permission to appeal has been served on the registrar in accordance with regulation 41(4) as soon as reasonably practicable after—

(i) the court has dismissed the application for permission to appeal or the appeal and there is no further appeal pending; or

(ii) the registrar becomes aware that the application for permission to appeal or the appeal has been subsequently withdrawn or abandoned.

(3) Where the registrar makes secured information available for public inspection on the register under this regulation, the registrar must notify the person to whom the secured information relates and the company to which the application under regulation 36, 37 or 38 related of that action as soon as reasonably practicable.

43 Duration of a determination under regulation 36, 37 or 38

(1) A determination under regulation 36(5), 37(5) or 38(5) that an application is successful continues to have effect until—

(a) either—

(i) the person to whom the determination relates; or

(ii) that person's personal representative,

notifies the registrar in writing that he or she wishes the determination to cease to have effect; or

(b) the registrar revokes the determination under regulation 44.

(2) Where a notice is given under paragraph (1)(a), the person giving the notice must also notify the LLP to which the application that was determined relates of the notice given to the registrar.

44 Revocation of a determination under regulation 36(5), 37(5) or 38(5)

(1) The registrar may revoke a determination made under regulation 36(5), 37(5) or 38(5) that an application is successful if—

(a) the applicant in relation to the determination or (if different) any person to whom the application relates has been found guilty of an offence under section 1112 of the Act (general false statement offence) in respect of purported compliance with any provision of this Part;

(b) the registrar has sent a notice in accordance with paragraph (2) to the applicant in relation to the determination and (if different) the person to whom the determination relates; and

(c) the period of 28 days beginning with the date of that notice has expired.

(2) The notice mentioned in paragraph (1)(b) must inform the addressee—

(a) of the registrar's intention to revoke the determination;

(b) that the addressee may, within 28 days beginning with the date of the notice, deliver representations in writing to the registrar as to why the registrar should not revoke the determination; and

(c) that if the registrar receives such representations within that period, the registrar will have regard to the representations in deciding whether to revoke the determination.

(3) If within the period specified in paragraph (2)(b) an addressee of the notice delivers representations in writing to the registrar as to why the registrar should not revoke the determination, the registrar must have regard to the representations in deciding whether to revoke the determination.

(4) The registrar must send notice of the registrar's decision as to whether to revoke a determination to the applicant in relation to the determination and (if different) the person to whom the determination relates within 7 days beginning with the date of the decision.

(5) Where the registrar has made a decision to revoke a determination, the registrar must make secured information on the register to which the determination relates available for public inspection as soon as reasonably practicable after sending the notice mentioned in paragraph (4).

(6) Where the registrar makes secured information available for public inspection on the register under this regulation, the registrar must notify the person to whom the secured information relates and the LLP to which the application under regulation 36, 37 or 38 related of that action as soon as reasonably practicable.

45 Protection by an LLP of secured information

(1) Subject to paragraph (2), an LLP must not use or disclose secured information relating to a person ("S") if—

(a) in relation to that information an application has been made under regulation 36, 37 or 38 and

(b) the LLP has not received notification under regulation 40(2), 40(3), 42(3), 43(2), 44(6) or 46(5)(b).

(2) The LLP may use or disclose secured information relating to S—

(a) for communicating with S;

(b) in order to comply with a requirement of the 2006 Act or these Regulations as to particulars to be sent to the registrar; . . .

(c) where S has given consent for the LLP to use or disclose secured information relating to S[; or

(d) to the extent necessary in order to comply with regulation 43 (corporate bodies: obligations) of the Money Laundering Terrorist Financing and Transfer of Funds (Information on the Payer) Regulations 2017].

(3) For the purposes of this regulation, an application has been made—

(a) under regulation 36(1)(a) or 36(1)(c) when the applicant has informed the LLP under regulation 36(4) that the applicant has made an application;

(b) under regulation 36(1)(b) when the LLP has received the particular required by section 790K(l)(i) of the Act in relation to that individual;

(c) under regulation 37 when the LLP sends the application to the registrar; or

(d) under regulation 38 when the proposed member of a proposed LLP sends an application to the registrar.

(4) Where an LLP is prohibited under paragraph (1) from using or disclosing any secured information, the LLP's PSC register is to be treated as not including that information for the purposes of sections 790N(1), 790O(1) and 790O(2) of the Act.

PART 8
TRANSITIONAL PROVISIONS, AMENDMENTS TO THE 2009 REGULATIONS AND REVIEW

46 Transitional provision regarding the protection of secured information

(1) This regulation applies where—

(a) an individual is a registrable person on 6th April 2016 (a "protectable person");

(b) an application under regulation 36 or 37 is made in relation to the protectable person's secured information on or before 30th June 2016; and

(c) the registrar makes a determination that the application is unsuccessful.

(2) Subject to paragraph (4)—

(a) for the protected period, the registrar must not use or disclose that secured information and must omit that secured information from the material on the register that is available for public inspection; and

(b) where, before the expiry of the protected period, the protectable person ceases to be a registrable person in relation to the LLP to which the application relates and notifies the registrar in writing of that fact, after the expiry of the protected period the registrar must not use or disclose the secured information and must omit that secured information from the material on the register that is available for public inspection.

(3) A protectable person who sends a notice to the registrar under paragraph (2)(b) must—

(a) include in the notice the date on which that protectable person ceased to be a registrable person in relation to the LLP; and

(b) send a copy of the notice to the LLP.

(4) The registrar may use or disclose the secured information for communicating with the protectable person and, where the application was made under regulation 37, the LLP which made the application.

(5) Where the registrar has not received a notice under paragraph (2)(b) before the expiry of the protected period, the registrar must, as soon as reasonably practicable after the expiry of that period—

(a) make the secured information on the register available for public inspection; and

(b) notify the protectable person and the LLP to which the application under regulation 36 or 37 related of that action.

(6) For the purposes of this regulation—

(a) an application under regulation 36 or 37 is made when it is registered by the registrar; and

(b) "protected period" means—

(i) where an appeal under regulation 41 has not been brought, 12 weeks beginning with the date of the notice sent under regulation 36(5) or 37(5);

(ii) where an appeal under regulation 41 has been brought and dismissed, 12 weeks beginning with the date the court dismissed the appeal in accordance with regulation 41(5); and

(iii) where an appeal under regulation 41 has been brought and subsequently withdrawn or abandoned, 12 weeks beginning with the date of the registrar becoming aware that such appeal has been withdrawn or abandoned.

47 Transitional provision for the purpose of section 790K

Where an individual or a relevant legal entity is registrable in relation to an LLP on 6th April 2016, the date on which the individual or entity became a registrable person or a registrable relevant legal entity, as the case may be, in relation to the LLP in question is deemed to be 6th April 2016 for the purposes of sections 790K(1)(g), 790K(2)(d) and 790K(3)(e) of the Act."

4. Schedules 1, 3 and 4 to the PSC Regulations apply to LLPs, [with the references to a company in Part 2A of Schedule 4 read as references to an LLP,] and Schedule 2 to the PSC Regulations applies to LLPs modified so that it reads as follows—

"SCHEDULE 2

PARTICULARS REQUIRED AS TO NATURE OF CONTROL.

Regulation 7

PART 1 FIRST CONDITION

1

A statement that the person holds or is treated as holding, directly or indirectly, the right to share in more than 25% but not more than 50% of any surplus assets of the LLP on a winding up.

2

A statement that the person holds, directly or indirectly, the right to share in more than 50% but less than 75% of any surplus assets of the LLP on a winding up.

3

A statement that the person holds, directly or indirectly, the right to share in 75% or more of any surplus assets of the LLP on a winding up.

PART 2 SECOND CONDITION

4

A statement that the person holds, directly or indirectly, more than 25% but not more than 50% of the LLP voting rights in the LLP.

5

A statement that the person holds, directly or indirectly, more than 50% but less than 75% of the LLP voting rights in the LLP.

6

A statement that the person holds, directly or indirectly, 75% or more of the LLP voting rights in the LLP.

PART 3 THIRD CONDITION

7

A statement that the person holds the right, directly or indirectly, to appoint or remove a majority of the persons who are entitled to take part in the management of the LLP.

PART 4 FOURTH CONDITION

8

A statement that the person has the right to exercise, or actually exercises, significant influence or control over the LLP.

PART 5 FIFTH CONDITION AND TRUSTS

9

A statement that—

(a) the person has the right to exercise, or actually exercises, significant influence or control over the activities of a trust; and

(b) the trustees of that trust (in their capacity as such) hold or are treated as holding, directly or indirectly, the right to share in more than 25% but not more than 50% of any surplus assets on a winding up of the LLP.

10

A statement that—

(a) the person has the right to exercise, or actually exercises, significant influence or control over the activities of a trust; and

(b) the trustees of that trust (in their capacity as such) hold, directly or indirectly, the right to share in more than 50% but less than 75% of any surplus assets on a winding up of the LLP.

11

A statement that—

(a) the person has the right to exercise, or actually exercises, significant influence or control over the activities of a trust; and

(b) the trustees of that trust (in their capacity as such) hold, directly or indirectly, the right to share in more than 75% of any surplus assets on a winding up of the LLP.

12

A statement that—

(a) the person has the right to exercise, or actually exercises, significant influence or control over the activities of a trust; and

(b) the trustees of that trust (in their capacity as such) hold, directly or indirectly, more than 25% but not more than 50% of the voting rights in the LLP.

13

A statement that—

(a) the person has the right to exercise, or actually exercises, significant influence or control over the activities of a trust; and

(b) the trustees of that trust (in their capacity as such) hold, directly or indirectly, more than 50% but less than 75% of the voting rights in the LLP.

14

A statement that—

(a) the person has the right to exercise, or actually exercises, significant influence or control over the activities of a trust; and

(b) the trustees of that trust (in their capacity as such) hold, directly or indirectly, 75% or more of the voting rights in the LLP.

15

A statement that—

(a) the person has the right to exercise, or actually exercises, significant influence or control over the activities of a trust; and

(b) the trustees of that trust (in their capacity as such) hold the right, directly or indirectly, to appoint or remove a majority of the members who are entitled to take part in the management of the LLP.

16

A statement that—

(a) the person has the right to exercise, or actually exercises, significant influence or control over the activities of a trust; and

(b) the trustees of that trust (in their capacity as such) have the right to exercise, or actually exercise, significant influence or control over the LLP.

PART 6 FIFTH CONDITION AND FIRMS

17

A statement that—

(a) the person has the right to exercise, or actually exercises, significant influence or control over the activities of a firm that, under the law by which it is governed, is not a legal person; and

(b) the members of that firm (in their capacity as such) hold or are treated as holding, directly or indirectly, the right to share in more than 25% but not more than 50% of any surplus assets of the LLP on a winding up.

18

A statement that—

(a) the person has the right to exercise, or actually exercises, significant influence or control over the activities of a firm that, under the law by which it is governed, is not a legal person; and

(b) the members of that firm (in their capacity as such) hold, directly or indirectly, the right to share in more than 50% but less than 75% of any surplus assets of the LLP on a winding up.

19

A statement that—

(a) the person has the right to exercise, or actually exercises, significant influence or control over the activities of a firm that, under the law by which it is governed, is not a legal person; and

(b) the members of that firm (in their capacity as such) hold, directly or indirectly, the right to share in 75% or more of any surplus assets of the LLP on a winding up.

20

A statement that—

(a) the person has the right to exercise, or actually exercises, significant influence or control over the activities of a firm that, under the law by which it is governed, is not a legal person; and

(b) the members of that firm (in their capacity as such) hold, directly or indirectly, more than 25% but not more than 50% of the voting rights in the LLP.

21

A statement that—

(a) the person has the right to exercise, or actually exercises, significant influence or control over the activities of a firm that, under the law by which it is governed, is not a legal person; and

(b) the members of that firm (in their capacity as such) hold, directly or indirectly, more than 50% but less than 75% of the voting rights in the LLP.

22

A statement that—

(a) the person has the right to exercise, or actually exercises, significant influence or control over the activities of a firm that, under the law by which it is governed, is not a legal person; and

(b) the members of that firm (in their capacity as such) hold, directly or indirectly, 75% or more of the voting rights in the LLP.

23

A statement that—

(a) the person has the right to exercise, or actually exercises, significant influence or control over the activities of a firm that, under the law by which it is governed, is not a legal person; and

(b) the members of that firm (in their capacity as such) hold the right, directly or indirectly, to appoint or remove a majority of the members who are entitled to take part in the management of the LLP.

24

A statement that—

(a) the person has the right to exercise, or actually exercises, significant influence or control over the activities of a firm that, under the law by which it is governed, is not a legal person; and

(b) the members of that firm (in their capacity as such) have the right to exercise, or actually exercise, significant influence or control over the LLP.".

NOTES

All amendments to this Schedule were made by the Information about People with Significant Control (Amendment) Regulations 2017, SI 2017/693, regs 28–31, as from 26 June 2017.

SCHEDULE 3

CONSEQUENTIAL AND SUPPLEMENTARY AMENDMENTS

(*Sch 3 contains consequential amendments to the Limited Liability Partnerships Act 2000, the Limited Liability Partnerships (Application of Companies Act 2006) Regulations 2009, SI 2009/1804, and the Companies (Disclosure of Address) Regulations 2009, SI 2009/214, which have been incorporated at the appropriate place.*)

Part 10 Miscellaneous other SIs

INSOLVENCY PROCEEDINGS (FEES) ORDER 2016

(SI 2016/692)

NOTES

Made: 29 June 2016.
Authority: Insolvency Act 1986, ss 414, 415.
Commencement: 21 July 2016.

ARRANGEMENT OF ARTICLES

SCHEDULES

[10.457]
1 Citation and commencement

This Order may be cited as the Insolvency Proceedings (Fees) Order 2016 and comes into force twenty-one days after the day on which it is laid.

[10.458]
2 Interpretation

In this Order—

"the Act" means the Insolvency Act 1986;

"chargeable receipts" means the sums which are paid into the Insolvency Services Account after deducting any amounts which are paid out to secured creditors or paid out in carrying on the business of the bankrupt or the company;

"the commencement date" means the date this Order comes into force;

"deposit" means—

(a) on the making of a bankruptcy application, the sum of £550,

(b) on the presentation of a bankruptcy petition, the sum of £990,

(c) on the presentation of a winding up petition, other than a petition presented under section 124A of the Act, the sum of £1,600,

(d) on the presentation of a winding-up petition under section 124A of the Act, the sum of £5,000;

"official receiver's administration fee" means the fee payable to the official receiver on the making of a bankruptcy or winding up order out of the chargeable receipts of the estate of the bankrupt or, as the case may be, the assets of the insolvent company for the performance of the official receiver's functions under the Act.

[10.459]

3 Fees payable in connection with individual voluntary arrangements, debt relief orders and bankruptcy and winding up

The fees payable to the Secretary of State in respect of the matters specified in column 1 of the Table of Fees in Schedule 1 (Fees payable in insolvency proceedings) are the fees specified in column 2 to that Table.

[10.460]

4 Deposit

(1) On the making of a bankruptcy application, the debtor will pay a deposit to the adjudicator as security for the payment of the official receiver's administration fee.

(2) On the presentation of a bankruptcy petition or a winding-up petition, the petitioner will pay a deposit to the court as security for the payment of the official receiver's administration fee.

(3) Where a deposit is paid to the court, the court will transmit the deposit paid to the official receiver attached to the court.

(4) The deposit will be used to discharge the official receiver's administration fee to the extent that the assets comprised in the estate of the bankrupt or, as the case may be, the assets of the company are insufficient to discharge the official receiver's administration fee.

(5) Where a bankruptcy order or a winding up order is made (including any case where a bankruptcy order or a winding up is subsequently annulled, rescinded or recalled), the deposit will be returned to the person who paid it save to the extent that the assets comprised in the estate of the bankrupt or, as the case may be, the assets of the company are insufficient to discharge the official receiver's administration fee.

(6) The deposit will be repaid to the debtor where—

(a) the adjudicator has refused to make a bankruptcy order,

(b) 14 days have elapsed from the date of delivery of the notice of refusal, and

(c) the debtor has not made a request to the adjudicator to review the decision.

(7) Where the debtor has made a request to the adjudicator to review the decision to refuse to make a bankruptcy order the deposit will be repaid to the debtor where—

(a) the adjudicator has confirmed the refusal to make a bankruptcy order,

(b) 28 days have elapsed from the date of delivery of the confirmation of the notice of refusal, and

(c) the debtor has not appealed to the court against the refusal to make a bankruptcy order.

(8) Where the debtor has appealed to the court against the refusal to make a bankruptcy order the deposit will be repaid to the debtor where the appeal is dismissed or withdrawn.

(9) Where—

(a) a deposit was paid by the petitioner to the court, and

(b) the petition is withdrawn or dismissed by the court

that deposit, less an administration fee of £50, will be repaid to the petitioner.

[10.461]

5 Value Added Tax

Where Value Added Tax is chargeable in respect of the provision of a service for which a fee is payable by virtue of any provision of this Order, Value Added Tax must be paid on that fee.

[10.462]

6 Revocation

The enactments listed in Schedule 2 are revoked.

[10.463]

7 Transitional and saving provisions

(1) This Order has no effect in respect of any fees payable in respect of—

(a) the preparation and submission of a report under section 274 (action on report of insolvency practitioner) of the Act; and

(b) bankruptcy orders and winding-up orders made following the making of a bankruptcy application or presentation of a petition before the commencement date.

(2) This Order has no effect in respect of any deposit paid on the making of a bankruptcy application or the presentation of a petition for bankruptcy or winding up before the commencement date.

SCHEDULES

SCHEDULE 1
FEES PAYABLE IN INSOLVENCY PROCEEDINGS

Article 3

Table of Fees

[10.464]

Description of fee and circumstances in which it is charged	*Amount of fee or applicable %*
Individual voluntary arrangement registration fee On the registration by the Secretary of State of an individual voluntary arrangement made under Part 8 of the Act, the fee of—	£15
Application for a debt relief order—official receiver's administration fee and costs of persons acting as approved intermediaries On the application for a debt relief order, for the performance of the official receiver's functions and for the payment of an amount not exceeding £10 in respect of the costs of persons acting as approved intermediaries under Part 7A of the Act, the fee of—	£90
Application for a bankruptcy order—adjudicator's administration fee On the application to the adjudicator for a bankruptcy order, for the performance of the adjudicator functions, the fee of—	£130
Bankruptcy—official receiver's administration fee following debtor's application On the making of a bankruptcy order on a debtor's application, for the performance of the official receiver's duties as official receiver the fee of—	£1,990
Bankruptcy—official receiver's administration fee following creditor's petition On the making of a bankruptcy order on a creditor's petition, for the performance of the official receiver's duties as official receiver the fee of—	£2,775
Bankruptcy—trustee in bankruptcy fee For the performance of the official receiver's duties while acting as trustee in bankruptcy of the bankrupt's estate a fee calculated as a percentage of chargeable receipts realised by the official receiver in the capacity of trustee in bankruptcy at the rate of—	15%
Bankruptcy—income payments agreement fee On entering into an income payments agreement with the official receiver under section 310A of the Act, the fee of—	£150
Bankruptcy—income payments order fee On the making of an income payments order by the court under section 310 of the Act, the fee of—	£150
Winding up by the court other than a winding up on a petition presented under section 124A—official receiver's administration fee On the making of a winding-up order, other than on a petition presented under section 124A, for the performance of the official receiver's duties as official receiver, including the duty to investigate and report on the affairs of bodies in liquidation, the fee of—	£5,000
Winding up by the court on a petition presented under section 124A—official receiver's administration fee On the making of a winding-up order on a petition presented under section 124A, for the performance of the official receiver's duties as official receiver, including the duty to investigate and report on the affairs of bodies in liquidation, the fee of—	£7,500
Winding up—liquidator fee For the performance of the official receiver's duties while acting as liquidator of the insolvent estate a fee calculated as a percentage of chargeable receipts realised by the official receiver in the capacity of liquidator at the rate of—	15%
Official receiver's general fee On the making of a bankruptcy order or the making of a winding up order by the court for the costs not recovered out of the official receiver's administration fee of administering— (a) bankruptcy orders, (b) winding up orders made by the court the fee of—	£6,000

SCHEDULE 2
REVOCATIONS

(Revokes the Insolvency Proceedings (Fees) Order 2004, SI 2004/593 and various other Orders that have amended the 2004 Fees Order.)

COMPENSATION ORDERS (DISQUALIFIED DIRECTORS) PROCEEDINGS (ENGLAND AND WALES) RULES 2016

(SI 2016/890)

NOTES

Made: 7 September 2016.

Authority: Insolvency Act 1986, s 411(1).

Commencement: 1 October 2016.

These Rules are reproduced as amended by: the Insolvency (England and Wales) Rules 2016 (Consequential Amendments and Savings) Rules 2017, SI 2017/369.

ARRANGEMENT OF RULES

[10.465]
1 Citation, commencement and interpretation

(1) These Rules may be cited as the Compensation Orders (Disqualified Directors) Proceedings (England and Wales) Rules 2016.

(2) These Rules come into force on 1st October 2016.

(3) In these Rules—

"the Act" means the Company Directors Disqualification Act 1986 and a reference to a numbered section is to that section of that Act;

"CPR" followed by a Part or rule by number means that Part or rule with that number in the Civil Procedure Rules 1998;

"practice direction" means a direction as to the practice and procedure of any court within the scope of the Civil Procedure Rules 1998;

["registrar" has the same meaning as in rule 1.2(2) of the Insolvency (England and Wales) Rules 2016; and

"relevant party" means—

(a) the defendant (in the case of an application under section 15A(1)); or

(b) the Secretary of State (in the case of an application under section 15C(1)).

NOTES

Para (3): definition "registrar" substituted by the Insolvency (England and Wales) Rules 2016 (Consequential Amendments and Savings) Rules 2017, SI 2017/369, r 2(2), Sch 2, para 12(1), (2), as from 6 April 2017.

[10.466]
2 Application

(1) Subject to paragraph (2), these Rules apply to an application under the Act made on or after 1st October 2016—

(a) by the Secretary of State for a compensation order against a person under section 15A(1); and

(b) by a person who is subject to a compensation undertaking under section 15A(2) for variation or revocation of that undertaking under section 15C(1).

(2) These Rules apply to applications where the courts in England and Wales—

(a) have made a disqualification order against the person;

(b) have jurisdiction to make a disqualification order against the person (in a case where proceedings for a disqualification order have or are being commenced); or

(c) would have had jurisdiction to make a disqualification order against the person (in a case where the person is subject to disqualification undertaking).

[10.467]
3 Form and conduct of applications

(1) The Civil Procedure Rules 1998, and any relevant practice direction, apply in respect of applications under these Rules, except where these Rules make different provision.

(2) An application must be made by claim form and the claimant must use the CPR Part 8 (alternative procedure for claims) procedure.

(3) In the case of an application under section 15C(1), the Secretary of State is the defendant for the purposes of the Civil Procedure Rules 1998.

(4) CPR rule 8.1(3) (power of the court to order the claim to continue as if the claimant had not used the Part 8 procedure), CPR rule 8.2 (contents of the claim form) and CPR rule 8.7 (Part 20 claims) do not apply to applications under these Rules.

[(5) Rule 12.49 (appeals and reviews of court orders in corporate insolvency) and rule 12.61 (procedure on appeal) of the Insolvency (England and Wales) Rules 2016 apply to applications under these rules.]

NOTES

Para (5): substituted by the Insolvency (England and Wales) Rules 2016 (Consequential Amendments and Savings) Rules 2017, SI 2017/369, r 2(2), Sch 2, para 12(1), (3), as from 6 April 2017.

[10.468]

4 The claimant's case

(1) The claimant must, at the time when the claim form is issued, file in court evidence in support of the application.

(2) The claimant must serve on the relevant party with the claim form copies of the evidence under paragraph (1).

(3) The evidence must be by one or more affidavits or witness statements, which must include—

- (a) in the case of an application under section 15A(1), a statement—
  - (i) of the disqualification order or undertaking in respect of which the application is being brought, or of the proceedings for a disqualification order either commenced or being commenced alongside the application;
  - (ii) of the loss it is alleged has been caused by the conduct in respect of which—
    - (aa) the defendant is subject to the disqualification order or undertaking, or
    - (bb) proceedings for a disqualification order have been or are being commenced;
  - (iii) identifying the creditor or creditors to whom it is alleged loss has been caused;
  - (iv) identifying particulars of the order the claimant is seeking under section 15B(1); and
  - (v) of any other matters considered to be of relevance to the application; and
- (b) in the case of an application under section 15C(1), the compensation undertaking (or a copy).

(4) In the case of an application under section 15A(1), where the insolvent company as referred to in section 15A(3)(b) is in administration or liquidation, or there is an administrative receiver of that company, the claimant must also give notice of the claim to the administrator, liquidator or administrative receiver within 14 days of the claim form being issued.

(5) The notice under paragraph (4) must identify particulars of the order the claimant is seeking under section 15B(1).

[10.469]

5 Endorsements etc on claim form

(1) The following information must be endorsed on the claim form—

- (a) that the application is made in accordance with these Rules;
- (b) in the case of an application under section 15A(1), that the court has the power to make such an order in respect of loss it is alleged has been caused by the defendant's conduct;
- (c) in the case of an application under 15C(1), that the court has the power to reduce the amount of a compensation undertaking offered and accepted under section 15A(2) or to provide that such an undertaking is not to have effect; and
- (d) that any evidence which the relevant party wishes the court to take into consideration must be filed in court in accordance with the time limit under rule 7(1).

(2) The time limit referred to in paragraph (1)(d) must be set out in the claim form.

[10.470]

6 Acknowledgment of service

(1) The claim form served on the relevant party must be accompanied by an acknowledgment of service and CPR rule 8.3(2) (dealing with the contents of an acknowledgment of service) does not apply.

(2) In the case of an application under section 15A(1), the acknowledgment of service must state that the defendant should indicate—

- (a) whether the defendant is contesting the disqualification on which the application is based by—
  - (i) contesting the making of a disqualification order (either before it has been made or by way of an appeal), or
  - (ii) applying for a disqualification undertaking to cease to be in force;
- (b) whether the defendant disputes that the conduct on which the application is based caused the loss alleged in the application; or
- (c) whether the defendant, while not resisting the application, intends to adduce mitigating factors with a view to justifying a reduced level of compensation.

(3) In the case of an application under section 15C(1)—

- (a) the acknowledgment of service must state whether or not the Secretary of State intends to file any evidence relating to the application; and
- (b) CPR rule 8.4 (consequence of not filing an acknowledgment of service) does not apply.

[10.471]

7 Evidence

(1) The relevant party must, within 28 days from the date of service of the claim form, file in court any evidence relating to the application which the relevant party wishes the court to take into consideration.

(2) The relevant party must, at the same time, serve on the claimant a copy of any such evidence.

(3) The claimant must, within 14 days of receiving the copy of the relevant party's evidence, file in court any further evidence in reply which the claimant wishes the court to take into consideration.

(4) The claimant must, at the same time, serve a copy of any such further evidence on the relevant party.

(5) Any evidence filed and served under this rule must be by either affidavit or witness statement.

(6) CPR rules 8.5 (filing and serving written evidence) and 8.6(1) (requirements where written evidence is to be relied on) do not apply.

[10.472]
8 The hearing of the application

(1) When the claim form is issued, the court must fix a date for the first hearing of the claim for a date not less than 8 weeks from the date of issue of the claim form.

(2) The hearing must in the first instance be before the registrar in open court.

(3) Without prejudice to the Secretary of State's rights and obligations under sections 15C(2) and 16(3) on the hearing of an application, subject to the direction of the court, any of the parties may give evidence, call and cross-examine witnesses at the hearing.

(4) The registrar must either determine the case on the date fixed or adjourn it.

(5) If the registrar adjourns the case for further consideration the registrar must—

- (a) direct whether the case is to be heard by a registrar or, if the registrar thinks it appropriate, for determination by the judge;
- (b) state the reasons for the adjournment; and
- (c) give directions as to the following matters—
  - (i) the manner in which and the time within which notice of the adjournment and the reasons for it are to be given to the relevant party,
  - (ii) any order for the provision of further information or for disclosure by the parties,
  - (iii) the filing in court and the service of further evidence (if any) by the parties,
  - (iv) such other matters as the registrar thinks necessary or expedient with a view to an expeditious disposal of the application, and
  - (v) the time and place of the adjourned hearing.

(6) Where a case is adjourned other than to the judge, it may be heard by the registrar who originally dealt with the case or by another registrar.

[10.473]
9 Compensation orders: making and setting aside of an order

(1) The court may make a compensation order under section 15A(1) against the defendant whether or not the defendant—

- (a) appears,
- (b) has completed and returned the acknowledgment of service of the claim form, or
- (c) has filed evidence in accordance with rule 7.

(2) Any compensation order made in the absence of the defendant may be set aside or varied by the court on such terms as it thinks just.

INSOLVENCY (ENGLAND AND WALES) RULES 2016

(SI 2016/1024)

NOTES

Made: 18 October 2016.
Authority: Insolvency Act 1986, ss 411, 412.
Commencement: 6 April 2017.
Note: these Rules are reproduced as per the original Queen's Printer's version (as subsequently amended). The original version uses square brackets in the text of the rules (particularly in certain notes). The use of square brackets in the text is therefore not necessarily indicative of the fact that the rule has been amended. Users of this Handbook should consult the notes to each provision to ascertain if the original rule has been subsequently amended.

Note that the Insolvency Act 1986 and these Rules are applied (with modifications) to various types of insolvency proceedings. See, for examples, the introductory notes to the 1986 Act in Part 9 *ante*. These are not noted here.

These Rules are reproduced as amended by: the Insolvency (England and Wales) (Amendment) Rules 2017, SI 2017/366; the Insolvency Amendment (EU 2015/848) Regulations 2017, SI 2017/702; the Insolvency (England and Wales) and Insolvency (Scotland) (Miscellaneous and Consequential Amendments) Rules 2017, SI 2017/1115; the Alteration of Judicial Titles (Registrar in Bankruptcy of the High Court) Order 2018, SI 2018/130; the Insolvency (Amendment) (EU Exit) Regulations 2019, SI 2019/146; the Insolvency (England and Wales) (No 2) (Amendment) Rules 2021, SI 2021/1028.

Application of these Rules:
(1) these Rules are applied and modified in relation to their application to moratoriums under Part A1 of the Insolvency Act 1986. See Sch 4 to the Corporate Insolvency and Governance Act 2020 (Moratoriums in Great Britain: Temporary Provision) at **[9.561]**; and, in particular, Part 3 of that Schedule (Temporary Rules: England and Wales) at **[9.563]**. Note that the modifications apply for the "relevant period" as defined in Sch 4, Pt 1, para 1 to the 2020 Act (as amended); ie, the period beginning on 26 June 2020, and ending on 30 September 2021.
(2) these Rules are applied and modified in relation to their application to winding up petitions under the Insolvency Act 1986. See Sch 10 to the Corporate Insolvency and Governance Act 2020 (Winding-up Petitions: Great Britain) at **[9.566]**. Note that the modifications apply for the "relevant period" as defined in Sch 10, para 4 to the 2020 Act (as amended); ie, the period beginning 1 October 2021 and ending 31 March 2022.

ARRANGEMENT OF RULES

INTRODUCTORY RULES

PART 1
SCOPE, INTERPRETATION, TIME AND RULES ABOUT DOCUMENTS

CHAPTER 1 SCOPE OF THESE RULES

CHAPTER 2 INTERPRETATION

CHAPTER 3 FORM AND CONTENT OF DOCUMENTS

CHAPTER 4 STANDARD CONTENTS OF GAZETTE NOTICES AND THE GAZETTE AS EVIDENCE ETC

CHAPTER 5 STANDARD CONTENTS OF NOTICES ADVERTISED OTHERWISE THAN IN THE GAZETTE

CHAPTER 6 STANDARD CONTENTS OF DOCUMENTS TO BE DELIVERED TO THE REGISTRAR OF COMPANIES

CHAPTER 7 STANDARD CONTENTS OF NOTICES FOR DELIVERY TO OTHER PERSONS ETC

CHAPTER 8 APPLICATIONS TO THE COURT

CHAPTER 9 DELIVERY OF DOCUMENTS AND OPTING OUT (SECTIONS 246C, 248A, 379C AND 383A)

CHAPTER 10 INSPECTION OF DOCUMENTS, COPIES AND PROVISION OF INFORMATION

PART 1A
MORATORIUMS

CHAPTER 1 PRELIMINARY

CHAPTER 2 OBTAINING MORATORIUM BY FILING NOTICE AT COURT

CHAPTER 3 OBTAINING A MORATORIUM BY APPLICATION TO THE COURT

CHAPTER 4 OBLIGATIONS TO NOTIFY WHERE MORATORIUM COMES INTO FORCE

CHAPTER 5 EXTENDING MORATORIUM BY FILING NOTICE WITH THE COURT

CHAPTER 6 EXTENDING MORATORIUM BY APPLICATION TO THE COURT

CHAPTER 5 CONSIDERATION OF THE PROPOSAL BY THE COMPANY MEMBERS AND CREDITORS

CHAPTER 6 ADDITIONAL MATTERS CONCERNING AND FOLLOWING APPROVAL OF CVA

CHAPTER 7 TIME RECORDING INFORMATION

PART 3
ADMINISTRATION

CHAPTER 1 INTERPRETATION FOR THIS PART

CHAPTER 2 APPOINTMENT OF ADMINISTRATOR BY COURT

CHAPTER 3 APPOINTMENT OF ADMINISTRATOR BY HOLDER OF FLOATING CHARGE

CHAPTER 4 APPOINTMENT OF ADMINISTRATOR BY COMPANY OR DIRECTORS

CHAPTER 5 NOTICE OF ADMINISTRATOR'S APPOINTMENT

Part 10 Miscellaneous other SIs

CHAPTER 2 ADMINISTRATIVE RECEIVERS (OTHER THAN IN SCOTTISH RECEIVERSHIPS)

CHAPTER 3 NON-ADMINISTRATIVE RECEIVERS AND THE PRESCRIBED PART

PART 5
MEMBERS' VOLUNTARY WINDING UP

CHAPTER 1 STATUTORY DECLARATION OF SOLVENCY (SECTION 89)

CHAPTER 2 THE LIQUIDATOR

CHAPTER 3 SPECIAL MANAGER

CHAPTER 4 CONVERSION TO CREDITORS' VOLUNTARY WINDING UP

PART 6
CREDITORS' VOLUNTARY WINDING UP

CHAPTER 1 APPLICATION OF PART 6

CHAPTER 2 STATEMENT OF AFFAIRS AND OTHER INFORMATION

PART 7
WINDING UP BY THE COURT

CHAPTER 1 APPLICATION OF PART

CHAPTER 2 THE STATUTORY DEMAND (SECTIONS 123(1)(A) AND 222(1)(A))

CHAPTER 3 PETITION FOR WINDING-UP ORDER

CHAPTER 4 PETITION BY A CONTRIBUTORY OR A RELEVANT OFFICE-HOLDER

CHAPTER 5 PROVISIONAL LIQUIDATOR

CHAPTER 6 STATEMENT OF AFFAIRS AND OTHER INFORMATION

CHAPTER 7 REPORTS AND INFORMATION TO CREDITORS AND CONTRIBUTORIES

CHAPTER 8 THE LIQUIDATOR

CHAPTER 9 DUTIES AND POWERS OF LIQUIDATOR

CHAPTER 10 SETTLEMENT OF LIST OF CONTRIBUTORIES

CHAPTER 11 CALLS ON CONTRIBUTORIES

CHAPTER 12 SPECIAL MANAGER

CHAPTER 13 PUBLIC EXAMINATION OF COMPANY OFFICERS AND OTHERS (SECTION 133)

Part 10 Miscellaneous other SIs

PART 14
CLAIMS BY AND DISTRIBUTIONS TO CREDITORS IN A MORATORIUM, ADMINISTRATION, WINDING UP AND BANKRUPTCY

CHAPTER 1 APPLICATION AND INTERPRETATION

CHAPTER 2 CREDITORS' CLAIMS IN A MORATORIUM, ADMINISTRATION, WINDING UP AND BANKRUPTCY

CHAPTER 3 DISTRIBUTION TO CREDITORS IN ADMINISTRATION, WINDING UP AND BANKRUPTCY

PART 15
DECISION MAKING

CHAPTER 1 APPLICATION OF PART

CHAPTER 2 DECISION PROCEDURES

CHAPTER 3 NOTICES, VOTING AND VENUES FOR DECISIONS

CHAPTER 4 DECISION MAKING IN PARTICULAR PROCEEDINGS

CHAPTER 5 REQUISITIONED DECISIONS

CHAPTER 6 CONSTITUTION OF MEETINGS

CHAPTER 7 ADJOURNMENT AND SUSPENSION OF MEETINGS

CHAPTER 8 CREDITORS' VOTING RIGHTS AND MAJORITIES

CHAPTER 9 EXCLUSIONS FROM MEETINGS

CHAPTER 10 CONTRIBUTORIES' VOTING RIGHTS AND MAJORITIES

CHAPTER 11 RECORDS

CHAPTER 12 COMPANY MEETINGS

PART 16
PROXIES AND CORPORATE REPRESENTATION

PART 17
CREDITORS' AND LIQUIDATION COMMITTEES

CHAPTER 1 INTRODUCTORY

CHAPTER 2 FUNCTIONS OF A COMMITTEE

CHAPTER 3 MEMBERSHIP AND FORMALITIES OF FORMATION OF A COMMITTEE

CHAPTER 4 MEETINGS OF COMMITTEE

CHAPTER 5 SUPPLY OF INFORMATION BY THE OFFICE-HOLDER TO THE COMMITTEE

CHAPTER 6 MISCELLANEOUS

CHAPTER 7 WINDING UP BY THE COURT FOLLOWING AN ADMINISTRATION

PART 18
REPORTING AND REMUNERATION OF OFFICE-HOLDERS

CHAPTER 1 INTRODUCTORY

CHAPTER 2 PROGRESS REPORTS

PART 22
PERMISSION TO ACT AS DIRECTOR ETC OF COMPANY WITH A PROHIBITED NAME (SECTION 216)

SCHEDULES

INTRODUCTORY RULES

[10.474]

1 Citation and commencement

These Rules may be cited as the Insolvency (England and Wales) Rules 2016 and come into force on 6th April 2017.

[10.475]

2 Revocations

The Rules listed in Schedule 1 are revoked.

[10.476]

3 Extent and application

(1) These Rules extend to England and Wales only.

(2) These Rules as they relate to company voluntary arrangements under Part 1 of the Act, administration under Part 2 of the Act and winding up under Parts 4 and 5 of the Act apply in relation to companies which the courts in England and Wales have jurisdiction to wind up.

(3) These Rules do not apply to receivers appointed under section 51 (Scottish receivership).

[10.477]

4 Transitional and savings provisions

The transitional and savings provisions set out in Schedule 2 have effect.

[10.478]

5 Power of the Secretary of State to regulate certain matters

(1) Under paragraph 27 of Schedule 8 and paragraph 30 of Schedule 9 to the Act, the Secretary of State may, subject to the Act and the Rules made under it, make regulations with respect to any matter provided for in the Rules relating to the carrying out of the functions of—

(a) a liquidator, provisional liquidator, administrator or administrative receiver of a company;
(b) an interim receiver appointed under section 286; and
(c) a trustee of a bankrupt's estate.

(2) The regulations that may be made may include, without prejudice to the generality of paragraph (1), provision with respect to the following matters arising in companies winding up and individual bankruptcy—

(a) the preparation and keeping by liquidators, trustees, provisional liquidators, interim receivers and the official receiver, of books, accounts and other records, and their production to such persons as may be authorised or required to inspect them;
(b) the auditing of liquidators' and trustees' accounts;
(c) the manner in which liquidators and trustees are to act in relation to the insolvent company's or bankrupt's books, papers and other records, and the manner of their disposal by the responsible office-holder or others;
(d) the supply of copies of documents relating to the insolvency and the affairs of the insolvent company or individual (on payment, in such cases as may be specified by the regulations, of the specified fee)—
    (i) by the liquidator in company insolvency to creditors and members of the company, contributories in its winding up and the liquidation committee; and
    (ii) by the trustee in bankruptcy to creditors and the creditors' committee;
(e) the manner in which insolvent estates are to be distributed by liquidators and trustees, including provision with respect to unclaimed funds and dividends;
(f) the manner in which moneys coming into the hands of a liquidator or trustee in the course of the administration of the proceedings are to be handled and invested, and the payment of interest on sums which have been paid into the Insolvency Services Account under regulations made by virtue of this sub-paragraph;

(g) the amount (or the manner of determining the amount) to be paid to the official receiver as remuneration when acting as provisional liquidator, liquidator, interim receiver or trustee.

(3) Regulations made under this rule may—

(a) confer a discretion on the court;

(b) make non-compliance with any of the regulations a criminal offence;

(c) make different provision for different cases, including different provision for different areas; and

(d) contain such incidental, supplemental and transitional provisions as may appear to the Secretary of State necessary or expedient.

[10.479]

6 Punishment of offences

Schedule 3 sets out the punishments for certain contraventions of these Rules.

[10.480]

7 Review

(1) The Secretary of State must from time to time—

(a) carry out a review of these Rules;

(b) set out the conclusions of the review in a report; and

(c) publish the report.

(2) The report must in particular—

(a) set out the objectives intended to be achieved by the regulatory system established by these Rules;

(b) assess the extent to which those objectives are achieved; and

(c) assess whether those objectives remain appropriate and, if so, the extent to which they could be achieved with a system that imposes less regulation.

(3) The first report under this rule must be published before the end of the period of five years beginning with the day on which these Rules come into force.

(4) Reports under this rule are afterwards to be published at intervals not exceeding five years.

PART 1 SCOPE, INTERPRETATION, TIME AND RULES ABOUT DOCUMENTS

CHAPTER 1 SCOPE OF THESE RULES

[10.481]

1.1 Scope

(1) These Rules are made to give effect to [Parts A1] to 11 of the Insolvency Act 1986 and to the [EU Regulation].

(2) Consequently references to insolvency proceedings and requirements relating to such proceedings are, unless the context requires otherwise, limited to proceedings in respect of [Parts A1] to 11 of the Act and the [EU Regulation] (whether or not court proceedings).

NOTES

Words "Parts A1" in square brackets substituted (for the original words "Parts 1") by the Insolvency (England and Wales) (No 2) (Amendment) Rules 2021, SI 2021/1028, r 80, Sch 1, as from 1 October 2021 (for savings provisions see the note to r 1A.1 at **[10.539]**).

Words "EU Regulation" in square brackets substituted by the Insolvency (England and Wales) and Insolvency (Scotland) (Miscellaneous and Consequential Amendments) Rules 2017, SI 2017/1115, rr 22, 23(1), as from 8 December 2017.

CHAPTER 2 INTERPRETATION

[Note: the terms which are defined in rule 1.2 include some terms defined by the Act for limited purposes which are applied generally by these Rules. Such terms have the meaning given by the Act for those limited purposes.]

[10.482]

1.2 Defined terms

(1) In these Rules, unless otherwise stated, a reference to a Part or a Schedule is to a Part of, or Schedule to, these Rules.

(2) In these Rules—

"the Act" means the Insolvency Act 1986, and—

(a) a reference to a numbered section without mention of another Act is to that section of the Act; and

(b) a reference to [Schedule ZA1, ZA2,] B1, 4ZA, 4ZB or 4A is to that Schedule to the Act;

"appointed person" means a person as described in paragraph (3) who is appointed by an office-holder (other than the official receiver);

"Article 1.2 undertaking" means one of the following within the meaning of Article 1.2 of [Regulation (EU) 2015/848 of the European Parliament and of the Council ("the EU Regulations")]—

(a) an insurance undertaking;

(b) a credit institution;

(c) an investment undertaking which provides services involving the holding of funds or securities for third parties;

(d) a collective investment undertaking;

[Note: "associate" is defined by section 435];

["attendance" and "attend" a person attends, or is in attendance at, a meeting who is present or attends remotely in accordance with section 246A or rule 15.6, or who participates in a virtual meeting, whether that person attends the meeting or virtual meeting in person, by proxy, or by corporate representative (in accordance with section 434B or section 323 of the Companies Act, as applicable);]

"authenticate" means to authenticate in accordance with rule 1.5;

"authorised deposit-taker" means a person with permission under Part 4A of the Financial Services and Markets Act 2000 to accept deposits; this definition must be read with—
 (a) section 22 of that Act and any relevant order under that section; and
 (b) Schedule 2 to that Act;
[Note: "bankrupt's estate" is defined in section 283];
"bankruptcy application" means the bankruptcy application submitted by the debtor to the adjudicator requesting the making of a bankruptcy order against the debtor;
"bankruptcy file" means the file opened by the adjudicator in accordance with rule 10.47;
"bankruptcy restrictions register" means the register referred to in rule 11.13(2) of matters relating to bankruptcy restrictions orders, interim bankruptcy restrictions orders and bankruptcy restrictions undertakings;
"business day" means, for the purposes of these Rules as they relate to Parts 7A to 10 of the Act (insolvency of individuals; bankruptcy), any day other than a Saturday, a Sunday, Christmas Day, Good Friday or a day which is a bank holiday in England and Wales [Note: for the purposes of these Rules as they relate to [Parts A1] to 7 of the Act (company insolvency; company winding up) section 251 defines "business day" as including additionally a day which is a bank holiday in Scotland];
"centre of main interests" has the same meaning as in the [EU Regulation];
"certificate of service" means a certificate of service which complies with the requirements in Schedule 4;
["COMI proceedings" means insolvency proceedings in England and Wales to which the EU Regulation applies where the centre of the debtor's main interests is in the United Kingdom;]
"Companies Act" means the Companies Act 2006;
[Note: the term "connected" used of a person in relation to a company is defined in section 249 of the Act];
"consumer" means an individual acting for purposes that are wholly or mainly outside that individual's trade, business, craft or profession;
[Note: "contributory" is defined by section 79];
"convener" means an office-holder or other person who seeks a decision in accordance with Part 15 of these Rules;
[Note: "the court" is defined by section 251 for the purposes of these Rules as they relate to Parts 1 to 7 of the Act (company insolvency; company winding up) and by section 385(1) for the purposes of these Rules as they relate to Parts 7A to 10 of the Act (insolvency of individuals; bankruptcy);
"CPR" means the Civil Procedure Rules 1998;
"credit reference agency" means a person authorised or permitted by the Financial Conduct Authority to carry on the regulated activity of providing credit references;
"CVA" means a voluntary arrangement in relation to a company under Part 1 of the Act;
"debt" is defined in rule 14.1(3) for the purposes of administration and winding up and "small debt" is also defined in rule 14.1(3) for administration, winding up and bankruptcy [Note: debt is defined in section 385(1) for the purposes of these Rules as they relate to Parts 7A to 10 of the Act (insolvency of individuals; bankruptcy)];
"debt relief restrictions register" means the register referred to in rule 11.13(2) of matters relating to debt relief restrictions orders and debt relief restrictions undertakings;
"decision date" and "decision procedure" are to be interpreted in accordance with rule 15.2 and Part 15;
"decision procedure" means a decision procedure prescribed by rule 15.3;
[Note: "deemed consent procedure" is defined in section 246ZF for corporate insolvency and 379ZB for individual insolvency; rule 15.7 makes further provision about deemed consent];
"deliver" and "delivery" are to be interpreted in accordance with Chapter 9 of Part 1;
"deliver to the creditors" and similar expressions in these Rules and the Act are to be interpreted in accordance with rule 1.37;
[Note: "distress" is defined in section 436 as including the procedure in Schedule 12 to the Tribunals, Courts and Enforcement Act 2007 (c 15), and references to levying distress, seizing goods and related expressions are to be construed accordingly];
"document" includes a written notice or statement or anything else in writing capable of being delivered to a recipient;
[[Note: EU Regulation is defined for the purposes of these Rules by section 436 of the Act as Regulation (EU) No 2015/848 of the European Parliament and of the Council]].
"enforcement agent" means a person authorised by section 63(2) of the Tribunals, Courts and Enforcement Act 2007 to act as an enforcement agent;
"enforcement officer" means an individual who is authorised to act as an enforcement officer under the Courts Act 2003;
["establishment" has the same meaning as in Article 2(10) of the EU Regulation;]
["establishment proceedings" means insolvency proceedings in England and Wales to which the EU Regulation applies where the debtor has an establishment in the United Kingdom;]
"fees estimate" means a written estimate that specifies—
 (a) details of the work the insolvency practitioner ("the IP") and the IP's staff propose to undertake;
 (b) the hourly rate or rates the IP and the IP's staff propose to charge for each part of that work;
 (c) the time the IP anticipates each part of that work will take;
 (d) whether the IP anticipates it will be necessary to seek approval or further approval under Chapter 4 of Part 18; and
 (e) the reasons it will be necessary to seek such approval under these Rules;
"file with the court" and similar expressions in these Rules means deliver to the court for filing and such references are to be read as including "submit" and "submission" to the court in the Act (except in sections 236 and 366);
"the Gazette", which has the meaning given in section 251 for the purposes of these Rules as they relate to [Parts A1] to 7 of the Act (company insolvency; company winding up), has that meaning for the purposes of these Rules as they relate to Parts 7A to 10 of the Act;
"Gazette notice" means a notice which is, has been or is to be gazetted;

"to gazette" means to advertise once in the Gazette;

"general regulations" means regulations made by the Secretary of State under introductory rule 5;

"hearing centre" means a hearing centre of the County Court;

[Note: "hire-purchase agreement" is defined by section 436(1) as having the same meaning as in the Consumer Credit Act 1974 for the *purposes of the Act and by paragraph 1 of Schedule A1 (company voluntary arrangement) for the purposes of that Schedule and by paragraph 111(1) of Schedule B1* (administration) for the purposes of that Schedule];

"identification details" and similar references to information identifying persons, proceedings, etc are to be interpreted in accordance with rule 1.6;

"individual insolvency register" means the register referred to in rule 11.13(1) of matters relating to bankruptcies, debt relief orders and IVAs;

"individual register" has the meaning given by rule 217(1) of the Land Registration Rules 2003;

"insolvent estate" means—

(a) in relation to a company insolvency, the company's assets;

(b) in relation to a bankruptcy, a petition or an application for bankruptcy, the bankrupt's estate (as defined in section 283);

(c) or otherwise the debtor's property;

"IP number" means the number assigned to an office-holder as an insolvency practitioner by the Secretary of State;

"IVA" means a voluntary arrangement in relation to an individual under Part 8 of the Act;

"judge" includes [an Insolvency and Companies Court Judge] unless the context otherwise requires;

"London Insolvency District" has the meaning given by section 374 of the Act and the London Insolvency District (County Court at Central London) Order 2014;

. . .

"meeting" in relation to a person's creditors or contributories means either a "physical meeting" or a "virtual meeting" as defined in rule 15.2, unless the contrary intention is given;

. . .

"nominated person" means a person who has been required under section 47 or 131 to make out and submit a statement as to the affairs of a company in administrative receivership or being wound up by the court;

[Note: "nominee" is defined in section 1(2) in relation to company voluntary arrangements and section 253(2) in relation to individual voluntary arrangements];

. . .

"office-holder" means a person who under the Act or these Rules holds an office in relation to insolvency proceedings and includes a nominee;

"permission" of the court is to be read as including "leave of the court" in the Act and in the Company Directors' Disqualification Act 1986;

"petitioner" or "petitioning creditor" includes a person who has been substituted as such or has been given carriage of the petition;

"physical meeting" means a meeting as described in section 246ZE(9) or 379ZA(9);

"Practice Direction" means a direction as to the practice and procedure of a court within the scope of the CPR;

"prescribed order of priority" means the order of priority of payments of expenses set out in—

(a) Chapter 10 of Part 3 for administration proceedings;

(b) Chapter 6 of Part 6 for creditors' voluntary winding up proceedings;

(c) Chapter 14 of Part 7 for winding up by the court proceedings; and

(d) Chapter 18 of Part 10 for bankruptcy proceedings;

"prescribed part" has the same meaning as in section 176A(2)(a) and the Insolvency Act 1986 (Prescribed Part) Order 2003;

"progress report" means a report which complies with Chapter 2 of Part 18;

[Note: "property" is defined by section 436(1) of the Act];

"prove" and "proof" have the following meaning—

(a) a creditor who claims for a debt in writing is referred to as proving that debt;

(b) the document by which the creditor makes the claim is referred to as that creditor's proof; and

(c) for the purpose of voting, or objecting to a deemed consent, in an administration, an administrative receivership, a creditors' voluntary winding up, a CVA or an IVA, the requirements for a proof are satisfied by the convener or chair having been notified by the creditor in writing of a debt;

"proxy" and "blank proxy" are to be interpreted in accordance with Part 16;

"qualified to act as an insolvency practitioner" in relation to a company, debtor or bankrupt has the meaning given by section 390 of the Act;

[Note: "records" are defined in section 436(1) of the Act]

"registered land" has the meaning given by section 132(1) of the Land Registration Act 2002;

"registrar" means [an Insolvency and Companies Court Judge] and unless the context requires otherwise includes a District Judge—

(a) in a District Registry of the High Court; and

(b) in a hearing centre with relevant insolvency jurisdiction;

"residential address" means the current residential address of an individual or, if that is not known, the last known residential address;

. . .

"solicitor" means a solicitor of the Senior Courts and, in relation to England and Wales, includes any other person who, for the purpose of the Legal Services Act 2007 is an authorised person in relation to an activity which constitutes the conduct of litigation (within the meaning of that Act);

"standard contents" means—

(a) for a Gazette notice, the standard contents set out in Chapter 4 of this Part;

(b) for a notice to be advertised other than in the Gazette, the standard contents set out in Chapter 5 of Part 1;

(c) for a document to be delivered to the registrar of companies, the standard contents set out in Chapter 6 of Part 1;

(d) for notices to be delivered to other persons, the standard contents set out in Chapter 7 of Part 1;

(e) for applications to the court the standard contents set out in Chapter 8 of Part 1;

"standard fee for copies" means 15 pence per A4 or A5 page or 30 pence per A3 page;

"statement of proposals" means a statement made by an administrator under paragraph 49 of Schedule B1 setting out proposals for achieving the purpose of an administration;

"statement of truth" means a statement of truth made in accordance with Part 22 of the CPR;

. . .

"trustee" has the same meaning throughout these Rules as they relate to the insolvency of individuals as it has for bankruptcy in section 385(1);

"venue" in relation to any proceedings, attendance before the court, decision procedure or meeting means the time, date and place or platform for the proceedings, attendance, decision procedure or meeting;

"virtual meeting" has the meaning given by rule 15.2(2);

"winding up by the court" means a winding up under section 122(1), 124A or 221;

"witness statement" means a witness statement verified by a statement of truth made in accordance with Part 32 of the CPR;

[Note: "writing": section 436B(1) of the Act provides that a reference to a thing in writing includes that thing in electronic form; subsection (2) excludes certain documents from the application of subsection (1); and

"written resolution" in respect of a private company refers to a written resolution passed in accordance with Chapter 2 of Part 13 of the Companies Act].

(3) An appointed person in relation to a company, debtor or bankrupt must be—

(a) qualified to act as an insolvency practitioner in relation to that company, debtor or bankrupt; or

(b) a person experienced in insolvency matters who is—

(i) a member or employee of the office-holder's firm, or

(ii) an employee of the office-holder.

(4) A fee or remuneration is charged when the work to which it relates is done.

NOTES

Para (2) is amended as follows:

In the definition "the Act", words in square brackets substituted (for the original words "Schedule A1") by the Insolvency (England and Wales) (No 2) (Amendment) Rules 2021, SI 2021/1028, r 81, Sch 2, as from 1 October 2021 (for savings provisions see the note to r 1A.1 at **[10.539]**).

Definitions "attendance" and "attend" substituted by the Insolvency (England and Wales) (Amendment) Rules 2017, SI 2017/366, rr 3, 4, as from 6 April 2017.

In the definition "Article 1.2 undertaking" the words in square brackets were substituted by the Insolvency Amendment (EU 2015/848) Regulations 2017, SI 2017/702, regs 2, 3, Schedule, Pt 2, paras 32, 33(a), as from 26 June 2017, except in relation to proceedings opened before that date.

In the definitions "business day" and "the Gazette", words "Parts A1" in square brackets substituted (for the original words "Parts 1") by SI 2021/1028, r 80, Sch 1, as from 1 October 2021 (for savings provisions see the note to r 1A.1 at **[10.539]**).

Words in square brackets in the definition "centre of main interests" substituted by the Insolvency (England and Wales) and Insolvency (Scotland) (Miscellaneous and Consequential Amendments) Rules 2017, SI 2017/1115, rr 22, 23(2), as from 8 December 2017.

Definitions "COMI proceedings", "establishment" and "establishment proceedings" inserted, and definitions "main proceedings", "member State liquidator", "non-EU proceedings"', "secondary proceedings", "temporary administrator" and "territorial proceedings" (all omitted) revoked, by the Insolvency (Amendment) (EU Exit) Regulations 2019, SI 2019/146, reg 2, Schedule, Pt 4, paras 46, 47, as from IP completion day (as defined in the European Union (Withdrawal Agreement) Act 2020, s 39) (for savings, see reg 4 of the 2019 Regulations at **[12.82]**).

The note following the definition of "document" was substituted by SI 2017/702, regs 2, 3, Schedule, Pt 2, para 32, as from 26 June 2017, except in relation to proceedings opened before that date.

In note relating to the definition of "hire-purchase agreement", the words in italics were revoked by SI 2021/1028, r 81, Sch 2, as from 1 October 2021 (for savings provisions see the note to r 1A.1 at **[10.539]**). Note that the relevant provision of Sch 2 to the 2021 Rules provides as follows—

> "In paragraph (2) in the definition of "hire-purchase agreement" — Omit the words from "purposes of the Act and" to "Schedule B1".".

It is assumed that this is an error as the remaining words in the definition would therefore read as follows—

> "Note: "hire-purchase agreement" is defined by section 436(1) as having the same meaning as in the Consumer Credit Act 1974 for the . . . (administration) for the purposes of that Schedule.".

Words in square brackets the definitions "judge" and "registrar" substituted by the Alteration of Judicial Titles (Registrar in Bankruptcy of the High Court) Order 2018, SI 2018/130, art 2, Schedule, para 14(a)(i), as from 26 February 2018.

[10.483]

1.3 Calculation of time periods

The rules set out in Schedule 5 apply to the calculation of the beginning and end of time periods under these Rules.

CHAPTER 3 FORM AND CONTENT OF DOCUMENTS

[10.484]

1.4 Requirement for writing and form of documents

(1) A notice or statement must be in writing unless the Act or these Rules provide otherwise.

(2) A document in electronic form must be capable of being—

(a) read by the recipient in electronic form; and

(b) reproduced by the recipient in hard-copy form.

[10.485]

1.5 Authentication

(1) A document in electronic form is sufficiently authenticated—

(a) if the identity of the sender is confirmed in a manner specified by the recipient; or

(b) where the recipient has not so specified, if the communication contains or is accompanied by a statement of the identity of the sender and the recipient has no reason to doubt the truth of that statement.

(2) A document in hard-copy form is sufficiently authenticated if it is signed.

(3) If a document is authenticated by the signature of an individual on behalf of—

(a) a body of persons, the document must also state the position of that individual in relation to the body;

(b) a body corporate of which the individual is the sole member, the document must also state that fact.

[10.486]

1.6 Information required to identify persons and proceedings etc

(1) Where the Act or these Rules require a document to identify, or to contain identification details in respect of, a person or proceedings, or to provide contact details for an office-holder, the information set out in the table must be given.

(2) Where a requirement relates to a proposed office-holder, the information set out in the table in respect of an office-holder must be given with any necessary adaptations.

Bankrupt	(a) full name; and (b) residential address (subject to any order for limited disclosure made under Part 20).
Company where it is the subject of the proceedings	In the case of a registered company— (c) the registered name; (d) for a company incorporated in England and Wales under the Companies Act or a previous Companies Act, its registered number; (e) for a company incorporated outside the United Kingdom— (i) the country or territory in which it is incorporated, (ii) the number, if any, under which it is registered, and (iii) the number, if any, under which it is registered as an overseas company under Part 34 of the Companies Act. In the case of an unregistered company— (f) its name; and (g) the postal address of any principal place of business.
Company other than one which is the subject of the proceedings	In the case of a registered company— (h) the registered name; (i) for a company incorporated in any part of the United Kingdom under the Companies Act or a previous Companies Act, its registered number; (j) for a company incorporated outside the United Kingdom— (i) the country or territory in which it is incorporated, (ii) the number, if any, under which it is registered; and (k) the number, if any, under which it is registered as an overseas company under Part 34 of the Companies Act; (l) In the case of an unregistered company— (i) its name, and (ii) the postal address of any principal place of business.
Debtor	(m) full name; and (n) residential address (subject to any order for limited disclosure made under Part 20).
Office-holder	(o) the name of the office-holder; and (p) the nature of the appointment held by the office-holder.
Contact details for an office-holder	(q) a postal address for the office-holder; and (r) either an email address, or a telephone number, through which the office-holder may be contacted.
Proceedings	(s) for proceedings relating to a company, the information identifying the company; (t) for proceedings relating to an individual, the full name of the bankrupt or debtor; (u) the full name of the court or hearing centre in which the proceedings are, or are to be, conducted or where documents relating to the proceedings have been or will be filed; and, if applicable, (v) any number assigned to those proceedings by the court, the hearing centre or the adjudicator.

[10.487]

1.7 [Reasons for stating whether proceedings are or will be COMI proceedings, establishment proceedings etc]

Where these Rules require reasons to be given for a statement that proceedings are or will be [COMI proceedings, establishment proceedings or proceedings to which the EU Regulation as it has effect in the law of the United Kingdom does not apply], the reasons must include [as applicable]—

(a) for a company—

(i) the centre of main interests,

Part 10 Miscellaneous other SIs

(ii) the place of the registered office within the meaning of Article 3(1) of the [EU Regulation] and where appropriate an explanation why this is not the same as the centre of main interests, . . .
[(iia) the place where there is an establishment within the jurisdiction, or]
(iii) that there is no registered office if that be the case in [proceedings to which the EU Regulation as it has effect in the law of the United Kingdom does not apply];
[(b) for a debtor—
(i) the centre of main interests, or
(ii) the place where there is an establishment within the jurisdiction.]

NOTES

The rule heading and the words in the first pair of square brackets were substituted, the words in the second pair of square brackets were inserted, the word omitted from sub-para (a)(ii) was revoked, sub-para (a)(iia) was inserted, the words in square brackets in sub-para (a)(iii) were substituted, and para (b) was substituted, by the Insolvency (Amendment) (EU Exit) Regulations 2019, SI 2019/146, reg 2, Schedule, Pt 4, paras 46, 48, as from IP completion day (as defined in the European Union (Withdrawal Agreement) Act 2020, s 39) (for savings, see reg 4 of the 2019 Regulations at **[12.82]**).

The words in square brackets In sub-para (a)(ii) were substituted by the Insolvency (England and Wales) and Insolvency (Scotland) (Miscellaneous and Consequential Amendments) Rules 2017, SI 2017/1115, rr 22, 23(4), as from 8 December 2017.

[10.488]
1.8 Prescribed format of documents

(1) Where a rule sets out requirements as to the contents of a document any title required by the rule must appear at the beginning of the document.

(2) Any other contents required by the rule (or rules where more than one apply to a particular document) must be provided in the order listed in the rule (or rules) or in another order which the maker of the document considers would be convenient for the intended recipient.

[10.489]
1.9 Variations from prescribed contents

(1) Where a rule sets out the required contents of a document, the document may depart from the required contents if—
(a) the circumstances require such a departure (including where the requirement is not applicable in the particular case); or
(b) the departure (whether or not intentional) is immaterial.

(2) However this rule does not apply to the required content of a statutory demand on a company set out in rule 7.3 and on an individual set out in rule 10.1.

CHAPTER 4 STANDARD CONTENTS OF GAZETTE NOTICES AND THE GAZETTE AS EVIDENCE ETC

[Note: (1) the requirements in Chapter 4 must be read with rule 1.6 which sets out the information required to identify an office-holder, a company etc;

(2) this Chapter does not apply to the notice of a liquidator's appointment prescribed under section 109 by SI 1987/752.]

[10.490]
1.10 Contents of notices to be gazetted under the Act or Rules

(1) Where the Act or these Rules require or permit a notice to be gazetted, the notice must also contain the standard contents set out in this Chapter in addition to any content specifically required by the Act or any other provision of these Rules.

(2) Information which this Chapter requires to be included in a Gazette notice may be omitted if it is not reasonably practicable to obtain it.

[10.491]
1.11 Standard contents of all notices

(1) A notice must identify the proceedings, if it is relevant to the particular notice, identify the office-holder and state—
(a) the office-holder's contact details;
(b) the office-holder's IP number (except for the official receiver);
(c) the name of any person other than the office-holder who may be contacted about the proceedings; and
(d) the date of the office-holder's appointment.

(2) This rule does not apply to a notice under rule 22.4(3) (Permission to act as a director: first excepted case).

[10.492]
1.12 Gazette notices relating to a company

(1) A notice relating to a registered company must also state—
(a) its registered office;
(b) any principal trading address if this is different from its registered office;
(c) any name under which it was registered in the period of 12 months before the date of the commencement of the proceedings which are the subject of the Gazette notice; and
(d) any other name or style (not being a registered name)—
(i) under which the company carried on business, and
(ii) in which any debt owed to a creditor was incurred.

(2) A notice relating to an unregistered company must also identify the company and specify any name or style—
(a) under which the company carried on business; and
(b) in which any debt owed to a creditor was incurred.

[10.493]

1.13 Gazette notices relating to a bankruptcy

A notice relating to a bankruptcy must also identify the bankrupt and state—

(a) any other address at which the bankrupt has resided in the period of 12 months before the making of the bankruptcy order;

(b) any principal trading address if different from the bankrupt's residential address;

(c) the bankrupt's date of birth;

(d) the bankrupt's occupation;

(e) any other name by which the bankrupt has been known; and

(f) any name or style (other than the bankrupt's own name) under which—

  (i) the bankrupt carried on business, and

  (ii) any debt owed to a creditor was incurred.

[10.494]

1.14 The Gazette: evidence, variations and errors

(1) A copy of the Gazette containing a notice required or permitted by the Act or these Rules to be gazetted is evidence of any facts stated in the notice.

(2) Where the Act or these Rules require an order of the court or of the adjudicator to be gazetted, a copy of the Gazette containing the notice may be produced in any proceedings as conclusive evidence that the order was made on the date specified in the notice.

(3) Where an order of the court or of the adjudicator which is gazetted has been varied, or any matter has been erroneously or inaccurately gazetted, the person whose responsibility it was to gazette the order or other matter must as soon as is reasonably practicable cause the variation to be gazetted or a further entry to be made in the Gazette for the purpose of correcting the error or inaccuracy.

CHAPTER 5 STANDARD CONTENTS OF NOTICES ADVERTISED OTHERWISE THAN IN THE GAZETTE

[Note: the requirements in Chapter 5 must be read with rule 1.6 which sets out the information required to identify an office-holder, a company etc]

[10.495]

1.15 Standard contents of notices advertised otherwise than in the Gazette

(1) Where the Act or these Rules provide that a notice may be advertised otherwise than in the Gazette the notice must contain the standard contents set out in this Chapter (in addition to any content specifically required by the Act or any other provision of these Rules).

(2) A notice must, if it is relevant to the particular notice, identify the office-holder and specify the office-holder's contact details.

(3) Information which this Chapter requires to be included in a notice may be omitted if it is not reasonably practicable to obtain it.

[10.496]

1.16 Non-Gazette notices relating to a company

A notice relating to a company must also identify the proceedings and state—

(a) the company's principal trading address;

(b) any name under which the company was registered in the 12 months before the date of the commencement of the proceedings which are the subject of the notice; and

(c) any name or style (not being a registered name) under which—

  (i) the company carried on business, and

  (ii) any debt owed to a creditor was incurred.

[10.497]

1.17 Non-Gazette notices relating to a bankruptcy

A notice relating to a bankruptcy must also identify the proceedings, identify the bankrupt and state—

(a) any other address at which the bankrupt has resided in the period of 12 months before the making of the bankruptcy order;

(b) any principal trading address if different from the bankrupt's residential address;

(c) the bankrupt's date of birth;

(d) the bankrupt's occupation;

(e) any other name by which the bankrupt has been known; and

(f) any name or style (other than the bankrupt's own name) under which—

  (i) the bankrupt carried on business, and

  (ii) any debt owed to a creditor was incurred.

[10.498]

1.18 Non-Gazette notices: other provisions

Information which this Chapter requires to be stated in a notice must be included in an advertisement of that notice in a way that is clear and comprehensible.

CHAPTER 6 STANDARD CONTENTS OF DOCUMENTS TO BE DELIVERED TO THE REGISTRAR OF COMPANIES

[Note: the requirements in Chapter 6 must be read with rule 1.6 which sets out the information required to identify an office-holder, a company etc]

[10.499]

1.19 Standard contents of documents delivered to the registrar of companies

(1) Where the Act or these Rules require a document to be delivered to the registrar of companies the document must contain the standard contents set out in this Chapter (in addition to any content specifically required by the Act or any other provision of these Rules).

(2) A document of more than one type must satisfy the requirements which apply to each.

(3) However requirements as to the contents of a document which is to be delivered to another person at the same time as the registrar of companies may be satisfied by delivering to that other person a copy of the document delivered to the registrar.

[10.500]

1.20 Registrar of companies: covering notices

[(1) This rule applies where—

(a) the Act or these Rules require an office-holder to deliver any of the documents specified in paragraph (1A) to the registrar of companies, or

(b) the directors are required to deliver a copy of a court order to the registrar of companies in accordance with sections A31(7) or A32(5).]

[(1A) The documents specified in this paragraph are—

(a) a notice under section A38 bringing a moratorium under Part A1 of the Act to an end;

(b) an account (including a final report) or a summary of receipts and payments;

(c) an administrative receiver's report under section 48(1);

(d) a court order;

(e) a declaration of solvency;

(f) a direction of the Secretary of State under section 203 or 205;

(g) a notice of disclaimer;

(h) a statement of administrator's proposals (including a statement of revised proposals);

(i) a statement of affairs;

(j) a statement of concurrence;

(k) a notice of an administrator's resignation under paragraph 87(2) of Schedule B1;

(l) a notice of a liquidator's death which the official receiver is required to deliver under rule 7.67(3)(b);

(m) a notice that a liquidator has vacated office on loss of qualification to act which the official receiver is required to deliver under rule 7.68(4)(b);

(n) any report including—

(i) a final report,

(ii) a progress report (including a final progress report),

(iii) a report of a creditor's decision under paragraph 53(2) or 54(6) of Schedule B1, and

(iv) a report of a decision approving a CVA under section 4(6) and (6A) or paragraph 30(3) and (4) of Schedule A1 to the Act;

(o) a copy of the notice that a CVA has been fully implemented or terminated that the supervisor is required to deliver under rule 2.44(3).]

(2) The office-holder [or the directors (as the case may be)] must deliver to the registrar of companies with a document mentioned in paragraph (1) a notice containing the standard contents required by this Part.

(3) Such a notice may relate to more than one document where those documents relate to the same proceedings and are delivered together to the registrar of companies.

NOTES

Para (1): substituted by the Insolvency (England and Wales) (No 2) (Amendment) Rules 2021, SI 2021/1028, r 7(1), (2), as from 1 October 2021 (for savings provisions see the note to r 1A.1 at **[10.539]**). The previous text read as follows—

"(1) This rule applies where the Act or these Rules require an office-holder to deliver any of the following documents to the registrar of companies—

(a) an account (including a final report) or a summary of receipts and payments;

(b) an administrative receiver's report under section 48(1);

(c) a court order;

(d) a declaration of solvency;

(e) a direction of the Secretary of State under section 203 or 205;

(f) a notice of disclaimer;

(g) a statement of administrator's proposals (including a statement of revised proposals);

(h) a statement of affairs;

(i) a statement of concurrence;

(j) a notice of an administrator's resignation under paragraph 87(2) of Schedule B1;

(k) a notice of a liquidator's death which the official receiver is required to deliver under rule [7.67(3)(b)];

(l) a notice that a liquidator has vacated office on loss of qualification to act which the official receiver is required to deliver under rule [7.68(4)(b)];

(m) any report including—

(i) a final report,

(ii) a progress report (including a final progress report),

(iii) a report of a creditors' decision under paragraph 53(2) or 54(6) of Schedule B1, and

(iv) a report of a decision approving a CVA under section 4(6) and [(6A)] *or paragraph 30(3) and (4) of Schedule A1 to the Act*;

(n) a copy of the notice that a CVA has been fully implemented or terminated that the supervisor is required to deliver under rule 2.44(3);

[(o) . . .]".

Note that para (1) as set out above was previously amended as follows: the figures in square brackets in sub-paras (k), (l), (m) were substituted by the Insolvency (England and Wales) (Amendment) Rules 2017, SI 2017/366, rr 3, 6, as from 6 April 2017; sub-para (o) originally added by the Insolvency Amendment (EU 2015/848) Regulations 2017, SI 2017/702, regs 2, 3, Schedule, Pt 2, paras 32, 34, as from 26 June 2017, except in relation to proceedings opened before that date, and subsequently revoked by the Insolvency (Amendment) (EU Exit) Regulations 2019, SI 2019/146, reg 2, Schedule, Pt 4, paras 46, 49, as from IP completion day (as defined in the European Union (Withdrawal Agreement) Act 2020, s 39) (for savings, see reg 4 of the 2019 Regulations at **[12.82]**). Note also that SI 2021/1028, r 81, Sch 2 also provides that the words "or paragraph 30(3) and (4) of Schedule A1 to the Act" in italics in para (1)(m)(iv) above are revoked, as from 1 October 2021 (for savings provisions see the note to r 1A.1 at **[10.539]**).

Para (1A): inserted by SI 2021/1028, r 7(1), (3), as from 1 October 2021 (for savings provisions see the note to r 1A.1 at **[10.539]**).

Para (2): words in square brackets inserted by SI 2021/1028, r 7(1), (4), as from 1 October 2021 (for savings provisions see the note to r 1A.1 at **[10.539]**).

[10.501]

1.21 Standard contents of all documents

(1) A document to be delivered to the registrar of companies must—

(a) identify the company;

(b) state—

(i) the nature of the document,

(ii) the section of the Act, the paragraph of Schedule *A1 or* B1 or the rule under which the document is delivered,

(iii) the date of the document,

(iv) the name and address of the person delivering the document, and

(v) the capacity in which that person is acting in relation to the company; and

(c) be authenticated by the person delivering the document.

(2) Where the person delivering the document is the office-holder, the address may be omitted if it has previously been notified to the registrar of companies in the proceedings and is unchanged.

NOTES

Para (1): words in italics in sub-para (b)(i) revoked by the Insolvency (England and Wales) (No 2) (Amendment) Rules 2021, SI 2021/1028, r 81, Sch 2, as from 1 October 2021 (for savings provisions see the note to r 1A.1 at **[10.539]**).

[10.502]

1.22 Standard contents of documents relating to the office of office-holders

(1) A document relating to the office of the office-holder must also identify the office-holder and state—

(a) the date of the event of which notice is delivered or of the notice (as applicable);

[(b) where the document relates to—

(i) an appointment, (other than an appointment to which sub-paragraph (b)(ii) refers), the person, body or court making the appointment; or

(ii) in the case of an appointment of a person as a monitor in respect of a moratorium for a company to which section A3 applies, the court with which the relevant documents, within the meaning given by section A6, were filed;]

(c) where the document relates to the termination of an appointment, the reason for that termination; and

(d) the contact details for the office-holder.

(2) Where the person delivering the document is the office-holder, the address may be omitted if it has previously been notified to the registrar of companies in the proceedings and is unchanged.

NOTES

Para (1): sub-para (b) substituted by the Insolvency (England and Wales) (No 2) (Amendment) Rules 2021, SI 2021/1028, r 8, as from 1 October 2021 (for savings provisions see the note to r 1A.1 at **[10.539]**). Sub-para (b) previously read as follows—

"(b) where the document relates to an appointment, the person, body or court making the appointment;".

[10.503]

1.23 Standard contents of documents relating to other documents

A document relating to another document must also state—

(a) the nature of the other document;

(b) the date of the other document; and

(c) where the other document relates to a period of time, the period of time to which it relates.

[10.504]

1.24 Standard contents of documents relating to court orders

A document relating to a court order must also specify—

(a) the nature of the order; and

(b) the date of the order.

[10.505]

1.25 Standard contents of returns or reports of decisions

A return or report of a decision procedure, deemed consent procedure or meeting must also state—

(a) the purpose of the procedure or meeting;

(b) a description of the procedure or meeting used;

(c) in the case of a decision procedure or meeting, the venue;

(d) whether, in the case of a meeting, the required quorum was in place;

(e) the outcome (including any decisions made or resolutions passed); and

(f) the date of any decision made or resolution passed.

[10.506]

1.26 Standard contents of returns or reports of matters considered by company members by correspondence

A return or report of a matter, consideration of which has been sought from the members of a company by correspondence, must also state—

(a) the purpose of the consideration; and

(b) the outcome of the consideration (including any resolutions passed or deemed to be passed).

[10.507]

1.27 Standard contents of documents relating to other events

A document relating to any other event must also state—

(a) the nature of the event, including the section of the Act, the paragraph of Schedule *A1 or* B1 or the rule under which it took place; and

(b) the date on which the event occurred.

NOTES

Words in italics in para (a) revoked by the Insolvency (England and Wales) (No 2) (Amendment) Rules 2021, SI 2021/1028, r 81, Sch 2, as from 1 October 2021 (for savings provisions see the note to r 1A.1 at **[10.539]**).

CHAPTER 7 STANDARD CONTENTS OF NOTICES FOR DELIVERY TO OTHER PERSONS ETC

[Note: the requirements in Chapter 7 must be read with rule 1.6 which sets out the information required to identify an office-holder, a company etc]

[10.508]

1.28 Standard contents of notices to be delivered to persons other than the registrar of companies

(1) Where the Act or these Rules require a notice to be delivered to a person other than the registrar of companies in respect of proceedings under [Parts A1] to 11 of the Act or the [EU Regulation], the notice must contain the standard contents set out in this Chapter (in addition to any content specifically required by the Act or another provision of these Rules).

(2) A notice of more than one type must satisfy the requirements which apply to each.

(3) However, the requirements in respect of a document which is to be delivered to another person at the same time as the registrar of companies may be satisfied by delivering to that other person a copy of the document delivered to the registrar.

NOTES

Para (1): words "Parts A1" in first pair of square brackets substituted (for the original words "Parts 1") by the Insolvency (England and Wales) (No 2) (Amendment) Rules 2021, SI 2021/1028, r 80, Sch 1, as from 1 October 2021 (for savings provisions see the note to r 1A.1 at **[10.539]**). Words in second pair of square brackets substituted by the Insolvency (England and Wales) and Insolvency (Scotland) (Miscellaneous and Consequential Amendments) Rules 2017, SI 2017/1115, rr 22, 23(5), as from 8 December 2017.

[10.509]

1.29 Standard contents of all notices

A notice must—

(a) state the nature of the notice;

(b) identify the proceedings;

(c) in the case of proceedings relating to an individual, identify the bankrupt or debtor;

(d) state the section of the Act, the paragraph of Schedule *A1 or* B1 or the rule under which the notice is given; and

(e) in the case of a notice delivered by the office-holder, state the contact details for the office-holder.

NOTES

Words in italics in para (d) revoked by the Insolvency (England and Wales) (No 2) (Amendment) Rules 2021, SI 2021/1028, r 81, Sch 2, as from 1 October 2021 (for savings provisions see the note to r 1A.1 at **[10.539]**).

[10.510]

1.30 Standard contents of notices relating to the office of office-holders

A notice relating to the office of the office-holder must also identify the office-holder and state—

(a) the date of the event of which notice is delivered;

[(b) where the document relates to—

(i) an appointment, (other than an appointment to which sub-paragraph (b)(ii) refers), the person, body or court making the appointment; or

(ii) in the case of an appointment of a person as a monitor in respect of a moratorium for a company to which section A3 applies, the court with which the relevant documents, within the meaning given by section A6, were filed.]

(c) where the notice relates to the termination of an appointment, the reason for that termination.

NOTES

Para (1): sub-para (b) substituted by the Insolvency (England and Wales) (No 2) (Amendment) Rules 2021, SI 2021/1028, r 9, as from 1 October 2021 (for savings provisions see the note to r 1A.1 at **[10.539]**). Sub-para (b) previously read as follows—

"(b) where the notice relates to an appointment, the person, body or court making the appointment; and".

[10.511]

1.31 Standard contents of notices relating to documents

A notice relating to a document must also state—

(a) the nature of the document;

(b) the date of the document; and

(c) where the document relates to a period of time the period of time to which the document relates.

[10.512]

1.32 Standard contents of notices relating to court proceedings or orders

A notice relating to court proceedings must also identify those proceedings and if the notice relates to a court order state—

(a) the nature of the order; and

(b) the date of the order.

[10.513]

1.33 Standard contents of notices of the results of decisions

A notice of the result of a decision procedure, deemed consent procedure or meeting must also state—

(a) the purpose of the procedure or meeting;

(b) a description of the procedure or meeting used;

(c) in the case of a decision procedure or meeting, the venue;

(d) whether, in the case of a meeting, the required quorum was in place; and

(e) the outcome (including any decisions made or resolutions passed).

[10.514]

1.34 Standard contents of returns or reports of matters considered by company members by correspondence

A return or report of a matter, consideration of which has been sought from the members of a company by correspondence, must also specify—

(a) the purpose of the consideration; and

(b) the outcome of the consideration (including any resolutions passed or deemed to be passed).

CHAPTER 8 APPLICATIONS TO THE COURT

[Note: the requirements in Chapter 8 must be read with rule 1.6 which sets out the information required to identify an office-holder, a company etc]

[10.515]

1.35 Standard contents and authentication of applications to the court under [Parts A1] to 11 of the Act

(1) This rule applies to applications to court under [Parts A1] to 11 of the Act (other than an application for an administration order, a winding up petition or a bankruptcy petition).

(2) The application must state—

(a) that the application is made under the Act or these Rules (as applicable);

(b) the section of the Act or paragraph of a Schedule to the Act or the number of the rule under which it is made;

(c) the names of the parties;

(d) the name of the bankrupt, debtor or company which is the subject of the insolvency proceedings to which the application relates;

(e) the court (and where applicable, the division or district registry of that court) or hearing centre in which the application is made;

(f) where the court has previously allocated a number to the insolvency proceedings within which the application is made, that number;

(g) the nature of the remedy or order applied for or the directions sought from the court;

(h) the names and addresses of the persons on whom it is intended to serve the application or that no person is intended to be served;

(i) where the Act or Rules require that notice of the application is to be delivered to specified persons, the names and addresses of all those persons (so far as known to the applicant); and

(j) the applicant's address for service.

(3) The application must be authenticated by or on behalf of the applicant or the applicant's solicitor.

NOTES

Words "Parts A1" in square brackets in the rule heading and para (1) substituted (for the original words "Parts 1") by the Insolvency (England and Wales) (No 2) (Amendment) Rules 2021, SI 2021/1028, r 80, Sch 1, as from 1 October 2021 (for savings provisions see the note to r 1A.1 at **[10.539]**).

CHAPTER 9 DELIVERY OF DOCUMENTS AND OPTING OUT (SECTIONS 246C, 248A, 379C AND 383A)

[10.516]

1.36 Application of Chapter

[Note: the registrar's rules include provision for the electronic delivery of documents.]

(1) This Chapter applies where a document is required under the Act or these Rules to be delivered, filed, forwarded, furnished, given, sent, or submitted in respect of proceedings under Parts 1 to 11 of the Act or the [EU Regulation] unless the Act, a rule or an order of the court makes different provision including one requiring service of the document.

(2) However in respect of delivery of a document to the registrar of companies—

(a) subject to sub-paragraph (b) only the following rules in this Chapter apply: rules 1.42 (postal delivery of documents), 1.43 (delivery by document exchange), 1.44 (personal delivery) and 1.52 (proof of delivery of documents);

(b) the registrar's rules made under sections 1068 and 1117 of the Companies Act apply to determine the date when any document is received by the registrar of companies.

NOTES

Para (1): words in square brackets substituted by the Insolvency (England and Wales) and Insolvency (Scotland) (Miscellaneous and Consequential Amendments) Rules 2017, SI 2017/1115, rr 22, 23(6), as from 8 December 2017.

[10.517]

1.37 Delivery to the creditors and opting out

(1) Where the Act or a rule requires an office-holder to deliver a document to the creditors, or the creditors in a class, the requirement is satisfied by the delivery of the document to all such creditors of whose address the office-holder is aware other than opted-out creditors [unless the opt out does not apply].

(2) Where a creditor has opted out from receiving documents, the opt out does not apply to—

(a) a notice which the Act requires to be delivered to all creditors without expressly excluding opted-out creditors;
(b) a notice of a change in the office-holder or the contact details for the office-holder;
(c) a notice as provided for by sections 246C(2) or 379C(2) (notices of distributions, intended distributions and notices required to be given by court order); or
(d) a document which these Rules requires to accompany a notice within sub-paragraphs (a) to (c).

(3) The office-holder must begin to treat a creditor as an opted-out creditor as soon as reasonably practicable after delivery of the creditor's election to opt out.

(4) An office-holder in any consecutive insolvency proceedings of a different kind under Parts 1 to 11 of the Act in respect of the same company or individual who is aware that a creditor was an opted-out creditor in the earlier proceedings must treat the creditor as an opted out creditor in the consecutive proceedings.

NOTES

Para (1): words in square brackets substituted by the Insolvency (England and Wales) (Amendment) Rules 2017, SI 2017/366, rr 3, 5. as from 6 April 2017.

[10.518]

1.38 Creditor's election to opt out

[(A1) This rule does not apply in relation to a moratorium under Part A1 of the Act.]

(1) A creditor may at any time elect to be an opted-out creditor.

(2) The creditor's election to opt out must be by a notice in writing authenticated and dated by the creditor.

(3) The creditor must deliver the notice to the office-holder.

(4) A creditor becomes an opted-out creditor when the notice is delivered to the office-holder.

(5) An opted-out creditor—

(a) will remain an opted-out creditor for the duration of the proceedings unless the opt out is revoked; and
(b) is deemed to be an opted-out creditor in respect of any consecutive insolvency proceedings under Parts 1 to 11 of the Act of a different kind relating to the same company or individual.

(6) The creditor may at any time revoke the election to opt out by a further notice in writing, authenticated and dated by the creditor and delivered to the office-holder.

(7) The creditor ceases to be an opted-out creditor from the date the notice is received by the office-holder.

NOTES

Para (A1): inserted by the Insolvency (England and Wales) (No 2) (Amendment) Rules 2021, SI 2021/1028, r 10, as from 1 October 2021 (for savings provisions see the note to r 1A.1 at **[10.539]**).

[10.519]

1.39 Office-holder to provide information to creditors on opting-out

[(A1) This rule does not apply in relation to a moratorium under Part A1 of the Act.]

(1) The office-holder must, in the first communication with a creditor, inform the creditor in writing that the creditor may elect to opt out of receiving further documents relating to the proceedings.

(2) The communication must contain—

(a) identification and contact details for the office-holder;
(b) a statement that the creditor has the right to elect to opt out of receiving further documents about the proceedings unless—
    (i) the Act requires a document to be delivered to all creditors without expressly excluding opted-out creditors,
    (ii) it is a notice relating to a change in the office-holder or the office-holder's contact details, or
    (iii) it is a notice of a dividend or proposed dividend or a notice which the court orders to be sent to all creditors or all creditors of a particular category to which the creditor belongs;
(c) a statement that opting-out will not affect the creditor's entitlement to receive dividends should any be paid to creditors;
(d) a statement that unless these Rules provide to the contrary opting-out will not affect any right the creditor may have to vote in a decision procedure or a participate in a deemed consent procedure in the proceedings although the creditor will not receive notice of it;
(e) a statement that a creditor who opts out will be treated as having opted out in respect of any consecutive insolvency proceedings of a different kind in respect of the same company or individual; and
(f) information about how the creditor may elect to be or cease to be an opted-out creditor.

NOTES

Para (A1): inserted by the Insolvency (England and Wales) (No 2) (Amendment) Rules 2021, SI 2021/1028, r 11, as from 1 October 2021 (for savings provisions see the note to r 1A.1 at **[10.539]**).

[10.520]

1.40 Delivery of documents to authorised recipients

Where under the Act or these Rules a document is to be delivered to a person (other than by being served on that person), it may be delivered instead to any other person authorised in writing to accept delivery on behalf of the first-mentioned person.

[10.521]

1.41 Delivery of documents to joint office-holders

Where there are joint office-holders in insolvency proceedings, delivery of a document to one of them is to be treated as delivery to all of them.

[10.522]

1.42 Postal delivery of documents

(1) A document is delivered if it is sent by post in accordance with the provisions of this rule.

(2) First class or second class post may be used to deliver a document except where these Rules require first class post to be used.

(3) Unless the contrary is shown—

(a) a document sent by first class post is treated as delivered on the second business day after the day on which it is posted;

(b) a document sent by second class post is treated as delivered on the fourth business day after the day on which it is posted;

(c) where a post-mark appears on the envelope in which a document was posted, the date of that post-mark is to be treated as the date on which the document was posted.

(4) In this rule "post-mark" means a mark applied by a postal operator which records the date on which a letter entered the postal system of the postal operator.

[10.523]

1.43 Delivery by document exchange

(1) A document is delivered to a member of a document exchange if it is delivered to that document exchange.

(2) Unless the contrary is shown, a document is treated as delivered—

(a) one business day after the day it is delivered to the document exchange where the sender and the intended recipient are members of the same document exchange; or

(b) two business days after the day it is delivered to the departure facility of the sender's document exchange where the sender and the intended recipient are members of different document exchanges.

[10.524]

1.44 Personal delivery of documents

A document is delivered if it is personally delivered in accordance with the rules for personal service in CPR Part 6.

[10.525]

1.45 Electronic delivery of documents

(1) A document is delivered if it is sent by electronic means and the following conditions apply.

(2) The conditions are that the intended recipient of the document has—

(a) given actual or deemed consent for the electronic delivery of the document;

(b) not revoked that consent before the document is sent; and

(c) provided an electronic address for the delivery of the document.

(3) Consent may relate to a specific case or generally.

(4) For the purposes of paragraph (2)(a) an intended recipient is deemed to have consented to the electronic delivery of a document by the office-holder where the intended recipient and the person who is the subject of the insolvency proceedings had customarily communicated with each other by electronic means before the proceedings commenced.

(5) Unless the contrary is shown, a document is to be treated as delivered by electronic means to an electronic address where the sender can produce a copy of the electronic communication which—

(a) contains the document; and

(b) shows the time and date the communication was sent and the electronic address to which it was sent.

(6) Unless the contrary is shown, a document sent electronically is treated as delivered to the electronic address to which it is sent at 9.00 am on the next business day after it was sent.

[10.526]

1.46 Electronic delivery of documents to the court

(1) A document may not be delivered to a court by electronic means unless this is expressly permitted by the CPR, a Practice Direction, or these Rules.

(2) A document delivered by electronic means is to be treated as delivered to the court at the time it is recorded by the court as having been received or otherwise as the CPR, a Practice Direction or these Rules provide.

[10.527]

1.47 Electronic delivery of notices to enforcement officers

Where anything in the Act or these Rules provides for the delivery of a notice to an enforcement officer or enforcement agent, it may be delivered by electronic means to a person who has been authorised to receive such a notice on behalf of a specified enforcement officer or enforcement agent or on behalf of enforcement officers or enforcement agents generally.

[10.528]

1.48 Electronic delivery by office-holders

(1) Where an office-holder delivers a document by electronic means, the document must contain, or be accompanied by, a statement that the recipient may request a hard copy of the document and a telephone number, email address and postal address that may be used to make that request.

(2) An office-holder who receives such a request must deliver a hard copy of the document to the recipient free of charge within five business days of receipt of the request.

[10.529]

1.49 Use of website by office-holder to deliver a particular document (sections 246B and 379B)

[Note: rule 3.54(3) allows notice of an extension to an administration to be given on a website, and rules 2.25(6) and 8.22(5) do likewise in respect of notice of the result of the consideration of a proposal for a CVA and an IVA respectively.]

(1) This rule applies for the purposes of sections 246B and 379B (use of websites).

(2) An office-holder who is required to deliver a document to any person may (except where personal delivery is required) satisfy that requirement by delivering a notice to that person which contains—

- (a) a statement that the document is available for viewing and downloading on a website;
- (b) the website's address and any password necessary to view and download the document; and
- (c) a statement that the person to whom the notice is delivered may request a hard copy of the document with a telephone number, email address and postal address which may be used to make that request.

(3) An office-holder who receives such a request must deliver a hard copy of the document to the recipient free of charge within five business days of receipt of the request.

(4) A document to which a notice under paragraph (2) relates must—

- (a) remain available on the website for the period required by rule 1.51; and
- (b) be in a format that enables it to be downloaded within a reasonable time of an electronic request being made for it to be downloaded.

(5) A document which is delivered to a person by means of a website in accordance with this rule, is deemed to have been delivered—

- (a) when the document is first made available on the website; or
- (b) when the notice under paragraph (2) is delivered to that person, if that is later.

[10.530]

1.50 General use of website to deliver documents

(1) The office-holder may deliver a notice to each person to whom a document will be required to be delivered in the insolvency proceedings which contains—

- (a) a statement that future documents in the proceedings other than those mentioned in paragraph (2) will be made available for viewing and downloading on a website without notice to the recipient and that the office-holder will not be obliged to deliver any such documents to the recipient of the notice unless it is requested by that person;
- (b) a telephone number, email address and postal address which may be used to make a request for a hard copy of a document;
- (c) a statement that the recipient of the notice may at any time request a hard copy of any or all of the following—
  - (i) all documents currently available for viewing on the website,
  - (ii) all future documents which may be made available there, and
- (d) the address of the website, any password required to view and download a relevant document from that site.

(2) A statement under paragraph (1)(a) does not apply to the following documents—

- (a) a document for which personal delivery is required;
- (b) a notice under rule 14.29 of intention to declare a dividend; and
- (c) a document which is not delivered generally.

(3) A document is delivered generally if it is delivered to some or all of the following classes of persons—

- (a) members,
- (b) contributories,
- (c) creditors;
- (d) any class of members, contributories or creditors.

(4) An office-holder who has delivered a notice under paragraph (1) is under no obligation—

- (a) to notify a person to whom the notice has been delivered when a document to which the notice applies has been made available on the website; or
- (b) to deliver a hard copy of such a document unless a request is received under paragraph (1)(c).

(5) An office-holder who receives such a request—

- (a) in respect of a document which is already available on the website must deliver a hard copy of the document to the recipient free of charge within five business days of receipt of the request; and
- (b) in respect of all future documents must deliver each such document in accordance with the requirements for delivery of such a document in the Act and these Rules.

(6) A document to which a statement under paragraph (1)(a) applies must—

(a) remain available on the website for the period required by rule 1.51; and
(b) must be in such a format as to enable it to be downloaded within a reasonable time of an electronic request being made for it to be downloaded.

(7) A document which is delivered to a person by means of a website in accordance with this rule, is deemed to have been delivered—
(a) when the relevant document was first made available on the website; or
(b) if later, when the notice under paragraph (1) was delivered to that person.

(8) Paragraph (7) does not apply in respect of a person who has made a request under paragraph (1)(c)(ii) for hard copies of all future documents.

[10.531]
1.51 Retention period for documents made available on websites

(1) This rule applies to a document which is made available on a website under rules 1.49, 1.50, 2.25(6) (notice of the result of the consideration of a proposal for a CVA), 3.54(3) (notice of an extension to an administration) and 8.22(4) (notice of the result of the consideration of a proposal for an IVA).

(2) Such a document must continue to be made available on the website until two months after the end of the particular insolvency proceedings or the release of the last person to hold office as the office-holder in those proceedings.

[10.532]
1.52 Proof of delivery of documents

(1) A certificate complying with this rule is proof that a document has been duly delivered to the recipient in accordance with this Chapter unless the contrary is shown.

(2) A certificate must state the method of delivery and the date of the sending, posting or delivery (as the case may be).

(3) In the case of the official receiver or the adjudicator the certificate must be given by—
(a) the official receiver or the adjudicator; or
(b) a member of the official receiver's or adjudicator's staff.

(4) In the case of an office-holder other than the official receiver or the adjudicator the certificate must be given by—
(a) the office-holder;
(b) the office-holder's solicitor; or
(c) a partner or an employee of either of them.

(5) In the case of a person other than an office-holder the certificate must be given by that person and must state—
(a) that the document was delivered by that person; or
(b) that another person (named in the certificate) was instructed to deliver it.

(6) A certificate under this rule may be endorsed on a copy of the document to which it relates.

[10.533]
1.53 Delivery of proofs and details of claims

(1) Once a proof has, or details of a claim have, been delivered to an office-holder in accordance with these Rules that proof or those details need not be delivered again; and accordingly, where a provision of these Rules requires delivery of a proof or details of a claim by a certain time, that requirement is satisfied if the proof has or the details have already been delivered.

(2) Paragraph (1) also applies to those cases set out in rule 14.3(2)(a) and (b) where a creditor who has proved in insolvency proceedings is deemed to have proved in an insolvency proceedings which immediately follows that proceeding.

CHAPTER 10 INSPECTION OF DOCUMENTS, COPIES AND PROVISION OF INFORMATION

[10.534]
1.54 Right to copies of documents

Where the Act, in relation to proceedings under [Parts A1] to 11 of the Act, or these Rules give a person the right to inspect documents, that person has a right to be supplied on request with copies of those documents on payment of the standard fee for copies.

NOTES

Words in square brackets substituted (for the original words "Parts 1") by the Insolvency (England and Wales) (No 2) (Amendment) Rules 2021, SI 2021/1028, r 80, Sch 1, as from 1 October 2021 (for savings provisions see the note to r 1A.1 at **[10.539]**).

[10.535]
1.55 Charges for copies of documents provided by the office-holder

Except where prohibited by these Rules, an office-holder is entitled to require the payment of the standard fee for copies of documents requested by a creditor, member, contributory or member of a liquidation or creditors' committee.

[10.536]
1.56 Offence in relation to inspection of documents

(1) It is an offence for a person who does not have a right under these Rules to inspect a relevant document falsely to claim to be a creditor, a member of a company or a contributory of a company with the intention of gaining sight of the document.

(2) A relevant document is one which is on the court file, the bankruptcy file or held by the office-holder or any other person and which a creditor, a member of a company or a contributory of a company has the right to inspect under these Rules.

(3) A person guilty of an offence under this rule is liable to imprisonment or a fine, or both.

[10.537]
1.57 Right to list of creditors

(1) This rule applies to—
[(za) a moratorium under Part A1 of the Act;]
(a) administration;
(b) creditors' voluntary winding up;
(c) winding up by the court; and
(d) bankruptcy.

(2) A creditor has the right to require the office-holder to provide a list of the names and addresses of the creditors and the amounts of their respective debts unless—
(a) a statement of affairs has been filed with the court or delivered to the registrar of companies; or
(b) the information is available for inspection on the bankruptcy file.

(3) The office-holder on being required to provide such a list—
(a) must deliver it to the person requiring the list as soon as reasonably practicable; and
(b) may charge the standard fee for copies for a hard copy.

(4) The office-holder may omit the name and address of a creditor if the office-holder thinks its disclosure would be prejudicial to the conduct of the proceedings or might reasonably be expected to lead to violence against any person.

(5) In such a case the list must include—
(a) the amount of that creditor's debt; and
(b) a statement that the name and address of the creditor has been omitted for that debt.

NOTES

Para (1): sub-para (za) inserted by the Insolvency (England and Wales) (No 2) (Amendment) Rules 2021, SI 2021/1028, r 12, as from 1 October 2021 (for savings provisions see the note to r 1A.1 at **[10.539]**).

[10.538]
1.58 Confidentiality of documents: grounds for refusing inspection

(1) Where an office-holder considers that a document forming part of the records of the insolvency proceedings—
(a) should be treated as confidential; or
(b) is of such a nature that its disclosure would be prejudicial to the conduct of the proceedings or might reasonably be expected to lead to violence against any person;

the office-holder may decline to allow it to be inspected by a person who would otherwise be entitled to inspect it.

(2) The persons to whom the office-holder may refuse inspection include members of a liquidation committee or a creditors' committee.

(3) Where the office-holder refuses inspection of a document, the person wishing to inspect it may apply to the court which may reconsider the office-holder's decision.

(4) The court's decision may be subject to such conditions (if any) as it thinks just.

[PART 1A MORATORIUMS

CHAPTER 1 PRELIMINARY

[Note: in accordance with rules 4 and 5 of the Insolvency (England and Wales) (No 2) (Amendment) Rules 2021 this Part applies only in relation to moratoriums under section A3 of the Act that come into force on or after 1st October 2021 and in relation to moratoriums under sections A4 and A5 of the Act where the application to the court is made on or after 1st October 2021.]

[10.539]
1A.1 Application of Part 1A

This Part applies for the purposes of a moratorium under Part A1 of the Act.]

NOTES

Commencement: 1 October 2021.

Part 1A (rr 1A.1–1A.32) inserted by the Insolvency (England and Wales) (No 2) (Amendment) Rules 2021, SI 2021/1028, r 6, as from 1 October 2021, subject to savings in rr 4, 5 thereof as noted below.

Savings: the Insolvency (England and Wales) (No 2) (Amendment) Rules 2021, SI 2021/1028, rr 4, 5 provide as follows—

"Saving provisions

4.

(1) This rule applies where before 1st October 2021—
(a) a moratorium under Part A1 of the Insolvency Act 1986 has come into force, or
(b) in the case of a moratorium for a company to which either section A4 or A5 of the Insolvency Act 1986 applies, an application has been made to the court.

(2) Where this rule applies—
(a) the amendments made by Parts 2 to 4 of these Rules do not apply, and
(b) Part 3 of Schedule 4 to the Corporate Insolvency and Governance Act 2020 continues to have effect,

in relation to that moratorium.

5. Nothing in Parts 2 to 4 of these Rules affects the operation of the Insolvency Rules in relation to a moratorium under Schedule A1 to the Insolvency Act 1986 which has come into force before 1st October 2021.".

[CHAPTER 2 OBTAINING MORATORIUM BY FILING NOTICE AT COURT

[Note: a document required by the Act or these Rules must also contain the standard contents set out in Part 1.]

[10.540]

1A.2 Application of Chapter

This Chapter applies for the purposes of obtaining a moratorium under section A3.]

NOTES

Commencement: 1 October 2021.

Part 1A (rr 1A.1–1A.32) inserted by the Insolvency (England and Wales) (No 2) (Amendment) Rules 2021, SI 2021/1028, r 6, as from 1 October 2021 (for savings provisions see the note to r 1A.1 at **[10.539]**).

[10.541]

[1A.3 Obtaining a moratorium by filing documents at court (section A3): notice of filing

(1) The directors must (in addition to the relevant documents referred to in section A6) file a notice with the court (referred to as a "notice of filing").

(2) The notice of filing must—

(a) be accompanied by the relevant documents,

(b) be headed "Moratorium under section A3 of the Insolvency Act 1986: notice of filing",

(c) state—

(i) that the directors wish to obtain a moratorium under section A3 of the Act,

(ii) the names of the persons filing the notice,

(iii) the identification details for the company,

(iv) the court (and where applicable the division or district registry of that court) or hearing centre in which the notice is filed,

(v) where the court has previously allocated a number to the insolvency proceedings within which the notice is filed, that number, and

(vi) the date on which the notice is filed, and

(d) be authenticated by, or on behalf of, the person filing the notice.

(3) The notice of filing must be endorsed by the court with the date and time of filing.]

NOTES

Commencement: 1 October 2021.

Part 1A (rr 1A.1–1A.32) inserted by the Insolvency (England and Wales) (No 2) (Amendment) Rules 2021, SI 2021/1028, r 6, as from 1 October 2021 (for savings provisions see the note to r 1A.1 at **[10.539]**).

[10.542]

[1A.4 The relevant documents: contents and requirements (section A6)

(1) Each relevant document must—

(a) state the nature of the document,

(b) identify the proceedings,

(c) contain the identification details for the company, and

(d) be authenticated by, or on behalf of, the person giving the notice or making the statement (as the case may be).

(2) The statements under section A6(1)(b) to (e) must—

(a) be made within the period of five business days ending with the day on which the notice of filing is filed with the court, and

(b) specify the date on which the statement is made.]

NOTES

Commencement: 1 October 2021.

Part 1A (rr 1A.1–1A.32) inserted by the Insolvency (England and Wales) (No 2) (Amendment) Rules 2021, SI 2021/1028, r 6, as from 1 October 2021 (for savings provisions see the note to r 1A.1 at **[10.539]**).

[10.543]

[1A.5 The relevant documents: further requirements relating to the proposed monitor's statement and consent to act (section A6(1)(b))

A statement under section A6(1)(b) must—

(a) be headed "Proposed monitor's statement and consent to act", and

(b) contain—

(i) a certificate that the proposed monitor is qualified to act as an insolvency practitioner in relation to the company,

(ii) the name of the relevant recognised professional body which is the source of the proposed monitor's authorisation,

(iii) the proposed monitor's IP number, and

(iv) a statement that the proposed monitor consents to act as monitor in relation to the company.]

NOTES

Commencement: 1 October 2021.

Part 1A (rr 1A.1–1A.32) inserted by the Insolvency (England and Wales) (No 2) (Amendment) Rules 2021, SI 2021/1028, r 6, as from 1 October 2021 (for savings provisions see the note to r 1A.1 at **[10.539]**).

[10.544]

[1A.6 Directions

The court may at any time give such directions as it thinks just as to service of the notice of filing on any person.]

NOTES

Commencement: 1 October 2021.

Part 1A (rr 1A.1–1A.32) inserted by the Insolvency (England and Wales) (No 2) (Amendment) Rules 2021, SI 2021/1028, r 6, as from 1 October 2021 (for savings provisions see the note to r 1A.1 at **[10.539]**).

[CHAPTER 3 OBTAINING A MORATORIUM BY APPLICATION TO THE COURT

[Note: a document required by the Act or these Rules must also contain the standard contents set out in Part 1.]

[10.545]

1A.7 Application of Chapter

This Chapter applies for the purposes of an application to the court to obtain a moratorium—

(a) for a company subject to a winding-up petition under section A4, or

(b) for an overseas company under section A5.]

NOTES

Commencement: 1 October 2021.

Part 1A (rr 1A.1–1A.32) inserted by the Insolvency (England and Wales) (No 2) (Amendment) Rules 2021, SI 2021/1028, r 6, as from 1 October 2021 (for savings provisions see the note to r 1A.1 at **[10.539]**).

[10.546]

[1A.8 Moratorium application (sections A4 and A5)

(1) An application for a moratorium under sections A4 or A5 must—

(a) specify the date on which the application is filed, and

(b) be accompanied by the relevant documents (as to which see section A6).

(2) The application must be endorsed by the court with the date and time of filing.]

NOTES

Commencement: 1 October 2021.

Part 1A (rr 1A.1–1A.32) inserted by the Insolvency (England and Wales) (No 2) (Amendment) Rules 2021, SI 2021/1028, r 6, as from 1 October 2021 (for savings provisions see the note to r 1A.1 at **[10.539]**).

[10.547]

[1A.9 The relevant documents: contents and requirements (section A6)

(1) Each relevant document must—

(a) state the nature of the document,

(b) identify the proceedings,

(c) contain the identification details for the company, and

(d) be authenticated by, or on behalf of, the person giving the notice or making the statement (as the case may be).

(2) The statements under section A6(1)(b) to (e) must—

(a) be made within the period of five business days ending with the day on which the application is filed with the court, and

(b) specify the date on which the statement is made.]

NOTES

Commencement: 1 October 2021.

Part 1A (rr 1A.1–1A.32) inserted by the Insolvency (England and Wales) (No 2) (Amendment) Rules 2021, SI 2021/1028, r 6, as from 1 October 2021 (for savings provisions see the note to r 1A.1 at **[10.539]**).

[10.548]

[1A.10 The relevant documents: further requirements relating to the monitor's statement and consent to act (section A6(1)(b))

A statement under section A6(1)(b) must—

(a) be headed "Proposed monitor's statement and consent to act for the purposes of a moratorium under Part A1 of the Insolvency Act 1986" and

(b) contain—

(i) a certificate that the proposed monitor is qualified to act as an insolvency practitioner in relation to the company,

(ii) the name of the relevant recognised professional body which is the source of the proposed monitor's authorisation,

(iii) the proposed monitor's IP number, and

(iv) a statement that the proposed monitor consents to act as monitor in relation to the company.]

NOTES

Commencement: 1 October 2021.

Part 1A (rr 1A.1–1A.32) inserted by the Insolvency (England and Wales) (No 2) (Amendment) Rules 2021, SI 2021/1028, r 6, as from 1 October 2021 (for savings provisions see the note to r 1A.1 at **[10.539]**).

[CHAPTER 4 OBLIGATIONS TO NOTIFY WHERE MORATORIUM COMES INTO FORCE

[Note: a document required by the Act or these Rules must also contain the standard contents set out in Part 1.]

[10.549]

1A.11 Notice given by court where moratorium comes into force:

As soon as reasonably practicable after the coming into force of a moratorium the court must deliver to the directors a sealed copy of the document referred to in paragraph (a) or (b) (as the case may be) endorsed with the date and time of filing—

(a) in the case of a moratorium under section A3, the notice of filing referred to in rule 1A.3, or
(b) in the case of a moratorium under section A4 or A5, the application referred to in rule 1A.8.]

NOTES

Commencement: 1 October 2021.

Part 1A (rr 1A.1–1A.32) inserted by the Insolvency (England and Wales) (No 2) (Amendment) Rules 2021, SI 2021/1028, r 6, as from 1 October 2021 (for savings provisions see the note to r 1A.1 at **[10.539]**).

[10.550]

[1A.12 Notice given by monitor where moratorium comes into force: standard contents and requirements

(1) Notification of the coming into force of a moratorium required by section A8(1) must be delivered—

(a) to the persons specified in section A8(2), and
(b) where paragraph (2) applies, in accordance with that paragraph.

(2) Paragraph (3) applies where—

(a) notification is required to be given to any of the persons referred to in section A8(2)(b) to (d), or
(b) the moratorium is for a company which is a regulated company within the meaning given by section A49.

(3) Where this paragraph applies—

(a) rule 1.19(3) (copy of a document delivered to registrar of companies may be used to satisfy requirements for delivery to other persons) does not apply, and
(b) the monitor must deliver a copy of the document delivered to the registrar of companies to—
   (i) the persons referred to in section A8(2)(b) to (d), for the purpose of giving the notification required by those paragraphs, and
   (ii) the appropriate regulator, for the purpose of giving the notification required by section A49(3).]

NOTES

Commencement: 1 October 2021.

Part 1A (rr 1A.1–1A.32) inserted by the Insolvency (England and Wales) (No 2) (Amendment) Rules 2021, SI 2021/1028, r 6, as from 1 October 2021 (for savings provisions see the note to r 1A.1 at **[10.539]**).

[CHAPTER 5 EXTENDING MORATORIUM BY FILING NOTICE WITH THE COURT

[Note: a document required by the Act or these Rules must also contain the standard contents set out in Part 1.]

[10.551]

1A.13 Application of Chapter

This Chapter applies for the purposes of extending a moratorium under sections A10 and A11.]

NOTES

Commencement: 1 October 2021.

Part 1A (rr 1A.1–1A.32) inserted by the Insolvency (England and Wales) (No 2) (Amendment) Rules 2021, SI 2021/1028, r 6, as from 1 October 2021 (for savings provisions see the note to r 1A.1 at **[10.539]**).

[10.552]

[1A.14 Extending a moratorium by filing notice with the court (sections A10 and A11): notice of extension

(1) The directors must file a notice with the court (referred to as a "notice of extension").

(2) The notice of extension must—

(a) be accompanied by the documents referred to in section A10(1) or A11(1) (as the case may be),
(b) be headed "Notice of extension of a moratorium under section A10/A11 of the Insolvency Act 1986",
(c) state—
   (i) that the notice is filed for the purpose of extending a moratorium,
   (ii) whether the extension is under section A10 or section A11 of the Insolvency Act 1986,
   (iii) the names of the persons filing the notice,
   (iv) the identification details of the company,
   (v) the court (and where applicable the division or district registry of that court) or hearing centre in which the notice is filed,
   (vi) where the court has previously allocated a number to the insolvency proceedings in which the notice is filed, that number, and
   (viii) the date on which the notice is filed, and
(d) be authenticated by, or on behalf of, the person filing the notice.

(3) The notice of extension must be endorsed by the court with the date and time of filing.]

NOTES

Commencement: 1 October 2021.

Part 1A (rr 1A.1–1A.32) inserted by the Insolvency (England and Wales) (No 2) (Amendment) Rules 2021, SI 2021/1028, r 6, as from 1 October 2021 (for savings provisions see the note to r 1A.1 at **[10.539]**).

[10.553]

[1A.15 Documents filed with the court under sections A10(1) or A11(1) of the Act: contents and requirements

(1) Each document filed with the court under section A10(1) or A11(1) must—

(a) state the nature of the document,
(b) identify the proceedings,
(c) contain the identification details for the company,
(d) be authenticated by, or on behalf of, the person giving the notice or making the statement (as the case may be).

(2) The statement under section A11(1)(e) must also state—

(a) a description of the procedure used,
(b) the venue,
(c) whether, in the case of a meeting, the required quorum was in place, and
(d) the outcome.

(3) The statements under section A10(1)(b) to (d) or A11(1)(b) to (e) (as the case may be) must—
(a) be made within the period of three business days ending with the day on which the notice of extension is filed with the court, and
(b) specify the date on which the statement is made.]

NOTES

Commencement: 1 October 2021.

Part 1A (rr 1A.1–1A.32) inserted by the Insolvency (England and Wales) (No 2) (Amendment) Rules 2021, SI 2021/1028, r 6, as from 1 October 2021 (for savings provisions see the note to r 1A.1 at **[10.539]**).

[10.554]
[1A.16 Directions

The court may at any time give such directions as it thinks just as to service of the notice of extension on or to any person.]

NOTES

Commencement: 1 October 2021.

Part 1A (rr 1A.1–1A.32) inserted by the Insolvency (England and Wales) (No 2) (Amendment) Rules 2021, SI 2021/1028, r 6, as from 1 October 2021 (for savings provisions see the note to r 1A.1 at **[10.539]**).

[CHAPTER 6 EXTENDING MORATORIUM BY APPLICATION TO THE COURT

[Note: a document required by the Act or these Rules must also contain the standard contents set out in Part 1.]

[10.555]
1A.17 Application of Chapter

This Chapter applies for the purposes of extending a moratorium by application to the court under section A13.]

NOTES

Commencement: 1 October 2021.

Part 1A (rr 1A.1–1A.32) inserted by the Insolvency (England and Wales) (No 2) (Amendment) Rules 2021, SI 2021/1028, r 6, as from 1 October 2021 (for savings provisions see the note to r 1A.1 at **[10.539]**).

[10.556]
[1A.18 Extending a moratorium by application to the court (section A13)

(1) An application for an extension to a moratorium under section A13 must—
(a) specify the date on which the application is filed, and
(b) be accompanied by the documents referred to in section A13(2).

(2) The application must be endorsed by the court with the date and time of filing.]

NOTES

Commencement: 1 October 2021.

Part 1A (rr 1A.1–1A.32) inserted by the Insolvency (England and Wales) (No 2) (Amendment) Rules 2021, SI 2021/1028, r 6, as from 1 October 2021 (for savings provisions see the note to r 1A.1 at **[10.539]**).

[10.557]
[1A.19 Documents filed with the court under section A13(2): contents and requirements

(1) Each document filed with the court under section A13(2) must—
(a) state the nature of the document,
(b) identify the proceedings,
(c) contain the identification details for the company, and
(d) be authenticated by, or on behalf of, the person making the statement.

(2) The statements comprised in a document filed with the court under section A13(2) must—
(a) be made within the period of three business days ending with the day on which the application is filed with the court, and
(b) specify the date on which the statement is made.]

NOTES

Commencement: 1 October 2021.

Part 1A (rr 1A.1–1A.32) inserted by the Insolvency (England and Wales) (No 2) (Amendment) Rules 2021, SI 2021/1028, r 6, as from 1 October 2021 (for savings provisions see the note to r 1A.1 at **[10.539]**).

[CHAPTER 7 NOTICES ABOUT CHANGE IN THE END OF MORATORIUM

[Note: a document required by the Act or these Rules must also contain the standard contents set out in Part 1.]

[10.558]
1A.20 Notification by directors to the monitor under section A17(1) of the Act: contents and requirements

(1) A notice under section A17(1) must be delivered to the monitor.

(2) The notice must—
(a) be delivered within the period of three business days beginning with the day on which the duty to give the notice arises, and
(b) contain—

(i) the identification details for the company,
(ii) a statement specifying the provision in Part A1 of the Insolvency Act 1986 by virtue of which the moratorium was extended or came to an end (as the case may be) and
(iii) if the moratorium has come to an end by virtue of section A16(1)(a) or (b) (company enters into insolvency procedure etc) the additional information required by paragraph (3).

(3) The additional information that is required if a moratorium has come to an end by virtue of—
(a) section A16(1)(a), is the date on which the compromise or arrangement came into effect, or
(b) section A16(1)(b), is—
(i) the date on which the company entered into the relevant insolvency procedure, and
(ii) the contact details for the office-holder for that procedure.]

NOTES

Commencement: 1 October 2021.

Part 1A (rr 1A.1–1A.32) inserted by the Insolvency (England and Wales) (No 2) (Amendment) Rules 2021, SI 2021/1028, r 6, as from 1 October 2021 (for savings provisions see the note to r 1A.1 at **[10.539]**).

[10.559]

[1A.21 Notification by the monitor to the relevant persons under sections A17(2) or (3) of the Act: contents and requirements

(1) Notification under section A17(2) or (3) must—
(a) be delivered—
(i) to the relevant persons specified in section A17(8)(a) to (d), and
(ii) where paragraph (4) applies, in accordance with that paragraph, and
(b) if the moratorium has come to an end by virtue of section A16(1)(b), contain the additional information referred to in paragraph (5).

(2) Notification delivered under this rule must be delivered within the period of five business days beginning with the day on which the duty to give the notice arises.

(3) Paragraph (4) applies where—
(a) notification is required to be given to any of the relevant persons referred to in section A17(8)(b) to (d), or
(b) the moratorium is for a company which is a regulated company within the meaning given by section A49(13).

(4) Where this paragraph applies—
(a) rule 1.19(3) (copy of a document delivered to registrar of companies may be used to satisfy requirements for delivery to other persons) does not apply, and
(b) the monitor must deliver a copy of the document delivered to the registrar of companies to—
(i) the persons referred to in section A17(8)(b) to (d), for the purpose of giving the notification required by those paragraphs, and
(ii) the appropriate regulator, for the purpose of giving the notification required by section A49(3).

(5) The additional information that is required if a moratorium has come to an end by virtue of section A16(1)(b) is—
(a) the date on which the company entered into the relevant insolvency procedure, and
(b) the contact details for the office-holder for that procedure.

[Note: Chapter 9 includes provision about notification by the monitor to the company etc where the end of the moratorium changes by virtue of a notice given to the court under section A38 (termination of moratorium by monitor).]]

NOTES

Commencement: 1 October 2021.

Part 1A (rr 1A.1–1A.32) inserted by the Insolvency (England and Wales) (No 2) (Amendment) Rules 2021, SI 2021/1028, r 6, as from 1 October 2021 (for savings provisions see the note to r 1A.1 at **[10.539]**).

[CHAPTER 8 NOTIFICATION BY DIRECTORS OF INSOLVENCY PROCEEDINGS

[Note: a document required by the Act or these Rules must also contain the standard contents set out in Part 1.]

[10.560]

1A.22 Notification by directors to the monitor of insolvency proceedings (section A24)

Notice by the directors of certain insolvency proceedings under section A24 must be delivered within the period of—
(a) in the case of a notice under subsection (1), three business days ending with the day on which any of the steps mentioned in paragraphs (a) to (c) of that subsection is to be taken, and
(b) in the case of a notice under sub-section (2), three business days beginning with the day on which the duty to give the notice arises.]

NOTES

Commencement: 1 October 2021.

Part 1A (rr 1A.1–1A.32) inserted by the Insolvency (England and Wales) (No 2) (Amendment) Rules 2021, SI 2021/1028, r 6, as from 1 October 2021 (for savings provisions see the note to r 1A.1 at **[10.539]**).

[CHAPTER 9 TERMINATION OF MORATORIUM BY MONITOR

[Note: a document required by the Act or these Rules must also contain the standard contents set out in Part 1.]

[10.561]

1A.23 Notice bringing moratorium to an end (section A38)

(1) Notice bringing the moratorium to an end under section A38 must—
(a) be filed with the court—
(i) as soon as practicable after the duty to bring the moratorium to an end arises, and

(ii) together with one copy for the company.

(b) be headed "Notice of termination of moratorium by monitor under section A38 of the Insolvency Act 1986",

(c) state—

(i) that the notice is filed for the purpose of terminating a moratorium under section A38 of the Insolvency Act 1986,

(ii) the identification details of the company,

(iii) the name and contact details of the monitor,

(iv) the court (and where applicable the division or district registry of that court) or hearing centre in which the notice is filed,

(v) where the court has previously allocated a number to the insolvency proceedings within which the notice is filed, that number,

(vi) the date on which the notice is filed,

(vii) the grounds on which the moratorium is to be terminated,

(viii) the monitor's reasons for concluding that those grounds are made out, and

(ix) the date on which the monitor concluded that those grounds were made out, and

(d) be authenticated by, or on behalf of, the monitor.

(3) The court must endorse both the notice and the copy of the notice with the date and time of filing.

(4) The copy of the notice must have the seal of the court applied to it and must be delivered to the monitor.

(5) The monitor must deliver—

(a) the sealed copy of the notice to the company, and

(b) further copies of that notice to—

(i) the registrar of companies, and

(ii) where paragraph (7) applies, the persons specified in paragraph 7(b),

within the period of three business days beginning with the day on which the sealed copy of the notice is delivered to the monitor.

(6) Paragraph (7) applies where—

(a) notification is required to be given to any of the relevant persons referred to in section A17(8)(b) to (d), or

(b) the moratorium is for a company which is a regulated company within the meaning given by section A49(13).

(7) Where this paragraph applies—

(a) rule 1.19(3) (copy of document delivered to registrar of companies may be used to satisfy requirements for delivery to other persons) does not apply, and

(b) the monitor must deliver a copy of the document delivered to the registrar of companies to—

(i) the persons referred to in section A17(8)(b) to (d) for the purpose of giving the notification required by those paragraphs, and

(ii) the appropriate regulator, for the purpose of giving the notification required by section A49(3).]

NOTES

Commencement: 1 October 2021.

Part 1A (rr 1A.1–1A.32) inserted by the Insolvency (England and Wales) (No 2) (Amendment) Rules 2021, SI 2021/1028, r 6, as from 1 October 2021 (for savings provisions see the note to r 1A.1 at **[10.539]**).

[10.562]

[1A.24 Debts that are to be disregarded for the purposes of section A38(1)(d) of the Act

For the purposes of deciding whether to bring a moratorium to an end under section A38(1)(d) the monitor must disregard—

(a) any debts that the monitor has reasonable grounds for thinking are likely to be—

(i) paid, or

(ii) compounded to the satisfaction of the creditor,

within five business days of the decision, and

(b) any debts in respect of which the creditor has agreed to defer payment until a time that is later than the decision.]

NOTES

Commencement: 1 October 2021.

Part 1A (rr 1A.1–1A.32) inserted by the Insolvency (England and Wales) (No 2) (Amendment) Rules 2021, SI 2021/1028, r 6, as from 1 October 2021 (for savings provisions see the note to r 1A.1 at **[10.539]**).

[CHAPTER 10 REPLACEMENT OF MONITOR OR APPOINTMENT OF ADDITIONAL MONITOR

[Note: a document required by the Act or these Rules must also contain the standard contents set out in Part 1.]

[10.563]

1A.25 Replacement of monitor or appointment of additional monitor, monitor's statement and consent to act: contents and requirements (section A39(4))

(1) A statement by a proposed replacement or additional monitor under section A39(4) must be filed with the court.

(2) The statement must—

(a) be headed "Proposed monitor's statement and consent to act for the purposes of a moratorium under Part A1 of the Insolvency Act 1986",

(b) contain—

(i) a certificate that the proposed monitor is qualified to act as an insolvency practitioner in relation to the company,

(ii) the name of the relevant recognised professional body which is the source of the proposed monitor's authorisation,

(iii) the proposed monitor's IP number, and

(iv) a statement that the proposed monitor consents to act as a replacement monitor or an additional monitor (as the case may be) in relation to the company,

(c) specify the date on which the statement was made,

(d) be authenticated by the proposed replacement monitor or the proposed additional monitor, and

(e) be made within the period of five business days ending with the day on which the statement is filed with the court.]

NOTES

Commencement: 1 October 2021.

Part 1A (rr 1A.1–1A.32) inserted by the Insolvency (England and Wales) (No 2) (Amendment) Rules 2021, SI 2021/1028, r 6, as from 1 October 2021 (for savings provisions see the note to r 1A.1 at **[10.539]**).

[10.564]

[1A.26 Notice to be given by monitor of replacement of monitor or appointment of additional monitor (section A39(8))

(1) Notification of the appointment of a replacement monitor or the appointment of an additional monitor by virtue of an order under section A39(1) must be delivered—

(a) to the persons specified in section A39(8), and

(b) where paragraph (2) applies, in accordance with that paragraph.

(2) Paragraph (3) applies where—

(a) notification is required to be given to any of the persons referred to in section A39(8)(b) to (d), or

(b) the moratorium is for a company which is a regulated company within the meaning given by section A49(13).

(3) Where this paragraph applies—

(a) rule 1.19(3) (copy of document delivered to registrar of companies may be used to satisfy requirements for delivery to other persons) does not apply, and

(b) the monitor must deliver a copy of the document delivered to the registrar of companies to—

(i) for the purpose of giving the notification required by section A39(8)(b) to (d), each of the persons referred to in those paragraphs (as applicable), and

(ii) for the purpose of giving the notification required by section A49(3), the appropriate regulator.]

NOTES

Commencement: 1 October 2021.

Part 1A (rr 1A.1–1A.32) inserted by the Insolvency (England and Wales) (No 2) (Amendment) Rules 2021, SI 2021/1028, r 6, as from 1 October 2021 (for savings provisions see the note to r 1A.1 at **[10.539]**).

[CHAPTER 11 CHALLENGES TO MONITOR REMUNERATION

[Note: a document required by the Act or these Rules must also contain the standard contents set out in Part 1.]

[10.565]

1A.27 Challenges to monitor remuneration in subsequent insolvency proceedings

(1) An administrator or liquidator may apply to the court on the grounds that remuneration charged by the monitor in relation to a prior moratorium was excessive.

(2) An application under paragraph (1) may not be made after the end of the period of 2 years beginning with the day after the day on which the moratorium ends.

(3) On an application under paragraph (1) the court may—

(a) dismiss the application,

(b) order the monitor—

(i) to repay some or all of the remuneration, and

(ii) to pay interest on that sum at the rate specified in paragraph (4) for the period beginning with the date on which the remuneration was paid to the monitor and ending with the date of repayment, or

(c) make such other order as it sees fit.

(4) The rate specified for the purpose of paragraph (3)(b)(ii) is the rate specified in section 17 of the Judgments Act 1838 on the date on which the remuneration was paid to the monitor.]

NOTES

Commencement: 1 October 2021.

Part 1A (rr 1A.1–1A.32) inserted by the Insolvency (England and Wales) (No 2) (Amendment) Rules 2021, SI 2021/1028, r 6, as from 1 October 2021 (for savings provisions see the note to r 1A.1 at **[10.539]**).

[CHAPTER 12 APPLICATIONS TO COURT

[Note: a document required by the Act of these Rules must also contain the standard contents set out in Part 1.]

[10.566]

1A.28 Application of Chapter

This Chapter applies where an application is made to the court under—

(a) section A21 (restrictions on enforcement and legal proceedings),

(b) section A31 (disposal of charged property free from charge),

(c) section A32 (disposal of hire-purchase property),

(d) section A37 (application by monitor for directions),

(e) section A39 (replacement of monitor or appointment of additional monitor),

(f) section A42 (challenge to monitor's actions),

(g) section A43 and rule 1A.27(1) (challenges to monitor remuneration in insolvency proceedings), or

(h) section A44 (challenge to directors' actions).]

NOTES

Commencement: 1 October 2021.

Part 1A (rr 1A.1–1A.32) inserted by the Insolvency (England and Wales) (No 2) (Amendment) Rules 2021, SI 2021/1028, r 6, as from 1 October 2021 (for savings provisions see the note to r 1A.1 at **[10.539]**).

[10.567]

[1A.29 Procedure for filing of application

(1) An application to which this Chapter applies must—

(a) identify the date on which the application is filed, and

(b) be filed at the court together with copies for—

(i) each of the persons specified in the third column of the Table in rule 1A.30(2), and

(ii) where the application is made in respect of a regulated company within the meaning given by section A49, the appropriate regulator (as defined in that section).

(2) The date and time of filing of the application must be endorsed on the application and on the copies.

(3) Each copy of the application must have the seal of the court applied to it and must be delivered to the applicant.]

NOTES

Commencement: 1 October 2021.

Part 1A (rr 1A.1–1A.32) inserted by the Insolvency (England and Wales) (No 2) (Amendment) Rules 2021, SI 2021/1028, r 6, as from 1 October 2021 (for savings provisions see the note to r 1A.1 at **[10.539]**).

[10.568]

[1A.30 Service of the application

(1) The applicant must serve a sealed copy of the application—

(a) in accordance with—

(i) Schedule 4, and

(ii) the Table in paragraph (2),

(b) in a case where the application is made in respect of a regulated company within the meaning given by section A49, on the appropriate regulator, and

(c) at least 14 days before the date fixed for the hearing unless—

(i) the case is urgent and the court acts under rule 12.10, or

(ii) the court extends or abridges the time limit.

(2) This is the Table referred to in paragraph (1)—

Section of the Act	*Topic*	*Persons on whom application must be served*
A21	Restrictions on enforcement and legal proceedings	The company and the monitor
A31	Disposal of charged property free from charge	The holder of the security interest and the monitor
A32	Disposal of hire-purchase property	The owner of the property and the monitor
A37	Application by monitor for directions	The company
A39	Replacement of monitor or appointment of additional monitor	The monitor, in cases where the application is made by the directors. The directors in cases where the application is made by the monitor.
A42	Challenge to monitor's actions	The company and the monitor
A43 and rule 1A.27(1)	Challenges to monitor remuneration in insolvency proceedings	The directors and the monitor
A44	Challenge to director's actions	The directors and the monitor]

NOTES

Commencement: 1 October 2021.

Part 1A (rr 1A.1–1A.32) inserted by the Insolvency (England and Wales) (No 2) (Amendment) Rules 2021, SI 2021/1028, r 6, as from 1 October 2021 (for savings provisions see the note to r 1A.1 at **[10.539]**).

[10.569]

[1A.31 Notice of opposition

(1) A person on whom an application has been served who intends to oppose the application must, not less than three business days before the day fixed for the hearing—

(a) file a notice with the court which complies with the requirements of paragraph (2), and

(b) deliver a copy of the notice to—

(i) the applicant or the applicant's solicitor, and

(ii) (where applicable) each of the other persons specified in the third column of the Table in rule 1A.30(2) on whom notice of the application is required to be served.

(2) The notice must—

(a) identify the proceedings,

(b) state that the person intends to oppose the application,

(c) state the grounds on which the person opposes the application, and

(d) state whether the person intends to appear on the hearing of the application.]

NOTES

Commencement: 1 October 2021.

Part 1A (rr 1A.1–1A.32) inserted by the Insolvency (England and Wales) (No 2) (Amendment) Rules 2021, SI 2021/1028, r 6, as from 1 October 2021 (for savings provisions see the note to r 1A.1 at **[10.539]**).

[10.570]
[1A.32 Notice where the court grants permission under section A31 or A32

(1) This rule applies where the court grants permission on an application in respect of—
 (a) the disposal of charged property by a company free from charge under section A31, or
 (b) the disposal of hire-purchase property by a company under section A32.

(2) Where this rule applies the court must deliver two sealed copies of the order to the company as soon as reasonably practicable after the order is made.

(3) As soon as reasonably practicable after receiving copies of the order under paragraph (2) the company must deliver one copy to the holder of the security or the owner of the hire-purchase goods (as the case may be).]

NOTES

Commencement: 1 October 2021.

Part 1A (rr 1A.1–1A.32) inserted by the Insolvency (England and Wales) (No 2) (Amendment) Rules 2021, SI 2021/1028, r 6, as from 1 October 2021 (for savings provisions see the note to r 1A.1 at **[10.539]**).

PART 2 COMPANY VOLUNTARY ARRANGEMENTS (CVA)

CHAPTER 1 PRELIMINARY

[10.571]
2.1 Interpretation

In this Part—

"nominee" and "supervisor" include the proposed nominee or supervisor in relation to a proposal for a CVA; and
"proposal" means a proposal for a CVA.

CHAPTER 2 THE PROPOSAL FOR A CVA (SECTION 1)

[Note: (1) section 1 of the Act sets out who may propose a CVA;

(2) a document required by the Act or these Rules must also contain the standard contents set out in Part 1.]

[10.572]
2.2 Proposal for a CVA: general principles and amendment

(1) A proposal must—
 (a) contain identification details for the company;
 (b) explain why the proposer thinks a CVA is desirable;
 (c) explain why the creditors are expected to agree to a CVA; and
 (d) be authenticated and dated by the proposer.

[(2) The proposal may be amended with the nominee's agreement in writing where—
 (a) the nominee is not the liquidator or administrator of the company; and
 (b) the nominee's report has not been filed with the court under section 2(2).]

(3) The first case is where—
 (a) no steps have been taken to obtain a moratorium;
 (b) the nominee is not the liquidator or administrator of the company; and
 (c) the nominee's report has not been filed with the court under section 2(2).

(4) The second case is where—
 (a) the proposal is made with a view to obtaining a moratorium; and
 (b) the nominee's statement under paragraph 6(2) of Schedule A1 (nominee's opinion on prospects of CVA being approved etc) has not yet been submitted to the directors.

NOTES

Para (2): substituted by the Insolvency (England and Wales) (No 2) (Amendment) Rules 2021, SI 2021/1028, r 13(1), (2), as from 1 October 2021 (for savings provisions see the note to r 1A.1 at **[10.539]**). Para (2) previously read as follows—

"(2) The proposal may be amended with the nominee's agreement in writing in the following cases.".

Paras (3), (4): revoked by SI 2021/1028, r 13(1), (3), as from 1 October 2021 (for savings provisions see the note to r 1A.1 at **[10.539]**).

[10.573]
2.3 Proposal: contents

(1) The proposal must set out the following so far as known to the proposer—

Assets	(a) the company's assets, with an estimate of their respective values; (b) which assets are charged and the extent of the charge; (c) which assets are to be excluded from the CVA; and (d) particulars of any property to be included in the CVA which is not owned by the company, including details of who owns such property, and the terms on which it will be available for inclusion;
Liabilities	(e) the nature and amount of the company's liabilities; (f) how the company's liabilities will be met, modified, postponed or otherwise dealt with by means of the CVA and in particular— (i) how preferential creditors and creditors who are, or claim to be, secured will be dealt with, (ii) how creditors who are connected with the company will be dealt with,

Part 10 Miscellaneous other SIs

	(iii) if the company is not in administration or liquidation whether, if the company did go into administration or liquidation, there are circumstances which might give rise to claims under section 238 (transactions at an undervalue), section 239 (preferences), section 244 (extortionate credit transactions), or section 245 (floating charges invalid), and (iv) where there are circumstances that might give rise to such claims, whether, and if so what, provision will be made to indemnify the company in respect of them;
Nominee's fees and expenses	(g) the amount proposed to be paid to the nominee by way of fees and expenses;
Supervisor	(h) identification and contact details for the supervisor; (i) confirmation that the supervisor is qualified to act as an insolvency practitioner in relation to the company and the name of the relevant recognised professional body which is the source of the supervisor's authorisation; (j) how the fees and expenses of the supervisor will be determined and paid; (k) the functions to be performed by the supervisor; (l) where it is proposed that two or more supervisors be appointed a statement whether acts done in connection with the CVA may be done by any one or more of them or must be done by all of them;
Guarantees and proposed guarantees	(m) whether any, and if so what, guarantees have been given in respect of the company's debts, specifying which of the guarantors are persons connected with the company; (n) whether any, and if so what, guarantees are proposed to be offered for the purposes of the CVA and, if so, by whom and whether security is to be given or sought;
Timing	(o) the proposed duration of the CVA; (p) the proposed dates of distributions to creditors, with estimates of their amounts;
Type of proceedings	[(q) whether the proceedings will be COMI proceedings, establishment proceedings or proceedings to which the EU Regulation as it has effect in the law of the United Kingdom does not apply with reasons;]
Conduct of the business	(r) how the business of the company will be conducted during the CVA;
Further credit facilities	(s) details of any further proposed credit facilities for the company, and how the debts so arising are to be paid;
Handling of funds arising	(t) the manner in which funds held for the purposes of the CVA are to be banked, invested or otherwise dealt with pending distribution to creditors; (u) how funds held for the purpose of payment to creditors, and not so paid on the termination of the CVA, will be dealt with; (v) how the claim of any person bound by the CVA by virtue of section 5(2)(b)(ii) *or paragraph 37(2)(b)(ii) of Schedule A1* will be dealt with;
[Matters relating to a moratorium	(va) whether a moratorium is, or has been, in force for the company under Part A1 of the Act and, if so, the date that moratorium came into force and, (if applicable), the date it ended;]
Other matters	(x) any other matters that the proposer considers appropriate to enable members and creditors to reach an informed decision on the proposal.

(2) Where the proposal is made by the directors, an estimate so far as known to them of—

(a) the value of the prescribed part if the proposal for the CVA is not accepted and the company goes into liquidation (whether or not the liquidator might be required under section 176A to make the prescribed part available for the satisfaction of unsecured debts); and

(b) the value of the company's net property (as defined by section 176A(6)) on the date that the estimate is made.

(3) Where the proposal is made by the administrator or liquidator the following so far as known to the office-holder—

(a) an estimate of—

(i) the value of the prescribed part (whether or not the administrator or liquidator might be required under section 176A to make the prescribed part available for the satisfaction of unsecured debts), and

(ii) the value of the company's net property (as defined by section 176A(6)); and

(b) a statement as to whether the administrator or liquidator proposes to make an application to the court under section 176A(5) and if so the reasons for the application; and

(c) details of the nature and amount of the company's preferential creditors.

(4) Information may be excluded from an estimate under paragraph (2) or (3)(a) if the inclusion of the information could seriously prejudice the commercial interests of the company.

(5) If the exclusion of such information affects the calculation of the estimate, the proposal must include a statement to that effect.

NOTES

Para (1) is amended as follows:

In the table, para (q) was substituted by the Insolvency (Amendment) (EU Exit) Regulations 2019, SI 2019/146, reg 2, Schedule, Pt 4, paras 46, 50, as from IP completion day (as defined in the European Union (Withdrawal Agreement) Act 2020, s 39) (for savings, see reg 4 of the 2019 Regulations at **[12.82]**).

In the table, the words in italics in para (v) were revoked by the Insolvency (England and Wales) (No 2) (Amendment) Rules 2021, SI 2021/1028, r 81, Sch 2, as from 1 October 2021 (for savings provisions see the note to r 1A.1 at **[10.539]**).

In the table, the entry "Matters relating to a moratorium" was substituted for the original entry "Address (where moratorium proposed)", by SI 2021/1028, r 14, as from 1 October 2021 (for savings provisions see the note to r 1A.1 at **[10.539]**). The original entry read as follows—

“Address (where moratorium proposed)	(w) where the proposal is made in relation to a company that is eligible for a moratorium (in accordance with paragraphs 2 and 3 of Schedule A1) with a view to obtaining a moratorium under Schedule A1, the address to which the documents referred to in paragraph 6(1) of that Schedule must be delivered; and”.

CHAPTER 3 PROCEDURE FOR A CVA *WITHOUT A MORATORIUM*

[Note: a document required by the Act or these Rules must also contain the standard contents set out in Part 1.]

NOTES

The words in italics in the preceding Chapter heading were revoked by the Insolvency (England and Wales) (No 2) (Amendment) Rules 2021, SI 2021/1028, r 81, Sch 2, as from 1 October 2021 (for savings provisions see the note to r 1A.1 at **[10.539]**).

[10.574]

2.4 Procedure for proposal where the nominee is not the liquidator or the administrator (section 2)

(1) This rule applies where the nominee is not the same person as the liquidator or the administrator.

(2) A nominee who consents to act must deliver a notice of that consent to the proposer as soon as reasonably practicable after the proposal has been submitted to the nominee under section 2(3).

(3) The notice must state the date the nominee received the proposal.

(4) The period of 28 days in which the nominee must submit a report to the court under section 2(2) begins on the date the nominee received the proposal as stated in the notice.

[10.575]

2.5 Information for the official receiver

Where the company is being wound up by the court, the liquidator must deliver to the official receiver—

(a) a copy of the proposal; and
(b) the name and address of the nominee (if the nominee is not the liquidator).

[10.576]

2.6 Statement of affairs (section 2(3))

(1) The statement of the company's affairs required by section 2(3) must contain the following [and, in addition, where paragraph (1B) applies, the information specified in that paragraph]—

(a) a list of the company's assets, divided into such categories as are appropriate for easy identification, and with each category given an estimated value;
(b) in the case of any property on which a claim against the company is wholly or partly secured, particulars of the claim, and of how and when the security was created;
(c) the names and addresses of the preferential creditors, with the amounts of their respective claims;
(d) the names and addresses of the unsecured creditors with the amounts of their respective claims;
(e) particulars of any debts owed by the company to persons connected with it;
(f) particulars of any debts owed to the company by persons connected with it;
(g) the names and addresses of the company's members, with details of their respective shareholdings; and
(h) any other particulars that the nominee in writing requires to be provided for the purposes of making the nominee's report on the proposal to the court.

[(1A) Paragraph (1B) applies if a moratorium under Part A1 of the Act is, or has been, in force for the company at any time within the period of 12 weeks ending with the day on which the statement of affairs is made up.

(1B) Where this paragraph applies the statement of affairs must identify which of the debts owed by the company are—

(a) moratorium debts, and
(b) priority pre-moratorium debts,

within the meaning given by section 174A; and

(c) sub-paragraph(1)(c) has effect as if the reference to preferential creditors included references to moratorium debts and priority pre-moratorium debts within the meaning given by section 174A.]

(2) The statement must be made up to a date not earlier than two weeks before the date of the proposal.

(3) However the nominee may allow the statement to be made up to an earlier date (but not more than two months before the date of the proposal) where that is more practicable.

(4) Where the statement is made up to an earlier date, the nominee's report to the court on the proposal must explain why.

(5) The statement of affairs must be verified by a statement of truth made by the proposer.

(6) Where the proposal is made by the directors, only one director need make the statement of truth.

NOTES

Para (1): words in square brackets inserted by the Insolvency (England and Wales) (No 2) (Amendment) Rules 2021, SI 2021/1028, r 15(1), (2), as from 1 October 2021 (for savings provisions see the note to r 1A.1 at **[10.539]**).

Paras (1A), (1B): inserted by SI 2021/1028, r 15(1), (3), as from 1 October 2021 (for savings provisions see the note to r 1A.1 at **[10.539]**).

[10.577]

2.7 Application to omit information from statement of affairs delivered to creditors

The nominee, the directors or any person appearing to the court to have an interest, may apply to the court for a direction that specified information be omitted from the statement of affairs as delivered to the creditors where disclosure of that information would be likely to prejudice the conduct of the CVA or might reasonably be expected to lead to violence against any person.

[10.578]

2.8 Additional disclosure for assistance of nominee where the nominee is not the liquidator or administrator

(1) This rule applies where the nominee is not the administrator or the liquidator of the company.

(2) If it appears to the nominee that the nominee's report to the court cannot properly be prepared on the basis of information in the proposal and statement of affairs, the nominee may require the proposer to provide—

(a) more information about the circumstances in which, and the reasons why, a CVA is being proposed;
(b) particulars of any previous proposals which have been made in relation to the company under Part 1 of the Act; and
(c) any further information relating to the company's affairs which the nominee thinks necessary for the purposes of the report.

(3) The nominee may require the proposer to inform the nominee whether, and if so in what circumstances, any person who is, or has been at any time in the two years before the date the nominee received the proposal, a director or officer of the company has—

(a) been concerned in the affairs of any other company (whether or not incorporated in England and Wales) or limited liability partnership which has been the subject of insolvency proceedings;
(b) been made bankrupt;
(c) been the subject of a debt relief order; or
(d) entered into an arrangement with creditors.

(4) The proposer must give the nominee such access to the company's accounts and records as the nominee may require to enable the nominee to consider the proposal and prepare the nominee's report.

[10.579]

2.9 Nominee's report on proposal where the nominee is not the liquidator or administrator (section 2(2))

(1) The nominee's report must be filed with the court under section 2(2) accompanied by—

(a) a copy of the report;
(b) a copy of the proposal (as amended under rule 2.2(2), if that is the case); and
(c) a copy of the statement of the company's affairs or a summary of it.

(2) The report must state—

(a) why the nominee considers the proposal does or does not have a reasonable prospect of being approved and implemented; and
(b) why the members and the creditors should or should not be invited to consider the proposal.

(3) The court must endorse the nominee's report and the copy of it with the date of filing and deliver the copy to the nominee.

(4) The nominee must deliver a copy of the report to the company.

[10.580]

2.10 Replacement of nominee (section 2(4))

(1) A person (other than the nominee) who intends to apply to the court under section 2(4) for the nominee to be replaced must deliver a notice that such an application is intended to be made to the nominee at least five business days before filing the application with the court.

(2) A nominee who intends to apply under that section to be replaced must deliver a notice that such an application is intended to be made to the person intending to make the proposal, or the proposer, at least five business days before filing the application with the court.

(3) The court must not appoint a replacement nominee unless a statement by the replacement nominee has been filed with the court confirming that person—

(a) consents to act; and
(b) is qualified to act as an insolvency practitioner, in relation to the company.

CHAPTER 4 PROCEDURE FOR A CVA WITH A MORATORIUM

[Note: a document required by the Act or these Rules must also contain the standard contents set out in Part 1.]

[10.581]

2.11 Statement of affairs (paragraph 6(1)(b) of Schedule A1)

(1) The statement of affairs required by paragraph 6(1)(b) of Schedule A1 must contain the same information as is required by rule 2.6.

(2) The statement must be made up to a date not earlier than two weeks before the date of the proposal.

(3) However the nominee may allow the statement to be made up to an earlier date (but not more than two months before the proposal) where that is more practicable.

(4) Where the statement is made up to an earlier date, the nominee's statement to the directors on the proposal must explain why.

(5) The statement of affairs must be verified by a statement of truth made by at least one director.

NOTES

Chapter 4 (rr 2.11–2.24) was revoked by the Insolvency (England and Wales) (No 2) (Amendment) Rules 2021, SI 2021/1028, r 81, Sch 2, as from 1 October 2021 (for savings provisions see the note to r 1A.1 at **[10.539]**).

[10.582]

2.12 Application to omit information from a statement of affairs

The nominee, the directors or any person appearing to the court to have an interest, may apply to the court for a direction that specified information be omitted from the statement of affairs as delivered to the creditors where disclosure of that information would be likely to prejudice the conduct of the CVA or might reasonably be expected to lead to violence against any person.

NOTES

Chapter 4 (rr 2.11–2.24) was revoked by the Insolvency (England and Wales) (No 2) (Amendment) Rules 2021, SI 2021/1028, r 81, Sch 2, as from 1 October 2021 (for savings provisions see the note to r 1A.1 at **[10.539]**).

[10.583]

2.13 The nominee's statement (paragraph 6(2) of Schedule A1)

(1) The nominee must submit to the directors the statement required by paragraph 6(2) of Schedule A1 within 28 days of the submission to the nominee of the proposal.

(2) The statement must—

(a) include the name and address of the nominee; and

(b) be authenticated and dated by the nominee.

(3) A statement which contains an opinion on all the matters referred to in paragraph 6(2) must—

(a) explain why the nominee has formed that opinion; and

(b) if the nominee is willing to act, be accompanied by a statement of the nominee's consent to act in relation to the proposed CVA.

(4) The statement of the nominee's consent must—

(a) include the name and address of the nominee;

(b) state that the nominee is qualified to act as an insolvency practitioner in relation to the company; and

(c) be authenticated and dated by the nominee.

NOTES

Chapter 4 (rr 2.11–2.24) was revoked by the Insolvency (England and Wales) (No 2) (Amendment) Rules 2021, SI 2021/1028, r 81, Sch 2, as from 1 October 2021 (for savings provisions see the note to r 1A.1 at **[10.539]**).

[10.584]

2.14 Documents filed with court to obtain a moratorium (paragraph 7(1) of Schedule A1)

(1) The statement of the company's affairs which the directors file with the court under paragraph 7(1)(b) of Schedule A1 must be the same as the statement they submit to the nominee under paragraph 6(1)(b) of that Schedule.

(2) The statement required by paragraph 7(1)(c) of that Schedule that the company is eligible for a moratorium must—

(a) be made by the directors;

(b) state that the company meets the requirements of paragraph 3 of Schedule A1 and is not a company which falls within paragraph 2(2) of that Schedule;

(c) confirm that the company is not ineligible for a moratorium under paragraph 4 of that Schedule; and

(d) be authenticated and dated by the directors.

[(2A) A statement from the nominee whether the proceedings will be [COMI proceedings, establishment proceedings or proceedings to which the EU Regulation as it has effect in the law of the United Kingdom does not apply] with the reasons for so stating must also be filed with the court.]

(3) The statement required by paragraph 7(1)(d) of that Schedule that the nominee has consented to act must be in the same terms as the statement referred to in rule 2.13(3)(b) and (4).

(4) The statement of the nominee's opinion required by paragraph 7(1)(e) of that Schedule—

(a) must be the same as the statement of opinion required by paragraph 6(2) of that Schedule; and

(b) must be filed with the court not later than ten business days after it was submitted to the directors.

(5) The documents filed with the court under paragraph 7(1) of that Schedule must be accompanied by four copies of a schedule, authenticated and dated by the directors, identifying the company and listing all the documents filed.

(6) The court must endorse the copies of the schedule with the date on which the documents were filed and deliver three copies of the endorsed schedule to the directors.

NOTES

Chapter 4 (rr 2.11–2.24) was revoked by the Insolvency (England and Wales) (No 2) (Amendment) Rules 2021, SI 2021/1028, r 81, Sch 2, as from 1 October 2021 (for savings provisions see the note to r 1A.1 at **[10.539]**).

Para (2A): inserted by the Insolvency Amendment (EU 2015/848) Regulations 2017, SI 2017/702, regs 2, 3, Schedule, Pt 2, paras 32, 35, as from 26 June 2017, except in relation to proceedings opened before that date. Words in square brackets substituted by the Insolvency (Amendment) (EU Exit) Regulations 2019, SI 2019/146, reg 2, Schedule, Pt 4, paras 46, 51, as from IP completion day (as defined in the European Union (Withdrawal Agreement) Act 2020, s 39) (for savings, see reg 4 of the 2019 Regulations at **[12.82]**).

[10.585]

2.15 Notice and advertisement of beginning of a moratorium

(1) The directors must as soon as reasonably practicable after delivery to them of the endorsed copies of the schedule deliver two copies of the schedule to the nominee and one to the company.

(2) After delivery of the copies of the schedule, the nominee—

(a) must as soon as reasonably practicable gazette a notice of the coming into force of the moratorium; and

(b) may advertise the notice in such other manner as the nominee thinks fit.

(3) The notice must specify—

(a) the nature of the business of the company;
(b) that a moratorium under section 1A has come into force; and
(c) the date on which it came into force.

(4) The nominee must as soon as reasonably practicable deliver a notice of the coming into force of the moratorium to—
(a) the registrar of companies;
(b) the company; and
(c) any petitioning creditor of whose address the nominee is aware.

(5) The notice must specify—
(a) the date on which the moratorium came into force; and
(b) the court with which the documents to obtain the moratorium were filed.

(6) The nominee must deliver a notice of the coming into force of the moratorium and the date on which it came into force to—
(a) any enforcement agent or other officer who to the knowledge of the nominee is charged with distress or other legal process, against the company or its property; and
(b) any person who to the nominee's knowledge has distrained against the company or its property.

NOTES

Chapter 4 (rr 2.11–2.24) was revoked by the Insolvency (England and Wales) (No 2) (Amendment) Rules 2021, SI 2021/1028, r 81, Sch 2, as from 1 October 2021 (for savings provisions see the note to r 1A.1 at **[10.539]**).

[10.586]

2.16 Notice of continuation of a moratorium where physical meeting of creditors is summoned (paragraph 8(3B) of Schedule A1)

(1) This rule applies where under paragraph 8(3B)(b) and (3C) of Schedule A1 the moratorium continues after the initial period of 28 days referred to in paragraph 8(3) of that Schedule because a physical meeting of the company's creditors is first summoned to take place after the end of that period.

(2) The nominee must file with the court and deliver to the registrar of companies a notice of the continuation as soon as reasonably practicable after summoning such a meeting of the company's creditors.

(3) The notice must—
(a) identify the company;
(b) give the name and address of the nominee;
(c) state the date on which the notice of the meeting was sent to the creditors under rule 15.6;
(d) state the date for which the meeting is summoned;
(e) state that under paragraph 8(3B)(b) and (3C) of Schedule A1 the moratorium will be continued to that date; and
(f) be authenticated and dated by the nominee.

NOTES

Chapter 4 (rr 2.11–2.24) was revoked by the Insolvency (England and Wales) (No 2) (Amendment) Rules 2021, SI 2021/1028, r 81, Sch 2, as from 1 October 2021 (for savings provisions see the note to r 1A.1 at **[10.539]**).

[10.587]

2.17 Notice of decision extending or further extending a moratorium (paragraph 36 of Schedule A1)

(1) This rule applies where the moratorium is extended, or further extended by a decision which takes effect under paragraph 36 of Schedule A1.

(2) The nominee must, as soon as reasonably practicable, file with the court and deliver to the registrar of companies a notice of the decision.

(3) The notice must—
(a) identify the company;
(b) give the name and address of the nominee;
(c) state the date on which the moratorium was extended or further extended;
(d) state the new expiry date of the moratorium; and
(e) be authenticated and dated by the nominee.

NOTES

Chapter 4 (rr 2.11–2.24) was revoked by the Insolvency (England and Wales) (No 2) (Amendment) Rules 2021, SI 2021/1028, r 81, Sch 2, as from 1 October 2021 (for savings provisions see the note to r 1A.1 at **[10.539]**).

[10.588]

2.18 Notice of court order extending or further extending or continuing or renewing a moratorium (paragraph 34(2) of Schedule A1)

Where the court makes an order extending, further extending, renewing or continuing a moratorium, the nominee must, as soon as reasonably practicable, deliver to the registrar of companies a notice stating the new expiry date of the moratorium.

NOTES

Chapter 4 (rr 2.11–2.24) was revoked by the Insolvency (England and Wales) (No 2) (Amendment) Rules 2021, SI 2021/1028, r 81, Sch 2, as from 1 October 2021 (for savings provisions see the note to r 1A.1 at **[10.539]**).

[10.589]

2.19 Advertisement of end of a moratorium (paragraph 11(1) of Schedule A1)

(1) After the moratorium ends, the nominee—

(a) must, as soon as reasonably practicable, gazette a notice of its coming to an end; and
(b) may advertise the notice in such other manner as the nominee thinks fit.

(2) The notice must state—
(a) the nature of the company's business;
(b) that a moratorium under section 1A has ended; and
(c) the date on which it came to an end.

(3) The nominee must, as soon as reasonably practicable—
(a) file with the court a notice specifying the date on which the moratorium ended; and
(b) deliver such a notice to—
(i) the registrar of companies,
(ii) the company, and
(iii) the creditors.

(4) The notice to the court must—
(a) identify the company;
(b) give the name and address of the nominee; and
(c) be authenticated and dated by the nominee.

NOTES

Chapter 4 (rr 2.11–2.24) was revoked by the Insolvency (England and Wales) (No 2) (Amendment) Rules 2021, SI 2021/1028, r 81, Sch 2, as from 1 October 2021 (for savings provisions see the note to r 1A.1 at **[10.539]**).

[10.590]

2.20 Disposal of charged property etc during a moratorium

(1) This rule applies where the company applies to the court under paragraph 20 of Schedule A1 for permission to dispose of—
(a) property subject to a security; or
(b) goods under a hire-purchase agreement.

(2) The court must fix a venue for hearing the application.

(3) The company must as soon as reasonably practicable deliver a notice of the venue to the holder of the security or the owner of the goods under the agreement.

(4) If an order is made, the court must deliver two sealed copies of the order to the company and the company must deliver one of them to the holder or owner as soon as reasonably practicable.

NOTES

Chapter 4 (rr 2.11–2.24) was revoked by the Insolvency (England and Wales) (No 2) (Amendment) Rules 2021, SI 2021/1028, r 81, Sch 2, as from 1 October 2021 (for savings provisions see the note to r 1A.1 at **[10.539]**).

[10.591]

2.21 Withdrawal of nominee's consent to act (paragraph 25(5) of Schedule A1)

(1) A nominee who withdraws consent to act, must file with the court and otherwise deliver a notice under paragraph 25(5) of Schedule A1 as soon as reasonably practicable.

(2) The notice filed with the court must—
(a) identify the company;
(b) give the name and address of the nominee;
(c) specify the date on which the nominee withdrew consent;
(d) state, with reference to the reasons at paragraph 25(2) of that Schedule, why the nominee withdrew consent; and
(e) be authenticated and dated by the nominee.

NOTES

Chapter 4 (rr 2.11–2.24) was revoked by the Insolvency (England and Wales) (No 2) (Amendment) Rules 2021, SI 2021/1028, r 81, Sch 2, as from 1 October 2021 (for savings provisions see the note to r 1A.1 at **[10.539]**).

[10.592]

2.22 Application to the court to replace the nominee (paragraph 28 of Schedule A1)

(1) Directors who intend to make an application under paragraph 28 of Schedule A1 for the nominee to be replaced must deliver a notice of the intention to make the application to the nominee at least five business days before filing the application with the court.

(2) A nominee who intends to make an application under that paragraph to be replaced must deliver notice of the intention to make the application to the directors at least five business days before filing the application with the court.

(3) The court must not appoint a replacement nominee unless a statement by the replacement nominee has been filed with the court confirming that person—
(a) consents to act; and
(b) is qualified to act as an insolvency practitioner in relation to the company.

NOTES

Chapter 4 (rr 2.11–2.24) was revoked by the Insolvency (England and Wales) (No 2) (Amendment) Rules 2021, SI 2021/1028, r 81, Sch 2, as from 1 October 2021 (for savings provisions see the note to r 1A.1 at **[10.539]**).

[10.593]

2.23 Notice of appointment of replacement nominee

(1) A person appointed as a replacement nominee must as soon as reasonably practicable deliver a notice of the appointment to the registrar of companies and the former nominee and, where the appointment is not by the court, file a notice of the appointment with the court.

(2) The notice filed with the court must—

(a) identify the company;

(b) give the name and address of the replacement nominee;

(c) specify the date on which the replacement nominee was appointed to act; and

(d) be authenticated and dated by the replacement nominee.

NOTES

Chapter 4 (rr 2.11–2.24) was revoked by the Insolvency (England and Wales) (No 2) (Amendment) Rules 2021, SI 2021/1028, r 81, Sch 2, as from 1 October 2021 (for savings provisions see the note to r 1A.1 at **[10.539]**).

[10.594]

2.24 Applications to court to challenge nominee's actions etc (paragraphs 26 and 27 of Schedule A1)

A person intending to make an application to the court under paragraph 26 or 27 of Schedule A1 must deliver a notice of the intention to make the application to the nominee at least five business days before filing the application with the court.

NOTES

Chapter 4 (rr 2.11–2.24) was revoked by the Insolvency (England and Wales) (No 2) (Amendment) Rules 2021, SI 2021/1028, r 81, Sch 2, as from 1 October 2021 (for savings provisions see the note to r 1A.1 at **[10.539]**).

CHAPTER 5 CONSIDERATION OF THE PROPOSAL BY THE COMPANY MEMBERS AND CREDITORS

[Note: a document required by the Act or these Rules must also contain the standard contents set out in Part 1.]

[10.595]

2.25 Consideration of proposal: common requirements (section 3)

(1) The nominee must invite the members of the company to consider a proposal by summoning a meeting of the company as required by section 3.

(2) The nominee must invite the creditors to consider the proposal by way of a decision procedure.

[(2A) The nominee must examine whether there is jurisdiction to open the proceedings and must specify in the nominee's comments on the proposal required by paragraphs (3)(d)(iii) and (5)(a)(iii) whether the proceedings will be [COMI proceedings, establishment proceedings or proceedings to which the EU Regulation as it has effect in the law of the United Kingdom does not apply] with the reasons for so stating.]

(3) In the case of the members, the nominee must deliver to every person whom the nominee believes to be a member a notice which must—

(a) identify the proceedings;

(b) state the venue for the meeting;

(c) state the effect of the following—

(i) rule 2.35 about members' voting rights,

(ii) rule 2.36 about the requisite majority of members for passing resolutions, and

(iii) rule 15.35 about rights of appeal; and

(d) be accompanied by—

(i) a copy of the proposal,

(ii) a copy of the statement of affairs, or if the nominee thinks fit a summary including a list of creditors with the amounts of their debts,

(iii) the nominee's comments on the proposal, unless the nominee is the administrator or liquidator [in which case the comments required are limited to stating whether the proceedings will be main, secondary, territorial or non-EU proceedings with the reasons for so stating], and

(iv) details of each resolution to be voted on.

(4) In the case of the creditors, the nominee must deliver to each creditor a notice in respect of the decision procedure which complies with rule 15.8 so far as is relevant.

(5) The notice must also—

(a) be accompanied by—

(i) a copy of the proposal,

(ii) a copy of the statement of affairs, or if the nominee thinks fit a summary including a list of creditors with the amounts of their debts, and

(iii) the nominee's comments on the proposal, unless the nominee is the administrator or liquidator; and

(b) state how a creditor may propose a modification to the proposal, and how the nominee will deal with such a proposal for a modification.

(6) The notice may also state that the results of the consideration of the proposal will be made available for viewing and downloading on a website and that no other notice will be delivered to the creditors or members (as the case may be).

(7) Where the results of the consideration of the proposal are to be made available for viewing and downloading on a website the nominee must comply with the requirements for use of a website to deliver a document set out in rule 1.49(2)(a) to (c), (3) and (4) with any necessary adaptations and rule 1.49(5)(a) applies to determine the time of delivery of the document.

NOTES

Para (2A): inserted by the Insolvency Amendment (EU 2015/848) Regulations 2017, SI 2017/702, regs 2, 3, Schedule, Pt 2, paras 32, 36(1), (2), as from 26 June 2017, except in relation to proceedings opened before that date. Words in square brackets substituted by the Insolvency (Amendment) (EU Exit) Regulations 2019, SI 2019/146, reg 2, Schedule, Pt 4, paras 46, 52, as from IP completion day (as defined in the European Union (Withdrawal Agreement) Act 2020, s 39) (for savings, see reg 4 of the 2019 Regulations at **[12.82]**).

Para (3): words in square brackets in sub-para (d)(iii) inserted by SI 2017/702, regs 2, 3, Schedule, Pt 2, paras 32, 36(1), (3), as from 26 June 2017, except in relation to proceedings opened before that date.

[10.596]

2.26 Members' consideration at a meeting

(1) Where the nominee invites the members to consider the proposal at a meeting the notice to members under rule 2.25(3) must also—

(a) specify the purpose of and venue for the meeting; and

(b) be accompanied by a blank proxy.

(2) The nominee must have regard to the convenience of those invited to attend when fixing the venue for a meeting (including the resumption of an adjourned meeting).

[(3) The date of the meeting (except where the nominee is the administrator or liquidator of the company) must not be more than 28 days from the date on which the nominee's report is filed with the court under rule 2.9.]

NOTES

Para (3): substituted by the Insolvency (England and Wales) (No 2) (Amendment) Rules 2021, SI 2021/1028, r 16, as from 1 October 2021 (for savings provisions see the note to r 1A.1 at **[10.539]**). Para (3) previously read as follows—

"(3) The date of the meeting (except where the nominee is the administrator or liquidator of the company) must not be more than 28 days from the date on which—

(a) the nominee's report is filed with the court under rule 2.9; or

(b) the moratorium came into force.".

[10.597]

[2.27 Creditors' consideration by a decision procedure

Where the nominee is inviting the creditors to consider the proposal by a decision procedure, the decision date must be not less than 14 days from the date of delivery of the notice and not more than 28 days from the date the nominee's report is filed with the court under rule 2.9.]

NOTES

Commencement: 1 October 2021.

Substituted by the Insolvency (England and Wales) (No 2) (Amendment) Rules 2021, SI 2021/1028, r 17, as from 1 October 2021 (for savings provisions see the note to r 1A.1 at **[10.539]**). Rule 2.27 previously read as follows—

"2.27 Creditors' consideration by a decision procedure

Where the nominee is inviting the creditors to consider the proposal by a decision procedure, the decision date must be not less than 14 days from the date of delivery of the notice and not more than 28 days from the date—

(a) the nominee's report is filed with the court under rule 2.9; or

(b) the moratorium came into force.".

[10.598]

2.28 Timing of decisions on proposal

(1) The decision date for the creditors' decision procedure may be on the same day as, or on a different day to, the meeting of the company.

(2) But the creditors' decision on the proposal must be made before the members' decision.

(3) The members' decision must be made not later than five business days after the creditors' decision.

(4) For the purpose of this rule, the timing of the members' decision is either the date and time of the meeting of the company or, where the nominee invites members to consider the proposal by correspondence, the deadline for receipt of members' votes.

[10.599]

2.29 Creditors' approval of modified proposal

(1) This rule applies where a decision is sought from the creditors following notice to the nominee of proposed modifications to the proposal from the company's directors under paragraph 31(7) of Schedule A1.

(2) The decision must be sought by a decision procedure with a decision date within 14 days of the date on which the directors gave notice to the nominee of the modifications.

(3) The creditors must be given at least seven days' notice of the decision date.

NOTES

Revoked by the Insolvency (England and Wales) (No 2) (Amendment) Rules 2021, SI 2021/1028, r 81, Sch 2, as from 1 October 2021 (for savings provisions see the note to r 1A.1 at **[10.539]**).

[10.600]

2.30 Notice of members' meeting and attendance of officers

(1) A notice under rule [2.25(3)] summoning a meeting of the company must be delivered at least 14 days before the day fixed for the meeting to all the members and to—

(a) every officer or former officer of the company whose presence the nominee thinks is required; and

(b) all other directors of the company.

(2) Every officer or former officer who receives such a notice stating that the nominee thinks that person's attendance is required is required to attend the meeting.

NOTES

Figure in square brackets substituted by the Insolvency (England and Wales) and Insolvency (Scotland) (Miscellaneous and Consequential Amendments) Rules 2017, SI 2017/1115, rr 2, 3, as from 8 December 2017.

[10.601]

2.31 Requisition of physical meeting by creditors

(1) This rule applies where the creditors requisition a physical meeting to consider a proposal (with or without modifications) in accordance with section 246ZE and rule 15.6.

(2) The meeting must take place within 14 days of the date on which the prescribed proportion of creditors have required the meeting to take place.

[(3) A notice summoning a meeting of the creditors must be delivered to the creditors at least seven days before the day fixed for the meeting.]

NOTES

Para (3): substituted by the Insolvency (England and Wales) (Amendment) Rules 2017, SI 2017/366, rr 3, 7, as from 6 April 2017.

[10.602]

2.32 Non-receipt of notice by members

Where in accordance with the Act or these Rules the members are invited to consider a proposal, the consideration is presumed to have duly taken place even if not everyone to whom the notice is to be delivered receives it.

[10.603]

2.33 Proposal for alternative supervisor

(1) If in response to a notice inviting—

(a) members to consider the proposal by correspondence; or

(b) creditors to consider the proposal other than at a meeting,

a member or creditor proposes that a person other than the nominee be appointed as supervisor, that person's consent to act and confirmation of being qualified to act as an insolvency practitioner in relation to the company must be delivered to the nominee by the deadline in the notice of the decision by correspondence or by the decision date (as the case may be).

(2) If, at either a meeting of the company or the creditors to consider the proposal, a resolution is moved for the appointment of a person other than the nominee to be supervisor, the person moving the resolution must produce to the chair at or before the meeting—

(a) confirmation that the person proposed as supervisor is qualified to act as an insolvency practitioner in relation to the company; and

(b) that person's written consent to act (unless that person is present at the meeting and there signifies consent to act).

[10.604]

2.34 Chair at meetings

The chair of a meeting under this Part must be the nominee or an appointed person.

[10.605]

2.35 Members' voting rights

(1) A member is entitled to vote according to the rights attaching to the member's shares in accordance with the articles of the company.

(2) A member's shares include any other interest that person may have as a member of the company.

(3) The value of a member for the purposes of voting is determined by reference to the number of votes conferred on that member by the company's articles.

[10.606]

2.36 Requisite majorities of members

(1) A resolution is passed by members by correspondence or at a meeting of the company when a majority (in value) of those voting have voted in favour of it.

(2) This is subject to any express provision to the contrary in the articles.

(3) A resolution is not passed by correspondence unless at least one member has voted in favour of it.

[10.607]

2.37 Notice of order made under section 4A(6) *or paragraph 36(5) of Schedule A1*

(1) This rule applies where the court makes an order under section 4A(6) *or paragraph 36(5) of Schedule A1*.

(2) The member who applied for the order must deliver a sealed copy of it to—

(a) the proposer; and

(b) the supervisor (if there is one different to the proposer).

(3) If the directors are the proposer a single copy may be delivered to the company at its registered office.

(4) The supervisor, or the proposer where there is no supervisor, must as soon as reasonably practicable deliver a notice that the order has been made to every person who had received a notice to vote on the matter or who is affected by the order.

(5) The member who applied for the order must, within five business days of the order, deliver a copy to the registrar of companies.

NOTES

The words in italics in the rule heading and para (1) were revoked by the Insolvency (England and Wales) (No 2) (Amendment) Rules 2021, SI 2021/1028, r 81, Sch 2, as from 1 October 2021 (for savings provisions see the note to r 1A.1 at **[10.539]**).

[10.608]

2.38 Report of consideration of proposal under section 4(6) and (6A) *or paragraph 30(3) and (4) of Schedule A1*

(1) A report [or reports as the case may be] must be prepared of the consideration of a proposal under section 4(6) and (6A) *or paragraph 30(3) and (4) of Schedule A1* by the convener or, in the case of a meeting, the chair.

(2) The report must—

- (a) state whether the proposal was approved or rejected and whether by the creditors alone or by both the creditors and members and, in either case, whether any approval was with any modifications;
- (b) list the creditors and members who voted or attended or who were represented at the meeting or decision procedure (as applicable) used to consider the proposal, setting out (with their respective values) how they voted on each resolution [or whether they abstained];
- (c) identify which of those creditors were considered to be connected with the company;
- (d) if the proposal was approved, state with reasons whether the proceedings are [COMI proceedings, establishment proceedings or proceedings to which the EU Regulation as it has effect in the law of the United Kingdom does not apply]; and
- (e) include such further information as the nominee or the chair thinks it appropriate to make known to the court.

(3) A copy of the report must be filed with the court, within four business days of . . . or the date of the company meeting.

(4) The court must endorse the copy of the report with the date of filing.

(5) The chair (in the case of a company meeting) or otherwise the convener must give notice of the result of the consideration of the proposal to everyone who was invited to consider the proposal or to whom notice of a decision procedure or meeting was delivered as soon as reasonably practicable after a copy of the report is filed with the court.

(6) Where the decision approving the CVA has effect under section 4A *or paragraph 36 of Schedule A1* with or without modifications, the supervisor must as soon as reasonably practicable deliver a copy of the convener's report or, in the case of a meeting, the chair's report to the registrar of companies.

NOTES

Rule heading: words in italics revoked by the Insolvency (England and Wales) (No 2) (Amendment) Rules 2021, SI 2021/1028, r 81, Sch 2, as from 1 October 2021 (for savings provisions see the note to r 1A.1 at **[10.539]**).

Para (1): words in square brackets inserted by the Insolvency (England and Wales) (Amendment) Rules 2017, SI 2017/366, rr 3, 8(1), as from 6 April 2017. Words in italics revoked by SI 2021/1028, r 81, Sch 2, as from 1 October 2021 (for savings provisions see the note to r 1A.1 at **[10.539]**).

Para (2): words in square brackets in sub-para (b) inserted by SI 2017/366, rr 3, 8(2), as from 6 April 2017. Words in square brackets in sub-para (d) substituted by the Insolvency (Amendment) (EU Exit) Regulations 2019, SI 2019/146, reg 2, Schedule, Pt 4, paras 46, 53, as from IP completion day (as defined in the European Union (Withdrawal Agreement) Act 2020, s 39) (for savings, see reg 4 of the 2019 Regulations at **[12.82]**).

Para (3): words omitted revoked by SI 2017/366, rr 3, 8(3), as from 6 April 2017.

Para (6): words in italics revoked by SI 2021/1028, r 81, Sch 2, as from 1 October 2021 (for savings provisions see the note to r 1A.1 at **[10.539]**).

CHAPTER 6 ADDITIONAL MATTERS CONCERNING AND FOLLOWING APPROVAL OF CVA

[Note: a document required by the Act or these Rules must also contain the standard contents set out in Part 1.]

[10.609]

2.39 Hand-over of property etc to supervisor

(1) Where the decision approving a CVA has effect under section 4A *or paragraph 36 of Schedule A1*, and the supervisor is not the same person as the proposer, the proposer must, as soon as reasonably practicable, do all that is required to put the supervisor in possession of the assets included in the CVA.

(2) Where the company is in administration or liquidation and the supervisor is not the same person as the administrator or liquidator, the supervisor must—

- (a) before taking possession of the assets included in the CVA, deliver to the administrator or liquidator an undertaking to discharge the balance referred to in paragraph (3) out of the first realisation of assets; or
- (b) upon taking possession of the assets included in the CVA, discharge such balance.

(3) The balance is any balance due to the administrator or liquidator, or to the official receiver not acting as liquidator—

- (a) by way of fees or expenses properly incurred and payable under the Act or these Rules; and
- (b) on account of any advances made in respect of the company together with interest on such advances at the rate specified in section 17 of the Judgments Act 1838 at the date on which the company entered administration or went into liquidation.

(4) The administrator or liquidator, or the official receiver not acting as liquidator, has a charge on the assets included in the CVA in respect of any sums comprising such balance, subject only to the deduction from realisations by the supervisor of the proper costs and expenses of such realisations.

(5) The supervisor must from time to time out of the realisation of assets—

- (a) discharge all guarantees properly given by the administrator or liquidator for the benefit of the company; and
- (b) pay all the expenses of the administrator or liquidator or of the official receiver not acting as liquidator.

(6) Sums due to the official receiver take priority over those due to any other person under this rule.

NOTES

Para (1): words in italics revoked by the Insolvency (England and Wales) (No 2) (Amendment) Rules 2021, SI 2021/1028, r 81, Sch 2, as from 1 October 2021 (for savings provisions see the note to r 1A.1 at **[10.539]**).

[10.610]

2.40 Revocation or suspension of CVA

(1) This rule applies where the court makes an order of revocation or suspension under section 6 *or paragraph 38 of Schedule A1*.

(2) The applicant for the order must deliver a sealed copy of it to—

(a) the proposer; and

(b) the supervisor (if different).

(3) If the directors are the proposer a single copy of the order may be delivered to the company at its registered office.

(4) If the order includes a direction by the court under section 6(4)(b) or (c) *or under paragraph 38(4)(b) or (c) of Schedule A1* for [action to be taken], the applicant for the order must deliver a notice that the order has been made to the person who is directed to take such action.

(5) The proposer must—

(a) as soon as reasonably practicable deliver a notice that the order has been made to all of those persons to whom a notice to consider the matter was delivered or who appear to be affected by the order;

(b) within five business days of delivery of a copy of the order (or within such longer period as the court may allow), deliver (if applicable) a notice to the court advising that it is intended to make a revised proposal to the company and its creditors, or to invite re-consideration of the original proposal.

(6) The applicant for the order must deliver a copy of the order to the registrar of companies within five business days of the making of the order with a notice which must contain the date on which the voluntary arrangement took effect.

NOTES

Para (1): words in italics revoked by the Insolvency (England and Wales) (No 2) (Amendment) Rules 2021, SI 2021/1028, r 81, Sch 2, as from 1 October 2021 (for savings provisions see the note to r 1A.1 at **[10.539]**).

Para (4): words in italics revoked by SI 2021/1028, r 81, Sch 2, as from 1 October 2021 (for savings provisions see the note to r 1A.1 at **[10.539]**). Words in square brackets substituted by the Insolvency (England and Wales) (Amendment) Rules 2017, SI 2017/366, rr 3, 9, as from 6 April 2017.

[10.611]

2.41 Supervisor's accounts and reports

(1) The supervisor must keep accounts and records where the CVA authorises or requires the supervisor—

(a) to carry on the business of the company;

(b) to realise assets of the company; or

(c) otherwise to administer or dispose of any of its funds.

(2) The accounts and records which must be kept are of the supervisor's acts and dealings in, and in connection with, the CVA, including in particular records of all receipts and payments of money.

(3) The supervisor must preserve any such accounts and records which were kept by any other person who has acted as supervisor of the CVA and are in the supervisor's possession.

(4) The supervisor must deliver reports on the progress and prospects for the full implementation of the CVA to—

(a) the registrar of companies;

(b) the company;

(c) the creditors bound by the CVA;

(d) subject to paragraph (10) below, the members; and

(e) if the company is not in liquidation, the company's auditors (if any) for the time being.

(5) The notice which accompanies the report when delivered to the registrar of companies must contain the date on which the voluntary arrangement took effect.

(6) The first report must cover the period of 12 months commencing on the date on which the CVA was approved and a further report must be made for each subsequent period of 12 months.

(7) Each report must be delivered within the period of two months after the end of the 12 month period.

(8) Such a report is not required if the obligation to deliver a final report under rule 2.44 . . . arises in the two month period.

(9) Where the supervisor is authorised or required to do any of the things mentioned in paragraph (1), the report must—

(a) include or be accompanied by a summary of receipts and payments required to be recorded by virtue of paragraph (2); or

(b) state that there have been no such receipts and payments.

(10) The court may, on application by the supervisor, dispense with the delivery of such reports or summaries to members, either altogether or on the basis that the availability of the report to members is to be advertised by the supervisor in a specified manner.

NOTES

Para (8): figure omitted revoked by the Insolvency (England and Wales) (Amendment) Rules 2017, SI 2017/366, rr 3, 10, as from 6 April 2017.

[10.612]

2.42 Production of accounts and records to the Secretary of State

(1) The Secretary of State may during the CVA, or after its full implementation or termination, require the supervisor to produce for inspection (either at the premises of the supervisor or elsewhere)—

(a) the supervisor's accounts and records in relation to the CVA; and

(b) copies of reports and summaries prepared in compliance with rule 2.41.

(2) The Secretary of State may require the supervisor's accounts and records to be audited and, if so, the supervisor must provide such further information and assistance as the Secretary of State requires for the purposes of audit.

[10.613]

2.43 Fees and expenses

The fees and expenses that may be incurred for the purposes of the CVA are—

(a) fees for the nominee's services agreed with the company (or, as the case may be, the administrator or liquidator) and disbursements made by the nominee before the decision approving the CVA takes effect under section 4A *or paragraph 36 of Schedule A1*;

(b) fees or expenses which—

(i) are sanctioned by the terms of the CVA, or

(ii) where they are not sanctioned by the terms of the CVA would be payable, or correspond to those which would be payable, in an administration or winding up.

NOTES

Words in italics revoked by the Insolvency (England and Wales) (No 2) (Amendment) Rules 2021, SI 2021/1028, r 81, Sch 2, as from 1 October 2021 (for savings provisions see the note to r 1A.1 at **[10.539]**).

[10.614]

2.44 Termination or full implementation of CVA

(1) Not more than 28 days after the full implementation or termination of the CVA the supervisor must deliver a notice that the CVA has been fully implemented or terminated to all the members and those creditors who are bound by the arrangement.

(2) The notice must state the date the CVA took effect and must be accompanied by a copy of a report by the supervisor which—

(a) summarises all receipts and payments in relation to the CVA;

(b) explains any departure from the terms of the CVA as it originally had effect;

(c) if the CVA has terminated, sets out the reasons why; and

(d) includes (if applicable) a statement as to the amount paid to any unsecured creditors by virtue of section 176A.

(3) The supervisor must within the 28 days mentioned above send to the registrar of companies and file with the court a copy of the notice to creditors and of the supervisor's report.

(4) The supervisor must not vacate office until after the copies of the notice and report have been delivered to the registrar of companies and filed with the court.

CHAPTER 7 TIME RECORDING INFORMATION

[Note: a document required by the Act or these Rules must also contain the standard contents set out in Part 1.]

[10.615]

2.45 Provision of information

(1) This rule applies where the remuneration of the nominee or the supervisor has been fixed on the basis of the time spent.

(2) A person who is acting, or has acted within the previous two years, as—

(a) a nominee in relation to a proposal; or

(b) the supervisor in relation to a CVA;

must, within 28 days of receipt of a request from a person mentioned in paragraph (3), deliver free of charge to that person a statement complying with paragraphs (4) and (5).

(3) The persons are—

(a) any director of the company; and

(b) where the proposal has been approved, any creditor or member.

(4) The statement must cover the period which—

(a) in the case of a person who has ceased to act as nominee or supervisor in relation to a company, begins with the date of appointment as nominee or supervisor and ends with the date of ceasing to act; and

(b) in any other case, consists of one or more complete periods of six months beginning with the date of appointment and ending most nearly before the date of receiving the request.

(5) The statement must set out—

(a) the total number of hours spent on the matter during that period by the nominee or supervisor, and any staff;

(b) for each grade of staff engaged on the matter, the average hourly rate at which work carried out by staff in that grade is charged; and

(c) the number of hours spent on the matter by each grade of staff during that period.

PART 3 ADMINISTRATION

CHAPTER 1 INTERPRETATION FOR THIS PART

[Note: a document required by the Act or these Rules must also contain the standard contents set out in Part 1.]

[10.616]
3.1 Interpretation for Part 3

In this Part—

"pre-administration costs" means fees charged, and expenses incurred by the administrator, or another person qualified to act as an insolvency practitioner in relation to the company, before the company entered administration but with a view to it doing so; and

"unpaid pre-administration costs" means pre-administration costs which had not been paid when the company entered administration.

[10.617]
3.2 Proposed administrator's statement and consent to act

(1) References in this Part to a consent to act are to a statement by a proposed administrator headed "Proposed administrator's statement and consent to act" which contains the following—

- (a) identification details for the company immediately below the heading;
- (b) a certificate that the proposed administrator is qualified to act as an insolvency practitioner in relation to the company;
- (c) the proposed administrator's IP number;
- (d) the name of the relevant recognised professional body which is the source of the proposed administrator's authorisation to act in relation to the company;
- (e) a statement that the proposed administrator consents to act as administrator of the company;
- (f) a statement whether or not the proposed administrator has had any prior professional relationship with the company and if so a short summary of the relationship;
- (g) the name of the person by whom the appointment is to be made or the applicant in the case of an application to the court for an appointment; and
- (h) a statement that the proposed administrator is of the opinion that the purpose of administration is reasonably likely to be achieved in the particular case.

(2) The statement and consent to act must be authenticated and dated by the proposed administrator.

(3) Where a number of persons are proposed to be appointed to act jointly or concurrently as the administrator of a company, each must make a separate statement and consent to act.

CHAPTER 2 APPOINTMENT OF ADMINISTRATOR BY COURT

[Note: a document required by the Act or these Rules must also contain the standard contents set out in Part 1.]

[10.618]
3.3 Administration application (paragraph 12 of Schedule B1)

(1) An administration application in relation to a company must be headed "Administration application" and must identify the company immediately below the heading.

(2) The application must contain—

- (a) the name of the applicant;
- (b) a statement whether the application is being made by—
  - (i) the company under paragraph 12(1)(a) of Schedule B1,
  - (ii) the directors of the company under paragraph 12(1)(b) of Schedule B1,
  - (iii) a single creditor under paragraph 12(1)(c) of Schedule B1,
  - (iv) a creditor under paragraph 12(1)(c) of Schedule B1 on behalf of that creditor and others,
  - (v) the holder of a qualifying floating charge under paragraph 35 or 37 of Schedule B1 (specifying which),
  - (vi) the liquidator of the company under paragraph 38 of Schedule B1,
  - (vii) the supervisor of a CVA under section 7(4)(b), or
  - (viii) a designated officer of a magistrates' court under section 87A of the Magistrates' Courts Act 1980;
- (c) if the application is made by a creditor on behalf of that creditor and others, the names of the others;
- (d) if the application is made by the holder of a qualifying floating charge, details of the charge including the date of the charge, the date on which it was registered and the maximum amount if any secured by the charge;
- (e) if the company is registered under the Companies Act—
  - (i) any issued and called-up capital, the number of shares into which the capital is divided, the nominal value of each share and the amount of capital paid up or treated as paid up; or
  - (ii) that it is a company limited by guarantee;
- (f) particulars of the principal business carried on by the company;
- (g) a statement whether the company is an Article 1.2 undertaking;
- (h) a statement whether the proceedings flowing from the appointment will be [COMI proceedings, establishment proceedings or proceedings to which the EU Regulation as it has effect in the law of the United Kingdom does not apply] and that the reasons for the statement are set out in the witness statement in support of the application made under rule 3.6;
- (i) except where the applicant is the holder of a qualifying floating charge and is making the application under paragraph 35 of Schedule B1, a statement that the applicant believes, for the reasons set out in the witness statement in support of the application that the company is, or is likely to become, unable to pay its debts;
- (j) the name and address of the proposed administrator;
- (k) the address for service of the applicant;
- (l) the statement that the applicant requests the court—
  - (i) to make an administration order in relation to the company,
  - (ii) to appoint the proposed person to be administrator, and
  - (iii) to make such ancillary order as the applicant may request, and such other order as the court thinks appropriate.

(3) The application must be authenticated by the applicant or the applicant's solicitor and dated.

NOTES

Para (2): words in square brackets in sub-para (h) substituted by the Insolvency (Amendment) (EU Exit) Regulations 2019, SI 2019/146, reg 2, Schedule, Pt 4, paras 46, 54, as from IP completion day (as defined in the European Union (Withdrawal Agreement) Act 2020, s 39) (for savings, see reg 4 of the 2019 Regulations at **[12.82]**).

[10.619]

3.4 Administration application made by the directors

After an application by the directors for an administration order is filed it is to be treated for all purposes as an application by the company.

[10.620]

3.5 Administration application by the supervisor of a CVA

After an application by the supervisor of a CVA for an administration order in respect of the company has been served on the company as required by rule 3.8(3)(d) it is to be treated for all purposes as an application by the company.

[10.621]

3.6 Witness statement in support of administration application

(1) If an administration application is to be made by—

(a) the company, a witness statement must be made by one of the following stating that the person making the statement does so on behalf of the company—
 (i) one of the directors,
 (ii) the secretary of the company, or
 (iii) the supervisor of a CVA;

(b) the company's directors, a witness statement must be made by one of the following stating that the person making it does so on behalf of the directors—
 (i) one of the directors, or
 (ii) the secretary of the company;

(c) a single creditor, a witness statement must be made by—
 (i) that creditor, or
 (ii) a person acting under that creditor's authority;

(d) two or more creditors, a witness statement must be made by a person acting under the authority of them all, whether or not one of their number.

(2) In a case falling within paragraph (1)(c)(ii) or (d), the witness statement must state the nature of the authority of the person making it and the means of that person's knowledge of the matters to which the witness statement relates.

(3) The witness statement must contain—

(a) a statement of the company's financial position, specifying (to the best of the applicant's knowledge and belief) the company's assets and liabilities, including contingent and prospective liabilities;

(b) details of any security known or believed to be held by creditors of the company, and whether in any case the security is such as to confer power on the holder to appoint an administrative receiver or to appoint an administrator under paragraph 14 of Schedule B1;

(c) a statement that an administrative receiver has been appointed if that is the case;

(d) details of any insolvency proceedings in relation to the company, including any petition that has been presented for the winding up of the company so far as known to the applicant;

(e) where it is intended to appoint a number of persons as administrators, a statement of the matters relating to the exercise of their functions set out in paragraph 100(2) of Schedule B1;

(f) the reasons for the statement that the proceedings will be [COMI proceedings, establishment proceedings or proceedings to which the EU Regulation as it has effect in the law of the United Kingdom does not apply]; and

(g) any other matters which, in the applicant's opinion, will assist the court in deciding whether to make such an order.

(4) Where the application is made by the holder of a qualifying floating charge under paragraph 35 or 37 of Schedule B1, the witness statement must give sufficient details to satisfy the court that the applicant is entitled to appoint an administrator under paragraph 14 of Schedule B1.

(5) Where the application is made under paragraph 37 or 38 of Schedule B1 in relation to a company in liquidation, the witness statement must also contain—

(a) details of the existing insolvency proceedings, the name and address of the liquidator, the date the liquidator was appointed and by whom;

(b) the reasons why it has subsequently been considered appropriate that an administration application should be made; and

(c) any other matters that would, in the applicant's opinion, assist the court in deciding whether to make provision in relation to matters arising in connection with the liquidation.

NOTES

Para (3): words in square brackets in sub-para (f) substituted by the Insolvency (Amendment) (EU Exit) Regulations 2019, SI 2019/146, reg 2, Schedule, Pt 4, paras 46, 55, as from IP completion day (as defined in the European Union (Withdrawal Agreement) Act 2020, s 39) (for savings, see reg 4 of the 2019 Regulations at **[12.82]**).

[10.622]

3.7 Filing of application

(1) The application must be filed with the court together with the witness statement in support and the proposed administrator's consent to act.

(2) The court must fix a venue for the hearing of the application.

(3) There must also be filed, at the same time as the application or at any time after that, a sufficient number of copies of the application and the statement for service in accordance with rule 3.8.

(4) Each of the copies filed must—

(a) have applied to it the seal of the court;

(b) be endorsed with—

(i) the date and time of filing, and

(ii) the venue fixed by the court; and

(c) be delivered by the court to the applicant.

[10.623]
3.8 Service of application

(1) In this rule, references to the application are to a copy of the application and witness statement delivered by the court under rule 3.7(4)(c).

(2) Notification for the purposes of paragraph 12(2) of Schedule B1 must be by service of the application.

(3) The applicant must serve the application on the following (in addition to serving it on the persons referred to in paragraph 12(2)(a) to (c) of Schedule B1)—

[(za) if there is a moratorium in force for the company under Part A1 of the Act, the monitor;]

(a) any administrative receiver of the company;

(b) if there is a petition pending for the winding up of the company on—

(i) the petitioner, and

(ii) any provisional liquidator;

(c) . . .

(d) the company, if the application is made by anyone other than the company or its directors;

(e) any supervisor of a CVA in relation to the company; and

(f) the proposed administrator.

(4) The certificate of service must be filed with the court as soon as reasonably practicable after service and in any event not later than the business day before the hearing of the application.

NOTES

Para (3): sub-para (za) inserted by the Insolvency (England and Wales) (No 2) (Amendment) Rules 2021, SI 2021/1028, r 18, as from 1 October 2021 (for savings provisions see the note to r 1A.1 at **[10.539]**). Sub-para (c) revoked by the Insolvency (Amendment) (EU Exit) Regulations 2019, SI 2019/146, reg 2, Schedule, Pt 4, paras 46, 56, as from IP completion day (as defined in the European Union (Withdrawal Agreement) Act 2020, s 39) (for savings, see reg 4 of the 2019 Regulations at **[12.82]**).

[10.624]
3.9 Notice to enforcement agents charged with distress or other legal process, etc

The applicant must as soon as reasonably practicable after filing the application deliver a notice of its being made to—

(a) any enforcement agent or other officer who to the knowledge of the applicant is charged with distress or other legal process against the company or its property; and

(b) any person who to the knowledge of the applicant has distrained against the company or its property.

[10.625]
3.10 Notice of other insolvency proceedings

After the application has been filed and until an order is made, it is the duty of the applicant to file with the court notice of the existence of any insolvency proceedings in relation to the company, as soon as the applicant becomes aware of them—

(a) anywhere in the world, in the case of a company registered under the Companies Act in England and Wales;

(b) in any EEA State . . . , in the case of a company incorporated in an EEA State . . . ; or

(c) in any member State other than Denmark, in the case of a company not incorporated in an EEA State.

NOTES

Words omitted from para (b) revoked by the Insolvency (Amendment) (EU Exit) Regulations 2019, SI 2019/146, reg 2, Schedule, Pt 4, paras 46, 57, as from IP completion day (as defined in the European Union (Withdrawal Agreement) Act 2020, s 39) (for savings, see reg 4 of the 2019 Regulations at **[12.82]**).

[10.626]
3.11 Intervention by holder of qualifying floating charge (paragraph 36(1)(b) of Schedule B1)

(1) Where the holder of a qualifying floating charge applies to the court under paragraph 36(1)(b) of Schedule B1 to have a specified person appointed as administrator, the holder must produce to the court—

(a) the written consent of the holder of any prior qualifying floating charge;

(b) the proposed administrator's consent to act; and

(c) sufficient evidence to satisfy the court that the holder is entitled to appoint an administrator under paragraph 14 of Schedule B1.

(2) If an administration order is made appointing the specified person, the costs of the person who made the administration application and of the applicant under paragraph 36(1)(b) of Schedule B1 are, unless the court orders otherwise, to be paid as an expense of the administration.

[10.627]
3.12 The hearing

(1) At the hearing of the administration application, any of the following may appear or be represented—

(a) the applicant;

(b) the company;

(c) one or more of the directors;

[(ca) if there is a moratorium in force for the company under Part A1 of the Act, the monitor;]
(d) any administrative receiver;
(e) any person who has presented a petition for the winding up of the company;
(f) the proposed administrator;
(g) . . .
(h) the holder of any qualifying floating charge;
(i) any supervisor of a CVA;
(j) with the permission of the court, any other person who appears to have an interest which justifies appearance.

(2) If the court makes an administration order, the costs of the applicant, and of any other person whose costs are allowed by the court, are payable as an expense of the administration.

NOTES

Para (1): sub-para (ca) inserted by the Insolvency (England and Wales) (No 2) (Amendment) Rules 2021, SI 2021/1028, r 19, as from 1 October 2021 (for savings provisions see the note to r 1A.1 at **[10.539]**). Sub-para (g) revoked by the Insolvency (Amendment) (EU Exit) Regulations 2019, SI 2019/146, reg 2, Schedule, Pt 4, paras 46, 58, as from IP completion day (as defined in the European Union (Withdrawal Agreement) Act 2020, s 39) (for savings, see reg 4 of the 2019 Regulations at **[12.82]**).

[10.628]
3.13 The order

(1) Where the court makes an administration order the court's order must be headed "Administration order" and must contain the following—
(a) identification details for the proceedings;
(b) the name and title of the judge making the order;
(c) the address for service of the applicant;
(d) details of any other parties (including the company) appearing and by whom represented;
(e) an order that during the period the order is in force the affairs, business and property of the company is to be managed by the administrator;
(f) the name of the person appointed as administrator;
(g) an order that that person is appointed as administrator of the company;
(h) a statement that the court is satisfied either that the [EU Regulation] [as it has effect in the law of the United Kingdom] does not apply or that it does;
(i) where the [EU Regulation] does apply, a statement whether the proceedings are [COMI proceedings or establishment proceedings];
(j) the date of the order (and if the court so orders the time); and
(k) such other provisions if any as the court thinks just.

(2) Where two or more administrators are appointed the order must also specify (as required by paragraph 100(2) of Schedule B1)—
(a) which functions (if any) are to be exercised by those persons acting jointly; and
(b) which functions (if any) are to be exercised by any or all of those persons.

NOTES

Para (1): words in first pair of square brackets in sub-paras (h), (i) substituted by the Insolvency (England and Wales) and Insolvency (Scotland) (Miscellaneous and Consequential Amendments) Rules 2017, SI 2017/1115, rr 22, 23(7), as from 8 December 2017. Words in second pair of square brackets in sub-para (h) inserted, and words in second pair of square brackets in sub-para (i) substituted, by the Insolvency (Amendment) (EU Exit) Regulations 2019, SI 2019/146, reg 2, Schedule, Pt 4, paras 46, 59, as from IP completion day (as defined in the European Union (Withdrawal Agreement) Act 2020, s 39) (for savings, see reg 4 of the 2019 Regulations at **[12.82]**).

[10.629]
3.14 Order on an application under paragraph 37 or 38 of Schedule B1

Where the court makes an administration order in relation to a company on an application under paragraph 37 or 38 of Schedule B1, the court must also include in the order—
(a) in the case of a liquidator appointed in a voluntary winding up, the removal of that liquidator from office;
(b) provision for payment of the expenses of the winding up;
(c) such provision as the court thinks just relating to—
   (i) any indemnity given to the liquidator,
   (ii) the release of the liquidator,
   (iii) the handling or realisation of any of the company's assets in the hands of or under the control of the liquidator, and
   (iv) other matters arising in connection with the winding up; and
(d) such other provisions if any as the court thinks just.

[10.630]
3.15 Notice of administration order

(1) If the court makes an administration order, it must as soon as reasonably practicable deliver two sealed copies of the order to the applicant.

(2) The applicant must as soon as reasonably practicable deliver a sealed copy of the order to the person appointed as administrator.

(3) If the court makes an order under sub-paragraph (d) or (f) of paragraph 13(1) of Schedule B1, it must give directions as to the persons to whom, and how, notice of that order is to be delivered.

CHAPTER 3 APPOINTMENT OF ADMINISTRATOR BY HOLDER OF FLOATING CHARGE

[Note: a document required by the Act or these Rules must also contain the standard contents set out in Part 1.]

[10.631]

3.16 Notice of intention to appoint

(1) This rule applies where the holder of a qualifying floating charge ("the appointer") gives a notice under paragraph 15(1)(a) of Schedule B1 of intention to appoint an administrator under paragraph 14 and files a copy of the notice with the court under paragraph 44(2).

(2) The notice filed with the court must be headed "Notice of intention to appoint an administrator by holder of qualifying floating charge" and must contain the following—

(a) identification details for the proceedings;

(b) the name and address of the appointer;

(c) a statement that the appointer intends to appoint an administrator of the company;

(d) the name and address of the proposed administrator;

(e) a statement that the appointer is the holder of the qualifying floating charge in question and that it is now enforceable;

(f) details of the charge, the date upon which it was registered and the maximum amount if any secured by the charge;

(g) a statement that the notice is being given in accordance with paragraph 15(1)(a) of Schedule B1 to the holder of every prior floating charge which satisfies paragraph 14(2) of that Schedule;

(h) the names and addresses of the holders of such prior floating charges and details of the charges;

(i) a statement whether the company is or is not subject to insolvency proceedings at the date of the notice, and details of the proceedings if it is;

(j) a statement whether the company is an Article 1.2 undertaking; and

(k) a statement whether the proceedings flowing from the appointment will be [COMI proceedings, establishment proceedings or proceedings to which the EU Regulation as it has effect in the law of the United Kingdom does not apply] with reasons for the statement.

(3) The notice must be authenticated by the appointer or the appointer's solicitor and dated.

(4) The filing of the copy with the court under paragraph 44(2) of Schedule B1 must be done at the same time as notice is given in accordance with paragraph 15(1)(a).

(5) The giving of notice under paragraph 15(1)(a) must be by service of the notice.

NOTES

Para (2): words in square brackets in sub-para (k) substituted by the Insolvency (Amendment) (EU Exit) Regulations 2019, SI 2019/146, reg 2, Schedule, Pt 4, paras 46, 60, as from IP completion day (as defined in the European Union (Withdrawal Agreement) Act 2020, s 39) (for savings, see reg 4 of the 2019 Regulations at **[12.82]**).

[10.632]

3.17 Notice of appointment

(1) Notice of an appointment under paragraph 14 of Schedule B1 must be headed "Notice of appointment of an administrator by holder of a qualifying floating charge" and must contain—

(a) identification details for the proceedings;

(b) the name and address of the appointer;

(c) a statement that the appointer has appointed the person named as administrator of the company;

(d) the name and address of the person appointed as administrator;

(e) a statement that a copy of the administrator's consent to act accompanies the notice;

(f) a statement that the appointer is the holder of the qualifying floating charge in question and that it is now enforceable;

(g) details of the charge including the date of the charge, the date on which it was registered and the maximum amount if any secured by the charge;

(h) one of the following statements—

(i) that notice has been given in accordance with paragraph 15(1)(a) of Schedule B1 to the holder of every prior floating charge which satisfies paragraph 14(2) of that Schedule, that two business days have elapsed from the date the last such notice was given (if more than one) and—

(aa) that a copy of every such notice was filed with the court under paragraph 44(2) of Schedule B1, and the date of that filing (or the latest date of filing if more than one), or

(bb) that a copy of every such notice accompanies the notice of appointment but was not filed with the court under paragraph 44(2) of Schedule B1,

(ii) that the holder of every such floating charge to whom notice was given has consented in writing to the making of the appointment and that a copy of every consent accompanies the notice of appointment,

(iii) that the holder of every such floating charge has consented in writing to the making of the appointment without notice having been given to all and that a copy of every consent accompanies the notice of appointment, or

(iv) that there is no such floating charge;

(i) a statement whether the company is or is not subject to insolvency proceedings at the date of the notice, and details of the proceedings if it is;

(j) a statement whether the company is an Article 1.2 undertaking;

(k) a statement whether the proceedings flowing from the appointment will be [COMI proceedings, establishment proceedings or proceedings to which the EU Regulation as it has effect in the law of the United Kingdom does not apply] and the reasons for so stating; and

(l) a statement that the appointment is in accordance with Schedule B1.

(2) Where two or more administrators are appointed the notice must also specify (as required by paragraph 100(2) of Schedule B1)—

(a) which functions (if any) are to be exercised by those persons acting jointly; and

(b) which functions (if any) are to be exercised by any or all of those persons.

(3) The statutory declaration included in the notice in accordance with paragraph 18(2) of Schedule B1 must be made not more than five business days before the notice is filed with the court.

NOTES

Para (1): words in square brackets in sub-para (k) substituted by the Insolvency (Amendment) (EU Exit) Regulations 2019, SI 2019/146, reg 2, Schedule, Pt 4, paras 46, 61, as from IP completion day (as defined in the European Union (Withdrawal Agreement) Act 2020, s 39) (for savings, see reg 4 of the 2019 Regulations at **[12.82]**).

[10.633]

3.18 Filing of notice with the court

(1) Three copies of the notice of appointment must be filed with the court, accompanied by—

(a) the administrator's consent to act; and

(b) either—

(i) evidence that the appointer has given notice as required by paragraph 15(1)(a) of Schedule B1; or

(ii) copies of the written consent of all those required to give consent in accordance with paragraph 15(1)(b) of Schedule B1.

(2) The court must apply the seal of the court to the copies of the notice, endorse them with the date and time of filing and deliver two of the sealed copies to the appointer.

(3) The appointer must as soon as reasonably practicable deliver one of the sealed copies to the administrator.

(4) This rule is subject to rules 3.20 and 3.21 (appointment made out of court business hours).

[10.634]

3.19 Appointment by floating charge holder after administration application made

(1) This rule applies where the holder of a qualifying floating charge, after receiving notice that an administration application has been made, appoints an administrator under paragraph 14 of Schedule B1.

(2) The holder must as soon as reasonably practicable deliver a copy of the notice of appointment to—

(a) the person making the administration application; and

(b) the court in which the application has been made.

[10.635]

3.20 Appointment taking place out of court business hours: procedure

(1) When (but only when) the court is closed, the holder of a qualifying floating charge may file a notice of appointment with the court by—

(a) faxing it to a designated telephone number; or

(b) emailing it, or attaching it to an email, to a designated email address.

(2) The notice must specify the name of the court (and hearing centre if applicable) that has jurisdiction.

(3) The Lord Chancellor must designate the telephone number and email address.

(4) The Secretary of State must publish the designated telephone number and email address on the Insolvency Service webpages and deliver notice of them to any person requesting them from the Insolvency Service.

(5) The appointer must ensure that—

(a) a fax transmission report giving the time and date of the fax transmission and the telephone number to which the notice was faxed and containing a copy of the first page (in part or in full) of the document faxed is created by the fax machine that is used to fax the notice; or

(b) a hard copy of the email is created giving the time and date of the email and the address to which it was sent.

(6) The appointer must retain the fax transmission report or hard copy of the email.

(7) The appointer must deliver a notice to the administrator of the filing of the notice of appointment as soon as reasonably practicable.

(8) The copy of the faxed or emailed notice of appointment as received by the Courts Service must be delivered by the Lord Chancellor as soon as reasonably practicable to the court specified in the notice as the court having jurisdiction in the case, to be placed on the relevant court file.

(9) The appointer must take to the court on the next occasion that the court is open for business—

(a) three copies of the faxed or emailed notice of appointment;

(b) the fax transmission report or hard copy required by paragraph (5);

(c) all supporting documents referred to in the notice in accordance with rule 3.21(1) which are in the appointer's possession; and

(d) a statement providing reasons for the out-of-hours filing of the notice of appointment, including why it would have been damaging to the company or its creditors not to have so acted.

(10) The copies of the notice must be sealed by the court and endorsed with—

(a) the date and time when, according to the appointer's fax transmission report or hard copy of the email, the notice was faxed or sent; and

(b) the date when the notice and accompanying documents were delivered to the court.

(11) The court must deliver two of the sealed copies of the notice of appointment to the appointer.

(12) The appointer must, as soon as reasonably practicable, deliver one of the copies to the administrator.

(13) The reference—

(a) to the Insolvency Service in paragraph (4) means the Secretary of State acting by means of the Insolvency Service; and

(b) to the Courts Service in paragraph (8) means the Lord Chancellor acting by means of Her Majesty's Courts and Tribunals Service.

[10.636]

3.21 Appointment taking place out of court business hours: content of notice

(1) Notice of an appointment filed in accordance with rule 3.20 must be headed "Notice of appointment of an administrator by holder of a qualifying floating charge", identify the company immediately below the heading and must contain—

(a) the name and address of the appointer;

(b) a statement that the appointer has appointed the person named as administrator of the company;

(c) the name and address of the person appointed as administrator;

(d) a statement that the appointer is the holder of the qualifying floating charge in question and that it is now enforceable;

(e) details of the charge, the date upon which it was registered and the maximum amount secured by the charge;

(f) one of the following statements—

(i) that notice has been given in accordance with paragraph 15(1)(a) of Schedule B1 to the holder of every prior floating charge which satisfies paragraph 14(2) of that Schedule, that a copy of every such notice was filed with the court under paragraph 44(2) of that Schedule, the date of that filing (or the latest date of filing if more than one) and that two business days have elapsed [since notice was given under paragraph 15(1)(a) of Schedule B1],

(ii) that notice has been given in accordance with paragraph 15(1)(a) of Schedule B1 to the holder of every prior floating charge which satisfies paragraph 14(2) of that Schedule and that a copy of every such notice is in the appointer's possession but was not filed with the court under paragraph 44(2) of that Schedule,

(iii) that the holder of every such floating charge to whom notice was given has consented to the making of the appointment and that a copy of every consent [in writing] is in the appointer's possession,

(iv) that the holder of every such floating charge has consented to the making of the appointment without notice having been given to all and that a copy of every consent [in writing] is in the appointer's possession, or

(v) that there is no such floating charge;

(g) a statement whether the company is or is not subject to insolvency proceedings at the date of the notice, and details of the proceedings if it is;

(h) a statement whether the company is an Article 1.2 undertaking . . . ;

(i) a statement whether the proceedings flowing from the appointment will be [COMI proceedings, establishment proceedings or proceedings to which the EU Regulation as it has effect in the law of the United Kingdom does not apply] [and that a statement of the reasons for stating this is in the appointer's possession];

(j) an undertaking that the following will be delivered to the court on the next occasion on which the court is open—

(i) any document referred to in the notice in accordance with rule 3.20 as being in the appointer's possession,

(ii) the fax transmission report or hard copy of the email, and

(iii) the statement of reasons for out-of-hours filing;

(k) a statement that the proposed administrator consents to act; and

(l) a statement that the appointment is in accordance with Schedule B1.

(2) Where two or more administrators are appointed the notice must also specify (as required by paragraph 100(2) of Schedule B1)—

(a) which functions (if any) are to be exercised by those persons acting jointly; and

(b) which functions (if any) are to be exercised by any or all of those persons.

(3) The statutory declaration included in the notice in accordance with paragraph 18(2) of Schedule B1 must be made not more than five business days before the notice is filed with the court.

NOTES

Para (1) is amended as follows:

Words in square brackets in sub-para (f)(i) substituted, words in square brackets in sub-paras (f)(iii), (iv) inserted, words omitted from sub-para (h) revoked, and words in second pair of square brackets in sub-para (i) inserted, by the Insolvency (England and Wales) (Amendment) Rules 2017, SI 2017/366, rr 3, 12, as from 6 April 2017.

Words in first pair of square brackets in sub-para (i) substituted by the Insolvency (Amendment) (EU Exit) Regulations 2019, SI 2019/146, reg 2, Schedule, Pt 4, paras 46, 62, as from IP completion day (as defined in the European Union (Withdrawal Agreement) Act 2020, s 39) (for savings, see reg 4 of the 2019 Regulations at **[12.82]**).

[10.637]

3.22 Appointment taking place out of court business hours: legal effect

(1) The filing of a notice in accordance with rule 3.20 has the same effect for all purposes as the filing of a notice of appointment in accordance with rule 3.18.

(2) The appointment—

(a) takes effect from the date and time of the fax transmission or sending of the email; but

(b) ceases to have effect if the requirements of rule 3.20(9) are not completed on the next occasion the court is open for business.

(3) Where any question arises in relation to the date and time that the notice of appointment was filed with the court, it is a presumption capable of rebuttal that the date and time shown on the appointer's fax transmission report or hard copy of the email is the date and time at which the notice was filed.

CHAPTER 4 APPOINTMENT OF ADMINISTRATOR BY COMPANY OR DIRECTORS

[Note: a document required by the Act or these Rules must also contain the standard contents set out in Part 1.]

[10.638]

3.23 Notice of intention to appoint

(1) If paragraph 26 of Schedule B1 requires a notice of intention to appoint an administrator under paragraph 22 of that Schedule then the notice must be headed "Notice of intention to appoint an administrator by company or directors" and must contain the following—

(a) identification details for the proceedings;

(b) a statement that the company or the directors, as the case may be, intend to appoint an administrator of the company;

(c) the name and address of the proposed administrator;

(d) the names and addresses of the persons to whom notice is being given in accordance with paragraph 26(1) of Schedule B1;

(e) a statement that each of those persons is or may be entitled to appoint—

(i) an administrative receiver of the company, or

(ii) an administrator of the company under paragraph 14 of Schedule B1;

[(ea) a statement as to whether there is a moratorium in force for the company under Part A1 of the Act;]

[(f) a statement that the company has not within the preceding 12 months been in administration;]

(g) a statement that in relation to the company there is no—

(i) petition for winding up which has been presented but not yet disposed of,

(ii) administration application which has not yet been disposed of, or

(iii) administrative receiver in office;

(h) a statement whether the company is an Article 1.2 undertaking;

(i) a statement whether the proceedings flowing from the appointment will be [COMI proceedings, establishment proceedings or proceedings to which the EU Regulation as it has effect in the law of the United Kingdom does not apply] and the reasons for so stating;

(j) a statement that the notice is accompanied (as appropriate) by either—

(i) a copy of the resolution of the company to appoint an administrator, or

(ii) a record of the decision of the directors to appoint an administrator; and

(k) a statement that if a recipient of the notice who is named in paragraph (e) wishes to consent in writing to the appointment that person may do so but that after five business days have expired from delivery of the notice the appointer may make the appointment although such a recipient has not replied.

(2) The notice must be accompanied by—

(a) a copy of the resolution of the company to appoint an administrator, where the company intends to make the appointment, or

(b) a record of the decision of the directors, where the directors intend to make the appointment.

(3) The giving of notice under paragraph 26(1) of Schedule B1 must be by service of the notice.

(4) If notice of intention to appoint is given under paragraph 26(1) of Schedule B1, a copy of the notice under paragraph 26(2) must be [sent] at the same time to—

(a) any enforcement agent or other officer who, to the knowledge of the person giving the notice, is charged with distress or other legal process against the company;

(b) any person who, to the knowledge of the person giving the notice, has distrained against the company or its property;

(c) any supervisor of a CVA; and

(d) the company, if the company is not intending to make the appointment.

(5) The giving of notice under paragraph 26(2) of Schedule B1 must be by service of the notice.

(6) The statutory declaration accompanying the notice in accordance with paragraph 27(2) of Schedule B1 must—

(a) if it is not made by the person making the appointment, indicate the capacity in which the person making the declaration does so; and

(b) be made not more than five business days before the notice is filed with the court.

NOTES

Para (1) is amended as follows:

Sub-para (ea) inserted, and sub-para (f) substituted, by the Insolvency (England and Wales) (No 2) (Amendment) Rules 2021, SI 2021/1028, r 20, as from 1 October 2021 (for savings provisions see the note to r 1A.1 at **[10.539]**). Sub-para (f) previously read as follows—

"(f) a statement that the company has not within the preceding 12 months been—

(i) in administration;

(ii) the subject of a moratorium under Schedule A1 which ended on a date when no CVA was in force; or

(iii) the subject of a CVA which was made during a moratorium under Schedule A1 and which ended prematurely within the meaning of section 7B;".

Words in square brackets in sub-para (i) substituted by the Insolvency (Amendment) (EU Exit) Regulations 2019, SI 2019/146, reg 2, Schedule, Pt 4, paras 46, 63, as from IP completion day (as defined in the European Union (Withdrawal Agreement) Act 2020, s 39) (for savings, see reg 4 of the 2019 Regulations at **[12.82]**).

Para (4): word in square brackets substituted by the Insolvency (England and Wales) (Amendment) Rules 2017, SI 2017/366, rr 3, 13, as from 6 April 2017.

[10.639]

3.24 Notice of appointment after notice of intention to appoint

(1) Notice of an appointment under paragraph 22 of Schedule B1 (when notice of intention to appoint has been given under paragraph 26) must be headed "Notice of appointment of an administrator by a company (where a notice of intention to appoint has been given)" or "Notice of appointment of an administrator by the directors of a company (where a notice of intention to appoint has been given)" and must contain—

(a) identification details for the company immediately below the heading;

(b) a statement that the company has, or the directors have, as the case may be, appointed the person named as administrator of the company;
(c) the name and address of the person appointed as administrator;
(d) a statement that a copy of the administrator's consent to act accompanies the notice;
(e) a statement that the company is, or the directors are, as the case may be, entitled to make an appointment under paragraph 22 of Schedule B1;
(f) a statement that the appointment is in accordance with Schedule B1;
(g) a statement whether the company is an Article 1.2 undertaking;
(h) a statement whether the proceedings flowing from the appointment will be [COMI proceedings, establishment proceedings or proceedings to which the EU Regulation as it has effect in the law of the United Kingdom does not apply] and the reasons for so stating;
(i) a statement that the company has, or the directors have, as the case may be, given notice of their intention to appoint in accordance with paragraph 26(1) of Schedule B1, that a copy of the notice was filed with the court, the date of that filing and either—
 (i) that five business days have elapsed [since notice was given under paragraph 26 of Schedule B1], or
 (ii) that each person to whom the notice was given has consented to the appointment; and
(j) the date and time of the appointment.

(2) Where two or more administrators are appointed the notice must also specify (as required by paragraph 100(2) of Schedule B1)—
(a) which functions (if any) are to be exercised by those persons acting jointly; and
(b) which functions (if any) are to be exercised by any or all of those persons.

(3) The statutory declaration included in the notice in accordance with paragraph 29(2) of Schedule B1 must be made not more than five business days before the notice is filed with the court.

(4) If the statutory declaration is not made by the person making the appointment it must indicate the capacity in which the person making the declaration does so.

NOTES

Para (1): words in square brackets in sub-para (h) substituted by the Insolvency (Amendment) (EU Exit) Regulations 2019, SI 2019/146, reg 2, Schedule, Pt 4, paras 46, 64, as from IP completion day (as defined in the European Union (Withdrawal Agreement) Act 2020, s 39) (for savings, see reg 4 of the 2019 Regulations at **[12.82]**). Words in square brackets in sub-para (i) substituted by the Insolvency (England and Wales) (Amendment) Rules 2017, SI 2017/366, rr 3, 14, as from 6 April 2017.

[10.640]
3.25 Notice of appointment without prior notice of intention to appoint

(1) Notice of an appointment under paragraph 22 of Schedule B1 (when notice of intention to appoint has not been given under paragraph 26) must be headed "Notice of appointment of an administrator by a company (where a notice of intention to appoint has not been given)" or "Notice of appointment of an administrator by the directors of a company (where a notice of intention to appoint has not been given)" and must identify the company immediately below the heading.

(2) The notice must state the following—
(a) that the company has, or the directors have, as the case may be, appointed the person specified under sub-paragraph (b) as administrator of the company;
(b) the name and address of the person appointed as administrator;
(c) that a copy of the administrator's consent to act accompanies the notice;
(d) that the company is or the directors are, as the case may be, entitled to make an appointment under paragraph 22 of Schedule B1;
(e) that the appointment is in accordance with Schedule B1;
[(ea) a statement as to whether there is a moratorium in force for the company under Part A1 of the Act;]
[(f) a statement that the company has not within the preceding 12 months been in administration;]
(g) that in relation to the company there is no—
 (i) petition for winding up which has been presented but not yet disposed of,
 (ii) administration application which has not yet been disposed of, or
 (iii) administrative receiver in office;
(h) whether the company is an Article 1.2 undertaking;
(i) whether the proceedings flowing from the appointment will be [COMI proceedings, establishment proceedings or proceedings to which the EU Regulation as it has effect in the law of the United Kingdom does not apply] and the reasons for so stating;
(j) that the notice is accompanied by—
 (i) a copy of the resolution of the company to appoint an administrator, or
 (ii) a record of the decision of the directors to appoint an administrator; and
(k) the date and time of the appointment.

(3) Where two or more administrators are appointed the notice must also specify (as required by paragraph 100(2) of Schedule B1)—
(a) which functions (if any) are to be exercised by those persons acting jointly; and
(b) which functions (if any) are to be exercised by any or all of those persons.

(4) The statutory declaration included in the notice in accordance with paragraphs 29(2) and 30 of Schedule B1 must—
(a) if the declaration is made on behalf of the person making the appointment, indicate the capacity in which the person making the declaration does so; and
(b) be made not more than five business days before the notice is filed with the court.

NOTES

Para (2) is amended as follows:

Sub-para (ea) inserted, and sub-para (f) substituted, by the Insolvency (England and Wales) (No 2) (Amendment) Rules 2021, SI 2021/1028, r 21, as from 1 October 2021 (for savings provisions see the note to r 1A.1 at **[10.539]**). Sub-para (f) previously read as follows—

"(f) that the company has not within the preceding 12 months been—
(i) in administration,
(ii) the subject of a moratorium under Schedule A1 which ended on a date when no CVA was in force, or
(iii) the subject of a CVA which was made during a moratorium under Schedule A1 and which ended prematurely within the meaning of section 7B;".

Words in square brackets in sub-para (i) substituted by the Insolvency (Amendment) (EU Exit) Regulations 2019, SI 2019/146, reg 2, Schedule, Pt 4, paras 46, 65, as from IP completion day (as defined in the European Union (Withdrawal Agreement) Act 2020, s 39) (for savings, see reg 4 of the 2019 Regulations at **[12.82]**).

[10.641]
3.26 Notice of appointment: filing with the court

(1) Three copies of the notice of appointment must be filed with the court, accompanied by—
(a) the administrator's consent to act; and
(b) the written consent of all those persons to whom notice was given in accordance with paragraph 26(1) of Schedule B1 unless the period of notice set out in paragraph 26(1) has expired.

(2) Where a notice of intention to appoint an administrator has not been given, the copies of the notice of appointment must also be accompanied by—
(a) a copy of the resolution of the company to appoint an administrator, where the company is making the appointment; or
(b) a record of the decision of the directors, where the directors are making the appointment.

(3) The court must apply to the copies the seal of the court, endorse them with the date and time of filing and deliver two of the sealed copies to the appointer.

(4) The appointer must as soon as reasonably practicable deliver one of the sealed copies to the administrator.

CHAPTER 5 NOTICE OF ADMINISTRATOR'S APPOINTMENT

[Note: a document required by the Act or these Rules must also contain the standard contents set out in Part 1.]

[10.642]
3.27 Publication of administrator's appointment

(1) The notice of appointment, to be published by the administrator as soon as reasonably practicable after appointment under paragraph 46(2)(b) of Schedule B1, must be gazetted and may be advertised in such other manner as the administrator thinks fit.

(2) The notice of appointment must state the following—
(a) that an administrator has been appointed;
(b) the date of the appointment; and
(c) the nature of the business of the company.

(3) The administrator must, as soon as reasonably practicable after the date specified in paragraph 46(6) of Schedule B1, deliver a notice of the appointment—
[(za) if there is a moratorium in force for the company under Part A1 of the Act, to the monitor;]
(a) if a receiver or an administrative receiver has been appointed, to that person;
(b) if there is pending a petition for the winding up of the company, to the petitioner (and also to the provisional liquidator, if any);
(c) to any enforcement officer, enforcement agent or other officer who, to the administrator's knowledge, is charged with distress or other legal process against the company or its property;
(d) to any person who, to the administrator's knowledge, has distrained against the company or its property; and
(e) any supervisor of a CVA.

(4) Where, under Schedule B1 or these Rules, the administrator is required to deliver a notice of the appointment to the registrar of companies or any other person, it must be headed "Notice of administrator's appointment" and must contain—
(a) the administrator's name and address and IP number;
(b) identification details for the proceedings; and
(c) a statement that the administrator has been appointed as administrator of the company;

(5) The notice must be authenticated and dated by the administrator.

NOTES

Para (3): sub-para (za) inserted by the Insolvency (England and Wales) (No 2) (Amendment) Rules 2021, SI 2021/1028, r 22, as from 1 October 2021 (for savings provisions see the note to r 1A.1 at **[10.539]**).

CHAPTER 6 STATEMENT OF AFFAIRS

[Note: a document required by the Act or these Rules must also contain the standard contents set out in Part 1.]

[10.643]
3.28 Interpretation

In this Chapter—

"nominated person" means a relevant person who has been required by the administrator to make out and deliver to the administrator a statement of affairs; and

"relevant person" means a person mentioned in paragraph 47(3) of Schedule B1.

[10.644]
3.29 Statement of affairs: notice requiring and delivery to the administrator (paragraph 47(1) of Schedule B1)

[Note: see section 234(1) and 235(1) for the application of section 235 to administrators.]

(1) A requirement under paragraph 47(1) of Schedule B1 for one or more relevant persons to provide the administrator with a statement of the affairs of the company must be made by a notice delivered to each such person.

(2) The notice must be headed "Notice requiring statement of affairs" and must—
- (a) require each nominated person to whom the notice is delivered to prepare and submit to the administrator a statement of the affairs of the company;
- (b) inform each nominated person of—
  - (i) the names and addresses of all others (if any) to whom the same notice has been delivered,
  - [(ii) the requirement to deliver the statement of affairs to the administrator no later than eleven days after receipt of the notice requiring the statement of affairs;] and
  - (iii) the effect of paragraph 48(4) of Schedule B1 (penalty for non-compliance) and section 235 (duty to co-operate with the office-holder).

(3) The administrator must inform each nominated person to whom notice is delivered that a document for the preparation of the statement of affairs capable of completion in compliance with rule 3.30 will be supplied if requested.

(4) The nominated person (or one of them, if more than one) must deliver the statement of affairs to the administrator with the statement of truth required by paragraph 47(2)(a) of Schedule B1 and a copy of each statement.

NOTES

Para (2): sub-para (b)(ii) substituted by the Insolvency (England and Wales) (Amendment) Rules 2017, SI 2017/366, rr 3, 15, as from 6 April 2017.

[10.645]
3.30 Statement of affairs: content (paragraph 47 of Schedule B1)

[Note: paragraph 47(2)(a) of Schedule B1 requires the statement of affairs to be verified by a statement of truth.]

(1) The statement of the company's affairs must be headed "Statement of affairs" and must—
- (a) identify the company immediately below the heading; and
- (b) state that it is a statement of the affairs of the company on a specified date, being the date on which it entered administration.

(2) The statement of affairs must contain (in addition to the matters required by paragraph 47(2) of Schedule B1) [the following, and, in addition, where paragraph (2B) applies, the information specified in that paragraph]—
- (a) a summary of the assets of the company, setting out the book value and the estimated realisable value of—
  - (i) any assets subject to a fixed charge,
  - (ii) any assets subject to a floating charge,
  - (iii) any uncharged assets, and
  - (iv) the total value of all the assets available for preferential creditors;
- (b) a summary of the liabilities of the company, setting out—
  - (i) the amount of preferential debts,
  - (ii) an estimate of the deficiency with respect to preferential debts or the surplus available after paying the preferential debts,
  - (iii) an estimate of the prescribed part, if applicable,
  - (iv) an estimate of the total assets available to pay debts secured by floating charges,
  - (v) the amount of debts secured by floating charges,
  - (vi) an estimate of the deficiency with respect to debts secured by floating charges or the surplus available after paying the debts secured by fixed or floating charges,
  - (vii) the amount of unsecured debts (excluding preferential debts),
  - (viii) an estimate of the deficiency with respect to unsecured debts or the surplus available after paying unsecured debts,
  - (ix) any issued and called-up capital, and
  - (x) an estimate of the deficiency with respect to, or surplus available to, members of the company;
- (c) a list of the company's creditors with the further particulars required by paragraph (3) indicating—
  - (i) any creditors under hire-purchase, chattel leasing or conditional sales agreements, and
  - (ii) any creditors claiming retention of title over property in the company's possession; and
- (d) the name and address of each member of the company and the number, nominal value and other details of the shares held by each member.

[(2A) Paragraph (2B) applies if a moratorium under Part A1 of the Act is, or has been, in force for the company at any time within the period of 12 weeks ending with the day on which it entered administration.

(2B) Where this paragraph applies the statement of affairs must identify which of the debts owed by the company are—
- (a) moratorium debts, and
- (b) priority pre-moratorium debts,

within the meaning given by section 174A; and
- (c) sub-paragraph (2)(a)(iv) has effect as if the reference to preferential creditors included references to moratorium debts and priority pre-moratorium debts within the meaning given by section 174A.
- (d) sub-paragraph (2)(b)(i), (ii) and (vii) has effect as if the reference to preferential debts included references to moratorium debts and priority pre-moratorium debts within the meaning given by section 174A.]

(3) The list of creditors required by paragraph 47(2) of Schedule B1 and paragraph (2)(c) of this rule must contain the details required by paragraph (4) except where paragraphs (5) and (6) apply.

(4) The particulars required by paragraph (3) are as follows—

(a) the name and postal address of the creditor;
(b) the amount of the debt owed to the creditor;
(c) details of any security held by the creditor;
(d) the date on which the security was given; and
(e) the value of any such security.

(5) Paragraph (6) applies where the particulars required by paragraph (4) relate to creditors who are either—
(a) employees or former employees of the company; or
(b) consumers claiming amounts paid in advance for the supply of goods or services.

(6) Where this paragraph applies—
(a) the statement of affairs itself must state separately for each of paragraph (5)(a) and (b) the number of such creditors and the total of the debts owed to them; and
(b) the particulars required by paragraph (4) must be set out in separate schedules to the statement of affairs for each of paragraphs (5)(a) and (b).

NOTES

Para (2): words in square brackets inserted by the Insolvency (England and Wales) (No 2) (Amendment) Rules 2021, SI 2021/1028, r 23(1), (2), as from 1 October 2021 (for savings provisions see the note to r 1A.1 at **[10.539]**).

Paras (2A), (2B): inserted by SI 2021/1028, r 23(1), (3), as from 1 October 2021 (for savings provisions see the note to r 1A.1 at **[10.539]**).

[10.646]
3.31 Statement of affairs: statement of concurrence

(1) The administrator may require a relevant person to deliver to the administrator a statement of concurrence.

(2) A statement of concurrence is a statement, verified by a statement of truth, that that person concurs in the statement of affairs submitted by a nominated person.

(3) The administrator must inform the nominated person who has been required to submit a statement of affairs that the relevant person has been required to deliver a statement of concurrence.

(4) The nominated person must deliver a copy of the statement of affairs to every relevant person who has been required to submit a statement of concurrence.

(5) A statement of concurrence—
(a) must identify the company; and
(b) may be qualified in relation to matters dealt with in the statement of affairs where the relevant person—
(i) is not in agreement with the statement of affairs,
(ii) considers the statement of affairs to be erroneous or misleading, or
(iii) is without the direct knowledge necessary for concurring with it.

(6) The relevant person must deliver the required statement of concurrence together with a copy to the administrator before the end of the period of five business days (or such other period as the administrator may agree) beginning with the day on which the relevant person receives the statement of affairs.

[10.647]
3.32 Statement of affairs: filing

(1) The administrator must as soon as reasonably practicable deliver to the registrar of companies a copy of—
(a) the statement of affairs; and
(b) any statement of concurrence.

(2) However, the administrator must not deliver to the registrar of companies with the statement of affairs any schedule required by rule 3.30(6)(b).

(3) The requirement to deliver the statement of affairs is subject to any order of the court made under rule 3.45 that the statement of affairs or a specified part must not be delivered to the registrar of companies.

[10.648]
3.33 Statement of affairs: release from requirement and extension of time

(1) The power of the administrator under paragraph 48(2) of Schedule B1 to revoke a requirement to provide a statement of affairs or to extend the period within which it must be submitted may be exercised upon the administrator's own initiative or at the request of a nominated person who has been required to provide it.

(2) The nominated person may apply to the court if the administrator refuses that person's request for a revocation or extension.

(3) On receipt of an application, the court may, if it is satisfied that no sufficient cause is shown for it, dismiss it without giving notice to any party other than the applicant.

(4) Unless the application is dismissed, the court must fix a venue for it to be heard.

(5) The applicant must, at least 14 days before any hearing, deliver to the administrator a notice stating the venue with a copy of the application and of any evidence on which the applicant intends to rely.

(6) The administrator may do either or both of the following—
(a) file a report of any matters which the administrator thinks ought to be drawn to the court's attention; or
(b) appear and be heard on the application.

(7) If a report is filed, the administrator must deliver a copy of it to the applicant not later than five business days before the hearing.

(8) Sealed copies of any order made on the application must be delivered by the court to the applicant and the administrator.

(9) On an application under this rule, the applicant's costs must be paid by the applicant in any event, but the court may order that an allowance of all or part of them be payable as an expense of the administration.

[10.649]

3.34 Statement of affairs: expenses

(1) The expenses of a nominated person which the administrator considers to have been reasonably incurred in making a statement of affairs or of a relevant person in making a statement of concurrence must be paid by the administrator as an expense of the administration.

(2) A decision by the administrator that expenses were not reasonably incurred (and are therefore not payable as an expense of the administration) may be appealed to the court.

CHAPTER 7 ADMINISTRATOR'S PROPOSALS

[Note: a document required by the Act or these Rules must also contain the standard contents set out in Part 1.]

[10.650]

3.35 Administrator's proposals: additional content

(1) The administrator's statement of proposals made under paragraph 49 of Schedule B1 (which is required by paragraph 49(4) to be delivered to the registrar of companies, creditors and members) must identify the proceedings and, in addition to the matters set out in paragraph 49, contain—

(a) any other trading names of the company;
(b) details of the administrator's appointment, including—
  (i) the date of appointment,
  (ii) the person making the application or appointment, and
  (iii) where a number of persons have been appointed as administrators, details of the matters set out in paragraph 100(2) of Schedule B1 relating to the exercise of their functions;
(c) the names of the directors and secretary of the company and details of any shareholdings in the company which they may have;
(d) an account of the circumstances giving rise to the appointment of the administrator;
[(da) a statement as to whether a moratorium under Part A1 of the Act has been in force for the company at any time within the period of 2 years ending with the day on which it entered administration and, if so—
  (i) the date on which it came into force,
  (ii) the date on which it ended, and
  (iii) particulars of the purposes for which it was entered into and whether, and to what extent, those purposes were achieved;]
(e) the date the proposals are delivered to the creditors;
(f) if a statement of the company's affairs has been submitted—
  (i) a copy or summary of it, except so far as an order under rule 3.45 or 3.46 limits disclosure of it, and excluding any schedule referred to in rule 3.30(6)(b), or the particulars relating to individual creditors contained in any such schedule,
  (ii) details of who provided the statement of affairs, and
  (iii) any comments which the administrator may have upon the statement of affairs;
(g) if an order under rule 3.45 or 3.46 has been made—
  (i) a statement of that fact, and
  (ii) the date of the order;
(h) if no statement of affairs has been submitted—
  (i) details of the financial position of the company [(as to which see paragraph (1A))] at the latest practicable date (which must, unless the court orders otherwise, be a date not earlier than that on which the company entered administration), and
  (ii) an explanation as to why there is no statement of affairs;
(i) a full list of the company's creditors in accordance with paragraph (2) if either—
  (i) no statement of affairs has been submitted, or
  (ii) a statement of affairs has been submitted but it does not include such a list, or the administrator believes the list included is less than full;
(j) a statement of—
  (i) how it is envisaged the purpose of the administration will be achieved, and
  (ii) how it is proposed that the administration will end, including, where it is proposed that the administration will end by the company moving to a creditors' voluntary winding up—
    (aa) details of the proposed liquidator,
    (bb) where applicable, the declaration required by section 231, and
    (cc) a statement that the creditors may, before the proposals are approved, nominate a different person as liquidator in accordance with paragraph 83(7)(a) of Schedule B1 and rule 3.60(6)(b);
(k) a statement of either—
  (i) the method by which the administrator has decided to seek a decision from creditors as to whether they approve the proposals, or
  (ii) the administrator's reasons for not seeking a decision from creditors;
(l) the manner in which the affairs and business of the company—
  (i) have, since the date of the administrator's appointment, been managed and financed, including, where any assets have been disposed of, the reasons for the disposals and the terms upon which the disposals were made, and
  (ii) will, if the administrator's proposals are approved, continue to be managed and financed;
(m) a statement whether the proceedings are [COMI proceedings, establishment proceedings or proceedings to which the EU Regulation as it has effect in the law of the United Kingdom does not apply]; and
(n) any other information that the administrator thinks necessary to enable creditors to decide whether or not to approve the proposals.

[(1A) For the purposes of paragraph (1)(h)(i) if a moratorium has been in force at any time within the period of 12 weeks ending with the day on which the company entered administration then the details of the financial position of the company must identify which of the debts owed by the company are—

(a) moratorium debts, and

(b) priority pre-moratorium debts,

within the meaning given by section 174A.]

(2) The list of creditors required by paragraph (1)(i) must contain the details required by sub-paragraph (3) except where paragraphs (4) and (5) apply;

(3) The particulars required by paragraph (2) are as follows and must be given in this order—

(a) the name and postal address of the creditor;

(b) the amount of the debt owed to the creditor;

(c) details of any security held by the creditor;

(d) the date on which any such security was given; and

(e) the value of any such security;

(4) This paragraph applies where the particulars required by paragraph (3) relate to creditors who are either—

(a) employees or former employees of the company; or

(b) consumers claiming amounts paid in advance for the supply of goods and services.

(5) Where paragraph (4) applies—

(a) the list of creditors required by paragraph (1)(i) must state separately for each of paragraphs (4)(a) and (b) the number of the creditors and the total of the debts owed to them; and

(b) the particulars required by paragraph (3) in respect of such creditors must be set out in separate schedules to the list of creditors for each of sub-paragraphs (4)(a) and (b); and

(c) the administrator must not deliver any such schedule to the registrar of companies with the statement of proposals.

(6) Except where the administrator proposes a CVA in relation to the company, the statement made by the administrator under paragraph 49 of Schedule B1 must also include—

(a) to the best of the administrator's knowledge and belief, an estimate of the value of—

(i) the prescribed part (whether or not the administrator might be required under section 176A to make the prescribed part available for the satisfaction of unsecured debts), and

(ii) the company's net property (as defined by section 176A(6)); and

(b) a statement whether the administrator proposes to make an application to the court under section 176A(5) and if so the reason for the application.

(7) The administrator may exclude from an estimate under paragraph (6)(a) information the disclosure of which could seriously prejudice the commercial interests of the company.

(8) If the exclusion of such information affects the calculation of an estimate, the report must say so.

(9) The document containing the statement of proposals must include a statement of the basis on which it is proposed that the administrator's remuneration should be fixed by a decision in accordance with Chapter 4 of Part 18 of these Rules.

(10) Where applicable the document containing the statement of proposals must include—

(a) a statement of any pre-administration costs charged or incurred by the administrator or, to the administrator's knowledge, by any other person qualified to act as an insolvency practitioner in relation to the company;

(b) a statement that the payment of any unpaid pre-administration costs as an expense of the administration is—

(i) subject to approval under rule 3.52, and

(ii) not part of the proposals subject to approval under paragraph 53 of Schedule B1.

NOTES

Para (1): sub-para (da) and words in square brackets in sub-para (h) inserted by the Insolvency (England and Wales) (No 2) (Amendment) Rules 2021, SI 2021/1028, r 24(1), (2), as from 1 October 2021 (for savings provisions see the note to r 1A.1 at **[10.539]**). Words in square brackets in sub-para (m) substituted by the Insolvency (Amendment) (EU Exit) Regulations 2019, SI 2019/146, reg 2, Schedule, Pt 4, paras 46, 66, as from IP completion day (as defined in the European Union (Withdrawal Agreement) Act 2020, s 39) (for savings, see reg 4 of the 2019 Regulations at **[12.82]**).

Para (1A): inserted by SI 2021/1028, r 24(1), (3), as from 1 October 2021 (for savings provisions see the note to r 1A.1 at **[10.539]**).

[10.651]

3.36 Administrator's proposals: statement of pre-administration costs

A statement of pre-administration costs under rule 3.35(10)(a) must include—

(a) details of any agreement under which the fees were charged and expenses incurred, including the parties to the agreement and the date on which the agreement was made;

(b) details of the work done for which the fees were charged and expenses incurred;

(c) an explanation of why the work was done before the company entered administration and how it had been intended to further the achievement of an objective in paragraph 3(1) of Schedule B1 in accordance with sub-paragraphs (2) to (4) of that paragraph;

(d) a statement of the amount of the pre-administration costs, setting out separately—

(i) the fees charged by the administrator,

(ii) the expenses incurred by the administrator,

(iii) the fees charged (to the administrator's knowledge) by any other person qualified to act as an insolvency practitioner in relation to the company (and, if more than one, by each separately), and

(iv) the expenses incurred (to the administrator's knowledge) by any other person qualified to act as an insolvency practitioner in relation to the company (and, if more than one, by each separately);

(e) a statement of the amounts of pre-administration costs which have already been paid (set out separately as under sub-paragraph (d));

(f) the identity of the person who made the payment or, if more than one person made the payment, the identity of each such person and of the amounts paid by each such person set out separately as under sub-paragraph (d); and

(g) a statement of the amounts of unpaid pre-administration costs (set out separately as under sub-paragraph (d)).

[10.652]

3.37 Advertising administrator's proposals and notices of extension of time for delivery of proposals (paragraph 49 of Schedule B1)

(1) A notice published by the administrator under paragraph 49(6) of Schedule B1 must—

(a) identify the proceedings and contain the registered office of the company;

(b) be advertised in such manner as the administrator thinks fit; and

(c) be published as soon as reasonably practicable after the administrator has delivered the statement of proposals to the company's creditors but no later than eight weeks (or such other period as may be agreed by the creditors or as the court may order) from the date on which the company entered administration.

(2) Where the court orders, on an application by the administrator under paragraph 107 of Schedule B1, an extension of the period in paragraph 49(5) of Schedule B1 for delivering copies of the statement of proposals, the administrator must as soon as reasonably practicable after the making of the order deliver a notice of the extension to—

(a) the creditors of the company;

(b) the members of the company of whose address the administrator is aware; and

(c) the registrar of companies.

(3) The notice must—

(a) identify the proceedings;

(b) state the date to which the court has ordered an extension; and

(c) contain the registered office of the company.

(4) The administrator is taken to comply with paragraph [(2)(b)] if the administrator publishes a notice complying with paragraph (5).

(5) The notice must—

(a) contain the information required by paragraph (3);

(b) be advertised in such manner as the administrator thinks fit;

(c) state that members may request in writing a copy of the notice of the extension, and state the address to which to write; and

(d) be published as soon as reasonably practicable after the administrator has delivered the notice of the extension to the company's creditors.

NOTES

Para (4): figure in square brackets substituted by the Insolvency (England and Wales) and Insolvency (Scotland) (Miscellaneous and Consequential Amendments) Rules 2017, SI 2017/1115, rr 2, 4, as from 8 December 2017.

[10.653]

3.38 Seeking approval of the administrator's proposals

(1) This rule applies where the administrator is required by paragraph 51 of Schedule B1 to seek approval from the company's creditors of the statement of proposals made under paragraph 49 of that Schedule.

(2) The statement of proposals delivered under paragraph 49(4) of Schedule B1 must be accompanied by a notice to the creditors of the decision procedure in accordance with rule 15.8.

(3) The administrator may seek a decision using deemed consent in which case the requirements in rule 15.7 also apply to the notice.

(4) Where the administrator has made a statement under paragraph 52(1) of Schedule B1 and has not sought a decision on approval from creditors, the proposal will be deemed to have been approved unless a decision has been requested under paragraph 52(2) of Schedule B1.

(5) Where under paragraph (4) the proposal is deemed to have been approved the administrator must, as soon as reasonably practicable after the expiry of the period for requisitioning a decision set out in rule 15.18(2), deliver a notice of the date of deemed approval to the registrar of companies, the court and any creditor to whom the administrator has not previously delivered the proposal.

(6) The notice must contain—

(a) identification details for the proceedings;

(b) the name of the administrator;

(c) the date the administrator was appointed; and

(d) the date on which the statement of proposals was delivered to the creditors.

(7) A copy of the statement of proposals, with the statements required by rule 3.35(5), must accompany the notice given to the court and to any creditors to whom a copy of the statement of proposals has not previously been delivered.

[10.654]

3.39 Invitation to creditors to form a creditors' committee

(1) Where the administrator is required to seek a decision from the company's creditors under rule 3.38, the administrator must at the same time deliver to the creditors a notice inviting them to decide whether a creditors' committee should be established if sufficient creditors are willing to be members of the committee.

(2) The notice must also invite nominations for membership of the committee, such nominations to be received by the administrator by a date to be specified in the notice.

(3) The notice must state that any nominations—

(a) must be delivered to the administrator by the specified date; and

(b) can only be accepted if the administrator is satisfied as to the creditor's eligibility under rule 17.4.

(4) A notice under this rule must also be delivered to the creditors at any other time when the administrator seeks a decision from creditors and a creditors' committee has not already been established at that time.

[10.655]

3.40 Notice of extension of time to seek approval

(1) Where the court orders an extension to the period set out in paragraph 51(2) of Schedule B1, the administrator must deliver a notice of the extension as soon as reasonably practicable to each person mentioned in paragraph 49(4) of Schedule B1.

(2) The notice must contain identification details for the proceedings and the date to which the court has ordered an extension.

(3) The administrator is taken to have complied with paragraph (1) as regards members of the company if the administrator publishes a notice complying with paragraph (4).

(4) The notice must—

(a) be advertised in such manner as the administrator thinks fit;

(b) state that members may request in writing a copy of the notice of the extension, and state the address to which to write; and

(c) be published as soon as reasonably practicable after the administrator has delivered the notice of the extension to the company's creditors.

[10.656]

3.41 Notice of the creditors' decision on the administrator's proposals (paragraph 53(2))

(1) In addition to delivering a report to the court and the registrar of companies (in accordance with paragraph 53(2) of Schedule B1) the administrator must deliver a report to—

(a) the company's creditors (accompanied by a copy of the statement of proposals, with the statement required by rule 3.35(10)(a) and (b), if it has not previously been delivered to the creditor); and

(b) every other person to whom a copy of the statement of proposals was delivered.

(2) A report mentioned in paragraph (1) must contain—

(a) identification details for the proceedings;

(b) details of decisions taken by the creditors including details of any modifications to the proposals which were approved by the creditors; and

(c) the date such decisions were made.

(3) A copy of the statement of proposals, with any statements required by rule 3.35(9) and (10), must accompany the report to the court.

[10.657]

3.42 Administrator's proposals: revision

(1) Where paragraph 54(1) of Schedule B1 applies, the statement of the proposed revision which is required to be delivered to the creditors must be delivered with a notice of the decision procedure in accordance with rule 15.8.

(2) The statement must identify the proceedings and include—

(a) any other trading names of the company;

(b) details of the administrator's appointment, including—

(i) the date of appointment, and

(ii) the person making the application or appointment;

(c) the names of the directors and secretary of the company and details of any shareholdings in the company which they may have;

(d) a summary of the original proposals and the reason or reasons for proposing a revision;

(e) details of the proposed revision, including details of the administrator's assessment of the likely impact of the proposed revision upon creditors generally or upon each class of creditors;

(f) where the proposed revision relates to the ending of the administration by a creditors' voluntary winding up and the nomination of a person to be the proposed liquidator of the company—

(i) details of the proposed liquidator,

(ii) where applicable, the declaration required by section 231, and

(iii) a statement that the creditors may, before the proposals are approved, nominate a different person as liquidator in accordance with paragraph 83(7)(a) of Schedule B1 and rule 3.60(6)(b); and

(g) any other information that the administrator thinks necessary to enable creditors to decide whether or not to vote for the proposed revisions.

(3) The administrator may seek a decision using deemed consent in which case the requirements in rule 15.7 also apply to the notice.

(4) The period within which, subject to paragraph 54(3) of Schedule B1, the administrator must send a copy of the statement to every member of the company of whose address the administrator is aware is five business days after sending the statement of the proposed revision to the creditors.

(5) Notice under paragraph 54(3) and (4) of Schedule B1 must—

(a) be advertised in such manner as the administrator thinks fit as soon as reasonably practicable after the administrator has sent the statement to the creditors; and

(b) state that members may request in writing a copy of the proposed revision, and state the address to which to write.

[(6) A copy of the statement of revised proposals under rule 3.43(3) must be delivered to the registrar of companies not later than five days after the report under rule 3.43(1) is delivered.]

NOTES

Para (6): added by the Insolvency (England and Wales) (Amendment) Rules 2017, SI 2017/366, rr 3, 16, as from 6 April 2017.

[10.658]

3.43 Notice of result of creditors' decision on revised proposals (paragraph 54(6))

(1) In addition to delivering a report to the court and the registrar of companies (in accordance with paragraph 54(6) of Schedule B1) the administrator must deliver a report to—

- (a) the company's creditors (accompanied by a copy of the original statement of proposals and the revised statement of proposals if the administrator had not delivered notice of the decision procedure or deemed consent procedure to the creditor); and
- (b) every other person to whom a copy of the original statement of proposals was delivered.

(2) A report mentioned in paragraph (1) must contain—

- (a) identification details for the proceedings;
- (b) the date of the revised proposals;
- (c) details of decisions taken by the creditors including details of any modifications to the revised proposals which were approved by the creditors; and
- (d) the date such decisions were made.

(3) A copy of the statement of revised proposals must accompany the notice to the court.

CHAPTER 8 LIMITED DISCLOSURE OF STATEMENTS OF AFFAIRS AND PROPOSALS

[Note: a document required by the Act or these Rules must also contain the standard contents set out in Part 1.]

[10.659]

3.44 Application of Chapter

This Chapter applies to the disclosure of information which would be likely to prejudice the conduct of the administration or might reasonably be expected to lead to violence against any person.

[10.660]

3.45 Orders limiting disclosure of statement of affairs etc

(1) If the administrator thinks that the circumstances in rule 3.44 apply in relation to the disclosure of—

- (a) the whole or part of the statement of the company's affairs;
- (b) any of the matters specified in rule 3.35(1)(h) and (i) (administrator's proposals); or
- (c) a statement of concurrence,

the administrator may apply to the court for an order in relation to the particular document or a specified part of it.

(2) The court may order that the whole of or a specified part of a document referred to in paragraph (1)(a) to (c) must not be delivered to the registrar of companies or, in the case of the statement of proposals, to creditors or members of the company.

(3) The administrator must as soon as reasonably practicable deliver to the registrar of companies—

- (a) a copy of the order;
- (b) the statement of affairs, statement of proposals and any statement of concurrence to the extent provided by the order; and
- (c) if the order relates to the statement of proposals, an indication of the nature of the matter in relation to which the order was made.

(4) If the order relates to the statement of proposals, the administrator must as soon as reasonably practicable also deliver to the creditors and members of the company—

- (a) the statement of proposals to the extent provided by the order; and
- (b) an indication of the nature of the matter in relation to which the order was made.

[10.661]

3.46 Order for disclosure by administrator

(1) A creditor may apply to the court for an order that the administrator disclose any of the following in relation to which an order has been made under rule 3.45(2)—

- (a) a statement of affairs;
- (b) a specified part of it;
- (c) a part of a statement of proposals; or
- (d) statement of concurrence.

(2) The application must be supported by a witness statement.

(3) The applicant must deliver to the administrator notice of the application at least three business days before the hearing.

(4) In an order for disclosure, the court may include conditions as to confidentiality, duration, the scope of the order in the event of any change of circumstances or such other matters as it thinks just.

[10.662]

3.47 Rescission or amendment of order for limited disclosure

(1) If there is a material change in circumstances rendering an order for limited disclosure under rule 3.45(2) wholly or partially unnecessary, the administrator must, as soon as reasonably practicable after the change, apply to the court for the order to be rescinded or amended.

(2) If the court makes such an order, the administrator must as soon as reasonably practicable deliver to the registrar of companies—

- (a) a copy of the order; and

(b) the statement of affairs, the statement of proposals and any statement of concurrence to the extent provided by the order.

(3) If the order relates to the statement of proposals, the administrator must as soon as reasonably practicable also deliver to the creditors and members the statement of proposals to the extent allowed by the order.

[10.663]

3.48 Publication etc of statement of affairs or statement of proposals

(1) CPR Part 31 does not apply to an application under rule 3.45, 3.46 or 3.47.

(2) If, after the administrator has sent a statement of proposals under paragraph 49(4) of Schedule B1, a statement of affairs is delivered to the registrar of companies in accordance with rule 3.47(2) as the result of the rescission or amendment of an order, the administrator must deliver to the creditors a copy or summary of the statement of affairs as delivered to the registrar of companies.

(3) The administrator is taken to comply with the requirements for delivery to members of the company in rule 3.45(4) or 3.47(3) if the administrator publishes the required notice.

(4) The required notice must—

(a) be advertised in such manner as the administrator thinks fit;

(b) state that members can request in writing—

(i) a copy of the statement of proposals to the extent provided by the order, and

(ii) an indication of the nature of the matter in relation to which the order was made;

(c) state the address to which to such a written request is to be made; and

(d) be published as soon as reasonably practicable after the administrator has delivered the statement of proposals to the extent provided by the order to the company's creditors.

CHAPTER 9 DISPOSAL OF CHARGED PROPERTY

[Note: a document required by the Act or these Rules must also contain the standard contents set out in Part 1.]

[10.664]

3.49 Disposal of charged property

(1) This rule applies where the administrator applies to the court under paragraph 71 or 72 of Schedule B1 for authority to dispose of—

(a) property which is subject to a security other than a floating charge; or

(b) goods in the possession of the company under a hire-purchase agreement.

(2) The court must fix a venue for the hearing of the application.

(3) As soon as reasonably practicable after the court has done so, the administrator must deliver notice of the venue to the holder of the security or the owner of the goods.

(4) If an order is made under paragraph 71 or 72 of Schedule B1, the court must deliver two sealed copies to the administrator.

(5) The administrator must deliver—

(a) one of the sealed copies to the holder of the security or the owner of the goods; and

(b) a copy of the sealed order to the registrar of companies.

CHAPTER 10 EXPENSES OF THE ADMINISTRATION

[Note: a document required by the Act or these Rules must also contain the standard contents set out in Part 1.]

[10.665]

3.50 Expenses

(1) All fees, costs, charges and other expenses incurred in the course of the administration are to be treated as expenses of the administration.

(2) The expenses associated with the prescribed part must be paid out of the prescribed part.

(3) The cost of the security required by section 390(3) for the proper performance of the administrator's functions is an expense of the administration.

(4) For the purposes of paragraph 99 of Schedule B1, a former administrator's remuneration and expenses comprise all the items in rule 3.51(2).

[(5) The costs of an application by the administrator under rule 1A.27 are to be treated as an expense of the administration unless the court orders otherwise.]

NOTES

Para (5): added by the Insolvency (England and Wales) (No 2) (Amendment) Rules 2021, SI 2021/1028, r 25, as from 1 October 2021 (for savings provisions see the note to r 1A.1 at **[10.539]**).

[10.666]

3.51 Order of priority

[(1) Where paragraph 64A or paragraph 99(1) of Schedule B1 applies, the items specified in paragraph 64A or paragraph 99 (as the case may be) are payable in priority to the expenses in this rule.]

(2) Subject to paragraph (1) and to any court order under paragraph (3) the expenses of the administration are payable in the following order of priority—

(a) expenses properly incurred by the administrator in performing the administrator's functions;

(b) the cost of any security provided by the administrator in accordance with the Act or these Rules;

(c) where an administration order was made, the costs of the applicant and any person appearing on the hearing of the application whose costs were allowed by the court;

(d) where the administrator was appointed otherwise than by order of the court—

(i) the costs and expenses of the appointer in connection with the making of the appointment, and

Part 10 Miscellaneous other SIs

(ii) the costs and expenses incurred by any other person in giving notice of intention to appoint an administrator;

(e) any amount payable to a person in respect of assistance in the preparation of a statement of affairs or statement of concurrence;

(f) any allowance made by order of the court in respect of the costs on an application for release from the obligation to submit a statement of affairs or deliver a statement of concurrence;

(g) any necessary disbursements by the administrator in the course of the administration (including any [. . .] expenses incurred by members of the creditors' committee or their representatives and allowed for by the administrator under rule 17.24, but not including any payment of corporation tax in circumstances referred to in sub-paragraph (j) below);

(h) the remuneration or emoluments of any person who has been employed by the administrator to perform any services for the company, as required or authorised under the Act or these Rules;

(i) the administrator's remuneration the basis of which has been fixed under Part 18 and unpaid pre-administration costs approved under rule 3.52; and

(j) the amount of any corporation tax on chargeable gains accruing on the realisation of any asset of the company (irrespective of the person by whom the realisation is effected).

(3) If the assets are insufficient to satisfy the liabilities, the court may make an order as to the payment out of the assets of the expenses incurred in the administration in such order of priority as the court thinks just.

NOTES

Para (1): substituted by the Insolvency (England and Wales) (No 2) (Amendment) Rules 2021, SI 2021/1028, r 26, as from 1 October 2021 (for savings provisions see the note to r 1A.1 at **[10.539]**). Para (1) previously read as follows—

"(1) Where there is a former administrator, the items in paragraph 99 of Schedule B1 are payable in priority to the expenses in this rule.".

Para (2): words omitted from sub-para (g) originally inserted by the Insolvency Amendment (EU 2015/848) Regulations 2017, SI 2017/702, regs 2, 3, Schedule, Pt 2, paras 32, 37, as from 26 June 2017, except in relation to proceedings opened before that date; and subsequently revoked by the Insolvency (Amendment) (EU Exit) Regulations 2019, SI 2019/146, reg 2, Schedule, Pt 4, paras 46, 67, as from IP completion day (as defined in the European Union (Withdrawal Agreement) Act 2020, s 39) (for savings, see reg 4 of the 2019 Regulations at **[12.82]**).

[10.667]

[3.51A Priority of moratorium debts in subsequent administration

Where paragraph 64A(1) of Schedule B1 applies, the moratorium debts and priority pre-moratorium debts mentioned in paragraph 64A(2) of that Schedule are payable in the following order of priority—

(a) amounts payable in respect of goods or services supplied during the moratorium under a contract where, but for section 233B(3) or (4), the supplier would not have had to make that supply;

(b) wages or salary arising under a contract of employment, so far as relating to a period of employment before or during the moratorium;

(c) other debts or other liabilities apart from the monitor's remuneration or expenses; and

(d) the monitor's remuneration or expenses.]

NOTES

Commencement: 1 October 2021.

Inserted by the Insolvency (England and Wales) (No 2) (Amendment) Rules 2021, SI 2021/1028, r 27, as from 1 October 2021 (for savings provisions see the note to r 1A.1 at **[10.539]**).

[10.668]

3.52 Pre-administration costs

(1) Where the administrator has made a statement of pre-administration costs under rule 3.35(10)(a), the creditors' committee may determine whether and to what extent the unpaid pre-administration costs set out in the statement are approved for payment.

(2) Paragraph (3) applies where—

(a) there is no creditors' committee;

(b) there is a creditors' committee but it does not make the necessary determination; or

(c) the creditors' committee does make the necessary determination but the administrator or other insolvency practitioner who has charged fees or incurred expenses as pre-administration costs considers the amount determined to be insufficient.

(3) When this paragraph applies, determination of whether and to what extent the unpaid pre-administration costs are approved for payment must be—

(a) by a decision of the creditors through a decision procedure; or

(b) in a case where the administrator has made a statement under paragraph 52(1)(b) of Schedule B1, by—

(i) the consent of each of the secured creditors, or

(ii) if the administrator has made, or intends to make, a distribution to preferential creditors, by—

(aa) the consent of each of the secured creditors, and

(bb) a decision of the preferential creditors in a decision procedure.

(4) The administrator must call a meeting of the creditors' committee or seek a decision of creditors by a decision procedure if so requested for the purposes of paragraphs (1) to (3) by another insolvency practitioner who has charged fees or incurred expenses as pre-administration costs; and the administrator must deliver notice of the meeting or decision procedure within 28 days of receipt of the request.

(5) The administrator (where the fees were charged or expenses incurred by the administrator) or other insolvency practitioner (where the fees were charged or expenses incurred by that practitioner) may apply to the court for a determination of whether and to what extent the unpaid pre-administration costs are approved for payment if either—

(a) there is no determination under paragraph (1) or (3); or
(b) there is such a determination but the administrator or other insolvency practitioner who has charged fees or incurred expenses as pre-administration costs considers the amount determined to be insufficient.

(6) Where there is a creditors' committee the administrator or other insolvency practitioner must deliver at least 14 days' notice of the hearing to the members of the committee; and the committee may nominate one or more of its members to appear, or be represented, and to be heard on the application.

(7) If there is no creditors' committee, notice of the application must be delivered to such one or more of the company's creditors as the court may direct, and those creditors may nominate one or more of their number to appear or be represented, and to be heard on the application.

(8) The court may, if it appears to be a proper case, order the costs of the application, including the costs of any member of the creditors' committee appearing or being represented on it, or of any creditor so appearing or being represented, to be paid as an expense of the administration.

(9) Where the administrator fails to call a meeting of the creditors' committee or seek a decision from creditors in accordance with paragraph (4), the other insolvency practitioner may apply to the court for an order requiring the administrator to do so.

CHAPTER 11 EXTENSION AND ENDING OF ADMINISTRATION

[Note: a document required by the Act or these Rules must also contain the standard contents set out in Part 1.]

[10.669]
3.53 Interpretation

"Final progress report" means in this Chapter, and in Part 18 in so far as it relates to final progress reports in an administration, a progress report which includes a summary of—
(a) the administrator's proposals;
(b) any major amendments to, or deviations from, those proposals;
(c) the steps taken during the administration; and
(d) the outcome.

[10.670]
3.54 Application to extend an administration and extension by consent (paragraph 76(2) of Schedule B1)

(1) This rule applies where an administrator makes an application to the court for an order, or delivers a notice to the creditors requesting their consent, to extend the administrator's term of office under paragraph 76(2) of Schedule B1.

(2) The application or the notice must state the reasons why the administrator is seeking an extension.

(3) A request to the creditors may contain or be accompanied by a notice that if the extension is granted a notice of the extension will be made available for viewing and downloading on a website and that no other notice will be delivered to the creditors.

(4) Where the result of a request to the creditors is to be made available for viewing and downloading on a website, the notice must comply with the requirements for use of a website to deliver documents set out in rule 1.49(2)(a) to (c), (3) and (4) with any necessary modifications and rule 1.49(5)(a) applies to determine the time of delivery of the document.

(5) Where the court makes an order extending the administrator's term of office, the administrator must as soon as reasonably practicable deliver to the creditors a notice of the order together with the reasons for seeking the extension given in the application to the court.

(6) Where the administrator's term of office has been extended with the consent of creditors, the administrator must as soon as reasonably practicable deliver a notice of the extension to the creditors except where paragraph (3) applies.

(7) The notices which paragraph 78(5)(b) of Schedule B1 require to be delivered to the registrar of companies must also identify the proceedings.

[10.671]
3.55 Notice of automatic end of administration (paragraph 76 of Schedule B1)

(1) This rule applies where—
(a) the appointment of an administrator has ceased to have effect; and
(b) the administrator is not required by any other rule to give notice of that fact.

(2) The former administrator must, as soon as reasonably practicable, and in any event within five business days of the date on which the appointment has ceased, deliver to the registrar of companies and file with the court a notice accompanied by a final progress report.

(3) The notice must be headed "Notice of automatic end of administration" and identify the company immediately below the heading.

(4) The notice must contain—
(a) identification details for the proceedings;
(b) the former administrator's name and address;
(c) a statement that that person had been appointed administrator of the company;
(d) the date of the appointment;
(e) the name of the person who made the appointment or the administration application, as the case may be;
(f) a statement that the appointment has ceased to have effect;
(g) the date on which the appointment ceased to have effect; and
(h) a statement that a copy of the final progress report accompanies the notice.

(5) The notice must be authenticated by the administrator and dated.

(6) A copy of the notice and accompanying final progress report must be delivered as soon as reasonably practicable to—

(a) the directors of the company; and
(b) all other persons to whom notice of the administrator's appointment was delivered.

(7) A former administrator who makes default in complying with this rule is guilty of an offence and liable to a fine and, for continued contravention, to a daily default fine.

[10.672]
3.56 Notice of end of administration when purposes achieved (paragraph 80(2) of Schedule B1)

(1) Where an administrator who was appointed under paragraph 14 or 22 of Schedule B1 thinks that the purpose of administration has been sufficiently achieved, the notice ("notice of end of administration") which the administrator may file with the court and deliver to the registrar of companies under paragraph 80(2) of Schedule B1 must be headed "Notice of end of administration" and identify the company immediately below the heading.

(2) The notice must contain—
(a) identification details for the proceedings;
(b) the administrator's name and address;
(c) a statement that that person has been appointed administrator of the company;
(d) the date of the appointment;
(e) the name of the person who made the appointment or the administration application, as the case may be;
(f) a statement that the administrator thinks that the purpose of the administration has been sufficiently achieved;
(g) a statement that a copy of the final progress report accompanies the notice; and
(h) a statement that the administrator is filing the notice with the court and delivering a copy to the registrar of companies.

(3) The notice must be authenticated by the administrator and dated.

(4) The notice must be accompanied by a final progress report.

(5) The notice filed with the court must also be accompanied by a copy of the notice.

(6) The court must endorse the notice and the copy with the date and time of filing, seal the copy and deliver it to the administrator.

(7) The prescribed period within which the administrator, under paragraph 80(4) of Schedule B1, must send a copy of the notice to the creditors is five business days from the filing of the notice.

(8) The copy notice sent to creditors must be accompanied by the final progress report.

(9) The administrator must within the same period deliver a copy of the notice and the final progress report to all other persons (other than the creditors and the registrar of companies) to whom notice of the administrator's appointment was delivered.

(10) The administrator is taken to have complied with the requirement in paragraph 80(4) of Schedule B1 to give notice to the creditors if, within five business days of filing the notice with the court, the administrator gazettes a notice which—
(a) states that the administration has ended, and the date on which it ended;
(b) undertakes that the administrator will provide a copy of the notice of end of administration to any creditor of the company who applies in writing; and
(c) specifies the address to which to write.

(11) The Gazette notice may be advertised in such other manner as the administrator thinks fit.

[10.673]
3.57 Administrator's application for order ending administration (paragraph 79 of Schedule B1)

(1) An application to court by the administrator under paragraph 79 of Schedule B1 for an order ending an administration must be accompanied by—
(a) a progress report for the period since—
(i) the last progress report (if any), or
(ii) if there has been no previous progress report, the date on which the company entered administration;
(b) a statement indicating what the administrator thinks should be the next steps for the company (if applicable); and
(c) where the administrator makes the application because of a requirement decided by the creditors, a statement indicating with reasons whether or not the administrator agrees with the requirement.

(2) Where the application is made other than because of a requirement by a decision of the creditors—
(a) the administrator must, at least five business days before the application is made, deliver notice of the administrator's intention to apply to court to—
(i) the person who made the administration application or appointment, and
(ii) the creditors; and
(b) the application must be accompanied by—
(i) a statement that notice has been delivered to the creditors, and
(ii) copies of any response from creditors to that notice.

(3) Where the application is in conjunction with a petition under section 124 for an order to wind up the company, the administrator must, at least five business days before the application is filed, deliver notice to the creditors as to whether the administrator intends to seek appointment as liquidator.

[10.674]
3.58 Creditor's application for order ending administration (paragraph 81 of Schedule B1)

(1) Where a creditor applies to the court under paragraph 81 of Schedule B1 for an order ending an administration, a copy of the application must be delivered, not less than five business days before the date fixed for the hearing, to—
(a) the administrator;
(b) the person who made the administration application or appointment; and

(c) where the appointment was made under paragraph 14 of Schedule B1, the holder of the floating charge by virtue of which the appointment was made (if different to (b)).

(2) Any of those persons may appear at the hearing of the application.

(3) Where the court makes an order under paragraph 81 ending the administration, the court must deliver a copy of the order to the administrator.

[10.675]
3.59 Notice by administrator of court order

Where the court makes an order ending the administration, the administrator must as soon as reasonably practicable deliver a copy of the order and of the final progress report to—

(a) the registrar of companies;
(b) the directors of the company; and
(c) all other persons to whom notice of the administrator's appointment was delivered.

[10.676]
3.60 Moving from administration to creditors' voluntary winding up (paragraph 83 of Schedule B1)

[Note: the information referred to in paragraph (5) is required to be included in the first progress report of the liquidator. See rule 18.3(5).]

(1) This rule applies where the administrator delivers to the registrar of companies a notice under paragraph 83(3) of Schedule B1 of moving from administration to creditors' voluntary winding up.

(2) The notice must contain—

(a) identification details for the proceedings;
(b) the name of the person who made the appointment or the administration application, as the case may be; and
(c) the name and IP number of the proposed liquidator.

(3) The notice to the registrar of companies must be accompanied by a copy of the administrator's final progress report.

(4) A copy of the notice and the final progress report must be sent as soon as reasonably practicable after delivery of the notice to all those persons to whom notice of the administrator's appointment was delivered in addition to the creditors (as required by paragraph 83(5)(b)).

(5) The person who ceases to be administrator on the registration of the notice must inform the person who becomes liquidator of anything which happens after the date of the final progress report and before the registration of the notice which the administrator would have included in the final report had it happened before the date of the report.

(6) For the purposes of paragraph 83(7)(a) of Schedule B1, a person is nominated by the creditors as liquidator by—

(a) their approval of the statement of the proposed liquidator in the administrator's proposals or revised proposals; or
(b) their nomination of a different person, through a decision procedure, before their approval of the proposals or revised proposals.

(7) Where the creditors nominate a different person, the nomination must, where applicable, include the declaration required by section 231.

[10.677]
3.61 Moving from administration to dissolution (paragraph 84 of Schedule B1)

(1) This rule applies where the administrator delivers to the registrar of companies a notice under paragraph 84(1) of Schedule B1 of moving from administration to dissolution.

(2) The notice must identify the proceedings.

(3) As soon as reasonably practicable after sending the notice, the administrator must deliver a copy of the notice to all persons to whom notice of the administrator's appointment was delivered (in addition to the creditors mentioned in paragraph 84(5)(b) [but excluding opted-out creditors]).

(4) A final progress report must accompany the notice to the registrar of companies and every copy filed or otherwise delivered.

(5) Where a court makes an order under paragraph 84(7) of Schedule B1 it must, where the applicant is not the administrator, deliver a copy of the order to the administrator.

(6) The administrator must deliver a copy of the order to the registrar of companies with the notice required by paragraph 84(8).

NOTES

Para (3): words in square brackets inserted by the Insolvency (England and Wales) and Insolvency (Scotland) (Miscellaneous and Consequential Amendments) Rules 2017, SI 2017/1115, rr 2, 5, as from 8 December 2017.

CHAPTER 12 REPLACING THE ADMINISTRATOR

[Note: a document required by the Act or these Rules must also contain the standard contents set out in Part 1.]

[10.678]
3.62 Grounds for resignation

(1) The administrator may resign—

(a) on grounds of ill health;
(b) because of the intention to cease to practise as an insolvency practitioner; or
(c) because the further discharge of the duties of administrator is prevented or made impractical by—
    (i) a conflict of interest, or
    (ii) a change of personal circumstances.

(2) The administrator may, with the permission of the court, resign on other grounds.

[10.679]
3.63 Notice of intention to resign

(1) The administrator must give at least five business days' notice of intention—
- (a) to resign in a case falling within rule 3.62(1); or
- (b) to apply for the court's permission to resign in a case falling within rule 3.62(2).

(2) The notice must contain—
- (a) identification details for the proceedings;
- (b) the date of the appointment of the administrator;
- (c) the name of the person who made the appointment or the administration application, as the case may be.

(3) The notice must also contain—
- (a) the date with effect from which the administrator intends to resign; or
- (b) where the administrator was appointed by an administration order, the date on which the administrator intends to file with the court an application for permission to resign.

(4) The notice must be delivered—
- (a) to any continuing administrator of the company;
- (b) to the creditors' committee (if any);
- (c) if there is neither a continuing administrator nor a creditors' committee, to—
  - (i) the company, and
  - (ii) the company's creditors;
- (d) . . .
- (e) where the administrator was appointed by the holder of a qualifying floating charge under paragraph 14 of Schedule B1, to—
  - (i) the person who appointed the administrator, and
  - (ii) all holders of prior qualifying floating charges;
- (f) where the administrator was appointed by the company or the directors of the company under paragraph 22 of Schedule B1, to—
  - (i) the appointer, and
  - (ii) all holders of qualifying floating charges.

(5) The notice must be accompanied by a summary of the administrator's receipts and payments.

NOTES

Para (4): sub-para (d) revoked by the Insolvency (Amendment) (EU Exit) Regulations 2019, SI 2019/146, reg 2, Schedule, Pt 4, paras 46, 68, as from IP completion day (as defined in the European Union (Withdrawal Agreement) Act 2020, s 39) (for savings, see reg 4 of the 2019 Regulations at **[12.82]**).

[10.680]
3.64 Notice of resignation (paragraph 87 of Schedule B1)

(1) A resigning administrator must, within five business days of delivering the notice under paragraph 87(2) of Schedule B1, deliver a copy of the notice to—
- (a) the registrar of companies;
- (b) all persons, other than the person who made the appointment, to whom notice of intention to resign was delivered under rule 3.63; and
- (c) except where the appointment was by administration order, file a copy of the notice with the court.

(2) The notice must contain—
- (a) identification details for the proceedings;
- (b) the date of the appointment of the administrator; and
- (c) the name of the person who made the appointment or the administration application, as the case may be.

(3) The notice must state—
- (a) the date from which the resignation is to have effect; and
- (b) where the resignation is with the permission of the court, the date on which permission was given.

(4) Where an administrator was appointed by an administration order, notice of resignation under paragraph 87(2)(a) of Schedule B1 must be given by filing the notice with the court.

[10.681]
3.65 Application to court to remove administrator from office

(1) An application for an order under paragraph 88 of Schedule B1 that the administrator be removed from office must state the grounds on which the order is requested.

(2) A copy of the application must be delivered, not less than five business days before the date fixed for the hearing—
- (a) to the administrator;
- (b) to the person who—
  - (i) made the application for the administration order, or
  - (ii) appointed the administrator;
- (c) to the creditors' committee (if any);
- (d) to any continuing administrator appointed to act jointly or concurrently; and
- (e) where there is neither a creditors' committee nor a continuing administrator appointed, to the company and the creditors, including any floating charge holders.

(3) The court must deliver to the applicant a copy of any order removing the administrator.

(4) The applicant must deliver a copy—
- (a) as soon as reasonably practicable, and in any event within five business days of the copy order being delivered, to the administrator; and

(b) within five business days of the copy order being delivered, to—
   (i) all other persons to whom notice of the application was delivered, and
   (ii) the registrar of companies.

[10.682]

3.66 Notice of vacation of office when administrator ceases to be qualified to act

An administrator who has ceased to be qualified to act as an insolvency practitioner in relation to the company and gives notice in accordance with paragraph 89 of Schedule B1 must also deliver notice to the registrar of companies.

[10.683]

3.67 Deceased administrator

(1) If the administrator dies a notice of the fact and date of death must be filed with the court.

(2) The notice must be filed as soon as reasonably practicable by one of the following—
   (a) a surviving administrator;
   (b) a member of the deceased administrator's firm (if the deceased was a member or employee of a firm);
   (c) an officer of the deceased administrator's company (if the deceased was an officer or employee of a company); or.
   (d) a personal representative of the deceased administrator.

(3) If such a notice has not been filed within the 21 days following the administrator's death then any other person may file the notice.

(4) The person who files the notice must also deliver a notice to the registrar of companies which contains—
   (a) identification details for the proceedings;
   (b) the name of the person who made the appointment or the administration application, as the case may be;
   (c) the date of the appointment of the administrator; and
   (d) the fact and date of death.

[10.684]

3.68 Application to replace

(1) Where an application to court is made under paragraph 91(1) or 95 of Schedule B1 to appoint a replacement administrator, the application must be accompanied by the proposed replacement administrator's consent to act.

(2) Where the application is made under paragraph 91(1), a copy of the application must be delivered—
   (a) to the person who made the application for the administration order;
   (b) to any person who has appointed an administrative receiver of the company;
   (c) to any person who is or may be entitled to appoint an administrative receiver of the company;
   (d) to any person who is or may be entitled to appoint an administrator of the company under paragraph 14 of Schedule B1;
   (e) to any administrative receiver of the company;
   (f) if there is pending a petition for the winding up of the company, to—
      (i) the petitioner, and
      (ii) any provisional liquidator;
   (g) . . .
   (h) to the company, if the application is made by anyone other than the company;
   (i) to any supervisor of any CVA in relation to the company; and
   (j) to the proposed administrator.

(3) Where the application is made under paragraph 95, the application must be accompanied by a witness statement setting out the applicant's belief as to the matters set out in that paragraph.

(4) Rules 3.12, 3.13, and 3.15(1) and (2) apply to applications made under paragraph 91(1) and 95 of Schedule B1, with any necessary modifications.

NOTES

Para (2): sub-para (g) revoked by the Insolvency (Amendment) (EU Exit) Regulations 2019, SI 2019/146, reg 2, Schedule, Pt 4, paras 46, 69, as from IP completion day (as defined in the European Union (Withdrawal Agreement) Act 2020, s 39) (for savings, see reg 4 of the 2019 Regulations at **[12.82]**).

[10.685]

3.69 Appointment of replacement or additional administrator

Where a replacement administrator is appointed or an additional administrator is appointed to act—
   (a) the following apply—
      (i) rule 3.17 (notice of appointment) the requirement as to the heading in paragraph (1) and paragraphs (1)(a) to (f), and (2),
      (ii) rule 3.18 (filing of notice with court) paragraphs (1)(a) and (b)(ii), (2) and (3),
      (iii) rule 3.24 (notice of appointment after notice of intention to appoint) paragraphs (1)(a) to (d) and (2),
      (iv) rule 3.25 (notice of appointment without prior notice of intention to appoint) paragraphs (1), (2)(a) to (c) and (3),
      (v) rule 3.26 (notice of appointment: filing with the court) paragraphs (1)(a), (3) and (4), and
      (vi) rule 3.27 (publication of administrator's appointment) paragraphs (1), (2)(a) and (b), (3) and (4);
   (b) the replacement or additional administrator must deliver notice of the appointment to the registrar of companies; and
   (c) all documents must clearly identify the appointment as of a replacement administrator or an additional administrator.

[10.686]

3.70 Administrator's duties on vacating office

(1) An administrator who ceases to be in office as a result of removal, resignation or ceasing to be qualified to act as an insolvency practitioner in relation to the company must as soon as reasonably practicable deliver to the person succeeding as administrator—

(a) the assets (after deduction of any expenses properly incurred and distributions made by the departing administrator);

(b) the records of the administration, including correspondence, proofs and other documents relating to the administration while it was within the responsibility of the departing administrator; and

(c) the company's records.

(2) An administrator who makes default in complying with this rule is guilty of an offence and liable to a fine and, for continued contravention, to a daily default fine.

PART 4 RECEIVERSHIP

[Note: for the application of this Part see introductory rule 3.]

CHAPTER 1 APPOINTMENT OF JOINT RECEIVERS OR MANAGERS TO WHOM PART 3 OF THE ACT APPLIES (OTHER THAN THOSE APPOINTED UNDER SECTION 51 (SCOTTISH RECEIVERSHIPS))

[Note: a document required by the Act or these Rules must also contain the standard contents set out in Part 1.]

[10.687]

4.1 Receivers or managers appointed under an instrument: acceptance of appointment (section 33)

(1) This Chapter applies to all receivers to whom Part 3 of the Act applies [(other than those appointed under section 51 (Scottish Receiverships))].

(2) Where two or more persons are appointed as joint receivers or managers of a company's property under powers contained in an instrument—

(a) each of them must accept the appointment in accordance with section 33 as if each were a sole appointee;

(b) the joint appointment takes effect only when all of them have accepted; and

(c) the joint appointment is deemed to have been made at the time at which the instrument of appointment was received by or on behalf of all of them.

(3) A person who is appointed as the sole or joint receiver or manager of a company's property under powers contained in an instrument and accepts the appointment in accordance with section 33(1)(a), but not in writing, must confirm the acceptance in writing to the person making the appointment within five business days.

(4) The written acceptance or confirmation of acceptance must contain—

(a) the name and address of the appointer;

(b) the name and address of the appointee;

(c) the name of the company concerned;

(d) the time and date of receipt of the instrument of appointment; and

(e) the time and date of acceptance.

(5) Acceptance or confirmation of acceptance of appointment as a receiver or manager of a company's property, whether under the Act or these Rules, may be given by any person (including, in the case of a joint appointment, any joint appointee) duly authorised for that purpose on behalf of the receiver or manager.

NOTES

Para (1): words in square brackets inserted by the Insolvency (England and Wales) (Amendment) Rules 2017, SI 2017/366, rr 3, 17, as from 6 April 2017.

CHAPTER 2 ADMINISTRATIVE RECEIVERS (OTHER THAN IN SCOTTISH RECEIVERSHIPS)

[Note: a document required by the Act or these Rules must also contain the standard contents set out in Part 1.]

[10.688]

4.2 Application of Chapter 2

This Chapter applies to administrative receivers (other than those appointed under section 51 (Scottish receiverships)).

[10.689]

4.3 Interpretation

In this Chapter—

"nominated person" means a relevant person who has been required by the administrative receiver to make out and deliver to the administrative receiver a statement of affairs; and

"relevant person" means a person mentioned in section 47(3).

[10.690]

4.4 Administrative receiver's security

The cost of the administrative receiver's security required by section 390(3) for the proper performance of the administrative receiver's functions is an expense of the administrative receivership.

[10.691]

4.5 Publication of appointment of administrative receiver (section 46(1))

(1) The notice which an administrative receiver is required by section 46(1) to send to the company and the creditors on being appointed must contain—

(a) identification details for the company;

(b) any other registered name of the company in the 12 months before the date of the appointment;

(c) any name under which the company has traded at any time in those 12 months, if substantially different from its then registered name;

(d) the name and address of the person appointed;
(e) the date of the appointment;
(f) the name of the person who made the appointment;
(g) the date of the instrument conferring the power under which the appointment was made;
(h) a brief description of the instrument; and
(i) a brief description of any assets of the company in relation to which the appointment is not made.

(2) The notice which an administrative receiver is required by section 46(1) to publish—
(a) must be gazetted;
(b) may be advertised in such other manner as the administrative receiver thinks fit; and
(c) must state—
(i) that an administrative receiver has been appointed,
(ii) the date of the appointment,
(iii) the name of the person who made the appointment, and
(iv) the nature of the business of the company.

[10.692]
4.6 Requirement to provide a statement of affairs (section 47(1))

[Note: see sections 234(1) and 235(1) for the application of section 235 to administrative receivers.]

(1) A requirement under section 47(1) for a nominated person to make out and submit to the administrative receiver a statement of the affairs of the company must be made by a notice delivered to such a person.

(2) The notice must be headed "Notice requiring statement of affairs" and must—
(a) identify the company immediately below the heading;
(b) require the recipient to prepare and submit to the administrative receiver a statement of the affairs of the company; and
(c) inform each recipient of—
(i) the name and address of any other nominated person to whom a notice has been delivered,
(ii) the date by which the statement must be delivered to the administrative receiver, and
(iii) the effect of sections 47(6) (penalty for non-compliance) and 235 (duty to co-operate with the office-holder).

(3) The administrative receiver must inform each nominated person that a document for the preparation of the statement of affairs capable of completion in compliance with rule 4.7 can be supplied if requested.

[10.693]
4.7 Statement of affairs: contents and delivery of copy (section 47(2))

[Note: section 47(2) requires the statement of affairs to be verified by a statement of truth.]

(1) The statement of affairs must be headed "Statement of affairs" and must state that it is a statement of the affairs of the company on a specified date, being the date on which the administrative receiver was appointed.

(2) The statement of affairs must contain, in addition to the matters required by section 47(2)—
(a) a summary of the assets of the company, setting out the book value and the estimated realisable value of—
(i) any assets subject to a fixed charge,
(ii) any assets subject to a floating charge,
(iii) any uncharged assets, and
(iv) the total assets available for preferential creditors;
(b) a summary of the liabilities of the company, setting out—
(i) the amount of preferential debts,
(ii) an estimate of the deficiency with respect to preferential debts or the surplus available after paying the preferential debts,
(iii) an estimate of the prescribed part, if applicable,
(iv) an estimate of the total assets available to pay debts secured by floating charges,
(v) the amount of debts secured by floating charges,
(vi) an estimate of the deficiency with respect to debts secured by floating charges or the surplus available after paying the debts secured by floating charges,
(vii) the amount of unsecured debts (excluding preferential debts and any deficiency with respect to debts secured by floating charges),
(viii) an estimate of the deficiency with respect to unsecured debts or the surplus available after paying unsecured debts (excluding preferential debts and any deficiency with respect to debts secured by fixed and floating charges),
(ix) any issued and called-up capital, and
(x) an estimate of the deficiency with respect to, or surplus available to, members of the company;
(c) a list of the company's creditors with the further particulars required by paragraph (3) indicating—
(i) any creditors under hire-purchase, chattel leasing or conditional sale agreements,
(ii) any creditors who are consumers claiming amounts paid in advance for the supply of goods or services, and
(iii) any creditors claiming retention of title over property in the company's possession.

(3) The particulars required by section 47(2) and paragraph (2)(c) of this rule to be included in the statement of affairs relating to each creditor are as follows—
(a) the name and postal address;
(b) the amount of the debt owed to the creditor;
(c) details of any security held by the creditor;
(d) the date the security was given; and
(e) the value of any such security.

(4) Paragraph (5) applies where the particulars required by paragraph (3) relate to creditors who are either—

(a) employees or former employees of the company; or
(b) consumers claiming amounts paid in advance for the supply of goods or services.

(5) Where this paragraph applies—
(a) the statement of affairs must state separately for each of paragraphs (4)(a) and (b) the number of such creditors and the total of the debts owed to them; and
(b) the particulars required by paragraph (3) must be set out in separate schedules to the statement of affairs for each of paragraphs (4)(a) and (b).

(6) The nominated person who makes the statement of truth required by section 47(2) (or, if more than one, by one of them,) must deliver the statement of affairs together with a copy to the administrative receiver.

[10.694]
4.8 Statement of affairs: statement of concurrence

(1) The administrative receiver may require a relevant person to deliver to the administrative receiver a statement of concurrence.

(2) A statement of concurrence is a statement, verified by a statement of truth, that that person concurs in the statement of affairs submitted by a nominated person.

(3) The administrative receiver must inform the nominated person who has been required to submit a statement of affairs that the relevant person has been required to deliver a statement of concurrence.

(4) The nominated person must deliver a copy of the statement of affairs to every relevant person who has been required to deliver a statement of concurrence.

(5) A statement of concurrence—
(a) must identify the company; and
(b) may be qualified in relation to matters dealt with in the statement of affairs where the relevant person—
(i) is not in agreement with the statement of affairs,
(ii) considers the statement to be erroneous or misleading, or
(iii) is without the direct knowledge necessary for concurring in it.

(6) The relevant person must deliver the required statement of concurrence together with a copy to the administrative receiver before the end of the period of five business days (or such other period as the administrative receiver may agree) beginning with the day on which the relevant person receives the statement of affairs.

[10.695]
4.9 Statement of affairs: retention by administrative receiver

The administrative receiver must retain the verified statement of affairs and each statement of concurrence as part of the records of the receivership.

[10.696]
4.10 Statement of affairs: release from requirement and extension of time (section 47(5))

(1) The administrative receiver may exercise the power in section 47(5) to release a person from an obligation to submit a statement of affairs imposed under section 47(1) or (2), or to grant an extension of time, either on the administrative receiver's own discretion or at the request of a nominated person.

(2) A nominated person may apply to the court if the administrative receiver refuses that person's request.

(3) On receipt of an application, the court may, if it is satisfied that no sufficient cause is shown for it, dismiss it without giving notice to any party other than the applicant.

(4) The applicant must, at least 14 days before any hearing, deliver to the administrative receiver a notice stating the venue with a copy of the application and of any evidence on which the applicant intends to rely.

(5) The administrative receiver may do either or both of the following—
(a) file a report of any matters which the administrative receiver thinks ought to be drawn to the court's attention; or
(b) appear and be heard on the application.

(6) If a report is filed, the administrative receiver must deliver a copy of it to the applicant not later than five business days before the hearing.

(7) Sealed copies of any order made on the application must be delivered by the court to the applicant and the administrative receiver.

(8) On any application under this rule, the applicant's costs must be paid by the applicant in any event; but the court may order that an allowance of all or part of them be payable out of the assets under the administrative receiver's control.

[10.697]
4.11 Statement of affairs: expenses

(1) The administrative receiver must pay, out of the assets under the administrative receiver's control, the expenses which the administrative receiver considers to have been reasonably incurred by—
(a) a nominated person in making a statement of affairs and statement of truth; or
(b) a relevant person in making a statement of concurrence.

(2) Any decision by the administrative receiver under this rule is subject to appeal to the court.

[10.698]
4.12 Limited disclosure

(1) This rule applies where the administrative receiver thinks that disclosure of the whole or part of a statement of the company's affairs or a statement of concurrence would be likely to prejudice the conduct of the receivership or might reasonably be expected to lead to violence against any person.

(2) The administrative receiver may apply to the court for an order in respect of—

(a) the statement of affairs; or

(b) a statement of concurrence;

and the court may order that the whole or any specified part of the statement of affairs or a statement of concurrence must not be open to inspection except with permission of the court.

(3) The court's order may include directions regarding the delivery of documents to the registrar of companies and the disclosure of relevant information to other persons.

[10.699]

4.13 Administrative receiver's report to the registrar of companies and secured creditors (section 48(1))

(1) The report which under section 48(1) an administrative receiver is to send to the registrar of companies must be accompanied by a copy of any statement of affairs under section 47 and any statement of concurrence under rule 4.8.

(2) However the administrative receiver must not deliver to the registrar of companies with the statement of affairs any schedule required by rule 4.7(5)(b).

(3) The duty to send a copy of the report to the registrar of companies is subject to any order for limited disclosure made under rule 4.12.

(4) If a statement of affairs or statement of concurrence is submitted to the administrative receiver after the report is sent to the registrar of companies, the administrative receiver must deliver a copy of it to the registrar of companies as soon as reasonably practicable after its receipt by the administrative receiver.

(5) The report must contain (in addition to the matters required by section 48(1)) estimates to the best of the administrative receiver's knowledge and belief of—

(a) the value of the prescribed part (whether or not the administrative receiver might be required under section 176A to make the prescribed part available for the satisfaction of unsecured debts); and

(b) the value of the company's net property (as defined by section 176A(6)).

(6) The administrative receiver may exclude from an estimate under paragraph (5) information the disclosure of which could seriously prejudice the commercial interests of the company.

(7) If the exclusion of such information affects the calculation of an estimate, the report must say so.

(8) If the administrative receiver proposes to make an application to court under section 176A(5) the report must say so and give the reason for the application.

[10.700]

4.14 Copy of report for unsecured creditors (section 48(2))

A notice under section 48(2)(b) stating an address to which unsecured creditors should write for copies of an administrative receiver's report under that section—

(a) must be gazetted;

(b) may be advertised in such other manner as the administrative receiver thinks fit; and

(c) must be accompanied by a notice under rule 4.15.

[10.701]

4.15 Invitation to creditors to form a creditors' committee

(1) An administrative receiver must deliver to the creditors with the report under section 48(1) a notice inviting the creditors to decide whether a creditors' committee should be established if sufficient creditors are willing to be members of the committee.

(2) The notice must also invite nominations for membership of the committee, such nominations to be received by the administrative receiver by a date to be specified in the notice.

(3) The notice must state that any nominations—

(a) must be delivered to the administrative receiver by the specified date; and

(b) can only be accepted if the administrative receiver is satisfied as to the creditor's eligibility under rule 17.4.

[10.702]

4.16 Disposal of charged property (section 43(1))

(1) This rule applies where an administrative receiver applies to the court under section 43(1) for authority to dispose of property of the company which is subject to a security.

(2) The court must fix a venue for the hearing of the application.

(3) As soon as reasonably practicable after the court has fixed the venue, the administrative receiver must deliver notice of the venue to the person who is the holder of the security.

(4) If an order is made under section 43(1), the court must deliver two sealed copies to the administrative receiver and the administrative receiver must deliver one of them to the holder of the security.

[10.703]

4.17 Summary of receipts and payments

(1) The administrative receiver must deliver a summary of receipts and payments as receiver to the registrar of companies, the company and to the person who made the appointment, and to each member of the creditors' committee.

(2) The notice delivered to the registrar of companies under rule 1.20 must contain the date of the appointment of the administrative receiver.

(3) The summary must be delivered to those persons within two months after—

(a) the end of the period of 12 months from the date of being appointed;

(b) the end of every subsequent period of 12 months; and

(c) ceasing to act as administrative receiver (unless there is a joint administrative receiver who continues in office).

(4) The summary must show receipts and payments—
  (a) during the relevant period of 12 months; or
  (b) where the administrative receiver has ceased to act, during the period—
    (i) from the end of the last 12-month period to the time when the administrative receiver so ceased, or
    (ii) if there has been no previous summary, since being appointed.

(5) This rule is without prejudice to the administrative receiver's duty to produce proper accounts otherwise than as above.

(6) An administrative receiver who makes default in complying with this rule is guilty of an offence and liable to a fine and, for continued contravention, to a daily default fine.

[10.704]
4.18 Resignation

(1) An administrative receiver must deliver notice of intention to resign at least five business days before the date the resignation is intended to take effect to—
  (a) the person by whom the appointment was made;
  (b) the company or, if it is then in liquidation, the liquidator; and
  (c) the members of the creditors' committee.

(2) The notice must specify the date on which the administrative receiver intends the resignation to take effect.

[10.705]
4.19 Deceased administrative receiver

(1) If the administrative receiver dies a notice of the fact and date of death must be delivered as soon as reasonably practicable to—
  (a) the person by whom the appointment was made;
  (b) the registrar of companies;
  (c) the company or, if it is in liquidation, the liquidator; and
  (d) the members of the creditors' committee.

(2) The notice must be delivered by one of the following—
  (a) a surviving joint administrative receiver;
  (b) a member of the deceased administrative receiver's firm (if the deceased was a member or employee of a firm);
  (c) an officer of the deceased administrative receiver's company (if the deceased was an officer or employee of a company); or
  (d) a personal representative of the deceased administrative receiver.

(3) If such a notice has not been delivered within 21 days following the administrative receiver's death then any other person may deliver the notice.

[10.706]
4.20 Other vacation of office

An administrative receiver, on vacating office on completion of the administrative receivership, or in consequence of ceasing to be qualified to act as an insolvency practitioner in relation to the company, must as soon as reasonably practicable deliver a notice of doing so to—
  (a) the person by whom the appointment was made;
  (b) the company or, if it is then in liquidation, the liquidator; and
  (c) the members of the creditors' committee.

[10.707]
4.21 Notice to registrar of companies (section 45(4))

Where an administrative receiver's office is vacated other than by death, the notice to the registrar of companies required by section 45(4) may be given by delivering to the registrar of companies the notice required by section 859K(3) of the Companies Act.

CHAPTER 3 NON-ADMINISTRATIVE RECEIVERS AND THE PRESCRIBED PART

[Note: a document required by the Act or these Rules must also contain the standard contents set out in Part 1.]

[10.708]
4.22 Application of Chapter 3

This Chapter applies where a receiver (other than an administrative receiver) is appointed by the court or otherwise under a charge which was created as a floating charge; and section 176A applies.

[10.709]
4.23 Report to creditors

(1) Within three months (or such longer period as the court may allow) of the date of the appointment, the receiver must deliver to the creditors—
  (a) a notice of the appointment; and
  (b) a report.

(2) The report must contain estimates to the best of the receiver's knowledge and belief of—
  (a) the value of the prescribed part (whether or not the receiver might be required under section 176A to make the prescribed part available for the satisfaction of unsecured debts); and
  (b) the value of company's net property (as defined by section 176A(6)).

(3) The receiver may exclude from an estimate under paragraph (2) information the disclosure of which could seriously prejudice the commercial interests of the company.

(4) If the exclusion of such information affects the calculation of an estimate, the report must say so.

(5) If the receiver proposes to make an application to court under section 176A(5) the report must say so and give the reason for the application.

(6) The report must also state whether, and if so why, the receiver proposes to present a petition for the winding up of the company.

(7) The receiver may, instead of delivering the report under paragraph (1), cause a notice to be gazetted and may advertise that notice in such other manner as the receiver thinks fit where—

(a) full details of the unsecured creditors of the company are not available to the receiver; or
(b) the receiver thinks it is otherwise impracticable to deliver such a report.

(8) A notice under paragraph (7) must contain the matters required to be included in the receiver's report.

[10.710]
4.24 Receiver to deal with prescribed part

(1) The receiver—

(a) may present a petition for the winding up of the company if the ground of the petition is that in section 122(1)(f); and
(b) must deliver to any administrator or liquidator the sums representing the prescribed part.

(2) If there is no administrator or liquidator the receiver must—

(a) apply to the court for directions as to the manner in which to discharge the duty under section 176A(2)(a); and
(b) act in accordance with any directions given.

PART 5 MEMBERS' VOLUNTARY WINDING UP

CHAPTER 1 STATUTORY DECLARATION OF SOLVENCY (SECTION 89)

[Note: a document required by the Act or these Rules must also contain the standard contents set out in Part 1.]

[10.711]
5.1 Statutory declaration of solvency: requirements additional to those in section 89

[Note: the "official rate" referred to in paragraph (1)(b) is defined in section 251 as being the rate referred to in section 189(4).]

(1) The statutory declaration of solvency required by section 89 must identify the company and state—

(a) the name and a postal address for each director making the declaration (which may be the director's service address provided for by section 163 of the Companies Act);
(b) either—
  (i) that all of the directors, or
  (ii) that a majority of the directors,
  have made a full inquiry into the company's affairs and that, having done so, they have formed the opinion that the company will be able to pay its debts in full together with interest at the official rate within a specified period (which must not exceed 12 months) from the commencement of the winding up; and
(c) that the declaration is accompanied by a statement of the company's assets and liabilities as at a date which is stated (being the latest practicable date before the making of the declaration as required by section 89(2)(b)).

(2) The statement of the company's assets and liabilities must contain—

(a) the date of the statement;
(b) a statement that the statement shows the assets of the company at estimated realisable values and liabilities of the company expected to rank as at the date referred to in sub-paragraph (1)(c);
(c) a summary of the assets of the company, setting out the estimated realisable value of—
  (i) any assets subject to a fixed charge,
  (ii) any assets subject to a floating charge,
  (iii) any uncharged assets; and
  (iv) the total value of all the assets available to preferential creditors;
(d) the value of each of the following secured liabilities of the company expected to rank for payment—
  (i) liabilities secured on specific assets, and
  (ii) liabilities secured by floating charges;
(e) a summary of the unsecured liabilities of the company expected to rank for payment;
(f) the estimated costs of the winding up and other expenses;
(g) the estimated amount of interest accruing until payment of debts in full; and
(h) the estimated value of any surplus after paying debts in full together with interest at the official rate.

CHAPTER 2 THE LIQUIDATOR

[Note: a document required by the Act or these Rules must also contain the standard contents set out in Part 1.]

[10.712]
5.2 Appointment by the company

(1) This rule applies where the liquidator is appointed by the company.

(2) The chair of the meeting, or a director or the secretary of the company in the case of a written resolution of a private company, must certify the appointment when the appointee has provided to the person certifying the appointment a statement to the effect that the appointee is an insolvency practitioner qualified under the Act to be the liquidator and consents to act.

(3) The certificate must be authenticated and dated by the person who certifies the appointment and must contain—

(a) identification details for the company;
(b) identification and contact details for the person appointed as liquidator;
(c) the date the liquidator was appointed; and

(d) a statement that the appointee—
   (i) provided a statement of being qualified to act as an insolvency practitioner in relation to the company,
   (ii) has consented to act, and
   (iii) was appointed liquidator of the company.

(4) Where two or more liquidators are appointed the certificate must also specify (as required by section 231) whether any act required or authorised under any enactment to be done by the liquidator is to be done by all or any one or more of them.

(5) The person who certifies the appointment must deliver the certificate as soon as reasonably practicable to the liquidator, who must keep it as part of the records of the winding up.

(6) Not later than 28 days from the liquidator's appointment, the liquidator must deliver notice of the appointment to the creditors of the company.

[10.713]
5.3 Meetings in members' voluntary winding up of authorised deposit-takers

(1) This rule applies to a meeting of the members of an authorised deposit-taker at which it is intended to propose a resolution for its winding up.

(2) Notice of such a meeting of the company must be delivered by the directors to the Financial Conduct Authority and to the scheme manager established under section 212(1) of the Financial Services and Markets Act 2000.

(3) The notice to the Financial Conduct Authority and the scheme manager must be the same as delivered to members of the company.

(4) The scheme manager is entitled to be represented at any meeting of which it is required by this rule to be given notice.

[10.714]
5.4 Appointment by the court (section 108)

(1) This rule applies where the liquidator is appointed by the court under section 108.

(2) The order of the court must contain—
(a) the name of the court (and hearing centre if applicable) in which the order is made;
(b) the name and title of the judge making the order;
(c) identification details for the company;
(d) the name and address of the applicant;
(e) the capacity in which the applicant made the application;
(f) identification details for the proposed liquidator;
(g) a statement that the appointee has filed with the court a statement to the effect that the appointee is an insolvency practitioner qualified to act as the liquidator and consents to act;
(h) an order that the proposed liquidator, having filed a statement of being qualified to act as an insolvency practitioner in relation to the company and having consented to act, is appointed liquidator of the company from the date of the order, or such other date as the court orders; and
(i) the date of the order.

(3) Where two or more liquidators are appointed the order must also specify (as required by section 231) whether any act required or authorised under any enactment to be done by the liquidator is to be done by all or any one or more of them.

(4) The court must deliver a sealed copy of the order to the liquidator, whose appointment takes effect from the date of the order or from such other date as the court orders.

(5) Not later than 28 days from the liquidator's appointment, the liquidator must deliver notice of the appointment to the creditors of the company.

[10.715]
5.5 Cost of liquidator's security (section 390(3))

The cost of the liquidator's security required by section 390(3) for the proper performance of the liquidator's functions is an expense of the winding up.

[10.716]
5.6 Liquidator's resignation

(1) A liquidator may resign only—
(a) on grounds of ill health;
(b) because of the intention to cease to practise as an insolvency practitioner;
(c) because the further discharge of the duties of liquidator is prevented or made impractical by—
   (i) a conflict of interest, or
   (ii) a change of personal circumstances;
(d) where two or more persons are acting as liquidator jointly and it is the opinion of both or all of them that it is no longer expedient that there should continue to be that number of joint liquidators.

(2) Before resigning, the liquidator must deliver a notice to the members of the company—
(a) stating the liquidator's intention to resign; and
(b) calling a meeting for the members to consider whether a replacement should be appointed;

except where the resignation is under sub-paragraph (1)(d).

(3) The notice must be accompanied by a summary of the liquidator's receipts and payments.

(4) The notice may suggest the name of a replacement liquidator.

(5) The date of the meeting must be not more than five business days before the date on which the liquidator intends to give notice of resignation to the registrar of companies under section 171(5).

(6) The resigning liquidator's release is effective 21 days after the date of delivery of the notice of resignation to the registrar of companies under section 171(5), unless the court orders otherwise.

[10.717]

5.7 Removal of liquidator by the court

(1) This rule applies where an application is made to the court for the removal of the liquidator, or for an order directing the liquidator to summon a company meeting for the purpose of removing the liquidator.

(2) On receipt of an application, the court may, if it is satisfied that no sufficient cause is shown for it, dismiss it without giving notice to any party other than the applicant.

(3) Unless the application is dismissed, the court must fix a venue for it to be heard.

(4) The applicant must, at least 14 days before any hearing, deliver to the liquidator a notice stating the venue with a copy of the application and of any evidence on which the applicant intends to rely.

(5) A respondent may apply for security for the costs of the application and the court may make such an order if it is satisfied, having regard to all the circumstances of the case, that it is just to make such an order.

(6) The liquidator may do either or both of the following at such a hearing—
- (a) file a report of any matters which the liquidator thinks ought to be drawn to the court's attention; or
- (b) appear and be heard on the application.

(7) On a successful application the court's order must contain the following—
- (a) the name of the court (and hearing centre if applicable) in which the order is made;
- (b) the name and title of the judge making the order;
- (c) identification details for the company;
- (d) the name and address of the applicant;
- (e) the capacity in which the applicant made the application;
- (f) identification and contact details for the liquidator (or former liquidator);
- (g) an order either—
  - (i) that the liquidator is removed from office, or
  - (ii) that the liquidator must summon a [company meeting] on or before a date which is stated in the order for the purpose of considering the liquidator's removal from office; and
- (h) the date of the order.

(8) The order of the court may include such provision as the court thinks just relating to matters arising in connection with the removal.

(9) The costs of the application are not payable as an expense of the winding up unless the court orders otherwise.

(10) Where the court removes the liquidator—
- (a) it must deliver the sealed order of removal to the former liquidator; and
- (b) the former liquidator must deliver a copy of the order to the registrar of companies as soon as reasonably practicable.

(11) If the court appoints a new liquidator, rule 5.4 applies.

NOTES

Para (7): words in square brackets in sub-para (g)(ii) substituted by the Insolvency (England and Wales) (Amendment) Rules 2017, SI 2017/366, rr 3, 18, as from 6 April 2017.

[10.718]

5.8 Removal of liquidator by company meeting

A liquidator removed by a meeting of the company must as soon as reasonably practicable deliver notice of the removal to the registrar of companies.

[10.719]

5.9 Delivery of proposed final account to members (section 94)

(1) The liquidator must deliver a notice to the members accompanied by the proposed final account required by section 94(1) and rule 18.14 giving them a minimum of eight weeks' notice of a specified date on which the liquidator intends to deliver the final account as required by section 94(2).

(2) The notice must inform the members that when the company's affairs are fully wound up—
- (a) the liquidator will make up the final account and deliver it to the members; and
- (b) when the final account is delivered to the registrar of companies the liquidator will be released under section 171(6).

(3) The affairs of the company are not fully wound up until the latest of—
- (a) the period referred to in paragraph (1) having expired without the liquidator receiving any request for information under rule 18.9 or the filing of any application to court under that rule or under rule 18.34 (application to court on the grounds that the liquidator's remuneration or expenses are excessive);
- (b) any request for information under rule 18.9 having been finally determined (including any applications to court under that rule); or
- (c) any application to the court under rule 18.34 having been finally determined.

(4) However the liquidator may conclude that the company's affairs are fully wound up before the period referred to in paragraph (1) has expired if every member confirms in writing to the liquidator that they do not intend to make any such request or application.

[10.720]

5.10 Final account prior to dissolution (section 94)

(1) The contents of the final account which the liquidator is required to make up under section 94 must comply with the requirements of rule 18.14.

(2) When the account is delivered to the members under section 94(2) it must be accompanied by a notice which states that—

(a) the company's affairs are fully wound up;

(b) the liquidator having delivered copies of the account to the members must, within 14 days of the date on which the account is made up, deliver a copy of the account to the registrar of companies; and

(c) the liquidator will vacate office and be released under section 171 on delivering the final account to the registrar of companies.

(3) The copy of the account which the liquidator must deliver to the registrar of companies under section 94(3) must be accompanied by a notice stating that the liquidator has delivered the final account of the winding up to the members in accordance with section 94(2).

[10.721]
5.11 Deceased liquidator

(1) If the liquidator dies a notice of the fact and date of death must be delivered as soon as reasonably practicable to—

(a) one of the company's directors; and

(b) the registrar of companies.

(2) One of the following must deliver the notice—

(a) a surviving joint liquidator;

(b) a member of the deceased liquidator's firm (if the deceased was a member or employee of a firm);

(c) an officer of the deceased liquidator's company (if the deceased was an officer or employee of a company); or

(d) a personal representative of the deceased liquidator.

(3) If such notice has not been delivered within the 21 days following the liquidator's death then any other person may deliver the notice.

[10.722]
5.12 Loss of qualification as insolvency practitioner

(1) This rule applies where the liquidator vacates office on ceasing to be qualified to act as an insolvency practitioner in relation to the company.

(2) A notice of the fact must be delivered as soon as reasonably practicable to the registrar of companies and the Secretary of State by one of the following—

(a) the liquidator who has vacated office;

(b) a continuing joint liquidator; or

(c) the recognised professional body which was the source of the vacating liquidator's authorisation to act in relation to the company.

(3) Each notice must be authenticated and dated by the person delivering the notice.

[10.723]
5.13 Liquidator's duties on vacating office

A liquidator who ceases to be in office as a result of removal, resignation or ceasing to be qualified to act as an insolvency practitioner in relation to the company, must as soon as reasonably practicable deliver to the succeeding liquidator—

(a) the assets (after deduction of any expenses properly incurred, and distributions made, by the former liquidator);

(b) the records of the winding up, including correspondence, proofs and other documents relating to the winding up; and

(c) the company's documents and other records.

[10.724]
5.14 Application by former liquidator to the Secretary of State for release (section 173(2)(b))

(1) This rule applies to a liquidator who—

(a) is removed by the court;

(b) vacates office on ceasing to be qualified to act as an insolvency practitioner in relation to the company; or

(c) vacates office in consequence of the court making a winding-up order against the company.

(2) Where the former liquidator applies to the Secretary of State for release the application must contain—

(a) identification details for the former liquidator;

(b) identification details for the company;

(c) the circumstances under which the former liquidator ceased to act as liquidator; and

(d) a statement that the former liquidator is applying to the Secretary of State for release.

(3) The application must be authenticated and dated by the former liquidator.

(4) When the Secretary of State gives a release, the Secretary of State must deliver—

(a) a certificate of the release to the former liquidator; and

(b) a notice of the release to the registrar of companies.

(5) Release is effective from the date of the certificate or such other date as the certificate specifies.

[10.725]
5.15 Power of court to set aside certain transactions entered into by liquidator

(1) If in dealing with the estate the liquidator enters into any transaction with a person who is an associate of the liquidator, the court may, on the application of any interested person, set the transaction aside and order the liquidator to compensate the company for any loss suffered in consequence of it.

(2) This does not apply if either—

(a) the transaction was entered into with the prior consent of the court; or

(b) it is shown to the court's satisfaction that the transaction was for value, and that it was entered into by the liquidator without knowing, or having any reason to suppose, that the person concerned was an associate.

(3) Nothing in this rule is to be taken as prejudicing the operation of any rule of law or equity relating to a liquidator's dealings with trust property, or the fiduciary obligations of any person.

[10.726]

5.16 Rule against improper solicitation by or on behalf of the liquidator

(1) Where the court is satisfied that any improper solicitation has been used by or on behalf of the liquidator in obtaining proxies or procuring the liquidator's appointment, it may order that no remuneration be allowed as an expense of the winding up to any person by whom, or on whose behalf, the solicitation was exercised.

(2) An order of the court under this Rule overrides any resolution of the members, or any other provision of these Rules relating to the liquidator's remuneration.

CHAPTER 3 SPECIAL MANAGER

[Note: a document required by the Act or these Rules must also contain the standard contents set out in Part 1.]

[10.727]

5.17 Application for and appointment of special manager (section 177)

(1) An application by the liquidator under section 177 for the appointment of a special manager must be supported by a report setting out the reasons for the application.

(2) The report must include the applicant's estimate of the value of the business or property in relation to which the special manager is to be appointed.

(3) The court's order appointing a special manager must have the title "Order of Appointment of Special Manager" and must contain—

(a) the name of the court (and hearing centre if applicable) in which the order is made;
(b) the name and title of the judge making the order;
(c) identification details for the proceedings;
(d) the name and address of the applicant;
(e) the name and address of the proposed special manager;
(f) an order that the proposed special manager is appointed as special manager of the company;
(g) details of the special manager's responsibility over the company's business or property;
(h) the powers to be entrusted to the special manager under section [177(3)];
(i) the time allowed for the special manager to give the required security for the appointment;
(j) the duration of the special manager's appointment, being one of the following—
  (i) for a fixed period stated in the order;
  (ii) until the occurrence of a specified event; or
  (iii) until the court makes a further order;
(k) the order that the special manager's remuneration will be fixed from time to time by the court; and
(l) the date of the order and the date on which it takes effect if different.

(4) The appointment of the special manager may be renewed by order of the court.

(5) The acts of the special manager are valid notwithstanding any defect in the special manager's appointment or qualifications.

NOTES

Para (3): figure in square brackets in sub-para (h) substituted by the Insolvency (England and Wales) (Amendment) Rules 2017, SI 2017/366, rr 3, 19, as from 6 April 2017.

[10.728]

5.18 Security

(1) The appointment of the special manager does not take effect until the person appointed has given (or, if the court allows, undertaken to give) security to the liquidator for the appointment.

(2) A person appointed as special manager may give security either specifically for a particular winding up, or generally for any winding up in relation to which that person may be appointed as special manager.

(3) The amount of the security must be not less than the value of the business or property in relation to which the special manager is appointed, as estimated in the liquidator's report which accompanied the application for appointment.

(4) When the special manager has given security to the liquidator, the liquidator must file with the court a certificate as to the adequacy of the security.

(5) The cost of providing the security must be paid in the first instance by the special manager, but the special manager is entitled to be reimbursed as an expense of the winding up.

[10.729]

5.19 Failure to give or keep up security

(1) If the special manager fails to give the required security within the time stated in the order of appointment, or any extension of that time that may be allowed, the liquidator must report the failure to the court, which may discharge the order appointing the special manager.

(2) If the special manager fails to keep up the security, the liquidator must report the failure to the court, which may remove the special manager, and make such order as it thinks just as to costs.

(3) If the court discharges the order appointing the special manager, or makes an order removing the special manager, the court must give directions as to whether any, and if so what, steps should be taken for the appointment of another special manager.

[10.730]
5.20 Accounting

(1) The special manager must produce accounts, containing details of the special manager's receipts and payments, for the approval of the liquidator.

(2) The accounts must be for—

(a) each three month period for the duration of the special manager's appointment; and
(b) any shorter period ending with the termination of the special manager's appointment.

(3) When the accounts have been approved, the special manager's receipts and payments must be added to those of the liquidator.

[10.731]
5.21 Termination of appointment

(1) If the liquidator thinks that the appointment of the special manager is no longer necessary or beneficial for the company, the liquidator must apply to the court for directions, and the court may order the special manager's appointment to be terminated.

(2) The liquidator must also make such an application if the members pass a resolution requesting that the appointment be terminated.

CHAPTER 4 CONVERSION TO CREDITORS' VOLUNTARY WINDING UP

[10.732]
5.22 Statement of affairs (section 95(3))

The rules in Chapter 2 of Part 6 apply to the statement of affairs made out by the liquidator under section 95(1A) where the liquidator is of the opinion that the company will be unable to pay its debts in full (together with interest at the official rate) within the period stated in the directors' declaration under section 89.

PART 6 CREDITORS' VOLUNTARY WINDING UP

CHAPTER 1 APPLICATION OF PART 6

[10.733]
6.1 Application of Part 6

(1) This Part applies to a creditors' voluntary winding up.

(2) However where a company moves from administration to creditors' voluntary winding up by the registration of a notice under paragraph 83(3) of Schedule B1 the following rules do not apply—

6.2 to 6.7 (statement of affairs etc);
6.11 to 6.15 (information to creditors and contributories and appointment of liquidator);
6.17 (report by directors etc);
6.18 (decisions on nomination);
6.20 (appointment by creditors or by the company);
6.22 (appointment by the court (section 100(3) or 108), other than in respect of appointments under section 108); and
6.23 (advertisement of appointment).

CHAPTER 2 STATEMENT OF AFFAIRS AND OTHER INFORMATION

[Note: a document required by the Act or these Rules must also contain the standard contents set out in Part 1.]

[10.734]
6.2 Statement of affairs made out by the liquidator under section 95(1A)

[Note: (1) section 95(4A) requires the statement of affairs to be verified by a statement of truth;

(2) the "official rate" referred to in paragraph (2)(c) is defined in section 251 as being the rate referred to in section 189(4)).]

(1) This rule applies to the statement of affairs made out by the liquidator under section 95(1A) (effect of company's insolvency in members' voluntary winding up).

(2) The statement of affairs must be headed "Statement of affairs" and must contain—

(a) identification details for the company;
(b) a statement that it is a statement of the affairs of the company on a date which is specified, being the date of the opinion formed by the liquidator under section 95(1);
(c) a statement that as at that date, the liquidator formed the opinion that the company would be unable to pay its debts in full (together with interest at the official rate) within the period stated in the directors' declaration of solvency made under section 89; and
(d) the date it is made.

(3) The statement of affairs must be delivered by the liquidator to the registrar of companies within five business days after the completion of the decision procedure or deemed consent procedure referred to in rule 6.11 in respect of the appointment of the liquidator.

(4) However the liquidator must not deliver to the registrar of companies with the statement of affairs any schedule required by rule 6.4(4)(b).

[10.735]
6.3 Statement of affairs made out by the directors under section 99(1)

[Note: section 99(2A) requires the statement of affairs to be verified by a statement of truth.]

(1) This rule applies to the statement of affairs made out by the directors under section 99(1).

(2) The statement of affairs must be headed "Statement of affairs" and must contain—

(a) identification details for the company;
(b) a statement that it is a statement of the affairs of the company on a date which is specified, being a date not more than 14 days before the date of the resolution for winding up; and
(c) the date it is made.

(3) If a creditor requests a copy of the statement of affairs at a time when no liquidator is appointed the directors must deliver a copy to the creditor.

(4) The directors must deliver the statement of affairs to the liquidator as soon as reasonably practicable after the liquidator is appointed.

(5) The liquidator must deliver the statement of affairs to the registrar of companies within five business days after the completion of the decision procedure or deemed consent procedure referred to in rule 6.14 in respect of the appointment of the liquidator.

(6) However the liquidator must not deliver to the registrar of companies with the statement of affairs any schedule required by rule 6.4(4)(b).

[10.736]

6.4 Additional requirements as to statements of affairs

(1) A statement of affairs under section 95(1A) or 99(1) must also contain [the following, and, in addition, where paragraph (1B) applies, the information specified in that paragraph]—
(a) a list of the company's shareholders, with the following details about each shareholder—
(i) name and postal address,
(ii) the type of shares held,
(iii) the nominal amount of the shares held,
(iv) the number of shares held,
(v) the amount per share called up, and
(vi) the total amount called up;
(b) the total amount of shares called up held by all shareholders;
(c) a summary of the assets of the company, setting out the book value and estimated realisable value of—
(i) any assets subject to a fixed charge,
(ii) any assets subject to a floating charge,
(iii) any uncharged assets, and
(iv) the total value of all the assets available for preferential creditors;
(d) a summary of the liabilities of the company, setting out—
(i) the amount of preferential debts,
(ii) an estimate of the deficiency with respect to preferential debts or the surplus available after paying the preferential debts,
(iii) an estimate of the prescribed part, if applicable,
(iv) an estimate of the total assets available to pay debts secured by floating charges,
(v) the amount of debts secured by floating charges,
(vi) an estimate of the deficiency with respect to debts secured by floating charges or the surplus available after paying the debts secured by fixed or floating charges,
(vii) the amount of unsecured debts (excluding preferential debts),
(viii) an estimate of the deficiency with respect to unsecured debts or the surplus available after paying unsecured debts,
(ix) any issued and called-up capital, and
(x) an estimate of the deficiency with respect to, or surplus available to, members of the company;
(e) a list of the company's creditors with the further particulars required by paragraph (2) indicating—
(i) any creditors under hire-purchase, chattel leasing or conditional sale agreements,
(ii) any creditors who are consumers claiming amounts paid in advance of the supply of goods or services, and
(iii) any creditors claiming retention of title over property in the company's possession.

[(1A) Paragraph (1B) applies if a moratorium under Part A1 of the Act is, or has been, in force for the company at any time within the period of 12 weeks ending with the day on which the resolution for a voluntary winding up is passed.

(1B) Where this paragraph applies the statement of affairs must identify which of the debts owed by the company are—
(a) moratorium debts, and
(b) priority pre-moratorium debts,

within the meaning given by section 174A; and
(c) sub-paragraph (1)(c)(iv) has effect as if the reference to preferential creditors included references to moratorium debts and priority pre-moratorium debts within the meaning given by section 174A.
(d) sub-paragraph (1)(d)(i), (ii) and (vii) has effect as if the reference to preferential debts included references to moratorium debts and priority pre-moratorium debts within the meaning given by section 174A.]

(2) The further particulars required by this paragraph relating to each creditor are as follows—
(i) the name and postal address,
(ii) amount of the debt owed to the creditor, (as required by section 95(4) or 99(2)),
(iii) details of any security held by the creditor,
(iv) the date the security was given, and
(v) the value of any such security.

(3) Paragraph (4) applies where the particulars required by paragraph (2) relate to creditors who are either—
(a) employees or former employees of the company; or
(b) consumers claiming amounts paid in advance for the supply of goods or services.

(4) Where this paragraph applies—

(a) the statement of affairs must state separately for each of paragraphs (3)(a) and (b) the number of such creditors and the total of the debts owed to them; and

(b) the particulars required by paragraph (2) must be set out in separate schedules to the statement of affairs for each of paragraphs (3)(a) and (b).

NOTES

Para (1): words in square brackets inserted by the Insolvency (England and Wales) (No 2) (Amendment) Rules 2021, SI 2021/1028, r 28(1), (2), as from 1 October 2021 (for savings provisions see the note to r 1A.1 at **[10.539]**).

Paras (1A), (1B): inserted by SI 2021/1028, r 28(1), (3), as from 1 October 2021 (for savings provisions see the note to r 1A.1 at **[10.539]**).

[10.737]

6.5 Statement of affairs: statement of concurrence

(1) The liquidator may require a director ("the relevant person") to deliver to the liquidator a statement of concurrence.

(2) A statement of concurrence is a statement that the relevant person concurs in the statement of affairs submitted by another director.

(3) The liquidator must inform the director who has been required to submit a statement of affairs that the relevant person has been required to deliver a statement of concurrence.

(4) The director who has been required to submit the statement of affairs must deliver a copy to every relevant person who has been required to submit a statement of concurrence.

(5) A statement of concurrence—

(a) must identify the company; and

(b) may be qualified in relation to matters dealt with in the statement of affairs, where the maker of the statement of concurrence—

(i) is not in agreement with the statement of affairs,

(ii) considers the statement of affairs to be erroneous or misleading, or

(iii) is without the direct knowledge necessary for concurring with it.

(6) The relevant person must deliver the required statement of concurrence, verified by a statement of truth, to the liquidator together with a copy before the end of the period of five business days (or such other period as the liquidator may agree) beginning with the day on which the relevant person receives the statement of affairs.

(7) The liquidator must deliver the verified statement of concurrence to the registrar of companies.

[10.738]

6.6 Order limiting disclosure of statement of affairs etc

(1) Where the liquidator thinks that disclosure of the whole or part of the statement of affairs or of any statement of concurrence would be likely to prejudice the conduct of the winding up or might reasonably be expected to lead to violence against any person, the liquidator may apply to the court for an order that the statement of affairs, statement of concurrence or any specified part of them must not be delivered to the registrar of companies.

(2) The court may order that the whole or a specified part of the statement of affairs or a statement of concurrence must not be delivered to the registrar of companies.

(3) The liquidator must as soon as reasonably practicable deliver to the registrar of companies a copy of the order, the statement of affairs and any statement of concurrence to the extent allowed by the order.

[10.739]

6.7 Expenses of statement of affairs and decisions sought from creditors

(1) Any reasonable and necessary expenses of preparing the statement of affairs under section 99 may be paid out of the company's assets, either before or after the commencement of the winding up, as an expense of the winding up.

(2) Any reasonable and necessary expenses of the decision procedure or deemed consent procedure to seek a decision from the creditors on the nomination of a liquidator under rule 6.14 may be paid out of the company's assets, either before or after the commencement of the winding up, as an expense of the winding up.

(3) Where payment under paragraph (1) or (2) is made before the commencement of the winding up, the directors must deliver to the creditors with the statement of affairs a statement of the amount of the payment and the identity of the person to whom it was made.

(4) The liquidator appointed under section 100 may make such a payment, but if there is a liquidation committee, the liquidator must deliver to the committee at least five business days' notice of the intention to make it.

(5) However such a payment may not be made to the liquidator, or to any associate of the liquidator, otherwise than with the approval of the liquidation committee, the creditors, or the court.

(6) This is without prejudice to the court's powers under rule 7.109 (voluntary winding up superseded by winding up by the court).

[10.740]

6.8 Delivery of accounts to liquidator (section 235)

(1) A person who is specified in section 235(3) must deliver to the liquidator accounts of the company of such nature, as at such date, and for such period, as the liquidator requires.

(2) The period for which the liquidator may require accounts may begin from a date up to three years before the date of the resolution for winding up, or from an earlier date to which audited accounts of the company were last prepared.

(3) The accounts must, if the liquidator so requires, be verified by a statement of truth.

(4) The accounts (verified by a statement of truth if so required) must be delivered to the liquidator within 21 days from the liquidator's request, or such longer period as the liquidator may allow.

[10.741]

6.9 Expenses of assistance in preparing accounts

(1) Where the liquidator requires a person to deliver accounts under rule 6.8 the liquidator may, with the approval of the liquidation committee (if there is one) and as an expense of the winding up, employ a person or firm to assist that person in the preparation of the accounts.

(2) The person who is required to deliver accounts may request an allowance of all or part of the expenses to be incurred in employing a person or firm to assist in preparing the accounts.

(3) A request for an allowance must be accompanied by an estimate of the expenses involved.

(4) The liquidator must only authorise the employment of a named person or a named firm approved by the liquidator.

(5) The liquidator may, with the approval of the liquidation committee (if there is one), authorise such an allowance, payable as an expense of the winding up.

CHAPTER 3 NOMINATION AND APPOINTMENT OF LIQUIDATORS AND INFORMATION TO CREDITORS

[Note: a document required by the Act or these Rules must also contain the standard contents set out in Part 1.]

[10.742]

6.10 Application of the rules in this Chapter

(1) The rules in this Chapter apply as follows.

(2) Rules 6.11 to 6.13 only apply to a conversion from a members' voluntary winding up to a creditors' voluntary winding up.

(3) Rule 6.16 only applies where the administrator becomes the liquidator in a voluntary winding up which follows an administration.

(4) Rules 6.14, 6.15 and 6.17 only apply to a creditors' voluntary winding up which has not been commenced by a conversion from a members' voluntary winding up or an administration.

(5) Rules 6.18 and 6.19 apply to all creditors' voluntary windings up.

[10.743]

6.11 Nomination of liquidator and information to creditors on conversion from members' voluntary winding up (section 96)

(1) This rule applies in respect of the conversion of a members' voluntary winding up to a creditors' voluntary winding up under section 96.

(2) The liquidator must seek a nomination from the creditors for a liquidator in the creditors' voluntary winding up by—

(a) a decision procedure; or

(b) the deemed consent procedure.

(3) The liquidator must deliver to the creditors a copy of the statement of affairs required by section 95(1A) and Chapter 2 of this Part together with a notice which complies with rules 15.7 or 15.8 so far as are relevant.

(4) The notice must also contain—

(a) identification and contact details for the existing liquidator; and

(b) a statement that if no person is nominated by the creditors then the existing liquidator will be the liquidator in the creditors' voluntary winding up.

(5) The decision date in the notice must be not later than 28 days from the date under section 95(1) that the liquidator formed the opinion that the company will be unable to pay its debts in full.

(6) Subject to paragraph (9), the creditors must be given at least 14 days' notice of the decision date.

(7) Paragraph (8) applies where—

(a) the liquidator has sought a decision from creditors on the nomination of a liquidator by the deemed consent procedure; but

(b) the level of objections to the proposed nomination have meant, under section 246ZF, that no nomination is deemed to have been made.

(8) Where this paragraph applies, the liquidator must seek a nomination from creditors by way of a decision procedure in accordance with this rule, the decision date to be as soon as reasonably practicable, but no more than 28 days from the date that the level of objections had the effect that no nomination was deemed to have been made.

(9) Where paragraph (8) applies, the creditors must be given at least seven days' notice of the decision date.

(10) Where the liquidator is required by rule 15.6 to summon a physical meeting as a result of requests from creditors received in response to a notice delivered under this rule, the physical meeting must be summoned to take place—

(a) within 28 days of the date on which the threshold for requiring a physical meeting was met; and

(b) with at least 14 days' notice.

[10.744]

6.12 Creditors' decision on appointment other than at a meeting (conversion from members' voluntary winding up)

(1) This rule applies where the creditors' decision on the nomination of a liquidator in a conversion of a members' into a creditors' voluntary winding up is intended to be sought otherwise than through a meeting or through the deemed consent procedure, including where the conditions in rule 6.11(7) are met and the liquidator, under rule 6.11(8), goes on to seek a nomination from creditors by way of a decision procedure other than a meeting.

(2) Instead of delivering a notice of the decision procedure or deemed consent procedure under rule 6.11, the liquidator must deliver a notice to creditors inviting them to make proposals for the nomination of a liquidator.

(3) Such a notice must—

(a) identify any liquidator for whom a proposal which is in compliance with paragraph 4 has already been received;

(b) explain that the liquidator is not obliged to seek the creditors' views on any proposal that does not meet the requirements of paragraphs (4) and (5); and

(c) be accompanied by the statement of affairs unless that has previously been delivered to the creditor.

(4) Any proposal must state the name and contact details of the proposed liquidator, and contain a statement that the proposed liquidator is qualified to act as an insolvency practitioner in relation to the company and has consented to act as liquidator of the company.

(5) Any proposal must be received by the liquidator within five business days of the date of the notice under paragraph (2).

(6) Within two business days of the end of the period referred to in paragraph (5), the liquidator must [send] a notice to creditors of a decision procedure under rule 6.11.

NOTES

Para (6): word in square brackets substituted by the Insolvency (England and Wales) (Amendment) Rules 2017, SI 2017/366, rr 3, 23, as from 6 April 2017.

[10.745]

6.13 Information to creditors and contributories (conversion of members' voluntary winding up into creditors' voluntary winding up)

(1) The liquidator must deliver to the creditors and contributories within 28 days of the conversion of a members' voluntary winding up into a creditors' voluntary winding up under section 96 a notice which must contain—

(a) the date the winding up became a creditors' voluntary winding up;

(b) a report of the decision procedure or deemed consent procedure which took place under rule [6.11]; and

(c) the information required by paragraph (3).

(2) The notice must be accompanied by a copy of the statement of affairs or a summary except where the notice is being delivered to a creditor to whom a copy of the statement of affairs has previously been delivered under section 95(1A).

(3) The required information is an estimate to the best of the liquidator's knowledge and belief of—

(a) the value of the prescribed part (whether or not the liquidator might be required under section 176A to make the prescribed part available for the satisfaction of unsecured debts); and

(b) the value of the company's net property (as defined by section 176A(6)).

(4) The liquidator may exclude from an estimate under paragraph (3) information the disclosure of which could seriously prejudice the commercial interests of the company.

(5) If the exclusion of such information affects the calculation of an estimate, the report must say so.

(6) If the liquidator proposes to make an application to court under section 176A(5) the report must say so and give the reason for the application.

NOTES

Para (1): figure in square brackets in sub-para (b) substituted by the Insolvency (England and Wales) (Amendment) Rules 2017, SI 2017/366, rr 3, 22, as from 6 April 2017.

[10.746]

6.14 Information to creditors and appointment of liquidator

(1) This rule applies in respect of the appointment of a liquidator under section 100.

(2) The directors of the company must deliver to the creditors a notice seeking their decision on the nomination of a liquidator by—

(a) the deemed consent procedure; or

(b) a virtual meeting.

(3) The decision date for the decision of the creditors on the nomination of a liquidator must be not earlier than three business days after the notice under paragraph (2) is delivered but not later than 14 days after the resolution is passed to wind up the company.

(4) Where the directors have sought a decision from the creditors through the deemed consent procedure under paragraph (2)(a) but, pursuant to section 246ZF(5)(a) (deemed consent procedure), more than the specified number of creditors object so that the decision cannot be treated as having been made, the directors must then seek a decision from the creditors on the nomination of a liquidator by holding a physical meeting under rule 15.6 (physical meetings) as if a physical meeting had been required under section 246ZE(4) (decisions by creditors and contributories: general).

(5) Where paragraph (4) applies, the meeting must not be held earlier than three business days after the notice under rule 15.6(3) is delivered or later than 14 days after the level of objections reach that described in paragraph (4).

(6) A request for a physical meeting under section 246ZE must be made in accordance with rule 15.6 except that—

(a) such a request may be made at any time between the delivery of the notice under paragraph (2) and the decision date under paragraph (3); and

(b) the decision date where this paragraph applies must be not earlier than three business days after the notice under rule 15.6(3) is delivered and not later than 14 days after the level of requests reach that described in section 246ZE.

(7) The directors must deliver to the creditors a copy of the statement of affairs required under section 99 of the Act not later than on the business day before the decision date.

(8) A notice delivered under paragraph (2), in addition to the information required by rules 15.7 (deemed consent) and 15.8 (notices to creditors of decision procedure), must contain—

(a) the date the resolution to wind up is to be considered or was passed;

(b) identification and contact details of any liquidator nominated by the company;

(c) a statement of either—

(i) the name and address of a person qualified to act as an insolvency practitioner in relation to the company who during the period before the decision date, will furnish creditors free of charge with such information concerning the company's affairs as they may reasonably require, or

(ii) a place in the relevant locality where, on the two business days falling next before the decision date, a list of the names and addresses of the company's creditors will be available for inspection free of charge; and

(d) where the notice is sent to creditors in advance of the copy of the statement of affairs, a statement that the directors, before the decision date and before the end of the period of seven days beginning with the day after the day on which the company passed a resolution for winding up, are required by section 99 of the Insolvency Act 1986—

(i) to make out a statement in the prescribed form as to the affairs of the company, and

(ii) send the statement to the company's creditors.

(9) Where the company's principal place of business in England or Wales was situated in different localities at different times during the relevant period, the duty imposed by sub-paragraph (8)(c)(ii) above applies separately in relation to each of those localities.

(10) Where the company had no place of business in England or Wales during the relevant period, the reference in paragraph (9) to the company's principal place of business in England or Wales are replaced by references to its registered office.

(11) In paragraph (9), "the relevant period" means the period of six months immediately preceding the day on which the notices referred to in paragraph (2) were delivered.

(12) Where a virtual or physical meeting is held under this rule and a liquidator has already been nominated by the company, the liquidator or an appointed person must attend any meeting held under this rule and report on any exercise of the liquidator's powers under section 112, 165 or 166 of the Act.

(13) A director who is in default in seeking a decision on the nomination of a liquidator in accordance with this rule is guilty of an offence and is liable to a fine.

[10.747]

6.15 Information to creditors and contributories

(1) The liquidator must deliver to the creditors and contributories within 28 days of the appointment of the liquidator under section 100 a notice which must—

(a) be accompanied by a statement of affairs or a summary where the notice is delivered to any contributory or creditor to whom the notice under rule 6.14 was not delivered;

(b) [be accompanied by] a report on the decision procedure or deemed consent procedure under rule 6.14; and

(c) be accompanied by the information required by paragraph (2).

(2) The required information is an estimate to the best of the liquidator's knowledge and belief of—

(a) the value of the prescribed part (whether or not the liquidator might be required under section 176A to make the prescribed part available for the satisfaction of unsecured debts); and

(b) the value of the company's net property (as defined by section 176A(6)).

(3) The liquidator may exclude from an estimate under paragraph (2) information the disclosure of which could seriously prejudice the commercial interests of the company.

(4) If the exclusion of such information affects the calculation of an estimate, the report must say so.

(5) If the liquidator proposes to make an application to court under section 176A(5) the report must say so and give the reason for the application.

NOTES

Para (1): words in square brackets inserted by the Insolvency (England and Wales) and Insolvency (Scotland) (Miscellaneous and Consequential Amendments) Rules 2017, SI 2017/1115, rr 2, 6, as from 8 December 2017.

[10.748]

6.16 Further information where administrator becomes liquidator (paragraph 83(3) of Schedule B1)

(1) This rule applies where an administrator becomes liquidator on the registration of a notice under paragraph 83(3) of Schedule B1, and becomes aware of creditors not formerly known to that person as administrator.

(2) The liquidator must deliver to those creditors a copy of any statement delivered by the administrator to creditors in accordance with paragraph 49(4) of Schedule B1 and rule 3.35.

[10.749]

6.17 Report by director etc

(1) Where the statement of affairs sent to creditors under section 99(1) does not, or will not, state the company's affairs at the decision date for the creditors' nomination of a liquidator, the directors of the company must cause a report (written or oral) to be made to the creditors in accordance with this rule on any material transactions relating to the company occurring between the date of the making of the statement and the decision date.

(2) In the case of a decision being taken through a meeting, the report must be made at the meeting by the director chairing the meeting or by another person with knowledge of the relevant matters.

(3) Where the deemed consent procedure is used, the report must be delivered to creditors as soon as reasonably practicable after the material transaction takes place in the same manner as the deemed consent procedure.

(4) Where the decision date is within the period of three business days from the delivery of a report under paragraph (3), this rule extends the decision date until the end of that period notwithstanding the requirement in rule 6.14(3) relating to the timing of the decision date.

(5) On delivery of a report under paragraph (3), the directors must notify the creditors of the effects of paragraph (4).

(6) A report under this rule must be recorded in the record of the decision under rule 15.40.

[10.750]

6.18 Decisions on nomination

(1) In the case of a decision on the nomination of a liquidator—

(a) if on any vote there are two nominees, the person who obtains the most support is appointed;

(b) if there are three or more nominees, and one of them has a clear majority over both or all the others together, that one is appointed; and

(c) in any other case, the convener or chair must continue to take votes (disregarding at each vote any nominee who has withdrawn and, if no nominee has withdrawn, the nominee who obtained the least support last time) until a clear majority is obtained for any one nominee.

(2) In the case of a decision being made at a meeting, the chair may at any time put to the meeting a resolution for the joint nomination of any two or more nominees.

[10.751]

6.19 Invitation to creditors to form a liquidation committee

(1) Where any decision is sought from the company's creditors—

(a) in a creditors' voluntary winding up; or

(b) where a members' voluntary winding up is converting in a creditors' voluntary winding up;

the convener of the decision must at the same time deliver to the creditors a notice inviting them to decide whether a liquidation committee should be established if sufficient creditors are willing to be members of the committee.

(2) The notice must also invite nominations for membership of the committee, such nominations to be received by a date specified in the notice.

(3) The notice must state that nominations—

(a) must be delivered to the convener by the specified date; and

(b) can only be accepted if the convener is satisfied as to the creditor's eligibility under rule 17.4.

CHAPTER 4 THE LIQUIDATOR

[Note: a document required by the Act or these Rules must also contain the standard contents set out in Part 1.]

[10.752]

6.20 Appointment by creditors or by the company

(1) This rule applies where a person is appointed as liquidator by creditors or the company.

[(2) The liquidator's appointment takes effect from the date of the passing of the resolution of the company or, where the creditors decide to appoint a person who is not the person appointed by the company, from the relevant decision date.]

(3) Their appointment must be certified by—

(a) the convener or chair of the decision procedure or deemed consent procedure; or

(b) in respect of an appointment by the company the chair of the company meeting or a director or the secretary of the company (in the case of a written resolution).

(4) The person who certifies the appointment must not do so unless and until the proposed liquidator ("the appointee") has provided that person with a statement of being an insolvency practitioner qualified under the Act to be the liquidator and of consenting to act.

(5) The certificate must be authenticated and dated by the person who certifies the appointment and must contain—

(a) identification details for the company;

(b) identification and contact details for the person appointed as liquidator;

(c) the date of the meeting of the company or conclusion of the decision procedure or deemed consent procedure when the liquidator was appointed;

(d) a statement that the appointee—

(i) has provided a statement of being qualified to act as an insolvency practitioner in relation to the company,

(ii) has consented to act, and

(iii) was appointed liquidator of the company.

(6) Where two or more liquidators are appointed the certificate must also specify (as required by section 231) whether any act required or authorised under any enactment to be done by the liquidator is to be done by all or any one or more of them.

(7) The person who certifies the appointment must deliver the certificate as soon as reasonably practicable to the liquidator, who must keep it as part of the records of the winding up.

NOTES

Para (2): substituted by the Insolvency (England and Wales) (Amendment) Rules 2017, SI 2017/366, rr 3, 24, as from 6 April 2017.

[10.753]

6.21 Power to fill vacancy in office of liquidator

Where a vacancy in the office of liquidator occurs in the manner mentioned in section 104 a decision procedure to fill the vacancy may be initiated by any creditor or, if there was more than one liquidator, by the continuing liquidator or liquidators.

[10.754]

6.22 Appointment by the court (section 100(3) or 108)

(1) This rule applies where the liquidator is appointed by the court under section 100(3) or 108.

(2) The court's order must not be made unless and until the proposed liquidator has filed with the court a statement of being qualified under the Act to act as an insolvency practitioner in relation to the company and of consenting to act.

(3) The order of the court must contain—

- (a) the name of the court (and hearing centre if applicable) in which the order is made;
- (b) the name and title of the judge making the order;
- (c) the date on which it is made;
- (d) identification details for the company;
- (e) the name and postal address of the applicant;
- (f) the capacity in which the applicant made the application;
- (g) identification details for the proposed liquidator; and
- (h) an order that the proposed liquidator, having filed a statement of being qualified to act as an insolvency practitioner in relation to the company and having consented to act, is appointed liquidator of the company from the date of the order, or such other date as the court orders.

(4) Where two or more liquidators are appointed the order must also specify (as required by section 231) whether any act required or authorised under any enactment to be done by the liquidator is to be done by all or any one or more of them.

(5) The court must deliver a sealed copy of the order to the liquidator.

(6) Within 28 days from appointment, the liquidator must—

- (a) deliver a notice of the appointment to creditors of the company; or
- (b) advertise the appointment in accordance with any directions given by the court.

[10.755]
6.23 Advertisement of appointment

(1) A liquidator appointed in a voluntary winding up in addition to delivering a notice of the appointment in accordance with section 109(1) may advertise the notice in such other manner as the liquidator thinks fit.

(2) The notice must state—

- (a) that a liquidator has been appointed; and
- (b) the date of the appointment.

(3) The liquidator must initially bear the expense of giving notice under this rule but is entitled to be reimbursed for the expenditure as an expense of the winding up.

[10.756]
[6.23A Additional requirements as to advertisement where moratorium under Part A1 of the Act in force

(1) This rule applies in the case of a voluntary winding up where, immediately before the company goes into liquidation, a moratorium under Part A1 of the Act is in force for that company.

(2) Where this rules applies the liquidator must, in addition to delivering a notice of the appointment in accordance with section 109(1), deliver notice of the liquidator's appointment to the monitor.

(3) Notice under this rule must be given within the period of 14 days beginning with the day on which the liquidator is appointed.]

NOTES

Commencement: 1 October 2021.

Inserted by the Insolvency (England and Wales) (No 2) (Amendment) Rules 2021, SI 2021/1028, r 29, as from 1 October 2021 (for savings provisions see the note to r 1A.1 at **[10.539]**).

[10.757]
6.24 Cost of liquidator's security (section 390(3))

The cost of the liquidator's security required by section 390(3) for the proper performance of the liquidator's functions is an expense of the winding up.

[10.758]
6.25 Liquidator's resignation and replacement

(1) A liquidator may resign only—

- (a) on grounds of ill health;
- (b) because of the intention to cease to practise as an insolvency practitioner;
- (c) because the further discharge of the duties of liquidator is prevented or made impractical by—
  - (i) a conflict of interest, or
  - (ii) or a change of personal circumstances; or
- (d) where two or more persons are acting as liquidator jointly and it is the opinion of both or all of them that it is no longer expedient that there should continue to be that number of joint liquidators.

(2) Before resigning the liquidator must invite the creditors by a decision procedure, or by deemed consent, to consider whether a replacement should be appointed except where the resignation is under paragraph (1)(d).

(3) The notice of the decision procedure or of deemed consent must—

- (a) state the liquidator's intention to resign;
- (b) state that under rule 6.25(7) of these Rules the liquidator will be released 21 days after the date of delivery of the notice of resignation to the registrar of companies under section 171(5), unless the court orders otherwise; and
- (c) comply with rules 15.7 and 15.8 so far as are relevant.

(4) The notice may suggest the name of a replacement liquidator.

(5) The notice must be accompanied by a summary of the liquidator's receipts and payments.

(6) The decision date must be not more than five business days before the date on which the liquidator intends to give notice of resignation to the registrar of companies under section 171(5).

(7) The resigning liquidator's release is effective 21 days after the date of delivery of the notice of resignation to the registrar of companies under section 171(5), unless the court orders otherwise.

[10.759]

6.26 Removal of liquidator by creditors

(1) Where the creditors decide that the liquidator be removed, the convener of the decision procedure or the chair of the meeting (as the case may be) must as soon as reasonably practicable deliver the certificate of the liquidator's removal to the removed liquidator.

(2) The removed liquidator must deliver a notice of the removal to the registrar of companies as soon as reasonably practicable.

[10.760]

6.27 Removal of liquidator by the court

(1) This rule applies where an application is made to the court for the removal of the liquidator, or for an order directing the liquidator to initiate a decision procedure of creditors for the purpose of removing the liquidator.

(2) On receipt of an application, the court may, if it is satisfied that no sufficient cause is shown for it, dismiss it without giving notice to any party other than the applicant.

(3) Unless the application is dismissed, the court must fix a venue for it to be heard.

(4) The applicant must, at least 14 days before any hearing, deliver to the liquidator a notice stating the venue with a copy of the application and of any evidence on which the applicant intends to rely.

(5) A respondent may apply for security for the costs of the application and the court may make such an order if it is satisfied, having regard to all the circumstances of the case, that it is just to make such an order.

(6) The liquidator may do either or both of the following—

- (a) file a report of any matters which the liquidator thinks ought to be drawn to the court's attention; or
- (b) appear and be heard on the application.

(7) The costs of the application are not payable as an expense of the winding up unless the court orders otherwise.

(8) On a successful application the court's order must contain the following—

- (a) the name of the court (and hearing centre if applicable) in which the order is made;
- (b) the name and title of the judge making the order;
- (c) identification details for the company;
- (d) the name and postal address of the applicant;
- (e) the capacity in which the applicant made the application;
- (f) identification and contact details for the liquidator;
- (g) an order either—
  - (i) that the liquidator is removed from office from the date of the order (unless the order specifies otherwise), or
  - (ii) that the liquidator must initiate a decision procedure of the company's creditors (specifying which procedure is to be used) on or before a date stated in the order for the purpose of considering the liquidator's removal from office; and
- (h) the date of the order.

(9) Where the court removes the liquidator—

- (a) it must deliver the sealed order of removal to the former liquidator; and
- (b) the former liquidator must deliver a copy of the order to the registrar of companies as soon as reasonably practicable.

(10) If the court appoints a new liquidator rule 6.22 applies.

[10.761]

6.28 Final account prior to dissolution (section 106)

(1) The final account which the liquidator is required to make up under section 106(1) and deliver to members and creditors must comply with the requirements of rule 18.14.

(2) When the account is delivered to the creditors it must be accompanied by a notice which states—

- (a) that the company's affairs are fully wound up;
- (b) that the creditors have the right to request information from the liquidator under rule 18.9;
- (c) that the creditors have the right to challenge the liquidator's remuneration and expenses under rule 18.34;
- (d) that a creditor may object to the release of the liquidator by giving notice in writing to the liquidator before the end of the prescribed period;
- (e) that the prescribed period is the period ending at the later of—
  - (i) eight weeks after delivery of the notice, or
  - (ii) if any request for information under rule 18.9 or any application to court under that rule or rule 18.34 is made, when that request or application is finally determined;
- (f) that the liquidator will vacate office under section 171 on delivering to the registrar of companies the final account and notice saying whether any creditor has objected to release; and
- (g) that the liquidator will be released under section 173 at the same time as vacating office unless any of the company's creditors objected to the liquidator's release.

(3) The copy of the account which the liquidator delivers to the registrar of companies under section 106(3) must be accompanied by a notice containing the statement required by section 106(3)(a) of whether any creditors have objected to the liquidator's release.

(4) Where a creditor has objected to the liquidator's release rule 6.33 applies to an application by the liquidator to the Secretary of State for release.

(5) The liquidator is not obliged to prepare or deliver any progress report which may become due under these Rules in the period between the date to which the final account is made up and the date when the account is delivered to the registrar of companies under section 106(3)(a).

[10.762]
6.29 Deceased liquidator

(1) If the liquidator dies a notice of the fact and date of death must be delivered as soon as reasonably practicable—
- (a) where there is a liquidation committee, to the members of that committee; and
- (b) to the registrar of companies.

(2) The notice must be delivered by one of the following—
- (a) a surviving joint liquidator;
- (b) a member of the deceased liquidator's firm (if the deceased was a member or employee of a firm);
- (c) an officer of the deceased liquidator's company (if the deceased was an officer or employee of a company); or
- (d) a personal representative of the deceased liquidator.

(3) If such a notice has not been delivered within the 21 days following the liquidator's death then any other person may deliver the notice.

[10.763]
6.30 Loss of qualification as insolvency practitioner

(1) This rule applies where the liquidator vacates office on ceasing to be qualified to act as an insolvency practitioner in relation to the company.

(2) A notice of the fact must be delivered as soon as reasonably practicable to the registrar of companies and the Secretary of State by one of the following—
- (a) the liquidator who has vacated office;
- (b) a continuing joint liquidator;
- (c) the recognised professional body which was the source of the vacating liquidator's authorisation to act in relation to the company.

(3) Each notice must be authenticated and dated by the person delivering the notice.

[10.764]
6.31 Vacation of office on making of winding-up order

Where the liquidator vacates office in consequence of the court making a winding-up order against the company, rule 6.33 applies in relation to the application to the Secretary of State for release of the liquidator.

[10.765]
6.32 Liquidator's duties on vacating office

A liquidator who ceases to be in office in consequence of removal, resignation or ceasing to be qualified as an insolvency practitioner in relation to the company, must as soon as reasonably practicable deliver to the succeeding liquidator—
- (a) the assets (after deduction of any expenses properly incurred, and distributions made, by the former liquidator);
- (b) the records of the winding up, including correspondence, proofs and other documents; and
- (c) the company's records.

[10.766]
6.33 Application by former liquidator for release (section 173(2)(b))

(1) An application to the Secretary of State by a former liquidator for release under section 173(2)(b) must contain—
- (a) identification and contact details for the former liquidator;
- (b) identification details for the company;
- (c) details of the circumstances under which the liquidator has ceased to act as liquidator;
- (d) a statement that the former liquidator of the company is applying to the Secretary of State for a certificate of release as liquidator as a result of the circumstances specified in the application.

(2) The application must be authenticated and dated by the former liquidator.

(3) When the Secretary of State releases the former liquidator, the Secretary of State must certify the release and deliver the certificate to the former liquidator whose release is effective from the date of the certificate or such other date as the certificate specifies.

(4) The Secretary of State must deliver a notice of the release to the registrar of companies.

[10.767]
6.34 Power of court to set aside certain transactions

(1) If in dealing with the insolvent estate the liquidator enters into any transaction with a person who is an associate of the liquidator, the court may, on the application of any interested person, set the transaction aside and order the liquidator to compensate the company for any loss suffered in consequence of it.

(2) This does not apply if either—
- (a) the transaction was entered into with the prior consent of the court; or
- (b) it is shown to the court's satisfaction that the transaction was for value, and that it was entered into by the liquidator without knowing, or having any reason to suppose, that the person concerned was an associate.

(3) Nothing in this rule is to be taken as prejudicing the operation of any rule of law or equity relating to a liquidator's dealings with trust property or the fiduciary obligations of any person.

[10.768]
6.35 Rule against improper solicitation

(1) Where the court is satisfied that any improper solicitation has been used by or on behalf of the liquidator in obtaining proxies or procuring the liquidator's appointment, it may order that no remuneration be allowed as an expense of the winding up to any person by whom, or on whose behalf, the solicitation was exercised.

(2) An order of the court under this rule overrides any resolution of the liquidation committee or the creditors, or any other provision of these Rules relating to the liquidator's remuneration.

[10.769]
6.36 Permission for exercise of powers by liquidator

(1) Where these Rules require permission for the liquidator to exercise a power any permission given must not be a general permission but must relate to a particular proposed exercise of the liquidator's power.

(2) A person dealing with the liquidator in good faith and for value is not concerned to enquire whether any such permission has been given.

(3) Where the liquidator has done anything without such permission, the court or the liquidation committee may, for the purpose of enabling the liquidator to meet the liquidator's expenses out of the assets, ratify what the liquidator has done; but neither may do so unless satisfied that the liquidator has acted in a case of urgency and has sought ratification without undue delay.

(4) In this rule "permission" includes "sanction".

CHAPTER 5 SPECIAL MANAGER

[Note: a document required by the Act or these Rules must also contain the standard contents set out in Part 1.]

[10.770]
6.37 Application for and appointment of special manager (section 177)

(1) An application by the liquidator under section 177 for the appointment of a special manager must be supported by a report setting out the reasons for the application.

(2) The report must include the applicant's estimate of the value of the business or property in relation to which the special manager is to be appointed.

(3) The court's order appointing a special manager must have the title "Order of Appointment of Special Manager" and must contain—

- (a) the name of the court (and hearing centre if applicable) in which the order is made;
- (b) the name and title of the judge making the order;
- (c) identification details for the proceedings;
- (d) the name and address of the applicant;
- (e) the name and address of the proposed special manager;
- (f) the order that that the proposed special manager is appointed as special manager of the company from the date of the order (or otherwise as the order provides);
- (g) details of the special manager's responsibility over the company's business or property;
- (h) the powers entrusted to the special manager under section [177(3)];
- (i) the time allowed for the special manager to give the required security for the appointment;
- (j) the duration of the special manager's appointment, being one of the following—
  - (i) for a fixed period stated in the order,
  - (ii) until the occurrence of a specified event, or
  - (iii) until the court makes a further order;
- (k) the order that the special manager's remuneration will be fixed from time to time by the court; and
- (l) the date of the order.

(4) The appointment of the special manager may be renewed by order of the court.

(5) The acts of the special manager are valid notwithstanding any defect in the special manager's appointment or qualifications.

NOTES

Para (3): figure in square brackets in sub-para (h) substituted by the Insolvency (England and Wales) (Amendment) Rules 2017, SI 2017/366, rr 3, 20, as from 6 April 2017.

Note: sub-para (3)(f) above is reproduced as per the original Queen's Printer's version of these Rules.

[10.771]
6.38 Security

(1) The appointment of the special manager does not take effect until the person appointed has given (or, if the court allows, undertaken to give) security to the applicant for the appointment.

(2) A person appointed as special manager may give security either specifically for a particular winding up, or generally for any winding up in relation to which that person may be appointed as special manager.

(3) The amount of the security must be not less than the value of the business or property in relation to which the special manager is appointed, as estimated in the applicant's report which accompanied the application for appointment.

(4) When the special manager has given security to the applicant, the applicant must file with the court a certificate as to the adequacy of the security.

(5) The cost of providing the security must be paid in the first instance by the special manager; but the special manager is entitled to be reimbursed as an expense of the winding up, in the prescribed order of priority.

[10.772]
6.39 Failure to give or keep up security

(1) If the special manager fails to give the required security within the time stated in the order of appointment, or any extension of that time that may be allowed, the liquidator must report the failure to the court which may discharge the order appointing the special manager.

(2) If the special manager fails to keep up the security, the liquidator must report the failure to the court, which may remove the special manager, and make such order as it thinks just as to costs.

(3) If the court discharges the order appointing the special manager or makes an order removing the special manager, the court must give directions as to whether any, and if so what, steps should be taken for the appointment of another special manager.

[10.773]
6.40 Accounting

(1) The special manager must produce accounts, containing details of the special manager's receipts and payments, for the approval of the liquidator.

(2) The account must be for—
- (a) each three month period for the duration of the special manager's appointment;
- (b) any shorter period ending with the termination of the special manager's appointment.

(3) When the accounts have been approved, the special manager's receipts and payments must be added to those of the liquidator.

[10.774]
6.41 Termination of appointment

(1) If the liquidator thinks that the employment of the special manager is no longer necessary or beneficial for the company, the liquidator must apply to the court for directions, and the court may order the special manager's appointment to be terminated.

(2) The liquidator must also make such an application if the creditors decide that the appointment should be terminated.

CHAPTER 6 PRIORITY OF PAYMENT OF COSTS AND EXPENSES, ETC

[10.775]
6.42 General rule as to priority

(1) All fees, costs, charges and other expenses incurred in the course of the winding up are to be treated as expenses of the winding up.

(2) The expenses of the winding up are payable out of—
- (a) assets of the company available for the payment of general creditors, including—
  - (i) proceeds of any legal action which the liquidator has power to bring in the liquidator's own name or in the name of the company,
  - (ii) proceeds arising from any award made under any arbitration or other dispute resolution procedure which the liquidator has power to bring in the liquidator's own name or in the name of the company,
  - (iii) any payments made under any compromise or other agreement intended to avoid legal action or recourse to arbitration or to any other dispute resolution procedure, and
  - (iv) payments made as a result of an assignment or a settlement of any such action, arbitration or other dispute resolution procedure in lieu of or before any judgment being given or award being made; and
- (b) subject as provided in rules 6.44 to 6.48, property comprised in or subject to a floating charge created by the company.

(3) The expenses associated with the prescribed part must be paid out of the prescribed part.

(4) Subject as provided in rules 6.44 to 6.48, the expenses are payable in the following order of priority—
- (a) expenses which are properly chargeable or incurred by the liquidator in preserving, realising or getting in any of the assets of the company or otherwise in the preparation, conduct or assignment of any legal proceedings, arbitration or other dispute resolution procedures, which the liquidator has power to bring in the liquidator's own name or bring or defend in the name of the company or in the preparation or conduct of any negotiations intended to lead or leading to a settlement or compromise of any legal action or dispute to which the proceedings or procedures relate;
- (b) the cost of any security provided by the liquidator or special manager under the Act or these Rules;
- (c) the remuneration of the special manager (if any);
- (d) any amount payable to a person employed or authorised, under Chapter 2 of this Part, to assist in the preparation of a statement of affairs or of accounts;
- (e) the costs of employing a shorthand writer on the application of the liquidator;
- (f) any necessary disbursements by the liquidator in the course of the administration of the winding up (including any [. . .] expenses incurred by members of the liquidation committee or their representatives and allowed by the liquidator under rule 17.24, but not including any payment of corporation tax in circumstances referred to in sub-paragraph (i));
- (g) the remuneration or emoluments of any person who has been employed by the liquidator to perform any services for the company, as required or authorised by or under the Act or these Rules;
- (h) the remuneration of the liquidator, up to an amount not exceeding that which is payable under Schedule 11 (determination of insolvency office-holder's remuneration);
- (i) the amount of any corporation tax on chargeable gains accruing on the realisation of any asset of the company (irrespective of the person by whom the realisation is effected);
- (j) the balance, after payment of any sums due under sub-paragraph (h) above, of any remuneration due to the liquidator; and

(k) any other expenses properly chargeable by the liquidator in carrying out the liquidator's functions in the winding up.

NOTES

Para (4): words omitted from sub-para (f) originally inserted by the Insolvency Amendment (EU 2015/848) Regulations 2017, SI 2017/702, regs 2, 3, Schedule, Pt 2, paras 32, 38, as from 26 June 2017, except in relation to proceedings opened before that date; and subsequently revoked by the Insolvency (Amendment) (EU Exit) Regulations 2019, SI 2019/146, reg 2, Schedule, Pt 4, paras 46, 70, as from IP completion day (as defined in the European Union (Withdrawal Agreement) Act 2020, s 39) (for savings, see reg 4 of the 2019 Regulations at **[12.82]**).

[10.776]

[6.42A Priority of moratorium debts in subsequent winding up

Where section 174A applies the moratorium debts and priority pre-moratorium debts mentioned in subsection (2)(b) of that section are payable in the following order of priority—

(a) amounts payable in respect of goods or services supplied during the moratorium under a contract where, but for section 233B(3) or (4), the supplier would not have had to make that supply;
(b) wages or salary arising under a contract of employment;
(c) other debts or other liabilities apart from the monitor's remuneration or expenses; and
(d) the monitor's remuneration or expenses.]

NOTES

Commencement: 1 October 2021.

Inserted by the Insolvency (England and Wales) (No 2) (Amendment) Rules 2021, SI 2021/1028, r 30, as from 1 October 2021 (for savings provisions see the note to r 1A.1 at **[10.539]**).

[10.777]

6.43 Saving for powers of the court

Nothing in these Rules—

(a) applies to or affects the powers of any court, in proceedings by or against the company, to order costs to be paid by the company, or the liquidator; or
(b) affects the rights of any person to whom such costs are ordered to be paid.

CHAPTER 7 LITIGATION EXPENSES AND PROPERTY SUBJECT TO A FLOATING CHARGE

[Note: a document required by the Act or these Rules must also contain the standard contents set out in Part 1.]

[10.778]

6.44 Interpretation

(1) In this Chapter—

"approval" and "authorisation" respectively mean—

(a) where yet to be incurred, the approval; and
(b) where already incurred, the authorisation;

of expenses specified in section [176ZA(1)];

"the creditor" means—

[(za) a creditor in respect of a debt which is a moratorium debt or a priority pre-moratorium debt within the meaning given by section 174A;]
(a) a preferential creditor of the company; or
(b) a holder of a debenture secured by, or a holder of, a floating charge created by the company;

"legal proceedings" means—

(a) proceedings under sections 212, 213, 214, 238, 239, 244 and 423 and any arbitration or other dispute resolution proceedings invoked for purposes corresponding to those to which the sections relate and any other proceedings, including arbitration or other dispute resolution procedures, which a liquidator has power to bring in the liquidator's own name for the purpose of preserving, realising, or getting in any of the assets of the company;
(b) legal actions and proceedings, arbitration or any other dispute resolution procedures which a liquidator has power to bring or defend in the name of the company; and
(c) negotiations intended to lead or leading to a settlement or compromise of any action, proceeding or procedure to which sub-paragraphs (a) or (b) relate;

"litigation expenses" means expenses of a winding up which—

(a) are properly chargeable or incurred in the preparation or conduct of any legal proceedings; and
(b) as expenses in the winding up, exceed, or in the opinion of the liquidator are likely to exceed (and only in so far as they exceed or are likely to exceed), in the aggregate £5,000; and

"specified creditor" means a creditor identified under rule 6.45(2).

(2) Litigation expenses will not have the priority provided by section 176ZA over any claims to property comprised in or subject to a floating charge created by the company and must not be paid out of any such property unless and until approved or authorised in accordance with rules 6.45 to 6.48.

NOTES

Para (1): figure in square brackets in the definitions "approval" and "authorisation" substituted by the Insolvency (England and Wales) (Amendment) Rules 2017, SI 2017/366, rr 3, 25, as from 6 April 2017. In the definition "creditor" para (za) was inserted by the Insolvency (England and Wales) (No 2) (Amendment) Rules 2021, SI 2021/1028, r 31, as from 1 October 2021 (for savings provisions see the note to r 1A.1 at **[10.539]**).

[10.779]

6.45 Requirement for approval or authorisation

(1) Subject to rules 6.46 to 6.48, either paragraphs (3) and (4) apply or paragraph (5) applies where, in the course of winding up a company, the liquidator—

(a) ascertains that property is comprised in or subject to a floating charge;

(b) has personally instituted or proposes to institute or continue legal proceedings or is in the process of defending or proposes to defend any legal proceeding brought or likely to be brought against the company; and

(c) before or at any stage in those proceedings, is of the opinion that—

(i) the assets of the company available for payment of general creditors are or will be insufficient to pay litigation expenses; and

(ii) in order to pay litigation expenses the liquidator will have to have recourse to property comprised in or subject to a floating charge created by the company.

(2) As soon as reasonably practicable after the date on which the liquidator forms the opinion referred to in paragraph (1), the liquidator must identify the creditor who, in the liquidator's opinion at that time—

(a) has a claim to property comprised in or subject to a floating charge created by the company; and

(b) taking into account the value of that claim and any subsisting property then comprised in or secured by such a charge, appears to the liquidator to be the creditor most immediately likely of any persons having such claims to receive some payment in respect of a claim but whose claim would not be paid in full.

(3) The liquidator must request from the specified creditor the approval or authorisation of such amount for litigation expenses as the liquidator thinks fit.

(4) Where the liquidator identifies two or more specified creditors, the liquidator must seek from each of them approval or authorisation of such amount of litigation expenses as the liquidator thinks fit, apportioned between them ("the apportioned amount") according to the value of the property to the extent covered by their charges.

(5) For so long as the conditions specified in paragraph (1) subsist, the liquidator may, in the course of a winding up, make such further requests to the specified creditor or creditors for approval or authorisation of such further amount for litigation expenses as the liquidator thinks fit to be paid out of property comprised in or subject to a floating charge created by the company, taking into account any amount for litigation expenses previously approved or authorised and the value of the property comprised in or subject to the floating charge.

[10.780]

6.46 Request for approval or authorisation

(1) All requests made by the liquidator for approval or authorisation must include the following—

(a) a statement describing the nature of the legal proceedings, including, where relevant, the statutory provision under which proceedings are or are to be brought and the grounds upon which the liquidator relies;

(b) a statement specifying the amount or apportioned amount of litigation expenses for which approval or authorisation is sought ("the specified amount");

(c) notice that approval or authorisation or other reply to the request must be made in writing within 28 days from the date of its being received ("the specified time limit"); and

(d) a statement explaining the consequences of a failure to reply within the specified time limit.

(2) Where anything in paragraph (1) requires the inclusion of any information, the disclosure of which could be seriously prejudicial to the winding up of the company, the liquidator may—

(a) exclude such information from any of the above statements or notices if accompanied by a statement to that effect; or

(b) include it on terms—

(i) that bind the creditor to keep the information confidential; and

(ii) that include an undertaking on the part of the liquidator to apply to the court for an order that so much of the information as may be kept in the files of the court is not to be open to public inspection.

(3) The creditor may within the specified time limit apply to the liquidator in writing for such further particulars as is reasonable and in such a case, the time limit specified in paragraph (1)(c) will apply from the date of the creditor's receipt of the liquidator's response to any such request.

(4) Where the liquidator requires the approval or authorisation of two or more creditors, the liquidator must deliver a request to each creditor, containing the matters listed in paragraph (1) and also giving—

(a) the number of creditors concerned;

(b) the total value of their claims, or if not known, as it is estimated to be by the liquidator immediately before delivering any such request; and

[(c) notice to—

(i) each preferential creditor, and

(ii) each creditor of the kind described in rule 6.44(1)(za),

that approval or authorisation of the specified amount will be taken to be given where a majority in value of those creditors referred to in sub-paragraphs (i) and (ii) who respond within the specified time limit are in favour of it; or]

(d) where rule 6.45 applies, notice to the specified creditors that the amount of litigation expenses will be apportioned between them in accordance with that rule and notice of the value of the portion allocated to, and the identity of, the specified creditors affected by that apportionment.

NOTES

Para (4): sub-para (c) substituted by the Insolvency (England and Wales) (No 2) (Amendment) Rules 2021, SI 2021/1028, r 32, as from 1 October 2021 (for savings provisions see the note to r 1A.1 at **[10.539]**). Sub-para (c) previously read as follows—

"(c) to each preferential creditor, notice that approval or authorisation of the specified amount will be taken to be given where a majority in value of those preferential creditors who respond within the specified time limit are in favour of it; or".

[10.781]

6.47 Grant of approval or authorisation

(1) Where the liquidator fails to include in the liquidator's request any one of the matters, statements or notices required to be specified by paragraph (1) or paragraphs (1) and (4), of rule 6.46, the request for approval or authorisation will be treated as not having been made.

(2) Subject to paragraphs (3), (4) and (5), approval or authorisation will be taken to have been given where the specified amount has been requested by the liquidator, and—

(a) that amount is approved or authorised within the specified time limit; or

(b) a different amount is approved or authorised within the specified time limit and the liquidator considers it sufficient.

[(3) Paragraph (3A) applies where the liquidator requires the approval or authorisation of—

(a) two or more—

(i) preferential creditors, or

(ii) creditors of the kind described in rule 6.44(1)(za); or

(b) one or more preferential creditors together with one or more creditors of the kind described in rule 6.44(1)(za).]

[(3A) Where this paragraph applies approval or authorisation will be taken to be given where a majority in value of those creditors referred to in sub-paragraph (3)(a)(i) or (ii) or sub-paragraph (3)(b) (as the case may be) who respond within the specified time approve or authorise—

(a) the specified amount; or

(b) a different amount which the liquidator considers sufficient.]

[(4) Where a majority in value of—

(a) two or more—

(i) preferential creditors, or

(ii) creditors of the kind described in rule 6.44(1)(za); or

(b) one or more preferential creditors together with one or more creditors of the kind described in rule 6.44(1)(za),

propose an amount other than that specified by the liquidator, they will be taken to have approved or authorised an amount equal to the lowest of the amounts so proposed.]

(5) In any case in which there is no response in writing within the specified time limit to the liquidator's request—

(a) at all, or

(b) at any time following the liquidator's provision of further particulars under rule 6.46(3),

the liquidator's request will be taken to have been approved or authorised from the date of the expiry of that time limit.

NOTES

Paras (3), (4): substituted by the Insolvency (England and Wales) (No 2) (Amendment) Rules 2021, SI 2021/1028, r 33(1), (2), (4), as from 1 October 2021 (for savings provisions see the note to r 1A.1 at **[10.539]**). Paras (3), (4) previously read as follows—

"(3) Where the liquidator requires the approval or authorisation of two or more preferential creditors, approval or authorisation will be taken to be given where a majority in value of those who respond within the specified time limit approve or authorise—

(a) the specified amount; or

(b) a different amount which the liquidator considers sufficient.

(4) Where a majority in value of two or more preferential creditors propose an amount other than that specified by the liquidator, they will be taken to have approved or authorised an amount equal to the lowest of the amounts so proposed.".

Para (3A): inserted by SI 2021/1028, r 33(1), (3), as from 1 October 2021 (for savings provisions see the note to r 1A.1 at **[10.539]**).

[10.782]

6.48 Application to the court by the liquidator

(1) In the circumstances specified below the court may, on the application of the liquidator, approve or authorise such amount of litigation expenses as it thinks just.

(2) Except where paragraph (3) applies, the liquidator may apply to the court for an order approving or authorising an amount for litigation expenses only where the specified creditor (or, if more than one, any one of them)—

(a) is or is intended to be a defendant in the legal proceedings in relation to which the litigation expenses have been or are to be incurred; or

(b) has been requested to approve or authorise the amount specified under rule 6.46(1)(b) and has—

(i) declined to approve or authorise, as the case may be, the specified amount;

(ii) approved or authorised an amount which is less than the specified amount and which lesser amount the liquidator considers insufficient; or

(iii) made such application for further particulars or other response to the liquidator's request as is, in the liquidator's opinion, unreasonable.

(3) Where the liquidator thinks that circumstances are such that the liquidator requires urgent approval or authorisation of litigation expenses, the liquidator may apply to the court for approval or authorisation either—

(a) without seeking approval or authorisation from the specified creditor; or

(b) if sought, before the expiry of the specified time limit.

(4) The court may grant such application for approval or authorisation—

(a) if the liquidator satisfies the court of the urgency of the case; and
(b) subject to such terms and conditions as the court thinks just.

(5) The liquidator must, at the same time as making any application to the court under this rule, deliver copies of it to the specified creditor, unless the court orders otherwise.

(6) The specified creditor (or, if more than one, any one of them) is entitled to be heard on any such application unless the court orders otherwise.

(7) The court may grant approval or authorisation subject to such terms and conditions as it may think just, including terms and conditions relating to the amount or nature of the litigation expenses and as to any obligation to make further applications to the court under this rule.

(8) The costs of the liquidator's application under this rule, including the costs of any specified creditor appearing or represented on it, are an expense of the winding up unless the court orders otherwise.

PART 7 WINDING UP BY THE COURT

CHAPTER 1 APPLICATION OF PART

[10.783]
7.1 Application of Part 7

This Part applies to winding up by the court.

CHAPTER 2 THE STATUTORY DEMAND (SECTIONS 123(1)(A) AND 222(1)(A))

[10.784]
7.2 Interpretation

A demand served by a creditor on a company under section 123(1)(a) (registered companies) or 222(1)(a) (unregistered companies) is referred to in this Part as "a statutory demand".

[10.785]
7.3 The statutory demand

(1) A statutory demand must be headed either "Statutory Demand under section 123(1)(a) of the Insolvency Act 1986" or "Statutory Demand under section 222(1)(a) of the Insolvency Act 1986" (as applicable) and must contain—

(a) identification details for the company;
(b) the registered office of the company (if any);
(c) the name and address of the creditor;
(d) either a statement that the demand is made under section 123(1)(a) or a statement that it is made under section 222(1)(a);
(e) the amount of the debt and the consideration for it (or, if there is no consideration, the way in which it arises);
(f) if the demand is founded on a judgment or order of a court, details of the judgment or order;
(g) if the creditor is entitled to the debt by way of assignment, details of the original creditor and any intermediary assignees;
(h) a statement that the company must pay the debt claimed in the demand within 21 days of service of the demand on the company after which the creditor may present a winding-up petition unless the company offers security for the debt and the creditor agrees to accept security or the company compounds the debt with the creditor's agreement;
(i) the name of an individual with whom an officer or representative of the company may communicate with a view to securing or compounding the debt to the creditor's satisfaction;
(j) the named individual's address, electronic address and telephone number (if any);
(k) a statement that the company has the right to apply to the court for an injunction restraining the creditor from presenting or advertising a petition for the winding up of the company; and
(l) the name of the court (and hearing centre if applicable) to which, according to the present information, the company must make the application (ie, the High Court, the County Court at Central London or a named hearing centre of the County Court, as the case may be).

(2) The following must be separately identified in the demand (if claimed) with the amount or rate of the charge and the grounds on which payment is claimed—

(a) any charge by way of interest of which notice had not previously been delivered to the company as included in its liability; and
(b) any other charge accruing from time to time.

(3) The amount claimed for such charges must be limited to that which has accrued due at the date of the demand.

(4) The demand must be dated, and authenticated either by the creditor, or a person authorised to make the demand on the creditor's behalf.

(5) A demand which is authenticated by a person other than the creditor must state that the person is authorised to make the demand on the creditor's behalf and state the person's relationship to the creditor.

CHAPTER 3 PETITION FOR WINDING-UP ORDER

[Notes: (1) for petitions by a contributory or relevant office-holder (an administrator, administrative receiver or supervisor of a CVA) see Chapter 4;

(2) a document required by the Act or these Rules must also contain the standard contents set out in Part 1.]

[10.786]
7.4 Application of this Chapter

(1) This Chapter applies subject to rule 7.25 to—

(a) a petition for winding up presented by a contributory; or
(b) a petition for winding up presented by a relevant office-holder of the company.

(2) "Relevant office-holder" in this Part means an administrator, administrative receiver and supervisor of a CVA.

[10.787]
7.5 Contents of petition

(1) The petition must contain [the following, and, in addition, where paragraph (1B) applies, the information specified in that paragraph]—
- (a) the name of the court (and hearing centre if applicable);
- (b) the name and address of the petitioner;
- (c) identification details for the company subject to the petition;
- (d) the company's registered office (if any);
- (e) the date the company was incorporated and the enactment under which it was incorporated;
- (f) the total number of issued shares of the company and the manner in which they are divided up;
- (g) the aggregate nominal value of those shares;
- (h) the amount of capital paid up or credited as paid up;
- (i) a statement of the nature of the company's business if known;
- (j) the grounds on which the winding-up order is sought;
- (k) where the ground for the winding-up order is section 122(1)(a), a statement that the company has by special resolution resolved that the company be wound up by the court and the date of such resolution;
- (l) where the ground for the winding-up order is section 122(1)(f) or 221(5)(b) and a statutory demand has been served on the company, a statement that such a demand has been served and the date of service and that the company is insolvent and unable to pay its debts;
- (m) a statement whether the company is an Article 1.2 undertaking;
- (n) a statement whether the proceedings will be [COMI proceedings, establishment proceedings or proceedings to which the EU Regulation as it has effect in the law of the United Kingdom does not apply] and that the reasons for so stating are given in a witness statement;
- (o) a statement that in the circumstances it is just and equitable that the company should be wound up;
- (p) a statement that the petitioner therefore applies for an order that the company may be wound up by the court under the Act, or that such other order may be made as the court thinks just;
- (q) the name and address of any person on whom the petitioner intends to serve the petition; and
- (r) the contact details of the petitioner's solicitor (if any).

[(1A) Paragraph (1B) applies if a moratorium under Part A1 is in force.

(1B) Where this paragraph applies the petition must contain—
- (a) a statement that a moratorium under Part A1 of the Act is in force for the company;
- (b) a statement as to which of the permitted exceptions to the restriction on winding up during a moratorium specified in section A20 applies; and
- (c) the name and contact details of the monitor.]

(2) The petition must also contain a blank box for the court to complete with the details of the venue for hearing the petition.

NOTES

Para (1): words in first pair of square brackets inserted by the Insolvency (England and Wales) (No 2) (Amendment) Rules 2021, SI 2021/1028, r 34(1), (2), as from 1 October 2021 (for savings provisions see the note to r 1A.1 at **[10.539]**). Words in square brackets in sub-para (n) substituted by the Insolvency (Amendment) (EU Exit) Regulations 2019, SI 2019/146, reg 2, Schedule, Pt 4, paras 46, 71, as from IP completion day (as defined in the European Union (Withdrawal Agreement) Act 2020, s 39) (for savings, see reg 4 of the 2019 Regulations at **[12.82]**).

Paras (1A), (1B): inserted by SI 2021/1028, r 34(1), (3), as from 1 October 2021 (for savings provisions see the note to r 1A.1 at **[10.539]**).

[10.788]
7.6 Verification of petition

(1) The petition must be verified by a statement of truth.

(2) Where the petition is in respect of debts due to different creditors then the debt to each creditor must be verified separately.

(3) A statement of truth which is not contained in or endorsed upon the petition must identify the petition and must contain—
- (a) identification details for the company;
- (b) the name of the petitioner; and
- (c) the name of the court (and hearing centre if applicable) in which the petition is to be presented.

(4) The statement of truth must be authenticated and dated by or on behalf of the petitioner.

(5) Where the person authenticating the statement of truth is not the petitioner, or one of the petitioners, the statement of truth must state—
- (a) the name and postal address of the person making the statement;
- (b) the capacity in which, and the authority by which, the person authenticates the statement; and
- (c) the means of that person's knowledge of the matters verified in the statement of truth.

(6) If the petition is based on a statutory demand, and more than four months have elapsed between the service of the demand and the presentation of the petition, a witness statement must explain the reasons for the delay.

(7) A statement of truth verifying more than one petition must include in its title the names of the companies to which it relates and must set out, in relation to each company, the statements relied on by the petitioner; and a clear and legible photocopy of the statement of truth must be filed with each petition which it verifies.

(8) The witness statement must give the reasons for the statement that the proceedings will be [COMI proceedings, establishment proceedings or proceedings to which the EU Regulation as it has effect in the law of the United Kingdom does not apply].

NOTES

Para (8): words in square brackets substituted by the Insolvency (Amendment) (EU Exit) Regulations 2019, SI 2019/146, reg 2, Schedule, Pt 4, paras 46, 72, as from IP completion day (as defined in the European Union (Withdrawal Agreement) Act 2020, s 39) (for savings, see reg 4 of the 2019 Regulations at **[12.82]**).

[10.789]

7.7 Petition: presentation and filing

(1) The petition must be filed with the court.

(2) A petition may not be filed unless—

(a) a receipt for the deposit payable to the official receiver is produced on presentation of the petition; or

(b) the Secretary of State has given notice to the court that the petitioner has made suitable alternative arrangements for the payment of the deposit and that notice has not been revoked.

(3) A notice of alternative arrangements for the deposit may be revoked by a further notice filed with the court.

(4) The court must fix a venue for hearing the petition, and this must be endorsed on the petition and the copies.

(5) Each copy of the petition must have the seal of the court applied to it, and must be delivered to the petitioner.

[10.790]

7.8 Court to which petition is to be presented where the company is subject to a CVA or is in administration

(1) A petition which is filed in relation to a company for which there is in force a CVA must be presented to the court or hearing centre to which the nominee's report under section 2 was submitted *or where the documents for a moratorium under section 1A were filed*.

(2) A petition which is filed in relation to a company which is in administration must be presented to the court or hearing centre of the court having jurisdiction for the administration.

NOTES

Para (1): words in italics revoked by the Insolvency (England and Wales) (No 2) (Amendment) Rules 2021, SI 2021/1028, r 81, Sch 2, as from 1 October 2021 (for savings provisions see the note to r 1A.1 at **[10.539]**).

[10.791]

7.9 Copies of petition to be served on company or delivered to other persons

(1) Where this rule requires the petitioner to serve a copy of the petition on the company or deliver a copy to another person the petitioner must, when filing the petition with the court, file an additional copy with the court for each such person.

(2) Where the petitioner is not the company the petitioner must serve a sealed copy of the petition on the company in accordance with Schedule 4.

(3) If, to the petitioner's knowledge—

(a) the company is in the course of being wound up voluntarily, the petitioner must deliver a copy of the petition to the liquidator;

(b) an administrative receiver has been appointed in relation to the company, or the company is in administration, the petitioner must deliver a copy of the petition to the receiver or the administrator; [or]

(c) there is in force for the company a CVA, the petitioner must deliver a copy of the petition to the supervisor of the CVA; . . .

(d) . . .

(4) If either the Financial Conduct Authority or Prudential Regulation Authority is entitled to be heard at the hearing of the petition in accordance with section 371 of the Financial Services and Markets Act 2000, the petitioner must deliver a copy of the petition to the Financial Conduct Authority or Prudential Regulation Authority (as appropriate).

(5) Where this rule requires the petitioner to deliver a copy of the petition to any other person that copy must be delivered within three business days after the day on which the petition is served on the company or where the petitioner is the company within three business days of the company receiving the sealed petition.

NOTES

Para (3): word in square brackets in sub-para (b) inserted, and sub-para (d) and the word immediately preceding it revoked, by the Insolvency (Amendment) (EU Exit) Regulations 2019, SI 2019/146, reg 2, Schedule, Pt 4, paras 46, 73, as from IP completion day (as defined in the European Union (Withdrawal Agreement) Act 2020, s 39) (for savings, see reg 4 of the 2019 Regulations at **[12.82]**).

[10.792]

7.10 Notice of petition

(1) Unless the court otherwise directs, the petitioner must give notice of the petition.

(2) The notice must state—

(a) that a petition has been presented for the winding up of the company;

(b) in the case of an overseas company, the address at which service of the petition was effected;

(c) the name and address of the petitioner;

(d) the date on which the petition was presented;

(e) the venue fixed for the hearing of the petition;

(f) the name and address of the petitioner's solicitor (if any); and

(g) that any person intending to appear at the hearing (whether to support or oppose the petition) must give notice of that intention in accordance with rule 7.14.

(3) The notice must be gazetted.

(4) The notice must be made to appear—

(a) if the petitioner is the company itself, not less than seven business days before the day appointed for the hearing; and
(b) otherwise, not less than seven business days after service of the petition on the company, nor less than seven business days before the day appointed for the hearing.

(5) The court may dismiss the petition if notice of it is not given in accordance with this rule.

[10.793]
7.11 Persons entitled to request a copy of petition

If a director, contributory [creditor, or, (if a moratorium under Part A1 of the Act is in force for the company), the monitor] requests a hard copy of the petition from the solicitor for the petitioner, or the petitioner, if acting in person, and pays the standard fee for copies the solicitor or petitioner must deliver the copy within two business days.

NOTES

Words in square brackets substituted (for the original words "or creditor") by the Insolvency (England and Wales) (No 2) (Amendment) Rules 2021, SI 2021/1028, r 35, as from 1 October 2021 (for savings provisions see the note to r 1A.1 at **[10.539]**).

[10.794]
7.12 Certificate of compliance

(1) The petitioner or the petitioner's solicitor must, at least five business days before the hearing of the petition, file with the court a certificate of compliance with rules 7.9 and 7.10 relating to service and notice of the petition.

(2) The certificate must be authenticated and dated by the petitioner or the petitioner's solicitor and must state—
(a) the date of presentation of the petition;
(b) the date fixed for the hearing; and
(c) the date or dates on which the petition was served and notice of it was given in compliance with rules 7.9 and 7.10.

(3) A copy of or, where that is not reasonably practicable, a statement of the content of, any notice given must be filed with the court with the certificate.

(4) The court may, if it thinks just, dismiss the petition if this rule is not complied with.

[10.795]
7.13 Permission for the petitioner to withdraw

(1) The court may order that the petitioner has permission to withdraw the petition on such terms as to costs as the parties may agree if at least five business days before the first hearing the petitioner, on an application without notice to any other party, satisfies the court that—
(a) notice of the petition has not been given under rule 7.10;
(b) no notices in support or in opposition to the petition have been received by the petitioner; and
(c) the company consents to an order being made under this rule.

(2) The order must contain—
(a) identification details for the company;
(b) the date the winding-up petition was presented;
(c) the name and postal address of the applicant;
(d) a statement that upon the application made without notice to any other party by the applicant named in the order the court is satisfied that notice of the petition has not been given, that no notices in support of or in opposition to the petition have been received by the petitioner and that the company consents to this order; and
(e) an order that, with the permission of the court, the petition is withdrawn.

[10.796]
7.14 Notice by persons intending to appear

(1) A creditor or contributory who intends to appear on the hearing of the petition must deliver a notice of intention to appear to the petitioner.

(2) The notice must contain—
(a) the name and address of the creditor or contributory, and any telephone number and reference which may be required for communication with that person or with any other person (also to be specified in the notice) authorised to speak or act on the creditor's or contributory's behalf;
(b) the date of the presentation of the petition and a statement that the notice relates to the matter of that petition;
(c) the date of the hearing of the petition;
(d) for a creditor, the amount and nature of the debt due from the company to the creditor;
(e) for a contributory, the number of shares held in the company;
(f) a statement whether the creditor or contributory intends to support or oppose the petition;
(g) where the creditor or contributory is represented by a solicitor or other agent, the name, postal address, telephone number and any reference number of that person and details of that person's position with or relationship to the creditor or contributory; and
(h) the name and postal address of the petitioner.

(3) The notice must be authenticated and dated by or on behalf of the creditor or contributory delivering it.

(4) Where the person authenticating the notice is not the creditor or contributory the notice must state the name and postal address of the person making the statement and the capacity in which, and the authority by which, the person authenticates the notice.

(5) The notice must be delivered to the petitioner or the petitioner's solicitor at the address shown in the court records, or in the notice of the petition required by rule 7.10.

(6) The notice must be delivered so as to reach the petitioner (or the petitioner's solicitor) not later than 4pm on the business day before that which is appointed for the hearing (or, where the hearing has been adjourned, for the adjourned hearing).

(7) A person who fails to comply with this rule may appear on the hearing of the petition only with the permission of the court.

[10.797]

7.15 List of appearances

(1) The petitioner must prepare for the court a list of the creditors and contributories who have given notice under rule 7.14.

(2) The list must contain—

(a) the date of the presentation of the petition;

(b) the date of the hearing of the petition;

(c) a statement that the creditors and contributories listed have delivered notice that they intend to appear at the hearing of the petition;

(d) their names and addresses;

(e) the amount each creditor claims to be owed;

(f) the number of shares claimed to be held by each contributory;

(g) the name and postal address of any solicitor for a person listed; and

(h) whether each person listed intends to support the petition, or to oppose it.

(3) On the day appointed for the hearing of the petition, a copy of the list must be handed to the court before the hearing commences.

(4) If the court gives a person permission to appear under rule 7.14(7), then the petitioner must add that person to the list with the same particulars.

[10.798]

7.16 Witness statement in opposition

(1) If the company intends to oppose the petition, it must not later than five business days before the date fixed for the hearing—

(a) file with the court a witness statement in opposition; and

(b) deliver a copy of the witness statement to the petitioner or the petitioner's solicitor.

(2) The witness statement must contain—

(a) identification details for the proceedings;

(b) a statement that the company intends to oppose the making of a winding-up order; and

(c) a statement of the grounds on which the company opposes the making of the order.

[10.799]

7.17 Substitution of creditor or contributory for petitioner

(1) This rule applies where the petitioner—

(a) is subsequently found not to have been entitled to present the petition;

(b) fails to give notice of the petition in accordance with rule 7.10;

(c) consents to withdraw the petition, or to allow it to be dismissed, consents to an adjournment, or fails to appear in support of the petition when it is called on in court on the day originally fixed for the hearing, or on a day to which it is adjourned; or

(d) appears, but does not apply for an order in the terms requested in the petition.

(2) The court may, on such terms as it thinks just, substitute as petitioner—

(a) a creditor or contributory who in its opinion would have a right to present a petition and who wishes to prosecute it; . . .

(b) . . .

NOTES

Para (2): words omitted revoked by the Insolvency (Amendment) (EU Exit) Regulations 2019, SI 2019/146, reg 2, Schedule, Pt 4, paras 46, 74, as from IP completion day (as defined in the European Union (Withdrawal Agreement) Act 2020, s 39) (for savings, see reg 4 of the 2019 Regulations at **[12.82]**).

[10.800]

7.18 Order for substitution of petitioner

An order for substitution of a petitioner must contain—

(a) identification details for the proceedings;

(b) the name of the original petitioner;

(c) the name of the creditor, [or] contributory . . . ("the named person") who is substituted as petitioner;

(d) a statement that the named person has requested to be substituted as petitioner under rule 7.17;

(e) the following orders—

(i) either—

(aa) that the named person must pay the statutory deposit to the court and that, upon such payment being made, the statutory deposit paid by the original petitioner is to be repaid to the original petitioner by the official receiver, or

(bb) where the named person is the subject of a notice to the court by the Secretary of State under rule 7.7(2)(b) (notice of alternative arrangements for the payment of deposit) that the statutory deposit paid by the original petitioner is to be repaid to the original petitioner by the official receiver;

(ii) that the named person be substituted as petitioner in place of the original petitioner and that the named person may amend the petition accordingly,

(iii) that the named person must within a period specified in the order file a statement of truth of the statements in the amended petition,
(iv) that not later than before the adjourned hearing of the petition, by a date specified in the order, the named person must serve a sealed copy of the amended petition on the company and deliver a copy to any other person to whom the original petition was delivered,
(v) that the hearing of the amended petition be adjourned to the venue specified in the order, and
(vi) that the question of the costs of the original petitioner and of the statutory deposit (if appropriate) be reserved until the final determination of the amended petition;

(f) the venue of the adjourned hearing; and
(g) the date of the order.

NOTES

Para (c): word in square brackets inserted, and words omitted revoked, by the Insolvency (Amendment) (EU Exit) Regulations 2019, SI 2019/146, reg 2, Schedule, Pt 4, paras 46, 75, as from IP completion day (as defined in the European Union (Withdrawal Agreement) Act 2020, s 39) (for savings, see reg 4 of the 2019 Regulations at **[12.82]**).

[10.801]
7.19 Notice of adjournment

(1) If the court adjourns the hearing of the petition the petitioner must as soon as reasonably practicable deliver a notice of the making of the order of adjournment and of the venue for the adjourned hearing to—
(a) the company; and
(b) any creditor or contributory who has given notice under rule 7.14 but was not present at the hearing.

(2) The notice must identify the proceedings.

[10.802]
7.20 Order for winding up by the court

(1) An order for winding-up by the court must contain—
(a) identification details for the proceedings;
(b) the name and title of the judge making the order;
(c) the name and postal address of the petitioner;
(d) the nature of the petitioner which entitles that person to present the petition (eg the company, a creditor, or a regulator);
(e) the date of presentation of the petition;
(f) an order that the company be wound up by the court under the Act;
(g) a statement whether the proceedings are [COMI proceedings, establishment proceedings or proceedings to which the EU Regulation as it has effect in the law of the United Kingdom does not apply];
(h) an order that the petitioner's costs of the petition be paid out of the assets of the company (unless the court determines otherwise);
(i) if applicable, an order that the costs of other persons as specified in the order be paid out of the assets of the company;
(j) the date of the order; and
(k) a statement that an official receiver attached to the court is by virtue of the order liquidator of the company, or

(2) The order may contain such additional terms concerning costs as the court thinks just.

NOTES

Para (1): words in square brackets in sub-para (g) substituted by the Insolvency (Amendment) (EU Exit) Regulations 2019, SI 2019/146, reg 2, Schedule, Pt 4, paras 46, 76, as from IP completion day (as defined in the European Union (Withdrawal Agreement) Act 2020, s 39) (for savings, see reg 4 of the 2019 Regulations at **[12.82]**).

[10.803]
7.21 Notice to official receiver of winding-up order

(1) When a winding-up order has been made, the court must deliver notice of the fact to the official receiver as soon as reasonably practicable.

(2) The notice must have the title "Notice to Official Receiver of Winding-up Order" and must contain—
(a) identification details for the proceedings;
(b) the company's registered office;
(c) the date of presentation of the petition;
(d) the date of the winding-up order; and
(e) the name and postal address of the petitioner or the petitioner's solicitor.

[10.804]
7.22 Delivery and notice of the order

(1) As soon as reasonably practicable after making a winding-up order, the court must deliver to the official receiver two copies of the order sealed with the seal of the court.

(2) The official receiver must deliver—
(a) a sealed copy of the order to the company; and
[(b) a copy of the order to—
(i) the registrar of companies (in compliance with section 130(1)); and
(ii) if a moratorium under Part A1 of the Act was in force for the company at the time the petition for the winding up of the company was presented, the monitor.]

(3) As an alternative to delivering a sealed copy of the order to the company, the court may direct that the sealed copy be delivered to such other person or persons, as the court directs.

(4) The official receiver—
(a) must cause a notice of the order to be gazetted as soon as reasonably practicable; and
(b) may advertise a notice of the order in such other manner as the official receiver thinks fit.

(5) The notice must state—
(a) that a winding-up order has been made in relation to the company; and
(b) the date of the order.

NOTES

Para (2): sub-para (b) substituted by the Insolvency (England and Wales) (No 2) (Amendment) Rules 2021, SI 2021/1028, r 36, as from 1 October 2021 (for savings provisions see the note to r 1A.1 at **[10.539]**). Sub-para (b) previously read as follows—

"(b) a copy of the order to the registrar of companies (in compliance with section 130(1)).".

[10.805]
7.23 Petition dismissed

(1) Unless the court otherwise directs, when a petition is dismissed the petitioner must give a notice of the dismissal as soon as reasonably practicable.

(2) The notice must be—
(a) gazetted; or
(b) advertised in accordance with any directions of the court.

(3) The notice must contain—
(a) a statement that a petition for the winding up of the company has been dismissed;
(b) in the case of an overseas company, the address at which service of the petition was effected;
(c) the name and address of the petitioner;
(d) the date on which the petition was presented;
(e) the date on which the petition was gazetted or otherwise advertised; and
(f) the date of the hearing at which the petition was dismissed.

(4) The company may itself gazette notice of the dismissal where—
(a) the petitioner is not the company; and
(b) the petitioner has not given notice in accordance with paragraphs (1) to (3) within 21 days of the date of the hearing at which the petition was dismissed.

[10.806]
7.24 Injunction to restrain presentation or notice of petition

(1) An application by a company for an injunction restraining a creditor from presenting a petition for the winding up of the company must be made to a court having jurisdiction to wind up the company.

(2) An application by a company for an injunction restraining a creditor from giving notice of a petition for the winding up of a company must be made to the court or hearing centre in which the petition is pending.

CHAPTER 4 PETITION BY A CONTRIBUTORY OR A RELEVANT OFFICE-HOLDER

[Note: (1) "relevant office-holder" is defined in rule 7.4(2);

(2) a document required by the Act or these Rules must also contain the standard contents set out in Part 1.]

[10.807]
7.25 Interpretation and application of rules in Chapter 3

(1) The following rules in Chapter 3 apply subject to paragraph (2), with the necessary modifications, to a petition under this Chapter by a contributory or a relevant office-holder—
rule 7.8 (court to which petition is to be presented where the company is subject to a CVA or is in administration);
rule 7.9(1), (4) and (5) (copies of petition to be served on other persons);
rule 7.11 (persons entitled to request a copy of petition);
rule 7.14 (notice by persons intending to appear);
rule 7.15 (list of appearances);
rule 7.19 (notice of adjournment);
rule 7.20 (order for winding up by the court) except where rule 7.32 applies (petition by administrator or where there is a supervisor);
rule 7.21 (notice to official receiver of winding-up order); and
rule 7.22 (delivery and notice of the order).

(2) The following rules apply to petitions under this Chapter presented by a relevant office-holder—
rule 7.23 (petition dismissed); and
rule 7.24 (injunction to restrain presentation or notice of petition).

[10.808]
7.26 Contents of petition for winding-up order by a contributory

(1) A petition presented by a contributory must contain—
(a) the name of the court (and hearing centre if applicable);
(b) the name and postal address of the petitioner;
(c) identification details for the company subject to the petition;
(d) the company's registered office (if any);
(e) the date the company was incorporated and the enactment under which it was incorporated;
(f) the total number of issued shares of the company and the manner in which they are divided up;
(g) the aggregate nominal value of those shares;

(h) the amount of capital paid up or credited as paid up;
(i) a statement of the nature of the company's business if known;
(j) the number and total value of the shares held by the petitioner;
(k) a statement whether the shares held by the petitioner—
  (i) were allotted to the petitioner on the incorporation of the company,
  (ii) have been registered in the name of the petitioner for more than six months in the last 18 months, or
  (iii) devolved upon the petitioner through the death of the former holder of the shares;
(l) the grounds on which the winding-up order is sought;
(m) a statement whether the company is an Article 1.2 undertaking;
(n) a statement whether the proceedings will be [COMI proceedings, establishment proceedings or proceedings to which the EU Regulation as it has effect in the law of the United Kingdom does not apply] and that the reasons for so stating are given in the form of a witness statement;
(o) a statement that in the circumstances it is just and equitable that the company should be wound up;
(p) a statement that the petitioner therefore applies for an order that the company may be wound up by the court under the Act, or that such other order may be made as the court thinks just;
(q) the name and postal address of any person on whom the petitioner intends to serve the petition; and
(r) the contact details of the petitioner's solicitor (if any).

(2) The petition must also contain a blank box for the court to complete with the details of the venue for hearing the petition.

NOTES

Para (1): words in square brackets in sub-para (n) substituted by the Insolvency (Amendment) (EU Exit) Regulations 2019, SI 2019/146, reg 2, Schedule, Pt 4, paras 46, 77, as from IP completion day (as defined in the European Union (Withdrawal Agreement) Act 2020, s 39) (for savings, see reg 4 of the 2019 Regulations at **[12.82]**).

[10.809]
7.27 Petition presented by a relevant office-holder

(1) A petition by a relevant office-holder must be expressed to be the petition of the company by the office-holder.

(2) The petition must contain the particulars required by rule 7.26 (other than paragraph (1)(j) and (k) and the following (as applicable)—
(a) identification details for the office-holder;
(b) the full name of the court or hearing centre in which the proceedings are being conducted or where documents relating to the proceedings are filed;
(c) the court case number;
(d) the date the insolvency proceedings in respect of which the office-holder holds office commenced; and
(e) where the office-holder is an administrator, an application under paragraph 79 of Schedule B1, requesting that the appointment of the administrator should cease to have effect.

[10.810]
7.28 Verification of petition

(1) The petition must be verified by a statement of truth.

(2) A statement of truth which is not contained in or endorsed upon the petition must identify the petition and must contain—
(a) identification details for the company;
(b) the name of the petitioner; and
(c) the name of the court (and hearing centre if applicable) in which the petition is to be presented.

(3) The statement of truth must be authenticated and dated by or on behalf of the petitioner.

(4) Where the person authenticating the statement of truth is not the petitioner, or one of the petitioners, the statement of truth must state—
(a) the name and postal address of the person making the statement;
(b) the capacity in which, and the authority by which, the person authenticates the statement; and
(c) the means of the person's knowledge of the matters verified in the statement of truth.

(5) A statement of truth verifying more than one petition must include in its title the names of the companies to which it relates and must set out, in relation to each company, the statements relied on by the petitioner; and a clear and legible photocopy of the statement of truth must be filed with each petition which it verifies.

(6) The reasons for the statement that the proceedings will be [COMI proceedings, establishment proceedings or proceedings to which the EU Regulation as it has effect in the law of the United Kingdom does not apply] must be given in a witness statement.

NOTES

Para (6): words in square brackets substituted by the Insolvency (Amendment) (EU Exit) Regulations 2019, SI 2019/146, reg 2, Schedule, Pt 4, paras 46, 78, as from IP completion day (as defined in the European Union (Withdrawal Agreement) Act 2020, s 39) (for savings, see reg 4 of the 2019 Regulations at **[12.82]**).

[10.811]
7.29 Presentation and service of petition

(1) The petition with one copy must be filed with the court.

(2) The petition may not be filed unless a receipt for the deposit payable to the official receiver is produced on presentation of the petition.

(3) The court must fix a hearing for a return day on which, unless the court otherwise directs, the petitioner and the company must attend before the court for—
(a) directions to be given in relation to the procedure on the petition; or

(b) the hearing of the petition where—
   (i) it is presented by a relevant office-holder, and
   (ii) the court considers it just in all the circumstances.

(4) On fixing the return day, the court must deliver to the petitioner a sealed copy of the petition endorsed with the return day and time of hearing.

(5) The petitioner must serve a sealed copy of the petition on the company at least 14 days before the return day.

(6) . . .

NOTES

Para (6): revoked by the Insolvency (Amendment) (EU Exit) Regulations 2019, SI 2019/146, reg 2, Schedule, Pt 4, paras 46, 79, as from IP completion day (as defined in the European Union (Withdrawal Agreement) Act 2020, s 39) (for savings, see reg 4 of the 2019 Regulations at **[12.82]**).

[10.812]

7.30 Request to appoint former administrator or supervisor as liquidator (section 140)

(1) This rule applies where a petition requests under section 140 the appointment of a former administrator or supervisor as liquidator.

(2) The person whose appointment is sought ("the appointee") must, not less than two business days before the return day fixed under rule 7.29(3), file with the court a report including particulars of—

(a) the date on which the appointee delivered notice to creditors of the company, of the appointee's intention to seek appointment as liquidator, such date to be at least seven business days before the day on which the report is filed; and

(b) details of any response from creditors to that notice, including any objections to the proposed appointment.

[10.813]

7.31 Hearing of petition

(1) On the return day, or at any time after it, the court—

(a) must, where the petition is presented by a person who is not a relevant office-holder, give directions;

(b) may, in any other case, give directions; or

(c) may, in either case, make any such order as it sees fit.

(2) In particular, the court may give directions relating to the following matters—

(a) service or delivery of the petition, whether in connection with the venue for a further hearing, or for any other purpose;

(b) whether particulars of claim and defence are to be delivered, and generally as to the procedure on the petition;

(c) whether and if so by what means, notice of the petition is to be given;

(d) the manner in which any evidence is to be provided at any hearing before the judge and in particular (but without prejudice to the generality of the above) as to—
   (i) the taking of evidence wholly or in part by witness statement or orally,
   (ii) the cross-examination of any person who has made a witness statement, and
   (iii) the matters to be dealt with in evidence; and

(e) any other matter affecting the procedure on the petition or in connection with the hearing and disposal of the petition.

(3) In giving directions the court must consider whether a copy of the petition should be served on or delivered to any of the persons specified in rule 7.9.

[10.814]

7.32 Order for winding up by the court of a company in administration or where there is a supervisor of a CVA in relation to the company

(1) An order for winding-up by the court of a company in administration or where there is a supervisor of a CVA in relation to the company must contain—

(a) identification details for the proceedings;

(b) the name and title of the judge making the order;

(c) the name and postal address of the administrator or supervisor of the company;

(d) the date of the administrator's or supervisor's appointment;

(e) the date of presentation of the petition;

(f) where there is an administrator, an order that the administrator's appointment ceases to have effect;

(g) an order that the company be wound up by the court under the Act;

(h) a statement whether the proceedings are [COMI proceedings, establishment proceedings or proceedings to which the EU Regulation as it has effect in the law of the United Kingdom does not apply]; and

(i) the name and address of the person appointed as liquidator of the company (if applicable);

(j) an order that—
   (i) an official receiver attached to the court is by virtue of the order liquidator of the company, or
   (ii) that the administrator or the supervisor (as the case may be) specified in the order is appointed liquidator of the company; and

(k) the date of the order.

(2) The order may contain such additional terms as to the costs as the court thinks just.

(3) Where the court appoints the former administrator or the supervisor as liquidator paragraphs (3)(c), (4), (7), (8) and (9) of rule 7.56 apply.

NOTES

Para (1): words in square brackets in sub-para (h) substituted by the Insolvency (Amendment) (EU Exit) Regulations 2019, SI 2019/146, reg 2, Schedule, Pt 4, paras 46, 80, as from IP completion day (as defined in the European Union (Withdrawal

Agreement) Act 2020, s 39) (for savings, see reg 4 of the 2019 Regulations at **[12.82]**).

CHAPTER 5 PROVISIONAL LIQUIDATOR

[Note: a document required by the Act or these Rules must also contain the standard contents set out in Part 1.]

[10.815]
7.33 Application for appointment of provisional liquidator (section 135)

(1) An application to the court for the appointment of a provisional liquidator under section 135 may be made by—
- (a) the petitioner;
- (b) a creditor of the company;
- (c) a contributory;
- (d) the company;
- (e) the Secretary of State;
- (f) a temporary administrator; [or]
- (g) . . .
- (h) any person who under any enactment would be entitled to present a petition for the winding up of the company.

(2) The application must be supported by a witness statement stating—
- (a) the grounds on which it is proposed that a provisional liquidator should be appointed;
- (b) if some person other than the official receiver is proposed to be appointed, that that person has consented to act and, to the best of the applicant's belief, is qualified to act as an insolvency practitioner in relation to the company;
- (c) whether or not the official receiver has been informed of the application and, if so, whether a copy of it has been delivered to the official receiver;
- (d) whether to the applicant's knowledge—
  - [(zi) a moratorium under Part A1 of the Act is in force for the company;]
  - (i) there has been proposed or is in force for the company a CVA;
  - (ii) an administrator or administrative receiver is acting in relation to the company; or
  - (iii) a liquidator has been appointed for its voluntary winding up; and
- (e) the applicant's estimate of the value of the assets in relation to which the provisional liquidator is to be appointed;
- [(f) a statement whether the proceedings will be [COMI proceedings, establishment proceedings or proceedings to which the EU Regulation as it has effect in the law of the United Kingdom does not apply] with the reasons for so stating.]

(3) The applicant must deliver copies of the application and the witness statement in support to the official receiver, who may attend the hearing and make any representations which the official receiver thinks appropriate.

(4) If for any reason it is not practicable to deliver copies of the application and statement to the official receiver before the hearing, the applicant must inform the official receiver of the application in sufficient time for the official receiver to be able to attend.

(5) If satisfied that sufficient grounds are shown for the appointment the court may appoint a provisional liquidator on such terms as it thinks just.

NOTES

Para (1): word in square brackets in sub-para (f) inserted, and sub-para (g) revoked, by the Insolvency (Amendment) (EU Exit) Regulations 2019, SI 2019/146, reg 2, Schedule, Pt 4, paras 46, 81(a), (b), as from IP completion day (as defined in the European Union (Withdrawal Agreement) Act 2020, s 39) (for savings, see reg 4 of the 2019 Regulations at **[12.82]**).

Para (2): sub-para (d)(zi) inserted by the Insolvency (England and Wales) (No 2) (Amendment) Rules 2021, SI 2021/1028, r 37, as from 1 October 2021 (for savings provisions see the note to r 1A.1 at **[10.539]**). Sub-para (f) added by the Insolvency Amendment (EU 2015/848) Regulations 2017, SI 2017/702, regs 2, 3, Schedule, Pt 2, paras 32, 39, as from 26 June 2017, except in relation to proceedings opened before that date. Words in square brackets in sub-para (f) substituted by SI 2019/146, reg 2, Schedule, Pt 4, paras 46, 81(c), as from IP completion day (as defined in the European Union (Withdrawal Agreement) Act 2020, s 39) (for savings, see reg 4 of the 2019 Regulations at **[12.82]**).

[10.816]
7.34 Deposit by applicant

(1) An applicant for an order appointing the official receiver as provisional liquidator must, before the order is made, deposit with the official receiver, or otherwise secure to the official receiver's satisfaction, such sum as the court directs to cover the official receiver's remuneration and expenses.

(2) If the sum deposited or secured proves to be insufficient, the court may, on the application of the official receiver, order the applicant for the appointment to deposit or secure an additional sum.

(3) If such additional sum is not deposited or secured within two business days after service of the order on the applicant then the court may discharge the order appointing the official receiver as provisional liquidator.

(4) If a winding-up order is made after a provisional liquidator has been appointed, any money deposited under this rule must (unless it is required because the assets are insufficient to pay the remuneration and expenses of the provisional liquidator) be repaid to the person depositing it (or as that person may direct) as an expense of the winding up, in the prescribed order of priority.

[10.817]
7.35 Order of appointment of provisional liquidator

(1) The order appointing the provisional liquidator must have the title "Order of appointment of Provisional Liquidator" and contain—
- (a) the name of the court (and hearing centre if applicable) in which the order is made;
- (b) the name and title of the judge making the order;

(c) the name and postal address of the applicant;
(d) identification details for the company;
(e) the statement that the court is satisfied—
  (i) that the company is unable to pay its debts (if applicable), and
  (ii) that the proceedings are [COMI proceedings, establishment proceedings or proceedings to which the EU Regulation as it has effect in the law of the United Kingdom does not apply], as the case may be;
(f) an order either that—
  (i) upon the sum, which is specified in the order, being deposited by the applicant with the official receiver, the official receiver is appointed provisional liquidator of the company, or
  (ii) the person specified in the order is appointed provisional liquidator of the company;
(g) identification and contact details for the provisional liquidator, where the provisional liquidator is not the official receiver;
(h) details of the functions to be carried out by the provisional liquidator in relation to the company's affairs;
(i) a notice to the officers of the company that they are required by section 235 to give the provisional liquidator all the information the provisional liquidator may reasonably require relating to the company's property and affairs and to attend upon the provisional liquidator at such times as the provisional liquidator may reasonably require; and
(j) the date of the order.

(2) Where two or more provisional liquidators are appointed the order must also specify (as required by section 231) whether any act required or authorised under any enactment to be done by the provisional liquidator is to be done by all or any one or more of them.

(3) The court must, as soon as reasonably practicable after the order is made, deliver copies of the order as follows—
(a) if the official receiver is the provisional liquidator, two sealed copies to the official receiver;
(b) if another person is appointed as provisional liquidator—
  (i) two sealed copies to that person, and
  (ii) one copy to the official receiver;
(c) if there is an administrative receiver acting in relation to the company, one sealed copy to the administrative receiver.

(4) The official receiver or other person appointed as provisional liquidator must as soon as reasonably practicable deliver a sealed copy of the order to either—
(a) the company, or
(b) the liquidator, if a liquidator was appointed for the company's voluntary winding-up.

[(4A) Where a moratorium under Part A1 of the Act is in force for the company the official receiver or other person appointed as provisional liquidator must as soon as reasonably practicable deliver a sealed copy of the order to the monitor.]

(5) The official receiver or other person appointed as provisional liquidator must as soon as reasonably practicable deliver a copy of the order to the registrar of companies.

NOTES

Para (1): words in square brackets in sub-para (e)(ii) substituted by the Insolvency (Amendment) (EU Exit) Regulations 2019, SI 2019/146, reg 2, Schedule, Pt 4, paras 46, 82, as from IP completion day (as defined in the European Union (Withdrawal Agreement) Act 2020, s 39) (for savings, see reg 4 of the 2019 Regulations at **[12.82]**).

Para (4A): inserted by the Insolvency (England and Wales) (No 2) (Amendment) Rules 2021, SI 2021/1028, r 38, as from 1 October 2021 (for savings provisions see the note to r 1A.1 at **[10.539]**).

[10.818]

7.36 Notice of appointment of provisional liquidator

(1) The provisional liquidator must as soon as reasonably practicable after receipt of the copy of the order of appointment give notice of appointment unless the court directs otherwise.

(2) The notice—
(a) must be gazetted; and
(b) may be advertised in such other manner as the provisional liquidator thinks fit.

(3) The notice must state—
(a) that a provisional liquidator has been appointed; and
(b) the date of the appointment.

[10.819]

7.37 Security

(1) This rule applies where an insolvency practitioner is appointed as provisional liquidator.

(2) The cost of providing the security required under the Act must be paid in the first instance by the provisional liquidator, however—
(a) if a winding-up order is not made, the person appointed is entitled to be reimbursed out of the property of the company, and the court may make an order on the company accordingly; and
(b) if a winding-up order is made, the person appointed is entitled to be reimbursed as an expense of the winding up in the prescribed order of priority.

(3) If the provisional liquidator fails to give or keep up the required security, the court may remove the provisional liquidator, and make such order as it thinks just as to costs.

(4) If an order is made under this rule removing the provisional liquidator, or discharging the order appointing the provisional liquidator, the court must give directions as to whether any, and if so what, steps should be taken for the appointment of another person in the place of the removed or discharged provisional liquidator.

[10.820]
7.38 Remuneration

(1) The remuneration of the provisional liquidator (other than the official receiver) is to be fixed by the court from time to time on the application of the provisional liquidator.

(2) In fixing the remuneration of the provisional liquidator, the court must take into account—

(a) the time properly given by the provisional liquidator and the staff of the provisional liquidator in attending to the company's affairs;

(b) the complexity of the case;

(c) any respects in which, in connection with the company's affairs, there falls on the provisional liquidator any responsibility of an exceptional kind or degree;

(d) the effectiveness with which the provisional liquidator appears to be carrying out, or to have carried out, the duties of the provisional liquidator; and

(e) the value and nature of the property with which the provisional liquidator has to deal.

(3) Without prejudice to any order the court may make as to costs, the remuneration of the provisional liquidator (whether the official receiver or another) must be paid to the provisional liquidator, and the amount of any expenses incurred by the provisional liquidator (including the remuneration and expenses of any special manager appointed under section 177) reimbursed—

(a) if a winding-up order is not made, out of the property of the company;

(b) if a winding-up order is made, as an expense of the winding up, in the prescribed order of priority; and

(c) in either case (if the relevant funds are insufficient), out of the deposit under rule 7.34.

(4) Unless the court otherwise directs, where a winding up order is not made, the provisional liquidator may retain out of the company's property such sums or property as are or may be required for meeting the remuneration and expenses of the provisional liquidator.

(5) Where a person other than the official receiver has been appointed provisional liquidator, and the official receiver has taken any steps for the purpose of obtaining a statement of affairs or has performed any other duty under these Rules, the provisional liquidator must pay the official receiver such sum (if any) as the court may direct.

[10.821]
7.39 Termination of appointment

(1) The appointment of the provisional liquidator may be terminated by the court on the application of the provisional liquidator, or a person specified in rule 7.33(1).

(2) If the provisional liquidator's appointment terminates, in consequence of the dismissal of the winding-up petition or otherwise, the court may give such directions as it thinks just relating to the accounts of the provisional liquidator's administration or any other matters which it thinks appropriate.

(3) The provisional liquidator must give notice of termination of the appointment as provisional liquidator, unless the termination is on the making of a winding-up order or the court directs otherwise.

(4) The notice referred to in paragraph (3)—

[(a) must be delivered as soon as reasonably practicable to—

(i) the registrar of companies; and

(ii) if a moratorium under Part A1 of the Act is in force for the company, the monitor;]

(b) must be gazetted as soon as reasonably practicable; and

(c) may be advertised in such other manner as the provisional liquidator thinks fit.

(5) The notice under paragraph (3) must state—

(a) that the appointment as provisional liquidator has been terminated;

(b) the date of that termination; and

(c) that the appointment terminated otherwise than on the making of a winding-up order.

NOTES

Para (4): sub-para (a) substituted by the Insolvency (England and Wales) (No 2) (Amendment) Rules 2021, SI 2021/1028, r 39, as from 1 October 2021 (for savings provisions see the note to r 1A.1 at **[10.539]**). Sub-para (a) previously read as follows—

"(a) must be delivered to the registrar of companies as soon as reasonably practicable;".

CHAPTER 6 STATEMENT OF AFFAIRS AND OTHER INFORMATION

[Note: a document required by the Act or these Rules must also contain the standard contents set out in Part 1.]

[10.822]
7.40 Notice requiring statement of affairs (section 131)

(1) Where, under section 131, the official receiver requires a nominated person to provide the official receiver with a statement of the affairs of the company, the official receiver must deliver a notice to that person.

(2) The notice must be headed "Notice requiring statement of affairs" and must—

(a) identify the company immediately below the heading;

(b) require a nominated person to prepare and submit to the official receiver a statement of affairs of the company;

(c) inform the nominated person—

(i) of the names and addresses of any other nominated person to whom such a notice has been delivered, and

(ii) of the date by which the statement must be delivered; and

(d) state the effect of section 131(7) (penalty for non-compliance) and section 235 (duty to co-operate) as it applies to the official receiver.

(3) The official receiver must inform the nominated person that a document for the preparation of the statement of affairs capable of completion in compliance with rule 7.41 can be supplied by the official receiver if requested.

[10.823]

7.41 Statement of affairs

(1) The statement of affairs must be headed "Statement of affairs" and must contain [the following, or, where paragraph (1B) applies, the information specified in that paragraph]—

- (a) identification details for the company;
- (b) a statement that it is a statement of the affairs of the company on a date which is specified, being—
  - (i) the date of the winding-up order, or
  - (ii) the date directed by the official receiver;
- (c) a list of the company's shareholders with the following information about each one—
  - (i) name and postal address,
  - (ii) the type of shares held,
  - (iii) the nominal amount of the shares held,
  - (iv) the number of shares held,
  - (v) the amount per share called up, and
  - (vi) the total amount of shares called up;
- (d) the total amount of shares called up held by all shareholders;
- (e) a summary of the assets of the company, setting out the book value and estimated realisable value of—
  - (i) any assets subject to a fixed charge,
  - (ii) any assets subject to a floating charge,
  - (iii) any uncharged assets, and
  - (iv) the total value of all the assets available for preferential creditors;
- (f) a summary of the liabilities of the company, setting out—
  - (i) the amount of preferential debts,
  - (ii) an estimate of the deficiency with respect to preferential debts or the surplus available after paying the preferential debts,
  - (iii) an estimate of the prescribed part, if applicable,
  - (iv) an estimate of the total assets available to pay debts secured by floating charges,
  - (v) the amount of debts secured by floating charges,
  - (vi) an estimate of the deficiency with respect to debts secured by floating charges or the surplus available after paying the debts secured by fixed or floating charges,
  - (vii) the amount of unsecured debts (excluding preferential debts),
  - (viii) an estimate of the deficiency with respect to unsecured debts or the surplus available after paying unsecured debts,
  - (ix) any issued and called-up capital, and
  - (x) an estimate of the deficiency with respect to, or surplus available to, members of the company;
- (g) a list of the company's creditors (as required by section 131(2)) with the following particulars required by paragraph (2) indicating—
  - (i) any creditors under hire-purchase, chattel leasing or conditional sale agreements,
  - (ii) any creditors who are consumers claiming amounts paid in advance of the supply of goods or services, and
  - (iii) any creditors claiming retention of title over property in the company's possession.

[(1A) Paragraph (1B) applies if a moratorium under Part A1 of the Act is or has been in force for the company at any time within the period of 12 weeks ending with the day on which the winding up petition is presented.

(1B) Where this paragraph applies the statement of affairs must contain—

- (a) the matters specified in paragraph (1)(a) to (e) and (g); and
- (b) the information specified in paragraph (1)(f) but with the modifications specified in paragraph (1C).

(1C) The modifications referred to in paragraph (1B)(b) are that—

- (a) the summary of the liabilities of the company must, in addition, set out which of the debts owed by the company are—
  - (i) moratorium debts, and
  - (ii) priority pre-moratorium debts,

  within the meaning given by section 174A, and
- (b) sub-paragraph 1(e)(iv) has effect as if the reference to preferential creditors included references to moratorium debts and priority pre-moratorium debts within the meaning given by section 174A.
- (c) paragraph (1)(f)(i), (ii) and (vii) has effect as if the reference to preferential debts included references to moratorium debts and priority pre-moratorium debts within the meaning given by section 174A.]

(2) The particulars required by this paragraph are as follows—

- (i) the name and postal address,
- (ii) the amount of the debt owed to the creditor,
- (iii) details of any security held by the creditor,
- (iv) the date the security was given, and
- (v) the value of any such security.

(3) Paragraph (4) applies where the particulars required by paragraph (2) relate to creditors who are either—

- (a) employees or former employees of the company; or
- (b) consumers claiming amounts paid in advance for the supply of goods or services.

(4) Where this paragraph applies—

- (a) the statement of affairs itself must state separately for each of paragraph (3)(a) and (b) the number of such creditors and the total of the debts owed to them; and
- (b) the particulars required by paragraph (2) in respect of those creditors must be set out in separate schedules to the statement of affairs for each of paragraph (3)(a) and (b).

(5) The statement of affairs must be verified by a statement of truth by the nominated person, or all of them if more than one, making the statement of affairs.

(6) The nominated person (or one of them, if more than one) must deliver the statement of affairs verified as required by paragraph (5) to the official receiver together with a copy.

(7) The official receiver must deliver the verified copy of the statement of affairs and any statements of concurrence delivered under rule 7.42 to the registrar of companies.

(8) However the official receiver must not deliver to the registrar of companies with the statement of affairs any schedule required by paragraph (4)(b).

NOTES

Para (1): words in square brackets inserted by the Insolvency (England and Wales) (No 2) (Amendment) Rules 2021, SI 2021/1028, r 40(1), (2), as from 1 October 2021 (for savings provisions see the note to r 1A.1 at **[10.539]**).

Paras (1A)–(1C): inserted by SI 2021/1028, r 40(1), (3), as from 1 October 2021 (for savings provisions see the note to r 1A.1 at **[10.539]**).

[10.824]

7.42 Statement of affairs: statement of concurrence

(1) The official receiver may require a person mentioned in section 131(3) ("a relevant person") to deliver to the official receiver a statement of concurrence.

(2) A statement of concurrence is a statement, verified by a statement of truth, that that person concurs in the statement of affairs submitted by a nominated person.

(3) The official receiver must inform the nominated person who has been required to submit a statement of affairs that the relevant person has been required to deliver a statement of concurrence.

(4) The nominated person must deliver a copy of the statement of affairs to every relevant person who has been required to submit a statement of concurrence.

(5) A statement of concurrence—
- (a) must identify the company; and
- (b) may be qualified in relation to matters dealt with in the statement of affairs, where the relevant person—
  - (i) is not in agreement with the statement of affairs,
  - (ii) considers the statement of affairs to be erroneous or misleading, or
  - (iii) is without the direct knowledge necessary for concurring in it.

(6) The relevant person must deliver the required statement of concurrence (with a copy) to the official receiver before the end of the period of five business days (or such other period as the official receiver may agree) beginning with the day on which the relevant person receives the statement of affairs.

[10.825]

7.43 Order limiting disclosure of statement of affairs etc

(1) Where the official receiver thinks that disclosure of the whole or part of the statement of affairs or of any statement of concurrence would be likely to prejudice the conduct of the winding up or might reasonably be expected to lead to violence against any person, the official receiver may apply to the court for an order that the statement of affairs, statement of concurrence or any specified part of them must not be filed with the registrar of companies.

(2) The court may order that the whole or a specified part of the statement of affairs or of a statement of concurrence must not be delivered to the registrar of companies.

(3) The official receiver must as soon as reasonably practicable deliver to the registrar of companies a copy of the order, and the statement of affairs and any statement of concurrence to the extent allowed by the order.

[10.826]

7.44 Release from duty to submit statement of affairs: extension of time (section 131)

(1) The official receiver may exercise the power in section 131(5) to release a person from an obligation to submit a statement of affairs imposed under section 131(1) or (2), or to grant an extension of time, either at the official receiver's own discretion, or at the request of a nominated person.

(2) A nominated person may apply to the court for a release or an extension of time if the official receiver refuses that person's request.

(3) On receipt of an application, the court may, if it is satisfied that no sufficient cause is shown for it, dismiss it without giving notice to any party other than the applicant.

(4) Unless the application is dismissed, the court must fix a venue for it to be heard.

(5) The applicant must, at least 14 days before any hearing, deliver to the official receiver a notice stating the venue with a copy of the application and of any evidence on which the applicant intends to rely.

(6) The official receiver may do either or both of the following—
- (a) file a report of any matters which the official receiver thinks ought to be drawn to the court's attention; or
- (b) appear and be heard on the application.

(7) If a report is filed, the official receiver must deliver a copy of it to the applicant not later than five business days before the hearing.

(8) The court must deliver sealed copies of any order made on the application to the nominated person and the official receiver.

(9) The applicant must pay the applicant's own costs in any event and, unless and to the extent that the court orders otherwise those costs will not be an expense of the winding up.

[10.827]

7.45 Statement of affairs: expenses

(1) If a nominated person cannot personally prepare a proper statement of affairs, the official receiver may, as an expense of the winding up, employ a person or firm to assist in the preparation of the statement.

(2) At the request of a nominated person, made on the grounds that the nominated person cannot personally prepare a proper statement, the official receiver may authorise an allowance, payable as an expense of the winding up, of all or part of the expenses to be incurred by the nominated person in employing a person or firm to assist the nominated person in preparing it.

(3) Any such request by the nominated person must be accompanied by an estimate of the expenses involved; and the official receiver must only authorise the employment of a named person or a named firm, approved by the official receiver.

(4) An authorisation given by the official receiver under this rule must be subject to such conditions (if any) as the official receiver thinks fit to impose relating to the manner in which any person may obtain access to relevant documents and other records.

(5) Nothing in this rule relieves a nominated person from any obligation relating to the preparation, verification and submission of the statement of affairs, or to the provision of information to the official receiver or the liquidator.

(6) Any payment made as an expense of the winding up under this rule must be made in the prescribed order of priority.

(7) Paragraphs (2) to (6) of this rule may be applied, on application to the official receiver by any nominated person, in relation to the making of a statement of concurrence.

[10.828]

7.46 Delivery of accounts to official receiver

(1) Any of the persons specified in section 235(3) must, at the request of the official receiver, deliver to the official receiver accounts of the company of such nature, as at such date, and for such period, as the official receiver may specify.

(2) The period specified may begin from a date up to three years before the date of the presentation of the winding-up petition, or from an earlier date to which audited accounts of the company were last prepared.

(3) The court may, on the official receiver's application, require accounts for any earlier period.

(4) Rule 7.45 applies (with the necessary modifications) in relation to accounts to be delivered under this rule as it applies in relation to the statement of affairs.

(5) The accounts must, if the official receiver so requires, be verified by a statement of truth and (whether or not so verified) be delivered to the official receiver within 21 days of the request under paragraph (1), or such longer period as the official receiver may allow.

[10.829]

7.47 Further disclosure

(1) The official receiver may at any time require a nominated person to deliver (in writing) further information amplifying, modifying or explaining any matter contained in the statement of affairs, or in accounts delivered under the Act or these Rules.

(2) The information must, if the official receiver so directs, be verified by a statement of truth, and (whether or not so verified) be delivered to the official receiver within 21 days of the requirement under paragraph (1), or such longer period as the official receiver may allow.

CHAPTER 7 REPORTS AND INFORMATION TO CREDITORS AND CONTRIBUTORIES

[Note: a document required by the Act or these Rules must also contain the standard contents set out in Part 1.]

[10.830]

7.48 Reports by official receiver

(1) The official receiver must deliver a report on the winding up and the state of the company's affairs to the creditors and contributories at least once after the making of the winding-up order.

(2) The report must contain—

(a) identification details for the proceedings;
(b) contact details for the official receiver;
(c) a summary of the assets and liabilities of the company as known to the official receiver at the date of the report;
(d) such comments on the summary and the company's affairs as the official receiver thinks fit; and
(e) any other information of relevance to the creditors or contributories.

(3) The official receiver may apply to the court to be relieved of any duty imposed by this rule or to be authorised to carry out the duty in another way.

(4) On such an application the court must have regard to the cost of carrying out the duty, to the amount of the assets available, and to the extent of the interest of creditors or contributories, or any particular class of them.

(5) If proceedings in a winding-up are stayed by order of the court any duty of the official receiver to deliver a report under this rule ceases.

[10.831]

7.49 Reports by official receiver: estimate of prescribed part

(1) The official receiver must include in a report under rule 7.48(1) estimates to the best of the official receiver's knowledge and belief of the value of—

(a) the prescribed part (whether or not the official receiver might be required under section 176A to make the prescribed part available for the satisfaction of unsecured debts); and
(b) the company's net property (as defined by section 176A(6)).

(2) If the official receiver (as liquidator) proposes to make an application to court under section 176A(5) the report must say so and give the reason for the application.

(3) The official receiver may exclude from an estimate under paragraph (1) information the disclosure of which could seriously prejudice the commercial interests of the company.

(4) If the exclusion of such information affects the calculation of the estimate, the report must say so.

[10.832]
7.50 Further information where winding up follows administration

(1) This rule applies where an administrator is appointed by the court under section 140 as the company's liquidator and becomes aware of creditors not formerly known to that person as administrator.

(2) The liquidator must deliver to those creditors a copy of any statement previously sent by the administrator to creditors in accordance with paragraph 49(4) of Schedule B1 and rule 3.35.

[10.833]
7.51 Notice of stay of winding up

Where the court grants a stay in a winding up it may include in its order such requirements on the company as it thinks just with a view to bringing the stay to the notice of creditors and contributories.

CHAPTER 8 THE LIQUIDATOR

[Note: a document required by the Act or these Rules must also contain the standard contents set out in Part 1.]

[10.834]
7.52 Choosing a person to be liquidator

(1) This rule applies where nominations are sought by the official receiver from the company's creditors and contributories under section 136 for the purpose of choosing a person to be liquidator of the company in place of the official receiver.

(2) The official receiver must deliver to the creditors and contributories a notice inviting proposals for a liquidator.

(3) The notice must explain that the official receiver is not obliged to seek the creditors' views on any proposals that do not meet the requirements of paragraphs (4) and (5).

(4) A proposal must state the name and contact details of the proposed liquidator, and contain a statement that the proposed liquidator is qualified to act as an insolvency practitioner in relation to the company and has consented to act as liquidator of the company.

(5) A proposal must be received by the official receiver within five business days of the date of the notice under paragraph (2).

(6) Following the end of the period for inviting proposals under paragraph (2), where any proposals are received the official receiver must seek a decision on the nomination of a liquidator from the creditors (on any proposals received from creditors) and from the contributories (on any proposals received from contributories) by—
(a) a decision procedure; or
(b) the deemed consent procedure.

(7) Where a decision is sought under paragraph (6) following the official receiver's decision under section 136(5)(a) to seek a nomination, the decision date must be not more than four months from the date of the winding-up order.

(8) Where the official receiver is required under section 136(5)(c) to seek such a decision, the official receiver must send a notice to the creditors and contributories which complies with rule 15.7 or 15.8 so far as relevant.

(9) The notice must also—
(a) identify any liquidator proposed to be nominated by a creditor (in the case of a notice to creditors) or by a contributory (in the case of a notice to contributories) in accordance with this rule; and
(b) contain a statement explaining the effect of section 137(2) (duty of official receiver to consider referral of need for appointment of liquidator to the Secretary of State where no person is chosen to be liquidator).

(10) The decision date in the notice must be no later than 21 days after the date for receiving proposals has passed.

(11) The creditors and contributories must be given at least 14 days' notice of the decision date.

(12) Where no proposal is received by the official receiver under paragraph (2), the official receiver has no obligation to seek a decision from creditors or contributories on a liquidator.

(13) Nothing in this rule affects the official receiver's ability under section 137(1), at any time when liquidator of the company, to apply to the Secretary of State to appoint a liquidator in place of the official receiver.

[10.835]
7.53 Appointment of liquidator by creditors or contributories

(1) This rule applies where a person is appointed as liquidator by the creditors or contributories.

(2) The convener of the decision procedure or deemed consent procedure, or the chair in the case of a meeting must certify the appointment, but not unless and until the appointee has provided to the convener or the chair a statement to the effect that the appointee is an insolvency practitioner qualified under the Act to be the liquidator and consents to act.

(3) The certificate must be authenticated and dated by the convener or chair and must—
(a) identify the company;
(b) identify and provide contact details for the person appointed as liquidator;
(c) state the date on which the liquidator was appointed;
(d) state that the appointee—

(i) has provided a statement of being qualified to act as an insolvency practitioner in relation to the company,

(ii) has consented to act, and

(iii) was appointed as liquidator of the company.

(4) Where two or more liquidators are appointed the certificate must also specify (as required by section 231) whether any act required or authorised under any enactment to be done by the liquidator is to be done by all or any one or more of them.

(5) The liquidator's appointment is effective from the date on which the appointment is certified, that date to be endorsed on the certificate.

(6) The convener or chair (if that person is not the official receiver) must deliver the certificate to the official receiver.

(7) The official receiver must in any case deliver the certificate to the liquidator.

[10.836]

7.54 Decision on nomination

(1) In the case of a decision on the nomination of a liquidator—

(a) if on any vote there are two nominees, the person who obtains the most support is appointed;

(b) if there are three or more nominees, and one of them has a clear majority over both or all the others together, that one is appointed; and

(c) in any other case, the convener or chair must continue to take votes (disregarding at each vote any nominee who has withdrawn and, if no nominee has withdrawn, the nominee who obtained the least support last time) until a clear majority is obtained for any one nominee.

(2) In the case of a decision being made at a meeting, the chair may at any time put to the meeting a resolution for the joint nomination of any two or more nominees.

[10.837]

7.55 Invitation to creditors and contributories to form a liquidation committee

(1) Where a decision is sought from the company's creditors and contributories on the appointment of a liquidator, the convener of the decision must at the same time deliver to the creditors and contributories a notice inviting them to decide whether a liquidation committee should be established if sufficient creditors are willing to be members of the committee.

(2) The notice must also invite nominations for membership of the committee, such nominations to be received by a date specified in the notice.

(3) The notice must—

(a) state that nominations must be delivered to the convener by the specified date;

(b) state, in the case of creditors, that nominations can only be accepted if the convener is satisfied as to the creditors' eligibility under rule 17.4; and

(c) explain the effect of section 141(2) and (3) on whether a committee is to be established under Part 17.

[10.838]

7.56 Appointment by the court

(1) This rule applies where the liquidator is appointed by the court under section 139(4) (different persons nominated by creditors and contributories) or section 140 (winding up following administration or CVA).

(2) The court must not make the order unless and until the person being appointed has filed with the court a statement to the effect that that person is an insolvency practitioner, duly qualified under the Act to be the liquidator, and consents to act.

(3) The order of the court must contain—

(a) identification details for the proceedings;

(b) the name and title of the judge making the order;

(c) the name and postal address of the applicant;

(d) the capacity in which the applicant made the application;

(e) identification and contact details for the proposed liquidator;

(f) a statement that the proposed liquidator has filed—

(i) a statement of qualification to act as an insolvency practitioner in relation to the company, and

(ii) a consent to act;

(g) the order that the proposed liquidator is appointed liquidator of the company; and

(h) the date on which the order is made.

(4) Where two or more liquidators are appointed the order must also specify (as required by section 231) whether any act required or authorised under any enactment to be done by the liquidator is to be done by all or any one or more of them.

(5) The court must deliver two copies of the order to the official receiver one of which must be sealed.

(6) The official receiver must deliver the sealed copy of the order to the person appointed as liquidator.

(7) The liquidator's appointment takes effect from the date of the order or such other date as the court orders.

(8) Within 28 days from appointment, the liquidator must—

(a) deliver notice of the appointment to the creditors and to the contributories of the company of whom the liquidator is aware; or

(b) advertise the appointment in accordance with any directions given by the court.

(9) In the notice under this rule the liquidator must—

(a) state whether the liquidator proposes to seek decisions from creditors and contributories for the purpose of establishing a liquidation committee, or proposes only to seek a decision from creditors for that purpose; and

(b) if the liquidator does not propose to seek any such decision, set out the powers of the creditors under the Act to require the liquidator to seek one.

[10.839]
7.57 Appointment by the Secretary of State

(1) This rule applies where the official receiver applies to the Secretary of State to appoint a liquidator in place of the official receiver, or refers to the Secretary of State the need for an appointment.

(2) If the Secretary of State makes an appointment, the Secretary of State must deliver a copy of the certificate of appointment to the official receiver, who must deliver it to the person appointed.

(3) The certificate must specify the date from which the liquidator's appointment is to be effective.

[10.840]
7.58 Cost of liquidator's security (section 390(3))

The cost of the liquidator's security required by section 390(3) for the proper performance of the liquidator's functions is an expense of the winding up.

[10.841]
7.59 Appointment to be gazetted and notice given to registrar of companies

(1) The liquidator—
- (a) must gazette a notice of the appointment as soon as reasonably practicable after appointment; and
- (b) may advertise the notice in such other manner as the liquidator thinks fit.

(2) The notice must state—
- (a) that a liquidator has been appointed; and
- (b) the date of the appointment.

(3) As soon as reasonably practicable the liquidator must deliver notice of the appointment to the registrar of companies.

[10.842]
7.60 Hand-over of assets by official receiver to liquidator

(1) This rule only applies where the liquidator is appointed in succession to the official receiver acting as liquidator.

(2) When the liquidator's appointment takes effect, the official receiver must as soon as reasonably practicable do all that is required for putting the liquidator into possession of the assets.

(3) On taking possession of the assets, the liquidator must discharge any balance due to the official receiver on account of—
- (a) expenses properly incurred by the official receiver and payable under the Act or these Rules; and
- (b) any advances made by the official receiver in respect of the assets, together with interest on such advances at the rate specified in section 17 of the Judgments Act 1838 at the date of the winding-up order.

(4) Alternatively, the liquidator may (before taking office) give to the official receiver a written undertaking to discharge any such balance out of the first realisation of assets.

(5) The official receiver has a charge on the assets in respect of any sums due to the official receiver under paragraph (3) until they have been discharged, subject only to the deduction from realisations by the liquidator of the proper costs and expenses of such realisations.

(6) The liquidator must from time to time out of the realisation of assets discharge all guarantees properly given by the official receiver for the benefit of the insolvent estate, and must pay all the official receiver's expenses.

(7) The official receiver must give to the liquidator all such information relating to the affairs of the company and the course of the winding up as the official receiver considers to be reasonably required for the effective discharge by the liquidator of the liquidator's duties.

(8) The official receiver must also deliver to the liquidator a copy of any report made by the official receiver under Chapter 7 of Part 7.

[10.843]
7.61 Liquidator's resignation

(1) A liquidator may resign only—
- (a) on grounds of ill health;
- (b) because of the intention to cease to practise as an insolvency practitioner;
- (c) because the further discharge of the duties of liquidator is prevented or made impracticable by—
  - (i) a conflict of interest, or
  - (ii) a change of personal circumstances;
- (d) where two or more persons are acting as liquidator jointly, and it is the opinion of both or all of them that it is no longer expedient that there should continue to be that number of joint liquidators.

(2) Before resigning, the liquidator must deliver a notice to creditors, and invite the creditors by a decision procedure, or by deemed consent procedure, to consider whether a replacement should be appointed, except where the resignation is under sub-paragraph (1)(d).

(3) The notice must—
- (a) state the liquidator's intention to resign;
- (b) state that under rule 7.61(7) of these Rules the liquidator will be released 21 days after the date of delivery of the notice of resignation to the court under section 172(6), unless the court orders otherwise; and
- (c) comply with rule 15.7 or 15.8 so far as applicable.

(4) The notice may suggest the name of a replacement liquidator.

(5) The notice must be accompanied by a summary of the liquidator's receipts and payments.

(6) The decision date must be not more than five business days before the date on which the liquidator intends to give notice under section 172(6).

(7) The resigning liquidator's release is effective 21 days after the date on which the notice of resignation under section 172(6) is filed with the court.

[10.844]
7.62 Notice to official receiver of intention to vacate office

(1) This rule applies where the liquidator intends to vacate office, whether by resignation or otherwise, and as a result there will be a vacancy in the office of liquidator (so that by virtue of section 136(3) the official receiver is liquidator until the vacancy is filled).

(2) The liquidator must deliver notice of that intention to the official receiver at least 21 days before the liquidator intends to vacate office.

(3) The liquidator must include in the notice to the official receiver the following details of any property of the company which has not been realised, applied, distributed or otherwise fully dealt with in the winding up—

- (a) the nature of the property;
- (b) its value (or the fact that it has no value);
- (c) its location;
- (d) any action taken by the liquidator to deal with the property or any reason for the liquidator not dealing with it; and
- (e) the current position in relation to it.

[10.845]
7.63 Decision of creditors to remove liquidator

(1) This rule applies where the convener of the decision procedure or chair of the meeting (as the case may be) is other than the official receiver, and a decision is made, using a decision procedure, to remove the liquidator

(2) The convener or chair must within three business days of the decision to remove the liquidator deliver a certificate to that effect to the official receiver.

(3) If the creditors decided to appoint a new liquidator, the certificate of the new liquidator's appointment must also be delivered to the official receiver within that time; and the certificate must comply with the requirements in rule 7.53.

(4) The certificate of the liquidator's removal must—

- (a) identify the company;
- (b) identify and provide contact details for the removed liquidator;
- (c) state that the creditors of the company decided on the date specified in the certificate that the liquidator specified in the certificate be removed from office as liquidator of the company;
- (d) state the decision procedure used, and the decision date;
- (e) state that the creditors either—
  - (i) did not decide against the liquidator being released, or
  - (ii) decided that the liquidator should not be released; and
- (f) be authenticated and dated by the convener or chair.

(5) The liquidator's removal is effective from the date of the certificate of removal.

[10.846]
7.64 Procedure on removal by creditors

(1) Where the creditors have decided that the liquidator be removed, the official receiver must file the certificate of removal with the court.

(2) The official receiver must deliver a copy of the certificate as soon as reasonably practicable to the removed liquidator and deliver a notice of the removal to the registrar of companies.

[10.847]
7.65 Removal of liquidator by the court (section 172(2))

(1) This rule applies where an application is made to the court under section 172(2) for the removal of the liquidator, or for an order directing the liquidator to initiate a decision procedure of creditors for the purpose of removing the liquidator.

(2) On receipt of an application, the court may, if it is satisfied that no sufficient cause is shown for it, dismiss it without giving notice to any party other than the applicant.

(3) Unless the application is dismissed, the court must fix a venue for it to be heard.

(4) The applicant must, at least 14 days before any hearing, deliver to the liquidator and the official receiver a notice stating the venue with a copy of the application and of any evidence on which the applicant intends to rely.

(5) A respondent may apply for security for costs of the application and the court may make such an order if it is satisfied, having regard to all the circumstances of the case, that it is just to make such an order.

(6) The liquidator and the official receiver may do either or both of the following—

- (a) file a report of any matters which the liquidator or the official receiver thinks ought to be drawn to the court's attention; or
- (b) appear and be heard on the application.

(7) On a successful application the court's order must contain—

- (a) the name of the court (and hearing centre if applicable) in which the order is made;
- (b) the name and title of the judge making the order;
- (c) the name and postal address of the applicant;
- (d) the capacity in which the applicant made the application;
- (e) identification and contact details for the liquidator;

(f) identification details for the company;

(g) an order either—

(i) that that the liquidator is removed from office; or

(ii) that the liquidator must initiate a decision procedure of the company's creditors (specifying which procedure is to be used) on or before the date specified in the order for the purpose of considering the liquidator's removal from office; and

(h) the date the order is made.

(8) The costs of the application are not payable as an expense of the winding up unless the court orders otherwise.

(9) Where the court removes the liquidator—

(a) it must deliver the sealed order of removal to the former liquidator and a copy of the order to the official receiver; and

(b) the former liquidator must deliver a copy of the order to the registrar of companies as soon as reasonably practicable.

(10) If the court appoints a new liquidator, rule 7.56 applies.

NOTES

Note: sub-para (7)(g)(i) above is reproduced as per the original Queen's Printer's version of these Rules.

[10.848]

7.66 Removal of liquidator by the Secretary of State (section 172(4))

(1) This rule applies where the Secretary of State decides to direct under section 172(4) the removal of a liquidator appointed by the Secretary of State.

(2) Before doing so the Secretary of State must deliver to the liquidator and the official receiver a notice of the Secretary of State's decision and the grounds for the decision.

(3) The notice must specify a period within which the liquidator may make representations against implementation of the decision.

(4) If the Secretary of State directs the removal of the liquidator, the Secretary of State must as soon as reasonably practicable—

(a) deliver notice of the Secretary of State's decision to the registrar of companies, the liquidator and the official receiver; and

(b) file notice of the decision with the court.

(5) Where the Secretary of State directs the liquidator be removed the court may make any order that it could have made if the liquidator had been removed by the court.

[10.849]

7.67 Deceased liquidator

(1) If the liquidator (not being the official receiver) dies a notice of the fact and date of death must be delivered to the official receiver by one of the following—

(a) a surviving joint liquidator;

(b) a member of the deceased liquidator's firm (if the deceased was a member or employee of a firm);

(c) an officer of the deceased liquidator's company (if the deceased was an officer or employee of a company);

(d) a personal representative of the deceased liquidator.

(2) If no such notice has been delivered within the 21 days following the liquidator's death then any other person may deliver the notice.

(3) The official receiver must—

(a) file notice of the death with the court, for the purpose of fixing the date of the deceased liquidator's release under section 174(4)(a); and

(b) deliver a copy of the notice to the registrar of companies.

[10.850]

7.68 Loss of qualification as insolvency practitioner

(1) This rule applies where the liquidator vacates office on ceasing to be qualified to act as an insolvency practitioner in relation to the company.

(2) A notice of the fact must be delivered as soon as reasonably practicable to the official receiver by one of the following—

(a) the liquidator who has vacated office;

(b) a continuing joint liquidator;

(c) the recognised professional body which was the source of the vacating liquidator's authorisation to act in relation to the company.

(3) The notice must be authenticated and dated by the person delivering the notice.

(4) The official receiver must—

(a) deliver a notice of receiving such a notice to the Secretary of State; and

(b) deliver a copy to the registrar of companies.

[10.851]

7.69 Application by liquidator for release (section 174(4)(b) or (d))

(1) An application by a liquidator to the Secretary of State for release under section 174(4)(b) or (d) must contain—

(a) identification details for the proceedings;

(b) identification and contact details for the liquidator;

(c) a statement that the liquidator of the company is applying to the Secretary of State to grant the liquidator with a certificate of the liquidator's release as liquidator as a result of the circumstances specified in the application;

(d) details of the circumstances referred to in sub-paragraph (c) under which the liquidator has ceased to act as liquidator.

(2) The application must be authenticated and dated by the liquidator.

(3) When the Secretary of State releases the former liquidator, the Secretary of State must certify the release and deliver the certificate to the former liquidator whose release is effective from the date of the certificate or such other date as the certificate specifies.

(4) The Secretary of State must deliver notice of the release to the registrar of companies.

[10.852]
7.70 Release of official receiver

(1) The official receiver must, before giving notice to the Secretary of State under section 174(3) (that the winding up is for practical purposes complete), deliver notice of intention to do so to the creditors.

(2) The notice must be accompanied by a summary of the official receiver's receipts and payments as liquidator.

(3) The summary of receipts and payments must also include a statement as to the amount paid to unsecured creditors under section 176A (prescribed part).

(4) When the Secretary of State has determined the date from which the official receiver's release is to be effective, the Secretary of State must—

(a) notify the official receiver of the release; and
(b) deliver a notice of the release to the registrar of companies accompanied by the summary of the official receiver's receipts and payments.

[10.853]
7.71 Final account prior to dissolution (section 146)

(1) The final account which the liquidator is required to make up under section 146(2) and deliver to creditors must comply with the requirements of rule 18.14.

(2) When the account is delivered to the creditors it must be accompanied by a notice which states—

(a) that the company's affairs are fully wound up;
(b) that the creditor has the right to request information from the liquidator under rule 18.9;
(c) that a creditor has the right to challenge the liquidator's remuneration and expenses under rule 18.34;
(d) that a creditor may object to the release of the liquidator by giving notice in writing to the liquidator before the end of the prescribed period;
(e) that the prescribed period is the period ending at the later of—
  (i) eight weeks after delivery of the notice, or
  (ii) if any request for information under rule 18.9 or any application to court under that rule or rule 18.34 is made when that request or application is finally determined;
(f) that the liquidator will vacate office under section 172(8) as soon as the liquidator has complied with section 146(4) by filing with the court and delivering to the registrar of companies the final account and notice containing the statement required by section 146(4)(b) of whether any creditors have objected to the liquidator's release; and
(g) that the liquidator will be released under section 174(4)(d)(ii) at the same time as vacating office unless any of the creditors objected to the release.

(3) The liquidator must deliver a copy of the notice under section 146(4) to the Secretary of State.

(4) Rule 7.69 applies to an application by the liquidator to the Secretary of State for release.

[10.854]
7.72 Relief from, or variation of, duty to report

(1) The court may, on the application of the liquidator or the official receiver, relieve the liquidator or official receiver of any duty imposed on the liquidator or official receiver by rule 7.70 or rule 7.71, or authorise the liquidator or official receiver to carry out the duty in a way other than required by either of those rules.

(2) In considering whether to act under this rule, the court must have regard to the cost of carrying out the duty, to the amount of the assets available, and to the extent of the interest of creditors or contributories, or any particular class of them.

[10.855]
7.73 Liquidator's duties on vacating office

(1) A liquidator who ceases to be in office in consequence of removal, resignation or ceasing to be qualified to act as an insolvency practitioner in relation to the company, must as soon as reasonably practicable deliver to the successor as liquidator—

(a) the assets (after deduction of any expenses properly incurred, and distributions made, by the previous liquidator);
(b) the records of the winding up, including correspondence, proofs and other documents relating to the winding up while it was within the former liquidator's responsibility; and
(c) the company's documents and other records.

(2) Where the liquidator vacates office under section 172(8) (final report to creditors), the liquidator must deliver to the official receiver the company's documents and other records which have not already been disposed of in accordance with general regulations in the course of the winding up.

[10.856]
7.74 Power of court to set aside certain transactions

(1) If in dealing with the insolvent estate the liquidator enters into any transaction with a person who is an associate of the liquidator, the court may, on the application of any interested person, set the transaction aside and order the liquidator to compensate the company for any loss suffered in consequence of it.

(2) This does not apply if either—

(a) the transaction was entered into with the prior consent of the court; or

(b) it is shown to the court's satisfaction that the transaction was for value, and that it was entered into by the liquidator without knowing, or having any reason to suppose, that the person concerned was an associate.

(3) Nothing in this rule is to be taken as prejudicing the operation of any rule of law or equity relating to a liquidator's dealings with trust property, or the fiduciary obligations of any person.

[10.857]
7.75 Rule against improper solicitation

(1) Where the court is satisfied that any improper solicitation has been used by or on behalf of the liquidator in obtaining proxies or procuring the liquidator's appointment, it may order that no remuneration be allowed as an expense of the winding up to any person by whom, or on whose behalf, the solicitation was exercised.

(2) An order of the court under this rule overrides any resolution of the liquidation committee or the creditors, or any other provision of these Rules relating to the liquidator's remuneration.

CHAPTER 9 DUTIES AND POWERS OF LIQUIDATOR

[Note: a document required by the Act or these Rules must also contain the standard contents set out in Part 1.]

[10.858]
7.76 General duties of liquidator

(1) The duties which the Act imposes on the court relating to the collection of the company's assets and their application in discharge of the company's liabilities are discharged by the liquidator as an officer of the court subject to its control.

(2) In the discharge of the liquidator's duties, the liquidator, for the purposes of acquiring and retaining possession of the company's property, has the same powers as a receiver appointed by the High Court, and the court may on the application of the liquidator enforce such acquisition or retention accordingly.

[10.859]
7.77 Permission for exercise of powers by liquidator

(1) Where the Act or these Rules require permission for the liquidator to exercise a power any permission given must not be a general permission but must relate to a particular proposed exercise of the liquidator's power.

(2) A person dealing with the liquidator in good faith and for value is not concerned to enquire whether any such permission has been given.

(3) Where the liquidator has done anything without such permission, the court or the liquidation committee may, for the purpose of enabling the liquidator to meet the liquidator's expenses out of the assets, ratify what the liquidator has done; but neither must do so unless satisfied that the liquidator has acted in a case of urgency and has sought ratification without undue delay.

(4) In this rule "permission" includes "sanction".

[10.860]
7.78 Enforced delivery up of company's property (section 234)

(1) The powers conferred on the court by section 234 (enforced delivery of company property) are exercisable by the liquidator or, where a provisional liquidator has been appointed, by the provisional liquidator.

(2) Any person on whom a requirement under section 234(2) is imposed by the liquidator or provisional liquidator must, without avoidable delay, comply with it.

CHAPTER 10 SETTLEMENT OF LIST OF CONTRIBUTORIES

[Note: a document required by the Act or these Rules must also contain the standard contents set out in Part 1.]

[10.861]
7.79 Delegation to liquidator of power to settle list of contributories

(1) The duties of the court under section 148 in relation to settling the list of contributories are, by virtue of these Rules and in accordance with section 160, delegated to the liquidator.

(2) The liquidator's duties in settling the list of contributories are performed as an officer of the court subject to the court's control.

[10.862]
7.80 Duty of liquidator to settle list (section 148)

The liquidator must, as soon as reasonably possible after the liquidator's appointment, exercise the court's power to settle a list of the company's contributories for the purposes of section 148 and, with the court's approval, rectify the register of members.

[10.863]
7.81 Contents of list

(1) The list must identify—

(a) the several classes of the company's shares (if more than one); and

(b) the several classes of contributories, distinguishing between those who are contributories in their own right and those who are so as representatives of, or liable for the debts of, others.

(2) In the case of each contributory the list must state—

(a) the address of the contributory;

(b) the number and class of shares, or the extent of any other interest to be attributed to the contributory; and

(c) if the shares are not fully paid up, the amounts which have been called up and paid in respect of them (and the equivalent, if any, where the interest of the contributory is other than shares).

[10.864]

7.82 Procedure for settling list

(1) Having settled the list, the liquidator must as soon as reasonably practicable deliver a notice, to each person included in the list, that this has been done.

(2) The notice given to each person must state—

(a) in what character, and for what number of shares or what interest, that person is included in the list;

(b) what amounts have been called up and paid up in respect of the shares or interest; and

(c) that in relation to any shares or interest not fully paid up, that person's inclusion in the list may result in the unpaid capital being called.

(3) The notice must inform a person to whom it is given that, if that person objects to any entry in, or omission from, the list, that person should so inform the liquidator in writing within 21 days from the date of the notice.

(4) On receipt of an objection, the liquidator must within 14 days deliver a notice to the objector either—

(a) that the liquidator has amended the list (specifying the amendment); or

(b) that the liquidator considers the objection to be not well-founded and declines to amend the list.

(5) The notice must in either case inform the objector of the effect of rule 7.83.

[10.865]

7.83 Application to court for variation of the list

(1) If a person ("the objector") objects to any entry in, or exclusion from, the list of contributories as settled by the liquidator and, notwithstanding notice by the liquidator declining to amend the list, the objector maintains the objection, the objector may apply to the court for an order removing the entry objected to or (as the case may be) otherwise amending the list.

(2) The application must be made within 21 days of the delivery to the applicant of the liquidator's notice under rule 7.82(4).

[10.866]

7.84 Variation of, or addition to, the list

The liquidator may from time to time vary or add to the list of contributories as previously settled by the liquidator, but subject in all respects to the preceding rules in this Chapter.

[10.867]

7.85 Costs of applications to vary etc the list of contributories

Where a person applies to set aside or vary any act or decision of the liquidator in settling the list of contributories then—

(a) the liquidator (if other than the official receiver) is not liable for any costs incurred by that person in relation to the application unless the court makes an order to that effect; and

(b) the official receiver is not personally liable for such costs.

CHAPTER 11 CALLS ON CONTRIBUTORIES

[Note: a document required by the Act or these Rules must also contain the standard contents set out in Part 1.]

[10.868]

7.86 Making of calls by the liquidator (sections 150 and 160)

(1) Subject as follows the powers relating to the making of calls on contributories are exercisable by the liquidator as an officer of the court.

(2) However as provided by section 160(2) the making of a call requires either the sanction of the liquidation committee or the court's special permission.

[10.869]

7.87 Sanction of the liquidation committee for making a call

(1) Where the liquidator proposes to make a call, and there is a liquidation committee, the liquidator may summon a meeting of the committee for the purpose of obtaining its sanction.

(2) The liquidator must deliver a notice of the meeting to each member of the committee giving at least five business days' notice of the meeting.

(3) The notice must state the purpose of making the call and the proposed amount of the call.

[10.870]

7.88 Application to court for permission to make a call (sections 150 and 160)

(1) Where the liquidator proposes to make a call the liquidator may apply to the court without notice to any other party for permission to make a call on any contributories of the company.

(2) The application must state the amount of the proposed call, and the contributories on whom it is to be made.

(3) The application must be supported by a witness statement accompanied by a schedule.

(4) The witness statement must have the title "Witness statement of liquidator in support of application for call" and must contain—

(a) identification and contact details for the liquidator;

(b) identification details for the company;

(c) the number of persons on the list of contributories settled by the liquidator;
(d) the total number of shares to which the proposed call relates;
(e) the statement that in addition to the amount of the assets of the company mentioned in the schedule the liquidator believes a further sum will be required to satisfy the debts and liabilities of the company, and pay the expenses of and incidental to the winding up;
(f) the additional sum required;
(g) a statement that in order to provide the additional sum it is necessary to make a call upon the persons on the settled list of contributories, and that as it is probable that some of those contributories will partly or wholly fail to pay the amount of the call, the liquidator believes that it is necessary that a call of a specified amount per share be made in order to realise the amount required;
(h) the specified amount per share.

(5) The accompanying schedule must show—
(a) the amount due in respect of debts already proved;
(b) the estimated amount of—
  (i) further liabilities of the company, and
  (ii) the expenses of the winding up;
(c) the total of the amounts referred to in sub-paragraphs (a) and (b); and
(d) a list of the assets in hand belonging to the company with their total value.

(6) The schedule must be verified by a statement of truth made by the liquidator.

[10.871]
7.89 Order giving permission to make a call

(1) The court's order giving permission to make a call must have the title "Order giving permission to make a call" and must contain—
(a) the name of the court (and hearing centre if applicable) in which the order is made;
(b) the name and title of the judge making the order;
(c) identification and contact details for the liquidator;
(d) identification details for the company;
(e) an order that the liquidator may make a call of the amount per share specified in the order on the contributories who are specified in the order;
(f) the amount per share of the call;
(g) the names of the contributories of the company on whom the liquidator is to make the call;
(h) an order that each such contributory must on or before the date specified in the order pay to the liquidator of the company the amount due from that contributory in respect of the call; and
(i) the date of the order.

(2) The court may direct that notice of the order be delivered to the contributories concerned, or to other contributories, or may direct that the notice be publicly advertised.

[10.872]
7.90 Making and enforcement of the call

(1) The liquidator must deliver a notice of the call to each of the contributories concerned.

(2) The notice must contain—
(a) identification details for the company;
(b) identification and contact details for the liquidator;
(c) a statement that a call on the contributories specified in the notice of the amount per share stated in the notice was sanctioned by—
  (i) a resolution of the liquidation committee of the company passed on the date which is stated in the notice, or
  (ii) an order of the court named in the notice on the date which is stated in the notice;
(d) the amount per share of the call;
(e) the amount or balance due from the contributory to whom the notice is addressed in respect of the call;
(f) the date by which the sum must be paid;
(g) a warning to the contributory that, if the required sum is not paid by the date specified in the notice, interest at the rate specified in the notice will be charged on the unpaid amount from that date until payment; and
(h) the specified annual interest rate.

(3) The notice must be accompanied by a copy of the resolution of the liquidation committee sanctioning the call or of the court's order giving permission as the case may be.

[10.873]
7.91 Court order to enforce payment of call by a contributory

(1) The court may make an order to enforce payment of the amount due from a contributory.

(2) The order must have the title "Order for payment of call due from contributory" and must contain—
(a) the name of the court (and hearing centre if applicable) in which the order is made;
(b) identification and contact details for the liquidator who made the application;
(c) the name and title of the judge making the order;
(d) identification details for the company;
(e) the name and postal address of the contributory who is the subject of the order;
(f) the amount per share of the call;
(g) an order that the contributory pay the liquidator the sum stated in the order in respect of the call on or before the date stated in the order or within four business days after service of the order whichever is the later;
(h) an order that the contributory pay the liquidator interest at the rate stated in the order for the period commencing from the date specified in the order to the date of payment;

(i) an order that the contributory pay the liquidator a stated sum in respect of the liquidator's costs of the application within the same period as the amount of the call must be paid;

(j) a warning to the contributory that if the required sums are not paid within the time specified in the order further steps will be taken to compel the contributory to comply with the order; and

(k) the date of the order.

CHAPTER 12 SPECIAL MANAGER

[Note: a document required by the Act or these Rules must also contain the standard contents set out in Part 1.]

[10.874]

7.92 Application of this Chapter and interpretation

This Chapter applies to applications for the appointment of a special manager by a liquidator and by a provisional liquidator (where one has been appointed), and so references to the liquidator are to be read as including a provisional liquidator.

[10.875]

7.93 Appointment and remuneration of special manager (section 177)

(1) An application made by the liquidator under section 177 for the appointment of a special manager must be supported by a report setting out the reasons for the application.

(2) The report must include the applicant's estimate of the value of the business or property in relation to which the special manager is to be appointed.

(3) The court's order appointing the special manager must have the title "Order of appointment of special manager" and must contain—

(a) identification details for the proceedings;

(b) the name and address of the person who made the application;

(c) the name and title of the judge making the order;

(d) the name and address of the proposed special manager;

(e) the order that the proposed special manager is appointed as special manager of the company;

(f) details of the special manager's responsibility over the company's business or property;

(g) the powers to be entrusted to the special manager under section [177(3)];

(h) the time allowed for the special manager to give the required security for the appointment;

(i) the duration of the special manager's appointment being one of the following—

(i) for a fixed period stated in the order,

(ii) until the occurrence of a specified event, or

(iii) until the court makes a further order;

(j) an order that the special manager's remuneration will be fixed from time to time by the court; and

(k) the date of the order.

(4) The appointment of a special manager may be renewed by order of the court.

(5) The special manager's remuneration will be fixed from time to time by the court.

(6) The acts of the special manager are valid notwithstanding any defect in the special manager's appointment or qualifications.

NOTES

Para (3): figure in square brackets in sub-para (g) substituted by the Insolvency (England and Wales) (Amendment) Rules 2017, SI 2017/366, rr 3, 21, as from 6 April 2017.

[10.876]

7.94 Security

(1) The appointment of the special manager does not take effect until the person appointed has given (or, if the court allows, undertaken to give) security to the applicant for the appointment.

(2) A person appointed as a special manager may give security either specifically for a particular winding up, or generally for any winding up in relation to which that person may be employed as special manager.

(3) The amount of the security must be not less than the value of the business or property in relation to which the special manager is appointed, as estimated in the applicant's report which accompanied the application for appointment.

(4) When the special manager has given security to the applicant that person must file with the court a certificate as to the adequacy of the security.

(5) The cost of providing the security must be paid in the first instance by the special manager; but—

(a) where a winding-up order is not made, the special manager is entitled to be reimbursed out of the property of the company, and the court may order accordingly; and

(b) where a winding-up order is made, the special manager is entitled to be reimbursed as an expense of the winding up in the prescribed order of priority.

[10.877]

7.95 Failure to give or keep up security

(1) If the special manager fails to give the required security within the time allowed for that purpose by the order of appointment, or any extension of that time that may be allowed, the liquidator must report the failure to the court, which may discharge the order appointing the special manager.

(2) If the special manager fails to keep up the security, the liquidator must report the failure to the court, which may remove the special manager, and make such order as it thinks just as to costs.

(3) If the court discharges the order appointing the special manager or makes an order removing the special manager, the court must give directions as to whether any, and if so what, steps should be taken for the appointment of another special manager.

[10.878]
7.96 Accounting

(1) The special manager must produce accounts, containing details of the special manager's receipts and payments, for the approval of the liquidator.

(2) The accounts must be for—
- (a) each three month period for the duration of the special manager's appointment; or
- (b) any shorter period ending with the termination of the special manager's appointment.

(3) When the accounts have been approved, the special manager's receipts and payments must be added to those of the liquidator.

[10.879]
7.97 Termination of appointment

(1) The special manager's appointment terminates—
- (a) if the winding-up petition is dismissed; or
- (b) in a case where a provisional liquidator was appointed under section 135, if the appointment is discharged without a winding-up order having been made.

(2) If the liquidator is of the opinion that the employment of the special manager is no longer necessary or beneficial for the company, the liquidator must apply to the court for directions, and the court may order the special manager's appointment to be terminated.

(3) The liquidator must make the same application if the creditors decide that the appointment should be terminated.

CHAPTER 13 PUBLIC EXAMINATION OF COMPANY OFFICERS AND OTHERS (SECTION 133)

[Note: a document required by the Act or these Rules must also contain the standard contents set out in Part 1.]

[10.880]
7.98 Applications relating to promoters, past managers etc (section 133(1)(c))

(1) An application under section 133(1) for the public examination of a person falling within paragraph (c) of subsection (1) (promoters, past managers, etc) must be accompanied by a report by the official receiver indicating—
- (a) the grounds on which the official receiver thinks the person is within that paragraph; and
- (b) whether the official receiver thinks it is likely that the order can be served on the person at a known address and, if so, by what means.

(2) If the official receiver thinks that there is no reasonable certainty that service at a known address will be effective, the court may direct that the order be served by some means other than, or in addition to, service in such manner.

[10.881]
7.99 Request by a creditor for a public examination (section 133(2))

(1) A request made under section 133(2) by a creditor to the official receiver for the public examination of a person must contain—
- (a) identification details for the company;
- (b) the name and postal address of the creditor;
- (c) the name and postal address of the proposed examinee;
- (d) a description of the relationship which the proposed examinee has, or has had, with the company;
- (e) a request by the creditor to the official receiver to apply to the court for a public examination of the proposed examinee under section 133(2);
- (f) the amount of the creditor's claim in the winding up;
- (g) a statement that the total amount of the creditor's and any concurring creditors' claims is believed to represent not less than one-half in value of the debts of the company;
- (h) a statement that the creditor understands the requirement to deposit with the official receiver such sum as the official receiver may determine to be appropriate by way of security for the expenses of holding a public examination; and
- (i) a statement that the creditor believes that a public examination is required for the reason stated in the request.

(2) The request must be authenticated and dated by the creditor.

(3) The request must be accompanied by—
- (a) a list of the creditors concurring with the request and the amounts of their respective claims in the winding up, with their respective values; and
- (b) from each concurring creditor, confirmation of the creditor's concurrence.

[10.882]
7.100 Request by a contributory for a public examination

(1) A request made under section 133(2) by a contributory to the official receiver for the public examination of a person must contain—
- (a) identification details for the company;
- (b) the name and postal address of the contributory;
- (c) the name and postal address of the proposed examinee;
- (d) a description of the relationship which the proposed examinee has, or has had, with the company;
- (e) a request by the contributory to the official receiver to apply to the court for a public examination of the proposed examinee under section 133(2);
- (f) the number of shares held in the company by the contributory;
- (g) the number of votes to which the contributory is entitled;

(h) a statement that the total amount of the contributory's and any concurring contributories' shares and votes is believed to represent not less than three-quarters in value of the company's contributories;
(i) a statement that the contributory understands the requirement to deposit with the official receiver such sum as the official receiver may determine to be appropriate by way of security for the expenses of holding a public examination; and
(j) a statement that the contributory believes that a public examination is required for the reason specified in the request.

(2) The request must be authenticated and dated by the contributory.

(3) The request must be accompanied by—
(a) a list of the contributories concurring with the request and the number of shares and votes each holds in the company; and
(b) from each concurring contributory, confirmation of the concurrence and of the number of shares and votes held in the company.

[10.883]
7.101 Further provisions about requests by a creditor or contributory for a public examination

(1) A request by a creditor or contributory for a public examination does not require the support of concurring creditors or contributories if the requisitioning creditor's debt or, as the case may be, requisitioning contributory's shares, is sufficient alone under section 133(2).

(2) Before the official receiver makes the requested application, the creditor or contributory requesting the examination must deposit with the official receiver such sum (if any) as the official receiver determines is appropriate as security for the expenses of the public examination (if ordered).

(3) The official receiver must make the application for the examination—
(a) within 28 days of receiving the creditor's or contributory's request (if no security is required under paragraph (2); or
(b) within 28 days of the creditor or contributory (as the case may be) depositing the required security.

(4) However if the official receiver thinks the request is unreasonable, the official receiver may apply to the court for an order to be relieved from making the application.

(5) If the application for an order under paragraph (4) is made without notice to any other party and the court makes such an order then the official receiver must deliver a notice of the order as soon as reasonably practicable to the creditors or contributories who requested the examination.

(6) If the court dismisses the official receiver's application under paragraph (4), the official receiver must make the application under section 133(2) as soon as reasonably practicable.

[10.884]
7.102 Order for public examination

(1) An order for a public examination must have the title "Order for Public Examination" and must contain the following—
(a) identification details for the proceedings;
(b) the name and title of the judge making the order;
(c) the name and postal address of the person to be examined;
(d) the venue for the public examination;
(e) the order that the person named in the order must attend the specified venue for the purpose of being publicly examined;
(f) the date of the order; and
(g) a warning to the person to be examined that failure without reasonable excuse to attend the public examination at the time and place specified in the order will make the person liable to be arrested without further notice under section 134(2); and that the person will also be guilty of contempt of court under section 134(1) and be liable to be committed to prison or fined.

(2) The official receiver must serve a copy of the order on the person to be examined as soon as reasonably practicable after the order is made.

(3) The court must rescind an order for the public examination of a person who was said to fall within section 133(1)(c) if that person satisfies the court that it is not so.

[Note: rule 81.9 (as amended) of the CPR requires a warning as mentioned in paragraph (1)(g) to be displayed prominently on the front of the order.]

[10.885]
7.103 Notice of the public examination

(1) The official receiver must give at least 14 days' notice of the public examination to—
(a) the liquidator (if a liquidator has been nominated or appointed);
(b) the special manager (if a special manager has been appointed); and
(c) the creditors and all the contributories of the company who are known to the official receiver (subject to any contrary direction of the court).

(2) Where the official receiver thinks fit additional notice of the order may be given by gazetting the notice.

(3) The official receiver may in addition to gazetting the notice advertise it in such other manner as the official receiver thinks fit;

(4) The notice must state—
(a) the purpose of the public examination; and
(b) the venue.

(5) Unless the court directs otherwise, the official receiver must not give notice under paragraph (2) of an order relating to a person falling within section 133(1)(c) until at least five business days have elapsed since the examinee was served with the order.

[10.886]
7.104 Examinee unfit for examination

(1) Where the examinee is a person who lacks capacity within the meaning of the Mental Capacity Act 2005 or is unfit to undergo or attend for public examination, the court may—
  (a) stay the order for the examinee's public examination; or
  (b) order that it is to be conducted in such manner and at such place as it thinks just.

(2) The applicant for an order under paragraph (1) must be—
  (a) a person who has been appointed by a court in the United Kingdom or elsewhere to manage the affairs of, or to represent, the examinee;
  (b) a person who appears to the court to be a suitable person to make the application; or
  (c) the official receiver.

(3) Where the application is made by a person other than the official receiver, then—
  (a) the application must, unless the examinee is a person who lacks capacity within the meaning of the Mental Capacity Act 2005, be supported by the witness statement of a registered medical practitioner as to the examinee's mental and physical condition;
  (b) at least five business days' notice of the application must be given to the official receiver and the liquidator (if other than the official receiver); and
  (c) before any order is made on the application, the applicant must deposit with the official receiver such sum as the latter certifies to be necessary for the additional expenses of an examination.

(4) An order must contain—
  (a) identification details for the proceedings;
  (b) the name and postal address of the applicant;
  (c) the name and title of the judge making the order;
  (d) the capacity in which the applicant (other than the official receiver) made the application;
  (e) the name and postal address of the examinee;
  (f) the date of the order for the examinee's public examination ("the original order");
  (g) a statement that the court is satisfied that the examinee specified in the order lacks capacity within the meaning of the Mental Capacity Act 2005 to manage and administer the examinee's property and affairs or is unfit to undergo a public examination;
  (h) an order that—
    (i) the original order is to be stayed on the grounds that the examinee is unfit to undergo a public examination, or
    (ii) the original order is varied (as specified in this order) on the grounds that the examinee is unfit to attend the public examination fixed by the original order; and
  (i) the date of the order.

(5) Where a person other than the official receiver makes the application, the court may order that some or all of the expenses of the examination are to be payable out of the deposit under paragraph (3)(c), instead of as an expense of the winding up.

(6) Where the application is made by the official receiver it may be made without notice to any other party, and may be supported by evidence set out in a report by the official receiver to the court.

[10.887]
7.105 Procedure at public examination

(1) At the public examination the examinee must—
  (a) be examined on oath; and
  (b) answer all the questions which the court puts, or allows to be put.

(2) A person allowed by section 133(4) to question the examinee may—
  (a) with the approval of the court appear by an appropriately qualified legal representative; or
  (b) in writing authorise another person to question the examinee on that person's behalf.

(3) The examinee may at the examinee's own expense employ an appropriately qualified legal representative, who may put to the examinee such questions as the court may allow for the purpose of enabling the examinee to explain or qualify any answers given by the examinee, and may make representations on behalf of the examinee.

(4) The court must have such record made of the examination as the court thinks proper.

(5) The record may, in any proceedings (whether under the Act or otherwise) be used as evidence of any statement made by the examinee in the course of the public examination.

(6) If criminal proceedings have been instituted against the examinee, and the court is of the opinion that continuing the hearing might prejudice a fair trial of those proceedings, the hearing may be adjourned.

[10.888]
7.106 Adjournment

[Note: rule 81.9 (as amended) of the CPR requires a warning as mentioned in paragraph (3) to be displayed prominently on the front of the order.]

(1) The court may adjourn the public examination from time to time, either to a fixed date or generally.

(2) Where the examination has been adjourned generally, the court may at any time on the application of the official receiver or of the examinee—
  (a) fix a venue for the resumption of the examination; and

(b) give directions as to the manner in which, and the time within which, notice of the resumed public examination is to be given to persons entitled to take part in it.

(3) An order adjourning the public examination to a fixed date must contain a warning to the examinee that failure without reasonable excuse to attend the public examination at the time and place specified in the order will make the examinee liable to be arrested without further notice under section 134(2); and that the examinee will also be guilty of contempt of court under section 134(1) and be liable to be committed to prison or fined.

(4) Where an application to resume an examination is made by the examinee, the court may grant it on terms that the examinee must pay the expenses of giving the notices required by paragraph (2) and that, before a venue for the resumed public examination is fixed, the examinee must deposit with the official receiver such sum as the official receiver considers necessary to cover those expenses.

[10.889]
7.107 Expenses of examination

(1) Where a public examination of the examinee has been ordered by the court on a request by a creditor under rule 7.99 or by a contributory under rule 7.100, the court may order that some or all of the expenses of the examination are to be paid out of the deposit required under those rules, instead of as an expense of the winding up.

(2) The costs and expenses of a public examination do not fall on the official receiver personally.

CHAPTER 14 PRIORITY OF PAYMENT OF COSTS AND EXPENSES, ETC

[10.890]
7.108 General rule as to priority

(1) All fees, costs, charges and other expenses incurred in the course of the winding up are to be treated as expenses of the winding up.

[(1A) The costs of an application by the liquidator under rule 1A.27 are to be treated as an expense of the winding up unless the court orders otherwise.]

[(2) The expenses of the winding up are payable out of—

(a) assets of the company available for the payment of general creditors, including—
  (i) proceeds of any legal action which the liquidator has power to bring in the liquidator's own name or in the name of the company;
  (ii) proceeds arising from any award made under any arbitration or other dispute resolution procedure which the liquidator has power to bring in the liquidator's own name or in the name of the company;
  (iii) any payments made under any compromise or other agreement intended to avoid legal action or recourse to arbitration or to any other dispute resolution procedure;
  (iv) payments made as a result of an assignment or a settlement of any such action, arrangement or procedure in lieu of or before any judgment being given or award being made; and
(b) subject as provided in rules 7.111 to 7.116, property comprised in or subject to a floating charge created by the company.]

(3) The expenses associated with the prescribed part must be paid out of the prescribed part.

(4) Subject as provided in [paragraphs (5) and (6), rule 7.108A, and] rules 7.112 to 7.116, the expenses are payable in the following order of priority—

(a) the following expenses, which rank equally in order of priority—
  (i) expenses that are properly chargeable or incurred by the provisional liquidator in carrying out the functions conferred on the provisional liquidator by the court,
  (ii) expenses that are properly chargeable or incurred by the official receiver or the liquidator in preserving, realising or getting in any of the assets of the company or otherwise in the preparation, conduct or assignment of any legal proceedings, arbitration or other dispute resolution procedures, which the official receiver or liquidator has power to bring in the official receiver's or liquidator's own name or bring or defend in the name of the company or in the preparation or conduct of any negotiations intended to lead or leading to a settlement or compromise of any legal action or dispute to which the proceedings or procedures relate,
  (iii) expenses that relate to the employment of a shorthand writer, if appointed by an order of the court made at the instance of the official receiver in connection with an examination, and
  (iv) expenses that are incurred in holding a hearing under rule 7.104 (examinee unfit) where the application for it was made by the official receiver;
(b) any other expenses incurred or disbursements made by the official receiver or under the official receiver's authority, including those incurred or made in carrying on the business of the company;
(c) the fees payable under any order made under section 414 or section 415A, including those payable to the official receiver (other than the fee referred to in sub-paragraph (d)), and any remuneration payable to the official receiver under general regulations;
(d) the fee payable under any order made under section 414 for the performance by the official receiver of the general duties of the official receiver and any repayable sum deposited under any such order as security for the fee;
(e) the cost of any security provided by a provisional liquidator, liquidator or special manager in accordance with the Act or these Rules;
(f) the remuneration of the provisional liquidator (if any);
(g) any sum deposited on an application for the appointment of a provisional liquidator;
(h) the costs of the petitioner, and of any person appearing on the petition whose costs are allowed by the court;
(i) the remuneration of the special manager (if any);
(j) any amount payable to a person employed or authorised, under Chapter 6 of this Part, to assist in the preparation of a statement of affairs or of accounts;

Part 10 Miscellaneous other SIs

(k) any allowance made, by order of the court, in respect of costs on an application for release from the obligation to submit a statement of affairs, or for an extension of time for submitting such a statement;

(l) the costs of employing a shorthand writer in any case other than one appointed by an order of the court at the instance of the official receiver in connection with an examination;

(m) any necessary disbursements by the liquidator in the course of the administration of the winding up (including any [. . .] expenses incurred by members of the liquidation committee or their representatives and allowed by the liquidator under rule 17.24, but not including any payment of corporation tax in circumstances referred to in sub-paragraph (p));

(n) the remuneration or emoluments of any person who has been employed by the liquidator to perform any services for the company, as required or authorised by or under the Act or these Rules;

(o) the remuneration of the liquidator, up to an amount not exceeding that which is payable under Schedule 11 (determination of insolvency office-holder's remuneration);

(p) the amount of any corporation tax on chargeable gains accruing on the realisation of any asset of the company (irrespective of the person by whom the realisation is effected);

(q) the balance, after payment of any sums due under sub-paragraph (o) above, of any remuneration due to the liquidator; and

(r) any other expenses properly chargeable by the liquidator in carrying out the liquidator's functions in the winding up.

[(5) This paragraph applies where—

(a) a moratorium has been in force for a company under Part A1 of the Act,

(b) proceedings for the winding up of the company are begun before the end of the period of 12 weeks beginning with the day after the end of the moratorium, and

(c) there are claims in respect of any prescribed fees or expenses of the official receiver which, in accordance with section 174A(2), fall to be paid in preference to all other claims.

(6) Where paragraph (5) applies, then, in consequence of those claims of the official receiver falling to be paid in preference to all other claims by virtue of section 174A(2), the order of priority referred to in paragraph (4) is modified as follows—

(a) sub-paragraph (a)(ii) is omitted in relation to any expenses chargeable or incurred by the official receiver,

(b) sub-paragraph (a)(iii) and (iv) are omitted, and

(c) sub-paragraphs (b) to (d) are omitted in relation to any expenses incurred by, or fee payable to, the official receiver.]

NOTES

Para (1A): inserted by the Insolvency (England and Wales) (No 2) (Amendment) Rules 2021, SI 2021/1028, r 41(1), (2), as from 1 October 2021 (for savings provisions see the note to r 1A.1 at **[10.539]**).

Para (2): substituted by the Insolvency (England and Wales) (Amendment) Rules 2017, SI 2017/366, rr 3, 26, as from 6 April 2017.

Para (4): words in first pair of square brackets inserted by SI 2021/1028, r 41(1), (3), as from 1 October 2021 (for savings provisions see the note to r 1A.1 at **[10.539]**). Words omitted from sub-para (m) originally inserted by the Insolvency Amendment (EU 2015/848) Regulations 2017, SI 2017/702, regs 2, 3, Schedule, Pt 2, paras 32, 40, as from 26 June 2017, except in relation to proceedings opened before that date; and subsequently revoked by the Insolvency (Amendment) (EU Exit) Regulations 2019, SI 2019/146, reg 2, Schedule, Pt 4, paras 46, 83, as from IP completion day (as defined in the European Union (Withdrawal Agreement) Act 2020, s 39) (for savings, see reg 4 of the 2019 Regulations at **[12.82]**).

Paras (5), (6): added by SI 2021/1028, r 41(1), (4), as from 1 October 2021 (for savings provisions see the note to r 1A.1 at **[10.539]**).

[10.891]
[7.108A Priority of moratorium debts in subsequent winding up

(1) Where section 174A applies the moratorium debts and priority pre-moratorium debts mentioned in subsection (2)(b) of that section are payable in the following order of priority—

(a) amounts payable in respect of goods or services supplied during the moratorium under a contract where, but for section 233B(3) or (4), the supplier would not have had to make that supply,

(b) wages or salary arising under contract of employment,

(c) other debts or other liabilities apart from the monitor's remuneration or expenses, and

(d) the monitor's remuneration or expenses.]

NOTES

Commencement: 1 October 2021.

Inserted by the Insolvency (England and Wales) (No 2) (Amendment) Rules 2021, SI 2021/1028, r 42, as from 1 October 2021 (for savings provisions see the note to r 1A.1 at **[10.539]**).

[10.892]
7.109 Winding up commencing as voluntary

Where the winding up by the court immediately follows a voluntary winding up (whether members' voluntary or creditors' voluntary), such remuneration of the voluntary liquidator and costs and expenses of the voluntary winding up as the court may allow are to rank in priority with the expenses specified in rule 7.108(4)(a).

[10.893]
7.110 Saving for powers of the court (section 156)

(1) The priorities laid down by rules 7.108 and 7.109 are subject to the power of the court to make orders under section 156, where the assets are insufficient to satisfy the liabilities.

(2) Nothing in those rules—

(a) applies to or affects the power of any court, in proceedings by or against the company, to order costs to be paid by the company, or the liquidator; or

(b) affects the rights of any person to whom such costs are ordered to be paid.

CHAPTER 15 LITIGATION EXPENSES AND PROPERTY SUBJECT TO A FLOATING CHARGE

[Note: a document required by the Act or these Rules must also contain the standard contents set out in Part 1.]

[10.894]

7.111 Interpretation

In this Chapter—

"approval" and "authorisation" respectively mean—

(a) where yet to be incurred, the approval, and

(b) where already incurred, the authorisation,

of expenses specified in section 176ZA(3);

"the creditor" means—

[(za) a creditor in respect of a debt which is a moratorium debt or a priority pre-moratorium debt within the meaning given by section 174A;]

(a) a preferential creditor of the company; or

(b) a holder of a debenture secured by, or a holder of, a floating charge created by the company;

"legal proceedings" means—

(a) proceedings under sections 212, 213, 214, 238, 239, 244 and 423 and any arbitration or other dispute resolution proceedings invoked for purposes corresponding to those to which the sections relate and any other proceedings, including arbitration or other dispute resolution procedures, which a liquidator has power to bring in the liquidator's own name for the purpose of preserving, realising, or getting in any of the assets of the company;

(b) legal actions and proceedings, arbitration or any other dispute resolution procedures which a liquidator has power to bring or defend in the name of the company; and

(c) negotiations intended to lead or leading to a settlement or compromise of any action, proceeding or procedure to which sub-paragraphs (a) or (b) relate;

"litigation expenses" means expenses of a winding up which—

(a) are properly chargeable or incurred in the preparation or conduct of any legal proceedings; and

(b) as expenses in the winding up, exceed, or in the opinion of the liquidator are likely to exceed (and only in so far as they exceed or are likely to exceed), in the aggregate £5,000; and

"specified creditor" means a creditor identified under rule 7.113(2).

NOTES

In the definition "the creditor", para (za) was inserted by the Insolvency (England and Wales) (No 2) (Amendment) Rules 2021, SI 2021/1028, r 43, as from 1 October 2021 (for savings provisions see the note to r 1A.1 at **[10.539]**).

[10.895]

7.112 Priority of litigation expenses

Litigation expenses will not have the priority provided by section 176ZA over any claims to property comprised in or subject to a floating charge created by the company and must not be paid out of any such property unless and until approved or authorised in accordance with rules 7.113 to 7.116.

[10.896]

7.113 Requirement for approval or authorisation of litigation expenses

(1) Subject to rules 7.114 to 7.116 either paragraphs (3) and (4) apply or paragraph (5) applies where, in the course of winding up a company, the liquidator—

(a) ascertains that property is comprised in or subject to a floating charge;

(b) has personally instituted or proposes to institute or continue legal proceedings or is in the process of defending or proposes to defend any legal proceeding brought or likely to be brought against the company; and

(c) before or at any stage in those proceedings, is of the opinion that—

(i) the assets of the company available for payment of general creditors are or will be insufficient to pay litigation expenses, and

(ii) in order to pay litigation expenses the liquidator will have to have recourse to property comprised in or subject to a floating charge created by the company.

(2) As soon as reasonably practicable after the date on which the liquidator forms the opinion referred to in paragraph (1), the liquidator must identify the creditor who, in the liquidator's opinion at that time—

(a) has a claim to property comprised in or subject to a floating charge created by the company; and

(b) taking into account the value of that claim and any subsisting property then comprised in or secured by such a charge, appears to the liquidator to be the creditor most immediately likely of any persons having such claims to receive some payment in respect of a claim but whose claim would not be paid in full.

(3) The liquidator must request from the specified creditor the approval or authorisation of such amount for litigation expenses as the liquidator thinks fit.

(4) Where the liquidator identifies two or more specified creditors, the liquidator must seek from each of them approval or authorisation of such amount of litigation expenses as the liquidator thinks fit, apportioned between them ("the apportioned amount") according to the value of the property to the extent covered by their charges.

(5) For so long as the conditions specified in paragraph (1) subsist, the liquidator may, in the course of a winding up, make such further requests to the specified creditor or creditors for approval or authorisation of such further amount for litigation expenses as the liquidator thinks fit to be paid out of property comprised in or subject to a floating charge created by the company, taking into account any amount for litigation expenses previously approved or authorised and the value of the property comprised in or subject to the floating charge.

Part 10 Miscellaneous other SIs

[10.897]

7.114 Requests for approval or authorisation

(1) All requests made by the liquidator for approval or authorisation must include the following—

(a) a statement describing the nature of the legal proceedings, including, where relevant, the statutory provision under which proceedings are or are to be brought and the grounds upon which the liquidator relies;

(b) a statement specifying the amount or apportioned amount of litigation expenses for which approval or authorisation is sought ("the specified amount");

(c) notice that approval or authorisation or other reply to the request must be made in writing within 28 days from the date of its being received ("the specified time limit"); and

(d) a statement explaining the consequences of a failure to reply within the specified time limit.

(2) Where anything in paragraph (1) requires the inclusion of any information, the disclosure of which could be seriously prejudicial to the winding up of the company, the liquidator may—

(a) exclude such information from any of the above statements or notices if accompanied by a statement to that effect; or

(b) include it on terms—

(i) that bind the creditor to keep the information confidential, and

(ii) that include an undertaking on the part of the liquidator to apply to the court for an order that so much of the information as may be kept in the files of the court, is not be open to public inspection.

(3) The creditor may within the specified time limit apply to the liquidator in writing for such further particulars as is reasonable and in such a case, the time limit specified in paragraph (1)(c) will apply from the date of the creditor's receipt of the liquidator's response to any such request.

(4) Where the liquidator requires the approval or authorisation of two or more creditors, the liquidator must deliver a request to each creditor, containing the matters listed in paragraph (1) and also giving—

(a) the number of creditors concerned;

(b) the total value of their claims, or if not known, as it is estimated to be by the liquidator immediately before delivering any such request; and

[(c) notice to—

(i) each preferential creditor, and

(ii) each creditor of the kind described in rule 7.111(za),

that approval or authorisation of the specified amount will be taken to be given where a majority in value of those creditors referred to in sub-paragraphs (i) and (ii) who respond within the specified time limit are in favour of it; or]

(d) where rule 7.113 applies, notice to the specified creditors that the amount of litigation expenses will be apportioned between them in accordance with that rule and notice of the value of the portion allocated to, and the identity of, the specified creditors affected by that apportionment.

NOTES

Para (4): sub-para (c) substituted by the Insolvency (England and Wales) (No 2) (Amendment) Rules 2021, SI 2021/1028, r 44, as from 1 October 2021 (for savings provisions see the note to r 1A.1 at **[10.539]**). Sub-para (c) previously read as follows—

"(c) to each preferential creditor, notice that approval or authorisation of the specified amount will be taken to be given where a majority in value of those preferential creditors who respond within the specified time limit are in favour of it; or".

[10.898]

7.115 Grant of approval or authorisation

(1) Where the liquidator fails to include in the liquidator's request any one of the matters, statements or notices required by paragraph (1) or paragraphs (1) and (4), of rule 7.114, the request for approval or authorisation will be treated as not having been made.

(2) Subject to paragraphs (3), (4) and (5), approval or authorisation will be taken to have been given where the specified amount has been requested by the liquidator, and—

(a) that amount is approved or authorised within the specified time limit; or

(b) a different amount is approved or authorised within the specified time limit and the liquidator considers it sufficient.

[(3) Paragraph (3A) applies where the liquidator requires the approval or authorisation of—

(a) two or more—

(i) preferential creditors, or

(ii) creditors of the kind described in rule 7.111(za); or

(b) one or more preferential creditors together with one or more creditors of the kind described in rule 7.111(za).]

[(3A) Where this paragraph applies approval or authorisation will be taken to be given where a majority in value of those creditors referred to in sub-paragraphs (3)(a)(i) or (ii) or (3)(b) (as the case may be) who respond within the specified time limit approve or authorise—

(a) the specified amount; or

(b) a different amount which the liquidator considers sufficient.]

[(4) Where a majority in value of—

(a) two or more—

(i) preferential creditors, or

(ii) creditors of the kind described in rule 7.111(za); or

(b) one or more preferential creditors together with one or more creditors of the kind described in rule 7.111(za), propose an amount other than that specified by the liquidator, they will be taken to have approved or authorised an amount equal to the lowest of the amounts so proposed.]

(5) In any case in which there is no response in writing within the specified time limit to the liquidator's request—

(a) at all; or

(b) at any time following the liquidator's provision of further particulars under rule 7.114(3);

the liquidator's request will be taken to have been approved or authorised from the date of the expiry of that time limit.

NOTES

Paras (3), (4): substituted by the Insolvency (England and Wales) (No 2) (Amendment) Rules 2021, SI 2021/1028, r 45(1), (2), (4), as from 1 October 2021 (for savings provisions see the note to r 1A.1 at **[10.539]**). Paras (3), (4) previously read as follows—

"(3) Where the liquidator requires the approval or authorisation of two or more preferential creditors, approval or authorisation will be taken to be given where a majority in value of those who respond within the specified time limit approve or authorise—

(a) the specified amount; or

(b) a different amount which the liquidator considers sufficient.

(4) Where a majority in value of two or more preferential creditors propose an amount other than that specified by the liquidator, they will be taken to have approved or authorised an amount equal to the lowest of the amounts so proposed.".

Para (3A): inserted by SI 2021/1028, r 45(1), (3), as from 1 October 2021 (for savings provisions see the note to r 1A.1 at **[10.539]**).

[10.899]

7.116 Application to the court by the liquidator

(1) In the circumstances specified below the court may, upon the application of the liquidator, approve or authorise such amount of litigation expenses as it thinks just.

(2) Except where paragraph (3) applies, the liquidator may apply to the court for an order approving or authorising an amount for litigation expenses only where the specified creditor (or, if more than one, any of them)—

(a) is or is intended to be a defendant in the legal proceedings in relation to which the litigation expenses have been or are to be incurred; or

(b) has been requested to approve or authorise the amount specified under rule 7.114(1)(b) and has—

(i) declined to approve or authorise, as the case may be, the specified amount,

(ii) approved or authorised an amount which is less than the specified amount and which lesser amount the liquidator considers insufficient, or

(iii) made such application for further particulars or other response to the liquidator's request as is, in the liquidator's opinion, unreasonable.

(3) Where the liquidator thinks that circumstances are such that the liquidator requires urgent approval or authorisation of litigation expenses, the liquidator may apply to the court for approval or authorisation either—

(a) without seeking approval or authorisation from the specified creditor; or

(b) if sought, before the expiry of the specified time limit.

(4) The court may grant such application for approval or authorisation—

(a) if the liquidator satisfies the court of the urgency of the case; and

(b) subject to such terms and conditions as the court thinks just.

(5) The liquidator must, at the same time as making any application to the court under this rule, deliver copies of it to the specified creditor, unless the court orders otherwise.

(6) The specified creditor (or, if more than one, any of them) is entitled to be heard on any such application unless the court orders otherwise.

(7) The court may grant approval or authorisation subject to such terms and conditions as it may think just, including terms and conditions relating to the amount or nature of the litigation expenses and as to any obligation to make further applications to the court under this rule.

(8) The costs of the liquidator's application under this rule, including the costs of any specified creditor appearing or represented on it, will be an expense of the winding up unless the court orders otherwise.

CHAPTER 16 MISCELLANEOUS RULES

[Note: a document required by the Act or these Rules must also contain the standard contents set out in Part 1.]

Sub-division A: Return of capital

[10.900]

7.117 Application to court for order authorising return of capital

(1) This rule applies where the liquidator intends to apply to the court for an order authorising a return of capital.

(2) The application must be accompanied by a list of the persons to whom the return is to be made.

(3) The list must include the same details of those persons as appears in the settled list of contributories, with any necessary alterations to take account of matters after settlement of the list, and the amount to be paid to each person.

(4) Where the court makes an order authorising the return, it must deliver a sealed copy of the order to the liquidator.

[10.901]

7.118 Procedure for return

(1) The liquidator must inform each person to whom a return is made of the rate of return per share, and whether it is expected that any further return will be made.

(2) Any payments made by the liquidator by way of the return may be delivered by post, unless for any reason another method of making the payment has been agreed with the payee.

Sub-division B: Dissolution after winding up

[10.902]

7.119 Secretary of State's directions under sections 203 and 205 and appeal

(1) This rule applies where the Secretary of State gives a direction under—

(a) section 203 (where official receiver applies to the registrar of companies for a company's early dissolution); or

(b) section 205 (application by interested person for postponement of dissolution).

(2) The Secretary of State must deliver the direction to the applicant for it.

(3) The applicant must deliver a copy of the direction to the registrar of companies, to comply with section 203(5) or, as the case may be, section 205(6).

(4) Following an appeal under section 203(4) or 205(4) (against a decision of the Secretary of State under the applicable section) the court must deliver a sealed copy of its order to the person in whose favour the appeal was determined.

(5) That person must deliver a copy to the registrar of companies to comply with section 203(5) or, as the case may be, section 205(6).

PARTS 8–11

(*Parts 8–11 concern personal insolvency and are outside the scope of this work.*)

PART 12 COURT PROCEDURE AND PRACTICE

CHAPTER 1 GENERAL

Application of the Civil Procedure Rules 1998

[10.903]

12.1 Court rules and practice to apply

(1) The provisions of the CPR (including any related Practice Directions) apply for the purposes of proceedings under [Parts A1] to 11 of the Act with any necessary modifications, except so far as disapplied by or inconsistent with these Rules.

(2) All insolvency proceedings must be allocated to the multi-track for which CPR Part 29 makes provision, and accordingly those provisions of the CPR which provide for directions questionnaires and track allocation do not apply.

(3) CPR Part 32 applies to a false statement in a document verified by a statement of truth made under these Rules as it applies to a false statement in a document verified by a statement of truth made under CPR Part 22.

NOTES

Para (1): words in square brackets substituted (for the original words "Parts 1") by the Insolvency (England and Wales) (No 2) (Amendment) Rules 2021, SI 2021/1028, r 80, Sch 1, as from 1 October 2021 (for savings provisions see the note to r 1A.1 at **[10.539]**).

[10.904]

12.2 Performance of functions by the Court

(1) Anything to be done under or by virtue of the Act or these Rules by, to or before the court may be done by, to or before a judge, District Judge or a registrar.

(2) The registrar or District Judge may authorise any act of a formal or administrative character which is not by statute that person's responsibility to be carried out by the chief clerk or any other officer of the court acting on that person's behalf, in accordance with directions given by the Lord Chancellor.

(3) The hearing of an application must be in open court unless the court directs otherwise.

CHAPTER 2 COMMENCEMENT OF INSOLVENCY PROCEEDINGS IN THE COUNTY COURT

[A document required by the Act or these Rules must also contain the standard contents set out in Part 1.]

[10.905]

12.3 Commencement of insolvency proceedings under [Parts A1] to 7 of the Act (corporate insolvency proceedings)

(1) Where section 117 of the Act, as extended in its application by section 251, gives jurisdiction to the County Court in respect of proceedings under [Parts A1] to 7 of the Act any such proceedings when they are commenced in the County Court may only be commenced in the hearing centre which serves the area in which the company's registered office is situated.

(2) However if the registered office is situated in an area served by a hearing centre for which Schedule 6 lists an alternative court or hearing centre then any such proceedings in the County Court may only be commenced in that alternative court or hearing centre.

NOTES

Words "Parts A1" in square brackets in the rule heading and in para (1) substituted (for the original words "Parts 1") by the Insolvency (England and Wales) (No 2) (Amendment) Rules 2021, SI 2021/1028, r 80, Sch 1, as from 1 October 2021 (for savings provisions see the note to r 1A.1 at **[10.539]**).

[10.906]

12.4 Commencement of insolvency proceedings under Parts 7A to 11 of the Act (personal insolvency proceedings; bankruptcy)

(1) Proceedings under Parts 7A to 11 of the Act that are allocated in accordance with rule 12.5 to the London Insolvency District when they are commenced in the County Court may only be commenced in the County Court at Central London.

(2) Elsewhere such proceedings when they are commenced in the County Court may only be commenced in the hearing centre determined in accordance with these Rules.

(3) However if the hearing centre so determined is one for which Schedule 6 lists an alternative hearing centre then such proceedings when they are commenced in the County Court may only be commenced in that alternative hearing centre.

[10.907]

12.5 Allocation of proceedings to the London Insolvency District

The following proceedings are allocated to the London Insolvency District—

(a) bankruptcy petitions or applications in relation to a debt relief order under section 251M (powers of court in relation to debt relief orders) or 251N (inquiry into debtor's dealings and property) where—

(i) the debtor is resident in England and Wales and within the six months immediately preceding the presentation of the petition or the making of the application the debtor carried on business within the area of the London Insolvency District—

(aa) for the greater part of those six months, or

(bb) for a longer period in those six months than in any other insolvency district,

(ii) the debtor is resident in England and Wales and within the six months immediately preceding the presentation of the petition or the making of the application the debtor did not carry on business in England and Wales but resided within the area of the London Insolvency District for—

(aa) the greater part of those six months, or

(bb) a longer period in those six months than in any other insolvency district,

(iii) the debtor is not resident in England and Wales but within the six months immediately preceding the presentation of the petition or the making of the application carried on business within the area of the London Insolvency District,

(iv) the debtor is not resident in England and Wales and within the 6 months immediately preceding the presentation of the petition or the making of the application did not carry on business in England and Wales but resided within the area of the London Insolvency District, or

(v) the debtor is not resident in England and Wales and within the 6 months immediately preceding the presentation of the petition or the making of the application the debtor neither carried on business nor resided in England and Wales;

(b) creditors' bankruptcy petitions presented by a Minister of the Crown or a Government Department, where either—

(i) in any statutory demand on which the petition is based the creditor has indicated the intention to present a bankruptcy petition to a court exercising jurisdiction in relation to the London Insolvency District, or

(ii) the petition is presented under section 267(2)(c) on the grounds specified in section 268(1)(b);

(c) bankruptcy petitions—

(i) where the petitioner is unable to ascertain the place where the debtor resides or, if the debtor carries on business in England and Wales, both where the debtor resides and where the debtor carries on business, or

(ii) where the debtor is a member of a partnership and—

(aa) the partnership is being wound up by the High Court sitting in London; or

(bb) a petition for the winding up of the partnership has been presented to the High Court sitting in London and at the time of the presentation of the bankruptcy petition, the petition for the winding up of the partnership has not been fully disposed of; and

(d) bankruptcy petitions based on criminal bankruptcy orders under section 264(1)(d).

CHAPTER 3 MAKING APPLICATIONS TO COURT: GENERAL

[Note: (1) a document required by the Act or these Rules must also contain the standard contents set out in Part 1 and an application to court must also contain the standard contents set out in rule 1.35;

(2) Paragraphs 3 and 4 of Schedule 5 make provision in relation to the court's power to extend the time for doing anything required by these Rules;

(3) the rules about the applications referred to in rule 12.6 are found in Chapter 2 of Part 3 (administration applications); Chapter 3 of Part 7 (petition for winding up order by creditor) and Chapter 4 of Part 7 (petition for winding up by contributory or office-holder) and Chapter 2 of Part 10 (creditor's bankruptcy petitions).]

[10.908]

12.6 Preliminary

This Chapter applies to an application made to the court except—

(a) an administration application under Part 2 of the Act;

(b) a petition for a winding-up order under Part 4 of the Act; and

(c) a creditor's petition for a bankruptcy order under Part 9 of the Act.

[10.909]

12.7 Filing of application

[Note: see rule 1.46 for electronic delivery of documents to the court.]

An application filed with the court in hard-copy form must be accompanied by one copy and a number of additional copies equal to the number of persons who are to be served with the application.

[10.910]

12.8 Fixing the venue

When an application is filed the court must fix a venue for it to be heard unless—

(a) it considers it is not appropriate to do so;
(b) the rule under which the application is brought provides otherwise; or
(c) the case is one to which rule 12.12 applies.

[10.911]

12.9 Service or delivery of application

[(1) The applicant must serve a sealed copy of the application, endorsed with the venue for the hearing on—

(a) the respondent named in the application; and
(b) where an application is made under Part A1 of the Act relating to a regulated company within the meaning given by section A49, the appropriate regulator (within the meaning given by that section),

unless the court directs or these Rules provide otherwise.]

(2) The court may also give one or more of the following directions—

(a) that the application be served upon persons other than those specified by the relevant provision of the Act or these Rules;
(b) that service upon, or the delivery of a notice to any person may be dispensed with;
(c) that such persons be notified of the application and venue in such other a way as the court specifies; or
(d) such other directions as the court sees fit.

(3) A sealed copy of the application must be served, or notice of the application and venue must be delivered, at least 14 days before the date fixed for its hearing unless—

(a) the provision of the Act or these Rules under which the application is made makes different provision;
(b) the case is urgent and the court acts under rule 12.10; or
(c) the court extends or abridges the time limit.

NOTES

Para (1): substituted by the Insolvency (England and Wales) (No 2) (Amendment) Rules 2021, SI 2021/1028, r 46, as from 1 October 2021 (for savings provisions see the note to r 1A.1 at **[10.539]**). Para (1) previously read as follows—

"(1) The applicant must serve a sealed copy of the application, endorsed with the venue for the hearing, on the respondent named in the application unless the court directs or these Rules provide otherwise.".

[10.912]

12.10 Hearing in urgent case

(1) Where the case is urgent, the court may (without prejudice to its general power to extend or abridge time limits) hear the application immediately with or without notification to, or the attendance of, other parties.

(2) The application may be heard on terms providing for the filing or service of documents, notification, or the carrying out of other formalities as the court thinks just.

[10.913]

12.11 Directions

The court may at any time give such directions as it thinks just as to—

(a) service or notice of the application on or to any person;
(b) whether particulars of claim and defence are to be delivered and generally as to the procedure on the application including whether a hearing is necessary;
(c) the matters to be dealt with in evidence; and
(d) the manner in which any evidence is to be provided and in particular as to—
    (i) the taking of evidence wholly or partly by witness statement or orally,
    (ii) any report to be made by an office-holder, and
    (iii) the cross-examination of the maker of a witness statement or of a report.

[10.914]

12.12 Hearing and determination without notice

(1) Where the Act and these Rules do not require service of a sealed copy of the application on, or notice of it to be delivered to, any person, the court may—

(a) hear the application as soon as reasonably practicable;
(b) fix a venue for the application to be heard, in which case rule 12.9 applies to the extent that it is relevant; or
(c) determine the application without a hearing.

(2) However nothing in the Act or these Rules is to be taken as prohibiting the applicant from giving notice.

[10.915]

12.13 Adjournment of the hearing of an application

(1) The court may adjourn the hearing of an application on such terms as it thinks just.

(2) The court may give directions as to the manner in which any evidence is to be provided at a resumed hearing and in particular as to—

(a) the taking of evidence wholly or partly by witness statement or orally;
(b) the cross-examination of the maker of a witness statement; or

(c) any report to be made by an office-holder.

CHAPTER 4 MAKING APPLICATIONS TO COURT: SPECIFIC APPLICATIONS

[Note: a document required by the Act or these Rules must also contain the standard contents set out in Part 1.]

Sub-division A: Applications in connection with section 176A (prescribed part)

[10.916]

12.14 Applications under section 176A(5) to disapply section 176A

(1) An application under section 176A(5) must be accompanied by a witness statement of the liquidator, administrator or receiver.

(2) The witness statement must state—

(a) the type of insolvency proceedings in which the application arises;
(b) a summary of the financial position of the company;
(c) the information substantiating the applicant's view that the cost of making a distribution to unsecured creditors would be disproportionate to the benefits; and
(d) whether any other office-holder is acting in relation to the company and, if so, that office-holder's address.

[10.917]

12.15 Notice of application under section 176A(5)

(1) An application under section 176A(5) may be made without the application being served upon, or notification to any other party.

(2) However the office-holder making the application must notify any other office-holder who is acting in relation to the company . . .

NOTES

Para (2): words omitted revoked by the Insolvency (Amendment) (EU Exit) Regulations 2019, SI 2019/146, reg 2, Schedule, Pt 4, paras 46, 97, as from IP completion day (as defined in the European Union (Withdrawal Agreement) Act 2020, s 39) (for savings, see reg 4 of the 2019 Regulations at **[12.82]**).

[10.918]

12.16 Notice of an order under section 176A(5)

(1) Where the court makes an order under section 176A(5), the court must, as soon as reasonably practicable, deliver the sealed order to the applicant and a sealed copy to any other office-holder.

(2) The liquidator, administrator or receiver must, as soon as reasonably practicable, deliver notice of the order to each creditor unless the court directs otherwise.

(3) The court may direct that the requirement in paragraph (2) is complied with if a notice is published by the liquidator, administrator or receiver which states that the court has made an order disapplying the requirement to set aside the prescribed part.

(4) As soon as reasonably practicable the notice—

(a) must be gazetted; and
(b) may be advertised in such other manner as the liquidator, administrator, or receiver thinks fit.

(5) The liquidator, administrator or receiver must deliver a copy of the order to the registrar of companies as soon as reasonably practicable after the making of the order.

Sub-division B: Applications for private examination (sections 236, 251N and 366)

[Note: for rules about public examinations see Chapter 13 of Part 7 and Chapter 8 of Part 10.]

[10.919]

12.17 Application of this sub-division and interpretation

(1) The rules in this sub-division apply to applications to the court for an order under—

(a) section 236 (inquiry into company's dealings);
(b) section 251N (debt relief orders—inquiry into dealings and property of debtor); and
(c) section 366 (inquiry into bankrupt's dealings and property) including section 366 as it applies by virtue of section 368.

(2) In this sub-division—

"applicable section" means section 236, 251N or 366; and
"the insolvent" means the company, the debtor or the bankrupt as the case may be.

[10.920]

12.18 Contents of application

(1) An application to the court under section 236, 251N or 366 must state—

(a) the grounds on which it is made; and
(b) which one or more of the following orders is sought—
  (i) for the respondent to appear before the court,
  (ii) for the respondent to clarify any matter which is in dispute in the proceedings or to give additional information in relation to any such matter (if so Part 18 CPR (further information) applies to any such order),
  (iii) for the respondent to submit witness statements (if so, particulars must be given of the matters to be included), or
  (iv) for the respondent to produce books, papers or other records (if so, the items in question to be specified).

(2) An application under an applicable section may be made without notice to any other party.

(3) The court may, whatever the order sought in the application, make any order which it has power to make under the applicable section.

[10.921]
12.19 Order for examination etc

(1) Where the court orders the respondent to appear before it, it must specify the venue for the appearance.

(2) The date must not be less than 14 days from the date of the order.

(3) If the respondent is ordered to file with the court a witness statement or a written account, the order must specify—

(a) the matters which are to be dealt with in it; and
(b) the time within which it is to be delivered.

(4) If the order is to produce documents or other records, the time and manner of compliance must be specified.

(5) The applicant must serve a copy of the order on the respondent as soon as reasonably practicable.

[10.922]
12.20 Procedure for examination

(1) The applicant may attend an examination of the respondent, in person, or be represented by an appropriately qualified legal representative, and may put such questions to the respondent as the court may allow.

(2) Unless the applicant objects, the following persons may attend the examination with the permission of the court and may put questions to the respondent (but only through the applicant)—

(a) any person who could have applied for an order under the applicable section; and
(b) any creditor who has provided information on which the application was made under section 236 or 366.

(3) If the respondent is ordered to clarify any matter or to give additional information, the court must direct the respondent as to the questions which the respondent is required to answer, and as to whether the respondent's answers (if any) are to be made in a witness statement.

(4) The respondent may employ an appropriately qualified legal representative at the respondent's own expense, who may—

(a) put to the respondent such questions as the court may allow for the purpose of enabling the respondent to explain or qualify any answers given by the respondent; and
(b) make representations on the respondent's behalf.

(5) Such written record of the examination must be made as the court thinks proper and such record must be read either to or by the respondent and authenticated by the respondent at a venue fixed by the court.

(6) The record may, in any proceedings (whether under the Act or otherwise), be used as evidence against the respondent of any statement made by the respondent in the course of the respondent's examination.

[10.923]
12.21 Record of examination

(1) Unless the court otherwise directs, the record of questions put to the respondent, the respondent's answers and any witness statement or written account delivered to the court by the respondent in compliance with an order of the court under the applicable section are not to be filed with the court.

(2) The documents listed in paragraph (3) may not be inspected without the permission of the court, except by—

(a) the applicant for an order under the applicable section; or
(b) any person who could have applied for such an order in relation to the affairs of the same insolvent.

(3) The documents are—

(a) the record of the respondent's examination;
(b) copies of questions put to the respondent or proposed to be put to the respondent and answers to questions given by the respondent;
(c) any witness statement by the respondent; and
(d) any document on the court file that shows the grounds for the application for the order.

(4) The court may from time to time give directions as to the custody and inspection of any documents to which this rule applies, and as to the provision of copies of, or extracts from, such documents.

[10.924]
12.22 Costs of proceedings under sections 236, 251N and 366

(1) Where the court has ordered an examination of a person under an applicable section, and it appears to it that the examination was made necessary because information had been unjustifiably refused by the respondent, it may order that the respondent pay the costs of the examination.

(2) Where the court makes an order against a person under—

(a) section 237(1) or 367(1) (to deliver up property in any person's possession which belongs to the insolvent estate); or
(b) section 237(2) or 367(2) (to pay any amount in discharge of a debt due to the insolvent);

the costs of the application for the order may be ordered by the court to be paid by the respondent.

(3) Subject to paragraphs (1) and (2), the applicant's costs must, unless the court orders otherwise, be paid—

(a) in relation to a company insolvency, as an expense of the insolvency proceedings; and
(b) in relation to an individual insolvency, but not in proceedings relating to debt relief orders or applications for debt relief orders, out of the bankrupt's estate or (as the case may be) the debtor's property.

(4) A person summoned to attend for examination must be tendered a reasonable sum for travelling expenses incurred in connection with that person's attendance but any other costs falling on that person are at the court's discretion.

(5) Where the examination is on the application of the official receiver otherwise than in the capacity of liquidator or trustee, no order may be made for the payment of costs by the official receiver.

Sub-division C: Persons unable to manage own property or affairs

[10.925]

12.23 Application and interpretation

(1) This sub-division applies where it appears to the court in insolvency proceedings that a person affected by the proceedings is unable to manage and administer that person's own property and affairs by reason of—

(a) lacking capacity within the meaning of the Mental Capacity Act 2005;
(b) suffering from a physical affliction; or
(c) disability.

(2) Such a person is referred to in this sub-division as "the incapacitated person".

[10.926]

12.24 Appointment of another person to act

(1) The court may appoint such person as it thinks just to appear for, represent or act for the incapacitated person.

(2) The appointment may be made either generally or for the purpose of a particular application or proceeding, or for the exercise of particular rights or powers which the incapacitated person might have exercised but for that person's incapacity.

(3) The court may make the appointment either of its own motion or on application by—

(a) a person who has been appointed by a court in the United Kingdom or elsewhere to manage the affairs of, or to represent, the incapacitated person;
(b) any person who appears to the court to be a suitable person to make the application;
(c) the official receiver; or
(d) the office-holder.

(4) An application may be made without notice to any other party.

(5) However the court may require such notice of the application as it thinks necessary to be delivered to the incapacitated person, or any other person, and may adjourn the hearing of the application to enable the notice to be delivered.

[10.927]

12.25 Witness statement in support of application

An application under rule 12.24(3) must be supported by a witness statement made by a registered medical practitioner as to the mental or physical condition of the incapacitated person.

[10.928]

12.26 Service of notices following appointment

Any notice served on, or sent to, a person appointed under rule 12.24 has the same effect as if it had been served on, or delivered to, the incapacitated person.

CHAPTER 5 OBTAINING INFORMATION AND EVIDENCE

[Note: a document required by the Act or these Rules must also contain the standard contents set out in Part 1.]

[10.929]

12.27 Further information and disclosure

(1) A party to insolvency proceedings in court may apply to court for an order—

(a) that in accordance with CPR Part 18 (further information) another party—
    (i) clarify a matter that is in dispute in the proceedings, or
    (ii) give additional information in relation to such a matter; or
(b) for disclosure from any person in accordance with CPR Part 31 (disclosure and inspection of documents).

(2) An application under this rule may be made without notice to any other party.

[10.930]

12.28 Witness statements and reports

(1) Where the Act or these Rules require evidence as to a matter, such evidence may be given by witness statement unless—

(a) in a specific case a rule or the Act makes different provision; or
(b) the court otherwise directs.

(2) Unless either the provision of the Act or rule under which the application is made provides otherwise, or the court directs otherwise—

(a) if the applicant intends to rely at the first hearing on evidence in a witness statement or report, the applicant must file the witness statement or report with the court and serve a copy of it on the respondent not less than 14 days before the date fixed for the hearing; and
(b) where the respondent intends to oppose the application and rely for that purpose on evidence contained in a witness statement or report, the respondent must file the witness statement or report with the court and serve a copy on the applicant not less than five business days before the date fixed for the hearing.

(3) The court may order a person who has made a witness statement or report to attend for cross-examination.

(4) Where a person who has been ordered to attend fails to do so the witness statement or report must not be used in evidence without the court's permission.

[10.931]

12.29 Evidence provided by the official receiver, an insolvency practitioner or a special manager

(1) Where in insolvency proceedings a witness statement is made by an office-holder, the office-holder must state—

(a) the capacity in which the office-holder is acting; and
(b) the office-holder's address.

(2) The following may file a report with the court instead of a witness statement in all insolvency proceedings—
(a) the official receiver; and
(b) the adjudicator.

(3) The following may file a report with the court instead of a witness statement unless the application involves other parties or the court otherwise directs—
(a) an administrator;
(b) a provisional liquidator;
(c) a liquidator;
(d) an interim receiver;
(e) a trustee; *and*
(f) a special manager[; and
(g) a monitor.]

(4) Where a report is filed instead of a witness statement, the report must be treated for the purpose of rule 12.28 and any hearing before the court as if it were a witness statement.

NOTES

Para (3): the word "and" in italics in sub-para (e) was revoked, and sub-para (g) and the preceding word were inserted, by the Insolvency (England and Wales) (No 2) (Amendment) Rules 2021, SI 2021/1028, r 47, as from 1 October 2021 (for savings provisions see the note to r 1A.1 at **[10.539]**).

CHAPTER 6 TRANSFER OF PROCEEDINGS

[Note: a document required by the Act or these Rules must also contain the standard contents set out in Part 1.]

Sub-division A: General

[10.932]
12.30 General power of transfer

(1) The High Court may order insolvency proceedings which are pending in that court to be transferred to a specified hearing centre.

(2) The County Court may order insolvency proceedings which are pending in a hearing centre to be transferred either to the High Court or another hearing centre.

(3) A judge of the High Court may order insolvency proceedings which are pending in the County Court to be transferred to the High Court.

(4) The court may order a transfer of proceedings—
(a) of its own motion;
(b) on the application of the official receiver; or
(c) on the application of a person appearing to the court to have an interest in the proceedings.

(5) Winding-up proceedings may only be transferred to a hearing centre in which proceedings to wind up companies may be commenced under the Act or to the County Court at Central London.

(6) Bankruptcy proceedings or proceedings relating to a debt relief order may only be transferred to a hearing centre in which bankruptcy proceedings may be commenced under the Act.

(7) A case in a schedule under rule 12.37(8) may be transferred solely for the purposes of rule 12.38 (action following application for a block transfer order) by—
(a) the registrar to or from the High Court; and
(b) the District Judge of the hearing centre to which the application is made, to or from that hearing centre.

[10.933]
12.31 Proceedings commenced in the wrong court

Where insolvency proceedings are commenced in the wrong court or hearing centre, that court may order—
(a) the proceedings be transferred to the court or hearing centre in which they ought to have been commenced;
(b) the proceedings be continued in the court in which they have been commenced; or
(c) the proceedings be struck out.

[10.934]
12.32 Applications for transfer

(1) An application by the official receiver for proceedings to be transferred must be accompanied by a report by the official receiver.

(2) The report must set out the reasons for the transfer, and include a statement either that—
(a) the petitioner, or the debtor in proceedings relating to a debt relief order, consents to the transfer; or
(b) the petitioner or such a debtor has been given at least 14 days' notice of the official receiver's application.

(3) If the court is satisfied from the report that the proceedings can be conducted more conveniently in another court or hearing centre, it must order that the proceedings be transferred to that court or hearing centre.

(4) A person other than the official receiver who applies for the transfer of winding up or bankruptcy proceedings or proceedings relating to a debt relief order must deliver a notice that such an application is intended to be made at least 14 days' before filing the application with the court to—
(a) the official receiver attached to the court or hearing centre in which the proceedings are pending; and
(b) the official receiver attached to the court or hearing centre to which it is proposed that they should be transferred.

[10.935]

12.33 Procedure following order for transfer

(1) Where a court makes an order for the transfer of proceedings under rule 12.30 (other than paragraph (7) of that rule), it must as soon as reasonably practicable deliver to the transferee court or hearing centre a sealed copy of the order, and the file of the proceedings.

(2) A transferee court (or hearing centre) which receives such an order and the file in winding up or bankruptcy proceedings or proceedings relating to a debt relief order must, as soon as reasonably practicable, deliver notice of the transfer to the official receiver attached to that court or hearing centre and the transferor court respectively.

(3) Where the High Court makes a transfer order under rule 12.30(7)—

(a) it must deliver sealed copies of the order—

(i) to the hearing centre from which the proceedings are transferred, and

(ii) in winding up or bankruptcy proceedings or proceedings relating to a debt relief order, to the official receiver attached to that hearing centre and the High Court respectively; and

(b) the hearing centre must deliver the file of the proceedings to the High Court.

[10.936]

12.34 Consequential transfer of other proceedings

(1) This rule applies where—

(a) the High Court has—

(i) made a winding-up order,

(ii) appointed a provisional liquidator,

(iii) made a bankruptcy order, or

(iv) appointed an interim receiver; or

(b) winding-up or bankruptcy proceedings have been transferred to the High Court from the County Court.

(2) A judge of any division of the High Court may, of that judge's own motion, order the transfer to that division of any such proceedings as are mentioned below and are pending against the company or individual concerned ("the insolvent") either in another division of the High Court or in a court in England and Wales other than the High Court.

(3) Paragraph (2) is subject to rule 30.5(4) CPR (transfer between divisions and to and from a specialist list).

(4) The proceedings which may be transferred are those brought by or against the insolvent for the purpose of enforcing a claim against the insolvent estate, or brought by a person other than the insolvent for the purpose of enforcing any such claim (including in either case proceedings of any description by a debenture-holder or mortgagee).

(5) Where any such proceedings are transferred, they must be listed before a registrar for directions or final disposal as the registrar sees fit.

Sub-division B: Block transfer of cases where insolvency practitioner has died etc

[10.937]

12.35 Interpretation

In this Sub-division—

"outgoing office-holder" has the meaning given in rule 12.36(1);

"replacement office-holder" has the meaning given in rule 12.36(1);

"block transfer order" has the meaning given in rule 12.36(2);

"substantive application" is that part of the application in rule 12.37(1)(c) and (d).

[10.938]

12.36 Power to make a block transfer order

(1) This rule applies where an office-holder ('the outgoing office-holder')—

(a) dies;

(b) retires from practice; or

(c) is otherwise unable or unwilling to continue in office;

and it is expedient to transfer some or all of the cases in which the outgoing office-holder holds office to one or more office-holders ('the replacement office-holder') in a single transaction.

(2) In a case to which this rule applies the court has the power to make an order ('a block transfer order') appointing a replacement office-holder in the place of the outgoing office-holder to be—

(a) liquidator in any winding up (including a case where the official receiver is the liquidator by virtue of section 136);

(b) administrator in any administration;

(c) trustee in a bankruptcy (including a case where the official receiver is the trustee by virtue of section 300); *or*

(d) supervisor of a CVA or an IVA[; or

(e) a monitor in respect of a moratorium under Part A1 of the Act.]

(3) The replacement office-holder must be—

(a) qualified to act as an insolvency practitioner in relation to the company or bankrupt; or

(b) where the replacement office-holder is to be appointed supervisor of an IVA—

(i) qualified to act as an insolvency practitioner in relation to the debtor, or

(ii) a person authorised so to act.

NOTES

Para (2): the word "or" in italics in sub-para (c) was revoked, and sub-para (e) and the preceding word were inserted, by the Insolvency (England and Wales) (No 2) (Amendment) Rules 2021, SI 2021/1028, r 48, as from 1 October 2021 (for savings provisions see the note to r 1A.1 at **[10.539]**).

Part 10 Miscellaneous other SIs

[10.939]
12.37 Application for a block transfer order

(1) An application for a block transfer order may be made to the registrar or District Judge for—

(a) the transfer to the High Court of the cases specified in the schedule to the application under paragraph (8);
(b) the transfer of the cases back to the court or hearing centre from which they were transferred when a replacement office-holder has been appointed;
(c) the removal of the outgoing office-holder by the exercise of any of the powers in paragraph (2);
(d) the appointment of a replacement office-holder by the exercise of any of the powers in paragraph (3); or
(e) such other order or direction as may be necessary or expedient in connection with any of the matters referred to above.

(2) The powers referred to in paragraph (1)(c) are those in—

[(za) section A39 (moratorium under Part A1 of the Act);]
(a) section 7(5) *and paragraph 39(6) of Schedule A1 (CVA)*;
(b) section 19, paragraph 88 of Schedule B1 and rule 12.36(2) (administration);
(c) section 108 (voluntary winding up);
(d) section 172(2) and rule 12.36(2) (winding up by the court);
(e) section 263(5) (IVA); and
(f) section 298 and rule 12.36(2) (bankruptcy).

(3) The powers referred to in paragraph (1)(d) are those in—

[(za) section A39 (moratorium under Part A1 of the Act);]
(a) section 7(5) *and paragraph 39(6) of Schedule A1 (CVA)*;
(b) section 13, paragraphs 63, 91 and 95 of Schedule B1 and rule 12.36(2) (administration);
(c) section 108 (voluntary winding up);
(d) section 168(3) and (5) and rule 12.36(2) (winding up by the court);
(e) section 263(5) (IVA); and
(f) sections 298 and 303(2) and rule 12.36(2) (bankruptcy).

(4) Subject to paragraph (5), the application may be made by any of the following—

(a) the outgoing office-holder (if able and willing to do so);
(b) any person who holds office jointly with the outgoing office-holder;
(c) any person who is proposed to be appointed as the replacement office-holder;
(d) any creditor in a case subject to the application;
(e) the recognised professional body which was the source of the outgoing office-holder's authorisation; or
(f) the Secretary of State.

(5) Where one or more outgoing office-holder in the schedule under paragraph (8) is an administrator, an application may not be made unless the applicant is a person permitted to apply to replace that office-holder under section 13 or paragraph 63, 91 or 95 of Schedule B1 or such a person is joined as applicant in relation to the replacement of that office-holder.

(6) An applicant (other than the Secretary of State) must deliver a notice of the intended application to the Secretary of State on or before the date the application is made.

(7) The following must be made a respondent to the application and served with it—

(a) the outgoing office-holder (if not the applicant or deceased);
(b) any person who holds office jointly with the outgoing office-holder; and
(c) such other person as the registrar or District Judge directs.

(8) The application must contain a schedule setting out—

(a) identification details for the proceedings; and
(b) the capacity in which the outgoing office-holder was appointed.

(9) The application must be supported by evidence—

(a) setting out the circumstances as a result of which it is expedient to appoint a replacement office-holder; and
(b) exhibiting the consent to act of each person who is proposed to be appointed as replacement office-holder.

(10) Where all the cases in the schedule under paragraph (8) are in the County Court—

(a) the application may be made to a District Judge of a convenient hearing centre in which insolvency proceedings of such type may be commenced; and
(b) this rule applies with appropriate modifications.

NOTES

Paras (2), (3): sub-para (za) was inserted, and the words in italics in sub-para (a) were revoked, by the Insolvency (England and Wales) (No 2) (Amendment) Rules 2021, SI 2021/1028, rr 49, 81, Sch 2, as from 1 October 2021 (for savings provisions see the note to r 1A.1 at **[10.539]**).

[10.940]
12.38 Action following application for a block transfer order

(1) The registrar or District Judge may in the first instance consider the application without a hearing and make such order as the registrar or District Judge thinks just.

(2) In the first instance, the registrar or District Judge may do any of the following—

(a) make an order directing the transfer to the High Court of those cases not already within its jurisdiction for the purpose only of the substantive application;
(b) if the documents are considered to be in order and the matter is considered straightforward, make an order on the substantive application;
(c) give any directions which are considered to be necessary including (if appropriate) directions for the joinder of any additional respondents or requiring the service of the application on any person or requiring additional evidence to be provided; or

(d) if an order is not made on the substantive application, give directions for the further consideration of the substantive application by the registrar or District Judge or a judge of the Chancery Division.

(3) The applicant must ensure that a sealed copy of every order transferring any case to the High Court and of every order which is made on a substantive application is filed with the court having jurisdiction over each case affected by such order.

(4) In any case other than an application relating to the appointment of an administrator, in deciding to what extent (if any) the costs of making an application under this rule should be paid as an expense of the insolvency proceedings to which the application relates, the factors to which the court must have regard include—

(a) the reasons for the making of the application;
(b) the number of cases to which the application relates;
(c) the value of assets comprised in those cases; and
(d) the nature and extent of the costs involved.

(5) Where an application relates to the appointment of an administrator and is made by a person under section 13 or paragraph 63, 91 or 95 of Schedule B1, the costs of making that application are to be paid as an expense of the administration to which the application relates unless the court directs otherwise.

(6) Notice of any appointment made under this rule must be delivered—

(a) to the Secretary of State as soon as reasonably practicable; and
(b) to—
  (i) the creditors, and
  (ii) such other persons as the court may direct, in such manner as the court may direct.

(7) Where the application was made to the District Judge under rule 12.37(10) this rule applies with appropriate modifications.

CHAPTER 7 THE COURT FILE

[Note: a document required by the Act or these Rules must also contain the standard contents set out in Part 1.]

[10.941]
12.39 The court file

(1) Where documents are filed with the court under the Act or these Rules, the court must open and maintain a court file and place those documents on the file.

(2) However where a bankruptcy file has been opened under rule 10.47, documents filed with the court under the Act or these Rules must be placed on the bankruptcy file.

(3) The following may inspect the court file, or obtain from the court a copy of the court file, or of any document in the court file—

(a) the office-holder in the proceedings;
(b) the Secretary of State; and
(c) a creditor who provides the court with a statement confirming that that person is a creditor of the company or the individual to whom the proceedings relate.

(4) The same right to inspect and obtain copies is exercisable—

(a) in proceedings under [Parts A1] to 7 of the Act, by—
  (i) an officer or former officer of the company to which the proceedings relate, or
  (ii) a member of the company or a contributory in its winding up;
(b) in proceedings relating to an IVA, by the debtor;
(c) in bankruptcy proceedings, by—
  (i) the bankrupt,
  (ii) a person against whom a bankruptcy petition has been presented, or
  (iii) a person who has been served with a statutory demand under section 268;
(d) in proceedings relating to a debt relief order, by the debtor.

(5) The right to inspect and obtain copies may be exercised on a person's behalf by someone authorised to do so by that person.

(6) Other persons may inspect the file or obtain copies if the court gives permission.

(7) The right to a copy of a document is subject to payment of the fee chargeable under an order made under section 92 of the Courts Act 2003.

(8) Inspection of the file, with permission if required, may be at any reasonable time.

(9) The court may direct that the file, a document (or part of it) or a copy of a document (or part of it) must not be made available under paragraph (3), (4) or (5) without the permission of the court.

(10) An application for a direction under paragraph (9) may be made by—

(a) the official receiver;
(b) the office-holder in the proceedings; or
(c) any person appearing to the court to have an interest.

(11) The following applications may be made without notice to any other party, but the court may direct that notice must be delivered to any person who would be affected by its decision—

(a) an application for permission to inspect the file or obtain a copy of a document under paragraph (6); and
(b) an application for a direction under paragraph (9).

(12) If, for the purposes of powers conferred by the Act or these Rules, the Secretary of State or the official receiver makes a request to inspect or requests the transmission of the file of insolvency proceedings, the court must comply with the request (unless the file is for the time being in use for the court's own purposes).

NOTES

Para (4): words in square brackets in sub-para (a) substituted (for the original words "Parts 1") by the Insolvency (England and Wales) (No 2) (Amendment) Rules 2021, SI 2021/1028, r 80, Sch 1, as from 1 October 2021 (for savings provisions see the note to r 1A.1 at **[10.539]**).

[10.942]

12.40 Office copies of documents

(1) The court must provide an office copy of a document from the court file to a person who has under these Rules the right to inspect the court file where that person has requested such a copy and paid the appropriate fee under rule 12.39(7).

(2) A person's right under this rule may be exercised on that person's behalf by someone authorised to do so by that person.

(3) An office copy must be in such form as the registrar or District Judge thinks appropriate, and must bear the court's seal.

CHAPTER 8 COSTS

[Note: a document required by the Act or these Rules must also contain the standard contents set out in Part 1.]

[10.943]

12.41 Application of Chapter and interpretation

(1) This Chapter applies to costs of and in connection with insolvency proceedings.

(2) In this Chapter "costs" includes charges and expenses.

(3) CPR Parts 44 and 47 (which relate to costs) apply to such costs.

[10.944]

12.42 Requirement to assess costs by the detailed procedure

(1) Where the costs of any person are payable as an expense out of the insolvent estate, the amount payable must be decided by detailed assessment unless agreed between the office-holder and the person entitled to payment.

(2) In the absence of agreement, the office-holder—

(a) may serve notice requiring the person entitled to payment to commence detailed assessment proceedings in accordance with CPR Part 47; and

(b) must serve such notice (except in an administrative receivership) where a liquidation or creditors' committee formed in relation to the insolvency proceedings resolves that the amount of the costs must be decided by detailed assessment.

(3) Detailed assessment proceedings must be commenced in the court to which the insolvency proceedings are allocated or, where in relation to a company there is no such court, any court having jurisdiction to wind up the company.

(4) Where the costs of any person employed by an office-holder in insolvency proceedings are required to be decided by detailed assessment or fixed by order of the court, the office-holder may make payments on account to such person in respect of those costs if that person undertakes in writing—

(a) to repay as soon as reasonably practicable any money which may, when detailed assessment is made, prove to have been overpaid; and

(b) to pay interest on any such sum as is mentioned in sub-paragraph (a) at the rate specified in section 17 of the Judgments Act 1838 on the date payment was made and for the period beginning with the date of payment and ending with the date of repayment.

(5) In any proceedings before the court (including proceedings on a petition), the court may order costs to be decided by detailed assessment.

(6) Unless otherwise directed or authorised, the costs of a trustee in bankruptcy or a liquidator are to be allowed on the standard basis for which provision is made in—

(a) CPR rule 44.3 (basis of assessment); and

(b) CPR rule 44.4 (factors to be taken into account when deciding the amount of costs).

[10.945]

12.43 Procedure where detailed assessment is required

(1) The costs officer must require a certificate of employment before making a detailed assessment of the costs of a person employed in insolvency proceedings by the office-holder.

(2) The certificate must be endorsed on the bill and signed by the office-holder and must include—

(a) the name and address of the person employed;

(b) details of the functions to be carried out under the employment; and

(c) a note of any special terms of remuneration which have been agreed.

(3) A person whose costs in insolvency proceedings are required to be decided by detailed assessment must, on being required in writing to do so by the office-holder, commence detailed assessment proceedings in accordance with CPR Part 47 (procedure for detailed assessment of costs and default provisions).

(4) If that person does not commence such proceedings within 3 months of being required to do so under paragraph (3), or within such further time as the court, on application, may permit, the office-holder may deal with the insolvent estate without regard to any claim for costs by that person, whose claim is forfeited by such failure to commence proceedings.

(5) Where in any such case such a claim for costs lies additionally against an office-holder in the office-holder's personal capacity, that claim is also forfeited by such failure to commence proceedings.

(6) Where costs have been incurred in insolvency proceedings in the High Court and those proceedings are subsequently transferred to the County Court, all costs of those proceedings directed by the court or otherwise required to be assessed may nevertheless, on the application of the person who incurred the costs, be ordered to be decided by detailed assessment in the High Court.

[10.946]

12.44 Costs of officers charged with execution of writs or other process

(1) This rule applies where an enforcement officer, or other officer charged with execution of the writ or other process—

- (a) is required under section 184(2) or 346(2) to deliver up goods or money; or
- (b) has under section 184(3) or 346(3) deducted costs from the proceeds of an execution or money paid to that officer.

(2) The office-holder may require in writing that the amount of the enforcement officer's or other officer's bill of costs be decided by detailed assessment and where such a requirement is made rule 12.43 (procedure where detailed assessment is required) applies.

(3) Where, in the case of a deduction of the kind mentioned in paragraph (1)(b), any amount deducted is disallowed at the conclusion of the detailed assessment proceedings, the enforcement officer must as soon as reasonably practicable pay a sum equal to that disallowed to the office-holder for the benefit of the insolvent estate.

[10.947]

12.45 Petitions presented by insolvent companies

(1) This rule applies where a winding-up petition is presented by a company against itself.

(2) A solicitor acting for the company must in the solicitor's bill of costs give credit for any sum or security received by the solicitor as a deposit from the company on account of the costs and expenses to be incurred in respect of the filing and prosecution of the petition and the deposit must be noted by the costs officer on the final costs certificate.

(3) Where an order is made on a petition presented by the company and before the presentation of that petition a petition had been presented by a creditor, no costs are to be allowed to the company or that company's solicitor out of the insolvent estate unless the court considers that—

- (a) the insolvent estate has benefited by the company's conduct; or
- (b) there are otherwise special circumstances justifying the allowance of costs.

[10.948]

12.46 Costs paid otherwise than out of the insolvent estate

Where the amount of costs is decided by detailed assessment under an order of the court directing that those costs are to be paid otherwise than out of the insolvent estate, the costs officer must note on the final costs certificate by whom, or the manner in which, the costs are to be paid.

[10.949]

12.47 Awards of costs against an office-holder, the adjudicator or the official receiver

Without prejudice to any provision of the Act or Rules by virtue of which the official receiver or the adjudicator is not in any event to be liable for costs and expenses, where an office-holder, the adjudicator or the official receiver (where the official receiver is not acting as an office-holder) is made a party to any proceedings on the application of another party to the proceedings, the office-holder, the adjudicator or official receiver is not to be personally liable for the costs unless the court otherwise directs.

[10.950]

12.48 Applications for costs

(1) This rule applies where a party to, or person affected by, any proceedings in an insolvency applies to the court for an order allowing their costs, or part of them, of or incidental to the proceedings, and that application is not made at the time of the proceedings.

(2) The applicant must serve a sealed copy of the application—

[(a) in proceedings other than those relating to a debt relief order, on the office-holder and—
 (i) in a winding up by the court or a bankruptcy, on the official receiver; or
 (ii) in proceedings under Part A1 of the Act, on the company to which the moratorium relates; or]
(b) in proceedings relating to a debt relief order, on the official receiver.

(3) The office-holder and, where appropriate, the official receiver may appear on an application to which paragraph (2)(a) applies.

(4) The official receiver may appear on an application to which paragraph (2)(b) applies.

(5) No costs of or incidental to the application are to be allowed to the applicant unless the court is satisfied that the application could not have been made at the time of the proceedings.

NOTES

Para (2): sub-para (a) substituted by the Insolvency (England and Wales) (No 2) (Amendment) Rules 2021, SI 2021/1028, r 50, as from 1 October 2021 (for savings provisions see the note to r 1A.1 at **[10.539]**). Sub-para (a) previously read as follows—

"(a) in proceedings other than proceedings relating to a debt relief order—
 (i) on the office-holder, and
 (ii) in a winding up by the court or a bankruptcy, on the official receiver; or".

Part 10 Miscellaneous other SIs

[10.951]
12.49 Costs and expenses of petitioners and other specified persons

(1) The petitioner is not to receive an allowance as a witness for attending the hearing of the petition.

(2) However the costs officer may allow that person's expenses of travelling and subsistence in attending the hearing.

(3) The bankrupt, the debtor or an officer of the insolvent company to which the proceedings relate is not to receive an allowance as a witness in an examination or other proceedings before the court except as directed by the court.

[10.952]
12.50 Final costs certificate

(1) A final costs certificate of the costs officer is final and conclusive as to all matters which have not been objected to in the manner provided for under the rules of the court.

(2) Where it is proved to the satisfaction of a costs officer that a final costs certificate has been lost or destroyed, the costs officer may issue a duplicate.

CHAPTER 9 ENFORCEMENT PROCEDURES

[Note: a document required by the Act or these Rules must also contain the standard contents set out in Part 1.]

[10.953]
12.51 Enforcement of court orders

(1) In any insolvency proceedings, orders of the court may be enforced in the same manner as a judgment to the same effect.

(2) Where an order in insolvency proceedings is made, or any process is issued, by the County Court, the order or process may be enforced, executed and dealt with by any hearing centre, as if it had been made or issued for the enforcement of a judgment or order to the same effect made by that hearing centre.

(3) Paragraph (2) applies whether or not the other hearing centre is one in which such insolvency proceedings may be commenced.

(4) Where a warrant for the arrest of a person is issued by the High Court, the warrant may be discharged by the County Court where the person who is the subject of the warrant—

(a) has been brought before a hearing centre in which insolvency proceedings may be commenced; and
(b) has given to the County Court a satisfactory undertaking to comply with the obligations that apply to that person under the Act or these Rules.

[10.954]
12.52 Orders enforcing compliance

(1) The court may, on application by the competent person, make such orders as it thinks necessary for the enforcement of obligations falling on any person in accordance with—

[(za) section A36 (provision of information to monitor);]
(a) paragraph 47 of Schedule B1 (duty to submit statement of affairs in administration);
(b) section 47(duty to submit statement of affairs in administrative receivership);
(c) section 131 (duty to submit statement of affairs in a winding up);
(d) section 143(2) (liquidator to furnish information, books, papers, etc); or
(e) section 235 (duty of various persons to co-operate with office-holder).

(2) The competent person for this purpose is—

[(za) under section A36, the monitor;]
(a) under paragraph 47 of Schedule B1, the administrator;
(b) under section 47, the administrative receiver;
(c) under section 131 or 143(2), the official receiver; and
(d) under section 235, the official receiver, the administrator, the administrative receiver, the liquidator or the provisional liquidator, as the case may be.

(3) An order of the court under this rule may provide that all costs of and incidental to the application for it are to be borne by the person against whom the order is made.

NOTES

Paras (1), (2): sub-para (za) inserted by the Insolvency (England and Wales) (No 2) (Amendment) Rules 2021, SI 2021/1028, r 51, as from 1 October 2021 (for savings provisions see the note to r 1A.1 at **[10.539]**).

[10.955]
12.53 Warrants (general provisions)

(1) A warrant issued by the court under any provision of the Act must be addressed to such officer of the High Court or of the County Court as the warrant specifies, or to any constable.

(2) The persons referred to in sections 134(2), 236(5), 251N(5), 364(1), 365(3) and 366(3) (court's powers of enforcement) as the prescribed officer of the court are—

(a) in the case of the High Court, the tipstaff and the tipstaff's assistants of the court; and
(b) in the case of the County Court, a bailiff.

(3) In this Chapter references to property include books, papers and other documents and records.

[10.956]
12.54 Warrants under sections 134 and 364

When a person ("the arrested person") is arrested under a warrant issued by the court under section 134 (officer of company failing to attend for public examination), or section 364 (arrest of debtor or bankrupt)—

(a) the arresting officer must give the arrested person into the custody of—
  (i) the court in a case where the court is ready and able to deal with the arrested person, or

(ii) where the court is not ready and able, the governor of the prison named in the warrant (or where that prison is not able to accommodate the arrested person, the governor of such other prison with appropriate facilities which is able to accommodate the arrested person), who must keep the arrested person in custody until such time as the court orders otherwise and must produce that person before the court at its next sitting; and

(b) any property in the arrested person's possession which may be seized must, as directed by the warrant, be—

(i) delivered to whoever is specified in the warrant as authorised to receive it, or otherwise dealt with in accordance with the directions in the warrant, or

(ii) kept by the officer seizing it pending the receipt of written orders from the court as to its disposal.

[10.957]

12.55 Warrants under sections 236, 251N and 366

(1) When a person is arrested under a warrant issued under section 236 (inquiry into insolvent company's dealings), 251N (the equivalent in relation to debt relief orders) or 366 (the equivalent in bankruptcy), the arresting officer must as soon as reasonably practicable bring the arrested person before the court issuing the warrant in order that the arrested person may be examined.

(2) If the arrested person cannot immediately be brought up for examination, the officer must deliver that person into the custody of the governor of the prison named in the warrant (or where that prison is not able to accommodate the arrested person, the governor of such other prison with appropriate facilities which is able to accommodate the arrested person), who must keep the arrested person in custody and produce that person before the court as it may from time to time direct.

(3) After arresting the person named in the warrant, the officer must as soon as reasonably practicable report to the court the arrest or delivery into custody (as the case may be) and apply to the court to fix a venue for the arrested person's examination.

(4) The court must appoint the earliest practicable time for the examination, and must—

(a) direct the governor of the prison to produce the arrested person for examination at the time and place appointed; and

(b) as soon as reasonably practicable deliver notice of the venue to the applicant for the warrant.

(5) Where any property in the arrested person's possession is seized, the property must, as directed by the warrant, be—

(a) delivered to whoever is specified in the warrant as authorised to receive it, or otherwise dealt with in accordance with the directions in the warrant; or

(b) kept by the officer seizing it pending the receipt of written orders from the court as to its disposal.

[10.958]

12.56 Warrants under section 365

(1) A warrant issued under section 365(3) (search of premises not belonging to the bankrupt) must authorise any person executing it to seize any property of the bankrupt found as a result of the execution of the warrant.

(2) Any property seized under a warrant issued under section 365(2) or (3) must, as directed by the warrant, be—

(a) delivered to whoever is specified in the warrant as authorised to receive it, or otherwise dealt with in accordance with the directions in the warrant; or

(b) kept by the officer seizing it pending the receipt of written orders from the court as to its disposal.

[10.959]

12.57 Execution overtaken by judgment debtor's insolvency

(1) This rule applies where execution has been taken out against property of a judgment debtor, and notice is delivered to the enforcement officer or other officer charged with the execution—

(a) under section 184(1) (that a winding-up order has been made against the debtor, or that a provisional liquidator has been appointed, or that a resolution for voluntary winding up has been passed);

(b) under section 184(4) (that a winding-up petition has been presented, or a winding-up order made, or that a meeting has been called at which there is to be proposed a resolution for voluntary winding up, or that such a resolution has been passed);

(c) under section 346(2) (that a judgment debtor has been made bankrupt); or

(d) under section 346(3)(b) (that a bankruptcy petition has been presented or a bankruptcy application has been made in relation to the debtor).

(2) Subject to paragraph (3) and rule 1.47, the notice must be delivered to the office of the enforcement officer or of the officer charged with the execution—

(a) by hand; or

(b) by any other means of delivery which enables proof of receipt of the document at the relevant address.

(3) Where the execution is in the County Court then if—

(a) there is filed with the hearing centre in charge of such execution in relation to the judgment debtor a winding-up or bankruptcy petition; or

(b) there is made by the hearing centre in charge of such execution in relation to the judgment debtor a winding-up order or an order appointing a provisional liquidator, or a bankruptcy order or an order appointing an interim receiver;

section 184 or 346 is deemed satisfied in relation to the requirement of a notice to be served on, or delivered to, the officer in charge of the execution.

CHAPTER 10 APPEALS

[Note: a document required by the Act or these Rules must also contain the standard contents set out in Part 1.]

[10.960]

12.58 Application of Chapter

CPR Part 52 (appeals) applies to appeals under this Chapter as varied by any applicable Practice Direction.

[10.961]

12.59 Appeals and reviews of court orders in corporate insolvency

(1) Every court having jurisdiction for the purposes of [Parts A1] to 7 of the Act and the corresponding Parts of these Rules, may review, rescind or vary any order made by it in the exercise of that jurisdiction.

(2) Appeals in civil matters in proceedings under [Parts A1] to 7 of the Act and the corresponding Parts of these Rules lie as follows—

(a) where the decision appealed against is made by a District Judge sitting in a hearing centre specified in the first column of the table in Schedule 10—

(i) to a High Court Judge sitting in a district registry, or

(ii) to [an Insolvency and Companies Court Judge];

as specified in the second column of the table;

(b) to a High Court Judge where the decision appealed against is made by—

(i) a Circuit Judge sitting in the County Court,

(ii) a Master,

(iii) [an Insolvency and Companies Court Judge], if that decision is made at first instance, or

(iv) a District Judge sitting in a district registry;

(c) to the Civil Division of the Court of Appeal where the decision appealed against is made by [an Insolvency and Companies Court Judge], if that decision is an appeal from a decision made by a District Judge; and

(d) to the Civil Division of the Court of Appeal where the decision is made by a High Court Judge.

(3) Any application for the rescission of a winding-up order must be made within five business days after the date on which the order was made.

(4) In this rule—

"Circuit Judge sitting in the county court" means a judge sitting pursuant to section 5(1)(a) of the County Courts Act 1984;

"Civil Division of the Court of Appeal" means the division of the Court of Appeal established by section 3(1) of the Senior Courts Act 1981;

"county court" means the court established by section A1 of the County Courts Act 1984;

"District Judge" means a person appointed a District Judge under section 6(1) of the County Courts Act 1984;

"District Judge sitting in a district registry" means a District Judge sitting in an assigned district registry as a District Judge of the High Court under section 100 of the Senior Courts Act 1981;

"district registry" means a district registry of the High Court under section 99 of the Senior Courts Act 1981;

"High Court Judge" means a judge listed in section 4(1) of the Senior Courts Act 1981;

["Insolvency and Companies Court Judge" means a person appointed to the office of Insolvency and Companies Court Judge under section 89(1) of the Senior Courts Act 1981;]

"Master" means a person appointed to the office of Master, Chancery Division under section 89(1) of the Senior Courts Act 1981;

. . .

and for the purposes of each definition a person appointed to act as a deputy for any person holding that office is included.

NOTES

Words "Parts A1" in square brackets paras (1), (2) substituted (for the original words "Parts 1") by the Insolvency (England and Wales) (No 2) (Amendment) Rules 2021, SI 2021/1028, r 80, Sch 1, as from 1 October 2021 (for savings provisions see the note to r 1A.1 at **[10.539]**).

Words in square brackets in sub-paras (2)(a)(ii), (b)(iii) and (c) substituted by the Alteration of Judicial Titles (Registrar in Bankruptcy of the High Court) Order 2018, SI 2018/130, art 2, Schedule, para 14(a)(ii), as from 26 February 2018.

In para (4), the definition "Insolvency and Companies Court Judge" was inserted, and the definition "Registrar in Bankruptcy of the High Court" (omitted) was revoked, by SI 2018/130, art 2, Schedule, para 14(b), as from 26 February 2018.

[10.962]

12.60 Appeals in bankruptcy by the Secretary of State

In bankruptcy proceedings, an appeal lies at the instance of the Secretary of State from any order of the court made on an application for the rescission or annulment of a bankruptcy order, or for the bankrupt's discharge.

[10.963]

12.61 Procedure on appeal

(1) An appeal against a decision at first instance may be brought only with the permission of the court which made the decision or of the court that has jurisdiction to hear the appeal.

(2) An appellant must file an appellant's notice within 21 days after the date of the decision of the court that the appellant wishes to appeal.

[10.964]

12.62 Appeals against decisions of the Secretary of State or official receiver

An appeal under the Act or these Rules against a decision of the Secretary of State or the official receiver must be brought within 28 days of delivery of notice of the decision.

CHAPTER 11 COURT ORDERS, FORMAL DEFECTS AND SHORTHAND WRITERS

[Note: a document required by the Act or these Rules must also contain the standard contents set out in Part 1.]

[10.965]

12.63 Court orders

Notwithstanding any requirement in these Rules as to the contents of a court order the court may make such other order or in such form as the court thinks just.

[10.966]

12.64 Formal defects

No insolvency proceedings will be invalidated by any formal defect or any irregularity unless the court before which objection is made considers that substantial injustice has been caused by the defect or irregularity and that the injustice cannot be remedied by any order of the court.

[10.967]

12.65 Shorthand writers: nomination etc

(1) The court may in writing nominate a person to be official shorthand writer to the court.

(2) The court may, at any time in the course of insolvency proceedings, appoint a shorthand writer to take down evidence of a person examined under section 133, 236, 251N, 290 or 366.

(3) Where the official receiver applies to the court for an order appointing a shorthand writer, the official receiver must name the person the official receiver proposes for the appointment.

(4) The remuneration of a shorthand writer appointed in insolvency proceedings must be paid by the party at whose instance the appointment was made, or out of the insolvent estate, or otherwise, as the court may direct.

(5) Any question arising as to the rates of remuneration payable under this rule must be determined by the court.

PART 13 OFFICIAL RECEIVERS

[10.968]

13.1 Official receivers in court

(1) Judicial notice must be taken of the appointment under sections 399 to 401 of official receivers and deputy official receivers.

(2) Official receivers and deputy official receivers have a right of audience in insolvency proceedings, whether in the High Court or the County Court.

[10.969]

13.2 Persons entitled to act on official receiver's behalf

(1) In the absence of the official receiver authorised to act in a particular case, an officer authorised in writing for the purpose by the Secretary of State, or by the official receiver, may with the permission of the court, act on the official receiver's behalf and in the official receiver's place—

(a) in any examination under section 133, 236, 251N, 290 or 366; and

(b) in relation to any application to the court.

(2) In case of emergency, where there is no official receiver capable of acting, anything to be done by, to or before the official receiver may be done by, to or before the registrar or District Judge.

[10.970]

13.3 Application for directions

The official receiver may apply to the court for directions in relation to any matter arising in insolvency proceedings.

[10.971]

13.4 Official receiver's expenses

(1) Any expenses (including damages) incurred by the official receiver (in whatever capacity the official receiver may be acting) in connection with proceedings taken against the official receiver in insolvency proceedings are to be treated as expenses of the insolvency proceedings.

(2) The official receiver has a charge on the insolvent estate in respect of any sums due to the official receiver under paragraph (1) in connection with insolvency proceedings other than proceedings relating to debt relief orders or applications for debt relief orders.

[10.972]

13.5 Official receiver not to be appointed liquidator or trustee

The official receiver may not be appointed as liquidator or trustee by any decision of creditors or (in a winding up) contributories or the company.

PART 14 CLAIMS BY AND DISTRIBUTIONS TO CREDITORS IN [A MORATORIUM,] ADMINISTRATION, WINDING UP AND BANKRUPTCY

NOTES

Words in square brackets in the Part heading inserted by the Insolvency (England and Wales) (No 2) (Amendment) Rules 2021, SI 2021/1028, r 52, as from 1 October 2021 (for savings provisions see the note to r 1A.1 at **[10.539]**).

CHAPTER 1 APPLICATION AND INTERPRETATION

[10.973]

14.1 Application of Part 14 and interpretation

[Note: "bankruptcy debt" and related expressions are defined in relation to bankruptcy in section 382.]

(1) This Part applies to [decision procedures in respect of a moratorium under Part A1 of the Act,] administration, winding up and bankruptcy proceedings.

(2) The definitions in this rule apply to [decision procedures in respect of a moratorium under Part A1 of the Act,] administration, winding up and bankruptcy proceedings except as otherwise stated.

(3) "Debt", in relation to [decision procedures in respect of a moratorium under Part A1 of the Act,] winding up and administration, means (subject to the next paragraph) any of the following—

(a) any debt or liability to which the company is subject at the relevant date;

(b) any debt or liability to which the company may become subject after the relevant date by reason of any obligation incurred before that date;

(c) any interest provable as mentioned in rule 14.23;

"small debt" means a debt (being the total amount owed to a creditor) which does not exceed £1,000 (which amount is prescribed for the purposes of paragraph 13A of Schedule 8 to the Act and paragraph 18A of Schedule 9 to the Act);

"dividend", in relation to a members' voluntary winding up, includes a distribution;

"provable debt" has the meaning given in rule 14.2; and

"relevant date" means—

[(za) in the case of decision procedures in respect of a moratorium under Part A1 of the Act, the date of the decision procedure;]

(a) in the case of an administration which was not immediately preceded by a winding up, the date on which the company entered administration,

(b) in the case of an administration which was immediately preceded by a winding up, the date on which the company went into liquidation,

(c) in the case of a winding up which was not immediately preceded by an administration, the date on which the company went into liquidation,

(d) in the case of a winding up which was immediately preceded by an administration, the date on which the company entered administration, and

(e) in the case of a bankruptcy, the date of the bankruptcy order.

[(3A) For the purpose of decision procedures in respect of a moratorium under Part A1 of the Act references in this Part to an "office-holder" are treated as references to the "convener".]

(4) For the purposes of any provision of the Act or these Rules about [moratoriums under Part A1 of the Act,] winding up or administration, any liability in tort is a debt provable in [the moratorium] the winding up or administration, if either—

(a) the cause of action has accrued at the relevant date; or

(b) all the elements necessary to establish the cause of action exist at that date except for actionable damage.

(5) For the purposes of references in any provision of the Act or these Rules about [moratoriums under Part A1 of the Act] winding up or administration to a debt or liability, it is immaterial whether the debt or liability is present or future, whether it is certain or contingent, or whether its amount is fixed or liquidated, or is capable of being ascertained by fixed rules or as a matter of opinion; and references in any such provision to owing a debt are to be read accordingly.

(6) In any provision of the Act or these Rules about [moratoriums under Part A1 of the Act] winding up or administration, except in so far as the context otherwise requires, "liability" means (subject to paragraph (4)) a liability to pay money or money's worth, including any liability under an enactment, a liability for breach of trust, any liability in contract, tort or bailment, and any liability arising out of an obligation to make restitution.

NOTES

The words in square brackets in paras (1)–(6) and paras (3)(za), (3A) were inserted by the Insolvency (England and Wales) (No 2) (Amendment) Rules 2021, SI 2021/1028, r 53, as from 1 October 2021 (for savings provisions see the note to r 1A.1 at **[10.539]**).

CHAPTER 2 CREDITORS' CLAIMS IN [A MORATORIUM,] ADMINISTRATION, WINDING UP AND BANKRUPTCY

[Note: a document required by the Act or these Rules must also contain the standard contents set out in Part 1.]

NOTES

Words in square brackets in the Chapter heading inserted by the Insolvency (England and Wales) (No 2) (Amendment) Rules 2021, SI 2021/1028, r 54, as from 1 October 2021 (for savings provisions see the note to r 1A.1 at **[10.539]**).

[10.974]

14.2 Provable debts

(1) All claims by creditors except as provided in this rule, are provable as debts against the company or bankrupt, whether they are present or future, certain or contingent, ascertained or sounding only in damages.

(2) The following are not provable—

(a) an obligation arising under a confiscation order made under—

(i) section 1 of the Drug Trafficking Offences Act 1986,

(ii) section 1 of the Criminal Justice (Scotland) Act 1987,

(iii) section 71 of the Criminal Justice Act 1988, or

(iv) Parts 2, 3 or 4 of the Proceeds of Crime Act 2002;

(b) an obligation arising from a payment out of the social fund under section 138(1)(b) of the Social Security Contributions and Benefits Act 1992 by way of crisis loan or budgeting loan.

(c) in bankruptcy—

(i) a fine imposed for an offence,

(ii) an obligation (other than an obligation to pay a lump sum or to pay costs) arising under an order made in family proceedings, or

(iii) an obligation arising under a maintenance assessment made under the Child Support Act 1991.

(3) In paragraph (2)(c), "fine" and "family proceedings" have the meanings given by section 281(8) (which applies the Magistrates Courts Act 1980 and the Matrimonial and Family Proceedings Act 1984).

(4) The following claims are not provable until after all other claims of creditors have been paid in full with interest under sections 189(2) (winding up), section 328(4) (bankruptcy) and rule 14.23 (payment of interest)—

(a) a claim arising by virtue of section 382(1)(a) of the Financial Services and Markets Act 2000 (restitution orders), unless it is also a claim arising by virtue of sub-paragraph (b) of that section (a person who has suffered loss etc); or

(b) in administration and winding up, a claim which by virtue of the Act or any other enactment is a claim the payment of which in a bankruptcy, an administration or a winding up is to be postponed.

(5) Nothing in this rule prejudices any enactment or rule of law under which a particular kind of debt is not provable, whether on grounds of public policy or otherwise.

[10.975]
14.3 Proving a debt

(1) A creditor wishing to recover a debt must submit a proof to the office-holder unless—

(a) this rule or an order of the court provides otherwise; or

(b) it is a members' voluntary winding up in which case the creditor is not required to submit a proof unless the liquidator requires one to be submitted.

(2) A creditor is deemed to have proved—

(a) in a winding up immediately preceded by an administration, where the creditor has already proved in the administration; or

(b) in an administration immediately preceded by a winding up, where the creditor has already proved in the winding up.

(3) A creditor is deemed to have proved for the purposes of determination and payment of a dividend but not otherwise where—

(a) the debt is a small debt;

(b) a notice has been delivered to the creditor of intention to declare a dividend or make a distribution under rule 14.29 which complies with rule 14.31 (further contents of notice to creditors owed small debts); and

(c) the creditor has not advised the office-holder that the debt is incorrect or not owed in response to the notice.

[10.976]
14.4 Requirements for proof

(1) A proof must—

(a) be made out by, or under the direction of, the creditor and authenticated by the creditor or a person authorised on the creditor's behalf;

(b) state the creditor's name and address;

(c) if the creditor is a company, identify the company;

(d) state the total amount of the creditor's claim (including any value added tax) as at the relevant date, less any payments made after that date in relation to the claim, any deduction under rule 14.20 and any adjustment by way of set-off in accordance with rules 14.24 and 14.25;

(e) state whether or not the claim includes any outstanding uncapitalised interest;

(f) contain particulars of how and when the debt was incurred by the company or the bankrupt;

(g) contain particulars of any security held, the date on which it was given and the value which the creditor puts on it;

(h) provide details of any reservation of title in relation to goods to which the debt relates;

(i) provide details of any document by reference to which the debt can be substantiated;

(j) be dated and authenticated; and

(k) state the name, postal address and authority of the person authenticating the proof (if someone other than the creditor).

(2) Where sub-paragraph (i) applies the document need not be delivered with the proof unless the office-holder has requested it.

(3) The office-holder may call for the creditor to produce any document or other evidence which the office-holder considers is necessary to substantiate the whole or any part of a claim.

[10.977]
14.5 Costs of proving

Unless the court orders otherwise—

(a) each creditor bears the cost of proving for that creditor's own debt, including costs incurred in providing documents or evidence under rule 14.4 (3);

(b) in an administration or winding up, costs incurred by the office-holder in estimating the value of a debt under rule 14.14 are payable out of the assets as an expense of the administration or winding up; and

(c) in a bankruptcy, costs incurred by the office-holder in estimating the value of a debt under section 322(3) fall on the bankrupt's estate as an expense of the bankruptcy.

[10.978]
14.6 Allowing inspection of proofs

The office-holder must, so long as proofs delivered to the office-holder are in the possession of the office-holder, allow them to be inspected, at all reasonable times on any business day, by the following—

(a) a creditor who has delivered a proof (unless the proof has been wholly rejected for purposes of dividend or otherwise, or withdrawn);

(b) a member or contributory of the company or, in the case of a bankruptcy, the bankrupt; and

(c) a person acting on behalf of any of the above.

[10.979]
14.7 Admission and rejection of proofs for dividend

(1) The office-holder may admit or reject a proof for dividend (in whole or in part).

(2) If the office-holder rejects a proof in whole or in part, the office-holder must deliver to the creditor a statement of the office-holder's reasons for doing so, as soon as reasonably practicable.

[10.980]
14.8 Appeal against decision on proof

(1) If a creditor is dissatisfied with the office-holder's decision under rule 14.7 in relation to the creditor's own proof (including a decision whether the debt is preferential), the creditor may apply to the court for the decision to be reversed or varied.

(2) The application must be made within 21 days of the creditor receiving the statement delivered under rule 14.7(2).

(3) A member, a contributory, any other creditor or, in a bankruptcy, the bankrupt, if dissatisfied with the office-holder's decision admitting, or rejecting the whole or any part of, a proof or agreeing to revalue a creditor's security under rule 14.15, may make such an application within 21 days of becoming aware of the office-holder's decision.

(4) The court must fix a venue for the application to be heard.

(5) The applicant must deliver notice of the venue to the creditor who delivered the proof in question (unless it is the applicant's own proof) and the office-holder.

(6) The office-holder must, on receipt of the notice, file the relevant proof with the court, together (if appropriate) with a copy of the statement sent under rule 14.7(2).

(7) After the application has been heard and determined, a proof which was submitted by the creditor in hard copy form must be returned by the court to the office-holder.

[10.981]
14.9 Office-holder not liable for costs under rule 14.8

(1) The official receiver is not personally liable for costs incurred by any person in respect of an application under rule 14.8.

(2) An office-holder other than the official receiver is not personally liable for costs incurred by any person in respect of an application under rule 14.8 unless the court orders otherwise.

[10.982]
14.10 Withdrawal or variation of proof

(1) A creditor may withdraw a proof at any time by delivering a written notice to the office-holder.

(2) The amount claimed by a creditor's proof may be varied at any time by agreement between the creditor and the office-holder.

[10.983]
14.11 Exclusion of proof by the court

(1) The court may exclude a proof or reduce the amount claimed—
- (a) on the office-holder's application, where the office-holder thinks that the proof has been improperly admitted, or ought to be reduced; or
- (b) on the application of a creditor, a member, a contributory or a bankrupt, if the office-holder declines to interfere in the matter.

(2) Where application is made under paragraph (1), the court must fix a venue for the application to be heard.

(3) The applicant must deliver notice of the venue—
- (a) in the case of an application by the office-holder, to the creditor who submitted the proof; and
- (b) in the case of an application by a creditor, a member, a contributory or a bankrupt, to the office-holder and to the creditor who made the proof (if not the applicant).

[10.984]
14.12 Administration and winding up by the court: debts of insolvent company to rank equally

[Note: for the equivalent rule for voluntary liquidation see section 107 of the Act and for bankruptcy section 328 of the Act.]

(1) This rule applies in an administration and a winding up by the court.

(2) Debts other than preferential debts rank equally between themselves and, after the preferential debts, must be paid in full unless the assets are insufficient for meeting them, in which case they abate in equal proportions between themselves.

[10.985]
14.13 Administration and winding up: division of unsold assets

[Note: in respect of bankruptcy see section 326 (distribution of property in specie).]

(1) This rule applies in an administration or in a winding up of a company (other than a members' voluntary winding up) to any property which from its peculiar nature or other special circumstances cannot be readily or advantageously sold.

(2) The office-holder may with the required permission divide the property in its existing form among the company's creditors according to its estimated value.

(3) The required permission is—
- (a) the permission of the creditors' committee in an administration or, if there is no creditors' committee, the creditors; and

(b) the permission of the liquidation committee in a winding up, or, if there is no liquidation committee, the creditors (without prejudice to provisions of the Act about disclaimer).

[10.986]

14.14 [Moratorium, administration] and winding up: estimate of value of debt

(1) In [the case of a decision procedure in respect of a moratorium under Part A1 of the Act,] an administration or in a winding up, the office-holder must estimate the value of a debt that does not have a certain value because it is subject to a contingency or for any other reason.

(2) The office-holder may revise such an estimate by reference to a change of circumstances or to information becoming available to the office-holder.

(3) The office-holder must inform the creditor of the office-holder's estimate and any revision.

(4) Where the value of a debt is estimated under this rule or by the court under section 168(3) or (5), the amount provable in the case of that debt is that of the estimate for the time being.

NOTES

Rule heading: words in square brackets substituted (for the original word "Administration") by the Insolvency (England and Wales) (No 2) (Amendment) Rules 2021, SI 2021/1028, r 55(1), (2), as from 1 October 2021 (for savings provisions see the note to r 1A.1 at **[10.539]**).

Para (1): words in square brackets inserted by SI 2021/1028, r 55(1), (3), as from 1 October 2021 (for savings provisions see the note to r 1A.1 at **[10.539]**).

[10.987]

14.15 Secured creditor: value of security

(1) A secured creditor may, with the agreement of the office-holder or the permission of the court, at any time alter the value which that creditor has put upon a security in a proof.

(2) Paragraph (3) applies where a secured creditor—

(a) being the applicant for the administration order or the appointer of the administrator, has in the application or the notice of appointment put a value on the security;

(b) being the petitioner in winding-up or bankruptcy proceedings, has put a value on the security in the petition; or

(c) has voted in respect of the unsecured balance of the debt.

(3) Where this paragraph applies—

(a) the secured creditor may re-value the security only with the agreement of the office-holder or the permission of the court; and

(b) where the revaluation was by agreement, the office-holder must deliver a notice of the revaluation to the creditors within five business days after the office-holder's agreement.

[10.988]

14.16 Secured creditor: surrender for non-disclosure

[(A1) This rule does not apply where a proof is submitted for the purpose of a decision procedure in respect of a moratorium under Part A1 of the Act.]

(1) If a secured creditor fails to disclose a security in a proof, the secured creditor must surrender that security for the general benefit of creditors, unless the court, on application by the secured creditor, relieves the secured creditor from the effect of this rule on the grounds that the omission was inadvertent or the result of honest mistake.

(2) If the court grants that relief, it may require or allow the creditor's proof to be amended, on such terms as may be just.

(3) . . .

NOTES

Para (A1): inserted by the Insolvency (England and Wales) (No 2) (Amendment) Rules 2021, SI 2021/1028, r 56, as from 1 October 2021 (for savings provisions see the note to r 1A.1 at **[10.539]**).

Para (3): revoked by the Insolvency (Amendment) (EU Exit) Regulations 2019, SI 2019/146, reg 2, Schedule, Pt 4, paras 46, 98, as from IP completion day (as defined in the European Union (Withdrawal Agreement) Act 2020, s 39) (for savings, see reg 4 of the 2019 Regulations at **[12.82]**).

[10.989]

14.17 Secured creditor: redemption by office-holder

[(A1) This rule does not apply where a proof is submitted for the purpose of a decision procedure in respect of a moratorium under Part A1 of the Act.]

(1) The office-holder may at any time deliver a notice to a creditor whose debt is secured that the office-holder proposes, at the expiration of 28 days from the date of the notice, to redeem the security at the value put upon it in the creditor's proof.

(2) The creditor then has 21 days (or such longer period as the office-holder may allow) in which to alter the value of the security in accordance with rule 14.15.

(3) If the creditor alters the value of the security with the permission of the office-holder or the court then the office-holder may only redeem at the new value.

(4) If the office-holder redeems the security the cost of transferring it is payable as an expense out of the insolvent estate.

(5) A creditor whose debt is secured may at any time deliver a notice to the office-holder requiring the office-holder to elect whether or not to redeem the security at the value then placed on it.

(6) The office-holder then has three months in which to redeem the security or elect not to redeem the security.

NOTES

Para (A1): inserted by the Insolvency (England and Wales) (No 2) (Amendment) Rules 2021, SI 2021/1028, r 57, as from 1 October 2021 (for savings provisions see the note to r 1A.1 at **[10.539]**).

[10.990]
14.18 Secured creditor: test of security's value

[(A1) This rule does not apply where a proof is submitted for the purpose of a decision procedure in respect of a moratorium under Part A1 of the Act.]

(1) If the office-holder is dissatisfied with the value which a secured creditor puts on a security in the creditor's proof the office-holder may require any property comprised in the security to be offered for sale.

(2) The terms of sale will be as agreed between the office-holder and the secured creditor, or as the court may direct.

(3) If the sale is by auction, the office-holder on behalf of the company or the insolvent estate and the creditor may bid.

(4) This rule does not apply if the value of the security has been altered with the court's permission.

NOTES

Para (A1): inserted by the Insolvency (England and Wales) (No 2) (Amendment) Rules 2021, SI 2021/1028, r 58, as from 1 October 2021 (for savings provisions see the note to r 1A.1 at **[10.539]**).

[10.991]
14.19 Realisation or surrender of security by creditor

(1) If a creditor who has valued a security subsequently realises the security (whether or not at the instance of the office-holder)—

(a) the net amount realised must be treated in all respects (including in relation to any valuation in a proof) as an amended valuation made by the creditor; and
(b) the creditor may prove for the balance of the creditor's debt.

(2) A creditor who voluntarily surrenders a security may prove for the whole of the creditor's debt as if it were unsecured.

[10.992]
14.20 Discounts

All trade and other discounts (except a discount for immediate or early settlement) which would have been available to the company or the debtor but for the insolvency proceedings must be deducted from the claim.

[10.993]
14.21 Debts in foreign currency

(1) A proof for a debt incurred or payable in a foreign currency must state the amount of the debt in that currency.

(2) The office-holder must convert all such debts into sterling at a single rate for each currency determined by the office-holder by reference to the exchange rates prevailing on the relevant date.

(3) On the next occasion when the office-holder communicates with the creditors the office-holder must advise them of any rate so determined.

(4) A creditor who considers that the rate determined by the office-holder is unreasonable may apply to the court.

(5) If on hearing the application the court finds that the rate is unreasonable it may itself determine the rate.

(6) This rule does not apply to the conversion of foreign currency debts in an application for a debt relief order.

[10.994]
14.22 Payments of a periodical nature

(1) In the case of rent and other payments of a periodical nature, the creditor may prove for any amounts due and unpaid up to the relevant date.

(2) Where at that date any payment was accruing due, the creditor may prove for so much as would have been due at that date, if accruing from day to day.

[10.995]
14.23 Interest

[Note: provision for the payment of interest out of a surplus remaining after payment of the debts is made by section 189(2) in respect of winding up and section 328(4) in respect of bankruptcy.]

(1) Where a debt proved in insolvency proceedings bears interest, that interest is provable as part of the debt except in so far as it is payable in respect of any period after the relevant date.

(2) In the circumstances set out below the creditor's claim may include interest on the debt for periods before the relevant date although not previously reserved or agreed.

(3) If the debt is due by virtue of a written instrument and payable at a certain time, interest may be claimed for the period from that time to the relevant date.

(4) If the debt is due otherwise, interest may only be claimed if demand for payment of the debt was made in writing by or on behalf of the creditor, and notice was delivered that interest would be payable from the date of the demand to the date of the payment, before—

(a) the relevant date, in respect of [a decision procedure in respect of a moratorium under Part A1 of the Act,] administration or winding up; or
(b) the presentation of the bankruptcy petition or the bankruptcy application.

(5) Interest under paragraph (4) may only be claimed for the period from the date of the demand to the relevant date and, for the purposes of the Act and these Rules, must be charged at a rate not exceeding that mentioned in paragraph (6).

(6) The rate of interest to be claimed under paragraphs (3) and (4) is the rate specified in section 17 of the Judgments Act 1838 on the relevant date.

(7) In an administration—

(a) any surplus remaining after payment of the debts proved must, before being applied for any other purpose, be applied in paying interest on those debts in respect of the periods during which they have been outstanding since the relevant date;

(b) all interest payable under sub-paragraph (a) ranks equally whether or not the debts on which it is payable rank equally; and

(c) the rate of interest payable under sub-paragraph (a) is whichever is the greater of the rate specified under paragraph (6) and the rate applicable to the debt apart from the administration.

NOTES

Para (4): words in square brackets in sub-para (a) substituted by the Insolvency (England and Wales) (No 2) (Amendment) Rules 2021, SI 2021/1028, r 59, as from 1 October 2021 (for savings provisions see the note to r 1A.1 at **[10.539]**).

[10.996]

[14.23A Moratoriums under Part A1 of the Act: mutual dealings and set off

(1) This rule applies for the purposes of a decision procedure in respect of a moratorium under Part A1 of the Act.

(2) An account must be taken of what is due from the company and the creditor to each other in respect of their mutual dealings and the sums due from the one must be set off against the sums due from the other.

(3) If there is a balance owed to the creditor then only that balance is provable for the purposes of the decision procedure.

(4) For the purpose of this rule, "mutual dealings" means mutual credits, mutual debts or other mutual dealings between the company and a creditor proving or claiming to prove for a debt in the decision procedure but—

(a) in the case of a decision under section A11, only includes those debts which are pre-moratorium debts within the meaning given by section A53, and

(b) in the case of a decision which is required by virtue of an order under section A44(3), only includes those debts which are pre-moratorium debts (within the meaning given by section A53) unless the court orders otherwise.

(5) A sum must be treated as being due to or from the company for the purposes of paragraph (2) whether—

(a) it is payable at present or in the future,

(b) the obligation by virtue of which it is payable is certain or contingent, or

(c) its amount is fixed or liquidated, or is capable of being ascertained by fixed rules or as a matter of opinion.

(6) For the purposes of this rule—

(a) rule 14.14 applies to an obligation which, by reason of its being subject to a contingency or for any other reason, does not bear a certain value, and

(b) rules 14.21 to 14.23 apply to sums due to the company which—

(i) are payable in a currency other than sterling,

(ii) are of a periodical nature, or

(iii) bear interest.]

NOTES

Commencement: 1 October 2021.

Inserted by the Insolvency (England and Wales) (No 2) (Amendment) Rules 2021, SI 2021/1028, r 60, as from 1 October 2021 (for savings provisions see the note to r 1A.1 at **[10.539]**).

[10.997]

14.24 Administration: mutual dealings and set-off

(1) This rule applies in an administration where the administrator intends to make a distribution and has delivered a notice under rule 14.29.

(2) An account must be taken as at the date of the notice of what is due from the company and a creditor to each other in respect of their mutual dealings and the sums due from the one must be set off against the sums due from the other.

(3) If there is a balance owed to the creditor then only that balance is provable in the administration.

(4) If there is a balance owed to the company that must be paid to the administrator as part of the assets.

(5) However if all or part of the balance owed to the company results from a contingent or prospective debt owed by the creditor then the balance (or that part of it which results from the contingent or prospective debt) must be paid in full (without being discounted under rule 14.44) if and when that debt becomes due and payable.

(6) In this rule—

"obligation" means an obligation however arising, whether by virtue of an agreement, rule of law or otherwise; and

"mutual dealings" means mutual credits, mutual debts or other mutual dealings between the company and a creditor proving or claiming to prove for a debt in the administration but does not include any of the following—

(a) a debt arising out of an obligation incurred after the company entered administration;

(b) a debt arising out of an obligation incurred at a time when the creditor had notice that—

(i) an application for an administration order was pending, or

(ii) any person had delivered notice of intention to appoint an administrator;

Part 10 Miscellaneous other SIs

(c) a debt arising out of an obligation where—
(i) the administration was immediately preceded by a winding up, and
(ii) at the time when the obligation was incurred the creditor had notice that a decision had been sought from creditors under section 100 on the nomination of a liquidator or that a winding-up petition was pending;
(d) a debt arising out of an obligation incurred during a winding up which immediately preceded the administration; or
(e) a debt which has been acquired by a creditor by assignment or otherwise, under an agreement between the creditor and another party where that agreement was entered into—
(i) after the company entered administration,
(ii) at a time when the creditor had notice that an application for an administration order was pending,
(iii) at a time when the creditor had notice that any person had given notice of intention to appoint an administrator,
(iv) where the administration was immediately preceded by a winding up, at a time when the creditor had notice that a decision had been sought from creditors under section 100 on the nomination of a liquidator or that a winding-up petition was pending, or
(v) during a winding up which immediately preceded the administration.

(7) A sum must be treated as being due to or from the company for the purposes of paragraph (2) whether—
(a) it is payable at present or in the future;
(b) the obligation by virtue of which it is payable is certain or contingent; or
(c) its amount is fixed or liquidated, or is capable of being ascertained by fixed rules or as a matter of opinion.

(8) For the purposes of this rule—
(a) rule 14.14 applies to an obligation which, by reason of its being subject to a contingency or for any other reason, does not bear a certain value;
(b) rules 14.21 to 14.23 apply to sums due to the company which—
(i) are payable in a currency other than sterling,
(ii) are of a periodical nature, or
(iii) bear interest; and
(c) rule 14.44 applies to a sum due to or from the company which is payable in the future.

[10.998]
14.25 Winding up: mutual dealings and set-off

(1) This rule applies in a winding up where, before the company goes into liquidation, there have been mutual dealings between the company and a creditor of the company proving or claiming to prove for a debt in the liquidation.

(2) An account must be taken of what is due from the company and the creditor to each other in respect of their mutual dealings and the sums due from the one must be set off against the sums due from the other.

(3) If there is a balance owed to the creditor then only that balance is provable in the winding up.

(4) If there is a balance owed to the company then that must be paid to the liquidator as part of the assets.

(5) However if all or part of the balance owed to the company results from a contingent or prospective debt owed by the creditor then the balance (or that part of it which results from the contingent or prospective debt) must be paid in full (without being discounted under rule 14.44) if and when that debt becomes due and payable.

(6) In this rule—

"obligation" means an obligation however arising, whether by virtue of an agreement, rule of law or otherwise; and

"mutual dealings" means mutual credits, mutual debts or other mutual dealings between the company and a creditor proving or claiming to prove for a debt in the winding up but does not include any of the following—
(a) a debt arising out of an obligation incurred at a time when the creditor had notice that—
(i) a decision had been sought from creditors on the nomination of a liquidator under section 100, or
(ii) a petition for the winding up of the company was pending;
(b) a debt arising out of an obligation where—
(i) the liquidation was immediately preceded by an administration, and
(ii) at the time the obligation was incurred the creditor had notice that an application for an administration order was pending or a person had delivered notice of intention to appoint an administrator; and
(c) a debt arising out of an obligation incurred during an administration which immediately preceded the liquidation;
(d) a debt which has been acquired by a creditor by assignment or otherwise, under an agreement between the creditor and another party where that agreement was entered into—
(i) after the company went into liquidation,
(ii) at a time when the creditor had notice that a decision had been sought from creditors under section 100 on the nomination of a liquidator,
(iii) at a time when the creditor had notice that a winding-up petition was pending,
(iv) where the winding up was immediately preceded by an administration at a time when the creditor had notice that an application for an administration order was pending or a person had delivered notice of intention to appoint an administrator, or
(v) during an administration which immediately preceded the winding up.

(7) A sum must be treated as being due to or from the company for the purposes of paragraph (2) whether—
- (a) it is payable at present or in the future;
- (b) the obligation by virtue of which it is payable is certain or contingent; or
- (c) its amount is fixed or liquidated, or is capable of being ascertained by fixed rules or as a matter of opinion.

(8) For the purposes of this rule—
- (a) rule 14.14 applies to an obligation which, by reason of its being subject to a contingency or for any other reason, does not bear a certain value;
- (b) rules 14.21 to 14.23 apply to sums due to the company which—
  - (i) are payable in a currency other than sterling,
  - (ii) are of a periodical nature, or
  - (iii) bear interest; and
- (c) rule 14.44 applies to a sum due to or from the company which is payable in the future.

CHAPTER 3 DISTRIBUTION TO CREDITORS IN ADMINISTRATION, WINDING UP AND BANKRUPTCY

[Note: a document required by the Act or these Rules must also contain the standard contents set out in Part 1.]

[10.999]

14.26 Application of Chapter to a particular class of creditors and to distributions

(1) This Chapter applies where the office-holder makes, or proposes to make, a distribution to any class of creditors other than secured creditors.

(2) Where the distribution is to a particular class of creditors in an administration, a reference in this Chapter to creditors is a reference to that class of creditors only.

[10.1000]

14.27 Declaration and distribution of dividends in a winding up

[Note: section 324 makes provision in respect of such a declaration and distribution in a bankruptcy.]

Whenever a liquidator in a creditors' voluntary winding up or a winding up by the court has sufficient funds in hand for the purpose the liquidator must, while retaining such sums as may be necessary for the expenses of the winding up, declare and distribute dividends among the creditors in respect of the debts which they have proved.

[10.1001]

14.28 Gazette notice of intended first dividend or distribution

(1) Subject to paragraphs (2) and (4) where the office-holder intends to declare a first dividend or distribution the office-holder must gazette a notice containing—
- (a) a statement that the office-holder intends to declare a first dividend or distribution;
- (b) the date by which and place to which proofs must be delivered; and
- (c) in the case of a members' voluntary winding up, where the dividend or distribution is to be a sole or final distribution, a statement that the distribution may be made without regard to the claim of any person in respect of a debt not proved.

(2) Where the intended dividend is only to preferential creditors [or creditors in respect of a debt which is a moratorium debt or priority pre-moratorium debt within the meaning given by section 174A] the office-holder need only gazette a notice if the office-holder thinks fit.

(3) The office-holder may in addition advertise such a notice in such other manner (if any) as the office-holder thinks fit.

(4) Paragraph (1) does not apply where the office-holder has previously, by a notice which has been gazetted, invited creditors to prove their debts.

NOTES

Para (2): words in square brackets inserted by the Insolvency (England and Wales) (No 2) (Amendment) Rules 2021, SI 2021/1028, r 61, as from 1 October 2021 (for savings provisions see the note to r 1A.1 at **[10.539]**).

[10.1002]

14.29 Individual notices to creditors etc of intended dividend or distribution

(1) The office-holder must deliver a notice of the intention to make a distribution to creditors or declare a dividend—
- (a) to the creditors in an administration; and
- (b) to all creditors in a winding up or a bankruptcy who have not proved (including any creditors who are owed small debts and are not deemed under rule 14.3(3) to have proved as a result of a previous notice under rule 14.29).

[(2) Paragraph (2A) applies where the intended dividend is only for one or both of the following—
- (a) preferential creditors, or
- (b) creditors in respect of a debt which is a moratorium debt or a priority pre-moratorium debt within the meaning given by section 174A.]

[(2A) Where this paragraph applies the office-holder is only required to deliver the notice to those creditors referred to in sub-paragraph (2)(a) or (b) for whom the dividend is intended.]

(3) Where the office-holder intends to declare a dividend to unsecured creditors in an administration or winding-up the notice must also state the value of the prescribed part unless there is no prescribed part or the court has made an order under section 176A(5).

NOTES

Para (2): substituted by the Insolvency (England and Wales) (No 2) (Amendment) Rules 2021, SI 2021/1028, r 62(1), (2), as from 1 October 2021 (for savings provisions see the note to r 1A.1 at **[10.539]**). Para (2) previously read as follows—

"(2) Where the intended dividend is only for preferential creditors, the office-holder is only required to deliver such a notice to the preferential creditors.".

Para (2A): inserted by SI 2021/1028, r 62(1), (3), as from 1 October 2021 (for savings provisions see the note to r 1A.1 at **[10.539]**).

[10.1003]

14.30 Contents of notice of intention to declare a dividend or make a distribution

A notice under rule 14.29 must contain the following—

(a) a statement that the office-holder intends to make a distribution to creditors or declare a dividend (as the case may be) within the period of two months from the last date for proving;

(b) a statement whether the proposed distribution or dividend is interim or final;

(c) the last date by which proofs may be delivered which must be—

(i) the same date for all creditors who prove, and

(ii) not less than 21 days from the date of notice;

(d) a statement of the place to which proofs must be delivered;

(e) the additional information required by rule 14.31 where the office-holder intends to treat a small debt as proved for the purposes of paying a dividend; and

(f) in the case of a members' voluntary winding up, where the distribution is to be a sole or final distribution, a statement that the distribution may be made without regard to the claim of any person in respect of a debt not proved.

[10.1004]

14.31 Further contents of notice to creditors owed small debts etc

(1) The office-holder may treat a debt, which is a small debt according to the accounting records or the statement of affairs of the company or bankrupt, as if it were proved for the purpose of paying a dividend.

(2) Where the office-holder intends to treat such a debt as if it were proved the notice delivered under rule 14.29 must—

(a) state the amount of the debt which the office-holder believes to be owed to the creditor according to the accounting records or statement of affairs of the company or the bankrupt (as the case may be);

(b) state that the office-holder will treat the debt which is stated in notice, being for £1,000 or less, as proved for the purposes of paying a dividend unless the creditor advises the office-holder that the amount of the debt is incorrect or that no debt is owed;

(c) require the creditor to notify the office-holder by the last date for proving if the amount of the debt is incorrect or if no debt is owed; and

(d) inform the creditor that where the creditor advises the office-holder that the amount of the debt is incorrect the creditor must also submit a proof in order to receive a dividend.

(3) The information required by paragraph (2)(a) may take the form of a list of small debts which the office-holder intends to treat as proved which includes that owed to the particular creditor to whom the notice is being delivered.

[10.1005]

14.32 Admission or rejection of proofs following last date for proving

(1) Unless the office-holder has already dealt with them, the office-holder must within 14 days of the last date for proving set out in the notice under rule 14.29—

(a) admit or reject (in whole or in part) proofs delivered to the office-holder; or

(b) make such provision in relation to them as the office-holder thinks fit.

(2) The office-holder is not obliged to deal with a proof delivered after the last date for proving, but the office-holder may do so if the office-holder thinks fit.

(3) In the declaration of a dividend a payment must not be made more than once in respect of the same debt.

(4) . . .

NOTES

Para (4): revoked by the Insolvency (Amendment) (EU Exit) Regulations 2019, SI 2019/146, reg 2, Schedule, Pt 4, paras 46, 99, as from IP completion day (as defined in the European Union (Withdrawal Agreement) Act 2020, s 39) (for savings, see reg 4 of the 2019 Regulations at **[12.82]**).

[10.1006]

14.33 Postponement or cancellation of dividend

(1) The office-holder may postpone or cancel the dividend in the period of two months from the last date for proving if an application is made to the court for the office-holder's decision on a proof to be reversed or varied, or for a proof to be excluded, or for a reduction of the amount claimed.

(2) The office-holder may postpone a dividend if the office-holder considers that due to the nature of the affairs of the person to whom the proceedings relate there is real complexity in admitting or rejecting proofs of claims submitted.

(3) Where the dividend is postponed or cancelled a new notice under rule 14.29 will be required if the dividend is paid subsequently.

[10.1007]

14.34 Declaration of dividend

(1) The office-holder must declare the dividend in the two month period referred to in rule 14.30(a) in accordance with the notice of intention to declare a dividend unless the office-holder has had cause to postpone or cancel the dividend.

(2) The office-holder must not declare a dividend so long as there is pending an application to the court to reverse or vary a decision of the office-holder on a proof, or to exclude a proof or to reduce the amount claimed unless the court gives permission.

(3) If the court gives such permission, the office-holder must make such provision in relation to the proof as the court directs.

[10.1008]
14.35 Notice of declaration of a dividend

(1) Where the office-holder declares a dividend the office-holder must deliver notice of that fact to all creditors who have proved for their debts (subject to paragraph (5) [and (6)]).

(2) The notice declaring a dividend may be delivered at the same time as the dividend is distributed.

(3) The notice must include the following in relation to the insolvency proceedings—

(a) the amounts raised from the sale of assets, indicating (so far as practicable) amounts raised by the sale of particular assets;
(b) the payments made by the office-holder in carrying out the office-holder's functions;
(c) the provision (if any) made for unsettled claims, and funds (if any) retained for particular purposes;
(d) the total amount to be distributed and the rate of dividend; and
(e) whether, and if so when, any further dividend is expected to be declared.

(4) In an administration, a creditors' voluntary winding-up or a winding up by the court, where the administrator or liquidator intends to make a distribution to unsecured creditors, the notice must also state the value of the prescribed part unless there is no prescribed part or the court has made an order under section 176A(5).

[(5) Paragraph (6) applies where the office-holder declares a dividend which is only for one or both of the following—

(a) preferential creditors, or
(b) creditors in respect of a debt which is a moratorium debt or priority pre-moratorium debt within the meaning given by section 174A.]

[(6) Where this paragraph applies the notice under paragraph (1) need only be delivered to those creditors referred to in sub-paragraph (5)(a) or (b) (as the case may be) who have proved for their debts.]

NOTES

The words in square brackets in para (1) were inserted, para (5) was substituted, and para (6) added, by the Insolvency (England and Wales) (No 2) (Amendment) Rules 2021, SI 2021/1028, r 63, as from 1 October 2021 (for savings provisions see the note to r 1A.1 at **[10.539]**). Para (5) previously read as follows—

> "(5) Where the office-holder declares a dividend for preferential creditors only, the notice under paragraph (1) need only be delivered to those preferential creditors who have proved for their debts.".

[10.1009]
14.36 Last notice about dividend in a winding up

[Note: section 330 contains the requirement to deliver such a notice in a bankruptcy.]

(1) When the liquidator in a winding up has realised all the company's assets or so much of them as can, in the liquidator's opinion, be realised without needlessly prolonging the winding up, the liquidator must deliver a notice as provided for in this Chapter, either—

(a) of intention to declare a final dividend; or
(b) that no dividend, or further dividend, will be declared.

(2) The notice must contain the particulars required by rule 14.30, 14.31, 14.37 or 14.38 as the case may be and must require claims against the assets to be established by a date set out in the notice.

[10.1010]
14.37 Contents of last notice about dividend (administration, winding up and bankruptcy)

(1) This rule applies in an administration, winding up or bankruptcy.

(2) If the office-holder delivers notice to creditors that the office-holder is unable to declare any dividend or (as the case may be) any further dividend, the notice must contain a statement to the effect either—

(a) that no funds have been realised; or
(b) that the funds realised have already been distributed or used or allocated for paying the expenses of the insolvency proceedings.

(3) The information required by paragraph (2) may be included in a progress report.

[10.1011]
14.38 Sole or final dividend

[Note: see section 330 in respect of a dividend in a bankruptcy.]

(1) Where, in an administration or winding up, it is intended that the distribution is to be a sole or final dividend, after the date specified as the last date for proving in the notice under rule 14.29, the office-holder—

(a) in a winding up, must pay any outstanding expenses of the winding up out of the assets;
(b) in an administration, must—
    (i) pay any outstanding expenses of a winding up (including any of the items mentioned in rule 6.42 or 7.108 (as appropriate)) or provisional winding up that immediately preceded the administration,
    (ii) pay any items payable in accordance with the provisions of paragraph 99 of Schedule B1,
    (iii) pay any amount outstanding (including debts or liabilities and the administrator's own remuneration and expenses) which would, if the administrator were to cease to be the administrator of the company, be payable out of the property of which he had custody or control in accordance with the provisions of paragraph 99, and
    (iv) declare and distribute that dividend without regard to the claim of any person in respect of a debt not already proved; or

(c) in a members' voluntary winding up may, and in every other case must, declare and distribute that dividend without regard to the claim of any person in respect of a debt not already proved.

(2) The reference in paragraph (1)(b)(iv) and (c) to debts that have not been proved does not include small debts treated as proved by the office-holder.

(3) The court may, on the application of any person, postpone the date specified in the notice.

[10.1012]
14.39 Administration and winding up: provisions as to dividends

[Note: see section 324(4) in respect of such provisions in bankruptcy.]

In an administration or winding up, in the calculation and distribution of a dividend the office-holder must make provision for—

(a) any debts which are the subject of claims which have not yet been determined; and
(b) disputed proofs and claims.

[10.1013]
14.40 Supplementary provisions as to dividends and distributions

(1) A creditor is not entitled to disturb the payment of any dividend or making of any distribution because—

(a) the amount claimed in the creditor's proof is increased after payment of the dividend;
(b) in an administration, a creditors' voluntary winding up or a winding up by the court the creditor did not prove for a debt before the declaration of the dividend; or
(c) in a members' voluntary winding up, the creditor did not prove for a debt before the last date for proving or increases the claim in proof after that date.

(2) However the creditor is entitled to be paid a dividend or receive a distribution which the creditor has failed to receive out of any money for the time being available for the payment of a further dividend or making a further distribution.

(3) Such a dividend must be paid or distribution made before that money is applied to the payment of any further dividend or making of any further distribution.

(4) If, after a creditor's proof has been admitted, the proof is withdrawn or excluded, or the amount of it is reduced, the creditor is liable to repay to the office-holder, for the credit of the insolvency proceedings, any amount overpaid by way of dividend.

[10.1014]
14.41 Secured creditors

(1) The following applies where a creditor alters the value of a security after a dividend has been declared.

(2) If the alteration reduces the creditor's unsecured claim ranking for dividend, the creditor must as soon as reasonably practicable repay to the office-holder, for the credit of the administration or of the insolvent estate, any amount received by the creditor as dividend in excess of that to which the creditor would be entitled, having regard to the alteration of the value of the security.

(3) If the alteration increases the creditor's unsecured claim, the creditor is entitled to receive from the office-holder, out of any money for the time being available for the payment of a further dividend, before any such further dividend is paid, any dividend or dividends which the creditor has failed to receive, having regard to the alteration of the value of the security.

(4) The creditor is not entitled to disturb any dividend declared (whether or not distributed) before the date of the alteration.

[10.1015]
14.42 Disqualification from dividend

If a creditor contravenes any provision of the Act or these Rules relating to the valuation of securities, the court may, on the application of the office-holder, order that the creditor be wholly or partly disqualified from participation in any dividend.

[10.1016]
14.43 Assignment of right to dividend

(1) If a person entitled to a dividend ("the entitled person") delivers notice to the office-holder that the entitled person wishes the dividend to be paid to another person, or that the entitled person has assigned the entitlement to another person, the office-holder must pay the dividend to that other person accordingly.

(2) A notice delivered under this rule must specify the name and address of the person to whom payment is to be made.

[10.1017]
14.44 Debt payable at future time

(1) Where a creditor has proved for a debt of which payment is not due at the date of the declaration of a dividend, the creditor is entitled to the dividend equally with other creditors, but subject as follows.

(2) For the purpose of dividend (and no other purpose) the amount of the creditor's admitted proof must be discounted by applying the following formula—

$$\frac{X}{1.05^n}$$

where—

(a) "X" is the value of the admitted proof; and

(b) "n" is the period beginning with the relevant date and ending with the date on which the payment of the creditor's debt would otherwise be due, expressed in years (part of a year being expressed as a decimal fraction of a year).

[10.1018]
14.45 Administration and winding up: non-payment of dividend

[Note: see section 325(2) for equivalent provisions in respect of bankruptcy.]

(1) No action lies against the office-holder in an administration or winding up for payment of a dividend.

(2) However, if the office-holder refuses to pay a dividend the court may, if it thinks just, order the office-holder to pay it and also to pay, out of the office-holder's own money—

(a) interest on the dividend, at the rate for the time being specified in section 17 of the Judgments Act 1838, from the time when it was withheld; and

(b) the costs of the proceedings in which the order to pay is made.

PART 15 DECISION MAKING

CHAPTER 1 APPLICATION OF PART

[10.1019]
15.1 Application of Part

In this Part—

(a) Chapters 2 to 11 apply where the Act or these Rules require a decision to be made by a qualifying decision procedure, or by a creditors' decision procedure or permit a decision to be made by the deemed consent procedure; and

(b) Chapter 12 applies to company meetings.

CHAPTER 2 DECISION PROCEDURES

[Note: a document required by the Act or these Rules must also contain the standard contents set out in Part 1.]

[10.1020]
15.2 Interpretation

(1) In these Rules—

["creditor", in relation to a decision procedure under section A11 (extension by directors with creditor consent), means a creditor who is a pre-moratorium creditor within the meaning given by section A12;]

"decision date" means—

(a) in the case of a decision to be made at a meeting, the date of the meeting;

(b) in the case of a decision to be made either by a decision procedure other than a meeting or by the deemed consent procedure, the date the decision is to be made or deemed to have been made;

and a decision falling within paragraph (b) is to be treated as made at 23:59 on the decision date;

"decision procedure" means a qualifying decision procedure or a creditors' decision procedure as prescribed by rule 15.3;

"electronic voting" includes any electronic system which enables a person to vote without the need to attend at a particular location to do so;

"physical meeting" means a meeting as described in section 246ZE(9) or 379ZA(9);

"virtual meeting" means a meeting where persons who are not invited to be physically present together may participate in the meeting including communicating directly with all the other participants in the meeting and voting (either directly or via a proxy-holder);

(2) The decision date is to be set at the discretion of the convener, but must be not less than 14 days from the date of delivery of the notice, except where the table in rule 15.11 requires a different period or the court directs otherwise.

(3) The rules in Chapters 2 to 11 about decision procedures of creditors apply with any necessary modifications to decision making by contributories.

(4) In particular, in place of the requirement for percentages or majorities in decision making by creditors to be determined by value, where the procedure seeks a decision from contributories value must be determined on the percentage of voting rights in accordance with rule 15.39.

NOTES

Para (1): definition "creditor" inserted by the Insolvency (England and Wales) (No 2) (Amendment) Rules 2021, SI 2021/1028, r 64, as from 1 October 2021 (for savings provisions see the note to r 1A.1 at **[10.539]**).

[10.1021]
15.3 The prescribed decision procedures

[Note: under sections 246ZE and 379ZA a decision may not be made by a creditors' meeting (a physical meeting) unless the prescribed proportion of the creditors request in writing that the decision be made by such a meeting.]

The following decision procedures are prescribed as decision procedures under sections 246ZE and 379ZA by which a convener may seek a decision under the Act or these Rules from creditors—

(a) correspondence;

(b) electronic voting;

(c) virtual meeting;

(d) physical meeting; . . .

(e) any other decision making procedure which enables all creditors who are entitled to participate in the making of the decision to participate equally.

NOTES

Word omitted from para (d) revoked by the Insolvency (England and Wales) (Amendment) Rules 2017, SI 2017/366, rr 3, 35, as from 6 April 2017.

[10.1022]
15.4 Electronic voting

Where the decision procedure uses electronic voting—

(a) the notice delivered to creditors must give them any necessary information as to how to access the voting system including any password required;

(b) except where electronic voting is being used at a meeting, the voting system must be a system capable of enabling a creditor to vote at any time between the notice being delivered and the decision date; and

(c) in the course of a vote the voting system must not provide any creditor with information concerning the vote cast by any other creditor.

[10.1023]
15.5 Virtual meetings

Where the decision procedure uses a virtual meeting the notice delivered to creditors must contain—

(a) any necessary information as to how to access the virtual meeting including any telephone number, access code or password required; and

(b) a statement that the meeting may be suspended or adjourned by the chair of the meeting (and must be adjourned if it is so resolved at the meeting).

[10.1024]
15.6 Physical meetings

(1) A request for a physical meeting may be made before or after the notice of the decision procedure or deemed consent procedure has been delivered, but must be made not later than five business days [or, in the case of a decision procedure in respect of a moratorium under Part A1 of the Act, three days] after the date on which the convener delivered the notice of the decision procedure or deemed consent procedure unless these Rules provide to the contrary.

(2) It is the convener's responsibility to check whether any requests for a physical meeting are submitted before the deadline and if so whether in aggregate they meet or surpass one of the thresholds requiring a physical meeting under sections 246ZE(7) or 379ZA(7).

(3) Where the prescribed proportion of creditors require a physical meeting the convener must summon the meeting by giving notice which complies with rule 15.8 so far as applicable and which must also contain a statement that the meeting may be suspended or adjourned by the chair of the meeting (and must be adjourned if it is so resolved at the meeting).

(4) In addition, the notice under paragraph (3) must inform the creditors that as a result of the requirement to hold a physical meeting the original decision procedure or the deemed consent procedure is superseded.

(5) The convener must send the notice under paragraph (3) not later than three business days after one of the thresholds requiring a physical meeting has been met or surpassed.

(6) The convener—

(a) may permit a creditor to attend a physical meeting remotely if the convener receives a request to do so in advance of the meeting; and

(b) must include in the notice of the meeting a statement explaining the convener's discretion to permit remote attendance.

(7) In this rule, attending a physical meeting "remotely" means attending and being able to participate in the meeting without being in the place where the meeting is being held.

[(8) For the purpose of determining whether the thresholds under section 246ZE(7) or 379ZA(7) are met, the convener must calculate the value of the creditor's debt by reference to rule 15.31.]

NOTES

Para (1): words in square brackets inserted by the Insolvency (England and Wales) (No 2) (Amendment) Rules 2021, SI 2021/1028, r 65, as from 1 October 2021 (for savings provisions see the note to r 1A.1 at **[10.539]**).

Para (8): added by the Insolvency (England and Wales) (Amendment) Rules 2017, SI 2017/366, rr 3, 36, as from 6 April 2017.

[10.1025]
15.7 Deemed consent (sections 246ZF and 379ZB)

[Note: the deemed consent procedure cannot be used to make a decision on remuneration of any person, or where the Act, these Rules or any other legislation requires a decision to be made by a decision procedure.]

(1) This rule makes further provision about the deemed consent procedure to that set out in sections 246ZF and 379ZB.

(2) A notice seeking deemed consent must, in addition to the requirements of section 246ZF or 379ZB (as applicable) comply with the requirements of rule 15.8 so far as applicable and must also contain—

(a) a statement that in order to object to the proposed decision a creditor must have delivered a notice, stating that the creditor so objects, to the convener not later than the decision date together with a proof in respect of the creditor's claim in accordance with these Rules failing which the objection will be disregarded;

(b) a statement that it is the convener's responsibility to aggregate any objections to see if the threshold is met for the decision to be taken as not having been made; and

(c) a statement that if the threshold is met the deemed consent procedure will terminate without a decision being made and if a decision is sought again on the same matter it will be sought by a decision procedure.

(3) In this rule, the threshold is met where the appropriate number of relevant creditors (as defined in sections 246ZF and 379ZB) have objected to the proposed decision.

(4) For the purpose of aggregating objections, the convener may presume the value of relevant creditors' claims to be the value of claims by those creditors who, in the convener's view, would have been entitled to vote had the decision been sought by a decision procedure in accordance with this Part, even where those creditors had not already met the criteria for such entitlement to vote.

(5) The provisions of rules 15.31(2) (calculation of voting rights), 15.32 (calculation of voting rights: special cases) and 15.33 (procedure for admitting creditors' claims for voting) apply to the admission or rejection of a claim for the purpose of the convener deciding whether or not an objection should count towards the total aggregated objections.

(6) A decision of the convener on the aggregation of objections under this rule is subject to appeal under rule 15.35 as if it were a decision under Chapter 8 of this Part.

CHAPTER 3 NOTICES, VOTING AND VENUES FOR DECISIONS

[Note: a document required by the Act or these Rules must also contain the standard contents set out in Part 1.]

[10.1026]
15.8 Notices to creditors of decision procedure

(1) This rule sets out the requirements for notices to creditors where a decision is sought by a decision procedure.

(2) The convener must deliver a notice to every creditor who is entitled to notice of the procedure.

(3) The notice must contain the following—

(a) identification details for the proceedings;

(b) details of the decision to be made or of any resolution on which a decision is sought;

(c) a description of the decision procedure which the convener is using, and arrangements, including the venue, for the decision procedure;

(d) a statement of the decision date;

(e) . . . a statement of by when the creditor must have delivered a proof in respect of the creditor's claim in accordance with these Rules failing which a vote by the creditor will be disregarded;

(f) [except in the case of a decision procedure in respect of a moratorium under Part A1 of the Act] a statement that a creditor whose debt is treated as a small debt in accordance with rule 14.31(1) must still deliver a proof if that creditor wishes to vote;

(g) [except in the case of a decision procedure in respect of a moratorium under Part A1 of the Act] a statement that a creditor who has opted out from receiving notices may nevertheless vote if the creditor provides a proof in accordance with paragraph (e);

(h) in the case of a decision to remove a liquidator in a creditors' voluntary winding-up or a winding up by the court, a statement drawing the attention of creditors to section 173(2)[, 174(2)] or 174(4) (which relate to the release of the liquidator), as appropriate;

(i) in the case of a decision to remove a trustee in a bankruptcy, a statement drawing the attention of creditors to section [299(1) or] 299(3) (which relates to the release of the trustee);

(j) in the case of a decision in relation to a proposed CVA or IVA, a statement of the effects of the relevant provisions of the following—

  (i) rule 15.28 about creditors' voting rights,

  (ii) rule 15.31 about the calculation of creditors' voting rights, and

  (iii) rule 15.34 about the requisite majority of creditors for making decisions;

(k) except in the case of a physical meeting, a statement that creditors who meet the thresholds in sections 246ZE(7) or 379ZA(7) may, within five business days from the date of delivery of the notice, require a physical meeting to be held to consider the matter;

(l) in the case of a meeting, a statement that any proxy must be delivered to the convener or chair before it may be used at the meeting;

(m) in the case of a meeting, a statement that, where applicable, a complaint may be made in accordance with rule 15.38 and the period within which such a complaint may be made; and

(n) a statement that a creditor may appeal a decision in accordance with rule 15.35, and the relevant period under rule 15.35 within which such an appeal may be made.

(4) The notice must be authenticated and dated by the convener.

(5) Where the decision procedure is a meeting the notice must be accompanied by a blank proxy complying with rule 16.3.

(6) This rule does not apply if the court orders under rule 15.12 that notice of a decision procedure be given by advertisement only.

NOTES

Para (3): words omitted from sub-para (e) revoked, and words in square brackets in sub-paras (h), (i) substituted, by the Insolvency (England and Wales) (Amendment) Rules 2017, SI 2017/366, rr 3, 37, as from 6 April 2017. Words in square brackets in sub-paras (f), (g) inserted by the Insolvency (England and Wales) (No 2) (Amendment) Rules 2021, SI 2021/1028, r 66, as from 1 October 2021 (for savings provisions see the note to r 1A.1 at **[10.539]**).

[10.1027]
15.9 Voting in a decision procedure

(1) In order to be counted in a decision procedure other than where votes are cast at a meeting, votes must—

(a) be received by the convener on or before the decision date; and

(b) in the case of a vote cast by a creditor, be accompanied by a proof in respect of the creditor's claim unless it has already been given to the convener.

(2) In [a decision procedure in respect of a moratorium under Part A1 of the Act,] an administration, an administrative receivership, a creditors' voluntary winding up, a winding up by the court or a bankruptcy a vote must be disregarded if—

(a) a proof in respect of the claim is not received by the convener on or before the decision date or, in the case of a meeting, 4pm on the business day before the decision date unless under rule 15.26 or 15.28(1)(b)(ii) (as applicable) the chair is content to accept the proof later; or

(b) the convener decides, in the application of Chapter 8 of this Part, that the creditor is not entitled to cast the vote.

(3) For the decision to be made, the convener must receive at least one valid vote on or before the decision date.

NOTES

Para (2): words in square brackets inserted by the Insolvency (England and Wales) (No 2) (Amendment) Rules 2021, SI 2021/1028, r 67, as from 1 October 2021 (for savings provisions see the note to r 1A.1 at **[10.539]**).

[10.1028]
15.10 Venue for decision procedure

The convener must have regard to the convenience of those invited to participate when fixing the venue for a decision procedure (including the resumption of an adjourned meeting).

[10.1029]
15.11 Notice of decision procedures or of seeking deemed consent: when and to whom delivered

[Note: when an office-holder is obliged to give notice to "the creditors", this is subject to rule 1.37, which limits the obligation to giving notice to those creditors of whose address the office-holder is aware.]

(1) Notices of decision procedures, and notices seeking deemed consent, must be delivered in accordance with the following table.

Proceedings	*Decisions*	*Persons to whom notice must be delivered*	*Minimum notice required*
[moratorium under Part A1 of the Act	decision of pre-moratorium creditors under section A11 and decision of creditors required by virtue of an order under section A44(3)	in the case of a decision under section A11 the pre-moratorium creditors, or, where the decision is required by virtue of an order under section A44(3), the creditors	5 days]
administration	decisions of creditors	the creditors who had claims against the company at the date when the company entered administration (except for those who have subsequently been paid in full)	14 days
administrative receivership	decisions of creditors	the creditors	14 days
creditors' voluntary winding up	decisions of creditors for appointment of liquidator (including any decision made at the same time on the liquidator's remuneration or the establishment of a liquidation committee)	the creditors	14 days on conversion from members' voluntary liquidation, 7 days on conversion from member's voluntary liquidation where deemed consent has been objected to and in other cases, 3 business days
creditors' voluntary winding up or a winding up by the court	decisions of creditors to consider whether a replacement should be appointed after a liquidator's resignation	the creditors	28 days
winding up by the court	decisions of creditors to consider whether to remove or replace the liquidator (other than after a liquidator's resignation)	the creditors and the official receiver	14 days
creditors' voluntary winding up or a winding up by the court	other decisions of creditors	the creditors	14 days
winding up by the court	decisions of contributories	every person appearing (by the company's records or otherwise) to be a contributory	14 days
proposed CVA	decisions of creditors	the creditors	*7 days for a decision on proposed modifications to the proposal from the*

Proceedings	*Decisions*	*Persons to whom notice must be delivered*	*Minimum notice required*
			company's directors under paragraph 31(7) of Schedule A1; 7 days for consideration of proposal where physical meeting requisitioned; in other cases, 14 days
proposed IVA	decisions of creditors	the creditors	14 days
bankruptcy	decisions of creditors to consider whether a replacement should be appointed after the resignation of a trustee	the creditors and the official receiver	28 days
bankruptcy	decisions of creditors to consider removing the trustee	the creditors and the official receiver	14 days
bankruptcy	decisions of creditors on appointment of new trustee following removal of previous trustee (including any decision made at the same time on the establishment of a creditors' committee)	the creditors	7 days
bankruptcy	other decisions of creditors	the creditors	14 days
[. . .	. . .	. . .	]

(2) This rule does not apply where the court orders under rule 15.12 that notice of a decision procedure be given by advertisement only.

NOTES

The table in para (1) is amended as follows:

The entry "moratorium under Part A1 of the Act" was inserted, and the words in italics in the fourth column of the entry "proposed CVA" were revoked, by the Insolvency (England and Wales) (No 2) (Amendment) Rules 2021, SI 2021/1028, rr 68, 81, Sch 2, as from 1 October 2021 (for savings provisions see the note to r 1A.1 at **[10.539]**).

The words omitted from the table were originally added by the Insolvency Amendment (EU 2015/848) Regulations 2017, SI 2017/702, regs 2, 3, Schedule, Pt 2, paras 32, 44, as from 26 June 2017, except in relation to proceedings opened before that date; and were subsequently revoked by the Insolvency (Amendment) (EU Exit) Regulations 2019, SI 2019/146, reg 2, Schedule, Pt 4, paras 46, 100, as from IP completion day (as defined in the European Union (Withdrawal Agreement) Act 2020, s 39) (for savings, see reg 4 of the 2019 Regulations at **[12.82]**).

[10.1030]

15.12 Notice of decision procedure by advertisement only

(1) The court may order that notice of a decision procedure is to be given by advertisement only and not by individual notice to the persons concerned.

(2) In considering whether to make such an order, the court must have regard to the relative cost of advertisement as against the giving of individual notices, the amount of assets available and the extent of the interest of creditors, members and contributories or any particular class of them.

(3) The advertisement must meet the requirements for a notice under rule 15.8(3), and must also state—

(a) that the court ordered that notice of the decision procedure be given by advertisement only; and
(b) the date of the court's order.

[10.1031]

15.13 Gazetting and advertisement of meeting

(1) In an administration, a creditors' voluntary winding up, a winding up by the court, or a bankruptcy, where a decision is being sought by a meeting the convener must gazette a notice of the procedure stating—

(a) that a meeting of creditors or contributories is to take place;
(b) the venue for the meeting;
(c) the purpose of the meeting; and
(d) the time and date by which, and place at which, those attending must deliver proxies and proofs (if not already delivered) in order to be entitled to vote.

(2) The notice must also state—

(a) who is the convener in respect of the decision procedure; and
(b) if the procedure results from a request of one or more creditors, the fact that it was so summoned and the section of the Act under which it was summoned.

(3) The notice must be gazetted before or as soon as reasonably practicable after notice of the meeting is delivered in accordance with these Rules.

(4) Information to be gazetted under this rule may also be advertised in such other manner as the convener thinks fit.

(5) The convener may gazette other decision procedures or the deemed consent procedure in which case the equivalent information to that required by this rule must be stated in the notice.

[10.1032]

15.14 Notice to company officers, bankrupts etc in respect of meetings

(1) In [a decision procedure in respect of a moratorium under Part A1 of the Act,] a proposal for a CVA, an administration, a creditors' voluntary winding up or a winding up by the court notice to participate in a creditors' meeting must be delivered to every present or former officer of the company whose presence the convener thinks is required and that person is required to attend the meeting.

(2) In a bankruptcy, notice of a meeting must be delivered to the bankrupt who is required to attend the meeting unless paragraph (3) applies.

(3) In a bankruptcy, where the bankrupt is not required to attend the meeting, the notice must state—

(a) that the bankrupt is not required to attend the meeting;

(b) that if the bankrupt wishes to attend, the bankrupt should tell the convener as soon as reasonably practicable;

(c) that whether the bankrupt will be allowed to participate in the meeting is at the discretion of the chair; and

(d) that the decision of the chair as to what intervention, if any, the bankrupt may make is final.

(4) Notices under this rule must be delivered in compliance with the minimum notice requirements set out in rule 15.2(2) or in compliance with an order of the court under rule 15.12.

NOTES

Para (1): words in square brackets inserted by the Insolvency (England and Wales) (No 2) (Amendment) Rules 2021, SI 2021/1028, r 69, as from 1 October 2021 (for savings provisions see the note to r 1A.1 at **[10.539]**).

[10.1033]

15.15 Non-receipt of notice of decision

Where a decision is sought by a notice in accordance with the Act or these Rules, the decision procedure or deemed consent procedure is presumed to have been duly initiated and conducted, even if not everyone to whom the notice is to be delivered has received it.

[10.1034]

15.16 Decisions on remuneration and conduct

(1) This rule applies in relation to a decision or resolution which is proposed in an administration, a creditors' voluntary winding up, a winding up by the court or a bankruptcy and which affects a person in relation to that person's remuneration or conduct as administrator, liquidator or trustee (actual, proposed or former).

(2) The following may not vote on such a decision or resolution whether as a creditor, contributory, proxy-holder or corporate representative, except so far as permitted by rule 16.7 (proxy-holder with financial interest)—

(a) that person;

(b) the partners and employees of that person; and

(c) the officers and employees of the company of which that person is a director, officer or employee.

CHAPTER 4 DECISION MAKING IN PARTICULAR PROCEEDINGS

[Note: a document required by the Act or these Rules must also contain the standard contents set out in Part 1.]

[10.1035]

15.17 Decisions in winding up of authorised deposit-takers

(1) This rule applies in a creditors' voluntary winding up or a winding up by the court of an authorised deposit-taker.

(2) The directors of a company must deliver a notice of a meeting of the company at which it is intended to propose a resolution for its winding up to the Financial Conduct Authority and to the scheme manager established under section 212(1) of the Financial Services and Markets Act 2000.

(3) These notices must be the same as those delivered to members of the company.

(4) Where any decision is sought for the purpose of considering whether a replacement should be appointed after the liquidator's resignation, removing the liquidator or appointing a new liquidator, the convener must also deliver a copy of the notice by which such a decision is sought to the Financial Conduct Authority and the scheme manager.

(5) A scheme manager who is required by this rule to be given notice of a meeting is entitled to be represented at the meeting.

CHAPTER 5 REQUISITIONED DECISIONS

[Note: a document required by the Act or these Rules must also contain the standard contents set out in Part 1.]

[10.1036]

15.18 Requisitions of decision

[Note: this rule is concerned with requests by creditors or contributories for a decision, rather than requests for decisions to be made by way of a physical meeting under sections 246ZE(3) or 379ZA(3).]

(1) In this Chapter, "requisitioned decision" means a decision on nominations requested to be sought under section 136(5)(c) or a decision requested to be sought under section 168(2), 171(2)(b), 171(3A), 172(3), 298(4)(c) or 314(7) or paragraph 52(2) or 56(1) of Schedule B1.

(2) A request for a decision to be sought under paragraph 52(2) of Schedule B1 must be delivered within 8 business days of the date on which the administrator's statement of proposals is delivered.

(3) The request for a requisitioned decision must include a statement of the purpose of the proposed decision and either—

(a) a statement of the requesting creditor's claim or contributory's value, together with—

(i) a list of the creditors or contributories concurring with the request and of the amounts of their respective claims or values, and

(ii) confirmation of concurrence from each creditor or contributory concurring; or

(b) a statement of the requesting creditor's debt or contributory's value and that that alone is sufficient without the concurrence of other creditors or contributories.

(4) A decision procedure must be instigated under section 171(2)(b) for the removal of the liquidator, other than a liquidator appointed by the court under section 108, if 25% in value of the company's creditors, excluding those who are connected with the company, request it.

(5) Where a decision procedure under section 171(2)(b), 171(3), 171(3A) or 298(4)(c) is to be instigated, or is proposed to be instigated, the court may, on the application of any creditor, give directions as to the decision procedure to be used and any other matter which appears to the court to require regulation or control.

(6) Where the official receiver receives a request under section 136(5)(c) and it appears that it is properly made, the official receiver must withdraw any notices previously given under section 136(5)(b) and act in accordance with Chapter 2 as if the official receiver had decided under section 136 to seek nominations.

[10.1037]
15.19 Expenses and timing of requisitioned decision

(1) The convener must, not later than 14 days from receipt of a request for a requisitioned decision, provide the requesting creditor with itemised details of the sum to be deposited as security for payment of the expenses of such procedure.

(2) The convener is not obliged to initiate the decision procedure or deemed consent procedure (where applicable) until either—

(a) the convener has received the required sum; or

(b) the period of 14 days has expired without the convener having informed the requesting creditor or contributory of the sum required to be deposited as security.

(3) A requisitioned decision must be made—

(a) where requested under section 136(5)(c), within three months; or

(b) in any other case, within 28 days;

of the date on which the earlier of the events specified in paragraph (2) of this rule occurs.

(4) The expenses of a requisitioned decision must be paid out of the deposit (if any) unless—

(a) the creditors decide that they are to be payable as an expense of the administration, winding up or bankruptcy, as the case may be; and

(b) in the case of a decision of contributories, the creditors are first paid in full, with interest.

(5) The notice of a requisitioned decision of creditors must contain a statement that the creditors may make a decision as in paragraph (4)(a) of this rule.

(6) Where the creditors do not so decide, the expenses must be paid by the requesting creditor or contributory to the extent that the deposit (if any) is not sufficient.

(7) To the extent that the deposit (if any) is not required for payment of the expenses, it must be repaid to the requesting creditor or contributory.

CHAPTER 6 CONSTITUTION OF MEETINGS

[10.1038]
15.20 Quorum at meetings

(1) A meeting is not competent to act unless a quorum is in attendance.

(2) A quorum is—

(a) in the case of a meeting of creditors, at least one creditor entitled to vote; and

(b) in the case of a meeting of contributories, at least two contributories entitled to vote, or all the contributories, if their number does not exceed two.

(3) Where the provisions of this rule as to quorum are satisfied by the attendance of the chair alone or the chair and one additional person, but the chair is aware, either by virtue of proofs and proxies received or otherwise, that one or more additional persons would, if attending, be entitled to vote, the chair must delay the start of the meeting by at least 15 minutes after the appointed time.

[10.1039]
15.21 Chair at meetings

[(1)] The chair of a meeting must be—

(a) the convener;

(b) an appointed person; or

(c) in cases where the convener is the official receiver, a person appointed by the official receiver.

[(2) However, where a decision on the appointment of a liquidator under rule 6.14(2)(b), 6.14(4) or 6.14(6) is made by a meeting or a virtual meeting, the chair of the meeting must be the convener.]

NOTES

Para (1) numbered as such, and para (2) added, by the Insolvency (England and Wales) (Amendment) Rules 2017, SI 2017/366, rr 3, 38, as from 6 April 2017.

[10.1040]
15.22 The chair—attendance, interventions and questions

The chair of a meeting may—

(a) allow any person who has given reasonable notice of wishing to attend to participate in a virtual meeting or to be admitted to a physical meeting;

(b) decide what intervention, if any, may be made at—
  (i) a meeting of creditors by any person attending who is not a creditor, or
  (ii) a meeting of contributories by any person attending who is not a contributory; and
(c) decide what questions may be put to—
  (i) any present or former officer of the company, or
  (ii) the bankrupt or debtor.

CHAPTER 7 ADJOURNMENT AND SUSPENSION OF MEETINGS

[10.1041]
15.23 Adjournment by chair

(1) The chair may (and must if it is so resolved) adjourn a meeting for not more than 14 days, but subject to any direction of the court and to rule [15.23A or] 15.24.

(2) Further adjournment under this rule must not be to a day later than 14 days after the date on which the meeting was originally held (subject to any direction by the court).

(3) But in a case relating to a proposed CVA, the chair may, and must if the meeting so resolves, adjourn a meeting held under paragraph 29(1) of Schedule A1 to a day which is not more than 14 days after the date on which the moratorium (including any extension) ends.

NOTES

Para (1): words in square brackets inserted by the Insolvency (England and Wales) (No 2) (Amendment) Rules 2021, SI 2021/1028, r 70, as from 1 October 2021 (for savings provisions see the note to r 1A.1 at **[10.539]**).

Para (3): revoked by SI 2021/1028, r 81, Sch 2, as from 1 October 2021 (for savings provisions see the note to r 1A.1 at **[10.539]**).

[10.1042]
[15.23A Adjournment of meeting in, or for the purposes of, a moratorium under Part A1 of the Act

(1) This rule applies where a meeting is for the purpose of a decision procedure in respect of a moratorium under Part A1 of the Act.

(2) Where this rule applies the chair may, (and must if it is so resolved), adjourn a meeting.

(3) A meeting may be adjourned under this rule on more than one occasion.

(4) An adjournment under this rule—
  (a) must not be—
    (i) for a period which is more than 14 days, or
    (ii) to a date which is more than 14 days after the first day on which the meeting was held, and
  (b) where a meeting is for the purpose of seeking a decision of creditors to a revised end date for a moratorium under section A11, must be to a date which is before the end of the moratorium.

(5) This rule is subject to any direction of the court.]

NOTES

Commencement: 1 October 2021.

Inserted by the Insolvency (England and Wales) (No 2) (Amendment) Rules 2021, SI 2021/1028, r 71, as from 1 October 2021 (for savings provisions see the note to r 1A.1 at **[10.539]**).

[10.1043]
15.24 Adjournment of meetings to remove a liquidator or trustee

If the chair of a meeting to remove the liquidator or trustee in a creditors' voluntary winding up, a winding up by the court or a bankruptcy is the liquidator or trustee or the liquidator's or trustee's nominee and a resolution has been proposed for the liquidator's or trustee's removal, the chair must not adjourn the meeting without the consent of at least one-half (in value) of the creditors attending and entitled to vote.

[10.1044]
15.25 Adjournment in absence of chair

(1) In [a decision procedure in respect of a moratorium under Part A1 of the Act,] an administration, administrative receivership, a creditors' voluntary winding up, a winding up by the court or a bankruptcy, if no one attends to act as chair within 30 minutes of the time fixed for a meeting to start, then the meeting is adjourned to the same time and place the following week or, if that is not a business day, to the business day immediately following.

(2) If no one attends to act as chair within 30 minutes of the time fixed for the meeting after a second adjournment under this rule, then the meeting comes to an end.

NOTES

Para (1): words in square brackets inserted by the Insolvency (England and Wales) (No 2) (Amendment) Rules 2021, SI 2021/1028, r 72, as from 1 October 2021 (for savings provisions see the note to r 1A.1 at **[10.539]**).

[10.1045]
15.26 Proofs in adjournment

Where a meeting [for the purpose of a decision procedure in respect of a moratorium under Part A1 of the Act or,] in an administration, an administrative receivership, a creditors' voluntary winding-up, a winding up by the court or a bankruptcy is adjourned, proofs may be used if delivered not later than 4pm on the business day immediately before resumption of the adjourned meeting, or later than that time where the chair is content to accept the proof.

NOTES

Words in square brackets inserted by the Insolvency (England and Wales) (No 2) (Amendment) Rules 2021, SI 2021/1028, r 73, as from 1 October 2021 (for savings provisions see the note to r 1A.1 at **[10.539]**).

[10.1046]
15.27 Suspension

The chair of a meeting may, without an adjournment, declare the meeting suspended for one or more periods not exceeding one hour in total (or, in exceptional circumstances, such longer total period during the same day at the chair's discretion).

CHAPTER 8 CREDITORS' VOTING RIGHTS AND MAJORITIES

[Note: a document required by the Act or these Rules must also contain the standard contents set out in Part 1.]

[10.1047]
15.28 Creditors' voting rights

[(A1) In a decision procedure in respect of a moratorium under Part A1 of the Act a creditor is entitled to vote only if the requirements in paragraph (1)(a) to (c) are satisfied in relation to that decision procedure.]

(1) In an administration, an administrative receivership, a creditors' voluntary winding up, a winding up by the court and a bankruptcy, a creditor is entitled to vote in a decision procedure or to object to a decision proposed using the deemed consent procedure only if—

(a) the creditor has, subject to rule 15.29, delivered to the convener a proof of the debt claimed in accordance with paragraph (3), including any calculation for the purposes of rule 15.31 or 15.32, and

(b) the proof was received by the convener—

(i) not later than the decision date, or in the case of a meeting, 4pm on the business day before the meeting, or

(ii) in the case of a meeting, later than the time given in sub-paragraph (i) where the chair is content to accept the proof; and

(c) the proof has been admitted for the purposes of entitlement to vote.

(2) In the case of a meeting, a proxy-holder is not entitled to vote on behalf of a creditor unless the convener or chair has received the proxy intended to be used on behalf of that creditor.

(3) A debt is claimed in accordance with this paragraph if it is—

(a) claimed as due from the company or bankrupt to the person seeking to be entitled to vote . . .

(b) . . .

(4) The convener or chair may call for any document or other evidence to be produced if the convener or chair thinks it necessary for the purpose of substantiating the whole or any part of a claim.

(5) In a decision relating to a proposed CVA or IVA every creditor, secured or unsecured, who has notice of the decision procedure is entitled to vote in respect of that creditor's debt.

(6) Where a decision is sought in an administration under rule 3.52(3)(b) (pre-administration costs), rule 18.18(4) (remuneration: procedure for initial determination in an administration) or rule 18.26(2) (first exception: administrator has made statement under paragraph 52(1)(b) of Schedule B1), creditors are entitled to participate to the extent stated in those paragraphs.

NOTES

Para (A1): inserted by the Insolvency (England and Wales) (No 2) (Amendment) Rules 2021, SI 2021/1028, r 74, as from 1 October 2021 (for savings provisions see the note to r 1A.1 at **[10.539]**).

Para (3): sub-para (b) and the word immediately preceding it revoked by the Insolvency (Amendment) (EU Exit) Regulations 2019, SI 2019/146, reg 2, Schedule, Pt 4, paras 46, 101, as from IP completion day (as defined in the European Union (Withdrawal Agreement) Act 2020, s 39) (for savings, see reg 4 of the 2019 Regulations at **[12.82]**).

[10.1048]
15.29 Scheme manager's voting rights

(1) For the purpose of voting in a creditors' voluntary winding up or a winding up by the court of an authorised deposit-taker at which the scheme manager established under section 212(1) of the Financial Services and Markets Act 2000 is entitled to be represented under rule 15.17 (but not for any other purpose), the manager may deliver, instead of a proof, a statement containing—

(a) the names of the creditors of the company in relation to whom an obligation of the scheme manager has arisen or may reasonably be expected to arise;

(b) the amount of each such obligation; and

(c) the total amount of all such obligations.

(2) The manager may from time to time deliver a further statement; and each such statement supersedes any previous statement.

15.30 *(Revoked by the Insolvency (Amendment) (EU Exit) Regulations 2019, SI 2019/146, reg 2, Schedule, Pt 4, paras 46, 102, as from IP completion day (as defined in the European Union (Withdrawal Agreement) Act 2020, s 39) (for savings, see reg 4 of the 2019 Regulations at* **[12.82]***).)*

[10.1049]
15.31 Calculation of voting rights

(1) Votes are calculated according to the amount of each creditor's claim—

[(za) in a decision procedure in respect of a moratorium under Part A1 of the Act, as at the decision date;]

(a) in an administration, as at the date on which the company entered administration, less—

(i) any payments that have been made to the creditor after that date in respect of the claim, and

(ii) any adjustment by way of set-off which has been made in accordance with rule 14.24 or would have been made if that rule were applied on the date on which the votes are counted;

(b) in an administrative receivership, as at the date of the appointment of the receiver, less any payments that have been made to the creditor after that date in respect of the claim;

(c) in a creditors' voluntary winding up, a winding up by the court or a bankruptcy, as set out in the creditor's proof to the extent that it has been admitted;

(d) in a proposed CVA—

(i) at the date the company went into liquidation where the company is being wound up,

(ii) at the date the company entered into administration (less any payments made to the creditor after that date in respect of the claim) where it is in administration,

[(iii) where (i) and (ii) do not apply, at the decision date;]

(iv) where (i) to (iii) do not apply, at the decision date;

(e) in a proposed IVA—

(i) where the debtor is not an undischarged bankrupt—

(aa) at the date of the interim order, where there is an interim order in force,

(bb) otherwise, at the decision date,

(ii) where the debtor is an undischarged bankrupt, at the date of the bankruptcy order.

(2) A creditor may vote in respect of a debt of an unliquidated or unascertained amount if the convener or chair decides to put upon it an estimated minimum value for the purpose of entitlement to vote and admits the claim for that purpose.

(3) But in relation to [a decision procedure in respect of a moratorium under Part A1 of the Act,] a proposed CVA or IVA, a debt of an unliquidated or unascertained amount is to be valued at £1 for the purposes of voting unless the convener or chair or an appointed person decides to put a higher value on it.

(4) Where a debt is wholly secured its value for voting purposes is nil.

(5) Where a debt is partly secured its value for voting purposes is the value of the unsecured part.

[(6) However, the value of the debt for voting purposes is its full value without deduction of the value of the security in the following cases—

(a) where, in respect of a moratorium under Part A1 of the Act, there is a decision of pre-moratorium creditors on whether to extend or further extend that moratorium under section A11; and

(b) where the administrator has made a statement under paragraph 52(1)(b) of Schedule B1 and the administrator has been requested to seek a decision under paragraph 52(2).]

(7) No vote may be cast in respect of a claim more than once on any resolution put to the meeting . . .

(8) A vote cast in a decision procedure which is not a meeting may not be changed.

(9) Paragraph (7) does not prevent a creditor . . . from—

(a) voting in respect of less than the full value of an entitlement to vote; or

(b) casting a vote one way in respect of part of the value of an entitlement and another way in respect of some or all of the balance of that value.

NOTES

Para (1): sub-para (za) inserted, sub-para (d)(iii) substituted, and sub-para (d)(iv) revoked, by the Insolvency (England and Wales) (No 2) (Amendment) Rules 2021, SI 2021/1028, r 75(1)–(3), as from 1 October 2021 (for savings provisions see the note to r 1A.1 at **[10.539]**). The original sub-para (d)(iii) read as follows—

"(iii) at the beginning of the moratorium where a moratorium has been obtained (less any payments made to the creditor after that date in respect of the claim), or".

Para (3): words in square brackets inserted by SI 2021/1028, r 75(1), (4), as from 1 October 2021 (for savings provisions see the note to r 1A.1 at **[10.539]**).

Para (6): substituted by SI 2021/1028, r 75(1), (5), as from 1 October 2021 (for savings provisions see the note to r 1A.1 at **[10.539]**). Para (6) previously read as follows—

"(6) However, the value of the debt for voting purposes is its full value without deduction of the value of the security in the following cases—

(a) where the administrator has made a statement under paragraph 52(1)(b) of Schedule B1 and the administrator has been requested to seek a decision under paragraph 52(2); and

(b) where, in a proposed CVA, there is a decision on whether to extend or further extend a moratorium or to bring a moratorium to an end before the end of the period of any extension.".

Paras (7), (9): words omitted revoked by the Insolvency (Amendment) (EU Exit) Regulations 2019, SI 2019/146, reg 2, Schedule, Pt 4, paras 46, 103, as from IP completion day (as defined in the European Union (Withdrawal Agreement) Act 2020, s 39) (for savings, see reg 4 of the 2019 Regulations at **[12.82]**).

[10.1050]

15.32 Calculation of voting rights: special cases

[(A1) In a decision procedure in respect of a moratorium under Part A1 of the Act, a creditor under a hire-purchase agreement is entitled to vote in respect of the debt due and payable by the company at the decision date.

(B1) In calculating the amount of any debt for the purpose of paragraph (A1) no account is to be taken of any amount attributable to the exercise of any right under the relevant agreement so far as the right has become exercisable solely by virtue of a moratorium for the company coming into force.]

(1) In an administration, a creditor under a hire-purchase agreement is entitled to vote in respect of the amount of the debt due and payable by the company on the date on which the company entered administration.

(2) In calculating the amount of any debt for the purpose of paragraph (1), no account is to be taken of any amount attributable to the exercise of any right under the relevant agreement so far as the right has become exercisable solely by virtue of—

(a) the making of an administration application;

(b) a notice of intention to appoint an administrator or any matter arising as a consequence of the notice; or

(c) the company entering administration.

(3) Any voting rights which a creditor might otherwise exercise in respect of a claim in a creditors' voluntary winding up or a winding up by the court of an authorised deposit-taker are reduced by a sum equal to the amount of that claim in relation to which the scheme manager, by virtue of its having delivered a statement under rule 15.29, is entitled to exercise voting rights.

NOTES

Paras (A1), (B1): inserted by the Insolvency (England and Wales) (No 2) (Amendment) Rules 2021, SI 2021/1028, r 76, as from 1 October 2021 (for savings provisions see the note to r 1A.1 at **[10.539]**).

[10.1051]
15.33 Procedure for admitting creditors' claims for voting

(1) The convener or chair in respect of a decision procedure must ascertain entitlement to vote and admit or reject claims accordingly.

(2) The convener or chair may admit or reject a claim in whole or in part.

(3) If the convener or chair is in any doubt whether a claim should be admitted or rejected, the convener or chair must mark it as objected to and allow votes to be cast in respect of it, subject to such votes being subsequently declared invalid if the objection to the claim is sustained.

[10.1052]
15.34 Requisite majorities

(1) A decision is made by creditors when a majority (in value) of those voting have voted in favour of the proposed decision, except where this rule provides otherwise.

[(1A) Subject to paragraphs (1B) and (1D), a decision in respect of a moratorium under Part A1 of the Act is made when a majority (in value) of those voting have voted in favour of the proposed decision.

(1B) A decision is not made if, of the total number of those creditors voting in respect of the proposed decision who are, to the best of the convener's belief, unconnected with the company, a majority vote against it.

(1C) For the purpose of paragraph (1B) a creditor is unconnected unless the convener decides that the creditor is connected.

(1D) In the case of a decision which is required by virtue of an order under section A44(3) paragraphs (1A) and (1B) have effect subject to such modifications as may be set out in the court's order.]

[(2) In the case of an administration, a decision is not made if those voting against it include more than half in value of the creditors to whom notice of the decision procedure was delivered who are not, to the best of the convener's or chair's belief, persons connected with the company.]

[(3) In the case of a proposed CVA a decision approving a proposal or a modification is made when three-quarters or more (in value) of those responding vote in favour of it.]

(4) In a proposed CVA a decision is not made if more than half of the total value of the unconnected creditors vote against it.

(5) For the purposes of paragraph (4)—

(a) a creditor is unconnected unless the convener or chair decides that the creditor is connected with the company;
(b) in deciding whether a creditor is connected reliance may be placed on the information provided by the company's statement of affairs or otherwise in accordance with these Rules; and
(c) the total value of the unconnected creditors is the total value of those unconnected creditors whose claims have been admitted for voting.

(6) In a case relating to a proposed IVA—

(a) a decision approving a proposal or a modification is made when three-quarters or more (in value) of those responding vote in favour of it;
(b) a decision is not made if more than half of the total value of creditors who are not associates of the debtor vote against it.

(7) For the purposes of paragraph (6)—

(a) a creditor is not an associate of the debtor unless the convener or chair decides that the creditor is an associate of the debtor;
(b) in deciding whether a creditor is an associate of the debtor, reliance may be placed on the information provided by the debtor's statement of affairs or otherwise in accordance with these Rules; and
(c) the total value of the creditors who are not associates of the debtor is the total value of the creditors who are not associates of the debtor whose claims have been admitted for voting.

NOTES

Paras (1A)–(1D): inserted by the Insolvency (England and Wales) (No 2) (Amendment) Rules 2021, SI 2021/1028, r 77(1), (2), as from 1 October 2021 (for savings provisions see the note to r 1A.1 at **[10.539]**).

Para (2): substituted by the Insolvency (England and Wales) (Amendment) Rules 2017, SI 2017/366, rr 3, 39, as from 6 April 2017.

Para (3): substituted by SI 2021/1028, r 77(1), (3), as from 1 October 2021 (for savings provisions see the note to r 1A.1 at **[10.539]**). Para (3) previously read as follows—

"(3) Each of the following decisions in a proposed CVA is made when three-quarters or more (in value) of those responding vote in favour of it—

(a) a decision approving a proposal or a modification;
(b) a decision extending or further extending a moratorium; or
(c) a decision bringing a moratorium to an end before the end of the period of any extension.".

[10.1053]

15.35 Appeals against decisions under this Chapter

(1) A decision of the convener or chair under this Chapter is subject to appeal to the court by a creditor, by a contributory, or by the bankrupt or debtor (as applicable).

(2) In a proposed CVA, an appeal against a decision under this Chapter may also be made by a member of the company.

(3) [In respect of a decision, other than one which is taken, or required, under Part A1 of the Act (as to which see paragraphs (3A) and (3B) if that] decision is reversed or varied, or votes are declared invalid, the court may order another decision procedure to be initiated or make such order as it thinks just but, in a CVA or IVA, the court may only make an order if it considers that the circumstances which led to the appeal give rise to unfair prejudice or material irregularity.

[(3A) Subject to paragraph (3B), on an appeal against a decision taken, or required, under Part A1 of the Act a court may—

(a) reverse the decision;
(b) vary the decision;
(c) declare certain votes to be invalid; or
(d) make such other order as it sees fit.

(3B) A court must not make an order of the kind referred to in paragraph (3A)(a) to (c) if—

(a) it is satisfied that the circumstances which led to the appeal did not give rise to unfair prejudice or material irregularity, or
(b) the decision was taken at a time when the moratorium was in force, and that moratorium has subsequently come to an end.]

(4) An appeal under this rule may not be made later than 21 days after the decision date.

(5) However, the previous paragraph does not apply in a proposed CVA or IVA, where an appeal may not be made after the end of the period of 28 days beginning with the day—

(a) in a proposed CVA, on which the first of the reports required by section 4(6) *or paragraph 30(3) of Schedule A1* was filed with the court; or
(b) in a proposed IVA—
    (i) where an interim order has not been obtained, on which the notice of the result of the consideration of the proposal required by section 259(1)(a) has been given, or
    (ii) otherwise, on which the report required by section 259(1)(b) is made to the court.

(6) The person who made the decision is not personally liable for costs incurred by any person in relation to an appeal under this rule unless the court makes an order to that effect.

(7) The court may not make an order under paragraph (6) if the person who made the decision in a winding up by the court or a bankruptcy is the official receiver or a person nominated by the official receiver.

NOTES

Para (3): words in square brackets substituted (for the original words "If the") by the Insolvency (England and Wales) (No 2) (Amendment) Rules 2021, SI 2021/1028, r 78(1), (2), as from 1 October 2021 (for savings provisions see the note to r 1A.1 at **[10.539]**).

Paras (3A), (3B): inserted by SI 2021/1028, r 78(1), (3), as from 1 October 2021 (for savings provisions see the note to r 1A.1 at **[10.539]**).

Para (5): the words in italics in sub-para (a) were revoked by SI 2021/1028, r 81, Sch 2, as from 1 October 2021 (for savings provisions see the note to r 1A.1 at **[10.539]**).

CHAPTER 9 EXCLUSIONS FROM MEETINGS

[Note: a document required by the Act or these Rules must also contain the standard contents set out in Part 1.]

[10.1054]

15.36 Action where person excluded

(1) In this rule and rules 15.37 and 15.38, an "excluded person" means a person who has taken all steps necessary to attend a virtual meeting or has been permitted by the convener to attend a physical meeting remotely under the arrangements which—

(a) have been put in place by the convener of the meeting; but
(b) do not enable that person to attend the whole or part of that meeting.

(2) Where the chair becomes aware during the course of the meeting that there is an excluded person, the chair may—

(a) continue the meeting;
(b) declare the meeting void and convene the meeting again; or
(c) declare the meeting valid up to the point where the person was excluded and adjourn the meeting.

(3) Where the chair continues the meeting, the meeting is valid unless—

(a) the chair decides in consequence of a complaint under rule 15.38 to declare the meeting void and hold the meeting again; or
(b) the court directs otherwise.

(4) Without prejudice to paragraph (2), where the chair becomes aware during the course of the meeting that there is an excluded person, the chair may, at the chair's discretion and without an adjournment, declare the meeting suspended for any period up to 1 hour.

[10.1055]

15.37 Indication to excluded person

(1) A creditor who claims to be an excluded person may request an indication of what occurred during the period of that person's claimed exclusion.

(2) A request under paragraph (1) must be made in accordance with paragraph (3) as soon as reasonably practicable, and in any event, not later than 4pm on the business day following the day on which the exclusion is claimed to have occurred.

(3) A request under paragraph (1) must be made to—

(a) the chair where it is made during the course of the business of the meeting; or

(b) the convener where it is made after the conclusion of the business of the meeting.

(4) Where satisfied that the person making the request is an excluded person, the person to whom the request is made under paragraph (3) must deliver the requested indication to the excluded person as soon as reasonably practicable, and in any event, not later than 4pm on the business day following the day on which the request was made under paragraph (1).

[10.1056]

15.38 Complaint

(1) A person may make a complaint who—

(a) is, or claims to be, an excluded person; or

(b) attends the meeting and claims to have been adversely affected by the actual, apparent or claimed exclusion of another person.

(2) The complaint must be made to the appropriate person who is—

(a) the chair, where the complaint is made during the course of the meeting; or

(b) the convener, where it is made after the meeting.

(3) The complaint must be made as soon as reasonably practicable and, in any event, no later than 4pm on the business day following—

(a) the day on which the person was, appeared or claimed to be excluded; or

(b) where an indication is sought under rule 15.37, the day on which the complainant received the indication.

(4) The appropriate person must, as soon as reasonably practicable following receipt of the complaint,—

(a) consider whether there is an excluded person;

(b) where satisfied that there is an excluded person, consider the complaint; and

(c) where satisfied that there has been prejudice, take such action as the appropriate person considers fit to remedy the prejudice.

(5) Paragraph (6) applies where the appropriate person is satisfied that the complainant is an excluded person and—

(a) a resolution was voted on at the meeting during the period of the person's exclusion; and

(b) the excluded person asserts how the excluded person intended to vote on the resolution.

(6) Where the appropriate person is satisfied that if the excluded person had voted as that person intended it would have changed the result of the resolution, then the appropriate person must, as soon as reasonably practicable,—

(a) count the intended vote as having been cast in that way;

(b) amend the record of the result of the resolution;

(c) where notice of the result of the resolution has been delivered to those entitled to attend the meeting, deliver notice to them of the change and the reason for it; and

(d) where notice of the result of the resolution has yet to be delivered to those entitled to attend the meeting, the notice must include details of the change and the reason for it.

(7) Where satisfied that more than one complainant is an excluded person, the appropriate person must have regard to the combined effect of the intended votes.

(8) The appropriate person must deliver notice to the complainant of any decision as soon as reasonably practicable.

(9) A complainant who is not satisfied by the action of the appropriate person may apply to the court for directions and any application must be made no more than two business days from the date of receiving the decision of the appropriate person.

CHAPTER 10 CONTRIBUTORIES' VOTING RIGHTS AND MAJORITIES

[10.1057]

15.39 Contributories' voting rights and requisite majorities

In a decision procedure for contributories—

(a) voting rights are as at a general meeting of the company, subject to any provision of the articles affecting entitlement to vote, either generally or at a time when the company is in liquidation; and

(b) a decision is made if more than one half of the votes cast by contributories are in favour.

CHAPTER 11 RECORDS

[10.1058]

15.40 Record of a decision

(1) The convener or chair must cause a record of the decision procedure to be kept.

(2) In the case of a meeting, the record must be in the form of a minute of the meeting.

(3) The record must be authenticated by the convener or chair and be retained by the office-holder as part of the records of the insolvency proceedings in question.

(4) The record must identify the proceedings, and must include—

(a) in the case of a decision procedure of creditors, a list of the names of the creditors who participated and their claims;

Part 10 Miscellaneous other SIs

(b) in the case of a decision procedure of contributories, a list of the names of the contributories who participated;
(c) where a decision is taken on the election of members of a creditors' committee or liquidation committee, the names and addresses of those elected;
(d) a record of any change to the result of the resolution made under rule 15.38(6) and the reason for any such change; and
(e) in any case, a record of every decision made and how creditors voted.

(5) Where a decision is sought using the deemed consent procedure, a record must be made of the procedure, authenticated by the convener, and must be retained by the office-holder as part of the records of the insolvency proceedings in question.

(6) The record under paragraph (5) must—
(a) identify the proceedings;
(b) state whether or not the decision was taken; and
(c) contain a list of the creditors or contributories who objected to the decision, and in the case of creditors, their claims.

(7) A record under this rule must also identify any decision procedure (or the deemed consent procedure) by which the decision had previously been sought.

CHAPTER 12 COMPANY MEETINGS

[10.1059]
15.41 Company meetings

(1) Unless the Act or these Rules provide otherwise, a company meeting must be called and conducted, and records of the meeting must be kept—
(a) in accordance with the law of England and Wales, including any applicable provision in or made under the Companies Act, in the case of a company incorporated—
  (i) in England and Wales, or
  (ii) outside the United Kingdom other than in an EEA state;
(b) in accordance with the law of that state applicable to meetings of the company in the case of a company incorporated in an EEA state other than the United Kingdom.

(2) For the purpose of this rule, reference to a company meeting called and conducted to resolve, decide or determine a particular matter includes a reference to that matter being resolved, decided or determined by written resolution of a private company passed in accordance with section 288 of the Companies Act.

(3) In an administration—
(a) in summoning any company meeting the administrator must have regard to the convenience of the members when fixing the venue; and
(b) the chair of the meeting must be either the administrator or an appointed person.

[10.1060]
15.42 Remote attendance: notification requirements

When a meeting is to be summoned and held in accordance with section 246A(3), the convener must notify all those to whom notice of the meeting is being given of—
(a) the ability of a person claiming to be an excluded person to request an indication in accordance with rule 15.45;
(b) the ability of a person within rule 15.46(1) to make a complaint in accordance with that rule; and
(c) in either case, the period within which a request or complaint must be made.

[10.1061]
15.43 Location of company meetings

(1) This rule applies to a request to the convener of a meeting under section 246A(9) to specify a place for the meeting.

(2) The request must be accompanied by
(a) a list of the members making or concurring with the request and their voting rights, and
(b) from each person concurring, confirmation of that person's concurrence.

(3) The request must be delivered to the convener within seven business days of the date on which the convener delivered the notice of the meeting in question.

(4) Where the convener considers that the request has been properly made in accordance with the Act and this rule, the convener must—
(a) deliver notice to all those previously given notice of the meeting—
  (i) that it is to be held at a specified place, and
  (ii) as to whether the date and time are to remain the same or not;
(b) set a venue (including specification of a place) for the meeting, the date of which must be not later than 28 days after the original date for the meeting; and
(c) deliver at least 14 days' notice of that venue to all those previously given notice of the meeting;
and the notices required by sub-paragraphs (a) and (c) may be delivered at the same or different times.

(5) Where the convener has specified a place for the meeting in response to a request to which this rule applies, the chair of the meeting must attend the meeting by being present in person at that place.

[10.1062]
15.44 Action where person excluded

(1) In this rule and rules 15.45 and 15.46, an "excluded person" means a person who has taken all steps necessary to attend a company meeting under the arrangements which—
(a) have been put in place by the convener of the meeting under section 246A(6); but

(b) do not enable that person to attend the whole or part of that meeting.

(2) Where the chair becomes aware during the course of the meeting that there is an excluded person, the chair may—

(a) continue the meeting;

(b) declare the meeting void and convene the meeting again; or

(c) declare the meeting valid up to the point where the person was excluded and adjourn the meeting.

(3) Where the chair continues the meeting, the meeting is valid unless—

(a) the chair decides in consequence of a complaint under rule 15.46 to declare the meeting void and hold the meeting again; or

(b) the court directs otherwise.

(4) Without prejudice to paragraph (2), where the chair becomes aware during the course of the meeting that there is an excluded person, the chair may, in the chair's discretion and without an adjournment, declare the meeting suspended for any period up to 1 hour.

[10.1063]

15.45 Indication to excluded person

(1) A person who claims to be an excluded person may request an indication of what occurred during the period of that person's claimed exclusion.

(2) A request under paragraph (1) must be made in accordance with paragraph (3) as soon as reasonably practicable, and in any event, not later than 4pm on the business day following the day on which the exclusion is claimed to have occurred.

(3) A request under paragraph (1) must be made to—

(a) the chair where it is made during the course of the business of the meeting; or

(b) the convener where it is made after the conclusion of the business of the meeting.

(4) Where satisfied that the person making the request is an excluded person, the person to whom the request is made under paragraph (3) must deliver the requested indication to the excluded person as soon as reasonably practicable, and in any event, not later than 4pm on the business day following the day on which the request was made under paragraph (1).

[10.1064]

15.46 Complaint

(1) A person may make a complaint who—

(a) is, or claims to be, an excluded person; or

(b) attends the meeting and claims to have been adversely affected by the actual, apparent or claimed exclusion of another person.

(2) The complaint must be made to the appropriate person who is—

(a) the chair, where the complaint is made during the course of the meeting; or

(b) the convener, where it is made after the meeting.

(3) The complaint must be made as soon as reasonably practicable and, in any event, no later than 4pm on the business day following—

(a) the day on which the person was, appeared or claimed to be excluded; or

(b) where an indication is sought under rule 15.45, the day on which the complainant received the indication.

(4) The appropriate person must, as soon as reasonably practicable following receipt of the complaint,—

(a) consider whether there is an excluded person;

(b) where satisfied that there is an excluded person, consider the complaint; and

(c) where satisfied that there has been prejudice, take such action as the appropriate person considers fit to remedy the prejudice.

(5) Paragraph (6) applies where the appropriate person is satisfied that the complainant is an excluded person and—

(a) a resolution was voted on at the meeting during the period of the person's exclusion; and

(b) the excluded person asserts how the excluded person intended to vote on the resolution.

(6) Where the appropriate person is satisfied that if the excluded person had voted as that person intended it would have changed the result of the resolution, then the appropriate person must, as soon as reasonably practicable,—

(a) count the intended vote as having been cast in that way;

(b) amend the record of the result of the resolution;

(c) where notice of the result of the resolution has been delivered to those entitled to attend the meeting, deliver notice to them of the change and the reason for it; and

(d) where notice of the result of the resolution has yet to be delivered to those entitled to attend the meeting, the notice must include details of the change and the reason for it.

(7) Where satisfied that more than one complainant is an excluded person, the appropriate person must have regard to the combined effect of the intended votes.

(8) The appropriate person must deliver notice to the complainant of any decision as soon as reasonably practicable.

(9) A complainant who is not satisfied by the action of the appropriate person may apply to the court for directions and any application must be made no more than two business days from the date of receiving the decision of the appropriate person.

PART 16 PROXIES AND CORPORATE REPRESENTATION

[Note: a document required by the Act or these Rules must also contain the standard contents set out in Part 1.]

[10.1065]

16.1 Application and interpretation

(1) This Part applies in any case where a proxy is given in relation to a meeting or proceedings under the Act or these Rules, or where a corporation authorises a person to represent it.

(2) References in this Part to "the chair" are to the chair of the meeting for which a specific proxy is given or at which a continuing proxy is exercised.

[10.1066]

16.2 Specific and continuing proxies

(1) A "proxy" is a document made by a creditor, member or contributory which directs or authorises another person ("the proxy-holder") to act as the representative of the creditor, member or contributory at a meeting or meetings by speaking, voting, abstaining, or proposing resolutions.

(2) A proxy may be either—

(a) a specific proxy which relates to a specific meeting; or
(b) a continuing proxy for the insolvency proceedings.

(3) A specific proxy must—

(a) direct the proxy-holder how to act at the meeting by giving specific instructions;
(b) authorise the proxy-holder to act at the meeting without specific instructions; or
(c) contain both direction and authorisation.

(4) A proxy is to be treated as a specific proxy for the meeting which is identified in the proxy unless it states that it is a continuing proxy for the insolvency proceedings.

(5) A continuing proxy must authorise the proxy-holder to attend, speak, vote or abstain, or to propose resolutions without giving the proxy-holder any specific instructions how to do so.

(6) A continuing proxy may be superseded by a proxy for a specific meeting or withdrawn by a written notice to the office-holder.

(7) A creditor, member or contributory may appoint more than one person to be proxy-holder but if so—

(a) their appointment is as alternates; and
(b) only one of them may act as proxy-holder at a meeting.

(8) The proxy-holder must be an individual.

[10.1067]

16.3 Blank proxy

(1) A "blank proxy" is a document which—

(a) complies with the requirements in this rule; and
(b) when completed with the details specified in paragraph (3) will be a proxy as described in rule 16.2.

[(2) A blank proxy must state that the creditor, member or contributory named in the document (when completed) appoints a person who is named or identified as the proxy-holder of the creditor, member or contributory.]

(3) The specified details are—

(a) the name and address of the creditor, member or contributory;
(b) either the name of the proxy-holder or the identification of the proxy-holder (eg the chair of the meeting or the official receiver); . . .
[(c) a statement that the proxy is either—
 (i) for a specific meeting, which is identified in the proxy, or
 (ii) a continuing proxy for the proceedings; and
(d) if the proxy is for a specific meeting, instructions as to the extent to which the proxy holder is directed to vote in a particular way, to abstain or to propose any resolution.]

[(4) When it is delivered, a blank proxy must not have inserted into it the name or description of any person as proxy-holder or as a nominee for the office-holder, or instructions as to how a person appointed as proxy-holder is to act.]

(5) A blank proxy must have a note to the effect that the proxy may be completed with the name of the person or the chair of the meeting who is to be proxy-holder.

NOTES

Para (2): substituted by the Insolvency (England and Wales) (Amendment) Rules 2017, SI 2017/366, rr 3, 40(a), as from 6 April 2017.

Para (3): word omitted from sub-para (b) revoked, and sub-paras (c), (d) substituted (for the original sub-para (c)), by SI 2017/366, rr 3, 40(b), as from 6 April 2017.

Para (4): substituted by the Insolvency (England and Wales) and Insolvency (Scotland) (Miscellaneous and Consequential Amendments) Rules 2017, SI 2017/1115, rr 2, 10, as from 8 December 2017.

[10.1068]

16.4 Use of proxies

(1) A proxy for a specific meeting must be delivered to the chair before the meeting.

(2) A continuing proxy must be delivered to the office-holder and may be exercised at any meeting which begins after the proxy is delivered.

(3) A proxy may be used at the resumption of the meeting after an adjournment, but if a different proxy is given for use at a resumed meeting, that proxy must be delivered to the chair before the start of the resumed meeting.

(4) Where a specific proxy directs a proxy-holder to vote for or against a resolution for the nomination or appointment of a person as office-holder, the proxy-holder may, unless the proxy states otherwise, vote for or against (as the proxy-holder thinks fit) a resolution for the nomination or appointment of that person jointly with another or others.

(5) A proxy-holder may propose a resolution which is one on which the proxy-holder could vote if someone else proposed it.

(6) Where a proxy gives specific directions as to voting, this does not, unless the proxy states otherwise, prohibit the proxy-holder from exercising discretion how to vote on a resolution which is not dealt with by the proxy.

(7) The chair may require a proxy used at a meeting to be the same as or substantially similar to the blank proxy delivered for that meeting or to a blank proxy previously delivered which has been completed as a continuing proxy.

[10.1069]
16.5 Use of proxies by the chair

(1) Where a proxy appoints the chair (however described in the proxy) as proxy-holder the chair may not refuse to be the proxy-holder.

(2) Where the office-holder is appointed as proxy-holder but another person acts as chair of the meeting, that other person may use the proxies as if that person were the proxy-holder.

(3) Where, in a meeting of creditors in an administration, creditors' voluntary winding up, winding up by the court or a bankruptcy, the chair holds a proxy which requires the proxy-holder to vote for a particular resolution and no other person proposes that resolution the chair must propose it unless the chair considers that there is good reason for not doing so.

(4) If the chair does not propose such a resolution, the chair must as soon as reasonably practicable after the meeting deliver a notice of the reason why that was not done to the creditor, member or contributory.

[10.1070]
16.6 Right of inspection and retention of proxies

(1) A person attending a meeting is entitled, immediately before or in the course of the meeting, to inspect proxies and associated documents delivered to the chair or to any other person in accordance with the notice convening the meeting.

(2) The chair must—
 (a) retain the proxies used for voting at a meeting where the chair is the office-holder, or
 (b) deliver them as soon as reasonably practicable after the meeting to the office-holder.

(3) The office-holder must allow proxies, so long as they remain in the office-holder's hands, to be inspected at all reasonable times on any business day by—
 (a) a creditor, in the case of proxies used at a meeting of creditors;
 (b) a member of the company or a contributory, in the case of proxies used at a meeting of the company, or a meeting of contributories;
 (c) a director of the company in the case of corporate insolvency proceedings; or
 (d) the debtor or the bankrupt in the case of personal insolvency proceedings.

(4) A creditor in paragraph (3)(a) is a person who has delivered a proof in the proceedings, but does not include a person whose claim has been wholly rejected.

(5) However the right of inspection is subject to rule 1.58 (confidentiality of documents—grounds for refusing inspection).

[10.1071]
16.7 Proxy-holder with financial interest

(1) A proxy-holder must not vote for a resolution which would—
 (a) directly or indirectly place the proxy-holder or any associate of the proxy-holder in a position to receive any remuneration, fees or expenses from the insolvent estate; or
 (b) fix or change the amount of or the basis of any remuneration, fees or expenses receivable by the proxy-holder or any associate of the proxy-holder out of the insolvent estate.

(2) However a proxy-holder may vote for such a resolution if the proxy specifically directs the proxy-holder to vote in that way.

(3) Where an office-holder is appointed as proxy-holder and that proxy is used under rule 16.5(2) by another person acting as chair, the office-holder is deemed to be an associate of the person acting as chair.

[10.1072]
16.8 Proxy-holder with financial interest

[Note: section 434B(a) makes similar provision for corporate representation in company insolvency proceedings.]

(1) If a corporation is a creditor in a bankruptcy or an IVA, it may by resolution of its directors or other governing body authorise a person or persons to act as its representative or representatives in relation to any decision procedure of the bankrupt or debtor's creditors held in pursuance of the Act or of these Rules.

(2) Where the corporation authorises only one person, that person is entitled to exercise the same powers on behalf of the corporation as the corporation could exercise if it were an individual creditor.

(3) Where the corporation authorises more than one person, any one of them is entitled to exercise the same powers on behalf of the corporation as the corporation could exercise if it were an individual creditor.

(4) Where the corporation authorises more than one person and more than one of them purport to exercise a power under paragraph (3)—
 (a) if they purport to exercise the power in the same way, the power is treated as exercised in that way; but
 (b) if they do not purport to exercise the power in the same way, the power is treated as not exercised.

[10.1073]
16.9 Instrument conferring authorisation to represent corporation

(1) A person authorised to represent a corporation (other than as a proxy-holder) at a meeting of creditors or contributories must produce to the chair—

(a) the instrument conferring the authority; or
(b) a copy of it certified as a true copy by—
(i) two directors,
(ii) a director and the secretary, or
(iii) a director in the presence of a witness who attests the director's signature.

(2) The instrument conferring the authority must have been executed in accordance with section 44(1) to (3) of the Companies Act unless the instrument is the constitution of the corporation.

PART 17 CREDITORS' AND LIQUIDATION COMMITTEES

CHAPTER 1 INTRODUCTORY

[10.1074]
17.1 Scope and interpretation

(1) This Part applies to the establishment and operation of—
(a) a creditors' committee in an administration;
(b) a creditors' committee in an administrative receivership;
(c) a liquidation committee in a creditors' voluntary winding up;
(d) a liquidation committee in a winding up by the court; and
(e) a creditors' committee in a bankruptcy.

(2) In this Part—
"contributory member" means a member of a liquidation committee appointed by the contributories; and
"creditor member" means a member of a liquidation committee appointed by the creditors.

CHAPTER 2 FUNCTIONS OF A COMMITTEE

[10.1075]
17.2 Functions of a committee

In addition to any functions conferred on a committee by any provision of the Act, the committee is to—
(a) assist the office-holder in discharging the office-holder's functions; and
(b) act in relation to the office-holder in such manner as may from time to time be agreed.

CHAPTER 3 MEMBERSHIP AND FORMALITIES OF FORMATION OF A COMMITTEE

[Note: (1) a document required by the Act or these Rules must also contain the standard contents set out in Part 1; (2) see sections 215, 362, 363, 365, 371 and 374 of the Financial Services and Markets Act 2000 (c 8) for the rights of persons appointed by a scheme manager, the Financial Conduct Authority and the Prudential Regulation Authority to attend committees and make representations.]

[10.1076]
17.3 Number of members of a committee

[Note: section 101(1) provides that a liquidation committee in a creditors' voluntary winding up may not have more than five members.]

(1) A committee in an administration, administrative receivership or a bankruptcy must have at least three members but not more than five members.

(2) A liquidation committee in a creditors' voluntary winding up appointed pursuant to section 101 must have at least three members.

(3) A liquidation committee in a winding up by the court established under section 141 must have—
(a) at least three and not more than five members elected by the creditors; and
(b) where the grounds on which the company was wound up do not include inability to pay its debts, and where the contributories so decide, up to three contributory members elected by the contributories.

[10.1077]
17.4 Eligibility for membership of creditors' or liquidation committee

(1) This rule applies to a creditors' committee in an administration, an administrative receivership, and a bankruptcy and to a liquidation committee in a creditors' voluntary winding up and a winding up by the court.

(2) A creditor is eligible to be a member of such a committee if—
(a) the person has proved for a debt;
(b) the debt is not fully secured; and
(c) neither of the following apply—
(i) the proof has been wholly disallowed for voting purposes, or
(ii) the proof has been wholly rejected for the purpose of distribution or dividend.

(3) No person can be a member as both a creditor and a contributory.

(4) A body corporate may be a member of a creditors' committee, but it cannot act otherwise than by a representative appointed under rule 17.17.

[10.1078]
17.5 Establishment of committees

(1) Where the creditors, or where applicable, contributories, decide that a creditors' or liquidation committee should be established, the convener or chair of the decision procedure [or convener of the deemed consent process] (if not the office-holder) must—
(a) as soon as reasonably practicable deliver a notice of the decision to the office-holder (or to the person appointed as office-holder); and
(b) where a decision has also been made as to membership of the committee, inform the office-holder of the names and addresses of the persons elected to be members of the committee.

(2) Before a person may act as a member of the committee that person must agree to do so.

(3) A person's proxy-holder attending a meeting establishing the committee or, in the case of a corporation, its duly appointed representative, may give such agreement (unless the proxy or instrument conferring authority contains a statement to the contrary).

(4) Where a decision has been made to establish a committee but not as to its membership, the office-holder must seek a decision from the creditors (about creditor members of the committee) and, where appropriate in a winding up by the court, a decision from contributories (about contributory members of the committee).

[(5) The committee is not established (and accordingly cannot act) until the office-holder has sent a notice of its membership in order to comply with paragraph (9) or (10).]

(6) The notice must contain the following—

(a) a statement that the committee has been duly constituted;

(b) identification details for any company that is a member of the committee;

(c) the full name and address of each member that is not a company.

(7) The notice must be authenticated and dated by the office-holder.

(8) The notice must be delivered as soon as reasonably practicable after the minimum number of persons required by rule 17.3 have agreed to act as members and been elected.

(9) Where the notice relates to a liquidation committee or a creditors' committee other than in a bankruptcy the office-holder must, as soon as reasonably practicable, deliver the notice to the registrar of companies.

(10) Where the notice relates to a creditors' committee in a bankruptcy the office-holder must, as soon as reasonably practicable—

(a) in bankruptcy proceedings based on a petition file the notice with the court; and

(b) in bankruptcy proceedings based on a bankruptcy application deliver the notice to the official receiver.

NOTES

Words in square brackets in para (1) inserted, and para (5) substituted, by the Insolvency (England and Wales) and Insolvency (Scotland) (Miscellaneous and Consequential Amendments) Rules 2017, SI 2017/1115, rr 2, 11, as from 8 December 2017.

[10.1079]

17.6 Liquidation committee established by contributories

(1) This rule applies where, under section 141, the creditors do not decide that a liquidation committee should be established, or decide that a committee should not be established.

(2) The contributories may decide to appoint one of their number to make application to the court for an order requiring the liquidator to seek a further decision from the creditors on whether to establish a liquidation committee; and—

(a) the court may, if it thinks that there are special circumstances to justify it, make such an order; and

(b) the creditors' decision sought by the liquidator in compliance with the order is deemed to have been a decision under section 141.

(3) If the creditors decide under paragraph (2)(b) not to establish a liquidation committee, the contributories may establish a committee.

(4) The committee must then consist of at least three, and not more than five, contributories elected by the contributories; and rule 17.5 applies, substituting for the reference to rule 17.3 in rule 17.5(8) a reference to this paragraph.

[10.1080]

17.7 Notice of change of membership of a committee

(1) The office-holder must deliver or file a notice if there is a change in membership of the committee.

(2) The notice must contain the following—

(a) the date of the original notice in respect of the constitution of the committee and the date of the last notice of membership given under this rule (if any);

(b) a statement that this notice of membership replaces the previous notice;

(c) identification details for any company that is a member of the committee;

(d) the full name and address of any member that is not a company;

(e) a statement whether any member has become a member since the issue of the previous notice;

(f) the identification details for a company or otherwise the full name of any member named in the previous notice who is no longer a member and the date the membership ended.

(3) The notice must be authenticated and dated by the office-holder.

(4) Where the notice relates to a liquidation committee or a creditors' committee other than in a bankruptcy the office-holder must, as soon as reasonably practicable, deliver the notice to the registrar of companies.

(5) Where the notice relates to a creditors' committee in a bankruptcy the office-holder must, as soon as reasonably practicable—

(a) in bankruptcy proceedings based on a petition file the notice with the court; and

(b) in bankruptcy proceedings based on a bankruptcy application deliver the notice to the official receiver.

[10.1081]

17.8 Vacancies: creditor members of creditors' or liquidation committee

(1) This rule applies if there is a vacancy among the creditor members of a creditors' or liquidation committee or where the number of creditor members of the committee is fewer than the maximum allowed.

(2) A vacancy need not be filled if—

(a) the office-holder and a majority of the remaining creditor members agree; and

(b) the total number of creditor members does not fall below three.

(3) The office-holder may appoint a creditor, who is qualified under rule 17.4 to be a member of the committee, to fill a vacancy or as an additional member of the committee, if—

(a) a majority of the remaining creditor members of the committee (provided there are at least two) agree to the appointment; and

(b) the creditor agrees to act.

(4) Alternatively, the office-holder may seek a decision from creditors to appoint a creditor (with that creditor's consent) to fill the vacancy.

(5) Where the vacancy is filled by an appointment made by a decision of creditors which is not convened or chaired by the office-holder, the convener or chair must report the appointment to the office-holder.

[10.1082]
17.9 Vacancies: contributory members of liquidation committee

(1) This rule applies if there is a vacancy among the contributory members of a liquidation committee or where the number of contributory members of the committee is fewer than the maximum allowed under rule 17.3(3)(b) or 17.6(4) as the case may be.

(2) A vacancy need not be filled if—

(a) the liquidator and a majority of the remaining contributory members agree; and

(b) in the case of a committee of contributories only, the number of members does not fall below three.

(3) The liquidator may appoint a contributory to be a member of the committee, to fill a vacancy or as an additional member of the committee, if—

(a) a majority of the remaining contributory members of the committee (provided there are at least two) agree to the appointment; and

(b) the contributory agrees to act.

(4) Alternatively, the office-holder may seek a decision from contributories to appoint a contributory (with that contributory's consent) to fill the vacancy.

(5) Where the vacancy is filled by an appointment made by a decision of contributories which is not convened or chaired by the office-holder, the convener or chair must report the appointment to the office-holder.

[10.1083]
17.10 Resignation

A member of a committee may resign by informing the office-holder in writing.

[10.1084]
17.11 Termination of membership

A person's membership of a committee is automatically terminated if that person—

(a) becomes bankrupt, in which case the person's trustee in bankruptcy replaces the bankrupt as a member of the committee;

(b) is a person to whom a moratorium period under a debt relief order applies;

(c) neither attends nor is represented at three consecutive meetings (unless it is resolved at the third of those meetings that this rule is not to apply in that person's case);

(d) has ceased to be eligible to be a member of the committee under rule 17.4;

(e) ceases to be a creditor or is found never to have been a creditor;

(f) ceases to be a contributory or is found never to have been a contributory.

[10.1085]
17.12 Removal

(1) A creditor member of a committee may be removed by a decision of the creditors through a decision procedure and in the case of a liquidation committee a contributory member of the committee may be removed by a decision of contributories through a decision procedure.

(2) At least 14 days' notice must be given of a decision procedure under this rule.

[10.1086]
17.13 Cessation of liquidation committee in a winding up when creditors are paid in full

(1) Where the creditors have been paid in full together with interest in accordance with section 189, the liquidator must deliver to the registrar of companies a notice to that effect.

(2) On the delivery of the notice the liquidation committee ceases to exist.

(3) The notice must—

(a) identify the liquidator;

(b) contain a statement by the liquidator certifying that the creditors of the company have been paid in full with interest in accordance with section 189; and

(c) be authenticated and dated by the liquidator.

CHAPTER 4 MEETINGS OF COMMITTEE

[Note: a document required by the Act or these Rules must also contain the standard contents set out in Part 1.]

[10.1087]
17.14 Meetings of committee

(1) Meetings of the committee must be held when and where determined by the office-holder.

(2) The office-holder must call a first meeting of the committee to take place within six weeks of the committee's establishment.

(3) After the calling of the first meeting, the office-holder must call a meeting—

(a) if so requested by a member of the committee or a member's representative (the meeting then to be held within 21 days of the request being received by the office-holder); and

(b) for a specified date, if the committee has previously resolved that a meeting be held on that date.

(4) The office-holder must give five business days' notice of the venue of a meeting to each member of the committee (or a member's representative, if designated for that purpose), except where the requirement for notice has been waived by or on behalf of a member.

(5) Waiver may be signified either at or before the meeting.

[10.1088]

17.15 The chair at meetings

The chair at a meeting of a committee must be the office-holder or an appointed person.

[10.1089]

17.16 Quorum

A meeting of a committee is duly constituted if due notice of it has been delivered to all the members, and at least two of the members are in attendance or represented.

[10.1090]

17.17 Committee-members' representatives

(1) A member of the committee may, in relation to the business of the committee, be represented by another person duly authorised by the member for that purpose.

(2) A person acting as a committee-member's representative must hold a letter of authority entitling that person to act (either generally or specifically) and authenticated by or on behalf of the committee-member.

(3) A proxy or an instrument conferring authority (in respect of a person authorised to represent a corporation) is to be treated as a letter of authority to act generally (unless the proxy or instrument conferring authority contains a statement to the contrary).

(4) The chair at a meeting of the committee may call on a person claiming to act as a committee-member's representative to produce a letter of authority, and may exclude that person if no letter of authority is produced at or by the time of the meeting or if it appears to the chair that the authority is deficient.

(5) A committee member may not be represented by—

(a) another member of the committee;

(b) a person who is at the same time representing another committee-member;

(c) a body corporate;

(d) an undischarged bankrupt;

(e) a person whose estate has been sequestrated and who has not been discharged;

(f) a person to whom a moratorium period under a debt relief order applies;

(g) a person who is subject to a company directors disqualification order or a company directors disqualification undertaking; or

(h) a person who is subject to a bankruptcy restrictions order (including an interim order), a bankruptcy restrictions undertaking, a debt relief restrictions order (including an interim order) or a debt relief restrictions undertaking.

(6) Where a representative authenticates any document on behalf of a committee-member the fact that the representative authenticates as a representative must be stated below the authentication.

[10.1091]

17.18 Voting rights and resolutions

(1) At a meeting of the committee, each member (whether the member is in attendance or is represented by a representative) has one vote.

(2) A resolution is passed when a majority of the members attending or represented have voted in favour of it.

(3) Every resolution passed must be recorded in writing and authenticated by the chair, either separately or as part of the minutes of the meeting, and the record must be kept with the records of the proceedings.

[10.1092]

17.19 Resolutions by correspondence

(1) The office-holder may seek to obtain the agreement of the committee to a resolution by delivering to every member (or the member's representative designated for the purpose) details of the proposed resolution.

(2) The details must be set out in such a way that the recipient may indicate agreement or dissent and where there is more than one resolution may indicate agreement to or dissent from each one separately.

(3) A member of the committee may, within five business days from the delivery of details of the proposed resolution, require the office-holder to summon a meeting of the committee to consider the matters raised by the proposed resolution.

(4) In the absence of such a request, the resolution is passed by the committee if a majority of the members (excluding any who are not permitted to vote by reason of rule 17.25(4)) deliver notice to the office-holder that they agree with the resolution.

(5) A copy of every resolution passed under this rule, and a note that the agreement of the committee was obtained, must be kept with the records of the proceedings.

[10.1093]

17.20 Remote attendance at meetings of committee

(1) Where the office-holder considers it appropriate, a meeting may be conducted and held in such a way that persons who are not present together at the same place may attend it.

(2) A person attends such a meeting who is able to exercise that person's right to speak and vote at the meeting.

(3) A person is able to exercise the right to speak at a meeting when that person is in a position to communicate during the meeting to all those attending the meeting any information or opinions which that person has on the business of the meeting.

(4) A person is able to exercise the right to vote at a meeting when—

(i) that person is able to vote, during the meeting, on resolutions or determinations put to the vote at the meeting, and

(ii) that person's vote can be taken into account in determining whether or not such resolutions or determinations are passed at the same time as the votes of all the other persons attending the meeting.

(5) Where such a meeting is to be held the office-holder must make whatever arrangements the office-holder considers appropriate to—

(a) enable those attending the meeting to exercise their rights to speak or vote; and

(b) verify the identity of those attending the meeting and to ensure the security of any electronic means used to enable attendance.

(6) A requirement in these Rules to specify a place for the meeting may be satisfied by specifying the arrangements the office-holder proposes to enable persons to exercise their rights to speak or vote where in the reasonable opinion of the office-holder—

(a) a meeting will be attended by persons who will not be present together at the same place; and

(b) it is unnecessary or inexpedient to specify a place for the meeting.

(7) In making the arrangements referred to in paragraph (6) and in forming the opinion referred to in paragraph (6)(b), the office-holder must have regard to the legitimate interests of the committee members or their representatives attending the meeting in the efficient despatch of the business of the meeting.

(8) Where the notice of a meeting does not specify a place for the meeting the office-holder must specify a place for the meeting if at least one member of the committee requests the office-holder to do so in accordance with rule 17.21.

[10.1094]

17.21 Procedure for requests that a place for a meeting should be specified

(1) This rule applies to a request to the office-holder under rule 17.20(8) to specify a place for the meeting.

(2) The request must be made within three business days of the date on which the office-holder delivered the notice of the meeting in question.

(3) Where the office-holder considers that the request has been properly made in accordance with this rule, the office-holder must—

(a) deliver notice to all those previously given notice of the meeting—

(i) that it is to be held at a specified place, and

(ii) as to whether the date and time are to remain the same or not;

(b) fix a venue for the meeting, the date of which must be not later than seven business days after the original date for the meeting; and

(c) give three business days' notice of the venue to all those previously given notice of the meeting.

(4) The notices required by sub-paragraphs (a) and (c) may be delivered at the same or different times.

(5) Where the office-holder has specified a place for the meeting in response to a request under rule 17.20(8), the chair of the meeting must attend the meeting by being present in person at that place.

CHAPTER 5 SUPPLY OF INFORMATION BY THE OFFICE-HOLDER TO THE COMMITTEE

[Note: a document required by the Act or these Rules must also contain the standard contents set out in Part 1.]

[10.1095]

17.22 Notice requiring office-holder to attend the creditors' committee (administration and administrative receivership) (paragraph 57(3)(a) of Schedule B1 and section 49(2))

[Note: in an administration paragraph 57(3) of Schedule B1 enables the creditors' committee to require the administrator to provide the committee with information: section 49(2) makes similar provision in an administrative receivership.]

(1) This rule applies where—

(a) a committee in an administration resolves under paragraph 57(3)(a) of Schedule B1 to require the attendance of an administrator; or

(b) a committee in an administrative receivership resolves under section 49(2) to require the attendance of the administrative receiver.

(2) The notice delivered to the office-holder requiring the office-holder's attendance must be—

(a) accompanied by a copy of the resolution; and

(b) authenticated by a member of the committee.

(3) A member's representative may authenticate the notice for the member.

(4) The meeting at which the office-holder's attendance is required must be fixed by the committee for a business day, and must be held at such time and place as the office-holder determines.

(5) Where the office-holder so attends, the committee may elect one of their number to be chair of the meeting in place of the office-holder or an appointed person.

[10.1096]

17.23 Office-holder's obligation to supply information to the committee (winding up and bankruptcy)

[Note: see section 49(2) and paragraph 57(3) of Schedule B1 for the office-holder's duty in an administrative receivership and an administration to supply information to the creditors' committee.]

(1) This rule applies in relation to a creditors' voluntary winding up, a winding up by the court and a bankruptcy.

(2) The office-holder must deliver a report to every member of the liquidation committee or the creditors' committee (as appropriate) containing the information required by paragraph (3)—

(a) not less than once in every period of six months (unless the committee agrees otherwise); and

(b) when directed to do so by the committee.

(3) The required information is a report setting out—

(a) the position generally in relation to the progress of the proceedings; and

(b) any matters arising in connection with them to which the office-holder considers the committee's attention should be drawn.

(4) The office-holder must, as soon as reasonably practicable after being directed by the committee—

(a) deliver any report directed under paragraph (2)(b);

(b) comply with a request by the committee for information.

(5) However the office-holder need not comply with such a direction where it appears to the office-holder that—

(a) the direction is frivolous or unreasonable;

(b) the cost of complying would be excessive, having regard to the relative importance of the information; or

(c) there are insufficient assets to enable the office-holder to comply.

(6) Where the committee has come into being more than 28 days after the appointment of the office-holder, the office-holder must make a summary report to the members of the committee of what actions the office-holder has taken since the office-holder's appointment, and must answer such questions as they may put to the office-holder relating to the office-holder's conduct of the proceedings so far.

(7) A person who becomes a member of the committee at any time after its first establishment is not entitled to require a report under this rule by the office-holder of any matters previously arising, other than a summary report.

(8) Nothing in this rule disentitles the committee, or any member of it, from having access to the office-holder's record of the proceedings, or from seeking an explanation of any matter within the committee's responsibility.

CHAPTER 6 MISCELLANEOUS

[Note: a document required by the Act or these Rules must also contain the standard contents set out in Part 1.]

[10.1097]

17.24 Expenses of members etc

(1) The office-holder must pay, as an expense of the insolvency proceedings, the reasonable travelling expenses directly incurred by members of the committee or their representatives in attending the committee's meetings or otherwise on the committee's business.

(2) The requirement for the office-holder to pay the expenses does not apply to a meeting of the committee held within six weeks of a previous meeting, unless the meeting is summoned by the office-holder.

[10.1098]

17.25 Dealings by committee members and others

(1) This rule applies in a creditors' voluntary winding up, a winding up by the court and a bankruptcy to a person who is, or has been in the preceding 12 months—

(a) a member of the committee;

(b) a member's representative; or

(c) an associate of a member, or of a member's representative.

(2) Such a person must not enter into a transaction as a result of which that person would—

(a) receive as an expense of the insolvency proceedings a payment for services given or goods supplied in connection with the administration of the insolvent estate;

(b) obtain a profit from the administration of the insolvent estate; or

(c) acquire an asset forming part of the insolvent estate.

(3) However such a transaction may be entered into—

(a) with the prior sanction of the committee, where it is satisfied (after full disclosure of the circumstances) that the person will be giving full value in the transaction;

(b) with the prior permission of the court; or

(c) if that person does so as a matter of urgency, or by way of performance of a contract in force before the start of the insolvency proceedings, and that person obtains the court's permission for the transaction, having applied for it without undue delay.

(4) Neither a member nor a representative of a member who is to participate directly or indirectly in a transaction may vote on a resolution to sanction that transaction.

(5) The court may, on the application of an interested person—

(a) set aside a transaction on the ground that it has been entered into in contravention of this rule; and

(b) make such other order about the transaction as it thinks just, including an order requiring a person to whom this rule applies to account for any profit obtained from the transaction and compensate the insolvent estate for any resultant loss.

(6) The court will not make an order under the previous paragraph in respect of an associate of a member of the committee or an associate of a member's representative, if satisfied that the associate or representative entered into the relevant transaction without having any reason to suppose that in doing so the associate or representative would contravene this rule.

(7) The costs of the application are not payable as an expense of the insolvency proceedings unless the court orders otherwise.

[10.1099]

17.26 Dealings by committee members and others: administration and administrative receivership

(1) This rule applies in an administration and administrative receivership.

(2) Membership of the committee does not prevent a person from dealing with the company provided that a transaction is in good faith and for value.

(3) The court may, on the application of an interested person—

(a) set aside a transaction which appears to it to be contrary to this rule; and

(b) make such other order about the transaction as it thinks just including an order requiring a person to whom this rule applies to account for any profit obtained from the transaction and compensate the company for any resultant loss.

[10.1100]

17.27 Formal defects

[Note: section 377 makes similar provision to paragraph (1) for the validity of acts of the creditors' committee in a bankruptcy.]

(1) The acts of a creditors' committee or a liquidation committee are valid notwithstanding any defect in the appointment, election or qualifications of a member of the committee or a committee-member's representative or in the formalities of its establishment.

(2) This rule does not apply to the creditors' committee in a bankruptcy.

[10.1101]

17.28 Special rule for winding up by the court and bankruptcy: functions vested in the Secretary of State

(1) At any time when the functions of a committee in a winding up by the court or a bankruptcy are vested in the Secretary of State under section 141(4) or (5) or section 302(1) or (2), requirements of the Act or these Rules about notices to be delivered, or reports to be made, to the committee by the office-holder do not apply, otherwise than as enabling the committee to require a report as to any matter.

(2) Where the committee's functions are so vested under section 141(5) or 302(2), they may be exercised by the official receiver.

CHAPTER 7 WINDING UP BY THE COURT FOLLOWING AN ADMINISTRATION

[Note: a document required by the Act or these Rules must also contain the standard contents set out in Part 1.]

[10.1102]

17.29 Continuation of creditors' committee

[Note: paragraph 83(8)(f) of Schedule B1 makes similar provision to this rule for the liquidation committee to continue where the administration is followed by a creditors' voluntary winding up.]

(1) This rule applies where—

(a) a winding-up order has been made by the court on the application of the administrator under paragraph 79 of Schedule B1;

(b) the court makes an order under section 140(1) appointing the administrator as the liquidator; and

(c) a creditors' committee was in existence immediately before the winding-up order was made.

(2) The creditors' committee shall continue in existence after the date of the order as if appointed as a liquidation committee under section 141.

(3) However, subject to rule 17.8(3)(a), the committee cannot act until—

(a) the minimum number of persons required by rule 17.3 have agreed to act as members of the liquidation committee (including members of the former creditors' committee and any other who may be appointed under rule 17.8); and

(b) the liquidator has delivered a notice of continuance of the committee to the registrar of companies.

(4) The notice must be delivered as soon as reasonably practicable after the minimum number of persons required have agreed to act as members or, if applicable, been appointed.

(5) The notice must contain—

(a) a statement that the former creditors' committee is continuing in existence;

(b) identification details for any company that is a member of the committee;

(c) the full name and address of each member that is not a company.

(6) The notice must be authenticated and dated by the office-holder.

PART 18 REPORTING AND REMUNERATION OF OFFICE-HOLDERS

[Note: this Part does not apply to the official receiver acting as an office-holder.]

CHAPTER 1 INTRODUCTORY

[10.1103]

18.1 Scope of Part 18 and interpretation

(1) This Part applies to administration, winding up and bankruptcy.

(2) However this Part does not apply to the official receiver as office-holder or in respect of any period for which the official receiver is the office-holder.

(3) In particular an office-holder other than the official receiver is not required to make any report in respect of a period during which the official receiver was office-holder.

(4) In this Part "committee" means either or both of a creditors' committee and a liquidation committee as the context requires.

CHAPTER 2 PROGRESS REPORTS

[Note: a document required by the Act or these Rules must also contain the standard contents set out in Part 1.]

[10.1104]

18.2 Reporting by the office-holder

The office-holder in an administration, winding up or bankruptcy must prepare and deliver reports in accordance with this Chapter.

[10.1105]

18.3 Contents of progress reports in administration, winding up and bankruptcy

[Note: see rule 3.53 for provisions about the contents of a final progress report in an administration.]

(1) The office-holder's progress report in an administration, winding up and bankruptcy must contain the following—

(a) identification details for the proceedings;

(b) identification details for the bankrupt;

(c) identification and contact details for the office-holder;

(d) the date of appointment of the office-holder and any changes in the office-holder in accordance with paragraphs (3) and (4);

(e) details of progress during the period of the report, including a summary account of receipts and payments during the period of the report;

(f) the information relating to remuneration and expenses required by rule 18.4;

(g) the information relating to distributions required by rules 18.10 to 18.13 as applicable;

(h) details of what remains to be done; and

(i) any other information of relevance to the creditors.

(2) The receipts and payments account in a final progress report must state the amount paid to unsecured creditors by virtue of the application of section 176A.

(3) A change in the office-holder is only required to be shown in the next report after the change.

(4) However if the current office-holder is seeking the repayment of pre-administration expenses from a former office-holder the change in office-holder must continue to be shown until the next report after the claim is settled.

(5) Where the period of an administrator's appointment is extended the next progress report after the date the extension is granted must contain details of the extension.

(6) Where an administration has converted to a voluntary winding up the first progress report by the liquidator must include a note of any information received by the liquidator from the former administrator under rule 3.60(5) (matters occurring after the date of the administrator's final progress report).

[10.1106]

18.4 Information about remuneration

(1) The information relating to remuneration and expenses referred to in rule 18.3(1)(f) is as follows—

(a) the basis fixed for the remuneration of the office-holder under rules 18.16 and 18.18 to 18.21 as applicable, (or, if not fixed at the date of the report, the steps taken during the period of the report to fix it);

(b) if the basis of remuneration has been fixed, a statement of—

(i) the remuneration charged by the office-holder during the period of the report, and

(ii) where the report is the first to be made after the basis has been fixed, the remuneration charged by the office-holder during the periods covered by the previous reports, together with a description of the things done by the office-holder during those periods in respect of which the remuneration was charged;

(c) where the basis of the remuneration is fixed as a set amount under rule 18.16(2)(c), it may be shown as that amount without any apportionment to the period of the report;

(d) a statement of the expenses incurred by the office-holder during the period of the report;

(e) a statement setting out whether at the date of the report—

[(i) in a case other than a members' voluntary winding up, the remuneration expected to be charged by the office-holder is likely to exceed the fees estimate under rule 18.16(4) or any approval given,]

(ii) the expenses incurred or expected to be incurred are likely to exceed, or have exceeded, the details given to the creditors prior to the determination of the basis of remuneration, and

(iii) the reasons for that excess; and

(f) a statement of the rights of creditors [or], in a members' voluntary winding up, of members—

(i) to request information about remuneration or expenses under rule 18.9, and

(ii) to challenge the office-holder's remuneration and expenses under rule 18.34.

(2) The information about remuneration and expenses is required irrespective of whether payment was made in respect of them during the period of the report.

NOTES

Para (1): sub-para (e)(i) and the word in square brackets in sub-para (f) substituted by the Insolvency (England and Wales) (Amendment) Rules 2017, SI 2017/366, rr 3, 41, as from 6 April 2017.

[10.1107]

18.5 Information about pre-administration costs

(1) Where the administrator has made a statement of pre-administration costs under rule 3.35(10)(a)—

(a) if they are approved under rule 3.52, the first progress report after the approval must include a statement setting out the date of the approval and the amounts approved;

(b) while any of the costs remain unapproved each successive report must include a statement of any steps taken to get approval.

(2) However if either the administrator has decided not to seek approval, or another insolvency practitioner entitled to seek approval has told the administrator of that practitioner's decision not to seek approval then—

(a) the next report after that must include a statement of whichever is the case; and
(b) no statement under paragraph (1)(b) is required in subsequent reports.

[10.1108]
18.6 Progress reports in administration: timing

(1) The administrator's progress report in an administration must cover the periods of—

(a) six months starting on the date the company entered administration; and
(b) each subsequent period of six months.

(2) The periods for which progress reports are required under paragraph (1) are unaffected by any change in the administrator.

(3) However where an administrator ceases to act the succeeding administrator must, as soon as reasonably practicable after being appointed, deliver a notice to the creditors of any matters about which the succeeding administrator thinks the creditors should be informed.

(4) The administrator must deliver a copy of a report to the registrar of companies and the creditors within one month of the end of the period covered by the report unless the report is a final progress report under rule 3.55.

(5) An administrator who makes default in delivering a progress report within the time limit in paragraph (4) is guilty of on offence and liable to a fine and, for continued contravention, to a daily default fine.

[10.1109]
18.7 Progress reports in voluntary winding up: timing

(1) This rule applies for the purposes of sections 92A and 104A and prescribes the periods for which reports must be made.

(2) The liquidator's progress reports in a voluntary winding up must cover the periods of—

(a) 12 months starting on the date the liquidator is appointed; and
(b) each subsequent period of 12 months.

(3) The periods for which progress reports are required under paragraph (2) are unaffected by any change in the liquidator.

(4) However where a liquidator ceases to act the succeeding liquidator must, as soon as reasonably practicable after being appointed, deliver a notice to the members (in a members' voluntary winding up) or to members and creditors (in a creditors' voluntary winding up) of any matters about which the succeeding liquidator thinks the members or creditors should be informed.

(5) A progress report is not required for any period which ends after [a notice is delivered under rule 5.9(1) (members' voluntary winding up) or after] the date to which a final account is made up under section . . . 106 and is delivered by the liquidator . . . to members and creditors (creditors' voluntary winding up).

(6) The liquidator must [deliver] a copy of each progress report within two months after the end of the period covered by the report to—

(a) the registrar of companies (who is a prescribed person for the purposes of sections 92A and 104A);
(b) the members; and
(c) in a creditors' voluntary liquidation, the creditors.

NOTES

Para (5): words in square brackets inserted, and words omitted revoked, by the Insolvency (England and Wales) (Amendment) Rules 2017, SI 2017/366, rr 3, 42(1), as from 6 April 2017.

Para (6): word in square brackets substituted by SI 2017/366, rr 3, 42(2), as from 6 April 2017.

[10.1110]
18.8 Progress reports in winding up by the court and bankruptcy: timing

(1) The liquidator or trustee's progress report in a winding up by the court or bankruptcy must cover the periods of—

(a) 12 months starting on the date a person other than the official receiver is appointed liquidator or trustee; and
(b) each subsequent period of 12 months.

(2) The periods for which progress reports are required under paragraph (1) are unaffected by any change in the liquidator or trustee unless at any time the official receiver becomes liquidator or trustee in succession to another person in which case—

(a) the current reporting period under paragraph (1) ends; and
(b) if a person other than the official receiver is subsequently appointed as liquidator or trustee a new period begins under paragraph (1)(a).

(3) Where a liquidator or trustee ceases to act the succeeding liquidator or trustee must as soon as reasonably practicable after being appointed, deliver a notice to the creditors of any matters about which the succeeding liquidator or trustee thinks the creditors should be informed.

(4) A progress report is not required for any period which ends after the date to which a final account or report is made up under section 146 (winding up by the court) or section 331 (bankruptcy) and is delivered by the liquidator or the trustee to the creditors.

(5) In a winding up by the court, the liquidator must deliver a copy of the progress report to the registrar of companies, the members of the company and the creditors within two months of the end of the period covered by the report.

(6) In a bankruptcy, the trustee must deliver a copy of the progress report to the creditors within two months of the end of the period covered by the report.

[10.1111]

18.9 Creditors' and members' requests for further information in administration, winding up and bankruptcy

(1) The following may make a written request to the office-holder for further information about remuneration or expenses (other than pre-administration costs in an administration) set out in a progress report under rule 18.4(1)(b), (c) or (d) or a final report [or account] under rule 18.14—

(a) a secured creditor;

(b) an unsecured creditor with the concurrence of at least 5% in value of the unsecured creditors (including the creditor in question);

(c) members of the company in a members' voluntary winding up with at least 5% of the total voting rights of all the members having the right to vote at general meetings of the company;

(d) any unsecured creditor with the permission of the court; or

(e) any member of the company in a members' voluntary winding up with the permission of the court.

(2) A request, or an application to the court for permission, by such a person or persons must be made or filed with the court (as applicable) within 21 days of receipt of the report [or account] by the person, or by the last of them in the case of an application by more than one member or creditor.

(3) The office-holder must, within 14 days of receipt of such a request respond to the person or persons who requested the information by—

(a) providing all of the information requested;

(b) providing some of the information requested; or

(c) declining to provide the information requested.

(4) The office-holder may respond by providing only some of the information requested or decline to provide the information if—

(a) the time or cost of preparation of the information would be excessive; or

(b) disclosure of the information would be prejudicial to the conduct of the proceedings;

(c) disclosure of the information might reasonably be expected to lead to violence against any person; or

(d) the office-holder is subject to an obligation of confidentiality in relation to the information.

(5) An office-holder who does not provide all the information or declines to provide the information must inform the person or persons who requested the information of the reasons for so doing.

(6) A creditor, and a member of the company in a members' voluntary winding up, who need not be the same as the creditor or members who requested the information, may apply to the court within 21 days of—

(a) the office-holder giving reasons for not providing all of the information requested; or

(b) the expiry of the 14 days within which an office-holder must respond to a request.

(7) The court may make such order as it thinks just on an application under paragraph (6).

NOTES

Paras (1), (2): words in square brackets inserted by the Insolvency (England and Wales) (Amendment) Rules 2017, SI 2017/366, rr 3, 43, as from 6 April 2017.

[10.1112]

18.10 Administration, creditors' voluntary liquidation and compulsory winding up: reporting distribution of property to creditors under rule 14.13

(1) This rule applies where in an administration, creditors' voluntary liquidation or compulsory winding up there has been a distribution of property to creditors under rule 14.13.

(2) In any account or summary of receipts and payments which is required to be included in an account or report prepared under a rule listed in paragraph (3) the office-holder must—

(a) state the estimated value of the property divided among the creditors of the company during the period to which the account or summary relates; and

(b) provide details of the basis of the valuation as a note to the account or summary of receipts and payments.

(3) Paragraph (2) applies to the following—

(a) rule 3.63 (administrator's intention to resign);

(b) rule 6.25 (liquidator's resignation and replacement);

(c) rule 7.61 (liquidator's resignation);

(d) rule 18.3 (contents of progress report); and

(e) rule 18.14 (contents of final account (winding up) and final report (bankruptcy)).

[10.1113]

18.11 Voluntary winding up: reporting arrangement under section 110

(1) This rule applies where in a voluntary winding up there has been an arrangement under section 110 and a distribution to members has taken place under section 110(2) or (4).

(2) In any account or summary of receipts and payments which is required to be included in an account or report prepared under a section or rule listed in paragraph (3) the liquidator must—

(a) state the estimated value during the period to which the account or report relates of—

(i) the property transferred to the transferee,

(ii) the property received from the transferee, and

(iii) the property distributed to members under section 110(2) or (4); and

(b) provide details of the basis of the valuation as a note to the account or summary of receipts and payments.

(3) Paragraph (2) applies to the following—

(a) section 92A and rule 18.7 (members' voluntary winding up: progress report to company at year's end);

(b) section 94 and rule 18.14 (members' voluntary winding up: final account prior to dissolution);

(c) section 104A (creditors' voluntary winding up: progress report to company and creditors at year's end);

(d) section 106 and rules 6.28 and 18.14 (creditors' voluntary winding up: final account prior to dissolution).

[10.1114]

18.12 Members' voluntary winding up: reporting distribution to members other than under section 110

(1) This rule applies where in a members' voluntary winding up there has been a distribution of property to members in its existing form other than under an arrangement under section 110.

(2) In any account or summary of receipts and payments which is required to be included in an account or report prepared under a section or rule listed in paragraph (3) the liquidator must—

(a) state the estimated value of the property distributed to the members of the company during the period to which the account or report relates; and

(b) provide details of the basis of the valuation as a note to the account or summary of receipts and payments.

(3) Paragraph (2) applies to the following—

(a) section 92A (progress report);

(b) section 94 (final account prior to dissolution);

(c) rule 5.6 (liquidator's resignation).

[10.1115]

18.13 Bankruptcy proceedings: reporting distribution of property to creditors under section 326

(1) This rule applies in bankruptcy where there has been a distribution of property to creditors under section 326.

(2) In an account or report which the trustee is required to prepare under a section or rule listed in paragraph (3) the trustee must—

(a) state the estimated value of the property distributed among the creditors during the period to which the account or report relates; and

(b) provide details of the basis of the valuation in a note to the account or report.

(3) Paragraph (2) applies to the following—

(a) section 331 (final report to creditors in bankruptcy);

(b) rule 10.77 (consideration of appointment of replacement trustee); and

(c) Chapters 2 and 3 of this Part.

CHAPTER 3 FINAL ACCOUNTS IN WINDING UP AND FINAL REPORTS IN BANKRUPTCY

[Note: a document required by the Act or these Rules must also contain the standard contents set out in Part 1.]

[10.1116]

18.14 Contents of final account (winding up) and final report (bankruptcy)

(1) The liquidator's final account under section 94, 106 or 146 or the trustee's final report under section 331 must contain an account of the liquidator's administration of the winding up or of the trustee's administration of the bankruptcy including——

(a) a summary of the office-holder's receipts and payments, including details of the office-holder's remuneration and expenses; and

(b) details of the basis fixed for the office-holder's remuneration.

(2) The liquidator's final account under section 106 or 146(1)(a) must also include a statement as to the amount paid to unsecured creditors by virtue of section 176A.

(3) The final account or report to creditors or members must also contain—

(a) details of the remuneration charged and expenses incurred by the office-holder during the period since the last progress report (if any);

(b) a description of the things done by the office-holder in that period in respect of which the remuneration was charged and the expenses incurred; and

(c) a summary of the receipts and payments during that period.

(4) If the basis of the office-holder's remuneration had not been fixed by the date to which the last progress report was made up, the final account or report must also include details of the remuneration charged in the period of any preceding progress report in which details of remuneration were not included.

(5) Where the basis of remuneration has been fixed as a set amount, it is sufficient for the office-holder to state that amount and to give details of the expenses charged within the period in question.

CHAPTER 4 REMUNERATION AND EXPENSES IN ADMINISTRATION, WINDING UP AND BANKRUPTCY

[Note: a document required by the Act or these Rules must also contain the standard contents set out in Part 1.]

[10.1117]

18.15 Application of Chapter

(1) This Chapter applies to the remuneration of—

(a) an administrator;

(a) a liquidator; and

(b) a trustee in bankruptcy.

(2) This Chapter does not apply to the remuneration of a provisional liquidator or an interim receiver.

[10.1118]

18.16 Remuneration: principles

(1) An administrator, liquidator or trustee in bankruptcy is entitled to receive remuneration for services as office-holder.

(2) The basis of remuneration must be fixed—

(a) as a percentage of the value of—

(i) the property with which the administrator has to deal, or
(ii) the assets which are realised, distributed or both realised and distributed by the liquidator or trustee;

(b) by reference to the time properly given by the office-holder and the office-holder's staff in attending to matters arising in the administration, winding up or bankruptcy; or

(c) as a set amount.

(3) The basis of remuneration may be one or a combination of the bases set out in paragraph (2) and different bases or percentages may be fixed in respect of different things done by the office-holder.

(4) Where an office-holder, other than in a members' voluntary winding up, proposes to take all or any part of the remuneration on the basis set out in paragraph (2)(b), the office-holder must, prior to the determination of which of the bases set out in paragraph (2) are to be fixed, deliver to the creditors—

(a) a fees estimate; and

(b) details of the expenses the office-holder considers will be, or are likely to be, incurred.

(5) The fees estimate and details of expenses given under paragraph (4) may include remuneration expected to be charged and expenses expected to be incurred if the administrator becomes the liquidator where the administration moves into winding up.

(6) An office-holder, other than in a members' voluntary winding up, must deliver to the creditors the information required under paragraph (7) before the determination of which of the bases set out in paragraph (2) is or are to be fixed, unless the information has already been delivered under paragraph (4).

(7) The information the office-holder is required to give under this paragraph is—

(a) the work the office-holder proposes to undertake; and

(b) details of the expenses the office-holder considers will be, or are likely to be, incurred.

(8) The matters to be determined in fixing the basis of remuneration are—

(a) which of the bases set out in paragraph (2) is or are to be fixed and (where appropriate) in what combination;

(b) the percentage or percentages (if any) to be fixed under paragraphs (2)(a) and (3);

(c) the amount (if any) to be set under paragraph (2)(c).

(9) In arriving at that determination, regard must be had to the following—

(a) the complexity (or otherwise) of the case;

(b) any respects in which, in connection with the company's or bankrupt's affairs, there falls on the office-holder, any responsibility of an exceptional kind or degree;

(c) the effectiveness with which the office-holder appears to be carrying out, or to have carried out, the office-holder's duties; and

(d) the value and nature of the property with which the office-holder has to deal.

(10) A proposed liquidator in respect of a creditors' voluntary winding up may deliver to the creditors the information required by paragraphs (4) or (6) before becoming liquidator in which case that person is not required to deliver that information again if that person is appointed as liquidator.

[10.1119]

18.17 Remuneration of joint office-holders

Where there are joint office-holders it is for them to agree between themselves how the remuneration payable should be apportioned; and any dispute arising between them may be referred—

(a) to the committee, to the creditors (by a decision procedure) or (in a members' voluntary winding up) the company in general meeting, for settlement by resolution; or

(b) to the court, for settlement by order.

[10.1120]

18.18 Remuneration: procedure for initial determination in an administration

(1) This rule applies to the determination of the officer-holder's remuneration in an administration.

(2) It is for the committee to determine the basis of remuneration.

(3) If the committee fails to determine the basis of the remuneration or there is no committee then the basis of remuneration must be fixed by a decision of the creditors by a decision procedure [except in a case under paragraph (4)].

(4) Where the administrator has made a statement under paragraph 52(1)(b) of Schedule B1 that there are insufficient funds for distribution to unsecured creditors other than out of the prescribed part and either there is no committee, or the committee fails to determine the basis of remuneration, the basis of the administrator's remuneration may be fixed by—

(a) the consent of each of the secured creditors; or

(b) if the administrator has made or intends to make a distribution to preferential creditors—

(i) the consent of each of the secured creditors, and
(ii) a decision of the preferential creditors in a decision procedure.

NOTES

Para (3): words in square brackets added by the Insolvency (England and Wales) (Amendment) Rules 2017, SI 2017/366, rr 3, 44, as from 6 April 2017.

[10.1121]

18.19 Remuneration: procedure for initial determination in a members' voluntary winding up

In a members' voluntary winding up, it is for the company in general meeting to determine the basis of remuneration.

[10.1122]
18.20 Remuneration: procedure for initial determination in a creditors' voluntary winding up or a winding up by the court

(1) This rule applies to the determination of the office-holder's remuneration in a creditors' voluntary winding up or a winding up by the court.

(2) It is for the committee to determine the basis of remuneration.

(3) If the committee fails to determine the basis of remuneration or there is no committee then the basis of remuneration may be fixed by a decision of the creditors by a decision procedure.

(4) However where an administrator becomes liquidator in either of the following two cases the basis of remuneration fixed under rule 18.18 for the administrator is treated as having been fixed for the liquidator, and paragraphs (2) and (3) do not apply.

(5) The two cases are where—
- (a) a company which is in administration moves into winding up under paragraph 83 of Schedule B1 and the administrator becomes the liquidator; and
- (b) a winding-up order is made immediately upon the appointment of an administrator ceasing to have effect and the court under section 140(1) appoints as liquidator the person whose appointment as administrator has ceased to have effect.

[10.1123]
18.21 Remuneration: procedure for initial determination in a bankruptcy

(1) This rule applies to the determination of the office-holder's remuneration in a bankruptcy.

(2) It is for the committee to determine the basis of remuneration.

(3) If the committee fails to determine the basis of the remuneration or there is no committee then the basis of the remuneration may be fixed by a decision of the creditors by a decision procedure.

[10.1124]
18.22 Application of scale fees where creditors fail to fix the basis of the office-holder's remuneration

(1) This rule applies where in a winding up by the court or bankruptcy, the liquidator or trustee—
- (a) has requested the creditors to fix the basis of remuneration under rule 18.20(3) or 18.21(3) as applicable and the creditors have not done so; or
- (b) in any event if the basis of remuneration is not fixed by the creditors within 18 months after the date of the liquidator's or trustee's appointment.

(2) The liquidator or trustee is entitled to such sum as is arrived at (subject to paragraph (3)) by—
- (a) applying the realisation scale set out in Schedule 11 to the moneys received by the liquidator or trustee from the realisation of the assets of the company or bankrupt (including any Value Added Tax on the realisation but after deducting any sums paid to secured creditors in respect of their securities and any sums spent out of money received in carrying on the business of the company or bankrupt); and
- (b) adding to the sum arrived at under sub-paragraph (a) such sum as is arrived at by applying the distribution scale set out in Schedule 11 to the value of assets distributed to creditors of the company or bankrupt (including payments made in respect of preferential debts) and to contributories.

(3) In a bankruptcy that part of the trustee's remuneration calculated under paragraph (2) by reference to the realisation scale must not exceed such sum as is arrived at by applying the realisation scale to such part of the bankrupt's assets as are required to pay—
- (a) the bankruptcy debts (including any interest payable by virtue of section 328(4)) to the extent required to be paid by these Rules (ignoring those debts paid otherwise than out of the proceeds of the realisation of the bankrupt's assets or which have been secured to the satisfaction of the court);
- (b) the expenses of the bankruptcy other than—
  - (i) fees or the remuneration of the official receiver, and
  - (ii) any sums spent out of money received in carrying on the business of the bankrupt;
- (c) fees payable by virtue of any order made under section 415; and
- (d) the remuneration of the official receiver.

[10.1125]
18.23 Remuneration: application to the court to fix the basis

(1) If the basis of the administrator's remuneration or the liquidator's remuneration in a voluntary winding up is not fixed under rules 18.18 to 18.20 (as applicable) then the administrator or liquidator must apply to the court for it to be fixed.

(2) Before making such an application the liquidator or administrator must attempt to fix the basis in accordance with rules 18.18 to 18.20.

(3) An application under this rule may not be made more than 18 months after the date of the administrator's or liquidator's appointment.

(4) In a members' voluntary winding up—
- (a) the liquidator must deliver at least 14 days' notice of such an application to the company's contributories, or such one or more of them as the court may direct; and
- (b) the contributories may nominate one or more of their number to appear, or be represented, and to be heard on the application.

[10.1126]
18.24 Remuneration: administrator, liquidator or trustee seeking increase etc

An office-holder who considers the rate or amount of remuneration fixed to be insufficient or the basis fixed to be inappropriate may—

(a) request the creditors to increase the rate or amount or change the basis in accordance with rules 18.25 to 18.27;

(b) apply to the court for an order increasing the rate or amount or changing the basis in accordance with rule 18.28.

[10.1127]

18.25 Application for an increase etc in remuneration: the general rule

(1) This rule applies to a request by an office-holder in accordance with rule 18.24 for an increase in the rate or amount of remuneration or a change in the basis.

(2) Subject to the exceptions set out in rules 18.26 and 18.27, where the basis of the office-holder's remuneration has been fixed by the committee an administrator, liquidator or trustee may make such a request to the creditors for approval by a decision procedure.

[10.1128]

18.26 First exception: administrator has made a statement under paragraph 52(1)(b) of Schedule B1

(1) This exception applies in an administration where—

(a) the basis of the administrator's remuneration has been fixed by the committee; and

(b) the administrator has made a statement under paragraph 52(1)(b) of Schedule B1.

(2) A request by the administrator for an increase in the rate or amount of remuneration or a change in the basis must be approved by—

(a) the consent of each of the secured creditors; or

(b) if the administrator has made or intends to make a distribution to preferential creditors—

(i) the consent of each of the secured creditors, and

(ii) a decision of the preferential creditors in a decision procedure.

[10.1129]

18.27 Second exception: administrator who had applied for increase etc under rule 18.24 becomes liquidator

(1) This exception applies in a liquidation where—

(a) an administrator has become the liquidator;

(b) the remuneration had been determined by the committee in the preceding administration;

(c) the basis of the liquidator's remuneration is treated under rule 18.20(4) and (5) as being that which was fixed in the administration; and

(d) the administrator had subsequently requested an increase under rule 18.24.

(2) A request by the liquidator for an increase in the rate or amount of remuneration or a change in the basis may only be made by application to the court.

(3) Rule 18.28(6) to (8) apply to such an application.

[10.1130]

18.28 Remuneration: recourse by administrator, liquidator or trustee to the court

(1) This rule applies to an application by an office-holder to the court in accordance with rule 18.24 for an increase in the rate or amount of remuneration or change in the basis.

(2) An administrator may make such an application where the basis of the administrator's remuneration has been fixed—

(a) by the committee and the administrator has requested that the rate or amount be increased or the basis changed by decision of the creditors (by a decision procedure), but the creditors have not changed it;

(b) by decision of the creditors (by decision procedure); or

(c) by the approval of either the secured creditors or the preferential creditors or both in a case where the administrator has made a statement under paragraph 52(1)(b) of Schedule B1.

(3) A liquidator may make such an application where the basis of the liquidator's remuneration has been fixed—

(a) by the committee, and the liquidator has requested that the rate or amount be increased or the basis changed by decision of the creditors (by a decision procedure), but the creditors have not changed it;

(b) by decision of the creditors (by a decision procedure);

(c) under rule 18.20(4) and (5) or 18.22; or

(d) in a members' voluntary winding up, by the company in general meeting.

(4) A trustee may make such an application where the trustee's remuneration has been fixed—

(a) by the committee and the trustee has requested that the amount be increased or the basis changed by decision of the creditors (by a decision procedure), but the creditors have not changed it;

(b) by decision of the creditors (by a decision procedure); or

(c) under rule 18.22.

(5) Where an application is made under paragraph (2)(c), the administrator must deliver notice to each of the creditors whose approval was sought under rule 18.18(4).

(6) The office-holder must deliver a notice of the application at least 14 days before the hearing as follows—

(a) in an administration, a creditors' voluntary winding up, a winding up by the court or a bankruptcy—

(i) to the members of the committee, or

(ii) if there is no committee to such one or more of the creditors as the court may direct;

(b) in a members' voluntary winding up, to the company's contributories, or such one or more of them as the court may direct.

(7) The committee, the creditors or the contributories (as the case may be) may nominate one or more of their number to appear or be represented and to be heard on the application.

Part 10 Miscellaneous other SIs

(8) The court may, if it appears to be a proper case (including in a members' voluntary winding up), order the costs of the office-holder's application, including the costs of any member of the committee appearing or being represented on it, or of any creditor or contributory so appearing or being represented on it, to be paid as an expense of the estate.

[10.1131]
18.29 Remuneration: review at request of administrator, liquidator or trustee

(1) Where, after the basis of the office-holder's remuneration has been fixed, there is a material and substantial change in the circumstances which were taken into account in fixing it, the office-holder may request that the basis be changed.

(2) The request must be made—
- (a) to the company, where in a members' voluntary liquidation the company fixed the basis in general meeting;
- (b) to the committee, where the committee fixed the basis;
- (c) to the creditors or a particular class of creditors where the creditors or that class of creditors fixed the basis;
- (d) by application to the court, where the court fixed the basis;
- (e) to the committee if there is one and otherwise to the creditors where, in a winding up or bankruptcy, the remuneration was determined under rule 18.22.

(3) The preceding provisions of this Chapter which apply to the fixing of the office-holder's remuneration apply to a request for a change as appropriate.

(4) However the exception in rule 18.27 which would require such an application to be made to the court in the circumstances there set out does not apply.

(5) Any change in the basis of remuneration applies from the date of the request under paragraph (2) and not for any earlier period.

[10.1132]
18.30 Remuneration: exceeding the fee estimate

(1) The office-holder must not draw remuneration in excess of the total amount set out in the fees estimate without approval.

(2) The request for approval must be made—
- (a) where the committee fixed the basis, to that committee;
- (b) where the creditors or a class of creditors fixed the basis, to the creditors or that class of creditors;
- (c) where the court fixed the basis, to the court;

and rules 18.16 to 18.23 apply as appropriate.

(3) The request for approval must specify—
- (a) the reasons why the office-holder has exceeded, or is likely to exceed, the fees estimate;
- (b) the additional work the office-holder has undertaken or proposes to undertake;
- (c) the hourly rate or rates the office-holder proposes to charge for each part of that additional work;
- (d) the time that additional work has taken or the office-holder expects that work will take;
- (e) whether the office-holder anticipates that it will be necessary to seek further approval; and
- (f) the reasons it will be necessary to seek further approval.

[10.1133]
18.31 Remuneration: new administrator, liquidator or trustee

(1) This rule applies where a new administrator, liquidator or trustee is appointed in place of another.

(2) Any decision, determination, resolution or court order in effect under the preceding provisions of this Chapter immediately before the former office-holder ceased to hold office (including any application of scale fees under rule 18.22) continues to apply in relation to the remuneration of the new office-holder until a further decision, determination, resolution or court order is made in accordance with those provisions.

[10.1134]
18.32 Remuneration: apportionment of set fees

(1) This rule applies where the basis of the office-holder's remuneration is a set amount under rule 18.16(2)(c) and the office-holder ceases (for whatever reason) to hold office before the time has elapsed or the work has been completed in respect of which the amount was set.

(2) A request or application may be made to determine what portion of the amount should be paid to the former office-holder or the former office-holder's personal representative in respect of the time which has actually elapsed or the work which has actually been done.

(3) The request or application may be made by—
- (a) the former office-holder or the former office-holder's personal representative within the period of 28 days beginning with the date upon which the former office-holder ceased to hold office; or
- (b) the office-holder for the time being in office, if the former office-holder or the former office-holder's personal representative has not applied by the end of that period.

(4) The request or application to determine the portion must be made to the relevant person being—
- (a) the company, where the company is in members' voluntary liquidation and it fixed the basis in general meeting;
- (b) the committee, where the committee fixed the basis;
- (c) the creditors or a class of creditors where the creditors or that class fixed the basis;
- (d) the court where the court fixed the basis.

(5) In an administration where the circumstances set out in rule 18.18(4) apply the relevant person is to be determined under that paragraph.

(6) The person making the request or application must deliver a copy of it to the office-holder for the time being or to the former office-holder or the former office-holder's personal representative, as the case may be ("the recipient").

(7) The recipient may, within 21 days of receipt of the copy of the request or application, deliver notice of intent to make representations to the relevant person or to appear or be represented before the court on an application to the court.

(8) No determination may be made upon the request or application until either—
 (a) the expiry of the 21 days, or
 (b) if the recipient delivers a notice of intent, the recipient has been given the opportunity to make representations or to appear or be represented.

(9) Where the former office-holder or the former office-holder's personal representative (whether or not the original person making the request or application) considers that the portion so determined is insufficient that person may apply—
 (a) to the creditors for a decision increasing the portion, in the case of a determination by the committee;
 (b) to the court, in the case of a decision or resolution (as the case may be) of—
  (i) the creditors (whether under paragraph (4)(c) or under sub-paragraph (a)), or
  (ii) the company in general meeting.

(10) Paragraphs (6) to (8) apply to an application under paragraph (9) as appropriate.

[10.1135]

18.33 Remuneration: variation of the application of rules 18.29, 18.30 and 18.32

(1) This rule applies where the basis of remuneration has been fixed in accordance with rule 18.18(4) and all of the following apply—
 (a) there is now, or is likely to be, sufficient property to enable a distribution to be made to unsecured creditors other than by virtue of section 176A(2)(a); and
 (b) the administrator or liquidator in a winding up which immediately follows an administration makes a request under rule 18.29, 18.30 or 18.32.

(2) A request under 18.29, 18.30 or 18.32, must be made—
 (a) where there is a committee, to the committee; or
 (b) where there is no committee, to the creditors for a decision by decision procedure.

[10.1136]

18.34 Remuneration and expenses: application to court by a creditor or member on grounds that remuneration or expenses are excessive

(1) This rule applies to an application in an administration, a winding-up or a bankruptcy made by a person mentioned in paragraph (2) on the grounds that—
 (a) the remuneration charged by the office-holder is in all the circumstances excessive;
 (b) the basis fixed for the office-holder's remuneration under rules 18.16, 18.18, 18.19, 18.20 and 18.21 (as applicable) is inappropriate; or
 (c) the expenses incurred by the office-holder are in all the circumstances excessive.

(2) The following may make such an application for one or more of the orders set out in rule 18.36 or 18.37 as applicable—
 (a) a secured creditor,
 (b) an unsecured creditor with either—
  (i) the concurrence of at least 10% in value of the unsecured creditors (including that creditor), or
  (ii) the permission of the court, or
 (c) in a members' voluntary winding up—
  (i) members of the company with at least 10% of the total voting rights of all the members having the right to vote at general meetings of the company, or
  (ii) a member of the company with the permission of the court.

(3) The application by a creditor or member must be made no later than eight weeks after receipt by the applicant of the progress report under rule 18.3, or final report or account under rule 18.14 which first reports the charging of the remuneration or the incurring of the expenses in question ("the relevant report").

[10.1137]

18.35 Remuneration and expenses: application to court by a bankrupt on grounds that remuneration or expenses are excessive

[Note: where a bankrupt is applying for an annulment under section 282(1)(b) the bankrupt may also make an application in respect of the trustee's remuneration or expenses. See rule 10.134.]

(1) A bankrupt may, with the permission of the court, make an application on the grounds that—
 (a) the remuneration charged by the office-holder is in all the circumstances excessive;
 (b) the expenses incurred by the office-holder are in all the circumstances excessive.

(2) The bankrupt may make such an application for one or more of the orders set out in rule 18.36(4).

(3) The application must be made no later than eight weeks after receipt by the bankrupt of the report under rule 10.87.

(4) The court must not give the bankrupt permission to make an application unless the bankrupt shows that—
 (a) there is (or would be but for the remuneration or expenses in question); or
 (b) it is likely that there will be (or would be but for the remuneration or expenses in question),

a surplus of assets to which the bankrupt would be entitled.

(5) Paragraph (4) is without prejudice to the generality of the matters which the court may take into account in determining whether to give the bankrupt permission.

[10.1138]

18.36 Applications under rules 18.34 and 18.35 where the court has given permission for the application

(1) This rule applies to applications made with permission under rules 18.34 and 18.35.

(2) Where the court has given permission, it must fix a venue for the application to be heard.

(3) The applicant must, at least 14 days before the hearing, deliver to the office-holder a notice stating the venue and accompanied by a copy of the application and of any evidence on which the applicant intends to rely.

(4) If the court considers the application to be well-founded, it must make one or more of the following orders—

(a) an order reducing the amount of remuneration which the office-holder is entitled to charge;

(b) an order reducing any fixed rate or amount;

(c) an order changing the basis of remuneration;

(d) an order that some or all of the remuneration or expenses in question is not to be treated as expenses of the administration, winding up or bankruptcy;

(e) an order for the payment of the amount of the excess of remuneration or expenses or such part of the excess as the court may specify by—

(i) the administrator or liquidator or the administrator's or liquidator's personal representative to the company, or

(ii) the trustee or the trustee's personal representative to such person as the court may specify as property comprised in the bankrupt's estate;

(f) any other order that it thinks just.

(5) An order under paragraph (4)(b) or (c) may only be made in respect of periods after the period covered by the relevant report.

(6) Unless the court orders otherwise the costs of the application must be paid by the applicant, and are not payable as an expense of the administration, winding up or bankruptcy.

[10.1139]

18.37 Applications under rule 18.34 where the court's permission is not required for the application

(1) On receipt of an application under rule 18.34 for which the court's permission is not required, the court may, if it is satisfied that no sufficient cause is shown for the application, dismiss it without giving notice to any party other than the applicant.

(2) Unless the application is dismissed, the court must fix a venue for it to be heard.

(3) The applicant must, at least 14 days before any hearing, deliver to the office-holder a notice stating the venue with a copy of the application and of any evidence on which the applicant intends to rely.

(4) If the court considers the application to be well-founded, it must make one or more of the following orders—

(a) an order reducing the amount of remuneration which the office-holder is entitled to charge;

(b) an order reducing any fixed rate or amount;

(c) an order changing the basis of remuneration;

(d) an order that some or all of the remuneration or expenses in question be treated as not being expenses of the administration or winding up or bankruptcy;

(e) an order for the payment of the amount of the excess of remuneration or expenses or such part of the excess as the court may specify by—

(i) the administrator or liquidator or the administrator's or liquidator's personal representative to the company, or

(ii) the trustee or the trustee's personal representative to such person as the court may specify as property comprised in the bankrupt's estate;

(f) any other order that it thinks just.

(5) An order under paragraph (4)(b) or (c) may only be made in respect of periods after the period covered by the relevant report.

(6) Unless the court orders otherwise the costs of the application must be paid by the applicant, and are not payable as an expense of the administration or as winding up or bankruptcy.

[10.1140]

18.38 Remuneration of a liquidator or trustee who realises assets on behalf of a secured creditor

(1) A liquidator or trustee who realises assets on behalf of a secured creditor is entitled to such sum by way of remuneration as is arrived at as follows, unless the liquidator or trustee has agreed otherwise with the secured creditor—

(a) in a winding up—

(i) where the assets are subject to a charge which when created was a mortgage or a fixed charge, such sum as is arrived at by applying the realisation scale in Schedule 11 to the monies received in respect of the assets realised (including any sums received in respect of Value Added Tax on them but after deducting any sums spent out of money received in carrying on the business of the company),

(ii) where the assets are subject to a charge which when created was a floating charge such sum as is arrived at by—

(aa) first applying the realisation scale in Schedule 11 to monies received by the liquidator from the realisation of the assets (including any Value Added Tax on the realisation but ignoring any sums received which are spent in carrying on the business of the company),

(bb) then by adding to the sum arrived at under sub-paragraph (a)(ii)(aa) such sum as is arrived at by applying the distribution scale in Schedule 11 to the value of the assets distributed to the holder of the charge and payments made in respect of preferential debts; or

(b) in a bankruptcy such sum as is arrived at by applying the realisation scale in Schedule 11 to the monies received in respect of the assets realised (including any Value Added Tax on them).

(2) The sum to which the liquidator or trustee is entitled must be taken out of the proceeds of the realisation.

PART 19 DISCLAIMER IN WINDING UP AND BANKRUPTCY

[Note: a document required by the Act or these Rules must also contain the standard contents set out in Part 1.]

[10.1141]

19.1 Application of this Part

This Part applies to disclaimer by a liquidator under section 178 (winding up) and by a trustee under section 315 (bankruptcy).

[10.1142]

19.2 Notice of disclaimer (sections 178 and 315)

(1) An office-holder's notice of disclaimer of property under section 178 (winding up) or section 315 (bankruptcy) must (as appropriate)—

- (a) have the title—
  - (i) "Notice of disclaimer under section 178 of the Insolvency Act 1986" (in the case of a winding up), or
  - (ii) "Notice of disclaimer under section 315 of the Insolvency Act 1986" (in the case of a bankruptcy);
- (b) identify the company or the bankrupt;
- (c) identify and provide contact details for the office-holder;
- (d) contain such particulars of the property disclaimed as will enable it to be easily identified;
- (e) state—
  - (i) that the liquidator of the company disclaims all the company's interest in the property, or
  - (ii) that the trustee of the bankrupt's estate disclaims all the bankrupt's interest in the property.

(2) The notice must be authenticated and dated by the office-holder.

(3) If the property consists of registered land—

- (a) the notice must state the registered title number; and
- (b) the office-holder must deliver a copy of the notice to the Chief Land Registrar as soon as reasonably practicable after authenticating the notice.

(4) The liquidator must, as soon as reasonably practicable after authenticating the notice, deliver a copy of the notice to the registrar of companies.

(5) The trustee must, as soon as reasonably practicable after authenticating the notice, file a copy of the notice—

- (a) with the court; or
- (b) where the bankruptcy is based on a bankruptcy application, on the bankruptcy file.

(6) If the property consists of land or buildings the nature of the interest must be stated in the notice.

(7) The date of disclaimer for the purposes of section 178(4)(a) (winding up) or section 315(3)(a) (bankruptcy) is the date on which the liquidator or trustee authenticated the notice.

[10.1143]

19.3 Notice of disclaimer to interested persons (sections 178 and 315)

(1) The office-holder must deliver a copy of the notice of disclaimer within seven business days after the date of the notice to every person who (to the office-holder's knowledge)—

- (a) claims an interest in the disclaimed property;
- (b) is under any liability in relation to the property, not being a liability discharged by the disclaimer; and
- (c) if the disclaimer is of an unprofitable contract, is a party to the contract or has an interest under it.

(2) If it subsequently comes to the office-holder's knowledge that a person has an interest in the disclaimed property which would have entitled that person to receive a copy of the notice under paragraph (1) then the office-holder must deliver a copy to that person as soon as reasonably practicable.

(3) If it subsequently comes to the office-holder's knowledge that a person has an interest in the disclaimed property which would have entitled that person to receive a copy of the notice under rule 19.4 or 19.5 then the office-holder must serve a copy on that person as soon as reasonably practicable.

(4) The office-holder is not required to deliver or serve a copy of a notice under paragraph (2) or (3) if—

- (a) the office-holder is satisfied that the person has already been made aware of the disclaimer and its date, or
- (b) the court, on the office-holder's application, orders that delivery or service of a copy is not required in the particular case.

[10.1144]

19.4 Notice of disclaimer of leasehold property (sections 179 and 317)

Where a notice of disclaimer relates to leasehold property the office-holder must serve any copies of the notice of disclaimer which are required by either section 179 (winding up) or section 317 (bankruptcy) within seven business days after the date of the notice of disclaimer.

[10.1145]

19.5 Notice of disclaimer in respect of a dwelling house (bankruptcy) (section 318)

(1) This rule applies in a bankruptcy where the disclaimer is of property in a dwelling house.

(2) The trustee must serve any copies of the notice of disclaimer which are required by section 318 within seven business days after the date of the notice of disclaimer.

(3) A notice, or copy notice in relation to the disclaimer by a trustee of property in a dwelling house which is to be served on a person under the age of 18 may be served on the person's parent or guardian.

[10.1146]
19.6 Additional notices of disclaimer

An office-holder who is disclaiming property may at any time deliver a copy of the notice of the disclaimer to any other person whom the office-holder thinks ought, in the public interest or otherwise, to be informed of the disclaimer.

[10.1147]
19.7 Records

The office-holder must include in the records of the insolvency a record of—

(a) the name and address of each person to whom a copy of the notice of disclaimer has been delivered or served under rules 19.3 to 19.6, with the nature of the person's interest;
(b) the date on which the copy of the notice was delivered to or served on that person;
(c) the date on which the liquidator delivered a copy of the notice to the registrar of companies;
(d) the date on which the trustee filed a copy of the notice with the court or on the bankruptcy file; and
(e) if applicable, the date on which a copy of the notice was delivered to the Chief Land Registrar.

[10.1148]
19.8 Application for permission to disclaim in bankruptcy (section 315(4))

(1) This rule applies where section 315(4) requires the trustee to obtain the court's permission to disclaim property claimed for the bankrupt's estate under section 307 or 308.

(2) The trustee may apply for permission without notice to any other party.

(3) The application must be accompanied by a report—

(a) containing such particulars of the property as will enable it to be easily identified;
(b) setting out the reasons why, the property having been claimed for the bankrupt's estate, the trustee is now applying for the court's permission to disclaim it; and
(c) stating the persons (if any) who have been informed of the trustee's intention to make the application.

(4) If the report says that any person has consented to the disclaimer, a copy of that consent must accompany the report.

(5) The court may grant the permission, and may, before doing so—

(a) order that notice of the application be delivered to all such persons who, if the property is disclaimed, will be entitled to apply for a vesting or other order under section 320; and
(b) fix a venue for the hearing of the application.

[10.1149]
19.9 Application by interested party for decision on disclaimer (sections 178(5) and 316)

(1) This rule applies where an interested party makes an application under section 178(5) (winding up) or section 316 (bankruptcy) to the office-holder in respect of any property.

(2) The applicant must deliver the application to the office-holder and must provide proof of delivery in accordance with rule 1.52 if requested.

(3) If in a bankruptcy the trustee cannot disclaim the property concerned without the court's permission and the trustee applies for permission within the period of 28 days mentioned in section 316(1)(b), then the court must extend the time allowed for giving notice of disclaimer to a date not earlier than the date fixed for hearing the application.

[10.1150]
19.10 Disclaimer presumed valid and effective

Any disclaimer of property by the office-holder is presumed valid and effective, unless it is proved that the office-holder has been in breach of the office-holder's duties relating to the giving of notice of disclaimer or otherwise under sections 178 to 180 (winding up) or sections 315 to 319 (bankruptcy), or under this Part.

[10.1151]
19.11 Application for exercise of court's powers under section 181 (winding up) or section 320 (bankruptcy)

(1) This rule applies to an application under section 181 (winding up) or section 320 (bankruptcy) for a court order to vest or deliver disclaimed property.

(2) The application must be made within three months of the applicant becoming aware of the disclaimer, or of the applicant receiving a copy of the office-holder's notice of disclaimer delivered under rule 19.3 to 19.6, whichever is the earlier.

(3) The applicant must file with the application a witness statement stating—

(a) whether the application is made under—
  (i) section 181(2)(a) (claim of interest in the property),
  (ii) section 181(2)(b) (liability not discharged),
  (iii) section 320(2)(a) (claim of interest in the property),
  (iv) section 320(2)(b) (liability not discharged), or
  (v) section 320(2)(c) (occupation of a dwelling-house);
(b) the date on which the applicant received a copy of the office-holder's notice of disclaimer, or otherwise became aware of the disclaimer; and
(c) the grounds of the application and the order sought.

(4) The court must fix a venue for hearing the application.

(5) The applicant must, not later than five business days before the date fixed, deliver to the office-holder notice of the venue, accompanied by copies of the application and the filed witness statement.

(6) On hearing the application, the court may give directions as to any other persons to whom notice of the application and the grounds on which it is made should be delivered.

(7) The court must deliver sealed copies of any order made on the application to the applicant and the office-holder.

(8) If the property disclaimed is of a leasehold nature, or in a bankruptcy is property in a dwelling house, and section 179 (winding up), 317 or 318 (bankruptcy) applies to suspend the effect of the disclaimer, the court's order must include a direction giving effect to the disclaimer.

(9) However, paragraph (8) does not apply if, before the order is drawn up, other applications under section 181 (winding up) or section 320 (bankruptcy) are pending in relation to the same property.

PART 20

(*Part 20 (Debtors and their Families at Risk of Violence: Orders not to Disclose Current Address) is outside the scope of this work.*)

PART 21 [THE EU REGULATION]

[Note: a document required by the Act or these Rules must also contain the standard contents set out in Part 1.]

NOTES

Part heading: substituted by the Insolvency Amendment (EU 2015/848) Regulations 2017, SI 2017/702, regs 2, 3, Schedule, Pt 2, paras 32, 45, as from 26 June 2017, except in relation to proceedings opened before that date.

21.1–21.3 (*Rule 21.1, r 21.1A (as inserted by the Insolvency Amendment (EU 2015/848) Regulations 2017, SI 2017/702, regs 2, 3, Schedule, Pt 2, paras 32, 47), and rr 21.2, 21.3 were revoked by the Insolvency (Amendment) (EU Exit) Regulations 2019, SI 2019/146, reg 2, Schedule, Pt 4, paras 46, 104, as from IP completion day (as defined in the European Union (Withdrawal Agreement) Act 2020, s 39) (for savings, see reg 4 of the 2019 Regulations at* **[12.82]**).)

[10.1152]

21.4 Confirmation of creditors' voluntary winding up: application

(1) This rule applies where—

(a) a company has passed a resolution for voluntary winding up, and either—

(i) no declaration of solvency has been made in accordance with section 89, or

(ii) a declaration made under section 89—

(aa) has no effect by virtue of section 89(2), or

(bb) is treated as not having been made by virtue of section 96; or

(b) a company has moved from administration to creditors' voluntary winding up in accordance with paragraph 83 of Schedule B1.

(2) The liquidator may apply to court for an order confirming the winding up as a creditors' voluntary winding up for the purposes of the [EU Regulation].

(3) The application must be supported by a witness statement made by the liquidator which must contain—

(a) identification details for the liquidator and the company;

(b) the date on which the resolution for voluntary winding up was passed;

(c) a statement that the application is accompanied by the documents required by paragraph (4);

(d) a statement that the documents required by paragraph (4)(c) and (d) are true copies of the originals; and

[(e) a statement whether the proceedings will be COMI proceedings, establishment proceedings or proceedings to which the EU Regulation as it has effect in the law of the United Kingdom does not apply and the reasons for so stating.]

(4) The liquidator must file with the court—

(a) two copies of the application;

(b) evidence of having been appointed liquidator of the company;

(c) a copy of—

(i) the resolution for voluntary winding up, or

(ii) the notice of moving from administration to creditors' voluntary winding up sent by the administrator to the registrar of companies under paragraph 83(3) of Schedule B1; and

(d) a copy of—

(i) the statement of affairs required by section 99 or under paragraph 47 of Schedule B1, or

(ii) the information included in the administrator's statement of proposals under rule 3.35(1)(h).

NOTES

Para (2): words in square brackets substituted by the Insolvency (England and Wales) and Insolvency (Scotland) (Miscellaneous and Consequential Amendments) Rules 2017, SI 2017/1115, rr 22, 23(10), as from 8 December 2017.

Para (3): sub-para (e) substituted by the Insolvency (Amendment) (EU Exit) Regulations 2019, SI 2019/146, reg 2, Schedule, Pt 4, paras 46, 105, as from IP completion day (as defined in the European Union (Withdrawal Agreement) Act 2020, s 39) (for savings, see reg 4 of the 2019 Regulations at **[12.82]**).

[10.1153]

21.5 Confirmation of creditors' voluntary winding up: court order

(1) On an application under the preceding rule, the court may make an order confirming the creditors' voluntary winding up.

(2) It may do so without a hearing.

(3) If the court makes an order confirming the creditors' voluntary winding up, it must affix its seal to the application.

(4) A member of the court staff may deal with an application under this rule.

21.6–21.17 (*Rules 21.6–21.8 and rr 21.9–21.17 (as added by the Insolvency Amendment (EU 2015/848) Regulations 2017, SI 2017/702, regs 2, 3, Schedule, Pt 2, paras 32, 52) were revoked by the Insolvency (Amendment) (EU Exit)*

Regulations 2019, SI 2019/146, reg 2, Schedule, Pt 4, paras 46, 106, as from IP completion day (as defined in the European Union (Withdrawal Agreement) Act 2020, s 39) (for savings, see reg 4 of the 2019 Regulations at **[12.82]***).)*

PART 22 PERMISSION TO ACT AS DIRECTOR ETC OF COMPANY WITH A PROHIBITED NAME (SECTION 216)

[Note: a document required by the Act or these Rules must also contain the standard contents set out in Part 1.]

[10.1154]
22.1 Preliminary

(1) The rules in this Part—
- (a) relate to permission required under section 216 (restriction on re-use of name of company in insolvent liquidation) for a person to act as mentioned in section 216(3) in relation to a company with a prohibited name;
- (b) prescribe the cases excepted from that provision, that is to say, in which a person to whom the section applies may so act without that permission; and
- (c) apply to all windings up to which section 216 applies.

[10.1155]
22.2 Application for permission under section 216(3)

(1) At least 14 days' notice of any application for permission to act in any of the circumstances which would otherwise be prohibited by section 216(3) must be given by the applicant to the Secretary of State, who may—
- (a) appear at the hearing of the application; and
- (b) whether or not appearing at the hearing, make representations.

[10.1156]
22.3 Power of court to call for liquidator's report

When considering an application for permission under section 216, the court may call on the liquidator, or any former liquidator, of the liquidating company for a report of the circumstances in which the company became insolvent and the extent (if any) of the applicant's apparent responsibility for its doing so.

[10.1157]
22.4 First excepted case

(1) This rule applies where—
- (a) a person ("the person") was within the period mentioned in section 216(1) a director, or shadow director, of an insolvent company that has gone into insolvent liquidation; and
- (b) the person acts in all or any of the ways specified in section 216(3) in connection with, or for the purposes of, the carrying on (or proposed carrying on) of the whole or substantially the whole of the business of the insolvent company where that business (or substantially the whole of it) is (or is to be) acquired from the insolvent company under arrangements—
  - (i) made by its liquidator, or
  - (ii) made before the insolvent company entered into insolvent liquidation by an office-holder acting in relation to it as administrator, administrative receiver or supervisor of a CVA.

(2) The person will not be taken to have contravened section 216 if prior to that person acting in the circumstances set out in paragraph (1) a notice is, in accordance with the requirements of paragraph (3),—
- (a) given by the person, to every creditor of the insolvent company whose name and address—
  - (i) is known by that person, or
  - (ii) is ascertainable by that person on the making of such enquiries as are reasonable in the circumstances; and
- (b) published in the Gazette.

(3) The notice referred to in paragraph (2)—
- (a) may be given and published before the completion of the arrangements referred to in paragraph (1)(b) but must be given and published no later than 28 days after their completion;
- (b) must contain—
  - (i) identification details for the company,
  - (ii) the name and address of the person,
  - (iii) a statement that it is the person's intention to act (or, where the insolvent company has not entered insolvent liquidation, to act or continue to act) in all or any of the ways specified in section 216(3) in connection with, or for the purposes of, the carrying on of the whole or substantially the whole of the business of the insolvent company,
  - (iv) the prohibited name or, where the company has not entered into insolvent liquidation, the name under which the business is being, or is to be, carried on which would be a prohibited name in respect of the person in the event of the insolvent company entering insolvent liquidation,
  - (v) a statement that the person would not otherwise be permitted to undertake those activities without the leave of the court or the application of an exception created by Rules made under the Insolvency Act 1986,
  - (vi) a statement that breach of the prohibition created by section 216 is a criminal offence, and
  - (vii) a statement as set out in rule 22.5 of the effect of issuing the notice under rule 22.4(2);
- (c) where the company is in administration, has an administrative receiver appointed or is subject to a CVA, must contain—
  - (i) the date that the company entered administration, had an administrative receiver appointed or a CVA approved (whichever is the earliest), and
  - (ii) a statement that the person was a director of the company on that date; and
- (d) where the company is in insolvent liquidation, must contain—
  - (i) the date that the company entered insolvent liquidation, and

(ii) a statement that the person was a director of the company during the 12 months ending with that date.

(4) Notice may in particular be given under this rule—

(a) prior to the insolvent company entering insolvent liquidation where the business (or substantially the whole of the business) is, or is to be, acquired by another company under arrangements made by an office-holder acting in relation to the insolvent company as administrator, administrative receiver or supervisor of a CVA (whether or not at the time of the giving of the notice the person is a director of that other company); or

(b) at a time when the person is a director of another company where—

(i) the other company has acquired, or is to acquire, the whole, or substantially the whole, of the business of the insolvent company under arrangements made by its liquidator, and

(ii) it is proposed that after the giving of the notice a prohibited name should be adopted by the other company.

(5) Notice may not be given under this rule by a person who has already acted in breach of section 216.

[10.1158]
22.5 Statement as to the effect of the notice under rule 22.4(2)

The statement as to the effect of the notice under rule 22.4(2) must be as set out below—

"Section 216(3) of the Insolvency Act 1986 lists the activities that a director of a company that has gone into insolvent liquidation may not undertake unless the court gives permission or there is an exception in the Insolvency Rules made under the Insolvency Act 1986. (This includes the exceptions in Part 22 of the Insolvency (England and Wales) Rules 2016.) These activities are—

(a) acting as a director of another company that is known by a name which is either the same as a name used by the company in insolvent liquidation in the 12 months before it entered liquidation or is so similar as to suggest an association with that company;

(b) directly or indirectly being concerned or taking part in the promotion, formation or management of any such company; or

(c) directly or indirectly being concerned in the carrying on of a business otherwise than through a company under a name of the kind mentioned in (a) above.

This notice is given under rule 22.4 of the Insolvency (England and Wales) Rules 2016 where the business of a company which is in, or may go into, insolvent liquidation is, or is to be, carried on otherwise than by the company in liquidation with the involvement of a director of that company and under the same or a similar name to that of that company.

The purpose of giving this notice is to permit the director to act in these circumstances where the company enters (or has entered) insolvent liquidation without the director committing a criminal offence and in the case of the carrying on of the business through another company, being personally liable for that company's debts.

Notice may be given where the person giving the notice is already the director of a company which proposes to adopt a prohibited name."

[10.1159]
22.6 Second excepted case

(1) Where a person to whom section 216 applies as having been a director or shadow director of the liquidating company applies for permission of the court under that section not later than seven business days from the date on which the company went into liquidation, the person may, during the period specified in paragraph (2) below, act in any of the ways mentioned in section 216(3), notwithstanding that the person does not have the permission of the court under that section.

(2) The period referred to in paragraph (1) begins with the day on which the company goes into liquidation and ends either on the day falling six weeks after that date or on the day on which the court disposes of the application for permission under section 216, whichever of those days occurs first.

[10.1160]
22.7 Third excepted case

The court's permission under section 216(3) is not required where the company there referred to though known by a prohibited name within the meaning of the section—

(a) has been known by that name for the whole of the period of 12 months ending with the day before the liquidating company went into liquidation; and

(b) has not at any time in those 12 months been dormant within the meaning of section 1169(1), (2) and (3)(a) of the Companies Act.

SCHEDULES

SCHEDULE 1
REVOCATIONS

Introductory rule 2

[10.1161]

The Insolvency Rules 1986	1986/1925
The Insolvency (Amendment) Rules 1987	1987/1919
The Insolvency (Amendment) Rules 1989	1989/397
The Insolvency (Amendment) Rules 1991	1991/495
The Insolvency (Amendment) Rules 1993	1993/602
The Insolvency (Amendment) Rules 1995	1995/586

The Insolvency (Amendment) Rules 1999	1999/359
The Insolvency (Amendment) (No 2) Rules 1999	1999/1022
The Insolvency (Amendment) Rules 2001	2001/763
The Insolvency (Amendment) Rules 2002	2002/1307
The Insolvency (Amendment) (No 2) Rules 2002	2002/2712
The Insolvency (Amendment) Rules 2003	2003/1730
The Insolvency (Amendment) Rules 2004	2004/584
The Insolvency (Amendment) (No 2) Rules 2004	2004/1070
The Insolvency (Amendment) Rules 2005	2005/527
The Insolvency (Amendment) Rules 2006	2006/1272
The Insolvency (Amendment) Rules 2007	2007/1974
The Insolvency (Amendment) Rules 2008	2008/737
The Insolvency (Amendment) Rules 2009	2009/642
The Insolvency (Amendment No 2) Rules 2009	2009/2472
The Insolvency (Amendment) Rules 2010	2010/686
The Insolvency (Amendment) (No 2) Rules 2010	2010/734
The Insolvency (Amendment) Rules 2011	2011/785
The Insolvency (Amendment) Rules 2012	2012/469
The Insolvency (Amendment) Rules 2013	2013/2135
The Insolvency (Commencement of Proceedings) and Insolvency Rules 1986 (Amendment) Rules 2014	2014/817
The Insolvency (Amendment) Rules 2015	2015/443
The Insolvency (Amendment) Rules 2016	2016/187
The Insolvency (Amendment) (No 2) Rules 2016	2016/903

SCHEDULE 2
TRANSITIONAL AND SAVINGS PROVISIONS

Introductory rule 4

General

[10.1162]

1. In this Schedule—

"the 1986 Rules" means the Insolvency Rules 1986 as they had effect immediately before the commencement date and a reference to "1986 rule" followed by a rule number is a reference to a rule in the 1986 Rules; and

"the commencement date" means the date these Rules come into force.

Requirement for office-holder to provide information to creditors on opting out

2. (1) Rule 1.39, which requires an office-holder to provide information to a creditor on the right to opt out under rule 1.38 in the first communication to the creditor, does not apply to an office-holder who has delivered the first communication before the commencement date.

(2) However, such an office-holder may choose to deliver information on the right to opt out in which case the communication to the creditor must contain the information required by rule 1.39(2).

Electronic communication

3. (1) Rule 1.45(4) does not apply where the relevant proceedings commenced before the commencement date.

(2) In this paragraph "commenced" means—

- (a) the delivery of a proposal for a voluntary arrangement to the intended nominee;
- (b) the appointment of an administrator under paragraph 14 or 22 of Schedule B1;
- (c) the making of an administration order;
- (d) the appointment of an administrative receiver;
- (e) the passing or deemed passing of a resolution to wind up a company;
- (f) the making of a winding-up order; or
- (g) the making of a bankruptcy order.

Statements of affairs

4. (1) The provisions of these Rules relating to statements of affairs in administration, administrative receivership, company winding up and bankruptcy do not apply and the following rules in the 1986 Rules continue to apply where relevant proceedings commenced before the commencement date and a person is required to provide a statement of affairs—

- (a) 1986 rules 2.28 to 2.32 (administration);
- (b) 1986 rules 3.3 to 3.8 (administrative receivership);
- (c) 1986 rules 4.32 to 4.42 (company winding up); and
- (d) 1986 rules 6.58 to 6.72 (bankruptcy).

(2) In this paragraph "commenced" means—

- (a) the appointment of an administrator under paragraph 14 or 22 of Schedule B1;
- (b) the making of an administration order;

(c) the appointment of an administrative receiver
(d) the passing or deemed passing of a resolution to wind up a company;
(e) the making of a winding-up order; or
(f) the making of a bankruptcy order.

Savings in respect of meetings taking place on or after the commencement date and resolutions by correspondence

5. (1) This paragraph applies where on or after the commencement date—
(a) a creditors' or contributories' meeting is to be held as a result of a notice issued before that date in relation to a meeting for which provision is made by the 1986 Rules or the 1986 Act;
(b) a meeting is to be held as a result of a requisition by a creditor or contributory made before that date;
(c) a meeting is to be held as a result of a statement made under paragraph 52(1)(b) of Schedule B1 and a request is made before that date which obliges the administrator to summon an initial creditors' meeting;
(d) a . . . meeting is required by [sections 93 or 105] of the 1986 Act in the winding up of a company where the resolution to wind up was passed before 6th April 2010.

(2) Where a meeting is to be held under sub-paragraph (1)(a) to (1)(d), Part 15 of these Rules does not apply and the 1986 Rules relating to the following continue to apply—
(a) the requirement to hold the meeting;
(b) notice and advertisement of the meeting;
(c) governance of the meeting;
(d) recording and taking minutes of the meeting;
(e) the report or return of the meeting;
(f) membership and formalities of establishment of liquidation and creditors' committees where the resolution to form the committee is passed at the meeting;
(g) the office-holder's resignation or removal at the meeting;
(h) the office-holder's release;
(i) fixing the office-holder's remuneration;
(j) . . .
(k) hand-over of assets to a supervisor of a voluntary arrangement where the proposal is approved at the meeting;
(l) the notice of the appointment of a supervisor of a voluntary arrangement where the appointment is made at the meeting;
(m) the advertisement of appointment of a trustee in bankruptcy where the appointment is made at the meeting;
(n) claims that remuneration is or that other expenses are excessive; and
(o) complaints about exclusion at the meeting.

(3) Where, before the commencement date, the office-holder sought to obtain a resolution by correspondence under 1986 rule 2.48, 4.63A or 6.88A, the 1986 Rules relating to resolutions by correspondence continue to apply and sub-paragraph (2) applies to any meeting that those rules require the office-holder to summon.

(4) However, any application to the court in respect of such a meeting or vote is to be made in accordance with Part 12 of these Rules.

Savings in respect of final meetings taking place on or after the commencement date

6. (1) This paragraph applies where—
(a) before the commencement date—
  (i) a final report to creditors has been sent under 1986 rule 4.49D (final report to creditors in liquidation),
  (ii) a final report to creditors and bankrupt has been sent under 1986 rule 6.78B (final report to creditors and bankrupt), or
  (iii) a meeting has been called under [sections 94, 106, 146 or 331] of the 1986 Act (final meeting . . .); and
(b) a meeting under section 94, 106, 146 or 331 of the 1986 Act is held on or after the commencement date.

(2) Where a meeting is held to which this paragraph applies, Part 15 of these Rules does not apply and the 1986 Rules relating to the following continue to apply—
(a) the requirement to hold the meeting;
(b) notice and advertisement of the meeting;
(c) governance of the meeting;
(d) recording and taking minutes of the meeting;
(e) the form and content of the final report;
(f) the office-holder's resignation or removal;
(g) the office-holder's release;
(h) fixing the office-holder's remuneration;
(i) requests for further information from creditors;
(j) claims that remuneration is or other expenses are excessive; and
(k) complaints about exclusion at the meeting.

(3) However, any application to the court in respect of such a meeting is to be made in accordance with Part 12 of these Rules.

Progress reports and statements to the registrar of companies

7. (1) Where an obligation to prepare a progress report arises before the commencement date but has not yet been fulfilled the following provisions of the 1986 Rules continue to apply—
(a) 1986 rule 2.47 (reports to creditors in administration;
(b) 1986 rules 4.49B and 4.49C (progress reports—winding up); and
(c) 1986 rule 6.78A (reports to creditors in bankruptcy).

(2) Where before the commencement date, a conversion notice under paragraph 83 of Schedule B1 was sent to the registrar of companies . . . , 1986 rule 2.117A(1) continues to apply . . . .

(3) The provisions of these Rules relating to progress reporting do not apply—

(a) in the case of a bankruptcy, where the bankruptcy order was made on a petition presented before 6th April 2010; or

(b) in the case of a winding up, where the winding-up order was made on a petition presented before 6th April 2010.

(4) Where a voluntary winding up commenced before 6th April 2010, 1986 rule 4.223-CVL as it had effect immediately before that date, continues to apply.

[(5) Where rules 18.6, 18.7 or 18.8 prescribe the periods for which progress reports must be made but before the commencement date an office-holder has ceased to act[, or an administrator has sent a progress report to creditors in support of a request for their consent to an extension of the administration,] resulting in a change in reporting period under 1986 rule 2.47(3A), 2.47(3B) 4.49B(5), 4.49C(3), or 6.78A(4), the period for which reports must be made is the period for which reports were required to be made under the 1986 Rules immediately before the commencement date.]"

Foreign currency

8. (1) Where, before the commencement date an amount stated in a foreign currency on an application, claim or proof of debt is converted into sterling by the office-holder under 1986 rule 2.86, 1986 rule 4.91, 1986 rule 5A.3 or 1986 rule 6.111, the office-holder and any successor to the office-holder must continue to use that exchange rate for subsequent conversions of that currency into sterling for the purpose of distributing any assets of the insolvent estate.

(2) However when an office-holder, convener, appointed person or chair uses an exchange rate to convert an application, claim or proof in a foreign currency into sterling solely for voting purposes before the commencement date, it does not prevent the office-holder from using an alternative rate for subsequent conversions.

CVA moratoria

9. Where, before the commencement date, the directors of a company submit to the nominee the documents required under paragraph 6(1) of Schedule A1, the 1986 Rules relating to moratoria continue to apply to that proposed voluntary arrangement.

Priority of expenses of voluntary arrangements

10. 1986 rule 4.21A (expenses of CVA in a liquidation) and 1986 rule 6.46A (expenses of IVA in a bankruptcy) continue to apply where a winding up or bankruptcy petition is presented or a bankruptcy application is made (as the case may be) before the commencement date.

General powers of liquidator

11. 1986 rule 4.184 (General powers of liquidator) continues to apply as regards a person dealing in good faith and for value with a liquidator and in respect of the power of the court or the liquidation committee to ratify anything done by the liquidator without permission before the amendments made to sections 165 and 167 of the Act by section 120(2) and (3) of the Small Business, Enterprise and Employment Act 2015 (which removed the requirements for the liquidator to obtain such permission) came into force.

Fast-track voluntary arrangements

12. Where a fast-track voluntary arrangement is in effect on the commencement date the following 1986 Rules continue to apply to it after the commencement date—

(a) 1986 rules 5.35 to 5.50 (fast-track voluntary arrangement);

(b) 1986 rules 5.57 to 5.59 (application by official receiver to annul a bankruptcy order under section 263D(3)); and

(c) 1986 rules 5.60 to 5.61 (other matters arising on annulments under sections 261(2)(a), 261(2)(b) or 263D(3)).

First trustee in bankruptcy

13. On the commencement date the official receiver becomes trustee of the bankrupt's estate where—

(a) a bankruptcy order was made before the commencement date; and

(b) no trustee has yet been appointed.

Applications before the court

14. (1) [Subject to paragraph (1A), where] an application to court is filed or a petition is presented under the Act or under the 1986 Rules before the commencement date and the court remains seised of that application or petition on the commencement date, the 1986 rules continue to apply to that application or petition.

[(1A) Where the 1986 Rules apply by virtue of paragraph (1) they are to apply as though—

(a) in rules 7.47(2)(a)(ii), (b)(iii) and (c) and 13.2(3A)(a) for "a Registrar in Bankruptcy of the High Court" there were substituted "an Insolvency and Companies Court Judge", and

(b) in rule 7.47(5), for the words "Registrar in Bankruptcy of the High Court" both times they appear there were substituted "Insolvency and Companies Court Judge.]

(2) For the purpose of paragraph (1), the court is no longer seised of an application when—

(a) it makes an order having the effect of determining of the application; or

(b) in relation to a petition for bankruptcy or winding up when—

(i) the court makes a bankruptcy order or a winding up order,

(ii) the court dismisses the petition, or

(iii) the petition is withdrawn.

(3) Any application to the court to review, rescind[, vary] or appeal an order made under paragraph [14(2)] is to be made in accordance with Part 12 of these Rules.

Forms

15. A form contained in Schedule 4 to the 1986 Rules may be used on or after the commencement date if—

(a) the form is used to provide a statement of affairs pursuant to paragraph 4 of this Schedule;

(b) the form relates to a meeting held under the 1986 Rules as described in paragraph 5(1) of this Schedule;
(c) the form is required for the administration of a fast-track voluntary arrangement pursuant to paragraph 12 of this Schedule;
(d) the form is required because before the commencement date, the office-holder sought to obtain the passing of a resolution by correspondence; or
(e) the form relates to any application to the court or petition presented before the commencement date.

Registers

16. (1) The Secretary of State must maintain on the individual insolvency register, the bankruptcy restrictions register and the debt relief restrictions register information which is on the registers immediately before the commencement date.

(2) The Secretary of State must also enter on the appropriate register referred to in paragraph (1) information received (but not yet entered on the register) before the commencement date.

(3) The Court's power under Part 20 to order that information must not be entered in those registers where there is a risk of violence applies equally to information received by the Secretary of State before the commencement date but not yet entered on a register.

(4) Any obligation in Part 11 to delete information from a register or to rectify a register applies equally to information entered on the register before these rules come into force.

Administrations commenced before 15th September 2003

17. The 1986 Rules continue to apply to administrations where the petition for an administration order was presented before 15th September 2003.

Set-off in insolvency proceedings commenced before 1st April 2005

18. Where before 1st April 2005 a company has entered administration or gone into liquidation, the office-holder, when calculating any set-off must apply the 1986 Rules as they had effect immediately before 1st April 2005.

Calculating the value of future debts in insolvency proceedings commenced before 1st April 2005

19. Where before 1st April 2005 a company has entered administration or gone into liquidation or a bankruptcy order has been made, the office-holder, when calculating the value of a future debt for the purpose of dividend (and no other purpose) must apply the 1986 Rules as they had effect immediately before 1st April 2005.

Obligations arising under family proceedings where bankruptcy order is made on or before 31 March 2005

20. Rule 12.3 of the 1986 Rules applies, without the amendments made by rule 44 of the Insolvency (Amendment) Rules 2005 to an obligation arising under an order made in family proceedings in any case where a bankruptcy order was made on or before 31 March 2005.

Insolvency practitioner [fees and expenses] estimates

21. (1) [Rules 18.4(1)(e), 18.16(4) to (10), and 18.30 do not apply in a case where before 1st October 2015—]
(a) the appointment of an administrator took effect;
(b) a liquidator was nominated under section 100(2), or 139(3) of the Act;
(c) a liquidator was appointed under section 139(4) or 140 of the Act;
(d) a person was directed by the court or appointed to be a liquidator under section 100(3) of the Act;
(e) a liquidator was nominated or the administrator became the liquidator under paragraph 83(7) of Schedule B1 to the Act; or
(f) a trustee of a bankrupt's estate was appointed.

(2) Paragraphs (4) and (5) of rule 18.20 do not apply where an administrator was appointed before 1st October 2015 and—
(a) the company is wound up under paragraph 83 of Schedule B1 on or after the commencement date and the administrator becomes the liquidator; or
(b) a winding-up order is made upon the appointment of an administrator ceasing to have effect on or after the commencement date and the court under section 140(1) appoints as liquidator the person whose appointment as administrator has ceased to have effect.

[Transitional provision for companies entering administration before 6th April 2010 and moving to voluntary liquidation between 6th April 2010 and 8th December 2017 inclusive of those dates]

[22. Where—
(a) a company goes into administration before 6th April 2010; and
(b) the company goes into voluntary liquidation under paragraph 83 of Schedule B1 between 6th April 2010 and 8th December 2017 inclusive of those dates;

the 1986 Rules as amended by the Insolvency (Amendment) Rules 2010( ) apply to the extent necessary to give effect to section 104A of the Act notwithstanding that by virtue of paragraph 1(6)(a) or (b) of Schedule 4 to the Insolvency (Amendment) Rules 2010 those amendments to the Insolvency Rules 1986 would otherwise not apply.]

NOTES

Para 5: word omitted from sub-para (1)(d) revoked, words in square brackets in that paragraph substituted, and sub-para (2)(j) revoked, by the Insolvency (England and Wales) (Amendment) Rules 2017, SI 2017/366, rr 3, 45, 46, as from 6 April 2017.

Para 6: words in square brackets in sub-para (1)(a)(iii) substituted, and words omitted from that paragraph revoked, by SI 2017/366, rr 3, 47, as from 6 April 2017.

Para 7: words omitted from sub-para (2) revoked, and sub-para (5) added, by SI 2017/366, rr 3, 48, 49, as from 6 April 2017. Words in square brackets in sub-paras (5) inserted by the Insolvency (England and Wales) and Insolvency (Scotland) (Miscellaneous and Consequential Amendments) Rules 2017, SI 2017/1115, rr 2, 13(1), (2), as from 8 December 2017.

Para 14: words in square brackets in para (1) substituted, and para (1A) inserted, by the Alteration of Judicial Titles (Registrar in Bankruptcy of the High Court) Order 2018, SI 2018/130, art 2, Schedule, para 14(c), as from 26 February 2018. Word in square brackets in sub-para (3) inserted, and figure in square brackets substituted, by SI 2017/1115, rr 2, 13(1), (3), as from 8 December 2017.

Para 21: word in square brackets in the paragraph heading and in sub-para (1) substituted by SI 2017/1115, rr 2, 13(1), (4), (5), as from 8 December 2017.

Para 22: substituted by SI 2017/1115, rr 2, 13(1), (6), (7), as from 8 December 2017.

SCHEDULE 3
PUNISHMENT OF OFFENCES UNDER THESE RULES

Introductory rule 6

[10.1163]

Rule creating offence	General nature of the offence	Mode of prosecution	Punishment	Daily default fine (if applicable)
1.56(3)	Falsely claiming to be a person entitled to inspect a document with the intention of gaining sight of it.	1 On indictment. 2 Summary.	2 years, or a fine, or both. 6 months, or a fine, or both.	Not applicable.
3.55(7)	Former administrator failing to file a notice of automatic end of administration and progress report.	Summary.	Level 3 on the standard scale.	One tenth of level 3 on the standard scale.
3.70(2)	Failing to comply with administrator's duties on vacating office.	Summary.	Level 3 on the standard scale.	One tenth of level 3 on the standard scale.
4.17(6)	Administrative receiver failing to deliver required accounts of receipts and payments.	Summary.	Level 3 on the standard scale.	One tenth of level 3 on the standard scale.
6.14(13)	Directors failing to seek a decision on the nomination of a liquidator.	1 On indictment. 2 Summary.	1 A fine. 2 A fine.	Not applicable.
18.6(5)	Administrator failing to deliver required progress reports in accordance with rule 18.6.	Summary.	Level 3 on the standard scale.	One tenth of level 3 on the standard scale.

SCHEDULE 4
SERVICE OF DOCUMENTS

Rule 1.2(2)

[10.1164]

1. (1) This Schedule sets out the requirements for service where a document is required to be served.

(2) Service is to be carried out in accordance with Part 6 of the CPR as that Part applies to either a "claim form" or a "document other than the claim form" except where this Schedule provides otherwise or the court otherwise approves or directs.

(3) However, where a document is required or permitted to be served at a company's registered office service may be effected at a previous registered office in accordance with section 87(2) of the Companies Act.

(4) In the case of an overseas company service may be effected in any manner provided for by section 1139(2) of the Companies Act.

(5) If for any reason it is impracticable to effect service as provided for in paragraphs (2) to (4) then service may be effected in such other manner as the court may approve or direct.

(6) The third column of the table below sets out which documents are treated as "claim forms" for the purposes of applying Part 6 of the CPR and which are "documents other than the claim form" (called in this Schedule "other documents").

(7) The fourth column of the table sets out modifications to Part 6 of the CPR which apply to the service of documents listed in the first and second columns.

(8) Part 6 of the CPR applies to the service of documents outside the jurisdiction with such modifications as the court may approve or direct.

Service of winding-up petitions

2. (1) A winding-up petition must be served at a company's registered office by handing it to a person at that address who—

(a) at the time of service acknowledges being a director, other officer or employee of the company;

(b) is, to the best of the knowledge and belief of the person serving the petition, a director, other officer or employee of the company; or

(c) acknowledges being authorised to accept service of documents on the company's behalf.

(2) However if there is no one of the kind mentioned in sub-paragraph (1) at the registered office, the petition may be served by depositing it at or about the registered office in such a way that it is likely to come to the notice of a person attending the office.

(3) Sub-paragraph (4) applies if—

(a) for any reason it is not practicable to serve a petition at a company's registered office;

(b) the company has no registered office; or

(c) the company is an unregistered company.

(4) Where this paragraph applies the petition may be served—

(a) by leaving it at the company's last known principal place of business in England and Wales in such a way that it is likely to come to the attention of a person attending there; or

(b) on the secretary or a director, manager or principal officer of the company, wherever that person may be found.

Service of administration application (paragraph 12 of Schedule B1)

3. (1) An application to the court for an administration order must be served by delivering the documents as follows—

(a) on the company at its registered office or if service at its registered office is not practicable at its last known principal place of business in England and Wales;

(b) on any other person at that person's proper address.

(2) A person's proper address is any which he has previously notified as the address for service, but if the person has not notified such an address then the documents may be served at that person's usual or last known address.

(3) Paragraph (4) sets out the proper address for service for an authorised deposit-taker who—

(a) has appointed, or is or may be entitled to appoint, an administrative receiver of the company; or

(b) is, or may be, entitled to appoint an administrative receiver of the company under paragraph 14 of Schedule B1; and

(c) has not notified an address for service.

(4) The proper address for service is—

(a) that of an office of the authorised-deposit taker where the applicant knows the company maintains a bank account; or

(b) where the applicant doesn't know of any such office, the registered office; or

(c) if there is no such registered office the usual or last known address.

Service on joint office-holders

4. Service of a document on one of joint office-holders is to be treated as service on all of them.

Service of orders staying proceedings

5. (1) This paragraph applies where the court makes an order staying an action, execution or other legal process against—

(a) the property of a company; or

(b) the property or person of an individual debtor or bankrupt.

(2) The order may be served within the jurisdiction by serving a sealed copy at the address for service of—

(a) the claimant; or

(b) another party having the carriage of the proceedings to be stayed.

Certificate of service

6. (1) The service of an application or petition must be verified by a certificate of service.

(2) The certificate of service must—

(a) identify the application or petition;

(b) identify the company, where the application or petition relates to a company;

(c) identify the debtor, where the application relates to an individual;

(d) identify the applicant or petitioner;

(e) specify—

(i) the court or hearing centre in which the application was made or at which the petition was filed, and the court reference number,

(ii) the date of the application or petition,

(iii) whether the copy served was a sealed copy,

(iv) the person(s) served, and

(v) the manner of service and the date of service; and

(f) be verified by a statement of truth.

[(3) Where the court has directed that service be effected in a particular manner, the certificate must be accompanied by a sealed copy of the order directing such manner of service.]

Table of requirements for service

Rule (or section)	*Document*	*Whether treated as claim form or other document*	*Modifications to Part 6 of the CPR which apply unless the court directs otherwise*
1A.28(h) and1A.30 (& section A44)	Challenge to directors' actions	Claim form	The applicant must serve the application.]
[1A.28(a) and 1A.30 (& section A21)	Application for permission of the court under section A21 to take enforcement action or to bring legal proceedings against the company during a moratorium	Claim form	The applicant must serve the application.
1A.28(b) and 1A.30 (& section A31)	Application for permission of the court under section A31 to dispose of charged property free from charge during a moratorium	Claim form	The applicant must serve the application.
1A.28(c) and 1A.30 (& section A32)	Application for permission of the court under section A32 to dispose of hire-purchase property during a	Claim form	The applicant must serve the application.

Part 10 Miscellaneous other SIs

Table of requirements for service			
Rule (or section)	***Document***	***Whether treated as claim form or other document***	***Modifications to Part 6 of the CPR which apply unless the court directs otherwise***
	moratorium		
1A.28(d) and 1A.30 (& section A37)	Application by monitor for directions	Claim form	The applicant must serve the application.
1A.28(e) and 1A.30 (& section A39)	Replacement of monitor or appointment of additional monitor	Claim form	The applicant must serve the application.
1A.28(f) and1A.30 (& section A42)	Challenge to monitor's actions	Claim form	The applicant must serve the application.
1A.28(g) and 1A.30 (& section A43)	Challenges to monitor remuneration in insolvency proceedings	Claim form	The applicant must serve the application.
3.8	Administration application	Claim form	Service in accordance with paragraph 3 of this Schedule. The applicant must serve the application.
3.16 (& Para 15 of Sch B1)	Notice of intention to appoint administrator by a floating charge holder	[Other document]	The appointer must serve the notice.
3.23 (& para 26 of Sch B1)	Notice of intention to appoint administrator by company or directors	[Other document]	Service on the company at its registered office or if that is not practicable, at its last known principal place of business in England and Wales.
7.3	Statutory demand on a company under section 123(1) or 222(1)(a) (unregistered companies)		[Note: the requirements for service of a statutory demand are set out in sections 123(1) and 222(1)(a) respectively.]
7.9 and 7.29	Winding-up petition	Claim form	Service in accordance with paragraph 2 of this Schedule. The petitioner must serve the petition.
7.34	Court order for additional deposit to be paid—provisional liquidator	Other document	
7.99	Court order to enforce payment of a call	Other document	
7.102	Court order for public examination served on examinee	Other document	
10.2	Statutory demand (bankruptcy)	Other document	Service in accordance with rule 10.2.
10.14	Bankruptcy petition (creditor's)	Claim form	Personal service. The petitioner must serve the petition.
10.29	Court order—change of carriage of petition	Other document	
10.50	Court order for additional deposit to be paid—interim receiver	Other document	
10.99	Court order for public examination served on bankrupt	Other document	
10.119	Court order for disclosure by HMRC	Other document	
10.126	Notice to recipient of after acquired property	Other document	
10.166	Court order for post redirection	Other document	
11.3	Application for debt relief restrictions order (DRRO) or bankruptcy restrictions order (BRO)	Claim form	The applicant must serve the application.
11.4	Service of evidence for DRRO or BRO	Other document	
12.9	Applications to court generally (where service required)	Claim form	The applicant must serve the application.
12.19	Court order for private examination	Other document	Personal service. The applicant must serve the order.
12.28(2)	Witness statement of evidence	Other document	

Table of requirements for service			
Rule (or section)	***Document***	***Whether treated as claim form or other document***	***Modifications to Part 6 of the CPR which apply unless the court directs otherwise***
12.37(7)	Application for block transfer order	Claim form	The applicant must serve the application.
12.42	Notice requiring person to assess costs by detailed assessment	Other document	
12.48	Application for costs	Claim form	The applicant must serve the application.
19.4 (& sections 179 and 317)	Notice of disclaimer (leasehold property)	Other document	
19.5 (& section 318)	Notice of disclaimer (dwelling house)	Other document	
. . .	. . .	. . .	. . .
Paragraph 5(1) of this Schedule	Order staying proceedings	Other document	The applicant must serve the order.

NOTES

Para 6 is amended as follows:

Sub-para (3) substituted by the Insolvency (England and Wales) and Insolvency (Scotland) (Miscellaneous and Consequential Amendments) Rules 2017, SI 2017/1115, rr 2, 14, as from 8 December 2017.

Table entries relating to rr 1A.28 and 1A. 30 inserted by the Insolvency (England and Wales) (No 2) (Amendment) Rules 2021, SI 2021/1028, r 79, as from 1 October 2021 (for savings provisions see the note to r 1A.1 at **[10.539]**).

Table entry relating to r 21.2 (omitted) revoked by the Insolvency (Amendment) (EU Exit) Regulations 2019, SI 2019/146, reg 2, Schedule, Pt 4, paras 46, 107, as from IP completion day (as defined in the European Union (Withdrawal Agreement) Act 2020, s 39) (for savings, see reg 4 of the 2019 Regulations at **[12.82]**).

The other words in square brackets in the table were substituted by the Insolvency (England and Wales) (Amendment) Rules 2017, SI 2017/366, rr 3, 50, as from 6 April 2017.

SCHEDULE 5
CALCULATION OF TIME PERIODS

Rule 1.3

[10.1165]

[Note: section 376 of the Act contains a power for the court to extend the time for doing anything required by the Act or these Rules under the Second Group of Parts (Insolvency of Individuals; bankruptcy).]

1. The rules in CPR 2.8 with the exception of paragraph (4) apply for the calculation of periods expressed in days in the Act and these Rules.

2. (1) This paragraph applies for the calculation of periods expressed in months.

(2) The beginning and the end of a period expressed in months is to be determined as follows—

(a) if the beginning of the period is specified—

(i) the month in which the period ends is the specified number of months after the month in which it begins, and

(ii) the date in the month on which the period ends is—

[(aa) the day before the date corresponding to the date in the month on which it begins, or]

(bb) if there is no such date in the month in which it ends, the last day of that month;

(b) if the end of the period is specified—

(i) the month in which the period begins is the specified number of months before the month in which it ends, and

(ii) the date in the month on which the period begins is—

[(aa) the day after the date corresponding to the date in the month on which it ends, or]

(bb) if there is no such date in the month in which it begins, the last day of that month.

3. The provisions of CPR rule 3.1(2)(a) (the court's general powers of management) apply so as to enable the court to extend or shorten the time for compliance with anything required or authorised to be done by these Rules.

4. Paragraph 3 is subject to any time limits expressly stated in the Act and to any specific powers in the Act or these Rules to extend or shorten the time for compliance.

NOTES

Para 2: sub-paras (2)(a)(ii)(aa) and (2)(b)(ii)(aa) substituted by the Insolvency (England and Wales) (Amendment) Rules 2017, SI 2017/366, rr 3, 51, as from 6 April 2017.

SCHEDULES 6–9

(*Schs 6–9 concern personal insolvency and are outside the scope of this work.*)

SCHEDULE 10
DESTINATION OF APPEALS FROM DECISIONS OF DISTRICT JUDGES IN CORPORATE INSOLVENCY MATTERS

Rule 12.59

[10.1166]

Country court hearing centre	***Destination of Appeal***
Aberystwyth	Cardiff or Caernarfon District Registry
Banbury	Birmingham District Registry
Barnsley	Leeds District Registry
Barnstaple	Bristol District Registry
Barrow-in-Furness	Liverpool District Registry or Manchester District Registry
Bath	Bristol District Registry
Bedford	Birmingham District Registry
Birkenhead	Liverpool District Registry or Manchester District Registry
Birmingham	Birmingham District Registry
Blackburn	Liverpool District Registry or Manchester District Registry
Blackpool	Liverpool District Registry or Manchester District Registry
Blackwood	Cardiff District Registry
Bolton	Liverpool District Registry or Manchester District Registry
Boston	Birmingham District Registry
Bournemouth and Poole	Registrar in Bankruptcy
Bradford	Leeds District Registry
Brighton	Registrar in Bankruptcy
Bristol	Bristol District Registry
Burnley	Liverpool District Registry or Manchester District Registry
Bury	Liverpool District Registry or Manchester District Registry
Bury St Edmunds	Registrar in Bankruptcy
Caernarfon	Cardiff District Registry
Cambridge	Registrar in Bankruptcy
Canterbury	Registrar in Bankruptcy
Cardiff	Cardiff District Registry
Carlisle	Liverpool District Registry or Manchester District Registry
Caernarfon	Cardiff District Registry or Caernarfon District Registry
County Court at Central London	Registrar in Bankruptcy
Chelmsford	Registrar in Bankruptcy
Chester	Liverpool District Registry or Manchester District Registry
Chesterfield	Leeds District Registry
Colchester	Registrar in Bankruptcy
Coventry	Birmingham District Registry
Crewe	Liverpool District Registry or Manchester District Registry
Croydon	Registrar in Bankruptcy
Darlington	Newcastle District Registry
Derby	Birmingham District Registry
Doncaster	Leeds District Registry
Dudley	Birmingham District Registry
Durham	Leeds District Registry or Newcastle District Registry
Eastbourne	Registrar in Bankruptcy
Exeter	Bristol District Registry
Gloucester and Cheltenham	Bristol District Registry
Great Grimsby	Leeds District Registry
Guildford	Registrar in Bankruptcy
Halifax	Leeds District Registry
Harrogate	Leeds District Registry
Hastings	Registrar in Bankruptcy
Haverfordwest	Cardiff District Registry
Hereford	Bristol District Registry
Hertford	Registrar in Bankruptcy

Country court hearing centre	***Destination of Appeal***
Huddersfield	Leeds District Registry
Ipswich	Registrar in Bankruptcy
Kendal	Liverpool District Registry or Manchester District Registry
Kingston-upon-Hull	Leeds District Registry
Kingston-upon-Thames	Registrar in Bankruptcy
Lancaster	Liverpool District Registry or Manchester District Registry
Leeds	Leeds District Registry
Leicester	Birmingham District Registry
Lincoln	Leeds District Registry or Birmingham District Registry
Liverpool	Liverpool District Registry or Manchester District Registry
Llangefni	Cardiff District Registry or Caernarfon District Registry
Luton	Registrar in Bankruptcy
Maidstone	Registrar in Bankruptcy
Manchester	Manchester District Registry
Merthyr Tydfil	Cardiff District Registry
Middlesbrough	Newcastle District Registry
Milton Keynes	Birmingham District Registry
Newcastle upon Tyne	Newcastle District Registry
Newport (Gwent)	Cardiff District Registry
Newport (Isle of Wight)	Registrar in Bankruptcy
Northampton	Birmingham District Registry
Norwich	Registrar in Bankruptcy
Nottingham	Birmingham District Registry
Oldham	Liverpool District Registry or Manchester District Registry
Oxford	Registrar in Bankruptcy
Peterborough	Registrar in Bankruptcy
Plymouth	Bristol District Registry
Pontypridd	Cardiff District Registry
Portsmouth	Registrar in Bankruptcy
Port Talbot	Cardiff District Registry
Prestatyn	Cardiff District Registry or Caernarfon District Registry
Preston	Liverpool District Registry or Manchester District Registry
Reading	Registrar in Bankruptcy
Rhyl	Cardiff District Registry or Caernarfon District Registry
Romford	Registrar in Bankruptcy
Salisbury	Registrar in Bankruptcy
Scarborough	Leeds District Registry
Scunthorpe	Leeds District Registry
Sheffield	Leeds District Registry
Slough	Registrar in Bankruptcy
Southampton	Registrar in Bankruptcy
Southend-on-Sea	Registrar in Bankruptcy
Stafford	Birmingham District Registry
St Albans	Registrar in Bankruptcy
Stockport	Liverpool District Registry or Manchester District Registry
Stoke-on-Trent	Manchester District Registry
Sunderland	Newcastle District Registry
Swansea	Cardiff District Registry
Swindon	Bristol District Registry
Taunton	Bristol District Registry
Telford	Birmingham District Registry
Torquay & Newton Abbot	Bristol District Registry
Truro	Bristol District Registry
Tunbridge Wells	Registrar in Bankruptcy
Wakefield	Leeds District Registry

Country court hearing centre	Destination of Appeal
Walsall	Birmingham District Registry
Warwick	Birmingham District Registry
Welshpool & Newton	Cardiff District Registry
West Cumbria	Liverpool District Registry or Manchester District Registry
Wigan	Liverpool District Registry or Manchester District Registry
Winchester	Registrar in Bankruptcy
Wolverhampton	Birmingham District Registry
Worcester	Birmingham District Registry
Wrexham	Cardiff District Registry or Caernarfon District Registry
Yeovil	Bristol District Registry
York	Leeds District Registry

SCHEDULE 11
DETERMINATION OF INSOLVENCY OFFICE-HOLDER'S REMUNERATION

Rule 18.22

[10.1167]
This table sets out the realisation and distribution scales for determining the remuneration of trustees and liquidators.

The realisation scale	
on the first £5,000	20%
on the next £5,000	15%
on the next £90,000	10%
on all further sums realised	5%

The distribution scale	
on the first £5,000	10%
on the next £5,000	7.5%
on the next £90,000	5%
on all further sums distributed	2.5%.

INSOLVENCY RULES 1986: DESTINATION TABLE

[10.1168]

NOTES

Editorial Note: this table is not part of the Insolvency (England and Wales) Rules 2016, but has been included here for convenience. It is taken from the gov.uk website at www.gov.uk/government/news/table-of-destinations-for-insolvency-rules-now-available. The derivation table for these Rules is not reproduced, but is available at assets.publishing.service.gov.uk/government/uploads/system/uploads/attachment_data/file/562471/Insolvency_Rules_2016_table_of_derivations.pdf. Note finally that provisions in the 1986 Rules relating to personal insolvency have been omitted from the table below.

The following table indicates the destination of provisions in the 1986 Rules. The 2016 Rules broadly derive from the 1986 Rules. However, there is rarely an exact match as the structure of the 2016 Rules is different, the language has been modernised and there have been significant changes, in particular as a result of amendments to the primary legislation made by the Enterprise and Regulatory Reform Act 2013, the Deregulation Act 2015, and the Small Business, Enterprise and Employment Act 2015. Furthermore, the information requirements previously contained in forms have now been imported into the relevant rule as specified content. Finally, the new Rules try to avoid copying out of the primary legislation. Instead, they contain many references to the Insolvency Act 1986 to enable the user to connect individual rules with the relevant provisions of the Act that the Rules supplement.

1986 Rule heading	1986 rule	2016 rule
Citation and commencement	0.1	1
Construction and interpretation	0.2	2
Extent	0.3	3
THE FIRST GROUP OF PARTS **PART 1 COMPANY VOLUNTARY ARRANGEMENTS** **CHAPTER 1 PRELIMINARY**		
Scope of this Part; interpretation	1.1	
CHAPTER 2 PROPOSAL BY DIRECTORS		
Preparation of proposal	1.2	
Contents of proposal	1.3	2.2, 2.3
Notice to intended nominee	1.4	
Statement of affairs	1.5	2.6
Additional disclosure for assistance of nominee	1.6	2.8
Nominee's report on the proposal	1.7	2.9
Replacement of nominee	1.8	2.10
Summoning of meetings under s 3	1.9	2.25–2.28
CHAPTER 3 PROPOSAL BY ADMINISTRATOR OR LIQUIDATOR (HIMSELF THE NOMINEE)		
Preparation of proposal	1.10	2.3, 2.5
Summoning of meetings under s 3	1.11	2.25–2.29, 2.31
CHAPTER 4 PROPOSAL BY ADMINISTRATOR OR LIQUIDATOR (ANOTHER INSOLVENCY PRACTITIONER THE NOMINEE)		
Preparation of proposal and notice to nominee	1.12	2.3
CHAPTER 5 PROCEEDINGS ON A PROPOSAL MADE BY THE DIRECTORS, OR BY THE ADMINISTRATOR, OR BY THE LIQUIDATOR		
Summoning of meetings	1.13	2.29, 15.8, 15.29
The chairman at meetings	1.14	15.21
The chairman as proxy-holder	1.15	16.5
Attendance by company officers	1.16	2.30, 15.14
Voting rights (creditors).	1.17	15.7, 15.29
Procedure for admission of creditors' claims for voting purposes	1.17A	15.33
Voting rights (members).	1.18	2.35
Requisite majorities (creditors).	1.19	15.31
Requisite majorities (members).	1.20	2.36
Proceedings to obtain agreement on the proposal	1.21	Part 15
Resolutions to follow approval	1.22	2.33
Notice of order made under section 4A(6)	1.22A	2.37
Hand-over of property etc to supervisor	1.23	2.39

1986 Rule heading	1986 rule	2016 rule
Report of meetings	1.24	2.38
Revocation or suspension of the arrangement	1.25	2.40
Supervisor's accounts and reports	1.26A	2.41
Production of accounts and records to Secretary of State	1.27	2.42
Fees, costs, charges and expenses	1.28	2.43
Completion of the arrangement	1.29	2.44
CHAPTER 7 EC REGULATION – CONVERSION OF VOLUNTARY ARRANGEMENT INTO WINDING UP		
Application for conversion into winding up	1.31	21.2
Contents of witness statement	1.32	21.2
Power of court	1.33	21.3
CHAPTER 8 EC REGULATION – MEMBER STATE LIQUIDATOR		
Interpretation of creditor and notice to member State liquidator	1.34	21.7, 21.8
CHAPTER 9 OBTAINING A MORATORIUM – PROCEEDINGS DURING A MORATORIUM – NOMINEES – CONSIDERATION OF PROPOSALS WHERE MORATORIUM OBTAINED		
Preparation of proposal by directors and submission to nominee	1.35	
Delivery of documents to the intended nominee etc	1.36	
Statement of affairs	1.37	2.11
The nominee's statement	1.38	2.13
Documents submitted to the court to obtain moratorium	1.39	2.14
Notice and advertisement of beginning of a moratorium	1.40	2.15
Notice of extension of moratorium	1.41	2.16, 2.17
Notice and advertisement of end of moratorium	1.42	2.18, 2.19
Disposal of charged property etc during a moratorium	1.43	2.18, 2.19
Withdrawal of nominee's consent to act	1.44	2.20
Replacement of nominee by the court	1.45	2.22
Notification of appointment of a replacement nominee	1.46	2.23
Applications to court under paragraphs 26 or 27 of Schedule A1 to the Act	1.47	2.24
Summoning of meetings; procedure at meetings etc	1.48	2.25–2.28, 2.30, Part 15
Entitlement to vote (creditors)	1.49	15.28
Procedure for admission of creditors' claims for voting purposes	1.50	15.33
Voting rights (members)	1.51	2.35
Requisite majorities (creditors)	1.52	15.31
Requisite majorities (members) and proceedings to obtain agreement	1.53	2.36, 15.21, 15.25
Implementation of the arrangement	1.54	2.39
CHAPTER 10 TIME RECORDING INFORMATION		
Provision by nominee or supervisor of information about time spent	1.55	2.45
CHAPTER 11 OMISSION OF INFORMATION FROM STATEMENT OF AFFAIRS.		
Omission of Information from Statement of Affairs	1.56	2.7, 2.12
PART 2 ADMINISTRATION PROCEDURE CHAPTER 1 APPLICATION FOR, AND MAKING OF, THE ORDER		
Introductory and interpretation	2.1	
CHAPTER 2 APPOINTMENT OF ADMINISTRATOR BY COURT		
Witness statement in support of administration application	2.2	3.6
Form of application	2.3	3.3, 3.4, 3.5
Contents of application and witness statement in support	2.4	3.6
Filing of application	2.5	3.7, 3.10
Service of application	2.6	3.7, Sch 4, para 3
Notice to officers charged with execution of writs or other process, etc	2.7	3.9
Manner in which service to be effected	2.8	Sch 4
Proof of service	2.9	Sch 4, para 6

1986 Rule heading	1986 rule	2016 rule
Application to appoint specified person as administrator by holder of qualifying floating charge	2.10	3.11
Application where company in liquidation	2.11	3.5
The hearing	2.12	3.11
Contents of court order	2.13	3.13, 3.14
Notice of administration order	2.14	3.15
CHAPTER 3 APPOINTMENT OF ADMINISTRATOR BY HOLDER OF FLOATING CHARGE		
Notice of intention to appoint	2.15	3.16
Notice of appointment	2.16	3.17
	2.17	3.18
	2.18	3.19
	2.19	3.20, 3.21, 3.22
CHAPTER 4 APPOINTMENT OF ADMINISTRATOR BY COMPANY OR DIRECTORS		
Notice of intention to appoint	2.20	3.23
	2.21	3.23
	2.22	3.23
Notice of appointment	2.23	3.24
	2.24	3.24
	2.25	3.25
	2.26	3.27
CHAPTER 5 PROCESS OF ADMINISTRATION		
Notification and advertisement of administrator's appointment	2.27	3.29
Notice requiring statement of affairs	2.28	3.27
Verification and filing	2.29	3.30, 3.31, 3.32
Limited disclosure	2.30	3.44, 3.45, 3.47
Release from duty to submit statement of affairs; extension of time	2.31	3.33, 3.37
Expenses of statement of affairs	2.32	3.34
Administrator's proposals	2.33	3.35, 3.36
Limited disclosure of para 49 statement 15	2.33A	3.45
CHAPTER 6 MEETINGS AND REPORTS		
Meetings to consider administrator's proposals	2.34	3.38, 15.7, 15.12, 15.13
Creditors' meetings generally	2.35	15.8, 15.9, 15.10, 15.23, 15.24, 15.25
The chairman at meetings	2.36	15.21, 16.5
Meeting requisitioned by creditors	2.37	15.18, 15.19
Notice of meetings by advertisement only	2.37A	15.12
Entitlement to vote	2.38	15.28, 15.31, 15.34
Admission and rejection of claims	2.39	15.33, 15.35
Secured creditors	2.40	15.31
Holders of negotiable instruments	2.41	
Hire-purchase, conditional sale and chattel leasing agreements	2.42	15.32
Resolutions	2.43	15.34
Minutes	2.44A	15.40
Revision of the administrator's proposals	2.45	3.42
Notice to creditors	2.46	3.43
Reports to creditors	2.47	18.6–18.10
Correspondence instead of creditors' meetings	2.48	
Creditors' request for further information	2.48A	18.9
Venue and conduct of company meeting	2.49	15.21, 15.25, 15.40, 15.41,
CHAPTER 7 THE CREDITORS' COMMITTEE		
Constitution of committee	2.50	17.3, 17.4
Formalities of establishment	2.51	17.5
Functions and meetings of the committee	2.52	17.2, 17.14
The chairman at meetings	2.53	17.15

1986 Rule heading	1986 rule	2016 rule
Quorum	2.54	17.16
Committee-members' representatives	2.55	17.17
Resignation	2.56	17.10
Termination of membership	2.57	17.11
Removal	2.58	17.12
Vacancies	2.59	17.8
Procedure at meetings	2.60	17.18
Resolutions of creditors' committee otherwise than at a meeting	2.61	17.19
Information from administrator	2.62	17.22
Expenses of members	2.63	17.24
Members' dealing with the company	2.64	17.25
Formal defects	2.65	17.27
CHAPTER 8 DISPOSAL OF CHARGED PROPERTY		
Disposal of charged property	2.66	3.49
CHAPTER 9 EXPENSES OF THE ADMINISTRATION		
Expenses of the administration	2.67	3.51
Pre-administration costs	2.67A	3.52
CHAPTER 10 DISTRIBUTIONS TO CREDITORS		
	2.68	14.28, 14.27, 14.38
Debts of insolvent company to rank equally	2.69	14.12
Supplementary provisions as to dividend	2.70	14.39
Division of unsold assets	2.71	14.13
Proving a debt	2.72	14.3, 14.4
Costs of proving	2.74	14.5
Administrator to allow inspection of proofs	2.75	14.6
New administrator appointed	2.76	3.70
Admission and rejection of proofs for dividend	2.77	14.7
Appeal against decision on proof	2.78	14.8, 14.9
Withdrawal or variation of proof	2.79	14.10
Expunging of proof by the court	2.80	14.11
Estimate of quantum	2.81	14.14
Negotiable instruments, etc	2.82	
Secured creditors	2.83	14.19
Discounts	2.84	14.20
Mutual credits and set-off	2.85	14.24
Debt in foreign currency	2.86	14.21
Payments of a periodical nature	2.87	14.22
Interest	2.88	14.23
Debt payable at future time	2.89	14.44
Value of security	2.90	14.15
Surrender for non-disclosure	2.91	14.16
Redemption by administrator	2.92	14.17
Test of security's value	2.93	14.18
Realisation of security by creditor	2.94	14.19
Notice of proposed distribution	2.95	14.26, 14.28, 14.29, 14.30
Admission or rejection of proofs	2.96	14.32
Postponement or cancellation of dividend	2.96A	14.33
Declaration of dividend	2.97	14.34
Notice of declaration of a dividend	2.98	14.35
Payments of dividends and related matters	2.99	14.35
Notice of no dividend, or no further dividend	2.100	14.37
Proof altered after payment of dividend	2.101	14.40
rule 2102 Secured creditors	2.102	14.41

1986 Rule heading	1986 rule	2016 rule
Disqualification from dividend	2.103	14.42
Assignment of right to dividend	2.104	14.43
Debt payable at future time	2.105	14.44
CHAPTER 11 THE ADMINISTRATOR		
Fixing of remuneration	2.106	18.16, 18.17, 18.18, 18.23
Recourse to meeting of creditors	2.107	18.24, 18.25
Recourse to the court	2.108	18.24–18.29
Creditors' claim that remuneration is or other expenses are excessive	2.109	18.34, 18.36, 18.37
Review of remuneration	2.109A	18.29
Remuneration of new administrator	2.109B	18.31
Apportionment of set fee remuneration	2.109C	18.32
CHAPTER 12 ENDING ADMINISTRATION		
Final progress reports	2.110	3.56, 18.3
Notice of automatic end of administration	2.111	3.55
Applications for extension of administration	2.112	3.54
Notice of end of administration	2.113	3.56
Application to court by administrator	2.114	3.57
Application to court by creditor	2.115	3.58
Notification by administrator of court order	2.116	3.59
Moving from administration to creditors' voluntary liquidation	2.117A	3.60
Moving from administration to dissolution	2.118	3.61
CHAPTER 13 REPLACING ADMINISTRATOR		
Grounds for resignation	2.119	3.62
Notice of intention to resign	2.120	3.63
Notice of resignation	2.121	3.64
Application to court to remove administrator from office	2.122	3.65
Notice of vacation of office when administrator ceases to be qualified to act	2.123	3.66
Administrator deceased	2.124	3.67
Application to replace	2.125	3.68
Notification and advertisement of appointment of replacement administrator	2.126	3.69
Notification and advertisement of appointment of joint administrator	2.127	3.69
	2.128	3.69
Administrator's duties on vacating office	2.129	3.70
CHAPTER 14 EC REGULATION: CONVERSION OF ADMINISTRATION INTO WINDING UP		
Application for conversion into winding up	2.130	21.2
Contents of witness statement	2.131	21.2
Power of court	2.132	21.3
CHAPTER 15 EC REGULATION: MEMBER STATE LIQUIDATOR		
Interpretation of creditor and notice to member State liquidator	2.133	21.8
PART 3 ADMINISTRATIVE RECEIVERSHIP **CHAPTER 1 APPOINTMENT OF ADMINISTRATIVE RECEIVER**		
Acceptance of appointment	3.1	4.1
Notice and advertisement of appointment	3.2	4.5
CHAPTER 2 STATEMENT OF AFFAIRS AND REPORT TO CREDITORS		
Notice requiring statement of affairs	3.3	4.6
Verification and filing	3.4	4.7, 4.8, 4.9
Limited disclosure	3.5	4.12
Release from duty to submit statement of affairs; extension of time	3.6	4.10
Expenses of statement of affairs	3.7	4.11
Report to creditors	3.8	4.13, 4.14
CHAPTER 3 CREDITORS' MEETING		

1986 Rule heading	1986 rule	2016 rule
Procedure for summoning meeting under s 48(2)	3.9	15.8, 15.9, 15.10
The chairman at the meeting	3.10	15.21
Voting rights	3.11	15.8, 15.28
Contents of claim	3.11A	1.2
Admission and rejection of claim	3.12	15.31, 15.33
Adjournment	3.14	15.23
Resolutions and minutes	3.15	15.34, 15.40
CHAPTER 4 THE CREDITORS' COMMITTEE		
Constitution of committee	3.16	17.3, 17.4
Formalities of establishment	3.17	17.5
Functions and meetings of the committee	3.18	17.14
The chairman at meetings	3.19	17.15
Quorum	3.20	17.16
Committee-members' representatives	3.21	17.17
Resignation	3.22	17.10
Termination of membership	3.23	17.11
Removal	3.24	17.12
Vacancies	3.25	17.8
Procedure at meetings	3.26	17.18
Resolutions by post	3.27	17.19
Information from receiver	3.28	17.22
Expenses of members	3.29	17.24
Members' dealings with the company	3.30	17.26
Formal defects	3.30A	17.27
CHAPTER 5 THE ADMINISTRATIVE RECEIVER (MISCELLANEOUS)		
Disposal of charged property	3.31	4.16
Abstract of receipts and payments	3.32	4.17
Resignation	3.33	4.18
Receiver deceased	3.34	4.19
Vacation of office	3.35	4.20, 4.21
CHAPTER 7 SECTION 176A THE REVISED PART		
Report for creditors	3.39	4.22, 4.23
Receiver to deal with prescribed part	3.40	4.24
PART 4 COMPANIES WINDING UP CHAPTER 1 THE SCHEME OF THIS PART OF THE RULES		
Voluntary winding up; winding up by the court	4.1	6.1
Winding up by the court: the various forms of petition	4.2	
Time-limits	4.3	
CHAPTER 2 THE STATUTORY DEMAND (NO CVL APPLICATION)		
Preliminary	4.4	7.2
Form and content of statutory demand	4.5	7.3
Information to be given in statutory demand	4.6	7.3
CHAPTER 3 PETITION TO WINDING-UP ORDER (NO CVL APPLICATION) (NO APPLICATION TO PETITION BY CONTRIBUTORIES)		
Injunction to restrain presentation or advertisement of petition	4.6A	7.24
Presentation and filing of petition	4.7	7.7
Service of petition	4.8	Sch 4, para 2
Proof of service	4.9A	Sch 4, para 6
Other persons to receive copies of petition	4.10	7.9
Advertisement of petition	4.11	7.10
Verification of petition	4.12	7.6
Persons entitled to copy of petition	4.13	7.11
Certificate of compliance	4.14	7.12
Leave for petitioner to withdraw	4.15	7.13
Notice of appearance	4.16	7.14

1986 Rule heading	1986 rule	2016 rule
List of appearances	4.17	7.15
Affidavit in opposition	4.18	7.16
Adjournment	4.18A	7.19
Substitution of creditor or contributory for petitioner	4.19	7.17
Notice and settling of winding-up order	4.20	7.21
Transmission and advertisement of order	4.21	7.22
Expenses of voluntary arrangement	4.21A	
Petition dismissed	4.21B	7.23
CHAPTER 4 PETITION BY CONTRIBUTORIES (NO CVL APPLICATION)		
Presentation and service of petition	4.22	7.29, Sch 4, para 2
Return of petition	4.23	7.31
Application of Rules in Chapter 3	4.24	
CHAPTER 5 PROVISIONAL LIQUIDATOR (NO CVL APPLICATION)		
Appointment of provisional liquidator	4.25	7.33
Notice of appointment	4.25A	7.36
Order of appointment	4.26	7.35
Deposit	4.27	7.34
Security	4.28	7.37
Failure to give or keep up security	4.29	7.37
Remuneration	4.30	7.38, 18.16, 18.20
Termination of appointment	4.31	7.39
CHAPTER 6 STATEMENT OF AFFAIRS AND OTHER INFORMATION		
Notice requiring statement of affairs	4.32	7.40
Verification and filing	4.33	7.41
Statement of affairs	4.34	6.2, 6.3, 6.4, 6.5
Copy statement of affairs	4.34A	
Limited disclosure	4.35	6.6, 7.43
Release from duty to submit statement of affairs; extension of time	4.36	7.44
Expenses of statement of affairs	4.37	7.45
Expenses of statement of affairs	4.38	6.7,
Submission of accounts	4.39	7.46
Submission of accounts	4.40	6.8
Expenses of preparing accounts	4.41	6.9
Further disclosure	4.42	7.47
CHAPTER 7 INFORMATION TO CREDITORS AND CONTRIBUTORIES		
Reports by official receiver	4.43	7.48
Meaning of "creditors"	4.44	1.37
Report where statement of affairs lodged	4.45	7.48
Statement of affairs dispensed with	4.46	7.48
General rule as to reporting	4.47	7.48
Winding up stayed	4.48	7.51, 7.52
Information to creditors and contributories	4.49	6.15
Further information where liquidation follows administration	4.49A	6.16, 7.50
Reports to creditors and members — winding up by the court	4.49B	18.3, 18.8
CVL Progress reports — voluntary winding up	4.49C	18.3, 18.7
Final report to creditors	4.49D	18.14
Creditors' and members' request for further information	4.49E	18.9
Arrangements under s 110 (acceptance of shares, etc, as consideration	4.49F	18.11
Other distributions to members in specie	4.49G	18.12
CHAPTER 8 MEETINGS OF CREDITORS AND CONTRIBUTORIES		
First meetings	4.50	7.52, 15.8, 15.11
First meeting of creditors	4.51	15.8
Business at first meetings in the liquidation	4.52	15.9

1986 Rule heading	1986 rule	2016 rule
Business at meeting under s 95 or 98	4.53	
Effect of adjournment on company meeting	4.53A	
Report by director, etc	4.53B	6.17
Additional contents of notices gazetted or advertised under s 95	4.53C	15.8
Additional contents of notices gazetted or advertised under s 98	4.53D	15.8
General power to call meetings	4.54	1.51, 15.3, 15.6
The chairman at meetings	4.55	15.21, 15.22
The chairman at meeting	4.56	15.21, 15.22
Requisitioned meetings	4.57	15.18, 15.19
Attendance at meetings of company's personnel	4.58	15.14, 15.22
Notice of meetings by advertisement only	4.59	15.12
Venue	4.60	15.10
Expenses of summoning meetings	4.61	15.19
Expenses of meeting under s 98	4.62	
Resolutions	4.63	6.18, 15.34, 15.39
Resolutions by correspondence	4.63A	15.3
Chairman of meeting as proxy-holder	4.64	16.5
Suspension and adjournment	4.65	15.23, 15.25, 15.26
Entitlement to vote (creditors)	4.67	15.28
Chairman's discretion to allow vote	4.68	15.28
Entitlement to vote (contributories)	4.69	15.39
Admission and rejection of proof (creditors' meeting)	4.70	15.33
Record of proceedings	4.71	15.40
Additional provisions as regards certain meetings	4.72	5.3, 15.17
CHAPTER 9 PROOF OF DEBTS IN A LIQUIDATION		
Meaning of "prove"	4.73	1.2, 14.3
Supply of forms	4.74	
Contents of proof	4.75	14.4
Particulars of creditor's claim	4.76	
Cost of proving	4.78	14.5
Liquidator to allow inspection of proofs	4.79	14.6
Transmission of proofs to liquidator	4.80	7.60
New liquidator appointed	4.81	7.73
Admission and rejection of proofs for dividend	4.82	14.7
Appeal against decision on proof	4.83	14.8, 14.9
Withdrawal or variation of proof	4.84	14.10
Expunging of proof by the court	4.85	14.11
Estimate of quantum	4.86	14.14
Negotiable instruments, etc	4.87	
Secured creditors	4.88	14.19
Discounts	4.89	14.20
Mutual credit and set-off	4.90	14.25
Debt in foreign currency	4.91	14.21
Payments of a periodical nature	4.92	14.22
Interest	4.93	14.23
Debt payable at future time	4.94	14.44
CHAPTER 10 SECURED CREDITORS		
Value of security	4.95	14.15
Surrender for non-disclosure	4.96	14.16
Redemption by liquidator	4.97	14.17
Test of security's value	4.98	14.18
Realisation of security by creditor	4.99	14.19
CHAPTER 11 THE LIQUIDATOR		

1986 Rule heading	1986 rule	2016 rule
Appointment by creditors or contributories	4.100	7.53
Appointment by creditors or by the company	4.101	6.20
Power to fill vacancy in office of liquidator	4.101A	6.21
Official Receiver not to be appointed liquidator	4.101B	
Appointment by the court	4.102	7.56
Appointment by the court	4.103	6.22
Appointment by Secretary of State	4.104	7.57
Authentication of liquidator's appointment	4.105	
Appointment to be gazetted and registered	4.106A	7.59
Hand-over of assets to liquidator	4.107	7.60
Creditors' meeting to receive liquidator's resignation	4.108	6.25, 7.61
Resignation (application under Rule 4.131)	4.108A	
Action following acceptance of resignation	4.109	
Action following acceptance of resignation	4.110	
Leave to resign granted by the court	4.111	
Advertisement of resignation	4.112	
Meeting of creditors to remove liquidator	4.113	7.63
Meeting of creditors to remove liquidator	4.114	15.7(3)
Court's power to regulate meetings under Rules 4.113, 4.114-CVL	4.115	
Procedure on removal	4.116	7.64
Procedure on removal	4.117	6.26
Advertisement of removal	4.118	
Removal of liquidator by the court	4.119	7.65
Removal of liquidator by the court	4.120	6.27
Release of resigning or removed liquidator	4.121	7.69
Release of resigning or removed liquidator	4.122	6.33
Removal of liquidator by Secretary of State	4.123	7.66
Release of official receiver	4.124	7.70
Final meeting	4.125	7.69, 7.71, 18.14
Rule as to reporting	4.125A	7.72
Final meeting	4.126	6.28. 18.14
Final meeting	4.126A	5.9, 5.10, 18.14
Fixing of remuneration	4.127	18.16, 18.19, 18.20
Liquidator's entitlement to remuneration where it is not fixed under Rule 4.127	4.127A	18.22
Liquidator's remuneration where he realises assets on behalf of chargeholder	4.127B	18.38
Other matters affecting remuneration	4.128	18.17
Recourse of liquidator to meeting of creditors	4.129A	18.24
Recourse to the court	4.130	18.23
Creditors' claim that remuneration is excessive	4.131	18.28, 18.34
Review of remuneration	4.131A	18.29
Remuneration of new liquidator	4.131B	18.31
Apportionment of set fee remuneration	4.131C	18.32
Liquidator deceased	4.132	7.67
Liquidator deceased	4.133	6.29
Loss of qualification as insolvency practitioner	4.134	7.68
Loss of qualification as insolvency practitioner	4.135	6.30
Vacation of office on making of winding-up order	4.136	6.31
Notice to official receiver of intention to vacate office	4.137	7.62
Liquidator's duties on vacating office	4.138	6.32, 7.73
Appointment by the company	4.139	5.2
Appointment by the court	4.140	5.4
Authentication of liquidator's appointment	4.141	

1986 Rule heading	1986 rule	2016 rule
Company meeting to receive liquidator's resignation	4.142	5.6, 5.8
Removal of liquidator by the court	4.143	5.7
Release of resigning or removed liquidator	4.144	5.14
Liquidator deceased	4.145	5.11,
Loss of qualification as insolvency practitioner	4.146	5.12
Vacation of office on making of winding-up order	4.147	5.14
Liquidator's duties on vacating office	4.148	5.13
Remuneration of liquidator in members' voluntary winding up	4.148A	18.16, 18.19
Members' claim that remuneration is excessive	4.148C	18.34
Remuneration of new liquidator	4.148D	18.31
Apportionment of fixed fee remuneration	4.148E	18.32
Power of court to set aside certain transactions	4.149	5.15, 6.34, 7.74
Rule against solicitation	4.150	5.16, 6.35, 7.75
CHAPTER 12 THE LIQUIDATION COMMITTEE		
Preliminary	4.151	
Membership of committee	4.152	17.3
Formalities of establishment	4.153	17.5
Committee established by contributories	4.154	17.6
Obligations of liquidator to committee	4.155	17.21
Meetings of the committee	4.156	17.12
The chairman at meetings	4.157	17.13
Quorum	4.158	17.14
Committee-members' representatives	4.159	17.15
Resignation	4.160	17.8
Termination of membership	4.161	17.9
Removal	4.162	17.10
Vacancy (creditor members)	4.163	17.8
Vacancy (contributory members)	4.164	17.9
Voting rights and resolutions	4.165	17.18
Voting rights and resolutions	4.166	17.18
Resolutions by post	4.167	17.19
Liquidator's reports	4.168	17.21
Expenses of members, etc	4.169	17.24
Dealings by committee-members and others	4.170	17.25
Composition of committee when creditors paid in full	4.171A	17.13
Committee's functions vested in Secretary of State	4.172	17.28
Formal defects	4.172A	17.27
CHAPTER 13 THE LIQUIDATION COMMITTEE WHERE WINDING UP FOLLOWS IMMEDIATELY ON ADMINISTRATION (NO CVL APPLICATION)		
Preliminary	4.173	17.29
Continuation of creditors' committee	4.174A	17.29
Liquidator's certificate	4.176	17.29
Obligations of liquidator to committee	4.177	17.23
Application of Chapter 12	4.178	17.29
CHAPTER 14 COLLECTION AND DISTRIBUTION OF COMPANY'S ASSETS BY LIQUIDATOR		
General duties of liquidator	4.179	7.76
Manner of distributing assets	4.180	14.27
Debts of insolvent company to rank equally	4.181	14.12
Supplementary provisions as to dividend	4.182	14.39, 14.40, 14.45
Distribution in members' voluntary winding up	4.182A	14.28
Division of unsold assets	4.183	14.13
General powers of liquidator	4.184	6.36, 7.77
Enforced delivery up of company's property	4.185	7.78
Final distribution	4.186	14.36, 14.37, 14.38
CHAPTER 15 DISCLAIMER		

1986 Rule heading	1986 rule	2016 rule
Liquidator's notice of disclaimer	4.187	19.1, 19.2
Communication of disclaimer to persons interested	4.188	19.3, 19.4
Additional notices	4.189	19.6
Records	4.190A	19.7
Application to interested party under s 178(5)	4.191A	19.9
Interest in property to be declared on request	4.192	
Disclaimer presumed valid and effective	4.193	19.10
Application for exercise of court's powers under s 181	4.194	19.11
CHAPTER 16 SETTLEMENT OF LIST OF CONTRIBUTORIES (NO CVL APPLICATION)		
Preliminary	4.195	7.79
Duty of liquidator to settle list	4.196	7.79, 7.80
Form of list	4.197	7.81
Procedure for settling list	4.198	7.82
Application to court for variation of the list	4.199	7.83
Variation of, or addition to, the list	4.200	7.84
Costs not to fall on official receiver	4.201	7.85
CHAPTER 17 CALLS (NO CVL APPLICATION)		
Calls by liquidator	4.202	7.86
Control by liquidation committee	4.203	7.87
Application to court for leave to make a call	4.204	7.88, 7.99
Making and enforcement of the call	4.205	7.90, 7.91
CHAPTER 18 SPECIAL MANAGER		
Appointment and remuneration	4.206	5.17, 6.37, 7.93
Security	4.207	5.18, 6.38, 7.94
Failure to give or keep up security	4.208	5.19, 6.39, 7.95
Accounting	4.209	5.20, 6.40, 7.96
Termination of appointment	4.210	5.21, 6.41, 7.97
CHAPTER 19 PUBLIC EXAMINATION OF COMPANY OFFICERS AND OTHERS		
Order for public examination	4.211	7.98, 7.102
Notice of hearing	4.212	7.103
Order on request by creditors or contributories	4.213	7.99, 7.100. 7.101
Witness unfit for examination	4.214	7.104
Procedure at hearing	4.215	7.105
Adjournment	4.216	7.106
Expenses of examination	4.217	7.107
CHAPTER 20 ORDER OF PAYMENT OF COSTS, ETC, OUT OF ASSETS		
General rule as to priority	4.218	6.42, 7.108
Litigation expenses and property subject to a floating charge — general provisions	4.218A	6.44, 7.111, 7.112
Litigation expenses and property subject to a floating charge — requirement for approval or authorisation	4.218B	6.45, 7.113
Litigation expenses and property subject to a floating charge — request for approval or authorisation	4.218C	6.46, 7.114
Litigation expenses and property subject to a floating charge — grant of approval or authorisation	4.218D	6.47, 7.115
Litigation expenses and property subject to a floating charge — application to court by the liquidator	4.218E	6.48, 7.116
Winding up commencing as voluntary	4.219	7.109
Saving for powers of the court	4.220	6.43, 7.110
CHAPTER 21 MISCELLANEOUS RULES		
Application to court for order authorising return	4.221	7.117
Procedure for return	4.222	7.118
Secretary of State's directions under ss203, 205	4.224	7.119
Procedure following appeal under s203(4) or 205(4)	4.225	7.119
CHAPTER 22 LEAVE TO ACT AS DIRECTOR, ETC., OF COMPANY WITH PROHIBITED NAME (SECTION 216 OF THE ACT)		

1986 Rule heading	1986 rule	2016 rule
Preliminary	4.226	22.1
Application for leave under s216(3)	4.227A	22.3
First excepted case	4.228	22.4, 22.5
Second excepted case	4.229	22.6
Third excepted case	4.230	22.7
CHAPTER 23 EC REGULATION–MEMBER STATE LIQUIDATOR		
Interpretation of creditor and notice to member State liquidator	4.231	21.9, 21.10
THE THIRD GROUP OF PARTS PART 7 COURT PROCEDURE AND PRACTICE CHAPTER 1 APPLICATIONS		
Preliminary	7.1	12.5
Form and contents of application	7.3	1.35
Application under section 176A(5) to disapply section 176A	7.3A	12.14
Filing and service of application	7.4	12.7 12.9, 12.10
Notice of application under section 176A(5)	7.4A	12.15
Hearings without notice	7.5A	12.12
Hearing of application	7.6A	12.2(3)
Witness statements–general	7.7A	12.28
Filing and service of witness statements	7.8	12.28
Use of reports	7.9	12.28
Adjournment of hearing; directions	7.10	12.9, 12.13
CHAPTER 1ZA THE LONDON INSOLVENCY DISTRICT		
Allocation of proceedings to the London insolvency district	7.10ZA	12.5
CHAPTER 1A BLOCK TRANSFER OF CASES WHERE INSOLVENCY PRACTITIONER		
Preliminary and interpretation	7.10A	12.35
Power to make a block transfer order	7.10B	12.36
Application for a block transfer order	7.10C	12.37
Action following application for a block transfer order	7.10D	12.38
CHAPTER 2 TRANSFER OF PROCEEDINGS BETWEEN COURTS		
General power of transfer	7.11	12.30
Proceedings commenced in wrong court	7.12	12.31
Applications for transfer	7.13	12.32
Procedure following order for transfer	7.14	12.33
Consequential transfer of other proceedings	7.15	12.34
CHAPTER 3 SHORTHAND WRITERS		
Nomination and appointment of shorthand writers	7.16	12.65
Remuneration	7.17	12.65
CHAPTER 4 ENFORCEMENT PROCEDURES		
Enforcement of court orders	7.19	12.51
Orders enforcing compliance with the Rules	7.20	12.52
Warrants (general provisions)	7.21	12.53
Warrants under ss134, 364	7.22	12.54
Warrants under ss236, 366	7.23	12.55
Warrants under s365	7.25	12.56
CHAPTER 5 COURT RECORDS AND RETURNS		
Court file	7.31A	12.39
CHAPTER 6 COSTS AND TAXATION		
Application of Chapter	7.33A	12.41
Requirement to assess costs by the detailed procedure	7.34A	12.42
Procedure where detailed assessment required	7.35	12.43
Costs of officers charged with execution of writs or other process	7.36	12.44
Petitions presented by insolvents	7.37A	12.45
Costs paid otherwise than out of the insolvent estate	7.38	12.46
Award of costs against official receiver or responsible insolvency practitioner	7.39	12.47

1986 Rule heading	1986 rule	2016 rule
Applications for costs	7.40	12.48
Costs and expenses of witnesses	7.41	12.49
Final costs certificate	7.42	12.50
CHAPTER 7 PERSONS WHO LACK CAPACITY TO MANAGE THEIR AFFAIRS		
Introductory	7.43	12.23
Appointment of another person to act	7.44	12.24
Witness statement in support of application	7.45A	12.25
Service of notices following appointment	7.46	12.26
CHAPTER 8 APPEALS IN INSOLVENCY PROCEEDINGS		
Appeals and reviews of court orders (winding up).	7.47	12.59
Appeals in bankruptcy	7.48	12.60
Procedure on appeal	7.49A	12.58, 12.61
Appeal against decision of Secretary of State or official receiver	7.50	12.62
CHAPTER 9 GENERAL		
Principal court rules and practice to apply	7.51A	12.1
Right of audience	7.52	13.1(2)
Formal defects	7.55	12.65
Service of orders staying proceedings	7.56	Sch 4, para 5
Payment into court	7.59	
Further information and disclosure	7.60	12.27
Office copies of documents	7.61	12.40
CHAPTER 10 EC REGULATION – CREDITORS' VOLUNTARY WINDING UP–CONFIRMATION BY THE COURT		
Application for confirmation	7.62	21.4, 21.5
Notice to Member State liquidator and creditors in member states	7.63	21.6
CHAPTER 11 EC REGULATION – MEMBER STATE LIQUIDATOR		
Interpretation of creditor	7.64	
PART 8 PROXIES AND COMPANY REPRESENTATION		
Definition of "proxy"	8.1	16.2
Issue and use of forms	8.2	16.3, 16.4
Use of proxies at meeting	8.3	16.4, 16.5
Retention of proxies	8.4	16.6
Right of inspection	8.5	16.6
Proxy-holder with financial interest	8.6	16.7
Company representation	8.7	16.8
Interpretation of creditor	8.8	
PART 9 EXAMINATION OF PERSONS CONCERNED IN COMPANY AND INDIVIDUAL INSOLVENCY		
Preliminary	9.1	12.17
Form and contents of application	9.2	12.18
Order for examination, etc	9.3	12.19
Procedure for examination	9.4	12.20
Record of examination	9.5	12.21
Costs of proceedings under ss236, 366	9.6	12.22
PART 10 OFFICIAL RECEIVERS		
Appointment of official receivers	10.1	13.1
Persons entitled to act on official receiver's behalf	10.2	13.3
Application for directions	10.3	13.4
Official receiver's expenses	10.4	13.5
PART 11 DECLARATION AND PAYMENT OF DIVIDEND (WINDING UP AND BANKRUPTCY)		
Preliminary		
Notice of intended dividend	11.2	14.28
Final admission/rejection of proofs	11.3	14.32
Postponement or cancellation of dividend	11.4	14.33

1986 Rule heading	1986 rule	2016 rule
Decision to declare dividend	11.5	14.34
Notice of declaration	11.6	14.35
Notice of no, or no further, dividend	11.7	14.37
Proof altered after payment of dividend	11.8	14.40
Secured creditors	11.9	14.41
Disqualification from dividend	11.10	14.42
Assignment of right to dividend	11.11	14.43
Preferential creditors	11.12	14.28(2), 14.29(2)
Debt payable at future time	11.13	14.44
PART 12 MISCELLANEOUS AND GENERAL		
Power of Secretary of State to regulate certain matters	12.1	0.5
Costs, expenses, etc	12.2	3.50, 6.42, 7.108, 10.147
Provable debts	12.3	14.2
False claim of status as creditor, etc	12.18	1.56
Punishment of offences	12.21	0.6
PART 12A PROVISIONS OF GENERAL EFFECT CHAPTER 1 THE GIVING OF NOTICE AND THE SUPPLY OF DOCUMENTS — GENERAL		
Application	12A.1	
Personal delivery of documents	12A.2	1.44
Postal delivery of documents	12A.3	1.42
Non-receipt of notice of meeting	12A.4	
Notice etc to solicitors	12A.5	1.40
CHAPTER 2 THE GIVING OF NOTICE AND THE SUPPLY OF DOCUMENTS BY OR TO OFFICE-HOLDERS		
Application	12A.6	
The form of notices and other documents	12A.7	1.4
Proof of sending etc	12A.8	1.52
Authentication	12A.9	1.5
Electronic delivery in insolvency proceedings — general	12A.10	1.45
Electronic delivery by office-holders	12A.11	1.48
Use of websites by office-holder	12A.12	1.47, 1.49
Special provision on account of expense as to website use	12A.13	1.49, 1.50
Electronic delivery of insolvency proceedings to courts	12A.14	1.46
Notice etc to joint office-holders	12A.15	1.41
CHAPTER 3 SERVICE OF COURT DOCUMENTS		
Application	12A.16	
Application of CPR Part 6 to service of court documents within the jurisdiction	12A.17	Sch 4, para 1
Service of orders staying proceedings	12A.18	Sch 4, para 5
Service on joint office-holders	12A.19	Sch 4, para 4
Application of CPR Part 6 to service of court documents outside the jurisdiction	12A.20	Sch 4, para 1
CHAPTER 4 MEETINGS		
Quorum at meeting of creditors or contributories	12A.21	15.20
Remote attendance at meetings of creditors	12A.22	15.6(6)
Action where person excluded	12A.23	15.36, 15.44
Indication to excluded person	12A.24	15.37, 15.45
Complaint	12A.25	15.38, 15.46
Remote attendance at meetings of creditors' committees and liquidation	12A.26	17.20
Procedure for requests that a place for a meeting should be specified 794	12A.27	17.21
CHAPTER 5 EFFECT OF INSOLVENCY ON EXECUTION — SPECIFIC PROVISIONS FOR NOTICES TO ENFORCEMENT OFFICERS ETC		
Execution overtaken by judgment debtor's insolvency	12A.28	12.57
Notice to enforcement officers	12A.29	1.47

1986 Rule heading	1986 rule	2016 rule
CHAPTER 6 FORMS		
Forms for use in insolvency proceedings	12A.30	
Electronic submission of information instead of submission of forms	12A.31	
Electronic submission of information instead of submission of forms	12A.32	
CHAPTER 7 GAZETTE NOTICES		
Contents of notices to be gazetted under the Act or Rules	12A.33	1.10
Gazette notices relating to companies	12A.34	1.12
Gazette notices relating to bankrupts	12A.35	1.13
Omission of unobtainable information	12A.36	1.10(2)
The Gazette — general	12A.37	1.14
CHAPTER 8 NOTICES ADVERTISED OTHERWISE THAN IN THE GAZETTE		
Notices otherwise advertised under the Act or Rules	12A.38	1.15
Non-Gazette notices relating to companies	12A.39	1.16
Non-Gazette notices relating to bankrupts	12A.40	1.17
Non-Gazette notices — other provisions	12A.41	1.18
CHAPTER 9 NOTIFICATIONS TO THE REGISTRAR OF COMPANIES		
Application of this Chapter	12A.42	1.19
Information to be contained in all notifications to the registrar	12A.43	1.20, 1.21
Notifications relating to the office of office-holders	12A.44	1.22
Notifications relating to documents	12A.45	1.23
Notifications relating to court orders	12A.46	1.24
Returns or reports of meetings	12A.47	1.25, 1.26
Notifications relating to other events	12A.48	1.27
Notifications of more than one nature	12A.49	1.19
Notifications made to other persons at the same time	12A.50	1.19
CHAPTER 10 INSPECTION OF DOCUMENTS AND THE PROVISION OF INFORMATION		
Confidentiality of documents — grounds for refusing inspection	12A.51	1.58
Right to copy documents	12A.52	12.39, 12.40, 12.54
Charges for copy documents	12A.53	1.55
Right to have list of creditors	12A.54	1.57
CHAPTER 11 COMPUTATION OF TIME AND TIME LIMITS		
Time limits	12A.55	1.3, Sch 5
CHAPTER 12 SECURITY		
Insolvency practitioners' security	12A.56	4.4, 5.5, 6.24, 7.37, 7.58, 10.52, 10.69
CHAPTER 13 NOTICE OF ORDER UNDER SECTION 176A(5)		
Notice of order under section 176A(5)	12A.57	12.15
PART 13 INTERPRETATION AND APPLICATION		
Introductory	13.1	
"The court"; "the registrar".	13.2	1.2
"Give notice", etc	13.3	
Notice, etc to solicitors	13.4	
Notice to joint liquidators, joint trustees, etc	13.5	
"Venue".	13.6	1.2
"Insolvency proceedings".	13.7	
"Insolvent estate".	13.8	1.2
"Responsible insolvency practitioner", etc	13.9	
"Office holder"	13.9A	1.2
"Petitioner".	13.10	1.2
"The appropriate fee".	13.11	
"Debt", "liability" (winding up).	13.12	14.1
"Authorised deposit-taker and former authorised deposit-taker"	13.12A	1.2
Expressions used generally	13.13	1.2

1986 Rule heading	1986 rule	2016 rule
Application	13.14	0.3
Application of Insolvency Act 1986 and Company Directors Disqualification Act 1986	13.15	
SCHEDULES		
Schedule 1 Scheme Manager's Voting Rights		15.29, 15.30, 15.31, 15.32
Schedule 4 Forms		
Schedule 5 Punishment of Offences under the Rules		Sch 3
Schedule 6 Determination of Insolvency Office Holder's Remuneration		Sch 11

REPORTING ON PAYMENT PRACTICES AND PERFORMANCE REGULATIONS 2017

(SI 2017/395)

NOTES

Made: 15 March 2017.

Authority: Small Business, Enterprise and Employment Act 2015, ss 3(1), (2), (4), (5), (7) and 161(2).

Commencement: 6 April 2017.

Application of these Regulations: note that these Regulations cease to have effect on 6 April 2024 (see reg 1 *post*).

Modification: these Regulations are applied and modified in relation to LLPs, by the Limited Liability Partnerships (Reporting on Payment Practices and Performance) Regulations 2017, SI 2017/425 at **[10.1181]**.

ARRANGEMENT OF REGULATIONS

[10.1169]

1 Citation and commencement

(1) These Regulations may be cited as the Reporting on Payment Practices and Performance Regulations 2017.

(2) These Regulations come into force on 6th April 2017.

(3) These Regulations cease to have effect on 6th April 2024.

NOTES

Note that these Regulations cease to have effect on 6 April 2024 (see above).

[10.1170]

2 Interpretation

In these Regulations—

"the 2006 Act" means the Companies Act 2006;

"director" includes any person occupying the position of director, by whatever name called;

"filing period" means 30 days beginning with the day after the last day of the reporting period to which a report relates;

"financial year" means a company's financial year determined in accordance with sections 390 to 392 of the 2006 Act;

"qualifying company" has the meaning given in regulation 5;

"qualifying contract" has the meaning given in regulation 6;

"reporting period" means a period determined in accordance with regulation 7.

NOTES

Note that these Regulations cease to have effect on 6 April 2024 (see reg 1 *ante*).

[10.1171]

3 Duty to publish information on payment practices, policies and performance

(1) For each reporting period, a qualifying company must publish a report containing the information set out in the Schedule.

(2) For the purposes of paragraph (1), to publish a report a qualifying company must publish it—

(a) within the filing period, and

(b) on the web-based service provided for the purposes of these Regulations by or on behalf of the Secretary of State.

NOTES

Note that these Regulations cease to have effect on 6 April 2024 (see reg 1 *ante*).

[10.1172]

4 Approval of the information

A qualifying company's information for a reporting period must be approved by a director of that company before it is published.

NOTES

Note that these Regulations cease to have effect on 6 April 2024 (see reg 1 *ante*).

[10.1173]

5 Companies to which the duty applies

(1) These Regulations apply to a company in relation to every financial year in which it is a qualifying company.

(2) A company is not a qualifying company in—

(a) its first financial year;

(b) a financial year which began before 6th April 2017.

(3) A company other than a parent company is a qualifying company—

(a) in its second financial year if on its last balance sheet date before that financial year it exceeded two or all three of the general thresholds;

(b) in a subsequent financial year if on both of the relevant balance sheet dates it exceeded two or all three of the general thresholds.

(4) A parent company is a qualifying company—

(a) in its second financial year if on its last balance sheet date before that financial year—

(i) it exceeded two or all three of the general thresholds, and

(ii) the group headed by it exceeded two or all three of the group thresholds;

(b) in a subsequent financial year if on both of the relevant balance sheet dates—

(i) it exceeded two or all three of the general thresholds, and

(ii) the group headed by it exceeded two or all three of the group thresholds.

(5) In this regulation—

(a) "balance sheet date" means the date as at which the company's balance sheet was made up;

(b) the "general thresholds" are the maximum figures for a company's turnover, balance sheet total and number of employees set out in subsection (3) of section 465 of the 2006 Act (companies qualifying as medium-sized: general), determined in accordance with subsections (4) to (6) of that section;

(c) "group" means a parent company and its subsidiary undertakings;

(d) the "group thresholds" are the maximum figures for a group's turnover, balance sheet total and number of employees set out in subsection (4) of section 466 of the 2006 Act (companies qualifying as medium-sized: parent companies), determined in accordance with subsections (5) to (7) of that section;

(e) "parent company" has the meaning given in section 1173 of the 2006 Act;

(f) the "relevant balance sheet dates" are—

(i) the company's last balance sheet date before the relevant financial year, and

(ii) the balance sheet date preceding that;

(g) "subsidiary undertaking" has the meaning given in section 1162 of, and Schedule 7 to, the 2006 Act.

(6) Paragraph (7) applies if the 2006 Act is amended so that the general thresholds or group thresholds which apply to a financial year ("X") differ from those which applied to either of the preceding two financial years.

(7) For the purpose of determining whether a company is a qualifying company in financial year X, the company is to be treated as if the general thresholds or group thresholds which apply to financial year X had also applied to the two preceding financial years.

NOTES

Note that these Regulations cease to have effect on 6 April 2024 (see reg 1 *ante*).

[10.1174]

6 Contracts to which the information relates

(1) A qualifying contract is a relevant contract which satisfies the conditions in paragraphs (2) and (3).

(2) The first condition is that the relevant contract is not a contract for financial services, as defined in section 2 of the Small Business, Enterprise and Employment Act 2015.

(3) The second condition is that the relevant contract is—

(a) governed by the law of a part of the United Kingdom otherwise than by choice of the parties;

(b) governed by the law of a part of the United Kingdom by choice of the parties, and—

(i) has a significant connection with that part of the United Kingdom, or

(ii) without that choice, its applicable law would still be the law of a part of the United Kingdom; or

(c) governed by a foreign law by choice of the parties and—

(i) without that choice, its applicable law would be the law of a part of the United Kingdom, and
(ii) has no significant connection with any country outside the United Kingdom.

(4) In this regulation "foreign law" means the law of a country outside the United Kingdom.

NOTES

Note that these Regulations cease to have effect on 6 April 2024 (see reg 1 *ante*).

[10.1175]
7 Periods in relation to which information must be published

(1) Subject to paragraphs (2) and (3), a qualifying company has two reporting periods in a financial year—
(a) the first reporting period is the six months beginning with the first day of that financial year;
(b) the second reporting period is the remainder of that financial year.

(2) In the event that a qualifying company's accounting reference period is shortened in accordance with section 392 (alteration of accounting reference date) of the 2006 Act so that a financial year lasts 9 months or less, the reporting period is that financial year.

(3) In the event that a qualifying company's accounting reference period is extended in accordance with section 392 (alteration of accounting reference date) of the 2006 Act so that a financial year lasts more than 15 months, there are three reporting periods—
(a) the first reporting period is the six months beginning with the first day of that financial year;
(b) the second reporting period is the six months beginning with the day after the last day of the first reporting period;
(c) the third reporting period is the remainder of that financial year.

(4) In this regulation "accounting reference period" has the meaning given in section 391 of the 2006 Act.

NOTES

Note that these Regulations cease to have effect on 6 April 2024 (see reg 1 *ante*).

[10.1176]
8 Failure to publish a report

(1) If the requirements of regulation 3 are not met in relation to a reporting period, the qualifying company and every person who was a director of the qualifying company immediately before the end of the filing period commits an offence.

(2) It is a defence for a director to prove that the director took all reasonable steps for securing that the requirements of regulation 3 would be complied with before the end of the filing period.

(3) A person guilty of an offence under this regulation is liable on summary conviction—
(a) in England and Wales, to a fine;
(b) in Scotland or Northern Ireland, to a fine not exceeding level 5 on the standard scale.

NOTES

Note that these Regulations cease to have effect on 6 April 2024 (see reg 1 *ante*).

[10.1177]
9 False statement offence

(1) It is an offence for a person knowingly or recklessly—
(a) to publish or cause to be published, for the purposes of these Regulations, a report or any information, or
(b) to make, for any such purpose, a statement,
that is misleading, false or deceptive in a material particular.

(2) A person guilty of an offence under this regulation is liable on summary conviction—
(a) in England and Wales, to a fine;
(b) in Scotland or Northern Ireland, to a fine not exceeding level 5 on the standard scale.

(3) No proceedings are to be brought under this regulation—
(a) in England and Wales except by or with consent of the Secretary of State or the Director of Public Prosecutions;
(b) in Northern Ireland except by or with consent of the Secretary of State or the Director of Public Prosecutions for Northern Ireland.

NOTES

Note that these Regulations cease to have effect on 6 April 2024 (see reg 1 *ante*).

[10.1178]
10 Summary proceedings: time limit for proceedings

(1) An information relating to an offence under these Regulations may be tried by a magistrates' court in England and Wales if it is laid—
(a) within three years beginning with the day after the commission of the offence, and
(b) within twelve months beginning with the day after the date on which evidence sufficient in the opinion of the Director of Public Prosecutions or the Secretary of State (as the case may be) to justify the proceedings comes to that person's knowledge.

(2) Summary proceedings in Scotland for an offence under these Regulations—
(a) must not be commenced after the expiration of three years beginning with the day after the commission of the offence;
(b) subject to that, may be commenced at any time—
(i) within twelve months beginning with the day after the date on which evidence sufficient in the Lord Advocate's opinion to justify the proceedings came to the knowledge of the Lord Advocate, or

(ii) where such evidence was reported to the Lord Advocate by the Secretary of State, within twelve months beginning with the day after the date on which it came to the knowledge of the Secretary of State.

(3) Section 136(3) of the Criminal Procedure (Scotland) Act 1995 (date when proceedings deemed to be commenced) applies for the purposes of this regulation as for the purposes of that section.

(4) A magistrates' court in Northern Ireland has jurisdiction to hear and determine a complaint charging the commission of an offence under these Regulations provided that the complaint is made—

(a) within three years beginning with the day after the commission of the offence, and

(b) within twelve months beginning with the day after the date on which evidence sufficient in the opinion of the Director of Public Prosecutions for Northern Ireland or the Secretary of State (as the case may be) to justify the proceedings comes to that person's knowledge.

(5) For the purposes of this regulation a certificate of the Director of Public Prosecutions, the Lord Advocate, the Director of Public Prosecutions for Northern Ireland or the Secretary of State (as the case may be) as to the date on which evidence came to that person's knowledge is conclusive evidence.

NOTES

Note that these Regulations cease to have effect on 6 April 2024 (see reg 1 *ante*).

[10.1179]

11 Review

(1) Before 6th April 2022 the Secretary of State must—

(a) carry out a review of these Regulations,

(b) set out the conclusions of the review in a report, and

(c) publish the report.

(2) The report must in particular—

(a) set out the objectives intended to be achieved by the regulatory provisions established by these Regulations,

(b) assess the extent to which those objectives are achieved, and

(c) assess whether those objectives remain appropriate and, if so, the extent to which they could be achieved with a system that imposes less regulation.

NOTES

Note that these Regulations cease to have effect on 6 April 2024 (see reg 1 *ante*).

SCHEDULE
INFORMATION

Regulation 3

[10.1180]

1. For the purposes of regulation 3, the information in relation to each reporting period that a qualifying company must publish is set out in paragraphs 2 to 12.

Information on payment terms

2. A description of the qualifying company's standard payment terms in relation to qualifying contracts, which must include—

(a) the payment period specified in those standard payment terms, expressed in days;

(b) where the qualifying company varied the standard payment terms in the reporting period—

(i) details of the variation, and

(ii) details of any notification or consultation conducted by the qualifying company with its suppliers before making the variation.

3. A description of the maximum payment period specified in a qualifying contract which the qualifying company has entered into during the reporting period.

Dispute resolution

4. An explanation of the qualifying company's process for resolving a dispute with a supplier in relation to payment under a qualifying contract.

Payment practices and policies

5. A statement as to whether the qualifying company's payment practices and policies in relation to qualifying contracts include an arrangement under which a supplier can receive payment of an invoiced sum from a finance provider before the end of the payment period, with the qualifying company paying the invoiced sum to the finance provider.

6. A statement as to whether the qualifying company's payment practices and policies in relation to qualifying contracts provide for the electronic submission and tracking of invoices.

7. A statement as to whether the qualifying company is a signatory to a code of conduct or standards on payment practices and, if so, the name of that code.

8. A statement as to whether the qualifying company's payment practices and policies allow the qualifying company to deduct a sum from a payment under a qualifying contract, as a charge to a supplier to remain on the qualifying company's list of suppliers or potential suppliers.

Payment performance

9. In relation to the payments made under qualifying contracts within the reporting period, a statement of—

(a) the average number of days taken to make such payments, where day 1 is the first day after the relevant day;

(b) the percentage of those payments which were made, where day 1 is the first day after the relevant day—

(i) within the period beginning on day 1 and ending with day 30;
(ii) within the period beginning on day 31 and ending with day 60;
(iii) on or after day 61.

10. In relation to the payments under qualifying contracts that fall due within the reporting period, a statement of the percentage of these payments which were not made within the payment period.

11. A statement as to whether the qualifying company has during the reporting period deducted a sum from a payment under a qualifying contract, as a charge to a supplier to remain on the qualifying company's list of suppliers or potential suppliers.

Approval

12. The name of the director of the qualifying company who has approved the information set out in paragraphs 2 to 11.

Interpretation

13. In this Schedule—

"average" means the arithmetic mean;

"payment period" means the period in which a company is contractually required to pay a sum;

"relevant day" means the day on which a company receives an invoice or otherwise has notice of an amount for payment;

"standard payment terms" means, in relation to a qualifying contract—

(a) the standard terms relating to payment that the qualifying company uses for that type of qualifying contract, or
(b) where the qualifying company does not use standard terms, the qualifying company's most frequently used payment terms for that type of qualifying contract.

14. For the purposes of this Schedule—

(a) a payment falls due on the last day of the payment period;
(b) a payment is made—
(i) when it is received by the supplier;
(ii) if there is any delay in the sum being received for which the qualifying company is not responsible, when it would have been received without that delay.

NOTES

Note that these Regulations cease to have effect on 6 April 2024 (see reg 1 *ante*).

LIMITED LIABILITY PARTNERSHIPS (REPORTING ON PAYMENT PRACTICES AND PERFORMANCE) REGULATIONS 2017

(SI 2017/425)

NOTES

Made: 15 March 2017.
Authority: Limited Liability Partnerships Act 2000, ss 15, 17(1), (2)(a), (3).
Commencement: 6 April 2017.
Application of these Regulations: note that these Regulations cease to have effect on 6 April 2024 (see reg 1 *post*).

[10.1181]

1 Citation and commencement

(1) These Regulations may be cited as the Limited Liability Partnerships (Reporting on Payment Practices and Performance) Regulations 2017.

(2) These Regulations come into force on 6th April 2017.

(3) These Regulations cease to have effect on 6th April 2024.

NOTES

Note that these Regulations cease to have effect on 6 April 2024 (see above).

[10.1182]

2 Interpretation

In these Regulations—

"limited liability partnership" means a limited liability partnership registered under the Limited Liability Partnerships Act 2000;

"the Principal Regulations" means the Reporting on Payment Practices and Performance Regulations 2017.

NOTES

Note that these Regulations cease to have effect on 6 April 2024 (see reg 1 *ante*).

[10.1183]

3 Application of the Principal Regulations to limited liability partnerships

The provisions of the Principal Regulations apply to limited liability partnerships with the modifications set out for this purpose in regulations 4 to 10.

NOTES

Note that these Regulations cease to have effect on 6 April 2024 (see reg 1 *ante*).

[10.1184]
4

Regulation 2 of the Principal Regulations (interpretation) shall read as if—

(a) the definition of "director" were omitted;
(b) the definition of "financial year" were—

""financial year" means an LLP's financial year determined in accordance with sections 390 to 392 of the 2006 Act (as applied and modified by regulation 7 of the 2008 Regulations);";

(c) the definition of "qualifying company" were omitted;
(d) there were, in the appropriate places alphabetically, the following definitions—

""the 2008 Regulations" means the Limited Liability Partnerships (Accounts and Audit) (Application of Companies Act 2006) Regulations 2008";

""designated member" has the meaning given in section 8 of the Limited Liability Partnerships Act 2000";

""LLP" means a limited liability partnership registered under the Limited Liability Partnerships Act 2000";

""qualifying LLP" has the meaning given in regulation 5".

NOTES

Note that these Regulations cease to have effect on 6 April 2024 (see reg 1 *ante*).

[10.1185]
5

Regulation 3 of the Principal Regulations (duty to publish information on payment practices, policies and performance) shall read as if references to "company" were to "LLP".

NOTES

Note that these Regulations cease to have effect on 6 April 2024 (see reg 1 *ante*).

[10.1186]
6

Regulation 4 of the Principal Regulations (approval of the information) shall read as if the words of that regulation were—

"4 Approval of the information

A qualifying LLP's information for a reporting period must be approved by a designated member of that LLP before it is published."

NOTES

Note that these Regulations cease to have effect on 6 April 2024 (see reg 1 *ante*).

[10.1187]
7

Regulation 5 of the Principal Regulations (companies to which the duty applies) shall read as if the words of that regulation were—

"5 LLPs to which the duty applies

(1) These Regulations apply to an LLP in relation to every financial year in which it is a qualifying LLP.
(2) An LLP is not a qualifying LLP in—
  (a) its first financial year;
  (b) a financial year which began before 6thApril 2017.
(3) An LLP other than a parent LLP is a qualifying LLP—
  (a) in its second financial year if on its last balance sheet date before that financial year it exceeded two or all three of the general thresholds;
  (b) in a subsequent financial year if on both of the relevant balance sheet dates it exceeded two or all three of the general thresholds.
(4) A parent LLP is a qualifying LLP—
  (a) in its second financial year if on its last balance sheet date before that financial year—
    (i) it exceeded two or all three of the general thresholds, and
    (ii) the group headed by it exceeded two or all three of the group thresholds;
  (b) in a subsequent financial year if on both of the relevant balance sheet dates—
    (i) it exceeded two or all three of the general thresholds, and
    (ii) the group headed by it exceeded two or all three of the group thresholds.
(5) In this regulation—
  (a) "balance sheet date" means the date as at which the LLP's balance sheet was made up;
  (b) the "general thresholds" are the maximum figures for an LLP's turnover, balance sheet total and number of employees set out in subsection (3) of section 465 of the 2006 Act (as applied and modified by regulation 26 of the 2008 Regulations), determined in accordance with subsections (4) to (6) of that section (as so applied and modified);
  (c) "group" means a parent LLP and its subsidiary undertakings;
  (d) the "group thresholds" are the maximum figures for a group's turnover, balance sheet total and number of employees set out in subsection (4) of section 466 of the 2006 Act (as applied and modified by regulation 26 of the 2008 Regulations), determined in accordance with subsections (5) to (7) of that section (as so applied and modified);

(e) "parent LLP" has the meaning given in section 1173 of the 2006 Act (as applied and modified by regulation 55 of the 2008 Regulations);

(f) the "relevant balance sheet dates" are—

(i) the LLP's last balance sheet date before the relevant financial year, and

(ii) the balance sheet date preceding that;

(g) "subsidiary undertaking" has the meaning given in section 1162 of, and Schedule 7 to, the 2006 Act (as applied and modified by regulation 52 of the 2008 Regulations).

(6) Paragraph (7) applies if the 2006 Act (as applied and modified by the 2008 Regulations) is amended so that the general thresholds or group thresholds which apply to a financial year ("X") differ from those which applied to either of the preceding two financial years.

(7) For the purposes of determining whether an LLP is a qualifying LLP in financial year X, the LLP is to be treated as if the general thresholds or group thresholds which apply to financial year X had also applied to the two preceding financial years."

NOTES

Note that these Regulations cease to have effect on 6 April 2024 (see reg 1 *ante*).

[10.1188]
8

Regulation 7 of the Principal Regulations (periods in relation to which information must be published) shall read as if—

(a) the words "company" and "company's", wherever they appear, were "LLP" and "LLP's";

(b) the references to sections 391 and 392 of the 2006 Act were to those sections as applied and modified by regulation 7 of the 2008 Regulations.

NOTES

Note that these Regulations cease to have effect on 6 April 2024 (see reg 1 *ante*).

[10.1189]
9

Regulation 8 of the Principal Regulations (failure to publish a report) shall read as if—

(a) the words of paragraph (1) were—

"(1) If the requirements of regulation 3 are not met in relation to a reporting period, the qualifying LLP and every person who was a designated member of the qualifying LLP immediately before the end of that filing period commits an offence.";

(b) in paragraph (2), the references to "director" were to "designated member".

NOTES

Note that these Regulations cease to have effect on 6 April 2024 (see reg 1 *ante*).

[10.1190]
10

The Schedule to the Principal Regulations (information) shall read as if—

(a) the words "a company", "company" and "company's" wherever they appear were "an LLP", "LLP" and "LLP's";

(b) in paragraph 12, the reference to the "director" were to the "designated member".

NOTES

Note that these Regulations cease to have effect on 6 April 2024 (see reg 1 *ante*).

[10.1191]
11 Review

(1) Before 6th April 2022 the Secretary of State must—

(a) carry out a review of these Regulations,

(b) set out the conclusions of the review in a report, and

(c) publish the report.

(2) The report must in particular—

(a) set out the objectives intended to be achieved by the regulatory provisions established by these Regulations,

(b) assess the extent to which those objectives are achieved, and

(c) assess whether those objectives remain appropriate and, if so, the extent to which they could be achieved with a system that imposes less regulation.

NOTES

Note that these Regulations cease to have effect on 6 April 2024 (see reg 1 *ante*).

INFORMATION ABOUT PEOPLE WITH SIGNIFICANT CONTROL (AMENDMENT) REGULATIONS 2017

(SI 2017/693)

NOTES

Made: 22 June 2017.

Authority: European Communities Act 1972, s 2(2) (see the note "Statutory Instruments made under the European Communities Act 1972" preceding paragraph **[4.1]** *ante*).

Commencement: 26 June 2017.

ARRANGEMENT OF REGULATIONS

PART 1
INTRODUCTION AND INTERPRETATION

SCHEDULES

PART 1 INTRODUCTION AND INTERPRETATION

[10.1192]
1 Citation

These Regulations may be cited as the Information about People with Significant Control (Amendment) Regulations 2017.

[10.1193]
2 Commencement

These Regulations come into force on 26th June 2017.

[10.1194]
3 Interpretation

In these Regulations—

"the Companies Act" means the Companies Act 2006;

"the 2009 LLP Regulations" means the Limited Liability Partnerships (Application of Companies Act 2006) Regulations 2009;

"the PSC Regulations" means the Register of People with Significant Control Regulations 2016;

"the commencement day" means the day set out in regulation 2;

"LLP" means a limited liability partnership registered under the Limited Liability Partnerships Act 2000;

"unregistered company" has the meaning given in regulation 2 of the Unregistered Companies Regulations 2009.

PARTS 2–5

(Part 2 provides as follows: regs 4–9 amend the Companies Act 2006, ss 790B, 790C, 790E, 790M, and inserts s 790VA (all in Part 21A at **[1.875]** *et seq); reg 10 amends ss 853A, 853B, 863H, 853J, 853K of the 2006 Act, and repeals s 853I (all in Part 24 at* **[1.971]** *et seq); regs 11–19 amend the Register of People with Significant Control Regulations 2016, SI 2016/339 at* **[4.559]**. *Part 3 provides as follows: regs 20–27 amend the Limited Liability Partnerships (Application of Companies Act 2006) Regulations 2009, SI 2009/1804 at* **[10.319]**; *regs 28–31 amend the Limited Liability Partnerships (Register of People with Significant Control) Regulations 2016, SI 2016/340 at* **[10.452]**. *Part 4 (regs 32–36) amends the Unregistered Companies Regulations 2009, SI 2009/2436 at* **[4.389]**. *Part 5 (regs 37–39) contains minor and consequential amendments, and introduces the Schedule to these Regulations (Transitional Arrangements).)*

SCHEDULE
TRANSITIONAL ARRANGEMENTS

Regulation 39

PART 1 TRANSITIONAL ARRANGEMENTS IN RELATION TO PART 2

Obligation to keep register of people with significant control

[10.1195]

1. (1) This paragraph applies where, as a result of the amendment of section 790B(1)(a) of the Companies Act made by regulation 5, Part 21A of the Companies Act applies on the commencement day to a company to which it did not apply immediately before that day.

(2) The company is not required to comply with Chapter 3 or 4 of Part 21A of the Companies Act (register of people with significant control and alternative method of record-keeping) until 24th July 2017.

Extension of new 14 day deadlines in section 790E and 790M of the Companies Act

2. (1) This paragraph applies where a company subject to an obligation to take an action under the old law has not complied with that obligation before the commencement day.

(2) The company must comply with the obligation to take the action referred to in paragraph (1) before the end of the period of 14 days beginning with the commencement day.

(3) In this paragraph "the old law" means section 790E and section 790M of the Companies Act without the amendments made by these Regulations.

Application of new section 790VA of the Companies Act

3. (1) Subject to sub-paragraph (2), section 790VA of the Companies Act (notification of changes to the registrar), inserted by regulation 9, applies to a change to a company's PSC register made before, on or after the commencement day.

(2) If, before the commencement day, a company has delivered to the registrar all the information that was stated in its PSC register in a confirmation period, in accordance with section 853I of the Companies Act, section 790VA of that Act does not apply to changes made to the company's PSC register on or before the confirmation date for that confirmation period.

(3) Where—

(a) a company has made a change to its PSC register before the commencement day, and

(b) the company is required by section 790VA of the Companies Act to give notice to the registrar before the end of the period of 14 days beginning with the day after it made the change,

the company is treated as having complied with the requirement if it gives notice to the registrar before the end of the period of 14 days beginning with the commencement day.

(4) In this paragraph—

"confirmation date" and "confirmation period" have the meaning given in section 853A(3) of the Companies Act;

"PSC register" has the meaning given in section 790C(10) of the Companies Act.

Application of amendments to Part 24 of the Companies Act

4. (1) The amendments to Part 24 of the Companies Act (annual confirmation of accuracy of information on register) made by regulation 10 apply to a company which delivers a confirmation statement to the registrar under section 853A of that Act on or after the commencement day, whether the confirmation period to which the statement relates ended before, on or after the commencement day.

(2) In this paragraph—

"confirmation statement" has the meaning given in section 853A(1)(b) of the Companies Act;

"confirmation period" has the meaning given in section 853A(3) of the Companies Act.

Protection for a registrable person applying for protection of secured information

5. (1) This paragraph applies where—

(a) as a result of the amendment of section 790B(1)(a) of the Companies Act made by regulation 5, Part 21A of the Companies Act applies on the commencement day to a company to which it did not apply immediately before that day,

(b) an individual is a registrable person in relation to the company on the commencement day,

(c) before 24th July 2017 an application is made under regulation 36 or 37 of the PSC Regulations for the protection of secured information relating to the individual, and

(d) the registrar determines that the application is unsuccessful.

(2) Subject to sub-paragraph (3), during the protected period, the registrar—

(a) must not use or disclose secured information relating to the individual, and

(b) must omit the information referred to in paragraph (a) from the material on the register that is available for public inspection.

(3) The registrar may use or disclose secured information relating to the individual—

(a) for communicating with the individual, and

(b) where the application was made under regulation 37 of the PSC Regulations, for communicating with the company which made the application.

(4) Sub-paragraph (5) applies where the individual ceases to be a registrable person in relation to the company before the end of the protected period.

(5) If, before the end of the protected period, the registrar receives notice from the individual setting out the date on which the individual ceased to be a registrable person in relation to the company, the registrar—

(a) must not use or disclose secured information relating to the individual which the registrar obtained before the end of the protected period, and

(b) must omit the information referred to in paragraph (a) from the material on the register that is available for public inspection.

(6) Where the registrar does not receive notice under sub-paragraph (5), the registrar must as soon as reasonably practicable after the end of the protected period—

(a) make the secured information on the register available for public inspection, and

(b) notify the individual and the company to which the application under regulation 36 or 37 related of the action taken under paragraph (a).

(7) In relation to an application to which this paragraph applies—

(a) regulation 42 (unsuccessful determination of application for protection of secured information) of the PSC Regulations does not apply, and

(b) in regulation 45 (protection by a company of secured information) of the PSC Regulations, paragraph (1)(b) (notifications which bring the protection to an end) has effect as if the reference to notification under regulation 42(3) were a reference to notification under sub-paragraph (6)(b) of this paragraph.

(8) For the purposes of this paragraph an application under regulation 36 or 37 of the PSC Regulations is made when it is registered by the registrar.

(9) In this paragraph—

"protected period" means—

(a) where an appeal under regulation 41 of the PSC Regulations (appeal against unsuccessful application under regulation 36, 37 or 38) has not been brought, 12 weeks beginning with the date on which notice of the registrar's determination was sent under regulation 36(5) or 37(5) of those regulations,

(b) where an appeal under regulation 41 of the PSC Regulations has been brought and dismissed, 12 weeks beginning with the date on which the court dismissed the appeal in accordance with regulation 41(5) of those regulations, or

(c) where an appeal under regulation 41 of the PSC Regulations has been brought and subsequently withdrawn or abandoned, 12 weeks beginning with the date on which the registrar became aware that the appeal had been withdrawn or abandoned;

"the register" has the meaning given in section 1080(2) of the Companies Act;

"registrable person" has the meaning given in section 790C(4) of the Companies Act;

"secured information" means the required particulars of a registrable person in relation to a company, other than the particular required by section 790K(1)(i) of the Companies Act.

6. In this Part of this Schedule "the registrar" has the meaning given in section 1060(3) of the Companies Act.

PART 2 TRANSITIONAL ARRANGEMENTS IN RELATION TO PART 3

Extension of the new 14 day deadlines in regulations 31C and 31E of the 2009 LLP Regulations

[10.1196]

7. (1) This paragraph applies where an LLP subject to an obligation to take an action under the old law has not complied with that obligation before the commencement day.

(2) The LLP must comply with the obligation to take the action referred to in paragraph (1) before the end of the period of 14 days beginning with the commencement day.

(3) In this paragraph "the old law" means—

(a) section 790E of the Companies Act without the amendments made to that section by these Regulations (as applied and modified in respect of LLPs by regulation 31C of the 2009 LLP Regulations), and

(b) section 790M of the Companies Act without the amendments made to that section by these Regulations (as applied and modified in respect of LLPs by regulation 31E of the 2009 LLP Regulations without the amendments made by these Regulations).

Application of new regulation 31JA to the 2009 LLP Regulations

8. (1) Subject to sub-paragraph (2), section 790VA of the Companies Act (notification of changes to the registrar) inserted by regulation 9 (and applied and modified in respect of LLPs by regulation 31JA of the 2009 LLP Regulations, inserted by regulation 26 of these Regulations), applies to a change made to an LLP's PSC register before, on or after the commencement day.

(2) If, before the commencement day, an LLP has delivered to the registrar all the information that was stated in its PSC register in a confirmation period, in accordance with section 853I of the Companies Act (as applied and modified by regulation 31 of the 2009 LLP Regulations), section 790VA of that Act (as applied and modified by regulation 31JA of the 2009 LLP Regulations) does not apply to changes made to the LLP's PSC register on or before the confirmation date for that confirmation period.

(3) Where—

(a) an LLP has made a change to its PSC register before the commencement day, and

(b) the LLP is required by section 790VA of the Companies Act (as applied and modified by regulation 31JA of the 2009 LLP Regulations) to give notice to the registrar before the end of the period of 14 days beginning with the day after it made the change,

the LLP is treated as having complied with the requirement if it gives notice to the registrar before the end of the period of 14 days beginning with the commencement day.

(4) In this paragraph—

"confirmation period" and "confirmation date" have the meanings given in section 853A(3) of the Companies Act (as applied and modified by regulation 30 of the 2009 LLP Regulations);

"PSC register" has the meaning given in section 790C(10) of the Companies Act (as applied and modified by regulation 31C of the 2009 LLP Regulations).

Application of amendments to Part 8 of the 2009 LLP Regulations

9. (1) The amendments to Part 24 of the Companies Act (annual confirmation by company of accuracy of information on register) made by regulation 10 of these Regulations (and applied and modified in respect of LLPs by regulations 20 to 22 of these Regulations), apply to an LLP which delivers a confirmation statement to the registrar under section 853A of the Act (as applied and modified by regulation 30 of the 2009 LLP Regulations) on or after the commencement day, whether the confirmation period to which the statement relates ended before, on or after the commencement day.

(2) In this paragraph—

"confirmation statement" has the meaning given in section 853A(1)(b) of the Companies Act (as applied and modified by regulation 30 of the 2009 LLP Regulations);

"confirmation period" has the meaning given in section 853A(3) of the Companies Act (as applied and modified by regulation 30 of the 2009 LLP Regulations).

10. In this Part of this Schedule, "the registrar" has the same meaning as in section 18 of the Limited Liability Partnerships Act 2000.

PART 3 TRANSITIONAL ARRANGEMENTS IN RELATION TO PART 4

Postponement of obligation to keep register of people with significant control

[10.1197]

11. An unregistered company is not required to comply with regulation 12B of the Unregistered Companies Regulations (register of people with significant control and alternative method of record-keeping) until 24th July 2017.

Application of amendments to Part 24 of the Companies Act

12. (1) The amendments to Part 24 of the Companies Act (annual confirmation of accuracy of information on register) made by regulation 10 apply to an unregistered company which delivers a confirmation statement to the registrar under section 853A of that Act on or after the commencement day, whether the confirmation period to which the statement relates ended before, on or after the commencement day.

(2) In this paragraph—

"confirmation statement" has the meaning given in section 853A(1)(b) of the Companies Act;

"confirmation period" has the meaning given in section 853A(3) of the Companies Act.

Protection for registrable persons applying for protection of secured information

13. (1) This paragraph applies where—

(a) an individual is a registrable person in relation to a unregistered company on the commencement day,

(b) before 24th July 2017 an application is made under regulation 36 or 37 of the PSC Regulations for the protection of secured information relating to the individual, and

(c) the registrar determines that the application is unsuccessful.

(2) Subject to sub-paragraph (3), during the protected period, the registrar—

(a) must not use or disclose secured information relating to the individual, and

(b) must omit the information referred to in paragraph (a) from the material on the register that is available for public inspection.

(3) The registrar may use or disclose secured information relating to the individual—

(a) for communicating with the individual, and

(b) where the application was made under regulation 37 of the PSC Regulations, for communicating with the unregistered company which made the application.

(4) Sub-paragraph (5) applies where the individual ceases to be a registrable person in relation to the unregistered company before the end of the protected period.

(5) If, before the end of the protected period, the registrar receives notice from the individual setting out the date on which the individual ceased to be a registrable person in relation to the unregistered company, the registrar—

(a) must not use or disclose secured information relating to the individual which the registrar obtained before the end of the protected period, and

(b) must omit the information referred to in paragraph (a) from the material on the register that is available for public inspection.

(6) Where the registrar does not receive notice under sub-paragraph (5), the registrar must as soon as reasonably practicable after the end of the protected period—

(a) make the secured information on the register available for public inspection, and

(b) notify the individual and the unregistered company to which the application under regulation 36 or 37 related of the action taken under paragraph (a).

(7) Where this paragraph applies—

(a) regulation 42 (unsuccessful determination of application for protection of secured information) of the PSC Regulations does not apply, and

(b) in regulation 45 (protection by a company of secured information) of the PSC Regulations, paragraph (1)(b) (notifications which bring the protection to an end) has effect as if the reference to notification under regulation 42(3) were a reference to notification under sub-paragraph (6)(b) of this paragraph.

(8) For the purposes of this paragraph an application under regulation 36 or 37 of the PSC Regulations is made when it is registered by the registrar.

(9) In this paragraph—

"protected period" means—

(a) where an appeal under regulation 41 of the PSC Regulations (appeal against unsuccessful application under regulation 36, 37 or 38) has not been brought, 12 weeks beginning with the date on which notice of the registrar's determination was sent under regulation 36(5) or 37(5) of those regulations,

(b) where an appeal under regulation 41 of the PSC Regulations has been brought and dismissed, 12 weeks beginning with the date on which the court dismissed the appeal in accordance with regulation 41(5) of those regulations, or

(c) where an appeal under regulation 41 of the PSC Regulations has been brought and subsequently withdrawn or abandoned, 12 weeks beginning with the date on which the registrar became aware that the appeal had been withdrawn or abandoned;

"the register" has the meaning given in section 1080(2) of the Companies Act;

"registrable person" has the meaning given in section 790C(4) of the Companies Act;

"secured information" means the required particulars of a registrable person in relation to a company, other than the particular required by section 790K(1)(i) of the Companies Act.

14. In this Part of this Schedule "the registrar" has the meaning given in section 1060(3) of the Companies Act.

SCOTTISH PARTNERSHIPS (REGISTER OF PEOPLE WITH SIGNIFICANT CONTROL) REGULATIONS 2017

(SI 2017/694)

NOTES

Made: 22 June 2017.

Authority: European Communities Act 1972, s 2(2) (see the note "Statutory Instruments made under the European Communities Act 1972" preceding paragraph **[4.1]** *ante*).

Commencement: 26 June 2017 (with the exception of regs 4 and 81 which come into force on 24 July 2017).

These Regulations are reproduced as amended by: the Data Protection Act 2018; the Companies (Disclosure of Address) (Amendment) Regulations 2018, SI 2018/528; the Companies, Limited Liability Partnerships and Partnerships (Amendment etc) (EU Exit) Regulations 2019, SI 2019/348; the Money Laundering and Terrorist Financing (Amendment) Regulations 2019, SI 2019/1511.

ARRANGEMENT OF REGULATIONS

PART 1 GENERAL INTRODUCTORY PROVISIONS

[10.1198]

1 Citation and commencement

(1) These Regulations may be cited as the Scottish Partnerships (Register of People with Significant Control) Regulations 2017 and, save as provided in paragraph (2), come into force on 26th June 2017.

(2) Regulation 4 and regulation 81 come into force on 24th July 2017.

[10.1199]

2 Interpretation

In these Regulations—

the "2017 Money Laundering Regulations" means the Money Laundering, Terrorist Financing and Transfer of Funds (Information on the Payer) Regulations 2017;

"additional matter" means information required to be delivered to the registrar under any of regulations 23 to 30;

"commencement day" is the day specified in regulation 1(1);

"confirmation date" has the meaning given in regulation 36;

"confirmation period" has the meaning given in regulation 36;

"confirmed" in relation to information has the meaning given in regulation 21;

"credit institution" has the same meaning as in regulation 10 of the 2017 Money Laundering Regulations;

"daily default fine" has the meaning given in section 1125 of the Companies Act 2006, as modified by regulation 70;

"DOB information" has the meaning given in regulation 62;

"eligible Scottish partnership" has the meaning given in regulation 3(2);

["EU regulated market" has the meaning given in regulation 3(12);]

"financial institution" has the same meaning as in regulation 10 of the 2017 Money Laundering, Regulations;

"firm" means any entity, whether or not a legal person, that is not an individual and includes a body corporate, a corporation sole and a partnership or other unincorporated association;

"former name", save where provided otherwise in regulation 64, means a name by which an individual was formerly known for business purposes;

"general partnership" is a partnership which is neither—

(a) a limited partnership; nor

(b) a limited liability partnership registered under the Limited Liability Partnerships Act 2000;

"legal entity" means a firm that is a legal person under the law by which it is governed;

"limited partnership" means a limited partnership registered under section 8(1) of the Limited Partnerships Act 1907;

"name" means a person's forename and surname, except that in the case of—

(a) a peer, or

(b) an individual usually known by a title,

the title may be stated instead of that person's forename and surname or in addition to either or both of them;

"nature of control" in relation to a person with significant control over an eligible Scottish partnership has the meaning given in regulation 18 and Schedule 3;

"officer", in relation to a partnership or a body corporate to which an offence under these Regulations applies, has the meaning given in regulation 3(3);

"partner", in relation to a limited partnership, has the same meaning as "general partner" in section 4(2) of the Limited Partnerships Act 1907;

"public authority" includes any person or body carrying out public functions;

"public function" has the meaning given in Part 3 of Schedule 5;

"qualifying partnership" has the meaning given in regulation 3 of the Partnership (Accounts) Regulations 2008;

"the register" means the register kept by the registrar under section 1080 of the Companies Act 2006;

"registrable person" has the meaning given in regulation 3(5);

"registrable relevant legal entity" has the meaning given in regulation 3(8);

"the registrar" means the registrar of companies for Scotland appointed under section 1060 of the Companies Act 2006;

"registration date" in relation to—

(a) a limited partnership means the registration date stated on the certificate issued to the limited partnership under section 8C of the Limited Partnerships Act 1907 and

(b) a Scottish qualifying partnership means the date notified to it by the registrar as the effective date of its registration under regulation 5;

"regulated market" has the meaning given in regulation 3(12);

"relevant body" means—

(a) a police force within the meaning of section 101(1) of the Police Act 1996;

(b) the Police Service of Northern Ireland; and

(c) the Police Service of Scotland;

"relevant change" has the meaning given in regulation 11;

"relevant legal entity" has the meaning given in regulation 3(6);

"required particulars" has the meaning given in regulation 17;

"review period" has the meaning given in regulation 37;

"Scottish limited partnership" has the meaning given in regulation 3(2)(a);

"Scottish qualifying partnership" has the meaning given in regulation 3(2)(b);

"secured information" has the meaning given in regulation 44;

"service address", in relation to a person, means an address at which documents may be effectively served on that person by physical delivery;

"significant control" has the meaning given in regulation 3(4);

"specified conditions", in relation to a person with or having significant control over an eligible Scottish partnership, means the conditions specified in Part 1 of Schedule 1;

"specified public authority" means a public authority listed in Schedule 4;

["UK regulated market" has the meaning given in regulation 3(12);]

"URA information" has the meaning given in regulation 39;

"withdrawal notice" has the meaning given in paragraph 14 of Schedule 2.

NOTES

Definitions "EU regulated market" and "UK regulated market" inserted by the Companies, Limited Liability Partnerships and Partnerships (Amendment etc) (EU Exit) Regulations 2019, SI 2019/348, reg 7, Sch 2, paras 15, 16, as from IP completion day (as defined in the European Union (Withdrawal Agreement) Act 2020, s 39).

[10.1200]

3 Key terms

(1) This regulation sets out some key terms used in these Regulations.

(2) An "eligible Scottish partnership" is—

(a) a limited partnership registered in Scotland (a "Scottish limited partnership"), or

(b) a general partnership constituted under the law of Scotland, during any period in which it is a qualifying partnership (a "Scottish qualifying partnership").

(3) Where these Regulations provide that an offence is committed by every officer of a partnership or body corporate who is in default—

(a) "officer" includes—

(i) any partner in the partnership or director of the body corporate, and

(ii) any manager, secretary or similar officer;

(b) an officer is "in default" for the purposes of the provision if the officer authorises or permits, participates in, or fails to take all reasonable steps to prevent, the contravention;

(c) a partnership or a body corporate which is an officer of the partnership or body corporate does not commit an offence as an officer in default unless one of its officers is in default; the officer in question also commits the offence and is liable to be proceeded against and punished accordingly.

(4) References to a person with or having "significant control" over an eligible Scottish partnership are to an individual who meets one or more of the specified conditions.

(5) Individuals with significant control over an eligible Scottish partnership are either "registrable" or "non-registrable" in relation to the eligible Scottish partnership—

(a) they are "non-registrable" if they do not hold any interest in the eligible Scottish partnership except through one or more other legal entities over each of which they have significant control and—

(i) as respects any right in the eligible Scottish partnership which they hold indirectly as described in paragraph 9(1)(b)(i) of Schedule 1, the legal entity through which the right is held is a relevant legal entity in relation to the eligible Scottish partnership; and

(ii) as respects any right in the eligible Scottish partnership which they hold indirectly as described in paragraph 9(1)(b)(ii) of Schedule 1, at least one of the legal entities in the chain is a relevant legal entity in relation to the eligible Scottish partnership;

(b) otherwise, they are "registrable",

and references to a "registrable person" in relation to an eligible Scottish partnership are to an individual with significant control over the eligible Scottish partnership who is registrable in relation to that eligible Scottish partnership.

(6) In relation to an eligible Scottish partnership, a legal entity is a "relevant legal entity" if—

(a) it would have come within the definition of a person with significant control over the eligible Scottish partnership if it had been an individual, and

(b) it is subject to its own disclosure requirements, as specified in paragraph (7).

(7) A legal entity is subject to its own disclosure requirements if—

(a) it is an eligible Scottish partnership;

(b) Part 21A of the Companies Act 2006 applies to it, whether by virtue of section 790B of that Act or another enactment that extends the application of that Part;

(c) it has voting shares admitted to trading on a [UK regulated market or an EU regulated market]; or

(d) it has voting shares admitted to trading on a market listed in Schedule 1 to the Register of People with Significant Control Regulations 2016.

(8) A relevant legal entity is either "registrable" or "non-registrable" in relation to an eligible Scottish partnership—

(a) it is "non-registrable" if it does not hold any interest in the eligible Scottish partnership except through one or more other legal entities in relation to each of which it would come within the definition of a person with significant control if it were an individual, and—

(i) as respects any right in the eligible Scottish partnership which it holds indirectly as described in paragraph 9(1)(b)(i) of Schedule 1, the legal entity through which the right is held is a relevant legal entity in relation to the eligible Scottish partnership; and

(ii) as respects any right in the eligible Scottish partnership which it holds indirectly as described in paragraph 9(1)(b)(ii) of Schedule 1, at least one of the legal entities in the chain is a relevant legal entity in relation to the eligible Scottish partnership;

(b) otherwise, it is "registrable",

and references to a "registrable relevant legal entity" in relation to an eligible Scottish partnership are to a relevant legal entity which is registrable in relation to that eligible Scottish partnership.

(9) For the purposes of paragraphs (5) and (8)—

(a) whether a person—

(i) holds an interest in an eligible Scottish partnership, or
(ii) holds that interest through another legal entity

is to be determined in accordance with Part 2 of Schedule 1; and

(b) whether a person has significant control over that other legal entity is to be determined in accordance with paragraph (3) and Part 1 of Schedule 1, reading references in those provisions to the eligible Scottish partnership as references to that other entity.

(10) Paragraphs (3) and (5) are to be read and have effect as if each of the following were an individual, even if they are legal persons under the laws by which they are governed—

(a) a corporation sole,
(b) a government or government department of a country or territory or a part of a country or territory,
(c) an international organisation whose members include two or more countries or territories (or their governments),
(d) a local authority or local government body in the United Kingdom or elsewhere.

(11) For the purposes of paragraph (7)(c) and (d)—

"voting shares" means shares carrying voting rights;

"voting rights" means rights to vote at general meetings of the legal entity in question, including rights that arise only in certain circumstances, and in relation to a legal entity that does not have general meetings at which matters are decided by the exercise of voting rights, a reference to voting rights is to be read as a reference to rights in relation to the entity that are equivalent to those of a person entitled to exercise voting rights in a company.

[(12) In paragraph (7), "UK regulated market" and "EU regulated market" have the meanings given in Article 2.1.13A and 2.1.13B respectively of Regulation (EU) No 600/2014 of the European Parliament and of the Council of 15 May 2014 and amending Regulation (EU) No 648/2012.]

NOTES

Para (7): words in square brackets in sub-para (c) substituted by the Companies, Limited Liability Partnerships and Partnerships (Amendment etc) (EU Exit) Regulations 2019, SI 2019/348, reg 7, Sch 2, paras 15, 17(a), as from IP completion day (as defined in the European Union (Withdrawal Agreement) Act 2020, s 39).

Para (12): substituted by SI 2019/348, reg 7, Sch 2, paras 15, 17(b), as from IP completion day (as defined in the European Union (Withdrawal Agreement) Act 2020, s 39).

PART 2 AMENDMENT OF REGISTRATION REQUIREMENT FOR SCOTTISH LIMITED PARTNERSHIPS

4 (*Reg 4 amends the Limited Partnerships Act 1907, s 8A at* **[9.63]**.)

PART 3 REGISTRATION OF SCOTTISH QUALIFYING PARTNERSHIPS

[10.1201]

5 Duty on Scottish qualifying partnerships to register

A Scottish qualifying partnership must deliver to the registrar the information set out in regulation 6, referred to in these Regulations as the "registration information", together with the information required by Part 5 (duty to deliver information to the registrar) within the period of 14 days beginning with—

(a) 24th July 2017, if it is a qualifying partnership on that day;
(b) any day after 24th July 2017 on which it becomes a qualifying partnership, either as a result of—
(i) its formation,
(ii) a change in its partners, or
(iii) a change in the partners in its partners.

[10.1202]

6 Registration information

(1) The registration information is set out in paragraphs (2) and (3).

(2) In relation to the Scottish qualifying partnership, the information is—

(a) its name;
(b) a service address for that partnership; and
(c) confirmation that it is a general partnership that is a qualifying partnership and is constituted under the law of Scotland.

(3) In relation to each partner in the Scottish qualifying partnership, the information is—

(a) the partner's full name, and
(b) if applicable, the register in which it is entered (including details of the state) and its registration number in that register.

(4) In paragraph (3)(b) "register" includes—

(a) the register maintained under section 1080(1) of the Companies Act 2006 elsewhere in the United Kingdom, and
(b) any comparable register maintained in a country or territory outside the United Kingdom.

[10.1203]

7 Notification of changes to the registration information

Save as provided in regulation 8(3), if any change is made or occurs as a result of which the registration information in relation to a Scottish qualifying partnership is incorrect or incomplete, the Scottish qualifying partnership must deliver to the registrar a notice setting out the correct and complete registration information within the period of 14 days beginning with the day on which the Scottish qualifying partnership becomes aware of the change.

NOTES

Temporary modification: this regulation was modified by the Companies etc (Filing Requirements) (Temporary Modifications) Regulations 2020, SI 2020/645, reg 22. By virtue of the Corporate Insolvency and Governance Act 2020, s 39(8), the modification applied from 27 June 2020 to the end of the day on 5 April 2021 (subject to the saving provision in s 39(9) which provides that the expiry of s 39 on 5 April 2021 does not affect the continued operation of any Regulations made under that section for the purpose of determining the length of any period that began before the expiry). As modified, this regulation had effect as if for the reference to "14 days" there were substituted a reference to "42 days".

[10.1204]

8 Effect of a partnership ceasing to be a Scottish qualifying partnership

(1) Subject to paragraph (2), a partnership which has ceased to be a Scottish qualifying partnership must deliver to the registrar within the period of 14 days beginning with the day it ceases to be a Scottish qualifying partnership a notice stating—

(a) that it has ceased to be a Scottish qualifying partnership, and

(b) the date on which it ceased to be a Scottish qualifying partnership.

(2) If the partnership ceases to be a qualifying partnership due to its dissolution, the former partners must deliver the notice in paragraph (1) to the registrar.

(3) A partnership which has delivered a notice under this regulation is not required to deliver to the registrar any notice in relation to any change or occurrence occurring after the day specified in the notice in paragraph (1)(b) under—

(a) regulation 7 (notification of changes to the registration information);

(b) Part 5 (duty to deliver information to the registrar); or

(c) Part 6 (confirmation statement).

(4) If a partnership which has delivered a notice under paragraph (1) subsequently becomes a Scottish qualifying partnership, the partnership—

(a) must register under regulation 5 (duty on Scottish qualifying partnerships to register) to receive a new registration number; and

(b) is not required to comply with regulation 11 (duty to keep information up to date) and 20 (duty to deliver information about a relevant change) in relation to any period during which it is not a Scottish qualifying partnership.

NOTES

Temporary modification: this regulation was modified by the Companies etc (Filing Requirements) (Temporary Modifications) Regulations 2020, SI 2020/645, reg 23. By virtue of the Corporate Insolvency and Governance Act 2020, s 39(8), the modification applied from 27 June 2020 to the end of the day on 5 April 2021 (subject to the saving provision in s 39(9) which provides that the expiry of s 39 on 5 April 2021 does not affect the continued operation of any Regulations made under that section for the purpose of determining the length of any period that began before the expiry). As modified, para (1) above had effect as if for the reference to "14 days" there were substituted a reference to "42 days".

[10.1205]

9 Offences in relation to registration

(1) If a Scottish qualifying partnership fails to comply with regulation 5, 7 or 8, an offence is committed by—

(a) the Scottish qualifying partnership, and

(b) every officer of the Scottish qualifying partnership who is in default.

(2) If an obligation under regulation 8(2) is not complied with, an offence is committed by every former partner who permits or fails to take all reasonable steps to prevent the non-compliance.

(3) A person guilty of an offence under this regulation is liable on summary conviction—

(a) in England and Wales to a fine, and, for continued contravention, a daily default fine not exceeding the greater of £500 and one-tenth of level 4 on the standard scale;

(b) in Scotland or Northern Ireland, to a fine not exceeding level 5 on the standard scale and, for continued contravention, a daily default fine not exceeding the greater of £500 and one-tenth of level 4 on the standard scale.

PART 4 INFORMATION DUTIES

[10.1206]

10 Duty to investigate and obtain information

(1) An eligible Scottish partnership must take reasonable steps—

(a) to find out if any person is a registrable person or a registrable relevant legal entity in relation to the eligible Scottish partnership, and

(b) if so, to identify them.

(2) Without limiting paragraph (1), an eligible Scottish partnership must give notice to any person whom it knows or has reasonable cause to believe to be a registrable person or a registrable relevant legal entity in relation to it.

(3) The notice, if addressed to an individual, must require the addressee—

(a) to state whether or not the individual is a registrable person in relation to the eligible Scottish partnership, and

(b) if so, to confirm or correct any particulars of the individual that are included in the notice, and supply any that are missing.

(4) The notice, if addressed to a legal entity, must require the addressee—

(a) to state whether or not it is a registrable relevant legal entity in relation to the eligible Scottish partnership, and

(b) if so, to confirm or correct any of its particulars that are included in the notice, and supply any that are missing.

(5) An eligible Scottish partnership may also give notice to a person under this regulation if it knows or has reasonable cause to believe that the person—

(a) knows the identity of a person who falls within paragraph (6), or

(b) knows the identity of a person likely to have that knowledge.

(6) The persons who fall within this paragraph are—

(a) any registrable person in relation to the eligible Scottish partnership;

(b) any relevant legal entity in relation to the eligible Scottish partnership;

(c) any entity which would be a relevant legal entity in relation to the eligible Scottish partnership if it were subject to its own disclosure requirements.

(7) A notice under paragraph (5) may require the addressee—

(a) to state whether or not the addressee knows the identity of—

(i) any person who falls within paragraph (6), or

(ii) any person likely to have that knowledge, and

(b) if so, to supply any particulars of theirs that are within the addressee's knowledge, and state whether or not the particulars are being supplied with the knowledge of each of the persons concerned.

(8) A notice under this regulation must state that the addressee is to comply with the notice by no later than the end of the period of one month beginning with the date of the notice.

(9) An eligible Scottish partnership is not required to take steps or give notice under this regulation with respect to a registrable person or registrable relevant legal entity if—

(a) the eligible Scottish partnership has already been informed of the person's status as a registrable person or registrable relevant legal entity in relation to it, and been supplied with all the particulars, and

(b) in the case of a registrable person, the information and particulars were provided either by the person concerned or with the person's knowledge.

(10) A person to whom a notice under paragraph (5) is given is not required by that notice to disclose any information in respect of which a claim to legal professional privilege (in Scotland, to confidentiality of communications) could be maintained in legal proceedings.

(11) In this regulation—

(a) a reference to knowing the identity of a person includes knowing information from which that person can be identified, and

(b) "particulars" means—

(i) in the case of a registrable person or a registrable relevant legal entity, the required particulars, and

(ii) in any other case, any particulars that will enable the person to be contacted by the eligible Scottish partnership.

(12) An eligible Scottish partnership is not by virtue of anything done for the purposes of these Regulations affected with notice of, or put upon inquiry as to, the rights of any person in relation to any rights in or with respect to the eligible Scottish partnership.

[10.1207]

11 Duty to keep information up to date

(1) This regulation applies if required particulars of a registrable person or registrable relevant legal entity have been delivered to the registrar by the eligible Scottish partnership in accordance with the requirements of regulation 19.

(2) The eligible Scottish partnership must give notice to the registrable person or registrable relevant legal entity if the eligible Scottish partnership knows or has reasonable cause to believe that a relevant change has occurred.

(3) In the case of a registrable person, a "relevant change" occurs if—

(a) the person ceases to be a registrable person in relation to the eligible Scottish partnership, or

(b) any other change occurs as a result of which the particulars stated for the registrable person in the register in respect of the eligible Scottish partnership are incorrect or incomplete.

(4) In the case of a registrable relevant legal entity, a "relevant change" occurs if—

(a) the entity ceases to be a registrable relevant legal entity in relation to the eligible Scottish partnership, or

(b) any other change occurs as a result of which the particulars stated for the registrable relevant legal entity in the register in respect of the eligible Scottish partnership are incorrect or incomplete.

(5) The eligible Scottish partnership must give the notice within the period of 14 days beginning with the day it—

(a) learns of the change, or

(b) if earlier, first has reasonable cause to believe that the change has occurred.

(6) The notice must require the addressee—

(a) to confirm whether or not the change has occurred, and

(b) if so—

(i) to state the date of the change, and

(ii) to confirm or correct the particulars included in the notice, and supply any that are missing from the notice.

(7) A notice under this regulation must state that the addressee is to comply with the notice by no later than the end of the period of one month beginning with the date of the notice.

(8) An eligible Scottish partnership is not required to give notice under this regulation if—

(a) the eligible Scottish partnership has already been informed of the relevant change, and

(b) in the case of a registrable person, that information was provided either by the person concerned or with the person's knowledge.

[10.1208]

12 Failure by an eligible Scottish partnership to comply with information duties

(1) If an eligible Scottish partnership fails to comply with a duty under regulation 10 or 11 to take steps or give notice, an offence is committed by—

(a) the eligible Scottish partnership, and

(b) every officer of the eligible Scottish partnership who is in default.

(2) A person guilty of an offence under this regulation is liable—

(a) on conviction on indictment, to imprisonment for a term not exceeding two years or a fine (or both);

(b) on summary conviction—

(i) in England and Wales, to imprisonment for a term not exceeding three months or a fine (or both);

(ii) in Scotland and Northern Ireland, to imprisonment for a term not exceeding three months or to a fine not exceeding the statutory maximum (or both).

[10.1209]

13 Duty on others to supply information

(1) This regulation applies to a person if—

(a) the person is a registrable person or a registrable relevant legal entity in relation to an eligible Scottish partnership;

(b) the person knows that to be the case or ought reasonably to do so,

(c) the required particulars of the person have not been delivered to the registrar in respect of the eligible Scottish partnership,

(d) the person has not received notice from the eligible Scottish partnership under regulation 10(2) (duty on eligible Scottish partnership to investigate and obtain information), and

(e) the circumstances described in sub-paragraphs (a) to (d) have continued for the period of at least one month.

(2) The person must—

(a) notify the eligible Scottish partnership of the person's status (as a registrable person or registrable relevant legal entity) in relation to the eligible Scottish partnership,

(b) state the date, to the best of the person's knowledge, on which the person acquired that status, and

(c) give the eligible Scottish partnership the person's required particulars.

(3) The duty under paragraph (2) must be complied with by the end of the period of one month beginning with the day on which all the conditions in paragraph (1)(a) to (e) were first met with respect to the person.

[10.1210]

14 Duty on others to update information

(1) This regulation applies to a person if—

(a) the required particulars of the person (whether a registrable person or a registrable relevant legal entity) have been delivered to the registrar in respect of the eligible Scottish partnership,

(b) a relevant change occurs,

(c) the person knows of the change or ought reasonably to do so,

(d) the register in respect of the eligible Scottish partnership has not been altered to reflect the change, and

(e) the person has not received notice from the eligible Scottish partnership under regulation 11(2) (duty to keep information up to date) by the end of the period of one month beginning with the day on which the change occurred.

(2) The person must—

(a) notify the eligible Scottish partnership of the change,

(b) state the date on which it occurred, and

(c) give the eligible Scottish partnership any information needed to update the register in respect of the eligible Scottish partnership.

(3) The duty under paragraph (2) must be complied with by the later of—

(a) the end of the period of two months beginning with the day on which the change occurred, and

(b) the end of the period of one month beginning with the day on which the person discovered the change.

[10.1211]

15 Enforcement of disclosure requirements

Schedule 2 makes provision for when a person fails to comply with a notice under regulation 10 or 11 (duty to investigate and obtain information and keep it up to date) or a duty under regulation 13 or 14 (duty on others to supply and update information).

[10.1212]

16 Power to make exemptions

(1) The Secretary of State may exempt a person under this regulation.

(2) The effect of an exemption is—

(a) the person is not required to comply with any notice under regulation 10(2) (duty on eligible Scottish partnership to investigate and obtain information) or 11 (eligible Scottish partnership's duty to keep information up to date), but if a notice is received, the person must bring the existence of the exemption to the attention of the eligible Scottish partnership that sent it;

(b) eligible Scottish partnerships are not obliged to take steps or give notice under the regulations specified in sub-paragraph (a) to or with respect to that person;

(c) a notice under regulation 10(5) does not require any other person to give any information about that person;

(d) the duties imposed by regulation 13 and 14 (duties to supply and update information) do not apply to that person, and

(e) the person does not count for the purposes of these Regulations as a registrable person or, as the case may be, a registrable relevant legal entity in relation to any eligible Scottish partnership.

(3) The Secretary of State must not grant an exemption under this regulation unless the Secretary of State is satisfied that, having regard to any undertaking given by the person to be exempted, there are special reasons why that person should be exempted.

[10.1213]

17 Required particulars

(1) The required particulars of an individual who is a registrable person are—

(a) the person's name,

(b) a service address,

(c) the country or territory (or part of the United Kingdom) in which the individual is usually resident,

(d) nationality,

(e) date of birth,

(f) usual residential address,

(g) subject to paragraph (5), the date on which the individual became a registrable person in relation to the eligible Scottish partnership in question,

(h) the nature of the individual's control over that eligible Scottish partnership, and

(i) if, in relation to that eligible Scottish partnership, restrictions on using or disclosing any of the individual's required particulars are in force under regulation 48, 49 or 50, that fact.

(2) In the case of a person in relation to which these Regulations have effect by virtue of regulation 3(10) (key terms) as if the person were an individual, the required particulars are—

(a) its name,

(b) its principal office,

(c) the legal form of the person and the law by which it is governed,

(d) subject to paragraph (5), the date on which it became a registrable person in relation to the eligible Scottish partnership in question, and

(e) the nature of its control over the eligible Scottish partnership.

(3) The required particulars of a registrable relevant legal entity are—

(a) its corporate or firm name,

(b) its registered or principal office,

(c) the legal form of the entity and the law by which it is governed,

(d) if applicable, the register in which it is entered (including details of the state) and its registration number in that register,

(e) subject to paragraph (5), the date on which it became a registrable relevant legal entity in relation to the eligible Scottish partnership in question, and

(f) the nature of its control over that eligible Scottish partnership.

(4) In paragraph (3)(d) "register" includes—

(a) the register maintained under section 1080(1) of the Companies Act 2006 elsewhere in the United Kingdom, and

(b) any comparable register maintained or in a country or territory outside the United Kingdom.

(5) In the case of a person who is a registrable person or a registrable relevant legal entity in relation to an eligible Scottish partnership on the commencement day, the date to be entered in the register as the date on which the individual became a registrable person, or the entity became a registrable relevant legal entity, is the commencement day.

[10.1214]

18 Nature of control over an eligible Scottish partnership

(1) The particulars required by paragraphs (1)(h), (2)(e) and (3)(f) of regulation 17 are—

(a) where the person meets the first specified condition, the statement listed in Part 1 of Schedule 3 which is applicable to that person;

(b) where the person meets the second specified condition, the statement listed in Part 2 of Schedule 3 which is applicable to that person;

(c) where the person meets the third specified condition, the statement listed in Part 3 of Schedule 3;

(d) where the person meets the fourth specified condition and does not meet the first, second or third specified condition, the statement listed in Part 4 of Schedule 3;

(e) where the person meets the fifth specified condition in connection with a trust, every statement listed in Part 5 of Schedule 3 which is applicable to that person;

(f) where the person meets the fifth specified condition in connection with a firm that, under the law by which it is governed is not a legal entity, every statement listed in Part 6 of Schedule 3 which is applicable to that person.

(2) Part 7 of Schedule 3 sets out rules for the interpretation of Schedule 3.

PART 5 DUTIES TO DELIVER INFORMATION TO THE REGISTRAR

[10.1215]

19 Duty to deliver information to the registrar

(1) An eligible Scottish partnership must deliver to the registrar the required particulars of any registrable person in relation to the eligible Scottish partnership within the period of 14 days beginning with the later of—

(a) 24th July 2017, and

(b) the day on which all the required particulars of the registrable person are first confirmed.

(2) The eligible Scottish partnership must not deliver any of the registrable person's particulars to the registrar until they have all been confirmed.

(3) Particulars of any individual with significant control over the eligible Scottish partnership who is non-registrable in relation to the eligible Scottish partnership must not be delivered to the registrar.

(4) An eligible Scottish partnership must deliver to the registrar the required particulars of any registrable relevant legal entity in relation to the eligible Scottish partnership within the period of 14 days beginning with the later of—

(a) 24th July 2017, and

(b) the day on which the eligible Scottish partnership has first obtained all the required particulars of the entity.

NOTES

Temporary modification: this regulation was modified by the Companies etc (Filing Requirements) (Temporary Modifications) Regulations 2020, SI 2020/645, reg 24. By virtue of the Corporate Insolvency and Governance Act 2020, s 39(8), the modification applied from 27 June 2020 to the end of the day on 5 April 2021 (subject to the saving provision in s 39(9) which provides that the expiry of s 39 on 5 April 2021 does not affect the continued operation of any Regulations made under that section for the purpose of determining the length of any period that began before the expiry). As modified, this regulation had effect as if for the references to "14 days" there were substituted references to "42 days".

[10.1216]

20 Duty to deliver information about a relevant change

(1) If an eligible Scottish partnership becomes aware of a relevant change with respect to a registrable person whose particulars have been delivered to the registrar, the eligible Scottish partnership must deliver to the registrar a statement specifying—

(a) the changes to the required particulars resulting from the relevant change, and

(b) the date on which the relevant change occurred,

within the period of 14 days beginning with the day on which all the changes to the required particulars and the date referred to in sub-paragraph (b) are confirmed to the eligible Scottish partnership.

(2) If an eligible Scottish partnership becomes aware of a relevant change with respect to a registrable relevant legal entity whose particulars have been delivered to the registrar, the eligible Scottish partnership must deliver to the registrar a statement specifying—

(a) the changes to the required particulars resulting from the relevant change, and

(b) the date on which the relevant change occurred,

within the period of 14 days beginning with the day on which the eligible Scottish partnership first has details of all of those changes and that date.

NOTES

Temporary modification: this regulation was modified by the Companies etc (Filing Requirements) (Temporary Modifications) Regulations 2020, SI 2020/645, reg 25. By virtue of the Corporate Insolvency and Governance Act 2020, s 39(8), the modification applied from 27 June 2020 to the end of the day on 5 April 2021 (subject to the saving provision in s 39(9) which provides that the expiry of s 39 on 5 April 2021 does not affect the continued operation of any Regulations made under that section for the purpose of determining the length of any period that began before the expiry). As modified, this regulation had effect as if for the references to "14 days" there were substituted references to "42 days".

[10.1217]

21 Meaning of "confirmed"

(1) A person's required particulars, and the details and date of any relevant change with respect to a person, are considered for the purposes of these Regulations to have been "confirmed" to an eligible Scottish partnership if—

(a) the person supplied or confirmed them to the eligible Scottish partnership (whether voluntarily, pursuant to a duty imposed by Part 4 or otherwise),

(b) another person did so but with that person's knowledge, or

(c) in relation to a limited partnership, the particulars were included in the statement of initial significant control delivered to the registrar under section 8A of the Limited Partnerships Act 1907.

(2) In the case of a person who is a registrable person in relation to an eligible Scottish partnership on the commencement day, that particular is deemed to have been "confirmed" to the eligible Scottish partnership.

[10.1218]

22 Usual residential address

(1) For the purposes of this Part, subject to paragraph (2), if a registrable person's usual residential address is the same as the service address for that individual, the particulars delivered to the registrar for that individual may state that fact instead of repeating the address.

(2) Paragraph (1) does not apply if a registrable person's service address is stated to be "the eligible Scottish partnership's service address".

[10.1219]

23 Additional matters to be notified to the registrar where there is no registrable person or registrable relevant legal entity

(1) This regulation applies where an eligible Scottish partnership knows or has reasonable cause to believe that there is no registrable person or registrable relevant legal entity in relation to the eligible Scottish partnership.

(2) The eligible Scottish partnership must deliver to the registrar a statement that it knows or has reasonable cause to believe that there is no registrable person or registrable relevant legal entity in relation to the eligible Scottish partnership within the period of 14 days beginning with the later of—

(a) 24th July 2017, and

(b) the day on which it first has the knowledge or reasonable cause for belief.

NOTES

Temporary modification: this regulation was modified by the Companies etc (Filing Requirements) (Temporary Modifications) Regulations 2020, SI 2020/645, reg 26. By virtue of the Corporate Insolvency and Governance Act 2020, s 39(8), the modification applied from 27 June 2020 to the end of the day on 5 April 2021 (subject to the saving provision in s 39(9) which provides that the expiry of s 39 on 5 April 2021 does not affect the continued operation of any Regulations made under that section for the purpose of determining the length of any period that began before the expiry). As modified, para (2) above had effect as if for the reference to "14 days" there were substituted a reference to "42 days".

[10.1220]

24 Additional matters where there is an unidentified registrable person

(1) This regulation applies where an eligible Scottish partnership—

(a) knows or has reasonable cause to believe that there is a registrable person in relation to the eligible Scottish partnership, and

(b) has not been able to identify the registrable person.

(2) The eligible Scottish partnership must deliver the information specified in paragraph (3) to the registrar within the period of 14 days beginning with the later of—

(a) 24th July 2017, and

(b) the day on which it first has the knowledge or reasonable cause for belief.

(3) The information required by paragraph (2) is a statement, in respect of each registrable person which the eligible Scottish partnership has been unable to identify, that it knows or has reasonable cause to believe that there is a registrable person in relation to the eligible Scottish partnership but has not identified the registrable person.

NOTES

Temporary modification: this regulation was modified by the Companies etc (Filing Requirements) (Temporary Modifications) Regulations 2020, SI 2020/645, reg 27. By virtue of the Corporate Insolvency and Governance Act 2020, s 39(8), the modification applied from 27 June 2020 to the end of the day on 5 April 2021 (subject to the saving provision in s 39(9) which provides that the expiry of s 39 on 5 April 2021 does not affect the continued operation of any Regulations made under that section for the purpose of determining the length of any period that began before the expiry). As modified, para (2) above had effect as if for the reference to "14 days" there were substituted a reference to "42 days".

[10.1221]

25 Additional matters where an identified registrable person's particulars are not confirmed

(1) This regulation applies where—

(a) an eligible Scottish partnership has identified a registrable person in relation to the eligible Scottish partnership, and

(b) all the required particulars of that person have not been confirmed for the purposes of regulation 19(1).

(2) The eligible Scottish partnership must deliver the information specified in paragraph (3) to the registrar within the period of 14 days beginning with the later of—

(a) 24th July 2017, and

(b) the day on which it identifies the registrable person as such.

(3) The information required by paragraph (2) is, in respect of each registrable person whose required particulars the eligible Scottish partnership has been unable to confirm, a statement that it knows or has reasonable cause to believe that there is a registrable person in relation to the eligible Scottish partnership but has been unable to confirm all the required particulars of that registrable person.

NOTES

Temporary modification: this regulation was modified by the Companies etc (Filing Requirements) (Temporary Modifications) Regulations 2020, SI 2020/645, reg 28. By virtue of the Corporate Insolvency and Governance Act 2020, s 39(8), the modification applied from 27 June 2020 to the end of the day on 5 April 2021 (subject to the saving provision in s 39(9) which provides that the expiry of s 39 on 5 April 2021 does not affect the continued operation of any Regulations made under that section for the purpose of determining the length of any period that began before the expiry). As modified, para (2) above had effect as if for the reference to "14 days" there were substituted a reference to "42 days".

[10.1222]

26 Additional matters where investigations by an eligible Scottish partnership are ongoing

(1) This regulation applies to an eligible Scottish partnership which—

(a) either—

(i) has not delivered any required particulars to the registrar, or

(ii) becomes aware that all the persons whose required particulars delivered by it to the registrar have ceased to be registrable persons or registrable relevant legal entities, as the case may be;

(b) is not required to deliver to the registrar any statement of additional matters under regulation 23, 24 or 25; and

(c) has not completed taking reasonable steps under regulation 10 to find out if any person is a registrable person or a registrable relevant legal entity in relation to the eligible Scottish partnership.

(2) The eligible Scottish partnership must comply with the requirement in paragraph (3) within the period of 14 days beginning with the day this regulation applies to it, unless any of sub-paragraphs (a)(i), (b) or (c) cease to apply to the eligible Scottish partnership before it complies with that requirement.

(3) The requirement is to deliver to the registrar a statement that the eligible Scottish partnership has not yet completed taking reasonable steps to find out if any person is a registrable person or a registrable relevant legal entity in relation to it.

NOTES

Temporary modification: this regulation was modified by the Companies etc (Filing Requirements) (Temporary Modifications) Regulations 2020, SI 2020/645, reg 29. By virtue of the Corporate Insolvency and Governance Act 2020, s 39(8), the modification applied from 27 June 2020 to the end of the day on 5 April 2021 (subject to the saving provision in s 39(9) which provides that the expiry of s 39 on 5 April 2021 does not affect the continued operation of any Regulations made under that section for the purpose of determining the length of any period that began before the expiry). As modified, para (2) above had effect as if for the reference to "14 days" there were substituted a reference to "42 days".

[10.1223]

27 Additional matters where there is a failure to comply with a notice given under regulation 10

(1) This regulation applies where—

(a) an eligible Scottish partnership has given a notice under regulation 10, and

(b) the addressee of the notice has failed to comply with the notice within the time specified in it (the "specified time").

(2) The eligible Scottish partnership must deliver to the registrar within the period of 14 days beginning with the day after the end of the specified time a statement that it has given a notice under regulation 10 which has not been complied with.

NOTES

Temporary modification: this regulation was modified by the Companies etc (Filing Requirements) (Temporary Modifications) Regulations 2020, SI 2020/645, reg 30. By virtue of the Corporate Insolvency and Governance Act 2020, s 39(8), the modification applied from 27 June 2020 to the end of the day on 5 April 2021 (subject to the saving provision in s 39(9) which provides that the expiry of s 39 on 5 April 2021 does not affect the continued operation of any Regulations made under that section for the purpose of determining the length of any period that began before the expiry). As modified, para (2) above had effect as if for the reference to "14 days" there were substituted a reference to "42 days".

[10.1224]

28 Additional matters where there is a failure to comply with a notice given under regulation 11

(1) This regulation applies where—

(a) an eligible Scottish partnership has given a notice under regulation 11, and

(b) the addressee of the notice has failed to comply with the notice within the time specified in it (the "specified time").

(2) The eligible Scottish partnership must deliver to the registrar within the period of 14 days beginning with the day after the end of the specified time a statement that it has given a notice under regulation 11 which has not been complied with.

NOTES

Temporary modification: this regulation was modified by the Companies etc (Filing Requirements) (Temporary Modifications) Regulations 2020, SI 2020/645, reg 31. By virtue of the Corporate Insolvency and Governance Act 2020, s 39(8), the modification applied from 27 June 2020 to the end of the day on 5 April 2021 (subject to the saving provision in s 39(9) which provides that the expiry of s 39 on 5 April 2021 does not affect the continued operation of any Regulations made under that section for the purpose of determining the length of any period that began before the expiry). As modified, para (2) above had effect as if for the reference to "14 days" there were substituted a reference to "42 days".

[10.1225]

29 Additional matters where a notice given under regulation 10 or 11 is complied with after the time specified in the notice

(1) This regulation applies where—

(a) a statement has been delivered to the registrar under regulation 27 or 28, and

(b) the addressee of the notice to which the statement relates has complied with the notice after the time specified in the notice.

(2) The eligible Scottish partnership must within the period of 14 days beginning with the day it becomes aware that the notice has been complied with deliver to the registrar a statement—

(a) that the notice has been complied with after the time specified in the notice, and

(b) providing the date on which the notice was complied with.

NOTES

Temporary modification: this regulation was modified by the Companies etc (Filing Requirements) (Temporary Modifications) Regulations 2020, SI 2020/645, reg 32. By virtue of the Corporate Insolvency and Governance Act 2020, s 39(8), the modification applied from 27 June 2020 to the end of the day on 5 April 2021 (subject to the saving provision in s 39(9) which provides that the expiry of s 39 on 5 April 2021 does not affect the continued operation of any Regulations made under that section for the purpose of determining the length of any period that began before the expiry). As modified, para (2) above had effect as if for the reference to "14 days" there were substituted a reference to "42 days".

[10.1226]

30 Additional matters where an eligible Scottish partnership has issued a restrictions notice

(1) This regulation applies where an eligible Scottish partnership has issued a restrictions notice under paragraph 1 of Schedule 2.

(2) The eligible Scottish partnership must within the period of 14 days beginning with the day on which it issues the restrictions notice deliver to the registrar a statement that it has issued a restrictions notice under paragraph 1 of Schedule 2.

(3) Where the eligible Scottish partnership withdraws the restrictions notice under paragraph 10 of Schedule 2, the eligible Scottish partnership must deliver to the registrar a statement—

(a) that it has withdrawn the restrictions notice by giving a withdrawal notice, and

(b) providing the date specified in the withdrawal notice as the date on which the withdrawal notice was given.

(4) Where a court makes an order under paragraph 7 of Schedule 2 directing that a relevant interest in the eligible Scottish partnership cease to be subject to restrictions, the eligible Scottish partnership must deliver to the registrar a statement—

(a) that the court has made an order under paragraph 7 of Schedule 2 directing that a relevant interest in the eligible Scottish partnership cease to be subject to restrictions; and

(b) providing the date on which that order takes effect.

NOTES

Temporary modification: this regulation was modified by the Companies etc (Filing Requirements) (Temporary Modifications) Regulations 2020, SI 2020/645, reg 33. By virtue of the Corporate Insolvency and Governance Act 2020, s 39(8), the modification applied from 27 June 2020 to the end of the day on 5 April 2021 (subject to the saving provision in s 39(9) which provides that the expiry of s 39 on 5 April 2021 does not affect the continued operation of any Regulations made under that section for the purpose of determining the length of any period that began before the expiry). As modified, para (2) above had effect as if for the reference to "14 days" there were substituted a reference to "42 days".

[10.1227]

31 End-dating of additional matters

Where a statement delivered to the registrar in accordance with regulation 23, 24, 25 or 26 ceases to be true, the eligible Scottish partnership must deliver to the registrar within the period of 14 days beginning with the day it becomes aware that the additional matter has ceased to be true, a statement—

(a) that the additional matter has ceased to be true, and
(b) providing the date on which the additional matter ceased to be true.

NOTES

Temporary modification: this regulation was modified by the Companies etc (Filing Requirements) (Temporary Modifications) Regulations 2020, SI 2020/645, reg 34. By virtue of the Corporate Insolvency and Governance Act 2020, s 39(8), the modification applied from 27 June 2020 to the end of the day on 5 April 2021 (subject to the saving provision in s 39(9) which provides that the expiry of s 39 on 5 April 2021 does not affect the continued operation of any Regulations made under that section for the purpose of determining the length of any period that began before the expiry). As modified, this regulation had effect as if for the reference to "14 days" there were substituted a reference to "42 days".

[10.1228]

32 Offences in relation to this Part

(1) If an eligible Scottish partnership makes any default in complying with any of the duties in regulation 19, 20, and 23 to 31, an offence is committed by—

(a) the eligible Scottish partnership, and
(b) every officer of the eligible Scottish partnership who is in default.

(2) A person guilty of an offence under this regulation is liable on summary conviction to a fine not exceeding level 3 on the standard scale and, for continued contravention, a daily default fine not exceeding one-tenth of level 3 on the standard scale.

[10.1229]

33 Information as to the state of the register

(1) When a person inspects or requests a copy of material on the register relating to an eligible Scottish partnership the person may ask the eligible Scottish partnership to confirm that all information that the eligible Scottish partnership is required to deliver to the registrar under this Part has been delivered.

(2) If an eligible Scottish partnership fails to respond to a request under paragraph (1) within the period of 14 days beginning with the day on which it receives the request, an offence is committed by—

(a) the eligible Scottish partnership, and
(b) every officer of the eligible Scottish partnership who is in default.

(3) A person guilty of an offence under this regulation is liable on summary conviction to a fine not exceeding level 3 on the standard scale.

[10.1230]

34 Power of court to order an eligible Scottish partnership to remedy default or delay

(1) This regulation applies if—

(a) the name of a person is without sufficient cause included in, or omitted from, information that an eligible Scottish partnership delivers to the registrar under this Part concerning persons who are registrable persons or registrable relevant legal entities in relation to the eligible Scottish partnership, or
(b) default is made or unnecessary delay takes place in informing the registrar under this Part that a person—
   (i) has become a registrable person or a registrable relevant legal entity in relation to the eligible Scottish partnership, or
   (ii) has ceased to be a registrable person or a registrable relevant legal entity in relation to it.

(2) The person aggrieved, or any other interested party, may apply to the court for an order requiring the eligible Scottish partnership to deliver to the registrar the information or statements necessary to rectify the position.

(3) The court may either refuse the application or may make the order and order the eligible Scottish partnership to pay any damages sustained by any party aggrieved.

(4) On such an application, the court may decide—

(a) any question as to whether the name of any person who is a party to the application should or should not be included in or omitted from information delivered to the registrar under this Part about persons who are a registrable person or a registrable relevant legal entity in relation to the eligible Scottish partnership, and
(b) any question necessary or expedient to be decided for rectifying the position.

(5) The reference in this regulation to "any other interested party" is to—

(a) any partner in the eligible Scottish partnership, and
(b) any other person who is a registrable person or a registrable relevant legal entity in relation to the eligible Scottish partnership.

PART 6 CONFIRMATION STATEMENT

[10.1231]

35 Duty to deliver a confirmation statement

(1) An eligible Scottish partnership must, within the period of 14 days beginning the day after the end of each review period, deliver to the registrar—

(a) such information as is necessary to ensure that the eligible Scottish partnership is able to make the statement referred to in sub-paragraph (b), and

(b) a statement (a "confirmation statement") confirming that all information required to be delivered by the eligible Scottish partnership to the registrar in relation to the confirmation period concerned under any duty mentioned in paragraph (2) either—

(i) has been delivered, or

(ii) is being delivered at the same time as the confirmation statement.

(2) The duties are—

(a) to deliver the information required in Part 5 (duty to deliver information to the registrar);

(b) in relation to a Scottish limited partnership, to deliver a change in the details required to be provided to the registrar pursuant to section 9 of the Limited Partnerships Act 1907 (registration of changes to partnerships); and

(c) in relation to a Scottish qualifying partnership, to notify a change in the details required to be provided to the registrar by regulation 7 (notification of changes to the registration information).

(3) A partnership which has served a notice under regulation 8 (effect of a Scottish general partnership ceasing to be a qualifying partnership) is not required to comply with paragraph (1) during any period in which it is not a qualifying partnership.

NOTES

Temporary modification: this regulation was modified by the Companies etc (Filing Requirements) (Temporary Modifications) Regulations 2020, SI 2020/645, reg 35. By virtue of the Corporate Insolvency and Governance Act 2020, s 39(8), the modification applied from 27 June 2020 to the end of the day on 5 April 2021 (subject to the saving provision in s 39(9) which provides that the expiry of s 39 on 5 April 2021 does not affect the continued operation of any Regulations made under that section for the purpose of determining the length of any period that began before the expiry). As modified, para (1) above had effect as if for the reference to "14 days" there were substituted a reference to "42 days".

[10.1232]

36 Meaning of "confirmation period" and "confirmation date"

In this Part—

"confirmation period" means—

(a) in relation to the first confirmation statement provided by a Scottish limited partnership registered before the commencement day, the period beginning with 24th July 2017 and ending with the confirmation date;

(b) in relation to the first confirmation statement provided by a Scottish limited partnership registered on or after the commencement day, the period beginning with its registration date and ending with the confirmation date;

(c) in relation to a Scottish limited partnership's subsequent confirmation statement, the period beginning with the day after the confirmation date of the previous confirmation statement, and ending with the confirmation date of the confirmation statement concerned;

(d) in relation to a Scottish qualifying partnership's first confirmation statement following a registration under regulation 5, the period beginning with the date of that registration under regulation 5 and ending with the confirmation date;

(e) in relation to a Scottish qualifying partnership's subsequent confirmation statement, the period beginning with the day after the confirmation date of the previous confirmation statement and ending with the confirmation date of the confirmation statement concerned;

"confirmation date" means the day specified as the confirmation date in the confirmation statement to which the confirmation period relates.

[10.1233]

37 Review period

(1) The confirmation date of a confirmation statement must be no later than the last day of the review period to which it relates.

(2) For the purposes of this Part, each of the following is a review period—

(a) in relation to a Scottish limited partnership—

(i) registered before the commencement day, the period beginning with 24th July 2017 and ending on the day before the first anniversary of its registration date occurring after the commencement day;

(ii) registered on or after the commencement day, the period of 12 months beginning on its registration date;

(b) in relation to a Scottish qualifying partnership, the period of 12 months beginning on its registration date;

(c) in relation to any eligible Scottish partnership, each period of 12 months beginning with the day after the end of the previous review period.

(3) But where an eligible Scottish partnership delivers a confirmation statement with a confirmation date which is earlier than the last day of the review period concerned, the next review period is the period of 12 months beginning with the day after the confirmation date.

(4) For the purpose of making a confirmation statement, an eligible Scottish partnership is entitled to assume that any information has been properly delivered to the registrar if it has been delivered within the period of 5 days ending with the day on which the statement is delivered.

(5) But paragraph (4) does not apply in a case where the eligible Scottish partnership has received notice from the registrar that such information has not been properly delivered.

[10.1234]

38 Failure to deliver a confirmation statement

(1) If an eligible Scottish partnership fails to deliver a confirmation statement before the end of the period of 14 days beginning the day after the end of a review period an offence is committed by—

(a) the eligible Scottish partnership, and

(b) every officer of the eligible Scottish partnership who is in default.

(2) A person guilty of an offence under subsection (1) is liable on summary conviction—

(a) in England and Wales to a fine, and, for continued contravention, a daily default fine not exceeding the greater of £500 and one-tenth of level 4 on the standard scale;

(b) in Scotland or Northern Ireland, to a fine not exceeding level 5 on the standard scale and, for continued contravention, a daily default fine not exceeding one-tenth of level 5 on the standard scale.

(3) The contravention continues until such time as a confirmation statement specifying a confirmation date no later than the last day of the review period concerned is delivered by the eligible Scottish partnership to the registrar.

(4) It is a defence for an officer charged with an offence under subsection (1) to prove that the person took all reasonable steps to avoid the commission or continuation of the offence.

(5) In the case of continued contravention, an offence is also committed by every officer of the eligible Scottish partnership who did not commit an offence under subsection (1) in relation to the initial contravention but who is in default in relation to the continued contravention.

(6) A person guilty of an offence under subsection (5) is liable on summary conviction—

(a) in England and Wales, to a fine not exceeding the greater of £500 and one-tenth of level 4 on the standard scale for each day on which the contravention continues and the person is in default;

(b) in Scotland or Northern Ireland, to a fine not exceeding one-tenth of level 5 on the standard scale for each day on which the contravention continues and the person is in default.

NOTES

Temporary modification: this regulation was modified by the Companies etc (Filing Requirements) (Temporary Modifications) Regulations 2020, SI 2020/645, reg 36. By virtue of the Corporate Insolvency and Governance Act 2020, s 39(8), the modification applied from 27 June 2020 to the end of the day on 5 April 2021 (subject to the saving provision in s 39(9) which provides that the expiry of s 39 on 5 April 2021 does not affect the continued operation of any Regulations made under that section for the purpose of determining the length of any period that began before the expiry). As modified, para (1) above had effect as if for the reference to "14 days" there were substituted a reference to "42 days".

PART 7 THE PROTECTION OF USUAL RESIDENTIAL ADDRESS INFORMATION

[10.1235]

39 Information as to usual residential address

(1) This Part makes provision for protecting, in relation to a registrable person, information—

(a) as to the usual residential address of the individual, and

(b) if applicable, that the individual's service address is the individual's usual residential address.

(2) The information in paragraph (1) is referred to in this Part as "URA information".

(3) An individual's information does not cease to be URA information on the individual ceasing to be a registrable person in relation to an eligible Scottish partnership.

(4) References in this Part to a registrable person include, for the purpose of this Part, a person who used to be a registrable person.

(5) This Part does not apply to URA information relating to a registrable person where an application under regulation 48, 49 or 50 has been granted with respect to that information and has not been revoked.

[10.1236]

40 Restriction on use or disclosure of URA information by an eligible Scottish partnership

(1) An eligible Scottish partnership must not use or disclose URA information relating to a registrable person in relation to the eligible Scottish partnership, other than—

(a) for communicating with the person;

(b) to comply with a requirement in these Regulations as to information to be delivered to the registrar;

(c) to comply with regulation 43 (corporate bodies: obligations) of the 2017 Money Laundering Regulations; or

(d) in accordance with regulation 43 (disclosure under court order) of these Regulations.

(2) Paragraph (1) does not prohibit any use or disclosure of URA information with the consent of the person concerned.

[10.1237]

41 Restriction on use or disclosure of URA information by the registrar

(1) The registrar must omit URA information from the material on the register that is available for inspection where—

(a) it is contained in a document delivered to the registrar in which such information is required to be stated, and

(b) in the case of a document having more than one part, it is contained in a part of the document in which such information is required to be stated.

(2) The registrar is not obliged to check other documents or (as the case may be) other parts of the document to ensure the absence of URA information.

(3) The registrar must not use or disclose URA information except—

(a) as permitted by regulation 42 (permitted use or disclosure), or

(b) in accordance with regulation 43 (disclosure under court order).

[10.1238]
42 Permitted use or disclosure by the registrar

(1) The registrar may use URA information relating to a registrable person for communicating with the person in question.

(2) The registrar may disclose URA information to one or more of the specified public authorities listed in Schedule 4 if in relation to the specified public authority the conditions in Part 1 of Schedule 5 are satisfied.

[10.1239]
43 Disclosure under court order

(1) The court may make an order for the disclosure by an eligible Scottish partnership or the registrar of URA information relating to a registrable person in relation to the eligible Scottish partnership if—

(a) there is evidence that the service of documents at a service address other than the person's usual residential address is not effective to bring them to the person's notice, or

(b) it is necessary or expedient for the information to be provided in connection with the enforcement of an order or decree of the court,

and the court is otherwise satisfied that it is appropriate to make the order.

(2) An order for disclosure by the registrar may only be made if the eligible Scottish partnership—

(a) does not have the person's usual residential address, or

(b) has been dissolved.

(3) The order may be made on the application of—

(a) a trustee or interim trustee in the sequestration under the Bankruptcy (Scotland) Act 2016 of the estate of the eligible Scottish partnership,

(b) a creditor or partner in the eligible Scottish partnership, or

(c) any other person appearing to the court to have a sufficient interest.

(4) The order must specify the persons to whom, and purposes for which, disclosure is authorised.

PART 8 THE PROTECTION OF SECURED INFORMATION

[10.1240]
44 Circumstances in which the registrar must omit secured information from material on the register available for public inspection

(1) In this Part and in Part 10 "secured information" means the required particulars of a registrable person in relation to an eligible Scottish partnership, other than the information that restrictions on using or disclosing the individual's required particulars are in force under this Part.

(2) The registrar must omit secured information from the material on the register that is available for public inspection if—

(a) in relation to that information an application has been made under regulation 48, 49 or 50 which—

(i) has not yet been determined by the registrar and has not been withdrawn under regulation 52 (withdrawal of an application);

(ii) has been determined by the registrar in favour of the applicant and the determination has not ceased to have effect under regulation 55 (duration of a determination);

(iii) was unsuccessful and the period of 42 days beginning with the date of the notice sent under regulation 48(5), 49(5) or 50(5) has not passed;

(iv) was unsuccessful and an appeal to the court in respect of that application under regulation 53 (appealing against an unsuccessful application) has not been determined by the court; or

(v) was unsuccessful and the applicant has successfully appealed the determination; and

(b) the information is contained in a document delivered to the registrar in which such information is required to be stated and, in the case of a document having more than one part, the information is contained in a part of the document in which such information is required to be stated.

(3) The registrar is not obliged to check documents, other than those described in paragraph (2)(b), to ensure the absence of secured information in relation to which an application under regulation 48, 49 or 50 has been made.

(4) If the secured information in relation to which an application under regulation 48, 49 or 50 is made is available for public inspection on the register at the time that the application is made, the registrar must comply with paragraph (2) as soon as reasonably practicable.

(5) For the purposes of this regulation an application under regulation 48, 49 or 50 is made when it has been registered by the registrar.

[10.1241]
45 Circumstances in which the registrar must not use or disclose secured information

(1) Save as permitted in paragraph (2), the registrar must not use or disclose secured information if an application under regulation 48, 49 or 50 has been made in relation to that information which—

(a) has not yet been determined by the registrar and has not been withdrawn under regulation 52 (withdrawal of an application);

(b) has been determined by the registrar in favour of the applicant and the determination has not ceased to have effect under regulation 55 (duration of a determination);

(c) was unsuccessful and the period of 42 days beginning with the date of the notice sent under regulation 48(5), 49(5) or 50(5) has not passed;

(d) was unsuccessful and an appeal to the court in respect of that application under regulation 53 (appealing against an unsuccessful application) has not been determined by the court; or

(e) was unsuccessful and the applicant has successfully appealed the determination.

(2) The registrar may—

(a) use or disclose secured information for communicating with the registrable person to whom the application under regulation 48, 49 or 50 relates and, if different, the applicant;

(b) disclose secured information on request to a specified public authority listed in Schedule 4 where the conditions specified in Part 1 of Schedule 5 are satisfied; and

(c) disclose the information specified in paragraph (3) on request to—

(i) a credit institution, or

(ii) a financial institution

which satisfies the conditions specified in Part 2 of Schedule 5.

(3) The secured information for disclosure under paragraph (2)(c) is, in relation to the registrable person—

(a) the individual's name,

(b) a service address,

(c) the country or territory (or part of the United Kingdom) in which the individual is usually resident,

(d) nationality,

(e) the month and year of birth,

(f) the date on which the individual became a registrable person in relation to the eligible Scottish partnership to which the secured information relates, and

(g) the nature of the individual's control over that eligible Scottish partnership.

(4) The registrar may rely on a statement delivered to the registrar by a credit institution or a financial institution under Part 2 of Schedule 5 as sufficient evidence of the matters stated therein.

(5) For the purposes of this regulation an application under regulation 48, 49 or 50 is made when it has been registered by the registrar.

[10.1242]

46 Fee payable for the disclosure by the registrar of secured information to a specified public authority

(1) On making a request for the disclosure of secured information under regulation 45(2)(b) the specified public authority must pay a fee to the registrar for the disclosure of that information.

(2) The fee payable under paragraph (1) is—

(a) where the request for secured information by the specified public authority is made by reference to an individual, £5.00 per individual specified in the request; or

(b) where the request for secured information by the specified public authority is made by reference to an eligible Scottish partnership, £5.00 per eligible Scottish partnership specified in the request.

[10.1243]

47 Fee payable for the disclosure by the registrar of secured information to a credit institution or a financial institution

(1) A credit institution or a financial institution which makes a request under regulation 45(2)(c) and Schedule 5 for the disclosure of information must pay a fee to the registrar for the disclosure of the information.

(2) The fee payable under paragraph (1) is—

(a) where the request for information is made by reference to an individual, £5.00 per individual specified in the request; or

(b) where the request for information is made by reference to an eligible Scottish partnership, £5.00 per eligible Scottish partnership specified in the request.

[10.1244]

48 Application by an individual requiring the registrar to refrain from using or disclosing that individual's secured information

(1) An individual may make an application to the registrar requiring the registrar to refrain from using or disclosing secured information relating to that individual if the individual—

(a) is a registrable person in relation to an eligible Scottish partnership;

(b) proposes to become a registrable person in relation to an eligible Scottish partnership; or

(c) used to be a registrable person in relation to an eligible Scottish partnership.

(2) The grounds on which an application may be made are that the applicant reasonably believes that if that secured information is disclosed by the registrar—

(a) the activities of the eligible Scottish partnership; or

(b) one or more characteristics or personal attributes of the applicant when associated with the eligible Scottish partnership,

will put the applicant or a person living with the applicant at serious risk of being subjected to violence or intimidation.

(3) The application must—

(a) contain—

(i) a statement of the grounds on which the application is made;

(ii) the name and any former name of the applicant;

(iii) the date of birth of the applicant;

(iv) the usual residential address of the applicant;

(v) the e-mail address of the applicant, if any; and

(vi) the name and, if applicable, the registered number of the eligible Scottish partnership in relation to which the applicant is, proposes to become, or used to be a registrable person.

(b) be accompanied by evidence which supports the applicant's statement of the grounds on which the application is made.

(4) Where an individual who is or used to be a registrable person in relation to an eligible Scottish partnership sends an application under paragraph (1) to the registrar in relation to the eligible Scottish partnership, that individual must inform that eligible Scottish partnership of that fact as soon as reasonably practicable.

(5) The registrar must determine the application and, within the period of 7 days beginning with the date on which the determination is made, send to the applicant notice of the determination.

(6) Where the application is unsuccessful, the notice under paragraph (5) must inform the applicant of the applicant's right to apply for permission to appeal against the determination within 28 days beginning with the date of the notice.

[10.1245]

49 Application by an eligible Scottish partnership requiring the registrar to refrain from using or disclosing an individual's secured information

(1) An eligible Scottish partnership ("the applicant") may make an application to the registrar requiring the registrar to refrain from using or disclosing secured information relating to an individual ("S") who—

- (a) is a registrable person;
- (b) proposes to become a registrable person; or
- (c) used to be a registrable person,

in relation to the applicant.

(2) An eligible Scottish partnership may only make an application under paragraph (1) where S has given consent for the eligible Scottish partnership to make the application on S's behalf.

(3) The grounds on which an application may be made are that the applicant reasonably believes that if the secured information is disclosed by the registrar—

- (a) the activities of the applicant; or
- (b) one or more characteristics or personal attributes of S when associated with the applicant,

will put S or a person living with S at serious risk of being subjected to violence or intimidation.

(4) The application must—

- (a) contain—
  - (i) a statement of the grounds on which the application is made;
  - (ii) confirmation that S consents to the making of the application;
  - (iii) the name and, if applicable, the registered number of the applicant;
  - (iv) an address at which documents may be effectively served on the applicant;
  - (v) the e-mail address of the applicant, if any;
  - (vi) the name and any former name of S;
  - (vii) the date of birth of S;
  - (viii) the usual residential address of S; and
  - (ix) the e-mail address of S, if any; and
- (b) be accompanied by evidence which supports the applicant's statement of the grounds on which the application is made.

(5) The registrar must determine the application and, within the period of 7 days beginning with the date on which that the determination is made, send to the applicant and to S notice of the determination.

(6) Where the application is unsuccessful, the notice under paragraph (5) must inform the applicant of the applicant's right to apply for permission to appeal against the determination within the period of 28 days beginning with the date of the notice.

[10.1246]

50 Application by a prospective partner in a prospective eligible Scottish partnership requiring the registrar to refrain from using or disclosing an individual's secured information

(1) A prospective partner in a prospective eligible Scottish partnership ("the applicant") may make an application to the registrar requiring the registrar to refrain from using or disclosing secured information relating to an individual ("S") who proposes to become, on or after the formation of the eligible Scottish partnership, a registrable person in relation to the prospective eligible Scottish partnership.

(2) A prospective partner in a prospective eligible Scottish partnership may only make an application under paragraph (1) where S has given consent for the prospective partner to make the application on S's behalf.

(3) The grounds on which an application may be made are that the applicant reasonably believes that if the secured information is disclosed by the registrar—

- (a) the proposed activities of the prospective eligible Scottish partnership, or
- (b) one or more characteristics or personal attributes of S when associated with the prospective eligible Scottish partnership,

will put S or a person living with S at serious risk of being subjected to violence or intimidation.

(4) The application must—

- (a) contain—
  - (i) a statement of the grounds on which the application is made;
  - (ii) confirmation that S consents to the making of the application;
  - (iii) the name and any former name of the applicant;
  - (iv) the usual residential address of the applicant;
  - (v) the e-mail address of the applicant, if any;
  - (vi) the proposed name of the eligible Scottish partnership to which the application relates;
  - (vii) the name and any former name of S;
  - (viii) the date of birth of S;
  - (ix) the usual residential address of S; and
  - (x) the e-mail address of S, if any; and

(b) be accompanied by evidence which supports the applicant's statement of the grounds on which the application is made.

(5) The registrar must determine the application and, within the period of 7 days beginning with the date on which the determination is made, send to the applicant and to S notice of the determination.

(6) Where the application is unsuccessful, the notice under paragraph (5) must inform the applicant of the applicant's right to apply for permission to appeal against the determination within the period of 28 days beginning with the date of the notice.

[10.1247]

51 Matters relating to an application made under regulation 48, 49 or 50

(1) For the purpose of determining an application made under regulation 48, 49 or 50 the registrar may—

(a) direct that additional information or evidence should be delivered to the registrar;

(b) refer any question relating to an assessment of the nature or extent of any risk of violence or intimidation to a relevant body or to any other person the registrar considers may be able to assist in making that assessment; and

(c) accept any answer to a question referred under paragraph (1)(b) as providing sufficient evidence of the nature or extent of any risk.

(2) The registrar must not make available for public inspection—

(a) any application made under regulation 48, 49 or 50;

(b) any documents provided in support of that application;

(c) any notice provided under regulation 52 (notice of withdrawal of application);

(d) any notice provided under regulation 53 (notice of an appeal);

(e) any notice provided under regulation 55 (notice that determination no longer wanted);

(f) any notice provided under regulation 56 (representations as to why determination should not be revoked); or

(g) any notice provided under regulation 82 (protection for registrable persons applying for protection of secured information).

(3) A person who makes an application under regulation 48, 49 or 50 must inform the registrar in writing without delay upon becoming aware of any change to any information or evidence provided to the registrar in connection with the application.

(4) For the purposes of this regulation an application under regulation 48, 49 or 50 is made when it has been registered by the registrar.

[10.1248]

52 Withdrawal of an application made under regulation 48, 49 or 50

(1) If an individual in relation to whom an application has been made under regulation 48, 49 or 50 that has not yet been determined notifies the registrar in writing that the individual no longer wishes the registrar to determine the application, the registrar is not required to determine the application under regulation 48(5), 49(5) or 50(5) (as the case may be).

(2) Where an individual in relation to whom an application under regulation 48 or 49 has been made sends a notice to the registrar under paragraph (1), that individual must notify the eligible Scottish partnership to which the application related of this fact as soon as reasonably practicable.

(3) Where an individual in relation to whom an application under regulation 50 has been made sends a notice to the registrar under paragraph (1), that individual must notify the prospective partners who made the application and, if formed, the eligible Scottish partnership to which the application related of this fact as soon as reasonably practicable.

(4) For the purposes of this regulation an application under regulation 48, 49 or 50 is made when it has been registered by the registrar.

[10.1249]

53 Appeal against an unsuccessful application made under regulation 48, 49 or 50

(1) Subject to paragraph (2), an applicant who has received notice under regulation 48(5), 49(5) or 50(5) that the applicant's application has been unsuccessful may appeal to the High Court or, in Scotland, the Court of Session on the grounds that the determination—

(a) is unlawful;

(b) is irrational or unreasonable; or

(c) has been made on the basis of a procedural impropriety or otherwise contravenes the rules of natural justice.

(2) No appeal may be brought unless the permission of the court has been obtained.

(3) No application for such permission may be made after 28 days beginning with the date of the notice under regulation 48(5), 49(5) or 50(5) unless the court is satisfied that there was good reason for the failure of the applicant to seek permission before the end of that period.

(4) An applicant who seeks permission to appeal must serve written notice of the application on the registrar within the period of 7 days beginning with the day on which the application for permission was issued.

(5) The court determining an appeal may—

(a) dismiss the appeal; or

(b) quash the determination.

(6) Where the court quashes a determination it may refer the matter to the registrar with a direction to reconsider it and make a determination in accordance with the findings of the court.

[10.1250]

54 Unsuccessful determination made under regulation 48, 49 or 50

(1) This regulation applies where the registrar has made a determination in respect of an application made under regulation 48, 49 or 50 which is not in favour of the applicant and to which regulation 82 does not apply.

(2) The registrar must make secured information on the register to which the application under regulation 48, 49 or 50 relates available for public inspection—

(a) where notice of an application for permission to appeal has not been served on the registrar in accordance with regulation 53(4), as soon as reasonably practicable after the end of the period of 42 days beginning with the date of the notice given under regulation 48(5), 49(5) or 50(5); or

(b) where notice of an application for permission to appeal has been served on the registrar in accordance with regulation 53(4), as soon as reasonably practicable after—

(i) the court has dismissed the application for permission to appeal or the appeal and there is no further appeal pending; or

(ii) the registrar becomes aware that the application for permission to appeal or the appeal has been subsequently withdrawn or abandoned.

(3) Where the registrar makes secured information available for public inspection on the register under this regulation, the registrar must notify the individual to whom the secured information relates and the eligible Scottish partnership to which the application under regulation 48, 49 or 50 related of that action as soon as reasonably practicable.

[10.1251]

55 Duration of a determination under regulation 48, 49 or 50

(1) A determination under regulation 48(5), 49(5) or 50(5) that an application is successful continues to have effect until—

(a) either—

(i) the individual to whom the determination relates; or

(ii) that individual's personal representative,

notifies the registrar in writing that the individual wishes the determination to cease to have effect; or

(b) the registrar revokes the determination under regulation 56.

(2) Where a notice is given under paragraph (1)(a), the person giving the notice must notify the eligible Scottish partnership to which the application that was determined relates of the notice given to the registrar.

(3) In this regulation "personal representative" means the executor or administrator for the time being of a deceased person.

[10.1252]

56 Revocation of a determination under regulation 48(5), 49(5) or 50(5)

(1) The registrar may revoke a determination made under regulation 48(5), 49(5) or 50(5) that an application is successful if—

(a) the applicant in relation to the determination or (if different) the individual to whom the application relates has been found guilty of an offence under section 1112 of the Companies Act 2006 (general false statement offence) in respect of purported compliance with any provision of this Part;

(b) the registrar has sent a notice in accordance with paragraph (2) to the applicant in relation to the determination and (if different) the individual to whom the determination relates; and

(c) the period of 28 days beginning with the date of that notice has expired.

(2) The notice mentioned in paragraph (1)(b) must inform the addressee—

(a) of the registrar's intention to revoke the determination;

(b) that the addressee may, within the period of 28 days beginning with the date of the notice, deliver representations in writing to the registrar as to why the registrar should not revoke the determination; and

(c) that if the registrar receives such representations within that period, the registrar will have regard to the representations in deciding whether to revoke the determination.

(3) If within the period specified in paragraph (2)(b) an addressee of the notice delivers representations in writing to the registrar as to why the registrar should not revoke the determination, the registrar must have regard to the representations in deciding whether to revoke the determination.

(4) The registrar must send notice of the registrar's decision as to whether to revoke a determination to the applicant in relation to the determination and (if different) the individual to whom the determination relates within the period of 7 days beginning with the date of the decision.

(5) Where the registrar has made a decision to revoke a determination, the registrar must make secured information on the register to which the determination relates available for public inspection as soon as reasonably practicable after sending the notice mentioned in paragraph (4).

(6) Where the registrar makes secured information available for public inspection on the register under this regulation, the registrar must notify the individual to whom the secured information relates and the eligible Scottish partnership to which the application under regulation 48, 49 or 50 related of that action as soon as reasonably practicable.

[10.1253]

57 Protection by an eligible Scottish partnership of secured information

(1) Subject to paragraph (2), an eligible Scottish partnership must not use or disclose secured information relating to an individual ("S") if—

(a) in relation to that information an application has been made under regulation 48, 49 or 50; and

(b) the eligible Scottish partnership has not received notification under regulation 52(2), 52(3), 54(3), 55(2), 56(6) or 82(6)(b).

(2) The eligible Scottish partnership may use or disclose secured information relating to S—

(a) for communicating with S;

(b) in order to comply with a requirement of these Regulations for information to be delivered to the registrar;

(c) where S has given consent for the eligible Scottish partnership to use or disclose secured information relating to S; or

(d) to the extent necessary in order to comply with regulation 43 of the 2017 Money Laundering Regulations (corporate bodies: obligations).

(3) For the purposes of this regulation, an application has been made—

(a) under regulation 48(1)(a) or 48(1)(c) when the applicant has informed the eligible Scottish partnership under regulation 48(4) that the applicant has made an application;

(b) under regulation 48(1)(b) when the eligible Scottish partnership has received the particular required by regulation 17(1)(i) (required particulars) in relation to that individual;

(c) under regulation 49 when the eligible Scottish partnership sends the application to the registrar; or

(d) under regulation 50 when the prospective partner sends the application to the registrar.

PART 9 APPLICATION OF THE COMPANIES ACT 2006

[10.1254]

58 Application of Part 35 of the Companies Act 2006

Section 1066 (registered numbers) of the Companies Act 2006 applies to Scottish qualifying partnerships with the following modifications—

(a) for references to a "company" substitute "Scottish qualifying partnership"; and

(b) omit subsections (5) and (6).

[10.1255]

59

Section 1081 (annotation of the register) of the Companies Act 2006 applies to eligible Scottish partnerships with the following modifications—

(a) in subsection (1), omit paragraphs (e) and (f);

(b) omit subsection (1A);

(c) for subsection (2), substitute—

"(2) Where it appears to the registrar that material on the register is misleading or confusing, the registrar may place a note in the register containing such information as appears to the registrar to be necessary to remedy, as far as possible, the misleading or confusing nature of the material.";

(d) omit subsection (5);

(e) in subsection (6)—

(i) omit "or (1A), or in pursuance of regulations under", and

(ii) for "all purposes of the Companies Acts" substitute "the purposes of the Scottish Partnerships (Register of People with Significant Control) Regulations 2017"; and

(f) omit subsection (7).

[10.1256]

60

The following provisions of the Companies Act 2006 apply to information on the register delivered to the registrar by eligible Scottish partnerships under these Regulations—

(a) section 1085 (inspection of the register);

(b) section 1086 (right to a copy of material on the register), with the omission of subsection (2).

[10.1257]

61

Section 1087 (material not available for public inspection) of the Companies Act 2006 applies in relation to information delivered to the registrar by eligible Scottish partnerships under these Regulations modified so that it reads as follows—

"1087 Material not available for public inspection

(1) The registrar must not make available for public inspection on the register material which is excluded from public inspection by or under any enactment.

(2) A restriction applying by reference to material deriving from a particular description of document does not affect the availability for public inspection of the same information contained in material derived from another description of document in relation to which no such restriction applies.

(3) Material to which this section applies need not be retained by the registrar for longer than appears to the registrar reasonably necessary for the purposes for which the material was delivered to the registrar."

[10.1258]

[61A

Section 1087ZA of the Companies Act 2006 (required particulars available for public inspection for limited period) applies to eligible Scottish partnerships, modified so that it reads as follows—

"1087ZA Required particulars available for public inspection for limited period

(1) This section applies where—

(a) a document is delivered to the registrar by an eligible Scottish partnership under regulation 19 (duty to deliver information to the registrar) of the Scottish partnerships regulations; or

(b) a document is delivered to the registrar by an eligible Scottish partnership under regulation 20 (duty to deliver information about a relevant change) of the Scottish partnerships regulations.

(2) The document, and any record of the information contained in the document, must not be made available by the registrar for public inspection after the expiration of ten years beginning with the date on which the registrar is notified of the dissolution of the eligible Scottish partnership.

(3) Subsection (2) does not affect the availability for public inspection of the same information contained in material derived from another description of document in relation to which no such restriction applies.

(4) For the purposes of this section—

"eligible Scottish partnership" has the meaning given in regulation 2 (interpretation) of the Scottish partnerships regulations.

"the Scottish partnerships regulations" means the Scottish Partnerships (Register of People with Significant Control) Regulations 2017."]

NOTES

Commencement: 10 January 2020.

Inserted by the Money Laundering and Terrorist Financing (Amendment) Regulations 2019, SI 2019/1511, reg 20(1), (2), as from 10 January 2020.

[10.1259]
62

Section 1087A of the Companies Act 2006 applies in relation to information delivered to the registrar by an eligible Scottish partnership under these Regulations modified so that it reads as follows—

"1087A Restricted DOB information

(1) Information is "restricted DOB information" if—

(a) it is DOB information,

(b) it is contained in a document delivered to the registrar,

(c) the document is one in which such information is required to be stated, and

(d) if the document has more than one part, the part in which the information is contained is a part in which such information is required to be stated.

(2) "DOB information" is information as to the day of the month (but not the month or year) on which an individual who is a registrable person in relation to an eligible Scottish partnership was born.

(3) Information about an individual does not cease to fall within subsection (1) when the individual ceases to be a registrable person.

(4) Nothing in subsection (1) obliges the registrar to check other documents or (as the case may be) other parts of the document to ensure the absence of DOB information."

[10.1260]
63

Section 1087B applies in relation to information delivered to the registrar by an eligible Scottish partnership under these Regulations modified so that it reads as follows—

"1087B Disclosure of restricted DOB information

(1) The registrar must not disclose an individual's restricted DOB information unless—

(a) the same information about the individual (whether in the same or a different capacity) is made available by the registrar for public inspection as a result of being contained in another description of document in relation to which no restriction under section 1087 of the Companies Act 2006 (as modified) applies (see subsection (2) of that section), or

(b) disclosure of the information by the registrar is permitted by subsection (2) or another provision of this Act.

(2) The registrar may disclose an individual's restricted DOB information to a public authority ("specified public authority") listed in Schedule 4 to the Scottish Partnerships (Register of People with Significant Control) Regulations 2017 if the conditions in Part 1 of Schedule 5 to those Regulations are satisfied."

[10.1261]
64

Section 1088 (application to registrar to make address unavailable for inspection) of the Companies Act 2006 applies to eligible Scottish partnerships, modified so that it reads as follows—

"1088 Modification of the Companies (Disclosure of Address) Regulations 2009

(1) The provisions of the Companies (Disclosure of Address) Regulations 2009 set out in subsection (2) apply with respect to applications to the registrar to make an address unavailable for public inspection, with the modifications specified in subsection (3).

(2) The provisions referred to in subsection (1) are—

(a) Part 3 (application to make an address unavailable for public inspection under section 1088);

(b) Part 4 (matters relating to applications under section 1088); and

(c) any other provisions of the Regulations having effect for the purposes of those provisions.

(3) Those provisions apply with the following modifications—

(a) in regulation 1(2) for the definition of "former name" substitute—

""former name" means a name by which the individual was formerly known and which has been notified to the registrar under section 8A(5) of the Limited Partnerships Act 1907 or under Part 5 of the Scottish Partnerships (Register of People with Significant Control) Regulations 2017;"

(b) [regulation 9 (application under section 1088 to make an address unavailable for public inspection by an individual)] substitute—

["9 (1) Where an individual's usual residential address is on the register, that individual may make a section 1088 application in respect of that address where, in the individual's capacity as a registrable person, that address was placed on the register either—

(a) as a service address in a statement of initial significant control delivered to the registrar under section 8A of the Limited Partnerships Act 1907, or

(b) as a service address included in the required particulars of a registrable person delivered to the registrar to comply with an obligation in Part 5 of the Scottish Partnerships (Register of People with Significant Control) Regulations 2017.

(2) The application must contain—

(a) the name and any former name of the applicant;

(b) the usual residential address of the applicant that is to be made unavailable for public inspection;

(c) an address for correspondence in respect of the application;

(d) the name and registered number of each eligible Scottish partnership in respect of which the applicant has indicated in the application that the applicant's usual residential address was placed on the register;

(e) in respect of each eligible Scottish partnership falling within sub-paragraph (d)—

(i) the name of the document in which that usual residential address appears on the register,

(ii) where that document is a form, the number and title of the form, and

(iii) the registration date of that document;

(f) where the application includes an eligible Scottish partnership which is required to maintain a current address for the applicant on the register, the service address which is to replace the usual residential address; and

(g) the date of birth of the applicant."];

(c) omit regulations [10, 11 and 12];

(d) . . .

(e) for regulation 13 (effect of a successful section 1088 application) substitute—

["13 (1) This regulation applies in relation to a section 1088 application made under regulation 9.

(2) The registrar must make the specified address unavailable for public inspection in the places on the register where the applicant has indicated, in the application, that it appears.

(3) Where the application relates to an entry concerning an eligible Scottish partnership which is required to maintain a current address on the register for the applicant, the registrar must make the specified address unavailable for public inspection by replacing it with the service address provided by the applicant.

(4) In any other case, the registrar must make the specified address unavailable for public inspection by removing all elements of that address except—

(a) for a United Kingdom address—

(i) the outward code from the postcode, or

(ii) where the address on the register does not include the outward code from the postcode, any information in that address that denotes a geographical area which is equivalent to or larger than the area represented by the outward code of the postcode which applies to that address; and

(b) for an address other than a United Kingdom address, the country or territory and the name of the next principal unit of geographical subdivision of that country or territory (eg the state, region, province, county, district, municipality or equivalent) if there is one included in that address as it appears on the register.

(5) In this regulation—

"specified address" means the address specified in the application as being the one to be made unavailable for public inspection; and

"outward code" means the part of a postcode before the internal space but not the number and letters which come after that space."];

[(i) omit regulations 14 to 16.]

NOTES

In s 1088 as set out above, the words in square brackets in sub-s (3)(b), (c) and (e) were substituted, sub-s (3)(d) was revoked, and sub-s (3)(i) was substituted (for the original sub-s (f)–(h)), by the Companies (Disclosure of Address) (Amendment) Regulations 2018, SI 2018/528, reg 6, as from 26 April 2018 (note that reg 8 of the 2018 Regulations provides that if a section 1088 application was received by the registrar before that date, the application must be dealt with by the registrar in accordance with these Regulations as they applied before that date).

[10.1262]

65

Section 1089 (form of application for inspection or copy) of the Companies Act 2006 applies in relation to information delivered to the registrar by an eligible Scottish partnership under these Regulations, with the omission of subsection (2).

[10.1263]

66

Section 1090 (form and manner in which copies to be provided) of the Companies Act 2006 applies in relation to information delivered to the registrar by an eligible Scottish partnership under these Regulations, modified so that it reads as follows—

"1099 Form and manner in which copies to be provided

The registrar may determine the form and manner in which copies are to be provided under section 1086."

[10.1264]

67

Section 1091 (certification of copies as accurate) of the Companies Act 2006 applies to information delivered to the registrar by an eligible Scottish partnership under these Regulations, modified so that it reads as follows—

"1091 Certification of copies as accurate

(1) Copies provided under section 1086 in hard copy form must be certified as true copies unless the applicant dispenses with such certification.

(2) A copy provided under section 1086, certified by the registrar (whose official position it is unnecessary to prove) to be an accurate record of the contents of the original document, is in all legal proceedings admissible in evidence—

(a) as of equal validity with the original document, and

(b) as evidence (in Scotland, sufficient evidence) of any fact stated in the original document of which direct oral evidence would be admissible.

(3) Copies provided by the registrar may, instead of being certified in writing to be an accurate record, be sealed with the registrar's official seal.

(4) In subsection (1) "hard copy form", in relation to a document or information sent or supplied, is a document or information sent or supplied in a paper copy or similar form capable of being read."

[10.1265]
[67A

Section 1095A of the Companies Act 2006 (rectification of register to resolve a discrepancy) applies to eligible Scottish partnerships, modified so that it reads as follows—

"1095A Rectification of register to resolve a discrepancy

(1) This section applies where—

(a) a discrepancy in information relating to an eligible Scottish partnership is reported to the registrar under regulation 30A(2) of the Money Laundering, Terrorist Financing and Transfer of Funds (Information on the Payer) Regulations 2017 (requirement to report discrepancies in information about beneficial ownership), and

(b) the registrar determines, having investigated the discrepancy under regulation 30A(5) of those Regulations, that there is a discrepancy.

(2) The registrar may remove material from the register if doing so is necessary to resolve the discrepancy.

(3) In this section "eligible Scottish partnership" has the meaning given in regulation 2 of the Scottish Partnerships (Register of People with Significant Control) Regulations 2017."]

NOTES

Commencement: 10 January 2020.

Inserted by the Money Laundering and Terrorist Financing (Amendment) Regulations 2019, SI 2019/1511, reg 20(1), (3), as from 10 January 2020.

[10.1266]
68

Section 1103 (documents to be drawn up and delivered in English) of the Companies Act 2006 applies to documents delivered to the registrar by an eligible Scottish partnership under these Regulations, modified so that it reads as follows—

"1103 Documents to be drawn up and delivered in English

All documents required to be delivered to the registrar must be drawn up and delivered in English."

[10.1267]
69

Section 1112 (general false statement offence) of the Companies Act 2006 applies in relation to information delivered to the registrar by an eligible Scottish partnership under these Regulations, with the following modifications—

(a) in subsection (1)(a), for "the Companies Acts" substitute "the Scottish Partnerships (Register of People with Significant Control) Regulations 2017"; and

(b) in subsection (2)(b)(i), omit "not exceeding the statutory maximum".

[10.1268]
70 Application of Part 36 of the Companies Act 2006

Section 1125 (meaning of "daily default fine") of the Companies Act 2006 applies in relation to these Regulations, modified so that in subsection (1) for "the Companies Acts" substitute "the Scottish Partnerships (Register of People with Significant Control) Regulations 2017".

[10.1269]
71

Section 1127 (summary proceedings: venue) of the Companies Act 2006 applies in relation to offences under these Regulations, with the following modifications in subsection (1)—

(a) for "the Companies Acts" substitute "the Scottish Partnerships (Register of People with Significant Control) Regulations 2017"; and

(b) for "body corporate" and "body" substitute "legal entity".

[10.1270]
72

Section 1128 (summary proceedings: time limit for proceedings) of the Companies Act 2006 applies, modified so that for every occurrence of "the Companies Acts" substitute "the Scottish Partnerships (Register of People with Significant Control) Regulations 2017".

[10.1271]
73

Section 1129 (legal professional privilege) of the Companies Act 2006 applies in relation to offences under these Regulations, modified so that for "the Companies Acts" and "those Acts" substitute "the Scottish Partnerships (Register of People with Significant Control) Regulations 2017".

[10.1272]
74

Section 1132 (production and inspection of documents where offence suspected) of the Companies Act 2006 applies, with the following modifications—

(a) for each occurrence of "a company" and "the company" substitute "an eligible Scottish partnership" or "the eligible Scottish partnership", as the case may be; and

(b) for "secretary of the company, or such other officer of it" substitute "such officer of the eligible Scottish partnership".

[10.1273]
75 Application of Part 37 of the Companies Act 2006

Section 1156 (meaning of "the court") of the Companies Act 2006 applies, modified so that for every occurrence of "the Companies Acts" substitute "the Scottish Partnerships (Register of People with Significant Control) Regulations 2017".

[10.1274]
76

Section 1157 (power of court to grant relief in certain cases) of the Companies Act 2006 applies, with the following modifications—

(a) in subsection (1)(a), for "a company" substitute "an eligible Scottish partnership";
(b) omit subsection (1)(b); and
(c) in subsection (1) and (2) omit "or person".

[10.1275]
77 Interpretation of this Part

(1) The provisions of this Part have effect together with any other provisions of the Companies Act 2006 having effect for the purposes of those provisions.

(2) Subject to paragraph (1), a term used in a provision of the Companies Act 2006 as applied by this Part which has a meaning given elsewhere in these Regulations has that meaning in this Part.

PART 10 CONSEQUENTIAL AMENDMENTS, TRANSITIONAL PROVISION, AND REVIEW

78, 79 (*Reg 78 amends the Companies Act 2006, s 790C(7) at* **[1.877]**. *Reg 79 amends the Limited Liability Partnerships (Application of Companies Act 2006) Regulations 2009, SI 2009/1804, reg 31B(3) at* **[10.354]**.)

[10.1276]
80 Transitional provision in relation to regulations 78 and 79

(1) Where as a result of the amendment made by regulation 78 and 79 an eligible Scottish partnership is a registrable relevant legal entity in relation to a company or a limited liability partnership on the commencement day, the date on which the eligible Scottish partnership became a registrable relevant legal entity is the commencement day.

(2) Where as a result of the amendment made by regulation 79 or 80 a relevant change occurs such that, with effect from the commencement day—

(a) an individual ceases to be a registrable person, or
(b) a legal entity ceases to be a registrable relevant legal entity,

the date of the relevant change is the commencement day.

(3) In paragraph (1), "limited liability partnership" means a limited liability partnership incorporated under the Limited Liability Partnerships Act 2000();

81 (*Amends the Limited Partnerships (Forms) Rules 2009, SI 2009/2160, and introduces Sch 6 to these Regulations.*)

[10.1277]
82 Protection for registrable persons applying for protection of secured information

(1) This regulation applies where—

(a) an individual is a registrable person in relation to an eligible Scottish partnership on the commencement day;
(b) before 24 July 2017 an application is made under regulation 48, 49 or 50 for the protection of secured information relating to the individual; and
(c) the registrar determines that the application is unsuccessful.

(2) Subject to paragraph (3), during the protected period, the registrar—

(a) must not use or disclose secured information relating to the individual, and
(b) must omit the information referred to in sub-paragraph (a) from the material on the register that is available for public inspection.

(3) The registrar may use or disclose secured information relating to the individual—

(a) for communicating with the individual, and
(b) where the application was made under regulation 49, for communicating with the eligible Scottish partnership which made the application.

(4) Paragraph (5) applies where the individual ceases to be a registrable person in relation to the eligible Scottish partnership before the end of the protected period.

(5) If, before the end of the protected period, the registrar receives notice from the individual setting out the date on which that individual ceased to be a registrable person in relation to the eligible Scottish partnership, the registrar—

(a) must not use or disclose secured information relating to the individual which the registrar obtained before the end of the protected period, and

(b) must omit the information referred to in sub-paragraph (a) from the material on the register that is available for public inspection.

(6) Where the registrar does not receive notice under paragraph (5), the registrar must as soon as reasonably practicable after the end of the protected period—

(a) make the secured information available on the register for public inspection, and

(b) notify the individual and the eligible Scottish partnership to which the application under regulation 48, 49 or 50 related of the action taken under sub-paragraph (a).

(7) In relation to an application to which this regulation applies regulation 54 (unsuccessful determination of application for protection of secured information) does not apply.

(8) For the purposes of this regulation an application under regulation 48, 49 or 50 is made when it is registered by the registrar.

(9) In this regulation—

"protected period" means, in relation to an appeal under regulation 53 (appeal against unsuccessful application under regulation 48, 49 or 50)—

(a) where no such appeal has been brought, 12 weeks beginning with the day on which notice of the registrar's determination was sent under regulation 48(5), 49(5) or 50(5) of those regulations,

(b) where such an appeal has been brought and dismissed, 12 weeks beginning with the day on which the court dismissed the appeal in accordance with regulation 53(5), or

(c) where such an appeal has been brought and subsequently withdrawn or abandoned, 12 weeks beginning with the day on which the registrar became aware that the appeal had been withdrawn or abandoned.

[10.1278]

83 Review

(1) The Secretary of State must from time to time—

(a) carry out a review of these Regulations;

(b) set out the conclusions of the review in a report; and

(c) publish the report.

(2) The report must in particular—

(a) set out the objectives intended to be achieved by the regulatory system established by these Regulations;

(b) assess the extent to which those objectives have been achieved; and

(c) assess whether those objectives remain appropriate and, if so, the extent to which they could be achieved in another way that imposed less regulation.

(3) Reports under this regulation are to be published at intervals not exceeding five years.

SCHEDULES

SCHEDULE 1
REFERENCES TO PEOPLE WITH SIGNIFICANT CONTROL OVER AN ELIGIBLE SCOTTISH PARTNERSHIP

Regulation 3

PART 1 THE SPECIFIED CONDITIONS

Introduction

[10.1279]

1. This Part of this Schedule specifies the conditions at least one of which must be met by an individual ("X") in relation to an eligible Scottish partnership ("eligible Scottish partnership Y") in order for the individual to be a person with "significant control" over the eligible Scottish partnership Y.

Ownership of right to surplus assets on a winding up

2. The first condition is that X holds, directly or indirectly, the right to more than 25% of any surplus assets in eligible Scottish partnership Y on a winding up.

Ownership of voting rights

3. The second condition is that X holds, directly or indirectly, more than 25% of the voting rights in eligible Scottish partnership Y.

Ownership of right to appoint or remove the persons entitled to manage the eligible Scottish partnership

4. The third condition is that X holds the right, directly or indirectly, to appoint or remove the majority of the persons who are entitled to take part in the management of eligible Scottish partnership Y.

Significant influence or control

5. The fourth condition is that X has the right to exercise, or actually exercises, significant influence or control over eligible Scottish partnership Y.

Trusts, partnerships etc

6. The fifth condition is that—

(a) the trustees of a trust or the members of a firm that, under the law by which it is governed, is not a legal person meet any of the other specified conditions (in their capacity as such) in relation to eligible Scottish partnership Y, or would do so if they were individuals, and

(b) X has the right to exercise, or actually exercises, significant influence or control over the activities of that trust or firm.

PART 2 HOLDING AN INTEREST IN AN ELIGIBLE SCOTTISH PARTNERSHIP ETC

Introduction

[10.1280]

7. This Part of this Schedule specifies the circumstances in which, for the purposes of paragraph (5) or (8) of regulation 3—

(a) a person ("V") is to be regarded as holding an interest in an eligible Scottish partnership ("eligible Scottish partnership W");

(b) an interest held by V in eligible Scottish partnership W is to be regarded as held through a legal entity.

Holding an interest

8. (1) V holds an interest in eligible Scottish partnership W if—

(a) V holds, directly or indirectly, the right to surplus assets of eligible Scottish partnership W on a winding up,

(b) V holds, directly or indirectly, voting rights in eligible Scottish partnership W,

(c) V holds, directly or indirectly, the right to appoint or remove any of the persons entitled to take part in the management of eligible Scottish partnership W,

(d) V has the right to exercise, or actually exercises, significant influence or control over eligible Scottish partnership W, or

(e) sub-paragraph (2) is satisfied.

(2) This sub-paragraph is satisfied where—

(a) the trustees of a trust or the members of a firm that, under the law by which it is governed, is not a legal person hold an interest in eligible Scottish partnership W in a way mentioned in sub-paragraph (1)(a) to (d), and

(b) V has the right to exercise, or actually exercises, significant influence or control over the activities of that trust or firm.

Interests held through a legal entity

9. (1) This paragraph applies where V—

(a) holds an interest in eligible Scottish partnership W by virtue of indirectly holding a right, and

(b) does so by virtue of having a majority stake in—

(i) a legal entity ("L") which holds the right directly, or

(ii) a legal entity that is part of a chain of legal entities such as is described in paragraph 13(1)(b) that includes L.

(2) Where this paragraph applies, V holds the interest in eligible Scottish partnership W—

(a) through L, and

(b) through each other legal entity in the chain mentioned in sub-paragraph (1)(b)(ii).

PART 3 INTERPRETATION OF SCHEDULE 1

Introduction

[10.1281]

10. This Part sets out rules for the interpretation of this Schedule, save that paragraph 17(1) does not apply to the interpretation of paragraph 2.

Joint interests and joint arrangements

11. (1) If two or more persons hold a right jointly, each of them is treated for the purposes of this Schedule as holding that right.

(2) If the right held by a person and the right held by another person are the subject of a joint arrangement between those persons, each of them is treated for the purposes of this Schedule as holding the combined rights of both of them.

(3) A "joint arrangement" is an arrangement between the holders of a right that they will exercise all or substantially all the rights conferred by their respective rights jointly in a way that is pre-determined by the arrangement.

(4) "Arrangement" has the meaning given by paragraph 16(3).

The right to surplus assets of an eligible Scottish partnership on a winding up

12. To the extent that the holding of a right to any surplus assets of an eligible Scottish partnership on a winding up is not expressly provided for, each partner in the eligible Scottish partnership shall be treated as holding the right to an equal share in any surplus assets on a winding up.

Right held "indirectly"

13. (1) A person holds a right "indirectly" if the person has a majority stake in a legal entity and that entity—

(a) holds that right, or

(b) is part of a chain of legal entities—

(i) each of which (other than the last) has a majority stake in the entity immediately below it in the chain, and

(ii) the last of which holds that right.

(2) For these purposes, A has a "majority stake" in B if—

(a) A holds a majority of the voting rights in B,

(b) A is a member of B and has the right to appoint or remove a majority of the board of directors of B,

(c) A is a member of B and controls alone, pursuant to an agreement with other shareholders or members, a majority of the voting rights in B, or

(d) A has the right to exercise, or actually exercises, dominant influence or control over B within the meaning of section 1162 of the Companies Act 2006.

(3) In the application of this paragraph to the right to appoint or remove a majority of the board of directors, a legal entity is to be treated as having the right to appoint a director if—

(a) a person's appointment as director follows necessarily from that person's appointment as director of the legal entity, or

(b) the directorship is held by the legal entity itself.

(4) In this paragraph—

(a) references to the right to appoint to or remove a majority of the board of directors of a legal entity are to the right to appoint or remove directors holding a majority of the voting rights at meetings of the board on all or substantially all matters, and

(b) references to a board of directors, in the case of an entity that does not have such a board, are to be read as references to the equivalent management body of that entity.

Voting rights and the right to appoint or remove persons entitled to take part in management

14. (1) A reference to the voting rights in a legal entity is to the rights conferred on shareholders in respect of their shares (or, in the case of an entity not having a share capital, on members) to vote at general meetings of the entity on all or substantially all matters.

(2) In relation to a legal entity that does not have general meetings at which matters are decided by the exercise of voting rights—

(a) a reference to exercising voting rights in the entity is to be read as a reference to exercising rights in relation to the entity that are equivalent to those of a person entitled to exercise voting rights in a company;

(b) a reference to exercising more than 25% of the voting rights in the entity is to read as a reference to exercising the right under the constitution of the entity to block changes to the overall policy of the entity or to the terms of its constitution.

(3) The voting rights in a legal entity are to be reduced by any rights held by the entity itself.

(4) The right to appoint or remove a majority of the persons who are entitled to take part in the management of an eligible Scottish partnership includes the right to appoint or remove those persons who hold a majority of the voting rights at meetings of the management body of the eligible Scottish partnership.

Rights held by nominees

15. A right held by a person as nominee for another is to be treated for the purposes of this Schedule as held by the other (and not by the nominee).

Rights treated as held by person who controls their exercise

16. (1) Where a person controls a right, the right is to be treated for the purposes of this Schedule as held by that person (and not by the person who in fact holds the right, unless that person also controls it).

(2) A person "controls" a right if, by virtue of any arrangement between that person and others, the right is exercisable only—

(a) by that person,

(b) in accordance with that person's directions or instructions, or

(c) with that person's consent or concurrence.

(3) "Arrangement" includes—

(a) any scheme, agreement or understanding, whether or not it is legally enforceable, and

(b) any convention, custom or practice of any kind.

(4) Something does not count as an arrangement unless there is at least some degree of stability about it (whether by its nature or terms, the time it has been in existence or otherwise).

Rights exercisable only in certain circumstances etc

17. (1) Rights that are exercisable only in certain circumstances are to be taken into account only—

(a) when the circumstances have arisen, and for so long as they continue to obtain, or

(b) when the circumstances are within the control of the person having the rights.

(2) But rights that are exercisable by an administrator or by creditors while a legal entity is in relevant insolvency proceedings are not to be taken into account even while the entity is in those proceedings.

(3) "Relevant insolvency proceedings" means—

(a) administration within the meaning of the Insolvency Act 1986,

(b) administration within the meaning of the Insolvency (Northern Ireland) Order 1989, or

(c) proceedings under the insolvency law of another country or territory during which an entity's assets and affairs are subject to the control or supervision of a third party or creditor.

(4) Rights that are normally exercisable but are temporarily incapable of exercise are to continue to be taken into account.

Rights attached to shares held by way of security

18. Rights attached to shares held by way of security provided by a person are to be treated for the purposes of this Schedule as held by that person—

(a) where apart from the right to exercise them for the purpose of preserving the value of the security, or of realising it, the rights are exercisable only in accordance with that person's instructions, and

(b) where the shares are held in connection with the granting of loans as part of normal business activities and apart from the right to exercise them for the purpose of preserving the value of the security, or of realising it, the rights are exercisable only in that person's interests.

Meaning of "significant influence or control"

19. Regard must be had to any guidance on the meaning of "significant influence and control" issued for the purposes of this Schedule by the Secretary of State.

SCHEDULE 2
ENFORCEMENT OF DISCLOSURE REQUIREMENTS

Regulation 15

Right to issue restrictions notice

[10.1282]

1. (1) This paragraph applies if—

(a) a notice under regulation 10 (duty to investigate) or 11 (duty to keep information up to date) is served by an eligible Scottish partnership on a person who has a relevant interest in the eligible Scottish partnership, and

(b) the person fails to comply with that notice within the time specified in it.

(2) The eligible Scottish partnership may give the person a notice under this paragraph (a "warning notice") informing the person that it is proposing to issue the person with a notice (a "restrictions notice") with respect to the relevant interest.

(3) The eligible Scottish partnership may issue the restrictions notice if, by the end of the period of one month beginning with the day on which the warning notice was given—

(a) the person has not complied with the notice served under regulation 10 or 11, and

(b) the eligible Scottish partnership has not been provided with a valid reason sufficient to justify the person's failure to comply with the notice served under that regulation.

(4) A restrictions notice is issued on a person by sending the notice to the person.

(5) The effect of a restrictions notice is set out in paragraph 3.

(6) In deciding whether to issue a restrictions notice, the eligible Scottish partnership must have regard to the effect of the notice on the rights of third parties in respect of the relevant interest.

Relevant interests

2. (1) For the purposes of this Schedule, a person has a relevant interest in an eligible Scottish partnership if the person—

(a) holds any interest in the eligible Scottish partnership,

(b) holds any voting rights in the eligible Scottish partnership, or

(c) holds the right to appoint or remove any of the persons who are entitled to take part in the management of the eligible Scottish partnership.

(2) References to the "relevant interest" are to the interest or right in question.

(3) Parts 2 and 3 of Schedule 1 apply for the interpretation of sub-paragraph (1) save that, where the relevant interest is by virtue of paragraph 15 or 16 of that Schedule treated for the purposes of that Schedule as held by a person other than the person who in fact holds the interest, both the holder and the other person are to be regarded for the purposes of this Schedule as having the relevant interest.

Effect of restrictions notice

3. (1) The effect of a restrictions notice issued under paragraph 1 with respect to a relevant interest is as follows—

(a) any transfer of the interest is void,

(b) no rights are exercisable in respect of the interest,

(c) except in a liquidation or a sequestration of the eligible Scottish partnership under the Bankruptcy (Scotland) Act 2016, no payment may be made of sums due from the eligible Scottish partnership in respect of the interest, whether in respect of capital or otherwise.

(2) An agreement to transfer an interest that is subject to the restriction in sub-paragraph (1)(a) is void.

(3) Sub-paragraph (2) does not apply to an agreement to transfer the interest on the making of an order under paragraph 7 made by virtue of sub-paragraph (3)(b) of that paragraph (removal of restrictions in case of court-approved transfer).

(4) An agreement to transfer any associated right (otherwise than in a liquidation) is void.

(5) Sub-paragraph (4) does not apply to an agreement to transfer any such right on the making of an order under paragraph 7 made by virtue of sub-paragraph (3)(b) of that paragraph (removal of restrictions in case of court-approved transfer).

(6) An "associated right", in relation to a relevant interest, is a right to receive payment of any sums due from the eligible Scottish partnership in respect of the relevant interest.

(7) The provisions of this paragraph are subject to any directions given under paragraph 4.

Protection of third party rights

4. (1) The court may give a direction under this paragraph if, on application by any person aggrieved, the court is satisfied that a restrictions notice issued by the eligible Scottish partnership under paragraph 1 unfairly affects the rights of third parties in respect of the relevant interest.

(2) The direction is given for the purpose of protecting those third party rights.

(3) The direction is a direction that certain acts will not constitute a breach of the restrictions placed on the relevant interest by the restrictions notice.

(4) An order containing a direction under this paragraph—

(a) must specify the acts that will not constitute a breach of the restrictions, and

(b) may confine the direction to cases where those acts are done by persons, or for purposes, described in the order.

(5) The direction may be given subject to such terms as the court thinks fit.

Breach of restrictions

5. (1) A person commits an offence if the person does anything listed in sub-paragraph (2) knowing that the interest is subject to restrictions.

(2) The things are—

(a) exercising or purporting to exercise any right to dispose of a relevant interest,

(b) exercising or purporting to exercise any right to dispose of any right to be issued with a relevant interest, or

(c) voting in respect of a relevant interest (whether as holder of the interest or as proxy) or appointing a proxy to vote in respect of a relevant interest.

(3) A person who has a relevant interest that the person knows to be subject to restrictions commits an offence if the person—

(a) knows a person to be entitled (apart from the restrictions) to vote in respect of the interest, whether as holder or as proxy,

(b) does not know the person to be aware of the fact that the interest is subject to restrictions, and

(c) fails to notify the person of that fact.

(4) A person commits an offence if the person—

(a) either has a relevant interest that the person knows to be subject to restrictions or is entitled to an associated right, and

(b) enters in that capacity into an agreement that is void by virtue of paragraph 3(2) or (4).

(5) References in this Schedule to an interest being "subject to restrictions" are to an interest being subject to restrictions by virtue of a restrictions notice under paragraph 1.

6. (1) A person guilty of an offence under paragraph 5 is liable—

(a) on conviction on indictment, to a fine;

(b) on summary conviction—

(i) in England and Wales, to a fine,

(ii) in Scotland or Northern Ireland, to a fine not exceeding the statutory maximum.

(2) The provisions of paragraph 5 are subject to any direction given under paragraph 4 or 7.

Relaxation of restrictions

7. (1) An application may be made to the court for an order directing that the relevant interest cease to be subject to restrictions.

(2) An application for an order under this paragraph may be made by the eligible Scottish partnership in question or by any person aggrieved.

(3) The court must not make an order under this paragraph unless—

(a) it is satisfied that the information required by the notice served under regulation 10 or 11 has been disclosed to the eligible Scottish partnership and no unfair advantage has accrued to any person as a result of the earlier failure to make that disclosure, or

(b) the relevant interest is to be transferred for valuable consideration and the court approves the transfer.

(4) An order under this paragraph made by virtue of sub-paragraph (3)(b) may continue, in whole or in part, the restriction mentioned in paragraph 3(1)(c) so far as it relates to a right acquired or offer made before the transfer.

(5) Where any restrictions continue in force under sub-paragraph (4)—

(a) an application may be made under this paragraph for an order directing that the relevant interest cease to be subject to those restrictions, and

(b) sub-paragraph (3) does not apply in relation to the making of such an order.

Orders for sale

8. (1) The court may order that the relevant interest subject to restrictions be sold subject to the court's approval as to the sale.

(2) An application for an order under sub-paragraph (1) may only be made by the eligible Scottish partnership in question.

(3) If the court makes an order under this paragraph, it may make such further order relating to the sale or transfer of the interest as it thinks fit.

(4) An application for an order under sub-paragraph (3) may be made—

(a) by the eligible Scottish partnership in question,

(b) by the person appointed by or in pursuance of the order to effect the sale, or

(c) by any person with an interest in the relevant interest.

(5) On making an order under sub-paragraph (1) or (3), the court may order that the applicant's costs (in Scotland, expenses) be paid out of the proceeds of sale.

9. (1) If a relevant interest is sold in pursuance of an order under paragraph 8, the proceeds of the sale, less the costs of the sale, must be paid into court for the benefit of those who are beneficially interested in the relevant interest.

(2) A person who is beneficially interested in the relevant interest may apply to the court for the whole or part of those proceeds to be paid to that person.

(3) On such an application, the court must order the payment to the applicant of—

(a) the whole of the proceeds of sale together with any interest on the proceeds, or

(b) if another person was also beneficially interested in the relevant interest at the time of the sale, such proportion of the proceeds (and any interest) as the value of the applicant's interest bears to the total value of the relevant interest.

(4) If the court has ordered under paragraph 8 that the costs (in Scotland, expenses) of an applicant under that paragraph are to be paid out of the proceeds of sale, the applicant is entitled to payment of those costs (or expenses) out of the proceeds before any person receives any part of the proceeds under this paragraph.

The power of an eligible Scottish partnership to withdraw restrictions notice

10. An eligible Scottish partnership that issues a person with a restrictions notice under paragraph 1 must by notice withdraw the restrictions notice if—

(a) it is satisfied that there is a valid reason sufficient to justify the person's failure to comply with the notice served under regulation 10 or 11,
(b) the notice served under regulation 10 or 11 is complied with,
(c) it discovers that the rights of a third party in respect of the relevant interest are being unfairly affected by the restrictions notice, or
(d) being a Scottish qualifying partnership, it delivers a notice to the registrar under regulation 8(1) (effect of a Scottish partnership ceasing to be a qualifying partnership).

Content of a warning notice

11. A warning notice given under paragraph 1 of this Schedule must—

(a) specify the date on which the warning notice is given;
(b) be accompanied by a copy of the notice given under regulation 10 or 11 to which the warning notice relates;
(c) identify the addressee's relevant interest in the eligible Scottish partnership by reference to the right in question;
(d) state that the eligible Scottish partnership will consider reasons provided to it as to why the addressee failed to comply with the notice given under regulation 10 or 11;
(e) explain the effect of a restrictions notice; and
(f) state that, by virtue of a restrictions notice, certain acts or failures to act may constitute an offence.

Content of a restrictions notice

12. A restrictions notice issued under paragraph 1 of this Schedule must—

(a) specify the date on which the restrictions notice is issued;
(b) be accompanied by a copy of the warning notice which preceded the restrictions notice;
(c) identify the addressee's relevant interest in the eligible Scottish partnership by reference to the right in question;
(d) explain the effect of the restrictions notice;
(e) state that, by virtue of the restrictions notice, certain acts or failures to act may constitute an offence; and
(f) state that an aggrieved person may apply to the court for an order directing that the relevant interest cease to be subject to restrictions.

Failure to comply with a regulation 10 or 11 notice: valid reason

13. An eligible Scottish partnership must take into account any incapacity of the addressee of a notice given under regulation 10 or 11 in deciding what counts as a "valid reason" sufficient to justify the addressee's failure to comply with the notice.

Withdrawal of a restrictions notice

14. Where an eligible Scottish partnership is required to withdraw a restrictions notice under paragraph 10 of this Schedule by notice (a "withdrawal notice"), the withdrawal notice must—

(a) be given within the period of 14 days beginning with the day the eligible Scottish partnership became required to withdraw the restrictions notice under that paragraph;
(b) specify the date on which the withdrawal notice is given;
(c) identify the addressee's relevant interest in the eligible Scottish partnership by reference to the right in question; and
(d) state that the relevant interest is no longer subject to restrictions.

Offences for failing to comply with notices

15. (1) A person to whom a notice under regulation 10 or 11 is addressed commits an offence if the person—

(a) fails to comply with the notice, or
(b) in purported compliance with the notice—
  (i) makes a statement that the person knows to be false in a material particular, or
  (ii) recklessly makes a statement that is false in a material particular.

(2) Where the person is a legal entity, an offence is also committed by every officer of the entity who is in default.

(3) A person does not commit an offence under sub-paragraph (1)(a) (or sub-paragraph (2) as it applies in relation to that sub-paragraph) if the person proves that the requirement to give information was frivolous or vexatious.

(4) A person guilty of an offence under this paragraph is liable—

(a) on conviction on indictment, to imprisonment for a term not exceeding two years or a fine (or both);
(b) on summary conviction—
  (i) in England and Wales, to imprisonment for a term not exceeding three months or to a fine (or both);
  (ii) in Scotland and Northern Ireland, to imprisonment for a term not exceeding three months or to a fine not exceeding the statutory maximum (or both).

Offences for failing to provide information

16. (1) A person commits an offence if the person—

(a) fails to comply with a duty under regulation 14 or 15, or
(b) in purported compliance with such a duty—
  (i) makes a statement that the person knows to be false in a material particular, or
  (ii) recklessly makes a statement that is false in a material particular.

(2) Where the person is a legal entity, an offence is also committed by every officer of the entity who is in default.

(3) A person guilty of an offence under this paragraph is liable—

(a) on conviction on indictment, to imprisonment for a term not exceeding two years or a fine (or both);

(b) on summary conviction—

(i) in England and Wales, to imprisonment for a term not exceeding three months or to a fine (or both);

(ii) in Scotland and Northern Ireland, to imprisonment for a term not exceeding three months or to a fine not exceeding the statutory maximum (or both).

SCHEDULE 3
STATEMENTS REQUIRED AS TO THE NATURE OF CONTROL

Regulation 18

PART 1 FIRST CONDITION

[10.1283]

1. A statement that the person holds, directly or indirectly, the right to more than 25% but not more than 50% of the surplus assets of the eligible Scottish partnership on a winding up.

2. A statement that the person holds, directly or indirectly, the right to more than 50% but less than 75% of the surplus assets of the eligible Scottish partnership on a winding up.

3. A statement that the person holds, directly or indirectly, the right to 75% or more of the surplus assets of the eligible Scottish partnership on a winding up.

PART 2 SECOND CONDITION

[10.1284]

4. A statement that the person holds, directly or indirectly, more than 25% but not more than 50% of any voting rights in the eligible Scottish partnership.

5. A statement that the person holds, directly or indirectly, more than 50% but less than 75% of any voting rights in the eligible Scottish partnership.

6. A statement that the person holds, directly or indirectly, 75% or more of any voting rights in the eligible Scottish partnership.

PART 3 THIRD CONDITION

[10.1285]

7. A statement that the person holds the right, directly or indirectly, to appoint or remove a majority of the persons who are entitled to take part in the management of the eligible Scottish partnership.

PART 4 FOURTH CONDITION

[10.1286]

8. A statement that the person has the right to exercise, or actually exercises, significant influence or control over the eligible Scottish partnership.

PART 5 FIFTH CONDITION AND TRUSTS

[10.1287]

9. A statement that—

(a) the person has the right to exercise, or actually exercises, significant influence or control over the activities of a trust; and

(b) the trustees of that trust (in their capacity as such) hold, directly or indirectly, the right to more than 25% but not more than 50% of any surplus assets of the eligible Scottish partnership on a winding up.

10. A statement that—

(a) the person has the right to exercise, or actually exercises, significant influence or control over the activities of a trust; and

(b) the trustees of that trust (in their capacity as such) hold, directly or indirectly, the right to more than 50% but less than 75% of any surplus assets of the eligible Scottish partnership on a winding up.

11. A statement that—

(a) the person has the right to exercise, or actually exercises, significant influence or control over the activities of a trust; and

(b) the trustees of that trust (in their capacity as such) hold, directly or indirectly, the right to 75% or more of any surplus assets of the eligible Scottish partnership on a winding up.

12. A statement that—

(a) the person has the right to exercise, or actually exercises, significant influence or control over the activities of a trust; and

(b) the trustees of that trust (in their capacity as such) hold, directly or indirectly, more than 25% but not more than 50% of any voting rights in the eligible Scottish partnership.

13. A statement that—

(a) the person has the right to exercise, or actually exercises, significant influence or control over the activities of a trust; and

(b) the trustees of that trust (in their capacity as such) hold, directly or indirectly, more than 50% but less than 75% of any voting rights in the eligible Scottish partnership.

14. A statement that—

(a) the person has the right to exercise, or actually exercises, significant influence or control over the activities of a trust; and

(b) the trustees of that trust (in their capacity as such) hold, directly or indirectly, 75% or more of any the voting rights in the eligible Scottish partnership.

15. A statement that—

(a) the person has the right to exercise, or actually exercises, significant influence or control over the activities of a trust; and

(b) the trustees of that trust (in their capacity as such) hold the right, directly or indirectly, to appoint or remove a majority of the persons who are entitled to take part in the management of the eligible Scottish partnership.

16. A statement that—

(a) the person has the right to exercise, or actually exercises, significant influence or control over the activities of a trust; and

(b) the trustees of that trust (in their capacity as such) have the right to exercise, or actually exercise, significant influence or control over the eligible Scottish partnership.

PART 6 FIFTH CONDITION AND FIRMS

[10.1288]

17. A statement that—

(a) the person has the right to exercise, or actually exercises, significant influence or control over the activities of a firm that, under the law by which it is governed, is not a legal person; and

(b) the members of that firm (in their capacity as such) hold, directly or indirectly, the right to more than 25% but not more than 50% of any surplus assets of the eligible Scottish partnership on a winding up.

18. A statement that—

(a) the person has the right to exercise, or actually exercises, significant influence or control over the activities of a firm that, under the law by which it is governed, is not a legal person; and

(b) the members of that firm (in their capacity as such) hold, directly or indirectly, the right to more than 50% but less than 75% of any surplus assets of the eligible Scottish partnership on a winding up.

19. A statement that—

(a) the person has the right to exercise, or actually exercises, significant influence or control over the activities of a firm that, under the law by which it is governed, is not a legal person; and

(b) the members of that firm (in their capacity as such) hold, directly or indirectly, the right to 75% or more of any surplus assets of the eligible Scottish partnership on a winding up.

20. A statement that—

(a) the person has the right to exercise, or actually exercises, significant influence or control over the activities of a firm that, under the law by which it is governed, is not a legal person; and

(b) the members of that firm (in their capacity as such) hold, directly or indirectly, more than 25% but not more than 50% of any voting rights in the eligible Scottish partnership.

21. A statement that—

(a) the person has the right to exercise, or actually exercises, significant influence or control over the activities of a firm that, under the law by which it is governed, is not a legal person; and

(b) the members of that firm (in their capacity as such) hold, directly or indirectly, more than 50% but less than 75% of any voting rights in the eligible Scottish partnership.

22. A statement that—

(a) the person has the right to exercise, or actually exercises, significant influence or control over the activities of a firm that, under the law by which it is governed, is not a legal person; and

(b) the members of that firm (in their capacity as such) hold, directly or indirectly, 75% or more of any voting rights in the eligible Scottish partnership.

23. A statement that—

(a) the person has the right to exercise, or actually exercises, significant influence or control over the activities of a firm that, under the law by which it is governed, is not a legal person; and

(b) the members of that firm (in their capacity as such) hold the right, directly or indirectly, to appoint or remove a majority of persons who are entitled to take part in the management of the eligible Scottish partnership.

24. A statement that—

(a) the person has the right to exercise, or actually exercises, significant influence or control over the activities of a firm that, under the law by which it is governed, is not a legal person; and

(b) the members of that firm (in their capacity as such) have the right to exercise, or actually exercise, significant influence or control over the eligible Scottish partnership.

PART 7 INTERPRETATION OF SCHEDULE 3

[10.1289]

25. In this Schedule—

(a) paragraph 12 of Schedule 1 has effect in relation to references to the right to surplus assets on the winding up of an eligible Scottish partnership;

(b) paragraph 14 of Schedule 1 has effect in relation to references to voting rights in an eligible Scottish partnership and to persons who are entitled to take part in the management of an eligible Scottish partnership;

(c) paragraph 19 of Schedule 1 has effect in relation to references to significant influence or control over an eligible Scottish partnership.

SCHEDULE 4
SPECIFIED PUBLIC AUTHORITIES

Regulation 42

[10.1290]

The Bank of England;

the Charity Commission;

the Charity Commission for Northern Ireland;

the Commissioners for Her Majesty's Revenue and Customs;

the Competition and Markets Authority;

the Crown Office and Procurator Fiscal Service;

the Director of Public Prosecutions;

the Director of Public Prosecutions for Northern Ireland;

the Financial Conduct Authority;

the Food Standards Agency;

the Gas and Electricity Markets Authority;

the Gambling Commission;

the Gangmasters Licensing Authority;

the Government Communications Headquarters;

the Health and Safety Executive;

the Health and Safety Executive for Northern Ireland;

the Marine Management Organisation;

the Minister for the Cabinet Office;

the National Crime Agency;

the Northern Ireland Authority for Utility Regulation;

any Northern Ireland Department;

the Office of Communications;

the Office of the Information Commissioner;

the Office for Nuclear Regulation;

the Office of the Scottish Charity Regulator;

the Official Receiver for Northern Ireland;

the Panel on Takeovers and Mergers;

the Pensions Regulator;

the Prudential Regulation Authority;

the Registry of Credit Unions and Industrial and Provident Societies for Northern Ireland;

the Regulator of Community Interest Companies;

the Scottish Housing Regulator;

the Scottish Ministers;

the Security Industry Authority;

the Secret Intelligence Service;

the Secretary of State;

the Security Service;

the Serious Fraud Office;

the Treasury;

the Treasury Solicitor;

the Welsh Ministers;

a local authority within the meaning of section 54(2) of the Companies Act 2006;

an official receiver appointed under section 399 of the Insolvency Act 1986 (appointment, etc, of official receivers);

a person acting as an insolvency practitioner within the meaning of section 388 of the Insolvency Act 1986 (meaning of "act as an insolvency practitioner") or article 3 of the Insolvency (Northern Ireland) Order 1989 ("act as an insolvency practitioner");

an inspector appointed under Part 14 of the Companies Act 1985 (investigation of companies and their affairs: requisition of documents) or a person appointed under regulation 30 of the Open-Ended Investment Companies Regulations 2001 (power to investigate) or regulation 30 of the Open-Ended Investment Companies Regulations (Northern Ireland) 2004;

any person authorised to exercise powers under section 447 of the Companies Act 1985 (power to require documents and information), or section 84 of the Companies Act 1989 (exercise of powers by partners, etc);

any person exercising functions conferred by Part 6 of the Financial Services and Markets Act 2000 (official listing);

a person appointed to make a report under section 166 or 166A (reports by skilled persons) of the Financial Services and Markets Act 2000;

a person appointed to conduct an investigation under section 167 (appointment of persons to carry out general investigations) or 168(3) or (5) (appointment of persons to carry out investigations in particular cases) of the Financial Services and Markets Act 2000;

a person appointed under section 284 (power to investigate) of the Financial Services and Markets Act 2000;

a police force within the meaning of section 101(1) of the Police Act 1996;

the Police Service of Northern Ireland;

the Police Service of Scotland;

the lead enforcement authority (as defined in section 33(1) of the Estate Agents Act 1979) exercising functions under the Estate Agents Act 1979.

SCHEDULE 5
CONDITIONS FOR PERMITTED DISCLOSURE

Regulations 42 and 45

PART 1 DISCLOSURE TO SPECIFIED PUBLIC AUTHORITIES

[10.1291]

1. The specified public authority has delivered to the registrar a statement that it intends to use the information only for the purpose of facilitating the carrying out by that specified public authority of a public function ("the permitted purpose").

2. Subject to paragraph 3, the specified public authority has delivered to the registrar a statement that, where it supplies a copy of the information to a processor for the purpose of processing the information for use in respect of the permitted purpose, the specified public authority will—

(a) ensure that the processor is one who carries on business [in the United Kingdom or] in the European Economic Area;

(b) require that the processor does not transmit the information outside the [area comprising the United Kingdom and the European Economic Area]; and

(c) require that the processor does not disclose the information except to that specified public authority or an employee of that specified public authority.

3. Paragraph 2 does not apply where the specified public authority is the National Crime Agency, Secret Intelligence Service, Security Service or Government Communications Headquarters.

4. The specified public authority has delivered any information or evidence required by the registrar for the purpose of enabling the registrar to determine in accordance with these Regulations whether to disclose the information.

5. The specified public authority has complied with any requirement by the registrar to confirm the accuracy of the statements, information or evidence delivered to the registrar pursuant to this Part of this Schedule.

NOTES

Para 2: words in square brackets in sub-para (a) inserted, and words in square brackets in sub-para (b) substituted, by the Companies, Limited Liability Partnerships and Partnerships (Amendment etc) (EU Exit) Regulations 2019, SI 2019/348, reg 7, Sch 2, paras 15, 18(a), as from IP completion day (as defined in the European Union (Withdrawal Agreement) Act 2020, s 39) (for transitional provisions see Sch 4, para 5 to the 2019 Regulations at **[12.106]**).

PART 2 DISCLOSURE TO A CREDIT INSTITUTION OR A FINANCIAL INSTITUTION

[10.1292]

6. [(1)] The credit institution or financial institution, referred to in this Part as the "relevant institution," maintains appropriate procedures to ensure that—

(a) an independent person can investigate and audit the measures maintained by the relevant institution for the purpose of ensuring the security of any information disclosed to that institution; and

[(b) for the purposes of ensuring that it complies with its [obligations under the data protection legislation (as defined in section 3 of the Data Protection Act 2018)].]

[(2) . . .]

7. The relevant institution has delivered to the registrar a statement confirming that it is a credit institution or a financial institution, as the case may be, and that it meets the conditions in paragraph 6.

8. The relevant institution has delivered to the registrar a statement that it intends to use information only for the purpose of applying customer due diligence measures to the eligible Scottish partnership to which the secured information relates, in compliance with the institution's obligations under Part 3 (customer due diligence) of the 2017 Money Laundering Regulations.

9. The relevant institution has delivered to the registrar a statement that confirms the name and registered number of the eligible Scottish partnership in respect of which it is required to apply customer due diligence measures under the 2017 Money Laundering Regulations.

10. The relevant institution has delivered to the registrar a statement that it intends to take delivery of and to use the information only in the United Kingdom . . . .

11. The relevant institution has delivered to the registrar a statement that it will, where it supplies a copy of the information to a processor for the purpose of processing the information for use in respect of the purpose referred to in paragraph 8—

(a) ensure that the processor is one who carries on business in the [United Kingdom];

(b) require that the processor does not transmit the information outside the [United Kingdom]; and

(c) require that the processor does not disclose the information except to that institution.

12. The relevant institution has delivered any information or evidence required by the registrar for the purpose of enabling the registrar to determine in accordance with these Regulations whether to disclose the information.

13. The relevant institution has complied with any requirement by the registrar to confirm the accuracy of the statements, information or evidence delivered to the registrar pursuant to this Part of this Schedule.

NOTES

Para 6: sub-para (1) numbered as such, para (b) of that sub-paragraph substituted, and sub-para (2) added, by the Data Protection Act 2018, s 211, Sch 19, Pt 2, para 420, as from 25 May 2018 (for transitional provisions and savings relating to the repeal of the Data Protection Act 1998, see Sch 20 to the 2018 Act). Words in square brackets in sub-para (1)(b) substituted, and sub-para (2) revoked, by the Companies, Limited Liability Partnerships and Partnerships (Amendment etc) (EU Exit) Regulations 2019, SI 2019/348, reg 7, Sch 2, paras 15, 18(b), as from IP completion day (as defined in the European Union (Withdrawal Agreement) Act 2020, s 39) (for transitional provisions see Sch 4, para 5 to the 2019 Regulations at **[12.106]**).

Para 10: words omitted revoked by SI 2019/348, reg 7, Sch 2, paras 15, 18(c), as from IP completion day (as defined in the European Union (Withdrawal Agreement) Act 2020, s 39) (for transitional provisions see Sch 4, para 5 to the 2019 Regulations at **[12.106]**).

Para 11: words in square brackets substituted by SI 2019/348, reg 7, Sch 2, paras 15, 18(d), as from IP completion day (as defined in the European Union (Withdrawal Agreement) Act 2020, s 39) (for transitional provisions see Sch 4, para 5 to the 2019 Regulations at **[12.106]**).

PART 3 INTERPRETATION OF SCHEDULE 5

[10.1293]

14. In this Schedule—

(a) "processor" means any person who provides a service which consists of putting information into data form or processing information in data form and any reference to a processor includes a reference to the processor's employees;

(b) "public function" includes—

(i) any function conferred by or in accordance with any provision contained in any enactment;

(ii) . . .

(iii) any similar function conferred on persons by or under provisions having effect as part of the law of a country or territory outside the United Kingdom; and

(iv) any function exercisable in relation to the investigation of any criminal offence or for the purpose of any criminal proceedings;

(c) any reference to an employee of any person who has access to information includes any person working or providing services for the purposes of that person or employed by or on behalf of, or working for, any person who is so working or who is supplying such a service; and

(d) any reference to the disclosure for the purpose of facilitating the carrying out of a public function includes disclosure in relation to, and for the purpose of, any proceedings whether civil, criminal or disciplinary in which the specified public authority engages while carrying out its public functions.

NOTES

Para 14: sub-para (b)(ii) revoked by the Companies, Limited Liability Partnerships and Partnerships (Amendment etc) (EU Exit) Regulations 2019, SI 2019/348, reg 7, Sch 2, paras 15, 18(e), as from IP completion day (as defined in the European Union (Withdrawal Agreement) Act 2020, s 39) (for transitional provisions see Sch 4, para 5 to the 2019 Regulations at **[12.106]**).

SCHEDULE 6

(*This Schedule substitutes the Limited Partnerships (Forms) Rules 2009, SI 2009/2160, Schedule.*)

INSOLVENCY (SCOTLAND) (COMPANY VOLUNTARY ARRANGEMENTS AND ADMINISTRATION) RULES 2018 (NOTE)

(SI 2018/1082)

[10.1294]

NOTES

These Rules were made on 11 October 2018 under the powers conferred by s 411 of the Insolvency Act 1986, and came into force on 6 April 2019.

These Rules set out the detailed procedures for the conduct of company voluntary arrangements and administration proceedings in Scotland under the Insolvency Act 1986. The Rules accordingly give effect, for Scotland, to Parts I and II of the 1986 Act (and, originally, to European Parliament and Council Regulation 2015/848/EU on insolvency proceedings ("the EU Insolvency Regulation")).

These Rules, in conjunction with a related Scottish Statutory Instrument – the Insolvency (Scotland) Receivership and Winding Up Rules 2018 *post* (which make provision in relation to winding up proceedings) – aim to modernise and consolidate the Insolvency (Scotland) Rules 1986 (SI 1986/1915, as amended). To the extent that they apply to CVAs and administration proceedings, the 1986 Rules are accordingly revoked by this instrument, along with a number of amending Rules and related instruments (as from 6 April 2019).

These Rules also give effect to amendments made to the 1986 Act by the Small Business, Enterprise and Employment Act 2015.

These Rules are structured as follows:

The Introductory Rules (rules 1–6) contain the citation, commencement, extent and application of these Rules. The Introductory Rules also introduce Schedule 1 (revocations), Schedule 2 (transitional and savings provisions) and Schedule 3 (punishment of offences).

Part 1 (rules 1.1–1.57) is a common part containing definitions and rules about the standard content of documents; the delivery of documents; the use of websites; and the keeping of records. Part 1 also gives effect to Schedule 4 which sets out the information to be contained in the Sederunt Book.

Part 1A (rules 1A.1–1A.36) was inserted by the Insolvency (Scotland) (Company Voluntary Arrangements and Administration) (Amendment) Rules 2021, SI 2021/1026, as from 1 October 2021. It sets out the detailed procedures for the conduct of the moratorium; in particular, it specifies the content and timing of the various notifications that are required to be given in connection with the obtaining, coming into force, extension and termination of the moratorium.

Part 2 (rules 2.1–2.44) contains rules about CVAs.

Part 3 (rules 3.1–3.119) contains rules about administration.

Part 4 (rules 4.1–4.3) contains rules about the block transfer of insolvency proceedings between insolvency practitioners.

Part 5 (rules 5.1–5.42) is a common part containing rules about decision making.

Part 6 (rules 6.1–6.8) is a common part containing rules about proxies and corporate representation.

Part 7 (rules 7.1–7.14) contained rules which gave effect to the EU Insolvency Regulation. This Part was revoked by the Insolvency (Amendment) (EU Exit) Regulations 2019, SI 2019/146, Schedule, as from IP completion day (as defined in the European Union (Withdrawal Agreement) Act 2020, s 39).

Schedule 1 contains revocations. Note that the Insolvency (Scotland) Rules 1986 (SI 1986/1905) are revoked as follows: Parts 1 and 2 are revoked in their entirety; and rr 0.1–0.3 and Part 7 (and Schedules 3 to 5) are revoked insofar as they apply to CVAs and administration. This Schedule also revoked various other statutory instruments that have amended the 1986 Rules.

Schedule 2 contains transitional and savings provisions; and provides that where an application to court is lodged or a petition is presented under the 1986 Act or under the 1986 Rules before the 6 April 2019 and the application or petition has not been determined or withdrawn, the 1986 Rules continue to apply to that application or petition.

Schedule 3 deals with punishment of offences under these Rules.

Schedule 4 contains information to be included in the sederunt book.

See also, as to the application of these Rules during the "relevant period", Sch 4 to the Corporate Insolvency and Governance Act 2020 (Moratoriums in Great Britain: Temporary Provision) at **[9.561]**; and, in particular, Part 4 of that Schedule (Temporary Rules: Scotland) at **[9.564]**. The "relevant period" is defined in Sch 4, Pt 1, para 1 to the Act (as amended) as the period beginning on 26 June 2020, and ending on 30 September 2021.

INSOLVENCY (SCOTLAND) (RECEIVERSHIP AND WINDING UP) RULES 2018 (NOTE)

(SSI 2018/347)

[10.1295]

NOTES

These Rules were made on 13 November 2018 under the powers conferred by s 411(1)(b), (2) and (2A) of the Insolvency Act 1986, and came into force on 6 April 2019.

These Rules set out the detailed procedures for the conduct of receivership and winding up proceedings in Scotland under the Insolvency Act 1986. The Rules accordingly give effect, for Scotland, to Parts 3–7 of the 1986 Act, and to European Parliament and Council Regulation 2015/848/EU on insolvency proceedings ("the EU Insolvency Regulation").

These Rules, in conjunction with the related Insolvency (Scotland) (Company Voluntary Arrangements and Administration) Rules 2018 (SI 2018/1082) *ante* – aim to modernise and consolidate the Insolvency (Scotland) Rules 1986 (SI 1986/1915). To the extent that they apply to receivership and winding up proceedings, the 1986 Rules are accordingly revoked by this instrument, along with a number of amending rules and related instruments, including the Receivers (Scotland) Regulations 1986.

These Rules also give effect to amendments made to the 1986 Act by the Enterprise and Regulatory Reform Act 2011, the Deregulation Act 2015, the Small Business, Enterprise and Employment Act 2015, the Public Services Reform (Insolvency) (Scotland) Order 2016 (SSI 2016/141), and the Public Services Reform (Corporate Insolvency and Bankruptcy) (Scotland) Order 2017 (SSI 2017/209).

The rules are structured as follows:

— The introductory rules 1 to 5 contain the citation, commencement, extent and application of these Rules. The introductory rules also introduce Schedule 1 (revocations), Schedule 2 (transitional and savings provisions) and Schedule 3 (punishment of offences).

— Part 1 (rules 1.1–1.57) is a common part containing definitions and rules about the standard contents of documents, the delivery and service of documents, the use of websites, and the keeping of records. Part 1 also gives effect to Schedule 4 which sets out minimum information to be contained in the Sederunt Book.

— Part 2 (rules 2.1–2.20) contains rules about receivership.

— Part 3 (rules 3.1–3.23) contains rules about members' voluntary winding up.

— Part 4 (rules 4.1–4.41) contains rules about creditors' voluntary winding up.

— Part 5 (rules 5.1–5.55) contains rules about winding up by the court.

— Part 6 (rules 6.1–6.3) contains rules about the block transfer of winding up proceedings between insolvency practitioners.

— Part 7 (rules 7.1–7.35) is a common part containing rules about reporting and remuneration of office-holders, accounts and claims by and distributions to creditors in winding up.

— Part 8 (rules 8.1–8.46) is a common part containing rules about decision making.

— Part 9 (rules 9.1–9.8) is a common part containing rules about proxies and corporate representation.

— Part 10 (rules 10.1–10.29) is a common part containing rules about creditors' and liquidation committees.

— Part 11 (rules 11.1–11.17) contains rules which gave effect to the EU Insolvency Regulation. Rules 11.1–11.3 and 11.6–11.17 were revoked by the Insolvency (Amendment) (EU Exit) Regulations 2019, SI 2019/146 (as from IP completion day (as defined in the European Union (Withdrawal Agreement) Act 2020, s 39)).

— Part 12 (rules 12.1–12.7) contains rules about obtaining permission to act as director of a company with a prohibited name.

PROXY ADVISORS (SHAREHOLDERS' RIGHTS) REGULATIONS 2019 (NOTE)

(SI 2019/926)

[10.1296]

NOTES

Made: 13 May 2019.

Authority: European Communities Act 1972, s 2(2) (see the note "Statutory Instruments made under the European Communities Act 1972" preceding paragraph **[4.1]** *ante*).

Commencement: 10 June 2019.

These Regulations implement the obligations of a Member State laid down in Article 3(j) of Directive 2007/36/EC of the European Parliament and of the Council on the exercise of certain rights of shareholders in listed companies (the Shareholder Rights Directive). Article 3j of Directive 2007/36/EC was inserted, together with Chapter 1a and the rest of Chapter 1b, by Article 1(3) of Directive 2017/828/EU of the European Parliament and of the Council amending Directive 2007/36/EC as regards the encouragement of long-term shareholder engagement (the Shareholder Rights Directive II).

Article 3j of the Shareholder Rights Directive seeks to improve the stewardship of EEA-based corporations by introducing the regulation of proxy advisors. Proxy advisors provide research, advice and recommendations to shareholders and their intermediaries. This may include advising shareholders on how to vote at an annual general meeting or translating documents. Proxy advisors primarily offer voting services to shareholders of publicly-listed companies, and therefore can have a considerable impact on how shareholders exercise their voting rights.

These Regulations require proxy advisors to disclose to the public any code of conduct they apply, information relating to how proxy advisors prepare their research, advice and voting recommendations, and whether there are any actual or potential conflicts of interest they may have whilst undertaking their activities.

These Regulations also provide the FCA with powers to enforce the obligations imposed on proxy advisors. Where the FCA considers that a proxy advisor has contravened a relevant requirement in the Regulations, the FCA may impose financial penalties or publish a statement outlining the contravention.

As originally enacted the Regulations created a regime applying to proxy advisors that: (a) provided services to a shareholder that has shares in a company registered in the UK, EEA or Gibraltar, and that company is trading on a UK, EEA or Gibraltarian regulated market; and (b) had a registered office in the UK, or a registered office in a non-EEA country or territory but provided services through a UK establishment.

At the end of the implementation period, it would be inappropriate to require proxy advisors that have a registered office or establishment in the UK, but that only offer services to shareholders with shares in companies with registered offices in an EEA State, and which are traded on EU-regulated markets, to fall under the UK proxy advisor regime. These Regulations were, accordingly, amended by the Financial Services (Miscellaneous Amendments) (EU Exit) Regulations 2020, SI 2020/628.

Regulation 15 of the 2020 Regulations amends the original scope of these Regulations so that, at the end of the implementation period, these Regulations apply only to proxy advisors that: (a) provide services to a shareholder that has shares in a company registered in the UK or Gibraltar, and that is trading on a UK or Gibraltarian regulated market; and, (b) have their registered office in the UK, or have their registered office outside of the UK or Gibraltar but provide services through a UK establishment.

The original definitions of "shareholder" and "regulated market" contained in the definition of "proxy advisor", were defined by reference to the Shareholders' Rights Directive. Regulation 15 of the 2020 Regulations also removes references to the Directive and replaces them with new definitions and references to related definitions in FSMA 2000, and the Financial Services (Markets in Financial Instruments) Act 2018 of Gibraltar, where appropriate. This reflects the UK-only scope of the regime that operates at the end of the implementation period.

See also the note relating to the Companies (Shareholders' Rights to Voting Confirmations) Regulations 2020 at **[10.1297]** *post*.

COMPANIES (SHAREHOLDERS' RIGHTS TO VOTING CONFIRMATIONS) REGULATIONS 2020 (NOTE)

(SI 2020/717)

[10.1297]

NOTES

Made: 6 July 2020.

Authority: European Communities Act 1972, s 2(2) (see the note "Statutory Instruments made under the European Communities Act 1972" preceding paragraph **[4.1]** *ante*).

Commencement: 3 September 2020.

These Regulations implement certain provisions contained in article 3c of Directive 2007/36/EC of the European Parliament and of the Council on the exercise of certain rights of shareholders in listed companies (the Shareholder Rights Directive). Article 3c of the Shareholder Rights Directive was inserted, together with the rest of Chapter 1a (and Chapter 1b), by Article 1(3) of Directive 2017/828/EU of the European Parliament and of the Council amending Directive 2007/36/EC as regards the encouragement of long-term shareholder engagement (the Shareholder Rights Directive II). Article 3c concerns the facilitation of the exercise of shareholder rights.

These Regulations apply to companies whose shares carry voting rights and are admitted to trading on a UK regulated market or an EU regulated market, defined as a "traded company" in section 360C of the Companies Act 2006.

Regulation 1 provides for citation and commencement.

Regulation 4 inserts section 360AA of the Companies Act 2006, to impose an obligation on a traded company to provide a confirmation of receipt of those votes which are cast electronically. Section 360A(2) of the 2006 Act enables a traded company to impose those requirements which are necessary to ensure the identification of those taking part in a general meeting of the company by electronic means. Regulation 2 of these Regulations provides that the new section 360AA has effect in relation to votes cast on or after 3 September 2020.

Regulation 5 inserts section 360BA of the 2006 Act, which provides a shareholder with the right to request information from the company which enables them to determine that their vote has been validly recorded and counted. Regulation 3 provides that this insertion has effect in relation to votes cast at a general meeting which takes place on or after 3 September 2020.

See also the note relating to the Proxy Advisors (Shareholders' Rights) Regulations 2019 at **[10.1296]** *ante*.

INSOLVENCY ACT 1986 (HMRC DEBTS: PRIORITY ON INSOLVENCY) REGULATIONS 2020

(SI 2020/983)

NOTES

Made: 11 September 2020.
Authority: Finance Act 2020, s 99(3).
Commencement: 2 December 2020.

[10.1298]

1 Citation and commencement

These Regulations may be cited as the Insolvency Act 1986 (HMRC Debts: Priority on Insolvency) Regulations 2020 and come into force on 1st December 2020.

NOTES

Commencement: 2 December 2020.

[10.1299]

2 Specified deductions

(1) The deductions set out in paragraph (2) are specified for the purposes of—
- (a) paragraph 15D(3)(c) of Schedule 6 to the Insolvency Act 1986,
- (b) paragraph 8A(3)(c) of Schedule 3 to the Bankruptcy (Scotland) Act 2016 (asp 21),
- (c) and paragraph 22(3)(c) of Schedule 4 to the Insolvency (Northern Ireland) Order 1989.

(2) The deductions are—
- (a) deductions under section 61 (deductions on account of tax from contract payments) of the Finance Act 2004,
- (b) deductions under paragraph 6(1)(b) (deduction of earnings-related contributions) of Schedule 4 to the Social Security (Contributions) Regulations 2001,
- (c) deductions under regulation 21 (deduction and repayment of tax by reference to employee's code) of the Income Tax (Pay As You Earn) Regulations 2003, and
- (d) deductions under regulation 50 (deductions of repayments) of the Education (Student Loans) (Repayment) Regulations 2009.

NOTES

Commencement: 2 December 2020.

CORPORATE INSOLVENCY AND GOVERNANCE ACT 2020 (CORONAVIRUS) (SUSPENSION OF LIABILITY FOR WRONGFUL TRADING AND EXTENSION OF THE RELEVANT PERIOD) REGULATIONS 2020

(SI 2020/1349)

NOTES

Made: 24 November 2020.
Authority: Corporate Insolvency and Governance Act 2020, s 20(1)(c), Sch 14, para 2(2).
Commencement: 26 November 2020.

These Regulations are reproduced as amended by: Corporate Insolvency and Governance Act 2020 (Coronavirus) (Extension of the Relevant Period) Regulations 2021, SI 2021/375.

[10.1300]

1 Citation and commencement

These Regulations may be cited as the Corporate Insolvency and Governance Act 2020 (Coronavirus) (Suspension of Liability for Wrongful Trading and Extension of the Relevant Period) Regulations 2020 and come into force on 26th November 2020.

NOTES

Commencement: 26 November 2020.

[10.1301]

2 Suspension of liability for wrongful trading: Great Britain

(1) In determining for the purposes of section 214 or 246ZB of the Insolvency Act 1986 (liability of director for wrongful trading) the contribution (if any) to a company's assets that it is proper for a person to make, the court is to assume that the person is not responsible for any worsening of the financial position of the company or its creditors that occurs during the relevant period.

(2) In this regulation the "relevant period" is the period which—
- (a) begins with 26th November 2020, and
- (b) ends with [30th June 2021].

(3) Paragraph (1) does not apply if at any time during the relevant period the company concerned is excluded from being eligible by any of the paragraphs of Schedule ZA1 to the Insolvency Act 1986 listed in paragraph (4), as they apply for the purposes of this paragraph (see paragraph (5)).

(4) The paragraphs of Schedule ZA1 to the Insolvency Act 1986 are—
- (a) paragraph 3 (insurance companies),
- (b) paragraph 4 (banks),
- (c) paragraph 5 (electronic money institutions),
- (d) paragraph 6 (investment banks and investment firms),
- (e) paragraph 9 (payment institutions),
- (f) paragraph 10 (operators of payment systems etc),
- (g) paragraph 11 (recognised investment exchanges, clearing houses, etc),
- (h) paragraph 12 (securitisation companies),
- (i) paragraph 13 (parties to capital market arrangements),
- (j) paragraph 15 (public-private partnership project companies), and
- (k) paragraph 18 (certain overseas companies).

(5) In their application for the purposes of paragraph (3)—
- (a) each of paragraphs 13 and 15 of Schedule ZA1 to the Insolvency Act 1986 has effect as if in sub-paragraph (1)—
  - (i) the words ", on the filing date" were omitted, and
  - (ii) paragraph (b) were omitted, and
- (b) paragraph 18 of that Schedule has effect as if for "paragraph 2" in both places, there were substituted "paragraphs 2, 7 and 8".

(6) Paragraph (1) also does not apply if at any time during the relevant period the company concerned—
- (a) has permission under Part 4A of the Financial Services and Markets Act 2000 to carry on a regulated activity, and
- (b) is not subject to a requirement imposed under that Act to refrain from holding money for clients.

(7) This regulation has effect—
- (a) in so far as it relates to section 214 of the Insolvency Act 1986, as if it were contained in Part 4 of that Act, and
- (b) in so far as it relates to section 246ZB of the Insolvency Act 1986, as if it were contained in Part 6 of that Act.

(8) But this regulation does not have effect in relation to the following bodies (which are bodies to which provisions contained in Parts 4 and 6 of the Insolvency Act 1986 apply)—
- (a) a society that is registered within the meaning of the Friendly Societies Act 1974 and that at any time during the relevant period carries on the regulated activity of effecting or carrying out contracts of insurance;
- (b) a building society within the meaning of the Building Societies Act 1986;
- (c) a society that is incorporated under the Friendly Societies Act 1992;
- (d) a registered society within the meaning of the Co-operative and Community Benefit Societies Act 2014 that is registered under that Act as a credit union;
- (e) a registered society within the meaning of the Co-operative and Community Benefit Societies Act 2014 that at any time during the relevant period carries on the regulated activity of effecting or carrying out contracts of insurance.

(9) In this regulation "regulated activity" has the meaning given by section 22 of the Financial Services and Markets Act 2000, taken with Schedule 2 to that Act and any order under that section.

NOTES

Commencement: 26 November 2020.

Para (2): words in square brackets substituted by the Corporate Insolvency and Governance Act 2020 (Coronavirus) (Extension of the Relevant Period) Regulations 2021, SI 2021/375, reg 2, as from 26 March 2021.

[10.1302]

3 Amendment of the Corporate Insolvency and Governance Act 2020

(1) (*Amends the Corporate Insolvency and Governance Act 2020, Sch 14, para 2(1) at* **[9.567]**.)

(2) Paragraph (1) applies only in relation to—
- (a) a building society within the meaning of the Building Societies Act 1986,
- (b) a society that is registered within the meaning of the Friendly Societies Act 1974 or incorporated under the Friendly Societies Act 1992,
- (c) a registered branch within the meaning of the Friendly Societies Act 1992,
- (d) a company within the meaning of section 1(1) of the Companies Act 2006,
- (e) a charitable incorporated organisation within the meaning of Part 11 of the Charities Act 2011, and
- (f) a registered society within the meaning of the Co-operative and Community Benefit Societies Act 2014.

NOTES

Commencement: 26 November 2020.

LIMITED LIABILITY PARTNERSHIPS (AMENDMENT ETC) REGULATIONS 2021

(SI 2021/60)

NOTES

Made: 15 January 2021.

Authority: Limited Liability Partnerships Act 2000, ss 14, 15, 16, 17(2), (3); Corporate Insolvency and Governance Act 2020, Sch 4, para 91, Sch 8, para 55.

Commencement: 16 February 2021.

Note that these Regulations revoke and replace the Limited Liability Partnerships (Amendment etc) Regulations 2020, SI 2020/643, which came into force on 26 June 2020. These Regulations replicate the provisions of the 2020 Regulations, with minor modifications (see the explanatory note to the 2021 Regulations at www.legislation.gov.uk/uksi/2021/60/pdfs/uksiem_20210060_en.pdf).

[10.1303]

1 Citation, commencement and interpretation

(1) These Regulations may be cited as the Limited Liability Partnerships (Amendment etc) Regulations 2021 and come into force on 16th February 2021.

(2) In these Regulations—

"the 1986 Act" means the Insolvency Act 1986;

"the 1989 Order" means the Insolvency (Northern Ireland) Order 1989;

"the 2001 Regulations" means the Limited Liability Partnerships Regulations 2001;

"the 2004 Regulations" means the Limited Liability Partnerships Regulations (Northern Ireland) 2004;

"the 2006 Act" means the Companies Act 2006;

"the 2009 Regulations" means the Limited Liability Partnerships (Application of Companies Act 2006) Regulations 2009;

"the 2020 Act" means the Corporate Insolvency and Governance Act 2020.

NOTES

Commencement: 16 February 2021.

2 (*Revokes the Limited Liability Partnerships (Amendment etc) Regulations 2020, SI 2020/643 (see further the introductory notes to these Regulations ante).*)

[10.1304]

3 Amendment of Schedule 3 to the 2001 Regulations

(1) (*Introduces Schedule 1 to these Regulations (Amendments to Schedule 3 to the 2001 Regulations).*)

(2) Nothing in these Regulations affects the operation of the 1986 Act, or any other enactment, in relation to a moratorium under Schedule A1 to that Act which comes into force before the repeal of that Schedule by Schedule 3 to the 2020 Act.

NOTES

Commencement: 16 February 2021.

4, 5 *(Reg 4 introduces Sch 2 to these Regulations (Amendments to the Limited Liability Partnerships Regulations (Northern Ireland) 2004) and is outside the scope of this work. Reg 5 introduces Sch 3 to these Regulations (Amendments to the Limited Liability Partnerships (Application of Companies Act 2006) Regulations 2009).)*

[10.1305]

6 Application of temporary provision in the 2020 Act to limited liability partnerships: Great Britain

Schedule 4 to the 2020 Act (moratoriums in Great Britain: temporary provision) applies to limited liability partnerships registered in Great Britain, except where the context otherwise requires, with the following modifications—

(a) references to a company include references to a limited liability partnership;

(b) references to a director of a company include references to a designated member of a limited liability partnership;

(c) such further modifications as the context requires for the purpose of giving effect to that Schedule as applied by these Regulations.

NOTES

Commencement: 16 February 2021.

7 (*This regulation is the Northern Ireland equivalent of reg 6 above and is outside the scope of this work.*)

SCHEDULES 1–3

(*Schedule 1 amends the Limited Liability Partnerships Regulations 2001, SI 2001/1090 at* **[10.99]**. *Schedule 2 amends the Limited Liability Partnerships Regulations (Northern Ireland) 2004 (outside the scope of this work). Schedule 3 amends the Limited Liability Partnerships (Application of Companies Act 2006) Regulations 2009, SI 2009/1804 at* **[10.319]**.)

ADMINISTRATION (RESTRICTIONS ON DISPOSAL ETC TO CONNECTED PERSONS) REGULATIONS 2021

(SI 2021/427)

NOTES

Made: 29 March 2021.

Authority: Insolvency Act 1986, Sch B1, para 60A(1), (2) and (7).

Commencement: 30 April 2021 (in relation to administrations that commence on or after that date).

ARRANGEMENT OF REGULATIONS

PART 1
INTRODUCTORY PROVISIONS

PART 2
RESTRICTIONS ON DISPOSAL OF PROPERTY BY ADMINISTRATORS

CHAPTER 1 GENERAL

CHAPTER 2 CONDITION AS TO CREDITOR APPROVAL

CHAPTER 3 CONDITION AS TO THE OBTAINING OF A QUALIFYING REPORT

CHAPTER 4 NOTIFICATION OF QUALIFYING REPORT TO REGISTRAR OF COMPANIES AND TO CREDITORS

PART 3
THE EVALUATOR

PART 1 INTRODUCTORY PROVISIONS

[10.1306]

1 Citation, commencement and application

(1) These Regulations may be cited as the Administration (Restrictions on Disposal etc to Connected Persons) Regulations 2021 and come into force on 30th April 2021.

(2) These Regulations apply only to administrations that commence on or after the day on which these Regulations come into force.

(3) For the purposes of this regulation an administration commences on—

(a) the appointment of an administrator under paragraph 14 or paragraph 22 of Schedule B1, or

(b) the making of an administration order.

NOTES

Commencement: 30 April 2021 (in relation to administrations that commence on or after that date).

[10.1307]

2 Interpretation

In these Regulations—

"the Act" means the Insolvency Act 1986;

"the company" means the company whose business or assets are the subject of the substantial disposal;

"qualifying report" has the meaning given to it in regulation 5;

"previous report" has the meaning given to it in regulation 8;

"relevant property" means the property being disposed of, hired out or sold by the substantial disposal;

"Schedule B1" means Schedule B1 to the Act; and

"substantial disposal" has the meaning given to it in regulation 3.

NOTES

Commencement: 30 April 2021 (in relation to administrations that commence on or after that date).

PART 2 RESTRICTIONS ON DISPOSAL OF PROPERTY BY ADMINISTRATORS

CHAPTER 1 GENERAL

[10.1308]

3 Conditions and requirements that apply in respect of a substantial disposal by the administrator

(1) An administrator must not make a substantial disposal unless either one of the following two conditions is met—

(a) the approval of the company's creditors for the making of that disposal has been obtained in accordance with regulation 4, or

(b) a qualifying report in respect of the making of that disposal has been obtained.

(2) Where the condition in paragraph (1)(b) is met and an administrator makes a substantial disposal the notification requirements in regulation 9 must be met.

(3) For the purposes of these Regulations a "substantial disposal"—

(a) means a disposal, hiring out or sale to one or more connected persons, during the period of 8 weeks beginning with the day on which the company enters administration, of what is, in the administrator's opinion, all or a substantial part of the company's business or assets, and

(b) includes a disposal which is effected by a series of transactions.

NOTES

Commencement: 30 April 2021 (in relation to administrations that commence on or after that date).

CHAPTER 2 CONDITION AS TO CREDITOR APPROVAL

[10.1309]

4 Creditor approval

(1) The approval of the company's creditors is obtained in accordance with this regulation if the requirements specified in paragraph (2) are met.

(2) The requirements specified in this paragraph are as follows—

(a) the administrator has—

(i) included proposals for making the disposal (referred to for the purposes of this paragraph as "the proposal") in the statement of administrator's proposals referred to in paragraph 49 of Schedule B1, and

(ii) subsequently sought a decision from the company's creditors as to whether they approve the proposal; and

(b) the company's creditors approve the proposal—

(i) without modification, or

(ii) with modifications to which the administrator consents.

NOTES

Commencement: 30 April 2021 (in relation to administrations that commence on or after that date).

CHAPTER 3 CONDITION AS TO THE OBTAINING OF A QUALIFYING REPORT

[10.1310]

5 Qualifying report: meaning of qualifying report

A qualifying report means a report—

(a) whose contents the administrator has considered, and

(b) which the administrator is satisfied—

(i) meets the requirements specified in regulation 6, and

(ii) includes the content specified in regulation 7.

NOTES

Commencement: 30 April 2021 (in relation to administrations that commence on or after that date).

[10.1311]

6 Qualifying report: requirements to be met in connection with obtaining and considering the report

(1) The requirements specified in this regulation are as follows—

(a) the report is—

(i) obtained by a connected person,

(ii) made by an individual who is an evaluator within the meaning given by Part 3 and in respect of whom the requirements specified in paragraph (2) are met, and

(iii) given to the administrator;

(b) the report—

(i) is in writing,

(ii) states the date on which it was made, and

(iii) is authenticated by the evaluator; and

(c) there have been no material changes since the date on which the report was made to—

(i) the relevant property,

(ii) the terms of the substantial disposal, or

(iii) any circumstances relating to the substantial disposal.

(2) The requirements specified in this paragraph are that the administrator, having regard to the date on which the report was made, is satisfied that the individual making that report had sufficient relevant knowledge and experience to make a qualifying report.

(3) For the purposes of paragraph (1)(a)(ii), the individual making the report is to be taken to have met the requirements for being an evaluator in regulation 10(b) and (c) if the administrator has no reason to believe that the individual did not meet those requirements.

(4) For the purposes of this regulation—

(a) the requirement that the report must be given to the administrator may be met by giving the administrator a copy of the report, and

(b) "authenticate" means to authenticate in accordance with rule 1.5 of the Insolvency (England and Wales) Rules 2016 or rule 1.6 of the Insolvency (Scotland) (Company Voluntary Arrangements and Administration) Rules 2018, as applicable.

NOTES

Commencement: 30 April 2021 (in relation to administrations that commence on or after that date).

[10.1312]

7 Qualifying report: required content

The report must contain the following—

(a) a statement that the person making the report is an evaluator within the meaning given by Part 3;

(b) a statement as to what relevant knowledge and experience the evaluator has to make the report;

(c) the following information concerning the professional indemnity insurance, within the meaning given by regulation 11, taken out by, or on behalf of, the evaluator—

(i) the name of the insurer;

(ii) the policy number;

(iii) the risks covered;

(iv) the amount covered; and

(v) exclusions from the cover;

(d) identification of the relevant property;

(e) either—

(i) the information specified in regulation 8(3) or, as the case may be,

(ii) a statement that the evaluator is satisfied that regulation 8 does not apply;

(f) a statement as to the nature of the consideration that is to be provided for the relevant property and the value of that consideration expressed in sterling;

(g) identification of the connected person and a statement as to their connection to the company;

(h) a statement that either—

(i) the evaluator is satisfied that the consideration to be provided for the relevant property and the grounds for the substantial disposal are reasonable in the circumstances or, as the case may be,

(ii) the evaluator is not satisfied that the consideration to be provided for the relevant property and the grounds for the substantial disposal are reasonable in the circumstances (a "case not made opinion"); and

(i) the evaluator's principal reasons for making the statement in sub-paragraph (h)(i) or (ii) and a summary of the evidence relied upon.

NOTES

Commencement: 30 April 2021 (in relation to administrations that commence on or after that date).

[10.1313]

8 Qualifying report: additional requirements where previous report obtained

(1) This regulation applies if, at any time before the date on which a report is made for the purpose of satisfying the condition in regulation 3(1)(b), the individual making that report—

(a) becomes aware that the connected person has obtained a previous report, or

(b) believes the connected person may have obtained a previous report (but this is subject to paragraph (2)).

(2) Where—

(a) the connected person makes a statement to the individual making the report as to whether they have obtained a previous report, or a specified number of previous reports, and

(b) the individual making the report has no reason to believe that statement is incorrect

the report must be made on the basis that the statement is correct.

(3) If this regulation applies, the report must contain the following—

(a) if the previous report has been given to the individual making the report, that previous report, a copy of that previous report, or details of the contents of that previous report which relate to the matters referred to in paragraph (6)(c), or

(b) if the previous report has not been given to the individual making the report—

(i) a statement that the previous report has not been obtained;

(ii) the reasons why the previous report has not been obtained;

(iii) details of any steps taken by the individual making the report to obtain the previous report; and

(iv) if this regulation applies by virtue of the individual making the report having formed the belief referred to in paragraph (1)(b), the reasons why the individual making the report formed that belief.

(4) The requirement in paragraph (3)(b)(ii) may be met by including, if applicable, in the report a statement that the connected person claims that no previous report exists.

(5) Where this regulation applies in respect of two or more previous reports, the report must contain the matters specified in paragraph (3) in relation to each of the previous reports.

(6) For the purposes of this regulation, a "previous report" means an opinion obtained by the connected person which—

(a) was obtained before the date on which the report is made,

(b) is concerned with a disposal of property that is the same, or substantially the same, as the relevant property identified in the report, and

(c) makes reference to whether the person making the previous report is satisfied that—

(i) the grounds for the disposal are reasonable or, as the case may be, unreasonable, in the circumstances, or

(ii) the consideration to be provided for the property is reasonable or, as the case may be, unreasonable, in the circumstances.

NOTES

Commencement: 30 April 2021 (in relation to administrations that commence on or after that date).

CHAPTER 4 NOTIFICATION OF QUALIFYING REPORT TO REGISTRAR OF COMPANIES AND TO CREDITORS

[10.1314]

9 Notification requirements where a qualifying report is obtained

(1) Where regulation 3(2) applies (administrator makes a substantial disposal following receipt of a qualifying report) the administrator must comply with the requirements specified in paragraphs (2) to (5).

(2) The administrator must send the following to the persons specified in paragraph (5)—

(a) a copy of the report (excluding any information that, in the administrator's opinion, is confidential or commercially sensitive); and

(b) where paragraph (3) applies, the information specified in paragraph (4).

(3) This paragraph applies where the qualifying report contains—

(a) a case not made opinion within the meaning given by regulation 7(h)(ii), or

(b) details of any previous report where the person making it was satisfied that—

(i) the grounds for the disposal were not reasonable in the circumstances, or

(ii) the consideration to be provided for the disposal was not reasonable in the circumstances.

(4) Where paragraph (3) applies the administrator must send together with each copy of the qualifying report a statement setting out their reasons for proceeding with the substantial disposal.

(5) A copy of the report and, where applicable, the additional information specified in paragraph (4) must be sent to—

(a) the registrar of companies, and

(b) every creditor of the company, other than an opted-out creditor, of whose claim and address the administrator is aware

at the same time as the administrator complies with the requirement in paragraph 49(4)(a) and (b) of Schedule B1 to send a copy of the statement of their proposals to the registrar of companies and to creditors.

NOTES

Commencement: 30 April 2021 (in relation to administrations that commence on or after that date).

PART 3 THE EVALUATOR

[10.1315]

10 Requirements for acting as evaluator

For the purposes of these Regulations an evaluator is an individual who—

(a) is satisfied that their relevant knowledge and experience is sufficient for the purposes of making a qualifying report,

(b) meets the—

(i) requirement as to insurance specified in regulation 11, and

(ii) requirement as to independence specified in regulation 12, and

(c) is not excluded from acting as an evaluator by virtue of regulation 13.

NOTES

Commencement: 30 April 2021 (in relation to administrations that commence on or after that date).

[10.1316]

11 The requirement as to insurance

(1) An individual meets the requirement as to insurance if there is in force professional indemnity insurance in respect of that individual.

(2) For the purposes of this regulation "professional indemnity insurance" means insurance taken out by, or on behalf of, an individual in respect of potential liabilities to the administrator, the connected person, creditors or any other person, as a result of, or arising from, any matter stated by the individual in a report made by them for the purpose of satisfying the condition in regulation 3(1)(b).

NOTES

Commencement: 30 April 2021 (in relation to administrations that commence on or after that date).

[10.1317]

12 Requirement as to independence

(1) An individual meets the requirement as to independence unless they—

(a) are connected with the company,

(b) are an associate of the connected person or connected with the connected person,

(c) know or have reason to believe that they have a conflict of interest with respect to the substantial disposal, or

(d) have, at any time during the period of 12 months ending with the date on which a report is made by that individual for the purpose of satisfying the condition in regulation 3(1)(b) provided advice to, and in respect of, the company or a connected person in relation to the company—
   (i) in connection with, or in anticipation of, the commencement of an insolvency procedure under Parts A1 to 5 of the Act, or
   (ii) in relation to corporate rescue or restructuring.

(2) In this regulation "conflict of interest" means a financial or other interest which is likely to affect prejudicially the independence of the individual in providing a report made for the purpose of satisfying the condition in regulation 3(1)(b).

(3) Nothing in this regulation limits the scope of an individual's obligation to comply with any professional or regulatory requirements to which that individual is subject.

NOTES

Commencement: 30 April 2021 (in relation to administrations that commence on or after that date).

[10.1318]

13 Exclusion from providing the report

An individual is excluded from acting as an evaluator if—

(a) the individual is—
   (i) the administrator,
   (ii) an associate of the administrator, or
   (iii) connected with a company with which the administrator is connected,
(b) the individual has at any time been convicted of an offence involving dishonesty or deception in the United Kingdom or any other jurisdiction and the conviction is not a spent conviction,
(c) the individual has at any time made a composition or arrangement with, or granted a trust deed for, the individual's creditors unless the individual has been discharged in respect of it,
(d) the individual has at any time been made bankrupt under the Act, the Bankruptcy (Scotland) Act 1985, the Bankruptcy (Scotland) Act 2016 or the Insolvency (Northern Ireland) Order 1989, or sequestration of the individual's estate has been awarded and in either case—
   (i) the individual has not been discharged, or
   (ii) the individual has been made the subject of a bankruptcy restrictions order or an interim bankruptcy restrictions order under the Act, the Bankruptcy (Scotland) Act 1985, the Bankruptcy (Scotland) Act 2016 or the Insolvency (Northern Ireland) Order 1989, unless that order has ceased to have effect or has been annulled,
(e) a moratorium period under a debt relief order under the Act or the Insolvency (Northern Ireland) Order 1989 applies in relation to the individual,
(f) a debt relief restrictions order under the Act or the Insolvency (Northern Ireland) Order 1989 is in force in respect of the individual,
(g) the individual is subject to—
   (i) a disqualification order under section 1 of the Company Directors Disqualification Act 1986,
   (ii) a disqualification undertaking under section 1A of that Act,
   (iii) a disqualification order under article 3 of the Company Directors Disqualification (Northern Ireland) Order 2002,
   (iv) a disqualification undertaking under article 4 of that Order, or
   (v) an order made under section 429(2)(b) of the Act (failure to pay under county court administration order),
(h) the individual has at any time been—
   (i) removed from the office of charity trustee or trustee for a charity by an order made by the Charity Commission for England and Wales or the High Court on the grounds of any misconduct or mismanagement in the administration of the charity for which the individual was responsible or to which the individual was privy, or which the individual by the individual's conduct contributed to or facilitated, or
   (ii) removed under section 34 of the Charities and Trustee Investment (Scotland) Act 2005 (powers of the Court of Session) from being concerned in the management or control of any charity or body,
(i) the individual is a patient within the meaning of section 329(1) of the Mental Health (Care and Treatment) (Scotland) Act 2003 or has had a guardian appointed under the Adults with Incapacity (Scotland) Act 2000,
(j) the individual lacks capacity, within the meaning of the Mental Capacity Act 2005, to provide the report, or
(k) the individual has at any time been subject to any measures in another jurisdiction equivalent to those set out in sub-paragraphs (d) to (h) above.

NOTES

Commencement: 30 April 2021 (in relation to administrations that commence on or after that date).

NATIONAL SECURITY AND INVESTMENT ACT 2021 (MONETARY PENALTIES) (TURNOVER OF A BUSINESS) REGULATIONS 2021

(SI 2021/1262)

NOTES

Made: 10 November 2021.

Authority: National Security and Investment Act 2021, s 41(8), (9).

Commencement: 4 January 2022.

[10.1319]

1 Citation, commencement, extent and interpretation

(1) These Regulations may be cited as the National Security and Investment Act 2021 (Monetary Penalties) (Turnover of a Business) Regulations 2021, and come into force on 4th January 2022.

(2) These Regulations extend to England and Wales, Scotland and Northern Ireland.

(3) In these Regulations, "the Act" means the National Security and Investment Act 2021.

NOTES

Commencement: 4 January 2022.

[10.1320]

2 Meaning of "business"

For the purposes of section 41 of the Act (permitted maximum penalties), "business" includes a sole trader.

NOTES

Commencement: 4 January 2022.

[10.1321]

3 Control of a business

(1) For the purposes of section 41 of the Act (permitted maximum penalties), a business is to be treated as controlled by another business ("A") where—

(a) the business is a body corporate in which A has a controlling interest;

(b) the business is a body corporate, and A is able to control directly or indirectly or materially to influence the policy of that body corporate without having a controlling interest in that body corporate;

(c) the business is a partnership or an unincorporated association or group of persons, and A (whether or not A is a member of that partnership, association or group) is able to control directly or indirectly or materially to influence the policy of that partnership, association or group; or

(d) the business is a sole trader, and A is able to control directly or indirectly or materially to influence the policy of that sole trader in carrying on the activities of the business.

(2) For the purposes of paragraph (1)(a) and (b), A has a controlling interest in a body corporate if A—

(a) is a parent undertaking of that body corporate within the meaning of section 1162 of the Companies Act 2006; or

(b) would be a parent undertaking of that body corporate within the meaning of that section if A were an undertaking within the meaning of section 1161 of that Act.

(3) For the purposes of paragraph (2), subsections (2)(c) and (4)(a) of section 1162 of the Companies Act 2006 are to be disregarded.

(4) For the purposes of paragraph (1)(b), (c) and (d), the Secretary of State may, having regard to all the circumstances, determine whether A is able to control directly or indirectly or materially to influence the policy of a body corporate or the policy of an individual or a partnership or an unincorporated association or group of persons in carrying on the activities of that business.

(5) References in this regulation—

(a) to a body corporate include a body incorporated outside the United Kingdom; and

(b) to a partnership or an unincorporated association or group of persons include a partnership or unincorporated association or group of persons formed or established, or having any members incorporated, formed or established, outside the United Kingdom.

NOTES

Commencement: 4 January 2022.

[10.1322]

4 Turnover of a business

(1) This regulation applies to determine the turnover of a business ("A") and any business owned or controlled by A for the purposes of section 41 of the Act (permitted maximum penalties).

(2) The turnover of a business is its turnover in—

(a) the complete accounting period immediately preceding the decision date (the "relevant accounting period") (subject to paragraph (3)); or

(b) if the business has no relevant accounting period, the period beginning with the date on which the activities of the business began to be carried on and ending with the last day of the month preceding the month in which the decision date falls.

(3) If the figures necessary to calculate turnover of the business in the relevant accounting period are not available to the Secretary of State on the decision date, the turnover is (subject to paragraph (4)) its turnover in—

(a) the complete accounting period immediately preceding the relevant accounting period (the "preceding accounting period"); or

(b) if the business has no preceding accounting period, the period beginning with the date on which the activities of the business began to be carried on and ending with the day immediately preceding the date on which the relevant accounting period began.

(4) If the figures necessary to calculate the turnover of the business under paragraph (3)(a) or (b) are not available to the Secretary of State on the decision date, the turnover of the business is its turnover in the period beginning with the day after the last day of the relevant accounting period and ending with the last day of the month preceding the month in which the decision date falls.

(5) Where a period described in this regulation does not equal 12 months, the turnover of the business is the turnover in that period divided by the number of days in that period and multiplied by 365 or, if the period includes 29th February, 366.

(6) The amount of a business's turnover for the purposes of this regulation is, in the event of a disagreement between that business and the Secretary of State, the amount determined by the Secretary of State.

(7) For the purposes of this regulation—

(a) an "accounting period" of a business is a period of more than six months in respect of which accounts are prepared or required to be prepared in relation to the business;

(b) the "decision date" means the date on which the Secretary of State decides to impose a monetary penalty;

(c) the provisions of the Schedule apply in the determination of turnover.

NOTES

Commencement: 4 January 2022.

SCHEDULE
TURNOVER OF A BUSINESS

Regulation 4

[10.1323]

1 Interpretation

(1) In this Schedule—

"credit institution" means a credit institution as defined in Article 4(1)(1) of Regulation (EU) No 575/2013 of the European Parliament and of the Council of 26 June 2013 on prudential requirements for credit institutions and investment firms and amending Regulation (EU) No 648/2012;

"financial institution" means a financial institution as defined in Article 4(1)(26) of Regulation (EU) No 575/2013 of the European Parliament and of the Council of 26 June 2013 on prudential requirements for credit institutions and investment firms and amending Regulation (EU) No 648/2012, or any undertaking located outside the United Kingdom which does not fall within the scope of that definition but which carries out equivalent activities;

"insurance undertaking" means—

(a) an undertaking which—

(i) has its head office in the United Kingdom;

(ii) has permission under Part 4A of the Financial Services and Markets Act 2000 to carry on one or more regulated activities; and

(iii) effects or carries out contracts of insurance or reinsurance; or

(b) a third-country insurance undertaking;

"third-country insurance undertaking" means an undertaking which, if its head office were in the United Kingdom, would require permission under Part 4A of the Financial Services and Markets Act 2000 to carry out regulated activities relating to insurance or reinsurance.

(2) The provisions of this Schedule are to be interpreted in accordance with generally accepted accounting principles and practices.

2 Turnover of a business

(1) The turnover of a business is the sum of all amounts derived from the sale of products and the provision of services falling within the ordinary activities of the business to businesses or consumers, after the deduction of sales rebates, value added tax and other taxes directly related to turnover.

(2) But where all or any of the activities of a business are the activities of a credit institution, a financial institution or an insurance undertaking, paragraph 3 or 4 (as the case may be) applies instead of sub-paragraph (1) to determine the turnover of the business in respect of those activities.

(3) Paragraph 5 also applies to determine the turnover of a business for the purposes of this Schedule.

3 Turnover in respect of activities of a credit institution or financial institution

(1) The turnover of a business in respect of the activities of a credit institution or financial institution is the sum of the following income items received by the institution, after deduction of value added tax and other taxes directly related to those items—

(a) interest income and similar income;

(b) the following income from securities—

(i) income from shares and other variable yield securities;

(ii) income from participating interests;

(iii) income from shares in affiliated undertakings;

(c) commissions receivable;

(d) net profit on financial operations;

(e) other operating income.

(2) Expressions used in sub-paragraph (1) have the meanings given by Council Directive (EEC) 86/635 of 8 December 1986 on the annual accounts and consolidated accounts of banks and other financial institutions.

4 Turnover in respect of activities of an insurance undertaking

The turnover of a business in respect of the activities of an insurance undertaking is the total value of gross premiums received, comprising all amounts received and receivable in respect of insurance contracts issued by or on behalf of the undertaking, including outgoing reinsurance premiums, and after deduction of taxes and parafiscal contributions or levies charged by reference to the amounts of individual premiums or the total volume of premiums.

5 Further provisions about determining turnover

(1) The turnover of a business is its turnover both in and outside the United Kingdom.

(2) The turnover of a business includes any subsidy given to the business, determined in accordance with paragraph 6.

(3) Where a business ("A") owns or controls one or more businesses, the turnover of the businesses owned or controlled by A does not include amounts derived from the sale of products or the provision of services between any of those businesses, or any of those businesses and A.

(4) Where in the accounts or other information used by the Secretary of State to calculate the turnover (or any part of the turnover) of a business any figure is expressed in a currency other than sterling, the Secretary of State may determine the equivalent in sterling, applying whatever rate or rates of exchange the Secretary of State considers appropriate and rounding the resulting figure up or down as the Secretary of State considers appropriate.

(5) Where an acquisition, divestment or other transaction or event has occurred since the end of the period in which the turnover of the business is determined in accordance with regulation 3 which the Secretary of State considers may have a significant impact on the turnover of the business, the Secretary of State may take account of that transaction or event if the Secretary of State considers it appropriate to do so and accordingly increase or (as the case may be) reduce by such amount as the Secretary of State considers appropriate the amount which would otherwise constitute the business's turnover.

6 Subsidies

(1) For the purposes of paragraph 5(2), "subsidy" means financial assistance which—

(a) is given, directly or indirectly, from public resources by a public authority;
(b) confers an economic advantage on one or more businesses; and
(c) is specific, that is, is such that it benefits one or more businesses over one or more other businesses with respect to the production of goods or the provision of services.

(2) For the purposes of sub-paragraph (1), the means by which financial assistance may be given include—

(a) a direct transfer of funds (such as grants or loans);
(b) a contingent transfer of funds (such as guarantees);
(c) the forgoing of revenue that is otherwise due;
(d) the provision of goods or services;
(e) the purchase of goods or services.

(3) For the purposes of sub-paragraph (1)(a), "public authority" means a person who exercises functions of a public nature.

(4) Financial assistance given from the person's resources by a person who is not a public authority is to be treated for the purposes of sub-paragraph (1)(a) as financial assistance given from public resources by a public authority if the involvement of a public authority in the decision to give financial assistance is such that the decision is, in substance, the decision of the public authority.

(5) For the purposes of sub-paragraph (4), the factors which may be taken into account when considering the involvement of a public authority in the decision of a person to give financial assistance include, in particular, factors relating to—

(a) the control exercised over that person by that public authority, or
(b) the relationship between that person and that public authority.

(6) For the purposes of this paragraph, financial assistance is to be treated as given to a business if the business has an enforceable right to the financial assistance.

NOTES

Commencement: 4 January 2022.

NATIONAL SECURITY AND INVESTMENT ACT 2021 (NOTIFIABLE ACQUISITION) (SPECIFICATION OF QUALIFYING ENTITIES) REGULATIONS 2021

(SI 2021/1264)

NOTES

Made: 10 November 2021.
Authority: National Security and Investment Act 2021, s 6(1), (2), (4), (8).
Commencement: 4 January 2022.

ARRANGEMENT OF REGULATIONS

SCHEDULES

[10.1324]
1 Citation, commencement and extent

(1) These Regulations may be cited as the National Security and Investment Act 2021 (Notifiable Acquisition) (Specification of Qualifying Entities) Regulations 2021.

(2) These Regulations come into force on 4th January 2022.

(3) These Regulations extend to England and Wales, Scotland and Northern Ireland.

NOTES
Commencement: 4 January 2022.

[10.1325]
2 Notifiable acquisitions

(1) Schedules 1 to 17 specify descriptions of qualifying entity for the purposes of section 6(2) of the National Security and Investment Act 2021 (notifiable acquisitions).

(2) A qualifying entity falls within a description in the Schedules by reason of the carrying on of an activity specified in the Schedules only if it carries on the activity in the United Kingdom.

NOTES
Commencement: 4 January 2022.

[10.1326]
3 Interpretation

In these Regulations—

"the Act" means the National Security and Investment Act 2021;

"development" means all stages prior to production, including design, design research, design analyses, design concepts, assembly and testing of prototypes, pilot production schemes, design data, process of transforming design data into goods or software, configuration design, integration design, layouts;

"production" means all production stages, including product engineering, manufacture, integration, assembly (mounting), inspection, testing and quality assurance.

NOTES
Commencement: 4 January 2022.

[10.1327]
4 Review

(1) The Secretary of State must from time to time—

(a) carry out a review of the regulatory provision contained in these Regulations; and
(b) publish a report setting out the conclusion of the review.

(2) The first report must be published before the end of the period of three years beginning with the day on which these Regulations come into force for any purpose.

(3) Subsequent reports must be published at intervals not exceeding three years.

(4) Section 30(4) of the Small Business, Enterprise and Employment Act 2015 requires that a report published under this regulation must, in particular—

(a) set out the objectives intended to be achieved by the regulatory provision referred to in paragraph (1)(a);
(b) assess the extent to which those objectives are achieved;
(c) assess whether those objectives remain appropriate; and
(d) if those objectives remain appropriate, assess the extent to which they could be achieved in another way which involves less onerous regulatory provision.

(5) In this regulation, "regulatory provision" has the same meaning as in sections 28 to 32 of the Small Business, Enterprise and Employment Act 2015 (see section 32 of that Act).

NOTES

Commencement: 4 January 2022.

SCHEDULES

SCHEDULE 1
ADVANCED MATERIALS

Regulation 2

[10.1328]

1 Interpretation

In this Schedule—

"2D" means two-dimensional;

"3D" means three-dimensional;

"advanced composites" relates to structural composite materials with either metallic or ceramic matrices and includes 3D reinforcing architectures for any matrix (polymer, metal or ceramic);

"advanced materials" means completely new materials and materials that are developments on traditional materials, where such materials provide any of the following—

- (a) targeted properties;
- (b) advantageous properties;
- (c) outstanding structural properties; or
- (d) outstanding functional properties;

"enabler" means any material or process which is not a material described in paragraph 2(3) or 3 but is used in the manufacture or application of such materials;

"fabrication" in sector (7) (semiconductors) of the table set out in paragraph 3 means the process of producing a microelectronic circuit on a semiconductor substrate or using other advanced materials;

"graphene and related 2D" are those materials with attributes as defined within ISO/TS 80004-13:2017;

"metamaterial"—

- (a) means a composite material in which the constituents are designed and spatially arranged through a rational design-led approach to change the manner in which electromagnetic, acoustic or vibrational energy interacts with the material, in order to achieve a property or performance that is not possible naturally and includes a metasurface and for this purpose "composite material" means a solid material formed from two or more constituents and "constituent" includes a region containing a vacuum, gas or liquid;
- (b) does not include the types of composite materials the advanced composites described in paragraph 5 and composites or coatings containing pigments or fillers that are mixed in or blended into a binder material where both of these types of composite materials can be a constituent from which a metamaterial may be formed;

"metasurface" means a two-dimensional form of metamaterial which includes one or more layers of material that are intentionally patterned or textured (irrespective of whether they are periodic or not) through a rational design-led approach;

"nanotechnology" means the manipulation and control of matter predominantly in the nanoscale to make use of size-and-structure-dependent properties and phenomena distinct from those associated with individual atoms or molecules, or extrapolation from larger sizes of the same material (where "manipulation and control" includes material synthesis in relation to nanotechnology) with current or potential utility for defence, including nanomaterials, nanodevices, nanocomponents and nanosystems (including nanomachines) in accordance with ISO/TR 10993-22:2017;

"nanomaterials" means materials with any external dimension in the nanoscale or having internal structure or surface structure in the nanoscale and include nano-objects, dispersions or mixtures containing nano-objects, and nanostructured material (including structuring at an interface between materials, including air, and within a material) in accordance with ISO/TR 10993-22:2017;

"packaging" in sector (7) (semiconductors) of the table set out in paragraph 3 means the process of turning a microelectronic circuit on an appropriate substrate into a package suitable for use in an electronic circuit but does not include the assembly and packaging of chips and devices into circuit boards;

"photonic and optoelectronic materials and devices" in sector (8) of the table set out in paragraph 3 relate to high power lasers that are characterised by a combination of power at the output apertures (values of 1 kilowatt and above), beam quality (M^2 of less than 1.2), intended operating ranges (greater than 1 kilometre) and at wavelengths compatible with propagation over those distances (typically 1 micrometre to 2 micrometres wavelengths);

"semiconductor" means—

- (a) semiconductors used to form radio frequency and microwave devices;
- (b) semiconductors used to realise imaging sensor arrays;
- (c) the accessibility of design and production for semiconductor devices and chips where "chips" include Field Programmable Gate Array devices, System on Chip, Application Specific Integrated Circuits and Readout Integrated Circuits and where "devices" includes radio and microwave frequency control circuitry, power amplifiers, low noise amplifiers and monolithic microwave integrated circuits and detectors;

"technical textiles" means textiles (and their processes and enablers) specifically developed for their functional performance including additional functionality (such as integrated computing, processing or data transmission), 3D architectures, protection against blast and ballistic events but does not include sportswear or clothing that is ordinarily available to consumers or household goods.

2 Activities

(1) A qualifying entity carrying on activities that consist of or include any of the activities set out in sub-paragraph (2) in relation to—

(a) any of the matters described in sub-paragraph (3); or

(b) any of the matters described in relation to the sectors set out in paragraph 3.

(2) The activities referred to in sub-paragraph (1) are—

(a) research;

(b) development or production;

(c) development or production of anything designed as an enabler;

(d) development or production of anything designed to be used for the purpose of production;

(e) the provision of qualified or certified designs, materials, parts or products;

(f) owning, creating, supplying or exploiting intellectual property;

(g) provision of know-how or services of enablers;

(h) recycling or re-using.

(3) The matters referred to in sub-paragraph (1)(a) are materials, the export or transfer of which is controlled by virtue of their being specified in—

(a) Schedule 2 to the Export Control Order 2008; or

(b) Annex I and Annex IV to Council Regulation (EC) No 2009/428 setting up a Community regime for the control of exports, transfer, brokering and transit of dual-use items.

3 Sectors and matters

The following Table sets out the sectors and matters referred to in paragraph 2(1)(b).

Table

Sector	*Matters*
(1) Advanced composites	1. The matters are, in relation to the sector of advanced composites, those set out in paragraphs 2 to 4.
	2. In relation to test, inspection and production equipment— (a) production technologies and capabilities for the manufacture of metal matrix composites; (b) production technologies and capabilities for the manufacture of ceramic matrix composites; (c) manufacture of 3D fibre architectures (that is with interlaminar reinforcement) for all composite types.
	3. In relation to materials— (a) metal matrix composites, powder-based metal matrix composites and continuous fibre reinforced metal matrix composites; (b) fibre reinforced ceramic matrix composites; (c) continuous silicon carbide fibres with diameters at and below 140 micrometres; (d) continuous oxide-based ceramic fibres with diameters at or below 20 micrometres; (e) coatings for the protection of ceramic matrix composites from degradation in the environment, for example ytterbium mono- and di-silicates;
	4. In relation to software and data— (a) capabilities for the design and design for manufacturing of metal matrix composites and fibre reinforced ceramic matrix composites; (b) software and computer-aided design for 3D fibre architectures and 3D preforms (with interlaminar reinforcement) for all composite types.
(2) Metals and alloys	1. The matters are, in relation to the sector of metal and alloys, those set out in paragraphs 2 to 5.
	2. In relation to systems, equipment and components, magnets utilising rare earth element-lean or element-free permanent magnetic materials with remanent magnetism, known as "B_r", greater than 1.0 Tesla and all rare-earth magnetic materials;
	3. In relation to testing, inspection and production equipment— (a) any processes that are involved in the reduction of either pure or mixed oxides in the solid state into either metals or alloys in or into crude or semi-fabricated forms, including powders, in batches of at least 1 kilogram; (b) hot isostatic pressing (also referred to as "HIP"); (c) spark plasma sintering (also referred to as "SPS") or field assisted sintering technology (also referred to as "FAST"); (d) diffusion and friction-based joining processes for steel for power transmission shafts described in paragraph 4(e) of this sector (metal and alloys), titanium alloys, nickel alloys or cobalt alloys; (e) friction-based processes to join metallic material layer by layer to create a structure; (f) superplastic forming of titanium and aluminium alloys; (g) electron beam, laser and weld arc-based metal additive manufacturing capabilities.
	4. In relation to materials— (a) any alloys that are formed by chemical or electrochemical reduction of feedstocks in the solid state directly from their oxides; (b) titanium alloys with continuous temperature-of-use capabilities above 350 Celsius; (c) powder metallurgy alloys; (d) nickel and cobalt based superalloys with continuous temperature-of-use capabilities above 700 Celsius; (e) steels for power transmission shafts with yield strengths of at least 1030 megapascals at 20 Celsius and 760 megapascals at 450 Celsius, ultimate tensile strengths of at least 1240 MPa at 20 Celsius and 950 megapascals at 450 Celsius and fracture toughnesses of at least 40 megapascals square root metres at 20 Celsius;

Sector	***Matters***
	(f) high strength high toughness weldable marine grade steels (toughness levels D, E and F); (g) armour grade steels; (h) armour grade aluminium alloys; (i) high entropy alloys and compositionally complex alloys (alloys that are formed by five or more elements where the composition is not dominated by one or two elements); (j) rare earth element-lean or element-free permanent magnetic materials with remanent magnetisation (also known as "B_r"), greater than 1.0 Tesla, and all rare-earth magnetic materials; (k) magnetic materials with high total saturation flux densities greater than 2.0 Tesla, which may include monolithic and laminate forms, and particulate and fibre reinforced composite materials.
	5.In relation to software and data— (a) computer models of complex metallic components, formed by powder-based additive manufacture, that embody a fluid and heat transfer function within their structure; (b) data on the performance of complex metallic components, formed by powder-based additive manufacture, that embody a fluid and heat transfer function within their structure.
(3) Engineering and technical polymers	1. The matters are, in relation to engineering and technical polymers, those set out in paragraphs 2 and 3.
	2. In relation to test, inspection and production equipment, machines for additively manufacturing the materials listed in paragraph 3 of this sector (Engineering and technical polymers), including loaded polymer filaments to enable electrically insulating and electrically conducting, thermally conducting and insulating, or magnetic and non-magnetic materials (or any further combination).
	3. In relation to materials— (a) engineering polymer materials and formulations with a glass transition temperature greater than 190 Celsius; (b) polymers responsive to external stimuli such as electromagnetic, load, chemical and biological stimuli (for example electroactive polymers, thermoactive polymers and self-healing systems) but not hydrogels in applications such as nappies; (c) high temperature, high pressure and chemically resistant elastomeric seals and systems; (d) polymer electrical insulation materials with high temperature (greater than 200 Celsius) and high voltage (above 1kilovolt)) capabilities for application in aviation electrical power management systems; (e) filaments and feedstocks for additive manufacturing or 3D printing with bespoke and elevated electrical, magnetic, or electromagnetic properties (typically formed from filled polymer compositions); (f) adhesives capable of retaining performance at high temperatures (above 190 Celsius); (g) adhesives with underwater curing capabilities; (h) void-filling viscoelastic polymers, created using at least a thermoplastic polyester and curing agent, intended for use to damp vibrations in metallic structures.
(4) Engineering and technical ceramics	1. The matters are, in relation to engineering and technical ceramics, those set out in paragraphs 2 and 3.
	2. In relation to test, inspection and production equipment, spark plasma sintering or field assisted sintering technology.
	3. In relation to materials— (a) boron carbide and silicon carbide ceramics for the manufacture of hard armour plates; (b) ultra-high temperature ceramics (with melting temperatures of at least 3000 Celsius) including transition metal diborides, either as monolithic or composite forms, including other ceramic monoliths or composites where ultra-high temperature ceramics have been added to their bulk or into surfaces; (c) magnetic materials, including fibres and particulates, for electromagnetic applications at frequencies above 500 megahertz; (d) functional ceramics (including ferroelectrics, magneto-dielectrics, or multi-ferroics) for acoustic applications, or electromagnetic applications above 100 megahertz; (e) dielectric and ferroelectric materials for use in the generation of, and manipulation of, high energy or high power radio frequency radiation, including functioning under high voltage conditions.
(5) Technical textiles	1. The matters are, in relation to technical textiles, those set out in paragraphs 2 to 6.
	2. In relation to systems, equipment and components, textile materials and products manufactured primarily for technical performance and functional properties rather than aesthetic or decorative characteristics but not sportswear or clothing ordinarily available to consumers or household goods;
	3. In relation to test, inspection and production equipment— (a) knitting, weaving, nonwoven or hybrid manufacturing processes related to the textile materials and products described in paragraph 2 of this sector; (b) fibre manufacturing processes related to the textile materials and products described in paragraph 2 of this sector (Technical textiles); (c) yarn manufacturing and texturing, dry fabric coating and laminating; (d) manufacture of 3D textiles; (e) closed loop recycling processes associated with the textile materials and products described in paragraph 2 of this sector.
	4. In relation to materials— (a) smart fabrics with fibres or yarns equipped with embedded sensors that respond to stimuli and perform a specific function; (b) fabrics made of smart polymers and textiles to protect and prevent injury or damage from

Sector	Matters
	blast and ballistic events; (c) energy harvesting fabrics; (d) textiles or fibres incorporating activated carbon; (e) fabrics with embedded devices for data storage and communication.
	5. In relation to software and data— (a) software and computer-aided design for 3D textiles and preforms; (b) machine learning software systems for smart textile manufacturing facilities, or for data-driven design and manufacturing of textile materials and systems.
	6. In relation to technology— (a) textile-based wearable electronics with potential to enable subtle integration of electronics with the human body for human-machine interfacing; (b) integration technologies to enable functionalities such as energy harvesting, data storage and communication, camouflage, structural and personnel health monitoring and protection.
(6) Metamaterials	1. The matters are, in relation to metamaterials, those set out in paragraphs 2 to 6.
	2. In relation to systems, equipment and components, metamaterials used in— (a) electromagnetic components including antennas, arrays, lens, devices; (b) electromagnetic applications including radio frequencies and microwave through to ultraviolet wavelengths; (c) nano-photonics or quantum technology as an enabler; (d) thermal control or protection; (e) airborne or underwater acoustics; or (f) structural applications.
	3. In relation to test, inspection and production equipment— (a) test, inspection and production equipment associated with the fabrication of 2D and 3D arrangements of one or more material and/or device constituents to form a metamaterial (including additive manufacturing, printed electronics methods, nano-fabrication, chemical self-assembly or engineering biology); (b) equipment associated with the non-destructive test and assurance of assembled or produced metamaterial, including composition, spatially varying composition and spatial arrangement parameters.
	4. In relation to materials— (a) a metamaterial; (b) tailored or bespoke feedstocks used in fabricating metamaterials including blended or formulated filaments referred to in paragraph 3(e) of sector (3) (engineering and technical polymers)), inks or dispersions used for additive manufacturing or printing but excluding inks or dispersions commercialised for forming electrically conducting pathways (known as "wires") in printed electronics.
	5. In relation to software and data, accumulations of metamaterial designs, or of elements comprising metamaterials, any of which that enable artificial intelligence, machine learning design or optimisation of metamaterials.
	6. In relation to technology, the inclusion with a metamaterial of technology in the form of systems or components, as well as material constituents, as part of the means and methods that enable metamaterials to alter their function and behaviour once installed or produced.
(7) Semiconductors	1. The matters are, in relation to semiconductors, those set out in paragraphs 2 to 5.
	2. In relation to systems, equipment and components— (a) high performance thermal imaging systems, equipment and components providing system sensitivity less than 30 milli-Kelvin for large format systems with more than 1 megapixels; (b) integrated systems having multiple operating wavebands on a single camera including mid-wavelength and long-wavelength infrared; (c) imaging systems with on-chip (smart) processing; (d) type II superlattice detectors; (e) single photon counting detector arrays operating at wavelengths longer than the visible band (wavelength greater than 750 nanometres), and with a size of at least 32x32 elements, or linear arrays with a size of at least 1x256 elements; (f) low noise CMOS (complementary metal-oxide-semiconductor) and EMCCD (electron multiplying charge coupled device) cameras where low noise would be less than 1 photoelectron/pixel/second; (g) technology and components for non-Von Neumann computing architectures, including but not limited to neuromorphic computing systems.
	3. In relation to test, inspection and production equipment— (a) the production of radio and microwave frequency systems, equipment and components incorporating compound semiconductors; example components include but are not limited to control circuitry, power amplifiers, low noise amplifiers and monolithic microwave integrated circuits, detectors and photonic devices; (b) facilities operating as a compound semiconductor foundry or providing compound semiconductor processing capability; (c) chip and device fabrication; (d) ceramic and polymeric packaging of processed semiconductor chips; (e) the production and integration capabilities for the high-performance imaging systems described in paragraph 2 of this sector (semiconductors).
	4. In relation to materials— (a) all compound semiconductors for radio frequency and microwave application including gallium nitride, gallium arsenide, gallium oxide, silicon germanium and indium phosphide;

Sector	*Matters*
	(b) imaging camera detector materials including cadmium mercury telluride, aluminium gallium arsenide, indium gallium arsenide and germanium silicon. 5. In relation to software and data, chip and device design
(8) Photonic and optoelectronic materials and devices	1. The matters are, in relation to photonic and optoelectronic materials and devices, those set out in paragraphs 2 to 6.
	2. In relation to systems, equipment and components— (a) polarisation control components including materials (solid and liquid) especially for high power applications (greater than 100 watts); (b) optical fibre designs mitigating nonlinear effects and enabling polarisation control of the output light for high power applications in both transverse single-mode and multimode optical fibre formats; (c) optical fibre based components such as light diodes, tap couplers and fibre Bragg gratings; (d) nonlinear components for nonlinear frequency conversion such as optical fibre geometries, crystal materials and optical patterning techniques; (e) low loss, high bandwidth optical fibre technologies (for laser sources and amplifier stages) and manufacturing techniques where the output power is capable of being scaled up for lasers that meet the characteristics set out in the description of "photonic and optoelectronic material and devices" in paragraph 1 of this Schedule (Interpretation); (f) phase modulators, where the spectral linewidth of fibre laser amplifiers is limited to no more than 16 gigahertz.
	3. In relation to test, inspection and production equipment— (a) optical fibre designs and production techniques, including coating techniques and test methodologies; (b) laser materials manufacturing techniques, host material doping techniques and characterisation techniques.
	4. In relation to materials— (a) materials that enable increased amplification, improved quality, improved robustness, improved increased electro-optical efficiency or reduced size or volume; (b) materials and or coatings or treatments that reduce optical losses of lenses or mirrors; (c) materials and or coatings or treatments that improve or increase the physical stability or robustness of lenses or mirrors; (d) materials enabling non-mechanical beam steering for detectors, sensors and imaging systems; (e) materials that reduce the size, weight and power requirements of optical detection, sensing and imaging systems; (f) materials suitable for aberration correction of high-power lasers (greater than 1 kilowatt) in the atmosphere.
	5. In relation to software and data— (a) algorithms, and their implementation in firmware, that compensate for the adverse atmospheric effects on laser beam propagation at distances greater than1 kilometre; (b) software, hardware and algorithm developments that improve phase control/coherent beam combination and efficiency.
	6. In relation to technology— (a) any approaches that enable high average optical power (greater than 3 kilowatts) combined with high quality (M2 <1.2) amplifiers; (b) any aspects that enable the propagation of light over significant distances (greater than 1 kilometre), including aberration correction devices.
(9) Graphene and related 2D materials	1. The matters are, in relation to graphene and related 2D materials, those set out in paragraphs 2 to 5.
	2. In relation to systems, equipment and components— (a) developing and operating equipment to synthesise single to few layer graphene and related 2D materials, including controlling the desired structure of the materials or their properties for application; (b) using processes including chemical exfoliation, electrochemical exfoliation, atom or molecule intercalation, surface growth, solution phase growth, vapour deposition and large area chemical vapour deposition.
	3. In relation to test, inspection and production equipment— (a) synthesis and manufacturing routes to either or both— (i) graphene and related 2D; or (ii) graphene and related 2D materials with bespoke or optimised functional properties, including but not limited to functioning as semi-conductors; (b) research, development and production of materials at scale for use as a filler or pigment including forming or using graphene and related two-dimensional materials in dispersions or mixed with other binders; (c) research, development and production to integrate the use of materials in devices and systems; (d) conversion of graphene and other 2D materials into intermediaries using processes including surface treatment and functionalisation, dispersion in matrices, mechanical and laser shaping, coating and ink printing processes.
	4. In relation to materials, all graphene and related 2D materials, including— (a) graphene, hexagonal boron nitride and transition metal dichalcogenides (such as MoS_2 and WS_2); (b) graphene and related 2D materials as thin films or coatings, powder form or mixtures with

Sector	Matters
	other materials; and (c) energetic materials (such as propellants or explosives).
	5. In relation to technology— (a) stacking of different 2D crystals resulting in either or both a charge redistribution between neighbouring crystals or causing structural changes; (b) components with finely tuned properties made by combining different 2D materials, including stacking different 2D materials.
(10) Nanotechnology	1. The matters are, in relation to nanotechnology, those set out in paragraphs 2 to 5.
	2. In relation to systems, equipment and components— (a) sensors or detectors including quantum dots with very high sensitivity to— (i) chemical, biological or nuclear materials (where the threshold is close to and including single molecule levels); or (ii) light or other forms of radiation (where the threshold is close to and including single photon levels); (b) autonomous remote or remotely activated sensing and reporting systems that are enabled by nanotechnology including Smart Dust; (c) nanomachines or nanoscale robots either with physically moving parts or capable of physical movement.
	3. In relation to test, inspection and production equipment— (a) test, inspection or production of nanotechnology or nanomaterials but not including services only offering test and inspection requiring the prior destruction of the produced nanotechnology or nanomaterials to form a test artefact (such as using Scanning Electron Microscopy or Atomic Force Microscopy); (b) methods to create or integrate nanotechnology for use in any of the following— (i) computer processing or memory devices (excluding commoditised silicon microelectronics technologies); (ii) communications or electronic warfare devices or components; (iii) precision navigation and timing systems; (iv) detectors, sensing or imaging systems; (v) counter-measure devices or systems; (vi) moving parts or soft robotics.
	4. In relation to materials, high-density nanoceramics and carbon nanotubes to reinforce ceramics for ballistic and blast protection.
	5. In relation to technology— (a) technology that exploits nanoscale phenomena or technology that is nano-enhanced or nanoscience that further enhances nanoscale phenomena; (b) materials possessing exploitable magnetic, quantum or atomic spin states, or in combination for spinwave effects or technologies including defect centres in nanomaterials or utilising skyrmions; (c) electro-optic, magneto-optic, photonic or nanophotonic effects or devices (including vertical cavity emitting lasers) and circuits; (d) micromechanical, nanomechanical, electromechanical, optomechanical, or electro-optomechanical effects or systems; (e) metamaterials.
(11) Critical materials	1. The matters are, in relation to critical materials, the extraction, refinement, processing, production and end of life recovery (in single element, compound or product form) of any the following— (i) activated carbon; (ii) antimony (iii) arsenic; (iv) beryllium; (v) bismuth; (vi) boron; (vii) cadmium; (viii) cerium; (ix) chromium; (x) cobalt; (xi) dysprosium; (xii) erbium; (xiii) europium; (xiv) fluorspar; (xv) gadolinium; (xvi) gallium; (xvii) germanium; (xviii) graphite; (xix) holmium; (xx) indium; (xxi) iridium; (xxii) lead; (xxiii) lithium; (xxiv) lutetium; (xxv) mercury; (xxvi) molybdenum; (xxvii) neodymium;

Sector	Matters
	(xxviii) niobium; (xxix) osmium; (xxx) palladium; (xxxi) platinum; (xxxii) praseodymium; (xxxiii) rhenium; (xxxiv) ruthenium; (xxxv) samarium; (xxxvi) scandium; (xxxvii) selenium; (xxxviii) tantalum; (xxxix) tellurium; (xl) terbium; (xli) thulium; (xlii) tungsten; (xliii) vanadium; (xliv) ytterbium; (xlv) yttrium.
(12) Other materials	1. The matters are, in relation to other materials, those set out in paragraphs 2 to 6.
	2. In relation to systems, equipment and components— (a) capacitors based on tantalum; (b) components used in equipment or systems for the purpose of protecting optical systems and human vision from dazzle or damage by lasers.
	3. In relation to test, inspection and production equipment— (a) machines for additively manufacturing fully-assembled robotic, soft-robotic, sub-systems and systems or autonomous robotic sub-systems, systems and vehicles but not including machines for additively manufacturing individual components for such sub-systems systems and vehicles; (b) circuit board manufacturing of pitch, track or gap dimensions less than 30 micrometres; (c) new component placement technologies, including multi-axis component placement; (d) additive manufacturing or printing of moving parts, components and machines (known as "4D printing"); (e) battery pack assembly specifically for defence and security applications at the stage of integration, not isolated battery cell construction.
	4. In relation to materials— (a) materials (including paints or other forms of coating or surface) that are capable of modifying (including in real time) the appearance, detectability, traceability or identification of any object to a human or to sensors within the range of 15 terahertz up to and including ultraviolet; (b) foams with designed electrical, electromagnetic or thermal protection properties; (c) honeycombs with designed electrical or electromagnetic properties; (d) smart materials (including micro-fluidic systems) the properties of which can be repeatedly altered once installed at rates exceeding 1 megahertz; (e) materials enabling extreme size, weight and power reduction for energy, power and propulsion sources, or sensing or communications devices and systems for use in micro or smaller unmanned systems; (f) materials used in equipment or systems for the purpose of protecting optical systems and human vision from dazzle or damage from lasers.
	5. In relation to software and data— (a) creative artificial intelligence algorithms for material discovery and optimisation; (b) quantum simulation for material discovery and optimisation.
	6. In relation to technology, neuromorphic or quantum technologies enabling creative artificial intelligence or quantum simulation for materials discovery.

NOTES

Commencement: 4 January 2022.

SCHEDULE 2
ADVANCED ROBOTICS

Regulation 2

[10.1329]

1 Interpretation

In this Schedule—

"cognitive" means having the abilities of reasoning, perception, communication, learning, planning, problem solving, abstract thinking, decision making or organisation;

"core components" means—

(a) sensors enabling advanced robotics to track and sense its environment;

(b) end effectors or other devices attached to advanced robotics allowing it to interact with its task or perform its operation;

(c) locomotion, where the advanced robotics is capable of moving in its environment;

(d) an energy source, including passive sources such as solar energy, providing power delivery enabling advanced robotics to move independently and to carry out its functions;

(e) hardware or software enabling sophisticated computational capabilities, including the use of artificial intelligence to process data and data sets received from the sensors and adapt the behaviour of the advanced robotics;

(f) communications capability, including the ability to communicate with a human operator or other advanced robotics.

2 Activities—advanced robotics

A qualifying entity carrying out any of the following activities—

(a) developing advanced robotics;

(b) producing advanced robotics;

(c) developing or producing core components specially designed or modified for use in advanced robotics.

3 Advanced robotics

Subject to paragraph 6, "advanced robotics" means a machine that meets either or both the descriptions set out in paragraph 4 and is capable of carrying out multifunctional physical actions, including positioning or orientating materials, parts, tools, special devices or itself through variable movements in three-dimensional space.

4 Description of advanced robotics

The descriptions referred to in paragraph 3 are—

(a) having the characteristic of autonomy set out in paragraph 5; and

(b) being capable of using its sensors to carry out sophisticated surveillance and data collection in respect of any aspects of its environment in order to collect, store or communicate to the operator, significant volumes of high-fidelity data.

5 Characteristic of autonomy

(1) Advanced robotics has the characteristic of autonomy where it is capable of performing actions—

(a) independent of human control; or

(b) independent of human control but complemented by—

(i) manual (including tele-operation) control;

(ii) pre-programmed operations or controls; or

(iii) control derived from other robotics or software control systems.

(2) The characteristics of autonomy may include either or both of the following—

(a) using physical, sensory and cognitive capabilities in combination, to decide on and implement a course of action that will vary depending on—

(i) the environment; or

(ii) the behaviour, dynamics, properties or arrangement of objects in the environment, which may include the ability to self-navigate or react to stimuli or changes in order to improve performance; or

(b) adapting or learning by carrying out actions to improve the performance of tasks from iteration and experience, which may include—

(i) the ability to self-heal;

(ii) the capability to identify and repair damaged robotics or components; or

(iii) having soft robotics capabilities (robotics made from compliant materials that mimic capabilities in living organisms that enable them to adapt or respond to their surroundings).

6 Exclusions

(1) Subject to sub-paragraph (2), "advanced robotics" does not include—

(a) machines containing robotic systems that are readily available for purchase by consumers, including robotic toys, domestic appliances described as "smart", vacuum cleaning robots and consumer-focussed drones, where "consumer" means an individual acting for purposes that are wholly or mainly outside of that individual's trade, business or craft;

(b) industrial automation systems that use mechanical tools performing repetitive functions with very basic or no sensors or cognitive ability, including—

(i) simple sensing or imaging devices that do not confer any ability to react or change their behaviour given a change in circumstances, without human intervention;

(ii) devices that carry out functions that require pre-set sequences of actions or require pre-set sensing of the environment;

(c) smart speakers or similar devices lacking end effectors or locomotion.

(2) The description of exceptions set out in sub-paragraph (1)(a) does not include self-driving vehicles.

NOTES

Commencement: 4 January 2022.

SCHEDULE 3
ARTIFICIAL INTELLIGENCE

Regulation 2

[10.1330]

1 Interpretation

In this Schedule—

"artificial intelligence" means technology enabling the programming or training of a device or software to—

(i) perceive environments through the use of data;

(ii) interpret data using automated processing designed to approximate cognitive abilities; and

(iii) make recommendations, predictions or decisions;

with a view to achieving a specific objective;

"advanced robotics" has the same meaning as in Schedule 2;

"cognitive abilities" means reasoning, perception, communication, learning, planning, problem solving, abstract thinking, decision-making or organisation;

"cyber security" means the activities necessary to protect network and information systems, the users of such systems, and other persons affected by cyber threats;

"cyber threat" means any potential circumstance, event or action that could damage, disrupt or otherwise adversely affect network and information systems, the users of such systems and other persons;

"network and information system" has the same meaning as in regulation 1 of the Network and Information Systems Regulations 2018;

"technology" has the same meaning as in Schedule 2 to the Export Control Order 2008.

2 Activities—artificial intelligence

(1) A qualifying entity carrying on any of the following activities for one or more of the purposes set out in sub-paragraph 2—

(a) research into artificial intelligence; or

(b) developing or producing goods, software or technology that use artificial intelligence.

(2) The purposes are—

(a) the identification or tracking of objects, people or events;

(b) advanced robotics;

(c) cyber security.

NOTES

Commencement: 4 January 2022.

SCHEDULE 4
CIVIL NUCLEAR

Regulation 2

[10.1331]

1 Activity—civil nuclear

A qualifying entity carrying on activities that consist of or include any of the following—

(a) subject to paragraph 2, holding a nuclear site licence granted in accordance with section 3 of the Nuclear Installations Act 1965 or applying for such a licence;

(b) subject to paragraph 2, being a tenant on a site in respect of which a nuclear site licence has been granted in accordance with section 3 of the Nuclear Installations Act 1965;

(c) holding either or both Category I/II or Category III nuclear material as defined in regulation 3(3) and (4) of the Nuclear Industries Security Regulations 2003;

(d) being a Class A carrier or a Class B carrier of nuclear material as approved under regulation 14 of the Nuclear Industries Security Regulations 2003;

(e) being in receipt of an order granting development consent under the Planning Act 2008 in relation to a nuclear reactor (as defined in section 26(1) of the Nuclear Installations Act 1965), or applying for such development consent;

(f) being, or having been, required to pay a fee to the Office for Nuclear Regulation under regulation 16(1) of the Health and Safety and Nuclear (Fees) Regulations 2021, where the outcome of the assessment for which that fee is to be, or has been, paid has not been determined;

(g) holding any equipment, software or information to which regulation 2(3) or (4), of the Uranium Enrichment Technology (Prohibition on Disclosure) Regulations 2004 applies;

(h) holding sensitive nuclear information as defined in section 77(7) of the Anti-Terrorism, Crime and Security Act 2001;

(i) being given financial support under section 5 of the Science and Technology Act 1965, or under section 93 of the Higher Education and Research Act 2017, for or in relation to nuclear reactors (as defined in section 26 of the Nuclear Installations Act 1965).

2 Exclusion

Paragraph 1(a) or (b) do not apply where the site to which the nuclear site licence relates is controlled or operated wholly or mainly for defence purposes as defined in section 70(3) of the Energy Act 2013.

NOTES

Commencement: 4 January 2022.

SCHEDULE 5
COMMUNICATIONS

Regulation 2

[10.1332]

1 Interpretation

In this Schedule—

"cable landing station" means a cable landing station for a submarine cable system;

"electronic communications service" has the meaning given by section 32(2) of the Communications Act 2003

"public electronic communications network" means a public electronic communications network as defined by section 151(1) of the Communications Act 2003 and includes a submarine cable system that is provided for purposes which include the purpose of making electronic communications services available to the public;

"public electronic communications service" means a public electronic communications service as defined by section 151(1) of the Communications Act 2003, and includes an electronic communications service that is provided by means of a submarine cable system so as to be available for use by members of the public;

"submarine cable system" means a system of fibre optic cables which—

(a) are beneath the sea (whether on or in the seabed or in a tunnel); and
(b) are used for the conveyance of signals.

2 Public electronic communications providers

(1) A qualifying entity which—
(a) carries on activities which consist of or include either or both of the following—
(i) providing a public electronic communications network;
(ii) providing a public electronic communications service; and
(b) meets the turnover condition in sub-paragraph (2).

(2) The turnover condition is that the turnover of the entity's relevant business for the relevant period is at least £50,000,000.

(3) In sub-paragraph (2)—
(a) "relevant business" means so much of any business carried on in the United Kingdom by the entity in question or any of its associated entities as consists of either or both of the following—
(i) the provision of a public electronic communications network;
(ii) the provision of a public electronic communications service;
(b) "relevant period" means—
(i) the period of one year ending with the 31st March last before the time when a person gains control of the qualifying entity, by virtue of one or more of the cases described in subsection (2), (5) or (6) of section 8 of the Act; and
(ii) in the case of an entity which at that time has been carrying on that business for a period of less than a year, the period, ending with that time, during which it has been carrying it on.

(4) For the purposes of sub-paragraph (3)(a), another qualifying entity is an associated entity of the entity in question if—
(a) the entity in question owns, or has a controlling interest in, the other qualifying entity;
(b) the other qualifying entity owns, or has a controlling interest in, the entity in question; or
(c) a person or group of persons owns, or has a controlling interest in, both entities.

(5) For the purposes of sub-paragraph (4), a person has a controlling interest in a qualifying entity if the person holds more than 50% of the shares or voting rights in the entity; and subsections (3), (4), and (7) of section 8 of the Act apply for the interpretation of this sub-paragraph.

(6) For the purposes of this paragraph—
(a) turnover is to be calculated in conformity with accounting practices and principles which are generally accepted in the United Kingdom;
(b) turnover is to be limited to the amounts derived by an entity from the relevant business after deduction of sales rebates, value added tax and other taxes directly related to amounts so derived;
(c) where the relevant business of the entity in question is carried on by two or more entities that each prepare accounts the turnover shall be calculated by adding together the turnover of each, except that no account shall be taken of any turnover resulting from the supply of goods or the provision of services between them.

3 Associated facilities

(1) A qualifying entity carrying on activities which consist of or include the making available of anything that—
(a) is an associated facility by reference to a qualifying network or qualifying service; and
(b) is not excluded by sub-paragraph (2) or (3).

(2) An associated facility consisting of a building or an entry to a building is excluded by this sub-paragraph unless the main purpose of the building is to host a network element that is active.

(3) An associated facility other than a building or an entry to a building is excluded by this sub-paragraph if the associated facility is an element (such as a pipe, mast, duct, antenna installation, tower or pole) which—
(a) is not itself active; and
(b) is designed merely to host either or both of the following—
(i) other network elements that are not active;
(ii) cables (including strands of optical fibre).

(4) In this paragraph—
"associated facility" has the meaning given by section 32(3) of the Communications Act 2003 but as if the reference in that provision to a "facility, element or service" included a reference to a cable landing station;
"qualifying network" means a public electronic communications network provided by a qualifying entity falling within paragraph 2;
"qualifying service" means a public electronic communications service provided by a qualifying entity falling within paragraph 2.

4 Repair or maintenance of submarine cable systems or cable landing stations

(1) A qualifying entity carrying on activities which consist of or include the provision of services for the repair or maintenance of—
(a) a submarine cable system (in the United Kingdom or elsewhere) forming part of a public electronic communications network that—
(i) is provided in the United Kingdom by a qualifying entity falling within paragraph 2; or
(ii) interconnects with a public electronic communications network provided in the United Kingdom by a qualifying entity falling within paragraph 2; or
(b) a cable landing station in the United Kingdom that is used in connection with a public electronic communications network or public electronic communications service provided in the United Kingdom by a qualifying entity falling within paragraph 2.

(2) In this paragraph "interconnect" is to be read in accordance with section 151(2) of the Communications Act 2003.

5 Information systems

(1) A qualifying entity carrying on activities that consist of or include supplying to persons in the United Kingdom services which consist of or include one or more of the following—

(a) providing a top-level domain name registry which, in any relevant 168-hour period, serviced 14 billion or more queries from devices located in the United Kingdom for domains registered within the Internet Corporation for Assigned Names and Numbers;

(b) providing a domain name system resolver service which, in any relevant 168-hour period, serviced 500,000 or more different Internet Protocol addresses used by persons in the United Kingdom;

(c) providing a domain name system authoritative hosting service servicing 100,000 or more domains registered to persons with an address in the United Kingdom.

(2) A qualifying entity which—

(a) carries on activities which consist of or include supplying to persons in the United Kingdom services which consist of or include providing an internet exchange point; and

(b) has 30% or more of the market share among operators of internet exchange points in the United Kingdom in terms of interconnected autonomous systems.

(3) In this paragraph—

"domain name system" has the meaning given to "Domain Name System" in paragraph 10(5)(a) of Schedule 2 to the Network and Information Systems Regulations 2018;

"internet exchange point" has the meaning given in paragraph 10(5)(c) of Schedule 2 to the Network and Information Systems Regulations 2018;

"relevant 168-hour period" means any consecutive period of 168 hours falling within the 12 months ending with the time when a person gains control of the qualifying entity by virtue of one or more of the cases described in subsection (2), (5) or (6) of section 8 of the Act;

"top-level domain name registry" has the meaning given in paragraph 10(5)(d) of Schedule 2 to the Network and Information Systems Regulations 2018.

NOTES

Commencement: 4 January 2022.

SCHEDULE 6
COMPUTING HARDWARE

Regulation 2

[10.1333]

1 Interpretation

In this Schedule—

"computer processing unit" means—

(a) a central processing unit (also referred to as "CPU");
(b) a field programmable gate array (also referred to as "FPGA");
(c) a microcontroller;
(d) a system on chip;
(e) a graphics processor unit; or
(f) a specialist processor for artificial intelligence applications;

"fabrication" means the process of producing a microelectronic circuit on a semiconductor substrate or using other advanced materials;

"packaging" means the process of turning a microelectronic circuit on an appropriate substrate into a package suitable for use in an electronic circuit but does not include the assembly and packaging of chips and devices into circuit boards;

"roots of trust" means hardware, firmware or software components that are inherently trusted to perform critical security functions.

2 Activity—computing hardware

A qualifying entity whose activities consist of one or more of the activities set out in paragraph 3.

3 The activities referred to in paragraph 2 are—

(a) the ownership, creation, supply or exploitation of intellectual property relating to any of the following—
(i) computer processing units;
(ii) architectural, logical or physical designs for such units;
(iii) the instruction set architecture for such units;
(iv) code, written in a low-level language, that can control how such units operate;
(v) integrated circuits with the purpose of providing memory;

(b) the design, maintenance or delivery of a service for the secure provisioning or management of either or both of the following—
(i) roots of trust of computer processing units;
(ii) code, written in a low level language, that can control how such units operate;

(c) the fabrication or packaging of either or both of the following—
(i) computer processing units;
(ii) integrated circuits with the purpose of providing memory.

NOTES

Commencement: 4 January 2022.

Part 10 Miscellaneous other SIs

SCHEDULE 7
CRITICAL SUPPLIERS TO GOVERNMENT

Regulation 2

[10.1334]

1 Interpretation

In this Schedule—

"government" has the same meaning as "contracting authorities" in regulation 2 of the Public Contracts Regulations 2015;

"relevant public contract" means a contract for pecuniary interest between one or more persons and government, where the contract has as its object the execution of works, the supply of products or the provision of services.

2 Activity—critical suppliers to government

A qualifying entity being a party to a relevant public contract where the contract contains one or more of the features set out in paragraph 2.

3 The features referred to in paragraph 1 are—

(a) either or both the processing or storage of material to which a security classification of SECRET or TOP SECRET has been applied in accordance with the document titled "Government Security Classifications Version 1.1—May 2018" published by the Cabinet Office;

(b) a requirement to have List X accreditation as described in the document titled "Security Requirements for List X Contractors Version 10.0—April 2014" published by the Cabinet Office;

(c) a requirement for employees of the qualifying entity to be vetted at or above 'Security Check' level as described in guidance titled "National security: vetting clearance levels" published on 12 February 2020 by the United Kingdom Security Vetting.

NOTES

Commencement: 4 January 2022.

SCHEDULE 8
CRYPTOGRAPHIC AUTHENTICATION

Regulation 2

[10.1335]

1 Interpretation

In this Schedule—

"consumer" means an individual acting for purposes that are wholly or mainly outside that individual's trade, business, craft or profession;

"authentication" means verifying—

(a) the identity of a user, process or device; or

(b) the origin or content of a message or other information;

"cryptography" means the discipline which embodies principles, means and methods for the transformation of data in order to hide its information content, prevent its undetected modification or prevent its unauthorised use and is limited to the transformation of information using one or more secret parameters or associated key management;

"secret parameter" means a variable, constant or key kept from the knowledge of others or shared only within a group.

2 Activity—cryptographic authentication

A qualifying entity carrying on activities consisting of or including research into, developing or producing, any product which—

(a) has authentication as a primary function;

(b) employs cryptography in performing that function; and

(c) is not ordinarily supplied to or made available for acquisition by consumers.

NOTES

Commencement: 4 January 2022.

SCHEDULE 9
DATA INFRASTRUCTURE

Regulation 2

[10.1336]

1 Interpretation

In this Schedule—

"administrative access" refers to either or both authorisation or access granted via either or both logical or administrative access controls by virtue of which an entity may access relevant data infrastructure or control access to relevant data infrastructure where such access would otherwise be restricted or compartmented and where such access would permit the modification of the relevant data infrastructure in a way that was not authorised;

"electronic communications network" has the meaning given in section 32(1) of the Communications Act 2003;

"public electronic communications network" has the meaning given in section 151(1) of the Communications Act 2003;

"public electronic communications service" has the meaning given in section 151(1) of the Communications Act 2003;

"public sector authority" means an authority listed in paragraph 2;

"relevant activity" means storing, processing or transmitting data in digital form which are used in connection with the administration and operation of a public sector authority;

"relevant data infrastructure" is physical or virtualised infrastructure, which—

(a) is used for a relevant activity and the qualifying entity—

(i) has a contract with a public sector authority to provide the relevant activity; or

(ii) is a sub-contractor who has been notified that it is in a chain of sub-contractors which begins with the contractor that has a contract with the public sector authority for the purpose of providing the relevant activity, where the sub-contractor is providing a relevant activity that would fulfil or contribute towards the fulfilment of the main contract;

(b) is provided for peering, interconnection or exchange of digital data between providers of public electronic communications networks and/or providers of public electronic communications services but which is not owned by a provider of public electronic communications networks or a provider of a public electronic communications service; or

(c) enables the interconnection of one or more public electronic communications networks with an electronic communications network where part of that network is provided by means of a submarine cable system;

"specialist or technical services" means either or both—

(a) equipment installation services;

(b) equipment repair and maintenance services;

"submarine cable system" means a system of fibre optic cables which—

(i) are beneath the sea (whether on or in the seabed or in a tunnel); and

(ii) are intended for the conveyance of signals.

2 Interpretation—public sector authority

The authorities referred to in the definition of a "public sector authority" in paragraph 1 are set out in the following Table.

Table

Public sector authority
Prime Minister's Office
Attorney General's Office
Crown Prosecution Service
Government Legal Department
Serious Fraud Office
Cabinet Office
Crown Commercial Service
Government Property Agency
The Electoral Commission
UK Statistics Authority
Department for Business, Energy and Industrial Strategy
Competition and Markets Authority
HM Land Registry
Intellectual Property Office
Meteorological Office
Nuclear Decommissioning Authority
Office of Gas and Electricity Markets (Ofgem)
United Kingdom Space Agency
Department for Digital, Culture, Media and Sport
Information Commissioner
The National Archives
Office of Communications (Ofcom)
Department for Education
Education and Skills Funding Agency
Office of Qualifications and Examinations Regulation (Ofqual)
Office for Standards in Education, Children's Services and Skills (Ofsted)
Teaching Regulation Agency

Public sector authority
Department for Environment, Food and Rural Affairs
Water Services Regulation Authority (Ofwat)
Department for International Trade
UK Export Finance (also known as the Exports Credit Guarantee Department)
Department for Transport
Civil Aviation Authority
Driver and Vehicle Licensing Agency
Maritime and Coastguard Agency
Office of Rail and Road
Department for Work and Pensions
Health and Safety Executive
Office for Nuclear Regulation
Department of Health and Social Care
Health and Social Care Information Centre
Joint Committee on Vaccination and Immunisation
Medicines and Healthcare products Regulatory Agency
Public Health England
UK Health Security Agency
Foreign, Commonwealth and Development Office
Wilton Park
GCHQ
HM Treasury
Bank of England
Financial Conduct Authority
Government Actuary's Department
Government Internal Audit Agency
HM Revenues and Customs
National Audit Office
National Infrastructure Commission
National Savings and Investments
Office for Budget Responsibility
UK Debt Management Office
Valuation Office Agency
Home Office
National Crime Agency
Investigatory Powers Commissioner's Office
Ministry of Defence
Defence Electronics and Components Agency
Defence Equipment and Support
Defence Science and Technology Laboratory
Submarine Delivery Agency
United Kingdom Hydrographic Office

Public sector authority
Ministry of Housing, Communities and Local Government
Queen Elizabeth II Centre
Ministry of Justice
Criminal Injuries Compensation Authority
HM Courts and Tribunals Service
HM Prison and Probation Service
Legal Aid Agency
Office of the Public Guardian
Supreme Court of the United Kingdom
Northern Ireland Office
Office of the Advocate General for Scotland
Office of the Leader of the House of Commons
Office of the Leader of the House of Lords
Office of the Secretary of State for Scotland
Office of the Secretary of State for Wales
Secret Intelligence Service
Security Service
Northern Ireland Executive
The Executive Office
Department of Agriculture, Environment and Rural Affairs
Department for Communities
Department for the Economy
Department of Education
Department of Finance
Department of Health
Department for Infrastructure
Department of Justice
Invest Northern Ireland
The Scottish Government
Crown Office and Procurator Fiscal Service
Disclosure Scotland
Education Scotland
Office of the Accountant in Bankruptcy
Registers of Scotland
Revenue Scotland
Scottish Courts and Tribunals Service
Scottish Fiscal Commission
Scottish National Investment Bank
Scottish Public Pensions Agency
Social Security Scotland
Student Awards Agency for Scotland
The Scottish Ministers

Public sector authority
Transport Scotland
The Welsh Government
Permanent Secretary's Group
Office of the First Minister Group
The Health and Social Services Group
The Economy, Skills and Natural Resources Group
The Education and Public Services Group

3 Activity—data infrastructure

A qualifying entity carrying on any of the activities set out in paragraph 4.

4 The activities referred to in paragraph 3 are—

(a) owning or operating relevant data infrastructure;
(b) managing relevant data infrastructure on behalf of other entities;
(c) managing facilities where relevant data infrastructure is located;
(d) providing specialist or technical services to entities carrying on activities described in sub-paragraphs (a), (b) or (c), which give the entity providing those specialist or technical services physical access to relevant data infrastructure;
(e) providing services where the provision of such services gives the entity providing those services administrative access to relevant data infrastructure;
(f) producing or developing software designed for use in the services in sub-paragraph (e) which configures or manages the provision of administrative access.

NOTES

Commencement: 4 January 2022.

SCHEDULE 10
DEFENCE

Regulation 2

[10.1337]

1 Interpretation

In this Schedule—

"defence" has the meaning given to it by section 2(4) of the Official Secrets Act 1989; and

"government contractor" has the meaning given to it by section 12 of the Official Secrets Act 1989.

2 Activity—defence

A qualifying entity carrying on activities that comprise or include the research, development, production, creation or application of goods or services which are used or provided for defence or national security purposes where that entity meets a condition in paragraph 3.

3 The conditions referred to in paragraph 2 are that the entity—

(a) is a government contractor or any sub-contractor in a chain of sub-contractors which begins with the government contractor which provides goods or services within the scope of paragraph 2; or
(b) has been notified by or on behalf of the Secretary of State of information, documents or other articles of a classified nature which the entity or an employee of the entity may hold or receive relating to the activities within the scope of paragraph 2.

NOTES

Commencement: 4 January 2022.

SCHEDULE 11
ENERGY

Regulation 2

[10.1338]

1 Interpretation

In this Schedule—

"aggregation" means combining multiple customer loads or generated electricity for sale, purchase or auction in the electricity market of Great Britain;

"downstream oil activity" means any of the following activities—

(a) the import of any of crude oil, intermediates, components and finished fuels;
(b) the storage of any of crude oil, intermediates, components and finished fuels;
(c) the production of intermediates, components and finished fuels through refining or blending processes;
(d) the distribution of petroleum-based fuels to storage sites by road, pipeline, rail or ship;
(e) the delivery of petroleum-based fuels to retail sites, airports or end users;

"existing upstream petroleum facility" means an upstream petroleum facility that began operating before the first day of the month that is 12 calendar months before the month in which a person gains control, by virtue of one or more of the cases described in subsection (2), (5) or (6) of section 8 of the Act, of the qualifying entity;

"gas" means any substance which is or (if it were in a gaseous state) would be gas within the meaning set out in section 48(1) of the Gas Act 1986;

"gas interconnector" has the meaning set out in section 5(8) of the Gas Act 1986;

"gas processing facility" has the meaning set out in section 90(1) of the Energy Act 2011;

"gas processing operation" has the meaning set out in section 90(2) of the Energy Act 2011;

"generate" in relation to electricity means carrying on an act within section 4(1)(a) of the Electricity Act 1989;

"generating asset" means an asset used to generate electricity;

"group undertaking" has the meaning set out in section 1161(5) of the Companies Act 2006;

"LNG import or export facility" has the meaning set out in section 12(6) of the Gas Act 1995 but does not include facilities in the territorial sea adjacent to Great Britain or the sea in any area designated under section 1(7) of the Continental Shelf Act 1964;

"new upstream petroleum facility" means an upstream petroleum facility that had not begun operating before the first day of the month that is 12 calendar months before the month in which a person gains control, by virtue of one or more of the cases described in subsection (2), (5) or (6) of section 8 of the Act, of the qualifying entity;

"oil equivalent" means petroleum and, for the purposes of assessments of throughput, where petroleum is in a gaseous state 1,100 cubic meters of this petroleum at a temperature of 15 degrees Celsius and pressure of one atmosphere is counted as equivalent to one tonne;

"petroleum" has the same meaning as in Part 1 of the Petroleum Act 1998, and includes petroleum that has undergone any processing;

"petroleum licence" means a licence granted under section 3 of the Petroleum Act 1998 or section 2 of the Petroleum (Production) Act 1934;

"petroleum production project" has the meaning set out in section 90(2) of the Energy Act 2011;

"terminal" has the meaning set out in section 90(2) of the Energy Act 2011, but does not include gas processing facilities in the United Kingdom or LNG import or export facilities;

"upstream petroleum facility" means a terminal, upstream petroleum pipeline or unit of infrastructure that is or will be necessary to a petroleum production project;

"upstream petroleum pipeline" has the meaning set out in section 90(2) of the Energy Act 2011, but does not include gas interconnectors.

2 Activity—energy

A qualifying entity carrying on any of the activities set out in paragraph 3.

3 The activities referred to in paragraph 2 are—

(a) in respect of any existing upstream petroleum facility that meets the conditions set out in paragraph 4(2)—
  (i) owning;
  (ii) operating;
  (iii) holding a petroleum licence in respect of; or
  (iv) where the qualifying entity meets the condition set out in paragraph 4(3), enabling the operation of;

(b) in respect of any new upstream petroleum facility that meets the conditions set out in paragraph 4(4)—
  (i) owning;
  (ii) operating;
  (iii) holding or applying for a petroleum licence in respect of; or
  (iv) where the qualifying entity meets the condition set out in paragraph 4(5)—
    (aa) developing;
    (bb) enabling the operation of; or
    (cc) enabling the development of;

(c) holding a transmission licence, distribution licence or interconnector licence under section 6 of the Electricity Act 1989 or carrying on any activity in pursuance of an exemption from section 4(1)(b), 4(1)(bb) or 4(1)(d) of the Electricity Act 1989 granted to the qualifying entity by order under section 5(1) of the Electricity Act 1989;

(d) where the qualifying entity meets the condition set out in paragraph 4(6)—
  (i) holding a generation licence under section 6 of the Electricity Act 1989 or carrying on any activity in pursuance of an exemption from section 4(1)(a) of the Electricity Act 1989 granted to the qualifying entity by order under section 5(1) of the Electricity Act 1989; or
  (ii) carrying on aggregation;

(e) holding a licence under section 7 or 7ZA of the Gas Act 1986 or carrying on any activity in pursuance of an exemption from sections 5(1)(a) or 5(1)(aa) of the Gas Act 1986 granted to the qualifying entity by order under section 6A(1) of the Gas Act 1986;

(f) owning or operating—
  (i) any gas processing facility in Great Britain that meets the condition set out in paragraph 4(8); or
  (ii) any LNG import or export facility that meets the condition set out in paragraph 4(9);

(g) where the qualifying entity meets the conditions set out in paragraph 4(10), supplying petroleum-based road, aviation or heating fuels (including liquefied petroleum gas) to persons in the United Kingdom.

4 Conditions

(1) This paragraph sets out the conditions referred to in paragraph 3.

(2) The conditions referred to in paragraph 3(a) are that the existing upstream petroleum facility—

(a) has a throughput of greater than 3,000,000 tonnes of oil equivalent over the 12 calendar months preceding the month in which a person gains control, by virtue of one or more of the cases described in subsection (2), (5) or (6) of section 8 of the Act, of the qualifying entity; and

(b) is—

(i) situated in whole or in part in the United Kingdom; or

(ii) used in connection with the supply of petroleum to persons in the United Kingdom.

(3) The condition referred to in paragraph (3)(a)(iv) is that the qualifying entity is an owner or operator of the existing upstream petroleum facility.

(4) The conditions referred to in paragraph 3(b) are that the new upstream petroleum facility—

(a) has an expected throughput of greater than 3,000,000 tonnes of oil equivalent in its first 12 calendar months of operation; and

(b) is or will be—

(i) situated in whole or in part in the United Kingdom; or

(ii) used in connection with the supply of petroleum to persons in the United Kingdom.

(5) The condition referred to in paragraph 3(b)(iv) is that the qualifying entity is or will be an owner or operator of the new upstream petroleum facility.

(6) The condition referred to in paragraph 3(d) is that—

(a) the qualifying entity is an owner or operator of any individual generating asset that has a total installed capacity equal to or greater than 100 megawatts; or

(b) the relevant capacity of the qualifying entity is equal to or greater than one gigawatt.

(7) For the purposes of sub-paragraph (6)(b), the "relevant capacity" of the qualifying entity is the total of—

(a) the total installed capacity of any generating assets owned or operated by the qualifying entity;

(b) the total installed capacity of any generating assets owned or operated by the acquirer or group undertakings of the acquirer;

(c) the amount of customer load and generated electricity available to the qualifying entity for aggregation; and

(d) the amount of customer load and generated electricity available to the acquirer or group undertakings of the acquirer for aggregation.

(8) The condition referred to in paragraph 3(f)(i) is that the gas processing facility has the technological capacity to carry on gas processing operations in relation to greater than 6 million cubic metres of gas per day.

(9) The condition referred in paragraph 3(f)(ii) is that the LNG import or export facility has the technological capacity to carry on the importation, regasification or liquefaction of greater than 6 million cubic metres of gas per day.

(10) The conditions referred to in paragraph 3(g) are that—

(a) the qualifying entity carries on any downstream oil activity; and

(b) the qualifying entity—

(i) has capacity of greater than 500,000 tonnes; or

(ii) owns a facility in the United Kingdom that has capacity of greater than 50,000 tonnes.

(11) For the purposes of sub-paragraph (10)—

(a) a qualifying entity "has capacity of greater than" a specified number of tonnes if any downstream oil activity was carried on in the United Kingdom by that qualifying entity in relation to greater than that number of tonnes of oil in at least one of the three calendar years preceding the year in which a person gains control, by virtue of one or more of the cases described in subsection (2), (5) or (6) of section 8 of the Act, of the qualifying entity; and

(b) a facility "has capacity of greater than" a specified number of tonnes if it was used for the purposes of any downstream oil activity in relation to greater than that number of tonnes of oil in at least one of the three calendar years preceding the year in which a person gains control, by virtue of one or more of the cases described in subsection (2), (5) or (6) of section 8 of the Act, of the qualifying entity.

NOTES

Commencement: 4 January 2022.

SCHEDULE 12
MILITARY AND DUAL-USE

Regulation 2

[10.1339]

1 Interpretation

In this Schedule—

"restricted goods" and "restricted technology" are respectively goods and technology, including software or information (other than information in the public domain), the export or transfer of which is controlled by virtue of their being specified in the relevant export control legislation;

"relevant export control legislation" means—

(a) Schedules 2 and 3 to the Export Control Order 2008;

(b) the Schedule to the Export of Radioactive Sources (Control) Order 2006;

(c) Annex I to Council Regulation (EC) No 2009/428 setting up a Community regime for the control of exports, transfer, brokering and transit of dual-use items.

2 Activity—military and dual-use

A qualifying entity carrying on activities that consist of or include researching, developing or producing restricted goods or restricted technology.

NOTES

Commencement: 4 January 2022.

SCHEDULE 13
QUANTUM TECHNOLOGIES

Regulation 2

[10.1340]

1 Interpretation

In this Schedule—

"quantum technology" means—

(a) quantum communications;
(b) quantum connectivity;
(c) quantum imaging, sensing, timing or navigation;
(d) quantum information processing, computing or simulation; or
(e) quantum resistant cryptography;

"quantum communications" means—

(a) the transmission of information, using the properties of quantum mechanics, specifically superposition, entanglement, single photon technology, the use of conjugate variable technologies or a combination of these;
(b) the use of a communication network (quantum or otherwise) to distribute quantum states or quantum state information; or
(c) the establishment of cryptographic keys or the generation of provably random numbers using a quantum physical process;

"quantum connectivity" means the ways in which quantum coherence, during processes such as transmission, propagation or amplification, is preserved;

"quantum imaging" means using the phase or amplitude properties of quantum mechanics, specifically superposition, entanglement, the use of sub-Poissonian sources or detectors of photons or a combination of these, to create images of objects;

"quantum information processing, computing or simulation" means—

(a) the simulation or realisation of systems that use certain properties of quantum mechanics, specifically superposition or entanglement, to acquire, encode, manipulate or process information, run algorithms or perform operations or measurements on data;
(b) algorithms, applications, software, error correction, noise reduction and operating systems that enable the functionality of the system;
(c) the capability of a classical computer to represent the internal state and operations of a quantum computer ("quantum emulation"); or
(d) the hosting or provision of third-party access of a quantum information processing, computing or simulation cloud-based service;

"quantum navigation" means using phase properties of quantum mechanics, specifically measurements of atoms or ions, or atom-ion interferometry, to establish the location or inertia of, and to guide, objects;

"quantum resistant cryptography" means methods of securing information or data being transmitted or stored, with a view to resisting attack by a quantum computing or simulation device;

"quantum sensing" means utilising the phase properties of quantum mechanics, specifically measurements of atoms or ions or atomic spin systems, to determine a property or rate of change in the property of an object, or the effect of an object on a measurable quantity;

"quantum timing" means using the phase properties of quantum mechanics, specifically measurements of atoms or ions or atomic gases, and the application of associated hardware including stable frequency mixers, optical or microwave sources, crystal oscillators and frequency combs, to provide a timing or synchronisation signal, or frequency reference.

2 Activity—quantum technology

A qualifying entity carrying on activities that consist of developing or producing quantum technology.

NOTES

Commencement: 4 January 2022.

SCHEDULE 14
SATELLITE AND SPACE TECHNOLOGY

Regulation 2

[10.1341]

1 Interpretation

In this Schedule—

"defence" has the meaning given to it by section 2(4) of the Official Secrets Act 1989;

"infrastructure" includes any of the following—

(a) command and control stations;
(b) ground stations, ground sites and ground support equipment;
(c) software (including analysis software);
(d) information technology and telecommunications networks (including fibre cables);
(e) uplink and downlink terminals;
(f) data processing and storage facilities (including databases);
(g) satellites;

Part 10 Miscellaneous other SIs

(h) technological systems and equipment deployed in outer space or on earth;

"outer space" has the meaning given to it by section 13(1) of the Outer Space Act 1986;

"space activity" and "sub-orbital activity" have the meaning given to them by section 1(4) of the Space Industry Act 2018;

"spacecraft" has the meaning given to it by section 2(6) of the Space Industry Act 2018;

"space derived data" means data obtained from space activity or from ground stations receiving data from outer space or from both space activity and ground stations receiving data from outer space, including data relating to—

(a) position, navigation and timing;
(b) earth observation;
(c) space situational awareness;
(d) telecommunications;
(e) signal intelligence;
(f) remote sensing; and
(g) research and development;

"space situational awareness" includes surveillance and tracking of satellites in outer space, monitoring and forecasting of weather in outer space, and mapping or detection of near earth objects or debris in outer space;

"testing" includes any service that provides quality assurance assessment of—

(a) equipment or systems for space activity or services derived from space activity, including engines, component parts, radio frequency, software and systems;
(b) facilities that manufacture, design or create any of the equipment set out in paragraph 3(e);
(c) launch site equipment or facilities; and
(d) equipment or facilities for transport of satellites, launch vehicles or their component parts between sites.

2 Activity—satellite and space technology

A qualifying entity carrying on activities that consist of or include operating, developing, producing, creating or using facilities for any of the activities set out in paragraph 3.

3 The activities referred to in paragraph 2 are—

(a) management of debris in outer space, including sending an object into outer space to remove debris;
(b) the provision of—
 (i) in-orbit servicing, maintenance or manoeuvring of satellites;
 (ii) in-orbit capabilities, including inspection services or life extension services, including refuelling, repair or relocation services; or
 (iii) any technology or system—
  (aa) that performs any of the activities set out in sub-paragraphs (a), (b)(i) and (b)(ii); or
  (bb) which is designed to, or may be used to, disrupt, modify or interfere with satellites;
(c) the provision of satellite communications links, including radio frequency or optical links—
 (i) between satellites in orbit;
 (ii) between spacecraft and satellites in orbit;
 (iii) between satellites in orbit and celestial bodies; or
 (iv) from earth to outer space, and from outer space to earth;
(d) operating or maintaining the capability of secure infrastructure related to—
 (i) space activity; or
 (ii) sub-orbital activity;
(e) the manufacture or testing of spacecraft, launch vehicles, satellites, planetary probes, orbital stations, ground support equipment, or component parts of, or materials used in, any equipment set out in this sub-paragraph;
(f) the use of space-derived data for a defence purpose;
(g) the operation or control of infrastructure;
(h) the provision or processing of space situational awareness data by activity on earth or by space activity or by means of infrastructure for any of the following—
 (i) sub-orbital activity;
 (ii) orbital activity;
 (iii) a defence purpose.

NOTES

Commencement: 4 January 2022.

SCHEDULE 15
SUPPLIERS TO THE EMERGENCY SERVICES

Regulation 2

[10.1342]

1 Interpretation

In this Schedule—

"ambulance services provider" means—

(a) in England—
 (i) an NHS trust or NHS foundation trust established pursuant to Part 2 of the National Health Service Act 2006 (or their subsidiaries), which has a function of providing ambulance services;
 (ii) any private, public or voluntary sector entity which has been commissioned under any

arrangement by or on behalf of the NHS Commissioning Board or [an integrated care board] pursuant to Parts 1 and 4 of the National Health Service Act 2006 to provide ambulance services;

(iii) any private, public or voluntary sector entity which has been commissioned under any arrangement by or on behalf of the Secretary of State pursuant to Part 1 of the National Health Service Act 2006 to provide ambulance services;

(b) in Wales, an NHS Trust established by the Welsh Ambulance Services National Health Service Trust (Establishment) Order 1998;

(c) in Northern Ireland, the Northern Ireland Ambulance Service Trust as defined in the Northern Ireland Ambulance Service Health and Social Services Trust (Establishment) Order (Northern Ireland) 1995;

(d) in Scotland, the Special Health Board constituted by the Scottish Ambulance Service Board Order 1999 or any other private, public or voluntary sector entity providing ambulances and other means of transport under section 45 of the National Health Service (Scotland) Act 1978 (ambulances);

"associated facility" has the meaning given in section 32(3) of the Communications Act 2003;

"the British Transport Police Force" means the police force established by Part 3 of the Railways and Transport Safety Act 2003;

"the Civil Nuclear Constabulary" means the constabulary established under section 52(1) of the Energy Act 2004 (the Civil Nuclear Constabulary);

"emergency service" means—

(a) Border Force;

(b) the British Transport Police Force;

(c) the Civil Nuclear Constabulary;

(d) a fire and rescue authority;

(e) the Ministry of Defence Police;

(f) the National Crime Agency;

(g) a police body;

"a fire and rescue authority" is—

(a) in England—

(i) an authority constituted by a scheme under section 2 of the Fire and Rescue Services Act 2004 (a combined fire and rescue authority);

(ii) an authority constituted by a scheme to which section 4 of the Fire and Rescue Services Act 2004 applies (a combined fire and rescue authority constituted under the Fire Services Act 1947);

(iii) an authority created by an order under section 4A of the Fire and Rescue Services Act 2004 (a police and crime commissioner as fire and rescue authority);

(iv) a metropolitan county fire and rescue authority;

(v) the London Fire Commissioner;

(vi) a combined authority established under section 103 of the Local Democracy, Economic Development and Construction Act 2009 (combined authorities and their areas);

(b) in Wales—

(i) for a county, a county council;

(ii) for a county borough, a county borough council;

(c) in Northern Ireland, the Northern Ireland Fire and Rescue Service Board, as defined in article 3 of the Fire and Rescue Services (Northern Ireland) Order 2006 (the Northern Ireland Fire and Rescue Service Board);

(d) in Scotland, the Scottish Fire and Rescue Service, as defined in section 1A the Fire (Scotland) Act 2005 (the Scottish Fire and Rescue Service);

"electronic communications network" has the meaning given in section 32(1) of the Communications Act 2003;

"electronic communications service" has the meaning given in section 32 of the Communications Act 2003;

"fuel card" means a card, the production of which enables the person to whom it is issued to discharge his obligation to a supplier of fuel in respect of payment for that fuel, the supplier being reimbursed by a person other than the person producing the card;

"Ministry of Defence Police" means the police force established under the Ministry of Defence Police Act 1987;

"National Crime Agency" means the agency established under the Crime and Courts Act 2013;

"personal data" has the meaning given in section 3(2) of the Data Protection Act 2018;

"police body" means—

(a) in England and Wales—

(i) a local policing body as defined in section 101 of the Police Act 1996 (interpretation); or

(ii) the chief officer of police as defined in section 101 of the Police Act 1996;

(b) in Northern Ireland, the Police Service of Northern Ireland and Police Service of Northern Ireland Reserve;

(c) in Scotland—

(i) the Scottish Police Authority, as defined in section 1 of the Police and Fire Reform (Scotland) Act 2012 (the Scottish Police Authority);

(ii) the Chief Constable of the Police Service of Scotland, as appointed under section 7 of the Police and Fire Reform (Scotland) Act 2012 (senior officers);

"public electronic communications network" has the meaning given in section 151(1) of the Communications Act 2003;

"public electronic communications service" has the meaning given in section 151(1) of the Communications Act 2003;

Part 10 Miscellaneous other SIs

"unmanned aircraft" means any aircraft operating or designed to operate autonomously or to be piloted remotely without a pilot on board.

2 Activity—suppliers to emergency services

A qualifying entity which supplies directly to—

(a) an emergency service of one or more of the goods and services set out in paragraph 3;

(b) an ambulance services provider of one or more of the goods and services set out in paragraph 4.

3 Good and services—emergency services

The goods and services referred to in paragraph 2(a) are the following—

(a) unmanned aircraft, any component, part or product of an unmanned aircraft, and any equipment, including an electronic device, relating to an unmanned aircraft;

(b) equipment designed to disrupt the operational system of an unmanned aircraft;

(c) equipment designed to detect, track or identify unmanned aircraft;

(d) firearms as defined in section 57(1) of the Firearms Act 1968 (interpretation: firearm);

(e) ammunition as defined in section 57(2) of the Firearms Act 1968 (interpretation: ammunition);

(f) certification, maintenance, support or repairs to vessels operated by Border Force for frontline operational purposes;

(g) maintenance or repairs of unmanned aircraft, any component, part or product of an unmanned aircraft, and any equipment, including an electronic device, relating to an unmanned aircraft;

(h) an electronic communications network, electronic communications service or associated facility, that—

(i) is not a public electronic communications network or public electronic communications service; and

(ii) is used by the emergency service for the purposes of—

(aa) the prevention or detection of crime; or

(bb) fulfilling the functions of a fire and rescue authority;

(i) hardware, systems or platforms to facilitate the storage of electronic data, used exclusively or primarily by the emergency service for the purposes of—

(i) the prevention or detection of crime;

(ii) fulfilling the functions of a fire and rescue authority; or

(iii) the storage of personal data, including personnel data;

(j) the maintenance and repair of the goods and services referred to in sub-paragraphs (g) and (h);

(k) fuel cards;

(l) services to control systems relating to access and security of buildings;

(m) front line operational delivery of firefighting services in the event of strike action.

4 Goods and services—ambulance services provider

The goods and services referred to in paragraph 2(b) are an electronic communications network or electronic communications service that—

(a) is not a public electronic communications network or a public electronic communications service; and

(b) is used by the ambulance services provider for the purposes of fulfilling its functions.

NOTES

Commencement: 4 January 2022.

Para 1: words in square brackets in sub-para (a)(ii) of the definition "ambulance services provider" substituted by the Health and Care Act 2022 (Consequential and Related Amendments and Transitional Provisions) Regulations 2022, SI 2022/634, reg 99, Schedule, as from 1 July 2022.

SCHEDULE 16
SYNTHETIC BIOLOGY

Regulation 2

[10.1343]

1 Interpretation

In this Schedule—

"basic scientific research" means experimental or theoretical work undertaken principally to acquire new knowledge of the fundamental principles of phenomena or observable facts and not primarily directed towards a specific practicable aim or objective;

"medicine" means—

(i) any substance or combination of substances presented as having properties of preventing or treating disease in human beings or animals;

(ii) any substance or combination of substances that may be used by or administered to human beings or animals with a view to—

(aa) restoring, correcting or modifying a physiological function by asserting a pharmacological, immunological or metabolic action;

(bb) making a medical diagnosis;

"services" means routine synthetic biology processes that are outsourced to specialist providers for completion before being re-integrated into the original work stream to assemble into an experiment or goods, including making a specific strand of DNA or running a proprietary algorithm on a dataset.

2 Activities

Subject to the exceptions referred to in paragraphs 5 and 6, a qualifying entity carrying on activities that consist of or include any of the following—

(a) carrying on basic scientific research into synthetic biology;

(b) the development of synthetic biology;

(c) the production of goods using synthetic biology;

(d) the formulation of synthetic biology to enable the degradation of materials;
(e) the provision of services that enable the activities in paragraphs (a) to (d).

3 Meaning of synthetic biology

In this Schedule, "synthetic biology" means the process of applying engineering principles to biology to design, redesign or make biological components or systems that do not exist in the natural world.

4 Synthetic biology includes but is not limited to—

(a) the design and engineering of biological-based parts of—
 (i) enzymes;
 (ii) genetic circuits and cells;
 (iii) novel devices and systems;
(b) redesigning existing natural biological systems;
(c) using microbes to template materials;
(d) cell-free systems;
(e) gene editing and gene therapy;
(f) the use of DNA for data storage, encryption and bio-enabled computing.

5 Exceptions—general

Exceptions to the activities described in paragraph 2 are—

(a) general services or servicing not related to core synthetic biology, where "core" means those activities without which experiments cannot be conducted, such as DNA synthesis or cloning;
(b) the use of microorganisms to remove harmful contaminants, pollutants or toxins from the environment (known as bioremediation), including bio-based reagents that allow for testing for contaminants;
(c) any approach used to gather clinical information for the purpose of making a clinical decision or making a diagnosis (known as diagnostics) but not the storage or ownership of sensitive human genetic information that enables the identification of an individual;
(d) industrial biotechnology research, development or production using enzymes or organisms that have not been modified through the application of synthetic biology;
(e) the production of substances ordinarily consumed as food or used as feed, including any ingredient or component of such substances;
(f) gene therapy, where it is used solely for the purpose of replacing missing or defective genes to restore phenotypes to achieve a therapeutic effect;
(g) cell therapy, where cells are modified by genetic engineering and then introduced into a patient to treat disease.

6 Exceptions—human or veterinary medicines or immunomodulatory approaches

(1) Exceptions to the activities described in paragraph 2 are the ownership, ownership of intellectual property or development of the matters set out in sub-paragraph (2) that employ synthetic biology at any stage of the development or production, unless the circumstances set out in sub-paragraph (3) apply.

(2) The matters referred to in sub-paragraph (1) are—

(a) human or veterinary medicines;
(b) immunomodulatory approaches.

(3) The circumstances referred to in sub-paragraph (1) are where the matter described in sub-paragraph (2)—

(a) has a synthetic biology technology that could be employed or modified to produce, deliver or produce and deliver—
 (i) toxic chemicals to achieve an incapacitating or lethal effect on humans or animals;
 (ii) materials restricted under Schedule 5 to the Anti-terrorism, Crime and Security Act 2001; or
(b) uses substances or pathogens set out in Schedule 5 to the Anti-terrorism, Crime and Security Act 2001.

NOTES

Commencement: 4 January 2022.

SCHEDULE 17
TRANSPORT

Regulation 2

[10.1344]

1 Interpretation—ports and harbours

In paragraph 2—

"harbour" is to be construed in accordance with section 313(1) of the Merchant Shipping Act 1995;

"infrastructure" means infrastructure, facilities and equipment within a port or harbour directly related to the movement of freight, passengers or seafarers;

"operating" means controlling the functioning of the port, harbour, terminal, wharf or other infrastructure;

"port" means an area of land and water made up of infrastructure which permits—
 (a) the receiving and departing of ships;
 (b) the loading and unloading of ships;
 (c) the storage of cargo;
 (d) the receipt and delivery of cargo; or
 (e) the embarkation and disembarkation of passengers, crew and other persons;

"ship" is to be construed in accordance with section 313(1) of the Merchant Shipping Act 1995.

2 Activity—ports and harbours

A qualifying entity carrying on activities that consist of or include—

(a) owning or operating a port or harbour in the United Kingdom that handled 1 million tonnes or more of cargo as recorded in the Port Freight Annual Statistics published by the Department for Transport, in the year preceding the year in which the acquisition is due to be completed; or

(b) owning and operating terminals, wharves or other infrastructure situated in a port or harbour described in sub-paragraph (a).

3 Interpretation—airports and air traffic control

(1) In paragraph 4—

"airport" has the meaning set out in section 66(1) of the Civil Aviation Act 2012;

"en route air traffic control services" mean services provided pursuant to a licence under section 6 of the Transport Act 2000;

"operating an airport" means having overall responsibility for its management;

"parent undertaking" has the meaning set out in section 1162 of the Companies Act 2006;

(2) The entities that are to be regarded as owning an airport for the purposes of paragraph 4 are—

(a) a company which owns the airport ("C"); and

(b) any parent undertaking of C ;

(3) The entities that are to be regarded as owning a provider of en route air traffic control services for the purposes of paragraph 4 are—

(a) a company which owns such a provider ("C"); and

(b) any parent undertaking of C.

4 Activity—airports and air traffic control

A qualifying entity carrying on activities that consist of or include—

(a) owning or operating an airport in the United Kingdom that handled at least six million passenger movements or 100,000 tonnes of freight in 2018, as recorded in the UK Airports Annual Statements of Movements, Passengers and Cargo published by the Civil Aviation Authority;

(b) providing en route air traffic control services in the United Kingdom;

(c) owning a provider of en route air traffic control services in the United Kingdom.

NOTES

Commencement: 4 January 2022.

NATIONAL SECURITY AND INVESTMENT ACT 2021 (PROCEDURE FOR SERVICE) REGULATIONS 2021

(SI 2021/1267)

NOTES

Made: 15 November 2021.
Authority: National Security and Investment Act 2021, s 53(1), (2).
Commencement: 4 January 2022.

ARRANGEMENT OF REGULATIONS

PART 1 INTRODUCTION

[10.1345]

1 Citation, commencement, extent and application

(1) These Regulations may be cited as the National Security and Investment Act 2021 (Procedure for Service) Regulations 2021, and come into force on 4th January 2022.

(2) These Regulations extend to England and Wales, Scotland and Northern Ireland.

(3) These Regulations do not apply to a document if rules of court make provision about its service.

NOTES

Commencement: 4 January 2022.

[10.1346]

2 Interpretation

(1) In these Regulations—

"the Act" means the National Security and Investment Act 2021;

"the NSI electronic portal" means an online facility provided by the Secretary of State for sending documents required or allowed to be given in connection with the Act;

"representative" means a person who has been appointed to act on behalf of another person in connection with the giving of documents under the Act.

(2) In these Regulations—

(a) references to the giving of a document (however expressed) include references to the service of a document;

(b) references to documents include references to orders, notices, notifications and applications required or allowed to be given under the Act.

NOTES

Commencement: 4 January 2022.

PART 2 SERVICE BY THE SECRETARY OF STATE

[10.1347]

3 Service of documents by the Secretary of State

(1) A document required or allowed by the Act to be given to a person by the Secretary of State must be given—

(a) by sending it by email to that person's email address (or the email address of their representative), as provided for in regulation 4, or

(b) by posting it to that person's postal address (or the postal address of that person's representative), as provided for in regulation 5.

(2) For the purposes of paragraph (1)(b), "posting" a document means sending that document pre-paid by a postal service intended to ensure expeditious delivery.

(3) A document sent by email in accordance with paragraph (1)(a) is to be treated as having been given immediately after it is sent.

(4) A document posted in accordance with paragraph (1)(b)—

(a) to an address within the United Kingdom, is to be treated as having been given on the second working day after posting;

(b) to an address outside the United Kingdom, is to be treated as having been given on the fifth working day after posting.

(5) When giving a document under this regulation, the Secretary of State must mark it as being for the attention of the person to whom it is required or allowed to be given under the Act.

(6) Where the person referred to in paragraph (5) is a body corporate or unincorporate, the document being given to that person must additionally be marked as being for the attention of an officer or member of that body (as the case may be) whom the Secretary of State considers to be appropriate.

NOTES

Commencement: 4 January 2022.

[10.1348]

4 Address for service by email under regulation 3(1)(a)

(1) For the purposes of regulation 3(1)(a), a person's email address (or the email address of their representative) is the email address provided by that person to the Secretary of State in connection with the giving of documents under the Act.

(2) Where an email address as referred to in paragraph (1) has not been provided, a person's email address is—

(a) in the case of an individual, an email address published for the time being by that person as an email address for contacting that person, or

(b) in the case of a body corporate or unincorporate, the general email address published for the time being by that body.

(3) Where an email address as referred to in paragraphs (1) and (2) has not been provided or published (as the case may be), or if the Secretary of State has reason to believe that such an address is unsuitable or inadequate, a person's email address is any email address by means of which the Secretary of State reasonably believes that the document will come to the attention of that person (or their representative).

NOTES

Commencement: 4 January 2022.

[10.1349]

5 Address for service by post under regulation 3(1)(b)

(1) For the purposes of regulation 3(1)(b), a person's postal address (or the postal address of their representative) is the postal address provided by that person to the Secretary of State in connection with the giving of documents under the Act.

(2) Where a postal address as referred to in paragraph (1) has not been provided, a person's postal address is—

(a) where that person is a body corporate, the address of its registered office or principal office, or

(b) where that person is a partnership or an unincorporated association or body, the address of its principal office.

(3) In the case of—

(a) a body corporate registered outside the United Kingdom,

(b) a partnership carrying on business outside the United Kingdom, or

(c) an unincorporated association or body with offices outside the United Kingdom,

the references in paragraph (2) to its principal office include references to its principal office in the United Kingdom (if any).

(4) Where a postal address as referred to in paragraphs (1) and (2) has not been provided or is not known (as the case may be), or if the Secretary of State has reason to believe that such an address is unsuitable or inadequate, a person's postal address is any postal address by means of which the Secretary of State reasonably believes that the document will come to the attention of that person (or their representative).

NOTES

Commencement: 4 January 2022.

PART 3 SERVICE ON THE SECRETARY OF STATE

[10.1350]

6 Service of documents on the Secretary of State

(1) The following documents required or allowed by the Act to be given by a person to the Secretary of State must be sent using the NSI electronic portal—

(a) a mandatory notice under section 14(1) of the Act;
(b) a validation application under section 16(1) of the Act;
(c) a voluntary notice under section 18(2) of the Act.

(2) Where a document is given to the Secretary of State in accordance with paragraph (1), the document is to be treated as having been given once it is registered on the NSI electronic portal.

(3) A document not covered by paragraph (1) which is required or allowed by the Act to be given by a person to the Secretary of State must be sent by email, to the email address specified for that purpose on the gov.uk website.

(4) Where a document is given to the Secretary of State in accordance with paragraph (3), the document is not to be treated as having been given until it is received by the Secretary of State in a form which is legible and capable of being used for subsequent reference.

(5) A document required or allowed by the Act to be given by a person to the Secretary of State may be given by that person's representative.

(6) This regulation is subject to regulation 7.

NOTES

Commencement: 4 January 2022.

[10.1351]

7 Exceptions to regulation 6 requirements

(1) Paragraph (2) applies where a person who is required or allowed by the Act to give a document to the Secretary of State (or where that person's representative) considers that—

(a) they are unable to comply with the requirements in regulation 6, or
(b) there is a good reason not to comply with the requirements in regulation 6.

(2) The person (or their representative) must—

(a) establish contact with the Secretary of State by alternative means, within the time limit (if any) for giving the document to the Secretary of State, and
(b) propose to the Secretary of State an alternative means for giving the document to the Secretary of State (which may or may not be the same as the alternative means referred to in sub-paragraph (a)).

(3) Where the Secretary of State has been contacted in accordance with paragraph (2) and is satisfied that the person (or their representative) is unable or has good reason not to comply with the requirements in regulation 6, the Secretary of State must agree to be given the document by alternative means (which may or may not be the same as the alternative means referred to in paragraph (2)(a) or (b)).

(4) Where the Secretary of State agrees to be given a document by alternative means under this regulation—

(a) if there is a time limit for giving the document under the Act, that remains unchanged, and
(b) the document is not to be treated as having been given until it is received by the Secretary of State in a form which is legible and capable of being used for subsequent reference.

NOTES

Commencement: 4 January 2022.

NATIONAL SECURITY AND INVESTMENT ACT 2021 (PRESCRIBED FORM AND CONTENT OF NOTICES AND VALIDATION APPLICATIONS) REGULATIONS 2021

(SI 2021/1272)

NOTES

Made: 15 November 2021.
Authority: National Security and Investment Act 2021, ss 14(4), 16(3), 18(4).
Commencement: 4 January 2022.
These Regulations are reproduced as amended by: the National Security and Investment Act 2021 (Prescribed Form and Content of Notices and Validation Applications) (Amendment) Regulations 2022, SI 2022/398.

ARRANGEMENT OF REGULATIONS

SCHEDULES

[10.1352]
1 Citation, commencement and extent

(1) These Regulations may be cited as the National Security and Investment Act 2021 (Prescribed Form and Content of Notices and Validation Applications) Regulations 2021 and come into force on 4th January 2022.

(2) These Regulations extend to England and Wales, Scotland and Northern Ireland.

NOTES

Commencement: 4 January 2022.

[10.1353]
2 Interpretation

In these Regulations—

"the Act" means the National Security and Investment Act 2021;

"body" means a body corporate, a partnership or an unincorporated association other than a partnership;

"dual-use items" means goods and technology, including software or information (other than information in the public domain), the export or transfer of which is controlled by virtue of their being specified in the relevant export control legislation;

"national infrastructure sector" means one of the following sectors listed by the Centre for the Protection of National Infrastructure as being sectors capable of containing critical national infrastructure—

(a) chemicals,
(b) civil nuclear,
(c) communications,
(d) defence,
(e) emergency services,
(f) energy,
(g) finance,
(h) food,
(i) government,
(j) health,
(k) space,
(l) transport, and
(m) water;

"notifying party" means the person who submits a mandatory notice, a validation application or a voluntary notice;

"relevant export control legislation" means—

(n) Annex 1 to Council Regulation (EC) No 428/2009 of 5 May 2009 setting up a Community regime for the control of exports, transfer, brokering and transit of dual-use items,
(o) the Schedule to the Export of Radioactive Sources (Control) Order 2006, and
(p) Schedules 2 and 3 to the Export Control Order 2008,

"representative" means a person who has been appointed to act on behalf of another person in connection with the giving of documents under the Act.

NOTES

Commencement: 4 January 2022.

[10.1354]
3 Prescribed form and content of a mandatory notice

A mandatory notice must be in writing and contain—

(a) the information specified in Part 1 of Schedule 1,
(b) a declaration that the information provided in the notification is true and complete to the notifying party's knowledge, in the form set out in paragraph 39 of Part 2 of Schedule 1 and referred to as Declaration A, and

(c) where the notifying party has appointed a representative, a declaration that the notifying party confirms that the representative is authorised to submit the notice and to accept service, in the form set out in paragraph 40 of Part 2 of Schedule 1 and referred to as Declaration B.

NOTES

Commencement: 4 January 2022.

[10.1355]

4 Prescribed form and content of a voluntary notice

A voluntary notice must be in writing and contain—

(a) the information specified in Part 1 of Schedule 2,

(b) a declaration that the information provided in the notification is true and complete to the notifying party's knowledge, in the form set out in paragraph 58 of Part 2 of Schedule 2 and referred to as Declaration A, and

(c) where the notifying party has appointed a representative, a declaration that the notifying party confirms that the representative is authorised to submit the notice and to accept service, in the form set out in paragraph 59 of Part 2 of Schedule 2 and referred to as Declaration B.

NOTES

Commencement: 4 January 2022.

[10.1356]

5 Prescribed form and content of a validation application

A validation application must be in writing and—

(a) contain the information specified in Part 1 of Schedule 3,

(b) a declaration that the information provided in the application is true and complete to the notifying party's knowledge, in the form set out in paragraph 48 of Part 2 of Schedule 3 and referred to as Declaration A, and

(c) where the notifying party has appointed a representative, a declaration that the notifying party confirms that the representative is authorised to submit the application and to accept service, in the format set out in paragraph 49 of Part 2 of Schedule 3 and referred to as Declaration B.

NOTES

Commencement: 4 January 2022.

SCHEDULES

SCHEDULE 1

Regulation 3

PART 1 INFORMATION REQUIRED IN A MANDATORY NOTICE

Notifying party name and contact details

[10.1357]

1. The acquirer's full name.

2. The acquirer's address.

3. Where the acquirer is an entity, the full name of an individual who holds or occupies a position in relation to the entity and who can be contacted in relation to the notice and the following information in relation to that individual—

(a) the position held in the entity,

(b) email address, and

(c) telephone number.

4. Where the acquirer has authorised a representative to submit the form and to accept service under the Act, the following information in relation to the representative—

(a) full name,

(b) business name,

(c) address,

(d) email address,

(e) telephone number, and

(f) details of the relationship between the representative and the acquirer.

Additional acquirers

5. (1) Where there is more than one acquirer involved in the acquisition, the information set out in subparagraphs (2) to (4), if known.

(2) The following information about each additional acquirer—

(a) name,

(b) address, and

(c) telephone number.

(3) Where an additional acquirer is an entity, the full name, of an individual who holds or occupies a position in relation to the entity and who can be contacted in relation to the notice, and the following information in relation to that individual—

(a) the position held in the entity,

(b) email address, and

(c) telephone number.

(4) The control thresholds set out in subsections (2), (5) and (6) of section 8 of the Act which are expected to be met by the additional acquirer and a description of the shares or voting rights expected to be acquired by the additional acquirer.

Related notifications

6. A statement of whether the acquirer (or in a case where there is more than one acquirer any of the acquirers) has submitted a notification to any overseas investment screening regimes within the last 12 months and specifying, if applicable, the following information about the notification—

(a) the name of the investment screening regime,
(b) the country, and
(c) any applicable case numbers or reference numbers.

Acquisition details

7. The areas of the economy as set out in the headings to the Schedules to the National Security and Investment Act 2021 (Notifiable Acquisition) (Specification of Qualifying Entities) Regulations 2021 in which the qualifying entity carries on activities and a description of those activities.

8. The control thresholds set out in subsections (2), (5) and (6) of section 8 of the Act which are expected to be met and provide a description of the shares or voting rights expected to be acquired by the acquirer.

9. The expected date of completion of the acquisition being notified.

Regulatory approvals

10. If applicable, the following information about any approvals given by a regulatory authority in the United Kingdom (including any approvals already given) required prior to completion of the acquisition—

(a) the name of the regulatory authority,
(b) details of the nature of the approval, and
(c) any key dates associated with those approvals.

Details of the qualifying entity

11. The qualifying entity's full name.

12. The qualifying entity's address.

13. If applicable, the qualifying entity's website address.

14. If known, the full name of an individual who holds or occupies a position in relation to the qualifying entity and who can be contacted in relation to the notice and the following information about that person—

(a) the position held in the qualifying entity,
(b) email address, and
(c) telephone number.

15. If the qualifying entity is registered in the United Kingdom, the following information—

(a) the Companies House registration number, and
(b) the Standard Industrial Classification code.

16. If the qualifying entity is formed or recognised under the law of a country or territory outside the United Kingdom, the following information in relation to the qualifying entity—

(a) the country of incorporation, and
(b) the full registration details within the country of incorporation.

17. A description of the activities which the qualifying entity carries out.

18. If known, a statement as to whether the qualifying entity is authorised to receive and/or store information which has been given a United Kingdom government security classification and, if it is, the following information—

(a) the classification level,
(b) the government department, agency or public body from which the information came, and
(c) a description of the information held by the qualifying entity under the authorisation.

19. A statement as to whether the qualifying entity requires any licences to operate within the areas of the economy as set out in the headings to the Schedules to the National Security and Investment Act 2021 (Notifiable Acquisition) (Specification of Qualifying Entities) Regulations 2021in the United Kingdom and, if it does, the following information in relation to each licence—

(a) the licence name,
(b) the name of the issuer of the licence, and
(c) the date when the licence was issued.

20. If known, a statement as to whether the qualifying entity owns or holds any dual-use items and, if it does, the name of each item and a description.

21. A statement as to whether the qualifying entity currently supplies, or in the past five years, has supplied, goods or services to a United Kingdom government department, agency or public body that relates to any one or more of the following areas—

(a) defence,
(b) national security responsibilities,
(c) law enforcement,
(d) national infrastructure [sector].

22. If the qualifying entity supplies, or has supplied, goods or services for the purposes of paragraph 21, the following information—

(a) the name of the government department, agency or public body,
(b) a description of the supply relationship, and
(c) a statement of which of the areas referred to in paragraph 21 the supply relationship relates to.

23. A statement as to whether the qualifying entity currently, or in the past five years, has undertaken any research and development project that has been partly or wholly funded by any United Kingdom government department, agency or public body that relates to any one or more of the areas referred to in paragraph 21.

24. If the qualifying entity undertakes, or has undertaken, a research and development project as described in paragraph 23, the following information—

(a) the name of the research and development project,
(b) a description of the research and development undertaken,
(c) a statement of which area in paragraph 21 it relates to, and
(d) the name of the United Kingdom government department, agency or public body that provided the funding.

25. A statement as to whether, if known, the qualifying entity is party to any contracts which require personnel of the qualifying entity to hold national security vetting security clearance and, if so, the following information, if known—

(a) the level of clearances held, and
(b) the number of personnel holding that level of clearance.

Ownership and structure of the qualifying entity

26. The following information about the pre-acquisition structure of the qualifying entity which must be provided in a chart attached to the notice—

(a) the full names of shareholders with share ownership or voting rights of 5% or more specifying the percentage held by each, and
(b) the nationality (for individuals) or country of incorporation or constitution (for entities) of any shareholder listed in subparagraph (a).

27. The following details of the expected post-acquisition structure of the qualifying entity which must be provided in a chart attached to the notice—

(a) the full names of shareholders with share ownership or voting rights of 5% or more specifying the percentage held by each, and
(b) the nationality (for individuals) or country of incorporation or constitution (for entities) of any shareholders listed in subparagraph (a).

28. A statement as to whether any non-United Kingdom government has a direct or indirect role in the operation or decision making of the qualifying entity and, if it has, the following information in relation to each non-United Kingdom government—

(a) the name of the non-United Kingdom government or representative, and
(b) a description of the non-United Kingdom government's role and interests.

Details of the acquirer

29. A statement as to whether the acquirer is an individual or an entity.

30. The acquirer's nationality (for individuals) or country of incorporation or constitution (for entities).

31. Where the acquirer is an entity, the following information—

(a) if the acquirer is registered in the United Kingdom, the following information—
  (i) the Companies House registration number, and
  (ii) the Standard Industrial Classification code.
(b) if the acquirer is formed or recognised under the law of a country or territory outside the United Kingdom, the following information—
  (i) the country of incorporation, and
  (ii) the full registration details within the country of incorporation.

32. A description of the activities that the acquirer carries out.

33. A statement as to whether any non-United Kingdom government or any person acting on behalf of a non-United Kingdom government has any share ownership or voting rights in the acquirer and, if it has, the following information—

(a) the name of the non-United Kingdom government or the full name of the person acting on behalf of the non-United Kingdom government, and
(b) information on the amount of share ownership or voting rights held in the acquirer.

34. A statement of whether any non-United Kingdom government has a direct or indirect role in the operation or decision-making of the acquirer and, if it has, the following information in relation to each non-United Kingdom government—

(a) the name of the non-United Kingdom government or the full name of the person acting on behalf of the non-United Kingdom government, and
(b) a description of the government's role and interests.

35. A statement as to whether there will be any contractual arrangements in place regarding share ownership or voting rights between the acquirer and any other party in relation to the qualifying entity once the proposed acquisition has been completed and a description of any such contractual arrangements.

36. If applicable, the following information about the structure of the acquirer which must be provided in a chart attached to the notice—

(a) the full names of shareholders with share ownership or voting rights of 5% or more specifying the percentage held by each, and
(b) the country of nationality (for individuals) or country of incorporation or constitution (for entities) of any shareholders listed in subparagraph (a).

37. Where the acquirer will be acquiring indirect control over the qualifying entity, a statement—

(a) confirming that indirect control is to be acquired, and

(b) specifying the chain of entities which holds an interest or right in the acquirer, up to the last entity which holds the interest or right.

38. A statement of whether the acquirer has a board of directors and if applicable, the following information about each of the members of the board of directors or equivalent within the acquirer at the time of submitting the notification—

(a) the individual's full name,
(b) the individual's date of birth,
(c) the position held within the acquirer, and
(d) whether the person is classified as a politically exposed person (PEP) within the meaning given in regulation 35(12)(a) and (14) of the Money Laundering, Terrorist Financing and Transfer of Funds (Information on the Payer) Regulations 2017/692.

NOTES

Commencement: 4 January 2022.

Para 21: word in square brackets in sub-para (d) inserted by the National Security and Investment Act 2021 (Prescribed Form and Content of Notices and Validation Applications) (Amendment) Regulations 2022, SI 2022/398, reg 2(a), as from 20 April 2022.

PART 2 DECLARATIONS

Form of Declaration A

[10.1358]

39. The form of Declaration A is—

"Declaration A

I declare that, to the best of my knowledge and belief, the information given in response to the questions in this Notice is true, correct, and complete in all material respects.

I understand that:

It is a criminal offence under section 34 of the National Security and Investment Act 2021 for a person recklessly or knowingly to supply to the Secretary of State information which is false or misleading in any material respect. This includes supplying such information to another person knowing that the information is to be used for the purpose of supplying information to the Secretary of State.

Signed:
Name: (block letters)
Position: (block letters)
Date:"

Form of Declaration B

40. The form of Declaration B is—

"Declaration B

I confirm that [full name of the representative] is authorised for the purpose of the acquisition described in this mandatory notice to submit this notice I hereby specify [the [email] address of the representative named in the notification] as an [email] address at which [name of the notifying party] will accept service of documents of any kind in connection with the National Security and Investment Act 2021 in relation to this Notice.

Signed:
Name: (block letters)
Position: (block letters)
Date:"

NOTES

Commencement: 4 January 2022.

SCHEDULE 2

Regulation 4

PART 1 INFORMATION REQUIRED IN A VOLUNTARY NOTICE

Notifying party name and contact details

[10.1359]

1. A statement setting out whether the notifying party is the acquirer, seller or qualifying entity.

2. The notifying party's full name.

3. The notifying party's address.

4. Where the notifying party is an entity, the full name of an individual who holds or occupies a position in relation to the entity and who can be contacted in relation to the notice and the following information in relation to that individual—

(a) the position held in the notifying party,
(b) email address, and
(c) telephone number.

5. Where the notifying party has authorised a representative to submit the form and accept service, the following information in relation to the representative—

(a) full name,
(b) business name,
(c) address,
(d) email address,
(e) telephone number, and

Part 10 Miscellaneous other SIs

(f) the relationship between the representative and the notifying party.

Acquirer's name and contact details

6. A statement as to whether there is more than one acquirer.

7. If the notifying party is not the acquirer, the following information in relation to the acquirer—

(a) full name, and

(b) address.

8. Where the acquirer is an entity, the full name, if known, of an individual who holds or occupies a position in relation to the entity and who can be contacted in relation to the notice, and the following information in relation to that individual—

(a) the position held in the entity,

(b) email address, and

(c) telephone number.

9. The control thresholds set out in subsections (2), (5) and (6) of section 8 or section 9 of the Act which are or are expected to be met by the acquirer and a description of the shares or voting rights being acquired by the acquirer.

10. Where the acquirer has authorised a representative to accept service under the Act on behalf of the acquirer, the following information in relation to the representative—

(a) full name,

(b) business name,

(c) address,

(d) email address,

(e) telephone number, and

(f) details of the relationship between the representative and the acquirer.

11. Where there is more than one acquirer involved in this acquisition, the information specified in paragraphs 7 to 10 must be provided in relation to each additional acquirer.

Related notifications

12. If known, a statement of whether the acquirer (or in a case where there is more than one acquirer, any of the acquirers) has submitted a notification to any overseas investment screening regimes within the last 12 months and specifying, if applicable, the following information about the notification—

(a) the name of the investment screening regime,

(b) the country, and

(c) any case numbers or reference numbers given.

Acquisition details

13. A statement specifying—

(a) whether the acquisition is in contemplation, in progress or has taken place,

(b) whether the notice is related to the acquisition of a qualifying asset or a qualifying entity, and

(c) if known, the date or the expected date of completion of the acquisition being notified.

14. If applicable, the following information about any approvals from a regulatory authority in the United Kingdom (including any approvals already given) required prior to completion of the acquisition—

(a) the name of the regulatory authority, and

(b) details of the nature of the approval, and

(c) any key dates associated with those approvals.

Details of the qualifying entity being acquired (to be provided in relation to an entity acquisition only)

15. The qualifying entity's full name.

16. The qualifying entity's address.

17. If applicable, the qualifying entity's website address.

18. If known, the full name of an individual who holds or occupies a position in relation to the qualifying entity and who can be contacted in relation to the notice and the following information about that person—

(a) the position held in the qualifying entity,

(b) email address, and

(c) telephone number.

19. If the qualifying entity is registered in the United Kingdom, the following information—

(a) the Companies House registration number, and

(b) the Standard Industrial Classification code.

20. If the qualifying entity is formed or recognised under the law of a country or territory outside the United Kingdom, the following information in relation to the qualifying entity—

(a) the country of incorporation, and

(b) the full registration details within the country of incorporation.

21. A description of the activities or services the qualifying entity provides or carries out.

22. If known, a statement as to whether the qualifying entity is authorised to receive and/or store information which has been given a United Kingdom government security classification and, if it is, the following information—

(a) the classification level,

(b) the government department, agency or public body from which the information came, and

(c) a description of the information held by the qualifying entity under the authorisation.

23. If known, a statement as to whether the qualifying entity holds any licences to operate in the United Kingdom and, if it does, the following information—

(a) the licence name,
(b) the name of the issuer of the licence, and
(c) the date when the licence was issued.

24. If known, a statement as to whether the qualifying entity owns or holds any dual-use items and, if it does, provide the name of each item and a description.

25. If known, a statement as to whether the qualifying entity currently supplies, or in the past five years, has supplied goods or services to a United Kingdom government department, agency or public body that relates to any one or more of the following areas—
(a) defence,
(b) national security responsibilities,
(c) law enforcement, or
(d) national infrastructure [sector].

26. If the entity does supply, or has supplied, goods or services for the purposes of paragraph 25, the following information—
(a) the name of the department, agency or public body,
(b) a description of the supply relationship, and
(c) a statement of which of the areas referred to in paragraph 25 the supply relationship relates to.

27. If known, a statement as to whether the qualifying entity currently, or in the past five years, has undertaken any research and development project that has been partly or wholly funded by any United Kingdom government department, agency or public body that relates to any one or more of the areas referred to in paragraph 25.

28. If the qualifying entity undertakes, or has undertaken a research and development project for the purposes of paragraph 27, the following information—
(a) the name of the research and development project,
(b) a description of the research and development undertaken,
(c) a statement of which area in paragraph 25 it relates to, and
(d) the name of the United Kingdom government department, agency or public body that provided the funding.

29. If known, a statement as to whether, the qualifying entity is party to any contracts which require personnel of the qualifying entity to hold national security vetting security clearance and, if so, the following information—
(a) the level of clearances held; and
(b) the number of personnel holding that level of clearance.

Ownership and structure of the qualifying entity

30. The following information about the pre-acquisition structure of the qualifying entity which must be provided in a chart attached to the notice—
(a) the full names of shareholders with share ownership or voting rights of 5% or more specifying the percentage held by each, and
(b) the nationality (for individuals) or country of incorporation or constitution (for entities) of any shareholder listed in subparagraph (a).

31. The following details of the expected post-acquisition structure of the qualifying entity which must be provided in a chart attached to the notice—
(a) the full names of shareholders with share ownership or voting rights of 5% or more specifying the percentage held by each, and
(b) the nationality (for individuals) or country of incorporation or constitution (for entities) of any shareholders listed in subparagraph (a).

32. If known, a statement as to whether any non-United Kingdom government has a direct or indirect role in the operation or decision making of the qualifying entity and, if it has, the following information in relation to each non-United Kingdom government—
(a) the name of the non-United Kingdom government or representative, and
(b) a description of the non-United Kingdom government's role and interests.

Details of the qualifying asset being acquired (to be provided in relation to an asset acquisition only)

33. The category of a qualifying asset set out in subsection (4) of section 7 of the Act that the asset belongs to.

34. The location of the qualifying asset.

35. A description of the qualifying asset.

36. If known, a statement as to whether the qualifying asset has been given a United Kingdom government security classification and if it has, the following information—
(a) the classification level,
(b) the government department, agency or public body from which the classification came, and
(c) the reasons why the qualifying asset has a United Kingdom government security classification.

37. If a licence is required to operate the qualifying asset in the United Kingdom, details of—
(a) the licence name,
(b) the name of the issuer of the licence, and
(c) the date when the licence was issued.

38. If known, a statement as to whether the qualifying asset is considered a dual-use item and if it is, provide the name of the item and a description.

39. If known, a statement as to whether the qualifying asset is used to gather and/or hold data on United Kingdom citizens and, if it does, provide a description of the data gathered or held.

40. If known, a statement as to whether the qualifying asset holds any United Kingdom or internationally recognised standards, accreditations or certification.

41. If known, in case of a qualifying asset which is land or tangible (or, in Scotland, corporeal) moveable property, the full names of any person who has previously gained control over the qualifying asset before the acquisition takes place, which must be provided in a chart attached to the notice.

42. Specify the following information on the structure of the qualifying asset after the acquisition, in a chart attached to the notification—

(a) full names of those with rights or interests in the qualifying asset before the acquisition (if known), and
(b) specify the changes in rights or interests held in the qualifying asset as a result of the acquisition.

43. If known, a statement as to whether any non-United Kingdom government has a direct or indirect role in the control of the asset and, if it has, provide the name of the non-United Kingdom government and describe their role and interests.

44. If known, a statement as to whether there will be any contractual arrangements in place regarding share ownership or voting rights between the acquirer and any other party once the acquisition will have been completed.

Details of the acquirer

45. The acquirer's full name.

46. A statement as to whether the acquirer is an individual or an entity.

47. The country of incorporation or constitution (for entities) or the country of nationality (for individuals) of the acquirer.

48. If the acquirer is a qualifying entity registered in the United Kingdom, the following information—

(a) the Companies House registration number, and
(b) the Standard Industrial Classification code.

49. If the acquirer is formed or recognised under the law of a country or territory outside the United Kingdom, the following information—

(a) the country of incorporation, and
(b) the full registration details within the country of incorporation.

50. A description of the acquirer's main activities, products or services.

51. If known, a statement as to whether any non-United Kingdom government or any person acting on behalf of a non-United Kingdom government has any share ownership or voting rights in the acquirer and, if it has, the following information—

(a) the name of the non-United Kingdom government or the full name of the person acting on behalf of the non-United Kingdom government, and
(b) information on share ownership or voting rights held in the acquirer.

52. If known, a statement as to whether any non-United Kingdom government has a direct or indirect role in the operation or decision making of the acquirer and, if it has, the following information in relation to each non-United Kingdom government—

(a) the name of the non-United Kingdom government or the full name of the person acting on behalf of the non-United Kingdom government, and
(b) a description of the non-United Kingdom government's role and interests.

53. If known, a statement as to whether there will be any contractual arrangements in place regarding share ownership or voting rights between the acquirer and any other party in relation to the qualifying entity once the proposed acquisition has been completed and a description of any such contractual arrangements.

54. If applicable, the following information about the structure of the acquirer which must be provided in a chart attached to the notice—

(a) the full names of shareholders with share ownership or voting rights of 5% or more specifying the percentage held by each, and
(b) the country of nationality (for individuals) or country of incorporation or constitution (for entities) of any shareholders listed in subparagraph (a).

55. A statement as to whether any individual or entity is acquiring indirect control over the qualifying entity and if this is the case, provide details of the chain of individuals or entities that hold an interest or right.

56. A statement as to whether the acquirer has a board of directors and, if applicable, the following information about each of the members of the board of directors or equivalent within the acquirer at the time of submitting the notification—

(a) the individual's full name,
(b) the individual's date of birth,
(c) the position held within the acquirer, and
(d) whether the person is classified as a politically exposed person within the meaning given in regulation 35(12)(1)(a) and (14) of the Money Laundering, Terrorist Financing and Transfer of Funds (Information on the Payer) Regulations 2017/692.

Other

57. Any additional information the notifying party considers relevant to the notification.

NOTES

Commencement: 4 January 2022.

Para 25: word in square brackets in sub-para (d) inserted by the National Security and Investment Act 2021 (Prescribed Form and Content of Notices and Validation Applications) (Amendment) Regulations 2022, SI 2022/398, reg 2(b), as from 20 April 2022.

PART 2 DECLARATIONS

Form of Declaration A

[10.1360]

58. The form of Declaration A is—

"Declaration A

I declare that, to the best of my knowledge and belief, the information given in response to the questions in this Notice is true, correct, and complete in all material respects.

I understand that:

It is a criminal offence under section 34 of the National Security and Investment Act 2021 for a person recklessly or knowingly to supply to the Secretary of State information which is false or misleading in any material respect. This includes supplying such information to another person knowing that the information is to be used for the purpose of supplying information to the Secretary of State.

Signed:

Name: (block letters)

Position: (block letters)

Date:"

Form of Declaration B

59. The form of Declaration B is—

"Declaration B

I confirm that [full name of the representative (if any)] is authorised for the purpose of the acquisition described in this form to act on behalf of the notifying party and to submit this form. I hereby specify [the [email] address of the representative named in the notification] as an [email] address at which [name of the notifying party] will accept correspondence and accept service of documents in accordance with the National Security and Investment Act 2021 (Procedure for Service) Regulations 2021.

Signed:

Name: (block letters)

Position: (block letters)

Date:"

NOTES

Commencement: 4 January 2022.

SCHEDULE 3

Regulation 5

PART 1 INFORMATION REQUIRED IN A VALIDATION APPLICATION

Notifying party name and contact details

[10.1361]

1. A statement setting out whether the notifying party is the acquirer, seller, the qualifying entity or otherwise materially affected by the fact that the notifiable acquisition to which the application relates is void.

2. Details of how the notifying party has been materially affected by the fact that the notifiable acquisition to which the application relates is void.

3. A statement as to whether the information is provided by the notifying party or a representative.

4. The notifying party's full name.

5. The notifying party's address.

6. If applicable, where the notifying party is an entity, the full name of an individual who holds or occupies a position in relation to the entity and who can be contacted in relation to the notice and the following information in relation to that individual—

(a) the position held in the notifying party,

(b) email address, and

(c) telephone number.

7. Where the notifying party has authorised a representative to submit the application and to accept service under the Act, the following information in relation to the representative—

(a) full name,

(b) business name,

(c) address,

(d) email address,

(e) telephone number, and

(f) details of the relationship between the representative and the notifying party.

Acquirer's name and contact details

8. A statement as to whether there was more than one acquirer.

9. If the notifying party was not the acquirer, the following information in relation to the acquirer—

(a) name, and

(b) address,

10. Where the acquirer is an entity, the full name, if known, of an individual who holds or occupies a position in relation to the entity and who can be contacted in relation to the notice, and the following information in relation to that individual—

(a) the position held in the body,

(b) email address, and
(c) telephone number.

11. Details of which of the control thresholds set out in subsections (2), (5) and (6) of section 8 or section 9 of the Act that were met by the acquirer and a description of the shares or voting rights acquired by the acquirer.

12. If the notifying party was not the acquirer, and the acquirer has authorised a representative to accept service under the Act, the following information in relation to the acquirer's representative—
(a) full name,
(b) business name,
(c) registered address,
(d) email address,
(e) telephone number, and
(f) the relationship between the representative and the acquirer.

13. Where there was more than one acquirer involved in the acquisition, the information specified in paragraphs 9 to 12 in relation to each additional acquirer, if known.

Related notifications

14. A statement of whether the acquirer (or in a case where there is more than one acquirer any of the acquirers) has submitted a notification to any other overseas investment screening regimes within the last 12 months and specifying, if applicable the following information about the notification—
(a) the name of the investment screening regime,
(b) the country, and
(c) any case numbers or reference numbers given.

Acquisition details

15. If known, the reasons why the notifiable acquisition was not notified to the Secretary of State as required by section 14(1) of the Act.

16. The areas of the economy as set out in the headings to the Schedules in the National Security and Investment Act 2021 (Notifiable Acquisition) (Specification of Entities) Regulations 2021 in which the qualifying entity carries on activities and provide a description of those activities.

17. The control thresholds set out in subsections (2), (5) and (6) of section 8 of the Act 2021 that would have been met and provide a description of the shares or voting rights that would have been acquired by the acquirer had the notifiable acquisition not been void

18. The date that the notifiable acquisition completed.

Regulatory approvals

19. If applicable, the following information about any approvals given by a regulatory authority in the United Kingdom (including any approvals already given) that were required prior to completion of the acquisition—
(a) the name of the United Kingdom regulator,
(b) details of the nature of the approval, and
(c) any key dates associated with those approvals.

Details of the qualifying entity

20. The qualifying entity's full name.

21. The qualifying entity's address.

22. If known, the full name of an individual who holds or occupies a position in relation to the qualifying entity and the following information about that individual—
(a) the position held in the qualifying entity,
(b) email address, and
(c) telephone number.

23. If the qualifying entity is registered in the United Kingdom, the following information—
(a) the Companies House registration number, and
(b) the Standard Industrial Classification code.

24. If the qualifying entity is formed or recognised under the law of a country or territory outside the United Kingdom, the following information—
(a) the country of incorporation, and
(b) the full registration details within the country of incorporation.

25. A description of the activities which the qualifying entity carries out.

26. If known, a statement of whether the qualifying entity is authorised to receive and/or store information which has been given a United Kingdom government security classification and, if it is, the following information—
(a) the classification level,
(b) the government department, agency or public body from which the information came, and
(c) a description of the information held by the qualifying entity under the authorisation.

27. If known, a statement as to whether the qualifying entity requires any licences to operate within the areas of the economy as set out in the headings to the Schedules to the National Security and Investment Act 2021 (Notifiable Acquisition) (Specification of Qualifying Entities) Regulations 2021 in the United Kingdom and, if it does, the following information in relation to each licence—
(a) the licence name,
(b) the name of the issuer of the licence, and
(c) the date when the licence was issued.

28. If known, a statement as to whether the qualifying entity owns or holds any dual-use items and, if it does, the name of each item and a description.

29. If known, a statement as to whether the qualifying entity currently supplies, or in the past five years, has supplied, goods or services to a United Kingdom government department, agency or public body that relates to any one or more of the following areas—

(a) defence,
(b) national security responsibilities,
(c) law enforcement,
(d) [national infrastructure sector].

30. If the entity does supply, or has supplied, goods or services for the purposes of paragraph 29, the following information—

(a) the name of the government department, agency or public body,
(b) a description of the supply relationship, and
(c) a statement of which of the areas referred to in paragraph 29 the supply relationship relates to.

31. If known, a statement as to whether the qualifying entity currently, or in the past five years, has undertaken any research and development project that has been partly or wholly funded by any United Kingdom government department, agency or public body that relates to any one or more of the areas referred to in paragraph 29.

32. If the qualifying entity undertakes, or has undertaken, a research and development project for the purposes of paragraph 31, the following information—

(a) the name of the research and development project,
(b) a description of the research and development undertaken,
(c) a statement of which area in paragraph 29 it relates to, and
(d) the name of the United Kingdom government department, agency or public body that provided the funding.

33. If known, a statement as to whether the qualifying entity is party to any contracts which require personnel of the qualifying entity to hold national security vetting security clearance and, if so, the following information, if known—

(a) the level of clearances held; and
(b) the number of personnel holding that level of clearance.

Ownership and structure of the qualifying entity

34. The following information about the pre-acquisition structure of the qualifying entity which must be provided in a chart attached to the notice—

(a) the full names of shareholders with share ownership or voting rights of 5% or more specifying the percentage held by each, and
(b) the nationality (for individuals) or country of incorporation or constitution (for entities) of any shareholder listed in subparagraph (a).

35. The following details of the post-acquisition structure of the qualifying entity which must be provided in a chart attached to the notice—

(a) the full names of shareholders with share ownership or voting rights of 5% or more specifying the percentage held by each, and
(b) the nationality (for individuals) or country of incorporation or constitution (for entities) of any shareholders listed in subparagraph (a).

36. If known, a statement as to whether any non-United Kingdom government has a direct or indirect role in the operation or decision making of the qualifying entity and, if it has, the following information in relation to each non-United Kingdom government—

(a) the name of the non-United Kingdom government or representative, and
(b) a description of the non-United Kingdom government's role and interests.

Details of the acquirer

37. A statement as to whether the acquirer is an individual or an entity.

38. The acquirer's nationality (for individuals) or country of incorporation or constitution (for entities).

39. Where the acquirer is an entity, the following information—

(a) if the acquirer is registered in the United Kingdom—
 (i) the Companies House registration number, and
 (ii) the Standard Industrial Classification code.
(b) if the acquirer is formed or recognised under the law of a country or territory outside the United Kingdom—
 (i) the country of incorporation, and
 (ii) the full registration details within the country of incorporation.

40. A description of the activities that the acquirer carries out.

41. If known, a statement as to whether any non-United Kingdom government or any person acting on behalf of a non-United Kingdom government has any share ownership or voting rights in the acquirer and, if it has, the following information—

(a) the name of the non-United Kingdom government or the full name of the person acting on behalf of the non-United Kingdom government, and
(b) information on the amount of share ownership or voting rights held in the acquirer.

42. If known, statement whether any non-United Kingdom government has a direct or indirect role in the operation or decision making of the acquirer and, if it has, the following information in relation to each non-United Kingdom government—

(a) the name of the non-United Kingdom government or the full name of the person acting on behalf of the non-United Kingdom government, and
(b) a description of the non-United Kingdom government's role and interests.

43. A statement as to whether there are any contractual arrangements in place regarding share ownership or voting rights between the acquirer and any other party in relation to the qualifying entity and a description of any such contractual arrangements.

44. The following information about the structure of the acquirer which must be provided in a chart attached to the application—

(a) the full names of shareholders with share ownership or voting rights of 5% or more specifying the percentage held by each, and

(b) the country of nationality (for individuals) or country of incorporation or constitution (for entities) of any shareholders listed in subparagraph (a).

45. Where the acquirer acquired indirect control over the qualifying entity, a statement—

(a) confirming that indirect control was acquired, and

(b) specifying the chain of entities which hold an interest or right in the acquirer, up to the last entity which holds the interest or right.

46. A statement as to whether the acquirer has a board of directors and, if applicable, the following information about each of the members of the board of directors or equivalent within the acquirer at the time of submitting this application—

(a) the individual's full name,

(b) the individual's date of birth,

(c) the position held within the acquirer, and

(d) whether the individual is classified as a politically exposed person within the meaning given in regulation 35(12)(a) and (14) of the Money Laundering, Terrorist Financing and Transfer of Funds (Information on the Payer) Regulations 2017.

Other

47. Any additional information the notifying party considers relevant to the application.

NOTES

Commencement: 4 January 2022.

Para 21: words in square brackets in sub-para (d) inserted by the National Security and Investment Act 2021 (Prescribed Form and Content of Notices and Validation Applications) (Amendment) Regulations 2022, SI 2022/398, reg 2(c), as from 20 April 2022.

PART 2 DECLARATIONS

Form of Declaration A

[10.1362]

48. The content of Declaration A is—

"Declaration A

I declare that, to the best of my knowledge and belief, the information given in response to the questions in this Application is true, correct, and complete in all material respects.

I understand that:

It is a criminal offence under section 34 of the National Security and Investment Act 2021 for a person recklessly or knowingly to supply to the Secretary of State information which is false or misleading in any material respect. This includes supplying such information to another person knowing that the information is to be used for the purpose of supplying information to the Secretary of State.

Signed:

Name: (block letters)

Position: (block letters)

Date:"

Form of Declaration B

49. The content of Declaration B is—

"Declaration B

I confirm that [full name of the representative] is authorised for the purpose of the acquisition described in this form to act on behalf of the notifying party and to submit this form. I hereby specify [the [email] address of the representative named in the application] as an [email] address at which [name of the notifying party] will accept correspondence and accept service of documents in accordance with the National Security and Investment Act 2021 (Procedure for Service) Regulations 2021.

Signed:

Name: (block letters)

Position: (block letters)

Date:"

NOTES

Commencement: 4 January 2022.

REGISTER OF OVERSEAS ENTITIES (VERIFICATION AND PROVISION OF INFORMATION) REGULATIONS 2022

(SI 2022/725)

NOTES

Made: 29 June 2022.

Authority: Economic Crime (Transparency and Enforcement) Act 2022, ss 16, 43(2), 67(2).

Commencement: see reg 1 at **[10.1363]**.

ARRANGEMENT OF REGULATIONS

PART 1
INTRODUCTORY

PART 2
VERIFICATION

PART 3
INFORMATION PROVIDED UNDER SECTION 42(1)(C) OF THE ECTEA

PART 1 INTRODUCTORY

[10.1363]
1 Citation, commencement and extent

(1) These Regulations may be cited as the Register of Overseas Entities (Verification and Provision of Information) Regulations 2022 and come into force on the day section 3 of the ECTEA comes into force.

(2) These Regulations extend to England and Wales, Scotland and Northern Ireland.

NOTES

Commencement: to be appointed (see above).

[10.1364]
2 Interpretation

In these Regulations—

"the ECTEA" means the Economic Crime (Transparency and Enforcement) Act 2022;

"the Money Laundering Regulations" means the Money Laundering, Terrorist Financing and Transfer of Funds (Information on the Payer) Regulations 2017;

"relevant activity" has the meaning given in regulation 4;

"relevant information" has the meaning given in regulation 5;

"relevant person" has the meaning given in regulation 3;

"section 42(1)(c) information" is information delivered to the registrar under section 42(1)(c) of the ECTEA (requirement for certain unregistered overseas entities to provide information).

NOTES

Commencement: to be appointed (see reg 1 at **[10.1363]**).

[10.1365]
3 Meaning of "relevant person"

(1) Subject to paragraph (2), a "relevant person" is a person who is a relevant person for the purposes of the Money Laundering Regulations.

(2) A person is not a relevant person where that person—

(a) is a high value dealer within the meaning given in regulation 14(1)(a) of the Money Laundering Regulations;

(b) is a casino within the meaning given in regulation 14(1)(b) of the Money Laundering Regulations;

(c) is an art market participant within the meaning given in regulation 14(1)(d) of the Money Laundering Regulations;

(d) is a cryptoasset exchange provider within the meaning given in regulation 14A(1) of the Money Laundering Regulations;

(e) is a custodian wallet provider within the meaning given in regulation 14A(2) of the Money Laundering Regulations;

(f) has been convicted of an offence—

(i) in Great Britain under section 32 of ECTEA (general false statement offence), and that conviction has not yet become spent within the meaning of the Rehabilitation of Offenders Act 1974, or

(ii) in Northern Ireland under section 32 of ECTEA, and that person's conviction has not yet become spent within the meaning of the Rehabilitation of Offenders (Northern Ireland) Order 1978;

(g) has been convicted of an offence—

Part 10 Miscellaneous other SIs

(i) in Great Britain under regulation 86, 87 or 88 of the Money Laundering Regulations, and that conviction has not yet become spent within the meaning of the Rehabilitation of Offenders Act 1974; or

(ii) in Northern Ireland under regulation 86, 87 or 88 of the Money Laundering Regulations, and that conviction has not yet become spent within the meaning of the Rehabilitation of Offenders (Northern Ireland) Order 1978.

NOTES

Commencement: to be appointed (see reg 1 at **[10.1363]**).

[10.1366]

4 Meaning of "relevant activity"

(1) A "relevant activity" is an activity described in paragraph (2) that is to be undertaken by an overseas entity.

(2) The activities described in this paragraph are—

(a) making an application under section 4 of the ECTEA (application for registration);

(b) complying with section 7 of that Act (updating duty);

(c) making an application under section 9 of that Act (application for removal);

(d) complying with a notice under section 27 of that Act (resolving inconsistencies in the register), but only in so far as it relates to any of paragraphs (a), (b) or (c);

(e) making an application under any regulations made under section 29 of that Act (application to rectify register), but only in so far as it relates to any of paragraphs (a), (b), or (c); and

(f) complying with section 42(1)(c) of that Act (requirement for certain unregistered overseas entities to provide information).

NOTES

Commencement: to be appointed (see reg 1 at **[10.1363]**).

[10.1367]

5 Meaning of "relevant information"

(1) "Relevant information" is information described in any of paragraphs (2), (3), (4), (5), (6) or (7).

(2) Where an overseas entity seeks to undertake a relevant activity within regulation 4(2)(a) (application for registration), the information is—

(a) the information specified in the column headed "Information" in the table in section 4(2) of the ECTEA, as that information corresponds to whichever statement is being made as part of the relevant activity in question; and

(b) where relevant, the information mentioned in section 4(3) of that Act.

(3) Where an overseas entity seeks to undertake a relevant activity within regulation 4(2)(b) (updating duty), the information is—

(a) the information mentioned in sub-paragraphs (a) and (b) of paragraph (2) of this regulation;

(b) the information specified in the column headed "Information" in the table in section 7(2) of the ECTEA, as that information corresponds to whichever statement is being made as part of the relevant activity in question; and

(c) where relevant—

(i) the information mentioned in section 7(3) of the ECTEA;

(ii) the information mentioned in section 7(4) of the ECTEA.

(4) Where an overseas entity seeks to undertake a relevant activity within regulation 4(2)(c) (application for removal), the information is—

(a) the information mentioned in sub-paragraphs (a) and (b) of paragraph (2) of this regulation;

(b) the information specified in the column headed "Information" in the table in section 9(2) of the ECTEA, as that information corresponds to whichever statement is being made as part of the relevant activity in question; and

(c) where relevant—

(i) the information mentioned in section 9(3) of the ECTEA;

(ii) the information mentioned in section 9(4) of the ECTEA.

(5) Where an overseas entity seeks to undertake a relevant activity within regulation 4(2)(d) (complying with a notice under section 27 of the ECTEA), the information is such information as the registrar may by notice request.

(6) Where an overseas entity seeks to undertake a relevant activity within regulation 4(2)(e) (making an application under any regulations made under section 29 of the ECTEA), the information is such information as regulations made under section 29 of the ECTEA may specify as required when making that application.

(7) Where an overseas entity seeks to undertake a relevant activity within regulation 4(2)(f) (requirement for certain unregistered overseas entities to provide information), the information is the information mentioned in section 42(1)(c) of the ECTEA.

NOTES

Commencement: to be appointed (see reg 1 at **[10.1363]**).

PART 2 VERIFICATION

[10.1368]

6 Verification: general

(1) An overseas entity may only undertake a relevant activity after a relevant person has verified the relevant information.

(2) Where a relevant person verifies information under paragraph (1), the verification is valid for the period of three months beginning with the day on which the relevant person verifies the information.

(3) Where a relevant person—

(a) has verified relevant information on behalf of an overseas entity; and

(b) delivers the relevant information to the registrar themselves,

they must deliver the statement referred to in paragraph (5) at the same time.

(4) Where a relevant person—

(a) has verified relevant information on behalf of an overseas entity; and

(b) does not deliver that relevant information to the registrar themselves,

they must deliver the statement referred to in paragraph (5) to the registrar within 14 days of that information being delivered to the registrar.

(5) The statement is a statement to the registrar providing—

(a) confirmation that—

(i) the relevant person has undertaken the verification of the relevant information; and

(ii) that verification has complied with the requirements of these Regulations and the ECTEA;

(b) the date on which the verification was undertaken;

(c) the names of the registrable beneficial owners, and as the case may be, the managing officers whose identity has been verified, but where it has not been possible to obtain full names, so much of that information as it has been possible to obtain;

(d) the relevant person's service address;

(e) the relevant person's email address;

(f) the name of the relevant person's supervisory authority;

(g) where available, the relevant person's registration number, or a copy of the certification details, given to the relevant person by their supervisory authority; and

(h) the name of the individual with overall responsibility for identity checks, where that is different to the name of the relevant person.

(6) For the purposes of this regulation—

(a) "supervisory authority" in relation to any relevant person, means the supervisory authority specified for such a person by regulation 7 of the Money Laundering Regulations;

(b) "verify" means verify on the basis of documents or information in either case obtained from a reliable source which is independent of the person whose identity is being verified, and "verified" and "verification" are to be interpreted accordingly;

(c) documents issued or made available by an official body are to be regarded as being independent of a person even if they are provided or made available to the relevant person by or on behalf of that person.

NOTES

Commencement: to be appointed (see reg 1 at **[10.1363]**).

[10.1369]

7 Verification: individuals

(1) This regulation applies where a relevant person seeks to verify relevant information relating to an individual.

(2) A relevant person must not be—

(a) a family member of the individual;

(b) a known close associate of the individual;

(c) the same individual as the information relates to.

(3) An individual's family members include—

(a) their spouse or civil partner;

(b) any other person (whether of a different sex or the same sex) with whom the individual lives as partner in an enduring family relationship;

(c) their grandparent or grandchild, sister, brother, aunt or uncle, or nephew or niece;

(d) their children or step-children;

(e) the spouses or civil partners of those children or step-children;

(f) any other person (whether of a different sex or the same sex) with whom any of those children or step-children lives as partner in an enduring family relationship;

(g) the children or step-children of a person within paragraph (b) (and who are not children or step-children of the individual) who live with the individual and have not attained the age of 18;

(h) their parents.

(4) A known close associate of an individual means—

(a) an individual known to have joint beneficial ownership of a legal entity or a legal arrangement or any other close business relations with the individual;

(b) an individual who has sole beneficial ownership of a legal entity or a legal arrangement which is known to have been set up for the benefit of the individual.

NOTES

Commencement: to be appointed (see reg 1 at **[10.1363]**).

[10.1370]

8 Retention of information

(1) This regulation applies in respect of any material provided to a relevant person by or on behalf of an overseas entity for the purpose of verifying relevant information.

(2) The relevant person must keep copies of the material mentioned in paragraph (1) for the period of five years beginning with the day on which that person verifies the information.

NOTES

Commencement: to be appointed (see reg 1 at **[10.1363]**).

PART 3 INFORMATION PROVIDED UNDER SECTION 42(1)(C) OF THE ECTEA

[10.1371]

9 Provision of information under section 42(1)(c)

(1) Subject to paragraph (2), a person who delivers section 42(1)(c) information to the registrar must do so by email.

(2) Paragraph (1) does not apply in respect of information to which the exception in regulation 4 of the Register of Overseas Entities (Delivery, Protection and Trust Services) Regulations 2022 applies.

NOTES

Commencement: to be appointed (see reg 1 at **[10.1363]**).

[10.1372]

10 Publication of section 42(1)(c) information

(1) Subject to paragraph (2), section 4(2)(1)(c) information must be made available for public inspection for a period of no less than two years, following which the registrar may transfer any such information to the Public Record Office.

(2) The registrar must not make any section 42(1)(c) information available for public inspection where that information comprises material of a type described in section 22 of the ECTEA (material unavailable for inspection).

NOTES

Commencement: to be appointed (see reg 1 at **[10.1363]**).

[10.1373]

11 Modification of section 20 of the ECTEA

Section 20 of the ECTEA (annotation of the register) applies in respect of section 42(1)(c) information as if—

(a) for the heading there were substituted "Annotation of section 42(1)(c) information";

(b) in subsection (1)—

(i) for the words before paragraph (a) there were substituted—

"The registrar may place a note on a document containing section 42(1)(c) information recording";

(ii) for paragraph (a), there were substituted—

"(a) the date on which a document containing section 42(1)(c) information is delivered to the registrar or otherwise in connection with the information";

(c) subsections (2) and (6) were omitted;

(d) in subsection (5), for the words before paragraph (a) there were substituted—

"The exercise of the registrar's power under subsection (1) with respect to annotation of section 42(1)(c) information is subject to the court's power under section 31 (power of court on ordering removal of material) to direct".

(e) after subsection (5) there were inserted—

"(5A) In this section and sections 28 and 30, "section 42(1)(c) information" is information delivered to the registrar under section 42(1)(c) of this Act (requirement for certain unregistered overseas entities to provide information).".

NOTES

Commencement: to be appointed (see reg 1 at **[10.1363]**).

[10.1374]

12 Modification of section 28 of the ECTEA

Section 28 of the ECTEA (administrative removal of material from register) applies in respect of section 42(1)(c) information provided to the registrar as if—

(a) for the heading there were substituted "Administrative removal of section 42(1)(c) information from public inspection";

(b) in subsection (1) in the words before paragraph (a), for "the register" there were substituted "public inspection";

(c) in subsection (2)—

(i) at the end of paragraph (a) there were inserted "or";

(ii) paragraph (c) were omitted.

NOTES

Commencement: to be appointed (see reg 1 at **[10.1363]**).

[10.1375]

13 Modification of section 30 of the ECTEA

Section 30 of the ECTEA (court order to rectify register) applies in respect of section 42(1)(c) information as if—

(a) for the heading there were substituted "Court order to remove section 42(1)(c) information from public inspection";

(b) in subsection (1)—

(i) in the words before paragraph (a), for "the register" there were substituted "public inspection";

(ii) in the words after paragraph (b), for "the register" there were substituted "public inspection";

(c) subsections (2) and (3) were omitted.

NOTES
Commencement: to be appointed (see reg 1 at **[10.1363]**).

REGISTER OF OVERSEAS ENTITIES (DELIVERY, PROTECTION AND TRUST SERVICES) REGULATIONS 2022

(SI 2022/870)

NOTES
Made: 25 July 2022.
Authority: Economic Crime (Transparency and Enforcement) Act 2022, ss 25(1), (3)(a)–(d), (f), (4), 67(2), Sch 2, para 7(1)(f); Companies Act 2006, ss 1069(1), 1292(1)(a), (b).
Commencement: to be appointed (see reg 1 at **[10.1376]**).

ARRANGEMENT OF REGULATIONS

PART 1 INTRODUCTORY

[10.1376]
1 Citation, commencement and extent

(1) These Regulations may be cited as the Register of Overseas Entities (Delivery, Protection and Trust Services) Regulations 2022 and come into force on the day section 3 of the ECTEA comes into force.

(2) These Regulations extend to England and Wales, Scotland and Northern Ireland.

NOTES
Commencement: to be appointed (see above).

[10.1377]
2 Interpretation

In these Regulations—

"the ECTEA" means the Economic Crime (Transparency and Enforcement) Act 2022;

"former name" means a name by which an individual was formerly known for business purposes;

"managing officer", in respect of an overseas entity, has the meaning given in section 44(1) of the ECTEA;

"name" means a person's first name (or other forename) and surname, except in the case of—

(a) a peer; or
(b) an individual usually known by a title,

the title may be stated instead of that person's first name (or other forename) and surname or in addition to either or both of them;

"overseas entity" has the meaning given in section 2 of the ECTEA;

"overseas entity ID" means an overseas entity ID allocated in accordance with section 5 of the ECTEA;

"protected information", in relation to a relevant individual, means—

(a) the name, any former name, date of birth and nationality of the relevant individual;
(b) the usual residential address of the relevant individual;
(c) a service address of the applicant;
(d) the e-mail address of the applicant, if any;
(e) the fact that the relevant individual is, or used to be, a relevant individual in respect of the overseas entity;

"registrable beneficial owner", in relation to an overseas entity, has the meaning given in Schedule 2 to the ECTEA;

"the registrar" means the registrar of companies for England and Wales;

"relevant individual" has the meaning given in section 25(2) of the ECTEA;

"specified public authority" means a public authority specified in Schedule 1.

NOTES

Commencement: to be appointed (see reg 1 at **[10.1376]**).

PART 2 ELECTRONIC DELIVERY OF DOCUMENTS

[10.1378]

3 Duty to deliver documents by electronic means

Subject to regulation 4 (exception to the duty to deliver documents by electronic means), the following documents must be delivered to the registrar by electronic means—

(a) an application for registration made under section 4 of the ECTEA (application for registration);
(b) the statements, information and any other thing required to be delivered to the registrar and referred to in section 7 of the ECTEA (updating duty);
(c) an application for removal made under section 9 of the ECTEA (application for removal);
(d) the replacement or additional documents referred to in section 27(2)(b) of the ECTEA (resolving inconsistencies in the register); and
(e) an application to rectify the register made under any regulations made under section 29 of the ECTEA (application to rectify register).

NOTES

Commencement: to be appointed (see reg 1 at **[10.1376]**).

[10.1379]

4 Exception to the duty to deliver documents by electronic means

(1) The duty to deliver a document by electronic means in regulation 3 does not apply where the document relates to an application which has been made under regulation 7 and that application—

(a) has not yet been determined by the registrar and has not been withdrawn under regulation 9;
(b) has been determined by the registrar in favour of the applicant (but see paragraph (3));
(c) was unsuccessful and a period of 42 days beginning with the date of the notice sent under regulation 7(7) has not passed;
(d) was unsuccessful and an appeal to the court in respect of that application under regulation 10 has not been determined by the court; or
(e) was unsuccessful but the applicant has successfully appealed the determination and the final determination is that the application is successful (but see paragraph (3)).

(2) For the purposes of paragraph (1), a document relates to such an application where the document is to be delivered by or in respect of the same overseas entity in relation of which P is or used to be a registerable beneficial owner or a managing officer, where P is the relevant individual in respect of whom the application under regulation 7 has been made.

(3) Paragraph (1)(b) and (e) do not apply where the determination has ceased to have effect under regulation 12 (duration of a determination under regulation 7).

NOTES

Commencement: to be appointed (see reg 1 at **[10.1376]**).

PART 3 PROTECTION OF INFORMATION

[10.1380]

5 Circumstances where the registrar must make information relating to a relevant individual unavailable for public inspection

(1) The registrar must make protected information relating to a relevant individual (whether that information is on the register or otherwise) unavailable for public inspection if—

(a) in relation to that information, an application has been made under regulation 7 which—
   (i) has not yet been determined by the registrar and has not been withdrawn under regulation 9;
   (ii) has been determined by the registrar in favour of the applicant (but see paragraph (4));
   (iii) was unsuccessful and a period of 42 days beginning with the date of the notice sent under regulation 7(7) has not passed;
   (iv) was unsuccessful and an appeal to the court in respect of that application under regulation 10 has not been determined by the court; or
   (v) was unsuccessful but the applicant has successfully appealed the determination and the final determination is that the application is successful (but see paragraph (4); and

(b) that information is contained in a document delivered to the registrar in which such information is required to be stated and, in the case of a document having more than one part, the protected information is contained in a part of the document in which such information is required to be stated.

(2) The registrar is not obliged to check documents, other than those described in paragraph (1)(b), to ensure the absence of protected information in relation to which an application under regulation 7 has been made.

(3) If the protected information in relation to which an application under regulation 7 is made is available for public inspection at the time that the application is made, the registrar must comply with paragraph (1) as soon as reasonably practicable.

(4) Paragraphs (ii) and (v) of paragraph (1)(a) do not apply where the determination has ceased to have effect under regulation 12 (duration of a determination under regulation 7).

(5) For the purposes of this regulation, an application under regulation 7 is made when it has been registered by the registrar.

NOTES

Commencement: to be appointed (see reg 1 at **[10.1376]**).

[10.1381]

6 Circumstances where the registrar must not disclose protected information

(1) Subject to paragraph (3), the registrar must not disclose protected information if in relation to that information an application has been made under regulation 7 which—

(a) has not yet been determined by the registrar and has not been withdrawn under regulation 9;

(b) has been determined by the registrar in favour of the applicant (but see paragraph (2));

(c) was unsuccessful and a period of 42 days beginning with the date of the notice sent under regulation 7(7) has not passed;

(d) was unsuccessful and an appeal to the court in respect of that application under regulation 10 has not been determined by the court; or

(e) was unsuccessful but the applicant has successfully appealed the determination and the final determination is that the application is successful (but see paragraph (2)).

(2) Sub-paragraphs (b) and (e) of paragraph (1) do not apply where the determination has ceased to have effect under regulation 12 (duration of a determination under regulation 7).

(3) Where the prohibition in paragraph (1) applies, the registrar may disclose that protected information—

(a) for communicating with the person to whom the application under regulation 7 relates and, if different, the applicant;

(b) to a specified public authority where the conditions specified in Schedule 2 are satisfied; and

(c) for the purposes of referring any question under regulation 8(1)(b).

(4) For the purposes of this regulation, an application under regulation 7 is made when it has been registered by the registrar.

NOTES

Commencement: to be appointed (see reg 1 at **[10.1376]**).

[10.1382]

7 Application to protect information relating to a relevant individual

(1) A relevant individual, or an overseas entity on behalf of a relevant individual, may make an application to the registrar requiring the registrar to—

(a) make protected information relating to that relevant individual unavailable for public inspection; and

(b) refrain from disclosing protected information relating to that relevant individual.

(2) An overseas entity may only make an application under paragraph (1) where the relevant individual has given consent for the overseas entity to make the application on their behalf.

(3) The grounds on which an application may be made are that the applicant reasonably believes that if that protected information is available for public inspection or disclosed by the registrar—

(a) the activities of that overseas entity; or

(b) one or more characteristics or personal attributes of the relevant individual when associated with that overseas entity,

will put the relevant individual or a person living with the relevant individual at serious risk of being subjected to violence or intimidation.

(4) The application must contain—

(a) a statement of the grounds on which the application is made;

(b) the name, any former name, date of birth and nationality of the relevant individual;

(c) the usual residential address of the relevant individual;

(d) a service address of the applicant, which may be stated as the entity's registered or principal office where the applicant is or used to be a managing officer;

(e) the e-mail address of the applicant, if any;

(f) the name, registered number, overseas entity ID if any and address of the overseas entity in respect of which the relevant individual is or used to be a registerable beneficial owner or managing officer;

(g) where the relevant individual is or used to be a registerable beneficial owner, a statement as to—

(i) the date on which the individual became a registrable beneficial owner in respect of the overseas entity;

(ii) which of the conditions in paragraph 6 of Schedule 2 to the ECTEA is met in relation to the registrable beneficial owner and a statement as to why the condition is met;

(iii) whether the relevant individual meets that condition by virtue of being a trustee;

(iv) whether the relevant individual is a designated person within the meaning of section 9(2) of the Sanctions and Anti-Money Laundering Act 2018, where that information is publicly available;

(h) where the relevant individual is or used to be a managing officer—

(i) the business occupation of the relevant individual;

(ii) a description of the officer's roles and responsibilities in respect of the overseas entity;

(i) where the application is made by an overseas entity, confirmation that the relevant individual consents to the making of the application.

(5) The application must be accompanied by evidence which supports the applicant's statement of the grounds on which the application is made.

(6) Where a relevant individual makes an application under paragraph (1) to the registrar, that individual must inform the overseas entity in respect of which the relevant individual is or used to be a registerable beneficial owner or managing officer of that fact as soon as reasonably practicable.

(7) The registrar must determine the application and, within 7 days beginning with the date that the determination is made, send notice of the determination to the applicant and, where they are not the applicant, the relevant individual or overseas entity (as the case may be).

(8) Where the application is unsuccessful, the notice under paragraph (7) must inform the relevant individual and the overseas entity of the right to apply for permission to appeal against the determination within 28 days beginning with the date of the notice.

NOTES

Commencement: to be appointed (see reg 1 at **[10.1376]**).

[10.1383]

8 Matters relating to an application made under regulation 7

(1) For the purpose of determining an application made under regulation 7 the registrar may—

(a) direct that additional information or evidence should be delivered to the registrar;

(b) refer any question relating to an assessment of the nature or extent of any risk of violence or intimidation to any person the registrar considers may be able to assist in making that assessment; and

(c) accept any answer to a question referred under paragraph (1)(b) as providing sufficient evidence of the nature or extent of any risk.

(2) The registrar must not make available for public inspection—

(a) any application made under regulation 7;

(b) any documents provided in support of that application;

(c) any notice provided under regulation 9 (notice of withdrawal of application);

(d) any notice provided under regulation 10 (notice of an appeal);

(e) any notice provided under regulation 12 (notice that determination no longer wanted);

(f) any representations delivered under regulation 13 (representations as to why determination should not be revoked); or

(g) any notice provided under regulation 13(1)(a)(ii) and (4) (notices of revocation).

(3) A person who makes an application under regulation 7 must inform the registrar in writing without delay upon becoming aware of any change to any information or evidence provided to the registrar in connection with the application.

(4) When a relevant individual makes an application under regulation 7, the registrar must inform in writing without delay the overseas entity in respect of which the relevant individual is or used to be a registrable beneficial owner or a managing officer that the exception in regulation 4(1)(a) (exceptions to the duty to deliver documents by electronic means) applies.

(5) For the purposes of this regulation, an application under regulation 7 is made when it has been registered by the registrar.

NOTES

Commencement: to be appointed (see reg 1 at **[10.1376]**).

[10.1384]

9 Withdrawal of an application made under regulation 7

(1) The registrar is not required to determine an application which has not yet been determined under regulation 7(7) where—

(a) the applicant, or

(b) where not the applicant, a relevant individual in respect of whom the application has been made,

notifies the registrar in writing that they no longer wish the registrar to determine the application.

(2) An overseas entity may only notify the registrar under paragraph (1) where the relevant individual has given consent for the overseas entity to make the notification on their behalf.

(3) Where a relevant individual in respect of whom an application under regulation 7 has been made sends a notification to the registrar under paragraph (1), that relevant individual must notify the overseas entity in respect of which that relevant individual is or used to be a registrable beneficial owner or a managing officer as soon as reasonably practicable.

(4) Where the registrar receives a notification under paragraph (1), the registrar must send a confirmation of receipt of that notification to the person who notified the registrar and must include in that confirmation a statement that—

(a) the application will not be determined; and

(b) information relating to the relevant individual will be available for public inspection and can be disclosed by the registrar.

NOTES

Commencement: to be appointed (see reg 1 at **[10.1376]**).

[10.1385]

10 Appealing against an unsuccessful application made under regulation 7

(1) Subject to paragraph (3)—

(a) an applicant who has received notice under regulation 7(7) that the application has been unsuccessful, or

(b) where such an applicant was an overseas entity, the relevant individual to which the application related,

may appeal to the High Court or, in Scotland, the Court of Session on the grounds mentioned in paragraph (2).

(2) The grounds referred to in paragraph (1) are that the determination—

(a) is unlawful;

(b) is irrational or unreasonable; or

(c) has been made on the basis of a procedural impropriety or otherwise contravenes the rules of natural justice.

(3) No appeal may be brought unless the permission of the court has been obtained.

(4) No application for such permission may be made after 28 days beginning with the date of the notice under regulation 7(7) unless the court is satisfied that there was good reason for the failure of the applicant to seek permission before the end of that period.

(5) An applicant who seeks permission to appeal must serve written notice of the application on the registrar within 7 days beginning with the date on which the application for permission was issued.

(6) The court determining an appeal may—

(a) dismiss the appeal; or

(b) quash the determination.

(7) Where the court quashes a determination it may refer the matter to the registrar with a direction to reconsider it and make a further determination under regulation 7(7) in accordance with the findings of the court.

NOTES

Commencement: to be appointed (see reg 1 at **[10.1376]**).

[10.1386]

11 Unsuccessful determination made under regulation 7

(1) This regulation applies where the registrar has made a determination in respect of an application made under regulation 7 that is not in favour of the applicant (an unsuccessful application).

(2) The registrar must make available for public inspection protected information to which the application under regulation 7 relates—

(a) where notice of an application for permission to appeal has not been served on the registrar in accordance with regulation 10(5), as soon as reasonably practicable after the end of the period of 42 days beginning with the date of the notice given under regulation 7(7); or

(b) where notice of an application for permission to appeal has been served on the registrar in accordance with regulation 10(5), as soon as reasonably practicable after—

(i) the court has dismissed the application for permission to appeal or has dismissed the appeal and there is no further appeal pending; or

(ii) the registrar becomes aware that the application for permission to appeal or the appeal has been subsequently withdrawn or abandoned.

(3) Where the registrar makes protected information available for public inspection under this regulation, the registrar must notify the relevant individual to whom the protected information relates and the overseas entity in respect of which the relevant individual is or used to be a registrable beneficial owner or a managing officer of that action as soon as reasonably practicable.

NOTES

Commencement: to be appointed (see reg 1 at **[10.1376]**).

[10.1387]

12 Duration of a determination under regulation 7

(1) A determination under regulation 7(7) that an application is successful continues to have effect until—

(a) the person to whom the determination relates notifies the registrar in writing that they wish the determination to cease to have effect; or

(b) the registrar revokes the determination under regulation 13.

(2) Where a notice is given under paragraph (1)(a), the person giving the notice must also notify the overseas entity to which the application that was determined relates of the notice given to the registrar.

NOTES

Commencement: to be appointed (see reg 1 at **[10.1376]**).

[10.1388]

13 Revocation of a determination under regulation 7(7)

(1) The registrar may revoke a determination made under regulation 7(7) that an application is successful if—

(a)

(i) the applicant in relation to the determination or (if different) any person to whom the application relates has been found guilty of an offence under section 32 of the ECTEA (general false statement offence) in respect of purported compliance with any provision of this Part;

(ii) the registrar has sent a notice in accordance with paragraph (2) to the applicant in relation to the determination and (if different) the relevant individual to whom the determination relates; and

(iii) the period of 28 days beginning with the date of that notice has expired; or

(b) the registrar is notified, or otherwise becomes aware, that the relevant individual has died or become incapacitated.

(2) The notice mentioned in paragraph (1)(a)(ii) must inform the addressee—

(a) of the registrar's intention to revoke the determination;

(b) that the addressee may, within 28 days beginning with the date of the notice, deliver representations in writing to the registrar as to why the registrar should not revoke the determination; and

(c) that if the registrar receives such representations within that period, the registrar will have regard to the representations in deciding whether to revoke the determination.

(3) If within the period specified in paragraph (2)(b) an addressee of the notice delivers representations in writing to the registrar as to why the registrar should not revoke the determination, the registrar must have regard to the representations in deciding whether to revoke the determination.

(4) The registrar must send notice of the registrar's decision as to whether to revoke a determination to the applicant in relation to the determination and (if different) the relevant individual to whom the determination relates within 7 days beginning with the date of the decision.

(5) Where the registrar has made a decision to revoke a determination, the registrar must make protected information to which the determination relates available for public inspection as soon as reasonably practicable after sending the notice mentioned in paragraph (4).

(6) Where the registrar makes protected information available for public inspection under this regulation, the registrar must notify the person to whom the protected information relates and the overseas entity to which the application under regulation 7 related of that action as soon as reasonably practicable.

NOTES

Commencement: to be appointed (see reg 1 at **[10.1376]**).

PART 4 REGISTRABLE BENEFICIAL OWNERS: SCHEDULE 2 TO THE ECTEA

[10.1389]

14 Description of legal entity subject to its own disclosure requirements

(1) A legal entity is specified for the purposes of paragraph 7(1)(f) of Schedule 2 (registrable beneficial owners) to the ECTEA as "subject to its own disclosure requirements", if—

(a) it is a legal entity governed by the law of a country or territory outside the United Kingdom;

(b) it provides trust services; and

(c) the provision of trust services is regulated in that country or territory by a supervisory authority.

(2) In this regulation "trust services" means acting as a trustee of a trust or similar legal arrangement.

NOTES

Commencement: to be appointed (see reg 1 at **[10.1376]**).

SCHEDULES

SCHEDULE 1
SPECIFIED PUBLIC AUTHORITIES

Regulation 2

[10.1390]

1. The Bank of England.

2. The Charity Commission.

3. The Charity Commission for Northern Ireland.

4. The Commissioners for Her Majesty's Revenue and Customs.

5. The Competition and Markets Authority.

6. The Crown Office and Procurator Fiscal Services.

7. The Director of Public Prosecutions.

8. The Director of Public Prosecutions for Northern Ireland.

9. The Financial Conduct Authority.

10. The Food Standards Agency.

11. The Gas and Electricity Markets Authority.

12. The Gambling Commission.

13. The Gangmasters Licensing Authority.

14. The Government Communications Headquarters.

15. The Health and Safety Executive.

16. The Health and Safety Executive for Northern Ireland.

17. The Marine Management Organisation.

18. The Minister for the Cabinet Office.

19. The National Crime Agency.

20. The Northern Ireland Authority for Utility Regulation.

21. Any Northern Ireland Department.

22. The Office of Communications.

23. The Office of the Information Commissioner.

24. The Office for Nuclear Regulation.

25. The Office of the Scottish Charity Regulator.

26. The Official Receiver for Northern Ireland.

27. The Panel on Takeovers and Mergers.

28. The Pensions Regulator.

29. The Prudential Regulation Authority.

30. The Registry of Credit Unions and Industrial and Provident Societies for Northern Ireland.

31. The Regulator of Community Interest Companies.

32. The Scottish Housing Regulator.

33. The Scottish Ministers.

34. The Security Industry Authority.

35. The Secret Intelligence Service.

36. The Secretary of State.

37. The Security Service.

38. The Serious Fraud Office.

39. The Treasury.

40. The Treasury Solicitor.

41. The Welsh Ministers.

42. A local authority within the meaning of section 54(2) of the Companies Act 2006.

43. An official receiver appointed under section 399 of the Insolvency Act 1986 (appointment, etc, of official receivers).

44. A person acting as an insolvency practitioner within the meaning of section 388 of the Insolvency Act 1986 (meaning of "act as an insolvency practitioner") or Article 3 of the Insolvency (Northern Ireland) Order 1989 ("act as an insolvency practitioner").

45. An inspector appointed under Part 14 of the Companies Act 1985 (investigation of companies and their affairs: requisition of documents) or a person appointed under regulation 30 of the Open-Ended Investment Companies Regulations 2001 (power to investigate) or regulation 30 of the Open-Ended Investment Companies Regulations (Northern Ireland) 2004.

46. Any person authorised to exercise powers under section 447 of the Companies Act 1985 (power to require documents and information), or section 84 of the Companies Act 1989 (exercise of powers by officers, etc).

47. Any person exercising functions conferred by Part 6 of the Financial Services and Markets Act 2000 (official listing).

48. A person appointed to make a report under section 166 or 166A (reports by skilled persons) of the Financial Services and Markets Act 2000.

49. A person appointed to conduct an investigation under section 167 (appointment of persons to carry out general investigations) or 168(3) or (5) (appointment of persons to carry out investigations in particular cases) of the Financial Services and Markets Act 2000.

50. A person appointed under section 284 (power to investigate) of the Financial Services and Markets Act 2000.

51. A police force within the meaning of section 101(1) of the Police Act 1996.

52. The Police Service of Northern Ireland.

53. The Police Service of Scotland.

54. The lead enforcement authority (as defined in section 24A of the Estate Agents Act 1979) exercising functions under the Estate Agents Act 1979.

NOTES

Commencement: to be appointed (see reg 1 at **[10.1376]**).

SCHEDULE 2
CONDITIONS FOR PERMITTED DISCLOSURE

Regulation 6(3)(b)

[10.1391]

1. The specified public authority has delivered to the registrar a statement that it intends to use the information only for the purpose of facilitating the carrying out by that specified public authority of a public function ("the permitted purpose").

2. Subject to paragraph 3, the specified public authority has delivered to the registrar a statement that, where it supplies a copy of the information to a processor for the purpose of processing the information for use in respect of the permitted purpose, the specified public authority will—

(a) ensure that the processor is one who carries on business in the United Kingdom or the European Economic Area;

(b) require that the processor does not transmit the information outside the area comprising the United Kingdom and the European Economic Area; and

(c) require that the processor does not disclose the information except to that specified public authority or an employee of that specified public authority.

3. Paragraph 2 does not apply where the specified public authority is the National Crime Agency, Secret Intelligence Service, Security Service or Government Communications Headquarters.

4. The specified public authority has delivered any information or evidence required by the registrar for the purpose of enabling the registrar to determine in accordance with these Regulations whether to disclose the information.

5. The specified public authority has complied with any requirement by the registrar to confirm the accuracy of the statements, information or evidence delivered to the registrar pursuant to this Schedule.

6. In this Schedule—

(a) "processor" means any person who provides a service which consists of putting information into data form or processing information in data form and any reference to a processor includes a reference to the processor's employees;

(b) "public function" includes—

  (i) any function conferred by or in accordance with any provision contained in any enactment;

  (ii) any similar function conferred on persons by or under provisions having effect as part of the law of a country or territory outside the United Kingdom; and

  (iii) any function exercisable in relation to the investigation of any criminal offence or for the purpose of any criminal proceedings; and

(c) any reference to the disclosure for the purpose of facilitating the carrying out of a public function includes disclosure in relation to, and for the purpose of, any proceedings whether civil, criminal or disciplinary in which the specified public authority engages while carrying out its public functions.

NOTES

Commencement: to be appointed (see reg 1 at **[10.1376]**).

PART 11
SELECTED EU LEGISLATION & RETAINED EU LEGISLATION

GENERAL NOTE – GENERAL SCHEME OF LEGISLATION CONTAINED IN THIS PART

CONTENT OF THIS PART

This Part contains:

(i) European Union Directives;

(ii) European Union Regulations – which divide into two categories, Regulations adopted or which apply only post-IP completion date (11pm, 31 December 2020), and Regulations which fall into the category of Retained EU Law, and which continue to apply with modifications to the UK.

STYLE OF NOTES USED IN THIS PART ETC

This Part contains the current texts of relevant EU Directives. It should be emphasised that these EU Directives no longer apply to the UK, but continue to apply to the EU, and remain of importance to those conducting business in the EU, hence their continued inclusion. Note that, although EU Directives are no longer applicable in the UK, legislation that is derived from such Directives (as transposed into UK law before Brexit) continues to apply. As to the status of "EU-derived domestic legislation" after IP completion day, see s 2 of the 2018 Act at **[12.4]**. "EU-derived domestic legislation" is defined in s 1B(7) of the 2018 Act, and includes all UK legislation made under s 2(2) of the European Communities Act 1972.

This Part also contains the current texts of relevant EU Regulations. The position with respect to EU Regulations is that the European Union (Withdrawal) Act 2018 directly incorporated into UK law specified elements of what was, before IP completion day, European Union law. See s 3 of the 2018 Act at **[12.5]** (Incorporation of direct EU legislation). As a consequence, The Regulations included in this Part, therefore fall into two categories:

• Firstly, Regulations that were fully operative before IP completion day. These Regulations continue to apply directly in the EU, and also apply (as Retained EU legislation) in the UK. The main version of the text is that applicable in the EU, and all amendments that apply to the UK are set out in the Notes to the affected provision.

With regard to such provisions, note the following:

— a bold heading, "**Application of this Article in relation to the UK**", has been added to all Part 11 materials to indicate where amendments have been made to Retained EU Legislation which are applicable only to the UK.

— Where an Article (etc) has been repealed in relation to the UK only, a bold heading, "**Repeal of this Article in relation to the UK**", has been added, along with details of the repealing instrument, and any applicable savings and transitional provisions.

— For ease of reference, in circumstances where there have been substantial amendments to an Article (etc) made by the various UK Exiting the EU Regulations (or Technical Standards Instruments made by the Financial Conduct Authority), the whole provision, as amended, has been reproduced in the Notes. This is the version of the provision that applied in the UK on IP completion day, with all subsequent (ie, post-IP completion day) amendments noted in the usual Handbook style.

• Secondly, Regulations which either come into force, or are specified to apply, after IP completion day. These Regulations do not apply in the UK, but are reproduced in this edition because the broader picture of EU regulation of company law remains of interest and importance, especially to those advising companies operating within the EU. In such cases, the following note is included in the introductory notes to the Regulation concerned:

"**This Regulation does not apply to the United Kingdom:** this Regulation was not "operative immediately before IP completion day" within the meaning of the European Union (Withdrawal) Act 2018, s 3 at **[12.5]** and, therefore, does not form part of domestic law on and after IP completion day.".

DIRECTIVE OF THE EUROPEAN PARLIAMENT AND OF THE COUNCIL

(2001/34/EC)

of 28 May 2001

on the admission of securities to official stock exchange listing and on information to be published on those securities

[11.1]

NOTES

Date of publication in OJ: OJ L184, 6.7.2001, p 1.

This Directive is reproduced as amended by: European Parliament and Council Directive 2003/6/EC (transposition date 12 October 2004); European Parliament and Council Directive 2003/71/EC (transposition date 1 July 2005); European Parliament and Council Directive 2004/109/EC (transposition date 20 January 2007); European Parliament and Council Directive 2005/1/EC (transposition date 13 May 2005).

Editorial note (legal status of EU Directives in the UK): note that EU Directives are not "direct EU legislation" within the meaning of the European Union (Withdrawal) Act 2018, s 3 at **[12.5]** and, accordingly, do not apply to the UK. As to the status of EU-derived domestic legislation after IP completion day (11pm on 31 December 2020), see s 2 of the 2018 Act at **[12.4]**. As to the UK implementation of this Directive, see the note below.

UK Implementation: in the UK this Directive was implemented by the Financial Services and Markets Act 2000 (Disclosure of Confidential Information) (Amendment) (No 2) Regulations 2001, SI 2001/3624 which amended the Financial Services and Markets Act 2000 (Disclosure of Confidential Information) Regulations 2001, SI 2001/2188.

THE EUROPEAN PARLIAMENT AND THE COUNCIL OF THE EUROPEAN UNION,

Having regard to the Treaty establishing the European Economic Community, and in particular Articles 44 and 95 thereof,

Having regard to the proposal from the Commission,

Having regard to the Opinion of the Economic and Social Committee,[1]

Acting in accordance with the procedure laid down in Article 251 of the Treaty,[2]

Whereas—

(1) Council Directive 79/279/EEC of 5 March 1979 coordinating the conditions for the admission of securities to official stock exchange listing,[3] Council Directive 80/390/EEC of 17 March 1980 coordinating the requirements for the drawing up, scrutiny and distribution of the listing particulars to be published for the admission of securities to official stock exchange listing,[4] Council Directive 82/121/EEC of 15 February 1982 on information to be published on a regular basis by companies the shares of which have been admitted to official stock-exchange listing[5] and Council Directive 88/627/EEC of 12 December 1988 on the information to be published when a major holding in a listed company is acquired or disposed of[6] have been substantially amended several times. In the interests of clarity and rationality, the said Directives should therefore be codified by grouping them together in a single text.

(2) The coordination of the conditions for the admission of securities to official listing on stock exchanges situated or operating in the Member States is likely to provide equivalent protection for investors at Community level, because of the more uniform guarantees offered to investors in the various Member States, it will facilitate both the admission to official stock exchange listing, in each such State, of securities from other Member States and the listing of any given security on a number of stock exchanges in the Community; it will accordingly make for greater interpenetration of national securities markets by removing those obstacles that may prudently be removed and therefore contribute to the prospect of establishing a European capital market.

(3) Such coordination must therefore apply to securities, independently of the legal status of their issuers, and must therefore also apply to securities issued by non-member States or their regional or local authorities or international public bodies; this Directive therefore covers entities not covered by the second paragraph of Article 48 of the Treaty.

(4) There should be the possibility of a right to apply to the courts against decisions by the competent national authorities in respect of the application of this Directive, concerning the admission of securities to official listing, although such right to apply must not be allowed to restrict the discretion of these authorities.

(5) Initially, this coordination of the conditions for admission of securities to official listing should be sufficiently flexible to enable account to be taken of present differences in the structures of securities markets in the Member States and to enable the Member States to take account of any specific situations with which they may be confronted.

(6) For this reason, coordination should first be limited to the establishment of minimum conditions for the admission of securities to official listing on stock exchanges situated or operating in the Member States, without however giving issuers any right to listing.

(7) This partial coordination of the conditions for admission to official listing constitutes a first step towards subsequent closer alignment of the rules of Member States in this field.

(8) The market in which undertakings operate has been enlarged to embrace the whole Community and this enlargement involves a corresponding increase in their financial requirements and extension of the capital markets on which they must call to satisfy them; admission to official listing on stock exchanges of Member States of securities issued by undertakings constitutes an important means of access to these capital markets; furthermore exchange restrictions on the purchase of securities traded on the stock exchanges of another Member State have been eliminated as part of the liberalisation of capital movements.

(9) Safeguards for the protection of the interests of actual and potential investors are required in most Member States of undertakings offering their securities to the public, either at the time of their offer or of their admission to official stock exchange listing; such safeguards require the provision of information which is sufficient

and as objective as possible concerning the financial circumstances of the issuer and particulars of the securities for which admission to official listing is requested; the form under which this information is required usually consists of the publication of listing particulars.

(10) The safeguards required differ from Member State to Member State, both as regards the contents and the layout of the listing particulars and the efficacy, methods and timing of the check on the information given therein; the effect of these differences is not only to make it more difficult for undertakings to obtain admission of securities to official listing on stock exchanges of several Member States but also to hinder the acquisition by investors residing in one Member State of securities listed on stock exchanges of other Member States and thus to inhibit the financing of the undertakings and investment throughout the Community.

(11) These differences should be eliminated by coordinating the rules and regulations without necessarily making them completely uniform, in order to achieve an adequate degree of equivalence in the safeguards required in each Member State to ensure the provision of information which is sufficient and as objective as possible for actual or potential security holders.

(12) Such coordination must apply to securities independently of the legal status of the issuing undertaking; this Directive applies to entities to which no reference is made in the second paragraph of Article 48 of the Treaty.

(13) Mutual recognition of listing particulars to be published for the admission of securities to official listing represents an important step forward in the creation of the Community's internal market.

(14) In this connection, it is necessary to specify which authorities are competent to check and approve listing particulars to be published for the admission of securities to official listing in the event of simultaneous applications for admission to official listing in two or more Member States.

(15) Article 21 of Council Directive 89/298/EEC of 17 April 1989 coordinating the requirements for the drawing-up, scrutiny and distribution of the prospectus to be published when transferable securities are offered to the public[7] provides that where public offers are made simultaneously or within short intervals of one another in two or more Member States, a public-offer prospectus drawn up and approved in accordance with Article 7, 8 or 12 of that Directive must be recognised as a public-offer prospectus in the other Member States concerned on the basis of mutual recognition.

(16) It is also desirable to provide the recognition of a public-offer prospectus as listing particulars where admission to official stock-exchange listing is requested within a short period of the public offer.

(17) The mutual recognition of a public-offer prospectus and admission to official listings does not in itself confer a right to admissions.

(18) It is advisable to provide for the extension, by means of agreements to be concluded by the Community with non-member countries, of the recognition of listing particulars for admission to official listings from those countries on a reciprocal basis.

(19) It seems appropriate to provide for the possibility for the Member State in which admission to official listing is sought in certain cases to grant partial or complete exemption from the obligation to publish listing particulars for admission to official listings to issuers the securities of which have already been admitted to official stock-exchange listing in another Member State.

(20) Companies which have already been listed in the Community for some time and are of high quality and international standing are the most likely candidates for cross-border listing. Those companies are generally well known in most Member States: information concerning them is widely circulated and available.

(21) The aim of this Directive is to ensure that sufficient information is provided for investors; therefore, when such a company seeks to have its securities admitted to listing in a host Member State, investors operating on the market in that country may be sufficiently protected by receiving only simplified information rather than full listing particulars.

(22) Member States may find it useful to establish non-discriminatory minimum quantitative criteria, such as the current equity market capitalisation, which issuers must fulfil to be eligible to benefit from the possibilities for exemption provided for in this Directive; given the increasing integration of securities markets, it should equally be open to the competent authorities to give smaller companies similar treatment.

(23) Furthermore, many stock exchanges have second-tier markets in order to deal in shares of companies not admitted to official listing; in some cases the second-tier markets are regulated and supervised by authorities recognised by public bodies that impose on companies disclosure requirements equivalent in substance to those imposed on officially listed companies; therefore, the principle underlying Article 23 of this Directive could also be applied when such companies seek to have their securities admitted to official listing.

(24) In order to protect investors the documents intended to be made available to the public must first be sent to the competent authorities in the Member State in which admission to official listing is sought; it is for that Member State to decide whether those documents should be scrutinised by its competent authorities and to determine, if necessary, the nature and the manner in which that scrutiny should be carried out.

(25) In the case of securities admitted to official stock-exchange listing, the protection of investors requires that the latter be supplied with appropriate regular information throughout the entire period during which the securities are listed; coordination of requirements for this regular information has similar objectives to those envisaged for the listing particulars, namely to improve such protection and to make it more equivalent, to facilitate the listing of these securities on more than one stock exchange in the Community, and in so doing to contribute towards the establishment of a genuine Community capital market by permitting a fuller inter-penetration of securities markets.

(26) Under this Directive, listed companies must as soon as possible make available to investors their annual accounts and report giving information on the company for the whole of the financial year; whereas the Fourth Council Directive 78/660/EEC[8] has coordinated the laws, regulations and administrative provisions of the Member States concerning the annual accounts of certain types of companies.

(27) Companies should also, at least once during each financial year, make available to investors reports on their activities; this Directive can, consequently, be confined to coordinating the content and distribution of a single report covering the first six months of the financial year.

(28) However, in the case of ordinary debentures, because of the rights they confer on their holders, the protection

of investors by means of the publication of a half-yearly report is not essential; by virtue of this Directive, convertible or exchangeable debentures and debentures with warrants may be admitted to official listing only if the related shares are already listed on the same stock exchange or on another regulated, regularly operating, recognised open market or are so admitted simultaneously; the Member States may derogate from this principle only if their competent authorities are satisfied that holders have at their disposal all the information necessary to form an opinion concerning the value of the shares to which these debentures relate; consequently, regular information needs to be coordinated only for companies whose shares are admitted to official stock-exchange listing.

(29) The half-yearly report must enable investors to make an informed appraisal of the general development of the company's activities during the period covered by the report; however, this report need contain only the essential details on the financial position and general progress of the business of the company in question.

(30) So as to ensure the effective protection of investors and the proper operation of stock exchanges, the rules relating to regular information to be published by companies, the shares of which are admitted to official stock-exchange listing within the Community, should apply not only to companies from Member States, but also to companies from non-member countries.

(31) A policy of adequate information of investors in the field of transferable securities is likely to improve investor protection, to increase investors' confidence in securities markets and thus to ensure that securities markets function correctly.

(32) By making such protection more equivalent, coordination of that policy at Community level is likely to make for greater inter-penetration of the Member States' transferable securities markets and therefore help to establish a true European capital market.

(33) To that end investors should be informed of major holdings and of changes in those holdings in Community companies the shares of which are officially listed on stock exchanges situated or operating within the Community.

(34) Coordinated rules should be laid down concerning the detailed content and the procedure for applying that requirement.

(35) Companies, the shares of which are officially listed on a Community stock exchange, can inform the public of changes in major holdings only if they have been informed of such changes by the holders of those holdings.

(36) Most Member States do not subject holders to such a requirement and where such a requirement exists there are appreciable differences in the procedures for applying it; coordinated rules should therefore be adopted at Community level in this field.

(37) This Directive should not affect the obligations of the Member States concerning the deadlines for transposition set out in Annex II, Part B,

NOTES

[1] OJ C116, 20.4.2001, p 69.

[2] Opinion of the European Parliament of 14 March 2001 (not yet published in the Official Journal) and Council Decision of 7 May 2001.

[3] OJ L66, 16.3.1979, p 21. Directive as last amended by Directive 88/627/EEC (OJ L348, 17.12.1988, p 62).

[4] OJ L100, 17.4.1980, p 1. Directive as last amended by European Parliament and Council Directive 94/18/EC (OJ L135, 31.5.1994, p 1).

[5] OJ L48, 20.2.1982, p 26.

[6] OJ L348, 17.12.1988, p 62.

[7] OJ L124, 5.5.1989, p 8.

[8] OJ L222, 14.8.1978, p 11. Directive as last amended by Directive 1999/60/EC (OJ L162, 26.6.1999, p 65).

HAVE ADOPTED THIS DIRECTIVE—

TITLE I DEFINITIONS AND SCOPE OF APPLICATION

CHAPTER I DEFINITIONS

[11.2]
Article 1

For the purposes of this Directive—

(a) "issuers" shall mean companies and other legal persons and any undertaking whose securities are the subject of an application for admission to official listing on a stock exchange;

(b) "collective investment undertakings other than the closed-end type" shall mean unit trusts and investment companies—

  (i) the object of which is the collective investment of capital provided by the public, and which operate on the principle of risk spreading, and

  (ii) the units of which are, at the holders' request, repurchased or redeemed, directly or indirectly, out of the assets of these undertakings. Action taken by such undertakings to ensure that the stock exchange value of its units does not significantly vary from their net asset value shall be regarded as equivalent to such repurchase or redemption;

(c) for the purposes of this Directive "investment companies other than those of the closed-end type" shall mean investment companies—

  (i) the object of which is the collective investment of capital provided by the public, and which operate on the principle of risk spreading, and

  (ii) the shares of which are, at the holders' request, repurchased or redeemed, directly or indirectly, out of those companies' assets. Action taken by such companies to ensure that the stock exchange value operating of their shares does not significantly vary from their net asset value shall be regarded as equivalent to such repurchase or redemption;

(d) "credit institution" shall mean an undertaking whose business is to receive deposits or other repayable funds from the public and to grant credits for its own account;

(e) "units of a collective investment undertaking" shall mean securities issued by a collective investment undertaking as representing the rights of participants in the assets of such undertaking;

(f) "participating interest" shall mean rights in the capital of other undertakings, whether or not represented by certificates, which, by creating a durable link with those undertakings, are intended to contribute to the activities of the undertaking which holds these rights;

(g), (h). . .

NOTES

Points (g), (h) repealed by European Parliament and Council Directive 2004/109/EC, Art 32(1), as from 20 January 2007.

CHAPTER II SCOPE OF APPLICATION

[11.3]
Article 2

1. Articles 5 to 19, 42 to 69, and 78 to 84 shall apply to securities which are admitted to official listing or are the subject of an application for admission to official listing on a stock exchange situated or operating within a Member State.

2. Member States may decide not to apply the provisions mentioned in paragraph 1 to—

(a) units issued by collective investment undertakings other than the closed-end type,

(b) securities issued by a Member State or its regional or local authorities.

Articles 3, 4 (*Article 3 repealed by European Parliament and Council Directive 2003/71/EC, Art 27(2), as from 1 July 2005; Article 4 repealed by European Parliament and Council Directive 2004/109/EC, Art 32(2), as from 20 January 2007.*)

TITLE II GENERAL PROVISIONS CONCERNING THE OFFICIAL LISTING OF SECURITIES

CHAPTER I GENERAL CONDITIONS FOR ADMISSION

[11.4]
Article 5

Member States shall ensure—

(a) securities may not be admitted to official listing on any stock exchange situated or operating within their territory unless the conditions laid down by this Directive are satisfied, and

(b) that issuers of securities admitted to such official listing, to regardless of the date on which this admission takes place, are subject to the obligations provided for by this Directive.

[11.5]
Article 6

1. The admission of securities to official listing shall be subject to the conditions set out in Articles 42 to 51, or 52 to 63, relating to shares and debt securities respectively.

2. . . .

3. Certificates representing shares may be admitted to official listing only if the issuer of the shares represented fulfils the conditions set out in Articles 42 to 44 and the obligations set out in Articles 64 to 69 and if the certificates fulfil the conditions set out in Articles 45 to 50.

NOTES

Para 2: repealed by European Parliament and Council Directive 2004/109/EC, Art 32(3), as from 20 January 2007.

[11.6]
Article 7

Member States may not make the admission to official listing of securities issued by companies or other legal persons which are nationals of another Member State subject to the condition that the securities must already have been admitted to official listing on a stock exchange situated or operating in one of the Member States.

CHAPTER II MORE STRINGENT OR ADDITIONAL CONDITIONS AND OBLIGATIONS

[11.7]
Article 8

1. Subject to the prohibitions provided for in Article 7 and in Articles 42 to 63, the Member States may make the admission of securities to official listing subject to more stringent conditions than those set out in Articles 42 to 63 or to additional conditions, provided that these more stringent and additional conditions apply generally for all issuers or for individual classes of issuer and that they have been published before application for admission of such securities is made.

[2. Member States may make the issuers of securities admitted to official listing subject to additional obligations, provided that those additional obligations apply generally for all issuers or for individual classes of issuers.]

3. Member States may, under the same conditions as those laid down in Article 9, authorise derogations from the additional or more stringent conditions and obligations referred to in paragraphs 1 and 2 hereof.

4. Member States may, in accordance with the applicable national rules require issuers of securities admitted to official listing to inform the public on a regular basis of their financial position and the general course of their business.

NOTES

Para 2: substituted by European Parliament and Council Directive 2004/109/EC, Art 32(4), as from 20 January 2007.

CHAPTER III DEROGATIONS

[11.8]
Article 9
Any derogations from the conditions for the admission of securities to official listing which may be authorised in accordance with Articles 42 to 63 must apply generally for all issuers where the circumstances justifying them are similar.

[11.9]
Article 10
Member States may decide not to apply the conditions set out in Articles 52 to 63 and the obligations set out in Article 81(1) and (3) in respect of applications for admission to official listing of debt securities issued by companies and other legal persons which are nationals of a Member State and which are set up by, governed by or managed pursuant to a special law where repayments and interest payments in respect of those securities are guaranteed by a Member State or one of its federal states.

CHAPTER IV POWERS OF THE NATIONAL COMPETENT AUTHORITIES

SECTION 1 DECISION OF ADMISSION

[11.10]
Article 11
1. The competent authorities referred to in Article 105 shall decide on the admission of securities to official listing on a stock exchange situated or operating within their territories.
2. Without prejudice to the other powers conferred upon them, the competent authorities may reject an application for the admission of a security to official listing if, in their opinion, the issuer's situation is such that admission would be detrimental to investors' interests.

[11.11]
Article 12
By way of derogation from Article 8, Member States may, solely in the interests of protecting the investors, give the competent authorities power to make the admission of a security to official listing subject to any special condition which the competent authorities consider appropriate and of which they have explicitly informed the applicant.

[11.12]
Article 13
1. Where applications are to be made simultaneously or within short intervals of one another for admission of the same securities to official listing on stock exchanges situated or operating in more than one Member State, or where an application for admission is made in respect of a security already listed on a stock exchange in another Member State, the competent authorities shall communicate with each other and make such arrangements as may be necessary to expedite the procedure and simplify as far as possible the formalities and any additional conditions required for admission of the security concerned.
2. In order to facilitate the work of the competent authorities, any application for the admission of a security to official listing on a stock exchange situated or operating in a Member State must state whether a similar application is being or has been made in another Member State, or will be made in the near future.

[11.13]
Article 14
The competent authorities may refuse to admit to official listing a security already officially listed in another Member State where the issuer fails to comply with the obligations resulting from admission in that Member State.

[11.14]
Article 15
Where an application for admission to official listing relates to certificates representing shares, the application shall be considered only if the competent authorities are of the opinion that the issuer of the certificates is offering adequate safeguards for the protection of investors.

SECTION 2 INFORMATION REQUESTED BY THE COMPETENT AUTHORITIES

[11.15]
Article 16
1. An issuer whose securities are admitted to official listing shall provide the competent authorities with all the information which the latter consider appropriate in order to protect investors or ensure the smooth operation of the market.
2. Where protection of investors or the smooth operation of the market so requires, an issuer may be required by the competent authorities to publish such information in such a form and within such time limits as they consider appropriate. Should the issuer fail to comply with such requirement, the competent authorities may themselves publish such information after having heard the issuer.

SECTION 3 ACTION AGAINST AN ISSUER FAILING TO COMPLY WITH THE OBLIGATIONS RESULTING FROM ADMISSION

[11.16]
Article 17
Without prejudice to any other action or penalties which they may contemplate in the event of failure on the part of the issuer to comply with the obligations resulting from admission to official listing, the competent authorities may make public the fact that an issuer is failing to comply with those obligations.

SECTION 4 SUSPENSION AND DISCONTINUANCE

[11.17]
Article 18
1. The competent authorities may decide to suspend the listing of a security where the smooth operation of the market is, or may be, temporarily jeopardised or where protection of investors so requires.
2. The competent authorities may decide that the listing of the security be discontinued where they are satisfied that, owing to special circumstances, normal regular dealings in a security are no longer possible.

SECTION 5 RIGHT TO APPLY TO THE COURTS IN CASE OF REFUSAL OF ADMISSION OR DISCONTINUANCE

[11.18]
Article 19
1. Member States shall ensure decisions of the competent authorities refusing the admission of a security to official listing or discontinuing such a listing shall be subject to the right to apply to the courts.
2. An applicant shall be notified of a decision regarding his application for admission to official listing within six months of receipt of the application or, should the competent authority require any further information within that period, within six months of the applicant's supplying such information.
3. Failure to give a decision within the time limit specified in paragraph 2 shall be deemed a rejection of the application. Such rejection shall give rise to the right to apply to the courts provided for in paragraph 1.

TITLE III PARTICULAR CONDITIONS RELATING TO OFFICIAL LISTINGS OF SECURITIES

Articles 20–41 (*Articles 20–41 (Chapter I) repealed by European Parliament and Council Directive 2003/71/EC, Art 27(1), as from 1 July 2005.*)

CHAPTER II SPECIFIC CONDITIONS FOR THE ADMISSION OF SHARES

SECTION 1 CONDITIONS RELATING TO COMPANIES FOR THE SHARES OF WHICH ADMISSION TO OFFICIAL LISTING IS SOUGHT

[11.19]
Article 42
The legal position of the company must be in conformity with the laws and Regulations to which it is subject, as regards both its formation and its operation under its statutes.

[11.20]
Article 43
1. The foreseeable market capitalisation of the shares for which admission to official listing is sought or, if this cannot be assessed, the company's capital and reserves, including profit or loss, from the last financial year, must be at least one million euro.
2. Member States may provide for admission to official listing, even when this condition is not fulfilled, provided that the competent authorities are satisfied that there will be an adequate market for the shares concerned.
3. A higher foreseeable market capitalisation or higher capital and reserves may be required by a Member State for admission to official listing only if another regulated, regularly operating, recognised open market exists in that State and the requirements for it are equal to or less than those referred to in paragraph 1.
4. The condition set out in paragraph 1 shall not be applicable for the admission to official listing of a further block of shares of the same class as those already admitted.
5. The equivalent in national currency of one million euro shall initially be the equivalent in national currency of one million European units of account that were applicable on 5 March 1979.
6. If, as a result of adjustment of the equivalent of the euro in national currency, the market capitalisation expressed in national currency remains for a period of one year at least 10% more or less than the value of one million euro the Member state must, within the 12 months following the expiry of that period, adjust its laws, regulations or administrative provisions to comply with paragraph 1.

[11.21]
Article 44
A company must have published or filed its annual accounts in accordance with national law for the three financial years preceding the application for official listing. By way of exception, the competent authorities may derogate from this condition where such derogation is desirable in the interests of the company or of investors and where the competent authorities are satisfied that investors have the necessary information available to be able to arrive at an informed judgement on the company and the shares for which admission to official listing is sought.

SECTION 2 CONDITIONS RELATING TO THE SHARES FOR WHICH ADMISSION IS SOUGHT

[11.22]
Article 45
The legal position of the shares must be in conformity with the laws and regulations to which they are subject.

[11.23]
Article 46
1. The shares must be freely negotiable.
2. The competent authorities may treat shares which are not fully paid up as freely negotiable, if arrangements have been made to ensure that the negotiability of such shares is not restricted and that dealing is made open and proper by providing the public with all appropriate information.
3. The competent authorities may, in the case of the admission to official listing of shares which may be acquired only subject to approval, derogate from paragraph 1 only if the use of the approval clause does not disturb the market.

[11.24]
Article 47
Where public issue precedes admission to official listing, the first listing may be made only after the end of the period during which subscription applications may be submitted.

[11.25]
Article 48
1. A sufficient number of shares must be distributed to the public in one or more Member States not later than the time of admission.
2. The condition set out in paragraph 1 shall not apply where shares are to be distributed to the public through the stock exchange. In that event, admission to official listing may be granted only if the competent authorities are satisfied that a sufficient number of shares will be distributed through the stock exchange within a short period.
3. Where admission to official listing is sought for a further block of shares of the same class, the competent authorities may assess whether a sufficient number of shares has been distributed to the public in relation to all the shares issued and not only in relation to this further block.
4. By way of derogation from paragraph 1, if the shares are admitted to official listing in one or more non-member countries, the competent authorities may provide for their admission to official listing if a sufficient number of shares is distributed to the public in the non-Member State or States where they are listed.
5. A sufficient number of shares shall be deemed to have been distributed either when the shares in respect of which application for admission has been made are in the hands of the public to the extent of a least 25% of the subscribed capital represented by the class of shares concerned or when, in view of the large number of shares of the same class and the extent of their distribution to the public, the market will operate properly with a lower percentage.

[11.26]
Article 49
1. The application for admission to official listing must cover all the shares of the same class already issued.
2. Member States may provide that this condition shall not apply to applications for admission not covering all the shares of the same class already issued where the shares of that class for which admission is not sought belong to blocks serving to maintain control of the company or are not negotiable for a certain time under agreements, provided that the public is informed of such situations and that there is no danger of such situations prejudicing the interests of the holders of the shares for which admission to official listing is sought.

[11.27]
Article 50
1. For the admission to official listing of shares issued by companies which are nationals of another Member State and which shares have a physical form it is necessary and sufficient that their physical form comply with the standards laid down in that other Member State. Where the physical form does not conform to the standards in force in the Member State in which admission to official listing is applied for, the competent authorities of that state shall make that fact known to the public.
2. The physical form of shares issued by companies which are nationals of a non-member country must afford sufficient safeguard for the protection of the investors.

[11.28]
Article 51
If the shares issued by a company which is a national of a non-member country are not listed in either the country of origin or in the country in which the major proportion of the shares is held, they may not be admitted to official listing unless the competent authorities are satisfied that the absence of a listing the in the country of origin or in the country in which the major proportion is held is not due to the need to protect investors.

CHAPTER III PARTICULAR CONDITIONS RELATING TO THE ADMISSION TO OFFICIAL LISTING OF DEBT SECURITIES ISSUED BY AN UNDERTAKING

SECTION 1 CONDITIONS RELATING TO UNDERTAKINGS FOR THE DEBT SECURITIES OF WHICH ADMISSION TO OFFICIAL LISTING IS SOUGHT

[11.29]
Article 52
The legal position of the undertaking must be in conformity with the laws and regulations to which it is subject, as regards both its formation and its operation under its statutes.

SECTION 2 CONDITIONS RELATING TO THE DEBT SECURITIES FOR WHICH ADMISSION TO OFFICIAL LISTING IS SOUGHT

[11.30]
Article 53
The legal position of the debt securities must be in conformity with the laws and regulations to which they are subject.

[11.31]
Article 54
1. The debt securities must be freely negotiable.
2. The competent authorities may treat debt securities which are not fully paid up as freely negotiable if arrangements have been made to ensure that the negotiability of these debt securities is not restricted and that dealing is made open and proper by providing the public with all appropriate information.

[11.32]
Article 55
Where public issue precedes admission to official listing, the first listing may be made only after the end of the period during which subscription applications may be submitted. This provision shall not apply in the case of tap issues of

debt securities when the closing date for subscription is not fixed.

[11.33]
Article 56
The application for admission to official listing must cover all debt securities ranking *pari passu*.

[11.34]
Article 57
1. For the admission to official listing of debt securities issued by undertakings which are nationals of another Member State and which debt securities have a physical form, it is necessary and sufficient that their physical form comply with the standards laid down in that other Member State. Where the physical form does not conform to the standards in force in the Member State in which admission to official listing is applied for, the competent authorities of that State shall make that fact known to the public.
2. The physical form of debt securities issued in a single Member State must conform to the standards in force in that State.
3. The physical form of debt securities issued by undertakings which are nationals of a non-member country must afford sufficient safeguard for the protection of the investors.

SECTION 3 OTHER CONDITIONS

[11.35]
Article 58
1. The amount of the loan may not be less than EUR 200,000. This provision shall not be applicable in the case of tap issues where the amount of the loan is not fixed.
2. Member States may provide for admission to official listing even when this condition is not fulfilled, where the competent authorities are satisfied that there will be a sufficient market for the debt securities concerned.
3. The equivalent in national currency of EUR 200,000 shall initially be the equivalent in national currency of 200,000 units of account that were applicable on 5 March 1979.
4. If as a result of adjustment of the equivalent of the euro in national currency the minimum amount of the loan expressed in national currency remains, for a period of one year, at least 10% less than the value of EUR 200,000 the Member State must, within the 12 months following the expiry of that period, amend its laws, regulations and administrative provisions to comply with paragraph 1.

[11.36]
Article 59
1. Convertible or exchangeable debentures and debentures with warrants may be admitted to official listing only if the related shares are already listed on the same stock exchange or on another regulated, regularly operating, recognised open market or are so admitted simultaneously.
2. Member States may, by way of derogation from paragraph 1, provide for the admission to official listing of convertible or exchangeable debentures or debentures with warrants, if the competent authorities are satisfied that holders have at their disposal all the information necessary to form an opinion concerning the value of the shares to which these debt securities relate.

CHAPTER IV PARTICULAR CONDITIONS RELATING TO THE ADMISSION TO OFFICIAL LISTING OF DEBT SECURITIES ISSUED BY A STATE, ITS REGIONAL OR LOCAL AUTHORITIES OR A PUBLIC INTERNATIONAL BODY

[11.37]
Article 60
The debt securities must be freely negotiable.

[11.38]
Article 61
Where public issue precedes admission to official listing, the first listing may be made only after the end of the period during which subscription applications may be submitted. This provision shall not apply where the closing date for subscription is not fixed.

[11.39]
Article 62
The application for admission to official listing must cover all the securities ranking *pari passu*.

[11.40]
Article 63
1. For the admission to official listing of debt securities which are issued by a Member State or its regional or local authorities in a physical form, it is necessary and sufficient that such physical form comply with the standards in force in that Member State. Where the physical form does not comply with the standards in force in the Member State where admission to official listing is applied for, the competent authorities of that state shall bring this situation to the attention of the public.
2. The physical form of debt securities issued by non-member countries or their regional or local authorities or by public international bodies must afford sufficient safeguard for the protection of the investors.

TITLE IV OBLIGATIONS RELATING TO SECURITIES ADMITTED TO OFFICIAL LISTING

CHAPTER I OBLIGATIONS OF COMPANIES WHOSE SHARES ARE ADMITTED TO OFFICIAL LISTING

SECTION 1 LISTING OF NEWLY ISSUED SHARES OF THE SAME CLASS

[11.41]
Article 64
Without prejudice to Article 49(2), in the case of a new public issue of shares of the same class as those already officially listed, the company shall be required, where the new shares are not automatically admitted, to apply for their admission to the same listing, either not more than a year after their issue or when they become freely negotiable.

Articles 65–104 (*Articles 65–97 (Title IV, Chapter I, Sections 2–8, and Chapters II, III) repealed by European Parliament and Council Directive 2004/109/EC, Art 32(5), as from 20 January 2007; Articles 98–104 (Title V), Arts 98–101, 104 repealed by European Parliament and Council Directive 2003/71/EC, Art 27(2), as from 1 July 2005; Arts 102, 103 repealed by European Parliament and Council Directive 2004/109/EC, Art 32(6), as from 20 January 2007.*)

TITLE VI COMPETENT AUTHORITIES AND COOPERATION BETWEEN MEMBER STATES

[11.42]
Article 105
1. Member States shall ensure that this Directive is applied and shall appoint one or more competent authorities for the purposes of the Directive. They shall notify the Commission thereof, giving details of any division of powers among them.
2. Member States shall ensure that the competent authorities have the powers necessary for them to carry out their task.
3. This Directive shall not affect the competent authorities' liability, which shall continue to be governed solely by national law.

[11.43]
Article 106
The competent authorities shall cooperate whenever necessary for the purpose of carrying out their duties and shall exchange any information useful for that purpose.

[11.44]
Article 107
1. Member States shall provide that all persons employed or formerly employed by the competent authorities shall be bound by professional secrecy. This means that any confidential information received in the course of their duties may not be divulged to any person or authority except by virtue of provisions laid down by law.
2. Paragraph 1 shall not, however, preclude the competent authorities of the various Member States from exchanging information as provided for in this Directive. Information thus exchanged shall be covered by the obligation of professional secrecy to which the persons employed or formerly employed by the competent authorities receiving the information are subject.
3. . . .

NOTES

Para 3: repealed by a combination of European Parliament and Council Directive 2003/71/EC, Art 27(2), as from 1 July 2005, and European Parliament and Council Directive 2004/109/EC, Art 32(7), as from 20 January 2007.

TITLE VII CONTACT COMMITTEE

CHAPTER I COMPOSITION, WORKING AND TASKS OF THE COMMITTEE

Article 108 (*Repealed by European Parliament and Council Directive 2005/1/EC, Art 10(1), as from 13 April 2005.*)

CHAPTER II ADAPTATION OF THE AMOUNT OF EQUITY MARKET CAPITALISATION

[11.45]
[Article 109
1. For the purpose of adjusting, in the light of the requirements of the economic situation, the minimum amount of the foreseeable market capitalisation laid down in Article 43(1), the Commission shall submit to the European Securities Committee instituted by Commission Decision 2001/528/EC of 6 June 2001[1] a draft of the measures to be taken.
2. Where reference is made to this paragraph, Articles 5 and 7 of Council Decision 1999/468/EC of 28 June 1999 laying down the procedures for the exercise of implementing powers conferred on the Commission[2] shall apply, having regard to Article 8 thereof.
The period laid down in Article 5(6) of Decision 1999/468/EC shall be set at three months.
3. The Committee shall adopt its rules of procedure.]

NOTES

Substituted by European Parliament and Council Directive 2005/1/EC, Art 10(2), as from 13 April 2005.

[1] OJ L191, 13.7.2001, p 45. Decision as amended by Decision 2004/8/EC (OJ L3, 7.1.2004, p 33).

[2] OJ L184, 17.7.1999, p 23.

TITLE VIII FINAL PROVISIONS

[11.46]
Article 110
The Member States shall communicate to the Commission the texts of the main laws, regulations and administrative provisions which they adopt in the field covered by this Directive.

[11.47]
Article 111
1. Directives 79/279/EEC, 80/390/EEC, 82/121/EEC and 88/627/EEC, as amended by the acts listed in Annex II Part A, are hereby repealed without prejudice to the obligations of the Member States concerning the time-limits for transposition set out in Annex II Part B.
2. References to the repealed Directives shall be construed as references to this Directive and should be read in accordance with the correlation table shown in Annex III.

[11.48]
Article 112
This Directive shall enter into force the twentieth day following that of its publication in the *Official Journal of the European Communities*.

[11.49]
Article 113
This Directive is addressed to the Member States.

ANNEXES

ANNEX I

(*Annex I repealed by European Parliament and Council Directive 2003/71/EC, Art 27(4), as from 1 July 2005.*)

ANNEX II

PART A REPEALED DIRECTIVES AND THEIR SUCCESSIVE AMENDMENTS
(REFERRED TO IN ARTICLE 111)

[11.50]

Council Directive 79/279/EEC	(OJ L66, 16.3.1979, p 21)
Council Directive 82/148/EEC	(OJ L62, 5.3.1982, p 22)
Council Directive 88/627/EEC	(OJ L348, 17.12.1988, p 62)
Council Directive 80/390/EEC	(OJ L100, 17.4.1980, p 1)
Council Directive 82/148/EEC	(OJ L62, 5.3.1982, p 22)
Council Directive 87/345/EEC	(OJ L185, 4.7.1987, p 81)
Council Directive 90/211/EEC	(OJ L112, 3.5.1990, p 24)
European Parliament and Council Directive 94/18/EC	(OJ L135, 31.5.1994, p 1)
Council Directive 82/121/EEC	(OJ L48, 20.2.1982, p 26)
Council Directive 88/627/EEC	(OJ L348, 17.12.1988, p 62)

PART B TIME-LIMITS FOR TRANSPOSITION INTO NATIONAL LAW
(REFERRED TO IN ARTICLE 111)

Directive	***Time-limit for transposition***
79/279/EEC	8 March 1981[1, 2]
80/390/EEC	19 September 1982[2]
82/121/EEC; 82/148/EEC	30 June 1983[3]
87/345/EEC	1 January 1990 1 January 1991 for Spain 1 January 1992 for Portugal
88/627/EEC	1 January 1991
90/211/EEC; 94/18/EC	17 April 1991

NOTES

1 8.3.1982 for the Member States which introduce simultaneously Directives 79/279/EEC and 80/390/EEC.

2 30.6.1983 for the Member States which introduce simultaneously Directives 79/279/EEC, 80/390/EEC and 82/121/EEC.

3 Time-limit for application: 30.6.1986.

ANNEX III

(*Annex III (Correlation Table) has been omitted because of space considerations.*)

DIRECTIVE OF THE EUROPEAN PARLIAMENT AND OF THE COUNCIL

(2004/25/EC)
of 21 April 2004

on takeover bids

(Text with EEA relevance)

[11.51]

NOTES

Date of publication in OJ: OJ L142, 30.4.2004, p 12.

This Directive is reproduced as amended by: European Parliament and Council Regulation 219/2009/EC; European Parliament and Council Directive 2014/59/EU (transposition date 1 January 2015); European Parliament and Council Regulation 2021/23/EU.

Editorial note (legal status of EU Directives in the UK): note that EU Directives are not "direct EU legislation" within the meaning of the European Union (Withdrawal) Act 2018, s 3 at **[12.5]** and, accordingly, do not apply to the UK. As to the status of EU-derived domestic legislation after IP completion day (11pm on 31 December 2020), see s 2 of the 2018 Act at **[12.4]**. As to the UK implementation of this Directive, see the note below.

UK Implementation: in the UK this Directive was implemented by Part 28 of the Companies Act 2006, the Takeovers Directive (Interim Implementation) Regulations 2006, SI 2006/1183 (revoked with savings), and the Companies Acts (Unregistered Companies) Regulations 2007, SI 2007/318 (revoked).

THE EUROPEAN PARLIAMENT AND THE COUNCIL OF THE EUROPEAN UNION,

Having regard to the Treaty establishing the European Community, and in particular Article 44(1) thereof,

Having regard to the proposal from the Commission,[1]

Having regard to the opinion of the European Economic and Social Committee,[2]

Acting in accordance with the procedure laid down in Article 251 of the Treaty,[3]

Whereas:

(1) In accordance with Article 44(2)(g) of the Treaty, it is necessary to coordinate certain safeguards which, for the protection of the interests of members and others, Member States require of companies governed by the law of a Member State the securities of which are admitted to trading on a regulated market in a Member State, with a view to making such safeguards equivalent throughout the Community.

(2) It is necessary to protect the interests of holders of the securities of companies governed by the law of a Member State when those companies are the subject of takeover bids or of changes of control and at least some of their securities are admitted to trading on a regulated market in a Member State.

(3) It is necessary to create Community-wide clarity and transparency in respect of legal issues to be settled in the event of takeover bids and to prevent patterns of corporate restructuring within the Community from being distorted by arbitrary differences in governance and management cultures.

(4) In view of the public-interest purposes served by the central banks of the Member States, it seems inconceivable that they should be the targets of takeover bids. Since, for historical reasons, the securities of some of those central banks are listed on regulated markets in Member States, it is necessary to exclude them explicitly from the scope of this Directive.

(5) Each Member State should designate an authority or authorities to supervise those aspects of bids that are governed by this Directive and to ensure that parties to takeover bids comply with the rules made pursuant to this Directive. All those authorities should cooperate with one another.

(6) In order to be effective, takeover regulation should be flexible and capable of dealing with new circumstances as they arise and should accordingly provide for the possibility of exceptions and derogations. However, in applying any rules or exceptions laid down or in granting any derogations, supervisory authorities should respect certain general principles.

(7) Self-regulatory bodies should be able to exercise supervision.

(8) In accordance with general principles of Community law, and in particular the right to a fair hearing, decisions of a supervisory authority should in appropriate circumstances be susceptible to review by an independent court or tribunal. However, Member States should be left to determine whether rights are to be made available which may be asserted in administrative or judicial proceedings, either in proceedings against a supervisory authority or in proceedings between parties to a bid.

(9) Member States should take the necessary steps to protect the holders of securities, in particular those with minority holdings, when control of their companies has been acquired. The Member States should ensure such protection by obliging the person who has acquired control of a company to make an offer to all the holders of that company's securities for all of their holdings at an equitable price in accordance with a common definition. Member States should be free to establish further instruments for the protection of the interests of the holders of securities, such as the obligation to make a partial bid where the offeror does not acquire control of the company or the obligation to announce a bid at the same time as control of the company is acquired.

(10) The obligation to make a bid to all the holders of securities should not apply to those controlling holdings already in existence on the date on which the national legislation transposing this Directive enters into force.

(11) The obligation to launch a bid should not apply in the case of the acquisition of securities which do not carry the right to vote at ordinary general meetings of shareholders. Member States should, however, be able to provide that the obligation to make a bid to all the holders of securities relates not only to securities carrying voting rights but also to securities which carry voting rights only in specific circumstances or which do not carry voting rights.

(12) To reduce the scope for insider dealing, an offeror should be required to announce his/her decision to launch a bid as soon as possible and to inform the supervisory authority of the bid.

(13) The holders of securities should be properly informed of the terms of a bid by means of an offer document. Appropriate information should also be given to the representatives of the company's employees or, failing that, to the employees directly.

(14) The time allowed for the acceptance of a bid should be regulated.

(15) To be able to perform their functions satisfactorily, supervisory authorities should at all times be able to require the parties to a bid to provide information concerning themselves and should cooperate and supply information in an efficient and effective manner, without delay, to other authorities supervising capital markets.

(16) In order to prevent operations which could frustrate a bid, the powers of the board of an offeree company to engage in operations of an exceptional nature should be limited, without unduly hindering the offeree company in carrying on its normal business activities.

(17) The board of an offeree company should be required to make public a document setting out its opinion of the bid and the reasons on which that opinion is based, including its views on the effects of implementation on all the company's interests, and specifically on employment.

(18) In order to reinforce the effectiveness of existing provisions concerning the freedom to deal in the securities of companies covered by this Directive and the freedom to exercise voting rights, it is essential that the defensive structures and mechanisms envisaged by such companies be transparent and that they be regularly presented in reports to general meetings of shareholders.

(19) Member States should take the necessary measures to afford any offeror the possibility of acquiring majority interests in other companies and of fully exercising control of them. To that end, restrictions on the transfer of securities, restrictions on voting rights, extraordinary appointment rights and multiple voting rights should be removed or suspended during the time allowed for the acceptance of a bid and when the general meeting of shareholders decides on defensive measures, on amendments to the articles of association or on the removal or appointment of board members at the first general meeting of shareholders following closure of the bid. Where the holders of securities have suffered losses as a result of the removal of rights, equitable compensation should be provided for in accordance with the technical arrangements laid down by Member States.

(20) All special rights held by Member States in companies should be viewed in the framework of the free movement of capital and the relevant provisions of the Treaty. Special rights held by Member States in companies which are provided for in private or public national law should be exempted from the 'breakthrough' rule if they are compatible with the Treaty.

(21) Taking into account existing differences in Member States' company law mechanisms and structures, Member States should be allowed not to require companies established within their territories to apply the provisions of this Directive limiting the powers of the board of an offeree company during the time allowed for the acceptance of a bid and those rendering ineffective barriers, provided for in the articles of association or in specific agreements. In that event Member States should at least allow companies established within their territories to make the choice, which must be reversible, to apply those provisions. Without prejudice to international agreements to which the European Community is a party, Member States should be allowed not to require companies which apply those provisions in accordance with the optional arrangements to apply them when they become the subject of offers launched by companies which do not apply the same provisions, as a consequence of the use of those optional arrangements.

(22) Member States should lay down rules to cover the possibility of a bid's lapsing, the offeror's right to revise his/her bid, the possibility of competing bids for a company's securities, the disclosure of the result of a bid, the irrevocability of a bid and the conditions permitted.

(23) The disclosure of information to and the consultation of representatives of the employees of the offeror and the offeree company should be governed by the relevant national provisions, in particular those adopted pursuant to Council Directive 94/45/EC of 22 September 1994 on the establishment of a European Works Council or a procedure in Community-scale undertakings and Community-scale groups of undertakings for the purposes of informing and consulting employees,[4] Council Directive 98/59/EC of 20 July 1998 on the approximation of the laws of the Member States relating to collective redundancies,[5] Council Directive 2001/86/EC of 8 October 2001 supplementing the statute for a European Company with regard to the involvement of employees[6] and Directive 2002/14/EC of the European Parliament and of the Council of 11 March 2002 establishing a general framework for informing and consulting employees in the European Community — Joint declaration of the European Parliament, the Council and the Commission on employee representation.[7] The employees of the companies concerned, or their representatives, should nevertheless be given an opportunity to state their views on the foreseeable effects of the bid on employment. Without prejudice to the rules of Directive 2003/6/EC of the European Parliament and of the Council of 28 January 2003 on insider dealing and market manipulation (market abuse),[8] Member States may always apply or introduce national provisions concerning the disclosure of information to and the consultation of representatives of the employees of the offeror before an offer is launched.

(24) Member States should take the necessary measures to enable an offeror who, following a takeover bid, has acquired a certain percentage of a company's capital carrying voting rights to require the holders of the remaining securities to sell him/her their securities. Likewise, where, following a takeover bid, an offeror has acquired a certain percentage of a company's capital carrying voting rights, the holders of the remaining securities should be able to require him/her to buy their securities. These squeeze-out and sell-out procedures should apply only under specific conditions linked to takeover bids. Member States may continue to apply national rules to squeeze-out and sell-out procedures in other circumstances.

(25) Since the objectives of the action envisaged, namely to establish minimum guidelines for the conduct of takeover bids and ensure an adequate level of protection for holders of securities throughout the Community, cannot be sufficiently achieved by the Member States because of the need for transparency and legal certainty in the case of cross-border takeovers and acquisitions of control, and can therefore, by reason of the scale and effects of the action, be better achieved at Community level, the Community may adopt measures, in accordance with the principle of

subsidiarity as set out in Article 5 of the Treaty. In accordance with the principle of proportionality as set out in that Article, this Directive does not go beyond what is necessary to achieve those objectives.

(26) The adoption of a Directive is the appropriate procedure for the establishment of a framework consisting of certain common principles and a limited number of general requirements which Member States are to implement through more detailed rules in accordance with their national systems and their cultural contexts.

(27) Member States should, however, provide for sanctions for any infringement of the national measures transposing this Directive.

(28) Technical guidance and implementing measures for the rules laid down in this Directive may from time to time be necessary, to take account of new developments on financial markets. For certain provisions, the Commission should accordingly be empowered to adopt implementing measures, provided that these do not modify the essential elements of this Directive and the Commission acts in accordance with the principles set out in this Directive, after consulting the European Securities Commission established by Commission Directive 2001/528/EC.[9] The measures necessary for the implementation of this Directive should be adopted in accordance with the Council Decision 1999/468/EC of 28 June 1999 laying down the procedures for the exercise of implementing powers conferred on the Commission[10] and with due regard to the declaration made by the Commission in the European Parliament on 5 February 2002 concerning the implementation of financial services legislation. For the other provisions, it is important to entrust a contact committee with the task of assisting Member States and the supervisory authorities in the implementation of this Directive and of advising the Commission, if necessary, on additions or amendments to this Directive. In so doing, the contact committee may make use of the information which Member States are to provide on the basis of this Directive concerning takeover bids that have taken place on their regulated markets.

(29) The Commission should facilitate movement towards the fair and balanced harmonisation of rules on takeovers in the European Union. To that end, the Commission should be able to submit proposals for the timely revision of this Directive,

NOTES

1 OJ C45E, 25.2.2003, p 1.

2 OJ C208, 3.9.2003, p 55.

3 Opinion of the European Parliament of 16 December 2003 (not yet published in the Official Journal) and Council decision of 30 March 2004.

4 OJ L254, 30.9.1994, p 64. Directive as amended by Directive 97/74/EC (OJ L10, 16.1.1998, p 22).

5 OJ L225, 12.8.1998, p 16.

6 OJ L294, 10.11.2001, p 22.

7 OJ L80, 23.3.2002, p 29.

8 OJ L96, 12.4.2003, p 16.

9 OJ L191, 13.7.2001, p 45. Decision as amended by Decision 2004/8/EC (OJ L3, 7.1.2004, p 33).

10 OJ L184, 17.7.1999, p 23.

HAVE ADOPTED THIS DIRECTIVE:

[11.52]

Article 1 Scope

1. This Directive lays down measures coordinating the laws, regulations, administrative provisions, codes of practice and other arrangements of the Member States, including arrangements established by organisations officially authorised to regulate the markets (hereinafter referred to as 'rules'), relating to takeover bids for the securities of companies governed by the laws of Member States, where all or some of those securities are admitted to trading on a regulated market within the meaning of Directive 93/22/EEC[1] in one or more Member States (hereinafter referred to as a 'regulated market').

2. This Directive shall not apply to takeover bids for securities issued by companies, the object of which is the collective investment of capital provided by the public, which operate on the principle of risk-spreading and the units of which are, at the holders' request, repurchased or redeemed, directly or indirectly, out of the assets of those companies. Action taken by such companies to ensure that the stock exchange value of their units does not vary significantly from their net asset value shall be regarded as equivalent to such repurchase or redemption.

3. This Directive shall not apply to takeover bids for securities issued by the Member States' central banks.

NOTES

1 Council Directive 93/22/EEC of 10 May 1993 on investment services in the securities field (OJ L141, 11.6.1993, p 27). Directive as last amended by Directive 2002/87/EC of the European Parliament and of the Council (OJ L35, 11.2.2003, p 1).

[11.53]

Article 2 Definitions

1. For the purposes of this Directive:

(a) 'takeover bid' or 'bid' shall mean a public offer (other than by the offeree company itself) made to the holders of the securities of a company to acquire all or some of those securities, whether mandatory or voluntary, which follows or has as its objective the acquisition of control of the offeree company in accordance with national law;

(b) 'offeree company' shall mean a company, the securities of which are the subject of a bid;

(c) 'offeror' shall mean any natural or legal person governed by public or private law making a bid;

(d) 'persons acting in concert' shall mean natural or legal persons who cooperate with the offeror or the offeree company on the basis of an agreement, either express or tacit, either oral or written, aimed either at acquiring control of the offeree company or at frustrating the successful outcome of a bid;

(e) 'securities' shall mean transferable securities carrying voting rights in a company;

(f) 'parties to the bid' shall mean the offeror, the members of the offeror's board if the offeror is a company, the offeree company, holders of securities of the offeree company and the members of the board of the offeree company, and persons acting in concert with such parties;

(g) 'multiple vote securities' shall mean securities included in a distinct and separate class and carrying more than one vote each.

2. For the purposes of paragraph 1(d), persons controlled by another person within the meaning of Article 87 of Directive 2001/34/EC[1] shall be deemed to be persons acting in concert with that other person and with each other.

NOTES

[1] Directive 2001/34/EC of the European Parliament and of the Council of 28 May 2001 on the admission of securities to official stock exchange listing and on information to be published on those securities (OJ L184, 6.7.2001, p 1). Directive as last amended by Directive 2003/71/EC (OJ L345, 31.12.2003, p 64).

[11.54]

Article 3 General Principles

1. For the purpose of implementing this Directive, Member States shall ensure that the following principles are complied with:

(a) all holders of the securities of an offeree company of the same class must be afforded equivalent treatment; moreover, if a person acquires control of a company, the other holders of securities must be protected;

(b) the holders of the securities of an offeree company must have sufficient time and information to enable them to reach a properly informed decision on the bid; where it advises the holders of securities, the board of the offeree company must give its views on the effects of implementation of the bid on employment, conditions of employment and the locations of the company's places of business;

(c) the board of an offeree company must act in the interests of the company as a whole and must not deny the holders of securities the opportunity to decide on the merits of the bid;

(d) false markets must not be created in the securities of the offeree company, of the offeror company or of any other company concerned by the bid in such a way that the rise or fall of the prices of the securities becomes artificial and the normal functioning of the markets is distorted;

(e) an offeror must announce a bid only after ensuring that he/she can fulfil in full any cash consideration, if such is offered, and after taking all reasonable measures to secure the implementation of any other type of consideration;

(f) an offeree company must not be hindered in the conduct of its affairs for longer than is reasonable by a bid for its securities.

2. With a view to ensuring compliance with the principles laid down in paragraph 1, Member States:

(a) shall ensure that the minimum requirements set out in this Directive are observed;

(b) may lay down additional conditions and provisions more stringent than those of this Directive for the regulation of bids.

[11.55]

Article 4 Supervisory authority and applicable law

1. Member States shall designate the authority or authorities competent to supervise bids for the purposes of the rules which they make or introduce pursuant to this Directive. The authorities thus designated shall be either public authorities, associations or private bodies recognised by national law or by public authorities expressly empowered for that purpose by national law. Member States shall inform the Commission of those designations, specifying any divisions of functions that may be made. They shall ensure that those authorities exercise their functions impartially and independently of all parties to a bid.

2.

(a) The authority competent to supervise a bid shall be that of the Member State in which the offeree company has its registered office if that company's securities are admitted to trading on a regulated market in that Member State.

(b) If the offeree company's securities are not admitted to trading on a regulated market in the Member State in which the company has its registered office, the authority competent to supervise the bid shall be that of the Member State on the regulated market of which the company's securities are admitted to trading.

If the offeree company's securities are admitted to trading on regulated markets in more than one Member State, the authority competent to supervise the bid shall be that of the Member State on the regulated market of which the securities were first admitted to trading.

(c) If the offeree company's securities were first admitted to trading on regulated markets in more than one Member State simultaneously, the offeree company shall determine which of the supervisory authorities of those Member States shall be the authority competent to supervise the bid by notifying those regulated markets and their supervisory authorities on the first day of trading.

If the offeree company's securities have already been admitted to trading on regulated markets in more than one Member State on the date laid down in Article 21(1) and were admitted simultaneously, the supervisory authorities of those Member States shall agree which one of them shall be the authority competent to supervise the bid within four weeks of the date laid down in Article 21(1). Otherwise, the offeree company shall determine which of those authorities shall be the competent authority on the first day of trading following that four-week period.

(d) Member States shall ensure that the decisions referred to in (c) are made public.

(e) In the cases referred to in (b) and (c), matters relating to the consideration offered in the case of a bid, in particular the price, and matters relating to the bid procedure, in particular the information on the offeror's decision to make a bid, the contents of the offer document and the disclosure of the bid, shall be dealt with in accordance with the rules of the Member State of the competent authority. In matters relating to the information to be provided to the employees of the offeree company and in matters relating to company law, in particular the percentage of voting rights which confers control and any derogation from the obligation to launch a bid, as well as the conditions under which the board of the offeree company may undertake any action which might result in the frustration of the bid, the applicable rules and the competent authority shall be those of the Member State in which the offeree company has its registered office.

3. Member States shall ensure that all persons employed or formerly employed by their supervisory authorities are bound by professional secrecy. No information covered by professional secrecy may be divulged to any person or authority except under provisions laid down by law.

4. The supervisory authorities of the Member States for the purposes of this Directive and other authorities supervising capital markets, in particular in accordance with Directive 93/22/EEC, Directive 2001/34/EC, Directive 2003/6/EC and Directive 2003/71/EC of the European Parliament and of the Council of 4 November 2003 on the prospectus to be published when securities are offered to the public or admitted to trading shall cooperate and supply each other with information wherever necessary for the application of the rules drawn up in accordance with this Directive and in particular in cases covered by paragraph 2(b), (c) and (e). Information thus exchanged shall be covered by the obligation of professional secrecy to which persons employed or formerly employed by the supervisory authorities receiving the information are subject. Cooperation shall include the ability to serve the legal documents necessary to enforce measures taken by the competent authorities in connection with bids, as well as such other assistance as may reasonably be requested by the supervisory authorities concerned for the purpose of investigating any actual or alleged breaches of the rules made or introduced pursuant to this Directive.

5. The supervisory authorities shall be vested with all the powers necessary for the purpose of carrying out their duties, including that of ensuring that the parties to a bid comply with the rules made or introduced pursuant to this Directive.

Provided that the general principles laid down in Article 3(1) are respected, Member States may provide in the rules that they make or introduce pursuant to this Directive for derogations from those rules:

(i) by including such derogations in their national rules, in order to take account of circumstances determined at national level

and/or

(ii) by granting their supervisory authorities, where they are competent, powers to waive such national rules, to take account of the circumstances referred to in (i) or in other specific circumstances, in which case a reasoned decision must be required.

[Member States shall ensure that Article 5(1) of this Directive does not apply in the case of application of resolution tools, powers and mechanisms provided for in Title IV of Directive 2014/59/EU of the European Parliament and of the Council[1] or in Title V of Regulation (EU) 2021/23 of the European Parliament and of the Council'.[2]]

6. This Directive shall not affect the power of the Member States to designate judicial or other authorities responsible for dealing with disputes and for deciding on irregularities committed in the course of bids or the power of Member States to regulate whether and under which circumstances parties to a bid are entitled to bring administrative or judicial proceedings. In particular, this Directive shall not affect the power which courts may have in a Member State to decline to hear legal proceedings and to decide whether or not such proceedings affect the outcome of a bid. This Directive shall not affect the power of the Member States to determine the legal position concerning the liability of supervisory authorities or concerning litigation between the parties to a bid.

NOTES

Para 5: third sub-paragraph originally inserted by European Parliament and Council Directive 2014/59/EU, Art 119, as from 2 July 2014. Subsequently substituted by European Parliament and Council Regulation 2021/23/EU, Art 90, as from 12 August 2022.

[1] Directive 2014/59/EU of the European Parliament and of the Council of 15 May 2014 establishing a framework for the recovery and resolution of credit institutions and investment firms and amending Council Directive 82/891/EEC and Directives 2001/24/EC, 2002/47/EC, 2004/25/EC, 2005/56/EC, 2007/36/EC, 2011/35/EU, 2012/30/EU and 2013/36/EU, and Regulations (EU) No 1093/2010 and (EU) No 648/2012, of the European Parliament and of the Council (OJ L173, 12.6.2014, p 190).

[2] Regulation (EU) 2021/23 of the European Parliament and of the Council of 16 December 2020 on a framework for the recovery and resolution of central counterparties and amending Regulations (EU) No 1095/2010, (EU) No 648/2012, (EU) No 600/2014, (EU) No 806/2014 and (EU) 2015/2365 and Directives 2002/47/EC, 2004/25/EC, 2007/36/EC, 2014/59/EU and (EU) 2017/1132 (OJ L022, 22.1.2021, p 1).

[11.56]

Article 5 Protection of minority shareholders, the mandatory bid and the equitable price

1. Where a natural or legal person, as a result of his/her own acquisition or the acquisition by persons acting in concert with him/her, holds securities of a company as referred to in Article 1(1) which, added to any existing holdings of those securities of his/hers and the holdings of those securities of persons acting in concert with him/her, directly or indirectly give him/her a specified percentage of voting rights in that company, giving him/her control of that company, Member States shall ensure that such a person is required to make a bid as a means of protecting the minority shareholders of that company. Such a bid shall be addressed at the earliest opportunity to all the holders of those securities for all their holdings at the equitable price as defined in paragraph 4.

2. Where control has been acquired following a voluntary bid made in accordance with this Directive to all the holders of securities for all their holdings, the obligation laid down in paragraph 1 to launch a bid shall no longer apply.

3. The percentage of voting rights which confers control for the purposes of paragraph 1 and the method of its calculation shall be determined by the rules of the Member State in which the company has its registered office.

4. The highest price paid for the same securities by the offeror, or by persons acting in concert with him/her, over a period, to be or determined by Member States, of not less than six months and not more than 12 before the bid referred to in paragraph 1 shall be regarded as the equitable price. If, after the bid has been made public and before the offer closes for acceptance, the offeror or any person acting in concert with him/her purchases securities at a price higher than the offer price, the offeror shall increase his/her offer so that it is not less than the highest price paid for the securities so acquired.

Provided that the general principles laid down in Article 3(1) are respected, Member States may authorise their supervisory authorities to adjust the price referred to in the first subparagraph in circumstances and in accordance with criteria that are clearly determined. To that end, they may draw up a list of circumstances in which the highest price may be adjusted either upwards or downwards, for example where the highest price was set by agreement between the purchaser and a seller, where the market prices of the securities in question have been manipulated, where market prices in general or certain market prices in particular have been affected by exceptional occurrences, or in order to enable a firm in difficulty to be rescued. They may also determine the criteria to be applied in such cases, for example the average market value over a particular period, the break-up value of the company or other objective valuation criteria generally used in financial analysis.

Any decision by a supervisory authority to adjust the equitable price shall be substantiated and made public.

5. By way of consideration the offeror may offer securities, cash or a combination of both.

However, where the consideration offered by the offeror does not consist of liquid securities admitted to trading on a regulated market, it shall include a cash alternative.

In any event, the offeror shall offer a cash consideration at least as an alternative where he/she or persons acting in concert with him/her, over a period beginning at the same time as the period determined by the Member State in accordance with paragraph 4 and ending when the offer closes for acceptance, has purchased for cash securities carrying 5% or more of the voting rights in the offeree company.

Member States may provide that a cash consideration must be offered, at least as an alternative, in all cases.

6. In addition to the protection provided for in paragraph 1, Member States may provide for further instruments intended to protect the interests of the holders of securities in so far as those instruments do not hinder the normal course of a bid.

[11.57]

Article 6 Information concerning bids

1. Member States shall ensure that a decision to make a bid is made public without delay and that the supervisory authority is informed of the bid. They may require that the supervisory authority must be informed before such a decision is made public. As soon as the bid has been made public, the boards of the offeree company and of the offeror shall inform the representatives of their respective employees or, where there are no such representatives, the employees themselves.

2. Member States shall ensure that an offeror is required to draw up and make public in good time an offer document containing the information necessary to enable the holders of the offeree company's securities to reach a properly informed decision on the bid. Before the offer document is made public, the offeror shall communicate it to the supervisory authority. When it is made public, the boards of the offeree company and of the offeror shall communicate it to the representatives of their respective employees or, where there are no such representatives, to the employees themselves.

Where the offer document referred to in the first subparagraph is subject to the prior approval of the supervisory authority and has been approved, it shall be recognised, subject to any translation required, in any other Member State on the market of which the offeree company's securities are admitted to trading, without its being necessary to obtain the approval of the supervisory authorities of that Member State. Those authorities may require the inclusion of additional information in the offer document only if such information is specific to the market of a Member State or Member States on which the offeree company's securities are admitted to trading and relates to the formalities to be complied with to accept the bid and to receive the consideration due at the close of the bid as well as to the tax arrangements to which the consideration offered to the holders of the securities will be subject.

3. The offer document referred to in paragraph 2 shall state at least:

(a) the terms of the bid;
(b) the identity of the offeror and, where the offeror is a company, the type, name and registered office of that company;
(c) the securities or, where appropriate, the class or classes of securities for which the bid is made;
(d) the consideration offered for each security or class of securities and, in the case of a mandatory bid, the method employed in determining it, with particulars of the way in which that consideration is to be paid;
(e) the compensation offered for the rights which might be removed as a result of the breakthrough rule laid down in Article 11(4), with particulars of the way in which that compensation is to be paid and the method employed in determining it;
(f) the maximum and minimum percentages or quantities of securities which the offeror undertakes to acquire;
(g) details of any existing holdings of the offeror, and of persons acting in concert with him/her, in the offeree company;
(h) all the conditions to which the bid is subject;
(i) the offeror's intentions with regard to the future business of the offeree company and, in so far as it is affected by the bid, the offeror company and with regard to the safeguarding of the jobs of their employees and management, including any material change in the conditions of employment, and in particular the offeror's strategic plans for the two companies and the likely repercussions on employment and the locations of the companies' places of business;
(j) the time allowed for acceptance of the bid;
(k) where the consideration offered by the offeror includes securities of any kind, information concerning those securities;
(l) information concerning the financing for the bid;
(m) the identity of persons acting in concert with the offeror or with the offeree company and, in the case of companies, their types, names, registered offices and relationships with the offeror and, where possible, with the offeree company;
(n) the national law which will govern contracts concluded between the offeror and the holders of the offeree company's securities as a result of the bid and the competent courts.

[4. The Commission may adopt rules modifying the list in paragraph 3. Those measures, designed to amend non-essential elements of this Directive, shall be adopted in accordance with the regulatory procedure with scrutiny referred to in Article 18(2).]

5. Member States shall ensure that the parties to a bid are required to provide the supervisory authorities of their Member State at any time on request with all the information in their possession concerning the bid that is necessary for the supervisory authority to discharge its functions.

NOTES

Para 4: substituted by European Parliament and Council Regulation 219/2009/EC, Annex, para 5(1), as from 20 April 2009.

[11.58]

Article 7 Time allowed for acceptance

1. Member States shall provide that the time allowed for the acceptance of a bid may not be less than two weeks nor more than 10 weeks from the date of publication of the offer document. Provided that the general principle laid down in Article 3(1)(f) is respected, Member States may provide that the period of 10 weeks may be extended on condition that the offeror gives at least two weeks' notice of his/her intention of closing the bid.

2 Member States may provide for rules changing the period referred to in paragraph 1 in specific cases. A Member State may authorise a supervisory authority to grant a derogation from the period referred to in paragraph 1 in order to allow the offeree company to call a general meeting of shareholders to consider the bid.

[11.59]

Article 8 Disclosure

1. Member States shall ensure that a bid is made public in such a way as to ensure market transparency and integrity for the securities of the offeree company, of the offeror or of any other company affected by the bid, in particular in order to prevent the publication or dissemination of false or misleading information.

2. Member States shall provide for the disclosure of all information and documents required by Article 6 in such a manner as to ensure that they are both readily and promptly available to the holders of securities at least in those Member States on the regulated markets of which the offeree company's securities are admitted to trading and to the representatives of the employees of the offeree company and the offeror or, where there are no such representatives, to the employees themselves.

[11.60]

Article 9 Obligations of the board of the offeree company

1. Member States shall ensure that the rules laid down in paragraphs 2 to 5 are complied with.

2. During the period referred to in the second subparagraph, the board of the offeree company shall obtain the prior authorisation of the general meeting of shareholders given for this purpose before taking any action, other than seeking alternative bids, which may result in the frustration of the bid and in particular before issuing any shares which may result in a lasting impediment to the offeror's acquiring control of the offeree company.

Such authorisation shall be mandatory at least from the time the board of the offeree company receives the information referred to in the first sentence of Article 6(1) concerning the bid and until the result of the bid is made public or the bid lapses. Member States may require that such authorisation be obtained at an earlier stage, for example as soon as the board of the offeree company becomes aware that the bid is imminent.

3. As regards decisions taken before the beginning of the period referred to in the second subparagraph of paragraph 2 and not yet partly or fully implemented, the general meeting of shareholders shall approve or confirm any decision which does not form part of the normal course of the company's business and the implementation of which may result in the frustration of the bid.

4. For the purpose of obtaining the prior authorisation, approval or confirmation of the holders of securities referred to in paragraphs 2 and 3, Member States may adopt rules allowing a general meeting of shareholders to be called at short notice, provided that the meeting does not take place within two weeks of notification's being given.

5. The board of the offeree company shall draw up and make public a document setting out its opinion of the bid and the reasons on which it is based, including its views on the effects of implementation of the bid on all the company's interests and specifically employment, and on the offeror's strategic plans for the offeree company and their likely repercussions on employment and the locations of the company's places of business as set out in the offer document in accordance with Article 6(3)(i). The board of the offeree company shall at the same time communicate that opinion to the representatives of its employees or, where there are no such representatives, to the employees themselves. Where the board of the offeree company receives in good time a separate opinion from the representatives of its employees on the effects of the bid on employment, that opinion shall be appended to the document.

6. For the purposes of paragraph 2, where a company has a two-tier board structure 'board' shall mean both the management board and the supervisory board.

[11.61]

Article 10 Information on companies as referred to in Article 1(1)

1. Member States shall ensure that companies as referred to in Article 1(1) publish detailed information on the following:

(a) the structure of their capital, including securities which are not admitted to trading on a regulated market in a Member State, where appropriate with an indication of the different classes of shares and, for each class of shares, the rights and obligations attaching to it and the percentage of total share capital that it represents;

(b) any restrictions on the transfer of securities, such as limitations on the holding of securities or the need to obtain the approval of the company or other holders of securities, without prejudice to Article 46 of Directive 2001/34/EC;

(c) significant direct and indirect shareholdings (including indirect shareholdings through pyramid structures and cross-shareholdings) within the meaning of Article 85 of Directive 2001/34/EC;

(d) the holders of any securities with special control rights and a description of those rights;

(e) the system of control of any employee share scheme where the control rights are not exercised directly by the employees;

(f) any restrictions on voting rights, such as limitations of the voting rights of holders of a given percentage or number of votes, deadlines for exercising voting rights, or systems whereby, with the company's cooperation, the financial rights attaching to securities are separated from the holding of securities;
(g) any agreements between shareholders which are known to the company and may result in restrictions on the transfer of securities and/or voting rights within the meaning of Directive 2001/34/EC;
(h) the rules governing the appointment and replacement of board members and the amendment of the articles of association;
(i) the powers of board members, and in particular the power to issue or buy back shares;
(j) any significant agreements to which the company is a party and which take effect, alter or terminate upon a change of control of the company following a takeover bid, and the effects thereof, except where their nature is such that their disclosure would be seriously prejudicial to the company; this exception shall not apply where the company is specifically obliged to disclose such information on the basis of other legal requirements;
(k) any agreements between the company and its board members or employees providing for compensation if they resign or are made redundant without valid reason or if their employment ceases because of a takeover bid.

2. The information referred to in paragraph 1 shall be published in the company's annual report as provided for in Article 46 of Directive 78/660/EEC[1] and Article 36 of Directive 83/349/EEC.[2]
3. Member States shall ensure, in the case of companies the securities of which are admitted to trading on a regulated market in a Member State, that the board presents an explanatory report to the annual general meeting of shareholders on the matters referred to in paragraph 1.

NOTES

1 Fourth Council Directive 78/660/EEC of 25 July 1978 on the annual accounts of certain types of companies (OJ L222, 14.8.1978, p 11). Directive as last amended by Directive 2003/51/EC of the European Parliament and of the Council (OJ L178, 17.7.2003, p 16).

2 Seventh Council Directive 83/349/EEC of 13 June 1983 on consolidated accounts (OJ L193, 18.7.1983, p 1). Directive as last amended by Directive 2003/51/EC.

[11.62]
Article 11 Breakthrough

1. Without prejudice to other rights and obligations provided for in Community law for the companies referred to in Article 1(1), Member States shall ensure that the provisions laid down in paragraphs 2 to 7 apply when a bid has been made public.
2. Any restrictions on the transfer of securities provided for in the articles of association of the offeree company shall not apply vis-à-vis the offeror during the time allowed for acceptance of the bid laid down in Article 7(1).

Any restrictions on the transfer of securities provided for in contractual agreements between the offeree company and holders of its securities, or in contractual agreements between holders of the offeree company's securities entered into after the adoption of this Directive, shall not apply vis-à-vis the offeror during the time allowed for acceptance of the bid laid down in Article 7(1).

3. Restrictions on voting rights provided for in the articles of association of the offeree company shall not have effect at the general meeting of shareholders which decides on any defensive measures in accordance with Article 9.

Restrictions on voting rights provided for in contractual agreements between the offeree company and holders of its securities, or in contractual agreements between holders of the offeree company's securities entered into after the adoption of this Directive, shall not have effect at the general meeting of shareholders which decides on any defensive measures in accordance with Article 9.

Multiple-vote securities shall carry only one vote each at the general meeting of shareholders which decides on any defensive measures in accordance with Article 9.

4. Where, following a bid, the offeror holds 75% or more of the capital carrying voting rights, no restrictions on the transfer of securities or on voting rights referred to in paragraphs 2 and 3 nor any extraordinary rights of shareholders concerning the appointment or removal of board members provided for in the articles of association of the offeree company shall apply; multiple-vote securities shall carry only one vote each at the first general meeting of shareholders following closure of the bid, called by the offeror in order to amend the articles of association or to remove or appoint board members.

To that end, the offeror shall have the right to convene a general meeting of shareholders at short notice, provided that the meeting does not take place within two weeks of notification.

5. Where rights are removed on the basis of paragraphs 2, 3, or 4 and/or Article 12, equitable compensation shall be provided for any loss suffered by the holders of those rights. The terms for determining such compensation and the arrangements for its payment shall be set by Member States.
6. Paragraphs 3 and 4 shall not apply to securities where the restrictions on voting rights are compensated for by specific pecuniary advantages.
7. This Article shall not apply either where Member States hold securities in the offeree company which confer special rights on the Member States which are compatible with the Treaty, or to special rights provided for in national law which are compatible with the Treaty or to cooperatives.

[11.63]
Article 12 Optional arrangements

1. Member States may reserve the right not to require companies as referred to in Article 1(1) which have their registered offices within their territories to apply Article 9(2) and (3) and/or Article 11.
2. Where Member States make use of the option provided for in paragraph 1, they shall nevertheless grant companies which have their registered offices within their territories the option, which shall be reversible, of applying Article 9(2) and (3) and/or Article 11, without prejudice to Article 11(7).

The decision of the company shall be taken by the general meeting of shareholders, in accordance with the law of the Member State in which the company has its registered office in accordance with the rules applicable to amendment of the articles of association. The decision shall be communicated to the supervisory authority of the Member State in which the company has its registered office and to all the supervisory authorities of Member States in which its securities are admitted to trading on regulated markets or where such admission has been requested.

3. Member States may, under the conditions determined by national law, exempt companies which apply Article 9(2) and (3) and/or Article 11 from applying Article 9(2) and (3) and/or Article 11 if they become the subject of an offer launched by a company which does not apply the same Articles as they do, or by a company controlled, directly or indirectly, by the latter, pursuant to Article 1 of Directive 83/349/EEC.

4. Member States shall ensure that the provisions applicable to the respective companies are disclosed without delay.

5. Any measure applied in accordance with paragraph 3 shall be subject to the authorisation of the general meeting of shareholders of the offeree company, which must be granted no earlier than 18 months before the bid was made public in accordance with Article 6(1).

[11.64]

Article 13 Other rules applicable to the conduct of bids

Member States shall also lay down rules which govern the conduct of bids, at least as regards the following:

(a) the lapsing of bids;
(b) the revision of bids;
(c) competing bids;
(d) the disclosure of the results of bids;
(e) the irrevocability of bids and the conditions permitted.

[11.65]

Article 14 Information for and consultation of employees' representatives

This Directive shall be without prejudice to the rules relating to information and to consultation of representatives of and, if Member States so provide, co-determination with the employees of the offeror and the offeree company governed by the relevant national provisions, and in particular those adopted pursuant to Directives 94/45/EC, 98/59/EC, 2001/86/EC and 2002/14/EC.

[11.66]

Article 15 The right of squeeze-out

1. Member States shall ensure that, following a bid made to all the holders of the offeree company's securities for all of their securities, paragraphs 2 to 5 apply.

2. Member States shall ensure that an offeror is able to require all the holders of the remaining securities to sell him/her those securities at a fair price. Member States shall introduce that right in one of the following situations:

(a) where the offeror holds securities representing not less than 90% of the capital carrying voting rights and 90% of the voting rights in the offeree company,

or

(b) where, following acceptance of the bid, he/she has acquired or has firmly contracted to acquire securities representing not less than 90% of the offeree company's capital carrying voting rights and 90% of the voting rights comprised in the bid.

In the case referred to in (a), Member States may set a higher threshold that may not, however, be higher than 95% of the capital carrying voting rights and 95% of the voting rights.

3. Member States shall ensure that rules are in force that make it possible to calculate when the threshold is reached.

Where the offeree company has issued more than one class of securities, Member States may provide that the right of squeeze- out can be exercised only in the class in which the threshold laid down in paragraph 2 has been reached.

4. If the offeror wishes to exercise the right of squeeze-out he/she shall do so within three months of the end of the time allowed for acceptance of the bid referred to in Article 7.

5. Member States shall ensure that a fair price is guaranteed. That price shall take the same form as the consideration offered in the bid or shall be in cash. Member States may provide that cash shall be offered at least as an alternative.

Following a voluntary bid, in both of the cases referred to in paragraph 2(a) and (b), the consideration offered in the bid shall be presumed to be fair where, through acceptance of the bid, the offeror has acquired securities representing not less than 90% of the capital carrying voting rights comprised in the bid.

Following a mandatory bid, the consideration offered in the bid shall be presumed to be fair.

[11.67]

Article 16 The right of sell-out

1. Member States shall ensure that, following a bid made to all the holders of the offeree company's securities for all of their securities, paragraphs 2 and 3 apply.

2. Member States shall ensure that a holder of remaining securities is able to require the offeror to buy his/her securities from him/her at a fair price under the same circumstances as provided for in Article 15(2).

3. Article 15(3) to (5) shall apply *mutatis mutandis*.

[11.68]

Article 17 Sanctions

Member States shall determine the sanctions to be imposed for infringement of the national measures adopted pursuant to this Directive and shall take all necessary steps to ensure that they are put into effect. The sanctions thus provided for shall be effective, proportionate and dissuasive. Member States shall notify the Commission of those measures no later than the date laid down in Article 21(1) and of any subsequent change thereto at the earliest opportunity.

[11.69]

Article 18 Committee procedure

1. The Commission shall be assisted by the European Securities Committee established by Decision 2001/528/EC (hereinafter referred to as 'the Committee').

[2. Where reference is made to this paragraph, Article 5a(1) to (4) and Article 7 of Decision 1999/468/EC shall apply, having regard to the provisions of Article 8 thereof.]

3. . . .

NOTES

Para 2 substituted, and para 3 repealed, by European Parliament and Council Regulation 219/2009/EC, Annex, para 5(2), (3), as from 20 April 2009.

[11.70]

Article 19 Contact committee

1. A contact committee shall be set up which has as its functions:
   (a) to facilitate, without prejudice to Articles 226 and 227 of the Treaty, the harmonised application of this Directive through regular meetings dealing with practical problems arising in connection with its application;
   (b) to advise the Commission, if necessary, on additions or amendments to this Directive.
2. It shall not be the function of the contact committee to appraise the merits of decisions taken by the supervisory authorities in individual cases.

[11.71]

Article 20 Revision

Five years after the date laid down in Article 21(1), the Commission shall examine this Directive in the light of the experience acquired in applying it and, if necessary, propose its revision. That examination shall include a survey of the control structures and barriers to takeover bids that are not covered by this Directive.

To that end, Member States shall provide the Commission annually with information on the takeover bids which have been launched against companies the securities of which are admitted to trading on their regulated markets. That information shall include the nationalities of the companies involved, the results of the offers and any other information relevant to the understanding of how takeover bids operate in practice.

[11.72]

Article 21 Transposition

1. Member States shall bring into force the laws, regulations and administrative provisions necessary to comply with this Directive no later than 20 May 2006. They shall forthwith inform the Commission thereof.

When Member States adopt those provisions, they shall contain a reference to this Directive or shall be accompanied by such reference on the occasion of their official publication. The methods of making such reference shall be laid down by the Member States.

2. Member States shall communicate to the Commission the text of the main provisions of national law that they adopt in the fields covered by this Directive.

[11.73]

Article 22 Entry into force

This Directive shall enter into force on the 20th day after that of its publication in the *Official Journal of the European Union*.

[11.74]

Article 23 Addressees

This Directive is addressed to Member States.

DIRECTIVE OF THE EUROPEAN PARLIAMENT AND OF THE COUNCIL

(2004/109/EC)

of 15 December 2004

on the harmonisation of transparency requirements in relation to information about issuers whose securities are admitted to trading on a regulated market and amending Directive 2001/34/EC

[11.75]

NOTES

Date of publication in OJ: OJ L390, 31.12.2004, p 38.

This Directive is reproduced as amended by: European Parliament and Council Directive 2008/22/EC (no transposition necessary); European Parliament and Council Directive 2010/73/EU (transposition date 1 July 2012); European Parliament and Council Directive 2010/78/EU (where transposition was required, the relevant date was 31 December 2011); European Parliament and Council Directive 2013/50/EU (transposition date 26 November 2015); European Parliament and Council Regulation 2021/337/EU.

Editorial note (legal status of EU Directives in the UK): note that EU Directives are not "direct EU legislation" within the meaning of the European Union (Withdrawal) Act 2018, s 3 at **[12.5]** and, accordingly, do not apply to the UK. As to the status of EU-derived domestic legislation after IP completion day (11pm on 31 December 2020), see s 2 of the 2018 Act at **[12.4]**. As to the UK implementation of this Directive, see the note below.

UK Implementation: in the UK this Directive was implemented by the Companies Act 2006 (Part 43), the Supervision of Accounts and Reports (Prescribed Body) Order 2007, SI 2007/2583 (revoked), the Companies (Defective Accounts and Directors' Reports) (Authorised Person) and Supervision of Accounts and Reports (Prescribed Body) Order 2008, SI 2008/623 (revoked), and FSA Disclosure Rules and Transparency Rules (DTR 1A, DTR 4, DTR 5, and DTR 6).

THE EUROPEAN PARLIAMENT AND THE COUNCIL OF THE EUROPEAN UNION,

Having regard to the Treaty establishing the European Community, and in particular Articles 44 and 95 thereof,

Having regard to the proposal from the Commission,

Having regard to the opinion of the European Economic and Social Committee,[1]

Having regard to the opinion of the European Central Bank,[2]

Acting in accordance with the procedure laid down in Article 251 of the Treaty,[3]

Whereas:

(1) Efficient, transparent and integrated securities markets contribute to a genuine single market in the Community and foster growth and job creation by better allocation of capital and by reducing costs. The disclosure of accurate, comprehensive and timely information about security issuers builds sustained investor confidence and allows an informed assessment of their business performance and assets. This enhances both investor protection and market efficiency.

(2) To that end, security issuers should ensure appropriate transparency for investors through a regular flow of information. To the same end, shareholders, or natural persons or legal entities holding voting rights or financial instruments that result in an entitlement to acquire existing shares with voting rights, should also inform issuers of the acquisition of or other changes in major holdings in companies so that the latter are in a position to keep the public informed.

(3) The Commission Communication of 11 May 1999, entitled "Implementing the framework for financial markets: Action Plan", identifies a series of actions that are needed in order to complete the single market for financial services. The Lisbon European Council of March 2000 calls for the implementation of that Action Plan by 2005. The Action Plan stresses the need to draw up a Directive upgrading transparency requirements. That need was confirmed by the Barcelona European Council of March 2002.

(4) This Directive should be compatible with the tasks and duties conferred upon the European System of Central Banks (ESCB) and the Member States' central banks by the Treaty and the Statute of the European System of Central Banks and of the European Central Bank; particular attention in this regard needs to be given to the Member States' central banks whose shares are currently admitted to trading on a regulated market, in order to guarantee the pursuit of primary Community law objectives.

(5) Greater harmonisation of provisions of national law on periodic and ongoing information requirements for security issuers should lead to a high level of investor protection throughout the Community. However, this Directive does not affect existing Community legislation on units issued by collective investment undertakings other than the closed-end type, or on units acquired or disposed of in such undertakings.

(6) Supervision of an issuer of shares, or of debt securities the denomination per unit of which is less than EUR 1,000, for the purposes of this Directive, would be best effected by the Member State in which the issuer has its registered office. In that respect, it is vital to ensure consistency with Directive 2003/71/EC of the European Parliament and of the Council of 4 November 2003 on the prospectus to be published when securities are offered to the public or admitted to trading.[4] Along the same lines, some flexibility should be introduced allowing third country issuers and Community companies issuing only securities other than those mentioned above a choice of home Member State.

(7) A high level of investor protection throughout the Community would enable barriers to the admission of securities to regulated markets situated or operating within a Member State to be removed. Member States other than the home Member State should no longer be allowed to restrict admission of securities to their regulated markets by imposing more stringent requirements on periodic and ongoing information about issuers whose securities are admitted to trading on a regulated market.

(8) The removal of barriers on the basis of the home Member State principle under this Directive should not affect areas not covered by this Directive, such as rights of shareholders to intervene in the management of an issuer. Nor should it affect the home Member State's right to request the issuer to publish, in addition, parts of or all regulated information through newspapers.

(9) Regulation (EC) No 1606/2002 of the European Parliament and of the Council of 19 July 2002 on the application of international accounting standards[5] has already paved the way for a convergence of financial reporting standards throughout the Community for issuers whose securities are admitted to trading on a regulated market and who are required to prepare consolidated accounts. Thus, a specific regime for security issuers beyond the general system for all companies, as laid down in the Company Law Directives, is already established. This Directive builds on this approach with regard to annual and interim financial reporting, including the principle of providing a true and fair view of an issuer's assets, liabilities, financial position and profit or loss. A condensed set of financial statements, as part of a half-yearly financial report, also represents a sufficient basis for giving such a true and fair view of the first six months of an issuer's financial year.

(10) An annual financial report should ensure information over the years once the issuer's securities have been admitted to a regulated market. Making it easier to compare annual financial reports is only of use to investors in securities markets if they can be sure that this information will be published within a certain time after the end of the financial year. As regards debt securities admitted to trading on a regulated market prior to 1 January 2005 and issued by issuers incorporated in a third country, the home Member State may under certain conditions allow issuers not to prepare annual financial reports in accordance with the standards required under this Directive.

(11) This Directive introduces more comprehensive half-yearly financial reports for issuers of shares admitted to trading on a regulated market. This should allow investors to make a more informed assessment of the issuer's situation.

(12) A home Member State may provide for exemptions from half-yearly reporting by issuers of debt securities in the case of:

— credit institutions acting as small-size issuers of debt securities, or

— issuers already existing on the date of the entry into force of this Directive who exclusively issue debt securities unconditionally and irrevocably guaranteed by the home Member State or by one of its regional or local authorities, or

— during a transitional period of ten years, only in respect of those debt securities admitted to trading on a regulated market prior to 1 January 2005 which may be purchased by professional investors only. If such an exemption is given by the home Member State, it may not be extended in respect of any debt securities admitted to a regulated market thereafter.

(13) The European Parliament and the Council welcome the Commission's commitment rapidly to consider enhancing the transparency of the remuneration policies, total remuneration paid, including any contingent or deferred compensation, and benefits in kind granted to each member of administrative, management or supervisory bodies under its Action Plan for "Modernising Company Law and Enhancing Corporate Governance in the European Union" of 21 May 2003 and the Commission's intention to make a Recommendation on this topic in the near future.

(14) The home Member State should encourage issuers whose shares are admitted to trading on a regulated market and whose principal activities lie in the extractive industry to disclose payments to governments in their annual financial report. The home Member State should also encourage an increase in the transparency of such payments within the framework established at various international financial fora.

(15) This Directive will also make half-yearly reporting mandatory for issuers of only debt securities on regulated markets. Exemptions should only be provided for wholesale markets on the basis of a denomination per unit starting at EUR 50,000, as under Directive 2003/71/EC. Where debt securities are issued in another currency, exemptions should only be possible where the denomination per unit in such a currency is, at the date of the issue, at least equivalent to EUR 50,000.

(16) More timely and more reliable information about the share issuer's performance over the financial year also requires a higher frequency of interim information. A requirement should therefore be introduced to publish an interim management statement during the first six months and a second interim management statement during the second six months of a financial year. Share issuers who already publish quarterly financial reports should not be required to publish interim management statements.

(17) Appropriate liability rules, as laid down by each Member State under its national law or regulations, should be applicable to the issuer, its administrative, management or supervisory bodies, or persons responsible within the issuer. Member States should remain free to determine the extent of the liability.

(18) The public should be informed of changes to major holdings in issuers whose shares are traded on a regulated market situated or operating within the Community. This information should enable investors to acquire or dispose of shares in full knowledge of changes in the voting structure; it should also enhance effective control of share issuers and overall market transparency of important capital movements. Information about shares or financial instruments as determined by Article 13, lodged as collateral, should be provided in certain circumstances.

(19) Articles 9 and 10(c) should not apply to shares provided to or by the members of the ESCB in carrying out their functions as monetary authorities provided that the voting rights attached to such shares are not exercised; the reference to a "short period" in Article 11 should be understood with reference to credit operations carried out in accordance with the Treaty and the European Central Bank (ECB) legal acts, in particular the ECB Guidelines on monetary policy instruments and procedures and TARGET, and to credit operations for the purpose of performing equivalent functions in accordance with national provisions.

(20) In order to avoid unnecessary burdens for certain market participants and to clarify who actually exercises influence over an issuer, there is no need to require notification of major holdings of shares, or other financial instruments as determined by Article 13 that result in an entitlement to acquire shares with regard to market makers or custodians, or of holdings of shares or such financial instruments acquired solely for clearing and settlement purposes, within limits and guarantees to be applied throughout the Community. The home Member State should be allowed to provide limited exemptions as regards holdings of shares in trading books of credit institutions and investment firms.

(21) In order to clarify who is actually a major holder of shares or other financial instruments in the same issuer throughout the Community, parent undertakings should not be required to aggregate their own holdings with those managed by undertakings for collective investment in transferable securities (UCITS) or investment firms, provided that such undertakings or firms exercise voting rights independently from their parent undertakings and fulfil certain further conditions.

(22) Ongoing information to holders of securities admitted to trading on a regulated market should continue to be based on the principle of equal treatment. Such equal treatment only relates to shareholders in the same position and does not therefore prejudice the issue of how many voting rights may be attached to a particular share. By the same token, holders of debt securities ranking pari passu should continue to benefit from equal treatment, even in the case of sovereign debt. Information to holders of shares and/or debt securities in general meetings should be facilitated. In particular, holders of shares and/or debt securities situated abroad should be more actively involved in that they should be able to mandate proxies to act on their behalf. For the same reasons, it should be decided in a general meeting of holders of shares and/or debt securities whether the use of modern information and communication technologies should become a reality. In that case, issuers should put in place arrangements in order effectively to inform holders of their shares and/or debt securities, insofar as it is possible for them to identify those holders.

(23) Removal of barriers and effective enforcement of new Community information requirements also require adequate control by the competent authority of the home Member State. This Directive should at least provide for a minimum guarantee for the timely availability of such information. For this reason, at least one filing and storage system should exist in each Member State.

(24) Any obligation for an issuer to translate all ongoing and periodic information into all the relevant languages in all the Member States where its securities are admitted to trading does not foster integration of securities markets, but has deterrent effects on cross-border admission of securities to trading on regulated markets. Therefore, the issuer should in certain cases be entitled to provide information drawn up in a language that is customary in the sphere of international finance. Since a particular effort is needed to attract investors from other Member States and third countries, Member States should no longer prevent shareholders, persons exercising voting rights, or holders of financial instruments, from making the required notifications to the issuer in a language that is customary in the sphere of international finance.

(25) Access for investors to information about issuers should be more organised at a Community level in order to actively promote integration of European capital markets. Investors who are not situated in the issuer's home Member State should be put on an equal footing with investors situated in the issuer's home Member State, when seeking access to such information. This could be achieved if the home Member State ensures compliance with minimum quality standards for disseminating information throughout the Community, in a fast manner on a non-discriminatory basis and depending on the type of regulated information in question. In addition, information which has been disseminated should be available in the home Member State in a centralised way allowing a European network to be built up, accessible at affordable prices for retail investors, while not leading to unnecessary duplication of filing requirements for issuers. Issuers should benefit from free competition when choosing the media or operators for disseminating information under this Directive.

(26) In order to further simplify investor access to corporate information across Member States, it should be left to the national supervisory authorities to formulate guidelines for setting up electronic networks, in close consultation with the other parties concerned, in particular security issuers, investors, market participants, operators of regulated markets and financial information providers.

(27) So as to ensure the effective protection of investors and the proper operation of regulated markets, the rules relating to information to be published by issuers whose securities are admitted to trading on a regulated market should also apply to issuers which do not have a registered office in a Member State and which do not fall within the scope of Article 48 of the Treaty. It should also be ensured that any additional relevant information about Community issuers or third country issuers, disclosure of which is required in a third country but not in a Member State, is made available to the public in the Community.

(28) A single competent authority should be designated in each Member State to assume final responsibility for supervising compliance with the provisions adopted pursuant to this Directive, as well as for international cooperation. Such an authority should be of an administrative nature, and its independence from economic players should be ensured in order to avoid conflicts of interest. Member States may however designate another competent authority for examining that information referred to in this Directive is drawn up in accordance with the relevant reporting framework and taking appropriate measures in case of discovered infringements; such an authority need not be of an administrative nature.

(29) Increasing cross-border activities require improved cooperation between national competent authorities, including a comprehensive set of provisions for the exchange of information and for precautionary measures. The organisation of the regulatory and supervisory tasks in each Member State should not hinder efficient cooperation between the competent national authorities.

(30) At its meeting on 17 July 2000, the Council set up the Committee of Wise Men on the Regulation of European securities markets. In its final report, that Committee proposed the introduction of new legislative techniques based on a four-level approach, namely essential principles, technical implementing measures, cooperation amongst national securities regulators, and enforcement of Community law. This Directive should confine itself to broad "framework" principles, while implementing measures to be adopted by the Commission with the assistance of the European Securities Committee established by Commission Decision 2001/528/EC[6] should lay down the technical details.

(31) The Resolution adopted by the Stockholm European Council of March 2001 endorsed the final report of the Committee of Wise Men and the proposed four-level approach to make the regulatory process for Community securities legislation more efficient and transparent.

(32) According to that Resolution, implementing measures should be used more frequently, to ensure that technical provisions can be kept up to date with market and supervisory developments, and deadlines should be set for all stages of implementing rules.

(33) The Resolution of the European Parliament of 5 February 2002 on the implementation of financial services legislation also endorsed the Committee of Wise Men's report, on the basis of the solemn declaration made before the European Parliament the same day by the President of the Commission and the letter of 2 October 2001 addressed by the Internal Market Commissioner to the Chairman of the Parliament's Committee on Economic and Monetary Affairs with regard to safeguards for the European Parliament's role in this process.

(34) The European Parliament should be given a period of three months from the first transmission of draft implementing measures to allow it to examine them and to give its opinion. However, in urgent and duly justified cases, that period may be shortened. If, within that period, a Resolution is passed by the European Parliament, the Commission should re-examine the draft measures.

(35) Technical implementing measures for the rules laid down in this Directive may be necessary to take account of new developments on securities markets. The Commission should accordingly be empowered to adopt implementing measures, provided that they do not modify the essential elements of this Directive and provided that the Commission acts in accordance with the principles set out therein, after consulting the European Securities Committee.

(36) In exercising its implementing powers in accordance with this Directive, the Commission should respect the following principles:

- the need to ensure confidence in financial markets among investors by promoting high standards of transparency in financial markets;
- the need to provide investors with a wide range of competing investments and a level of disclosure and protection tailored to their circumstances;
- the need to ensure that independent regulatory authorities enforce the rules consistently, especially as regards the fight against economic crime;
- the need for high levels of transparency and consultation with all market participants and with the European Parliament and the Council;
- the need to encourage innovation in financial markets if they are to be dynamic and efficient;
- the need to ensure market integrity by close and reactive monitoring of financial innovation;
- the importance of reducing the cost of, and increasing access to, capital;
- the balance of costs and benefits to market participants on a long-term basis, including small and medium-sized businesses and small investors, in any implementing measures;

— the need to foster the international competitiveness of Community financial markets without prejudice to a much-needed extension of international cooperation;
— the need to achieve a level playing field for all market participants by establishing Community-wide regulations wherever appropriate;
— the need to respect differences in national markets where these do not unduly impinge on the coherence of the single market;
— the need to ensure coherence with other Community legislation in this area, as imbalances in information and a lack of transparency may jeopardise the operation of the markets and above all harm consumers and small investors.

(37) In order to ensure that the requirements set out in this Directive or the measures implementing this Directive are fulfilled, any infringement of those requirements or measures should be promptly detected and, if necessary, subject to penalties. To that end, measures and penalties should be sufficiently dissuasive, proportionate and consistently enforced. Member States should ensure that decisions taken by the competent national authorities are subject to the right of appeal to the courts.

(38) This Directive aims to upgrade the current transparency requirements for security issuers and investors acquiring or disposing of major holdings in issuers whose shares are admitted to trading on a regulated market. This Directive replaces some of the requirements set out in Directive 2001/34/EC of the European Parliament and of the Council of 28 May 2001 on the admission of securities to official stock exchange listing and on information to be published on those securities.[7] In order to gather transparency requirements in a single act it is necessary to amend it accordingly. Such an amendment however should not affect the ability of Member States to impose additional requirements under Articles 42 to 63 of Directive 2001/34/EC, which remain valid.

(39) This Directive is in line with Directive 95/46/EC of the European Parliament and of the Council of 24 October 1995 on the protection of individuals with regard to the processing of personal data and on the free movement of such data.[8]

(40) This Directive respects fundamental rights and observes the principles recognised in particular by the Charter of the Fundamental Rights of the European Union.

(41) Since the objectives of this Directive, namely to ensure investor confidence through equivalent transparency throughout the Community and thereby to complete the internal market, cannot be sufficiently achieved by the Member States on the basis of the existing Community legislation and can therefore be better achieved at Community level, the Community may adopt measures, in accordance with the principle of subsidiarity as set out in Article 5 of the Treaty. In accordance with the principle of proportionality, as set out in that Article, this Directive does not go beyond what is necessary in order to achieve these objectives.

(42) The measures necessary for implementing this Directive should be adopted in accordance with Council Decision 1999/468/EC of 28 June 1999 laying down the procedures for the exercise of implementing powers conferred on the Commission,[9]

NOTES

1 OJ C80, 30.3.2004, p 128.
2 OJ C242, 9.10.2003, p 6.
3 Opinion of the European Parliament of 30 March 2004 (not yet published in the Official Journal) and Council Decision of 2 December 2004.
4 OJ L345, 31.12.2003, p 64.
5 OJ L243, 11.9.2002, p 1.
6 OJ L191, 13.7.2001, p 45. Decision as amended by Decision 2004/8/EC (OJ L3, 7.1.2004, p 33).
7 OJ L184, 6.7.2001, p 1. Directive as last amended by Directive 2003/71/EC.
8 OJ L281, 23.11.1995, p 31. Directive as amended by Regulation (EC) No 1882/2003 (OJ L284, 31.10.2003, p 1).
9 OJ L184, 17.7.1999, p 23.

HAVE ADOPTED THIS DIRECTIVE:

CHAPTER I GENERAL PROVISIONS

[11.76]
Article 1 Subject matter and scope

1. This Directive establishes requirements in relation to the disclosure of periodic and ongoing information about issuers whose securities are already admitted to trading on a regulated market situated or operating within a Member State.
2. This Directive shall not apply to units issued by collective investment undertakings other than the closed-end type, or to units acquired or disposed of in such collective investment undertakings.
3. Member States may decide not to apply the provisions mentioned in Article 16(3) and in paragraphs 2, 3 and 4 of Article 18 to securities which are admitted to trading on a regulated market issued by them or their regional or local authorities.
4. Member States may decide not to apply Article 17 to their national central banks in their capacity as issuers of shares admitted to trading on a regulated market if this admission took place before 20 January 2005.

[11.77]
Article 2 Definitions

1. For the purposes of this Directive the following definitions shall apply:
(a) "securities" means transferable securities as defined in Article 4(1), point 18, of Directive 2004/39/EC of the European Parliament and of the Council of 21 April 2004 on markets in financial instruments[1] with the exception of money-market instruments, as defined in Article 4(1), point 19, of that Directive having a maturity of less than 12 months, for which national legislation may be applicable;

(b) "debt securities" means bonds or other forms of transferable securitised debts, with the exception of securities which are equivalent to shares in companies or which, if converted or if the rights conferred by them are exercised, give rise to a right to acquire shares or securities equivalent to shares;

(c) "regulated market" means a market as defined in Article 4(1), point 14, of Directive 2004/39/EC;

[(d) "issuer" means a natural person, or a legal entity governed by private or public law, including a State, whose securities are admitted to trading on a regulated market.

In the case of depository receipts admitted to trading on a regulated market, the issuer means the issuer of the securities represented, whether or not those securities are admitted to trading on a regulated market;]

(e) "shareholder" means any natural person or legal entity governed by private or public law, who holds, directly or indirectly:

(i) shares of the issuer in its own name and on its own account;

(ii) shares of the issuer in its own name, but on behalf of another natural person or legal entity;

(iii) depository receipts, in which case the holder of the depository receipt shall be considered as the shareholder of the underlying shares represented by the depository receipts;

(f) "controlled undertaking" means any undertaking

(i) in which a natural person or legal entity has a majority of the voting rights; or

(ii) of which a natural person or legal entity has the right to appoint or remove a majority of the members of the administrative, management or supervisory body and is at the same time a shareholder in, or member of, the undertaking in question; or

(iii) of which a natural person or legal entity is a shareholder or member and alone controls a majority of the shareholders' or members' voting rights, respectively, pursuant to an agreement entered into with other shareholders or members of the undertaking in question; or

(iv) over which a natural person or legal entity has the power to exercise, or actually exercises, dominant influence or control;

(g) "collective investment undertaking other than the closed-end type" means unit trusts and investment companies:

(i) the object of which is the collective investment of capital provided by the public, and which operate on the principle of risk spreading; and

(ii) the units of which are, at the request of the holder of such units, repurchased or redeemed, directly or indirectly, out of the assets of those undertakings;

(h) "units of a collective investment undertaking" means securities issued by a collective investment undertaking and representing rights of the participants in such an undertaking over its assets;

(i) "home Member State" means

[(i) in the case of an issuer of debt securities the denomination per unit of which is less than EUR 1000 or an issuer of shares:

— where the issuer is incorporated in the Union, the Member State in which it has its registered office,

[— where the issuer is incorporated in a third country, the Member State chosen by the issuer from amongst the Member States where its securities are admitted to trading on a regulated market. The choice of home Member State shall remain valid unless the issuer has chosen a new home Member State under point (iii) and has disclosed the choice in accordance with the second paragraph of this point [letter] (i);]

The definition of "home" Member State shall be applicable to debt securities in a currency other than euro, provided that the value of such denomination per unit is, at the date of the issue, less than EUR 1000, unless it is nearly equivalent to EUR 1000;]

[(ii) for any issuer not covered by point (i), the Member State chosen by the issuer from among the Member State in which the issuer has its registered office, where applicable, and those Member States where its securities are admitted to trading on a regulated market. The issuer may choose only one Member State as its home Member State. Its choice shall remain valid for at least three years unless its securities are no longer admitted to trading on any regulated market in the Union or unless the issuer becomes covered by points (i) or (iii) during the three-year period;]

[(iii) for an issuer whose securities are no longer admitted to trading on a regulated market in its home Member State as defined by the second indent of point (i) or (ii) but instead are admitted to trading in one or more other Member States, such new home Member State as the issuer may choose from amongst the Member States where its securities are admitted to trading on a regulated market and, where applicable, the Member State where the issuer has its registered office;]

[An issuer shall disclose its home Member State as referred to in points (i), (ii) or (iii) in accordance with Articles 20 and 21. In addition, an issuer shall disclose its home Member State to the competent authority of the Member State where it has its registered office, where applicable, to the competent authority of the home Member State and to the competent authorities of all host Member States.

In the absence of disclosure by the issuer of its home Member State as defined by the second indent of point (i) or (ii) within a period of three months from the date the issuers' securities are first admitted to trading on a regulated market, the home Member State shall be the Member State where the issuer's securities are admitted to trading on a regulated market. Where the issuer's securities are admitted to trading on regulated markets situated or operating within more than one Member State, those Member States shall be the issuer's home Member States until a subsequent choice of a single home Member State has been made and disclosed by the issuer.

For an issuer whose securities are already admitted to trading on a regulated market and whose choice of home Member State as referred to in the second indent of point (i) or in point (ii) has not been disclosed prior to 27 November 2015, the period of three months shall start on 27 November 2015.

An issuer that has made a choice of a home Member State as referred to in the second indent of point (i) or in point (ii) or (iii) and has communicated that choice to the competent authorities of the home Member State prior to 27 November 2015 shall be exempted from the requirement under the second paragraph of this point [letter] (i), unless such issuer chooses another home Member State after 27 November 2015];

(j) "host Member State" means a Member State in which securities are admitted to trading on a regulated market, if different from the home Member State;

(k) "regulated information" means all information which the issuer, or any other person who has applied for the admission of securities to trading on a regulated market without the issuer's consent, is required to disclose under this Directive, under Article 6 of Directive 2003/6/EC of the European Parliament and of the Council of 28 January 2003 on insider dealing and market manipulation (market abuse),[2] or under the laws, regulations or administrative provisions of a Member State adopted under Article 3(1) of this Directive;

(l) "electronic means" are means of electronic equipment for the processing (including digital compression), storage and transmission of data, employing wires, radio, optical technologies, or any other electromagnetic means;

(m) "management company" means a company as defined in Article 1a(2) of Council Directive 85/611/EEC of 20 December 1985 on the coordination of laws, regulations and administrative provisions relating to undertakings for collective investment in transferable securities (UCITS);[3]

(n) "market maker" means a person who holds himself out on the financial markets on a continuous basis as being willing to deal on own account by buying and selling financial instruments against his proprietary capital at prices defined by him;

(o) "credit institution" means an undertaking as defined in Article 1(1)(a) of Directive 2000/12/EC of the European Parliament and of the Council of 20 March 2000 relating to the taking up and pursuit of the business of credit institutions;[4]

(p) "securities issued in a continuous or repeated manner" means debt securities of the same issuer on tap or at least two separate issues of securities of a similar type and/or class;

[(q) "formal agreement" means an agreement which is binding under the applicable law.]

2. For the purposes of the definition of "controlled undertaking" in paragraph 1(f)(ii), the holder's rights in relation to voting, appointment and removal shall include the rights of any other undertaking controlled by the shareholder and those of any natural person or legal entity acting, albeit in its own name, on behalf of the shareholder or of any other undertaking controlled by the shareholder.

[2a. Any reference to legal entities in this Directive shall be understood as including registered business associations without legal personality and trusts.]

[[3. In order to take account of technical developments on financial markets, to specify the requirements and to ensure the uniform application of paragraph 1, the Commission shall adopt, in accordance with Article 27(2a), (2b) and (2c), and subject to the conditions of Articles 27a and 27b, measures concerning the definitions set out in paragraph 1.]

The Commission shall, in particular:

(a) establish, for the purposes of paragraph 1(i)(ii), the procedural arrangements in accordance with which an issuer may make the choice of the home Member State;

(b) adjust, where appropriate for the purposes of the choice of the home Member State referred to in paragraph 1(i)(ii), the three-year period in relation to the issuer's track record in the light of any new requirement under Community law concerning admission to trading on a regulated market; and

(c) establish, for the purposes of paragraph 1(l), an indicative list of means which are not to be considered as electronic means, thereby taking into account Annex V to Directive 98/34/EC of the European Parliament and of the Council of 22 June 1998 laying down a procedure for the provision of information in the field of technical standards and regulations and of rules on Information Society services[5] in accordance with the regulatory procedure referred to in Article 27(2).

[The measures referred to in points (a) and (b) of the second subparagraph shall be laid down by means of delegated acts in accordance with Article 27(2a), (2b) and (2c), and subject to the conditions of Articles 27a and 27b.]]

NOTES

Para 1: point (i)(i) substituted by European Parliament and Council Directive 2010/73/EU, Art 2(1), as from 31 December 2010. All other words in square brackets inserted or substituted by European Parliament and Council Directive 2013/50/EU, Art 1(1)(a), as from 26 November 2013.

Para 2a: inserted by European Parliament and Council Directive 2013/50/EU, Art 1(1)(b), as from 26 November 2013.

Para 3: substituted by European Parliament and Council Directive 2008/22/EC, Art 1(1), as from 20 March 2008. First and third sub-paragraphs further substituted by European Parliament and Council Directive 2010/78/EU, Art 7(1), as from 4 January 2011.

Implementing Act for the purposes of para 3(a): see Commission Directive 2007/14/EC laying down detailed rules for the implementation of certain provisions of Directive 2004/109/EC on the harmonisation of transparency requirements in relation to information about issuers whose securities are admitted to trading on a regulated market. See the EUR-Lex website at eur-lex.europa.eu/legal-content/EN/TXT/?uri=CELEX:32007L0014.

1 OJ L145, 30.4.2004, p 1.

2 OJ L96, 12.4.2003, p 16.

3 OJ L375, 31.12.1985, p 3. Directive as last amended by Directive 2004/39/EC.

4 OJ L126, 26.5.2000, p 1. Directive as last amended by Commission Directive 2004/69/EC (OJ L125, 28.4.2004, p 44).

5 OJ L 204, 21.7.1998, p 37. Directive as last amended by Council Directive 2006/96/EC (OJ L 363, 20.12.2006, p 81).

[11.78]

Article 3 Integration of securities markets

[1. The home Member State may make an issuer subject to requirements more stringent than those laid down in this Directive, except that it may not require issuers to publish periodic financial information on a more frequent basis than the annual financial reports referred to in Article 4 and the half-yearly financial reports referred to in Article 5.]

[1a. By way of derogation from paragraph 1, the home Member States may require issuers to publish additional periodic financial information on a more frequent basis than the annual financial reports referred to in Article 4 and the half-yearly financial reports referred to in Article 5, where the following conditions are met:

— the additional periodic financial information does not constitute a disproportionate financial burden in the Member State concerned, in particular for the small and medium-sized issuers concerned, and

— the content of the additional periodic financial information required is proportionate to the factors that contribute to investment decisions by the investors in the Member State concerned.

Before taking a decision requiring issuers to publish additional periodic financial information, Member States shall assess both whether such additional requirements may lead to an excessive focus on the issuers' short-term results and performance and whether they may impact negatively on the ability of small and medium-sized issuers to have access to the regulated markets.

This is without prejudice to the ability of Member States to require the publication of additional periodic financial information by issuers who are financial institutions.

The home Member State may not make a holder of shares, or a natural person or legal entity referred to in Article 10 or 13, subject to requirements more stringent than those laid down in this Directive, except when:

(i) setting lower or additional notification thresholds than those laid down in Article 9(1) and requiring equivalent notifications in relation to thresholds based on capital holdings;

(ii) applying more stringent requirements than those referred to in Article 12; or

(iii) applying laws, regulations or administrative provisions adopted in relation to takeover bids, merger transactions and other transactions affecting the ownership or control of companies, supervised by the authorities appointed by Member States pursuant to Article 4 of Directive 2004/25/EC of the European Parliament and of the Council of 21 April 2004 on takeover bids.[1]]

2. A host Member State may not:

(a) as regards the admission of securities to a regulated market in its territory, impose disclosure requirements more stringent than those laid down in this Directive or in Article 6 of Directive 2003/6/EC;

(b) as regards the notification of information, make a holder of shares, or a natural person or legal entity referred to in Articles 10 or 13, subject to requirements more stringent than those laid down in this Directive.

NOTES

Para 1: substituted by European Parliament and Council Directive 2013/50/EU, Art 1(2)(a), as from 26 November 2013.

Para 1a: inserted by European Parliament and Council Directive 2013/50/EU, Art 1(2)(b), as from 26 November 2013.

[1] OJ L142, 30.4.2004, p 12.

CHAPTER II PERIODIC INFORMATION

[11.79]

Article 4 Annual financial reports

[1. The issuer shall make public its annual financial report at the latest four months after the end of each financial year and shall ensure that it remains publicly available for at least 10 years.]

2. The annual financial report shall comprise:

(a) the audited financial statements;

(b) the management report; and

(c) statements made by the persons responsible within the issuer, whose names and functions shall be clearly indicated, to the effect that, to the best of their knowledge, the financial statements prepared in accordance with the applicable set of accounting standards give a true and fair view of the assets, liabilities, financial position and profit or loss of the issuer and the undertakings included in the consolidation taken as a whole and that the management report includes a fair review of the development and performance of the business and the position of the issuer and the undertakings included in the consolidation taken as a whole, together with a description of the principal risks and uncertainties that they face.

3. Where the issuer is required to prepare consolidated accounts according to the Seventh Council Directive 83/349/EEC of 13 June 1983 on consolidated accounts,[1] the audited financial statements shall comprise such consolidated accounts drawn up in accordance with Regulation (EC) No 1606/2002 and the annual accounts of the parent company drawn up in accordance with the national law of the Member State in which the parent company is incorporated.

Where the issuer is not required to prepare consolidated accounts, the audited financial statements shall comprise the accounts prepared in accordance with the national law of the Member State in which the company is incorporated.

4. The financial statements shall be audited in accordance with Articles 51 and 51a of the Fourth Council Directive 78/660/EEC of 25 July 1978 on the annual accounts of certain types of companies[2] and, if the issuer is required to prepare consolidated accounts, in accordance with Article 37 of Directive 83/349/EEC.

The audit report, signed by the person or persons responsible for auditing the financial statements, shall be disclosed in full to the public together with the annual financial report.

5. The management report shall be drawn up in accordance with Article 46 of Directive 78/660/EEC and, if the issuer is required to prepare consolidated accounts, in accordance with Article 36 of Directive 83/349/EEC.

6. The Commission shall, in accordance with the procedure referred to in Article 27(2), adopt implementing measures in order to take account of technical developments in financial markets and to ensure the uniform application of paragraph 1. The Commission shall in particular specify the technical conditions under which a published annual financial report, including the audit report, is to remain available to the public. Where appropriate, the Commission may also adapt the five-year period referred to in paragraph 1.

[7. [For financial years beginning on or after 1 January 2020, all annual financial reports shall be prepared in a single electronic reporting format provided that a cost-benefit analysis has been undertaken by the European Supervisory Authority (European Securities and Markets Authority) (ESMA) established by Regulation (EU) No 1095/2010 of the European Parliament and of the Council.[3] However, a Member State may allow issuers to apply that reporting requirement for financial years beginning on or after 1 January 2021, provided that that Member State notifies the Commission of its intention to allow such a delay by 19 March 2021, and that its intention is duly justified.]

ESMA shall develop draft regulatory technical standards to specify the electronic reporting format, with due reference to current and future technological options. Before the adoption of the draft regulatory technical standards, ESMA shall carry out an adequate assessment of possible electronic reporting formats and conduct appropriate field tests. ESMA shall submit those draft regulatory technical standards to the Commission at the latest by 31 December 2016.

Power is delegated to the Commission to adopt the regulatory technical standards referred to in the second subparagraph in accordance with Articles 10 to 14 of Regulation (EU) No 1095/2010.]

NOTES

Para 1: substituted by European Parliament and Council Directive 2013/50/EU, Art 1(3)(a), as from 26 November 2013.

Para 7: added by European Parliament and Council Directive 2013/50/EU, Art 1(3)(b), as from 26 November 2013. Words in square brackets substituted by European Parliament and Council Regulation 2021/337/EU, Art 2, as from 18 March 2021.

Regulatory technical standards for the purposes of para 7: see Commission Delegated Regulation 2019/815/EU supplementing Directive 2004/109/EC of the European Parliament and of the Council with regard to regulatory technical standards on the specification of a single electronic reporting format. See the EUR-Lex website at eur-lex.europa.eu/legal-content/EN/TXT/?uri=CELEX:32019R0815. See also (i) Commission Delegated Regulation 2019/2100/EU amending Delegated Regulation (EU) 2019/815 with regard to updates of the taxonomy to be used for the single electronic reporting format; (ii) Commission Delegated Regulation 2020/1989/EU amending Delegated Regulation (EU) 2019/815 as regards the 2020 update of the taxonomy laid down in the regulatory technical standards for the single electronic reporting format; (iii) Commission Delegated Regulation 2022/352/EU amending Delegated Regulation (EU) 2019/815 as regards the 2021 update of the taxonomy laid down in the regulatory technical standards on the single electronic reporting format.

[1] OJ L193, 18.7.1983, p 1. Directive as last amended by Directive 2003/51/EC of the European Parliament and of the Council (OJ L178, 17.7.2003, p 16).

[2] OJ L222, 14.8.1978, p 11. Directive as last amended by Directive 2003/51/EC.

[3] OJ L331, 15.12.2010, p 84.

[11.80]

Article 5 Half-yearly financial reports

[1. The issuer of shares or debt securities shall make public a half-yearly financial report covering the first six months of the financial year as soon as possible after the end of the relevant period, but at the latest three months thereafter. The issuer shall ensure that the half-yearly financial report remains available to the public for at least 10 years.]

2. The half-yearly financial report shall comprise:

(a) the condensed set of financial statements;

(b) an interim management report; and

(c) statements made by the persons responsible within the issuer, whose names and functions shall be clearly indicated, to the effect that, to the best of their knowledge, the condensed set of financial statements which has been prepared in accordance with the applicable set of accounting standards gives a true and fair view of the assets, liabilities, financial position and profit or loss of the issuer, or the undertakings included in the consolidation as a whole as required under paragraph 3, and that the interim management report includes a fair review of the information required under paragraph 4.

3. Where the issuer is required to prepare consolidated accounts, the condensed set of financial statements shall be prepared in accordance with the international accounting standard applicable to the interim financial reporting adopted pursuant to the procedure provided for under Article 6 of Regulation (EC) No 1606/2002.

Where the issuer is not required to prepare consolidated accounts, the condensed set of financial statements shall at least contain a condensed balance sheet, a condensed profit and loss account and explanatory notes on these accounts. In preparing the condensed balance sheet and the condensed profit and loss account, the issuer shall follow the same principles for recognising and measuring as when preparing annual financial reports.

4. The interim management report shall include at least an indication of important events that have occurred during the first six months of the financial year, and their impact on the condensed set of financial statements, together with a description of the principal risks and uncertainties for the remaining six months of the financial year. For issuers of shares, the interim management report shall also include major related parties transactions.

5. If the half-yearly financial report has been audited, the audit report shall be reproduced in full. The same shall apply in the case of an auditors' review. If the half-yearly financial report has not been audited or reviewed by auditors, the issuer shall make a statement to that effect in its report.

[6. The Commission shall adopt, in accordance with Article 27(2) or Article 27(2a), (2b) and (2c), in order to take account of technical developments on financial markets, measures to specify the requirements and ensure the uniform application of paragraphs 1 to 5 of this Article.]

The Commission shall, in particular:

(a) specify the technical conditions under which a published half-yearly financial report, including the auditors' review, is to remain available to the public;

(b) clarify the nature of the auditors' review;

(c) specify the minimum content of the condensed balance sheet and profit and loss accounts and explanatory notes on these accounts, where they are not prepared in accordance with the international accounting standards adopted pursuant to the procedure provided for under Article 6 of Regulation (EC) No 1606/2002.

[The measures referred to in point (a) shall be adopted in accordance with the regulatory procedure referred to in Article 27(2). The measures referred to in points (b) and (c) shall be laid down by means of delegated acts in accordance with Article 27(2a), (2b) and (2c), and subject to the conditions of Articles 27a and 27b.]

[Where appropriate, the Commission may also adapt the five-year period referred to in paragraph 1 by means of a delegated act in accordance with Article 27(2a), (2b) and (2c), and subject to the conditions of Articles 27a and 27b.]

NOTES

Para 1: substituted by European Parliament and Council Directive 2013/50/EU, Art 1(4), as from 26 November 2013.

Para 6: words in square brackets substituted by European Parliament and Council Directive 2010/78/EU, Art 7(2), as from 4 January 2011.

Implementing Act for the purposes of para 6: see Commission Directive 2007/14/EC laying down detailed rules for the implementation of certain provisions of Directive 2004/109/EC on the harmonisation of transparency requirements in relation to information about issuers whose securities are admitted to trading on a regulated market. See the EUR-Lex website at eur-lex.europa.eu/legal-content/EN/TXT/?uri=CELEX:32007L0014.

[11.81]

[Article 6 Report on payments to governments

Member States shall require issuers active in the extractive or logging of primary forest industries, as defined in Article 41(1) and (2) of Directive 2013/34/EU of the European Parliament and of the Council of 26 June 2013 on the annual financial statements, consolidated financial statements and related reports of certain types of undertakings, amending Directive 2006/43/EC of the European Parliament and of the Council and repealing Council Directives 78/660/EEC and 83/349/EEC,[1] to prepare on an annual basis, in accordance with Chapter 10 of that Directive, a report on payments made to governments. The report shall be made public at the latest six months after the end of each financial year and shall remain publicly available for at least 10 years. Payments to governments shall be reported at consolidated level.]

NOTES

Substituted by European Parliament and Council Directive 2013/50/EU, Art 1(5), as from 26 November 2013.

[1] OJ L182, 29.6.2013, p 19.

[11.82]

Article 7 Responsibility and liability

Member States shall ensure that responsibility for the information to be drawn up and made public in accordance with Articles 4, 5, 6 and 16 lies at least with the issuer or its administrative, management or supervisory bodies and shall ensure that their laws, regulations and administrative provisions on liability apply to the issuers, the bodies referred to in this Article or the persons responsible within the issuers.

[11.83]

Article 8 Exemptions

[1. Articles 4 and 5 shall not apply to the following issuers:

(a) a State, a regional or local authority of a State, a public international body of which at least one Member State is a member, the European Central Bank (ECB), the European Financial Stability Facility (EFSF) established by the EFSF Framework Agreement and any other mechanism established with the objective of preserving the financial stability of European monetary union by providing temporary financial assistance to the Member States whose currency is the euro and Member States' national central banks whether or not they issue shares or other securities; and

(b) an issuer exclusively of debt securities admitted to trading on a regulated market, the denomination per unit of which is at least EUR 100,000 or, in the case of debt securities denominated in a currency other than euro, the value of such denomination per unit is, at the date of the issue, equivalent to at least EUR 100,000.]

2. The home Member State may choose not to apply Article 5 to credit institutions whose shares are not admitted to trading on a regulated market and which have, in a continuous or repeated manner, only issued debt securities provided that the total nominal amount of all such debt securities remains below EUR 100,000,000 and that they have not published a prospectus under Directive 2003/71/EC.

3. The home Member State may choose not to apply Article 5 to issuers already existing at the date of the entry into force of Directive 2003/71/EC which exclusively issue debt securities unconditionally and irrevocably guaranteed by the home Member State or by one of its regional or local authorities, on a regulated market.

[4. By way of derogation from point (b) of paragraph 1 of this Article, Articles 4 and 5 shall not apply to issuers exclusively of debt securities the denomination per unit of which is at least EUR 50,000 or, in the case of debt securities denominated in a currency other than euro, the value of such denomination per unit is, at the date of the issue, equivalent to at least EUR 50,000, which have already been admitted to trading on a regulated market in the Union before 31 December 2010, for as long as such debt securities are outstanding.]

NOTES

Para 1: substituted by European Parliament and Council Directive 2013/50/EU, Art 1(6)(a), as from 26 November 2013.

Para 4: originally added by European Parliament and Council Directive 2010/73/EU, Art 2(2)(b), as from 31 December 2010. Subsequently substituted by European Parliament and Council Directive 2013/50/EU, Art 1(6)(b), as from 26 November 2013.

CHAPTER III ONGOING INFORMATION

SECTION I INFORMATION ABOUT MAJOR HOLDINGS

[11.84]

Article 9 Notification of the acquisition or disposal of major holdings

1. The home Member State shall ensure that, where a shareholder acquires or disposes of shares of an issuer whose shares are admitted to trading on a regulated market and to which voting rights are attached, such shareholder notifies the issuer of the proportion of voting rights of the issuer held by the shareholder as a result of the acquisition or disposal where that proportion reaches, exceeds or falls below the thresholds of 5%, 10%, 15%, 20%, 25%, 30%, 50% and 75%.

The voting rights shall be calculated on the basis of all the shares to which voting rights are attached even if the exercise thereof is suspended. Moreover this information shall also be given in respect of all the shares which are in the same class and to which voting rights are attached.

2. The home Member States shall ensure that the shareholders notify the issuer of the proportion of voting rights, where that proportion reaches, exceeds or falls below the thresholds provided for in paragraph 1, as a result of events changing the breakdown of voting rights, and on the basis of the information disclosed pursuant to Article 15. Where the issuer is incorporated in a third country, the notification shall be made for equivalent events.

3. The home Member State need not apply:
- (a) the 30% threshold, where it applies a threshold of one-third;
- (b) the 75% threshold, where it applies a threshold of two-thirds.

4. This Article shall not apply to shares acquired for the sole purpose of clearing and settling within the usual short settlement cycle, or to custodians holding shares in their custodian capacity provided such custodians can only exercise the voting rights attached to such shares under instructions given in writing or by electronic means.

5. This Article shall not apply to the acquisition or disposal of a major holding reaching or crossing the 5% threshold by a market maker acting in its capacity of a market maker, provided that:
- (a) it is authorised by its home Member State under Directive 2004/39/EC; and
- (b) it neither intervenes in the management of the issuer concerned nor exerts any influence on the issuer to buy such shares or back the share price.

[6. This Article shall not apply to voting rights held in the trading book, as defined in Article 11 of Directive 2006/49/EC of the European Parliament and of the Council of 14 June 2006 on the capital adequacy of investment firms and credit institutions,[1] of a credit institution or investment firm provided that:
- (a) the voting rights held in the trading book do not exceed 5%; and
- (b) the voting rights attached to shares held in the trading book are not exercised or otherwise used to intervene in the management of the issuer.]

[6a. This Article shall not apply to voting rights attached to shares acquired for stabilisation purposes in accordance with Commission Regulation (EC) No 2273/2003 of 22 December 2003 implementing Directive 2003/6/EC of the European Parliament and of the Council as regards exemptions for buy-back programmes and stabilisation of financial instruments,[2] provided the voting rights attached to those shares are not exercised or otherwise used to intervene in the management of the issuer.

6b. ESMA shall develop draft regulatory technical standards to specify the method of calculation of the 5% threshold referred to in paragraphs 5 and 6, including in the case of a group of companies, taking into account Article 12(4) and (5).

ESMA shall submit those draft regulatory technical standards to the Commission by 27 November 2014.

Power is delegated to the Commission to adopt the regulatory technical standards referred to in the first subparagraph in accordance with Articles 10 to 14 of Regulation (EU) No 1095/2010.]

[[7. The Commission shall adopt, by means of delegated acts in accordance with Article 27(2a), (2b) and (2c), and subject to the conditions of Articles 27a and 27b, measures in order to take account of technical developments on financial markets and to specify the requirements laid down in paragraphs 2, 4 and 5.]

[The Commission shall specify, by means of delegated acts in accordance with Article 27(2a), (2b) and (2c), and subject to the conditions of Articles 27a and 27b, the maximum length of the "short settlement cycle" referred to in paragraph 4 of this Article, as well as the appropriate control mechanisms by the competent authority of the home Member State.]

In addition, the Commission may draw up a list of the events referred to in paragraph 2 of this Article, in accordance with the regulatory procedure referred to in Article 27(2).]

NOTES

Para 6: substituted by European Parliament and Council Directive 2013/50/EU, Art 1(7)(a), as from 26 November 2013.

Paras 6a, 6b: inserted by European Parliament and Council Directive 2013/50/EU, Art 1(7)(b), as from 26 November 2013.

Para 7: substituted by European Parliament and Council Directive 2008/22/EC, Art 1(3), as from 20 March 2008. First and second sub-paragraphs further substituted by European Parliament and Council Directive 2010/78/EU, Art 7(3), as from 4 January 2011.

Implementing Act for the purposes of para 7: see Commission Directive 2007/14/EC laying down detailed rules for the implementation of certain provisions of Directive 2004/109/EC on the harmonisation of transparency requirements in relation to information about issuers whose securities are admitted to trading on a regulated market. See the EUR-Lex website at eur-lex.europa.eu/legal-content/EN/TXT/?uri=CELEX:32007L0014.

[1] OJ L177, 30.6.2006, p 201.

[2] OJ L336, 23.12.2003, p 33.

[11.85]

Article 10 Acquisition or disposal of major proportions of voting rights

The notification requirements defined in paragraphs 1 and 2 of Article 9 shall also apply to a natural person or legal entity to the extent it is entitled to acquire, to dispose of, or to exercise voting rights in any of the following cases or a combination of them:
- (a) voting rights held by a third party with whom that person or entity has concluded an agreement, which obliges them to adopt, by concerted exercise of the voting rights they hold, a lasting common policy towards the management of the issuer in question;
- (b) voting rights held by a third party under an agreement concluded with that person or entity providing for the temporary transfer for consideration of the voting rights in question;
- (c) voting rights attaching to shares which are lodged as collateral with that person or entity, provided the person or entity controls the voting rights and declares its intention of exercising them;
- (d) voting rights attaching to shares in which that person or entity has the life interest;
- (e) voting rights which are held, or may be exercised within the meaning of points (a) to (d), by an undertaking controlled by that person or entity;

(f) voting rights attaching to shares deposited with that person or entity which the person or entity can exercise at its discretion in the absence of specific instructions from the shareholders;
(g) voting rights held by a third party in its own name on behalf of that person or entity;
(h) voting rights which that person or entity may exercise as a proxy where the person or entity can exercise the voting rights at its discretion in the absence of specific instructions from the shareholders.

[11.86]
Article 11
1. Articles 9 and 10(c) shall not apply to shares provided to or by the members of the ESCB in carrying out their functions as monetary authorities, including shares provided to or by members of the ESCB under a pledge or repurchase or similar agreement for liquidity granted for monetary policy purposes or within a payment system.
2. The exemption shall apply to the above transactions lasting for a short period and provided that the voting rights attaching to such shares are not exercised.

[11.87]
Article 12 Procedures on the notification and disclosure of major holdings
1. The notification required under Articles 9 and 10 shall include the following information:
(a) the resulting situation in terms of voting rights;
(b) the chain of controlled undertakings through which voting rights are effectively held, if applicable;
(c) the date on which the threshold was reached or crossed; and
(d) the identity of the shareholder, even if that shareholder is not entitled to exercise voting rights under the conditions laid down in Article 10, and of the natural person or legal entity entitled to exercise voting rights on behalf of that shareholder.
2. [The notification to the issuer shall be effected promptly, but not later than four trading days after the date on which the shareholder, or the natural person or legal person referred to in Article 10,]
(a) learns of the acquisition or disposal or of the possibility of exercising voting rights, or on which, having regard to the circumstances, should have learned of it, regardless of the date on which the acquisition, disposal or possibility of exercising voting rights takes effect; or
(b) is informed about the event mentioned in Article 9(2).
3. An undertaking shall be exempted from making the required notification in accordance with paragraph 1 if the notification is made by the parent undertaking or, where the parent undertaking is itself a controlled undertaking, by its own parent undertaking.
4. The parent undertaking of a management company shall not be required to aggregate its holdings under Articles 9 and 10 with the holdings managed by the management company under the conditions laid down in Directive 85/611/EEC, provided such management company exercises its voting rights independently from the parent undertaking.
However, Articles 9 and 10 shall apply where the parent undertaking, or another controlled undertaking of the parent undertaking, has invested in holdings managed by such management company and the management company has no discretion to exercise the voting rights attached to such holdings and may only exercise such voting rights under direct or indirect instructions from the parent or another controlled undertaking of the parent undertaking.
5. The parent undertaking of an investment firm authorised under Directive 2004/39/EC shall not be required to aggregate its holdings under Articles 9 and 10 with the holdings which such investment firm manages on a client-by-client basis within the meaning of Article 4(1), point 9, of Directive 2004/39/EC, provided that:
— the investment firm is authorised to provide such portfolio management under point 4 of Section A of Annex I to Directive 2004/39/EC;
— it may only exercise the voting rights attached to such shares under instructions given in writing or by electronic means or it ensures that individual portfolio management services are conducted independently of any other services under conditions equivalent to those provided for under Directive 85/611/EEC by putting into place appropriate mechanisms; and
— the investment firm exercises its voting rights independently from the parent undertaking.
However, Articles 9 and 10 shall apply where the parent undertaking, or another controlled undertaking of the parent undertaking, has invested in holdings managed by such investment firm and the investment firm has no discretion to exercise the voting rights attached to such holdings and may only exercise such voting rights under direct or indirect instructions from the parent or another controlled undertaking of the parent undertaking.
6. Upon receipt of the notification under paragraph 1, but no later than three trading days thereafter, the issuer shall make public all the information contained in the notification.
7. A home Member State may exempt issuers from the requirement in paragraph 6 if the information contained in the notification is made public by its competent authority, under the conditions laid down in Article 21, upon receipt of the notification, but no later than three trading days thereafter.
[8. In order to take account of technical developments on financial markets and to specify the requirements laid down in paragraphs 1, 2, 4, 5 and 6 of this Article, the Commission shall adopt, in accordance with Article 27(2a), (2b) and (2c), and subject to the conditions of Articles 27a and 27b, measures:]
(a) . . .
(b) to determine a calendar of "trading days" for all Member States;
(c) to establish in which cases the shareholder, or the natural person or legal entity referred to in Article 10, or both, shall effect the necessary notification to the issuer;
(d) to clarify the circumstances under which the shareholder, or the natural person or legal entity referred to in Article 10, should have learned of the acquisition or disposal;
(e) to clarify the conditions of independence to be complied with by management companies and their parent undertakings or by investment firms and their parent undertakings to benefit from the exemptions in paragraphs 4 and 5.

. . .

[9. In order to ensure the uniform conditions of application of this Article and to take account of technical developments on financial markets, the European Supervisory Authority (European Securities and Markets Authority) (hereinafter "ESMA"), established by Regulation (EU) No 1095/2010 of the European Parliament and of the Council[1] may develop draft implementing technical standards to establish standard forms, templates and procedures to be used when notifying the required information to the issuer under paragraph 1 of this Article or when filing information under Article 19(3).

Power is conferred on the Commission to adopt the implementing technical standards referred to in the first subparagraph in accordance with Article 15 of Regulation (EU) No 1095/2010.]

NOTES

Words in square brackets in para 2 substituted by European Parliament and Council Directive 2013/50/EU, Art 1(8), as from 26 November 2013.

Words in square brackets in para 8 substituted, words omitted from that paragraph repealed, and para 9 added, by European Parliament and Council Directive 2010/78/EU, Art 7(4), as from 4 January 2011.

Implementing Act for the purposes of para 8: see Commission Directive 2007/14/EC laying down detailed rules for the implementation of certain provisions of Directive 2004/109/EC on the harmonisation of transparency requirements in relation to information about issuers whose securities are admitted to trading on a regulated market. See the EUR-Lex website at eur-lex.europa.eu/legal-content/EN/TXT/?uri=CELEX:32007L0014.

[1] OJ L331, 15.12.2010, p 84.

[11.88]

Article 13

[1. The notification requirements laid down in Article 9 shall also apply to a natural person or legal entity who holds, directly or indirectly:

(a) financial instruments that, on maturity, give the holder, under a formal agreement, either the unconditional right to acquire or the discretion as to his right to acquire, shares to which voting rights are attached, already issued, of an issuer whose shares are admitted to trading on a regulated market;

(b) financial instruments which are not included in point (a) but which are referenced to shares referred to in that point and with economic effect similar to that of the financial instruments referred to in that point, whether or not they confer a right to a physical settlement.

The notification required shall include the breakdown by type of financial instruments held in accordance with point (a) and financial instruments held in accordance with point (b) of that subparagraph, distinguishing between the financial instruments which confer a right to a physical settlement and the financial instruments which confer a right to a cash settlement.]

[1a. The number of voting rights shall be calculated by reference to the full notional amount of shares underlying the financial instrument except where the financial instrument provides exclusively for a cash settlement, in which case the number of voting rights shall be calculated on a "delta-adjusted" basis, by multiplying the notional amount of underlying shares by the delta of the instrument. For this purpose, the holder shall aggregate and notify all financial instruments relating to the same underlying issuer. Only long positions shall be taken into account for the calculation of voting rights. Long positions shall not be netted with short positions relating to the same underlying issuer.

ESMA shall develop draft regulatory technical standards to specify:

(a) the method for calculating the number of voting rights referred to in the first subparagraph in the case of financial instruments referenced to a basket of shares or an index; and

(b) the methods for determining delta for the purposes of calculating voting rights relating to financial instruments which provide exclusively for a cash settlement as required by the first subparagraph.

ESMA shall submit those draft regulatory technical standards to the Commission by 27 November 2014.

Power is delegated to the Commission to adopt the regulatory technical standards referred to in the second subparagraph of this paragraph in accordance with Articles 10 to 14 of Regulation (EU) No 1095/2010.

[1b. For the purposes of paragraph 1, the following shall be considered to be financial instruments, provided they satisfy any of the conditions set out in points (a) or (b) of the first subparagraph of paragraph 1:

(a) transferable securities;

(b) options;

(c) futures;

(d) swaps;

(e) forward rate agreements;

(f) contracts for differences; and

(g) any other contracts or agreements with similar economic effects which may be settled physically or in cash.

ESMA shall establish and periodically update an indicative list of financial instruments that are subject to notification requirements pursuant to paragraph 1, taking into account technical developments on financial markets.]

[2. The Commission shall be empowered to adopt, by means of delegated acts in accordance with Article 27(2a), (2b) and (2c), and subject to the conditions laid down by Articles 27a and 27b, the measures to specify the contents of the notification to be made, the notification period and to whom the notification is to be made as referred to in paragraph 1.]

[3. In order to ensure uniform conditions of application of paragraph 1 of this Article and to take account of technical developments on financial markets, ESMA may develop draft implementing technical standards to establish standard forms, templates and procedures to be used when notifying the required information to the issuer under paragraph 1 of this Article or when filing information under Article 19(3).

Power is conferred on the Commission to adopt the implementing technical standards referred to in the first subparagraph in accordance with Article 15 of Regulation (EU) No 1095/2010.]

[4. The exemptions laid down in Article 9(4), (5) and (6) and in Article 12(3), (4) and (5) shall apply *mutatis mutandis* to the notification requirements under this Article.

ESMA shall develop draft regulatory technical standards to specify the cases in which the exemptions referred to in the first subparagraph apply to financial instruments held by a natural person or a legal entity fulfilling orders received from clients or responding to a client's requests to trade otherwise than on a proprietary basis, or hedging positions arising out of such dealings.

ESMA shall submit those draft regulatory technical standards to the Commission by 27 November 2014.

Power is delegated to the Commission to adopt the regulatory technical standards referred to in the second subparagraph of this paragraph in accordance with Articles 10 to 14 of Regulation (EU) No 1095/2010.]

NOTES

Para 1: substituted by European Parliament and Council Directive 2013/50/EU, Art 1(9)(a), as from 26 November 2013.

Paras 1a, 1b: inserted by European Parliament and Council Directive 2013/50/EU, Art 1(9)(b), as from 26 November 2013.

Para 2: substituted by European Parliament and Council Directive 2013/50/EU, Art 1(9)(c), as from 26 November 2013.

Para 3: added by European Parliament and Council Directive 2010/78/EU, Art 7(5), as from 4 January 2011.

Para 4: added by European Parliament and Council Directive 2013/50/EU, Art 1(9)(c), as from 26 November 2013.

Implementing Act for the purposes of para 2: see Commission Directive 2007/14/EC laying down detailed rules for the implementation of certain provisions of Directive 2004/109/EC on the harmonisation of transparency requirements in relation to information about issuers whose securities are admitted to trading on a regulated market. See the EUR-Lex website at eur-lex.europa.eu/legal-content/EN/TXT/?uri=CELEX:32007L0014.

Regulatory technical standards for the purposes of para 4: see Commission Delegated Regulation 2015/761/EU supplementing Directive 2004/109/EC of the European Parliament and of the Council with regard to certain regulatory technical standards on major holdings. See the EUR-Lex website at eur-lex.europa.eu/legal-content/EN/TXT/?uri=CELEX:32015R0761.

[11.89]

[Article 13a Aggregation

1. The notification requirements laid down in Articles 9, 10 and 13 shall also apply to a natural person or a legal entity when the number of voting rights held directly or indirectly by such person or entity under Articles 9 and 10 aggregated with the number of voting rights relating to financial instruments held directly or indirectly under Article 13 reaches, exceeds or falls below the thresholds set out in Article 9(1).

The notification required under the first subparagraph of this paragraph shall include a breakdown of the number of voting rights attached to shares held in accordance with Articles 9 and 10 and voting rights relating to financial instruments within the meaning of Article 13.

2. Voting rights relating to financial instruments that have already been notified in accordance with Article 13 shall be notified again when the natural person or the legal entity has acquired the underlying shares and such acquisition results in the total number of voting rights attached to shares issued by the same issuer reaching or exceeding the thresholds laid down by Article 9(1).]

NOTES

Inserted by European Parliament and Council Directive 2013/50/EU, Art 1(10), as from 26 November 2013.

[11.90]

Article 14

1. Where an issuer of shares admitted to trading on a regulated market acquires or disposes of its own shares, either itself or through a person acting in his own name but on the issuer's behalf, the home Member State shall ensure that the issuer makes public the proportion of its own shares as soon as possible, but not later than four trading days following such acquisition or disposal where that proportion reaches, exceeds or falls below the thresholds of 5% or 10% of the voting rights. The proportion shall be calculated on the basis of the total number of shares to which voting rights are attached.

[2. The Commission shall adopt, by means of delegated acts in accordance with Article 27(2a), (2b) and (2c), and subject to the conditions of Articles 27a and 27b, measures in order to take account of technical developments on financial markets and to specify the requirements laid down in paragraph 1.]

NOTES

Para 2: substituted by European Parliament and Council Directive 2010/78/EU, Art 7(6), as from 4 January 2011.

Implementing Act for the purposes of para 2: see Commission Directive 2007/14/EC laying down detailed rules for the implementation of certain provisions of Directive 2004/109/EC on the harmonisation of transparency requirements in relation to information about issuers whose securities are admitted to trading on a regulated market. See the EUR-Lex website at eur-lex.europa.eu/legal-content/EN/TXT/?uri=CELEX:32007L0014.

[11.91]

Article 15

For the purpose of calculating the thresholds provided for in Article 9, the home Member State shall at least require the disclosure to the public by the issuer of the total number of voting rights and capital at the end of each calendar month during which an increase or decrease of such total number has occurred.

[11.92]

Article 16 Additional information

1. The issuer of shares admitted to trading on a regulated market shall make public without delay any change in the rights attaching to the various classes of shares, including changes in the rights attaching to derivative securities issued by the issuer itself and giving access to the shares of that issuer.

2. The issuer of securities, other than shares admitted to trading on a regulated market, shall make public without delay any changes in the rights of holders of securities other than shares, including changes in the terms and conditions of these securities which could indirectly affect those rights, resulting in particular from a change in loan terms or in interest rates.

3. . . .

NOTES

Para 3: repealed by European Parliament and Council Directive 2013/50/EU, Art 1(11), as from 26 November 2013.

SECTION II INFORMATION FOR HOLDERS OF SECURITIES ADMITTED TO TRADING ON A REGULATED MARKET

[11.93]

Article 17 Information requirements for issuers whose shares are admitted to trading on a regulated market

1. The issuer of shares admitted to trading on a regulated market shall ensure equal treatment for all holders of shares who are in the same position.

2. The issuer shall ensure that all the facilities and information necessary to enable holders of shares to exercise their rights are available in the home Member State and that the integrity of data is preserved. Shareholders shall not be prevented from exercising their rights by proxy, subject to the law of the country in which the issuer is incorporated. In particular, the issuer shall:

(a) provide information on the place, time and agenda of meetings, the total number of shares and voting rights and the rights of holders to participate in meetings;

(b) make available a proxy form, on paper or, where applicable, by electronic means, to each person entitled to vote at a shareholders' meeting, together with the notice concerning the meeting or, on request, after an announcement of the meeting;

(c) designate as its agent a financial institution through which shareholders may exercise their financial rights; and

(d) publish notices or distribute circulars concerning the allocation and payment of dividends and the issue of new shares, including information on any arrangements for allotment, subscription, cancellation or conversion.

3. For the purposes of conveying information to shareholders, the home Member State shall allow issuers the use of electronic means, provided such a decision is taken in a general meeting and meets at least the following conditions:

(a) the use of electronic means shall in no way depend upon the location of the seat or residence of the shareholder or, in the cases referred to in Article 10(a) to (h), of the natural persons or legal entities;

(b) identification arrangements shall be put in place so that the shareholders, or the natural persons or legal entities entitled to exercise or to direct the exercise of voting rights, are effectively informed;

(c) shareholders, or in the cases referred to in Article 10(a) to (e) the natural persons or legal entities entitled to acquire, dispose of or exercise voting rights, shall be contacted in writing to request their consent for the use of electronic means for conveying information and, if they do not object within a reasonable period of time, their consent shall be deemed to be given. They shall be able to request, at any time in the future, that information be conveyed in writing, and

(d) any apportionment of the costs entailed in the conveyance of such information by electronic means shall be determined by the issuer in compliance with the principle of equal treatment laid down in paragraph 1.

[4. The Commission shall adopt, by means of delegated acts in accordance with Article 27(2a), (2b) and (2c), and subject to the conditions of Articles 27a and 27b, measures in order to take account of technical developments on financial markets, to take account of developments in information and communication technology and to specify the requirements laid down in paragraphs 1, 2 and 3. The Commission shall, in particular, specify the types of financial institution through which a shareholder may exercise the financial rights provided for in paragraph 2(c).]

NOTES

Para 4: substituted by European Parliament and Council Directive 2010/78/EU, Art 7(7), as from 4 January 2011.

[11.94]

Article 18 Information requirements for issuers whose debt securities are admitted to trading on a regulated market

1. The issuer of debt securities admitted to trading on a regulated market shall ensure that all holders of debt securities ranking pari passu are given equal treatment in respect of all the rights attaching to those debt securities.

2. The issuer shall ensure that all the facilities and information necessary to enable debt securities holders to exercise their rights are publicly available in the home Member State and that the integrity of data is preserved. Debt securities holders shall not be prevented from exercising their rights by proxy, subject to the law of country in which the issuer is incorporated. In particular, the issuer shall:

(a) publish notices, or distribute circulars, concerning the place, time and agenda of meetings of debt securities holders, the payment of interest, the exercise of any conversion, exchange, subscription or cancellation rights, and repayment, as well as the right of those holders to participate therein;

(b) make available a proxy form on paper or, where applicable, by electronic means, to each person entitled to vote at a meeting of debt securities holders, together with the notice concerning the meeting or, on request, after an announcement of the meeting; and

(c) designate as its agent a financial institution through which debt securities holders may exercise their financial rights.

[3. Where only holders of debt securities whose denomination per unit amounts to at least EUR 100,000 or, in the case of debt securities denominated in a currency other than euro whose denomination per unit is, at the date of the issue, equivalent to at least EUR 100,000, are to be invited to a meeting, the issuer may choose as venue any Member State, provided that all the facilities and information necessary to enable such holders to exercise their rights are made available in that Member State.

The choice referred to in the first subparagraph shall also apply with regard to holders of debt securities whose denomination per unit amounts to at least EUR 50,000 or, in the case of debt securities denominated in a currency other than euro, the value of such denomination per unit is, at the date of the issue, equivalent to at least EUR 50,000, which have already been admitted to trading on a regulated market in the Union before 31 December 2010, for as long as such debt securities are outstanding, provided that all the facilities and information necessary to enable such holders to exercise their rights are made available in the Member State chosen by the issuer.]

4. For the purposes of conveying information to debt securities holders, the home Member State, or the Member State chosen by the issuer pursuant to paragraph 3, shall allow issuers the use of electronic means, provided such a decision is taken in a general meeting and meets at least the following conditions:

(a) the use of electronic means shall in no way depend upon the location of the seat or residence of the debt security holder or of a proxy representing that holder;

(b) identification arrangements shall be put in place so that debt securities holders are effectively informed;

(c) debt securities holders shall be contacted in writing to request their consent for the use of electronic means for conveying information and if they do not object within a reasonable period of time, their consent shall be deemed to be given. They shall be able to request, at any time in the future, that information be conveyed in writing; and

(d) any apportionment of the costs entailed in the conveyance of information by electronic means shall be determined by the issuer in compliance with the principle of equal treatment laid down in paragraph 1.

[5. The Commission shall adopt, by means of delegated acts in accordance with Article 27(2a), (2b) and (2c), and subject to the conditions of Articles 27a and 27b, measures in order to take account of technical developments on financial markets, to take account of developments in information and communication technology and to specify the requirements laid down in paragraphs 1 to 4. The Commission shall, in particular, specify the types of financial institution through which a debt security holder may exercise the financial rights provided for in paragraph 2(c).]

NOTES

Para 3: substituted by European Parliament and Council Directive 2010/73/EU, Art 2(3), as from 31 December 2010.

Para 5: substituted by European Parliament and Council Directive 2010/78/EU, Art 7(8), as from 4 January 2011.

CHAPTER IV GENERAL OBLIGATIONS

[11.95]

Article 19 Home Member State control

1. Whenever the issuer, or any person having requested, without the issuer's consent, the admission of its securities to trading on a regulated market, discloses regulated information, it shall at the same time file that information with the competent authority of its home Member State. That competent authority may decide to publish such filed information on its Internet site.

. . .

2. The home Member State may exempt an issuer from the requirement under paragraph 1 in respect of information disclosed in accordance with Article 6 of Directive 2003/6/EC or Article 12(6) of this Directive.

3. Information to be notified to the issuer in accordance with Articles 9, 10, 12 and 13 shall at the same time be filed with the competent authority of the home Member State.

[4. The Commission shall adopt, by means of delegated acts in accordance with Article 27(2a), (2b) and (2c), and subject to the conditions of Articles 27a and 27b, measures in order to specify the requirements laid down in paragraphs 1, 2 and 3.

The Commission shall, in particular, specify the procedure in accordance with which an issuer, a holder of shares or other financial instruments, or a person or entity referred to in Article 10, is to file information with the competent authority of the home Member State under paragraph 1 or 3, respectively, in order to enable filing by electronic means in the home Member State.]

NOTES

Para 1: second sub-paragraph repealed by European Parliament and Council Directive 2013/50/EU, Art 1(12), as from 26 November 2013.

Para 4: substituted by European Parliament and Council Directive 2010/78/EU, Art 7(9), as from 4 January 2011.

[11.96]

Article 20 Languages

1. Where securities are admitted to trading on a regulated market only in the home Member State, regulated information shall be disclosed in a language accepted by the competent authority in the home Member State.

2. Where securities are admitted to trading on a regulated market both in the home Member State and in one or more host Member States, regulated information shall be disclosed:

(a) in a language accepted by the competent authority in the home Member State; and

(b) depending on the choice of the issuer, either in a language accepted by the competent authorities of those host Member States or in a language customary in the sphere of international finance.

3. Where securities are admitted to trading on a regulated market in one or more host Member States, but not in the home Member State, regulated information shall, depending on the choice of the issuer, be disclosed either in a language accepted by the competent authorities of those host Member States or in a language customary in the sphere of international finance.

In addition, the home Member State may lay down in its law, regulations or administrative provisions that the regulated information shall, depending on the choice of the issuer, be disclosed either in a language accepted by its competent authority or in a language customary in the sphere of international finance.

4. Where securities are admitted to trading on a regulated market without the issuer's consent, the obligations under paragraphs 1, 2 and 3 shall be incumbent not upon the issuer, but upon the person who, without the issuer's consent, has requested such admission.

5. Member States shall allow shareholders and the natural person or legal entity referred to in Articles 9, 10 and 13 to notify information to an issuer under this Directive only in a language customary in the sphere of international finance. If the issuer receives such a notification, Member States may not require the issuer to provide a translation into a language accepted by the competent authorities.

[6. By way of derogation from paragraphs 1 to 4, where securities whose denomination per unit amounts to at least EUR 100,000 or, in the case of debt securities denominated in a currency other than euro equivalent to at least EUR 100,000 at the date of the issue, are admitted to trading on a regulated market in one or more Member States, regulated information shall be disclosed to the public either in a language accepted by the competent authorities of the home and host Member States or in a language customary in the sphere of international finance, at the choice of the issuer or of the person who, without the issuer's consent, has requested such admission.

The derogation referred to in the first subparagraph shall also apply to debt securities the denomination per unit of which is at least EUR 50,000 or, in the case of debt securities denominated in a currency other than euro, the value of such denomination per unit is, at the date of the issue, equivalent to at least EUR 50,000, which have already been admitted to trading on a regulated market in one or more Member States before 31 December 2010, for as long as such debt securities are outstanding.]

7. If an action concerning the content of regulated information is brought before a court or tribunal in a Member State, responsibility for the payment of costs incurred in the translation of that information for the purposes of the proceedings shall be decided in accordance with the law of that Member State.

NOTES

Para 6: substituted by European Parliament and Council Directive 2010/73/EU, Art 2(4), as from 31 December 2010.

[11.97]

Article 21 Access to regulated information

1. The home Member State shall ensure that the issuer, or the person who has applied for admission to trading on a regulated market without the issuer's consent, discloses regulated information in a manner ensuring fast access to such information on a non-discriminatory basis and makes it available to the officially appointed mechanism referred to in paragraph 2. The issuer, or the person who has applied for admission to trading on a regulated market without the issuer's consent, may not charge investors any specific cost for providing the information. The home Member State shall require the issuer to use such media as may reasonably be relied upon for the effective dissemination of information to the public throughout the Community. The home Member State may not impose an obligation to use only media whose operators are established on its territory.

2. The home Member State shall ensure that there is at least one officially appointed mechanism for the central storage of regulated information. These mechanisms should comply with minimum quality standards of security, certainty as to the information source, time recording and easy access by end users and shall be aligned with the filing procedure under Article 19(1).

3. Where securities are admitted to trading on a regulated market in only one host Member State and not in the home Member State, the host Member State shall ensure disclosure of regulated information in accordance with the requirements referred to in paragraph 1.

[4. The Commission shall be empowered to adopt, by means of delegated acts in accordance with Article 27(2a), (2b) and (2c), and subject to the conditions laid down in Articles 27a and 27b, measures to specify the following:

(a) minimum standards for the dissemination of regulated information, as referred to in paragraph 1;
(b) minimum standards for the central storage mechanisms as referred to in paragraph 2;
(c) rules to ensure the interoperability of the information and communication technologies used by the mechanisms referred to in paragraph 2 and access to regulated information at the Union level, referred to therein.

The Commission may also specify and update a list of media for the dissemination of information to the public.]

NOTES

Para 4: substituted by European Parliament and Council Directive 2013/50/EU, Art 1(13), as from 26 November 2013.

Implementing Act for the purposes of para 4: see Commission Directive 2007/14/EC laying down detailed rules for the implementation of certain provisions of Directive 2004/109/EC on the harmonisation of transparency requirements in relation to information about issuers whose securities are admitted to trading on a regulated market. See the EUR-Lex website at eur-lex.europa.eu/legal-content/EN/TXT/?uri=CELEX:32007L0014.

[11.98]

[Article 21a European electronic access point

1. A web portal serving as a European electronic access point ("the access point") shall be established by 1 January 2018. ESMA shall develop and operate the access point.

2. The system of interconnection of officially appointed mechanisms shall be composed of:

— the mechanisms referred to in Article 21(2),
— the portal serving as the European electronic access point.

3. Member States shall ensure access to their central storage mechanisms via the access point.]

NOTES

Inserted by European Parliament and Council Directive 2013/50/EU, Art 1(14), as from 26 November 2013.

[11.99]

[Article 22 Access to regulated information at Union level

1. ESMA shall develop draft regulatory technical standards setting technical requirements regarding access to regulated information at Union level in order to specify the following:

(a) the technical requirements regarding communication technologies used by the mechanisms referred to in Article 21(2);
(b) the technical requirements for the operation of the central access point for the search for regulated information at Union level;
(c) the technical requirements regarding the use of a unique identifier for each issuer by the mechanisms referred to in Article 21(2);
(d) the common format for the delivery of regulated information by the mechanisms referred to in Article 21(2);
(e) the common classification of regulated information by the mechanisms referred to in Article 21(2) and the common list of types of regulated information.

2. In developing the draft regulatory technical standards, ESMA shall take into account the technical requirements for the system of interconnection of business registers established by Directive 2012/17/EU of the European Parliament and of the Council.[1]

ESMA shall submit those draft regulatory technical standards to the Commission by 27 November 2015.

Power is delegated to the Commission to adopt the regulatory technical standards referred to in the first subparagraph of this paragraph in accordance with Articles 10 to 14 of Regulation (EU) No 1095/2010.]

NOTES

Substituted by European Parliament and Council Directive 2013/50/EU, Art 1(15), as from 26 November 2013.

Regulatory technical standards for the purposes of this Article: see Commission Delegated Regulation 2016/1437/EU supplementing Directive 2004/109/EC of the European Parliament and of the Council with regard to regulatory technical standards on access to regulated information at Union level. It is available on the EUR-Lex website at eur-lex.europa.eu/legal-content/EN/TXT/?uri=CELEX:32016R1437.

[1] OJ L156, 16.6.2012, p 1.

[11.100]

Article 23 Third countries

[1. Where the registered office of an issuer is situated in a third country, the competent authority of the home Member State may exempt that issuer from requirements under Articles 4 to 7, Article 12(6) and Articles 14 to 18, provided that the law of the third country in question lays down equivalent requirements or such an issuer complies with requirements of the law of a third country that the competent authority of the home Member State considers as equivalent.

The competent authority shall then inform ESMA of the exemption granted.]

[The information covered by the requirements laid down in the third country shall be filed in accordance with Article 19 and disclosed in accordance with Articles 20 and 21.]

2. By way of derogation from paragraph 1, an issuer whose registered office is in a third country shall be exempted from preparing its financial statement in accordance with Article 4 or Article 5 prior to the financial year starting on or after 1 January 2007, provided such issuer prepares its financial statements in accordance with internationally accepted standards referred to in Article 9 of Regulation (EC) No 1606/2002.

3. The competent authority of the home Member State shall ensure that information disclosed in a third country which may be of importance for the public in the Community is disclosed in accordance with Articles 20 and 21, even if such information is not regulated information within the meaning of Article 2(1)(k).

[4. In order to ensure the uniform conditions of application of paragraph 1, the Commission shall adopt, in accordance with the procedure referred to in Article 27(2), implementing measures:

(i) setting up a mechanism ensuring the establishment of equivalence of information required under this Directive, including financial statements and information, required under the law, regulations or administrative provisions of a third country;

(ii) stating that, by reason of its domestic law, regulations, administrative provisions, or of the practices or procedures based on the international standards set by international organisations, the third country where the issuer is registered ensures the equivalence of the information requirements provided for in this Directive.

In the context of point (ii) of the first subparagraph, the Commission shall also adopt, by means of delegated acts in accordance with Article 27(2a), (2b) and (2c), and subject to the conditions of Articles 27a and 27b, measures concerning the assessment of standards relevant to the issuers of more than one country.

The Commission shall, in accordance with the procedure referred to in Article 27(2), take the necessary decisions on the equivalence of accounting standards which are used by third-country issuers under the conditions set out in Article 30(3). If the Commission decides that the accounting standards of a third country are not equivalent, it may allow the issuers concerned to continue using such accounting standards during an appropriate transitional period.

In the context of the third subparagraph, the Commission shall also adopt, by means of delegated acts in accordance with Article 27(2a), (2b) and (2c), and subject to the conditions of Articles 27a and 27b, measures aimed at establishing general equivalence criteria regarding accounting standards relevant to issuers of more than one country.]

[5. In order to specify the requirements laid down in paragraph 2, the Commission may adopt, by means of delegated acts in accordance with Article 27(2a), (2b) and (2c), and subject to the conditions of Articles 27a and 27b, measures defining the type of information disclosed in a third country that is of importance to the public in the Union.]

6. Undertakings whose registered office is in a third country which would have required an authorisation in accordance with Article 5(1) of Directive 85/611/EEC or, with regard to portfolio management under point 4 of section A of Annex I to Directive 2004/39/EC if it had its registered office or, only in the case of an investment firm, its head office within the Community, shall also be exempted from aggregating holdings with the holdings of its parent undertaking under the requirements laid down in Article 12(4) and (5) provided that they comply with equivalent conditions of independence as management companies or investment firms.

7. In order to take account of technical developments in financial markets and to ensure the uniform application of paragraph 6, the Commission shall, in accordance with the procedure referred to in Article 27(2), adopt implementing measures stating that, by reason of its domestic law, regulations, or administrative provisions, a third country ensures the equivalence of the independence requirements provided for under this Directive and its implementing measures.

[The Commission shall also adopt, by means of delegated acts in accordance with Article 27(2a), (2b) and (2c), and subject to the conditions of Articles 27a and 27b, measures aimed at establishing general equivalence criteria for the purpose of the first subparagraph.]

[8. ESMA shall assist the Commission in carrying out its tasks under this Article in accordance with Article 33 of Regulation (EU) No 1095/2010.]

NOTES

Paras 1, 4, 5 substituted, words in square brackets in para 7 substituted, and para 8 added, by European Parliament and Council Directive 2010/78/EU, Art 7(12), as from 4 January 2011.

The third sub-paragraph of para 1 was added by European Parliament and Council Directive 2013/50/EU, Art 1(16), as from 26 November 2013.

Regulatory technical standards for the purposes of para 4(i): see Commission Regulation 1569/2007/EU establishing a mechanism for the determination of equivalence of accounting standards applied by third country issuers of securities pursuant to Directives 2003/71/EC and 2004/109/EC of the European Parliament and of the Council. See the EUR-Lex website at eur-lex.europa.eu/legal-content/EN/TXT/?uri=CELEX:32007R1569. See also (i) Commission Delegated Regulation 310/2012/EU amending Regulation (EC) No 1569/2007 establishing a mechanism for the determination of equivalence of accounting standards applied by third country issuers of securities pursuant to Directives 2003/71/EC and 2004/109/EC of the European Parliament and of the Council; (ii) Commission Delegated Regulation 2015/1605/EU amending Regulation (EC) No 1569/2007 establishing a mechanism for the determination of equivalence of accounting standards applied by third country issuers of securities pursuant to Directives 2003/71/EC and 2004/109/EC of the European Parliament and of the Council.

Implementing Act for the purposes of paras 4(ii), 7: see Commission Directive 2007/14/EC laying down detailed rules for the implementation of certain provisions of Directive 2004/109/EC on the harmonisation of transparency requirements in relation to information about issuers whose securities are admitted to trading on a regulated market. See the EUR-Lex website at eur-lex.europa.eu/legal-content/EN/TXT/?uri=CELEX:32007L0014.

CHAPTER V COMPETENT AUTHORITIES

[11.101]

Article 24 Competent authorities and their powers

[1. Each Member State shall designate the central authority referred to in Article 21(1) of Directive 2003/71/EC as the central competent administrative authority responsible for carrying out the obligations provided for in this Directive and for ensuring that the provisions adopted pursuant to this Directive are applied. Member States shall inform the Commission and ESMA accordingly.]

However, for the purpose of paragraph 4(h) Member States may designate a competent authority other than the central competent authority referred to in the first subparagraph.

2. Member States may allow their central competent authority to delegate tasks. Except for the tasks referred to in paragraph 4(h), any delegation of tasks relating to the obligations provided for in this Directive and in its implementing measures shall be reviewed five years after the entry into force of this Directive and shall end eight years after the entry into force of this Directive. Any delegation of tasks shall be made in a specific manner stating the tasks to be undertaken and the conditions under which they are to be carried out.

Those conditions shall include a clause requiring the entity in question to be organised in a manner such that conflicts of interest are avoided and information obtained from carrying out the delegated tasks is not used unfairly or to prevent competition. In any case, the final responsibility for supervising compliance with the provisions of this Directive and implementing measures adopted pursuant thereto shall lie with the competent authority designated in accordance with paragraph 1.

[3. Member States shall inform the Commission, ESMA in accordance with Article 28(4) of Regulation(EU) No 1095/2010, and competent authorities of other Member States of any arrangements entered into with regard to the delegation of tasks, including the precise conditions for regulating the delegations.]

4. Each competent authority shall have all the powers necessary for the performance of its functions. It shall at least be empowered to:

(a) require auditors, issuers, holders of shares or other financial instruments, or persons or entities referred to in Articles 10 or 13, and the persons that control them or are controlled by them, to provide information and documents;

(b) require the issuer to disclose the information required under point (a) to the public by the means and within the time limits the authority considers necessary. It may publish such information on its own initiative in the event that the issuer, or the persons that control it or are controlled by it, fail to do so and after having heard the issuer;

(c) require managers of the issuers and of the holders of shares or other financial instruments, or of persons or entities referred to in Articles 10 or 13, to notify the information required under this Directive, or under national law adopted in accordance with this Directive, and, if necessary, to provide further information and documents;

(d) suspend, or request the relevant regulated market to suspend, trading in securities for a maximum of ten days at a time if it has reasonable grounds for suspecting that the provisions of this Directive, or of national law adopted in accordance with this Directive, have been infringed by the issuer;

(e) prohibit trading on a regulated market if it finds that the provisions of this Directive, or of national law adopted in accordance with this Directive, have been infringed, or if it has reasonable grounds for suspecting that the provisions of this Directive have been infringed;

(f) monitor that the issuer discloses timely information with the objective of ensuring effective and equal access to the public in all Member States where the securities are traded and take appropriate action if that is not the case;

(g) make public the fact that an issuer, or a holder of shares or other financial instruments, or a person or entity referred to in Articles 10 or 13, is failing to comply with its obligations;

(h) examine that information referred to in this Directive is drawn up in accordance with the relevant reporting framework and take appropriate measures in case of discovered infringements; and

(i) carry out on-site inspections in its territory in accordance with national law, in order to verify compliance with the provisions of this Directive and its implementing measures. Where necessary under national law, the competent authority or authorities may use this power by applying to the relevant judicial authority and/or in cooperation with other authorities.

[4a. Without prejudice to paragraph 4, competent authorities shall be given all investigative powers that are necessary for the exercise of their functions. Those powers shall be exercised in conformity with national law.

4b. Competent authorities shall exercise their sanctioning powers, in accordance with this Directive and national law, in any of the following ways:

— directly,
— in collaboration with other authorities,
— under their responsibility by delegation to such authorities,

— by application to the competent judicial authorities.]

5. Paragraphs 1 to 4 shall be without prejudice to the possibility for a Member State to make separate legal and administrative arrangements for overseas European territories for whose external relations that Member State is responsible.

6. The disclosure to competent authorities by the auditors of any fact or decision related to the requests made by the competent authority under paragraph (4)(a) shall not constitute a breach of any restriction on disclosure of information imposed by contract or by any law, regulation or administrative provision and shall not involve such auditors in liability of any kind.

NOTES

The first sub-paragraph of para 1, and all of para 3, were substituted by European Parliament and Council Directive 2010/78/EU, Art 7(13), as from 4 January 2011.

Paras 4a, 4b were inserted by European Parliament and Council Directive 2013/50/EU, Art 1(17), as from 26 November 2013.

[11.102]

Article 25 Professional secrecy and cooperation between Member States

1. The obligation of professional secrecy shall apply to all persons who work or who have worked for the competent authority and for entities to which competent authorities may have delegated certain tasks. Information covered by professional secrecy may not be disclosed to any other person or authority except by virtue of the laws, regulations or administrative provisions of a Member State.

2. Competent authorities of the Member States shall cooperate with each other, whenever necessary, for the purpose of carrying out their duties and making use of their powers, whether set out in this Directive or in national law adopted pursuant to this Directive. Competent authorities shall render assistance to competent authorities of other Member States.

[In the exercise of their sanctioning and investigative powers, competent authorities shall cooperate to ensure that sanctions or measures produce the desired results, and shall coordinate their action when dealing with cross-border cases.]

[2a. The competent authorities may refer to ESMA situations where a request for cooperation has been rejected or has not been acted upon within a reasonable time. Without prejudice to the Article 258 of the Treaty on the Functioning of the European Union (TFEU), ESMA may, in situations referred to in the first sentence, act in accordance with the powers conferred on it under Article 19 of Regulation (EU) No 1095/2010.

2b. The competent authorities shall cooperate with ESMA for the purposes of this Directive, in accordance with Regulation (EU) No 1095/2010.

2c. The competent authorities shall without delay provide ESMA with all information necessary to carryout its duties under this Directive and under Regulation(EU) No 1095/2010, in accordance with Article 35 of that Regulation.]

3. [Paragraph 1 shall not prevent the competent authorities from exchanging confidential information with, or from transmitting information to, other competent authorities, ESMA and the European Systemic Risk Board (ESRB) established by Regulation (EU) No 1092/2010 of the European Parliament and of the Council of 24 November 2010 on European Union macro-prudential oversight of the financial system and establishing a European Systemic Risk Board.[1]] Information thus exchanged shall be covered by the obligation of professional secrecy to which the persons employed or formerly employed by the competent authorities receiving the information are subject.

[4. Member States and ESMA in accordance with Article 33 of Regulation (EU) No 1095/2010, may conclude cooperation agreements providing for the exchange of information with the competent authorities or bodies of third countries enabled by their respective legislation to carry out any tasks under this Directive in accordance with Article 24. Member States shall notify ESMA when they conclude cooperation agreements. Such an exchange of information is subject to guarantees of professional secrecy at least equivalent to those referred to in this Article. Such an exchange of information shall be intended for the performance of the supervisory task of the authorities or bodies mentioned. Where the information originates in another Member State, it shall not be disclosed without the express agreement of the competent authorities which disclosed it and, where appropriate, solely for the purposes for which those authorities gave their agreement.]

NOTES

Second sub-paragraph of para 2 inserted by European Parliament and Council Directive 2013/50/EU, Art 1(18), as from 26 November 2013.

Paras 2a–2c inserted, words in square brackets in para 3 substituted, and para 4 substituted, by European Parliament and Council Directive 2010/78/EU, Art 7(14), as from 4 January 2011.

[1] OJ L331, 15.12.2010, p 1.

[11.103]

[Article 26 Precautionary measures

1. Where the competent authority of a host Member State finds that the issuer or the holder of shares or other financial instruments, or the person or entity referred to in Article 10, has committed irregularities or infringed its obligations, it shall refer its findings to the competent authority of the home Member State and to ESMA.

2. If, despite the measures taken by the competent authority of the home Member State, or because such measures prove inadequate, the issuer or the security holder persists in infringing the relevant legal or regulatory provisions, the competent authority of the host Member State shall, after informing the competent authority of the home Member State, take, in accordance with Article 3(2), all the appropriate measures in order to protect investors, informing the Commission and ESMA thereof at the earliest opportunity.]

NOTES

Substituted by European Parliament and Council Directive 2010/78/EU, Art 7(15), as from 4 January 2011.

CHAPTER VI [DELEGATED ACTS AND IMPLEMENTING MEASURES]

NOTES

Words in square brackets in the preceding heading substituted by European Parliament and Council Directive 2010/78/EU, Art 7(16), as from 4 January 2011.

[11.104]

Article 27 Committee procedure

1. The Commission shall be assisted by the European Securities Committee, instituted by Article 1 of Decision 2001/528/EC.

2. Where reference is made to this paragraph, Articles 5 and 7 of Decision 1999/468/EC shall apply, having regard to the provisions of Article 8 thereof, provided that the implementing measures adopted in accordance with that procedure do not modify the essential provisions of this Directive.

The period laid down in Article 5(6) of Decision 1999/468/EC shall be set at three months.

[2a. The power to adopt the delegated acts referred to in Article 2(3), Article 5(6), Article 9(7), Article 12(8), Article 13(2), Article 14(2), Article 17(4), Article 18(5), Article 19(4), Article 21(4), Article 23(4), Article 23(5) and Article 23(7) shall be conferred on the Commission for a period of 4 years from 4 January 2011. The Commission shall draw up a report in respect of delegated power at the latest 6 months before the end of the four-year period. The delegation of power shall be automatically extended for periods of an identical duration, unless the European Parliament or the Council revokes it in accordance with Article 27a.]

[2b. As soon as it adopts a delegated act, the Commission shall notify it simultaneously to the European Parliament and to the Council.

2c. The power to adopt delegated acts is conferred on the Commission subject to the conditions laid down in Articles 27a and 27b.]

[3. By 31 December 2010, and, thereafter, at least every three years, the Commission shall review the provisions concerning its implementing powers and present a report to the European Parliament and to the Council on the functioning of those powers. The report shall examine, in particular, the need for the Commission to propose amendments to this Directive in order to ensure the appropriate scope of the implementing powers conferred on the Commission. The conclusion as to whether or not amendment is necessary shall be accompanied by a detailed statement of reasons. If necessary, the report shall be accompanied by a legislative proposal to amend the provisions conferring implementing powers on the Commission.]

NOTES

Para 2a originally inserted, and para 3 substituted (for the original paras 3, 4), by European Parliament and Council Directive 2008/22/EC, Art 1(10), as from 20 March 2008.

Para 2a subsequently substituted, and paras 2b, 2c inserted, by European Parliament and Council Directive 2010/78/EU, Art 7(17), as from 4 January 2011.

[11.105]

[Article 27a Revocation of the delegation

1. The delegation of power referred to in Article 2(3), Article 5(6), Article 9(7), Article 12(8), Article 13(2), Article 14(2), Article 17(4), Article 18(5), Article 19(4) article 21(4), Article 23(4), Article 23(5) and Article 23(7)may be revoked at any time by the European Parliament or by the Council.

2. The institution which has commenced an internal procedure for deciding whether to revoke a delegation of power shall endeavour to inform the other institution and the Commission within a reasonable time before the final decision is taken, indicating the delegated power which could be subject to revocation.

3. The decision of revocation shall put an end to the delegation of the power specified in that decision. It shall take effect immediately or at a later date specified therein. It shall not affect the validity of the delegated acts already in force. It shall be published in the Official Journal of the European Union.]

NOTES

Inserted by European Parliament and Council Directive 2010/78/EU, Art 7(18), as from 4 January 2011.

[11.106]

[Article 27b Objections to delegated acts

1. The European Parliament or the Council may object to a delegated act within a period of 3 months from the date of notification. At the initiative of the European Parliament or the Council that period shall be extended by 3 months.

2. If, on the expiry of the period referred to in paragraph 1, neither the European Parliament nor the Council has objected to the delegated act, it shall be published in the *Official Journal of the European Union* and shall enter into force on the date stated therein.

The delegated act may be published in the *Official Journal of the European Union* and enter into force before the expiry of that period if the European Parliament and the Council have both informed the Commission of their intention not to raise objections.

3. If either the European Parliament or the Council objects to a delegated act within the period referred to in paragraph 1, it shall not enter into force. In accordance with Article 296 TFEU, the institution which objects shall state the reasons for objecting to the delegated act.]

NOTES

Inserted by European Parliament and Council Directive 2010/78/EU, Art 7(18), as from 4 January 2011.

[CHAPTER VIA SANCTIONS AND MEASURES]

NOTES

Chapter title inserted by European Parliament and Council Directive 2013/50/EU, Art 1(19), as from 26 November 2013.

[11.107]

[28 Administrative measures and sanctions

1. Without prejudice to the powers of competent authorities in accordance with Article 24 and the right of Member States to provide for and impose criminal sanctions, Member States shall lay down rules on administrative measures and sanctions applicable to breaches of the national provisions adopted in transposition of this Directive and shall take all measures necessary to ensure that they are implemented. Those administrative measures and sanctions shall be effective, proportionate and dissuasive.

2. Without prejudice to Article 7, Member States shall ensure that where obligations apply to legal entities, in the event of a breach, sanctions can be applied, subject to the conditions laid down in national law, to the members of administrative, management or supervisory bodies of the legal entity concerned, and to other individuals who are responsible for the breach under national law.]

NOTES

Substituted by European Parliament and Council Directive 2013/50/EU, Art 1(20), as from 26 November 2013.

[11.108]

[28a Breaches

Article 28b shall apply at least to the following breaches:

(a) failure by the issuer to make public, within the required time limit, information required under the national provisions adopted in transposition of Articles 4, 5, 6, 14 and 16;

(b) failure by the natural or the legal person to notify, within the required time limit, the acquisition or disposal of a major holding in accordance with the national provisions adopted in transposition of Articles 9, 10, 12, 13 and 13a.]

NOTES

Inserted by European Parliament and Council Directive 2013/50/EU, Art 1(21), as from 26 November 2013.

[11.109]

[28b Sanctioning powers

1. In the case of breaches referred to in Article 28a, competent authorities shall have the power to impose at least the following administrative measures and sanctions:

(a) a public statement indicating the natural person or the legal entity responsible and the nature of the breach;

(b) an order requiring the natural person or the legal entity responsible to cease the conduct constituting the breach and to desist from any repetition of that conduct;

(c) administrative pecuniary sanctions of;

(i) in the case of a legal entity,

— up to EUR 10,000,000 or up to 5% of the total annual turnover according to the last available annual accounts approved by the management body; where the legal entity is a parent undertaking or a subsidiary of a parent undertaking which has to prepare consolidated financial accounts pursuant to Directive 2013/34/EU, the relevant total turnover shall be the total annual turnover or the corresponding type of income pursuant to the relevant accounting Directives according to the last available consolidated annual accounts approved by the management body of the ultimate parent undertaking, or

— up to twice the amount of the profits gained or losses avoided because of the breach, where those can be determined,

whichever is higher;

(ii) in the case of a natural person:

— up to EUR 2,000,000, or

— up to twice the amount of the profits gained or losses avoided because of the breach, where those can be determined,

whichever is higher;

In Member States where the euro is not the official currency, the corresponding value to euro in the national currency shall be calculated taking into account the official exchange rate on the date of entry into force of Directive 2013/50/EU of the European Parliament and of the Council of 22 October 2013 amending Directive 2004/109/EC of the European Parliament and of the Council on the harmonisation of transparency requirements in relation to information about issuers whose securities are admitted to trading on a regulated market, Directive 2003/71/EC of the European Parliament and of the Council on the prospectus to be published when securities are offered to the public or admitted to trading and Commission Directive 2007/14/EC laying down detailed rules for the implementation of certain provisions of Directive 2004/109/EC.[1]

2. Without prejudice to the powers of competent authorities under Article 24 and the right of Member States to impose criminal sanctions, Member States shall ensure that their laws, regulations or administrative provisions provide for the possibility of suspending the exercise of voting rights attached to shares in the event of breaches as referred to in point (b) of Article 28a. Member States may provide that the suspension of voting rights is to apply only to the most serious breaches.

3. Member States may provide for additional sanctions or measures and for higher levels of administrative pecuniary sanctions than those provided for in this Directive.]

NOTES

Inserted by European Parliament and Council Directive 2013/50/EU, Art 1(21), as from 26 November 2013.

[1] OJ L294, 6.11.2013, p 13.

[11.110]

[28c Exercise of sanctioning powers

1. Member States shall ensure that, when determining the type and level of administrative sanctions or measures, the competent authorities take into account all relevant circumstances, including where appropriate:

(a) the gravity and the duration of the breach;

(b) the degree of responsibility of the natural person or legal entity responsible;

(c) the financial strength of the natural person or legal entity responsible, for example as indicated by the total turnover of the legal entity responsible or the annual income of the natural person responsible;

(d) the importance of profits gained or losses avoided by the natural person or legal entity responsible, in so far as they can be determined;

(e) the losses sustained by third parties as a result of the breach, in so far as they can be determined;

(f) the level of cooperation of the natural person or legal entity responsible with the competent authority;

(g) previous breaches by the natural person or legal entity responsible.

2. The processing of personal data collected in or for the exercise of the supervisory and investigatory powers in accordance with this Directive shall be carried out in accordance with Directive 95/46/EC and Regulation (EC) No 45/2001 where relevant.]

NOTES

Inserted by European Parliament and Council Directive 2013/50/EU, Art 1(21), as from 26 November 2013.

[CHAPTER VIB PUBLICATION OF DECISIONS]

NOTES

Chapter title inserted by European Parliament and Council Directive 2013/50/EU, Art 1(22), as from 26 November 2013.

[11.111]

[29 Publication of decisions

1. Member States shall provide that competent authorities are to publish every decision on sanctions and measures imposed for a breach of this Directive without undue delay, including at least information on the type and nature of the breach and the identity of natural persons or legal entities responsible for it.

However, competent authorities may delay publication of a decision, or may publish the decision on an anonymous basis in a manner which is in conformity with national law, in any of the following circumstances:

(a) where, in the event that the sanction is imposed on a natural person, publication of personal data is found to be disproportionate by an obligatory prior assessment of the proportionality of such publication;

(b) where publication would seriously jeopardise the stability of the financial system or an ongoing official investigation;

(c) where publication would, in so far as can be determined, cause disproportionate and serious damage to the institutions or natural persons involved.

2. If an appeal is submitted against the decision published under paragraph 1, the competent authority shall be obliged either to include information to that effect in the publication at the time of the publication or to amend the publication if the appeal is submitted after the initial publication.]

NOTES

Substituted by European Parliament and Council Directive 2013/50/EU, Art 1(23), as from 26 November 2013.

CHAPTER VII TRANSITIONAL AND FINAL PROVISIONS

[11.112]

Article 30 Transitional provisions

1. By way of derogation from Article 5(3) of this Directive, the home Member State may exempt from disclosing financial statements in accordance with Regulation (EC) No 1606/2002 issuers referred to in Article 9 of that Regulation for the financial year starting on or after 1 January 2006.

2. Notwithstanding Article 12(2), a shareholder shall notify the issuer at the latest two months after the date in Article 31(1) of the proportion of voting rights and capital it holds, in accordance with Articles 9, 10 and 13, with issuers at that date, unless it has already made a notification containing equivalent information before that date.

Notwithstanding Article 12(6), an issuer shall in turn disclose the information received in those notifications no later than three months after the date in Article 31(1).

3. Where an issuer is incorporated in a third country, the home Member State may exempt such issuer only in respect of those debt securities which have already been admitted to trading on a regulated market in the Community prior to 1 January 2005 from drawing up its financial statements in accordance with Article 4(3) and its management report in accordance with Article 4(5) as long as

(a) the competent authority of the home Member State acknowledges that annual financial statements prepared by issuers from such a third country give a true and fair view of the issuer's assets and liabilities, financial position and results;

(b) the third country where the issuer is incorporated has not made mandatory the application of international accounting standards referred to in Article 2 of Regulation (EC) No 1606/2002; and

(c) the Commission has not taken any decision in accordance with Article 23(4)(ii) as to whether there is an equivalence between the abovementioned accounting standards and

— the accounting standards laid down in the law, regulations or administrative provisions of the third country where the issuer is incorporated, or

— the accounting standards of a third country such an issuer has elected to comply with.

4. The home Member State may exempt issuers only in respect of those debt securities which have already been admitted to trading on a regulated market in the Community prior to 1 January 2005 from disclosing half-yearly financial report in accordance with Article 5 for 10 years following 1 January 2005, provided that the home Member State had decided to allow such issuers to benefit from the provisions of Article 27 of Directive 2001/34/EC at the point of admission of those debt securities.

[11.113]

Article 31 Transposition

1. Member States shall take the necessary measures to comply with this Directive by 20 January 2007. They shall forthwith inform the Commission thereof.

When Member States adopt these measures, they shall contain a reference to this Directive or shall be accompanied by such reference on the occasion of their official publication. The methods of making such reference shall be laid down by Member States.

[2. Where Member States adopt measures pursuant to Article 3(1), 8(2) or 8(3) or Article 30, they shall immediately communicate those measures to the Commission and to the other Member States.]

NOTES

Para 2: substituted by European Parliament and Council Directive 2013/50/EU, Art 1(24), as from 26 November 2013.

Article 32 Amendments

(*This Article amends Directive 2001/34/EC ante.*)

[11.114]

Article 33 Review

The Commission shall by 30 June 2009 report on the operation of this Directive to the European Parliament and to the Council including the appropriateness of ending the exemption for existing debt securities after the 10-year period as provided for by Article 30(4) and its potential impact on the European financial markets.

[11.115]

Article 34 Entry into force

This Directive shall enter into force on the twentieth day following that of its publication in the Official Journal of the European Union.

[11.116]

Article 35 Addressees

This Directive is addressed to the Member States.

DIRECTIVE OF THE EUROPEAN PARLIAMENT AND OF THE COUNCIL

(2006/43/EC)

of 17 May 2006

on statutory audits of annual accounts and consolidated accounts, amending Council Directives 78/660/EEC and 83/349/EEC and repealing Council Directive 84/253/EEC (Note)

[11.117]

NOTES

Date of publication in OJ: OJ L157, 9.6.2006, p 87.

This Directive clarifies the duties of statutory auditors, their independence and ethics, by introducing a requirement for external quality assurance and by ensuring robust public oversight over the audit profession. This considerably broadens the scope of the former Eighth Council Directive on Company Law, which only dealt with the approval of statutory auditors. The Directive also provides a basis for effective and balanced international co-operation between regulators in the EU and with regulators in third countries, such as the US Public Company Accounting Oversight Board (PCAOB).

The following measures apply to all statutory auditors and audit firms:

— update of the educational curriculum for auditors, which must now also include knowledge of international accounting standards (IAS) and international auditing standards (ISA)

— liberalisation of the ownership and the management of audit firms by opening up the ownership and the management to statutory auditors of all Member States

— introduction of an electronic registration system for auditors and audit firms in all Member States, with a catalogue of registration information that has to be permanently updated

— definition of basic principles of professional ethics

— legal underpinning of principles of auditor independence including the duty of the statutory auditor or audit firm to document factors which may affect auditors' independence (such as performing other work for the companies they audit) and safeguards against these sorts of risks

— obligation for Member States to set rules for audit fees that ensure audit quality and prevent "low-balling"; in other words preventing audit firms from offering the audit service for a marginal fee and compensating this with the fee income from other non-audit services

— requirement to use international auditing standards for all EU statutory audits once those standards have been endorsed under an EU procedure; Member States can only impose additional requirements in certain defined circumstances

— possibility for the adoption of a common audit report for financial statements that have been prepared on the basis of International Accounting Standards (IAS). This would ensure that all audit reports for financial statements prepared on the basis of IAS are identical throughout the EU

— introduction of a requirement for Member States to organise an audit quality assurance system that has to comply with clearly defined principles, such as the independence of reviewers and secure funding

— obligation for Member States to introduce effective investigative and disciplinary systems

— adoption of common rules concerning the appointment and the resignation of statutory auditors and audit firms (for example, statutory auditors to be dismissed only if there is a significant reason why they cannot finalise the audit) and introduction of a requirement for companies to document their communication with the statutory auditor or audit firm

— disclosure by companies, in the notes to their financial statements, of the audit fee and other fees for non-audit services delivered by the auditor.

In addition, there are specific measures applying to statutory auditors and audit firms of public-interest entities:

— introduction of an annual transparency report for audit firms that includes information on the governance of the audit firm, its international network, its quality assurance systems and the fees collected for audit and non-audit services (to demonstrate the relative importance of audit in the firm's overall business)

— auditor "rotation" - Member States to have the option of requiring either a change of key audit partner dealing with an audited company every five years, if the same audit firm keeps the work, or a change of audit firm every seven years

— shortening of the period when an audit quality review must be carried out from five to three years

— appointment of the statutory auditor or audit firm on the basis of a selection by the audit committee which must be set up in all public-interest entities

— obligation for the statutory auditor or audit firm to report to the audit committee on key matters arising from the statutory audit, particularly on material weaknesses of the internal control system

— disclosure to and discussion with the audit committee of any threats to the auditor's independence and confirmation in writing to the audit committee of his independence.

The Directive (as amended) defines public-interest entities as: (a) entities governed by the law of a Member State whose transferable securities are admitted to trading on a regulated market of any Member State within the meaning of point 14 of Article 4(1) of Directive 2004/39/EC (repealed by Directive 2014/65/EU of the European Parliament and of the Council of 15 May 2014 on markets in financial instruments and amending Directive 2002/92/EC and Directive 2011/61/EU); (b) credit institutions as defined in point 1 of Article 3(1) of Directive 2013/36/EU of the European Parliament and of the Council, other than those referred to in Article 2 of that Directive; (c) insurance undertakings within the meaning of Article 2(1) of Directive 91/674/EEC; or (d) entities designated by Member States as public-interest entities, for instance undertakings that are of significant public relevance because of the nature of their business, their size or the number of their employees.

Editorial note (legal status of EU Directives in the UK): note that EU Directives are not "direct EU legislation" within the meaning of the European Union (Withdrawal) Act 2018, s 3 at **[12.5]** and, accordingly, do not apply to the UK. As to the status of EU-derived domestic legislation after IP completion day (11pm on 31 December 2020), see s 2 of the 2018 Act at **[12.4]**. As to the UK implementation of this Directive, see the note below.

UK Implementation: in the UK this Directive has been implemented by the following:

Companies Act 2006 Part 16 (Audit) and Part 42 (Statutory Auditors) (see **[1.541]** et seq and **[1.1380]** et seq)

SI 2007/3494 Statutory Auditors and Third Country Auditors Regulations 2007

SI 2008/489 Companies (Disclosure of Auditor Remuneration and Liability Limitation Agreements) Regulations 2008 (see **[4.115]**)

SI 2008/496 Statutory Auditors (Delegation of Functions etc) Order 2008 (revoked)

SI 2008/499 Statutory Auditors and Third Country Auditors (Amendment) Regulations 2008 (revoked)

SI 2008/565 Insurance Accounts Directive (Miscellaneous Insurance Undertakings) Regulations 2008

SI 2008/567 Bank Accounts Directive (Miscellaneous Banks) Regulations 2008 (revoked)

SI 2008/569 Partnerships (Accounts) Regulations 2008 (see **[10.202]**)

SI 2008/1140 Friendly Societies Act 1992 (Accounts, Audit and EEA State Amendments) Order 2008

SI 2008/1143 Building Societies (Accounts and related Provisions) (Amendment) Regulations 2008

SI 2008/1144 Friendly Societies (Accounts and Related Provisions) (Amendment) Regulations 2008

SI 2008/1519 Building Societies Act 1986 (Accounts, Audit and EEA State Amendments) Order 2008

SI 2008/1950 Insurance Accounts Directive (Lloyd's Syndicate and Aggregate Accounts) Regulations 2008

SI 2009/2798 Statutory Auditors and Third Country Auditors (Amendment) Regulations 2009 (revoked)

SI 2010/2537 Companies Act 2006 (Transfer of Audit Working Papers to Third Countries) Regulations 2010

SI 2011/1856 Statutory Auditors and Third Country Auditors (Amendment) Regulations 2011

SI 2011/2198 Companies (Disclosure of Auditor Remuneration and Liability Limitation Agreements) (Amendment) Regulations 2011

SI 2012/1741 Statutory Auditors (Amendment of Companies Act 2006 and Delegation of Functions etc) Order 2012 (see **[4.430]**)

SI 2013/1672 Statutory Auditors and Third Country Auditors Regulations 2013 (see **[4.482]**)

SI 2013/2005 Companies and Partnerships (Accounts and Audit) Regulations 2013

SI 2017/1164 Statutory Auditors Regulations 2017

SI 2019/177 Statutory Auditors and Third Country Auditors (Amendment) (EU Exit) Regulations 2019

POB Instrument 01/2008 Statutory Auditors (Transparency) Instrument 2008

POB Instrument 02/2008 Statutory Auditors (Registration) Instrument 2008

POB Instrument 03/2008 Statutory Auditors (Examinations) Instrument 2008

FSA 2008/32 Disclosure Rules and Transparency Rules Sourcebook (Corporate Governance Rules) Instrument 2008.

For a summary of the implementing Orders and Regulations listed above (in so far as they are made under the Companies Act 2006), see Appendix 4 at **[A4]**.

The Directive is available on the EUR-Lex website at: eur-lex.europa.eu/legal-content/EN/TXT/?uri=CELEX:32006L0043. It has been amended by the following:

Directive 2008/30/EC of the European Parliament and of the Council amending Directive 2006/43/EC on statutory audits of annual accounts and consolidated accounts, as regards the implementing powers conferred on the Commission;

Directive 2013/34/EU of the European Parliament and of the Council on the annual financial statements, consolidated financial statements and related reports of certain types of undertakings, amending Directive 2006/43/EC of the European Parliament and of the Council and repealing Council Directives 78/660/EEC and 83/349/EEC;

Directive 2014/56/EU of the European Parliament and of the Council amending Directive 2006/43/EC on statutory audits of annual accounts and consolidated accounts.

DIRECTIVE OF THE EUROPEAN PARLIAMENT AND OF THE COUNCIL

(2007/36/EC)

of 11 July 2007

on the exercise of certain rights of shareholders in listed companies

[11.118]

NOTES

Date of publication in OJ: OJ L184, 14.07.2007, p 17.

This Directive is reproduced as amended by: European Parliament and Council Directive 2014/59/EU (transposition date 1 January 2015); European Parliament and Council Directive 2017/828/EU (transposition date 10 June 2019 (subject to exceptions)); European Parliament and Council Regulation 2021/23/EU.

Editorial note (legal status of EU Directives in the UK): note that EU Directives are not "direct EU legislation" within the meaning of the European Union (Withdrawal) Act 2018, s 3 at **[12.5]** and, accordingly, do not apply to the UK. As to the status of EU-derived domestic legislation after IP completion day (11pm on 31 December 2020), see s 2 of the 2018 Act at **[12.4]**. As to the UK implementation of this Directive, see the note below.

UK Implementation: in the UK this Directive was implemented by the Companies (Shareholders' Rights) Regulations 2009, SI 2009/1632 (see **[10.318]**), and the Proxy Advisors (Shareholders' Rights) Regulations 2019, SI 2019/926 (see **[10.1296]**).

THE EUROPEAN PARLIAMENT AND THE COUNCIL OF THE EUROPEAN UNION,

Having regard to the Treaty establishing the European Community, and in particular Articles 44 and 95 thereof,

Having regard to the proposal from the Commission,

Having regard to the opinion of the European Economic and Social Committee,[1]

Acting in accordance with the procedure laid down in Article 251 of the Treaty,[2]

Whereas:

(1) In its Communication to the Council and the European Parliament of 21 May 2003, entitled "Modernising Company Law and enhancing Corporate Governance in the European Union — A Plan to Move Forward", the Commission indicated that new tailored initiatives should be taken with a view to enhancing shareholders' rights in listed companies and that problems relating to cross-border voting should be solved as a matter of urgency.

(2) In its Resolution of 21 April 2004,[3] the European Parliament expressed its support for the Commission's intention to strengthen shareholders' rights, in particular through the extension of the rules on transparency, proxy voting rights, the possibility of participating in general meetings via electronic means and ensuring that cross-border voting rights are able to be exercised.

(3) Holders of shares carrying voting rights should be able to exercise those rights given that they are reflected in the price that has to be paid at the acquisition of the shares. Furthermore, effective shareholder control is a prerequisite to sound corporate governance and should, therefore, be facilitated and encouraged. It is therefore necessary to adopt measures to approximate the laws of the Member States to this end. Obstacles which deter shareholders from voting, such as making the exercise of voting rights subject to the blocking of shares during a certain period before the general meeting, should be removed. However, this Directive does not affect existing Community legislation on units issued by collective investment undertakings or on units acquired or disposed of in such undertakings.

(4) The existing Community legislation is not sufficient to achieve this objective. Directive 2001/34/EC of the European Parliament and of the Council of 28 May 2001 on the admission of securities to official stock exchange listing and on information to be published on those securities[4] focuses on the information issuers have to disclose to the market and accordingly does not deal with the shareholder voting process itself. Moreover, Directive 2004/109/EC of the European Parliament and of the Council of 15 December 2004 on the harmonisation of transparency requirements in relation to information about issuers whose securities are admitted to trading on a regulated market[5] imposes on issuers an obligation to make available certain information and documents relevant to general meetings, but such information and documents are to be made available in the issuer's home Member State. Therefore, certain minimum standards should be introduced with a view to protecting investors and promoting the smooth and effective exercise of shareholder rights attaching to voting shares. As regards rights other than the right to vote, Member States are free to extend the application of these minimum standards also to non-voting shares, to the extent that those shares do not enjoy such standards already.

(5) Significant proportions of shares in listed companies are held by shareholders who do not reside in the Member State in which the company has its registered office. Non-resident shareholders should be able to exercise their rights in relation to the general meeting as easily as shareholders who reside in the Member State in which the company has its registered office. This requires that existing obstacles which hinder the access of non-resident shareholders to the information relevant to the general meeting and the exercise of voting rights without physically attending the general meeting be removed. The removal of these obstacles should also benefit resident shareholders who do not or cannot attend the general meeting.

(6) Shareholders should be able to cast informed votes at, or in advance of, the general meeting, no matter where they reside. All shareholders should have sufficient time to consider the documents intended to be submitted to the general meeting and determine how they will vote their shares. To this end, timely notice should be given of the general meeting, and shareholders should be provided with the complete information intended to be submitted to the general meeting. The possibilities which modern technologies offer to make information instantly accessible should be exploited. This Directive presupposes that all listed companies already have an Internet site.

(7) Shareholders should, in principle, have the possibility to put items on the agenda of the general meeting and to table draft resolutions for items on the agenda. Without prejudice to different time-frames and modalities which are currently in use across the Community, the exercise of those rights should be made subject to two basic rules, namely

that any threshold required for the exercise of those rights should not exceed 5% of the company's share capital and that all shareholders should in every case receive the final version of the agenda in sufficient time to prepare for the discussion and voting on each item on the agenda.

(8) Every shareholder should, in principle, have the possibility to ask questions related to items on the agenda of the general meeting and to have them answered, while the rules on how and when questions are to be asked and answered should be left to be determined by Member States.

(9) Companies should face no legal obstacles in offering to their shareholders any means of electronic participation in the general meeting. Voting without attending the general meeting in person, whether by correspondence or by electronic means, should not be subject to constraints other than those necessary for the verification of identity and the security of electronic communications. However, this should not prevent Member States from adopting rules aimed at ensuring that the results of the voting reflect the intentions of the shareholders in all circumstances, including rules aimed at addressing situations where new circumstances occur or are revealed after a shareholder has cast his vote by correspondence or by electronic means.

(10) Good corporate governance requires a smooth and effective process of proxy voting. Existing limitations and constraints which make proxy voting cumbersome and costly should therefore be removed. But good corporate governance also requires adequate safeguards against a possible abuse of proxy voting. The proxy holder should therefore be bound to observe any instructions he may have received from the shareholder and Member States should be able to introduce appropriate measures ensuring that the proxy holder does not pursue any interest other than that of the shareholder, irrespective of the reason that has given rise to the conflict of interests. Measures against possible abuse may, in particular, consist of regimes which Member States may adopt in order to regulate the activity of persons who actively engage in the collection of proxies or who have in fact collected more than a certain significant number of proxies, notably to ensure an adequate degree of reliability and transparency. Shareholders have an unfettered right under this Directive to appoint such persons as proxy holders to attend and vote at general meetings in their name. This Directive does not, however, affect any rules or sanctions that Member States may impose on such persons where votes have been cast by making fraudulent use of proxies collected. Moreover, this Directive does not impose any obligation on companies to verify that proxy holders cast votes in accordance with the voting instructions of the appointing shareholders.

(11) Where financial intermediaries are involved, the effectiveness of voting upon instructions relies, to a great extent, on the efficiency of the chain of intermediaries, given that investors are frequently unable to exercise the voting rights attached to their shares without the cooperation of every intermediary in the chain, who may not have an economic stake in the shares. In order to enable the investor to exercise his voting rights in cross-border situations, it is therefore important that intermediaries facilitate the exercise of voting rights. Further consideration should be given to this issue by the Commission in the context of a Recommendation, with a view to ensuring that investors have access to effective voting services and that voting rights are exercised in accordance with the instructions given by those investors.

(12) While the timing of disclosure to the administrative, management or supervisory body as well as to the public of votes cast in advance of the general meeting electronically or by correspondence is an important matter of corporate governance, it can be determined by Member States.

(13) Voting results should be established through methods that reflect the voting intentions expressed by shareholders, and they should be made transparent after the general meeting at least through the company's Internet site.

(14) Since the objective of this Directive, namely to allow shareholders effectively to make use of their rights throughout the Community, cannot be sufficiently achieved by the Member States on the basis of the existing Community legislation and can therefore, by reason of the scale and effects of the measures, be better achieved at Community level, the Community may adopt measures, in accordance with the principle of subsidiarity as set out in Article 5 of the Treaty. In accordance with the principle of proportionality, as set out in that Article, this Directive does not go beyond what is necessary in order to achieve that objective.

(15) In accordance with paragraph 34 of the Interinstitutional Agreement on better law-making,[6] Member States are encouraged to draw up, for themselves and in the interests of the Community, their own tables illustrating, as far as possible, the correlation between this Directive and the transposition measures, and to make them public,

NOTES

1 OJ C318, 23.12.2006, p 42.

2 Opinion of the European Parliament of 15 February 2007 (not yet published in the Official Journal) and Council Decision of 12 June 2007.

3 OJ C104E, 30.4.2004, p 714.

4 OJ L184, 6.7.2001, p 1. Directive as last amended by Directive 2005/1/EC (OJ L79, 24.3.2005, p 9).

5 OJ L390, 31.12.2004, p 38.

6 OJ C321, 31.12.2003, p 1.

HAVE ADOPTED THIS DIRECTIVE:

CHAPTER I GENERAL PROVISIONS

[11.119]

Article 1 Subject-matter and scope

[1. This Directive establishes requirements in relation to the exercise of certain shareholder rights attached to voting shares in relation to general meetings of companies which have their registered office in a Member State and the shares of which are admitted to trading on a regulated market situated or operating within a Member State. It also establishes specific requirements in order to encourage shareholder engagement, in particular in the long term. Those specific requirements apply in relation to identification of shareholders, transmission of information, facilitation of exercise of shareholders rights, transparency of institutional investors, asset managers and proxy advisors, remuneration of directors and related party transactions.

2. The Member State competent to regulate matters covered in this Directive shall be the Member State in which the company has its registered office, and references to the "applicable law" are references to the law of that Member State.

For the purpose of application of Chapter Ib, the competent Member State shall be defined as follows:

(a) for institutional investors and asset managers, the home Member State as defined in any applicable sector-specific Union legislative act;

(b) for proxy advisors, the Member State in which the proxy advisor has its registered office, or, where the proxy advisor does not have its registered office in a Member State, the Member State in which the proxy advisor has its head office, or, where the proxy advisor has neither its registered office nor its head office in a Member State, the Member State in which the proxy advisor has an establishment.]

3. Member States may exempt from this Directive the following types of companies:

[(a) undertakings for collective investment in transferable securities (UCITS) within the meaning of Article 1(2) of Directive 2009/65/EC of the European Parliament and of the Council;[1]

(b) collective investment undertakings within the meaning of point (a) of Article 4(1) of Directive 2011/61/EU of the European Parliament and of the Council;[*]]

(c) cooperative societies.

[3a. The companies referred to in paragraph 3 shall not be exempted from the provisions laid down in Chapter Ib.]

[4. Member States shall ensure that this Directive does not apply in the case of the application of resolution tools, powers and mechanisms provided for in Title IV of Directive 2014/59/EU of the European Parliament and of the Council[2] or in Title V of Regulation (EU) 2021/23 of the European Parliament and of the Council.'[3]]

[5. Chapter Ia shall apply to intermediaries in so far they provide services to shareholders or other intermediaries with respect to shares of companies which have their registered office in a Member State and the shares of which are admitted to trading on a regulated market situated or operating within a Member State.

6. Chapter Ib shall apply to:

(a) institutional investors, to the extent that they invest directly or through an asset manager in shares traded on a regulated market;

(b) asset managers, to the extent that they invest in such shares on behalf of investors; and

(c) proxy advisors, to the extent that they provide services to shareholders with respect to shares of companies which have their registered office in a Member State and the shares of which are admitted to trading on a regulated market situated or operating within a Member State.

7. The provisions of this Directive are without prejudice to the provisions laid down in any sector-specific Union legislative act regulating specific types of company or specific types of entity. Where this Directive provides for more specific rules or adds requirements compared to the provisions laid down by any sector-specific Union legislative act, those provisions shall be applied in conjunction with the provisions of this Directive.]

NOTES

Paras 1, 2: substituted by European Parliament and Council Directive 2017/828/EU, Art 1(1)(a), as from 9 June 2017.

Para 3: points (a), (b) substituted by European Parliament and Council Directive 2017/828/EU, Art 1(1)(b), as from 9 June 2017.

Para 3a: inserted by European Parliament and Council Directive 2017/828/EU, Art 1(1)(c), as from 9 June 2017.

Para 4: originally added by European Parliament and Council Directive 2014/59/EU, Art 121(1), as from 2 July 2014. Subsequently substituted by European Parliament and Council Regulation 2021/23/EU, Art 91(1), as from 12 August 2022.

Paras 5–7: added by European Parliament and Council Directive 2017/828/EU, Art 1(1)(d), as from 9 June 2017.

1 Directive 2009/65/EC of the European Parliament and of the Council of 13 July 2009 on the coordination of laws, regulations and administrative provisions relating to undertakings for collective investment in transferable securities (UCITS) (OJ L302, 17.11.2009, p 32).

* Directive 2011/61/EU of the European Parliament and of the Council of 8 June 2011 on Alternative Investment Fund Managers and amending Directives 2003/41/EC and 2009/65/EC and Regulations (EC) No 1060/2009 and (EU) No 1095/2010 (OJ L174, 1.7.2011, p 1).';

2 Directive 2014/59/EU of the European Parliament and of the Council of 15 May 2014 establishing a framework for the recovery and resolution of credit institutions and investment firms and amending Council Directive 82/891/EEC and Directives 2001/24/EC, 2002/47/EC, 2004/25/EC, 2005/56/EC, 2007/36/EC, 2011/35/EU, 2012/30/EU and 2013/36/EU, and Regulations (EU) No 1093/2010 and (EU) No 648/2012, of the European Parliament and of the Council (OJ L173, 12.6.2014, p 190).

3 Regulation (EU) 2021/23 of the European Parliament and of the Council of 16 December 2020 on a framework for the recovery and resolution of central counterparties and amending Regulations (EU) No 1095/2010, (EU) No 648/2012, (EU) No 600/2014, (EU) No 806/2014 and (EU) 2015/2365 and Directives 2002/47/EC, 2004/25/EC, 2007/36/EC, 2014/59/EU and (EU) 2017/1132 (OJ L022, 22.1.2021, p 1).

[11.120]

Article 2 Definitions

For the purposes of this Directive the following definitions shall apply:

[(a) "regulated market" means a regulated market as defined in point (21) of Article 4(1) of Directive 2014/65/EU of the European Parliament and of the Council;[1]]

(b) "shareholder" means the natural or legal person that is recognised as a shareholder under the applicable law;

(c) "proxy" means the empowerment of a natural or legal person by a shareholder to exercise some or all rights of that shareholder in the general meeting in his name;

[(d) "intermediary" means a person, such as an investment firm as defined in point (1) of Article 4(1) of Directive 2014/65/EU, a credit institution as defined in point (1) of Article 4(1) of Regulation (EU) No 575/2013 of the European Parliament and of the Council[2] and a central securities depository as defined in point (1) of Article 2(1) of Regulation (EU) No 909/2014 of the European Parliament and of the Council,[3] which provides services of safekeeping of shares, administration of shares or maintenance of securities accounts on behalf of shareholders or other persons;

(e) "institutional investor" means:

(i) an undertaking carrying out activities of life assurance within the meaning of points (a), (b) and (c) of Article 2(3) of Directive 2009/138/EC of the European Parliament and of the Council,[4] and of reinsurance as defined in point (7) of Article 13 of that Directive provided that those activities cover life-insurance obligations, and which is not excluded pursuant to that Directive;

(ii) an institution for occupational retirement provision falling within the scope of Directive (EU) 2016/2341 of the European Parliament and of the Council[5] in accordance with Article 2 thereof, unless a Member State has chosen not to apply that Directive in whole or in parts to that institution in accordance with Article 5 of that Directive;

(f) "asset manager" means an investment firm as defined in point (1) of Article 4(1) of Directive 2014/65/EU that provides portfolio management services to investors, an AIFM (alternative investment fund manager) as defined in point (b) of Article 4(1) of Directive 2011/61/EU that does not fulfil the conditions for an exemption in accordance with Article 3 of that Directive or a management company as defined in point (b) of Article 2(1) of Directive 2009/65/EC, or an investment company that is authorised in accordance with Directive 2009/65/EC provided that it has not designated a management company authorised under that Directive for its management;

(g) "proxy advisor" means a legal person that analyses, on a professional and commercial basis, the corporate disclosure and, where relevant, other information of listed companies with a view to informing investors' voting decisions by providing research, advice or voting recommendations that relate to the exercise of voting rights;

(h) "related party" has the same meaning as in the international accounting standards adopted in accordance with Regulation (EC) No 1606/2002 of the European Parliament and of the Council;[6]

(i) "director" means:

(i) any member of the administrative, management or supervisory bodies of a company;

(ii) where they are not members of the administrative, management or supervisory bodies of a company, the chief executive officer and, if such function exists in a company, the deputy chief executive officer;

(iii) where so determined by a Member State, other persons who perform functions similar to those performed under point (i) or (ii);

(j) "information regarding shareholder identity" means information allowing the identity of a shareholder to be established, including at least the following information:

(i) name and contact details (including full address and, where available, email address) of the shareholder, and, where it is a legal person, its registration number, or, if no registration number is available, its unique identifier, such as legal entity identifier;

(ii) the number of shares held; and

(iii) only insofar they are requested by the company, one or more of the following details: the categories or classes of the shares held or the date from which the shares have been held.]

NOTES

Point (a) substituted, and points (d)–(j) added, by European Parliament and Council Directive 2017/828/EU, Art 1(2)(a), as from 9 June 2017.

1 Directive 2014/65/EU of the European Parliament and of the Council of 15 May 2014 on markets in financial instruments and amending Directive 2002/92/EC and Directive 2011/61/EU (OJ L173, 12.6.2014, p 349).';

2 Regulation (EU) No 575/2013 of the European Parliament and of the Council of 26 June 2013 on prudential requirements for credit institutions and investment firms and amending Regulation (EU) No 648/2012 (OJ L176, 27.6.2013, p 1).

3 Regulation (EU) No 909/2014 of the European Parliament and of the Council of 23 July 2014 on improving securities settlement in the European Union and on central securities depositories and amending Directives 98/26/EC and 2014/65/EU and Regulation (EU) No 236/2012 (OJ L257, 28.8.2014, p 1).

4 Directive 2009/138/EC of the European Parliament and of the Council of 25 November 2009 on the taking-up and pursuit of the business of Insurance and Reinsurance (Solvency II) (OJ L335, 17.12.2009, p 1).

5 Directive (EU) 2016/2341 of the European Parliament and of the Council of 14 December 2016 on the activities and supervision of institutions for occupational retirement provision (IORPs) (OJ L354, 23.12.2016, p 37).

6 Regulation (EC) No 1606/2002 of the European Parliament and of the Council of 19 July 2002 on the application of international accounting standards (OJ L243, 11.9.2002, p 1).

[11.121]

Article 3 Further national measures

This Directive shall not prevent Member States from imposing further obligations on companies or from otherwise taking further measures to facilitate the exercise by shareholders of the rights referred to in this Directive.

[CHAPTER IA IDENTIFICATION OF SHAREHOLDERS, TRANSMISSION OF INFORMATION AND FACILITATION OF EXERCISE OF SHAREHOLDER RIGHTS

[11.122]

Article 3a Identification of shareholders

1. Member States shall ensure that companies have the right to identify their shareholders. Member States may provide for companies having a registered office on their territory to be only allowed to request the identification of shareholders holding more than a certain percentage of shares or voting rights. Such a percentage shall not exceed 0.5%.

2. Member States shall ensure that, on the request of the company or of a third party nominated by the company, the intermediaries communicate without delay to the company the information regarding shareholder identity.

3. Where there is more than one intermediary in a chain of intermediaries, Member States shall ensure that the request of the company, or of a third party nominated by the company, is transmitted between intermediaries without delay and that the information regarding shareholder identity is transmitted directly to the company or to a third party

nominated by the company without delay by the intermediary who holds the requested information. Member States shall ensure that the company is able to obtain information regarding shareholder identity from any intermediary in the chain that holds the information.

Member States may provide for the company to be allowed to request the central securities depository or another intermediary or service provider to collect the information regarding shareholder identity, including from the intermediaries in the chain of intermediaries and to transmit the information to the company.

Member States may additionally provide that, at the request of the company, or of a third party nominated by the company, the intermediary is to communicate to the company without delay the details of the next intermediary in the chain of intermediaries.

4. The personal data of shareholders shall be processed pursuant to this Article in order to enable the company to identify its existing shareholders in order to communicate with them directly with the view to facilitating the exercise of shareholder rights and shareholder engagement with the company.

Without prejudice to any longer storage period laid down by any sector-specific Union legislative act, Member States shall ensure that companies and intermediaries do not store the personal data of shareholders transmitted to them in accordance with this Article for the purpose specified in this Article for longer than 12 months after they have become aware that the person concerned has ceased to be a shareholder.

Member States may provide by law for processing of the personal data of shareholders for other purposes.

5. Member States shall ensure that legal persons have the right of rectification of incomplete or inaccurate information regarding their shareholder identity.

6. Member States shall ensure that an intermediary that discloses information regarding shareholder identity in accordance with the rules laid down in this Article is not considered to be in breach of any restriction on disclosure of information imposed by contract or by any legislative, regulatory or administrative provision.

7. By 10 June 2019, Member States shall provide the European Supervisory Authority (European Securities and Markets Authority) (ESMA), established by Regulation (EU) No 1095/2010 of the European Parliament and of the Council[1] with information on whether they have limited shareholder identification to shareholders holding more than a certain percentage of the shares or voting rights in accordance with paragraph 1 and, if so, the applicable percentage. ESMA shall publish that information on its website.

8. The Commission shall be empowered to adopt implementing acts to specify the minimum requirements to transmit the information laid down in paragraph 2 as regards the format of information to be transmitted, the format of the request, including their security and interoperability, and the deadlines to be complied with. Those implementing acts shall be adopted by 10 September 2018 in accordance with the examination procedure referred to in Article 14a(2).]

NOTES

Chapters Ia and Ib were inserted by European Parliament and Council Directive 2017/828/EU, Art 1(3), as from 9 June 2017.

Implementing Act for the purpose of para 8 above: see the note relating to Commission Implementing Regulation 2018/1212/EU laying down minimum requirements implementing the provisions of Directive 2007/36/EC of the European Parliament and of the Council as regards shareholder identification, the transmission of information and the facilitation of the exercise of shareholders rights (at **[11.615]**). Note that the 2018 Regulation was repealed, in relation to the UK, by the European Grouping of Territorial Cooperation and Limited Liability Partnerships etc (Revocations and Amendments) (EU Exit) Regulations 2021, SI 2021/153, reg 2, Schedule, as from 8 March 2021.

[1] Regulation (EU) No 1095/2010 of the European Parliament and of the Council of 24 November 2010 establishing a European Supervisory Authority (European Securities and Markets Authority), amending Decision No 716/2009/EC and repealing Commission Decision 2009/77/EC (OJ L331, 15.12.2010, p 84).

[11.123]

[Article 3b Transmission of information

1. Member States shall ensure that the intermediaries are required to transmit the following information, without delay, from the company to the shareholder or to a third party nominated by the shareholder:

(a) the information which the company is required to provide to the shareholder, to enable the shareholder to exercise rights flowing from its shares, and which is directed to all shareholders in shares of that class; or

(b) where the information referred to in point (a) is available to shareholders on the website of the company, a notice indicating where on the website that information can be found.

2. Member States shall require companies to provide intermediaries in a standardised and timely manner with the information referred to in point (a) of paragraph 1 or the notice referred to in point (b) of that paragraph.

3. However, Member States shall not require that the information referred to in point (a) of paragraph 1 or the notice referred to in point (b) of that paragraph be transmitted or provided in accordance with paragraphs 1 and 2 where companies send that information or that notice directly to all their shareholders or to a third party nominated by the shareholder.

4. Member States shall oblige intermediaries to transmit, without delay, to the company, in accordance with the instructions received from the shareholders, the information received from the shareholders related to the exercise of the rights flowing from their shares.

5. Where there is more than one intermediary in a chain of intermediaries, information referred to in paragraphs 1 and 4 shall be transmitted between intermediaries without delay, unless the information can be directly transmitted by the intermediary to the company or to the shareholder or to a third party nominated by the shareholder.

6. The Commission shall be empowered to adopt implementing acts to specify the minimum requirements to transmit information laid down in paragraphs 1 to 5 of this Article as regards the types and format of information to be transmitted, including their security and interoperability, and the deadlines to be complied with. Those implementing acts shall be adopted by 10 September 2018 in accordance with the examination procedure referred to in Article 14a(2).]

NOTES

Inserted as noted to Article 3a at **[11.122]**.

Implementing Act for the purpose of para 6 above: see the note relating to Commission Implementing Regulation 2018/1212/EU laying down minimum requirements implementing the provisions of Directive 2007/36/EC of the European Parliament and of the Council as regards shareholder identification, the transmission of information and the facilitation of the exercise of shareholders rights (at **[11.615]**). Note that the 2018 Regulation was repealed, in relation to the UK, by the European Grouping of Territorial Cooperation and Limited Liability Partnerships etc (Revocations and Amendments) (EU Exit) Regulations 2021, SI 2021/153, reg 2, Schedule, as from 8 March 2021.

[11.124]

[Article 3c Facilitation of the exercise of shareholder rights

1. Member States shall ensure that the intermediaries facilitate the exercise of the rights by the shareholder, including the right to participate and vote in general meetings, which shall comprise at least one of the following:

(a) the intermediary makes the necessary arrangements for the shareholder or a third party nominated by the shareholder to be able to exercise themselves the rights;

(b) the intermediary exercises the rights flowing from the shares upon the explicit authorisation and instruction of the shareholder and for the shareholder's benefit.

2. Member States shall ensure that when votes are cast electronically an electronic confirmation of receipt of the votes is sent to the person that casts the vote.

Member States shall ensure that after the general meeting the shareholder or a third party nominated by the shareholder can obtain, at least upon request, confirmation that their votes have been validly recorded and counted by the company, unless that information is already available to them. Member States may establish a deadline for requesting such confirmation. Such a deadline shall not be longer than three months from the date of the vote.

Where the intermediary receives confirmation as referred to in the first or second subparagraph, it shall transmit it without delay to the shareholder or a third party nominated by the shareholder. Where there is more than one intermediary in the chain of intermediaries the confirmation shall be transmitted between intermediaries without delay, unless the confirmation can be directly transmitted to the shareholder or a third party nominated by the shareholder.

3. The Commission shall be empowered to adopt implementing acts to specify the minimum requirements to facilitate the exercise of shareholder rights laid down in paragraphs 1 and 2 of this Article as regards the types of the facilitation, the format of the electronic confirmation of receipt of the votes, the format for the transmission of the confirmation that the votes have been validly recorded and counted through the chain of intermediaries, including their security and interoperability, and the deadlines to be complied with. Those implementing acts shall be adopted by 10 September 2018 in accordance with the examination procedure referred to in Article 14a(2).]

NOTES

Inserted as noted to Article 3a at **[11.122]**.

Implementing Act for the purpose of para 3 above: see the note relating to Commission Implementing Regulation 2018/1212/EU laying down minimum requirements implementing the provisions of Directive 2007/36/EC of the European Parliament and of the Council as regards shareholder identification, the transmission of information and the facilitation of the exercise of shareholders rights (at **[11.615]**). Note that the 2018 Regulation was repealed, in relation to the UK, by the European Grouping of Territorial Cooperation and Limited Liability Partnerships etc (Revocations and Amendments) (EU Exit) Regulations 2021, SI 2021/153, reg 2, Schedule, as from 8 March 2021.

[11.125]

[Article 3d Non-discrimination, proportionality and transparency of costs

1. Member States shall require intermediaries to disclose publicly any applicable charges for services provided for under this Chapter separately for each service.

2. Member States shall ensure that any charges levied by an intermediary on shareholders, companies and other intermediaries shall be non-discriminatory and proportionate in relation to the actual costs incurred for delivering the services. Any differences between the charges levied between domestic and cross-border exercise of rights shall be permitted only where duly justified and where they reflect the variation in actual costs incurred for delivering the services.

3. Member States may prohibit intermediaries from charging fees for the services provided for under this Chapter.]

NOTES

Inserted as noted to Article 3a at **[11.122]**.

[11.126]

[Article 3e Third-country intermediaries

This Chapter also applies to intermediaries which have neither their registered office nor their head office in the Union when they provide services referred to in Article 1(5).]

NOTES

Inserted as noted to Article 3a at **[11.122]**.

[11.127]

[Article 3f Information on implementation

1. Competent authorities shall inform the Commission of substantial practical difficulties in enforcement of the provisions of this Chapter or non-compliance with the provisions of this Chapter by Union or third-country intermediaries.

2. The Commission shall, in close cooperation with ESMA and the European Supervisory Authority (European Banking Authority), established by Regulation (EU) No 1093/2010 of the European Parliament and of the Council,[1] submit a report to the European Parliament and to the Council on the implementation of this Chapter, including its effectiveness, difficulties in practical application and enforcement, while taking into account relevant market developments at the Union and international level. The report shall also address the appropriateness of the scope of application of this Chapter in relation to third-country intermediaries. The Commission shall publish the report by 10 June 2023.]

NOTES

Inserted as noted to Article 3a at **[11.122]**.

[1] Regulation (EU) No 1093/2010 of the European Parliament and of the Council of 24 November 2010 establishing a

European Supervisory Authority (European Banking Authority), amending Decision No 716/2009/EC and repealing Commission Decision 2009/78/EC (OJ L331, 15.12.2010, p 12).'.

[CHAPTER IB TRANSPARENCY OF INSTITUTIONAL INVESTORS, ASSET MANAGERS AND PROXY ADVISORS

[11.128]

Article 3g Engagement policy

1. Member States shall ensure that institutional investors and asset managers either comply with the requirements set out in points (a) and (b) or publicly disclose a clear and reasoned explanation why they have chosen not to comply with one or more of those requirements.

(a) Institutional investors and asset managers shall develop and publicly disclose an engagement policy that describes how they integrate shareholder engagement in their investment strategy. The policy shall describe how they monitor investee companies on relevant matters, including strategy, financial and non-financial performance and risk, capital structure, social and environmental impact and corporate governance, conduct dialogues with investee companies, exercise voting rights and other rights attached to shares, cooperate with other shareholders, communicate with relevant stakeholders of the investee companies and manage actual and potential conflicts of interests in relation to their engagement.

(b) Institutional investors and asset managers shall, on an annual basis, publicly disclose how their engagement policy has been implemented, including a general description of voting behaviour, an explanation of the most significant votes and the use of the services of proxy advisors. They shall publicly disclose how they have cast votes in the general meetings of companies in which they hold shares. Such disclosure may exclude votes that are insignificant due to the subject matter of the vote or the size of the holding in the company.

2. The information referred to in paragraph 1 shall be available free of charge on the institutional investor's or asset manager's website. Member States may provide for the information to be published, free of charge, by other means that are easily accessible online.

Where an asset manager implements the engagement policy, including voting, on behalf of an institutional investor, the institutional investor shall make a reference as to where such voting information has been published by the asset manager.

3. Conflicts of interests rules applicable to institutional investors and asset managers, including Article 14 of Directive 2011/61/EU, point (b) of Article 12(1) and point (d) of 14(1) of Directive 2009/65/EC and the relevant implementing rules, and Article 23 of Directive 2014/65/EU shall also apply with regard to engagement activities.]

NOTES

Inserted as noted to Article 3a at **[11.122]**.

[11.129]

[Article 3h Investment strategy of institutional investors and arrangements with asset managers

1. Member States shall ensure that institutional investors publicly disclose how the main elements of their equity investment strategy are consistent with the profile and duration of their liabilities, in particular long-term liabilities, and how they contribute to the medium to long-term performance of their assets.

2. Member States shall ensure that where an asset manager invests on behalf of an institutional investor, whether on a discretionary client-by-client basis or through a collective investment undertaking, the institutional investor publicly discloses the following information regarding its arrangement with the asset manager:

(a) how the arrangement with the asset manager incentivises the asset manager to align its investment strategy and decisions with the profile and duration of the liabilities of the institutional investor, in particular long-term liabilities;

(b) how that arrangement incentivises the asset manager to make investment decisions based on assessments about medium to long-term financial and non-financial performance of the investee company and to engage with investee companies in order to improve their performance in the medium to long-term;

(c) how the method and time horizon of the evaluation of the asset manager's performance and the remuneration for asset management services are in line with the profile and duration of the liabilities of the institutional investor, in particular long-term liabilities, and take absolute long-term performance into account;

(d) how the institutional investor monitors portfolio turnover costs incurred by the asset manager and how it defines and monitors a targeted portfolio turnover or turnover range;

(e) the duration of the arrangement with the asset manager.

Where the arrangement with the asset manager does not contain one or more of such elements, the institutional investor shall give a clear and reasoned explanation why this is the case.

3. The information referred to in paragraphs 1 and 2 of this Article shall be available, free of charge, on the institutional investor's website and shall be updated annually unless there is no material change. Member States may provide for that information to be available, free of charge, through other means that are easily accessible online.

Member States shall ensure that institutional investors regulated by Directive 2009/138/EC are allowed to include this information in their report on solvency and financial condition referred to in Article 51 of that Directive.]

NOTES

Inserted as noted to Article 3a at **[11.122]**.

[11.130]

[Article 3i Transparency of asset managers

1. Member States shall ensure that asset managers disclose, on an annual basis, to the institutional investor with which they have entered into the arrangements referred to in Article 3h how their investment strategy and implementation thereof complies with that arrangement and contributes to the medium to long-term performance of the assets of the institutional investor or of the fund. Such disclosure shall include reporting on the key material medium to long-term risks associated with the investments, on portfolio composition, turnover and turnover costs, on the use of proxy advisors for the purpose of engagement activities and their policy on securities lending and how it is

applied to fulfil its engagement activities if applicable, particularly at the time of the general meeting of the investee companies. Such disclosure shall also include information on whether and, if so, how, they make investment decisions based on evaluation of medium to long-term performance of the investee company, including non-financial performance, and on whether and, if so, which conflicts of interests have arisen in connection with engagements activities and how the asset managers have dealt with them.

2. Member States may provide for the information in paragraph 1 to be disclosed together with the annual report referred to in Article 68 of Directive 2009/65/EC or in Article 22 of Directive 2011/61/EU, or periodic communications referred to in Article 25(6) of Directive 2014/65/EU.

Where the information disclosed pursuant to paragraph 1 is already publicly available, the asset manager is not required to provide the information to the institutional investor directly.

3. Member States may where the asset manager does not manage the assets on a discretionary client-by-client basis, require that the information disclosed pursuant to paragraph 1 also be provided to other investors of the same fund at least upon request.]

NOTES

Inserted as noted to Article 3a at **[11.122]**.

[11.131]

[Article 3j Transparency of proxy advisors

1. Member States shall ensure that proxy advisors publicly disclose reference to a code of conduct which they apply and report on the application of that code of conduct.

Where proxy advisors do not apply a code of conduct, they shall provide a clear and reasoned explanation why this is the case. Where proxy advisors apply a code of conduct but depart from any of its recommendations, they shall declare from which parts they depart, provide explanations for doing so and indicate, where appropriate, any alternative measures adopted.

Information referred to in this paragraph shall be made publicly available, free of charge, on the websites of proxy advisors and shall be updated on an annual basis.

2. Member States shall ensure that, in order to adequately inform their clients about the accuracy and reliability of their activities, proxy advisors publicly disclose on an annual basis at least all of the following information in relation to the preparation of their research, advice and voting recommendations:

(a) the essential features of the methodologies and models they apply;

(b) the main information sources they use;

(c) the procedures put in place to ensure quality of the research, advice and voting recommendations and qualifications of the staff involved;

(d) whether and, if so, how they take national market, legal, regulatory and company-specific conditions into account;

(e) the essential features of the voting policies they apply for each market;

(f) whether they have dialogues with the companies which are the object of their research, advice or voting recommendations and with the stakeholders of the company, and, if so, the extent and nature thereof;

(g) the policy regarding the prevention and management of potential conflicts of interests.

The information referred to in this paragraph shall be made publicly available on the websites of proxy advisors and shall remain available free of charge for at least three years from the date of publication. The information does not need to be disclosed separately where it is available as part of the disclosure under paragraph 1.

3. Member States shall ensure that proxy advisors identify and disclose without delay to their clients any actual or potential conflicts of interests or business relationships that may influence the preparation of their research, advice or voting recommendations and the actions they have undertaken to eliminate, mitigate or manage the actual or potential conflicts of interests.

4. This Article also applies to proxy advisors that have neither their registered office nor their head office in the Union which carry out their activities through an establishment located in the Union.]

NOTES

Inserted as noted to Article 3a at **[11.122]**.

[11.132]

[Article 3k Review

1. The Commission shall submit a report to the European Parliament and to the Council on the implementation of Articles 3g, 3h and 3i, including the assessment of the need to require asset managers to publicly disclose certain information under Article 3i, taking into account relevant Union and international market developments. The report shall be published by 10 June 2022 and shall be accompanied, if appropriate, by legislative proposals.

2. The Commission shall, in close cooperation with ESMA, submit a report to the European Parliament and to the Council on the implementation of Article 3j, including the appropriateness of its scope of application and its effectiveness and the assessment of the need for establishing regulatory requirements for proxy advisors, taking into account relevant Union and international market developments. The report shall be published by 10 June 2023 and shall be accompanied, if appropriate, by legislative proposals.]

NOTES

Inserted as noted to Article 3a at **[11.122]**.

CHAPTER II GENERAL MEETINGS OF SHAREHOLDERS

[11.133]

Article 4 Equal treatment of shareholders

The company shall ensure equal treatment for all shareholders who are in the same position with regard to participation and the exercise of voting rights in the general meeting.

Part 11 EU & Retained EU Legislation

[11.134]

Article 5 Information prior to the general meeting

1. Without prejudice to Articles 9(4) and 11(4) of Directive 2004/25/EC of the European Parliament and of the Council of 21 April 2004 on takeover bids,[1] Member States shall ensure that the company issues the convocation of the general meeting in one of the manners specified in paragraph 2 of this Article not later than on the 21st day before the day of the meeting.

Member States may provide that, where the company offers the facility for shareholders to vote by electronic means accessible to all shareholders, the general meeting of shareholders may decide that it shall issue the convocation of a general meeting which is not an annual general meeting in one of the manners specified in paragraph 2 of this Article not later than on the 14th day before the day of the meeting. This decision is to be taken by a majority of not less than two thirds of the votes attaching to the shares or the subscribed capital represented and for a duration not later than the next annual general meeting.

Member States need not apply the minimum periods referred to in the first and second subparagraphs for the second or subsequent convocation of a general meeting issued for lack of a quorum required for the meeting convened by the first convocation, provided that this Article has been complied with for the first convocation and no new item is put on the agenda, and that at least 10 days elapse between the final convocation and the date of the general meeting.

2. Without prejudice to further requirements for notification or publication laid down by the competent Member State as defined in Article 1(2), the company shall be required to issue the convocation referred to in paragraph 1 of this Article in a manner ensuring fast access to it on a non-discriminatory basis. The Member State shall require the company to use such media as may reasonably be relied upon for the effective dissemination of information to the public throughout the Community. The Member State may not impose an obligation to use only media whose operators are established on its territory.

The Member State need not apply the first subparagraph to companies that are able to identify the names and addresses of their shareholders from a current register of shareholders, provided that the company is under an obligation to send the convocation to each of its registered shareholders.

In either case the company may not charge any specific cost for issuing the convocation in the prescribed manner.

3. The convocation referred to in paragraph 1 shall at least:

(a) indicate precisely when and where the general meeting is to take place, and the proposed agenda for the general meeting;

(b) contain a clear and precise description of the procedures that shareholders must comply with in order to be able to participate and to cast their vote in the general meeting. This includes information concerning:

   (i) the rights available to shareholders under Article 6, to the extent that those rights can be exercised after the issuing of the convocation, and under Article 9, and the deadlines by which those rights may be exercised; the convocation may confine itself to stating only the deadlines by which those rights may be exercised, provided it contains a reference to more detailed information concerning those rights being made available on the Internet site of the company;

   (ii) the procedure for voting by proxy, notably the forms to be used to vote by proxy and the means by which the company is prepared to accept electronic notifications of the appointment of proxy holders; and

   (iii) where applicable, the procedures for casting votes by correspondence or by electronic means;

(c) where applicable, state the record date as defined in Article 7(2) and explain that only those who are shareholders on that date shall have the right to participate and vote in the general meeting;

(d) indicate where and how the full, unabridged text of the documents and draft resolutions referred to in points (c) and (d) of paragraph 4 may be obtained;

(e) indicate the address of the Internet site on which the information referred to in paragraph 4 will be made available.

4. Member States shall ensure that, for a continuous period beginning not later than on the 21 day before the day of the general meeting and including the day of the meeting, the company shall make available to its shareholders on its Internet site at least the following information:

(a) the convocation referred to in paragraph 1;

(b) the total number of shares and voting rights at the date of the convocation (including separate totals for each class of shares where the company's capital is divided into two or more classes of shares);

(c) the documents to be submitted to the general meeting;

(d) a draft resolution or, where no resolution is proposed to be adopted, a comment from a competent body within the company, to be designated by the applicable law, for each item on the proposed agenda of the general meeting; moreover, draft resolutions tabled by shareholders shall be added to the Internet site as soon as practicable after the company has received them;

(e) where applicable, the forms to be used to vote by proxy and to vote by correspondence, unless those forms are sent directly to each shareholder.

Where the forms referred to in point (e) cannot be made available on the Internet for technical reasons, the company shall indicate on its Internet site how the forms can be obtained on paper. In this case the company shall be required to send the forms by postal services and free of charge to every shareholder who so requests.

Where, pursuant to Articles 9(4) or 11(4) of Directive 2004/25/EC, or to the second subparagraph of paragraph 1 of this Article, the convocation of the general meeting is issued later than on the 21st day before the meeting, the period specified in this paragraph shall be shortened accordingly.

[5. Member States shall ensure that for the purposes of Directive 2014/59/EU and Regulation (EU) 2021/23 the general meeting may, by a majority of two-thirds of the votes validly cast, issue a convocation to a general meeting, or modify the statutes to prescribe that a convocation to a general meeting is issued, at shorter notice than as laid down in paragraph 1 of this Article, to decide on a capital increase, provided that that meeting does not take place within ten calendar days of the convocation, that the conditions of Article 27 or 29 of Directive 2014/59/EU or of Article 18 of Regulation (EU) 2021/23 are met, and that the capital increase is necessary to avoid the conditions for resolution laid down in Articles 32 and 33 of Directive 2014/59/EU or in Article 22 of Regulation (EU) 2021/23.]

6. For the purposes of paragraph 5, the obligation on each Member State to set a single deadline in Article 6(3), the obligation to ensure timely availability of a revised agenda in Article 6(4) and the obligation on each Member State to set a single record date in Article 7(3) shall not apply.]

NOTES

Paras 5, 6: added by European Parliament and Council Directive 2014/59/EU, Art 121(2), as from 2 July 2014. Para 5 subsequently substituted by European Parliament and Council Regulation 2021/23/EU, Art 91(2), as from 12 August 2022.

[1] OJ L142, 30.4.2004, p 12.

[11.135]

Article 6 Right to put items on the agenda of the general meeting and to table draft resolutions

1. Member States shall ensure that shareholders, acting individually or collectively:

(a) have the right to put items on the agenda of the general meeting, provided that each such item is accompanied by a justification or a draft resolution to be adopted in the general meeting; and

(b) have the right to table draft resolutions for items included or to be included on the agenda of a general meeting.

Member States may provide that the right referred to in point (a) may be exercised only in relation to the annual general meeting, provided that shareholders, acting individually or collectively, have the right to call, or to require the company to call, a general meeting which is not an annual general meeting with an agenda including at least all the items requested by those shareholders.

Member States may provide that those rights shall be exercised in writing (submitted by postal services or electronic means).

2. Where any of the rights specified in paragraph 1 is subject to the condition that the relevant shareholder or shareholders hold a minimum stake in the company, such minimum stake shall not exceed 5% of the share capital.

3. Each Member State shall set a single deadline, with reference to a specified number of days prior to the general meeting or the convocation, by which shareholders may exercise the right referred to in paragraph 1, point (a). In the same manner each Member State may set a deadline for the exercise of the right referred to in paragraph 1, point (b).

4. Member States shall ensure that, where the exercise of the right referred to in paragraph 1, point (a) entails a modification of the agenda for the general meeting already communicated to shareholders, the company shall make available a revised agenda in the same manner as the previous agenda in advance of the applicable record date as defined in Article 7(2) or, if no record date applies, sufficiently in advance of the date of the general meeting so as to enable other shareholders to appoint a proxy or, where applicable, to vote by correspondence.

[11.136]

Article 7 Requirements for participation and voting in the general meeting

1. Member States shall ensure:

(a) that the rights of a shareholder to participate in a general meeting and to vote in respect of any of his shares are not subject to any requirement that his shares be deposited with, or transferred to, or registered in the name of, another natural or legal person before the general meeting; and

(b) that the rights of a shareholder to sell or otherwise transfer his shares during the period between the record date, as defined in paragraph 2, and the general meeting to which it applies are not subject to any restriction to which they are not subject at other times.

2. Member States shall provide that the rights of a shareholder to participate in a general meeting and to vote in respect of his shares shall be determined with respect to the shares held by that shareholder on a specified date prior to the general meeting (the record date).

Member States need not apply the first subparagraph to companies that are able to identify the names and addresses of their shareholders from a current register of shareholders on the day of the general meeting.

3. Each Member State shall ensure that a single record date applies to all companies. However, a Member State may set one record date for companies which have issued bearer shares and another record date for companies which have issued registered shares, provided that a single record date applies to each company which has issued both types of shares. The record date shall not lie more than 30 days before the date of the general meeting to which it applies. In implementing this provision and Article 5(1), each Member State shall ensure that at least eight days elapse between the latest permissible date for the convocation of the general meeting and the record date. In calculating that number of days those two dates shall not be included. In the circumstances described in Article 5(1), third subparagraph, however, a Member State may require that at least six days elapse between the latest permissible date for the second or subsequent convocation of the general meeting and the record date. In calculating that number of days those two dates shall not be included.

4. Proof of qualification as a shareholder may be made subject only to such requirements as are necessary to ensure the identification of shareholders and only to the extent that they are proportionate to achieving that objective.

[11.137]

Article 8 Participation in the general meeting by electronic means

1. Member States shall permit companies to offer to their shareholders any form of participation in the general meeting by electronic means, notably any or all of the following forms of participation:

(a) real-time transmission of the general meeting;

(b) real-time two-way communication enabling shareholders to address the general meeting from a remote location;

(c) a mechanism for casting votes, whether before or during the general meeting, without the need to appoint a proxy holder who is physically present at the meeting.

2. The use of electronic means for the purpose of enabling shareholders to participate in the general meeting may be made subject only to such requirements and constraints as are necessary to ensure the identification of shareholders and the security of the electronic communication, and only to the extent that they are proportionate to achieving those objectives.

This is without prejudice to any legal rules which Member States have adopted or may adopt concerning the decision-making process within the company for the introduction or implementation of any form of participation by electronic means.

[11.138]

Article 9 Right to ask questions

1. Every shareholder shall have the right to ask questions related to items on the agenda of the general meeting. The company shall answer the questions put to it by shareholders.

2. The right to ask questions and the obligation to answer are subject to the measures which Member States may take, or allow companies to take, to ensure the identification of shareholders, the good order of general meetings and their preparation and the protection of confidentiality and business interests of companies. Member States may allow companies to provide one overall answer to questions having the same content.

Member States may provide that an answer shall be deemed to be given if the relevant information is available on the company's Internet site in a question and answer format.

[11.139]

[Article 9a Right to vote on the remuneration policy

1. Member States shall ensure that companies establish a remuneration policy as regards directors and that shareholders have the right to vote on the remuneration policy at the general meeting.

2. Member States shall ensure that the vote by the shareholders at the general meeting on the remuneration policy is binding. Companies shall pay remuneration to their directors only in accordance with a remuneration policy that has been approved by the general meeting.

Where no remuneration policy has been approved and the general meeting does not approve the proposed policy, the company may continue to pay remuneration to its directors in accordance with its existing practices and shall submit a revised policy for approval at the following general meeting.

Where an approved remuneration policy exists and the general meeting does not approve the proposed new policy, the company shall continue to pay remuneration to its directors in accordance with the existing approved policy and shall submit a revised policy for approval at the following general meeting.

3. However, Member States may provide for the vote at the general meeting on the remuneration policy to be advisory. In that case, companies shall pay remuneration to their directors only in accordance with a remuneration policy that has been submitted to such a vote at the general meeting. Where the general meeting rejects the proposed remuneration policy, the company shall submit a revised policy to a vote at the following general meeting.

4. Member States may allow companies, in exceptional circumstances, to temporarily derogate from the remuneration policy, provided that the policy includes the procedural conditions under which the derogation can be applied and specifies the elements of the policy from which a derogation is possible.

Exceptional circumstances as referred to in the first subparagraph shall cover only situations in which the derogation from the remuneration policy is necessary to serve the long-term interests and sustainability of the company as a whole or to assure its viability.

5. Member States shall ensure that companies submit the remuneration policy to a vote by the general meeting at every material change and in any case at least every four years.

6. The remuneration policy shall contribute to the company's business strategy and long-term interests and sustainability and shall explain how it does so. It shall be clear and understandable and describe the different components of fixed and variable remuneration, including all bonuses and other benefits in whatever form, which can be awarded to directors and indicate their relative proportion.

The remuneration policy shall explain how the pay and employment conditions of employees of the company were taken into account when establishing the remuneration policy.

Where a company awards variable remuneration, the remuneration policy shall set clear, comprehensive and varied criteria for the award of the variable remuneration. It shall indicate the financial and non-financial performance criteria, including, where appropriate, criteria relating to corporate social responsibility, and explain how they contribute to the objectives set out in the first subparagraph, and the methods to be applied to determine to which extent the performance criteria have been fulfilled. It shall specify information on any deferral periods and on the possibility for the company to reclaim variable remuneration.

Where the company awards share-based remuneration, the policy shall specify vesting periods and where applicable retention of shares after vesting and explain how the share based remuneration contributes to the objectives set out in the first subparagraph.

The remuneration policy shall indicate the duration of the contracts or arrangements with directors and the applicable notice periods, the main characteristics of supplementary pension or early retirement schemes and the terms of the termination and payments linked to termination.

The remuneration policy shall explain the decision-making process followed for its determination, review and implementation, including, measures to avoid or manage conflicts of interests and, where applicable, the role of the remuneration committee or other committees concerned. Where the policy is revised, it shall describe and explain all significant changes and how it takes into account the votes and views of shareholders on the policy and reports since the most recent vote on the remuneration policy by the general meeting of shareholders.

7. Member States shall ensure that after the vote on the remuneration policy at the general meeting the policy together with the date and the results of the vote is made public without delay on the website of the company and remains publicly available, free of charge, at least as long as it is applicable.]

NOTES

Articles 9a–9c inserted by European Parliament and Council Directive 2017/828/EU, Art 1(4), as from 9 June 2017.

[11.140]

[Article 9b Information to be provided in and right to vote on the remuneration report

1. Member States shall ensure that the company draws up a clear and understandable remuneration report, providing a comprehensive overview of the remuneration, including all benefits in whatever form, awarded or due during the most recent financial year to individual directors, including to newly recruited and to former directors, in accordance with the remuneration policy referred to in Article 9a.

Where applicable, the remuneration report shall contain the following information regarding each individual director's remuneration:

(a) the total remuneration split out by component, the relative proportion of fixed and variable remuneration, an explanation how the total remuneration complies with the adopted remuneration policy, including how it contributes to the long-term performance of the company, and information on how the performance criteria were applied;

(b) the annual change of remuneration, of the performance of the company, and of average remuneration on a full-time equivalent basis of employees of the company other than directors over at least the five most recent financial years, presented together in a manner which permits comparison;

(c) any remuneration from any undertaking belonging to the same group as defined in point (11) of Article 2 of Directive 2013/34/EU of the European Parliament and of the Council;[1]

(d) the number of shares and share options granted or offered, and the main conditions for the exercise of the rights including the exercise price and date and any change thereof;

(e) information on the use of the possibility to reclaim variable remuneration;

(f) information on any deviations from the procedure for the implementation of the remuneration policy referred to in Article 9a(6) and on any derogations applied in accordance with Article 9a(4), including the explanation of the nature of the exceptional circumstances and the indication of the specific elements derogated from.

2. Member States shall ensure that companies do not include in the remuneration report special categories of personal data of individual directors within the meaning of Article 9(1) of Regulation (EU) 2016/679 of the European Parliament and of the Council[2] or personal data which refer to the family situation of individual directors.

3. Companies shall process the personal data of directors included in the remuneration report pursuant to this Article for the purpose of increasing corporate transparency as regards directors' remuneration with the view to enhancing directors' accountability and shareholder oversight over directors' remuneration.

Without prejudice to any longer period laid down by any sector-specific Union legislative act, Member States shall ensure that companies no longer make publicly available pursuant to paragraph 5 of this Article the personal data of directors included in the remuneration report in accordance with this Article after 10 years from the publication of the remuneration report.

Member States may provide by law for processing of the personal data of directors for other purposes.

4. Member States shall ensure that the annual general meeting has the right to hold an advisory vote on the remuneration report of the most recent financial year. The company shall explain in the following remuneration report how the vote by the general meeting has been taken into account.

However, for small and medium-sized companies as defined, respectively, in Article 3(2) and (3) of Directive 2013/34/EU, Member States may provide, as an alternative to a vote, for the remuneration report of the most recent financial year to be submitted for discussion in the annual general meeting as a separate item of the agenda. The company shall explain in the following remuneration report how the discussion in the general meeting has been taken into account.

5. Without prejudice to Article 5(4), after the general meeting the companies shall make the remuneration report publicly available on their website, free of charge, for a period of 10 years, and may choose to keep it available for a longer period provided it no longer contains the personal data of directors. The statutory auditor or audit firm shall check that the information required by this Article has been provided.

Member States shall ensure that the directors of the company, acting within its field of competence assigned to them by national law, have collective responsibility for ensuring that the remuneration report is drawn up and published in accordance with the requirements of this Directive. Member States shall ensure that their laws, regulations and administrative provisions on liability, at least towards the company, apply to the directors of the company for breach of the duties referred to in this paragraph.

6. The Commission shall, with a view to ensuring harmonisation in relation to this Article, adopt guidelines to specify the standardised presentation of the information laid down in paragraph 1.]

NOTES

Inserted as noted to Article 9a at **[11.139]**.

[1] Directive 2013/34/EU of the European Parliament and of the Council of 26 June 2013 on the annual financial statements, consolidated financial statements and related reports of certain types of undertakings, amending Directive 2006/43/EC of the European Parliament and of the Council and repealing Council Directives 78/660/EEC and 83/349/EEC (OJ L182, 29.6.2013, p 19).

[2] Regulation (EU) 2016/679 of the European Parliament and of the Council of 27 April 2016 on the protection of natural persons with regard to the processing of personal data and on the free movement of such data, and repealing Directive 95/46/EC (General Data Protection Regulation) (OJ L119, 4.5.2016, p 1).

[11.141]

[Article 9c Transparency and approval of related party transactions

1. Member States shall define material transactions for the purposes of this Article, taking into account:

(a) the influence that the information about the transaction may have on the economic decisions of shareholders of the company;

(b) the risk that the transaction creates for the company and its shareholders who are not a related party, including minority shareholders.

When defining material transactions Member States shall set one or more quantitative ratios based on the impact of the transaction on the financial position, revenues, assets, capitalisation, including equity, or turnover of the company or take into account the nature of transaction and the position of the related party.

Member States may adopt different materiality definitions for the application of paragraph 4 than those for the application of paragraphs 2 and 3 and may differentiate the definitions according to the company size.

2. Member States shall ensure that companies publicly announce material transactions with related parties at the latest at the time of the conclusion of the transaction. The announcement shall contain at least information on the nature of the related party relationship, the name of the related party, the date and the value of the transaction and other information necessary to assess whether or not the transaction is fair and reasonable from the perspective of the company and of the shareholders who are not a related party, including minority shareholders.

3. Member States may provide for the public announcement referred to in paragraph 2 to be accompanied by a report assessing whether or not the transaction is fair and reasonable from the perspective of the company and of the shareholders who are not a related party, including minority shareholders, and explaining the assumptions it is based upon together with the methods used.

The report shall be produced by one of the following:

(a) an independent third party;

(b) the administrative or supervisory body of the company;

(c) the audit committee or any committee the majority of which is composed of independent directors.

Member States shall ensure that the related parties do not take part in the preparation of the report.

4. Member States shall ensure that material transactions with related parties are approved by the general meeting or by the administrative or supervisory body of the company according to procedures which prevent the related party from taking advantage of its position and provide adequate protection for the interests of the company and of the shareholders who are not a related party, including minority shareholders.

Member States may provide for shareholders in the general meeting to have the right to vote on material transactions with related parties which have been approved by the administrative or supervisory body of the company.

Where the related party transaction involves a director or a shareholder, the director or shareholder shall not take part in the approval or the vote.

Member States may allow the shareholder who is a related party to take part in the vote provided that national law ensures appropriate safeguards which apply before or during the voting process to protect the interests of the company and of the shareholders who are not a related party, including minority shareholders, by preventing the related party from approving the transaction despite the opposing opinion of the majority of the shareholders who are not a related party or despite the opposing opinion of the majority of the independent directors.

5. Paragraphs 2, 3 and 4 shall not apply to transactions entered into in the ordinary course of business and concluded on normal market terms. For such transactions the administrative or supervisory body of the company shall establish an internal procedure to periodically assess whether these conditions are fulfilled. The related parties shall not take part in that assessment.

However, Member States may provide for companies to apply the requirements in paragraph 2, 3 or 4 to transactions entered into in the ordinary course of business and concluded on normal market terms.

6. Member States may exclude, or may allow companies to exclude, from the requirements in paragraphs 2, 3 and 4:

(a) transactions entered into between the company and its subsidiaries provided that they are wholly owned or that no other related party of the company has an interest in the subsidiary undertaking or that national law provides for adequate protection of interests of the company, of the subsidiary and of their shareholders who are not a related party, including minority shareholders in such transactions;

(b) clearly defined types of transactions for which national law requires approval by the general meeting, provided that fair treatment of all shareholders and the interests of the company and of the shareholders who are not a related party, including minority shareholders, are specifically addressed and adequately protected in such provisions of law;

(c) transactions regarding remuneration of directors, or certain elements of remuneration of directors, awarded or due in accordance with Article 9a;

(d) transactions entered into by credit institutions on the basis of measures, aiming at safeguarding their stability, adopted by the competent authority in charge of the prudential supervision within the meaning of Union law;

(e) transactions offered to all shareholders on the same terms where equal treatment of all shareholders and protection of the interests of the company is ensured.

7. Member States shall ensure that companies publicly announce material transactions concluded between the related party of the company and that company's subsidiary. Member States may also provide that the announcement is accompanied by a report assessing whether or not the transaction is fair and reasonable from the perspective of the company and of the shareholders who are not a related party, including minority shareholders and explaining the assumptions it is based upon together with the methods used. The exemptions provided in paragraph 5 and 6 shall also apply to the transactions specified in this paragraph.

8. Member States shall ensure that transactions with the same related party that have been concluded in any 12-month period or in the same financial year and have not been subject to the obligations listed in paragraph 2, 3 or 4 are aggregated for the purposes of those paragraphs.

9. This Article is without prejudice to the rules on public disclosure of inside information as referred to in Article 17 of Regulation (EU) No 596/2014 of the European Parliament and of the Council.[1]]

NOTES

Inserted as noted to Article 9a at **[11.139]**.

[1] Regulation (EU) No 596/2014 of the European Parliament and of the Council of 16 April 2014 on market abuse (market abuse regulation) and repealing Directive 2003/6/EC of the European Parliament and of the Council and Commission Directives 2003/124/EC, 2003/125/EC and 2004/72/EC (OJ L173, 12.6.2014, p 1).'.

[11.142]

Article 10 Proxy voting

1. Every shareholder shall have the right to appoint any other natural or legal person as a proxy holder to attend and vote at a general meeting in his name. The proxy holder shall enjoy the same rights to speak and ask questions in the general meeting as those to which the shareholder thus represented would be entitled.

Apart from the requirement that the proxy holder possess legal capacity, Member States shall abolish any legal rule which restricts, or allows companies to restrict, the eligibility of persons to be appointed as proxy holders.

2. Member States may limit the appointment of a proxy holder to a single meeting, or to such meetings as may be held during a specified period.

Without prejudice to Article 13(5), Member States may limit the number of persons whom a shareholder may appoint as proxy holders in relation to any one general meeting. However, if a shareholder has shares of a company held in more than one securities account, such limitation shall not prevent the shareholder from appointing a separate proxy holder as regards shares held in each securities account in relation to any one general meeting. This does not affect rules prescribed by the applicable law that prohibit the casting of votes differently in respect of shares held by one and the same shareholder.

3. Apart from the limitations expressly permitted in paragraphs 1 and 2, Member States shall not restrict or allow companies to restrict the exercise of shareholder rights through proxy holders for any purpose other than to address potential conflicts of interest between the proxy holder and the shareholder, in whose interest the proxy holder is bound to act, and in doing so Member States shall not impose any requirements other than the following:

(a) Member States may prescribe that the proxy holder disclose certain specified facts which may be relevant for the shareholders in assessing any risk that the proxy holder might pursue any interest other than the interest of the shareholder;

(b) Member States may restrict or exclude the exercise of shareholder rights through proxy holders without specific voting instructions for each resolution in respect of which the proxy holder is to vote on behalf of the shareholder;

(c) Member States may restrict or exclude the transfer of the proxy to another person, but this shall not prevent a proxy holder who is a legal person from exercising the powers conferred upon it through any member of its administrative or management body or any of its employees.

A conflict of interest within the meaning of this paragraph may in particular arise where the proxy holder:

(i) is a controlling shareholder of the company, or is another entity controlled by such shareholder;

(ii) is a member of the administrative, management or supervisory body of the company, or of a controlling shareholder or controlled entity referred to in point (i);

(iii) is an employee or an auditor of the company, or of a controlling shareholder or controlled entity referred to in (i);

(iv) has a family relationship with a natural person referred to in points (i) to (iii).

4. The proxy holder shall cast votes in accordance with the instructions issued by the appointing shareholder.

Member States may require proxy holders to keep a record of the voting instructions for a defined minimum period and to confirm on request that the voting instructions have been carried out.

5. A person acting as a proxy holder may hold a proxy from more than one shareholder without limitation as to the number of shareholders so represented. Where a proxy holder holds proxies from several shareholders, the applicable law shall enable him to cast votes for a certain shareholder differently from votes cast for another shareholder.

[11.143]

Article 11 Formalities for proxy holder appointment and notification

1. Member States shall permit shareholders to appoint a proxy holder by electronic means. Moreover, Member States shall permit companies to accept the notification of the appointment by electronic means, and shall ensure that every company offers to its shareholders at least one effective method of notification by electronic means.

2. Member States shall ensure that proxy holders may be appointed, and that such appointment be notified to the company, only in writing. Beyond this basic formal requirement, the appointment of a proxy holder, the notification of the appointment to the company and the issuance of voting instructions, if any, to the proxy holder may be made subject only to such formal requirements as are necessary to ensure the identification of the shareholder and of the proxy holder, or to ensure the possibility of verifying the content of voting instructions, respectively, and only to the extent that they are proportionate to achieving those objectives.

3. The provisions of this Article shall apply mutatis mutandis for the revocation of the appointment of a proxy holder.

[11.144]

Article 12 Voting by correspondence

Member States shall permit companies to offer their shareholders the possibility to vote by correspondence in advance of the general meeting. Voting by correspondence may be made subject only to such requirements and constraints as are necessary to ensure the identification of shareholders and only to the extent that they are proportionate to achieving that objective.

[11.145]

Article 13 Removal of certain impediments to the effective exercise of voting rights

1. This Article applies where a natural or legal person who is recognised as a shareholder by the applicable law acts in the course of a business on behalf of another natural or legal person (the client).

2. Where the applicable law imposes disclosure requirements as a prerequisite for the exercise of voting rights by a shareholder referred to in paragraph 1, such requirements shall not go beyond a list disclosing to the company the identity of each client and the number of shares voted on his behalf.

3. Where the applicable law imposes formal requirements on the authorisation of a shareholder referred to in paragraph 1 to exercise voting rights, or on voting instructions, such formal requirements shall not go beyond what is necessary to ensure the identification of the client, or the possibility of verifying the content of voting instructions, respectively, and is proportionate to achieving those objectives.

4. A shareholder referred to in paragraph 1 shall be permitted to cast votes attaching to some of the shares differently from votes attaching to the other shares.

5. Where the applicable law limits the number of persons whom a shareholder may appoint as proxy holders in accordance with Article 10(2), such limitation shall not prevent a shareholder referred to in paragraph 1 of this Article from granting a proxy to each of his clients or to any third party designated by a client.

[11.146]

Article 14 Voting results

1. The company shall establish for each resolution at least the number of shares for which votes have been validly cast, the proportion of the share capital represented by those votes, the total number of votes validly cast as well as the number of votes cast in favour of and against each resolution and, where applicable, the number of abstentions.

However, Member States may provide or allow companies to provide that if no shareholder requests a full account of the voting, it shall be sufficient to establish the voting results only to the extent needed to ensure that the required majority is reached for each resolution.

2. Within a period of time to be determined by the applicable law, which shall not exceed 15 days after the general meeting, the company shall publish on its Internet site the voting results established in accordance with paragraph 1.

3. This Article is without prejudice to any legal rules that Member States have adopted or may adopt concerning the formalities required in order for a resolution to become valid or the possibility of a subsequent legal challenge to the voting result.

[CHAPTER IIA IMPLEMENTING ACTS AND PENALTIES

[11.147]

Article 14a Committee procedure

1. The Commission shall be assisted by the European Securities Committee established by Commission Decision 2001/528/EC.[1] That committee shall be a committee within the meaning of Regulation (EU) No 182/2011 of the European Parliament and of the Council.[2]

2. Where reference is made to this paragraph, Article 5 of Regulation (EU) No 182/2011 shall apply.]

NOTES

Chapter IIa inserted by European Parliament and Council Directive 2017/828/EU, Art 1(5), as from 9 June 2017.

[1] Commission Decision 2001/528/EC of 6 June 2001 establishing the European Securities Committee (OJ L191, 13.7.2001, p 45).

[2] Regulation (EU) No 182/2011 of the European Parliament and of the Council of 16 February 2011 laying down the rules and general principles concerning mechanisms for control by Member States of the Commission's exercise of implementing powers (OJ L55, 28.2.2011, p 13).'.

[11.148]

[Article 14b Measures and penalties

Member States shall lay down the rules on measures and penalties applicable to infringements of national provisions adopted pursuant to this Directive and shall take all measures necessary to ensure that they are implemented.

The measures and penalties provided for shall be effective, proportionate and dissuasive. Member States shall, by 10 June 2019, notify the Commission of those rules and of those implementing measures and shall notify it, without delay, of any subsequent amendment affecting them.]

NOTES

Inserted as noted to Article 14a at **[11.147]**.

CHAPTER III FINAL PROVISIONS

[11.149]

Article 15 Transposition

Member States shall bring into force the laws, regulations and administrative provisions necessary to comply with this Directive by 3 August 2009 at the latest. They shall forthwith communicate to the Commission the text of those measures.

Notwithstanding the first paragraph, Member States which on 1 July 2006 had in force national measures restricting or prohibiting the appointment of a proxy holder in the case of Article 10(3), second subparagraph, point (ii), shall bring into force the laws, regulations and administrative provisions necessary in order to comply with Article 10(3) as concerns such restriction or prohibition by 3 August 2012 at the latest.

Member States shall forthwith communicate the number of days specified under Articles 6(3) and 7(3), and any subsequent changes thereof, to the Commission, which shall publish this information in the Official Journal of the European Union.

When Member States adopt the measures referred to in the first paragraph, they shall contain a reference to this Directive or shall be accompanied by such reference on the occasion of their official publication. The methods of making such reference shall be laid down by the Member States.

[11.150]

Article 16 Entry into force

This Directive shall enter into force on the 20th day following its publication in the Official Journal of the European Union.

[11.151]

Article 17 Addressees

This Directive is addressed to the Member States.

DIRECTIVE OF THE EUROPEAN PARLIAMENT AND OF THE COUNCIL

(2013/34/EU)

of 26 June 2013

on the annual financial statements, consolidated financial statements and related reports of certain types of undertakings, amending Directive 2006/43/EC of the European Parliament and of the Council and repealing Council Directives 78/660/EEC and 83/349/EEC

(Text with EEA relevance)

[11.152]

NOTES

Date of publication in OJ: OJ L182, 29.6.2013, p 19.

This Directive is reproduced as amended by: European Parliament and Council Directive 2014/95/EU (transposition date 1 January 2017); European Parliament and Council Directive 2021/2101/EU (transposition date 22 June 2023). Amendments to provisions of the Annexes that are not reproduced are not noted.

Editorial note (legal status of EU Directives in the UK): note that EU Directives are not "direct EU legislation" within the meaning of the European Union (Withdrawal) Act 2018, s 3 at **[12.5]** and, accordingly, do not apply to the UK. As to the status of EU-derived domestic legislation after IP completion day (11pm on 31 December 2020), see s 2 of the 2018 Act at **[12.4]**. As to the UK implementation of this Directive, see the note below.

UK Implementation: in the UK this Directive was implemented by the Small Companies (Micro-Entities' Accounts) Regulations 2013, SI 2013/3008; the Reports on Payments to Governments Regulations 2014, SI 2014/3209; the Companies, Partnerships and Groups (Accounts and Reports) Regulations 2015, SI 2015/980 (see **[4.548]**); the Companies, Partnerships and Groups (Accounts and Reports) Regulations 2015, 2015/1672; the Limited Liability Partnerships, Partnerships and Groups (Accounts and Audit) Regulations 2016, SI 2016/575; and the Companies, Partnerships and Groups (Accounts and Non-Financial Reporting) Regulations 2016, SI 2016/1245. For a summary of the Regulations listed above, see Appendix 4 at **[A4]**.

THE EUROPEAN PARLIAMENT AND THE COUNCIL OF THE EUROPEAN UNION,

Having regard to the Treaty on the Functioning of the European Union, and in particular Article 50(1) thereof,

Having regard to the proposal from the European Commission,

After transmission of the draft legislative act to the national parliaments,

Having regard to the opinion of the European Economic and Social Committee,[1]

Acting in accordance with the ordinary legislative procedure,[2]

Whereas:

(1) This Directive takes into account the Commission's better regulation programme, and, in particular, the Commission Communication entitled "Smart Regulation in the European Union", which aims at designing and delivering regulation of the highest quality whilst respecting the principles of subsidiarity and proportionality and ensuring that the administrative burdens are proportionate to the benefits they bring. The Commission Communication entitled "Think Small First – Small Business Act for Europe", adopted in June 2008 and revised in February 2011, recognises the central role played by small and medium-sized enterprises (SMEs) in the Union economy and aims to improve the overall approach to entrepreneurship and to anchor the "think small first" principle in policy-making from regulation to public service. The European Council of 24 and 25 March 2011 welcomed the Commission's intention to present the "Single Market Act" with measures creating growth and jobs, bringing tangible results to citizens and businesses.

The Commission Communication entitled "Single Market Act", adopted in April 2011, proposes to simplify the Fourth Council Directive 78/660/EEC of 25 July 1978 based on Article 54(3)(g) of the Treaty on the annual accounts of certain types of companies[3] and the Seventh Council Directive 83/349/EEC of 13 June 1983 based on the Article 54(3)(g) of the Treaty on consolidated accounts[4] (the Accounting Directives) as regards financial information obligations and to reduce administrative burdens, in particular for SMEs. "The Europe 2020 Strategy" for smart, sustainable and inclusive growth aims to reduce administrative burdens and improve the business environment, in particular for SMEs, and to promote the internationalisation of SMEs. The European Council of 24 and 25 March 2011 also called for the overall regulatory burden, in particular for SMEs, to be reduced at both Union and national level and suggested measures to increase productivity, such as the removal of red tape and the improvement of the regulatory framework for SMEs.

(2) On 18 December 2008 the European Parliament adopted a non-legislative resolution on accounting requirements as regards small and medium-sized companies, particularly micro-entities,[5] stating that the Accounting Directives are often very burdensome for small and medium-sized companies, and in particular for micro-entities, and asking the Commission to continue its efforts to review those Directives.

(3) The coordination of national provisions concerning the presentation and content of annual financial statements and management reports, the measurement bases used therein and their publication in respect of certain types of undertakings with limited liability is of special importance for the protection of shareholders, members and third parties. Simultaneous coordination is necessary in those fields for such types of undertakings because, on the one hand, some undertakings operate in more than one Member State and, on the other hand, such undertakings offer no safeguards to third parties beyond the amounts of their net assets.

(4) Annual financial statements pursue various objectives and do not merely provide information for investors in capital markets but also give an account of past transactions and enhance corporate governance. Union accounting legislation needs to strike an appropriate balance between the interests of the addressees of financial statements and the interest of undertakings in not being unduly burdened with reporting requirements.

(5) The scope of this Directive should include certain undertakings with limited liability such as public and private

Part 11 EU & Retained EU Legislation

limited liability companies. Additionally, there is a substantial number of partnerships and limited partnerships all the fully liable members of which are constituted either as public or as private limited liability companies, and such partnerships should therefore be subject to the coordination measures of this Directive. This Directive should also ensure that partnerships fall within its scope where members of a partnership which are not constituted as private or public limited companies in fact have limited liability for the partnership's obligations because that liability is limited by other undertakings within the scope of this Directive. The exclusion of not-for-profit undertakings from the scope of this Directive is consistent with its purpose, in line with point (g) of Article 50(2) of the Treaty on the Functioning of the European Union (TFEU).

(6) The scope of this Directive should be principles-based and should ensure that it is not possible for an undertaking to exclude itself from that scope by creating a group structure containing multiple layers of undertakings established inside or outside the Union.

(7) The provisions of this Directive should apply only to the extent that they are not inconsistent with, or contradicted by, provisions on the financial reporting of certain types of undertakings or provisions regarding the distribution of an undertaking's capital which are laid down in other legislative acts in force adopted by one or more Union institutions.

(8) It is necessary, moreover, to establish minimum equivalent legal requirements at Union level as regards the extent of the financial information that should be made available to the public by undertakings that are in competition with one another.

(9) Annual financial statements should be prepared on a prudent basis and should give a true and fair view of an undertaking's assets and liabilities, financial position and profit or loss. It is possible that, in exceptional cases, a financial statement does not give such a true and fair view where provisions of this Directive are applied. In such cases, the undertaking should depart from such provisions in order to give a true and fair view. The Member States should be allowed to define such exceptional cases and to lay down the relevant special rules which are to apply in those cases. Those exceptional cases should be understood to be only very unusual transactions and unusual situations and should, for instance, not be related to entire specific sectors.

(10) This Directive should ensure that the requirements for small undertakings are to a large extent harmonised throughout the Union. This Directive is based on the "think small first" principle. In order to avoid disproportionate administrative burdens on those undertakings, Member States should only be allowed to require a few disclosures by way of notes that are additional to the mandatory notes. In the case of a single filing system, however, Member States may in certain cases require a limited number of additional disclosures where these are explicitly required by their national tax legislation and are strictly necessary for the purposes of tax collection. It should be possible for Member States to impose requirements on medium-sized and large undertakings that go further than the minimum requirements prescribed by this Directive.

(11) Where this Directive allows Member States to impose additional requirements on, for instance, small undertakings, this means that Member States can make use of this option in full or in part by requiring less than the option allows for. In the same way, where this Directive allows Member States to make use of an exemption in relation to, for instance, small undertakings, this means that Member States can exempt such undertakings wholly or in part.

(12) Small, medium-sized and large undertakings should be defined and distinguished by reference to balance sheet total, net turnover and the average number of employees during the financial year, as those criteria typically provide objective evidence as to the size of an undertaking. However, where a parent undertaking is not preparing consolidated financial statements for the group, Member States should be allowed to take steps they deem necessary to require that such an undertaking be classified as a larger undertaking by determining its size and resulting category on a consolidated or aggregated basis. Where a Member State applies one or more of the optional exemptions for micro-undertakings, micro-undertakings should also be defined by reference to balance sheet total, net turnover and the average number of employees during the financial year. Member States should not be obliged to define separate categories for medium-sized and large undertakings in their national legislation if medium-sized undertakings are subject to the same requirements as large undertakings.

(13) Micro-undertakings have limited resources with which to comply with demanding regulatory requirements. Where no specific rules are in place for micro-undertakings, the rules applying to small undertakings apply to them. Those rules place on them administrative burdens which are disproportionate to their size and are, therefore, relatively more onerous for micro-undertakings as compared to other small undertakings. Therefore, it should be possible for Member States to exempt micro-undertakings from certain obligations applying to small undertakings that would impose excessive administrative burdens on them. However, micro-undertakings should still be subject to any national obligation to keep records showing their business transactions and financial position. Moreover, investment undertakings and financial holding undertakings should be excluded from the benefits of simplifications applicable to micro-undertakings.

(14) Member States should take into account the specific conditions and needs of their own markets when making a decision about whether or how to implement a distinct regime for micro-undertakings within the context of this Directive.

(15) Publication of financial statements can be burdensome for micro-undertakings. At the same time, Member States need to ensure compliance with this Directive. Accordingly, Member States making use of the exemptions for micro-undertakings provided for in this Directive should be allowed to exempt micro-undertakings from a general publication requirement, provided that balance sheet information is duly filed, in accordance with national law, with at least one designated competent authority and that the information is forwarded to the business register, so that a copy should be obtainable upon application. In such cases, the obligation laid down in this Directive to publish any accounting document in accordance with Article 3(5) of Directive 2009/101/EC of the European Parliament and of the Council of 16 September 2009 on coordination of safeguards which, for the protection of the interests of members and third parties, are required by Member States of companies within the meaning of the second paragraph of Article 48 of the Treaty, with a view to making such safeguards equivalent,[6] should not apply.

(16) To ensure the disclosure of comparable and equivalent information, recognition and measurement principles should include the going concern, the prudence, and the accrual bases. Set-offs between asset and liability items and income and expense items should not be allowed and components of assets and liabilities should be valued separately.

In specific cases, however, Member States should be allowed to permit or require undertakings to perform set-offs between asset and liability items and income and expense items. The presentation of items in financial statements should have regard to the economic reality or commercial substance of the underlying transaction or arrangement. Member States should, however, be allowed to exempt undertakings from applying that principle.

(17) The principle of materiality should govern recognition, measurement, presentation, disclosure and consolidation in financial statements. According to the principle of materiality, information that is considered immaterial may, for instance, be aggregated in the financial statements. However, while a single item might be considered to be immaterial, immaterial items of a similar nature might be considered material when taken as a whole. Member States should be allowed to limit the mandatory application of the principle of materiality to presentation and disclosure. The principle of materiality should not affect any national obligation to keep complete records showing business transactions and financial position.

(18) Items recognised in annual financial statements should be measured on the basis of the principle of purchase price or production cost to ensure the reliability of information contained in financial statements. However, Member States should be allowed to permit or require undertakings to revalue fixed assets in order that more relevant information may be provided to the users of financial statements.

(19) The need for comparability of financial information throughout the Union makes it necessary to require Member States to allow a system of fair value accounting for certain financial instruments. Furthermore, systems of fair value accounting provide information that can be of more relevance to the users of financial statements than purchase price or production cost-based information. Accordingly, Member States should permit the adoption of a fair value system of accounting by all undertakings or classes of undertaking, other than micro-undertakings making use of the exemptions provided for in this Directive, in respect of both annual and consolidated financial statements or, if a Member State so chooses, in respect of consolidated financial statements only. Furthermore, Member States should be allowed to permit or require fair value accounting for assets other than financial instruments.

(20) A limited number of layouts for the balance sheet is necessary to allow users of financial statements to better compare the financial position of undertakings within the Union. Member States should require the use of one layout for the balance sheet and should be allowed to offer a choice from amongst permitted layouts. However, Member States should be able to permit or require undertakings to modify the layout and present a balance sheet distinguishing between current and non-current items. A profit and loss account layout showing the nature of expenses and a profit and loss account layout showing the function of expenses should be permitted. Member States should require the use of one layout for the profit and loss account and should be allowed to offer a choice from amongst permitted layouts. Member States should also be able to allow undertakings to present a statement of performance instead of a profit and loss account prepared in accordance with one of the permitted layouts. Simplifications of the required layouts may be made available for small and medium-sized undertakings. However, Member States should be allowed to restrict layouts of the balance sheet and profit and loss account if necessary for the electronic filing of financial statements.

(21) For comparability reasons, a common framework for recognition, measurement and presentation of, *inter alia*, value adjustments, goodwill, provisions, stocks of goods and fungible assets, and income and expenditure of exceptional size or incidence should be provided.

(22) The recognition and measurement of some items in financial statements are based on estimates, judgements and models rather than exact depictions. As a result of the uncertainties inherent in business activities, certain items in financial statements cannot be measured precisely but can only be estimated. Estimation involves judgements based on the latest available reliable information. The use of estimates is an essential part of the preparation of financial statements. This is especially true in the case of provisions, which by their nature are more uncertain than most other items in the balance sheet. Estimates should be based on a prudent judgement of the management of the undertaking and calculated on an objective basis, supplemented by experience of similar transactions and, in some cases, even reports from independent experts. The evidence considered should include any additional evidence provided by events after the balance-sheet date.

(23) The information presented in the balance sheet and in the profit and loss account should be supplemented by disclosures by way of notes to the financial statements. Users of financial statements typically have a limited need for supplementary information from small undertakings, and it can be costly for small undertakings to collate that supplementary information. A limited disclosure regime for small undertakings is, therefore, justified. However, where a micro- or small undertaking considers that it is beneficial to provide additional disclosures of the types required of medium-sized and large undertakings, or other disclosures not provided for in this Directive, it should not be prevented from doing so.

(24) Disclosure in respect of accounting policies is one of the key elements of the notes to the financial statements. Such disclosure should include, in particular, the measurement bases applied to various items, a statement on the conformity of those accounting policies with the going concern concept and any significant changes to the accounting policies adopted.

(25) Users of financial statements prepared by medium-sized and large undertakings typically have more sophisticated needs. Therefore, further disclosures should be provided in certain areas. Exemption from certain disclosure obligations is justified where such disclosure would be prejudicial to certain persons or to the undertaking.

(26) The management report and the consolidated management report are important elements of financial reporting. A fair review of the development of the business and of its position should be provided, in a manner consistent with the size and complexity of the business. The information should not be restricted to the financial aspects of the undertaking's business, and there should be an analysis of environmental and social aspects of the business necessary for an understanding of the undertaking's development, performance or position. In cases where the consolidated management report and the parent undertaking management report are presented in a single report, it may be appropriate to give greater emphasis to those matters which are significant to the undertakings included in the consolidation taken as a whole. However, having regard to the potential burden placed on small and medium-sized undertakings, it is appropriate to provide that Member States may choose to waive the obligation to provide non-financial information in the management report of such undertakings.

(27) Member States should have the possibility of exempting small undertakings from the obligation to draw up a management report provided that such undertakings include, in the notes to the financial statements, the data

concerning the acquisition of own shares referred to in Article 24(2) of Directive 2012/30/EU of the European Parliament and of the Council of 25 October 2012 on coordination of safeguards which, for the protection of the interests of members and others, are required by Member States of companies within the meaning of the second paragraph of Article 54 of the Treaty on the Functioning of the European Union, in respect of the formation of public limited liability companies and the maintenance and alteration of their capital, with a view to making such safeguards equivalent.[7]

(28) Given that listed undertakings can have a prominent role in the economies in which they operate, the provisions of this Directive concerning the corporate governance statement should apply to undertakings whose transferable securities are admitted to trading on a regulated market.

(29) Many undertakings own other undertakings and the aim of coordinating the legislation governing consolidated financial statements is to protect the interests subsisting in companies with share capital. Consolidated financial statements should be drawn up so that financial information concerning such undertakings may be conveyed to members and third parties. National law governing consolidated financial statements should therefore be coordinated in order to achieve the objectives of comparability and equivalence in the information which undertakings should publish within the Union. However, given the lack of an arm's-length transaction price, Member States should be allowed to permit intra-group transfers of participating interests, so-called common control transactions, to be accounted for using the pooling of interests method of accounting, in which the book value of shares held in an undertaking included in a consolidation is set off against the corresponding percentage of capital only.

(30) In Directive 83/349/EEC there was a requirement to prepare consolidated financial statements for groups in cases where either the parent undertaking or one or more of the subsidiary undertakings was established as one of the types of undertakings listed in Annex I or Annex II to this Directive. Member States had the option of exempting parent undertakings from the requirement to draw up consolidated accounts in cases where the parent undertaking was not of the type listed in Annex I or Annex II. This Directive requires only parent undertakings of the types listed in Annex I or, in certain circumstances, Annex II to draw up consolidated financial statements, but does not preclude Member States from extending the scope of this Directive to cover other situations as well. In substance there is therefore no change, as it remains up to the Member States to decide whether to require undertakings which do not fall within the scope of this Directive to prepare consolidated financial statements.

(31) Consolidated financial statements should present the activities of a parent undertaking and its subsidiaries as a single economic entity (a group). Undertakings controlled by the parent undertaking should be considered as subsidiary undertakings. Control should be based on holding a majority of voting rights, but control may also exist where there are agreements with fellow shareholders or members. In certain circumstances control may be effectively exercised where the parent holds a minority or none of the shares in the subsidiary. Member States should be entitled to require that undertakings not subject to control, but which are managed on a unified basis or have a common administrative, managerial or supervisory body, be included in consolidated financial statements.

(32) A subsidiary undertaking which is itself a parent undertaking should draw up consolidated financial statements. Nevertheless, Member States should be entitled to exempt such a parent undertaking from the obligation to draw up such consolidated financial statements in certain circumstances, provided that its members and third parties are sufficiently protected.

(33) Small groups should be exempt from the obligation to prepare consolidated financial statements as the users of small undertakings' financial statements do not have sophisticated information needs and it can be costly to prepare consolidated financial statements in addition to the annual financial statements of the parent and subsidiary undertakings. Member States should be able to exempt medium-sized groups from the obligation to prepare consolidated financial statements on the same cost/benefit grounds unless any of the affiliated undertakings is a public-interest entity.

(34) Consolidation requires the full incorporation of the assets and liabilities and of the income and expenditure of group undertakings, the separate disclosure of non-controlling interests in the consolidated balance sheet within capital and reserves and the separate disclosure of non-controlling interests in the profit and loss of the group in the consolidated profit and loss accounts. However, the necessary corrections should be made to eliminate the effects of the financial relations between the undertakings consolidated.

(35) Recognition and measurement principles applicable to the preparation of annual financial statements should also apply to the preparation of consolidated financial statements. However, Member States should be allowed to permit the general provisions and principles stated in this Directive to be applied differently in annual financial statements than in consolidated financial statements.

(36) Associated undertakings should be included in consolidated financial statements by means of the equity method. The provisions on measurement of associated undertakings should in substance remain unchanged from Directive 83/349/EEC, and the methods allowed under that Directive can still be applied. Member States should also be able to permit or require that a jointly managed undertaking be proportionately consolidated within consolidated financial statements.

(37) Consolidated financial statements should include all disclosures by way of notes to the financial statements for the undertakings included in the consolidation taken as a whole. The names, registered offices and group interest in the undertakings' capital should also be disclosed in respect of subsidiaries, associated undertakings, jointly managed undertakings and participating interests.

(38) The annual financial statements of all undertakings to which this Directive applies should be published in accordance with Directive 2009/101/EC. It is, however, appropriate to provide that certain derogations may be granted in this area for small and medium-sized undertakings.

(39) The Member States are strongly encouraged to develop electronic publication systems that allow undertakings to file accounting data, including statutory financial statements, only once and in a form that allows multiple users to access and use the data easily. With regard to the reporting of financial statements, the Commission is encouraged to explore means for a harmonised electronic format. Such systems should, however, not be burdensome to small and medium-sized undertakings.

(40) The Members of the administrative, management and supervisory bodies of an undertaking should, as a

minimum requirement, be collectively responsible to the undertaking for drawing up and publishing annual financial statements and management reports. The same approach should also apply to members of the administrative, management and supervisory bodies of undertakings drawing up consolidated financial statements. Those bodies act within the competences assigned to them by national law. This should not prevent Member States from going further and providing for direct responsibility to shareholders or even other stakeholders.

(41) Liability for drawing up and publishing annual financial statements and consolidated financial statements, as well as management reports and consolidated management reports, is based on national law. Appropriate liability rules, as laid down by each Member State under its national law, should be applicable to members of the administrative, management and supervisory bodies of an undertaking. Member States should be allowed to determine the extent of the liability.

(42) In order to promote credible financial reporting processes across the Union, members of the body within an undertaking that is responsible for the preparation of the undertaking's financial statements should ensure that the financial information included in the undertaking's annual financial statement and the group's consolidated financial statement gives a true and fair view.

(43) Annual financial statements and consolidated financial statements should be audited. The requirement that an audit opinion should state whether annual or consolidated financial statements give a true and fair view in accordance with the relevant financial reporting framework should not be understood as restricting the scope of that opinion but as clarifying the context in which it is expressed. The annual financial statements of small undertakings should not be covered by this audit obligation, as audit can be a significant administrative burden for that category of undertaking, while for many small undertakings the same persons are both shareholders and managers and, therefore, have limited need for third-party assurance on financial statements. However, this Directive should not prevent Member States from imposing an audit on their small undertakings, taking into account the specific conditions and needs of small undertakings and the users of their financial statements. Furthermore, it is more appropriate to define the content of the audit report in Directive 2006/43/EC of the European Parliament and of the Council of 17 May 2006 on statutory audits of annual accounts and consolidated accounts.[8] Therefore that directive should be amended accordingly.

(44) In order to provide for enhanced transparency of payments made to governments, large undertakings and public-interest entities which are active in the extractive industry or logging of primary forests[9] should disclose material payments made to governments in the countries in which they operate in a separate report, on an annual basis. Such undertakings are active in countries rich in natural resources, in particular minerals, oil, natural gas and primary forests. The report should include types of payments comparable to those disclosed by an undertaking participating in the Extractive Industries Transparency Initiative (EITI). The initiative is also complementary to the Forest Law Enforcement, Governance and Trade Action Plan of the European Union (EU FLEGT) and the provisions of Regulation (EU) No 995/2010 of the European Parliament and of the Council of 20 October 2010 laying down the obligations of operators who place timber and timber products on the market,[10] which require traders of timber products to exercise due diligence in order to prevent illegal wood from entering the Union market.

(45) The report should serve to help governments of resource-rich countries to implement the EITI principles and criteria and account to their citizens for payments such governments receive from undertakings active in the extractive industry or loggers of primary forests operating within their jurisdiction. The report should incorporate disclosures on a country and project basis. A project should be defined as the operational activities that are governed by a single contract, license, lease, concession or similar legal agreements and form the basis for payment liabilities to a government. Nonetheless, if multiple such agreements are substantially interconnected, this should be considered a project. 'Substantially interconnected' legal agreements should be understood as a set of operationally and geographically integrated contracts, licenses, leases or concessions or related agreements with substantially similar terms that are signed with a government, giving rise to payment liabilities. Such agreements can be governed by a single contract, joint venture, production sharing agreement, or other overarching legal agreement.

(46) Any payment, whether made as a single payment or as a series of related payments, need not be taken into account in the report if it is below EUR 100,000 within a financial year. This means that, in the case of any arrangement providing for periodic payments or instalments (e.g. rental fees), the undertaking must consider the aggregate amount of the related periodic payments or instalments of the related payments in determining whether the threshold has been met for that series of payments, and accordingly, whether disclosure is required.

(47) Undertakings active in the extractive industry or the logging of primary forests should not be required to disaggregate and allocate payments on a project basis where payments are made in respect of obligations imposed on the undertakings at the entity level rather than the project level. For instance, if an undertaking has more than one project in a host country, and that country's government levies corporate income taxes on the undertaking with respect to the undertaking's income in the country as a whole, and not with respect to a particular project or operation within the country, the undertaking would be permitted to disclose the resulting income tax payment or payments without specifying a particular project associated with the payment.

(48) An undertaking active in the extractive industry or in the logging of primary forests generally does not need to disclose dividends paid to a government as a common or ordinary shareholder of that undertaking as long as the dividend is paid to the government on the same terms as to other shareholders. However, the undertaking will be required to disclose any dividends paid in lieu of production entitlements or royalties.

(49) In order to address the potential for circumvention of disclosure requirements, this Directive should specify that payments are to be disclosed with respect to the substance of the activity or payment concerned. Therefore, the undertaking should not be able to avoid disclosure by, for example, re-characterising an activity that would otherwise be covered by this Directive. In addition, payments or activities should not be artificially split or aggregated with a view to evading such disclosure requirements.

(50) In order to ascertain the circumstances in which undertakings should be exempted from the reporting requirements provided for in Chapter 10, the power to adopt delegated acts in accordance with Article 290 of the TFEU should be delegated to the Commission in respect of determining the criteria to be applied when assessing whether third country reporting requirements are equivalent to the requirements of that Chapter. It is of particular importance that the Commission carry out appropriate consultations during its preparatory work, including at expert level.

The Commission, when preparing and drawing up delegated acts, should ensure a simultaneous, timely and appropriate transmission of relevant documents to the European Parliament and to the Council.

(51) In order to ensure uniform conditions for the implementation of Article 46(1), implementing powers should be conferred upon the Commission. Those powers should be exercised in accordance with Regulation (EU) No 182/2011 of the European Parliament and of the Council of 16 February 2011 laying down the rules and general principles concerning mechanisms for the control by Member States of the Commission's exercise of implementing powers.[11]

(52) The reporting regime should be subject to a review and a report by the Commission within three years of the expiry of the deadline for transposition of this Directive by the Member States. That review should consider the effectiveness of the regime and take into account international developments, including issues of competitiveness and energy security. The review should also consider the extension of reporting requirements to additional industry sectors and whether the report should be audited. In addition, the review should take into account the experience of preparers and users of the payments information and consider whether it would be appropriate to include additional payment information such as effective tax rates and recipient details such as bank account information.

(53) In line with the conclusions of the G8 Summit in Deauville in May 2011 and in order to promote a level international playing field, the Commission should continue to encourage all the international partners to introduce similar requirements concerning reporting on payments to governments. Continued work on the relevant international accounting standard is particularly important in this context.

(54) In order to take account of future changes to the laws of the Member States and to Union legislation concerning company types, the Commission should be empowered to adopt delegated acts in accordance with Article 290 of the TFEU in order to update the lists of undertakings contained in Annexes I and II. The use of delegated acts is also necessary in order to adapt the undertaking size criteria, as with the passage of time inflation will erode their real value. It is of particular importance that the Commission carry out appropriate consultations during its preparatory work, including at expert level. The Commission, when preparing and drawing up delegated acts, should ensure a simultaneous, timely and appropriate transmission of relevant documents to the European Parliament and to the Council.

(55) Since the objectives of this Directive, namely facilitating cross-border investment and improving Union-wide comparability and public confidence in financial statements and reports through enhanced and consistent specific disclosures, cannot be sufficiently achieved by the Member States and can therefore, by reason of the scale and the effects of this Directive, be better achieved at Union level, the Union may adopt measures, in accordance with the principle of subsidiarity as set out in Article 5 of the Treaty on European Union. In accordance with the principle of proportionality, as set out in that Article, this Directive does not go beyond what is necessary in order to achieve those objectives.

(56) This Directive replaces Directives 78/660/EEC and 83/349/EEC. Therefore, those Directives should be repealed.

(57) This Directive respects fundamental rights and observes the principles recognised, in particular, by the Charter of Fundamental Rights of the European Union.

(58) In accordance with the Joint Political Declaration of Member States and the Commission on explanatory documents of 28 September 2011, Member States have undertaken to accompany, in justified cases, the notification of their transposition measures with one or more documents explaining the relationship between the components of a directive and the corresponding parts of national transposition instruments. With regard to this Directive, the legislator considers the transmission of correlation tables to be justified,

NOTES

1 OJ C181, 21.6.2012, p 84.

2 Position of the European Parliament of 12 June 2013 (not yet published in the Official Journal) and decision of the Council of 20 June 2013.

3 OJ L222, 14.8.1978, p 11.

4 OJ L193, 18.7.1983, p 1.

5 OJ C45 E, 23.2.2010, p 58.

6 OJ L258, 1.10.2009, p 11.

7 OJ L315, 14.11.2012, p 74.

8 OJ L157, 9.6.2006, p 87.

9 Defined in Directive 2009/28/EC as "forest of native species, where there is no clearly visible indication of human activities and the ecological processes are not significantly disturbed.".

10 OJ L295, 12.11.2010, p 23.

11 OJ L55, 28.2.2011, p 13.

HAVE ADOPTED THIS DIRECTIVE:

CHAPTER 1 SCOPE, DEFINITIONS AND CATEGORIES OF UNDERTAKINGS AND GROUPS

[11.153]

Article 1 Scope

1. The coordination measures prescribed by this Directive shall apply to the laws, regulations and administrative provisions of the Member States relating to the types of undertakings listed:

(a) in Annex I;

(b) in Annex II, where all of the direct or indirect members of the undertaking having otherwise unlimited liability in fact have limited liability by reason of those members being undertakings which are:

  (i) of the types listed in Annex I; or

  (ii) not governed by the law of a Member State but which have a legal form comparable to those listed in Annex I.

[1a. The coordination measures prescribed by Articles 48a to 48e and Article 51 shall also apply to the laws, regulations and administrative provisions of the Member States relating to branches opened in a Member State by an undertaking which is not governed by the law of a Member State but which is of a legal form comparable with the types of undertakings listed in Annex I. Article 2 shall apply in respect of those branches to the extent that Articles 48a to 48e and Article 51 are applicable to such branches.]

2. Member States shall inform the Commission within a reasonable period of time of changes in the types of undertakings in their national law that may affect the accuracy of Annex I or Annex II. In such a case, the Commission shall be empowered to adapt, by means of delegated acts in accordance with Article 49, the lists of undertakings contained in Annexes I and II.

NOTES

Para 1a: inserted by European Parliament and Council Directive 2021/2101/EU, Art 1(1), as from 21 December 2021; note that the 2021 Directive has a transposition date of 22 June 2023.

[11.154]

Article 2 Definitions

For the purposes of this Directive, the following definitions shall apply:

(1) 'public-interest entities' means undertakings within the scope of Article 1 which are:

(a) governed by the law of a Member State and whose transferable securities are admitted to trading on a regulated market of any Member State within the meaning of point (14) of Article 4(1) of Directive 2004/39/EC of the European Parliament and of the Council of 21 April 2004 on markets in financial instruments;[1]

(b) credit institutions as defined in point (1) of Article 4 of Directive 2006/48/EC of the European Parliament and of the Council of 14 June 2006 relating to the taking up and pursuit of the business of credit institutions,[2] other than those referred to in Article 2 of that Directive;

(c) insurance undertakings within the meaning of Article 2(1) of Council Directive 91/674/EEC of 19 December 1991 on the annual accounts of insurance undertakings;[3] or

(d) designated by Member States as public-interest entities, for instance undertakings that are of significant public relevance because of the nature of their business, their size or the number of their employees;

(2) 'participating interest' means rights in the capital of other undertakings, whether or not represented by certificates, which, by creating a durable link with those undertakings, are intended to contribute to the activities of the undertaking which holds those rights. The holding of part of the capital of another undertaking is presumed to constitute a participating interest where it exceeds a percentage threshold fixed by the Member States which is lower than or equal to 20%;

(3) 'related party' has the same meaning as in the international accounting standards adopted in accordance with Regulation (EC) No 1606/2002 of the European Parliament and of the Council of 19 July 2002 on the application of international accounting standards;[4]

(4) 'fixed assets' means those assets which are intended for use on a continuing basis for the undertaking's activities;

(5) 'net turnover' means the amounts derived from the sale of products and the provision of services after deducting sales rebates and value added tax and other taxes directly linked to turnover;

(6) 'purchase price' means the price payable and any incidental expenses minus any incidental reductions in the cost of acquisition;

(7) 'production cost' means the purchase price of raw materials, consumables and other costs directly attributable to the item in question. Member States shall permit or require the inclusion of a reasonable proportion of fixed or variable overhead costs indirectly attributable to the item in question, to the extent that they relate to the period of production. Distribution costs shall not be included;

(8) 'value adjustment' means the adjustments intended to take account of changes in the values of individual assets established at the balance sheet date, whether the change is final or not;

(9) 'parent undertaking' means an undertaking which controls one or more subsidiary undertakings;

(10) 'subsidiary undertaking' means an undertaking controlled by a parent undertaking, including any subsidiary undertaking of an ultimate parent undertaking;

(11) 'group' means a parent undertaking and all its subsidiary undertakings;

(12) 'affiliated undertakings' means any two or more undertakings within a group;

(13) 'associated undertaking' means an undertaking in which another undertaking has a participating interest, and over whose operating and financial policies that other undertaking exercises significant influence. An undertaking is presumed to exercise a significant influence over another undertaking where it has 20% or more of the shareholders' or members' voting rights in that other undertaking;

(14) 'investment undertakings' means:

(a) undertakings the sole object of which is to invest their funds in various securities, real property and other assets, with the sole aim of spreading investment risks and giving their shareholders the benefit of the results of the management of their assets,

(b) undertakings associated with investment undertakings with fixed capital, if the sole object of those associated undertakings is to acquire fully paid shares issued by those investment undertakings without prejudice to point (h) of Article 22(1) of Directive 2012/30/EU;

(15) 'financial holding undertakings' means undertakings the sole object of which is to acquire holdings in other undertakings and to manage such holdings and turn them to profit, without involving themselves directly or indirectly in the management of those undertakings, without prejudice to their rights as shareholders;

(16) 'material' means the status of information where its omission or misstatement could reasonably be expected to influence decisions that users make on the basis of the financial statements of the undertaking. The materiality of individual items shall be assessed in the context of other similar items.

NOTES

[1] OJ L145, 30.4.2004, p 1.
[2] OJ L177, 30.6.2006, p 1.
[3] OJ L374, 31.12.1991, p 7.
[4] OJ L243, 11.9.2002, p 1.

[11.155]
Article 3 Categories of undertakings and groups

1. In applying one or more of the options in Article 36, Member States shall define micro-undertakings as undertakings which on their balance sheet dates do not exceed the limits of at least two of the three following criteria:
  (a) balance sheet total: EUR 350,000;
  (b) net turnover: EUR 700,000;
  (c) average number of employees during the financial year: 10.

2. Small undertakings shall be undertakings which on their balance sheet dates do not exceed the limits of at least two of the three following criteria:
  (a) balance sheet total: EUR 4,000,000;
  (b) net turnover: EUR 8,000,000;
  (c) average number of employees during the financial year: 50.

Member States may define thresholds exceeding the thresholds in points (a) and (b) of the first subparagraph. However, the thresholds shall not exceed EUR 6,000,000 for the balance sheet total and EUR 12,000,000 for the net turnover.

3. Medium-sized undertakings shall be undertakings which are not micro-undertakings or small undertakings and which on their balance sheet dates do not exceed the limits of at least two of the three following criteria:
  (a) balance sheet total: EUR 20,000,000;
  (b) net turnover: EUR 40,000,000;
  (c) average number of employees during the financial year: 250.

4. Large undertakings shall be undertakings which on their balance sheet dates exceed at least two of the three following criteria:
  (a) balance sheet total: EUR 20,000,000;
  (b) net turnover: EUR 40,000,000;
  (c) average number of employees during the financial year: 250.

5. Small groups shall be groups consisting of parent and subsidiary undertakings to be included in a consolidation and which, on a consolidated basis, do not exceed the limits of at least two of the three following criteria on the balance sheet date of the parent undertaking:
  (a) balance sheet total: EUR 4,000,000;
  (b) net turnover: EUR 8,000,000;
  (c) average number of employees during the financial year: 50.

Member States may define thresholds exceeding the thresholds in points (a) and (b) of the first subparagraph. However, the thresholds shall not exceed EUR 6,000,000 for the balance sheet total and EUR 12,000,000 for the net turnover.

6. Medium-sized groups shall be groups which are not small groups, which consist of parent and subsidiary undertakings to be included in a consolidation and which, on a consolidated basis, do not exceed the limits of at least two of the three following criteria on the balance sheet date of the parent undertaking:
  (a) balance sheet total: EUR 20,000,000;
  (b) net turnover: EUR 40,000,000;
  (c) average number of employees during the financial year: 250.

7. Large groups shall be groups consisting of parent and subsidiary undertakings to be included in a consolidation and which, on a consolidated basis, exceed the limits of at least two of the three following criteria on the balance sheet date of the parent undertaking:
  (a) balance sheet total: EUR 20,000,000;
  (b) net turnover: EUR 40,000,000;
  (c) average number of employees during the financial year: 250.EN L 182/28 Official Journal of the European Union 29.6.2013

8. Member States shall permit the set-off referred to in Article 24(3) and any elimination as a consequence of Article 24(7) not to be effected when the limits in paragraphs 5 to 7 of this Article are calculated. In such cases, the limits for the balance sheet total and net turnover criteria shall be increased by 20%.

9. In the case of those Member States which have not adopted the euro, the amount in national currency equivalent to the amounts set out in paragraphs 1 to 7 shall be that obtained by applying the exchange rate published in the *Official Journal of the European Union* as at the date of the entry into force of any Directive setting those amounts. For the purposes of conversion into the national currencies of those Member States which have not adopted the euro, the amounts in euro specified in paragraphs 1, 3, 4, 6 and 7 may be increased or decreased by not more than 5% in order to produce round sum amounts in the national currencies.

10. Where, on its balance sheet date, an undertaking or a group exceeds or ceases to exceed the limits of two of the three criteria set out in paragraphs 1 to 7, that fact shall affect the application of the derogations provided for in this Directive only if it occurs in two consecutive financial years.

11. The balance sheet total referred to in paragraphs 1 to 7 of this Article shall consist of the total value of the assets in A to E under 'Assets' in the layout set out in Annex III or of the assets in A to E in the layout set out in Annex IV.

12. When calculating the thresholds in paragraphs 1 to 7, Member States may require the inclusion of income from other sources for undertakings for which "net turnover" is not relevant. Member States may require parent undertakings to calculate their thresholds on a consolidated basis rather than on an individual basis. Member States may also require affiliated undertakings to calculate their thresholds on a consolidated or aggregated basis where such undertakings have been established for the sole purpose of avoiding the reporting of certain information.

13. In order to adjust for the effects of inflation, the Commission shall at least every five years review and, where appropriate, amend, by means of delegated acts in accordance with Article 49, the thresholds referred to in paragraphs 1 to 7 of this Article, taking into account measures of inflation as published in the *Official Journal of the European Union*.

CHAPTER 2 GENERAL PROVISIONS AND PRINCIPLES

[11.156]
Article 4 General provisions

1. The annual financial statements shall constitute a composite whole and shall for all undertakings comprise, as a minimum, the balance sheet, the profit and loss account and the notes to the financial statements.

Member States may require undertakings other than small undertakings to include other statements in the annual financial statements in addition to the documents referred to in the first subparagraph.

2. The annual financial statements shall be drawn up clearly and in accordance with the provisions of this Directive.

3. The annual financial statements shall give a true and fair view of the undertaking's assets, liabilities, financial position and profit or loss. Where the application of this Directive would not be sufficient to give a true and fair view of the undertaking's assets, liabilities, financial position and profit or loss, such additional information as is necessary to comply with that requirement shall be given in the notes to the financial statements.

4. Where in exceptional cases the application of a provision of this Directive is incompatible with the obligation laid down in paragraph 3, that provision shall be disapplied in order to give a true and fair view of the undertaking's assets, liabilities, financial position and profit or loss. The disapplication of any such provision shall be disclosed in the notes to the financial statements together with an explanation of the reasons for it and of its effect on the undertaking's assets, liabilities, financial position and profit or loss.

The Member States may define the exceptional cases in question and lay down the relevant special rules which are to apply in those cases.

5. Member States may require undertakings other than small undertakings to disclose information in their annual financial statements which is additional to that required pursuant to this Directive.

6. By way of derogation from paragraph 5, Member States may require small undertakings to prepare, disclose and publish information in the financial statements which goes beyond the requirements of this Directive, provided that any such information is gathered under a single filing system and the disclosure requirement is contained in the national tax legislation for the strict purposes of tax collection. The information required in accordance with this paragraph shall be included in the relevant part of the financial statements.

7. Member States shall communicate to the Commission any additional information they require in accordance with paragraph 6 upon the transposition of this Directive and when they introduce new requirements in accordance with paragraph 6 in national law.

8. Member States using electronic solutions for filing and publishing annual financial statements shall ensure that small undertakings are not required to publish, in accordance with Chapter 7, the additional disclosures required by national tax legislation, as referred to in paragraph 6.

[11.157]
Article 5 General disclosure

The document containing the financial statements shall state the name of the undertaking and the information prescribed by points (a) and (b) of Article 5 of Directive 2009/101/EC.

[11.158]
Article 6 General financial reporting principles

1. Items presented in the annual and consolidated financial statements shall be recognised and measured in accordance with the following general principles:

(a) the undertaking shall be presumed to be carrying on its business as a going concern;

(b) accounting policies and measurement bases shall be applied consistently from one financial year to the next;

(c) recognition and measurement shall be on a prudent basis, and in particular:

  (i) only profits made at the balance sheet date may be recognised,

  (ii) all liabilities arising in the course of the financial year concerned or in the course of a previous financial year shall be recognised, even if such liabilities become apparent only between the balance sheet date and the date on which the balance sheet is drawn up, and

  (iii) all negative value adjustments shall be recognised, whether the result of the financial year is a profit or a loss;

(d) amounts recognised in the balance sheet and profit and loss account shall be computed on the accrual basis;

(e) the opening balance sheet for each financial year shall correspond to the closing balance sheet for the preceding financial year;

(f) the components of asset and liability items shall be valued separately;

(g) any set-off between asset and liability items, or between income and expenditure items, shall be prohibited;

(h) items in the profit and loss account and balance sheet shall be accounted for and presented having regard to the substance of the transaction or arrangement concerned;

(i) items recognised in the financial statements shall be measured in accordance with the principle of purchase price or production cost; and

(j) the requirements set out in this Directive regarding recognition, measurement, presentation, disclosure and consolidation need not be complied with when the effect of complying with them is immaterial.

2. Notwithstanding point (g) of paragraph 1, Member States may in specific cases permit or require undertakings to perform a set-off between asset and liability items, or between income and expenditure items, provided that the amounts which are set off are specified as gross amounts in the notes to the financial statements.

3. Member States may exempt undertakings from the requirements of point (h) of paragraph 1.

4. Member States may limit the scope of point (j) of paragraph 1 to presentation and disclosures.

5. In addition to those amounts recognised in accordance with point (c)(ii) of paragraph 1, Member States may permit or require the recognition of all foreseeable liabilities and potential losses arising in the course of the financial year concerned or in the course of a previous financial year, even if such liabilities or losses become apparent only between the balance sheet date and the date on which the balance sheet is drawn up.

[11.159]
Article 7 Alternative measurement basis of fixed assets at revalued amounts
1. By way of derogation from point (i) of Article 6(1), Member States may permit or require, in respect of all undertakings or any classes of undertaking, the measurement of fixed assets at revalued amounts. Where national law provides for the revaluation basis of measurement, it shall define its content and limits and the rules for its application.
2. Where paragraph 1 is applied, the amount of the difference between measurement on a purchase price or production cost basis and measurement on a revaluation basis shall be entered in the balance sheet in the revaluation reserve under 'Capital and reserves'.
The revaluation reserve may be capitalised in whole or in part at any time.
The revaluation reserve shall be reduced where the amounts transferred to that reserve are no longer necessary for the implementation of the revaluation basis of accounting. The Member States may lay down rules governing the application of the revaluation reserve, provided that transfers to the profit and loss account from the revaluation reserve may be made only where the amounts transferred have been entered as an expense in the profit and loss account or reflect increases in value which have actually been realised. No part of the revaluation reserve may be distributed, either directly or indirectly, unless it represents a gain actually realised.
Save as provided under the second and third subparagraphs of this paragraph, the revaluation reserve may not be reduced.
3. Value adjustments shall be calculated each year on the basis of the revalued amount. However, by way of derogation from Articles 9 and 13, Member States may permit or require that only the amount of the value adjustments arising as a result of the purchase price or production cost measurement basis be shown under the relevant items in the layouts set out in Annexes V and VI and that the difference arising as a result of the measurement on a revaluation basis under this Article be shown separately in the layouts.

[11.160]
Article 8 Alternative measurement basis of fair value
1. By way of derogation from point (i) of Article 6(1) and subject to the conditions set out in this Article:
(a) Member States shall permit or require, in respect of all undertakings or any classes of undertaking, the measurement of financial instruments, including derivative financial instruments, at fair value; and
(b) Member States may permit or require, in respect of all undertakings or any classes of undertaking, the measurement of specified categories of assets other than financial instruments at amounts determined by reference to fair value.

Such permission or requirement may be restricted to consolidated financial statements.
2. For the purpose of this Directive, commodity-based contracts that give either contracting party the right to settle in cash or some other financial instrument shall be considered to be derivative financial instruments, except where such contracts:
(a) were entered into and continue to meet the undertaking's expected purchase, sale or usage requirements at the time they were entered into and subsequently;
(b) were designated as commodity-based contracts at their inception; and
(c) are expected to be settled by delivery of the commodity.

3. Point (a) of paragraph 1 shall apply only to the following liabilities:
(a) liabilities held as part of a trading portfolio; and
(b) derivative financial instruments.

4. Measurement according to point (a) of paragraph 1 shall not apply to the following:
(a) non-derivative financial instruments held to maturity;
(b) loans and receivables originated by the undertaking and not held for trading purposes; and
(c) interests in subsidiaries, associated undertakings and joint ventures, equity instruments issued by the undertaking, contracts for contingent consideration in a business combination, and other financial instruments with such special characteristics that the instruments, according to what is generally accepted, are accounted for differently from other financial instruments.

5. By way of derogation from point (i) of Article 6(1), Member States may, in respect of any assets and liabilities which qualify as hedged items under a fair value hedge accounting system, or identified portions of such assets or liabilities, permit measurement at the specific amount required under that system.
6. By way of derogation from paragraphs 3 and 4, Member States may permit or require the recognition, measurement and disclosure of financial instruments in conformity with international accounting standards adopted in accordance with Regulation (EC) No 1606/2002.
7. The fair value within the meaning of this Article shall be determined by reference to one of the following values:
(a) in the case of financial instruments for which a reliable market can readily be identified, the market value. Where the market value is not readily identifiable for an instrument but can be identified for its components or for a similar instrument, the market value may be derived from that of its components or of the similar instrument;
(b) in the case of financial instruments for which a reliable market cannot be readily identified, a value resulting from generally accepted valuation models and techniques, provided that such valuation models and techniques ensure a reasonable approximation of the market value.

Financial instruments that cannot be measured reliably by any of the methods described in points (a) and (b) of the first subparagraph shall be measured in accordance with the principle of purchase price or production cost in so far as measurement on that basis is possible.
8. Notwithstanding point (c) of Article 6(1), where a financial instrument is measured at fair value, a change in value shall be included in the profit and loss account, except in the following cases, where such a change shall be included directly in a fair value reserve:

(a) the instrument accounted for is a hedging instrument under a system of hedge accounting that allows some or all of the change in value not to be shown in the profit and loss account; or

(b) the change in value relates to an exchange difference arising on a monetary item that forms part of an undertaking's net investment in a foreign entity.

Member States may permit or require a change in the value of an available for sale financial asset, other than a derivative financial instrument, to be included directly in a fair value reserve. That fair value reserve shall be adjusted when amounts shown therein are no longer necessary for the implementation of points (a) and (b) of the first subparagraph.

9. Notwithstanding point (c) of Article 6(1), Member States may permit or require, in respect of all undertakings or any classes of undertaking, that, where assets other than financial instruments are measured at fair value, a change in the value be included in the profit and loss account.

CHAPTER 3 BALANCE SHEET AND PROFIT AND LOSS ACCOUNT

[11.161]

Article 9 General provisions concerning the balance sheet and the profit and loss account

1. The layout of the balance sheet and of the profit and loss account shall not be changed from one financial year to the next. Departures from that principle shall, however, be permitted in exceptional cases in order to give a true and fair view of the undertaking's assets, liabilities, financial position and profit or loss. Any such departure and the reasons therefor shall be disclosed in the notes to the financial statements.

2. In the balance sheet and in the profit and loss account the items set out in Annexes III to VI shall be shown separately in the order indicated. Member States shall permit a more detailed subdivision of those items, subject to adherence to the prescribed layouts. Member States shall permit the addition of subtotals and of new items, provided that the contents of such new items are not covered by any of the items in the prescribed layouts. Member States may require such subdivision or subtotals or new items.

3. The layout, nomenclature and terminology of items in the balance sheet and profit and loss account that are preceded by Arabic numerals shall be adapted where the special nature of an undertaking so requires. Member States may require such adaptations for undertakings which form part of a particular economic sector.

Member States may permit or require balance sheet and profit and loss account items that are preceded by Arabic numerals to be combined where they are immaterial in amount for the purposes of giving a true and fair view of the undertaking's assets, liabilities, financial position and profit or loss or where such combination makes for greater clarity, provided that the items so combined are dealt with separately in the notes to the financial statements.

4. By way of derogation from paragraphs 2 and 3 of this Article, Member States may limit the undertaking's ability to depart from the layouts set out in Annexes III to VI to the extent that this is necessary in order for the financial statements to be filed electronically.

5. In respect of each balance sheet and profit and loss account item, the figure for the financial year to which the balance sheet and the profit and loss account relate and the figure relating to the corresponding item for the preceding financial year shall be shown. Where those figures are not comparable, Member States may require the figure for the preceding financial year to be adjusted. Any case of non-comparability or any adjustment of the figures shall be disclosed, with explanations, in the notes to the financial statements.

6. Member States may permit or require adaptation of the layout of the balance sheet and profit and loss account in order to include the appropriation of profit or the treatment of loss.

7. In respect of the treatment of participating interests in annual financial statements:

(a) Member States may permit or require participating interests to be accounted for using the equity method as provided for in Article 27, taking account of the essential adjustments resulting from the particular characteristics of annual financial statements as compared to consolidated financial statements;

(b) Member States may permit or require that the proportion of the profit or loss attributable to the participating interest be recognised in the profit and loss account only to the extent of the amount corresponding to dividends already received or the payment of which can be claimed; and

(c) where the profit attributable to the participating interest and recognised in the profit and loss account exceeds the amount of dividends already received or the payment of which can be claimed, the amount of the difference shall be placed in a reserve which cannot be distributed to shareholders.

[11.162]

Article 10 Presentation of the balance sheet

For the presentation of the balance sheet, Member States shall prescribe one or both of the layouts set out in Annexes III and IV. If a Member State prescribes both layouts, it shall permit undertakings to choose which of the prescribed layouts to adopt.

[11.163]

Article 11 Alternative presentation of the balance sheet

Member States may permit or require undertakings, or certain classes of undertaking, to present items on the basis of a distinction between current and non-current items in a different layout from that set out in Annexes III and IV, provided that the information given is at least equivalent to that otherwise to be provided in accordance with Annexes III and IV.

[11.164]

Article 12 Special provisions relating to certain balance sheet items

1. Where an asset or liability relates to more than one layout item, its relationship to other items shall be disclosed either under the item where it appears or in the notes to the financial statements.

2. Own shares and shares in affiliated undertakings shall be shown only under the items prescribed for that purpose.

3. Whether particular assets are to be shown as fixed assets or current assets shall depend upon the purpose for which they are intended.

4. Rights to immovables and other similar rights as defined by national law shall be shown under 'Land and buildings'.

5. The purchase price or production cost or revalued amount, where Article 7(1) applies, of fixed assets with limited useful economic lives shall be reduced by value adjustments calculated to write off the value of such assets systematically over their useful economic lives.
6. Value adjustments to fixed assets shall be subject to the following:
   (a) Member States may permit or require value adjustments to be made in respect of financial fixed assets, so that they are valued at the lower figure to be attributed to them at the balance sheet date;
   (b) value adjustments shall be made in respect of fixed assets, whether their useful economic lives are limited or not, so that they are valued at the lower figure to be attributed to them at the balance sheet date if it is expected that the reduction in their value will be permanent;
   (c) the value adjustments referred to in points (a) and (b) shall be charged to the profit and loss account and disclosed separately in the notes to the financial statements if they have not been shown separately in the profit and loss account;
   (d) measurement at the lower of the values provided for in points (a) and (b) may not continue if the reasons for which the value adjustments were made have ceased to apply; this provision shall not apply to value adjustments made in respect of goodwill.
7. Value adjustments shall be made in respect of current assets with a view to showing them at the lower market value or, in particular circumstances, another lower value to be attributed to them at the balance sheet date.
Measurement at the lower value provided for in the first subparagraph may not continue if the reasons for which the value adjustments were made no longer apply.
8. Member States may permit or require that interest on capital borrowed to finance the production of fixed or current assets be included within production costs, to the extent that it relates to the period of production. Any application of this provision shall be disclosed in the notes to the financial statements.
9. Member States may permit the purchase price or production cost of stocks of goods of the same category and all fungible items including investments to be calculated either on the basis of weighted average prices, on the basis of the 'first in, first out' (FIFO) method, the 'last in, first out' (LIFO) method, or a method reflecting generally accepted best practice.
10. Where the amount repayable on account of any debt is greater than the amount received, Member States may permit or require that the difference be shown as an asset. It shall be shown separately in the balance sheet or in the notes to the financial statements. The amount of that difference shall be written off by a reasonable amount each year and completely written off no later than at the time of repayment of the debt.
11. Intangible assets shall be written off over the useful economic life of the intangible asset.
In exceptional cases where the useful life of goodwill and development costs cannot be reliably estimated, such assets shall be written off within a maximum period set by the Member State. That maximum period shall not be shorter than five years and shall not exceed 10 years. An explanation of the period over which goodwill is written off shall be provided within the notes to the financial statements.
Where national law authorises the inclusion of costs of development under 'Assets' and the costs of development have not been completely written off, Member States shall require that no distribution of profits take place unless the amount of the reserves available for distribution and profits brought forward is at least equal to that of the costs not written off.
Where national law authorises the inclusion of formation expenses under 'Assets', they shall be written off within a period of maximum five years. In that case, Member States shall require that the third subparagraph apply mutatis mutandis to formation expenses.
In exceptional cases, the Member States may permit derogations from the third and fourth subparagraphs. Such derogations and the reasons therefor shall be disclosed in the notes to the financial statements.
12. Provisions shall cover liabilities the nature of which is clearly defined and which at the balance sheet date are either likely to be incurred or certain to be incurred, but uncertain as to their amount or as to the date on which they will arise.
The Member States may also authorise the creation of provisions intended to cover expenses the nature of which is clearly defined and which at the balance sheet date are either likely to be incurred or certain to be incurred, but uncertain as to their amount or as to the date on which they will arise.
At the balance sheet date, a provision shall represent the best estimate of the expenses likely to be incurred or, in the case of a liability, of the amount required to meet that liability. Provisions shall not be used to adjust the values of assets.

[11.165]
Article 13 Presentation of the profit and loss account
1. For the presentation of the profit and loss account, Member States shall prescribe one or both of the layouts set out in Annexes V and VI. If a Member State prescribes both layouts, it may permit undertakings to choose which of the prescribed layouts to adopt.
2. By way of derogation from Article 4(1), Member States may permit or require all undertakings, or any classes of undertaking, to present a statement of their performance instead of the presentation of profit and loss items in accordance with Annexes V and VI, provided that the information given is at least equivalent to that otherwise required by Annexes V and VI.

[11.166]
Article 14 Simplifications for small and medium-sized undertakings
1. Member States may permit small undertakings to draw up abridged balance sheets showing only those items in Annexes III and IV preceded by letters and roman numerals, disclosing separately:
   (a) the information required in brackets in D (II) under 'Assets' and C under 'Capital, reserves and liabilities' of Annex III, but in the aggregate for each; or
   (b) the information required in brackets in D (II) of Annex IV.
2. Member States may permit small and medium-sized undertakings to draw up abridged profit and loss accounts within the following limits:
   (a) in Annex V, items 1 to 5 may be combined under one item called 'Gross profit or loss';

(b) in Annex VI, items 1, 2, 3 and 6 may be combined under one item called 'Gross profit or loss'.

CHAPTER 4 NOTES TO THE FINANCIAL STATEMENTS

[11.167]

Article 15 General provisions concerning the notes to the financial statements

Where notes to the balance sheet and profit and loss account are presented in accordance with this Chapter, the notes shall be presented in the order in which items are presented in the balance sheet and in the profit and loss account.

[11.168]

Article 16 Content of the notes to the financial statements relating to all undertakings

1. In the notes to the financial statements all undertakings shall, in addition to the information required under other provisions of this Directive, disclose information in respect of the following:

- (a) accounting policies adopted;
- (b) where fixed assets are measured at revalued amounts, a table showing:
  - (i) movements in the revaluation reserve in the financial year, with an explanation of the tax treatment of items therein, and
  - (ii) the carrying amount in the balance sheet that would have been recognised had the fixed assets not been revalued;
- (c) where financial instruments and/or assets other than financial instruments are measured at fair value:
  - (i) the significant assumptions underlying the valuation models and techniques where fair values have been determined in accordance with point (b) of Article 8(7),
  - (ii) for each category of financial instrument or asset other than financial instruments, the fair value, the changes in value included directly in the profit and loss account and changes included in fair value reserves,
  - (iii) for each class of derivative financial instrument, information about the extent and the nature of the instruments, including significant terms and conditions that may affect the amount, timing and certainty of future cash flows, and
  - (iv) a table showing movements in fair value reserves during the financial year;
- (d) the total amount of any financial commitments, guarantees or contingencies that are not included in the balance sheet, and an indication of the nature and form of any valuable security which has been provided; any commitments concerning pensions and affiliated or associated undertakings shall be disclosed separately;
- (e) the amount of advances and credits granted to members of the administrative, managerial and supervisory bodies, with indications of the interest rates, main conditions and any amounts repaid or written off or waived, as well as commitments entered into on their behalf by way of guarantees of any kind, with an indication of the total for each category;
- (f) the amount and nature of individual items of income or expenditure which are of exceptional size or incidence;
- (g) amounts owed by the undertaking becoming due and payable after more than five years, as well as the undertaking's entire debts covered by valuable security furnished by the undertaking, with an indication of the nature and form of the security; and
- (h) the average number of employees during the financial year.

2. Member States may require mutatis mutandis that small undertakings are to disclose information as required in points (a), (m), (p), (q) and (r) of Article 17(1).

For the purposes of applying the first subparagraph, the information required in point (p) of Article 17(1) shall be limited to the nature and business purpose of the arrangements referred to in that point.

For the purposes of applying the first subparagraph, the disclosure of the information required in point (r) of Article 17(1) shall be limited to transactions entered into with the parties listed in the fourth subparagraph of that point.

3. Member States shall not require disclosure for small undertakings beyond what is required or permitted by this Article.

[11.169]

Article 17 Additional disclosures for medium-sized and large undertakings and public-interest entities

1. In the notes to the financial statements, medium-sized and large undertakings and public-interest entities shall, in addition to the information required under Article 16 and any other provisions of this Directive, disclose information in respect of the following matters:

- (a) for the various fixed asset items:
  - (i) the purchase price or production cost or, where an alternative basis of measurement has been followed, the fair value or revalued amount at the beginning and end of the financial year,
  - (ii) additions, disposals and transfers during the financial year,
  - (iii) the accumulated value adjustments at the beginning and end of the financial year,
  - (iv) value adjustments charged during the financial year,
  - (v) movements in accumulated value adjustments in respect of additions, disposals and transfers during the financial year, and
  - (vi) where interest is capitalised in accordance with Article 12(8), the amount capitalised during the financial year.
- (b) if fixed or current assets are the subject of value adjustments for taxation purposes alone, the amount of the adjustments and the reasons for making them;
- (c) where financial instruments are measured at purchase price or production cost:
  - (i) for each class of derivative financial instrument:
    - — the fair value of the instruments, if such a value can be determined by any of the methods prescribed in point (a) of Article 8(7), and
    - — information about the extent and nature of the instruments,

Part 11 EU & Retained EU Legislation

(ii) for financial fixed assets carried at an amount in excess of their fair value:

— the book value and the fair value of either the individual assets or appropriate groupings of those individual assets, and

— the reasons for not reducing the book value, including the nature of the evidence underlying the assumption that the book value will be recovered;

(d) the amount of the emoluments granted in respect of, the financial year to the members of administrative, managerial and supervisory bodies by reason of their responsibilities and any commitments arising or entered into in respect of retirement pensions of former members of those bodies, with an indication of the total for each category of body.

Member States may waive the requirement to disclose such information where its disclosure would make it possible to identify the financial position of a specific member of such a body;

(e) the average number of employees during the financial year, broken down by categories and, if they are not disclosed separately in the profit and loss account, the staff costs relating to the financial year, broken down between wages and salaries, social security costs and pension costs;

(f) where a provision for deferred tax is recognised in the balance sheet, the deferred tax balances at the end of the financial year, and the movement in those balances during the financial year;

(g) the name and registered office of each of the undertakings in which the undertaking, either itself or through a person acting in his own name but on the undertaking's behalf, holds a participating interest, showing the proportion of the capital held, the amount of capital and reserves, and the profit or loss for the latest financial year of the undertaking concerned for which financial statements have been adopted; the information concerning capital and reserves and the profit or loss may be omitted where the undertaking concerned does not publish its balance sheet and is not controlled by the undertaking.

Member States may allow the information required to be disclosed by the first subparagraph of this point to take the form of a statement filed in accordance with Article 3(1) and (3) of Directive 2009/101/EC; the filing of such a statement shall be disclosed in the notes to the financial statements. Member States may also allow that information to be omitted when its nature is such that it would be seriously prejudicial to any of the undertakings to which it relates. Member States may make such omissions subject to prior administrative or judicial authorisation. Any such omission shall be disclosed in the notes to the financial statements;

(h) the number and the nominal value or, in the absence of a nominal value, the accounting par value of the shares subscribed during the financial year within the limits of the authorised capital, without prejudice as far as the amount of that capital is concerned to point (e) of Article 2 of Directive 2009/101/EC or to points (c) and (d) of Article 2 of Directive 2012/30/EU;

(i) where there is more than one class of shares, the number and the nominal value or, in the absence of a nominal value, the accounting par value for each class;

(j) the existence of any participation certificates, convertible debentures, warrants, options or similar securities or rights, with an indication of their number and the rights they confer;

(k) the name, the head or registered office and the legal form of each of the undertakings of which the undertaking is a member having unlimited liability;

(l) the name and registered office of the undertaking which draws up the consolidated financial statements of the largest body of undertakings of which the undertaking forms part as a subsidiary undertaking;

(m) the name and registered office of the undertaking which draws up the consolidated financial statements of the smallest body of undertakings of which the undertaking forms part as a subsidiary undertaking and which is also included in the body of undertakings referred to in point (l);

(n) the place where copies of the consolidated financial statements referred to in points (l) and (m) may be obtained, provided that they are available;

(o) the proposed appropriation of profit or treatment of loss, or where applicable, the appropriation of the profit or treatment of the loss;

(p) the nature and business purpose of the undertaking's arrangements that are not included in the balance sheet and the financial impact on the undertaking of those arrangements, provided that the risks or benefits arising from such arrangements are material and in so far as the disclosure of such risks or benefits is necessary for the purposes of assessing the financial position of the undertaking;

(q) the nature and the financial effect of material events arising after the balance sheet date which are not reflected in the profit and loss account or balance sheet; and

(r) transactions which have been entered into with related parties by the undertaking, including the amount of such transactions, the nature of the related party relationship and other information about the transactions necessary for an understanding of the financial position of the undertaking. Information about individual transactions may be aggregated according to their nature except where separate information is necessary for an understanding of the effects of related party transactions on the financial position of the undertaking.

Member States may permit or require that only transactions with related parties that have not been concluded under normal market conditions be disclosed.

Member States may permit that transactions entered into between one or more members of a group be not disclosed, provided that subsidiaries which are party to the transaction are wholly owned by such a member.

Member States may permit that a medium-sized undertaking limit the disclosure of transactions with related parties to transactions entered into with:

(i) owners holding a participating interest in the undertaking;

(ii) undertakings in which the undertaking itself has a participating interest; and

(iii) members of the administrative, management or supervisory bodies of the undertaking.

2. Member States shall not be required to apply point (g) of paragraph 1 to an undertaking which is a parent undertaking governed by their national laws in the following cases:

(a) where the undertaking in which that parent undertaking holds a participating interest for the purposes of point (g) of paragraph 1 is included in consolidated financial statements drawn up by that parent undertaking, or in the consolidated financial statements of a larger body of undertakings as referred to in Article 23(4);
(b) where that participating interest has been dealt with by that parent undertaking in its annual financial statements in accordance with Article 9(7), or in the consolidated financial statements drawn up by that parent undertaking in accordance with Article 27(1) to (8).

[11.170]
Article 18 Additional disclosures for large undertakings and public-interest entities
1. In the notes to the financial statements, large undertakings and public-interest entities shall, in addition to the information required under Articles 16 and 17 and any other provisions of this Directive, disclose information in respect of the following matters:
(a) the net turnover broken down by categories of activity and into geographical markets, in so far as those categories and markets differ substantially from one another, taking account of the manner in which the sale of products and the provision of services are organised; and
(b) the total fees for the financial year charged by each statutory auditor or audit firm for the statutory audit of the annual financial statements, and the total fees charged by each statutory auditor or audit firm for other assurance services, for tax advisory services and for other non-audit services.
2. Member States may allow the information referred to in point (a) of paragraph 1to be omitted where the disclosure of that information would be seriously prejudicial to the undertaking. Member States may make such omissions subject to prior administrative or judicial authorisation. Any such omission shall be disclosed in the notes to the financial statements.
3. Member States may provide that point (b) of paragraph 1 is not to apply to the annual financial statements of an undertaking where that undertaking is included within the consolidated financial statements required to be drawn up under Article 22, provided that such information is given in the notes to the consolidated financial statements.

CHAPTER 5 MANAGEMENT REPORT

[11.171]
Article 19 Contents of the management report
1. The management report shall include a fair review of the development and performance of the undertaking's business and of its position, together with a description of the principal risks and uncertainties that it faces.
The review shall be a balanced and comprehensive analysis of the development and performance of the undertaking's business and of its position, consistent with the size and complexity of the business.
To the extent necessary for an understanding of the undertaking's development, performance or position, the analysis shall include both financial and, where appropriate, non-financial key performance indicators relevant to the particular business, including information relating to environmental and employee matters. In providing the analysis, the management report shall, where appropriate, include references to, and additional explanations of, amounts reported in the annual financial statements.
2. The management report shall also give an indication of:
(a) the undertaking's likely future development;
(b) activities in the field of research and development;
(c) the information concerning acquisitions of own shares prescribed by Article 24(2) of Directive 2012/30/EU;
(d) the existence of branches of the undertaking; and
(e) in relation to the undertaking's use of financial instruments and where material for the assessment of its assets, liabilities, financial position and profit or loss:
(i) the undertaking's financial risk management objectives and policies, including its policy for hedging each major type of forecasted transaction for which hedge accounting is used; and
(ii) the undertaking's exposure to price risk, credit risk, liquidity risk and cash flow risk.
3. Member States may exempt small undertakings from the obligation to prepare management reports, provided that they require the information referred to in Article 24(2) of Directive 2012/30/EU concerning the acquisition by an undertaking of its own shares to be given in the notes to the financial statements.
4. Member States may exempt small and medium-sized undertakings from the obligation set out in the third subparagraph of paragraph 1 in so far as it relates to non-financial information.

[11.172]
[Article 19a Non-financial statement
1. Large undertakings which are public-interest entities exceeding on their balance sheet dates the criterion of the average number of 500 employees during the financial year shall include in the management report a non-financial statement containing information to the extent necessary for an understanding of the undertaking's development, performance, position and impact of its activity, relating to, as a minimum, environmental, social and employee matters, respect for human rights, anti-corruption and bribery matters, including:
(a) a brief description of the undertaking's business model;
(b) a description of the policies pursued by the undertaking in relation to those matters, including due diligence processes implemented;
(c) the outcome of those policies;
(d) the principal risks related to those matters linked to the undertaking's operations including, where relevant and proportionate, its business relationships, products or services which are likely to cause adverse impacts in those areas, and how the undertaking manages those risks;
(e) non-financial key performance indicators relevant to the particular business.

Where the undertaking does not pursue policies in relation to one or more of those matters, the non-financial statement shall provide a clear and reasoned explanation for not doing so.

The non-financial statement referred to in the first subparagraph shall also, where appropriate, include references to, and additional explanations of, amounts reported in the annual financial statements.

Member States may allow information relating to impending developments or matters in the course of negotiation to be omitted in exceptional cases where, in the duly justified opinion of the members of the administrative, management and supervisory bodies, acting within the competences assigned to them by national law and having collective responsibility for that opinion, the disclosure of such information would be seriously prejudicial to the commercial position of the undertaking, provided that such omission does not prevent a fair and balanced understanding of the undertaking's development, performance, position and impact of its activity.

In requiring the disclosure of the information referred to in the first subparagraph, Member States shall provide that undertakings may rely on national, Union-based or international frameworks, and if they do so, undertakings shall specify which frameworks they have relied upon.

2. Undertakings fulfilling the obligation set out in paragraph 1 shall be deemed to have fulfilled the obligation relating to the analysis of non-financial information set out in the third subparagraph of Article 19(1).

3. An undertaking which is a subsidiary undertaking shall be exempted from the obligation set out in paragraph 1 if that undertaking and its subsidiary undertakings are included in the consolidated management report or the separate report of another undertaking, drawn up in accordance with Article 29 and this Article.

4. Where an undertaking prepares a separate report corresponding to the same financial year whether or not relying on national, Union-based or international frameworks and covering the information required for the nonfinancial statement as provided for in paragraph 1, Member States may exempt that undertaking from the obligation to prepare the non-financial statement laid down in paragraph 1, provided that such separate report:

(a) is published together with the management report in accordance with Article 30; or

(b) is made publicly available within a reasonable period of time, not exceeding six months after the balance sheet date, on the undertaking's website, and is referred to in the management report.

Paragraph 2 shall apply *mutatis mutandis* to undertakings preparing a separate report as referred to in the first subparagraph of this paragraph.

5. Member States shall ensure that the statutory auditor or audit firm checks whether the non-financial statement referred to in paragraph 1 or the separate report referred to in paragraph 4 has been provided.

6. Member States may require that the information in the non-financial statement referred to in paragraph 1 or in the separate report referred to in paragraph 4 be verified by an independent assurance services provider.]

NOTES

Inserted by European Parliament and Council Directive 2014/95/EU, Art 1(1), as from 5 December 2014.

[11.173]

Article 20 Corporate governance statement

1. Undertakings referred to in point (1)(a) of Article 2 shall include a corporate governance statement in their management report. That statement shall be included as a specific section of the management report and shall contain at least the following information:

(a) a reference to the following, where applicable:

  (i) the corporate governance code to which the undertaking is subject,

  (ii) the corporate governance code which the undertaking may have voluntarily decided to apply,

  (iii) all relevant information about the corporate governance practices applied over and above the requirements of national law.

  Where reference is made to a corporate governance code referred to in points (i) or (ii), the undertaking shall also indicate where the relevant texts are publicly available. Where reference is made to the information referred to in point (iii), the undertaking shall make details of its corporate governance practices publicly available;

(b) where an undertaking, in accordance with national law, departs from a corporate governance code referred to in points (a)(i) or (ii), an explanation by the undertaking as to which parts of the corporate governance code it departs from and the reasons for doing so; where the undertaking has decided not to refer to any provisions of a corporate governance code referred to in points (a)(i) or (ii), it shall explain its reasons for not doing so;

(c) a description of the main features of the undertaking's internal control and risk management systems in relation to the financial reporting process;

(d) the information required by points (c), (d), (f), (h) and (i) of Article 10(1) of Directive 2004/25/EC of the European Parliament and of the Council of 21 April 2004 on takeover bids,[1] where the undertaking is subject to that Directive;

(e) unless the information is already fully provided for in national law, a description of the operation of the shareholder meeting and its key powers and a description of shareholders' rights and how they can be exercised; and

(f) the composition and operation of the administrative, management and supervisory bodies and their committees;

[(g) a description of the diversity policy applied in relation to the undertaking's administrative, management and supervisory bodies with regard to aspects such as, for instance, age, gender, or educational and professional backgrounds, the objectives of that diversity policy, how it has been implemented and the results in the reporting period. If no such policy is applied, the statement shall contain an explanation as to why this is the case.]

2. Member States may permit the information required by paragraph 1 of this Article to be set out in:

(a) a separate report published together with the management report in the manner set out in Article 30; or

(b) a document publicly available on the undertaking's website, to which reference is made in the management report.

That separate report or that document referred to in points (a) and (b), respectively, may cross-refer to the management report, where the information required by point (d) of paragraph 1 of this Article is made available in that management report.

[3. The statutory auditor or audit firm shall express an opinion in accordance with the second subparagraph of Article 34(1) regarding information prepared under points (c) and (d) of paragraph 1 of this Article and shall check that the information referred to in points (a), (b), (e), (f) and (g) of paragraph 1 of this Article has been provided.]

[4. Member States may exempt undertakings referred to in paragraph 1 which have only issued securities other than shares admitted to trading on a regulated market within the meaning of point (14) of Article 4(1) of Directive 2004/39/EC from the application of points (a), (b), (e), (f) and (g) of paragraph 1 of this Article, unless such undertakings have issued shares which are traded in a multilateral trading facility within the meaning of point (15) of Article 4(1) of Directive 2004/39/EC.]

[5. Notwithstanding Article 40, point (g) of paragraph 1 shall not apply to small and medium-sized undertakings.]

NOTES

Point (g) of para 1 was inserted, paras 3, 4 were substituted, and para 5 was added, by European Parliament and Council Directive 2014/95/EU, Art 1(2), as from 5 December 2014.

[1] OJ L142, 30.4.2004, p 12.

CHAPTER 6 CONSOLIDATED FINANCIAL STATEMENTS AND REPORTS

[11.174]

Article 21 Scope of the consolidated financial statements and reports

For the purposes of this Chapter, a parent undertaking and all of its subsidiary undertakings shall be undertakings to be consolidated where the parent undertaking is an undertaking to which the coordination measures prescribed by this Directive apply by virtue of Article 1(1).

[11.175]

Article 22 The requirement to prepare consolidated financial statements

1. A Member State shall require any undertaking governed by its national law to draw up consolidated financial statements and a consolidated management report if that undertaking (a parent undertaking):

(a) has a majority of the shareholders' or members' voting rights in another undertaking (a subsidiary undertaking);

(b) has the right to appoint or remove a majority of the members of the administrative, management or supervisory body of another undertaking (a subsidiary undertaking) and is at the same time a shareholder in or member of that undertaking;

(c) has the right to exercise a dominant influence over an undertaking (a subsidiary undertaking) of which it is a shareholder or member, pursuant to a contract entered into with that undertaking or to a provision in its memorandum or articles of association, where the law governing that subsidiary undertaking permits its being subject to such contracts or provisions.

A Member State need not prescribe that a parent undertaking must be a shareholder in or member of its subsidiary undertaking. Those Member States the laws of which do not provide for such contracts or clauses shall not be required to apply this provision; or

(d) is a shareholder in or member of an undertaking, and:

(i) a majority of the members of the administrative, management or supervisory bodies of that undertaking (a subsidiary undertaking) who have held office during the financial year, during the preceding financial year and up to the time when the consolidated financial statements are drawn up, have been appointed solely as a result of the exercise of its voting rights; or

(ii) controls alone, pursuant to an agreement with other shareholders in or members of that undertaking (a subsidiary undertaking), a majority of shareholders' or members' voting rights in that undertaking. The Member States may introduce more detailed provisions concerning the form and contents of such agreements.

Member States shall prescribe at least the arrangements referred to in point (ii). They may subject the application of point (i) to the requirement that the voting rights represent at least 20% of the total.

However, point (i) shall not apply where a third party has the rights referred to in points (a), (b) or (c) with regard to that undertaking.

2. In addition to the cases mentioned in paragraph 1, Member States may require any undertaking governed by their national law to draw up consolidated financial statements and a consolidated management report if:

(a) that undertaking (a parent undertaking) has the power to exercise, or actually exercises, dominant influence or control over another undertaking (the subsidiary undertaking); or

(b) that undertaking (a parent undertaking) and another undertaking (the subsidiary undertaking) are managed on a unified basis by the parent undertaking.

3. For the purposes of points (a), (b) and (d) of paragraph 1, the voting rights and the rights of appointment and removal of any other subsidiary undertaking as well as those of any person acting in his own name but on behalf of the parent undertaking or of another subsidiary undertaking shall be added to those of the parent undertaking.

4. For the purposes of points (a), (b) and (d) of paragraph 1, the rights mentioned in paragraph 3 shall be reduced by the rights:

(a) attaching to shares held on behalf of a person who is neither the parent undertaking nor a subsidiary of that parent undertaking; or

(b) attaching to shares:

(i) held by way of security, provided that the rights in question are exercised in accordance with the instructions received, or

(ii) held in connection with the granting of loans as part of normal business activities, provided that the voting rights are exercised in the interests of the person providing the security.

5. For the purposes of points (a) and (d) of paragraph 1, the total of the shareholders' or members' voting rights in the subsidiary undertaking shall be reduced by the voting rights attaching to the shares held by that undertaking itself, by a subsidiary undertaking of that undertaking or by a person acting in his own name but on behalf of those undertakings.

6. Without prejudice to Article 23(9), a parent undertaking and all of its subsidiary undertakings shall be undertakings to be consolidated regardless of where the registered offices of such subsidiary undertakings are situated.
7. Without prejudice to this Article and Articles 21 and 23, a Member State may require any undertaking governed by its national law to draw up consolidated financial statements and a consolidated management report if:
(a) that undertaking and one or more other undertakings to which it is not related as described in paragraphs 1 or 2, are managed on a unified basis in accordance with:
(i) a contract concluded with that undertaking, or
(ii) the memorandum or articles of association of those other undertakings; or
(b) the administrative, management or supervisory bodies of that undertaking and of one or more other undertakings to which it is not related, as described in paragraphs 1 or 2, consist in the majority of the same persons in office during the financial year and until the consolidated financial statements are drawn up.
8. Where the Member State option referred to in paragraph 7 is exercised, the undertakings described in that paragraph and all of their subsidiary undertakings shall be consolidated, where one or more of those undertakings is established as one of the types of undertaking listed in Annex I or Annex II.
9. Paragraph 6 of this Article, Article 23(1), (2), (9) and (10) and Articles 24 to 29 shall apply to the consolidated financial statements and the consolidated management report referred to in paragraph 7 of this Article, subject to the following modifications:
(a) references to parent undertakings shall be understood to refer to all of the undertakings specified in paragraph 7 of this Article; and
(b) without prejudice to Article 24(3), the items 'capital', 'share premium account', 'revaluation reserve', 'reserves', 'profit or loss brought forward', and 'profit or loss for the financial year' to be included in the consolidated financial statements shall be the aggregate amounts attributable to each of the undertakings specified in paragraph 7 of this Article.

[11.176]
Article 23 Exemptions from consolidation
1. Small groups shall be exempted from the obligation to draw up consolidated financial statements and a consolidated management report, except where any affiliated undertaking is a public-interest entity.
2. Member States may exempt medium-sized groups from the obligation to draw up consolidated financial statements and a consolidated management report, except where any affiliated undertaking is a public-interest entity.
3. Notwithstanding paragraphs 1 and 2 of this Article, a Member State shall, in the following cases, exempt from the obligation to draw up consolidated financial statements and a consolidated management report any parent undertaking (the exempted undertaking) governed by its national law which is also a subsidiary undertaking, including a public-interest entity unless that public-interest entity falls under point (1)(a) of Article 2, the own parent undertaking of which is governed by the law of a Member State and:
(a) the parent undertaking of the exempted undertaking holds all of the shares in the exempted undertaking. The shares in the exempted undertaking held by members of its administrative, management or supervisory bodies pursuant to a legal obligation or an obligation in its memorandum or articles of association shall be ignored for this purpose; or
(b) the parent undertaking of the exempted undertaking holds 90% or more of the shares in the exempted undertaking and the remaining shareholders in or members of the exempted undertaking have approved the exemption.
4. The exemptions referred to in paragraph 3 shall fulfil all of the following conditions:
(a) the exempted undertaking and, without prejudice to paragraph 9, all of its subsidiary undertakings are consolidated in the financial statements of a larger body of undertakings, the parent undertaking of which is governed by the law of a Member State;
(b) the consolidated financial statements referred to in point (a) and the consolidated management report of the larger body of undertakings are drawn up by the parent undertaking of that body, in accordance with the law of the Member State by which that parent undertaking is governed, in accordance with this Directive or international accounting standards adopted in accordance with Regulation (EC) No 1606/2002;
(c) in relation to the exempted undertaking the following documents are published in the manner prescribed by the law of the Member State by which that exempted undertaking is governed, in accordance with Article 30:
(i) the consolidated financial statements referred to in point (a) and the consolidated management report referred to in point (b),
(ii) the audit report, and
(iii) where appropriate, the appendix referred to in paragraph 6.
That Member State may require that the documents referred to in points (i), (ii) and (iii) be published in its official language and that the translation be certified;
(d) the notes to the annual financial statements of the exempted undertaking disclose the following:
(i) the name and registered office of the parent undertaking that draws up the consolidated financial statements referred to in point (a), and
(ii) the exemption from the obligation to draw up consolidated financial statements and a consolidated management report.
5. In cases not covered by paragraph 3, a Member State may, without prejudice to paragraphs 1, 2 and 3 of this Article, exempt from the obligation to draw up consolidated financial statements and a consolidated management report any parent undertaking (the exempted undertaking) governed by its national law which is also a subsidiary undertaking, including a public-interest entity unless that public-interest entity falls under point (1)(a) of Article 2, the parent undertaking of which is governed by the law of a Member State, provided that all the conditions set out in paragraph 4 are fulfilled and provided further:
(a) that the shareholders in or members of the exempted undertaking who own a minimum proportion of the subscribed capital of that undertaking have not requested the preparation of consolidated financial statements at least six months before the end of the financial year;
(b) that the minimum proportion referred to in point (a) does not exceed the following limits:

(i) 10% of the subscribed capital in the case of public limited liability companies and limited partnerships with share capital; and
(ii) 20% of the subscribed capital in the case of undertakings of other types;

(c) that the Member State does not make the exemption subject to:
(i) the condition that the parent undertaking, which prepared the consolidated financial statements referred to in point (a) of paragraph 4, is governed by the national law of the Member State granting the exemption, or
(ii) conditions relating to the preparation and auditing of those financial statements.

6. A Member State may make the exemptions provided for in paragraphs 3 and 5 subject to the disclosure of additional information, in accordance with this Directive, in the consolidated financial statements referred to in point (a) of paragraph 4, or in an appendix thereto, if that information is required of undertakings governed by the national law of that Member State which are obliged to prepare consolidated financial statements and are in the same circumstances.

7. Paragraphs 3 to 6 shall apply without prejudice to Member State legislation on the drawing-up of consolidated financial statements or consolidated management reports in so far as those documents are required:
(a) for the information of employees or their representatives; or
(b) by an administrative or judicial authority for its own purposes.

8. Without prejudice to paragraphs 1, 2, 3 and 5 of this Article, a Member State which provides for exemptions under paragraphs 3 and 5 of this Article may also exempt from the obligation to draw up consolidated financial statements and a consolidated management report any parent undertaking (the exempted undertaking) governed by its national law which is also a subsidiary undertaking, including a public-interest entity unless that public-interest entity falls under point (1)(a) of Article 2, the parent undertaking of which is not governed by the law of a Member State, if all of the following conditions are fulfilled:
(a) the exempted undertaking and, without prejudice to paragraph 9, all of its subsidiary undertakings are consolidated in the financial statements of a larger body of undertakings;
(b) the consolidated financial statements referred to in point (a) and, where appropriate, the consolidated management report are drawn up:
(i) in accordance with this Directive,
(ii) in accordance with international accounting standards adopted pursuant to Regulation (EC) No 1606/2002,
(iii) in a manner equivalent to consolidated financial statements and consolidated management reports drawn up in accordance with this Directive, or
(iv) in a manner equivalent to international accounting standards as determined in accordance with Commission Regulation (EC) No 1569/2007 of 21 December 2007 establishing a mechanism for the determination of equivalence of accounting standards applied by third country issuers of securities pursuant to Directives 2003/71/EC and 2004/109/EC of the European Parliament and of the Council;[1]
(c) the consolidated financial statements referred to in point (a) have been audited by one or more statutory auditor(s) or audit firm(s) authorised to audit financial statements under the national law governing the undertaking which drew up those statements.

Points (c) and (d) of paragraph 4 and paragraphs 5, 6 and 7 shall apply.

9. An undertaking, including a public-interest entity, need not be included in consolidated financial statements where at least one of the following conditions is fulfilled:
(a) in extremely rare cases where the information necessary for the preparation of consolidated financial statements in accordance with this Directive cannot be obtained without disproportionate expense or undue delay;
(b) the shares of that undertaking are held exclusively with a view to their subsequent resale; or
(c) severe long-term restrictions substantially hinder:
(i) the parent undertaking in the exercise of its rights over the assets or management of that undertaking; or
(ii) the exercise of unified management of that undertaking where it is in one of the relationships defined in Article 22(7).

10. Without prejudice to point (b) of Article 6(1), Article 21 and paragraphs 1 and 2 of this Article, any parent undertaking, including a public-interest entity, shall be exempted from the obligation imposed in Article 22 if:
(a) it only has subsidiary undertakings which are immaterial, both individually and collectively; or
(b) all its subsidiary undertakings can be excluded from consolidation by virtue of paragraph 9 of this Article.

NOTES

[1] OJ L340, 22.12.2007, p 66.

[11.177]

Article 24 The preparation of consolidated financial statements

1. Chapters 2 and 3 shall apply in respect of consolidated financial statements, taking into account the essential adjustments resulting from the particular characteristics of consolidated financial statements as compared to annual financial statements.

2. The assets and liabilities of undertakings included in a consolidation shall be incorporated in full in the consolidated balance sheet.

3. The book values of shares in the capital of undertakings included in a consolidation shall be set off against the proportion which they represent of the capital and reserves of those undertakings in accordance with the following:
(a) except in the case of shares in the capital of the parent undertaking held either by that undertaking itself or by another undertaking included in the consolidation, which shall be treated as own shares in accordance with

Chapter 3, that set-off shall be effected on the basis of book values as they stand on the date on which those undertakings are included in a consolidation for the first time. Differences arising from that set-off shall, as far as possible, be entered directly against those items in the consolidated balance sheet which have values above or below their book values;

(b) a Member State may permit or require set-offs on the basis of the values of identifiable assets and liabilities as at the date of acquisition of the shares or, in the event of acquisition in two or more stages, as at the date on which the undertaking became a subsidiary;

(c) any difference remaining after the application of point (a) or resulting from the application of point (b) shall be shown as goodwill in the consolidated balance sheet;

(d) the methods used to calculate the value of goodwill and any significant changes in value in relation to the preceding financial year shall be explained in the notes to the financial statements;

(e) where the offsetting of positive and negative goodwill is authorised by a Member State, the notes to the financial statements shall include an analysis of the goodwill;

(f) negative goodwill may be transferred to the consolidated profit and loss account where such a treatment is in accordance with the principles set out in Chapter 2.

4. Where shares in subsidiary undertakings included in the consolidation are held by persons other than those undertakings, the amount attributable to those shares shall be shown separately in the consolidated balance sheet as non-controlling interests.

5. The income and expenditure of undertakings included in a consolidation shall be incorporated in full in the consolidated profit and loss account.

6. The amount of any profit or loss attributable to the shares referred to in paragraph 4 shall be shown separately in the consolidated profit and loss account as the profit or loss attributable to non-controlling interests.

7. Consolidated financial statements shall show the assets, liabilities, financial positions, profits or losses of the undertakings included in a consolidation as if they were a single undertaking. In particular, the following shall be eliminated from the consolidated financial statements:

(a) debts and claims between the undertakings;

(b) income and expenditure relating to transactions between the undertakings; and

(c) profits and losses resulting from transactions between the undertakings, where they are included in the book values of assets.

8. Consolidated financial statements shall be drawn up as at the same date as the annual financial statements of the parent undertaking.

A Member State may, however, permit or require consolidated financial statements to be drawn up as at another date in order to take account of the balance sheet dates of the largest number or the most important of the undertakings included in the consolidation, provided that:

(a) that fact shall be disclosed in the notes to the consolidated financial statements and reasons given;

(b) account shall be taken, or disclosure made, of important events concerning the assets and liabilities, the financial position and the profit or loss of an undertaking included in a consolidation which have occurred between that undertaking's balance sheet date and the consolidated balance sheet date; and

(c) where an undertaking's balance sheet date precedes or follows the consolidated balance sheet date by more than three months, that undertaking shall be consolidated on the basis of interim financial statements drawn up as at the consolidated balance sheet date.

9. If the composition of the undertakings included in a consolidation has changed significantly in the course of a financial year, the consolidated financial statements shall include information which makes the comparison of successive sets of consolidated financial statements meaningful. This obligation may be fulfilled by the preparation of an adjusted comparative balance sheet and an adjusted comparative profit and loss account.

10. Assets and liabilities included in consolidated financial statements shall be measured on a uniform basis and in accordance with Chapter 2.

11. An undertaking which draws up consolidated financial statements shall apply the same measurement bases as are applied in its annual financial statements. However, Member States may permit or require that other measurement bases in accordance with Chapter 2 be used in consolidated financial statements. Where use is made of this derogation, that fact shall be disclosed in the notes to the consolidated financial statements and reasons given.

12. Where assets and liabilities included in consolidated financial statements have been measured by undertakings included in the consolidation using bases differing from those used for the purposes of the consolidation, those assets and liabilities shall be re-measured in accordance with the bases used for the consolidation. Departures from this requirement shall be permitted in exceptional cases. Any such departures shall be disclosed in the notes to the consolidated financial statements and reasons given.

13. Deferred tax balances shall be recognised on consolidation provided that it is probable that a charge to tax will arise within the foreseeable future for one of the undertakings included in the consolidation.

14. Where assets included in consolidated financial statements have been the subject of value adjustments solely for tax purposes, they shall be incorporated in the consolidated financial statements only after those adjustments have been eliminated.

[11.178]

Article 25 Business combinations within a group

1. A Member State may permit or require the book values of shares held in the capital of an undertaking included in the consolidation to be set off against the corresponding percentage of capital only, provided that the undertakings in the business combination are ultimately controlled by the same party both before and after the business combination, and that control is not transitory.

2. Any difference arising under paragraph 1 shall be added to or deducted from consolidated reserves, as appropriate.

3. The application of the method described in paragraph 1, the resulting movement in reserves and the names and registered offices of the undertakings concerned shall be disclosed in the notes to the consolidated financial statements.

[11.179]

Article 26 Proportional consolidation

1. Where an undertaking included in a consolidation manages another undertaking jointly with one or more undertakings not included in that consolidation, Member States may permit or require the inclusion of that other undertaking in the consolidated financial statements in proportion to the rights in its capital held by the undertaking included in the consolidation.

2. Article 23(9) and (10) and Article 24 shall apply mutatis mutandis to the proportional consolidation referred to in paragraph 1 of this Article.

[11.180]

Article 27 Equity accounting of associated undertakings

1. Where an undertaking included in a consolidation has an associated undertaking, that associated undertaking shall be shown in the consolidated balance sheet as a separate item with an appropriate heading.

2. When this Article is applied for the first time to an associated undertaking, that associated undertaking shall be shown in the consolidated balance sheet either:

(a) at its book value calculated in accordance with the measurement rules laid down in Chapters 2 and 3. The difference between that value and the amount corresponding to the proportion of capital and reserves represented by the participating interest in that associated undertaking shall be disclosed separately in the consolidated balance sheet or in the notes to the consolidated financial statements. That difference shall be calculated as at the date on which that method is used for the first time; or

(b) at an amount corresponding to the proportion of the associated undertaking's capital and reserves represented by the participating interest in that associated undertaking. The difference between that amount and the book value calculated in accordance with the measurement rules laid down in Chapters 2 and 3 shall be disclosed separately in the consolidated balance sheet or in the notes to the consolidated financial statements. That difference shall be calculated as at the date on which that method is used for the first time.

A Member State may prescribe the application of one or other of the options provided for in points (a) and (b). In such cases, the consolidated balance sheet or the notes to the consolidated financial statements shall indicate which of those options has been used.

In addition, for the purposes of points (a) and (b), a Member State may permit or require the calculation of the difference as at the date of acquisition of the shares or, where they were acquired in two or more stages, as at the date on which the undertaking became an associated undertaking.

3. Where an associated undertaking's assets or liabilities have been valued by methods other than those used for consolidation in accordance with Article 24(11), they may, for the purpose of calculating the difference referred to in points (a) and (b) of paragraph 2, be revalued by the methods used for consolidation. Where such revaluation has not been carried out, that fact shall be disclosed in the notes to the consolidated financial statements. A Member State may require such revaluation.

4. The book value referred to in point (a) of paragraph 2, or the amount corresponding to the proportion of the associated undertaking's capital and reserves referred to in point (b) of paragraph 2, shall be increased or reduced by the amount of any variation which has taken place during the financial year in the proportion of the associated undertaking's capital and reserves represented by that participating interest; it shall be reduced by the amount of the dividends relating to that participating interest.

5. In so far as the positive difference referred to in points (a) and (b) of paragraph 2 cannot be related to any category of assets or liabilities, it shall be treated in accordance with the rules applicable to the item 'goodwill' as set out in point (d) of Article 12(6), the first subparagraph of Article 12(11), point (c) of Article 24(3), and Annex III and Annex IV.

6. The proportion of the profit or loss of the associated undertakings attributable to the participating interests in such associated undertakings shall be shown in the consolidated profit and loss account as a separate item under an appropriate heading.

7. The eliminations referred to in Article 24(7) shall be effected in so far as the facts are known or can be ascertained.

8. Where an associated undertaking draws up consolidated financial statements, paragraphs 1 to 7 shall apply to the capital and reserves shown in such consolidated financial statements.

9. This Article need not be applied where the participating interest in the capital of the associated undertaking is not material.

[11.181]

Article 28 The notes to the consolidated financial statements

1. The notes to the consolidated financial statements shall set out the information required by Articles 16, 17 and 18, in addition to any other information required under other provisions of this Directive, in a way which facilitates the assessment of the financial position of the undertakings included in the consolidation taken as a whole, taking account of the essential adjustments resulting from the particular characteristics of consolidated financial statements as compared to annual financial statements, including the following:

(a) in disclosing transactions between related parties, transactions between related parties included in a consolidation that are eliminated on consolidation shall not be included;

(b) in disclosing the average number of employees employed during the financial year, there shall be separate disclosure of the average number of employees employed by undertakings that are proportionately consolidated; and

(c) in disclosing the amounts of emoluments and advances and credits granted to members of the administrative, managerial and supervisory bodies, only amounts granted by the parent undertaking and its subsidiary undertakings to members of the administrative, managerial and supervisory bodies of the parent undertaking shall be disclosed.

2. The notes to the consolidated financial statements shall, in addition to the information required under paragraph 1, set out the following information:

(a) in relation to undertakings included in the consolidation:

(i) the names and registered offices of those undertakings,

(ii) the proportion of the capital held in those undertakings, other than the parent undertaking, by the undertakings included in the consolidation or by persons acting in their own names but on behalf of those undertakings, and

(iii) information as to which of the conditions referred to in Article 22(1), (2) and (7) following the application of Article 22(3), (4) and (5) has formed the basis on which the consolidation has been carried out. That disclosure may, however, be omitted where consolidation has been carried out on the basis of point (a) of Article 22(1) and where the proportion of the capital and the proportion of the voting rights held are the same.

The same information shall be given in respect of undertakings excluded from a consolidation on the grounds of immateriality pursuant to point (j) of Article 6(1) and Article 23(10), and an explanation shall be given for the exclusion of the undertakings referred to in Article 23(9);

(b) the names and registered offices of associated undertakings included in the consolidation as described in Article 27(1) and the proportion of their capital held by undertakings included in the consolidation or by persons acting in their own names but on behalf of those undertakings;

(c) the names and registered offices of undertakings proportionally consolidated under Article 26, the factors on which joint management of those undertakings is based, and the proportion of their capital held by the undertakings included in the consolidation or by persons acting in their own names but on behalf of those undertakings; and

(d) in relation to each of the undertakings, other than those referred to in points (a), (b) and (c), in which undertakings included in the consolidation, either themselves or through persons acting in their own names but on behalf of those undertakings, hold a participating interest:

(i) the name and registered office of those undertakings,

(ii) the proportion of the capital held,

(iii) the amount of the capital and reserves, and the profit or loss for the latest financial year of the undertaking concerned for which financial statements have been adopted.

The information concerning capital and reserves and the profit or loss may also be omitted where the undertaking concerned does not publish its balance sheet.

3. Member States may allow the information required by points (a) to (d) of paragraph 2 to take the form of a statement filed in accordance with Article 3(3) of Directive 2009/101/EC. The filing of such a statement shall be disclosed in the notes to the consolidated financial statements. Member States may also allow that information to be omitted when its nature is such that its disclosure would be seriously prejudicial to any of the undertakings to which it relates. Member States may make such omissions subject to prior administrative or judicial authorisation. Any such omission shall be disclosed in the notes to the consolidated financial statements.

[11.182]

Article 29 The consolidated management report

1. The consolidated management report shall, as a minimum, in addition to any other information required under other provisions of this Directive, set out the information required by Articles 19 and 20, taking account of the essential adjustments resulting from the particular characteristics of a consolidated management report as compared to a management report in a way which facilitates the assessment of the position of the undertakings included in the consolidation taken as a whole.

2. The following adjustments to the information required by Articles 19 and 20 shall apply:

(a) in reporting details of own shares acquired, the consolidated management report shall indicate the number and nominal value or, in the absence of a nominal value, the accounting par value of all of the parent undertaking's shares held by that parent undertaking, by subsidiary undertakings of that parent undertaking or by a person acting in his own name but on behalf of any of those undertakings. A Member State may permit or require the disclosure of those particulars in the notes to the consolidated financial statements;

(b) in reporting on internal control and risk management systems, the corporate governance statement shall refer to the main features of the internal controls and risk management systems for the undertakings included in the consolidation, taken as a whole.

3. Where a consolidated management report is required in addition to the management report, the two reports may be presented as a single report.

[11.183]

[Article 29a Consolidated non-financial statement

1. Public-interest entities which are parent undertakings of a large group exceeding on its balance sheet dates, on a consolidated basis, the criterion of the average number of 500 employees during the financial year shall include in the consolidated management report a consolidated non-financial statement containing information to the extent necessary for an understanding of the group's development, performance, position and impact of its activity, relating to, as a minimum, environmental, social and employee matters, respect for human rights, anti-corruption and bribery matters, including:

(a) a brief description of the group's business model;

(b) a description of the policies pursued by the group in relation to those matters, including due diligence processes implemented;

(c) the outcome of those policies;

(d) the principal risks related to those matters linked to the group's operations including, where relevant and proportionate, its business relationships, products or services which are likely to cause adverse impacts in those areas, and how the group manages those risks;

(e) non-financial key performance indicators relevant to the particular business.

Where the group does not pursue policies in relation to one or more of those matters, the consolidated non-financial statement shall provide a clear and reasoned explanation for not doing so.

The consolidated non-financial statement referred to in the first subparagraph shall also, where appropriate, include references to, and additional explanations of, amounts reported in the consolidated financial statements.

Member States may allow information relating to impending developments or matters in the course of negotiation to be omitted in exceptional cases where, in the duly justified opinion of the members of the administrative, management and supervisory bodies, acting within the competences assigned to them by national law and having collective responsibility for that opinion, the disclosure of such information would be seriously prejudicial to the commercial position of the group, provided that such omission does not prevent a fair and balanced understanding of the group's development, performance, position and impact of its activity

In requiring the disclosure of the information referred to in the first subparagraph, Member States shall provide that the parent undertaking may rely on national, Union-based or international frameworks, and if it does so, the parent undertaking shall specify which frameworks it has relied upon.

2. A parent undertaking fulfilling the obligation set out in paragraph 1 shall be deemed to have fulfilled the obligation relating to the analysis of non-financial information set out in the third subparagraph of Article 19(1) and in Article 29.

3. A parent undertaking which is also a subsidiary undertaking shall be exempted from the obligation set out in paragraph 1 if that exempted parent undertaking and its subsidiaries are included in the consolidated management report or the separate report of another undertaking, drawn up in accordance with Article 29 and this Article.

4. Where a parent undertaking prepares a separate report corresponding to the same financial year, referring to the whole group, whether or not relying on national, Union-based or international frameworks and covering the information required for the consolidated non-financial statement as provided for in paragraph 1, Member States may exempt that parent undertaking from the obligation to prepare the consolidated non-financial statement laid down in paragraph 1, provided that such separate report:

(a) is published together with the consolidated management report in accordance with Article 30; or

(b) is made publicly available within a reasonable period of time, not exceeding six months after the balance sheet date, on the parent undertaking's website, and is referred to in the consolidated management report.

Paragraph 2 shall apply *mutatis mutandis* to parent undertakings preparing a separate report as referred to in the first subparagraph of this paragraph.

5. Member States shall ensure that the statutory auditor or audit firm checks whether the consolidated non-financial statement referred to in paragraph 1 or the separate report referred to in paragraph 4 has been provided.

6. Member States may require that the information in the consolidated non-financial statement referred to in paragraph 1 or in the separate report referred to in paragraph 4 be verified by an independent assurance services provider.]

NOTES

Inserted by European Parliament and Council Directive 2014/95/EU, Art 1(3), as from 5 December 2014.

CHAPTER 7 PUBLICATION

[11.184]

Article 30 General publication requirement

1. Member States shall ensure that undertakings publish within a reasonable period of time, which shall not exceed 12 months after the balance sheet date, the duly approved annual financial statements and the management report, together with the opinion submitted by the statutory auditor or audit firm referred to in Article 34 of this Directive, as laid down by the laws of each Member State in accordance with Chapter 2 of Directive 2009/101/EC.

Member States may, however, exempt undertakings from the obligation to publish the management report where a copy of all or part of any such report can be easily obtained upon request at a price not exceeding its administrative cost.

2. Member States may exempt an undertaking referred to in Annex II to which the coordination measures prescribed by this Directive apply by virtue of point (b) of Article 1(1) from publishing its financial statements in accordance with Article 3 of Directive 2009/101/EC, provided that those financial statements are available to the public at its head office, in the following cases:

(a) all the members of the undertaking concerned that have unlimited liability are undertakings referred to in Annex I governed by the laws of Member States other than the Member State whose law governs that undertaking, and none of those undertakings publishes the financial statements of the undertaking concerned with its own financial statements;

(b) all the members of the undertaking concerned that have unlimited liability are undertakings which are not governed by the laws of a Member State but which have a legal form comparable to those referred to in Directive 2009/101/EC.

Copies of the financial statements shall be obtainable upon request. The price of such a copy may not exceed its administrative cost.

3. Paragraph 1 shall apply with respect to consolidated financial statements and consolidated management reports. Where the undertaking drawing up the consolidated financial statements is established as one of the types of undertaking listed in Annex II and is not required by the national law of its Member State to publish the documents referred to in paragraph 1 in the same manner as prescribed in Article 3 of Directive 2009/101/EC, it shall, as a minimum, make those documents available to the public at its head office and a copy shall be provided upon request, the price of which shall not exceed its administrative cost.

[11.185]

Article 31 Simplifications for small and medium-sized undertakings

1. Member States may exempt small undertakings from the obligation to publish their profit and loss accounts and management reports.

2. Member States may permit medium-sized undertakings to publish:

(a) abridged balance sheets showing only those items preceded by letters and roman numerals in Annexes III and IV and disclosing separately, either in the balance sheet or in the notes to the financial statements:

(i) C (I) (3), C (II) (1), (2), (3) and (4), C (III) (1), (2), (3) and (4), D (II) (2), (3) and (6) and D (III) (1) and (2) under 'Assets' and C, (1), (2), (6), (7) and (9) under 'Capital, reserves and liabilities' in Annex III,

(ii) C (I) (3), C (II) (1), (2), (3) and (4), C (III) (1), (2), (3) and (4), D (II) (2), (3) and (6), D (III) (1) and (2), F (1), (2), (6), (7) and (9) and (I) (1), (2), (6), (7) and (9) in Annex IV,

(iii) the information required as indicated in brackets in D (II) under 'Assets' and C under 'Capital, reserves and liabilities' in Annex III, in total for all the items concerned and separately for D (II) (2) and (3) under 'Assets' and C (1), (2), (6), (7) and (9) under 'Capital, reserves and liabilities',

(iv) the information required as indicated in brackets in D (II) in Annex IV, in total for all the items concerned, and separately for D (II) (2) and (3);

(b) abridged notes to their financial statements without the information required in points (f) and (j) of Article 17(1).

This paragraph shall be without prejudice to Article 30(1), in so far as that Article relates to the profit and loss account, the management report and the opinion of the statutory auditor or audit firm.

[11.186]

Article 32 Other publication requirements

1. Where the annual financial statements and the management report are published in full, they shall be reproduced in the form and text on the basis of which the statutory auditor or audit firm has drawn up his/her/its opinion. They shall be accompanied by the full text of the audit report.

2. If the annual financial statements are not published in full, the abridged version of those financial statements, which shall not be accompanied by the audit report, shall:

(a) indicate that the version published is abridged;

(b) refer to the register in which the financial statements have been filed in accordance with Article 3 of Directive 2009/101/EC or, where the financial statements have not yet been filed, disclose that fact;

(c) disclose whether an unqualified, qualified or adverse audit opinion was expressed by the statutory auditor or audit firm, or whether the statutory auditor or audit firm was unable to express an audit opinion;

(d) disclose whether the audit report included a reference to any matters to which the statutory auditor or audit firm drew attention by way of emphasis without qualifying the audit opinion.

[11.187]

Article 33 Responsibility and liability for drawing up and publishing the financial statements and the management report

[1. Member States shall ensure that the members of the administrative, management and supervisory bodies of an undertaking, acting within the competences assigned to them by national law, have collective responsibility for ensuring that:

(a) the annual financial statements, the management report, the corporate governance statement when provided separately and the report referred to in Article 19a(4); and

(b) the consolidated financial statements, the consolidated management reports, the consolidated corporate governance statement when provided separately and the report referred to in Article 29a(4),

are drawn up and published in accordance with the requirements of this Directive and, where applicable, with the international accounting standards adopted in accordance with Regulation (EC) No 1606/2002.']

2. Member States shall ensure that their laws, regulations and administrative provisions on liability, at least towards the undertaking, apply to the members of the administrative, management and supervisory bodies of the undertakings for breach of the duties referred to in paragraph 1.

NOTES

Para 1: substituted by European Parliament and Council Directive 2014/95/EU, Art 1(4), as from 5 December 2014.

CHAPTER 8 AUDITING

[11.188]

Article 34 General requirement

1. Member States shall ensure that the financial statements of public-interest entities, medium-sized and large undertakings are audited by one or more statutory auditors or audit firms approved by Member States to carry out statutory audits on the basis of Directive 2006/43/EC.

The statutory auditor(s) or audit firm(s) shall also:

(a) express an opinion on:

(i) whether the management report is consistent with the financial statements for the same financial year, and

(ii) whether the management report has been prepared in accordance with the applicable legal requirements;

(b) state whether, in the light of the knowledge and understanding of the undertaking and its environment obtained in the course of the audit, he, she or it has identified material misstatements in the management report, and shall give an indication of the nature of any such misstatements.

2. The first subparagraph of paragraph 1 shall apply mutatis mutandis with respect to consolidated financial statements. The second subparagraph of paragraph 1 shall apply mutatis mutandis with respect to consolidated financial statements and consolidated management reports.

[3. This Article shall not apply to the non-financial statement referred to in Article 19a(1) and the consolidated non-financial statement referred to in Article 29a(1) or to the separate reports referred to in Articles 19a(4) and 29a(4).]

NOTES

Para 3: added by European Parliament and Council Directive 2014/95/EU, Art 1(5), as from 5 December 2014.

Article 35 Amendment of Directive 2006/43/EC as regards the audit report

(*This Article substitutes Directive 2006/43/EC, Article 28.*)

CHAPTER 9 PROVISIONS CONCERNING EXEMPTIONS AND RESTRICTIONS ON EXEMPTIONS

[11.189]

Article 36 Exemptions for micro-undertakings

1. Member States may exempt micro-undertakings from any or all of the following obligations:
   (a) the obligation to present 'Prepayments and accrued income' and 'Accruals and deferred income'. Where a Member State makes use of that option, it may permit those undertakings, only in respect of other charges as referred to in point (b)(vi) of paragraph 2 of this Article, to depart from point (d) of Article 6(1) with regard to the recognition of 'Prepayments and accrued income' and 'Accruals and deferred income', provided that this fact is disclosed in the notes to the financial statements or, in accordance with point (b) of this paragraph, at the foot of the balance sheet;
   (b) the obligation to draw up notes to the financial statements in accordance with Article 16, provided that the information required by points (d) and (e) of Article 16(1) of this Directive and by Article 24(2) of Directive 2012/30/EU is disclosed at the foot of the balance sheet;
   (c) the obligation to prepare a management report in accordance with Chapter 5, provided that the information required by Article 24(2) of Directive 2012/30/EU is disclosed in the notes to the financial statements or, in accordance with point (b) of this paragraph, at the foot of the balance sheet;
   (d) the obligation to publish annual financial statements in accordance with Chapter 7 of this Directive, provided that the balance sheet information contained therein is duly filed, in accordance with national law, with at least one competent authority designated by the Member State concerned. Whenever the competent authority is not the central register, commercial register or companies register, as referred to in Article 3(1) of Directive 2009/101/EC, the competent authority is required to provide the register with the information filed.
2. Member States may permit micro-undertakings:
   (a) to draw up only an abridged balance sheet showing separately at least those items preceded by letters in Annexes III or IV, where applicable. In cases where point (a) of paragraph 1 of this Article applies, items E under 'Assets' and D under 'Liabilities' in Annex III or items E and K in Annex IV shall be excluded from the balance sheet;
   (b) to draw up only an abridged profit and loss account showing separately at least the following items, where applicable:
      (i) net turnover,
      (ii) other income,
      (iii) cost of raw materials and consumables,
      (iv) staff costs,
      (v) value adjustments,
      (vi) other charges,
      (vii) tax,
      (viii) profit or loss.
3. Member States shall not permit or require the application of Article 8 to any micro-undertaking making use of any of the exemptions provided for in paragraphs 1 and 2 of this Article.
4. In respect of micro-undertakings, annual financial statements drawn up in accordance with paragraphs 1, 2 and 3 of this Article shall be regarded as giving the true and fair view required by Article 4(3), and consequently Article 4(4) shall not apply to such financial statements.
5. If point (a) of paragraph 1 of this Article applies, the balance sheet total referred to in point (a) of Article 3(1) shall consist of the assets referred to in items A to D under 'Assets' in Annex III or items A to D in Annex IV.
6. Without prejudice to this Article, Member States shall ensure that micro-undertakings are otherwise regarded as small undertakings.
7. Member States shall not make available the derogations provided for in paragraphs 1, 2 and 3 in respect of investment undertakings or financial holding undertakings.
8. Member States which at 19 July 2013 have brought into force laws, regulations or administrative provisions in compliance with Directive 2012/6/EU of the European Parliament and of the Council of 14 March 2012 amending Council Directive 78/660/EEC on the annual accounts of certain types of companies as regards micro-entities,[1] may be exempted from the requirements set out in Article 3(9) with regard to the conversion into national currencies of thresholds set out in Article 3(1) when applying the first sentence of Article 53(1).
9. By 20 July 2018 the Commission shall submit to the European Parliament, to the Council and to the European Economic and Social Committee a report on the situation of micro-undertakings taking account, in particular, of the situation at national level regarding the number of undertakings covered by the size criteria and the reduction of administrative burdens resulting from the exemption from the publication requirement.

NOTES

[1] OJ L81, 21.3.2012, p 3.

[11.190]

Article 37 Exemption for subsidiary undertakings

Notwithstanding the provisions of Directives 2009/101/EC and 2012/30/EU, a Member State shall not be required to apply the provisions of this Directive concerning the content, auditing and publication of the annual financial statements and the management report to undertakings governed by their national laws which are subsidiary undertakings, where the following conditions are fulfilled:

(1) the parent undertaking is subject to the laws of a Member State;
(2) all shareholders or members of the subsidiary undertaking have, in respect of each financial year in which the exemption is applied, declared their agreement to the exemption from such obligation;
(3) the parent undertaking has declared that it guarantees the commitments entered into by the subsidiary undertaking;
(4) the declarations referred to in points (2) and (3) of this Article are published by the subsidiary undertaking as laid down by the laws of the Member State in accordance with Chapter 2 of Directive 2009/101/EC;

(5) the subsidiary undertaking is included in the consolidated financial statements drawn up by the parent undertaking in accordance with this Directive;

(6) the exemption is disclosed in the notes to the consolidated financial statements drawn up by the parent undertaking; and

(7) the consolidated financial statements referred to in point (5) of this Article, the consolidated management report, and the audit report are published for the subsidiary undertaking as laid down by the laws of the Member State in accordance with Chapter 2 of Directive 2009/101/EC.

[11.191]

Article 38 Undertakings which are members having unlimited liability of other undertakings

1. Member States may require undertakings referred to in point (a) of Article 1(1) which are governed by their laws and which are members having unlimited liability of any undertaking referred to in point (b) of Article 1(1) ('the undertaking concerned'), to draw up, have audited and publish, with their own financial statements, the financial statements of the undertaking concerned in accordance with this Directive; in such case the requirements of this Directive shall not apply to the undertaking concerned.

2. Member States shall not be required to apply the requirements of this Directive to the undertaking concerned where:

(a) the financial statements of the undertaking concerned are drawn up, audited and published in accordance with the provisions of this Directive by an undertaking which:
   (i) is a member having unlimited liability of that undertaking concerned, and
   (ii) is governed by the laws of another Member State;

(b) the undertaking concerned is included in consolidated financial statements drawn up, audited and published in accordance with this Directive by:
   (i) a member having unlimited liability, or
   (ii) where the undertaking concerned is included in the consolidated financial statements of a larger body of undertakings drawn up, audited and published in conformity with this Directive, a parent undertaking governed by the laws of a Member State. This exemption shall be disclosed in the notes to the consolidated financial statements.

3. In the cases referred to in paragraph 2, the undertaking concerned shall, upon request, reveal the name of the undertaking publishing the financial statements.

[11.192]

Article 39 Profit and loss account exemption for parent undertakings preparing consolidated financial statements

A Member State shall not be required to apply the provisions of this Directive concerning the auditing and publication of the profit and loss account to undertakings governed by its national laws which are parent undertakings, provided that the following conditions are fulfilled:

(1) the parent undertaking draws up consolidated financial statements in accordance with this Directive and is included in those consolidated financial statements;

(2) the exemption is disclosed in the notes to the annual financial statements of the parent undertaking;

(3) the exemption is disclosed in the notes to the consolidated financial statements drawn up by the parent undertaking; and

(4) the profit or loss of the parent undertaking, determined in accordance with this Directive, is shown in its balance sheet.

[11.193]

Article 40 Restriction of exemptions for public-interest entities

Unless expressly provided for in this Directive, Member States shall not make the simplifications and exemptions set out in this Directive available to public-interest entities. A public-interest entity shall be treated as a large undertaking regardless of its net turnover, balance sheet total or average number of employees during the financial year.

CHAPTER 10 REPORT ON PAYMENTS TO GOVERNMENTS

[11.194]

Article 41 Definitions relating to reporting on payments to governments

For the purpose of this Chapter, the following definitions shall apply:

(1) 'undertaking active in the extractive industry' means an undertaking with any activity involving the exploration, prospection, discovery, development, and extraction of minerals, oil, natural gas deposits or other materials, within the economic activities listed in Section B, Divisions 05 to 08 of Annex I to Regulation (EC) No 1893/2006 of the European Parliament and of the Council of 20 December 2006 establishing the statistical classification of economic activities NACE Revision 2;[1]

(2) 'undertaking active in the logging of primary forests' means an undertaking with activities as referred to in Section A, Division 02, Group 02.2 of Annex I to Regulation (EC) No 1893/2006, in primary forests;

(3) 'government' means any national, regional or local authority of a Member State or of a third country. It includes a department, agency or undertaking controlled by that authority as laid down in Article 22(1) to (6) of this Directive;

(4) 'project' means the operational activities that are governed by a single contract, license, lease, concession or similar legal agreements and form the basis for payment liabilities with a government. None the less, if multiple such agreements are substantially interconnected, this shall be considered a project;

(5) 'payment' means an amount paid, whether in money or in kind, for activities, as described in points 1 and 2, of the following types:
   (a) production entitlements;
   (b) taxes levied on the income, production or profits of companies, excluding taxes levied on consumption such as value added taxes, personal income taxes or sales taxes;
   (c) royalties;

(d) dividends;
(e) signature, discovery and production bonuses;
(f) licence fees, rental fees, entry fees and other considerations for licences and/or concessions; and
(g) payments for infrastructure improvements.

NOTES

[1] OJ L393, 30.12.2006, p 1.

[11.195]
Article 42 Undertakings required to report on payments to governments

1. Member States shall require large undertakings and all public-interest entities active in the extractive industry or the logging of primary forests to prepare and make public a report on payments made to governments on an annual basis.

2. That obligation shall not apply to any undertaking governed by the law of a Member State which is a subsidiary or parent undertaking, where both of the following conditions are fulfilled:

(a) the parent undertaking is subject to the laws of a Member State; and
(b) the payments to governments made by the undertaking are included in the consolidated report on payments to governments drawn up by that parent undertaking in accordance with Article 44.

[11.196]
Article 43 Content of the report

1. Any payment, whether made as a single payment or as a series of related payments, need not be taken into account in the report if it is below EUR 100,000 within a financial year.

2. The report shall disclose the following information in relation to activities as described in points (1) and (2) of Article 41 in respect of the relevant financial year:

(a) the total amount of payments made to each government;
(b) the total amount per type of payment as specified in points (5)(a) to (g) of Article 41 made to each government;
(c) where those payments have been attributed to a specific project, the total amount per type of payment as specified in point (5)(a) to (g) of Article 41, made for each such project and the total amount of payments for each such project.

Payments made by the undertaking in respect of obligations imposed at entity level may be disclosed at the entity level rather than at project level.

3. Where payments in kind are made to a government, they shall be reported in value and, where applicable, in volume. Supporting notes shall be provided to explain how their value has been determined.

4. The disclosure of the payments referred to in this Article shall reflect the substance, rather than the form, of the payment or activity concerned. Payments and activities may not be artificially split or aggregated to avoid the application of this Directive.

5. In the case of those Member States which have not adopted the euro, the euro threshold identified in paragraph 1 shall be converted into national currency by:

(a) applying the exchange rate published in the *Official Journal of the European Union* as at the date of the entry into force of any Directive fixing that threshold, and
(b) rounding to the nearest hundred.

[11.197]
Article 44 Consolidated report on payments to governments

1. A Member State shall require any large undertaking or any public-interest entity active in the extractive industry or the logging of primary forests and governed by its national law to draw up a consolidated report on payments to governments in accordance with Articles 42 and 43 if that parent undertaking is under the obligation to prepare consolidated financial statements as laid down in Article 22(1) to (6).

A parent undertaking is considered to be active in the extractive industry or the logging of primary forests if any of its subsidiary undertakings are active in the extractive industry or the logging of primary forests.

The consolidated report shall only include payments resulting from extractive operations and/or operations relating to the logging of primary forests.

2. The obligation to draw up the consolidated report referred to in paragraph 1 shall not apply to:

(a) a parent undertaking of a small group, as defined in Article 3(5), except where any affiliated undertaking is a public-interest entity;
(b) a parent undertaking of a medium-sized group, as defined in Article 3(6), except where any affiliated undertaking is a public-interest entity; and
(c) a parent undertaking governed by the law of a Member State which is also a subsidiary undertaking, if its own parent undertaking is governed by the law of a Member State.

3. An undertaking, including a public-interest entity, need not be included in a consolidated report on payments to governments where at least one of the following conditions is fulfilled:

(a) severe long-term restrictions substantially hinder the parent undertaking in the exercise of its rights over the assets or management of that undertaking;
(b) extremely rare cases where the information necessary for the preparation of the consolidated report on payments to governments in accordance with this Directive cannot be obtained without disproportionate expense or undue delay;
(c) the shares of that undertaking are held exclusively with a view to their subsequent resale.

The above exemptions shall apply only if they are also used for the purposes of the consolidated financial statements.

[11.198]

Article 45 Publication

1. The report referred to in Article 42 and the consolidated report referred to in Article 44 on payments to governments shall be published as laid down by the laws of each Member State in accordance with Chapter 2 of Directive 2009/101/EC.

2. Member States shall ensure that the members of the responsible bodies of an undertaking, acting within the competences assigned to them by national law, have responsibility for ensuring that, to the best of their knowledge and ability, the report on payments to governments is drawn up and published in accordance with the requirements of this Directive.

[11.199]

Article 46 Equivalence criteria

1. Undertakings referred to in Articles 42 and 44 that prepare and make public a report complying with third-country reporting requirements assessed, in accordance with Article 47, as equivalent to the requirements of this Chapter are exempt from the requirements of this Chapter except for the obligation to publish this report as laid down by the laws of each Member State in accordance with Chapter 2 of Directive 2009/101/EC.

2. The Commission shall be empowered to adopt delegated acts in accordance with Article 49 identifying the criteria to be applied when assessing, for the purposes of paragraph 1 of this Article, the equivalence of third-country reporting requirements and the requirements of this Chapter.

3. The criteria identified by the Commission in accordance with paragraph 2 shall:

(a) include the following:

(i) target undertakings,
(ii) target recipients of payments,
(iii) payments captured,
(iv) attribution of payments captured,
(v) breakdown of payments captured,
(vi) triggers for reporting on a consolidated basis,
(vii) reporting medium,
(viii) frequency of reporting, and
(ix) anti-evasion measures;

(b) otherwise be limited to criteria which facilitate a direct comparison of third-country reporting requirements with the requirements of this Chapter.

[11.200]

Article 47 Application of equivalence criteria

The Commission shall be empowered to adopt implementing acts identifying those third-country reporting requirements which, after applying the equivalence criteria identified in accordance with Article 46, it considers equivalent to the requirements of this Chapter. Those implementing acts shall be adopted in accordance with the examination procedure referred to in Article 50(2).

[11.201]

Article 48 Review

The Commission shall review and report on the implementation and effectiveness of this Chapter, in particular as regards the scope of, and compliance with, the reporting obligations and the modalities of the reporting on a project basis.

The review shall take into account international developments, in particular with regard to enhancing transparency of payments to governments, assess the impacts of other international regimes and consider the effects on competitiveness and security of energy supply. It shall be completed by 21 July 2018.

The report shall be submitted to the European Parliament and to the Council, together with a legislative proposal, if appropriate. That report shall consider the extension of the reporting requirements to additional industry sectors and whether the report on payments to governments should be audited. The report shall also consider the disclosure of additional information on the average number of employees, the use of subcontractors and any pecuniary penalties administered by a country.

[The report shall also consider, taking into account developments in the OECD and the results of related European initiatives, the possibility of introducing an obligation requiring large undertakings to produce on an annual basis a country-by-country report for each Member State and third country in which they operate, containing information on, as a minimum, profits made, taxes paid on profits and public subsidies received.]

In addition, the report shall analyse the feasibility of the introduction of an obligation for all Union issuers to carry out due diligence when sourcing minerals to ensure that supply chains have no connection to conflict parties and respect the EITI and OECD recommendations on responsible supply chain management.

NOTES

The penultimate paragraph was inserted by European Parliament and Council Directive 2014/95/EU, Art 1(6), as from 5 December 2014.

[CHAPTER 10A REPORT ON INCOME TAX INFORMATION

[11.202]

Article 48a Definitions relating to reporting on income tax information

1. For the purposes of this Chapter, the following definitions apply:

(1) "ultimate parent undertaking" means an undertaking which draws up the consolidated financial statements of the largest body of undertakings;

(2) "consolidated financial statements" means the financial statements prepared by a parent undertaking of a group, in which the assets, liabilities, equity, income and expenses are presented as those of a single economic entity;

(3) "tax jurisdiction" means a State or non-State jurisdiction which has fiscal autonomy in respect of corporate income tax;

(4) "standalone undertaking" means an undertaking which is not part of a group as defined in Article 2, point (11).

2. For the purposes of Article 48b of this Directive, "revenue" has the same meaning as:

(a) "net turnover", for undertakings governed by the law of a Member State that do not apply international accounting standards adopted on the basis of Regulation (EC) No 1606/2002; or

(b) "revenue" as defined by or within the meaning of the financial reporting framework on the basis of which the financial statements are prepared, for other undertakings.]

NOTES

Chapter 10a (Articles 48a–48h) was inserted by European Parliament and Council Directive 2021/2101/EU, Art 1(2), as from 21 December 2021; note that the 2021 Directive has a transposition date of 22 June 2023.

[11.203]

[Article 48b Undertakings and branches required to report on income tax information

1. Member States shall require ultimate parent undertakings governed by their national laws, where the consolidated revenue on their balance sheet date exceeded for each of the last two consecutive financial years a total of EUR 750,000,000, as reflected in their consolidated financial statements, to draw up, publish and make accessible a report on income tax information as regards the latter of those two consecutive financial years.

Member States shall provide for an ultimate parent undertaking to no longer be subject to the reporting obligations set out in the first subparagraph where the total consolidated revenue on its balance sheet date falls below EUR 750,000,000 for each of the last two consecutive financial years as reflected in its consolidated financial statements.

Member States shall require standalone undertakings governed by their national laws, where the revenue on their balance sheet date exceeded for each of the last two consecutive financial years a total of EUR 750,000,000, as reflected in their annual financial statements, to draw up, publish and make accessible a report on income tax information as regards the latter of those two consecutive financial years.

Member States shall provide for a standalone undertaking to no longer be subject to the reporting obligations set out in the third subparagraph where the total revenue on its balance sheet date falls below EUR 750,000,000 for each of the last two consecutive financial years as reflected in its financial statements.

2. Member States shall provide that the rule set out in paragraph 1 does not apply to standalone undertakings or ultimate parent undertakings and their affiliated undertakings where such undertakings, including their branches, are established, or have their fixed places of business or permanent business activity, within the territory of a single Member State and no other tax jurisdiction.

3. Member States shall provide that the rule set out in paragraph 1 of this Article does not apply to standalone undertakings and ultimate parent undertakings where such undertakings or their affiliated undertakings disclose a report, in accordance with Article 89 of Directive 2013/36/EU of the European Parliament and of the Council,[1] that encompasses information on all of their activities and, in the case of ultimate parent undertakings, on all the activities of all the affiliated undertakings included in the consolidated financial statements.

4. Member States shall require medium-sized and large subsidiary undertakings as referred to in Article 3(3) and (4) that are governed by their national laws and controlled by an ultimate parent undertaking that is not governed by the law of a Member State, where the consolidated revenue on its balance sheet date exceeded for each of the last two consecutive financial years a total of EUR 750,000,000, as reflected in its consolidated financial statements, to publish and make accessible a report on income tax information concerning that ultimate parent undertaking as regards the latter of those two consecutive financial years.

Where that information or report is not available, the subsidiary undertaking shall request its ultimate parent undertaking to provide it with all information required to enable it to meet its obligations under the first subparagraph. If the ultimate parent undertaking does not provide all the required information, the subsidiary undertaking shall draw up, publish and make accessible a report on income tax information containing all information in its possession, obtained or acquired, and a statement indicating that its ultimate parent undertaking did not make the necessary information available.

Member States shall provide for medium-sized and large subsidiary undertakings to no longer be subject to the reporting obligations set out in this paragraph where the total consolidated revenue of the ultimate parent undertaking on its balance sheet date falls below EUR 750,000,000 for each of the last two consecutive financial years as reflected in its consolidated financial statements.

5. Member States shall require branches opened in their territories by undertakings that are not governed by the law of a Member State to publish and make accessible a report on income tax information concerning the ultimate parent undertaking or the standalone undertaking referred to in the sixth subparagraph, point (a), as regards the latter of the last two consecutive financial years.

Where that information or report is not available, the person or persons designated to carry out the disclosure formalities referred to in Article 48e(2) shall request the ultimate parent undertaking or the standalone undertaking referred to in the sixth subparagraph, point (a), of this paragraph to provide them with all information necessary to enable them to meet their obligations.

In the event that not all the required information is provided, the branch shall draw up, publish and make accessible a report on income tax information, containing all information in its possession, obtained or acquired, and a statement indicating that the ultimate parent undertaking or the standalone undertaking did not make the necessary information available.

Member States shall provide for the reporting obligations set out in this paragraph to apply only to branches which have a net turnover that exceeded the threshold as transposed pursuant to Article 3(2) for each of the last two consecutive financial years.

Member States shall provide for a branch subject to the reporting obligations under this paragraph to no longer be subject to those obligations where its net turnover falls below the threshold as transposed pursuant to Article 3(2) for each of the last two consecutive financial years.

Part 11 EU & Retained EU Legislation

Member States shall provide that the rules set out in this paragraph apply to a branch only where the following criteria are met:

(a) the undertaking that opened the branch is either an affiliated undertaking of a group whose ultimate parent undertaking is not governed by the law of a Member State and the consolidated revenue of which on its balance sheet date exceeded for each of the last two consecutive financial years a total of EUR 750,000,000, as reflected in its consolidated financial statements, or a standalone undertaking the revenue of which on its balance sheet date exceeded for each of the last two consecutive financial years a total of EUR 750,000,000 as reflected in its financial statements; and

(b) the ultimate parent undertaking referred to in point (a) of this subparagraph does not have a medium-sized or large subsidiary undertaking as referred to in paragraph 4.

Member States shall provide for a branch to no longer be subject to the reporting obligations set out in this paragraph where the criterion provided for in point (a) ceases to be met for two consecutive financial years.

6. Member States shall not apply the rules set out in paragraphs 4 and 5 of this Article where a report on income tax information is drawn up by an ultimate parent undertaking or standalone undertaking that is not governed by the law of a Member State, in a manner that is consistent with Article 48c, and meets the following criteria:

(a) it is made accessible to the public, free of charge and in an electronic reporting format which is machine-readable:
   (i) on the website of that ultimate parent undertaking or of that standalone undertaking;
   (ii) in at least one of the official languages of the Union;
   (iii) no later than 12 months after the balance sheet date of the financial year for which the report is drawn up; and

(b) it identifies the name and the registered office of a single subsidiary undertaking, or the name and the address of a single branch governed by the law of a Member State, which has published a report in accordance with Article 48d(1).

7. Member States shall require subsidiary undertakings or branches not subject to the provisions of paragraphs 4 and 5 of this Article to publish and make accessible a report on income tax information where such subsidiary undertakings or branches serve no other objective than to circumvent the reporting requirements set out in this Chapter.]

NOTES

Chapter 10a (Articles 48a–48h) was inserted by European Parliament and Council Directive 2021/2101/EU, Art 1(2), as from 21 December 2021; note that the 2021 Directive has a transposition date of 22 June 2023.

[1] Directive 2013/36/EU of the European Parliament and of the Council of 26 June 2013 on access to the activity of credit institutions and the prudential supervision of credit institutions, amending Directive 2002/87/EC and repealing Directives 2006/48/EC and 2006/49/EC (OJ L176, 27.6.2013, p 338).

[11.204]

[Article 48c Content of the report on income tax information

1. The report on income tax information required under Article 48b shall include information relating to all the activities of the standalone undertaking or ultimate parent undertaking, including those of all affiliated undertakings consolidated in the financial statements in respect of the relevant financial year.

2. The information referred to in paragraph 1 shall consist of:

(a) the name of the ultimate parent undertaking or the standalone undertaking, the financial year concerned, the currency used for the presentation of the report and, where applicable, a list of all subsidiary undertakings consolidated in the financial statements of the ultimate parent undertaking, in respect of the relevant financial year, established in the Union or in tax jurisdictions included in Annexes I and II to the Council conclusions on the revised EU list of non-cooperative jurisdictions for tax purposes;

(b) a brief description of the nature of their activities;

(c) the number of employees on a full-time equivalent basis;

(d) revenues, which are to be calculated as:
   (i) the sum of the net turnover, other operating income, income from participating interests, excluding dividends received from affiliated undertakings, income from other investments and loans forming part of the fixed assets, other interest receivable and similar income as listed in Annexes V and VI to this Directive; or
   (ii) the income as defined by the financial reporting framework on the basis of which the financial statements are prepared, excluding value adjustments and dividends received from affiliated undertakings;

(e) the amount of profit or loss before income tax;

(f) the amount of income tax accrued during the relevant financial year, which is to be calculated as the current tax expense recognised on taxable profits or losses of the financial year by undertakings and branches in the relevant tax jurisdiction;

(g) the amount of income tax paid on a cash basis, which is to be calculated as the amount of income tax paid during the relevant financial year by undertakings and branches in the relevant tax jurisdiction; and

(h) the amount of accumulated earnings at the end of the relevant financial year.

For the purposes of point (d), the revenues shall include transactions with related parties.

For the purposes of point (f), the current tax expense shall relate only to the activities of an undertaking in the relevant financial year and shall not include deferred taxes or provisions for uncertain tax liabilities.

For the purposes of point (g), taxes paid shall include withholding taxes paid by other undertakings with respect to payments to undertakings and branches within a group.

For the purposes of point (h), the accumulated earnings shall mean the sum of the profits from past financial years and the relevant financial year, the distribution of which has not yet been decided upon. With regard to branches, accumulated earnings shall be those of the undertaking which opened the branch.

3. Member States shall permit the information listed in paragraph 2 of this Article to be reported on the basis of the reporting instructions referred to in Section III, Parts B and C, of Annex III to Council Directive 2011/16/EU.[1]

4. The information referred to in paragraphs 2 and 3 of this Article shall be presented using a common template and electronic reporting formats which are machine-readable. The Commission shall, by means of implementing acts, lay down that common template and those electronic reporting formats. Those implementing acts shall be adopted in accordance with the examination procedure referred to in Article 50(2).

5. The report on income tax information shall present the information referred to in paragraph 2 or 3 separately for each Member State. Where a Member State comprises several tax jurisdictions, the information shall be aggregated at Member State level.

The report on income tax information shall also present the information referred to in paragraph 2 or 3 of this Article separately for each tax jurisdiction which, on 1 March of the financial year for which the report is to be drawn up, is listed in Annex I to the Council conclusions on the revised EU list of non-cooperative jurisdictions for tax purposes, and shall provide such information separately for each tax jurisdiction which, on 1 March of the financial year for which the report is to be drawn up and on 1 March of the preceding financial year, was mentioned in Annex II to the Council conclusions on the revised EU list of non-cooperative jurisdictions for tax purposes.

The report on income tax information shall also present the information referred to in paragraph 2 or 3 on an aggregated basis for other tax jurisdictions.

The information shall be attributed to each relevant tax jurisdiction on the basis of establishment, the existence of a fixed place of business or of a permanent business activity which, given the activities of the group or standalone undertaking, can be subject to income tax in that tax jurisdiction.

Where the activities of several affiliated undertakings can be subject to income tax within a single tax jurisdiction, the information attributed to that tax jurisdiction shall represent the sum of the information relating to such activities of each affiliated undertaking and their branches in that tax jurisdiction.

Information on any particular activity shall not be attributed simultaneously to more than one tax jurisdiction.

6. Member States may allow for one or more specific items of information otherwise required to be disclosed in accordance with paragraph 2 or 3 to be temporarily omitted from the report where their disclosure would be seriously prejudicial to the commercial position of the undertakings to which the report relates. Any omission shall be clearly indicated in the report together with a duly reasoned explanation regarding the reasons therefor.

Member States shall ensure that all information omitted pursuant to the first subparagraph is made public in a later report on income tax information, within no more than five years of the date of its original omission.

Member States shall ensure that information pertaining to tax jurisdictions included in Annexes I and II to the Council conclusions on the revised EU list of non-cooperative jurisdictions for tax purposes, as referred to in paragraph 5 of this Article, may never be omitted.

7. The report on income tax information may include, where applicable at group level, an overall narrative providing explanations for any material discrepancies between the amounts disclosed pursuant to paragraph 2, points (f) and (g), taking into account, if appropriate, corresponding amounts concerning previous financial years.

8. The currency used in the report on income tax information shall be the currency in which the consolidated financial statements of the ultimate parent undertaking or the annual financial statements of the standalone undertaking are presented. Member States shall not require this report to be published in a currency other than the currency used in the financial statements.

However, in the case mentioned in the second subparagraph of Article 48b(4), the currency used in the report on income tax information shall be the currency in which the subsidiary undertaking publishes its annual financial statements.

9. Member States that have not adopted the euro may convert the threshold of EUR 750,000,000 into their national currency. In making that conversion, those Member States shall apply the exchange rate as at 21 December 2021 published in the Official Journal of the European Union. Those Member States may increase or decrease the thresholds by up to 5% in order to produce a round sum in the national currencies.

The thresholds referred to in Article 48b(4) and (5) shall be converted to an equivalent amount in the national currency of any relevant third countries by applying the exchange rate as at 21 December 2021, rounded off to the nearest thousand.

10. The report on income tax information shall specify whether it was prepared in accordance with paragraph 2 or 3 of this Article.]

NOTES

Chapter 10a (Articles 48a–48h) was inserted by European Parliament and Council Directive 2021/2101/EU, Art 1(2), as from 21 December 2021; note that the 2021 Directive has a transposition date of 22 June 2023.

[1] Council Directive 2011/16/EU of 15 February 2011 on administrative cooperation in the field of taxation and repealing Directive 77/799/EEC (OJ L64, 11.3.2011, p 1).

[11.205]

[Article 48d Publication and accessibility

1. The report on income tax information and the statement mentioned in Article 48b of this Directive shall be published within 12 months of the balance sheet date of the financial year for which the report is drawn up as provided for by each Member State in accordance with Articles 14 to 28 of Directive (EU) 2017/1132 of the European Parliament and of the Council[1] and, where relevant, in accordance with Article 36 of Directive (EU) 2017/1132.

2. Member States shall ensure that the report on income tax information and the statement published by the undertakings in accordance with paragraph 1 of this Article are made accessible to the public in at least one of the official languages of the Union, free of charge, no later than 12 months after the balance sheet date of the financial year for which the report is drawn up, on the website of:

(a) the undertaking, where Article 48b(1) applies;
(b) the subsidiary undertaking or an affiliated undertaking, where Article 48b(4) applies; or
(c) the branch or the undertaking which opened the branch, or an affiliated undertaking, where Article 48b(5) applies.

3. Member States may exempt undertakings from applying the rules set out in paragraph 2 of this Article where the report on income tax information published in accordance with paragraph 1 of this Article is simultaneously made accessible to the public in an electronic reporting format which is machine-readable, on the website of the register

referred to in Article 16 of Directive (EU) 2017/1132, and free of charge to any third party located within the Union. The website of the undertakings and branches, as referred to in paragraph 2 of this Article, shall contain information on that exemption and a reference to the website of the relevant register.

4. The report referred to in Article 48b(1), (4), (5), (6) and (7) and, where applicable, the statement referred to in paragraphs 4 and 5 of that Article, shall remain accessible on the relevant website for a minimum of five consecutive years.]

NOTES

Chapter 10a (Articles 48a–48h) was inserted by European Parliament and Council Directive 2021/2101/EU, Art 1(2), as from 21 December 2021; note that the 2021 Directive has a transposition date of 22 June 2023.

[1] Directive (EU) 2017/1132 of the European Parliament and of the Council of 14 June 2017 relating to certain aspects of company law (OJ L169, 30.6.2017, p 46).

[11.206]

[Article 48e Responsibility for drawing up, publishing and making accessible the report on income tax information

1. Member States shall provide that the members of the administrative, management and supervisory bodies of the ultimate parent undertakings or the standalone undertakings referred to in Article 48b(1), acting within the competences assigned to them under national law, have collective responsibility for ensuring that the report on income tax information is drawn up, published and made accessible in accordance with Articles 48b, 48c and 48d.

2. Member States shall provide that the members of the administrative, management and supervisory bodies of the subsidiary undertakings referred to in Article 48b(4) of this Directive and the person or persons designated to carry out the disclosure formalities provided for in Article 41 of Directive (EU) 2017/1132 for the branches referred to in Article 48b(5) of this Directive, acting within the competences assigned to them by national law, have collective responsibility for ensuring, to the best of their knowledge and ability, that the report on income tax information is drawn up in a manner that is consistent with or in accordance with, as relevant, Articles 48b and 48c, and that it is published and made accessible in accordance with Article 48d.]

NOTES

Chapter 10a (Articles 48a–48h) was inserted by European Parliament and Council Directive 2021/2101/EU, Art 1(2), as from 21 December 2021; note that the 2021 Directive has a transposition date of 22 June 2023.

[11.207]

[Article 48f Statement by statutory auditor

Member States shall require that, where the financial statements of an undertaking governed by the law of a Member State are required to be audited by one or more statutory auditors or audit firms, the audit report shall state whether, for the financial year preceding the financial year for which the financial statements under audit were prepared, the undertaking was required under Article 48b to publish a report on income tax information and, if so, whether the report was published in accordance with Article 48d.]

NOTES

Chapter 10a (Articles 48a–48h) was inserted by European Parliament and Council Directive 2021/2101/EU, Art 1(2), as from 21 December 2021; note that the 2021 Directive has a transposition date of 22 June 2023.

[11.208]

[Article 48g Commencement date for reporting on income tax information

Member States shall ensure that laws, regulations and administrative provisions transposing Articles 48a to 48f apply, at the latest, from the commencement date of the first financial year starting on or after 22 June 2024.]

NOTES

Chapter 10a (Articles 48a–48h) was inserted by European Parliament and Council Directive 2021/2101/EU, Art 1(2), as from 21 December 2021; note that the 2021 Directive has a transposition date of 22 June 2023.

[11.209]

[Article 48h Review clause

By 22 June 2027, the Commission shall submit a report on compliance with, and the impact of, the reporting obligations set out in Articles 48a to 48f and, taking into account the situation at OECD level, the need to ensure that there is a sufficient level of transparency and the need to preserve and ensure a competitive environment for undertakings and private investment, it shall review and assess, in particular, whether it would be appropriate to extend the obligation to report on income tax information set out in Article 48b to large undertakings and large groups, as defined in Article 3(4) and (7) respectively, and to extend the content of the report on income tax information set out in Article 48c to include additional items. In that report, the Commission shall also assess the impact that presenting the tax information on an aggregated basis for third-country tax jurisdictions as provided for in Article 48c(5) and the temporary omission of information provided for in Article 48c(6) has on the effectiveness of this Directive.

The Commission shall submit the report to the European Parliament and to the Council, together, where appropriate, with a legislative proposal.]

NOTES

Chapter 10a (Articles 48a–48h) was inserted by European Parliament and Council Directive 2021/2101/EU, Art 1(2), as from 21 December 2021; note that the 2021 Directive has a transposition date of 22 June 2023.

CHAPTER 11 FINAL PROVISIONS

[11.210]

Article 49 Exercise of delegated powers

1. The power to adopt delegated acts is conferred on the Commission subject to the conditions laid down in this Article.

2. The power to adopt delegated acts referred to in Article 1(2), Article 3(13) and Article 46(2) shall be conferred on the Commission for an indeterminate period of time from the date referred to in Article 54.

3. The delegation of power referred to in Article 1(2), Article 3(13) and Article 46(2) may be revoked at any time by the European Parliament or by the Council. A decision to revoke shall put an end to the delegation of the power specified in that decision. It shall take effect the day following the publication of that decision in the *Official Journal of the European Union* or at a later date specified therein. It shall not affect the validity of any delegated acts already in force.

[3a. Before adopting a delegated act, the Commission shall consult experts designated by each Member State in accordance with the principles laid down in the Interinstitutional Agreement of 13 April 2016 on Better Law-Making.[1]]

4. As soon as it adopts a delegated act, the Commission shall notify it simultaneously to the European Parliament and to the Council.

5. A delegated act adopted pursuant to Article 1(2), Article 3(13) or Article 46(2) shall enter into force only if no objection has been expressed either by the European Parliament or the Council within a period of two months of notification of that act to the European Parliament and the Council or if, before the expiry of that period, the European Parliament and the Council have both informed the Commission that they will not object. That period shall be extended by two months at the initiative of the European Parliament or the Council.

NOTES

Para 3a: inserted by European Parliament and Council Directive 2021/2101/EU, Art 1(3), as from 21 December 2021; note that the 2021 Directive has a transposition date of 22 June 2023.

[1] OJ L123, 12.5.2016, p 1.

[11.211]

Article 50 Committee procedure

1. The Commission shall be assisted by a committee. That committee shall be a committee within the meaning of Regulation (EU) No 182/2011.

2. Where reference is made to this paragraph, Article 5 of Regulation (EU) No 182/2011 shall apply.

[11.212]

Article 51 Penalties

Member States shall provide for penalties applicable to infringements of the national provisions adopted in accordance with this Directive and shall take all the measures necessary to ensure that those penalties are enforced. The penalties provided for shall be effective, proportionate and dissuasive.

[11.213]

Article 52 Repeal of Directives 78/660/EEC and 83/349/EEC

Directives 78/660/EEC and 83/349/EEC are repealed.

References to the repealed Directives shall be construed as references to this Directive and shall be read in accordance with the correlation table in Annex VII.

[11.214]

Article 53 Transposition

1. Member States shall bring into force the laws, regulations and administrative provisions necessary to comply with this Directive by 20 July 2015. They shall immediately inform the Commission thereof.

Member States may provide that the provisions referred to in the first subparagraph are first to apply to financial statements for financial years beginning on 1 January 2016 or during the calendar year 2016.

When Member States adopt those provisions, they shall contain a reference to this Directive or be accompanied by such a reference on the occasion of their official publication. The methods of making such reference shall be laid down by Member States.

2. Member States shall communicate to the Commission the text of the main provisions of national law which they adopt in the field covered by this Directive.

[11.215]

Article 54 Entry into force

This Directive shall enter into force on the twentieth day following that of its publication in the *Official Journal of the European Union*.

[11.216]

Article 55 Addressees

This Directive is addressed to the Member States.

ANNEX I
TYPES OF UNDERTAKING REFERRED TO IN POINT (A) OF ARTICLE 1(1)

[11.217]

— the United Kingdom:

public companies limited by shares or by guarantee, private companies limited by shares or by guarantee

NOTES

Note: entries other than for the UK have been omitted. Amendments to those entries are not noted.

ANNEX II
TYPES OF UNDERTAKING REFERRED TO IN POINT (B) OF ARTICLE 1(1)

[11.218]

— the United Kingdom:
  partnerships, limited partnerships, unlimited companies.

NOTES

Note: entries other than for the UK have been omitted. Amendments to those entries are not noted.

ANNEX III
HORIZONTAL LAYOUT OF THE BALANCE SHEET PROVIDED FOR IN ARTICLE 10

ASSETS

[11.219]

A. Subscribed capital unpaid
  of which there has been called
  (unless national law provides that called-up capital is to be shown under 'Capital and reserves', in which case the part of the capital called but not yet paid shall appear as an asset either under A or under D (II) (5)).

B. Formation expenses
  as defined by national law, and in so far as national law permits their being shown as an asset. National law may also provide for formation expenses to be shown as the first item under 'Intangible assets'.

C. Fixed assets
  I. Intangible assets
    1. Costs of development, in so far as national law permits their being shown as assets.
    2. Concessions, patents, licences, trade marks and similar rights and assets, if they were:
      (a) acquired for valuable consideration and need not be shown under C (I) (3); or
      (b) created by the undertaking itself, in so far as national law permits their being shown as assets.
    3. Goodwill, to the extent that it was acquired for valuable consideration.
    4. Payments on account.
  II. Tangible assets
    1. Land and buildings.
    2. Plant and machinery.
    3. Other fixtures and fittings, tools and equipment.
    4. Payments on account and tangible assets in the course of construction.
  III. Financial assets
    1. Shares in affiliated undertakings.
    2. Loans to affiliated undertakings.
    3. Participating interests.
    4. Loans to undertakings with which the undertaking is linked by virtue of participating interests.
    5. Investments held as fixed assets.
    6. Other loans.

D. Current assets
  I. Stocks
    1. Raw materials and consumables.
    2. Work in progress.
    3. Finished goods and goods for resale.
    4. Payments on account.
  II. Debtors
  (Amounts becoming due and payable after more than one year shall be shown separately for each item.)
    1. Trade debtors.
    2. Amounts owed by affiliated undertakings.
    3. Amounts owed by undertakings with which the undertaking is linked by virtue of participating interests.
    4. Other debtors.
    5. Subscribed capital called but not paid (unless national law provides that called-up capital is to be shown as an asset under A).
    6. Prepayments and accrued income (unless national law provides that such items are to be shown as assets under E).
  III. Investments
    1. Shares in affiliated undertakings.
    2. Own shares (with an indication of their nominal value or, in the absence of a nominal value, their accounting par value), to the extent that national law permits their being shown in the balance sheet.
    3. Other investments.
  IV. Cash at bank and in hand

E. Prepayments and accrued income
  (Unless national law provides that such items are to be shown as assets under D (II) (6).)

CAPITAL, RESERVES AND LIABILITIES

A. Capital and reserves
  I. Subscribed capital

(Unless national law provides that called-up capital is to be shown under this item, in which case the amounts of subscribed capital and paid-up capital shall be shown separately.)

II. Share premium account

III. Revaluation reserve

IV. Reserves

1. Legal reserve, in so far as national law requires such a reserve.
2. Reserve for own shares, in so far as national law requires such a reserve, without prejudice to point (b) of Article 24(1) of Directive 2012/30/EU.
3. Reserves provided for by the articles of association.
4. Other reserves, including the fair value reserve.

V. Profit or loss brought forward

VI. Profit or loss for the financial year

B. Provisions

1. Provisions for pensions and similar obligations.
2. Provisions for taxation.
3. Other provisions.

C. Creditors

(Amounts becoming due and payable within one year and amounts becoming due and payable after more than one year shall be shown separately for each item and for the aggregate of those items.)

1. Debenture loans, showing convertible loans separately.
2. Amounts owed to credit institutions.
3. Payments received on account of orders, in so far as they are not shown separately as deductions from stocks.
4. Trade creditors.
5. Bills of exchange payable.
6. Amounts owed to affiliated undertakings.
7. Amounts owed to undertakings with which the undertaking is linked by virtue of participating interests.
8. Other creditors, including tax and social security authorities.
9. Accruals and deferred income (unless national law provides that such items are to be shown under D).

D. Accruals and deferred income

(Unless national law provides that such items are to be shown under C (9) under 'Creditors'.)

ANNEX IV
VERTICAL LAYOUT OF THE BALANCE SHEET PROVIDED FOR IN ARTICLE 10

[11.220]

A. Subscribed capital unpaid

of which there has been called

(unless national law provides that called-up capital is to be shown under L, in which case the part of the capital called but not yet paid must appear either under A or under D (II) (5).)

B. Formation expenses

as defined by national law, and in so far as national law permits their being shown as an asset. National law may also provide for formation expenses to be shown as the first item under 'Intangible assets'.

C. Fixed assets

I. Intangible assets

1. Costs of development, in so far as national law permits their being shown as assets.
2. Concessions, patents, licences, trade marks and similar rights and assets, if they were:
   (a) acquired for valuable consideration and need not be shown under C (I) (3); or
   (b) created by the undertaking itself, in so far as national law permits their being shown as assets.
3. Goodwill, to the extent that it was acquired for valuable consideration.
4. Payments on account.

II. Tangible assets

1. Land and buildings.
2. Plant and machinery.
3. Other fixtures and fittings, tools and equipment.
4. Payments on account and tangible assets in the course of construction.

III. Financial assets

1. Shares in affiliated undertakings.
2. Loans to affiliated undertakings.
3. Participating interests.
4. Loans to undertakings with which the undertaking is linked by virtue of participating interests.
5. Investments held as fixed assets.
6. Other loans.

D. Current assets

I. Stocks

1. Raw materials and consumables.
2. Work in progress.
3. Finished goods and goods for resale.

4. Payments on account.

II. Debtors

(Amounts becoming due and payable after more than one year must be shown separately for each item.)

1. Trade debtors.
2. Amounts owed by affiliated undertakings.
3. Amounts owed by undertakings with which the company is linked by virtue of participating interests.
4. Other debtors.
5. Subscribed capital called but not paid (unless national law provides that called-up capital is to be shown as an asset under A).
6. Prepayments and accrued income (unless national law provides that such items are to be shown as assets under E).

III. Investments

1. Shares in affiliated undertakings.
2. Own shares (with an indication of their nominal value or, in the absence of a nominal value, their accounting par value), to the extent that national law permits their being shown in the balance sheet.
3. Other investments.

IV. Cash at bank and in hand

E. Prepayments and accrued income

(Unless national law provides that such items are to be shown under D (II) (6).)

F. Creditors: amounts becoming due and payable within one year

1. Debenture loans, showing convertible loans separately.
2. Amounts owed to credit institutions.
3. Payments received on account of orders, in so far as they are not shown separately as deductions from stocks.
4. Trade creditors.
5. Bills of exchange payable.
6. Amounts owed to affiliated undertakings.
7. Amounts owed to undertakings with which the company is linked by virtue of participating interests.
8. Other creditors, including tax and social security authorities.
9. Accruals and deferred income (unless national law provides that such items are to be shown under K).

G. Net current assets/liabilities

(Taking into account prepayments and accrued income when shown under E and accruals and deferred income when shown under K.)

H. Total assets less current liabilities

I. Creditors: amounts becoming due and payable after more than one year

1. Debenture loans, showing convertible loans separately.
2. Amounts owed to credit institutions.
3. Payments received on account of orders, in so far as they are not shown separately as deductions from stocks.
4. Trade creditors.
5. Bills of exchange payable.
6. Amounts owed to affiliated undertakings.
7. Amounts owed to undertakings with which the company is linked by virtue of participating interests.
8. Other creditors, including tax and social security authorities.
9. Accruals and deferred income (unless national law provides that such items are to be shown under K).

J. Provisions

1. Provisions for pensions and similar obligations.
2. Provisions for taxation.
3. Other provisions.

K. Accruals and deferred income

(Unless national law provides that such items are to be shown under F (9) or I (9) or both.)

L. Capital and reserves

I. Subscribed capital

(Unless national law provides that called-up capital is to be shown under this item, in which case the amounts of subscribed capital and paid-up capital must be shown separately.)

II. Share premium account

III. Revaluation reserve

IV. Reserves

1. Legal reserve, in so far as national law requires such a reserve.
2. Reserve for own shares, in so far as national law requires such a reserve, without prejudice to point (b) of Article 24(1) of Directive 2012/30/EU.
3. Reserves provided for by the articles of association.
4. Other reserves, including the fair value reserve.

V. Profit or loss brought forward

VI. Profit or loss for the financial year

ANNEX V
LAYOUT OF THE PROFIT AND LOSS ACCOUNT – BY NATURE OF EXPENSE, PROVIDED FOR IN ARTICLE 13

[11.221]

1. Net turnover.
2. Variation in stocks of finished goods and in work in progress.
3. Work performed by the undertaking for its own purposes and capitalised.
4. Other operating income.
5.
   (a) Raw materials and consumables.
   (b) Other external expenses.
6. Staff costs:
   (a) wages and salaries;
   (b) social security costs, with a separate indication of those relating to pensions.
7.
   (a) Value adjustments in respect of formation expenses and of tangible and intangible fixed assets.
   (b) Value adjustments in respect of current assets, to the extent that they exceed the amount of value adjustments which are normal in the undertaking concerned.
8. Other operating expenses.
9. Income from participating interests, with a separate indication of that derived from affiliated undertakings.
10. Income from other investments and loans forming part of the fixed assets, with a separate indication of that derived from affiliated undertakings.
11. Other interest receivable and similar income, with a separate indication of that derived from affiliated undertakings.
12. Value adjustments in respect of financial assets and of investments held as current assets.
13. Interest payable and similar expenses, with a separate indication of amounts payable to affiliated undertakings.
14. Tax on profit or loss.
15. Profit or loss after taxation.
16. Other taxes not shown under items 1 to 15.
17. Profit or loss for the financial year.

ANNEX VI
LAYOUT OF THE PROFIT AND LOSS ACCOUNT – BY FUNCTION OF EXPENSE, PROVIDED FOR IN ARTICLE 13

[11.222]

1. Net turnover.
2. Cost of sales (including value adjustments).
3. Gross profit or loss.
4. Distribution costs (including value adjustments).
5. Administrative expenses (including value adjustments).
6. Other operating income.
7. Income from participating interests, with a separate indication of that derived from affiliated undertakings.
8. Income from other investments and loans forming part of the fixed assets, with a separate indication of that derived from affiliated undertakings.
9. Other interest receivable and similar income, with a separate indication of that derived from affiliated undertakings.
10. Value adjustments in respect of financial assets and of investments held as current assets.
11. Interest payable and similar expenses, with a separate indication of amounts payable to affiliated undertakings.
12. Tax on profit or loss.
13. Profit or loss after taxation.
14. Other taxes not shown under items 1 to 13.
15. Profit or loss for the financial year.

ANNEX VII

The correlation table (Annex VII) has been omitted because of space considerations.

REGULATION OF THE EUROPEAN PARLIAMENT AND OF THE COUNCIL

(537/2014/EU)

of 16 April 2014

on specific requirements regarding statutory audit of public-interest entities and repealing Commission Decision 2005/909/EC (Note)

[11.223]

NOTES

Date of publication in OJ: OJ L158, 27.5.2014, p 77.

The main objectives of this Regulation and the 2014 Audit Directive (Directive 2014/56/EU amending Directive 2006/43/EC on statutory audits of annual accounts and consolidated accounts) are:

1. Further clarify the role of the statutory auditor
2. Reinforce the independence and the professional scepticism of the statutory auditor
3. Facilitate the cross-border provision of statutory audit services in the EU
4. Contribute to a more dynamic audit market in the EU
5. Improve the supervision of statutory auditors and the coordination of audit supervision by competent authorities in the EU.

This Regulation provides for specific requirements regarding statutory audit of public-interest entities ("PIEs"), ie, listed companies, credit institutions and insurance undertakings.

The following measures apply to all statutory auditors and audit firms, regardless of whether the audited entity is a public-interest entity or not:

— Introducing stronger requirements on independence, notably by improving the organisational requirements of statutory auditors and audit firms

— Making the audit report more informative for investors, providing them with relevant information about the audited company beyond a mere standardised opinion on the financial statements

— Reinforcing the competences and powers of the competent authorities responsible for the public oversight of the audit profession

— Establishing a more effective sanctioning regime by harmonising the types and addressees of sanctions as well as, for instance, the criteria to be taken into account by competent authorities when applying sanctions

— Conferring on the European Commission the competence to adopt the International Standards on Auditing (ISAs) at EU level.

In addition, the following stricter requirements apply to the statutory audit of PIEs:

— Introducing mandatory rotation of statutory auditors and audit firms every 10 years;

— Establishing a list of non-audit services that cannot be provided by the statutory auditor or audit firm to the audited entity;

— Imposing limitations on the fees charged for non-audit services;

— Reinforcing the role and competences of the audit committee, enhancing its composition and giving it a prominent direct role in the appointment of the statutory auditor or the audit firm, as well as in the monitoring of the audit;

— Strengthening the requirements on the audit report, and introducing an additional, more detailed, report to the audit committee, containing thorough information about the performance of the audit;

— Establishing a dialogue between the statutory auditor or audit firm of a PIE on the one hand and the supervisor of that given PIE on the other hand.

The new framework covers all statutory audits required by EU law. In addition, the new framework also covers audits for small undertakings and audits voluntarily conducted by small undertakings, where defined by national legislation as statutory audits. This Regulation applies from 17 June 2016.

This Regulation can be viewed on the EUR-Lex website at: eur-lex.europa.eu/legal-content/EN/TXT/?uri=CELEX:32014R0537.

Application of this Regulation in relation to the UK: in accordance with the European Union (Withdrawal) Act 2018, s 3 at **[12.5]**, this Regulation became domestic law on IP completion day (as defined in the European Union (Withdrawal Agreement) Act 2020, s 39). For post IP completion day amendments to this Regulation, see (i) the Statutory Auditors and Third Country Auditors (Amendment) (EU Exit) Regulations 2019, SI 2019/177 (for transitional provisions, see Sch 4 to the 2019 Regulations at **[12.88]**); (ii) the European Grouping of Territorial Cooperation and Limited Liability Partnerships etc (Revocations and Amendments) (EU Exit) Regulations 2021, SI 2021/153; and (iii) the Financial Services Act 2021 (Prudential Regulation of Credit Institutions and Investment Firms) (Consequential Amendments and Miscellaneous Provisions) Regulations 2022, SI 2022/838.

DIRECTIVE OF THE EUROPEAN PARLIAMENT AND OF THE COUNCIL

(2014/95/EU)

of 22 October 2014

amending Directive 2013/34/EU as regards disclosure of non-financial and diversity information by certain large undertakings and groups (Note)

[11.224]

NOTES

Date of publication in OJ: OJ L330, 15.11.2014, p 1.

Editorial note (legal status of EU Directives in the UK): note that EU Directives are not "direct EU legislation" within the meaning of the European Union (Withdrawal) Act 2018, s 3 at **[12.5]** and, accordingly, do not apply to the UK. As to the status of EU-derived domestic legislation after IP completion day (11pm on 31 December 2020), see s 2 of the 2018 Act at **[12.4]**. As to the UK implementation of this Directive, see the note below.

Article 1 amends Directive 2013/34/EU (the New EU Accounting Directive at **[11.152]**).

Article 2 (Guidance on reporting) provides that the Commission shall prepare non-binding guidelines on methodology for reporting non-financial information, including non-financial key performance indicators, general and sectoral, with a view to facilitating relevant, useful and comparable disclosure of non-financial information by undertakings. In doing so, the Commission shall consult relevant stakeholders. They shall do this by 6 December 2016.

Article 3 (Review) provides that the Commission shall submit a report to the European Parliament and to the Council on the implementation of this Directive, including, among other aspects, its scope, particularly as regards large non-listed undertakings, its effectiveness and the level of guidance and methods provided. The report shall be published by 6 December 2018 and shall be accompanied, if appropriate, by legislative proposals.

Article 4 (Transposition) provides that Member States shall bring into force the laws, regulations and administrative provisions necessary to comply with this Directive by 6 December 2016; and that they are to apply to all undertakings within the scope of Article 1 for the financial year starting on 1 January 2017 or during the calendar year 2017.

Article 5 provides that this Regulation enters into force on 5 December 2014.

UK Implementation: in the UK this Directive was implemented by the Companies, Partnerships and Groups (Accounts and Non-Financial Reporting) Regulations 2016, SI 2016/1245. For a summary of the Regulations, see Appendix 4 at **[A4]**.

REGULATION OF THE EUROPEAN PARLIAMENT AND OF THE COUNCIL

(2015/848/EU)

of 20 May 2015

on insolvency proceedings

(recast)

[11.225]

NOTES

Date of publication in OJ: OJ L141, 5.6.2015, p 19. The text of this Regulation incorporates the corrigendum published in OJ L349, 21.12.2016, p 9.

This Regulation is reproduced as amended by: European Parliament and Council Regulation 2018/946/EU (note that amendments made by European Parliament and Council Regulation 2017/353/EU are superseded by the 2018 Regulation); European Parliament and Council Regulation 2021/2260/EU (see the note below).

In previous editions of this Handbook, only the entries relating to the UK in Annexes A and B were reproduced. Those Annexes were substituted by European Parliament and Council Regulation 2021/2260/EU amending Regulation (EU) 2015/848 on insolvency proceedings to replace its Annexes A and B, with effect from 9 January 2022. Following the UK's exit from the EU, the new Annexes do not contain entries for the UK and, accordingly, they have now been omitted.

Application of this Regulation in relation to the UK: in accordance with the European Union (Withdrawal) Act 2018, s 3 at **[12.5]**, this Regulation became domestic law on IP completion day (as defined in the European Union (Withdrawal Agreement) Act 2020, s 39). In so far as applying to the UK, this Regulation is amended by the Insolvency (Amendment) (EU Exit) Regulations 2019, SI 2019/146, as from IP completion day. The amendments are set out below. With regard to these amendments, note that Articles that are repealed are reproduced in italics. In the case of other amendments, the relevant amending provision from SI 2019/146 is set out in full in the Notes to the amended Article, and the text of the amended Article has not been altered.

THE EUROPEAN PARLIAMENT AND THE COUNCIL OF THE EUROPEAN UNION,

Having regard to the Treaty on the Functioning of the European Union, and in particular Article 81 thereof,

Having regard to the proposal from the European Commission,

After transmission of the draft legislative act to the national parliaments,

Having regard to the opinion of the European Economic and Social Committee,[1]

Acting in accordance with the ordinary legislative procedure,[2]

Whereas:

(1) On 12 December 2012, the Commission adopted a report on the application of Council Regulation (EC) No 1346/2000.[3] The report concluded that the Regulation is functioning well in general but that it would be desirable to improve the application of certain of its provisions in order to enhance the effective administration of cross-border insolvency proceedings. Since that Regulation has been amended several times and further amendments are to be made, it should be recast in the interest of clarity.

(2) The Union has set the objective of establishing an area of freedom, security and justice.

(3) The proper functioning of the internal market requires that cross-border insolvency proceedings should operate efficiently and effectively. This Regulation needs to be adopted in order to achieve that objective, which falls within the scope of judicial cooperation in civil matters within the meaning of Article 81 of the Treaty.

(4) The activities of undertakings have more and more cross-border effects and are therefore increasingly being regulated by Union law. The insolvency of such undertakings also affects the proper functioning of the internal market, and there is a need for a Union act requiring coordination of the measures to be taken regarding an insolvent debtor's assets.

(5) It is necessary for the proper functioning of the internal market to avoid incentives for parties to transfer assets or judicial proceedings from one Member State to another, seeking to obtain a more favourable legal position to the detriment of the general body of creditors (forum shopping).

(6) This Regulation should include provisions governing jurisdiction for opening insolvency proceedings and actions which are directly derived from insolvency proceedings and are closely linked with them. This Regulation should also contain provisions regarding the recognition and enforcement of judgments issued in such proceedings, and

provisions regarding the law applicable to insolvency proceedings. In addition, this Regulation should lay down rules on the coordination of insolvency proceedings which relate to the same debtor or to several members of the same group of companies.

(7) Bankruptcy, proceedings relating to the winding-up of insolvent companies or other legal persons, judicial arrangements, compositions and analogous proceedings and actions related to such proceedings are excluded from the scope of Regulation (EU) No 1215/2012 of the European Parliament and of the Council.[4] Those proceedings should be covered by this Regulation. The interpretation of this Regulation should as much as possible avoid regulatory loopholes between the two instruments. However, the mere fact that a national procedure is not listed in Annex A to this Regulation should not imply that it is covered by Regulation (EU) No 1215/2012.

(8) In order to achieve the aim of improving the efficiency and effectiveness of insolvency proceedings having cross- border effects, it is necessary, and appropriate, that the provisions on jurisdiction, recognition and applicable law in this area should be contained in a Union measure which is binding and directly applicable in Member States.

(9) This Regulation should apply to insolvency proceedings which meet the conditions set out in it, irrespective of whether the debtor is a natural person or a legal person, a trader or an individual. Those insolvency proceedings are listed exhaustively in Annex A. In respect of the national procedures contained in Annex A, this Regulation should apply without any further examination by the courts of another Member State as to whether the conditions set out in this Regulation are met. National insolvency procedures not listed in Annex A should not be covered by this Regulation.

(10) The scope of this Regulation should extend to proceedings which promote the rescue of economically viable but distressed businesses and which give a second chance to entrepreneurs. It should, in particular, extend to proceedings which provide for restructuring of a debtor at a stage where there is only a likelihood of insolvency, and to proceedings which leave the debtor fully or partially in control of its assets and affairs. It should also extend to proceedings providing for a debt discharge or a debt adjustment in relation to consumers and self- employed persons, for example by reducing the amount to be paid by the debtor or by extending the payment period granted to the debtor. Since such proceedings do not necessarily entail the appointment of an insolvency practitioner, they should be covered by this Regulation if they take place under the control or supervision of a court. In this context, the term 'control' should include situations where the court only intervenes on appeal by a creditor or other interested parties.

(11) This Regulation should also apply to procedures which grant a temporary stay on enforcement actions brought by individual creditors where such actions could adversely affect negotiations and hamper the prospects of a restructuring of the debtor's business. Such procedures should not be detrimental to the general body of creditors and, if no agreement on a restructuring plan can be reached, should be preliminary to other procedures covered by this Regulation.

(12) This Regulation should apply to proceedings the opening of which is subject to publicity in order to allow creditors to become aware of the proceedings and to lodge their claims, thereby ensuring the collective nature of the proceedings, and in order to give creditors the opportunity to challenge the jurisdiction of the court which has opened the proceedings.

(13) Accordingly, insolvency proceedings which are confidential should be excluded from the scope of this Regulation. While such proceedings may play an important role in some Member States, their confidential nature makes it impossible for a creditor or a court located in another Member State to know that such proceedings have been opened, thereby making it difficult to provide for the recognition of their effects throughout the Union.

(14) The collective proceedings which are covered by this Regulation should include all or a significant part of the creditors to whom a debtor owes all or a substantial proportion of the debtor's outstanding debts provided that the claims of those creditors who are not involved in such proceedings remain unaffected. Proceedings which involve only the financial creditors of a debtor should also be covered. Proceedings which do not include all the creditors of a debtor should be proceedings aimed at rescuing the debtor. Proceedings that lead to a definitive cessation of the debtor's activities or the liquidation of the debtor's assets should include all the debtor's creditors. Moreover, the fact that some insolvency proceedings for natural persons exclude specific categories of claims, such as maintenance claims, from the possibility of a debt-discharge should not mean that such proceedings are not collective.

(15) This Regulation should also apply to proceedings that, under the law of some Member States, are opened and conducted for a certain period of time on an interim or provisional basis before a court issues an order confirming the continuation of the proceedings on a non-interim basis. Although labelled as 'interim', such proceedings should meet all other requirements of this Regulation.

(16) This Regulation should apply to proceedings which are based on laws relating to insolvency. However, proceedings that are based on general company law not designed exclusively for insolvency situations should not be considered to be based on laws relating to insolvency. Similarly, the purpose of adjustment of debt should not include specific proceedings in which debts of a natural person of very low income and very low asset value are written off, provided that this type of proceedings never makes provision for payment to creditors.

(17) This Regulation's scope should extend to proceedings which are triggered by situations in which the debtor faces non-financial difficulties, provided that such difficulties give rise to a real and serious threat to the debtor's actual or future ability to pay its debts as they fall due. The time frame relevant for the determination of such threat may extend to a period of several months or even longer in order to account for cases in which the debtor is faced with non-financial difficulties threatening the status of its business as a going concern and, in the medium term, its liquidity. This may be the case, for example, where the debtor has lost a contract which is of key importance to it.

(18) This Regulation should be without prejudice to the rules on the recovery of State aid from insolvent companies as interpreted by the case-law of the Court of Justice of the European Union.

(19) Insolvency proceedings concerning insurance undertakings, credit institutions, investment firms and other firms, institutions or undertakings covered by Directive 2001/24/EC of the European Parliament and of the Council[5] and collective investment undertakings should be excluded from the scope of this Regulation, as they are all subject to special arrangements and the national supervisory authorities have wide-ranging powers of intervention.

(20) Insolvency proceedings do not necessarily involve the intervention of a judicial authority. Therefore, the term 'court' in this Regulation should, in certain provisions, be given a broad meaning and include a person or body

empowered by national law to open insolvency proceedings. In order for this Regulation to apply, proceedings (comprising acts and formalities set down in law) should not only have to comply with the provisions of this Regulation, but they should also be officially recognised and legally effective in the Member State in which the insolvency proceedings are opened.

(21) Insolvency practitioners are defined in this Regulation and listed in Annex B. Insolvency practitioners who are appointed without the involvement of a judicial body should, under national law, be appropriately regulated and authorised to act in insolvency proceedings. The national regulatory framework should provide for proper arrangements to deal with potential conflicts of interest.

(22) This Regulation acknowledges the fact that as a result of widely differing substantive laws it is not practical to introduce insolvency proceedings with universal scope throughout the Union. The application without exception of the law of the State of the opening of proceedings would, against this background, frequently lead to difficulties. This applies, for example, to the widely differing national laws on security interests to be found in the Member States. Furthermore, the preferential rights enjoyed by some creditors in insolvency proceedings are, in some cases, completely different. At the next review of this Regulation, it will be necessary to identify further measures in order to improve the preferential rights of employees at European level. This Regulation should take account of such differing national laws in two different ways. On the one hand, provision should be made for special rules on the applicable law in the case of particularly significant rights and legal relationships (e.g. rights *in rem* and contracts of employment). On the other hand, national proceedings covering only assets situated in the State of the opening of proceedings should also be allowed alongside main insolvency proceedings with universal scope.

(23) This Regulation enables the main insolvency proceedings to be opened in the Member State where the debtor has the centre of its main interests. Those proceedings have universal scope and are aimed at encompassing all the debtor's assets. To protect the diversity of interests, this Regulation permits secondary insolvency proceedings to be opened to run in parallel with the main insolvency proceedings. Secondary insolvency proceedings may be opened in the Member State where the debtor has an establishment. The effects of secondary insolvency proceedings are limited to the assets located in that State. Mandatory rules of coordination with the main insolvency proceedings satisfy the need for unity in the Union.

(24) Where main insolvency proceedings concerning a legal person or company have been opened in a Member State other than that of its registered office, it should be possible to open secondary insolvency proceedings in the Member State of the registered office, provided that the debtor is carrying out an economic activity with human means and assets in that State, in accordance with the case-law of the Court of Justice of the European Union.

(25) This Regulation applies only to proceedings in respect of a debtor whose centre of main interests is located in the Union.

(26) The rules of jurisdiction set out in this Regulation establish only international jurisdiction, that is to say, they designate the Member State the courts of which may open insolvency proceedings. Territorial jurisdiction within that Member State should be established by the national law of the Member State concerned.

(27) Before opening insolvency proceedings, the competent court should examine of its own motion whether the centre of the debtor's main interests or the debtor's establishment is actually located within its jurisdiction.

(28) When determining whether the centre of the debtor's main interests is ascertainable by third parties, special consideration should be given to the creditors and to their perception as to where a debtor conducts the administration of its interests. This may require, in the event of a shift of centre of main interests, informing creditors of the new location from which the debtor is carrying out its activities in due course, for example by drawing attention to the change of address in commercial correspondence, or by making the new location public through other appropriate means.

(29) This Regulation should contain a number of safeguards aimed at preventing fraudulent or abusive forum shopping.

(30) Accordingly, the presumptions that the registered office, the principal place of business and the habitual residence are the centre of main interests should be rebuttable, and the relevant court of a Member State should carefully assess whether the centre of the debtor's main interests is genuinely located in that Member State. In the case of a company, it should be possible to rebut this presumption where the company's central administration is located in a Member State other than that of its registered office, and where a comprehensive assessment of all the relevant factors establishes, in a manner that is ascertainable by third parties, that the company's actual centre of management and supervision and of the management of its interests is located in that other Member State. In the case of an individual not exercising an independent business or professional activity, it should be possible to rebut this presumption, for example where the major part of the debtor's assets is located outside the Member State of the debtor's habitual residence, or where it can be established that the principal reason for moving was to file for insolvency proceedings in the new jurisdiction and where such filing would materially impair the interests of creditors whose dealings with the debtor took place prior to the relocation.

(31) With the same objective of preventing fraudulent or abusive forum shopping, the presumption that the centre of main interests is at the place of the registered office, at the individual's principal place of business or at the individual's habitual residence should not apply where, respectively, in the case of a company, legal person or individual exercising an independent business or professional activity, the debtor has relocated its registered office or principal place of business to another Member State within the 3-month period prior to the request for opening insolvency proceedings, or, in the case of an individual not exercising an independent business or professional activity, the debtor has relocated his habitual residence to another Member State within the 6-month period prior to the request for opening insolvency proceedings.

(32) In all cases, where the circumstances of the matter give rise to doubts about the court's jurisdiction, the court should require the debtor to submit additional evidence to support its assertions and, where the law applicable to the insolvency proceedings so allows, give the debtor's creditors the opportunity to present their views on the question of jurisdiction.

(33) In the event that the court seised of the request to open insolvency proceedings finds that the centre of main interests is not located on its territory, it should not open main insolvency proceedings.

(34) In addition, any creditor of the debtor should have an effective remedy against the decision to open insolvency proceedings. The consequences of any challenge to the decision to open insolvency proceedings should be governed by national law.

(35) The courts of the Member State within the territory of which insolvency proceedings have been opened should also have jurisdiction for actions which derive directly from the insolvency proceedings and are closely linked with them. Such actions should include avoidance actions against defendants in other Member States and actions concerning obligations that arise in the course of the insolvency proceedings, such as advance payment for costs of the proceedings. In contrast, actions for the performance of the obligations under a contract concluded by the debtor prior to the opening of proceedings do not derive directly from the proceedings. Where such an action is related to another action based on general civil and commercial law, the insolvency practitioner should be able to bring both actions in the courts of the defendant's domicile if he considers it more efficient to bring the action in that forum. This could, for example, be the case where the insolvency practitioner wishes to combine an action for director's liability on the basis of insolvency law with an action based on company law or general tort law.

(36) The court having jurisdiction to open the main insolvency proceedings should be able to order provisional and protective measures as from the time of the request to open proceedings. Preservation measures both prior to and after the commencement of the insolvency proceedings are important to guarantee the effectiveness of the insolvency proceedings. In that connection, this Regulation should provide for various possibilities. On the one hand, the court competent for the main insolvency proceedings should also be able to order provisional and protective measures covering assets situated in the territory of other Member States. On the other hand, an insolvency practitioner temporarily appointed prior to the opening of the main insolvency proceedings should be able, in the Member States in which an establishment belonging to the debtor is to be found, to apply for the preservation measures which are possible under the law of those Member States.

(37) Prior to the opening of the main insolvency proceedings, the right to request the opening of insolvency proceedings in the Member State where the debtor has an establishment should be limited to local creditors and public authorities, or to cases in which main insolvency proceedings cannot be opened under the law of the Member State where the debtor has the centre of its main interests. The reason for this restriction is that cases in which territorial insolvency proceedings are requested before the main insolvency proceedings are intended to be limited to what is absolutely necessary.

(38) Following the opening of the main insolvency proceedings, this Regulation does not restrict the right to request the opening of insolvency proceedings in a Member State where the debtor has an establishment. The insolvency practitioner in the main insolvency proceedings or any other person empowered under the national law of that Member State may request the opening of secondary insolvency proceedings.

(39) This Regulation should provide for rules to determine the location of the debtor's assets, which should apply when determining which assets belong to the main or secondary insolvency proceedings, or to situations involving third parties' rights *in rem*. In particular, this Regulation should provide that European patents with unitary effect, a Community trade mark or any other similar rights, such as Community plant variety rights or Community designs, should only be included in the main insolvency proceedings.

(40) Secondary insolvency proceedings can serve different purposes, besides the protection of local interests. Cases may arise in which the insolvency estate of the debtor is too complex to administer as a unit, or the differences in the legal systems concerned are so great that difficulties may arise from the extension of effects deriving from the law of the State of the opening of proceedings to the other Member States where the assets are located. For that reason, the insolvency practitioner in the main insolvency proceedings may request the opening of secondary insolvency proceedings where the efficient administration of the insolvency estate so requires.

(41) Secondary insolvency proceedings may also hamper the efficient administration of the insolvency estate. Therefore, this Regulation sets out two specific situations in which the court seised of a request to open secondary insolvency proceedings should be able, at the request of the insolvency practitioner in the main insolvency proceedings, to postpone or refuse the opening of such proceedings.

(42) First, this Regulation confers on the insolvency practitioner in main insolvency proceedings the possibility of giving an undertaking to local creditors that they will be treated as if secondary insolvency proceedings had been opened. That undertaking has to meet a number of conditions set out in this Regulation, in particular that it be approved by a qualified majority of local creditors. Where such an undertaking has been given, the court seised of a request to open secondary insolvency proceedings should be able to refuse that request if it is satisfied that the undertaking adequately protects the general interests of local creditors. When assessing those interests, the court should take into account the fact that the undertaking has been approved by a qualified majority of local creditors.

(43) For the purposes of giving an undertaking to local creditors, the assets and rights located in the Member State where the debtor has an establishment should form a sub-category of the insolvency estate, and, when distributing them or the proceeds resulting from their realisation, the insolvency practitioner in the main insolvency proceedings should respect the priority rights that creditors would have had if secondary insolvency proceedings had been opened in that Member State.

(44) National law should be applicable, as appropriate, in relation to the approval of an undertaking. In particular, where under national law the voting rules for adopting a restructuring plan require the prior approval of creditors' claims, those claims should be deemed to be approved for the purpose of voting on the undertaking. Where there are different procedures for the adoption of restructuring plans under national law, Member States should designate the specific procedure which should be relevant in this context.

(45) Second, this Regulation should provide for the possibility that the court temporarily stays the opening of secondary insolvency proceedings, when a temporary stay of individual enforcement proceedings has been granted in the main insolvency proceedings, in order to preserve the efficiency of the stay granted in the main insolvency proceedings. The court should be able to grant the temporary stay if it is satisfied that suitable measures are in place to protect the general interest of local creditors. In such a case, all creditors that could be affected by the outcome of the negotiations on a restructuring plan should be informed of the negotiations and be allowed to participate in them.

(46) In order to ensure effective protection of local interests, the insolvency practitioner in the main insolvency proceedings should not be able to realise or re-locate, in an abusive manner, assets situated in the Member State where

an establishment is located, in particular, with the purpose of frustrating the possibility that such interests can be effectively satisfied if secondary insolvency proceedings are opened subsequently.

(47) This Regulation should not prevent the courts of a Member State in which secondary insolvency proceedings have been opened from sanctioning a debtor's directors for violation of their duties, provided that those courts have jurisdiction to address such disputes under their national law.

(48) Main insolvency proceedings and secondary insolvency proceedings can contribute to the efficient administration of the debtor's insolvency estate or to the effective realisation of the total assets if there is proper cooperation between the actors involved in all the concurrent proceedings. Proper cooperation implies the various insolvency practitioners and the courts involved cooperating closely, in particular by exchanging a sufficient amount of information. In order to ensure the dominant role of the main insolvency proceedings, the insolvency practitioner in such proceedings should be given several possibilities for intervening in secondary insolvency proceedings which are pending at the same time. In particular, the insolvency practitioner should be able to propose a restructuring plan or composition or apply for a suspension of the realisation of the assets in the secondary insolvency proceedings. When cooperating, insolvency practitioners and courts should take into account best practices for cooperation in cross-border insolvency cases, as set out in principles and guidelines on communication and cooperation adopted by European and international organisations active in the area of insolvency law, and in particular the relevant guidelines prepared by the United Nations Commission on International Trade Law (Uncitral).

(49) In light of such cooperation, insolvency practitioners and courts should be able to enter into agreements and protocols for the purpose of facilitating cross-border cooperation of multiple insolvency proceedings in different Member States concerning the same debtor or members of the same group of companies, where this is compatible with the rules applicable to each of the proceedings. Such agreements and protocols may vary in form, in that they may be written or oral, and in scope, in that they may range from generic to specific, and may be entered into by different parties. Simple generic agreements may emphasise the need for close cooperation between the parties, without addressing specific issues, while more detailed, specific agreements may establish a framework of principles to govern multiple insolvency proceedings and may be approved by the courts involved, where the national law so requires. They may reflect an agreement between the parties to take, or to refrain from taking, certain steps or actions.

(50) Similarly, the courts of different Member States may cooperate by coordinating the appointment of insolvency practitioners. In that context, they may appoint a single insolvency practitioner for several insolvency proceedings concerning the same debtor or for different members of a group of companies, provided that this is compatible with the rules applicable to each of the proceedings, in particular with any requirements concerning the qualification and licensing of the insolvency practitioner.

(51) This Regulation should ensure the efficient administration of insolvency proceedings relating to different companies forming part of a group of companies.

(52) Where insolvency proceedings have been opened for several companies of the same group, there should be proper cooperation between the actors involved in those proceedings. The various insolvency practitioners and the courts involved should therefore be under a similar obligation to cooperate and communicate with each other as those involved in main and secondary insolvency proceedings relating to the same debtor. Cooperation between the insolvency practitioners should not run counter to the interests of the creditors in each of the proceedings, and such cooperation should be aimed at finding a solution that would leverage synergies across the group.

(53) The introduction of rules on the insolvency proceedings of groups of companies should not limit the possibility for a court to open insolvency proceedings for several companies belonging to the same group in a single jurisdiction if the court finds that the centre of main interests of those companies is located in a single Member State. In such cases, the court should also be able to appoint, if appropriate, the same insolvency practitioner in all proceedings concerned, provided that this is not incompatible with the rules applicable to them.

(54) With a view to further improving the coordination of the insolvency proceedings of members of a group of companies, and to allow for a coordinated restructuring of the group, this Regulation should introduce procedural rules on the coordination of the insolvency proceedings of members of a group of companies. Such coordination should strive to ensure the efficiency of the coordination, whilst at the same time respecting each group member's separate legal personality.

(55) An insolvency practitioner appointed in insolvency proceedings opened in relation to a member of a group of companies should be able to request the opening of group coordination proceedings. However, where the law applicable to the insolvency so requires, that insolvency practitioner should obtain the necessary authorisation before making such a request. The request should specify the essential elements of the coordination, in particular an outline of the coordination plan, a proposal as to whom should be appointed as coordinator and an outline of the estimated costs of the coordination.

(56) In order to ensure the voluntary nature of group coordination proceedings, the insolvency practitioners involved should be able to object to their participation in the proceedings within a specified time period. In order to allow the insolvency practitioners involved to take an informed decision on participation in the group coordination proceedings, they should be informed at an early stage of the essential elements of the coordination. However, any insolvency practitioner who initially objects to inclusion in the group coordination proceedings should be able to subsequently request to participate in them. In such a case, the coordinator should take a decision on the admissibility of the request. All insolvency practitioners, including the requesting insolvency practitioner, should be informed of the coordinator's decision and should have the opportunity of challenging that decision before the court which has opened the group coordination proceedings.

(57) Group coordination proceedings should always strive to facilitate the effective administration of the insolvency proceedings of the group members, and to have a generally positive impact for the creditors. This Regulation should therefore ensure that the court with which a request for group coordination proceedings has been filed makes an assessment of those criteria prior to opening group coordination proceedings.

(58) The advantages of group coordination proceedings should not be outweighed by the costs of those proceedings. Therefore, it is necessary to ensure that the costs of the coordination, and the share of those costs that each group member will bear, are adequate, proportionate and reasonable, and are determined in accordance with the national law of the Member State in which group coordination proceedings have been opened. The insolvency

practitioners involved should also have the possibility of controlling those costs from an early stage of the proceedings. Where the national law so requires, controlling costs from an early stage of proceedings could involve the insolvency practitioner seeking the approval of a court or creditors' committee.

(59) Where the coordinator considers that the fulfilment of his or her tasks requires a significant increase in costs compared to the initially estimated costs and, in any case, where the costs exceed 10% of the estimated costs, the coordinator should be authorised by the court which has opened the group coordination proceedings to exceed such costs. Before taking its decision, the court which has opened the group coordination proceedings should give the possibility to the participating insolvency practitioners to be heard before it in order to allow them to communicate their observations on the appropriateness of the coordinator's request.

(60) For members of a group of companies which are not participating in group coordination proceedings, this Regulation should also provide for an alternative mechanism to achieve a coordinated restructuring of the group. An insolvency practitioner appointed in proceedings relating to a member of a group of companies should have standing to request a stay of any measure related to the realisation of the assets in the proceedings opened with respect to other members of the group which are not subject to group coordination proceedings. It should only be possible to request such a stay if a restructuring plan is presented for the members of the group concerned, if the plan is to the benefit of the creditors in the proceedings in respect of which the stay is requested, and if the stay is necessary to ensure that the plan can be properly implemented.

(61) This Regulation should not prevent Member States from establishing national rules which would supplement the rules on cooperation, communication and coordination with regard to the insolvency of members of groups of companies set out in this Regulation, provided that the scope of application of those national rules is limited to the national jurisdiction and that their application would not impair the efficiency of the rules laid down by this Regulation.

(62) The rules on cooperation, communication and coordination in the framework of the insolvency of members of a group of companies provided for in this Regulation should only apply to the extent that proceedings relating to different members of the same group of companies have been opened in more than one Member State.

(63) Any creditor which has its habitual residence, domicile or registered office in the Union should have the right to lodge its claims in each of the insolvency proceedings pending in the Union relating to the debtor's assets. This should also apply to tax authorities and social insurance institutions. This Regulation should not prevent the insolvency practitioner from lodging claims on behalf of certain groups of creditors, for example employees, where the national law so provides. However, in order to ensure the equal treatment of creditors, the distribution of proceeds should be coordinated. Every creditor should be able to keep what it has received in the course of insolvency proceedings, but should be entitled only to participate in the distribution of total assets in other proceedings if creditors with the same standing have obtained the same proportion of their claims.

(64) It is essential that creditors which have their habitual residence, domicile or registered office in the Union be informed about the opening of insolvency proceedings relating to their debtor's assets. In order to ensure a swift transmission of information to creditors, Regulation (EC) No 1393/2007 of the European Parliament and of the Council[6] should not apply where this Regulation refers to the obligation to inform creditors. The use of standard forms available in all official languages of the institutions of the Union should facilitate the task of creditors when lodging claims in proceedings opened in another Member State. The consequences of the incomplete filing of the standard forms should be a matter for national law.

(65) This Regulation should provide for the immediate recognition of judgments concerning the opening, conduct and closure of insolvency proceedings which fall within its scope, and of judgments handed down in direct connection with such insolvency proceedings. Automatic recognition should therefore mean that the effects attributed to the proceedings by the law of the Member State in which the proceedings were opened extend to all other Member States. The recognition of judgments delivered by the courts of the Member States should be based on the principle of mutual trust. To that end, grounds for non-recognition should be reduced to the minimum necessary. This is also the basis on which any dispute should be resolved where the courts of two Member States both claim competence to open the main insolvency proceedings. The decision of the first court to open proceedings should be recognised in the other Member States without those Member States having the power to scrutinise that court's decision.

(66) This Regulation should set out, for the matters covered by it, uniform rules on conflict of laws which replace, within their scope of application, national rules of private international law. Unless otherwise stated, the law of the Member State of the opening of proceedings should be applicable (*lex concursus*). This rule on conflict of laws should be valid both for the main insolvency proceedings and for local proceedings. The *lex concursus* determines all the effects of the insolvency proceedings, both procedural and substantive, on the persons and legal relations concerned. It governs all the conditions for the opening, conduct and closure of the insolvency proceedings.

(67) Automatic recognition of insolvency proceedings to which the law of the State of the opening of proceedings normally applies may interfere with the rules under which transactions are carried out in other Member States. To protect legitimate expectations and the certainty of transactions in Member States other than that in which proceedings are opened, provision should be made for a number of exceptions to the general rule.

(68) There is a particular need for a special reference diverging from the law of the opening State in the case of rights *in rem*, since such rights are of considerable importance for the granting of credit. The basis, validity and extent of rights *in rem* should therefore normally be determined according to the *lex situs* and not be affected by the opening of insolvency proceedings. The proprietor of a right *in rem* should therefore be able to continue to assert its right to segregation or separate settlement of the collateral security. Where assets are subject to rights *in rem* under the *lex situs* in one Member State but the main insolvency proceedings are being carried out in another Member State, the insolvency practitioner in the main insolvency proceedings should be able to request the opening of secondary insolvency proceedings in the jurisdiction where the rights *in rem* arise if the debtor has an establishment there. If secondary insolvency proceedings are not opened, any surplus on the sale of an asset covered by rights *in rem* should be paid to the insolvency practitioner in the main insolvency proceedings.

(69) This Regulation lays down several provisions for a court to order a stay of opening proceedings or a stay of enforcement proceedings. Any such stay should not affect the rights *in rem* of creditors or third parties.

(70) If a set-off of claims is not permitted under the law of the State of the opening of proceedings, a creditor should nevertheless be entitled to the set-off if it is possible under the law applicable to the claim of the insolvent

debtor. In this way, set-off would acquire a kind of guarantee function based on legal provisions on which the creditor concerned can rely at the time when the claim arises.

(71) There is also a need for special protection in the case of payment systems and financial markets, for example in relation to the position-closing agreements and netting agreements to be found in such systems, as well as the sale of securities and the guarantees provided for such transactions as governed in particular by Directive 98/26/EC of the European Parliament and of the Council.[7] For such transactions, the only law which is relevant should be that applicable to the system or market concerned. That law is intended to prevent the possibility of mechanisms for the payment and settlement of transactions, and provided for in payment and set-off systems or on the regulated financial markets of the Member States, being altered in the case of insolvency of a business partner. Directive 98/26/EC contains special provisions which should take precedence over the general rules laid down in this Regulation.

(72) In order to protect employees and jobs, the effects of insolvency proceedings on the continuation or termination of employment and on the rights and obligations of all parties to such employment should be determined by the law applicable to the relevant employment agreement, in accordance with the general rules on conflict of laws. Moreover, in cases where the termination of employment contracts requires approval by a court or administrative authority, the Member State in which an establishment of the debtor is located should retain jurisdiction to grant such approval even if no insolvency proceedings have been opened in that Member State. Any other questions relating to the law of insolvency, such as whether the employees' claims are protected by preferential rights and the status such preferential rights may have, should be determined by the law of the Member State in which the insolvency proceedings (main or secondary) have been opened, except in cases where an undertaking to avoid secondary insolvency proceedings has been given in accordance with this Regulation.

(73) The law applicable to the effects of insolvency proceedings on any pending lawsuit or pending arbitral proceedings concerning an asset or right which forms part of the debtor's insolvency estate should be the law of the Member State where the lawsuit is pending or where the arbitration has its seat. However, this rule should not affect national rules on recognition and enforcement of arbitral awards.

(74) In order to take account of the specific procedural rules of court systems in certain Member States flexibility should be provided with regard to certain rules of this Regulation. Accordingly, references in this Regulation to notice being given by a judicial body of a Member State should include, where a Member State's procedural rules so require, an order by that judicial body directing that notice be given.

(75) For business considerations, the main content of the decision opening the proceedings should be published, at the request of the insolvency practitioner, in a Member State other than that of the court which delivered that decision. If there is an establishment in the Member State concerned, such publication should be mandatory. In neither case, however, should publication be a prior condition for recognition of the foreign proceedings.

(76) In order to improve the provision of information to relevant creditors and courts and to prevent the opening of parallel insolvency proceedings, Member States should be required to publish relevant information in cross- border insolvency cases in a publicly accessible electronic register. In order to facilitate access to that information for creditors and courts domiciled or located in other Member States, this Regulation should provide for the interconnection of such insolvency registers via the European e-Justice Portal. Member States should be free to publish relevant information in several registers and it should be possible to interconnect more than one register per Member State.

(77) This Regulation should determine the minimum amount of information to be published in the insolvency registers. Member States should not be precluded from including additional information. Where the debtor is an individual, the insolvency registers should only have to indicate a registration number if the debtor is exercising an independent business or professional activity. That registration number should be understood to be the unique registration number of the debtor's independent business or professional activity published in the trade register, if any.

(78) Information on certain aspects of insolvency proceedings is essential for creditors, such as time limits for lodging claims or for challenging decisions. This Regulation should, however, not require Member States to calculate those time-limits on a case-by-case basis. Member States should be able to fulfil their obligations by adding hyperlinks to the European e-Justice Portal, where self-explanatory information on the criteria for calculating those time-limits is to be provided.

(79) In order to grant sufficient protection to information relating to individuals not exercising an independent business or professional activity, Member States should be able to make access to that information subject to supplementary search criteria such as the debtor's personal identification number, address, date of birth or the district of the competent court, or to make access conditional upon a request to a competent authority or upon the verification of a legitimate interest.

(80) Member States should also be able not to include in their insolvency registers information on individuals not exercising an independent business or professional activity. In such cases, Member States should ensure that the relevant information is given to the creditors by individual notice, and that claims of creditors who have not received the information are not affected by the proceedings.

(81) It may be the case that some of the persons concerned are not aware that insolvency proceedings have been opened, and act in good faith in a way that conflicts with the new circumstances. In order to protect such persons who, unaware that foreign proceedings have been opened, make a payment to the debtor instead of to the foreign insolvency practitioner, provision should be made for such a payment to have a debt-discharging effect.

(82) In order to ensure uniform conditions for the implementation of this Regulation, implementing powers should be conferred on the Commission. Those powers should be exercised in accordance with Regulation (EU) No 182/2011 of the European Parliament and of the Council.[8]

(83) This Regulation respects the fundamental rights and observes the principles recognised in the Charter of Fundamental Rights of the European Union. In particular, this Regulation seeks to promote the application of Articles 8, 17 and 47 concerning, respectively, the protection of personal data, the right to property and the right to an effective remedy and to a fair trial.

(84) Directive 95/46/EC of the European Parliament and of the Council[9] and Regulation (EC) No 45/2001 of the European Parliament and of the Council[10] apply to the processing of personal data within the framework of this Regulation.

(85) This Regulation is without prejudice to Regulation (EEC, Euratom) No 1182/71 of the Council.[11]

(86) Since the objective of this Regulation cannot be sufficiently achieved by the Member States but can rather, by reason of the creation of a legal framework for the proper administration of cross-border insolvency proceedings, be better achieved at Union level, the Union may adopt measures in accordance with the principle of subsidiarity as set out in Article 5 of the Treaty on European Union. In accordance with the principle of proportionality, as set out in that Article, this Regulation does not go beyond what is necessary in order to achieve that objective.

(87) In accordance with Article 3 and Article 4a(1) of Protocol No 21 on the position of the United Kingdom and Ireland in respect of the area of freedom, security and justice, annexed to the Treaty on European Union and the Treaty on the Functioning of the European Union, the United Kingdom and Ireland have notified their wish to take part in the adoption and application of this Regulation.

(88) In accordance with Articles 1 and 2 of Protocol No 22 on the position of Denmark annexed to the Treaty on European Union and the Treaty on the Functioning of the European Union, Denmark is not taking part in the adoption of this Regulation and is not bound by it or subject to its application.

(89) The European Data Protection Supervisor was consulted and delivered an opinion on 27 March 2013,[12]

NOTES

1 OJ C271, 19.9.2013, p 55.

2 Position of the European Parliament of 5 February 2014 (not yet published in the Official Journal) and position of the Council at first reading of 12 March 2015 (not yet published in the Official Journal). Position of the European Parliament of 20 May 2015 (not yet published in the Official Journal).

3 Council Regulation (EC) No 1346/2000 of 29 May 2000 on insolvency proceedings (OJ L160, 30.6.2000, p 1).

4 Regulation (EU) No 1215/2012 of the European Parliament and of the Council of 12 December 2012 on jurisdiction and the recognition and enforcement of judgments in civil and commercial matters (OJ L351, 20.12.2012, p 1).

5 Directive 2001/24/EC of the European Parliament and of the Council of 4 April 2001 on the reorganisation and winding-up of credit institutions (OJ L125, 5.5.2001, p 15).

6 Regulation (EC) No 1393/2007 of the European Parliament and of the Council of 13 November 2007 on the service in the Member States of judicial and extrajudicial documents in civil and commercial matters (service of documents), and repealing Council Regulation (EC) No 1348/2000 (OJ L324, 10.12.2007, p 79).

7 Directive 98/26/EC of the European Parliament and of the Council of 19 May 1998 on settlement finality in payment and securities settlement systems (OJ L166, 11.6.1998, p 45).

8 Regulation (EU) No 182/2011 of the European Parliament and of the Council of 16 February 2011 laying down the rules and general principles concerning mechanisms for control by the Member States of the Commission's exercise of implementing powers (OJ L55, 28.2.2011, p 13).

9 Directive 95/46/EC of the European Parliament and of the Council of 24 October 1995 on the protection of individuals with regard to the processing of personal data and on the free movement of such data (OJ L281, 23.11.1995, p 31).

10 Regulation (EC) No 45/2001 of the European Parliament and of the Council of 18 December 2000 on the protection of individuals with regard to the processing of personal data by the Community institutions and bodies and on the free movement of such data (OJ L8, 12.1.2001, p 1).

11 Regulation (EEC, Euratom) No 1182/71 of the Council of 3 June 1971 determining the rules applicable to periods, dates and time limits (OJ L124, 8.6.1971, p 1).

12 OJ C358, 7.12.2013, p 15.

HAVE ADOPTED THIS REGULATION:

CHAPTER I GENERAL PROVISIONS

[11.226]

Article 1 Scope

1. This Regulation shall apply to public collective proceedings, including interim proceedings, which are based on laws relating to insolvency and in which, for the purpose of rescue, adjustment of debt, reorganisation or liquidation:

(a) a debtor is totally or partially divested of its assets and an insolvency practitioner is appointed;

(b) the assets and affairs of a debtor are subject to control or supervision by a court; or

(c) a temporary stay of individual enforcement proceedings is granted by a court or by operation of law, in order to allow for negotiations between the debtor and its creditors, provided that the proceedings in which the stay is granted provide for suitable measures to protect the general body of creditors, and, where no agreement is reached, are preliminary to one of the proceedings referred to in point (a) or (b).

Where the proceedings referred to in this paragraph may be commenced in situations where there is only a likelihood of insolvency, their purpose shall be to avoid the debtor's insolvency or the cessation of the debtor's business activities.

The proceedings referred to in this paragraph are listed in Annex A.

2. This Regulation shall not apply to proceedings referred to in paragraph 1 that concern:

(a) insurance undertakings;

(b) credit institutions;

(c) investment firms and other firms, institutions and undertakings to the extent that they are covered by Directive 2001/24/EC; or

(d) collective investment undertakings.

NOTES

Application of this Article in relation to the UK: this Article is amended, in relation to the UK only, by the Insolvency (Amendment) (EU Exit) Regulations 2019, SI 2019/146, reg 2, Schedule, Pt 1, paras 1, 2, as from IP completion day (as defined in the European Union (Withdrawal Agreement) Act 2020, s 39), as follows (for transitional provisions and savings, see reg 4 of the 2019 Regulations at **[12.82]**)—

"(1) Article 1 is amended as follows.

(2) For the heading substitute "Application and jurisdiction".

(3) For paragraph 1 substitute—

"1. The grounds for jurisdiction to open insolvency proceedings set out in paragraph 1B are in addition to any grounds for jurisdiction to open such proceedings which apply in the laws of any part of the United Kingdom.

1A. There is jurisdiction to open insolvency proceedings listed in paragraph 1B where the proceedings are opened for the purposes of rescue, adjustment of debt, reorganisation or liquidation and—

(a) the centre of the debtor's main interests is in the United Kingdom; or

(b) the centre of the debtor's main interests is in a Member State and there is an establishment in the United Kingdom.

1B. The proceedings referred to in paragraph 1 are—

(a) winding up by or subject to the supervision of the court;

(b) creditors' voluntary winding up with confirmation by the court;

(c) administration, including appointments made by filing prescribed documents with the court;

(d) voluntary arrangements under insolvency legislation; and

(e) bankruptcy or sequestration.".

(4) In paragraph 2 for "Directive 2001/24/EC" substitute "the Credit Institutions (Reorganisation and Winding up) Regulations 2004".".

[11.227]

Article 2 Definitions

For the purposes of this Regulation:

(1) 'collective proceedings' means proceedings which include all or a significant part of a debtor's creditors, provided that, in the latter case, the proceedings do not affect the claims of creditors which are not involved in them;

(2) 'collective investment undertakings' means undertakings for collective investment in transferable securities (UCITS) as defined in Directive 2009/65/EC of the European Parliament and of the Council[1] and alternative investment funds (AIFs) as defined in Directive 2011/61/EU of the European Parliament and of the Council;[2]

(3) 'debtor in possession' means a debtor in respect of which insolvency proceedings have been opened which do not necessarily involve the appointment of an insolvency practitioner or the complete transfer of the rights and duties to administer the debtor's assets to an insolvency practitioner and where, therefore, the debtor remains totally or at least partially in control of its assets and affairs;

(4) 'insolvency proceedings' means the proceedings listed in Annex A;

(5) 'insolvency practitioner' means any person or body whose function, including on an interim basis, is to:

(i) verify and admit claims submitted in insolvency proceedings;

(ii) represent the collective interest of the creditors;

(iii) administer, either in full or in part, assets of which the debtor has been divested;

(iv) liquidate the assets referred to in point (iii); or

(v) supervise the administration of the debtor's affairs.

The persons and bodies referred to in the first subparagraph are listed in Annex B;

(6) 'court' means:

(i) in points (b) and (c) of Article 1(1), Article 4(2), Articles 5 and 6, Article 21(3), point (j) of Article 24(2), Articles 36 and 39, and Articles 61 to 77, the judicial body of a Member State;

(ii) in all other articles, the judicial body or any other competent body of a Member State empowered to open insolvency proceedings, to confirm such opening or to take decisions in the course of such proceedings;

(7) 'judgment opening insolvency proceedings' includes:

(i) the decision of any court to open insolvency proceedings or to confirm the opening of such proceedings; and

(ii) the decision of a court to appoint an insolvency practitioner;

(8) 'the time of the opening of proceedings' means the time at which the judgment opening insolvency proceedings becomes effective, regardless of whether the judgment is final or not;

(9) 'the Member State in which assets are situated' means, in the case of:

(i) registered shares in companies other than those referred to in point (ii), the Member State within the territory of which the company having issued the shares has its registered office;

(ii) financial instruments, the title to which is evidenced by entries in a register or account maintained by or on behalf of an intermediary ('book entry securities'), the Member State in which the register or account in which the entries are made is maintained;

(iii) cash held in accounts with a credit institution, the Member State indicated in the account's IBAN, or, for cash held in accounts with a credit institution which does not have an IBAN, the Member State in which the credit institution holding the account has its central administration or, where the account is held with a branch, agency or other establishment, the Member State in which the branch, agency or other establishment is located;

(iv) property and rights, ownership of or entitlement to which is entered in a public register other than those referred to in point (i), the Member State under the authority of which the register is kept;

(v) European patents, the Member State for which the European patent is granted;

(vi) copyright and related rights, the Member State within the territory of which the owner of such rights has its habitual residence or registered office;

(vii) tangible property, other than that referred to in points (i) to (iv), the Member State within the territory of which the property is situated;

(viii) claims against third parties, other than those relating to assets referred to in point (iii), the Member State within the territory of which the third party required to meet the claims has the centre of its main interests, as determined in accordance with Article 3(1);

(10) 'establishment' means any place of operations where a debtor carries out or has carried out in the 3-month period prior to the request to open main insolvency proceedings a non-transitory economic activity with human means and assets;

(11) 'local creditor' means a creditor whose claims against a debtor arose from or in connection with the operation of an establishment situated in a Member State other than the Member State in which the centre of the debtor's main interests is located;

(12) 'foreign creditor' means a creditor which has its habitual residence, domicile or registered office in a Member State other than the State of the opening of proceedings, including the tax authorities and social security authorities of Member States;
(13) 'group of companies' means a parent undertaking and all its subsidiary undertakings;
(14) 'parent undertaking' means an undertaking which controls, either directly or indirectly, one or more subsidiary undertakings. An undertaking which prepares consolidated financial statements in accordance with Directive 2013/34/EU of the European Parliament and of the Council[3] shall be deemed to be a parent undertaking.

NOTES

Application of this Article in relation to the UK: this Article is amended, in relation to the UK only, by the Insolvency (Amendment) (EU Exit) Regulations 2019, SI 2019/146, reg 2, Schedule, Pt 1, paras 1, 3, as from IP completion day (as defined in the European Union (Withdrawal Agreement) Act 2020, s 39), as follows (for transitional provisions and savings, see reg 4 of the 2019 Regulations at **[12.82]**)—

"In Article 2—

(a) insert the following paragraph—

"1A. "Member State" means a state which is a member of the EU other than Denmark;";

(b) omit paragraphs (1) and (3);
(c) in paragraph (4) for "listed in Annex A" substitute "listed in Article 1(1B) which there is jurisdiction to open under Article 1(1A) and includes interim proceedings";
(d) in paragraph (6)—
(i) omit point (i); and
(ii) in point (ii) omit "in all other articles," and "of a Member State";
(e) omit paragraph (9);
(f) in paragraph (10) omit "main";
(g) omit paragraphs (11) to (14).".

1 Directive 2009/65/EC of the European Parliament and of the Council of 13 July 2009 on the coordination of laws, regulations and administrative provisions relating to undertakings for collective investment in transferable securities (UCITS) (OJ L302, 17.11.2009, p 32).

2 Directive 2011/61/EU of the European Parliament and of the Council of 8 June 2011 on Alternative Investment Fund Managers and amending Directives 2003/41/EC and 2009/65/EC and Regulations (EC) No 1060/2009 and (EU) No 1095/2010 (OJ L174, 1.7.2011, p 1).

3 Directive 2013/34/EU of the European Parliament and of the Council of 26 June 2013 on the annual financial statements, consolidated financial statements and related reports of certain types of undertaking, amending Directive 2006/43/EC of the European Parliament and of the Council and repealing Council Directives 78/660/EEC and 83/349/EEC (OJ L182, 29.6.2013, p 19).

[11.228]
Article 3 International jurisdiction

1. The courts of the Member State within the territory of which the centre of the debtor's main interests is situated shall have jurisdiction to open insolvency proceedings ('main insolvency proceedings'). The centre of main interests shall be the place where the debtor conducts the administration of its interests on a regular basis and which is ascertainable by third parties.
In the case of a company or legal person, the place of the registered office shall be presumed to be the centre of its main interests in the absence of proof to the contrary. That presumption shall only apply if the registered office has not been moved to another Member State within the 3-month period prior to the request for the opening of insolvency proceedings.
In the case of an individual exercising an independent business or professional activity, the centre of main interests shall be presumed to be that individual's principal place of business in the absence of proof to the contrary. That presumption shall only apply if the individual's principal place of business has not been moved to another Member State within the 3-month period prior to the request for the opening of insolvency proceedings.
In the case of any other individual, the centre of main interests shall be presumed to be the place of the individual's habitual residence in the absence of proof to the contrary. This presumption shall only apply if the habitual residence has not been moved to another Member State within the 6-month period prior to the request for the opening of insolvency proceedings.
2. Where the centre of the debtor's main interests is situated within the territory of a Member State, the courts of another Member State shall have jurisdiction to open insolvency proceedings against that debtor only if it possesses an establishment within the territory of that other Member State. The effects of those proceedings shall be restricted to the assets of the debtor situated in the territory of the latter Member State.
3. Where insolvency proceedings have been opened in accordance with paragraph 1, any proceedings opened subsequently in accordance with paragraph 2 shall be secondary insolvency proceedings.
4. The territorial insolvency proceedings referred to in paragraph 2 may only be opened prior to the opening of main insolvency proceedings in accordance with paragraph 1 where
(a) insolvency proceedings under paragraph 1 cannot be opened because of the conditions laid down by the law of the Member State within the territory of which the centre of the debtor's main interests is situated; or
(b) the opening of territorial insolvency proceedings is requested by:
(i) a creditor whose claim arises from or is in connection with the operation of an establishment situated within the territory of the Member State where the opening of territorial proceedings is requested; or
(ii) a public authority which, under the law of the Member State within the territory of which the establishment is situated, has the right to request the opening of insolvency proceedings.
When main insolvency proceedings are opened, the territorial insolvency proceedings shall become secondary insolvency proceedings.

NOTES

Application of this Article in relation to the UK: this Article is amended, in relation to the UK only, by the Insolvency (Amendment) (EU Exit) Regulations 2019, SI 2019/146, reg 2, Schedule, Pt 1, paras 1, 4, as from IP completion day (as defined in the European Union (Withdrawal Agreement) Act 2020, s 39), as follows (for transitional provisions and savings, see reg 4 of the 2019 Regulations at **[12.82]**)—

"(1) Article 3 is amended as follows.

(2) For the heading "International jurisdiction" substitute "Centre of main interests".

(3) In paragraph 1—

(a) in the first sub-paragraph omit the first sentence;

(b) in the second sub-paragraph for "to another Member State" substitute "from the United Kingdom to a Member State or to the United Kingdom from a Member State";

(c) in the third sub-paragraph for "to another Member State" substitute "from the United Kingdom to a Member State or to the United Kingdom from a Member State";

(d) in the fourth sub-paragraph for "to another Member State" substitute "from the United Kingdom to a Member State or to the United Kingdom from a Member State";

(4) Omit paragraphs 2 to 4.".

[11.229]

Article 4 Examination as to jurisdiction

1. A court seised of a request to open insolvency proceedings shall of its own motion examine whether it has jurisdiction pursuant to Article 3. The judgment opening insolvency proceedings shall specify the grounds on which the jurisdiction of the court is based, and, in particular, whether jurisdiction is based on Article 3 (1) or (2).

2. Notwithstanding paragraph 1, where insolvency proceedings are opened in accordance with national law without a decision by a court, Member States may entrust the insolvency practitioner appointed in such proceedings to examine whether the Member State in which a request for the opening of proceedings is pending has jurisdiction pursuant to Article 3. Where this is the case, the insolvency practitioner shall specify in the decision opening the proceedings the grounds on which jurisdiction is based and, in particular, whether jurisdiction is based on Article 3(1) or (2).

NOTES

Application of this Article in relation to the UK: this Article is amended, in relation to the UK only, by the Insolvency (Amendment) (EU Exit) Regulations 2019, SI 2019/146, reg 2, Schedule, Pt 1, paras 1, 5, as from IP completion day (as defined in the European Union (Withdrawal Agreement) Act 2020, s 39), as follows (for transitional provisions and savings, see reg 4 of the 2019 Regulations at **[12.82]**)—

"(1) Article 4 is amended as follows.

(2) In paragraph 1—

(a) in the first sentence for "Article 3" substitute "Article 1(1A) (a) or (b)"; and

(b) for the second sentence substitute "Where there is jurisdiction to open insolvency proceedings on either of the grounds specified in Article 1(1A)(a) or (b), the judgment opening such proceedings must state which of those grounds is applicable.".

(3) In paragraph 2—

(a) in the first sentence—

(i) omit "in accordance with national law" and "Member States may entrust";

(ii) for the words from "to examine" to the end of the sentence substitute "must examine the grounds on which there is jurisdiction to open the proceedings under Article 1(1A)."; and

(b) for the second sentence substitute "Where this is the case and there is jurisdiction to open insolvency proceedings on either of the grounds specified in Article 1(1A)(a) or (b), the insolvency practitioner must specify in the decision opening the proceedings which of those grounds is applicable.".".

[11.230]

Article 5 Judicial review of the decision to open main insolvency proceedings

1. The debtor or any creditor may challenge before a court the decision opening main insolvency proceedings on grounds of international jurisdiction.

2. The decision opening main insolvency proceedings may be challenged by parties other than those referred to in paragraph 1 or on grounds other than a lack of international jurisdiction where national law so provides.

NOTES

Application of this Article in relation to the UK: this Article is amended, in relation to the UK only, by the Insolvency (Amendment) (EU Exit) Regulations 2019, SI 2019/146, reg 2, Schedule, Pt 1, paras 1, 6, as from IP completion day (as defined in the European Union (Withdrawal Agreement) Act 2020, s 39), as follows (for transitional provisions and savings, see reg 4 of the 2019 Regulations at **[12.82]**)—

"(1) Article 5 is amended as follows.

(2) In the heading omit "main".

(3) In paragraph 1—

(a) omit "main" after "the decision opening"; and

(b) for "grounds of international jurisdiction" substitute "the grounds of jurisdiction under Article 1(1A)(a)".

(4) In paragraph 2—

(a) omit "main" after "the decision opening";

(b) omit "international";

(c) after "jurisdiction" insert "under Article 1(1A)(a)"; and

(d) for "national law so provides" substitute "the relevant law (other than this Regulation) of the part of the United Kingdom in which the matter is being determined so provides".".

[11.231]

Article 6 Jurisdiction for actions deriving directly from insolvency proceedings and closely linked with them

1. The courts of the Member State within the territory of which insolvency proceedings have been opened in accordance with Article 3 shall have jurisdiction for any action which derives directly from the insolvency proceedings and is closely linked with them, such as avoidance actions.

2. Where an action referred to in paragraph 1 is related to an action in civil and commercial matters against the same defendant, the insolvency practitioner may bring both actions before the courts of the Member State within the territory of which the defendant is domiciled, or, where the action is brought against several defendants, before the courts of the Member State within the territory of which any of them is domiciled, provided that those courts have jurisdiction pursuant to Regulation (EU) No 1215/2012.

The first subparagraph shall apply to the debtor in possession, provided that national law allows the debtor in possession to bring actions on behalf of the insolvency estate.

3. For the purpose of paragraph 2, actions are deemed to be related where they are so closely connected that it is expedient to hear and determine them together to avoid the risk of irreconcilable judgments resulting from separate proceedings.

NOTES

Repeal of this Article in relation to the UK: this Article is repealed, in relation to the UK only, by the Insolvency (Amendment) (EU Exit) Regulations 2019, SI 2019/146, reg 2, Schedule, Pt 1, paras 1, 7, as from IP completion day (as defined in the European Union (Withdrawal Agreement) Act 2020, s 39) (for transitional provisions and savings, see reg 4 of the 2019 Regulations at **[12.82]**).

[11.232]

Article 7 Applicable law

1. Save as otherwise provided in this Regulation, the law applicable to insolvency proceedings and their effects shall be that of the Member State within the territory of which such proceedings are opened (the 'State of the opening of proceedings').

2. The law of the State of the opening of proceedings shall determine the conditions for the opening of those proceedings, their conduct and their closure. In particular, it shall determine the following:

- *(a) the debtors against which insolvency proceedings may be brought on account of their capacity;*
- *(b) the assets which form part of the insolvency estate and the treatment of assets acquired by or devolving on the debtor after the opening of the insolvency proceedings;*
- *(c) the respective powers of the debtor and the insolvency practitioner;*
- *(d) the conditions under which set-offs may be invoked;*
- *(e) the effects of insolvency proceedings on current contracts to which the debtor is party;*
- *(f) the effects of the insolvency proceedings on proceedings brought by individual creditors, with the exception of pending lawsuits;*
- *(g) the claims which are to be lodged against the debtor's insolvency estate and the treatment of claims arising after the opening of insolvency proceedings;*
- *(h) the rules governing the lodging, verification and admission of claims;*
- *(i) the rules governing the distribution of proceeds from the realisation of assets, the ranking of claims and the rights of creditors who have obtained partial satisfaction after the opening of insolvency proceedings by virtue of a right in rem or through a set-off;*
- *(j) the conditions for, and the effects of closure of, insolvency proceedings, in particular by composition;*
- *(k) creditors' rights after the closure of insolvency proceedings;*
- *(l) who is to bear the costs and expenses incurred in the insolvency proceedings;*
- *(m) the rules relating to the voidness, voidability or unenforceability of legal acts detrimental to the general body of creditors.*

NOTES

Repeal of this Article in relation to the UK: this Article is repealed, in relation to the UK only, by the Insolvency (Amendment) (EU Exit) Regulations 2019, SI 2019/146, reg 2, Schedule, Pt 1, paras 1, 7, as from IP completion day (as defined in the European Union (Withdrawal Agreement) Act 2020, s 39) (for transitional provisions and savings, see reg 4 of the 2019 Regulations at **[12.82]**).

[11.233]

Article 8 Third parties' rights in rem

1. The opening of insolvency proceedings shall not affect the rights in rem of creditors or third parties in respect of tangible or intangible, moveable or immoveable assets, both specific assets and collections of indefinite assets as a whole which change from time to time, belonging to the debtor which are situated within the territory of another Member State at the time of the opening of proceedings.

2. The rights referred to in paragraph 1 shall, in particular, mean:

- *(a) the right to dispose of assets or have them disposed of and to obtain satisfaction from the proceeds of or income from those assets, in particular by virtue of a lien or a mortgage;*
- *(b) the exclusive right to have a claim met, in particular a right guaranteed by a lien in respect of the claim or by assignment of the claim by way of a guarantee;*
- *(c) the right to demand assets from, and/or to require restitution by, anyone having possession or use of them contrary to the wishes of the party so entitled;*
- *(d) a right in rem to the beneficial use of assets.*

3. The right, recorded in a public register and enforceable against third parties, based on which a right in rem within the meaning of paragraph 1 may be obtained shall be considered to be a right in rem.

4. Paragraph 1 shall not preclude actions for voidness, voidability or unenforceability as referred to in point (m) of Article 7(2).

NOTES

Repeal of this Article in relation to the UK: this Article is repealed, in relation to the UK only, by the Insolvency (Amendment) (EU Exit) Regulations 2019, SI 2019/146, reg 2, Schedule, Pt 1, paras 1, 7, as from IP completion day (as defined in the European Union (Withdrawal Agreement) Act 2020, s 39) (for transitional provisions and savings, see reg 4 of the 2019 Regulations at **[12.82]**).

[11.234]

Article 9 Set-off

1. The opening of insolvency proceedings shall not affect the right of creditors to demand the set-off of their claims against the claims of a debtor, where such a set-off is permitted by the law applicable to the insolvent debtor's claim.

2. Paragraph 1 shall not preclude actions for voidness, voidability or unenforceability as referred to in point (m) of Article 7(2).

NOTES

Repeal of this Article in relation to the UK: this Article is repealed, in relation to the UK only, by the Insolvency (Amendment) (EU Exit) Regulations 2019, SI 2019/146, reg 2, Schedule, Pt 1, paras 1, 7, as from IP completion day (as defined in the European Union (Withdrawal Agreement) Act 2020, s 39) (for transitional provisions and savings, see reg 4 of the 2019 Regulations at **[12.82]**).

[11.235]

Article 10 Reservation of title

1. The opening of insolvency proceedings against the purchaser of an asset shall not affect sellers' rights that are based on a reservation of title where at the time of the opening of proceedings the asset is situated within the territory of a Member State other than the State of the opening of proceedings.

2. The opening of insolvency proceedings against the seller of an asset, after delivery of the asset, shall not constitute grounds for rescinding or terminating the sale and shall not prevent the purchaser from acquiring title where at the time of the opening of proceedings the asset sold is situated within the territory of a Member State other than the State of the opening of proceedings.

3. Paragraphs 1 and 2 shall not preclude actions for voidness, voidability or unenforceability as referred to in point (m) of Article 7(2).

NOTES

Repeal of this Article in relation to the UK: this Article is repealed, in relation to the UK only, by the Insolvency (Amendment) (EU Exit) Regulations 2019, SI 2019/146, reg 2, Schedule, Pt 1, paras 1, 7, as from IP completion day (as defined in the European Union (Withdrawal Agreement) Act 2020, s 39) (for transitional provisions and savings, see reg 4 of the 2019 Regulations at **[12.82]**).

[11.236]

Article 11 Contracts relating to immoveable property

1. The effects of insolvency proceedings on a contract conferring the right to acquire or make use of immoveable property shall be governed solely by the law of the Member State within the territory of which the immoveable property is situated.

2. The court which opened main insolvency proceedings shall have jurisdiction to approve the termination or modification of the contracts referred to in this Article where:

- *(a) the law of the Member State applicable to those contracts requires that such a contract may only be terminated or modified with the approval of the court opening insolvency proceedings; and*
- *(b) no insolvency proceedings have been opened in that Member State.*

NOTES

Repeal of this Article in relation to the UK: this Article is repealed, in relation to the UK only, by the Insolvency (Amendment) (EU Exit) Regulations 2019, SI 2019/146, reg 2, Schedule, Pt 1, paras 1, 7, as from IP completion day (as defined in the European Union (Withdrawal Agreement) Act 2020, s 39) (for transitional provisions and savings, see reg 4 of the 2019 Regulations at **[12.82]**).

[11.237]

Article 12 Payment systems and financial markets

1. Without prejudice to Article 8, the effects of insolvency proceedings on the rights and obligations of the parties to a payment or settlement system or to a financial market shall be governed solely by the law of the Member State applicable to that system or market.

2. Paragraph 1 shall not preclude any action for voidness, voidability or unenforceability which may be taken to set aside payments or transactions under the law applicable to the relevant payment system or financial market.

NOTES

Repeal of this Article in relation to the UK: this Article is repealed, in relation to the UK only, by the Insolvency (Amendment) (EU Exit) Regulations 2019, SI 2019/146, reg 2, Schedule, Pt 1, paras 1, 7, as from IP completion day (as defined in the European Union (Withdrawal Agreement) Act 2020, s 39); for transitional provisions and savings, see reg 4 of the 2019 Regulations at **[12.82]**.

[11.238]

Article 13 Contracts of employment

1. The effects of insolvency proceedings on employment contracts and relationships shall be governed solely by the law of the Member State applicable to the contract of employment.

2. The courts of the Member State in which secondary insolvency proceedings may be opened shall retain jurisdiction to approve the termination or modification of the contracts referred to in this Article even if no insolvency proceedings have been opened in that Member State.

The first subparagraph shall also apply to an authority competent under national law to approve the termination or modification of the contracts referred to in this Article.

NOTES

Repeal of this Article in relation to the UK: this Article is repealed, in relation to the UK only, by the Insolvency (Amendment) (EU Exit) Regulations 2019, SI 2019/146, reg 2, Schedule, Pt 1, paras 1, 7, as from IP completion day (as defined in the European Union (Withdrawal Agreement) Act 2020, s 39) (for transitional provisions and savings, see reg 4 of the 2019 Regulations at **[12.82]**).

[11.239]

Article 14 Effects on rights subject to registration

The effects of insolvency proceedings on the rights of a debtor in immoveable property, a ship or an aircraft subject to registration in a public register shall be determined by the law of the Member State under the authority of which the register is kept.

NOTES

Repeal of this Article in relation to the UK: this Article is repealed, in relation to the UK only, by the Insolvency (Amendment) (EU Exit) Regulations 2019, SI 2019/146, reg 2, Schedule, Pt 1, paras 1, 7, as from IP completion day (as defined in the European Union (Withdrawal Agreement) Act 2020, s 39) (for transitional provisions and savings, see reg 4 of the 2019 Regulations at **[12.82]**).

[11.240]

Article 15 European patents with unitary effect and Community trade marks

For the purposes of this Regulation, a European patent with unitary effect, a Community trade mark or any other similar right established by Union law may be included only in the proceedings referred to in Article 3(1).

NOTES

Repeal of this Article in relation to the UK: this Article is repealed, in relation to the UK only, by the Insolvency (Amendment) (EU Exit) Regulations 2019, SI 2019/146, reg 2, Schedule, Pt 1, paras 1, 7, as from IP completion day (as defined in the European Union (Withdrawal Agreement) Act 2020, s 39) (for transitional provisions and savings, see reg 4 of the 2019 Regulations at **[12.82]**).

[11.241]

Article 16 Detrimental acts

Point (m) of Article 7(2) shall not apply where the person who benefited from an act detrimental to all the creditors provides proof that:

(a) the act is subject to the law of a Member State other than that of the State of the opening of proceedings; and

(b) the law of that Member State does not allow any means of challenging that act in the relevant case.

NOTES

Repeal of this Article in relation to the UK: this Article is repealed, in relation to the UK only, by the Insolvency (Amendment) (EU Exit) Regulations 2019, SI 2019/146, reg 2, Schedule, Pt 1, paras 1, 7, as from IP completion day (as defined in the European Union (Withdrawal Agreement) Act 2020, s 39) (for transitional provisions and savings, see reg 4 of the 2019 Regulations at **[12.82]**).

[11.242]

Article 17 Protection of third-party purchasers

Where, by an act concluded after the opening of insolvency proceedings, a debtor disposes, for consideration, of:

(a) an immoveable asset;

(b) a ship or an aircraft subject to registration in a public register; or

(c) securities the existence of which requires registration in a register laid down by law;

the validity of that act shall be governed by the law of the State within the territory of which the immoveable asset is situated or under the authority of which the register is kept.

NOTES

Repeal of this Article in relation to the UK: this Article is repealed, in relation to the UK only, by the Insolvency (Amendment) (EU Exit) Regulations 2019, SI 2019/146, reg 2, Schedule, Pt 1, paras 1, 7, as from IP completion day (as defined in the European Union (Withdrawal Agreement) Act 2020, s 39) (for transitional provisions and savings, see reg 4 of the 2019 Regulations at **[12.82]**).

[11.243]

Article 18 Effects of insolvency proceedings on pending lawsuits or arbitral proceedings

The effects of insolvency proceedings on a pending lawsuit or pending arbitral proceedings concerning an asset or a right which forms part of a debtor's insolvency estate shall be governed solely by the law of the Member State in which that lawsuit is pending or in which the arbitral tribunal has its seat.

NOTES

Repeal of this Article in relation to the UK: this Article is repealed, in relation to the UK only, by the Insolvency (Amendment) (EU Exit) Regulations 2019, SI 2019/146, reg 2, Schedule, Pt 1, paras 1, 7, as from IP completion day (as defined in the European Union (Withdrawal Agreement) Act 2020, s 39) (for transitional provisions and savings, see reg 4 of the 2019 Regulations at **[12.82]**).

CHAPTER II RECOGNITION OF INSOLVENCY PROCEEDINGS

[11.244]

Article 19 Principle

1. Any judgment opening insolvency proceedings handed down by a court of a Member State which has jurisdiction pursuant to Article 3 shall be recognised in all other Member States from the moment that it becomes effective in the State of the opening of proceedings.

The rule laid down in the first subparagraph shall also apply where, on account of a debtor's capacity, insolvency proceedings cannot be brought against that debtor in other Member States.

2. Recognition of the proceedings referred to in Article 3 (1) shall not preclude the opening of the proceedings referred to in Article 3 (2) by a court in another Member State. The latter proceedings shall be secondary insolvency proceedings within the meaning of Chapter III.

NOTES

Repeal of this Article in relation to the UK: this Article is repealed, in relation to the UK only, by the Insolvency (Amendment) (EU Exit) Regulations 2019, SI 2019/146, reg 2, Schedule, Pt 1, paras 1, 7, as from IP completion day (as defined in the European Union (Withdrawal Agreement) Act 2020, s 39) (for transitional provisions and savings, see reg 4 of the 2019 Regulations at **[12.82]**).

[11.245]

Article 20 Effects of recognition

1. The judgment opening insolvency proceedings as referred to in Article 3 (1) shall, with no further formalities, produce the same effects in any other Member State as under the law of the State of the opening of proceedings, unless this Regulation provides otherwise and as long as no proceedings referred to in Article 3(2) are opened in that other Member State.

2. The effects of the proceedings referred to in Article 3(2) may not be challenged in other Member States. Any restriction of creditors' rights, in particular a stay or discharge, shall produce effects vis-à-vis assets situated within the territory of another Member State only in the case of those creditors who have given their consent.

NOTES

Repeal of this Article in relation to the UK: this Article is repealed, in relation to the UK only, by the Insolvency (Amendment) (EU Exit) Regulations 2019, SI 2019/146, reg 2, Schedule, Pt 1, paras 1, 7, as from IP completion day (as defined in the European Union (Withdrawal Agreement) Act 2020, s 39); for transitional provisions and savings, see reg 4 of the 2019 Regulations at **[12.82]**.

[11.246]

Article 21 Powers of the insolvency practitioner

1. The insolvency practitioner appointed by a court which has jurisdiction pursuant to Article 3(1) may exercise all the powers conferred on it, by the law of the State of the opening of proceedings, in another Member State, as long as no other insolvency proceedings have been opened there and no preservation measure to the contrary has been taken there further to a request for the opening of insolvency proceedings in that State. Subject to Articles 8 and 10, the insolvency practitioner may, in particular, remove the debtor's assets from the territory of the Member State in which they are situated.

2. The insolvency practitioner appointed by a court which has jurisdiction pursuant to Article 3(2) may in any other Member State claim through the courts or out of court that moveable property was removed from the territory of the State of the opening of proceedings to the territory of that other Member State after the opening of the insolvency proceedings. The insolvency practitioner may also bring any action to set aside which is in the interests of the creditors.

3. In exercising its powers, the insolvency practitioner shall comply with the law of the Member State within the territory of which it intends to take action, in particular with regard to procedures for the realisation of assets. Those powers may not include coercive measures, unless ordered by a court of that Member State, or the right to rule on legal proceedings or disputes.

NOTES

Repeal of this Article in relation to the UK: this Article is repealed, in relation to the UK only, by the Insolvency (Amendment) (EU Exit) Regulations 2019, SI 2019/146, reg 2, Schedule, Pt 1, paras 1, 7, as from IP completion day (as defined in the European Union (Withdrawal Agreement) Act 2020, s 39) (for transitional provisions and savings, see reg 4 of the 2019 Regulations at **[12.82]**).

[11.247]

Article 22 Proof of the insolvency practitioner's appointment

The insolvency practitioner's appointment shall be evidenced by a certified copy of the original decision appointing it or by any other certificate issued by the court which has jurisdiction.

A translation into the official language or one of the official languages of the Member State within the territory of which it intends to act may be required. No legalisation or other similar formality shall be required.

NOTES

Repeal of this Article in relation to the UK: this Article is repealed, in relation to the UK only, by the Insolvency (Amendment) (EU Exit) Regulations 2019, SI 2019/146, reg 2, Schedule, Pt 1, paras 1, 7, as from IP completion day (as defined in the European Union (Withdrawal Agreement) Act 2020, s 39); for transitional provisions and savings, see reg 4 of the 2019 Regulations at **[12.82]**.

[11.248]

Article 23 Return and imputation

1. A creditor which, after the opening of the proceedings referred to in Article 3(1), obtains by any means, in particular through enforcement, total or partial satisfaction of its claim on the assets belonging to a debtor situated within the territory of another Member State, shall return what it has obtained to the insolvency practitioner, subject to Articles 8 and 10.

2. In order to ensure the equal treatment of creditors, a creditor which has, in the course of insolvency proceedings, obtained a dividend on its claim shall share in distributions made in other proceedings only where creditors of the same ranking or category have, in those other proceedings, obtained an equivalent dividend.

NOTES

Repeal of this Article in relation to the UK: this Article is repealed, in relation to the UK only, by the Insolvency (Amendment) (EU Exit) Regulations 2019, SI 2019/146, reg 2, Schedule, Pt 1, paras 1, 7, as from IP completion day (as defined in the European Union (Withdrawal Agreement) Act 2020, s 39); for transitional provisions and savings, see reg 4 of the 2019 Regulations at **[12.82]**.

[11.249]

Article 24 Establishment of insolvency registers

1. Member States shall establish and maintain in their territory one or several registers in which information concerning insolvency proceedings is published ('insolvency registers'). That information shall be published as soon as possible after the opening of such proceedings.

2. The information referred to in paragraph 1 shall be made publicly available, subject to the conditions laid down in Article 27, and shall include the following ('mandatory information'):

(a) the date of the opening of insolvency proceedings;
(b) the court opening insolvency proceedings and the case reference number, if any;
(c) the type of insolvency proceedings referred to in Annex A that were opened and, where applicable, any relevant subtype of such proceedings opened in accordance with national law;
(d) whether jurisdiction for opening proceedings is based on Article 3(1), 3(2) or 3(4);
(e) if the debtor is a company or a legal person, the debtor's name, registration number, registered office or, if different, postal address;
(f) if the debtor is an individual whether or not exercising an independent business or professional activity, the debtor's name, registration number, if any, and postal address or, where the address is protected, the debtor's place and date of birth;
(g) the name, postal address or e-mail address of the insolvency practitioner, if any, appointed in the proceedings;
(h) the time limit for lodging claims, if any, or a reference to the criteria for calculating that time limit;
(i) the date of closing main insolvency proceedings, if any;
(j) the court before which and, where applicable, the time limit within which a challenge of the decision opening insolvency proceedings is to be lodged in accordance with Article 5, or a reference to the criteria for calculating that time limit.

3. Paragraph 2 shall not preclude Member States from including documents or additional information in their national insolvency registers, such as directors' disqualifications related to insolvency.

4. Member States shall not be obliged to include in the insolvency registers the information referred to in paragraph 1 of this Article in relation to individuals not exercising an independent business or professional activity, or to make such information publicly available through the system of interconnection of those registers, provided that known foreign creditors are informed, pursuant to Article 54, of the elements referred to under point (j) of paragraph 2 of this Article.

Where a Member State makes use of the possibility referred to in the first subparagraph, the insolvency proceedings shall not affect the claims of foreign creditors who have not received the information referred to in the first subparagraph.

5. The publication of information in the registers under this Regulation shall not have any legal effects other than those set out in national law and in Article 55(6).

NOTES

Repeal of this Article in relation to the UK: this Article is repealed, in relation to the UK only, by the Insolvency (Amendment) (EU Exit) Regulations 2019, SI 2019/146, reg 2, Schedule, Pt 1, paras 1, 7, as from IP completion day (as defined in the European Union (Withdrawal Agreement) Act 2020, s 39); for transitional provisions and savings, see reg 4 of the 2019 Regulations at **[12.82]**.

[11.250]

Article 25 Interconnection of insolvency registers

1. The Commission shall establish a decentralised system for the interconnection of insolvency registers by means of implementing acts. That system shall be composed of the insolvency registers and the European e-Justice Portal, which shall serve as a central public electronic access point to information in the system. The system shall provide a search service in all the official languages of the institutions of the Union in order to make available the mandatory information and any other documents or information included in the insolvency registers which the Member States choose to make available through the European e-Justice Portal.

2. By means of implementing acts in accordance with the procedure referred to in Article 87, the Commission shall adopt the following by 26 June 2019:

(a) the technical specification defining the methods of communication and information exchange by electronic means on the basis of the established interface specification for the system of interconnection of insolvency registers;
(b) the technical measures ensuring the minimum information technology security standards for communication and distribution of information within the system of interconnection of insolvency registers;
(c) minimum criteria for the search service provided by the European e-Justice Portal based on the information set out in Article 24;
(d) minimum criteria for the presentation of the results of such searches based on the information set out in Article 24;
(e) the means and the technical conditions of availability of services provided by the system of interconnection; and
(f) a glossary containing a basic explanation of the national insolvency proceedings listed in Annex A.

NOTES

Repeal of this Article in relation to the UK: this Article is repealed, in relation to the UK only, by the Insolvency (Amendment) (EU Exit) Regulations 2019, SI 2019/146, reg 2, Schedule, Pt 1, paras 1, 7, as from IP completion day (as defined

in the European Union (Withdrawal Agreement) Act 2020, s 39); for transitional provisions and savings, see reg 4 of the 2019 Regulations at **[12.82]**. Note that SI 2019/146, Schedule, Pt 1, para 7 was amended by the Insolvency (Amendment) (EU Exit) (No 2) Regulations 2019, SI 2019/1459, reg 2, Schedule, para 4, as from IP completion day (as defined in the European Union (Withdrawal Agreement) Act 2020, s 39). The effect of that amendment was to include this Article in the list of provisions repealed by Schedule, Pt 1, para 7.

Implementing Act for the purposes of para 2: see Commission Implementing Regulation 2019/917/EU establishing technical specifications, measures and other requirements required for the system of interconnection of insolvency registers in accordance with Article 25 of Regulation (EU) 2015/848 of the European Parliament and of the Council. It is available on the EUR-Lex website at eur-lex.europa.eu/legal-content/EN/TXT/?uri=CELEX:32019R0917.

[11.251]

Article 26 Costs of establishing and interconnecting insolvency registers

1. The establishment, maintenance and future development of the system of interconnection of insolvency registers shall be financed from the general budget of the Union.

2. Each Member State shall bear the costs of establishing and adjusting its national insolvency registers to make them interoperable with the European e-Justice Portal, as well as the costs of administering, operating and maintaining those registers. This shall be without prejudice to the possibility to apply for grants to support such activities under the Union's financial programmes.

NOTES

Repeal of this Article in relation to the UK: this Article is repealed, in relation to the UK only, by the Insolvency (Amendment) (EU Exit) Regulations 2019, SI 2019/146, reg 2, Schedule, Pt 1, paras 1, 7, as from IP completion day (as defined in the European Union (Withdrawal Agreement) Act 2020, s 39); for transitional provisions and savings, see reg 4 of the 2019 Regulations at **[12.82]**.

[11.252]

Article 27 Conditions of access to information via the system of interconnection

1. Member States shall ensure that the mandatory information referred to in points (a) to (j) of Article 24(2) is available free of charge via the system of interconnection of insolvency registers.

2. This Regulation shall not preclude Member States from charging a reasonable fee for access to the documents or additional information referred to in Article 24(3) via the system of interconnection of insolvency registers.

3. Member States may make access to mandatory information concerning individuals who are not exercising an independent business or professional activity, and concerning individuals exercising an independent business or professional activity when the insolvency proceedings are not related to that activity, subject to supplementary search criteria relating to the debtor in addition to the minimum criteria referred to in point (c) of Article 25(2).

4. Member States may require that access to the information referred to in paragraph 3 be made conditional upon a request to the competent authority. Member States may make access conditional upon the verification of the existence of a legitimate interest for accessing such information. The requesting person shall be able to submit the request for information electronically by means of a standard form via the European e-Justice Portal. Where a legitimate interest is required, it shall be permissible for the requesting person to justify his request by electronic copies of relevant documents. The requesting person shall be provided with an answer by the competent authority within 3 working days.

The requesting person shall not be obliged to provide translations of the documents justifying his request, or to bear any costs of translation which the competent authority may incur.

NOTES

Repeal of this Article in relation to the UK: this Article is repealed, in relation to the UK only, by the Insolvency (Amendment) (EU Exit) Regulations 2019, SI 2019/146, reg 2, Schedule, Pt 1, paras 1, 7, as from IP completion day (as defined in the European Union (Withdrawal Agreement) Act 2020, s 39); for transitional provisions and savings, see reg 4 of the 2019 Regulations at **[12.82]**.

[11.253]

Article 28 Publication in another Member State

1. The insolvency practitioner or the debtor in possession shall request that notice of the judgment opening insolvency proceedings and, where appropriate, the decision appointing the insolvency practitioner be published in any other Member State where an establishment of the debtor is located in accordance with the publication procedures provided for in that Member State. Such publication shall specify, where appropriate, the insolvency practitioner appointed and whether the jurisdiction rule applied is that pursuant to Article 3(1) or (2).

2. The insolvency practitioner or the debtor in possession may request that the information referred to in paragraph 1 be published in any other Member State where the insolvency practitioner or the debtor in possession deems it necessary in accordance with the publication procedures provided for in that Member State.

NOTES

Repeal of this Article in relation to the UK: this Article is repealed, in relation to the UK only, by the Insolvency (Amendment) (EU Exit) Regulations 2019, SI 2019/146, reg 2, Schedule, Pt 1, paras 1, 7, as from IP completion day (as defined in the European Union (Withdrawal Agreement) Act 2020, s 39); for transitional provisions and savings, see reg 4 of the 2019 Regulations at **[12.82]**.

[11.254]

Article 29 Registration in public registers of another Member State

1. Where the law of a Member State in which an establishment of the debtor is located and this establishment has been entered into a public register of that Member State, or the law of a Member State in which immovable property belonging to the debtor is located, requires information on the opening of insolvency proceedings referred to in Article 28 to be published in the land register, company register or any other public register, the insolvency practitioner or the debtor in possession shall take all the necessary measures to ensure such a registration.

2. The insolvency practitioner or the debtor in possession may request such registration in any other Member State, provided that the law of the Member State where the register is kept allows such registration.

NOTES

Repeal of this Article in relation to the UK: this Article is repealed, in relation to the UK only, by the Insolvency (Amendment) (EU Exit) Regulations 2019, SI 2019/146, reg 2, Schedule, Pt 1, paras 1, 7, as from IP completion day (as defined in the European Union (Withdrawal Agreement) Act 2020, s 39); for transitional provisions and savings, see reg 4 of the 2019 Regulations at **[12.82]**.

[11.255]

Article 30 Costs

The costs of the publication and registration provided for in Articles 28 and 29 shall be regarded as costs and expenses incurred in the proceedings.

NOTES

Repeal of this Article in relation to the UK: this Article is repealed, in relation to the UK only, by the Insolvency (Amendment) (EU Exit) Regulations 2019, SI 2019/146, reg 2, Schedule, Pt 1, paras 1, 7, as from IP completion day (as defined in the European Union (Withdrawal Agreement) Act 2020, s 39); for transitional provisions and savings, see reg 4 of the 2019 Regulations at **[12.82]**.

[11.256]

Article 31 Honouring of an obligation to a debtor

1. Where an obligation has been honoured in a Member State for the benefit of a debtor who is subject to insolvency proceedings opened in another Member State, when it should have been honoured for the benefit of the insolvency practitioner in those proceedings, the person honouring the obligation shall be deemed to have discharged it if he was unaware of the opening of the proceedings.

2. Where such an obligation is honoured before the publication provided for in Article 28 has been effected, the person honouring the obligation shall be presumed, in the absence of proof to the contrary, to have been unaware of the opening of insolvency proceedings. Where the obligation is honoured after such publication has been effected, the person honouring the obligation shall be presumed, in the absence of proof to the contrary, to have been aware of the opening of proceedings.

NOTES

Repeal of this Article in relation to the UK: this Article is repealed, in relation to the UK only, by the Insolvency (Amendment) (EU Exit) Regulations 2019, SI 2019/146, reg 2, Schedule, Pt 1, paras 1, 7, as from IP completion day (as defined in the European Union (Withdrawal Agreement) Act 2020, s 39); for transitional provisions and savings, see reg 4 of the 2019 Regulations at **[12.82]**.

[11.257]

Article 32 Recognition and enforceability of other judgments

1. Judgments handed down by a court whose judgment concerning the opening of proceedings is recognised in accordance with Article 19 and which concern the course and closure of insolvency proceedings, and compositions approved by that court, shall also be recognised with no further formalities. Such judgments shall be enforced in accordance with Articles 39 to 44 and 47 to 57 of Regulation (EU) No 1215/2012.

The first subparagraph shall also apply to judgments deriving directly from the insolvency proceedings and which are closely linked with them, even if they were handed down by another court.

The first subparagraph shall also apply to judgments relating to preservation measures taken after the request for the opening of insolvency proceedings or in connection with it.

2. The recognition and enforcement of judgments other than those referred to in paragraph 1 of this Article shall be governed by Regulation (EU) No 1215/2012 provided that that Regulation is applicable.

NOTES

Repeal of this Article in relation to the UK: this Article is repealed, in relation to the UK only, by the Insolvency (Amendment) (EU Exit) Regulations 2019, SI 2019/146, reg 2, Schedule, Pt 1, paras 1, 7, as from IP completion day (as defined in the European Union (Withdrawal Agreement) Act 2020, s 39); for transitional provisions and savings, see reg 4 of the 2019 Regulations at **[12.82]**.

[11.258]

Article 33 Public policy

Any Member State may refuse to recognise insolvency proceedings opened in another Member State or to enforce a judgment handed down in the context of such proceedings where the effects of such recognition or enforcement would be manifestly contrary to that State's public policy, in particular its fundamental principles or the constitutional rights and liberties of the individual.

NOTES

Repeal of this Article in relation to the UK: this Article is repealed, in relation to the UK only, by the Insolvency (Amendment) (EU Exit) Regulations 2019, SI 2019/146, reg 2, Schedule, Pt 1, paras 1, 7, as from IP completion day (as defined in the European Union (Withdrawal Agreement) Act 2020, s 39); for transitional provisions and savings, see reg 4 of the 2019 Regulations at **[12.82]**.

CHAPTER III SECONDARY INSOLVENCY PROCEEDINGS

[11.259]

Article 34 Opening of proceedings

Where main insolvency proceedings have been opened by a court of a Member State and recognised in another Member State, a court of that other Member State which has jurisdiction pursuant to Article 3(2) may open secondary insolvency proceedings in accordance with the provisions set out in this Chapter. Where the main insolvency proceedings required that the debtor be insolvent, the debtor's insolvency shall not be re-examined in the Member State in which secondary insolvency proceedings may be opened. The effects of secondary insolvency proceedings shall be restricted to the assets of the debtor situated within the territory of the Member State in which those proceedings have been opened.

NOTES

Repeal of this Article in relation to the UK: this Article is repealed, in relation to the UK only, by the Insolvency (Amendment) (EU Exit) Regulations 2019, SI 2019/146, reg 2, Schedule, Pt 1, paras 1, 7, as from IP completion day (as defined in the European Union (Withdrawal Agreement) Act 2020, s 39); for transitional provisions and savings, see reg 4 of the 2019 Regulations at **[12.82]**.

[11.260]

Article 35 Applicable law

Save as otherwise provided for in this Regulation, the law applicable to secondary insolvency proceedings shall be that of the Member State within the territory of which the secondary insolvency proceedings are opened.

NOTES

Repeal of this Article in relation to the UK: this Article is repealed, in relation to the UK only, by the Insolvency (Amendment) (EU Exit) Regulations 2019, SI 2019/146, reg 2, Schedule, Pt 1, paras 1, 7, as from IP completion day (as defined in the European Union (Withdrawal Agreement) Act 2020, s 39); for transitional provisions and savings, see reg 4 of the 2019 Regulations at **[12.82]**.

[11.261]

Article 36 Right to give an undertaking in order to avoid secondary insolvency proceedings

1. In order to avoid the opening of secondary insolvency proceedings, the insolvency practitioner in the main insolvency proceedings may give a unilateral undertaking (the 'undertaking') in respect of the assets located in the Member State in which secondary insolvency proceedings could be opened, that when distributing those assets or the proceeds received as a result of their realisation, it will comply with the distribution and priority rights under national law that creditors would have if secondary insolvency proceedings were opened in that Member State. The undertaking shall specify the factual assumptions on which it is based, in particular in respect of the value of the assets located in the Member State concerned and the options available to realise such assets.

2. Where an undertaking has been given in accordance with this Article, the law applicable to the distribution of proceeds from the realisation of assets referred to in paragraph 1, to the ranking of creditors' claims, and to the rights of creditors in relation to the assets referred to in paragraph 1 shall be the law of the Member State in which secondary insolvency proceedings could have been opened. The relevant point in time for determining the assets referred to in paragraph 1 shall be the moment at which the undertaking is given.

3. The undertaking shall be made in the official language or one of the official languages of the Member State where secondary insolvency proceedings could have been opened, or, where there are several official languages in that Member State, the official language or one of the official languages of the place in which secondary insolvency proceedings could have been opened.

4. The undertaking shall be made in writing. It shall be subject to any other requirements relating to form and approval requirements as to distributions, if any, of the State of the opening of the main insolvency proceedings.

5. The undertaking shall be approved by the known local creditors. The rules on qualified majority and voting that apply to the adoption of restructuring plans under the law of the Member State where secondary insolvency proceedings could have been opened shall also apply to the approval of the undertaking. Creditors shall be able to participate in the vote by distance means of communication, where national law so permits. The insolvency practitioner shall inform the known local creditors of the undertaking, of the rules and procedures for its approval, and of the approval or rejection of the undertaking.

6. An undertaking given and approved in accordance with this Article shall be binding on the estate. If secondary insolvency proceedings are opened in accordance with Articles 37 and 38, the insolvency practitioner in the main insolvency proceedings shall transfer any assets which it removed from the territory of that Member State after the undertaking was given or, where those assets have already been realised, their proceeds, to the insolvency practitioner in the secondary insolvency proceedings.

7. Where the insolvency practitioner has given an undertaking, it shall inform local creditors about the intended distributions prior to distributing the assets and proceeds referred to in paragraph 1. If that information does not comply with the terms of the undertaking or the applicable law, any local creditor may challenge such distribution before the courts of the Member State in which main insolvency proceedings have been opened in order to obtain a distribution in accordance with the terms of the undertaking and the applicable law. In such cases, no distribution shall take place until the court has taken a decision on the challenge.

8. Local creditors may apply to the courts of the Member State in which main insolvency proceedings have been opened, in order to require the insolvency practitioner in the main insolvency proceedings to take any suitable measures necessary to ensure compliance with the terms of the undertaking available under the law of the State of the opening of main insolvency proceedings.

9. Local creditors may also apply to the courts of the Member State in which secondary insolvency proceedings could have been opened in order to require the court to take provisional or protective measures to ensure compliance by the insolvency practitioner with the terms of the undertaking.

10. The insolvency practitioner shall be liable for any damage caused to local creditors as a result of its non-compliance with the obligations and requirements set out in this Article.

11. For the purpose of this Article, an authority which is established in the Member State where secondary insolvency proceedings could have been opened and which is obliged under Directive 2008/94/EC of the European Parliament and of the Council[1] to guarantee the payment of employees' outstanding claims resulting from contracts of employment or employment relationships shall be considered to be a local creditor, where the national law so provides.

NOTES

Repeal of this Article in relation to the UK: this Article is repealed, in relation to the UK only, by the Insolvency (Amendment) (EU Exit) Regulations 2019, SI 2019/146, reg 2, Schedule, Pt 1, paras 1, 7, as from IP completion day (as defined in the European Union (Withdrawal Agreement) Act 2020, s 39); for transitional provisions and savings, see reg 4 of the 2019 Regulations at **[12.82]**.

[1] Directive 2008/94/EC of the European Parliament and of the Council of 22 October 2008 on the protection of employees in the event of the insolvency of their employer (OJ L283, 28.10.2008, p 36).

[11.262]

Article 37 Right to request the opening of secondary insolvency proceedings

1. The opening of secondary insolvency proceedings may be requested by:

(a) the insolvency practitioner in the main insolvency proceedings;

(b) any other person or authority empowered to request the opening of insolvency proceedings under the law of the Member State within the territory of which the opening of secondary insolvency proceedings is requested.

2. Where an undertaking has become binding in accordance with Article 36, the request for opening secondary insolvency proceedings shall be lodged within 30 days of having received notice of the approval of the undertaking.

NOTES

Repeal of this Article in relation to the UK: this Article is repealed, in relation to the UK only, by the Insolvency (Amendment) (EU Exit) Regulations 2019, SI 2019/146, reg 2, Schedule, Pt 1, paras 1, 7, as from IP completion day (as defined in the European Union (Withdrawal Agreement) Act 2020, s 39); for transitional provisions and savings, see reg 4 of the 2019 Regulations at **[12.82]**.

[11.263]

Article 38 Decision to open secondary insolvency proceedings

1. A court seised of a request to open secondary insolvency proceedings shall immediately give notice to the insolvency practitioner or the debtor in possession in the main insolvency proceedings and give it an opportunity to be heard on the request.

2. Where the insolvency practitioner in the main insolvency proceedings has given an undertaking in accordance with Article 36, the court referred to in paragraph 1 of this Article shall, at the request of the insolvency practitioner, not open secondary insolvency proceedings if it is satisfied that the undertaking adequately protects the general interests of local creditors.

3. Where a temporary stay of individual enforcement proceedings has been granted in order to allow for negotiations between the debtor and its creditors, the court, at the request of the insolvency practitioner or the debtor in possession, may stay the opening of secondary insolvency proceedings for a period not exceeding 3 months, provided that suitable measures are in place to protect the interests of local creditors.

The court referred to in paragraph 1 may order protective measures to protect the interests of local creditors by requiring the insolvency practitioner or the debtor in possession not to remove or dispose of any assets which are located in the Member State where its establishment is located unless this is done in the ordinary course of business. The court may also order other measures to protect the interest of local creditors during a stay, unless this is incompatible with the national rules on civil procedure.

The stay of the opening of secondary insolvency proceedings shall be lifted by the court of its own motion or at the request of any creditor if, during the stay, an agreement in the negotiations referred to in the first subparagraph has been concluded.

The stay may be lifted by the court of its own motion or at the request of any creditor if the continuation of the stay is detrimental to the creditor's rights, in particular if the negotiations have been disrupted or it has become evident that they are unlikely to be concluded, or if the insolvency practitioner or the debtor in possession has infringed the prohibition on disposal of its assets or on removal of them from the territory of the Member State where the establishment is located.

4. At the request of the insolvency practitioner in the main insolvency proceedings, the court referred to in paragraph 1 may open a type of insolvency proceedings as listed in Annex A other than the type initially requested, provided that the conditions for opening that type of proceedings under national law are fulfilled and that that type of proceedings is the most appropriate as regards the interests of the local creditors and coherence between the main and secondary insolvency proceedings. The second sentence of Article 34 shall apply.

NOTES

Repeal of this Article in relation to the UK: this Article is repealed, in relation to the UK only, by the Insolvency (Amendment) (EU Exit) Regulations 2019, SI 2019/146, reg 2, Schedule, Pt 1, paras 1, 7, as from IP completion day (as defined in the European Union (Withdrawal Agreement) Act 2020, s 39); for transitional provisions and savings, see reg 4 of the 2019 Regulations at **[12.82]**.

[11.264]

Article 39 Judicial review of the decision to open secondary insolvency proceedings

The insolvency practitioner in the main insolvency proceedings may challenge the decision to open secondary insolvency proceedings before the courts of the Member State in which secondary insolvency proceedings have been opened on the ground that the court did not comply with the conditions and requirements of Article 38.

NOTES

Repeal of this Article in relation to the UK: this Article is repealed, in relation to the UK only, by the Insolvency (Amendment) (EU Exit) Regulations 2019, SI 2019/146, reg 2, Schedule, Pt 1, paras 1, 7, as from IP completion day (as defined in the European Union (Withdrawal Agreement) Act 2020, s 39); for transitional provisions and savings, see reg 4 of the 2019 Regulations at **[12.82]**.

[11.265]

Article 40 Advance payment of costs and expenses

Where the law of the Member State in which the opening of secondary insolvency proceedings is requested requires that the debtor's assets be sufficient to cover in whole or in part the costs and expenses of the proceedings, the court may, when it receives such a request, require the applicant to make an advance payment of costs or to provide appropriate security.

NOTES

Repeal of this Article in relation to the UK: this Article is repealed, in relation to the UK only, by the Insolvency (Amendment) (EU Exit) Regulations 2019, SI 2019/146, reg 2, Schedule, Pt 1, paras 1, 7, as from IP completion day (as defined in the European Union (Withdrawal Agreement) Act 2020, s 39); for transitional provisions and savings, see reg 4 of the 2019 Regulations at **[12.82]**.

[11.266]

Article 41 Cooperation and communication between insolvency practitioners

1. The insolvency practitioner in the main insolvency proceedings and the insolvency practitioner or practitioners in secondary insolvency proceedings concerning the same debtor shall cooperate with each other to the extent such cooperation is not incompatible with the rules applicable to the respective proceedings. Such cooperation may take any form, including the conclusion of agreements or protocols.

2. In implementing the cooperation set out in paragraph 1, the insolvency practitioners shall:

- *(a) as soon as possible communicate to each other any information which may be relevant to the other proceedings, in particular any progress made in lodging and verifying claims and all measures aimed at rescuing or restructuring the debtor, or at terminating the proceedings, provided appropriate arrangements are made to protect confidential information;*
- *(b) explore the possibility of restructuring the debtor and, where such a possibility exists, coordinate the elaboration and implementation of a restructuring plan;*
- *(c) coordinate the administration of the realisation or use of the debtor's assets and affairs; the insolvency practitioner in the secondary insolvency proceedings shall give the insolvency practitioner in the main insolvency proceedings an early opportunity to submit proposals on the realisation or use of the assets in the secondary insolvency proceedings.*

3. Paragraphs 1 and 2 shall apply mutatis mutandis to situations where, in the main or in the secondary insolvency proceedings or in any territorial insolvency proceedings concerning the same debtor and open at the same time, the debtor remains in possession of its assets.

NOTES

Repeal of this Article in relation to the UK: this Article is repealed, in relation to the UK only, by the Insolvency (Amendment) (EU Exit) Regulations 2019, SI 2019/146, reg 2, Schedule, Pt 1, paras 1, 7, as from IP completion day (as defined in the European Union (Withdrawal Agreement) Act 2020, s 39); for transitional provisions and savings, see reg 4 of the 2019 Regulations at **[12.82]**.

[11.267]

Article 42 Cooperation and communication between courts

1. In order to facilitate the coordination of main, territorial and secondary insolvency proceedings concerning the same debtor, a court before which a request to open insolvency proceedings is pending, or which has opened such proceedings, shall cooperate with any other court before which a request to open insolvency proceedings is pending, or which has opened such proceedings, to the extent that such cooperation is not incompatible with the rules applicable to each of the proceedings. For that purpose, the courts may, where appropriate, appoint an independent person or body acting on its instructions, provided that it is not incompatible with the rules applicable to them.

2. In implementing the cooperation set out in paragraph 1, the courts, or any appointed person or body acting on their behalf, as referred to in paragraph 1, may communicate directly with, or request information or assistance directly from, each other provided that such communication respects the procedural rights of the parties to the proceedings and the confidentiality of information.

3. The cooperation referred to in paragraph 1 may be implemented by any means that the court considers appropriate. It may, in particular, concern:

- *(a) coordination in the appointment of the insolvency practitioners;*
- *(b) communication of information by any means considered appropriate by the court;*
- *(c) coordination of the administration and supervision of the debtor's assets and affairs;*
- *(d) coordination of the conduct of hearings;*
- *(e) coordination in the approval of protocols, where necessary.*

NOTES

Repeal of this Article in relation to the UK: this Article is repealed, in relation to the UK only, by the Insolvency (Amendment) (EU Exit) Regulations 2019, SI 2019/146, reg 2, Schedule, Pt 1, paras 1, 7, as from IP completion day (as defined in the European Union (Withdrawal Agreement) Act 2020, s 39); for transitional provisions and savings, see reg 4 of the 2019 Regulations at **[12.82]**.

[11.268]

Article 43 Cooperation and communication between insolvency practitioners and courts

1. In order to facilitate the coordination of main, territorial and secondary insolvency proceedings opened in respect of the same debtor:

- *(a) an insolvency practitioner in main insolvency proceedings shall cooperate and communicate with any court before which a request to open secondary insolvency proceedings is pending or which has opened such proceedings;*

(b) *an insolvency practitioner in territorial or secondary insolvency proceedings shall cooperate and communicate with the court before which a request to open main insolvency proceedings is pending or which has opened such proceedings; and*

(c) *an insolvency practitioner in territorial or secondary insolvency proceedings shall cooperate and communicate with the court before which a request to open other territorial or secondary insolvency proceedings is pending or which has opened such proceedings;*

to the extent that such cooperation and communication are not incompatible with the rules applicable to each of the proceedings and do not entail any conflict of interest.

2. The cooperation referred to in paragraph 1 may be implemented by any appropriate means, such as those set out in Article 42(3).

NOTES

Repeal of this Article in relation to the UK: this Article is repealed, in relation to the UK only, by the Insolvency (Amendment) (EU Exit) Regulations 2019, SI 2019/146, reg 2, Schedule, Pt 1, paras 1, 7, as from IP completion day (as defined in the European Union (Withdrawal Agreement) Act 2020, s 39); for transitional provisions and savings, see reg 4 of the 2019 Regulations at **[12.82]**.

[11.269]

Article 44 Costs of cooperation and communication

The requirements laid down in Articles 42 and 43 shall not result in courts charging costs to each other for cooperation and communication.

NOTES

Repeal of this Article in relation to the UK: this Article is repealed, in relation to the UK only, by the Insolvency (Amendment) (EU Exit) Regulations 2019, SI 2019/146, reg 2, Schedule, Pt 1, paras 1, 7, as from IP completion day (as defined in the European Union (Withdrawal Agreement) Act 2020, s 39); for transitional provisions and savings, see reg 4 of the 2019 Regulations at **[12.82]**.

[11.270]

Article 45 Exercise of creditors' rights

1. Any creditor may lodge its claim in the main insolvency proceedings and in any secondary insolvency proceedings.

2. The insolvency practitioners in the main and any secondary insolvency proceedings shall lodge in other proceedings claims which have already been lodged in the proceedings for which they were appointed, provided that the interests of creditors in the latter proceedings are served by doing so, subject to the right of creditors to oppose such lodgement or to withdraw the lodgement of their claims where the law applicable so provides.

3. The insolvency practitioner in the main or secondary insolvency proceedings shall be entitled to participate in other proceedings on the same basis as a creditor, in particular by attending creditors' meetings.

NOTES

Repeal of this Article in relation to the UK: this Article is repealed, in relation to the UK only, by the Insolvency (Amendment) (EU Exit) Regulations 2019, SI 2019/146, reg 2, Schedule, Pt 1, paras 1, 7, as from IP completion day (as defined in the European Union (Withdrawal Agreement) Act 2020, s 39); for transitional provisions and savings, see reg 4 of the 2019 Regulations at **[12.82]**.

[11.271]

Article 46 Stay of the process of realisation of assets

1. The court which opened the secondary insolvency proceedings shall stay the process of realisation of assets in whole or in part on receipt of a request from the insolvency practitioner in the main insolvency proceedings. In such a case, it may require the insolvency practitioner in the main insolvency proceedings to take any suitable measure to guarantee the interests of the creditors in the secondary insolvency proceedings and of individual classes of creditors. Such a request from the insolvency practitioner may be rejected only if it is manifestly of no interest to the creditors in the main insolvency proceedings. Such a stay of the process of realisation of assets may be ordered for up to 3 months. It may be continued or renewed for similar periods.

2. The court referred to in paragraph 1 shall terminate the stay of the process of realisation of assets:

(a) *at the request of the insolvency practitioner in the main insolvency proceedings;*

(b) *of its own motion, at the request of a creditor or at the request of the insolvency practitioner in the secondary insolvency proceedings if that measure no longer appears justified, in particular, by the interests of creditors in the main insolvency proceedings or in the secondary insolvency proceedings.*

NOTES

Repeal of this Article in relation to the UK: this Article is repealed, in relation to the UK only, by the Insolvency (Amendment) (EU Exit) Regulations 2019, SI 2019/146, reg 2, Schedule, Pt 1, paras 1, 7, as from IP completion day (as defined in the European Union (Withdrawal Agreement) Act 2020, s 39); for transitional provisions and savings, see reg 4 of the 2019 Regulations at **[12.82]**.

[11.272]

Article 47 Power of the insolvency practitioner to propose restructuring plans

1. Where the law of the Member State where secondary insolvency proceedings have been opened allows for such proceedings to be closed without liquidation by a restructuring plan, a composition or a comparable measure, the insolvency practitioner in the main insolvency proceedings shall be empowered to propose such a measure in accordance with the procedure of that Member State.

2. Any restriction of creditors' rights arising from a measure referred to in paragraph 1 which is proposed in secondary insolvency proceedings, such as a stay of payment or discharge of debt, shall have no effect in respect of assets of a debtor that are not covered by those proceedings, without the consent of all the creditors having an interest.

NOTES

Repeal of this Article in relation to the UK: this Article is repealed, in relation to the UK only, by the Insolvency (Amendment) (EU Exit) Regulations 2019, SI 2019/146, reg 2, Schedule, Pt 1, paras 1, 7, as from IP completion day (as defined in the European Union (Withdrawal Agreement) Act 2020, s 39); for transitional provisions and savings, see reg 4 of the 2019 Regulations at **[12.82]**.

[11.273]

Article 48 Impact of closure of insolvency proceedings

1. Without prejudice to Article 49, the closure of insolvency proceedings shall not prevent the continuation of other insolvency proceedings concerning the same debtor which are still open at that point in time.

2. Where insolvency proceedings concerning a legal person or a company in the Member State of that person's or company's registered office would entail the dissolution of the legal person or of the company, that legal person or company shall not cease to exist until any other insolvency proceedings concerning the same debtor have been closed, or the insolvency practitioner or practitioners in such proceedings have given consent to the dissolution.

NOTES

Repeal of this Article in relation to the UK: this Article is repealed, in relation to the UK only, by the Insolvency (Amendment) (EU Exit) Regulations 2019, SI 2019/146, reg 2, Schedule, Pt 1, paras 1, 7, as from IP completion day (as defined in the European Union (Withdrawal Agreement) Act 2020, s 39); for transitional provisions and savings, see reg 4 of the 2019 Regulations at **[12.82]**.

[11.274]

Article 49 Assets remaining in the secondary insolvency proceedings

If, by the liquidation of assets in the secondary insolvency proceedings, it is possible to meet all claims allowed under those proceedings, the insolvency practitioner appointed in those proceedings shall immediately transfer any assets remaining to the insolvency practitioner in the main insolvency proceedings.

NOTES

Repeal of this Article in relation to the UK: this Article is repealed, in relation to the UK only, by the Insolvency (Amendment) (EU Exit) Regulations 2019, SI 2019/146, reg 2, Schedule, Pt 1, paras 1, 7, as from IP completion day (as defined in the European Union (Withdrawal Agreement) Act 2020, s 39); for transitional provisions and savings, see reg 4 of the 2019 Regulations at **[12.82]**.

[11.275]

Article 50 Subsequent opening of the main insolvency proceedings

Where the proceedings referred to in Article 3(1) are opened following the opening of the proceedings referred to in Article 3(2) in another Member State, Articles 41, 45, 46, 47 and 49 shall apply to those opened first, in so far as the progress of those proceedings so permits.

NOTES

Repeal of this Article in relation to the UK: this Article is repealed, in relation to the UK only, by the Insolvency (Amendment) (EU Exit) Regulations 2019, SI 2019/146, reg 2, Schedule, Pt 1, paras 1, 7, as from IP completion day (as defined in the European Union (Withdrawal Agreement) Act 2020, s 39); for transitional provisions and savings, see reg 4 of the 2019 Regulations at **[12.82]**.

[11.276]

Article 51 Conversion of secondary insolvency proceedings

1. At the request of the insolvency practitioner in the main insolvency proceedings, the court of the Member State in which secondary insolvency proceedings have been opened may order the conversion of the secondary insolvency proceedings into another type of insolvency proceedings listed in Annex A, provided that the conditions for opening that type of proceedings under national law are fulfilled and that that type of proceedings is the most appropriate as regards the interests of the local creditors and coherence between the main and secondary insolvency proceedings.

2. When considering the request referred to in paragraph 1, the court may seek information from the insolvency practitioners involved in both proceedings.

NOTES

Repeal of this Article in relation to the UK: this Article is repealed, in relation to the UK only, by the Insolvency (Amendment) (EU Exit) Regulations 2019, SI 2019/146, reg 2, Schedule, Pt 1, paras 1, 7, as from IP completion day (as defined in the European Union (Withdrawal Agreement) Act 2020, s 39); for transitional provisions and savings, see reg 4 of the 2019 Regulations at **[12.82]**.

[11.277]

Article 52 Preservation measures

Where the court of a Member State which has jurisdiction pursuant to Article 3(1) appoints a temporary administrator in order to ensure the preservation of a debtor's assets, that temporary administrator shall be empowered to request any measures to secure and preserve any of the debtor's assets situated in another Member State, provided for under the law of that Member State, for the period between the request for the opening of insolvency proceedings and the judgment opening the proceedings.

NOTES

Repeal of this Article in relation to the UK: this Article is repealed, in relation to the UK only, by the Insolvency (Amendment) (EU Exit) Regulations 2019, SI 2019/146, reg 2, Schedule, Pt 1, paras 1, 7, as from IP completion day (as defined in the European Union (Withdrawal Agreement) Act 2020, s 39); for transitional provisions and savings, see reg 4 of the 2019 Regulations at **[12.82]**.

CHAPTER IV PROVISION OF INFORMATION FOR CREDITORS AND LODGEMENT OF THEIR CLAIMS

[11.278]

Article 53 Right to lodge claims

Any foreign creditor may lodge claims in insolvency proceedings by any means of communication, which are accepted by the law of the State of the opening of proceedings. Representation by a lawyer or another legal professional shall not be mandatory for the sole purpose of lodging of claims.

NOTES

Repeal of this Article in relation to the UK: this Article is repealed, in relation to the UK only, by the Insolvency (Amendment) (EU Exit) Regulations 2019, SI 2019/146, reg 2, Schedule, Pt 1, paras 1, 7, as from IP completion day (as defined in the European Union (Withdrawal Agreement) Act 2020, s 39); for transitional provisions and savings, see reg 4 of the 2019 Regulations at **[12.82]**.

[11.279]

Article 54 Duty to inform creditors

1. As soon as insolvency proceedings are opened in a Member State, the court of that State having jurisdiction or the insolvency practitioner appointed by that court shall immediately inform the known foreign creditors.

2. The information referred to in paragraph 1, provided by an individual notice, shall in particular include time limits, the penalties laid down with regard to those time limits, the body or authority empowered to accept the lodgement of claims and any other measures laid down. Such notice shall also indicate whether creditors whose claims are preferential or secured in rem need to lodge their claims. The notice shall also include a copy of the standard form for lodging of claims referred to in Article 55 or information on where that form is available.

3. The information referred to in paragraphs 1 and 2 of this Article shall be provided using the standard notice form to be established in accordance with Article 88. The form shall be published in the European e-Justice Portal and shall bear the heading 'Notice of insolvency proceedings' in all the official languages of the institutions of the Union. It shall be transmitted in the official language of the State of the opening of proceedings or, if there are several official languages in that Member State, in the official language or one of the official languages of the place where insolvency proceedings have been opened, or in another language which that State has indicated it can accept, in accordance with Article 55(5), if it can be assumed that that language is easier to understand for the foreign creditors.

4. In insolvency proceedings relating to an individual not exercising a business or professional activity, the use of the standard form referred to in this Article shall not be obligatory if creditors are not required to lodge their claims in order to have their claims taken into account in the proceedings.

NOTES

Repeal of this Article in relation to the UK: this Article is repealed, in relation to the UK only, by the Insolvency (Amendment) (EU Exit) Regulations 2019, SI 2019/146, reg 2, Schedule, Pt 1, paras 1, 7, as from IP completion day (as defined in the European Union (Withdrawal Agreement) Act 2020, s 39); for transitional provisions and savings, see reg 4 of the 2019 Regulations at **[12.82]**.

[11.280]

Article 55 Procedure for lodging claims

1. Any foreign creditor may lodge its claim using the standard claims form to be established in accordance with Article 88. The form shall bear the heading 'Lodgement of claims' in all the official languages of the institutions of the Union.

2. The standard claims form referred to in paragraph 1 shall include the following information:

(a) the name, postal address, e-mail address, if any, personal identification number, if any, and bank details of the foreign creditor referred to in paragraph 1;

(b) the amount of the claim, specifying the principal and, where applicable, interest and the date on which it arose and the date on which it became due, if different;

(c) if interest is claimed, the interest rate, whether the interest is of a legal or contractual nature, the period of time for which the interest is claimed and the capitalised amount of interest;

(d) if costs incurred in asserting the claim prior to the opening of proceedings are claimed, the amount and the details of those costs;

(e) the nature of the claim;

(f) whether any preferential creditor status is claimed and the basis of such a claim;

(g) whether security in rem or a reservation of title is alleged in respect of the claim and if so, what assets are covered by the security interest being invoked, the date on which the security was granted and, where the security has been registered, the registration number; and

(h) whether any set-off is claimed and, if so, the amounts of the mutual claims existing on the date when insolvency proceedings were opened, the date on which they arose and the amount net of set-off claimed.

The standard claims form shall be accompanied by copies of any supporting documents.

3. The standard claims form shall indicate that the provision of information concerning the bank details and the personal identification number of the creditor referred to in point (a) of paragraph 2 is not compulsory.

4. When a creditor lodges its claim by means other than the standard form referred to in paragraph 1, the claim shall contain the information referred to in paragraph 2.

5. Claims may be lodged in any official language of the institutions of the Union. The court, the insolvency practitioner or the debtor in possession may require the creditor to provide a translation in the official language of the State of the opening of proceedings or, if there are several official languages in that Member State, in the official language or one of the official languages of the place where insolvency proceedings have been opened, or in another language which that Member State has indicated it can accept. Each Member State shall indicate whether it accepts any official language of the institutions of the Union other than its own for the purpose of the lodging of claims.

6. Claims shall be lodged within the period stipulated by the law of the State of the opening of proceedings. In the case of a foreign creditor, that period shall not be less than 30 days following the publication of the opening of insolvency proceedings in the insolvency register of the State of the opening of proceedings. Where a Member State relies on Article 24(4), that period shall not be less than 30 days following a creditor having been informed pursuant to Article 54.

7. Where the court, the insolvency practitioner or the debtor in possession has doubts in relation to a claim lodged in accordance with this Article, it shall give the creditor the opportunity to provide additional evidence on the existence and the amount of the claim.

NOTES

Repeal of this Article in relation to the UK: this Article is repealed, in relation to the UK only, by the Insolvency (Amendment) (EU Exit) Regulations 2019, SI 2019/146, reg 2, Schedule, Pt 1, paras 1, 7, as from IP completion day (as defined in the European Union (Withdrawal Agreement) Act 2020, s 39); for transitional provisions and savings, see reg 4 of the 2019 Regulations at **[12.82]**.

CHAPTER V INSOLVENCY PROCEEDINGS OF MEMBERS OF A GROUP OF COMPANIES

SECTION 1 COOPERATION AND COMMUNICATION

[11.281]

Article 56 Cooperation and communication between insolvency practitioners

1. Where insolvency proceedings relate to two or more members of a group of companies, an insolvency practitioner appointed in proceedings concerning a member of the group shall cooperate with any insolvency practitioner appointed in proceedings concerning another member of the same group to the extent that such cooperation is appropriate to facilitate the effective administration of those proceedings, is not incompatible with the rules applicable to such proceedings and does not entail any conflict of interest. That cooperation may take any form, including the conclusion of agreements or protocols.

2. In implementing the cooperation set out in paragraph 1, insolvency practitioners shall:

(a) as soon as possible communicate to each other any information which may be relevant to the other proceedings, provided appropriate arrangements are made to protect confidential information;

(b) consider whether possibilities exist for coordinating the administration and supervision of the affairs of the group members which are subject to insolvency proceedings, and if so, coordinate such administration and supervision;

(c) consider whether possibilities exist for restructuring group members which are subject to insolvency proceedings and, if so, coordinate with regard to the proposal and negotiation of a coordinated restructuring plan.

For the purposes of points (b) and (c), all or some of the insolvency practitioners referred to in paragraph 1 may agree to grant additional powers to an insolvency practitioner appointed in one of the proceedings where such an agreement is permitted by the rules applicable to each of the proceedings. They may also agree on the allocation of certain tasks amongst them, where such allocation of tasks is permitted by the rules applicable to each of the proceedings.

NOTES

Repeal of this Article in relation to the UK: this Article is repealed, in relation to the UK only, by the Insolvency (Amendment) (EU Exit) Regulations 2019, SI 2019/146, reg 2, Schedule, Pt 1, paras 1, 7, as from IP completion day (as defined in the European Union (Withdrawal Agreement) Act 2020, s 39); for transitional provisions and savings, see reg 4 of the 2019 Regulations at **[12.82]**.

[11.282]

Article 57 Cooperation and communication between courts

1. Where insolvency proceedings relate to two or more members of a group of companies, a court which has opened such proceedings shall cooperate with any other court before which a request to open proceedings concerning another member of the same group is pending or which has opened such proceedings to the extent that such cooperation is appropriate to facilitate the effective administration of the proceedings, is not incompatible with the rules applicable to them and does not entail any conflict of interest. For that purpose, the courts may, where appropriate, appoint an independent person or body to act on its instructions, provided that this is not incompatible with the rules applicable to them.

2. In implementing the cooperation set out in paragraph 1, courts, or any appointed person or body acting on their behalf, as referred to in paragraph 1, may communicate directly with each other, or request information or assistance directly from each other, provided that such communication respects the procedural rights of the parties to the proceedings and the confidentiality of information.

3. The cooperation referred to in paragraph 1 may be implemented by any means that the court considers appropriate. It may, in particular, concern:

(a) coordination in the appointment of insolvency practitioners;

(b) communication of information by any means considered appropriate by the court;

(c) coordination of the administration and supervision of the assets and affairs of the members of the group;

(d) coordination of the conduct of hearings;

(e) coordination in the approval of protocols where necessary.

NOTES

Repeal of this Article in relation to the UK: this Article is repealed, in relation to the UK only, by the Insolvency (Amendment) (EU Exit) Regulations 2019, SI 2019/146, reg 2, Schedule, Pt 1, paras 1, 7, as from IP completion day (as defined in the European Union (Withdrawal Agreement) Act 2020, s 39); for transitional provisions and savings, see reg 4 of the 2019 Regulations at **[12.82]**.

[11.283]

Article 58 Cooperation and communication between insolvency practitioners and courts

An insolvency practitioner appointed in insolvency proceedings concerning a member of a group of companies:

(a) *shall cooperate and communicate with any court before which a request for the opening of proceedings in respect of another member of the same group of companies is pending or which has opened such proceedings; and*

(b) *may request information from that court concerning the proceedings regarding the other member of the group or request assistance concerning the proceedings in which he has been appointed;*

to the extent that such cooperation and communication are appropriate to facilitate the effective administration of the proceedings, do not entail any conflict of interest and are not incompatible with the rules applicable to them.

NOTES

Repeal of this Article in relation to the UK: this Article is repealed, in relation to the UK only, by the Insolvency (Amendment) (EU Exit) Regulations 2019, SI 2019/146, reg 2, Schedule, Pt 1, paras 1, 7, as from IP completion day (as defined in the European Union (Withdrawal Agreement) Act 2020, s 39); for transitional provisions and savings, see reg 4 of the 2019 Regulations at **[12.82]**.

[11.284]

Article 59 Costs of cooperation and communication in proceedings concerning members of a group of companies

The costs of the cooperation and communication provided for in Articles 56 to 60 incurred by an insolvency practitioner or a court shall be regarded as costs and expenses incurred in the respective proceedings.

NOTES

Repeal of this Article in relation to the UK: this Article is repealed, in relation to the UK only, by the Insolvency (Amendment) (EU Exit) Regulations 2019, SI 2019/146, reg 2, Schedule, Pt 1, paras 1, 7, as from IP completion day (as defined in the European Union (Withdrawal Agreement) Act 2020, s 39); for transitional provisions and savings, see reg 4 of the 2019 Regulations at **[12.82]**.

[11.285]

Article 60 Powers of the insolvency practitioner in proceedings concerning members of a group of companies

1. An insolvency practitioner appointed in insolvency proceedings opened in respect of a member of a group of companies may, to the extent appropriate to facilitate the effective administration of the proceedings:

(a) *be heard in any of the proceedings opened in respect of any other member of the same group;*

(b) *request a stay of any measure related to the realisation of the assets in the proceedings opened with respect to any other member of the same group, provided that:*

  (i) *a restructuring plan for all or some members of the group for which insolvency proceedings have been opened has been proposed under point (c) of Article 56(2) and presents a reasonable chance of success;*

  (ii) *such a stay is necessary in order to ensure the proper implementation of the restructuring plan;*

  (iii) *the restructuring plan would be to the benefit of the creditors in the proceedings for which the stay is requested; and*

  (iv) *neither the insolvency proceedings in which the insolvency practitioner referred to in paragraph 1 of this Article has been appointed nor the proceedings in respect of which the stay is requested are subject to coordination under Section 2 of this Chapter;*

(c) *apply for the opening of group coordination proceedings in accordance with Article 61.*

2. The court having opened proceedings referred to in point (b) of paragraph 1 shall stay any measure related to the realisation of the assets in the proceedings in whole or in part if it is satisfied that the conditions referred to in point (b) of paragraph 1 are fulfilled.

Before ordering the stay, the court shall hear the insolvency practitioner appointed in the proceedings for which the stay is requested. Such a stay may be ordered for any period, not exceeding 3 months, which the court considers appropriate and which is compatible with the rules applicable to the proceedings.

The court ordering the stay may require the insolvency practitioner referred to in paragraph 1 to take any suitable measure available under national law to guarantee the interests of the creditors in the proceedings.

The court may extend the duration of the stay by such further period or periods as it considers appropriate and which are compatible with the rules applicable to the proceedings, provided that the conditions referred to in points (b)(ii) to (iv) of paragraph 1 continue to be fulfilled and that the total duration of the stay (the initial period together with any such extensions) does not exceed 6 months.

NOTES

Repeal of this Article in relation to the UK: this Article is repealed, in relation to the UK only, by the Insolvency (Amendment) (EU Exit) Regulations 2019, SI 2019/146, reg 2, Schedule, Pt 1, paras 1, 7, as from IP completion day (as defined in the European Union (Withdrawal Agreement) Act 2020, s 39); for transitional provisions and savings, see reg 4 of the 2019 Regulations at **[12.82]**.

SECTION 2 COORDINATION

SUBSECTION 1 PROCEDURE

[11.286]

Article 61 Request to open group coordination proceedings

1. Group coordination proceedings may be requested before any court having jurisdiction over the insolvency proceedings of a member of the group, by an insolvency practitioner appointed in insolvency proceedings opened in relation to a member of the group.

2. The request referred to in paragraph 1 shall be made in accordance with the conditions provided for by the law applicable to the proceedings in which the insolvency practitioner has been appointed.

3. The request referred to in paragraph 1 shall be accompanied by:

(a) a proposal as to the person to be nominated as the group coordinator ('the coordinator'), details of his or her eligibility pursuant to Article 71, details of his or her qualifications and his or her written agreement to act as coordinator;

(b) an outline of the proposed group coordination, and in particular the reasons why the conditions set out in Article 63(1) are fulfilled;

(c) a list of the insolvency practitioners appointed in relation to the members of the group and, where relevant, the courts and competent authorities involved in the insolvency proceedings of the members of the group;

(d) an outline of the estimated costs of the proposed group coordination and the estimation of the share of those costs to be paid by each member of the group.

NOTES

Repeal of this Article in relation to the UK: this Article is repealed, in relation to the UK only, by the Insolvency (Amendment) (EU Exit) Regulations 2019, SI 2019/146, reg 2, Schedule, Pt 1, paras 1, 7, as from IP completion day (as defined in the European Union (Withdrawal Agreement) Act 2020, s 39); for transitional provisions and savings, see reg 4 of the 2019 Regulations at **[12.82]**.

[11.287]

Article 62 Priority rule

Without prejudice to Article 66, where the opening of group coordination proceedings is requested before courts of different Member States, any court other than the court first seised shall decline jurisdiction in favour of that court.

NOTES

Repeal of this Article in relation to the UK: this Article is repealed, in relation to the UK only, by the Insolvency (Amendment) (EU Exit) Regulations 2019, SI 2019/146, reg 2, Schedule, Pt 1, paras 1, 7, as from IP completion day (as defined in the European Union (Withdrawal Agreement) Act 2020, s 39); for transitional provisions and savings, see reg 4 of the 2019 Regulations at **[12.82]**.

[11.288]

Article 63 Notice by the court seised

1. The court seised of a request to open group coordination proceedings shall give notice as soon as possible of the request for the opening of group coordination proceedings and of the proposed coordinator to the insolvency practitioners appointed in relation to the members of the group as indicated in the request referred to in point (c) of Article 61(3), if it is satisfied that:

(a) the opening of such proceedings is appropriate to facilitate the effective administration of the insolvency proceedings relating to the different group members;

(b) no creditor of any group member expected to participate in the proceedings is likely to be financially disadvantaged by the inclusion of that member in such proceedings; and

(c) the proposed coordinator fulfils the requirements laid down in Article 71.

2. The notice referred to in paragraph 1 of this Article shall list the elements referred to in points (a) to (d) of Article 61(3).

3. The notice referred to in paragraph 1 shall be sent by registered letter, attested by an acknowledgment of receipt.

4. The court seised shall give the insolvency practitioners involved the opportunity to be heard.

NOTES

Repeal of this Article in relation to the UK: this Article is repealed, in relation to the UK only, by the Insolvency (Amendment) (EU Exit) Regulations 2019, SI 2019/146, reg 2, Schedule, Pt 1, paras 1, 7, as from IP completion day (as defined in the European Union (Withdrawal Agreement) Act 2020, s 39); for transitional provisions and savings, see reg 4 of the 2019 Regulations at **[12.82]**.

[11.289]

Article 64 Objections by insolvency practitioners

1. An insolvency practitioner appointed in respect of any group member may object to:

(a) the inclusion within group coordination proceedings of the insolvency proceedings in respect of which it has been appointed; or

(b) the person proposed as a coordinator.

2. Objections pursuant to paragraph 1 of this Article shall be lodged with the court referred to in Article 63 within 30 days of receipt of notice of the request for the opening of group coordination proceedings by the insolvency practitioner referred to in paragraph 1 of this Article.

The objection may be made by means of the standard form established in accordance with Article 88.

3. Prior to taking the decision to participate or not to participate in the coordination in accordance with point (a) of paragraph 1, an insolvency practitioner shall obtain any approval which may be required under the law of the State of the opening of proceedings for which it has been appointed.

NOTES

Repeal of this Article in relation to the UK: this Article is repealed, in relation to the UK only, by the Insolvency (Amendment) (EU Exit) Regulations 2019, SI 2019/146, reg 2, Schedule, Pt 1, paras 1, 7, as from IP completion day (as defined in the European Union (Withdrawal Agreement) Act 2020, s 39); for transitional provisions and savings, see reg 4 of the 2019 Regulations at **[12.82]**.

[11.290]

Article 65 Consequences of objection to the inclusion in group coordination

1. Where an insolvency practitioner has objected to the inclusion of the proceedings in respect of which it has been appointed in group coordination proceedings, those proceedings shall not be included in the group coordination proceedings.

2. The powers of the court referred to in Article 68 or of the coordinator arising from those proceedings shall have no effect as regards that member, and shall entail no costs for that member.

NOTES

Repeal of this Article in relation to the UK: this Article is repealed, in relation to the UK only, by the Insolvency (Amendment) (EU Exit) Regulations 2019, SI 2019/146, reg 2, Schedule, Pt 1, paras 1, 7, as from IP completion day (as defined in the European Union (Withdrawal Agreement) Act 2020, s 39); for transitional provisions and savings, see reg 4 of the 2019 Regulations at **[12.82]**.

[11.291]

Article 66 Choice of court for group coordination proceedings

1. Where at least two-thirds of all insolvency practitioners appointed in insolvency proceedings of the members of the group have agreed that a court of another Member State having jurisdiction is the most appropriate court for the opening of group coordination proceedings, that court shall have exclusive jurisdiction.

2. The choice of court shall be made by joint agreement in writing or evidenced in writing. It may be made until such time as group coordination proceedings have been opened in accordance with Article 68.

3. Any court other than the court seised under paragraph 1 shall decline jurisdiction in favour of that court.

4. The request for the opening of group coordination proceedings shall be submitted to the court agreed in accordance with Article 61.

NOTES

Repeal of this Article in relation to the UK: this Article is repealed, in relation to the UK only, by the Insolvency (Amendment) (EU Exit) Regulations 2019, SI 2019/146, reg 2, Schedule, Pt 1, paras 1, 7, as from IP completion day (as defined in the European Union (Withdrawal Agreement) Act 2020, s 39); for transitional provisions and savings, see reg 4 of the 2019 Regulations at **[12.82]**.

[11.292]

Article 67 Consequences of objections to the proposed coordinator

Where objections to the person proposed as coordinator have been received from an insolvency practitioner which does not also object to the inclusion in the group coordination proceedings of the member in respect of which it has been appointed, the court may refrain from appointing that person and invite the objecting insolvency practitioner to submit a new request in accordance with Article 61(3).

NOTES

Repeal of this Article in relation to the UK: this Article is repealed, in relation to the UK only, by the Insolvency (Amendment) (EU Exit) Regulations 2019, SI 2019/146, reg 2, Schedule, Pt 1, paras 1, 7, as from IP completion day (as defined in the European Union (Withdrawal Agreement) Act 2020, s 39); for transitional provisions and savings, see reg 4 of the 2019 Regulations at **[12.82]**.

[11.293]

Article 68 Decision to open group coordination proceedings

1. After the period referred to in Article 64(2) has elapsed, the court may open group coordination proceedings where it is satisfied that the conditions of Article 63(1) are met. In such a case, the court shall:

- *(a) appoint a coordinator;*
- *(b) decide on the outline of the coordination; and*
- *(c) decide on the estimation of costs and the share to be paid by the group members.*

2. The decision opening group coordination proceedings shall be brought to the notice of the participating insolvency practitioners and of the coordinator.

NOTES

Repeal of this Article in relation to the UK: this Article is repealed, in relation to the UK only, by the Insolvency (Amendment) (EU Exit) Regulations 2019, SI 2019/146, reg 2, Schedule, Pt 1, paras 1, 7, as from IP completion day (as defined in the European Union (Withdrawal Agreement) Act 2020, s 39); for transitional provisions and savings, see reg 4 of the 2019 Regulations at **[12.82]**.

[11.294]

Article 69 Subsequent opt-in by insolvency practitioners

1. In accordance with its national law, any insolvency practitioner may request, after the court decision referred to in Article 68, the inclusion of the proceedings in respect of which it has been appointed, where:

- *(a) there has been an objection to the inclusion of the insolvency proceedings within the group coordination proceedings; or*
- *(b) insolvency proceedings with respect to a member of the group have been opened after the court has opened group coordination proceedings.*

2. Without prejudice to paragraph 4, the coordinator may accede to such a request, after consulting the insolvency practitioners involved, where

- *(a) he or she is satisfied that, taking into account the stage that the group coordination proceedings has reached at the time of the request, the criteria set out in points (a) and (b) of Article 63(1) are met; or*
- *(b) all insolvency practitioners involved agree, subject to the conditions in their national law.*

3. The coordinator shall inform the court and the participating insolvency practitioners of his or her decision pursuant to paragraph 2 and of the reasons on which it is based.

4. Any participating insolvency practitioner or any insolvency practitioner whose request for inclusion in the group coordination proceedings has been rejected may challenge the decision referred to in paragraph 2 in accordance with the procedure set out under the law of the Member State in which the group coordination proceedings have been opened.

NOTES

Repeal of this Article in relation to the UK: this Article is repealed, in relation to the UK only, by the Insolvency (Amendment) (EU Exit) Regulations 2019, SI 2019/146, reg 2, Schedule, Pt 1, paras 1, 7, as from IP completion day (as defined in the European Union (Withdrawal Agreement) Act 2020, s 39); for transitional provisions and savings, see reg 4 of the 2019 Regulations at **[12.82]**.

[11.295]

Article 70 Recommendations and group coordination plan

1. When conducting their insolvency proceedings, insolvency practitioners shall consider the recommendations of the coordinator and the content of the group coordination plan referred to in Article 72(1).

2. An insolvency practitioner shall not be obliged to follow in whole or in part the coordinator's recommendations or the group coordination plan.

If it does not follow the coordinator's recommendations or the group coordination plan, it shall give reasons for not doing so to the persons or bodies that it is to report to under its national law, and to the coordinator.

NOTES

Repeal of this Article in relation to the UK: this Article is repealed, in relation to the UK only, by the Insolvency (Amendment) (EU Exit) Regulations 2019, SI 2019/146, reg 2, Schedule, Pt 1, paras 1, 7, as from IP completion day (as defined in the European Union (Withdrawal Agreement) Act 2020, s 39); for transitional provisions and savings, see reg 4 of the 2019 Regulations at **[12.82]**.

SUBSECTION 2 GENERAL PROVISIONS

[11.296]

Article 71 The coordinator

1. The coordinator shall be a person eligible under the law of a Member State to act as an insolvency practitioner.

2. The coordinator shall not be one of the insolvency practitioners appointed to act in respect of any of the group members, and shall have no conflict of interest in respect of the group members, their creditors and the insolvency practitioners appointed in respect of any of the group members.

NOTES

Repeal of this Article in relation to the UK: this Article is repealed, in relation to the UK only, by the Insolvency (Amendment) (EU Exit) Regulations 2019, SI 2019/146, reg 2, Schedule, Pt 1, paras 1, 7, as from IP completion day (as defined in the European Union (Withdrawal Agreement) Act 2020, s 39); for transitional provisions and savings, see reg 4 of the 2019 Regulations at **[12.82]**.

[11.297]

Article 72 Tasks and rights of the coordinator

1. The coordinator shall:

(a) identify and outline recommendations for the coordinated conduct of the insolvency proceedings;

(b) propose a group coordination plan that identifies, describes and recommends a comprehensive set of measures appropriate to an integrated approach to the resolution of the group members' insolvencies. In particular, the plan may contain proposals for:

(i) the measures to be taken in order to re-establish the economic performance and the financial soundness of the group or any part of it;

(ii) the settlement of intra-group disputes as regards intra-group transactions and avoidance actions;

(iii) agreements between the insolvency practitioners of the insolvent group members.

2. The coordinator may also:

(a) be heard and participate, in particular by attending creditors' meetings, in any of the proceedings opened in respect of any member of the group;

(b) mediate any dispute arising between two or more insolvency practitioners of group members;

(c) present and explain his or her group coordination plan to the persons or bodies that he or she is to report to under his or her national law;

(d) request information from any insolvency practitioner in respect of any member of the group where that information is or might be of use when identifying and outlining strategies and measures in order to coordinate the proceedings; and

(e) request a stay for a period of up to 6 months of the proceedings opened in respect of any member of the group, provided that such a stay is necessary in order to ensure the proper implementation of the plan and would be to the benefit of the creditors in the proceedings for which the stay is requested; or request the lifting of any existing stay. Such a request shall be made to the court that opened the proceedings for which a stay is requested.

3. The plan referred to in point (b) of paragraph 1 shall not include recommendations as to any consolidation of proceedings or insolvency estates.

4. The coordinator's tasks and rights as defined under this Article shall not extend to any member of the group not participating in group coordination proceedings.

5. The coordinator shall perform his or her duties impartially and with due care.

6. Where the coordinator considers that the fulfilment of his or her tasks requires a significant increase in the costs compared to the cost estimate referred to in point (d) of Article 61(3), and in any case, where the costs exceed 10% of the estimated costs, the coordinator shall:

(a) inform without delay the participating insolvency practitioners; and

(b) seek the prior approval of the court opening group coordination proceedings.

NOTES

Repeal of this Article in relation to the UK: this Article is repealed, in relation to the UK only, by the Insolvency (Amendment) (EU Exit) Regulations 2019, SI 2019/146, reg 2, Schedule, Pt 1, paras 1, 7, as from IP completion day (as defined

in the European Union (Withdrawal Agreement) Act 2020, s 39); for transitional provisions and savings, see reg 4 of the 2019 Regulations at **[12.82]**.

[11.298]

Article 73 Languages

1. The coordinator shall communicate with the insolvency practitioner of a participating group member in the language agreed with the insolvency practitioner or, in the absence of an agreement, in the official language or one of the official languages of the institutions of the Union, and of the court which opened the proceedings in respect of that group member.

2. The coordinator shall communicate with a court in the official language applicable to that court.

NOTES

Repeal of this Article in relation to the UK: this Article is repealed, in relation to the UK only, by the Insolvency (Amendment) (EU Exit) Regulations 2019, SI 2019/146, reg 2, Schedule, Pt 1, paras 1, 7, as from IP completion day (as defined in the European Union (Withdrawal Agreement) Act 2020, s 39); for transitional provisions and savings, see reg 4 of the 2019 Regulations at **[12.82]**.

[11.299]

Article 74 Cooperation between insolvency practitioners and the coordinator

1. Insolvency practitioners appointed in relation to members of a group and the coordinator shall cooperate with each other to the extent that such cooperation is not incompatible with the rules applicable to the respective proceedings.

2. In particular, insolvency practitioners shall communicate any information that is relevant for the coordinator to perform his or her tasks.

NOTES

Repeal of this Article in relation to the UK: this Article is repealed, in relation to the UK only, by the Insolvency (Amendment) (EU Exit) Regulations 2019, SI 2019/146, reg 2, Schedule, Pt 1, paras 1, 7, as from IP completion day (as defined in the European Union (Withdrawal Agreement) Act 2020, s 39); for transitional provisions and savings, see reg 4 of the 2019 Regulations at **[12.82]**.

[11.300]

Article 75 Revocation of the appointment of the coordinator

The court shall revoke the appointment of the coordinator of its own motion or at the request of the insolvency practitioner of a participating group member where:

(a) the coordinator acts to the detriment of the creditors of a participating group member; or

(b) the coordinator fails to comply with his or her obligations under this Chapter.

NOTES

Repeal of this Article in relation to the UK: this Article is repealed, in relation to the UK only, by the Insolvency (Amendment) (EU Exit) Regulations 2019, SI 2019/146, reg 2, Schedule, Pt 1, paras 1, 7, as from IP completion day (as defined in the European Union (Withdrawal Agreement) Act 2020, s 39); for transitional provisions and savings, see reg 4 of the 2019 Regulations at **[12.82]**.

[11.301]

Article 76 Debtor in possession

The provisions applicable, under this Chapter, to the insolvency practitioner shall also apply, where appropriate, to the debtor in possession.

NOTES

Repeal of this Article in relation to the UK: this Article is repealed, in relation to the UK only, by the Insolvency (Amendment) (EU Exit) Regulations 2019, SI 2019/146, reg 2, Schedule, Pt 1, paras 1, 7, as from IP completion day (as defined in the European Union (Withdrawal Agreement) Act 2020, s 39); for transitional provisions and savings, see reg 4 of the 2019 Regulations at **[12.82]**.

[11.302]

Article 77 Costs and distribution

1. The remuneration for the coordinator shall be adequate, proportionate to the tasks fulfilled and reflect reasonable expenses.

2. On having completed his or her tasks, the coordinator shall establish the final statement of costs and the share to be paid by each member, and submit this statement to each participating insolvency practitioner and to the court opening coordination proceedings.

3. In the absence of objections by the insolvency practitioners within 30 days of receipt of the statement referred to in paragraph 2, the costs and the share to be paid by each member shall be deemed to be agreed. The statement shall be submitted to the court opening coordination proceedings for confirmation.

4. In the event of an objection, the court that opened the group coordination proceedings shall, upon the application of the coordinator or any participating insolvency practitioner, decide on the costs and the share to be paid by each member in accordance with the criteria set out in paragraph 1 of this Article, and taking into account the estimation of costs referred to in Article 68 (1) and, where applicable, Article 72(6).

5. Any participating insolvency practitioner may challenge the decision referred to in paragraph 4 in accordance with the procedure set out under the law of the Member State where group coordination proceedings have been opened.

NOTES

Repeal of this Article in relation to the UK: this Article is repealed, in relation to the UK only, by the Insolvency (Amendment) (EU Exit) Regulations 2019, SI 2019/146, reg 2, Schedule, Pt 1, paras 1, 7, as from IP completion day (as defined

in the European Union (Withdrawal Agreement) Act 2020, s 39); for transitional provisions and savings, see reg 4 of the 2019 Regulations at **[12.82]**.

CHAPTER VI DATA PROTECTION

[11.303]

Article 78 Data protection

1. National rules implementing Directive 95/46/EC shall apply to the processing of personal data carried out in the Member States pursuant to this Regulation, provided that processing operations referred to in Article 3(2) of Directive 95/46/EC are not concerned.

2. Regulation (EC) No 45/2001 shall apply to the processing of personal data carried out by the Commission pursuant to this Regulation.

NOTES

Repeal of this Article in relation to the UK: this Article is repealed, in relation to the UK only, by the Insolvency (Amendment) (EU Exit) Regulations 2019, SI 2019/146, reg 2, Schedule, Pt 1, paras 1, 7, as from IP completion day (as defined in the European Union (Withdrawal Agreement) Act 2020, s 39); for transitional provisions and savings, see reg 4 of the 2019 Regulations at **[12.82]**.

[11.304]

Article 79 Responsibilities of Member States regarding the processing of personal data in national insolvency registers

1. Each Member State shall communicate to the Commission the name of the natural or legal person, public authority, agency or any other body designated by national law to exercise the functions of controller in accordance with point (d) of Article 2 of Directive 95/46/EC, with a view to its publication on the European e-Justice Portal.

2. Member States shall ensure that the technical measures for ensuring the security of personal data processed in their national insolvency registers referred to in Article 24 are implemented.

3. Member States shall be responsible for verifying that the controller, designated by national law in accordance with point (d) of Article 2 of Directive 95/46/EC, ensures compliance with the principles of data quality, in particular the accuracy and the updating of data stored in national insolvency registers.

4. Member States shall be responsible, in accordance with Directive 95/46/EC, for the collection and storage of data in national databases and for decisions taken to make such data available in the interconnected register that can be consulted via the European e-Justice Portal.

5. As part of the information that should be provided to data subjects to enable them to exercise their rights, and in particular the right to the erasure of data, Member States shall inform data subjects of the accessibility period set for personal data stored in insolvency registers.

NOTES

Repeal of this Article in relation to the UK: this Article is repealed, in relation to the UK only, by the Insolvency (Amendment) (EU Exit) Regulations 2019, SI 2019/146, reg 2, Schedule, Pt 1, paras 1, 7, as from IP completion day (as defined in the European Union (Withdrawal Agreement) Act 2020, s 39); for transitional provisions and savings, see reg 4 of the 2019 Regulations at **[12.82]**.

[11.305]

Article 80 Responsibilities of the Commission in connection with the processing of personal data

1. The Commission shall exercise the responsibilities of controller pursuant to Article 2(d) of Regulation (EC) No 45/2001 in accordance with its respective responsibilities defined in this Article.

2. The Commission shall define the necessary policies and apply the necessary technical solutions to fulfil its responsibilities within the scope of the function of controller.

3. The Commission shall implement the technical measures required to ensure the security of personal data while in transit, in particular the confidentiality and integrity of any transmission to and from the European e-Justice Portal.

4. The obligations of the Commission shall not affect the responsibilities of the Member States and other bodies for the content and operation of the interconnected national databases run by them.

NOTES

Repeal of this Article in relation to the UK: this Article is repealed, in relation to the UK only, by the Insolvency (Amendment) (EU Exit) Regulations 2019, SI 2019/146, reg 2, Schedule, Pt 1, paras 1, 7, as from IP completion day (as defined in the European Union (Withdrawal Agreement) Act 2020, s 39); for transitional provisions and savings, see reg 4 of the 2019 Regulations at **[12.82]**.

[11.306]

Article 81 Information obligations

Without prejudice to the information to be given to data subjects in accordance with Articles 11 and 12 of Regulation (EC) No 45/2001, the Commission shall inform data subjects, by means of publication through the European e-Justice Portal, about its role in the processing of data and the purposes for which those data will be processed.

NOTES

Repeal of this Article in relation to the UK: this Article is repealed, in relation to the UK only, by the Insolvency (Amendment) (EU Exit) Regulations 2019, SI 2019/146, reg 2, Schedule, Pt 1, paras 1, 7, as from IP completion day (as defined in the European Union (Withdrawal Agreement) Act 2020, s 39); for transitional provisions and savings, see reg 4 of the 2019 Regulations at **[12.82]**.

[11.307]

Article 82 Storage of personal data

As regards information from interconnected national databases, no personal data relating to data subjects shall be stored in the European e-Justice Portal. All such data shall be stored in the national databases operated by the Member States or other bodies.

NOTES

Repeal of this Article in relation to the UK: this Article is repealed, in relation to the UK only, by the Insolvency (Amendment) (EU Exit) Regulations 2019, SI 2019/146, reg 2, Schedule, Pt 1, paras 1, 7, as from IP completion day (as defined in the European Union (Withdrawal Agreement) Act 2020, s 39); for transitional provisions and savings, see reg 4 of the 2019 Regulations at **[12.82]**.

[11.308]

Article 83 Access to personal data via the European e-Justice Portal

Personal data stored in the national insolvency registers referred to in Article 24 shall be accessible via the European e-Justice Portal for as long as they remain accessible under national law.

NOTES

Repeal of this Article in relation to the UK: this Article is repealed, in relation to the UK only, by the Insolvency (Amendment) (EU Exit) Regulations 2019, SI 2019/146, reg 2, Schedule, Pt 1, paras 1, 7, as from IP completion day (as defined in the European Union (Withdrawal Agreement) Act 2020, s 39); for transitional provisions and savings, see reg 4 of the 2019 Regulations at **[12.82]**.

CHAPTER VII TRANSITIONAL AND FINAL PROVISIONS

[11.309]

Article 84 Applicability in time

1. The provisions of this Regulation shall apply only to insolvency proceedings opened from 26 June 2017. Acts committed by a debtor before that date shall continue to be governed by the law which was applicable to them at the time they were committed.
2. Notwithstanding Article 91 of this Regulation, Regulation (EC) No 1346/2000 shall continue to apply to insolvency proceedings which fall within the scope of that Regulation and which have been opened before 26 June 2017.

NOTES

Application of this Article in relation to the UK: this Article is amended, in relation to the UK only, by the Insolvency (Amendment) (EU Exit) Regulations 2019, SI 2019/146, reg 2, Schedule, Pt 1, paras 1, 8, as from IP completion day (as defined in the European Union (Withdrawal Agreement) Act 2020, s 39), as follows (for transitional provisions and savings, see reg 4 of the 2019 Regulations at **[12.82]**)—

"In Article 84 omit—

(a) the second sentence of paragraph 1, and
(b) paragraph 2.".

[11.310]

Article 85 Relationship to Conventions

1. This Regulation replaces, in respect of the matters referred to therein, and as regards relations between Member States, the Conventions concluded between two or more Member States, in particular:

(a) the Convention between Belgium and France on Jurisdiction and the Validity and Enforcement of Judgments, Arbitration Awards and Authentic Instruments, signed at Paris on 8 July 1899;
(b) the Convention between Belgium and Austria on Bankruptcy, Winding-up, Arrangements, Compositions and Suspension of Payments (with Additional Protocol of 13 June 1973), signed at Brussels on 16 July 1969;
(c) the Convention between Belgium and the Netherlands on Territorial Jurisdiction, Bankruptcy and the Validity and Enforcement of Judgments, Arbitration Awards and Authentic Instruments, signed at Brussels on 28 March 1925;
(d) the Treaty between Germany and Austria on Bankruptcy, Winding-up, Arrangements and Compositions, signed at Vienna on 25 May 1979;
(e) the Convention between France and Austria on Jurisdiction, Recognition and Enforcement of Judgments on Bankruptcy, signed at Vienna on 27 February 1979;
(f) the Convention between France and Italy on the Enforcement of Judgments in Civil and Commercial Matters, signed at Rome on 3 June 1930;
(g) the Convention between Italy and Austria on Bankruptcy, Winding-up, Arrangements and Compositions, signed at Rome on 12 July 1977;
(h) the Convention between the Kingdom of the Netherlands and the Federal Republic of Germany on the Mutual Recognition and Enforcement of Judgments and other Enforceable Instruments in Civil and Commercial Matters, signed at The Hague on 30 August 1962;
(i) the Convention between the United Kingdom and the Kingdom of Belgium providing for the Reciprocal Enforcement of Judgments in Civil and Commercial Matters, with Protocol, signed at Brussels on 2 May 1934;
(j) the Convention between Denmark, Finland, Norway, Sweden and Iceland on Bankruptcy, signed at Copenhagen on 7 November 1933;
(k) the European Convention on Certain International Aspects of Bankruptcy, signed at Istanbul on 5 June 1990;
(l) the Convention between the Federative People's Republic of Yugoslavia and the Kingdom of Greece on the Mutual Recognition and Enforcement of Judgments, signed at Athens on 18 June 1959;
(m) the Agreement between the Federative People's Republic of Yugoslavia and the Republic of Austria on the Mutual Recognition and Enforcement of Arbitral Awards and Arbitral Settlements in Commercial Matters, signed at Belgrade on 18 March 1960;

(n) the Convention between the Federative People's Republic of Yugoslavia and the Italian Republic on Mutual Judicial Cooperation in Civil and Administrative Matters, signed at Rome on 3 December 1960;

(o) the Agreement between the Socialist Federative Republic of Yugoslavia and the Kingdom of Belgium on Judicial Cooperation in Civil and Commercial Matters, signed at Belgrade on 24 September 1971;

(p) the Convention between the Governments of Yugoslavia and France on the Recognition and Enforcement of Judgments in Civil and Commercial Matters, signed at Paris on 18 May 1971;

(q) the Agreement between the Czechoslovak Socialist Republic and the Hellenic Republic on Legal Aid in Civil and Criminal Matters, signed at Athens on 22 October 1980, still in force between the Czech Republic and Greece;

(r) the Agreement between the Czechoslovak Socialist Republic and the Republic of Cyprus on Legal Aid in Civil and Criminal Matters, signed at Nicosia on 23 April 1982, still in force between the Czech Republic and Cyprus;

(s) the Treaty between the Government of the Czechoslovak Socialist Republic and the Government of the Republic of France on Legal Aid and the Recognition and Enforcement of Judgments in Civil, Family and Commercial Matters, signed at Paris on 10 May 1984, still in force between the Czech Republic and France;

(t) the Treaty between the Czechoslovak Socialist Republic and the Italian Republic on Legal Aid in Civil and Criminal Matters, signed at Prague on 6 December 1985, still in force between the Czech Republic and Italy;

(u) the Agreement between the Republic of Latvia, the Republic of Estonia and the Republic of Lithuania on Legal Assistance and Legal Relationships, signed at Tallinn on 11 November 1992;

(v) the Agreement between Estonia and Poland on Granting Legal Aid and Legal Relations on Civil, Labour and Criminal Matters, signed at Tallinn on 27 November 1998;

(w) the Agreement between the Republic of Lithuania and the Republic of Poland on Legal Assistance and Legal Relations in Civil, Family, Labour and Criminal Matters, signed at Warsaw on 26 January 1993;

(x) the Convention between the Socialist Republic of Romania and the Hellenic Republic on legal assistance in civil and criminal matters and its Protocol, signed at Bucharest on 19 October 1972;

(y) the Convention between the Socialist Republic of Romania and the French Republic on legal assistance in civil and commercial matters, signed at Paris on 5 November 1974;

(z) the Agreement between the People's Republic of Bulgaria and the Hellenic Republic on Legal Assistance in Civil and Criminal Matters, signed at Athens on 10 April 1976;

(aa) the Agreement between the People's Republic of Bulgaria and the Republic of Cyprus on Legal Assistance in Civil and Criminal Matters, signed at Nicosia on 29 April 1983;

(ab) the Agreement between the Government of the People's Republic of Bulgaria and the Government of the French Republic on Mutual Legal Assistance in Civil Matters, signed at Sofia on 18 January 1989;

(ac) the Treaty between Romania and the Czech Republic on judicial assistance in civil matters, signed at Bucharest on 11 July 1994;

(ad) the Treaty between Romania and the Republic of Poland on legal assistance and legal relations in civil cases, signed at Bucharest on 15 May 1999.

2. The Conventions referred to in paragraph 1 shall continue to have effect with regard to proceedings opened before the entry into force of Regulation (EC) No 1346/2000.

3. This Regulation shall not apply:

(a) in any Member State, to the extent that it is irreconcilable with the obligations arising in relation to bankruptcy from a convention concluded by that Member State with one or more third countries before the entry into force of Regulation (EC) No 1346/2000;

(b) in the United Kingdom of Great Britain and Northern Ireland, to the extent that is irreconcilable with the obligations arising in relation to bankruptcy and the winding-up of insolvent companies from any arrangements with the Commonwealth existing at the time Regulation (EC) No 1346/2000 entered into force.

NOTES

Application of this Article in relation to the UK: this Article is amended, in relation to the UK only, by the Insolvency (Amendment) (EU Exit) Regulations 2019, SI 2019/146, reg 2, Schedule, Pt 1, paras 1, 9, as from IP completion day (as defined in the European Union (Withdrawal Agreement) Act 2020, s 39), as follows (for transitional provisions and savings, see reg 4 of the 2019 Regulations at **[12.82]**)—

"In Article 85—

(a) omit paragraphs 1 and 2;

(b) in paragraph 3—

(i) in point (a) omit "in any Member State"; and

(ii) for "that Member State" substitute "the United Kingdom".".

[11.311]

Article 86 Information on national and Union insolvency law

1. The Member States shall provide, within the framework of the European Judicial Network in civil and commercial matters established by Council Decision 2001/470/EC,[1] and with a view to making the information available to the public, a short description of their national legislation and procedures relating to insolvency, in particular relating to the matters listed in Article 7(2).

2. The Member States shall update the information referred to in paragraph 1 regularly.

3. The Commission shall make information concerning this Regulation available to the public.

NOTES

Repeal of this Article in relation to the UK: this Article is repealed, in relation to the UK only, by the Insolvency (Amendment) (EU Exit) Regulations 2019, SI 2019/146, reg 2, Schedule, Pt 1, paras 1, 10, as from IP completion day (as defined in the European Union (Withdrawal Agreement) Act 2020, s 39); for transitional provisions and savings, see reg 4 of the 2019 Regulations at **[12.82]**.

[1] Council Decision 2001/470/EC of 28 May 2001 establishing a European Judicial Network in civil and commercial matters

(OJ L174, 27.6.2001, p 25).

[11.312]
Article 87 Establishment of the interconnection of registers
The Commission shall adopt implementing acts establishing the interconnection of insolvency registers as referred to in Article 25. Those implementing acts shall be adopted in accordance with the examination procedure referred to in Article 89(3).

NOTES

Repeal of this Article in relation to the UK: this Article is repealed, in relation to the UK only, by the Insolvency (Amendment) (EU Exit) Regulations 2019, SI 2019/146, reg 2, Schedule, Pt 1, paras 1, 10, as from IP completion day (as defined in the European Union (Withdrawal Agreement) Act 2020, s 39); for transitional provisions and savings, see reg 4 of the 2019 Regulations at **[12.82]**.

[11.313]
Article 88 Establishment and subsequent amendment of standard forms
The Commission shall adopt implementing acts establishing and, where necessary, amending the forms referred to in Article 27(4), Articles 54 and 55 and Article 64(2). Those implementing acts shall be adopted in accordance with the advisory procedure referred to in Article 89(2).

NOTES

Repeal of this Article in relation to the UK: this Article is repealed, in relation to the UK only, by the Insolvency (Amendment) (EU Exit) Regulations 2019, SI 2019/146, reg 2, Schedule, Pt 1, paras 1, 10, as from IP completion day (as defined in the European Union (Withdrawal Agreement) Act 2020, s 39); for transitional provisions and savings, see reg 4 of the 2019 Regulations at **[12.82]**.

Implementing Act for the purposes of this Article: see Commission Implementing Regulation 2017/1105/EU establishing the forms referred to in Regulation (EU) 2015/848 of the European Parliament and of the Council on insolvency proceedings. It is available on the EUR-Lex website at eur-lex.europa.eu/legal-content/EN/TXT/?uri=CELEX:32017R1105.

[11.314]
Article 89 Committee procedure
1. The Commission shall be assisted by a committee. That committee shall be a committee within the meaning of Regulation (EU) No 182/2011.
2. Where reference is made to this paragraph, Article 4 of Regulation (EU) No 182/2011 shall apply.
3. Where reference is made to this paragraph, Article 5 of Regulation (EU) No 182/2011 shall apply.

NOTES

Repeal of this Article in relation to the UK: this Article is repealed, in relation to the UK only, by the Insolvency (Amendment) (EU Exit) Regulations 2019, SI 2019/146, reg 2, Schedule, Pt 1, paras 1, 10, as from IP completion day (as defined in the European Union (Withdrawal Agreement) Act 2020, s 39); for transitional provisions and savings, see reg 4 of the 2019 Regulations at **[12.82]**.

[11.315]
Article 90 Review clause
1. No later than 27 June 2027, and every 5 years thereafter, the Commission shall present to the European Parliament, the Council and the European Economic and Social Committee a report on the application of this Regulation. The report shall be accompanied where necessary by a proposal for adaptation of this Regulation.
2. No later than 27 June 2022, the Commission shall present to the European Parliament, the Council and the European Economic and Social Committee a report on the application of the group coordination proceedings. The report shall be accompanied where necessary by a proposal for adaptation of this Regulation.
3. No later than 1 January 2016, the Commission shall submit to the European Parliament, the Council and the European Economic and Social Committee a study on the cross-border issues in the area of directors' liability and disqualifications.
4. No later than 27 June 2020, the Commission shall submit to the European Parliament, the Council and the European Economic and Social Committee a study on the issue of abusive forum shopping.

NOTES

Repeal of this Article in relation to the UK: this Article is repealed, in relation to the UK only, by the Insolvency (Amendment) (EU Exit) Regulations 2019, SI 2019/146, reg 2, Schedule, Pt 1, paras 1, 10, as from IP completion day (as defined in the European Union (Withdrawal Agreement) Act 2020, s 39); for transitional provisions and savings, see reg 4 of the 2019 Regulations at **[12.82]**.

[11.316]
Article 91 Repeal
Regulation (EC) No 1346/2000 is repealed.
References to the repealed Regulation shall be construed as references to this Regulation and shall be read in accordance with the correlation table set out in Annex D to this Regulation.

NOTES

Application of this Article in relation to the UK: this Article is amended, in relation to the UK only, by the Insolvency (Amendment) (EU Exit) Regulations 2019, SI 2019/146, reg 2, Schedule, Pt 1, paras 1, 11, as from IP completion day (as defined in the European Union (Withdrawal Agreement) Act 2020, s 39), as follows (for transitional provisions and savings, see reg 4 of the 2019 Regulations at **[12.82]**)—

"In Article 91 omit the second sentence.".

[11.317]

Article 92 Entry into force

This Regulation shall enter into force on the twentieth day following that of its publication in the *Official Journal of the European Union*.

It shall apply from 26 June 2017, with the exception of:

(a) Article 86, which shall apply from 26 June 2016;

(b) Article 24(1), which shall apply from 26 June 2018; and

(c) Article 25, which shall apply from 26 June 2019.

This Regulation shall be binding in its entirety and directly applicable in the Member States in accordance with the Treaties.

NOTES

Application of this Article in relation to the UK: this Article is amended, in relation to the UK only, by the Insolvency (Amendment) (EU Exit) Regulations 2019, SI 2019/146, reg 2, Schedule, Pt 1, paras 1, 12, 13, as from IP completion day (as defined in the European Union (Withdrawal Agreement) Act 2020, s 39), as follows (for transitional provisions and savings, see reg 4 of the 2019 Regulations at **[12.82]**)—

"In Article 92 omit point (c).

Omit the sentence immediately following Article 92 which begins "This Regulation shall be binding".".

ANNEXES

ANNEXES A AND B

(In previous editions of this Handbook, only the entries relating to the UK in Annexes A and B were reproduced. Those Annexes were substituted by European Parliament and Council Regulation 2021/2260/EU amending Regulation (EU) 2015/848 on insolvency proceedings to replace its Annexes A and B, with effect from 9 January 2022. Following the UK's exit from the EU, the new Annexes do not contain entries for the UK and, accordingly, they have now been omitted.)

ANNEX C
REPEALED REGULATION WITH LIST OF THE SUCCESSIVE AMENDMENTS THERETO

[11.318]

Council Regulation (EC) No 1346/2000

(OJ L160, 30.6.2000, p 1)

Council Regulation (EC) No 603/2005

(OJ L100, 20.4.2005, p 1)

Council Regulation (EC) No 694/2006

(OJ L121, 6.5.2006, p 1)

Council Regulation (EC) No 1791/2006

(OJ L363, 20.12.2006, p 1)

Council Regulation (EC) No 681/2007

(OJ L159, 20.6.2007, p 1)

Council Regulation (EC) No 788/2008

(OJ L213, 8.8.2008, p 1)

Implementing Regulation of the Council (EU) No 210/2010

(OJ L65, 13.3.2010, p 1)

Council Implementing Regulation (EU) No 583/2011

(OJ L160, 18.6.2011, p 52)

Council Regulation (EU) No 517/2013

(OJ L158, 10.6.2013, p 1)

Council Implementing Regulation (EU) No 663/2014

(OJ L179, 19.6.2014, p 4)

Act concerning the conditions of accession of the Czech Republic, the Republic of Estonia, the Republic of Cyprus, the Republic of Latvia, the Republic of Lithuania, the Republic of Hungary, the Republic of Malta, the Republic of Poland, the Republic of Slovenia and the Slovak Republic and the adjustments to the Treaties on which the European Union is founded

(OJ L236, 23.9.2003, p 33)

ANNEX D
CORRELATION TABLE

[11.319]

Regulation (EC) No 1346/2000	This Regulation
Article 1	Article 1
Article 2, introductory words	Article 2, introductory words

Regulation (EC) No 1346/2000	This Regulation
Article 2, point (a)	Article 2, point (4)
Article 2, point (b)	Article 2, point (5)
Article 2, point (c)	—
Article 2, point (d)	Article 2, point (6)
Article 2, point (e)	Article 2, point (7)
Article 2, point (f)	Article 2, point (8)
Article 2, point (g), introductory words	Article 2, point (9), introductory words
Article 2, point (g), first indent	Article 2, point (9)(vii)
Article 2, point (g), second indent	Article 2, point (9)(iv)
Article 2, point (g), third indent	Article 2, point (9)(viii)
Article 2, point (h)	Article 2, point 10
—	Article 2, points (1) to (3) and (11) to (13)
—	Article 2, point (9)(i) to (iii), (v), (vi)
Article 3	Article 3
—	Article 4
—	Article 5
—	Article 6
Article 4	Article 7
Article 5	Article 8
Article 6	Article 9
Article 7	Article 10
Article 8	Article 11(1)
—	Article 11(2)
Article 9	Article 12
Article 10	Article 13(1)
—	Article 13(2)
Article 11	Article 14
Article 12	Article 15
Article 13, first indent	Article 16, point (a)
Article 13, second indent	Article 16, point (b)
Article 14, first indent	Article 17, point (a)
Article 14, second indent	Article 17, point (b)
Article 14, third indent	Article 17, point (c)
Article 15	Article 18
Article 16	Article 19
Article 17	Article 20
Article 18	Article 21
Article 19	Article 22
Article 20	Article 23
—	Article 24
—	Article 25
—	Article 26
—	Article 27
Article 21(1)	Article 28(2)
Article 21(2)	Article 28(1)
Article 22	Article 29
Article 23	Article 30
Article 24	Article 31
Article 25	Article 32
Article 26	Article 33
Article 27	Article 34
Article 28	Article 35
—	Article 36
Article 29	Article 37(1)
—	Article 37(2)

Regulation (EC) No 1346/2000	This Regulation
—	Article 38
—	Article 39
Article 30	Article 40
Article 31	Article 41
—	Article 42
—	Article 43
—	Article 44
Article 32	Article 45
Article 33	Article 46
Article 34(1)	Article 47(1)
Article 34(2)	Article 47(2)
Article 34(3)	—
—	Article 48
Article 35	Article 49
Article 36	Article 50
Article 37	Article 51
Article 38	Article 52
Article 39	Article 53
Article 40	Article 54
Article 41	Article 55
Article 42	—
—	Article 56
—	Article 57
—	Article 58
—	Article 59
—	Article 60
—	Article 61
—	Article 62
—	Article 63
—	Article 64
—	Article 65
—	Article 66
—	Article 67
—	Article 68
—	Article 69
—	Article 70
—	Article 71
—	Article 72
—	Article 73
—	Article 74
—	Article 75
—	Article 76
—	Article 77
—	Article 78
—	Article 79
—	Article 80
—	Article 81
—	Article 82
—	Article 83
Article 43	Article 84(1)
—	Article 84(2)
Article 44	Article 85
—	Article 86
Article 45	—
—	Article 87

Regulation (EC) No 1346/2000	This Regulation
—	Article 88
—	Article 89
Article 46	Article 90(1)
—	Article 90(2) to (4)
—	Article 91
Article 47	Article 92
Annex A	Annex A
Annex B	—
Annex C	Annex B
—	Annex C
—	Annex D

REGULATION OF THE EUROPEAN PARLIAMENT AND OF THE COUNCIL

(2017/1129/EU)

of 14 June 2017

on the prospectus to be published when securities are offered to the public or admitted to trading on a regulated market, and repealing Directive 2003/71/EC

(Text with EEA relevance)

[11.320]

NOTES

Date of publication in OJ: OJ L168, 30.6.2017, p 12.

This Regulation is reproduced as amended by: European Parliament and Council Regulation 2019/2115/EU; European Parliament and Council Regulation 2020/1503/EU; European Parliament and Council Regulation 2021/337/EU.

Application of this Regulation in relation to the UK: in accordance with the European Union (Withdrawal) Act 2018, s 3 at **[12.5]**, this Regulation became domestic law on IP completion day (as defined in the European Union (Withdrawal Agreement) Act 2020, s 39). In so far as applying to the UK, this Regulation is amended by the Official Listing of Securities, Prospectus and Transparency (Amendment etc) (EU Exit) Regulations 2019, SI 2019/707, the Prospectus (Amendment etc) (EU Exit) Regulations 2019, SI 2019/1234, and the Financial Services (Miscellaneous Amendments) (EU Exit) Regulations 2020, SI 2020/628 (all as from IP completion day). The amendments are set out below. With regard to these amendments, note that new Articles are inserted, and Articles that are repealed are reproduced in italics. In the case of other amendments, the amending provisions from the Regulations listed *ante* are set out in full in the Notes to the amended Article, and the text of the amended Article has not been altered. Post-IP completion day, this Regulation has been amended, in relation to the UK only, by the Financial Services Act 2021 (Prudential Regulation of Credit Institutions and Investment Firms) (Consequential Amendments and Miscellaneous Provisions) Regulations 2021, SI 2021/1376.

THE EUROPEAN PARLIAMENT AND THE COUNCIL OF THE EUROPEAN UNION,

Having regard to the Treaty on the Functioning of the European Union, and in particular Article 114 thereof,

Having regard to the proposal from the European Commission,

After transmission of the draft legislative act to the national parliaments,

Having regard to the opinion of the European Central Bank,[1]

Having regard to the opinion of the European Economic and Social Committee,[2]

After consulting the Committee of the Regions,

Acting in accordance with the ordinary legislative procedure,[3]

Whereas:

(1) This Regulation constitutes an essential step towards the completion of the Capital Markets Union as set out in the Communication of the Commission of 30 September 2015, entitled 'Action Plan on Building a Capital Markets Union'. The aim of the Capital Markets Union is to help businesses tap into more diverse sources of capital from anywhere within the European Union ('the Union'), make markets work more efficiently and offer investors and savers additional opportunities to put their money to work, in order to enhance growth and create jobs.

(2) Directive 2003/71/EC of the European Parliament and of the Council[4] laid down harmonised principles and rules on the prospectus to be drawn up, approved and published when securities are offered to the public or admitted to trading on a regulated market. Given the legislative and market developments since its entry into force, that Directive should be repealed and replaced by this Regulation.

(3) Disclosure of information in cases of offers of securities to the public or admission of securities to trading on a regulated market is vital to protect investors by removing asymmetries of information between them and issuers. Harmonising such disclosure allows for the establishment of a cross-border passport mechanism which facilitates the effective functioning of the internal market in a wide variety of securities.

(4) Divergent approaches would result in fragmentation of the internal market since issuers, offerors and persons asking for admission to trading on a regulated market would be subject to different rules in different Member States and prospectuses approved in one Member State could be prevented from being used in other Member States. In the

absence of a harmonised framework to ensure uniformity of disclosure and the functioning of the passport in the Union it is therefore likely that differences in Member States' laws would create obstacles to the smooth functioning of the internal market for securities. Therefore, to ensure the proper functioning of the internal market and improve the conditions of its functioning, in particular with regard to capital markets, and to guarantee a high level of consumer and investor protection, it is appropriate to lay down a regulatory framework for prospectuses at Union level.

(5) It is appropriate and necessary for the rules on disclosure when securities are offered to the public or admitted to trading on a regulated market to take the legislative form of a regulation in order to ensure that provisions directly imposing obligations on persons involved in offers of securities to the public and in admissions of securities to trading on a regulated market are applied in a uniform manner throughout the Union. Since a legal framework for the provisions on prospectuses necessarily involves measures specifying precise requirements for all different aspects inherent to prospectuses, even small divergences on the approach taken regarding one of those aspects could result in significant impediments to cross-border offers of securities, to multiple listings on regulated markets and to Union consumer protection rules. Therefore, the use of a regulation, which is directly applicable without requiring national law, should reduce the possibility of divergent measures being taken at national level, and should ensure a consistent approach, greater legal certainty and prevent such significant impediments. The use of a regulation will also strengthen confidence in the transparency of markets across the Union, and reduce regulatory complexity as well as search and compliance costs for companies.

(6) The assessment of Directive 2010/73/EU of the European Parliament and of the Council[5] has revealed that certain changes introduced by that Directive have not met their original objectives and that further amendments to the prospectus regime in the Union are necessary to simplify and improve its application, increase its efficiency and enhance the international competitiveness of the Union, thereby contributing to the reduction of administrative burdens.

(7) The aim of this Regulation is to ensure investor protection and market efficiency, while enhancing the internal market for capital. The provision of information which, according to the nature of the issuer and of the securities, is necessary to enable investors to make an informed investment decision ensures, together with rules on the conduct of business, the protection of investors. Moreover, such information provides an effective means of increasing confidence in securities and thus of contributing to the proper functioning and development of securities markets. The appropriate way to make that information available is to publish a prospectus.

(8) The disclosure requirements of this Regulation do not prevent a Member State or a competent authority or an exchange, through its rulebook, from imposing other particular requirements in the context of the admission to trading of securities on a regulated market, notably regarding corporate governance. Such requirements should not directly or indirectly restrict the drawing up, the content and the dissemination of a prospectus approved by a competent authority.

(9) Non-equity securities issued by a Member State or by one of a Member State's regional or local authorities, by public international bodies of which one or more Member States are members, by the European Central Bank or by the central banks of the Member States should not be covered by this Regulation and thus should remain unaffected by this Regulation.

(10) The obligation to publish a prospectus should apply to both equity and non-equity securities offered to the public or admitted to trading on regulated markets in order to ensure investor protection. Some of the securities covered by this Regulation entitle the holder to acquire transferable securities or to receive a cash amount through a cash settlement determined by reference to other instruments, notably transferable securities, currencies, interest rates or yields, commodities or other indices or measures. This Regulation covers in particular warrants, covered warrants, certificates, depositary receipts and convertible notes, such as securities convertible at the option of the investor.

(11) To ensure the approval and passporting of the prospectus as well as the supervision of compliance with this Regulation, a competent authority needs to be identified for each prospectus. Thus, this Regulation should clearly determine the home Member State best placed to approve the prospectus.

(12) For offers of securities to the public with a total consideration in the Union of less than EUR 1,000,000, the cost of producing a prospectus in accordance with this Regulation is likely to be disproportionate to the envisaged proceeds of the offer. It is therefore appropriate that the obligation to draw up a prospectus under this Regulation should not apply to offers of such small scale. Member States should not extend the obligation to draw up a prospectus in accordance with this Regulation to offers of securities to the public with a total consideration below that threshold. However, Member States should be able to require other disclosure requirements at national level to the extent that such requirements do not constitute a disproportionate or unnecessary burden in relation to such offers of securities.

(13) Furthermore, in view of the varying sizes of financial markets across the Union, it is appropriate to give Member States the option of exempting offers of securities to the public not exceeding EUR 8,000,000 from the obligation to publish a prospectus as provided for in this Regulation. In particular, Member States should be free to set out in their national law a threshold between EUR 1,000,000 and EUR 8,000,000, expressed as the total consideration of the offer in the Union over a period of 12 months, below which the exemption should apply taking into account the level of domestic investor protection they deem to be appropriate. However, such exempted offers of securities to the public should not benefit from the passporting regime under this Regulation. Below that threshold, Member States should be able to require other disclosure requirements at national level to the extent that such requirements do not constitute a disproportionate or unnecessary burden in relation to such exempted offers of securities. Nothing in this Regulation should prevent those Member States from introducing rules at national level which allow the operators of multilateral trading facilities (MTFs) to determine the content of the admission document which an issuer is required to produce upon initial admission to trading of its securities or the modalities of its review.

(14) The mere admission of securities to trading on a MTF or the publication of bid and offer prices is not to be regarded in itself as an offer of securities to the public and is therefore not subject to the obligation to draw up a prospectus under this Regulation. A prospectus should only be required where those situations are accompanied by a communication constituting an 'offer of securities to the public' as defined in this Regulation.

(15) Where an offer of securities is addressed exclusively to a restricted circle of investors who are not qualified investors, drawing up a prospectus represents a disproportionate burden in view of the small number of persons targeted by the offer, thus no prospectus should be required. That would apply for example in the case of an offer addressed to a limited number of relatives or personal acquaintances of the managers of a company.

(16) This Regulation should be interpreted in a manner consistent with Directive 2004/25/EC of the European Parliament and of the Council,[6] where applicable, in the context of takeover bids, merger transactions and other transactions affecting the ownership or control of companies.

(17) Incentivising directors and employees to hold securities of their own company can have a positive impact on companies' governance and help create long-term value by fostering employees' dedication and sense of ownership, aligning the respective interests of shareholders and employees, and providing the latter with investment opportunities. Participation of employees in the ownership of their company is particularly important for small and medium-sized enterprises (SMEs), in which individual employees are likely to play a significant role in the success of the company. Therefore, there should be no obligation to publish a prospectus for offers made in the context of an employee-share scheme within the Union, provided a document is made available containing information on the number and nature of the securities and the reasons for and details of the offer or allotment, to safeguard investor protection. To ensure equal access to employee-share schemes for all directors and employees, independently of whether their employer is established in or outside the Union, no equivalence decision of third country markets should be required any longer, as long as such information document is made available. Thus, all participants in employee-share schemes will benefit from equal treatment and information.

(18) Dilutive issuances of shares or securities giving access to shares often indicate transactions with a significant impact on the issuer's capital structure, prospects and financial situation, for which the information contained in a prospectus is needed. In contrast, where an issuer has shares already admitted to trading on a regulated market, a prospectus should not be required for any subsequent admission of the shares of the same class on the same regulated market, including where such shares result from the conversion or exchange of other securities or from the exercise of the rights conferred by other securities, provided that the newly admitted shares represent a limited proportion in relation to shares of the same class already admitted to the same regulated market, unless such admission is combined with an offer of securities to the public falling within the scope of this Regulation. The same principle should apply more generally to securities fungible with securities already admitted to trading on a regulated market.

(19) This Regulation is without prejudice to the laws, regulations and administrative provisions adopted pursuant to Directive 2014/59/EU of the European Parliament and of the Council[7] in relation to the resolution of credit institutions, in particular Articles 53(2), 59(2) and 63(1) and (2) thereof, in cases where there is no obligation to publish a prospectus.

(20) Exemptions from the obligation to publish a prospectus under this Regulation should be able to be combined for an offer of securities to the public and/or an admission to trading on a regulated market, where the conditions for those exemptions are fulfilled at the same time. For example, where an offer is addressed simultaneously to qualified investors, to non-qualified investors that commit to invest at least EUR 100,000 each, to the employees of the issuer and, in addition, to a limited number of non-qualified investors not exceeding the number set out in this Regulation, that offer should be exempt from the obligation to publish a prospectus.

(21) In order to ensure the proper functioning of the wholesale market for non-equity securities and increase market liquidity, it is important to set out a distinct alleviated treatment for non-equity securities admitted to trading on a regulated market and designed for qualified investors. Such alleviated treatment should comprise minimum information requirements that are less onerous than those applying to non-equity securities offered to retail investors, no requirement to include a summary in the prospectus, and more flexible language requirements. The alleviated treatment should be applicable to, firstly, non-equity securities, regardless of their denomination, which are traded only on a regulated market, or a specific segment thereof, to which only qualified investors can have access for the purposes of trading in such securities and, secondly, to non-equity securities with a denomination per unit of at least EUR 100,000, which reflects the higher investment capacity of the investors concerned by the prospectus. No resale to non-qualified investors should be allowed for non-equity securities that are traded only on a regulated market, or a specific segment thereof, to which only qualified investors can have access for the purposes of trading in such securities, unless a prospectus is drawn up in accordance with this Regulation that is appropriate for non-qualified investors. To that end, it is essential that market operators, when establishing such regulated markets, or a specific segment thereof, do not allow direct or indirect access by non-qualified investors to that regulated market or specific segment.

(22) Where securities are allocated without an element of individual choice on the part of the recipient, including allocations of securities where there is no right to repudiate the allocation or where allocation is automatic following a decision by a court, such as an allocation of securities to existing creditors in the course of a judicial insolvency proceeding, such allocation should not qualify as an offer of securities to the public.

(23) Issuers, offerors or persons asking for the admission to trading on a regulated market of securities which are not subject to the obligation to publish a prospectus should benefit from the single passport where they choose to comply with this Regulation on a voluntary basis.

(24) In view of the specificities of different types of securities, issuers, offers and admissions, this Regulation sets out rules for different forms of prospectuses — a standard prospectus, a wholesale prospectus for non-equity securities, a base prospectus, a simplified prospectus for secondary issuances and an EU Growth prospectus. Therefore, all references to 'prospectus' under this Regulation are to be understood as referring to all those forms of prospectuses, unless explicitly stated otherwise.

(25) Disclosure provided by a prospectus should not be required for offers of securities to the public which are limited to qualified investors. In contrast, any resale to the public or public trading through admission to trading on a regulated market should require the publication of a prospectus.

(26) A valid prospectus, drawn up by the issuer or the person responsible for drawing up the prospectus and available to the public at the time of the final placement of securities through financial intermediaries or in any subsequent resale of securities, provides sufficient information for investors to make informed investment decisions. Therefore, financial intermediaries placing or subsequently reselling the securities should be entitled to rely upon the initial prospectus published by the issuer or the person responsible for drawing up the prospectus as long as it is valid and duly supplemented and the issuer or the person responsible for drawing up the prospectus consents to its use. The issuer or the person responsible for drawing up the prospectus should be allowed to attach conditions to such consent. The consent to use the prospectus, including any conditions attached thereto, should be given in a written agreement

enabling assessment by relevant parties of whether the resale or final placement of securities complies with the agreement. In the event that consent to use the prospectus has been given, the issuer or person responsible for drawing up the initial prospectus should be liable for the information stated therein and in the case of a base prospectus, for providing and filing final terms and no other prospectus should be required. However, in the event that the issuer or the person responsible for drawing up such initial prospectus does not consent to its use, the financial intermediary should be required to publish a new prospectus. In that case, the financial intermediary should be liable for the information in the prospectus, including all information incorporated by reference and, in the case of a base prospectus, in the final terms.

(27) Harmonisation of the information contained in the prospectus should provide equivalent investor protection at Union level. In order to enable investors to make an informed investment decision, that information should be sufficient and objective and should be written and presented in an easily analysable, concise and comprehensible form. The information which is included in a prospectus should be adapted to the type of prospectus, the nature and circumstances of the issuer, the type of securities, and whether the investors targeted by the offer are solely qualified investors. A prospectus should not contain information which is not material or specific to the issuer and the securities concerned, as that could obscure the information relevant to the investment decision and thus undermine investor protection.

(28) The summary of the prospectus should be a useful source of information for investors, in particular retail investors. It should be a self-contained part of the prospectus and should focus on key information that investors need in order to be able to decide which offers and admissions to trading of securities they want to study further by reviewing the prospectus as a whole to take their decision. Such key information should convey the essential characteristics of, and risks associated with, the issuer, any guarantor, and the securities offered or admitted to trading on a regulated market. It should also provide the general terms and conditions of the offer.

(29) The presentation of risk factors in the summary should consist of a limited selection of specific risks which the issuer considers to be of most relevance to the investor when the investor is making an investment decision. The description of the risk factors in the summary should be of relevance to the specific offer and should be prepared solely for the benefit of investors and not give general statements on investment risk, or limit the liability of the issuer, offeror or any persons acting on their behalf. Those risk factors should, where applicable, highlight the risks, in particular for retail investors, in the case of securities issued by credit institutions that are subject to bail-in under Directive 2014/59/EU.

(30) The summary of the prospectus should be short, simple and easy for investors to understand. It should be written in plain, non-technical language, presenting the information in an easily accessible way. It should not be a mere compilation of excerpts from the prospectus. It is appropriate to set a maximum length for the summary in order to ensure that investors are not deterred from reading it and to encourage issuers to select the information which is essential for investors. In certain circumstances set out in this Regulation, the maximum length of the summary should be extended.

(31) To ensure the uniform structure of the prospectus summary, general sections and sub-headings should be provided, with indicative contents which the issuer should fill in with brief, narrative descriptions including figures where appropriate. As long as they present it in a fair and balanced way, issuers should be given discretion to select the information that they deem to be material and meaningful.

(32) The prospectus summary should be modelled as much as possible on the key information document required under Regulation (EU) No 1286/2014 of the European Parliament and of the Council.[8] Where securities fall under the scope of both this Regulation and Regulation (EU) No 1286/2014, full reuse in the summary of the contents of the key information document would minimise compliance costs and administrative burdens for issuers, and this Regulation therefore facilitates such reuse. The requirement to produce a summary should however not be waived when a key information document is required, as the latter does not contain key information on the issuer and the offer to the public or admission to trading on a regulated market of the securities concerned.

(33) No civil liability should be attached to any person solely on the basis of the summary, including any translation thereof, unless it is misleading, inaccurate or inconsistent with the relevant parts of the prospectus or where it does not provide, when read together with the other parts of the prospectus, key information in order to aid investors when considering whether to invest in such securities. The summary should contain a clear warning to that effect.

(34) Issuers which repeatedly raise financing on capital markets should be offered specific formats of registration documents and prospectuses as well as specific procedures for their filing and approval, in order to provide them with more flexibility and enable them to seize market windows. In any case, those formats and procedures should be optional and at the choice of issuers.

(35) For all non-equity securities, including those that are issued in a continuous or repeated manner or as part of an offering programme, issuers should be allowed to draw up a prospectus in the form of a base prospectus.

(36) It is appropriate to clarify that final terms to a base prospectus should contain only information relating to the securities note which is specific to the individual issue and which can be determined only at the time of the individual issue. Such information may, for example, include the international securities identification number (ISIN), the issue price, the date of maturity, any coupon, the exercise date, the exercise price, the redemption price and other terms not known at the time of drawing up the base prospectus. Where the final terms are not included in the base prospectus they should not have to be approved by the competent authority, but should only be filed with it. Other new information which is capable of affecting the assessment of the issuer and of the securities should be included in a supplement to the base prospectus. Neither the final terms nor a supplement should be used to include a type of securities not already described in the base prospectus.

(37) Under a base prospectus, a summary should only be drawn up by the issuer in relation to each individual issue, in order to reduce administrative burdens and to enhance the readability for investors. That issue-specific summary should be annexed to the final terms and should only be approved by the competent authority where the final terms are included in the base prospectus or in a supplement thereto.

(38) In order to enhance the flexibility and cost-effectiveness of the base prospectus, an issuer should be allowed to draw up a base prospectus as separate documents.

(39) Frequent issuers should be incentivised to draw up their prospectus as separate documents, since that can reduce their cost of compliance with this Regulation and enable them to swiftly react to market windows. Thus, issuers whose securities are admitted to trading on regulated markets or MTFs should have the option, but not the obligation, to draw up and publish every financial year a universal registration document containing legal, business, financial, accounting and shareholding information and providing a description of the issuer for that financial year. On the condition that an issuer fulfils the criteria set out in this Regulation, the issuer should be deemed to be a frequent issuer as from the moment when the issuer submits the universal registration document for approval to the competent authority. Drawing up a universal registration document should enable the issuer to keep the information up-to-date and to draw up a prospectus when market conditions become favourable for an offer of securities to the public or an admission to trading on a regulated market by adding a securities note and a summary. The universal registration document should be multi-purpose insofar as its content should be the same irrespective of whether the issuer subsequently uses it for an offer of securities to the public or an admission to trading on a regulated market of equity or non-equity securities. Therefore, the disclosure standards for the universal registration document should be based on those for equity securities. The universal registration document should act as a source of reference on the issuer, supplying investors and analysts with the minimum information needed to make an informed judgement on the company's business, financial position, earnings and prospects, governance and shareholding.

(40) An issuer which has filed and received approval for a universal registration document for two consecutive years can be considered well-known to the competent authority. All subsequent universal registration documents and any amendments thereto should therefore be allowed to be filed without prior approval and reviewed on an ex-post basis by the competent authority where that competent authority deems it necessary. Each competent authority should decide the frequency of such review taking into account for example its assessment of the risks of the issuer, the quality of its past disclosures, or the length of time elapsed since a filed universal registration document has been last reviewed.

(41) As long as it has not become a constituent part of an approved prospectus, it should be possible for the universal registration document to be amended, either voluntarily by the issuer — for example in the event of a material change in the organisation or financial situation of the issuer — or upon request by the competent authority in the context of an ex-post filing review where it is concluded that the standards of completeness, comprehensibility and consistency are not met. Such amendments should be published according to the same arrangements that apply to the universal registration document. In particular, when the competent authority identifies a material omission, a material mistake or a material inaccuracy, the issuer should amend its universal registration document and make that amendment publicly available without undue delay. As neither an offer to the public nor an admission to trading of securities is taking place, the procedure for amending a universal registration document should be distinct from the procedure for supplementing a prospectus, which should apply only after the approval of the prospectus.

(42) Where an issuer draws up a prospectus consisting of separate documents, all constituent parts of the prospectus should be subject to approval, including, where applicable, the universal registration document and any amendments thereto, where they have been previously filed with the competent authority but not approved. Amendments to the universal registration document should not be subject to approval by the competent authority at the time of filing but should only be approved when all the constituent parts of the prospectus are submitted for approval.

(43) To speed up the process of preparing a prospectus and to facilitate access to capital markets in a cost-effective way, frequent issuers who produce a universal registration document should be granted the benefit of a faster approval process, since the main constituent part of the prospectus has either already been approved or is already available for the review by the competent authority. The time needed to obtain approval of the prospectus should therefore be shortened when the registration document takes the form of a universal registration document.

(44) Frequent issuers should be allowed to use a universal registration document and any amendments thereto as a constituent part of a base prospectus. Where a frequent issuer is eligible to draw up an EU Growth prospectus, a simplified prospectus under the simplified disclosure regime for secondary issuances or a wholesale prospectus for non-equity securities, it should be allowed to use its universal registration document and any amendments thereto as a constituent part of any such prospectus, instead of the specific registration document required under those disclosure regimes.

(45) Provided that an issuer complies with the procedures for the filing, dissemination and storage of regulated information and with the deadlines set out in Articles 4 and 5 of Directive 2004/109/EC of the European Parliament and of the Council,[9] it should be allowed to publish the annual and half-yearly financial reports required under Directive 2004/109/EC as parts of the universal registration document, unless the home Member States of the issuer are different for the purposes of this Regulation and Directive 2004/109/EC and unless the language of the universal registration document does not fulfil the conditions of Article 20 of Directive 2004/109/EC. That should alleviate administrative burdens linked to multiple filings, without affecting the information available to the public or the supervision of those reports under Directive 2004/109/EC.

(46) A clear time limit should be set for the validity of a prospectus in order to avoid investment decisions based on outdated information. In order to improve legal certainty, the validity of a prospectus should commence at its approval, a point in time which is easily verified by the competent authority. An offer of securities to the public under a base prospectus should only extend beyond the validity of the base prospectus where a succeeding base prospectus is approved and published before such validity expires and covers the continuing offer.

(47) By nature, information on taxes on the income from the securities in a prospectus can only be generic, adding little informational value for the individual investor. Since such information is to cover not only the country of registered office of the issuer but also the countries where the offer is being made or admission to trading on a regulated market is being sought, where a prospectus is passported, it is costly to produce and might hamper cross-border offers. Therefore, a prospectus should only contain a warning that the tax laws of the investor's Member State and of the issuer's Member State of incorporation might have an impact on the income received from the securities. However, the prospectus should still contain appropriate information on taxation where the proposed investment entails a specific tax regime, for instance in the case of investments in securities granting investors a favourable tax treatment.

(48) Once a class of securities is admitted to trading on a regulated market, investors are provided with ongoing disclosures by the issuer under Regulation (EU) No 596/2014 of the European Parliament and of the Council[10] and

Directive 2004/109/EC. The need for a full prospectus is therefore less acute in cases of subsequent offers to the public or admissions to trading on a regulated market by such an issuer. A distinct simplified prospectus should therefore be available for use in cases of secondary issuances and its content should be alleviated compared to the normal regime, taking into account the information already disclosed. Still, investors need to be provided with consolidated and well-structured information, especially where such information is not required to be disclosed on an ongoing basis under Regulation (EU) No 596/2014 and Directive 2004/109/EC.

(49) The simplified disclosure regime for secondary issuances should be available for offers to the public by issuers whose securities are traded on SME growth markets, as their operators are required under Directive 2014/65/EU of the European Parliament and of the Council[11] to establish and apply rules ensuring appropriate ongoing disclosure.

(50) The simplified disclosure regime for secondary issuances should only be available for use after a minimum period has elapsed since the initial admission to trading on a regulated market or an SME growth market of a class of securities of an issuer. A delay of 18 months should ensure that the issuer has complied at least once with its obligation to publish an annual financial report under Directive 2004/109/EC or under the rules of the market operator of an SME growth market.

(51) One of the core objectives of the Capital Markets Union is to facilitate access to financing on capital markets for SMEs in the Union. It is appropriate to extend the definition of SMEs to include SMEs as defined in Directive 2014/65/EU to ensure consistency between this Regulation and Directive 2014/65/EU. As SMEs usually need to raise relatively lower amounts than other issuers, the cost of drawing up a standard prospectus can be disproportionately high and might deter them from offering their securities to the public. At the same time, because of their size and potentially shorter track record, SMEs might carry a specific investment risk compared to larger issuers and should disclose sufficient information for investors to take their investment decision. Furthermore, in order to encourage the use of capital market financing by SMEs, this Regulation should ensure that special consideration is given to SME growth markets, which are a promising tool to allow smaller, growing companies to raise capital. The success of such venues depends, however, on their ability to cater for the financing needs of growing SMEs. Similarly, certain companies offering securities to the public with a total consideration in the Union not exceeding EUR 20,000,000 would benefit from easier access to capital market financing in order to be able to grow and should be able to raise funds at costs that are not disproportionately high. Therefore, it is appropriate that this Regulation establishes a specific proportionate EU Growth prospectus regime which is available to such companies. A proper balance should be struck between cost-efficient access to financial markets and investor protection when calibrating the content of an EU Growth prospectus. As is the case for other types of prospectus under this Regulation, once approved, an EU Growth prospectus should benefit from the passporting regime under this Regulation and should therefore be valid for any offer of securities to the public across the Union.

(52) The reduced information required to be disclosed in EU Growth prospectuses should be calibrated in a way that focuses on information that is material and relevant when investing in the securities offered, and on the need to ensure proportionality between the size of the company and its fundraising needs, on the one hand, and the cost of producing a prospectus, on the other hand.

(53) The proportionate disclosure regime for EU Growth prospectuses should not be available where a company already has securities admitted to trading on regulated markets, so that investors on regulated markets feel confident that the issuers whose securities they invest in are subject to one single set of disclosure rules. Therefore, there should not be a two-tier disclosure standard on regulated markets depending on the size of the issuer.

(54) The primary purpose of including risk factors in a prospectus is to ensure that investors make an informed assessment of such risks and thus take investment decisions in full knowledge of the facts. Risk factors should therefore be limited to those risks which are material and specific to the issuer and its securities and which are corroborated by the content of the prospectus. A prospectus should not contain risk factors which are generic and only serve as disclaimers, as those could obscure more specific risk factors that investors should be aware of, thereby preventing the prospectus from presenting information in an easily analysable, concise and comprehensible form. Among others, environmental, social and governance circumstances can also constitute specific and material risks for the issuer and its securities and, in that case, should be disclosed. To help investors identify the most material risks, the issuer should adequately describe and present each risk factor in the prospectus. A limited number of risk factors selected by the issuer should be included in the summary.

(55) The market practice whereby an approved prospectus does not include the final offer price and/or the amount of securities to be offered to the public, whether expressed in number of securities or as an aggregate nominal amount, should be acceptable when such final offer price and/or amount cannot be included in the prospectus, provided that protection is granted to investors in that case. Investors should either be entitled to a right of withdrawal once the final offer price or amount of securities is known, or, alternatively, the prospectus should disclose the maximum price investors might have to pay for the securities, or the maximum amount of securities, or the valuation methods and criteria, and/or conditions, in accordance with which the price of the securities is to be determined and an explanation of any valuation methods used, such as the discounted cash flow method, a peer group analysis or any other commonly accepted valuation methods. The valuation methods and criteria should be precise enough to make the price predictable and ensure a level of investor protection that is similar to the disclosure of the maximum price of the offer. In that respect, a mere reference to the bookbuilding method would not be acceptable as valuation method or criteria where no maximum price is included in the prospectus.

(56) Omission of sensitive information in a prospectus, or in constituent parts thereof, should be allowed in certain circumstances by means of a derogation granted by the competent authority in order to avoid detrimental situations for an issuer.

(57) Member States publish abundant information on their financial situation which is, in general, available in the public domain. Thus, where a Member State guarantees an offer of securities, such information should not need to be provided in the prospectus.

(58) Allowing issuers to incorporate by reference documents containing the information to be disclosed in a prospectus, subject to the requirement that such documents have been published electronically, should facilitate the procedure of drawing up a prospectus and lower the costs for the issuers without endangering investor protection. However, the aim of simplifying and reducing the costs of drafting a prospectus should not be achieved to the detriment

of other interests the prospectus is meant to protect, including the accessibility of the information. The language used for information incorporated by reference should follow the language regime applying to prospectuses. Information incorporated by reference should be able to refer to historical data. However, where such information is no longer relevant due to material change, that should be clearly stated in the prospectus and the updated information should also be provided.

(59) Any regulated information, as defined in point (k) of Article 2(1) of Directive 2004/109/EC, should be eligible for incorporation by reference in a prospectus. Issuers whose securities are traded on an MTF, and issuers which are exempted from publishing annual and half-yearly financial reports pursuant to point (b) of Article 8(1) of Directive 2004/109/EC, should also be allowed to incorporate by reference in a prospectus all or part of their annual and interim financial information, audit reports, financial statements, management reports or corporate governance statements, subject to their electronic publication.

(60) Not all issuers have access to adequate information and guidance about the scrutiny and approval process and the necessary steps to follow to get a prospectus approved, as different approaches by competent authorities exist in Member States. This Regulation should eliminate those differences by harmonising the criteria for the scrutiny of the prospectus and harmonising the rules applying to the approval processes of competent authorities by streamlining them. It is important to ensure that all competent authorities take a convergent approach when scrutinising the completeness, consistency and comprehensibility of the information contained in a prospectus taking into account the need for a proportionate approach in the scrutiny of prospectuses based on the circumstances of the issuer and of the issuance. Guidance on how to seek the approval of a prospectus should be publicly available on the websites of the competent authorities. The European Securities and Markets Authority (ESMA) should play a key role in fostering supervisory convergence in that field by using its powers under Regulation (EU) No 1095/2010 of the European Parliament and of the Council.[12] In particular, ESMA should conduct peer reviews covering activities of the competent authorities under this Regulation within an appropriate time-frame before the review of this Regulation and in accordance with Regulation (EU) No 1095/2010.

(61) To facilitate access to the markets of Member States, it is important that fees charged by competent authorities for the approval and filing of prospectuses and their related documents are reasonable, proportionate and publicly disclosed.

(62) Since the internet ensures easy access to information, and in order to ensure better accessibility for investors, the approved prospectus should always be published in an electronic form. The prospectus should be published on a dedicated section of the website of the issuer, the offeror or the person asking for admission to trading on a regulated market, or, where applicable, on the website of the financial intermediaries placing or selling the securities, including paying agents, or on the website of the regulated market where the admission to trading is sought, or of the operator of the MTF.

(63) All prospectuses approved, or alternatively a list of those prospectuses with hyperlinks to the relevant dedicated website sections, should be published on the website of the competent authority of the issuer's home Member State, and each prospectus should be transmitted by the competent authority to ESMA along with the relevant data enabling its classification. ESMA should provide a centralised storage mechanism of prospectuses allowing access free of charge and appropriate search facilities for the public. To ensure that investors have access to reliable data that can be used and analysed in a timely and efficient matter, certain information contained in the prospectuses, such as the ISINs identifying the securities and the legal entity identifiers (LEIs) identifying the issuers, offerors and guarantors, should be machine readable including when metadata is used. Prospectuses should remain publicly available for at least 10 years after their publication, to ensure that their period of public availability is aligned with that of annual and half-yearly financial reports under Directive 2004/109/EC. Prospectuses should always be available to investors on a durable medium, free of charge, upon request. Where a potential investor makes a specific demand for a paper copy, that investor should be able to receive a printed version of the prospectus. However, that does not require the issuer, the offeror, the person asking for admission to trading on a regulated market or the financial intermediary to keep in reserve printed copies of the prospectus to satisfy such potential requests.

(64) It is also necessary to harmonise advertisements in order to avoid undermining public confidence and prejudicing the proper functioning of financial markets. The fairness and accuracy of advertisements, as well as their consistency with the content of the prospectus are of utmost importance for the protection of investors, including retail investors. Without prejudice to the passporting regime under this Regulation, the supervision of such advertisements is an integral part of the role of competent authorities. The requirements on advertisements in this Regulation should be without prejudice to other applicable provisions of Union law, in particular relating to consumer protection and unfair commercial practices.

(65) Any significant new factor, material mistake or material inaccuracy which could influence the assessment of the investment, arising after the publication of the prospectus but before the closing of the offer or the start of trading on a regulated market, should be properly evaluated by investors and, therefore, requires the approval and dissemination of a supplement to the prospectus without undue delay.

(66) In order to improve legal certainty, the respective time limits within which an issuer is to publish a supplement to the prospectus and within which investors have a right to withdraw their acceptance of the offer following the publication of a supplement should be clarified. On the one hand, the obligation to supplement a prospectus should apply when the significant new factor, material mistake or material inaccuracy occurs before the closing of the offer period or the time when trading of such securities on a regulated market begins, whichever occurs later. On the other hand, the right to withdraw an acceptance should apply only where the prospectus relates to an offer of securities to the public and the significant new factor, material mistake or material inaccuracy arose or was noted before the closing of the offer period and the delivery of the securities. Hence, the right of withdrawal should be linked to the timing of the significant new factor, material mistake or material inaccuracy that gives rise to a supplement, and should apply provided that such triggering event has occurred while the offer is open and before the securities are delivered. The right of withdrawal granted to investors owing to a significant new factor, material mistake or material inaccuracy that arose or was noted during the validity period of a prospectus is not affected by the fact that the corresponding supplement is published after the validity period of that prospectus. In the particular case of an offer that continues under two successive base prospectuses, the fact that the issuer is in the process of having a succeeding base

prospectus approved does not remove the obligation to supplement the previous base prospectus until the end of its validity and grant the associated rights of withdrawal. To improve legal certainty, the supplement to the prospectus should specify when the right of withdrawal ends. Financial intermediaries should inform investors of their rights and facilitate proceedings when investors exert their right to withdraw acceptances.

(67) The obligation for an issuer to translate the entire prospectus into all the relevant official languages discourages cross-border offers or multiple trading. To facilitate cross-border offers, only the summary should be available in the official language or at least one of the official languages of the host Member State or in another language accepted by the competent authority of that Member State.

(68) The competent authority of the host Member State should be entitled to receive a certificate from the competent authority of the home Member State which states that the prospectus has been drawn up in accordance with this Regulation. The competent authority of the home Member State should also notify the issuer or the person responsible for drawing up the prospectus of the certificate of approval of the prospectus that is addressed to the authority of the host Member State in order to provide the issuer or the person responsible for drawing up the prospectus with certainty as to whether and when a notification has in fact been made. All transfers of documents between competent authorities for the purpose of notifications should take place through a notification portal to be established by ESMA.

(69) Where this Regulation allows an issuer to choose its home Member State for the purpose of the prospectus approval, it is appropriate to ensure that such issuer can use as a constituent part of its prospectus a registration document, or a universal registration document, which has already been approved by the competent authority of another Member State. A system of notification between competent authorities should therefore be introduced to ensure that such registration document, or universal registration document, is not subject to a scrutiny or approval by the competent authority approving the prospectus, and that competent authorities remain responsible only for the constituent part of a prospectus which they have approved, including in the event that a supplement is subsequently drawn up.

(70) In order to ensure that the purposes of this Regulation will be fully achieved, it is also necessary to include within its scope securities issued by issuers governed by the laws of third countries. In order to ensure exchanges of information and cooperation with third-country authorities in relation to the effective enforcement of this Regulation, competent authorities should conclude cooperation arrangements with their counterparts in third countries. Any transfer of personal data carried out on the basis of those arrangements should comply with Regulation (EU) 2016/679 of the European Parliament and of the Council[13] and with Regulation (EC) No 45/2001 of the European Parliament and of the Council.[14]

(71) A variety of competent authorities in Member States, with different responsibilities, might create unnecessary costs and overlapping of responsibilities without providing any additional benefit. In each Member State, a single competent authority should be designated to approve prospectuses and to assume responsibility for supervising compliance with this Regulation. That competent authority should be established as an administrative authority and in such a form that their independence from economic actors is guaranteed and conflicts of interest are avoided. The designation of a competent authority for prospectus approval should not exclude cooperation between that competent authority and third parties, such as banking and insurance regulators or listing authorities, with a view to guaranteeing efficient scrutiny and approval of prospectuses in the interest of issuers, investors, markets participants and markets alike. Delegation of tasks by a competent authority to third parties should only be permitted where it relates to the publication of approved prospectuses.

(72) A set of effective tools and powers and resources for the competent authorities of Member States guarantees supervisory effectiveness. This Regulation should therefore in particular provide for a minimum set of supervisory and investigative powers with which competent authorities of Member States should be entrusted in accordance with national law. Those powers should be exercised, where the national law so requires, by application to the competent judicial authorities. When exercising their powers under this Regulation, competent authorities and ESMA should act objectively and impartially and remain autonomous in their decision-making.

(73) For the purpose of detecting infringements of this Regulation, it is necessary for competent authorities to be able to access sites other than the private residences of natural persons in order to seize documents. Access to such premises is necessary when there is reasonable suspicion that documents and other data related to the subject matter of an inspection or investigation exist and might be relevant to prove an infringement of this Regulation. Additionally, access to such premises is necessary where the person to whom a demand for information has already been made fails to comply with it, or where there are reasonable grounds for believing that, if a demand were to be made, it would not be complied with or that the documents or information to which the information requirement relates would be removed, tampered with or destroyed.

(74) In line with the Communication of the Commission of 8 December 2010 on Reinforcing sanctioning regimes in the financial services sector and in order to ensure that the requirements of this Regulation are fulfilled, it is important that Member States take necessary steps to ensure that infringements of this Regulation are subject to appropriate administrative sanctions and other administrative measures. Those sanctions and measures should be effective, proportionate and dissuasive and ensure a common approach in Member States and a deterrent effect. This Regulation should not limit Member States in their ability to provide for higher levels of administrative sanctions.

(75) In order to ensure that decisions imposing administrative sanctions or other administrative measures taken by competent authorities have a deterrent effect on the public at large, they should normally be published unless the competent authority in accordance with this Regulation deems it necessary to opt for a publication on an anonymous basis, to delay the publication or not to publish.

(76) Although Member States should be able to lay down rules for administrative and criminal sanctions for the same infringements, Member States should not be required to lay down rules for administrative sanctions for the infringements of this Regulation which are subject to criminal sanctions in their national law by 21 July 2018. In accordance with national law, Member States are not obliged to impose both administrative and criminal sanctions for the same offence, but they should be able to do so if their national law so permits. However, the maintenance of criminal sanctions instead of administrative sanctions for infringements of this Regulation should not reduce or otherwise affect the ability of competent authorities to cooperate, access and exchange information in a timely way with

competent authorities in other Member States for the purposes of this Regulation, including after any referral of the relevant infringements to the competent judicial authorities for criminal prosecution.

(77) Whistleblowers might bring new information to the attention of competent authorities which assists them in detecting and imposing sanctions in cases of infringements of this Regulation. This Regulation should therefore ensure that adequate arrangements are in place to enable whistleblowers to alert competent authorities to actual or potential infringements of this Regulation and to protect them from retaliation.

(78) In order to specify the requirements set out in this Regulation, the power to adopt acts in accordance with Article 290 of the Treaty on the Functioning of the European Union (TFEU) should be delegated to the Commission in respect of the minimum information content of certain documents to be made available to the public in connection with a takeover by means of an exchange offer, a merger or a division, the scrutiny, approval, filing and review of the universal registration document and any amendments thereto as well as the conditions under which the status of frequent issuer is lost, the format of the prospectus, the base prospectus and the final terms, and the specific information which must be included in a prospectus, the minimum information to be included in the universal registration document, the reduced information to be included in the simplified prospectus in cases of secondary issuances and by SMEs, the specific reduced content and standardised format and sequence of the EU Growth prospectus and its specific summary, the criteria for assessment and presentation of risk factors by the issuer, the scrutiny and approval of prospectuses and the general equivalence criteria for prospectuses drawn up by third country issuers. It is of particular importance that the Commission carry out appropriate consultations during its preparatory work, including at expert level, and that those consultations be conducted in accordance with the principles laid down in the Interinstitutional Agreement of 13 April 2016 on Better Law-Making.[15] In particular, to ensure equal participation in the preparation of delegated acts, the European Parliament and the Council receive all documents at the same time as Member States' experts, and their experts systematically have access to meetings of Commission expert groups dealing with the preparation of delegated acts.

(79) In order to ensure uniform conditions for the implementation of this Regulation in respect of equivalence of the prospectus laws of third countries, implementing powers should be conferred on the Commission to take a decision on such equivalence. Those powers should be exercised in accordance with Regulation (EU) No 182/2011 of the European Parliament and of the Council.[16]

(80) Technical standards in financial services should ensure adequate protection of investors and consumers across the Union. As a body with highly specialised expertise, it would be efficient and appropriate to entrust ESMA with the elaboration of draft regulatory technical standards which do not involve policy choices, for submission to the Commission.

(81) The Commission should be empowered to adopt regulatory technical standards developed by ESMA, with regard to the content and format of presentation of the key financial information to be included in the summary, the cases where it is possible for certain information to be omitted from the prospectus, the information to be incorporated by reference and further types of documents required under Union law, the publication of the prospectus, the data necessary for the classification of prospectuses in the storage mechanism operated by ESMA, the provisions concerning advertisements, the situations where a significant new factor, material mistake or material inaccuracy relating to the information included in the prospectus requires a supplement to the prospectus to be published, the technical arrangements necessary for the functioning of the ESMA notification portal, the minimum content of the cooperation arrangements with supervisory authorities in third countries and the templates to be used therefor, and the information exchanged between competent authorities and ESMA in the context of the obligation to cooperate. The Commission should adopt those draft regulatory technical standards by means of delegated acts pursuant to Article 290 TFEU and in accordance with Articles 10 to 14 of Regulation (EU) No 1095/2010.

(82) The Commission should also be empowered to adopt implementing technical standards developed by ESMA, with regard to the standard forms, templates and procedures for the notification of the certificate of approval, the prospectus, registration document, universal registration document, any supplement thereto and the translation thereof, the supplement of the prospectus, and the translation of the prospectus and/or summary, the standard forms, templates and procedures for the cooperation and exchange of information between competent authorities, and the procedures and forms for exchange of information between competent authorities and ESMA. The Commission should adopt those implementing technical standards by means of implementing acts pursuant to Article 291 TFEU and in accordance with Article 15 of Regulation (EU) No 1095/2010.

(83) In exercising its delegated and implementing powers in accordance with this Regulation, the Commission should respect the following principles:

— the need to ensure confidence in financial markets among retail investors and SMEs by promoting high standards of transparency in financial markets,

— the need to calibrate the disclosure requirements of a prospectus taking into account the size of the issuer and the information which an issuer is already required to disclose under Directive 2004/109/EC and Regulation (EU) No 596/2014,

— the need to facilitate access to capital markets for SMEs while ensuring investor confidence in investing in such companies,

— the need to provide investors with a wide range of competing investment opportunities and a level of disclosure and protection tailored to their circumstances,

— the need to ensure that independent regulatory authorities enforce the rules consistently, especially as regards the fight against white-collar crime,

— the need for a high level of transparency and consultation with all market participants and with the European Parliament and the Council,

— the need to encourage innovation in financial markets if they are to be dynamic and efficient,

— the need to ensure systemic stability of the financial system by close and reactive monitoring of financial innovation,

— the importance of reducing the cost of, and increasing access to, capital,

— the need to balance, on a long-term basis, the costs and benefits to all market participants of any implementing measure,

— the need to foster the international competitiveness of the Union's financial markets without prejudice to a much-needed extension of international cooperation,

— the need to achieve a level playing field for all market participants by establishing Union law every time it is appropriate,

— the need to ensure coherence with other Union law in the same area, as imbalances in information and a lack of transparency might jeopardise the operation of the markets and above all harm consumers and small investors.

(84) Any processing of personal data carried out within the framework of this Regulation, such as the exchange or transmission of personal data by the competent authorities, should be undertaken in accordance with Regulation (EU) 2016/679 and any exchange or transmission of information by ESMA should be undertaken in accordance with Regulation (EC) No 45/2001.

(85) The Commission should, by 21 July 2022, review the application of this Regulation and assess in particular whether the disclosure regimes for secondary issuances and for the EU Growth prospectus, the universal registration document and the prospectus summary remain appropriate to meet the objectives pursued by this Regulation. In particular, the report should analyse the relevant figures and trends concerning the EU Growth prospectus and assess whether the new regime strikes a proper balance between investor protection and the reduction of administrative burdens for the companies entitled to use it. Such a review should also assess whether issuers, in particular SMEs, can obtain LEIs and ISINs at a reasonable cost and within a reasonable period.

(86) The application of the requirements in this Regulation should be deferred in order to allow for the adoption of delegated and implementing acts and to allow competent authorities and market participants to assimilate and plan for the application of the new measures.

(87) Since the objectives of this Regulation, namely to enhance investor protection and market efficiency while establishing the Capital Markets Union, cannot be sufficiently achieved by the Member States but can rather, by reason of its effects, be better achieved at Union level, the Union may adopt measures in accordance with principle of subsidiarity as set out in Article 5 of the Treaty on European Union. In accordance with the principle of proportionality as set out in that Article, this Regulation does not go beyond what is necessary in order to achieve those objectives.

(88) This Regulation respects the fundamental rights and observes the principles recognised in particular by the Charter of Fundamental Rights of the European Union. Therefore, this Regulation should be interpreted and applied in accordance with those rights and principles.

(89) The European Data Protection Supervisor was consulted in accordance with Article 28(2) of Regulation (EC) No 45/2001,

NOTES

1 OJ C195, 2.6.2016, p 1.

2 OJ C177, 18.5.2016, p 9.

3 Position of the European Parliament of 5 April 2017 (not yet published in the Official Journal) and decision of the Council of 16 May 2017.

4 Directive 2003/71/EC of the European Parliament and of the Council of 4 November 2003 on the prospectus to be published when securities are offered to the public or admitted to trading and amending Directive 2001/34/EC (OJ L345, 31.12.2003, p 64).

5 Directive 2010/73/EU of the European Parliament and of the Council of 24 November 2010 amending Directives 2003/71/EC on the prospectus to be published when securities are offered to the public or admitted to trading and 2004/109/EC on the harmonisation of transparency requirements in relation to information about issuers whose securities are admitted to trading on a regulated market (OJ L327, 11.12.2010, p 1).

6 Directive 2004/25/EC of the European Parliament and of the Council of 21 April 2004 on takeover bids (OJ L142, 30.4.2004, p 12).

7 Directive 2014/59/EU of the European Parliament and of the Council of 15 May 2014 establishing a framework for the recovery and resolution of credit institutions and investment firms and amending Council Directive 82/891/EEC, and Directives 2001/24/EC, 2002/47/EC, 2004/25/EC, 2005/56/EC, 2007/36/EC, 2011/35/EU, 2012/30/EU and 2013/36/EU, and Regulations (EU) No 1093/ 2010 and (EU) No 648/2012, of the European Parliament and of the Council (OJ L173, 12.6.2014, p 190).

8 Regulation (EU) No 1286/2014 of the European Parliament and of the Council of 26 November 2014 on key information documents for packaged retail and insurance-based investment products (PRIIPs) (OJ L352, 9.12.2014, p 1).

9 Directive 2004/109/EC of the European Parliament and of the Council of 15 December 2004 on the harmonisation of transparency requirements in relation to information about issuers whose securities are admitted to trading on a regulated market and amending Directive 2001/34/EC (OJ L390, 31.12.2004, p 38).

10 Regulation (EU) No 596/2014 of the European Parliament and of the Council of 16 April 2014 on market abuse (market abuse regulation) and repealing Directive 2003/6/EC of the European Parliament and of the Council and Commission Directives 2003/124/EC, 2003/125/EC and 2004/72/EC (OJ L173, 12.6.2014, p 1).

11 Directive 2014/65/EU of the European Parliament and of the Council of 15 May 2014 on markets in financial instruments and amending Directive 2002/92/EC and Directive 2011/61/EU (OJ L173, 12.6.2014, p 349).

12 Regulation (EU) No 1095/2010 of the European Parliament and of the Council of 24 November 2010 establishing a European Supervisory Authority (European Securities and Markets Authority), amending Decision No 716/2009/EC and repealing Commission Decision 2009/77/EC (OJ L331, 15.12.2010, p 84).

13 Regulation (EU) 2016/679 of the European Parliament and of the Council of 27 April 2016 on the protection of natural persons with regard to the processing of personal data and on the free movement of such data, and repealing Directive 95/46/EC (General Data Protection Regulation) (OJ L119, 4.5.2016, p 1).

14 Regulation (EC) No 45/2001 of the European Parliament and of the Council of 18 December 2000 on the protection of individuals with regard to the processing of personal data by the Community institutions and bodies and on the free movement of such data (OJ L8, 12.1.2001, p 1).

15 OJ L123, 12.5.2016, p 1.

16 Regulation (EU) No 182/2011 of the European Parliament and of the Council of 16 February 2011 laying down the rules and general principles concerning mechanisms for control by the Member States of the Commission's exercise of implementing powers (OJ L55, 28.2.2011, p 13).

HAVE ADOPTED THIS REGULATION:

CHAPTER I GENERAL PROVISIONS

[11.321]

Article 1 Subject matter, scope and exemptions

1. This Regulation lays down requirements for the drawing up, approval and distribution of the prospectus to be published when securities are offered to the public or admitted to trading on a regulated market situated or operating within a Member State.

2. This Regulation shall not apply to the following types of securities:

(a) units issued by collective investment undertakings other than the closed-end type;

(b) non-equity securities issued by a Member State or by one of a Member State's regional or local authorities, by public international bodies of which one or more Member States are members, by the European Central Bank or by the central banks of the Member States;

(c) shares in the capital of central banks of the Member States;

(d) securities unconditionally and irrevocably guaranteed by a Member State or by one of a Member State's regional or local authorities;

(e) securities issued by associations with legal status or non-profit-making bodies, recognised by a Member State, for the purposes of obtaining the funding necessary to achieve their non-profit-making objectives;

(f) non-fungible shares of capital whose main purpose is to provide the holder with a right to occupy an apartment, or other form of immovable property or a part thereof and where the shares cannot be sold on without that right being given up.

3. Without prejudice to the second subparagraph of this paragraph and to Article 4, this Regulation shall not apply to an offer of securities to the public with a total consideration in the Union of less than EUR 1,000,000, which shall be calculated over a period of 12 months.

Member States shall not extend the obligation to draw up a prospectus in accordance with this Regulation to offers of securities to the public referred to in the first subparagraph of this paragraph. However, in those cases, Member States may require other disclosure requirements at national level to the extent that such requirements do not constitute a disproportionate or unnecessary burden.

4. The obligation to publish a prospectus set out in Article 3(1) shall not apply to any of the following types of offers of securities to the public:

(a) an offer of securities addressed solely to qualified investors;

(b) an offer of securities addressed to fewer than 150 natural or legal persons per Member State, other than qualified investors;

(c) an offer of securities whose denomination per unit amounts to at least EUR 100,000;

(d) an offer of securities addressed to investors who acquire securities for a total consideration of at least EUR 100,000 per investor, for each separate offer;

(e) shares issued in substitution for shares of the same class already issued, if the issuing of such new shares does not involve any increase in the issued capital;

(f) securities offered in connection with a takeover by means of an exchange offer, provided that a document is made available to the public in accordance with the arrangements set out in Article 21(2), containing information describing the transaction and its impact on the issuer;

(g) securities offered, allotted or to be allotted in connection with a merger or division, provided that a document is made available to the public in accordance with the arrangements set out in Article 21(2), containing information describing the transaction and its impact on the issuer;

(h) dividends paid out to existing shareholders in the form of shares of the same class as the shares in respect of which such dividends are paid, provided that a document is made available containing information on the number and nature of the shares and the reasons for and details of the offer;

(i) securities offered, allotted or to be allotted to existing or former directors or employees by their employer or by an affiliated undertaking provided that a document is made available containing information on the number and nature of the securities and the reasons for and details of the offer or allotment;

(j) non-equity securities issued in a continuous or repeated manner by a credit institution, where the total aggregated consideration in the Union for the securities offered is less than EUR 75,000,000 per credit institution calculated over a period of 12 months, provided that those securities:

(i) are not subordinated, convertible or exchangeable; and

(ii) do not give a right to subscribe for or acquire other types of securities and are not linked to a derivative instrument;

[(k) an offer of securities to the public from a crowdfunding service provider authorised under Regulation (EU) 2020/1503 of the European Parliament and of the Council*, provided that it does not exceed the threshold laid down in point (c) of Article 1(2) of that Regulation];

[(l) from 18 March 2021 to 31 December 2022, non-equity securities issued in a continuous or repeated manner by a credit institution, where the total aggregated consideration in the Union for the securities offered is less than EUR 150,000,000 per credit institution calculated over a period of 12 months, provided that those securities:

(i) are not subordinated, convertible or exchangeable; and

(ii) do not give a right to subscribe for or acquire other types of securities and are not linked to a derivative instrument.]

5. The obligation to publish a prospectus set out in Article 3(3) shall not apply to the admission to trading on a regulated market of any of the following:

(a) securities fungible with securities already admitted to trading on the same regulated market, provided that they represent, over a period of 12 months, less than 20% of the number of securities already admitted to trading on the same regulated market;

(b) shares resulting from the conversion or exchange of other securities or from the exercise of the rights conferred by other securities, where the resulting shares are of the same class as the shares already admitted to trading on the same regulated market, provided that the resulting shares represent, over a period of 12 months, less than 20% of the number of shares of the same class already admitted to trading on the same regulated market, subject to the second subparagraph of this paragraph;

(c) securities resulting from the conversion or exchange of other securities, own funds or eligible liabilities by a resolution authority due to the exercise of a power referred to in Article 53(2), 59(2) or Article 63(1) or (2) of Directive 2014/59/ EU;

(d) shares issued in substitution for shares of the same class already admitted to trading on the same regulated market, where the issuing of such shares does not involve any increase in the issued capital;

(e) securities offered in connection with a takeover by means of an exchange offer, provided that a document is made available to the public in accordance with the arrangements set out in Article 21(2), containing information describing the transaction and its impact on the issuer;

(f) securities offered, allotted or to be allotted in connection with a merger or a division, provided that a document is made available to the public in accordance with the arrangements set out in Article 21(2), containing information describing the transaction and its impact on the issuer;

(g) shares offered, allotted or to be allotted free of charge to existing shareholders, and dividends paid out in the form of shares of the same class as the shares in respect of which such dividends are paid, provided that the said shares are of the same class as the shares already admitted to trading on the same regulated market and that a document is made available containing information on the number and nature of the shares and the reasons for and details of the offer or allotment;

(h) securities offered, allotted or to be allotted to existing or former directors or employees by their employer or an affiliated undertaking, provided that the said securities are of the same class as the securities already admitted to trading on the same regulated market and that a document is made available containing information on the number and nature of the securities and the reasons for and detail of the offer or allotment;

(i) non-equity securities issued in a continuous or repeated manner by a credit institution, where the total aggregated consideration in the Union for the securities offered is less than EUR 75,000,000 per credit institution calculated over a period of 12 months, provided that those securities:

  (i) are not subordinated, convertible or exchangeable; and

  (ii) do not give a right to subscribe for or acquire other types of securities and are not linked to a derivative instrument;

(j) securities already admitted to trading on another regulated market, on the following conditions:

  (i) that those securities, or securities of the same class, have been admitted to trading on that other regulated market for more than 18 months;

  (ii) that, for securities first admitted to trading on a regulated market after 1 July 2005, the admission to trading on that other regulated market was subject to a prospectus approved and published in accordance with Directive 2003/71/EC;

  (iii) that, except where point (ii) applies, for securities first admitted to listing after 30 June 1983, listing particulars were approved in accordance with the requirements of Council Directive 80/390/EEC[1] or Directive 2001/34/EC of the European Parliament and of the Council;[2]

  (iv) that the ongoing obligations for trading on that other regulated market have been fulfilled;

  (v) that the person seeking the admission of a security to trading on a regulated market under the exemption set out in this point (j) makes available to the public in the Member State of the regulated market where admission to trading is sought, in accordance with the arrangements set out in Article 21(2), a document the content of which complies with Article 7, except that the maximum length set out in Article 7(3) shall be extended by two additional sides of A4-sized paper, drawn up in a language accepted by the competent authority of the Member State of the regulated market where admission is sought; and

  (vi) that the document referred to in point (v) states where the most recent prospectus can be obtained and where the financial information published by the issuer pursuant to ongoing disclosure obligations is available;

[(k) from 18 March 2021 to 31 December 2022, non-equity securities issued in a continuous or repeated manner by a credit institution, where the total aggregated consideration in the Union for the securities offered is less than EUR 150,000,000 per credit institution calculated over a period of 12 months, provided that those securities:

  (i) are not subordinated, convertible or exchangeable; and

  (ii) do not give a right to subscribe for or acquire other types of securities and are not linked to a derivative instrument.]

The requirement that the resulting shares represent, over a period of 12 months, less than 20% of the number of shares of the same class already admitted to trading on the same regulated market as referred to in point (b) of the first subparagraph shall not apply in any of the following cases:

(a) where a prospectus was drawn up in accordance with either this Regulation or Directive 2003/71/EC upon the offer to the public or admission to trading on a regulated market of the securities giving access to the shares;

(b) where the securities giving access to the shares were issued before 20 July 2017;

(c) where the shares qualify as Common Equity Tier 1 items as laid down in Article 26 of Regulation (EU) No 575/2013 of the European Parliament and of the Council[3] of an institution as defined in point (3) of Article 4(1) of that Regulation and result from the conversion of Additional Tier 1 instruments issued by that institution due to the occurrence of a trigger event as laid down in point (a) of Article 54(1) of that Regulation;

(d) where the shares qualify as eligible own funds or eligible basic own funds as defined in Section 3 of Chapter VI of Title I of Directive 2009/138/EC of the European Parliament and of the Council,[4] and result from the conversion of other securities which was triggered for the purposes of fulfilling the obligations to comply with the Solvency Capital Requirement or Minimum Capital Requirement as laid down in Sections 4 and 5 of Chapter VI of Title I of Directive 2009/138/EC or the group solvency requirement as laid down in Title III of Directive 2009/138/EC.

6. The exemptions from the obligation to publish a prospectus that are set out in paragraphs 4 and 5 may be combined together. However, the exemptions in points (a) and (b) of the first subparagraph of paragraph 5 shall not be combined together if such combination could lead to the immediate or deferred admission to trading on a regulated market over a period of 12 months of more than 20% of the number of shares of the same class already admitted to trading on the same regulated market, without a prospectus being published.

[6a. The exemptions set out in point (f) of paragraph 4 and in point (e) of paragraph 5 shall only apply to equity securities, and only in the following cases:.

(a) the equity securities offered are fungible with existing securities already admitted to trading on a regulated market prior to the takeover and its related transaction, and the takeover is not considered to be a reverse acquisition transaction within the meaning of paragraph B19 of international financial reporting standard (IFRS) 3, Business Combinations, adopted by Commission Regulation (EC) No 1126/2008;[5] or

(b) the supervisory authority that has the competence, where applicable, to review the offer document under Directive 2004/25/EC of the European Parliament and of the Council[6] has issued a prior approval of the document referred to in point (f) of paragraph 4 or point (e) of paragraph 5 of this Article.

6b. The exemptions set out in point (g) of paragraph 4 and in point (f) of paragraph 5 shall apply only to equity securities in respect of which the transaction is not considered to be a reverse acquisition transaction within the meaning of paragraph B19 of IFRS 3, Business Combinations, and only in the following cases:

(a) the equity securities of the acquiring entity have already been admitted to trading on a regulated market prior to the transaction; or

(b) the equity securities of the entities subject to the division have already been admitted to trading on a regulated market prior to the transaction.]

7. The Commission is empowered to adopt delegated acts in accordance with Article 44 supplementing this Regulation by setting out the minimum information content of the documents referred to in points (f) and (g) of paragraph 4 and points (e) and (f) of the first subparagraph of paragraph 5 of this Article.

7. The Commission is empowered to adopt delegated acts in accordance with Article 44 supplementing this Regulation by setting out the minimum information content of the documents referred to in points (f) and (g) of paragraph 4 and points (e) and (f) of the first subparagraph of paragraph 5 of this Article.

NOTES

Para 4: point (k) inserted by European Parliament and Council Regulation 2020/1503/EU, Art 46, as from 10 November 2021. Point (l) inserted by European Parliament and Council Regulation 2021/337/EU, Art 1(1), as from 18 March 2021.

Para 5: point (k) inserted by European Parliament and Council Regulation 2021/337/EU, Art 1(2), as from 18 March 2021.

Paras 6a, 6b: inserted by European Parliament and Council Regulation 2019/2115/EU, Art 2(1), as from 31 December 2019.

Application of this Article in relation to the UK: note that substantial amendments have been made to this Article, in relation to the UK only, by the Prospectus (Amendment etc) (EU Exit) Regulations 2019, SI 2019/1234, reg 32, as from IP completion day (as defined in the European Union (Withdrawal Agreement) Act 2020, s 39) (subject to transitional provisions in regs 74, 75 of the 2019 Regulations at **[12.165]** et seq), and by the Financial Services (Miscellaneous Amendments) (EU Exit) Regulations 2020, SI 2020/628, reg 18, as from IP completion day. For ease of reference, the Article as so amended is set out below. With regard to the text as set out below note also that (i) it includes all amendments made by the Prospectus (Amendment etc) (EU Exit) Regulations 2019, SI 2019/1234, the Financial Services (Miscellaneous Amendments) (EU Exit) Regulations 2020, SI 2020/628, and amendments made by in force and operative EU legislation within the meaning of the European Union (Withdrawal) Act 2018, s 3 at **[12.5]** (as noted above); (ii) it does not include amendments made by EU legislation that falls outside of the definition of "direct EU legislation" in s 3 of the 2018 Act (as noted above); (iii) the Prospectus (Amendment etc) (EU Exit) Regulations 2019, SI 2019/1234, reg 32 was amended by the Financial Services (Miscellaneous Amendments) (EU Exit) Regulations 2020, SI 2020/628, reg 17(1), (3), as from immediately before IP completion day; and the effect of the amendments has been incorporated in the text set out below. For subsequent amendments to this Article (ie, post-IP completion day), see the notes that follow the Article set out below—

"Article 1 Subject matter, scope and exemptions

1. This Regulation lays down requirements for the drawing up, approval and distribution of the prospectus to be published when securities are offered to the public or admitted to trading on a regulated market situated or operating within the United Kingdom.

2. This Regulation shall not apply to the following types of securities:

(a) units issued by collective investment undertakings other than the closed-end type;

(b) non-equity securities issued by—

(i) the government of any country or territory,

(ii) a local or regional authority of any country or territory,

(iii) a public international body of which any state is a member,

(iv) the European Central Bank or the central bank of any state;

(c) shares in the capital of central banks of any state;

(d) securities unconditionally and irrevocably guaranteed by the government or a local or regional authority of any country or territory;

(e) securities issued by associations with legal status or non-profit-making bodies, recognised by a state, for the purposes of obtaining the funding necessary to achieve their non-profit-making objectives;

(f) non-fungible shares of capital whose main purpose is to provide the holder with a right to occupy an apartment, or other form of immovable property or a part thereof and where the shares cannot be sold on without that right being given up.

3. Without prejudice to Article 4, this Regulation shall not apply to an offer of securities to the public with a total consideration in the United Kingdom of less than EUR 1,000,000, which shall be calculated over a period of 12 months.

4. The obligation to publish a prospectus set out in Article 3(1) shall not apply to any of the following types of offers of securities to the public:

(a) an offer of securities addressed solely to qualified investors;

(b) an offer of securities addressed to fewer than 150 natural or legal persons in the United Kingdom, other than qualified investors;
(c) an offer of securities whose denomination per unit amounts to at least EUR 100,000;
(d) an offer of securities addressed to investors who acquire securities for a total consideration of at least EUR 100,000 per investor, for each separate offer;
(e) shares issued in substitution for shares of the same class already issued, if the issuing of such new shares does not involve any increase in the issued capital;
(f) subject to paragraph 6a, securities offered in connection with a takeover by means of an exchange offer, provided that a document is made available to the public in accordance with the arrangements set out in Article 21(2), containing information describing the transaction and its impact on the issuer;
(g) subject to paragraph 6b, securities offered, allotted or to be allotted in connection with a merger or division, provided that a document is made available to the public in accordance with the arrangements set out in Article 21(2), containing information describing the transaction and its impact on the issuer;
(h) dividends paid out to existing shareholders in the form of shares of the same class as the shares in respect of which such dividends are paid, provided that a document is made available containing information on the number and nature of the shares and the reasons for and details of the offer;
(i) securities offered, allotted or to be allotted to existing or former directors or employees by their employer or by an affiliated undertaking provided that a document is made available containing information on the number and nature of the securities and the reasons for and details of the offer or allotment;
(j) non-equity securities issued in a continuous or repeated manner by a credit institution, where the total aggregated consideration in the United Kingdom for the securities offered is less than EUR 75,000,000 per credit institution calculated over a period of 12 months, provided that those securities:
  (i) are not subordinated, convertible or exchangeable; and
  (ii) do not give a right to subscribe for or acquire other types of securities and are not linked to a derivative instrument.

5. The obligation to publish a prospectus set out in Article 3(3) shall not apply to the admission to trading on a regulated market of any of the following:
(a) securities fungible with securities already admitted to trading on the same regulated market, provided that they represent, over a period of 12 months, less than 20% of the number of securities already admitted to trading on the same regulated market;
(b) shares resulting from the conversion or exchange of other securities or from the exercise of the rights conferred by other securities, where the resulting shares are of the same class as the shares already admitted to trading on the same regulated market, provided that the resulting shares represent, over a period of 12 months, less than 20% of the number of shares of the same class already admitted to trading on the same regulated market, subject to the second subparagraph of this paragraph;
(c) securities resulting from the conversion or exchange of other securities, own funds or eligible liabilities by a resolution authority due to the exercise of a power referred to in the UK law which implemented Article 53(2), 59(2) or Article 63(1) or (2) of Directive 2014/59/ EU;
(d) shares issued in substitution for shares of the same class already admitted to trading on the same regulated market, where the issuing of such shares does not involve any increase in the issued capital;
(e) subject to paragraph 6a, securities offered in connection with a takeover by means of an exchange offer, provided that a document is made available to the public in accordance with the arrangements set out in Article 21(2), containing information describing the transaction and its impact on the issuer;
(f) subject to paragraph 6b, securities offered, allotted or to be allotted in connection with a merger or a division, provided that a document is made available to the public in accordance with the arrangements set out in Article 21(2), containing information describing the transaction and its impact on the issuer;
(g) shares offered, allotted or to be allotted free of charge to existing shareholders, and dividends paid out in the form of shares of the same class as the shares in respect of which such dividends are paid, provided that the said shares are of the same class as the shares already admitted to trading on the same regulated market and that a document is made available containing information on the number and nature of the shares and the reasons for and details of the offer or allotment;
(h) securities offered, allotted or to be allotted to existing or former directors or employees by their employer or an affiliated undertaking, provided that the said securities are of the same class as the securities already admitted to trading on the same regulated market and that a document is made available containing information on the number and nature of the securities and the reasons for and detail of the offer or allotment;
(i) non-equity securities issued in a continuous or repeated manner by a credit institution, where the total aggregated consideration in the Union for the securities offered is less than EUR 75,000,000 per credit institution calculated over a period of 12 months, provided that those securities:
  (i) are not subordinated, convertible or exchangeable; and
  (ii) do not give a right to subscribe for or acquire other types of securities and are not linked to a derivative instrument;
(j) securities already admitted to trading on another regulated market, on the following conditions:
  (i) that those securities, or securities of the same class, have been admitted to trading on that other regulated market for more than 18 months;
  (ii) that, for securities first admitted to trading on a regulated market after 1 July 2005, the admission to trading on that other regulated market was subject to a prospectus approved and published in accordance with Directive 2003/71/EC;
  (iii) that, except where point (ii) applies, for securities first admitted to listing after 30 June 1983, listing particulars were approved in accordance with the requirements of Council Directive 80/390/EEC[1] or Directive 2001/34/EC of the European Parliament and of the Council;[2]
  (iv) that the ongoing obligations for trading on that other regulated market have been fulfilled;
  (v) that the person seeking the admission of a security to trading on a regulated market under the exemption set out in this point (j) makes available to the public, in accordance with the arrangements set out in Article 21(2), a document the content of which complies with Article 7, except that the maximum length set out in Article 7(3) shall be extended by two additional sides of A4-sized paper, drawn up in a language accepted by the competent authority; and
  (vi) that the document referred to in point (v) states where the most recent prospectus can be obtained and where

the financial information published by the issuer pursuant to ongoing disclosure obligations is available.

The requirement that the resulting shares represent, over a period of 12 months, less than 20% of the number of shares of the same class already admitted to trading on the same regulated market as referred to in point (b) of the first subparagraph shall not apply in any of the following cases:

(a) where a prospectus was drawn up in accordance with—

(i) before IP completion day, either this Regulation as it had effect immediately before IP completion day or Directive 2003/71/EC, or

(ii) on or after IP completion day, this Regulation,

upon the offer to the public or admission to trading on a regulated market of the securities giving access to the shares;

(b) where the securities giving access to the shares were issued before 20 July 2017;

(c) where the shares qualify as Common Equity Tier 1 items as laid down in Article 26 of Regulation (EU) No 575/2013 of the European Parliament and of the Council[3] of an institution as defined in point (3) of Article 4(1) of that Regulation and result from the conversion of Additional Tier 1 instruments issued by that institution due to the occurrence of a trigger event as laid down in point (a) of Article 54(1) of that Regulation;

[(ca) where the shares of an FCA investment firm result from the conversion of one class of instrument into another class of instrument because of rules made by the FCA under Part 9C of FSMA;];

(d) where the shares qualify as eligible own funds or eligible basic own funds as defined in the UK law which implemented Section 3 of Chapter VI of Title I of Directive 2009/138/EC of the European Parliament and of the Council,[4] and result from the conversion of other securities which was triggered for the purposes of fulfilling the obligations to comply with the UK law which implemented the Solvency Capital Requirement or Minimum Capital Requirement as laid down in Sections 4 and 5 of Chapter VI of Title I of Directive 2009/138/EC or the UK law which implemented the group solvency requirement as laid down in Title III of Directive 2009/138/EC.

6. The exemptions from the obligation to publish a prospectus that are set out in paragraphs 4 and 5 may be combined together. However, the exemptions in points (a) and (b) of the first subparagraph of paragraph 5 shall not be combined together if such combination could lead to the immediate or deferred admission to trading on a regulated market over a period of 12 months of more than 20% of the number of shares of the same class already admitted to trading on the same regulated market, without a prospectus being published.

6a. The exemptions set out in point (f) of paragraph 4 and in point (e) of paragraph 5 shall only apply to equity securities, and only in the following cases:.

(a) the equity securities offered are fungible with existing securities already admitted to trading on a regulated market prior to the takeover and its related transaction, and the takeover is not considered to be a reverse acquisition transaction within the meaning of paragraph B19 of international financial reporting standard (IFRS) 3, Business Combinations, adopted by Commission Regulation (EC) No 1126/2008;[5] or

(b) the FCA has issued a prior approval, under paragraph 6c of this Article, for the documents referred to in point (f) of paragraph 4 or point (e) of paragraph 5 of this Article.

6b. The exemptions set out in point (g) of paragraph 4 and in point (f) of paragraph 5 shall apply only to equity securities in respect of which the transaction is not considered to be a reverse acquisition transaction within the meaning of paragraph B19 of IFRS 3, Business Combinations, and only in the following cases:

(a) the equity securities of the acquiring entity have already been admitted to trading on a regulated market prior to the transaction; or

(b) the equity securities of the entities subject to the division have already been admitted to trading on a regulated market prior to the transaction.

6c. The FCA may issue prior approval for the documents referred to in point (f) of paragraph 4 or point (e) of paragraph 5 of this Article.

7. The Treasury may by regulations specify the minimum information content of the documents referred to in points (f) and (g) of paragraph 4 and points (e) and (f) of the first subparagraph of paragraph 5 of this Article.".

Para 1: point (ca) inserted by the Financial Services Act 2021 (Prudential Regulation of Credit Institutions and Investment Firms) (Consequential Amendments and Miscellaneous Provisions) Regulations 2021, SI 2021/1376, reg 28(2), as from 1 January 2022.

Delegated Act for the purposes of para 7: see Commission Delegated Regulation 2021/528/EU supplementing Regulation (EU) 2017/1129 of the European Parliament and of the Council as regards the minimum information content of the document to be published for a prospectus exemption in connection with a takeover by means of an exchange offer, a merger or a division at **[11.815]**.

* Regulation (EU) 2020/1503 of the European Parliament and of the Council of 7 October 2020 on European crowdfunding service providers for business and amending Regulation (EU) 2017/1129 and Directive (EU) 2019/1937 (OJ L347, 20.10.2020, p 1).

1 Council Directive 80/390/EEC of 17 March 1980 coordinating the requirements for the drawing up, scrutiny and distribution of the listing particulars to be published for the admission of securities to official stock exchange listing (OJ L100, 17.4.1980, p 1).

2 Directive 2001/34/EC of the European Parliament and of the Council of 28 May 2001 on the admission of securities to official stock exchange listing and on information to be published on those securities (OJ L184, 6.7.2001, p 1).

3 Regulation (EU) No 575/2013 of the European Parliament and of the Council of 26 June 2013 on prudential requirements for credit institutions and investment firms and amending Regulation (EU) No 648/2012 (OJ L176, 27.6.2013, p 1).

4 Directive 2009/138/EC of the European Parliament and of the Council of 25 November 2009 on the taking-up and pursuit of the business of Insurance and Reinsurance (Solvency II) (OJ L335, 17.12.2009, p 1).

5 Commission Regulation (EC) No 1126/2008 of 3 November 2008 adopting certain international accounting standards in accordance with Regulation (EC) No 1606/2002 of the European Parliament and of the Council (OJ L320, 29.11.2008, p 1).

6 Directive 2004/25/EC of the European Parliament and of the Council of 21 April 2004 on takeover bids (OJ L142, 30.4.2004, p 12).

[11.322]

Article 2 Definitions

For the purposes of this Regulation, the following definitions apply:

(a) 'securities' means transferable securities as defined in point (44) of Article 4(1) of Directive 2014/65/EU with the exception of money market instruments as defined in point (17) of Article 4(1) of Directive 2014/65/EU, having a maturity of less than 12 months;

(b) 'equity securities' means shares and other transferable securities equivalent to shares in companies, as well as any other type of transferable securities giving the right to acquire any of the aforementioned securities as a consequence of their being converted or the rights conferred by them being exercised, provided that securities of the latter type are issued by the issuer of the underlying shares or by an entity belonging to the group of the said issuer;

(c) 'non-equity securities' means all securities that are not equity securities;

(d) 'offer of securities to the public' means a communication to persons in any form and by any means, presenting sufficient information on the terms of the offer and the securities to be offered, so as to enable an investor to decide to purchase or subscribe for those securities. This definition also applies to the placing of securities through financial intermediaries;

(e) 'qualified investors' means persons or entities that are listed in points (1) to (4) of Section I of Annex II to Directive 2014/65/EU, and persons or entities who are, on request, treated as professional clients in accordance with Section II of that Annex, or recognised as eligible counterparties in accordance with Article 30 of Directive 2014/65/ EU unless they have entered into an agreement to be treated as non-professional clients in accordance with the fourth paragraph of Section I of that Annex. For the purposes of applying the first sentence of this point, investment firms and credit institutions shall, upon request from the issuer, communicate the classification of their clients to the issuer subject to compliance with the relevant laws on data protection;

(f) 'small and medium-sized enterprises' or 'SMEs' means any of the following:

(i) companies, which, according to their last annual or consolidated accounts, meet at least two of the following three criteria: an average number of employees during the financial year of less than 250, a total balance sheet not exceeding EUR 43,000,000 and an annual net turnover not exceeding EUR 50,000,000;

(ii) small and medium-sized enterprises as defined in point (13) of Article 4(1) of Directive 2014/65/EU.

(g) 'credit institution' means a credit institution as defined in point (1) of Article 4(1) of Regulation (EU) No 575/2013;

(h) 'issuer' means a legal entity which issues or proposes to issue securities;

(i) 'offeror' means a legal entity or individual which offers securities to the public;

(j) 'regulated market' means a regulated market as defined in point (21) of Article 4(1) of Directive 2014/65/EU;

(k) 'advertisement' means a communication with both of the following characteristics:

(i) relating to a specific offer of securities to the public or to an admission to trading on a regulated market;

(ii) aiming to specifically promote the potential subscription or acquisition of securities;

(l) 'regulated information' means regulated information as defined in point (k) of Article 2(1) of Directive 2004/109/EC;

(m) 'home Member State' means:

(i) for all issuers of securities established in the Union which are not mentioned in point (ii), the Member State where the issuer has its registered office;

(ii) for any issues of non-equity securities whose denomination per unit amounts to at least EUR 1,000, and for any issues of non-equity securities giving the right to acquire any transferable securities or to receive a cash amount, as a consequence of their being converted or the rights conferred by them being exercised, provided that the issuer of the non-equity securities is not the issuer of the underlying securities or an entity belonging to the group of the latter issuer, the Member State where the issuer has its registered office, or where the securities were or are to be admitted to trading on a regulated market or where the securities are offered to the public, at the choice of the issuer, the offeror or the person asking for admission to trading on a regulated market. The same shall apply to non-equity securities in a currency other than euro, provided that the value of such minimum denomination is nearly equivalent to EUR 1,000;

(iii) for all issuers of securities established in a third country which are not mentioned in point (ii), the Member State where the securities are intended to be offered to the public for the first time or where the first application for admission to trading on a regulated market is made, at the choice of the issuer, the offeror or the person asking for admission to trading on a regulated market, subject to a subsequent choice by issuers established in a third country in either of the following circumstances:

— where the home Member State was not determined by the choice of those issuers;

— in accordance with point (i)(iii) of Article 2(1) of Directive 2004/109/EC;

(n) 'host Member State' means the Member State where an offer of securities to the public is made or admission to trading on a regulated market is sought, when different from the home Member State;

(o) 'competent authority' means the authority designated by each Member State in accordance with Article 31, unless otherwise specified in this Regulation;

(p) 'collective investment undertaking other than the closed-end type' means unit trusts and investment companies with both of the following characteristics:

(i) they raise capital from a number of investors, with a view to investing it in accordance with a defined investment policy for the benefit of those investors;

(ii) their units are, at the holder's request, repurchased or redeemed, directly or indirectly, out of their assets;

(q) 'units of a collective investment undertaking' means securities issued by a collective investment undertaking as representing the rights of the participants in such an undertaking over its assets;

(r) 'approval' means the positive act at the outcome of the scrutiny by the home Member State's competent authority of the completeness, the consistency and the comprehensibility of the information given in the prospectus;

(s) 'base prospectus' means a prospectus that complies with Article 8, and, at the choice of the issuer, the final terms of the offer;
(t) 'working days' means working days of the relevant competent authority excluding Saturdays, Sundays and public holidays, as defined in the national law applicable to that competent authority;
(u) 'multilateral trading facility' or 'MTF' means a multilateral trading facility as defined in point (22) of Article 4(1) of Directive 2014/65/EU;
(v) 'organised trading facility' or 'OTF' means an organised trading facility as defined in point (23) of Article 4(1) of Directive 2014/65/EU;
(w) 'SME growth market' means an SME growth market as defined in point (12) of Article 4(1) of Directive 2014/65/EU;
(x) 'third country issuer' means an issuer established in a third country;
(y) 'offer period' means the period during which potential investors may purchase or subscribe for the securities concerned;
(z) 'durable medium' means any instrument which:
  (i) enables a customer to store information addressed personally to that customer in a way accessible for future reference and for a period adequate for the purposes of the information; and
  (ii) allows the unchanged reproduction of the information stored.

NOTES

Application of this Article in relation to the UK: note that substantial amendments have been made to this Article, in relation to the UK only, by the Prospectus (Amendment etc) (EU Exit) Regulations 2019, SI 2019/1234, reg 33, as from IP completion day (as defined in the European Union (Withdrawal Agreement) Act 2020, s 39) (subject to transitional provisions in regs 74, 75 of the 2019 Regulations at **[12.165]** et seq). For ease of reference, the Article as so amended is set out below. With regard to the text as set out below, note also that reg 33 of the 2019 Regulations was amended by the Financial Services and Economic and Monetary Policy (Consequential Amendments) (EU Exit) Regulations 2020, SI 2020/1301, reg 3, Schedule, para 48(c), as from 30 December 2020; and the effect of the amendments has been incorporated in the text set out below. For subsequent amendments to this Article (ie, post-IP completion day), see the notes that follow the Article set out below—

"Article 2 Definitions

For the purposes of this Regulation, the following definitions apply:
(za) 'FCA' means the Financial Conduct Authority;
(zb) 'FSMA' means the Financial Services and Markets Act 2000;
(zc) 'markets in financial instruments regulation' means Regulation (EU) No 600/2014 of the European Parliament and of the Council of 15 May 2014 on markets in financial instruments and amending Regulation (EU) No 648/2012;
(zd) references to a 'third country' (including in expressions including the words 'third country') are to be read as references to a country other than the United Kingdom;
(ze) any reference in this Regulation to a sourcebook is to a sourcebook in the Handbook of Rules and Guidance published by the FCA containing rules made by the FCA under FSMA, as the sourcebook has effect on IP completion day;
(zf) a reference to the UK law which implemented a Directive, or a provision thereof, is to the law of the United Kingdom which was relied on by the United Kingdom immediately before IP completion day to implement that Directive and its implementing measures—
  (i) as they have effect on IP completion day, in the case of rules made by the FCA under FSMA, and
  (ii) as amended from time to time, in all other cases;
[(zg) 'FCA investment firm' has the meaning given in section 143A(1) of FSMA;]
(a) 'securities' means transferable securities as defined in Article 2(1)(24) of the markets in financial instruments regulation, other than money market instruments as defined in Article 2(1)(25A) of that regulation that have a maturity of less than 12 months;
(b) 'equity securities' means shares and other transferable securities equivalent to shares in companies, as well as any other type of transferable securities giving the right to acquire any of the aforementioned securities as a consequence of their being converted or the rights conferred by them being exercised, provided that securities of the latter type are issued by the issuer of the underlying shares or by an entity belonging to the group of the said issuer;
(c) 'non-equity securities' means all securities that are not equity securities;
(d) 'offer of securities to the public' means a communication to persons in any form and by any means, presenting sufficient information on the terms of the offer and the securities to be offered, so as to enable an investor to decide to purchase or subscribe for those securities. This definition also applies to the placing of securities through financial intermediaries;
(e) 'qualified investor', in relation to an offer of transferable securities, means—
  (i) a person described in paragraph 3 of Schedule 1 to the markets in financial instruments regulation, other than a person who, before the making of the offer, has agreed in writing with the relevant firm (or each of the relevant firms) to be treated as a non-professional client in accordance with paragraph 4 of that Schedule;
  (ii) a person who has made a request to one or more relevant firms to be treated as a professional client in accordance with paragraphs 5 and 6 of that Schedule and has not subsequently, but before the making of the offer, agreed in writing with that relevant firm (or each of those relevant firms) to be treated as a non-professional client in accordance with paragraph 4 of that Schedule;
  (iii) a person who—
    (aa) is an eligible counterparty for the purposes of Section 6 of Chapter 3 of the Conduct of Business sourcebook, and
    (bb) has not, before the making of the offer, agreed in writing with the relevant firm (or each of the relevant firms) to be treated as a non-professional client in accordance with paragraph 4 of Schedule 1 to the markets in financial instruments regulation; or
  (iv) a person whom—
    (aa) any relevant firm was authorised to continue to treat as a professional client immediately before 3 January 2018 by virtue of Article 71.6 (transitional provisions) of Directive 2004/39/EC on markets in financial instruments; and
    (bb) the firm was entitled immediately before IP completion day to continue to treat as a professional client by virtue of Section II.2 of Annex II to the markets in financial instruments directive,

and for the purposes of this definition, 'relevant firm" means an investment firm (within the meaning of section 424A of FSMA) or qualifying credit institution (within the meaning in section 417 of FSMA) acting in connection with the offer;

(f) 'small and medium-sized enterprises' or 'SMEs' means any of the following:
 (i) companies, which, according to their last annual or consolidated accounts, meet at least two of the following three criteria: an average number of employees during the financial year of less than 250, a total balance sheet not exceeding EUR 43,000,000 and an annual net turnover not exceeding EUR 50,000,000;
 (ii) small and medium-sized enterprises as defined in point (13) of Article 4(1) of Directive 2014/65/EU.

(g) 'credit institution' has the meaning given in Article 2(1)(19) of the markets in financial instruments regulation;

(h) 'issuer' means a legal entity which issues or proposes to issue securities;

(i) 'offeror' means a legal entity or individual which offers securities to the public;

(j) 'regulated market' means a regulated market as defined in Article 2(1)(13) of the markets in financial instruments regulation;

(k) 'advertisement' means a communication with both of the following characteristics:
 (i) relating to a specific offer of securities to the public or to an admission to trading on a regulated market;
 (ii) aiming to specifically promote the potential subscription or acquisition of securities;

(l) 'regulated information' means all information which an issuer, or any other person who has applied for the admission of securities to trading on a regulated market without the issuer's consent, is required to disclose under—
 (i) qualifying transparency legislation;
 (ii) Articles 17 to 19 of Regulation (EU) No 596/2014 of the European Parliament and of the Council of 16 April 2014 on market abuse (market abuse regulation) and repealing Directive 2003/6/EC of the European Parliament and of the Council and Commission Directives 2003/124/EC, 2003/125/EC and 2004/72/EC;
 (iii) listing rules,

 and for the purposes of this definition, 'listing rules' and 'qualifying transparency legislation' have the same meaning as in Part 6 of FSMA;

(o) 'competent authority' means the FCA;

(p) 'collective investment undertaking other than the closed-end type' means unit trusts and investment companies with both of the following characteristics:
 (i) they raise capital from a number of investors, with a view to investing it in accordance with a defined investment policy for the benefit of those investors;
 (ii) their units are, at the holder's request, repurchased or redeemed, directly or indirectly, out of their assets;

(q) 'units of a collective investment undertaking' means securities issued by a collective investment undertaking as representing the rights of the participants in such an undertaking over its assets;

(r) 'approval' means the positive act at the outcome of the scrutiny by the competent authority of the completeness, the consistency and the comprehensibility of the information given in the prospectus;

(s) 'base prospectus' means a prospectus that complies with Article 8, and, at the choice of the issuer, the final terms of the offer;

(t) 'working day' has the same meaning as in section 103 of FSMA;

(u) 'multilateral trading facility' or 'MTF' means a UK multilateral trading facility as defined by Article 2(1)(14A) of the markets in financial instruments regulation;

(v) 'organised trading facility' or 'OTF' means a UK organised trading facility as defined by Article 2(1)(15A) of the markets in financial instruments regulation;

(w) 'SME growth market' means a multilateral trading facility that is registered as an SME growth market in accordance with Section 10 of Part 5 of the Market Conduct sourcebook;

(x) 'third country issuer' means an issuer established in a third country;

(y) 'offer period' means the period during which potential investors may purchase or subscribe for the securities concerned;

(z) 'durable medium' means any instrument which:
 (i) enables a customer to store information addressed personally to that customer in a way accessible for future reference and for a period adequate for the purposes of the information; and
 (ii) allows the unchanged reproduction of the information stored.".

Point (zg) inserted by the Financial Services Act 2021 (Prudential Regulation of Credit Institutions and Investment Firms) (Consequential Amendments and Miscellaneous Provisions) Regulations 2021, SI 2021/1376, reg 28(3), as from 1 January 2022.

[11.323]

Article 3 Obligation to publish a prospectus and exemption

1. Without prejudice to Article 1(4), securities shall only be offered to the public in the Union after prior publication of a prospectus in accordance with this Regulation.

2. Without prejudice to Article 4, a Member State may decide to exempt offers of securities to the public from the obligation to publish a prospectus set out in paragraph 1 provided that:
 (a) such offers are not subject to notification in accordance with Article 25; and
 (b) the total consideration of each such offer in the Union is less than a monetary amount calculated over a period of 12 months which shall not exceed EUR 8,000,000.

Member States shall notify the Commission and ESMA whether and how they decide to apply the exemption pursuant to the first subparagraph, including the monetary amount below which the exemption for offers in that Member State applies. They shall also notify the Commission and ESMA of any subsequent changes to that monetary amount.

3. Without prejudice to Article 1(5), securities shall only be admitted to trading on a regulated market situated or operating within the Union after prior publication of a prospectus in accordance with this Regulation.

NOTES

Application of this Article in relation to the UK: this Article is amended (as follows), in relation to the UK only, by the Official Listing of Securities, Prospectus and Transparency (Amendment etc) (EU Exit) Regulations 2019, SI 2019/707, reg 69, as from IP completion day (as defined in the European Union (Withdrawal Agreement) Act 2020, s 39)—

"In Regulation (EU) 2017/1129 of the European Parliament and of the Council of 14 June 2017 on the prospectus to be published when securities are offered to the public or admitted to trading on a regulated market, and repealing Directive 2003/71/EC, omit Article 3(2).

Note that the Official Listing of Securities, Prospectus and Transparency (Amendment etc) (EU Exit) Regulations 2019, SI 2019/707, reg 69 was amended by the Financial Services (Miscellaneous Amendments) (EU Exit) Regulations 2020, SI 2020/628, reg 14, as from immediately before IP completion day; and the effect of that amendment has been incorporated in the text as set out above. Note also that para 2 is also repealed as noted below.

This Article is also amended (as follows), in relation to the UK only, by the Prospectus (Amendment etc) (EU Exit) Regulations 2019, SI 2019/1234, reg 34, as from IP completion day (as defined in the European Union (Withdrawal Agreement) Act 2020, s 39); for transitional provisions, see regs 74, 75 of the 2019 Regulations at **[12.165]** et seq—

"In Article 3—

(a) in paragraphs 1 and 3, for "Union" substitute "United Kingdom";

(b) omit paragraph 2.".

[11.324]

Article 4 Voluntary prospectus

1. Where an offer of securities to the public or an admission of securities to trading on a regulated market is outside the scope of this Regulation in accordance with Article 1(3), or exempted from the obligation to publish a prospectus in accordance with Article 1(4), 1(5) or 3(2), an issuer, an offeror or a person asking for admission to trading on a regulated market shall be entitled to voluntarily draw up a prospectus in accordance with this Regulation.

2. Such voluntarily drawn up prospectus approved by the competent authority of the home Member State, as determined in accordance with point (m) of Article 2, shall entail all the rights and obligations provided for a prospectus required under this Regulation and shall be subject to all provisions of this Regulation, under the supervision of that competent authority.

NOTES

Application of this Article in relation to the UK:this Article is amended (as follows), in relation to the UK only, by the Prospectus (Amendment etc) (EU Exit) Regulations 2019, SI 2019/1234, reg 35, as from IP completion day (as defined in the European Union (Withdrawal Agreement) Act 2020, s 39); for transitional provisions, see regs 74, 75 of the 2019 Regulations at **[12.165]** et seq—

"In Article 4(2), omit the words from "of the home" to "Article 2,".".

[11.325]

Article 5 Subsequent resale of securities

1. Any subsequent resale of securities which were previously the subject of one or more of the types of offer of securities to the public listed in points (a) to (d) of Article 1(4) shall be considered as a separate offer and the definition set out in point (d) of Article 2 shall apply for the purpose of determining whether that resale is an offer of securities to the public. The placement of securities through financial intermediaries shall be subject to publication of a prospectus unless one of the exemptions listed in points (a) to (d) of Article 1(4) applies in relation to the final placement.

No additional prospectus shall be required in any such subsequent resale of securities or final placement of securities through financial intermediaries as long as a valid prospectus is available in accordance with Article 12 and the issuer or the person responsible for drawing up such prospectus consents to its use by means of a written agreement.

2. Where a prospectus relates to the admission to trading on a regulated market of non-equity securities that are to be traded only on a regulated market, or a specific segment thereof, to which only qualified investors can have access for the purposes of trading in such securities, the securities shall not be resold to non-qualified investors, unless a prospectus is drawn up in accordance with this Regulation that is appropriate for non-qualified investors.

CHAPTER II DRAWING UP OF THE PROSPECTUS

[11.326]

Article 6 The prospectus

[1. Without prejudice to Articles 14(2), 14a(2) and 18(1), a prospectus shall contain the necessary information which is material to an investor for making an informed assessment of:]

(a) the assets and liabilities, profits and losses, financial position, and prospects of the issuer and of any guarantor;

(b) the rights attaching to the securities; and

(c) the reasons for the issuance and its impact on the issuer.

That information may vary depending on any of the following:

(a) the nature of the issuer;

(b) the type of securities;

(c) the circumstances of the issuer;

(d) where relevant, whether or not the non-equity securities have a denomination per unit of at least EUR 100,000 or are to be traded only on a regulated market, or a specific segment thereof, to which only qualified investors can have access for the purposes of trading in the securities.

2. The information in a prospectus shall be written and presented in an easily analysable, concise and comprehensible form, taking into account the factors set out in the second subparagraph of paragraph 1.

3. The issuer, offeror or person asking for the admission to trading on a regulated market may draw up the prospectus as a single document or as separate documents.

Without prejudice to Article 8(8) and the second subparagraph of Article 7(1), a prospectus composed of separate documents shall divide the required information into a registration document, a securities note and a summary. The registration document shall contain the information relating to the issuer. The securities note shall contain the information concerning the securities offered to the public or to be admitted to trading on a regulated market.

NOTES

Para 1: words in square brackets substituted by European Parliament and Council Regulation 2021/337/EU, Art 1(3), as from 18 March 2021.

Application of this Article in relation to the UK: note that Regulation 2021/337/EU (which amends this Article as noted above) is not "direct EU legislation" within the meaning of the European Union (Withdrawal) Act 2018, s 3 at **[12.5]** and, therefore, the amendment made by it does not apply to the UK. Note also that the original words were "Without prejudice to Article 14(2) and Article 18(1), a prospectus shall contain the necessary information which is material to an investor for making an informed assessment of:".

[11.327]

Article 7 The prospectus summary

1. The prospectus shall include a summary that provides the key information that investors need in order to understand the nature and the risks of the issuer, the guarantor and the securities that are being offered or admitted to trading on a regulated market, and that is to be read together with the other parts of the prospectus to aid investors when considering whether to invest in such securities.

By way of derogation from the first subparagraph, no summary shall be required where the prospectus relates to the admission to trading on a regulated market of non-equity securities provided that:

(a) such securities are to be traded only on a regulated market, or a specific segment thereof, to which only qualified investors can have access for the purposes of trading in such securities; or

(b) such securities have a denomination per unit of at least EUR 100,000.

2. The content of the summary shall be accurate, fair and clear and shall not be misleading. It is to be read as an introduction to the prospectus and it shall be consistent with the other parts of the prospectus.

3. The summary shall be drawn up as a short document written in a concise manner and of a maximum length of seven sides of A4-sized paper when printed. The summary shall:

(a) be presented and laid out in a way that is easy to read, using characters of readable size;

(b) be written in a language and a style that facilitate the understanding of the information, in particular, in language that is clear, non-technical, concise and comprehensible for investors.

4. The summary shall be made up of the following four sections:

(a) an introduction, containing warnings;

(b) key information on the issuer;

(c) key information on the securities;

(d) key information on the offer of securities to the public and/or the admission to trading on a regulated market.

5. The section referred to in point (a) of paragraph 4 shall contain:

(a) the name and international securities identification number (ISIN) of the securities;

(b) the identity and contact details of the issuer, including its legal entity identifier (LEI);

(c) where applicable, the identity and contact details of the offeror, including its LEI if the offeror has legal personality, or of the person asking for admission to trading on a regulated market;

(d) the identity and contact details of the competent authority approving the prospectus and, where different, the competent authority that approved the registration document or the universal registration document;

(e) the date of approval of the prospectus;

It shall contain the following warnings:

(a) the summary should be read as an introduction to the prospectus;

(b) any decision to invest in the securities should be based on a consideration of the prospectus as a whole by the investor;

(c) where applicable, that the investor could lose all or part of the invested capital and, where the investor's liability is not limited to the amount of the investment, a warning that the investor could lose more than the invested capital and the extent of such potential loss;

(d) where a claim relating to the information contained in a prospectus is brought before a court, the plaintiff investor might, under national law, have to bear the costs of translating the prospectus before the legal proceedings are initiated;

(e) civil liability attaches only to those persons who have tabled the summary including any translation thereof, but only where the summary is misleading, inaccurate or inconsistent, when read together with the other parts of the prospectus, or where it does not provide, when read together with the other parts of the prospectus, key information in order to aid investors when considering whether to invest in such securities;

(f) where applicable, the comprehension alert required in accordance with point (b) of Article 8(3) of Regulation (EU) No 1286/2014.

6. The section referred to in point (b) of paragraph 4 shall contain the following information:

(a) under a sub-section entitled 'Who is the issuer of the securities?', a brief description of the issuer of the securities, including at least the following:

(i) its domicile and legal form, its LEI, the law under which it operates and its country of incorporation;

(ii) its principal activities;

(iii) its major shareholders, including whether it is directly or indirectly owned or controlled and by whom;

(iv) the identity of its key managing directors;

(v) the identity of its statutory auditors;

(b) under a sub-section entitled 'What is the key financial information regarding the issuer?' a selection of historical key financial information presented for each financial year of the period covered by the historical financial information, and any subsequent interim financial period accompanied by comparative data from the same period in the prior financial year. The requirement for comparative balance sheet information shall be satisfied by presenting the year-end balance sheet information. Key financial information shall, where applicable, include:

(i) pro forma financial information;

Part 11 EU & Retained EU Legislation

(ii) a brief description of any qualifications in the audit report relating to the historical financial information;

(c) under a sub-section entitled 'What are the key risks that are specific to the issuer?' a brief description of the most material risk factors specific to the issuer contained in the prospectus, while not exceeding the total number of risk factors set out in paragraph 10.

7. The section referred to in point (c) of paragraph 4 shall contain the following information:

(a) under a sub-section entitled 'What are the main features of the securities?', a brief description of the securities being offered to the public and/or admitted to trading on a regulated market including at least:

(i) their type, class and ISIN;

(ii) where applicable, their currency, denomination, par value, the number of securities issued and the term of the securities;

(iii) the rights attached to the securities;

(iv) the relative seniority of the securities in the issuer's capital structure in the event of insolvency, including, where applicable, information on the level of subordination of the securities and the potential impact on the investment in the event of a resolution under Directive 2014/59/EU;

(v) any restrictions on the free transferability of the securities;

(vi) where applicable, the dividend or payout policy;

(b) under a sub-section entitled 'Where will the securities be traded?', an indication as to whether the securities are or will be subject to an application for admission to trading on a regulated market or for trading on an MTF and the identity of all the markets where the securities are or are to be traded;

(c) where there is a guarantee attached to the securities, under a sub-section entitled 'Is there a guarantee attached to the securities?', the following information:

(i) a brief description of the nature and scope of the guarantee;

(ii) a brief description of the guarantor, including its LEI;

(iii) the relevant key financial information for the purpose of assessing the guarantor's ability to fulfil its commitments under the guarantee; and

(iv) a brief description of the most material risk factors pertaining to the guarantor contained in the prospectus in accordance with Article 16(3), while not exceeding the total number of risk factors set out in paragraph 10;

(d) under a sub-section entitled 'What are the key risks that are specific to the securities?', a brief description of the most material risk factors specific to the securities contained in the prospectus, while not exceeding the total number of risk factors set out in paragraph 10.

Where a key information document is required to be prepared under Regulation (EU) No 1286/2014, the issuer, the offeror or the person asking for admission to trading on a regulated market may substitute the content set out in this paragraph with the information set out in points (c) to (i) of Article 8(3) of Regulation (EU) No 1286/2014. Where Regulation (EU) No 1286/2014 applies, each Member State acting as a home Member State for the purpose of this Regulation may require issuers, offerors or persons asking for admission to trading on a regulated market to substitute the content set out in this paragraph with the information set out in points (c) to (i) of Article 8(3) of Regulation (EU) No 1286/2014 in the prospectuses approved by its competent authority.

Where there is a substitution of content pursuant to the second subparagraph, the maximum length set out in paragraph 3 shall be extended by three additional sides of A4-sized paper. The content of the key information document shall be included as a distinct section of the summary. The page layout of that section shall clearly identify it as the content of the key information document as set out in points (c) to (i) of Article 8(3) of Regulation (EU) No 1286/2014.

Where, in accordance with the third subparagraph of Article 8(9), a single summary covers several securities which differ only in some very limited details, such as the issue price or maturity date, the maximum length set out in paragraph 3 shall be extended by two additional sides of A4-sized paper. However, in the event that a key information document is required to be prepared for those securities under Regulation (EU) No 1286/2014 and the issuer, the offeror or the person asking for admission to trading on a regulated market proceeds with the substitution of content referred to in the second subparagraph of this paragraph, the maximum length shall be extended by three additional sides of A4-sized paper for each additional security.

Where the summary contains the information referred to in point (c) of the first subparagraph, the maximum length set out in paragraph 3 shall be extended by one additional side of A4-sized paper.

8. The section referred to in point (d) of paragraph 4 shall contain the following information:

(a) under a sub-section entitled 'Under which conditions and timetable can I invest in this security?', where applicable, the general terms, conditions and expected timetable of the offer, the details of the admission to trading on a regulated market, the plan for distribution, the amount and percentage of immediate dilution resulting from the offer and an estimate of the total expenses of the issue and/or offer, including estimated expenses charged to the investor by the issuer or the offeror;

(b) if different from the issuer, under a sub-section entitled 'Who is the offeror and/or the person asking for admission to trading?', a brief description of the offeror of the securities and/or the person asking for admission to trading on a regulated market, including its domicile and legal form, the law under which it operates and its country of incorporation;

(c) under a sub-section entitled 'Why is this prospectus being produced?', a brief description of the reasons for the offer or for the admission to trading on a regulated market, as well as, where applicable:

(i) the use and estimated net amount of the proceeds;

(ii) an indication of whether the offer is subject to an underwriting agreement on a firm commitment basis, stating any portion not covered;

(iii) an indication of the most material conflicts of interest pertaining to the offer or the admission to trading.

9. Under each of the sections described in paragraphs 6, 7 and 8, the issuer may add sub-headings where deemed necessary.

10. The total number of risk factors included in the sections of the summary referred to in point (c) of paragraph 6 and point (c)(iv) and point (d) of the first subparagraph of paragraph 7 shall not exceed 15.

11. The summary shall not contain cross-references to other parts of the prospectus or incorporate information by reference.

12. Where a key information document is required to be prepared for securities offered to the public under Regulation (EU) No 1286/2014 and a home Member State requires the issuer, the offeror or the person asking for admission to trading on a regulated market to substitute the content of the key information document in accordance with the second sentence of the second subparagraph of paragraph 7 of this Article, the persons advising on or selling the securities on behalf of the issuer, the offeror or the person asking for admission to trading on a regulated market shall be deemed to have fulfilled, during the offer period, the obligation to provide the key information document in accordance with Article 13 of Regulation (EU) No 1286/2014, provided that they instead provide the investors concerned with the summary of the prospectus under the timing and conditions set out in Articles 13 and 14 of that Regulation.

[12a. By way of derogation from paragraphs 3 to 12 of this Article, an EU Recovery prospectus drawn up in accordance with Article 14a shall include a summary drawn up in accordance with this paragraph.

The summary of an EU Recovery prospectus shall be drawn up as a short document written in a concise manner and of a maximum length of two sides of A4-sized paper when printed.

The summary of an EU Recovery prospectus shall not contain cross-references to other parts of the prospectus or incorporate information by reference and shall:

(a) be presented and laid out in a way that is easy to read, using characters of readable size;

(b) be written in a language and a style that facilitate the understanding of the information, in particular, in language that is clear, non-technical, concise and comprehensible for investors;

(c) be made up of the following four sections:

  (i) an introduction, containing all of the information referred to in paragraph 5 of this Article, including warnings and the date of approval of the EU Recovery prospectus;

  (ii) key information on the issuer, including, if applicable, a specific reference of not less than 200 words to the business and financial impact on the issuer of the COVID-19 pandemic;

  (iii) key information on the shares, including the rights attached to those shares and any limitations on those rights;

  (iv) key information on the offer of shares to the public and/or the admission to trading on a regulated market.]

13. ESMA shall develop draft regulatory technical standards to specify the content and format of presentation of the key financial information referred to in point (b) of paragraph 6, and the relevant key financial information referred to in point (c)(iii) of paragraph 7, taking into account the various types of securities and issuers and ensuring that the information produced is concise and understandable.

ESMA shall submit those draft regulatory technical standards to the Commission by 21 July 2018.

Power is delegated to the Commission to adopt the regulatory technical standards referred to in the first subparagraph in accordance with Articles 10 to 14 of Regulation (EU) No 1095/2010.

NOTES

Para 12a: inserted by European Parliament and Council Regulation 2021/337/EU, Art 1(4), as from 18 March 2021.

Application of this Article in relation to the UK: this Article is amended (as follows), in relation to the UK only, by the Prospectus (Amendment etc) (EU Exit) Regulations 2019, SI 2019/1234, reg 36, as from IP completion day (as defined in the European Union (Withdrawal Agreement) Act 2020, s 39); for transitional provisions, see regs 74, 75 of the 2019 Regulations at **[12.165]** et seq—

"In Article 7—

(a) in paragraph 5, in the second subparagraph, omit point (d);

(b) in paragraph 7—

  (i) in the first subparagraph, in point (a)(iv), before "Directive 2014/59/EU" insert "the UK law which implemented";

  (ii) in the second subparagraph, omit the second sentence;

(c) omit paragraph 12;

(d) in paragraph 13—

  (i) in the first subparagraph, for "ESMA shall develop draft regulatory" substitute "The FCA may make";

  (ii) omit the second and third subparagraphs.".

Note also that Regulation 2021/337/EU (which amends this Article as noted above) is not "direct EU legislation" within the meaning of the European Union (Withdrawal) Act 2018, s 3 at **[12.5]** and, therefore, the amendment made by it does not apply to the UK.

Regulatory technical standards for the purposes of para 13: see Commission Delegated Regulation 2019/979/EU supplementing Regulation (EU) 2017/1129 of the European Parliament and of the Council with regard to regulatory technical standards on key financial information in the summary of a prospectus, the publication and classification of prospectuses, advertisements for securities, supplements to a prospectus, and the notification portal, and repealing Commission Delegated Regulation (EU) No 382/2014 and Commission Delegated Regulation (EU) 2016/301 at **[11.616]**.

See also Commission Delegated Regulation 2020/1272/EU amending and correcting Delegated Regulation (EU) 2019/979 supplementing Regulation (EU) 2017/1129 of the European Parliament and of the Council with regard to regulatory technical standards on key financial information in the summary of a prospectus, the publication and classification of prospectuses, advertisements for securities, supplements to a prospectus, and the notification portal.

[11.328]

Article 8 The base prospectus

1. For non-equity securities, including warrants in any form, the prospectus may, at the choice of the issuer, offeror or person asking for the admission to trading on a regulated market, consist of a base prospectus containing the necessary information concerning the issuer and the securities offered to the public or to be admitted to trading on a regulated market.

2. A base prospectus shall include the following information:

(a) a template, entitled 'form of the final terms', to be filled out for each individual issue and indicating the available options with regard to the information to be determined in the final terms of the offer;

(b) the address of the website where the final terms will be published.

3. Where a base prospectus contains options with regard to the information required by the relevant securities note, the final terms shall determine which of the options is applicable to the individual issue by referring to the relevant sections of the base prospectus or by replicating such information.

4. The final terms shall be presented in the form of a separate document or shall be included in the base prospectus or in any supplement thereto. The final terms shall be prepared in an easily analysable and comprehensible form.

The final terms shall only contain information that relates to the securities note and shall not be used to supplement the base prospectus. Point (b) of Article 17(1) shall apply in such cases.

5. Where the final terms are neither included in the base prospectus, nor in a supplement, the issuer shall make them available to the public in accordance with the arrangements set out in Article 21 and file them with the competent authority of the home Member State, as soon as practicable upon offering securities to the public and, where possible, before the beginning of the offer of securities to the public or admission to trading on a regulated market.

A clear and prominent statement shall be inserted in the final terms indicating:

(a) that the final terms have been prepared for the purpose of this Regulation and must be read in conjunction with the base prospectus and any supplement thereto in order to obtain all the relevant information;

(b) where the base prospectus and any supplement thereto are published in accordance with the arrangements set out in Article 21;

(c) that a summary of the individual issue is annexed to the final terms.

6. A base prospectus may be drawn up as a single document or as separate documents.

Where the issuer, the offeror or the person asking for admission to trading on a regulated market has filed a registration document for non-equity securities, or a universal registration document in accordance with Article 9, and chooses to draw up a base prospectus, the base prospectus shall consist of the following:

(a) the information contained in the registration document, or in the universal registration document;

(b) the information which would otherwise be contained in the relevant securities note, with the exception of the final terms where the final terms are not included in the base prospectus.

7. The specific information on each of the different securities included in a base prospectus shall be clearly segregated.

8. A summary shall only be drawn up once the final terms are included in the base prospectus, or in a supplement, or are filed, and that summary shall be specific to the individual issue.

9. The summary of the individual issue shall be subject to the same requirements as the final terms, as set out in this Article, and shall be annexed to them.

The summary of the individual issue shall comply with Article 7 and shall provide the following:

(a) the key information in the base prospectus, including the key information on the issuer;

(b) the key information in the appropriate final terms, including the key information which was not included in the base prospectus.

Where the final terms relate to several securities which differ only in some very limited details, such as the issue price or maturity date, a single summary of the individual issue may be attached for all those securities, provided the information referring to the different securities is clearly segregated.

10. The information contained in the base prospectus shall, where necessary, be supplemented in accordance with Article 23.

11. An offer of securities to the public may continue after the expiration of the base prospectus under which it was commenced provided that a succeeding base prospectus is approved and published no later than the last day of validity of the previous base prospectus. The final terms of such an offer shall contain a prominent warning on their first page indicating the last day of validity of the previous base prospectus and where the succeeding base prospectus will be published. The succeeding base prospectus shall include or incorporate by reference the form of the final terms from the initial base prospectus and refer to the final terms that are relevant for the continuing offer.

A right of withdrawal pursuant to Article 23(2) shall also apply to investors who have agreed to purchase or subscribe for the securities during the validity period of the previous base prospectus, unless the securities have already been delivered to them.

NOTES

Application of this Article in relation to the UK: this Article is amended (as follows), in relation to the UK only, by the Prospectus (Amendment etc) (EU Exit) Regulations 2019, SI 2019/1234, reg 37, as from IP completion day (as defined in the European Union (Withdrawal Agreement) Act 2020, s 39); for transitional provisions, see regs 74, 75 of the 2019 Regulations at **[12.165]** et seq—

"In Article 8, in paragraph 5, omit "of the home Member State".".

[11.329]

Article 9 The universal registration document

1. Any issuer whose securities are admitted to trading on a regulated market or an MTF may draw up every financial year a registration document in the form of a universal registration document describing the company's organisation, business, financial position, earnings and prospects, governance and shareholding structure.

2. Any issuer that chooses to draw up a universal registration document every financial year shall submit it for approval to the competent authority of its home Member State in accordance with the procedure set out in Article 20(2) and (4).

After the issuer has had a universal registration document approved by the competent authority for two consecutive financial years, subsequent universal registration documents may be filed with the competent authority without prior approval.

Where the issuer thereafter fails to file a universal registration document for one financial year, the benefit of filing without prior approval shall be lost and all subsequent universal registration documents shall be submitted to the competent authority for approval until the condition set out in the second subparagraph is met again.

The issuer shall indicate in its application to the competent authority whether the universal registration document is submitted for approval or filed without prior approval.

Where the issuer referred to in the second subparagraph of this paragraph requests the notification of its universal registration document pursuant to Article 26, it shall submit its universal registration document for approval, including any amendments thereto which were previously filed.

3. Issuers which, prior to 21 July 2019, have had a registration document, drawn up in accordance with Annex I to Commission Regulation (EC) No 809/2004,[1] approved by a competent authority for at least two consecutive financial years and have thereafter filed, in accordance with Article 12(3) of Directive 2003/71/EC, or got approved such a registration document every year, shall be allowed to file a universal registration document without prior approval in accordance with the second subparagraph of paragraph 2 of this Article from 21 July 2019.

4. Once approved or filed without prior approval, the universal registration document, as well as the amendments thereto referred to in paragraphs 7 and 9 of this Article, shall be made available to the public without undue delay, in accordance with the arrangements set out in Article 21.

5. The universal registration document shall comply with the language requirements laid down in Article 27.

6. Information may be incorporated by reference into a universal registration document under the conditions set out in Article 19.

7. Following the filing or approval of a universal registration document, the issuer may at any time update the information it contains by filing an amendment thereto with the competent authority. Subject to the first and second subparagraphs of Article 10(3), the filing of the amendment with the competent authority shall not require approval.

8. The competent authority may at any time review the content of any universal registration document which has been filed without prior approval, as well as the content of any amendments thereto.

The review by the competent authority shall consist in scrutinising the completeness, the consistency and the comprehensibility of the information given in the universal registration document and any amendments thereto.

9. Where the competent authority, in the course of the review, finds that the universal registration document does not meet the standards of completeness, comprehensibility and consistency, or that amendments or supplementary information are needed, it shall notify it to the issuer.

A request for amendment or supplementary information addressed by the competent authority to the issuer needs only be taken into account by the issuer in the next universal registration document filed for the following financial year, except where the issuer wishes to use the universal registration document as a constituent part of a prospectus submitted for approval. In that case, the issuer shall file an amendment to the universal registration document at the latest upon submission of the application referred to in Article 20(6).

By way of derogation from the second subparagraph, where the competent authority notifies the issuer that its request for amendment or supplementary information concerns a material omission or a material mistake or material inaccuracy, which is likely to mislead the public with regard to facts and circumstances essential for an informed assessment of the issuer, the issuer shall file an amendment to the universal registration document without undue delay.

The competent authority may request that the issuer produces a consolidated version of the amended universal registration document, where such a consolidated version is necessary to ensure comprehensibility of the information provided in that document. An issuer may voluntarily include a consolidated version of its amended universal registration document in an annex to the amendment.

10. Paragraphs 7 and 9 shall only apply where the universal registration document is not in use as a constituent part of a prospectus. Whenever a universal registration document is in use as a constituent part of a prospectus, only Article 23 on supplementing the prospectus shall apply between the time when the prospectus is approved and the final closing of the offer of securities to the public or, as the case may be, the time when trading on a regulated market begins, whichever occurs later.

11. An issuer fulfilling the conditions set out in the first or second subparagraph of paragraph 2 or in paragraph 3 of this Article shall have the status of frequent issuer and shall benefit from the faster approval process in accordance with Article 20(6), provided that:

(a) upon the filing or submission for approval of each universal registration document, the issuer provides written confirmation to the competent authority that, to the best of its knowledge, all regulated information which it was required to disclose under Directive 2004/109/EC, if applicable, and under Regulation (EU) No 596/2014 has been filed and published in accordance with those acts over the last 18 months or over the period since the obligation to disclose regulated information commenced, whichever is the shorter; and

(b) where the competent authority has undertaken a review as referred to in paragraph 8, the issuer has amended its universal registration document in accordance with paragraph 9.

Where any of the above conditions is not fulfilled by the issuer, the status of frequent issuer shall be lost.

12. Where the universal registration document filed with or approved by the competent authority is made public at the latest four months after the end of the financial year, and contains the information required to be disclosed in the annual financial report referred to in Article 4 of Directive 2004/109/EC, the issuer shall be deemed to have fulfilled its obligation to publish the annual financial report required under that Article.

Where the universal registration document, or an amendment thereto, is filed or approved by the competent authority and made public at the latest three months after the end of the first six months of the financial year, and contains the information required to be disclosed in the half-yearly financial report referred to in Article 5 of Directive 2004/109/EC, the issuer shall be deemed to have fulfilled its obligation to publish the half-yearly financial report required under that Article.

In the cases referred to in the first and second subparagraph, the issuer:

(a) shall include in the universal registration document a cross reference list identifying where each item required in the annual and half-yearly financial reports can be found in the universal registration document;

(b) shall file the universal registration document in accordance with Article 19(1) of Directive 2004/109/EC and make it available to the officially appointed mechanism referred to in Article 21(2) of that Directive;

Part 11 EU & Retained EU Legislation

(c) shall include in the universal registration document a responsibility statement using the terms required under point (c) of Article 4(2) and point (c) of Article 5(2) of Directive 2004/109/EC.

13. Paragraph 12 shall only apply where the home Member State of the issuer for the purposes of this Regulation is also the home Member State for the purposes of Directive 2004/109/EC, and where the language of the universal registration document fulfils the conditions set out in Article 20 of that Directive.

14. The Commission shall, by 21 January 2019, adopt delegated acts in accordance with Article 44 to supplement this Regulation by specifying the criteria for the scrutiny and review of the universal registration document and any amendments thereto, and the procedures for the approval and filing of those documents as well as the conditions under which the status of frequent issuer is lost.

NOTES

Application of this Article in relation to the UK: note that substantial amendments have been made to this Article, in relation to the UK only, by the Prospectus (Amendment etc) (EU Exit) Regulations 2019, SI 2019/1234, reg 38, as from IP completion day (as defined in the European Union (Withdrawal Agreement) Act 2020, s 39) (subject to transitional provisions in regs 74, 75 of the 2019 Regulations at **[12.165]** et seq). For ease of reference, the Article as so amended is set out below—

"Article 9 The universal registration document

1. Any issuer whose securities are admitted to trading on a regulated market or an MTF may draw up every financial year a registration document in the form of a universal registration document describing the company's organisation, business, financial position, earnings and prospects, governance and shareholding structure.

2. Any issuer that chooses to draw up a universal registration document every financial year shall submit it for approval to the competent authority in accordance with the procedure set out in Article 20(2) and (4).

After the issuer has had a universal registration document approved by the competent authority for two consecutive financial years, subsequent universal registration documents may be filed with the competent authority without prior approval.

Where the issuer thereafter fails to file a universal registration document for one financial year, the benefit of filing without prior approval shall be lost and all subsequent universal registration documents shall be submitted to the competent authority for approval until the condition set out in the second subparagraph is met again.

The issuer shall indicate in its application to the competent authority whether the universal registration document is submitted for approval or filed without prior approval.

3. Issuers which, prior to 21 July 2019, have had a registration document, drawn up in accordance with Annex I to Commission Regulation (EC) No 809/2004,[1] approved by the competent authority for at least two consecutive financial years and have thereafter filed, in accordance with Article 12(3) of Directive 2003/71/EC, or got approved such a registration document every year, shall be allowed to file a universal registration document without prior approval in accordance with the second subparagraph of paragraph 2 of this Article from 21 July 2019. This paragraph does not apply in relation to a registration document forming part of a prospectus deemed to be approved by the competent authority in accordance with regulation 73 of the Official Listing of Securities, Prospectus and Transparency (Amendment etc) (EU Exit) Regulations 2019.

4. Once approved or filed without prior approval, the universal registration document, as well as the amendments thereto referred to in paragraphs 7 and 9 of this Article, shall be made available to the public without undue delay, in accordance with the arrangements set out in Article 21.

6. Information may be incorporated by reference into a universal registration document under the conditions set out in Article 19.

7. Following the filing or approval of a universal registration document, the issuer may at any time update the information it contains by filing an amendment thereto with the competent authority. Subject to the first and second subparagraphs of Article 10(3), the filing of the amendment with the competent authority shall not require approval.

8. The competent authority may at any time review the content of any universal registration document which has been filed without prior approval, as well as the content of any amendments thereto.

The review by the competent authority shall consist in scrutinising the completeness, the consistency and the comprehensibility of the information given in the universal registration document and any amendments thereto.

9. Where the competent authority, in the course of the review, finds that the universal registration document does not meet the standards of completeness, comprehensibility and consistency, or that amendments or supplementary information are needed, it shall notify it to the issuer.

A request for amendment or supplementary information addressed by the competent authority to the issuer needs only be taken into account by the issuer in the next universal registration document filed for the following financial year, except where the issuer wishes to use the universal registration document as a constituent part of a prospectus submitted for approval. In that case, the issuer shall file an amendment to the universal registration document at the latest upon submission of the application referred to in Article 20(6).

By way of derogation from the second subparagraph, where the competent authority notifies the issuer that its request for amendment or supplementary information concerns a material omission or a material mistake or material inaccuracy, which is likely to mislead the public with regard to facts and circumstances essential for an informed assessment of the issuer, the issuer shall file an amendment to the universal registration document without undue delay.

The competent authority may request that the issuer produces a consolidated version of the amended universal registration document, where such a consolidated version is necessary to ensure comprehensibility of the information provided in that document. An issuer may voluntarily include a consolidated version of its amended universal registration document in an annex to the amendment.

10. Paragraphs 7 and 9 shall only apply where the universal registration document is not in use as a constituent part of a prospectus. Whenever a universal registration document is in use as a constituent part of a prospectus, only Article 23 on supplementing the prospectus shall apply between the time when the prospectus is approved and the final closing of the offer of securities to the public or, as the case may be, the time when trading on a regulated market begins, whichever occurs later.

11. An issuer fulfilling the conditions set out in the first or second subparagraph of paragraph 2 or in paragraph 3 of this Article shall have the status of frequent issuer and shall benefit from the faster approval process in accordance with Article 20(6), provided that:

(a) upon the filing or submission for approval of each universal registration document, the issuer provides written confirmation to the competent authority that, to the best of its knowledge, all regulated information which it was required to disclose under the UK law which implemented Directive 2004/109/EC, if applicable, and under

Regulation (EU) No 596/2014 has been filed and published in accordance with those acts over the last 18 months or over the period since the obligation to disclose regulated information commenced, whichever is the shorter; and

(b) where the competent authority has undertaken a review as referred to in paragraph 8, the issuer has amended its universal registration document in accordance with paragraph 9.

Where any of the above conditions is not fulfilled by the issuer, the status of frequent issuer shall be lost.

12. Where the universal registration document filed with or approved by the competent authority is made public at the latest four months after the end of the financial year, and contains the information required to be disclosed in the annual financial report referred to in Section 1 of Chapter 4 of the Disclosure Guidance and Transparency Rules Sourcebook, the issuer shall be deemed to have fulfilled its obligation to publish the annual financial report required under that Article.

Where the universal registration document, or an amendment thereto, is filed or approved by the competent authority and made public at the latest three months after the end of the first six months of the financial year, and contains the information required to be disclosed in the half-yearly financial report referred to in Section 2 of Chapter 4 of the Disclosure Guidance and Transparency Rules Sourcebook, the issuer shall be deemed to have fulfilled its obligation to publish the half-yearly financial report required under that Article.

In the cases referred to in the first and second subparagraph, the issuer:

(a) shall include in the universal registration document a cross reference list identifying where each item required in the annual and half-yearly financial reports can be found in the universal registration document;

(b) shall file the universal registration document in accordance with Article 19(1) of Directive 2004/109/EC and make it available to the officially appointed mechanism referred to in Article 21(2) of that Directive;

(c) shall include in the universal registration document a responsibility statement using the terms required under point (c) of Article 4(2) and point (c) of Article 5(2) of Directive 2004/109/EC.

14. The Treasury may make regulations to supplement this Regulation by specifying the criteria for the scrutiny and review of the universal registration document and any amendments thereto, and the procedures for the approval and filing of those documents as well as the conditions under which the status of frequent issuer is lost.".

Delegated Act for the purposes of para 14: see Commission Delegated Regulation 2019/980/EU supplementing Regulation (EU) 2017/1129 of the European Parliament and of the Council as regards the format, content, scrutiny and approval of the prospectus to be published when securities are offered to the public or admitted to trading on a regulated market, and repealing Commission Regulation (EC) No 809/2004 at **[11.648]**.

[1] Commission Regulation (EC) No 809/2004 of 29 April 2004 implementing Directive 2003/71/EC of the European Parliament and of the Council as regards information contained in prospectuses as well as the format, incorporation by reference and publication of such prospectuses and dissemination of advertisements (OJ L149, 30.4.2004, p 1).

[11.330]

Article 10 Prospectuses consisting of separate documents

1. An issuer that has already had a registration document approved by a competent authority shall be required to draw up only the securities note and the summary, where applicable, when securities are offered to the public or admitted to trading on a regulated market. In that case, the securities note and the summary shall be subject to a separate approval.

Where, since the approval of the registration document, there has been a significant new factor, material mistake or material inaccuracy relating to the information included in the registration document which is capable of affecting the assessment of the securities, a supplement to the registration document shall be submitted for approval, at the latest at the same time as the securities note and the summary. The right to withdraw acceptances in accordance with Article 23(2) shall not apply in that case.

The registration document and its supplement, where applicable, accompanied by the securities note and the summary shall constitute a prospectus, once approved by the competent authority.

2. Once approved, the registration document shall be made available to the public without undue delay and in accordance with the arrangements set out in Article 21.

3. An issuer that has already had a universal registration document approved by the competent authority, or that has filed a universal registration document without prior approval pursuant to the second subparagraph of Article 9(2), shall be required to draw up only the securities note and the summary when securities are offered to the public or admitted to trading on a regulated market.

Where the universal registration document has already been approved, the securities note, the summary and all amendments to the universal registration document filed since the approval of the universal registration document shall be subject to a separate approval.

Where an issuer has filed a universal registration document without prior approval, the entire documentation, including amendments to the universal registration document, shall be subject to approval, notwithstanding the fact that those documents remain separate.

The universal registration document, amended in accordance with Article 9(7) or (9), accompanied by the securities note and the summary shall constitute a prospectus, once approved by the competent authority.

NOTES

Application of this Article in relation to the UK: this Article is amended (as follows), in relation to the UK only, by the Prospectus (Amendment etc) (EU Exit) Regulations 2019, SI 2019/1234, reg 39, as from IP completion day (as defined in the European Union (Withdrawal Agreement) Act 2020, s 39); for transitional provisions, see regs 74, 75 of the 2019 Regulations at **[12.165]** et seq—

"In Article 10, in paragraph 1, in the first subparagraph, for "a competent" insert "the competent".".

[11.331]

Article 11 Responsibility attaching to the prospectus

1. Member States shall ensure that responsibility for the information given in a prospectus, and any supplement thereto, attaches to at least the issuer or its administrative, management or supervisory bodies, the offeror, the person asking for the admission to trading on a regulated market or the guarantor, as the case may be. The persons responsible for the prospectus, and any supplement thereto, shall be clearly identified in the prospectus by their names and functions or, in the case of legal persons, their names and registered offices, as well as declarations by them that, to the best of their knowledge, the information contained in the prospectus is in accordance with the facts and that the prospectus makes no omission likely to affect its import.

2. Member States shall ensure that their laws, regulations and administrative provisions on civil liability apply to those persons responsible for the information given in a prospectus.

However, Member States shall ensure that no civil liability shall attach to any person solely on the basis of the summary pursuant to Article 7 or the specific summary of an EU Growth prospectus pursuant to the second subparagraph of Article 15(1), including any translation thereof, unless:

- *(a) it is misleading, inaccurate or inconsistent, when read together with the other parts of the prospectus; or*
- *(b) it does not provide, when read together with the other parts of the prospectus, key information in order to aid investors when considering whether to invest in the securities.*

3. The responsibility for the information given in a registration document or in a universal registration document shall attach to the persons referred to in paragraph 1 only in cases where the registration document or the universal registration document is in use as a constituent part of an approved prospectus.

The first subparagraph shall apply without prejudice to Articles 4 and 5 of Directive 2004/109/EC where the information under those Articles is included in a universal registration document.

NOTES

Repeal of this Article in relation to the UK: this Article is repealed, in relation to the UK only, by the Prospectus (Amendment etc) (EU Exit) Regulations 2019, SI 2019/1234, reg 40, as from IP completion day (as defined in the European Union (Withdrawal Agreement) Act 2020, s 39); for transitional provisions, see regs 74, 75 of the 2019 Regulations at **[12.165]** et seq.

[11.332]

Article 12 Validity of a prospectus, registration document and universal registration document

1. A prospectus, whether a single document or consisting of separate documents, shall be valid for 12 months after its approval for offers to the public or admissions to trading on a regulated market, provided that it is completed by any supplement required pursuant to Article 23.

Where a prospectus consists of separate documents, the period of validity shall begin upon approval of the securities note.

2. A registration document which has been previously approved shall be valid for use as a constituent part of a prospectus for 12 months after its approval.

The end of the validity of such a registration document shall not affect the validity of a prospectus of which it is a constituent part.

3. A universal registration document shall be valid for use as a constituent part of a prospectus for 12 months after its approval as referred to in the first subparagraph of Article 9(2) or after its filing as referred to in the second subparagraph of Article 9(2).

The end of the validity of such a universal registration document shall not affect the validity of a prospectus of which it is a constituent part.

CHAPTER III THE CONTENT AND FORMAT OF THE PROSPECTUS

[11.333]

Article 13 Minimum information and format

1. The Commission shall adopt delegated acts in accordance with Article 44 to supplement this Regulation regarding the format of the prospectus, the base prospectus and the final terms, and the schedules defining the specific information to be included in a prospectus, including LEIs and ISINs, avoiding duplication of information when a prospectus is composed of separate documents.

In particular, when setting out the various prospectus schedules, account shall be taken of the following:

- (a) the various types of information needed by investors relating to equity securities as compared with non-equity securities; a consistent approach shall be taken with regard to information required in a prospectus for securities which have a similar economic rationale, notably derivative securities;
- (b) the various types and characteristics of offers and admissions to trading on a regulated market of non-equity securities;
- (c) the format used and the information required in base prospectuses relating to non-equity securities, including warrants in any form;
- (d) where applicable, the public nature of the issuer;
- (e) where applicable, the specific nature of the activities of the issuer.

For the purposes of point (b) of the second subparagraph, when setting out the various prospectus schedules, the Commission shall set out specific information requirements for prospectuses that relate to the admission to trading on a regulated market of non-equity securities which:

- (a) are to be traded only on a regulated market, or a specific segment thereof, to which only qualified investors can have access for the purposes of trading in such securities; or
- (b) have a denomination per unit of at least EUR 100,000.

Those information requirements shall be appropriate, taking into account the information needs of the investors concerned.

2. The Commission shall, by 21 January 2019, adopt delegated acts in accordance with Article 44 to supplement this Regulation by setting out the schedule defining the minimum information to be included in the universal registration document.

Such a schedule shall ensure that the universal registration document contains all the necessary information on the issuer so that the same universal registration document can be used equally for the subsequent offer to the public or admission to trading on a regulated market of equity or non-equity securities. With regard to the financial information, the operating and financial review and prospects and the corporate governance, such information shall be aligned as much as possible with the information required to be disclosed in the annual and half-yearly financial reports referred to in Articles 4 and 5 of Directive 2004/109/EC, including the management report and the corporate governance statement.

3. The delegated acts referred to in paragraphs 1 and 2 shall be based on the standards in the field of financial and non-financial information set out by international securities commission organisations, in particular by the International Organisation of Securities Commissions (IOSCO), and on Annexes I, II and III to this Regulation.

NOTES

Application of this Article in relation to the UK: this Article is amended (as follows), in relation to the UK only, by the Prospectus (Amendment etc) (EU Exit) Regulations 2019, SI 2019/1234, reg 41, as from IP completion day (as defined in the European Union (Withdrawal Agreement) Act 2020, s 39); for transitional provisions, see regs 74, 75 of the 2019 Regulations at **[12.165]** et seq—

"In Article 13—
(a) in paragraph 1—
(i) in the first subparagraph, for "The Commission shall adopt delegated acts in accordance with Article 44 to" substitute "The Treasury may by regulations";
(ii) in the third subparagraph, for "Commission" substitute "Treasury";
(b) in paragraph 2, in the first subparagraph, for "The Commission shall, by 21 January 2019, adopt delegated acts in accordance with Article 44 to" substitute "The Treasury may by regulations";
(c) in paragraph 3, for "The delegated acts" substitute "Regulations".".

Delegated Act for the purposes of paras 1, 2: see Commission Delegated Regulation 2019/980/EU supplementing Regulation (EU) 2017/1129 of the European Parliament and of the Council as regards the format, content, scrutiny and approval of the prospectus to be published when securities are offered to the public or admitted to trading on a regulated market, and repealing Commission Regulation (EC) No 809/2004 at **[11.648]**. See also Commission Delegated Regulation 2020/1273/EU amending and correcting Delegated Regulation (EU) 2019/980 supplementing Regulation (EU) 2017/1129 of the European Parliament and of the Council as regards the format, content, scrutiny and approval of the prospectus to be published when securities are offered to the public or admitted to trading on a regulated market.

[11.334]

Article 14 Simplified disclosure regime for secondary issuances

1. The following persons may choose to draw up a simplified prospectus under the simplified disclosure regime for secondary issuances, in the case of an offer of securities to the public or of an admission to trading of securities on a regulated market:

(a) issuers whose securities have been admitted to trading on a regulated market or an SME growth market continuously for at least the last 18 months and who issue securities fungible with existing securities which have been previously issued;
[(b) without prejudice to Article 1(5), issuers whose equity securities have been admitted to trading on a regulated market or an SME growth market continuously for at least the last 18 months and who issue non-equity securities or securities giving access to equity securities fungible with the existing equity securities of the issuer already admitted to trading;]
(c) offerors of securities admitted to trading on a regulated market or an SME growth market continuously for at least the last 18 months;
[(d) issuers whose securities have been offered to the public and admitted to trading on an SME growth market continuously for at least two years, and who have fully complied with reporting and disclosure obligations throughout the period of being admitted to trading, and who seek admission to trading on a regulated market of securities fungible with existing securities which have been previously issued].

The simplified prospectus shall consist of a summary in accordance with Article 7, a specific registration document which may be used by persons referred to in points (a), (b) and (c) of the first subparagraph of this paragraph and a specific securities note which may be used by persons referred to in points (a) and (c) of that subparagraph.

2. By way of derogation from Article 6(1), and without prejudice to Article 18(1), the simplified prospectus shall contain the relevant reduced information which is necessary to enable investors to understand:

(a) the prospects of the issuer and the significant changes in the business and the financial position of the issuer and the guarantor that have occurred since the end of the last financial year, if any;
(b) the rights attaching to the securities;
(c) the reasons for the issuance and its impact on the issuer, including on its overall capital structure, and the use of the proceeds.

The information contained in the simplified prospectus shall be written and presented in an easily analysable, concise and comprehensible form and shall enable investors to make an informed investment decision. It shall also take into account the regulated information that has already been disclosed to the public pursuant to Directive 2004/109/EC, where applicable, and Regulation (EU) No 596/2014. [Those issuers referred to in point (d) of the first subparagraph of paragraph 1 of this Article that are required to prepare consolidated accounts in line with Directive 2013/34/EU of the European Parliament and of the Council[1] after their securities' admission to trading on a regulated market shall compile the most recent financial information pursuant to point (a) of the second subparagraph of paragraph 3 of this Article, containing comparative information for the previous year included in the simplified prospectus, in accordance with the International Financial Reporting Standards referred to in Regulation (EC) No 1606/2002 of the European Parliament and of the Council.[2]]

[Those issuers referred to in point (d) of the first subparagraph of paragraph 1 of this Article that are not required to prepare consolidated accounts in line with Directive 2013/34/EU after their securities' admission to trading on a regulated market shall compile the most recent financial information pursuant to point (a) of the second subparagraph of paragraph 3 of this Article, containing comparative information for the previous year included in the simplified prospectus, in accordance with the national law of the Member State in which the issuer is incorporated.

Third country issuers whose securities have been admitted to trading on an SME growth market shall compile the most recent financial information pursuant to point (a) of the second subparagraph of paragraph 3 of this Article, containing comparative information for the previous year included in the simplified prospectus, in accordance with their national accounting standards, provided that those standards are equivalent to Regulation (EC) No 1606/2002. If those national accounting standards are not equivalent to the International Financial Reporting Standards, the financial information shall be restated pursuant to Regulation (EC) No 1606/2002.]

3. The Commission shall, by 21 January 2019, adopt delegated acts in accordance with Article 44 to supplement this Regulation by setting out the schedules specifying the reduced information to be included under the simplified disclosure regime referred to in paragraph 1.

The schedules shall include in particular:

(a) the annual and half-yearly financial information published over the 12 months prior to the approval of the prospectus;

(b) where applicable, profit forecasts and estimates;

(c) a concise summary of the relevant information disclosed under Regulation (EU) No 596/2014 over the 12 months prior to the approval of the prospectus;

(d) risk factors;

[(e) for equity securities, including securities giving access to equity securities, the working capital statement, the statement of capitalisation and indebtedness, a disclosure of relevant conflicts of interest and related-party transactions, major shareholders and, where applicable, pro forma financial information.]

When specifying the reduced information to be included under the simplified disclosure regime, the Commission shall take into account the need to facilitate fundraising on capital markets and the importance of reducing the cost of capital. In order to avoid imposing unnecessary burdens on issuers, when specifying the reduced information, the Commission shall also take into account the information which an issuer is already required to disclose under Directive 2004/109/EC, where applicable, and Regulation (EU) No 596/2014. The Commission shall also calibrate the reduced information so that it focuses on the information that is relevant for secondary issuances and is proportionate.

NOTES

All words in square brackets were inserted or substituted by European Parliament and Council Regulation 2019/2115/EU, Art 2(2), as from 31 December 2019.

Application of this Article in relation to the UK: this Article is amended (as follows), in relation to the UK only, by the Prospectus (Amendment etc) (EU Exit) Regulations 2019, SI 2019/1234, reg 42, as from IP completion day (as defined in the European Union (Withdrawal Agreement) Act 2020, s 39); for transitional provisions, see regs 74, 75 of the 2019 Regulations at **[12.165]** et seq—

"In Article 14—

(a) for paragraph 2 substitute—

"2. By way of derogation from Article 6(1), and without prejudice to Article 18(1), the simplified prospectus shall contain the relevant reduced information which is necessary to enable investors to understand—

(a) the prospects of the issuer and the significant changes in the business and the financial position of the issuer and the guarantor that have occurred since the end of the last financial year, if any;

(b) the rights attaching to the securities;

(c) the reasons for the issuance and its impact on the issuer, including on its overall capital structure, and the use of the proceeds.

The information contained in the simplified prospectus shall be written and presented in an easily analysable, concise and comprehensible form and shall enable investors to make an informed investment decision. It shall also take into account the regulated information that has already been disclosed to the public pursuant to—

(a) provisions of the law of the United Kingdom relied on at the time of the disclosure in question to implement Directive 2004/109/EC, where applicable, in relation to disclosures made before IP completion day,

(b) the UK law which implemented Directive 2004/109/EC, where applicable, in relation to disclosures after IP completion day, and

(c) Regulation (EU) No 596/2014.

Those issuers referred to in point (d) of the first subparagraph of paragraph 1 of this Article that are or are not required to prepare consolidated accounts in line with section 399 of the Companies Act 2006 after their securities' admission to trading on a regulated market shall compile the most recent financial information pursuant to point (a) of the second subparagraph of paragraph 3 of this Article, containing comparative information for the previous year included in the simplified prospectus, in accordance with Article 23a of Regulation (EU) 2019/980.

Third country issuers whose securities have been admitted to trading on an SME growth market shall compile the most recent financial information pursuant to point (a) of the second subparagraph of paragraph 3 of this Article, containing comparative information for the previous year included in the simplified prospectus in accordance with Article 23a of Regulation (EU) 2019/980.".

(b) in paragraph 3—

(i) in the first subparagraph, for "The Commission shall, by 21 January 2019, adopt delegated acts in accordance with Article 44 to" substitute "The Treasury may by regulations";

(ii) in the third subparagraph—

(aa) for "Commission" in each place it occurs, substitute "Treasury";

(bb) for "Directive 2004/109/EC, where applicable, and Regulation (EU) No 596/2014" substitute "the provisions referred to in the second sentence of paragraph 2 of this Article".".

Note that the Prospectus (Amendment etc) (EU Exit) Regulations 2019, SI 2019/1234, reg 42 was amended by the Financial Services (Miscellaneous Amendments) (EU Exit) Regulations 2020, SI 2020/628, reg 17(1), (4), as from immediately before IP completion day; and the effect of the amendment has been incorporated in the text set out above.

Delegated Act for the purposes of para 3: see Commission Delegated Regulation 2019/980/EU supplementing Regulation (EU) 2017/1129 of the European Parliament and of the Council as regards the format, content, scrutiny and approval of the prospectus to be published when securities are offered to the public or admitted to trading on a regulated market, and repealing Commission Regulation (EC) No 809/2004 at **[11.648]**. See also Commission Delegated Regulation 2020/1273/EU amending and correcting Delegated Regulation (EU) 2019/980 supplementing Regulation (EU) 2017/1129 of the European

Parliament and of the Council as regards the format, content, scrutiny and approval of the prospectus to be published when securities are offered to the public or admitted to trading on a regulated market.

[1] Directive 2013/34/EU of the European Parliament and of the Council of 26 June 2013 on the annual financial statements, consolidated financial statements and related reports of certain types of undertakings, amending Directive 2006/43/EC of the European Parliament and of the Council and repealing Council Directives 78/660/EEC and 83/349/EEC (OJ L182, 29.6.2013, p 19).

[2] Regulation (EC) No 1606/2002 of the European Parliament and of the Council of 19 July 2002 on the application of international accounting standards (OJ L243, 11.9.2002, p 1).

[11.335]

[Article 14a EU Recovery prospectus

1. The following persons may choose to draw up an EU Recovery prospectus under the simplified disclosure regime set out in this Article in the case of an offer of shares to the public or of an admission to trading of shares on a regulated market:

(a) issuers whose shares have been admitted to trading on a regulated market continuously for at least the last 18 months and who issue shares fungible with existing shares which have been previously issued;

(b) issuers whose shares have already been traded on an SME growth market continuously for at least the last 18 months, provided that a prospectus has been published for the offer of those shares, and who issue shares fungible with existing shares which have been previously issued;

(c) offerors of shares admitted to trading on a regulated market or an SME growth market continuously for at least the last 18 months.

Issuers may only draw up an EU Recovery prospectus provided that the number of shares intended to be offered represents, together with the number of shares already offered via an EU Recovery prospectus over a period of 12 months, if any, no more than 150% of the number of shares already admitted to trading on a regulated market or an SME growth market, as the case may be, on the date of approval of the EU Recovery prospectus.

The period of 12 months referred to in the second subparagraph shall begin on the date of approval of the EU Recovery prospectus.

2. By way of derogation from Article 6(1), and without prejudice to Article 18(1), the EU Recovery prospectus shall contain the relevant reduced information which is necessary to enable investors to understand:

(a) the prospects and financial performance of the issuer and the significant changes in the financial and business position of the issuer that have occurred since the end of the last financial year, if any, as well as its financial and non-financial long-term business strategy and objectives, including, if applicable, a specific reference of not less than 400 words to the business and financial impact of the COVID-19 pandemic on the issuer and the anticipated future impact of the same;

(b) the essential information on the shares, including the rights attached to those shares and any limitations on those rights, the reasons for the issuance and its impact on the issuer, including on the overall capital structure of the issuer, as well as a disclosure of capitalisation and indebtedness, a working capital statement, and the use of proceeds.

3. The information contained in the EU Recovery prospectus shall be written and presented in an easily analysable, concise and comprehensible form and shall enable investors, especially retail investors, to make an informed investment decision, taking into account the regulated information that has already been disclosed to the public pursuant to Directive 2004/109/EC, where applicable, Regulation (EU) No 596/2014 and, where applicable, information referred to in Commission Delegated Regulation (EU) 2017/565.[1]

4. The EU Recovery prospectus shall be drawn up as a single document containing the minimum information set out in Annex Va. It shall be of a maximum length of 30 sides of A4-sized paper when printed and shall be presented and laid out in a way that is easy to read, using characters of readable size.

5. Neither the summary nor the information incorporated by reference in accordance with Article 19 shall be taken into account as regards the maximum length referred to in paragraph 4 of this Article.

6. Issuers may decide the order in which the information set out in Annex Va is set out in the EU Recovery prospectus.]

NOTES

Inserted by European Parliament and Council Regulation 2021/337/EU, Art 1(5), as from 18 March 2021.

Application of this Article in relation to the UK: note that Regulation 2021/337/EU (which inserts this Article as noted above) is not "direct EU legislation" within the meaning of the European Union (Withdrawal) Act 2018, s 3 at **[12.5]** and, therefore, this Article does not apply to the UK.

[1] Commission Delegated Regulation (EU) 2017/565 of 25 April 2016 supplementing Directive 2014/65/EU of the European Parliament and of the Council as regards organisational requirements and operating conditions for investment firms and defined terms for the purposes of that Directive (OJ L87, 31.3.2017, p 1).

[11.336]

Article 15 EU Growth prospectus

1. The following persons may choose to draw up an EU Growth prospectus under the proportionate disclosure regime set out in this Article in the case of an offer of securities to the public provided that they have no securities admitted to trading on a regulated market:

(a) SMEs;

(b) issuers, other than SMEs, whose securities are traded or are to be traded on an SME growth market, provided that those issuers had an average market capitalisation of less than EUR 500,000,000 on the basis of end-year quotes for the previous three calendar years;

(c) issuers, other than those referred to in points (a) and (b), where the offer of securities to the public is of a total consideration in the Union that does not exceed EUR 20,000,000 calculated over a period of 12 months, and provided that such issuers have no securities traded on an MTF and have an average number of employees during the previous financial year of up to 499;

[(ca) issuers, other than SMEs, offering shares to the public at the same time as seeking admission of those shares to trading on an SME growth market, provided that such issuers have no shares already admitted to trading on an SME growth market and the combined value of the following two items is less than EUR 200,000,000:

(i) the final offer price, or the maximum price in the case referred to in point (b)(i) of Article 17(1);

(ii) he total number of shares outstanding immediately after the share offer to the public, calculated either on the basis of the amount of shares offered to the public or, in the case referred to in point (b)(i) of Article 17(1), on the basis of the maximum amount of shares offered to the public.]

(d) offerors of securities issued by issuers referred to in points (a) and (b).

An EU Growth prospectus under the proportionate disclosure regime shall be a document of a standardised format, written in a simple language and which is easy for issuers to complete. It shall consist of a specific summary based on Article 7, a specific registration document and a specific securities note. The information in the EU Growth prospectus shall be presented in a standardised sequence in accordance with the delegated act referred to in paragraph 2.

2. The Commission shall, by 21 January 2019, adopt delegated acts in accordance with Article 44 to supplement this Regulation by specifying the reduced content and the standardised format and sequence for the EU Growth prospectus, as well as the reduced content and the standardised format of the specific summary.

The specific summary shall not impose any additional burdens or costs on issuers insofar as it shall only require the relevant information already included in the EU Growth prospectus. When specifying the standardised format of the specific summary, the Commission shall calibrate the requirements to ensure that it is shorter than the summary provided for in Article 7.

When specifying the reduced content and standardised format and sequence of the EU Growth prospectus, the Commission shall calibrate the requirements to focus on:

(a) the information that is material and relevant for investors when making an investment decision;

(b) the need to ensure proportionality between the size of the company and the cost of producing a prospectus.

In doing so, the Commission shall take into account the following:

(a) the need to ensure that the EU Growth prospectus is significantly lighter than the standard prospectus, in terms of administrative burdens and costs to issuers;

(b) the need to facilitate access to capital markets for SMEs and minimise costs for SMEs while ensuring investor confidence in investing in such companies;

(c) the various types of information relating to equity and non-equity securities needed by investors.

Those delegated acts shall be based on Annexes IV and V.

NOTES

Para 1: point (ca) inserted by European Parliament and Council Regulation 2019/2115/EU, Art 2(3), as from 31 December 2019.

Application of this Article in relation to the UK: note that substantial amendments have been made to this Article, in relation to the UK only, by the Prospectus (Amendment etc) (EU Exit) Regulations 2019, SI 2019/1234, reg 43, as from IP completion day (as defined in the European Union (Withdrawal Agreement) Act 2020, s 39) (subject to transitional provisions in regs 74, 75 of the 2019 Regulations at **[12.165]** et seq). For ease of reference, the Article as so amended is set out below. With regard to the text as set out below note that it also includes amendments made by in force and operative EU legislation within the meaning of the European Union (Withdrawal) Act 2018, s 3 at **[12.5]** (as noted above)—

"Article 15 UK Growth prospectus

1. The following persons may choose to draw up a UK Growth prospectus under the proportionate disclosure regime set out in this Article in the case of an offer of securities to the public provided that they have no securities admitted to trading on a regulated market:

(a) SMEs;

(b) issuers, other than SMEs, whose securities are traded or are to be traded on an SME growth market, provided that those issuers had an average market capitalisation of less than EUR 500,000,000 on the basis of end-year quotes for the previous three calendar years;

(c) issuers, other than those referred to in points (a) and (b), where the offer of securities to the public is of a total consideration in the United Kingdom that does not exceed EUR 20,000,000 calculated over a period of 12 months, and provided that such issuers have no securities traded on an MTF and have an average number of employees during the previous financial year of up to 499;

(ca) issuers, other than SMEs, offering shares to the public at the same time as seeking admission of those shares to trading on an SME growth market, provided that such issuers have no shares already admitted to trading on an SME growth market and the combined value of the following two items is less than EUR 200,000,000:

(i) the final offer price, or the maximum price in the case referred to in point (b)(i) of Article 17(1);

(ii) he total number of shares outstanding immediately after the share offer to the public, calculated either on the basis of the amount of shares offered to the public or, in the case referred to in point (b)(i) of Article 17(1), on the basis of the maximum amount of shares offered to the public.

(d) offerors of securities issued by issuers referred to in points (a) and (b).

A UK Growth prospectus under the proportionate disclosure regime shall be a document of a standardised format, written in a simple language and which is easy for issuers to complete. It shall consist of a specific summary based on Article 7, a specific registration document and a specific securities note. The information in the UK Growth prospectus shall be presented in a standardised sequence in accordance with the regulations referred to in paragraph 2.

2. The Treasury may by regulations supplement this Regulation by specifying the reduced content and the standardised format and sequence for the UK Growth prospectus, as well as the reduced content and the standardised format of the specific summary.

The specific summary shall not impose any additional burdens or costs on issuers insofar as it shall only require the relevant information already included in the UK Growth prospectus. When specifying the standardised format of the specific summary, the Treasury shall calibrate the requirements to ensure that it is shorter than the summary provided for in Article 7.

When specifying the reduced content and standardised format and sequence of the UK Growth prospectus, the Treasury shall calibrate the requirements to focus on:

(a) the information that is material and relevant for investors when making an investment decision;

(b) the need to ensure proportionality between the size of the company and the cost of producing a prospectus.

In doing so, the Treasury shall take into account the following:

(a) the need to ensure that the UK Growth prospectus is significantly lighter than the standard prospectus, in terms of administrative burdens and costs to issuers;

(b) the need to facilitate access to capital markets for SMEs and minimise costs for SMEs while ensuring investor confidence in investing in such companies;

(c) the various types of information relating to equity and non-equity securities needed by investors.

Those regulations shall be based on Annexes IV and V.".

Delegated Act for the purposes of para 2: see Commission Delegated Regulation 2019/980/EU supplementing Regulation (EU) 2017/1129 of the European Parliament and of the Council as regards the format, content, scrutiny and approval of the prospectus to be published when securities are offered to the public or admitted to trading on a regulated market, and repealing Commission Regulation (EC) No 809/2004 at **[11.648]**. See also Commission Delegated Regulation 2020/1273/EU amending and correcting Delegated Regulation (EU) 2019/980 supplementing Regulation (EU) 2017/1129 of the European Parliament and of the Council as regards the format, content, scrutiny and approval of the prospectus to be published when securities are offered to the public or admitted to trading on a regulated market.

[11.337]

Article 16 Risk factors

1. The risk factors featured in a prospectus shall be limited to risks which are specific to the issuer and/or to the securities and which are material for taking an informed investment decision, as corroborated by the content of the registration document and the securities note.

When drawing up the prospectus, the issuer, the offeror or the person asking for admission to trading on a regulated market shall assess the materiality of the risk factors based on the probability of their occurrence and the expected magnitude of their negative impact.

Each risk factor shall be adequately described, explaining how it affects the issuer or the securities being offered or to be admitted to trading. The assessment of the materiality of the risk factors provided for in the second subparagraph may also be disclosed by using a qualitative scale of low, medium or high.

The risk factors shall be presented in a limited number of categories depending on their nature. In each category the most material risk factors shall be mentioned first according to the assessment provided for in the second subparagraph.

2. Risk factors shall also include those resulting from the level of subordination of a security and the impact on the expected size or timing of payments to holders of the securities in the event of bankruptcy, or any other similar procedure, including, where relevant, the insolvency of a credit institution or its resolution or restructuring in accordance with Directive 2014/59/EU.

3. Where there is a guarantee attached to the securities, the prospectus shall contain the specific and material risk factors pertaining to the guarantor to the extent that they are relevant to the guarantor's ability to fulfil its commitment under the guarantee.

4. In order to encourage appropriate and focused disclosure of risk factors, ESMA shall develop guidelines to assist competent authorities in their review of the specificity and materiality of risk factors and of the presentation of risk factors across categories depending on their nature.

5. The Commission is empowered to adopt delegated acts in accordance with Article 44 to supplement this Regulation by specifying criteria for the assessment of the specificity and materiality of risk factors and for the presentation of risk factors across categories depending on their nature.

NOTES

Application of this Article in relation to the UK: this Article is amended (as follows), in relation to the UK only, by the Prospectus (Amendment etc) (EU Exit) Regulations 2019, SI 2019/1234, reg 44, as from IP completion day (as defined in the European Union (Withdrawal Agreement) Act 2020, s 39); for transitional provisions, see regs 74, 75 of the 2019 Regulations at **[12.165]** et seq—

"In Article 16—

(a) in paragraph 2, before "Directive 2014/59/EU" insert "the UK law which implemented";

(b) omit paragraph 4;

(c) in paragraph 5, for "The Commission is empowered to adopt delegated acts in accordance with Article 44 to" substitute "The Treasury may by regulations".".

[11.338]

Article 17 Final offer price and amount of securities

1. Where the final offer price and/or amount of securities to be offered to the public, whether expressed in number of securities or as an aggregate nominal amount, cannot be included in the prospectus:

(a) the acceptances of the purchase or subscription of securities may be withdrawn for not less than two working days after the final offer price and/or amount of securities to be offered to the public has been filed; or

(b) the following shall be disclosed in the prospectus:

 (i) the maximum price and/or the maximum amount of securities, as far as they are available; or

 (ii) the valuation methods and criteria, and/or conditions, in accordance with which the final offer price is to be determined and an explanation of any valuation methods used.

2. The final offer price and amount of securities shall be filed with the competent authority of the home Member State and made available to the public in accordance with the arrangements set out in Article 21(2).

NOTES

Application of this Article in relation to the UK: this Article is amended (as follows), in relation to the UK only, by the Prospectus (Amendment etc) (EU Exit) Regulations 2019, SI 2019/1234, reg 45, as from IP completion day (as defined in the European Union (Withdrawal Agreement) Act 2020, s 39); for transitional provisions, see regs 74, 75 of the 2019 Regulations at **[12.165]** et seq—

"In Article 17, in paragraph 2, omit "of the home Member State".".

[11.339]

Article 18 Omission of information

1. The competent authority of the home Member State may authorise the omission from the prospectus, or constituent parts thereof, of certain information to be included therein, where it considers that any of the following conditions is met:

(a) disclosure of such information would be contrary to the public interest;

(b) disclosure of such information would be seriously detrimental to the issuer or to the guarantor, if any, provided that the omission of such information would not be likely to mislead the public with regard to facts and circumstances essential for an informed assessment of the issuer or guarantor, if any, and of the rights attached to the securities to which the prospectus relates;

(c) such information is of minor importance in relation to a specific offer or admission to trading on a regulated market and would not influence the assessment of the financial position and prospects of the issuer or guarantor, if any.

The competent authority shall submit a report to ESMA on a yearly basis regarding the information the omission of which it has authorised.

2. Subject to adequate information being provided to investors, where, exceptionally, certain information required to be included in a prospectus, or constituent parts thereof, is inappropriate to the sphere of activity or to the legal form of the issuer or of the guarantor, if any, or to the securities to which the prospectus relates, the prospectus, or constituent parts thereof, shall contain information equivalent to the required information, unless no such information exists.

3. Where securities are guaranteed by a Member State, an issuer, an offeror or a person asking for admission to trading on a regulated market, when drawing up a prospectus in accordance with Article 4, shall be entitled to omit information pertaining to that Member State.

4. ESMA may, or where the Commission so requests shall, develop draft regulatory technical standards to specify the cases where information may be omitted in accordance with paragraph 1, taking into account the reports of competent authorities to ESMA referred to in paragraph 1.

NOTES

Application of this Article in relation to the UK: this Article is amended (as follows), in relation to the UK only, by the Prospectus (Amendment etc) (EU Exit) Regulations 2019, SI 2019/1234, reg 46, as from IP completion day (as defined in the European Union (Withdrawal Agreement) Act 2020, s 39); for transitional provisions, see regs 74, 75 of the 2019 Regulations at **[12.165]** et seq—

"In Article 18—

(a) in paragraph 1—

(i) in the first subparagraph, omit "of the home Member State";

(ii) omit the second subparagraph;

(b) in paragraph 3, for "Member State", both times it occurs, substitute "state";

(c) for paragraph 4, substitute—

4. The FCA may make technical standards to specify the cases where information may be omitted in accordance with paragraph 1.".".

[11.340]

Article 19 Incorporation by reference

1. Information may be incorporated by reference in a prospectus where it has been previously or simultaneously published electronically, drawn up in a language fulfilling the requirements of Article 27 and where it is contained in one of the following documents:

(a) documents which have been approved by a competent authority, or filed with it, in accordance with this Regulation or Directive 2003/71/EC;

(b) documents referred to in points (f) to (i) of Article 1(4) and points (e) to (h) and point (j)(v) of the first subparagraph of Article 1(5);

(c) regulated information;

(d) annual and interim financial information;

(e) audit reports and financial statements;

(f) management reports as referred to in Chapter 5 of Directive 2013/34/EU of the European Parliament and of the Council;[1]

(g) corporate governance statements as referred to in Article 20 of Directive 2013/34/EU;

(h) reports on the determination of the value of an asset or a company;

(i) remuneration reports as referred to in Article 9b of Directive 2007/36/EC of the European Parliament and of the Council;[2]

(j) annual reports or any disclosure of information required under Articles 22 and 23 of Directive 2011/61/EU of the European Parliament and of the Council;[3]

(k) memorandum and articles of association.

Such information shall be the most recent available to the issuer.

Where only certain parts of a document are incorporated by reference, a statement shall be included in the prospectus that the non-incorporated parts are either not relevant for the investor or covered elsewhere in the prospectus.

2. When incorporating information by reference, issuers, offerors or persons asking for admission to trading on a regulated market shall ensure accessibility of the information. In particular, a cross-reference list shall be provided in the prospectus in order to enable investors to identify easily specific items of information, and the prospectus shall contain hyperlinks to all documents containing information which is incorporated by reference.

3. Where possible alongside the first draft of the prospectus submitted to the competent authority, and in any case during the prospectus review process, the issuer, the offeror or the person asking for admission to trading on a regulated market shall submit in searchable electronic format any information which is incorporated by reference into the prospectus, unless such information has already been approved by or filed with the competent authority approving the prospectus.

4. ESMA may, or where the Commission so requests shall, develop draft regulatory technical standards to update the list of documents set out in paragraph 1 of this Article by including additional types of documents required under Union law to be filed with or approved by a public authority.

Power is delegated to the Commission to adopt the regulatory technical standards referred to in the first subparagraph of this paragraph in accordance with Articles 10 to 14 of Regulation (EU) No 1095/2010.

NOTES

Application of this Article in relation to the UK: this Article is amended (as follows), in relation to the UK only, by the Prospectus (Amendment etc) (EU Exit) Regulations 2019, SI 2019/1234, reg 47, as from IP completion day (as defined in the European Union (Withdrawal Agreement) Act 2020, s 39); for transitional provisions, see regs 74, 75 of the 2019 Regulations at **[12.165]** et seq—

"In Article 19—

(a) in paragraph 1, in the first subparagraph—

(i) in the opening words, after "Article 27" insert "as it had effect immediately before IP completion day where the information was published before IP completion day,";

(ii) for point (a) substitute—

"(a) a document which has—

(i) before IP completion day, been approved by or filed with a competent authority (as defined in this Regulation as it had effect immediately before IP completion day) in accordance with this Regulation (as it had effect immediately before IP completion day), or a competent authority (as defined in Directive 2003/71/EC) in accordance with that Directive; or

(ii) on or after IP completion day, been approved by or filed with the competent authority in accordance with this Regulation or the UK law implementing Directive 2003/71/EC;";

(iii) for point (j), substitute—

"(j) annual reports or any disclosure of information required under—

—provisions of the law of the United Kingdom relied on at the time of the disclosure in question to implement Articles 22 and 23 of Directive 2011/61/EU, in relation to disclosures made before IP completion day,

—the UK law which implemented Articles 22 and 23 of Directive 2011/61/EC, in relation to disclosures after IP completion day.";

(b) in paragraph 4—

(i) in the first subparagraph—

(aa) for "ESMA may, or where the Commission so requests shall, develop draft regulatory" substitute "The FCA may make";

(bb) for "Union law" substitute "the law of the United Kingdom".

(ii) omit the second subparagraph.".

Note that the Prospectus (Amendment etc) (EU Exit) Regulations 2019, SI 2019/1234, reg 47 was amended by the Financial Services and Economic and Monetary Policy (Consequential Amendments) (EU Exit) Regulations 2020, SI 2020/1301, reg 3, Schedule, para 48(d), as from 30 December 2020 (and the effect of the amendments has been incorporated in the text set out above).

[1] Directive 2013/34/EU of the European Parliament and of the Council of 26 June 2013 on the annual financial statements, consolidated financial statements and related reports of certain types of undertakings, amending Directive 2006/43/EC of the European Parliament and of the Council and repealing Council Directives 78/660/EEC and 83/349/EEC (OJ L182, 29.6.2013, p 19).

[2] Directive 2007/36/EC of the European Parliament and of the Council of 11 July 2007 on the exercise of certain rights of shareholders in listed companies (OJ L184, 14.7.2007, p 17).

[3] Directive 2011/61/EU of the European Parliament and of the Council of 8 June 2011 on Alternative Investment Fund Managers and amending Directives 2003/41/EC and 2009/65/EC and Regulations (EC) No 1060/2009 and (EU) No 1095/2010 (OJ L174, 1.7.2011, p 1).

CHAPTER IV ARRANGEMENTS FOR APPROVAL AND PUBLICATION OF THE PROSPECTUS

[11.341]

Article 20 Scrutiny and approval of the prospectus

1. A prospectus shall not be published unless the relevant competent authority has approved it, or all of its constituent parts in accordance with Article 10.

2. The competent authority shall notify the issuer, the offeror or the person asking for admission to trading on a regulated market of its decision regarding the approval of the prospectus within 10 working days of the submission of the draft prospectus.

Where the competent authority fails to take a decision on the prospectus within the time limits laid down in the first subparagraph of this paragraph and paragraphs 3 and 6, such failure shall not be deemed to constitute approval of the application.

The competent authority shall notify ESMA of the approval of the prospectus and any supplement thereto as soon as possible and in any event by no later than the end of the first working day after that approval is notified to the issuer, the offeror or the person asking for admission to trading on a regulated market.

3. The time limit set out in the first subparagraph of paragraph 2 shall be extended to 20 working days where the offer to the public involves securities issued by an issuer that does not have any securities admitted to trading on a regulated market and that has not previously offered securities to the public.

The time limit of 20 working days shall only be applicable for the initial submission of the draft prospectus. Where subsequent submissions are necessary in accordance with paragraph 4, the time limit set out in the first subparagraph of paragraph 2 shall apply.

4. Where the competent authority finds that the draft prospectus does not meet the standards of completeness, comprehensibility and consistency necessary for its approval and/or that changes or supplementary information are needed:

(a) it shall inform the issuer, the offeror or the person asking for admission to trading on a regulated market of that fact promptly and at the latest within the time limits set out in the first subparagraph of paragraph 2 or, as applicable, paragraph 3, as calculated from the submission of the draft prospectus and/or the supplementary information; and

(b) it shall clearly specify the changes or supplementary information that are needed.

In such cases, the time limit set out in the first subparagraph of paragraph 2 shall then apply only from the date on which a revised draft prospectus or the supplementary information requested are submitted to the competent authority.

5. Where the issuer, the offeror or the person asking for admission to trading on a regulated market is unable or unwilling to make the necessary changes or to provide the supplementary information requested in accordance with paragraph 4, the competent authority shall be entitled to refuse the approval of the prospectus and terminate the review process. In such case, the competent authority shall notify the issuer, the offeror or the person asking for admission to trading on a regulated market of its decision and indicate the reasons for such refusal.

6. By way of derogation from paragraphs 2 and 4, the time limits set out in the first subparagraph of paragraph 2 and paragraph 4 shall be reduced to five working days for a prospectus consisting of separate documents drawn up by frequent issuers referred to in Article 9(11), including frequent issuers using the notification procedure provided for in Article 26. The frequent issuer shall inform the competent authority at least five working days before the date envisaged for the submission of an application for approval.

A frequent issuer shall submit an application to the competent authority containing the necessary amendments to the universal registration document, where applicable, the securities note and the summary submitted for approval.

[6a. By way of derogation from paragraphs 2 and 4, the time limits set out in the first subparagraph of paragraph 2 and paragraph 4 shall be reduced to seven working days for an EU Recovery prospectus. The issuer shall inform the competent authority at least five working days before the date envisaged for the submission of an application for approval.]

7. Competent authorities shall provide on their websites guidance on the scrutiny and approval process in order to facilitate efficient and timely approval of prospectuses. Such guidance shall include contact details for the purposes of approvals. The issuer, the offeror, the person asking for admission to trading on a regulated market or the person responsible for drawing up the prospectus shall have the possibility to directly communicate and interact with the staff of the competent authority throughout the process of approval of the prospectus.

8. On request of the issuer, the offeror or the person asking for admission to trading on a regulated market, the competent authority of the home Member State may transfer the approval of a prospectus to the competent authority of another Member State, subject to prior notification to ESMA and the agreement of that competent authority. The competent authority of the home Member State shall transfer the documentation filed, together with its decision to grant the transfer, in electronic format, to the competent authority of the other Member State on the date of its decision. Such a transfer shall be notified to the issuer, the offeror or the person asking for admission to trading on a regulated market within three working days from the date of the decision taken by the competent authority of the home Member State. The time limits set out in the first subparagraph of paragraph 2 and paragraph 3 shall apply from the date the decision was taken by the competent authority of the home Member State. Article 28(4) of Regulation (EU) No 1095/2010 shall not apply to the transfer of the approval of the prospectus in accordance with this paragraph. Upon completion of the transfer of the approval, the competent authority to whom the approval of the prospectus has been transferred shall be deemed to be the competent authority of the home Member State for that prospectus for the purposes of this Regulation.

9. This Regulation shall not affect the competent authority's liability, which shall continue to be governed solely by national law.

Member States shall ensure that their national provisions on the liability of competent authorities apply only to approvals of prospectuses by their competent authority.

10. The level of fees charged by the competent authority of the home Member State for the approval of prospectuses, of documents that are intended to become constituent parts of prospectuses in accordance with Article 10 or of supplements to prospectuses as well as for the filing of universal registration documents, amendments thereto and final terms, shall be reasonable and proportionate and shall be disclosed to the public at least on the website of the competent authority.

11. The Commission shall, by 21 January 2019, adopt delegated acts in accordance with Article 44 to supplement this Regulation by specifying the criteria for the scrutiny of prospectuses, in particular the completeness, comprehensibility and consistency of the information contained therein, and the procedures for the approval of the prospectus.

12. ESMA shall use its powers under Regulation (EU) No 1095/2010 to promote supervisory convergence with regard to the scrutiny and approval processes of competent authorities when assessing the completeness, consistency and comprehensibility of the information contained in a prospectus. To that end, ESMA shall develop guidelines addressed to the competent authorities on the supervision and enforcement with regard to prospectuses, covering the examination of compliance with this Regulation and with any delegated and implementing acts adopted pursuant thereto. In particular, ESMA shall foster convergence regarding the efficiency, methods and timing of the scrutiny by the competent authorities of the information given in a prospectus, using in particular the peer reviews pursuant to paragraph 13.

13. Without prejudice to Article 30 of Regulation (EU) No 1095/2010, ESMA shall organise and conduct at least one peer review of the scrutiny and approval procedures of competent authorities, including notifications of approval between competent authorities. The peer review shall also assess the impact of different approaches with regard to

scrutiny and approval by competent authorities on issuers' ability to raise capital in the Union. The report on the peer review shall be published by 21 July 2022. In the context of the peer review, ESMA shall take into account the opinions or advice from the Securities and Markets Stakeholder Group referred to in Article 37 of Regulation (EU) No 1095/2010.

NOTES

Para 6a: inserted by European Parliament and Council Regulation 2021/337/EU, Art 1(6), as from 18 March 2021.

Application of this Article in relation to the UK: this Article is amended (as follows), in relation to the UK only, by the Prospectus (Amendment etc) (EU Exit) Regulations 2019, SI 2019/1234, reg 48, as from IP completion day (as defined in the European Union (Withdrawal Agreement) Act 2020, s 39); for transitional provisions, see regs 74, 75 of the 2019 Regulations at **[12.165]** et seq—

"In Article 20—

(a) in paragraph 1, omit "relevant";
(b) in paragraph 2, omit the third subparagraph;
(c) in paragraph 6, omit ", including frequent issuers using the notification procedure provided for in Article 26";
(d) in paragraph 7, for "Competent authorities shall provide on their websites" substitute "The competent authority must provide on its website";
(e) omit paragraphs 8 and 9;
(f) in paragraph 10, omit "of the home Member State";
(g) in paragraph 11, for "The Commission shall, by 21 January 2019, adopt delegated acts in accordance with Article 44 to", substitute "The Treasury may by regulations";
(h) omit paragraphs 12 and 13.".

Note also that Regulation 2021/337/EU (which amends this article as noted above) is not "direct EU legislation" within the meaning of the European Union (Withdrawal) Act 2018, s 3 at **[12.5]** and, therefore, the amendment made by it does not apply to the UK.

Delegated Act for the purposes of para 11: see Commission Delegated Regulation 2019/980/EU supplementing Regulation (EU) 2017/1129 of the European Parliament and of the Council as regards the format, content, scrutiny and approval of the prospectus to be published when securities are offered to the public or admitted to trading on a regulated market, and repealing Commission Regulation (EC) No 809/2004 at **[11.648]**.

[11.342]

Article 21 Publication of the prospectus

1. Once approved, the prospectus shall be made available to the public by the issuer, the offeror or the person asking for admission to trading on a regulated market at a reasonable time in advance of, and at the latest at the beginning of, the offer to the public or the admission to trading of the securities involved.

In the case of an initial offer to the public of a class of shares that is admitted to trading on a regulated market for the first time, the prospectus shall be made available to the public at least six working days before the end of the offer.

2. The prospectus, whether a single document or consisting of separate documents, shall be deemed available to the public when published in electronic form on any of the following websites:

(a) the website of the issuer, the offeror or the person asking for admission to trading on a regulated market;
(b) the website of the financial intermediaries placing or selling the securities, including paying agents;
(c) the website of the regulated market where the admission to trading is sought, or where no admission to trading on a regulated market is sought, the website of the operator of the MTF.

3. The prospectus shall be published on a dedicated section of the website which is easily accessible when entering the website. It shall be downloadable, printable and in searchable electronic format that cannot be modified.

The documents containing information incorporated by reference in the prospectus, the supplements and/or final terms related to the prospectus and a separate copy of the summary shall be accessible under the same section alongside the prospectus, including by way of hyperlinks where necessary.

The separate copy of the summary shall clearly indicate the prospectus to which it relates.

4. Access to the prospectus shall not be subject to the completion of a registration process, the acceptance of a disclaimer limiting legal liability or the payment of a fee. Warnings specifying the jurisdiction(s) in which an offer or an admission to trading is being made shall not be considered to be disclaimers limiting legal liability.

5. The competent authority of the home Member State shall publish on its website all the prospectuses approved or at least the list of prospectuses approved, including a hyperlink to the dedicated website sections referred to in paragraph 3 of this Article as well as an identification of the host Member State or States where prospectuses are notified in accordance with Article 25. The published list, including the hyperlinks, shall be kept up-to-date and each item shall remain on the website at least for the period referred to in paragraph 7 of this Article.

At the same time as it notifies ESMA of the approval of a prospectus or of any supplement thereto, the competent authority shall provide ESMA with an electronic copy of the prospectus and any supplement thereto, as well as the data necessary for its classification by ESMA in the storage mechanism referred to in paragraph 6 and for the report referred to in Article 47.

The competent authority of the host Member State shall publish information on all notifications received in accordance with Article 25 on its website.

[5a. An EU Recovery prospectus shall be classified in the storage mechanism referred to in paragraph 6 of this Article. The data used for the classification of prospectuses drawn up in accordance with Article 14 may be used for the classification of EU Recovery prospectuses drawn up in accordance with Article 14a, provided that the two types of prospectuses are differentiated in that storage mechanism.]

6. ESMA shall, without undue delay, publish all prospectuses received from the competent authorities on its website, including any supplements thereto, final terms and related translations where applicable, as well as information on the host Member State(s) where prospectuses are notified in accordance with Article 25. Publication shall be ensured through a storage mechanism providing the public with free of charge access and search functions.

7. All prospectuses approved shall remain publicly available in electronic form for at least 10 years after their publication on the websites referred to in paragraphs 2 and 6.

Where hyperlinks are used for information incorporated by reference in the prospectus, and the supplements and/or final terms related to the prospectus, such hyperlinks shall be functional for the period referred to in the first subparagraph.

8. An approved prospectus shall contain a prominent warning stating when the validity of the prospectus will expire. The warning shall also state that the obligation to supplement a prospectus in the event of significant new factors, material mistakes or material inaccuracies does not apply when a prospectus is no longer valid.

9. In the case of a prospectus comprising several documents and/or incorporating information by reference, the documents and information that constitute the prospectus may be published and distributed separately provided that those documents are made available to the public in accordance with paragraph 2. Where a prospectus consists of separate documents in accordance with Article 10, each of those constituent documents, except for documents incorporated by reference, shall indicate that it is only one part of the prospectus and where the other constituent documents may be obtained.

10. The text and the format of the prospectus, and any supplement to the prospectus made available to the public, shall at all times be identical to the original version approved by the competent authority of the home Member State.

11. A copy of the prospectus on a durable medium shall be delivered to any potential investor, upon request and free of charge, by the issuer, the offeror, the person asking for admission to trading on a regulated market or the financial intermediaries placing or selling the securities. In the event that a potential investor makes a specific demand for a paper copy, the issuer, the offeror, the person asking for admission to trading on a regulated market or a financial intermediary placing or selling the securities shall deliver a printed version of the prospectus. Delivery shall be limited to jurisdictions in which the offer of securities to the public is made or where the admission to trading on a regulated market is taking place under this Regulation.

12. ESMA may, or where the Commission so requests shall, develop draft regulatory technical standards to specify further the requirements relating to the publication of the prospectus.

Power is delegated to the Commission to adopt the regulatory technical standards referred to in the first subparagraph in accordance with Articles 10 to 14 of Regulation (EU) No 1095/2010.

13. ESMA shall develop draft regulatory technical standards to specify the data necessary for the classification of prospectuses referred to in paragraph 5 and the practical arrangements to ensure that such data, including the ISINs of the securities and the LEIs of the issuers, offerors and guarantors, is machine readable.

ESMA shall submit those draft regulatory technical standards to the Commission by 21 July 2018.

Power is delegated to the Commission to adopt the regulatory technical standards referred to in the first subparagraph in accordance with Articles 10 to 14 of Regulation (EU) No 1095/2010.

NOTES

Para 5a: inserted by European Parliament and Council Regulation 2021/337/EU, Art 1(7), as from 18 March 2021.

Application of this Article in relation to the UK: note that substantial amendments have been made to this Article, in relation to the UK only, by the Prospectus (Amendment etc) (EU Exit) Regulations 2019, SI 2019/1234, reg 49, as from IP completion day (as defined in the European Union (Withdrawal Agreement) Act 2020, s 39) (subject to transitional provisions in regs 74, 75 of the 2019 Regulations at **[12.165]** et seq). For ease of reference, the Article as so amended is set out below. Note also that Regulation 2021/337/EU (which amends this article as noted above) is not "direct EU legislation" within the meaning of the European Union (Withdrawal) Act 2018, s 3 at **[12.5]** and, therefore, the amendment made by it does not apply to the UK—

"Article 21 Publication of the prospectus

1. Once approved, the prospectus shall be made available to the public by the issuer, the offeror or the person asking for admission to trading on a regulated market at a reasonable time in advance of, and at the latest at the beginning of, the offer to the public or the admission to trading of the securities involved.

In the case of an initial offer to the public of a class of shares that is admitted to trading on a regulated market for the first time, the prospectus shall be made available to the public at least six working days before the end of the offer.

2. The prospectus, whether a single document or consisting of separate documents, shall be deemed available to the public when published in electronic form on any of the following websites:

(a) the website of the issuer, the offeror or the person asking for admission to trading on a regulated market;

(b) the website of the financial intermediaries placing or selling the securities, including paying agents;

(c) the website of the regulated market where the admission to trading is sought, or where no admission to trading on a regulated market is sought, the website of the operator of the MTF.

3. The prospectus shall be published on a dedicated section of the website which is easily accessible when entering the website. It shall be downloadable, printable and in searchable electronic format that cannot be modified.

The documents containing information incorporated by reference in the prospectus, the supplements and/or final terms related to the prospectus and a separate copy of the summary shall be accessible under the same section alongside the prospectus, including by way of hyperlinks where necessary.

The separate copy of the summary shall clearly indicate the prospectus to which it relates.

4. Access to the prospectus shall not be subject to the completion of a registration process, the acceptance of a disclaimer limiting legal liability or the payment of a fee. Warnings specifying the jurisdiction(s) in which an offer or an admission to trading is being made shall not be considered to be disclaimers limiting legal liability.

5. The competent authority shall publish on its website all the prospectuses approved or at least the list of prospectuses approved, including a hyperlink to the dedicated website sections referred to in paragraph 3 of this Article. The published list, including the hyperlinks, shall be kept up-to-date and each item shall remain on the website at least for the period referred to in paragraph 7 of this Article.

7. All prospectuses approved shall remain publicly available in electronic form for at least 10 years after their publication on the websites referred to in paragraph 2.

Where hyperlinks are used for information incorporated by reference in the prospectus, and the supplements and/or final terms related to the prospectus, such hyperlinks shall be functional for the period referred to in the first subparagraph.

8. An approved prospectus shall contain a prominent warning stating when the validity of the prospectus will expire. The warning shall also state that the obligation to supplement a prospectus in the event of significant new factors, material mistakes or material inaccuracies does not apply when a prospectus is no longer valid.

9. In the case of a prospectus comprising several documents and/or incorporating information by reference, the documents and information that constitute the prospectus may be published and distributed separately provided that those documents are made available to the public in accordance with paragraph 2. Where a prospectus consists of separate documents in accordance with Article 10, each of those constituent documents, except for documents incorporated by reference, shall indicate that it is only one part of the prospectus and where the other constituent documents may be obtained.

10. The text and the format of the prospectus, and any supplement to the prospectus made available to the public, shall at all times be identical to the original version approved by the competent authority.

11. A copy of the prospectus on a durable medium shall be delivered to any potential investor, upon request and free of charge, by the issuer, the offeror, the person asking for admission to trading on a regulated market or the financial intermediaries placing or selling the securities. In the event that a potential investor makes a specific demand for a paper copy, the issuer, the offeror, the person asking for admission to trading on a regulated market or a financial intermediary placing or selling the securities shall deliver a printed version of the prospectus. Delivery shall be limited to jurisdictions in which the offer of securities to the public is made.

12. The FCA may make technical standards to specify further the requirements relating to the publication of the prospectus.

13. The FCA may make technical standards to specify the data necessary for the classification of prospectuses referred to in paragraph 5 and the practical arrangements to ensure that such data, including the ISINs of the securities and the LEIs of the issuers, offerors and guarantors, is machine readable.".

Regulatory technical standards for the purposes of paras 12, 13: see Commission Delegated Regulation 2019/979/EU supplementing Regulation (EU) 2017/1129 of the European Parliament and of the Council with regard to regulatory technical standards on key financial information in the summary of a prospectus, the publication and classification of prospectuses, advertisements for securities, supplements to a prospectus, and the notification portal, and repealing Commission Delegated Regulation (EU) No 382/2014 and Commission Delegated Regulation (EU) 2016/301 at **[11.616]**.

See also Commission Delegated Regulation 2020/1272/EU amending and correcting Delegated Regulation (EU) 2019/979 supplementing Regulation (EU) 2017/1129 of the European Parliament and of the Council with regard to regulatory technical standards on key financial information in the summary of a prospectus, the publication and classification of prospectuses, advertisements for securities, supplements to a prospectus, and the notification portal.

[11.343]

Article 22 Advertisements

1. Any advertisement relating either to an offer of securities to the public or to an admission to trading on a regulated market shall comply with the principles contained in paragraphs 2 to 5. Paragraphs 2 to 4 and point (b) of paragraph 5 shall apply only to cases where the issuer, the offeror or the person asking for admission to trading on a regulated market is subject to the obligation to draw up a prospectus.

2. Advertisements shall state that a prospectus has been or will be published and indicate where investors are or will be able to obtain it.

3. Advertisements shall be clearly recognisable as such. The information contained in an advertisement shall not be inaccurate or misleading and shall be consistent with the information contained in the prospectus, where already published, or with the information required to be in the prospectus, where the prospectus is yet to be published.

4. All information disclosed in an oral or written form concerning the offer of securities to the public or the admission to trading on a regulated market, even where not for advertising purposes, shall be consistent with the information contained in the prospectus.

5. In the event that material information is disclosed by an issuer or an offeror and addressed to one or more selected investors in oral or written form, such information shall, as applicable, either:

(a) be disclosed to all other investors to whom the offer is addressed, in the event that a prospectus is not required to be published in accordance with Article 1(4) or (5); or

(b) be included in the prospectus or in a supplement to the prospectus in accordance with Article 23(1), in the event that a prospectus is required to be published.

6. The competent authority of the Member State where the advertisements are disseminated shall have the power to exercise control over the compliance of advertising activity, relating to an offer of securities to the public or an admission to trading on a regulated market, with paragraphs 2 to 4.

Where necessary, the competent authority of the home Member State shall assist the competent authority of the Member State where the advertisements are disseminated with assessing the consistency of the advertisements with the information in the prospectus.

Without prejudice to Article 32(1), scrutiny of the advertisements by a competent authority shall not constitute a precondition for the offer of securities to the public or the admission to trading to a regulated market to take place in any host Member State.

The use of any of the supervisory and investigatory powers set out in Article 32 in relation to the enforcement of this Article by the competent authority of a host Member State shall be communicated without undue delay to the competent authority of the home Member State of the issuer.

7. Competent authorities of host Member States may only charge fees that are linked to the performance of their supervisory tasks pursuant to this Article. The level of fees shall be disclosed on the websites of the competent authorities. Fees shall be non-discriminatory, reasonable and proportionate to the supervisory task. Competent authorities of host Member States shall not impose any requirements or administrative procedures in addition to those required for the exercise of their supervisory tasks pursuant to this Article.

8. By way of derogation from paragraph 6, any two competent authorities may conclude an agreement whereby, for the purposes of exercising control over compliance of advertising activity in cross-border situations, the competent authority of the home Member State is to retain control over that compliance. Any such agreement shall be notified to ESMA. ESMA shall publish and regularly update a list of such agreements.

9. ESMA shall develop draft regulatory technical standards to specify further the provisions concerning advertisements laid down in paragraphs 2 to 4, including to specify the provisions concerning the dissemination of advertisements and to establish procedures on the cooperation between the competent authorities of the home Member State and of the Member State where the advertisements are disseminated.

ESMA shall submit those draft regulatory technical standards to the Commission by 21 July 2018.

Power is delegated to the Commission to adopt the regulatory technical standards referred to in the first subparagraph in accordance with Articles 10 to 14 of Regulation (EU) No 1095/2010.

10. Pursuant to Article 16 of Regulation (EU) No 1095/2010, ESMA shall develop guidelines and recommendations addressed to competent authorities relating to the control exercised under paragraph 6 of this Article. Those guidelines and recommendations shall take into account the need to ensure that such control does not hamper the functioning of the notification procedure set out in Article 25, while minimising the administrative burdens on issuers making cross-border offers in the Union.

11. This Article is without prejudice to other applicable provisions of Union law.

NOTES

Application of this Article in relation to the UK: this Article is amended (as follows), in relation to the UK only, by the Prospectus (Amendment etc) (EU Exit) Regulations 2019, SI 2019/1234, reg 50, as from IP completion day (as defined in the European Union (Withdrawal Agreement) Act 2020, s 39); for transitional provisions, see regs 74, 75 of the 2019 Regulations at **[12.165]** et seq—

"In Article 22—

(a) in paragraph 6—
- (i) in the first subparagraph, omit "of the Member State where the advertisements are disseminated";
- (ii) omit the second subparagraph;
- (iii) in the third subparagraph—
  - (aa) for "a competent" substitute "the competent";
  - (bb) for "any host Member State" substitute "the United Kingdom";
- (iv) omit the fourth subparagraph;

(b) omit paragraphs 7 and 8;

(c) for paragraph 9 substitute—

9. The FCA may make technical standards to specify further the provisions concerning advertisements laid down in paragraphs 2 to 4, including to specify the provisions concerning the dissemination of advertisements.";

(d) omit paragraph 10;

(e) in paragraph 11, for "Union law" substitute "the law of the United Kingdom"."

Regulatory technical standards for the purposes of para 9: see Commission Delegated Regulation 2019/979/EU supplementing Regulation (EU) 2017/1129 of the European Parliament and of the Council with regard to regulatory technical standards on key financial information in the summary of a prospectus, the publication and classification of prospectuses, advertisements for securities, supplements to a prospectus, and the notification portal, and repealing Commission Delegated Regulation (EU) No 382/2014 and Commission Delegated Regulation (EU) 2016/301 at **[11.616]**.

[11.344]

Article 23 Supplements to the prospectus

1. Every significant new factor, material mistake or material inaccuracy relating to the information included in a prospectus which may affect the assessment of the securities and which arises or is noted between the time when the prospectus is approved and the closing of the offer period or the time when trading on a regulated market begins, whichever occurs later, shall be mentioned in a supplement to the prospectus without undue delay.

Such a supplement shall be approved in the same way as a prospectus in a maximum of five working days and published in accordance with at least the same arrangements as were applied when the original prospectus was published in accordance with Article 21. The summary, and any translations thereof, shall also be supplemented, where necessary, to take into account the new information included in the supplement.

2. Where the prospectus relates to an offer of securities to the public, investors who have already agreed to purchase or subscribe for the securities before the supplement is published shall have the right, exercisable within two working days after the publication of the supplement, to withdraw their acceptances, provided that the significant new factor, material mistake or material inaccuracy referred to in paragraph 1 arose or was noted before the closing of the offer period or the delivery of the securities, whichever occurs first. That period may be extended by the issuer or the offeror. The final date of the right of withdrawal shall be stated in the supplement.

The supplement shall contain a prominent statement concerning the right of withdrawal, which clearly states:

(a) that a right of withdrawal is only granted to those investors who had already agreed to purchase or subscribe for the securities before the supplement was published and where the securities had not yet been delivered to the investors at the time when the significant new factor, material mistake or material inaccuracy arose or was noted;

(b) the period in which investors can exercise their right of withdrawal; and

(c) whom investors may contact should they wish to exercise the right of withdrawal.

[2a. By way of derogation from paragraph 2, from 18 March 2021 to 31 December 2022, where the prospectus relates to an offer of securities to the public, investors who have already agreed to purchase or subscribe for the securities before the supplement is published shall have the right, exercisable within three working days after the publication of the supplement, to withdraw their acceptances, provided that the significant new factor, material mistake or material inaccuracy referred to in paragraph 1 arose or was noted before the closing of the offer period or the delivery of the securities, whichever occurs first. That period may be extended by the issuer or the offeror. The final date of the right of withdrawal shall be stated in the supplement.

The supplement shall contain a prominent statement concerning the right of withdrawal, which clearly states:

(a) that a right of withdrawal is only granted to those investors who had already agreed to purchase or subscribe for the securities before the supplement was published and where the securities had not yet been delivered to the investors at the time when the significant new factor, material mistake or material inaccuracy arose or was noted;

(b) the period in which investors can exercise their right of withdrawal; and

(c) whom investors may contact should they wish to exercise the right of withdrawal.]

3. Where the securities are purchased or subscribed through a financial intermediary, that financial intermediary shall inform investors of the possibility of a supplement being published, where and when it would be published and that the financial intermediary would assist them in exercising their right to withdraw acceptances in such case.

The financial intermediary shall contact investors on the day when the supplement is published. Where the securities are purchased or subscribed directly from the issuer, that issuer shall inform investors of the possibility of a supplement being published and where it would be published and that in such case, they could have a right to withdraw the acceptance.

[3a. By way of derogation from paragraph 3, from 18 March 2021 to 31 December 2022, where investors purchase or subscribe securities through a financial intermediary between the time when the prospectus for those securities is approved and the closing of the initial offer period, that financial intermediary shall inform those investors of the possibility of a supplement being published, where and when it would be published and that the financial intermediary would assist them in exercising their right to withdraw acceptances in such a case.

Where the investors referred to in the first subparagraph of this paragraph have the right of withdrawal referred to in paragraph 2a, the financial intermediary shall contact those investors by the end of the first working day following that on which the supplement is published.

Where the securities are purchased or subscribed directly from the issuer, that issuer shall inform investors of the possibility of a supplement being published and where it would be published and that, in such a case, they could have a right to withdraw the acceptance.]

4. Where the issuer prepares a supplement concerning information in the base prospectus that relates to only one or several individual issues, the right of investors to withdraw their acceptances pursuant to paragraph 2 shall only apply to the relevant issue(s) and not to any other issue of securities under the base prospectus.

5. In the event that the significant new factor, material mistake or material inaccuracy referred to in paragraph 1 concerns only the information contained in a registration document or a universal registration document and that registration document or universal registration document is simultaneously used as a constituent part of several prospectuses, only one supplement shall be drawn up and approved. In that case, the supplement shall mention all the prospectuses to which it relates.

6. When scrutinising a supplement before approval, the competent authority may request that the supplement contains a consolidated version of the supplemented prospectus, registration document or universal registration document in an annex, where such consolidated version is necessary to ensure comprehensibility of the information given in the prospectus. Such a request shall be deemed to be a request for supplementary information under Article 20(4). An issuer may in any event voluntarily include a consolidated version of the supplemented prospectus, registration document or universal registration document in an annex to the supplement.

7. ESMA shall develop draft regulatory technical standards to specify situations where a significant new factor, material mistake or material inaccuracy relating to the information included in the prospectus requires a supplement to the prospectus to be published.

ESMA shall submit those draft regulatory technical standards to the Commission by 21 July 2018.

Power is delegated to the Commission to adopt the regulatory technical standards referred to in the first subparagraph in accordance with Articles 10 to 14 of Regulation (EU) No 1095/2010.

NOTES

Paras 2a, 3a: inserted by European Parliament and Council Regulation 2021/337/EU, Art 1(8), as from 18 March 2021.

Application of this Article in relation to the UK: this Article is amended (as follows), in relation to the UK only, by the Prospectus (Amendment etc) (EU Exit) Regulations 2019, SI 2019/1234, reg 51, as from IP completion day (as defined in the European Union (Withdrawal Agreement) Act 2020, s 39); for transitional provisions, see regs 74, 75 of the 2019 Regulations at **[12.165]** et seq—

"In Article 23—

(a) in paragraph 1, in the second subparagraph, omit ", and any translations thereof,";

(b) in paragraph 7—

(i) in the first subparagraph, for "ESMA shall develop draft regulatory" substitute "The FCA may make";

(ii) omit the second and third subparagraphs.".

Note also that Regulation 2021/337/EU (which amends this article as noted above) is not "direct EU legislation" within the meaning of the European Union (Withdrawal) Act 2018, s 3 at **[12.5]** and, therefore, the amendments made by it do not apply to the UK.

Regulatory technical standards for the purposes of para 7: see Commission Delegated Regulation 2019/979/EU supplementing Regulation (EU) 2017/1129 of the European Parliament and of the Council with regard to regulatory technical standards on key financial information in the summary of a prospectus, the publication and classification of prospectuses, advertisements for securities, supplements to a prospectus, and the notification portal, and repealing Commission Delegated Regulation (EU) No 382/2014 and Commission Delegated Regulation (EU) 2016/301 at **[11.616]**.

See also Commission Delegated Regulation 2020/1272/EU amending and correcting Delegated Regulation (EU) 2019/979 supplementing Regulation (EU) 2017/1129 of the European Parliament and of the Council with regard to regulatory technical standards on key financial information in the summary of a prospectus, the publication and classification of prospectuses, advertisements for securities, supplements to a prospectus, and the notification portal.

CHAPTER V CROSS-BORDER OFFERS AND ADMISSIONS TO TRADING ON A REGULATED MARKET AND USE OF LANGUAGES

[11.345]

Article 24 Union scope of approvals of prospectuses

1. Without prejudice to Article 37, where an offer of securities to the public or admission to trading on a regulated market occurs in one or more Member States, or in a Member State other than the home Member State, the prospectus approved by the home Member State and any supplements thereto shall be valid for the offer to the public or the admission to trading in any number of host Member States, provided that ESMA and the competent authority of each host Member State are notified in accordance with Article 25. Competent authorities of host Member States shall not undertake any approval or administrative procedures relating to prospectuses and supplements approved by the competent authorities of other Member States, and relating to final terms.

2. Where a significant new factor, material mistake or material inaccuracy arises or is noted within the timeframe specified in Article 23(1), the competent authority of the home Member State shall require that the publication of a supplement be approved in accordance with Article 20(1). ESMA and the competent authority of the host Member State may inform the competent authority of the home Member State of the need for new information.

NOTES

Repeal of this Article in relation to the UK: this Article is repealed, in relation to the UK only, by the Prospectus (Amendment etc) (EU Exit) Regulations 2019, SI 2019/1234, reg 52, as from IP completion day (as defined in the European Union (Withdrawal Agreement) Act 2020, s 39); for transitional provisions, see regs 74, 75 of the 2019 Regulations at **[12.165]** et seq.

[11.346]

Article 25 Notification of prospectuses and supplements and communication of final terms

1. The competent authority of the home Member State shall, at the request of the issuer, the offeror, the person asking for admission to trading on a regulated market or the person responsible for drawing up the prospectus and within one working day following receipt of that request or, where the request is submitted together with the draft prospectus, within one working day following the approval of the prospectus, notify the competent authority of the host Member State with a certificate of approval attesting that the prospectus has been drawn up in accordance with this Regulation and with an electronic copy of that prospectus.

Where applicable, the notification referred to in the first subparagraph shall be accompanied by a translation of the prospectus and any summary, produced under the responsibility of the issuer, the offeror, the person asking for admission to trading on a regulated market or the person responsible for drawing up the prospectus.

The same procedure shall be followed for any supplement to the prospectus.

The issuer, the offeror, the person asking for admission to trading on a regulated market or the person responsible for drawing up the prospectus shall be notified of the certificate of approval at the same time as the competent authority of the host Member State.

2. Any application of the provisions of Article 18(1) and (2) shall be stated in the certificate of approval, as well as its justification.

3. The competent authority of the home Member State shall notify ESMA of the certificate of approval of the prospectus or any supplement thereto at the same time as it is notified to the competent authority of the host Member State.

4. Where the final terms of a base prospectus which has been previously notified are neither included in the base prospectus, nor in a supplement, the competent authority of the home Member State shall communicate them electronically to the competent authority of the host Member State(s) and to ESMA as soon as practicable after they are filed.

5. No fee shall be charged by competent authorities for the notification, or receipt of notification, of prospectuses and supplements thereto, or any related supervisory activity, whether in the home Member State or in the host Member State(s).

6. ESMA shall establish a notification portal into which each competent authority shall upload the certificates of approval and electronic copies referred to in paragraph 1 of this Article and in Article 26(2), and the final terms of base prospectuses, for the purpose of the notifications and communications referred to in paragraphs 1, 3 and 4 of this Article and in Article 26.

All transfers of those documents between competent authorities shall take place through that notification portal.

7. ESMA shall develop draft regulatory technical standards to specify the technical arrangements necessary for the functioning of the notification portal referred to in paragraph 6.

ESMA shall submit those draft regulatory technical standards to the Commission by 21 July 2018.

Power is delegated to the Commission to adopt the regulatory technical standards referred to in the first subparagraph in accordance with Articles 10 to 14 of Regulation (EU) No 1095/2010.

8. In order to ensure uniform conditions of application of this Regulation and to take account of technical developments on financial markets, ESMA may develop draft implementing technical standards to establish standard forms, templates and procedures for the notification of the certificate of approval, the prospectus, any supplement thereto and the translation of the prospectus and/or summary.

Power is conferred on the Commission to adopt the implementing technical standards referred to in the first subparagraph in accordance with Article 15 of Regulation (EU) No 1095/2010.

NOTES

Repeal of this Article in relation to the UK: this Article is repealed, in relation to the UK only, by the Prospectus (Amendment etc) (EU Exit) Regulations 2019, SI 2019/1234, reg 52, as from IP completion day (as defined in the European Union (Withdrawal Agreement) Act 2020, s 39); for transitional provisions, see regs 74, 75 of the 2019 Regulations at **[12.165]** et seq.

Regulatory technical standards for the purposes of para 7: see Commission Delegated Regulation 2019/979/EU supplementing Regulation (EU) 2017/1129 of the European Parliament and of the Council with regard to regulatory technical standards on key financial information in the summary of a prospectus, the publication and classification of prospectuses, advertisements for securities, supplements to a prospectus, and the notification portal, and repealing Commission Delegated Regulation (EU) No 382/2014 and Commission Delegated Regulation (EU) 2016/301 at **[11.616]**.

[11.347]

Article 26 Notification of registration documents or universal registration documents

1. This Article shall only apply to issues of non-equity securities referred to in point (m)(ii) of Article 2 and to issuers established in a third country referred to in point (m)(iii) of Article 2, where the home Member State chosen for the prospectus approval pursuant to those provisions is different from the Member State whose competent authority has approved the registration document or universal registration document drawn up by the issuer, the offeror or the person asking for admission to trading on a regulated market.

2. A competent authority that has approved a registration document, or a universal registration document and any amendments thereto, shall, at the request of the issuer, the offeror, the person asking for admission to trading on a regulated market or the person responsible for drawing up such document, notify the competent authority of the home Member State for the prospectus approval with a certificate of approval attesting that the registration document, or universal registration document and any amendments thereto, has been drawn up in accordance with this Regulation and with an electronic copy of that document. That notification shall be made within one working day following receipt of the request or, where the request is submitted together with the draft registration document or draft universal registration document, within one working day following the approval of that document.

Where applicable, the notification referred to in the first subparagraph shall be accompanied by a translation of the registration document, or universal registration document and any amendments thereto, produced under the responsibility of the issuer, the offeror, the person asking for admission to trading on a regulated market or the person responsible for drawing up such documents.

The issuer, the offeror, the person asking for admission to trading on a regulated market or the person responsible for drawing up the registration document, or the universal registration document and any amendments thereto, shall be notified of the certificate of approval at the same time as the competent authority of the home Member State for the prospectus approval.

Any application of the provisions of Article 18(1) and (2) shall be stated in the certificate, as well as its justification.

The competent authority that has approved the registration document, or the universal registration document and any amendments thereto, shall notify ESMA of the certificate of approval of those documents at the same time as it is notified to the competent authority of the home Member State for the prospectus approval.

No fee shall be charged by those competent authorities for the notification, or receipt of notification, of registration documents, or universal registration documents and any amendments thereto, or any related supervisory activity.

3. A registration document or universal registration document notified pursuant to paragraph 2 may be used as a constituent part of a prospectus submitted for approval to the competent authority of the home Member State for the prospectus approval.

The competent authority of the home Member State for the prospectus approval shall not undertake any scrutiny nor approval relating to the notified registration document, or universal registration document and any amendments thereto, and shall approve only the securities note and the summary, and only after receipt of the notification.

4. A registration document or a universal registration document notified pursuant to paragraph 2 shall contain an appendix setting out the key information on the issuer referred to in Article 7(6). The approval of the registration document or universal registration document shall encompass the appendix.

Where applicable pursuant to the second subparagraph of Article 27(2) and the second subparagraph of Article 27(3), the notification shall be accompanied by a translation of the appendix to the registration document or universal registration document produced under the responsibility of the issuer, offeror or person responsible for drawing up the registration document or the universal registration document.

When drawing up the summary, the issuer, offeror or person responsible for drawing up the prospectus shall reproduce the content of the appendix without any changes in the section referred to in point (b) of Article 7(4). The competent authority of the home Member State for the prospectus approval shall not scrutinise that section of the summary.

5. Where a significant new factor, material mistake or material inaccuracy arises or is noted within the timeframe specified in Article 23(1) and relates to the information contained in the registration document or the universal registration document, the supplement required pursuant to Article 23 shall be submitted for approval to the competent authority which approved the registration document or the universal registration document. That supplement shall be notified to the competent authority of the home Member State for the prospectus approval within one working day following its approval, under the procedure set out in paragraphs 2 and 3 of this Article.

Where a registration document or a universal registration document is simultaneously used as a constituent part of several prospectuses, as provided for in Article 23(5), the supplement shall be notified to each competent authority which has approved such prospectuses.

6. In order to ensure uniform conditions of application of this Regulation and to take account of technical developments on financial markets, ESMA may develop draft implementing technical standards to establish standard forms, templates and procedures for the notification of the certificate of approval relating to the registration document, the universal registration document, any supplement thereto and the translation thereof.

Power is conferred on the Commission to adopt the implementing technical standards referred to in the first subparagraph in accordance with Article 15 of Regulation (EU) No 1095/2010.

NOTES

Repeal of this Article in relation to the UK: this Article is repealed, in relation to the UK only, by the Prospectus (Amendment etc) (EU Exit) Regulations 2019, SI 2019/1234, reg 52, as from IP completion day (as defined in the European Union (Withdrawal Agreement) Act 2020, s 39); for transitional provisions, see regs 74, 75 of the 2019 Regulations at **[12.165]** et seq.

[11.348]

Article 27 Use of language

1. Where an offer of securities to the public is made or admission to trading on a regulated market is sought only in the home Member State, the prospectus shall be drawn up in a language accepted by the competent authority of the home Member State.

Part 11 EU & Retained EU Legislation

2. Where an offer of securities to the public is made or admission to trading on a regulated market is sought in one or more Member States excluding the home Member State, the prospectus shall be drawn up either in a language accepted by the competent authorities of those Member States or in a language customary in the sphere of international finance, at the choice of the issuer, the offeror or the person asking for admission to trading on a regulated market.

The competent authority of each host Member State shall require that the summary referred to in Article 7 be available in its official language, or at least one of its official languages, or in another language accepted by the competent authority of that Member State, but it shall not require the translation of any other part of the prospectus.

For the purpose of the scrutiny and approval by the competent authority of the home Member State, the prospectus shall be drawn up either in a language accepted by that authority or in a language customary in the sphere of international finance, at the choice of the issuer, the offeror or the person asking for admission to trading on a regulated market.

3. Where an offer of securities to the public is made or an admission to trading on a regulated market is sought in more than one Member State including the home Member State, the prospectus shall be drawn up in a language accepted by the competent authority of the home Member State, and shall also be made available either in a language accepted by the competent authorities of each host Member State or in a language customary in the sphere of international finance, at the choice of the issuer, the offeror, or the person asking for admission to trading on a regulated market.

The competent authority of each host Member State shall require that the summary referred to in Article 7 be available in its official language or at least one of its official languages, or in another language accepted by the competent authority of that Member State, but it shall not require the translation of any other part of the prospectus.

4. The final terms and the summary of the individual issue shall be drawn up in the same language as the language of the approved base prospectus.

When, in accordance with Article 25(4), the final terms are communicated to the competent authority of the host Member State or, if there is more than one host Member State, to the competent authorities of the host Member States, the following language rules shall apply to the final terms and the summary annexed thereto:

- *(a) the summary of the individual issue annexed to the final terms shall be available in the official language or at least one of the official languages of the host Member State, or in another language accepted by the competent authority of the host Member State in accordance with the second subparagraph of paragraph 2 or the second subparagraph of paragraph 3, as applicable;*
- *(b) where the base prospectus is to be translated pursuant to paragraph 2 or 3, as applicable, the final terms and the summary of the individual issue annexed thereto, shall be subject to the same translation requirements as the base prospectus.*

5. Where a prospectus relates to the admission to trading on a regulated market of non-equity securities and admission to trading on a regulated market is sought in one or more Member States, the prospectus shall be drawn up either in a language accepted by the competent authorities of the home and host Member States or in a language customary in the sphere of international finance, at the choice of the issuer, the offeror or the person asking for admission to trading on a regulated market, provided that either:

- *(a) such securities are to be traded only on a regulated market, or a specific segment thereof, to which only qualified investors can have access for the purposes of trading such securities; or*
- *(b) such securities have a denomination per unit of at least EUR 100,000.*

NOTES

Repeal of this Article in relation to the UK: this Article is repealed, in relation to the UK only, by the Prospectus (Amendment etc) (EU Exit) Regulations 2019, SI 2019/1234, reg 52, as from IP completion day (as defined in the European Union (Withdrawal Agreement) Act 2020, s 39); for transitional provisions, see regs 74, 75 of the 2019 Regulations at **[12.165]** et seq.

CHAPTER VI SPECIFIC RULES IN RELATION TO ISSUERS ESTABLISHED IN THIRD COUNTRIES

[11.349]

Article 28 Offer of securities to the public or admission to trading on a regulated market made under a prospectus drawn up in accordance with this Regulation

Where a third country issuer intends to offer securities to the public in the Union or to seek admission to trading of securities on a regulated market established in the Union under a prospectus drawn up in accordance with this Regulation, it shall obtain approval of its prospectus, in accordance with Article 20, from the competent authority of its home Member State.

Once a prospectus is approved in accordance with the first subparagraph, it shall entail all the rights and obligations provided for a prospectus under this Regulation and the prospectus and the third country issuer shall be subject to all of the provisions of this Regulation under the supervision of the competent authority of the home Member State.

NOTES

Application of this Article in relation to the UK: this Article is amended (as follows), in relation to the UK only, by the Prospectus (Amendment etc) (EU Exit) Regulations 2019, SI 2019/1234, reg 53, as from IP completion day (as defined in the European Union (Withdrawal Agreement) Act 2020, s 39); for transitional provisions, see regs 74, 75 of the 2019 Regulations at **[12.165]** et seq—

"In Article 28—

- (a) in the first subparagraph—
  - (i) for "Union", in both places it occurs, substitute "United Kingdom";
  - (ii) omit "of its home Member State";
- (b) in the second subparagraph, omit "of the home Member State".".

[11.350]

Article 29 Offer of securities to the public or admission to trading on a regulated market made under a prospectus drawn up in accordance with the laws of a third country

1. The competent authority of the home Member State of a third country issuer may approve a prospectus for an offer of securities to the public or for admission to trading on a regulated market, drawn up in accordance with, and which is subject to, the national laws of the third country issuer, provided that:

(a) the information requirements imposed by those third country laws are equivalent to the requirements under this Regulation; and

(b) the competent authority of the home Member State has concluded cooperation arrangements with the relevant supervisory authorities of the third country issuer in accordance with Article 30.

2. In the case of an offer to the public or admission to trading on a regulated market of securities issued by a third country issuer, in a Member State other than the home Member State, the requirements set out in Articles 24, 25 and 27 shall apply.

3. The Commission is empowered to adopt delegated acts in accordance with Article 44 to supplement this Regulation by establishing general equivalence criteria, based on the requirements laid down in Articles 6, 7, 8 and 13.

On the basis of the above criteria, the Commission may adopt an implementing decision stating that the information requirements imposed by the national law of a third country are equivalent to the requirements under this Regulation. Such implementing decision shall be adopted in accordance with the examination procedure referred to in Article 45(2).

NOTES

Application of this Article in relation to the UK: this Article is amended (as follows), in relation to the UK only, by the Prospectus (Amendment etc) (EU Exit) Regulations 2019, SI 2019/1234, reg 54, as from IP completion day (as defined in the European Union (Withdrawal Agreement) Act 2020, s 39); for transitional provisions, see regs 74, 75 of the 2019 Regulations at **[12.165]** et seq—

"In Article 29—

(a) in paragraph 1—

(i) in the opening words, omit "of the home Member state of a third country issuer";

(ii) in point (b), omit "of the home Member State";

(b) omit paragraph 2;

(c) in paragraph 3—

(i) in the first subparagraph, for "The Commission is empowered to adopt delegated acts in accordance with Article 44 to" substitute "The Treasury may by regulations";

(ii) in the second subparagraph—

(aa) for "the Commission may adopt an implementing decision stating" substitute "the Treasury may by regulations state";

(bb) omit the last sentence.".

[11.351]

Article 30 Cooperation with third countries

1. For the purpose of Article 29 and, where deemed necessary, for the purpose of Article 28, the competent authorities of Member States shall conclude cooperation arrangements with supervisory authorities of third countries concerning the exchange of information with supervisory authorities in third countries and the enforcement of obligations arising under this Regulation in third countries unless that third country, in accordance with a delegated act in force adopted by the Commission pursuant to Article 9 of Directive (EU) 2015/849 of the European Parliament and of the Council,[1] is on the list of jurisdictions which have strategic deficiencies in their national anti-money laundering and countering the financing of terrorism regimes that pose significant threats to the financial system of the Union. Those cooperation arrangements shall ensure at least an efficient exchange of information that allows the competent authorities to carry out their duties under this Regulation.

A competent authority shall inform ESMA and the other competent authorities where it proposes to enter into such an arrangement.

2. For the purpose of Article 29 and, where deemed necessary, for the purpose of Article 28, ESMA shall facilitate and coordinate the development of cooperation arrangements between the competent authorities and the relevant supervisory authorities of third countries.

ESMA shall also, where necessary, facilitate and coordinate the exchange between competent authorities of information obtained from supervisory authorities of third countries that may be relevant to the taking of measures under Articles 38 and 39.

3. The competent authorities shall conclude cooperation arrangements on exchange of information with the supervisory authorities of third countries only where the information disclosed is subject to guarantees of professional secrecy which are at least equivalent to those set out in Article 35. Such exchange of information must be intended for the performance of the tasks of those competent authorities.

4. ESMA may, or where the Commission so requests shall, develop draft regulatory technical standards to determine the minimum content of the cooperation arrangements referred to in paragraph 1 and the template document to be used therefor.

Power is delegated to the Commission to adopt the regulatory technical standards referred to in the first subparagraph in accordance with Articles 10 to 14 of Regulation (EU) No 1095/2010.

NOTES

Application of this Article in relation to the UK: this Article is amended (as follows), in relation to the UK only, by the Prospectus (Amendment etc) (EU Exit) Regulations 2019, SI 2019/1234, reg 55, as from IP completion day (as defined in the European Union (Withdrawal Agreement) Act 2020, s 39); for transitional provisions, see regs 74, 75 of the 2019 Regulations at **[12.165]** et seq—

"In Article 30—

(a) for paragraph 1, substitute—

1. For the purpose of Article 29 and, where deemed necessary, for the purpose of Article 28, the competent authority shall conclude cooperation arrangements with supervisory authorities of third countries concerning the exchange of information with supervisory authorities in third countries and the enforcement of obligations arising under this Regulation in third countries unless that third country is a high-risk third country within the meaning of regulation 33 of the Money Laundering, Terrorist Financing and Transfer of Funds (Information on the Payer) Regulations 2017. Those cooperation arrangements shall at least ensure an efficient exchange of information that allows the competent authority to carry out its duties under this Regulation.";

(b) omit paragraph 2;
(c) in paragraph 3—
  (i) for "The competent authorities" substitute "The competent authority";
  (ii) for "those competent authorities" substitute "the competent authority";
(d) in paragraph 4—
  (i) in the first subparagraph, for "ESMA may, or where the Commission so requests shall, develop draft regulatory" substitute "The FCA may make";
  (ii) omit the second subparagraph.".

[1] Directive (EU) 2015/849 of the European Parliament and of the Council of 20 May 2015 on the prevention of the use of the financial system for the purposes of money laundering or terrorist financing, amending Regulation (EU) No 648/2012 of the European Parliament and of the Council, and repealing Directive 2005/60/EC of the European Parliament and of the Council and Commission Directive 2006/70/EC (OJ L141, 5.6.2015, p 73).

CHAPTER VII ESMA AND COMPETENT AUTHORITIES

NOTES

Application in relation to the UK: the preceding Chapter heading is amended (as follows), in relation to the UK only, by the Prospectus (Amendment etc) (EU Exit) Regulations 2019, SI 2019/1234, reg 56, as from IP completion day (as defined in the European Union (Withdrawal Agreement) Act 2020, s 39); for transitional provisions, see regs 74, 75 of the 2019 Regulations at **[12.165]** et seq—

"For the heading of Chapter 7, substitute "The competent authority".".

[11.352]

Article 31 Competent authorities

1. Each Member State shall designate a single competent administrative authority responsible for carrying out the duties resulting from this Regulation and for ensuring that the provisions of this Regulation are applied. Member States shall inform the Commission, ESMA and the competent authorities of other Member States accordingly.

The competent authority shall be independent from market participants.

2. Member States may allow their competent authority to delegate to third parties the tasks of electronic publication of approved prospectuses and related documents.

Any such delegation of tasks shall be made in a specific decision setting out the following:

(a) the tasks to be undertaken and the conditions under which they are to be carried out;

(b) a clause obliging the third party in question to act and be organised in such a manner as to avoid conflicts of interest and to ensure that information obtained while carrying out the delegated tasks is not used unfairly or to prevent competition; and

(c) all arrangements entered into between the competent authority and the third party to which tasks are delegated.

The final responsibility for supervising compliance with this Regulation and for approving the prospectus shall lie with the competent authority designated in accordance with paragraph 1.

The Member States shall inform the Commission, ESMA and the competent authorities of other Member States of any decision to delegate tasks as referred to in the second subparagraph, including the precise conditions regulating such delegation.

3. Paragraphs 1 and 2 are without prejudice to the possibility for a Member State to make separate legal and administrative arrangements for overseas European territories for whose external relations that Member State is responsible.

NOTES

Repeal of this Article in relation to the UK: this Article is repealed, in relation to the UK only, by the Prospectus (Amendment etc) (EU Exit) Regulations 2019, SI 2019/1234, reg 57, as from IP completion day (as defined in the European Union (Withdrawal Agreement) Act 2020, s 39); for transitional provisions, see regs 74, 75 of the 2019 Regulations at **[12.165]** et seq.

[11.353]

Article 32 Powers of competent authorities

1. In order to fulfil their duties under this Regulation, competent authorities shall have, in accordance with national law, at least the following supervisory and investigatory powers:

(a) to require issuers, offerors or persons asking for admission to trading on a regulated market to include in the prospectus supplementary information, where necessary for investor protection;

(b) to require issuers, offerors or persons asking for admission to trading on a regulated market, and the persons that control them or are controlled by them, to provide information and documents;

(c) to require auditors and managers of the issuer, offeror or person asking for admission to trading on a regulated market, as well as financial intermediaries commissioned to carry out the offer of securities to the public or ask for admission to trading on a regulated market, to provide information;

(d) to suspend an offer of securities to the public or admission to trading on a regulated market for a maximum of 10 consecutive working days on any single occasion where there are reasonable grounds for suspecting that this Regulation has been infringed;

(e) to prohibit or suspend advertisements or require issuers, offerors or persons asking for admission to trading on a regulated market, or relevant financial intermediaries to cease or suspend advertisements for a maximum of 10 consecutive working days on any single occasion where there are reasonable grounds for believing that this Regulation has been infringed;
(f) to prohibit an offer of securities to the public or admission to trading on a regulated market where they find that this Regulation has been infringed or where there are reasonable grounds for suspecting that it would be infringed;
(g) to suspend or require the relevant regulated markets, MTFs or OTFs to suspend trading on a regulated market, an MTF or an OTF for a maximum of 10 consecutive working days on any single occasion where there are reasonable grounds for believing that this Regulation has been infringed;
(h) to prohibit trading on a regulated market, an MTF or an OTF where they find that this Regulation has been infringed;
(i) to make public the fact that an issuer, an offeror or a person asking for admission to trading on a regulated market is failing to comply with its obligations;
(j) to suspend the scrutiny of a prospectus submitted for approval or suspend or restrict an offer of securities to the public or admission to trading on a regulated market where the competent authority is making use of the power to impose a prohibition or restriction pursuant to Article 42 of Regulation (EU) No 600/2014 of the European Parliament and of the Council,[1] until such prohibition or restriction has ceased;
(k) to refuse approval of any prospectus drawn up by a certain issuer, offeror or person asking for admission to trading on a regulated market for a maximum of five years, where that issuer, offeror or person asking for admission to trading on a regulated market has repeatedly and severely infringed this Regulation;
(l) to disclose, or to require the issuer to disclose, all material information which may have an effect on the assessment of the securities offered to the public or admitted to trading on a regulated market in order to ensure investor protection or the smooth operation of the market;
(m) to suspend or require the relevant regulated market, MTF or OTF to suspend the securities from trading where it considers that the issuer's situation is such that trading would be detrimental to investors' interests;
(n) to carry out on-site inspections or investigations at sites other than the private residences of natural persons, and for that purpose to enter premises in order to access documents and other data in any form, where a reasonable suspicion exists that documents and other data related to the subject-matter of the inspection or investigation may be relevant to prove an infringement of this Regulation.

Where necessary under national law, the competent authority may ask the relevant judicial authority to decide on the use of the powers referred to in the first subparagraph.

In the event that approval of a prospectus has been refused pursuant to point (k) of the first subparagraph, the competent authority shall inform ESMA thereof, which shall then inform the competent authorities of other Member States.

In accordance with Article 21 of Regulation (EU) No 1095/2010, ESMA shall be entitled to participate in on-site inspections referred to in point (n) of the first subparagraph where those inspections are carried out jointly by two or more competent authorities.

2. Competent authorities shall exercise their functions and powers referred to in paragraph 1 in any of the following ways:
(a) directly;
(b) in collaboration with other authorities;
(c) under their responsibility by delegation to such authorities;
(d) by application to the competent judicial authorities.

3. Member States shall ensure that appropriate measures are in place so that competent authorities have all the supervisory and investigatory powers that are necessary to fulfil their duties.

4. This Regulation is without prejudice to laws and regulations on takeover bids, merger transactions and other transactions affecting the ownership or control of companies that transpose Directive 2004/25/EC and that impose requirements in addition to the requirements of this Regulation.

5. A person making information available to the competent authority in accordance with this Regulation shall not be considered to be infringing any restriction on disclosure of information imposed by contract or by any legislative, regulatory or administrative provision, and shall not be subject to liability of any kind related to such notification.

6. Paragraphs 1 to 3 are without prejudice to the possibility for a Member State to make separate legal and administrative arrangements for overseas European territories for whose external relations that Member State is responsible.

NOTES

Application of this Article in relation to the UK: this Article is amended (as follows), in relation to the UK only, by the Prospectus (Amendment etc) (EU Exit) Regulations 2019, SI 2019/1234, reg 58, as from IP completion day (as defined in the European Union (Withdrawal Agreement) Act 2020, s 39); for transitional provisions, see regs 74, 75 of the 2019 Regulations at **[12.165]** et seq—

"In Article 32—
(a) in the heading, for "competent authorities" substitute "the competent authority";
(b) omit paragraphs 1 to 3;
(c) in paragraph 4—
(i) for "laws and regulations" substitute "the law of the United Kingdom";
(ii) for "that transpose" substitute "which implemented";
(d) omit paragraph 6.".

[1] Regulation (EU) No 600/2014 of the European Parliament and of the Council of 15 May 2014 on markets in financial instruments and amending Regulation (EU) No 648/2012 (OJ L173, 12.6.2014, p 84).

[11.354]

Article 33 Cooperation between competent authorities

1. Competent authorities shall cooperate with each other and with ESMA for the purposes of this Regulation. They shall exchange information without undue delay and cooperate in investigation, supervision and enforcement activities.

Where Member States have chosen, in accordance with Article 38, to lay down criminal sanctions for infringements of this Regulation, they shall ensure that appropriate measures are in place so that competent authorities have all the necessary powers to liaise with judicial authorities within their jurisdiction to receive specific information related to criminal investigations or proceedings commenced for possible infringements of this Regulation and provide the same to other competent authorities and ESMA to fulfil their obligation to cooperate with each other and ESMA for the purposes of this Regulation.

2. A competent authority may refuse to act on a request for information or a request to cooperate with an investigation only in any of the following exceptional circumstances:

(a) where complying with the request is likely to adversely affect its own investigation, enforcement activities or a criminal investigation;

(b) where judicial proceedings have already been initiated in respect of the same actions and against the same persons before the authorities of the Member State addressed;

(c) where a final judgment has already been delivered in relation to such persons for the same actions in the Member State addressed.

3. Competent authorities shall, on request, immediately supply any information required for the purposes of this Regulation.

4. The competent authority may request assistance from the competent authority of another Member State with regard to on-site inspections or investigations.

A requesting competent authority shall inform ESMA of any request referred to in the first subparagraph. In the case of an on-site inspection or investigation with cross-border effect, ESMA shall, where requested to do so by one of the competent authorities, coordinate the inspection or investigation.

Where a competent authority receives a request from a competent authority of another Member State to carry out an on-site inspection or an investigation, it may do any of the following:

(a) carry out the on-site inspection or investigation itself;

(b) allow the competent authority which submitted the request to participate in an on-site inspection or investigation;

(c) allow the competent authority which submitted the request to carry out the on-site inspection or investigation itself;

(d) appoint auditors or experts to carry out the on-site inspection or investigation;

(e) share specific tasks related to supervisory activities with the other competent authorities.

5. The competent authorities may refer to ESMA situations where a request for cooperation, in particular to exchange information, has been rejected or has not been acted upon within a reasonable time. Without prejudice to Article 258 TFEU, ESMA may, in the situations referred to in the first sentence of this paragraph, act in accordance with the power conferred on it under Article 19 of Regulation (EU) No 1095/2010.

6. ESMA may, or where the Commission so requests shall, develop draft regulatory technical standards to specify the information to be exchanged between competent authorities in accordance with paragraph 1.

Power is delegated to the Commission to adopt the regulatory technical standards referred to in the first subparagraph in accordance with Articles 10 to 14 of Regulation (EU) No 1095/2010.

7. ESMA may develop draft implementing technical standards to establish standard forms, templates and procedures for the cooperation and exchange of information between competent authorities.

Power is conferred on the Commission to adopt the implementing technical standards referred to in the first subparagraph in accordance with Article 15 of Regulation (EU) No 1095/2010.

NOTES

Repeal of this Article in relation to the UK: this Article is repealed, in relation to the UK only, by the Prospectus (Amendment etc) (EU Exit) Regulations 2019, SI 2019/1234, reg 59, as from IP completion day (as defined in the European Union (Withdrawal Agreement) Act 2020, s 39); for transitional provisions, see regs 74, 75 of the 2019 Regulations at **[12.165]** et seq.

[11.355]

Article 34 Cooperation with ESMA

1. The competent authorities shall cooperate with ESMA for the purposes of this Regulation, in accordance with Regulation (EU) No 1095/2010.

2. The competent authorities shall without delay provide ESMA with all information necessary to carry out its duties, in accordance with Article 35 of Regulation (EU) No 1095/2010.

3. In order to ensure uniform conditions of application of this Article, ESMA may develop draft implementing technical standards to determine the procedures and forms for exchange of information as referred to in paragraph 2.

Power is conferred on the Commission to adopt the implementing technical standards referred to in the first subparagraph in accordance with Article 15 of Regulation (EU) No 1095/2010.

NOTES

Repeal of this Article in relation to the UK: this Article is repealed, in relation to the UK only, by the Prospectus (Amendment etc) (EU Exit) Regulations 2019, SI 2019/1234, reg 59, as from IP completion day (as defined in the European Union (Withdrawal Agreement) Act 2020, s 39); for transitional provisions, see regs 74, 75 of the 2019 Regulations at **[12.165]** et seq.

[11.356]

Article 35 Professional secrecy

1. All information exchanged between the competent authorities under this Regulation that concerns business or operational conditions and other economic or personal affairs shall be considered to be confidential and shall be subject to the requirements of professional secrecy, except where the competent authority states at the time of communication that such information may be disclosed or such disclosure is necessary for legal proceedings.

2. The obligation of professional secrecy shall apply to all persons who work or who have worked for the competent authority or for any third party to whom the competent authority has delegated its powers. Information covered by professional secrecy may not be disclosed to any other person or authority except by virtue of provisions laid down by Union or national law.

NOTES

Application of this Article in relation to the UK: this Article is amended (as follows), in relation to the UK only, by the Prospectus (Amendment etc) (EU Exit) Regulations 2019, SI 2019/1234, reg 60, as from IP completion day (as defined in the European Union (Withdrawal Agreement) Act 2020, s 39); for transitional provisions, see regs 74, 75 of the 2019 Regulations at **[12.165]** et seq—

"In Article 35—

(a) in paragraph 1—

(i) for "competent authorities" substitute "competent authority, the Treasury and any other authority (including a third country authority), or received by the competent authority, the Treasury or any other authority (including a third country authority) from another authority"

(ii) for "competent authority" substitute "authority from which the information is received";

(b) in paragraph 2, for "Union or national law" substitute "the law of the United Kingdom or any part of the United Kingdom".".

[11.357]

Article 36 Data protection

With regard to the processing of personal data within the framework of this Regulation, competent authorities shall carry out their tasks for the purposes of this Regulation in accordance with Regulation (EU) 2016/679.

With regard to the processing of personal data by ESMA within the framework of this Regulation, it shall comply with Regulation (EC) No 45/2001.

NOTES

Application of this Article in relation to the UK: this Article is amended (as follows), in relation to the UK only, by the Prospectus (Amendment etc) (EU Exit) Regulations 2019, SI 2019/1234, reg 61, as from IP completion day (as defined in the European Union (Withdrawal Agreement) Act 2020, s 39); for transitional provisions, see regs 74, 75 of the 2019 Regulations at **[12.165]** et seq—

"In Article 36—

(a) in the first paragraph—

(i) for "competent authorities shall carry out their" substitute "the competent authority shall carry out its";

(ii) at the end insert "and the Data Protection Act 2018";

(b) omit the second subparagraph.".

[11.358]

Article 37 Precautionary measures

1. Where the competent authority of the host Member State has clear and demonstrable grounds for believing that irregularities have been committed by the issuer, the offeror or the person asking for admission to trading on a regulated market or by the financial intermediaries in charge of the offer of securities to the public or that those persons have infringed their obligations under this Regulation, it shall refer those findings to the competent authority of the home Member State and to ESMA.

2. Where, despite the measures taken by the competent authority of the home Member State, the issuer, the offeror or the person asking for admission to trading on a regulated market or the financial intermediaries in charge of the offer of securities to the public persists in infringing this Regulation, the competent authority of the host Member State, after informing the competent authority of the home Member State and ESMA, shall take all appropriate measures in order to protect investors and shall inform the Commission and ESMA thereof without undue delay.

3. Where a competent authority disagrees with any of the measures taken by another competent authority pursuant to paragraph 2, it may bring the matter to the attention of ESMA. ESMA may act in accordance with the powers conferred on it under Article 19 of Regulation (EU) No 1095/2010.

NOTES

Repeal of this Article in relation to the UK: this Article is repealed, in relation to the UK only, by the Prospectus (Amendment etc) (EU Exit) Regulations 2019, SI 2019/1234, reg 62, as from IP completion day (as defined in the European Union (Withdrawal Agreement) Act 2020, s 39); for transitional provisions, see regs 74, 75 of the 2019 Regulations at **[12.165]** et seq.

CHAPTER VIII ADMINISTRATIVE SANCTIONS AND OTHER ADMINISTRATIVE MEASURES

[11.359]

Article 38 Administrative sanctions and other administrative measures

1. Without prejudice to the supervisory and investigatory powers of competent authorities under Article 32, and the right of Member States to provide for and impose criminal sanctions, Member States shall, in accordance with national law, provide for competent authorities to have the power to impose administrative sanctions and take appropriate other administrative measures which shall be effective, proportionate and dissuasive. Those administrative sanctions and other administrative measures shall apply at least to:

(a) *infringements of Article 3, Article 5, Article 6, Article 7(1) to (11), Article 8, Article 9, Article 10, Article 11(1) and (3), Article 14(1) and (2), Article 15(1), Article 16(1), (2) and (3), Article 17, Article 18, Article 19(1) to (3), Article 20(1), Article 21(1) to (4) and (7) to (11), Article 22(2) to (5), Article 23 (1), (2), (3) and (5), and Article 27;*

(b) *failure to cooperate or comply in an investigation or with an inspection or request covered by Article 32.*

Member States may decide not to lay down rules for administrative sanctions as referred to in the first subparagraph where the infringements referred to in point (a) or point (b) of that subparagraph are already subject to criminal sanctions in their national law by 21 July 2018. Where they so decide, Member States shall notify, in detail, to the Commission and to ESMA, the relevant parts of their criminal law.

By 21 July 2018, Member States shall notify, in detail, the rules referred to in the first and second subparagraph to the Commission and to ESMA. They shall notify the Commission and ESMA without delay of any subsequent amendment thereto.

2. Member States shall, in accordance with national law, ensure that competent authorities have the power to impose at least the following administrative sanctions and other administrative measures in relation to the infringements listed in point (a) of paragraph 1:

(a) *a public statement indicating the natural person or the legal entity responsible and the nature of the infringement in accordance with Article 42;*

(b) *an order requiring the natural person or legal entity responsible to cease the conduct constituting the infringement;*

(c) *maximum administrative pecuniary sanctions of at least twice the amount of the profits gained or losses avoided because of the infringement where those can be determined;*

(d) *in the case of a legal person, maximum administrative pecuniary sanctions of at least EUR 5,000,000, or, in the Member States whose currency is not the euro, the corresponding value in the national currency on 20 July 2017, or 3% of the total annual turnover of that legal person according to the last available financial statements approved by the management body.*

Where the legal person is a parent undertaking or a subsidiary of a parent undertaking which is required to prepare consolidated financial accounts in accordance with Directive 2013/34/EU, the relevant total annual turnover shall be the total annual turnover or the corresponding type of income in accordance with the relevant Union law in the area of accounting according to the last available consolidated accounts approved by the management body of the ultimate parent undertaking;

(e) *in the case of a natural person, maximum administrative pecuniary sanctions of at least EUR 700,000, or, in the Member States whose currency is not the euro, the corresponding value in the national currency on 20 July 2017.*

3. Member States may provide for additional sanctions or measures and for higher levels of administrative pecuniary sanctions than those provided for in this Regulation.

NOTES

Repeal of this Article in relation to the UK: this Article is repealed, in relation to the UK only, by the Prospectus (Amendment etc) (EU Exit) Regulations 2019, SI 2019/1234, reg 62, as from IP completion day (as defined in the European Union (Withdrawal Agreement) Act 2020, s 39); for transitional provisions, see regs 74, 75 of the 2019 Regulations at **[12.165]** et seq.

[11.360]

Article 39 Exercise of supervisory powers and powers to impose sanctions

1. Competent authorities, when determining the type and level of administrative sanctions and other administrative measures, shall take into account all relevant circumstances including, where appropriate:

(a) *the gravity and the duration of the infringement;*

(b) *the degree of responsibility of the person responsible for the infringement;*

(c) *the financial strength of the person responsible for the infringement, as indicated by the total turnover of the responsible legal person or the annual income and net assets of the responsible natural person;*

(d) *the impact of the infringement on retail investors' interests;*

(e) *the importance of the profits gained, losses avoided by the person responsible for the infringement or the losses for third parties derived from the infringement, insofar as they can be determined;*

(f) *the level of cooperation of the person responsible for the infringement with the competent authority, without prejudice to the need to ensure disgorgement of profits gained or losses avoided by that person;*

(g) *previous infringements by the person responsible for the infringement;*

(h) *measures taken after the infringement by the person responsible for the infringement to prevent its repetition.*

2. In the exercise of their powers to impose administrative sanctions and other administrative measures under Article 38, competent authorities shall cooperate closely to ensure that the exercise of their supervisory and investigative powers and the administrative sanctions and other administrative measures that they impose are effective and appropriate under this Regulation. They shall coordinate their action in order to avoid duplication and overlaps when exercising their supervisory and investigative powers and when imposing administrative sanctions and other administrative measures in cross-border cases.

NOTES

Repeal of this Article in relation to the UK: this Article is repealed, in relation to the UK only, by the Prospectus (Amendment etc) (EU Exit) Regulations 2019, SI 2019/1234, reg 62, as from IP completion day (as defined in the European Union (Withdrawal Agreement) Act 2020, s 39); for transitional provisions, see regs 74, 75 of the 2019 Regulations at **[12.165]** et seq.

[11.361]

Article 40 Right of appeal

Member States shall ensure that decisions taken under this Regulation are properly reasoned and subject to a right of appeal before a tribunal.

For the purposes of Article 20, a right of appeal shall also apply where the competent authority has neither taken a decision to approve or to refuse an application for approval nor has made any request for changes or supplementary information within the time limits set out in Article 20(2), (3) and (6) in respect of that application.

NOTES

Repeal of this Article in relation to the UK: this Article is repealed, in relation to the UK only, by the Prospectus (Amendment etc) (EU Exit) Regulations 2019, SI 2019/1234, reg 62, as from IP completion day (as defined in the European Union (Withdrawal Agreement) Act 2020, s 39); for transitional provisions, see regs 74, 75 of the 2019 Regulations at **[12.165]** et seq.

[11.362]

Article 41 Reporting of infringements

1. Competent authorities shall establish effective mechanisms to encourage and enable reporting of actual or potential infringements of this Regulation to them.

2. The mechanisms referred to in paragraph 1 shall include at least:

- *(a) specific procedures for the receipt of reports of actual or potential infringements and their follow-up, including the establishment of secure communication channels for such reports;*
- *(b) appropriate protection for employees working under a contract of employment who report infringements at least against retaliation, discrimination and other types of unfair treatment by their employer or third parties;*
- *(c) protection of the identity and personal data of both the person who reports the infringements and the natural person who is allegedly responsible for an infringement, at all stages of the procedure unless such disclosure is required by national law in the context of further investigation or subsequent judicial proceedings.*

3. Member States may provide for financial incentives to persons who offer relevant information about actual or potential infringements of this Regulation to be granted in accordance with national law where such persons do not have other pre-existing legal or contractual duties to report such information, and provided that the information is new, and that it results in the imposition of an administrative or criminal sanction, or the taking of another administrative measure, for an infringement of this Regulation.

4. Member States shall require employers engaged in activities that are regulated for financial services purposes to have in place appropriate procedures for their employees to report actual or potential infringements internally through a specific, independent and autonomous channel.

NOTES

Repeal of this Article in relation to the UK: this Article is repealed, in relation to the UK only, by the Prospectus (Amendment etc) (EU Exit) Regulations 2019, SI 2019/1234, reg 62, as from IP completion day (as defined in the European Union (Withdrawal Agreement) Act 2020, s 39); for transitional provisions, see regs 74, 75 of the 2019 Regulations at **[12.165]** et seq.

[11.363]

Article 42 Publication of decisions

1. A decision imposing an administrative sanction or other administrative measure for infringement of this Regulation shall be published by competent authorities on their official websites immediately after the person subject to that decision has been informed of that decision. The publication shall include at least information on the type and nature of the infringement and the identity of the persons responsible. That obligation does not apply to decisions imposing measures that are of an investigatory nature.

2. Where the publication of the identity of the legal entities, or identity or personal data of natural persons, is considered by the competent authority to be disproportionate following a case-by-case assessment conducted on the proportionality of the publication of such data, or where such publication would jeopardise the stability of financial markets or an on-going investigation, Member States shall ensure that the competent authorities do one of the following:

- (a) defer the publication of the decision to impose a sanction or a measure until the moment where the reasons for non-publication cease to exist;
- (b) publish the decision to impose a sanction or a measure on an anonymous basis in a manner which is in conformity with national law, where such anonymous publication ensures an effective protection of the personal data concerned;
- (c) not publish the decision to impose a sanction or measure in the event that the options laid down in points (a) and (b) are considered to be insufficient to ensure:
  - (i) that the stability of financial markets would not be put in jeopardy;
  - (ii) the proportionality of the publication of such decisions with regard to measures which are deemed to be of a minor nature.

In the case of a decision to publish a sanction or measure on an anonymous basis, as referred to in point (b) of the first subparagraph, the publication of the relevant data may be deferred for a reasonable period where it is foreseen that within that period the reasons for anonymous publication shall cease to exist.

3. Where the decision to impose a sanction or measure is subject to appeal before the relevant judicial or other authorities, competent authorities shall also publish, immediately, on their official website such information and any subsequent information on the outcome of such appeal. Moreover, any decision annulling a previous decision to impose a sanction or a measure shall also be published.

4. Competent authorities shall ensure that any publication, in accordance with this Article shall remain on their official website for a period of at least five years after its publication. Personal data contained in the publication shall be kept on the official website of the competent authority only for the period which is necessary in accordance with the applicable data protection rules.

NOTES

Application of this Article in relation to the UK: this Article is amended (as follows), in relation to the UK only, by the Prospectus (Amendment etc) (EU Exit) Regulations 2019, SI 2019/1234, reg 63, as from IP completion day (as defined in the European Union (Withdrawal Agreement) Act 2020, s 39); for transitional provisions, see regs 74, 75 of the 2019 Regulations

Part 11 EU & Retained EU Legislation

at **[12.165]** et seq—

"In Article 42—

(a) omit paragraphs 1 to 3;

(b) in paragraph 4, for the first sentence substitute "The competent authority shall ensure that any information about an infringement of this Regulation which the authority publishes under section 391(4) of FSMA is published on its website (whether or not also published in any other way) and then remains on that website for a period of at least five years after its publication".".

[11.364]

Article 43 Reporting sanctions to ESMA

1. The competent authority shall, on an annual basis, provide ESMA with aggregate information regarding all administrative sanctions and other administrative measures imposed in accordance with Article 38. ESMA shall publish that information in an annual report.

Where Member States have chosen, in accordance with Article 38(1), to lay down criminal sanctions for the infringements of the provisions referred to in that paragraph, their competent authorities shall provide ESMA annually with anonymised and aggregated data regarding all criminal investigations undertaken and criminal sanctions imposed. ESMA shall publish data on criminal sanctions imposed in an annual report.

2. Where the competent authority has disclosed administrative sanctions, other administrative measures or criminal sanctions to the public, it shall simultaneously report them to ESMA.

3. Competent authorities shall inform ESMA of all administrative sanctions or other administrative measures imposed but not published in accordance with point (c) of the first subparagraph of Article 42(2) including any appeal in relation thereto and the outcome thereof. Member States shall ensure that competent authorities receive information and the final judgment in relation to any criminal sanction imposed and submit it to ESMA. ESMA shall maintain a central database of sanctions communicated to it solely for the purposes of exchanging information between competent authorities. That database shall be accessible only to competent authorities and it shall be updated on the basis of the information provided by the competent authorities.

NOTES

Repeal of this Article in relation to the UK: this Article is repealed, in relation to the UK only, by the Prospectus (Amendment etc) (EU Exit) Regulations 2019, SI 2019/1234, reg 64, as from IP completion day (as defined in the European Union (Withdrawal Agreement) Act 2020, s 39); for transitional provisions, see regs 74, 75 of the 2019 Regulations at **[12.165]** et seq.

CHAPTER IX DELEGATED AND IMPLEMENTING ACTS

NOTES

Application to the UK: this preceding Chapter heading is amended (as follows), in relation to the UK only, by the Prospectus (Amendment etc) (EU Exit) Regulations 2019, SI 2019/1234, reg 65, as from IP completion day (as defined in the European Union (Withdrawal Agreement) Act 2020, s 39); for transitional provisions, see regs 74, 75 of the 2019 Regulations at **[12.165]** et seq—

"For the heading of Chapter 9, substitute "Treasury regulations".".

[11.365]

Article 44 Exercise of the delegation

1. The power to adopt delegated acts is conferred on the Commission subject to the conditions laid down in this Article.

2. The power to adopt delegated acts referred to in Article 1(7), Article 9(14), Article 13(1) and (2), Article 14(3), Article 15(2), Article 16(5), Article 20(11) and Article 29(3) shall be conferred on the Commission for an indeterminate period from 20 July 2017.

3. The delegation of powers referred to in Article 1(7), Article 9(14), Article 13(1) and (2), Article 14(3), Article 15(2), Article 16(5), Article 20(11) and Article 29(3) may be revoked at any time by the European Parliament or by the Council. A decision to revoke shall put an end to the delegation of the power specified in that decision. It shall take effect the day following the publication of the decision in the Official Journal of the European Union or at a later date specified therein. It shall not affect the validity of any delegated acts already in force.

4. Before adopting a delegated act, the Commission shall consult experts designated by each Member State in accordance with the principles laid down in the Interinstitutional Agreement of 13 April 2016 on Better Law-Making.

5. As soon as it adopts a delegated act, the Commission shall notify it simultaneously to the European Parliament and to the Council.

6. A delegated act adopted pursuant to Article 1(7), Article 9(14), Article 13(1) and (2), Article 14(3), Article 15(2), Article 16(5), Article 20(11) and Article 29(3) shall enter into force only if no objection has been expressed either by the European Parliament or the Council within a period of three months of notification of that act to the European Parliament and the Council or if, before the expiry of that period, the European Parliament and the Council have both informed the Commission that they will not object. That period shall be extended by three months at the initiative of the European Parliament or of the Council.

NOTES

Repeal of this Article in relation to the UK: this Article is repealed, in relation to the UK only, by the Prospectus (Amendment etc) (EU Exit) Regulations 2019, SI 2019/1234, reg 66(1), as from IP completion day (as defined in the European Union (Withdrawal Agreement) Act 2020, s 39); for transitional provisions, see regs 74, 75 of the 2019 Regulations at **[12.165]** et seq.

[11.366]

Article 45 Committee procedure

1. The Commission shall be assisted by the European Securities Committee established by Commission Decision 2001/ 528/EC.[1] That committee shall be a committee within the meaning of Regulation (EU) No 182/2011.

2. Where reference is made to this paragraph, Article 5 of Regulation (EU) No 182/2011 shall apply.

NOTES

Repeal of this Article in relation to the UK: this Article is repealed, in relation to the UK only, by the Prospectus (Amendment etc) (EU Exit) Regulations 2019, SI 2019/1234, reg 66(1), as from IP completion day (as defined in the European Union (Withdrawal Agreement) Act 2020, s 39); for transitional provisions, see regs 74, 75 of the 2019 Regulations at **[12.165]** et seq.

[1] Commission Decision 2001/528/EC of 6 June 2001 establishing the European Securities Committee (OJ L191, 13.7.2001, p 45).

[11.367]

[Article 45a Treasury regulations

1. Any power to make regulations conferred on the Treasury by this Regulation is exercisable by statutory instrument.

2. Such regulations may—

(a) contain incidental, supplemental, consequential, transitional and saving provision; and

(b) make different provision for different purposes.

3. A statutory instrument containing regulations under this Regulation is subject to annulment in pursuance of a resolution of either House of Parliament.]

NOTES

Application of this Article in relation to the UK: this Article is inserted, in relation to the UK only, by the Prospectus (Amendment etc) (EU Exit) Regulations 2019, SI 2019/1234, reg 66(2), as from IP completion day (as defined in the European Union (Withdrawal Agreement) Act 2020, s 39); for transitional provisions, see regs 74, 75 of the 2019 Regulations at **[12.165]** et seq.

CHAPTER X FINAL PROVISIONS

[11.368]

Article 46 Repeal

1. Directive 2003/71/EC is repealed with effect from 21 July 2019, except for:

(a) points (a) and (g) of Article 4(2) of Directive 2003/71/EC, which are repealed with effect from 20 July 2017; and

(b) point (h) of Article 1(2) and point (e) of the first subparagraph of Article 3(2) of Directive 2003/71/EC, which are repealed with effect from 21 July 2018.

2. References to Directive 2003/71/EC shall be construed as references to this Regulation and shall be read in accordance with the correlation table in Annex VI to this Regulation.

3. Prospectuses approved in accordance with the national laws transposing Directive 2003/71/EC before 21 July 2019 shall continue to be governed by that national law until the end of their validity, or until twelve months have elapsed after 21 July 2019, whichever occurs first.

[11.369]

Article 47 ESMA report on prospectuses

1. Based on the documents made public through the mechanism referred to in Article 21(6), ESMA shall publish every year a report containing statistics on the prospectuses approved and notified in the Union and an analysis of trends taking into account:

(a) the types of issuers, in particular the categories of persons referred to in points (a) to (d) of Article 15(1); and

(b) the types of issuances, in particular the total consideration of the offers, the types of transferable securities, the types of trading venue and the denominations.

2. The report referred to in paragraph 1 shall contain in particular:

(a) an analysis of the extent to which the disclosure regimes set out in Articles 14 and 15 and the universal registration document referred to in Article 9 are used throughout the Union;

(b) statistics on base prospectuses and final terms, and on prospectuses drawn up as separate documents or as a single document;

(c) statistics on the average and overall consideration of offers of securities to the public subject to this Regulation, by unlisted companies, companies whose securities are traded on MTFs, including SME growth markets, and companies whose securities are admitted to trading on regulated markets. Where applicable, such statistics shall provide a breakdown between initial public offerings and subsequent offers, and between equity and non-equity securities;

(d) statistics on the use of the notification procedures of Articles 25 and 26, including a breakdown per Member State of the number of certificates of approval notified in relation to prospectuses, registration documents and universal registration documents.

NOTES

Repeal of this Article in relation to the UK: this Article is repealed, in relation to the UK only, by the Prospectus (Amendment etc) (EU Exit) Regulations 2019, SI 2019/1234, reg 67, as from IP completion day (as defined in the European Union (Withdrawal Agreement) Act 2020, s 39); for transitional provisions, see regs 74, 75 of the 2019 Regulations at **[12.165]** et seq.

[11.370]

[Article 47a Time limitation of the EU Recovery prospectus regime

The EU Recovery prospectus regime set out in Article 7(12a), Article 14a, Article 20(6a) and Article 21(5a) expires on 31 December 2022.

EU Recovery prospectuses approved between 18 March 2021 and 31 December 2022 shall continue to be governed in accordance with Article 14a until the end of their validity or until 12 months have elapsed after 31 December 2022, whichever occurs first.]

NOTES

Inserted by European Parliament and Council Regulation 2021/337/EU, Art 1(9), as from 18 March 2021.

Application of this Article in relation to the UK: note that Regulation 2021/337/EU (which inserts this Article as noted above) is not "direct EU legislation" within the meaning of the European Union (Withdrawal) Act 2018, s 3 at **[12.5]** and, therefore, this Article does not apply to the UK.

[11.371]

Article 48 Review

1. Before 21 July 2022 the Commission shall present a report to the European Parliament and the Council on the application of this Regulation, accompanied where appropriate by a legislative proposal.

[2. The report shall assess, inter alia, whether the prospectus summary, the disclosure regimes set out in Articles 14, 14a and 15 and the universal registration document referred to in Article 9 remain appropriate in light of their pursued objectives. In particular, the report shall include the following:

- *(a) the number of EU Growth prospectuses of persons in each of the categories referred to in points (a) to (d) of Article 15(1) and an analysis of the evolution of each such number and of the trends in the choice of trading venues by the persons entitled to use the EU Growth prospectus;*
- *(b) an analysis of whether the EU Growth prospectus strikes a proper balance between investor protection and the reduction of administrative burdens for the persons entitled to use it;*
- *(c) the number of EU Recovery prospectuses approved and an analysis of the evolution of such number, as well as an estimate of the actual additional market capitalisation mobilised by EU Recovery prospectuses at the date of issue in order to gather experience about the EU Recovery prospectus for post-evaluation;*
- *(d) the cost of preparing and having an EU Recovery prospectus approved compared to the current costs for the preparation and approval of a standard prospectus, a secondary issuance prospectus and an EU Growth prospectus, together with an indication of the overall financial savings achieved and of which costs could be further reduced, and the total costs of complying with this Regulation for issuers, offerors and financial intermediaries together with a calculation of those costs as a percentage of operational costs;*
- *(e) an analysis of whether the EU Recovery prospectus strikes the proper balance between investor protection and the reduction of administrative burden for the persons entitled to use it, and of the accessibility of essential information for investments;*
- *(f) an analysis of whether it would be appropriate to extend the duration of the EU Recovery prospectus regime, including whether the threshold referred to in the second subparagraph of Article 14a(1), beyond which an EU Recovery prospectus may not be used, is appropriate;*
- *(g) an analysis of whether the measures laid down in Articles 23(2a) and 23(3a) achieved the objective of providing additional clarity and flexibility to both financial intermediaries and investors and whether it would be appropriate to make those measures permanent.]*

3. Based on the analysis referred to in paragraph 2, the report shall assess whether any amendments to this Regulation are necessary in order to further facilitate capital-raising by smaller companies, while ensuring a sufficient level of investor protection, including whether the relevant thresholds need to be adjusted.

4. Furthermore, the report shall evaluate whether LEIs and ISINs can be obtained at a reasonable cost and within a reasonable period by issuers, in particular SMEs. The report shall take into account the results of the peer review referred to in Article 20(13).

NOTES

Para 2: substituted by European Parliament and Council Regulation 2021/337/EU, Art 1(10), as from 18 March 2021.

Repeal of this Article in relation to the UK: this Article is repealed, in relation to the UK only, by the Prospectus (Amendment etc) (EU Exit) Regulations 2019, SI 2019/1234, reg 67, as from IP completion day (as defined in the European Union (Withdrawal Agreement) Act 2020, s 39); for transitional provisions, see regs 74, 75 of the 2019 Regulations at **[12.165]** et seq.

[11.372]

Article 49 Entry into force and application

1. This Regulation shall enter into force on the twentieth day following that of its publication in the *Official Journal of the European Union*.

2. Without prejudice to Article 44(2), this Regulation shall apply from 21 July 2019, except for Article 1(3) and Article 3(2) which shall apply from 21 July 2018 and points (a), (b) and (c) of the first subparagraph of Article 1(5) and the second subparagraph of Article 1(5) which shall apply from 20 July 2017.

3. Member States shall take the necessary measures to comply with Article 11, Article 20(9), Article 31, Article 32 and Articles 38 to 43 by 21 July 2019.

This Regulation shall be binding in its entirety and directly applicable in all Member States.

NOTES

Application of this Article in relation to the UK: this Article is amended (as follows), in relation to the UK only, by the Prospectus (Amendment etc) (EU Exit) Regulations 2019, SI 2019/1234, reg 68, 69, as from IP completion day (as defined in the European Union (Withdrawal Agreement) Act 2020, s 39); for transitional provisions, see regs 74, 75 of the 2019 Regulations at **[12.165]** et seq—

"In Article 49, omit paragraph 3.

Omit the words "This Regulation shall be binding in its entirety and directly applicable in all Member States." following Article 49.".

ANNEXES

ANNEX I
PROSPECTUS

[11.373]

I. Summary

II. Identity of directors, senior management, advisers and auditors

The purpose is to identify the company representatives and other individuals involved in the company's offer or admission to trading; these are the persons responsible for drawing up the prospectus and those responsible for auditing the financial statements.

III. Offer statistics and expected timetable

The purpose is to provide essential information regarding the conduct of any offer and the identification of important dates relating to that offer.

A. Offer statistics
B. Method and expected timetable

IV. Essential information

The purpose is to summarise essential information about the company's financial condition, capitalisation and risk factors. If the financial statements included in the document are restated to reflect material changes in the company's group structure or accounting policies, the selected financial data must also be restated.

A. Selected financial data
B. Capitalisation and indebtedness (for equity securities only)
C. Reasons for the offer and use of proceeds
D. Risk factors

V. Information on the company

The purpose is to provide information about the company's business operations, the products it makes or the services it provides, and the factors which affect the business. It is also intended to provide information regarding the adequacy and suitability of the company's properties, plant and equipment, as well as its plans for future capacity increases or decreases.

A. History and development of the company
B. Business overview
C. Organisational structure
D. Property, plant and equipment

VI. Operating and financial review and prospects

The purpose is to provide the management's explanation of factors that have affected the company's financial condition and results of operations for the historical periods covered by the financial statements, and management's assessment of factors and trends which are expected to have a material effect on the company's financial condition and results of operations in future periods.

A. Operating results
B. Liquidity and capital resources
C. Research and development, patents and licences, etc.
D. Trends

VII. Directors, senior management and employees

The purpose is to provide information concerning the company's directors and managers that will allow investors to assess their experience, qualifications and levels of remuneration, as well as their relationship with the company.

A. Directors and senior management
B. Remuneration
C. Board practices
D. Employees
E. Share ownership

VIII. Major shareholders and related-party transactions

The purpose is to provide information regarding the major shareholders and others that may control or have an influence on the company. It also provides information regarding the transactions the company has entered into with persons affiliated with the company and whether the terms of such transactions are fair to the company.

A. Major shareholders
B. Related-party transactions
C. Interests of experts and advisers

IX. Financial information

The purpose is to specify which financial statements must be included in the document, as well as the periods to be covered, the age of the financial statements and other information of a financial nature. The accounting and auditing principles that will be accepted for use in preparation and audit of the financial statements will be determined in accordance with international accounting and auditing standards.

A. Consolidated statements and other financial information
B. Significant changes

X. Details of the offer and admission to trading details

The purpose is to provide information regarding the offer and the admission to trading of securities, the plan for distribution of the securities and related matters.

A. Offer and admission to trading
B. Plan for distribution
C. Markets

D. Holders of securities who are selling
E. Dilution (for equity securities only)
F. Expenses of the issue

XI. Additional information

The purpose is to provide information, most of which is of a statutory nature, that is not covered elsewhere in the prospectus.

A. Share capital
B. Memorandum and articles of association
C. Material contracts
D. Exchange controls
E. Warning on tax consequences
F. Dividends and paying agents
G. Statement by experts
H. Documents on display
I. Subsidiary information

ANNEX II
REGISTRATION DOCUMENT

[11.374]

I. Identity of directors, senior management, advisers and auditors

The purpose is to identify the company representatives and other individuals involved in the company's offer or admission to trading; these are the persons responsible for drawing up the prospectus and those responsible for auditing the financial statements.

II. Essential information about the issuer

The purpose is to summarise essential information about the company's financial condition, capitalisation and risk factors. If the financial statements included in the document are restated to reflect material changes in the company's group structure or accounting policies, the selected financial data must also be restated.

A. Selected financial data
B. Capitalisation and indebtedness (for equity securities only)
C. Risk factors relating to the issuer

III. Information on the company

The purpose is to provide information about the company's business operations, the products it makes or the services it provides and the factors which affect the business. It is also intended to provide information regarding the adequacy and suitability of the company's properties, plants and equipment, as well as its plans for future capacity increases or decreases.

A. History and development of the company
B. Business overview
C. Organisational structure
D. Property, plants and equipment

IV. Operating and financial review and prospects

The purpose is to provide the management's explanation of factors that have affected the company's financial condition and results of operations for the historical periods covered by the financial statements, and management's assessment of factors and trends which are expected to have a material effect on the company's financial condition and results of operations in future periods.

A. Operating results
B. Liquidity and capital resources
C. Research and development, patents and licences, etc.
D. Trends

V. Directors, senior management and employees

The purpose is to provide information concerning the company's directors and managers that will allow investors to assess their experience, qualifications and levels of remuneration, as well as their relationship with the company.

A. Directors and senior management
B. Remuneration
C. Board practices
D. Employees
E. Share ownership

VI. Major shareholders and related-party transactions

The purpose is to provide information regarding the major shareholders and others that may control or have an influence on the company. It also provides information regarding the transactions the company has entered into with persons affiliated with the company and whether the terms of such transactions are fair to the company.

A. Major shareholders
B. Related-party transactions
C. Interests of experts and advisers

VII. Financial information

The purpose is to specify which financial statements must be included in the document, as well as the periods to be covered, the age of the financial statements and other information of a financial nature. The accounting and auditing principles that will be accepted for use in preparation and audit of the financial statements will be determined in accordance with international accounting and auditing standards.

A. Consolidated statements and other financial information

B. Significant changes

VIII. Additional information

The purpose is to provide information, most of which is of a statutory nature, that is not covered elsewhere in the prospectus.

A. Share capital
B. Memorandum and articles of association
C. Material contracts
D. Statement by experts
E. Documents on display
F. Subsidiary information

ANNEX III
SECURITIES NOTE

[11.375]

I. Identity of directors, senior management, advisers and auditors

The purpose is to identify the company representatives and other individuals involved in the company's offer or admission to trading; these are the persons responsible for drawing up the prospectus and those responsible for auditing the financial statements.

II. Offer statistics and expected timetable

The purpose is to provide essential information regarding the conduct of any offer and the identification of important dates relating to that offer.

A. Offer statistics
B. Method and expected timetable

III. Essential information about the issuer

The purpose is to summarise essential information about the company's financial condition, capitalisation and risk factors. If the financial statements included in the document are restated to reflect material changes in the company's group structure or accounting policies, the selected financial data must also be restated.

A. Capitalisation and indebtedness (for equity securities only)
B. Information concerning working capital (for equity securities only)
C. Reasons for the offer and use of proceeds
D. Risk factors

IV. Essential information about the securities

The purpose is to provide essential information about the securities to be offered to the public and/or admitted to trading.

A. A description of the type and class of the securities being offered to the public and/or admitted to trading
B. Currency of the securities issued
C. The relative seniority of the securities in the issuer's capital structure in the event of the issuer's insolvency, including, where applicable, information on the level of subordination of the securities and the potential impact on the investment in the event of a resolution under Directive 2014/59/EU
D. The dividend payout policy, provisions relating to interest payable or a description of the underlying, including the method used to relate the underlying and the rate, and an indication where information about the past and future performance of the underlying and its volatility can be obtained
E. A description of any rights attached to the securities, including any limitations of those rights, and the procedure for the exercise of those rights

V. Interests of experts

The purpose is to provide information regarding transactions the company has entered into with experts or advisers employed on a contingent basis.

VI. Details of the offer and admission to trading

The purpose is to provide information regarding the offer and the admission to trading of securities, the plan for distribution of the securities and related matters.

A. Offer and admission to trading
B. Plan for distribution
C. Markets
D. Selling securities holders
E. Dilution (for equity securities only)
F. Expenses of the issue

VII. Additional information

The purpose is to provide information, most of which is of a statutory nature, that is not covered elsewhere in the prospectus.

A. Exchange controls
B. Warning on tax consequences
C. Dividends and paying agents
D. Statement by experts
E. Documents on display

NOTES

Application of this Annex in relation to the UK: this Annex is amended (as follows), in relation to the UK only, by the Prospectus (Amendment etc) (EU Exit) Regulations 2019, SI 2019/1234, reg 70(2), as from IP completion day (as defined in the European Union (Withdrawal Agreement) Act 2020, s 39); for transitional provisions, see regs 74, 75 of the 2019 Regulations at **[12.165]** et seq—

Part 11 EU & Retained EU Legislation

"(2) In Annex 3, point 4C, before "Directive" insert "the UK law which implemented".".

ANNEX IV
REGISTRATION DOCUMENT FOR THE EU GROWTH PROSPECTUS

[11.376]

I. Responsibility for the registration document

The purpose is to identify the issuer and its representatives and other individuals involved in the company's offer; these are the persons responsible for drawing up the registration document.

II. Strategy, performance and business environment

The purpose is to inform about the company's strategy and objectives related to development and future performance and to provide information about the company's business operations, the products it makes or the services it provides, its investments and the factors which affect the business. Furthermore, the risk factors specific to the company and relevant trend information must be included.

III. Corporate governance

The purpose is to provide information concerning the company's directors and managers that will allow investors to assess their experience, qualifications and levels of remuneration, as well as their relationship with the company.

IV. Financial statements and key performance indicators

The purpose is to specify which financial statements and key performance indicators must be included in the document covering the two latest financial years (for equity securities) or the last financial year (for non-equity securities) or such shorter period during which the issuer has been in operation.

V. Operating and financial review (only for equity securities issued by companies with market capitalisation above EUR 200,000,000).

The purpose is to provide information about the financial condition and operating results if the reports, presented and prepared in accordance with Articles 19 and 29 of Directive 2013/34/EU for the periods covered by the historical financial information, are not included in the EU Growth prospectus.

VI. Shareholders' information

The purpose is to provide information about legal and arbitration proceedings, conflicts of interest and related-party transactions as well as information on the share capital.

NOTES

Application of this Annex in relation to the UK: this Annex is amended (as follows), in relation to the UK only, by the Prospectus (Amendment etc) (EU Exit) Regulations 2019, SI 2019/1234, reg 70(3), as from IP completion day (as defined in the European Union (Withdrawal Agreement) Act 2020, s 39); for transitional provisions, see regs 74, 75 of the 2019 Regulations at **[12.165]** et seq—

"(3) In Annex 4—
(a) in the heading, for "EU Growth" substitute "UK Growth";
(b) in point 5—
(i) for "Articles 19 and 29 of Directive 2013/34/EU" substitute "rules 4.1.8 and 4.1.11 of the Disclosure Guidance and Transparency Rules Sourcebook";
(ii) for "EU Growth" substitute "UK Growth".".

ANNEX V
SECURITIES NOTE FOR THE EU GROWTH PROSPECTUS

[11.377]

I. Responsibility for the securities note

The purpose is to identify the issuer and its representatives and other individuals involved in the company's offer or admission to trading; these are the persons responsible for drawing up the prospectus.

[II. Statement of capitalisation and indebtedness (only for equity securities issued by companies with market capitalisation above EUR 200,000,000) and working capital statement (only for equity securities).

The purpose is to provide information on the issuer's capitalisation and indebtedness and information as to whether the working capital is sufficient to meet the issuer's present requirements or, if not, how the issuer proposes to provide the additional working capital needed.]

III. Terms and conditions of the securities

The purpose is to provide essential information regarding the terms and conditions of the securities and a description of any rights attached to the securities. Furthermore, the risk factors specific to the securities must be included.

IV. Details of the offer and expected timetable

The purpose is to provide information regarding the offer and, where applicable, the admission to trading on an MTF, including the final offer price and amount of securities (whether in number of securities or aggregate nominal amount) which will be offered, the reasons for the offer, the plan for distribution of the securities, the use of proceeds of the offer, the expenses of the issuance and offer, and dilution (for equity securities only).

V. Information on the guarantor

The purpose is to provide information on the guarantor of the securities where applicable, including essential information about the guarantee attached to the securities, the risk factors and financial information specific to the guarantor.

NOTES

Point II substituted by European Parliament and Council Regulation 2019/2115/EU, Art 2(4), as from 31 December 2019.

Application of this Annex in relation to the UK: this Annex is amended (as follows), in relation to the UK only, by the Prospectus (Amendment etc) (EU Exit) Regulations 2019, SI 2019/1234, reg 70(4), as from IP completion day (as defined in the European Union (Withdrawal Agreement) Act 2020, s 39); for transitional provisions, see regs 74, 75 of the 2019 Regulations at **[12.165]** et seq—

"(4) In Annex 5, in the heading for "EU Growth" substitute "UK Growth".".

[ANNEX VA
MINIMUM INFORMATION TO BE INCLUDED IN THE EU RECOVERY PROSPECTUS

[11.378]

I. Summary

The EU Recovery prospectus must include a summary drawn up in accordance with Article 7(12a).

II. Name of the issuer, country of incorporation, link to the issuer's website

Identify the company issuing shares, including its legal entity identifier (LEI), its legal and commercial name, its country of incorporation and the website where investors can find information on the company's business operations, the products it makes or the services it provides, the principal markets where it competes, its major shareholders, the composition of its administrative, management and supervisory bodies and of its senior management and, where applicable, information incorporated by reference (with a disclaimer that the information on the website does not form part of the prospectus unless that information is incorporated by reference into the prospectus).

III. Responsibility statement and statement on the competent authority

1. Responsibility statement

Identify the persons responsible for drawing up the EU Recovery prospectus and include a statement by those persons that, to the best of their knowledge, the information contained in the EU Recovery prospectus is in accordance with the facts and that the EU Recovery prospectus makes no omission likely to affect its import.

Where applicable, the statement must contain information sourced from third parties, including the source(s) of that information, and statements or reports attributed to a person as an expert and the following details of that person:

(a) name;
(b) business address;
(c) qualifications; and
(d) material interest (if any) in the issuer.

2. Statement on the competent authority

The statement must indicate the competent authority that has approved, in accordance with this Regulation, the EU Recovery prospectus, specify that such approval is not an endorsement of the issuer nor of the quality of the shares to which the EU Recovery prospectus relates, that the competent authority has only approved the EU Recovery prospectus as meeting the standards of completeness, comprehensibility and consistency imposed by this Regulation, and specify that the EU Recovery prospectus has been drawn up in accordance with Article 14a.

IV. Risk factors

A description of the material risks that are specific to the issuer and a description of the material risks that are specific to the shares being offered to the public and/or admitted to trading on a regulated market, in a limited number of categories, in a section headed "Risk Factors".

In each category, the most material risks, in the assessment undertaken by the issuer, offeror or person asking for admission to trading on a regulated market, taking into account the negative impact on the issuer as well as on the shares being offered to the public and/or admitted to trading on a regulated market and the probability of their occurrence, shall be set out first. The risks shall be corroborated by the content of the EU Recovery prospectus.

V. Financial statements

The EU Recovery prospectus must include the financial statements (annual and half-yearly) published over the period of 12 months prior to the approval of the EU Recovery prospectus. Where both annual and half-yearly financial statements have been published, only the annual statements must be required where they postdate the half-yearly financial statements.

The annual financial statements must be independently audited. The audit report must be prepared in accordance with Directive 2006/43/EC of the European Parliament and of the Council (1) and Regulation (EU) No 537/2014 of the European Parliament and of the Council (2).

Where Directive 2006/43/EC and Regulation (EU) No 537/2014 do not apply, the annual financial statements must be audited or reported on as to whether or not, for the purposes of the EU Recovery prospectus, they give a true and fair view in accordance with auditing standards applicable in a Member State or an equivalent standard. Otherwise, the following information must be included in the EU Recovery prospectus:

(a) a prominent statement disclosing which auditing standards have been applied;
(b) an explanation of any significant departures from International Standards on Auditing.

Where audit reports on the annual financial statements have been refused by the statutory auditors or where they contain qualifications, modifications of opinion, disclaimers or an emphasis of matter, the reason must be given, and such qualifications, modifications, disclaimers or emphasis of matter must be reproduced in full.

A description of any significant change in the financial position of the group which has occurred since the end of the last financial period for which either audited financial statements or interim financial information have been published, must also be included, or an appropriate negative statement must be included.

Where applicable, pro forma information must also be included.

VI. Dividend policy

A description of the issuer's policy on dividend distributions and any current restrictions thereon, as well as on share repurchases.

VII. Trend information

A description of:

(a) the most significant recent trends in production, sales and inventory, and costs and selling prices since the end of the last financial year to the date of the EU Recovery prospectus;

(b) information on any known trends, uncertainties, demands, commitments or events that are reasonably likely to have a material effect on the issuer's prospects for at least the current financial year;

(c) information on the issuer's short and long-term financial and non-financial business strategy and objectives, including, if applicable, a specific reference of not less than 400 words to the business and financial impact of the COVID-19 pandemic on the issuer and the anticipated future impact of the same.

If there is no significant change in either of the trends referred to in points (a) or (b) of this section, a statement to that effect is to be made.

VIII. Terms and conditions of the offer, firm commitments and intentions to subscribe and key features of the underwriting and placement agreements

Set out the offer price, the number of shares offered, the amount of the issue/offer, the conditions to which the offer is subject, and the procedure for the exercise of any right of pre-emption.

To the extent known to the issuer, provide information on whether major shareholders or members of the issuer's management, supervisory or administrative bodies intend to subscribe for the offer, or whether any person intends to subscribe for more than 5% of the offer.

Present any firm commitments to subscribe for more than 5% of the offer and all material features of the underwriting and placement agreements, including the name and address of the entities agreeing to underwrite or place the issue on a firm commitment basis or under "best efforts" arrangements and the quotas.

IX. Essential information on the shares and on their subscription

Provide the following essential information about the shares offered to the public or admitted to trading on a regulated market:

(a) the international security identification number (ISIN);

(b) the rights attached to the shares, the procedure for the exercise of those rights and any limitations of those rights;

(c) where the shares can be subscribed as well as on the time period, including any possible amendments, during which the offer will be open and a description of the application process together with the issue date of new shares.

X. Reasons for the offer and use of proceeds

Provide information on the reasons for the offer and, where applicable, the estimated net amount of the proceeds broken into each principal intended use and presented in order of priority of such uses.

Where the issuer is aware that the anticipated proceeds will not be sufficient to fund all the proposed uses, it must state the amount and sources of other funds needed. Details must also be given with regard to the use of the proceeds, in particular where proceeds are being used to acquire assets, other than in the ordinary course of business, to finance announced acquisitions of other business, or to discharge, reduce or retire indebtedness.

XI. Receipt of state aid support

Provide a statement with information as to whether the issuer has benefited from state aid in whatever form in the context of the recovery as well as the purpose of the aid, type of instrument and amount of the aid received and conditions attached to it, if any.

The statement as to whether the issuer received state aid must contain a declaration that the information is provided solely under the responsibility of the persons responsible for the prospectus, as referred to in Article 11(1), that the competent authority's role in approving the prospectus is to scrutinise its completeness, comprehensibility and consistency, and that therefore in respect of the statement on state aid the competent authority is not obliged to independently verify that statement.

XII. Working capital statement

Statement by the issuer that, in its opinion, the working capital is sufficient for the issuer's present requirements or, if not, how the issuer proposes to provide the additional working capital needed.

XIII. Capitalisation and indebtedness

A statement of capitalisation and indebtedness (distinguishing between guaranteed and unguaranteed, secured and unsecured indebtedness) as of a date no earlier than 90 days prior to the date of the EU Recovery prospectus. The term "indebtedness" also includes indirect and contingent indebtedness.

In the case of material changes in the capitalisation and indebtedness position of the issuer within the 90 day period, additional information must be given through the presentation of a narrative description of such changes or through the updating of those figures.

XIV. Conflicts of interest

Provide information about any interests related to the issuance, including conflicts of interest, and details of the persons involved and the nature of the interests.

XV. Dilution and shareholding after the issuance

Present a comparison of participation in share capital and voting rights for existing shareholders before and after the capital increase resulting from the public offer, with the assumption that existing shareholders do not subscribe for the new shares and, separately, with the assumption that existing shareholders do take up their entitlement.

XVI. Documents available

A statement that for the term of the EU Recovery prospectus the following documents, where applicable, can be inspected:

(a) the up to date memorandum and articles of association of the issuer;
(b) all reports, letters, and other documents, valuations and statements prepared by an expert at the issuer's request any part of which is included or referred to in the EU Recovery prospectus.

An indication of the website on which the documents may be inspected.]

NOTES

Inserted by European Parliament and Council Regulation 2021/337/EU, Art 1(11), Annex, as from 18 March 2021.

Application of this Annex in relation to the UK: note that Regulation 2021/337/EU (which inserts this Annex as noted above) is not "direct EU legislation" within the meaning of the European Union (Withdrawal) Act 2018, s 3 at **[12.5]** and, therefore, this Annex does not apply to the UK.

ANNEX VI
CORRELATION TABLE

(referred to in Article 46)

[11.379]

Directive 2003/71/EC	**This Regulation**
Article 1(1)	Article 1(1)
Article 1(2)(a)	Article 1(2)(a)
Article 1(2)(b)	Article 1(2)(b)
Article 1(2)(c)	Article 1(2)(c)
Article 1(2)(d)	Article 1(2)(d)
Article 1(2)(e)	Article 1(2)(e)
Article 1(2)(f)	—
Article 1(2)(g)	Article 1(2)(f)
Article 1(2)(h)	Article 1(3)
Article 1(2)(i)	—
Article 1(2)(j)	Article 1(4)(j) and Article 1(5), first subparagraph, point (i)
Article 1(3)	Article 4
Article 1(4)	—
Article 2(1)(a)	Article 2(a)
Article 2(1)(b)	Article 2(b)
Article 2(1)(c)	Article 2(c)
Article 2(1)(d)	Article 2(d)
Article 2(1)(e)	Article 2(e)
Article 2(1)(f)	Article 2(f)
Article 2(1)(g)	Article 2(g)
Article 2(1)(h)	Article 2(h)
Article 2(1)(i)	Article 2(i)
Article 2(1)(j)	Article 2(j)
Article 2(1)(k)	—
Article 2(1)(l)	—
Article 2(1)(m)	Article 2(m)
Article 2(1)(n)	Article 2(n)
Article 2(1)(o)	Article 2(p)
Article 2(1)(p)	Article 2(q)
Article 2(1)(q)	Article 2(r)
Article 2(1)(r)	Article 2(s)
Article 2(1)(s)	—
Article 2(1)(t)	—
Article 2(4)	—
Article 3(1)	Article 3(1)
Article 3(2)(a)	Article 1(4)(a)
Article 3(2)(b)	Article 1(4)(b)
Article 3(2)(c)	Article 1(4)(d)
Article 3(2)(d)	Article 1(4)(c)
Article 3(2)(e)	—

Directive 2003/71/EC	This Regulation
Article 3(2), second and third subparagraphs	Article 5(1)
Article 3(3)	Article 3(3)
Article 3(4)	—
Article 4(1)(a)	Article 1(4)(e)
Article 4(1)(b)	Article 1(4)(f)
Article 4(1)(c)	Article 1(4)(g)
Article 4(1)(d)	Article 1(4)(h)
Article 4(1)(e)	Article 1(4)(i)
Article 4(1), second to fifth subparagraphs	—
Article 4(2)(a)	Article 1(5), first subparagraph, point (a)
Article 4(2)(b)	Article 1(5), first subparagraph, point (d)
Article 4(2)(c)	Article 1(5), first subparagraph, point (e)
Article 4(2)(d)	Article 1(5), first subparagraph, point (f)
Article 4(2)(e)	Article 1(5), first subparagraph, point (g)
Article 4(2)(f)	Article 1(5), first subparagraph, point (h)
Article 4(2)(g)	Article 1(5), first subparagraph, points (b) and (c)
Article 4(2)(h)	Article 1(5), first subparagraph, point (j)
Article 4(3)	Article 1(7)
Article 5(1)	Article 6(1) and (2), Article 14(2)
Article 5(2)	Article 7
Article 5(3)	Article 6(3)
Article 5(4), first subparagraph	Article 8(1)
Article 5(4), second subparagraph	Article 8(10)
Article 5(4), third subparagraph, first sentence	Article 8(5) and Article 25(4)
Article 5(4), third subparagraph, second sentence	Article 8(4)
Article 5(5)	Article 13(1) and Article 7(13)
Article 6(1)	Article 11(1)
Article 6(2)	Article 11(2)
Article 7(1)	Article 13(1), first subparagraph
Article 7(2)(a)	Article 13(1), second subparagraph, point (a)
Article 7(2)(b)	Article 13(1), second subparagraph, point (b)
Article 7(2)(c)	Article 13(1), second subparagraph, point (c)
Article 7(2)(d)	Article 13(1), second subparagraph, point (c)
Article 7(2)(e)	Article 15(2)
Article 7(2)(f)	Article 13(1), second subparagraph, point (d)
Article 7(2)(g)	Article 14(3)
Article 7(3)	Article 13(3)
Article 7(4)	—
Article 8(1), first subparagraph, point (a)	Article 17(1), first subparagraph, point (b)
Article 8(1), first subparagraph, point (b)	Article 17(1), first subparagraph, point (a)
Article 8(1), second subparagraph	Article 17(2)
Article 8(2)	Article 18(1)
Article 8(3)	Article 18(2)
Article 8(3a)	Article 18(3)
Article 8(4)	Article 18(4), first subparagraph
Article 8(5), first subparagraph	—
Article 8(5), second subparagraph	—
Article 9(1)	Article 12(1)
Article 9(2)	Article 12(1)
Article 9(3)	Article 12(1)
Article 9(4)	Article 12(2)
Article 11(1)	Article 19(1)
Article 11(2)	Article 19(2)
Article 11(3)	Article 19(4)
Article 12(1)	Article 10(1), first subparagraph

Directive 2003/71/EC	This Regulation
Article 12(2)	Article 10(1), second subparagraph
Article 12(3)	—
Article 13(1)	Article 20(1)
Article 13(2)	Article 20(2)
Article 13(3)	Article 20(3)
Article 13(4)	Article 20(4)
Article 13(5)	Article 20(8)
Article 13(6)	Article 20(9)
Article 13(7)	—
Article 14(1)	Article 21(1)
Article 14(2)	Article 21(2)
Article 14(3)	—
Article 14(4)	Article 21(5)
Article 14(4a)	Article 21(6)
Article 14(5)	Article 21(9)
Article 14(6)	Article 21(10)
Article 14(7)	Article 21(11)
Article 14(8)	Article 21(12)
Article 15(1)	Article 22(1)
Article 15(2)	Article 22(2)
Article 15(3)	Article 22(3)
Article 15(4)	Article 22(4)
Article 15(5)	Article 22(5)
Article 15(6)	Article 22(6)
Article 15(7)	Article 22(9)
Article 16(1)	Article 23(1)
Article 16(2)	Article 23(2)
Article 16(3)	Article 23(7)
Article 17(1)	Article 24(1)
Article 17(2)	Article 24(2)
Article 18(1)	Article 25(1)
Article 18(2)	Article 25(2)
Article 18(3), first subparagraph	Article 25(3)
Article 18(3), second subparagraph	Article 21(5)
Article 18(4)	Article 25(8)
Article 19(1)	Article 27(1)
Article 19(2)	Article 27(2)
Article 19(3)	Article 27(3)
Article 19(4)	Article 27(5)
Article 20(1)	Article 29(1)
Article 20(2)	Article 29(2)
Article 20(3)	Article 29(3)
Article 21(1)	Article 31(1)
Article 21(1a)	Article 34(1)
Article 21(1b)	Article 34(2)
Article 21(2)	Article 31(2)
Article 21(3)(a)	Article 32(1)(a)
Article 21(3)(b)	Article 32(1)(b)
Article 21(3)(c)	Article 32(1)(c)
Article 21(3)(d)	Article 32(1)(d)
Article 21(3)(e)	Article 32(1)(e)
Article 21(3)(f)	Article 32(1)(f)
Article 21(3)(g)	Article 32(1)(g)
Article 21(3)(h)	Article 32(1)(h)
Article 21(3)(i)	Article 32(1)(i)

Directive 2003/71/EC	This Regulation
Article 21(3), second subparagraph	Article 32(1), second subparagraph
Article 21(4)(a)	Article 32(1)(l)
Article 21(4)(b)	Article 32(1)(m)
Article 21(4)(c)	—
Article 21(4)(d)	Article 32(1)(n)
Article 21(4), second subparagraph	Article 32(1), fourth subparagraph
Article 21(5)	Article 31(3) and Article 32(6)
Article 22(1)	Article 35(2)
Article 22(2), first subparagraph	Article 33(1)
Article 22(2), second subparagraph	—
Article 22(2), third subparagraph	Article 33(5)
Article 22(3)	—
Article 22(4)	Article 33(6) and (7)
Article 23(1)	Article 37(1)
Article 23(2)	Article 37(2)
Article 24(1)	Article 45(1)
Article 24(2)	Article 45(2)
Article 24(2a)	—
Article 24(3)	—
Article 24a	Article 44
Article 24b	Article 44
Article 24c	Article 44
Article 25(1)	Article 38(1)
Article 25(2)	Article 42
Article 26	Article 40
Article 27	—
Article 28	Article 46
Article 29	—
Article 30	—
Article 31	Article 48
Article 31a	—
Article 32	Article 49
Article 33	—

DIRECTIVE OF THE EUROPEAN PARLIAMENT AND OF THE COUNCIL

(2017/1132/EU)

of 14 June 2017

relating to certain aspects of company law (codification)

(Text with EEA relevance)

[11.380]

NOTES

Date of publication in OJ: OJ L169, 30.6.2017, p 46.

This Directive is reproduced as amended by: European Parliament and Council Directive 2019/1023/EU (transposition date 17 July 2021 (but see also **[11.761]**)); European Parliament and Council Directive 2019/1151/EU (transposition date 1 August 2021 and 1 August 2023 (and see further Article 2 of the Directive)); European Parliament and Council Directive 2019/2121/EU (transposition date 31 January 2023); European Parliament and Council Regulation 2021/23/EU.

Editorial note (legal status of EU Directives in the UK): note that EU Directives are not "direct EU legislation" within the meaning of the European Union (Withdrawal) Act 2018, s 3 at **[12.5]** and, accordingly, do not apply to the UK. As to the status of EU-derived domestic legislation after IP completion day (11pm on 31 December 2020), see s 2 of the 2018 Act at **[12.4]**. As to the UK implementation of this Directive, see the note below.

UK Implementation: this is a codification of previous law. The Directives repealed by this Directive (see Article 166 *post*) were implemented in the UK as follows:

Council Directive 82/891/EEC: implemented by the Companies (Mergers and Divisions) Regulations 1987, SI 1987/1991 (revoked).

Council Directive 89/666/EEC: implemented by the Companies Act 1985 (Disclosure of Branches and Bank Accounts) Regulations 1992, SI 1992/3178 (revoked); the Overseas Companies and Credit and Financial Institutions (Branch Disclosure) Regulations 1992, SI 1992/3179 (revoked); the Overseas Companies Regulations 2009, SI 2009/1801.

European Parliament and Council Directive 2005/56/EC: implemented by the Companies (Cross-Border Mergers) Regulations 2007, SI 2007/2974 (revoked); the Companies (Cross-Border Mergers) (Amendment) Regulations 2008, SI 2008/583 (revoked).

European Parliament and Council Directive 2009/101/EC: implemented by the Companies Act 2006 (Interconnection of Registers) Order 2014, SI 2014/1557.

European Parliament and Council Directive 2011/35/EU: no specific implementation measures in the UK.

European Parliament and Council Directive 2012/30/EU: no specific implementation measures in the UK.

THE EUROPEAN PARLIAMENT AND THE COUNCIL OF THE EUROPEAN UNION,

Having regard to the Treaty on the Functioning of the European Union, and in particular Article 50(1) and (2)(g) thereof,

Having regard to the proposal from the European Commission,

After transmission of the draft legislative act to the national parliaments,

Having regard to the opinion of the European Economic and Social Committee,[1]

Acting in accordance with the ordinary legislative procedure,[2]

Whereas:

(1) Council Directives 82/891/EEC[3] and 89/666/EEC[4] and Directives 2005/56/EC,[5] 2009/101/EC,[6] 2011/35/EU[7] and 2012/30/EU[8] of the European Parliament and of the Council have been substantially amended several times.[9] In the interests of clarity and rationality those Directives should be codified.

(2) The coordination provided for in Article 50(2)(g) of the Treaty and in the General Programme for the abolition of restrictions on freedom of establishment, which was begun by the First Council Directive 68/151/EEC,[10] is especially important in relation to public limited liability companies because their activities predominate in the economy of the Member States and frequently extend beyond their national boundaries.

(3) In order to ensure minimum equivalent protection for both shareholders and creditors of public limited liability companies, the coordination of national provisions relating to the formation of such companies and to the maintenance, increase or reduction of their capital is particularly important.

(4) In the Union, the statutes or instrument of incorporation of a public limited liability company must make it possible for any interested person to acquaint oneself with the basic particulars of the company, including the exact composition of its capital.

(5) The protection of third parties should be ensured by provisions which restrict to the greatest possible extent the grounds on which obligations entered into in the name of companies limited by shares or otherwise having limited liability are not valid.

(6) It is necessary, in order to ensure certainty in the law as regards relations between companies and third parties, and also between members, to limit the cases in which nullity can arise and the retroactive effect of a declaration of nullity, and to fix a short time limit within which third parties may enter an objection to any such declaration.

(7) The coordination of national provisions concerning disclosure, the validity of obligations entered into by, and the nullity of, companies limited by shares or otherwise having limited liability, is of special importance, particularly for the purpose of protecting the interests of third parties.

(8) The basic documents of a company should be disclosed in order for third parties to be able to ascertain their contents and other information concerning the company, especially particulars of the persons who are authorised to bind the company.

(9) Without prejudice to substantive requirements and formalities established by the national law of the Member States, companies should be able to choose to file their compulsory documents and particulars by paper means or by electronic means.

(10) Interested parties should be able to obtain from the register a copy of such documents and particulars by paper means as well as by electronic means.

(11) Member States should be allowed to decide to keep the national gazette, designated for publication of compulsory documents and particulars, in paper form or electronic form, or to provide for disclosure by equally effective means.

(12) Cross-border access to company information should be facilitated by allowing, in addition to the compulsory disclosure made in one of the languages permitted in the company's Member State, the voluntary registration in additional languages of the required documents and particulars. Third parties acting in good faith should be able to rely on the translations thereof.

(13) It is appropriate to clarify that the statement of the compulsory particulars set out in this Directive should be included in all company letters and order forms, whether they are in paper form or use any other medium. In the light of technological developments, it is also appropriate to provide that that statement of compulsory particulars be placed on any company website.

(14) The opening of a branch, like the creation of a subsidiary, is one of the possibilities currently open to companies in the exercise of their right of establishment in another Member State.

(15) In respect of branches, the lack of coordination, in particular concerning disclosure, gives rise to some disparities, in the protection of shareholders and third parties, between companies which operate in other Member States by opening branches and those which operate there by creating subsidiaries.

(16) To ensure the protection of persons who deal with companies through the intermediary of branches, measures in respect of disclosure are required in the Member State in which a branch is situated. In certain respects, the economic and social influence of a branch can be comparable to that of a subsidiary company, so that there is public interest in disclosure of the company at the branch. To effect such disclosure, it is necessary to make use of the procedure already instituted for companies with share capital within the Union.

(17) Such disclosure relates to a range of important documents and particulars and amendments thereto.

(18) Such disclosure, with the exception of the powers of representation, the name and legal form, and the winding- up of the company and the insolvency proceedings to which it is subject, can be confined to information concerning a branch itself together with a reference to the register of the company of which that branch is part, since under existing Union rules, all information covering the company as such is available in that register.

(19) National provisions in respect of the disclosure of accounting documents relating to a branch can no longer be justified following the coordination of national law in respect of the drawing up, audit and disclosure of companies' accounting documents. It is accordingly sufficient to disclose, in the register of the branch, the accounting documents as audited and disclosed by the company.

(20) Letters and order forms used by a branch should give at least the same information as letters and order forms used by the company, and state the register in which the branch is entered.

(21) To ensure that the purposes of this Directive are fully realised and to avoid any discrimination on the basis of a company's country of origin, this Directive should also cover branches opened by companies governed by the law of third countries and set up in legal forms comparable to companies to which this Directive applies. For such branches it is necessary to apply specific provisions that are different from those that apply to the branches of companies governed by the law of other Member States since this Directive does not apply to companies from third countries.

(22) This Directive in no way affects the disclosure requirements for branches under other provisions of, for example, employment law on workers' rights to information and tax law, or for statistical purposes.

(23) The interconnection of central, commercial and companies registers is a measure required to create a more business-friendly legal and fiscal environment. It should contribute to fostering the competitiveness of European business by reducing administrative burdens and increasing legal certainty and thus contributing to an exit from the global economic and financial crisis, which is one of the priorities of the agenda of Europe 2020. It should also improve cross-border communication between registers by using innovations in information and communication technology.

(24) The Multiannual European e-Justice action plan 2009–2013[11] provided for the development of a European e-Justice portal ('the portal') as the single European electronic access point for legal information, judicial and administrative institutions, registers, databases and other services and considers the interconnection of central, commercial and companies registers to be important.

(25) Cross-border access to business information on companies and their branches opened in other Member States can only be improved if all Member States engage in enabling electronic communication to take place between registers and transmitting information to individual users in a standardised way, by means of identical content and interoperable technologies, throughout the Union. This interoperability of registers should be ensured by the registers of Member States ('domestic registers') providing services, which should constitute interfaces with the European central platform ('the platform'). The platform should be a centralised set of information technology tools integrating services and should form a common interface. That interface should be used by all domestic registers. The platform should also provide services constituting an interface with the portal serving as the European electronic access point, and to the optional access points established by Member States. The platform should be conceived only as an instrument for the interconnection of registers and not as a distinct entity possessing legal personality. On the basis of unique identifiers, the platform should be capable of distributing information from each of the Member States' registers to the competent registers of other Member States in a standard message format (an electronic form of messages exchanged between information technology systems, such as, for example, xml) and in the relevant language version.

(26) This Directive is not aimed at establishing any centralised registers database storing substantive information about companies. At the stage of implementation of the system of interconnection of central, commercial and companies registers ('the system of interconnection of registers'), only the set of data necessary for the correct functioning of the platform should be defined. The scope of those data should include, in particular, operational data, dictionaries and glossaries. It should be determined taking also into account the need to ensure the efficient operation of the system of interconnection of registers. Those data should be used for the purpose of enabling the platform to perform its functions and should never be made publicly available in a direct form. Moreover, the platform should modify neither the content of the data on companies stored in domestic registers nor the information about companies transmitted through the system of interconnection of registers.

(27) Since the objective of Directive 2012/17/EU of the European Parliament and of the Council[12] was not to harmonise national systems of central, commercial and companies registers, that Directive did not impose any obligation on Member States to change their internal systems of registers, in particular as regards the management and storage of data, fees, and the use and disclosure of information for national purposes.

(28) The portal should deal, through the use of the platform, with queries submitted by individual users concerning the information on companies and their branches opened in other Member States which is stored in the domestic registers. That should enable the search results to be presented on the portal, including the explanatory labels in all the official languages of the Union, listing the information provided. In addition, in order to improve the protection of third parties in other Member States, basic information on the legal value of documents and particulars disclosed pursuant to the laws of Member States adopted in accordance with this Directive should be available on the portal.

(29) Member States should be able to establish one or more optional access points, which may have an impact on the use and operation of the platform. Therefore, the Commission should be notified of their establishment and of any significant changes to their operation, in particular of their closure. Such notification should not in any way restrict the powers of Member States as to the establishment and operation of the optional access points.

(30) Companies and their branches opened in other Member States should have a unique identifier allowing them to be unequivocally identified within the Union. The identifier is intended to be used for communication between registers through the system of interconnection of registers. Therefore, companies and branches should not be obliged to include the unique identifier in the company letters or order forms mentioned in this Directive. They should continue to use their domestic registration number for their own communication purposes.

(31) It should be made possible to establish a clear connection between the register of a company and the registers of its branches opened in other Member States, consisting of the exchange of information on the opening and

termination of any winding-up or insolvency proceedings of the company and on the striking-off of the company from the register, if this entails legal consequences in the Member State of the register of the company. While Member States should be able to decide on the procedures they follow with respect to the branches registered in their territory, they should ensure, at least, that the branches of a dissolved company are struck off the register without undue delay and, if applicable, after liquidation proceedings of the branch concerned. This obligation should not apply to branches of companies that have been struck off the register but which have a legal successor, such as in the case of any change in the legal form of the company, a merger or division, or a cross-border transfer of its registered office.

(32) The provisions of this Directive relating to the interconnection of registers should not apply to a branch opened in a Member State by a company which is not governed by the law of a Member State.

(33) Member States should ensure that, in the event of any changes to information entered in the registers concerning companies, the information is updated without undue delay. The update should be disclosed, normally, within 21 days of receipt of the complete documentation regarding those changes, including the legality check in accordance with national law. That time limit should be interpreted as requiring Member States to make reasonable efforts to meet the deadline laid down in this Directive. It should not be applicable as regards the accounting documents which companies are obliged to submit for each financial year. That exclusion is justified by the overload of work on domestic registers during reporting periods. In accordance with general legal principles common to all Member States, the time limit of 21 days should be suspended in cases of *force majeure*.

(34) If the Commission decides to develop and/or operate the platform through a third party, this should be done in accordance with Regulation (EU, Euratom) No 966/2012 of the European Parliament and of the Council.[13] An appropriate degree of Member States' involvement in this process should be ensured by establishing the technical specifications for the purpose of the public procurement procedure by means of implementing acts adopted in accordance with the examination procedure referred to in Article 5 of Regulation (EU) No 182/2011 of the European Parliament and of the Council.[14]

(35) If the Commission decides to operate the platform through a third party, the continuity of the provision of services by the system of interconnection of registers and a proper public supervision of the functioning of the platform should be ensured. Detailed rules on the operational management of the platform should be adopted by means of implementing acts adopted in accordance with the examination procedure referred to in Article 5 of Regulation (EU) No 182/2011. In any case, the involvement of Member States in the functioning of the whole system should be ensured by means of a regular dialogue between the Commission and the representatives of Member States on the issues concerning the operation of the system of interconnection of registers and its future development.

(36) The interconnection of central, commercial and companies registers necessitates the coordination of national systems having varying technical characteristics. This entails the adoption of technical measures and specifications which need to take account of differences between registers. In order to ensure uniform conditions for the implementation of this Directive, implementing powers should be conferred on the Commission to tackle those technical and operational issues. Those powers should be exercised in accordance with the examination procedure referred to in Article 5 of Regulation (EU) No 182/2011.

(37) This Directive should not limit the right of Member States to charge fees for obtaining information on companies through the system of interconnection of registers, if such fees are required under national law. Therefore, technical measures and specifications for the system of interconnection of registers should allow for the establishment of payment modalities. In this respect, this Directive should not prejudge any specific technical solution as the payment modalities should be determined at the stage of adoption of the implementing acts, taking into account widely available online payment facilities.

(38) It could be desirable for third countries to be able, in the future, to participate in the system of interconnection of registers.

(39) An equitable solution regarding the funding of the system of interconnection of registers entails participation both by the Union and by its Member States in the financing of that system. Member States should bear the financial burden of adjusting their domestic registers to that system, while the central elements, namely the platform and the portal serving as the European electronic access point, should be funded from an appropriate budget line in the general budget of the Union. In order to supplement non-essential elements of this Directive, the power to adopt acts in accordance with Article 290 of the Treaty should be delegated to the Commission in respect of the charging of fees for obtaining company information. This does not affect the possibility for the domestic registers to charge fees, but it could involve an additional fee in order to co-finance the maintenance and functioning of the platform. It is of particular importance that the Commission carry out appropriate consultations during its preparatory work, including at expert level. The Commission, when preparing and drawing up delegated acts, should ensure a simultaneous, timely and appropriate transmission of relevant documents to the European Parliament and to the Council.

(40) Union provisions are necessary for maintaining the capital, which constitutes the creditors' security, in particular by prohibiting any reduction thereof by distribution to shareholders where the latter are not entitled to it and by imposing limits on the right of public limited liability companies to acquire their own shares.

(41) The restrictions on a public limited liability company's acquisition of its own shares apply not only to acquisitions made by a company itself but also to those made by any person acting in his own name but on the company's behalf.

(42) In order to prevent a public limited liability company from using another company in which it holds a majority of the voting rights or on which it can exercise a dominant influence to make such acquisitions without complying with the restrictions imposed in that respect, the arrangements governing a company's acquisition of its own shares should cover the most important and most frequent cases of the acquisition of shares by such other companies. Those arrangements should cover subscription for shares in the public limited liability company.

(43) In order to prevent the circumvention of this Directive, companies limited by shares or otherwise having limited liability governed by this Directive and companies governed by the laws of third countries, and having comparable legal forms, should also be covered by the arrangements referred to in recital 42.

(44) Where the relationship between a public limited liability company and another company such as referred to in recital 42 is only indirect, it would appear to be justified to relax the provisions applicable when that relationship

is direct, by providing for the suspension of voting rights as a minimum measure, for the purpose of achieving the aims of this Directive.

(45) Furthermore, it is justifiable to exempt cases in which the specific nature of a professional activity rules out the possibility of the attainment of the objectives of this Directive being endangered.

(46) It is necessary, having regard to the objectives of Article 50(2)(g) of the Treaty, that the Member States' laws relating to the increase or reduction of capital ensure that the principles of equal treatment of shareholders in the same position and of protection of creditors whose claims exist prior to the decision on reduction are observed and harmonised.

(47) In order to enhance standardised creditor protection in all Member States, creditors should be able to resort, under certain conditions, to judicial or administrative proceedings where their claims are at stake, as a consequence of a reduction in the capital of a public limited liability company.

(48) In order to ensure that market abuse is prevented, Member States should take into account, for the purpose of the implementation of this Directive, the provisions of Regulation (EU) No 596/2014 of the European Parliament and of the Council.[15]

(49) The protection of the interests of members and third parties requires that the laws of the Member States relating to mergers of public limited liability companies be coordinated, and that provision for mergers be made in the laws of all the Member States.

(50) In the context of such coordination, it is particularly important that the shareholders of merging companies be kept adequately informed in as objective a manner as possible, and that their rights be suitably protected. However, there is no reason to require an examination of the draft terms of a merger by an independent expert for the shareholders if all the shareholders agree that it can be dispensed with.

(51) Creditors, including debenture holders, and persons having other claims on the merging companies should be protected so that the merger does not adversely affect their interests.

(52) The disclosure requirements for the protection of the interests of members and third parties should include mergers so that third parties are kept adequately informed.

(53) The safeguards afforded to members and third parties in connection with mergers of public limited liability companies should cover certain legal practices which in important respects are similar to merger, so that the obligation to provide such protection cannot be evaded.

(54) To ensure certainty in the law as regards relations between the companies concerned, between them and third parties, and between the members, it is necessary to limit the cases in which nullity can arise by providing that defects be remedied wherever that is possible, and by restricting the period within which nullification proceedings can be commenced.

(55) This Directive also facilitates the cross-border merger of limited liability companies. The laws of the Member States should allow the cross-border merger of a national limited liability company with a limited liability company from another Member State if the national law of the relevant Member States permits mergers between such types of company.

(56) In order to facilitate cross-border merger operations, it should be specified that, unless this Directive provides otherwise, each company taking part in a cross-border merger, and each third party concerned, remains subject to the provisions and formalities of the national law which would be applicable in the case of a national merger. None of the provisions and formalities of national law, to which reference is made in this Directive, should introduce restrictions on freedom of establishment or on the free movement of capital, save where these can be justified in accordance with the case-law of the Court of Justice of the European Union and in particular, by requirements of the general interest and are both necessary for, and proportionate to, the attainment of such overriding requirements.

(57) The common draft terms of a cross-border merger should be drawn up in the same terms for each of the companies concerned in the various Member States. The minimum content of such common draft terms should therefore be specified, while leaving the companies free to agree on other terms.

(58) In order to protect the interests of members and others, both the common draft terms of the cross-border merger and the completion of the cross-border merger should be publicised for each merging company via an entry in the appropriate public register.

(59) The laws of all the Member States should provide for the drawing-up at national level of a report on the common draft terms of the cross-border merger by one or more experts on behalf of each of the companies that are merging. In order to limit experts' costs connected with cross-border mergers, provision should be made for the possibility of drawing up a single report intended for all members of companies taking part in a cross-border merger operation. The common draft terms of the cross-border merger should be approved by the general meeting of each of those companies.

(60) In order to facilitate cross-border merger operations, it should be provided that monitoring of the completion and legality of the decision-making process in each merging company should be carried out by the national authority having jurisdiction over each of those companies, whereas monitoring of the completion and legality of the cross-border merger should be carried out by the national authority having jurisdiction over the company resulting from the cross-border merger. The national authority in question could be a court, a notary or any other competent authority appointed by the Member State concerned. The national law determining the date on which the cross-border merger takes effect, this being the law to which the company resulting from the cross- border merger is subject, should also be specified.

(61) In order to protect the interests of members and others, the legal effects of the cross-border merger, distinguishing as to whether the company resulting from the cross-border merger is an acquiring company or a new company, should be specified. In the interests of legal certainty, it should no longer be possible, after the date on which a cross-border merger takes effect, to declare the merger null and void.

(62) This Directive is without prejudice to the application of the legislation on the control of concentrations between undertakings, both at Union level, by Council Regulation (EC) No 139/2004,[16] and at Member State level.

(63) This Directive does not affect Union legislation regulating credit intermediaries and other financial undertakings and national rules made or introduced pursuant to such Union legislation.

(64) This Directive is without prejudice to Member State legislation demanding information on the place of central administration or the principal place of business proposed for the company resulting from the cross-border merger.

(65) Employees' rights, other than rights of participation, should remain subject to the national provisions referred to in Council Directives 98/59/EC[17] and 2001/23/EC,[18] and in Directives 2002/14/EC[19] and 2009/38/EC[20] of the European Parliament and of the Council.

(66) If employees have participation rights in one of the merging companies under the circumstances set out in this Directive and, if the national law of the Member State in which the company resulting from the cross-border merger has its registered office does not provide for the same level of participation as operated in the relevant merging companies, including in committees of the supervisory board that have decision-making powers, or does not provide for the same entitlement to exercise rights for employees of establishments resulting from the cross- border merger, the participation of employees in the company resulting from the cross-border merger and their involvement in the definition of such rights should be regulated. To that end, the principles and procedures provided for in Council Regulation (EC) No 2157/2001[21] and in Council Directive 2001/86/EC,[22] should be taken as a basis, subject, however, to modifications that are deemed necessary because the resulting company will be subject to the national laws of the Member State where it has its registered office. A prompt start to negotiations under Article 133 of this Directive, with a view to not unnecessarily delaying mergers, may be ensured by Member States in accordance with Article 3(2)(b) of Directive 2001/86/EC.

(67) For the purpose of determining the level of employee participation operated in the relevant merging companies, account should also be taken of the proportion of employee representatives amongst the members of the management group, which covers the profit units of the companies, subject to employee participation.

(68) The protection of the interests of members and third parties requires that the laws of the Member States relating to divisions of public limited liability companies be coordinated where Member States permit such operations.

(69) In the context of such coordination, it is particularly important that the shareholders of the companies involved in a division be kept adequately informed in as objective a manner as possible, and that their rights be suitably protected.

(70) Creditors, including debenture holders, and persons having other claims on the companies involved in a division of public limited liability companies, should be protected so that the division does not adversely affect their interests.

(71) Disclosure requirements under Section 1 of Chapter III of Title I of this Directive should include divisions so that third parties are kept adequately informed.

(72) The safeguards afforded to members and third parties in connection with divisions should cover certain legal practices which in important respects are similar to division, so that the obligation to provide such protection cannot be evaded.

(73) To ensure certainty in the law as regards relations between the public limited liability companies involved in the division, between them and third parties, and between the members, the cases in which nullity can arise should be limited by providing that defects should be remedied wherever that is possible and by restricting the period within which nullification proceedings can be commenced.

(74) Company websites or other websites offer, in certain cases, an alternative to publication via the companies registers. Member States should be able to designate those other websites which companies can use free of charge for such publication, such as websites of business associations or chambers of commerce or the central electronic platform referred to in this Directive. Where the possibility exists of using company or other websites for publication of draft terms of merger and/or division and of other documents that have to be made available to shareholders and creditors in the process, guarantees relating to the security of the website and the authenticity of the documents should be met.

(75) Member States should be able to provide that the extensive reporting or information requirements relating to the merger or division of companies, laid down in Chapter I and Chapter III of Title II, need not be complied with where all the shareholders of the companies involved in the merger or division agree that such compliance can be dispensed with.

(76) Any modification of Chapter I and Chapter III of Title II allowing such agreement by shareholders, should be without prejudice to the systems of protection of the interests of creditors of the companies involved, and to rules aimed at ensuring the provision of necessary information to the employees of those companies and to public authorities, such as tax authorities, controlling the merger or division in accordance with existing Union law.

(77) It is not necessary to impose the requirement to draw up an accounting statement where an issuer whose securities are admitted to trading on a regulated market publishes half-yearly financial reports in accordance with Directive 2004/109/EC of the European Parliament and of the Council.[23]

(78) An independent expert's report on consideration other than in cash is often not needed where an independent expert's report protecting the interests of shareholders or creditors also has to be drawn up in the context of the merger or the division. Member States should therefore have the possibility in such cases of dispensing companies from the reporting requirement regarding consideration other than in cash or of providing that both reports can be drawn up by the same expert.

(79) Directive 95/46/EC of the European Parliament and of the Council[24] and Regulation (EC) No 45/2001 of the European Parliament and of the Council[25] govern the processing of personal data, including the electronic transmission of personal data within the Member States. Any processing of personal data by the registers of Member States, by the Commission and, if applicable, by any third party involved in operating the platform should take place in compliance with those acts. The implementing acts to be adopted in relation to the system of interconnection of registers should, where appropriate, ensure such compliance, in particular by establishing the relevant tasks and responsibilities of all the participants concerned and the organisational and technical rules applicable to them.

(80) This Directive respects fundamental rights and observes the principles enshrined in the Charter of Fundamental Rights of the European Union, in particular Article 8 thereof, which states that everyone has the right to the protection of personal data concerning him or her.

(81) This Directive should be without prejudice to the obligations of the Member States relating to the time limits

for the transposition into national law and the dates of application of the directives set out in Annex III, Part B,

NOTES

[1] OJ C264, 20.7.2016, p 82.

[2] Position of the European Parliament of 5 April 2017 (not yet published in the Official Journal) and decision of the Council of 29 May 2017.

[3] Sixth Council Directive 82/891/EEC of 17 December 1982 based on Article 54(3)(g) of the Treaty, concerning the division of public limited liability companies (OJ L378, 31.12.1982, p 47).

[4] Eleventh Council Directive 89/666/EEC of 21 December 1989 concerning disclosure requirements in respect of branches opened in a Member State by certain types of company governed by the law of another State (OJ L395, 30.12.1989, p 36).

[5] Directive 2005/56/EC of the European Parliament and of the Council of 26 October 2005 on cross-border mergers of limited liability companies (OJ L310, 25.11.2005, p 1).

[6] Directive 2009/101/EC of the European Parliament and of the Council of 16 September 2009 on coordination of safeguards which, for the protection of the interests of members and third parties, are required by Member States of companies within the meaning of the second paragraph of Article 48 of the Treaty, with a view to making such safeguards equivalent (OJ L258, 1.10.2009, p 11).

[7] Directive 2011/35/EU of the European Parliament and of the Council of 5 April 2011 concerning mergers of public limited liability companies (OJ L110, 29.4.2011, p 1).

[8] Directive 2012/30/EU of the European Parliament and of the Council of 25 October 2012 on coordination of safeguards which, for the protection of the interests of members and others, are required by Member States of companies within the meaning of the second paragraph of Article 54 of the Treaty on the Functioning of the European Union, in respect of the formation of public limited liability companies and the maintenance and alteration of their capital, with a view to making such safeguards equivalent (OJ L315, 14.11.2012, p 74).

[9] See Annex III, Part A.

[10] First Council Directive 68/151/EEC of 9 March 1968 on coordination of safeguards which, for the protection of the interests of members and others, are required by Member States of companies within the meaning of the second paragraph of Article 58 of the Treaty, with a view to making such safeguards equivalent throughout the Community (OJ L65, 14.3.1968, p 8).

[11] OJ C75, 31.3.2009, p 1.

[12] Directive 2012/17/EU of the European Parliament and of the Council of 13 June 2012 amending Council Directive 89/666/EEC and Directives 2005/56/EC and 2009/101/EC of the European Parliament and of the Council as regards the interconnection of central, commercial and companies registers (OJ L156, 16.6.2012, p 1).

[13] Regulation (EU, Euratom) No 966/2012 of the European Parliament and of the Council of 25 October 2012 on the financial rules applicable to the general budget of the Union and repealing Council Regulation (EC, Euratom) No 1605/2002 (OJ L298, 26.10.2012, p 1).

[14] Regulation (EU) No 182/2011 of the European Parliament and of the Council of 16 February 2011 laying down the rules and general principles concerning mechanisms for control by Member States of the Commission's exercise of implementing powers (OJ L55, 28.2.2011, p 13).

[15] Regulation (EU) No 596/2014 of the European Parliament and of the Council of 16 April 2014 on market abuse (market abuse regulation) and repealing Directive 2003/6/EC of the European Parliament and of the Council and Commission Directives 2003/124/EC, 2003/125/EC and 2004/72/EC (OJ L173, 12.6.2014, p 1).

[16] Council Regulation (EC) No 139/2004 of 20 January 2004 on the control of concentrations between undertakings (the EC Merger Regulation) (OJ L24, 29.1.2004, p 1).

[17] Council Directive 98/59/EC of 20 July 1998 on the approximation of the laws of the Member States relating to collective redundancies (OJ L225, 12.8.1998, p 16).

[18] Council Directive 2001/23/EC of 12 March 2001 on the approximation of the laws of the Member States relating to the safeguarding of employees' rights in the event of transfers of undertakings, businesses or parts of undertakings or businesses (OJ L82, 22.3.2001, p 16).

[19] Directive 2002/14/EC of the European Parliament and of the Council of 11 March 2002 establishing a general framework for informing and consulting employees in the European Community (OJ L80, 23.3.2002, p 29).

[20] Directive 2009/38/EC of the European Parliament and of the Council of 6 May 2009 on the establishment of a European Works Council or a procedure in Community-scale undertakings and Community-scale groups of undertakings for the purposes of informing and consulting employees (OJ L122, 16.5.2009, p 28).

[21] Council Regulation (EC) No 2157/2001 of 8 October 2001 on the Statute for a European company (SE) (OJ L294, 10.11.2001, p 1).

[22] Council Directive 2001/86/EC of 8 October 2001 supplementing the Statute for a European company with regard to the involvement of employees (OJ L294, 10.11.2001, p 22).

[23] Directive 2004/109/EC of the European Parliament and of the Council of 15 December 2004 on the harmonisation of transparency requirements in relation to information about issuers whose securities are admitted to trading on a regulated market and amending Directive 2001/34/EC (OJ L390, 31.12.2004, p 38).

[24] Directive 95/46/EC of the European Parliament and of the Council of 24 October 1995 on the protection of individuals with regard to the processing of personal data and on the free movement of such data (OJ L281, 23.11.1995, p 31).

[25] Regulation (EC) No 45/2001 of the European Parliament and of the Council of 18 December 2000 on the protection of individuals with regard to the processing of personal data by the Community institutions and bodies and on the free movement of such data (OJ L8, 12.1.2001, p 1).

HAVE ADOPTED THIS DIRECTIVE:

TITLE I GENERAL PROVISIONS AND THE ESTABLISHMENT AND FUNCTIONING OF LIMITED LIABILITY COMPANIES

CHAPTER I SUBJECT MATTER

[11.381]

Article 1 Subject matter

This Directive lays down measures concerning the following:

— the coordination of safeguards which, for the protection of the interests of members and others, are required by Member States of companies within the meaning of the second paragraph of Article 54 of the Treaty, in respect of the formation of public limited liability companies and the maintenance and alteration of their capital, with a view to making such safeguards equivalent,
— the coordination of safeguards which, for the protection of the interests of members and third parties, are required by Member States of companies within the meaning of the second paragraph of Article 54 of the Treaty, in respect of disclosure, the validity of obligations entered into by, and the nullity of, companies limited by shares or otherwise having limited liability, with a view to making such safeguards equivalent,
[— the rules on online formation of companies, on online registration of branches and on online filing of documents and information by companies and branches,]
— the disclosure requirements in respect of branches opened in a Member State by certain types of company governed by the law of another State,
— mergers of public limited liability companies,
— [cross-border conversions, cross-border mergers and cross-border divisions of limited liability companies,]
— the division of public limited liability companies.

NOTES

Words in first pair of square brackets inserted by European Parliament and Council Directive 2019/1151/EU, Art 1(1), as from 31 July 2019.

Words in second pair of square brackets substituted by European Parliament and Council Directive 2019/2121/EU, Art 1(1), as form 1 January 2020. Note that the 2019 Directive has a transposition date of 31 January 2023.

CHAPTER II INCORPORATION AND NULLITY OF THE COMPANY AND VALIDITY OF ITS OBLIGATIONS

SECTION 1 INCORPORATION OF THE PUBLIC LIABILITY COMPANY

[11.382]

Article 2 Scope

1. The coordination measures prescribed by this Section shall apply to the provisions laid down by law, regulation or administrative action in Member States relating to the types of company listed in Annex I. The name for any company of the types listed in Annex I shall comprise or be accompanied by a description which is distinct from the description required of other types of companies.

2. Member States may decide not to apply this Section to investment companies with variable capital and to cooperatives incorporated as one of the types of company listed in Annex I. In so far as the laws of the Member States make use of this option, they shall require such companies to include the words 'investment company with variable capital', or 'cooperative' in all documents indicated in Article 26.

The term 'investment company with variable capital', within the meaning of this Directive, means only those companies:
— the exclusive object of which is to invest their funds in various stocks and shares, land or other assets with the sole aim of spreading investment risks and giving their shareholders the benefit of the results of the management of their assets,
— which offer their own shares for subscription by the public, and
— the statutes of which provide that, within the limits of a minimum and maximum capital, they may at any time issue, redeem or resell their shares.

[11.383]

Article 3 Compulsory information to be provided in the statutes or instruments of incorporation

The statutes or the instrument of incorporation of a company shall always give at least the following information:
(a) the type and name of the company;
(b) the objects of the company;
(c) where the company has no authorised capital, the amount of the subscribed capital;
(d) where the company has an authorised capital, the amount thereof and also the amount of the capital subscribed at the time the company is incorporated or is authorised to commence business, and at the time of any change in the authorised capital, without prejudice to Article 14(e);
(e) in so far as they are not legally determined, the rules governing the number of, and the procedure for, appointing members of the bodies responsible for representing the company vis-à-vis third parties, administration, management, supervision or control of the company and the allocation of powers among those bodies;
(f) the duration of the company, except where this is indefinite.

[11.384]

Article 4 Compulsory information to be provided in the statutes or instruments of incorporation or separate documents

The following information at least shall appear in either the statutes or the instrument of incorporation or a separate document published in accordance with the procedure laid down in the laws of each Member State in accordance with Article 16:
(a) the registered office;
(b) the nominal value of the shares subscribed and, at least once a year, the number thereof;
(c) the number of shares subscribed without stating the nominal value, where such shares may be issued under national law;
(d) the special conditions, if any, limiting the transfer of shares;
(e) where there are several classes of shares, the information referred to in points (b), (c) and (d) for each class and the rights attaching to the shares of each class;
(f) whether the shares are registered or bearer, where national law provides for both types, and any provisions relating to the conversion of such shares unless the procedure is laid down by law;

(g) the amount of the subscribed capital paid up at the time the company is incorporated or is authorised to commence business;
(h) the nominal value of the shares or, where there is no nominal value, the number of shares issued for a consideration other than in cash, together with the nature of the consideration and the name of the person providing the consideration;
(i) the identity of the natural or legal persons or companies or firms by which or in whose name the statutes or the instrument of incorporation, or where the company was not formed at the same time, the drafts of those documents, have been signed;
(j) the total amount, or at least an estimate, of all the costs payable by the company or chargeable to it by reason of its formation and, where appropriate, before the company is authorised to commence business;
(k) any special advantage granted, at the time the company is formed or up to the time it receives authorisation to commence business, to anyone who has taken part in the formation of the company or in transactions leading to the grant of such authorisation.

[11.385]

Article 5 Authorisation for commencing business

1. Where the laws of a Member State prescribe that a company may not commence business without authorisation, they shall also make provision for responsibility for liabilities incurred by or on behalf of the company during the period before such authorisation is granted or refused.
2. Paragraph 1 shall not apply to liabilities under contracts concluded by the company conditionally upon its being granted authorisation to commence business.

[11.386]

Article 6 Multiple-member companies

1. Where the laws of a Member State require a company to be formed by more than one member, the fact that all the shares are held by one person or that the number of members has fallen below the legal minimum after incorporation of the company shall not lead to the automatic dissolution of the company.
2. If, in the cases referred to in paragraph 1, the laws of a Member State permit the company to be wound up by order of the court, the judge having jurisdiction shall be able to give the company sufficient time to regularise its position.
3. Where a winding-up order as referred to in paragraph 2 is made, the company shall enter into liquidation.

SECTION 2 NULLITY OF THE LIMITED LIABILITY COMPANY AND VALIDITY OF ITS OBLIGATIONS

[11.387]

Article 7 General provisions and joint and several liability

1. The coordination measures prescribed by this Section shall apply to the laws, regulations and administrative provisions of the Member States relating to the types of company listed in Annex II.
2. If, before a company being formed has acquired legal personality, action has been carried out in its name and the company does not assume the obligations arising from such action, the persons who acted shall, without limit, be jointly and severally liable therefor, unless otherwise agreed.

[11.388]

Article 8 Effects of disclosure with respect to third parties

Completion of the formalities of disclosure of the particulars concerning the persons who, as an organ of the company, are authorised to represent it, shall constitute a bar to any irregularity in their appointment being relied upon as against third parties, unless the company proves that such third parties had knowledge thereof.

[11.389]

Article 9 Acts of the organs of a company and its representation

1. Acts done by the organs of the company shall be binding upon it even if those acts are not within the objects of the company, unless such acts exceed the powers that the law confers or allows to be conferred on those organs.
However, Member States may provide that the company shall not be bound where such acts are outside the objects of the company, if it proves that the third party knew that the act was outside those objects or could not in view of the circumstances have been unaware of it. Disclosure of the statutes shall not of itself be sufficient proof thereof.
2. The limits on the powers of the organs of the company, arising under the statutes or from a decision of the competent organs, may not be relied on as against third parties, even if they have been disclosed.
3. If national law provides that authority to represent a company may, in derogation from the legal rules governing the subject, be conferred by the statutes on a single person or on several persons acting jointly, that law may provide that such a provision in the statutes may be relied on as against third parties on condition that it relates to the general power of representation; the question whether such a provision in the statutes can be relied on as against third parties shall be governed by Article 16.

[11.390]

Article 10 Drawing up and certification of the instrument of constitution and the company statutes in due legal form

In all Member States whose laws do not provide for preventive administrative or judicial control, at the time of formation of a company, the instrument of constitution, the company statutes and any amendments to those documents shall be drawn up and certified in due legal form.

[11.391]

Article 11 Conditions for nullity of a company

The laws of the Member States may not provide for the nullity of companies otherwise than in accordance with the following provisions:
(a) nullity must be ordered by decision of a court of law;
(b) nullity may be ordered only on the grounds:

(i) that no instrument of constitution was executed or that the rules of preventive control or the requisite legal formalities were not complied with;
(ii) that the objects of the company are unlawful or contrary to public policy;
(iii) that the instrument of constitution or the statutes do not state the name of the company, the amount of the individual subscriptions of capital, the total amount of the capital subscribed or the objects of the company;
(iv) of failure to comply with provisions of national law concerning the minimum amount of capital to be paid up;
(v) of the incapacity of all the founder members;
(vi) that, contrary to the national law governing the company, the number of founder members is less than two.

Apart from the grounds of nullity referred to in the first paragraph, a company shall not be subject to any cause of non-existence, absolute nullity, relative nullity or declaration of nullity.

[11.392]
Article 12 Consequences of nullity
1. The question whether a decision of nullity pronounced by a court of law may be relied on as against third parties shall be governed by Article 16. Where the national law entitles a third party to challenge the decision, he may do so only within six months of public notice of the decision of the court being given.
2. Nullity shall entail the winding-up of the company, as may dissolution.
3. Nullity shall not of itself affect the validity of any commitments entered into by or with the company, without prejudice to the consequences of the company's being wound up.
4. The laws of each Member State may make provision for the consequences of nullity as between members of the company.
5. Holders of shares in the capital of a company shall remain obliged to pay up the capital agreed to be subscribed by them but which has not been paid up, to the extent that commitments entered into with creditors so require.

CHAPTER III [ONLINE PROCEDURES (FORMATION, REGISTRATION AND FILING), DISCLOSURE AND REGISTERS]

NOTES
Chapter III heading substituted by European Parliament and Council Directive 2019/1151/EU, Art 1(2), as from 31 July 2019.

SECTION 1 GENERAL PROVISIONS

[11.393]
[Article 13 Scope
The coordination measures prescribed by this Section and by Section 1A shall apply to the laws, regulations and administrative provisions of the Member States relating to the types of companies listed in Annex II and, where specified, to the types of companies listed in Annexes I and IIA.]

NOTES
Substituted by European Parliament and Council Directive 2019/1151/EU, Art 1(3), as from 31 July 2019.

[11.394]
[Article 13a Definitions
For the purposes of this Chapter:
(1) "electronic identification means" means an electronic identification means as defined in point (2) of Article 3 of Regulation (EU) No 910/2014 of the European Parliament and of the Council;[1]
(2) "electronic identification scheme" means an electronic identification scheme as defined in point (4) of Article 3 of Regulation (EU) No 910/2014;
(3) "electronic means" means electronic equipment used for the processing, including digital compression, and the storage of data, and through which information is initially sent and received at its destination; that information being entirely transmitted, conveyed and received in a manner to be determined by Member States;
(4) "formation" means the whole process of establishing a company in accordance with national law, including the drawing up of the company's instrument of constitution and all the necessary steps for the entry of the company in the register;
(5) "registration of a branch" means a process leading to disclosure of documents and information relating to a branch newly opened in a Member State;
(6) "template" means a model for the instrument of constitution of a company which is drawn up by Member States in compliance with national law and is used for the online formation of a company in accordance with Article 13g.]

NOTES
Articles 13a–13f inserted by European Parliament and Council Directive 2019/1151/EU, Art 1(4), as from 31 July 2019.
[1] Regulation (EU) No 910/2014 of the European Parliament and of the Council of 23 July 2014 on electronic identification and trust services for electronic transactions in the internal market and repealing Directive 1999/93/EC (OJ L257, 28.8.2014, p 73).

[11.395]
[Article 13b Recognition of identification means for the purposes of online procedures
1. Member States shall ensure that the following electronic identification means can be used by applicants who are Union citizens in the online procedures referred to in this Chapter:
(a) an electronic identification means issued under an electronic identification scheme approved by their own Member State;
(b) an electronic identification means issued in another Member State and recognised for the purpose of cross-border authentication in accordance with Article 6 of Regulation (EU) No 910/2014.

2. Member States may refuse to recognise electronic identification means where the assurance levels of those electronic identification means do not comply with the conditions set out in Article 6(1) of Regulation (EU) No 910/2014.
3. All identification means recognised by Member States shall be made publicly available.
4. Where justified by reason of the public interest in preventing identity misuse or alteration, Member States may, for the purposes of verifying an applicant's identity, take measures which could require the physical presence of that applicant before any authority or person or body mandated under national law to deal with any aspect of the online procedures referred to in this Chapter, including the drawing up of the instrument of constitution of a company. Member States shall ensure that the physical presence of an applicant may only be required on a case-by-case basis where there are reasons to suspect identity falsification, and that any other steps of the procedure can be completed online.]

NOTES

Inserted as noted to Article 13a at **[11.394]**.

[11.396]

[Article 13c General provisions on online procedures

1. This Directive shall be without prejudice to national laws that, in accordance with Member States] legal systems and legal traditions, designate any authority or person or body mandated under national law to deal with any aspect of online formation of companies, online registration of branches and online filing of documents and information.
2. This Directive shall also be without prejudice to the procedures and requirements laid down by national law, including those relating to legal procedures for the drawing up of instruments of constitution, provided that online formation of a company, as referred to in Article 13g, and online registration of a branch, as referred to in Article 28a, as well as online filing of documents and information, as referred to in Articles 13j and 28b, is possible.
3. The requirements under applicable national law concerning the authenticity, accuracy, reliability, trustworthiness and the appropriate legal form of documents or information that are submitted shall remain unaffected by this Directive, provided that online formation, as referred to in Article 13g, and online registration of a branch, as referred to in Article 28a, as well as online filing of documents and information, as referred to in Articles 13j and 28b, is possible.]

NOTES

Inserted as noted to Article 13a at **[11.394]**.

[11.397]

[Article 13d Fees for online procedures

1. Member States shall ensure that the rules on fees applicable to the online procedures referred to in this Chapter are transparent and are applied in a non-discriminatory manner.
2. Any fees for online procedures charged by the registers referred to in Article 16 shall not exceed the recovery of the costs of providing such services.]

NOTES

Inserted as noted to Article 13a at **[11.394]**.

[11.398]

[Article 13e Payments

Where the completion of a procedure laid down in this Chapter requires a payment, Member States shall ensure that that payment can be made by means of a widely available online payment service that can be used for cross-border payments, that permits identification of the person that made the payment and is provided by a financial institution or payment service provider established in a Member State.]

NOTES

Inserted as noted to Article 13a at **[11.394]**.

[11.399]

[Article 13f Information requirements

Member States shall ensure that concise and user-friendly information, provided free of charge and at least in a language broadly understood by the largest possible number of cross-border users, is made available on registration portals or websites that are accessible by means of the Single Digital Gateway to assist in the formation of companies and the registration of branches. The information shall cover at least the following:

(a) rules on the formation of companies, including online procedures referred to in Articles 13g and 13j, and requirements relating to the use of templates and to other formation documents, identification of persons, the use of languages and to applicable fees;
(b) rules on the registration of branches, including online procedures referred to in Articles 28a and 28b, and requirements relating to registration documents, identification of persons and the use of languages;
(c) an outline of the applicable rules on becoming a member of the administrative body, the management body or the supervisory body of a company, including of the rules on disqualification of directors, and on the authorities or bodies responsible for keeping information about disqualified directors;
(d) an outline of the powers and responsibilities of the administrative body, the management body and the supervisory body of a company, including the authority to represent a company in dealings with third parties.]

NOTES

Inserted as noted to Article 13a at **[11.394]**.

[SECTION 1A ONLINE FORMATION, ONLINE FILING AND DISCLOSURE

[11.400]

Article 13g Online formation of companies

1. Member States shall ensure that the online formation of companies may be carried out fully online without the necessity for the applicants to appear in person before any authority or person or body mandated under national law to deal with any aspect of the online formation of companies, including drawing up the instrument of constitution of a company, subject to the provisions laid down in Article 13b(4) and paragraph (8) of this Article.

However, Member States may decide not to provide for online formation procedures for types of companies other than those listed in Annex IIA.

2. Member States shall lay down detailed rules for the online formation of companies, including rules on the use of templates as referred to in Article 13h, and on the documents and information required for the formation of a company. As part of those rules, Member States shall ensure that such online formation may be carried out by submitting documents or information in electronic form, including electronic copies of the documents and information referred to in Article 16a(4).

3. The rules referred to in paragraph 2 shall at least provide for the following:

(a) the procedures to ensure that the applicants have the necessary legal capacity and have authority to represent the company;

(b) the means to verify the identity of the applicants in accordance with Article 13b;

(c) the requirements for the applicants to use trust services referred to in Regulation (EU) No 910/2014;

(d) the procedures to verify the legality of the object of the company, insofar as such checks are provided for under national law;

(e) the procedures to verify the legality of the name of the company, insofar as such checks are provided for under national law;

(f) the procedures to verify the appointment of directors.

4. The rules referred to in paragraph 2 may, in particular, also provide for the following:

(a) the procedures to ensure the legality of the company instruments of constitution, including verifying the correct use of templates;

(b) the consequences of the disqualification of a director by the competent authority in any Member State;

(c) the role of a notary or any other person or body mandated under national law to deal with any aspect of the online formation of a company;

(d) the exclusion of online formation in cases where the share capital of the company is paid by way of contributions in kind.

5. Member States shall not make the online formation of a company conditional on obtaining a licence or authorisation before the company is registered, unless such a condition is indispensable for the proper oversight laid down in national law of certain activities.

6. Member States shall ensure that where the payment of share capital is required as part of the procedure to form a company, such payment can be made online, in accordance with Article 13e, to a bank account of a bank operating in the Union. In addition, Member States shall ensure that proof of such payments can also be provided online.

7. Member States shall ensure that the online formation is completed within five working days where a company is formed exclusively by natural persons who use the templates referred to in Article 13h, or within ten working days in other cases, from the later of the following:

(a) the date of the completion of all formalities required for the online formation, including the receipt of all documents and information, which comply with national law, by an authority or a person or body mandated under national law to deal with any aspect of the formation of a company;

(b) the date of the payment of a registration fee, the payment in cash for share capital, or the payment for the share capital by way of a contribution in kind, as provided for under national law.

Where it is not possible to complete the procedure within the deadlines referred to in this paragraph, Member States shall ensure that the applicant is notified of the reasons for the delay.

8. Where justified by reason of the public interest in ensuring compliance with the rules on legal capacity and on the authority of applicants to represent a company, any authority or person or body mandated under national law to deal with any aspect of the online formation of a company, including the drawing up of the instrument of constitution, may request the physical presence of the applicant. Member States shall ensure that, in such cases, the physical presence of an applicant may only be required on a case-by-case basis where there are reasons to suspect non-compliance with the rules referred to in point (a) of paragraph 3. Member States shall ensure that any other steps of the procedure can nonetheless be completed online.]

NOTES

Section 1A (Articles 13g–13j) was inserted by European Parliament and Council Directive 2019/1151/EU, Art 1(5), as from 31 July 2019.

[11.401]

[Article 13h Templates for online formation of companies

1. Member States shall make templates available, for the types of companies listed in Annex IIA, on registration portals or websites that are accessible by means of the Single Digital Gateway. Member States may also make templates available online for the formation of other types of companies.

2. Member States shall ensure that the templates, referred to in paragraph 1 of this Article, may be used by applicants as part of the online formation procedure referred to in Article 13g. Where those templates are used by applicants in compliance with the rules referred to in point (a) of Article 13g(4), the requirement to have the company instruments of constitution drawn up and certified in due legal form where preventive administrative or judicial control is not provided for, as laid down in Article 10, shall be deemed to have been fulfilled.

This Directive shall not affect any requirement under national law to have the drawing up of instruments of constitution done in due legal form, as long as the online formation referred to in Article 13g is possible.

3. Member States shall at least make the templates available in an official Union language broadly understood by the largest possible number of cross-border users. The availability of templates in languages other than the official language or languages of the Member State concerned shall be for information purposes only, unless that Member State decides that it is also possible to form a company with templates in such other languages.
4. The content of the templates shall be governed by national law.]

NOTES

Inserted as noted to Article 13g at **[11.400]**.

[11.402]

[Article 13i Disqualified directors

1. Member States shall ensure that they have rules on disqualification of directors. Those rules shall include providing for the possibility to take into account any disqualification that is in force, or information relevant for disqualification, in another Member State. For the purpose of this Article, directors shall at least include the persons referred to in point (i) of Article 14(d).
2. Member States may require that persons applying to become directors declare whether they are aware of any circumstances which could lead to a disqualification in the Member State concerned.
Member States may refuse the appointment of a person as a director of a company where that person is currently disqualified from acting as a director in another Member State.
3. Member States shall ensure that they are able to reply to a request from another Member State for information relevant for the disqualification of directors under the law of the Member State replying to the request.
4. In order to reply to a request referred to in paragraph 3 of this Article, Member States shall at least make the necessary arrangements to ensure that they are able to provide without delay information on whether a given person is disqualified or is recorded in any of their registers that contain information relevant for disqualification of directors, by means of the system referred to in Article 22. Member States may also exchange further information, such as on the period and grounds of disqualification. Such exchange shall be governed by national law.
5. The Commission shall lay down detailed arrangements and technical details for the exchange of the information referred to in paragraph 4 of this Article, by means of the implementing acts referred to in Article 24.
6. Paragraphs 1 to 5 of this Article shall apply mutatis mutandis where a company files information concerning the appointment of a new director in the register referred to in Article 16.
7. The personal data of persons referred to in this Article shall be processed in accordance with Regulation (EU) 2016/679 and national law, in order to enable the authority or the person or body mandated under national law to assess necessary information relating to the disqualification of a person as a director, with a view to preventing fraudulent or other abusive behaviour and ensuring that all persons interacting with companies or branches are protected.
Member States shall ensure that the registers referred to in Article 16, authorities or persons or bodies mandated under national law to deal with any aspect of online procedures do not store personal data transmitted for the purposes of this Article any longer than is necessary, and in any event no longer than any personal data related to the formation of a company, the registration of a branch or a filing by a company or branch are stored.]

NOTES

Inserted as noted to Article 13g at **[11.400]**. Note that this Article has a transposition date of 1 August 2023.

Implementing Act for the purposes of para 5: see Commission Implementing Regulation 2021/1042/EU laying down rules for the application of Directive (EU) 2017/1132 of the European Parliament and of the Council as regards technical specifications and procedures for the system of interconnection of registers and repealing Commission Implementing Regulation (EU) 2020/2244. It is available on the EUR-Lex website at eur-lex.europa.eu/legal-content/EN/TXT/?uri=CELEX:32021R1042.

[11.403]

[Article 13j Online filing of company documents and information

1. Member States shall ensure that documents and information referred to in Article 14, including any modification thereof, can be filed online with the register within the time limit provided by the laws of the Member State where the company is registered. Member States shall ensure that such filing can be completed online in its entirety without the necessity for an applicant to appear in person before any authority or person or body mandated under national law to deal with the online filing, subject to the provisions laid down in Article 13b(4) and, where applicable, Article 13g(8).
2. Member States shall ensure that the origin and integrity of the documents filed online may be verified electronically.
3. Member States may require that certain companies or that all companies file certain or all of the documents and information referred to in paragraph 1 online.
4. Article 13g (2) to (5) shall apply mutatis mutandis to online filing of documents and information.
5. Member States may continue to allow forms of filing other than those referred to in paragraph 1, including by electronic or by paper means, by companies, by notaries or by any other persons or bodies mandated under national law to deal with such forms of filing.]

NOTES

Inserted as noted to Article 13g at **[11.400]**. Note that in so far as relating to para 2 of this Article, the transposition date is 1 August 2023.

[11.404]

Article 14 Documents and particulars to be disclosed by companies

Member States shall take the measures required to ensure compulsory disclosure by companies of at least the following documents and particulars:

(a) the instrument of constitution, and the statutes if they are contained in a separate instrument;
(b) any amendments to the instruments referred to in point (a), including any extension of the duration of the company;

(c) after every amendment of the instrument of constitution or of the statutes, the complete text of the instrument or statutes as amended to date;

(d) the appointment, termination of office and particulars of the persons who either as a body constituted pursuant to law or as members of any such body:

   (i) are authorised to represent the company in dealings with third parties and in legal proceedings; it shall be apparent from the disclosure whether the persons authorised to represent the company may do so alone or are required to act jointly;

   (ii) take part in the administration, supervision or control of the company;

(e) at least once a year, the amount of the capital subscribed, where the instrument of constitution or the statutes mention an authorised capital, unless any increase in the capital subscribed necessitates an amendment of the statutes;

(f) the accounting documents for each financial year which are required to be published in accordance with Council Directives 86/635/EEC[1] and 91/674/EEC[2] and Directive 2013/34/EU of the European Parliament and of the Council;[3]

(g) any change of the registered office of the company;

(h) the winding-up of the company;

(i) any declaration of nullity of the company by the courts;

(j) the appointment of liquidators, particulars concerning them, and their respective powers, unless such powers are expressly and exclusively derived from law or from the statutes of the company;

(k) any termination of a liquidation and, in Member States where striking off the register entails legal consequences, the fact of any such striking off.

NOTES

[1] Council Directive 86/635/EEC of 8 December 1986 on the annual accounts and consolidated accounts of banks and other financial institutions (OJ L372, 31.12.1986, p 1).

[2] Council Directive 91/674/EEC of 19 December 1991 on the annual accounts and consolidated accounts of insurance undertakings (OJ L374, 31.12.1991, p 7).

[3] Directive 2013/34/EU of the European Parliament and of the Council of 26 June 2013 on the annual financial statements, consolidated financial statements and related reports of certain types of undertakings, amending Directive 2006/43/EC of the European Parliament and of the Council and repealing Council Directives 78/660/EEC and 83/349/EEC (OJ L182, 29.6.2013, p 19).

[11.405]

Article 15 Changes in documents and particulars

1. Member States shall take the measures required to ensure that any changes in the documents and particulars referred to in Article 14 are entered in the competent register referred to in the first subparagraph of Article 16(1) and are disclosed, in accordance with Article 16(3) and (5), normally within 21 days of receipt of the complete documentation regarding those changes including, if applicable, the legality check as required under national law for entry in the file.

2. Paragraph 1 shall not apply to the accounting documents referred to in Article 14(f).

[11.406]

[Article 16 Disclosure in the register

1. In each Member State, a file shall be opened in a central, commercial or companies register ("the register"), for each of the companies registered therein.

Member States shall ensure that companies have a European unique identifier ("EUID"), referred to in point (8) of the Annex to Commission Implementing Regulation (EU) 2015/884,[1] allowing them to be unequivocally identified in communications between registers through the system of interconnection of registers established in accordance with Article 22 ("the system of interconnection of registers"). That unique identifier shall comprise, at least, elements making it possible to identify the Member State of the register, the domestic register of origin and the company number in that register and, where appropriate, features to avoid identification errors.

2. All documents and information that are required to be disclosed pursuant to Article 14 shall be kept in the file referred to in paragraph 1 of this Article, or entered directly in the register, and the subject matter of the entries in the register shall be recorded in the file.

All documents and information referred to in Article 14, irrespective of the means by which they are filed, shall be kept in the file in the register or entered directly into it in electronic form. Member States shall ensure that all documents and information that are filed by paper means are converted by the register to electronic form as quickly as possible.

Member States shall ensure that documents and information referred to in Article 14 that were filed by paper means before 31 December 2006 are converted into electronic form by the register upon receipt of an application for disclosure by electronic means.

3. Member States shall ensure that the disclosure of the documents and information referred to in Article 14 is effected by making them publicly available in the register. In addition, Member States may also require that some or all of those documents and information are published in a national gazette designated for that purpose, or by equally effective means. Those means shall entail at least the use of a system whereby the documents or information published can be accessed in chronological order through a central electronic platform. In such cases, the register shall ensure that those documents and information are sent electronically by the register to the national gazette or to a central electronic platform.

4. Member States shall take the necessary measures to avoid any discrepancy between what is in the register and in the file.

Member States that require the publication of documents and information in a national gazette or on a central electronic platform shall take the necessary measures to avoid any discrepancy between what is disclosed in accordance with paragraph 3 and what is published in the gazette or on the platform.

In cases of any discrepancies under this Article, the documents and information made available in the register shall prevail.

5. The documents and information referred to in Article 14 may be relied on by the company as against third parties only after they have been disclosed in accordance with paragraph 3 of this Article, unless the company proves that the third parties had knowledge thereof.

However, with regard to transactions taking place before the sixteenth day following the disclosure, the documents and information shall not be relied on as against third parties who prove that it was impossible for them to have had knowledge thereof.

Third parties may always rely on any documents and information in respect of which the disclosure formalities have not yet been completed, save where non-disclosure causes such documents or information to have no effect.

6. Member States shall ensure that all documents and information submitted as part of the formation of a company, the registration of a branch, or a filing by a company or a branch, is stored by the registers in a machine-readable and searchable format or as structured data.]

NOTES

Substituted by European Parliament and Council Directive 2019/1151/EU, Art 1(6), as from 31 July 2019. Note that in so far as relating to para 6 of this Article, the transposition date is 1 August 2023.

[1] Commission Implementing Regulation (EU) 2015/884 of 8 June 2015 establishing technical specifications and procedures required for the system of interconnection of registers established by Directive 2009/101/EC of the European Parliament and of the Council (OJ L144, 10.6.2015, p 1).

[*] Directive 1999/93/EC of the European Parliament and of the Council of 13 December 1999 on a Community framework for electronic signatures (OJ L13, 19.1.2000, p 12).

[11.407]

[Article 16a Access to disclosed information

1. Member States shall ensure that copies of all or any part of the documents and information, referred to in Article 14, may be obtained from the register on application, and that such an application may be submitted to the register by either paper or electronic means.

However, Member States may decide that certain types or parts of the documents and information, which were filed by paper means on or before 31 December 2006, cannot be obtained by electronic means where a specified period has elapsed between the date of filing and the date of the application. Such a specified period shall not be less than 10 years.

2. The price of obtaining a copy of all or any part of the documents and information referred to in Article 14, whether by paper or electronic means, shall not exceed the administrative costs thereof, including the costs of development and maintenance of registers.

3. Electronic and paper copies supplied to an applicant shall be certified as "true copies" unless the applicant dispenses with such certification.

4. Member States shall ensure that electronic copies and extracts of the documents and information provided by the register have been authenticated by means of trust services referred to in Regulation (EU) No 910/2014, in order to guarantee that the electronic copies or extracts have been provided by the register and that their content is a true copy of the document held by the register or that it is consistent with the information contained therein.]

NOTES

Inserted by European Parliament and Council Directive 2019/1151/EU, Art 1(7), as from 31 July 2019.

[11.408]

Article 17 Up-to-date information on national law with regard to the rights of third parties

[1. Member States shall ensure that up-to-date information is made available explaining the provisions of national law pursuant to which third parties may rely on information and each type of document referred to in Article 14, in accordance with Article 16(3), (4) and (5).]

2. Member States shall provide the information required for publication on the European e-Justice portal ('the portal') in accordance with the portal's rules and technical requirements.

3. The Commission shall publish that information on the portal in all the official languages of the Union.

NOTES

Para 1: substituted by European Parliament and Council Directive 2019/1151/EU, Art 1(8), as from 31 July 2019.

[11.409]

Article 18 Availability of electronic copies of documents and particulars

[1. Electronic copies of the documents and information referred to in Article 14 shall also be made publicly available through the system of interconnection of registers. Member States may also make available documents and information referred to in Article 14 for types of companies other than those listed in Annex II.]

2. Member States shall ensure that the documents and particulars referred to in Article 14 are available through the system of interconnection of registers in a standard message format and accessible by electronic means. Member States shall also ensure that minimum standards for the security of data transmission are respected.

3. The Commission shall provide a search service in all the official languages of the Union in respect of companies registered in the Member States, in order to make available through the portal:

[(a) the documents and information referred to in Article 14, including for types of companies other than those listed in Annex II, where such documents are made available by Member States;]

[(aa) the documents and information referred to in Articles 86g, 86n, 86p, 123, 127a, 130, 160g, 160n and 160p;]

(b) the explanatory labels, available in all the official languages of the Union, listing those particulars and the types of those documents.

NOTES

Para 1: substituted by European Parliament and Council Directive 2019/1151/EU, Art 1(9)(a), as from 31 July 2019.

Para 3 is amended as follows:

Point (a) substituted by European Parliament and Council Directive 2019/1151/EU, Art 1(9)(b), as from 31 July 2019.

Point (aa) inserted by European Parliament and Council Directive 2019/2121/EU, Art 1(2), as form 1 January 2020. Note that the 2019 Directive has a transposition date of 31 January 2023.

[11.410]

[Article 19 Fees chargeable for documents and information

1. The fees charged for obtaining documents and information referred to in Article 14 through the system of interconnection of registers shall not exceed the administrative costs thereof, including the costs of development and maintenance of registers.

2. Member States shall ensure that at least the following information and documents are available free of charge through the system of interconnection of registers:

(a) the name or names and legal form of the company;

(b) the registered office of the company and the Member State where it is registered;

(c) the registration number of the company and its EUID;

(d) details of the company website, where such details are recorded in the national register;

(e) the status of the company, such as when it is closed, struck off the register, wound up, dissolved, economically active or inactive as defined in national law and where recorded in the national registers;

(f) the object of the company, where it is recorded in the national register;

(g) the particulars of any persons who either as a body or as members of any such body are currently authorised by the company to represent it in dealing with third parties and in legal proceedings and information as to whether the persons authorised to represent the company may do so alone or are required to act jointly;

(h) information on any branches opened by the company in another Member State including the name, registration number, EUID and the Member State where the branch is registered.

3. The exchange of any information through the system of interconnection of registers shall be free of charge for the registers.

4. Member States may decide that the information referred to in points (d) and (f) is to be made available free of charge only for the authorities of other Member States.]

NOTES

Substituted by European Parliament and Council Directive 2019/1151/EU, Art 1(10), as from 31 July 2019.

[11.411]

Article 20 Information on the opening and termination of winding-up or insolvency proceedings and on striking-off of a company from the register

1. The register of a company shall, through the system of interconnection of registers, make available, without delay, the information on the opening and termination of any winding-up or insolvency proceedings of the company and on the striking-off of the company from the register, if this entails legal consequences in the Member State of the register of the company.

2. The register of the branch shall, through the system of interconnection of registers, ensure receipt, without delay, of the information referred to in paragraph 1.

3. . . .

NOTES

Para 3: repealed by European Parliament and Council Directive 2019/1151/EU, Art 1(11), as from 31 July 2019.

[11.412]

Article 21 Language of disclosure and translation of documents and particulars to be disclosed

1. Documents and particulars to be disclosed pursuant to Article 14 shall be drawn up and filed in one of the languages permitted by the language rules applicable in the Member State in which the file referred to in Article 16(1) is opened.

2. In addition to the compulsory disclosure referred to in Article 16, Member States shall allow translations of documents and particulars referred to in Article 14 to be disclosed voluntarily in accordance with Article 16 in any official language(s) of the Union.

Member States may prescribe that the translation of such documents and particulars be certified.

Member States shall take the necessary measures to facilitate access by third parties to the translations voluntarily disclosed.

3. In addition to the compulsory disclosure referred to in Article 16, and to the voluntary disclosure provided for under paragraph 2 of this Article, Member States may allow the documents and particulars concerned to be disclosed, in accordance with Article 16, in any other language(s).

Member States may prescribe that the translation of such documents and particulars be certified.

4. In cases of discrepancy between the documents and particulars disclosed in the official languages of the register and the translation voluntarily disclosed, the latter may not be relied upon as against third parties. Third parties may nevertheless rely on the translations voluntarily disclosed, unless the company proves that the third parties had knowledge of the version which was the subject of the compulsory disclosure.

[11.413]

Article 22 System of interconnection of registers

1. A European central platform ('the platform') shall be established.

2. The system of interconnection of registers shall be composed of:

— the registers of Member States,

— the platform,

— the portal serving as the European electronic access point.

3. Member States shall ensure the interoperability of their registers within the system of interconnection of registers via the platform.

4. Member States may establish optional access points to the system of interconnection of registers. They shall notify the Commission without undue delay of the establishment of such access points and of any significant changes to their operation.

[The Commission may also establish optional access points to the system of interconnection of registers. Such access points shall consist of systems developed and operated by the Commission or other Union institutions, bodies, offices or agencies in order to perform their administrative functions or to comply with provisions of Union law. The Commission shall notify the Member States without undue delay of the establishment of such access points and of any significant changes to their operation.]

[5. Access to information from the system of interconnection of registers shall be provided through the portal and through the optional access points established by the Member States and by the Commission.]

6. The establishment of the system of interconnection of registers shall not affect existing bilateral agreements concluded between Member States concerning the exchange of information on companies.

NOTES

Words in square brackets in para 4 inserted, and para 5 substituted, by European Parliament and Council Directive 2019/1151/EU, Art 1(12), as from 31 July 2019.

[11.414]

Article 23 Development and operation of the platform

1. The Commission shall decide to develop and/or operate the platform either by its own means or through a third party.

If the Commission decides to develop and/or operate the platform through a third party, the choice of the third party and the enforcement by the Commission of the agreement concluded with that third party shall be done in accordance with Regulation (EU, Euratom) No 966/2012.

2. If the Commission decides to develop the platform through a third party, it shall, by means of implementing acts, establish the technical specifications for the purpose of the public procurement procedure and the duration of the agreement to be concluded with that third party.

3. If the Commission decides to operate the platform through a third party, it shall, by means of implementing acts, adopt detailed rules on the operational management of the platform.

The operational management of the platform shall include, in particular:

— the supervision of the functioning of the platform,
— the security and protection of data distributed and exchanged using the platform,
— the coordination of relations between Member States' registers and the third party.

The supervision of the functioning of the platform shall be carried out by the Commission.

4. The implementing acts referred to in Paragraphs 2 and 3 shall be adopted in accordance with the examination procedure referred to in Article 164(2).

[11.415]

Article 24 Implementing acts

By means of implementing acts, the Commission shall adopt the following:

(a) the technical specification defining the methods of communication by electronic means for the purpose of the system of interconnection of registers;
(b) the technical specification of the communication protocols;
(c) the technical measures ensuring the minimum information technology security standards for communication and distribution of information within the system of interconnection of registers;
[(d) the technical specification defining the methods of exchange of information between the register of the company and the register of the branch as referred to in Articles 20, 28a, 28c, 30a and 34;]
[(e) the detailed list of data to be transmitted for the purpose of exchanging information between registers, as referred to in Articles 20, 28a, 28c, 30a and 34;]
[(ea) the detailed list of data to be transmitted for the purpose of exchanging information between registers and for the purposes of disclosure, as referred to in Articles 86g, 86n, 86p, 123, 127a, 130, 160g, 160n and 160p;]
(f) the technical specification defining the structure of the standard message format for the purpose of the exchange of information between the registers, the platform and the portal;
(g) the technical specification defining the set of the data necessary for the platform to perform its functions as well as the method of storage, use and protection of such data;
(h) the technical specification defining the structure and use of the unique identifier for communication between registers;
(i) the specification defining the technical methods of operation of the system of interconnection of registers as regards the distribution and exchange of information, and the specification defining the information technology services, provided by the platform, ensuring the delivery of messages in the relevant language version;
(j) the harmonised criteria for the search service provided by the portal;
(k) the payment modalities, taking into account available payment facilities such as online payment;
(l) the details of the explanatory labels listing the particulars and the types of documents referred to in Article 14;
(m) the technical conditions of availability of services provided by the system of interconnection of registers;
[(n) the procedure and technical requirements for the connection of the optional access points to the platform as referred to in Article 22;]
[(o) the detailed arrangements for and technical details of the exchange between registers of the information referred to in Article 13i.]

Those implementing acts shall be adopted in accordance with the examination procedure referred to in Article 164(2).

[The Commission shall adopt the implementing acts pursuant to points (d), (e), (n) and (o) by 1 February 2021.]

[The Commission shall adopt the implementing acts referred to in point (ea) by 2 July 2021.]

NOTES

Points (d), (e) and (n) substituted, and point (o) and the penultimate words in square brackets added, by European Parliament and Council Directive 2019/1151/EU, Art 1(13), as from 31 July 2019.

Point (e) was further substituted, point (ea) was inserted, and the final words in square brackets were added, by European Parliament and Council Directive 2019/2121/EU, Art 1(3), as form 1 January 2020. Note that the 2019 Directive has a transposition date of 31 January 2023.

Note also that the date in the final paragraph above was changed from 2 July 2020 to 2 July 2021 by a corrigendum published in OJ L20, 24.1.2020.

Implementing Act for the purposes of this Article: see Commission Implementing Regulation 2021/1042/EU laying down rules for the application of Directive (EU) 2017/1132 of the European Parliament and of the Council as regards technical specifications and procedures for the system of interconnection of registers and repealing Commission Implementing Regulation (EU) 2020/2244. It is available on the EUR-Lex website at eur-lex.europa.eu/legal-content/EN/TXT/?uri=CELEX:32021R1042.

[11.416]
Article 25 Financing

1. The establishment and future development of the platform and the adjustments to the portal resulting from this Directive shall be financed from the general budget of the Union.
2. The maintenance and functioning of the platform shall be financed from the general budget of the Union and may be co-financed by fees for access to the system of interconnection of registers charged to its individual users. Nothing in this paragraph shall affect fees at the national level.
3. By means of delegated acts and in accordance with Article 163, the Commission may adopt rules on whether to co-finance the platform by charging fees, and, in that case, the amount of the fees charged to individual users in accordance with paragraph 2 of this Article.
4. Any fees imposed in accordance with paragraph 2 of this Article shall be without prejudice to the fees, if any, charged by Member States for obtaining documents and particulars as referred to in Article 19(1).
5. Any fees imposed in accordance with paragraph 2 of this Article shall not be charged for obtaining the particulars referred to in Article 19(2)(a), (b) and (c).
6. Each Member State shall bear the costs of adjusting its domestic registers, as well as their maintenance and functioning costs resulting from this Directive.

[11.417]
Article 26 Information on letters and order forms

Member States shall prescribe that letters and order forms, whether they are in paper form or use any other medium, are to state the following particulars:

(a) the information necessary in order to identify the register in which the file referred to in Article 16 is kept, together with the number of the company in that register;
(b) the legal form of the company, the location of its registered office and, where appropriate, the fact that the company is being wound up.

Where, in those documents, mention is made of the capital of the company, the reference shall be to the capital subscribed and paid up.

Member States shall prescribe that company websites are to contain at least the particulars referred to in the first paragraph and, if applicable, a reference to the capital subscribed and paid up.

[11.418]
Article 27 Persons carrying out disclosure formalities

Each Member State shall determine by which persons the disclosure formalities are to be carried out.

[11.419]
Article 28 Penalties

Member States shall provide for appropriate penalties at least in the case of:

(a) failure to disclose accounting documents as required by Article 14(f);
(b) omission from commercial documents or from any company website of the compulsory particulars provided for in Article 26.

SECTION 2 [REGISTRATION AND DISCLOSURE RULES APPLICABLE TO BRANCHES OF COMPANIES FROM OTHER MEMBER STATES]

NOTES

The section heading was substituted by European Parliament and Council Directive 2019/1151/EU, Art 1(14), as from 31 July 2019.

[11.420]
[Article 28a Online registration of branches

1. Member States shall ensure that the registration in a Member State of a branch of a company that is governed by the law of another Member State may be fully carried out online without the necessity for the applicants to appear in person before any authority or any person or body mandated under national law to deal with any aspect of the application for registration of branches, subject to Article 13b(4) and mutatis mutandis to Article 13g(8).
2. Member States shall lay down detailed rules for the online registration of branches, including rules on the documents and information required to be submitted to a competent authority. As part of those rules, Member States shall ensure that online registration may be carried out by submitting information or documents in electronic form, including electronic copies of the documents and information referred to in Article 16a(4), or by making use of the information or documents previously submitted to a register.
3. The rules referred to in paragraph 2 shall at least provide for the following:

(a) the procedure to ensure that the applicants have the necessary legal capacity and that they have authority to represent the company;

(b) the means for verifying the identity of the person or persons registering the branch or their representatives;
(c) the requirements for the applicants to use the trust services referred to in Regulation (EU) No 910/2014.

4. The rules referred to in paragraph 2 may also provide for procedures to do the following:
(a) verify the legality of the object of the branch;
(b) verify the legality of the name of the branch;
(c) verify the legality of the documents and information submitted for the registration of the branch;
(d) provide for the role of a notary or any other person or body involved in the process of registration of the branch under the applicable national provisions.

5. Member States may verify the information about the company by means of the system of interconnection of registers when registering a branch of a company established in another Member State.

Member States shall not make the online registration of a branch conditional on obtaining any licence or authorisation before the branch is registered, unless such a condition is indispensable for the proper oversight laid down in national law of certain activities.

6. Member States shall ensure that the online registration of a branch is completed within 10 working days of the completion of all formalities, including the receipt of all the necessary documents and information which comply with national law by an authority or a person or body mandated under national law to deal with any aspect of the registration of a branch.

Where it is not possible to register a branch within the deadlines referred to in this paragraph, Member States shall ensure that the applicant is notified of the reasons for the delay.

7. Following the registration of a branch of a company established under the laws of another Member State, the register of the Member State where that branch is registered shall notify the Member State where the company is registered that the branch has been registered by means of the system of interconnection of registers. The Member State where the company is registered shall acknowledge receipt of such notification and shall record the information in their register without delay.]

NOTES

Inserted by European Parliament and Council Directive 2019/1151/EU, Art 1(15), as from 31 July 2019.

[11.421]

[Article 28b Online filing of documents and information for branches

1. Member States shall ensure that documents and information referred to in Article 30 or any modification thereof may be filed online within the period provided by the laws of the Member State where the branch is established. Member States shall ensure that such filing may be completed online in its entirety without the necessity for the applicants to appear in person before any authority or person or body mandated under national law to deal with the online filing, subject to the provisions laid down in Article 13b(4) and mutatis mutandis in Article 13g(8).

2. Article 28a (2) to (5) shall apply mutatis mutandis to online filing for branches.

3. Member States may require that certain or all documents and information referred to in paragraph 1 are only filed online.]

NOTES

Inserted by European Parliament and Council Directive 2019/1151/EU, Art 1(15), as from 31 July 2019.

[11.422]

[Article 28c Closure of branches

Member States shall ensure that, upon receipt of the documents and information referred to in point (h) of Article 30(1), the register of a Member State where a branch of a company is registered informs, by means of the system of interconnection of registers, the register of the Member State where the company is registered that its branch has been closed and struck off the register. The register of the Member State of the company shall acknowledge receipt of such notification also by means of that system and shall record the information without delay.]

NOTES

Inserted by European Parliament and Council Directive 2019/1151/EU, Art 1(15), as from 31 July 2019.

[11.423]

Article 29 Disclosure of documents and particulars relating to a branch

1. Documents and particulars relating to a branch opened in a Member State by a company of a type listed in Annex II, which is governed by the law of another Member State, shall be disclosed pursuant to the law of the Member State of the branch, in accordance with Article 16.

2. Where disclosure requirements in respect of the branch differ from those in respect of the company, the branch's disclosure requirements shall take precedence with regard to transactions carried out with the branch.

3. The documents and particulars referred to in Article 30(1) shall be made publicly available through the system of interconnection of registers. Article 18 and Article 19(1) shall apply *mutatis mutandis*.

4. Member States shall ensure that branches have a unique identifier allowing them to be unequivocally identified in communications between registers through the system of interconnection of registers. That unique identifier shall comprise, at least, elements making it possible to identify the Member State of the register, the domestic register of origin and the branch number in that register, and, where appropriate, features to avoid identification errors.

[11.424]

Article 30 Documents and particulars to be disclosed

1. The compulsory disclosure provided for in Article 29 shall cover the following documents and particulars only:
(a) the address of the branch;
(b) the activities of the branch;
(c) the register in which the company file referred to in Article 16 is kept, together with the registration number in that register;

(d) the name and legal form of the company and the name of the branch, if that is different from the name of the company;

(e) the appointment, termination of office and particulars of the persons who are authorised to represent the company in dealings with third parties and in legal proceedings:

— as a company organ constituted pursuant to law or as members of any such organ, in accordance with the disclosure by the company as provided for in Article 14(d),

— as permanent representatives of the company for the activities of the branch, with an indication of the extent of their powers;

(f)

— the winding-up of the company, the appointment of liquidators, particulars concerning them and their powers and the termination of the liquidation in accordance with disclosure by the company as provided for in Article 14(h), (j) and (k),

— insolvency proceedings, arrangements, compositions, or any analogous proceedings to which the company is subject;

(g) the accounting documents in accordance with Article 31;

(h) the closure of the branch.

2. The Member State in which the branch has been opened may provide for the disclosure, as referred to in Article 29, of

(a) the signature of the persons referred to in points (e) and (f) of paragraph 1 of this Article;

(b) the instruments of constitution and the memorandum and articles of association if they are contained in a separate instrument, in accordance with points (a), (b) and (c) of Article 14, together with amendments to those documents;

(c) an attestation from the register referred to in point (c) of paragraph 1 of this Article relating to the existence of the company;

(d) an indication of the securities on the company's property situated in that Member State, provided such disclosure relates to the validity of those securities.

[11.425]

[Article 30a Changes to documents and information of the company

The Member State where a company is registered shall notify, by means of the system of interconnection of registers, without delay, the Member State where a branch of the company is registered, in the event that a change has been filed with regard to any of the following:

(a) the company's name;

(b) the company's registered office;

(c) the company's registration number in the register;

(d) the company's legal form;

(e) the documents and information referred to in points (d) and (f) of Article 14.

Upon receipt of the notification referred to in the first paragraph of this Article, the register in which the branch is registered shall, by means of the system of interconnection of registers, acknowledge receipt of such notification and shall ensure that the documents and information referred to in Article 30(1) are updated without delay.]

NOTES

Inserted by European Parliament and Council Directive 2019/1151/EU, Art 1(16), as from 31 July 2019.

[11.426]

Article 31 Limits on the compulsory disclosure of accounting documents

The compulsory disclosure provided for by Article 30(1)(g) shall be limited to the accounting documents of the company as drawn up, audited and disclosed pursuant to the law of the Member State by which the company is governed in accordance with Directive 2006/43/EC of the European Parliament and of the Council[1] and Directive 2013/34/EU.

[Member States may provide that the mandatory disclosure of accounting documents referred to in point (g) of Article 30(1) may be considered fulfilled by the disclosure in the register of the Member State in which the company is registered in accordance with point (f) of Article 14.]

NOTES

Words in square brackets added by European Parliament and Council Directive 2019/1151/EU, Art 1(17), as from 31 July 2019.

[1] Directive 2006/43/EC of the European Parliament and of the Council of 17 May 2006 on statutory audits of annual accounts and consolidated accounts, amending Council Directives 78/660/EEC and 83/349/EEC and repealing Council Directive 84/253/EEC (OJ L157, 9.6.2006, p 87).

[11.427]

Article 32 Language of disclosure and translation of documents to be disclosed

The Member State in which the branch has been opened may stipulate that the documents referred to in Article 30(2)(b) and Article 31 are to be published in another official language of the Union and that the translations of such documents are to be certified.

[11.428]

Article 33 Disclosure in cases of multiple branches in a Member State

Where a company has opened more than one branch in a Member State, the disclosure referred to in Article 30(2)(b) and Article 31 may be made in the register of the branch of the company's choice.

In the case referred to in the first paragraph, compulsory disclosure by the other branches shall cover the particulars of the branch register of which disclosure was made, together with the number of that branch in that register.

[11.429]
Article 34 Information on the opening and termination of winding-up or insolvency proceedings and on striking-off of the company from the register
1. Article 20 shall apply to the register of the company and to the register of the branch respectively.
2. Member States shall determine the procedure to be followed upon receipt of the information referred to in Article 20(1) and (2). Such procedure shall ensure that, where a company has been dissolved or otherwise struck off the register, its branches are likewise struck off the register without undue delay.
3. The second sentence of paragraph 2 shall not apply to branches of companies that have been struck off the register as a consequence of any change in the legal form of the company concerned, a merger or division, or a cross- border transfer of its registered office.

[11.430]
Article 35 Information on letters and order forms
Member States shall prescribe that letters and order forms used by a branch shall state, in addition to the information prescribed by Article 26, the register in which the file in respect of the branch is kept together with the number of the branch in that register.

SECTION 3 DISCLOSURE RULES APPLICABLE TO BRANCHES OF COMPANIES FROM THIRD COUNTRIES

[11.431]
Article 36 Disclosure of documents and particulars relating to a branch
1. Documents and particulars concerning a branch opened in a Member State by a company which is not governed by the law of a Member State but which is of a legal form comparable with the types of company listed in Annex II, shall be disclosed in accordance with the law of the Member State of the branch as laid down in Article 16.
2. Article 29(2) shall apply.

[11.432]
Article 37 Compulsory documents and particulars to be disclosed
The compulsory disclosure provided for in Article 36 shall cover at least the following documents and particulars:
(a) the address of the branch;
(b) the activities of the branch;
(c) the law of the State by which the company is governed;
(d) where that law so provides, the register in which the company is entered and the registration number of the company in that register;
(e) the instruments of constitution, and memorandum and articles of association if they are contained in a separate instrument, with all amendments to those documents;
(f) the legal form of the company, its principal place of business and its object and, at least annually, the amount of subscribed capital if those particulars are not given in the documents referred to in point (e);
(g) the name of the company and the name of the branch if that is different from the name of the company;
(h) the appointment, termination of office and particulars of the persons who are authorised to represent the company in dealings with third parties and in legal proceedings:
— as a company organ constituted pursuant to law or as members of any such organ,
— as permanent representatives of the company for the activities of the branch.
The extent of the powers of the persons authorised to represent the company shall be stated, as well as whether those persons may represent the company alone or are required to act jointly;
(i)
— the winding-up of the company and the appointment of liquidators, particulars concerning them and their powers and the termination of the liquidation,
— insolvency proceedings, arrangements, compositions or any analogous proceedings to which the company is subject;
(j) the accounting documents in accordance with Article 38;
(k) the closure of the branch.

[11.433]
Article 38 Limits of compulsory disclosure of accounting documents
1. The compulsory disclosure provided for by Article 37(j) shall apply to the accounting documents of the company as drawn up, audited and disclosed pursuant to the law of the State which governs the company. Where they are not drawn up in accordance with or in a manner equivalent to Directive 2013/34/EU, Member States may require that accounting documents relating to the activities of the branch be drawn up and disclosed.
2. Articles 32 and 33 shall apply.

[11.434]
Article 39 Information on letters and order forms
Member States shall prescribe that letters and order forms used by a branch state the register in which the file in respect of the branch is kept together with the number of the branch in that register. Where the law of the State by which the company is governed requires entry in a register, the register in which the company is entered, and the registration number of the company in that register shall also be stated.

SECTION 4 APPLICATION AND IMPLEMENTING ARRANGEMENTS

[11.435]
Article 40 Penalties
Member States shall provide for appropriate penalties in the event of failure to disclose the matters set out in Articles 29, 30, 31, 36, 37 and 38 and of omission from letters and order forms of the compulsory particulars provided for in Articles 35 and 39.

[11.436]

Article 41 Persons carrying out disclosure formalities

Each Member State shall determine who shall carry out the disclosure formalities provided for in Sections 2 and 3.

[11.437]

Article 42 Exemptions to provisions on disclosure of accounting documents for branches

1. Articles 31 and 38 shall not apply to branches opened by credit institutions and financial institutions covered by Council Directive 89/117/EEC.[1]

2. Pending subsequent coordination, the Member States need not apply Articles 31 and 38 to branches opened by insurance companies.

NOTES

[1] Council Directive 89/117/EEC of 13 February 1989 on the obligations of branches established in a Member State of credit institutions and financial institutions having their head offices outside that Member State regarding the publication of annual accounting documents (OJ L44, 16.2.1989, p 40).

43 *(Article 43 (Contact Committee) was repealed by European Parliament and Council Directive 2019/1151/EU, Art 1(18), as from 31 July 2019.)*

CHAPTER IV CAPITAL MAINTENANCE AND ALTERATION

SECTION 1 CAPITAL REQUIREMENTS

[11.438]

Article 44 General provisions

1. The coordination measures prescribed by this Chapter shall apply to the provisions laid down by law, regulation or administrative action in Member States relating to the types of company listed in Annex I.

2. The Member States may decide not to apply the provisions of this Chapter to investment companies with variable capital and to cooperatives incorporated as one of the types of company listed in Annex I. In so far as the laws of the Member States make use of this option, they shall require such companies to include the words 'investment company with variable capital', or 'cooperative' in all documents indicated in Article 26.

[11.439]

Article 45 Minimum capital

1. The laws of the Member States shall require that, in order for a company to be incorporated or obtain authorisation to commence business, a minimum capital shall be subscribed the amount of which shall be not less than EUR 25,000.

2. Every five years the European Parliament and the Council, acting on a proposal from the Commission in accordance with Article 50(1) and Article 50(2)(g) of the Treaty, shall examine and, if need be, revise the amount expressed in paragraph 1 in euro in the light of economic and monetary trends in the Union and of the tendency to allow only large and medium-sized undertakings to opt for the types of company listed in Annex I.

[11.440]

Article 46 Assets

Subscribed capital may be formed only of assets capable of economic assessment. However, an undertaking to perform work or supply services may not form part of those assets.

[11.441]

Article 47 Issuing price of shares

Shares may not be issued at a price lower than their nominal value, or, where there is no nominal value, their accountable par.

However, Member States may allow those who undertake to place shares in the exercise of their profession to pay less than the total price of the shares for which they subscribe in the course of this transaction.

[11.442]

Article 48 Paying up of shares issued for a consideration

Shares issued for consideration shall be paid up at the time the company is incorporated or is authorised to commence business at not less than 25% of their nominal value or, in the absence of a nominal value, their accountable par.

However, where shares are issued for consideration other than in cash at the time the company is incorporated or is authorised to commence business, the consideration shall be transferred in full within five years of that time.

SECTION 2 SAFEGUARDS AS REGARDS STATUTORY CAPITAL

[11.443]

Article 49 Experts' report on consideration other than in cash

1. A report on any consideration other than in cash shall be drawn up before the company is incorporated or is authorised to commence business, by one or more independent experts appointed or approved by an administrative or judicial authority. Such experts may be natural persons as well as legal persons and companies or firms under the laws of each Member State.

2. The experts' report referred to in paragraph 1 shall contain at least a description of each of the assets comprising the consideration as well as of the methods of valuation used and shall state whether the values arrived at by the application of those methods correspond at least to the number and nominal value or, where there is no nominal value, to the accountable par and, where appropriate, to the premium on the shares to be issued for them.

3. The experts' report shall be published in the manner laid down by the laws of each Member State, in accordance with Article 16.

4. Member States may decide not to apply this Article where 90% of the nominal value, or where there is no nominal value, of the accountable par, of all the shares is issued to one or more companies for a consideration other than in cash, and where the following requirements are met:

(a) with regard to the company in receipt of such consideration, the persons referred to in point (i) of Article 4 have agreed to dispense with the experts' report;
(b) such agreement has been published as provided for in paragraph 3;
(c) the companies furnishing such consideration have reserves which may not be distributed under the law or the statutes and which are at least equal to the nominal value or, where there is no nominal value, the accountable par of the shares issued for consideration other than in cash;
(d) the companies furnishing such consideration guarantee, up to an amount equal to that indicated in point (c), the debts of the recipient company arising between the time the shares are issued for a consideration other than in cash and one year after the publication of that company's annual accounts for the financial year during which such consideration was furnished. Any transfer of such shares shall be prohibited during that period;
(e) the guarantee referred to in point (d) has been published as provided for in paragraph 3; and
(f) the companies furnishing such consideration shall place a sum equal to that indicated in point (c) into a reserve which may not be distributed until three years after publication of the annual accounts of the recipient company for the financial year during which such consideration was furnished or, if necessary, until such later date as all claims relating to the guarantee referred to in point (d) which are submitted during this period have been settled.

5. Member States may decide not to apply this Article to the formation of a new company by way of merger or division where a report by one or more independent experts on the draft terms of merger or division is drawn up.

Where Member States decide to apply this Article in the cases referred to in the first subparagraph, they may provide that the report drawn up under paragraph 1 of this Article and the report by one or more independent experts on the draft terms of merger or division may be drawn up by the same expert or experts.

[11.444]

Article 50 Derogation from the requirement for an experts' report

1. Member States may decide not to apply Article 49(1), (2) and (3) where, upon a decision of the administrative or management body, transferable securities as defined in point 44 of Article 4(1) of Directive 2014/65/EU of the European Parliament and of the Council[1] or money-market instruments as defined in point 17 of Article 4(1) of that Directive are contributed as consideration other than in cash, and those securities or money-market instruments are valued at the weighted average price at which they have been traded on one or more regulated markets as defined in point 21 of Article 4(1) of that Directive during a sufficient period, to be determined by national law, preceding the effective date of the contribution of the respective consideration other than in cash.

However, where that price has been affected by exceptional circumstances that would significantly change the value of the asset at the effective date of its contribution, including situations where the market for such transferable securities or money-market instruments has become illiquid, a revaluation shall be carried out on the initiative and under the responsibility of the administrative or management body.

For the purposes of such revaluation, Article 49(1), (2) and (3) shall apply.

2. Member States may decide not to apply Article 49(1), (2) and (3) where, upon a decision of the administrative or management body, assets, other than the transferable securities and money-market instruments referred to in paragraph 1 of this Article, are contributed as consideration other than in cash which have already been subject to a fair value opinion by a recognised independent expert and where the following conditions are fulfilled:
(a) the fair value is determined for a date not more than six months before the effective date of the asset contribution; and
(b) the valuation has been performed in accordance with generally accepted valuation standards and principles in the Member State which are applicable to the kind of assets to be contributed.

In the case of new qualifying circumstances that would significantly change the fair value of the asset at the effective date of its contribution, a revaluation shall be carried out on the initiative and under the responsibility of the administrative or management body.

For the purposes of the revaluation referred to in the second subparagraph, Article 49(1), (2) and (3) shall apply.

In the absence of such a revaluation, one or more shareholders holding an aggregate percentage of at least 5% of the company's subscribed capital on the date the decision on the increase in the capital is taken, may demand a valuation by an independent expert, in which case Article 49(1), (2) and (3) shall apply.

Such shareholder(s) may submit a demand up until the effective date of the asset contribution, provided that, at the date of the demand, the shareholder(s) in question still hold(s) an aggregate percentage of at least 5% of the company's subscribed capital, as it was on the date the decision on the increase in the capital was taken.

3. Member States may decide not to apply Article 49(1), (2) and (3) where, upon a decision of the administrative or management body, assets, other than the transferable securities and money-market instruments referred to in paragraph 1 of this Article, are contributed as consideration other than in cash the fair value of which is derived from the value of an individual asset from the statutory accounts of the previous financial year provided that the statutory accounts have been subject to an audit in accordance with Directive 2006/43/EC.

The second to fifth subparagraphs of paragraph 2 of this Article shall apply *mutatis mutandis*.

NOTES

[1] Directive 2014/65/EU of the European Parliament and of the Council of 15 May 2014 on markets in financial instruments and amending Directive 2002/92/EC and Directive 2011/61/EU (OJ L173, 12.6.2014, p 349).

[11.445]

Article 51 Consideration other than in cash without an experts' report

1. Where consideration other than in cash as referred to in Article 50 is provided without an experts' report as referred to in Article 49(1), (2) and (3), in addition to the requirements set out in point (h) of Article 4 and within one month of the effective date of the asset contribution, a declaration containing the following shall be published:
(a) a description of the consideration other than in cash at issue;
(b) its value, the source of this valuation and, where appropriate, the method of valuation;

(c) a statement whether the value arrived at corresponds at least to the number, to the nominal value or, where there is no nominal value, the accountable par and, where appropriate, to the premium on the shares to be issued for such consideration; and

(d) a statement that no new qualifying circumstances with regard to the original valuation have occurred.

The publication of the declaration shall be effected in the manner laid down by the laws of each Member State in accordance with Article 16.

2. Where consideration other than in cash is proposed to be provided without an experts' report, as referred to in Article 49(1), (2) and (3), in relation to an increase in the capital proposed to be made under Article 68(2), an announcement containing the date when the decision on the increase was taken and the information listed in paragraph 1 of this Article shall be published, in the manner laid down by the laws of each Member State in accordance with Article 16, before the contribution of the asset as consideration other than in cash is to become effective. In that event, the declaration pursuant to paragraph 1 of this Article shall be limited to the statement that no new qualifying circumstances have occurred since the aforementioned announcement was published.

3. Each Member State shall provide for adequate safeguards ensuring compliance with the procedure set out in Article 50 and in this Article where a contribution for a consideration other than in cash is provided without an experts' report as referred to in Article 49(1), (2) and (3).

[11.446]

Article 52 Substantial acquisitions after incorporation or authorisation to commence business

1. If, before the expiry of a time limit laid down by national law of at least two years from the time the company is incorporated or is authorised to commence business, the company acquires any asset belonging to a person or company or firm referred to in point (i) of Article 4 for a consideration of not less than one-tenth of the subscribed capital, the acquisition shall be examined and details of it published in the manner provided for in Article 49(1), (2) and (3), and it shall be submitted for the approval of a general meeting.

Articles 50 and 51 shall apply *mutatis mutandis*.

Member States may also require these provisions to be applied when the assets belong to a shareholder or to any other person.

2. Paragraph 1 shall not apply to acquisitions effected in the normal course of the company's business, to acquisitions effected at the instance or under the supervision of an administrative or judicial authority, or to stock exchange acquisitions.

[11.447]

Article 53 Shareholders' obligation to pay up contributions

Subject to the provisions relating to the reduction of subscribed capital, the shareholders may not be released from the obligation to pay up their contributions.

[11.448]

Article 54 Safeguards in the event of conversion

Pending coordination of national laws at a subsequent date, Member States shall adopt the measures necessary to require provision of at least the same safeguards as are laid down in Articles 3 to 6 and Articles 45 to 53 in the event of the conversion of another type of company into a public limited liability company.

[11.449]

Article 55 Modification of the statutes or of the instrument of incorporation

Articles 3 to 6 and Articles 45 to 54 shall be without prejudice to the provisions of Member States on competence and procedure relating to the modification of the statutes or of the instrument of incorporation.

SECTION 3 RULES ON DISTRIBUTION

[11.450]

Article 56 General rules on distribution

1. Except for cases of reductions of subscribed capital, no distribution to shareholders may be made when on the closing date of the last financial year the net assets as set out in the company's annual accounts are or, following such a distribution, would become, lower than the amount of the subscribed capital plus those reserves which may not be distributed under the law or the statutes of the company.

2. Where the uncalled part of the subscribed capital is not included in the assets shown in the balance sheet, that amount shall be deducted from the amount of subscribed capital referred to in paragraph 1.

3. The amount of a distribution to shareholders may not exceed the amount of the profits at the end of the last financial year plus any profits brought forward and sums drawn from reserves available for this purpose, less any losses brought forward and sums placed to reserve in accordance with the law or the statutes.

4. The term 'distribution' used in Paragraphs 1 and 3 includes, in particular, the payment of dividends and of interest relating to shares.

5. When the laws of a Member State allow the payment of interim dividends, at least the following conditions shall apply:

(a) interim accounts shall be drawn up showing that the funds available for distribution are sufficient;

(b) the amount to be distributed may not exceed the total profits made since the end of the last financial year for which the annual accounts have been drawn up, plus any profits brought forward and sums drawn from reserves available for this purpose, less losses brought forward and sums to be placed to reserve pursuant to the requirements of the law or the statutes.

6. Paragraphs 1 to 5 shall not affect the provisions of the Member States as regards increases in subscribed capital by capitalisation of reserves.

7. The laws of a Member State may provide for derogation from paragraph 1 in the case of investment companies with fixed capital.

For the purposes of this paragraph, the term 'investment company with fixed capital' means only companies:

(a) the exclusive object of which is to invest their funds in various stocks and shares, land or other assets with the sole aim of spreading investment risks and giving their shareholders the benefit of the results of the management of their assets; and

(b) which offer their own shares for subscription by the public.

In so far as the laws of Member States make use of the option they shall:

(a) require such companies to include the term 'investment company' in all documents indicated in Article 26;

(b) not permit any such company whose net assets fall below the amount specified in paragraph 1 to make a distribution to shareholders when on the closing date of the last financial year the company's total assets as set out in the annual accounts are, or following such distribution would become, less than one-and-a-half times the amount of the company's total liabilities to creditors as set out in the annual accounts; and

(c) require any such company which makes a distribution when its net assets fall below the amount specified in paragraph 1 to include in its annual accounts a note to that effect.

[11.451]
Article 57 Recovery of distributions unlawfully made

Any distribution made contrary to Article 56 shall be returned by shareholders who have received it if the company proves that those shareholders knew of the irregularity of the distributions made to them, or could not in view of the circumstances have been unaware of it.

[11.452]
Article 58 Serious loss of the subscribed capital

1. In the case of a serious loss of the subscribed capital, a general meeting of shareholders shall be called within the period laid down by the laws of the Member States, to consider whether the company should be wound up or any other measures taken.

2. The amount of a loss deemed to be serious within the meaning of paragraph 1 shall not be set by the laws of Member States at a figure higher than half the subscribed capital.

SECTION 4 RULES ON COMPANIES' ACQUISITIONS OF THEIR OWN SHARES

[11.453]
Article 59 No subscription of own shares

1. The shares of a company may not be subscribed for by the company itself.

2. If the shares of a company have been subscribed for by a person acting in his or her own name, but on behalf of the company, the subscriber shall be deemed to have subscribed for them for his or her own account.

3. The persons or companies or firms referred to in point (i) of Article 4 or, in cases of an increase in subscribed capital, the members of the administrative or management body shall be liable to pay for shares subscribed in contravention of this Article.

However, the laws of a Member State may provide that any such person may be released from his or her obligation if they prove that no fault is attributable to them personally.

[11.454]
Article 60 Acquisition of own shares

1. Without prejudice to the principle of equal treatment of all shareholders who are in the same position, and to Regulation (EU) No 596/2014, Member States may permit a company to acquire its own shares, either itself or through a person acting in his or her own name but on the company's behalf. To the extent that the acquisitions are permitted, Member States shall make such acquisitions subject to the following conditions:

(a) authorisation is given by the general meeting, which shall determine the terms and conditions of such acquisitions, and, in particular, the maximum number of shares to be acquired, the duration of the period for which the authorisation is given, the maximum length of which shall be determined by national law without, however, exceeding five years, and, in the case of acquisition for value, the maximum and minimum consideration. Members of the administrative or management body shall satisfy themselves that, at the time when each authorised acquisition is effected, the conditions referred to in points (b) and (c) are respected;

(b) the acquisitions, including shares previously acquired by the company and held by it, and shares acquired by a person acting in his or her own name but on the company's behalf, cannot have the effect of reducing the net assets below the amount referred to in Article 56(1) and (2); and

(c) only fully paid-up shares can be included in the transaction.

Furthermore, Member States may subject acquisitions within the meaning of the first subparagraph to any of the following conditions:

(a) the nominal value or, in the absence thereof, the accountable par of the acquired shares, including shares previously acquired by the company and held by it, and shares acquired by a person acting in his own name but on the company's behalf, does not exceed a limit to be determined by Member States; this limit may not be lower than 10% of the subscribed capital;

(b) the power of the company to acquire its own shares within the meaning of the first subparagraph, the maximum number of shares to be acquired, the duration of the period for which the power is given and the maximum or minimum consideration are laid down in the statutes or in the instrument of incorporation of the company;

(c) the company complies with appropriate reporting and notification requirements;

(d) certain companies, as determined by Member States, can be required to cancel the acquired shares provided that an amount equal to the nominal value of the shares cancelled is included in a reserve which cannot be distributed to the shareholders, except in the event of a reduction in the subscribed capital; this reserve may be used only for the purposes of increasing the subscribed capital by the capitalisation of reserves;

(e) the acquisition does not prejudice the satisfaction of creditors' claims.

2. The laws of a Member State may provide for derogations from the first sentence of point (a) of the first subparagraph of paragraph 1 where the acquisition of a company's own shares is necessary to prevent serious and imminent harm to the company. In such a case, the next general meeting shall be informed by the administrative or

management body of the reasons for and nature of the acquisitions effected, of the number and nominal value or, in the absence of a nominal value, the accountable par, of the shares acquired, of the proportion of the subscribed capital which they represent, and of the consideration for those shares.

3. Member States may decide not to apply the first sentence of point (a) of the first subparagraph of paragraph 1 to shares acquired by either the company itself or by a person acting in his or her own name but on the company's behalf, for distribution to that company's employees or to the employees of an associate company. Such shares shall be distributed within 12 months of their acquisition.

[11.455]

Article 61 Derogation from rules on acquisition of own shares

1. Member States may decide not to apply Article 60 to:

(a) shares acquired in carrying out a decision to reduce capital, or in the circumstances referred to in Article 82;
(b) shares acquired as a result of a universal transfer of assets;
(c) fully paid-up shares acquired free of charge or by, banks and other financial institutions as purchasing commission;
(d) shares acquired by virtue of a legal obligation or resulting from a court ruling for the protection of minority shareholders in the event, particularly, of a merger, a change in the company's object or form, transfer abroad of the registered office, or the introduction of restrictions on the transfer of shares;
(e) shares acquired from a shareholder in the event of failure to pay them up;
(f) shares acquired in order to indemnify minority shareholders in associated companies;
(g) fully paid-up shares acquired under a sale enforced by a court order for the payment of a debt owed to the company by the owner of the shares; and
(h) fully paid-up shares issued by an investment company with fixed capital, as defined in the second subparagraph of Article 56(7), and acquired at the investor's request by that company or by an associate company. point (a) of the third subparagraph of Article 56(7) shall apply. Such acquisitions may not have the effect of reducing the net assets below the amount of the subscribed capital plus any reserves the distribution of which is forbidden by law.

2. Shares acquired in the cases listed in points (b) to (g) of paragraph 1 shall, however, be disposed of within not more than three years of their acquisition unless the nominal value or, in the absence of a nominal value, the accountable par of the shares acquired, including shares which the company may have acquired through a person acting in his own name but on the company's behalf, does not exceed 10% of the subscribed capital.

3. If the shares are not disposed of within the period laid down in paragraph 2, they shall be cancelled. The laws of a Member State may make this cancellation subject to a corresponding reduction in the subscribed capital. Such a reduction shall be prescribed where the acquisition of shares to be cancelled results in the net assets having fallen below the amount specified in Article 56(1) and (2).

[11.456]

Article 62 Consequences of illegal acquisition of own shares

Shares acquired in contravention of Articles 60 and 61 shall be disposed of within one year of their acquisition. If they are not disposed of within that period, Article 61(3) shall apply.

[11.457]

Article 63 Holding of own shares and annual report in case of acquisition of own shares

1. Where the laws of a Member State permit a company to acquire its own shares, either itself or through a person acting in his or her own name but on the company's behalf, they shall make the holding of these shares at all times subject to at least the following conditions:

(a) among the rights attaching to the shares, the right to vote attaching to the company's own shares must in any event be suspended;
(b) if the shares are included among the assets shown in the balance sheet, a reserve of the same amount, unavailable for distribution, shall be included among the liabilities.

2. Where the laws of a Member State permit a company to acquire its own shares, either itself or through a person acting in his or her own name but on the company's behalf, they shall require the annual report to state at least:

(a) the reasons for acquisitions made during the financial year;
(b) the number and nominal value or, in the absence of a nominal value, the accountable par of the shares acquired and disposed of during the financial year and the proportion of the subscribed capital which they represent;
(c) in the case of acquisition or disposal for a value, the consideration for the shares;
(d) the number and nominal value or, in the absence of a nominal value, the accountable par of all the shares acquired and held by the company and the proportion of the subscribed capital which they represent.

[11.458]

Article 64 Financial assistance by a company for acquisition of its shares by a third party

1. Where Member States permit a company to, either directly or indirectly, advance funds or make loans or provide security, with a view to the acquisition of its shares by a third party, they shall make such transactions subject to the conditions set out in Paragraphs 2 to 5.

2. The transactions shall take place under the responsibility of the administrative or management body at fair market conditions, especially with regard to interest received by the company and with regard to security provided to the company for the loans and advances referred to in paragraph 1.

The credit standing of the third party or, in the case of multiparty transactions, of each counterparty thereto shall have been duly investigated.

3. The transactions shall be submitted by the administrative or management body to the general meeting for prior approval, whereby the general meeting shall act in accordance with the rules for a quorum and a majority laid down in Article 83.

The administrative or management body shall present a written report to the general meeting, indicating:

(a) the reasons for the transaction;

Part 11 EU & Retained EU Legislation

- (b) the interest of the company in entering into such a transaction;
- (c) the conditions on which the transaction is entered into;
- (d) the risks involved in the transaction for the liquidity and solvency of the company; and
- (e) the price at which the third party is to acquire the shares.

This report shall be submitted to the register for publication in accordance with Article 16.

4. The aggregate financial assistance granted to third parties shall at no time result in the reduction of the net assets below the amount specified in Article 56(1) and (2), taking into account also any reduction of the net assets that may have occurred through the acquisition, by the company or on behalf of the company, of its own shares in accordance with Article 60(1).

The company shall include, among the liabilities in the balance sheet, a reserve, unavailable for distribution, of the amount of the aggregate financial assistance.

5. Where a third party by means of financial assistance from a company acquires that company's own shares within the meaning of Article 60(1) or subscribes for shares issued in the course of an increase in the subscribed capital, such acquisition or subscription shall be made at a fair price.

6. Paragraphs 1 to 5 shall not apply to transactions concluded by banks and other financial institutions in the normal course of business, nor to transactions effected with a view to the acquisition of shares by or for the company's employees or the employees of an associate company.

However, these transactions may not have the effect of reducing the net assets below the amount specified in Article 56(1).

7. Paragraphs 1 to 5 shall not apply to transactions effected with a view to acquisition of shares as described in of Article 61(1)(h).

[11.459]

Article 65 Additional safeguards in case of related party transactions

In cases where individual members of the administrative or management body of the company being party to a transaction referred to in Article 64(1) of this Directive, or of the administrative or management body of a parent undertaking within the meaning of Article 22 of Directive 2013/34/EU or such parent undertaking itself, or individuals acting in their own name, but on behalf of the members of such bodies or on behalf of such undertaking, are counterparties to such a transaction, Member States shall ensure through adequate safeguards that such transaction does not conflict with the company's best interests.

[11.460]

Article 66 Acceptance of the company's own shares as security

1. The acceptance of the company's own shares as security, either by the company itself or through a person acting in his own name but on the company's behalf, shall be treated as an acquisition for the purposes of Article 60, Article 61(1), and Articles 63 and 64.

2. The Member States may decide not to apply paragraph 1 to transactions concluded by banks and other financial institutions in the normal course of business.

[11.461]

Article 67 Subscription, acquisition or holding of shares by a company in which the public limited liability company holds a majority of the voting rights or on which it can exercise a dominant influence

1. The subscription, acquisition or holding of shares in a public limited liability company by another company of a type listed in Annex II in which the public limited liability company directly or indirectly holds a majority of the voting rights or on which it can directly or indirectly exercise a dominant influence shall be regarded as having been effected by the public limited liability company itself.

The first subparagraph shall also apply where the other company is governed by the law of a third country and has a legal form comparable to those listed in Annex II.

However, where the public limited liability company holds a majority of the voting rights indirectly or can exercise a dominant influence indirectly, Member States need not apply the first and the second subparagraphs if they provide for the suspension of the voting rights attached to the shares in the public limited liability company held by the other company.

2. In the absence of coordination of national legislation on groups of companies, Member States may:

- (a) define the cases in which a public limited liability company shall be regarded as being able to exercise a dominant influence on another company; if a Member State exercises this option, its national law shall in any event provide that a dominant influence can be exercised if a public limited liability company:
  - (i) has the right to appoint or dismiss a majority of the members of the administrative organ, of the management organ or of the supervisory organ, and is at the same time a shareholder or member of the other company; or
  - (ii) is a shareholder or member of the other company and has sole control of a majority of the voting rights of its shareholders or members under an agreement concluded with other shareholders or members of that company.

  Member States shall not be obliged to make provision for any cases other than those referred to in points (i) and (ii) of the first subparagraph;
- (b) define the cases in which a public limited liability company shall be regarded as indirectly holding voting rights or as able indirectly to exercise a dominant influence;
- (c) specify the circumstances in which a public limited liability company shall be regarded as holding voting rights.

3. Member States need not apply the first and second subparagraphs of paragraph 1 where the subscription, acquisition or holding is effected on behalf of a person other than the person subscribing, acquiring or holding the shares, who is neither the public limited liability company referred to in paragraph 1 nor another company in which the public limited liability company directly or indirectly holds a majority of the voting rights or on which it can directly or indirectly exercise a dominant influence.

4. Member States need not apply the first and second subparagraphs of paragraph 1 where the subscription, acquisition or holding is effected by the other company in its capacity and in the context of its activities as a professional dealer in securities, provided that it is a member of a stock exchange situated or operating within a Member State, or is approved or supervised by an authority of a Member State competent to supervise professional dealers in securities which, within the meaning of this Directive, may include credit institutions.

5. Member States need not apply the first and second subparagraphs of paragraph 1 where shares in a public limited liability company held by another company were acquired before the relationship between the two companies corresponded to the criteria laid down in paragraph 1.

However, the voting rights attached to those shares shall be suspended and the shares shall be taken into account when it is determined whether the condition laid down in Article 60(1)(b) is fulfilled.

6. Member States need not apply Article 61(2) or (3) or Article 62 where shares in a public limited liability company are acquired by another company on condition that they provide for:

(a) the suspension of the voting rights attached to the shares in the public limited liability company held by the other company; and

(b) the members of the administrative or the management organ of the public limited liability company to be obliged to buy back from the other company the shares referred to in Article 61(2) and (3) and Article 62 at the price at which the other company acquired them; this sanction shall be inapplicable only where the members of the administrative or the management organ of the public limited liability company prove that that company played no part whatsoever in the subscription for or acquisition of the shares in question.

SECTION 5 RULES FOR THE INCREASE AND REDUCTION OF CAPITAL

[11.462]

Article 68 Decision by the general meeting on the increase of capital

1. Any increase in capital shall be decided upon by the general meeting. Both that decision and the increase in the subscribed capital shall be published in the manner laid down by the laws of each Member State, in accordance with Article 16.

2. Nevertheless, the statutes or instrument of incorporation or the general meeting, the decision of which is to be published in accordance with the rules referred to in paragraph 1, may authorise an increase in the subscribed capital up to a maximum amount which they shall fix with due regard for any maximum amount provided for by law. Where appropriate, the increase in the subscribed capital shall be decided on within the limits of the amount fixed by the company body empowered to do so. The power of such body in this respect shall be for a maximum period of five years and may be renewed one or more times by the general meeting, each time for a period not exceeding five years.

3. Where there are several classes of shares, the decision by the general meeting concerning the increase in capital referred to in paragraph 1 or the authorisation to increase the capital referred to in paragraph 2, shall be subject to a separate vote at least for each class of shareholder whose rights are affected by the transaction.

4. This Article shall apply to the issue of all securities which are convertible into shares or which carry the right to subscribe for shares, but not to the conversion of such securities, nor to the exercise of the right to subscribe.

[11.463]

Article 69 Paying up shares issued for consideration

Shares issued for consideration, in the course of an increase in subscribed capital, shall be paid up to at least 25% of their nominal value or, in the absence of a nominal value, of their accountable par. Where provision is made for an issue premium, it shall be paid in full.

[11.464]

Article 70 Shares issued for consideration other than in cash

1. Where shares are issued for consideration other than in cash in the course of an increase in the subscribed capital, the consideration shall be transferred in full within a period of five years from the decision to increase the subscribed capital.

2. The consideration referred to in paragraph 1 shall be the subject of a report drawn up before the increase in capital is made by one or more experts who are independent of the company and appointed or approved by an administrative or judicial authority. Such experts may be natural persons as well as legal persons and companies and firms under the laws of each Member State.

Article 49(2) and (3) and Articles 50 and 51 shall apply.

3. Member States may decide not to apply paragraph 2 in the event of an increase in subscribed capital made in order to give effect to a merger, a division or a public offer for the purchase or exchange of shares and to pay the shareholders of the company which is being absorbed or divided, or which is the object of the public offer for the purchase or exchange of shares.

In the case of a merger or a division, however, Member States shall apply the first subparagraph only where a report by one or more independent experts on the draft terms of merger or division is drawn up.

Where Member States decide to apply paragraph 2 in the case of a merger or a division, they may provide that the report under this Article and the report by one or more independent experts on the draft terms of merger or division may be drawn up by the same expert or experts.

4. Member States may decide not to apply paragraph 2 if all the shares issued in the course of an increase in subscribed capital are issued for a consideration other than in cash to one or more companies, on condition that all the shareholders in the company which receive the consideration have agreed not to have an experts' report drawn up and that the requirements of points (b) to (f) of Article 49(4) are met.

[11.465]

Article 71 Increase in capital not fully subscribed

Where an increase in capital is not fully subscribed, the capital will be increased by the amount of the subscriptions received only if the conditions of the issue so provide.

[11.466]

Article 72 Increase in capital by consideration in cash

1. Whenever the capital is increased by consideration in cash, the shares shall be offered on a pre-emptive basis to shareholders in proportion to the capital represented by their shares.

2. The laws of a Member State:

(a) need not apply paragraph 1 to shares which carry a limited right to participate in distributions within the meaning of Article 56 and/or in the company's assets in the event of liquidation; or

(b) may permit, where the subscribed capital of a company having several classes of shares carrying different rights with regard to voting, or participation in distributions within the meaning of Article 56 or in assets in the event of liquidation, is increased by issuing new shares in only one of these classes, the right of pre-emption of shareholders of the other classes to be exercised only after the exercise of this right by the shareholders of the class in which the new shares are being issued.

3. Any offer of subscription on a pre-emptive basis and the period within which this right shall be exercised shall be published in the national gazette appointed in accordance with Article 16. However, the laws of a Member State need not provide for such publication where all of a company's shares are registered. In such case, all the company's shareholders shall be informed in writing. The right of pre-emption shall be exercised within a period which shall not be less than 14 days from the date of publication of the offer or from the date of dispatch of the letters to the shareholders.

4. The right of pre-emption may not be restricted or withdrawn by the statutes or instrument of incorporation. This may, however, be done by decision of the general meeting. The administrative or management body shall be required to present to such a meeting a written report indicating the reasons for restriction or withdrawal of the right of pre-emption, and justifying the proposed issue price. The general meeting shall act in accordance with the rules for a quorum and a majority laid down in Article 83. Its decision shall be published in the manner laid down by the laws of each Member State, in accordance with Article 16.

5. The laws of a Member State may provide that the statutes, the instrument of incorporation or the general meeting, acting in accordance with the rules for a quorum, a majority and publication set out in paragraph 4 of this Article, may give the power to restrict or withdraw the right of pre-emption to the company body which is empowered to decide on an increase in subscribed capital within the limit of the authorised capital. This power may not be granted for a longer period than the power for which provision is made in Article 68(2).

6. Paragraphs 1 to 5 shall apply to the issue of all securities which are convertible into shares or which carry the right to subscribe for shares, but not to the conversion of such securities, nor to the exercise of the right to subscribe.

7. The right of pre-emption is not excluded for the purposes of Paragraphs 4 and 5 where, in accordance with the decision to increase the subscribed capital, shares are issued to banks or other financial institutions with a view to their being offered to shareholders of the company in accordance with Paragraphs 1 and 3.

[11.467]

Article 73 Decision by the general meeting on reduction in the subscribed capital

Any reduction in the subscribed capital, except under a court order, shall be subject at least to a decision of the general meeting acting in accordance with the rules for a quorum and a majority laid down in Article 83 without prejudice to Articles 79 and 80. Such decision shall be published in the manner laid down by the laws of each Member State in accordance with Article 16.

The notice convening the meeting shall specify at least the purpose of the reduction and the way in which it is to be carried out.

[11.468]

Article 74 Reduction in the subscribed capital in case of several classes of shares

Where there are several classes of shares, the decision by the general meeting concerning a reduction in the subscribed capital shall be subject to a separate vote, at least for each class of shareholders whose rights are affected by the transaction.

[11.469]

Article 75 Safeguards for creditors in case of reduction in the subscribed capital

1. In the event of a reduction in the subscribed capital, at least the creditors whose claims antedate the publication of the decision on the reduction shall at least have the right to obtain security for claims which have not fallen due by the date of that publication. Member States may not set aside such a right unless the creditor has adequate safeguards, or unless such safeguards are not necessary having regard to the assets of the company.

Member States shall lay down the conditions for the exercise of the right provided for in the first subparagraph. In any event, Member States shall ensure that the creditors are authorised to apply to the appropriate administrative or judicial authority for adequate safeguards provided that they can credibly demonstrate that due to the reduction in the subscribed capital the satisfaction of their claims is at stake, and that no adequate safeguards have been obtained from the company.

2. The laws of the Member States shall also stipulate at least that the reduction shall be void, or that no payment may be made for the benefit of the shareholders, until the creditors have obtained satisfaction or a court has decided that their application should not be acceded to.

3. This Article shall apply where the reduction in the subscribed capital is brought about by the total or partial waiving of the payment of the balance of the shareholders' contributions.

[11.470]

Article 76 Derogation from safeguards for creditors in case of reduction in the subscribed capital

1. Member States need not apply Article 75 to a reduction in the subscribed capital the purpose of which is to offset losses incurred or to include sums of money in a reserve provided that, following this operation, the amount of such reserve is not more than 10% of the reduced subscribed capital. Except in the event of a reduction in the subscribed capital, this reserve may not be distributed to shareholders; it may be used only for offsetting losses incurred or for increasing the subscribed capital by the capitalisation of such reserve, in so far as the Member States permit such an operation.

2. In the cases referred to in paragraph 1, the laws of the Member States shall at least provide for the measures necessary to ensure that the amounts deriving from the reduction of subscribed capital may not be used for making payments or distributions to shareholders, or discharging shareholders from the obligation to make their contributions.

[11.471]

Article 77 Reduction in the subscribed capital and the minimum capital

The subscribed capital may not be reduced to an amount less than the minimum capital laid down in accordance with Article 45.

However, Member States may permit such a reduction if they also provide that the decision to reduce the subscribed capital may take effect only when the subscribed capital is increased to an amount at least equal to the prescribed minimum.

[11.472]

Article 78 Redemption of subscribed capital without reduction

Where the laws of a Member State authorise total or partial redemption of the subscribed capital without reduction of the latter, they shall at least require that the following conditions are observed:

(a) where the statutes or instrument of incorporation provide for redemption, the latter shall be decided on by the general meeting voting at least under the usual conditions of quorum and majority; where the statutes or instrument of incorporation do not provide for redemption, the latter shall be decided upon by the general meeting acting at least under the conditions of quorum and majority laid down in Article 83; the decision shall be published in the manner prescribed by the laws of Member States, in accordance with Article 16;

(b) only sums which are available for distribution within the meaning of Article 56(1) to (4) may be used for redemption purposes;

(c) shareholders whose shares are redeemed shall retain their rights in the company, with the exception of their rights to the repayment of their investment and participation in the distribution of an initial dividend on unredeemed shares.

[11.473]

Article 79 Reduction in the subscribed capital by compulsory withdrawal of shares

1. Where the laws of a Member State allow companies to reduce their subscribed capital by compulsory withdrawal of shares, they shall require that at least the following conditions are observed:

(a) compulsory withdrawal must be prescribed or authorised by the statutes or instrument of incorporation before the shares which are to be withdrawn are subscribed for;

(b) where the compulsory withdrawal is authorised merely by the statutes or instrument of incorporation, it shall be decided upon by the general meeting unless it has been unanimously approved by the shareholders concerned;

(c) the company body deciding on the compulsory withdrawal shall fix the terms and manner thereof, where they have not already been fixed by the statutes or instrument of incorporation;

(d) Article 75 shall apply except in the case of fully paid-up shares which are made available to the company free of charge or are withdrawn using sums available for distribution in accordance with Article 56(1) to (4); in these cases, an amount equal to the nominal value or, in the absence thereof, to the accountable par of all the withdrawn shares must be included in a reserve; except in the event of a reduction in the subscribed capital, this reserve may not be distributed to shareholders; it can be used only for offsetting losses incurred or for increasing the subscribed capital by the capitalisation of such reserve, in so far as Member States permit such an operation; and

(e) the decision on compulsory withdrawal shall be published in the manner laid down by the laws of each Member State in accordance with Article 16.

2. The first paragraph of Article 73 and Articles 74, 76 and 83 shall not apply to the cases to which paragraph 1 of this Article refers.

[11.474]

Article 80 Reduction in the subscribed capital by the withdrawal of shares acquired by the company itself or on its behalf

1. In the case of a reduction in the subscribed capital by the withdrawal of shares acquired by the company itself or by a person acting in his own name but on behalf of the company, the withdrawal shall always be decided on by the general meeting.

2. Article 75 shall apply unless the shares are fully paid up and are acquired free of charge or using sums available for distribution in accordance with Article 56(1) to (4); in these cases an amount equal to the nominal value or, in the absence thereof, to the accountable par of all the shares withdrawn shall be included in a reserve. Except in the event of a reduction in the subscribed capital, this reserve may not be distributed to shareholders. It may be used only for offsetting losses incurred or for increasing the subscribed capital by the capitalisation of such reserve, in so far as the Member States permit such an operation.

3. Articles 74, 76 and 83 shall not apply to the cases to which paragraph 1 of this Article refers.

[11.475]

Article 81 Redemption of the subscribed capital or its reduction by withdrawal of shares in case of several classes of shares

In the cases covered by Article 78, Article 79(1)(b) and Article 80(1), when there are several classes of shares, the decision by the general meeting concerning redemption of the subscribed capital or its reduction by withdrawal of shares shall be subject to a separate vote, at least for each class of shareholders whose rights are affected by the transaction.

[11.476]

Article 82 Conditions for redemption of shares

Where the laws of a Member State authorise companies to issue redeemable shares, they shall require that the following conditions, at least, are complied with for the redemption of such shares:

(a) redemption must be authorised by the company's statutes or instrument of incorporation before the redeemable shares are subscribed for;
(b) the shares must be fully paid up;
(c) the terms and the manner of redemption must be laid down in the company's statutes or instrument of incorporation;
(d) redemption can be only effected by using sums available for distribution in accordance with Article 56(1) to (4) or the proceeds of a new issue made with a view to effecting such redemption;
(e) an amount equal to the nominal value or, in the absence thereof, to the accountable par of all the redeemed shares must be included in a reserve which cannot be distributed to the shareholders, except in the event of a reduction in the subscribed capital; it may be used only for the purpose of increasing the subscribed capital by the capitalisation of reserves;
(f) point (e) shall not apply to redemption using the proceeds of a new issue made with a view to effecting such redemption;
(g) where provision is made for the payment of a premium to shareholders in consequence of a redemption, the premium may be paid only from sums available for distribution in accordance with Article 56(1) to (4), or from a reserve other than that referred to in point (e) of this Article which may not be distributed to shareholders except in the event of a reduction in the subscribed capital; this reserve may be used only for the purposes of increasing the subscribed capital by the capitalisation of reserves or for covering the costs referred to in point (j) of Article 4 or the cost of issuing shares or debentures or for the payment of a premium to holders of redeemable shares or debentures;
(h) notification of redemption shall be published in the manner laid down by the laws of each Member State in accordance with Article 16.

[11.477]
Article 83 Voting requirements for the decisions of the general meeting
The laws of the Member States shall provide that the decisions referred to in Article 72(4) and (5) and Articles 73, 74, 78 and 81 are to be taken at least by a majority of not less than two thirds of the votes attaching to the securities or the subscribed capital represented.
The laws of the Member States may, however, lay down that a simple majority of the votes specified in the first paragraph is sufficient when at least half the subscribed capital is represented.

SECTION 6 APPLICATION AND IMPLEMENTING ARRANGEMENTS

[11.478]
Article 84 Derogation from certain requirements
1. Member States may derogate from the first paragraph of Article 48, the first sentence of Article 60(1)(a) and Articles 68, 69 and 72 to the extent that such derogations are necessary for the adoption or application of provisions designed to encourage the participation of employees, or other groups of persons defined by national law, in the capital of undertakings.
2. Member States may decide not to apply the first sentence of Article 60(1)(a) and Articles 73, 74 and 79 to 82 to companies incorporated under a special law which issue both capital shares and workers' shares, the latter being issued to the company's employees as a body, who are represented at general meetings of shareholders by delegates having the right to vote.
[3. Member States shall ensure that Article 49, Article 58(1), Article 68(1), (2) and (3), the first subparagraph of Article 70(2), Articles 72 to 75, 79, 80 and 81 of this Directive do not apply in the case of application of the resolution tools, powers and mechanisms provided for in Title IV of Directive 2014/59/EU of the European Parliament and of the Council[1] or in Title V of Regulation (EU) 2021/23 of the European Parliament and of the Council.[*]]
[4. Member States shall derogate from Article 58(1), Article 68, Articles 72, 73, and 74, point (b) of Article 79(1), Article 80(1) and Article 81 to the extent and for the period that such derogations are necessary for the establishment of the preventive restructuring frameworks provided for in Directive (EU) 2019/1023 of the European Parliament and of the Council.[2]
The first subparagraph shall be without prejudice to the principle of equal treatment of shareholders.]

NOTES
Para 3: substituted by European Parliament and Council Regulation 2021/23/EU, Art 92(1), as from 12 August 2022.
Para 4: added by European Parliament and Council Directive 2019/1023/EU, Art 32, as from 16 July 2019.
[1] Directive 2014/59/EU of the European Parliament and of the Council of 15 May 2014 establishing a framework for the recovery and resolution of credit institutions and investment firms and amending Council Directive 82/891/EEC, and Directives 2001/24/EC, 2002/47/EC, 2004/25/EC, 2005/56/EC, 2007/36/EC, 2011/35/EU, 2012/30/EU and 2013/36/EU, and Regulations (EU) No 1093/2010 and (EU) No 648/2012, of the European Parliament and of the Council (OJ L173, 12.6.2014, p 190).
[*] Regulation (EU) 2021/23 of the European Parliament and of the Council of 16 December 2020 on a framework for the recovery and resolution of central counterparties and amending Regulations (EU) No 1095/2010, (EU) No 648/2012, (EU) No 600/2014, (EU) No 806/2014 and (EU) 2015/2365 and Directives 2002/47/EC, 2004/25/EC, 2007/36/EC, 2014/59/EU and (EU) 2017/1132 (OJ L022, 22.1.2021, p 1).
[2] Directive (EU) 2019/1023 of the European Parliament and of the Council of 20 June 2019 on preventive restructuring frameworks, on discharge of debt and disqualifications and on measures to increase the efficiency of procedures concerning restructuring, insolvency and discharge of debt, and amending Directive (EU) 2017/1132 (Directive on restructuring and insolvency) (OJ L172, 26.6.2019, p 18).

[11.479]
Article 85 Equal treatment of all shareholders who are in the same position
For the purposes of the implementation of this Chapter, the laws of the Member States shall ensure equal treatment to all shareholders who are in the same position.

[11.480]

Article 86 Transitional provisions

Member States may decide not to apply points (g), (i), (j) and (k) of Article 4 to companies already in existence at the date of entry into force of the laws, regulations and administrative provisions adopted in order to comply with Council Directive 77/91/EEC.[1]

NOTES

[1] Second Council Directive 77/91/EEC of 13 December 1976 on coordination of safeguards which, for the protection of the interests of members and others, are required by Member States of companies within the meaning of the second paragraph of Article 58 of the Treaty, in respect of the formation of public limited liability companies and the maintenance and alteration of their capital, with a view to making such safeguards equivalent (OJ L26, 31.1.1977, p 1).

TITLE II [CONVERSIONS, MERGERS AND DIVISIONS OF LIMITED LIABILITY COMPANIES]

NOTES

The Title II heading was substituted by European Parliament and Council Directive 2019/2121/EU, Art 1(4), as form 1 January 2020. Note that the 2019 Directive has a transposition date of 31 January 2023.

[CHAPTER –I CROSS-BORDER CONVERSIONS

[11.481]

Article 86a Scope

1. This Chapter shall apply to conversions of limited liability companies formed in accordance with the law of a Member State and having their registered office, central administration or principal place of business within the Union, into limited liability companies governed by the law of another Member State.

2. This Chapter shall not apply to cross-border conversions involving a company the object of which is the collective investment of capital provided by the public, which operates on the principle of risk-spreading and the units of which are, at the holders' request, repurchased or redeemed, directly or indirectly, out of the assets of that company. Action taken by such a company to ensure that the stock exchange value of its units does not vary significantly from its net asset value shall be regarded as equivalent to such repurchase or redemption.

3. Member States shall ensure that this Chapter does not apply to companies in either of the following circumstances:
 (a) the company is in liquidation and has begun to distribute assets to its members;
 [(b) the company is subject to resolution tools, powers and mechanisms provided for in Title IV of Directive 2014/59/EU or in Title V of Regulation (EU) 2021/23.]

4. Member States may decide not to apply this Chapter to companies which are:
 (a) the subject of insolvency proceedings or subject to preventive restructuring frameworks;
 (b) the subject of liquidation proceedings other than those referred to in point (a) of paragraph 3, or
 [(c) the subject of crisis prevention measures as defined in point (101) of Article 2(1) of Directive 2014/59/EU or in point (48) of Article 2 of Regulation (EU) 2021/23.]]

NOTES

Chapter –I (Arts 86a–86t) inserted by European Parliament and Council Directive 2019/2121/EU, Art 1(5), as form 1 January 2020. Note that the 2019 Directive has a transposition date of 31 January 2023.

Para 3: point (b) substituted by European Parliament and Council Regulation 2021/23/EU, Art 92(2)(a), as from 12 August 2022.

Para 4: point (c) substituted by European Parliament and Council Regulation 2021/23/EU, Art 92(2)(b), as from 12 August 2022.

[11.482]

[Article 86b Definitions

For the purposes of this Chapter:

(1) "company" means a limited liability company of a type listed in Annex II that carries out a cross-border conversion;

(2) "cross-border conversion" means an operation whereby a company, without being dissolved or wound up or going into liquidation, converts the legal form under which it is registered in a departure Member State into a legal form of the destination Member State, as listed in Annex II, and transfers at least its registered office to the destination Member State, while retaining its legal personality;

(3) "departure Member State" means a Member State in which a company is registered prior to a cross-border conversion;

(4) "destination Member State" means a Member State in which a converted company is registered as a result of a cross-border conversion;

(5) "converted company" means a company formed in a destination Member State as a result of a cross-border conversion.]

NOTES

Inserted as noted to Art 86a at **[11.481]**.

[11.483]

[Article 86c Procedures and formalities

In compliance with Union law, the law of the departure Member State shall govern those parts of the procedures and formalities to be complied with in connection with the cross-border conversion in order to obtain the pre-conversion certificate, and the law of the destination Member State shall govern those parts of the procedures and formalities to be complied with following receipt of the pre-conversion certificate.]

NOTES

Inserted as noted to Art 86a at **[11.481]**.

[11.484]

[Article 86d Draft terms of cross-border conversions

The administrative or management body of the company shall draw up the draft terms of a cross-border conversion. The draft terms of a cross-border conversion shall include at least the following particulars:

(a) the legal form and name of the company in the departure Member State and the location of its registered office in that Member State;
(b) the legal form and name proposed for the converted company in the destination Member State and the proposed location of its registered office in that Member State;
(c) the instrument of constitution of the company in the destination Member State, where applicable, and the statutes if they are contained in a separate instrument;
(d) the proposed indicative timetable for the cross-border conversion;
(e) the rights conferred by the converted company on members enjoying special rights or on holders of securities other than shares representing the company capital, or the measures proposed concerning them;
(f) any safeguards offered to creditors, such as guarantees or pledges;
(g) any special advantages granted to members of the administrative, management, supervisory or controlling bodies of the company;
(h) whether any incentives or subsidies were received by the company in the departure Member State in the preceding five years;
(i) details of the offer of cash compensation for members in accordance with Article 86i;
(j) the likely repercussions of the cross-border conversion on employment;
(k) where appropriate, information on the procedures by which arrangements for the involvement of employees in the definition of their rights to participation in the converted company are determined pursuant to Article 86l.]

NOTES

Inserted as noted to Art 86a at **[11.481]**.

[11.485]

[Article 86e Report of the administrative or management body for members and employees

1. The administrative or management body of the company shall draw up a report for members and employees, explaining and justifying the legal and economic aspects of the cross-border conversion, as well as explaining the implications of the cross-border conversion for employees.

It shall, in particular, explain the implications of the cross-border conversion for the future business of the company.

2. The report shall also include a section for members and a section for employees.

The company may decide either to draw up one report containing those two sections or to draw up separate reports for members and employees, respectively, containing the relevant section.

3. The section of the report for members shall, in particular, explain the following:

(a) the cash compensation and the method used to determine the cash compensation;
(b) the implications of the cross-border conversion for members;
(c) the rights and remedies available to members in accordance with Article 86i.

4. The section of the report for members shall not be required where all the members of the company have agreed to waive that requirement. Member States may exclude single-member companies from the provisions of this Article.

5. The section of the report for employees shall, in particular, explain the following:

(a) the implications of the cross-border conversion for employment relationships, as well as, where applicable, any measures for safeguarding those relationships;
(b) any material changes to the applicable conditions of employment or to the location of the company's places of business;
(c) how the factors set out in points (a) and (b) affect any subsidiaries of the company.

6. The report or reports shall be made available in any case electronically, together with the draft terms of the cross-border conversion, if available, to the members and to the representatives of the employees or, where there are no such representatives, to the employees themselves, not less than six weeks before the date of the general meeting referred to in Article 86h.

7. Where the administrative or management body of the company receives an opinion on the information referred to in paragraphs 1 and 5 in good time from the representatives of the employees or, where there are no such representatives, from the employees themselves, as provided for under national law, the members shall be informed thereof and that opinion shall be appended to the report.

8. The section of the report for employees shall not be required where a company and its subsidiaries, if any, have no employees other than those who form part of the administrative or management body.

9. Where the section of the report for members referred to in paragraph 3 is waived in accordance with paragraph 4 and the section for employees referred to in paragraph 5 is not required under paragraph 8, the report shall not be required.

10. Paragraphs 1 to 9 of this Article shall be without prejudice to the applicable information and consultation rights and procedures provided for at national level following the transposition of Directives 2002/14/EC and 2009/38/EC.]

NOTES

Inserted as noted to Art 86a at **[11.481]**.

[11.486]

[Article 86f Independent expert report

1. Member States shall ensure that an independent expert examines the draft terms of cross-border conversion and draws up a report for members. That report shall be made available to the members not less than one month before the date of the general meeting referred to in Article 86h. Depending on the law of the Member State, the expert may be a natural or legal person.

2. The report referred to in paragraph 1 shall in any case include the expert's opinion as to whether the cash compensation is adequate. When assessing the cash compensation, the expert shall consider any market price of the shares in the company prior to the announcement of the conversion proposal or the value of the company excluding the effect of the proposed conversion, as determined in accordance with generally accepted valuation methods. The report shall at least:

(a) indicate the method or methods used to determine the cash compensation proposed;

(b) state whether the method or methods used are adequate for the assessment of the cash compensation, indicate the value arrived at using such methods and give an opinion on the relative importance attributed to those methods in arriving at the value decided on; and

(c) describe any special valuation difficulties which have arisen.

The expert shall be entitled to obtain from the company all information necessary for the discharge of the duties of the expert.

3. Neither an examination of the draft terms of cross-border conversion by an independent expert nor an independent expert report shall be required if all the members of the company have so agreed.

Member States may exclude single-member companies from the application of this Article.]

NOTES

Inserted as noted to Art 86a at **[11.481]**.

[11.487]

[Article 86g Disclosure

1. Member States shall ensure that the following documents are disclosed by the company and made publicly available in the register of the departure Member State, at least one month before the date of the general meeting referred to in Article 86h:

(a) the draft terms of the cross-border conversion; and

(b) a notice informing the members, creditors and representatives of the employees of the company, or, where there are no such representatives, the employees themselves, that they may submit to the company, at the latest five working days before the date of the general meeting, comments concerning the draft terms of the cross-border conversion.

Member States may require that the independent expert report be disclosed and made publicly available in the register.

Member States shall ensure that the company is able to exclude confidential information from the disclosure of the independent expert report.

The documents disclosed in accordance with this paragraph shall also be accessible through the system of interconnection of registers.

2. Member States may exempt a company from the disclosure requirement referred to in paragraph 1 of this Article where, for a continuous period beginning at least one month before the date fixed for the general meeting referred to in Article 86h and ending not earlier than the conclusion of that meeting, that company makes the documents referred to in paragraph 1 of this Article available on its website free of charge to the public.

However, Member States shall not subject that exemption to any requirements or constraints other than those which are necessary to ensure the security of the website and the authenticity of the documents, and which are proportionate to achieving those objectives.

3. Where the company makes the draft terms of the cross-border conversion available in accordance with paragraph 2 of this Article, it shall submit to the register of the departure Member State, at least one month before the date of the general meeting referred to in Article 86h, the following information:

(a) the legal form and name of the company and the location of its registered office in the departure Member State and the legal form and name proposed for the converted company in the destination Member State and the proposed location of its registered office in that Member State;

(b) the register in which the documents referred to in Article 14 are filed in respect of the company and its registration number in that register;

(c) an indication of the arrangements made for the exercise of the rights of creditors, employees and members; and

(d) details of the website from which the draft terms of the cross-border conversion, the notice referred to in paragraph 1, the independent expert report and complete information on the arrangements referred to in point (c) of this paragraph may be obtained online and free of charge.

The register of the departure Member State shall make publicly available the information referred to in points (a) to (d) of the first subparagraph.

4. Member States shall ensure that the requirements referred to in paragraphs 1 and 3 can be fulfilled fully online without the necessity for the applicants to appear in person before any competent authority in the departure Member State, in accordance with the relevant provisions of Chapter III of Title I.

5. Member States may require, in addition to the disclosure referred to in paragraphs 1, 2 and 3 of this Article, that the draft terms of the cross-border conversion, or the information referred to in paragraph 3 of this Article, be published in their national gazette or through a central electronic platform in accordance with Article 16(3). In that instance, Member States shall ensure that the register transmits the relevant information to the national gazette or to a central electronic platform.

6. Member States shall ensure that the documentation referred to in paragraph 1 or the information referred to in paragraph 3 is accessible to the public free of charge through the system of interconnection of registers.

Member States shall further ensure that any fees charged to the company by the registers for the disclosure referred to in paragraphs 1 and 3 and, where applicable, for the publication referred to in paragraph 5 do not exceed the recovery of the cost of providing such services.]

NOTES

Inserted as noted to Art 86a at **[11.481]**.

[11.488]

[Article 86h Approval by the general meeting

1. After taking note of the reports referred to in Articles 86e and 86f, where applicable, employees' opinions submitted in accordance with Article 86e and comments submitted in accordance with Article 86g, the general meeting of the company shall decide, by means of a resolution, whether to approve the draft terms of the cross- border conversion and whether to adapt the instrument of constitution, and the statutes if they are contained in a separate instrument.

2. The general meeting of the company may reserve the right to make implementation of the cross-border conversion conditional on express ratification by it of the arrangements referred to in Article 86l.

3. Member States shall ensure that the approval of the draft terms of the cross-border conversion, and of any amendment to those draft terms, requires a majority of not less than two thirds but not more than 90% of the votes attached either to the shares or to the subscribed capital represented at the general meeting. In any event, the voting threshold shall not be higher than that provided for in national law for the approval of cross-border mergers.

4. Where a clause in the draft terms of the cross-border conversion or any amendment to the instrument of constitution of the converting company leads to an increase of the economic obligations of a member towards the company or third parties, Member States may require, in such specific circumstances, that such clause or the amendment to the instrument of constitution be approved by the member concerned, provided that such member is unable to exercise the rights laid down in Article 86i.

5. Member States shall ensure that the approval of the cross-border conversion by the general meeting cannot be challenged solely on the following grounds:

(a) the cash compensation referred to in point (i) of Article 86d has been inadequately set; or

(b) the information given with regard to the cash compensation referred to in point (a) did not comply with the legal requirements.]

NOTES

Inserted as noted to Art 86a at **[11.481]**.

[11.489]

[Article 86i Protection of members

1. Member States shall ensure that at least the members of a company who voted against the approval of the draft terms of the cross-border conversion have the right to dispose of their shares for adequate cash compensation, under the conditions laid down in paragraphs 2 to 5.

Member States may also provide for other members of the company to have the right referred to in the first subparagraph.

Member States may require that express opposition to the draft terms of the cross-border conversion, the intention of members to exercise their right to dispose of their shares, or both, be appropriately documented, at the latest at the general meeting referred to in Article 86h. Member States may allow the recording of opposition to the draft terms of the cross-border conversion to be considered proper documentation of a negative vote.

2. Member States shall establish the period within which the members referred to in paragraph 1 have to declare to the company their decision to exercise the right to dispose of their shares. That period shall not exceed one month after the general meeting referred to in Article 86h. Member States shall ensure that the company provides an electronic address for receiving that declaration electronically.

3. Member States shall further establish the period within which the cash compensation specified in the draft terms of the cross-border conversion is to be paid. That period shall not end later than two months after the cross- border conversion takes effect in accordance with Article 86q.

4. Member States shall ensure that any members who have declared their decision to exercise the right to dispose of their shares, but who consider that the cash compensation offered by the company has not been adequately set, are entitled to claim additional cash compensation before the competent authority or body mandated under national law. Member States shall establish a time limit for the claim for additional cash compensation.

Member States may provide that the final decision to provide additional cash compensation is valid for all members who have declared their decision to exercise the right to dispose of their shares in accordance with paragraph 2.

5. Member States shall ensure that the law of the departure Member State governs the rights referred to in paragraphs 1 to 4 and that the exclusive competence to resolve any disputes relating to those rights lies within the jurisdiction of that departure Member State.]

NOTES

Inserted as noted to Art 86a at **[11.481]**.

[11.490]

[Article 86j Protection of creditors

1. Member States shall provide for an adequate system of protection of the interests of creditors whose claims antedate the disclosure of the draft terms of the cross-border conversion and have not fallen due at the time of such disclosure.

Member States shall ensure that creditors who are dissatisfied with the safeguards offered in the draft terms of the cross-border conversion, as provided for in point (f) of Article 86d, may apply, within three months of the disclosure of the draft terms of the cross-border conversion referred to in Article 86g, to the appropriate administrative or judicial authority for adequate safeguards, provided that such creditors can credibly demonstrate that, due to the cross-border conversion, the satisfaction of their claims is at stake and that they have not obtained adequate safeguards from the company.

Member States shall ensure that the safeguards are conditional on the cross-border conversion taking effect in accordance with Article 86q.

2. Member States may require that the administrative or management body of the company provide a declaration that accurately reflects its current financial status at a date no earlier than one month before the disclosure of that declaration. The declaration shall state that, on the basis of the information available to the administrative or

management body of the company at the date of that declaration, and after having made reasonable enquiries, that administrative or management body is unaware of any reason why the company would, after the conversion takes effect, be unable to meet its liabilities when those liabilities fall due. The declaration shall be disclosed together with the draft terms of the cross-border conversion in accordance with Article 86g.

3. Paragraphs 1 and 2 shall be without prejudice to the application of the law of the departure Member State concerning the satisfaction or securing of pecuniary or non-pecuniary obligations due to public bodies.

4. Member States shall ensure that creditors whose claims antedate the disclosure of the draft terms of the cross-border conversion are able to institute proceedings against the company also in the departure Member State within two years of the date the conversion has taken effect, without prejudice to the jurisdiction rules arising from Union or national law or from a contractual agreement. The option of instituting such proceedings shall be in addition to other rules on the choice of jurisdiction that are applicable pursuant to Union law.]

NOTES

Inserted as noted to Art 86a at **[11.481]**.

[11.491]

[Article 86k Employee information and consultation

1. Member States shall ensure that employees' rights to information and consultation are respected in relation to the cross-border conversion and are exercised in accordance with the legal framework provided for in Directive 2002/14/EC and, where applicable for Community-scale undertakings or Community-scale groups of undertakings, in accordance with Directive 2009/38/EC. Member States may decide that employees' rights to information and consultation apply with respect to the employees of companies other than those referred to in Article 3(1) of Directive 2002/14/EC.

2. Notwithstanding Article 86e(7) and point (b) of Article 86g(1), Member States shall ensure that employees' rights to information and consultation are respected, at least before the draft terms of the cross-border conversion or the report referred to in Article 86e are decided upon, whichever is earlier, in such a way that a reasoned response is given to the employees before the general meeting referred to in Article 86h.

3. Without prejudice to any provisions or practices in force more favourable to employees, Member States shall determine the practical arrangements for exercising the right to information and consultation in accordance with Article 4 of Directive 2002/14/EC.]

NOTES

Inserted as noted to Art 86a at **[11.481]**.

[11.492]

[Article 86l Employee participation

1. Without prejudice to paragraph 2, the converted company shall be subject to the rules in force concerning employee participation, if any, in the destination Member State.

2. However, the rules in force concerning employee participation, if any, in the destination Member State shall not apply where the company has, in the six months prior to the disclosure of the draft terms of the cross-border conversion, an average number of employees equivalent to four fifths of the applicable threshold, as laid down in the law of the departure Member State, for triggering the participation of employees within the meaning of point (k) of Article 2 of Directive 2001/86/EC, or where the law of the destination Member State does not:

(a) provide for at least the same level of employee participation as operated in the company prior to the cross-border conversion, measured by reference to the proportion of employee representatives among the members of the administrative or supervisory body or their committees or of the management group which covers the profit units of the company, subject to employee representation; or

(b) provide for employees of establishments of the converted company that are situated in other Member States the same entitlement to exercise participation rights as is enjoyed by those employees employed in the destination Member State.

3. In the cases referred to in paragraph 2 of this Article, the participation of employees in the converted company and their involvement in the definition of such rights shall be regulated by the Member States, mutatis mutandis and subject to paragraphs 4 to 7 of this Article, in accordance with the principles and procedures laid down in Article 12(2) and (4) of Regulation (EC) No 2157/2001 and the following provisions of Directive 2001/86/EC:

(a) Article 3(1), points (a)(i) and (b) of Article 3(2), Article 3(3), the first two sentences of Article 3(4), and Article 3(5) and (7);
(b) Article 4(1), points (a), (g) and (h) of Article 4(2), and Article 4(3) and (4);
(c) Article 5;
(d) Article 6;
(e) Article 7(1), with the exception of the second indent of point (b);
(f) Articles 8, 10, 11 and 12; and
(g) point (a) of Part 3 of the Annex.

4. When regulating the principles and procedures referred to in paragraph 3, Member States:

(a) shall confer on the special negotiating body the right to decide, by a majority of two thirds of its members representing at least two thirds of the employees, not to open negotiations or to terminate negotiations already opened and to rely on the rules on participation in force in the destination Member State;

(b) may, in the case where, following prior negotiations, standard rules for participation apply and notwithstanding such rules, decide to limit the proportion of employee representatives in the administrative body of the converted company. However, if, in the company, employee representatives constituted at least one third of the administrative or supervisory body, the limitation may never result in a lower proportion of employee representatives in the administrative body than one third;

(c) shall ensure that the rules on employee participation that applied prior to the cross-border conversion continue to apply until the date of application of any subsequently agreed rules or, in the absence of agreed rules, until the application of standard rules in accordance with point (a) of Part 3 of the Annex to Directive 2001/86/EC.

Part 11 EU & Retained EU Legislation

5. The extension of participation rights to employees of the converted company employed in other Member States, as referred to in point (b) of paragraph 2, shall not entail any obligation for Member States which choose to do so to take those employees into account when calculating the size of workforce thresholds giving rise to participation rights under national law.
6. Where the converted company is to be governed by an employee participation system, in accordance with the rules referred to in paragraph 2, it shall be obliged to take a legal form allowing for the exercise of participation rights.
7. Where the converted company is operating under an employee participation system, it shall be obliged to take measures to ensure that employees' participation rights are protected in the event of any subsequent conversion, merger or division, be it cross-border or domestic, for a period of four years after the cross-border conversion has taken effect, by applying mutatis mutandis the rules laid down in paragraphs 1 to 6.
8. A company shall communicate to its employees or their representatives the outcome of the negotiations concerning employee participation without undue delay.]

NOTES

Inserted as noted to Art 86a at **[11.481]**.

[11.493]

[Article 86m Pre-conversion certificate

1. Member States shall designate the court, notary or other authority or authorities competent to scrutinise the legality of cross-border conversions as regards those parts of the procedure which are governed by the law of the departure Member State and to issue a pre-conversion certificate attesting to compliance with all relevant conditions and to the proper completion of all procedures and formalities in the departure Member State ("the competent authority").
Such completion of procedures and formalities may comprise the satisfaction or securing of pecuniary or non-pecuniary obligations due to public bodies or compliance with specific sectoral requirements, including securing obligations arising from ongoing proceedings.
2. Member States shall ensure that the application to obtain a pre-conversion certificate by the company is accompanied by the following:
 (a) the draft terms of the cross-border conversion;
 (b) the report and the appended opinion, if any, referred to in Article 86e, as well as the report referred to in Article 86f, where they are available;
 (c) any comments submitted in accordance with Article 86g(1); and
 (d) information on the approval by the general meeting referred to in Article 86h.
3. Member States may require that the application to obtain a pre-conversion certificate by the company is accompanied by additional information, such as, in particular:
 (a) the number of employees at the time of the drawing up of the draft terms of the cross-border conversion;
 (b) the existence of subsidiaries and their respective geographical location;
 (c) information regarding the satisfaction of obligations due to public bodies by the company.
For the purposes of this paragraph, competent authorities may request such information, if not provided by the company, from other relevant authorities.
4. Member States shall ensure that the application referred to in paragraphs 2 and 3, including the submission of any information and documents, may be completed fully online without the necessity for the applicants to appear in person before the competent authority, in accordance with the relevant provisions of Chapter III of Title I.
5. In respect of compliance with the rules concerning employee participation as laid down in Article 86l, the competent authority of the departure Member State shall verify that the draft terms of the cross-border conversion include information on the procedures by which the relevant arrangements are determined and on the possible options for such arrangements.
6. As part of the scrutiny referred to in paragraph 1, the competent authority shall examine the following:
 (a) all documents and information submitted to the competent authority in accordance with paragraphs 2 and 3;
 (b) an indication by the company that the procedure referred to in Article 86l(3) and (4) has started, where relevant.
7. Member States shall ensure that the scrutiny referred to in paragraph 1 is carried out within three months of the date of receipt of the documents and information concerning the approval of the cross-border conversion by the general meeting of the company. That scrutiny shall have one of the following outcomes:
 (a) where it is determined that the cross-border conversion complies with all the relevant conditions and that all necessary procedures and formalities have been completed, the competent authority shall issue the pre-conversion certificate;
 (b) where it is determined that the cross-border conversion does not comply with all the relevant conditions or that not all necessary procedures and formalities have been completed, the competent authority shall not issue the pre-conversion certificate and shall inform the company of the reasons for its decision; in that case, the competent authority may give the company the opportunity to fulfil the relevant conditions or to complete the procedures and formalities within an appropriate period of time.
8. Member States shall ensure that the competent authority does not issue the pre-conversion certificate where it is determined in compliance with national law that a cross-border conversion is set up for abusive or fraudulent purposes leading to or aimed at the evasion or circumvention of Union or national law, or for criminal purposes.
9. Where the competent authority, during the scrutiny referred to in paragraph 1, has serious doubts indicating that the cross-border conversion is set up for abusive or fraudulent purposes leading to or aimed at the evasion or circumvention of Union or national law, or for criminal purposes, it shall take into consideration relevant facts and circumstances, such as, where relevant and not considered in isolation, indicative factors of which the competent authority has become aware, in the course of the scrutiny referred to in paragraph 1, including through consultation of relevant authorities. The assessment for the purposes of this paragraph shall be conducted on a case-by-case basis, through a procedure governed by national law.
10. Where it is necessary for the purposes of the assessment under paragraphs 8 and 9 to take into account additional information or to perform additional investigative activities, the period of three months provided for in paragraph 7 may be extended by a maximum of three months.

11. Where, due to the complexity of the cross-border procedure, it is not possible to carry out the assessment within the deadlines provided for in paragraphs 7 and 10, Member States shall ensure that the applicant is notified of the reasons for any delay before the expiry of those deadlines.

12. Member States shall ensure that the competent authority may consult other relevant authorities with competence in the different fields concerned by the cross-border conversion, including those of the destination Member State, and obtain from those authorities and from the company information and documents necessary to scrutinise the legality of the cross-border conversion, within the procedural framework laid down in national law. For the purposes of the assessment, the competent authority may have recourse to an independent expert.]

NOTES

Inserted as noted to Art 86a at **[11.481]**.

[11.494]

[Article 86n Transmission of the pre-conversion certificate

1. Member States shall ensure that the pre-conversion certificate is shared with the authorities referred to in Article 86o(1) through the system of interconnection of registers.

Member States shall also ensure that the pre-conversion certificate is available through the system of interconnection of registers.

2. Access to the pre-conversion certificate shall be free of charge for the authorities referred to in Article 86o(1) and for the registers.]

NOTES

Inserted as noted to Art 86a at **[11.481]**.

[11.495]

[Article 86o Scrutiny of the legality of the cross-border conversion by the destination Member State

1. Member States shall designate the court, notary or other authority competent to scrutinise the legality of the cross-border conversion as regards that part of the procedure which is governed by the law of the destination Member State and to approve the cross-border conversion.

That authority shall in particular ensure that the converted company complies with provisions of national law on the incorporation and registration of companies and, where appropriate, that arrangements for employee participation have been determined in accordance with Article 86l.

2. For the purposes of paragraph 1 of this Article, the company shall submit to the authority referred to in paragraph 1 of this Article the draft terms of the cross-border conversion approved by the general meeting referred to in Article 86h.

3. Each Member State shall ensure that any application for the purposes of paragraph 1, by the company, including the submission of any information and documents, may be completed fully online without the necessity for the applicants to appear in person before the authority referred to in paragraph 1, in accordance with the relevant provisions of Chapter III of Title I.

4. The authority referred to in paragraph 1 shall approve the cross-border conversion as soon as it has determined that all relevant conditions have been properly fulfilled and formalities properly completed in the destination Member State.

5. The pre-conversion certificate shall be accepted by the authority referred to in paragraph 1 as conclusively attesting to the proper completion of the applicable pre-conversion procedures and formalities in the departure Member State, without which the cross-border conversion cannot be approved.]

NOTES

Inserted as noted to Art 86a at **[11.481]**.

[11.496]

[Article 86p Registration

1. The laws of the departure Member State and of the destination Member State shall determine, with regard to their respective territories, the arrangements, in accordance with Article 16, for disclosing the completion of the cross-border conversion in their registers.

2. Member States shall ensure that at least the following information is entered in their registers:

(a) in the register of the destination Member State, that the registration of the converted company is the result of a cross-border conversion;

(b) in the register of the destination Member State, the date of registration of the converted company;

(c) in the register of the departure Member State, that the striking off or removal of the company from the register is the result of a cross-border conversion;

(d) in the register of the departure Member State, the date of striking off or removal of the company from the register;

(e) in the registers of the departure Member State and of the destination Member State, respectively, the registration number, name and legal form of the company and the registration number, name and legal form of the converted company.

The registers shall make the information referred to in the first subparagraph publicly available and accessible through the system of interconnection of registers.

3. Member States shall ensure that the register in the destination Member State notifies the register in the departure Member State, through the system of interconnection of registers, that the cross-border conversion has taken effect. Member States shall also ensure that the registration of the company is struck off or removed from the register immediately upon receipt of that notification.]

NOTES

Inserted as noted to Art 86a at **[11.481]**.

[11.497]

[Article 86q Date on which the cross-border conversion takes effect

The law of the destination Member State shall determine the date on which the cross-border conversion takes effect. That date shall be after the scrutiny referred to in Articles 86m and 86o has been carried out.]

NOTES

Inserted as noted to Art 86a at **[11.481]**.

[11.498]

[Article 86r Consequences of a cross-border conversion

A cross-border conversion shall, from the date referred to in Article 86q, have the following consequences:

(a) all the assets and liabilities of the company, including all contracts, credits, rights and obligations, shall be those of the converted company;

(b) the members of the company shall continue to be members of the converted company, unless they have disposed of their shares as referred to in Article 86i(1);

(c) the rights and obligations of the company arising from contracts of employment or from employment relationships and existing at the date on which the cross-border conversion takes effect shall be those of the converted company.]

NOTES

Inserted as noted to Art 86a at **[11.481]**.

[11.499]

[Article 86s Independent experts

1. Member States shall lay down rules governing at least the civil liability of the independent expert responsible for drawing up the report referred to in Article 86f.

2. Member States shall have rules in place to ensure that:

(a) the expert, or the legal person on whose behalf the expert is operating, is independent from and has no conflict of interest with the company applying for the pre-conversion certificate; and

(b) the expert's opinion is impartial and objective, and is given with a view to providing assistance to the competent authority in accordance with the independence and impartiality requirements under the law and professional standards to which the expert is subject.]

NOTES

Inserted as noted to Art 86a at **[11.481]**.

[11.500]

[Article 86t Validity

A cross-border conversion which has taken effect in compliance with the procedures transposing this Directive may not be declared null and void.

The first paragraph does not affect Member States' powers, inter alia, in relation to criminal law, the prevention and combatting of terrorist financing, social law, taxation and law enforcement, to impose measures and penalties, under national law, after the date on which the cross-border conversion took effect.]

NOTES

Inserted as noted to Art 86a at **[11.481]**.

CHAPTER I

SECTION 1 GENERAL PROVISIONS ON MERGERS

[11.501]

Article 87 General provisions

1. The coordination measures laid down by this Chapter shall apply to the laws, regulations and administrative provisions of the Member States relating to the types of company listed in Annex I.

2. Member States need not apply this Chapter to cooperatives incorporated as one of the types of company listed in Annex I. In so far as the laws of the Member States make use of this option, they shall require such companies to include the word 'cooperative' in all the documents referred to in Article 26.

3. Member States need not apply this Chapter In cases where the company or companies which are being acquired or will cease to exist are the subject of bankruptcy proceedings, proceedings relating to the winding-up of insolvent companies, judicial arrangements, compositions and analogous proceedings.

[4. Member States shall ensure that this Chapter does not apply to companies which are the subject of the application of resolution tools, powers and mechanisms provided for in Title IV of Directive 2014/59/EU or in Title V of Regulation (EU) 2021/23.]

NOTES

Para 4: substituted by European Parliament and Council Regulation 2021/23/EU, Art 92(3), as from 12 August 2022.

[11.502]

Article 88 Rules governing mergers by acquisition and mergers by formation of a new company

Member States shall, as regards companies governed by their national laws, make provision for rules governing mergers by the acquisition of one or more companies by another company and merger by the formation of a new company.

[11.503]

Article 89 Definition of a 'merger by acquisition'

1. For the purposes of this Chapter, 'merger by acquisition' shall mean the operation whereby one or more companies are wound up without going into liquidation and transfer to another all their assets and liabilities in exchange for the issue to the shareholders of the company or companies being acquired of shares in the acquiring company and a cash payment, if any, not exceeding 10% of the nominal value of the shares so issued or, where they have no nominal value, of their accounting par value.

2. A Member State's laws may provide that merger by acquisition may also be effected where one or more of the companies being acquired is in liquidation, provided that this option is restricted to companies which have not yet begun to distribute their assets to their shareholders.

[11.504]

Article 90 Definition of a 'merger by the formation of a new company'

1. For the purposes of this Chapter, 'merger by the formation of a new company' shall mean the operation whereby several companies are wound up without going into liquidation and transfer to a company that they set up all their assets and liabilities in exchange for the issue to their shareholders of shares in the new company and a cash payment, if any, not exceeding 10% of the nominal value of the shares so issued or, where they have no nominal value, of their accounting par value.

2. A Member State's laws may provide that merger by the formation of a new company may also be effected where one or more of the companies which are ceasing to exist is in liquidation, provided that this option is restricted to companies which have not yet begun to distribute their assets to their shareholders.

SECTION 2 MERGER BY ACQUISITION

[11.505]

Article 91 Draft terms of merger

1. The administrative or management bodies of the merging companies shall draw up draft terms of merger in writing.

2. Draft terms of merger shall specify at least:

(a) the type, name and registered office of each of the merging companies;
(b) the share exchange ratio and the amount of any cash payment;
(c) the terms relating to the allotment of shares in the acquiring company;
(d) the date from which the holding of such shares entitles the holders to participate in profits and any special conditions affecting that entitlement;
(e) the date from which the transactions of the company being acquired shall be treated for accounting purposes as being those of the acquiring company;
(f) the rights conferred by the acquiring company on the holders of shares to which special rights are attached and the holders of securities other than shares, or the measures proposed concerning them;
(g) any special advantage granted to the experts referred to in Article 96(1) and members of the merging companies' administrative, management, supervisory or controlling bodies.

[11.506]

Article 92 Publication of the draft terms of merger

Draft terms of merger shall be published in the manner prescribed by the laws of the Member States in accordance with Article 16, for each of the merging companies, at least one month before the date fixed for the general meeting which is to decide thereon.

Any of the merging companies shall be exempt from the publication requirement laid down in Article 16 if, for a continuous period beginning at least one month before the date fixed for the general meeting which is to decide on the draft terms of merger and ending not earlier than the conclusion of that meeting, it makes the draft terms of such merger available on its website free of charge for the public. Member States shall not subject that exemption to any requirements or constraints other than those which are necessary in order to ensure the security of the website and the authenticity of the documents, and may impose such requirements or constraints only to the extent that they are proportionate in order to achieve those objectives.

By way of derogation from the second paragraph of this Article, Member States may require that publication be effected via the central electronic platform referred to in Article 16(5). Member States may alternatively require that such publication be made on any other website designated by them for that purpose. Where Member States avail themselves of one of those possibilities, they shall ensure that companies are not charged a specific fee for such publication.

Where a website other than the central electronic platform is used, a reference giving access to that website shall be published on the central electronic platform at least one month before the date fixed for the general meeting. That reference shall include the date of publication of the draft terms of merger on the website and shall be accessible to the public free of charge. Companies shall not be charged a specific fee for such publication.

The prohibition precluding the charging of companies of a specific fee for publication, laid down in the third and fourth paragraphs, shall not affect the ability of Member States to pass on to companies the costs in respect of the central electronic platform.

Member States may require companies to maintain the information for a specific period after the general meeting on their website or, where applicable, on the central electronic platform or the other website designated by the Member State concerned. Member States may determine the consequences of temporary disruption of access to the website or to the central electronic platform, caused by technical or other factors.

[11.507]

Article 93 Approval by the general meeting of each of the merging companies

1. A merger shall require at least the approval of the general meeting of each of the merging companies. The laws of the Member States shall provide that this approval decision shall require a majority of not less than two thirds of the votes attached either to the shares or to the subscribed capital represented.

The laws of a Member State may, however, provide that a simple majority of the votes specified in the first subparagraph shall be sufficient when at least half of the subscribed capital is represented. Moreover, where appropriate, the rules governing alterations to the memorandum and articles of association shall apply.
2. Where there is more than one class of shares, the decision concerning a merger shall be subject to a separate vote by at least each class of shareholders whose rights are affected by the transaction.
3. The decision shall cover both the approval of the draft terms of merger and any alterations to the memorandum and articles of association necessitated by the merger.

[11.508]
Article 94 Derogation from the requirement of approval by the general meeting of the acquiring company
The laws of a Member State need not require approval of the merger by the general meeting of the acquiring company where the following conditions are fulfilled:
(a) the publication provided for in Article 92 is effected, for the acquiring company, at least one month before the date fixed for the general meeting of the company or companies being acquired which is to decide on the draft terms of merger;
(b) at least one month before the date specified in point (a), all shareholders of the acquiring company are entitled to inspect the documents specified in Article 97(1) at the registered office of the acquiring company;
(c) one or more shareholders of the acquiring company holding a minimum percentage of the subscribed capital is entitled to require that a general meeting of the acquiring company be called to decide whether to approve the merger; this minimum percentage may not be fixed at more than 5%. Member States may, however, provide for the exclusion of non-voting shares from this calculation.

For the purposes of point (b) of the first paragraph, Article 97(2), (3) and (4) shall apply.

[11.509]
Article 95 Detailed written report and information on a merger
1. The administrative or management bodies of each of the merging companies shall draw up a detailed written report explaining the draft terms of merger and setting out the legal and economic grounds for them, in particular the share exchange ratio.
That report shall also describe any special valuation difficulties which have arisen.
2. The administrative or management bodies of each of the companies involved shall inform the general meeting of their company, and the administrative or management bodies of the other companies involved, so that the latter may inform their respective general meetings of any material change in the assets and liabilities between the date of preparation of the draft terms of merger and the date of the general meetings which are to decide on the draft terms of merger.
3. Member States may provide that the report referred to in paragraph 1 and/or the information referred to in paragraph 2 shall not be required if all the shareholders and the holders of other securities conferring the right to vote of each of the companies involved in the merger have so agreed.

[11.510]
Article 96 Examination of the draft terms of merger by experts
1. One or more experts, acting on behalf of each of the merging companies but independent of them, appointed or approved by a judicial or administrative authority, shall examine the draft terms of merger and draw up a written report to the shareholders. However, the laws of the Member States may provide for the appointment of one or more independent experts for all the merging companies, if such appointment is made by a judicial or administrative authority at the joint request of those companies. Such experts may, depending on the laws of each Member State, be natural or legal persons or companies or firms.
2. In the report referred to in paragraph 1, the experts shall in any case state whether in their opinion the share exchange ratio is fair and reasonable. Their statement shall at least:
(a) indicate the method or methods used to arrive at the share exchange ratio proposed;
(b) state whether such method or methods are adequate in the case in question, indicate the values arrived at using each such methods and give an opinion on the relative importance attributed to such methods in arriving at the value decided on.

The report shall also describe any special valuation difficulties which have arisen.
3. Each expert shall be entitled to obtain from the merging companies all relevant information and documents and to carry out all necessary investigations.
4. Neither an examination of the draft terms of merger nor an expert report shall be required if all the shareholders and the holders of other securities conferring the right to vote of each of the companies involved in the merger have so agreed.

[11.511]
Article 97 Availability of documents for inspection by shareholders
1. All shareholders shall be entitled to inspect at least the following documents at the registered office at least one month before the date fixed for the general meeting which is to decide on the draft terms of merger:
(a) the draft terms of merger;
(b) the annual accounts and annual reports of the merging companies for the preceding three financial years;
(c) where applicable, an accounting statement drawn up on a date which shall not be earlier than the first day of the third month preceding the date of the draft terms of merger, if the latest annual accounts relate to a financial year which ended more than six months before that date;
(d) where applicable, the reports of the administrative or management bodies of the merging companies provided for in Article 95;
(e) where applicable, the report referred to in Article 96(1).

For the purposes of point (c) of the first subparagraph, an accounting statement shall not be required if the company publishes a half-yearly financial report in accordance with Article 5 of Directive 2004/109/EC and makes it available to shareholders in accordance with this paragraph. Furthermore, Member States may provide that an accounting statement shall not be required if all the shareholders and the holders of other securities conferring the right to vote of each of the companies involved in the merger have so agreed.

2. The accounting statement provided for in point (c) of the first subparagraph of paragraph 1 shall be drawn up using the same methods and the same layout as the last annual balance sheet.

However, the laws of a Member State may provide that:

(a) it is not necessary to take a fresh physical inventory;

(b) the valuations shown in the last balance sheet are to be altered only to reflect entries in the books of account; the following shall nevertheless be taken into account:

— interim depreciation and provisions,

— material changes in actual value not shown in the books.

3. Every shareholder shall be entitled to obtain, on request and free of charge, full or, if so desired, partial copies of the documents referred to in paragraph 1.

Where a shareholder has consented to the use by the company of electronic means for conveying information, such copies may be provided by electronic mail.

4. A company shall be exempt from the requirement to make the documents referred to in paragraph 1 available at its registered office if, for a continuous period beginning at least one month before the date fixed for the general meeting which is to decide on the draft terms of merger and ending not earlier than the conclusion of that meeting, it makes them available on its website. Member States shall not subject that exemption to any requirements or constraints other than those which are necessary in order to ensure the security of the website and the authenticity of the documents and may impose such requirements or constraints only to the extent that they are proportionate in order to achieve those objectives.

Paragraph 3 shall not apply if the website gives shareholders the possibility, throughout the period referred to in the first subparagraph of this paragraph, of downloading and printing the documents referred to in paragraph 1. However, in that case Member States may provide that the company is to make those documents available at its registered office for consultation by the shareholders.

Member States may require companies to maintain the information on their website for a specific period after the general meeting. Member States may determine the consequences of temporary disruption of access to the website caused by technical or other factors.

[11.512]

Article 98 Protection of employees' rights

Protection of the rights of the employees of each of the merging companies shall be regulated in accordance with Directive 2001/23/EC.

[11.513]

Article 99 Protection of the interests of creditors of the merging companies

1. The laws of the Member States shall provide for an adequate system of protection of the interests of creditors of the merging companies whose claims antedate the publication of the draft terms of merger and have not fallen due at the time of such publication.

2. For the purposes of paragraph 1, the laws of the Member States shall at least provide that such creditors shall be entitled to obtain adequate safeguards where the financial situation of the merging companies makes such protection necessary and where those creditors do not already have such safeguards.

Member States shall lay down the conditions for the protection provided for in paragraph 1 and in the first subparagraph of this paragraph. In any event, Member States shall ensure that the creditors are authorised to apply to the appropriate administrative or judicial authority for adequate safeguards provided that they can credibly demonstrate that due to the merger the satisfaction of their claims is at stake and that no adequate safeguards have been obtained from the company.

3. Such protection may be different for the creditors of the acquiring company and for those of the company being acquired.

[11.514]

Article 100 Protection of the interests of debenture holders of the merging companies

Without prejudice to the rules governing the collective exercise of their rights, Article 99 shall apply to the debenture holders of the merging companies, except where the merger has been approved by a meeting of the debenture holders, if such a meeting is provided for under national laws, or by the debenture holders individually.

[11.515]

Article 101 Protection of holders of securities, other than shares, to which special rights are attached

Holders of securities, other than shares, to which special rights are attached shall be given rights in the acquiring company at least equivalent to those they possessed in the company being acquired, unless the alteration of those rights has been approved by a meeting of the holders of such securities, if such a meeting is provided for under national laws, or by the holders of those securities individually, or unless the holders are entitled to have their securities repurchased by the acquiring company.

[11.516]

Article 102 Drawing up and certification of documents in due legal form

1. Where the laws of a Member State do not provide for judicial or administrative preventive supervision of the legality of mergers, or where such supervision does not extend to all the legal acts required for a merger, the minutes of the general meetings which decide on the merger and, where appropriate, the merger contract subsequent to such general meetings shall be drawn up and certified in due legal form. In cases where the merger need not be approved by the general meetings of all the merging companies, the draft terms of merger shall be drawn up and certified in due legal form.

2. The notary or the authority competent to draw up and certify the document in due legal form shall check and certify the existence and validity of the legal acts and formalities required of the company for which that notary or authority is acting and of the draft terms of merger.

[11.517]
Article 103 Date on which a merger takes effect
The laws of the Member States shall determine the date on which a merger takes effect.

[11.518]
Article 104 Publication formalities
1. A merger shall be publicised in the manner prescribed by the laws of each Member State, in accordance with Article 16, in respect of each of the merging companies.
2. The acquiring company may itself carry out the publication formalities relating to the company or companies being acquired.

[11.519]
Article 105 Consequences of a merger
1. A merger shall have the following consequences *ipso jure* and simultaneously:
(a) the transfer, both as between the company being acquired and the acquiring company and, as regards third parties, to the acquiring company of all the assets and liabilities of the company being acquired;
(b) the shareholders of the company being acquired become shareholders of the acquiring company; and
(c) the company being acquired ceases to exist.
2. No shares in the acquiring company shall be exchanged for shares in the company being acquired held either:
(a) by the acquiring company itself or through a person acting in his own name but on its behalf; or
(b) by the company being acquired itself or through a person acting in his own name but on its behalf.
3. The foregoing shall not affect the laws of Member States which require the completion of special formalities for the transfer of certain assets, rights and obligations by the acquired company to be effective as against third parties. The acquiring company may carry out such formalities itself; however, the laws of the Member States may permit the company being acquired to continue to carry out such formalities for a limited period which may not, save in exceptional cases, be fixed at more than six months from the date on which the merger takes effect.

[11.520]
Article 106 Civil liability of members of the administrative or management bodies of the company being acquired
The laws of the Member States shall at least lay down rules governing the civil liability, towards the shareholders of the company being acquired, of the members of the administrative or management bodies of that company in respect of misconduct on the part of members of those bodies in preparing and implementing the merger.

[11.521]
Article 107 Civil liability of the experts responsible for drawing up the expert report on behalf of the company being acquired
The laws of the Member States shall at least lay down rules governing the civil liability, towards the shareholders of the company being acquired, of the experts responsible for drawing up on behalf of that company the report referred to in Article 96(1), in respect of misconduct on the part of those experts in the performance of their duties.

[11.522]
Article 108 Conditions for nullity of a merger
1. The laws of the Member States may lay down nullity rules for mergers in accordance with the following conditions only:
(a) nullity is to be ordered in a court judgment;
(b) mergers which have taken effect pursuant to Article 103 may be declared void only if there has been no judicial or administrative preventive supervision of their legality, or if they have not been drawn up and certified in due legal form, or if it is shown that the decision of the general meeting is void or voidable under national law;
(c) nullification proceedings may not be initiated more than six months after the date on which the merger becomes effective as against the person alleging nullity or where the situation has been rectified;
(d) where it is possible to remedy a defect liable to render a merger void, the competent court is to grant the companies involved a period of time within which to rectify the situation;
(e) a judgment declaring a merger void is to be published in the manner prescribed by the laws of each Member State in accordance with Article 16;
(f) where the laws of a Member State permit a third party to challenge such a judgment, that party may only do so within six months of publication of the judgment in the manner prescribed by Section 1 of Chapter III of Title I;
(g) a judgment declaring a merger void does not of itself affect the validity of obligations owed by or in relation to the acquiring company which arose before the judgment was published and after the date on which the merger takes effect; and
(h) companies which have been parties to a merger are jointly and severally liable in respect of the obligations of the acquiring company referred to in point (g).
2. By way of derogation from point (a) of paragraph 1, the laws of a Member State may also provide for the nullity of a merger to be ordered by an administrative authority if an appeal against such a decision lies to a court. point (b) and points (d) to (h) of paragraph 1shall apply by analogy to the administrative authority. Such nullification proceedings may not be initiated more than six months after the date on which the merger takes effect.
3. The laws of the Member States on the nullity of a merger pronounced following any supervision other than judicial or administrative preventive supervision of legality shall not be affected.

SECTION 3 MERGER BY FORMATION OF A NEW COMPANY

[11.523]
Article 109 Merger by formation of a new company

1. Articles 91, 92, 93 and 95 to 108 shall apply, without prejudice to Articles 11 and 12, to merger by formation of a new company. For this purpose, 'merging companies' and 'company being acquired' shall mean the companies which will cease to exist, and 'acquiring company' shall mean the new company.

Article 91(2)(a) shall also apply to the new company.

2. The draft terms of merger and, if they are contained in a separate document, the memorandum or draft memorandum of association and the articles or draft articles of association of the new company shall be approved at a general meeting of each of the companies that will cease to exist.

SECTION 4 ACQUISITION OF ONE COMPANY BY ANOTHER WHICH HOLDS 90% OR MORE OF ITS SHARES

[11.524]
Article 110 Transfer of all assets and liabilities by one or more companies to another company which is the holder of all their shares

Member States shall make provision, in respect of companies governed by their laws, for the operation whereby one or more companies are wound up without going into liquidation and transfer all their assets and liabilities to another company which is the holder of all their shares and other securities conferring the right to vote at general meetings. Such operations shall be regulated by the provisions of Section 2 of this Chapter. However, Member States shall not impose the requirements set out in points (b), (c) and (d) of Article 91(2), Articles 95 and 96, points (d) and (e) of Article 97(1), point (b) of Article 105(1) and Articles 106 and 107.

[11.525]
Article 111 Exemption from the requirement of approval by the general meeting

Member States shall not apply Article 93 to the operations referred to in Article 110 if the following conditions are fulfilled:

(a) the publication provided for in Article 92 is effected, as regards each company involved in the operation, at least one month before the operation takes effect;

(b) at least one month before the operation takes effect, all shareholders of the acquiring company are entitled to inspect the documents referred to in points (a), (b) and (c) of Article 97(1) at the company's registered office;

(c) point (c) of the first paragraph of Article 94 applies.

For the purposes of point (b) of the first paragraph of this Article, Article 97(2), (3) and (4) shall apply.

[11.526]
Article 112 Shares held by or on behalf of the acquiring company

The Member States may apply Articles 110 and 111 to operations whereby one or more companies are wound up without going into liquidation and transfer all their assets and liabilities to another company, if all the shares and other securities specified in Article 110 of the company or companies being acquired are held by the acquiring company and/or by persons holding those shares and securities in their own names but on behalf of that company.

[11.527]
Article 113 Merger by acquisition by a company which holds 90% or more of the shares of a company being acquired

Where a merger by acquisition is carried out by a company which holds 90% or more, but not all, of the shares and other securities conferring the right to vote at general meetings of the company or companies being acquired, Member States shall not require approval of the merger by the general meeting of the acquiring company if the following conditions are fulfilled:

(a) the publication provided for in Article 92 is effected, as regards the acquiring company, at least one month before the date fixed for the general meeting of the company or companies being acquired which is to decide on the draft terms of merger;

(b) at least one month before the date specified in point (a), all shareholders of the acquiring company are entitled to inspect the documents specified in points (a) and (b) and, where applicable, points (c), (d) and (e) of Article 97(1) at the company's registered office;

(c) point (c) of the first paragraph of Article 94 applies.

For the purposes of point (b) of the first paragraph of this Article, Article 97(2), (3) and (4) shall apply.

[11.528]
Article 114 Exemption from requirements applicable to mergers by acquisition

Member States shall not impose the requirements set out in Articles 95, 96 and 97 in the case of a merger within the meaning of Article 113 if the following conditions are fulfilled:

(a) the minority shareholders of the company being acquired are entitled to have their shares acquired by the acquiring company;

(b) if they exercise that right, they are entitled to receive consideration corresponding to the value of their shares;

(c) in the event of disagreement regarding such consideration, it is possible for the value of the consideration to be determined by a court or by an administrative authority designated by the Member State for that purpose.

A Member State need not apply the first paragraph if the laws of that Member State entitle the acquiring company, without a previous public takeover offer, to require all the holders of the remaining securities of the company or companies to be acquired, to sell those securities to it prior to the merger at a fair price.

[11.529]
Article 115 Transfer of all assets and liabilities by one or more companies to another company which is the holder of 90% or more of their shares

The Member States may apply Articles 113 and 114 to operations whereby one or more companies are wound up without going into liquidation and transfer all their assets and liabilities to another company, if 90% or more, but not all, of the shares and other securities referred to in Article 113 of the company or companies being acquired are held by that acquiring company and/or by persons holding those shares and securities in their own names but on behalf of that company.

SECTION 5 OTHER OPERATIONS TREATED AS MERGERS

[11.530]
Article 116 Mergers with cash payment exceeding 10%
Where in the case of one of the operations referred to in Article 88 the laws of a Member State permit a cash payment to exceed 10%, Sections 2 and 3 of this Chapter and Articles 113, 114 and 115 shall apply.

[11.531]
Article 117 Mergers without all of the transferring companies ceasing to exist
Where the laws of a Member State permit one of the operations referred to in Articles 88, 110 and 116, without all of the transferring companies thereby ceasing to exist, Section 2, except for point (c) of Article 105(1), and Section 3 or 4 of this Chapter shall apply as appropriate.

CHAPTER II CROSS-BORDER MERGERS OF LIMITED LIABILITY COMPANIES

[11.532]
Article 118 General provisions
This Chapter shall apply to mergers of limited liability companies formed in accordance with the law of a Member State and having their registered office, central administration or principal place of business within the Union, provided at least two of them are governed by the laws of different Member States (hereinafter referred to as 'cross-border mergers').

[11.533]
Article 119 Definitions
For the purposes of this Chapter:

(1) 'limited liability company', hereinafter referred to as 'company', means:
   (a) a company of a type listed in Annex II; or
   (b) a company with share capital and having legal personality, possessing separate assets which alone serve to cover its debts and that is subject, under the national law governing it, to conditions concerning guarantees such as are provided for by Section 2 of Chapter II of Title I and Section 1 of Chapter III of Title I for the protection of the interests of members and others;
(2) 'merger' means an operation whereby:
   (a) one or more companies, on being dissolved without going into liquidation, transfer all their assets and liabilities to another existing company, the acquiring company, in exchange for the issue to their members of securities or shares representing the capital of that other company and, if applicable, a cash payment not exceeding 10% of the nominal value, or, in the absence of a nominal value, of the accounting par value of those securities or shares; or
   (b) two or more companies, on being dissolved without going into liquidation, transfer all their assets and liabilities to a company that they form, the new company, in exchange for the issue to their members of securities or shares representing the capital of that new company and, if applicable, a cash payment not exceeding 10% of the nominal value, or in the absence of a nominal value, of the accounting par value of those securities or shares; or
   (c) a company, on being dissolved without going into liquidation, transfers all its assets and liabilities to the company holding all the securities or shares representing its capital[; or]
   [(d) one or more companies, on being dissolved without going into liquidation, transfer all their assets and liabilities to another existing company, the acquiring company, without the issue of any new shares by the acquiring company, provided that one person holds directly or indirectly all the shares in the merging companies or the members of the merging companies hold their securities and shares in the same proportion in all merging companies].

NOTES

Para 2: point (d) and the preceding word were added by European Parliament and Council Directive 2019/2121/EU, Art 1(6), as form 1 January 2020. Note that the 2019 Directive has a transposition date of 31 January 2023.

[11.534]
Article 120 Further provisions concerning scope
1. Notwithstanding Article 119(2), this Chapter shall also apply to cross-border mergers where the law of at least one of the Member States concerned allows the cash payment referred to in Article 119(2)(a) and (b) to exceed 10% of the nominal value, or, in the absence of a nominal value, of the accounting par value of the securities or shares representing the capital of the company resulting from the cross-border merger.
2. Member States may decide not to apply this Chapter to cross-border mergers involving a cooperative society even in the cases where the latter would fall within the definition of a limited liability company as laid down in Article 119(1).
3. This Chapter shall not apply to cross-border mergers involving a company the object of which is the collective investment of capital provided by the public, which operates on the principle of risk-spreading and the units of which are, at the holders' request, repurchased or redeemed, directly or indirectly, out of the assets of that company. Action taken by such a company to ensure that the stock exchange value of its units does not vary significantly from its net asset value shall be regarded as equivalent to such repurchase or redemption.
[4. Member States shall ensure that this Chapter does not apply to companies in either of the following circumstances:
(a) the company is in liquidation and has begun to distribute assets to its members;

[(b) the company is subject to resolution tools, powers and mechanisms provided for in Title IV of Directive 2014/59/EU or in Title V of Regulation (EU) 2021/23.]]

[5. Member States may decide not to apply this Chapter to companies which are:

(a) the subject of insolvency proceedings or subject to preventive restructuring frameworks;

(b) the subject of liquidation proceedings other than those referred to in point (a) of paragraph 4, or

[(c) the subject of crisis prevention measures as defined in point (101) of Article 2(1) of Directive 2014/59/EU or in point (48) of Article 2 of Regulation (EU) 2021/23.]]

NOTES

Para 4 was substituted, and para 5 was added, by European Parliament and Council Directive 2019/2121/EU, Art 1(7), as form 1 January 2020. Note that the 2019 Directive has a transposition date of 31 January 2023.

Point (b) of para 4 and point (c) of para 5 were further substituted by European Parliament and Council Regulation 2021/23/EU, Art 92(4), as from 12 August 2022.

[11.535]

Article 121 Conditions relating to cross-border mergers

1. Save as otherwise provided in this Chapter,

(a) . . .

(b) a company taking part in a cross-border merger shall comply with the provisions and formalities of the national law to which it is subject. The laws of a Member State enabling its national authorities to oppose a given internal merger on grounds of public interest shall also be applicable to a cross-border merger where at least one of the merging companies is subject to the law of that Member State. This provision shall not apply to the extent that Article 21 of Regulation (EC) No 139/2004 is applicable.

[2. The provisions and formalities referred to in point (b) of paragraph 1 of this Article shall, in particular, include those concerning the decision-making process relating to the merger and the protection of employees as regards rights other than those governed by Article 133.]

NOTES

Point (a) of para 1 was repealed, and para 2 was substituted, by European Parliament and Council Directive 2019/2121/EU, Art 1(8), as form 1 January 2020. Note that the 2019 Directive has a transposition date of 31 January 2023.

[11.536]

Article 122 Common draft terms of cross-border mergers

The management or administrative organ of each of the merging companies shall draw up the common draft terms of a cross-border merger. The common draft terms of a cross-border merger shall include at least the following particulars:

[(a) for each of the merging companies, its legal form and name, and the location of its registered office, and the legal form and name proposed for the company resulting from the cross-border merger and the proposed location of its registered office;

(b) the ratio applicable to the exchange of securities or shares representing the company capital and the amount of any cash payment, where appropriate;]

(c) the terms for the allotment of securities or shares representing the capital of the company resulting from the cross- border merger;

(d) the likely repercussions of the cross-border merger on employment;

(e) the date from which the holding of such securities or shares representing the company capital will entitle the holders to share in profits and any special conditions affecting that entitlement;

(f) the date from which the transactions of the merging companies will be treated for accounting purposes as being those of the company resulting from the cross-border merger;

(g) the rights conferred by the company resulting from the cross-border merger on members enjoying special rights or on holders of securities other than shares representing the company capital, or the measures proposed concerning them;

[(h) any special advantages granted to members of the administrative, management, supervisory or controlling bodies of the merging companies;

(i) the instrument of constitution of the company resulting from the cross-border merger, where applicable, and the statutes if they are contained in a separate instrument;]

(j) where appropriate, information on the procedures by which arrangements for the involvement of employees in the definition of their rights to participation in the company resulting from the cross-border merger are determined pursuant to Article 133;

(k) information on the evaluation of the assets and liabilities which are transferred to the company resulting from the cross-border merger;

(l) dates of the merging companies' accounts used to establish the conditions of the cross-border merger;

(m) details of the offer of cash compensation for members in accordance with Article 126a;

(n) any safeguards offered to creditors, such as guarantees or pledges].

NOTES

Points (a), (b) and (h), (i) were substituted, and points (m) and (n) were added, by European Parliament and Council Directive 2019/2121/EU, Art 1(9), as form 1 January 2020. Note that the 2019 Directive has a transposition date of 31 January 2023.

[11.537]

[Article 123 Disclosure

1. Member States shall ensure that the following documents are disclosed by the company and made publicly available in the register of the Member State of each of the merging companies, at least one month before the date of the general meeting referred to in Article 126:

(a) the common draft terms of the cross-border merger; and

(b) a notice informing the members, creditors and representatives of the employees of the merging company, or, where there are no such representatives, the employees themselves, that they may submit to their respective company, at the latest five working days before the date of the general meeting, comments concerning the common draft terms of the cross-border merger.

Member States may require that the independent expert report be disclosed and made publicly available in the register. Member States shall ensure that the company is able to exclude confidential information from the disclosure of the independent expert report.

The documents disclosed in accordance with this paragraph shall also be accessible through the system of interconnection of registers.

2. Member States may exempt merging companies from the disclosure requirement referred to in paragraph 1 of this Article where, for a continuous period beginning at least one month before the date fixed for the general meeting referred to in Article 126 and ending not earlier than the conclusion of that meeting, those companies make the documents referred to in paragraph 1 of this Article available on their websites free of charge to the public.

However, Member States shall not subject that exemption to any requirements or constraints other than those which are necessary to ensure the security of the website and the authenticity of the documents, and which are proportionate to achieving those objectives.

3. Where merging companies make the common draft terms of the cross-border merger available in accordance with paragraph 2 of this Article, they shall submit to their respective register, at least one month before the date of the general meeting referred to in Article 126, the following information:

(a) for each of the merging companies its legal form and name and the location of its registered office and the legal form and name proposed for any newly created company and the proposed location of its registered office;

(b) the register in which the documents referred to in Article 14 are filed in respect of each of the merging companies, and the registration number of the respective company in that register;

(c) an indication, for each of the merging companies, of the arrangements made for the exercise of the rights of creditors, employees and members; and

(d) details of the website from which the common draft terms of the cross-border merger, the notice referred to in paragraph 1, the independent expert report and complete information on the arrangements referred to in point (c) of this paragraph may be obtained online and free of charge.

The register of the Member State of each of the merging companies shall make publicly available the information referred to in points (a) to (d) of the first subparagraph.

4. Member States shall ensure that the requirements referred to in paragraphs 1 and 3 can be fulfilled fully online without the necessity for the applicants to appear in person before any competent authority in the Member States of the merging companies, in accordance with the relevant provisions of Chapter III of Title I.

5. Where the approval of the merger is not required by the general meeting of the acquiring company in accordance with Article 126(3), the disclosure referred to in paragraphs 1, 2 and 3 of this Article shall be made at least one month before the date of the general meeting of the other merging company or companies.

6. Member States may require, in addition to the disclosure referred to in paragraphs 1, 2 and 3 of this Article, that the common draft terms of the cross-border merger, or the information referred to in paragraph 3 of this Article, be published in their national gazette or through a central electronic platform in accordance with Article 16(3). In that instance, Member States shall ensure that the register transmits the relevant information to the national gazette or to a central electronic platform.

7. Member States shall ensure that the documentation referred to in paragraph 1 or the information referred to in paragraph 3 is accessible to the public free of charge through the system of interconnection of registers.

Member States shall further ensure that any fees charged to the company by the registers for the disclosure referred to in paragraphs 1 and 3 and, where applicable, for the publication referred to in paragraph 6 do not exceed the recovery of the cost of providing such services.]

NOTES

Substituted by European Parliament and Council Directive 2019/2121/EU, Art 1(10), as form 1 January 2020. Note that the 2019 Directive has a transposition date of 31 January 2023.

[11.538]

[Article 124 Report of the administrative or management body for members and employees

1. The administrative or management body of each of the merging companies shall draw up a report for members and employees explaining and justifying the legal and economic aspects of the cross-border merger, as well as explaining the implications of the cross-border merger for employees.

It shall, in particular, explain the implications of the cross-border merger for the future business of the company.

2. The report shall also include a section for members and a section for employees.

The company may decide either to draw up one report containing those two sections or to draw up separate reports for members and employees, respectively, containing the relevant section.

3. The section of the report for members shall, in particular, explain the following:

(a) the cash compensation and the method used to determine the cash compensation;

(b) the share exchange ratio and the method or methods used to arrive at the share exchange ratio, where applicable;

(c) the implications of the cross-border merger for members;

(d) the rights and remedies available to members in accordance with Article 126a.

4. The section of the report for members shall not be required where all the members of the company have agreed to waive that requirement. Member States may exclude single-member companies from the provisions of this Article.

5. The section of the report for employees shall, in particular, explain the following:

(a) the implications of the cross-border merger for employment relationships, as well as, where applicable, any measures for safeguarding those relationships;

(b) any material changes to the applicable conditions of employment or to the location of the company's places of business;

(c) how the factors set out in points (a) and (b) affect any subsidiaries of the company.

6. The report or reports shall be made available in any case electronically, together with the common draft terms of the cross-border merger, if available, to the members and to the representatives of the employees of each of the merging companies or, where there are no such representatives, to the employees themselves, not less than six weeks before the date of the general meeting referred to in Article 126.

However, where the approval of the merger is not required by the general meeting of the acquiring company in accordance with Article 126(3), the report shall be made available at least six weeks before the date of the general meeting of the other merging company or companies.

7. Where the administrative or management body of the merging company receives an opinion on the information referred to in paragraphs 1 and 5 in good time from the representatives of the employees or, where there are no such representatives, from the employees themselves, as provided for under national law, the members shall be informed thereof and that opinion shall be appended to the report.

8. The section of the report for employees shall not be required where a merging company and its subsidiaries, if any, have no employees other than those who form part of the administrative or management body.

9. Where the section of the report for members referred to in paragraph 3 is waived in accordance with paragraph 4 and the section for employees referred to in paragraph 5 is not required under paragraph 8, the report shall not be required.

10. Paragraphs 1 to 9 of this Article shall be without prejudice to the applicable information and consultation rights and procedures provided for at national level following the transposition of Directives 2002/14/EC and 2009/38/EC.]

NOTES

Substituted by European Parliament and Council Directive 2019/2121/EU, Art 1(10), as form 1 January 2020. Note that the 2019 Directive has a transposition date of 31 January 2023.

[11.539]

Article 125 Independent expert report

1. An independent expert report intended for members and made available not less than one month before the date of the general meeting referred to in Article 126 shall be drawn up for each merging company. Depending on the law of each Member State, such experts may be natural persons or legal persons.

[However, where the approval of the merger is not required by the general meeting of the acquiring company in accordance with Article 126(3), the report shall be made available at least one month before the date of the general meeting of the other merging company or companies.]

2. As an alternative to experts operating on behalf of each of the merging companies, one or more independent experts, appointed for that purpose at the joint request of the companies by a judicial or administrative authority in the Member State of one of the merging companies or of the company resulting from the cross-border merger or approved by such an authority, may examine the common draft terms of cross-border merger and draw up a single written report to all the members.

[3. The report referred to in paragraph 1 shall in any case include the expert's opinion as to whether the cash compensation and the share exchange ratio are adequate. When assessing the cash compensation, the expert shall consider any market price of the shares in the merging companies prior to the announcement of the merger proposal or the value of the companies excluding the effect of the proposed merger, as determined in accordance with generally accepted valuation methods. The report shall at least:

(a) indicate the method or methods used to determine the cash compensation proposed;

(b) indicate the method or methods used to arrive at the share exchange ratio proposed;

(c) state whether the method or methods used are adequate for the assessment of the cash compensation and the share exchange ratio, indicate the value arrived at using such methods and give an opinion on the relative importance attributed to those methods in arriving at the value decided on, and in the event that different methods are used in the merging companies, state also whether the use of different methods was justified; and

(d) describe any special valuation difficulties which have arisen.

The expert shall be entitled to obtain from the merging companies all information necessary for the discharge of the duties of the expert.]

4. Neither an examination of the common draft terms of cross-border merger by independent experts nor an expert report shall be required if all the members of each of the companies involved in the cross-border merger have so agreed.

[Member States may exclude single-member companies from the application of this Article.]

NOTES

Words in square brackets in paras 1 and 4 added, and para 3 substituted, by European Parliament and Council Directive 2019/2121/EU, Art 1(11), as form 1 January 2020. Note that the 2019 Directive has a transposition date of 31 January 2023.

[11.540]

Article 126 Approval by the general meeting

[1. After taking note of the reports referred to in Articles 124 and 125, where applicable, employees' opinions submitted in accordance with Article 124 and comments submitted in accordance with Article 123, the general meeting of each of the merging companies shall decide, by means of a resolution, whether to approve the common draft terms of the cross-border merger and whether to adapt the instrument of constitution, and the statutes if they are contained in a separate instrument.

2. The general meeting of each of the merging companies may reserve the right to make implementation of the cross-border merger conditional on express ratification by it of the arrangements decided on with respect to the participation of employees in the company resulting from the cross-border merger.

3. The laws of a Member State need not require approval of the merger by the general meeting of the acquiring company if the conditions laid down in Article 94 are fulfilled.

[4. Member States shall ensure that the approval of the cross-border merger by the general meeting cannot be challenged solely on the following grounds:

(a) the share exchange ratio referred to in point (b) of Article 122 has been inadequately set;

(b) the cash compensation referred to in point (m) of Article 122 has been inadequately set; or

(c) the information given with regard to the share exchange ratio referred to in point (a) or the cash compensation referred to in point (b) did not comply with the legal requirements.]

NOTES

Para 1 was substituted, and para 4 was added, by European Parliament and Council Directive 2019/2121/EU, Art 1(12), as form 1 January 2020. Note that the 2019 Directive has a transposition date of 31 January 2023.

[11.541]

[Article 126a Protection of members

1. Member States shall ensure that at least the members of the merging companies who voted against the approval of the common draft-terms of the cross-border merger have the right to dispose of their shares for adequate cash compensation, under the conditions laid down in paragraphs 2 to 6, provided that as a result of the merger they would acquire shares in the company resulting from the merger which would be governed by the law of a Member State other than the Member State of their respective merging company.

Member States may also provide for other members of the merging companies to have the right referred to in the first subparagraph.

Member States may require that express opposition to the common draft terms of the cross-border merger, the intention of members to exercise their right to dispose of their shares, or both, be appropriately documented, at the latest at the general meeting referred to in Article 126. Member States may allow the recording of opposition to the common draft terms of the cross-border merger to be considered proper documentation of a negative vote.

2. Member States shall establish the period within which the members referred to in paragraph 1 have to declare to the merging company concerned their decision to exercise the right to dispose of their shares. That period shall not exceed one month after the general meeting referred to in Article 126. Member States shall ensure that the merging companies provide an electronic address for receiving that declaration electronically.

3. Member States shall further establish the period within which the cash compensation specified in the common draft terms of the cross-border merger is to be paid. That period shall not end later than two months after the cross-border merger takes effect in accordance with Article 129.

4. Member States shall ensure that any members who have declared their decision to exercise the right to dispose of their shares, but who consider that the cash compensation offered by the merging company concerned has not been adequately set, are entitled to claim additional cash compensation before the competent authority or body mandated under national law. Member States shall establish a time limit for the claim for additional cash compensation.

Member States may provide that the final decision to provide additional cash compensation is valid for all members of the merging company concerned who have declared their decision to exercise the right to dispose of their shares in accordance with paragraph 2.

5. Member States shall ensure that the law of the Member State to which a merging company is subject governs the rights referred to in paragraphs 1 to 4 and that the exclusive competence to resolve any disputes relating to those rights lies within the jurisdiction of that Member State.

6. Member States shall ensure that members of the merging companies who did not have or did not exercise the right to dispose of their shares, but who consider that the share exchange ratio set out in the common draft terms of the cross-border merger is inadequate, may dispute that ratio and claim a cash payment. Proceedings in that regard shall be initiated before the competent authority or body mandated under the law of the Member State to which the relevant merging company is subject, within the time limit laid down in that national law and such proceedings shall not prevent the registration of the cross-border merger. The decision shall be binding on the company resulting from the cross-border merger.

Member States may also provide that the share exchange ratio as established in that decision is valid for any members of the merging company concerned who did not have or did not exercise their right to dispose of their shares.

7. Member States may also provide that the company resulting from the cross-border merger can provide shares or other compensation instead of a cash payment.]

NOTES

Inserted, together with Articles 126b and 126c, by European Parliament and Council Directive 2019/2121/EU, Art 1(13), as form 1 January 2020. Note that the 2019 Directive has a transposition date of 31 January 2023.

[11.542]

[Article 126b Protection of creditors

1. Member States shall provide for an adequate system of protection of the interests of creditors whose claims antedate the disclosure of the common draft terms of the cross-border merger and have not fallen due at the time of such disclosure.

Member States shall ensure that creditors who are dissatisfied with the safeguards offered in the common draft terms of the cross-border merger, as provided for in point (n) of Article 122, may apply, within three months of the disclosure of the common draft terms of the cross-border merger referred to in Article 123, to the appropriate administrative or judicial authority for adequate safeguards, provided that such creditors can credibly demonstrate that, due to the cross-border merger, the satisfaction of their claims is at stake and that they have not obtained adequate safeguards from the merging companies.

Member States shall ensure that the safeguards are conditional on the cross-border merger taking effect in accordance with Article 129.

2. Member States may require that the administrative or management body of each of the merging companies provides a declaration that accurately reflects its current financial status at a date no earlier than one month before the disclosure of that declaration. The declaration shall state that, on the basis of the information available to the administrative or management body of the merging companies at the date of that declaration, and after having made

reasonable enquiries, that administrative or management body is unaware of any reason why the company resulting from the merger would be unable to meet its liabilities when those liabilities fall due. The declaration shall be disclosed together with the common draft terms of the cross-border merger in accordance with Article 123.

3. Paragraphs 1 and 2 shall be without prejudice to the application of the laws of the Member States of the merging companies concerning the satisfaction or securing of pecuniary or non-pecuniary obligations due to public bodies.]

NOTES

Inserted as noted to Art 126a at **[11.541]**.

[11.543]

[Article 126c Employee information and consultation

1. Member States shall ensure that employees' rights to information and consultation are respected in relation to the cross-border merger and are exercised in accordance with the legal framework provided for in Directive 2002/14/EC, and Directive 2001/23/EC where the cross-border merger is considered to be a transfer of an undertaking within the meaning of Directive 2001/23/EC, and, where applicable for Community-scale undertakings or Community-scale groups of undertakings, in accordance with Directive 2009/38/EC. Member States may decide that employees' rights to information and consultation apply with respect to the employees of companies other than those referred to in Article 3(1) of Directive 2002/14/EC.

2. Notwithstanding point (b) of Article 123(1) and Article 124(7), Member States shall ensure that employees' rights to information and consultation are respected, at least before the common draft terms of the cross-border merger or the report referred to in Article 124 are decided upon, whichever is earlier, in such a way that a reasoned response is given to the employees before the general meeting referred to in Article 126.

3. Without prejudice to any provisions or practices in force more favourable to employees, Member States shall determine the practical arrangements for exercising the right to information and consultation in accordance with Article 4 of Directive 2002/14/EC.]

NOTES

Inserted as noted to Art 126a at **[11.541]**.

[11.544]

[Article 127 Pre-merger certificate

1. Member States shall designate the court, notary or other authority or authorities competent to scrutinise the legality of cross-border mergers as regards those parts of the procedure which are governed by the law of the Member State of the merging company and to issue a pre-merger certificate attesting to compliance with all relevant conditions and to the proper completion of all procedures and formalities in the Member State of the merging company ("the competent authority").

Such completion of procedures and formalities may comprise the satisfaction or securing of pecuniary or non-pecuniary obligations due to public bodies or compliance with specific sectoral requirements, including securing obligations arising from ongoing proceedings.

2. Member States shall ensure that the application to obtain a pre-merger certificate by the merging company is accompanied by the following:

(a) the common draft terms of the cross-border merger;

(b) the report and the appended opinion, if any, referred to in Article 124, as well as the report referred to in Article 125, where they are available;

(c) any comments submitted in accordance with Article 123(1); and

(d) information on the approval by the general meeting referred to in Article 126.

3. Member States may require that the application to obtain a pre-merger certificate by the merging company is accompanied by additional information, such as, in particular:

(a) the number of employees at the time of the drawing up of the common draft terms of the cross-border merger;

(b) the existence of subsidiaries and their respective geographical location;

(c) information regarding the satisfaction of obligations due to public bodies by the merging company.

For the purposes of this paragraph, competent authorities may request such information, if not provided by the merging company, from other relevant authorities.

4. Member States shall ensure that the application referred to in paragraphs 2 and 3, including the submission of any information and documents, may be completed fully online without the necessity for the applicants to appear in person before the competent authority, in accordance with the relevant provisions of Chapter III of Title I.

5. In respect of compliance with the rules concerning employee participation as laid down in Article 133, the competent authority in the Member State of the merging company shall verify that the common draft terms of the cross-border merger include information on the procedures by which the relevant arrangements are determined and on the possible options for such arrangements.

6. As part of the scrutiny referred to in paragraph 1, the competent authority shall examine the following:

(a) all documents and information submitted to the competent authority in accordance with paragraphs 2 and 3;

(b) an indication by the merging companies that the procedure referred to in Article 133(3) and (4) has started, where relevant.

7. Member States shall ensure that the scrutiny referred to in paragraph 1 is carried out within three months of the date of receipt of the documents and information concerning the approval of the cross-border merger by the general meeting of the merging company. That scrutiny shall have one of the following outcomes:

(a) where it is determined that the cross-border merger complies with all the relevant conditions and that all necessary procedures and formalities have been completed, the competent authority shall issue the pre-merger certificate;

(b) where it is determined that the cross-border merger does not comply with all the relevant conditions or that not all necessary procedures and formalities have been completed, the competent authority shall not issue the pre-merger certificate and shall inform the company of the reasons for its decision; in that case, the competent authority may give the company the opportunity to fulfil the relevant conditions or to complete the procedures and formalities within an appropriate period of time.

8. Member States shall ensure that the competent authority does not issue the pre-merger certificate where it is determined in compliance with national law that a cross-border merger is set up for abusive or fraudulent purposes leading to or aimed at the evasion or circumvention of Union or national law, or for criminal purposes.

9. Where the competent authority, during the scrutiny referred to in paragraph 1, has serious doubts indicating that the cross-border merger is set up for abusive or fraudulent purposes leading to or aimed at the evasion or circumvention of Union or national law, or for criminal purposes, it shall take into consideration relevant facts and circumstances, such as, where relevant and not considered in isolation, indicative factors of which the competent authority has become aware, in the course of the scrutiny referred to in paragraph 1, including through consultation of relevant authorities. The assessment for the purposes of this paragraph shall be conducted on a case-by-case basis, through a procedure governed by national law.

10. Where it is necessary for the purposes of the assessment under paragraphs 8 and 9 to take into account additional information or to perform additional investigative activities, the period of three months provided for in paragraph 7 may be extended by a maximum of three months.

11. Where, due to the complexity of the cross-border procedure, it is not possible to carry out the assessment within the deadlines provided for in paragraphs 7 and 10, Member States shall ensure that the applicant is notified of the reasons for any delay before the expiry of those deadlines.

12. Member States shall ensure that the competent authority may consult other relevant authorities with competence in the different fields concerned by the cross-border merger, including those of the Member State of the company resulting from the merger, and obtain from those authorities and from the merging company information and documents necessary to scrutinise the legality of the cross-border merger, within the procedural framework laid down in national law. For the purposes of the assessment, the competent authority may have recourse to an independent expert.]

NOTES

Substituted by European Parliament and Council Directive 2019/2121/EU, Art 1(14), as form 1 January 2020. Note that the 2019 Directive has a transposition date of 31 January 2023.

[11.545]

[Article 127a Transmission of the pre-merger certificate

1. Member States shall ensure that the pre-merger certificate is shared with the authorities referred to in Article 128(1) through the system of interconnection of registers.

Member States shall also ensure that the pre-merger certificate is available through the system of interconnection of registers.

2. Access to the pre-merger certificate shall be free of charge for the authorities referred to in Article 128(1) and for the registers.]

NOTES

Inserted by European Parliament and Council Directive 2019/2121/EU, Art 1(15), as form 1 January 2020. Note that the 2019 Directive has a transposition date of 31 January 2023.

[11.546]

Article 128 Scrutiny of the legality of the cross-border merger

1. Each Member State shall designate the court, notary or other authority competent to scrutinise the legality of the cross-border merger as regards that part of the procedure which concerns the completion of the cross-border merger and, where appropriate, the formation of a new company resulting from the cross-border merger where the company created by the cross-border merger is subject to its national law. The said authority shall in particular ensure that the merging companies have approved the common draft terms of cross-border merger in the same terms and, where appropriate, that arrangements for employee participation have been determined in accordance with Article 133.

[2. For the purposes of paragraph 1 of this Article, each merging company shall submit to the authority referred to in paragraph 1 of this Article the common draft terms of the cross-border merger approved by the general meeting referred to in Article 126 or, in the event that the approval by the general meeting is not required in accordance with Article 132(3), the common draft terms of the cross-border merger approved by each merging company in accordance with national law.]

[3. Each Member State shall ensure that any application for the purposes of paragraph 1, by any of the merging companies, including the submission of any information and documents, may be completed fully online without the necessity for the applicants to appear in person before the authority referred to in paragraph 1, in accordance with the relevant provisions of Chapter III of Title I.

4. The authority referred to in paragraph 1 shall approve the cross-border merger as soon as it has determined that all relevant conditions have been fulfilled.

5. The pre-merger certificate shall be accepted by the authority referred to in paragraph 1 as conclusively attesting to the proper completion of the applicable pre-merger procedures and formalities in its respective Member State, without which the cross-border merger cannot be approved.]

NOTES

Para 2 substituted, and paras 3–5 added, by European Parliament and Council Directive 2019/2121/EU, Art 1(16), as form 1 January 2020. Note that the 2019 Directive has a transposition date of 31 January 2023.

[11.547]

Article 129 Date on which the cross-border merger takes effect

The law of the Member State to whose jurisdiction the company resulting from the cross-border merger is subject shall determine the date on which the cross-border merger takes effect. That date shall be after the scrutiny referred to in Article 128 has been carried out.

[11.548]

[Article 130 Registration

1. The laws of the Member States of the merging companies and of the company resulting from the merger shall determine, with regard to their respective territories, the arrangements, in accordance with Article 16, for disclosing the completion of the cross-border merger in their registers.

2. Member States shall ensure that at least the following information is entered in their registers:

(a) in the register of the Member State of the company resulting from the merger, that the registration of the company resulting from the merger is the result of a cross-border merger;

(b) in the register of the Member State of the company resulting from the merger, the date of registration of the company resulting from the merger;

(c) in the register of the Member State of each merging company, that the striking off or removal of the merging company from the register is the result of a cross-border merger;

(d) in the register of the Member State of each merging company, the date of striking off or removal of the merging company from the register;

(e) in the registers of the Member States of each merging company and of the Member State of the company resulting from the merger, respectively, the registration number, name and legal form of each merging company and of the company resulting from the merger.

The registers shall make the information referred to in the first subparagraph publicly available and accessible through the system of interconnection of registers.

3. Member States shall ensure that the register in the Member State of the company resulting from the cross- border merger notifies the register in the Member State of each of the merging companies, through the system of interconnection of registers, that the cross-border merger has taken effect. Member States shall also ensure that the registration of the merging company is struck off or removed from the register immediately upon receipt of that notification.]

NOTES

Substituted by European Parliament and Council Directive 2019/2121/EU, Art 1(17), as form 1 January 2020. Note that the 2019 Directive has a transposition date of 31 January 2023.

[11.549]

Article 131 Consequences of a cross-border merger

[1. A cross-border merger carried out as laid down in subpoints (a), (c) and (d) of point (2) of Article 119 shall, from the date referred to in Article 129, have the following consequences:

(a) all the assets and liabilities of the company being acquired, including all contracts, credits, rights and obligations, shall be transferred to the acquiring company;

(b) the members of the company being acquired shall become members of the acquiring company, unless they have disposed of their shares as referred to in Article 126a(1);

(c) the company being acquired shall cease to exist.]

2. A cross-border merger carried out as laid down in subpoint (b) of point 2 Article 119 shall, from the date referred to in Article 129, have the following consequences:

[(a) all the assets and liabilities of the merging companies, including all contracts, credits, rights and obligations, shall be transferred to the new company;

(b) the members of the merging companies shall become members of the new company, unless they have disposed of their shares as referred to in Article 126a(1);]

(c) the merging companies shall cease to exist.

3. Where, in the case of a cross-border merger of companies covered by this Chapter, the laws of the Member States require the completion of special formalities before the transfer of certain assets, rights and obligations by the merging companies becomes effective against third parties, those formalities shall be carried out by the company resulting from the cross-border merger.

4. The rights and obligations of the merging companies arising from contracts of employment or from employment relationships and existing at the date on which the cross-border merger takes effect shall, by reason of that cross-border merger taking effect, be transferred to the company resulting from the cross-border merger on the date on which the cross-border merger takes effect.

5. No shares in the acquiring company shall be exchanged for shares in the company being acquired held either:

(a) by the acquiring company itself or through a person acting in his or her own name but on its behalf;

(b) by the company being acquired itself or through a person acting in his or her own name but on its behalf.

NOTES

Para 1: substituted by European Parliament and Council Directive 2019/2121/EU, Art 1(18)(a), as form 1 January 2020. Note that the 2019 Directive has a transposition date of 31 January 2023.

Para 2: points (a) and (b) substituted by European Parliament and Council Directive 2019/2121/EU, Art 1(18)(b), as form 1 January 2020. Note that the 2019 Directive has a transposition date of 31 January 2023.

[11.550]

Article 132 Simplified formalities

[1. Where a cross-border merger by acquisition is carried out either by a company which holds all the shares and other securities conferring the right to vote at general meetings of the company or companies being acquired or by a person who holds directly or indirectly all the shares in the acquiring company and in the company or companies being acquired, and the acquiring company does not allot any shares under the merger:

— points (b), (c), (e) and (m) of Article 122, Article 125, and point (b) of Article 131(1) shall not apply;

— Article 124 and Article 126(1) shall not apply to the company or companies being acquired.]

Part 11 EU & Retained EU Legislation

2. Where a cross-border merger by acquisition is carried out by a company which holds 90% or more, but not all, of the shares and other securities conferring the right to vote at general meetings of the company or companies being acquired, reports by an independent expert or experts and the documents necessary for scrutiny shall be required only to the extent that the national law governing either the acquiring company or the company or companies being acquired so requires, in accordance with Chapter I of Title II.

[3. Where the laws of the Member States of all of the merging companies provide for the exemption from the approval by the general meeting in accordance with Article 126(3) and paragraph 1 of this Article, the common draft terms of cross-border merger or the information referred to in Article 123(1) to (3) respectively and the reports referred to in Articles 124 and 125, shall be made available at least one month before the decision on the merger is taken by the company in accordance with national law.]

NOTES

Para 1 substituted, and para 3 added, by European Parliament and Council Directive 2019/2121/EU, Art 1(19), as form 1 January 2020. Note that the 2019 Directive has a transposition date of 31 January 2023.

[11.551]

Article 133 Employee participation

1. Without prejudice to paragraph 2, the company resulting from the cross-border merger shall be subject to the rules in force concerning employee participation, if any, in the Member State where it has its registered office.

[2. However, the rules in force concerning employee participation, if any, in the Member State where the company resulting from the cross-border merger has its registered office shall not apply where at least one of the merging companies has, in the six months prior to the disclosure of the common draft terms of the cross-border merger, an average number of employees equivalent to four fifths of the applicable threshold, as laid down in the law of the Member State to whose jurisdiction the merging company is subject, for triggering the participation of employees within the meaning of point (k) of Article 2 of Directive 2001/86/EC, or where the national law applicable to the company resulting from the cross-border merger does not:

(a) provide for at least the same level of employee participation as operated in the relevant merging companies, measured by reference to the proportion of employee representatives amongst the members of the administrative or supervisory organ or their committees or of the management group which covers the profit units of the company, subject to employee representation; or

(b) provide for employees of establishments of the company resulting from the cross-border merger that are situated in other Member States the same entitlement to exercise participation rights as is enjoyed by those employees employed in the Member State where the company resulting from the cross-border merger has its registered office.

3. In the cases referred to in paragraph 2, the participation of employees in the company resulting from the cross-border merger and their involvement in the definition of such rights shall be regulated by the Member States, *mutatis mutandis* and subject to Paragraphs 4 to 7, in accordance with the principles and procedures laid down in Article 12(2), (3) and (4) of Regulation (EC) No 2157/2001 and the following provisions of Directive 2001/86/EC:

(a) Article 3(1), (2) and (3), the first indent of the first subparagraph of Article 3(4), the second subparagraph of Article 3(4) and Article 3(5) and (7);

(b) Article 4(1), Article 4(2)(a), (g) and (h) and Article 4(3);

(c) Article 5;

(d) Article 6;

(e) Article 7(1), point (b) of the first subparagraph of Article 7(2), the second subparagraph of Article 7(2) and Article 7(3). However, for the purposes of this Chapter, the percentages required by point (b) of the first subparagraph of Article 7(2) of Directive 2001/86/EC for the application of the standard rules contained in Part 3 of the Annex to that Directive shall be raised from 25 to 33⅓%;

(f) Articles 8, 10 and 12;

(g) Article 13(4);

(h) point (b) of Part 3 of the Annex.

4. When regulating the principles and procedures referred to in paragraph 3, Member States:

[(a) shall confer on the relevant bodies of the merging companies, in the event that at least one of the merging companies is operating under an employee participation system within the meaning of point (k) of Article 2 of Directive 2001/86/EC, the right to choose without any prior negotiation to be directly subject to the standard rules for participation referred to in point (b) of Part 3 of the Annex to that Directive, as laid down by the legislation of the Member State in which the company resulting from the cross-border merger is to have its registered office, and to abide by those rules from the date of registration;]

(b) shall confer on the special negotiating body the right to decide, by a majority of two thirds of its members representing at least two thirds of the employees, including the votes of members representing employees in at least two different Member States, not to open negotiations or to terminate negotiations already opened and to rely on the rules on participation in force in the Member State where the registered office of the company resulting from the cross-border merger will be situated;

(c) may, in the case where, following prior negotiations, standard rules for participation apply and notwithstanding such rules, decide to limit the proportion of employee representatives in the administrative organ of the company resulting from the cross-border merger. However, if in one of the merging companies employee representatives constituted at least one third of the administrative or supervisory board, the limitation may never result in a lower proportion of employee representatives in the administrative organ than one third.

5. The extension of participation rights to employees of the company resulting from the cross-border merger employed in other Member States, referred to in point (b) of paragraph 2, shall not entail any obligation for Member States which choose to do so to take those employees into account when calculating the size of workforce thresholds giving rise to participation rights under national law.

6. Where at least one of the merging companies is operating under an employee participation system and the company resulting from the cross-border merger is to be governed by such a system in accordance with the rules referred to in paragraph 2, that company shall be obliged to take a legal form allowing for the exercise of participation rights.

[7. Where the company resulting from the cross-border merger is operating under an employee participation system, that company shall be obliged to take measures to ensure that employees' participation rights are protected in the event of any subsequent conversion, merger or division, be it cross-border or domestic, for a period of four years after the cross-border merger has taken effect, by applying *mutatis mutandis* the rules laid down in paragraphs 1 to 6.]

[8. A company shall communicate to its employees or their representatives whether it chooses to apply standard rules for participation referred to in point (h) of paragraph 3 or whether it enters into negotiations within the special negotiating body. In the latter case, the company shall communicate to its employees or their representatives the outcome of the negotiations without undue delay.]

NOTES

All amendments to this Article were made by European Parliament and Council Directive 2019/2121/EU, Art 1(20), as form 1 January 2020. Note that the 2019 Directive has a transposition date of 31 January 2023.

[11.552]

[Article 133a Independent experts

1. Member States shall lay down rules governing at least the civil liability of the independent expert responsible for drawing up the report referred to in Article 125.

2. Member States shall have rules in place to ensure that:

(a) the expert, or the legal person on whose behalf the expert is operating, is independent from and has no conflict of interest with the company applying for the pre-merger certificate; and

(b) the expert's opinion is impartial and objective, and is given with a view to providing assistance to the competent authority in accordance with the independence and impartiality requirements under the law and professional standards to which the expert is subject.]

NOTES

Inserted by European Parliament and Council Directive 2019/2121/EU, Art 1(21), as form 1 January 2020. Note that the 2019 Directive has a transposition date of 31 January 2023.

[11.553]

Article 134 Validity

A cross-border merger which has taken effect as provided for in Article 129 may not be declared null and void.

[The first paragraph does not affect Member States' powers, inter alia, in relation to criminal law, the prevention and combatting of terrorist financing, social law, taxation and law enforcement, to impose measures and penalties, under national law, after the date on which the cross-border merger took effect.]

NOTES

Words in square brackets added by European Parliament and Council Directive 2019/2121/EU, Art 1(22), as form 1 January 2020. Note that the 2019 Directive has a transposition date of 31 January 2023.

CHAPTER III DIVISIONS OF PUBLIC LIMITED LIABILITY COMPANIES

SECTION 1 GENERAL PROVISIONS

[11.554]

Article 135 General provisions on division operations

1. Where Member States permit the types of companies listed in Annex I coming under their laws to carry out division operations by acquisition as defined in Article 136, they shall make those operations subject to Section 2 of this Chapter.

2. Where Member States permit the types of companies referred to in paragraph 1 to carry out division operations by the formation of new companies as defined in Article 155, they shall make those operations subject to Section 3 of this Chapter.

3. Where Member States permit the types of companies referred to in paragraph 1 to carry out operations, whereby a division by acquisition as defined in Article 136(1) is combined with a division by the formation of one or more new companies as defined in Article 155(1), they shall make those operations subject to Section 2 of this Chapter and Article 156.

4. Article 87(2), (3) and (4) shall apply.

SECTION 2 DIVISION BY ACQUISITION

[11.555]

Article 136 Definition of a 'division by acquisition'

1. For the purposes of this Chapter, 'division by acquisition' shall mean the operation whereby, after being wound up without going into liquidation, a company transfers to more than one company all its assets and liabilities in exchange for the allocation to the shareholders of the company being divided of shares in the companies receiving contributions as a result of the division (hereinafter referred to as 'recipient companies') and possibly a cash payment not exceeding 10% of the nominal value of the shares allocated or, where they have no nominal value, of their accounting par value.

2. Article 89(2) shall apply.

3. In so far as this Chapter refers to provisions of Chapter I of Title II, the term 'merging companies' shall mean 'the companies involved in a division', the term 'company being acquired' shall mean 'the company being divided', the term 'acquiring company' shall mean 'each of the recipient companies' and the term 'draft terms of merger' shall mean 'draft terms of division'.

[11.556]
Article 137 Draft terms of division

1. The administrative or management bodies of the companies involved in a division shall draw up draft terms of division in writing.

2. Draft terms of division shall specify at least:

(a) the type, name and registered office of each of the companies involved in the division;
(b) the share exchange ratio and the amount of any cash payment;
(c) the terms relating to the allotment of shares in the recipient companies;
(d) the date from which the holding of such shares entitles the holders to participate in profits and any special conditions affecting that entitlement;
(e) the date from which the transactions of the company being divided shall be treated for accounting purposes as being those of one or other of the recipient companies;
(f) the rights conferred by the recipient companies on the holders of shares to which special rights are attached and the holders of securities other than shares, or the measures proposed concerning them;
(g) any special advantage granted to the experts referred to in Article 142(1) and members of the administrative, management, supervisory or controlling bodies of the companies involved in the division;
(h) the precise description and allocation of the assets and liabilities to be transferred to each of the recipient companies;
(i) the allocation to the shareholders of the company being divided of shares in the recipient companies and the criterion upon which such allocation is based.

3. Where an asset is not allocated by the draft terms of division and where the interpretation of those terms does not make a decision on its allocation possible, the asset or the consideration therefor shall be allocated to all the recipient companies in proportion to the share of the net assets allocated to each of those companies under the draft terms of division.

Where a liability is not allocated by the draft terms of division and where the interpretation of those terms does not make a decision on its allocation possible, each of the recipient companies shall be jointly and severally liable for it. Member States may provide that such joint and several liability be limited to the net assets allocated to each company.

[11.557]
Article 138 Publication of the draft terms of division

Draft terms of division shall be published in the manner prescribed by the laws of each Member State in accordance with Article 16 for each of the companies involved in a division, at least one month before the date of the general meeting which is to decide thereon.

Any of the companies involved in the division shall be exempt from the publication requirement laid down in Article 16 if, for a continuous period beginning at least one month before the date fixed for the general meeting which is to decide on the draft terms of division and ending not earlier than the conclusion of that meeting, it makes the draft terms of division available on its website free of charge for the public. Member States shall not subject that exemption to any requirements or constraints other than those which are necessary in order to ensure the security of the website and the authenticity of the documents and may impose such requirements or constraints only to the extent that they are proportionate in order to achieve those objectives.

By way of derogation from the second paragraph, Member States may require that publication be effected via the central electronic platform referred to in Article 16(5). Member States may alternatively require that such publication be made on any other website designated by them for that purpose. Where Member States avail themselves of one of those possibilities, they shall ensure that companies are not charged a specific fee for such publication.

Where a website other than the central electronic platform is used, a reference giving access to that website shall be published on that central electronic platform at least one month before the date fixed for the general meeting. That reference shall include the date of publication of the draft terms of division on the website and shall be accessible to the public free of charge. Companies shall not be charged a specific fee for such publication.

The prohibition precluding the charging to companies of a specific fee for publication, laid down in the third and fourth paragraphs, shall not affect the ability of Member States to pass on to companies the costs in respect of the central electronic platform.

Member States may require companies to maintain the information for a specific period after the general meeting on their website or, where applicable, on the central electronic platform or the other website designated by the Member State concerned. Member States may determine the consequences of temporary disruption of access to the website or to the central electronic platform, caused by technical or other factors.

[11.558]
Article 139 Approval by the general meeting of each company involved in a division

1. A division shall require at least the approval of a general meeting of each company involved in the division. Article 93 shall apply with regard to the majority required for such decisions, their scope and the need for separate votes.

2. Where shares in the recipient companies are allocated to the shareholders of the company being divided otherwise than in proportion to their rights in the capital of that company, Member States may provide that the minority shareholders of that company may exercise the right to have their shares purchased. In such case, they shall be entitled to receive consideration corresponding to the value of their shares. In the event of a dispute concerning such consideration, it shall be possible for the consideration to be determined by a court.

[11.559]
Article 140 Derogation from the requirement of approval by the general meeting of a recipient company

The laws of a Member State need not require approval of a division by a general meeting of a recipient company if the following conditions are fulfilled:

(a) the publication provided for in Article 138 is effected, for each recipient company, at least one month before the date fixed for the general meeting of the company being divided which is to decide on the draft terms of division;

(b) at least one month before the date specified in point (a), all shareholders of each recipient company are entitled to inspect the documents specified in Article 143(1) at the registered office of that company;

(c) one or more shareholders of any recipient company holding a minimum percentage of the subscribed capital is entitled to require that a general meeting of such recipient company be called to decide whether to approve the division. Such minimum percentage may not be fixed at more than 5%. Member States may, however, provide for the exclusion of non-voting shares from this calculation.

For the purposes of point (b) of the first paragraph, Article 143(2), (3) and (4) shall apply.

[11.560]

Article 141 Detailed written report and information on a division

1. The administration or management bodies of each of the companies involved in the division shall draw up a detailed written report explaining the draft terms of division and setting out the legal and economic grounds for them, in particular the share exchange ratio and the criterion determining the allocation of shares.

2. The report shall also describe any special valuation difficulties which have arisen.

Where applicable, it shall disclose the preparation of the report on the consideration other than in cash referred to in Article 70(2) for recipient companies and the register where that report must be lodged.

3. The administrative or management bodies of a company being divided shall inform the general meeting of that company and the administrative or management bodies of the recipient companies so that they can inform their respective general meetings of any material change in the assets and liabilities between the date of preparation of the draft terms of division and the date of the general meeting of the company being divided which is to decide on the draft terms of division.

[11.561]

Article 142 Examination of the draft terms of division by experts

1. One or more experts acting on behalf of each of the companies involved in the division but independent of them, appointed or approved by a judicial or administrative authority, shall examine the draft terms of division and draw up a written report to the shareholders. However, the laws of a Member State may provide for the appointment of one or more independent experts for all of the companies involved in a division if such appointment is made by a judicial or administrative authority at the joint request of those companies. Such experts may, depending on the laws of each Member State, be natural or legal persons or companies or firms.

2. Article 96(2) and (3) shall apply.

[11.562]

Article 143 Availability of documents for inspection by shareholders

1. All shareholders shall be entitled to inspect at least the following documents at the registered office at least one month before the date of the general meeting which is to decide on the draft terms of division:

(a) the draft terms of division;

(b) the annual accounts and annual reports of the companies involved in the division for the preceding three financial years;

(c) where applicable, an accounting statement drawn up as at a date which shall not be earlier than the first day of the third month preceding the date of the draft terms of division, if the latest annual accounts relate to a financial year which ended more than six months before that date;

(d) where applicable, the reports of the administrative or management bodies of the companies involved in the division provided for in Article 141(1);

(e) where applicable, the reports provided for in Article 142.

For the purposes of point (c) of the first subparagraph, an accounting statement shall not be required if the company publishes a half-yearly financial report in accordance with Article 5 of Directive 2004/109/EC and makes it available to shareholders in accordance with this paragraph.

2. The accounting statement provided for in point (c) of paragraph 1 shall be drawn up using the same methods and the same layout as the last annual balance sheet.

However, the laws of a Member State may provide that:

(a) it shall not be necessary to take a fresh physical inventory;

(b) the valuations shown in the last balance sheet shall be altered only to reflect entries in the books of account; the following shall nevertheless be taken into account:

 (i) interim depreciation and provisions,

 (ii) material changes in actual value not shown in the books.

3. Every shareholder shall be entitled to obtain, on request and free of charge, full or, if so desired, partial copies of the documents referred to in paragraph 1.

Where a shareholder has consented to the use by the company of electronic means for conveying information, such copies may be provided by electronic mail.

4. A company shall be exempt from the requirement to make the documents referred to in paragraph 1 available at its registered office if, for a continuous period beginning at least one month before the date fixed for the general meeting which is to decide on the draft terms of division and ending not earlier than the conclusion of that meeting, it makes them available on its website. Member States shall not subject that exemption to requirements or constraints other than those which are necessary in order to ensure the security of the website and the authenticity of the documents, and may impose such requirements or constraints only to the extent that they are proportionate in order to achieve those objectives.

Paragraph 3 shall not apply if the website gives shareholders the possibility, throughout the period referred to in the first subparagraph of this paragraph, of downloading and printing the documents referred to in paragraph 1. However, in that case Member States may provide that the company is to make those documents available at its registered office for consultation by the shareholders.

Member States may require companies to maintain the information on their website for a specific period after the general meeting. Member States may determine the consequences of temporary disruption of access to the website caused by technical or other factors.

[11.563]

Article 144 Simplified formalities

1. Neither an examination of the draft terms of division nor an expert report as provided for in Article 142(1) shall be required if all the shareholders and the holders of other securities conferring the right to vote of each of the companies involved in the division have so agreed.

2. Member States may permit the non-application of Article 141 and points (c) and (d) of Article 143(1) if all the shareholders and the holders of other securities conferring the right to vote of each of the companies involved in the division have so agreed.

[11.564]

Article 145 Protection of employees' rights

Protection of the rights of the employees of each of the companies involved in a division shall be regulated in accordance with Directive 2001/23/EC.

[11.565]

Article 146 Protection of the interests of creditors of companies involved in a division; joint and several liability of the recipient companies

1. The laws of Member States shall provide for an adequate system of protection for the interests of the creditors of the companies involved in a division whose claims antedate publication of the draft terms of division and have not yet fallen due at the time of such publication.

2. For the purpose of paragraph 1, the laws of the Member States shall at least provide that such creditors shall be entitled to obtain adequate safeguards where the financial situation of the company being divided, and that of the company to which the obligation is to be transferred in accordance with the draft terms of division, make such protection necessary, and where those creditors do not already have such safeguards.

Member States shall lay down the conditions for the protection provided for in paragraph 1 and in the first subparagraph of this paragraph. In any event, Member States shall ensure that the creditors are authorised to apply to the appropriate administrative or judicial authority for adequate safeguards provided that they can credibly demonstrate that due to the division the satisfaction of their claims is at stake and that no adequate safeguards have been obtained from the company.

3. In so far as a creditor of the company to which the obligation has been transferred in accordance with the draft terms of division has not obtained satisfaction, the recipient companies shall be jointly and severally liable for that obligation. Member States may limit that liability to the net assets allocated to each of those companies other than the one to which the obligation has been transferred. However, they need not apply this paragraph where the division operation is subject to the supervision of a judicial authority in accordance with Article 157 and a majority in number representing three-quarters in value of the creditors or any class of creditors of the company being divided have agreed to forego such joint and several liability at a meeting held pursuant to point (c) of Article 157(l).

4. Article 99(3) shall apply.

5. Without prejudice to the rules governing the collective exercise of their rights, Paragraphs 1 to 4 shall apply to the debenture holders of the companies involved in the division except where the division has been approved by a meeting of the debenture holders, if such a meeting is provided for under national laws, or by the debenture holders individually.

6. Member States may provide that the recipient companies shall be jointly and severally liable for the obligations of the company being divided. In such case they need not apply Paragraphs 1 to 5.

7. Where a Member State combines the system of creditor protection set out in Paragraphs 1 to 5 with the joint and several liability of the recipient companies as referred to in paragraph 6, it may limit such joint and several liability to the net assets allocated to each of those companies.

[11.566]

Article 147 Protection of holders of securities, other than shares, to which special rights are attached

Holders of securities, other than shares, to which special rights are attached, shall be given rights in the recipient companies against which such securities may be invoked in accordance with the draft terms of division, at least equivalent to the rights they possessed in the company being divided, unless the alteration of those rights has been approved by a meeting of the holders of such securities, if such a meeting is provided for under national laws, or by the holders of those securities individually, or unless the holders are entitled to have their securities repurchased.

[11.567]

Article 148 Drawing up and certification of documents in due legal form

Where the laws of a Member State do not provide for judicial or administrative preventive supervision of the legality of divisions or where such supervision does not extend to all the legal acts required for a division, Article 102 shall apply.

[11.568]

Article 149 Date on which a division takes effect

The laws of Member States shall determine the date on which a division takes effect.

[11.569]

Article 150 Publication formalities

1. A division shall be published in the manner prescribed by the laws of each Member State in accordance with Article 16 in respect of each of the companies involved in a division.

2. Any recipient company may itself carry out the publication formalities relating to the company being divided.

[11.570]

Article 151 Consequences of a division

1. A division shall have the following consequences *ipso jure* and simultaneously:
  (a) the transfer, both as between the company being divided and the recipient companies and as regards third parties, to each of the recipient companies of all the assets and liabilities of the company being divided; such transfer shall take effect with the assets and liabilities being divided in accordance with the allocation laid down in the draft terms of division or in Article 137(3);
  (b) the shareholders of the company being divided become shareholders of one or more of the recipient companies in accordance with the allocation laid down in the draft terms of division;
  (c) the company being divided ceases to exist.
2. No shares in a recipient company shall be exchanged for shares held in the company being divided either:
  (a) by that recipient company itself or by a person acting in his own name but on its behalf; or
  (b) by the company being divided itself or by a person acting in his own name but on its behalf.
3. The foregoing shall not affect the laws of Member States which require the completion of special formalities for the transfer of certain assets, rights and obligations by a company being divided to be effective as against third parties. The recipient company or companies to which such assets, rights or obligations are transferred in accordance with the draft terms of division or with Article 137(3) may carry out those formalities themselves; however, the laws of Member States may permit a company being divided to continue to carry out those formalities for a limited period which may not, save in exceptional circumstances, be fixed at more than six months from the date on which the division takes effect.

[11.571]

Article 152 Civil liability of members of the administrative or management bodies of a company being divided

The laws of Member States shall at least lay down rules governing the civil liability of members of the administrative or management bodies of a company being divided towards the shareholders of that company in respect of misconduct on the part of members of those bodies in preparing and implementing the division and the civil liability of the experts responsible for drawing up for that company the report provided for in Article 142 in respect of misconduct on the part of those experts in the performance of their duties.

[11.572]

Article 153 Conditions for nullity of a division

1. The laws of Member States may lay down nullity rules for divisions in accordance with the following conditions only:
  (a) nullity must be ordered in a court judgment;
  (b) divisions which have taken effect pursuant to Article 149 are declared void only if there has been no judicial or administrative preventive supervision of their legality, or if they have not been drawn up and certified in due legal form, or if it is shown that the decision of the general meeting is void or voidable under national law;
  (c) nullification proceedings are not initiated more than six months after the date on which the division becomes effective as against the person alleging nullity or if the situation has been rectified;
  (d) where it is possible to remedy a defect liable to render a division void, the competent court grants the companies involved a period of time within which to rectify the situation;
  (e) a judgment declaring a division void is published in the manner prescribed by the laws of each Member State in accordance with Article 16;
  (f) where the laws of a Member State permit a third party to challenge such a judgment, he does so only within six months of publication of the judgment in the manner prescribed by Chapter III of Title I;
  (g) a judgment declaring a division void does not of itself affect the validity of obligations owed by or in relation to the recipient companies which arose before the judgment was published and after the date referred to in Article 149;
  (h) each of the recipient companies is liable for its obligations arising after the date on which the division took effect and before the date on which the decision pronouncing the nullity of the division was published. The company being divided shall also be liable for such obligations; Member States may provide that this liability be limited to the share of net assets transferred to the recipient company on whose account such obligations arose.
2. By way of derogation from point (a) of paragraph 1 of this Article, the laws of a Member State may also provide for the nullity of a division to be ordered by an administrative authority if an appeal against such a decision lies to a court. point (b) and points (d) to (h) of paragraph 1 of this Article shall apply by analogy to the administrative authority. Such nullification proceedings may not be initiated more than six months after the date referred to in Article 149.
3. The foregoing shall not affect the laws of the Member States on the nullity of a division pronounced following any supervision of legality.

[11.573]

Article 154 Exemption from the requirement of approval by the general meeting of the company being divided

Without prejudice to Article 140, Member States shall not require approval of the division by the general meeting of the company being divided if the recipient companies together hold all the shares of the company being divided and all other securities conferring the right to vote at general meetings of the company being divided, and the following conditions are fulfilled:
  (a) each of the companies involved in the operation carries out the publication provided for in Article 138 at least one month before the operation takes effect;
  (b) at least one month before the operation takes effect, all shareholders of companies involved in the operation are entitled to inspect the documents specified in Article 143(1), at their company's registered office;

(c) where a general meeting of the company being divided, required for the approval of the division, is not summoned, the information provided for in Article 141(3) covers any material change in the asset and liabilities after the date of preparation of the draft terms of division.

For the purposes of point (b) of the first paragraph, Article 143(2), (3) and (4) and Article 144 shall apply.

SECTION 3 DIVISION BY THE FORMATION OF NEW COMPANIES

[11.574]
Article 155 Definition of a 'division by the formation of new companies'

1. For the purposes of this Chapter, 'division by the formation of new companies' means the operation whereby, after being wound up without going into liquidation, a company transfers to more than one newly-formed company all its assets and liabilities in exchange for the allocation to the shareholders of the company being divided of shares in the recipient companies, and possibly a cash payment not exceeding 10% of the nominal value of the shares allocated or, where they have no nominal value, of their accounting par value.
2. Article 90(2) shall apply.

[11.575]
Article 156 Application of rules on divisions by acquisition

1. Articles 137, 138, 139, and 141, Article 142(1) and (2) and Articles 143 to 153 shall apply, without prejudice to Articles 11 and 12, to division by the formation of new companies. For this purpose, the term 'companies involved in a division' shall refer to the company being divided and the term 'recipient companies' shall refer to each of the new companies.
2. In addition to the information specified in Article 137(2), the draft terms of division shall indicate the form, name and registered office of each of the new companies.
3. The draft terms of division and, if they are contained in a separate document, the memorandum or draft memorandum of association and the articles or draft articles of association of each of the new companies shall be approved at a general meeting of the company being divided.
4. Member States shall not impose the requirements set out in Articles 141 and 142 and in points (c), (d) and (e) of Article 143(1) where the shares in each of the new companies are allocated to the shareholders of the company being divided in proportion to their rights in the capital of that company.

SECTION 4 DIVISIONS UNDER THE SUPERVISION OF A JUDICIAL AUTHORITY

[11.576]
Article 157 Divisions under the supervision of a judicial authority

1. Member States may apply paragraph 2 where division operations are subject to the supervision of a judicial authority having the power:
   (a) to call a general meeting of the shareholders of the company being divided in order to decide upon the division;
   (b) to ensure that the shareholders of each of the companies involved in a division have received or can obtain at least the documents referred to in Article 143 in time to examine them before the date of the general meeting of their company called to decide upon the division. Where a Member State makes use of the option provided for in Article 140, the period shall be long enough for the shareholders of the recipient companies to be able to exercise the rights conferred on them by that Article;
   (c) to call any meeting of creditors of each of the companies involved in a division in order to decide upon the division;
   (d) to ensure that the creditors of each of the companies involved in a division have received or can obtain at least the draft terms of division in time to examine them before the date referred to in point (b);
   (e) to approve the draft terms of division.
2. Where the judicial authority establishes that the conditions referred to in points (b) and (d) of paragraph 1 have been fulfilled and that no prejudice would be caused to shareholders or creditors, it may relieve the companies involved in the division from applying:
   (a) Article 138, on condition that the adequate system of protection of the interest of the creditors referred to in Article 146(1) covers all claims regardless of their date;
   (b) the conditions referred to in points (a) and (b) of Article 140 where a Member State makes use of the option provided for in Article 140;
   (c) Article 143, as regards the period and the manner prescribed for the inspection of the documents referred to therein.

SECTION 5 OTHER OPERATIONS TREATED AS DIVISIONS

[11.577]
Article 158 Divisions with cash payment exceeding 10%

Where, in the case of one of the operations specified in Article 135, the laws of a Member State permit the cash payment to exceed 10%, Sections 2, 3 and 4 of this Chapter shall apply.

[11.578]
Article 159 Divisions without the company being divided ceasing to exist

Where the laws of a Member State permit one of the operations specified in Article 135 without the company being divided ceasing to exist, Sections 2, 3 and 4 of this Chapter shall apply, except for point (c) of Article 151(1).

SECTION 6 APPLICATION ARRANGEMENTS

[11.579]
Article 160 Transitional provisions

Member States need not apply Articles 146 and 147 as regards the holders of convertible debentures and other securities convertible into shares if, at the time when the provisions referred to in Article 26(1) or (2) of Directive

82/891/EEC came into force, the position of those holders in the event of a division had previously been determined by the conditions of issue.

[CHAPTER IV CROSS-BORDER DIVISIONS OF LIMITED LIABILITY COMPANIES

[11.580]

Article 160a Scope

1. This Chapter shall apply to cross-border divisions of limited liability companies formed in accordance with the law of a Member State and having their registered office, central administration or principal place of business within the Union, provided that at least two of the limited liability companies involved in the division are governed by the laws of different Member States (hereinafter referred to as "cross-border division").

2. Notwithstanding point 4 of Article 160b, this Chapter shall also apply to cross-border divisions where the law of at least one of the Member States concerned allows the cash payment referred to in points (a) and (b) of point 4 of Article 160b to exceed 10% of the nominal value, or, in the absence of a nominal value, 10% of the accounting par value of the securities or shares representing the capital of the recipient companies.

3. This Chapter shall not apply to cross-border divisions involving a company the object of which is the collective investment of capital provided by the public, which operates on the principle of risk-spreading and the units of which are, at the holders' request, repurchased or redeemed, directly or indirectly, out of the assets of that company. Action taken by such a company to ensure that the stock exchange value of its units does not vary significantly from its net asset value shall be regarded as equivalent to such repurchase or redemption.

4. Member States shall ensure that this Chapter does not apply to companies in either of the following circumstances:
- (a) the company is in liquidation and has begun to distribute assets to its members;
- [(b) the company is subject to resolution tools, powers and mechanisms provided for in Title IV of Directive 2014/59/EU or in Title V of Regulation (EU) 2021/23.]

5. Member States may decide not to apply this Chapter to companies which are:
- (a) the subject of insolvency proceedings or subject to preventive restructuring frameworks;
- (b) the subject of liquidation proceedings other than those referred to in point (a) of paragraph 4; or
- [(c) the subject of crisis prevention measures as defined in point (101) of Article 2(1) of Directive 2014/59/EU or in point (48) of Article 2 of Regulation (EU) 2021/23.]]

NOTES

Chapter IV (Arts 160a–160U) was inserted by European Parliament and Council Directive 2019/2121/EU, Art 1(23), as form 1 January 2020. Note that the 2019 Directive has a transposition date of 31 January 2023.

Para 4: point (b) substituted by European Parliament and Council Regulation 2021/23/EU, Art 92(5)(a), as from 12 August 2022.

Para 5: point (c) substituted by European Parliament and Council Regulation 2021/23/EU, Art 92(5)(b), as from 12 August 2022.

[11.581]

[Article 160b Definitions

For the purposes of this Chapter:

(1) "company" means a limited liability company of a type listed in Annex II;

(2) "company being divided" means a company which, in the process of a cross-border division, transfers all its assets and liabilities to two or more companies in the case of a full division, or transfers part of its assets and liabilities to one or more companies in the case of a partial division or division by separation;

(3) "recipient company" means a company newly formed in the course of a cross-border division;

(4) "division" means an operation whereby:
- (a) a company being divided, on being dissolved without going into liquidation, transfers all its assets and liabilities to two or more recipient companies, in exchange for the issue to the members of the company being divided of securities or shares in the recipient companies and, if applicable, a cash payment not exceeding 10% of the nominal value, or, in the absence of a nominal value, a cash payment not exceeding 10% of the accounting par value of those securities or shares ("full division");
- (b) a company being divided transfers part of its assets and liabilities to one or more recipient companies, in exchange for the issue to the members of the company being divided of securities or shares in the recipient companies, in the company being divided or in both the recipient companies and the company being divided, and, if applicable, a cash payment not exceeding 10% of the nominal value, or, in the absence of a nominal value, a cash payment not exceeding 10% of the accounting par value of those securities or shares ("partial division"); or
- (c) a company being divided transfers part of its assets and liabilities to one or more recipient companies, in exchange for the issue to the company being divided of securities or shares in the recipient companies ("division by separation").]

NOTES

Inserted as noted to Art 160a at **[11.580]**.

[11.582]

[Article 160c Procedures and formalities

In compliance with Union law, the law of the Member State of the company being divided shall govern those parts of the procedures and formalities to be complied with in connection with the cross-border division in order to obtain the pre-division certificate, and the laws of the Member States of the recipient companies shall govern those parts of the procedures and formalities to be complied with following receipt of the pre-division certificate.]

NOTES

Inserted as noted to Art 160a at **[11.580]**.

[11.583]

[Article 160d Draft terms of cross-border divisions

The administrative or management body of the company being divided shall draw up the draft terms of a cross-border division. The draft terms of a cross-border division shall include at least the following particulars:

(a) the legal form and name of the company being divided and the location of its registered office, and the legal form and name proposed for the new company or companies resulting from the cross-border division and the proposed location of their registered offices;
(b) the ratio applicable to the exchange of securities or shares representing the companies' capital and the amount of any cash payment, where appropriate;
(c) the terms for the allotment of securities or shares representing the capital of the recipient companies or of the company being divided;
(d) the proposed indicative timetable for the cross-border division;
(e) the likely repercussions of the cross-border division on employment;
(f) the date from which the holding of securities or shares representing the companies' capital will entitle the holders to share in profits, and any special conditions affecting that entitlement;
(g) the date or dates from which the transactions of the company being divided will be treated for accounting purposes as being those of the recipient companies;
(h) any special advantages granted to members of the administrative, management, supervisory or controlling bodies of the company being divided;
(i) the rights conferred by the recipient companies on members of the company being divided enjoying special rights or on holders of securities other than shares representing the divided company capital, or the measures proposed concerning them;
(j) the instruments of constitution of the recipient companies, where applicable, and the statutes if they are contained in a separate instrument, and any changes to the instrument of constitution of the company being divided in the case of a partial division or a division by separation;
(k) where appropriate, information on the procedures by which arrangements for the involvement of employees in the definition of their rights to participation in the recipient companies are determined pursuant to Article 160l;
(l) a precise description of the assets and liabilities of the company being divided and a statement of how those assets and liabilities are to be allocated between the recipient companies, or are to be retained by the company being divided in the case of a partial division or a division by separation, including provisions on the treatment of assets or liabilities not explicitly allocated in the draft terms of cross-border division, such as assets or liabilities which are unknown on the date on which the draft terms of cross-border division are drawn up;
(m) information on the evaluation of the assets and liabilities which are to be allocated to each company involved in the cross-border division;
(n) the date of the accounts of the company being divided used to establish the conditions of the cross-border division;
(o) where appropriate, the allocation to the members of the company being divided of shares and securities in the recipient companies, in the company being divided or in both, and the criterion upon which such allocation is based;
(p) details of the offer of cash compensation for members in accordance with Article 160i;
(q) any safeguards offered to creditors, such as guarantees or pledges.]

NOTES

Inserted as noted to Art 160a at **[11.580]**.

[11.584]

[Article 160e Report of the administrative or management body for members and employees

1. The administrative or management body of the company being divided shall draw up a report for members and employees, explaining and justifying the legal and economic aspects of the cross-border division, as well as explaining the implications of the cross-border division for employees.

It shall, in particular, explain the implications of the cross-border division for the future business of the companies.

2. The report shall also include a section for members and a section for employees.

The company may decide either to draw up one report containing those two sections or to draw up separate reports for members and employees, respectively, containing the relevant section.

3. The section of the report for members shall, in particular, explain the following:
(a) the cash compensation and the method used to determine the cash compensation;
(b) the share exchange ratio and the method or methods used to arrive at the share exchange ratio, where applicable;
(c) the implications of the cross-border division for members;
(d) the rights and remedies available to members in accordance with Article 160i.

4. The section of the report for members shall not be required where all the members of the company have agreed to waive that requirement. Member States may exclude single-member companies from the provisions of this Article.

5. The section of the report for employees shall, in particular, explain the following:
(a) the implications of the cross-border division for employment relationships, as well as, where applicable, any measures for safeguarding those relationships;
(b) any material changes to the applicable conditions of employment or to the location of the company's places of business;
(c) how the factors set out in points (a) and (b) affect any subsidiaries of the company.

6. The report or reports shall be made available in any case electronically, together with the draft terms of the cross-border division, if available, to the members and to the representatives of the employees of the company being divided or, where there are no such representatives, to the employees themselves, not less than six weeks before the date of the general meeting referred to in Article 160h.

7. Where the administrative or management body of the company being divided receives an opinion on the information referred to in paragraphs 1 and 5 in good time from the representatives of the employees or, where there are no such representatives, from the employees themselves, as provided for under national law, the members shall be informed thereof and that opinion shall be appended to the report.

8. The section of the report for employees shall not be required where a company being divided and its subsidiaries, if any, have no employees other than those who form part of the administrative or management body.

9. Where the section of the report for members referred to in paragraph 3 is waived in accordance with paragraph 4 and the section for employees referred to in paragraph 5 is not required under paragraph 8, the report shall not be required.

10. Paragraphs 1 to 9 of this Article shall be without prejudice to the applicable information and consultation rights and procedures provided for at national level following the transposition of Directives 2002/14/EC and 2009/38/EC.]

NOTES

Inserted as noted to Art 160a at **[11.580]**.

[11.585]

[Article 160f Independent expert report

1. Member States shall ensure that an independent expert examines the draft terms of the cross-border division and draws up a report for members. That report shall be made available to the members not less than one month before the date of the general meeting referred to in Article 160h. Depending on the law of the Member State, the expert may be a natural or legal person.

2. The report referred to in paragraph 1 shall in any case include the expert's opinion as to whether the cash compensation and the share exchange ratio are adequate. When assessing the cash compensation, the expert shall consider any market price of the shares in the company being divided prior to the announcement of the division proposal or the value of the company excluding the effect of the proposed division, as determined in accordance with generally accepted valuation methods. The report shall at least:

(a) indicate the method or methods used to determine the cash compensation proposed;
(b) indicate the method or methods used to arrive at the share exchange ratio proposed;
(c) state whether the method or methods are adequate for the assessment of the cash compensation and the share exchange ratio, indicate the value arrived at using such methods and give an opinion on the relative importance attributed to those methods in arriving at the value decided on; and
(d) describe any special valuation difficulties which have arisen.

The expert shall be entitled to obtain from the company being divided all information necessary for the discharge of the duties of the expert.

3. Neither an examination of the draft terms of cross-border division by an independent expert nor an independent expert report shall be required if all the members of the company being divided have so agreed.

Member States may exclude single-member companies from the application of this Article.]

NOTES

Inserted as noted to Art 160a at **[11.580]**.

[11.586]

[Article 160g Disclosure

1. Member States shall ensure that the following documents are disclosed by the company and made publicly available in the register of the Member State of the company being divided, at least one month before the date of the general meeting referred to in Article 160h:

(a) the draft terms of the cross-border division; and
(b) a notice informing the members, creditors and representatives of the employees of the company being divided, or, where there are no such representatives, the employees themselves, that they may submit to the company, at the latest five working days before the date of the general meeting, comments concerning the draft terms of the cross-border division.

Member States may require that the independent expert report be disclosed and made publicly available in the register.

Member States shall ensure that the company is able to exclude confidential information from the disclosure of the independent expert report.

The documents disclosed in accordance with this paragraph shall be also accessible through the system of interconnection of registers.

2. Member States may exempt a company being divided from the disclosure requirement referred to in paragraph 1 of this Article where, for a continuous period beginning at least one month before the date fixed for the general meeting referred to in Article 160h and ending not earlier than the conclusion of that meeting, that company makes the documents referred to in paragraph 1 of this Article available on its website free of charge to the public.

However, Member States shall not subject that exemption to any requirements or constraints other than those which are necessary to ensure the security of the website and the authenticity of the documents, and which are proportionate to achieving those objectives.

3. Where the company being divided makes the draft terms of the cross-border division available in accordance with paragraph 2 of this Article, it shall submit to the register, at least one month before the date of the general meeting referred to in Article 160h, the following information:

(a) the legal form and name of the company being divided and the location of its registered office and the legal form and name proposed for the newly created company or companies resulting from the cross-border division and the proposed location of their registered office;
(b) the register in which the documents referred to in Article 14 are filed in respect of the company being divided, and its registration number in that register;
(c) an indication of the arrangements made for the exercise of the rights of creditors, employees and members; and

(d) details of the website from which the draft terms of the cross-border division, the notice referred to in paragraph 1, the independent expert report and complete information on the arrangements referred to in point (c) of this paragraph may be obtained online and free of charge.

The register shall make publicly available the information referred to in points (a) to (d) of the first subparagraph.

4. Member States shall ensure that the requirements referred to in paragraphs 1 and 3 can be fulfilled fully online without the necessity for the applicants to appear in person before any competent authority in the Member State concerned, in accordance with the relevant provisions of Chapter III of Title I.

5. Member States may require, in addition to the disclosure referred to in paragraphs 1, 2 and 3 of this Article, that the draft terms of the cross-border division, or the information referred to in paragraph 3 of this Article, be published in their national gazette or through a central electronic platform in accordance with Article 16(3). In that instance, Member States shall ensure that the register transmits the relevant information to the national gazette or to a central electronic platform.

6. Member States shall ensure that the documentation referred to in paragraph 1 or the information referred to in paragraph 3 is accessible to the public free of charge through the system of interconnection of registers.

Member States shall further ensure that any fees charged to the company by the registers for the disclosure referred to in paragraphs 1 and 3 and, where applicable, for the publication referred to in paragraph 5 do not exceed the recovery of the cost of providing such services.]

NOTES

Inserted as noted to Art 160a at **[11.580]**.

[11.587]

[Article 160h Approval by the general meeting

1. After taking note of the reports referred to in Articles 160e and 160f, where applicable, employees' opinions submitted in accordance with Article 160e and comments submitted in accordance with Article 160g, the general meeting of the company being divided shall decide, by means of a resolution, whether to approve the draft terms of cross-border division and whether to adapt the instrument of constitution, and the statutes if they are contained in a separate instrument.

2. The general meeting of the company being divided may reserve the right to make implementation of the cross-border division conditional on express ratification by it of the arrangements referred to in Article 160l.

3. Member States shall ensure that the approval of the draft terms of the cross-border division, and of any amendment to those draft terms, requires a majority of not less than two thirds but not more than 90% of the votes attached either to the shares or to the subscribed capital represented at the general meeting. In any event, the voting threshold shall not be higher than that provided for in national law for the approval of cross-border mergers.

4. Where a clause in the draft terms of the cross-border division or any amendment to the instrument of constitution of the company being divided leads to an increase of the economic obligations of a member towards the company or third parties, Member States may require, in such specific circumstances, that such clause or the amendment to the instrument of constitution of the company being divided be approved by the member concerned, provided that such member is unable to exercise the rights laid down in Article 160i.

5. Member States shall ensure that the approval of the cross-border division by the general meeting cannot be challenged solely on the following grounds:

(a) the share exchange ratio referred to in point (b) of Article 160d has been inadequately set;

(b) the cash compensation referred to in point (p) of Article 160d has been inadequately set; or

(c) the information given with regard to the share exchange ratio referred to in point (a) or the cash compensation referred to in point (b) did not comply with the legal requirements.]

NOTES

Inserted as noted to Art 160a at **[11.580]**.

[11.588]

[Article 160i Protection of members

1. Member States shall ensure that at least the members of a company being divided who voted against the approval of the draft terms of the cross-border division have the right to dispose of their shares for adequate cash compensation, under the conditions laid down in paragraphs 2 to 6, provided that, as a result of the cross-border division, they would acquire shares in the recipient companies which would be governed by the law of a Member State other than the Member State of the company being divided.

Member States may also provide for other members of the company being divided to have the right referred to in the first subparagraph.

Member States may require that express opposition to the draft terms of the cross-border division, the intention of members to exercise their right to dispose of their shares, or both, be appropriately documented at the latest at the general meeting referred to in Article 160h. Member States may allow the recording of opposition to the draft terms of the cross-border division to be considered proper documentation of a negative vote.

2. Member States shall establish the period within which the members referred to in paragraph 1 have to declare to the company being divided their decision to exercise the right to dispose of their shares. That period shall not exceed one month after the general meeting referred to in Article 160h. Member States shall ensure that the company being divided provides an electronic address for receiving that declaration electronically.

3. Member States shall further establish the period within which the cash compensation specified in the draft terms of the cross-border division is to be paid. That period shall not end later than two months after the cross- border division takes effect in accordance with Article 160q.

4. Member States shall ensure that any members who have declared their decision to exercise the right to dispose of their shares, but who consider that the cash compensation offered by the company being divided has not been adequately set, are entitled to claim additional cash compensation before the competent authority or body mandated under national law. Member States shall establish a time limit for the claim for additional cash compensation.

Member States may provide that the final decision to provide additional cash compensation is valid for all members of the company being divided who have declared their decision to exercise the right to dispose of their shares in accordance with paragraph 2.

5. Member States shall ensure that the law of the Member State of a company being divided governs the rights referred to in paragraphs 1 to 4 and that the exclusive competence to resolve any disputes relating to those rights lies within the jurisdiction of that Member State.

6. Member States shall ensure that members of the company being divided who did not have or did not exercise the right to dispose of their shares, but who consider that the share-exchange ratio set out in the draft terms of the cross-border division is inadequate, may dispute that ratio and claim a cash payment. Proceedings in that regard shall be initiated before the competent authority or body mandated under the law of the Member State to which the company being divided is subject, within the time limit laid down in that national law and such proceedings shall not prevent the registration of the cross-border division. The decision shall be binding on the recipient companies and, in the event of a partial division, also on the company being divided.

7. Member States may also provide that the recipient company concerned and, in the event of a partial division, also the company being divided, can provide shares or other compensation instead of a cash payment.]

NOTES

Inserted as noted to Art 160a at **[11.580]**.

[11.589]

[Article 160j Protection of creditors

1. Member States shall provide for an adequate system of protection of the interests of creditors whose claims antedate the disclosure of the draft terms of the cross-border division and have not fallen due at the time of such disclosure.

Member States shall ensure that creditors who are dissatisfied with the safeguards offered in the draft terms of the cross-border division, as provided for in point (q) of Article 160d, may apply, within three months of the disclosure of the draft terms of cross-border division referred to in Article 160g, to the appropriate administrative or judicial authority for adequate safeguards, provided that such creditors can credibly demonstrate that, due to the cross-border division, the satisfaction of their claims is at stake and that they have not obtained adequate safeguards from the company.

Member States shall ensure that the safeguards are conditional on the cross-border division taking effect in accordance with Article 160q.

2. Where a creditor of the company being divided does not obtain satisfaction from the company to which the liability is allocated, the other recipient companies, and in the case of a partial division or a division by separation, the company being divided, shall be jointly and severally liable with the company to which the liability is allocated for that obligation. However, the maximum amount of joint and several liability of any company involved in the division shall be limited to the value, at the date on which the division takes effect, of the net assets allocated to that company.

3. Member States may require that the administrative or management body of the company being divided provide a declaration that accurately reflects its current financial status at a date no earlier than one month before the disclosure of that declaration. The declaration shall state that, on the basis of the information available to the administrative or management body of the company being divided at the date of that declaration, and after having made reasonable enquiries, that administrative or management body is unaware of any reason why any recipient company and, in the case of a partial division, the company being divided, would, after the division takes effect, be unable to meet the liabilities allocated to them under the draft terms of the cross-border division when those liabilities fall due. The declaration shall be disclosed together with the draft terms of the cross-border division in accordance with Article 160g.

4. Paragraphs 1, 2 and 3 shall be without prejudice to the application of the law of the Member State of the company being divided concerning the satisfaction or securing of pecuniary or non-pecuniary obligations due to public bodies.]

NOTES

Inserted as noted to Art 160a at **[11.580]**.

[11.590]

[Article 160k Employee information and consultation

1. Member States shall ensure that employees' rights to information and consultation are respected in relation to the cross-border division and are exercised in accordance with the legal framework provided for in Directive 2002/14/EC, and Directive 2001/23/EC where the cross-border division is considered to be a transfer of an undertaking within the meaning of Directive 2001/23/EC, and, where applicable for Community-scale undertakings or Community-scale groups of undertakings, in accordance with Directive 2009/38/EC. Member States may decide that employees' rights to information and consultation apply with respect to the employees of companies other than those referred to in Article 3(1) of Directive 2002/14/EC.

2. Notwithstanding Article 160e(7) and point (b) of Article 160g(1), Member States shall ensure that employees' rights to information and consultation are respected, at least before the draft terms of the cross-border division or the report referred to in Article 160e are decided upon, whichever is earlier, in such a way that a reasoned response is given to the employees before the general meeting referred to in Article 160h.

3. Without prejudice to any provisions or practices in force more favourable to employees, Member States shall determine the practical arrangements for exercising the right to information and consultation in accordance with Article 4 of Directive 2002/14/EC.]

NOTES

Inserted as noted to Art 160a at **[11.580]**.

[11.591]

[Article 160l Employee participation

1. Without prejudice to paragraph 2, each recipient company shall be subject to the rules in force concerning employee participation, if any, in the Member State where it has its registered office.

2. However, the rules in force concerning employee participation, if any, in the Member State where the company resulting from the cross-border division has its registered office shall not apply where the company being divided has, in the six months prior to the disclosure of the draft terms of the cross-border division, an average number of employees equivalent to four fifths of the applicable threshold, as laid down in the law of the Member State of the company being divided, for triggering the participation of employees within the meaning of point (k) of Article 2 of Directive 2001/86/EC, or where the national law applicable to each of the recipient companies does not:

(a) provide for at least the same level of employee participation as operated in the company being divided prior to its cross-border division, measured by reference to the proportion of employee representatives among the members of the administrative or supervisory body or their committees or of the management group which covers the profit units of the company, subject to employee representation; or
(b) provide for employees of establishments of the recipient companies that are situated in other Member States the same entitlement to exercise participation rights as is enjoyed by those employees employed in the Member State where the recipient company has its registered office.

3. In the cases referred to in paragraph 2 of this Article, the participation of employees in the companies resulting from the cross-border division and their involvement in the definition of such rights shall be regulated by the Member States, mutatis mutandis and subject to paragraphs 4 to 7 of this Article, in accordance with the principles and procedures laid down in Article 12(2) and (4) of Regulation (EC) No 2157/2001 and the following provisions of Directive 2001/86/EC:

(a) Article 3(1), points (a)(i) and (b) of Article 3(2), Article 3(3), the first two sentences of Article 3(4), and Article 3(5) and (7);
(b) Article 4(1), points (a), (g) and (h) of Article 4(2), and Article 4(3) and (4);
(c) Article 5;
(d) Article 6;
(e) Article 7(1), with the exception of the second indent of point (b);
(f) Articles 8, 10, 11 and 12; and
(g) point (a) of Part 3 of the Annex.

4. When regulating the principles and procedures referred to in paragraph 3, Member States:

(a) shall confer on the special negotiating body the right to decide, by a majority of two thirds of its members representing at least two thirds of the employees, not to open negotiations or to terminate negotiations already opened and to rely on the rules on participation in force in the Member States of each of the recipient companies;
(b) may, in the case where, following prior negotiations, standard rules for participation apply and notwithstanding such rules, decide to limit the proportion of employee representatives in the administrative body of the recipient companies. However, if, in the company being divided, employee representatives constituted at least one third of the administrative or supervisory body, the limitation may never result in a lower proportion of employee representatives in the administrative body than one third;
(c) shall ensure that the rules on employee participation that applied prior to the cross-border division continue to apply until the date of application of any subsequently agreed rules or, in the absence of agreed rules, until the application of standard rules in accordance with point (a) of Part 3 of the Annex to Directive 2001/86/EC.

5. The extension of participation rights to employees of the recipient companies employed in other Member States, as referred to in point (b) of paragraph 2, shall not entail any obligation for Member States which choose to do so to take those employees into account when calculating the size of workforce thresholds giving rise to participation rights under national law.

6. Where any of the recipient companies is to be governed by an employee participation system in accordance with the rules referred to in paragraph 2, that company shall be obliged to take a legal form allowing for the exercise of participation rights.

7. Where the recipient company is operating under an employee participation system, that company shall be obliged to take measures to ensure that employees' participation rights are protected in the event of any subsequent conversion, merger or division, be it cross-border or domestic, for a period of four years after the cross-border division has taken effect, by applying, mutatis mutandis, the rules laid down in paragraphs 1 to 6.

8. A company shall communicate to its employees or their representatives the outcome of the negotiations concerning employee participation without undue delay.]

NOTES

Inserted as noted to Art 160a at **[11.580]**.

[11.592]

[Article 160m Pre-division certificate

1. Member States shall designate the court, notary or other authority or authorities competent to scrutinise the legality of cross-border divisions as regards those parts of the procedure which are governed by the law of the Member State of the company being divided, and to issue a pre-division certificate attesting to compliance with all relevant conditions and to the proper completion of all procedures and formalities in that Member State ("the competent authority").

Such completion of procedures and formalities may comprise the satisfaction or securing of pecuniary or non-pecuniary obligations due to public bodies or compliance with specific sectoral requirements, including securing obligations arising from ongoing proceedings.

2. Member States shall ensure that the application to obtain a pre-division certificate by the company being divided is accompanied by the following:

(a) the draft terms of the cross-border division;
(b) the report and the appended opinion, if any, referred to in Article 160e, as well as the report referred to in Article 160f, where they are available;
(c) any comments submitted in accordance with Article 160g(1); and
(d) information on the approval by the general meeting referred to in Article 160h.

3. Member States may require that the application to obtain a pre-division certificate by the company being divided is accompanied by additional information, such as, in particular:
  (a) the number of employees at the time of the drawing up of the draft terms of the cross-border division;
  (b) the existence of subsidiaries and their respective geographical location;
  (c) information regarding the satisfaction of obligations due to public bodies by the company being divided.

For the purposes of this paragraph, competent authorities may request such information, if not provided by the company being divided, from other relevant authorities.

4. Member States shall ensure that the application referred to in paragraphs 2 and 3, including the submission of any information and documents, may be completed fully online without the necessity for the applicants to appear in person before the competent authority, in accordance with the relevant provisions of Chapter III of Title I.

5. In respect of compliance with the rules concerning employee participation as laid down in Article 160l, the competent authority of the Member State of the company being divided shall verify that the draft terms of the cross-border division include information on the procedures by which the relevant arrangements are determined and on the possible options for such arrangements.

6. As part of the scrutiny referred to in paragraph 1, the competent authority shall examine the following:
  (a) all documents and information submitted to the competent authority in accordance with paragraphs 2 and 3;
  (b) an indication by the company being divided that the procedure referred to in Article 160l(3) and (4) has started, where relevant.

7. Member States shall ensure that the scrutiny referred to in paragraph 1 is carried out within three months of the date of receipt of the documents and information concerning the approval of the cross-border division by the general meeting of the company being divided. That scrutiny shall have one of the following outcomes:
  (a) where it is determined that the cross-border division complies with all the relevant conditions and that all necessary procedures and formalities have been completed, the competent authority shall issue the pre-division certificate;
  (b) where it is determined that the cross-border division does not comply with all the relevant conditions or that not all necessary procedures and formalities have been completed, the competent authority shall not issue the pre-division certificate and shall inform the company of the reasons for its decision; in that case, the competent authority may give the company the opportunity to fulfil the relevant conditions or to complete the procedures and formalities within an appropriate period of time.

8. Member States shall ensure that the competent authority does not issue the pre-division certificate where it is determined in compliance with national law that a cross-border division is set up for abusive or fraudulent purposes leading to or aimed at the evasion or circumvention of Union or national law, or for criminal purposes.

9. Where the competent authority, during the scrutiny referred to in paragraph 1, has serious doubts indicating that the cross-border division is set up for abusive or fraudulent purposes leading to or aimed at the evasion or circumvention of Union or national law, or for criminal purposes, it shall take into consideration relevant facts and circumstances, such as, where relevant and not considered in isolation, indicative factors of which the competent authority has become aware, in the course of the scrutiny referred to in paragraph 1, including through consultation of relevant authorities. The assessment for the purposes of this paragraph shall be conducted on a case-by-case basis, through a procedure governed by national law.

10. Where it is necessary for the purposes of the assessment under paragraphs 8 and 9 to take into account additional information or to perform additional investigative activities, the period of three months provided for in paragraph 7 may be extended by a maximum of three months.

11. Where, due to the complexity of the cross-border procedure, it is not possible to carry out the assessment within the deadlines provided for in paragraphs 7 and 10, Member States shall ensure that the applicant is notified of the reasons for any delay before the expiry of those deadlines.

12. Member States shall ensure that the competent authority may consult other relevant authorities with competence in the different fields concerned by the cross-border division, including those of the Member State of the recipient companies, and obtain from those authorities and from the company being divided information and documents necessary to scrutinise the legality of the cross-border division, within the procedural framework laid down in national law. For the purposes of the assessment, the competent authority may have recourse to an independent expert.]

NOTES

Inserted as noted to Art 160a at **[11.580]**.

[11.593]

[Article 160n Transmission of the pre-division certificate

1. Member States shall ensure that the pre-division certificate is shared with the authorities referred to in Article 160o(1) through the system of interconnection of registers.

Member States shall also ensure that the pre-division certificate is available through the system of interconnection of registers.

2. Access to the pre-division certificate shall be free of charge for the authorities referred to in Article 160o(1) and for the registers.]

NOTES

Inserted as noted to Art 160a at **[11.580]**.

[11.594]

[Article 160o Scrutiny of the legality of the cross-border division

1. Member States shall designate the court, notary or other authority competent to scrutinise the legality of the cross-border division as regards that part of the procedure which concerns the completion of the cross-border division governed by the law of the Member States of the recipient companies and to approve the cross-border division.

That authority or authorities shall in particular ensure that the recipient companies comply with provisions of national law on the incorporation and registration of companies and, where appropriate, that arrangements for employee participation have been determined in accordance with Article 160l.

2. For the purposes of paragraph 1 of this Article, the company being divided shall submit to each authority referred to in paragraph 1 of this Article the draft terms of the cross-border division approved by the general meeting referred to in Article 160h.
3. Each Member State shall ensure that any application for the purposes of paragraph 1, by the company being divided, including the submission of any information and documents, may be completed fully online without the necessity for the applicants to appear in person before the authority referred to in paragraph 1, in accordance with the relevant provisions of Chapter III of Title I.
4. The authority referred to in paragraph 1 shall approve the cross-border division as soon as it has determined that all relevant conditions have been properly fulfilled and formalities properly completed in the Member States of the recipient companies.
5. The pre-division certificate shall be accepted by the authority referred to in paragraph 1 as conclusively attesting to the proper completion of the applicable pre-division procedures and formalities in the Member State of the company being divided, without which the cross-border division cannot be approved.]

NOTES

Inserted as noted to Art 160a at **[11.580]**.

[11.595]

[Article 160p Registration

1. The laws of the Member States of the company being divided and of the recipient companies shall determine, with regard to their respective territories, the arrangements, in accordance with Article 16, for disclosing the completion of the cross-border division in their registers.
2. Member States shall ensure that at least the following information is entered in their registers:
   (a) in the register of the Member States of the recipient companies, that the registration of the recipient company is the result of a cross-border division;
   (b) in the register of the Member States of the recipient companies, the dates of registration of the recipient companies;
   (c) in the register of the Member State of the company being divided in the event of a full division, that the striking off or removal of the company being divided from the register is the result of a cross-border division;
   (d) in the register of the Member State of the company being divided in the event of a full division, the date of striking off or removal of the company being divided from the register;
   (e) in the registers of the Member State of the company being divided and of the Member States of the recipient companies, respectively, the registration number, name and legal form of the company being divided and of the recipient companies.

The registers shall make the information referred to in the first subparagraph publicly available and accessible through the system of interconnection of registers.
3. Member States shall ensure that the registers in the Member States of the recipient companies notify the register in the Member State of the company being divided, through the system of interconnection of registers, that the recipient companies have been registered. Member States shall also ensure that, in the event of a full division, the company being divided is struck off or removed from the register immediately upon receipt of all those notifications.
4. Member States shall ensure that the register in the Member State of the company being divided notifies the registers in the Member States of the recipient companies, through the system of interconnection of registers, that the cross-border division has taken effect.]

NOTES

Inserted as noted to Art 160a at **[11.580]**.

[11.596]

[Article 160q Date on which the cross-border division takes effect

The law of the Member State of the company being divided shall determine the date on which the cross-border division takes effect. That date shall be after the scrutiny referred to in Articles 160m and 160o has been carried out and after the registers have received all notifications referred to in Article 160p(3).]

NOTES

Inserted as noted to Art 160a at **[11.580]**.

[11.597]

[Article 160r Consequences of a cross-border division

1. A cross-border full division shall, from the date referred to in Article 160q, have the following consequences:
   (a) all the assets and liabilities of the company being divided, including all contracts, credits, rights and obligations, shall be transferred to the recipient companies in accordance with the allocation specified in the draft terms of the cross-border division;
   (b) the members of the company being divided shall become members of the recipient companies in accordance with the allocation of shares specified in the draft terms of the cross-border division, unless they have disposed of their shares as referred to in Article 160i(1);
   (c) the rights and obligations of the company being divided arising from contracts of employment or from employment relationships and existing at the date on which the cross-border division takes effect shall be transferred to the recipient companies;
   (d) the company being divided shall cease to exist.
2. A cross-border partial division shall, from the date referred to in Article 160q, have the following consequences:
   (a) part of the assets and liabilities of the company being divided, including contracts, credits, rights and obligations, shall be transferred to the recipient company or companies, while the remaining part shall continue to be that of the company being divided in accordance with the allocation specified in the draft terms of the cross-border division;

(b) at least some of the members of the company being divided shall become members of the recipient company or companies and at least some of the members shall remain in the company being divided or shall become members of both in accordance with the allocation of shares specified in the draft terms of the cross-border division, unless those members have disposed of their shares as referred to in Article 160i(1);

(c) the rights and obligations of the company being divided arising from contracts of employment or from employment relationships and existing at the date on which the cross-border division takes effect, allocated to the recipient company or companies under the draft terms of the cross-border division, shall be transferred to the respective recipient company or companies.

3. A cross-border division by separation shall, from the date referred to in Article 160q, have the following consequences:

(a) part of the assets and liabilities of the company being divided, including contracts, credits, rights and obligations, shall be transferred to the recipient company or companies, while the remaining part shall continue to be that of the company being divided, in accordance with the allocation specified in the draft terms of the cross-border division;

(b) the shares of the recipient company or companies shall be allocated to the company being divided;

(c) the rights and obligations of the company being divided arising from contracts of employment or from employment relationships and existing at the date on which the cross-border division takes effect, allocated to the recipient company or companies under the draft terms of the cross-border division, shall be transferred to the respective recipient company or companies.

4. Without prejudice to Article 160j(2), Member States shall ensure that where an asset or a liability of the company being divided is not explicitly allocated under the draft terms of the cross-border division, as referred to in point (l) of Article 160d, and where the interpretation of those terms does not make a decision on its allocation possible, the asset, the consideration therefor or the liability is allocated to all the recipient companies or, in the case of a partial division or a division by separation, to all the recipient companies and the company being divided in proportion to the share of the net assets allocated to each of those companies under the draft terms of the cross- border division.

5. Where, in the case of a cross-border division, the laws of the Member States require the completion of special formalities before the transfer of certain assets, rights and obligations by the company being divided becomes effective as against third parties, those formalities shall be carried out by the company being divided or by the recipient companies, as appropriate.

6. Member States shall ensure that shares in a recipient company cannot be exchanged for shares in the company being divided which are either held by the company itself or through a person acting in his or her own name but on behalf of the company.]

NOTES

Inserted as noted to Art 160a at **[11.580]**.

[11.598]

[Article 160s Simplified formalities

Where a cross-border division is carried out as a division by separation, points (b), (c), (f), (i), (o) and (p) of Article 160d and Articles 160e, 160f and 160i shall not apply.]

NOTES

Inserted as noted to Art 160a at **[11.580]**.

[11.599]

[Article 160t Independent experts

1. Member States shall lay down rules governing at least the civil liability of the independent expert responsible for drawing up the report referred to in Article 160f.

2. Member States shall have rules in place to ensure that:

(a) the expert, or the legal person on whose behalf the expert is operating, is independent from and has no conflict of interest with the company applying for the pre-division certificate; and

(b) the expert's opinion is impartial and objective, and is given with a view to providing assistance to the competent authority in accordance with the independence and impartiality requirements under the law and professional standards to which the expert is subject.]

NOTES

Inserted as noted to Art 160a at **[11.580]**.

[11.600]

[Article 160u Validity

A cross-border division which has taken effect in compliance with the procedures transposing this Directive may not be declared null and void.

The first paragraph does not affect Member States' powers, inter alia, in relation to criminal law, the prevention and combatting of terrorist financing, social law, taxation and law enforcement, to impose measures and penalties, under national law, after the date on which the cross-border division took effect.]

NOTES

Inserted as noted to Art 160a at **[11.580]**.

TITLE III FINAL PROVISIONS

[11.601]

[Article 161 Data protection

The processing of any personal data carried out in the context of this Directive shall be subject to Regulation (EU) 2016/679.]

NOTES

Substituted by European Parliament and Council Directive 2019/1151/EU, Art 1(19), as from 31 July 2019.

[11.602]

Article 162 Report, regular dialogue on the system of interconnection of registers and review

1. The Commission shall, not later than 8 June 2022, publish a report concerning the functioning of the system of interconnection of registers, in particular examining its technical operation and its financial aspects.

2. That report shall be accompanied, if appropriate, by proposals for amending provisions of this Directive relating to the system of interconnection of registers.

3. The Commission and the representatives of the Member States shall regularly convene to discuss matters covered by this Directive relating to the system of interconnection of registers in any appropriate forum.

4. By 30 June 2016, the Commission shall review the functioning of those provisions which concern the reporting and documentation requirements in the case of mergers and divisions and which have been amended or added by Directive 2009/109/EC of the European Parliament and of the Council,[1] and in particular their effects on the reduction of administrative burdens on companies, in the light of experience acquired in their application, and shall present a report to the European Parliament and the Council, accompanied if necessary by proposals to amend those provisions.

NOTES

[1] Directive 2009/109/EC of the European Parliament and of the Council of 16 September 2009 amending Council Directives 77/91/EEC, 78/855/EEC and 82/891/EEC, and Directive 2005/56/EC as regards reporting and documentation requirements in the case of mergers and divisions (OJ L259, 2.10.2009, p 14).

[11.603]

[Article 162a Amendments to the Annexes

Member States shall inform the Commission without delay of any changes to the types of limited liability companies provided for in their national law which would affect the contents of Annexes I, II and IIA.

Where a Member State informs the Commission pursuant to the first paragraph of this Article, the Commission shall be empowered to adapt the list of the types of the companies contained in Annexes I, II and IIA in line with the information referred to in the first paragraph of this Article, by means of delegated acts in accordance with Article 163.]

NOTES

Inserted by European Parliament and Council Directive 2019/1151/EU, Art 1(20), as from 31 July 2019.

[11.604]

[Article 163 Exercise of the delegation

1. The power to adopt delegated acts is conferred on the Commission subject to the conditions laid down in this Article.

2. The power to adopt delegated acts referred to in Article 25(3) and Article 162a shall be conferred on the Commission for an indeterminate period of time from 31 July 2019.

3. The delegation of power referred to in Article 25(3) and Article 162a may be revoked at any time by the European Parliament or by the Council. A decision to revoke shall put an end to the delegation of the power specified in that decision. It shall take effect the day following the publication of the decision in the Official Journal of the European Union or at a later date specified therein. It shall not affect the validity of any delegated acts already in force.

4. Before adopting a delegated act, the Commission shall consult experts designated by each Member State in accordance with the principles laid down in the Interinstitutional Agreement of 13 April 2016 on Better Law-Making.

5. As soon as it adopts a delegated act, the Commission shall notify it simultaneously to the European Parliament and to the Council.

6. A delegated act adopted pursuant to Article 25(3) or Article 162a shall enter into force only if no objection has been expressed either by the European Parliament or by the Council within a period of three months of notification of that act to the European Parliament and to the Council or if, before the expiry of that period, the European Parliament and the Council have both informed the Commission that they will not object. That period shall be extended by three months at the initiative of the European Parliament or of the Council.]

NOTES

Substituted by European Parliament and Council Directive 2019/1151/EU, Art 1(21), as from 31 July 2019.

[11.605]

Article 164 Committee procedure

1. The Commission shall be assisted by a committee. That committee shall be a committee within the meaning of Regulation (EU) No 182/2011.

2. Where reference is made to this paragraph, Article 5 of Regulation (EU) No 182/2011 shall apply.

[11.606]

Article 165 Communication

Member States shall communicate to the Commission the text of the main provisions of national law which they adopt in the fields covered by this Directive.

[11.607]

Article 166 Repeal

Directives 82/891/EEC, 89/666/EEC, 2005/56/EC, 2009/101/EC, 2011/35/EU and 2012/30/EU, as amended by the Directives listed in Part A of Annex III, are repealed, without prejudice to the obligations of the Member States relating to the time limits for the transposition into national law and the dates of application of the Directives set out in Part B of Annex III.

References to the repealed Directives shall be construed as references to this Directive and shall be read in accordance with the correlation table in Annex IV.

[11.608]

Article 167 Entry into force

This Directive shall enter into force on the twentieth day following that of its publication in the *Official Journal of the European Union*.

[11.609]

Article 168 Addressees

This Directive is addressed to the Member States.

ANNEXES

ANNEX I
TYPES OF COMPANIES REFERRED TO IN ARTICLE 2(1) AND (2), ARTICLE 44(1) AND (2), ARTICLE 45(2), ARTICLE 87(1) AND (2) AND ARTICLE 135(1)

[11.610]

— the United Kingdom:

public company limited by shares,

public company limited by guarantee and having a share capital.

NOTES

Note that only the text relating to the UK is reproduced here.

Note also that this Annex was amended by European Parliament and Council Directive 2019/1151/EU, Art 1(22), as from 31 July 2019 (the provision has a transposition date of 1 August 2021).

ANNEX II
[TYPES OF COMPANIES REFERRED TO IN ARTICLES 7(1), 13, 29(1), 36(1), 67(1), POINTS (1) AND (2) OF ARTICLE 86B, POINT (A) OF ARTICLE 119(1), AND POINT (1) OF ARTICLE 160B]

[11.611]

— United Kingdom:

companies incorporated with limited liability.

NOTES

Note that only the text relating to the UK is reproduced here.

The Annex title was substituted by European Parliament and Council Directive 2019/2121/EU, Art 1(24), as form 1 January 2020. Note that the 2019 Directive has a transposition date of 31 January 2023.

Note also that this Annex was amended by European Parliament and Council Directive 2019/1151/EU, Art 1(23), as from 31 July 2019.

[ANNEX IIA
TYPES OF COMPANIES REFERRED TO IN ARTICLES 13, 13F, 13G, 13H, AND 162A

[11.612]

— United Kingdom:

private company limited by shares or guarantee.]

NOTES

Note that only the text relating to the UK is reproduced here.

Note also that this Annex was inserted by European Parliament and Council Directive 2019/1151/EU, Art 1(24), Annex, as from 31 July 2019.

ANNEX III

PART A REPEALED DIRECTIVES WITH LIST OF THE SUCCESSIVE AMENDMENTS THERETO (REFERRED TO IN ARTICLE 166)

[11.613]

Council Directive 82/891/EEC	
(OJ L378, 31.12.1982, p 47).	
Directive 2007/63/EC of the European Parliament and of the Council	Article 3
(OJ L300, 17.11.2007, p 47).	
Directive 2009/109/EC of the European Parliament and of the Council	Article 3
(OJ L259, 2.10.2009, p 14).	
Directive 2014/59/EU of the European Parliament and of the Council	Article 116
(OJ L173, 12.6.2014, p 190).	
Council Directive 89/666/EEC	
(OJ L395, 30.12.1989, p 36).	
Directive 2012/17/EU of the European Parliament and of the Council	Article 1

Part 11 EU & Retained EU Legislation

(OJ L156, 16.6.2012, p 1).	
Directive 2005/56/EC of the European Parliament and of the Council	
(OJ L310, 25.11.2005, p 1).	
Directive 2009/109/EC of the European Parliament and of the Council	Article 4
(OJ L259, 2.10.2009, p 14).	
Directive 2012/17/EU of the European Parliament and of the Council	Article 2
(OJ L156, 16.6.2012, p 1).	
Directive 2014/59/EU of the European Parliament and of the Council	Article 120
(OJ L173, 12.6.2014, p 190).	
Directive 2009/101/EC of the European Parliament and of the Council	
(OJ L258, 1.10.2009, p 11).	
Directive 2012/17/EU of the European Parliament and of the Council	Article 3
(OJ L156, 16.6.2012, p 1).	
Council Directive 2013/24/EU	Article 1 and point 1 of Part A of the Annex
(OJ L158, 10.6.2013, p 365).	
Directive 2011/35/EU of the European Parliament and of the Council	
(OJ L110, 29.4.2011, p 1).	
Council Directive 2013/24/EU	Article 1 and point 3 of Part A of the Annex
(OJ L158, 10.6.2013, p 365).	
Directive 2014/59/EU of the European Parliament and of the Council	Article 122
(OJ L173, 12.6.2014, p 190).	
Directive 2012/30/EU of the European Parliament and of the Council	
(OJ L315, 14.11.2012, p 74).	
Council Directive 2013/24/EU	Article 1 and point 4 of Part A of the Annex
(OJ L158, 10.6.2013, p 365).	
Directive 2014/59/EU of the European Parliament and of the Council	Article 123
(OJ L173, 12.6.2014, p 190).	

PART B TIME LIMITS FOR TRANSPOSITION INTO NATIONAL LAW AND DATES OF APPLICATION (REFERRED TO IN ARTICLE 166)

Directive	Time limit for transposition	Date of application
82/891/EEC	1 January 1986	—
89/666/EEC	1 January 1992	1 January 1993[1]
2005/56/EC	15 December 2007	—
2007/63/EC	31 December 2008	—
2009/109/EC	30 July 2011	—
2012/17/EU	7 July 2014[2]	—
2013/24/EU	1 July 2013	—
2014/59/EU	31 December 2014	1 January 2015[3]

NOTES

[1] Under Article 16(2) of Directive 89/666/EC, Member States are required to stipulate that the provisions referred to in paragraph 1 shall apply from 1 January 1993 and, with regard to accounting documents, shall apply for the first time to annual accounts for the financial year beginning on 1 January 1993 or during 1993.

[2] Under Article 5(2) of Directive 2012/17/EU Member States are required to, not later than 8 June 2017, adopt, publish and apply the provisions necessary to comply with:

— Article 1(3) and (4) and Article 5a of Directive 89/666/EEC,

— Article 13 of Directive 2005/56/EC,

— Article 3(1), second subparagraph, Article 3b, Article 3c, Article 3d and Article 4a(3) to (5) of Directive 2009/101/EC.

[3] Under the third subparagraph of Article 130(1) of Directive 2014/59/EU, Member States are required to apply provisions adopted in order to comply with Section 5 of Chapter IV of Title IV of that Directive from 1 January 2016 at the latest.

ANNEX IV
CORRELATION TABLE

[11.614]

Directive 82/891/EEC	Directive 89/666/EEC	Directive 2005/56/EC	Directive 2009/101/EC	Directive 2011/35/EU	Directive 2012/30/EU	This Directive
—	—	—	—	—	—	Article 1
Article 1						Article 135
Article 2						Article 136
Article 3(1) and (2)						Article 137(1) and (2)
Article 3(3)(a)						Article 137(3) first subparagraph
Article 3(3)(b)						Article 137(3) second subparagraph
Article 4						Article 138
Article 5						Article 139
Article 6						Article 140
Article 7						Article 141
Article 8						Article 142
Article 9						Article 143
Article 10						Article 144
Article 11						Article 145
Article 12						Article 146
Article 13						Article 147
Article 14						Article 148
Article 15						Article 149
Article 16						Article 150
Article 17						Article 151
Article 18						Article 152
Article 19						Article 153
Article 20(a) and (b)						Article 154(a) and (b)
Article 20(d)						Article 154(c)
Article 21						Article 155
Article 22(1), (2) and (3)						Article 156(1), (2) and (3)
Article 22(5)						Article 156(4)
Article 23						Article 157
Article 24						Article 158
Article 25						Article 159
Article 26(1)						—
Article 26(2)						Article 160(1)
Article 26(3)						—
Article 26(4)						Article 160(2)
Article 26(5)						—
Article 27						—
	Article 1					Article 29
	Article 2					Article 30
	Article 3					Article 31
	Article 4					Article 32
	Article 5					Article 33
	—					Article 34(1)
	Article 5a(1), (2) and (3)					Article 20(1), (2) and (3)
						Article 33(1)
	Article 5a(4)					Article 34(2)
	Article 5a(5)					Article 34(3)
	Article 6					Article 35

Directive 82/891/EEC	Directive 89/666/EEC	Directive 2005/56/EC	Directive 2009/101/EC	Directive 2011/35/EU	Directive 2012/30/EU	This Directive
	Article 7					Article 36
	Article 8					Article 37
	Article 9					Article 38
	Article 10					Article 39
	Article 11					—
	Article 11a					Article 161
	Article 12					Article 40
	Article 13					Article 41
	Article 14					Article 42
	Article 15					—
	Article 16					—
	Article 17					Article 43
	Article 18					—
		Article 1				Article 118
		Article 2				Article 119
		Article 3				Article 120
		Article 4				Article 121
		Article 5				Article 122
		Article 6				Article 123
		Article 7				Article 124
		Article 8				Article 125
		Article 9				Article 126
		Article 10				Article 127
		Article 11				Article 128
		Article 12				Article 129
		Article 13				Article 130
		Article 14				Article 131
		Article 15				Article 132
		Article 16				Article 133
		Article 17				Article 134
		Article 17a				Article 161
		Article 18				
		Article 19				—
		Article 20				—
		Article 21				—
			Article 1			Annex II
			Article 2			Article 14
			Article 2a			Article 15
			Article 3			Article 16
			Article 3a			Article 17
			Article 3b			Article 18
			Article 3c			Article 19
			Article 3d			Article 20
			Article 4			Article 21
			Article 4a			Article 22
			Article 4b			Article 23
			Article 4c first and second paragraphs			Article 24 first and second paragraphs
			Article 4c third paragraph			—
			Article 4d			Article 25
			Article 4e			Article 165
			Article 5			Article 26
			Article 6			Article 27
			Article 7			Article 28

Directive 82/891/EEC	Directive 89/666/EEC	Directive 2005/56/EC	Directive 2009/101/EC	Directive 2011/35/EU	Directive 2012/30/EU	This Directive
			Article 7a			Article 161
			—			Article 7(1)
			Article 8			Article 7(2)
			Article 9			Article 8
			Article 10			Article 9
			Article 11			Article 10
			Article 12			Article 11
			Article 13			Article 12
			Article 13a			Article 163
			Article 14			—
			Article 15			—
			Article 16			—
			Article 17			—
			Article 18			—
			Annex I			—
			Annex II			—
				Article 1		Article 87
				Article 2		Article 88
				Article 3		Article 89
				Article 4		Article 90
				Article 5		Article 91
				Article 6		Article 92
				Article 7		Article 93
				Article 8		Article 94
				Article 9		Article 95
				Article 10		Article 96
				Article 11		Article 97
				Article 12		Article 98
				Article 13		Article 99
				Article 14		Article 100
				Article 15		Article 101
				Article 16		Article 102
				Article 17		Article 103
				Article 18		Article 104
				Article 19		Article 105
				Article 20		Article 106
				Article 21		Article 107
				Article 22		Article 108
				Article 23		Article 109
				Article 24		Article 110
				Article 25		Article 111
				Article 26		Article 112
				Article 27		Article 113
				Article 28		Article 114
				Article 29		Article 115
				Article 30		Article 116
				Article 31		Article 117
				Article 32		—
				Article 33		—
				Article 34		—
				Annex I		—
				Annex II		—
					Article 1(1)	Article 2(1)
						Article 44(1)
					Article 1(2)	Article 2(2)

Directive 82/891/EEC	Directive 89/666/EEC	Directive 2005/56/EC	Directive 2009/101/EC	Directive 2011/35/EU	Directive 2012/30/EU	This Directive
						Article 44(2)
					Article 2	Article 44(2)
					Article 2	Article 3
					Article 3	Article 4
					Article 4	Article 5
					Article 5	Article 6
					—	Article 43
					Article 6	Article 45
					Article 7	Article 46
					Article 8	Article 47
					Article 9	Article 48
					Article 10	Article 49
					Article 11	Article 50
					Article 12	Article 51
					Article 13	Article 52
					Article 14	Article 53
					Article 15	Article 54
					Article 16	Article 55
					Article 17	Article 56
					Article 18	Article 57
					Article 19	Article 58
					Article 20	Article 59
					Article 21	Article 60
					Article 22	Article 61
					Article 23	Article 62
					Article 24	Article 63
					Article 25	Article 64
					Article 26	Article 65
					Article 27	Article 66
					Article 28	Article 67
					Article 29	Article 68
					Article 30	Article 69
					Article 31	Article 70
					Article 32	Article 71
					Article 33	Article 72
					Article 34	Article 73
					Article 35	Article 74
					Article 36	Article 75
					Article 37	Article 76
					Article 38	Article 77
					Article 39	Article 78
					Article 40	Article 79
					Article 41	Article 80
					Article 42	Article 81
					Article 43	Article 82
					Article 44	Article 83
					Article 45	Article 84
					Article 46	Article 85
					Article 47(1)	Article 86
					Article 47(2)	Article 165
					Article 48	—
					—	Article 166
					Article 49	Article 167
					Article 50	Article 168
					Annex I	Annex I

Directive 82/891/EEC	Directive 89/666/EEC	Directive 2005/56/EC	Directive 2009/101/EC	Directive 2011/35/EU	Directive 2012/30/EU	This Directive
					Annex II	—
					Annex III	—
					—	Annex III
					—	Annex IV

COMMISSION IMPLEMENTING REGULATION

(2018/1212/EU)

of 29 September 2018

laying down minimum requirements implementing the provisions of Directive 2007/36/EC of the European Parliament and of the Council as regards shareholder identification, the transmission of information and the facilitation of the exercise of shareholders rights (Note)

(Text with EEA relevance)

[11.615]

NOTES

Date of publication in OJ: OJ L223, 4.9.2018, p 1.

This Regulation is available on the EUR-Lex website at eur-lex.europa.eu/legal-content/EN/TXT/?uri=CELEX:32018R1212. A summary is below.

Directive 2017/828/EU (Shareholders Rights Directive 2) amended the Shareholders Rights Directive (Directive 2007/36/EC) with regard to the encouragement of long-term shareholder engagement. It gave the Commission the power to adopt implementing acts that specify minimum requirements in relation to shareholder identification, the transmission of information and the facilitation of the exercise of shareholder rights.

This Regulation specifies standardised formats and minimum content requirements for a number of documents including:

— requests to disclose information about a shareholder's identity and responses to such a request

— notices of general meetings

— confirmations of entitlement to exercise shareholders' rights at a general meeting and notices of participation by a shareholder at a general meeting

— the format of the confirmation of the receipt and recording and counting of votes at a general meeting

— the transmission of information specific to corporate events other than general meetings of shareholders.

The use of standardised formats and content requirements is intended to prevent diverging implementation of the provisions of the SRD, which could result in the adoption of incompatible national standards across Member States, and to enable efficient and reliable processing of information between intermediaries, issuers and shareholders.

The Regulation also sets out deadlines to be complied with by issuers and intermediaries in corporate events and in shareholder identification processes, as well as minimum security requirements.

The Regulation applies from 3 September 2020.

Repeal of this Regulation in relation to the UK: this Regulation was repealed, in relation to the UK, by the European Grouping of Territorial Cooperation and Limited Liability Partnerships etc (Revocations and Amendments) (EU Exit) Regulations 2021, SI 2021/153, reg 2, Schedule, as from 8 March 2021.

COMMISSION DELEGATED REGULATION

(2019/979/EU)

of 14 March 2019

supplementing Regulation (EU) 2017/1129 of the European Parliament and of the Council with regard to regulatory technical standards on key financial information in the summary of a prospectus, the publication and classification of prospectuses, advertisements for securities, supplements to a prospectus, and the notification portal, and repealing Commission Delegated Regulation (EU) No 382/2014 and Commission Delegated Regulation (EU) 2016/301

(Text with EEA relevance)

[11.616]

NOTES

Date of publication in OJ: OJ L166, 21.6.2019, p 1.

This Regulation is reproduced as amended by: Commission Delegated Regulation 2020/1272/EU.

Application of this Regulation in relation to the UK: in accordance with the European Union (Withdrawal) Act 2018, s 3 at **[12.5]**, this Regulation became domestic law on IP completion day (as defined in the European Union (Withdrawal Agreement) Act 2020, s 39). In so far as applying to the UK, this Regulation is amended by the Technical Standards (Prospectus Regulation) (EU Exit) Instrument 2020 (FCA 2020/50), as from that date. Articles that are repealed are reproduced in italics and, in the case of other amendments, the relevant details from FCA 2020/50 have been included in the Notes of the affected Articles below; but the text is unchanged.

Note also that the words "(Text with EEA relevance)" above are repealed, in relation to the UK only, by FCA 2020/50, as from IP completion day.

THE EUROPEAN COMMISSION,

Having regard to the Treaty on the Functioning of the European Union,

Having regard to Regulation (EU) 2017/1129 of the European Parliament and of the Council of 14 June 2017 on the prospectus to be published when securities are offered to the public or admitted to trading on a regulated market, and repealing Directive 2003/71/EC,[1] and in particular Articles 7(13), 21(12), 21(13), 22(9), 23(7) and 25(7) thereof,

Whereas:

(1) The key financial information in the summary of a prospectus should present the key financial figures that provide investors with a succinct overview of the issuer's assets, liabilities and profitability, as well as any other key financial information that is relevant for investors to make a preliminary assessment of the financial performance and financial position of the issuer. In order to ensure that this information is concise and relevant, it is therefore necessary to identify a limited number of disclosures, specify their layout and calibrate the financial information to take account of different types of issuers and securities.

(2) In order to avoid misleading investors, issuers should be entitled to include specific additional disclosures, including alternative performance measures, where they consider that the required disclosures do not provide a clear picture of their performance and financial position. However, to ensure that investors focus primarily on the figures stemming from financial statements, alternative performance measures should not be given more prominence in the prospectus than the figures extracted from the historical financial information.

(3) In order to reduce compliance costs and administrative burdens on issuers, the key financial information in the summary of a prospectus, including additional line items and alternative performance measures, should reproduce information disclosed in the body of the prospectus.

(4) It is appropriate that the key financial information in the summary of a prospectus is adapted to the economic activity of the issuer, its industrial sector, the major line items of its financial statements and the type of securities being issued or offered. However, it is not possible to provide specific templates for all types of issuers.

(5) To avoid misleading investors and ensure consistency with the information included in the prospectus, where the historical financial information included in the prospectus is restated in case of material errors contained in the financial statements or changes in accounting standards, the key financial information in the summary of a prospectus should reflect that restated historical financial information.

(6) Where an issuer has a complex financial history, it should, where appropriate, present both its financial information and the financial information relating to another entity or entities within a standalone section in the summary of the prospectus.

(7) Investors need clarity as regards which information forms part of the prospectus and to whom an offer of securities to the public is addressed. Therefore, with the exception of information incorporated by reference, where the prospectus contains hyperlinks, it should inform investors that the information on the related websites is not part of the prospectus and has not been scrutinised or approved by the competent authority. Furthermore, measures should be established to prevent websites used for the publication of the prospectus targeting residents in Member States or third countries where the offer of securities to the public does not take place, such as by including on the website a statement identifying the addressees of the offer.

(8) Reporting and publication of data in an electronic, machine-readable format facilitates the efficient use and exchange of that data. The list of data fields to be reported to the European Securities and Markets Authority (ESMA) for the classification of prospectuses should therefore be specified and the use of XML format templates should be required to ensure that such fields are machine-readable. The list of data should be sufficiently comprehensive to ensure that ESMA meets its mandate under Article 47 of Regulation (EU) 2017/1129 to publish a yearly report containing statistics on the prospectuses approved and notified in the Union, as well as an analysis of trends taking into account the type of issuers and the type of issuances.

(9) To avoid misleading retail investors during the process of marketing any security proposed for public offers or admission to trading on a regulated market, an advertisement should not purport to be the principal information document. Accordingly and in order to avoid confusion with the prospectus, advertisements should not be inappropriately long.

(10) Advertisements relating to an offer of securities to the public or an admission to trading on a regulated market can become inaccurate or misleading where a significant new factor, material mistake or material inaccuracy relating to the information in the corresponding prospectus arises. Requirements should be established to ensure that advertisements are amended without undue delay where they become inaccurate or misleading due to such a new factor, material mistake or material inaccuracy.

(11) To allow investors to take informed investment decisions, the information contained in advertisements should not present an unbalanced view for example by presenting negative aspects of such information with less prominence than the positive aspects.

(12) As alternative performance measures can disproportionally influence investment decisions, information about an offer to the public or an admission to trading on a regulated market circulated outside the prospectus should not be permitted to contain such measures, unless they are included in the body of the prospectus.

(13) Competent authorities in host Member States do not scrutinise prospectuses. Therefore, to ensure that investors in host Member States are adequately protected, when the competent authority of the host Member State seeks the assistance of the competent authority in the home Member State, it should communicate the information that is relevant for the competent authority in the home Member State to assess the consistency of the advertisement with the content of the prospectus. Such communication should occur within the appropriate timeframe to ensure that investors in host Member States are not penalised by the fact that host competent authorities do not scrutinise prospectuses and have sufficient time to analyse the underlying public offering. The competent authority in the host Member State should be informed to the degree necessary to exercise control over the compliance of advertising activity in its jurisdiction.

(14) To ensure a consistent application of Regulation (EU) 2017/1129 and to take account of technical developments on financial markets, it is necessary to specify situations where the publication of supplements to the

prospectus is required. It is not possible to identify all situations where a supplement to the prospectus is required as this may depend on the issuer and securities involved. Therefore, it is appropriate to specify the minimum situations where a supplement is required.

(15) Annual audited financial statements are crucial for investors when making investment decisions. To ensure that investors base their investment decisions on the most recent financial information, it is necessary to require the publication of a supplement incorporating new annual audited financial statements of issuers of equity securities and issuers of underlying shares where depository receipts are published after the approval of the prospectus.

(16) Given that profit forecasts and profit estimates can influence an investment decision, it is necessary to publish a supplement containing any amendments to implicit or explicit figures constituting profit forecasts or profit estimates or the withdrawal of a profit forecast or profit estimate already included in the prospectus. For the same reason, in case of equity securities and depositary receipts, it is also necessary to produce a supplement to the prospectus where a new profit forecast or profit estimate has been published before the end of the offer period or before admission to trading.

(17) Information concerning the identity of the main shareholders or any controlling entity of the issuer is vital for an informed assessment of the issuer. However, change of control of the issuer is particularly significant where the offer refers to equity securities, which are generally more price sensitive to changes of issuers. Therefore, a supplement should be published where there is a change of control of an issuer of equity securities or an issuer of underlying shares of depository receipts.

(18) It is essential that potential investors assessing an outstanding offer of equity securities are in a position to compare the terms and conditions of such an offer with the price or exchange terms attached to any public takeover bid announced during the offer period. Moreover, the result of a public takeover bid is significant for the investment decision as investors need to know whether it implies or not a change of control of the issuer. It is therefore necessary to publish a supplement in the case of any new public takeover bid.

(19) Where the working capital statement is no longer valid, investors are unable to make a fully informed investment decision about the issuer's financial situation. Investors should be in a position to reassess their investment decisions in light of the new information on the issuer's ability to access cash and other available liquid resources to meet its liabilities. In order to do so, a supplement is necessary.

(20) After the approval of a prospectus, an issuer or offeror may decide to offer the securities in Member States other than those referred to in the prospectus, or to apply for admission to trading of the securities on regulated markets in Member States other than those provided for in the prospectus. Information about such offers and admissions therein is important for the investor's assessment of certain aspects of the issuer's securities and it is therefore appropriate to require a supplement in such cases.

(21) The financial position or the business of the entity is likely to be affected by a significant financial commitment. Therefore, investors should be entitled to receive additional information on the consequences of that commitment in a supplement to the prospectus.

(22) An increase of the aggregate nominal amount of an offering programme provides information on issuers' increased financing needs or an increase in demands for the issuers' securities. In such a case, a supplement to the prospectus should be published.

(23) Relevant competent authorities should receive in a timely manner via the notification portal the prospectus and accompanying data, together with a certificate of approval that states that the prospectus has been drawn up in accordance with Regulation (EU) 2017/1129. ESMA should ensure that the notification portal preserves the security and integrity of the information exchanged between competent authorities. Competent authorities remain responsible for the submission of such information. In order to enable a smoothly and timely operation of the notification portal, it is necessary to specify the accompanying data that is to be uploaded to that notification portal.

(24) In accordance with Article 10 of Regulation (EU) No 1095/2010 of the European Parliament and of the Council,[2] ESMA has conducted open public consultations on such draft regulatory technical standards, analysed the potential related costs and benefits and requested the opinion of the Securities and Markets Stakeholder Group established in accordance with Article 37 of that Regulation. However, ESMA has not consulted that stakeholder group on the draft regulatory technical standards on the technical arrangements for the notification portal as those arrangements only affect ESMA and national competent authorities.

(25) This Regulation is based on the draft regulatory technical standards submitted by ESMA to the Commission.

(26) Since this Regulation replaces Commission Delegated Regulation (EU) No 382/2014[3] and Commission Delegated Regulation (EU) 2016/301,[4] those Delegated Regulations become obsolete and should therefore be repealed.

(27) As this Regulation supplements provisions of Regulation (EU) 2017/1129, its application should be deferred until the date of application of Regulation (EU) 2017/1129,

NOTES

[1] OJ L168, 30.6.2017, p 12.

[2] Regulation (EU) No 1095/2010 of the European Parliament and of the Council of 24 November 2010 establishing a European Supervisory Authority (European Securities and Markets Authority), amending Decision No 716/2009/EC and repealing Commission Decision 2009/77/EC (OJ L331, 15.12.2010, p 84).

[3] Commission Delegated Regulation (EU) No 382/2014 of 7 March 2014 supplementing Directive 2003/71/EC of the European Parliament and of the Council with regard to regulatory technical standards for publication of supplements to the prospectus (OJ L111, 15.4.2014, p 36).

[4] Commission Delegated Regulation (EU) 2016/301 of 30 November 2015 supplementing Directive 2003/71/EC of the European Parliament and of the Council with regard to regulatory technical standards for approval and publication of the prospectus and dissemination of advertisements and amending Commission Regulation (EC) No 809/2004 (OJ L58, 4.3.2016, p 13).

HAS ADOPTED THIS REGULATION:

CHAPTER I KEY FINANCIAL INFORMATION IN THE PROSPECTUS SUMMARY

SECTION 1 CONTENT OF THE KEY FINANCIAL INFORMATION IN THE PROSPECTUS SUMMARY

[11.617]
Article 1 Minimum content of the key financial information in the summary of a prospectus
1. The key financial information in the summary of a prospectus shall be made up of the financial information laid down in the Annexes to Commission Delegated Regulation 2019/980.[1]
2. Where any information referred to in the relevant tables set out in Annexes I to VI to this Regulation is not included in the financial statements of the issuer, the issuer shall disclose a corresponding item from its financial statements instead.
3. The issuer may include additional line items or alternative performance measures in the summary of a prospectus where these are key financial information on the issuer or on the securities being offered or admitted to trading on a regulated market. For the purposes of the first sentence, alternative performance measures shall be financial measures of historical or future financial performance, financial position or cash flows, other than financial measures defined in the applicable financial reporting framework.
4. Issuers who do not fall under any of the types of issuers identified in Articles 2 to 8 shall present the key financial information referred to in the tables that they consider correspond most closely to the type of securities issued.
5. The key financial information shall be presented for the number of years required by Delegated Regulation 2019/980 for the type of issuance and the type of securities being issued.

NOTES
[1] Commission Delegated Regulation 2019/980 of 14 March 2019 supplementing Regulation (EU) 2017/1129 of the European Parliament and of the Council as regards the format, content, scrutiny and approval of the prospectus to be published when securities are offered to the public or admitted to trading on a regulated market, and repealing Commission Regulation (EC) No 809/2004 (See page 26 of this Official Journal).

[11.618]
Article 2 Key financial information for non-financial entities issuing equity securities
Where the issuer is a non-financial entity issuing equity securities, the summary of a prospectus shall contain the key financial information referred to in the tables set out in Annex I.

[11.619]
Article 3 Key financial information for non-financial entities issuing non-equity securities
Where the issuer is a non-financial entity issuing non-equity securities, the summary of a prospectus shall contain the key financial information referred to in the tables set out in Annex II.

[11.620]
Article 4 Key financial information for credit institutions
Where the issuer is a credit institution, the summary of a prospectus shall contain the key financial information referred to in the tables set out in Annex III.

[11.621]
Article 5 Key financial information for insurance companies
Where the issuer is an insurance company, the summary of a prospectus shall contain the key financial information referred to in the tables set out in Annex IV.

[11.622]
Article 6 Key financial information for special purpose vehicles issuing asset backed securities
Where the issuer is a special purpose vehicle issuing asset backed securities, the prospectus summary shall contain the key financial information referred to in the tables set out in Annex V.

[11.623]
Article 7 Key financial information for closed end funds
Where the issuer is a closed end fund, the summary of a prospectus shall contain the key financial information referred to in the tables set out in Annex VI.

[11.624]
Article 8 Key financial information for guarantors
Where a guarantee is attached to the securities, the key financial information on the guarantor shall be presented as if the guarantor were the issuer of the same type of security that is the subject of the guarantee using the tables set out in Annexes I to VI. Where the guarantee is given for asset-backed securities, the key financial information on the guarantor shall be presented as if the guarantor were the issuer of the underlying securities.

SECTION 2 FORMAT OF THE KEY FINANCIAL INFORMATION IN THE PROSPECTUS SUMMARY

[11.625]
Article 9 Format of the key financial information in the summary of a prospectus
1. The key financial information shall be presented in tabular format in accordance with the tables of Annexes I to VI to this Regulation.
2. Any historical financial information in the summary of a prospectus, which is not extracted from the financial statements, shall be identified as such.
3. Where pro forma information to be included in the summary of a prospectus affects the key financial information referred to in the relevant table of Annexes I to VI to this Regulation, that pro forma information shall be presented in additional columns in the tables set out in Annexes I to VI to this Regulation or as a separate table. Where necessary for its understanding, the pro forma information shall be accompanied by a brief explanation of the figures presented in the additional columns or separate table.

Where in the case of a significant gross change only qualitative information is included in the prospectus, a statement to that effect shall be included in the summary of that prospectus.

4. Where the issuer has a complex financial history as set out in Article 18 of Delegated Regulation 2019/980, the key financial information in the summary of the prospectus shall be presented in a manner consistent with the prospectus and using the relevant tables in Annexes I to VI to this Regulation.

CHAPTER II PUBLICATION OF THE PROSPECTUS

[11.626]

Article 10 Publication of the prospectus

1. Where a prospectus, whether a single document or consisting of separate documents, contains hyperlinks to websites, it shall include a statement to the effect that the information on the websites does not form part of the prospectus and has not been scrutinised or approved by the competent authority. That requirement shall not apply to hyperlinks to information that is incorporated by reference.

2. Where a prospectus is published in accordance with Article 21(2) of Regulation (EU) 2017/1129, measures shall be taken on websites used for the publication of the prospectus to avoid targeting residents of Member States or third countries other than those where the securities are offered to the public.

NOTES

Application of this Article in relation to the UK: this Article is amended, in relation to the UK only, by the Technical Standards (Prospectus Regulation) (EU Exit) Instrument 2020 (FCA 2020/50), as from IP completion day (as defined in the European Union (Withdrawal Agreement) Act 2020, s 39), as follows—

— In para 2, the words "Member States or" are repealed.

CHAPTER III MACHINE READABLE DATA FOR THE CLASSIFICATION OF PROSPECTUSES

[11.627]

Article 11 Data for classification of prospectuses

When providing ESMA with an electronic copy of an approved prospectus, including any supplements thereto and final terms where applicable, the competent authority shall also provide to ESMA with the relevant accompanying data for the classification of prospectuses in accordance with the tables set out in Annex VII to this Regulation.

NOTES

Repeal of this Article in relation to the UK: this Article is repealed, in relation to the UK only, by the Technical Standards (Prospectus Regulation) (EU Exit) Instrument 2020 (FCA 2020/50), as from IP completion day (as defined in the European Union (Withdrawal Agreement) Act 2020, s 39).

[11.628]

Article 12 Practical arrangements to ensure the machine readability of the data

The competent authority shall provide the accompanying data referred to in Article 11 in a common XML format and in accordance with the format and standards set out in the tables in Annex VII.

NOTES

Repeal of this Article in relation to the UK: this Article is repealed, in relation to the UK only, by the Technical Standards (Prospectus Regulation) (EU Exit) Instrument 2020 (FCA 2020/50), as from IP completion day (as defined in the European Union (Withdrawal Agreement) Act 2020, s 39).

CHAPTER IV ADVERTISEMENTS

[11.629]

Article 13 Identification of the prospectus

Where the issuer, the offeror or the person asking for admission to trading on a regulated market is subject to the obligation to draw up a prospectus, an advertisement shall clearly identify that prospectus by:

(a) clearly identifying the website where the prospectus is published, or will be published, where the advertisement is disseminated in written form and by means other than electronic means;

(b) including a hyperlink to the prospectus and to the relevant final terms of a base prospectus where the advertisement is disseminated in written form by electronic means, or by including a hyperlink to the page of the website where the prospectus will be published if the prospectus has not yet been published;

(c) including accurate information on where the prospectus may be obtained, and accurate information on the offer of securities or the admission to trading on a regulated market to which it relates, where the advertisement is disseminated in a form or by means not falling within the scope of points (a) or (b).

[11.630]

Article 14 Required content

1. Advertisements disseminated to potential retail investors shall include the following elements:

(a) the word 'advertisement', in a prominent manner. Where an advertisement is disseminated in an oral form, the purpose of the communication shall be clearly identified at the beginning of the message;

(b) a statement that the approval of the prospectus should not be understood as an endorsement of the securities offered or admitted to trading on a regulated market where the advertisement contains a reference to a prospectus approved by a competent authority;

(c) a recommendation that potential investors read the prospectus before making an investment decision in order to fully understand the potential risks and rewards associated with the decision to invest in the securities where the advertisement contains a reference to a prospectus approved by a competent authority;

(d) the comprehension alert required pursuant to point (b) of Article 8(3) of Regulation (EU) No 1286/2014 of the European Parliament and of the Council[1] where:

(i) the advertisement relates to complex securities other than the financial instruments referred to in points (i), (ii) and (vi) of Article 25(4)(a) of Directive 2014/65/EU of the European Parliament and of the Council[2] and;

(ii) the comprehension alert is, or will be, included in the summary of the prospectus.

2. Advertisements in written form, which are disseminated to potential retail investors, shall be sufficiently different in format and length from the prospectus that no confusion with the prospectus is possible.

NOTES

Application of this Article in relation to the UK: this Article is amended, in relation to the UK only, by the Technical Standards (Prospectus Regulation) (EU Exit) Instrument 2020 (FCA 2020/50), as from IP completion day (as defined in the European Union (Withdrawal Agreement) Act 2020, s 39), as follows—

— For the words "a competent authority" in points (b) and (c) of para 1 there are substituted the words "the FCA".

— For the words "points (i), (ii) and (vi) of Article 25(4)(a) of Directive 2014/65/EU of the European Parliament and of the Council" in point (d)(i) of para 1 there are substituted the words "sub-paragraphs (a), (b) and (d) of rule 10A.4.1(2) of the Conduct of Business sourcebook in the Financial Conduct Authority's Handbook of rules and guidance".

1 Regulation (EU) No 1286/2014 of the European Parliament and of the Council of 26 November 2014 on key information documents for packaged retail and insurance-based investment products (PRIIPs) (OJ L352, 9.12.2014, p 1).

2 Directive 2014/65/EU of the European Parliament and of the Council of 15 May 2014 on markets in financial instruments and amending Directive 2002/92/EC and Directive 2011/61/EU (OJ L173, 12.6.2014, p 349).

[11.631]

Article 15 Dissemination of advertisements

1. Advertisements disseminated to potential investors shall be amended where:

(a) a supplement to the prospectus is subsequently published in accordance with Article 23 of Regulation (EU) 2017/1129;

(b) the significant new factor, material mistake or material inaccuracy mentioned in the supplement renders the previously disseminated advertisement materially inaccurate or misleading.

The first subparagraph shall not apply after the final closing of the offer period to the public or after the time when trading on a regulated market begins, whichever occurs later.

2. Advertisements amended as referred to in paragraph 1 shall be disseminated to potential investors without undue delay following the publication of the supplement to the prospectus and shall contain all of the following:

(a) a clear reference to the inaccurate or misleading version of the advertisement;

(b) an explanation that the advertisement has been amended as it contained materially inaccurate or misleading information;

(c) a clear description of the differences between the two versions of the advertisement.

3. With the exception of orally disseminated advertisements, advertisements amended pursuant to paragraph 1 shall be disseminated through at least the same means as the previous advertisement.

[11.632]

Article 16 Information concerning offers of securities

1. Information disclosed in oral or written form concerning an offer of securities to the public or an admission to trading on a regulated market, whether as an advertisement or for other purposes, shall not:

(a) contradict the information in the prospectus;

(b) refer to information which contradicts the information in the prospectus;

(c) present the information in the prospectus in a materially unbalanced way, including by way of presentation of negative aspects of such information with less prominence than the positive aspects, omission or selective presentation of certain information;

(d) contain alternative performance measures unless they are contained in the prospectus.

2. For the purposes of the paragraph 1, information in the prospectus shall consist of either information included in the prospectus, where already published, or information to be included in the prospectus, where the prospectus is to be published at a later date.

3. For the purposes of point (d) of the paragraph 1, alternative performance measures shall consist of financial measures of historical or future financial performance, financial position or cash flows, other than financial measures defined in the applicable financial reporting framework.

[11.633]

Article 17 Procedure for the cooperation between competent authorities

1. Where the competent authority of a Member State in which an advertisement is disseminated believes that the content of that advertisement is inconsistent with the information in the prospectus, it may request the assistance of the competent authority of the home Member State. Where requested, the competent authority in which the advertisement is disseminated shall communicate the following to the competent authority of the home Member State:

(a) its reasons for believing that the content of the advertisement is inconsistent with the information in the prospectus;

(b) the relevant advertisement and, where necessary, a translation of the advertisement in the language of the prospectus or in a language customary in the sphere of international finance.

2. The competent authority of the home Member State shall transmit to the competent authority in which the advertisement is disseminated as soon as possible the results of its assessment of the consistency of the advertisement with the information in the prospectus.

NOTES

Repeal of this Article in relation to the UK: this Article is repealed, in relation to the UK only, by the Technical Standards (Prospectus Regulation) (EU Exit) Instrument 2020 (FCA 2020/50), as from IP completion day (as defined in the European Union (Withdrawal Agreement) Act 2020, s 39).

CHAPTER V SUPPLEMENTS TO THE PROSPECTUS

[11.634]

Article 18 Publication of a supplement to the prospectus

1. A supplement to the prospectus shall be published where:

(a) new annual audited financial statements are published by any of the following:
  [(i) an issuer where a prospectus relates to shares or other transferable securities equivalent to shares;
  (ii) an issuer of the underlying shares or other transferable securities equivalent to shares in case of securities referred to in Articles 19(2) or 20(2) of Delegated Regulation (EU) 2019/980;]
  (iii) an issuer of the underlying shares of depository receipts referred to in Articles 6 and 14 of Delegated Regulation 2019/980;
(b) an issuer has published a profit forecast or estimate following the approval of the prospectus, where a profit forecast or estimate is required to be included in the prospectus pursuant to Delegated Regulation 2019/980;
(c) an amendment to, or a withdrawal of, a profit forecast or a profit estimate is included in the prospectus;
(d) a change in control occurs in respect of any of the following:
  [(i) an issuer where a prospectus relates to shares or other transferable securities equivalent to shares;
  (ii) an issuer of the underlying shares or other transferable securities equivalent to shares where a prospectus relates to securities referred to in Articles 19(2) or 20(2) of Delegated Regulation (EU) 2019/980;]
  (iii) an issuer of the underlying shares of depository receipts referred to in Articles 6 and 14 of Delegated Regulation 2019/980;
[(e) third parties make a new takeover bid as defined in Article 2(1)(a) of Directive 2004/25/EC of the European Parliament and of the Council[1] or the result of any takeover bid becomes available in respect of any of the following:
  (i) the equity of the issuer where a prospectus relates to shares or other transferable securities equivalent to shares;
  (ii) the equity of the issuer of the underlying shares or other transferable securities equivalent to shares where a prospectus relates to the securities referred to in Articles 19(2) or 20(2) of Delegated Regulation (EU) 2019/980;
  (iii) the equity of the issuer of the underlying shares of depository receipts where a prospectus is drawn up in accordance with Articles 6 and 14 of Delegated Regulation (EC) 2019/980;]
(f) the working capital statement included in a prospectus becomes sufficient or insufficient for the issuer's present requirements, in relation to:
  [(i) shares or other transferable securities equivalent to shares;
  (ii) securities as referred to in Article 19(2) of Delegated Regulation (EU) 2019/980;]
  (iii) depository receipts issued over shares as referred to in Articles 6 and 14 of Delegated Regulation 2019/980.
(g) an issuer is seeking admission to trading on at least one additional regulated market in at least one additional Member State or is intending to make an offer of securities to the public in at least one additional Member State that is not mentioned in the prospectus;
[(h) in the case of a prospectus relating to shares or other transferable securities equivalent to shares or to the securities referred to in Articles 19(2) or 20(2) of Delegated Regulation (EU) 2019/980, a new significant financial commitment is likely to give rise to a significant gross change as defined in Article 1, point (e), of that Delegated Regulation;]
(i) the aggregate nominal amount of the offering programme is increased.

NOTES

All words in square brackets were substituted by Commission Delegated Regulation 2020/1272/EU, Art 1(1), as from 21 July 2019.

Application of this Article in relation to the UK: this Article is amended, in relation to the UK only, by the Technical Standards (Prospectus Regulation) (EU Exit) Instrument 2020 (FCA 2020/50), as from IP completion day (as defined in the European Union (Withdrawal Agreement) Act 2020, s 39), as follows—

— For the words "Article 2(1)(a) of Directive 2004/25/EC of the European Parliament and of the Council" in point (e) of para 1 there are substituted the words "paragraph 20(1) of Schedule 1C to the Companies Act 2006".

— Point (g) of para 1 is repealed.

1 Directive 2004/25/EC of the European Parliament and of the Council of 21 April 2004 on takeover bids (OJ L142, 30.4.2004, p 12).

CHAPTER VI TECHNICAL ARRANGEMENTS FOR THE FUNCTIONING OF THE NOTIFICATION PORTAL

[11.635]

Article 19 Upload of documents and accompanying data

When uploading any documents referred to in Article 25(6) of Regulation (EU) 2017/1129 into the notification portal, the competent authority shall ensure those documents are in a searchable electronic format that cannot be modified and are accompanied by the data relating to those documents as specified in the tables of Annex VII to this Regulation in a common XML format.

NOTES

Repeal of this Article in relation to the UK: this Article is repealed, in relation to the UK only, by the Technical Standards (Prospectus Regulation) (EU Exit) Instrument 2020 (FCA 2020/50), as from IP completion day (as defined in the European Union (Withdrawal Agreement) Act 2020, s 39).

[11.636]

Article 20 Processing and notification of documents and accompanying data

1. ESMA shall ensure that the notification portal automatically processes and checks all uploaded documents and accompanying data and notifies the uploading competent authority of whether the upload was successful and whether the upload contained any error.

2. ESMA shall ensure that the notification portal sends notifications of uploaded documents and accompanying data to the relevant competent authorities.

NOTES

Repeal of this Article in relation to the UK: this Article is repealed, in relation to the UK only, by the Technical Standards (Prospectus Regulation) (EU Exit) Instrument 2020 (FCA 2020/50), as from IP completion day (as defined in the European Union (Withdrawal Agreement) Act 2020, s 39).

[11.637]

[Article 21 Download of documents and accompanying data

ESMA shall ensure that the notification portal makes any uploaded documents and accompanying data available to the relevant competent authorities.]

NOTES

Substituted by Commission Delegated Regulation 2020/1272/EU, Art 2, as from 21 July 2019.

Repeal of this Article in relation to the UK: this Article is repealed, in relation to the UK only, by the Technical Standards (Prospectus Regulation) (EU Exit) Instrument 2020 (FCA 2020/50), as from IP completion day (as defined in the European Union (Withdrawal Agreement) Act 2020, s 39).

CHAPTER VII FINAL PROVISIONS

[11.638]

Article 22 Repeal

Delegated Regulation (EU) No 382/2014 is repealed.

Delegated Regulation (EU) 2016/301 is repealed.

NOTES

Repeal of this Article in relation to the UK: this Article is repealed, in relation to the UK only, by the Technical Standards (Prospectus Regulation) (EU Exit) Instrument 2020 (FCA 2020/50), as from IP completion day (as defined in the European Union (Withdrawal Agreement) Act 2020, s 39).

[11.639]

[Article 22a Summaries of prospectuses approved between 21 July 2019 and 16 September 2020 for non-financial entities issuing equity securities

Summaries of prospectuses that contain information as referred to in Table 3 of Annex I and that have been approved between 21 July 2019 and 16 September 2020 shall continue to be valid until the end of the validity of those prospectuses.]

NOTES

Inserted by Commission Delegated Regulation 2020/1272/EU, Art 1(2), as from 17 September 2020.

[11.640]

Article 23 Entry into force

This Regulation shall enter into force on the twentieth day following that of its publication in the *Official Journal of the European Union*.

It shall apply from 21 July 2019.

This Regulation shall be binding in its entirety and directly applicable in all Member States.

NOTES

Application of this Article in relation to the UK: the words "This Regulation shall be binding in its entirety and directly applicable in all Member States." are repealed, in relation to the UK only, by the Technical Standards (Prospectus Regulation) (EU Exit) Instrument 2020 (FCA 2020/50), as from IP completion day (as defined in the European Union (Withdrawal Agreement) Act 2020, s 39)

[11.641]

ANNEX I
NON-FINANCIAL ENTITIES (EQUITY SECURITIES)

— An entry which is marked with '*' refers to mandatory information or corresponding information where the issuer does not use International Financial Reporting Standards (IFRS). The issuer can use a different title to present substantially the same information as set out in the table, where this alternative title is used in its financial statements.

— An entry which is marked with '#' denotes that if this information appears elsewhere in the prospectus, it is mandatory.

— An entry which is marked with '~' in relation to closed end funds refers to investments at fair value through profit or loss at the same date as the date of the net asset value (NAV).

Table 1
Income statement for non-financial entities (equity securities)

	Year	Year -1	Year -2	Interim	Comparative interim from same period in prior year
*Total revenue					

	Year	Year -1	Year -2	Interim	Comparative interim from same period in prior year
*Operating profit/loss or another similar measure of financial performance used by the issuer in the financial statements					
*Net profit or loss (for consolidated financial statements net profit or loss attributable to equity holders of the parent)					
#Year on year revenue growth					
#Operating profit margin					
#Net profit margin					
#Earnings per share					

Table 2
Balance sheet for non-financial entities (equity securities)

	Year	Year -1	Year -2	Interim
*Total assets				
*Total equity				
#Net financial debt (long term debt plus short term debt minus cash)				

[Table 3
Cash flow statement for non-financial entities (equity securities)

	Year	Year -1	Year -2	Interim	Comparative interim from same period in prior year
*Relevant net Cash flows from operating activities and/or cash flows from investing activities and/or cash from financing activities]					

NOTES

Table 3 substituted by Commission Delegated Regulation 2020/1272/EU, Art 1(3), Annex 1, as from 21 July 2019.

[11.642]

ANNEX II
NON-FINANCIAL ENTITIES (NON-EQUITY SECURITIES)

— An entry which is marked with '*' refers to mandatory information or corresponding information where the issuer does not use International Financial Reporting Standards (IFRS). The issuer can use a different title to present substantially the same information as set out in the table, where this alternative title is used in its financial statements.

— An entry which is marked with '#' denotes that if this information appears elsewhere in the prospectus, it is mandatory.

— An entry which is marked with '~' in relation to closed end funds refers to investments at fair value through profit or loss at the same date as the date of the net asset value (NAV).

Table 1
Income statement for non-equity securities

	Year	Year -1	Interim	Comparative interim from same period in prior year
*Operating profit/loss or another similar measure of financial performance used by the issuer in the financial statements				

Table 2

Balance sheet for non-equity securities

	Year	**Year -1**	**Interim**
*Net financial debt (long term debt plus short term debt minus cash)			
#Current ratio (current assets/current liabilities)			
#Debt to equity ratio (total liabilities/total shareholder equity)			
#Interest cover ratio (operating income/interest expense)			

Table 3

Cash flow statement for non-equity securities

	Year	**Year -1**	**Interim**	**Comparative interim from same period in prior year**
*Net Cash flows from operating activities				
*Net Cash flows from financing activities				
*Net Cash flow from investing activities				

[11.643]

ANNEX III
CREDIT INSTITUTIONS (EQUITY AND NON-EQUITY SECURITIES)

— An entry which is marked with '*' refers to mandatory information or corresponding information where the issuer does not use International Financial Reporting Standards (IFRS). The issuer can use a different title to present substantially the same information as set out in the table, where this alternative title is used in its financial statements.

— An entry which is marked with '#' denotes that if this information appears elsewhere in the prospectus, it is mandatory.

— An entry which is marked with '~' in relation to closed end funds refers to investments at fair value through profit or loss at the same date as the date of the net asset value (NAV).

Table 1

Income statement for credit institutions

	Year	**Year -1**	**Year -2**[1]	**Interim**	**Comparative interim from same period in prior year**
*Net interest income (or equivalent)					
*Net fee and commission income					
*Net impairment loss on financial assets					
*Net trading income					
*Measure of financial performance used by the issuer in the financial statements such as operating profit					
*Net profit or loss (for consolidated financial statements net profit or loss attributable to equity holders of the parent)					
#Earnings per share (for equity issuers only)					

Table 2
Balance sheet for credit institutions

	Year	Year -1	Year -2[1]	Interim	#Value as outcome from the most recent Supervisory Review and Evaluation Process ('SREP')
*Total assets					
*Senior debt					
*Subordinated debt					
*Loans and receivables from customers (net)					
*Deposits from customers					
*Total equity					
#Non-performing loans (based on net carrying amount)/Loans and receivables)					
#Common Equity Tier 1 capital (CET1) ratio or other relevant prudential capital adequacy ratio depending on the issuance					
#Total Capital Ratio					
#Leverage Ratio calculated under applicable regulatory framework					

NOTES

[1] Please indicate the key financial information for the number of years for which the relevant information requirement applies pursuant to Delegated Regulation 2019/980.

[11.644]

ANNEX IV
INSURANCE COMPANIES (EQUITY AND NON-EQUITY SECURITIES)

— An entry which is marked with '*' refers to mandatory information or corresponding information where the issuer does not use International Financial Reporting Standards (IFRS). The issuer can use a different title to present substantially the same information as set out in the table, where this alternative title is used in its financial statements.

— An entry which is marked with '#' denotes that if this information appears elsewhere in the prospectus, it is mandatory.

— An entry which is marked with '~' in relation to closed end funds refers to investments at fair value through profit or loss at the same date as the date of the net asset value (NAV).

Table 1
Income statement for insurance companies

	Year	Year -1	Year -2[1]	Interim	Comparative interim from same period in prior year
*Net premiums					
*Net benefits and claims					
*Earnings before tax					
*Operating profit (distinguishing between life and non-life insurance)					
*Net profit or loss (for consolidated financial statements net profit or loss attributable to equity holders of the parent)					
#Year on year revenue growth (net premiums)					
#Earnings per share (for equity issuers only)					

Table 2
Balance sheet for insurance companies

	Year	Year -1	Year -2[1]	Interim
*Investments including financial assets related to unit linked contracts				
*Total assets				
*Insurance contract liabilities				
*Financial liabilities				
*Total liabilities				
*Total equity				
#Solvency Cover Ratio (Solvency II ratio — SII ratio) or other relevant other relevant prudential capital requirement ratio depending on the issuance				
#Loss ratio				
#Combined ratio (claims + expenses/premiums for the period)				

NOTES

[1] Please indicate the key financial information for the number of years for which the relevant information requirement applies pursuant to Delegated Regulation 2019/980.

[11.645]

ANNEX V
SPECIAL PURPOSE VEHICLES ('SPVS') ISSUING ASSET BACKED SECURITIES

— An entry which is marked with '*' refers to mandatory information or corresponding information where the issuer does not use International Financial Reporting Standards (IFRS). The issuer can use a different title to present substantially the same information as set out in the table, where this alternative title is used in its financial statements.

— An entry which is marked with '#' denotes that if this information appears elsewhere in the prospectus, it is mandatory.

— An entry which is marked with '~' in relation to closed end funds refers to investments at fair value through profit or loss at the same date as the date of the net asset value (NAV).

Table 1
Income statement for SPVs in relation to asset backed securities

	Year	Year -1
*Net profit or loss		

Table 2
Balance sheet for SPVs in relation to asset backed securities

	Year	Year -1
*Total Assets		
*Total Liabilities		
*Financial Assets designated at fair value through profit or loss		
*Derivative financial assets		
*Non-financial assets if material to the entity's business		
*Financial Liabilities designated at fair value through profit or loss		
*Derivative financial liabilities		

[11.646]

ANNEX VI
CLOSED END FUNDS

— An entry which is marked with '*' refers to mandatory information or corresponding information where the issuer does not use International Financial Reporting Standards (IFRS). The issuer can use a different title to present substantially the same information as set out in the table, where this alternative title is used in its financial statements.

— An entry which is marked with '#' denotes that if this information appears elsewhere in the prospectus, it is mandatory.

— An entry which is marked with '~' in relation to closed end funds refers to investments at fair value through profit or loss at the same date as the date of the net asset value (NAV).

Table 1
Additional information relevant to closed end funds

Share Class	Total NAV	No. of shares/ units	~NAV/share or Market price/ share/unit	#Historical performance of the fund
A	XXX	XX	X	
	Overall Total	Overall Total		

Table 2
Income statement for closed end funds

	Year	Year -1	Year -2	Interim	Comparative interim from same period in prior year
*Total net Income/Net investment Income or total income before operating expenses					
*Net Profit/(Loss)					
*Performance fee (accrued/paid)					
*Investment management fee (accrued/paid)					
*Any other material fees (accrued/paid) to service providers					
#Earnings per share					

Table 3
Balance sheet for closed end funds

	Year	Year -1	Year -2	Interim
*Total Net Assets				
#Leverage ratio				

[11.647]

ANNEX VII
MACHINE-READABLE DATA TO BE PROVIDED TO ESMA

Table 1

Number	*Field*	*Content to be reported*	*Format and Standard to be used for reporting*
1.	*National identifier*	*Unique identifier of the uploaded record, assigned by the sending NCA*	*{ALPHANUM-50}*
2.	*Related national identifier*	*Unique identifier of the record to which the uploaded record relates, assigned by the sending NCA* *Not reported in case the related national identifier is not applicable*	*{ALPHANUM-50}*
3.	*Sending Member State*	*Country code of the Member State which approved the uploaded record or with which the uploaded record was filed*	*{COUNTRYCODE_2}*
4.	*Receiving Member State(s)*	*Country code of the Member State(s) to which uploaded record is to be notified or communicated* *When multiple Member States shall be communi-*	*{COUNTRYCODE_2}*

Number	*Field*	*Content to be reported*	*Format and Standard to be used for reporting*
		cated, field 4 shall be reported as many times as necessary	
5.	*Document type*	*The type of uploaded document(s)*	*Choice from list of predefined fields:* *— 'BPFT' — Base prospectus with final terms* *— 'BPWO' — Base prospectus without final terms* *— 'STDA' — Standalone prospectus* *— 'REGN' — Registration document* *— 'URGN' — Universal registration document* *— 'SECN' — Securities note* *— 'FTWS' — Final terms, including the summary of the individual issue annexed to them* *— 'SMRY' — Summary* *— 'SUPP' — Supplement* *— 'SUMT' — Translation of summary* *— 'COAP' — Certificate of Approval* *— 'AMND' — Amendment* *When multiple documents shall be communicated, field [5] shall be reported as many times as necessary to describe each document composing the record*
6.	*Structure type*	*The format chosen for the prospectus*	*Choice from list of predefined fields:* *— 'SNGL' — Single document prospectus* *— 'SPWS' — Prospectus consisting of separate documents with summary* *— 'SPWO' — Prospectus consisting of separate documents without summary*
7.	*Approval or filing date*	*The date on which the uploaded record was approved or filed*	*{DATEFORMAT}*
8.	*Language*	*The EU language in which the uploaded record is drafted*	*{LANGUAGE}*
9.	*Offeror standardised name*	*Name and surname of the offeror in case the offeror is a natural person* *When multiple offerors shall be communicated, field [9] shall be reported as many times as necessary*	*{ALPHANUM-280}*
10.	*Guarantor standardised name*	*Name and surname of the guarantor in case the guarantor is a natural person* *When multiple guarantors shall be communicated, field [10] shall be reported as many times as necessary*	*{ALPHANUM-280}*
11.	*Issuer LEI*	*Legal Entity Identifier of the issuer* *When multiple issuers shall be communicated, field [11] shall be reported as many times as necessary*	*{LEI}*
12.	*Offeror LEI*	*Legal Entity Identifier of the*	*{LEI}*

Number	*Field*	*Content to be reported*	*Format and Standard to be used for reporting*
		offeror *When multiple offerors shall be communicated, field [12] shall be reported as many times as necessary*	
13.	*Guarantor LEI*	*Legal Entity Identifier of the guarantor* *When multiple guarantors shall be communicated, field [13] shall be reported as many times as necessary*	*{LEI}*
14.	*Offeror residency*	*Offeror's residency in case the offeror is a natural person* *When multiple offerors shall be communicated, field [14] shall be reported as many times as necessary*	*{COUNTRYCODE_2}*
15.	*Guarantor residency*	*Guarantor's residency in case the guarantor is a natural person* *When multiple guarantors shall be communicated, field [15] shall be reported as many times as necessary*	*{COUNTRYCODE_2}*
16.	*FISN*	*Financial Instrument Short Name of the security* *This field should be repeated for each ISIN*	*{FISN}*
17.	*ISIN*	*International Securities Identification Number*	*{ISIN}*
18.	*CFI*	*Classification of Financial Instrument code* *This field should be repeated for each ISIN*	*{CFI_CODE}*
19.	*Issuance currency*	*Code representing the currency in which the nominal or notional value is denominated* *This field should be repeated for each ISIN*	*{CURRENCYCODE_3}*
20.	*Denomination per unit*	*Nominal value or notional value per unit in the issuance currency* *This field should be repeated for each ISIN* *Field applicable to securities with defined denomination*	*{DECIMAL-18/5}*
21.	*Identifier or name of the underlying*	*ISIN code of the underlying security/index or name of the underlying security/index if an ISIN does not exist* *When basket of securities, to be identified accordingly* *Field applicable to securities with defined underlying. This field should be repeated for each ISIN of such securities*	*For unique underlying:* *— In case of security or index with existing ISIN: {ISIN}* *— In case the index has no ISIN: {INDEX}* *— Otherwise: {ALPHANUM-50}* *For multiple underlyings (more than one): 'BSKT'*
22.	*Maturity or expiry date*	*Date of maturity or expiry date of the security, when applicable*	*{DATEFORMAT}*

Number	*Field*	*Content to be reported*	*Format and Standard to be used for reporting*
		This field should be repeated for each ISIN *Field applicable to securities with defined maturity*	*For perpetual debt securities field 22 should be populated with the value 9999-12-31.*
23.	*Volume offered*	*Number of securities offered* *Field applicable only to equity* *This field should be repeated for each applicable ISIN*	*{INTEGER-18}* *Either as single value, range of values, maximum*
24.	*Price offered*	*Price per security offered, in monetary value. The currency of the price is the issuance currency* *Field applicable only to equity* *This field should be repeated for each applicable ISIN*	*{DECIMAL-18/5}* *Either as single value, range of values, maximum* *'PNDG' in case the price offered is not available but pending* *'NOAP' in case the price offered is not applicable*
25.	*Consideration offered*	*Total amount offered, in monetary value of the issuance currency* *This field should be repeated for each ISIN*	*{DECIMAL-18/5}* *Either as single value, range of values, maximum* *'PNDG' in case the consideration offered is not available but pending* *'NOAP' in case the consideration offered is not applicable*
26.	*Type of security*	*Classification of categories of equity and non-equity securities* *This field should be repeated for each ISIN*	*Choice from list of predefined fields:* *Equity* *— 'SHRS': Share* *— 'UCEF': Unit or share in closed end funds* *— 'CVTS': Convertible security* *— '[DPRS]': Depository receipt* *— 'OTHR': Other equity* *Debt* *— 'DWLD': Debt with denomination per unit of at least EUR 100,000* *— 'DWHD': Debt with denomination per unit of less than EUR 100,000* *— 'DLRM': Debt with denomination per unit of less than EUR 100,000 traded on a regulated market to which only qualified investors have access to* *'ABSE': ABS* *'DERV': Derivative security*
27.	*Type of offer/admission*	*Taxonomy according to PR and MiFID/MIFIR*	*Choice from list of predefined fields:* *— 'IOWA': Initial offer without admission to trading/ listing* *— 'SOWA': Secondary offer without admission to trading/listing* *— 'IRMT': Initial admission to trading on regulated market* *— 'IPTM': Initial admission to trading on regulated market from previously*

Number	*Field*	*Content to be reported*	*Format and Standard to be used for reporting*
			being traded on MTF *— 'IMTF': Initial admission to trading on MTF with offer to the public* *— 'SIRM': Secondary issuance on a regulated market or MTF*
28.	*Characteristics of the trading venue where the security is initially admitted to trading*	*Taxonomy according to PR and MiFID/MIFIR*	*Choice from list of predefined fields:* *— 'RMKT': RM open to all investors* *— 'RMQI': RM, or segment thereof, limited to qualified investors* *— 'MSGM': MTF which is a SME growth market* *— 'MLTF': MTF which is not a SME growth market*
29.	*Disclosure regime*	*The annex number in accordance with which the prospectus is drafted under the Commission Delegated Regulation (EU) []* *When multiple annexes shall be communicated, field 29 shall be reported as many times as necessary*	*{INTEGER-2} From 1 to [29]*
30.	*EU Growth prospectus category*	*Reason based on which an EU Growth prospectus has been used*	*Choice from list of predefined fields:* *— 'S15A': SME under PR Article 15(1)(a)* *— 'I15B': Issuer other than SME under PR Article 15(1)(b)* *— 'I15C': Issuer other than SME under PR Article 15(1)(c)* *— 'O15D': Offeror of securities under PR Article 15(1)(d)*

Table 2

Symbol	*Data Type*	*Definition*
{ALPHANUM-n}	*Up to n alphanumerical characters*	*Free text field*
{CFI_CODE}	*6 characters*	*CFI code, as defined in ISO10962*
{COUNTRYCODE_2}	*2 alphanumerical characters*	*2 letter country code, as defined by ISO 3166-1 alfa-2 country code*
{DATEFORMAT}	*Dates in the following format: YYYY-MM-DD* *Dates shall be reported in UTC*	*ISO 8601 date format*
{LANGUAGE}	*2 letter code*	*ISO639-1*
{LEI}	*20 alphanumerical characters*	*Legal entity identifier as defined in ISO17442*
{FISN}	*35 alphanumerical characters with the following structure*	*FISN code, as defined in ISO 18774*
{ISIN}	*12 alphanumerical characters*	*ISIN code, as defined in ISO 6166*
{CURRENCYCODE_3}	*3 alphanumerical characters*	*3 letter currency code, as defined by ISO 4217 currency codes*
{DECIMAL-n/m}	*Decimal number of up to n digit in total, of which up to m digits can be fraction digits*	*Numerical field* *Decimal separator is '.' (full stop)* *Values are rounded and not truncated*
{INTEGER-n}	*Integer number of up to n digits in*	*Numerical field*

Symbol	*Data Type*	*Definition*
	total	
{INDEX}	*4 alphabetic characters*	*'EONA' — EONIA* *'EONS' — EONIA SWAP* *'EURI' — EURIBOR* *'EUUS' — EURODOLLAR* *'EUCH' — EuroSwiss* *'GCFR' — GCF REPO* *'ISDA' — ISDAFIX* *'LIBI' — LIBID* *'LIBO' — LIBOR* *'MAAA' — Muni AAA* *'PFAN' — Pfandbriefe* *'TIBO' — TIBOR* *'STBO' — STIBOR* *'BBSW' — BBSW* *'JIBA' — JIBAR* *'BUBO' — BUBOR* *'CDOR' — CDOR* *'CIBO' — CIBOR* *'MOSP' – MOSPRIM* *'NIBO' — NIBOR* *'PRBO' — PRIBOR* *'TLBO' — TELBOR* *'WIBO' — WIBOR* *'TREA' — Treasury* *'SWAP' — SWAP* *'FUSW' — Future SWA*

NOTES

In Table 1, in the column 'Format and Standard to be used for reporting', in entry 26, 'DPRS' was substituted by Commission Delegated Regulation 2020/1272/EU, Art 1(4), Annex 2, as from 21 July 2019.

Repeal of this Annex in relation to the UK: this Annex is repealed, in relation to the UK only, by the Technical Standards (Prospectus Regulation) (EU Exit) Instrument 2020 (FCA 2020/50), as from IP completion day (as defined in the European Union (Withdrawal Agreement) Act 2020, s 39).

COMMISSION DELEGATED REGULATION

(2019/980/EU)

of 14 March 2019

supplementing Regulation (EU) 2017/1129 of the European Parliament and of the Council as regards the format, content, scrutiny and approval of the prospectus to be published when securities are offered to the public or admitted to trading on a regulated market, and repealing Commission Regulation (EC) No 809/2004

(Text with EEA relevance)

[11.648]

NOTES

Date of publication in OJ: OJ L166, 21.6.2019, p 26.

This Regulation is reproduced as amended by: Commission Delegated Regulation 2020/1273/EU.

Application of this Regulation in relation to the UK: in accordance with the European Union (Withdrawal) Act 2018, s 3 at **[12.5]**, this Regulation became domestic law on IP completion day (as defined in the European Union (Withdrawal Agreement) Act 2020, s 39). In so far as applying to the UK, this Regulation is amended by the Prospectus (Amendment etc) (EU Exit) Regulations 2019, SI 2019/1234, as from IP completion day. The amendments are set out below. With regard to these amendments, note that new Articles are inserted, and Articles that are repealed are reproduced in italics. In the case of other amendments, the relevant amending provision from the 2019 Regulations is set out in the Notes to the amended Article, and the text of the amended Article has not been altered. Note also that post-IP completion day, this Regulation has been amended by the Financial Services Act 2021 (Prudential Regulation of Credit Institutions and Investment Firms) (Consequential Amendments and Miscellaneous Provisions) Regulations 2022, SI 2022/838.

THE EUROPEAN COMMISSION,

Having regard to the Treaty on the Functioning of the European Union,

Having regard to Regulation (EU) 2017/1129 of the European Parliament and of the Council of 14 June 2017 on the prospectus to be published when securities are offered to the public or admitted to trading on a regulated market, and repealing Directive 2003/71/EC,[1] and in particular Article 9(14), paragraphs (1) and (2) of Article 13, Articles 14(3), 15(2) and 20(11) thereof,

Whereas:

(1) Regulation (EU) 2017/1129 lays down requirements to be complied with when drawing up prospectuses. The requirements concerning the scrutiny, review, approval and filing of the universal registration document and any amendments thereto, the requirements concerning the format of the prospectus, the base prospectus and the final terms, the specific information to be included in a prospectus, the minimum information to be included in the universal registration document, the reduced information to be included under the simplified disclosure regime for secondary issuances, the reduced content, the standardised format and the sequence of the EU Growth prospectus, the reduced content and standardised format of the specific summary and the scrutiny and approval of prospectuses all need to be specified.

(2) The content and the format of a prospectus depend on a variety of factors, such as the type of issuer, type of security, type of issuance as well as the possible involvement of a third party as a guarantor and the question of whether or not there is an admission to trading. It is therefore not appropriate to lay down the same requirements for all types of prospectuses. Specific information requirements should be laid down instead and should be combined depending on those factors and the type of prospectus. This should however not prevent an issuer, offeror or person asking for admission to trading on a regulated market to provide in the prospectus the most comprehensive information available.

(3) To ensure legal certainty and increase transparency for investors, issuers should state in their universal registration document whether the universal registration document has been approved by the competent authority or merely has been filed and published without prior approval.

(4) The alleviated information requirements for secondary issuances should reflect the specificities of equity and non-equity securities.

(5) Collective investment undertakings of the close-end type pursue specific investment objectives and might be subject to specific investment restrictions. The registration documents for those undertakings should therefore be subject to specific information requirements.

(6) Due to the indirect link between the investor and the underlying shares of depository receipts, it is important that the investor is informed about the issuer of the underlying shares. The prospectus for depository receipts should therefore contain, apart from information about the depositary receipt and the issuer of the depository receipt, information about the underlying shares and the issuer of those underlying shares.

(7) The information contained in prospectuses for non-equity securities should be adapted to the level of knowledge and expertise of each type of investor. Prospectuses for non-equity securities in which retail investors can invest should therefore be subject to more comprehensive and distinct information requirements than prospectuses for non-equity securities that are reserved to qualified investors.

(8) The obligation to produce a prospectus applies to non-equity securities issued by third countries and their regional and local authorities in cases where those entities wish to make a public offer of securities in the Union or wish their securities to be admitted to trading on a regulated market. Due to the particular nature of those public entities, specific information requirements should be laid down.

(9) Investors should be able to understand the situation of an issuer with a complex financial history and the expected effects of a transaction involving a significant financial commitment. Those issuers should therefore be required to include additional information in the prospectus to that effect.

(10) Where securities are exchangeable for or convertible into shares that are already admitted to trading on a regulated market, shareholders and investors normally already have the information about the underlying shares of those securities. It is therefore sufficient to add to the prospectus a statement setting out the type of the underlying share and details of where information about the underlying share can be obtained.

(11) Investors may want to invest in securities that are exchangeable for or convertible into shares that are or will be issued by the issuer of those securities or by an entity belonging to that issuer's group and that have not yet been admitted to trading on a regulated market. Those investors should have the same information about the ability of the issuer of the underlying shares to continue its operations and about its indebtedness compared to its capitalisation as investors that have invested in those shares directly. The prospectus should therefore contain a working capital statement as well as a statement of capitalisation and indebtedness of the issuer of the underlying shares.

(12) Derivative securities entail particular risks for investors because, for instance, the losses might be higher than the investment made and because the underlying is not always admitted to trading on a regulated market and information about that underlying might therefore not be available. Some non-equity securities, such as structured bonds, also incorporate certain elements of a derivative security. Consequently, the securities note should contain additional information about the underlying of a derivative security or about the derivative component of the non-equity security and, where applicable, a statement about the potential losses that investors might face.

(13) Where a base prospectus is drawn up for securities linked to or backed by an underlying asset, that base prospectus should contain all information about the type of underlying asset where that underlying asset is known at the date of approval of the base prospectus. Market conditions may however change the choice of the underlying asset within a category of underlying assets. Only the final terms of the base prospectus should therefore contain specific details about that underlying asset.

(14) Guarantees are intended to ensure that the payments related to the security are duly serviced. Given the potential diversity in guarantees, clear information requirements related to the nature and the scope of those guarantees should be laid down.

(15) The format of the prospectus, base prospectus and final terms should be specified by determining the order in which the required information should be disclosed. However, due to the multipurpose character of the universal registration document, issuers who choose to draw up and publish a universal registration document every financial

year should be granted more flexibility as regards the order of information to be provided in the universal registration document.

(16) Whilst the base prospectus should contain all information available at the time of drawing up that base prospectus, it should be possible to leave blanks as regards specific information that only becomes available at a later stage and is to be found in the final terms, or to include a list of that missing information.

(17) It is not always required to include a summary into the prospectus. That should however not prevent the insertion of an overview section into the prospectus. To avoid confusion among investors, such overview section should however not be called a summary, unless it complies with all the requirements for summaries.

(18) The EU growth prospectus is intended to alleviate the administrative burden, in particular for SMEs. It is therefore appropriate to simplify the drafting of EU growth prospectuses by laying down a fixed order in which the information should be presented. However, to ensure that information is presented in a manner that is coherent and consistent with the different business models, flexibility should be allowed as regards the order of information items within each section of the EU growth prospectus.

(19) To allow for flexibility and to encourage the use of the EU growth prospectus, it should be possible that the EU growth prospectus is composed of separate documents. To avoid the risk of duplicating information, separate detailed information requirements for the specific registration document on the one hand and for the specific securities note on the other should be laid down and adapted to the type of securities concerned, differentiating between equity and non-equity securities.

(20) The specific summary of the EU Growth prospectus should provide investors with key information needed to decide which offers of securities they want to study further by reviewing the prospectus as a whole. It should therefore convey the essential characteristics of, and risks associated with, the issuer and the securities offered and contain the general terms and conditions of the offer. However, given that the specific summary is only an introduction to the EU Growth prospectus and must be read together with the other parts thereof, the content of the specific summary should be consistent with those other parts. To ensure that the size of the specific summary is tailored to the reduced size of the EU Growth prospectus, the length of the summary should be restricted.

(21) To ensure that competent authorities apply harmonised standards across the Union when scrutinising prospectuses, and in particular the completeness, comprehensibility and consistency of the information contained in draft prospectuses, criteria for prospectus scrutiny should be laid down. Those criteria should be applied for the entire draft prospectus and any of its constituent parts, including the universal registration document and any amendments and supplements to the prospectus.

(22) A high level of investor protection should be ensured. Competent authorities should therefore be allowed to consider, where necessary, additional criteria for the scrutiny of the completeness, consistency and comprehensibility of draft prospectuses in order to adapt that scrutiny to the specific characteristics of a prospectus.

(23) Some issuers are involved into very specific business activities that require a profound knowledge of the activities concerned to have a full understanding of the securities issued by those issuers. That would apply for example in the case of a property company that could be required to disclose a valuation report providing all relevant details in respect of material properties necessary for the purposes of the valuation. Competent authorities should therefore be able to take a proportionate approach and require, where appropriate, that those specialist issuers include in the prospectus specific and adapted information about those activities that goes beyond the information required from non-specialist issuers.

(24) Due to the rapid evolution of securities markets, there is the possibility that certain types of securities that are not covered by the Annexes to this Regulation will be offered to the public or admitted to trading. In such a case, to enable investors to make an informed investment decision, competent authorities should decide in consultation with the issuer, offeror or person asking for admission to trading on a regulated market which information should be included in the prospectus.

(25) To drive efficiency in the process of drawing up the prospectus and eliminate unnecessary burdens, it is appropriate to allow the omission of information items set out in the Annexes to this Regulation that are not pertinent to the issuer or to the securities being offered or admitted to trading on a regulated market.

(26) Scrutiny and approval of prospectuses is an iterative process. As such, the decision of the competent authority to approve the draft prospectus may involve several rounds of analysis of the draft prospectus and ensuing improvements by the issuer, offeror or person asking for admission to trading on a regulated market to ensure that the draft prospectus meets the standards of completeness, comprehensibility and consistency. To provide certainty about the approval process, it is necessary to specify which documents should be provided to competent authorities at the different stages of the approval process.

(27) For reasons of efficiency, competent authorities should be permitted to carry out a lighter scrutiny where a draft prospectus replicates information that has already been scrutinised or reviewed.

(28) To enable competent authorities to search for specific terms or words in submitted documents and thus to ensure an efficient and timely scrutiny process of the prospectuses, draft prospectuses and accompanying information should be submitted in searchable electronic format and through electronic means acceptable to the competent authority.

(29) Issuers, offerors or persons asking for admission to trading on a regulated market should be able to demonstrate to the competent authority how they addressed issues notified by that authority. Each draft of the prospectus submitted to the competent authority, with the exception of the first draft, should therefore contain both a marked-up version that clearly highlights all changes made to the previously submitted draft, and a clean version where such changes are not highlighted.

(30) To minimise delays in the scrutiny process, competent authorities should be able to identify quickly information requirements that are not applicable or not relevant. For that purpose, the competent authorities should be informed about the information that has not been included in the draft prospectus.

(31) To facilitate the drawing up of a prospectus and thus to facilitate the raising of capital by undertakings established in the Union, and to ensure that common standards are applied when scrutinizing and approving

prospectuses, all requirements related to the format, content, scrutiny and approval of prospectuses should be laid down in a single Regulation.

(32) Since this Delegated Regulation replaces Commission Regulation (EC) No 809/2004,[2] the latter has become obsolete and should therefore be repealed.

(33) For reasons of coherence, the application of this Regulation should be deferred until the date of application of Regulation (EU) 2017/1129,

NOTES

[1] OJ L168, 30.6.2017, p. 12.

[2] Commission Regulation (EC) No 809/2004 of 29 April 2004 implementing Directive 2003/71/EC of the European Parliament and of the Council as regards information contained in prospectuses as well as the format, incorporation by reference and publication of such prospectuses and dissemination of advertisements (OJ L149, 30.4.2004, p. 1).

HAS ADOPTED THIS REGULATION:

CHAPTER I DEFINITIONS

[11.649]

Article 1 Definitions

For the purposes of this Regulation, the following definitions shall apply:

(a) 'asset-backed securities' means non-equity securities which either:
 (i) represent an interest in assets, including any rights intended to ensure the servicing of those assets, the receipt or the timely receipt by holders of those assets of the amounts payable under those assets;
 (ii) are secured by assets and the terms of the securities provide for payments calculated by reference to those assets;

(b) 'equivalent third country market' means a third country market which has been deemed equivalent to a regulated market in accordance with the requirements set out in third and fourth subparagraphs of Article 25(4) of Directive 2014/65/EU of the European Parliament and of the Council;[1]

(c) 'profit estimate' means a profit forecast for a financial period which has expired and for which results have not yet been published;

(d) 'profit forecast' means a statement that expressly or by implication indicates a figure or a minimum or maximum figure for the likely level of profits or losses for current or future financial periods, or contains data from which a calculation of such a figure for future profits or losses can be made, even if no particular figure is mentioned and the word 'profit' is not used;

(e) 'significant gross change' means a variation of more than 25% to one or more indicators of the size of the issuer's business.

NOTES

Application of this Article in relation to the UK: this Article is amended (as follows), in relation to the UK only, by the Prospectus (Amendment etc) (EU Exit) Regulations 2019, SI 2019/1234, reg 71(2), as from IP completion day (as defined in the European Union (Withdrawal Agreement) Act 2020, s 39); for transitional provisions, see regs 74, 75 of the 2019 Regulations at **[12.165]** et seq—

"(2) In Article 1—

(a) for paragraph (b) substitute—

"(b) equivalent third country market" means a third country market which has been—
deemed equivalent to a regulated market by the Commission, in accordance with the third and fourth subparagraphs of Article 25(4) of Directive 2014/65/EU of the European Parliament and of the Council of 15 May 2014 on markets in financial instruments and amending Directive 2002/92/EC and Directive 2011/61/EU, before IP completion day in retained EU law, or
specified as equivalent to a regulated market in regulations made by the Treasury under paragraph 8 of Schedule 3 to Regulation (EU) No 600/2014 of the European Parliament and of the Council of 15 May 2014 on markets in financial instruments and amending Regulation (EU) No 648/2012;";

(b) after paragraph (e) insert—

"(f) 'competent authority' means the Financial Conduct Authority;
(g) 'UK accounting standards' means accounting standards as defined by section 464 of the Companies Act 2006;
(h) 'UK-adopted international accounting standards' has the meaning given by section 474(1) of the Companies Act 2006;
(i) a reference to the United Kingdom law which implemented a Directive, or a provision thereof, is to the law of the United Kingdom which was relied on by the United Kingdom immediately before IP completion day to implement that Directive and its implementing measures—
 (i) as they have effect on IP completion day, in the case of rules made by the Financial Conduct Authority under the Financial Services and Markets Act 2000, and
 (ii) as amended from time to time, in all other cases.".".

Note that the Prospectus (Amendment etc) (EU Exit) Regulations 2019, SI 2019/1234, reg 71(2) was amended by the Financial Services and Economic and Monetary Policy (Consequential Amendments) (EU Exit) Regulations 2020, SI 2020/1301, reg 3, Schedule, para 48(e), as from 30 December 2020 (and the effect of the amendments has been incorporated in the text set out above).

[1] Directive 2014/65/EU of the European Parliament and of the Council of 15 May 2014 on markets in financial instruments and amending Directive 2002/92/EC and Directive 2011/61/EU (OJ L173, 12.6.2014, p. 349).

CHAPTER II CONTENT OF THE PROSPECTUS

SECTION 1 MINIMUM INFORMATION TO BE INCLUDED IN THE REGISTRATION DOCUMENTS

[11.650]

[Article 2 Registration document for equity securities

1. For equity securities, the registration document shall contain the information referred to in Annex 1 to this Regulation, unless it is drawn up in accordance with Articles 9, 14 or 15 of Regulation (EU) 2017/1129.

2. By way of derogation from paragraph 1, the registration document for the following securities, where those securities are not shares or other transferable securities equivalent to shares, may be drawn up in accordance with Article 7 of this Regulation for retail securities or Article 8 of this Regulation for wholesale securities:

(a) the securities referred to in Articles 19(1) and 20(1) of this Regulation;

(b) the securities referred to in Article 19(2) of this Regulation, where those securities are exchangeable for or convertible into shares that are or will be issued by an entity belonging to the issuer's group and that are not admitted to trading on a regulated market;

(c) the securities referred to in Article 20(2) of this Regulation, where those securities give the right to subscribe or acquire shares that are or will be issued by an entity belonging to the issuer's group and that are not admitted to trading on a regulated market.]

NOTES

Substituted by Commission Delegated Regulation 2020/1273/EU, Art 1(1), as from 21 July 2019.

[11.651]

Article 3 Universal registration document

A registration document that is drawn up in accordance with Article 9 of Regulation (EU) 2017/1129 shall contain the information referred to in Annex 2 to this Regulation.

[11.652]

[Article 4 Registration document for secondary issuances of equity securities

1. A specific registration document for equity securities that is drawn up in accordance with Article 14 of Regulation (EU) 2017/1129 shall contain the information referred to in Annex 3 to this Regulation.

2. By way of derogation from paragraph 1, the registration document for the following securities, where those securities are not shares or other transferable securities equivalent to shares, may be drawn up in accordance with Article 9:

(a) the securities referred to in Articles 19(1) and 20(1) of this Regulation;

(b) the securities referred to in Article 19(2) of this Regulation, where those securities are exchangeable for or convertible into shares that are or will be issued by an entity belonging to the issuer's group and that are not admitted to trading on a regulated market;

(c) the securities referred to in Article 20(2) of this Regulation, where those securities give the right to subscribe or acquire shares that are or will be issued by an entity belonging to the issuer's group and that are not admitted to trading on a regulated market.]

NOTES

Substituted by Commission Delegated Regulation 2020/1273/EU, Art 1(2), as from 21 July 2019.

[11.653]

Article 5 Registration document for units of closed-end collective investment undertakings

For units issued by collective investment undertakings of the closed-end type, the registration document shall contain the information referred to in Annex 4.

[11.654]

Article 6 Registration document for depository receipts issued over shares

For depository receipts issued over shares, the registration document shall contain the information referred to in Annex 5.

[11.655]

Article 7 Registration document for retail non-equity securities

For non-equity securities other than those referred to in Article 8(2) of this Regulation, the registration document shall contain the information referred to in Annex 6 to this Regulation, unless it is drawn up in accordance with Articles 9, 14 or 15 of Regulation (EU) 2017/1129 or contains the information referred to in Annex 1 to this Regulation.

[11.656]

Article 8 Registration document for wholesale non-equity securities

1. For non-equity securities as referred to in paragraph 2, the registration document shall contain the information referred to in Annex 7 to this Regulation, unless the registration document is drawn up in accordance with Articles 9, 14 or 15 of Regulation (EU) 2017/1129 or contains the information referred to in Annexes 1 or 6 to this Regulation.

2. The requirement referred to in paragraph 1 shall apply to non-equity securities that comply with one of the following conditions:

(a) they are to be traded only on a regulated market, or a specific segment thereof, to which only qualified investors can have access for the purposes of trading in such securities;

(b) they have a denomination per unit of at least than EUR 100,000 or, where there is no individual denomination, can only be acquired on issue for at least EUR 100,000 per security.

[11.657]

Article 9 Registration document for secondary issuances of non-equity securities

A specific registration document for non-equity securities that is drawn up in accordance with Article 14 of Regulation (EU) 2017/1129 shall contain the information referred to in Annex 8 to this Regulation, unless it contains the information referred to in Annex 3 to this Regulation.

[11.658]

Article 10 Registration document for asset-backed securities

By way of derogation from Articles 7 and 8, a registration document that is drawn up for asset-backed securities, shall contain the information referred to in Annex 9.

[11.659]

Article 11 Registration document for non-equity securities issued by third countries and their regional and local authorities

By way of derogation from Articles 7 and 8, a registration document that is drawn up for non-equity securities issued by third countries or their regional or local authorities, shall contain the information referred to in Annex 10.

NOTES

Repeal of this Article in relation to the UK: this Article is repealed, in relation to the UK only, by the Prospectus (Amendment etc) (EU Exit) Regulations 2019, SI 2019/1234, reg 71(2A), as from IP completion day (as defined in the European Union (Withdrawal Agreement) Act 2020, s 39); for transitional provisions, see regs 74, 75 of the 2019 Regulations at **[12.165]** et seq. Note that reg 71(2A) of the 2019 Regulations was inserted by the Securities Financing Transactions, Securitisation and Miscellaneous Amendments (EU Exit) Regulations 2020, SI 2020/1385, reg 66(2)(a), with effect from immediately before IP completion day.

SECTION 2 MINIMUM INFORMATION TO BE INCLUDED IN THE SECURITIES NOTES

[11.660]

[Article 12 Securities note for equity securities or units issued by collective investment undertakings of the closed-end type

1. For equity securities or units issued by collective investment undertakings of the closed-end type, the securities note shall contain the information referred to in Annex 11 to this Regulation, unless it is drawn up in accordance with Articles 14 or 15 of Regulation (EU) 2017/1129.

2. By way of derogation from paragraph 1, the securities note for the securities referred to in paragraphs 1 and 2 of Article 19 and paragraphs 1 and 2 of Article 20 of this Regulation, where those securities are not shares or other transferable securities equivalent to shares, shall be drawn up in accordance with Article 15 of this Regulation for retail securities or Article 16 of this Regulation for wholesale securities.]

NOTES

Substituted by Commission Delegated Regulation 2020/1273/EU, Art 1(3), as from 21 July 2019.

[11.661]

[Article 13 Securities note for secondary issuances of equity securities or of units issued by collective investment undertakings of the closed-end type

1. A specific securities note for equity securities or units issued by collective investment undertakings of the closed-end type that is drawn up in accordance with Article 14 of Regulation (EU) 2017/1129 shall contain the information referred to in Annex 12 to this Regulation.

2. By way of derogation from paragraph 1, the specific securities note for the securities referred to in paragraphs 1 and 2 of Article 19 and paragraphs 1 and 2 of Article 20 of this Regulation, where those securities are not shares or other transferable securities equivalent to shares, shall be drawn up in accordance with Article 17 of this Regulation.]

NOTES

Substituted by Commission Delegated Regulation 2020/1273/EU, Art 1(4), as from 21 July 2019.

[11.662]

Article 14 Securities note for depository receipts issued over shares

For depository receipts issued over shares, the securities note shall contain the information referred to in Annex 13.

[11.663]

Article 15 Securities note for retail non-equity securities

For non-equity securities other than those referred to in Article 8(2) of this Regulation, the securities note shall contain the information referred to in Annex 14 to this Regulation, unless a specific securities note is drawn up in accordance with Articles 14 or 15 of Regulation (EU) 2017/1129.

[11.664]

Article 16 Securities note for wholesale non-equity securities

For non-equity securities as referred to in Article 8(2) of this Regulation, the securities note shall contain the information referred to in Annex 15 to this Regulation, unless it contains the information referred to in Annex 14 to this Regulation or unless a specific securities note is drawn up in accordance with Articles 14 or 15 of Regulation (EU) 2017/1129.

[11.665]

Article 17 Securities note for secondary issuances of non-equity securities

A specific securities note for non-equity securities that is drawn up in accordance with Article 14 of Regulation (EU) 2017/1129 shall contain the information referred to in Annex 16 to this Regulation.

SECTION 3 ADDITIONAL INFORMATION TO BE INCLUDED IN THE PROSPECTUS

[11.666]

Article 18 Complex financial history and significant financial commitment of issuers of equity securities

1. Where the issuer of an equity security has a complex financial history, or has made a significant financial commitment, additional information with respect to an entity other than the issuer shall be included in the prospectus, as referred to in paragraph 2.

2. With respect to an entity, other than the issuer, additional information shall be all information referred to in Annexes 1 and 20 to this Regulation that investors need to make an informed assessment as referred to in Article 6(1) and Article 14(2) of Regulation (EU) 2017/1129, as if that entity were the issuer of the equity security.

Such additional information shall be preceded by a clear explanation of why that information is needed for investors to make an informed assessment and shall specify the effects of the complex financial history or of the significant financial commitment on the issuer or on the issuer's business.

3. For the purposes of paragraph 1, an issuer shall be considered as having a complex financial history where all of the following conditions are fulfilled:

(a) at the time of drawing up the prospectus, the information referred to in the relevant Annexes does not represent the issuer's undertaking accurately;

(b) the inaccuracy referred to in point (a) affects the ability of investors to make an informed assessment as referred to in Article 6(1) and Article 14(2) of Regulation (EU) 2017/1129;

(c) additional information relating to an entity other than the issuer is needed for investors to make an informed assessment as referred to in Article 6(1) and Article 14(2) of Regulation (EU) 2017/1129.

4. For the purposes of paragraph 1, a significant financial commitment is a binding agreement to undertake a transaction that is likely to give rise to a variation of more than 25% relative to one or more indicators of the size of the issuer's business.

[11.667]

Article 19 Securities that are exchangeable for or convertible into shares

1. Where securities are exchangeable for or convertible into shares that are admitted to trading on a regulated market, the securities note shall contain as additional information the information referred to in item 2.2.2 of Annex 17.

2. Where securities are exchangeable for or convertible into shares that are or will be issued by the issuer or by an entity belonging to that issuer's group and that are not admitted to trading on a regulated market, the securities note shall also contain the following additional information:

(a) the information referred to in items 3.1 and 3.2 of Annex 11 in respect of that issuer or of that entity belonging to the issuer's group;

(b) the information referred to in Annex 18 in respect of the underlying share.

3. Where securities are exchangeable for or convertible into shares that are or will be issued by a third party issuer and that are not admitted to trading on a regulated market, the securities note shall contain as additional information the information referred to in Annex 18.

[11.668]

Article 20 Securities giving rise to payment or delivery obligations linked to an underlying asset

1. For securities other than those referred to in Article 19 that give the right to subscribe or to acquire shares that are or will be issued by the issuer or by an entity belonging to that issuer's group and that are admitted to trading on a regulated market, the securities note shall contain as additional information the information referred to in Annex 17.

2. For securities other than those referred to in Article 19 that give the right to subscribe or acquire shares that are or will be issued by the issuer or by an entity belonging to that issuer's group and that are not admitted to trading on a regulated market, the securities note shall also contain the following additional information

(a) the information referred to in Annex 17 except for the information referred to in item 2.2.2 of that Annex;

(b) the information referred to in Annex 18 in respect of the underlying share.

3. For securities other than those referred to in Article 19 that are linked to an underlying other than shares referred to in paragraphs 1 and 2 of this Article, the securities note shall contain as additional information the information referred to in Annex 17.

[11.669]

Article 21 Asset backed securities

For asset-backed securities, the securities notes shall also contain the additional information referred to in Annex 19.

[11.670]

Article 22 Guarantees

For non-equity securities that include guarantees, the securities notes shall also contain the additional information referred to in Annex 21.

[11.671]

Article 23 Consent

Where the issuer or the person responsible for drawing up a prospectus consents to its use as referred to in the second subparagraph of Article 5(1) of Regulation (EU) 2017/1129, the prospectus shall contain the following additional information:

(a) the information referred to in items 1 and 2A of Annex 22 to this Regulation where the consent is provided to one or more specified financial intermediaries;

(b) the information referred to in items 1 and 2B of Annex 22 to this Regulation where the consent is given to all financial intermediaries.

[11.672]

[Article 23a Historical financial information

1. In relation to any financial year beginning on or before the day on which [IP completion day] falls, issuers established in the United Kingdom must present their historical financial information in accordance with—

(a) International Financial Reporting Standards adopted pursuant to Regulation (EC) No 1606/2002 as it applies in the European Union;
(b) if those standards are not applicable, UK accounting standards.

2. In relation to any financial year beginning on or before the day on which [IP completion day] falls, issuers established in an EEA State must present their historical financial information in accordance with—
(a) International Financial Reporting Standards adopted pursuant to Regulation (EC) No 1606/2002 as it applies in the European Union; or
(b) if not applicable, national accounting standards of that EEA State.

3. In relation to any financial year beginning on or before the day on which [IP completion day] falls, issuers established outside the United Kingdom and the EEA States must present their historical financial information in accordance with one of the following accounting standards—
(a) International Financial Reporting Standards adopted pursuant to Regulation (EC) No 1606/2002 as it applies in the European Union;
(b) International Financial Reporting Standards provided that the notes to the audited financial statements that form part of the historical financial information contain an explicit and unreserved statement that these financial statements comply with International Financial Reporting Standards in accordance with IAS 1 Presentation of Financial Statements;
(c) Generally Accepted Accounting Principles of Japan;
(d) Generally Accepted Accounting Principles of the United States of America.
(e) Generally Accepted Accounting Principles of the People's Republic of China;
(f) Generally Accepted Accounting Principles of Canada;
(g) Generally Accepted Accounting Principles of the Republic of Korea.

4. In relation to a financial year beginning after the day on which [IP completion day] falls, issuers established in the United Kingdom, must present their historical financial information in accordance with—
(a) UK-adopted international accounting standards; or
(b) if those standards are not applicable, UK accounting standards.

5. In relation to a financial year beginning after the day on which [IP completion day] falls, issuers established in a country outside the United Kingdom must present their historical financial information in accordance with—
(a) UK-adopted international accounting standards;
(b) one of the accounting standards referred to in Article 23a(3); or
(c) national accounting standards of a country that are equivalent to UK-adopted international accounting standards in accordance with a determination made by the Treasury in regulations under Commission Regulation (EC) No 1569/2007 of 21 December 2007 establishing a mechanism for the determination of equivalence of accounting standards applied by third country issuers of securities pursuant to Directives 2003/71/EC and 2004/109/EC of the European Parliament and of the Council.

6. For an issuer established in a country outside the United Kingdom, if such financial information is not prepared in accordance with the required standards, the financial statements must be restated in compliance with UK-adopted international accounting standards.]

NOTES

Application of this Article in relation to the UK: this Article is inserted, in relation to the UK only, by the Prospectus (Amendment etc) (EU Exit) Regulations 2019, SI 2019/1234, reg 71(3), as from IP completion day (as defined in the European Union (Withdrawal Agreement) Act 2020, s 39); for transitional provisions, see regs 74, 75 of the 2019 Regulations at **[12.165]** et seq. Note that reg 71(3) of the 2019 Regulations was amended by the Financial Services and Economic and Monetary Policy (Consequential Amendments) (EU Exit) Regulations 2020, SI 2020/1301, reg 3, Schedule, para 48(e), as from 30 December 2020 (and the effect of the amendments has been incorporated in the text set out above)

CHAPTER III FORMAT OF THE PROSPECTUS

[11.673]

Article 24 Format of a prospectus

1. Where a prospectus is drawn up as a single document, it shall be composed of the following elements set out in the following order:
(a) a table of contents;
(b) a summary, where required by Article 7 of Regulation (EU) 2017/1129;
(c) the risk factors referred to in Article 16 of Regulation (EU) 2017/1129;
(d) any other information referred to in the Annexes to this Regulation that is to be included in that prospectus.

The issuer, offeror or person asking for admission to trading on a regulated market may decide the order in which the information referred to in the Annexes to this Regulation is set out in the prospectus.

2. Where a prospectus is drawn up as separate documents, the registration document and the securities note shall be composed of the following elements set out in the following order:
(a) a table of contents;
(b) the risk factors referred to in Article 16 of Regulation (EU) 2017/1129;
(c) any other information referred to in the Annexes to this Regulation that is to be included in that registration document or that securities note.

The issuer, offeror or person asking for admission to trading on a regulated market may decide the order in which the information referred to in the Annexes to this Regulation is set out in the registration document and the securities note.

3. Where the registration document is drawn up in the form of a universal registration document, the issuer may include the risks factors referred to in point (b) of paragraph 2 amongst the information referred to in point (c) of that paragraph provided that those risk factors remain identifiable as a single section.

[4. Where a universal registration document is used for the purposes of Article 9(12) of Regulation (EU) 2017/1129, the information referred to in that Article shall be presented in accordance with Commission Delegated Regulation (EU) 2019/815][1]

5. Where the order of the information referred to in point (d) of paragraph 1 and in point (c) of paragraph 2 is different from the order in which that information is presented in the Annexes to this Regulation, competent authorities may request to provide a list of cross references indicating the items of those Annexes to which that information corresponds.

The list of cross references referred to in the first subparagraph shall identify any items set out in the Annexes to this Regulation that have not been included in the draft prospectus due to the nature or type of issuer, securities, offer or admission to trading.

6. Where no list of cross-references is requested in accordance with paragraph 5 or is not voluntarily submitted by the issuer, offeror or person asking for admission to trading on a regulated market, it shall be indicated in the margin of the draft prospectus to which information in the draft prospectus the relevant information items set out in the Annexes to this Regulation correspond.

NOTES

Para 4: substituted by Commission Delegated Regulation 2020/1273/EU, Art 1(5), as from 21 July 2019.

Application of this Article in relation to the UK: this Article is amended (as follows), in relation to the UK only, by the Prospectus (Amendment etc) (EU Exit) Regulations 2019, SI 2019/1234, reg 71(4), as from IP completion day (as defined in the European Union (Withdrawal Agreement) Act 2020, s 39); for transitional provisions, see regs 74, 75 of the 2019 Regulations at **[12.165]** et seq—

"(4) In Article 24, in paragraph 5, for "competent authorities" substitute "the competent authority".".

Note that the Prospectus (Amendment etc) (EU Exit) Regulations 2019, SI 2019/1234, reg 71(4) was substituted by the Financial Services (Miscellaneous Amendments) (EU Exit) Regulations 2020, SI 2020/628, reg 17(1), (5)(a), with effect from immediately before IP completion day; and the effect of that amendment has been incorporated in the text as set out above. Note also that effectively the same amendment was made by the Securities Financing Transactions, Securitisation and Miscellaneous Amendments (EU Exit) Regulations 2020, SI 2020/1385, reg 66(2)(b), with effect from immediately before IP completion day.

[1] Commission Delegated Regulation (EU) 2019/815 of 17 December 2018 supplementing Directive 2004/109/EC of the European Parliament and of the Council with regard to regulatory technical standards on the specification of a single electronic reporting format (OJ L143, 29.5.2019, p. 1).

[11.674]

Article 25 Format of a base prospectus

1. A base prospectus drawn up as a single document shall be composed of the following elements set out in the following order:

(a) a table of contents;
(b) a general description of the offering programme;
(c) the risk factors referred to in Article 16 of Regulation (EU) 2017/1129;
(d) any other information referred to in the Annexes to this Regulation that is to be included in the base prospectus.

The issuer, offeror or person asking for admission to trading on a regulated market may decide the order in which the information referred to in the Annexes to this Regulation is set out in the base prospectus.

2. Where a base prospectus is drawn up as separate documents, the registration document and the securities note shall be composed of the following elements set out in the following order:

(a) a table of contents;
(b) in the securities note, a general description of the offering programme;
(c) the risk factors referred to in Article 16 of Regulation (EU) 2017/1129;
(d) any other information referred to in the Annexes to this Regulation that is to be included in the registration document and the securities note.

The issuer, offeror or person asking for admission to trading on a regulated market may decide the order in which the information referred to in the Annexes to this Regulation is set out in the registration document and the securities note.

3. An issuer, offeror or person asking for admission to trading on a regulated market may compile in one single document two or more base prospectuses.

4. Where the registration document is drawn up in the form of a universal registration document, the issuer may include the risks factors referred to in point (c) of paragraph 2 amongst the information referred to in point (d) of that paragraph provided that those risk factors remain identifiable as a single section.

[5. Where a universal registration document is used for the purposes of Article 9(12) of Regulation (EU) 2017/1129, the information referred to in that Article shall be presented in accordance with Commission Delegated Regulation (EU) 2019/815.]

6. Where the order of the information referred to in point (d) of paragraphs 1 and 2 is different from the order in which that information is presented in the Annexes to this Regulation, competent authorities may request to provide a list of cross references indicating the items of those Annexes to which that information corresponds.

The list of cross references referred to in the first subparagraph shall identify any items set out in the Annexes to this Regulation that have not been included in the draft base prospectus due to the nature or type of issuer, securities, offer or admission to trading.

7. Where no list of cross-references is requested in accordance with paragraph 6 or is not voluntarily submitted by the issuer, offeror or person asking for admission to trading on a regulated market, it shall be indicated in the margin of the draft base prospectus to which information in the draft base prospectus the relevant information items set out in the Annexes to this Regulation correspond.

NOTES

Para 5: substituted by Commission Delegated Regulation 2020/1273/EU, Art 1(6), as from 21 July 2019.

Application of this Article in relation to the UK: this Article is amended (as follows), in relation to the UK only, by the Prospectus (Amendment etc) (EU Exit) Regulations 2019, SI 2019/1234, reg 71(5), as from IP completion day (as defined in the European Union (Withdrawal Agreement) Act 2020, s 39); for transitional provisions, see regs 74, 75 of the 2019 Regulations at **[12.165]** et seq—

"(5) In Article 25, in paragraph 6, for "competent authorities" substitute "the competent authority".".

Note that the Prospectus (Amendment etc) (EU Exit) Regulations 2019, SI 2019/1234, reg 71(5) was substituted by the Financial Services (Miscellaneous Amendments) (EU Exit) Regulations 2020, SI 2020/628, reg 17(1), (5)(b), as from immediately before IP completion day; and the effect of that amendment has been incorporated in the text as set out above. Note also that effectively the same amendment was made by the Securities Financing Transactions, Securitisation and Miscellaneous Amendments (EU Exit) Regulations 2020, SI 2020/1385, reg 66(2)(c), with effect from immediately before IP completion day.

[11.675]

Article 26 Information to be included in the base prospectus and the final terms

1. The information referred to as 'Category A' in Annexes 14 to 19 and 27 to this Regulation shall be included in the base prospectus.

2. The information referred to as 'Category B' in Annexes 14 to 19 and 27 to this Regulation shall be included in the base prospectus except for details of that information that are not known at the time of approval of that base prospectus. Such details shall be inserted in the final terms.

3. The information referred to as 'Category C' in Annexes 14 to 19 and 27 to this Regulation shall be inserted in the final terms, unless it is known at the time of approval of the base prospectus, in which case it may be inserted in that base prospectus instead.

4. In addition to the information referred to in paragraphs 2 and 3 of this Article, the final terms may only contain the information referred to in Annex 28 to this Regulation. The form of the final terms referred to in Article 8(2)(a) of Regulation (EU) 2017/1129 shall indicate which of the information referred to in Annex 28 to this Regulation is to be determined in the final terms.

5. The final terms shall not contradict the information included in the base prospectus.

[11.676]

Article 27 Prospectus summary

1. An overview section of a prospectus shall only use the term 'summary' if it complies with the requirements laid down in Article 7 of Regulation (EU) 2017/1129.

2. Where the summary of a prospectus is to be supplemented in accordance with Article 23 of Regulation (EU) 2017/1129, the new information shall be integrated in the summary of that prospectus in a way that enables investors to easily identify the changes. The new information shall be integrated in the summary of the prospectus either by producing a new summary or by supplementing the original summary.

CHAPTER IV THE EU GROWTH PROSPECTUS

NOTES

Application in relation to the UK: the preceding Chapter heading is amended (as follows), in relation to the UK only, by the Prospectus (Amendment etc) (EU Exit) Regulations 2019, SI 2019/1234, reg 71(6), as from IP completion day (as defined in the European Union (Withdrawal Agreement) Act 2020, s 39); for transitional provisions, see regs 74, 75 of the 2019 Regulations at **[12.165]** et seq—

"(6) In the heading to Chapter 4 and the headings to Articles 28 to 31, for "EU" substitute "UK".".

[11.677]

[Article 28 EU growth registration document for equity securities

1. A specific registration document for equity securities drawn up in accordance with Article 15 of Regulation (EU) 2017/1129 shall contain the information referred to in Annex 24 to this Regulation.

2. By way of derogation from paragraph 1, the specific registration document for the following securities, where those securities are not shares or other transferable securities equivalent to shares, may be drawn up in accordance with Article 29 of this Regulation:

(a) the securities referred to in Articles 19(1) and 20(1) of this Regulation;

(b) the securities referred to in Article 19(2) of this Regulation, where those securities are exchangeable for or convertible into shares that are or will be issued by an entity belonging to the issuer's group and that are not admitted to trading on a regulated market;

(c) the securities referred to in Article 20(2) of this Regulation, where those securities give the right to subscribe or acquire shares that are or will be issued by an entity belonging to the issuer's group and that are not admitted to trading on a regulated market.]

NOTES

Substituted by Commission Delegated Regulation 2020/1273/EU, Art 1(7), as from 21 July 2019.

Application of this Article in relation to the UK: see the note following the Chapter IV heading *ante* (which provides that in the headings to Articles 28–31, for "EU" substitute "UK").

[11.678]

Article 29 EU growth registration document for non-equity securities

A specific registration document for non-equity securities that is drawn up in accordance with Article 15 of Regulation (EU) 2017/1129 shall contain the information referred to in Annex 25 to this Regulation.

NOTES

Application of this Article in relation to the UK: see the note following the Chapter IV heading *ante* (which provides that in the headings to Articles 28–31, for "EU" substitute "UK").

[11.679]

[Article 30 EU Growth securities note for equity securities

1. A specific securities note for equity securities drawn up in accordance with Article 15 of Regulation (EU) 2017/1129 shall contain the information referred to in Annex 26 to this Regulation.

2. By way of derogation from paragraph 1, the specific securities note for the securities referred to in paragraphs 1 and 2 of Article 19 and paragraphs 1 and 2 of Article 20 of this Regulation, where those securities are not shares or other transferable securities equivalent to shares, shall be drawn up in accordance with Article 31 of this Regulation.]

NOTES

Substituted by Commission Delegated Regulation 2020/1273/EU, Art 1(8), as from 21 July 2019.

Application of this Article in relation to the UK: see the note following the Chapter IV heading *ante* (which provides that in the headings to Articles 28–31, for "EU" substitute "UK").

[11.680]

Article 31 EU Growth securities note for non-equity securities

A specific securities note for non-equity securities that is drawn up in accordance with Article 15 of Regulation (EU) 2017/1129 shall contain the information referred to in Annex 27 to this Regulation.

NOTES

Application of this Article in relation to the UK: see the note following the Chapter IV heading *ante* (which provides that in the headings to Articles 28–31, for "EU" substitute "UK").

[11.681]

Article 32 Format of the EU Growth prospectus

1. An EU Growth prospectus that is drawn up as a single document shall be composed of the following elements in the following order:

(a) a table of contents;

(b) where applicable, all information incorporated by reference in accordance with Article 19 of Regulation (EU) 2017/1129;

(c) the specific summary;

(d) where the EU Growth prospectus is drawn up in the form of a base prospectus, a general description of the offering programme;

[(e) the information referred to in section 1 of Annex 24 and section 1 of Annex 26, or the information referred to in section 1 of Annex 25 and section 1 of Annex 27 to this Regulation, depending on the type of securities;]

(f) the information referred to in section 2 of Annex 24 or section 2 of Annex 25 to this Regulation, depending on the type of securities;

[(g) for equity securities, the information referred to in item 2.1 of Annex 26 and, where equity securities are issued by an issuer with a market capitalisation above EUR 200,000,000, the information referred to in item 2.2 of Annex 26 to this Regulation;]

(h) the information referred to in section 3 of Annex 24 and section 3 of Annex 26, or the information referred to in section 3 of Annex 25 and section 2 of Annex 27, depending on the type of securities;

(i) the information referred to in section 4 of Annex 26 or in section 3 of Annex 27 to this Regulation, depending on the type of securities;

(j) the information referred to in section 5 of Annex 26 or in section 4 of Annex 27 to this Regulation, depending on the type of securities;

(k) the information referred to in section 4 of Annex 24 or section 4 of Annex 25, depending on the type of securities;

(l) the information referred to in section 5 of Annex 24 or section 5 of Annex 25 to this Regulation, depending on the type of securities;

(m) the information referred to in section 6 of Annex 24 or section 6 of Annex 25 to this Regulation, depending on the type of securities;

(n) where non-equity securities include guarantees, the information referred to in section 5 of Annex 27 to this Regulation;

(o) the information referred to in section 7 of Annex 24 or section 7 of Annex 25 to this Regulation, depending on the type of securities;

[(p) where information on the underlying share is required pursuant to Article 19(2), point (b), Article 19(3) or Article 20(2), point (b) of this Regulation, the information referred to in section 6 of Annex 26 to this Regulation or the information referred to in section 6 of Annex 27 to this Regulation, depending on the type of securities;

(q) where the issuer or the person responsible for drawing up a prospectus consents to its use as referred to in the second subparagraph of Article 5(1) of Regulation (EU) 2017/1129, the information referred to in section 7 of Annex 26 or in section 7 of Annex 27 to this Regulation, depending on the type of securities].

2. Where an EU Growth prospectus is drawn up as separate documents, the EU Growth registration document and the EU Growth securities note shall contain the following elements in the following order:

(a) EU Growth registration document:

(i) a table of contents;

(ii) where applicable, all information incorporated by reference in accordance with Article 19 of Regulation (EU) 2017/1129;

(iii) any other information referred to in Annex 24 or 25 to this Regulation that, depending on the type of securities, is to be included in the EU Growth registration document following the order of the sections set out in those Annexes.

(b) EU Growth securities note:

(i) a table of contents;

(ii) where applicable, all information incorporated by reference in accordance with Article 19 of Regulation (EU) 2017/1129;

(iii) a general description of the programme, in the case of a base prospectus;

(iv) any other information referred to in Annex 26 or 27 to this Regulation that, depending on the type of securities, is to be included in the EU Growth securities note following the order of the sections set out in those Annexes.

3. An EU Growth prospectus drawn up either as a single document or as separate documents may take the form of a base prospectus.

4. The SMEs, issuers and offerors referred to in Article 15(1) of Regulation (EU) 2017/1129 shall follow the order of the sections of the Annexes to this Regulation. They may however deviate from the order of the information items within those sections.

NOTES

Para 1: points (e) and (g) substituted, and points (p) and (q) added, by Commission Delegated Regulation 2020/1273/EU, Art 1(9)–(11), as from 17 September 2020.

Application of this Article in relation to the UK: this Article is amended (as follows), in relation to the UK only, by the Prospectus (Amendment etc) (EU Exit) Regulations 2019, SI 2019/1234, reg 71(7), as from IP completion day (as defined in the European Union (Withdrawal Agreement) Act 2020, s 39); for transitional provisions, see regs 74, 75 of the 2019 Regulations at **[12.165]** et seq—

"(7) In Article 32—
(a) in the heading, for "EU" substitute "UK";
(b) in paragraph 1—
(i) in the opening words, for "An EU" substitute "A UK";
(ii) in point (d), for "EU" substitute "UK";
(c) in paragraph 2—
(i) for "an EU" substitute "a UK";
(ii) for "EU Growth" in each other place it occurs, substitute "UK Growth";
(iii) in paragraph 3, for "An EU" substitute "A UK".".

[11.682]

Article 33 Specific summary for the EU Growth prospectus

1. The specific summary for the EU Growth prospectus shall provide the key information that investors need to understand the nature and the risks of the issuer, of the guarantor and of the securities that are being offered.
2. The content of the specific summary shall be accurate, fair, clear and not misleading.
3. The specific summary shall be consistent with the other parts of the EU Growth prospectus.
4. The specific summary shall be drawn up as a short document written in a concise manner and shall have a maximum length of six sides of A4-sized paper when printed. The specific summary shall:
(a) be presented and laid out in a way that is easy to read, using characters of readable size;
(b) be written in a clear, non-technical and concise language that facilitates the understanding of the information and its comprehensibility by investors.

The first subparagraph shall also apply where information is presented in a tabular format.
5. The specific summary shall contain the information referred to in Annex 23 to this Regulation.
6. The specific summary shall not contain cross-references to other parts of the EU Growth prospectus or incorporate information by reference.
[7. The specific summary may use sub-headings to present the information referred to in sections 2, 3 and 4 of Annex 23 to this Regulation.]
8. The total number of risk factors referred to in items 2.3.1, 3.3(d) and 3.4.1 of Annex 23 to this Regulation and included in the specific summary shall not exceed 15.
9. Where securities are also subject to Regulation (EU) No 1286/2014 of the European Parliament and of the Council,[1] the competent authority of the home Member State may require the SMEs, the issuers and offerors referred to in Article 15(1) of Regulation (EU) 2017/1129 to substitute the information referred to in section 3 of Annex 23 to this Regulation with the information set out in points (c) to (i) of Article 8(3) of Regulation (EU) No 1286/2014.
10. Where the substitution referred to in paragraph 9 is not required by the competent authority of the home Member State, the SMEs, the issuers and offerors referred to in Article 15(1) of Regulation (EU) 2017/1129 may substitute the information referred to in section 3 of Annex 23 to this Regulation with the information set out in points (c) to (i) of Article 8(3) of Regulation (EU) No 1286/2014.
11. Where the information referred to in paragraphs 9 and 10 is substituted, it shall be included as a distinct section of the specific summary and that section shall clearly be identified as including the information set out in points (c) to (i) of Article 8(3) of Regulation (EU) No 1286/2014.
12. The maximum length of the specific summary referred to in paragraph 4 shall be extended by:
(a) one additional side of A4-sized paper where the specific summary contains information about a guarantee attached to the securities;
(b) two additional sides of A4-sized paper where a specific summary covers several securities which differ only in very limited details such as issue price or maturity date;
(c) three additional sides of A4-sized paper where there is a substitution of information as referred to in paragraphs 9 and 10.

For the purposes of point (c), three additional sides of A4-sized paper may be used for each security where the specific summary covers several securities which differ only in very limited details such as issue price or maturity date.

NOTES

Para 7: substituted by Commission Delegated Regulation 2020/1273/EU, Art 2(1), as from 21 July 2019.

Application of this Article in relation to the UK: this Article is amended (as follows), in relation to the UK only, by the Prospectus (Amendment etc) (EU Exit) Regulations 2019, SI 2019/1234, reg 71(8), as from IP completion day (as defined in the European Union (Withdrawal Agreement) Act 2020, s 39); for transitional provisions, see regs 74, 75 of the 2019 Regulations at **[12.165]** et seq—

"(8) In Article 33—
(a) in the heading and paragraphs 1, 3 and 6, for "EU Growth" substitute "UK Growth";
(b) in paragraphs 9 and 10, omit "of the home Member State".".

[1] Regulation (EU) No 1286/2014 of the European Parliament and of the Council of 26 November 2014 on key information documents for packaged retail and insurance-based investment products (PRIIPs) (OJ L352, 9.12.2014, p. 1).

[11.683]

Article 34 Supplements to the specific summary for the EU Growth prospectus

Where the specific summary of an EU Growth prospectus is to be supplemented in accordance with Article 23 of Regulation (EU) 2017/1129, the new information shall be integrated in the specific summary of that EU Growth prospectus in a way that enables investors to easily identify the changes. The new information shall be integrated in the specific summary of the EU Growth prospectus either by producing a new specific summary or by supplementing the original specific summary.

NOTES

Application of this Article in relation to the UK: this Article is amended (as follows), in relation to the UK only, by the Prospectus (Amendment etc) (EU Exit) Regulations 2019, SI 2019/1234, reg 71(9), as from IP completion day (as defined in the European Union (Withdrawal Agreement) Act 2020, s 39); for transitional provisions, see regs 74, 75 of the 2019 Regulations at **[12.165]** et seq—

"(9) In Article 34—
(a) in the heading, for "EU" substitute "UK";
(b) for "an EU" substitute "a UK";
(c) for "EU Growth" in each other place it occurs, substitute "UK Growth".".

CHAPTER V SCRUTINY AND APPROVAL OF THE PROSPECTUS AND REVIEW OF THE UNIVERSAL REGISTRATION DOCUMENT

[11.684]

Article 35 Scope of the scrutiny

For the purposes of the scrutiny of the prospectus and the review of the universal registration document, references to the prospectus shall mean the prospectus or any of its constituent parts, including a universal registration document whether submitted for approval or filed without prior approval and any amendments thereto as well as supplements to the prospectus.

[11.685]

Article 36 Criteria for the scrutiny of the completeness of the information contained in the prospectus

1. For the purposes of scrutinising the completeness of the information in a draft prospectus, competent authorities shall consider all of the following:
(a) whether the draft prospectus is drawn up in accordance with Regulation (EU) 2017/1129 and this Regulation, depending on the type of issuer, the type of issuance, the type of security and the type of offer or admission to trading;
(b) whether the issuer has a complex financial history or has made a significant financial commitment, as referred to in Article 18.

2. For the purposes of point (b) of paragraph 1, competent authorities may require the issuer to include, modify or remove information from a draft prospectus, taking into account the following:
(a) the type of securities;
(b) the information already included in the prospectus and the existence and content of information already included in a prospectus of the entity other than the issuer, as well as the applicable accounting and auditing principles;
(c) the economic nature of the transactions by which the issuer has acquired, or disposed of, its undertaking or any part of it, and the specific nature of that undertaking;
(d) whether the issuer can obtain with reasonable effort information about the entity other than the issuer.

NOTES

Application of this Article in relation to the UK: this Article is amended (as follows), in relation to the UK only, by the Prospectus (Amendment etc) (EU Exit) Regulations 2019, SI 2019/1234, reg 71(10), as from IP completion day (as defined in the European Union (Withdrawal Agreement) Act 2020, s 39); for transitional provisions, see regs 74, 75 of the 2019 Regulations at **[12.165]** et seq—

"(10) In Article 36, in paragraphs 1 and 2, for "competent authorities" substitute "the competent authority".".

[11.686]

Article 37 Criteria for the scrutiny of the comprehensibility of the information contained in the prospectus

1. For the purposes of scrutinising the comprehensibility of the information in a draft prospectus, competent authorities shall consider all of the following:
(a) whether the draft prospectus has a clear and detailed table of contents;
(b) whether the draft prospectus is free from unnecessary reiterations;
(c) whether related information is grouped together;
(d) whether the draft prospectus uses an easily readable font size;
(e) whether the draft prospectus has a structure that enables investors to understand its contents;
(f) whether the draft prospectus defines the components of mathematical formulas and, where applicable, clearly describes the product structure;
(g) whether the draft prospectus is written in plain language;
(h) whether the draft prospectus clearly describes the nature of the issuer's operations and its principal activities;
(i) whether the draft prospectus explains trade or industry specific terminology.

However, competent authorities shall not be required to consider points (g), (h) and (i) where a draft prospectus is to be used exclusively for the purposes of admission to trading on a regulated market of non-equity securities for which a summary is not required by Article 7 of Regulation (EU) 2017/1129.

2. For the purposes of the first paragraph, competent authorities may, on a case-by-case basis and in addition to the information referred to in Article 7 of Regulation (EU) 2017/1129 and Article 33 of this Regulation, require that certain information provided in the draft prospectus be included in the summary.

NOTES

Application of this Article in relation to the UK: this Article is amended (as follows), in relation to the UK only, by the Prospectus (Amendment etc) (EU Exit) Regulations 2019, SI 2019/1234, reg 71(11), as from IP completion day (as defined in the European Union (Withdrawal Agreement) Act 2020, s 39); for transitional provisions, see regs 74, 75 of the 2019 Regulations at **[12.165]** et seq—

"(11) In Article 37, in—

(a) both places it occurs in paragraph 1;

(b) paragraph 2,

for "competent authorities" substitute "the competent authority".".

[11.687]

Article 38 Criteria for the scrutiny of the consistency of the information contained in the prospectus

For the purposes of scrutinising the consistency of the information in a draft prospectus, the competent authority shall consider all of the following:

(a) whether the draft prospectus is free of material discrepancies between the different pieces of information provided therein, including any information incorporated by reference;

(b) whether any material and specific risks disclosed elsewhere in the draft prospectus are included in the risk factors section;

(c) whether the information in the summary is in line with information elsewhere in the draft prospectus;

(d) whether any figures on the use of proceeds correspond to the amount of proceeds being raised and whether the disclosed use of proceeds is in line with the disclosed strategy of the issuer;

(e) whether the description of the issuer in the operating and financial review, the historical financial information, the description of the issuer's activity and the description of the risk factors are consistent;

(f) whether the working capital statement is in line with the risk factors, the auditor's report, the use of proceeds and the disclosed strategy of the issuer and how that strategy will be funded.

[11.688]

Article 39 Scrutiny of the information contained in the prospectus of specialist issuers

Competent authorities may require additional information to be included in the prospectus based on the activities of the specialist issuers falling under one of the categories set out in Annex 29.

NOTES

Application of this Article in relation to the UK: this Article is amended (as follows), in relation to the UK only, by the Prospectus (Amendment etc) (EU Exit) Regulations 2019, SI 2019/1234, reg 71(12), as from IP completion day (as defined in the European Union (Withdrawal Agreement) Act 2020, s 39); for transitional provisions, see regs 74, 75 of the 2019 Regulations at **[12.165]** et seq—

"(12) In Article 39, for "Competent authorities" substitute "The competent authority".".

[11.689]

Article 40 Additional criteria for the scrutiny of the completeness, consistency and comprehensibility of the information contained in the prospectus

Where necessary for investor protection, the competent authority may apply criteria in addition to those laid down in Articles 36, 37 and 38 for the purposes of scrutinising the completeness, comprehensibility and consistency of the information in the draft prospectus.

[11.690]

Article 41 Proportionate approach in the scrutiny of draft prospectuses and review of the universal registration document

1. Where a first draft of a prospectus that is submitted to a competent authority is substantially similar to a prospectus that the same competent authority has already approved, and where that draft prospectus highlights all changes made to that approved prospectus, the competent authority shall only be required to apply the criteria laid down in Articles 36, 37 and 38 to scrutinise those changes and any other information affected by them.

2. For the purposes of scrutinizing a universal registration document filed without prior approval that has already been reviewed, or an amendment to such a document, competent authorities shall only be required to apply the criteria laid down in Article 36, 37 and 38 to those parts of the universal registration document or the amendment that have not been reviewed.

3. Where a first draft of a prospectus that incorporates information by reference to a document that has been approved in accordance with Regulation (EU) 2017/1129 or in accordance with the national provisions transposing Directive 2003/71/EC of the European Parliament and of the Council,[1] competent authorities shall only be required to apply the criteria laid down in Article 38 of this Regulation to scrutinise that information.

4. When applying paragraphs 1, 2 or 3, competent authorities shall request the issuer, offeror or person asking for admission to trading on a regulated market to confirm that all information in the final draft of the prospectus or universal registration document is up-to-date and contains all the information referred to in the Annexes to this Regulation applicable to that prospectus or universal registration document.

5. Where subsequent drafts of the prospectus are submitted to the competent authority, that competent authority, when scrutinising such subsequent drafts, shall only be required to apply the criteria laid down in Articles 36, 37 and 38 to changes made to the preceding draft and to any other information affected by those changes.

NOTES

Application of this Article in relation to the UK: this Article is amended (as follows), in relation to the UK only, by the Prospectus (Amendment etc) (EU Exit) Regulations 2019, SI 2019/1234, reg 71(13), as from IP completion day (as defined in the European Union (Withdrawal Agreement) Act 2020, s 39); for transitional provisions, see regs 74, 75 of the 2019 Regulations at **[12.165]** et seq—

"(13) In Article 41—

(a) in paragraph 1—
  (i) for "a competent" substitute "the competent";
  (ii) omit "same";
(b) in paragraph 2, for "competent authorities" substitute "the competent authority";
(c) for paragraph 3 substitute—

"3. Where a first draft of a prospectus that incorporates information by reference to a document that has been approved—
  (a) before IP completion day in accordance with Regulation (EU) 2017/1129 or in accordance with the UK law which implemented Directive 2003/71/EC of the European Parliament and of the Council by a competent authority (as defined in Regulation (EU) 2017/1129 as it had effect immediately before IP completion day); or
  (b) on or after IP completion day, by the competent authority in accordance with Regulation (EU) 2017/1129,

the competent authority shall only be required to apply the criteria laid down in Article 38 of this Regulation to scrutinise that information.";

(d) in paragraph 4, for "competent authorities" substitute "the competent authority".".

Note that the Prospectus (Amendment etc) (EU Exit) Regulations 2019, SI 2019/1234, reg 71(13) was amended by the Financial Services and Economic and Monetary Policy (Consequential Amendments) (EU Exit) Regulations 2020, SI 2020/1301, reg 3, Schedule, para 48(e), as from 30 December 2020 (and the effect of the amendments has been incorporated in the text set out above).

[1] Directive 2003/71/EC of the European Parliament and of the Council of 4 November 2003 on the prospectus to be published when securities are offered to the public or admitted to trading and amending Directive 2001/34/EC (OJ L345, 31.12.2003, p. 64).

[11.691]

Article 42 Submission of an application for approval of a draft prospectus or filing of a universal registration document or of amendments thereto

1. All drafts of a prospectus shall be submitted to the competent authority in searchable electronic format via electronic means.

When submitting the first draft of the prospectus, the issuer, offeror or person asking for admission to trading on a regulated market shall provide the competent authority with a contact point for the competent authority to submit all notifications in writing and by electronic means.

2. The following information shall also be submitted to the competent authority in searchable electronic format via electronic means:
  (a) the list of cross references, where requested by the competent authority in accordance with Article 24(5) of this Regulation, or when submitted on own initiative;
  (b) where no list of cross reference is requested, a document that identifies any items set out in the Annexes to this Regulation that, due to the nature or type of issuer, securities, offer or admission to trading, have not been included in the draft prospectus;
  (c) any information that is incorporated into the prospectus by reference as referred to in Article 19 of Regulation (EU) 2017/1129, unless such information has already been approved by or filed with the same competent authority in searchable electronic format;
  (d) any reasoned request to the competent authority to authorise the omission of information from the prospectus as referred to in Article 18 of Regulation (EU) 2017/1129;
  (e) any request to the competent authority to make a notification as referred to in Article 25(1) of Regulation (EU) 2017/1129;
  (f) any request to the competent authority to make a notification as referred to in Article 26(2) of Regulation (EU) 2017/1129;
  [(g) an appendix where required by Article 26(4) of Regulation (EU) 2017/1129, unless no summary is required pursuant to the second subparagraph of Article 7(1) of that Regulation;]
  (h) a confirmation that, to the best of the knowledge of the issuer, all regulated information which was required to be disclosed under the national provisions transposing Directive 2004/109/EC of the European Parliament and of the Council,[1] where applicable, and under Regulation (EU) No 596/2014 of the European Parliament and of the Council,[2] has been filed and published in accordance with those acts over the last 18 months or over the period since the obligation to disclose that regulated information commenced, whichever is the shorter, where the issuer is submitting for approval a draft universal registration document or filing a universal registration document without prior approval and seeks to obtain the status of frequent issuer;
    (i) where a universal registration document is filed without prior approval, an explanation as to how a request for amendment or supplementary information as referred to in the second subparagraph of Article 9(9) of Regulation (EU) 2017/1129 has been taken into account in the universal registration document;
    (j) any other information requested by the competent authority for the purposes of the scrutiny and approval of the prospectus or the scrutiny, review and approval of the universal registration document.

3. Where a universal registration document that is filed without prior approval is annotated in the margin in accordance with Article 24(6), it shall be accompanied by an identical version without annotations in the margin.

4. Where a universal registration document is filed without prior approval or where a universal registration document is amended, the information referred to in points (a), (b), (c), (d), (h) and (i) of paragraph 2 shall be submitted at the time when the universal registration document is filed with the competent authority whilst the information referred to in point (j) of paragraph 2 shall be submitted during the review process. In all other cases, the information referred to in paragraph 2 shall be submitted together with the first draft of the prospectus submitted to the competent authority or during the scrutiny process.

5. Where a frequent issuer informs the competent authority that it intends to submit an application for approval of a draft prospectus in accordance with the second sentence of the first subparagraph of Article 20(6) of Regulation (EU) 2017/1129, that frequent issuer shall do so in writing and by electronic means.

The information referred to in the first subparagraph shall indicate the Annexes to this Regulation relevant for that draft prospectus.

NOTES

Para 2: point (g) substituted by Commission Delegated Regulation 2020/1273/EU, Art 2(2), as from 21 July 2019.

Application of this Article in relation to the UK: this Article is amended (as follows), in relation to the UK only, by the Prospectus (Amendment etc) (EU Exit) Regulations 2019, SI 2019/1234, reg 71(14), as from IP completion day (as defined in the European Union (Withdrawal Agreement) Act 2020, s 39); for transitional provisions, see regs 74, 75 of the 2019 Regulations at **[12.165]** et seq—

"(14) In Article 42, in paragraph 2—
(a) omit points (e) and (f);
(b) in point (h), for "the national provisions transposing" substitute "the UK law which implemented".".

1 Directive 2004/109/EC of the European Parliament and of the Council of 15 December 2004 on the harmonisation of transparency requirements in relation to information about issuers whose securities are admitted to trading on a regulated market and amending Directive 2001/34/EC (OJ L390, 31.12.2004, p. 38).

2 Regulation (EU) No 596/2014 of the European Parliament and of the Council of 16 April 2014 on market abuse (market abuse regulation) and repealing Directive 2003/6/EC of the European Parliament and of the Council and Commission Directives 2003/124/EC, 2003/125/EC and 2004/72/EC (OJ L173, 12.6.2014, p. 1).

[11.692]

Article 43 Changes to a draft prospectus during the approval procedure

1. Each version of the draft prospectus submitted after the first draft prospectus shall highlight all changes made to the preceding draft and shall be accompanied by an unmarked draft. Competent authorities shall accept marked extracts of the preceding draft prospectus where only limited changes have been made.

2. Where competent authorities, in accordance with Article 45(2) of this Regulation, have notified the issuer, offeror or person asking for admission to trading on a regulated market that the draft prospectus does not meet the standards of completeness, comprehensibility and consistency as referred to in Article 20(4) of Regulation (EU) 2017/1129, the subsequently submitted draft of the prospectus shall be accompanied by an explanation as to how the outstanding issues notified by competent authorities have been addressed.

3. Where changes made to a draft prospectus are self-explanatory or clearly address the outstanding issues notified by the competent authority, an indication of where the changes have been made to address the outstanding issues shall be considered sufficient explanation for the purposes of paragraph 2.

NOTES

Application of this Article in relation to the UK: this Article is amended (as follows), in relation to the UK only, by the Prospectus (Amendment etc) (EU Exit) Regulations 2019, SI 2019/1234, reg 71(15), as from IP completion day (as defined in the European Union (Withdrawal Agreement) Act 2020, s 39); for transitional provisions, see regs 74, 75 of the 2019 Regulations at **[12.165]** et seq—

"(15) In Article 43—
(a) in paragraph 1;
(b) in both places it occurs in paragraph 2,
for "competent authorities" substitute "the competent authority".".

[11.693]

Article 44 Submission for approval of the final draft of the prospectus

1. The final draft of the prospectus shall be submitted for approval together with all the information referred to in Article 42(2) that has changed compared to the previous submission, with the exception of the information referred to in points (a) and (h) of that Article. The final draft of the prospectus shall not be annotated in the margin.

2. Where no changes have been made to the information referred to in Article 42(2), the issuer, offeror or person asking for admission to trading on a regulated market shall confirm so in writing and by electronic means.

[11.694]

Article 45 Acknowledgment of the receipt of an application for approval of a draft prospectus, or of the filing of a universal registration document or of an amendment thereto, and processing of an application for approval of a draft prospectus

1. Competent authorities shall acknowledge receipt of the initial application for approval of a draft prospectus or of the filing of a universal registration document as referred to in the second subparagraph of Article 9(2) of Regulation (EU) 2017/1129, or of an amendment to that universal registration document in writing and by electronic means as soon as possible and no later than by close of business on the second working day following the receipt of the application or filing.

Upon receipt of the initial application for approval of a draft prospectus and of the filing of a universal registration document, or of an amendment thereto, the competent authority shall inform the issuer, offeror or person asking for admission to trading on a regulated market of the following:

(a) the reference number of the application or of the filing;
(b) the contact point within the competent authority to which queries regarding the application or the filing may be addressed.

2. Where the draft prospectus does not meet the standards of completeness, comprehensibility and consistency necessary for its approval or where changes or supplementary information are needed, competent authorities shall inform the issuer, offeror or person asking for admission to trading on a regulated market thereof in writing and by electronic means.

Where the universal registration document referred to in the second subparagraph of Article 9(2) of Regulation (EU) 2017/1129, or an amendment to that universal registration document, does not meet the standards of completeness, comprehensibility and consistency or where amendments or supplementary information are needed, competent authorities shall inform the issuer thereof in writing and by electronic means. Where the shortcoming must be addressed without undue delay, as required by the third subparagraph of Article 9(9) of Regulation (EU) 2017/1129, the competent authority shall inform the issuer thereof.

3. The competent authority shall notify the issuer, offeror or person asking for admission to trading on a regulated market about its decision regarding the approval of the draft prospectus in writing and by electronic means as soon as possible and by no later than by close of business of the day on which that decision is taken.

NOTES

Application of this Article in relation to the UK: this Article is amended (as follows), in relation to the UK only, by the Prospectus (Amendment etc) (EU Exit) Regulations 2019, SI 2019/1234, reg 71(16), as from IP completion day (as defined in the European Union (Withdrawal Agreement) Act 2020, s 39); for transitional provisions, see regs 74, 75 of the 2019 Regulations at **[12.165]** et seq—

"(16) In Article 45—
(a) in paragraph 1;
(b) in both places it occurs in paragraph 2,
for "competent authorities" substitute "the competent authority".".

CHAPTER VI FINAL PROVISIONS

[11.695]

Article 46 Repeal

Regulation (EC) No 809/2004 is repealed.

[11.696]

[Article 46a Prospectuses approved between 21 July 2019 and 16 September 2020

Prospectuses that have been approved between 21 July 2019 and 16 September 2020 shall continue to be valid until the end of their validity.]

NOTES

Inserted by Commission Delegated Regulation 2020/1273/EU, Art 1(12), as from 17 September 2020.

[11.697]

Article 47 Entry into force and application

This Regulation shall enter into force on the twentieth day following that of its publication in the *Official Journal of the European Union*.

It shall apply from 21 July 2019.

This Regulation shall be binding in its entirety and directly applicable in all Member States.

NOTES

Application of this Article in relation to the UK: this Article is amended (as follows), in relation to the UK only, by the Prospectus (Amendment etc) (EU Exit) Regulations 2019, SI 2019/1234, reg 71(17), as from IP completion day (as defined in the European Union (Withdrawal Agreement) Act 2020, s 39); for transitional provisions, see regs 74, 75 of the 2019 Regulations at **[12.165]** et seq—

"(17) Omit the words "This Regulation shall be binding in its entirety and directly applicable in all Member States." following Article 47.".

[11.698]

LIST OF ANNEXES

PART A REGISTRATION DOCUMENTS

Annex 1:	Registration document for equity securities
Annex 2:	Universal registration document
Annex 3:	Registration document for secondary issuances of equity securities
Annex 4:	Registration document for units of closed-end collective investment undertakings
Annex 5:	Registration document for depository receipts issued over shares
Annex 6:	Registration document for retail non-equity securities
Annex 7:	Registration document for wholesale non-equity securities
Annex 8:	Registration document for secondary issuances of non-equity securities
Annex 9:	Registration document for asset-backed securities
Annex 10:	Registration documents for non-equity securities issued by third countries and their regional and local authorities

PART B SECURITIES NOTES

Annex 11:	Securities note for equity securities or units issued by collective investment undertakings of the closed- end type
Annex 12:	Securities note for secondary issuances of equity securities or of units issued by collective investment undertakings of the closed-end type
Annex 13:	Securities note for depository receipts issued over shares
Annex 14:	Securities note for retail non-equity securities

Annex 15:	Securities note for wholesale non-equity securities
Annex 16:	Securities note for secondary issuances of non-equity securities

PART C ADDITIONAL INFORMATION TO BE INCLUDED IN THE PROSPECTUS

Annex 17:	Securities giving rise to payment or delivery obligations linked to an underlying asset
Annex 18:	Underlying share
Annex 19:	Asset-backed securities
Annex 20:	Pro forma information
Annex 21:	Guarantees
Annex 22:	Consent

PART D EU GROWTH PROSPECTUS

Annex 23:	Specific summary for the EU Growth prospectus
Annex 24:	EU Growth registration document for equity securities
Annex 25:	EU Growth registration document for non-equity securities
Annex 26:	EU Growth securities note for equity securities
Annex 27:	EU Growth securities note for non-equity securities

PART E OTHER CATEGORIES OF INFORMATION

Annex 28:	List of additional information in final terms
Annex 29:	List of specialist issuers

NOTES

Application in relation to the UK: this list of Annexes is amended (as follows), in relation to the UK only, by the Prospectus (Amendment etc) (EU Exit) Regulations 2019, SI 2019/1234, Schedule, para 1, as from IP completion day (as defined in the European Union (Withdrawal Agreement) Act 2020, s 39); for transitional provisions, see regs 74, 75 of the 2019 Regulations at **[12.165]** et seq—

"1. In the List of Annexes, for each of the headings in Part D, for "EU" substitute "UK".".

[11.699]

ANNEX 1
REGISTRATION DOCUMENT FOR EQUITY SECURITIES

SECTION 1	PERSONS RESPONSIBLE, THIRD PARTY INFORMATION, EXPERTS' REPORTS AND COMPETENT AUTHORITY APPROVAL
Item 1.1	Identify all persons responsible for the information or any parts of it, given in the registration document with, in the latter case, an indication of such parts. In the case of natural persons, including members of the issuer's administrative, management or supervisory bodies, indicate the name and function of the person; in the case of legal persons indicate the name and registered office.
Item 1.2	A declaration by those responsible for the registration document that to the best of their knowledge, the information contained in the registration document is in accordance with the facts and that the registration document makes no omission likely to affect its import. Where applicable, a declaration by those responsible for certain parts of the registration document that, to the best of their knowledge, the information contained in those parts of the registration document for which they are responsible is in accordance with the facts and that those parts of the registration document make no omission likely to affect their import.
Item 1.3	Where a statement or report attributed to a person as an expert, is included in the registration document, provide the following details for that person: (a) name; (b) business address; (c) qualifications; (d) material interest if any in the issuer. If the statement or report has been produced at the issuer's request, state that such statement or report has been included in the registration document with the consent of the person who has authorised the contents of that part of the registration document for the purpose of the prospectus.
Item 1.4	Where information has been sourced from a third party, provide a confirmation that this information has been accurately reproduced and that as far as the issuer is aware and is able to ascertain from information published by that third party, no facts have been omitted which would render the reproduced information inaccurate or misleading. In addition, identify the source(s) of the information.
Item 1.5	A statement that:

	(a) the [registration document/prospectus] has been approved by the [name of the competent authority], as competent authority under Regulation (EU) 2017/1129; (b) the [name of competent authority] only approves this [registration document/prospectus] as meeting the standards of completeness, comprehensibility and consistency imposed by Regulation (EU) 2017/1129; (c) such approval should not be considered as an endorsement of the issuer that is the subject of this [registration document/prospectus].
SECTION 2	STATUTORY AUDITORS
Item 2.1	Names and addresses of the issuer's auditors for the period covered by the historical financial information (together with their membership in a professional body).
Item 2.2	If auditors have resigned, been removed or have not been re-appointed during the period covered by the historical financial information, indicate details if material.
SECTION 3	RISK FACTORS
Item 3.1	A description of the material risks that are specific to the issuer, in a limited number of categories, in a section headed 'Risk Factors'. In each category, the most material risks, in the assessment undertaken by the issuer, offeror or person asking for admission to trading on a regulated market, taking into account the negative impact on the issuer and the probability of their occurrence shall be set out first. The risks shall be corroborated by the content of the registration document.
SECTION 4	INFORMATION ABOUT THE ISSUER
Item 4.1	The legal and commercial name of the issuer.
Item 4.2	The place of registration of the issuer, its registration number and legal entity identifier ('LEI').
Item 4.3	The date of incorporation and the length of life of the issuer, except where the period is indefinite.
Item 4.4	The domicile and legal form of the issuer, the legislation under which the issuer operates, its country of incorporation, the address, telephone number of its registered office (or principal place of business if different from its registered office) and website of the issuer, if any, with a disclaimer that the information on the website does not form part of the prospectus unless that information is incorporated by reference into the prospectus.
SECTION 5	BUSINESS OVERVIEW
Item 5.1	Principal activities
Item 5.1.1	A description of, and key factors relating to, the nature of the issuer's operations and its principal activities, stating the main categories of products sold and/or services performed for each financial year for the period covered by the historical financial information;
Item 5.1.2	An indication of any significant new products and/or services that have been introduced and, to the extent the development of new products or services has been publicly disclosed, give the status of their development.
Item 5.2	Principal markets A description of the principal markets in which the issuer competes, including a breakdown of total revenues by operating segment and geographic market for each financial year for the period covered by the historical financial information.
Item 5.3	The important events in the development of the issuer's business.
Item 5.4	Strategy and objectives A description of the issuer's business strategy and objectives, both financial and non-financial (if any). This description shall take into account the issuer's future challenges and prospects.
Item 5.5	If material to the issuer's business or profitability, summary information regarding the extent to which the issuer is dependent, on patents or licences, industrial, commercial or financial contracts or new manufacturing processes.
Item 5.6	The basis for any statements made by the issuer regarding its competitive position.
Item 5.7	Investments
Item 5.7.1	A description, (including the amount) of the issuer's material investments for each financial year for the period covered by the historical financial information up to the date of the registration document.
Item 5.7.2	A description of any material investments of the issuer that are in progress or for which firm commitments have already been made, including the geographic distribution of these investments (home and abroad) and the method of financing (internal or external).
Item 5.7.3	Information relating to the joint ventures and undertakings in which the issuer holds a proportion of the capital likely to have a significant effect on the assessment of its own assets and liabilities, financial position or profits and losses.
Item 5.7.4	A description of any environmental issues that may affect the issuer's utilisation of the tangible fixed assets.
SECTION 6	ORGANISATIONAL STRUCTURE

Item 6.1	If the issuer is part of a group, a brief description of the group and the issuer's position within the group. This may be in the form of, or accompanied by, a diagram of the organisational structure if this helps to clarify the structure.
Item 6.2	A list of the issuer's significant subsidiaries, including name, country of incorporation or residence, the proportion of ownership interest held and, if different, the proportion of voting power held.
SECTION 7	OPERATING AND FINANCIAL REVIEW
Item 7.1	Financial condition
Item 7.1.1	To the extent not covered elsewhere in the registration document and to the extent necessary for an understanding of the issuer's business as a whole, a fair review of the development and performance of the issuer's business and of its position for each year and interim period for which historical financial information is required, including the causes of material changes. The review shall be a balanced and comprehensive analysis of the development and performance of the issuer's business and of its position, consistent with the size and complexity of the business. To the extent necessary for an understanding of the issuer's development, performance or position, the analysis shall include both financial and, where appropriate, non-financial Key Performance Indicators relevant to the particular business. The analysis shall, where appropriate, include references to, and additional explanations of, amounts reported in the annual financial statements.
Item 7.1.2	To the extent not covered elsewhere in the registration document and to the extent necessary for an understanding of the issuer's business as a whole, the review shall also give an indication of: (a) the issuer's likely future development; (b) activities in the field of research and development. The requirements set out in item 7.1 may be satisfied by the inclusion of the management report referred to in Articles 19 and 29 of Directive 2013/34/EU of the European Parliament and of the Council.[1]
Item 7.2	Operating results
Item 7.2.1	Information regarding significant factors, including unusual or infrequent events or new developments, materially affecting the issuer's income from operations and indicate the extent to which income was so affected.
Item 7.2.2	Where the historical financial information discloses material changes in net sales or revenues, provide a narrative discussion of the reasons for such changes.
SECTION 8	CAPITAL RESOURCES
Item 8.1	Information concerning the issuer's capital resources (both short term and long term).
Item 8.2	An explanation of the sources and amounts of and a narrative description of the issuer's cash flows.
Item 8.3	Information on the borrowing requirements and funding structure of the issuer.
Item 8.4	Information regarding any restrictions on the use of capital resources that have materially affected, or could materially affect, directly or indirectly, the issuer's operations.
Item 8.5	Information regarding the anticipated sources of funds needed to fulfil commitments referred to in item 5.7.2
SECTION 9	REGULATORY ENVIRONMENT
Item 9.1	A description of the regulatory environment that the issuer operates in and that may materially affect its business, together with information regarding any governmental, economic, fiscal, monetary or political policies or factors that have materially affected, or could materially affect, directly or indirectly, the issuer's operations.
SECTION 10	TREND INFORMATION
Item 10.1	A description of: (a) the most significant recent trends in production, sales and inventory, and costs and selling prices since the end of the last financial year to the date of the registration document; (b) any significant change in the financial performance of the group since the end of the last financial period for which financial information has been published to the date of the registration document, or provide an appropriate negative statement.
Item 10.2	Information on any known trends, uncertainties, demands, commitments or events that are reasonably likely to have a material effect on the issuer's prospects for at least the current financial year.
SECTION 11	PROFIT FORECASTS OR ESTIMATES
Item 11.1	Where an issuer has published a profit forecast or a profit estimate (which is still outstanding and valid) that forecast or estimate shall be included in the registration document. If a profit forecast or profit estimate has been published and is still outstanding, but no longer

	valid, then provide a statement to that effect and an explanation of why such forecast or estimate is no longer valid. Such an invalid forecast or estimate is not subject to the requirements in items 11.2 and 11.3.
Item 11.2	Where an issuer chooses to include a new profit forecast or a new profit estimate, or a previously published profit forecast or a previously published profit estimate pursuant to item 11.1, the profit forecast or estimate shall be clear and unambiguous and contain a statement setting out the principal assumptions upon which the issuer has based its forecast, or estimate. The forecast or estimate shall comply with the following principles: (a) there must be a clear distinction between assumptions about factors which the members of the administrative, management or supervisory bodies can influence and assumptions about factors which are exclusively outside the influence of the members of the administrative, management or supervisory bodies; (b) the assumptions must be reasonable, readily understandable by investors, specific and precise and not relate to the general accuracy of the estimates underlying the forecast; (c) in the case of a forecast, the assumptions shall draw the investor's attention to those uncertain factors which could materially change the outcome of the forecast.
Item 11.3	The prospectus shall include a statement that the profit forecast or estimate has been compiled and prepared on a basis which is both: (a) comparable with the historical financial information; (b) consistent with the issuer's accounting policies.
SECTION 12	ADMINISTRATIVE, MANAGEMENT AND SUPERVISORY BODIES AND SENIOR MANAGEMENT
Item 12.1	Names, business addresses and functions within the issuer of the following persons and an indication of the principal activities performed by them outside of that issuer where these are significant with respect to that issuer: (a) members of the administrative, management or supervisory bodies; (b) partners with unlimited liability, in the case of a limited partnership with a share capital; (c) founders, if the issuer has been established for fewer than five years; (d) any senior manager who is relevant to establishing that the issuer has the appropriate expertise and experience for the management of the issuer's business. Details of the nature of any family relationship between any of the persons referred to in points (a) to (d). In the case of each member of the administrative, management or supervisory bodies of the issuer and of each person referred to in points (b) and (d) of the first subparagraph, details of that person's relevant management expertise and experience and the following information: (a) the names of all companies and partnerships where those persons have been a member of the administrative, management or supervisory bodies or partner at any time in the previous five years, indicating whether or not the individual is still a member of the administrative, management or supervisory bodies or partner. It is not necessary to list all the subsidiaries of an issuer of which the person is also a member of the administrative, management or supervisory bodies; (b) details of any convictions in relation to fraudulent offences for at least the previous five years; (c) details of any bankruptcies, receiverships, liquidations or companies put into administration in respect of those persons described in points (a) and (d) of the first subparagraph who acted in one or more of those capacities for at least the previous five years; (d) details of any official public incrimination and/or sanctions involving such persons by statutory or regulatory authorities (including designated professional bodies) and whether they have ever been disqualified by a court from acting as a member of the administrative, management or supervisory bodies of an issuer or from acting in the management or conduct of the affairs of any issuer for at least the previous five years. If there is no such information required to be disclosed, a statement to that effect is to be made.
Item 12.2	Administrative, management and supervisory bodies and senior management conflicts of interests Potential conflicts of interests between any duties to the issuer, of the persons referred to in item 12.1, and their private interests and or other duties must be clearly stated. In the event that there are no such conflicts, a statement to that effect must be made. Any arrangement or understanding with major shareholders, customers, suppliers or others, pursuant to which any person referred to in item 12.1 was selected as a member of the

	administrative, management or supervisory bodies or member of senior management. Details of any restrictions agreed by the persons referred to in item 12.1 on the disposal within a certain period of time of their holdings in the issuer's securities.
SECTION 13	REMUNERATION AND BENEFITS
	In relation to the last full financial year for those persons referred to in points (a) and (d) of the first subparagraph of item 12.1:
Item 13.1	The amount of remuneration paid (including any contingent or deferred compensation), and benefits in kind granted to such persons by the issuer and its subsidiaries for services in all capacities to the issuer and its subsidiaries by any person. That information must be provided on an individual basis unless individual disclosure is not required in the issuer's home country and is not otherwise publicly disclosed by the issuer.
Item 13.2	The total amounts set aside or accrued by the issuer or its subsidiaries to provide for pension, retirement or similar benefits.
SECTION 14	BOARD PRACTICES In relation to the issuer's last completed financial year, and unless otherwise specified, with respect to those persons referred to in point (a) of the first subparagraph of item 12.1.
Item 14.1	Date of expiration of the current term of office, if applicable, and the period during which the person has served in that office.
Item 14.2	Information about members of the administrative, management or supervisory bodies' service contracts with the issuer or any of its subsidiaries providing for benefits upon termination of employment, or an appropriate statement to the effect that no such benefits exist.
Item 14.3	Information about the issuer's audit committee and remuneration committee, including the names of committee members and a summary of the terms of reference under which the committee operates.
Item 14.4	A statement as to whether or not the issuer complies with the corporate governance regime(s) applicable to the issuer. In the event that the issuer does not comply with such a regime, a statement to that effect must be included together with an explanation regarding why the issuer does not comply with such regime.
Item 14.5	Potential material impacts on the corporate governance, including future changes in the board and committees composition (in so far as this has been already decided by the board and/or shareholders meeting).
SECTION 15	EMPLOYEES
Item 15.1	Either the number of employees at the end of the period or the average for each financial year for the period covered by the historical financial information up to the date of the registration document (and changes in such numbers, if material) and, if possible and material, a breakdown of persons employed by main category of activity and geographic location. If the issuer employs a significant number of temporary employees, include disclosure of the number of temporary employees on average during the most recent financial year.
Item 15.2	Shareholdings and stock options With respect to each person referred to in points (a) and (d) of the first subparagraph of item 12.1 provide information as to their share ownership and any options over such shares in the issuer as of the most recent practicable date.
Item 15.3	Description of any arrangements for involving the employees in the capital of the issuer.
SECTION 16	MAJOR SHAREHOLDERS
Item 16.1	In so far as is known to the issuer, the name of any person other than a member of the administrative, management or supervisory bodies who, directly or indirectly, has an interest in the issuer's capital or voting rights which is notifiable under the issuer's national law, together with the amount of each such person's interest, as at the date of the registration document or, if there are no such persons, an appropriate statement to that effect that no such person exists.
Item 16.2	Whether the issuer's major shareholders have different voting rights, or an appropriate statement to the effect that no such voting rights exist.
Item 16.3	To the extent known to the issuer, state whether the issuer is directly or indirectly owned or controlled and by whom and describe the nature of such control and describe the measures in place to ensure that such control is not abused.
Item 16.4	A description of any arrangements, known to the issuer, the operation of which may at a subsequent date result in a change in control of the issuer.
SECTION 17	RELATED PARTY TRANSACTIONS
Item 17.1	Details of related party transactions (which for these purposes are those set out in the Standards adopted in accordance with the Regulation (EC) No 1606/2002 of the European Parliament and of the Council,[2] that the issuer has entered into during the period covered by the historical financial information and up to the date of the registration document, must be disclosed in accordance with the respective standard adopted under Regula-

	tion (EC) No 1606/2002 if applicable. If such standards do not apply to the issuer the following information must be disclosed: (a) the nature and extent of any transactions which are, as a single transaction or in their entirety, material to the issuer. Where such related party transactions are not concluded at arm's length provide an explanation of why these transactions were not concluded at arm's length. In the case of outstanding loans including guarantees of any kind indicate the amount outstanding; (b) the amount or the percentage to which related party transactions form part of the turnover of the issuer.
SECTION 18	FINANCIAL INFORMATION CONCERNING THE ISSUER'S ASSETS AND LIABILITIES, FINANCIAL POSITION AND PROFITS AND LOSSES
Item 18.1	Historical financial information
Item 18.1.1	Audited historical financial information covering the latest three financial years (or such shorter period as the issuer has been in operation) and the audit report in respect of each year.
Item 18.1.2	Change of accounting reference date If the issuer has changed its accounting reference date during the period for which historical financial information is required, the audited historical information shall cover at least 36 months, or the entire period for which the issuer has been in operation, whichever is shorter.
Item 18.1.3	Accounting standards The financial information must be prepared according to International Financial Reporting Standards as endorsed in the Union based on Regulation (EC) No 1606/2002. If Regulation (EC) No 1606/2002 is not applicable, the financial information must be prepared in accordance with: (a) a Member State's national accounting standards for issuers from the EEA, as required by Directive 2013/34/EU; (b) a third country's national accounting standards equivalent to Regulation (EC) No 1606/2002 for third country issuers. If such third country's national accounting standards are not equivalent to Regulation (EC) No 1606/2002 the financial statements shall be restated in compliance with that Regulation.
Item 18.1.4	Change of accounting framework The last audited historical financial information, containing comparative information for the previous year, must be presented and prepared in a form consistent with the accounting standards framework that will be adopted in the issuer's next published annual financial statements having regard to accounting standards and policies and legislation applicable to such annual financial statements. Changes within the accounting framework applicable to an issuer do not require the audited financial statements to be restated solely for the purposes of the prospectus. However, if the issuer intends to adopt a new accounting standards framework in its next published financial statements, at least one complete set of financial statements (as defined by IAS 1 Presentation of Financial Statements as set out in Regulation (EC) No 1606/2002), including comparatives, must be presented in a form consistent with that which will be adopted in the issuer's next published annual financial statements, having regard to accounting standards and policies and legislation applicable to such annual financial statements.
Item 18.1.5	Where the audited financial information is prepared according to national accounting standards, it must include at least the following: (a) the balance sheet; (b) the income statement; (c) a statement showing either all changes in equity or changes in equity other than those arising from capital transactions with owners and distributions to owners; (d) the cash flow statement; (e) the accounting policies and explanatory notes.
Item 18.1.6	Consolidated financial statements If the issuer prepares both stand-alone and consolidated financial statements, include at least the consolidated financial statements in the registration document.
Item 18.1.7	Age of financial information The balance sheet date of the last year of audited financial information may not be older than one of the following: (a) 18 months from the date of the registration document if the issuer includes audited interim financial statements in the registration document; (b) 16 months from the date of the registration document if the issuer includes unaudited interim financial statements in the registration document.

Item 18.2	Interim and other financial information
Item 18.2.1	If the issuer has published quarterly or half-yearly financial information since the date of its last audited financial statements, these must be included in the registration document. If the quarterly or half-yearly financial information has been audited or reviewed, the audit or review report must also be included. If the quarterly or half-yearly financial information is not audited or has not been reviewed, state that fact. If the registration document is dated more than nine months after the date of the last audited financial statements, it must contain interim financial information, which may be unaudited (in which case that fact must be stated) covering at least the first six months of the financial year. Interim financial information prepared in accordance with the requirements of Regulation (EC) No 1606/2002. For issuers not subject to Regulation (EC) No 1606/2002, the interim financial information must include comparative statements for the same period in the prior financial year, except that the requirement for comparative balance sheet information may be satisfied by presenting the year's end balance sheet in accordance with the applicable financial reporting framework.
Item 18.3	Auditing of historical annual financial information
Item 18.3.1	[The historical annual financial information must be independently audited. The audit report shall be prepared in accordance with Directive 2006/43/EC of the European Parliament and of the Council[3] and Regulation (EU) No 537/2014 of the European Parliament and of the Council.[4] Where Directive 2006/43/EC and Regulation (EU) No 537/2014 do not apply, the historical annual financial information must be audited or reported on as to whether or not, for the purposes of the registration document, it gives a true and fair view in accordance with auditing standards applicable in a Member State or an equivalent standard.]
[Item 18.3.1a	Where audit reports on the historical financial information have been refused by the statutory auditors or where they contain qualifications, modifications of opinion, disclaimers or an emphasis of matter, the reason must be given, and such qualifications, modifications, disclaimers or emphasis of matter must be reproduced in full.]
Item 18.3.2	Indication of other information in the registration document that has been audited by the auditors.
Item 18.3.3	Where financial information in the registration document is not extracted from the issuer's audited financial statements state the source of the information and state that the information is not audited.
Item 18.4	Pro forma financial information
Item 18.4.1	In the case of a significant gross change, a description of how the transaction might have affected the assets, liabilities and earnings of the issuer, had the transaction been undertaken at the commencement of the period being reported on or at the date reported. This requirement will normally be satisfied by the inclusion of pro forma financial information. This pro forma financial information is to be presented as set out in Annex 20 and must include the information indicated therein. Pro forma financial information must be accompanied by a report prepared by independent accountants or auditors.
Item 18.5	Dividend policy
Item 18.5.1	A description of the issuer's policy on dividend distributions and any restrictions thereon. If the issuer has no such policy, include an appropriate negative statement.
Item 18.5.2	The amount of the dividend per share for each financial year for the period covered by the historical financial information adjusted, where the number of shares in the issuer has changed, to make it comparable.
Item 18.6	Legal and arbitration proceedings
Item 18.6.1	Information on any governmental, legal or arbitration proceedings (including any such proceedings which are pending or threatened of which the issuer is aware), during a period covering at least the previous 12 months which may have, or have had in the recent past significant effects on the issuer and/or group's financial position or profitability, or provide an appropriate negative statement.
Item 18.7	Significant change in the issuer's financial position
Item 18.7.1	A description of any significant change in the financial position of the group which has occurred since the end of the last financial period for which either audited financial statements or interim financial information have been published, or provide an appropriate negative statement.
SECTION 19	ADDITIONAL INFORMATION
Item 19.1	Share capital The information in items 19.1.1 to 19.1.7 in the historical financial information as of the date of the most recent balance sheet:
Item 19.1.1	The amount of issued capital, and for each class of share capital:

	(a) the total of the issuer's authorised share capital; (b) the number of shares issued and fully paid and issued but not fully paid; (c) the par value per share, or that the shares have no par value; and (d) a reconciliation of the number of shares outstanding at the beginning and end of the year. If more than 10% of capital has been paid for with assets other than cash within the period covered by the historical financial information, state that fact.
Item 19.1.2	If there are shares not representing capital, state the number and main characteristics of such shares.
Item 19.1.3	The number, book value and face value of shares in the issuer held by or on behalf of the issuer itself or by subsidiaries of the issuer.
Item 19.1.4	The amount of any convertible securities, exchangeable securities or securities with warrants, with an indication of the conditions governing and the procedures for conversion, exchange or subscription.
Item 19.1.5	Information about and terms of any acquisition rights and or obligations over authorised but unissued capital or an undertaking to increase the capital.
Item 19.1.6	Information about any capital of any member of the group which is under option or agreed conditionally or unconditionally to be put under option and details of such options including those persons to whom such options relate.
Item 19.1.7	A history of share capital, highlighting information about any changes, for the period covered by the historical financial information.
Item 19.2	Memorandum and Articles of Association
Item 19.2.1	The register and the entry number therein, if applicable, and a brief description of the issuer's objects and purposes and where they can be found in the up to date memorandum and articles of association.
Item 19.2.2	Where there is more than one class of existing shares, a description of the rights, preferences and restrictions attaching to each class.
Item 19.2.3	A brief description of any provision of the issuer's articles of association, statutes, charter or bylaws that would have an effect of delaying, deferring or preventing a change in control of the issuer.
SECTION 20	MATERIAL CONTRACTS
Item 20.1	A summary of each material contract, other than contracts entered into in the ordinary course of business, to which the issuer or any member of the group is a party, for the two years immediately preceding publication of the registration document. A summary of any other contract (not being a contract entered into in the ordinary course of business) entered into by any member of the group which contains any provision under which any member of the group has any obligation or entitlement which is material to the group as at the date of the registration document.
SECTION 21	DOCUMENTS AVAILABLE
Item 21.1	A statement that for the term of the registration document the following documents, where applicable, can be inspected: (a) the up to date memorandum and articles of association of the issuer; (b) all reports, letters, and other documents, valuations and statements prepared by any expert at the issuer's request any part of which is included or referred to in the registration document. An indication of the website on which the documents may be inspected.

NOTES

Item 18.3.1 substituted, and item 18.3.1a inserted, by Commission Delegated Regulation 2020/1273/EU, Art 1(13), Annex I, as from 17 September 2020.

Application of this Annex in relation to the UK: this Annex is amended (as follows), in relation to the UK only, by the Prospectus (Amendment etc) (EU Exit) Regulations 2019, SI 2019/1234, Schedule, para 2, as from IP completion day (as defined in the European Union (Withdrawal Agreement) Act 2020, s 39); for transitional provisions, see regs 74, 75 of the 2019 Regulations at **[12.165]** et seq—

"2.—(1) Annex 1 is amended as follows.

(2) In item 7.1.2, for "management report referred to in Articles 19 and 29 of Directive 2013/34/EU" substitute "directors' report required by section 415 of the Companies Act 2006".

(3) In item 17.1, in the first paragraph—

(a) for "the Standards adopted in accordance with the Regulation (EC) No 1606/2002 of the European Parliament and of the Council" substitute "UK-adopted international accounting standards";

(b) for "the respective standard adopted under Regulation (EC) No 1606/2002" substitute "UK-adopted international accounting standards".

(4) In item 18.1.3, for the words from "according to International" to the end substitute "in accordance with Article 23a".

(5) In item 18.1.4, for "Regulation (EC) 1606/2002" substitute "UK-adopted international accounting standards".

(6) In item 18.2.1, for "Regulation (EC) 1606/2002" in both places it occurs, substitute "section 403 of the Companies Act 2006".

(7) In item 18.3.1—

(a) before "Directive" in both places it occurs, insert "the UK law which implemented";
(b) for "a Member State" substitute "the United Kingdom".".

1 Directive 2013/34/EU of the European Parliament and of the Council of 26 June 2013 on the annual financial statements, consolidated financial statements and related reports of certain types of undertakings, amending Directive 2006/43/EC of the European Parliament and of the Council and repealing Council Directives 78/660/EEC and 83/349/EEC (OJ L182, 29.6.2013, p.19).

2 Regulation (EC) No 1606/2002 of the European Parliament and of the Council of 19 July 2002 on the application of international accounting standards (OJ L243, 11.9.2002, p. 1).

3 Directive 2006/43/EC of the European Parliament and of the Council of 17 May 2006 on statutory audits of annual accounts and consolidated accounts, amending Council Directives 78/660/EEC and 83/349/EEC and repealing Council Directive 84/253/EEC (OJ L157, 9.6.2006, p 87).

4 Regulation (EU) No 537/2014 of the European Parliament and of the Council of 16 April 2014 on specific requirements regarding statutory audit of public-interest entities and repealing Commission Decision 2005/909/EC (OJ L158, 27.5.2014, p. 77).

[11.700]

ANNEX 2
UNIVERSAL REGISTRATION DOCUMENT

SECTION 1	INFORMATION TO BE DISCLOSED ABOUT THE ISSUER
Item 1.1	The issuer shall disclose information in accordance with the disclosure requirements for the registration document for equity securities laid down in Annex 1.
Item 1.2	When the universal registration document is approved, item 1.5 of Annex 1 shall be supplemented with a statement that the universal registration document may be used for the purposes of an offer to the public of securities or admission of securities to trading on a regulated market if completed by amendments, if applicable, and a securities note and summary approved in accordance with Regulation (EU) 2017/1129. When the universal registration document is filed and published without prior approval, item 1.5 of Annex 1 shall be replaced with a statement that: (a) the universal registration document has been filed with the [name of the competent authority] as competent authority under Regulation (EU) 2017/1129 without prior approval pursuant to Article 9 of Regulation (EU) 2017/1129; (a) the universal registration document may be used for the purposes of an offer to the public of securities or admission of securities to trading on a regulated market if approved by the [insert name of competent authority] together with any amendments, if applicable, and a securities note and summary approved in accordance with Regulation (EU) 2017/1129.

[11.701]

ANNEX 3
REGISTRATION DOCUMENT FOR SECONDARY ISSUANCES OF EQUITY SECURITIES

SECTION 1	PERSONS RESPONSIBLE, THIRD PARTY INFORMATION, EXPERTS' REPORTS AND COMPETENT AUTHORITY APPROVAL
Item 1.1	Identify all persons responsible for the information or any parts of it, given in the registration document with, in the latter case, an indication of such parts. In the case of natural persons, including members of the issuer's administrative, management or supervisory bodies, indicate the name and function of the person; in the case of legal persons indicate the name and registered office.
Item 1.2	A declaration by those responsible for the registration document that to the best of their knowledge, the information contained in the registration document is in accordance with the facts and that the registration document makes no omission likely to affect its import. Where applicable, a declaration by those responsible for certain parts of the registration document that, to the best of their knowledge, the information contained in those parts of the registration document for which they are responsible is in accordance with the facts and that those parts of the registration document make no omission likely to affect their import.
Item 1.3	Where a statement or report attributed to a person as an expert is included in the Registration Document, provide the following details for that person: (a) name; (b) business address; (c) qualifications; (d) material interest if any in the issuer. If the statement or report has been produced at the issuer's request, state that such statement or report has been included in the registration document with the consent of the person who has authorised the contents of that part of the registration document for the purpose of the prospectus.
Item 1.4	Where information has been sourced from a third party, provide a confirmation that this information has been accurately reproduced and that as far as the issuer is aware and is

	able to ascertain from information published by that third party, no facts have been omitted which would render the reproduced information inaccurate or misleading. In addition, identify the source(s) of the information.
Item 1.5	A statement that: (a) the [registration document/prospectus] has been approved by the [name of competent authority], as competent authority under Regulation (EU) 2017/1129; (b) the [name of competent authority] only approves this [registration document/prospectus] as meeting the standards of completeness, comprehensibility and consistency imposed by Regulation (EU) 2017/1129; (c) such approval shall not be considered as an endorsement of the issuer that it the subject of this [registration document/prospectus]. (d) that the [registration document/prospectus] has been drawn up as part of a simplified prospectus in accordance with Article 14 of Regulation (EU) 2017/1129.
SECTION 2	STATUTORY AUDITORS
Item 2.1	Names of the issuer's auditors for the period covered by the historical financial information (together with their membership in a professional body).
SECTION 3	RISK FACTORS
Item 3.1	A description of the material risks that are specific to the issuer, in a limited number of categories, in a section headed 'Risk Factors'. In each category, the most material risks, in the assessment undertaken by the issuer, offeror or person asking for admission to trading on a regulated market, taking into account the negative impact on the issuer and the probability of their occurrence shall be set out first. The risks shall be corroborated by the content of the registration document.
SECTION 4	INFORMATION ABOUT THE ISSUER
Item 4.1	The legal and commercial name of the issuer.
Item 4.2	The domicile and legal form of the issuer, legal entity identifier ('LEI'), the legislation under which the issuer operates, its country of incorporation, the address, telephone number of its registered office (or principal place of business if different from its registered office) and website of the issuer, if any, with a disclaimer that the information on the website does not form part of the prospectus unless that information is incorporated by reference into the prospectus.
SECTION 5	BUSINESS OVERVIEW
Item 5.1	A brief description of: (a) the key principal activities of the issuer; (b) of any significant changes impacting the issuer's operations and principal activities since the end of the period covered by the latest published audited financial statements, including the following: (i) an indication of any significant new products and services that have been introduced; (ii) the status of the development of new products or services to the extent that they have been publicly disclosed; (iii) any material changes in the issuer's regulatory environment since the period covered by the latest published audited financial statements.
Item 5.2	Investments
Item 5.2.1	A description of the issuer's material investments made since the date of the last published financial statements and which are in progress and/or for which firm commitments have already been made, together with the anticipated source of funds.
SECTION 6	TREND INFORMATION
Item 6.1	A description of: (a) the most significant recent trends in production, sales and inventory, and costs and selling prices since the end of the last financial year to the date of the registration document; (b) any significant change in the financial performance of the group since the end of the last financial period for which financial information has been published to the date of the registration document, or provide an appropriate negative statement; (c) information on any known trends, uncertainties, demands, commitments or events that are reasonably likely to have a material effect on the issuer's prospects for at least the current financial year.
SECTION 7	PROFIT FORECASTS OR ESTIMATES
Item 7.1	Where an issuer has published a profit forecast or a profit estimate (which is still outstanding and valid), that forecast or estimate shall be included in the registration document. If a profit forecast or profit estimate has been published and is still outstanding, but no longer valid, then provide a statement to that effect and an explanation of why such forecast or estimate is no longer valid. Such an invalid forecast or estimate is not subject to the re-

	quirements in items 7.2 and 7.3.
Item 7.2	Where an issuer chooses to include a new profit forecast or a new profit estimate, or where the issuer includes a previously published profit forecast or a previously published profit estimate pursuant to item 7.1, the profit forecast or estimate shall be clear and unambiguous and shall contain a statement setting out the principal assumptions upon which the issuer has based its forecast, or estimate. The forecast or estimate shall comply with the following principles: (a) there must be a clear distinction between assumptions about factors which the members of the administrative, management or supervisory bodies can influence and assumptions about factors which are exclusively outside the influence of the members of the administrative, management or supervisory bodies; (b) the assumptions must be reasonable, readily understandable by investors, specific and precise and not relate to the general accuracy of the estimates underlying the forecast; (c) in the case of a forecast, the assumptions shall draw the investor's attention to those uncertain factors which could materially change the outcome of the forecast.
Item 7.3	The prospectus shall include a statement that the profit forecast or estimate has been compiled and prepared on a basis which is both: (a) comparable with the historical financial information; (b) consistent with the issuer's accounting policies.
SECTION 8	ADMINISTRATIVE, MANAGEMENT AND SUPERVISORY BODIES AND SENIOR MANAGEMENT
Item 8.1	Names, business addresses and functions within the issuer of the following persons and an indication of the principal activities performed by them outside of that issuer where these are significant with respect to that issuer: (a) members of the administrative, management or supervisory bodies; (b) partners with unlimited liability, in the case of a limited partnership with a share capital; (c) founders, if the issuer has been established for fewer than five years; (d) any senior manager who is relevant to establishing that the issuer has the appropriate expertise and experience for the management of the issuer's business. Details of the nature of any family relationship between any of the persons referred to in points (a) to (d). To the extent not already disclosed, and in the case of new members of the administrative, management or supervisory bodies of the issuer (since the date of the latest audited annual financial statements) and of each person referred to in points (b) and (d) of the first subparagraph the following information: (a) the names of all companies and partnerships where those persons have been a member of the administrative, management or supervisory bodies or partner at any time in the previous five years, indicating whether or not the individual is still a member of the administrative, management or supervisory bodies or partner. It is not necessary to list all the subsidiaries of an issuer of which the person is also a member of the administrative, management or supervisory bodies; (b) details of any convictions in relation to fraudulent offences for at least the previous five years; (c) details of any bankruptcies, receiverships, liquidations or companies put into administration in respect of those persons described in points (a) and (d) of the first subparagraph who acted in one or more of those capacities for at least the previous five years; (d) details of any official public incrimination and/or sanctions involving such persons by statutory or regulatory authorities (including designated professional bodies) and whether they have ever been disqualified by a court from acting as a member of the administrative, management or supervisory bodies of an issuer or from acting in the management or conduct of the affairs of any issuer for at least the previous five years. If there is no such information required to be disclosed, a statement to that effect is to be made.
Item 8.2	Potential conflicts of interest between any duties carried out on behalf of the issuer by the persons referred to in item 8.1 and their private interests or other duties must be clearly stated. In the event that there are no such conflicts a statement to that effect must be made. Any arrangement or understanding with major shareholders, customers, suppliers or others, pursuant to which any person referred to in item 8.1 was selected as a member of the administrative, management or supervisory bodies or member of senior management. Details of any restrictions agreed by the persons referred to in item 8.1 on the disposal within a certain period of time of their holdings in the issuer's securities.

SECTION 9	MAJOR SHAREHOLDERS
Item 9.1	In so far as is known to the issuer, the name of any person other than a member of the administrative, management or supervisory bodies who, directly or indirectly, has an interest in the issuer's capital or voting rights which is notifiable under the issuer's national law, together with the amount of each such person's interest, as of the date of the registration document or, if there are no such persons, an appropriate statement to that effect that no such person exists.
Item 9.2	Whether the issuer's major shareholders have different voting rights, or an appropriate statement to the effect that no such voting rights exist.
Item 9.3	To the extent known to the issuer, state whether the issuer is directly or indirectly owned or controlled and by whom and describe the nature of such control and describe the measures in place to ensure that such control is not abused.
Item 9.4	A description of any arrangements, known to the issuer, the operation of which may at a subsequent date result in a change in control of the issuer.
SECTION 10	RELATED PARTY TRANSACTIONS
Item 10.1	Details of related party transactions (which for these purposes are those set out in the Standards adopted in accordance with Regulation (EC) No 1606/2002), that the issuer has entered into since the date of the last financial statements, must be disclosed in accordance with the respective standard adopted under Regulation (EC) No 1606/2002 if applicable. If such standards do not apply to the issuer the following information must be disclosed: (a) the nature and extent of any transactions which are, as a single transaction or in their entirety, material to the issuer. Where such related party transactions are not concluded at arm's length provide an explanation of why these transactions were not concluded at arm's length. In the case of outstanding loans including guarantees of any kind indicate the amount outstanding; (b) the amount or the percentage to which related party transactions form part of the turnover of the issuer.
SECTION 11	FINANCIAL INFORMATION CONCERNING THE ISSUER'S ASSETS AND LIABILITIES, FINANCIAL POSITION AND PROFITS, AND LOSSES
Item 11.1	Financial statements Financial statements (annual and half-yearly) are required to be published covering the period of 12 months prior to the approval of the prospectus. Where both annual and half-yearly financial statements have been published, only the annual statements shall be required where they postdate the half-yearly financial statements.
Item 11.2	Auditing of annual financial information
[Item 11.2.1	Audit report The annual financial statements must be independently audited. The audit report shall be prepared in accordance with Directive 2006/43/EC and Regulation (EU) No 537/2014. Where Directive 2006/43/EC and Regulation (EU) No 537/2014 do not apply, the annual financial statements must be audited or reported on as to whether or not, for the purposes of the registration document, it gives a true and fair view in accordance with auditing standards applicable in a Member State or an equivalent standard. Otherwise, the following information must be included in the registration document: (a) a prominent statement disclosing which auditing standards have been applied; (b) an explanation of any significant departures from International Standards on Auditing.]
[Item 11.2.1a	Where audit reports on the annual financial statements have been refused by the statutory auditors or where they contain qualifications, modifications of opinion, disclaimers or an emphasis of matter, the reason must be given, and such qualifications, modifications, disclaimers or emphasis of matter must be reproduced in full.]
Item 11.2.2	Indication of other information in the registration document which has been audited by the auditors.
Item 11.2.3	Where financial information in the registration document is not extracted from the issuer's audited financial statements state the source of the data and state that the data is not audited.
Item 11.3	Legal and arbitration proceedings Information on any governmental, legal or arbitration proceedings (including any such proceedings which are pending or threatened of which the issuer is aware), during a period covering at least the previous 12 months which may have, or have had in the recent past significant effects on the issuer and/or group's financial position or profitability, or provide an appropriate negative statement.
Item 11.4	Significant change in the issuer's financial position A description of any significant change in the financial position of the group which has occurred since the end of the last financial period for which either audited financial state-

	ments or interim financial information have been published, or provide an appropriate negative statement.
Item 11.5	Pro forma financial information This requirement will normally be satisfied by the inclusion of pro forma financial information. This pro forma financial information must be presented as set out in Annex 20 and must include the information indicated therein. Pro forma financial information must be accompanied by a report prepared by independent accountants or auditors.
Item 11.6	Dividend policy A description of the issuer's policy on dividend distributions and any restrictions thereon.
Item 11.6.1	The amount of the dividend per share for the last financial year adjusted, where the number of shares in the issuer has changed, to make it comparable.
SECTION 12	ADDITIONAL INFORMATION
Item 12.1	Share capital
Item 12.1.1	The amount of any convertible securities, exchangeable securities or securities with warrants, with an indication of the conditions governing and the procedures for conversion, exchange or subscription.
Item 12.1.2	Information about and terms of any acquisition rights and or obligations over authorised but unissued capital or an undertaking to increase the capital.
SECTION 13	REGULATORY DISCLOSURES
Item 13.1	A summary of the information disclosed under Regulation (EU) No 596/2014 over the last 12 months which is relevant as at the date of the prospectus. The summary shall be presented in an easily analysable, concise and comprehensible form and shall not be a replication of information already published under Regulation (EU) No 596/2014. The summary shall be presented in a limited number of categories depending on their subject.
SECTION 14	MATERIAL CONTRACTS
Item 14.1	A brief summary of each material contract, other than contracts entered into in the ordinary course of business, to which the issuer or any member of the group is a party, for the two years immediately preceding publication of the registration document. A brief summary of any other contract (not being a contract entered into in the ordinary course of business) entered into by any member of the group which contains any provision under which any member of the group has any obligation or entitlement which is material to the group as at the date of the registration document.
SECTION 15	DOCUMENTS AVAILABLE
Item 15.1	A statement that for the term of the registration document the following documents, where applicable, can be inspected: (a) the up to date memorandum and articles of association of the issuer; (b) all reports, letters, and other documents, valuations and statements prepared by any expert at the issuer's request any part of which is included or referred to in the registration document. An indication of the website on which the documents may be inspected.

NOTES

Item 11.2.1 substituted, and item 11.2.1a inserted, by Commission Delegated Regulation 2020/1273/EU, Art 1(14), Annex II, as from 17 September 2020.

Application of this Annex in relation to the UK: this Annex is amended (as follows), in relation to the UK only, by the Prospectus (Amendment etc) (EU Exit) Regulations 2019, SI 2019/1234, Schedule, para 3, as from IP completion day (as defined in the European Union (Withdrawal Agreement) Act 2020, s 39); for transitional provisions, see regs 74, 75 of the 2019 Regulations at **[12.165]** et seq—

"3.—(1) Annex 3 is amended as follows.

(2) In item 10.1, in the first paragraph—

(a) for "the Standards adopted in accordance with Regulation (EC) No 1606/2002" substitute "UK-adopted international accounting standards";

(b) for "the respective standard adopted according to Regulation (EC) No 1606/2002" substitute "UK-adopted international accounting standards".

(3) In item 11.2.1—

(i) before "Directive" in both places it occurs, insert "the UK law which implemented";

(ii) for "a Member State" substitute "the United Kingdom".".

[11.702]

ANNEX 4
REGISTRATION DOCUMENT FOR UNITS OF CLOSED-END COLLECTIVE INVESTMENT UNDERTAKINGS

	[In addition to the information required in this Annex, a collective investment undertaking must provide the information required in sections/items 1, 2, 3, 4, 6, 7.1, 7.2.1, 8.4, 9 (al-

	though the description of the regulatory environment that the issuer operates in, need only relate to the regulatory environment relevant to the issuer's investments), 11, 12, 13, 14, 15.2, 16, 17, 18 (except for pro forma financial information), 19, 20 and 21 of Annex 1 to this Regulation, or, where the collective investment undertaking meets the requirements of Article 14(1) of Regulation (EU) 2017/1129, the information required in sections/items 1, 2, 3, 4, 7, 8, 9, 10, 11 (except for pro forma financial information), 12, 13, 14 and 15 of Annex 3 to this Regulation. Where units are issued by a collective investment undertaking which is constituted as a common fund managed by a fund manager, the information referred to in sections/items 6, 12, 13, 14, 15.2, 16 and 20 of Annex 1 to this Regulation shall be disclosed in relation to the fund manager, while the information referred to in items 2, 4 and 18 of Annex 1 to this Regulation shall be disclosed in relation to both the fund and the fund manager.]
SECTION 1	INVESTMENT OBJECTIVE AND POLICY
Item 1.1	(a) description of the investment policy, strategy and objectives of the collective investment undertaking; (b) information on where the underlying collective investment undertaking(s) is/are established if the collective investment undertaking is a fund comprising of funds; (c) a description of the types of assets in which the collective investment undertaking may invest; (d) the techniques it may employ and all associated risks together with the circumstances in which the collective investment undertaking may use leverage; (e) the types and sources of leverage permitted and the associated risks; (f) any restrictions on the use of leverage and any collateral and asset reuse arrangements; (g) the maximum level of leverage which may be employed on behalf of the collective investment undertaking.
Item 1.2	A description of the procedures by which the collective investment undertaking may change its investment strategy or investment policy, or both.
Item 1.3	The leverage limits of the collective investment undertaking. If there are no such limits, include a statement to that effect.
Item 1.4	The regulatory status of the collective investment undertaking together with the name of any regulator in its country of incorporation.
Item 1.5	The profile of a typical investor for whom the collective investment undertaking is designed.
Item 1.6	A statement confirming the following: (a) the [registration document/prospectus] has been approved by the [name of competent authority], as competent authority under Regulation (EU) 2017/1129; (b) the [name of competent authority] only approves this [registration document/prospectus] as meeting the standards of completeness, comprehensibility and consistency imposed by Regulation (EU) 2017/1129; (c) such approval should not be considered as an endorsement of the issuer that is the subject of this [registration document/prospectus].
SECTION 2	INVESTMENT RESTRICTIONS
Item 2.1	A statement of the investment restrictions which apply to the collective investment undertaking, if any, and an indication of how the holders of securities will be informed of the actions that the investment manager will take in the event of a breach.
Item 2.2	Certain information is required to be disclosed, where more than 20% of the gross assets of any collective investment undertaking (except where the registration document is being prepared for an entity as a result of the application of item 2.3 or 2.5) may be either: (a) invested in, either directly or indirectly, or loaned to any single underlying issuer (including the underlying issuer's subsidiaries or affiliates); (b) invested in one or more collective investment undertakings which may invest in excess of 20% of its gross assets in other collective investment undertakings (open-end and/or closed-end type); (c) exposed to the creditworthiness or solvency of any one counterparty (including its subsidiaries or affiliates); The information, referred to in the introductory sentence, shall comprise the following in either of the following circumstances: (i) where the underlying securities are not admitted to trading on a regulated or equivalent third country market or an SME Growth Market, information relating to each underlying issuer/collective investment undertaking/counterparty as if it were an issuer for the purposes of the minimum disclosure requirements for the registration document for equity securities (in the case of point (a)) or minimum disclosure requirements for the registration document for units issued by closed-end collective investment undertakings (in the case of point (b)) or the minimum disclosure requirements for the registration document for wholesale non-equity securities (in the

	case of point (c)); (ii) if the securities issued by the underlying issuer/collective investment undertaking/counterparty have already been admitted to trading on a regulated or equivalent third country market or an SME Growth Market, or the obligations are guaranteed by an entity admitted to trading on a regulated or equivalent market or an SME Growth Market, the name, address, country of incorporation, nature of business and name of the market in which its securities are admitted. The disclosure requirement referred to in points (i) and (ii) shall not apply where the 20% threshold is exceeded due to appreciations or depreciations, changes in exchange rates, or by reason of the receipt of rights, bonuses, benefits in the nature of capital or by reason of any other action affecting every holder of that investment, provided the investment manager has regard to the threshold when considering changes in the investment portfolio. Where the collective investment undertaking can reasonably demonstrate to the competent authority that it is unable to access some or all of the information required under point (i), the collective investment undertaking must disclose all of the information that it is able to access, that it is aware of, and/or that it is able to ascertain from information published by the underlying issuer/ collective investment undertaking/counterparty in order to satisfy as far as is practicable the requirements laid down in point (i). In this case, the prospectus must include a prominent warning that the collective investment undertaking has been unable to access specified items of information that would otherwise be required to be included in the prospectus and therefore a reduced level of disclosure has been provided in relation to a specified underlying issuer, collective investment undertaking or counterparty.
Item 2.3	Where a collective investment undertaking invests in investments in excess of 20% of its gross assets in other collective investment undertakings (open ended and/or closed ended), a description of the investment and how the risk is spread in relation to those investments shall be disclosed. In addition, item 2.2 shall apply, in addition to all underlying investments of the collective investment undertaking as if those investments had been made directly.
Item 2.4	With reference to point (c) of item 2.2, if collateral is advanced to cover that portion of the exposure to any one counterparty in excess of 20% of the gross assets of the collective investment undertaking, set out the details of such collateral arrangements.
Item 2.5	Where a collective investment undertaking invests in investments in excess of 40% of its gross assets in another collective investment undertaking, then one of the following must be disclosed: (a) information relating to each underlying collective investment undertaking as if it were an issuer under minimum disclosure requirements as set out in this Annex; (b) if securities issued by an underlying collective investment undertaking have already been admitted to trading on a regulated or equivalent third country market or an SME Growth Market, or the obligations are guaranteed by an entity admitted to trading on a regulated or equivalent market or an SME Growth Market, then the name, address, country of incorporation, nature of business and name of the market in which its securities are admitted. Where the collective investment undertaking can reasonably demonstrate to the competent authority that it is unable to access some or all of the information required under point (i), the collective investment undertaking must disclose all of the information that it is able to access, that it is aware of, and/or that it is able to ascertain from information published by the underlying issuer/ collective investment undertaking/counterparty in order to satisfy as far as is practicable the requirements laid down in point (a). In this case, the prospectus must include a prominent warning that the collective investment undertaking has been unable to access specified items of information that would otherwise be required to be included in the prospectus and therefore a reduced level of disclosure has been provided in relation to a specified underlying issuer, collective investment undertaking or counterparty.
Item 2.6	Physical commodities Where a collective investment undertaking invests directly in physical commodities a disclosure of that fact and the percentage of the gross assets that will be so invested.
Item 2.7	Property collective investment undertakings Where a collective investment undertaking holds property as part of its investment objective, the percentage of the portfolio that is to be invested in property, the description of the property and any material costs relating to the acquisition and holding of such property shall be disclosed. In addition, a valuation report relating to the properties must be included. The disclosure requirements set out in item 4.1 shall apply to: (a) the entity producing the valuation report; (b) any other entity responsible for the administration of the property.
Item 2.8	Derivatives financial instruments/money market instruments/currencies Where a collective investment undertaking invests in derivatives, financial instruments, money market instruments or currencies other than for the purposes of efficient portfolio management namely solely for the purpose of reducing, transferring or eliminating invest-

	ment risk in the underlying investments of a collective investment undertaking, including any technique or instrument used to provide protection against exchange and credit risks, a statement of whether those investments are used for hedging or for investment purposes, and a description of where and how risk is spread in relation to those investments.
Item 2.9	Item 2.2 does not apply to investment in securities issued or guaranteed by a government, government agency or instrumentality of any Member State, its regional or local authorities, or of any OECD Member State.
Item 2.10	Point (a) of item 2.2 does not apply to a collective investment undertaking whose investment objective is to track, without material modification, a broadly based and recognised published index. A statement setting out details of where information about the index can be obtained shall be included.
SECTION 3	THE APPLICANT'S SERVICE PROVIDERS
Item 3.1	The actual or estimated maximum amount of all material fees payable directly or indirectly by the collective investment undertaking for any services provided under arrangements entered into on or prior to the date of the registration document and a description of how these fees are calculated.
Item 3.2	A description of any fee payable directly or indirectly by the collective investment undertaking which cannot be quantified under item 3.1 and which is or which may be material.
Item 3.3	If any service provider to the collective investment undertaking is in receipt of any benefits from third parties (other than the collective investment undertaking) by virtue of providing any services to the collective investment undertaking, and those benefits may not accrue to the collective investment undertaking, a statement of that fact, the name of that third party, if available, and a description of the nature of the benefits shall be disclosed.
Item 3.4	The identity of the service providers and a description of their duties and the investor's rights.
Item 3.5	A description of any material potential conflicts of interest which any of the service providers to the collective investment undertaking may have as between their duty to the collective investment undertaking and duties owed by them to third parties and their other interests. A description of any arrangements which are in place to address such potential conflicts.
SECTION 4	INVESTMENT MANAGER/ADVISERS
Item 4.1	In respect of any Investment Manager the information required to be disclosed under items 4.1 to 4.4 and, if material, under item 5.3 of Annex 1 together with a description of its regulatory status and experience.
Item 4.2	In respect of any entity providing investment advice in relation to the assets of the collective investment undertaking, the name and a brief description of the entity.
SECTION 5	CUSTODY
Item 5.1	A full description of how the assets of the collective investment undertaking will be held and by whom and any fiduciary or similar relationship between the collective investment undertaking and any third party in relation to custody: Where a depositary, trustee, or other fiduciary is appointed, the following shall be provided: (a) such information as is required to be disclosed under items 4.1 to 4.4 and, if material, under item 5.3 of Annex 1; (b) a description of the obligations of each party under the custody or similar agreement; (c) any delegated custody arrangements; (d) the regulatory status of each party and their delegates.
Item 5.2	Where any entity other than those entities referred to in item 5.1, holds any assets of the collective investment undertaking, a description of how these assets are held together with a description of any additional risks.
SECTION 6	VALUATION
Item 6.1	A description of the valuation procedure and of the pricing methodology for valuing assets.
Item 6.2	Details of all circumstances in which valuations may be suspended and a statement of how such suspension will be communicated or made available to investors.
SECTION 7	CROSS LIABILITIES
Item 7.1	In the case of an umbrella collective investment undertaking, a statement of any cross liability that may occur between classes of investments in other collective investment undertakings and any action taken to limit such liability.
SECTION 8	FINANCIAL INFORMATION
Item 8.1	Where a collective investment undertaking has not commenced operations and no financial statements have been made up as at the date of the registration document, since the date of incorporation or establishment, a statement to that effect. Where a collective investment undertaking has commenced operations, the provisions of

	section 18 of Annex 1 or section 11 of Annex 3 shall apply as appropriate.
Item 8.2	A comprehensive and meaningful analysis of the collective investment undertaking's portfolio. Where the portfolio is not audited, this must be clearly marked as such.
Item 8.3	An indication of the latest net asset value of the collective investment undertaking or the latest market price of the unit or share of the collective investment undertaking. Where the net asset value or the latest market price of the unit or share is not audited, this must be clearly marked as such.

NOTES

The words preceding Section 1 were substituted by Commission Delegated Regulation 2020/1273/EU, Art 1(15), Annex III, as from 17 September 2020.

[11.703]

ANNEX 5
REGISTRATION DOCUMENT FOR DEPOSITORY RECEIPTS ISSUED OVER SHARES

SECTION 1	INFORMATION ABOUT THE ISSUER OF THE UNDERLYING SHARES		
	For depository receipts issued over shares, the information about the issuer of the underlying share shall be provided in accordance with Annex 1 to this Regulation. For depository receipts issued over shares that meet the requirements of Article 14(1) of Regulation (EU) 2017/1129, the information about the issuer of the underlying share shall be provided in accordance with Annex 3 to this Regulation.		
SECTION 2	INFORMATION ABOUT THE ISSUER OF THE DEPOSITORY RECEIPTS	Primary Issuance	Secondary Issuances
Item 2.1	Name, registered office, legal entity identifier ('LEI') and principal administrative establishment if different from the registered office.	√	√
Item 2.2	Date of incorporation and length of life of the issuer, except where the period is indefinite.	√	√
Item 2.3	Legislation under which the issuer operates and legal form which it has adopted under that legislation.	√	√

[11.704]

ANNEX 6
REGISTRATION DOCUMENT FOR RETAIL NON-EQUITY SECURITIES

SECTION 1	PERSONS RESPONSIBLE, THIRD PARTY INFORMATION, EXPERTS' REPORTS AND COMPETENT AUTHORITY APPROVAL
Item 1.1	Identify all persons responsible for the information or any parts of it, given in the registration document with, in the latter case, an indication of such parts. In the case of natural persons, including members of the issuer's administrative, management or supervisory bodies, indicate the name and function of the person; in the case of legal persons indicate the name and registered office.
Item 1.2	A declaration by those responsible for the registration document that to the best of their knowledge, the information contained in the registration document is in accordance with the facts and that the registration document makes no omission likely to affect its import. Where applicable, a declaration by those responsible for certain parts of the registration document that, to the best of their knowledge, the information contained in those parts of the registration document for which they are responsible is in accordance with the facts and that those parts of the registration document make no omission likely to affect their import.
Item 1.3	Where a statement or report attributed to a person as an expert is included in the registration document, provide the following in relation to that person: (a) name; (b) business address; (c) qualifications; (d) material interest if any in the issuer. If the statement or report has been produced at the issuer's request, state that such statement or report has been included in the registration document with the consent of the person who has authorised the contents of that part of the registration document for the purpose of the prospectus.
Item 1.4	Where information has been sourced from a third party, provide a confirmation that this information has been accurately reproduced and that as far as the issuer is aware and is able to ascertain from information published by that third party, no facts have been omitted which would render the reproduced information inaccurate or misleading. In addition, identify the source(s) of the information.
Item 1.5	A statement that:

	(a) the [registration document/prospectus] has been approved by the [name of competent authority], as competent authority under Regulation (EU) 2017/1129; (b) the [name of competent authority] only approves this [registration document/prospectus] as meeting the standards of completeness, comprehensibility and consistency imposed by Regulation (EU) 2017/1129; (c) such approval should not be considered as an endorsement of the issuer that is the subject of this [registration document/prospectus].
SECTION 2	STATUTORY AUDITORS
Item 2.1	Names and addresses of the issuer's auditors for the period covered by the historical financial information (together with their membership in a professional body).
Item 2.2	If auditors have resigned, been removed or have not been re-appointed during the period covered by the historical financial information, indicate details if material.
SECTION 3	RISK FACTORS
Item 3.1	A description of the material risks that are specific to the issuer and that may affect the issuer's ability to fulfil its obligations under the securities, in a limited number of categories, in a section headed 'Risk Factors'. In each category the most material risks, in the assessment of the issuer, offeror or person asking for admission to trading on a regulated market, taking into account the negative impact on the issuer and the probability of their occurrence, shall be set out first. The risk factors shall be corroborated by the content of the registration document.
SECTION 4	INFORMATION ABOUT THE ISSUER
Item 4.1	History and development of the issuer
Item 4.1.1	The legal and commercial name of the issuer
Item 4.1.2	The place of registration of the issuer, its registration number and legal entity identifier ('LEI').
Item 4.1.3	The date of incorporation and the length of life of the issuer, except where the period is indefinite.
Item 4.1.4	The domicile and legal form of the issuer, the legislation under which the issuer operates, its country of incorporation, the address, telephone number of its registered office (or principal place of business if different from its registered office) and website of the issuer, if any, with a disclaimer that the information on the website does not form part of the prospectus unless that information is incorporated by reference into the prospectus.
Item 4.1.5	Details of any recent events particular to the issuer and which are to a material extent relevant to an evaluation of the issuer's solvency.
Item 4.1.6	Credit ratings assigned to an issuer at the request or with the cooperation of the issuer in the rating process. A brief explanation of the meaning of the ratings if this has previously been published by the rating provider.
Item 4.1.7	Information on the material changes in the issuer's borrowing and funding structure since the last financial year;
Item 4.1.8	Description of the expected financing of the issuer's activities
SECTION 5	BUSINESS OVERVIEW
Item 5.1	Principal activities
Item 5.1.1	A description of the issuer's principal activities, including: (a) the main categories of products sold and/or services performed; (b) an indication of any significant new products or activities; (c) the principal markets in which the issuer competes.
Item 5.2	The basis for any statements made by the issuer regarding its competitive position.
SECTION 6	ORGANISATIONAL STRUCTURE
Item 6.1	If the issuer is part of a group, a brief description of the group and the issuer's position within the group. This may be in the form of, or accompanied by, a diagram of the organisational structure if this helps to clarify the structure.
Item 6.2	If the issuer is dependent upon other entities within the group, this must be clearly stated together with an explanation of this dependence.
SECTION 7	TREND INFORMATION
Item 7.1	A description of: (a) any material adverse change in the prospects of the issuer since the date of its last published audited financial statements; (b) any significant change in the financial performance of the group since the end of the last financial period for which financial information has been published to the date of the registration document. If neither of the above are applicable then the issuer shall include an appropriate statement to the effect that no such changes exist.

Item 7.2	Information on any known trends, uncertainties, demands, commitments or events that are reasonably likely to have a material effect on the issuer's prospects for at least the current financial year.
SECTION 8	PROFIT FORECASTS OR ESTIMATES
Item 8.1	Where an issuer includes on a voluntary basis a profit forecast or a profit estimate (which is still outstanding and valid), that forecast or estimate included in the registration document must contain the information set out in items 8.2 and 8.3. If a profit forecast or profit estimate has been published and is still outstanding, but no longer valid, then provide a statement to that effect and an explanation of why such profit forecast or estimate is no longer valid. Such an invalid forecast or estimate is not subject to the requirements in items 8.2 and 8.3.
Item 8.2	Where an issuer chooses to include a new profit forecast or a new profit estimate, or where the issuer includes a previously published profit forecast or a previously published profit estimate pursuant to item 8.1, the profit forecast or estimate shall be clear and unambiguous and contain a statement setting out the principal assumptions upon which the issuer has based its forecast, or estimate. The forecast or estimate shall comply with the following principles: (a) there must be a clear distinction between assumptions about factors which the members of the administrative, management or supervisory bodies can influence and assumptions about factors which are exclusively outside the influence of the members of the administrative, management or supervisory bodies; (b) the assumptions must be reasonable, readily understandable by investors, specific and precise and not relate to the general accuracy of the estimates underlying the forecast; and (c) In the case of a forecast, the assumptions shall draw the investor's attention to those uncertain factors which could materially change the outcome of the forecast.
Item 8.3	The prospectus shall include a statement that the profit forecast or estimate has been compiled and prepared on a basis which is both: (a) comparable with the historical financial information; (b) consistent with the issuer's accounting policies.
SECTION 9	ADMINISTRATIVE, MANAGEMENT, AND SUPERVISORY BODIES
Item 9.1	Names, business addresses and functions within the issuer of the following persons and an indication of the principal activities performed by them outside of that issuer where these are significant with respect to that issuer: (a) members of the administrative, management or supervisory bodies; (b) partners with unlimited liability, in the case of a limited partnership with a share capital.
Item 9.2	Administrative, management, and supervisory bodies' conflicts of interests Potential conflicts of interests between any duties to the issuer, of the persons referred to in item 9.1, and their private interests and or other duties must be clearly stated. In the event that there are no such conflicts, a statement to that effect must be made.
SECTION 10	MAJOR SHAREHOLDERS
Item 10.1	To the extent known to the issuer, state whether the issuer is directly or indirectly owned or controlled and by whom and describe the nature of such control and describe the measures in place to ensure that such control is not abused.
Item 10.2	A description of any arrangements, known to the issuer, the operation of which may at a subsequent date result in a change in control of the issuer.
SECTION 11	FINANCIAL INFORMATION CONCERNING THE ISSUER'S ASSETS AND LIABILITIES, FINANCIAL POSITION AND PROFITS AND LOSSES
Item 11.1	Historical financial information
Item 11.1.1	Audited historical financial information covering the latest two financial years (or such shorter period as the issuer has been in operation) and the audit report in respect of each year.
Item 11.1.2	Change of accounting reference date If the issuer has changed its accounting reference date during the period for which historical financial information is required, the audited historical financial information shall cover at least 24 months, or the entire period for which the issuer has been in operation, whichever is shorter.
Item 11.1.3	Accounting Standards The financial information must be prepared according to International Financial Reporting Standards as endorsed in the Union based on Regulation (EC) No 1606/2002. If Regulation (EC) No 1606/2002 is not applicable, the financial information must be prepared in accordance with either: (a) a Member State's national accounting standards for issuers from the EEA, as re-

	quired by the Directive 2013/34/EU; (b) a third country's national accounting standards equivalent to Regulation (EC) No 1606/2002 for third country issuers. If such third country's national accounting standards are not equivalent to Regulation (EC) No 1606/2002, the financial statements shall be restated in compliance with that Regulation.
Item 11.1.4	Change of accounting framework The last audited historical financial information, containing comparative information for the previous year, must be presented and prepared in a form consistent with the accounting standards framework that will be adopted in the issuer's next published annual financial statements. Changes within the issuer's existing accounting framework do not require the audited financial statements to be restated. However, if the issuer intends to adopt a new accounting standards framework in its next published financial statements, the latest year of financial statements must be prepared and audited in line with the new framework.
Item 11.1.5	Where the audited financial information is prepared according to national accounting standards, the financial information required under this heading must include at least the following: (a) the balance sheet; (b) the income statement; (c) the cash flow statement; (d) the accounting policies and explanatory notes.
Item 11.1.6	Consolidated financial statements If the issuer prepares both stand-alone and consolidated financial statements, include at least the consolidated financial statements in the registration document.
Item 11.1.7	Age of financial information The balance sheet date of the last year of audited financial information statements may not be older than 18 months from the date of the registration document.
Item 11.2	Interim and other financial information
Item 11.2.1	If the issuer has published quarterly or half yearly financial information since the date of its last audited financial statements, these must be included in the registration document. If the quarterly or half yearly financial information has been reviewed or audited, the audit or review report must also be included. If the quarterly or half yearly financial information is not audited or has not been reviewed state that fact. If the registration document is dated more than nine months after the date of the last audited financial statements, it must contain interim financial information, which may be unaudited (in which case that fact must be stated) covering at least the first six months of the financial year. Interim financial information prepared in accordance with either the requirements of the Directive 2013/34/EU or Regulation (EC) No 1606/2002 as the case may be. For issuers not subject to either Directive 2013/34/EU or Regulation (EC) No 1606/2002, the interim financial information must include comparative statements for the same period in the prior financial year, except that the requirement for comparative balance sheet information may be satisfied by presenting the year's end balance sheet.
Item 11.3	Auditing of historical annual financial information
[Item 11.3.1	The historical annual financial information must be independently audited. The audit report shall be prepared in accordance with Directive 2006/43/EC and Regulation (EU) No 537/2014. Where Directive 2006/43/EC and Regulation (EU) No 537/2014 do not apply, the historical financial information must be audited or reported on as to whether or not, for the purposes of the registration document, it gives a true and fair view in accordance with auditing standards applicable in a Member State or an equivalent standard.]
[Item 11.3.1a	Where audit reports on the historical financial information have been refused by the statutory auditors or where they contain qualifications, modifications of opinion, disclaimers or an emphasis of matter, the reason must be given, and such qualifications, modifications, disclaimers or emphasis of matter must be reproduced in full.]
Item 11.3.2	Indication of other information in the registration document which has been audited by the auditors.
Item 11.3.3	Where financial information in the registration document is not extracted from the issuer's audited financial statements state the source of the data and state that the data is not audited.
Item 11.4	Legal and arbitration proceedings
Item 11.4.1	Information on any governmental, legal or arbitration proceedings (including any such proceedings which are pending or threatened of which the issuer is aware), during a period covering at least the previous 12 months which may have, or have had in the recent past significant effects on the issuer and/or group's financial position or profitability, or provide

	an appropriate negative statement.
Item 11.5	Significant change in the issuer's financial position
Item 11.5.1	A description of any significant change in the financial position of the group which has occurred since the end of the last financial period for which either audited financial information or interim financial information have been published, or provide an appropriate negative statement.
SECTION 12	ADDITIONAL INFORMATION
Item 12.1	Share capital The amount of the issued capital, the number and classes of the shares of which it is composed with details of their principal characteristics, the part of the issued capital still to be paid up with an indication of the number, or total nominal value and the type of the shares not yet fully paid up, broken down where applicable according to the extent to which they have been paid up.
Item 12.2	Memorandum and Articles of Association The register and the entry number therein, if applicable, and a description of the issuer's objects and purposes and where they can be found in the memorandum and articles of association.
SECTION 13	MATERIAL CONTRACTS
Item 13.1	A brief summary of all material contracts that are not entered into in the ordinary course of the issuer's business, which could result in any group member being under an obligation or an entitlement that is material to the issuer's ability to meet its obligations to security holders in respect of the securities being issued.
SECTION 14	DOCUMENTS AVAILABLE
Item 14.1	A statement that for the term of the registration document the following documents, where applicable, can be inspected: (a) the up to date memorandum and articles of association of the issuer; (b) all reports, letters, and other documents, valuations and statements prepared by any expert at the issuer's request any part of which is included or referred to in the registration document. An indication of the website on which the documents may be inspected.

NOTES

Item 11.3.1 substituted, and item 11.3.1a inserted, by Commission Delegated Regulation 2020/1273/EU, Art 1(16), Annex 4, as from 17 September 2020.

Application of this Annex in relation to the UK: this Annex is amended (as follows), in relation to the UK only, by the Prospectus (Amendment etc) (EU Exit) Regulations 2019, SI 2019/1234, Schedule, para 4, as from IP completion day (as defined in the European Union (Withdrawal Agreement) Act 2020, s 39); for transitional provisions, see regs 74, 75 of the 2019 Regulations at **[12.165]** et seq—

"4.—(1) Annex 6 is amended as follows.

(2) In item 11.1.3, for the words from "according to International" to the end substitute "in accordance with Article 23a".

(3) In item 11.2.1—

(a) before "Directive" in both places it occurs, insert "the UK law which implemented";

(b) for "Regulation (EC) 1606/2002" in both places it occurs, substitute "section 403 of the Companies Act 2006".

(4) In item 11.3.1—

(a) before "Directive" in both places it occurs, insert "the UK law which implemented";

(b) for "a Member State" substitute "the United Kingdom".".

[11.705]

ANNEX 7
REGISTRATION DOCUMENT FOR WHOLESALE NON-EQUITY SECURITIES

SECTION 1	PERSONS RESPONSIBLE, THIRD PARTY INFORMATION, EXPERTS' REPORTS AND COMPETENT AUTHORITY APPROVAL
Item 1.1	Identify all persons responsible for the information or any parts of it, given in the registration document with, in the latter case, an indication of such parts. In the case of natural persons, including members of the issuer's administrative, management or supervisory bodies, indicate the name and function of the person; in the case of legal persons indicate the name and registered office.
Item 1.2	A declaration by those responsible for the registration document that to the best of their knowledge, the information contained in the registration document is in accordance with the facts and that the registration document makes no omission likely to affect its import. Where applicable, a declaration by those responsible for certain parts of the registration document that, to the best of their knowledge, the information contained in those parts of the registration document for which they are responsible is in accordance with the facts and that those parts of the registration document make no omission likely to affect their import.
Item 1.3	Where a statement or report attributed to a person as an expert is included in the registration document, provide the following information in relation to that person:

	(a) name;
	(b) business address;
	(c) qualifications;
	(d) material interest if any in the issuer.
	If the statement or report has been produced at the issuer's request, state that such statement or report has been included in the registration document with the consent of the person who has authorised the contents of that part of the registration document for the purpose of the prospectus.
Item 1.4	Where information has been sourced from a third party, provide a confirmation that this information has been accurately reproduced and that as far as the issuer is aware and is able to ascertain from information published by that third party, no facts have been omitted which would render the reproduced information inaccurate or misleading. In addition, identify the source(s) of the information.
Item 1.5	A statement that:
	(a) the [registration document/prospectus] has been approved by the [name of competent authority], as competent authority under Regulation (EU) 2017/1129;
	(b) the [name of competent authority] only approves this [registration document/prospectus] as meeting the standards of completeness, comprehensibility and consistency imposed by Regulation (EU) 2017/1129;
	(c) such approval should not be considered as an endorsement of the issuer that is the subject of this [registration document/prospectus].
SECTION 2	STATUTORY AUDITORS
Item 2.1	Names and addresses of the issuer's auditors for the period covered by the historical financial information (together with their membership in a professional body).
Item 2.2	If auditors have resigned, been removed or have not been re-appointed during the period covered by the historical financial information, indicate details if material.
SECTION 3	RISK FACTORS
Item 3.1	A description of the material risks that are specific to the issuer and that may affect the issuer's ability to fulfil its obligations under the securities, in a limited number of categories, in a section headed 'Risk Factors'.
	In each category the most material risks, in the assessment of the issuer, offeror or person asking for admission to trading on a regulated market, taking into account the negative impact on the issuer and the probability of their occurrence, shall be set out first. The risk factors shall be corroborated by the content of the registration document.
SECTION 4	INFORMATION ABOUT THE ISSUER
Item 4.1	History and development of the Issuer
Item 4.1.1	The legal and commercial name of the issuer
Item 4.1.2	The place of registration of the issuer, its registration number and legal entity identifier ('LEI').
Item 4.1.3	The date of incorporation and the length of life of the issuer, except where the period is indefinite.
Item 4.1.4	The domicile and legal form of the issuer, the legislation under which the issuer operates, its country of incorporation, the address, telephone number of its registered office (or principal place of business if different from its registered office) and website of the issuer, if any, with a disclaimer that the information on the website does not form part of the prospectus unless that information is incorporated by reference into the prospectus.
Item 4.1.5	Any recent events particular to the issuer and which are to a material extent relevant to an evaluation of the issuer's solvency.
Item 4.1.6	Credit ratings assigned to the issuer at the request or with the cooperation of the issuer in the rating process.
SECTION 5	BUSINESS OVERVIEW
Item 5.1	Principal activities
Item 5.1.1	A brief description of the issuer's principal activities stating the main categories of products sold and/or services performed.
Item 5.1.2	The basis for any statements made by the issuer regarding its competitive position.
SECTION 6	ORGANISATIONAL STRUCTURE
Item 6.1	If the issuer is part of a group, a brief description of the group and the issuer's position within the group. This may be in the form of, or accompanied by, a diagram of the organisational structure if this helps to clarify the structure.
Item 6.2	If the issuer is dependent upon other entities within the group, this must be clearly stated together with an explanation of this dependence.
SECTION 7	TREND INFORMATION
Item 7.1	A description of:

	(a) any material adverse change in the prospects of the issuer since the date of its last published audited financial statements; and (b) any significant change in the financial performance of the group since the end of the last financial period for which financial information has been published to the date of the registration document. If neither of the above are applicable then the issuer should include (an) appropriate negative statement(s).
SECTION 8	PROFIT FORECASTS OR ESTIMATES
Item 8.1	Where an issuer includes on a voluntary basis a profit forecast or a profit estimate, that profit forecast or estimate shall be clear and unambiguous and contain a statement setting out the principal assumptions upon which the issuer has based its forecast or estimate. The forecast or estimate shall comply with the following principles: (a) there must be a clear distinction between assumptions about factors which the members of the administrative, management or supervisory bodies can influence and assumptions about factors which are exclusively outside the influence of the members of the administrative, management or supervisory bodies; (b) the assumptions must be reasonable, readily understandable by investors, specific and precise and not relate to the general accuracy of the estimates underlying the forecast. (c) in the case of a forecast, the assumptions shall draw the investor's attention to those uncertain factors which could materially change the outcome of the forecast.
Item 8.2	The prospectus shall include a statement that the profit forecast or estimate has been compiled and prepared on a basis which is both: (a) comparable with the historical financial information; (b) consistent with the issuer's accounting policies.
SECTION 9	ADMINISTRATIVE, MANAGEMENT, AND SUPERVISORY BODIES
Item 9.1	Names, business addresses and functions within the issuer of the following persons and an indication of the principal activities performed by them outside of that issuer where these are significant with respect to that issuer: (a) members of the administrative, management or supervisory bodies; (b) partners with unlimited liability, in the case of a limited partnership with a share capital.
Item 9.2	Administrative, management, and supervisory bodies conflicts of interests Potential conflicts of interests between any duties to the issuer, of the persons referred to in item 9.1, and their private interests and or other duties must be clearly stated. In the event that there are no such conflicts, a statement to that effect must be made.
SECTION 10	MAJOR SHAREHOLDERS
Item 10.1	To the extent known to the issuer, state whether the issuer is directly or indirectly owned or controlled and by whom and describe the nature of such control and describe the measures in place to ensure that such control is not abused.
Item 10.2	A description of any arrangements, known to the issuer, the operation of which may at a subsequent date result in a change in control of the issuer.
SECTION 11	FINANCIAL INFORMATION CONCERNING THE ISSUER'S ASSETS AND LIABILITIES, FINANCIAL POSITION AND PROFITS AND LOSSES
Item 11.1	Historical financial information
Item 11.1.1	Historical financial information covering the latest two financial years (at least 24 months) or such shorter period as the issuer has been in operation and the audit report in respect of each year.
Item 11.1.2	Change of accounting reference date If the issuer has changed its accounting reference date during the period for which historical financial information is required, the audited historical financial information shall cover at least 24 months, or the entire period for which the issuer has been in operation, whichever is shorter.
Item 11.1.3	Accounting standards The financial information must be prepared according to International Financial Reporting Standards as endorsed in the Union based on Regulation (EC) No 1606/2002. If Regulation (EC) No 1606/2002 is not applicable the financial statements must be prepared according to: (a) a Member State's national accounting standards for issuers from the EEA as required by Directive 2013/34/EU; (b) a third country's national accounting standards equivalent to Regulation (EC) No 1606/2002 for third country issuers. Otherwise the following information must be included in the registration document:

	(a) a prominent statement that the financial information included in the registration document has not been prepared in accordance with International Financial Reporting Standards as endorsed in the Union based on Regulation (EC) No 1606/2002 and that there may be material differences in the financial information had Regulation (EC) No 1606/2002 been applied to the historical financial information; (b) immediately following the historical financial information a narrative description of the differences between Regulation (EC) No 1606/2002 as adopted by the Union and the accounting principles adopted by the issuer in preparing its annual financial statements.
Item 11.1.4	Where the audited financial information is prepared according to national accounting standards, the financial information must include at least the following: (a) the balance sheet; (b) the income statement; (c) the accounting policies and explanatory notes.
Item 11.1.5	Consolidated financial statements If the issuer prepares both stand-alone and consolidated financial statements, include at least the consolidated financial statements in the registration document.
Item 11.1.6	Age of financial information The balance sheet date of the last year of audited financial information may not be older than 18 months from the date of the registration document
Item 11.2	Auditing of Historical financial information
[Item 11.2.1	The historical annual financial information must be independently audited. The audit report shall be prepared in accordance with Directive 2006/43/EC and Regulation (EU) No 537/2014. Where Directive 2006/43/EC and Regulation (EU) No 537/2014 do not apply, the historical financial information must be audited or reported on as to whether or not, for the purposes of the registration document, it gives a true and fair view in accordance with auditing standards applicable in a Member State or an equivalent standard. Otherwise, the following information must be included in the registration document: (a) a prominent statement disclosing which auditing standards have been applied; (b) an explanation of any significant departures from International Standards on Auditing.]
[Item 11.2.1a	Where audit reports on the historical financial information have been refused by the statutory auditors or where they contain qualifications, modifications of opinion, disclaimers or an emphasis of matter, the reason must be given, and such qualifications, modifications, disclaimers or emphasis of matter must be reproduced in full.]
Item 11.2.2	Indication of other information in the registration document which has been audited by the auditors.
Item 11.2.3	Where financial information in the registration document is not extracted from the issuer's audited financial statements state the source of the data and state that the data is not audited.
Item 11.3	Legal and arbitration proceedings
Item 11.3.1	Information on any governmental, legal or arbitration proceedings (including any such proceedings which are pending or threatened of which the issuer is aware), during a period covering at least the previous 12 months which may have, or have had in the recent past significant effects on the issuer and/or group's financial position or profitability, or provide an appropriate negative statement.
Item 11.4	Significant change in the issuer's financial position
Item 11.4.1	A description of any significant change in the financial position of the group which has occurred since the end of the last financial period for which either audited financial information or interim financial information have been published, or provide an appropriate negative statement.
SECTION 12	MATERIAL CONTRACTS
Item 12.1	A brief summary of all material contracts that are not entered into in the ordinary course of the issuer's business, which could result in any group member being under an obligation or entitlement that is material to the issuer's ability to meet its obligations to security holders in respect of the securities being issued.
SECTION 13	DOCUMENTS AVAILABLE
Item 13.1	A statement that for the term of the registration document the following documents, where applicable, can be inspected: (a) the up to date memorandum and articles of association of the issuer; (b) all reports, letters, and other documents, valuations and statements prepared by any expert at the issuer's request any part of which is included or referred to in the registration document.

	An indication of the website on which the documents may be inspected.

NOTES

Item 11.2.1 substituted, and item 11.2.1a inserted, by Commission Delegated Regulation 2020/1273/EU, Art 1(17), Annex V, as from 17 September 2020.

Application of this Annex in relation to the UK: this Annex is amended (as follows), in relation to the UK only, by the Prospectus (Amendment etc) (EU Exit) Regulations 2019, SI 2019/1234, Schedule, para 5, as from IP completion day (as defined in the European Union (Withdrawal Agreement) Act 2020, s 39); for transitional provisions, see regs 74, 75 of the 2019 Regulations at **[12.165]** et seq—

"5.—(1) Annex 7 is amended as follows.

(2) In item 11.1.3—

(a) in the first paragraph, for the words from "according to International" to the end of that paragraph substitute "in accordance with Article 23a(1) to (5)";

(b) omit the second paragraph;

(c) in the third paragraph—

(i) in point (a)—

(aa) for "International Financial Reporting Standards as endorsed in the Union based on Regulation (EC) 1606/2002" substitute "UK-adopted international accounting standards";

(bb) for "Regulation (EC) 1606/2002" the second time it occurs, substitute "UK-adopted international accounting standards";

(ii) in point (b), for "Regulation (EC) 1606/2002 as adopted by the Union" substitute "UK-adopted international accounting standards".

(3) In item 11.2.1—

(a) before "Directive" in both places it occurs, insert "the UK law which implemented";

(b) for "a Member State" substitute "the United Kingdom".".

[11.706]

ANNEX 8
REGISTRATION DOCUMENT FOR SECONDARY ISSUANCES OF NON-EQUITY SECURITIES

SECTION 1	PERSONS RESPONSIBLE, THIRD PARTY INFORMATION, EXPERTS' REPORTS AND COMPETENT AUTHORITY APPROVAL
Item 1.1	Identify all persons responsible for the information or any parts of it, given in the registration document with, in the latter case, an indication of such parts. In the case of natural persons, including members of the issuer's administrative, management or supervisory bodies, indicate the name and function of the person; in the case of legal persons indicate the name and registered office.
Item 1.2	A declaration by those responsible for the registration document that to the best of their knowledge, the information contained in the registration document is in accordance with the facts and that the registration document makes no omission likely to affect its import. Where applicable, a declaration by those responsible for certain parts of the registration document that, to the best of their knowledge, the information contained in those parts of the registration document for which they are responsible is in accordance with the facts and that those parts of the registration document make no omission likely to affect their import.
Item 1.3	Where a statement or report attributed to a person as an expert is included in the registration document, provide the following details for that person: (a) name; (b) business address; (c) qualifications; (d) material interest if any in the issuer. If the statement or report has been produced at the issuer's request, state that such statement or report has been included in the registration document with the consent of the person who has authorised the contents of that part of the registration document for the purpose of the prospectus.
Item 1.4	Where information has been sourced from a third party, provide a confirmation that this information has been accurately reproduced and that as far as the issuer is aware and is able to ascertain from information published by that third party, no facts have been omitted which would render the reproduced information inaccurate or misleading. In addition, identify the source(s) of the information.
Item 1.5	A statement that: (a) the [registration document/prospectus] has been approved by the [name of competent authority], as competent authority under Regulation (EU) 2017/1129; (b) the [name of competent authority] only approves this [registration document/prospectus] as meeting the standards of completeness, comprehensibility and consistency imposed by Regulation (EU) 2017/1129; (c) such approval shall not be considered as an endorsement of the issuer that it the subject of this [registration document/prospectus]. (d) that the [registration document/prospectus] has been drawn up as part of a simplified

	prospectus in accordance with Article 14 of Regulation (EU) 2017/1129.
SECTION 2	STATUTORY AUDITORS
Item 2.1	Names of the issuer's auditors for the period covered by the historical financial information (together with their membership in a professional body).
SECTION 3	RISK FACTORS
Item 3.1	A description of the material risks that, are specific to the issuer and that may affect the issuer's ability to fulfil its obligations under the securities, in a limited number of categories, in a section headed 'Risk Factors'. In each category the most material risks, in the assessment of the issuer, offeror or person asking for admission to trading on a regulated market, taking into account the negative impact on the issuer and the probability of their occurrence, shall be set out first. The risk factors shall be corroborated by the content of the registration document.
SECTION 4	INFORMATION ABOUT THE ISSUER
Item 4.1	The legal and commercial name of the issuer.
Item 4.2	The domicile and legal form of the issuer, legal entity identifier ('LEI'), the legislation under which the issuer operates, its country of incorporation, the address, telephone number of its registered office (or principal place of business if different from its registered office) and website of the issuer, if any, with a disclaimer that the information on the website does not form part of the prospectus unless that information is incorporated by reference into the prospectus.
SECTION 5	BUSINESS OVERVIEW
Item 5.1	A brief description of the issuer's principal activities stating the main categories of products sold and/or services performed.
SECTION 6	TREND INFORMATION
Item 6.1	A description of: (a) any material adverse change in the prospects of the issuer since the date of its last published audited financial statements; (b) any significant change in the financial performance of the group since the end of the last financial period for which financial information has been published to the date of the registration document. If neither of points (a) or (b) are applicable, then the issuer should include an appropriate negative statement.
Item 6.2 (Retail only)	Information on any known trends, uncertainties, demands, commitments or events that are reasonably likely to have a material effect on the issuer's prospects for at least the current financial year.
SECTION 7	PROFIT FORECASTS OR ESTIMATES
Item 7.1	Where an issuer includes on a voluntary basis a profit forecast or a profit estimate (which is still outstanding and valid) that forecast or estimate included in the registration document must contain the information set out in items 7.2 and 7.3. If a profit forecast or profit estimate has been published and is still outstanding, but no longer valid, then provide a statement to that effect and an explanation of why such profit forecast or estimate is no longer valid. Such an invalid forecast or estimate is not subject to the requirements in items 7.2 to 7.3. Inclusion of the profit forecast or estimate shall be at the discretion of the issuer. Where such a forecast or estimate is included, the registration document shall contain the information set out in items 7.2 and 7.3.
Item 7.2	Where an issuer chooses to include a new profit forecast or a new profit estimate, or where the issuer includes a previously published profit forecast or a previously published profit estimate pursuant to item 7.1, the profit forecast or estimate shall be clear and unambiguous and shall contain a statement setting out the principal assumptions upon which the issuer has based its forecast, or estimate. The forecast or estimate shall comply with the following principles: (a) there must be a clear distinction between assumptions about factors which the members of the administrative, management or supervisory bodies can influence and assumptions about factors which are exclusively outside the influence of the members of the administrative, management or supervisory bodies; (b) the assumptions must be reasonable, readily understandable by investors, specific and precise and not relate to the general accuracy of the estimates underlying the forecast; and (c) in the case of a forecast, the assumptions shall draw the investor's attention to those uncertain factors which could materially change the outcome of the forecast.
Item 7.3	The prospectus shall include a statement that the profit forecast or estimate has been compiled and prepared on a basis which is both: (a) comparable with the historical financial information; (b) consistent with the issuer's accounting policies.

SECTION 8	ADMINISTRATIVE, MANAGEMENT AND SUPERVISORY BODIES AND SENIOR MANAGEMENT
Item 8.1	Names, business addresses and functions within the issuer of the following persons and an indication of the principal activities performed by them outside of that issuer where these are significant with respect to that issuer: (a) members of the administrative, management or supervisory bodies; (b) partners with unlimited liability, in the case of a limited partnership with a share capital.
Item 8.2	Potential conflicts of interest between any duties carried out on behalf of the issuer, by the persons referred to in item 8.1 and their private interests or other duties must be clearly stated. In the event that there are no such conflicts a statement to that effect must be made.
SECTION 9	MAJOR SHAREHOLDERS
Item 9.1	To the extent known to the issuer, state whether the issuer is directly or indirectly owned or controlled and by whom and describe the nature of such control and describe the measures in place to ensure that such control is not abused.
Item 9.2	A description of any arrangements, known to the issuer, the operation of which may at a subsequent date result in a change in control of the issuer.
SECTION 10	FINANCIAL INFORMATION CONCERNING THE ISSUER'S ASSETS AND LIABILITIES, FINANCIAL POSITION AND PROFITS, AND LOSSES
Item 10.1	Financial statements Financial statements (annual and half-yearly) required to be published covering the period of 12 months prior to the approval of the prospectus. Where both annual and half-yearly financial statements have been published, only the annual statements shall be required where they postdate the half-yearly financial statements.
Item 10.2	Auditing of annual financial information
[Item 10.2.1	Audit report The annual financial statements must be independently audited. The audit report shall be prepared in accordance with Directive 2006/43/EC and Regulation (EU) No 537/2014. Where Directive 2006/43/EC and Regulation (EU) No 537/2014 do not apply, the annual financial statements must be audited or reported on as to whether or not, for the purposes of the registration document, it gives a true and fair view in accordance with auditing standards applicable in a Member State or an equivalent standard. Otherwise, the following information must be included in the registration document: (a) a prominent statement disclosing which auditing standards have been applied; (b) an explanation of any significant departures from International Standards on Auditing.]
[Item 10.2.1a	Where audit reports on the annual financial statements have been refused by the statutory auditors or where they contain qualifications, modifications of opinion, disclaimers or an emphasis of matter, the reason must be given, and such qualifications, modifications, disclaimers or emphasis of matter must be reproduced in full.]
Item 10.2.2	Indication of other information in the registration document which has been audited by the auditors.
Item 10.2.3	Where financial information in the registration document is not extracted from the issuer's audited financial statements, state the source of the data and identify the data that has not been audited.
Item 10.3	Legal and arbitration proceedings Information on any governmental, legal or arbitration proceedings (including any such proceedings which are pending or threatened of which the issuer is aware), during a period covering at least the previous 12 months which may have, or have had in the recent past significant effects on the issuer and/or group's financial position or profitability, or provide an appropriate negative statement.
Item 10.4	Significant change in the issuer's financial position A description of any significant change in the financial position of the group which has occurred since the end of the last financial period for which either audited financial statements or interim financial information have been published, or provide an appropriate negative statement.
SECTION 11	REGULATORY DISCLOSURES
Item 11.1	A summary of the information disclosed under Regulation (EU) No 596/2014 over the last 12 months which is relevant as at the date of the prospectus. The summary shall be presented in an easily analysable, concise and comprehensible form and shall not be a replication of information already published under Regulation (EU) No 596/2014. The summary shall be presented in a limited number of categories depending on their subject.

SECTION 12	MATERIAL CONTRACTS
Item 12.1	A brief summary of all material contracts that are not entered into in the ordinary course of the issuer's business, which could result in any group member being under an obligation or an entitlement that is material to the issuer's ability to meet its obligations to security holders in respect of the securities being issued.
SECTION 13	DOCUMENTS AVAILABLE
Item 13.1	A statement that for the term of the registration document the following documents, where applicable, can be inspected: (a) the up to date memorandum and articles of association of the issuer; (b) all reports, letters, and other documents, valuations and statements prepared by any expert at the issuer's request any part of which is included or referred to in the registration document. An indication of the website on which the documents may be inspected.

NOTES

Item 10.2.1 substituted, and item 10.2.1a inserted, by Commission Delegated Regulation 2020/1273/EU, Art 1(18), Annex VI, as from 17 September 2020.

Application of this Annex in relation to the UK: this Annex is amended (as follows), in relation to the UK only, by the Prospectus (Amendment etc) (EU Exit) Regulations 2019, SI 2019/1234, Schedule, para 6, as from IP completion day (as defined in the European Union (Withdrawal Agreement) Act 2020, s 39); for transitional provisions, see regs 74, 75 of the 2019 Regulations at **[12.165]** et seq—

"6. In Annex 8, in item 10.2.1—

(a) before "Directive" in both places it occurs, insert "the UK law which implemented";

(b) in the second paragraph, for "a Member State" substitute "the United Kingdom".".

Note that the Prospectus (Amendment etc) (EU Exit) Regulations 2019, SI 2019/1234, Schedule, para 6 was amended by the Financial Services (Miscellaneous Amendments) (EU Exit) Regulations 2020, SI 2020/628, reg 17(1), (6), as from immediately before IP completion day; and the effect of the amendment has been incorporated in the text set out above.

[11.707]

ANNEX 9
REGISTRATION DOCUMENT FOR ASSET-BACKED SECURITIES

SECTION 1	PERSONS RESPONSIBLE, THIRD PARTY INFORMATION, EXPERTS' REPORTS AND COMPETENT AUTHORITY APPROVAL
Item 1.1	Identify all persons responsible for the information or any parts of it, given in the registration document with, in the latter case, an indication of such parts. In the case of natural persons, including members of the issuer's administrative, management or supervisory bodies, indicate the name and function of the person; in the case of legal persons indicate the name and registered office.
Item 1.2	A declaration by those responsible for the registration document that to the best of their knowledge, the information contained in the registration document is in accordance with the facts and that the registration document makes no omission likely to affect its import. Where applicable, a declaration by those responsible for certain parts of the registration document that, to the best of their knowledge, the information contained in those parts of the registration document for which they are responsible is in accordance with the facts and that those parts of the registration document make no omission likely to affect their import.
Item 1.3	Where a statement or report attributed to a person as an expert is included in the registration document, provide the following details for that person: (a) name; (b) business address; (c) qualifications; (d) material interest if any in the issuer. If the statement or report has been produced at the issuer's request, state that such statement or report has been included in the registration document with the consent of the person who has authorised the contents of that part of the registration document for the purpose of the prospectus.
Item 1.4	Where information has been sourced from a third party, provide a confirmation that this information has been accurately reproduced and that as far as the issuer is aware and is able to ascertain from information published by that third party, no facts have been omitted which would render the reproduced information inaccurate or misleading In addition, the issuer shall identify the source(s) of the information.
Item 1.5	A statement that: (a) the [registration document/prospectus] has been approved by the [name of competent authority], as competent authority under Regulation (EU) 2017/1129; (b) the [name of competent authority] only approves this [registration document/prospectus] as meeting the standards of completeness, comprehensibility

	and consistency imposed by Regulation (EU) 2017/1129; (c) such approval should not be considered as an endorsement of the issuer that is the subject of this [registration document/prospectus].
SECTION 2	STATUTORY AUDITORS
Item 2.1	Names and addresses of the issuer's auditors for the period covered by the historical financial information (together with any membership in a professional body).
SECTION 3	RISK FACTORS
Item 3.1	A description of the material risks that are specific to the issuer in a limited number of categories, in a section headed 'Risk Factors'. In each category the most material risks, in the assessment of the issuer, offeror or person asking for admission to trading on a regulated market, taking into account the negative impact on the issuer and the probability of their occurrence, shall be set out first. The risk factors shall be corroborated by the content of the registration document.
SECTION 4	INFORMATION ABOUT THE ISSUER
Item 4.1	A statement whether the issuer has been established as a special purpose vehicle or entity for the purpose of issuing asset backed securities.
Item 4.2	The legal and commercial name of the issuer and the legal entity identifier ('LEI').
Item 4.3	The place of registration of the issuer and its registration number.
Item 4.4	The date of incorporation and the length of life of the issuer, except where the period is indefinite.
Item 4.5	The domicile and legal form of the issuer, the legislation under which the issuer operates, its country of incorporation, the address and telephone number of its registered office (or principal place of business if different from its registered office) and website of the issuer, if any, or website of a third party or guarantor, with a disclaimer that the information on the website does not form part of the prospectus unless that information is incorporated by reference into the prospectus.
Item 4.6	Description of the amount of the issuer's authorised and issued capital and the amount of any capital agreed to be issued, the number and classes of the securities of which it is composed.
SECTION 5	BUSINESS OVERVIEW
Item 5.1	A brief description of the issuer's principal activities.
SECTION 6	ADMINISTRATIVE, MANAGEMENT AND SUPERVISORY BODIES
Item 6.1	Names, business addresses and functions within the issuer of the following persons, and an indication of the principal activities performed by them outside of that issuer where these are significant with respect to that issuer: (a) members of the administrative, management or supervisory bodies; (b) partners with unlimited liability, in the case of a limited partnership with a share capital.
SECTION 7	MAJOR SHAREHOLDERS
Item 7.1	To the extent known to the issuer, state whether the issuer is directly or indirectly owned or controlled and by whom, and describe the nature of such control and describe the measures in place to ensure that such control is not abused.
SECTION 8	FINANCIAL INFORMATION CONCERNING THE ISSUER'S ASSETS AND LIABILITIES, FINANCIAL POSITION, AND PROFITS AND LOSSES
Item 8.1	Where, since the date of incorporation or establishment, an issuer has not commenced operations and no financial statements have been drawn up as at the date of the registration document, a statement to that effect shall be provided in the registration document.
Item 8.2	Historical Financial Information Where, since the date of incorporation or establishment, an issuer has commenced operations and financial statements have been drawn up, the registration document must contain audited historical financial information covering the latest two financial years (at least 24 months or such shorter period as the issuer has been in operation) and the audit report in respect of each year.
Item 8.2.1	Change of accounting reference date If the issuer has changed its accounting reference date during the period for which historical financial information is required, the historical financial information shall cover at least 24 months, or the entire period for which the issuer has been in operation, whichever is the shorter.
Item 8.2.2	Accounting standards The financial information must be prepared according to International Financial Reporting Standards as endorsed in the Union based on Regulation (EC) No 1606/2002. The financial information must be prepared according to International Financial Reporting Standards as endorsed in the Union based on Regulation (EC) No 1606/2002.

	(a) a Member State's national accounting standards for issuers from the EEA as required by Directive 2013/34/EU; (b) a third country's national accounting standards equivalent to Regulation (EC) No 1606/2002 for third country issuers. If such third country's national accounting standards are not equivalent to Regulation (EC) No 1606/2002 the financial statements shall be restated in compliance with Regulation (EC) No 1606/2002.
Item 8.2.3	Change of accounting framework The last year's historical financial information, containing comparative information for the previous year, must be presented and prepared in a form consistent with the accounting standards framework that will be adopted in the issuer's next annual published financial statements having regard to accounting standards and policies and legislation applicable to such annual financial statements. Changes within the issuer's existing accounting framework do not require the audited financial statements to be restated. However, if the issuer intends to adopt a new accounting standards framework in its next published financial statements, at least one complete set of financial statements, (as defined by IAS 1 Presentation of Financial Statements), including comparatives, must be presented in a form consistent with that which will be adopted in the issuer's next published annual financial statements, having regard to accounting standards and policies and legislation applicable to such annual financial statements.
Item 8.2.4	Where the audited financial information is prepared according to national accounting standards, financial information required under this heading must include at least the following: (a) the balance sheet; (b) the income statement; (c) the accounting policies and explanatory notes.
Item 8.2.a	This paragraph (items 8.2.a, 8.2.a.1, 8.2.a.2 and 8.2.a.3) may be used only for issues of asset-backed securities having a denomination per unit of at least EUR 100,000 or which are to be traded only on a regulated market, and/or a specific section thereof, to which only qualified investors have access for the purpose of trading in the securities. Historical financial information Where, since the date of incorporation or establishment, an issuer has commenced operations and financial statements have been drawn up, the registration document must contain historical financial information covering the latest two financial years (at least 24 month or such shorter period as the issuer has been in operation) and the audit report in respect of each year.
Item 8.2.a.1	Accounting standards The financial information must be prepared according to International Financial Reporting Standards as adopted by the Union based on Regulation (EC) No 1606/2002. If Regulation (EC) No 1606/2002 is not applicable, the financial statements must be prepared in accordance with: (a) a Member State's national accounting standards for issuers from the EEA as required by the Directive 2013/34/EU; (b) a third country's national accounting standards equivalent to Regulation (EC) No 1606/2002 for third country issuers. Otherwise the following information must be included in the registration document: (a) a prominent statement that the financial information included in the registration document has not been prepared in accordance with Regulation (EC) No 1606/2002 as adopted by the Union and that there may be material differences in the financial information had Regulation (EC) No 1606/2002 been applied to the historical financial information; (b) immediately following the historical financial information a narrative description of the differences between Regulation (EC) No 1606/2002 as adopted by the Union and the accounting principles adopted by the issuer in preparing its annual financial statements.
Item 8.2.a.2	Where the audited financial information is prepared according to national accounting standards, it must include at least the following: (a) the balance sheet; (b) the income statement; (c) the accounting policies and explanatory notes.
[Item 8.2.a.3	Audit report The historical annual financial information must be independently audited. The audit report shall be prepared in accordance with Directive 2006/43/EC and Regulation (EU) No 537/2014. Where Directive 2006/43/EC and Regulation (EU) No 537/2014 do not apply, the historical financial information must be audited or reported on as to whether or not, for the pur-

	poses of the registration document, it gives a true and fair view in accordance with auditing standards applicable in a Member State or an equivalent standard. Otherwise, the following information must be included in the registration document: (a) a prominent statement disclosing which auditing standards have been applied; (b) an explanation of any significant departures from International Standards on Auditing.]
[Item 8.2.a.4	A statement that the historical financial information has been audited. Where audit reports on the historical financial information have been refused by the statutory auditors or where they contain qualifications, modifications of opinion, disclaimers or an emphasis of matter, the reason must be given, and such qualifications, modifications, disclaimers or emphasis of matter must be reproduced in full.]
Item 8.3	Legal and arbitration proceedings Information on any governmental, legal or arbitration proceedings (including any such proceedings which are pending or threatened of which the company is aware), during a period covering at least the previous 12 months, which may have, or have had in the recent past, significant effects on the issuer and/or group's financial position or profitability, or provide an appropriate negative statement.
Item 8.4	Material adverse change in the issuer's financial position Where an issuer has prepared financial statements, include a statement that there has been no material adverse change in the financial position or prospects of the issuer since the date of its last published audited financial statements. Where a material adverse change has occurred, this must be disclosed in the registration document.
SECTION 9	DOCUMENTS AVAILABLE
Item 9.1	A statement that for the term of the registration document the following documents, where applicable, may be inspected: (a) the memorandum and up to date articles of association of the issuer; (b) all reports, letters, and other documents, historical financial information, valuations and statements prepared by any expert at the issuer's request any part of which is included or referred to in the registration document. An indication of the website on which the documents may be inspected.

NOTES

Item 8.2a.3 substituted, and item 8.2a.4 inserted, by Commission Delegated Regulation 2020/1273/EU, Art 1(19), Annex VII, as from 17 September 2020.

Application of this Annex in relation to the UK: this Annex is amended (as follows), in relation to the UK only, by the Prospectus (Amendment etc) (EU Exit) Regulations 2019, SI 2019/1234, Schedule, para 7, as from IP completion day (as defined in the European Union (Withdrawal Agreement) Act 2020, s 39); for transitional provisions, see regs 74, 75 of the 2019 Regulations at **[12.165]** et seq—

"7.—(1) Annex 9 is amended as follows.

(2) In item 8.2.2, for the words from "according to International" to the end substitute "in accordance with Article 23a".

(3) In item 8.2.a.1—

- (a) in the first paragraph, for the words from "according to International" to the end of that paragraph substitute "in accordance with Article 23a(1) to (5)";
- (b) omit the second paragraph;
- (c) in the third paragraph—
  - (i) in point (a)—
    - (aa) for "Regulation (EC) 1606/2002 as adopted by the Union" substitute "UK-adopted international accounting standards";
    - (bb) for "Regulation (EC) 1606/2002" the second time it occurs, substitute "UK-adopted international accounting standards";
  - (ii) in point (b), for "Regulation (EC) 1606/2002 as adopted by the Union" substitute "UK-adopted international accounting standards".

(4) In item 8.2.a.3—

- (i) before "Directive" in both places it occurs, insert "the UK law which implemented";
- (ii) for "a Member State" substitute "the United Kingdom".".

[11.708]

ANNEX 10

REGISTRATION DOCUMENTS FOR NON-EQUITY SECURITIES ISSUED BY THIRD COUNTRIES AND THEIR REGIONAL AND LOCAL AUTHORITIES

SECTION 1	*PERSONS RESPONSIBLE, THIRD PARTY INFORMATION, EXPERTS' REPORTS AND COMPETENT AUTHORITY APPROVAL*
Item 1.1	*Identify all persons responsible for the information or any parts of it, given in the registration document with, in the latter case, an indication of such parts. In the case of natural persons, including members of the issuer's administrative, management or supervisory bodies, indicate the name and function of the person; in the case of legal persons indicate the name and registered office.*
Item 1.2	*A declaration by those responsible for the registration document that to the best of their*

Part 11 EU & Retained EU Legislation

	knowledge, the information contained in the registration document is in accordance with the facts and that the registration document makes no omission likely to affect its import. *Where applicable, a declaration by those responsible for certain parts of the registration document that, to the best of their knowledge, the information contained in those parts of the registration document for which they are responsible is in accordance with the facts and that those parts of the registration document make no omission likely to affect their import.*
Item 1.3	*Where a statement or report, attributed to a person as an expert, is included in the registration document, provide the following details for that person:* *(a) such person's name;* *(b) business address;* *(c) qualifications;* *(d) material interest if any in the issuer.* *If the statement or report has been produced at the issuer's request, state that such statement or report has been included in the registration document with the consent of the person who has authorised the contents of that part of the registration document for the purpose of the prospectus.* *To the extent known to the issuer, provide information in respect of any interest relating to such expert which may affect the independence of the expert in the preparation of the report.*
Item 1.4	*A statement that:* *(a) the [registration document/prospectus] has been approved by the [name of competent authority], as competent authority under Regulation (EU) 2017/1129;* *(b) the [name of competent authority] only approves this [registration document/prospectus] as meeting the standards of completeness, comprehensibility and consistency imposed by Regulation (EU) 2017/1129;* *(c) such approval should not be considered as an endorsement of the issuer that is the subject of this [registration document/prospectus];*
SECTION 2	*RISK FACTORS*
Item 2.1	*A description of the material risks that are specific to the issuer in a limited number of categories, in a section headed 'Risk Factors'.* *In each category the most material risks, in the assessment of the issuer, offeror or person asking for admission to trading on a regulated market, taking into account the negative impact on the issuer and the probability of their occurrence, shall be set out first.* *The risk factors shall be corroborated by the content of the registration document.*
SECTION 3	*INFORMATION ABOUT THE ISSUER*
Item 3.1	*History and development of the issuer* *The legal name of the issuer and a brief description of the issuer's position within the national governmental framework.*
Item 3.2	*The domicile or geographical location and legal form of the issuer and its contact address, telephone number and website of the issuer, if any, with a disclaimer that the information on the website does not form part of the prospectus unless that information is incorporated by reference into the prospectus.*
Item 3.3	*Any recent events relevant to the evaluation of the issuer's solvency.*
Item 3.4	*A description of the issuer's economy including:* *(a) the structure of the economy with details of the main sectors of the economy;* *(b) gross domestic product with a breakdown by the issuer's economic sectors for the previous two fiscal years.*
Item 3.5	*A general description of the issuer's political system and government including details of the governing body of the issuer.*
Item 3.6	*Any credit ratings assigned to the issuer at the request or with the cooperation of the issuer in the rating process.*
SECTION 4	*PUBLIC FINANCE AND TRADE*
Item 4.1	*Information on the following for the two fiscal years prior to the date of the registration document:* *(a) the tax and budgetary systems;* *(b) gross public debt including a summary of the debt, the maturity structure of outstanding debt (particularly noting debt with a residual maturity of less than one year) and debt payment record, and of the parts of debt denominated in the domestic currency of the issuer and in foreign currencies;* *(c) foreign trade and balance of payment figures;* *(d) foreign exchange reserves including any potential encumbrances to such foreign exchange reserves as forward contracts or derivatives;*

	(e) financial position and resources including liquid deposits available in domestic currency; *(f) income and expenditure figures.* *Description of any auditing or independent review procedures on the accounts of the issuer.*
SECTION 5	*SIGNIFICANT CHANGE*
Item 5.1	*Details of any significant changes to the information provided pursuant to item 4 which have occurred since the end of the last fiscal year, or an appropriate negative statement.*
SECTION 6	*LEGAL AND ARBITRATION PROCEEDINGS*
Item 6.1	*Information on any governmental, legal or arbitration proceedings (including any such proceedings which are pending or threatened of which the issuer is aware), during a period covering at least the previous 12 months which may have, or have had in the recent past, significant effects on the issuer's financial position, or provide an appropriate negative statement.*
Item 6.2	*Information on any immunity the issuer may have from legal proceedings.*
SECTION 7	*DOCUMENTS AVAILABLE*
Item 7.1	*A statement that for the term of the registration document the following documents, where applicable, can be inspected:* *(a) financial and audit reports for the issuer covering the last two fiscal years and the budget for the current fiscal year;* *(b) all reports, letters, and other documents, valuations and statements prepared by any expert at the issuer's request any part of which is included or referred to in the registration document.* *An indication of the website on which the documents may be inspected.*

NOTES

Repeal of this Annex in relation to the UK: this Annex is repealed, in relation to the UK only, by the Prospectus (Amendment etc) (EU Exit) Regulations 2019, SI 2019/1234, Schedule, para 7A, as from IP completion day (as defined in the European Union (Withdrawal Agreement) Act 2020, s 39); for transitional provisions, see regs 74, 75 of the 2019 Regulations at **[12.165]** et seq. Note that Schedule, para 7A to the 2019 Regulations was inserted by the Securities Financing Transactions, Securitisation and Miscellaneous Amendments (EU Exit) Regulations 2020, SI 2020/1385, reg 66(2)(a), with effect from immediately before IP completion day (as defined in the European Union (Withdrawal Agreement) Act 2020, s 39).

[11.709]

ANNEX 11
SECURITIES NOTE FOR EQUITY SECURITIES OR UNITS ISSUED BY COLLECTIVE INVESTMENT UNDERTAKINGS OF THE CLOSED- END TYPE

SECTION 1	PERSONS RESPONSIBLE, THIRD PARTY INFORMATION, EXPERTS' REPORTS AND COMPETENT AUTHORITY APPROVAL
Item 1.1	Identify all persons responsible for the information or any parts of it, given in the securities note with, in the latter case, an indication of such parts. In the case of natural persons, including members of the issuer's administrative, management or supervisory bodies, indicate the name and function of the person; in the case of legal persons indicate the name and registered office.
Item 1.2	A declaration by those responsible for the securities note that to the best of their knowledge, the information contained in the securities note is in accordance with the facts and that the securities note makes no omission likely to affect its import. Where applicable, a declaration by those responsible for certain parts of the securities note that, to the best of their knowledge, the information contained in those parts of the securities note for which they are responsible is in accordance with the facts and that those parts of the securities note make no omission likely to affect their import.
Item 1.3	Where a statement or report attributed to a person as an expert, is included in the securities note, provide the following in relation to that person: (a) name; (b) business address; (c) qualifications; (d) material interest, if any, in the issuer. If the statement or report has been produced at the issuer's request, state that such statement or report has been included in the securities note with the consent of the person who has authorised the contents of that part of the securities note for the purpose of the prospectus.
Item 1.4	Where information has been sourced from a third party, provide a confirmation that this information has been accurately reproduced and that as far as the issuer is aware and is able to ascertain from information published by that third party, no facts have been omitted which would render the reproduced information inaccurate or misleading. In addition,

	identify the source(s) of the information.
Item 1.5	A statement that: (a) this [securities note/prospectus] has been approved by the name of competent authority], as competent authority under Regulation (EU) 2017/1129; (b) the [name of competent authority] only approves this [securities note/prospectus] as meeting the standards of completeness, comprehensibility and consistency imposed by Regulation (EU) 2017/1129; (c) such approval should not be considered as an endorsement of [the quality of the securities that are the subject of this [securities note/prospectus]; (d) investors should make their own assessment as to the suitability of investing in the securities.
SECTION 2	RISK FACTORS
Item 2.1	A description of the material risks that are specific to the securities being offered and/or admitted to trading in a limited number of categories, in a section headed 'Risk Factors'. In each category the most material risks, in the assessment of the issuer, offeror or person asking for admission to trading on a regulated market, taking into account the negative impact on the issuer and the securities and the probability of their occurrence, shall be set out first. The risks shall be corroborated by the content of the securities note.
SECTION 3	ESSENTIAL INFORMATION
Item 3.1	Working capital statement Statement by the issuer that, in its opinion, the working capital is sufficient for the issuer's present requirements or, if not, how it proposes to provide the additional working capital needed.
Item 3.2	Capitalisation and indebtedness A statement of capitalisation and indebtedness (distinguishing between guaranteed and unguaranteed, secured and unsecured indebtedness) as of a date no earlier than 90 days prior to the date of the document. The term 'indebtedness' also includes indirect and contingent indebtedness. In the case of material changes in the capitalisation and indebtedness position of the issuer within the 90 day period, additional information shall be given through the presentation of a narrative description of such changes or through the updating of those figures.
Item 3.3	Interest of natural and legal persons involved in the issue/offer A description of any interest, including a conflict of interest that is material to the issue/offer, detailing the persons involved and the nature of the interest.
Item 3.4	Reasons for the offer and use of proceeds Reasons for the offer and, where applicable, the estimated net amount of the proceeds broken into each principal intended use and presented in order of priority of such uses. If the issuer is aware that the anticipated proceeds will not be sufficient to fund all the proposed uses, then state the amount and sources of other funds needed. Details must be also given with regard to the use of the proceeds, in particular when they are being used to acquire assets, other than in the ordinary course of business, to finance announced acquisitions of other business, or to discharge, reduce or retire indebtedness.
SECTION 4	INFORMATION CONCERNING THE SECURITIES TO BE OFFERED/ADMITTED TO TRADING
Item 4.1	A description of the type and the class of the securities being offered and/or admitted to trading, including the international security identification number ('ISIN').
Item 4.2	Legislation under which the securities have been created.
Item 4.3	An indication whether the securities are in registered form or bearer form and whether the securities are in certificated form or book-entry form. In the latter case, name and address of the entity in charge of keeping the records.
Item 4.4	Currency of the securities issue.
Item 4.5	A description of the rights attached to the securities, including any limitations of those rights and procedure for the exercise of those rights: (a) dividend rights: (ii) fixed date(s) on which entitlement arises; (ii) time limit after which entitlement to dividend lapses and an indication of the person in whose favour the lapse operates; (iii) dividend restrictions and procedures for non-resident holders; (iv) rate of dividend or method of its calculation, periodicity and cumulative or non-cumulative nature of payments; (b) voting rights; (c) pre-emption rights in offers for subscription of securities of the same class; (d) right to share in the issuer's profits;

	(e) rights to share in any surplus in the event of liquidation; (f) redemption provisions; (g) conversion provisions.
Item 4.6	In the case of new issues, a statement of the resolutions, authorisations and approvals by virtue of which the securities have been or will be created and/or issued.
Item 4.7	In the case of new issues, the expected issue date of the securities.
Item 4.8	A description of any restrictions on the transferability of the securities.
Item 4.9	Statement on the existence of any national legislation on takeovers applicable to the issuer which may frustrate such takeovers if any. A brief description of the shareholders' rights and obligations in case of mandatory takeover bids and/or squeeze-out or sell-out rules in relation to the securities.
Item 4.10	An indication of public takeover bids by third parties in respect of the issuer's equity, which have occurred during the last financial year and the current financial year. The price or exchange terms attaching to such offers and the outcome thereof must be stated.
Item 4.11	A warning that the tax legislation of the investor's Member State and of the issuer's country of incorporation may have an impact on the income received from the securities. Information on the taxation treatment of the securities where the proposed investment attracts a tax regime specific to that type of investment.
Item 4.12	Where applicable, the potential impact on the investment in the event of resolution under Directive 2014/59/EU of the European Parliament and of the Council.[1]
Item 4.13	If different from the issuer, the identity and contact details of the offeror of the securities and/or the person asking for admission to trading, including the legal entity identifier ('LEI') where the offeror has legal personality.
SECTION 5	TERMS AND CONDITIONS OF THE OFFER OF SECURITIES TO THE PUBLIC
Item 5.1	Conditions, offer statistics, expected timetable and action required to apply for the offer.
Item 5.1.1	Conditions to which the offer is subject.
Item 5.1.2	Total amount of the issue/offer, distinguishing the securities offered for sale and those offered for subscription; if the amount is not fixed, an indication of the maximum amount of securities to be offered (if available) and a description of the arrangements and the time period for announcing to the public the definitive amount of the offer. Where the maximum amount of securities cannot be provided in the prospectus, the prospectus shall specify that acceptances of the purchase or subscription of securities may be withdrawn for not less than two working days after the amount of securities to be offered to the public has been filed.
Item 5.1.3	The time period, including any possible amendments, during which the offer will be open and description of the application process.
Item 5.1.4	An indication of when, and under which circumstances, the offer may be revoked or suspended and whether revocation can occur after dealing has begun.
Item 5.1.5	A description of any possibility to reduce subscriptions and the manner for refunding amounts paid in excess by applicants.
Item 5.1.6	Details of the minimum and/or maximum amount of application (whether in number of securities or aggregate amount to invest).
Item 5.1.7	An indication of the period during which an application may be withdrawn, provided that investors are allowed to withdraw their subscription.
Item 5.1.8	Method and time limits for paying up the securities and for delivery of the securities.
Item 5.1.9	A full description of the manner and date in which results of the offer are to be made public.
Item 5.1.10	The procedure for the exercise of any right of pre-emption, the negotiability of subscription rights and the treatment of subscription rights not exercised.
Item 5.2	Plan of distribution and allotment.
Item 5.2.1	The various categories of potential investors to which the securities are offered. If the offer is being made simultaneously in the markets of two or more countries and if a tranche has been or is being reserved for certain of these, indicate any such tranche.
Item 5.2.2	To the extent known to the issuer, an indication of whether major shareholders or members of the issuer's management, supervisory or administrative bodies intend to subscribe in the offer, or whether any person intends to subscribe for more than five per cent of the offer.
Item 5.2.3	Pre-allotment Disclosure: (a) the division into tranches of the offer including the institutional, retail and issuer's employee tranches and any other tranches; (b) the conditions under which the claw-back may be used, the maximum size of such claw-back and any applicable minimum percentages for individual tranches; (c) the allotment method or methods to be used for the retail and issuer's employee

Part 11 EU & Retained EU Legislation

	tranche in the event of an over-subscription of these tranches; (d) a description of any pre-determined preferential treatment to be accorded to certain classes of investors or certain affinity groups (including friends and family programmes) in the allotment, the percentage of the offer reserved for such preferential treatment and the criteria for inclusion in such classes or groups; (e) whether the treatment of subscriptions or bids to subscribe in the allotment may be determined on the basis of which firm they are made through or by; (f) a target minimum individual allotment if any within the retail tranche; (g) the conditions for the closing of the offer as well as the date on which the offer may be closed at the earliest; (h) whether or not multiple subscriptions are admitted, and where they are not, how any multiple subscriptions will be handled.
Item 5.2.4	Process for notifying applicants of the amount allotted and an indication whether dealing may begin before notification is made.
Item 5.3	Pricing
Item 5.3.1	An indication of the price at which the securities will be offered and the amount of any expenses and taxes charged to the subscriber or purchaser. If the price is not known, then pursuant to Article 17 of Regulation (EU) 2017/1129 indicate either: (a) the maximum price as far as it is available; (b) the valuation methods and criteria, and/or conditions, in accordance with which the final offer price has been or will be determined and an explanation of any valuation methods used. Where neither point (a) nor (b) can be provided in the securities note, the securities note shall specify that acceptances of the purchase or subscription of securities may be withdrawn up to two working days after the final offer price of securities to be offered to the public has been filed.
Item 5.3.2	Process for the disclosure of the offer price.
Item 5.3.3	If the issuer's equity holders have pre-emptive purchase rights and this right is restricted or withdrawn, an indication of the basis for the issue price if the issue is for cash, together with the reasons for and beneficiaries of such restriction or withdrawal.
Item 5.3.4	Where there is or could be a material disparity between the public offer price and the effective cash cost to members of the administrative, management or supervisory bodies or senior management, or affiliated persons, of securities acquired by them in transactions during the past year, or which they have the right to acquire, include a comparison of the public contribution in the proposed public offer and the effective cash contributions of such persons.
Item 5.4	Placing and underwriting
Item 5.4.1	Name and address of the coordinator(s) of the global offer and of single parts of the offer and, to the extent known to the issuer or to the offeror, of the placers in the various countries where the offer takes place.
Item 5.4.2	Name and address of any paying agents and depository agents in each country.
Item 5.4.3	Name and address of the entities agreeing to underwrite the issue on a firm commitment basis, and name and address of the entities agreeing to place the issue without a firm commitment or under best 'efforts' arrangements. Indication of the material features of the agreements, including the quotas. Where not all of the issue is underwritten, a statement of the portion not covered. Indication of the overall amount of the underwriting commission and of the placing commission.
Item 5.4.4	When the underwriting agreement has been or will be reached.
SECTION 6	ADMISSION TO TRADING AND DEALING ARRANGEMENTS
Item 6.1	An indication as to whether the securities offered are or will be the object of an application for admission to trading, with a view to their distribution in a regulated market or third country market, SME Growth Market or MTF with an indication of the markets in question. This circumstance must be set out, without creating the impression that the admission to trading will necessarily be approved. If known, the earliest dates on which the securities will be admitted to trading.
Item 6.2	All the regulated markets, third country markets, SME Growth Market or MTFs on which, to the knowledge of the issuer, securities of the same class of the securities to be offered or admitted to trading are already admitted to trading.
Item 6.3	If simultaneously or almost simultaneously with the application for the admission of the securities to a regulated market, securities of the same class are subscribed for or placed privately or if securities of other classes are created for public or private placing, give details of the nature of such operations and of the number, characteristics and price of the securities to which they relate.
Item 6.4	In case of an admission to trading on a regulated market, details of the entities which have given a firm commitment to act as intermediaries in secondary trading, providing liquidity

	through bid and offer rates and a description of the main terms of their commitment.
Item 6.5	Details of any stabilisation in line with items 6.5.1 to 6.6 in case of an admission to trading on a regulated market, third country market, SME Growth Market or MTF, where an issuer or a selling shareholder has granted an over-allotment option or it is otherwise proposed that price stabilising activities may be entered into in connection with an offer:
Item 6.5.1	The fact that stabilisation may be undertaken, that there is no assurance that it will be undertaken and that it may be stopped at any time;
Item 6.5.1.1	The fact that stabilisation transactions aim at supporting the market price of the securities during the stabilisation period;
Item 6.5.2	The beginning and the end of the period during which stabilisation may occur;
Item 6.5.3	The identity of the stabilisation manager for each relevant jurisdiction unless this is not known at the time of publication;
Item 6.5.4	The fact that stabilisation transactions may result in a market price that is higher than would otherwise prevail;
Item 6.5.5	The place where the stabilisation may be undertaken including, where relevant, the name of the trading venue(s).
Item 6.6	Over-allotment and 'green shoe': In case of an admission to trading on a regulated market, SME Growth Market or an MTF: (a) the existence and size of any over-allotment facility and/or 'green shoe'; (b) the existence period of the over-allotment facility and/or 'green shoe'; (c) any conditions for the use of the over-allotment facility or exercise of the 'green shoe'.
SECTION 7	SELLING SECURITIES HOLDERS
Item 7.1	Name and business address of the person or entity offering to sell the securities, the nature of any position office or other material relationship that the selling persons has had within the past three years with the issuer or any of its predecessors or affiliates.
Item 7.2	The number and class of securities being offered by each of the selling security holders.
Item 7.3	Where a major shareholder is selling the securities, the size of its shareholding both before and immediately after the issuance.
Item 7.4	In relation to lock-up agreements, provide details of the following: (a) the parties involved; (b) the content and exceptions of the agreement; (c) an indication of the period of the lock up.
SECTION 8	EXPENSE OF THE ISSUE/OFFER
Item 8.1	The total net proceeds and an estimate of the total expenses of the issue/offer.
SECTION 9	DILUTION
Item 9.1	A comparison of: (a) participation in share capital and voting rights for existing shareholders before and after the capital increase resulting from the public offer, with the assumption that existing shareholders do not subscribe for the new shares; (b) the net asset value per share as of the date of the latest balance sheet before the public offer (selling offer and/or capital increase) and the offering price per share within that public offer.
Item 9.2	Where existing shareholders will be diluted regardless of whether they subscribe for their entitlement, because a part of the relevant share issue is reserved only for certain investors (e.g. an institutional placing coupled with an offer to shareholders), an indication of the dilution existing shareholders will experience shall also be presented on the basis that they do take up their entitlement (in addition to the situation in item 9.1 where they do not).
SECTION 10	ADDITIONAL INFORMATION
Item 10.1	If advisors connected with an issue are referred to in the Securities Note, a statement of the capacity in which the advisors have acted.
Item 10.2	An indication of other information in the securities note which has been audited or reviewed by statutory auditors and where auditors have produced a report. Reproduction of the report or, with permission of the competent authority, a summary of the report.

NOTES

Application of this Annex in relation to the UK: this Annex is amended (as follows), in relation to the UK only, by the Prospectus (Amendment etc) (EU Exit) Regulations 2019, SI 2019/1234, Schedule, para 8, as from IP completion day (as defined in the European Union (Withdrawal Agreement) Act 2020, s 39); for transitional provisions, see regs 74, 75 of the 2019 Regulations at **[12.165]** et seq—

"8.—(1) Annex 11 is amended as follows.

(2) In item 4.11, for "Member State" insert "home country".

(3) In item 4.12, before "Directive" insert "the UK law which implemented".".

[1] Directive 2014/59/EU of the European Parliament and of the Council of 15 May 2014 establishing a framework for the recovery and resolution of credit institutions and investment firms and amending Council Directive 82/891/EEC, and Directives 2001/24/EC, 2002/47/EC, 2004/25/EC, 2005/56/EC, 2007/36/EC, 2011/35/EU, 2012/30/EU and 2013/36/EU, and Regulations (EU) No 1093/2010 and (EU) No 648/2012, of the European Parliament and of the Council (OJ L173, 12.6.2014, p. 190).

[11.710]

ANNEX 12
SECURITIES NOTE FOR SECONDARY ISSUANCES OF EQUITY SECURITIES OR OF UNITS ISSUED BY COLLECTIVE INVESTMENT UNDERTAKINGS OF THE CLOSED-END TYPE

SECTION 1	PERSONS RESPONSIBLE, THIRD PARTY INFORMATION, EXPERTS' REPORTS AND COMPETENT AUTHORITY APPROVAL
Item 1.1	Identify all persons responsible for the information or any parts of it, given in the securities note with, in the latter case, an indication of such parts. In the case of natural persons, including members of the issuer's administrative, management or supervisory bodies, indicate the name and function of the person; in the case of legal persons indicate the name and registered office.
Item 1.2	A declaration by those responsible for the securities note that to the best of their knowledge, the information contained in the securities note is in accordance with the facts and that the securities note makes no omission likely to affect its import. Where applicable, a declaration by those responsible for certain parts of the securities note that, to the best of their knowledge, the information contained in those parts of the securities note for which they are responsible is in accordance with the facts and that those parts of the securities note make no omission likely to affect their import.
Item 1.3	Where a statement or report attributed to a person as an expert is included in the securities note, provide the following details for that person: (a) name; (b) business address; (c) qualifications; (d) material interest if any in the issuer. If the statement or report has been produced at the issuer's request, state that such statement or report has been included in the securities note with the consent of the person who has authorised the contents of that part of the securities note for the purpose of the prospectus.
Item 1.4	Where information has been sourced from a third party, provide a confirmation that this information has been accurately reproduced and that as far as the issuer is aware and is able to ascertain from information published by that third party, no facts have been omitted which would render the reproduced information inaccurate or misleading. In addition, identify the source(s) of the information.
Item 1.5	A statement that: (a) this [securities note/prospectus] has been approved by the [name of competent authority], as competent authority under Regulation (EU) 2017/1129; (b) the [name of competent authority] only approves this [securities note/prospectus] as meeting the standards of completeness, comprehensibility and consistency imposed by Regulation (EU) 2017/1129; (c) such approval should not be considered as an endorsement of the quality of the securities that are the subject of this [securities note/prospectus]; (d) investors should make their own assessment as to the suitability of investing in the securities; (e) that the [securities note/prospectus] has been drawn up as part of a simplified prospectus in accordance with Article 14 of Regulation (EU) 2017/1129.
SECTION 2	RISK FACTORS
Item 2.1	A description of the material risks that are specific to the securities being offered and/or admitted to trading, in a limited number of categories, in a section headed 'Risk Factors'. In each category the most material risks, in the assessment of the issuer, offeror or person asking for admission to trading on a regulated market, taking into account the negative impact on the issuer and the securities and the probability of their occurrence, shall be set out first. The risks shall be corroborated by the content of the securities note.
SECTION 3	ESSENTIAL INFORMATION
Item 3.1	Interest of natural and legal persons involved in the issue/offer A description of any interest, including a conflict of interest that is material to the issue/offer, detailing the persons involved and the nature of the interest.
Item 3.2	Reasons for the offer and use of proceeds Reasons for the offer and, where applicable, the estimated net amount of the proceeds broken into each principal intended use and presented in order of priority of such uses. If the

	issuer is aware that the anticipated proceeds will not be sufficient to fund all the proposed uses, then state the amount and sources of other funds needed. Details must also be given with regard to the use of the proceeds, in particular when they are being used to acquire assets, other than in the ordinary course of business, to finance announced acquisitions of other business, or to discharge, reduce or retire indebtedness.
Item 3.3	Working capital statement Statement by the issuer that, in its opinion, the working capital is sufficient for the issuer's present requirements or, if not, how it proposes to provide the additional working capital needed.
Item 3.4	Capitalisation and indebtedness A statement of capitalisation and indebtedness (distinguishing between guaranteed and unguaranteed, secured and unsecured indebtedness) as of a date no earlier than 90 days prior to the date of the document. The term 'indebtedness' also includes indirect and contingent indebtedness. In the case of material changes in the capitalisation and indebtedness position of the issuer within the 90 day period additional information shall be given through the presentation of a narrative description of such changes or through the updating of those figures.
SECTION 4	INFORMATION CONCERNING THE SECURITIES TO BE OFFERED/ADMITTED TO TRADING
Item 4.1	A description of the type, class and amount of the securities being offered and/or admitted to trading, including the international security identification number ('ISIN').
Item 4.2	Currency of the securities issue.
Item 4.3	In the case of new issues, a statement of the resolutions, authorisations and approvals by virtue of which the securities have been or will be created and/or issued.
Item 4.4	A description of any restrictions on the transferability of the securities.
Item 4.5	A warning that the tax legislation of the investor's Member State and of the issuer's country of incorporation may have an impact on the income received from the securities. Information on the taxation treatment of the securities where the proposed investment attracts a tax regime specific to that type of investment.
Item 4.6	If different from the issuer, the identity and contact details of the offeror, of the securities and/or the person asking for admission to trading including the legal entity identifier ('LEI') where the offeror has legal personality.
Item 4.7	A description of the rights attached to the securities, including any limitations of those rights, and procedure for the exercise of those rights: (a) Dividend rights: (i) fixed date(s) on which the entitlement arises; (ii) time limit after which entitlement to dividend lapses and an indication of the person in whose favour the lapse operates; (iii) dividend restrictions and procedures for non-resident holders; (iv) rate of dividend or method of its calculation, periodicity and cumulative or non-cumulative nature of payments. (b) voting rights. (c) pre-emption rights in offers for subscription of securities of the same class. (d) right to share in the issuer's profits. (e) rights to share in any surplus in the event of liquidation. (f) redemption provisions. (g) conversion provisions.
Item 4.8	Statement on the existence of national legislation on takeovers applicable to the issuer which may frustrate such takeovers, if any.
Item 4.9	An indication of public takeover bids by third parties in respect of the issuer's equity, which have occurred during the last financial year and the current financial year. The price or exchange terms attaching to such offers and the outcome thereof must be stated.
SECTION 5	TERMS AND CONDITIONS OF THE OFFER
Item 5.1	Conditions, offer statistics, expected timetable and action required to apply for the offer
Item 5.1.1	Conditions to which the offer is subject.
Item 5.1.2	The time period, including any possible amendments, during which the offer will be open and a description of the application process together with the issue date of new securities.
Item 5.1.3	A description of any possibility to reduce subscriptions and the manner for refunding amounts paid in excess by applicants.
Item 5.1.4	Details of the minimum and/or maximum amount of application (whether in number of securities or aggregate amount to invest).
Item 5.1.5	Method and time limits for paying up the securities and for delivery of the securities.

Item 5.1.6	A full description of the manner and date in which results of the offer are to be made public.
Item 5.1.7	The procedure for the exercise of any right of pre-emption, the negotiability of subscription rights and the treatment of subscription rights not exercised.
Item 5.1.8	Total amount of the issue/offer, distinguishing the securities offered for sale and those offered for subscription; if the amount is not fixed, an indication of the amount of securities to be offered (if available) and a description of the arrangements and time for announcing to the public the definitive amount of the offer. Where the maximum amount of securities to be offered cannot be provided in the securities note, the securities note shall specify that acceptances of the purchase of subscription of securities may be withdrawn up to two working days after the amount of securities to be offered to the public has been filed.
Item 5.1.9	An indication of when, and under which circumstances, the offer may be revoked or suspended and whether revocation can occur after dealing has begun.
Item 5.1.10	An indication of the period during which an application may be withdrawn, provided that investors are allowed to withdraw their subscription.
Item 5.2	Plan of distribution and allotment
Item 5.2.1.	Process for notifying applicants of the amount allotted and an indication whether dealing may begin before notification is made.
Item 5.2.2	To the extent known to the issuer, an indication of whether major shareholders or members of the issuer's management, supervisory or administrative bodies intended to subscribe in the offer, or whether any person intends to subscribe for more than five per cent of the offer.
Item 5.3	Pricing
Item 5.3.1	An indication of the price at which the securities will be offered and the amount of any expenses and taxes charged to the subscriber or purchaser. If the price is not known, then pursuant to Article 17 of Regulation (EU) 2017/1129 indicate either: (a) the maximum price of securities, as far as they are available; (b) the valuation methods and criteria, and/or conditions, in accordance with which the final offer price is to be determined and an explanation of any valuation methods used. Where neither (a) nor (b) can be provided in the securities note, the securities note shall specify that acceptances of the purchase or subscription of securities may be withdrawn up to two working days after the final offer price of securities to be offered to the public has been filed.
Item 5.3.2	Process for the disclosure of the offer price.
Item 5.3.3	If the issuer's equity holders have pre-emptive purchase rights and this right is restricted or withdrawn, an indication of the basis for the issue price if the issue is for cash, together with the reasons for and beneficiaries of such restriction or withdrawal.
Item 5.4	Placing and underwriting
Item 5.4.1	Name and address of the coordinator(s) of the global offer and of single parts of the offer and, to the extent known by the issuer or to the offeror, of the placers in the various countries where the offer takes place
Item 5.4.2	Name and address of any paying agents and depository agents in each country.
Item 5.4.3	Name and address of the entities agreeing to underwrite the issue on a firm commitment basis, and name and address of the entities agreeing to place the issue without a firm commitment or under 'best efforts' arrangements. Indication of the material features of the agreements, including the quotas. Where not all of the issue is underwritten, a statement of the portion not covered. Indication of the overall amount of the underwriting commission and of the placing commission.
Item 5.4.4	When the underwriting agreement has been or will be reached.
SECTION 6	ADMISSION TO TRADING AND DEALING ARRANGEMENTS
Item 6.1	An indication as to whether the securities offered are or will be the object of an application for admission to trading, with a view to their distribution in a regulated market, other equivalent third country markets or an SME Growth Market with an indication of the markets in question. This circumstance must be set out, without creating the impression that the admission to trading will necessarily be approved. If known, the earliest dates on which the securities will be admitted to trading.
Item 6.2	All the regulated markets equivalent third country markets or SME Growth Markets on which, to the knowledge of the issuer, securities of the same class of the securities to be offered or admitted to trading are already admitted to trading.
Item 6.3	If simultaneously or almost simultaneously with the application for admission of the securities to a regulated market, securities of the same class are subscribed for or placed privately or if securities of other classes are created for public or private placing, give details of the nature of such operations and of the number, characteristics and price of the securi-

	ties to which they relate.
Item 6.4	Details of the entities which have given a firm commitment to act as intermediaries in secondary trading, providing liquidity through bid and offer rates and description of the main terms of their commitment.
SECTION 7	SELLING SECURITIES HOLDERS
Item 7.1	Lock-up agreements In relation to lock up agreements, provide details of the following: (a) the parties involved; (b) content and exceptions of the agreement; (c) an indication of the period of the lock up.
SECTION 8	EXPENSE OF THE ISSUE/OFFER
Item 8.1	The total net proceeds and an estimate of the total expenses of the issue/offer.
SECTION 9	DILUTION
Item 9.1	A comparison of (a) participation in share capital and voting rights for existing shareholders before and after the capital increase resulting from the public offer, with the assumption that existing shareholders do not subscribe for the new shares; (b) the net asset value per share as of the date of the latest balance sheet before the public offer (selling offer and/or capital increase) and the offering price per share within that public offer.
Item 9.2	Where existing shareholders will be diluted regardless of whether they subscribe for their entitlement, because a part of the relevant share issue is reserved only for certain investors (e.g. an institutional placing coupled with an offer to shareholders), an indication of the dilution existing shareholders will experience should also be presented on the basis that they do take up their entitlement (in addition to the situation where they do not).
SECTION 10	ADDITIONAL INFORMATION
Item 10.1	If advisors connected with an issue are referred to in the securities note, a statement of the capacity in which the advisors have acted.
Item 10.2	An indication of other information in the securities note which has been audited or reviewed by statutory auditors and where auditors have produced a report. Reproduction of the report or, with permission of the competent authority, a summary of the report.

NOTES

Application of this Annex in relation to the UK: this Annex is amended (as follows), in relation to the UK only, by the Prospectus (Amendment etc) (EU Exit) Regulations 2019, SI 2019/1234, Schedule, para 9, as from IP completion day (as defined in the European Union (Withdrawal Agreement) Act 2020, s 39); for transitional provisions, see regs 74, 75 of the 2019 Regulations at **[12.165]** et seq—

"9. In Annex 12, in item 4.5, for "Member State" insert "home country".".

[11.711]

ANNEX 13
SECURITIES NOTE FOR DEPOSITORY RECEIPTS ISSUED OVER SHARES

SECTION 1	ESSENTIAL INFORMATION	Primary Issuance	Secondary Issuances
Item 1.1	Working Capital Statement Statement by the issuer of the underlying securities that, in its opinion, the working capital is sufficient for the issuer of the underlying securities' present requirements or, if not, how it proposes to provide the additional working capital needed.	√	√
Item 1.2	Capitalisation and indebtedness A statement of capitalisation and indebtedness of the issuer of the underlying securities (distinguishing between guaranteed and unguaranteed, secured and unsecured indebtedness) as of a date no earlier than 90 days prior to the date of the document. The term 'indebtedness' also includes indirect and contingent indebtedness. In the case of material changes in the capitalisation and indebtedness position of the issuer within the 90 day period additional information shall be given through the presentation of a narrative description of such changes or through the updating of those figures.	√	√
Item 1.3	A description of the type and the class of the underlying shares including the international security identification number ('ISIN')	√	√
Item 1.4	Legislation under which the securities have been created.	√	√
Item 1.5	An indication whether the underlying shares are in registered form or	√	√

	bearer form and whether the underlying shares are in certificated form or book-entry form. In the latter case, name and address of the entity in charge of keeping the records.		
Item 1.6	Currency of the underlying shares.	√	√
Item 1.7	A description of the rights, including any limitations of these, attached to the underlying shares and procedure for the exercise of those rights.	√	√
Item 1.8	Dividend rights: (a) fixed date(s) on which the entitlement arises; (b) time limit after which entitlement to dividend lapses and an indication of the person in whose favour the lapse operates; (c) dividend restrictions and procedures for non-resident holders; (d) rate of dividend or method of its calculation, periodicity and cumulative or non-cumulative nature of payments.	√	√
Item 1.9	Voting rights. Pre-emption rights in offers for subscription of securities of the same class. Right to share in the issuer's profits. Rights to share in any surplus in the event of liquidation. Redemption provisions. Conversion provisions.	√	√
Item 1.10	The issue date of the underlying shares if new underlying shares are being created for the issue of depository receipts and they are not in existence at the time of issue of the depository receipts.	√	√
Item 1.11	If new underlying shares are being created for the issue of the depository receipts, state the resolutions, authorisations and approvals by virtue of which the new underlying shares have been or will be created or issued.	√	√
Item 1.12	A description of any restrictions on the transferability of the underlying shares.	√	√
Item 1.13	A warning that the tax legislation of the investor's Member State and of the issuer's country of incorporation may have an impact on the income received from the securities. Information on the taxation treatment of the securities where the proposed investment attracts a tax regime specific to that type of investment.	√	√
Item 1.14	(a) Statement on the existence of any national legislation on takeovers applicable to the issuer which may frustrate such takeovers, if any. (b) A brief description of the shareholders' rights and obligations in case of mandatory takeover bids and/or squeeze-out or sell-out rules in relation to the securities.	√ √	√
Item 1.15	An indication of public takeover bids by third parties in respect of the issuer's equity, which have occurred during the last financial year and the current financial year. The price or exchange terms attaching to such offers and the outcome thereof must be stated.	√	√
Item 1.16	Where applicable, the potential impact on the investment in the event of resolution under the Directive 2014/59/EU.	√	√
Item 1.17	Lock-up agreements (a) The parties involved. (b) Content and exceptions of the agreement. (c) An indication of the period of the lock up.	√	√
Item 1.18	Information about selling shareholders if any.	√	√
Item 1.18.1	Name and business address of the person or entity offering to sell the underlying shares, the nature of any position office or other material relationship that the selling persons has had within the past three years with the issuer or any of its predecessors or affiliates.	√	√
Item 1.19	Dilution		
Item 1.19.1	A comparison of: (a) participation in share capital and voting rights for existing shareholders before and after the capital increase resulting from the public offer, with the assumption that existing shareholders do not subscribe for the new shares; (b) the net asset value per share as of the date of the latest balance sheet before the public offer (selling offer and/or capital increase) and the offering price per share within that public offer.	√	√

Item 1.19.2	Where existing shareholders will be diluted regardless of whether they subscribe for their entitlement, because a part of the relevant share issue is reserved only for certain investors (e.g. an institutional placing coupled with an offer to shareholders), an indication of the dilution existing shareholders will experience shall also be presented on the basis that they do take up their entitlement (in addition to the situation in 1.19.1 where they do not).	√	√
Item 1.20	Additional information where there is a simultaneous or almost simultaneous offer or admission to trading of the same class of underlying shares as those underlying shares over which the depository receipts are being issued.	√	√
Item 1.20.1	If simultaneously or almost simultaneously with the creation of the depository receipts for which admission to a regulated market is being sought underlying shares of the same class as those over which the depository receipts are being issued are subscribed for or placed privately, details are to be given of the nature of such operations and of the number and characteristics of the underlying shares to which they relate.	√	√
Item 1.20.2	Disclose all regulated markets or equivalent markets on which, to the knowledge of the issuer of the depository receipts, underlying shares of the same class as those over which the depository receipts are being issued are offered or admitted to trading.	√	√
Item 1.20.3	To the extent known to the issuer of the depository receipts, indicate whether major shareholders, members of the administrative, management or supervisory bodies intended to subscribe in the offer, or whether any person intends to subscribe for more than five per cent of the offer.	√	√
SECTION 2	INFORMATION ABOUT THE DEPOSITORY RECEIPTS	Primary Issuance	Secondary Issuances
Item 2.1	Indicate the number of shares represented by each depository receipts	√	√
Item 2.2	A description of the type and class of depository receipts being offered and/or admitted to trading	√	√
Item 2.3	Legislation under which the depository receipts have been created.	√	√
Item 2.4	An indication whether the depository receipts are in registered or bearer form and whether the depository receipts are in certificated or book-entry form. In the latter case, include the name and address of the entity in charge of keeping the records.	√	√
Item 2.5	Currency of the depository receipts	√	√
Item 2.6	Describe the rights attaching to the depository receipts, including any limitations of these attached to the depository receipts and the procedure if any for the exercise of these rights.	√	√
Item 2.7	If the dividend rights attaching to depository receipts are different from the dividend rights disclosed in relation to the underlying shares, disclose the following information about dividend rights: (a) fixed date(s) on which the entitlement arises; (b) time limit after which entitlement to dividend lapses and an indication of the person in whose favour the lapse operates; (c) dividend restrictions and procedures for non-resident holders; (d) rate of dividend or method of its calculation, periodicity and cumulative or non-cumulative nature of payments.	√	√
Item 2.8	If the voting rights attaching to the depository receipts are different from the voting rights disclosed in relation to the underlying shares disclose the following about those rights: (a) voting rights; (b) pre-emption rights in offers for subscription of securities of the same class; (c) right to share in the issuer's profits; (d) rights to share in any surplus in the event of liquidation; (e) redemption provisions; (f) conversion provisions.	√	√
Item 2.9	Describe the exercise of and benefit from rights attaching to the underlying shares, in particular voting rights, the conditions on which the issuer of the depository receipts may exercise such rights, and measures envisaged to obtain the instructions of the depository receipt holders – and the right to share in profits and any liquidation surplus which are not passed on to the holder of the depository receipt.	√	√
Item 2.10	The expected issue date of the depository receipts.	√	√

Item 2.11	A description of any restrictions on the transferability of the depository receipts.	√	√
Item 2.12	A warning that the tax legislation of the investor's Member State and of the issuer's country of incorporation may have an impact on the income received from the securities. Information on the taxation treatment of the depository receipts where the proposed investment attracts a tax regime specific to that type of investment.	√	√
Item 2.13	Bank or other guarantees attached to the depository receipts and intended to underwrite the issuer's obligations.	√	√
Item 2.14	Possibility of obtaining the delivery of the depository receipts into original shares and procedure for such delivery.	√	√
SECTION 3	INFORMATION ABOUT THE TERMS AND CONDITIONS OF THE OFFER OF THE DEPOSITORY RECEIPTS	Primary Issuance	Secondary Issuances
Item 3.1	Conditions, offer statistics, expected timetable and action required to apply for the offer		
Item 3.1.1	Total amount of the issue/offer, distinguishing the securities offered for sale and those offered for subscription; if the amount is not fixed, an indication of the maximum amount of securities to be offered (if available) and a description of the arrangements and the time period for announcing to the public the definitive amount of the offer. Where the maximum amount of securities to be offered cannot be provided in the prospectus, the prospectus shall specify that acceptances of the purchase or subscription of securities may be withdrawn for not less than two working days after the amount of securities to be offered to the public has been filed.	√	√
Item 3.1.2	The time period, including any possible amendments, during which the offer will be open and description of the application process.	√	√
Item 3.1.3	An indication of when, and under which circumstances, the offer may be revoked or suspended and whether revocation can occur after dealing has begun.	√	√
Item 3.1.4	A description of the possibility to reduce subscriptions and the manner for refunding amounts paid in excess by applicants.	√	√
Item 3.1.5	Details of the minimum and/or maximum amount of application (whether in number of securities or aggregate amount to invest).	√	√
Item 3.1.6	An indication of the period during which an application may be withdrawn, provided that investors are allowed to withdraw their subscription.	√	√
Item 3.1.7	Method and time limits for paying up the securities and for delivery of the securities.	√	√
Item 3.1.8	A full description of the manner and date in which results of the offer are to be made public.	√	√
Item 3.1.9	The procedure for the exercise of any right of pre-emption, the negotiability of subscription rights and the treatment of subscription rights not exercised.	√	√
Item 3.2	Plan of distribution and allotment		
Item 3.2.1	The various categories of potential investors to which the securities are offered. If the offer is being made simultaneously in the markets of two or more countries and if a tranche has been or is being reserved for certain of these, indicate any such tranche.	√	√
Item 3.2.2	To the extent known to the issuer, an indication of whether major shareholders or members of the issuer's management, supervisory or administrative bodies intended to subscribe in the offer, or whether any person intends to subscribe for more than five per cent of the offer.	√	√
Item 3.2.3	Pre-allotment disclosure: (a) the division into tranches of the offer including the institutional, retail and issuer's employee tranches and any other tranches; (b) the conditions under which the claw- back may be used, the maximum size of such claw back and any applicable minimum percentages for individual tranches; (c) the allotment method or methods to be used for the retail and issuer's employee tranche in the event of an over-subscription of these tranches; (d) a description of any pre-determined preferential treatment to be accorded to certain classes of investors or certain affinity groups	√	√

	(including friends and family programmes) in the allotment, the percentage of the offer reserved for such preferential treatment and the criteria for inclusion in such classes or groups; (e) whether the treatment of subscriptions or bids to subscribe in the allotment may be determined on the basis of which firm they are made through or by; (f) a target minimum individual allotment if any within the retail tranche; (g) the conditions for the closing of the offer as well as the date on which the offer may be closed at the earliest; (h) whether or not multiple subscriptions are admitted, and where they are not, how any multiple subscriptions will be handled.		
Item 3.2.4	Process for notifying applicants of the amount allotted and an indication whether dealing may begin before notification is made.	√	√
Item 3.3	Pricing		
Item 3.3.1	An indication of the price at which the securities will be offered and the amount of any expenses and taxes charged to the subscriber or purchaser. If the price is not known, then pursuant to Article 17 of Regulation (EU) 2017/1129 indicate either: (a) the maximum price of the securities, as far as they are available; (b) the valuation methods and criteria, and/or conditions, in accordance with which the final offer price has been or will be determined and an explanation of any valuation methods used. Where neither (a) nor (b) can be provided in the prospectus, the prospectus shall specify that acceptances of the purchase or subscription of securities may be withdrawn for not less than two working days after the final offer price of securities to be offered to the public has been filed.	√	√
Item 3.3.2	Process for the disclosure of the offer price.	√	√
Item 3.3.3	Where there is or could be a material disparity between the public offer price and the effective cash cost to members of the administrative, management or supervisory bodies or senior management, or affiliated persons, of securities acquired by them in transactions during the past year, or which they have the right to acquire, include a comparison of the public contribution in the proposed public offer an the effective cash contributions of such persons.	√	√
Item 3.4	Placing and Underwriting		
Item 3.4.1	Name and address of the coordinator(s) of the global offer and of single parts of the offer and, to the extent known to the issuer or to the offeror, of the placers in the various countries where the offer takes place.	√	√
Item 3.4.2	Name and address of any paying agents and depository agents in each country.	√	√
Item 3.4.3	Name and address of the entities agreeing to underwrite the issue on a firm commitment basis, and name and address of the entities agreeing to place the issue without a firm commitment or under best efforts' arrangements. Indication of the material features of the agreements, including the quotas. Where not all of the issue is underwritten, a statement of the portion not covered. Indication of the overall amount of the underwriting commission and of the placing commission.	√	√
Item 3.4.4	When the underwriting agreement has been or will be reached.	√	√
SECTION 4	ADMISSION TO TRADING AND DEALING ARRANGEMENTS IN THE DEPOSITORY RECEIPTS	Primary Issuance	Secondary Issuances
Item 4.1	An indication as to whether the securities offered are or will be the object of an application for admission to trading, with a view to their distribution in a regulated market or equivalent third country market, SME Growth Market or MTF with an indication of the markets in question. This circumstance must be set out, without creating the impression that the admission to trading will necessarily be approved. If known, the earliest dates on which the securities will be admitted to trading.	√	√
Item 4.2	All the regulated markets or equivalent third country markets, SME Growth Market or MTFs on which, to the knowledge of the issuer, securities of the same class of the securities to be offered or admitted to trading are already admitted to trading.	√	√
Item 4.3	If simultaneously or almost simultaneously with the creation of the securities for which admission to a regulated market is being sought securities of the same class are subscribed for or placed privately or if securities of other classes are created for public or private placing, give details	√	√

	of the nature of such operations and of the number and characteristics of the securities to which they relate.		
	In case of an admission to trading on a regulated market, details of the entities which have a firm commitment to act as intermediaries in secondary trading, providing liquidity through bid and offer rates and description of the main terms of their commitment.	√	√
Item 4.4	The issue price of the securities	√	√
	Details of stabilisation: where an issuer or a selling shareholder has granted an over-allotment option or it is otherwise proposed that price stabilising activities may be entered into in connection with an offer:	√	√
	The fact that stabilisation may be undertaken, that there is no assurance that it will be undertaken and that it may be stopped at any time.	√	
Item 4.5	The fact that stabilisation transactions aim at supporting the market price of the securities during the stabilisation period.	√	
	The beginning and the end of the period during which stabilisation may occur.	√	
	The identity of the stabilisation manager for each relevant jurisdiction unless this is not known at the time of publication.	√	
	The fact that stabilisation transactions may result in a market price that is higher than would otherwise prevail.	√	
Item 4.6	The place where the stabilisation may be undertaken including, where relevant, the name of the trading venue(s).	√	
	Over-allotment and 'green shoe':	√	√
	In case of an admission to trading on a regulated market: (a) the existence and size of any over-allotment facility and/or 'green shoe'; (b) the existence period of the over-allotment facility and/or 'green shoe'; (c) any conditions for the use of the over-allotment facility or exercise of the 'green shoe'.		
SECTION 5	ESSENTIAL INFORMATION ABOUT THE ISSUANCE OF THE DEPOSITORY RECEIPTS	Primary Issuance	Secondary Issuances
Item 5.1	Reasons for the offer and use of proceeds		
Item 5.1.1	Reasons for the offer and, where applicable, the estimated net amount of the proceeds broken into each principal intended use and presented in order of priority of such uses. If the issuer is aware that the anticipated proceeds will not be sufficient to fund all the proposed uses, then state the amount and sources of other funds needed. Details must also be given with regard to the use of the proceeds, in particular when they are being used to acquire assets, other than in the ordinary course of business, to finance announced acquisitions of other business, or to discharge, reduce or retire indebtedness.	√	√
Item 5.2	Interest of natural and legal persons involved in the issuer/offer		
Item 5.2.1	A description of any interest, including a conflict of interest that is material to the issue/offer, detailing the persons involved and the nature of the interest.	√	√
Item 5.3	Risk Factors		
Item 5.3.1	A description of the material risks that are specific to the securities being offered and/or admitted to trading in a limited number of categories, in a section headed 'Risk Factors'.	√	√
	In each category the most material risks, in the assessment of the issuer, offeror or person asking for admission to trading on a regulated market, taking into account the negative impact on the issuer and the securities and the probability of their occurrence, shall be set out first. The risks shall be corroborated by the content of the prospectus.		
SECTION 6	EXPENSE OF THE ISSUE/OFFER OF THE DEPOSITORY RECEIPTS	Primary Issuance	Secondary Issuances
Item 6.1	The total net proceeds and an estimate of the total expenses of the issue/offer.	√	√

NOTES

Application of this Annex in relation to the UK: this Annex is amended (as follows), in relation to the UK only, by the Prospectus (Amendment etc) (EU Exit) Regulations 2019, SI 2019/1234, Schedule, para 10, as from IP completion day (as defined in the European Union (Withdrawal Agreement) Act 2020, s 39); for transitional provisions, see regs 74, 75 of the 2019

Regulations at **[12.165]** et seq—

"10.—(1) Annex 13 is amended as follows.

(2) In item 1.13, for "Member State" insert "home country".

(3) In item 1.16, before "Directive" insert "the UK law which implemented".

(4) In item 2.12, for "Member State" insert "home country".".

[11.712]

ANNEX 14
SECURITIES NOTE FOR RETAIL NON-EQUITY SECURITIES

SECTION 1	PERSONS RESPONSIBLE, THIRD PARTY INFORMATION, EXPERTS' REPORTS AND COMPETENT AUTHORITY APPROVAL	
Item 1.1	Identify all persons responsible for the information or any parts of it, given in the securities note with, in the latter case, an indication of such parts. In the case of natural persons, including members of the issuer's administrative, management or supervisory bodies, indicate the name and function of the person; in the case of legal persons indicate the name and registered office.	Category A
Item 1.2	A declaration by those responsible for the securities note that to the best of their knowledge, the information contained in the securities note is in accordance with the facts and that the securities note makes no omission likely to affect its import. Where applicable, a declaration by those responsible for certain parts of the securities note that, to the best of their knowledge, the information contained in those parts of the securities note for which they are responsible is in accordance with the facts and that those parts of the securities note make no omission likely to affect their import.	Category A
Item 1.3	Where a statement or report, attributed to a person as an expert, is included in the securities note, provide the following details for that person: (a) name; (b) business address; (c) qualifications; (d) material interest if any in the issuer. If the statement or report has been produced at the issuer's request, state that such statement or report has been included in the securities note with the consent of the person who has authorised the contents of that part of the securities note for the purpose of the prospectus.	Category A
Item 1.4	Where information has been sourced from a third party, provide a confirmation that this information has been accurately reproduced and that as far as the issuer is aware and is able to ascertain from information published by that third party, no facts have been omitted which would render the reproduced information inaccurate or misleading. In addition, identify the source(s) of the information.	Category C
Item 1.5	A statement that: (a) this [securities note/prospectus] has been approved by the [name of competent authority], as competent authority under Regulation (EU) 2017/1129. (b) the [name of competent authority] only approves this [securities note/prospectus] as meeting the standards of completeness, comprehensibility and consistency imposed by Regulation (EU) 2017/1129; (c) such approval should not be considered as an endorsement of [the quality of the securities that are the subject of this [securities note/prospectus]; (d) investors should make their own assessment as to the suitability of investing in the securities.	Category A
SECTION 2	RISK FACTORS	
Item 2.1	A description of the material risks that are specific to the securities being offered and/or admitted to trading in a limited number of categories, in a section headed 'Risk Factors'. Risks to be disclosed shall include: (a) those resulting from the level of subordination of a security and the impact on the expected size or timing of payments to holders of the securities under bankruptcy, or any other similar procedure, including, where relevant, the insolvency of a credit institution or its resolution or restructuring in accordance with Directive 2014/59/EU; (b) in cases where the securities are guaranteed, the specific and material risks related to the guarantor to the extent they are relevant to its ability to fulfil its commitment under the guarantee. In each category the most material risks, in the assessment of the issuer, offeror	Category A

	or person asking for admission to trading on a regulated market, taking into account the negative impact on the issuer and the securities and the probability of their occurrence, shall be set out first. The risks shall be corroborated by the content of the securities note.	
SECTION 3	ESSENTIAL INFORMATION	
Item 3.1	Interest of natural and legal persons involved in the issue/offer A description of any interest, including a conflict of interest that is material to the issue/offer, detailing the persons involved and the nature of the interest.	Category C
Item 3.2	Reasons for the offer and use of proceeds Reasons for the offer to the public or for the admission to trading. Where applicable, disclosure of the estimated total expenses of the issue/offer and the estimated net amount of the proceeds. These expenses and proceeds shall be broken into each principal intended use and presented in order of priority of such uses. If the issuer is aware that the anticipated proceeds will not be sufficient to fund all the proposed uses, then state the amount and sources of other funds needed.	Category C
SECTION 4	INFORMATION CONCERNING THE SECURITIES TO BE OFFERED TO THE PUBLIC/ADMITTED TO TRADING	
Item 4.1	(a) A description of the type and the class of the securities being offered to the public and/or admitted to trading.	Category B
	(b) The international security identification number ('ISIN') for those classes of securities referred to in (a).	Category C
Item 4.2	Legislation under which the securities have been created.	Category A
Item 4.3	(a) An indication of whether the securities are in registered form or bearer form and whether the securities are in certificated form or book-entry form.	Category A
	(b) In the case of securities registered in book-entry form, the name and address of the entity in charge of keeping the records.	Category C
Item 4.4	Total amount of the securities offered to the public/admitted to trading. If the amount is not fixed, an indication of the maximum amount of the securities to be offered (if available) and a description of the arrangements and time for announcing to the public the definitive amount of the offer. Where the maximum amount of securities to be offered cannot be provided in the securities note, the securities note shall specify that acceptances of the purchase or subscription of securities may be withdrawn up to two working days after the amount of securities to be offered to the public has been filed.	Category C
Item 4.5	Currency of the securities issue.	Category C
Item 4.6	The relative seniority of the securities in the issuer's capital structure in the event of insolvency, including, where applicable, information on the level of subordination of the securities and the potential impact on the investment in the event of a resolution under Directive 2014/59/EU.	Category A
Item 4.7	A description of the rights attached to the securities, including any limitations of those rights, and procedure for the exercise of those rights.	Category B
Item 4.8	(a) The nominal interest rate;	Category C
	(b) the provisions relating to interest payable;	Category B
	(c) the date from which interest becomes payable;	Category C
	(d) the due dates for interest;	Category C
	(e) the time limit on the validity of claims to interest and repayment of principal.	Category B
	Where the rate is not fixed:	
	(a) a statement setting out the type of underlying;	Category A
	(b) a description of the underlying on which the rate is based;	Category C
	(c) the method used to relate the rate with the underlying;	Category B
	(d) an indication where information about the past and the future performance of the underlying and its volatility can be obtained by electronic means and whether or not it can be obtained free of charge;	Category C
	(e) a description of any market disruption or settlement disruption events that affect the underlying;	Category B
	(f) any adjustment rules with relation to events concerning the underlying;	Category B
	(g) the name of the calculation agent;	Category C
	(h) if the security has a derivative component in the interest payment, a clear and comprehensive explanation to help investors understand how the value of their investment is affected by the value of the underlying instrument(s), especially under the circumstances when the risks are most evident.	Category B

Item 4.9	(a) Maturity date.	Category C
	(b) Details of the arrangements for the amortisation of the loan, including the repayment procedures. Where advance amortisation is contemplated, on the initiative of the issuer or of the holder, it shall be described, stipulating the amortisation terms and conditions.	Category B
Item 4.10	(a) An indication of yield.	Category C
	(b) Description of the method whereby the yield in point (a) is to be calculated in summary form.	Category B
Item 4.11	Representation of non-equity security holders including an identification of the organisation representing the investors and provisions applying to such representation. Indication of the website where the public may have free access to the contracts relating to these forms of representation.	Category B
Item 4.12	In the case of new issues, a statement of the resolutions, authorisations and approvals by virtue of which the securities have been or will be created and/or issued.	Category C
Item 4.13	The issue date or in the case of new issues, the expected issue date of the securities.	Category C
Item 4.14	A description of any restrictions on the transferability of the securities.	Category A
Item 4.15	A warning that the tax legislation of the investor's Member State and of the issuer's country of incorporation may have an impact on the income received from the securities. Information on the taxation treatment of the securities where the proposed investment attracts a tax regime specific to that type of investment.	Category A
Item 4.16	If different from the issuer, the identity and contact details of the offeror, of the securities and/or the person asking for admission to trading, including the legal entity identifier ('LEI') where the offeror has legal personality.	Category C
SECTION 5	TERMS AND CONDITIONS OF THE OFFER OF SECURITIES TO THE PUBLIC	
Item 5.1	Conditions, offer statistics, expected timetable and action required to apply for the offer.	
Item 5.1.1	Conditions to which the offer is subject.	Category C
Item 5.1.2	The time period, including any possible amendments, during which the offer will be open. A description of the application process.	Category C
Item 5.1.3	A description of the possibility to reduce subscriptions and the manner for refunding amounts paid in excess by applicants.	Category C
Item 5.1.4	Details of the minimum and/or maximum amount of the application, (whether in number of securities or aggregate amount to invest).	Category C
Item 5.1.5	Method and time limits for paying up the securities and for delivery of the securities.	Category C
Item 5.1.6	A full description of the manner and date in which results of the offer are to be made public.	Category C
Item 5.1.7	The procedure for the exercise of any right of pre-emption, the negotiability of subscription rights and the treatment of subscription rights not exercised.	Category C
Item 5.2	Plan of distribution and allotment.	
Item 5.2.1	The various categories of potential investors to which the securities are offered. If the offer is being made simultaneously in the markets of two or more countries and if a tranche has been or is being reserved for certain of these, indicate any such tranche.	Category C
Item 5.2.2	Process for notifying applicants of the amount allotted and an indication whether dealing may begin before notification is made.	Category C
Item 5.3	Pricing	
Item 5.3.1	(a) An indication of the expected price at which the securities will be offered.	Category C
	(b) Where an indication of the expected price cannot be given, a description of the method of determining the price, pursuant to Article 17 of Regulation (EU) 2017/1129, and the process for its disclosure.	Category B
	(c) Indication of the amount of any expenses, and taxes charged to the subscriber or purchaser. Where the issuer is subject to Regulation (EU) No 1286/2014 or Directive 2014/65/EU and to the extent that they are known, include those expenses contained in the price.	Category C
Item 5.4	Placing and Underwriting	
Item 5.4.1	Name and address of the coordinator(s) of the global offer and of single parts of the offer and, to the extent known to the issuer or to the offeror, of the placers in the various countries where the offer takes place.	Category C
Item 5.4.2	Name and address of any paying agents and depository agents in each country.	Category C

Item 5.4.3	Name and address of the entities agreeing to underwrite the issue on a firm commitment basis, and name and address of the entities agreeing to place the issue without a firm commitment or under 'best efforts' arrangements. Indication of the material features of the agreements, including the quotas. Where not all of the issue is underwritten, a statement of the portion not covered. Indication of the overall amount of the underwriting commission and of the placing commission.	Category C
Item 5.4.4	When the underwriting agreement has been or will be reached.	Category C
SECTION 6	ADMISSION TO TRADING AND DEALING ARRANGEMENTS	
Item 6.1	(a) an indication as to whether the securities offered are or will be the object of an application for admission to trading, with a view to their distribution in a regulated market, other third country markets, SME Growth Market or MTF with an indication of the markets in question. This circumstance must be set out, without creating the impression that the admission to trading will necessarily be approved.	Category B
	(b) If known, give the earliest dates on which the securities will be admitted to trading.	Category C
Item 6.2	All the regulated markets or third country markets, SME Growth Market or MTFs on which, to the knowledge of the issuer, securities of the same class of the securities to be offered to the public or admitted to trading are already admitted to trading.	Category C
Item 6.3	In the case of admission to trading on a regulated market, the name and address of the entities which have a firm commitment to act as intermediaries in secondary trading, providing liquidity through bid and offer rates and description of the main terms of their commitment.	Category C
Item 6.4	The issue price of the securities.	Category C
SECTION 7	ADDITIONAL INFORMATION	
Item 7.1	If advisors connected with an issue are referred to in the securities note, a statement of the capacity in which the advisors have acted.	Category C
Item 7.2	An indication of other information in the securities note which has been audited or reviewed by statutory auditors and where auditors have produced a report. Reproduction of the report or, with permission of the competent authority, a summary of the report.	Category A
Item 7.3	Credit ratings assigned to the securities at the request or with the cooperation of the issuer in the rating process. A brief explanation of the meaning of the ratings if this has previously been published by the rating provider.	Category C
Item 7.4	Where the summary is substituted in part with the information set out in points (c) to (i) of paragraph 3 of Article 8 of Regulation (EU) No 1286/2014, all such information to the extent it is not already disclosed elsewhere in the securities note, must be disclosed.	Category C

NOTES

Application of this Annex in relation to the UK: this Annex is amended (as follows), in relation to the UK only, by the Prospectus (Amendment etc) (EU Exit) Regulations 2019, SI 2019/1234, Schedule, para 11, as from IP completion day (as defined in the European Union (Withdrawal Agreement) Act 2020, s 39); for transitional provisions, see regs 74, 75 of the 2019 Regulations at **[12.165]** et seq—

"11.—(1) Annex 14 is amended as follows.

(2) In item 2.1, before "Directive" insert "the UK law which implemented".

(3) In item 4.6, before "Directive" insert "the UK law which implemented".

(4) In item 4.15, for "Member State" substitute "home country".

(5) In item 5.3.1, point (c), before "Directive" insert "the UK law which implemented".".

[11.713]

ANNEX 15
SECURITIES NOTE FOR WHOLESALE NON-EQUITY SECURITIES

SECTION 1	PERSONS RESPONSIBLE, THIRD PARTY INFORMATION, EXPERTS' REPORTS AND COMPETENT AUTHORITY APPROVAL	
Item 1.1	Identify all persons responsible for the information or any parts of it, given in the securities note with, in the latter case, an indication of such parts. In the case of natural persons, including members of the issuer's administrative, management or supervisory bodies, indicate the name and function of the person; in the case of legal persons indicate the name and registered office.	Category A
Item 1.2	A declaration by those responsible for the securities note that to the best of their knowledge, the information contained in the securities note is in accordance with the facts and that the securities note makes no omission likely to affect its import. Where applicable, a declaration by those responsible for certain parts of the securities note that, to the best of their knowledge, the information contained in	Category A

	those parts of the securities note for which they are responsible is in accordance with the facts and that those parts of the securities note make no omission likely to affect their import.	
Item 1.3	Where a statement or report, attributed to a person as an expert, is included in the securities note, provide the following details for that person: (a) name; (b) business address; (c) qualifications; (d) material interest if any in the issuer. If the statement or report has been produced at the issuer's request, state that such statement or report has been included in the securities note with the consent of the person who has authorised the contents of that part of the securities note for the purpose of the prospectus.	Category A
Item 1.4	Where information has been sourced from a third party, provide a confirmation that this information has been accurately reproduced and that as far as the issuer is aware and is able to ascertain from information published by that third party, no facts have been omitted which would render the reproduced information inaccurate or misleading. In addition, identify the source(s) of the information.	Category C
Item 1.5	A statement that: (a) this [securities note/prospectus] has been approved by the [name of competent authority], as competent authority under Regulation (EU) 2017/1129; (b) the [name of competent authority] only approves this [securities note/prospectus] as meeting the standards of completeness, comprehensibility and consistency imposed by Regulation (EU) 2017/1129; (c) such approval should not be considered as an endorsement of the quality of the securities that are the subject of this [securities note/prospectus]; and (d) investors should make their own assessment as to the suitability of investing in the securities.	Category A
SECTION 2	RISK FACTORS	
Item 2.1	A description of the material risks that are specific to the securities being offered and/or admitted to trading in a limited number of categories, in a section headed 'Risk Factors'. Risks to be disclosed shall include: (a) those resulting from the level of subordination of a security and the impact on the expected size or timing of payments to holders of the securities under bankruptcy, or any other similar procedure, including, where relevant, the insolvency of a credit institution or its resolution or restructuring in accordance with Directive 2014/59/EU; (b) in cases where the securities are guaranteed, the specific and material risks related to the guarantor to the extent they are relevant to its ability to fulfil its commitment under the guarantee. In each category the most material risks, in the assessment of the issuer, offeror or person asking for admission to trading on a regulated market, taking into account the negative impact on the issuer and the securities and the probability of their occurrence, shall be set out first. The risks shall be corroborated by the content of the securities note.	Category A
SECTION 3	ESSENTIAL INFORMATION	
Item 3.1	Interest of natural and legal persons involved in the issue. A description of any interest, including a conflict of interest that is material to the issue, detailing the persons involved and the nature of the interest.	Category C
Item 3.2	The use and estimated net amount of the proceeds.	Category C
SECTION 4	INFORMATION CONCERNING THE SECURITIES TO BE ADMITTED TO TRADING	
Item 4.1	Total amount of securities being admitted to trading.	Category C
Item 4.2	(a) A description of the type and the class of the securities being admitted to trading;	Category B
	(b) The international security identification number ('ISIN').	Category C
Item 4.3	Legislation under which the securities have been created.	Category A
Item 4.4	(a) An indication of whether the securities are in registered or bearer form and whether the securities are in certificated or book-entry form.	Category A
	(b) In the case of securities registered in book-entry form, the name and address of the entity in charge of keeping the records.	Category C
Item 4.5	Currency of the securities issue.	Category C

Item 4.6	The relative seniority of the securities in the issuer's capital structure in the event of insolvency, including, where applicable, information on the level of subordination of the securities and the potential impact on the investment in the event of a resolution under Directive 2014/59/EU.	Category A
Item 4.7	A description of the rights, including any limitations of these, attached to the securities and procedure for the exercise of said rights.	Category B
Item 4.8	(a) The nominal interest rate;	Category C
	(b) the provisions relating to interest payable;	Category B
	(c) the date from which interest becomes payable;	Category C
	(d) the due dates for interest;	Category C
	(e) the time limit on the validity of claims to interest and repayment of principal.	Category B
	Where the rate is not fixed:	
	(a) a statement setting out the type of underlying;	Category A
	(b) a description of the underlying on which the rate is based;	Category C
	(c) the method used to relate the rate with the underlying;	Category B
	(d) a description of any market disruption or settlement disruption events that affect the underlying;	Category B
	(e) any adjustment rules with relation to events concerning the underlying;	Category C
	(f) the name of the calculation agent.	Category C
Item 4.9	(a) Maturity date.	Category C
	(b) Details of the arrangements for the amortisation of the loan, including the repayment procedures. Where advance amortisation is contemplated, on the initiative of the issuer or of the holder, it shall be described, stipulating amortisation terms and conditions.	Category B
Item 4.10	An indication of yield.	Category C
Item 4.11	Representation of debt security holders including an identification of the organisation representing the investors and provisions applying to such representation. Indication of the website where investors may have free access to the contracts relating to these forms of representation.	Category B
Item 4.12	A statement of the resolutions, authorisations and approvals by virtue of which the securities have been created and/or issued.	Category C
Item 4.13	The issue date of the securities.	Category C
Item 4.14	A description of any restrictions on the transferability of the securities.	Category A
Item 4.15	If different from the issuer, the identity and contact details of the offeror of the securities and/or the person asking for admission to trading, including the legal entity identifier ('LEI') where the offeror has legal personality.	Category C
SECTION 5	ADMISSION TO TRADING AND DEALING ARRANGEMENTS	
Item 5.1	(a) An indication of the regulated market, or other third country market, SME Growth Market or MTF where the securities will be traded and for which a prospectus has been published.	Category B
	(b) If known, give the earliest dates on which the securities will be admitted to trading.	Category C
Item 5.2	Name and address of any paying agents and depository agents in each country.	Category C
SECTION 6	EXPENSE OF THE ADMISSION TO TRADING	
Item 6.1	An estimate of the total expenses related to the admission to trading.	Category C
SECTION 7	ADDITIONAL INFORMATION	
Item 7.1	If advisors are referred to in the Securities Note, a statement of the capacity in which the advisors have acted.	Category C
Item 7.2	An indication of other information in the Securities Note which has been audited or reviewed by auditors and where auditors have produced a report. Reproduction of the report or, with permission of the competent authority, a summary of the report.	Category A
Item 7.3	Credit ratings assigned to the securities at the request or with the cooperation of the issuer in the rating process. A brief explanation of the meaning of the ratings if this has previously been published by the rating provider.	Category C

NOTES

Application of this Annex in relation to the UK: this Annex is amended (as follows), in relation to the UK only, by the Prospectus (Amendment etc) (EU Exit) Regulations 2019, SI 2019/1234, Schedule, para 12, as from IP completion day (as defined in the European Union (Withdrawal Agreement) Act 2020, s 39); for transitional provisions, see regs 74, 75 of the 2019 Regulations at **[12.165]** et seq—

"12.—(1) Annex 15 is amended as follows.

(2) In item 2.1, before "Directive" insert "the UK law which implemented";
(3) In item 4.6, before "Directive" insert "the UK law which implemented".".

[11.714]

ANNEX 16
SECURITIES NOTE FOR SECONDARY ISSUANCES OF NON-EQUITY SECURITIES

SECTION 1	PERSONS RESPONSIBLE, THIRD PARTY INFORMATION, EXPERTS' REPORTS AND COMPETENT AUTHORITY APPROVAL	
Item 1.1	Identify all persons responsible for the information or any parts of it, given in the securities note with, in the latter case, an indication of such parts. In the case of natural persons, including members of the issuer's administrative, management or supervisory bodies, indicate the name and function of the person; in the case of legal persons indicate the name and registered office.	Category A
Item 1.2	A declaration by those responsible for the securities note that to the best of their knowledge, the information contained in the securities note is in accordance with the facts and that the securities note makes no omission likely to affect its import. Where applicable, a declaration by those responsible for certain parts of the securities note that, to the best of their knowledge, the information contained in those parts of the securities note for which they are responsible is in accordance with the facts and that those parts of the securities note make no omission likely to affect their import.	Category A
Item 1.3	Where a statement or report attributed to a person as an expert is included in the Securities Note, provide the following details for that person: (a) name; (b) business address; (c) qualifications; (d) material interest if any in the issuer. If the statement or report has been produced at the issuer's request, state that such statement or report has been included in the securities note with the consent of the person who has authorised the contents of that part of the securities note for the purpose of the prospectus.	Category A
Item 1.4	Where information has been sourced from a third party, provide a confirmation that this information has been accurately reproduced and that as far as the issuer is aware and is able to ascertain from information published by that third party, no facts have been omitted which would render the reproduced information inaccurate or misleading. In addition, identify the source(s) of the information.	Category C
Item 1.5	A statement that: (a) this [securities note/prospectus] has been approved by the [name of competent authority], as competent authority under Regulation (EU) 2017/1129; (b) the [name of competent authority] only approves this [securities note/prospectus] as meeting the standards of completeness, comprehensibility and consistency imposed by Regulation (EU) 2017/1129; (c) such approval should not be considered as an endorsement of the quality of the securities that are the subject of this [securities note/prospectus]; (d) investors should make their own assessment as to the suitability of investing in the securities; and (e) that the [securities note/prospectus] has been drawn up as a simplified prospectus in accordance with Article 14 of Regulation (EU) 2017/1129.	Category A
SECTION 2	RISK FACTORS	
Item 2.1	A description of the material risks that are specific to the securities being offered and/or admitted to trading, in a limited number of categories, in a section headed 'Risk Factors'. Risks to be disclosed shall include: (a) those resulting from the level of subordination of a security and the impact on the expected size or timing of payments to holders of the securities under bankruptcy, or any other similar procedure, including, where relevant, the insolvency of a credit institution or its resolution or restructuring in accordance with Directive 2014/59/EU; (b) in cases where the securities are guaranteed, the specific and material risks related to the guarantor to the extent they are relevant to its ability to fulfil its commitment under the guarantee. In each category the most material risks, in the assessment of the issuer, offeror or person asking for admission to trading on a regulated market, taking into ac-	Category A

	count the negative impact on the issuer and the securities and the probability of their occurrence, shall be set out first. The risks shall be corroborated by the content of the securities note.	
SECTION 3	ESSENTIAL INFORMATION	
Item 3.1	Interest of natural and legal persons involved in the issue/offer A description of any interest, including a conflict of interest that is material to the issue/offer, detailing the persons involved and the nature of the interest.	Category C
Item 3.2 (Retail only)	Reasons for the offer to the public or for the admission to trading if different from making profit and/or hedging certain risks. In case of an offer to the public, disclosure of the estimated total expenses of the issue/offer and the estimated net amount of the proceeds. These expenses and proceeds shall be broken into each principal intended use and presented in order of priority of such uses. If the issuer is aware that the anticipated proceeds will not be sufficient to fund all the proposed uses, then state the amount and sources of other funds needed.	Category C
Item 3.3 (Wholesale only)	Reasons for the issuance if different from making profit and/or hedging certain risks	Category C
SECTION 4	INFORMATION CONCERNING THE SECURITIES TO BE OFFERED/ADMITTED TO TRADING	
[Item 4.1	(a) a description of the type, class and amount of the securities being offered to the public and/or admitted to trading;	Category B
	(b) the international security identification number ('ISIN') of the securities being offered to the public and/or admitted to trading.	Category C]
Item 4.2	Currency of the securities issue.	Category C
Item 4.3	In the case of new issues, a statement of the resolutions, authorisations and approvals by virtue of which the securities have been or will be created and/or issued.	Category C
Item 4.4	A description of any restrictions on the transferability of the securities.	Category B
Item 4.5 (Retail only)	A warning that the tax legislation of the investor's Member State and of the issuer's country of incorporation may have an impact on the income received from the securities. Information on the taxation treatment of the securities where the proposed investment attracts a tax regime specific to that type of investment.	Category A
Item 4.6	If different from the issuer, the identity and contact details of the offeror, of the securities and/or the person asking for admission to trading including the legal entity identifier ('LEI') where the offeror has legal personality.	Category C
Item 4.7	The relative seniority of the securities in the issuer's capital structure in the event of insolvency, including, where applicable, information on the level of subordination of the securities and the potential impact on the investment in the event of a resolution under Directive 2014/59/EU.	Category A
Item 4.8	A description of the rights attached to the securities, including any limitations of those rights.	Category B
Item 4.9	(a) The nominal interest rate;	Category C
	(b) the provisions relating to interest payable;	Category B
	(c) the date from which interest becomes payable and the due dates for interest.	Category C
	(d) the time limit on the validity of claims to interest and repayment of principal.	Category B
	Where the rate is not fixed:	
	(a) a statement setting out the type of underlying;	Category A
	(b) a description of the underlying on which the rate is based and of the method used to relate the rate with the underlying;	Category C
	(c) in the case of retail non-equity securities, an indication where information about the past and the future performance of the underlying and its volatility can be obtained;	Category C
	(d) a description of any market disruption or settlement disruption events that affect the underlying;	Category B
	(e) any adjustment rules with relation to events concerning the underlying;	Category B
	(f) the name of the calculation agent;	Category C
	(g) in the case of retail non-equity securities, if the security has a derivative component in the interest payment, a clear and comprehensive explanation to help investors understand how the value of their investment is affected by the value of the underlying instrument(s), especially under the circumstances when the risks are most evident,.	Category B

Item 4.10	(a) Maturity date.	Category C
	(b) Details of the arrangements for the amortisation of the loan, including the repayment procedures.	Category B
	Where advance amortisation is contemplated, on the initiative of the issuer or of the holder, it shall be described, stipulating amortisation terms and conditions.	
Item 4.11	(a) An indication of yield.	Category C
	(b) In the case of retail non-equity securities, description of the method of how the yield is calculated in summary form.	Category B
Item 4.15	Representation of debt securities holders including an identification of the organisation representing the investors and provisions applying to such representation. Indication of the website where the public may have free access to the contracts relating to these forms of representation.	Category B
Item 4.16	Where there is no offer, the issue date of the securities.	Category C
SECTION 5	TERMS AND CONDITIONS OF THE OFFER (RETAIL ONLY)	
Item 5.1	Conditions, offer statistics, expected timetable and action required to apply for the offer	
Item 5.1.1	Conditions to which the offer is subject.	Category C
Item 5.1.2	The time period, including any possible amendments, during which the offer will be open and a description of the application process together with the issue date of new securities.	Category C
Item 5.1.3	A description of the possibility to reduce subscriptions and the manner for refunding amounts paid in excess by applicants.	Category C
Item 5.1.4	Details of the minimum and/or maximum amount of application (whether in number of securities or aggregate amount to invest).	Category C
Item 5.1.5	Method and time limits for paying up the securities and for delivery of the securities.	Category C
Item 5.1.6	A full description of the manner and date in which results of the offer are to be made public.	Category C
Item 5.1.7	The procedure for the exercise of any right of pre-emption, the negotiability of subscription rights and the treatment of subscription rights not exercised.	Category C
Item 5.1.8	Total amount of the issue/offer; if the amount is not fixed an indication of the amount of securities to be offered (if available) and a description of the arrangements and time for announcing to the public the definitive amount of the offer.	Category C
	Where the maximum amount of securities to be offered cannot be provided in the prospectus, the prospectus shall specify that acceptances of the purchase of subscription of securities may be withdrawn for not less than two working days after the amount of securities to be offered to the public has been filed.	
Item 5.2	Plan of distribution and allotment	
Item 5.2.1	Process notifying applicants of the amount allotted and an indication whether dealing may begin before notification is made.	Category C
Item 5.3	Pricing	
Item 5.3.1	(a) an indication of the price at which the securities will be offered; or	Category C
	(b) a description of the method for determining the price and the process for its disclosure.	Category B
	(c) Indication of the amount of any expenses and taxes charged to the subscriber or purchaser. Where the issuer is subject to Regulation (EU) No 1286/2014 or Directive 2014/65/EU and to the extent that they are known, include those expenses contained in the price.	Category C
Item 5.4.	Placing and underwriting	
Item 5.4.1	Name and address of the coordinator(s) of the global offer and of single parts of the offer and, to the extent known to the issuer or to the offeror, of the placers in the various countries where the offer takes place	Category C
Item 5.4.2	Name and address of any paying agents and depository agents in each country.	Category C
Item 5.4.3	Name and address of the entities agreeing to underwrite the issue on a firm commitment basis, and name and address of the entities agreeing to place the issue without a firm commitment or under 'best efforts' arrangements. Indication of the material features of the agreements, including the quotas. Where not all of the issue is underwritten, a statement of the portion not covered. Indication of the overall amount of the underwriting commission and of the placing commission.	Category C
Item 5.4.4	When the underwriting agreement has been or will be reached.	Category C
SECTION 6	ADMISSION TO TRADING AND DEALING ARRANGEMENTS	
Item 6.1	An indication as to whether the securities offered are or will be the object of an application for admission to trading, with a view to their distribution in a regulated market, other equivalent third country markets or an SME Growth Market	Category B

	with an indication of the markets in question. This circumstance must be set out, without creating the impression that the admission to trading will necessarily be approved. If known, the earliest dates on which the securities will be admitted to trading.	
Item 6.2 (Retail only)	All the regulated markets, equivalent third country markets or SME Growth Markets on which, to the knowledge of the issuer, securities of the same class of the securities to be offered or admitted to trading are already admitted to trading.	Category C
Item 6.3 (Retail only)	The issue price of the securities.	Category C
Item 6.4 (Wholesale only)	An estimate of the total expenses related to the admission to trading.	Category C
Item 6.5	Name and address of any paying agents and depositary agents in each country.	Category C
SECTION 7	ADDITIONAL INFORMATION	
Item 7.1	If advisors connected with an issue are referred to in the securities note, a statement of the capacity in which the advisors have acted.	Category C
Item 7.2	An indication of other information in the securities note which has been audited or reviewed by statutory auditors and where auditors have produced a report. Reproduction of the report or, with permission of the competent authority, a summary of the report.	Category A
Item 7.3 (Retail only)	Credit ratings assigned to the securities at the request or with the cooperation of the issuer in the rating process. A brief explanation of the meaning of the ratings if this has previously been published by the rating provider.	Category C
[Item 7.3a (Retail only)	Where the summary is substituted in part with the information set out in points (c) to (i) of paragraph 3 of Article 8 of Regulation (EU) No 1286/2014, all such information must be disclosed to the extent it is not already disclosed elsewhere in the securities note.	Category C]
Item 7.4 (Wholesale only)	An estimate of the total expenses related to the admission to trading.	Category C
Item 7.5 (Wholesale only)	Credit ratings assigned to the securities at the request or with the cooperation of the issuer in the rating process.	Category C

NOTES

Item 4.1 substituted, and item 7.3a inserted, by Commission Delegated Regulation 2020/1273/EU, Art 1(20), Annex 8, as from 17 September 2020.

Application of this Annex in relation to the UK: this Annex is amended (as follows), in relation to the UK only, by the Prospectus (Amendment etc) (EU Exit) Regulations 2019, SI 2019/1234, Schedule, para 13, as from IP completion day (as defined in the European Union (Withdrawal Agreement) Act 2020, s 39); for transitional provisions, see regs 74, 75 of the 2019 Regulations at **[12.165]** et seq—

"13.—(1) Annex 16 is amended as follows.

(2) In item 2.1, before "Directive" insert "the UK law which implemented".

(3) In item 4.5, for "Member State" insert "home country".

(4) In item 4.7, before "Directive" insert "the UK law which implemented".

(5) In item 5.3.1, in point (c), before "Directive" insert "the UK law which implemented".".

[11.715]

ANNEX 17
SECURITIES GIVING RISE TO PAYMENT OR DELIVERY OBLIGATIONS LINKED TO AN UNDERLYING ASSET

SECTION 1	RISK FACTORS	
Item 1.1	Prominent disclosure of risk factors that are material to the securities being offered and/or admitted to trading in order to assess the market risk associated with these securities in a section headed 'Risk Factors'. If applicable, this must include a risk warning to the effect that investors may lose the value of their entire investment or part of it, as the case may be, and, if the investor's liability is not limited to the value of his investment, a statement of that fact, together with a description of the circumstances in which such additional liability arises and the likely financial effect.	Category A
SECTION 2	INFORMATION CONCERNING THE SECURITIES TO BE OFFERED/ADMITTED TO TRADING	
Item 2.1	Information concerning the securities	
Item 2.1.1	A clear and comprehensive explanation to help investors understand how the value of their investment is affected by the value of the underlying instrument(s), especially in the circumstances where the risks are most evident, unless the securities have a denomination per unit of at least EUR 100,000, or	Category B

	can only be acquired for at least EUR 100,000 per security, or are to be traded on a regulated market or a specific segment of a regulated market to which only qualified investors can have access.	
Item 2.1.2	The expiration or maturity date of the derivative securities and their exercise date or final reference date.	Category C
Item 2.1.3	A description of the settlement procedure of the derivative securities.	Category B
Item 2.1.4	A description of:	
	(a) how any return on derivative securities takes place;	Category B
	(b) the payment or delivery date;	Category C
	(c) the way it is calculated.	Category B
Item 2.2	Information concerning the underlying	
Item 2.2.1	The exercise price or the final reference price of the underlying.	Category C
Item 2.2.2	A statement setting out the type of the underlying.	Category A
	Details of where information on the underlying can be obtained including an indication of where information about the past and the future performance of that underlying and its volatility can be obtained by electronic means, and whether or not it can be obtained free of charge.	Category C
	Where the underlying is a security:	
	(a) the name of the issuer of the security;	Category C
	(b) the international security identification number ('ISIN');	Category C
	where the underlying is a reference entity or reference obligation (for credit-linked securities):	
	(a) where the reference entity or reference obligation comprises of a single entity or obligation, or in the case of a pool of underlying where a single reference entity or reference obligation represents 20% or more of the pool:	
	(i) if the reference entity (or issuer of the reference obligation) has no securities admitted to trading on a regulated market, equivalent third country market or SME Growth Market, so far as the issuer is aware and/or able to ascertain from information published by the reference entity (or by the issuer of the reference obligation), information relating to the reference entity (or to the issuer of the reference obligation) as if it were the issuer (in accordance with the registration document for wholesale non-equity securities);	Category A
	(ii) if the reference entity (or the issuer of the reference obligation) has securities already admitted to trading on a regulated market, equivalent third country market or SME Growth Market, so far as the issuer is aware and/or able to ascertain from information published by the reference entity (or by the issuer of the reference obligation), its name, ISIN, address, country of incorporation, industry or industries in which the reference entity (or the issuer of the reference obligation) operates and the name of the market in which its securities are admitted.	Category C
	(b) in the case of a pool of underlying, where a single reference entity or reference obligation represents less than 20% of the pool:	
	(i) the names of the reference entities or issuers of the reference obligation; and	Category C
	(ii) the ISIN.	Category C
	Where the underlying is an index:	
	(a) the name of the index;	Category C
	(b) a description of the index if it is composed by the issuer or by any legal entity belonging to the same group;	Category A
	(c) a description of the index provided by a legal entity or a natural person acting in association with, or on behalf of, the issuer, unless the prospectus contains the following statements:	Category B
	(i) the complete set of rules of the index and information on the performance of the index are freely accessible on the issuer's or on the index provider's website;	
	(ii) the governing rules (including methodology of the index for the selection and the re-balancing of the components of the index, description of market disruption events and of adjustment rules) are based on predetermined and objective criteria.	
	Points (b) and (c) do not apply where the administrator of the index is included in the public register maintained by ESMA under Article 36 of Regulation (EU) 2016/1011.[1]	

Part 11 EU & Retained EU Legislation

	(d) Where the index is not composed by the issuer, an indication of where information about the index can be obtained.	Category C
	Where the underlying is an interest rate, a description of the interest rate.	Category C
	Where the underlying does not fall within the categories specified above, the securities note shall contain equivalent information.	Category C
	Where the underlying is a basket of underlying, a disclosure for each underlying as described above and disclosure of the relevant weightings of each underlying in the basket.	Category C
Item 2.2.3	A description of any market disruption or settlement disruption or credit events that affect the underlying.	Category B
Item 2.2.4	Adjustment rules with relation to events concerning the underlying.	Category B
SECTION 3	ADDITIONAL INFORMATION	
Item 3.1	An indication in the prospectus whether or not the issuer intends to provide post issuance information. Where the issuer has indicated that it intends to report such information, the issuer shall specify in the prospectus what information will be reported and where such information can be obtained.	Category C

NOTES

Application of this Annex in relation to the UK: this Annex is amended (as follows), in relation to the UK only, by the Prospectus (Amendment etc) (EU Exit) Regulations 2019, SI 2019/1234, Schedule, para 14, as from IP completion day (as defined in the European Union (Withdrawal Agreement) Act 2020, s 39); for transitional provisions, see regs 74, 75 of the 2019 Regulations at **[12.165]** et seq—

"14. In Annex 17, in item 2.2.2, in the 5th point before item 2.2.3, for "ESMA" substitute "the FCA".".

[1] Regulation (EU) 2016/1011 of the European Parliament and of the Council of 8 June 2016 on indices used as benchmarks in financial instruments and financial contracts or to measure the performance of investment funds and amending Directives 2008/48/EC and 2014/17/EU and Regulation (EU) No 596/2014 (OJ L171, 29.6.2016, p. 1).

[11.716]

ANNEX 18
UNDERLYING SHARE

SECTION 1	DESCRIPTION OF THE UNDERLYING SHARE	
Item 1.1	Description of the type and the class of the shares.	Category A
Item 1.2	Legislation under which the shares have been or will be created.	Category A
Item 1.3	(a) Indication whether the securities are in registered form or bearer form and whether the securities are in certificated form or book-entry form.	Category A
	(b) In the case of securities registered in book-entry form, the name and address of the entity in charge of keeping the records.	Category C
Item 1.4	Indication of the currency of the shares issue	Category A
Item 1.5	A description of the rights, including any limitations of these, attached to the securities and procedure for the exercise of those rights: (a) dividend rights: (i) fixed date(s) on which the entitlement arises; (ii) time limit after which entitlement to dividend lapses and an indication of the person in whose favour the lapse operates; (iii) dividend restrictions and procedures for non-resident holders; (iv) rate of dividend or method of its calculation, periodicity and cumulative or non-cumulative nature of payments. (b) voting rights; (c) pre-emption rights in offers for subscription of securities of the same class; (d) right to share in the issuer's profits; (e) rights to share in any surplus in the event of liquidation; (f) redemption provisions; (g) conversion provisions.	Category A
Item 1.6	In the case of new issues, a statement of the resolutions, authorisations and approvals by virtue of which the shares have been or will be created and/or issued and indication of the issue date.	Category C
Item 1.7	Where and when the shares will be or have been admitted to trading.	Category C
Item 1.8	Description of any restrictions on the transferability of the shares.	Category A
Item 1.9	Statement on the existence of any national legislation on takeovers applicable to the issuer which may frustrate such takeovers, if any. Brief description of the shareholders' rights and obligations in case of mandatory takeover bid, squeeze-out or sell-out.	Category A

Item 1.10	Indication of public takeover bids by third parties in respect of the issuer's equity, which have occurred during the last financial year and the current financial year. The price or exchange terms attaching to such offers and the outcome thereof must be stated.	Category C
Item 1.11	A comparison of: (a) participation in share capital and voting rights for existing shareholders before and after the capital increase resulting from the public offer, with the assumption that existing shareholders do not subscribe for the new shares; (b) the net asset value per share as of the date of the latest balance before the public offer (selling offer and/or capital increase) and the offering price per share within that public offer.	Category C Category C
SECTION 2	INFORMATION TO BE PROVIDED WHERE THE ISSUER OF THE UNDERLYING IS AN ENTITY BELONGING TO THE SAME GROUP	Category C
Item 2.1	When the issuer of the underlying is an entity belonging to the same group, the information to provide on this issuer is the one required by the registration document for equity securities or, if applicable, the registration document for secondary issuances of equity securities or the EU Growth registration document for equity securities.	Category A

NOTES

Application of this Annex in relation to the UK: this Annex is amended (as follows), in relation to the UK only, by the Prospectus (Amendment etc) (EU Exit) Regulations 2019, SI 2019/1234, Schedule, para 15, as from IP completion day (as defined in the European Union (Withdrawal Agreement) Act 2020, s 39); for transitional provisions, see regs 74, 75 of the 2019 Regulations at **[12.165]** et seq—

"15. In Annex 18. in item 2.1, for "EU" substitute "UK".".

[11.717]

ANNEX 19
ASSET-BACKED SECURITIES

SECTION 1	THE SECURITIES	
Item 1.1	A statement that a notification has been, or is intended to be communicated to ESMA, as regards simple, transparent and standardised securitisation ('STS') compliance, where applicable. This should be accompanied by an a explanation of the meaning of such notification together with a reference or hyperlink to ESMA's data base indicating that the STS-notification is available for download there if deemed necessary.	Category A
Item 1.2	Where the prospectus includes a statement that the transaction is STS compliant, a warning that the STS status of a transaction is not static and that investors should verify the current status of the transaction on ESMA's website.	Category B
Item 1.3	The minimum denomination of an issue.	Category C
Item 1.4	Where information is disclosed about an undertaking/obligor which is not involved in the issue, provide a confirmation that the information relating to the undertaking/obligor has been accurately reproduced from information published by the undertaking/obligor. So far as the issuer is aware and is able to ascertain from information published by the undertaking/obligor no facts have been omitted which would render the reproduced information misleading. In addition, identify the source(s) of information in the securities note that has been reproduced from information published by an undertaking/obligor.	Category C
SECTION 2	THE UNDERLYING ASSETS	
Item 2.1	Confirmation that the securitised assets backing the issue have characteristics that demonstrate capacity to produce funds to service any payments due and payable on the securities.	Category A
Item 2.2	In respect of a pool of discrete assets backing the issue:	
Item 2.2.1	The legal jurisdiction by which the pool of assets is governed.	Category C
Item 2.2.2	(a) In the case of a small number of easily identifiable obligors a general description of each obligor. (b) In all other cases, a description of the general characteristics of the obligors and the economic environment. (c) In relation to those obligors referred to in point (b), any global statistical data referred to the securitised assets.	Category C Category B Category C
Item 2.2.3	The legal nature of the assets.	Category C
Item 2.2.4	The expiry or maturity date(s) of the assets.	Category C
Item 2.2.5	The amount of the assets.	Category C

Item 2.2.6	Loan to value ratio or level of collateralisation.	Category B
Item 2.2.7	The method of origination or creation of the assets, and for loans and credit agreements, the principal lending criteria and an indication of any loans which do not meet these criteria and any rights or obligations to make further advances.	Category B
Item 2.2.8	An indication of significant representations and collateral given to the issuer relating to the assets.	Category C
Item 2.2.9	Any rights to substitute the assets and a description of the manner in which and the type of assets which may be so substituted; if there is any capacity to substitute assets with a different class or quality of assets a statement to that effect together with a description of the impact of such substitution.	Category B
Item 2.2.10	A description of any relevant insurance policies relating to the assets. Any concentration with one insurer must be disclosed if it is material to the transaction.	Category B
Item 2.2.11	Where the assets comprise obligations of 5 or fewer obligors which are legal persons or are guaranteed by 5 or fewer legal persons or where an obligor or entity guaranteeing the obligations accounts for 20% or more of the assets, or where 20% or more of the assets are guaranteed by a single guarantor, so far as the issuer is aware and/or is able to ascertain from information published by the obligor(s) or guarantor(s) indicate either of the following:	
	(a) information relating to each obligor or guarantor as if it were an issuer drafting a registration document for non-equity securities with an individual denomination of at least EUR 100,000 and/or that are to be traded only on a regulated market, or a specific segment thereof, to which only qualified investors can have access for the purposes of trading in such securities;	Category A
	(b) if an obligor or guarantor has securities already admitted to trading on a regulated or equivalent third country market or SME Growth Market its name, address, country of incorporation, significant business activities/investment policy and the name of the market in which its securities are admitted.	Category C
Item 2.2.12	If a relationship exists that is material to the issue, between the issuer, guarantor and obligor, details of the principal terms of that relationship.	Category C
Item 2.2.13	Where the assets comprise obligations that are traded on regulated or equivalent third country market or SME Growth Market, a brief description of the securities, the market and an electronic link where the documentation in relation to the obligations can be found on the regulated or equivalent third country market or SME Growth Market.	Category C
Item 2.2.14	Where the assets comprise obligations that are not traded on a regulated or equivalent third country market or SME Growth Market, a description of the principal terms and conditions in relation to the obligations.	Category B
Item 2.2.15	Where the assets comprise equity securities that are admitted to trading on a regulated or equivalent third country market or SME Growth Market indicate the following:	Category C
	(a) a description of the securities;	
	(b) a description of the market on which they are traded including its date of establishment, how price information is published, an indication of daily trading volumes, information as to the standing of the market in the country, the name of the market's regulatory authority and an electronic link where the documentation in relation to the securities can be found on the regulated or equivalent third country market or SME Growth Market;	Category C
	(c) the frequency with which prices of the relevant securities, are published.	Category C
Item 2.2.16	Where more than 10% of the assets comprise equity securities that are not traded on a regulated or equivalent third country market or SME Growth Market, a description of those equity securities and equivalent information to that contained in the registration document for equity securities or where applicable, the registration document for securities issued by closed-end collective investment undertakings in respect of each issuer of those securities.	Category A
Item 2.2.17	Where a material portion of the assets are secured on or backed by real property, a valuation report relating to the property setting out both the valuation of the property and cash flow/income streams. Compliance with this disclosure is not required if the issue is of securities backed by mortgage loans with property as security, where there has been no revaluation of the properties for the purpose of the issue, and it is clearly stated that the valuations quoted are as at the date of the original initial mortgage loan origination.	Category A
Item 2.3	In respect of an actively managed pool of assets backing the issue:	
Item 2.3.1	Equivalent information to that contained in items 2.1 and 2.2 to allow an assess-	See items 2.1

	ment of the type, quality, sufficiency and liquidity of the asset types in the portfolio which will secure the issue.	and 2.2
Item 2.3.2	The parameters within which investments can be made, the name and description of the entity responsible for such management including a description of that entity's expertise and experience, a summary of the provisions relating to the termination of the appointment of such entity and the appointment of an alternative management entity and a description of that entity's relationship with any other parties to the issue.	Category A
Item 2.4	Where an issuer proposes to issue further securities backed by the same assets, a prominent statement to that effect and unless those further securities are fungible with or are subordinated to those classes of existing debt, a description of how the holders of that class will be informed.	Category C
SECTION 3	STRUCTURE AND CASH FLOW	
Item 3.1	Description of the structure of the transaction containing an overview of the transaction and the cash flows, including a structure diagram.	Category A
Item 3.2	Description of the entities participating in the issue and description of the functions to be performed by them in addition to information on the direct and indirect ownership or control between those entities.	Category A
Item 3.3	Description of the method and date of the sale, transfer, novation or assignment of the assets or of any rights and/or obligations in the assets to the issuer or, where applicable, the manner and time period in which the proceeds from the issue will be fully invested by the issuer.	Category B
Item 3.4	An explanation of the flow of funds including:	
Item 3.4.1	(a) how the cash flow from the assets will meet the issuer's obligations to holders of the securities, including, if necessary:	Category A
	(b) a financial service table and a description of the assumptions used in developing that table;	Category C
Item 3.4.2	information on any credit enhancements, an indication of where potentially material liquidity shortfalls may occur and the availability of any liquidity supports and indication of provisions designed to cover interest/principal shortfall risks;	Category B
Item 3.4.3	(a) the risk retention requirement applicable to the transaction, where applicable;	Category A
	(b) the material net economic interest retained by the originator, the sponsor or the original lender;[1]	Category C
Item 3.4.4	without prejudice to item 3.4.2, details of any subordinated debt finance;	Category C
Item 3.4.5	an indication of any investment parameters for the investment of temporary liquidity surpluses and description of the parties responsible for such investment;	Category B
Item 3.4.6	how payments are collected in respect of the assets;	Category A
Item 3.4.7	the order of priority of payments made by the issuer to the holders of the class of securities in question;	Category A
Item 3.4.8	details of any other arrangements upon which payments of interest and principal to investors are dependent;	Category B
Item 3.5	the name, address and significant business activities of the originators of the securitised assets.	Category C
Item 3.6	Where the return on, and/or repayment of the security is linked to the performance or credit of other assets or underlyings which are not assets of the issuer, for each such reference asset or underlying furnish one of the following; (a) disclosure in accordance with items 2.2 and 2.3; (b) where the principal is not at risk, the name of the issuer of the reference asset, the international security identification number ('ISIN'), and an indication where information about the past and the current performance of the reference asset can be obtained; (c) where the reference asset is an index, parts 1 and 2 of Annex 17.	See Annex 17
Item 3.7	The name, address and significant business activities of the administrator, calculation agent or equivalent, together with a summary of the administrator's/calculation agents responsibilities, their relationship with the originator or the creator of the assets and a summary of the provisions relating to the termination of the appointment of the administrator/calculation agent and the appointment of an alternative administrator/calculation agent;	Category C
Item 3.8	The names and addresses and brief description of:	
	(a) any swap counterparties and any providers of other material forms of credit/ liquidity enhancement;	Category A
	(b) the banks with which the main accounts relating to the transaction are held.	Category C
SECTION 4	POST ISSUANCE REPORTING	

Item 4.1	An indication in the prospectus of where the issuer is under an obligation to, or where the issuer intends to, provide post-issuance transaction information regarding securities to be admitted to trading and the performance of the underlying collateral. The issuer shall indicate what information will be reported, where such information can be obtained, and the frequency with which such information will be reported.	Category C

NOTES

Application of this Annex in relation to the UK: this Annex is amended (as follows), in relation to the UK only, by the Prospectus (Amendment etc) (EU Exit) Regulations 2019, SI 2019/1234, Schedule, para 16, as from IP completion day (as defined in the European Union (Withdrawal Agreement) Act 2020, s 39); for transitional provisions, see regs 74, 75 of the 2019 Regulations at **[12.165]** et seq—

"16. In Annex 19, in items 1.1 and 1.2, for "ESMA" in each place it occurs, substitute "FCA".".

[1] This may change depending on the final securitisation regulation requirements.

[11.718]

ANNEX 20
PRO FORMA INFORMATION

SECTION 1	CONTENTS OF PRO FORMA FINANCIAL INFORMATION
Item 1.1	The pro forma financial information shall consist of: (a) an introduction setting out: (i) the purpose for which the pro forma financial information has been prepared, including a description of the transaction or significant commitment and the businesses or entities involved; (ii) the period or date covered by the pro forma financial information; (iii) the fact that the pro forma financial information has been prepared for illustrative purposes only; (iv) an explanation that: (i) the pro forma financial information illustrates the impact of the transaction as if the transaction had been undertaken at an earlier date; (ii) the hypothetical financial position or results included in the pro forma financial information may differ from the entity's actual financial position or results; (b) a profit and loss account, a balance sheet or both, depending on the circumstances presented in a columnar format composed of: (i) historical unadjusted information; (ii) accounting policy adjustments, where necessary; (iii) pro forma adjustments; (iv) the results of the pro forma financial information in the final column; (c) accompanying notes explaining: (i) the sources from which the unadjusted financial information has been extracted and whether or not an audit or review report on the source has been published; (ii) the basis upon which the pro forma financial information is prepared; (iii) source and explanation for each adjustment;
	(iv) whether each adjustment in respect of a pro forma profit and loss statement is expected to have a continuing impact on the issuer or not; (d) where applicable, the financial information and interim financial information of the (or to be) acquired businesses or entities used in the preparation of the pro forma financial information must be included in the prospectus.
SECTION 2	PRINCIPLES IN PREPARING AND PRESENTING PRO FORMA FINANCIAL INFORMATION
Item 2.1	The pro forma financial information shall be identified as such in order to distinguish it from historical financial information. The pro forma financial information must be prepared in a manner consistent with the accounting policies adopted by the issuer in its last or next financial statements.
Item 2.2	Pro forma information may only be published in respect of: (a) the last completed financial period; and/or (b) the most recent interim period for which relevant unadjusted information has been published or are included in the registration document/prospectus.
Item 2.3	Pro forma adjustments must comply with the following: (a) be clearly shown and explained; (b) present all significant effects directly attributable to the transaction;

	(c) be factually supportable.
SECTION 3	REQUIREMENTS FOR AN ACCOUNTANT/AUDIT REPORT The prospectus shall include a report prepared by the independent accountants or auditors stating that in their opinion: (a) the pro forma financial information has been properly compiled on the basis stated; (b) that the basis referred to in (a) is consistent with the accounting policies of the issuer.

[11.719]

ANNEX 21
GUARANTEES

SECTION 1	NATURE OF THE GUARANTEE
	A description of any arrangement intended to ensure that any obligation material to the issue will be duly serviced, whether in the form of guarantee, surety, Keep well Agreement, Mono-line Insurance policy or other equivalent commitment ('guarantees') and their provider ('guarantor'). Such arrangements encompass commitments, including those under conditions, to ensure that the obligations to repay non-equity securities and/or the payment of interest are fulfilled and their description shall set out how the arrangement is intended to ensure that the guaranteed payments will be duly serviced.
SECTION 2	SCOPE OF THE GUARANTEE
	Details shall be disclosed about the terms and conditions and scope of the guarantee. These details should cover any conditionality on the application of the guarantee in the event of any default under the terms of the security and the material terms of any Mono-line Insurance or Keep well Agreement between the issuer and the guarantor. Details must also be disclosed of any guarantor's power of veto in relation to changes to the security holder's rights, such as is often found in Mono-line Insurance.
SECTION 3	INFORMATION TO BE DISCLOSED ABOUT THE GUARANTOR
	The guarantor must disclose information about itself as if it were the issuer of that same type of security that is the subject of the guarantee.
SECTION 4	DOCUMENTS AVAILABLE
	Indication of the website where the public may have access to the material contracts and other documents relating to the guarantee.

[11.720]

ANNEX 22
CONSENT

SECTION 1	INFORMATION TO BE PROVIDED REGARDING CONSENT BY THE ISSUER OR PERSON RESPONSIBLE FOR DRAWING UP THE PROSPECTUS	
Item 1.1	Express consent by the issuer or person responsible for drawing up the prospectus to the use of the prospectus and a statement that such person accepts responsibility for the content of the prospectus also with respect to the subsequent resale or final placement of securities by any financial intermediary which was given consent to use the prospectus.	Category A
Item 1.2	Indication of the period for which consent to use the prospectus is given.	Category A
Item 1.3	Indication of the offer period upon which subsequent resale or final placement of the securities by financial intermediaries can be made.	Category C
Item 1.4	Indication of the Member States in which the financial intermediaries may use the prospectus for subsequent resale or final placement of the securities.	Category A
Item 1.5	Any other clear and objective conditions attached to the consent which are relevant for the use of the prospectus.	Category C
Item 1.6	Notice in bold informing investors that, in the event of an offer being made by a financial intermediary, the financial intermediary will provide information to investors on the terms and conditions of the offer at the time the offer is made.	Category A
SECTION 2A	ADDITIONAL INFORMATION TO BE PROVIDED WHERE CONSENT IS GIVEN TO ONE OR MORE SPECIFIED FINANCIAL INTERMEDIARIES	
Item 2A.1	List and identify (name and address) the financial intermediary or intermediaries that are allowed to use the prospectus.	Category C
Item 2A.2	Indication of how any new information with respect to the finan-	Category A

Part 11 EU & Retained EU Legislation

	cial intermediaries, unknown at the time of the approval of the prospectus, the base prospectus or the filing of the final terms, as the case may be, is to be published and where it can be found.	
SECTION 2B	ADDITIONAL INFORMATION TO BE PROVIDED WHERE CONSENT IS GIVEN TO ALL FINANCIAL INTERMEDIARIES	
Item 2B.1	Notice in bold informing investors that any financial intermediary using the prospectus has to state on its website that it uses the prospectus in accordance with the consent and the conditions attached thereto.	Category A

NOTES

Application of this Annex in relation to the UK: this Annex is amended (as follows), in relation to the UK only, by the Prospectus (Amendment etc) (EU Exit) Regulations 2019, SI 2019/1234, Schedule, para 17, as from IP completion day (as defined in the European Union (Withdrawal Agreement) Act 2020, s 39); for transitional provisions, see regs 74, 75 of the 2019 Regulations at **[12.165]** et seq—

"17. In Annex 22, omit item 1.4.".

[11.721]

ANNEX 23
SPECIFIC SUMMARY FOR THE EU GROWTH PROSPECTUS

SECTION 1	INTRODUCTION
Item 1.1	Name and international securities identification number ('ISIN') of the securities.
Item 1.2	Identity and contact details of the issuer, including its legal entity identifier ('LEI').
Item 1.3	Identity and contact details of the competent authority that approved the prospectus and, where different, the competent authority that approved the registration document.
Item 1.4	Date of approval of the EU Growth prospectus.
Item 1.5	Warnings
Item 1.5.1	Statements by the issuer with regard to the following: (a) the summary should be read as an introduction to the EU Growth prospectus and that any decision to invest in the securities should be based on a consideration of the EU Growth prospectus as a whole by the investor; (b) where applicable, that the investor could lose all or part of the invested capital and, where the investor's liability is not limited to the amount of the investment, a warning that the investor could lose more than the invested capital and the extent of such potential loss; (c) where a claim relating to the information contained in an EU Growth prospectus is brought before a court, the plaintiff investor may, under the national law of the Member States, have to bear the costs of translating the EU Growth prospectus before the legal proceedings are initiated; (d) the fact that civil liability attaches only to those persons who have tabled the summary including any translation thereof, but only where the summary is misleading, inaccurate or inconsistent when read together with the other parts of the EU Growth prospectus, or where it does not provide, when read together with the other parts of the EU Growth prospectus, key information in order to aid investors when considering whether to invest in such securities; (e) where applicable, the comprehension alert required in accordance with point (b) of Article 8(3) of Regulation (EU) No 1286/2014.
SECTION 2	KEY INFORMATION ON THE ISSUER
Item 2.1	Who is the issuer of the securities?
Item 2.1.1	Information about the issuer: (a) its legal form, the law under which it operates and its country of incorporation; (b) its principal activities; (c) its controlling shareholder(s), including whether it is directly or indirectly controlled; (d) name of the Chief Executive Officer (or equivalent).
Item 2.2	What is the key financial information regarding the issuer?
Item 2.2.1	Key financial information presented for each financial year of the period covered by the historical financial information, and if included in the prospectus any subsequent interim financial period accompanied by comparative data from the same period in the prior financial year. The requirement for comparative balance sheet information shall be satisfied by presenting the year-end balance sheet information. The key financial information shall include financial measures, which appear in the prospectus. These financial measures should provide information on: (a) revenue, profitability, assets, capital structure and, where included in the prospectus,

	cash flows; and (b) key performance indicators, where included in the prospectus. The key financial information shall, where applicable, include: (c) condensed pro forma financial information and a brief explanation of what the pro forma financial information illustrates and the material adjustments done; (d) a brief description of any qualifications in the audit report relating to the historical financial information.
Item 2.3	What are the key risks that are specific to the issuer?
Item 2.3.1	A brief description of the most material risk factors specific to the issuer contained in the EU Growth prospectus, while not exceeding the total number of risk factors set out in Article 33(8) of this Regulation.
SECTION 3	KEY INFORMATION ON THE SECURITIES
Item 3.1	What are the main features of the securities?
Item 3.1.1	Information about the securities: (a) their type and class; (b) where applicable, their currency, denomination, the number of securities issued and the term of the securities; (c) the rights attached to the securities; (d) the relative seniority of the securities in the issuer's capital structure in the event of insolvency including, where applicable, information on the level of subordination of the securities; (e) where applicable, the dividend or pay-out policy.
Item 3.2	Where will the securities be traded?
Item 3.2.1	Where applicable, information as to whether the securities are or will be the subject to an application for admission to trading on an MTF or an SME Growth market, the identity of all the markets where the securities are or are to be traded and the details of the admission to trading on an MTF or an SME Growth market.
Item 3.3	Is there a guarantee attached to the securities? (a) A brief description of the nature and scope of the guarantee; (b) a brief description of the guarantor, including its legal entity identifier (LEI); (c) the relevant key financial information for the purpose of assessing the guarantor's ability to fulfil its commitments under the guarantee; (d) a brief description of the most material risk factors pertaining to the guarantor contained in the EU Growth prospectus in accordance with Article 16(3) of Regulation (EU) 2017/1129, while not exceeding the total number of risk factors set out in Article 33(8) of this Regulation.
Item 3.4	What are the key risks that are specific to the securities?
Item 3.4.1	A brief description of the most material risk factors specific to the securities contained in the EU Growth prospectus, while not exceeding the total number of risk factors set out in Article 33(8) of this Regulation.
SECTION 4	KEY INFORMATION ON THE OFFER OF SECURITIES TO THE PUBLIC
Item 4.1	Under which conditions and timetable can I invest in this security?
	Where applicable, the general terms, conditions and expected timetable of the offer, the plan for distribution, the amount and percentage of immediate dilution resulting from the offer and an estimate of the total expenses of the issue and/or offer, including estimated expenses charged to the investor by the issuer or the offeror.
Item 4.2	Why is this EU Growth prospectus being produced?
Item 4.2.1	A brief description of the reasons for the offer as well as, where applicable: (a) the use and estimated net amount of the proceeds; (b) where the offer is subject to an underwriting agreement on a firm commitment basis, state any portion not covered; (c) a description of any material conflict of interest pertaining to the offer or the admission to trading that are described in the prospectus.
Item 4.3	Who is the offeror and/or the person asking for admission to trading?
Item 4.3.1	If different from the issuer, a brief description of the offeror of the securities and/or the person asking for admission to trading on an MTF or an SME Growth Market, including its domicile and legal form, the law under which it operates and its country of incorporation.

NOTES

Application of this Annex in relation to the UK: this Annex is amended (as follows), in relation to the UK only, by the Prospectus (Amendment etc) (EU Exit) Regulations 2019, SI 2019/1234, Schedule, para 18, as from IP completion day (as defined in the European Union (Withdrawal Agreement) Act 2020, s 39); for transitional provisions, see regs 74, 75 of the 2019 Regulations at **[12.165]** et seq—

"18.—(1) Annex 23 is amended as follows.

(2) In the heading and in item 1.4, for "EU" substitute "UK".

(3) In item 1.5.1—

(i) for "the EU" in each place it occurs, substitute "the UK"

(ii) omit point (c).

(4) In items 2.3.1, 3.3 and 3.4.1, for "the EU" in each place it occurs, substitute "the UK".

(5) In item 4.2, for "EU" substitute "UK".".

[11.722]

ANNEX 24
EU GROWTH REGISTRATION DOCUMENT FOR EQUITY SECURITIES

SECTION 1	PERSONS RESPONSIBLE, THIRD PARTY INFORMATION, EXPERTS' REPORTS AND COMPETENT AUTHORITY APPROVAL *This section shall provide information on the persons who are responsible for the content of the EU Growth registration document. The purpose of this section is to provide comfort to investors on the accuracy of the information disclosed in the prospectus. Moreover, this section provides information on the legal basis of the EU Growth registration document and its approval by the competent authority.*
Item 1.1	Identify all persons responsible for the information or any parts of it, given in the registration document with, in the latter case, an indication of such parts. In the case of natural persons, including members of the issuer's administrative, management or supervisory bodies, indicate the name and function of the person; in the case of legal persons indicate the name and registered office.
Item 1.2	A declaration by those responsible for the registration document that to the best of their knowledge, the information contained in the registration document is in accordance with the facts and that the registration document makes no omission likely to affect its import. Where applicable, a declaration by those responsible for certain parts of the registration document that, to the best of their knowledge, the information contained in those parts of the registration document for which they are responsible is in accordance with the facts and that those parts of the registration document make no omission likely to affect their import.
Item 1.3	Where a statement or report attributed to a person as an expert, is included in the registration document, provide the following details for that person: (a) name; (b) business address; (c) qualifications; (d) material interest if any in the issuer. If the statement or report has been produced at the issuer's request, state that such statement or report has been included in the registration document with the consent of the person who has authorised the contents of that part of the registration document for the purpose of the prospectus.
Item 1.4	Where information has been sourced from a third party, provide a confirmation that this information has been accurately reproduced and that as far as the issuer is aware and is able to ascertain from information published by that third party, no facts have been omitted which would render the reproduced information inaccurate or misleading. In addition, identify the source(s) of the information.
Item 1.5	A statement that: (a) the [registration document/prospectus] has been approved by the [name of the competent authority], as competent authority under Regulation (EU) 2017/1129; (b) the [name of the competent authority] only approves this [registration document/prospectus] as meeting the standards of completeness, comprehensibility and consistency imposed by Regulation (EU) 2017/1129; (c) such approval should not be considered as an endorsement of the issuer that is the subject of this [registration document/prospectus]; (d) the [registration document/prospectus] has been drawn up as part of an EU Growth prospectus in accordance with Article 15 of Regulation (EU) 2017/1129.
SECTION 2	STRATEGY, PERFORMANCE AND BUSINESS ENVIRONMENT *The purpose of this section is to disclose information on the identity of the issuer, its business, strategy and objectives. By reading this section, investors should have a clear understanding of the issuer's activities and the main trends affecting its performance, its organisational structure and material investments. Where applicable the issuer shall disclose in this section estimates or forecasts of its future performance. Moreover, issuers with market*

	capitalisation above EUR 200,000,000 shall provide a fair and balanced review of the company's past performance in this section.
Item 2.1	Information about the issuer: (a) the legal and commercial name of the issuer; (b) the place of registration of the issuer, its registration number and legal entity identifier ('LEI'); (c) the date of incorporation and the length of life of the issuer, except where the period is indefinite; (d) the domicile and legal form of the issuer, the legislation under which the issuer operates, its country of incorporation the address, telephone number of its registered office (or principal place of business if different from its registered office) and website of the issuer, if any, with a disclaimer that the information on the website does not form part of the prospectus unless that information is incorporated by reference into the prospectus.
Item 2.1.1	Information on the material changes in the issuer's borrowing and funding structure since the end of the last financial period for which information has been provided in the registration document. Where the registration document contains interim financial information, this information may be provided since the end of the last interim period for which financial information has been included in the registration document;
Item 2.1.2	A description of the expected financing of the issuer's activities
Item 2.2	Business overview
Item 2.2.1	Strategy and objectives A description of the issuer's business strategy and strategic objectives (both financial and non-financial, if any). This description shall take into account the issuer's future challenges and prospects. Where relevant the description shall take into account the regulatory environment in which the issuer operates.
Item 2.2.2	Principal Activities A description of the issuer's principal activities, including: (a) the main categories of products sold and/or services performed; (b) an indication of any significant new products, services or activities that have been introduced since the publication of the latest audited financial statements.
Item 2.2.3	Principal Markets A description of the principal markets in which the issuer competes.
Item 2.3	Organisational structure
Item 2.3.1	If the issuer is part of a group and where not covered elsewhere in the registration document and to the extent necessary for an understanding of the issuer's business as a whole, a diagram of the organisational structure. At the choice of the issuer, such diagram may be replaced, or accompanied, by a brief description of the group and the issuer's position within the group, if this helps to clarify the structure.
Item 2.3.2	If the issuer is dependent upon other entities within the group this must be clearly stated together with an explanation of this dependence.
Item 2.4	Investments
Item 2.4.1	To the extent not covered elsewhere in the registration document a description, (including the amount) of the issuer's material investments from the end of the period covered by the historical financial information included in the prospectus up to the date of the registration document.
Item 2.4.2	A description of any material investments of the issuer's that are in progress or for which firm commitments have already been made, including, if material to the issuer's business, the method of financing (internal or external).
Item 2.5	Operating and financial review (to be provided by equity issuers with market capitalisation above EUR 200,000,000 only when the Management Report presented and prepared in accordance with Articles 19 and 29 of Directive 2013/34/EU is not included in the EU Growth prospectus).
Item 2.5.1	To the extent not covered elsewhere in the registration document and to the extent necessary for an understanding of the issuer's business as a whole, provide the following: (a) a balanced and comprehensive analysis of the development and performance of the issuer's business and of its position consistent with the size and complexity of the business for each year for which historical financial information is required including the causes of material changes; (b) an indication of: (i) the issuer's likely future development; (ii) activities in the field of research and development.

	To the extent necessary for an understanding of the issuer's development, performance or position, the analysis shall include both financial and, where appropriate, non-financial Key Performance Indicators relevant to the particular business, including information relating to environmental and employee matters. This analysis shall, where appropriate, include references to, and additional explanations of, amounts reported in the annual financial statements.
Item 2.6	Trend information
Item 2.6.1	A description of the most significant recent trends in production, sales, inventory, costs and selling prices since the end of the last financial year to the date of the registration document.
Item 2.7	Profit forecasts or estimates
Item 2.7.1	Where an issuer has published a profit forecast or a profit estimate (which is still outstanding and valid) that forecast or estimate shall be included in the registration document. If a profit forecast or profit estimate has been published and is still outstanding, but no longer valid, then provide a statement to that effect and an explanation of why such forecast or estimate is no longer valid. Such an invalid forecast or estimate is not subject to the requirements in items 2.7.2 to 2.7.3.
Item 2.7.2	Where an issuer chooses to include a new profit forecast or a new profit estimate, or where the issuer includes a previously published profit forecast or a previously published profit estimate pursuant to item 2.7.1, the profit forecast or estimate shall be clear and unambiguous and shall contain a statement setting out the principal assumptions upon which the issuer has based its forecast, or estimate. The forecast or estimate shall comply with the following principles: (a) there must be a clear distinction between assumptions about factors which the members of the administrative, management or supervisory bodies can influence and assumptions about factors which are exclusively outside the influence of the members of the administrative, management or supervisory bodies; (b) the assumptions must be reasonable, readily understandable by investors, specific and precise and not relate to the general accuracy of the estimates underlying the forecast; (c) in the case of a forecast, the assumptions shall draw the investor's attention to those uncertain factors which could materially change the outcome of the forecast.
Item 2.7.3	The prospectus shall include a statement that the profit forecast or estimate has been compiled and prepared on a basis which is both: (a) comparable with the annual financial statements; (b) consistent with the issuer's accounting policies.
SECTION 3	RISK FACTORS *The purpose of this section is to describe the main risks faced by the issuer and their impact on the issuer's future performance.*
Item 3.1	A description of the material risks that are specific to the issuer, in a limited number of categories, in a section headed 'Risk Factors'. In each category, the most material risks in the assessment of the issuer or offeror, taking into account the negative impact on the issuer and the probability of their occurrence, shall be set out first. The risks shall be corroborated by the content of the registration document.
SECTION 4	CORPORATE GOVERNANCE *This section shall explain the issuer's administration and the role of the persons involved in the management of the company. It will furthermore provide information on the background of senior management, their remuneration and its potential link to the issuer's performance.*
Item 4.1	Administrative, management, and supervisory bodies and senior management
Item 4.1.1	Names, business addresses and functions within the issuer of the following persons and an indication of the principal activities performed by them outside of the issuer where these are significant with respect to that issuer: (a) members of the administrative, management and/or supervisory bodies; (b) partners with unlimited liability, in the case of a limited partnership with a share capital; (c) any senior manager who is relevant to establishing that the issuer has the appropriate expertise and experience for the management of the issuer's business. Details of the nature of any family relationship between any of the persons referred to in points (a) to (c).
Item 4.1.2	In the case of each member of the administrative, management or supervisory bodies of the issuer and of each person referred to in points (b) and (c) of the item 4.1.1, details of that person's relevant management expertise and experience and the following information: (a) details of any convictions in relation to fraudulent offences for at least the previous

	five years;
	(b) details of any official public incrimination and/or sanctions involving such persons by statutory or regulatory authorities (including designated professional bodies) and whether they have ever been disqualified by a court from acting as a member of the administrative, management or supervisory bodies of an issuer or from acting in the management or conduct of the affairs of any issuer for at least the previous five years. If there is no such information required to be disclosed, a statement to that effect is to be made.
Item 4.2	Remuneration and benefits To the extent not covered elsewhere in the registration document in relation to the last full financial year for those persons referred to in points (a) and (c) of item 4.1.1.
Item 4.2.1	The amount of remuneration paid (including any contingent or deferred compensation), and benefits in kind granted to such persons by the issuer and its subsidiaries for services in all capacities to the issuer and its subsidiaries by any person. That information must be provided on an individual basis unless individual disclosure is not required in the issuer's home country or is not otherwise publicly disclosed by the issuer.
Item 4.2.2	The total amounts set aside or accrued by the issuer or its subsidiaries to provide pension, retirement or similar benefits.
Item 4.3	Shareholdings and stock options With respect to each person referred to in points (a) and (c) of item 4.1.1 provide information as to their share ownership and any stock options in the issuer as of the most recent practicable date.
SECTION 5	FINANCIAL INFORMATION AND KEY PERFORMANCE INDICATORS (KPIs) *This section shall provide historical financial information by disclosing the issuer's financial information and key performance indicators. It shall also provide information on the issuer's dividend policy and where applicable it shall disclose pro forma financial information.*
Item 5.1	Historical financial information
Item 5.1.1	Audited historical financial information covering the latest two financial years (or such shorter period as the issuer has been in operation) and the audit report in respect of each year.
Item 5.1.2	Change of accounting reference date If the issuer has changed its accounting reference date during the period for which historical financial information is required, the audited historical information shall cover at least 24 months or the entire period for which the issuer has been in operation, whichever is shorter.
Item 5.1.3	Accounting Standards The financial information must be prepared according to International Financial Reporting Standards as endorsed in the Union based on Regulation (EC) No 1606/2002. If Regulation (EC) No 1606/2002 is not applicable the financial information must be prepared according to: (a) a Member State's national accounting standards for issuers from the EEA, as required by Directive 2013/34/EU; (b) a third country's national accounting standards equivalent to Regulation (EC) No 1606/2002 for third country issuers. If such third country's national accounting standards are not equivalent to Regulation (EC) No 1606/2002 the financial statements shall be restated in accordance with that Regulation.
Item 5.1.4	Change of accounting framework The last audited historical financial information, containing comparative information for the previous year, must be presented and prepared in a form consistent with the accounting standards framework that will be adopted in the issuer's next published annual financial statements having regard to accounting standards and policies and legislation applicable to such annual financial statements. Changes within the accounting framework applicable to the issuer do not require the audited financial statements to be restated. However, if the issuer intends to adopt a new accounting standards framework in its next published financial statements, at least one complete set of financial statements, (as defined by IAS 1 Presentation of Financial Statements), including comparatives, must be prepared in a form consistent with that which will be adopted in the issuer's next published annual financial statements, having regard to accounting standards and policies and legislation applicable to such annual financial statements.
Item 5.1.5	Where the audited financial information is prepared according to national accounting standards, they must include at least the following: (a) the balance sheet; (b) the income statement;

Part 11 EU & Retained EU Legislation

	(c) the accounting policies and explanatory notes.
Item 5.1.6	Consolidated financial statements If the issuer prepares both stand-alone and consolidated financial statements, include at least the consolidated financial statements in the registration document (a) 18 months from the date of the registration document if the issuer includes audited interim financial statements in the registration document; (b) 16 months from the date of the registration document if the issuer includes interim financial statements in the registration document which is not audited. Where the registration document contains no interim financial information, the balance sheet date of the last year of audited financial statements may not be older than 16 months from the date of the registration document.
Item 5.2	Interim and other financial information
Item 5.2.1	If the issuer has published quarterly or half-yearly financial information since the date of its last audited financial statements, these must be included in the registration document. If the quarterly or half-yearly financial information has been audited or reviewed, the audit or review report must also be included. If the quarterly or half-yearly financial information is not audited or has not been reviewed, state that fact. Interim financial information prepared in accordance with the requirements of the Directive 2013/34/EU or Regulation (EC) No 1606/2002 as the case may be. For issuers not subject to either the Directive 2013/34/EU or Regulation (EC) No 1606/2002, the interim financial information must include comparative statements for the same period in the prior financial year, except that the requirement for comparative balance sheet information may be satisfied by presenting the year's end balance sheet in accordance with the applicable financial reporting framework.
Item 5.3	Auditing of annual financial information
[Item 5.3.1	The historical annual financial information must be independently audited. The audit report shall be prepared in accordance with Directive 2006/43/EC and Regulation (EU) No 537/2014. Where Directive 2006/43/EC and Regulation (EU) No 537/2014 do not apply, the historical financial information must be audited or reported on as to whether or not, for the purposes of the registration document, it gives a true and fair view in accordance with auditing standards applicable in a Member State or an equivalent standard.]
[Item 5.3.1a	Where audit reports on the historical financial information have been refused by the statutory auditors or where they contain qualifications, modifications of opinion, disclaimers or an emphasis of matter, the reason must be given, and such qualifications, modifications, disclaimers or emphasis of matter must be reproduced in full.]
Item 5.3.2	Indication of other information in the registration document, which has been audited by the auditors.
Item 5.3.3	Where financial information in the registration document is not extracted from the issuer's audited financial statements state the source of the information and state that the information is not audited.
Item 5.4	Key Performance Indicators (KPIs)
Item 5.4.1	To the extent not disclosed elsewhere in the registration document and where an issuer has published KPIs, financial and/or operational, or chooses to include such in the registration document, a description of the issuer's KPIs for each financial year for the period covered by the historical financial information shall be included in the registration document. KPIs must be calculated on a comparable basis. Where the KPIs have been audited by the auditors, that fact must be stated.
Item 5.5	Significant change in the issuer's financial position A description of any significant change in the financial position of the group which has occurred since the end of the last financial period for which either audited financial statements or interim financial information have been published, or provide an appropriate negative statement.
Item 5.6	Dividend policy A description of the issuer's policy on dividend distributions and any restrictions thereon. If the issuer has no such policy, include an appropriate negative statement. the amount of the dividend per share for each financial year for the period covered by the annual financial statements adjusted, where the number of shares in the issuer has changed, to make it comparable, if not disclosed in the financial statements.
Item 5.7	Pro forma financial information In the case of a significant gross change, a description of how the transaction might have affected the assets and liabilities and earnings of the issuer, had the transaction been undertaken at the commencement of the period being reported on or at the date reported. This requirement will normally be satisfied by the inclusion of pro forma financial information. This pro forma financial information is to be presented as set out in Annex 20 and

	must include the information indicated therein. Pro forma financial information must be accompanied by a report prepared by independent accountants or auditors.
SECTION 6	SHAREHOLDER AND SECURITY HOLDER INFORMATION *This section shall provide information on the issuer's major shareholders, the existence of potential conflicts of interest between senior management and the issuer, the issuer's share capital as well as information on related party transactions, legal and arbitration proceedings and material contracts.*
Item 6.1	Major shareholders
Item 6.1.1	In so far as known to the issuer, the name of any person who, directly or indirectly, has an interest in the issuer's capital or voting rights which is equal or above 5% of capital or total voting rights, together with the amount of each such person's interest, as at the date of the registration document or, if there are no such persons, an appropriate negative statement.
Item 6.1.2	Whether the issuer's major shareholders have different voting rights, or an appropriate negative statement.
Item 6.1.3	To the extent known to the issuer, state whether the issuer is directly or indirectly owned or controlled and by whom and describe the nature of such control and describe the measures in place to ensure that such control is not abused.
Item 6.1.4	A description of any arrangements, known to the issuer, the operation of which may at a subsequent date result in or prevent a change in control of the issuer.
Item 6.2	Legal and arbitration proceedings
Item 6.2.1	Information on any governmental, legal or arbitration proceedings (including any such proceedings which are pending or threatened of which the issuer is aware), during a period covering at least the previous 12 months which may have, or have had in the recent past significant effects on the issuer and/or group's financial position or profitability, or provide an appropriate negative statement.
Item 6.3	Administrative, Management and Supervisory bodies' and Senior Management's conflicts of interests
Item 6.3.1	Potential conflicts of interests between any duties to the issuer, of the persons referred to in item 4.1.1, and their private interests and or other duties must be clearly stated. In the event that there are no such conflicts, a statement to that effect must be made. Any arrangement or understanding with major shareholders, customers, suppliers or others, pursuant to which any person referred to in item 4.1.1 was selected as a member of the administrative, management or supervisory bodies or member of senior management. Details of any restrictions agreed by the persons referred to in item 4.1.1 on the disposal within a certain period of time of their holdings in the issuer's securities.
Item 6.4	Related party transactions
Item 6.4.1	If the International Financial Reporting Standards adopted in accordance with Regulation (EC) No 1606/2002 do not apply to the issuer, the following information must be disclosed for the period covered by the historical financial information and up to the date of the registration document: (a) the nature and extent of any related party transactions[1] which are, as a single transaction or in their entirety, material to the issuer. Where such related party transactions are not concluded at arm's length provide an explanation of why these transactions were not concluded at arm's length. In the case of outstanding loans including guarantees of any kind indicate the amount outstanding; (b) the amount or the percentage to which related party transactions form part of the turnover of the issuer. If the International Financial Reporting Standards adopted in accordance with Regulation (EC) No 1606/2002 apply to the issuer, the information set out in points (a) and (b) must be disclosed only for transactions that have occurred since the end of the last financial period for which audited financial information have been published.
Item 6.5	Share capital
Item 6.5.1	The following information in items 6.5.2 to 6.5.7 in the annual financial statements as of the date of the most recent balance sheet:
Item 6.5.2	The amount of issued capital, and for each class of share capital: (a) the total of the issuer's authorised share capital; (b) the number of shares issued and fully paid and issued but not fully paid; (c) the par value per share, or that the shares have no par value; and (d) a reconciliation of the number of shares outstanding at the beginning and end of the year. If more than 10% of the capital has been paid for with assets other than cash within the period covered by the annual financial statements, state that fact.

Item 6.5.3	If there are shares not representing capital, state the number and main characteristics of such shares.
Item 6.5.4	The number, book value and face value of shares in the issuer held by or on behalf of the issuer itself or by subsidiaries of the issuer.
Item 6.5.5	The amount of any convertible securities, exchangeable securities or securities with warrants, with an indication of the conditions governing and the procedures for conversion, exchange or subscription.
Item 6.5.6	Information about and terms of any acquisition rights and or obligations over authorised but unissued capital or an undertaking to increase the capital.
Item 6.5.7	Information about any capital of any member of the group which is under option or agreed conditionally or unconditionally to be put under option and details of such options including those persons to whom such options relate.
Item 6.6	Memorandum and Articles of Association
Item 6.6.1	A brief description of any provision of the issuer's articles of association, statutes, charter or bylaws that would have an effect of delaying, deferring or preventing a change in control of the issuer.
Item 6.7	Material contracts
Item 6.7.1	A brief summary of any material contracts, other than contracts entered into in the ordinary course of business, to which the issuer or any member of the group is a party, for the last year immediately preceding publication of the registration document.
SECTION 7	DOCUMENTS AVAILABLE
Item 7.1	A statement that for the term of the registration document the following documents, where applicable, can be inspected: (a) the up to date memorandum and articles of association of the issuer; (b) all reports, letters, and other documents, valuations and statements prepared by any expert at the issuer's request any part of which is included or referred to in the registration document. An indication of the website on which the documents may be inspected.

NOTES

Item 5.3.1 substituted, and item 5.3.1a inserted, by Commission Delegated Regulation 2020/1273/EU, Art 1(21), Annex IX, as from 17 September 2020.

Application of this Annex in relation to the UK: this Annex is amended (as follows), in relation to the UK only, by the Prospectus (Amendment etc) (EU Exit) Regulations 2019, SI 2019/1234, Schedule, para 19, as from IP completion day (as defined in the European Union (Withdrawal Agreement) Act 2020, s 39); for transitional provisions, see regs 74, 75 of the 2019 Regulations at **[12.165]** et seq—

"19.—(1) Annex 24 is amended as follows.

(2) In the heading, and in section 1, for "EU" substitute "UK".

(3) In item 1.5, for "an EU" substitute "a UK".

(4) For item 2.5, substitute—

"Operating and financial review (to be provided by equity issuers with market capitalisation above EUR 200,000,000 only when the directors' report presented and prepared in accordance with section 415 of the Companies Act 2006 is not included in the UK Growth prospectus).";

(5) In item 5.1.3, for the words from "according to International" to the end substitute "in accordance with Article 23a".

(6) In item 5.2.1—

(a) before "Directive" in both places it occurs, insert "the UK law which implemented";

(b) for "Regulation (EC) 1606/2002" in both places it occurs, substitute "section 403 of the Companies Act 2006".

(7) In item 5.3.1—

(a) before "Directive" in both places it occurs, insert "the UK law which implemented";

(b) for "a Member State", substitute "the United Kingdom".

(8) In item 6.4.1, for "the International Financial Reporting Standards adopted in accordance with Regulation (EC) No 1606/2002" in both places it occurs, substitute "UK-adopted international accounting standards".".

Note that the Prospectus (Amendment etc) (EU Exit) Regulations 2019, SI 2019/1234, Schedule, para 19 was amended by the Securities Financing Transactions, Securitisation and Miscellaneous Amendments (EU Exit) Regulations 2020, SI 2020/1385, reg 66(3)(b), with effect from immediately before IP completion day (as defined in the European Union (Withdrawal Agreement) Act 2020, s 39); and the effect of the amendment has been incorporated in the text set out above.

[1] Related party transactions for these purposes are those set out in the standards adopted in accordance with Regulation (EC) No 1606/2002.

[11.723]

ANNEX 25
EU GROWTH REGISTRATION DOCUMENT FOR NON-EQUITY SECURITIES

SECTION 1	PERSONS RESPONSIBLE, THIRD PARTY INFORMATION, EXPERTS' REPORTS AND COMPETENT AUTHORITY APPROVAL *This section shall provide information on the persons who are responsible for the content of the EU Growth registration document. The purpose of this section is to provide comfort to investors on the accuracy of the information disclosed in the prospectus. Moreover, this*

	section provides information on the legal basis of the EU Growth registration document and its approval by the competent authority.
Item 1.1	Identify all persons responsible for the information or any parts of it, given in the registration document with, in the latter case, an indication of such parts. In the case of natural persons, including members of the issuer's administrative, management or supervisory bodies, indicate the name and function of the person; in the case of legal persons indicate the name and registered office.
Item 1.2	A declaration by those responsible for the registration document that to the best of their knowledge, the information contained in the registration document is in accordance with the facts and that the registration document makes no omission likely to affect its import. Where applicable, a declaration by those responsible for certain parts of the registration document that, to the best of their knowledge, the information contained in those parts of the registration document for which they are responsible is in accordance with the facts and that those parts of the registration document make no omission likely to affect their import.
Item 1.3	Where a statement or report attributed to a person as an expert is included in the registration document, provide the following details for that person: (a) name; (b) business address; (c) qualifications; (d) material interest if any in the issuer. If the report has been produced at the issuer's request, state that the report has been included in the registration document with the consent of the person who has authorised the contents of that part of the registration document for the purpose of the prospectus.
Item 1.4	Where information has been sourced from a third party, provide a confirmation that this information has been accurately reproduced and that as far as the issuer is aware and is able to ascertain from information published by that third party, no facts have been omitted which would render the reproduced information inaccurate or misleading. In addition, identify the source(s) of the information.
Item 1.5	A statement that: (a) the [registration document/prospectus] has been approved by the [name of the competent authority], as competent authority under Regulation (EU) 2017/1129; (b) the [name of the competent authority] only approves this [registration document/prospectus]as meeting the standards of completeness, comprehensibility and consistency imposed by Regulation (EU) 2017/1129; (c) such approval should not be considered as an endorsement of the issuer that is the subject of this [registration document/prospectus]; (d) the [registration document/prospectus] has been drawn up as part of an EU Growth prospectus in accordance with Article 15 of Regulation (EU) 2017/1129.
SECTION 2	STRATEGY, PERFORMANCE AND BUSINESS ENVIRONMENT *The purpose of this section is to disclose information on the identity of the issuer, its business, strategy and objectives. By reading this section, investors should have a clear understanding of the issuer's activities and the main trends affecting its performance, its organisational structure and material investments. Where applicable the issuer shall disclose in this section estimates or forecasts of its future performance.*
Item 2.1	Information about the issuer: (a) the legal and commercial name of the issuer; (b) the place of registration of the issuer, its registration number and legal entity identifier ('LEI'); (c) the date of incorporation and the length of life of the issuer, except where the period is indefinite; (d) the domicile and legal form of the issuer, the legislation under which the issuer operates, its country of incorporation, the address, telephone number of its registered office (or principal place of business if different from its registered office) and website of the issuer, if any, with a disclaimer that the information on the website does not form part of the prospectus unless that information is incorporated by reference into the prospectus; (e) any recent events particular to the issuer and which are to a material extent relevant to an evaluation of the issuer's solvency; (f) credit ratings assigned to an issuer at the request or with the cooperation of the issuer in the rating process.
Item 2.1.1	Information on the material changes in the issuer's borrowing and funding structure since the end of the last financial period for which information has been provided in the registration document. Where the registration document contains interim financial information, this information may be provided since the end of the last interim period for which finan-

	cial information has been included in the registration document;
Item 2.1.2	A description of the expected financing of the issuer's activities
Item 2.2	Business overview
Item 2.2.1	Principal Activities A description of the issuer's principal activities, including: (a) the main categories of products sold and/or services performed; (b) an indication of any significant new products, services or activities that have been introduced since the publication of the latest audited financial statements.
Item 2.2.2	Principal Markets A description of the principal markets in which the issuer competes.
Organisational structure	Item 2.3
Item 2.3.1	If the issuer is part of a group and where not covered elsewhere in the registration document and to the extent necessary for an understanding of the issuer's business as a whole, a diagram of the organisational structure. At the choice of the issuer, such diagram may be replaced, or accompanied, by a brief description of the group and the issuer's position within the group, if this helps to clarify the structure.
Item 2.3.2	If the issuer is dependent upon other entities within the group this must be clearly stated together with an explanation of this dependence.
Item 2.4	Trend information
Item 2.4.1	A description of: (a) any material adverse change in the prospects of the issuer since the date of its last published audited financial statements; (b) any significant change in the financial performance of the group since the end of the last financial period for which financial information has been published to the date of the registration document. If points (a) and (b) are not applicable then the issuer should include (an) appropriate negative statement(s) to that effect.
Item 2.5	Profit forecasts or estimates
Item 2.5.1	Where an issuer includes on a voluntary basis a profit forecast or estimate in the prospectus, the profit forecast or estimate shall be clear and unambiguous and shall contain a statement setting out the principal assumptions upon which the issuer has based its forecast, or estimate. The forecast or estimate shall comply with the following principles: (a) there must be a clear distinction between assumptions about factors which the members of the administrative, management or supervisory bodies can influence and assumptions about factors which are exclusively outside the influence of the members of the administrative, management or supervisory bodies; (b) the assumptions must be reasonable, readily understandable by investors, specific and precise and not relate to the general accuracy of the estimates underlying the forecast; (c) in the case of a forecast, the assumptions shall draw the investor's attention to those uncertain factors which could materially change the outcome of the forecast.
Item 2.5.2	The prospectus shall include a statement that the profit forecast or estimate has been compiled and prepared on a basis which is both: (a) comparable with the annual financial statements; (b) consistent with the issuer's accounting policies.
SECTION 3	RISK FACTORS *The purpose of this section is to describe the main risks faced by the issuer and their impact on the issuer's future performance.*
Item 3.1	A description of the material risks that are specific to the issuer and that may affect the issuer's ability to fulfil its obligations under the securities, in a limited number of categories, in a section headed 'Risk Factors'. In each category the most material risks, in the assessment of the issuer or offeror, taking into account the negative impact on the issuer and the probability of their occurrence, shall be set out first. The risks shall be corroborated by the content of the registration document.
SECTION 4	CORPORATE GOVERNANCE *This section shall explain the issuer's administration and the role of the persons involved in the management of the company.*

Item 4.1	Administrative, management, and supervisory bodies and senior management
Item 4.1.1	Names, business addresses and functions within the issuer of the following persons and an indication of the principal activities performed by them outside of that issuer where these are significant with respect to that issuer: (a) members of the administrative, management and/or supervisory bodies; (b) partners with unlimited liability, in the case of a limited partnership with a share capital.
SECTION 5	FINANCIAL INFORMATION AND KEY PERFORMANCE INDICATORS *This section shall provide historical financial information by disclosing the issuer's financial information and KPIs.*
Item 5.1	Historical financial information
Item 5.1.1	Audited historical financial information covering the last financial year (or such shorter period as the issuer has been in operation) and the audit report in respect of that year.
Item 5.1.2	Change of accounting reference date If the issuer has changed its accounting reference date during the period for which historical financial information is required, the audited historical information shall cover at least 12 months or the entire period for which the issuer has been in operation, whichever is shorter.
Item 5.1.3	Accounting Standards The financial information must be prepared according to International Financial Reporting Standards as endorsed in the Union based on Regulation (EC) No 1606/2002. If Regulation (EC) No 1606/2002 is not applicable the financial information must be prepared in accordance with: (a) a Member State's national accounting standards for issuers from the EEA, as required by 2013/34/EU; (b) a third country's national accounting standards equivalent to Regulation (EC) No 1606/2002 for third country issuers. If such third country's national accounting standards are not equivalent to Regulation (EC) No 1606/2002 the financial statements shall be restated in compliance with that Regulation.
Item 5.1.4	Change of accounting framework The last audited historical financial information must be presented and prepared in a form consistent with the accounting standards framework that will be adopted in the issuer's next published annual financial statements. Changes within the issuer's existing accounting framework do not require the audited financial statements to be restated. However, if the issuer intends to adopt a new accounting standards framework in its next published financial statements, the latest year of financial statements must be prepared and audited in line with the new framework.
Item 5.1.5	Where the audited financial information is prepared according to national accounting standards, they must include at least the following: (a) the balance sheet; (b) the income statement; (c) the accounting policies and explanatory notes.
Item 5.1.6	Consolidated financial statements If the issuer prepares both stand-alone and consolidated financial statements, include at least the consolidated financial statements in the registration document
Item 5.1.7	Age of Financial Information The balance sheet of the last year of audited financial information may not be older than 18 months from the date of the registration document.
Item 5.2	Interim and other financial information
Item 5.2.1	If the issuer has published quarterly or half-yearly financial information since the date of its last audited financial statements, these must be included in the registration document. If the quarterly or half-yearly financial information has been audited or reviewed, the audit or review report must also be included. If the quarterly or half-yearly financial information is not audited or has not been reviewed, state that fact. Interim financial information prepared in accordance with the requirements of the Directive 2013/34/EU or Regulation (EC) No 1606/2002 as the case may be. For issuers not subject to either the Directive 2013/34/EU or Regulation (EC) No 1606/2002, the interim financial information must include comparative statements for the same period in the prior financial year, except that the requirement for comparative balance sheet information may be satisfied by presenting the year's end balance sheet in accordance with the applicable financial reporting framework.
Item 5.3	Auditing of historical annual financial information
[Item 5.3.1	The historical annual financial information must be independently audited. The audit report

	shall be prepared in accordance with Directive 2006/43/EC and Regulation (EU) No 537/2014.
	Where Directive 2006/43/EC and Regulation (EU) No 537/2014 do not apply, the historical financial information must be audited or reported on as to whether or not, for the purposes of the registration document, it gives a true and fair view in accordance with auditing standards applicable in a Member State or an equivalent standard.]
[Item 5.3.1a	Where audit reports on the historical financial information have been refused by the statutory auditors or where they contain qualifications, modifications of opinion, disclaimers or an emphasis of matter, the reason must be given, and such qualifications, modifications, disclaimers or emphasis of matter must be reproduced in full.]
Item 5.3.2	Indication of other information in the registration document, which has been audited by the auditors.
Item 5.3.3	Where financial information in the registration document is not extracted from the issuer's audited financial statements state the source of the information and state that the information is not audited.
Item 5.4	Key Performance Indicators ('KPIs')
Item 5.4.1	To the extent not disclosed elsewhere in the registration document and where an issuer has published KPIs, financial and/or operational, or chooses to include such in the registration document a description of the issuer's key performance indicators for each financial year for the period covered by the historical financial information shall be included in the registration document. KPIs must be calculated on a comparable basis. Where the KPIs have been audited by the auditors, that fact must be stated.
Item 5.5	Significant change in the issuer's financial position A description of any significant change in the financial position of the group which has occurred since the end of the last financial period for which either audited financial statements or interim financial information have been published, or provide an appropriate negative statement.
SECTION 6	SHAREHOLDER AND SECURITY HOLDER INFORMATION *This section shall provide information on the issuer's major shareholders, the existence of potential conflicts of interest between senior management and the issuer, the issuer's share capital as well as information on related party transactions, legal and arbitration proceedings and material contracts.*
Item 6.1	Major shareholders
Item 6.1.1	To the extent known to the issuer, state whether the issuer is directly or indirectly owned or controlled and by whom and describe the nature of such control and describe the measures in place to ensure that such control is not abused.
Item 6.1.2	A description of any arrangements, known to the issuer, the operation of which may at a subsequent date result in or prevent a change in control of the issuer.
Item 6.2	Legal and arbitration proceedings
Item 6.2.1	Information on any governmental, legal or arbitration proceedings (including any such proceedings which are pending or threatened of which the issuer is aware), during a period covering at least the previous 12 months which may have, or have had in the recent past significant effects on the issuer and/or group's financial position or profitability, or provide an appropriate negative statement.
Item 6.3	Administrative, Management and Supervisory bodies' and Senior Management's conflicts of interests
Item 6.3.1	Potential conflicts of interests between any duties to the issuer, of the persons referred to in item 4.1.1., and their private interests and or other duties must be clearly stated. In the event that there are no such conflicts of interest, a statement to that effect must be made.
Item 6.4	Material contracts
Item 6.4.1	A brief summary of any material contract that are not entered into in the ordinary course of the issuer's business which could result in any group member being under an obligation or entitlement that is material to the issuer's ability to meet its obligations to security holders in respect of the securities being issued.
SECTION 7	DOCUMENTS AVAILABLE
Item 7.1	A statement that for the term of the registration document the following documents, where applicable, can be inspected: (a) the up to date memorandum and articles of association of the issuer; (b) all reports, letters, and other documents, valuations and statements prepared by any expert at the issuer's request any part of which is included or referred to in the registration document. An indication of the website on which the documents may be inspected.

NOTES

Item 5.3.1 substituted, and item 5.3.1a inserted, by Commission Delegated Regulation 2020/1273/EU, Art 1(22), Annex X, as from 17 September 2020.

Application of this Annex in relation to the UK: this Annex is amended (as follows), in relation to the UK only, by the Prospectus (Amendment etc) (EU Exit) Regulations 2019, SI 2019/1234, Schedule, para 20, as from IP completion day (as defined in the European Union (Withdrawal Agreement) Act 2020, s 39); for transitional provisions, see regs 74, 75 of the 2019 Regulations at **[12.165]** et seq—

"20.—(1) Annex 25 is amended as follows.

(2) In the heading, and in section 1, for "EU" substitute "UK".

(3) In item 1.5, for "an EU" substitute "a UK".

(4) In item 5.1.3, for the words from "according to International" to the end substitute "in accordance with Article 23a".

(5) In item 5.2.1—

(a) before "Directive" in both places it occurs, insert "the UK law which implemented";

(b) for "Regulation (EC) 1606/2002" in both places it occurs, substitute "section 403 of the Companies Act 2006".

(6) In item 5.3.1—

(a) before "Directive" in each place it occurs, insert "the UK law which implemented";

(b) for "a Member State", substitute "the United Kingdom".

Note that the Prospectus (Amendment etc) (EU Exit) Regulations 2019, SI 2019/1234, Schedule, para 20 was amended by the Securities Financing Transactions, Securitisation and Miscellaneous Amendments (EU Exit) Regulations 2020, SI 2020/1385, reg 66(3)(c), with effect from immediately before IP completion day (as defined in the European Union (Withdrawal Agreement) Act 2020, s 39); and the effect of the amendment has been incorporated in the text set out above.

[11.724]

ANNEX 26
EU GROWTH SECURITIES NOTE FOR EQUITY SECURITIES

SECTION 1	PURPOSE, PERSONS RESPONSIBLE, THIRD PARTY INFORMATION, EXPERTS' REPORTS AND COMPETENT AUTHORITY APPROVAL *This section shall provide information on the persons who are responsible for the content of the EU Growth securities note. The purpose of this section is to provide comfort to investors on the accuracy of the information disclosed in the prospectus. In addition, this section provides information on the interests of persons involved in the offer, as well as the reasons of the offer, the use of proceeds and the expenses of the offer. Moreover, the section provides information on the legal basis of the EU Growth securities note and its approval by the competent authority.*
Item 1.1	Identify all persons responsible for the information or any parts of it, given in the securities note with, in the latter case, an indication of such parts. In the case of natural persons, including members of the issuer's administrative, management or supervisory bodies, indicate the name and function of the person; in the case of legal persons indicate the name and registered office.
Item 1.2	A declaration by those responsible for the securities note that to the best of their knowledge, the information contained in the securities note is in accordance with the facts and that the securities note makes no omission likely to affect its import. Where applicable, a declaration by those responsible for certain parts of the securities note that, to the best of their knowledge, the information contained in those parts of the securities note for which they are responsible is in accordance with the facts and that those parts of the securities note make no omission likely to affect their import.
Item 1.3	Where a statement or report attributed to a person as an expert is included in the securities note, provide the following details for that person: (a) name; (b) business address; (c) qualifications; (d) material interest if any in the issuer. If the statement or report has been produced at the issuer's request, state that such statement or report has been included in the securities note with the consent of the person who has authorised the contents of that part of the securities note for the purpose of the prospectus.
Item 1.4	Where information has been sourced from a third party, provide a confirmation that this information has been accurately reproduced and that as far as the issuer is aware and is able to ascertain from information published by that third party, no facts have been omitted which would render the reproduced information inaccurate or misleading. In addition, identify the source(s) of the information.
Item 1.5	A statement that: (a) this [securities note/prospectus] has been approved by the [insert name of competent authority], as competent authority under Regulation (EU) 2017/1129; (b) the [name of competent authority] only approves this [securities note/prospectus] as meeting the standards of completeness, comprehensibility and consistency imposed by Regulation 2017/EU/1129; (c) such approval should not be considered as an endorsement of the quality of the securities that are the subject of this [securities note/prospectus]; (d) investors should make their own assessment as to the suitability of investing in the securities; and

	(e) that the [securities note/prospectus] has been drawn up as part of an EU Growth prospectus in accordance with Article 15 of Regulation (EU) 2017/1129.
Item 1.6	Interest of natural and legal persons involved in the issue/offer A description of any interest, including a conflict of interest that is material to the issue/offer, detailing the persons involved and the nature of the interest.
Item 1.7	Reasons for the offer, use of proceeds and expenses of the issue/offer
Item 1.7.1	Reasons for the offer and, where applicable, the estimated net amount of the proceeds broken into each principal intended use and presented in order of priority of such uses. If the issuer is aware that the anticipated proceeds will not be sufficient to fund all the proposed uses, then state the amount and sources of other funds needed. Details must also be given with regard to the use of the proceeds, in particular when they are being used to acquire assets, other than in the ordinary course of business, to finance announced acquisitions of other business, or to discharge, reduce or retire indebtedness. The total net proceeds and an estimate of the total expenses of the issue/offer.
Item 1.7.2	An explanation about how the proceeds from this offer align with the business strategy and strategic objectives described in the registration document.
Item 1.8	Additional information
Item 1.8.1	If advisors connected with an issue are referred to in the securities note, a statement of the capacity in which the advisors have acted.
Item 1.8.2	An indication of other information in the securities note which has been audited or reviewed by statutory auditors and where auditors have produced a report. Reproduction of the report or, with permission of the competent authority, a summary of the report.
[SECTION 2	WORKING CAPITAL STATEMENT AND STATEMENT OF CAPITALISATION AND INDEBTEDNESS *The disclosure under this section provides information on the issuer's working capital requirements and its capitalisation and indebtedness.*
Item 2.1	Working capital Statement Statement by the issuer that, in its opinion, the working capital is sufficient for the issuer's present requirements or, if not, how it proposes to provide the additional working capital needed.
Item 2.2	Capitalisation and indebtedness
Issuers with market capitalisation above EUR 200,000,000 only	A statement of capitalisation and indebtedness (distinguishing between guaranteed and unguaranteed, secured and unsecured indebtedness) as of a date no earlier than 90 days prior to the date of the document. The term 'indebtedness' also includes indirect and contingent indebtedness. In the case of material changes in the capitalisation and indebtedness position of the issuer within the 90 day period, additional information shall be given through the presentation of a narrative description of such changes or through the updating of those figures.]
SECTION 3	RISK FACTORS *The purpose of this section is to describe the main risks which are specific to the securities of the issuer.*
Item 3.1	A description of the material risks that are specific to the securities being offered in a limited number of categories, in a section headed 'Risk Factors'. In each category the most material risks, in the assessment of the issuer or offeror taking into account their impact on the issuer and the securities and the probability of their occurrence, shall be set out first. The risks shall be corroborated by the content of the securities note.
SECTION 4	TERMS AND CONDITIONS OF THE SECURITIES *The purpose of this section is to set out the terms and conditions of the securities and provides a detailed description of their characteristics.*
Item 4.1	Information concerning the securities to be offered.
Item 4.1.1	A description of the type and the class of the securities being offered, including the international security identification number ('ISIN').
Item 4.1.2	Legislation under which the securities have been created.
Item 4.1.3	An indication whether the securities are in registered form or bearer form and whether the securities are in certificated form or book-entry form. In the case of book-entry form, the name and address of the entity in charge of keeping the records.
Item 4.1.4	Currency of the securities issue.
Item 4.1.5	A description of the rights attached to the securities, including any limitations of those rights, and procedure for the exercise of those rights: (a) dividend rights: (i) fixed date(s) on which the entitlement arises;

	(ii) time limit after which entitlement to dividend lapses and an indication of the person in whose favour the lapse operates; (iii) dividend restrictions and procedures for non-resident holders; (iv) rate of dividend or method of its calculation, periodicity and cumulative or non-cumulative nature of payments; (b) voting rights; (c) pre-emption rights in offers for subscription of securities of the same class; (d) right to share in the issuer's profits; (e) right to share in any surplus in the event of liquidation; (f) redemption provisions; (g) conversion provisions.
Item 4.1.6	In the case of new issues a statement of the resolutions, authorisations and approvals by virtue of which the securities have been or will be created and/or issued.
Item 4.1.7	The issue date (for non-equity securities) or in the case of new issues the expected issue date of the securities.
Item 4.1.8	A description of any restrictions on the transferability of the securities.
Item 4.1.9	A warning that the tax legislation of the investor's Member State and of the issuer's country of incorporation may have an impact on the income received from the securities. Information on the taxation treatment of the securities where the proposed investment attracts a tax regime specific to that type of investment.
Item 4.1.10	If different from the issuer, the identity and contact details of the offeror of the securities and/or the person asking for admission to trading, including the legal entity identifier ('LEI') where the offeror has legal personality.
Item 4.1.11	(a) Statement on the existence of national legislation or rules on takeovers applicable to the issuer and the possibility for frustrating measures if any; (b) a brief description of the shareholders' rights and obligations in case of mandatory takeover bid, and/or squeeze-out or sell-out rules in relation to the securities; (c) an indication of public takeover bids by third parties in respect of the issuer's equity, which have occurred during the last financial year and the current financial year. The price or exchange terms attaching to such offers and the outcome thereof must also be stated.
Item 4.1.12	Where applicable, the potential impact on the investment in the event of resolution under Directive 2014/59/EU.
[Item 4.2	In the case of issuance of shares with warrants, the information referred to in Article 20(2).]
SECTION 5	DETAILS OF THE OFFER/ADMISSION TO TRADING *The purpose of this section is to set out the specific information on the offer of the securities, the plan for their distribution and allotment, an indication of their pricing. Moreover, it presents information on the placing of the securities, any underwriting agreements and arrangements relating to admission to trading. It also sets out information on the persons selling the securities and dilution to existing shareholders.*
Item 5.1	Terms and conditions of the offer of securities to the public. Conditions, offer statistics, expected timetable and action required to apply for the offer.
Item 5.1.1	Conditions to which the offer is subject.
Item 5.1.2	Total amount of the issue/offer distinguishing the securities offered for sale and those offered for subscription; if the amount is not fixed, an indication of the maximum amount of securities to be offered (if available) and a description of the arrangements and the time period for announcing to the public the definitive amount of the offer. Where the maximum amount of securities cannot be provided in the prospectus, the prospectus shall specify that acceptances of the purchase or subscription of securities may be withdrawn for not less than two working days after the amount of securities to be offered to the public has been filed.
Item 5.1.3	The time period, including any possible amendments, during which the offer will be open and description of the application process.
Item 5.1.4	An indication of when, and under which circumstances, the offer may be revoked or suspended and whether revocation can occur after dealing has begun.
Item 5.1.5	A description of any possibility to reduce subscriptions and the manner for refunding amounts paid in excess by applicants.
Item 5.1.6	Details of the minimum and/or maximum amount of application (whether in number of securities or aggregate amount to invest).
Item 5.1.7	An indication of the period during which an application may be withdrawn, provided that investors are allowed to withdraw their subscription.
Item 5.1.8	Method and time limits for paying up the securities and for delivery of the securities.
Item 5.1.9	A full description of the manner and date in which results of the offer are to be made public.

Item 5.1.10	The procedure for the exercise of any right of pre-emption, the negotiability of subscription rights and the treatment of subscription rights not exercised.
Item 5.2	Plan of distribution and allotment
Item 5.2.1	The various categories of potential investors to which the securities are offered. If the offer is being made simultaneously in the markets of two or more countries and if a tranche has been or is being reserved for certain of these, indicate any such tranche.
Item 5.2.2	To the extent known to the issuer, an indication of whether major shareholders or members of the issuer's management, supervisory or administrative bodies intended to subscribe in the offer, or whether any person intends to subscribe for more than five per cent of the offer.
Item 5.2.3	Pre-allotment Disclosure: (a) the division into tranches of the offer including the institutional, retail and issuer's employee tranches and any other tranches; (b) the conditions under which the claw-back may be used, the maximum size of such claw back and any applicable minimum percentages for individual tranches; (c) the allotment method or methods to be used for the retail and issuer's employee tranche in the event of an over-subscription of these tranches; (d) a description of any pre-determined preferential treatment to be accorded to certain classes of investors or certain affinity groups (including friends and family programmes) in the allotment, the percentage of the offer reserved for such preferential treatment and the criteria for inclusion in such classes or groups; (e) whether the treatment of subscriptions or bids to subscribe in the allotment may be determined on the basis of which firm they are made through or by; (f) a target minimum individual allotment if any within the retail tranche; (g) the conditions for the closing of the offer as well as the date on which the offer may be closed at the earliest; (h) whether or not multiple subscriptions are admitted, and where they are not, how any multiple subscriptions will be handled.
Item 5.3	Process for notifying applicants of the amount allotted and an indication whether dealing may begin before notification is made.
Item 5.4	Pricing
Item 5.4.1	An indication of the price at which the securities will be offered and the amount of any expenses and taxes charged to the subscriber or purchaser.
Item 5.4.2	If the price is not known, then pursuant to Article 17 of Regulation (EU) 2017/1129 indicate either: (a) the maximum price as far as it is available; (b) the valuation methods and criteria, and/or conditions, in accordance with which the final offer price has been or will be determined and an explanation of any valuation methods used. Where neither point (a) nor (b) can be provided in the securities note, the securities note shall specify that acceptances of the purchase or subscription of securities may be withdrawn up to two working days after the final offer price of securities to be offered to the public has been filed.
Item 5.4.3	Process for the disclosure of the offer price. If the issuer's equity holders have pre-emptive purchase rights and this right is restricted or withdrawn, an indication of the basis for the issue price if the issue is for cash, together with the reasons for and beneficiaries of such restriction or withdrawal. Where there is or could be a material disparity between the public offer price and the effective cash cost to members of the administrative, management or supervisory bodies or senior management, or affiliated persons, of securities acquired by them in transactions during the past year, or which they have the right to acquire, include a comparison of the public contribution in the proposed public offer and the effective cash contributions of such persons.
Item 5.5	Placing and Underwriting
Item 5.5.1	Name and address of the coordinator(s) of the global offer and of single parts of the offer and, to the extent known to the issuer or to the offeror, of the placers in the various countries where the offer takes place.
Item 5.5.2	Name and address of any paying agents and depository agents in each country.
Item 5.5.3	Name and address of the entities agreeing to underwrite the issue on a firm commitment basis, and name and address of the entities agreeing to place the issue without a firm commitment or under 'best efforts' arrangements. Indication of the material features of the agreements, including the quotas. Where not all of the issue is underwritten, a statement of the portion not covered. Indication of the overall amount of the underwriting commission and of the placing commission.
Item 5.5.4	When the underwriting agreement has been or will be reached.
Item 5.6	Admission to trading and dealing arrangements
Item 5.6.1	An indication as to whether the securities offered are or will be the object of an application for admission to trading on an SME growth Market or an MTF, with a view to their distribution in

	an SME Growth Market or an MTF with an indication of the markets in question. This circumstance must be set out, without creating the impression that the admission to trading will necessarily be approved. If known, the earliest dates on which the securities will be admitted to trading.
Item 5.6.2	All the SME growth markets or MTFs on which, to the knowledge of the issuer, securities of the same class of the securities to be offered tor admitted to trading are already admitted to trading.
Item 5.6.3	If simultaneously or almost simultaneously with the creation of the securities for which admission on an SME growth Market or MTF is being sought or which are offered to the public, securities of the same class are subscribed for or placed privately or if securities of other classes are created for public or private placing, give details of the nature of such operations and of the number and characteristics of the securities to which they relate.
Item 5.6.4	In case of an admission to trading on an SME growth market or an MTF, details of the entities which have a firm commitment to act as intermediaries in secondary trading, providing liquidity through bid and offer rates and description of the main terms of their commitment.
Item 5.6.5	Details of stabilisation in line with items 5.6.5.1 to 5.6.5.6 in the case of an admission to trading on an SME growth market or an MTF, where an issuer or a selling shareholder has granted an over-allotment option or it is otherwise proposed that price stabilising activities may be entered into in connection with an offer:
Item 5.6.5.1	The fact that stabilisation may be undertaken, that there is no assurance that it will be undertaken and that it may be stopped at any time;
Item 5.6.5.2	The fact that stabilisation transactions aim at supporting the market price of the securities during the stabilisation period;
Item 5.6.5.3	The beginning and the end of the period during which stabilisation may occur;
Item 5.6.5.4	The identity of the stabilisation manager for each relevant jurisdiction unless this is not known at the time of publication;
Item 5.6.5.5	The fact that stabilisation transactions may result in a market price that is higher than would otherwise prevail; and
Item 5.6.5.6	The place where the stabilisation may be undertaken including, where relevant, the name of the trading venue(s).
Item 5.6.6	Over-allotment and 'green shoe' In the case of an admission to trading on an SME growth market or an MTF: (a) the existence and size of any over-allotment facility and/or 'green shoe'; (b) the existence period of the over-allotment facility and/or 'green shoe'; and (c) any conditions for the use of the over-allotment facility or exercise of the 'green shoe'.
Item 5.7	Selling securities holders
Item 5.7.1	Name and business address of the person or entity offering to sell the securities, the nature of any position office or other material relationship that the selling persons has had within the past three years with the issuer or any of its predecessors or affiliates.
Item 5.7.2	The number and class of securities being offered by each of the selling security holders.
Item 5.7.3	In relation to lock-up agreements, provide details of the following: (a) the parties involved; (b) the content and exceptions of the agreement; (c) an indication of the period of the lock up.
Item 5.8	Dilution
Item 5.8.1	A comparison of participation in share capital and voting rights for existing shareholders before and after the capital increase resulting from the public offer, with the assumption that existing shareholders do not subscribe for the new shares.
Item 5.8.2	Where existing shareholders will be diluted regardless of whether they subscribe for their entitlement, because a part of the relevant share issue is reserved only for certain investors (e.g. an institutional placing coupled with an offer to shareholders), an indication of the dilution existing shareholders will experience should also be presented on the basis that they do take up their entitlement (in addition to the situation in item 5.8.1 where they do not).
[SECTION 6	UNDERLYING SHARE INFORMATION (WHERE APPLICABLE)
Item 6.1	Where applicable, the information referred to in Annex 18.
SECTION 7	CONSENT INFORMATION (WHERE APPLICABLE)
	Where the issuer or the person responsible for drawing up a prospectus consents to its use as referred to in the second subparagraph of Article 5(1) of Regulation (EU) 2017/1129, the following additional information:
	(a) the information referred to in sections 1 and 2A of Annex 22 to this Regulation where the consent is provided to one or more specified financial intermediaries;
	(b) the information referred to in sections 1 and 2B of Annex 22 to this Regulation where the consent is given to all financial intermediaries.]

NOTES

Section 2 was substituted, item 4.2 was inserted, and Sections 6 and 7 were added, by Commission Delegated Regulation 2020/1273/EU, Art 1(23), Annex XI, as from 17 September 2020.

Application of this Annex in relation to the UK: this Annex is amended (as follows), in relation to the UK only, by the Prospectus (Amendment etc) (EU Exit) Regulations 2019, SI 2019/1234, Schedule, para 21, as from IP completion day (as defined in the European Union (Withdrawal Agreement) Act 2020, s 39); for transitional provisions, see regs 74, 75 of the 2019 Regulations at **[12.165]** et seq—

"21.—(1) Annex 26 is amended as follows.
(2) In the heading and section 1, for "EU" substitute "UK".
(3) In item 1.5, for "an EU" substitute "a UK".
(4) *In item 4.1.12 before "Directive" substitute "the UK law which implemented".*".

This Annex is also amended by the Financial Services Act 2021 (Prudential Regulation of Credit Institutions and Investment Firms) (Consequential Amendments and Miscellaneous Provisions) Regulations 2022, SI 2022/838, reg 23, as from 17 August 2022. It is believed that this amendment aims to correct an error contained in the italicised text set out immediately above. Regulation 23 provides that for the entry in column 2 of the table relating to Item 4.1.12, substitute—

"Where applicable, the potential impact on the investment in the event of resolution under the UK law which implemented Directive 2014/59/EU.".

[11.725]

ANNEX 27
EU GROWTH SECURITIES NOTE FOR NON-EQUITY SECURITIES

SECTION 1	PURPOSE, PERSONS RESPONSIBLE, THIRD PARTY INFORMATION, EXPERTS' REPORTS AND COMPETENT AUTHORITY APPROVAL *This section shall provide information on the persons who are responsible for the content of the EU Growth securities note. The purpose of this section is to provide comfort to investors on the accuracy of the information disclosed in the prospectus. In addition, this section provides information on the interests of persons involved in the offer, as well as the reasons of the offer, the use of proceeds and the expenses of the offer. Moreover, the section provides information on the legal basis of the EU Growth securities note and its approval by the competent authority.*	
Item 1.1	Identify all persons responsible for the information or any parts of it, given in the securities note with, in the latter case, an indication of such parts. In the case of natural persons, including members of the issuer's administrative, management or supervisory bodies, indicate the name and function of the person; in the case of legal persons indicate the name and registered office.	Category A
Item 1.2	A declaration by those responsible for the securities note that to the best of their knowledge, the information contained in the securities note is in accordance with the facts and that the securities note makes no omission likely to affect its import. Where applicable, a declaration by those responsible for certain parts of the securities note that, to the best of their knowledge, the information contained in those parts of the securities note for which they are responsible is in accordance with the facts and that those parts of the securities note make no omission likely to affect their import.	Category A
Item 1.3	Where a statement or report attributed to a person as an expert is included in the securities note, provide the following in relation to that person: (a) name; (b) business address; (c) qualifications; (d) material interest if any in the issuer. If the statement or report has been produced at the issuer's request, state that such statement or report has been included in the securities note with the consent of the person who has authorised the contents of that part of the securities note for the purpose of the prospectus.	Category A
Item 1.4	Where information has been sourced from a third party, provide a confirmation that this information has been accurately reproduced and that as far as the issuer is aware and is able to ascertain from information published by that third party, no facts have been omitted which would render the reproduced information inaccurate or misleading. In addition, identify the source(s) of the information.	Category C
Item 1.5	A statement that: (a) this [securities note/prospectus] has been approved by the [insert name of the competent authority], as competent authority under Regulation (EU) 2017/1129; (b) /the [name of the competent authority] only approves this [se-	Category A

	curities note/prospectus] as meeting the standards of completeness, comprehensibility and consistency imposed by Regulation 2017/EU/1129; (c) such approval should not be considered as an endorsement of the quality of the securities that are the subject of this [securities note/prospectus]; (d) investors should make their own assessment as to the suitability of investing in the securities; and (e) that the [securities note/prospectus] has been drawn up as an EU Growth prospectus in accordance with Article 15 of Regulation (EU) 2017/1129.	
Item 1.6	Interest of natural and legal persons involved in the issue/offer A description of any interest, including a conflict of interest that is material to the issue/offer, detailing the persons involved and the nature of the interest.	Category C
Item 1.7	Reasons for the offer, use of proceeds and expenses of the issue/offer Reasons for the offer to the public or for the admission to trading. Where applicable, disclosure of the estimated total expenses of the issue/offer and the estimated net amount of the proceeds. These expenses and proceeds shall be broken into each principal intended use and presented in order of priority of such uses. If the issuer is aware that the anticipated proceeds will not be sufficient to fund all the proposed uses, then state the amount and sources of other funds needed.	Category C
Item 1.8	Additional information	
Item 1.8.1	If advisors connected with an issue are referred to in the securities note, a statement of the capacity in which the advisors have acted.	Category C
Item 1.8.2	An indication of other information in the securities note which has been audited or reviewed by statutory auditors and where auditors have produced a report. Reproduction of the report or, with permission of the competent authority, a summary of the report.	Category A
Item 1.8.3	Credit ratings assigned to the securities at the request or with the cooperation of the issuer in the rating process. A brief explanation of the meaning of the ratings if this has previously been published by the rating provider.	Category C
Item 1.8.4	Where the summary is substituted in part with the information set out in points (c) to (i) of paragraph 3 of Article 8 of Regulation (EU) No 1286/2014, all such information to the extent it is not already disclosed elsewhere in the securities note	Category C
SECTION 2	RISK FACTORS *The purpose of this section is to describe the main risks which are specific to the securities of the issuer.*	
Item 2.1	A description of the material risks that are specific to the securities being offered in a limited number of categories, in a section headed 'Risk Factors'. Risks to be disclosed shall include: (a) those resulting from the level of subordination of a security and the impact on the expected size or timing of payments to holders of the securities under bankruptcy, or any other similar procedure, including, where relevant, the insolvency of a credit institution or its resolution or restructuring in accordance with Directive 2014/59/EU; (b) in cases where the securities are guaranteed, the specific and material risks related to the guarantor to the extent they are relevant to its ability to fulfil its commitment under the guarantee. In each category the most material risks, in the assessment of the issuer or offeror taking into account their impact on the issuer and the securities and the probability of their occurrence, shall be set out first. The risks shall be corroborated by the content of the securities note.	Category A
SECTION 3	TERMS AND CONDITIONS OF THE SECURITIES	
Item 3.1	Information concerning the securities to be offered	
Item 3.1.1	A description of the type and the class of the securities being offered.	Category A

	The international security identification number ('ISIN') of the securities being offered.	Category C
Item 3.1.2	Legislation under which the securities have been created.	Category A
Item 3.1.3	An indication whether the securities are in registered form or bearer form and whether the securities are in certificated form or book-entry form.	Category A
	In the case of book-entry form, the name and address of the entity in charge of keeping the records.	Category C
Item 3.1.4	Currency of the securities issue.	Category C
Item 3.1.5	The relative seniority of the securities in the issuer's capital structure in the event of insolvency, including, where applicable, information on the level of subordination of the securities and the potential impact on the investment in the event of a resolution under Directive 2014/59/EU.	Category A
Item 3.1.6	A description of the rights attached to the securities, including any limitations of those rights, and procedure for the exercise of those rights.	Category B
Item 3.1.7	(a) The nominal interest rate;	Category C
	(b) the provisions relating to interest payable;	Category B
	(c) the date from which interest becomes payable;	Category C
	(d) the due dates for interest;	Category C
	(e) the time limit on the validity of claims to interest and repayment of principal.	Category B
	Where the rate is not fixed:	
	(a) a statement setting out the type of underlying;	Category A
	(b) a description of the underlying on which the rate is based;	Category C
	(c) of the method used to relate the rate with the underlying;	Category B
	(d) an indication where information about the past and the further performance of the underlying and its volatility can be obtained by electronic means and whether or not it can be obtained free of charge;	Category C
	(e) a description of any market disruption or settlement disruption events that affect the underlying;	Category B
	(f) any adjustment rules with relation to events concerning the underlying;	Category B
	(g) the name of the calculation agent;	Category C
	(h) if the security has a derivative component in the interest payment, a clear and comprehensive explanation to help investors understand how the value of their investment is affected by the value of the underlying instrument(s), especially under the circumstances when the risks are most evident.	Category B
Item 3.1.8	(a) Maturity date.	Category C
	(b) Details of the arrangements for the amortisation of the loan, including the repayment procedures. Where advance amortisation is contemplated, on the initiative of the issuer or of the holder, it shall be described, stipulating amortisation terms and conditions	Category B
Item 3.1.9	(a) An indication of yield.	Category C
	(b) A description of the method whereby that yield is calculated in summary form.	Category B
Item 3.1.10	Representation of non-equity security holders including an identification of the organisation representing the investors and provisions applying to such representation. Indication of the website where the public may have free access to the contracts relating to these forms of representation.	Category B
Item 3.1.11	In the case of new issues, a statement of the resolutions, authorisations and approvals by virtue of which the securities have been or will be created and/or issued.	Category C
Item 3.1.12	The issue date or in the case of new issues, the expected issue date of the securities.	Category C
Item 3.1.13	A description of any restrictions on the transferability of the securities.	Category A
Item 3.1.14	A warning that the tax legislation of the investor's Member State and of the issuer's country of incorporation may have an impact on	Category A

	the income received from the securities. Information on the taxation treatment of the securities where the proposed investment attracts a tax regime specific to that type of investment.	
Item 3.1.15	If different from the issuer, the identity and contact details of the offeror of the securities and/or the person asking for admission to trading, including the legal entity identifier ('LEI') where the offeror has legal personality.	Category C
Item 3.1.16	Where applicable, the potential impact on the investment in the event of resolution under Directive 2014/59/EU.	
. . .	. . .	
[Item 3.2	Information on derivative securities	
	In the case of issuance of derivative securities, the following information:	
	(a) for derivative securities referred to in Article 20(1), the information referred to in that paragraph;	
	(b) for derivative securities referred to in Article 20(2), the information referred to in that paragraph;	
	(c) for derivative securities referred to in Article 20(3), the information referred to in that paragraph.]	
SECTION 4	DETAILS OF THE OFFER/ADMISSION TO TRADING *The purpose of this section is to set out the specific information on the offer of the securities, the plan for their distribution and allotment, an indication of their pricing. Moreover, it presents information on the placing of the securities, any underwriting agreements and arrangements relating to admission to trading. It also sets out information on the persons selling the securities and dilution to existing shareholders.*	
Item 4.1	Terms and conditions of the offer of securities to the public (Conditions, offer statistics, expected timetable and action required to apply for the offer)	
Item 4.1.1	Conditions to which the offer is subject	Category C
Item 4.1.2	Total amount of the securities offered to the public. If the amount is not fixed, an indication of the maximum amount of the securities to be offered (if available) and a description of the arrangements and the time period for announcing to the public the definitive amount of the offer. Where the maximum amount of securities to be offered cannot be provided in the prospectus, the prospectus shall specify that acceptances of the purchase of subscription of securities may be withdrawn for not less than two working days after the amount of securities to be offered to the public has been filed.	Category C
Item 4.1.3	The time period, including any possible amendments, during which the offer will be open and description of the application process.	Category C
Item 4.1.4	A description of any possibility to reduce subscriptions and the manner for refunding amounts paid in excess by applicants.	Category C
Item 4.1.5	Details of the minimum and/or maximum amount of application (whether in number of securities or aggregate amount to invest).	Category C
Item 4.1.6	Method and time limits for paying up the securities and for delivery of the securities.	Category C
Item 4.1.7	A full description of the manner and date in which results of the offer are to be made public.	Category C
Item 4.1.8	The procedure for the exercise of any right of pre-emption, the negotiability of subscription rights and the treatment of subscription rights not exercised.	Category C
Item 4.2	Plan of distribution and allotment	
Item 4.2.1	The various categories of potential investors to which the securities are offered. If the offer is being made simultaneously in the markets of two or more countries and if a tranche has been or is being reserved for certain of these, indicate any such tranche.	Category C
Item 4.3	Process for notifying applicants of the amount allotted and an indication whether dealing may begin before notification is made.	Category C
Item 4.4	Pricing	
Item 4.4.1	An indication of the expected price at which the securities will be offered;	Category C

Item 4.4.2	In the alternative to item 4.4.1, a description of the method of for determining the price, pursuant to Article 17 of Regulation (EU) 2017/1129 and the process for its disclosure.	Category B
Item 4.4.3	Indicate the amount of any expenses and taxes charged to the subscriber or purchaser. Where the issuer is subject to Regulation (EU) No 1286/2014 and/or Directive 2014/65/EU, and to the extent that they are known, include those expenses contained in the price.	Category C
Item 4.5	Placing and underwriting	
Item 4.5.1	Name and address of the coordinator(s) of the global offer and of single parts of the offer and, to the extent known to the issuer or to the offeror, of the placers in the various countries where the offer takes place.	Category C
Item 4.5.2	Name and address of any paying agents and depository agents in each country.	Category C
Item 4.5.3	Name and address of the entities agreeing to underwrite the issue on a firm commitment basis, and name and address of the entities agreeing to place the issue without a firm commitment or under 'best efforts' arrangements. Indication of the material features of the agreements, including the quotas. Where not all of the issue is underwritten, a statement of the portion not covered. Indication of the overall amount of the underwriting commission and of the placing commission.	Category C
Item 4.5.4	When the underwriting agreement has been or will be reached.	Category C
Item 4.6	Admission to trading and dealing arrangements	
Item 4.6.1	An indication as to whether the securities offered are or will be the object of an application for admission to trading on an SME growth Market or an MTF, with a view to their distribution in an SME Growth Market or an MTF with an indication of the markets in question. This circumstance must be set out, without creating the impression that the admission to trading will necessarily be approved. If known, the earliest dates on which the securities will be admitted to trading.	Category B
Item 4.6.2	All the SME growth Markets or MTFs on which, to the knowledge of the issuer, securities of the same class of the securities to be offered tor admitted to trading are already admitted to trading.	Category C
Item 4.6.3	In the case of an admission to trading on an SME growth market or an MTF, details of the entities which have a firm commitment to act as intermediaries in secondary trading, providing liquidity through bid and offer rates and description of the main terms of their commitment.	Category C
Item 4.6.4	The issue price of the securities	Category C
SECTION 5	GUARANTOR INFORMATION (IF APPLICABLE)	
Item 5.1	In the case of a guarantee attached to the securities, the information that is required in Annex 21.	
[SECTION 6	UNDERLYING SHARE INFORMATION (WHERE APPLICABLE)	
Item 6.1	(a) Where applicable, the information referred to in items 2.1 and 2.2 of Annex 26 in respect of the issuer of the underlying share.	
	(b) Where applicable, the information referred to in Annex 18.	
SECTION 7	CONSENT INFORMATION (WHERE APPLICABLE)	
Item 7.1	Where the issuer or the person responsible for drawing up a prospectus consents to its use as referred to in the second subparagraph of Article 5(1) of Regulation (EU) 2017/1129, the following additional information:	
	(a) the information referred to in sections 1 and 2A of Annex 22 to this Regulation where the consent is provided to one or more specified financial intermediaries;	

NOTES

Item 3.1.17 is repealed, item 3.2 is inserted, and Sections 6 and 7 are added, by Commission Delegated Regulation 2020/1273/EU, Art 1(24), Annex XII, as from 17 September 2020.

Application of this Annex in relation to the UK: this Annex is amended (as follows), in relation to the UK only, by the Prospectus (Amendment etc) (EU Exit) Regulations 2019, SI 2019/1234, Schedule, para 22, as from IP completion day (as defined in the European Union (Withdrawal Agreement) Act 2020, s 39); for transitional provisions, see regs 74, 75 of the 2019 Regulations at **[12.165]** et seq—

"22.—(1) Annex 27 is amended as follows.

(2) In the heading and section 1, for "EU" substitute "UK".

(3) In item 1.5, for "an EU" substitute "a UK".

(4) In item 2.1, before "Directive" insert "the UK law which implemented".
(5) In item 3.1.5, before "Directive" insert "the UK law which implemented".
(6) In item 3.1.14, for "Member State" substitute "home country".
(7) In item 3.1.16. before "Directive" insert "the UK law which implemented".
(9) In item 4.4.3, before "Directive" insert "the UK law which implemented".".

Note that the Prospectus (Amendment etc) (EU Exit) Regulations 2019, SI 2019/1234, Schedule, para 22 was amended by the Financial Services (Miscellaneous Amendments) (EU Exit) Regulations 2020, SI 2020/628, reg 17(1), (6), as from immediately before IP completion day; and the effect of that amendment has been incorporated in the text as set out above. Note also that the same amendment (ie, the omission of para (8)) is also made by the Securities Financing Transactions, Securitisation and Miscellaneous Amendments (EU Exit) Regulations 2020, SI 2020/1385, reg 66(3)(d), with effect from immediately before IP completion day.

[11.726]

ANNEX 28
LIST OF ADDITIONAL INFORMATION IN FINAL TERMS

1. Example(s) relating to complex derivative securities to explain how the value of the investment is affected by the value of the underlying and the nature of those securities.
2. Additional provisions, not required by the relevant securities note annex, which relate to the underlying.
3. Country(ies) where the offer((s) to the public takes place.
4. Country(ies) where admission to trading on the regulated market(s) is being sought.
5. Country(ies) where the relevant base prospectus has been notified.
6. ECB eligibility.
7. Series number.
8. Tranche number.

NOTES

Application of this Annex in relation to the UK: this Annex is amended (as follows), in relation to the UK only, by the Prospectus (Amendment etc) (EU Exit) Regulations 2019, SI 2019/1234, Schedule, para 23, as from IP completion day (as defined in the European Union (Withdrawal Agreement) Act 2020, s 39); for transitional provisions, see regs 74, 75 of the 2019 Regulations at **[12.165]** et seq—

"23. In Annex 28, omit items 3, 4 and 5.".

[11.727]

ANNEX 29
LIST OF SPECIALIST ISSUERS

(a) Property companies;
(b) Mineral companies;
(c) Investment companies;
(d) Scientific research based companies;
(e) Start-up companies;
(f) Shipping companies.

DIRECTIVE OF THE EUROPEAN PARLIAMENT AND OF THE COUNCIL

(2019/1023/EU)

of 20 June 2019

on preventive restructuring frameworks, on discharge of debt and disqualifications, and on measures to increase the efficiency of procedures concerning restructuring, insolvency and discharge of debt, and amending Directive (EU) 2017/1132 (Directive on restructuring and insolvency)

(Text with EEA relevance)

[11.728]

NOTES

Date of publication in OJ: OJ L166, 21.6.2019, p 26.

Editorial note (legal status of EU Directives in the UK): note that EU Directives are not "direct EU legislation" within the meaning of the European Union (Withdrawal) Act 2018, s 3 at **[12.5]** and, accordingly, do not apply to the UK. As to the status of EU-derived domestic legislation after IP completion day (11pm on 31 December 2020), see s 2 of the 2018 Act at **[12.4]**. As to the UK implementation of this Directive, see the note below.

UK Implementation: the transposition of this Directive is provided for by Article 33 *post*. Member States were required to implement this Directive into national law by 17 July 2021, subject to a possible one-year extension. No specific implementation measures were enacted in the UK prior to the UK leaving the European Union on 31 December 2020. However, the UK restructuring regime already included many of the elements required by this Directive, and this has now been further supplemented by the enactment of the Corporate Insolvency and Governance Act 2020 (at **[9.533]**), which introduced wide-ranging reforms that are broadly consistent with the provisions of this Directive. See, in particular, Part 26A of the Companies Act 2006, as inserted by Sch 9 to the Corporate Insolvency and Governance Act 2020.

THE EUROPEAN PARLIAMENT AND THE COUNCIL OF THE EUROPEAN UNION,

Having regard to the Treaty on the Functioning of the European Union, and in particular Articles 53 and 114 thereof,

Having regard to the proposal from the European Commission,

After transmission of the draft legislative act to the national parliaments,

Having regard to the opinion of the European Economic and Social Committee,[1]

Having regard to the opinion of the Committee of the Regions,[2]

Acting in accordance with the ordinary legislative procedure,[3]

Whereas:

(1) The objective of this Directive is to contribute to the proper functioning of the internal market and remove obstacles to the exercise of fundamental freedoms, such as the free movement of capital and freedom of establishment, which result from differences between national laws and procedures concerning preventive restructuring, insolvency, discharge of debt, and disqualifications. Without affecting workers' fundamental rights and freedoms, this Directive aims to remove such obstacles by ensuring that: viable enterprises and entrepreneurs that are in financial difficulties have access to effective national preventive restructuring frameworks which enable them to continue operating; honest insolvent or over-indebted entrepreneurs can benefit from a full discharge of debt after a reasonable period of time, thereby allowing them a second chance; and that the effectiveness of procedures concerning restructuring, insolvency and discharge of debt is improved, in particular with a view to shortening their length.

(2) Restructuring should enable debtors in financial difficulties to continue business, in whole or in part, by changing the composition, conditions or structure of their assets and their liabilities or any other part of their capital structure — including by sales of assets or parts of the business or, where so provided under national law, the business as a whole — as well as by carrying out operational changes. Unless otherwise specifically provided for by national law, operational changes, such as the termination or amendment of contracts or the sale or other disposal of assets, should comply with the general requirements that are provided for under national law for such measures, in particular civil law and labour law rules. Any debt-to-equity swaps should also comply with safeguards provided for by national law. Preventive restructuring frameworks should, above all, enable debtors to restructure effectively at an early stage and to avoid insolvency, thus limiting the unnecessary liquidation of viable enterprises. Those frameworks should help to prevent job losses and the loss of know-how and skills, and maximise the total value to creditors — in comparison to what they would receive in the event of the liquidation of the enterprise's assets or in the event of the next-best-alternative scenario in the absence of a plan — as well as to owners and the economy as a whole.

(3) Preventive restructuring frameworks should also prevent the build-up of non-performing loans. The availability of effective preventive restructuring frameworks would ensure that action is taken before enterprises default on their loans, thereby helping to reduce the risk of loans becoming non-performing in cyclical downturns and mitigating the adverse impact on the financial sector. A significant percentage of businesses and jobs could be saved if preventive frameworks existed in all the Member States in which businesses' places of establishment, assets or creditors are situated. In restructuring frameworks the rights of all parties involved, including workers, should be protected in a balanced manner. At the same time, non-viable businesses with no prospect of survival should be liquidated as quickly as possible. Where a debtor in financial difficulties is not economically viable or cannot be readily restored to economic viability, restructuring efforts could result in the acceleration and accumulation of losses to the detriment of creditors, workers and other stakeholders, as well as the economy as a whole.

(4) There are differences between Member States as regards the range of the procedures available to debtors in financial difficulties in order to restructure their business. Some Member States have a limited range of procedures that allow the restructuring of businesses only at a relatively late stage, in the context of insolvency procedures. In other Member States, restructuring is possible at an earlier stage but the procedures available are not as effective as they could be, or they are very formal, in particular because they limit the use of out-of-court arrangements. Preventive solutions are a growing trend in insolvency law. The trend favours approaches that, unlike the traditional approach of liquidating a business in financial difficulties, have the aim of restoring it to a healthy state or, at least, saving those of its units which are still economically viable. That approach, among other benefits to the economy, often helps to maintain jobs or reduce job losses. Moreover, the degree of involvement of judicial or administrative authorities, or the persons appointed by them, varies from no involvement or minimal involvement in some Member States to full involvement in others. Similarly, national rules giving entrepreneurs a second chance, in particular by granting them discharge from the debts they have incurred in the course of their business, vary between Member States in respect of the length of the discharge period and the conditions for granting such a discharge.

(5) In many Member States, it takes more than three years for entrepreneurs who are insolvent but honest to be discharged from their debts and make a fresh start. Inefficient discharge of debt and disqualification frameworks result in entrepreneurs having to relocate to other jurisdictions in order to benefit from a fresh start in a reasonable period of time, at considerable additional cost to both their creditors and the entrepreneurs themselves. Long disqualification orders, which often accompany a procedure leading to discharge of debt, create obstacles to the freedom to take up and pursue a self-employed, entrepreneurial activity.

(6) The excessive length of procedures concerning restructuring, insolvency and discharge of debt in several Member States is an important factor triggering low recovery rates and deterring investors from carrying out business in jurisdictions where procedures risk taking too long and being unduly costly.

(7) Differences between Member States in relation to procedures concerning restructuring, insolvency and discharge of debt translate into additional costs for investors when assessing the risk of debtors getting into financial difficulties in one or more Member States, or of investing in viable businesses in financial difficulties, as well as additional costs of restructuring enterprises that have establishments, creditors or assets in other Member States. This is most notably the case with restructuring international groups of companies. Investors mention uncertainty about insolvency rules or the risk of lengthy or complex insolvency procedures in another Member State as being one of the main reasons for not investing or not entering into a business relationship with a counterpart outside the Member State where they are based. That uncertainty acts as a disincentive which obstructs the freedom of establishment of undertakings and the promotion of entrepreneurship and harms the proper functioning of the internal market. Micro,

small and medium-sized enterprises ('SMEs') in particular do not, for the most part, have the resources needed to assess risks related to cross-border activities.

(8) The differences among Member States in procedures concerning restructuring, insolvency and discharge of debt lead to uneven conditions for access to credit and to uneven recovery rates in the Member States. A higher degree of harmonisation in the field of restructuring, insolvency, discharge of debt and disqualifications is thus indispensable for a well-functioning internal market in general and for a working Capital Markets Union in particular, as well as for the resilience of European economies, including for the preservation and creation of jobs.

(9) The additional cost of risk-assessment and of cross-border enforcement of claims for creditors of over-indebted entrepreneurs who relocate to another Member State in order to obtain a discharge of debt in a much shorter period of time should also be reduced. The additional costs for entrepreneurs stemming from the need to relocate to another Member State in order to benefit from a discharge of debt should also be reduced. Furthermore, the obstacles stemming from long disqualification orders linked to an entrepreneur's insolvency or over-indebtedness inhibit entrepreneurship.

(10) Any restructuring operation, in particular one of major size which generates a significant impact, should be based on a dialogue with the stakeholders. That dialogue should cover the choice of the measures envisaged in relation to the objectives of the restructuring operation, as well as alternative options, and there should be appropriate involvement of employees' representatives as provided for in Union and national law.

(11) The obstacles to the exercise of fundamental freedoms are not limited to purely cross-border situations. An increasingly interconnected internal market, in which goods, services, capital and workers circulate freely, and which has an ever-stronger digital dimension, means that very few enterprises are purely national if all relevant elements are considered, such as their client base, supply chain, scope of activities, investor and capital base. Even purely national insolvencies can have an impact on the functioning of the internal market through the so-called domino effect of insolvencies, whereby a debtor's insolvency may trigger further insolvencies in the supply chain.

(12) Regulation (EU) 2015/848 of the European Parliament and of the Council[4] deals with issues of jurisdiction, recognition and enforcement, applicable law and cooperation in cross-border insolvency proceedings as well as with the interconnection of insolvency registers. Its scope covers preventive procedures which promote the rescue of economically viable debtors as well as discharge procedures for entrepreneurs and other natural persons. However, that Regulation does not tackle the disparities between national laws regulating those procedures. Furthermore, an instrument limited only to cross-border insolvencies would not remove all obstacles to free movement, nor would it be feasible for investors to determine in advance the cross-border or domestic nature of the potential financial difficulties of the debtor in the future. There is therefore a need to go beyond matters of judicial cooperation and to establish substantive minimum standards for preventive restructuring procedures as well as for procedures leading to a discharge of debt for entrepreneurs.

(13) This Directive should be without prejudice to the scope of Regulation (EU) 2015/848. It aims to be fully compatible with, and complementary to, that Regulation, by requiring Member States to put in place preventive restructuring procedures which comply with certain minimum principles of effectiveness. It does not change the approach taken in that Regulation of allowing Member States to maintain or introduce procedures which do not fulfil the condition of publicity for notification under Annex A to that Regulation. Although this Directive does not require that procedures within its scope fulfil all the conditions for notification under that Annex, it aims to facilitate the cross-border recognition of those procedures and the recognition and enforceability of judgments.

(14) The advantage of the application of Regulation (EU) 2015/848 is that it provides for safeguards against abusive relocation of the debtor's centre of main interests during cross-border insolvency proceedings. Certain restrictions should also apply to procedures not covered by that Regulation.

(15) It is necessary to lower the costs of restructuring for both debtors and creditors. Therefore, the differences between Member States which hamper the early restructuring of viable debtors in financial difficulties and the possibility of a discharge of debt for honest entrepreneurs should be reduced. Reducing such differences should bring greater transparency, legal certainty and predictability across the Union. It should maximise the returns to all types of creditors and investors and encourage cross-border investment. Greater coherence of restructuring and insolvency procedures should also facilitate the restructuring of groups of companies irrespective of where the members of the group are located in the Union.

(16) Removing the barriers to effective preventive restructuring of viable debtors in financial difficulties contributes to minimising job losses and losses of value for creditors in the supply chain, preserves know-how and skills and hence benefits the wider economy. Facilitating a discharge of debt for entrepreneurs would help to avoid their exclusion from the labour market and enable them to restart entrepreneurial activities, drawing lessons from past experience. Moreover, reducing the length of restructuring procedures would result in higher recovery rates for creditors as the passing of time would normally only result in a further loss of value of the debtor or the debtor's business. Finally, efficient preventive restructuring, insolvency and discharge procedures would enable a better assessment of the risks involved in lending and borrowing decisions and facilitate the adjustment for insolvent or over-indebted debtors, minimising the economic and social costs involved in their deleveraging process. This Directive should allow Member States flexibility to apply common principles while respecting national legal systems. Member States should be able to maintain or introduce in their national legal systems preventive restructuring frameworks other than those provided for by this Directive.

(17) Enterprises, and in particular SMEs, which represent 99% of all businesses in the Union, should benefit from a more coherent approach at Union level. SMEs are more likely to be liquidated than restructured, since they have to bear costs that are disproportionately higher than those faced by larger enterprises. SMEs, especially when facing financial difficulties, often do not have the necessary resources to cope with high restructuring costs and to take advantage of the more efficient restructuring procedures available only in some Member States. In order to help such debtors restructure at low cost, comprehensive check-lists for restructuring plans, adapted to the needs and specificities of SMEs, should be developed at national level and made available online. In addition, early warning tools should be put in place to warn debtors of the urgent need to act, taking into account the limited resources of SMEs for hiring experts.

(18) When defining SMEs, Member States could give due consideration to Directive 2013/34/EU of the European

Parliament and of the Council[5] or the Commission Recommendation of 6 May 2003 concerning the definition of micro, small and medium-sized enterprises.[6]

(19) It is appropriate to exclude from the scope of this Directive debtors which are insurance and re-insurance undertakings as defined in points (1) and (4) of Article 13 of Directive 2009/138/EC of the European Parliament and of the Council,[7] credit institutions as defined in point (1) of Article 4(1) of Regulation (EU) No 575/2013 of the European Parliament and of the Council,[8] investment firms and collective investment undertakings as defined in points (2) and (7) of Article 4(1) of Regulation (EU) No 575/2013, central counterparties as defined in point (1) of Article 2 of Regulation (EU) No 648/2012 of the European Parliament and of the Council,[9] central securities depositories as defined in point (1) of Article 2(1) of Regulation (EU) No 909/2014 of the European Parliament and of the Council[10] and other financial institutions and entities listed in the first subparagraph of Article 1(1) of Directive 2014/59/EU of the European Parliament and of the Council.[11] Such debtors are subject to special arrangements and the national supervisory and resolution authorities have wide-ranging powers of intervention in relation to them. Member States should be able to exclude other financial entities providing financial services which are subject to comparable arrangements and powers of intervention.

(20) For similar considerations, it is also appropriate to exclude from the scope of this Directive public bodies under national law. Member States should also be able to limit the access to preventive restructuring frameworks to legal persons, since the financial difficulties of entrepreneurs may be efficiently addressed not only by means of preventive restructuring procedures but also by means of procedures which lead to a discharge of debt or by means of informal restructurings based on contractual agreements. Member States with different legal systems, where the same type of entity has a different legal status in those legal systems, should be able to apply one uniform regime to such entities. A preventive restructuring framework laid down pursuant to this Directive should not affect claims and entitlements against a debtor that arise from occupational pension systems if those claims and entitlements accrued during a period prior to the restructuring.

(21) Consumer over-indebtedness is a matter of great economic and social concern and is closely related to the reduction of debt overhang. Furthermore, it is often not possible to draw a clear distinction between the debts incurred by entrepreneurs in the course of their trade, business, craft or profession and those incurred outside those activities. Entrepreneurs would not effectively benefit from a second chance if they had to go through separate procedures, with different access conditions and discharge periods, to discharge their business debts and other debts incurred outside their business. For those reasons, although this Directive does not include binding rules on consumer over-indebtedness, it would be advisable for Member States to apply also to consumers, at the earliest opportunity, the provisions of this Directive concerning discharge of debt.

(22) The earlier a debtor can detect its financial difficulties and can take appropriate action, the higher the probability of avoiding an impending insolvency or, in the case of a business the viability of which is permanently impaired, the more orderly and efficient the liquidation process would be. Clear, up-to-date, concise and user-friendly information on the available preventive restructuring procedures as well as one or more early warning tools should therefore be put in place to incentivise debtors that start to experience financial difficulties to take early action. Early warning tools which take the form of alert mechanisms that indicate when the debtor has not made certain types of payments could be triggered by, for example, non-payment of taxes or social security contributions. Such tools could be developed either by Member States or by private entities, provided that the objective is met. Member States should make information about early warning tools available online, for example on a dedicated website or webpage. Member States should be able to adapt the early warning tools depending on the size of the enterprise and to lay down specific provisions on early warning tools for large-sized enterprises and groups that take into account their peculiarities. This Directive should not impose any liability on Member States for potential damage incurred through restructuring procedures which are triggered by such early warning tools.

(23) In an effort to increase the support of employees and their representatives, Member States should ensure that employees' representatives are given access to relevant and up-to-date information regarding the availability of early warning tools and it should also be possible for them to provide support to employees' representatives in assessing the economic situation of the debtor.

(24) A restructuring framework should be available to debtors, including legal entities and, where so provided under national law, natural persons and groups of companies, to enable them to address their financial difficulties at an early stage, when it appears likely that their insolvency can be prevented and the viability of the business can be ensured. A restructuring framework should be available before a debtor becomes insolvent under national law, namely before the debtor fulfils the conditions under national law for entering collective insolvency proceedings, which normally entail a total divestment of the debtor and the appointment of a liquidator. In order to avoid restructuring frameworks being misused, the financial difficulties of the debtor should indicate a likelihood of insolvency and the restructuring plan should be capable of preventing the insolvency of the debtor and ensuring the viability of the business.

(25) Member States should be able to determine whether claims that fall due or that come into existence after an application to open a preventive restructuring procedure has been submitted or after the procedure has been opened are included in the preventive restructuring measures or the stay of individual enforcement actions. Member States should be able to decide whether the stay of individual enforcement actions has an effect on the interest due on claims.

(26) Member States should be able to introduce a viability test as a condition for access to the preventive restructuring procedure provided for by this Directive. Such a test should be carried out without detriment to the debtor's assets, which could take the form of, among other things, the granting of an interim stay or the carrying out without undue delay of the test. However, the absence of detriment should not prevent Member States from requiring debtors to prove their viability at their own cost.

(27) The fact that Member States can limit access to a restructuring framework with regard to debtors that have been sentenced for serious breaches of accounting or book-keeping obligations should not prevent Member States from also limiting the access of debtors to preventive restructuring frameworks where their books and records are incomplete or deficient to a degree that makes it impossible to ascertain the business and financial situation of the debtors.

(28) Member States should be able to extend the scope of preventive restructuring frameworks provided for by this Directive to situations in which debtors face non-financial difficulties, provided that such difficulties give rise to

a real and serious threat to a debtor's actual or future ability to pay its debts as they fall due. The time frame relevant for the determination of such threat may extend to a period of several months, or even longer, in order to account for cases in which the debtor is faced with non-financial difficulties threatening the status of its business as a going concern and, in the medium term, its liquidity. This may be the case, for example, where the debtor has lost a contract which is of key importance to it.

(29) To promote efficiency and reduce delays and costs, national preventive restructuring frameworks should include flexible procedures. Where this Directive is implemented by means of more than one procedure within a restructuring framework, the debtor should have access to all rights and safeguards provided for by this Directive with the aim of achieving an effective restructuring. Except in the event of mandatory involvement of judicial or administrative authorities as provided for under this Directive, Member States should be able to limit the involvement of such authorities to situations in which it is necessary and proportionate, while taking into consideration, among other things, the aim of safeguarding the rights and interests of debtors and of affected parties, as well as the aim of reducing delays and the cost of the procedures. Where creditors or employees' representatives are allowed to initiate a restructuring procedure under national law and where the debtor is an SME, Member States should require the agreement of the debtor as a precondition for the initiation of the procedure, and should also be able to extend that requirement to debtors which are large enterprises.

(30) To avoid unnecessary costs, to reflect the early nature of preventive restructuring and to encourage debtors to apply for preventive restructuring at an early stage of their financial difficulties, they should, in principle, be left in control of their assets and the day-to-day operation of their business. The appointment of a practitioner in the field of restructuring, to supervise the activity of a debtor or to partially take over control of a debtor's daily operations, should not be mandatory in every case, but made on a case-by-case basis depending on the circumstances of the case or on the debtor's specific needs. Nevertheless, Member States should be able to determine that the appointment of a practitioner in the field of restructuring is always necessary in certain circumstances, such as where: the debtor benefits from a general stay of individual enforcement actions; the restructuring plan needs to be confirmed by means of a cross-class cram-down; the restructuring plan includes measures affecting the rights of workers; or the debtor or its management have acted in a criminal, fraudulent, or detrimental manner in business relations.

(31) For the purpose of assisting the parties with negotiating and drafting a restructuring plan, Member States should provide for the mandatory appointment of a practitioner in the field of restructuring where: a judicial or administrative authority grants the debtor a general stay of individual enforcement actions, provided that in such case a practitioner is needed to safeguard the interests of the parties; the restructuring plan needs to be confirmed by a judicial or administrative authority by means of a cross-class cram-down; it was requested by the debtor; or it is requested by a majority of creditors provided that the creditors cover the costs and fees of the practitioner.

(32) A debtor should be able to benefit from a temporary stay of individual enforcement actions, whether granted by a judicial or administrative authority or by operation of law, with the aim of supporting the negotiations on a restructuring plan, in order to be able to continue operating or at least to preserve the value of its estate during the negotiations. Where so provided by national law, it should also be possible for the stay to apply for the benefit of third-party security providers, including guarantors and collateral givers. However, Member States should be able to provide that judicial or administrative authorities can refuse to grant a stay of individual enforcement actions where such a stay is not necessary or where it would not fulfil the objective of supporting the negotiations. Grounds for refusal might include a lack of support by the required majorities of creditors or, where so provided under national law, the debtor's actual inability to pay debts as they fall due.

(33) In order to facilitate and accelerate the course of proceedings, Member States should be able to establish, on a rebuttable basis, presumptions for the presence of grounds for refusal of the stay, where, for example, the debtor shows conduct that is typical of a debtor that is unable to pay debts as they fall due — such as a substantial default vis-à-vis workers or tax or social security agencies — or where a financial crime has been committed by the debtor or the current management of an enterprise which gives reason to believe that a majority of creditors would not support the start of the negotiations.

(34) A stay of individual enforcement actions could be general, in that it affects all creditors, or it could apply only to some individual creditors or categories of creditors. Member States should be able to exclude certain claims or categories of claims from the scope of the stay, in well-defined circumstances, such as claims which are secured by assets the removal of which would not jeopardise the restructuring of the business or claims of creditors in respect of which a stay would cause unfair prejudice, such as by way of an uncompensated loss or depreciation of collateral.

(35) In order to provide for a fair balance between the rights of the debtor and those of creditors, a stay of individual enforcement actions should apply for a maximum period of up to four months. Complex restructurings may, however, require more time. Member States should be able to provide that, in such cases, extensions of the initial period of the stay can be granted by the judicial or administrative authority. Where a judicial or administrative authority does not take a decision on the extension of a stay before it lapses, the stay should cease to have effect upon expiry of the stay period. In the interest of legal certainty, the total period of the stay should be limited to 12 months. Member States should be able to provide for an indefinite stay where the debtor becomes insolvent under national law. Member States should be able to decide whether a short interim stay pending a judicial or administrative authority's decision on access to the preventive restructuring framework is subject to the time limits under this Directive.

(36) To ensure that creditors do not suffer unnecessary detriment, Member States should provide that judicial or administrative authorities can lift a stay of individual enforcement actions if it no longer fulfils the objective of supporting negotiations, for example if it becomes apparent that the required majority of creditors does not support the continuation of the negotiations. The stay should also be lifted if creditors are unfairly prejudiced by it, where Member States provide for such a possibility. Member States should be allowed to limit the possibility to lift the stay to situations where creditors have not had the opportunity to be heard before it came into force or before it was extended. Member States should also be allowed to provide for a minimum period during which the stay cannot be lifted. In establishing whether there is unfair prejudice to creditors, judicial or administrative authorities should be able to take into account whether the stay would preserve the overall value of the estate, and whether the debtor acts in bad

faith or with the intention of causing prejudice or generally acts against the legitimate expectations of the general body of creditors.

(37) This Directive does not cover provisions on compensation or guarantees for creditors of which the collateral is likely to decrease in value during the stay. A single creditor or a class of creditors would be unfairly prejudiced by the stay if, for example, their claims would be made substantially worse-off as a result of the stay than if the stay did not apply, or if the creditor is put more at a disadvantage than other creditors in a similar position. Member States should be able to provide that, whenever unfair prejudice is established in respect of one or more creditors or one or more classes of creditors, the stay can be lifted in respect of those creditors or classes of creditors or in respect of all creditors. Member States should be able to decide who is entitled to request the lifting of the stay.

(38) A stay of individual enforcement actions should also result in the suspension of a debtor's obligation to file for, or the opening at a creditor's request of, an insolvency procedure which could end in liquidation of the debtor. Such insolvency procedures should, in addition to those limited by law to having as the only possible outcome the liquidation of the debtor, also include procedures that could lead to a restructuring of the debtor. The suspension of the opening of an insolvency procedure at the request of creditors should apply not only where Member States provide for a general stay of individual enforcement actions covering all creditors, but also where Member States provide for the option of a stay of individual enforcement actions covering only a limited number of creditors. Nevertheless, Member States should be able to provide that insolvency proceedings can be opened at the request of public authorities which are not acting in a creditor capacity, but in the general interest, such as a public prosecutor.

(39) This Directive should not prevent debtors from paying, in the ordinary course of business, claims of unaffected creditors, and claims of affected creditors that arise during the stay of individual enforcement actions. To ensure that creditors with claims that came into existence before the opening of a restructuring procedure or a stay of individual enforcement actions do not put pressure on the debtor to pay those claims, which otherwise would be reduced through the implementation of the restructuring plan, Member States should be able to provide for the suspension of the obligation on the debtor with respect to payment of those claims.

(40) When a debtor enters an insolvency procedure, some suppliers can have contractual rights, provided for in so-called ipso facto clauses, entitling them to terminate the supply contract solely on account of the insolvency, even if the debtor has duly met its obligations. Ipso facto clauses could also be triggered when a debtor applies for preventive restructuring measures. Where such clauses are invoked when the debtor is merely negotiating a restructuring plan or requesting a stay of individual enforcement actions or invoked in connection with any event connected with the stay, early termination can have a negative impact on the debtor's business and the successful rescue of the business. Therefore, in such cases, it is necessary to provide that creditors are not allowed to invoke ipso facto clauses which make reference to negotiations on a restructuring plan or a stay or any similar event connected to the stay.

(41) Early termination can endanger the ability of a business to continue operating during restructuring negotiations, especially when contracts for essential supplies such as gas, electricity, water, telecommunication and card payment services are concerned. Member States should provide that creditors to which a stay of individual enforcement actions applies, and whose claims came into existence prior to the stay and have not been paid by a debtor, are not allowed to withhold performance of, terminate, accelerate or, in any other way, modify essential executory contracts during the stay period, provided that the debtor complies with its obligations under such contracts which fall due during the stay. Executory contracts are, for example, lease and licence agreements, long-term supply contracts and franchise agreements.

(42) This Directive lays down minimum standards for the content of a restructuring plan. However, Member States should be able to require additional explanations in the restructuring plan, concerning for example the criteria according to which creditors have been grouped, which may be relevant in cases where a debt is only partially secured. Member States should not be obliged to require an expert opinion regarding the value of assets which need to be indicated in the plan.

(43) Creditors affected by a restructuring plan, including workers, and, where allowed under national law, equity-holders, should have a right to vote on the adoption of a restructuring plan. Member States should be able to provide for limited exceptions to this rule. Parties unaffected by the restructuring plan should have no voting rights in relation to the plan, nor should their support be required for the approval of any plan. The concept of 'affected parties' should only include workers in their capacity as creditors. Therefore, if Member States decide to exempt the claims of workers from the preventive restructuring framework, workers should not be considered as affected parties. The vote on the adoption of a restructuring plan could take the form of a formal voting process or of a consultation and agreement with the required majority of affected parties. However, where the vote takes the form of an agreement with the requisite majority, affected parties which were not involved in the agreement could nevertheless be offered the opportunity to join the restructuring plan.

(44) To ensure that rights which are substantially similar are treated equitably and that restructuring plans can be adopted without unfairly prejudicing the rights of affected parties, affected parties should be treated in separate classes which correspond to the class formation criteria under national law. 'Class formation' means the grouping of affected parties for the purposes of adopting a plan in such a way as to reflect their rights and the seniority of their claims and interests. As a minimum, secured and unsecured creditors should always be treated in separate classes. Member States should, however, be able to require that more than two classes of creditors are formed, including different classes of unsecured or secured creditors and classes of creditors with subordinated claims. Member States should also be able to treat types of creditors that lack a sufficient commonality of interest, such as tax or social security authorities, in separate classes. It should be possible for Member States to provide that secured claims can be divided into secured and unsecured parts based on collateral valuation. It should also be possible for Member States to lay down specific rules supporting class formation where non-diversified or otherwise especially vulnerable creditors, such as workers or small suppliers, would benefit from such class formation.

(45) Member States should be able to provide that debtors that are SMEs, can, on account of their relatively simple capital structure, be exempted from the obligation to treat affected parties in separate classes. In cases where SMEs have opted to create only one voting class and that class votes against the plan, it should be possible for debtors to submit another plan, in line with the general principles of this Directive.

(46) Member States should in any case ensure that adequate treatment is given in their national law to matters of

particular importance for class formation purposes, such as claims from connected parties, and that their national law contains rules that deal with contingent claims and contested claims. Member States should be allowed to regulate how contested claims are to be handled for the purposes of allocating voting rights. The judicial or administrative authority should examine class formation, including the selection of creditors affected by the plan, when a restructuring plan is submitted for confirmation. However, Member States should be able to provide that such authority can also examine class formation at an earlier stage should the proposer of the plan seek validation or guidance in advance.

(47) Requisite majorities should be established by national law to ensure that a minority of affected parties in each class cannot obstruct the adoption of a restructuring plan which does not unfairly reduce their rights and interests. Without a majority rule binding dissenting secured creditors, early restructuring would not be possible in many cases, for example where a financial restructuring is needed but the business is otherwise viable. To ensure that parties have a say on the adoption of restructuring plans proportionate to the stakes they have in the business, the required majority should be based on the amount of the creditors' claims or equity holders' interests in any given class. Member States should, in addition, be able to require a majority in the number of affected parties in each class. Member States should be able to lay down rules in relation to affected parties with a right to vote which do not exercise that right in a correct manner or are not represented, such as rules allowing those affected parties to be taken into account for a participation threshold or for the calculation of a majority. Member States should also be able to provide for a participation threshold for the vote.

(48) Confirmation of a restructuring plan by a judicial or administrative authority is necessary to ensure that the reduction of the rights of creditors or interests of equity holders is proportionate to the benefits of the restructuring and that they have access to an effective remedy. Confirmation is particularly necessary where: there are dissenting affected parties; the restructuring plan contains provisions on new financing; or the plan involves a loss of more than 25% of the work force. Member States should, however, be able to provide that confirmation by a judicial or administrative authority is necessary also in other cases. A confirmation of a plan which involves the loss of more than 25% of the work force should only be necessary where national law allows preventive restructuring frameworks to provide for measures that have a direct effect on employment contracts.

(49) Member States should ensure that a judicial or administrative authority is able to reject a plan where it has been established that it reduces the rights of dissenting creditors or equity holders either to a level below what they could reasonably expect to receive in the event of the liquidation of the debtor's business, whether by piecemeal liquidation or by a sale as a going concern, depending on the particular circumstances of each debtor, or to a level below what they could reasonably expect in the event of the next-best-alternative scenario where the restructuring plan is not confirmed. However, where the plan is confirmed through a cross-class cram-down, reference should be made to the protection mechanism used in such scenario. Where Member States opt to carry out a valuation of the debtor as a going concern, the going-concern value should take into account the debtor's business in the longer term, as opposed to the liquidation value. The going-concern value is, as a rule, higher than the liquidation value because it is based on the assumption that the business continues its activity with the minimum of disruption, has the confidence of financial creditors, shareholders and clients, continues to generate revenues, and limits the impact on workers.

(50) While compliance with the best-interests-of-creditors test should be examined by a judicial or administrative authority only if the restructuring plan is challenged on that ground in order to avoid a valuation being made in every case, Member States should be able to provide that other conditions for confirmation can be examined *ex officio*. Member States should be able to add other conditions which need to be complied with in order to confirm a restructuring plan, such as whether equity holders are adequately protected. Judicial or administrative authorities should be able to refuse to confirm restructuring plans which have no reasonable prospect of preventing the insolvency of the debtor or ensuring the viability of the business. However, Member States should not be required to ensure that such assessment is made *ex officio*.

(51) Notification to all affected parties should be one of the conditions for confirmation of a restructuring plan. Member States should be able to define the form of the notification, to identify the time when it is to be made, as well as to lay down provisions for the treatment of unknown claims as regards notification. They should also be able to provide that non-affected parties have to be informed about the restructuring plan.

(52) Satisfying the 'best-interest-of-creditors' test should be considered to mean that no dissenting creditor is worse off under a restructuring plan than it would be either in the case of liquidation, whether piecemeal liquidation or sale of the business as a going concern, or in the event of the next-best-alternative scenario if the restructuring plan were not to be confirmed. Member States should be able to choose one of those thresholds when implementing the best-interest-of-creditors test in national law. That test should be applied in any case where a plan needs to be confirmed in order to be binding for dissenting creditors or, as the case may be, dissenting classes of creditors. As a consequence of the best-interest-of-creditors test, where public institutional creditors have a privileged status under national law, Member States could provide that the plan cannot impose a full or partial cancellation of the claims of those creditors.

(53) While a restructuring plan should always be adopted if the required majority in each affected class supports the plan, it should still be possible for a restructuring plan which is not supported by the required majority in each affected class to be confirmed by a judicial or administrative authority, upon the proposal of a debtor or with the debtor's agreement. In the case of a legal person, Member States should be able to decide if, for the purpose of adopting or confirming a restructuring plan, the debtor is to be understood as the legal person's management board or a certain majority of shareholders or equity holders. For the plan to be confirmed in the case of a cross-class cram-down, it should be supported by a majority of voting classes of affected parties. At least one of those classes should be a secured creditor class or senior to the ordinary unsecured creditors class.

(54) It should be possible that, where a majority of voting classes does not support the restructuring plan, the plan can nevertheless be confirmed if it is supported by at least one affected or impaired class of creditors which, upon a valuation of the debtor as a going concern, receive payment or keep any interest, or, where so provided under national law, can reasonably be presumed to receive payment or keep any interest, if the normal ranking of liquidation priorities is applied under national law. In such a case, Member States should be able to increase the number of classes which are required to approve the plan, without necessarily requiring that all those classes should, upon a valuation of the debtor as a going concern, receive payment or keep any interest under national law. However, Member States should not require the consent of all classes. Accordingly, where there are only two classes of creditors, the consent of at least

one class should be deemed to be sufficient, if the other conditions for the application of a cross-class cram-down are met. The impairment of creditors should be understood to mean that there is a reduction in the value of their claims.

(55) In the case of a cross-class cram-down, Member States should ensure that dissenting classes of affected creditors are not unfairly prejudiced under the proposed plan and Member States should provide sufficient protection for such dissenting classes. Member States should be able to protect a dissenting class of affected creditors by ensuring that it is treated at least as favourably as any other class of the same rank and more favourably than any more junior class. Alternatively, Member States could protect a dissenting class of affected creditors by ensuring that such dissenting class is paid in full if a more junior class receives any distribution or keeps any interest under the restructuring plan (the 'absolute priority rule'). Member States should have discretion in implementing the concept of 'payment in full', including in relation to the timing of the payment, as long as the principal of the claim and, in the case of secured creditors, the value of the collateral are protected. Member States should also be able to decide on the choice of the equivalent means by which the original claim could be satisfied in full.

(56) Member States should be able to derogate from the absolute priority rule, for example where it is considered fair that equity holders keep certain interests under the plan despite a more senior class being obliged to accept a reduction of its claims, or that essential suppliers covered by the provision on the stay of individual enforcement actions are paid before more senior classes of creditors. Member States should be able to choose which of the above-mentioned protection mechanisms they put in place.

(57) While shareholders' or other equity holders' legitimate interests should be protected, Member States should ensure that they cannot unreasonably prevent the adoption of restructuring plans that would bring the debtor back to viability. Member States should be able to use different means to achieve that goal, for example by not giving equity holders the right to vote on a restructuring plan and by not making the adoption of a restructuring plan conditional on the agreement of equity holders that, upon a valuation of the enterprise, would not receive any payment or other consideration if the normal ranking of liquidation priorities were applied. However, where equity holders have the right to vote on a restructuring plan, a judicial or administrative authority should be able to confirm the plan by applying the rules on cross-class cram down notwithstanding the dissent of one or more classes of equity holders. Member States that exclude equity holders from voting should not be required to apply the absolute priority rule in the relationship between creditors and equity holders. Another possible means of ensuring that equity holders do not unreasonably prevent the adoption of restructuring plans would be to ensure that restructuring measures that directly affect equity holders' rights, and that need to be approved by a general meeting of shareholders under company law, are not subject to unreasonably high majority requirements and that equity holders have no competence in terms of restructuring measures that do not directly affect their rights.

(58) Several classes of equity holders can be needed where different classes of shareholdings with different rights exist. Equity holders of SMEs that are not mere investors, but are the owners of the enterprise and contribute to the enterprise in other ways, such as managerial expertise, might not have an incentive to restructure under such conditions. For this reason, the cross-class cram-down should remain optional for debtors that are SMEs.

(59) The restructuring plan should, for the purposes of its implementation, make it possible for equity holders of SMEs to provide non-monetary restructuring assistance by drawing on, for example, their experience, reputation or business contacts.

(60) Throughout the preventive restructuring procedures, workers should enjoy full labour law protection. In particular, this Directive should be without prejudice to workers' rights guaranteed by Council Directives 98/59/EC[12] and 2001/23/EC,[13] and Directives 2002/14/EC,[14] 2008/94/EC[15] and 2009/38/EC[16] of the European Parliament and of the Council. The obligations concerning information and consultation of employees under national law transposing those Directives remain fully intact. This includes obligations to inform and consult employees' representatives on the decision to have recourse to a preventive restructuring framework in accordance with Directive 2002/14/EC.

(61) Employees and their representatives should be provided with information regarding the proposed restructuring plan in so far as provided for in Union law, in order to allow them to undertake an in-depth assessment of the various scenarios. Furthermore, employees and their representatives should be involved to the extent necessary to fulfil the consultation requirements laid down in Union law. Given the need to ensure an appropriate level of protection of workers, Member States should be required to exempt workers' outstanding claims from any stay of individual enforcement actions, irrespective of the question of whether those claims arise before or after the stay is granted. A stay of enforcement of workers' outstanding claims should be allowed only for the amounts and for the period for which the payment of such claims is effectively guaranteed at a similar level by other means under national law. Where national law provides for limitations on the liability of guarantee institutions, either in terms of the length of the guarantee or the amount paid to workers, workers should be able to enforce any shortfall in their claims against the employer even during the stay period. Alternatively, Member States should be able to exclude workers' claims from the scope of the preventive restructuring frameworks and provide for their protection under national law.

(62) Where a restructuring plan entails the transfer of a part of an undertaking or business, workers' rights arising from a contract of employment or from an employment relationship, in particular the right to wages, should be safeguarded in accordance with Articles 3 and 4 of Directive 2001/23/EC, without prejudice to the specific rules applying in the event of insolvency proceedings under Article 5 of that Directive and in particular the possibilities provided for in Article 5(2) of that Directive. This Directive should be without prejudice to the rights to information and consultation, which are guaranteed by Directive 2002/14/EC, including on decisions likely to lead to substantial changes in work organisation or in contractual relations with a view to reaching an agreement on such decisions. Furthermore, under this Directive, workers whose claims are affected by a restructuring plan should have the right to vote on the plan. For the purposes of voting on the restructuring plan, Member States should be able to decide to place workers in a class separate from other classes of creditors.

(63) Judicial or administrative authorities should only decide on the valuation of a business — either in liquidation or in the next-best-alternative scenario, if the restructuring plan was not confirmed — if a dissenting affected party challenges the restructuring plan. This should not prevent Member States from carrying out valuations in another context under national law. However, it should be possible that such a decision also consists of an approval of a valuation by an expert or of a valuation submitted by the debtor or another party at an earlier stage of the process. Where the decision to carry out a valuation is taken, Member States should be able to provide for special rules, separate

from general civil procedural law, for a valuation in restructuring cases, with a view to ensuring that it is carried out in an expedited manner. Nothing in this Directive should affect the rules on burden of proof under national law in the case of a valuation.

(64) The binding effects of a restructuring plan should be limited to the affected parties that were involved in the adoption of the plan. Member States should be able to determine what it means for a creditor to be involved, including in the case of unknown creditors or creditors of future claims. For example, Member States should be able to decide how to deal with creditors that have been notified correctly but that did not participate in the procedures.

(65) Interested affected parties should be able to appeal a decision on the confirmation of a restructuring plan issued by an administrative authority. Member States should also be able to introduce the option of appealing a decision on the confirmation of a restructuring plan issued by a judicial authority. However, in order to ensure the effectiveness of the plan, to reduce uncertainty and to avoid unjustifiable delays, appeals should, as a rule, not have suspensive effects and therefore not preclude the implementation of a restructuring plan. Member States should be able to determine and limit the grounds for appeal. Where the decision on the confirmation of the plan is appealed, Member States should be able to allow the judicial authority to issue a preliminary or summary decision that protects the execution and implementation of the plan against the consequences of the pending appeal being upheld. Where an appeal is upheld, judicial or administrative authorities should be able to consider, as an alternative to setting aside the plan, an amendment of the plan, where Member States provide for such a possibility, as well as a confirmation of the plan without amendments. It should be possible for any amendments to the plan to be proposed or voted on by the parties, on their own initiative or at the request of the judicial authority. Member States could also provide for compensation for monetary losses for the party whose appeal was upheld. National law should be able to deal with a potential new stay or extension of the stay in event of the judicial authority deciding that the appeal has suspensive effect.

(66) The success of a restructuring plan often depends on whether financial assistance is extended to the debtor to support, firstly, the operation of the business during restructuring negotiations and, secondly, the implementation of the restructuring plan after its confirmation. Financial assistance should be understood in a broad sense, including the provision of money or third-party guarantees and the supply of stock, inventory, raw materials and utilities, for example through granting the debtor a longer repayment period. Interim financing and new financing should therefore be exempt from avoidance actions which seek to declare such financing void, voidable or unenforceable as an act detrimental to the general body of creditors in the context of subsequent insolvency procedures.

(67) National insolvency laws providing for avoidance actions of interim and new financing or providing that new lenders may incur civil, administrative or criminal sanctions for extending credit to debtors in financial difficulties could jeopardise the availability of financing necessary for the successful negotiation and implementation of a restructuring plan. This Directive should be without prejudice to other grounds for declaring new or interim financing void, voidable or unenforceable, or for triggering civil, criminal or administrative liability for providers of such financing, as laid down in national law. Such other grounds could include, among other things, fraud, bad faith, a certain type of relationship between the parties which could be associated with a conflict of interest, such as in the case of transactions between related parties or between shareholders and the company, and transactions where a party received value or collateral without being entitled to it at the time of the transaction or in the manner performed.

(68) When interim financing is extended, the parties do not know whether the restructuring plan will be eventually confirmed or not. Therefore, Member States should not be required to limit the protection of interim finance to cases where the plan is adopted by creditors or confirmed by a judicial or administrative authority. To avoid potential abuses, only financing that is reasonably and immediately necessary for the continued operation or survival of the debtor's business or the preservation or enhancement of the value of that business pending the confirmation of that plan should be protected. Furthermore, this Directive should not prevent Member States from introducing an ex ante control mechanism for interim financing. Member States should be able to limit the protection for new financing to cases where the plan is confirmed by a judicial or administrative authority and for interim financing to cases where it is subject to ex ante control. An ex ante control mechanism for interim financing or other transactions could be exercised by a practitioner in the field of restructuring, by a creditor's committee or by a judicial or administrative authority. Protection from avoidance actions and protection from personal liability are minimum guarantees that should be granted to interim financing and new financing. However, encouraging new lenders to take the enhanced risk of investing in a viable debtor in financial difficulties could require further incentives such as, for example, giving such financing priority at least over unsecured claims in subsequent insolvency procedures.

(69) In order to promote a culture that encourages early preventive restructuring, it is desirable that transactions which are reasonable and immediately necessary for the negotiation or implementation of a restructuring plan also be given protection from avoidance actions in subsequent insolvency procedures. Judicial or administrative authorities should be able, when determining the reasonableness and immediate necessity of costs and fees, for instance, to consider projections and estimates submitted to affected parties, a creditor's committee, a practitioner in the field of restructuring or the judicial or administrative authority itself. To this end, Member States should also be able to require debtors to provide and update relevant estimates. Such protection should enhance certainty in respect of transactions with businesses that are known to be in financial difficulties and remove the fear of creditors and investors that all such transactions could be declared void in the event that the restructuring fails. Member States should be able to provide for a point in time prior to the opening of a preventive restructuring procedure and to the granting of the stay of individual enforcement actions, from which fees and costs of negotiating, adopting, confirming or seeking professional advice for the restructuring plan start to benefit from protection against avoidance actions. In the case of other payments and disbursements and the protection of the payment of workers' wages, such a starting point could also be the granting of the stay or the opening of the preventive restructuring procedure.

(70) To further promote preventive restructuring, it is important to ensure that directors are not dissuaded from exercising reasonable business judgment or taking reasonable commercial risks, particularly where to do so would improve the chances of a restructuring of potentially viable businesses. Where the company experiences financial difficulties, directors should take steps to minimise losses and to avoid insolvency, such as: seeking professional advice, including on restructuring and insolvency, for instance by making use of early warning tools where applicable; protecting the assets of the company so as to maximise value and avoid loss of key assets; considering the structure and functions of the business to examine viability and reduce expenditure; refraining from committing the company

to the types of transaction that might be subject to avoidance unless there is an appropriate business justification; continuing to trade in circumstances where it is appropriate to do so in order to maximise going-concern value; holding negotiations with creditors and entering preventive restructuring procedures.

(71) Where the debtor is close to insolvency, it is also important to protect the legitimate interests of creditors from management decisions that may have an impact on the constitution of the debtor's estate, in particular where those decisions could have the effect of further diminishing the value of the estate available for restructuring efforts or for distribution to creditors. It is therefore necessary to ensure that, in such circumstances, directors avoid any deliberate or grossly negligent actions that result in personal gain at the expense of stakeholders, and avoid agreeing to transactions at below market value, or taking actions leading to unfair preference being given to one or more stakeholders. Member States should be able to implement the corresponding provisions of this Directive by ensuring that judicial or administrative authorities, when assessing whether a director is to be held liable for breaches of duty of care, take the rules on duties of directors laid down in this Directive into account. This Directive is not intended to establish any hierarchy among the different parties whose interests need to be given due regard. However, Member States should be able to decide on establishing such a hierarchy. This Directive should be without prejudice to Member States' national rules on the decision-making processes in a company.

(72) Entrepreneurs exercising a trade, business, craft or independent, self-employed profession can run the risk of becoming insolvent. The differences between the Member States in terms of opportunities for a fresh start could incentivise over-indebted or insolvent entrepreneurs to relocate to a Member State other than the Member State where they are established, in order to benefit from shorter discharge periods or more attractive conditions for discharge, leading to additional legal uncertainty and costs for the creditors when recovering their claims. Furthermore, the effects of insolvency, in particular the social stigma, the legal consequences, such as disqualifying entrepreneurs from taking up and pursuing entrepreneurial activity, and the continual inability to pay off debts, constitute important disincentives for entrepreneurs seeking to set up a business or have a second chance, even if evidence shows that entrepreneurs who have become insolvent have more chances of being successful the next time.

(73) Steps should therefore be taken to reduce the negative effects of over-indebtedness or insolvency on entrepreneurs, in particular by allowing for a full discharge of debt after a certain period of time and by limiting the length of disqualification orders issued in connection with a debtor's over-indebtedness or insolvency. The concept of 'insolvency' should be defined by national law and it could take the form of over-indebtedness. The concept of 'entrepreneur' within the meaning of this Directive should have no bearing on the position of managers or directors of a company, which should be treated in accordance with national law. Member States should be able to decide how to obtain access to discharge, including the possibility of requiring the debtor to request discharge.

(74) Member States should be able to provide for the possibility to adjust the repayment obligations of insolvent entrepreneurs when there is a significant change in their financial situation, regardless of whether it improves or deteriorates. This Directive should not require that a repayment plan be supported by a majority of creditors. Member States should be able to provide that entrepreneurs are not prevented from starting a new activity in the same or different field during the implementation of the repayment plan.

(75) A discharge of debt should be available in procedures that include a repayment plan, a realisation of assets, or a combination of both. In implementing those rules, Member States should be able to choose freely among those options. If more than one procedure leading to discharge of debt is available under national law, Member States should ensure that at least one of those procedures gives insolvent entrepreneurs the opportunity of having a full discharge of debt within a period that does not exceed three years. In the case of procedures which combine a realisation of assets and a repayment plan, the discharge period should start, at the latest, from the date the repayment plan is confirmed by a court or starts being implemented, for example from the first instalment under the plan, but it could also start earlier, such as when a decision to open the procedure is taken.

(76) In procedures that do not include a repayment plan, the discharge period should start, at the latest, from the date when a decision to open the procedure is taken by a judicial or administrative authority, or the date of the establishment of the insolvency estate. For the purposes of calculating the duration of the discharge period under this Directive, Member States should be able to provide that the concept of 'opening of procedure' does not include preliminary measures, such as preservation measures or the appointment of a preliminary insolvency practitioner, unless such measures allow for the realisation of assets, including the disposal and the distribution of assets to creditors. The establishment of the insolvency estate should not necessarily entail a formal decision or confirmation by a judicial or administrative authority, where such decision is not required under national law, and could consist in the submission of the inventory of assets and liabilities.

(77) Where the procedural path leading to a discharge of debt entails the realisation of an entrepreneur's assets, Member States should not be prevented from providing that the request for discharge is treated separately from the realisation of assets, provided that such request constitutes an integral part of the procedural path leading to the discharge under this Directive. Member States should be able to decide on the rules on the burden of proof in order for the discharge to operate, which means that it should be possible for entrepreneurs to be required by law to prove compliance with their obligations.

(78) A full discharge of debt or the ending of disqualifications after a period no longer than three years is not appropriate in all circumstances, therefore derogations from this rule which are duly justified by reasons laid down in national law might need to be introduced. For instance, such derogations should be introduced in cases where the debtor is dishonest or has acted in bad faith. Where entrepreneurs do not benefit from a presumption of honesty and good faith under national law, the burden of proof concerning their honesty and good faith should not make it unnecessarily difficult or onerous for them to enter the procedure.

(79) In establishing whether an entrepreneur was dishonest, judicial or administrative authorities might take into account circumstances such as: the nature and extent of the debt; the time when the debt was incurred; the efforts of the entrepreneur to pay the debt and comply with legal obligations, including public licensing requirements and the need for proper bookkeeping; actions on the entrepreneur's part to frustrate recourse by creditors; the fulfilment of duties in the likelihood of insolvency, which are incumbent on entrepreneurs who are directors of a company; and compliance with Union and national competition and labour law. It should also be possible to introduce derogations where the entrepreneur has not complied with certain legal obligations, including obligations to maximise returns to

creditors, which could take the form of a general obligation to generate income or assets. It should furthermore be possible to introduce specific derogations where it is necessary to guarantee the balance between the rights of the debtor and the rights of one or more creditors, such as where the creditor is a natural person who needs more protection than the debtor.

(80) A derogation could also be justified where the costs of the procedure leading to a discharge of debt, including the fees of judicial and administrative authorities and of practitioners, are not covered. Member States should be able to provide that the benefits of that discharge can be revoked where, for example, the financial situation of the debtor improves significantly due to unexpected circumstances, such as winning a lottery, or coming in the possession of an inheritance or a donation. Member States should not be prevented from providing additional derogations in well-defined circumstances and when duly justified.

(81) Where there is a duly justified reason under national law, it could be appropriate to limit the possibility of discharge for certain categories of debt. It should be possible for Member States to exclude secured debts from eligibility for discharge only up to the value of the collateral as determined by national law, while the rest of the debt should be treated as unsecured debt. Member States should be able to exclude further categories of debt when duly justified.

(82) Member States should be able to provide that judicial or administrative authorities can verify, either *ex officio* or at the request of a person with a legitimate interest, whether entrepreneurs have fulfilled the conditions for obtaining a full discharge of debt.

(83) If an entrepreneur's permit or licence to carry on a certain craft, business, trade or profession has been denied or revoked as a result of a disqualification order, this Directive should not prevent Member States from requiring the entrepreneur to submit an application for a new permit or licence after the disqualification has expired. Where a Member State authority adopts a decision concerning a specifically supervised activity, it should be possible to also take into account, even after the expiry of the disqualification period, the fact that the insolvent entrepreneur has obtained a discharge of debt in accordance with this Directive.

(84) Personal and professional debts that cannot be reasonably separated, for example where an asset is used in the course of the professional activity of the entrepreneur as well as outside that activity, should be treated in a single procedure. Where Member States provide that such debts are subject to different insolvency procedures, coordination of those procedures is needed. This Directive should be without prejudice to Member States being able to choose to treat all the debts of an entrepreneur in a single procedure. Member States in which entrepreneurs are allowed to continue their business on their own account during insolvency proceedings should not be prevented from providing that such entrepreneurs can be made subject to new insolvency proceedings, where such continued business becomes insolvent.

(85) It is necessary to maintain and enhance the transparency and predictability of the procedures in delivering outcomes that are favourable to the preservation of businesses and to allowing entrepreneurs to have a second chance or that permit the efficient liquidation of non-viable enterprises. It is also necessary to reduce the excessive length of insolvency procedures in many Member States, which results in legal uncertainty for creditors and investors and low recovery rates. Finally, given the enhanced cooperation mechanisms between courts and practitioners in cross-border cases, set up under Regulation (EU) 2015/848, the professionalism of all actors involved needs to be brought to comparable high levels across the Union. To achieve those objectives, Member States should ensure that members of the judicial and administrative authorities dealing with procedures concerning preventive restructuring, insolvency and discharge of debt are suitably trained and have the necessary expertise for their responsibilities. Such training and expertise could be acquired also during the exercise of the duties as a member of a judicial or administrative authority or, prior to appointment to such duties, during the exercise of other relevant duties.

(86) Such training and expertise should enable decisions with a potentially significant economic and social impact to be taken in an efficient manner, and should not be understood to mean that members of a judicial authority have to deal exclusively with matters concerning restructuring, insolvency and discharge of debt. Member States should ensure that procedures concerning restructuring, insolvency and discharge of debt can be carried out in an efficient and expeditious manner. The creation of specialised courts or chambers, or the appointment of specialised judges in accordance with national law, as well as concentrating jurisdiction in a limited number of judicial or administrative authorities would be efficient ways of achieving the objectives of legal certainty and effectiveness of procedures. Member States should not be obliged to require that procedures concerning restructuring, insolvency and discharge of debt be prioritised over other procedures.

(87) Member States should also ensure that practitioners in the field of restructuring, insolvency, and discharge of debt that are appointed by judicial or administrative authorities ('practitioners') are: suitably trained; appointed in a transparent manner with due regard to the need to ensure efficient procedures; supervised when carrying out their tasks; and perform their tasks with integrity. It is important that practitioners adhere to standards for such tasks, such as obtaining insurance for professional liability. Suitable training, qualifications and expertise for practitioners could also be acquired while practising their profession. Member States should not be obliged to provide the necessary training themselves, but this could be provided by, for example, professional associations or other bodies. Insolvency practitioners as defined in Regulation (EU) 2015/848 should be included in the scope of this Directive.

(88) This Directive should not prevent Member States from providing that practitioners are chosen by a debtor, by creditors or by a creditors' committee from a list or a pool that is pre-approved by a judicial or administrative authority. In choosing a practitioner, the debtor, the creditors or the creditors' committee could be granted a margin of appreciation as to the practitioner's expertise and experience in general and the demands of the particular case. Debtors who are natural persons could be exempted from such a duty altogether. In cases with cross-border elements, the appointment of the practitioner should take into account, among other things, the practitioner's ability to comply with the obligations, under Regulation (EU) 2015/848, to communicate and cooperate with insolvency practitioners and judicial and administrative authorities from other Member States, as well as their human and administrative resources to deal with potentially complex cases. Member States should not be prevented from providing for a practitioner to be selected by other methods, such as random selection by a software programme, provided that it is ensured that in using those methods due consideration is given to the practitioner's experience and expertise. Member States should be able to decide on the means for objecting to the selection or appointment of a practitioner or for requesting the replacement

of the practitioner, for example through a creditors' committee.

(89) Practitioners should be subject to oversight and regulatory mechanisms which should include effective measures regarding the accountability of practitioners who have failed in their duties, such as: a reduction in a practitioner's fee; the exclusion from the list or pool of practitioners who can be appointed in insolvency cases; and, where appropriate, disciplinary, administrative or criminal sanctions. Such oversight and regulatory mechanisms should be without prejudice to provisions under national law on civil liability for damages for breach of contractual or non-contractual obligations. Member States should not be required to set up specific authorities or bodies. Member States should ensure that information about the authorities or bodies exercising oversight over practitioners is publicly available. For instance, a mere reference to the judicial or administrative authority should be sufficient as information. It should be possible, in principle, to attain such standards without the need to create new professions or qualifications under national law. Member States should be able to extend the provisions on the training and supervision of practitioners to other practitioners not covered by this Directive. Member States should not be obliged to provide that disputes over remuneration of practitioners are to be prioritised over other procedures.

(90) To further reduce the length of procedures, to facilitate better participation of creditors in procedures concerning restructuring, insolvency and discharge of debt and to ensure similar conditions among creditors irrespective of where they are located in the Union, Member States should put in place provisions enabling debtors, creditors, practitioners and judicial and administrative authorities to use electronic means of communication. Therefore, it should be possible that procedural steps such as the filing of claims by creditors, the notification of creditors, or the lodging of challenges and appeals, can be carried out by electronic means of communication. Member States should be able to provide that notifications of a creditor can only be performed electronically if the creditor concerned has previously consented to electronic communication.

(91) Parties to procedures concerning restructuring, insolvency and discharge of debt should not be obliged to use electronic means of communication if such use is not mandatory under national law, without prejudice to Member States being able to establish a mandatory system of electronic filing and service of documents in procedures concerning restructuring, insolvency and discharge of debt. Member States should be able to choose the means of electronic communications. Examples of such means could include a purpose-built system for the electronic transmission of such documents or the use of email, without preventing Member States from being able to put in place features to ensure the security of electronic transmissions, such as electronic signature, or trust services, such as electronic registered delivery services, in accordance with Regulation (EU) No 910/2014 of the European Parliament and of the Council.[17]

(92) It is important to gather reliable and comparable data on the performance of procedures concerning restructuring, insolvency and discharge of debt in order to monitor the implementation and application of this Directive. Therefore, Member States should collect and aggregate data that are sufficiently granular to enable an accurate assessment of how the Directive is working in practice and should communicate those data to the Commission. The communication form for the transmission of such data to the Commission should be established by the Commission assisted by a Committee within the meaning of Regulation (EU) No 182/2011 of the European Parliament and of the Council.[18] The form should provide a shortlist of the main outcomes of procedures that are common to all Member States. For example, in the case of a restructuring procedure, those main outcomes could be the following: the plan being confirmed by a court; the plan not being confirmed by a court; the restructuring procedures being converted to liquidation procedures or closed because of the opening of liquidation procedures before the plan was confirmed by a court. Member States should not be required to provide a break-down by types of outcome in respect of the procedures which end before any relevant measures are taken, but could instead provide a common number for all procedures which are declared inadmissible, rejected or withdrawn before being opened.

(93) The communication form should provide a list of options which could be taken into account by the Member States when determining the size of a debtor, by reference to one or more of the elements of the definition of SMEs and large enterprises common to all Member States. The list should include the option of determining the size of a debtor based on the number of workers only. The form should: define the elements of average cost and average recovery rates for which Member States should be able to collect data voluntarily; provide guidance on elements which could be taken into account when Member States make use of a sampling technique, for example on sample sizes to ensure representativeness in terms of geographical distribution, size of debtors and industry; and include the opportunity for Member States to provide any additional information available, for example on the total amount of assets and liabilities of debtors.

(94) The stability of financial markets relies heavily on financial collateral arrangements, in particular, when collateral security is provided in connection with the participation in designated systems or in central bank operations and when margins are provided to central counterparties. As the value of financial instruments given as collateral security may be very volatile, it is crucial to realise their value quickly before it goes down. Therefore, the provisions of Directives 98/26/EC[19] and 2002/47/EC[20] of the European Parliament and of the Council and Regulation (EU) No 648/2012 should apply notwithstanding the provisions of this Directive. Member States should be allowed to exempt netting arrangements, including close-out netting, from the effects of the stay of individual enforcement actions even in circumstances where they are not covered by Directives 98/26/EC, 2002/47/EC and Regulation (EU) No 648/2012, if such arrangements are enforceable under the laws of the relevant Member State even if insolvency proceedings are opened.

This could be the case for a significant number of master agreements widely used in the financial, energy and commodity markets, both by non-financial and financial counterparties. Such arrangements reduce systemic risks especially in derivatives markets. Such arrangements might therefore be exempt from restrictions that insolvency laws impose on executory contracts. Accordingly, Member States should also be allowed to exempt from the effects of the stay of individual enforcement actions statutory netting arrangements, including close-out netting arrangements, which operate upon the opening of insolvency procedures. The amount resulting from the operation of netting arrangements, including close-out netting arrangements should, however, be subject to the stay of individual enforcement actions.

(95) Member States that are parties to the Convention on international interests in mobile equipment, signed at Cape Town on 16 November 2001, and its Protocols should be able to continue to comply with their existing

international obligations. The provisions of this Directive regarding preventive restructuring frameworks should apply with the derogations necessary to ensure an application of those provisions without prejudice to the application of that Convention and its Protocols.

(96) The effectiveness of the process of adoption and implementation of the restructuring plan should not be jeopardised by company law. Therefore, Member States should be able to derogate from the requirements laid down in Directive (EU) 2017/1132 of the European Parliament and of the Council[21] concerning the obligations to convene a general meeting and to offer on a pre-emptive basis shares to existing shareholders, to the extent and for the period necessary to ensure that shareholders do not frustrate restructuring efforts by abusing their rights under that Directive. For example, Member States might need to derogate from the obligation to convene a general meeting of shareholders or from the normal time periods, for cases where urgent action is to be taken by the management to safeguard the assets of the company, for instance through requesting a stay of individual enforcement actions and when there is a serious and sudden loss of subscribed capital and a likelihood of insolvency. Derogations from company law might also be required when the restructuring plan provides for the emission of new shares which could be offered with priority to creditors as debt-to-equity swaps, or for the reduction of the amount of subscribed capital in the event of a transfer of parts of the undertaking. Such derogations should be limited in time to the extent that Member States consider such derogations necessary for the establishment of a preventive restructuring framework. Member States should not be obliged to derogate from company law, wholly or partially, for an indefinite or for a limited period of time, if they ensure that their company law requirements do not jeopardise the effectiveness of the restructuring process or if Member States have other, equally effective tools in place to ensure that shareholders do not unreasonably prevent the adoption or implementation of a restructuring plan which would restore the viability of the business. In this context, Member States should attach particular importance to the effectiveness of provisions relating to a stay of individual enforcement actions and confirmation of the restructuring plan which should not be unduly impaired by calls for, or the results of, general meetings of shareholders. Directive (EU) 2017/1132 should therefore be amended accordingly. Member States should enjoy a margin of appreciation in assessing which derogations are needed in the context of national company law in order to effectively implement this Directive, and should also be able to provide for similar exemptions from Directive (EU) 2017/1132 in the case of insolvency proceedings not covered by this Directive but which allow for restructuring measures to be taken.

(97) In respect of the establishment of, and subsequent changes to, the data communication form, implementing powers should be conferred on the Commission. Those powers should be exercised in accordance with Regulation (EU) No 182/2011.

(98) A study should be carried out by the Commission in order to evaluate the necessity of submitting legislative proposals to deal with the insolvency of persons not exercising a trade, business, craft or profession, who, as consumers, in good faith, are temporarily or permanently unable to pay debts as they fall due. Such study should investigate whether access to basic goods and services needs to be safeguarded for those persons to ensure that they benefit from decent living conditions.

(99) In accordance with the Joint Political Declaration of 28 September 2011 of Member States and the Commission on explanatory documents,[22] Member States have undertaken to accompany, in justified cases, the notification of their transposition measures with one or more documents explaining the relationship between the components of a directive and the corresponding parts of national transposition instruments. With regard to this Directive, the legislator considers the transmission of such documents to be justified.

(100) Since the objectives of this Directive cannot be sufficiently achieved by the Member States because differences between national restructuring and insolvency frameworks would continue to raise obstacles to the free movement of capital and the freedom of establishment, but can rather be better achieved at Union level, the Union may adopt measures, in accordance with the principle of subsidiarity as set out in Article 5 of the Treaty on European Union. In accordance with the principle of proportionality, as set out in that Article, this Directive does not go beyond what is necessary in order to achieve those objectives.

(101) On 7 June 2017, the European Central Bank delivered an opinion,[23]

NOTES

1 OJ C209, 30.6.2017, p 21.

2 OJ C342, 12.10.2017, p 43.

3 Position of the European Parliament of 28 March 2019 (not yet published in the Official Journal) and decision of the Council of 6 June 2019.

4 Regulation (EU) 2015/848 of the European Parliament and of the Council of 20 May 2015 on insolvency proceedings (OJ L141, 5.6.2015, p 19).

5 Directive 2013/34/EU of the European Parliament and of the Council of 26 June 2013 on the annual financial statements, consolidated financial statements and related reports of certain types of undertakings, amending Directive 2006/43/EC of the European Parliament and of the Council and repealing Council Directives 78/660/EEC and 83/349/EEC (OJ L182, 29.6.2013, p 19).

6 Commission Recommendation of 6 May 2003 concerning the definition of micro, small and medium-sized enterprises (OJ L124, 20.5.2003, p 36).

7 Directive 2009/138/EC of the European Parliament and of the Council of 25 November 2009 on the taking-up and pursuit of the business of Insurance and Reinsurance (Solvency II) (OJ L335, 17.12.2009, p 1).

8 Regulation (EU) No 575/2013 of the European Parliament and of the Council of 26 June 2013 on prudential requirements for credit institutions and investment firms and amending Regulation (EU) No 648/2012 (OJ L176, 27.6.2013, p 1).

9 Regulation (EU) No 648/2012 of the European Parliament and of the Council of 4 July 2012 on OTC derivatives, central counterparties and trade repositories (OJ L201, 27.7.2012, p 1).

10 Regulation (EU) No 909/2014 of the European Parliament and of the Council of 23 July 2014 on improving securities settlement in the European Union and on central securities depositories and amending Directives 98/26/EC and 2014/65/EU and Regulation (EU) No 236/2012 (OJ L257, 28.8.2014, p 1).

11 Directive 2014/59/EU of the European Parliament and of the Council of 15 May 2014 establishing a framework for the recovery and resolution of credit institutions and investment firms and amending Council Directive 82/891/EEC, and Directives 2001/24/EC, 2002/47/EC, 2004/25/EC, 2005/56/EC, 2007/36/EC, 2011/35/EU, 2012/30/EU and 2013/36/EU,

and Regulations (EU) No 1093/2010 and (EU) No 648/2012, of the European Parliament and of the Council (OJ L173, 12.6.2014, p 190).

[12] Council Directive 98/59/EC of 20 July 1998 on the approximation of the laws of the Member States relating to collective redundancies (OJ L225, 12.8.1998, p 16).

[13] Council Directive 2001/23/EC of 12 March 2001 on the approximation of the laws of the Member States relating to the safeguarding of employees' rights in the event of transfers of undertakings, businesses or parts of undertakings or businesses (OJ L82, 22.3.2001, p 16).

[14] Directive 2002/14/EC of the European Parliament and of the Council of 11 March 2002 establishing a general framework for informing and consulting employees in the European Community (OJ L80, 23.3.2002, p 29).

[15] Directive 2008/94/EC of the European Parliament and of the Council of 22 October 2008 on the protection of employees in the event of the insolvency of their employer (OJ L283, 28.10.2008, p 36).

[16] Directive 2009/38/EC of the European Parliament and of the Council of 6 May 2009 on the establishment of a European Works council or a procedure in Community-scale undertakings and community-scale groups of undertakings for the purpose of informing and consulting employees (OJ L122, 16.5.2009, p 28).

[17] Regulation (EU) No 910/2014 of the European Parliament and of the Council of 23 July 2014 on electronic identification and trust services for electronic transactions in the internal market and repealing Directive 1999/93/EC (OJ L257, 28.8.2014, p 73).

[18] Regulation (EU) No 182/2011 of the European Parliament and of the Council of 16 February 2011 laying down the rules and general principles concerning mechanisms for control by the Member States of the Commission's exercise of implementing powers (OJ L55, 28.2.2011, p 13).

[19] Directive 98/26/EC of the European Parliament and of the Council of 19 May 1998 on settlement finality in payment and securities settlement systems (OJ L166, 11.6.1998, p 45).

[20] Directive 2002/47/EC of the European Parliament and of the Council of 6 June 2002 on financial collateral arrangements (OJ L168, 27.6.2002, p 43).

[21] Directive (EU) 2017/1132 of the European Parliament and of the Council of 14 June 2017 relating to certain aspects of company law (OJ L169, 30.6.2017, p 46).

[22] OJ C369, 17.12.2011, p 14.

[23] OJ C236, 21.7.2017, p 2.

HAVE ADOPTED THIS DIRECTIVE:

TITLE I GENERAL PROVISIONS

[11.729]

Article 1 Subject matter and scope

1. This Directive lays down rules on:
   (a) preventive restructuring frameworks available for debtors in financial difficulties when there is a likelihood of insolvency, with a view to preventing the insolvency and ensuring the viability of the debtor;
   (b) procedures leading to a discharge of debt incurred by insolvent entrepreneurs; and
   (c) measures to increase the efficiency of procedures concerning restructuring, insolvency and discharge of debt.
2. This Directive does not apply to procedures referred to in paragraph 1 of this Article that concern debtors that are:
   (a) insurance undertakings or reinsurance undertakings as defined in points (1) and (4) of Article 13 of Directive 2009/138/EC;
   (b) credit institutions as defined in point (1) of Article 4(1) of Regulation (EU) No 575/2013;
   (c) investment firms or collective investment undertakings as defined in points (2) and (7) of Article 4(1) of Regulation (EU) No 575/2013;
   (d) central counter parties as defined in point (1) of Article 2 of Regulation (EU) No 648/2012;
   (e) central securities depositories as defined in point (1) of Article 2(1) of Regulation (EU) No 909/2014;
   (f) other financial institutions and entities listed in the first subparagraph of Article 1(1) of Directive 2014/59/EU;
   (g) public bodies under national law; and
   (h) natural persons who are not entrepreneurs.
3. Member States may exclude from the scope of this Directive procedures referred to in paragraph 1 that concern debtors which are financial entities, other than those referred to in paragraph 2, providing financial services which are subject to special arrangements under which the national supervisory or resolution authorities have wide-ranging powers of intervention comparable to those laid down in Union and national law in relation to the financial entities referred to in paragraph 2. Member States shall communicate those special arrangements to the Commission.
4. Member States may extend the application of the procedures referred to in point (b) of paragraph 1 to insolvent natural persons who are not entrepreneurs.

Member States may restrict the application of point (a) of paragraph 1 to legal persons.

5. Member States may provide that the following claims are excluded from, or are not affected by, preventive restructuring frameworks referred to in point (a) of paragraph 1:
   (a) existing and future claims of existing or former workers;
   (b) maintenance claims arising from a family relationship, parentage, marriage or affinity; or
   (c) claims that arise from tortious liability of the debtor.
6. Member States shall ensure that preventive restructuring frameworks have no impact on accrued occupational pension entitlements.

[11.730]

Article 2 Definitions

1. For the purposes of this Directive, the following definitions apply:
   (1) 'restructuring' means measures aimed at restructuring the debtor's business that include changing the composition, conditions or structure of a debtor's assets and liabilities or any other part of the debtor's capital structure, such as sales of assets or parts of the business and, where so provided under national law, the sale of the business as a going concern, as well as any necessary operational changes, or a combination of those elements;

(2) 'affected parties' means creditors, including, where applicable under national law, workers, or classes of creditors and, where applicable, under national law, equity holders, whose claims or interests, respectively, are directly affected by a restructuring plan;

(3) 'equity holder' means a person that has an ownership interest in a debtor or a debtor's business, including a shareholder, in so far as that person is not a creditor;

(4) 'stay of individual enforcement actions' means a temporary suspension, granted by a judicial or administrative authority or applied by operation of law, of the right of a creditor to enforce a claim against a debtor and, where so provided for by national law, against a third-party security provider, in the context of a judicial, administrative or other procedure, or of the right to seize or realise out of court the assets or business of the debtor;

(5) 'executory contract' means a contract between a debtor and one or more creditors under which the parties still have obligations to perform at the time the stay of individual enforcement actions is granted or applied;

(6) 'best-interest-of-creditors test' means a test that is satisfied if no dissenting creditor would be worse off under a restructuring plan than such a creditor would be if the normal ranking of liquidation priorities under national law were applied, either in the event of liquidation, whether piecemeal or by sale as a going concern, or in the event of the next-best-alternative scenario if the restructuring plan were not confirmed;

(7) 'new financing' means any new financial assistance provided by an existing or a new creditor in order to implement a restructuring plan and that is included in that restructuring plan;

(8) 'interim financing' means any new financial assistance, provided by an existing or a new creditor, that includes, as a minimum, financial assistance during the stay of individual enforcement actions, and that is reasonable and immediately necessary for the debtor's business to continue operating, or to preserve or enhance the value of that business;

(9) 'entrepreneur' means a natural person exercising a trade, business, craft or profession;

(10) 'full discharge of debt' means that enforcement against entrepreneurs of their outstanding dischargeable debts is precluded or that outstanding dischargeable debts as such are cancelled, as part of a procedure which could include a realisation of assets or a repayment plan or both;

(11) 'repayment plan' means a programme of payments of specified amounts on specified dates by an insolvent entrepreneur to creditors, or a periodic transfer to creditors of a certain part of entrepreneur's disposable income during the discharge period;

(12) 'practitioner in the field of restructuring' means any person or body appointed by a judicial or administrative authority to carry out, in particular, one or more of the following tasks:

(a) assisting the debtor or the creditors in drafting or negotiating a restructuring plan;

(b) supervising the activity of the debtor during the negotiations on a restructuring plan, and reporting to a judicial or administrative authority;

(c) taking partial control over the assets or affairs of the debtor during negotiations.

2. For the purposes of this Directive, the following concepts are to be understood as defined by national law:

(a) insolvency;

(b) likelihood of insolvency;

(c) micro, small and medium-sized enterprises ('SMEs').

[11.731]

Article 3 Early warning and access to information

1. Member States shall ensure that debtors have access to one or more clear and transparent early warning tools which can detect circumstances that could give rise to a likelihood of insolvency and can signal to them the need to act without delay.

For the purposes of the first subparagraph, Member States may make use of up-to-date IT technologies for notifications and for communication.

2. Early warning tools may include the following:

(a) alert mechanisms when the debtor has not made certain types of payments;

(b) advisory services provided by public or private organisations.

(c) incentives under national law for third parties with relevant information about the debtor, such as accountants, tax and social security authorities, to flag to the debtor a negative development.

3. Member States shall ensure that debtors and employees' representatives have access to relevant and up-to-date information about the availability of early warning tools as well as of the procedures and measures concerning restructuring and discharge of debt.

4. Member States shall ensure that information on access to early warning tools is publicly available online and that, in particular for SMEs, it is easily accessible and presented in a user-friendly manner.

5. Member States may provide support to employees' representatives for the assessment of the economic situation of the debtor.

TITLE II PREVENTIVE RESTRUCTURING FRAMEWORKS

CHAPTER 1 AVAILABILITY OF PREVENTIVE RESTRUCTURING FRAMEWORKS

[11.732]

Article 4 Availability of preventive restructuring frameworks

1. Member States shall ensure that, where there is a likelihood of insolvency, debtors have access to a preventive restructuring framework that enables them to restructure, with a view to preventing insolvency and ensuring their viability, without prejudice to other solutions for avoiding insolvency, thereby protecting jobs and maintaining business activity.

2. Member States may provide that debtors that have been sentenced for serious breaches of accounting or bookkeeping obligations under national law are allowed to access a preventive restructuring framework only after those debtors have taken adequate measures to remedy the issues that gave rise to the sentence, with a view to providing creditors with the necessary information to enable them to take a decision during restructuring negotiations.

3. Member States may maintain or introduce a viability test under national law, provided that such a test has the purpose of excluding debtors that do not have a prospect of viability, and that it can be carried out without detriment to the debtors' assets.
4. Member States may limit the number of times within a certain period a debtor can access a preventive restructuring framework as provided for under this Directive.
5. The preventive restructuring framework provided for under this Directive may consist of one or more procedures, measures or provisions, some of which may take place out of court, without prejudice to any other restructuring frameworks under national law.
Member States shall ensure that such restructuring framework affords debtors and affected parties the rights and safeguards provided for in this Title in a coherent manner.
6. Member States may put in place provisions limiting the involvement of a judicial or administrative authority in a preventive restructuring framework to where it is necessary and proportionate while ensuring that rights of any affected parties and relevant stakeholders are safeguarded.
7. Preventive restructuring frameworks provided for under this Directive shall be available on application by debtors.
8. Member States may also provide that preventive restructuring frameworks provided for under this Directive are available at the request of creditors and employees' representatives, subject to the agreement of the debtor. Member States may limit that requirement to obtain the debtor's agreement to cases where debtors are SMEs.

CHAPTER 2 FACILITATING NEGOTIATIONS ON PREVENTIVE RESTRUCTURING PLANS

[11.733]
Article 5 Debtor in possession

1. Member States shall ensure that debtors accessing preventive restructuring procedures remain totally, or at least partially, in control of their assets and the day-to-day operation of their business.
2. Where necessary, the appointment by a judicial or administrative authority of a practitioner in the field of restructuring shall be decided on a case-by-case basis, except in certain circumstances where Member States may require the mandatory appointment of such a practitioner in every case.
3. Member States shall provide for the appointment of a practitioner in the field of restructuring, to assist the debtor and creditors in negotiating and drafting the plan, at least in the following cases:
- (a) where a general stay of individual enforcement actions, in accordance with Article 6(3), is granted by a judicial or administrative authority, and the judicial or administrative authority decides that such a practitioner is necessary to safeguard the interest of the parties;
- (b) where the restructuring plan needs to be confirmed by a judicial or administrative authority by means of a cross-class cram-down, in accordance with Article 11; or
- (c) where it is requested by the debtor or by a majority of the creditors, provided that, in the latter case, the cost of the practitioner is borne by the creditors.

[11.734]
Article 6 Stay of individual enforcement actions

1. Member States shall ensure that debtors can benefit from a stay of individual enforcement actions to support the negotiations of a restructuring plan in a preventive restructuring framework.
Member States may provide that judicial or administrative authorities can refuse to grant a stay of individual enforcement actions where such a stay is not necessary or where it would not achieve the objective set out in the first subparagraph.
2. Without prejudice to paragraphs 4 and 5, Member States shall ensure that a stay of individual enforcement actions can cover all types of claims, including secured claims and preferential claims.
3. Member States may provide that a stay of individual enforcement actions can be general, covering all creditors, or can be limited, covering one or more individual creditors or categories of creditors.
Where a stay is limited, the stay shall only apply to creditors that have been informed, in accordance with national law, of negotiations as referred to in paragraph 1 on the restructuring plan or of the stay.
4. Member States may exclude certain claims or categories of claims from the scope of the stay of individual enforcement actions, in well-defined circumstances, where such an exclusion is duly justified and where:
- (a) enforcement is not likely to jeopardise the restructuring of the business; or
- (b) the stay would unfairly prejudice the creditors of those claims.

5. Paragraph 2 shall not apply to workers' claims.
By way of derogation from the first subparagraph, Member States may apply paragraph 2 to workers' claims if, and to the extent that, Member States ensure that the payment of such claims is guaranteed in preventive restructuring frameworks at a similar level of protection.
6. The initial duration of a stay of individual enforcement actions shall be limited to a maximum period of no more than four months.
7. Notwithstanding paragraph 6, Member States may enable judicial or administrative authorities to extend the duration of a stay of individual enforcement actions or to grant a new stay of individual enforcement actions, at the request of the debtor, a creditor or, where applicable, a practitioner in the field of restructuring. Such extension or new stay of individual enforcement actions shall be granted only if well-defined circumstances show that such extension or new stay is duly justified, such as:
- (a) relevant progress has been made in the negotiations on the restructuring plan;
- (b) the continuation of the stay of individual enforcement actions does not unfairly prejudice the rights or interests of any affected parties; or
- (c) insolvency proceedings which could end in the liquidation of the debtor under national law have not yet been opened in respect of the debtor.

8. The total duration of the stay of individual enforcement actions, including extensions and renewals, shall not exceed 12 months.
Where Member States choose to implement this Directive by means of one or more procedures or measures which do not fulfil the conditions for notification under Annex A to Regulation (EU) 2015/848, the total duration of the stay

under such procedures shall be limited to no more than four months if the centre of main interests of the debtor has been transferred from another Member State within a three-month period prior to the filing of a request for the opening of preventive restructuring proceedings.

9. Member States shall ensure that judicial or administrative authorities can lift a stay of individual enforcement actions in the following cases:

(a) the stay no longer fulfils the objective of supporting the negotiations on the restructuring plan, for example if it becomes apparent that a proportion of creditors which, under national law, could prevent the adoption of the restructuring plan do not support the continuation of the negotiations;

(b) at the request of the debtor or the practitioner in the field of restructuring;

(c) where so provided for in national law, if one or more creditors or one or more classes of creditors are, or would be, unfairly prejudiced by a stay of individual enforcement actions; or

(d) where so provided for in national law, if the stay gives rise to the insolvency of a creditor.

Member States may limit the power, under the first subparagraph, to lift the stay of individual enforcement actions to situations where creditors had not had the opportunity to be heard before the stay came into force or before an extension of the period was granted by a judicial or administrative authority.

Member States may provide for a minimum period, which does not exceed the period referred to in paragraph 6, during which a stay of individual enforcement actions cannot be lifted.

[11.735]

Article 7 Consequences of the stay of individual enforcement actions

1. Where an obligation on a debtor, provided for under national law, to file for the opening of insolvency proceedings which could end in the liquidation of the debtor, arises during a stay of individual enforcement actions, that obligation shall be suspended for the duration of that stay.

2. A stay of individual enforcement actions in accordance with Article 6 shall suspend, for the duration of the stay, the opening, at the request of one or more creditors, of insolvency proceedings which could end in the liquidation of the debtor.

3. Member States may derogate from paragraphs 1 and 2 in situations where a debtor is unable to pay its debts as they fall due. In such cases, Member States shall ensure that a judicial or administrative authority can decide to keep in place the benefit of the stay of individual enforcement actions, if, taking into account the circumstances of the case, the opening of insolvency proceedings which could end in the liquidation of the debtor would not be in the general interest of creditors.

4. Member States shall provide for rules preventing creditors to which the stay applies from withholding performance or terminating, accelerating or, in any other way, modifying essential executory contracts to the detriment of the debtor, for debts that came into existence prior to the stay, solely by virtue of the fact that they were not paid by the debtor. 'Essential executory contracts' shall be understood to mean executory contracts which are necessary for the continuation of the day-to-day operations of the business, including contracts concerning supplies, the suspension of which would lead to the debtor's activities coming to a standstill.

The first subparagraph shall not preclude Member States from affording such creditors appropriate safeguards with a view to preventing unfair prejudice being caused to such creditors as a result of that subparagraph.

Member States may provide that this paragraph also applies to non-essential executory contracts.

5. Member States shall ensure that creditors are not allowed to withhold performance or terminate, accelerate or, in any other way, modify executory contracts to the detriment of the debtor by virtue of a contractual clause providing for such measures, solely by reason of:

(a) a request for the opening of preventive restructuring proceedings;

(b) a request for a stay of individual enforcement actions;

(c) the opening of preventive restructuring proceedings; or

(d) the granting of a stay of individual enforcement actions as such.

6. Member States may provide that a stay of individual enforcement actions does not apply to netting arrangements, including close-out netting arrangements, on financial markets, energy markets and commodity markets, even in circumstances where Article 31(1) does not apply, if such arrangements are enforceable under national insolvency law. The stay shall, however, apply to the enforcement by a creditor of a claim against a debtor arising as a result of the operation of a netting arrangement.

The first subparagraph shall not apply to contracts for the supply of goods, services or energy necessary for the operation of the debtor's business, unless such contracts take the form of a position traded on an exchange or other market, such that it can be substituted at any time at current market value.

7. Member States shall ensure that the expiry of a stay of individual enforcement actions without the adoption of a restructuring plan does not, of itself, give rise to the opening of an insolvency procedure which could end in the liquidation of the debtor, unless the other conditions for such opening laid down by national law are fulfilled.

CHAPTER 3 RESTRUCTURING PLANS

[11.736]

Article 8 Content of restructuring plans

1. Member States shall require that restructuring plans submitted for adoption in accordance with Article 9, or for confirmation by a judicial or administrative authority in accordance with Article 10, contain at least the following information:

(a) the identity of the debtor;

(b) the debtor's assets and liabilities at the time of submission of the restructuring plan, including a value for the assets, a description of the economic situation of the debtor and the position of workers, and a description of the causes and the extent of the difficulties of the debtor;

(c) the affected parties, whether named individually or described by categories of debt in accordance with national law, as well as their claims or interests covered by the restructuring plan;

(d) where applicable, the classes into which the affected parties have been grouped, for the purpose of adopting the restructuring plan, and the respective values of claims and interests in each class;

(e) where applicable, the parties, whether named individually or described by categories of debt in accordance with national law, which are not affected by the restructuring plan, together with a description of the reasons why it is proposed not to affect them;
(f) where applicable, the identity of the practitioner in the field of restructuring;
(g) the terms of the restructuring plan, including, in particular:
 (i) any proposed restructuring measures as referred to in point (1) of Article 2(1);
 (ii) where applicable, the proposed duration of any proposed restructuring measures;
 (iii) the arrangements with regard to informing and consulting the employees' representatives in accordance with Union and national law;
 (iv) where applicable, overall consequences as regards employment such as dismissals, short-time working arrangements or similar;
 (v) the estimated financial flows of the debtor, if provided for by national law; and
 (vi) any new financing anticipated as part of the restructuring plan, and the reasons why the new financing is necessary to implement that plan;
(h) a statement of reasons which explains why the restructuring plan has a reasonable prospect of preventing the insolvency of the debtor and ensuring the viability of the business, including the necessary pre-conditions for the success of the plan. Member States may require that that statement of reasons be made or validated either by an external expert or by the practitioner in the field of restructuring if such a practitioner is appointed.

2. Member States shall make available online a comprehensive check-list for restructuring plans, adapted to the needs of SMEs. The check-list shall include practical guidelines on how the restructuring plan has to be drafted under national law.
The check-list shall be made available in the official language or languages of the Member State. Member States shall consider making the check-list available in at least one other language, in particular in a language used in international business.

[11.737]
Article 9 Adoption of restructuring plans

1. Member States shall ensure that, irrespective of who applies for a preventive restructuring procedure in accordance with Article 4, debtors have the right to submit restructuring plans for adoption by the affected parties.
Member States may also provide that creditors and practitioners in the field of restructuring have the right to submit restructuring plans, and provide for conditions under which they may do so.
2. Member States shall ensure that affected parties have a right to vote on the adoption of a restructuring plan.
Parties that are not affected by a restructuring plan shall not have voting rights in the adoption of that plan.
3. Notwithstanding paragraph 2, Member States may exclude from the right to vote the following:
(a) equity holders;
(b) creditors whose claims rank below the claims of ordinary unsecured creditors in the normal ranking of liquidation priorities; or
(c) any related party of the debtor or the debtor's business, with a conflict of interest under national law.
4. Member States shall ensure that affected parties are treated in separate classes which reflect sufficient commonality of interest based on verifiable criteria, in accordance with national law. As a minimum, creditors of secured and unsecured claims shall be treated in separate classes for the purposes of adopting a restructuring plan.
Member States may also provide that workers' claims are treated in a separate class of their own.
Member States may provide that debtors that are SMEs can opt not to treat affected parties in separate classes.
Member States shall put in place appropriate measures to ensure that class formation is done with a particular view to protecting vulnerable creditors such as small suppliers.
5. Voting rights and the formation of classes shall be examined by a judicial or administrative authority when a request for confirmation of the restructuring plan is submitted.
Member States may require a judicial or administrative authority to examine and confirm the voting rights and formation of classes at an earlier stage than that referred to in the first subparagraph.
6. A restructuring plan shall be adopted by affected parties, provided that a majority in the amount of their claims or interests is obtained in each class. Member States may, in addition, require that a majority in the number of affected parties is obtained in each class.
Member States shall lay down the majorities required for the adoption of a restructuring plan. Those majorities shall not be higher than 75% of the amount of claims or interests in each class or, where applicable, of the number of affected parties in each class.
7. Notwithstanding paragraphs 2 to 6, Member States may provide that a formal vote on the adoption of a restructuring plan can be replaced by an agreement with the requisite majority.

[11.738]
Article 10 Confirmation of restructuring plans

1. Member States shall ensure that at least the following restructuring plans are binding on the parties only if they are confirmed by a judicial or administrative authority:
(a) restructuring plans which affect the claims or interests of dissenting affected parties;
(b) restructuring plans which provide for new financing;
(c) restructuring plans which involve the loss of more than 25% of the workforce, if such loss is permitted under national law.
2. Member States shall ensure that the conditions under which a restructuring plan can be confirmed by a judicial or administrative authority are clearly specified and include at least the following:
(a) the restructuring plan has been adopted in accordance with Article 9;
(b) creditors with sufficient commonality of interest in the same class are treated equally, and in a manner proportionate to their claim;
(c) notification of the restructuring plan has been given in accordance with national law to all affected parties;
(d) where there are dissenting creditors, the restructuring plan satisfies the best-interest-of-creditors test;

(e) where applicable, any new financing is necessary to implement the restructuring plan and does not unfairly prejudice the interests of creditors.

Compliance with point (d) of the first subparagraph shall be examined by a judicial or administrative authority only if the restructuring plan is challenged on that ground.

3. Member States shall ensure that judicial or administrative authorities are able to refuse to confirm a restructuring plan where that plan would not have a reasonable prospect of preventing the insolvency of the debtor or ensuring the viability of the business.

4. Member States shall ensure that where a judicial or administrative authority is required to confirm a restructuring plan in order for it to become binding, the decision is taken in an efficient manner with a view to expeditious treatment of the matter.

[11.739]

Article 11 Cross-class cram-down

1. Member States shall ensure that a restructuring plan which is not approved by affected parties, as provided for in Article 9(6), in every voting class, may be confirmed by a judicial or administrative authority upon the proposal of a debtor or with the debtor's agreement, and become binding upon dissenting voting classes where the restructuring plan fulfils at least the following conditions:

(a) it complies with Article 10(2) and (3);

(b) it has been approved by:

(i) a majority of the voting classes of affected parties, provided that at least one of those classes is a secured creditors class or is senior to the ordinary unsecured creditors class; or, failing that,

(ii) at least one of the voting classes of affected parties or where so provided under national law, impaired parties, other than an equity-holders class or any other class which, upon a valuation of the debtor as a going concern, would not receive any payment or keep any interest, or, where so provided under national law, which could be reasonably presumed not to receive any payment or keep any interest, if the normal ranking of liquidation priorities were applied under national law;

(c) it ensures that dissenting voting classes of affected creditors are treated at least as favourably as any other class of the same rank and more favourably than any junior class; and

(d) no class of affected parties can, under the restructuring plan, receive or keep more than the full amount of its claims or interests.

By way of derogation from the first subparagraph, Member States may limit the requirement to obtain the debtor's agreement to cases where debtors are SMEs.

Member States may increase the minimum number of classes of affected parties or, where so provided under national law, impaired parties, required to approve the plan as laid down in point (b)(ii) of the first subparagraph.

2. By way of derogation from point (c) of paragraph 1, Member States may provide that the claims of affected creditors in a dissenting voting class are satisfied in full by the same or equivalent means where a more junior class is to receive any payment or keep any interest under the restructuring plan.

Member States may maintain or introduce provisions derogating from the first subparagraph where they are necessary in order to achieve the aims of the restructuring plan and where the restructuring plan does not unfairly prejudice the rights or interests of any affected parties.

[11.740]

Article 12 Equity holders

1. Where Member States exclude equity holders from the application of Articles 9 to 11, they shall ensure by other means that those equity holders are not allowed to unreasonably prevent or create obstacles to the adoption and confirmation of a restructuring plan.

2. Member States shall also ensure that equity holders are not allowed to unreasonably prevent or create obstacles to the implementation of a restructuring plan.

3. Member States may adapt what it means to unreasonably prevent or create obstacles under this Article to take into account, inter alia: whether the debtor is an SME or a large enterprise; the proposed restructuring measures touching upon the rights of equity holders; the type of equity holder; whether the debtor is a legal or a natural person; or whether partners in a company have limited or unlimited liability.

[11.741]

Article 13 Workers

1. Members States shall ensure that individual and collective workers' rights, under Union and national labour law, such as the following, are not affected by the preventive restructuring framework:

(a) the right to collective bargaining and industrial action; and

(b) the right to information and consultation in accordance with Directive 2002/14/EC and Directive 2009/38/EC, in particular:

(i) information to employees' representatives about the recent and probable development of the undertaking's or the establishment's activities and economic situation, enabling them to communicate to the debtor concerns about the situation of the business and as regards the need to consider restructuring mechanisms;

(ii) information to employees' representatives about any preventive restructuring procedure which could have an impact on employment, such as on the ability of workers to recover their wages and any future payments, including occupational pensions;

(iii) information to and consultation of employees' representatives about restructuring plans before they are submitted for adoption in accordance with Article 9, or for confirmation by a judicial or administrative authority in accordance with Article 10;

(c) the rights guaranteed by Directives 98/59/EC, 2001/23/EC and 2008/94/EC.

2. Where the restructuring plan includes measures leading to changes in the work organisation or in contractual relations with workers, those measures shall be approved by those workers, if national law or collective agreements provide for such approval in such cases.

[11.742]
Article 14 Valuation by the judicial or administrative authority
1. The judicial or administrative authority shall take a decision on the valuation of the debtor's business only where a restructuring plan is challenged by a dissenting affected party on the grounds of either:
(a) an alleged failure to satisfy the best-interest-of-creditors test under point (6) of Article 2(1); or
(b) an alleged breach of the conditions for a cross-class cram-down under point (ii) of Article 11(1)(b).
2. Member States shall ensure that, for the purpose of taking a decision on a valuation in accordance with paragraph 1, judicial or administrative authorities may appoint or hear properly qualified experts.
3. For the purposes of paragraph 1, Member States shall ensure that a dissenting affected party may lodge a challenge with the judicial or administrative authority called upon to confirm the restructuring plan.
Member States may provide that such a challenge can be lodged in the context of an appeal against a decision on the confirmation of a restructuring plan.

[11.743]
Article 15 Effects of restructuring plans
1. Member States shall ensure that restructuring plans that are confirmed by a judicial or administrative authority are binding upon all affected parties named or described in accordance with point (c) of Article 8(1).
2. Member States shall ensure that creditors that are not involved in the adoption of a restructuring plan under national law are not affected by the plan.

[11.744]
Article 16 Appeals
1. Member States shall ensure that any appeal provided for under national law against a decision to confirm or reject a restructuring plan taken by a judicial authority is brought before a higher judicial authority.
Member States shall ensure that an appeal against a decision to confirm or reject a restructuring plan taken by an administrative authority is brought before a judicial authority.
2. Appeals shall be resolved in an efficient manner with a view to expeditious treatment.
3. An appeal against a decision confirming a restructuring plan shall have no suspensive effects on the execution of that plan.
By way of derogation from the first subparagraph, Member States may provide that judicial authorities can suspend the execution of the restructuring plan or parts thereof where necessary and appropriate to safeguard the interests of a party.
4. Member States shall ensure that, where an appeal pursuant to paragraph 3 is upheld, the judicial authority may either:
(a) set aside the restructuring plan; or
(b) confirm the restructuring plan, either with amendments, where so provided under national law, or without amendments.
Member States may provide that, where a plan is confirmed under point (b) of the first subparagraph, compensation is granted to any party that incurred monetary losses and whose appeal is upheld.

CHAPTER 4 PROTECTION FOR NEW FINANCING, INTERIM FINANCING AND OTHER RESTRUCTURING RELATED TRANSACTIONS

[11.745]
Article 17 Protection for new financing and interim financing
1. Member States shall ensure that new financing and interim financing are adequately protected. As a minimum, in the case of any subsequent insolvency of the debtor:
(a) new financing and interim financing shall not be declared void, voidable or unenforceable; and
(b) the grantors of such financing shall not incur civil, administrative or criminal liability, on the ground that such financing is detrimental to the general body of creditors, unless other additional grounds laid down by national law are present.
2. Member States may provide that paragraph 1 shall only apply to new financing if the restructuring plan has been confirmed by a judicial or administrative authority, and to interim financing which has been subject to ex ante control.
3. Member States may exclude from the application of paragraph 1 interim financing which is granted after the debtor has become unable to pay its debts as they fall due.
4. Member States may provide that grantors of new or interim financing are entitled to receive payment with priority in the context of subsequent insolvency procedures in relation to other creditors that would otherwise have superior or equal claims.

[11.746]
Article 18 Protection for other restructuring related transactions
1. Without prejudice to Article 17, Member States shall ensure that, in the event of any subsequent insolvency of a debtor, transactions that are reasonable and immediately necessary for the negotiation of a restructuring plan are not declared void, voidable or unenforceable on the ground that such transactions are detrimental to the general body of creditors, unless other additional grounds laid down by national law are present.
2. Member States may provide that paragraph 1 only applies where the plan is confirmed by a judicial or administrative authority or where such transactions were subject to *ex ante* control.
3. Member States may exclude from the application of paragraph 1 transactions that are carried out after the debtor has become unable to pay its debts as they fall due.
4. Transactions referred to in paragraph 1 shall include, as a minimum:
(a) the payment of fees for and costs of negotiating, adopting or confirming a restructuring plan;
(b) the payment of fees for and costs of seeking professional advice closely connected with the restructuring;
(c) the payment of workers' wages for work already carried out without prejudice to other protection provided in Union or national law;

(d) any payments and disbursements made in the ordinary course of business other than those referred to in points (a) to (c).

5. Without prejudice to Article 17, Member States shall ensure that, in the event of any subsequent insolvency of the debtor, transactions that are reasonable and immediately necessary for the implementation of a restructuring plan, and that are carried out in accordance with the restructuring plan confirmed by a judicial or administrative authority, are not declared void, voidable or unenforceable on the ground that such transactions are detrimental to the general body of creditors, unless other additional grounds laid down by national law are present.

CHAPTER 5 DUTIES OF DIRECTORS

[11.747]

Article 19 Duties of directors where there is a likelihood of insolvency

Member States shall ensure that, where there is a likelihood of insolvency, directors, have due regard, as a minimum, to the following:

(a) the interests of creditors, equity holders and other stakeholders;

(b) the need to take steps to avoid insolvency; and

(c) the need to avoid deliberate or grossly negligent conduct that threatens the viability of the business.

TITLE III DISCHARGE OF DEBT AND DISQUALIFICATIONS

[11.748]

Article 20 Access to discharge

1. Member States shall ensure that insolvent entrepreneurs have access to at least one procedure that can lead to a full discharge of debt in accordance with this Directive.

Member States may require that the trade, business, craft or profession to which an insolvent entrepreneur's debts are related has ceased.

2. Member States in which a full discharge of debt is conditional on a partial repayment of debt by the entrepreneur shall ensure that the related repayment obligation is based on the individual situation of the entrepreneur and, in particular, is proportionate to the entrepreneur's seizable or disposable income and assets during the discharge period, and takes into account the equitable interest of creditors.

3. Member States shall ensure that entrepreneurs who have been discharged from their debts may benefit from existing national frameworks providing for business support for entrepreneurs, including access to relevant and up-to-date information about these frameworks.

[11.749]

Article 21 Discharge period

1. Member States shall ensure that the period after which insolvent entrepreneurs are able to be fully discharged from their debts is no longer than three years starting at the latest from the date of either:

(a) in the case of a procedure which includes a repayment plan, the decision by a judicial or administrative authority to confirm the plan or the start of the implementation of the plan; or

(b) in the case of any other procedure, the decision by the judicial or administrative authority to open the procedure, or the establishment of the entrepreneur's insolvency estate.

2. Member States shall ensure that insolvent entrepreneurs who have complied with their obligations, where such obligations exist under national law, are discharged of their debt on expiry of the discharge period without the need to apply to a judicial or administrative authority to open a procedure additional to those referred to in paragraph 1.

Without prejudice to the first subparagraph, Member States may maintain or introduce provisions allowing the judicial or administrative authority to verify whether the entrepreneurs have fulfilled the obligations for obtaining a discharge of debt.

3. Member States may provide that a full discharge of debt does not hinder the continuation of an insolvency procedure that entails the realisation and distribution of assets of an entrepreneur that formed part of the insolvency estate of that entrepreneur as at the date of expiry of the discharge period.

[11.750]

Article 22 Disqualification period

1. Member States shall ensure that, where an insolvent entrepreneur obtains a discharge of debt in accordance with this Directive, any disqualifications from taking up or pursuing a trade, business, craft or profession on the sole ground that the entrepreneur is insolvent, shall cease to have effect, at the latest, at the end of the discharge period.

2. Member States shall ensure that, on expiry of the discharge period, the disqualifications referred to in paragraph 1 of this Article cease to have effect without the need to apply to a judicial or administrative authority to open a procedure additional to those referred to in Article 21(1).

[11.751]

Article 23 Derogations

1. By way of derogation from Articles 20 to 22, Member States shall maintain or introduce provisions denying or restricting access to discharge of debt, revoking the benefit of such discharge or providing for longer periods for obtaining a full discharge of debt or longer disqualification periods, where the insolvent entrepreneur acted dishonestly or in bad faith under national law towards creditors or other stakeholders when becoming indebted, during the insolvency proceedings or during the payment of the debt, without prejudice to national rules on burden of proof.

2. By way of derogation from Articles 20 to 22, Member States may maintain or introduce provisions denying or restricting access to discharge of debt, revoking the benefit of discharge or providing for longer periods for obtaining a full discharge of debt or longer disqualification periods in certain well-defined circumstances and where such derogations are duly justified, such as where:

(a) the insolvent entrepreneur has substantially violated obligations under a repayment plan or any other legal obligation aimed at safeguarding the interests of creditors, including the obligation to maximise returns to creditors;

(b) the insolvent entrepreneur has failed to comply with information or cooperation obligations under Union and national law;
(c) there are abusive applications for a discharge of debt;
(d) there is a further application for a discharge within a certain period after the insolvent entrepreneur was granted a full discharge of debt or was denied a full discharge of debt due to a serious violation of information or cooperation obligations;
(e) the cost of the procedure leading to the discharge of debt is not covered; or
(f) a derogation is necessary to guarantee the balance between the rights of the debtor and the rights of one or more creditors.

3. By way of derogation from Article 21, Member States may provide for longer discharge periods in cases where:
(a) protective measures are approved or ordered by a judicial or administrative authority in order to safeguard the main residence of the insolvent entrepreneur and, where applicable, of the entrepreneur's family, or the essential assets for the continuation of the entrepreneur's trade, business, craft or profession; or
(b) the main residence of the insolvent entrepreneur and, where applicable, of the entrepreneur's family, is not realised.

4. Member States may exclude specific categories of debt from discharge of debt, or restrict access to discharge of debt or lay down a longer discharge period where such exclusions, restrictions or longer periods are duly justified, such as in the case of:
(a) secured debts;
(b) debts arising from or in connection with criminal penalties;
(c) debts arising from tortious liability;
(d) debts regarding maintenance obligations arising from a family relationship, parentage, marriage or affinity;
(e) debts incurred after the application for or opening of the procedure leading to a discharge of debt; and
(f) debts arising from the obligation to pay the cost of the procedure leading to a discharge of debt.

5. By way of derogation from Article 22, Member States may provide for longer or indefinite disqualification periods where the insolvent entrepreneur is a member of a profession:
(a) to which specific ethical rules or specific rules on reputation or expertise apply, and the entrepreneur has infringed those rules; or
(b) dealing with the management of the property of others.

The first subparagraph shall also apply where an insolvent entrepreneur requests access to a profession as referred to in point (a) or (b) of that subparagraph.

6. This Directive is without prejudice to national rules regarding disqualifications ordered by a judicial or administrative authority other than those referred to in Article 22.

[11.752]
Article 24 Consolidation of proceedings regarding professional and personal debts

1. Member States shall ensure that, where insolvent entrepreneurs have professional debts incurred in the course of their trade, business, craft or profession as well as personal debts incurred outside those activities, which cannot be reasonably separated, such debts, if dischargeable, shall be treated in a single procedure for the purposes of obtaining a full discharge of debt.

2. Member States may provide that, where professional debts and personal debts can be separated, those debts are to be treated, for the purposes of obtaining a full discharge of debt, either in separate but coordinated procedures or in the same procedure.

TITLE IV MEASURES TO INCREASE THE EFFICIENCY OF PROCEDURES CONCERNING RESTRUCTURING, INSOLVENCY AND DISCHARGE OF DEBT

[11.753]
Article 25 Judicial and administrative authorities

Without prejudice to judicial independence and to any differences in the organisation of the judiciary across the Union, Member States shall ensure that:
(a) members of the judicial and administrative authorities dealing with procedures concerning restructuring, insolvency and discharge of debt receive suitable training and have the necessary expertise for their responsibilities; and
(b) procedures concerning restructuring, insolvency and discharge of debt are dealt with in an efficient manner, with a view to the expeditious treatment of procedures.

[11.754]
Article 26 Practitioners in procedures concerning restructuring, insolvency and discharge of debt

1. Member States shall ensure that:
(a) practitioners appointed by a judicial or administrative authority in procedures concerning restructuring, insolvency and discharge of debt ('practitioners') receive suitable training and have the necessary expertise for their responsibilities;
(b) the conditions for eligibility, as well as the process for the appointment, removal and resignation of practitioners are clear, transparent and fair;
(c) in appointing a practitioner for a particular case, including cases with cross-border elements, due consideration is given to the practitioner's experience and expertise, and to the specific features of the case; and
(d) in order to avoid any conflict of interest, debtors and creditors have the opportunity to either object to the selection or appointment of a practitioner or request the replacement of the practitioner.

2. The Commission shall facilitate the sharing of best practices between Member States with a view to improving the quality of training across the Union, including by means of the exchange of experiences and capacity building tools.

[11.755]

Article 27 Supervision and remuneration of practitioners

1. Member States shall put in place appropriate oversight and regulatory mechanisms to ensure that the work of practitioners is effectively supervised, with a view to ensuring that their services are provided in an effective and competent way, and, in relation to the parties involved, are provided impartially and independently. Those mechanisms shall also include measures for the accountability of practitioners who have failed in their duties.

2. Member States shall ensure that information about the authorities or bodies exercising oversight over practitioners is publicly available.

3. Member States may encourage the development of and adherence to codes of conduct by practitioners.

4. Member States shall ensure that the remuneration of practitioners is governed by rules that are consistent with the objective of an efficient resolution of procedures.

Member States shall ensure that appropriate procedures are in place to resolve any disputes over remuneration.

[11.756]

Article 28 Use of electronic means of communication

Member States shall ensure that, in procedures concerning restructuring, insolvency and discharge of debt, the parties to the procedure, the practitioner and the judicial or administrative authority are able to perform by use of electronic means of communication, including in cross-border situations, at least the following actions:

(a) filing of claims;
(b) submission of restructuring or repayment plans;
(c) notifications to creditors;
(d) lodging of challenges and appeals.

TITLE V MONITORING OF PROCEDURES CONCERNING RESTRUCTURING, INSOLVENCY AND DISCHARGE OF DEBT

[11.757]

Article 29 Data collection

1. Member States shall collect and aggregate, on an annual basis, at national level, data on procedures concerning restructuring, insolvency and discharge of debt, broken down by each type of procedure, and covering at least the following elements:

(a) the number of procedures that were applied for or opened, where such opening is provided for under national law, and of procedures that are pending or were closed;
(b) the average length of procedures from the submission of the application, or from the opening thereof, where such opening is provided for under national law, to their closure;
(c) the number of procedures other than those required under point (d), broken down by types of outcome;
(d) the number of applications for restructuring procedures that were declared inadmissible, were rejected or were withdrawn before being opened.

2. Member States shall collect and aggregate, on an annual basis, at national level, data on the number of debtors which were subject to restructuring procedures or insolvency procedures and which, within the three years prior to the submission of the application or the opening of such procedures, where such opening is provided for under national law, had a restructuring plan confirmed under a previous restructuring procedure implementing Title II.

3. Member States may collect and aggregate, on an annual basis, at national level, data on:

(a) the average cost of each type of procedure;
(b) the average recovery rates for secured and unsecured creditors and, where applicable, other types of creditors, separately;
(c) the number of entrepreneurs who, after having undergone a procedure under point (b) of Article 1(1), launch a new business;
(d) the number of job losses linked to restructuring and insolvency procedures.

4. Member States shall break down the data referred to in points (a) to (c) of paragraph 1 and, where applicable and available, the data referred to in paragraph 3 by:

(a) the size of the debtors that are not natural persons;
(b) whether debtors subject to procedures concerning restructuring or insolvency are natural or legal persons; and
(c) whether the procedures leading to a discharge of debt concern only entrepreneurs or all natural persons.

5. Member States may collect and aggregate the data referred to in paragraphs 1 to 4 through a sample technique that ensures that the samples are representative in terms of size and diversity.

6. Member States shall collect and aggregate the data referred to in paragraphs 1, 2, 4 and, where applicable, paragraph 3, for full calendar years ending on 31 December of each year, starting with the first full calendar year following the date of application of implementing acts referred to in paragraph 7. The data shall be communicated annually to the Commission, on the basis of a standard data communication form, by 31 December of the calendar year following the year for which data are collected.

7. The Commission shall establish the communication form referred to in paragraph 6 of this Article by way of implementing acts. Those implementing acts shall be adopted in accordance with the examination procedure referred to in Article 30(2).

8. The Commission shall publish on its website the data communicated in accordance with paragraph 6 in an accessible and user-friendly manner.

[11.758]

Article 30 Committee procedure

1. The Commission shall be assisted by a committee. That committee shall be a committee within the meaning of Regulation (EU) No 182/2011.

2. Where reference is made to this paragraph, Article 5 of Regulation (EU) No 182/2011 shall apply.

Where the committee delivers no opinion, the Commission shall not adopt the draft implementing act and the third subparagraph of Article 5(4) of Regulation (EU) No 182/2011 shall apply.

TITLE VI FINAL PROVISIONS

[11.759]

Article 31 Relationship with other acts and international instruments

1. The following acts shall apply notwithstanding this Directive:
   (a) Directive 98/26/EC;
   (b) Directive 2002/47/EC; and
   (c) Regulation (EU) No 648/2012.

2. This Directive shall be without prejudice to the safeguarding requirements of funds for payment institutions laid down under Directive (EU) 2015/2366 of the European Parliament and of the Council[1] and for electronic money institutions laid down under Directive 2009/110/EC of the European Parliament and of the Council.[2]

3. This Directive shall be without prejudice to the application of the Convention on international interests in mobile equipment and its Protocol on matters specific to aircraft equipment, signed at Cape Town on 16 November 2001, to which some Member States are party at the time of the adoption of this Directive.

NOTES

[1] Directive (EU) 2015/2366 of the European Parliament and of the Council of 25 November 2015 on payment services in the internal market, amending Directives 2002/65/EC, 2009/110/EC and 2013/36/EU and Regulation (EU) No 1093/2010, and repealing Directive 2007/64/EC (OJ L337, 23.12.2015, p 35).

[2] Directive 2009/110/EC of the European Parliament and of the Council of 16 September 2009 on the taking up, pursuit and prudential supervision of the business of electronic money institutions amending Directives 2005/60/EC and 2006/48/EC and repealing Directive 2000/46/EC (OJ L267, 10.10.2009, p 7).

Article 32 (*Amends European Parliament and Council Directive 2017/1132/EU relating to certain aspects of company law at* **[11.380]**.)

[11.760]

Article 33 Review clause

No later than 17 July 2026 and every five years thereafter, the Commission shall present to the European Parliament, the Council and the European Economic and Social Committee a report on the application and impact of this Directive, including on the application of the class formation and voting rules in respect of vulnerable creditors, such as workers. On the basis of that assessment, the Commission shall submit, if appropriate, a legislative proposal, considering additional measures to consolidate and harmonise the legal framework on restructuring, insolvency and discharge of debt.

[11.761]

Article 34 Transposition

1. Member States shall adopt and publish, by 17 July 2021, the laws, regulations and administrative provisions necessary to comply with this Directive, with the exception of the provisions necessary to comply with points (a), (b) and (c) of Article 28 which shall be adopted and published by 17 July 2024 and the provisions necessary to comply with point (d) of Article 28 which shall be adopted and published by 17 July 2026. They shall immediately communicate the text of those provisions to the Commission.
They shall apply the laws, regulations and administrative provisions necessary to comply with this Directive from 17 July 2021, with the exception of the provisions necessary to comply with points (a), (b) and (c) of Article 28, which shall apply from 17 July 2024 and of the provisions necessary to comply with point (d) of Article 28, which shall apply from 17 July 2026.

2. By way of derogation from paragraph 1, Member States that encounter particular difficulties in implementing this Directive shall be able to benefit from an extension of a maximum of one year of the implementation period provided for in paragraph 1. Member States shall notify to the Commission the need to make use of this option to extend the implementation period by 17 January 2021.

3. Member States shall communicate to the Commission the text of the main provisions of national law which they adopt in the field covered by this Directive.

[11.762]

Article 35 Entry into force

This Directive shall enter into force on the twentieth day following that of its publication in the *Official Journal of the European Union*.

[11.763]

Article 36

This Directive is addressed to the Member States.

REGULATION OF THE EUROPEAN PARLIAMENT AND OF THE COUNCIL

(2019/2088/EU)

of 27 November 2019

on sustainability-related disclosures in the financial services sector

(Text with EEA relevance)

[11.764]

NOTES

Date of publication in OJ: OJ L317, 9.12.2019, p 1.

This Regulation is reproduced as amended by: European Parliament and Council Regulation 2020/852/EU.

Repeal of this Regulation in relation to the UK: only Articles 2a, 4(6), (7), 8(3), (4), 9(5), (6), 10(2), 11(4), (5), 13(2) of this Regulation were in force and applied immediately before IP completion day within the meaning of the European Union (Withdrawal) Act 2018, s 3 at **[12.5]**. Accordingly, the remaining provisions of this Regulation did not became domestic law on IP completion day. In so far as applying to the UK, this Regulation was amended by the Financial Services (Miscellaneous Amendments) (EU Exit) Regulations 2020, SI 2020/628, and by the Securities Financing Transactions, Securitisation and Miscellaneous Amendments (EU Exit) Regulations 2020, SI 2020/1385. The combined effect of the two sets of Regulations was to repeal Articles 2a, 4(6), (7), 8(3), (4), 9(5), (6), 10(2), 11(4), (5), 13(2) (and the provisions in Article 20 that brought them into force). This Regulation, therefore, does not apply to the UK.

THE EUROPEAN PARLIAMENT AND THE COUNCIL OF THE EUROPEAN UNION,

Having regard to the Treaty on the Functioning of the European Union, and in particular Article 114 thereof,

Having regard to the proposal from the European Commission,

After transmission of the draft legislative act to the national parliaments,

Having regard to the opinion of the European Economic and Social Committee,[1]

Acting in accordance with the ordinary legislative procedure,[2]

Whereas:

(1) On 25 September 2015, the UN General Assembly adopted a new global sustainable development framework: the 2030 Agenda for Sustainable Development (the '2030 Agenda'), which has at its core the Sustainable Development Goals (SDGs). The Commission Communication of 22 November 2016 on the next steps for a sustainable European future links the SDGs to the Union policy framework to ensure that all Union actions and policy initiatives, both within the Union and globally, take the SDGs on board at the outset. In its conclusions of 20 June 2017, the Council confirmed the commitment of the Union and its Member States to the implementation of the 2030 Agenda in a full, coherent, comprehensive, integrated and effective manner, and in close cooperation with partners and other stakeholders.

(2) The transition to a low-carbon, more sustainable, resource-efficient and circular economy in line with the SDGs is key to ensuring long-term competitiveness of the economy of the Union. The Paris Agreement adopted under the United Nations Framework Convention on Climate Change (the 'Paris Agreement'), which was approved by the Union on 5 October 2016[3] *and which entered into force on 4 November 2016, seeks to strengthen the response to climate change by, inter alia, making finance flows consistent with a pathway towards low greenhouse gas emissions and climate-resilient development.*

(3) In order to reach the objectives of the Paris Agreement and significantly reduce the risks and impacts of climate change, the global target is to hold the increase in the global average temperature to well below 2°C above pre-industrial levels and to pursue efforts to limit the temperature increase to 1.5°C above pre-industrial levels.

(4) Directives 2009/65/EC,[4] *2009/138/EC,*[5] *2011/61/EU,*[6] *2013/36/EU,*[7] *2014/65/EU,*[8] *(EU) 2016/97,*[9] *(EU) 2016/2341*[10] *of the European Parliament and of the Council, and Regulations (EU) No 345/2013,*[11] *(EU) No 346/2013,*[12] *(EU) 2015/760*[13] *and (EU) 2019/1238*[14] *of the European Parliament and of the Council share the common objective of facilitating the uptake and pursuit of the activities of undertakings for collective investment in transferable securities (UCITS), credit institutions, alternative investment fund managers (AIFMs) which manage or market alternative investment funds, including European long-term investment funds (ELTIFs), insurance undertakings, investment firms, insurance intermediaries, institutions for occupational retirement provision (IORPs), managers of qualifying venture capital funds (EuVECA managers), managers of qualifying social entrepreneurship funds (EuSEF managers) and providers of pan-European personal pension products (PEPPs). Those Directives and Regulations ensure the more uniform protection of end investors and make it easier for them to benefit from a wide range of financial products, while at the same time providing rules that enable end investors to make informed investment decisions.*

(5) Disclosures to end investors on the integration of sustainability risks, on the consideration of adverse sustainability impacts, on sustainable investment objectives, or on the promotion of environmental or social characteristics, in investment decision-making and in advisory processes, are insufficiently developed because such disclosures are not yet subject to harmonised requirements.

(6) The exemption from this Regulation for financial advisers which employ fewer than three persons should be without prejudice to the application of the provisions of national law transposing Directives 2014/65/EU and (EU) 2016/97, in particular the rules on investment and insurance advice. Therefore, although such advisers are not required to provide information in accordance with this Regulation, they are required to consider and factor in sustainability risks in their advisory processes.

(7) Entities covered by this Regulation, depending on the nature of their activities, should comply with the rules on financial market participants where they manufacture financial products and should comply with the rules on financial advisers where they provide investment advice or insurance advice. Therefore, where such entities carry out activities of both financial market participants and financial advisers concurrently, such entities should be deemed to be financial

market participants where they act in the capacity of manufacturers of financial products, including portfolio management, and should be deemed to be financial advisers where they provide investment or insurance advice.

(8) As the Union is increasingly faced with the catastrophic and unpredictable consequences of climate change, resource depletion and other sustainability-related issues, urgent action is needed to mobilise capital not only through public policies but also by the financial services sector. Therefore, financial market participants and financial advisers should be required to disclose specific information regarding their approaches to the integration of sustainability risks and the consideration of adverse sustainability impacts.

(9) In the absence of harmonised Union rules on sustainability-related disclosures to end investors, it is likely that diverging measures will continue to be adopted at national level and different approaches in different financial services sectors might persist. Such divergent measures and approaches would continue to cause significant distortions of competition because of significant differences in disclosure standards. In addition, the parallel development of market-based practices that are based on commercially-driven priorities that produce divergent results currently causes further market fragmentation and might even further exacerbate inefficiencies in the functioning of the internal market in the future. Divergent disclosure standards and market-based practices make it very difficult to compare different financial products, create an uneven playing field for such products and for distribution channels, and erect additional barriers within the internal market. Such divergences could also be confusing for end investors and could distort their investment decisions. In ensuring compliance with the Paris Agreement, there is a risk that Member States adopt divergent national measures which could create obstacles to the smooth functioning of the internal market and be detrimental to financial market participants and financial advisers. Furthermore, the lack of harmonised rules relating to transparency makes it difficult for end investors to effectively compare different financial products in different Member States with respect to their environmental, social and governance risks and sustainable investment objectives. It is therefore necessary to address existing obstacles to the functioning of the internal market and to enhance the comparability of financial products in order to avoid likely future obstacles.

(10) This Regulation aims to reduce information asymmetries in principal-agent relationships with regard to the integration of sustainability risks, the consideration of adverse sustainability impacts, the promotion of environmental or social characteristics, and sustainable investment, by requiring financial market participants and financial advisers to make pre-contractual and ongoing disclosures to end investors when they act as agents of those end investors (principals).

(11) This Regulation supplements the disclosure requirements laid down in Directives 2009/65/EC, 2009/138/EC, 2011/61/EU, 2014/65/EU, (EU) 2016/97, (EU) 2016/2341, and Regulations (EU) No 345/2013, (EU) No 346/2013, (EU) 2015/760 and (EU) 2019/1238 as well as in national law governing personal and individual pension products. To ensure the orderly and effective monitoring of compliance with this Regulation, Member States should rely on the competent authorities already designated under those rules.

(12) This Regulation maintains the requirements for financial market participants and financial advisers to act in the best interest of end investors, including but not limited to, the requirement of conducting adequate due diligence prior to making investments, provided for in Directives 2009/65/EC, 2009/138/EC, 2011/61/EU, 2013/36/EU, 2014/65/EU, (EU) 2016/97, (EU) 2016/2341, and Regulations (EU) No 345/2013 and (EU) No 346/2013, as well as in national law governing personal and individual pension products. In order to comply with their duties under those rules, financial market participants and financial advisers should integrate in their processes, including in their due diligence processes, and should assess on a continuous basis not only all relevant financial risks but also including all relevant sustainability risks that might have a relevant material negative impact on the financial return of an investment or advice. Therefore, financial market participants and financial advisers should specify in their policies how they integrate those risks and publish those policies.

(13) This Regulation requires financial market participants and financial advisers which provide investment advice or insurance advice with regard to insurance-based investment products (IBIPs), regardless of the design of the financial product and the target market, to publish written policies on the integration of sustainability risks and ensure the transparency of such integration.

(14) A sustainability risk means an environmental, social or governance event or condition that, if it occurs, could cause a negative material impact on the value of the investment, as specified in sectoral legislation, in particular in Directives 2009/65/EC, 2009/138/EC, 2011/61/EU, 2013/36/EU, 2014/65/EU, (EU) 2016/97, (EU) 2016/2341, or delegated acts and regulatory technical standards adopted pursuant to them.

(15) This Regulation should be without prejudice to the rules on the risk integration under Directives 2009/65/EC, 2009/138/EC, 2011/61/EU, 2013/36/EU, (EU) 2016/97, (EU) 2016/2341, and Regulations (EU) No 345/2013 and (EU) No 346/2013 and as well as under national law governing personal and individual pension products, including but not limited to the relevant applicable proportionality criteria such as size, internal organisation and the nature, scope and complexity of the activities in question. This Regulation seeks to achieve more transparency regarding how financial market participants and financial advisers integrate sustainability risks into their investment decisions and investment or insurance advice. Where the sustainability risk assessment leads to the conclusion that there are no sustainability risks deemed to be relevant to the financial product, the reasons therefor should be explained. Where the assessment leads to the conclusion that those risks are relevant, the extent to which those sustainability risks might impact the performance of the financial product should be disclosed either in qualitative or quantitative terms. The sustainability risk assessments and related pre-contractual disclosures by financial market participants should feed into pre-contractual disclosures by financial advisers. Financial advisers should disclose how they take sustainability risks into account in the selection process of the financial product that is presented to the end investors before providing the advice, regardless of the sustainability preferences of the end investors. This should be without prejudice to the application of provisions of national law transposing Directives 2014/65/EU and (EU) 2016/97, in particular the obligations on financial market participants and financial advisers as regards product governance, assessments of suitability and appropriateness, and the demands-and-needs test.

(16) Investment decisions and advice might cause, contribute to or be directly linked to effects on sustainability factors that are negative, material or likely to be material.

(17) To ensure the coherent and consistent application of this Regulation, it is necessary to lay down a harmonised definition of 'sustainable investment' which provides that the investee companies follow good governance

practices and the precautionary principle of 'do no significant harm' is ensured, so that neither the environmental nor the social objective is significantly harmed.

(18) Where financial market participants, taking due account of their size, the nature and scale of their activities and the types of financial products they make available, consider principal adverse impacts, whether material or likely to be material, of investment decisions on sustainability factors, they should integrate in their processes, including in their due diligence processes, the procedures for considering the principal adverse impacts alongside the relevant financial risks and relevant sustainability risks. The information on such procedures might describe how financial market participants discharge their sustainability-related stewardship responsibilities or other shareholder engagements. Financial market participants should include on their websites information on those procedures and descriptions of the principal adverse impacts. In that respect, the Joint Committee of the European Banking Authority established by Regulation (EU) No 1093/2010 of the European Parliament and of the Council[15] (EBA), the European Insurance and Occupational Pensions Authority established by Regulation (EU) No 1094/2010 of the European Parliament and of the Council[16] (EIOPA) and the European Securities and Markets Authority established by Regulation (EU) No 1095/2010 of the European Parliament and of the Council[17] (ESMA) (the 'Joint Committee'), and financial market participants and financial advisers should consider the due diligence guidance for responsible business conduct developed by the Organisation for Economic Co-operation and Development (OECD) and the United Nations-supported Principles for Responsible Investment.

(19) The consideration of sustainability factors in the investment decision-making and advisory processes can realise benefits beyond financial markets. It can increase the resilience of the real economy and the stability of the financial system. In so doing, it can ultimately impact on the risk-return of financial products. It is therefore essential that financial market participants and financial advisers provide the information necessary to enable end investors to make informed investment decisions.

(20) Financial market participants which consider the principal adverse impacts of investment decisions on sustainability factors should disclose in the pre-contractual information for each financial product, concisely in qualitative or quantitative terms, how such impacts are considered as well as a statement that information on the principal adverse impacts on sustainability factors is available in the ongoing reporting. Principal adverse impacts should be understood as those impacts of investment decisions and advice that result in negative effects on sustainability factors.

(21) Sustainable products with various degrees of ambition have been developed to date. Therefore, for the purposes of pre-contractual disclosures and disclosures in periodical reports, it is necessary to distinguish between the requirements for financial products which promote environmental or social characteristics and those for financial products which have as an objective a positive impact on the environment and society. As a consequence, as regards the financial products with environmental or social characteristics, financial market participants should disclose whether and how the designated index, sustainability index or mainstream index, is aligned with those characteristics and where no benchmark is used, information on how the sustainability characteristics of the financial products are met. As regards financial products which have as an objective a positive impact on the environment and society, financial market participants should disclose which sustainable benchmark they use to measure the sustainable performance and where no benchmark is used, explain how the sustainable objective is met. Those disclosures by means of periodic reports should be carried out annually.

(22) This Regulation is without prejudice to the rules on remuneration or the assessment of the performance of staff of financial market participants and financial advisers under Directives 2009/65/EC, 2009/138/EC, 2011/61/EU, 2013/36/EU, 2014/65/EU, (EU) 2016/97, (EU) 2016/2341, and Regulations (EU) No 345/2013 and (EU) No 346/2013, or to implementing acts and national law governing personal and individual pension products, including but not limited to the relevant applicable proportionality criteria such as size, internal organisation and the nature, scope and complexity of the activities in question. It is, however, appropriate to achieve more transparency, in qualitative or quantitative terms, on the remuneration policies of financial market participants and financial advisers, with respect to their investment or insurance advice, that promote sound and effective risk management with respect to sustainability risks whereas the structure of remuneration does not encourage excessive risk-taking with respect to sustainability risks and is linked to risk-adjusted performance.

(23) To enhance transparency and inform end investors, access to information on how financial market participants and financial advisers integrate relevant sustainability risks, whether material or likely to be material, in their investment decision making processes, including the organisational, risk management and governance aspects of such processes, and in their advisory processes, respectively, should be regulated by requiring those entities to maintain concise information about those policies on their websites.

(24) The current disclosure requirements set out in Union law do not require the disclosure of all the information necessary to properly inform end investors about the sustainability-related impact of their investments in financial products with environmental or social characteristics or financial products which pursue sustainability objectives. Therefore, it is appropriate to set out more specific and standardised disclosure requirements with regard to such investments. For instance, the overall sustainability-related impact of financial products should be reported regularly by means of indicators relevant for measuring the chosen sustainable investment objective. Where an appropriate index has been designated as a reference benchmark, that information should also be provided for the designated index as well as for a broad market index to allow for comparison. Where EuSEF managers make available information on the positive social impact that is the objective of a given fund, on the overall social outcome achieved and on the related methods used in accordance with Regulation (EU) No 346/2013, they might, where appropriate, use such information for the purposes of the disclosures under this Regulation.

(25) Directive 2013/34/EU of the European Parliament and of the Council[18] imposes transparency obligations as regards environmental, social and corporate governance matters in non-financial reporting. However, the form and presentation required by that Directive is not, always suitable for direct use by financial market participants and financial advisers when dealing with end investors. Financial market participants and financial advisers should have the option to use information in management reports and non-financial statements for the purposes of this Regulation in accordance with that Directive, where appropriate.

(26) To ensure the reliability of information published on the websites of financial market participants and

financial advisers, such information should be kept up to date, and any revisions or changes to such information should be clearly explained.

(27) Even though this Regulation does not cover national social security schemes covered by Regulations (EC) No 883/2004 and (EC) No 987/2009, in view of the fact that Member States increasingly open up parts of the management of compulsory pension schemes within their social security systems to financial market participants or other entities under private law, and as such schemes are exposed to sustainability risks and might consider adverse sustainability impacts, promote environmental or social characteristics or pursue sustainable investment, Member States should have the option to apply this Regulation with regard to such schemes in order to mitigate information asymmetries.

(28) This Regulation should not prevent a Member State from adopting or maintaining in force more stringent provisions on the publication of climate change adaptation policies and on additional disclosures to end investors regarding sustainability risks provided that the affected financial market participants and financial advisers, have their head offices in its territory. However, such provisions should not impede the effective application of this Regulation or the achievement of its objectives.

(29) Under Directive (EU) 2016/2341, IORPs are already required to apply governance and risk-management rules to their investment decisions and risk assessments in order to ensure continuity and regularity. Investment decisions and the assessment of relevant risks, including environmental, social and governance risks, should be made in such a manner as to ensure compliance with the interests of members and beneficiaries of IORPs. EIOPA should issue guidelines specifying how investment decisions and risk assessments by IORPs are to take into account environmental, social and governance risks under that Directive.

(30) EBA, EIOPA and ESMA (collectively, the 'ESAs') should be mandated, through the Joint Committee, to develop draft regulatory technical standards to further specify the content, methodologies and presentation of information in relation to sustainability indicators with regard to climate and other environment-related adverse impacts, to social and employee matters, to respect for human rights, and to anti-corruption and anti-bribery matters, as well as to specify the presentation and content of the information with regard to the promotion of environmental or social characteristics and sustainable investment objectives to be disclosed in pre-contractual documents, annual reports and on websites of financial market participants in accordance with Articles 10 to 14 of Regulations (EU) No 1093/2010, (EU) No 1094/2010 and (EU) No 1095/2010. The Commission should be empowered to adopt those regulatory technical standards by means of delegated acts pursuant to Article 290 of the Treaty on the Functioning of the European Union (TFEU) and in accordance with Articles 10 to 14 of Regulations (EU) No 1093/2010, (EU) No 1094/2010 and (EU) No 1095/2010.

(31) The ESAs should be mandated, through the Joint Committee, to develop draft implementing technical standards to determine the standard presentation of information on the promotion of environmental or social characteristics and sustainable investments in marketing communications. The Commission should be empowered to adopt those implementing technical standards by means of an implementing act pursuant to Article 291 TFEU and in accordance with Article 15 of Regulations (EU) No 1093/2010, (EU) No 1094/2010 and (EU) No 1095/2010.

(32) Since annual reports in principle summarise business results for complete calendar years, the provisions of this Regulation regarding the transparency requirements for such reports should not apply until 1 January 2022.

(33) The disclosure rules contained in this Regulation should supplement the provisions of Directives 2009/65/EC, 2009/138/EC, 2011/61/EU, 2014/65/EU, (EU) 2016/97 and (EU) 2016/2341, and Regulations (EU) No 345/2013, (EU) No 346/2013, (EU) 2015/760 and (EU) 2019/1238.

(34) This Regulation respects fundamental rights and observes the principles recognised in particular by the Charter of the Fundamental Rights of the European Union.

(35) Since the objectives of this Regulation, namely to strengthen protection for end investors and improve disclosures to them, including in cases of cross-border purchases by end investors, cannot be sufficiently achieved by the Member States but can rather, by reason of the need to lay down uniform disclosure requirements, be better achieved at Union level, the Union may adopt measures, in accordance with the principle of subsidiarity as set out in Article 5 of the Treaty on European Union. In accordance with the principle of proportionality, as set out in that Article, this Regulation does not go beyond what is necessary in order to achieve those objectives,

NOTES

Repeal of this Regulation in relation to the UK: see the introductory notes to this Regulation *ante*.

1 OJ C62, 15.2.2019, p 97.

2 Position of the European Parliament of 18 April 2019 (not yet published in the Official Journal) and decision of the Council of 8 November 2019.

3 Council Decision (EU) 2016/1841 of 5 October 2016 on the conclusion, on behalf of the European Union, of the Paris Agreement adopted under the United Nations Framework Convention on Climate Change (OJ L282, 19.10.2016, p 1).

4 Directive 2009/65/EC of the European Parliament and of the Council of 13 July 2009 on the coordination of laws, regulations and administrative provisions relating to undertakings for collective investment in transferable securities (UCITS) (OJ L302, 17.11.2009, p 32).

5 Directive 2009/138/EC of the European Parliament and of the Council of 25 November 2009 on the taking-up and pursuit of the business of Insurance and Reinsurance (Solvency II) (OJ L335, 17.12.2009, p 1).

6 Directive 2011/61/EU of the European Parliament and of the Council of 8 June 2011 on Alternative Investment Fund Managers (OJ L174, 1.7.2011, p 1).

7 Directive 2013/36/EU of the European Parliament and of the Council of 26 June 2013 on access to the activity of credit institutions and the prudential supervision of credit institutions and investment firms, amending Directive 2002/87/EC and repealing Directives 2006/48/EC and 2006/49/EC (OJ L176, 27.6.2013, p 338).

8 Directive 2014/65/EU of the European Parliament and of the Council of 15 May 2014 on markets in financial instruments and amending Directive 2002/92/EC and Directive 2011/61/EU (OJ L173, 12.6.2014, p 349).

9 Directive (EU) 2016/97 of the European Parliament and of the Council of 20 January 2016 on insurance distribution (OJ L26, 2.2.2016, p 19).

10 Directive (EU) 2016/2341 of the European Parliament and of the Council of 14 December 2016 on the activities and supervision of institutions for occupational retirement provision (IORPs) (OJ L354, 23.12.2016, p 37).

[11] Regulation (EU) No 345/2013 of the European Parliament and of the Council of 17 April 2013 on European venture capital funds (OJ L115, 25.4.2013, p 1).

[12] Regulation (EU) No 346/2013 of the European Parliament and of the Council of 17 April 2013 on European social entrepreneurship funds (OJ L115, 25.4.2013, p 18).

[13] Regulation (EU) 2015/760 of the European Parliament and of the Council of 29 April 2015 on European long-term investment funds (OJ L123, 19.5.2015, p.98).

[14] Regulation (EU) 2019/1238 of the European Parliament and of the Council of 20 June 2019 on a Pan-European Personal Pension Product (PEPP) (OJ L198, 25.7.2019, p 1).

[15] Regulation (EU) No 1093/2010 of the European Parliament and of the Council of 24 November 2010 establishing a European Supervisory Authority (European Banking Authority), amending Decision No 716/2009/EC and repealing Commission Decision 2009/78/EC (OJ L331, 15.12.2010, p 12).

[16] Regulation (EU) No 1094/2010 of the European Parliament and of the Council of 24 November 2010 establishing a European Supervisory Authority (European Insurance and Occupational Pensions Authority), amending Decision No 716/2009/EC and repealing Commission Decision 2009/79/EC (OJ L331, 15.12.2010, p 48).

[17] Regulation (EU) No 1095/2010 of the European Parliament and of the Council of 24 November 2010 establishing a European Supervisory Authority (European Securities and Markets Authority), amending Decision No 716/2009/EC and repealing Commission Decision 2009/77/EC (OJ L331, 15.12.2010, p 84).

[18] Directive 2013/34/EU of the European Parliament and of the Council of 26 June 2013 on the annual financial statements, consolidated financial statements and related reports of certain types of undertakings, amending Directive 2006/43/EC of the European Parliament and of the Council and repealing Council Directives 78/660/EEC and 83/349/EEC (OJ L182, 29.6.2013, p 19).

HAVE ADOPTED THIS REGULATION:

[11.765]

Article 1 Subject matter

This Regulation lays down harmonised rules for financial market participants and financial advisers on transparency with regard to the integration of sustainability risks and the consideration of adverse sustainability impacts in their processes and the provision of sustainability-related information with respect to financial products.

NOTES

Repeal of this Regulation in relation to the UK: see the introductory notes to this Regulation *ante*.

[11.766]

Article 2 Definitions

For the purposes of this Regulation, the following definitions apply:

(1) 'financial market participant' means:
- *(a) an insurance undertaking which makes available an insurance-based investment product (IBIP);*
- *(b) an investment firm which provides portfolio management;*
- *(c) an institution for occupational retirement provision (IORP);*
- *(d) a manufacturer of a pension product;*
- *(e) an alternative investment fund manager (AIFM);*
- *(f) a pan-European personal pension product (PEPP) provider;*
- *(g) a manager of a qualifying venture capital fund registered in accordance with Article 14 of Regulation (EU) No 345/2013;*
- *(h) a manager of a qualifying social entrepreneurship fund registered in accordance with Article 15 of Regulation (EU) No 346/2013;*
- *(i) a management company of an undertaking for collective investment in transferable securities (UCITS management company); or*
- *(j) a credit institution which provides portfolio management;*

(2) 'insurance undertaking' means an insurance undertaking authorised in accordance with Article 18 of Directive 2009/138/EC;

(3) 'insurance-based investment product' or 'IBIP' means:
- *(a) an insurance-based investment product as defined in point (2) of Article 4 of Regulation (EU) No 1286/2014 of the European Parliament and of the Council;*[1] *or*
- *(b) an insurance product which is made available to a professional investor and which offers a maturity or surrender value that is wholly or partially exposed, directly or indirectly, to market fluctuations;*

(4) 'alternative investment fund manager' or 'AIFM' means an AIFM as defined in point (b) of Article 4(1) of Directive 2011/61/EU;

(5) 'investment firm' means an investment firm as defined in point (1) of Article 4(1) of Directive 2014/65/EU;

(6) 'portfolio management' means portfolio management as defined in point (8) of Article 4(1) of Directive 2014/65/EU; (7) 'institution for occupational retirement provision' or 'IORP' means an institution for occupational retirement provision authorised or registered in accordance with Article 9 of Directive (EU) 2016/2341 except an institution in respect of which a Member State has chosen to apply Article 5 of that Directive or an institution that operates pension schemes which together have less than 15 members in total;

(7) 'institution for occupational retirement provision' or 'IORP' means an institution for occupational retirement provision authorised or registered in accordance with Article 9 of Directive (EU) 2016/2341 except an institution in respect of which a Member State has chosen to apply Article 5 of that Directive or an institution that operates pension schemes which together have less than 15 members in total;

(8) 'pension product' means:
- *(a) a pension product as referred to in point (e) of Article 2(2) of Regulation (EU) No 1286/2014; or*
- *(b) an individual pension product as referred to in point (g) of Article 2(2) of Regulation (EU) No 1286/2014;*

(9) 'pan-European Personal Pension Product' or 'PEPP' means a product as referred to in point (2) of Article 2 of Regulation (EU) 2019/1238;

(10) 'UCITS management company' means:
- *(a) a management company as defined in point (b) of Article 2(1) of Directive 2009/65/EC; or*
- *(b) an investment company authorised in accordance with Directive 2009/65/EC which has not designated a management company authorised under that Directive for its management;*

(11) 'financial adviser' means:
- *(a) an insurance intermediary which provides insurance advice with regard to IBIPs;*
- *(b) an insurance undertaking which provides insurance advice with regard to IBIPs;*
- *(c) a credit institution which provides investment advice;*
- *(d) an investment firm which provides investment advice;*
- *(e) an AIFM which provides investment advice in accordance with point (b)(i) of Article 6(4) of Directive 2011/61/EU; or*
- *(f) a UCITS management company which provides investment advice in accordance with point (b)(i) of Article 6(3) of Directive 2009/65/EC;*

(12) 'financial product' means:
- *(a) a portfolio managed in accordance with point (6) of this Article;*
- *(b) an alternative investment fund (AIF);*
- *(c) an IBIP;*
- *(d) a pension product;*
- *(e) a pension scheme;*
- *(f) a UCITS; or*
- *(g) a PEPP;*

(13) 'alternative investment funds' or 'AIFs' means AIFs as defined in point (a) of Article 4(1) of Directive 2011/61/EU;

(14) 'pension scheme' means a pension scheme as defined in point (2) of Article 6 of Directive (EU) 2016/2341;

(15) 'undertaking for collective investment in transferable securities' or 'UCITS' means an undertaking authorised in accordance with Article 5 of Directive 2009/65/EC;

(16) 'investment advice' means investment advice as defined in point (4) of Article 4(1) of Directive 2014/65/EU;

(17) 'sustainable investment' means an investment in an economic activity that contributes to an environmental objective, as measured, for example, by key resource efficiency indicators on the use of energy, renewable energy, raw materials, water and land, on the production of waste, and greenhouse gas emissions, or on its impact on biodiversity and the circular economy, or an investment in an economic activity that contributes to a social objective, in particular an investment that contributes to tackling inequality or that fosters social cohesion, social integration and labour relations, or an investment in human capital or economically or socially disadvantaged communities, provided that such investments do not significantly harm any of those objectives and that the investee companies follow good governance practices, in particular with respect to sound management structures, employee relations, remuneration of staff and tax compliance;

(18) 'professional investor' means a client who meets the criteria laid down in Annex II to Directive 2014/65/EU;

(19) 'retail investor' means an investor who is not a professional investor;

(20) 'insurance intermediary' means an insurance intermediary as defined in point (3) of Article 2(1) of Directive (EU) 2016/97;

(21) 'insurance advice' means advice as defined in point (15) of Article 2(1) of Directive (EU) 2016/97;

(22) 'sustainability risk' means an environmental, social or governance event or condition that, if it occurs, could cause an actual or a potential material negative impact on the value of the investment;

(23) 'European long-term investment fund' or 'ELTIF' means a fund authorised in accordance with Article 6 of Regulation (EU) 2015/760;

(24) 'sustainability factors' mean environmental, social and employee matters, respect for human rights, anti-corruption and anti-bribery matters.

NOTES

Repeal of this Regulation in relation to the UK: see the introductory notes to this Regulation *ante*.

[1] Regulation (EU) No 1286/2014 of the European Parliament and of the Council of 26 November 2014 on key information documents for packaged retail and insurance-based investment products (PRIIPs) (OJ L352, 9.12.2014, p 1).

[11.767]

[Article 2a Principle of do no significant harm

1. The European Supervisory Authorities established by Regulations (EU) No 1093/2010, (EU) No 1094/2010 and (EU) No 1095/2010 of the European Parliament and of the Council (collectively, the 'ESAs') shall, through the Joint Committee, develop draft regulatory technical standards to specify the details of the content and presentation of the information in relation to the principle of 'do no significant harm' referred to in point (17) of Article 2 of this Regulation consistent with the content, methodologies, and presentation in respect of the sustainability indicators in relation to the adverse impacts referred to in paragraphs 6 and 7 of Article 4 of this Regulation.

2. The ESAs shall submit the draft regulatory technical standards referred to in paragraph 1 to the Commission by 30 December 2020.

3. Power is delegated to the Commission to supplement this Regulation by adopting the regulatory technical standards referred to in paragraph 1 of this Article in accordance with Articles 10 to 14 of Regulations (EU) No 1093/2010, (EU) No 1094/2010 and (EU) No 1095/2010.]

NOTES

Inserted by European Parliament and Council Regulation 2020/852/EU, Art 25(1), as from 12 July 2020.

Repeal of this Regulation in relation to the UK: see the introductory notes to this Regulation *ante*.

Regulatory technical standards for the purposes of para 3: see Commission Delegated Regulation 2022/1288/EU supplementing Regulation (EU) 2019/2088 of the European Parliament and of the Council with regard to regulatory technical standards specifying the details of the content and presentation of the information in relation to the principle of 'do no significant harm', specifying the content, methodologies and presentation of information in relation to sustainability indicators and adverse sustainability impacts, and the content and presentation of the information in relation to the promotion of environmental or social characteristics and sustainable investment objectives in pre-contractual documents, on websites and in periodic reports. See the EUR-Lex website at eur-lex.europa.eu/legal-content/EN/TXT/?uri=CELEX:32022R1288.

[11.768]

Article 3 Transparency of sustainability risk policies

1. Financial market participants shall publish on their websites information about their policies on the integration of sustainability risks in their investment decision-making process.

2. Financial advisers shall publish on their websites information about their policies on the integration of sustainability risks in their investment advice or insurance advice.

NOTES

Repeal of this Regulation in relation to the UK: see the introductory notes to this Regulation *ante*.

[11.769]

Article 4 Transparency of adverse sustainability impacts at entity level

1. Financial market participants shall publish and maintain on their websites:

(a) where they consider principal adverse impacts of investment decisions on sustainability factors, a statement on due diligence policies with respect to those impacts, taking due account of their size, the nature and scale of their activities and the types of financial products they make available; or

(b) where they do not consider adverse impacts of investment decisions on sustainability factors, clear reasons for why they do not do so, including, where relevant, information as to whether and when they intend to consider such adverse impacts.

2. Financial market participants shall include in the information provided in accordance with point (a) of paragraph 1 at least the following:

(a) information about their policies on the identification and prioritisation of principal adverse sustainability impacts and indicators;

(b) a description of the principal adverse sustainability impacts and of any actions in relation thereto taken or, where relevant, planned;

(c) brief summaries of engagement policies in accordance with Article 3g of Directive 2007/36/EC, where applicable;

(d) a reference to their adherence to responsible business conduct codes and internationally recognised standards for due diligence and reporting and, where relevant, the degree of their alignment with the objectives of the Paris Agreement.

3. By way of derogation from paragraph 1, from 30 June 2021, financial market participants exceeding on their balance sheet dates the criterion of the average number of 500 employees during the financial year shall publish and maintain on their websites a statement on their due diligence policies with respect to the principal adverse impacts of investment decisions on sustainability factors. That statement shall at least include the information referred to in paragraph 2.

4. By way of derogation from paragraph 1 of this Article, from 30 June 2021, financial market participants which are parent undertakings of a large group as referred to in Article 3(7) of Directive 2013/34/EU exceeding on the balance sheet date of the group, on a consolidated basis, the criterion of the average number of 500 employees during the financial year shall publish and maintain on their websites a statement on their due diligence policies with respect to the principal adverse impacts of investment decisions on sustainability factors. That statement shall at least include the information referred to in of paragraph 2.

5. Financial advisers shall publish and maintain on their websites:

(a) information as to whether, taking due account of their size, the nature and scale of their activities and the types of financial products they advise on, they consider in their investment advice or insurance advice the principal adverse impacts on sustainability factors; or

(b) information as to why they do not to consider adverse impacts of investment decisions on sustainability factors in their investment advice or insurance advice, and, where relevant, including information as to whether and when they intend to consider such adverse impacts.

6. By 30 December 2020, the ESAs shall develop, through the Joint Committee, draft regulatory technical standards in accordance with Articles 10 to 14 of Regulations (EU) No 1093/2010, (EU) No 1094/2010 and (EU) No 1095/2010 on the content, methodologies and presentation of information referred to in paragraphs 1 to 5 of this Article in respect of the sustainability indicators in relation to adverse impacts on the climate and other environment-related adverse impacts.

The ESAs shall, where relevant, seek input from the European Environment Agency and the Joint Research Centre of the European Commission.

Power is delegated to the Commission to supplement this Regulation by adopting the regulatory technical standards referred to in the first subparagraph in accordance with Articles 10 to 14 of Regulations (EU) No 1093/2010, (EU) No 1094/2010 and (EU) No 1095/2010.

7. By 30 December 2021, the ESAs shall develop, through the Joint Committee, draft regulatory technical standards in accordance with Articles 10 to 14 of Regulations (EU) No 1093/2010, (EU) No 1094/2010 and (EU) No 1095/2010 on the content, methodologies and presentation of information referred to in paragraphs 1 to 5 of this Article in respect of sustainability indicators in relation to adverse impacts in the field of social and employee matters, respect for human rights, anti-corruption and anti-bribery matters.

Power is delegated to the Commission to supplement this Regulation by adopting the regulatory technical standards referred to in the first subparagraph in accordance with Articles 10 to 14 of Regulations (EU) No 1093/2010, (EU) No 1094/2010 and (EU) No 1095/2010.

NOTES

Repeal of this Regulation in relation to the UK: see the introductory notes to this Regulation *ante*.

Regulatory technical standards for the purposes of paras 6, 7: see Commission Delegated Regulation 2022/1288/EU supplementing Regulation (EU) 2019/2088 of the European Parliament and of the Council with regard to regulatory technical standards specifying the details of the content and presentation of the information in relation to the principle of 'do no significant harm', specifying the content, methodologies and presentation of information in relation to sustainability indicators and adverse sustainability impacts, and the content and presentation of the information in relation to the promotion of environmental or social characteristics and sustainable investment objectives in pre-contractual documents, on websites and in periodic reports. See the EUR-Lex website at eur-lex.europa.eu/legal-content/EN/TXT/?uri=CELEX:32022R1288.

[11.770]

Article 5 Transparency of remuneration policies in relation to the integration of sustainability risks

1. Financial market participants and financial advisers shall include in their remuneration policies information on how those policies are consistent with the integration of sustainability risks, and shall publish that information on their websites.

2. The information referred to in paragraph 1 shall be included in remuneration policies that financial market participants and financial advisers are required to establish and maintain in accordance with sectoral legislation, in particular Directives 2009/65/EC, 2009/138/EC, 2011/61/EU, 2013/36/EU, 2014/65/EU, (EU) 2016/97 and (EU) 2016/2341.

NOTES

Repeal of this Regulation in relation to the UK: see the introductory notes to this Regulation *ante*.

[11.771]

Article 6 Transparency of the integration of sustainability risks

1. Financial market participants shall include descriptions of the following in pre-contractual disclosures:

(a) the manner in which sustainability risks are integrated into their investment decisions; and

(b) the results of the assessment of the likely impacts of sustainability risks on the returns of the financial products they make available.

Where financial market participants deem sustainability risks not to be relevant, the descriptions referred to in the first subparagraph shall include a clear and concise explanation of the reasons therefor.

2. Financial advisers shall include descriptions of the following in pre-contractual disclosures:

(a) the manner in which sustainability risks are integrated into their investment or insurance advice; and

(b) the result of the assessment of the likely impacts of sustainability risks on the returns of the financial products they advise on.

Where financial advisers deem sustainability risks not to be relevant, the descriptions referred to in the first subparagraph shall include a clear and concise explanation of the reasons therefor.

3. The information referred to in paragraphs 1 and 2 of this Article shall be disclosed in the following manner:

(a) for AIFMs, in the disclosures to investors referred to in Article 23(1) of Directive 2011/61/EU;

(b) for insurance undertakings, in the provision of information referred to in Article 185(2) of Directive 2009/138/EC or, where relevant, in accordance with Article 29(1) of Directive (EU) 2016/97;

(c) for IORPs, in the provision of information referred to in Article 41 of Directive (EU) 2016/2341;

(d) for managers of qualifying venture capital funds, in the provision of information referred to in Article 13(1) of Regulation (EU) No 345/2013;

(e) for managers of qualifying social entrepreneurship funds, in the provision of information referred to in Article 14(1) of Regulation (EU) No 346/2013;

(f) for manufacturers of pension products, in writing in good time before a retail investor is bound by a contract relating to a pension product;

(g) for UCITS management companies, in the prospectus referred to in Article 69 of Directive 2009/65/EC;

(h) for investment firms which provide portfolio management or provide investment advice, in accordance with Article 24 (4) of Directive 2014/65/EU;

(i) for credit institutions which provide portfolio management or provide investment advice, in accordance with Article 24(4) of Directive 2014/65/EU;

(j) for insurance intermediaries and insurance undertakings which provide insurance advice with regard to IBIPs and for insurance intermediaries which provide insurance advice with regard to pension products exposed to market fluctuations, in accordance with Article 29(1) of Directive (EU) 2016/97;

(k) for AIFMs of ELTIFs, in the prospectus referred to in Article 23 of Regulation (EU) 2015/760;

(l) for PEPP providers, in the PEPP key information document referred to in Article 26 of Regulation (EU) 2019/1238.

NOTES

Repeal of this Regulation in relation to the UK: see the introductory notes to this Regulation *ante*.

[11.772]

Article 7 Transparency of adverse sustainability impacts at financial product level

1. By 30 December 2022, for each financial product where a financial market participant applies point (a) of Article 4 (1) or Article 4(3) or (4), the disclosures referred to in Article 6(3) shall include the following:

(a) a clear and reasoned explanation of whether, and, if so, how a financial product considers principal adverse impacts on sustainability factors;

(b) a statement that information on principal adverse impacts on sustainability factors is available in the information to be disclosed pursuant to Article 11(2).

Where information in Article 11(2) includes quantifications of principal adverse impacts on sustainability factors, that information may rely on the provisions of the regulatory technical standards adopted pursuant to Article 4(6) and (7).

2. Where a financial market participant applies point (b) of Article 4(1), the disclosures referred to in Article 6(3) shall include for each financial product a statement that the financial market participant does not consider the adverse impacts of investment decisions on sustainability factors and the reasons therefor.

NOTES

Repeal of this Regulation in relation to the UK: see the introductory notes to this Regulation *ante*.

[11.773]

Article 8 Transparency of the promotion of environmental or social characteristics in pre-contractual disclosures

1. Where a financial product promotes, among other characteristics, environmental or social characteristics, or a combination of those characteristics, provided that the companies in which the investments are made follow good governance practices, the information to be disclosed pursuant to Article 6(1) and (3) shall include the following:

(a) information on how those characteristics are met;

(b) if an index has been designated as a reference benchmark, information on whether and how this index is consistent with those characteristics.

2. Financial market participants shall include in the information to be disclosed pursuant to Article 6(1) and (3) an indication of where the methodology used for the calculation of the index referred to in paragraph 1 of this Article is to be found.

[2a. Where financial market participants make available a financial product as referred to in Article 6 of Regulation (EU) 2020/852 of the European Parliament and of the Council,[1] they shall include in the information to be disclosed pursuant to Article 6(1) and (3) of this Regulation the information required under Article 6 of Regulation (EU) 2020/852].

[3. The ESAs shall, through the Joint Committee, develop draft regulatory technical standards to specify the details of the content and presentation of the information to be disclosed pursuant to paragraphs 1 and 2 of this Article.]

When developing the draft regulatory technical standards referred to in the first subparagraph, the ESAs shall take into account the various types of financial products, their characteristics and the differences between them, as well as the objective that disclosures are to be accurate, fair, clear, not misleading, simple and concise.

The ESAs shall submit the draft regulatory technical standards referred to in the first subparagraph to the Commission by 30 December 2020.

Power is delegated to the Commission to supplement this Regulation by adopting the regulatory technical standards referred to in the first subparagraph in accordance with Articles 10 to 14 of Regulations (EU) No 1093/2010, (EU) No 1094/2010 and (EU) No 1095/2010.

[4. The ESAs shall, through the Joint Committee, develop draft regulatory technical standards to specify the details of the content and presentation of the information referred to in paragraph 2a of this Article.

When developing the draft regulatory technical standards referred to in the first subparagraph of this paragraph, the ESAs shall take into account the various types of financial products, their characteristics and the differences between them, as well as the objective that disclosures are to be accurate, fair, clear, not misleading, simple and concise and, where necessary to achieve that objective, shall develop draft amendments to the regulatory technical standards referred to in paragraph 3 of this Article. The draft regulatory technical standards shall take into account the respective dates of application set out in points (a) and (b) of Article 27(2) of Regulation (EU) 2020/852 in respect of the environmental objectives set out in Article 9 of that Regulation.

The ESAs shall submit the draft regulatory technical standards referred to in the first subparagraph to the Commission:

(a) in respect of the environmental objectives referred to in points (a) and (b) of Article 9 of Regulation (EU) 2020/852, by 1 June 2021; and

(b) in respect of the environmental objectives referred to in points (c) to (f) of Article 9 of Regulation (EU) 2020/852, by 1 June 2022.

Power is delegated to the Commission to supplement this Regulation by adopting the regulatory technical standards referred to in the first subparagraph of this paragraph in accordance with Articles 10 to 14 of Regulations (EU) No 1093/2010, (EU) No 1094/2010 and (EU) No 1095/2010.]

NOTES

Para 2a inserted, words in square brackets in para 3 substituted, and para 4 added, by European Parliament and Council Regulation 2020/852/EU, Art 25(2), as from 12 July 2020.

Repeal of this Regulation in relation to the UK: see the introductory notes to this Regulation *ante*.

Regulatory technical standards for the purposes of paras 3, 4: see Commission Delegated Regulation 2022/1288/EU supplementing Regulation (EU) 2019/2088 of the European Parliament and of the Council with regard to regulatory technical standards specifying the details of the content and presentation of the information in relation to the principle of 'do no significant harm', specifying the content, methodologies and presentation of information in relation to sustainability indicators and adverse sustainability impacts, and the content and presentation of the information in relation to the promotion of environmental or social characteristics and sustainable investment objectives in pre-contractual documents, on websites and in periodic reports. See the EUR-Lex website at eur-lex.europa.eu/legal-content/EN/TXT/?uri=CELEX:32022R1288.

[1] Regulation (EU) 2020/852 of the European Parliament and of the Council of 18 June 2020 on the establishment of a framework to facilitate sustainable investment, and amending Regulation (EU) 2019/2088 (OJ L198, 22.6.2020, p 13).';

[11.774]

Article 9 Transparency of sustainable investments in pre-contractual disclosures

1. Where a financial product has sustainable investment as its objective and an index has been designated as a reference benchmark, the information to be disclosed pursuant to Article 6(1) and (3) shall be accompanied by the following:

(a) information on how the designated index is aligned with that objective;

(b) an explanation as to why and how the designated index aligned with that objective differs from a broad market index.

2. Where a financial product has sustainable investment as its objective and no index has been designated as a reference benchmark, the information to be disclosed pursuant to Article 6(1) and (3) shall include an explanation on how that objective is to be attained.

3. Where a financial product has a reduction in carbon emissions as its objective, the information to be disclosed pursuant to Article 6(1) and (3) shall include the objective of low carbon emission exposure in view of achieving the long-term global warming objectives of the Paris Agreement.

By way of derogation from paragraph 2 of this Article, where no EU Climate Transition Benchmark or EU Paris-aligned Benchmark in accordance with Regulation (EU) 2016/1011 of the European Parliament and of the Council[1] is available, the information referred to in Article 6 shall include a detailed explanation of how the continued effort of attaining the objective of reducing carbon emissions is ensured in view of achieving the long-term global warming objectives of the Paris Agreement.

4. Financial market participants shall include in the information to be disclosed pursuant to Article 6(1) and (3) an indication of where the methodology used for the calculation of the indices referred to in paragraph 1 of this Article and the benchmarks referred to in the second subparagraph of paragraph 3 of this Article are to be found.

[4a. Financial market participants shall include in the information to be disclosed pursuant to Article 6(1) and (3) of this Regulation the information required under Article 5 of Regulation (EU) 2020/852.]

[5. The ESAs shall, through the Joint Committee, develop draft regulatory technical standards to specify the details of the content and presentation of the information to be disclosed pursuant to paragraphs 1 to 4 of this Article.]

When developing the draft regulatory technical standards referred to in the first subparagraph of this paragraph, the ESAs shall take into account the various types of financial products, their objectives as referred to in paragraphs 1, 2 and 3 and the differences between them as well as the objective that disclosures are to be accurate, fair, clear, not misleading, simple and concise.

The ESAs shall submit the draft regulatory technical standards referred to in the first subparagraph to the Commission by 30 December 2020.

Power is delegated to the Commission to supplement this Regulation by adopting the regulatory technical standards referred to in the first subparagraph in accordance with Articles 10 to 14 of Regulations (EU) No 1093/2010, (EU) No 1094/2010 and (EU) No 1095/2010.

[6. The ESAs shall, through the Joint Committee, develop draft regulatory technical standards to specify the details of the content and presentation of the information referred to in paragraph 4a of this Article.

When developing the draft regulatory technical standards referred to in the first subparagraph of this paragraph, the ESAs shall take into account the various types of financial products, their objectives as referred to in paragraph 4a of this Article and the differences between them as well as the objective that disclosures are to be accurate, fair, clear, not misleading, simple and concise and, where necessary to achieve that objective, shall develop draft amendments to the regulatory technical standards referred to in paragraph 5 of this Article. The draft regulatory technical standards shall take into account the respective dates of application set out in points (a) and (b) of Article 27(2) of Regulation (EU) 2020/852 in respect of the environmental objectives set out in Article 9 of that Regulation.

The ESAs shall submit the draft regulatory technical standards referred to in the first subparagraph to the Commission:

- *(a) in respect of the environmental objectives referred to in points (a) and (b) of Article 9 of Regulation (EU) 2020/852, by 1 June 2021; and*
- *(b) in respect of the environmental objectives referred to in points (c) to (f) of Article 9 of Regulation (EU) 2020/852, by 1 June 2022.*

Power is delegated to the Commission to supplement this Regulation by adopting the regulatory technical standards referred to in the first subparagraph of this paragraph in accordance with Articles 10 to 14 of Regulations (EU) No 1093/2010, (EU) No 1094/2010 and (EU) No 1095/2010.]

NOTES

Para 4a inserted, words in square brackets in para 5 substituted, and para 6 added, by European Parliament and Council Regulation 2020/852/EU, Art 25(3), as from 12 July 2020.

Repeal of this Regulation in relation to the UK: see the introductory notes to this Regulation *ante*.

Regulatory technical standards for the purposes of paras 5, 6: see Commission Delegated Regulation 2022/1288/EU supplementing Regulation (EU) 2019/2088 of the European Parliament and of the Council with regard to regulatory technical standards specifying the details of the content and presentation of the information in relation to the principle of 'do no significant harm', specifying the content, methodologies and presentation of information in relation to sustainability indicators and adverse sustainability impacts, and the content and presentation of the information in relation to the promotion of environmental or social characteristics and sustainable investment objectives in pre-contractual documents, on websites and in periodic reports. See the EUR-Lex website at eur-lex.europa.eu/legal-content/EN/TXT/?uri=CELEX:32022R1288.

1 Regulation (EU) 2016/1011 of the European Parliament and of the Council of 8 June 2016 on indices used as benchmarks in financial instruments and financial contracts or to measure the performance of investment funds and amending Directives 2008/48/EC and 2014/17/EU and Regulation (EU) No 596/2014 (OJ L171, 29.6.2016, p 1).

[11.775]

Article 10 Transparency of the promotion of environmental or social characteristics and of sustainable investments on websites

1. Financial market participants shall publish and maintain on their websites the following information for each financial product referred to in Article 8(1) and Article 9(1), (2) and (3):

- *(a) a description of the environmental or social characteristics or the sustainable investment objective;*
- *(b) information on the methodologies used to assess, measure and monitor the environmental or social characteristics or the impact of the sustainable investments selected for the financial product, including its data sources, screening criteria for the underlying assets and the relevant sustainability indicators used to measure the environmental or social characteristics or the overall sustainable impact of the financial product;*
- *(c) the information referred to in Articles 8 and 9;*
- *(d) the information referred to in Article 11.*

The information to be disclosed pursuant to the first subparagraph shall be clear, succinct and understandable to investors. It shall be published in a way that is accurate, fair, clear, not misleading, simple and concise and in a prominent easily accessible area of the website.

2. The ESAs shall, through the Joint Committee, develop draft regulatory technical standards to specify the details of the content of the information referred to in points (a) and (b) of the first subparagraph of paragraph 1, and the presentation requirements referred to in the second subparagraph of that paragraph.

When developing the draft regulatory technical standards referred to in the first subparagraph of this paragraph, the ESAs shall take into account the various types of financial products, their characteristics and objectives as referred to in paragraph 1 and the differences between them. The ESAs shall update the regulatory technical standards in the light of regulatory and technological developments.

The ESAs shall submit the draft regulatory technical standards referred to in the first subparagraph to the Commission by 30 December 2020.

Power is delegated to the Commission to supplement this Regulation by adopting the regulatory technical standards referred to in the first subparagraph in accordance with Articles 10 to 14 of Regulations (EU) No 1093/2010, (EU) No 1094/2010 and (EU) No 1095/2010.

NOTES

Repeal of this Regulation in relation to the UK: see the introductory notes to this Regulation *ante*.

Regulatory technical standards for the purposes of para 2: see Commission Delegated Regulation 2022/1288/EU supplementing Regulation (EU) 2019/2088 of the European Parliament and of the Council with regard to regulatory technical standards specifying the details of the content and presentation of the information in relation to the principle of 'do no significant harm', specifying the content, methodologies and presentation of information in relation to sustainability indicators and adverse sustainability impacts, and the content and presentation of the information in relation to the promotion of environmental or social characteristics and sustainable investment objectives in pre-contractual documents, on websites and in periodic reports. See the EUR-Lex website at eur-lex.europa.eu/legal-content/EN/TXT/?uri=CELEX:32022R1288.

[11.776]

Article 11 Transparency of the promotion of environmental or social characteristics and of sustainable investments in periodic reports

1. Where financial market participants make available a financial product as referred to in Article 8(1) or in Article 9(1), (2) or (3), they shall include a description of the following in periodic reports:

(a) for a financial product as referred to in Article 8(1), the extent to which environmental or social characteristics are met;

(b) for a financial product as referred to in Article 9(1), (2) or (3):

(i) the overall sustainability-related impact of the financial product by means of relevant sustainability indicators; or

(ii) where an index has been designated as a reference benchmark, a comparison between the overall sustainability-related impact of the financial product with the impacts of the designated index and of a broad market index through sustainability indicators;

[(c) for a financial product subject to Article 5 of Regulation (EU) 2020/852, the information required under that Article;

(d) for a financial product subject to Article 6 of Regulation (EU) 2020/852, the information required under that Article.]

2. The information referred to in paragraph 1 of this Article shall be disclosed in the following manner:

(a) for AIFMs, in the annual report referred to in Article 22 of Directive 2011/61/EU;

(b) for insurance undertakings, annually in writing in accordance with Article 185(6) of Directive 2009/138/EC;

(c) for IORPs, in the annual report referred to in Article 29 of Directive (EU) 2016/2341;

(d) for managers of qualifying venture capital funds, in the annual report referred to in Article 12 of Regulation (EU) No 345/2013;

(e) for managers of qualifying social entrepreneurship funds, in the annual report referred to in Article 13 of Regulation (EU) No 346/2013;

(f) for manufacturers of pension products, in writing in the annual report or in a report in accordance with national law;

(g) for UCITS management companies, in the annual report referred to in Article 69 of Directive 2009/65/EC;

(h) for investment firms which provide portfolio management, in a periodic report as referred to in Article 25(6) of Directive 2014/65/EU;

(i) for credit institutions which provide portfolio management, in a periodic report as referred to in Article 25(6) of Directive 2014/65/EU;

(j) for PEPP providers, in the PEPP Benefit Statement referred to in Article 36 of Regulation (EU) 2019/1238.

3. For the purposes of paragraph 1 of this Article, financial market participants may use the information in management reports in accordance with Article 19 of Directive 2013/34/EU or the information in non-financial statements in accordance with Article 19a of that Directive where appropriate.

[4. The ESAs shall, through the Joint Committee, develop draft regulatory technical standards to specify the details of the content and presentation of the information referred to in points (a) and (b) of paragraph 1.]

When developing the draft regulatory technical standards referred to in the first subparagraph, the ESAs shall take into account the various types of financial products, their characteristics and objectives and the differences between them. The ESAs shall update the regulatory technical standards in the light of regulatory and technological developments.

The ESAs shall submit the draft regulatory technical standards referred to in the first subparagraph to the Commission by 30 December 2020.

Power is delegated to the Commission to supplement this Regulation by adopting the regulatory technical standards referred to in the first subparagraph in accordance with Articles 10 to 14 of Regulations (EU) No 1093/2010, (EU) No 1094/2010 and (EU) No 1095/2010.

[5. The ESAs shall, through the Joint Committee, develop draft regulatory technical standards to specify the details of the content and presentation of the information referred to in points (c) and (d) of paragraph 1.

When developing the draft regulatory technical standards referred to in the first subparagraph of this paragraph, the ESAs shall take into account the various types of financial products, their characteristics and objectives and the differences between them and, where necessary, shall develop draft amendments to the regulatory technical standards referred to in paragraph 4 of this Article. The draft regulatory technical standards shall take into account the respective dates of application set out in points (a) and (b) of Article 27(2) of Regulation (EU) 2020/852 in respect of the environmental objectives set out in Article 9 of that Regulation. The ESAs shall update the regulatory technical standards in the light of regulatory and technological developments.

The ESAs shall submit the draft regulatory technical standards referred to in the first subparagraph to the Commission:

- *(a) in respect of the environmental objectives referred to in points (a) and (b) of Article 9 of Regulation (EU) 2020/852, by 1 June 2021; and*
- *(b) in respect of the environmental objectives referred to in points (c) to (f) of Article 9 of Regulation (EU) 2020/852, by 1 June 2022.*

Power is delegated to the Commission to supplement this Regulation by adopting the regulatory technical standards referred to in the first subparagraph of this paragraph in accordance with Articles 10 to 14 of Regulations (EU) No 1093/2010, (EU) No 1094/2010 and (EU) No 1095/2010.]

NOTES

Points (c) and (d) of para 1 inserted, words in square brackets in para 4 substituted, and para 5 added, by European Parliament and Council Regulation 2020/852/EU, Art 25(4), as from 12 July 2020.

Repeal of this Regulation in relation to the UK: see the introductory notes to this Regulation *ante*.

Regulatory technical standards for the purposes of paras 4, 5: see Commission Delegated Regulation 2022/1288/EU supplementing Regulation (EU) 2019/2088 of the European Parliament and of the Council with regard to regulatory technical standards specifying the details of the content and presentation of the information in relation to the principle of 'do no significant harm', specifying the content, methodologies and presentation of information in relation to sustainability indicators and adverse sustainability impacts, and the content and presentation of the information in relation to the promotion of environmental or social characteristics and sustainable investment objectives in pre-contractual documents, on websites and in periodic reports. See the EUR-Lex website at eur-lex.europa.eu/legal-content/EN/TXT/?uri=CELEX:32022R1288.

[11.777]

Article 12 Review of disclosures

1. Financial market participants shall ensure that any information published in accordance with Article 3, 5 or 10 is kept up to date. Where a financial market participant amends such information, a clear explanation of such amendment shall be published on the same website.

2. Paragraph 1 shall apply mutatis mutandis to financial advisers with regard to any information published in accordance with Articles 3 and 5.

NOTES

Repeal of this Regulation in relation to the UK: see the introductory notes to this Regulation *ante*.

[11.778]

Article 13 Marketing communications

1. Without prejudice to stricter sectoral legislation, in particular Directives 2009/65/EC, 2014/65/EU and (EU) 2016/97 and Regulation (EU) No 1286/2014, financial market participants and financial advisers shall ensure that their marketing communications do not contradict the information disclosed pursuant to this Regulation.

2. The ESAs may develop, through the Joint Committee, draft implementing technical standards to determine the standard presentation of information on the promotion of environmental or social characteristics and sustainable investments.

Power is delegated to the Commission to adopt the implementing technical standards referred to in the first subparagraph in accordance with Article 15 of Regulations (EU) No 1093/2010, (EU) No 1094/2010 and (EU) No 1095/2010.

NOTES

Repeal of this Regulation in relation to the UK: see the introductory notes to this Regulation *ante*.

[11.779]

Article 14 Competent authorities

1. Member States shall ensure that the competent authorities designated in accordance with sectoral legislation, in particular the sectoral legislation referred to in Article 6(3) of this Regulation, and in accordance with Directive 2013/36/EU, monitor the compliance of financial market participants and financial advisers with the requirements of this Regulation. The competent authorities shall have all the supervisory and investigatory powers that are necessary for the exercise of their functions under this Regulation.

2. For the purposes of this Regulation, the competent authorities shall cooperate with each other and shall provide each other, without undue delay, with such information as is relevant for the purposes of carrying out their duties under this Regulation.

NOTES

Repeal of this Regulation in relation to the UK: see the introductory notes to this Regulation *ante*.

[11.780]

Article 15 Transparency by IORPs and insurance intermediaries

1. IORPs shall publish and maintain the information referred to in Articles 3 to 7 and the first subparagraph of Article 10(1), of this Regulation in accordance with point (f) of Article 36(2) of Directive (EU) 2016/2341.

2. Insurance intermediaries shall communicate the information referred to in Article 3, Article 4(5), Article 5, Article 6 and the first subparagraph of Article 10(1), of this Regulation in accordance with Article 23 of Directive (EU) 2016/97.

NOTES

Repeal of this Regulation in relation to the UK: see the introductory notes to this Regulation *ante*.

[11.781]

Article 16 Pension products covered by Regulations (EC) No 883/2004 and (EC) No 987/2009

1. Member States may decide to apply this Regulation to manufacturers of pension products operating national social security schemes which are covered by Regulations (EC) No 883/2004 and (EC) No 987/2009. In such cases, manufacturers of pension products as referred to in point (1)(d) of Article 2 of this Regulation shall include manufacturers of pension products operating national social security schemes and of pension products referred to in point (8) of Article 2 of this Regulation. In such case, the definition of pension product in point (8) of Article 2 of this Regulation shall be deemed to include the pension products referred to in the first sentence.

2. Member States shall notify the Commission and the ESAs of any decision taken pursuant to paragraph 1.

NOTES

Repeal of this Regulation in relation to the UK: see the introductory notes to this Regulation *ante*.

[11.782]

Article 17 Exemptions

1. This Regulation shall neither apply to insurance intermediaries which provide insurance advice with regard to IBIPs nor to investment firms which provide investment advice that are enterprises irrespective of their legal form, including natural persons and self-employed persons, provided that they employ fewer than three persons.

2. Member States may decide to apply this Regulation to insurance intermediaries which provide insurance advice with regard to IBIPs or investment firms which provide investment advice as referred to in paragraph 1.

3. Member States shall notify the Commission and the ESAs of any decision taken pursuant to paragraph 2.

NOTES

Repeal of this Regulation in relation to the UK: see the introductory notes to this Regulation *ante*.

[11.783]

Article 18 Report

The ESAs shall take stock of the extent of voluntary disclosures in accordance with point (a) of Article 4(1) and point (a) of Article 7(1). By 10 September 2022 and every year thereafter, the ESAs shall submit a report to the Commission on best practices and make recommendations towards voluntary reporting standards. That annual report shall consider the implications of due diligence practices on disclosures under this Regulation and shall provide guidance on this matter. That report shall be made public and be transmitted to the European Parliament and to the Council.

NOTES

Repeal of this Regulation in relation to the UK: see the introductory notes to this Regulation *ante*.

[11.784]

Article 19 Evaluation

1. By 30 December 2022, the Commission shall evaluate the application of this Regulation and shall in particular consider:

- *(a) whether the reference to the average number of employees in Article 4(3) and (4) should be maintained, replaced or accompanied by other criteria, and shall consider the benefits and proportionality of the related administrative burden;*
- *(b) whether the functioning of this Regulation is inhibited by the lack of data or their suboptimal quality, including indicators on adverse impacts on sustainability factors by investee companies.*

2. The evaluation referred to in paragraph 1 shall be accompanied, if appropriate, by a legislative proposal.

NOTES

Repeal of this Regulation in relation to the UK: see the introductory notes to this Regulation *ante*.

[11.785]

Article 20 Entry into force and application

1. This Regulation shall enter into force on the twentieth day following that of its publication in the Official Journal of the European Union.

2. This Regulation shall apply from 10 March 2021.

[3. By way of derogation from paragraph 2 of this Article:

- *(a) Articles 4(6) and (7), 8(3), 9(5), 10(2), 11(4) and 13(2) shall apply from 29 December 2019;*
- *(b) Articles 2a, 8(4), 9(6) and 11(5) shall apply from 12 July 2020;*
- *(c) Articles 8(2a) and 9(4a) shall apply:*
  - *(i) in respect of the environmental objectives referred to in points (a) and (b) of Article 9 of Regulation (EU) 2020/852, from 1 January 2022; and*
  - *(ii) in respect of the environmental objectives referred to in points (c) to (f) of Article 9 of Regulation (EU) 2020/852, from 1 January 2023;*
- *(d) Article 11(1), (2) and (3) shall apply from 1 January 2022.]*

This Regulation shall be binding in its entirety and directly applicable in all Member States.

NOTES

Para 3: substituted by European Parliament and Council Regulation 2020/852/EU, Art 25(5), as from 12 July 2020.

Repeal of this Regulation in relation to the UK: see the introductory notes to this Regulation *ante*.

DIRECTIVE OF THE EUROPEAN PARLIAMENT AND OF THE COUNCIL

(2019/2121/EU)

of 27 November 2019

amending Directive (EU) 2017/1132 as regards cross-border conversions, mergers and divisions

(Text with EEA relevance)

[11.786]

NOTES

Date of publication in OJ: OJ L321, 12.12.2019, p 1. Note that Article 1 of this Directive was corrected by a corrigendum published in OJ L20, 24.1.2020, p 24.

Editorial note (legal status of EU Directives in the UK): note that EU Directives are not "direct EU legislation" within the meaning of the European Union (Withdrawal) Act 2018, s 3 at **[12.5]** and, accordingly, do not apply to the UK. As to the status of EU-derived domestic legislation after IP completion day (11pm on 31 December 2020), see s 2 of the 2018 Act at **[12.4]**. Note that Article 3 below provides that this Directive is implemented by 1 January 2023, and note also that no specific implementation measures were enacted in the UK prior to the UK leaving the European Union on 31 December 2020.

THE EUROPEAN PARLIAMENT AND THE COUNCIL OF THE EUROPEAN UNION,

Having regard to the Treaty on the Functioning of the European Union, and in particular Article 50(1) and (2) thereof,

Having regard to the proposal from the European Commission,

After transmission of the draft legislative act to the national parliaments,

Having regard to the opinion of the European Economic and Social Committee,[1]

Acting in accordance with the ordinary legislative procedure,[2]

Whereas:

(1) Directive (EU) 2017/1132 of the European Parliament and of the Council[3] regulates cross-border mergers of limited liability companies. The rules on cross-border mergers represent a significant milestone in improving the functioning of the internal market for companies and firms and their exercise of the freedom of establishment. However, evaluation of those rules shows that they need to be changed. Furthermore, it is appropriate to provide for rules regulating cross-border conversions and divisions, since Directive (EU) 2017/1132 only provides for rules on domestic divisions of public limited liability companies.

(2) Freedom of establishment is one of the fundamental principles of Union law. Under the second paragraph of Article 49 of the Treaty on the Functioning of the European Union ('TFEU'), when read in conjunction with Article 54 of the TFEU, the freedom of establishment for companies or firms includes, inter alia, the right to form and manage such companies or firms under the conditions laid down by the legislation of the Member State of establishment. This has been interpreted by the Court of Justice of the European Union as encompassing the right of a company or firm formed in accordance with the legislation of a Member State to convert itself into a company or firm governed by the law of another Member State, provided that the conditions laid down by the legislation of that other Member State are satisfied and, in particular, that the test adopted by the latter Member State to determine the connection of a company or firm with its national legal order is satisfied.

(3) In the absence of harmonisation of Union law, defining the connecting factor that determines the national law applicable to a company or firm falls, in accordance with Article 54 of the TFEU, within the competence of each Member State. Article 54 of the TFEU places the connecting factors of the registered office, the central administration and the principal place of business of a company or firm on an equal footing. Therefore, as clarified in case-law, the fact that only the registered office, and not the central administration or principal place of business, is transferred does not as such exclude the applicability of the freedom of establishment under Article 49 of the TFEU.

(4) Developments in the case-law have opened up new opportunities for companies in the internal market to foster economic growth, effective competition and productivity. At the same time, the objective of an internal market without internal borders for companies has also to be reconciled with other objectives of European integration, such as social protection as set out in Article 3 of the Treaty on European Union (TEU) and Article 9 of the TFEU, as well as the promotion of social dialogue as set out in Articles 151 and 152 of the TFEU. The rights of companies to convert, merge and divide across borders should go hand in hand, and be properly balanced, with the protection of employees, creditors and members.

(5) The lack of a legal framework for cross-border conversions and divisions leads to legal fragmentation and legal uncertainty, and thus to barriers to the exercise of the freedom of establishment. It also leads to the suboptimal protection of employees, creditors and minority members within the internal market.

(6) The European Parliament has called upon the Commission to adopt harmonised rules on cross-border conversions and divisions. A harmonised legal framework would further contribute to the removal of restrictions on the freedom of establishment while at the same time providing adequate protection for stakeholders such as employees, creditors and members.

(7) The Commission announced in its Communication of 28 October 2015 entitled 'Upgrading the Single Market: more opportunities for people and business' that it would assess the need to update the existing rules on cross-border mergers in order to make it easier for SMEs to choose their preferred business strategies and to better adapt to changes in market conditions, but without weakening existing employment protection. In its Communication of 25 October 2016 entitled 'Commission Work Programme 2017: Delivering a Europe that protects, empowers and defends', the Commission announced an initiative to facilitate cross-border mergers.

(8) In addition to new rules on conversions, this Directive lays down rules on cross-border divisions, both for partial and full divisions, but those rules only relate to cross-border divisions that involve the formation of new companies. This Directive does not provide a harmonised framework for cross-border divisions in which a company transfers assets and liabilities to one or more existing companies, as such cases have been viewed as being very complex, requiring the involvement of competent authorities from several Member States and entailing additional risks in terms of the circumvention of Union and national rules. The possibility of forming a company through a division by separation as provided for in this Directive offers companies a new harmonised procedure in the internal market. However, companies should be free to directly set up subsidiaries in other Member States.

(9) This Directive should not apply to companies in liquidation where the distribution of assets has begun. In addition, Member States should be able to choose to exclude companies subject to other liquidation proceedings from the application of this Directive. Member States should also be able to choose not to apply this Directive to companies subject to insolvency proceedings, as defined by national law, or to preventive restructuring frameworks, as defined by national law, irrespective of whether such proceedings are part of a national insolvency framework or regulated outside of it. Also, Member States should be able to choose not to apply this Directive to companies that are subject to crisis prevention measures as defined in Directive 2014/59/EU of the European Parliament and of the Council.[4] This Directive should be without prejudice to Directive (EU) 2019/1023 of the European Parliament and of the Council.[5]

(10) Given the complexity of cross-border conversions, mergers and divisions (collectively, 'cross-border operations') and the multitude of the interests concerned, it is appropriate to provide for the scrutiny of the legality of cross-border operations before they take effect, in order to provide legal certainty. To that effect, the competent authorities of the Member States involved should ensure that a decision on the approval of a cross-border operation is taken in a fair, objective and non-discriminatory manner and on the basis of all relevant elements required by Union and national law.

(11) This Directive should be without prejudice to Member States' powers to provide strengthened protection for employees in accordance with the existing social acquis.

(12) To allow all stakeholders' legitimate interests to be taken into account in the procedure governing a cross-border operation, the company should draw up and disclose the draft terms of the proposed operation, containing the most important information about it. The administrative or management body should, where provided for in national law or in accordance with national practice, or both, include board level employee representatives in the decision on the draft terms of a cross-border operation. Such information should at least include the legal form envisaged for the company or companies, the instrument of constitution where applicable, the statutes, the proposed indicative timetable for the operation and details of any safeguards offered to members and creditors. A notice should be disclosed in the register informing the members, creditors and representatives of the employees, or, where there are no such representatives, the employees themselves, that they may submit comments with regard to the proposed operation. Member States could also decide that the independent expert report required by this Directive has to be disclosed.

(13) In order to provide information to its members and employees, the company carrying out the cross-border operation should prepare a report for them. The report should explain and justify the legal and economic aspects of the proposed cross-border operation and the implications of the proposed cross-border operation for employees. In particular, the report should explain the implications of the cross-border operation with regard to the future business of the company, including its subsidiaries. As far as members are concerned, the report should include remedies available to them, especially information about their right to exit the company. For employees, the report should explain the implications of the proposed cross-border operation on the employment situation. In particular, the report should explain whether there would be any material change to the employment conditions laid down by law, to collective agreements or to transnational company agreements, and in the locations of the company's places of business, such as the location of the head office. In addition, the report should include information on the management body and, where applicable, on staff, equipment, premises and assets before and after the cross-border operation and the likely changes to the organisation of work, wages and salaries, the location of specific posts and the expected consequences for the employees occupying those posts, as well as on the company-level social dialogue, including, where applicable, board level employee representation. The report should also explain how those changes would affect any subsidiaries of the company.

No section for employees should be required where the only employees of the company are in its administrative or management body. Furthermore, in order to enhance the protection afforded to employees, either the employees themselves or their representatives should be able to provide their opinion on the report's section setting out the implications of the cross-border operation for them. The provision of the report and of any opinion should be without prejudice to applicable information and consultation procedures provided for at national level including those following the implementation of Directive 2002/14/EC of the European Parliament and of the Council[6] or Directive 2009/38/EC of the European Parliament and of the Council.[7] The report or, where drawn up separately, the reports, should

Part 11 EU & Retained EU Legislation

be available to the members and to the representatives of the employees of the company carrying out the cross-border operation or, where there are no such representatives, the employees themselves.

(14) The draft terms of the cross-border operation, the offer of cash compensation made by the company to those members who wish to exit the company and, where applicable, the share-exchange ratio, including the amount of any complementary cash payment included in the draft terms, should be examined by an expert who is independent from the company. With regard to the independence of the expert, Member States should take into account the requirements laid down in Articles 22 and 22b of Directive 2006/43/EC of the European Parliament and of the Council.[8]

(15) The information disclosed by the company should be comprehensive and make it possible for stakeholders to assess the implications of the intended cross-border operation. However, companies should not be obliged to disclose confidential information, the disclosure of which would be prejudicial to their business position, in accordance with Union or national law. Such non-disclosure should not undermine the other requirements provided for in this Directive.

(16) On the basis of the draft terms and the reports, the general meeting of the members of the company or companies should decide on whether or not to approve those draft terms and the necessary amendments to the instruments of constitution, including the statutes. It is important that the required majority for the vote be sufficiently large in order to ensure that the decision is taken by a solid majority. In addition, members should also have the right to vote on any arrangements concerning employee participation, if they have reserved that right during the general meeting.

(17) The lack of harmonisation of safeguards for members has been identified as an obstacle to cross-border operations. Companies and their members face a wide variety of different forms of protection leading to complexity and legal uncertainty. Members should, therefore, be offered the same minimum level of protection regardless of the Member State in which the company is situated. Member States should be able therefore to maintain or introduce additional rules on protection for members, unless such rules conflict with those provided for under this Directive or with the freedom of establishment. Members' individual rights to information should remain unaffected.

(18) As a consequence of a cross-border operation, members often face a situation whereby the law applicable to their rights changes because they become members of a company governed by the law of a Member State other than the Member State the law of which was applicable to the company before the operation. Member States should, therefore, at least provide for members holding shares with voting rights and who voted against the approval of the draft terms to have the right to exit the company and receive cash compensation for their shares that is equivalent to the value of those shares. However, Member States should be free to decide to extend that right also to other members, for example, to members holding shares without voting rights or members who, as a result of a cross-border division, would acquire shares in the recipient company in proportions different from those they held before the operation, or to members for whom there would be no change of applicable law but for whom certain rights would change due to the operation. This Directive should not affect national rules on the validity of contracts for the sale and transfer of shares in companies or special legal form requirements. Member States should, for example, be able to require a notarial deed or a confirmation of signatures.

(19) Companies should be able to estimate, to the extent possible, the costs related to the cross-border operation. Members should, therefore, be required to declare to the company whether they have decided to exercise the right to dispose of their shares. That requirement should be without prejudice to any formal requirements laid down in national law. Members might also be required to indicate, together with that declaration or within a specific time limit, whether they intend to dispute the cash compensation offered and claim additional cash compensation.

(20) The calculation of the offer of cash compensation should be based on generally accepted valuation methods. Members should have a right to dispute the calculation and question the adequacy of the cash compensation before a competent administrative or judicial authority or a body mandated under national law, including arbitral tribunals. Member States should be able to provide that members who have declared their decision to exercise the right to dispose of their shares are entitled to join such proceedings. Member States should also be able to establish time limits in national law for joining those proceedings.

(21) As far as cross-border mergers or divisions are concerned, members who did not have or did not exercise the right to exit the company should, nevertheless, have a right to dispute the share-exchange ratio. When assessing the adequacy of the share-exchange ratio, the competent administrative or judicial authority or a body mandated under national law should also take into account the amount of any complementary cash payment included in the draft terms.

(22) Following a cross-border operation, the former creditors of the company or companies carrying out that operation could see their claims affected where the company that is liable for the debt is, following that operation, governed by the law of another Member State. Currently, creditor protection rules vary across Member States, which adds significant complexity to the cross-border operation process and leads to uncertainty both for the companies involved and for their creditors in relation to the recovery or satisfaction of their claim.

(23) In order to ensure that creditors have appropriate protection in cases where they are not satisfied with the protection offered by the company in the draft terms and where they may not have found a satisfactory solution with the company, creditors, who have notified the company beforehand, should be able to apply for safeguards to the appropriate authority. When assessing such safeguards, the appropriate authority should take into account whether a creditor's claim against the company or a third party is of at least an equivalent value and of a commensurate credit quality as it was before the cross-border operation and whether the claim may be brought in the same jurisdiction.

(24) Member States should ensure that creditors who entered into a relationship with the company before the company had made public its intention to carry out a cross-border operation have adequate protection. After the draft terms of the cross-border operation have been disclosed, creditors should be able to take into account the potential impact of the change of jurisdiction and applicable law as a result of the cross-border operation. Creditors to be protected could comprise current and former employees with occupational vested pension rights and persons receiving occupational pension benefits. In addition to the general rules set out in Regulation (EU) No 1215/2012 of the European Parliament and of the Council,[9] Member States should provide that such creditors have the right to file a claim in the departure Member State for a period of two years after a cross-border conversion has taken effect. The two-year protection period provided for in this Directive with respect to the jurisdiction to which creditors whose claims antedate the disclosure of the draft terms of the cross-border conversion may apply, should be without prejudice to national law determining the limitation periods for claims.

(25) In addition, in order to protect creditors against the risk of the insolvency of the company following a cross-border operation, Member States should be allowed to require the company or companies to make a declaration of solvency stating that they are not aware of any reason why the company or companies resulting from the cross-border operation would not be able to meet their liabilities. In those circumstances, Member States should be able to make the members of the management body personally liable for the accuracy of that declaration. As legal traditions vary amongst Member States with regard to the use of solvency declarations and their possible consequences, it should be up to the Member States to decide on the appropriate consequences of providing inaccurate or misleading declarations, which should include effective and proportionate penalties and liabilities in compliance with Union law.

(26) It is important to ensure that the rights of employees to be informed and consulted in the context of cross-border operations are fully respected. The information and consultation of employees in the context of cross-border operations should be carried out in accordance with the legal framework provided for in Directive 2002/14/EC and, where applicable for Community-scale undertakings or Community-scale groups of undertakings, in accordance with Directive 2009/38/EC, as well as, where the cross-border merger or cross-border division is considered to be a transfer of an undertaking within the meaning of Council Directive 2001/23/EC,[10] in accordance with Directive 2001/23/EC. This Directive does not affect Council Directive 98/59/EC,[11] Directive 2001/23/EC, Directive 2002/14/EC or Directive 2009/38/EC. However, given that this Directive lays down a harmonised procedure for cross-border operations, it is appropriate to specify, in particular, the time frame within which the information and consultation of employees related to the cross-border operation should take place.

(27) Employee representatives provided for in national law or, where applicable, in accordance with national practice should also include any relevant bodies established in accordance with Union law, such as the European Works Council established in accordance with Directive 2009/38/EC and the representative body established in accordance with Council Directive 2001/86/EC.[12]

(28) Member States should ensure that employee representatives, when carrying out their functions, enjoy adequate protection and guarantees in accordance with Article 7 of Directive 2002/14/EC to enable them to perform properly the duties which have been assigned to them.

(29) In order to conduct an analysis of the report for employees, a company carrying out a cross-border operation should provide employee representatives with the resources necessary to enable them to exercise the rights arising from this Directive in an appropriate manner.

(30) In order to ensure that employee participation is not unduly prejudiced as a result of the cross-border operation, where the company carrying out the cross-border operation has implemented an employee participation system, the company or companies resulting from the cross-border operation should be obliged to take a legal form allowing for the exercise of such participation rights, including through the presence of representatives of the employees in the appropriate management or supervisory body of the company or companies. Moreover, in such a case, where a bona fide negotiation between the company and its employees takes place, it should be carried out in line with the procedure provided for in Directive 2001/86/EC, with a view to finding an amicable solution that reconciles the right of the company to carry out a cross-border operation with the employees' rights of participation. As a result of those negotiations, either a bespoke and agreed solution or, in the absence of an agreement, standard rules as set out in the Annex to Directive 2001/86/EC should apply, mutatis mutandis. In order to protect the agreed solution or the application of those standard rules, the company should not be able to remove the participation rights through carrying out a subsequent conversion, merger or division, be it cross-border or domestic, within four years.

(31) In order to prevent the circumvention of employee participation rights by means of a cross-border operation, the company or companies carrying out the cross-border operation and registered in the Member State which provides for the employee participation rights, should not be able to perform a cross-border operation without first entering into negotiations with its employees or their representatives when the average number of employees employed by that company is equivalent to four fifths of the national threshold for triggering such employee participation.

(32) The involvement of all stakeholders in cross-border operations, in particular the involvement of employees, contributes to a long-term and sustainable approach being taken by companies across the internal market. In this regard, safeguarding and promoting the participation rights of employees within the board of a company plays an important role, in particular when a company moves or restructures across borders. Therefore, the successful completion of negotiations on participation rights in the context of cross-border operations is essential and should be encouraged.

(33) To ensure that there is proper allocation of tasks among Member States and an efficient and effective ex-ante control of cross-border operations, the competent authorities of the Member States of the company or companies carrying out the cross-border operation should have the power to issue a pre-

conversion, pre-merger or pre-division certificate (hereinafter referred to as 'pre-operation certificate'). The competent authorities of the Member States of the company or companies resulting from the cross-border operation should not be able to approve the cross-border operation without such a certificate.

(34) In order to issue a pre-operation certificate, the Member States of the company or companies carrying out the cross-border operation should designate, in accordance with national law, an authority or authorities competent to scrutinise the legality of the operation. The competent authority could comprise courts, notaries or other authorities, a tax authority or a financial service authority. Where there is more than one competent authority, the company should be able to apply for the pre-operation certificate to one single competent authority, as designated by the Member States, which should co-ordinate with the other competent authorities. The competent authority should assess compliance with all relevant conditions and the proper completion of all procedures and formalities in that Member State, and should decide whether to issue a pre-operation certificate within three months of the application by the company, unless the competent authority has serious doubts indicating that the cross-border operation is set up for abusive or fraudulent purposes leading to or aimed at the evasion or circumvention of Union or national law, or for criminal purposes, and the assessment requires additional information to be considered or additional investigative activities to be performed.

(35) In certain circumstances, the right of companies to carry out a cross-border operation could be used for abusive or fraudulent purposes, such as for the circumvention of the rights of employees, social security payments or tax obligations, or for criminal purposes. In particular, it is important to counteract 'shell' or 'front' companies set up for the purpose of evading, circumventing or infringing Union or national law. Where, in the course of the scrutiny of the legality of a cross-border operation, the competent authority becomes aware, including through consultation of relevant authorities, that the cross-border operation is set up for abusive or fraudulent purposes leading to or aimed at the evasion or circumvention of Union or national law, or for criminal purposes, it should not issue the pre-operation certificate. The relevant procedures, including any assessment, should be carried out in accordance with national law. In such cases, the competent authority should be able to extend the period of assessment by a maximum of three months.

(36) Where the competent authority has serious doubts indicating that the cross-border operation is set up for abusive or fraudulent purposes, the assessment should consider all relevant facts and circumstances, and should take into account, where relevant, at a minimum, indicative factors relating to the characteristics of the establishment in the Member State in which the company or companies are to be registered after the cross-border operation, including the intention of the operation, the sector, the investment, the net turnover and profit or loss, the number of employees, the composition of the balance sheet, the tax residence, the assets and their location, equipment, the beneficial owners of the company, the habitual places of work of the employees and of specific groups of employees, the place where social contributions are due, the number of employees posted in the year prior to the cross-border operation within the meaning of Regulation (EC) No 883/2004 of the European Parliament and of the Council[13] and of Directive 96/71/EC of the European Parliament and of the Council,[14] the number of employees working simultaneously in more than one Member State within the meaning of Regulation (EC) No 883/2004, and the commercial risks assumed by the company or companies before and after the cross-border operation.

The assessment should also take into account relevant facts and circumstances related to employee participation rights, in particular as regards negotiations on such rights where those negotiations were triggered by reaching four fifths of the applicable national threshold. All of those elements should be considered only as indicative factors in the overall assessment and therefore should not be regarded in isolation. The competent authority may consider that if the cross-border operation were to result in the company having its place of effective management or place of economic activity in the Member State in which the company or companies are to be registered after the cross-border operation, that would be an indication of an absence of circumstances leading to abuse or fraud.

(37) The competent authority should also be able to obtain from the company carrying out the cross-border operation, or from other competent authorities, including those of the destination Member State, all relevant information and documents, with a view to carrying out the scrutiny of the legality of the cross-border operation within the procedural framework laid down in national law. Member States should be able to stipulate the possible consequences for the issuance of the pre-operation certificate of the procedures initiated by members and creditors in accordance with this Directive.

(38) In the assessment required to obtain a pre-operation certificate, the competent authority should be able to have recourse to an independent expert. Member States should lay down rules to ensure that the expert, or the legal person on whose behalf the expert is operating, is independent from the company applying for the pre-operation certificate. The expert should be appointed by the competent authority and should have no past or current link with the company concerned which might affect the expert's independence.

(39) In order to ensure that the company carrying out the cross-border operation does not prejudice its creditors, the competent authority should be able to check, in particular, whether the company has fulfilled its obligations towards public creditors and whether any open obligations have been sufficiently secured. In particular, the competent authority should be able to check whether the company is the subject of any ongoing court proceedings concerning, for example, infringement of social, labour or environmental law, the outcome of which might lead to further obligations being imposed on the company, including in respect of citizens and private entities.

(40) Member States should provide for procedural safeguards in line with the general principles of access to justice, including providing for the possibility of reviewing the decisions of the competent authorities in the proceedings concerning cross-border operations, the possibility of delaying the time when a pre-operation certificate takes effect in order to allow parties to bring an action before the competent court and the possibility of having interim measures granted, where appropriate.

(41) Member States should ensure that the completion of certain procedural steps, namely, the disclosure of the draft terms, the application for a pre-operation certificate as well as the submission of any information and documents for the scrutiny of the legality of the cross-border operation by the destination Member State, can be completed fully online, without the necessity for the applicants to appear in person before a competent authority in the Member States. The rules on the use of digital tools and processes in company law, including the relevant safeguards, should apply as appropriate. The competent authority should be able to receive the application for the pre-operation certificate online, including the submission of any information and documents, unless, exceptionally, it is technically impossible for the competent authority.

(42) In order to cut costs and reduce the length of the procedures and administrative burden for companies, Member States should apply the 'once-only' principle in the area of company law, which entails that companies are not required to submit the same information to more than one public authority. For example, companies should not have to submit the same information both to the national register and to the national gazette.

(43) In order to provide for an appropriate level of transparency and the use of digital tools and processes, the pre-operation certificates issued by the competent authorities in different Member States should be shared through the system of interconnection of registers and should be made publicly available. In accordance with the general principle underlying Directive (EU) 2017/1132, such exchange of information should always be free of charge.

(44) The carrying out of a cross-border conversion entails a change of the legal form of a company without that company losing its legal personality. However, neither a cross-border conversion nor a cross-border merger or division should lead to the circumvention of the requirements for incorporation in the Member State in which the company is to be registered after that cross-border operation. Such conditions, including the requirements to have the head office in the destination Member State and those relating to the disqualification of directors, should be fully respected by the company. However, in the case of cross-border conversions, the application of such conditions by the destination Member State should not affect the continuity of the converted company's legal personality.

(45) Once a pre-operation certificate has been received, and after verifying that the legal requirements of the Member State in which the company is to be registered after the cross-border operation are fulfilled, including a possible check as to whether the cross-border operation constitutes a circumvention of Union or national law, the competent authorities should register the company in the register of that Member State. Only after this registration should the competent authority of the former Member State of the company or companies carrying out the cross-border operation strike the company off its own register. It should not be possible for the competent authorities of the Member State in which the company is to be registered after the cross-border operation to dispute the information provided by the pre-operation certificate.

(46) To enhance the transparency of cross-border operations, it is important that the registers of the Member States involved contain the necessary information from other registers about the companies involved in those operations in order to be able to track the history of those companies. In particular, the file in the register in which the company was registered prior to the cross-border operation should contain the new registration number attributed to that company after the cross-border operation. Similarly, the file in the register in which the company is registered after the cross-border operation should contain the initial registration number attributed to the company prior to the cross-border operation.

(47) As a consequence of the cross-border conversion, the company resulting from the conversion (the 'converted company') should retain its legal personality, its assets and liabilities, and all its rights and obligations, including any rights and obligations arising from contracts, acts or omissions. In particular, the converted company should respect any rights and obligations arising from contracts of employment or from employment relationships, including any collective agreements.

(48) As a consequence of the cross-border merger, the assets and liabilities and all rights and obligations, including any rights and obligations arising from contracts, acts or omissions, should be transferred to the acquiring company or to the new company, and the members of the merging companies who do not exercise their exit rights should become members of the acquiring company or the new company respectively. In particular, the acquiring company or the new company should respect any rights and obligations arising from contracts of employment or from employment relationships, including any collective agreements.

(49) As a consequence of the cross-border division, the assets and liabilities and all rights and obligations, including any rights and obligations arising from contracts, acts or omissions, should be transferred to the recipient companies in accordance with the allocation specified in the draft terms of division, and the members of the company being divided who do not exercise their exit rights should become members of the recipient companies, should remain members of the company being divided or should become members of both. In particular, recipient companies should respect any rights and obligations arising from contracts of employment or from employment relationships, including any collective agreements.

(50) In order to ensure legal certainty, it should not be possible to declare a cross-border operation which has taken effect in accordance with the procedure laid down in this Directive null and void. That restriction should be without prejudice to Member States' powers, inter alia, in relation to criminal law,

the prevention and combatting of terrorist financing, social law, taxation and law enforcement under national laws, in particular in the event that the competent or other relevant authorities establish, in particular through new substantive information, after the cross-border operation took effect, that the cross-border operation was set up for abusive or fraudulent purposes leading to or aimed at the evasion or circumvention of Union or national law or for criminal purposes. In this context, the competent authorities could also assess whether the applicable national threshold for employee participation of the Member State of the company carrying out the cross-border operation was met or exceeded in the years following the cross-border operation.

(51) Any cross-border operation should be without prejudice to liability for tax obligations related to a company's activity before that operation.

(52) To guarantee the rights of employees other than rights of participation, Directives 98/59/EC, 2001/23/EC, 2002/14/EC and 2009/38/EC are not affected by this Directive. National laws should also apply to matters outside the scope of this Directive such as tax or social security.

(53) This Directive does not affect the legal or administrative provisions of national law relating to the taxes of Member States or their territorial and administrative subdivisions, including the enforcement of tax rules in cross-border operations.

(54) This Directive is without prejudice to Council Directives 2009/133/EC,[15] (EU) 2015/2376,[16] (EU) 2016/881,[17] (EU) 2016/1164[18] and (EU) 2018/822.[19]

(55) This Directive is without prejudice to the provisions of Directive (EU) 2015/849 of the European Parliament and of the Council[20] that address risks of money laundering and terrorist financing, in particular the obligations provided for therein relating to the carrying out of appropriate customer due diligence measures on a risk-sensitive basis, and those relating to identifying and registering the beneficial owner of any newly created entity in the Member State of its incorporation.

(56) This Directive does not affect Union law concerning transparency and the rights of shareholders in listed companies, or national rules laid down or introduced pursuant to such Union law.

(57) This Directive does not affect Union law regulating credit intermediaries and other financial undertakings, or national rules laid down or introduced pursuant to such Union law.

(58) Since the objectives of this Directive, namely to facilitate and regulate cross-border conversions, mergers and divisions, cannot be sufficiently achieved by the Member States, but can rather, by reason of its scale and effects, be better achieved at Union level, the Union may adopt measures, in accordance with the principle of subsidiarity as set out in Article 5 of the TEU. In accordance with the principle of proportionality as set out in that Article, this Directive does not go beyond what is necessary in order to achieve those objectives.

(59) This Directive respects the fundamental rights and observes the principles recognised in particular by the Charter of Fundamental Rights of the European Union.

(60) In accordance with the Joint Political Declaration of 28 September 2011 of Member States and the Commission on explanatory documents,[21] Member States have undertaken to accompany, in justified cases, the notification of their transposition measures with one or more documents explaining the relationship between the components of a directive and the corresponding parts of national transposition instruments. With regard to this Directive, the legislator considers the transmission of such documents to be justified.

(61) The Commission should carry out an evaluation of this Directive, including an evaluation of the implementation of the provisions on employee information, consultation and participation in the context of cross-border operations. The evaluation should, in particular, aim to assess cross-border operations where negotiations on employee participation were triggered by reaching four fifths of the applicable threshold, and to see whether, after the cross-border operation, those companies met or exceeded the applicable threshold for employee participation of the Member State of the company which carried out the cross-border operation. Pursuant to paragraph 22 of the Interinstitutional Agreement of 13 April 2016 on Better Law-Making[22] (the 'Interinstitutional Agreement'), that evaluation should be based on the five criteria of efficiency, effectiveness, relevance, coherence and value added, and should provide the basis for impact assessments of possible further measures.

(62) Information should be collected in order to assess the performance of the provisions of this Directive in relation to the objectives it pursues and in order to provide the basis for an evaluation of Directive (EU) 2017/1132 in accordance with paragraph 22 of the Interinstitutional Agreement.

(63) Directive (EU) 2017/1132 should therefore be amended accordingly,

NOTES

1 OJ C62, 15.2.2019, p 24.

2 Position of the European Parliament of 18 April 2019 (not yet published in the Official Journal) and decision of the Council of 18 November 2019.

3 Directive (EU) 2017/1132 of the European Parliament and of the Council of 14 June 2017 relating to certain aspects of company law (OJ L169, 30.6.2017, p 46).

4 Directive 2014/59/EU of the European Parliament and of the Council of 15 May 2014 establishing a framework for the recovery and resolution of credit institutions and investment firms and amending Council Directive 82/891/EEC, and Directives 2001/24/EC, 2002/47/EC, 2004/25/EC, 2005/56/EC, 2007/36/EC, 2011/35/EU, 2012/30/EU and 2013/36/EU, and Regulations (EU) No 1093/2010 and (EU) No 648/2012, of the European Parliament and of the Council (OJ L173, 12.6.2014, p 190).

5 Directive (EU) 2019/1023 of the European Parliament and of the Council of 20 June 2019 on preventive restructuring frameworks, on discharge of debt and disqualifications, and on measures to increase the efficiency of procedures concerning restructuring, insolvency and discharge of debt, and amending Directive (EU) 2017/1132 (Directive on restructuring and insolvency) (OJ L172, 26.6.2019, p 18).

6 Directive 2002/14/EC of the European Parliament and of the Council of 11 March 2002 establishing a general framework

for informing and consulting employees in the European Community (OJ L80, 23.3.2002, p 29).

7 Directive 2009/38/EC of the European Parliament and of the Council of 6 May 2009 on the establishment of a European Works Council or a procedure in Community-scale undertakings and Community-scale groups of undertakings for the purposes of informing and consulting employees (OJ L122, 16.5.2009, p 28).

8 Directive 2006/43/EC of the European Parliament and of the Council of 17 May 2006 on statutory audits of annual accounts and consolidated accounts, amending Council Directives 78/660/EEC and 83/349/EEC and repealing Council Directive 84/253/EEC (OJ L157, 9.6.2006, p 87).

9 Regulation (EU) No 1215/2012 of the European Parliament and of the Council of 12 December 2012 on jurisdiction and the recognition and enforcement of judgments in civil and commercial matters (OJ L351, 20.12.2012, p 1).

10 Council Directive 2001/23/EC of 12 March 2001 on the approximation of the laws of the Member States relating to the safeguarding of employees' rights in the event of transfers of undertakings, businesses or parts of undertakings or businesses (OJ L82, 22.3.2001, p 16).

11 Council Directive 98/59/EC of 20 July 1998 on the approximation of the laws of the Member States relating to collective redundancies (OJ L225, 12.8.1998, p 16).

12 Council Directive 2001/86/EC of 8 October 2001 supplementing the Statute for a European company with regard to the involvement of employees (OJ L294, 10.11.2001, p 22).

13 Regulation (EC) No 883/2004 of the European Parliament and of the Council of 29 April 2004 on the coordination of social security systems (OJ L166, 30.4.2004, p 1).

14 Directive 96/71/EC of the European Parliament and of the Council of 16 December 1996 concerning the posting of workers in the framework of the provision of services (OJ L18, 21.1.1997, p 1).

15 Council Directive 2009/133/EC of 19 October 2009 on the common system of taxation applicable to mergers, divisions, partial divisions, transfers of assets and exchanges of shares concerning companies of different Member States and to the transfer of the registered office of an SE or SCE between Member States (OJ L310, 25.11.2009, p 34).

16 Council Directive (EU) 2015/2376 of 8 December 2015 amending Directive 2011/16/EU as regards mandatory automatic exchange of information in the field of taxation (OJ L332, 18.12.2015, p 1).

17 Council Directive (EU) 2016/881 of 25 May 2016 amending Directive 2011/16/EU as regards mandatory automatic exchange of information in the field of taxation (OJ L146, 3.6.2016, p 8).

18 Council Directive (EU) 2016/1164 of 12 July 2016 laying down rules against tax avoidance practices that directly affect the functioning of the internal market (OJ L193, 19.7.2016, p 1).

19 Council Directive (EU) 2018/822 of 25 May 2018 amending Directive 2011/16/EU as regards mandatory automatic exchange of information in the field of taxation in relation to reportable cross-border arrangements (OJ L139, 5.6.2018, p 1).

20 Directive (EU) 2015/849 of the European Parliament and of the Council of 20 May 2015 on the prevention of the use of the financial system for the purposes of money laundering or terrorist financing, amending Regulation (EU) No 648/2012 of the European Parliament and of the Council, and repealing Directive 2005/60/EC of the European Parliament and of the Council and Commission Directive 2006/70/EC (OJ L141, 5.6.2015, p 73).

21 OJ C369, 17.12.2011, p 14.

22 OJ L123, 12.5.2016, p 1.

HAVE ADOPTED THIS DIRECTIVE:

Articles 1, 2 *(Article 1 amends European Parliament and Council Directive 2017/1132/EU relating to certain aspects of company law (the Codified Company Law Directive) at* **[11.380]** *et seq. Article 2 provides that "Member States shall lay down the rules on measures and penalties to infringements of national provisions adopted pursuant to this Directive and shall take all measures necessary to ensure that they are implemented. Member States may provide for criminal penalties for serious infringements".)*

[11.787]

Article 3 Transposition

1. Member States shall bring into force the laws, regulations and administrative provisions necessary to comply with this Directive by 31 January 2023. They shall immediately inform the Commission thereof.

When Member States adopt those measures, they shall contain a reference to this Directive or shall be accompanied by such a reference on the occasion of their official publication. The methods of making such reference shall be laid down by Member States.

2. Member States shall communicate to the Commission the text of the main measures of national law which they adopt in the field covered by this Directive.

Articles 4–6 *(Article 4 concerns the review etc of this Directive by the Commission. Article 5 provides that this Directive shall enter into force on the twentieth day following that of its publication in the Official Journal. Article 6 provides that this Directive is addressed to the Member States.)*

REGULATION OF THE EUROPEAN PARLIAMENT AND OF THE COUNCIL

(2020/852/EU)

of 18 June 2020

on the establishment of a framework to facilitate sustainable investment, and amending Regulation (EU) 2019/2088

(Text with EEA relevance)

[11.788]

NOTES

Date of publication in OJ: OJ L198, 22.6.2020, p 13. The text of this Regulation incorporates the corrigendum published in OJ L156, 9.6.2022, p 159.

Application of this Regulation in relation to the UK: only provisions of this Regulation that were in force and applied immediately before IP completion day fall within the scope of the European Union (Withdrawal) Act 2018, s 3 at **[12.5]** (incorporation of direct EU legislation). Accordingly, the remaining provisions of this Regulation did not became domestic law on IP completion day. See further Article 27 of this Regulation (Entry into force and application) at **[11.814]**. In so far as applying to the UK, this Regulation is amended by the Securities Financing Transactions, Securitisation and Miscellaneous Amendments (EU Exit) Regulations 2020, SI 2020/1385. With regard to these amendments, note that Articles that are repealed are reproduced in italics. In the case of other amendments, the amending provision from the 2020 Regulations is set out in the Notes to the amended Article, and the text of the amended Article has not been changed.

THE EUROPEAN PARLIAMENT AND THE COUNCIL OF THE EUROPEAN UNION,

Having regard to the Treaty on the Functioning of the European Union, and in particular Article 114 thereof,

Having regard to the proposal from the European Commission,

After transmission of the draft legislative act to the national parliaments,

Having regard to the opinion of the European Economic and Social Committee,[1]

Acting in accordance with the ordinary legislative procedure,[2]

Whereas:

(1) Article 3(3) of the Treaty on European Union aims to establish an internal market that works for the sustainable development of Europe, based, among other things, on balanced economic growth and a high level of protection and the improvement of the quality of the environment.

(2) On 25 September 2015, the UN General Assembly adopted a new global sustainable development framework: the 2030 Agenda for Sustainable Development (the '2030 Agenda'). The 2030 Agenda has at its core the Sustainable Development Goals (SDGs) and covers the three dimensions of sustainability: economic, social and environmental. The Commission communication of 22 November 2016 on the next steps for a sustainable European future links the SDGs to the Union policy framework to ensure that all Union actions and policy initiatives, both within the Union and globally, take the SDGs on board at the outset. In its conclusions of 20 June 2017 the Council confirmed the commitment of the Union and its Member States to the implementation of the 2030 Agenda in a full, coherent, comprehensive, integrated and effective manner, in close cooperation with partners and other stakeholders. On 11 December 2019, the Commission published its communication on 'The European Green Deal'.

(3) The Paris Agreement adopted under the United Nations Framework Convention on Climate Change (the 'Paris Agreement') was approved by the Union on 5 October 2016.[3] Article 2(1)(c) of the Paris Agreement aims to strengthen the response to climate change by making finance flows consistent with a pathway towards low greenhouse gas emissions and climate-resilient development, among other means. In that context, on 12 December 2019, the European Council adopted conclusions on climate change. In light thereof, this Regulation represents a key step towards the objective of achieving a climate-neutral Union by 2050.

(4) Sustainability and the transition to a safe, climate-neutral, climate-resilient, more resource-efficient and circular economy are crucial to ensuring the long-term competitiveness of the Union economy. Sustainability has long been central to the Union project, and the Treaty on European Union and the Treaty on the Functioning of the European Union (TFEU) reflect its social and environmental dimensions.

(5) In December 2016, the Commission mandated a High-Level Expert Group to develop an overarching and comprehensive Union strategy on sustainable finance. The report of the High-Level Expert Group published on 31 January 2018 calls for the creation of a technically robust classification system at Union level to establish clarity on which activities qualify as 'green' or 'sustainable', starting with climate change mitigation.

(6) In its communication of 8 March 2018, the Commission published its action plan on financing sustainable growth, launching an ambitious and comprehensive strategy on sustainable finance. One of the objectives set out in that action plan is to reorient capital flows towards sustainable investment in order to achieve sustainable and inclusive growth. The establishment of a unified classification system for sustainable activities is the most important and urgent action envisaged by the action plan. The action plan recognises that the shift of capital flows towards more sustainable activities has to be underpinned by a shared, holistic understanding of the environmental sustainability of activities and investments. As a first step, clear guidance on activities that qualify as contributing to environmental objectives would help inform investors about the investments that fund environmentally sustainable economic activities. Further guidance on activities that contribute to other sustainability objectives, including social objectives, might be developed at a later stage.

(7) Given the systemic nature of global environmental challenges, there is a need for a systemic and forward-looking approach to environmental sustainability that addresses growing negative trends, such as climate change, the loss of biodiversity, the global overconsumption of resources, food scarcity, ozone depletion, ocean acidification, the deterioration of the fresh water system, and land system change as well as the appearance of new

threats, such as hazardous chemicals and their combined effects.

(8) Decision No 1386/2013/EU of the European Parliament and of the Council[4] calls for an increase in private sector funding for environmental and climate-related expenditure, in particular by putting in place incentives and methodologies that stimulate companies to measure the environmental costs of their business and profits derived from using environmental services.

(9) Achieving the SDGs in the Union requires the channelling of capital flows towards sustainable investments. It is important to fully exploit the potential of the internal market to achieve those goals. In that context, it is crucial to remove obstacles to the efficient movement of capital into sustainable investments in the internal market and to prevent new obstacles from emerging.

(10) In view of the scale of the challenge and the costs associated with inaction or delayed action, the financial system should be gradually adapted in order to support the sustainable functioning of the economy. To that end, sustainable finance needs to become mainstream and consideration needs to be given to the sustainability impact of financial products and services.

(11) Making available financial products which pursue environmentally sustainable objectives is an effective way of channelling private investments into sustainable activities. Requirements for marketing financial products or corporate bonds as environmentally sustainable investments, including requirements set by Member States and the Union to allow financial market participants and issuers to use national labels, aim to enhance investor confidence and awareness of the environmental impact of those financial products or corporate bonds, to create visibility and to address concerns about 'greenwashing'. In the context of this Regulation, greenwashing refers to the practice of gaining an unfair competitive advantage by marketing a financial product as environmentally friendly, when in fact basic environmental standards have not been met. Currently, a few Member States have labelling schemes in place. Those existing schemes build on different classification systems for environmentally sustainable economic activities. Given the political commitments under the Paris Agreement and at Union level, it is likely that more and more Member States will establish labelling schemes or impose other requirements on financial market participants or issuers in respect of promoting financial products or corporate bonds as environmentally sustainable. In such cases, Member States would use their own national classification systems for the purposes of determining which investments qualify as sustainable. If those national labelling schemes or requirements use different criteria to determine which economic activities qualify as environmentally sustainable, investors would be discouraged from investing across borders due to difficulties in comparing different investment opportunities. In addition, economic operators that wish to attract investment from across the Union would have to meet different criteria in different Member States in order for their activities to qualify as environmentally sustainable. The absence of uniform criteria would therefore increase costs and significantly disincentivise economic operators from accessing cross-border capital markets for the purposes of sustainable investment.

(12) The criteria for determining whether an economic activity qualifies as environmentally sustainable should be harmonised at Union level in order to remove barriers to the functioning of the internal market with regard to raising funds for sustainability projects, and to prevent the future emergence of barriers to such projects. With such harmonisation, economic operators would find it easier to raise funding across borders for their environmentally sustainable activities, as their economic activities could be compared against uniform criteria in order to be selected as underlying assets for environmentally sustainable investments. Such harmonisation would therefore facilitate cross-border sustainable investment in the Union.

(13) If financial market participants do not provide any explanation to investors about how the activities in which they invest contribute to environmental objectives, or if financial market participants use different concepts in their explanations of what an environmentally sustainable economic activity is, investors will find it disproportionately burdensome to check and compare different financial products. It has been found that such practices discourage investors from investing in environmentally sustainable financial products. Furthermore, a lack of investor confidence has a major detrimental impact on the market for sustainable investment. It has also been shown that national rules and market-based initiatives taken to tackle that issue within national borders lead to the fragmentation of the internal market. If financial market participants disclose how and to what extent the financial products that are made available as environmentally sustainable invest in activities that meet the criteria for environmentally sustainable economic activities under this Regulation, and if financial market participants use common criteria for such disclosures across the Union, that would help investors compare investment opportunities across borders and would incentivise investee companies to make their business models more environmentally sustainable. Additionally, investors would invest in environmentally sustainable financial products across the Union with higher confidence, thereby improving the functioning of the internal market.

(14) To address existing obstacles to the functioning of the internal market and to prevent the emergence of such obstacles in the future, Member States and the Union should be required to use a common concept of environmentally sustainable investment when introducing requirements at national and Union level regarding financial market participants or issuers for the purpose of labelling financial products or corporate bonds that are marketed as environmentally sustainable. To avoid market fragmentation and harm to the interests of consumers and investors as a result of diverging notions of environmentally sustainable economic activities, national requirements that financial market participants or issuers have to comply with in order to market financial products or corporate bonds as environmentally sustainable should build on the uniform criteria for environmentally sustainable economic activities. Such financial market participants and issuers include financial market participants that make available environmentally sustainable financial products and non-financial companies that issue environmentally sustainable corporate bonds.

(15) Establishing criteria for environmentally sustainable economic activities may encourage economic operators not covered by this Regulation, on a voluntary basis, to publish and disclose information on their websites regarding the environmentally sustainable economic activities they carry out. That information will not only help financial market participants and other relevant actors on the financial markets to easily identify which economic operators carry out environmentally sustainable economic activities, but will also make it easier for those economic operators to raise funding for their environmentally sustainable activities.

(16) A classification of environmentally sustainable economic activities at Union level should enable the

development of future Union policies in support of sustainable finance, including Union-wide standards for environmentally sustainable financial products and the eventual establishment of labels that formally recognise compliance with those standards across the Union. It could also serve as the basis for other economic and regulatory measures. Uniform legal requirements for determining the degree of environmental sustainability of investments, based on uniform criteria for environmentally sustainable economic activities, are necessary as a reference for future Union law that aims to facilitate the shift of investment towards environmentally sustainable economic activities.

(17) In the context of achieving the SDGs in the Union, policy choices such as the creation of a European Fund for Strategic Investment, have been effective in contributing to the channelling of private investment towards sustainable investments alongside public spending. Regulation (EU) 2015/1017 of the European Parliament and of the Council[5] specifies a 40% climate investment target for infrastructure and innovation projects under the European Fund for Strategic Investment. Common criteria for determining whether economic activities qualify as sustainable, including their impact on the environment, could underpin future similar initiatives of the Union to mobilise investment that pursues climate-related or other environmental objectives.

(18) To avoid harming investor interests, fund managers and institutional investors that make available financial products should disclose how and to what extent they use the criteria for environmentally sustainable economic activities to determine the environmental sustainability of their investments. The information disclosed should enable investors to understand the proportion of the investments underlying the financial product in environmentally sustainable economic activities as a percentage of all investments underlying that financial product, thereby enabling investors to understand the degree of environmental sustainability of the investment. Where the investments underlying the financial product are in economic activities that contribute to an environmental objective, the information to be disclosed should specify the environmental objective or objectives to which the investment underlying the financial product contributes, as well as how and to what extent the investments underlying the financial product fund environmentally sustainable economic activities, and should include details on the respective proportions of enabling and transitional activities. The Commission should specify the information that needs to be disclosed in that regard. That information should enable national competent authorities to easily verify compliance with that disclosure obligation, and to enforce such compliance in accordance with applicable national law. Where financial market participants do not take the criteria for environmentally sustainable investments into account, they should provide a statement to that end. To avoid the circumvention of the disclosure obligation, that obligation should also apply where financial products are marketed as promoting environmental characteristics, including financial products that have as their objective environmental protection in a broad sense.

(19) The disclosure obligations laid down in this Regulation supplement the rules on sustainability-related disclosures laid down in Regulation (EU) 2019/2088 of the European Parliament and of the Council.[6] To enhance transparency and to provide an objective point of comparison by financial market participants to end investors on the proportion of investments that fund environmentally sustainable economic activities, this Regulation supplements the rules on transparency in pre-contractual disclosures and in periodic reports laid down in Regulation (EU) 2019/2088. The definition of 'sustainable investment' in Regulation (EU) 2019/2088 includes investments in economic activities that contribute to an environmental objective which, amongst others, should include investments into 'environmentally sustainable economic activities' within the meaning of this Regulation. Moreover, Regulation (EU) 2019/2088 only considers an investment to be a sustainable investment if it does not significantly harm any environmental or social objective as set out in that Regulation.

(20) To ensure the reliability, consistency and comparability of sustainability-related disclosures in the financial services sector, disclosures pursuant to this Regulation should use existing sustainability indicators to the extent feasible as proposed by the European Parliament in its resolution of 29 May 2018 on sustainable finance.[7] In that context, the technical screening criteria should, to the extent feasible, be based on the sustainability indicators referred to in Regulation (EU) 2019/2088.

(21) Regarding economic activities carried out by undertakings that are not required to disclose information under this Regulation, there could be exceptional cases where financial market participants cannot reasonably obtain the relevant information to reliably determine the alignment with the technical screening criteria established pursuant to this Regulation. In such exceptional cases and only for those economic activities for which complete, reliable and timely information could not be obtained, financial market participants should be allowed to make complementary assessments and estimates on the basis of information from other sources. Such assessments and estimates should only compensate for limited and specific parts of the desired data elements, and produce a prudent outcome. In order to ensure that the disclosure to investors is clear and not misleading, financial market participants should clearly explain the basis for their conclusions as well as the reasons for having to make such complementary assessments and estimates for the purposes of disclosure to end investors.

(22) In its communication of 20 June 2019 on 'Guidelines on non-financial reporting: Supplement on reporting climate-related information', the Commission recommends that certain large companies report on certain climate-related key performance indicators (KPIs) that are based on the framework established by this Regulation. In particular, information on the proportion of the turnover, capital expenditure (CapEx) or operating expenditure (OpEx) of such large non-financial companies that is associated with environmentally sustainable economic activities, as well as KPIs that are tailored for large financial companies, is useful to investors who are interested in companies whose products and services contribute substantially to any one of the environmental objectives set out in this Regulation. It is therefore appropriate to require the annual publication of such KPIs by such large companies and to further define that requirement in delegated acts, in particular with regard to large financial companies. While it would be disproportionately burdensome to extend such a requirement to smaller companies, smaller companies may voluntarily decide to publish such information.

(23) For the purpose of determining the environmental sustainability of a given economic activity, an exhaustive list of environmental objectives should be laid down. The six environmental objectives that this Regulation should cover are: climate change mitigation; climate change adaptation; the sustainable use and protection of water and marine resources; the transition to a circular economy; pollution prevention and control; and the protection and restoration of biodiversity and ecosystems.

(24) An economic activity that pursues the environmental objective of climate change mitigation should

contribute substantially to the stabilisation of greenhouse gas emissions by avoiding or reducing them or by enhancing greenhouse gas removals. The economic activity should be consistent with the long-term temperature goal of the Paris Agreement. That environmental objective should be interpreted in accordance with relevant Union law, including Directive 2009/31/EC of the European Parliament and of the Council.[8]

(25) An economic activity that pursues the environmental objective of climate change adaptation should contribute substantially to reducing or preventing the adverse impact of the current or expected future climate, or the risks of such adverse impact, whether on that activity itself or on people, nature or assets. That environmental objective should be interpreted in accordance with relevant Union law and the Sendai Framework for Disaster Risk Reduction 2015–2030.

(26) The environmental objective of the sustainable use and protection of water and marine resources should be interpreted in accordance with relevant Union law, including Regulation (EU) No 1380/2013 of the European Parliament and of the Council[9] and Directives 2000/60/EC,[10] 2006/7/EC,[11] 2006/118/EC,[12] 2008/56/EC[13] and 2008/105/EC[14] of the European Parliament and of the Council, Council Directives 91/271/EEC,[15] 91/676/EEC[16] and 98/83/EC[17] and Commission Decision (EU) 2017/848,[18] and with the communications of the Commission of 18 July 2007 on 'Addressing the challenge of water scarcity and droughts in the European Union', of 14 November 2012 on 'A Blueprint to Safeguard Europe's Water Resources' and of 11 March 2019 on 'European Union Strategic Approach to Pharmaceuticals in the Environment'.

(27) The environmental objective of the transition to a circular economy should be interpreted in accordance with relevant Union law in the areas of the circular economy, waste and chemicals, including Regulations (EC) No 1013/2006,[19] (EC) No 1907/2006[20] and (EU) 2019/1021[21] of the European Parliament and of the Council and Directives 94/62/EC,[22] 2000/53/EC,[23] 2006/66/EC,[24] 2008/98/EC,[25] 2010/75/EU,[26] 2011/65/EU,[27] 2012/19/EU,[28] (EU) 2019/883[29] and (EU) 2019/904[30] of the European Parliament and of the Council, Council Directive 1999/31/EC,[31] Commission Regulation (EU) No 1357/2014[32] and Commission Decisions 2000/532/EC[33] and 2014/955/EU,[34] and with the communications of the Commission of 2 December 2015 on 'Closing the loop – An EU action plan for the Circular Economy' and of 16 January 2018 on 'A European Strategy for Plastics in a Circular Economy'.

(28) An economic activity can contribute substantially to the environmental objective of transitioning to a circular economy in several ways. It can, for example, increase the durability, reparability, upgradability and reusability of products, or can reduce the use of resources through the design and choice of materials, facilitating repurposing, disassembly and deconstruction in the buildings and construction sector, in particular to reduce the use of building materials and promote the reuse of building materials. It can also contribute substantially to the environmental objective of transitioning to a circular economy by developing 'product-as-a-service' business models and circular value chains, with the aim of keeping products, components and materials at their highest utility and value for as long as possible. Any reduction in the content of hazardous substances in materials and products throughout the life cycle, including by replacing them with safer alternatives, should, as a minimum, be in accordance with Union law. An economic activity can also contribute substantially to the environmental objective of transitioning to a circular economy by reducing food waste in the production, processing, manufacturing or distribution of food.

(29) The environmental objective of pollution prevention and control should be interpreted in accordance with relevant Union law, including Directives 2000/60/EC, 2004/35/EC,[35] 2004/107/EC,[36] 2006/118/EC, 2008/50/EC,[37] 2008/105/EC, 2010/75/EU, (EU) 2016/802[38] and (EU) 2016/2284[39] of the European Parliament and of the Council.

(30) The environmental objective of the protection and restoration of biodiversity and ecosystems should be interpreted in accordance with relevant Union law, including Regulations (EU) No 995/2010,[40] (EU) No 511/2014[41] and (EU) No 1143/2014[42] of the European Parliament and of the Council, Directive 2009/147/EC of the European Parliament and of the Council,[43] Council Regulation (EC) No 338/97,[44] Council Directives 91/676/EEC and 92/43/EEC,[45] and with the communications of the Commission of 21 May 2003 on 'Forest Law Enforcement, Governance and Trade (FLEGT)', of 3 May 2011 on 'Our life insurance, our natural capital: an EU biodiversity strategy to 2020', of 6 May 2013 on 'Green Infrastructure (GI) – Enhancing Europe's natural Capital', of 26 February 2016 on 'EU Action Plan against Wildlife Trafficking' and of 23 July 2019 on 'Stepping up EU Action to Protect and Restore the World's Forests'.

(31) An economic activity can contribute substantially to the environmental objective of the protection and restoration of biodiversity and ecosystems, in several ways, including by protecting, conserving or restoring biodiversity and ecosystems, and thereby enhancing ecosystem services. Such services are grouped into four categories, namely provisioning services, such as the provisioning of food and water; regulating services, such as the control of climate and disease; supporting services, such as nutrient cycles and oxygen production; and cultural services, such as providing spiritual and recreational benefits.

(32) For the purposes of this Regulation, the term 'sustainable forest management' should be construed by taking into account practices and uses of forests and forest land that contribute to enhancing biodiversity or to halting or preventing the degradation of ecosystems, deforestation and habitat loss, by taking into account the stewardship and use of forests and forest land in a way, and at a rate, that maintains their biodiversity, productivity, regeneration capacity, vitality and their potential to fulfil, now and in the future, relevant ecological, economic and social functions, at local, national, and global levels, and that does not cause damage to other ecosystems, as set out in Resolution H1 of the Second Ministerial Conference on the Protection of Forests in Europe of 16–17 June 1993 in Helsinki on General Guidelines for the Sustainable Management of Forests in Europe as well as by taking into account Regulations (EU) No 995/2010 and (EU) 2018/841[46] of the European Parliament and of the Council and Directive (EU) 2018/2001 of the European Parliament and of the Council[47] and the communication of the Commission of 20 September 2013 on 'A new EU Forest Strategy: for forests and the forest-based sector'.

(33) For the purposes of this Regulation, the term 'energy efficiency' is used in a broad sense and should be construed by taking into account relevant Union law, including Regulation (EU) 2017/1369 of the European Parliament and of the Council[48] and Directives 2012/27/EU[49] and (EU) 2018/844[50] of the European Parliament and of the Council, as well as the implementing measures adopted pursuant to Directive 2009/125/EC of the European Parliament and of the Council.[51]

(34) For each environmental objective, uniform criteria for determining whether economic activities contribute

substantially to that objective should be laid down. One element of the uniform criteria should be to avoid significant harm to any of the environmental objectives set out in this Regulation. This is in order to avoid that investments qualify as environmentally sustainable in cases where the economic activities benefitting from those investments cause harm to the environment to an extent that outweighs their contribution to an environmental objective. Such criteria should take into account the life cycle of the products and services provided by that economic activity in addition to the environmental impact of the economic activity itself, including taking into account evidence from existing life-cycle assessments, in particular by considering their production, use and end of life.

(35) Recalling the joint commitment of the European Parliament, the Council and the Commission to pursuing the principles enshrined in the European Pillar of Social Rights in support of sustainable and inclusive growth, and recognising the relevance of international minimum human and labour rights and standards, compliance with minimum safeguards should be a condition for economic activities to qualify as environmentally sustainable. For that reason, economic activities should only qualify as environmentally sustainable where they are carried out in alignment with the OECD Guidelines for Multinational Enterprises and UN Guiding Principles on Business and Human Rights, including the declaration on Fundamental Principles and Rights at Work of the International Labour Organisation (ILO), the eight fundamental conventions of the ILO and the International Bill of Human Rights. The fundamental conventions of the ILO define human and labour rights that undertakings should respect. Several of those international standards are enshrined the Charter of Fundamental Rights of the European Union, in particular the prohibition of slavery and forced labour and the principle of non-discrimination. Those minimum safeguards are without prejudice to the application of more stringent requirements related to the environment, health, safety and social sustainability set out in Union law, where applicable. When complying with those minimum safeguards, undertakings should adhere to the principle of 'do no significant harm' referred to in Regulation (EU) 2019/2088, and take into account the regulatory technical standards adopted pursuant to that Regulation that further specify that principle.

(36) In order to ensure consistency between this Regulation and Regulation (EU) 2019/2088, this Regulation should amend Regulation (EU) 2019/2088 to mandate the European Supervisory Authorities established by Regulations (EU) No 1093/2010,[52] (EU) No 1094/2010[53] and (EU) No 1095/2010[54] of the European Parliament and of the Council (collectively, the 'ESAs') to jointly develop regulatory technical standards to further specify the details of the content and presentation of the information in relation to the principle of 'do no significant harm'. Those regulatory technical standards should be consistent with the content, methodologies, and presentation of the sustainability indicators in relation to adverse impacts as referred to in Regulation (EU) 2019/2088. They should also be consistent with the principles enshrined in the European Pillar of Social Rights, the OECD Guidelines for Multinational Enterprises, the UN Guiding Principles on Business and Human Rights, including the ILO Declaration on Fundamental Principles and Rights at Work, the eight fundamental conventions of the ILO and the International Bill of Human Rights.

(37) Regulation (EU) 2019/2088 should further be amended to mandate the ESAs to develop, through the Joint Committee, draft regulatory technical standards to supplement the rules on transparency of the promotion of environmental characteristics and of environmentally sustainable investments in pre-contractual disclosures and in periodic reports.

(38) Given the specific technical details needed to assess the environmental impact of an economic activity and the fast-changing nature of both science and technology, the criteria for environmentally sustainable economic activities should be adapted regularly to reflect such changes. For the criteria to be up to date, based on scientific evidence and input from experts as well as relevant stakeholders, the conditions for 'substantial contribution' and 'significant harm' should be specified with more granularity for different economic activities and should be updated regularly. For that purpose, granular and calibrated technical screening criteria for the different economic activities should be established by the Commission on the basis of technical input from a multi-stakeholder platform on sustainable finance.

(39) Some economic activities have a negative impact on the environment, and reducing such negative impact can make a substantial contribution to one or more environmental objectives. For those economic activities, it is appropriate to establish technical screening criteria that require a substantial improvement in environmental performance compared with, inter alia, the industry average, but at the same time avoid environmentally harmful lock-in effects, including carbon-intensive lock-in effects, during the economic lifetime of the funded economic activity. Those criteria should also consider the long-term impact of a specific economic activity.

(40) An economic activity should not qualify as environmentally sustainable if it causes more harm to the environment than the benefits it brings. The technical screening criteria should identify the minimum requirements necessary to avoid significant harm to other objectives, including by building on any minimum requirements laid down pursuant to Union law. When establishing and updating the technical screening criteria, the Commission should ensure that those criteria are based on available scientific evidence, are developed by taking into account life-cycle considerations, including existing life-cycle assessments, and are updated regularly. Where scientific evaluation does not allow for a risk to be determined with sufficient certainty, the precautionary principle should apply in accordance with Article 191 TFEU.

(41) In establishing and updating the technical screening criteria for the environmental objective of climate change mitigation, the Commission should take into account and provide incentives for the ongoing and necessary transition towards a climate-neutral economy in accordance with Article 10(2) of this Regulation. In addition to the use of climate-neutral energy and more investments in already low-carbon economic activities and sectors, the transition requires substantial reductions in greenhouse gas emissions in other economic activities and sectors for which there are no technologically and economically feasible low-carbon alternatives. Those transitional economic activities should qualify as contributing substantially to climate change mitigation if their greenhouse gas emissions are substantially lower than the sector or industry average, they do not hamper the development and deployment of low-carbon alternatives and they do not lead to a lock-in of assets incompatible with the objective of climate-neutrality, considering the economic lifetime of those assets. The technical screening criteria for such transitional economic activities should ensure that those transitional activities have a credible path towards climate-neutrality, and should be adjusted accordingly at regular intervals.

(42) An economic activity should qualify as contributing substantially to one or more of the environmental

objectives set out in this Regulation where it directly enables other activities to make a substantial contribution to one or more of those objectives. Such enabling activities should not lead to a lock-in of assets that undermine long-term environmental goals, considering the economic lifetime of those assets, and should have a substantial positive environmental impact, on the basis of life-cycle considerations.

(43) When establishing and updating the technical screening criteria the Commission should take into account relevant Union law, including Regulations (EC) No 1221/2009[55] and (EC) No 66/2010[56] of the European Parliament and of the Council, as well as Commission Recommendation 2013/179/EU[57] and the communication of the Commission of 16 July 2008 on "Public procurement for a better environment". To avoid unnecessary inconsistencies with classifications of economic activities that already exist for other purposes, the Commission should also take into account the statistical classifications relating to the environmental goods and services sector, namely the classification of environmental protection activities (CEPA) and the classification of resource management activities (CReMA) of Regulation (EU) No 538/2014 of the European Parliament and of the Council.[58] When establishing and updating the technical screening criteria, the Commission should take into account existing environmental indicators and reporting frameworks, developed by, amongst others, the Commission and the European Environment Agency, and existing international standards, such as those developed by, amongst others, the OECD.

(44) When establishing and updating the technical screening criteria, the Commission should also take into account the specificities of the infrastructure sector and should take into account environmental, social and economic externalities within a cost-benefit analysis. In that regard, the Commission should take into account relevant Union law, including Directives 2001/42/EC,[59] 2011/92/EU,[60] 2014/23/EU,[61] 2014/24/EU[62] and 2014/25/EU[63] of the European Parliament and of the Council, standards and current methodology, as well as the work of international organisations, such as the OECD. In that context, the technical screening criteria should promote appropriate governance frameworks integrating environmental, social and governance factors as referred to in the United Nations-supported Principles for Responsible Investment at all stages of a project's life cycle.

(45) The technical screening criteria should ensure that relevant economic activities within a specific sector can qualify as environmentally sustainable and are treated equally if they contribute equally to one or more of the environmental objectives laid down in this Regulation. The potential capacity to contribute to those environmental objectives can vary across sectors, which should be reflected in those criteria. However, within each sector, those criteria should not unfairly disadvantage certain economic activities over others if the former contribute to the environmental objectives to the same extent as the latter.

(46) When establishing and updating technical screening criteria for environmentally sustainable activities, the Commission should assess whether the establishment of those criteria would give rise to stranded assets or would result in inconsistent incentives, or would have any other adverse impact on financial markets.

(47) To avoid overly burdensome compliance costs on economic operators, the Commission should establish technical screening criteria that provide for sufficient legal clarity, that are practicable and easy to apply, and for which compliance can be verified within reasonable cost-of-compliance boundaries, thereby avoiding unnecessary administrative burden. Technical screening criteria could require carrying out a life-cycle assessment where sufficiently practicable and where necessary.

(48) To ensure that investments are channelled towards economic activities that make the greatest positive impact on the environmental objectives, the Commission should give priority to the establishment of technical screening criteria for the economic activities that potentially contribute most to the environmental objectives.

(49) Appropriate technical screening criteria should be established for the transport sector, including for mobile assets. Those screening criteria should take into account the fact that the transport sector, including international shipping, contributes close to 26% of total greenhouse gas emissions in the Union. As stated in the Action Plan on Financing Sustainable Growth the transport sector represents about 30% of the additional annual investment needed for sustainable development in the Union, for example to increase electrification or to support the transition to cleaner modes of transport by promoting modal shift and better traffic management.

(50) When developing the technical screening criteria, it is of particular importance that the Commission carry out appropriate consultations in line with the Better Regulation Agenda. The process for the establishment and update of the technical screening criteria should involve relevant stakeholders and should build on the advice of experts who have proven knowledge and experience in the relevant areas. For that purpose, the Commission should set up a Platform on Sustainable Finance (the 'Platform'). The Platform should be composed of experts representing both the public and private sectors. Public-sector experts should include representatives of the European Environmental Agency, the ESAs, the European Investment Bank and the European Union Agency for Fundamental Rights. Private sector experts should include representatives of financial and non-financial market participants and business sectors, representing relevant industries, and persons with accounting and reporting expertise. The Platform should also include experts representing civil society, including experts in the field of environmental, social, labour and governance issues. Financial market participants should be encouraged to inform the Commission if they consider that an economic activity that does not meet the technical screening criteria, or for which such criteria have not yet been established, should qualify as environmentally sustainable, in order to help the Commission in evaluating the appropriateness of complementing or updating the technical screening criteria.

(51) The Platform should be constituted in accordance with the applicable horizontal rules on the creation and operation of Commission expert groups, including with regard to the selection process. The selection process should aim to ensure a high level of expertise, geographical and gender balance, as well as a balanced representation of relevant know-how, taking into account the specific tasks of the Platform. During the selection process, the Commission should perform an assessment in accordance with those horizontal rules to determine whether potential conflicts of interest exist and should take appropriate measures to resolve any such conflicts.

(52) The Platform should advise the Commission on the development, analysis and review of technical screening criteria, including the potential impact of such criteria on the valuation of assets that qualify as environmentally sustainable assets under existing market practices. The Platform should also advise the Commission on whether the technical screening criteria are suitable for use in future Union policy initiatives aimed at facilitating sustainable investment and on the possible role of sustainability accounting and reporting standards in supporting the application of the technical screening criteria. The Platform should advise the Commission on developing further measures to

improve data availability and quality, taking into account the objective of avoiding undue administrative burden, on addressing other sustainability objectives, including social objectives, and on the functioning of minimum safeguards and the possible need to supplement them.

(53) The Commission should continue the existing Member State Expert Group on Sustainable Finance and provide it with a formal status. The tasks of that expert group will, inter alia, consist of advising the Commission on the appropriateness of the technical screening criteria and the approach taken by the Platform with regard to developing those criteria. For that purpose, the Commission should keep the Member States informed through regular meetings of the Member State Expert Group on Sustainable Finance.

(54) In order to specify the requirements set out in this Regulation, and in particular to establish and update for different economic activities granular and calibrated technical screening criteria for what constitutes 'substantial contribution' and 'significant harm' to the environmental objectives, the power to adopt acts in accordance with Article 290 TFEU should be delegated to the Commission in respect of the information required to comply with the disclosure obligations pursuant to this Regulation, and in respect of the technical screening criteria. It is of particular importance that the Commission carry out appropriate consultations during its preparatory work, including at expert level, such as through the Platform and the Member State Expert Group on Sustainable Finance, and that those consultations be conducted in accordance with the principles laid down in the Interinstitutional Agreement of 13 April 2016 on Better Law-Making.[64] In particular, to ensure equal participation in the preparation of delegated acts, the European Parliament and the Council receive all documents at the same time as Member States' experts, and their experts systematically have access to meetings of Commission expert groups dealing with the preparation of delegated acts.

(55) This Regulation supplements the disclosure requirements laid down in Regulation (EU) 2019/2088. To ensure the orderly and effective monitoring of compliance by financial market participants with this Regulation, Member States should rely on the competent authorities designated in accordance with Regulation (EU) 2019/2088. To enforce compliance, Member States should in addition lay down rules on measures and penalties, which should be effective, proportionate and dissuasive. National competent authorities and the ESAs should exercise the product intervention powers laid down in Regulations (EU) No 600/2014,[65] (EU) No 1286/2014[66] and (EU) 2019/1238[67] of the European Parliament and of the Council also with respect to mis-selling practices or misleading disclosures of sustainability-related information, including the information required under this Regulation.

(56) In order to ensure the efficient and sustainable organisation of the work and meeting practices of both the Platform and the Member State Expert Group on Sustainable Finance, and in order to enable broad participation and efficient interaction within the groups, their subgroups, the Commission and stakeholders, the increased use of digital, including virtual, technologies should be considered, where appropriate.

(57) To give sufficient time to the relevant actors to familiarise themselves with the criteria for qualification as environmentally sustainable economic activities set out in this Regulation and to prepare for their application, the obligations set out in this Regulation should become applicable, for each environmental objective, 12 months after the relevant technical screening criteria have been established.

(58) The provision in this Regulation referring to certificate-based tax incentive schemes that exist prior to the entry into force of this Regulation is without prejudice to the respective competences of the Union and the Member States with respect to tax provisions, as set out by the Treaties.

(59) The application of this Regulation should be reviewed regularly in order to assess, inter alia: the progress with regard to the development of technical screening criteria for environmentally sustainable economic activities; the possible need to revise and complement those criteria for determining whether an economic activity qualifies as environmentally sustainable; the effectiveness of the classification system for environmentally sustainable economic activities in channelling private investment into such activities and in particular as regards the flow of capital into private enterprises and other legal entities; and the further development of that classification system, including by expanding its scope beyond environmentally sustainable economic activities, in order to cover activities that significantly harm the environment, as well as other sustainability objectives, including social objectives.

(60) Since the objectives of this Regulation cannot be sufficiently achieved by the Member States, but can rather, by reason of the need to introduce at Union level uniform criteria for environmentally sustainable economic activities, be better achieved at Union level, the Union may adopt measures, in accordance with the principle of subsidiarity as set out in Article 5 of the Treaty on European Union. In accordance with the principle of proportionality as set out in that Article, this Regulation does not go beyond what is necessary in order to achieve those objectives,

NOTES

1 OJ C62, 15.2.2019, p 103.

2 Position of the European Parliament of 28 March 2019 (not yet published in the Official Journal) and Position of the Council at first reading of 15 April 2020 (OJ C184, 3.6.2020, p 1). Position of the European Parliament of 17 June 2020 (not yet published in the Official Journal).

3 Council Decision (EU) 2016/1841 of 5 October 2016 on the conclusion, on behalf of the European Union, of the Paris Agreement adopted under the United Nations Framework Convention on Climate Change (OJ L282, 19.10.2016, p 1).

4 Decision No 1386/2013/EU of the European Parliament and of the Council of 20 November 2013 on a General Union Environment Action Programme to 2020 'Living well, within the limits of our planet' (OJ L354, 28.12.2013, p 171).

5 Regulation (EU) 2015/1017 of the European Parliament and of the Council of 25 June 2015 on the European Fund for Strategic Investments, the European Investment Advisory Hub and the European Investment Project Portal and amending Regulations (EU) No 1291/2013 and (EU) No 1316/2013 – the European Fund for Strategic Investments (OJ L169, 1.7.2015, p 1).

6 Regulation (EU) 2019/2088 of the European Parliament and of the Council of 27 November 2019 on sustainability-related disclosures in the financial services sector (OJ L317, 9.12.2019, p 1).

7 OJ C76, 9.3.2020, p 23.

8 Directive 2009/31/EC of the European Parliament and of the Council of 23 April 2009 on the geological storage of carbon dioxide and amending Council Directive 85/337/EEC, European Parliament and Council Directives 2000/60/EC, 2001/80/EC, 2004/35/EC, 2006/12/EC, 2008/1/EC and Regulation (EC) No 1013/2006 (OJ L140, 5.6.2009, p 114).

9 Regulation (EU) No 1380/2013 of the European Parliament and of the Council of 11 December 2013 on the Common

Fisheries Policy, amending Council Regulations (EC) No 1954/2003 and (EC) No 1224/2009 and repealing Council Regulations (EC) No 2371/2002 and (EC) No 639/2004 and Council Decision 2004/585/EC (OJ L354, 28.12.2013, p 22).

10 Directive 2000/60/EC of the European Parliament and of the Council of 23 October 2000 establishing a framework for Community action in the field of water policy (OJ L327, 22.12.2000, p 1).

11 Directive 2006/7/EC of the European Parliament and of the Council of 15 February 2006 concerning the management of bathing water quality and repealing Directive 76/160/EEC (OJ L64, 4.3.2006, p 37).

12 Directive 2006/118/EC of the European Parliament and of the Council of 12 December 2006 on the protection of groundwater against pollution and deterioration (OJ L372, 27.12.2006, p 19).

13 Directive 2008/56/EC of the European Parliament and of the Council of 17 June 2008 establishing a framework for community action in the field of marine environmental policy (Marine Strategy Framework Directive) (OJ L164, 25.6.2008, p 19).

14 Directive 2008/105/EC of the European Parliament and of the Council of 16 December 2008 on environmental quality standards in the field of water policy, amending and subsequently repealing Council Directives 82/176/EEC, 83/513/EEC, 84/156/EEC, 84/491/EEC, 86/280/EEC and amending Directive 2000/60/EC of the European Parliament and of the Council (OJ L348, 24.12.2008, p 84).

15 Council Directive 91/271/EEC of 21 May 1991 concerning urban waste water treatment (OJ L135, 30.5.1991, p 40).

16 Council Directive 91/676/EEC of 12 December 1991 concerning the protection of waters against pollution caused by nitrates from agricultural sources (OJ L375, 31.12.1991, p 1).

17 Council Directive 98/83/EC of 3 November 1998 on the quality of water intended for human consumption (OJ L330, 5.12.1998, p 32).

18 Commission Decision (EU) 2017/848 of 17 May 2017 laying down criteria and methodological standards on good environmental status of marine waters and specifications and standardised methods for monitoring and assessment, and repealing Decision 2010/477/EU (OJ L125, 18.5.2017, p 43).

19 Regulation (EC) No 1013/2006 of the European Parliament and of the Council of 14 June 2006 on shipments of waste (OJ L190, 12.7.2006, p 1).

20 Regulation (EC) No 1907/2006 of the European Parliament and of the Council of 18 December 2006 concerning the Registration, Evaluation, Authorisation and Restriction of Chemicals (REACH), establishing a European Chemicals Agency, amending Directive 1999/45/EC and repealing Council Regulation (EEC) No 793/93 and Commission Regulation (EC) No 1488/94 as well as Council Directive 76/769/EEC and Commission Directives 91/155/EEC, 93/67/EEC, 93/105/EC and 2000/21/EC (OJ L396, 30.12.2006, p 1).

21 Regulation (EU) 2019/1021 of the European Parliament and of the Council of 20 June 2019 on persistent organic pollutants (OJ L169, 25.6.2019, p 45).

22 European Parliament and Council Directive 94/62/EC of 20 December 1994 on packaging and packaging waste (OJ L365, 31.12.1994, p 10).

23 Directive 2000/53/EC of the European Parliament and of the Council of 18 September 2000 on end-of life vehicles (OJ L269, 21.10.2000, p 34).

24 Directive 2006/66/EC of the European Parliament and of the Council of 6 September 2006 on batteries and accumulators and waste batteries and accumulators and repealing Directive 91/157/EEC (OJ L266, 26.9.2006, p 1).

25 Directive 2008/98/EC of the European Parliament and of the Council of 19 November 2008 on waste and repealing certain Directives (OJ L312, 22.11.2008, p 3).

26 Directive 2010/75/EU of the European Parliament and of the Council of 24 November 2010 on industrial emissions (integrated pollution prevention and control) (OJ L334, 17.12.2010, p 17).

27 Directive 2011/65/EU of the European Parliament and of the Council of 8 June 2011 on the restriction of the use of certain hazardous substances in electrical and electronic equipment (OJ L174, 1.7.2011, p 88).

28 Directive 2012/19/EU of the European Parliament and of the Council of 4 July 2012 on waste electrical and electronic equipment (WEEE) (OJ L197, 24.7.2012, p 38).

29 Directive (EU) 2019/883 of the European Parliament and of the Council of 17 April 2019 on port reception facilities for the delivery of waste from ships, amending Directive 2010/65/EU and repealing Directive 2000/59/EC (OJ L151, 7.6.2019, p 116).

30 Directive (EU) 2019/904 of the European Parliament and of the Council of 5 June 2019 on the reduction of the impact of certain plastic products on the environment (OJ L155, 12.6.2019, p 1).

31 Council Directive 1999/31/EC of 26 April 1999 on the landfill of waste (OJ L182, 16.7.1999, p 1).

32 Commission Regulation (EU) No 1357/2014 of 18 December 2014 replacing Annex III to Directive 2008/98/EC of the European Parliament and of the Council on waste and repealing certain Directives (OJ L365, 19.12.2014, p 89).

33 Commission Decision 2000/532/EC of 3 May 2000 replacing Decision 94/3/EC establishing a list of wastes pursuant to Article 1(a) of Council Directive 75/442/EEC on waste and Council Decision 94/904/EC establishing a list of hazardous waste pursuant to Article 1 (4) of Council Directive 91/689/EEC on hazardous waste (OJ L226, 6.9.2000, p 3).

34 Commission Decision 2014/955/EU of 18 December 2014 amending Decision 2000/532/EC on the list of waste pursuant to Directive 2008/98/EC of the European Parliament and of the Council (OJ L370, 30.12.2014, p 44).

35 Directive 2004/35/EC of the European Parliament and of the Council of 21 April 2004 on environmental liability with regard to the prevention and remedying of environmental damage (OJ L143, 30.4.2004, p 56).

36 Directive 2004/107/EC of the European Parliament and of the Council of 15 December 2004 relating to arsenic, cadmium, mercury, nickel and polycyclic aromatic hydrocarbons in ambient air (OJ L23, 26.1.2005, p 3).

37 Directive 2008/50/EC of the European Parliament and of the Council of 21 May 2008 on ambient air quality and cleaner air for Europe (OJ L152, 11.6.2008, p 1).

38 Directive (EU) 2016/802 of the European Parliament and of the Council of 11 May 2016 relating to a reduction in the sulphur content of certain liquid fuels (OJ L132, 21.5.2016, p 58).

39 Directive (EU) 2016/2284 of the European Parliament and of the Council of 14 December 2016 on the reduction of national emissions of certain atmospheric pollutants, amending Directive 2003/35/EC and repealing Directive 2001/81/EC (OJ L344, 17.12.2016, p 1).

40 Regulation (EU) No 995/2010 of the European Parliament and of the Council of 20 October 2010 laying down the obligations of operators who place timber and timber products on the market (OJ L295, 12.11.2010, p 23).

41 Regulation (EU) No 511/2014 of the European Parliament and of the Council of 16 April 2014 on compliance measures for users from the Nagoya Protocol on Access to Genetic Resources and the Fair and Equitable Sharing of Benefits

Arising from their Utilization in the Union (OJ L150, 20.5.2014, p 59).

42 Regulation (EU) No 1143/2014 of the European Parliament and of the Council of 22 October 2014 on the prevention and management of the introduction and spread of invasive alien species (OJ L317, 4.11.2014, p 35).

43 Directive 2009/147/EC of the European Parliament and of the Council of 30 November 2009 on the conservation of wild birds (OJ L20, 26.1.2010, p 7).

44 Council Regulation (EC) No 338/97 of 9 December 1996 on the protection of species of wild fauna and flora by regulating trade therein (OJ L61, 3.3.1997, p 1).

45 Council Directive 92/43/EEC of 21 May 1992 on the conservation of natural habitats and of wild fauna and flora (OJ L206, 22.7.1992, p 7).

46 Regulation (EU) 2018/841 of the European Parliament and of the Council of 30 May 2018 on the inclusion of greenhouse gas emissions and removals from land use, land use change and forestry in the 2030 climate and energy framework, and amending Regulation (EU) No 525/2013 and Decision No 529/2013/EU (OJ L156, 19.6.2018, p 1).

47 Directive (EU) 2018/2001 of the European Parliament and of the Council of 11 December 2018 on the promotion of the use of energy from renewable sources (OJ L328, 21.12.2018, p 82).

48 Regulation (EU) 2017/1369 of the European Parliament and of the Council of 4 July 2017 setting a framework for energy labelling and repealing Directive 2010/30/EU (OJ L198, 28.7.2017, p 1).

49 Directive 2012/27/EU of the European Parliament and of the Council of 25 October 2012 on energy efficiency, amending Directives 2009/125/EC and 2010/30/EU and repealing Directives 2004/8/EC and 2006/32/EC(OJ L315, 14.11.2012, p 1).

50 Directive (EU) 2018/844 of the European Parliament and of the Council of 30 May 2018 amending Directive 2010/31/EU on the energy performance of buildings and Directive 2012/27/EU on energy efficiency (OJ L156, 19.6.2018, p 75).

51 Directive 2009/125/EC of the European Parliament and of the Council of 21 October 2009 establishing a framework for the setting of ecodesign requirements for energy-related products (OJ L285, 31.10.2009, p 10).

52 Regulation (EU) No 1093/2010 of the European Parliament and of the Council of 24 November 2010 establishing a European Supervisory Authority (European Banking Authority), amending Decision No 716/2009/EC and repealing Commission Decision 2009/78/EC (OJ L331, 15.12.2010, p 12).

53 Regulation (EU) No 1094/2010 of the European Parliament and of the Council of 24 November 2010 establishing a European Supervisory Authority (European Insurance and Occupational Pensions Authority), amending Decision No 716/2009/EC and repealing Commission Decision 2009/79/EC (OJ L331, 15.12.2010, p 48).

54 Regulation (EU) No 1095/2010 of the European Parliament and of the Council of 24 November 2010 establishing a European Supervisory Authority (European Securities and Markets Authority), amending Decision No 716/2009/EC and repealing Commission Decision 2009/77/EC (OJ L331, 15.12.2010, p 84).

55 Regulation (EC) No 1221/2009 of the European Parliament and of the Council of 25 November 2009 on the voluntary participation by organisations in a Community eco-management and audit scheme (EMAS), repealing Regulation (EC) No 761/2001 and Commission Decisions 2001/681/EC and 2006/193/EC (OJ L342, 22.12.2009, p 1).

56 Regulation (EC) No 66/2010 of the European Parliament and the Council of 25 November 2009 on the EU Ecolabel (OJ L27, 30.1.2010, p 1).

57 Commission Recommendation 2013/179/EU of 9 April 2013 on the use of common methods to measure and communicate the life cycle environmental performance of products and organisations (OJ L124, 4.5.2013, p 1).

58 Regulation (EU) No 538/2014 of the European Parliament and of the Council of 16 April 2014 amending Regulation (EU) No 691/2011 on European environmental economic accounts (OJ L158, 27.5.2014, p 113).

59 Directive 2001/42/EC of the European Parliament and of the Council of 27 June 2001 on the assessment of the effects of certain plans and programmes on the environment (OJ L197, 21.7.2001, p 30).

60 Directive 2011/92/EU of the European Parliament and of the Council of 13 December 2011 on the assessment of the effects of certain public and private projects on the environment (OJ L26, 28.1.2012, p 1).

61 Directive 2014/23/EU of the European Parliament and of the Council of 26 February 2014 on the award of concession contracts (OJ L94, 28.3.2014, p 1).

62 Directive 2014/24/EU of the European Parliament and of the Council of 26 February 2014 on public procurement and repealing Directive 2004/18/EC (OJ L94, 28.3.2014, p 65).

63 Directive 2014/25/EU of the European Parliament and of the Council of 26 February 2014 on procurement by entities operating in the water, energy, transport and postal services sectors and repealing Directive 2004/17/EC (OJ L94, 28.3.2014, p 243).

64 OJ L123, 12.5.2016, p 1.

65 Regulation (EU) No 600/2014 of the European Parliament and of the Council of 15 May 2014 on markets in financial instruments and amending Regulation (EU) No 648/2012 (OJ L173, 12.6.2014, p 84).

66 Regulation (EU) No 1286/2014 of the European Parliament and of the Council of 26 November 2014 on key information documents for packaged retail and insurance-based investment products (PRIIPs) (OJ L352, 9.12.2014, p 1).

67 Regulation (EU) 2019/1238 of the European Parliament and of the Council of 20 June 2019 on a pan-European Personal Pension Product (PEPP) (OJ L198, 25.7.2019, p 1).

HAVE ADOPTED THIS REGULATION:

CHAPTER I SUBJECT MATTER, SCOPE AND DEFINITIONS

[11.789]

Article 1 Subject matter and scope

1. This Regulation establishes the criteria for determining whether an economic activity qualifies as environmentally sustainable for the purposes of establishing the degree to which an investment is environmentally sustainable.

2. This Regulation applies to:

(a) measures adopted by Member States or by the Union that set out requirements for financial market participants or issuers in respect of financial products or corporate bonds that are made available as environmentally sustainable;

(b) financial market participants that make available financial products;

(c) undertakings which are subject to the obligation to publish a non-financial statement or a consolidated non-financial statement pursuant to Article 19a or Article 29a of Directive 2013/34/EU of the European Parliament and of the Council,[1] respectively.

NOTES

Application of this Article in relation to the UK: this Article is amended, in relation to the UK only, by the Securities Financing Transactions, Securitisation and Miscellaneous Amendments (EU Exit) Regulations 2020, SI 2020/1385, reg 78(2), as from IP completion day (as defined in the European Union (Withdrawal Agreement) Act 2020, s 39), as follows—

"(2) Omit Article 1, paragraph 2.".

[1] Directive 2013/34/EU of the European Parliament and of the Council of 26 June 2013 on the annual financial statements, consolidated financial statements and related reports of certain types of undertakings, amending Directive 2006/43/EC of the European Parliament and of the Council and repealing Council Directives 78/660/EEC and 83/349/EEC (OJ L182, 29.6.2013, p 19).

[11.790]

Article 2 Definitions

For the purposes of this Regulation, the following definitions apply:

(1) 'environmentally sustainable investment' means an investment in one or several economic activities that qualify as environmentally sustainable under this Regulation;

(2) 'financial market participant' means a financial market participant as defined in point (1) of Article 2 of Regulation (EU) 2019/2088 and includes a manufacturer of a pension product to which a Member State has decided to apply that Regulation in accordance with Article 16 of that Regulation;

(3) 'financial product' means a financial product as defined in point (12) of Article 2 of Regulation (EU) 2019/2088;

(4) 'issuer' means an issuer as defined in point (h) of Article 2 of Regulation (EU) 2017/1129 of the European Parliament and of the Council;[1]

(5) 'climate change mitigation' means the process of holding the increase in the global average temperature to well below 2°C and pursuing efforts to limit it to 1.5 C above pre-industrial levels, as laid down in the Paris Agreement;

(6) 'climate change adaptation' means the process of adjustment to actual and expected climate change and its impacts;

(7) 'greenhouse gas' means a greenhouse gas listed in Annex I to Regulation (EU) No 525/2013 of the European Parliament and of the Council;[2]

(8) 'waste hierarchy' means the waste hierarchy as laid down in Article 4 of Directive 2008/98/EC;

(9) 'circular economy' means an economic system whereby the value of products, materials and other resources in the economy is maintained for as long as possible, enhancing their efficient use in production and consumption, thereby reducing the environmental impact of their use, minimising waste and the release of hazardous substances at all stages of their life cycle, including through the application of the waste hierarchy;

(10) 'pollutant' means a substance, vibration, heat, noise, light or other contaminant present in air, water or land which may be harmful to human health or the environment, which may result in damage to material property, or which may impair or interfere with amenities and other legitimate uses of the environment;

(11) 'soil' means the top layer of the Earth's crust situated between the bedrock and the surface, which is composed of mineral particles, organic matter, water, air and living organisms;

(12) 'pollution' means:

(a) the direct or indirect introduction of pollutants into air, water or land as a result of human activity;
(b) in the context of the marine environment, pollution as defined in point 8 of Article 3 of Directive 2008/56/EC;
(c) in the context of the water environment, pollution as defined in point 33 of Article 2 of Directive 2000/60/EC;

(13) 'ecosystem' means a dynamic complex of plant, animal, and micro-organism communities and their non-living environment interacting as a functional unit;

(14) 'ecosystem services' means the direct and indirect contributions of ecosystems to the economic, social, cultural and other benefits that people derive from those ecosystems;

(15) 'biodiversity' means the variability among living organisms arising from all sources including terrestrial, marine and other aquatic ecosystems and the ecological complexes of which they are part and includes diversity within species, between species and of ecosystems;

(16) 'good condition' means, in relation to an ecosystem, that the ecosystem is in good physical, chemical and biological condition or of a good physical, chemical and biological quality with self-reproduction or self-restoration capability, in which species composition, ecosystem structure and ecological functions are not impaired;

(17) 'energy efficiency' means the more efficient use of energy at all the stages of the energy chain from production to final consumption;

(18) 'marine waters' means marine waters as defined in point 1 of Article 3 of Directive 2008/56/EC;

(19) 'surface water' means surface water as defined in point 1 of Article 2 of Directive 2000/60/EC;

(20) 'groundwater' means groundwater as defined in point 2 of Article 2 of Directive 2000/60/EC;

(21) 'good environmental status' means good environmental status as defined in point 5 of Article 3 of Directive 2008/56/EC;

(22) 'good status' means:

(a) for surface water, having both 'good ecological status' as defined in point 22 of Article 2 of Directive 2000/60/EC and 'good surface water chemical status' as defined in point 24 of Article 2 of that Directive;
(b) for groundwater, having both 'good groundwater chemical status' as defined in point 25 of Article 2 of Directive 2000/60/EC and 'good quantitative status' as defined in point 28 of Article 2 of that Directive;

(23) 'good ecological potential' means good ecological potential as defined in point 23 of Article 2 of Directive 2000/60/EC.

NOTES

Application of this Article in relation to the UK: note that substantial amendments have been made to this Article, in relation to the UK only, by the Securities Financing Transactions, Securitisation and Miscellaneous Amendments (EU Exit) Regulations 2020, SI 2020/1385, reg 78(3), as from IP completion day (as defined in the European Union (Withdrawal

Agreement) Act 2020, s 39). For ease of reference, the Article as so amended is set out below—

"Article 2 Definitions

For the purposes of this Regulation, the following definitions apply:

(1) 'environmentally sustainable investment' means an investment in one or several economic activities that qualify as environmentally sustainable under this Regulation;

(5) 'climate change mitigation' means the process of holding the increase in the global average temperature to well below 2°C and pursuing efforts to limit it to 1.5 C above pre-industrial levels, as laid down in the Paris Agreement;

(6) 'climate change adaptation' means the process of adjustment to actual and expected climate change and its impacts;

(7) "greenhouse gas" has the meaning given in section 92 of the Climate Change Act 2008;

(8) "waste hierarchy" has the meaning—

(a) in England and Wales, given in regulation 12 of the Waste (England and Wales) Regulations 2011;

(b) in Northern Ireland, given in regulation 9(1) of the Waste (Northern Ireland) Regulations 2011;

(c) in Scotland, given in section 34(2A) of the Environmental Protection Act 1990;

(9) 'circular economy' means an economic system whereby the value of products, materials and other resources in the economy is maintained for as long as possible, enhancing their efficient use in production and consumption, thereby reducing the environmental impact of their use, minimising waste and the release of hazardous substances at all stages of their life cycle, including through the application of the waste hierarchy;

(10) 'pollutant' means a substance, vibration, heat, noise, light or other contaminant present in air, water or land which may be harmful to human health or the environment, which may result in damage to material property, or which may impair or interfere with amenities and other legitimate uses of the environment;

(11) 'soil' means the top layer of the Earth's crust situated between the bedrock and the surface, which is composed of mineral particles, organic matter, water, air and living organisms;

(12) "pollution" means—

(a) the direct or indirect introduction of pollutants into air, water or land as a result of human activity;

(b) in the context of the marine environment, pollution as defined in Part 2 of Schedule 1 to the Marine Strategy Regulations 2010;

(c) in the context of the water environment—

(i) in England and Wales, pollution as defined in paragraph 1(2) of Schedule 1 to the Water Environment (Water Framework Directive) (England and Wales) Regulations 2017;

(ii) in Northern Ireland, pollution as defined in paragraph 1(2) of Schedule 1 to the Water Environment (Water Framework Directive) (Northern Ireland) Regulations 2017;

(iii) in Scotland, pollution as defined in regulation 20(6) of the Water Environment and Water Services (Scotland) Act 2003;

(13) 'ecosystem' means a dynamic complex of plant, animal, and micro-organism communities and their non-living environment interacting as a functional unit;

(14) 'ecosystem services' means the direct and indirect contributions of ecosystems to the economic, social, cultural and other benefits that people derive from those ecosystems;

(15) 'biodiversity' means the variability among living organisms arising from all sources including terrestrial, marine and other aquatic ecosystems and the ecological complexes of which they are part and includes diversity within species, between species and of ecosystems;

(16) 'good condition' means, in relation to an ecosystem, that the ecosystem is in good physical, chemical and biological condition or of a good physical, chemical and biological quality with self-reproduction or self-restoration capability, in which species composition, ecosystem structure and ecological functions are not impaired;

(17) 'energy efficiency' means the more efficient use of energy at all the stages of the energy chain from production to final consumption;

(18) "marine waters" means marine waters as defined in regulation 3(3) of the Marine Strategy Regulations 2010;

(19) "surface water" has the meaning—

(a) in England and Wales, given in paragraph 1(2) of Schedule 1 to the Water Environment (Water Framework Directive) (England and Wales) Regulations 2017;

(b) in Northern Ireland, given in paragraph 1(2) of Schedule 1 to the Water Environment (Water Framework Directive) (Northern Ireland) Regulations 2017;

(c) in Scotland, given in regulation 3(3) of the Water Environment and Water Services (Scotland) Act 2003;

(20) "groundwater" has the meaning—

(a) in England and Wales, given in paragraph 1(2) of Schedule 1 to the Water Environment (Water Framework Directive) (England and Wales) Regulations 2017;

(b) in Northern Ireland, given in paragraph 1(2) of Schedule 1 to the Water Environment (Water Framework Directive) (Northern Ireland) Regulations 2017;

(c) in Scotland, given in regulation 3(4) of the Water Environment and Water Services (Scotland) Act 2003;

(21) "good environmental status" has the meaning given in Part 2 of Schedule 1 to the Marine Strategy Regulations 2010;

(22) "good status" has the meaning—

(a) for surface water—

(i) in England and Wales, of having both "good ecological status" and "good surface water chemical status", as defined in paragraph 1(2) of Schedule 1 to the Water Environment (Water Framework Directive) (England and Wales) Regulations 2017;

(ii) in Northern Ireland, of having both "good ecological status" and "good surface water chemical status", as defined in paragraph 1(2) of Schedule 1 to the Water Environment (Water Framework Directive) (Northern Ireland) Regulations 2017;

(iii) in Scotland, of having both "good ecological status", as defined in paragraph 3(2)(b) of Part B of Schedule 1 to the Scotland River Basin District (Status) Directions 2014, and "good surface water chemical status", as defined in paragraph 5(2)(a) of Part C of Schedule 1 to the Scotland River Basin District (Status) Directions 2014;

(b) for groundwater—

(i) in England and Wales, of having both "good groundwater status" and "good quantitative status", as defined in paragraph 1(2) of Schedule 1 to the Water Environment (Water Framework Directive) (England and Wales) Regulations 2017;

(ii) in Northern Ireland, of having both "good groundwater status" and "good quantitative status", as defined in paragraph 1(2) of Schedule 1 to the Water Environment (Water Framework Directive) (Northern Ireland) Regulations 2017;

(iii) in Scotland, of having both "good groundwater chemical status", as defined in paragraph 2(2) of Part B of Schedule 4 to the Scotland River Basin District (Status) Directions 2014, and "good quantitative status", as defined in paragraph 3(2) of Part C of Schedule 4 to the Scotland River Basin District (Status) Directions 2014;

(23) "good ecological potential" has the meaning—

(a) in England and Wales, given in paragraph 1(2) of Schedule 1 to the Water Environment (Water Framework Directive) (England and Wales) Regulations 2017;

(b) in Northern Ireland, given in paragraph 1(2) of Schedule 1 to the Water Environment (Water Framework Directive) (Northern Ireland) Regulations 2017;

(b) in Scotland, given in paragraph 2(b) of Part B of Schedule 2 to the Scotland River Basin District (Status) Directions 2014.".

[1] Regulation (EU) 2017/1129 of the European Parliament and of the Council of 14 June 2017 on the prospectus to be published when securities are offered to the public or admitted to trading on a regulated market, and repealing Directive 2003/71/EC (OJ L168, 30.6.2017, p 12).

[2] Regulation (EU) No 525/2013 of the European Parliament and of the Council of 21 May 2013 on a mechanism for monitoring and reporting greenhouse gas emissions and for reporting other information at national and Union level relevant to climate change and repealing Decision No 280/2004/EC (OJ L165, 18.6.2013, p 13).

CHAPTER II ENVIRONMENTALLY SUSTAINABLE ECONOMIC ACTIVITIES

[11.791]

Article 3 Criteria for environmentally sustainable economic activities

For the purposes of establishing the degree to which an investment is environmentally sustainable, an economic activity shall qualify as environmentally sustainable where that economic activity:

(a) contributes substantially to one or more of the environmental objectives set out in Article 9 in accordance with Articles 10 to 16;

(b) does not significantly harm any of the environmental objectives set out in Article 9 in accordance with Article 17;

(c) is carried out in compliance with the minimum safeguards laid down in Article 18; and

(d) complies with technical screening criteria that have been established by the Commission in accordance with Article 10 (3), 11(3), 12(2), 13(2), 14(2) or 15(2).

NOTES

Application of this Article in relation to the UK: this Article is amended, in relation to the UK only, by the Securities Financing Transactions, Securitisation and Miscellaneous Amendments (EU Exit) Regulations 2020, SI 2020/1385, reg 78(4), as from IP completion day (as defined in the European Union (Withdrawal Agreement) Act 2020, s 39), as follows—

"(4) In Article 3(d) omit "by the Commission".".

[11.792]

Article 4 Use of the criteria for environmentally sustainable economic activities in public measures, in standards and in labels

Member States and the Union shall apply the criteria set out in Article 3 to determine whether an economic activity qualifies as environmentally sustainable for the purposes of any measure setting out requirements for financial market participants or issuers in respect of financial products or corporate bonds that are made available as environmentally sustainable.

[11.793]

Article 5 Transparency of environmentally sustainable investments in pre-contractual disclosures and in periodic reports

Where a financial product as referred to in Article 9(1), (2) or (3) of Regulation (EU) 2019/2088 invests in an economic activity that contributes to an environmental objective within the meaning of point (17) of Article 2 of that Regulation, the information to be disclosed in accordance with Articles 6(3) and 11(2) of that Regulation shall include the following:

(a) the information on the environmental objective or environmental objectives set out in Article 9 of this Regulation to which the investment underlying the financial product contributes; and

(b) a description of how and to what extent the investments underlying the financial product are in economic activities that qualify as environmentally sustainable under Article 3 of this Regulation.

The description referred to in point (b) of the first subparagraph of this Article shall specify the proportion of investments in environmentally sustainable economic activities selected for the financial product, including details on the proportions of enabling and transitional activities referred to in Article 16 and Article 10(2), respectively, as a percentage of all investments selected for the financial product.

[11.794]

Article 6 Transparency of financial products that promote environmental characteristics in pre-contractual disclosures and in periodic reports

Where a financial product as referred to in Article 8(1) of Regulation (EU) 2019/2088 promotes environmental characteristics, Article 5 of this Regulation shall apply *mutatis mutandis*.

The information to be disclosed in accordance with Articles 6(3) and 11(2) of Regulation (EU) 2019/2088 shall be accompanied by the following statement:

'The "do no significant harm" principle applies only to those investments underlying the financial product that take into account the EU criteria for environmentally sustainable economic activities.

The investments underlying the remaining portion of this financial product do not take into account the EU criteria for environmentally sustainable economic activities.'.

[11.795]
Article 7 Transparency of other financial products in pre-contractual disclosures and in periodic reports
Where a financial product is not subject to Article 8(1) or to Article 9(1), (2) or (3) of Regulation (EU) 2019/2088, the information to be disclosed in accordance with the provisions of sectoral legislation referred to in Articles 6(3) and 11(2) of that Regulation shall be accompanied by the following statement:

'The investments underlying this financial product do not take into account the EU criteria for environmentally sustainable economic activities.'.

[11.796]
Article 8 Transparency of undertakings in non-financial statements
1. Any undertaking which is subject to an obligation to publish non-financial information pursuant to Article 19a or Article 29a of Directive 2013/34/EU shall include in its non-financial statement or consolidated non-financial statement information on how and to what extent the undertaking's activities are associated with economic activities that qualify as environmentally sustainable under Articles 3 and 9 of this Regulation.
2. In particular, non-financial undertakings shall disclose the following:
(a) the proportion of their turnover derived from products or services associated with economic activities that qualify as environmentally sustainable under Articles 3 and 9; and
(b) the proportion of their capital expenditure and the proportion of their operating expenditure related to assets or processes associated with economic activities that qualify as environmentally sustainable under Articles 3 and 9.
3. If an undertaking publishes non-financial information pursuant to Article 19a or Article 29a of Directive 2013/34/EU in a separate report in accordance with Article 19a(4) or Article 29a(4) of that Directive, the information referred to in paragraphs 1 and 2 of this Article shall be published in that separate report.
4. The Commission shall adopt a delegated act in accordance with Article 23 to supplement paragraphs 1 and 2 of this Article to specify the content and presentation of the information to be disclosed pursuant to those paragraphs, including the methodology to be used in order to comply with them, taking into account the specificities of both financial and non-financial undertakings and the technical screening criteria established pursuant to this Regulation. The Commission shall adopt that delegated act by 1 June 2021.

NOTES

Application of this Article in relation to the UK: this Article is amended, in relation to the UK only, by the Securities Financing Transactions, Securitisation and Miscellaneous Amendments (EU Exit) Regulations 2020, SI 2020/1385, reg 78(5), as from IP completion day (as defined in the European Union (Withdrawal Agreement) Act 2020, s 39), as follows—

"(5) Omit Article 8(4).".

Delegated Act for the purposes of para 4: see Commission Delegated Regulation 2021/2178/EU supplementing Regulation (EU) 2020/852 of the European Parliament and of the Council by specifying the content and presentation of information to be disclosed by undertakings subject to Articles 19a or 29a of Directive 2013/34/EU concerning environmentally sustainable economic activities, and specifying the methodology to comply with that disclosure obligation. It is available on the EUR-Lex website at eur-lex.europa.eu/legal-content/EN/TXT/?uri=CELEX:32021R2178.

See also Commission Delegated Regulation 2022/1214/EU amending Delegated Regulation (EU) 2021/2139 as regards economic activities in certain energy sectors and Delegated Regulation (EU) 2021/2178 as regards specific public disclosures for those economic activities.

[11.797]
Article 9 Environmental objectives
For the purposes of this Regulation, the following shall be environmental objectives:
(a) climate change mitigation;
(b) climate change adaptation;
(c) the sustainable use and protection of water and marine resources;
(d) the transition to a circular economy;
(e) pollution prevention and control;
(f) the protection and restoration of biodiversity and ecosystems.

[11.798]
Article 10 Substantial contribution to climate change mitigation
1. An economic activity shall qualify as contributing substantially to climate change mitigation where that activity contributes substantially to the stabilisation of greenhouse gas concentrations in the atmosphere at a level which prevents dangerous anthropogenic interference with the climate system consistent with the long-term temperature goal of the Paris Agreement through the avoidance or reduction of greenhouse gas emissions or the increase of greenhouse gas removals, including through process innovations or product innovations, by:
(a) generating, transmitting, storing, distributing or using renewable energy in line with Directive (EU) 2018/2001, including through using innovative technology with a potential for significant future savings or through necessary reinforcement or extension of the grid;
(b) improving energy efficiency, except for power generation activities as referred to in Article 19(3);
(c) increasing clean or climate-neutral mobility;
(d) switching to the use of sustainably sourced renewable materials;
(e) increasing the use of environmentally safe carbon capture and utilisation (CCU) and carbon capture and storage (CCS) technologies that deliver a net reduction in greenhouse gas emissions;
(f) strengthening land carbon sinks, including through avoiding deforestation and forest degradation, restoration of forests, sustainable management and restoration of croplands, grasslands and wetlands, afforestation, and regenerative agriculture;
(g) establishing energy infrastructure required for enabling the decarbonisation of energy systems;
(h) producing clean and efficient fuels from renewable or carbon-neutral sources; or
(i) enabling any of the activities listed in points (a) to (h) of this paragraph in accordance with Article 16.

2. For the purposes of paragraph 1, an economic activity for which there is no technologically and economically feasible low-carbon alternative shall qualify as contributing substantially to climate change mitigation where it supports the transition to a climate-neutral economy consistent with a pathway to limit the temperature increase to 1.5 C above pre-industrial levels, including by phasing out greenhouse gas emissions, in particular emissions from solid fossil fuels, and where that activity:

(a) has greenhouse gas emission levels that correspond to the best performance in the sector or industry;
(b) does not hamper the development and deployment of low-carbon alternatives; and
(c) does not lead to a lock-in of carbon-intensive assets, considering the economic lifetime of those assets.

For the purpose of this paragraph and the establishment of technical screening criteria pursuant to Article 19, the Commission shall assess the potential contribution and feasibility of all relevant existing technologies.

3. The Commission shall adopt a delegated act in accordance with Article 23 to:

(a) supplement paragraphs 1 and 2 of this Article by establishing technical screening criteria for determining the conditions under which a specific economic activity qualifies as contributing substantially to climate change mitigation; and
(b) supplement Article 17 by establishing, for each relevant environmental objective, technical screening criteria for determining whether an economic activity in respect of which technical screening criteria have been established pursuant to point (a) of this paragraph causes significant harm to one or more of those objectives.

4. Prior to adopting the delegated act referred to in paragraph 3 of this Article, the Commission shall consult the Platform referred to in Article 20 regarding the technical screening criteria referred to in paragraph 3 of this Article.

5. The Commission shall establish the technical screening criteria referred to in paragraph 3 of this Article in one delegated act, taking into account the requirements of Article 19.

6. The Commission shall adopt the delegated act referred to in paragraph 3 by 31 December 2020, with a view to ensuring its application from 1 January 2022.

NOTES

Application of this Article in relation to the UK: this Article is amended, in relation to the UK only, by the Securities Financing Transactions, Securitisation and Miscellaneous Amendments (EU Exit) Regulations 2020, SI 2020/1385, reg 78(6), as from IP completion day (as defined in the European Union (Withdrawal Agreement) Act 2020, s 39), as follows—

"(6) In Article 10—

(a) in paragraph 1(a), omit "in line with Directive (EU) 2018/2011";
(b) in paragraph 2, for "the Commission" substitute "the Treasury";
(c) in paragraph 3, for "The Commission shall adopt a delegated act in accordance with Article 23" substitute "The Treasury must make regulations";
(d) omit paragraph 4;
(e) for paragraph 5 substitute—

"5. The Treasury must establish the technical screening criteria referred to in paragraph 3 of this Article taking into account the requirements of Article 19.";

(f) for paragraph 6 substitute—

"6. The Treasury must make the regulations in paragraph 3 above no later than 1 January 2023.".

Delegated Act for the purposes of para 3: see Commission Delegated Regulation 2021/2139/EU supplementing Regulation (EU) 2020/852 of the European Parliament and of the Council by establishing the technical screening criteria for determining the conditions under which an economic activity qualifies as contributing substantially to climate change mitigation or climate change adaptation and for determining whether that economic activity causes no significant harm to any of the other environmental objectives. It is available on the EUR-Lex website at: eur-lex.europa.eu/legal-content/EN/TXT/?uri=CELEX:32021R2139. See also Commission Delegated Regulation 2022/1214/EU amending Delegated Regulation (EU) 2021/2139 as regards economic activities in certain energy sectors and Delegated Regulation (EU) 2021/2178 as regards specific public disclosures for those economic activities.

[11.799]

Article 11 Substantial contribution to climate change adaptation

1. An economic activity shall qualify as contributing substantially to climate change adaptation where that activity:

(a) includes adaptation solutions that either substantially reduce the risk of the adverse impact of the current climate and the expected future climate on that economic activity or substantially reduce that adverse impact, without increasing the risk of an adverse impact on people, nature or assets; or
(b) provides adaptation solutions that, in addition to satisfying the conditions set out in Article 16, contribute substantially to preventing or reducing the risk of the adverse impact of the current climate and the expected future climate on people, nature or assets, without increasing the risk of an adverse impact on other people, nature or assets.

2. The adaptation solutions referred to in point (a) of paragraph 1 shall be assessed and ranked in order of priority using the best available climate projections and shall, at a minimum, prevent or reduce:

(a) the location-specific and context-specific adverse impact of climate change on the economic activity; or
(b) the potential adverse impact of climate change on the environment within which the economic activity takes place.

3. The Commission shall adopt a delegated act in accordance with Article 23 to:

(a) supplement paragraphs 1 and 2 of this Article by establishing technical screening criteria for determining the conditions under which a specific economic activity qualifies as contributing substantially to climate change adaptation; and
(b) supplement Article 17 by establishing, for each relevant environmental objective, technical screening criteria for determining whether an economic activity in respect of which technical screening criteria have been established pursuant to point (a) of this paragraph causes significant harm to one or more of those objectives.

4. Prior to adopting the delegated act referred to in paragraph 3 of this Article, the Commission shall consult the Platform referred to in Article 20 regarding the technical screening criteria referred to in paragraph 3 of this Article.

5. The Commission shall establish the technical screening criteria referred to in paragraph 3 of this Article in one delegated act, taking into account the requirements of Article 19.

6. The Commission shall adopt the delegated act referred to in paragraph 3 by 31 December 2020, with a view to ensuring its application from 1 January 2022.

NOTES

Application of this Article in relation to the UK: this Article is amended, in relation to the UK only, by the Securities Financing Transactions, Securitisation and Miscellaneous Amendments (EU Exit) Regulations 2020, SI 2020/1385, reg 78(7), as from IP completion day (as defined in the European Union (Withdrawal Agreement) Act 2020, s 39), as follows—

"(7) In Article 11—

(a) in paragraph 3 for "The Commission shall adopt a delegated act in accordance with Article 23" substitute "the Treasury must make regulations";

(b) omit paragraph 4;

(c) for paragraph 5 substitute—

"5. The Treasury must establish the technical screening criteria referred to in paragraph 3 of this Article taking into account the requirements of Article 19.";

(d) for paragraph 6 substitute—

"6. The Treasury must make the regulations in paragraph 3 above no later than 1 January 2023.".

Delegated Act for the purposes of para 3: see Commission Delegated Regulation 2021/2139/EU supplementing Regulation (EU) 2020/852 of the European Parliament and of the Council by establishing the technical screening criteria for determining the conditions under which an economic activity qualifies as contributing substantially to climate change mitigation or climate change adaptation and for determining whether that economic activity causes no significant harm to any of the other environmental objectives. It is available on the EUR-Lex website at: eur-lex.europa.eu/legal-content/EN/TXT/?uri=CELEX:32021R2139. See also Commission Delegated Regulation 2022/1214/EU amending Delegated Regulation (EU) 2021/2139 as regards economic activities in certain energy sectors and Delegated Regulation (EU) 2021/2178 as regards specific public disclosures for those economic activities.

[11.800]

Article 12 Substantial contribution to the sustainable use and protection of water and marine resources

1. An economic activity shall qualify as contributing substantially to the sustainable use and protection of water and marine resources where that activity either contributes substantially to achieving the good status of bodies of water, including bodies of surface water and groundwater or to preventing the deterioration of bodies of water that already have good status, or contributes substantially to achieving the good environmental status of marine waters or to preventing the deterioration of marine waters that are already in good environmental status, by:

(a) protecting the environment from the adverse effects of urban and industrial waste water discharges, including from contaminants of emerging concern such as pharmaceuticals and microplastics, for example by ensuring the adequate collection, treatment and discharge of urban and industrial waste waters;

(b) protecting human health from the adverse impact of any contamination of water intended for human consumption by ensuring that it is free from any micro-organisms, parasites and substances that constitute a potential danger to human health as well as increasing people's access to clean drinking water;

(c) improving water management and efficiency, including by protecting and enhancing the status of aquatic ecosystems, by promoting the sustainable use of water through the long-term protection of available water resources, inter alia, through measures such as water reuse, by ensuring the progressive reduction of pollutant emissions into surface water and groundwater, by contributing to mitigating the effects of floods and droughts, or through any other activity that protects or improves the qualitative and quantitative status of water bodies;

(d) ensuring the sustainable use of marine ecosystem services or contributing to the good environmental status of marine waters, including by protecting, preserving or restoring the marine environment and by preventing or reducing inputs in the marine environment; or

(e) enabling any of the activities listed in points (a) to (d) of this paragraph in accordance with Article 16.

2. The Commission shall adopt a delegated act in accordance with Article 23 to:

(a) supplement paragraph 1 of this Article by establishing technical screening criteria for determining the conditions under which a specific economic activity qualifies as contributing substantially to sustainable use and protection of water and marine resources; and

(b) supplement Article 17 by establishing, for each relevant environmental objective, technical screening criteria, for determining whether an economic activity in respect of which technical screening criteria have been established pursuant to point (a) of this paragraph causes significant harm to one or more of those objectives.

3. Prior to adopting the delegated act referred to in paragraph 2 of this Article, the Commission shall consult the Platform referred to in Article 20 regarding the technical screening criteria referred to in paragraph 2 of this Article.

4. The Commission shall establish the technical screening criteria referred to in paragraph 2 of this Article in one delegated act, taking into account the requirements of Article 19.

5. The Commission shall adopt the delegated act referred to in paragraph 2 by 31 December 2021, with a view to ensuring its application from 1 January 2023.

NOTES

Application of this Article in relation to the UK: this Article is amended, in relation to the UK only, by the Securities Financing Transactions, Securitisation and Miscellaneous Amendments (EU Exit) Regulations 2020, SI 2020/1385, reg 78(8), as from IP completion day (as defined in the European Union (Withdrawal Agreement) Act 2020, s 39), as follows—

"(8) In Article 12—

(a) in paragraph 2, for "The Commission shall adopt a delegated act in accordance with Article 23" substitute "the Treasury must make regulations";

(b) omit paragraph 3;

(c) for paragraph 4 substitute—

"4. The Treasury must establish the technical screening criteria referred to in paragraph 2 of this Article taking into account the requirements of Article 19.";

(d) for paragraph 5 substitute—

"5. The Treasury must make the regulations in paragraph 2 above no later than 1 January 2024.".".

[11.801]

Article 13 Substantial contribution to the transition to a circular economy

1. An economic activity shall qualify as contributing substantially to the transition to a circular economy, including waste prevention, re-use and recycling, where that activity:

(a) uses natural resources, including sustainably sourced bio-based and other raw materials, in production more efficiently, including by:

(i) reducing the use of primary raw materials or increasing the use of by-products and secondary raw materials; or

(ii) resource and energy efficiency measures;

(b) increases the durability, reparability, upgradability or reusability of products, in particular in designing and manufacturing activities;

(c) increases the recyclability of products, including the recyclability of individual materials contained in those products, inter alia, by substitution or reduced use of products and materials that are not recyclable, in particular in designing and manufacturing activities;

(d) substantially reduces the content of hazardous substances and substitutes substances of very high concern in materials and products throughout their life cycle, in line with the objectives set out in Union law, including by replacing such substances with safer alternatives and ensuring traceability;

(e) prolongs the use of products, including through reuse, design for longevity, repurposing, disassembly, remanufacturing, upgrades and repair, and sharing products;

(f) increases the use of secondary raw materials and their quality, including by high-quality recycling of waste;

(g) prevents or reduces waste generation, including the generation of waste from the extraction of minerals and waste from the construction and demolition of buildings;

(h) increases preparing for the re-use and recycling of waste;

(i) increases the development of the waste management infrastructure needed for prevention, for preparing for re-use and for recycling, while ensuring that the recovered materials are recycled as high-quality secondary raw material input in production, thereby avoiding downcycling;

(j) minimises the incineration of waste and avoids the disposal of waste, including landfilling, in accordance with the principles of the waste hierarchy;

(k) avoids and reduces litter; or

(l) enables any of the activities listed in points (a) to (k) of this paragraph in accordance with Article 16.

2. The Commission shall adopt a delegated act in accordance with Article 23 to:

(a) supplement paragraph 1 of this Article by establishing technical screening criteria for determining the conditions under which a specific economic activity qualifies as contributing substantially to the transition to a circular economy; and

(b) supplement Article 17 by establishing, for each relevant environmental objective, technical screening criteria for determining whether an economic activity in respect of which technical screening criteria have established pursuant to point (a) of this paragraph causes significant harm to one or more of those objectives.

3. Prior to adopting the delegated act referred to in paragraph 2 of this Article, the Commission shall consult the Platform referred to in Article 20 regarding the technical screening criteria referred to in paragraph 2 of this Article.

4. The Commission shall establish the technical screening criteria referred to in paragraph 2 of this Article in one delegated act, taking into account the requirements of Article 19.

5. The Commission shall adopt the delegated act referred to in paragraph 2 by 31 December 2021, with a view to ensuring its application from 1 January 2023.

NOTES

Application of this Article in relation to the UK: this Article is amended, in relation to the UK only, by the Securities Financing Transactions, Securitisation and Miscellaneous Amendments (EU Exit) Regulations 2020, SI 2020/1385, reg 78(9), as from IP completion day (as defined in the European Union (Withdrawal Agreement) Act 2020, s 39), as follows—

"(9) In Article 13—

(a) in paragraph 1(d) omit "in line with the objectives set out in Union law,";

(b) in paragraph 2 for "The Commission shall adopt a delegated act in accordance with Article 23" substitute "the Treasury must make regulations";

(c) omit paragraph 3;

(d) for paragraph 4 substitute—

"4. The Treasury must establish the technical screening criteria referred to in paragraph 2 of this Article taking into account the requirements of Article 19.";

(e) for paragraph 5 substitute—

"5. The Treasury must make the regulations in paragraph 2 above no later than 1 January 2024.".".

[11.802]

Article 14 Substantial contribution to pollution prevention and control

1. An economic activity shall qualify as contributing substantially to pollution prevention and control where that activity contributes substantially to environmental protection from pollution by:

(a) preventing or, where that is not practicable, reducing pollutant emissions into air, water or land, other than greenhouse gasses;

(b) improving levels of air, water or soil quality in the areas in which the economic activity takes place whilst minimising any adverse impact on, human health and the environment or the risk thereof;
(c) preventing or minimising any adverse impact on human health and the environment of the production, use or disposal of chemicals;
(d) cleaning up litter and other pollution; or
(e) enabling any of the activities listed in points (a) to (d) of this paragraph in accordance with Article 16.

2. The Commission shall adopt a delegated act in accordance with Article 23 to:
(a) supplement paragraph 1 of this Article by establishing technical screening criteria for determining the conditions under which a specific economic activity qualifies as contributing substantially to pollution prevention and control; and
(b) supplement Article 17 by establishing, for each relevant environmental objective, technical screening criteria for determining whether an economic activity in respect of which technical screening criteria have been established pursuant to point (a) of this paragraph causes significant harm to one or more of those objectives.

3. Prior to adopting the delegated act referred to in paragraph 2 of this Article, the Commission shall consult the Platform referred to in Article 20 regarding the technical screening criteria referred to in paragraph 2 of this Article.

4. The Commission shall establish the technical screening criteria referred to in paragraph 2 of this Article in one delegated act, taking into account the requirements of Article 19.

5. The Commission shall adopt the delegated act referred to in paragraph 2 by 31 December 2021, with a view to ensuring its application from 1 January 2023.

NOTES

Application of this Article in relation to the UK: this Article is amended, in relation to the UK only, by the Securities Financing Transactions, Securitisation and Miscellaneous Amendments (EU Exit) Regulations 2020, SI 2020/1385, reg 78(10), as from IP completion day (as defined in the European Union (Withdrawal Agreement) Act 2020, s 39), as follows—

"(10) In Article 14—
(a) in paragraph 2 for "The Commission shall adopt a delegated act in accordance with Article 23" substitute "the Treasury must make regulations";
(b) omit paragraph 3;
(c) for paragraph 4 substitute—

"4. The Treasury must establish the technical screening criteria referred to in paragraph 2 of this Article taking into account the requirements of Article 19."

(d) for paragraph 5 substitute—

"5. The Treasury must make the regulations in paragraph 2 above no later than 1 January 2024.".".

[11.803]

Article 15 Substantial contribution to the protection and restoration of biodiversity and ecosystems

1. An economic activity shall qualify as contributing substantially to the protection and restoration of biodiversity and ecosystems where that activity contributes substantially to protecting, conserving or restoring biodiversity or to achieving the good condition of ecosystems, or to protecting ecosystems that are already in good condition, through:
(a) nature and biodiversity conservation, including achieving favourable conservation status of natural and semi-natural habitats and species, or preventing their deterioration where they already have favourable conservation status, and protecting and restoring terrestrial, marine and other aquatic ecosystems in order to improve their condition and enhance their capacity to provide ecosystem services;
(b) sustainable land use and management, including adequate protection of soil biodiversity, land degradation neutrality and the remediation of contaminated sites;
(c) sustainable agricultural practices, including those that contribute to enhancing biodiversity or to halting or preventing the degradation of soils and other ecosystems, deforestation and habitat loss;
(d) sustainable forest management, including practices and uses of forests and forest land that contribute to enhancing biodiversity or to halting or preventing degradation of ecosystems, deforestation and habitat loss; or
(e) enabling any of the activities listed in points (a) to (d) of this paragraph in accordance with Article 16.

2. The Commission shall adopt a delegated act in accordance with Article 23 to:
(a) supplement paragraph 1 of this Article by establishing technical screening criteria for determining the conditions under which a specific economic activity qualifies as contributing substantially to the protection and restoration of biodiversity and ecosystems; and
(b) supplement Article 17 by establishing, for each relevant environmental objective, technical screening criteria for determining whether an economic activity in respect of which technical screening criteria have been established pursuant to point (a) of this paragraph causes significant harm to one or more of those objectives.

3. Prior to adopting the delegated act referred to in paragraph 2 of this Article, the Commission shall consult the Platform referred to in Article 20 regarding the technical screening criteria referred to in paragraph 2 of this Article.

4. The Commission shall establish the technical screening criteria referred to in paragraph 2 of this Article in one delegated act, taking into account the requirements of Article 19.

5. The Commission shall adopt the delegated act referred to in paragraph 2 by 31 December 2021, with a view to ensuring its application from 1 January 2023.

NOTES

Application of this Article in relation to the UK: this Article is amended, in relation to the UK only, by the Securities Financing Transactions, Securitisation and Miscellaneous Amendments (EU Exit) Regulations 2020, SI 2020/1385, reg 78(11), as from IP completion day (as defined in the European Union (Withdrawal Agreement) Act 2020, s 39), as follows—

"(11) In Article 15—
(a) in paragraph 2 for "The Commission shall adopt a delegated act in accordance with Article 23" substitute "the Treasury must make regulations";
(b) omit paragraph 3;
(c) for paragraph 4 substitute—

"4. The Treasury must establish the technical screening criteria referred to in paragraph 2 of this Article taking into account the requirements of Article 19.";

(d) for paragraph 5 substitute—

"5. The Treasury must make the regulations in paragraph 2 above no later than 1 January 2024.".".

[11.804]
Article 16 Enabling activities

An economic activity shall qualify as contributing substantially to one or more of the set out in Article 9 by directly enabling other activities to make a substantial contribution to one or more of those objectives, provided that such economic activity:

(a) does not lead to a lock-in of assets that undermine long-term environmental goals, considering the economic lifetime of those assets; and
(b) has a substantial positive environmental impact, on the basis of life-cycle considerations.

[11.805]
Article 17 Significant harm to environmental objectives

1. For the purposes of point (b) of Article 3, taking into account the life cycle of the products and services provided by an economic activity, including evidence from existing life-cycle assessments, that economic activity shall be considered to significantly harm:

(a) climate change mitigation, where that activity leads to significant greenhouse gas emissions;
(b) climate change adaptation, where that activity leads to an increased adverse impact of the current climate and the expected future climate, on the activity itself or on people, nature or assets;
(c) the sustainable use and protection of water and marine resources, where that activity is detrimental:
 (i) to the good status or the good ecological potential of bodies of water, including surface water and groundwater; or
 (ii) to the good environmental status of marine waters;
(d) the circular economy, including waste prevention and recycling, where:
 (i) that activity leads to significant inefficiencies in the use of materials or in the direct or indirect use of natural resources such as non-renewable energy sources, raw materials, water and land at one or more stages of the life cycle of products, including in terms of durability, reparability, upgradability, reusability or recyclability of products;
 (ii) that activity leads to a significant increase in the generation, incineration or disposal of waste, with the exception of the incineration of non-recyclable hazardous waste; or
 (iii) the long-term disposal of waste may cause significant and long-term harm to the environment;
(e) pollution prevention and control, where that activity leads to a significant increase in the emissions of pollutants into air, water or land, as compared with the situation before the activity started; or
(f) the protection and restoration of biodiversity and ecosystems, where that activity is:
 (i) significantly detrimental to the good condition and resilience of ecosystems; or
 (ii) detrimental to the conservation status of habitats and species, including those of Union interest.

2. When assessing an economic activity against the criteria set out in paragraph 1, both the environmental impact of the activity itself and the environmental impact of the products and services provided by that activity throughout their life cycle shall be taken into account, in particular by considering the production, use and end of life of those products and services.

NOTES

Application of this Article in relation to the UK: this Article is amended, in relation to the UK only, by the Securities Financing Transactions, Securitisation and Miscellaneous Amendments (EU Exit) Regulations 2020, SI 2020/1385, reg 78(12), as from IP completion day (as defined in the European Union (Withdrawal Agreement) Act 2020, s 39), as follows—

"(12) In Article 17, in paragraph 1(f)(ii), for "Union" substitute "United Kingdom".".

[11.806]
Article 18 Minimum safeguards

1. The minimum safeguards referred to in point (c) of Article 3 shall be procedures implemented by an undertaking that is carrying out an economic activity to ensure the alignment with the OECD Guidelines for Multinational Enterprises and the UN Guiding Principles on Business and Human Rights, including the principles and rights set out in the eight fundamental conventions identified in the Declaration of the International Labour Organisation on Fundamental Principles and Rights at Work and the International Bill of Human Rights.

2. When implementing the procedures referred to in paragraph 1 of this Article, undertakings shall adhere to the principle of 'do no significant harm' referred to in point (17) of Article 2 of Regulation (EU) 2019/2088.

NOTES

Application of this Article in relation to the UK: this Article is amended, in relation to the UK only, by the Securities Financing Transactions, Securitisation and Miscellaneous Amendments (EU Exit) Regulations 2020, SI 2020/1385, reg 78(13), as from IP completion day (as defined in the European Union (Withdrawal Agreement) Act 2020, s 39), as follows—

"(13) In Article 18, omit paragraph 2.

[11.807]
Article 19 Requirements for technical screening criteria

1. The technical screening criteria established pursuant to Articles 10(3), 11(3), 12(2), 13(2), 14(2) and 15(2) shall:

(a) identify the most relevant potential contributions to the given environmental objective while respecting the principle of technological neutrality, considering both the short- and long-term impact of a given economic activity;

(b) specify the minimum requirements that need to be met to avoid significant harm to any of the relevant environmental objectives, considering both the short- and long-term impact of a given economic activity;
(c) be quantitative and contain thresholds to the extent possible, and otherwise be qualitative;
(d) where appropriate, build upon Union labelling and certification schemes, Union methodologies for assessing environmental footprint, and Union statistical classification systems, and take into account any relevant existing Union legislation;
(e) where feasible, use sustainability indicators as referred to in Article 4(6) of Regulation (EU) 2019/2088;
(f) be based on conclusive scientific evidence and the precautionary principle enshrined in Article 191 TFEU;
(g) take into account the life cycle, including evidence from existing life-cycle assessments, by considering both the environmental impact of the economic activity itself and the environmental impact of the products and services provided by that economic activity, in particular by considering the production, use and end of life of those products and services;
(h) take into account the nature and the scale of the economic activity, including:
  (i) whether it is an enabling activity as referred to in Article 16; or
  (ii) whether it is a transitional activity as referred to in Article 10(2);
(i) take into account the potential market impact of the transition to a more sustainable economy, including the risk of certain assets becoming stranded as a result of such transition, as well as the risk of creating inconsistent incentives for investing sustainably;
(j) cover all relevant economic activities within a specific sector and ensure that those activities are treated equally if they contribute equally towards the environmental objectives set out in Article 9 of this Regulation, to avoid distorting competition in the market; and
(k) be easy to use and be set in a manner that facilitates the verification of their compliance.

Where the economic activity belongs to one of the categories referred to in point (h), the technical screening criteria shall clearly indicate that fact.

2. The technical screening criteria referred to in paragraph 1 shall also include criteria for activities related to the clean energy transition consistent with a pathway to limit the temperature increase to 1.5 C above pre-industrial levels, in particular energy efficiency and renewable energy, to the extent that those activities substantially contribute to any of the environmental objectives.

3. The technical screening criteria referred to in paragraph 1 shall ensure that power generation activities that use solid fossil fuels do not qualify as environmentally sustainable economic activities.

4. The technical screening criteria referred to in paragraph 1 shall also include criteria for activities related to the switch to clean or climate-neutral mobility, including through modal shift, efficiency measures and alternative fuels, to the extent that those are substantially contributing to any of the environmental objectives.

5. The Commission shall regularly review the technical screening criteria referred to in paragraph 1 and, where appropriate, amend the delegated acts adopted in accordance with this Regulation in line with scientific and technological developments.

In that context, before amending or replacing a delegated act, the Commission shall assess the implementation of those criteria taking into account the outcome of their application by financial market participants and their impact on capital markets, including on the channelling of investment into environmentally sustainable economic activities.

To ensure that economic activities as referred to in Article 10(2) remain on a credible transition pathway consistent with a climate-neutral economy, the Commission shall review the technical screening criteria for those activities at least every three years and, where appropriate, amend the delegated act referred to in Article 10(3) in line with scientific and technological developments.

NOTES

Application of this Article in relation to the UK: this Article is amended, in relation to the UK only, by the Securities Financing Transactions, Securitisation and Miscellaneous Amendments (EU Exit) Regulations 2020, SI 2020/1385, reg 78(14), as from IP completion day (as defined in the European Union (Withdrawal Agreement) Act 2020, s 39), as follows—

"(14) In Article 19—
(a) in paragraph 1, omit subparagraphs (d) and (e), and in subparagraph (f) omit "and the precautionary principle enshrined in Article 191 TFEU";
(b) in paragraph 5—
  (i) in the first subparagraph, for "The Commission shall regularly review the technical screening criteria referred to in paragraph 1 and, where appropriate, amend the delegated acts" substitute "The Treasury may by regulations amend the technical screening criteria set out in any regulations made under this Regulation.";
  (ii) omit the second subparagraph;
  (iii) in the third paragraph for "the Commission" substitute "the Treasury".".

[11.808]

Article 20 Platform on Sustainable Finance

1. The Commission shall establish a Platform on Sustainable Finance (the 'Platform'). It shall be composed in a balanced manner of the following groups:
(a) representatives of:
  (i) the European Environment Agency;
  (ii) the ESAs;
  (iii) the European Investment Bank and the European Investment Fund; and
  (iv) the European Union Agency for Fundamental Rights;
(b) experts representing relevant private stakeholders, including financial and non-financial market participants and business sectors, representing relevant industries, and persons with accounting and reporting expertise;
(c) experts representing civil society, including persons with expertise in the field of environmental, social, labour and governance issues;
(d) experts appointed in a personal capacity, who have proven knowledge and experience in the areas covered by this Regulation;

(e) experts representing academia, including universities, research institutes and other scientific organisations, including persons with global expertise.

2. The Platform shall:

(a) advise the Commission on the technical screening criteria referred to in Article 19, as well as on the possible need to update those criteria;

(b) analyse the impact of the technical screening criteria in terms of potential costs and benefits of their application;

(c) assist the Commission in analysing requests from stakeholders to develop or revise technical screening criteria for a given economic activity;

(d) advise the Commission, where appropriate, on the possible role of sustainability accounting and reporting standards in supporting the application of the technical screening criteria;

(e) monitor and regularly report to the Commission on trends at Union and Member State level regarding capital flows into sustainable investment;

(f) advise the Commission on the possible need to develop further measures to improve data availability and quality;

(g) advise the Commission on the usability of the technical screening criteria, taking into account the need to avoid undue administrative burdens;

(h) advise the Commission on the possible need to amend this Regulation;

(i) advise the Commission on the evaluation and development of sustainable finance policies, including with regard to policy coherence issues;

(j) advise the Commission on addressing other sustainability objectives, including social objectives;

(k) advise the Commission on the application of Article 18 and the possible need to supplement the requirements thereof.

3. The Platform shall take into account the views of a wide range of stakeholders.

4. The Platform shall be chaired by the Commission and constituted in accordance with the horizontal rules on the creation and operation of Commission expert groups. In that context the Commission may invite experts with specific expertise on an ad hoc basis.

5. The Platform shall carry out its tasks in accordance with the principle of transparency. The Commission shall publish the minutes of the meetings of the Platform and other relevant documents on the Commission website.

6. Where financial market participants consider that an economic activity which does not comply with the technical screening criteria established pursuant to this Regulation, or for which such technical screening criteria have not yet been established, should qualify as environmentally sustainable, they may inform the Platform thereof.

NOTES

Repeal of this Article in relation to the UK: this Article is repealed, in relation to the UK only, by the Securities Financing Transactions, Securitisation and Miscellaneous Amendments (EU Exit) Regulations 2020, SI 2020/1385, reg 78(15), as from IP completion day (as defined in the European Union (Withdrawal Agreement) Act 2020, s 39).

[11.809]

Article 21 Competent authorities

1. Member States shall ensure that the competent authorities referred to in Article 14(1) of Regulation (EU) 2019/2088 monitor the compliance of financial market participants with the requirements laid down in Articles 5, 6 and 7 of this Regulation. Member States shall ensure that their competent authorities have all the necessary supervisory and investigatory powers for the exercise of their functions under this Regulation.

2. For the purposes of this Regulation, the competent authorities shall cooperate with each other and shall provide each other, without undue delay, with such information as is relevant for the purposes of carrying out their duties under this Regulation.

NOTES

Repeal of this Article in relation to the UK: this Article is repealed, in relation to the UK only, by the Securities Financing Transactions, Securitisation and Miscellaneous Amendments (EU Exit) Regulations 2020, SI 2020/1385, reg 78(15), as from IP completion day (as defined in the European Union (Withdrawal Agreement) Act 2020, s 39).

[11.810]

Article 22 Measures and penalties

Member States shall lay down the rules on measures and penalties applicable to infringements of Articles 5, 6 and 7. The measures and penalties provided for shall be effective, proportionate and dissuasive.

NOTES

Repeal of this Article in relation to the UK: this Article is repealed, in relation to the UK only, by the Securities Financing Transactions, Securitisation and Miscellaneous Amendments (EU Exit) Regulations 2020, SI 2020/1385, reg 78(15), as from IP completion day (as defined in the European Union (Withdrawal Agreement) Act 2020, s 39).

[11.811]

Article 23 Exercise of the delegation

1. The power to adopt delegated acts is conferred on the Commission subject to the conditions laid down in this Article.

2. The power to adopt delegated acts referred to in Articles 8(4), 10(3), 11(3), 12(2), 13(2), 14(2) and 15(2) shall be conferred on the Commission for an indeterminate period from 12 July 2020.

3. The delegations of powers referred to in Articles 8(4), 10(3), 11(3), 12(2), 13(2), 14(2) and 15(2) may be revoked at any time by the European Parliament or by the Council. A decision to revoke shall put an end to the delegation of the power specified in that decision. It shall take effect the day following the publication of the decision in the *Official Journal of the European Union* or at a later date specified therein. It shall not affect the validity of any delegated acts already in force.

4. The Commission shall gather all necessary expertise, prior to the adoption and during the development of delegated acts, including through the consultation of the experts of the Member State Expert Group on Sustainable Finance referred to in Article 24. Before adopting a delegated act, the Commission shall act in accordance with the principles and procedures laid down in the Interinstitutional Agreement of 13 April 2016 on Better Law-Making.
5. As soon as it adopts a delegated act, the Commission shall notify it simultaneously to the European Parliament and to the Council.
6. A delegated act adopted pursuant to Article 8(4), 10(3), 11(3), 12(2), 13(2), 14(2) or 15(2) shall enter into force only if no objection has been expressed either by the European Parliament or by the Council within a period of four months of notification of that act to the European Parliament and the Council or if, before the expiry of that period, the European Parliament and the Council have both informed the Commission that they will not object. That period shall be extended by two months at the initiative of the European Parliament or of the Council.

NOTES

Application of this Article in relation to the UK: this Article is substituted, in relation to the UK only, by the Securities Financing Transactions, Securitisation and Miscellaneous Amendments (EU Exit) Regulations 2020, SI 2020/1385, reg 78(16), as from IP completion day (as defined in the European Union (Withdrawal Agreement) Act 2020, s 39), as follows—

"Article 23 Regulations

1. Any power to make regulations conferred on the Treasury by this Regulation is exercisable by statutory instrument.
2. Such regulations may—
   (a) contain incidental, supplemental, consequential, transitional, transitory or saving provision; and
   (b) make different provisions for different purposes.
3. A statutory instrument containing regulations made under this Regulation is subject to annulment in pursuance of a resolution of either House of Parliament.".

[11.812]

Article 24 Member State Expert Group on Sustainable Finance

1. A Member State Expert Group on Sustainable Finance (the 'Member State Expert Group') shall advise the Commission on the appropriateness of the technical screening criteria and the approach taken by the Platform regarding the development of those criteria in accordance with Article 19.
2. The Commission shall inform the Member States through meetings of the Member State Expert Group to facilitate an exchange of views between the Member States and the Commission on a timely basis, in particular as regards the main output of the Platform, such as new technical screening criteria or material updates thereof, or draft reports.

NOTES

Repeal of this Article in relation to the UK: this Article is repealed, in relation to the UK only, by the Securities Financing Transactions, Securitisation and Miscellaneous Amendments (EU Exit) Regulations 2020, SI 2020/1385, reg 78(17), as from IP completion day (as defined in the European Union (Withdrawal Agreement) Act 2020, s 39).

CHAPTER III FINAL PROVISIONS

Article 25 (*Amends European Parliament and Council Regulation 2019/2088/EU at* **[11.764]**. *This Article is amended, in relation to the UK only, by the Securities Financing Transactions, Securitisation and Miscellaneous Amendments (EU Exit) Regulations 2020, SI 2020/1385, reg 78(18), as from IP completion day (as defined in the European Union (Withdrawal Agreement) Act 2020, s 39).*)

[11.813]

Article 26 Review

1. By 13 July 2022, and subsequently every three years thereafter, the Commission shall publish a report on the application of this Regulation. That report shall evaluate the following:
   (a) the progress in implementing this Regulation with regard to the development of technical screening criteria for environmentally sustainable economic activities;
   (b) the possible need to revise and complement the criteria set out in Article 3 for an economic activity to qualify as environmentally sustainable;
   (c) the use of the definition of environmentally sustainable investment in Union law, and at Member State level, including the provisions required for setting up verification mechanisms of compliance with the criteria set out in this Regulation;
   (d) the effectiveness of the application of the technical screening criteria established pursuant to this Regulation in channelling private investments into environmentally sustainable economic activities and in particular as regards capital flows, including equity, into private enterprises and other legal entities, both through financial products covered by this Regulation and other financial products;
   (e) the access by financial market participants covered by this Regulation and by investors to reliable, timely and verifiable information and data regarding private enterprises and other legal entities, including investee companies within and outside the scope of this Regulation and, in both cases, as regards equity and debt capital, taking into account the associated administrative burden, as well as the procedures for the verification of the data that are necessary for the determination of the degree of alignment with the technical screening criteria and to ensure compliance with those procedures;
   (f) the application of Articles 21 and 22.
2. By 31 December 2021, the Commission shall publish a report describing the provisions that would be required to extend the scope of this Regulation beyond environmentally sustainable economic activities and describing the provisions that would be required to cover:
   (a) economic activities that do not have a significant impact on environmental sustainability and economic activities that significantly harm environmental sustainability, as well as a review of the appropriateness of specific disclosure requirements related to transitional and enabling activities; and
   (b) other sustainability objectives, such as social objectives.

3. By 13 July 2022, the Commission shall assess the effectiveness of the advisory procedures for the development of the technical screening criteria established under this Regulation.

NOTES

Application of this Article in relation to the UK: this Article is amended, in relation to the UK only, by the Securities Financing Transactions, Securitisation and Miscellaneous Amendments (EU Exit) Regulations 2020, SI 2020/1385, reg 78(19), as from IP completion day (as defined in the European Union (Withdrawal Agreement) Act 2020, s 39), as follows—

"(19) In Article 26—

(a) in paragraph 1, for "By 13 July 2022, and subsequently every three years thereafter, the Commission shall publish a report on the application of this Regulation" substitute "The Treasury must, no later than 1 January 2024, and every three years thereafter, review the functioning of this Regulation and lay a report before Parliament";

(b) omit paragraph 1(c), (d), (e) and (f);

(c) in paragraph 2, for "By 31 December 2021, the Commission shall publish a report describing the provisions that would be required to extend the scope of this Regulation beyond environmentally sustainable economic activities and describing the provisions that would be required to cover" substitute "The Treasury must, no later than 1 January 2024, lay a report before Parliament evaluating the appropriateness of extending the scope of this Regulation beyond environmentally sustainable economic activities, and considering the measures that would be required to cover";

(d) omit Article 26(3).".

[11.814]

Article 27 Entry into force and application

1. This Regulation shall enter into force on the twentieth day following that of its publication in the *Official Journal of the European Union*.

2. Articles 4, 5, 6 and 7 and Article 8(1), (2) and (3) shall apply:

(a) in respect of the environmental objectives referred to in points (a) and (b) of Article 9 from 1 January 2022; and

(b) in respect of the environmental objectives referred to in points (c) to (f) of Article 9 from 1 January 2023.

3. Article 4 shall not apply to certificate-based tax incentive schemes that exist prior to the entry into force of this Regulation and that set out requirements for financial products that aim to finance sustainable projects.

This Regulation shall be binding in its entirety and directly applicable in all Member States.

NOTES

Application of this Article in relation to the UK: this Article is amended, in relation to the UK only, by the Securities Financing Transactions, Securitisation and Miscellaneous Amendments (EU Exit) Regulations 2020, SI 2020/1385, reg 78(20), as from IP completion day (as defined in the European Union (Withdrawal Agreement) Act 2020, s 39), as follows—

"(20) After Article 27 omit the words "This Regulation shall be binding in its entirety and directly applicable in all member States.".".

COMMISSION DELEGATED REGULATION

(2021/528/EU)

of 16 December 2020

supplementing Regulation (EU) 2017/1129 of the European Parliament and of the Council as regards the minimum information content of the document to be published for a prospectus exemption in connection with a takeover by means of an exchange offer, a merger or a division

(Text with EEA relevance)

[11.815]

NOTES

Date of publication in OJ: OJ L106, 26.3.2021, p 36.

This Regulation does not apply to the United Kingdom: this Regulation was not "operative immediately before IP completion day" within the meaning of the European Union (Withdrawal) Act 2018, s 3 at **[12.5]** and, therefore, does not form part of domestic law on and after IP completion day.

THE EUROPEAN COMMISSION,

Having regard to Regulation (EU) 2017/1129 of the European Parliament and of the Council of 14 June 2017 on the prospectus to be published when securities are offered to the public or admitted to trading on a regulated market, and repealing Directive 2003/71/EC,[1] and in particular Article 1(7) thereof,

Whereas:

(1) In order to provide the highest standards of investor protection across the Union and to enable investors to make an informed investment decision, the document referred to in Article 1(4), points (f) and (g), and Article 1(5), first subparagraph, points (e) and (f), of Regulation (EU) 2017/1129 ('exemption document') should contain sufficient, objective and comprehensible information on the companies involved in the transaction, the rights attaching to the equity securities, the prospects of the issuer of those equity securities and, depending on the type of transaction, of the offeree company, of the company being acquired or of the company being divided.

(2) To ensure that investors are provided with the necessary information to take an informed investment decision, a more comprehensive exemption document should be required in case of a takeover by means of an exchange offer that meets the condition of Article 1(6a), point (b), of Regulation (EU) 2017/1129 when, in that case, the equity

Part 11 EU & Retained EU Legislation

securities offered are not fungible with existing securities already admitted to trading on a regulated market prior to the takeover and its related transaction, or the takeover is considered to be a reverse acquisition transaction. The expanded content of the exemption document in such situations should be specified.

(3) To limit unnecessary costs for issuers, an exemption document should be lighter where, in connection with a transaction, the equity securities offered to the public or to be admitted to trading on a regulated market are fungible with equity securities already admitted to trading on a regulated market, and represent a small percentage of those equity securities. The reduced content of the exemption document in such a situation should be specified. However, in such a situation an issuer should not be prevented from benefiting from the exemptions laid down in Article 1(5), first subparagraph, points (a) or (b), of Regulation (EU) 2017/1129.

(4) To simplify drafting and to reduce costs of producing an exemption document, issuers should be allowed to incorporate by reference into that document certain information that already has been published in electronic form, provided such information is easily accessible and is written in the same language as the exemption document.

(5) Investors should be able to understand the situation of an issuer with a complex financial history or that has made a significant financial commitment, in which case the disclosure of information about an entity other than the issuer may be necessary. Issuers should therefore be obliged to describe in the exemption document their complex financial history or the effects on the issuer or on the issuer's business of the significant financial commitment undertaken.

(6) In order to ensure that an exemption document is a workable document for investors, it is necessary to specify that it is for the national competent authority to determine in what language that document will be drafted,

NOTES

[1] OJ L168, 30.6.2017, p 12.

HAS ADOPTED THIS REGULATION:

[11.816]
Article 1 Definitions

For the purposes of this Regulation, the following definitions shall apply:

(a) 'transaction' means a takeover by means of an exchange offer, a merger or a division as referred to in Article 1(4), points (f) or (g), or Article 1(5), first subparagraph, points (e) or (f), of Regulation (EU) 2017/1129, in respect of which the conditions laid down in Article 1(6a) or Article 1(6b) of that Regulation have been fulfilled;

(b) 'exemption document' means a document to be made available to the public in accordance with Article 21(2) of Regulation (EU) 2017/1129 to be entitled to an exemption from the obligation to publish a prospectus in case of a transaction;

(c) 'offeree company' means an offeree company as defined in Article 2(1), point (b), of Directive 2004/25/EC of the European Parliament and of the Council;[2]

(d) 'company being acquired' means a company transferring assets and liabilities to an acquiring company as a result of any merger in respect of which the conditions laid down in Article 1(6b) of Regulation (EU) 2017/1129 have been fulfilled;

(e) 'company being divided' means a company transferring assets and liabilities to a company receiving contributions as a result of any division in respect of which the conditions laid down in Article 1(6b) of Regulation (EU) 2017/1129 have been fulfilled;

(f) 'offeror' means an offeror as defined in Article 2(i) of Regulation (EU) 2017/1129.

NOTES

[2] Directive 2004/25/EC of the European Parliament and of the Council of 21 April 2004 on takeover bids (OJ L142, 30.4.2004, p 12).

[11.817]
Article 2 Minimum information content of the exemption document

1. An exemption document shall contain the relevant information which is necessary to enable investors to understand:

(a) the prospects of the issuer, and, depending on the type of transaction, of the offeree company, of the company being acquired or of the company being divided, and any significant changes in the business and financial position of each of those companies that have occurred since the end of the previous financial year;

(b) the rights attaching to the equity securities;

(c) a description of the transaction and its impact on the issuer.

The information contained in an exemption document shall be written and presented in an easily analysable, concise and comprehensible form and shall enable investors to make an informed investment decision.

An exemption document shall include the minimum information referred to in Annex I to this Regulation.

An exemption document shall, however, include the minimum information referred to in Annex II to this Regulation where all of the following conditions are met:

(a) the exemption document relates to a takeover by means of an exchange offer in respect of which the conditions laid down in Article 1(6a), point (b), of Regulation (EU) 2017/1129 have been fulfilled;

(b) the equity securities offered are not fungible with existing securities already admitted to trading on a regulated market prior to the takeover and its related transaction, or the takeover is considered to be a reverse acquisition transaction within the meaning of paragraph B19 of international financial reporting standard (IFRS) 3, Business Combinations, adopted by Commission Regulation (EC) No 1126/2008.[3]

2. By way of derogation from paragraph 1 and without prejudice to Article 1(5), first subparagraph, points (a) or (b), of Regulation (EU) 2017/1129, where, in connection with a transaction, the equity securities are offered to the public or are to be admitted to trading on a regulated market and are fungible with and represent no more than 10% of equity securities already admitted to trading on a regulated market, the exemption document shall only contain the minimum information referred to in sections 1, 3 and 5 and in items 2.2 and 4.2 of Annex I to this Regulation.

NOTES

[3] Commission Regulation (EC) No 1126/2008 of 3 November 2008 adopting certain international accounting standards in accordance with Regulation (EC) No 1606/2002 of the European Parliament and of the Council (OJ L320, 29.11.2008, p 1).

[11.818]
Article 3 Incorporation by reference

1. Information may be incorporated by reference in an exemption document where that information has been previously or simultaneously published electronically, drawn up in a language fulfilling the requirements of Article 5 of this Regulation and where that information is contained in one of the following documents:

(a) documents as referred to in Article 19(1) of Regulation (EU) 2017/1129;
(b) documents required by national law transposing Directive 2004/25/EC;
(c) documents required by national law transposing Directive (EU) 2017/1132 of the European Parliament and of the Council;[4]
(d) other documents that are published in accordance with national law where those documents are relevant to the transaction.

The information referred to in the first subparagraph shall be the most recent that is available to the issuer, the offeree company, the company being acquired or the company being divided.

2. Where only certain items of information are incorporated by reference, the exemption document shall contain a statement that the non-incorporated parts are either not relevant for the investor or are included elsewhere in the exemption document.

3. Persons responsible for the exemption document shall ensure that information incorporated by reference in that exemption document is easily accessible.

4. An exemption document that contains information incorporated by reference shall contain a cross-reference list that enables investors to easily identify specific items of information and shall contain hyperlinks to all documents containing information that is incorporated by reference.

NOTES

[4] Directive (EU) 2017/1132 of the European Parliament and of the Council of 14 June 2017 relating to certain aspects of company law (OJ L169, 30.6.2017, p 46).

[11.819]
Article 4 Complex financial history and significant financial commitment

1. Where the issuer of equity securities has a complex financial history as referred to in Article 18(3) of Commission Delegated Regulation (EU) 2019/980,[5] or has made a significant financial commitment as referred to in Article 18(4) of that Regulation, the exemption document shall contain all information referred to in Annex I or, where applicable, Annex II to this Regulation about the entity other than the issuer as if that entity were the issuer of the equity securities, to the extent that investors need that information to make an informed investment decision as referred to in Article 2(1) of this Regulation.

Such additional information shall specify the anticipated effects of the transaction, as defined in Article 1(a) of this Regulation, on the issuer or on the issuer's business, and the effects of the complex financial history or of the significant financial commitment on the issuer or on the issuer's business.

2. The additional information referred to in paragraph 1 shall be accompanied by a clear explanation why investors need that information to make an informed investment decision.

3. An issuer that is unable to provide the additional information referred to in paragraph 1 shall explain in the exemption document why that is the case.

NOTES

[5] Commission Delegated Regulation (EU) 2019/980 of 14 March 2019 supplementing Regulation (EU) 2017/1129 of the European Parliament and of the Council as regards the format, content, scrutiny and approval of the prospectus to be published when securities are offered to the public or admitted to trading on a regulated market, and repealing Commission Regulation (EC) No 809/2004 (OJ L166, 21.6.2019, p 26).

[11.820]
Article 5 Use of languages

An exemption document shall be drawn up in a language accepted by the competent authority as defined in Article 2, point (o), of Regulation (EU) 2017/1129.

[11.821]
Article 6 Entry into force

This Regulation shall enter into force on the twentieth day following that of its publication in the *Official Journal of the European Union.*

This Regulation shall be binding in its entirety and directly applicable in all Member States.

ANNEXES

ANNEX I
MINIMUM INFORMATION CONTENT OF THE EXEMPTION DOCUMENT

Article 2(1), third subparagraph, and Article 2(2)

[11.822]

SECTION 1	**PERSONS RESPONSIBLE FOR DRAWING UP THE EXEMPTION DOCUMENT, THIRD PARTY INFORMATION AND EXPERTS REPORT**
Item 1.1	**Identification of persons responsible for drawing up the exemption document** Identify all persons responsible for the information or any parts of it, given in the exemption document with, in the latter case, an indication of such parts. In case of natural persons, including members of the issuer's administrative, management or supervisory bodies, indicate the name and function of the person; in case of legal persons indicate the name and registered office.
Item 1.2	**Responsibility statement** A declaration by those responsible for the exemption document that, to the best of their knowledge, the information contained in the exemption document is in accordance with the facts and that the exemption document makes no omission likely to affect its import. Where applicable, a declaration by those responsible for certain parts of the exemption document that, to the best of their knowledge, the information contained in those parts of the exemption document for which they are responsible is in accordance with the facts and that those parts of the exemption document make no omission likely to affect their import.
Item 1.3	**Expert's statement or report** Where a statement or report attributed to a person as an expert is included in the exemption document, provide the following details for that person: (a) name; (b) business address; (c) qualifications; (d) material interest, if any, in the issuer. Where the statement or report has been produced at the issuer's request, state that such statement or report has been included in the exemption document with the consent of the person who has authorised the contents of that part of the exemption document.
Item 1.4	**Information sourced by a third party** Where information has been sourced from a third party, provide a confirmation that that information has been accurately reproduced and that as far as the issuer is aware and is able to ascertain from information published by that third party, no facts have been omitted which would render the reproduced information inaccurate or misleading. In addition, identify the source(s) of the information.
Item 1.5	**Regulatory statements** A statement that: (a) the exemption document does not constitute a prospectus within the meaning of Regulation (EU) 2017/1129; (b) the exemption document has not been subject to the scrutiny and approval by the relevant competent authority in accordance with Article 20 of Regulation (EU) 2017/1129; (c) pursuant to Article 1(6a), point (b), of Regulation (EU) 2017/1129, where applicable, the supervisory authority that has the competence to review the offer document under Directive 2004/25/EC has issued a prior approval of the exemption document.
SECTION 2	**INFORMATION ON THE ISSUER AND ON THE OFFEREE COMPANY, COMPANY BEING ACQUIRED OR COMPANY BEING DIVIDED**

Unless stated otherwise, the items listed in Section 2 shall be provided for the issuer and, depending on the type of transaction, the offeree company, the company being acquired or the company being divided. Where one of the aforementioned entities is a group and the consolidated financial statements have already been published, the information listed in this section shall be presented on a consolidated basis.

For equity securities other than shares, the items listed in Section 2 shall also be provided for the issuer of the underlying shares, where different from the issuer of the equity securities.

In case of a takeover by means of an exchange offer, where the requested information on the offeree company is not available, a statement to that effect shall be provided.

Item 2.1	**General information**
Item 2.1.1	Legal and commercial name

SECTION 1	**PERSONS RESPONSIBLE FOR DRAWING UP THE EXEMPTION DOCUMENT, THIRD PARTY INFORMATION AND EXPERTS REPORT**
Item 2.1.2	(a) domicile and legal form; (b) legal entity identifier ('LEI'); (c) the law of the country of incorporation; (d) country of incorporation, and the address, telephone number of its registered office (or principal place of business where different from the registered office); (e) hyperlink to the website with a disclaimer that the information on the website does not form part of the exemption document unless that information is incorporated by reference into the exemption document.
Item 2.1.3	Names of the auditors for the period covered by the financial statements and the name of the professional body(ies) which they are members of.
Item 2.2	**Business overview**
Item 2.2.1	Principal activities, including the main categories of products sold and/or services performed in the last financial year.
Item 2.2.2	Any significant changes having an impact on the operations and principal activities since the end of the period covered by the latest published audited financial statements.
Item 2.2.3	A brief description of the principal markets, including a breakdown of total revenues by operating segment and geographic market for the last financial year. In case of a division, the description referred to in the first paragraph shall refer to the principal markets where the main assets and liabilities of the company being divided are located.
Item 2.3	**Investments** A description of the material investments made since the date of the last published financial statements and which are in progress and/or for which firm commitments have already been made, together with the anticipated source of funds.
Item 2.4	**Corporate governance**
Item 2.4.1	Names, business addresses and functions within the issuer or, depending on the type of transaction, the offeree company, the company being acquired or the company being divided, of the members of the administrative, management or supervisory bodies and, in case of a limited partnership with a share capital, of partners with unlimited liability.
Item 2.4.2	Identity of major shareholders
Item 2.4.3	Number of employees
Item 2.5	**Financial information**
Item 2.5.1	Financial statements Financial statements (annual and half-yearly) that were published over the 12 months prior to the publication of the exemption document. Where both annual and half-yearly financial statements have been published, only the annual statements shall be required where they postdate the half-yearly financial statements. The financial statements shall include the audit reports. Where statutory auditors have refused audit reports on the financial statements or where such audit reports contain qualifications, modifications of opinion, disclaimers or an emphasis of matter, the reason for this shall be given and such qualifications, modifications, disclaimers or emphasis of matter shall be reproduced in full.
Item 2.5.1.a (Mergers only)	By way of derogation from item 2.5.1, where the company being acquired does not have equity securities already admitted to trading on a regulated market, the company shall provide the audited financial statements (annual and half-yearly) that were adopted over the 12 months prior to the publication of the exemption document. Where both annual and half-yearly financial statements have been published, only the annual statements shall be required where they postdate the half-yearly financial statements. The financial statements shall include the audit reports. Where statutory auditors have refused audit reports on the financial statements or where such audit reports contain qualifications, modifications of opinion, disclaimers or an emphasis of matter, the reason for this shall be given and such qualifications, modifications, disclaimers or emphasis of matter shall be reproduced in full. Where the company being acquired does not have audited financial statements, it shall provide financial statements prepared during the past 12 months and a negative statement stating that the financial statements have not been reviewed or audited.

SECTION 1	PERSONS RESPONSIBLE FOR DRAWING UP THE EXEMPTION DOCUMENT, THIRD PARTY INFORMATION AND EXPERTS REPORT
Item 2.5.2	Accounting standards The financial information shall be prepared in accordance with the International Financial Reporting Standards as endorsed in the Union in accordance with Regulation (EC) No 1606/2002 of the European Parliament and of the Council.[1] Where Regulation (EC) No 1606/2002 is not applicable, the financial information shall be prepared in accordance with: (a) a Member State's national accounting standards for issuers from the EEA, as required by Directive 2013/34/EU of the European Parliament and of the Council;[2] (b) a third country's national accounting standards equivalent to Regulation (EC) No 1606/2002 for third country issuers. If such third country's national accounting standards are not equivalent to Regulation (EC) No 1606/2002 the financial statements shall be restated in compliance with that Regulation.
Item 2.5.3	A description of any significant change in the financial position which has occurred since the end of the last financial period for which either audited financial statements or interim financial information have been published, or where no such significant change has occurred, a statement to that effect. Where applicable, information on any known trends, uncertainties, demands, commitments or events that are reasonably likely to have a material effect on the issuer and, depending on the type of transaction, the offeree company, the company being acquired or the company being divided for at least the current financial year.
Item 2.5.4	Where applicable, the management report referred to in Articles 19 and 29 of Directive 2013/34/EU.
Item 2.6	**Legal and arbitration proceedings** Information on any governmental, legal or arbitration proceedings (including any such proceedings which are pending or threatened of which the issuer, the offeree company, the company being acquired or the company being divided is aware), during a period covering at least the previous 12 months which may have, or have had in the recent past, significant effects on the issuer, offeree company, company being acquired, company being divided or the group and/or group's financial position or profitability, or provide an appropriate negative statement. In case of a division, the information on legal and arbitration proceedings shall refer to the assets and liabilities that form the object of the division.
Item 2.7	**Summary of information disclosed under Regulation (EU) No 596/2014 of the European Parliament and of the Council[3]** For entities within the scope of Regulation (EU) No 596/2014, a summary of the information disclosed under that Regulation over the last 12 months, where that information is relevant at the date of the exemption document. The summary shall be presented in an easily analysable, concise and comprehensible form and shall not be a replication of information already published under Regulation (EU) No 596/2014. The summary shall be presented in a limited number of categories depending on their subject.
SECTION 3	**DESCRIPTION OF THE TRANSACTION**
Item 3.1	**Purpose and objectives of the transaction**
Item 3.1.1	Purpose of the transaction for the issuer and its shareholders.
Item 3.1.2	Purpose of the transaction for the offeree company, the company being acquired or the company being divided and its shareholders.
Item 3.1.3	Description of any anticipated benefits resulting from the transaction.
Item 3.2	**Conditions of the transaction**
Item 3.2.1	Information on the procedures and terms of the transaction and the governing law of the agreement executing the transaction. In case of a takeover by means of an exchange offer, the exemption document shall contain the information required by Article 6(3) of Directive 2004/25/EC, or an indication of where that information may be found for perusal. In case of a merger, the exemption document shall contain the information required by Article 91(2) or Article 122 of Directive (EU) 2017/1132, depending on the type of merger, or an indication of where that information may be found for perusal. In case of a division, the exemption document shall contain the information required by Article 137(2) of Directive (EU) 2017/1132 or an indication of where this information may be found for perusal.
Item 3.2.2	Where applicable, any conditions to which the effectiveness of the transaction is subject, including any guarantee.
Item 3.2.3	Where applicable, any information on break-up fees or other penalties which may be payable if the transaction is not completed.
Item 3.2.4	Where the transaction is subject to any notifications and/or requests for authorisations, a description of those notifications and/or requests for authorisations.

SECTION 1	**PERSONS RESPONSIBLE FOR DRAWING UP THE EXEMPTION DOCUMENT, THIRD PARTY INFORMATION AND EXPERTS REPORT**
Item 3.2.5	Where applicable, all information necessary to fully understand the financing structure of the transaction.
Item 3.2.6	Timetable of the transaction.
Item 3.3	**Risk factors** A description, in a limited number of categories, of the material risks that are specific to the transaction, in a section headed 'Risk factors relating to the transaction'. In each category, the most material risk factors in the assessment of the issuer, taking into account the negative impact on the issuer and the probability of their occurrence, shall be mentioned first. The risk factors shall be corroborated by the content of the exemption document.
Item 3.4	**Conflict of interests** Details on any conflict of interests that the issuer, offeree company, company being acquired or company being divided and any of its shareholders may have in respect of the transaction.
Item 3.5	Consideration of the offer
Item 3.5.1	The addressees of the offer or allotment of the equity securities connected with the transaction.
Item 3.5.2	The consideration offered for each equity security or class of equity securities, and in particular the exchange ratio and the amount of any cash payment.
Item 3.5.3	Information concerning any contingent consideration agreed in the context of the transaction, including, in case of a merger, any obligation of the acquiring company to transfer additional securities or cash to the former owners of the company being acquired if future events occur or conditions are met.
Item 3.5.4	The valuation methods and the assumptions employed to determine the consideration offered for each equity security or class of equity securities, and in particular regarding the exchange ratio.
Item 3.5.5	Indication of any appraisals or reports prepared by independent experts and information where these appraisals or reports may be found for perusal. In case of a merger, the exemption document shall contain the information required by Articles 96 or Article 125 of Directive (EU) 2017/1132, depending on the type of merger, or an indication of where that information may be found for perusal. In case of a division, the exemption document shall contain the information required by Article 142 of Directive (EU) 2017/1132 or an indication of where that information may be found for perusal.
SECTION 4	**EQUITY SECURITIES OFFERED TO THE PUBLIC OR ADMITTED TO TRADING ON A REGULATED MARKET FOR THE PURPOSE OF THE TRANSACTION**
For equity securities other than shares, the information given shall be comprehensive and include the information listed below for the underlying shares.	
Item 4.1	**Risk factors** A description of the material risks that are specific to the equity securities being offered and/or admitted to trading in a limited number of categories, in a section headed 'Risk factors relating to the equity securities'. In each category the most material risks, in the assessment of the issuer, offeror or person asking for admission to trading on a regulated market, shall be set out first, taking into account the negative impact on the issuer and the equity securities and the probability of their occurrence. The risk factors shall be corroborated by the content of the exemption document.
Item 4.2	**Working capital statement** Statement by the issuer that, in its opinion, the working capital is sufficient for the issuer's present requirements or, if not, how it proposes to provide the additional working capital needed.
Item 4.3	**Information concerning the equity securities to be offered and/or admitted to trading**
Item 4.3.1	General information to be provided: (a) a description of the type, class and amount of the equity securities being offered and/or admitted to trading, including the international security identification number ('ISIN'); (b) currency of the equity securities issued.
Item 4.3.2	A statement of the resolutions, authorisations and approvals by virtue of which the equity securities have been or will be created and/or issued.
Item 4.3.3	A description of any restrictions on the free transferability of the equity securities.
Item 4.3.4	An indication of public takeover bids by third parties in respect of the issuer's equity which have occurred during the last financial year and the current financial year. The price or exchange terms attaching to such offers and the outcome thereof shall be stated.
Item 4.4	Admission to trading and dealing arrangements

SECTION 1	PERSONS RESPONSIBLE FOR DRAWING UP THE EXEMPTION DOCUMENT, THIRD PARTY INFORMATION AND EXPERTS REPORT
Item 4.4.1	An indication as to whether the equity securities offered are or will be the object of an application for admission to trading, with a view to their distribution in a regulated market, or other equivalent third country markets as defined in Article 1, point (b) of Commission Delegated Regulation (EU) 2019/980,[4] with an indication of the markets in question. Where known, the earliest dates on which the equity securities will be admitted to trading.
Item 4.4.2	All the regulated markets, or equivalent third country markets as defined in Article 1, point (b), of Delegated Regulation (EU) 2019/980, on which, to the knowledge of the issuer, equity securities of the same class of the equity securities to be offered or to be admitted to trading are already admitted to trading including, where applicable, depository receipts and underlying shares.
Item 4.4.3	Details of the entities that have given a firm commitment to act as intermediaries in secondary trading, providing liquidity through bid and offer rates and a description of the main terms of their commitment.
Item 4.4.4	Lock-up agreements: (a) the parties involved; (b) content and exceptions of the agreement; (c) indication of the period of the lock-up.
Item 4.5	**Dilution**
Item 4.5.1	A comparison of the net asset value per share as of the date of the latest balance sheet before the transaction and the issue price per share within that transaction.
Item 4.5.2	Additional information where there is a simultaneous or almost simultaneous offer or admission to trading of equity securities of the same class.
Item 4.5.3	A table presenting the number of equity securities and voting rights as well as the share capital for both before and after the transaction. An indication of the dilution (including the dilution in voting rights) that existing shareholders of the issuer will experience as a result of the offer.
Item 4.6	**Advisors** Where advisors connected with an issue are referred to in the exemption document, a statement of the capacity in which the advisors have acted.
SECTION 5	**IMPACT OF THE TRANSACTION ON THE ISSUER**
Item 5.1	**Strategy and objectives** The issuer shall provide a description of its intentions with regard to the future business following the transaction, including an indication of any significant changes impacting the operations, principal activities as well as the products and services as a result of the transaction. Where applicable, that information shall include a description of the business prospects and any restructuring and/or reorganisation.
Item 5.2	**Material contracts** A brief summary of all material contracts of the issuer, offeree company, company being acquired or company being divided, other than contracts entered into in the ordinary course of business, which are materially affected by the transaction.
Item 5.3	**Disinvestment**
Item 5.3.1	To the extent known, information on material disinvestments such as material sales of subsidiaries or any major line(s) of business after the transaction becomes effective, together with a description of possible impacts on the issuer's group.
Item 5.3.2	Information on any material cancellation of future investments or disinvestments previously announced.
Item 5.4	**Corporate governance** (a) to the extent known by the issuer, names, business addresses and functions within the issuer of the persons that are going be, immediately after the transaction, members of the administrative, management or supervisory bodies and, in case of a limited partnership with a share capital, partners with unlimited liability; (b) any potential conflicts of interest that may arise as a result of the carrying out by the persons referred to in point (a) of any duties on behalf of the issuer and their private interests or other duties shall be clearly stated. Where there are no such conflicts, a statement to that effect shall be made; (c) details of any restrictions agreed by the persons referred to in point (a) on the disposal of their holdings in the issuer's equity securities within a certain period of time after the transaction.
Item 5.5	**Shareholding** The shareholding structure immediately after the transaction.
Item 5.6	**Pro forma financial information**

SECTION 1	PERSONS RESPONSIBLE FOR DRAWING UP THE EXEMPTION DOCUMENT, THIRD PARTY INFORMATION AND EXPERTS REPORT
Item 5.6.1	In case of a significant gross change as defined in Article 1, point (e), of Delegated Regulation (EU) 2019/980, a description of how the transaction might have affected the assets and liabilities and earnings of the issuer, had the transaction been undertaken at the commencement of the period being reported on or at the date reported. This requirement will normally be satisfied by the inclusion of pro forma financial information. Such pro forma financial information shall be presented as set out in items 5.7 to 5.9 and shall include the information indicated therein. Pro forma financial information shall be accompanied by a report prepared by independent accountants or auditors.
Item 5.6.2	Where pro forma financial information is not applicable, the issuer shall provide narrative and financial information about the material impacts that the transaction will have on the issuer's financial statements. That narrative and financial information shall not require auditing. The narrative and financial information shall be prepared in a manner consistent with the applicable financial reporting framework and accounting policies adopted by the issuer in its latest or next financial statements. Where that information is audited, it shall be disclosed in the exemption document that this information was audited as well as information about the auditors who proceeded with such audit.
Item 5.7	**Contents of the pro forma financial information** Pro forma financial information shall consist of: (a) an introduction setting out: (i) the purpose for which the pro forma financial information has been prepared, including a description of the takeover by means of an exchange offer, merger or division or significant commitment and businesses or entities involved; (ii) the period and/or date covered by the pro forma financial information; (iii) the fact that the pro forma financial information has been prepared for illustrative purposes only; (iv) an explanation that: (A) the pro forma financial information illustrates the impact of the transaction as if the transaction had been undertaken at an earlier date; (B) the hypothetical financial position or results included in the pro forma financial information may differ from the entity's actual financial position or results; (b) a profit and loss account, a balance sheet or both, depending on the circumstances, presented in a columnar format composed of: (i) historical unadjusted information; (ii) accounting policies adjustments, where necessary; (iii) pro forma adjustments; (iv) the results of the pro forma financial information in the final column; (c) accompanying notes explaining: (i) the sources from which the unadjusted financial information has been extracted and whether or not an audit or review report on the source has been published; (ii) the basis upon which the pro forma financial information is prepared; (iii) the source and explanation for each adjustment; (iv) whether each adjustment in respect of a pro forma profit and loss statement is expected to have a continuing impact on the issuer or not; (d) where applicable, to the extent not covered elsewhere in the exemption document, the financial information and interim financial information of the (to be) acquired businesses or entities used in the preparation of the pro forma financial information shall be included in the exemption document. Similarly, in case of a division, the financial information of the company being divided shall be included.
Item 5.8	**Principles in preparing and presenting pro forma financial information**
Item 5.8.1	The pro forma financial information shall be identified in order to distinguish it from historical financial information. The pro forma financial information shall be prepared in a manner consistent with the accounting policies adopted by the issuer in its last or next financial statements.
Item 5.8.2	Pro forma information may only be published in respect of either of the following: (a) the last completed financial period; (b) the most recent interim period for which relevant unadjusted information has been published or is included in the exemption document.

SECTION 1	PERSONS RESPONSIBLE FOR DRAWING UP THE EXEMPTION DOCUMENT, THIRD PARTY INFORMATION AND EXPERTS REPORT
Item 5.8.3	Pro forma adjustments shall: (a) be clearly shown and explained; (b) present all significant effects directly attributable to the transaction; (c) be factually supportable.
Item 5.9	**Requirements for an accountant/auditor report** The exemption document shall include a report prepared by independent accountants or auditors stating that in their opinion: (a) the pro forma financial information has been properly compiled on the basis stated; (b) that the basis referred to in point (a) is consistent with the accounting policies of the issuer.
SECTION 6	**DOCUMENTS AVAILABLE**
Item 6.1	Information on where the following documents, where applicable, can be perused in the 12 months following the publication of the exemption document: (a) the up-to-date memorandum and articles of association of the issuer; (b) all reports, letters, and other documents, historical financial information, valuations and statements prepared by any expert at the issuer's request any part of which is included or referred to in the exemption document; (c) all reports, letters, and other documents, valuations and statements not covered by points (a) or (b) of this item or by any other points in this Annex, prepared in accordance with Directive 2004/25/EC or Directive (EU) 2017/1132. An indication of the website on which the documents may be perused.

NOTES

1 Regulation (EC) No 1606/2002 of the European Parliament and of the Council of 19 July 2002 on the application of international accounting standards (OJ L243, 11.9.2002, p 1).

2 Directive 2013/34/EU of the European Parliament and of the Council of 26 June 2013 on the annual financial statements, consolidated financial statements and related reports of certain types of undertakings, amending Directive 2006/43/EC of the European Parliament and of the Council and repealing Council Directives 78/660/EEC and 83/349/EEC (OJ L182, 29.6.2013, p 19).

3 Regulation (EU) No 596/2014 of the European Parliament and of the Council of 16 April 2014 on market abuse (market abuse regulation) and repealing Directive 2003/6/EC of the European Parliament and of the Council and Commission Directives 2003/124/EC, 2003/125/EC and 2004/72/EC (OJ L173, 12.6.2014, p 1).

4 Commission Delegated Regulation (EU) 2019/980 of 14 March 2019 supplementing Regulation (EU) 2017/1129 of the European Parliament and of the Council as regards the format, content, scrutiny and approval of the prospectus to be published when securities are offered to the public or admitted to trading on a regulated market, and repealing Commission Regulation (EC) No 809/2004 (OJ L166, 21.6.2019, p 26).

ANNEX II
MINIMUM INFORMATION CONTENT OF THE EXEMPTION DOCUMENT

Article 2(1), fourth subparagraph

[11.823]

SECTION 1	INFORMATION ON THE ISSUER
	The following information shall be provided: (a) the information required in Section 1 of Annex I to this Regulation; (b) the information required in Annex 1 to Delegated Regulation (EU) 2019/980, with the exception of Section 1 of that Annex. Where applicable, that information shall also be provided for the issuer of the underlying shares, where different from the issuer of the equity securities. Any reference to 'registration document' or to 'prospectus' contained in Annex 1 to Delegated Regulation (EU) 2019/980 shall be construed as a reference to an exemption document as referred to in this Regulation.
SECTION 2	**INFORMATION ON THE OFFEREE COMPANY, THE COMPANY BEING ACQUIRED OR THE COMPANY BEING DIVIDED**
	The information required in Section 2 of Annex I to this Regulation shall be provided, depending on the type of transaction, for the offeree company, the company being acquired or the company being divided. Where one of the aforementioned entities is a group, and the consolidated financial statements have already been published, the information listed in this section shall be presented on a consolidated basis. In case of a takeover by means of an exchange offer, where the requested information on the offeree company is not available, a statement to that effect shall be provided.
SECTION 3	**INFORMATION ABOUT THE EQUITY SECURITIES OFFERED TO THE PUBLIC OR ADMITTED TO TRADING ON A REGULATED MARKET FOR THE PURPOSE OF THE TRANSACTION**

SECTION 1	**INFORMATION ON THE ISSUER**
Item 3.1	The information required in Annex 11 to Delegated Regulation (EU) 2019/980 shall be provided, with the exception of section 1 of that Annex. Where applicable, that information shall also be provided for the underlying shares. Any reference to 'securities note' or to 'prospectus' contained in Annex 11 to Delegated Regulation (EU) 2019/980 shall be construed as a reference to an exemption document as referred to in this Regulation.
Item 3.2	By way of derogation from item 3.1, the following information shall be provided in the following cases: (a) for the securities referred to in Article 19, paragraphs 1 or 2, or in Article 20, paragraphs 1 or 2, of Delegated Regulation (EU) 2019/980, where those securities are not shares or other transferable securities equivalent to shares, the information required in Annex 14 to that Regulation shall be provided (with the exception of section 1 of that Annex), as well as the additional information referred to in Article 19, paragraphs 1 or 2, or in Article 20, paragraphs 1 or 2; (b) for depository receipts issued over shares, the information required in Annex 13 of Delegated Regulation (EU) 2019/980 shall be provided. Any reference to 'securities note' or to 'prospectus' contained in the relevant Annexes to Delegated Regulation (EU) 2019/980 shall be construed as a reference to an exemption document as referred to in this Regulation.
SECTION 4	**DESCRIPTION OF THE TRANSACTION**
	The information required in Section 3 of Annex I to this Regulation shall be provided.
SECTION 5	**IMPACT OF THE TRANSACTION ON THE ISSUER**
	The information required in Section 5 of Annex I to this Regulation shall be provided.

PART 12
EXITING THE EU MATERIALS

EUROPEAN UNION (WITHDRAWAL) ACT 2018

(2018 c 16)

NOTES

This Act is reproduced as amended by: the European Union (Withdrawal) Act 2019; the European Union (Withdrawal) Act 2018 (Exit Day) (Amendment) (No 2) Regulations 2019, SI 2019/859; the European Union (Withdrawal) Act 2018 (Exit Day) (Amendment) (No 3) Regulations 2019, SI 2019/1423; the European Union (Withdrawal Agreement) Act 2020; the European Union Withdrawal (Consequential Modifications) (EU Exit) Regulations 2020, SI 2020/1447; the European Union (Future Relationship) Act 2020; the United Kingdom Internal Market Act 2020; the European Union (Withdrawal) Act 2018 (Repeal of EU Restrictions in Devolution Legislation, etc) Regulations 2022, SI 2022/357.

'Exit day' and 'IP completion day': 'exit day' is defined by section 20 of this Act (at **[12.28]**) as 31 January 2020 at 11pm. 'IP completion day' is defined by the European Union (Withdrawal Agreement) Act 2020, s 39 (at **[12.53]**) as 31 December 2020 at 11pm.

ARRANGEMENT OF SECTIONS

SCHEDULES

An Act to repeal the European Communities Act 1972 and make other provision in connection with the withdrawal of the United Kingdom from the EU.

[26 June 2018]

Repeal of the ECA

[12.1]

1 Repeal of the European Communities Act 1972

The European Communities Act 1972 is repealed on exit day.

NOTES

Commencement: 17 August 2019.

[Savings for implementation period

[12.2]

1A Saving for ECA for implementation period

(1)–(4) . . .

(5) Subsections (1) to (4) are repealed on IP completion day.

(6) In this Act—

"the implementation period" means the transition or implementation period provided for by Part 4 of the withdrawal agreement and beginning with exit day and ending on IP completion day;

"IP completion day" (and related expressions) have the same meaning as in the European Union (Withdrawal Agreement) Act 2020 (see section 39(1) to (5) of that Act);

"withdrawal agreement" has the same meaning as in that Act (see section 39(1) and (6) of that Act).

(7) In this Act—

(a) references to the European Communities Act 1972 are to be read, so far as the context permits or requires, as being or (as the case may be) including references to that Act as it continues to have effect by virtue of subsections (2) to (4) above, and

(b) references to any Part of the withdrawal agreement or the EEA EFTA separation agreement include references to any other provisions of that agreement so far as applying to that Part.]

NOTES

Commencement: exit day (as defined in s 20 of this Act).

Inserted, together with the previous heading, by the European Union (Withdrawal Agreement) Act 2020, s 1, as from exit day (as defined in s 20 of this Act).

Sub-ss (1)–(4): repealed by subsection (5) above, as from IP completion day (as defined in the European Union (Withdrawal Agreement) Act 2020, s 39).

[12.3]

[1B Saving for EU-derived domestic legislation for implementation period

(1)–(5) . . .

(6) Subsections (1) to (5) are repealed on IP completion day.

(7) In this Act "EU-derived domestic legislation" means any enactment so far as—

(a) made under section 2(2) of, or paragraph 1A of Schedule 2 to, the European Communities Act 1972,

(b) passed or made, or operating, for a purpose mentioned in section 2(2)(a) or (b) of that Act,

(c) relating to—

(i) anything which falls within paragraph (a) or (b), or

(ii) any rights, powers, liabilities, obligations, restrictions, remedies or procedures which are recognised and available in domestic law by virtue of section 2(1) of the European Communities Act 1972, or

(d) relating otherwise to the EU or the EEA,

but does not include any enactment contained in the European Communities Act 1972 or any enactment contained in this Act or the European Union (Withdrawal Agreement) Act 2020 or in regulations made under this Act or the Act of 2020.]

NOTES

Commencement: exit day (as defined in s 20 of this Act).

Inserted by the European Union (Withdrawal Agreement) Act 2020, s 2, as from exit day (as defined in s 20 of this Act).

Sub-ss (1)–(5): repealed by subsection (6) above, as from IP completion day (as defined in the European Union (Withdrawal Agreement) Act 2020, s 39).

Retention of [saved EU law at end of implementation period]

NOTES

Words in square brackets in the above heading substituted by the European Union (Withdrawal Agreement) Act 2020, s 41(4), Sch 5, Pt 2, paras 38, 39, as from IP completion day (as defined in the European Union (Withdrawal Agreement) Act 2020, s 39).

[12.4]

2 Saving for EU-derived domestic legislation

(1) EU-derived domestic legislation, as it has effect in domestic law immediately before [IP completion day], continues to have effect in domestic law on and after [IP completion day].

(2) . . .

(3) This section is subject to section 5 and Schedule 1 (exceptions to savings and incorporation) [and section 5A (savings and incorporation: supplementary)].

NOTES

Commencement: IP completion day (as defined in the European Union (Withdrawal Agreement) Act 2020, s 39).

Words in square brackets in sub-s (1) substituted, sub-s (2) repealed, and words in square brackets in sub-s (3) inserted, by the European Union (Withdrawal Agreement) Act 2020, s 25(1), as from IP completion day (as defined in the European Union (Withdrawal Agreement) Act 2020, s 39).

[12.5]

3 Incorporation of direct EU legislation

(1) Direct EU legislation, so far as operative immediately before [IP completion day], forms part of domestic law on and after [IP completion day].

(2) In this Act "direct EU legislation" means—

(a) any EU regulation, EU decision or EU tertiary legislation, as it has effect in EU law immediately before [IP completion day] and so far as—

[(ai) it is applicable to and in the United Kingdom by virtue of Part 4 of the withdrawal agreement,

(bi) it neither has effect nor is to have effect by virtue of section 7A or 7B,]

(i) it is not an exempt EU instrument (for which see section 20(1) and Schedule 6), [and]

(ii) . . .

(iii) its effect is not reproduced in an enactment to which section 2(1) applies,

(b) any Annex to the EEA agreement, as it has effect in EU law immediately before [IP completion day] and so far as—

[(ai) it is applicable to and in the United Kingdom by virtue of Part 4 of the withdrawal agreement,

(bi) it neither has effect nor is to have effect by virtue of section 7A or 7B,]

(i) it refers to, or contains adaptations of, anything falling within paragraph (a), and

(ii) its effect is not reproduced in an enactment to which section 2(1) applies, or

(c) Protocol 1 to the EEA agreement (which contains horizontal adaptations that apply in relation to EU instruments referred to in the Annexes to that agreement), as it has effect in EU law immediately before [IP completion day and so far as—

(i) it is applicable to and in the United Kingdom by virtue of Part 4 of the withdrawal agreement, and

(ii) it neither has effect nor is to have effect by virtue of section 7A or 7B,]

(3) For the purposes of this Act, any direct EU legislation is operative immediately before [IP completion day] if—

(a) in the case of anything which comes into force at a particular time and is stated to apply from a later time, it is in force and applies immediately before [IP completion day],

(b) in the case of a decision which specifies to whom it is addressed, it has been notified to that person before [IP completion day], and

(c) in any other case, it is in force immediately before [IP completion day].

(4) This section—

(a) brings into domestic law any direct EU legislation only in the form of the English language version of that legislation, and

(b) does not apply to any such legislation for which there is no such version,

but paragraph (a) does not affect the use of the other language versions of that legislation for the purposes of interpreting it.

(5) This section is subject to section 5 and Schedule 1 (exceptions to savings and incorporation) [and section 5A (savings and incorporation: supplementary)].

NOTES

Commencement: IP completion day (as defined in the European Union (Withdrawal Agreement) Act 2020, s 39).

All amendments to this section were made by the European Union (Withdrawal Agreement) Act 2020, s 25(2), as from IP completion day (as defined in the European Union (Withdrawal Agreement) Act 2020, s 39).

[12.6]

4 Saving for rights etc under section 2(1) of the ECA

(1) Any rights, powers, liabilities, obligations, restrictions, remedies and procedures which, immediately before [IP completion day]—

(a) are recognised and available in domestic law by virtue of section 2(1) of the European Communities Act 1972, and

(b) are enforced, allowed and followed accordingly,

continue on and after [IP completion day] to be recognised and available in domestic law (and to be enforced, allowed and followed accordingly).

(2) Subsection (1) does not apply to any rights, powers, liabilities, obligations, restrictions, remedies or procedures so far as they—

(a) form part of domestic law by virtue of section 3,

[(aa) are, or are to be, recognised and available in domestic law (and enforced, allowed and followed accordingly) by virtue of section 7A or 7B,] or

(b) arise under an EU directive (including as applied by the EEA agreement) and are not of a kind recognised by the European Court or any court or tribunal in the United Kingdom in a case decided before [IP completion day] (whether or not as an essential part of the decision in the case).

(3) This section is subject to section 5 and Schedule 1 (exceptions to savings and incorporation) [and section 5A (savings and incorporation: supplementary)].

NOTES

Commencement: IP completion day (as defined in the European Union (Withdrawal Agreement) Act 2020, s 39).

All amendments to this section were made by the European Union (Withdrawal Agreement) Act 2020, s 25(3), as from IP completion day (as defined in the European Union (Withdrawal Agreement) Act 2020, s 39).

Note that this section ceases to apply to rights, powers, liabilities, obligations, restrictions, remedies and procedures derived from the Trafficking Directive so far as their continued existence would otherwise be incompatible with provision made by or under the Nationality and Borders Act 2022 (see s 68 of that Act and note that the "Trafficking Directive" means Council Directive 2011/36/EU of the European Parliament and of the Council on preventing and combating trafficking in human beings and protecting its victims).

[12.7]

5 Exceptions to savings and incorporation

(1) The principle of the supremacy of EU law does not apply to any enactment or rule of law passed or made on or after [IP completion day].

(2) Accordingly, the principle of the supremacy of EU law continues to apply on or after [IP completion day] so far as relevant to the interpretation, disapplication or quashing of any enactment or rule of law passed or made before [IP completion day].

(3) Subsection (1) does not prevent the principle of the supremacy of EU law from applying to a modification made on or after [IP completion day] of any enactment or rule of law passed or made before [IP completion day] if the application of the principle is consistent with the intention of the modification.

(4) The Charter of Fundamental Rights is not part of domestic law on or after [IP completion day].

(5) Subsection (4) does not affect the retention in domestic law on or after [IP completion day] in accordance with this Act of any fundamental rights or principles which exist irrespective of the Charter (and references to the Charter in any case law are, so far as necessary for this purpose, to be read as if they were references to any corresponding retained fundamental rights or principles).

(6) Schedule 1 (which makes further provision about exceptions to savings and incorporation) has effect.

[(7) Subsections (1) to (6) and Schedule 1 are subject to relevant separation agreement law (for which see section 7C).]

NOTES

Commencement: 4 July 2018 (sub-s (6) certain purposes); IP completion day (as defined in the European Union (Withdrawal Agreement) Act 2020, s 39) (otherwise).

Sub-ss (1)–(5): words in square brackets substituted by the European Union (Withdrawal Agreement) Act 2020, s 25(4)(a), as from IP completion day (as defined in the European Union (Withdrawal Agreement) Act 2020, s 39).

Sub-s (7): added by the European Union (Withdrawal Agreement) Act 2020, s 25(4)(b), as from exit day (as defined in s 20 of this Act) (for the purposes of sub-s (6) above, and Sch 1 *post*, so far as they are in force on exit day), and as from IP completion day (as defined in the European Union (Withdrawal Agreement) Act 2020, s 39) (otherwise).

[12.8]

[5A Savings and incorporation: supplementary

The fact that anything which continues to be, or forms part of, domestic law on or after IP completion day by virtue of section 2, 3 or 4 has an effect immediately before IP completion day which is time-limited by reference to the implementation period does not prevent it from having an indefinite effect on and after IP completion day by virtue of section 2, 3 or 4.]

NOTES

Commencement: IP completion day (as defined in the European Union (Withdrawal Agreement) Act 2020, s 39).

Inserted by the European Union (Withdrawal Agreement) Act 2020, s 25(5), as from IP completion day (as defined in the European Union (Withdrawal Agreement) Act 2020, s 39).

Transitional provisions: nothing in this section prevents the modification on or after IP completion day of Retained EU law by an enactment passed or made before IP completion day and coming into force or otherwise having effect on or after IP completion day (whether or not that enactment is itself retained EU law). See the European Union (Withdrawal) Act 2018 and European Union (Withdrawal Agreement) Act 2020 (Commencement, Transitional and Savings Provisions) Regulations 2020, SI 2020/1622, reg 17.

[12.9]

6 Interpretation of retained EU law

(1) A court or tribunal—

(a) is not bound by any principles laid down, or any decisions made, on or after [IP completion day] by the European Court, and

(b) cannot refer any matter to the European Court on or after [IP completion day].

(2) Subject to this and subsections (3) to (6), a court or tribunal may have regard to anything done on or after [IP completion day] by the European Court, another EU entity or the EU so far as it is relevant to any matter before the court or tribunal.

(3) Any question as to the validity, meaning or effect of any retained EU law is to be decided, so far as that law is unmodified on or after [IP completion day] and so far as they are relevant to it—

(a) in accordance with any retained case law and any retained general principles of EU law, and

(b) having regard (among other things) to the limits, immediately before [IP completion day], of EU competences.

(4) But—

(a) the Supreme Court is not bound by any retained EU case law,

(b) the High Court of Justiciary is not bound by any retained EU case law when—

(i) sitting as a court of appeal otherwise than in relation to a compatibility issue (within the meaning given by section 288ZA(2) of the Criminal Procedure (Scotland) Act 1995) or a devolution issue (within the meaning given by paragraph 1 of Schedule 6 to the Scotland Act 1998), or

(ii) sitting on a reference under section 123(1) of the Criminal Procedure (Scotland) Act 1995,

[(ba) a relevant court or relevant tribunal is not bound by any retained EU case law so far as is provided for by regulations under subsection (5A),] and

(c) no court or tribunal is bound by any retained domestic case law that it would not otherwise be bound by.

(5) In deciding whether to depart from any retained EU case law [by virtue of subsection (4)(a) or (b)], the Supreme Court or the High Court of Justiciary must apply the same test as it would apply in deciding whether to depart from its own case law.

[(5A) A Minister of the Crown may by regulations provide for—

(a) a court or tribunal to be a relevant court or (as the case may be) a relevant tribunal for the purposes of this section,

(b) the extent to which, or circumstances in which, a relevant court or relevant tribunal is not to be bound by retained EU case law,

(c) the test which a relevant court or relevant tribunal must apply in deciding whether to depart from any retained EU case law, or

(d) considerations which are to be relevant to—

(i) the Supreme Court or the High Court of Justiciary in applying the test mentioned in subsection (5), or

(ii) a relevant court or relevant tribunal in applying any test provided for by virtue of paragraph (c) above.

(5B) Regulations under subsection (5A) may (among other things) provide for—

(a) the High Court of Justiciary to be a relevant court when sitting otherwise than as mentioned in subsection (4)(b)(i) and (ii),

(b) the extent to which, or circumstances in which, a relevant court or relevant tribunal not being bound by retained EU case law includes (or does not include) that court or tribunal not being bound by retained domestic case law which relates to retained EU case law,

(c) other matters arising in relation to retained domestic case law which relates to retained EU case law (including by making provision of a kind which could be made in relation to retained EU case law), or

(d) the test mentioned in paragraph (c) of subsection (5A) or the considerations mentioned in paragraph (d) of that subsection to be determined (whether with or without the consent of a Minister of the Crown) by a person mentioned in subsection (5C)(a) to (e) or by more than one of those persons acting jointly.

(5C) Before making regulations under subsection (5A), a Minister of the Crown must consult—

(a) the President of the Supreme Court,

(b) the Lord Chief Justice of England and Wales,

(c) the Lord President of the Court of Session,

(d) the Lord Chief Justice of Northern Ireland,

(e) the Senior President of Tribunals, and

(f) such other persons as the Minister of the Crown considers appropriate.

(5D) No regulations may be made under subsection (5A) after IP completion day.]

(6) Subsection (3) does not prevent the validity, meaning or effect of any retained EU law which has been modified on or after [IP completion day] from being decided as provided for in that subsection if doing so is consistent with the intention of the modifications.

[(6A) Subsections (1) to (6) are subject to relevant separation agreement law (for which see section 7C).]

(7) In this Act—

"retained case law" means—

(a) retained domestic case law, and

(b) retained EU case law;

"retained domestic case law" means any principles laid down by, and any decisions of, a court or tribunal in the United Kingdom, as they have effect immediately before [IP completion day] and so far as they—

(a) relate to anything to which section 2, 3 or 4 applies, and

(b) are not excluded by section 5 or Schedule 1,

(as those principles and decisions are modified by or under this Act or by other domestic law from time to time);

"retained EU case law" means any principles laid down by, and any decisions of, the European Court, as they have effect in EU law immediately before [IP completion day] and so far as they—

(a) relate to anything to which section 2, 3 or 4 applies, and
(b) are not excluded by section 5 or Schedule 1,

(as those principles and decisions are modified by or under this Act or by other domestic law from time to time);

"retained EU law" means anything which, on or after [IP completion day], continues to be, or forms part of, domestic law by virtue of section 2, 3 or 4 or subsection (3) or (6) above (as that body of law is added to or otherwise modified by or under this Act or by other domestic law from time to time);

"retained general principles of EU law" means the general principles of EU law, as they have effect in EU law immediately before [IP completion day] and so far as they—

(a) relate to anything to which section 2, 3 or 4 applies, and
(b) are not excluded by section 5 or Schedule 1,

(as those principles are modified by or under this Act or by other domestic law from time to time).

NOTES

Commencement: 4 July 2018 (sub-s (7)); IP completion day (as defined in the European Union (Withdrawal Agreement) Act 2020, s 39) (otherwise).

The words "IP completion day" in square brackets were substituted, sub-s (4)(ba) was inserted, the words "by virtue of subsection (4)(a) or (b)" in square brackets in sub-s (5) were inserted, and sub-s (6A) was inserted, by the European Union (Withdrawal Agreement) Act 2020, s 26(1)(a)–(c), (e), as from IP completion day (as defined in the European Union (Withdrawal Agreement) Act 2020, s 39).

Sub-ss (5A)–(5D) were inserted by the European Union (Withdrawal Agreement) Act 2020, s 26(1)(d), as from 19 May 2020.

The words "IP completion day" in square brackets in sub-s (7) (in each place that they occur) were substituted by the European Union (Withdrawal Agreement) Act 2020, s 26(1)(a), as from exit day (as defined in s 20 of this Act).

[12.10]

7 Status of retained EU law

(1) Anything which—

(a) was, immediately before exit day, primary legislation of a particular kind, subordinate legislation of a particular kind or another enactment of a particular kind, and
(b) continues to be domestic law on and after exit day by virtue of [section 1A(2) or 1B(2)],

continues to be domestic law as an enactment of the same kind.

[(1A) Anything which—

(a) was, immediately before IP completion day, primary legislation of a particular kind, subordinate legislation of a particular kind or another enactment of a particular kind, and
(b) continues to be domestic law on and after IP completion day by virtue of section 2,

continues to be domestic law as an enactment of the same kind.]

(2) Retained direct principal EU legislation cannot be modified by any primary or subordinate legislation other than—

(a) an Act of Parliament,
(b) any other primary legislation (so far as it has the power to make such a modification), or
(c) any subordinate legislation so far as it is made under a power which permits such a modification by virtue of—
 (i) paragraph 3, 5(3)(a) or (4)(a), 8(3), 10(3)(a) or (4)(a), 11(2)(a) or 12(3) of Schedule 8,
 (ii) any other provision made by or under this Act,
 (iii) any provision made by or under an Act of Parliament passed before, and in the same Session as, this Act, or
 (iv) any provision made on or after the passing of this Act by or under primary legislation.

(3) Retained direct minor EU legislation cannot be modified by any primary or subordinate legislation other than—

(a) an Act of Parliament,
(b) any other primary legislation (so far as it has the power to make such a modification), or
(c) any subordinate legislation so far as it is made under a power which permits such a modification by virtue of—
 (i) paragraph 3, 5(2) or (4)(a), 8(3), 10(2) or (4)(a) or 12(3) of Schedule 8,
 (ii) any other provision made by or under this Act,
 (iii) any provision made by or under an Act of Parliament passed before, and in the same Session as, this Act, or
 (iv) any provision made on or after the passing of this Act by or under primary legislation.

(4) Anything which is retained EU law by virtue of section 4 cannot be modified by any primary or subordinate legislation other than—

(a) an Act of Parliament,
(b) any other primary legislation (so far as it has the power to make such a modification), or
(c) any subordinate legislation so far as it is made under a power which permits such a modification by virtue of—
 (i) paragraph 3, 5(3)(b) or (4)(b), 8(3), 10(3)(b) or (4)(b), 11(2)(b) or 12(3) of Schedule 8,
 (ii) any other provision made by or under this Act,
 (iii) any provision made by or under an Act of Parliament passed before, and in the same Session as, this Act, or
 (iv) any provision made on or after the passing of this Act by or under primary legislation.

(5) For other provisions about the status of retained EU law, see—

(a) section 5(1) to (3) [and (7)] (status of retained EU law in relation to other enactments or rules of law),
(b) section 6 (status of retained case law and retained general principles of EU law),
[(ba) section 7C (status of case law of European Court etc in relation to retained EU law which is relevant separation agreement law),]
(c) section 15(2) and Part 2 of Schedule 5 (status of retained EU law for the purposes of the rules of evidence),

(d) paragraphs 13 to 16 of Schedule 8 (affirmative and enhanced scrutiny procedure for, and information about, instruments which amend or revoke subordinate legislation under section 2(2) of the European Communities Act 1972 including subordinate legislation implementing EU directives),

(e) paragraphs 19 and 20 of that Schedule (status of certain retained direct EU legislation for the purposes of the Interpretation Act 1978), and

(f) paragraph 30 of that Schedule (status of retained direct EU legislation for the purposes of the Human Rights Act 1998).

(6) In this Act—

"retained direct minor EU legislation" means any retained direct EU legislation which is not retained direct principal EU legislation;

"retained direct principal EU legislation" means—

(a) any EU regulation so far as it—

(i) forms part of domestic law on and after [IP completion day] by virtue of section 3, and

(ii) was not EU tertiary legislation immediately before [IP completion day], or

(b) any Annex to the EEA agreement so far as it—

(as modified by or under this Act or by other domestic law from time to time).

(i) forms part of domestic law on and after [IP completion day] by virtue of section 3, and

(ii) refers to, or contains adaptations of, any EU regulation so far as it falls within paragraph (a),

NOTES

Commencement: exit day (as defined in s 20 of this Act) (sub-ss (1) and (6)); IP completion day (as defined in the European Union (Withdrawal Agreement) Act 2020, s 39) (otherwise).

Sub-s (1): words in square brackets substituted by the European Union (Withdrawal Agreement) Act 2020, s 41(4), Sch 5, Pt 2, paras 38, 40(1), (2), as from exit day (as defined in s 20 of this Act).

Sub-s (1A): inserted by the European Union (Withdrawal Agreement) Act 2020, s 41(4), Sch 5, Pt 2, paras 38, 40(1), (3), as from IP completion day (as defined in the European Union (Withdrawal Agreement) Act 2020, s 39).

Sub-s (5): words in square brackets inserted by the European Union (Withdrawal Agreement) Act 2020, s 41(4), Sch 5, Pt 2, paras 38, 40(1), (4), as from IP completion day (as defined in the European Union (Withdrawal Agreement) Act 2020, s 39).

Sub-s (6): words in square brackets substituted by the European Union (Withdrawal Agreement) Act 2020, s 41(4), Sch 5, Pt 2, paras 38, 40(1), (5), as from exit day (as defined in s 20 of this Act).

[Further aspects of withdrawal

[12.11]

7A General implementation of remainder of withdrawal agreement

(1) Subsection (2) applies to—

(a) all such rights, powers, liabilities, obligations and restrictions from time to time created or arising by or under the withdrawal agreement, and

(b) all such remedies and procedures from time to time provided for by or under the withdrawal agreement,

as in accordance with the withdrawal agreement are without further enactment to be given legal effect or used in the United Kingdom.

(2) The rights, powers, liabilities, obligations, restrictions, remedies and procedures concerned are to be—

(a) recognised and available in domestic law, and

(b) enforced, allowed and followed accordingly.

(3) Every enactment (including an enactment contained in this Act) is to be read and has effect subject to subsection (2).

(4) This section does not apply in relation to Part 4 of the withdrawal agreement so far as section 2(1) of the European Communities Act 1972 applies in relation to that Part.

(5) See also (among other things)—

(a) Part 3 of the European Union (Withdrawal Agreement) Act 2020 (further provision about citizens' rights),

(b) section 20 of that Act (financial provision),

(c) section 7C of this Act (interpretation of law relating to withdrawal agreement etc),

(d) section 8B of this Act (power in connection with certain other separation issues),

(e) section 8C of this Act (power in connection with the Protocol on Ireland/Northern Ireland in withdrawal agreement), and

(f) Parts 1B and 1C of Schedule 2 to this Act (powers involving devolved authorities in connection with certain other separation issues and the Ireland/Northern Ireland Protocol).]

NOTES

Commencement: exit day (as defined in s 20 of this Act).

Inserted by the European Union (Withdrawal Agreement) Act 2020, s 5, as from exit day (as defined in s 20 of this Act).

[12.12]

[7B General implementation of EEA EFTA and Swiss agreements

(1) Subsection (2) applies to all such rights, powers, liabilities, obligations, restrictions, remedies and procedures as—

(a) would from time to time be created or arise, or (in the case of remedies or procedures) be provided for, by or under the EEA EFTA separation agreement or the Swiss citizens' rights agreement, and

(b) would, in accordance with Article 4(1) of the withdrawal agreement, be required to be given legal effect or used in the United Kingdom without further enactment,

if that Article were to apply in relation to the EEA EFTA separation agreement and the Swiss citizens' rights agreement, those agreements were part of EU law and the relevant EEA states and Switzerland were member States.

(2) The rights, powers, liabilities, obligations, restrictions, remedies and procedures concerned are to be—

(a) recognised and available in domestic law, and

(b) enforced, allowed and followed accordingly.

(3) Every enactment (other than section 7A but otherwise including an enactment contained in this Act) is to be read and has effect subject to subsection (2).

(4) See also (among other things)—

(a) Part 3 of the European Union (Withdrawal Agreement) Act 2020 (further provision about citizens' rights),

(b) section 7C of this Act (interpretation of law relating to the EEA EFTA separation agreement and the Swiss citizens' rights agreement etc),

(c) section 8B of this Act (power in connection with certain other separation issues), and

(d) Part 1B of Schedule 2 to this Act (powers involving devolved authorities in connection with certain other separation issues).

(5) In this section "the relevant EEA states" means Norway, Iceland and Liechtenstein.

(6) In this Act "EEA EFTA separation agreement" and "Swiss citizens' rights agreement" have the same meanings as in the European Union (Withdrawal Agreement) Act 2020 (see section 39(1) of that Act).]

NOTES

Commencement: exit day (as defined in s 20 of this Act).

Inserted by the European Union (Withdrawal Agreement) Act 2020, s 5, as from exit day (as defined in s 20 of this Act).

[12.13]

[7C Interpretation of relevant separation agreement law

(1) Any question as to the validity, meaning or effect of any relevant separation agreement law is to be decided, so far as they are applicable—

(a) in accordance with the withdrawal agreement, the EEA EFTA separation agreement and the Swiss citizens' rights agreement, and

(b) having regard (among other things) to the desirability of ensuring that, where one of those agreements makes provision which corresponds to provision made by another of those agreements, the effect of relevant separation agreement law in relation to the matters dealt with by the corresponding provision in each agreement is consistent.

(2) See (among other things)—

(a) Article 4 of the withdrawal agreement (methods and principles relating to the effect, the implementation and the application of the agreement),

(b) Articles 158 and 160 of the withdrawal agreement (jurisdiction of the European Court in relation to Part 2 and certain provisions of Part 5 of the agreement),

(c) Articles 12 and 13 of the Protocol on Ireland/Northern Ireland in the withdrawal agreement (implementation, application, supervision and enforcement of the Protocol and common provisions),

(d) Article 4 of the EEA EFTA separation agreement (methods and principles relating to the effect, the implementation and the application of the agreement), and

(e) Article 4 of the Swiss citizens' rights agreement (methods and principles relating to the effect, the implementation and the application of the agreement).

(3) In this Act "relevant separation agreement law" means—

(a) any of the following provisions or anything which is domestic law by virtue of any of them—

(i) section 7A, 7B, 8B or 8C or Part 1B or 1C of Schedule 2 or this section, or

(ii) Part 3, or section 20, of the European Union (Withdrawal Agreement) Act 2020 (citizens' rights and financial provision), or

(b) anything not falling within paragraph (a) so far as it is domestic law for the purposes of, or otherwise within the scope of—

(i) the withdrawal agreement (other than Part 4 of that agreement),

(ii) the EEA EFTA separation agreement, or

(iii) the Swiss citizens' rights agreement,

as that body of law is added to or otherwise modified by or under this Act or by other domestic law from time to time.]

NOTES

Commencement: exit day (as defined in s 20 of this Act).

Inserted by the European Union (Withdrawal Agreement) Act 2020, s 26(2), as from exit day (as defined in s 20 of this Act).

Main powers in connection with withdrawal

[12.14]

8 Dealing with deficiencies arising from withdrawal

(1) A Minister of the Crown may by regulations make such provision as the Minister considers appropriate to prevent, remedy or mitigate—

(a) any failure of retained EU law to operate effectively, or

(b) any other deficiency in retained EU law,

arising from the withdrawal of the United Kingdom from the EU.

(2) Deficiencies in retained EU law are where the Minister considers that retained EU law—

(a) contains anything which has no practical application in relation to the United Kingdom or any part of it or is otherwise redundant or substantially redundant,

(b) confers functions on, or in relation to, EU entities which no longer have functions in that respect under EU law in relation to the United Kingdom or any part of it,

(c) makes provision for, or in connection with, reciprocal arrangements between—

(i) the United Kingdom or any part of it or a public authority in the United Kingdom, and

(ii) the EU, an EU entity, a member State or a public authority in a member State,

which no longer exist or are no longer appropriate,

(d) makes provision for, or in connection with, other arrangements which—

(i) involve the EU, an EU entity, a member State or a public authority in a member State, or

(ii) are otherwise dependent upon the United Kingdom's membership of the EU [or Part 4 of the withdrawal agreement],

and which no longer exist or are no longer appropriate,

(e) makes provision for, or in connection with, any reciprocal or other arrangements not falling within paragraph (c) or (d) which no longer exist, or are no longer appropriate, as a result of the United Kingdom ceasing to be a party to any of the EU Treaties [or as a result of either the end of the implementation period or any other effect of the withdrawal agreement],

[(ea) is not clear in its effect as a result of the operation of any provision of sections 2 to 6 or Schedule 1,]

(f) does not contain any functions or restrictions which—

(i) were in an EU directive and in force immediately before [IP completion day] (including any power to make EU tertiary legislation), and

(ii) it is appropriate to retain, or

(g) contains EU references which are no longer appropriate.

(3) There is also a deficiency in retained EU law where the Minister considers that there is—

(a) anything in retained EU law which is of a similar kind to any deficiency which falls within subsection (2), or

(b) a deficiency in retained EU law of a kind described, or provided for, in regulations made by a Minister of the Crown.

(4) But retained EU law is not deficient merely because it does not contain any modification of EU law which is adopted or notified, comes into force or only applies on or after [IP completion day].

(5) Regulations under subsection (1) may make any provision that could be made by an Act of Parliament.

(6) Regulations under subsection (1) may (among other things) provide for functions of EU entities or public authorities in member States (including making an instrument of a legislative character or providing funding) to be—

(a) exercisable instead by a public authority (whether or not established for the purpose) in the United Kingdom, or

(b) replaced, abolished or otherwise modified.

(7) But regulations under subsection (1) may not—

(a) impose or increase taxation or fees,

(b) make retrospective provision,

(c) create a relevant criminal offence,

(d) establish a public authority,

(e) . . .

(f) amend, repeal or revoke the Human Rights Act 1998 or any subordinate legislation made under it, or

(g) amend or repeal the Scotland Act 1998, the Government of Wales Act 2006 or the Northern Ireland Act 1998 (unless the regulations are made by virtue of paragraph 21(b) of Schedule 7 to this Act or are amending or repealing any provision of those Acts which modifies another enactment).

(8) No regulations may be made under this section after the end of the period of two years beginning with [IP completion day].

(9) The reference in subsection (1) to a failure or other deficiency arising from the withdrawal of the United Kingdom from the EU includes a reference to any failure or other deficiency arising from[—

(a) any aspect of that withdrawal, including (among other things)—

(i) the end of the implementation period, or

(ii) any other effect of the withdrawal agreement, or

(b) that withdrawal, or any such aspect of it, taken together] with the operation of any provision, or the interaction between any provisions, made by or under this Act [or the European Union (Withdrawal Agreement) Act 2020].

NOTES

All amendments to this section were made by the European Union (Withdrawal Agreement) Act 2020, s 27(1), as from exit day (as defined in s 20 of this Act).

Regulations: the Financial Regulators' Powers (Technical Standards etc) (Amendment etc) (EU Exit) Regulations 2018, SI 2018/1115; the European Public Limited-Liability Company (Amendment etc) (EU Exit) Regulations 2018, SI 2018/1298 at **[12.61]**; the European Economic Interest Grouping (Amendment) (EU Exit) Regulations 2018, SI 2018/1299; the Accounts and Reports (Amendment) (EU Exit) Regulations 2019, SI 2019/145 at **[12.76]**; the Insolvency (Amendment) (EU Exit) Regulations 2019, SI 2019/146 at **[12.80]**; the Statutory Auditors and Third Country Auditors (Amendment) (EU Exit) Regulations 2019, SI 2019/177 at **[12.83]**; the Takeovers (Amendment) (EU Exit) Regulations 2019, SI 2019/217 at **[12.89]**; the Market Abuse (Amendment) (EU Exit) Regulations 2019, SI 2019/310; the Collective Investment Schemes (Amendment etc) (EU Exit) Regulations 2019, SI 2019/325; the Alternative Investment Fund Managers (Amendment etc) (EU Exit) Regulations 2019, SI 2019/328; the Financial Markets and Insolvency (Amendment and Transitional Provision) (EU Exit) Regulations 2019, SI 2019/341 at **[12.90]**; the Companies, Limited Liability Partnerships and Partnerships (Amendment etc) (EU Exit) Regulations 2019, SI 2019/348 at **[12.101]**; the Equivalence Determinations for Financial Services and Miscellaneous Provisions (Amendment etc) (EU Exit) Regulations 2019, SI 2019/541; the Financial Regulators' Powers (Technical Standards etc) and Markets in Financial Instruments (Amendment) (EU Exit) Regulations 2019, SI 2019/576; the European Union (Withdrawal) Act 2018 (Consequential Modifications and Repeals and Revocations) (EU Exit) Regulations 2019, SI 2019/628 at **[12.107]**; Financial Services and Markets Act 2000 (Amendment) (EU Exit) Regulations 2019, SI 2019/632 at **[12.109]**; the Investment Exchanges, Clearing Houses and Central Securities Depositories (Amendment) (EU Exit) Regulations 2019, SI 2019/662; the Uncertificated Securities (Amendment and EU Exit) Regulations 2019, SI 2019/679 at **[12.123]**; the Gibraltar (Miscellaneous Amendments) (EU Exit) Regulations 2019, SI 2019/680 at **[12.128]**; the Public Record, Disclosure of Information and Co-operation (Financial Services) (Amendment) (EU Exit) Regulations 2019, SI 2019/681; the International Accounting Standards and European Public Limited-Liability Company (Amendment etc) (EU Exit) Regulations 2019, SI 2019/685 at **[12.130]**; the Official Listing of Securities, Prospectus and Transparency (Amendment etc) (EU Exit) Regulations 2019, SI 2019/707 at **[12.153]**; the Financial Services (Miscellaneous) (Amendment) (EU Exit) Regulations 2019, SI 2019/710 at **[12.161]**; the Risk Transformation and Solvency 2 (Amendment) (EU Exit) Regulations 2019, SI 2019/1233; the Electronic Commerce and Solvency 2 (Amendment etc) (EU Exit) Regulations 2019, SI 2019/1361; the Financial Services (Miscellaneous) (Amendment) (EU Exit) (No 3) Regulations 2019, SI 2019/1390; the Statutory Auditors, Third Country Auditors and International Accounting Standards (Amendment) (EU Exit) Regulations 2019, SI 2019/1392; the

Freedom of Establishment and Free Movement of Services (EU Exit) Regulations 2019, SI 2019/1401 at **[12.167]**; the Over the Counter Derivatives, Central Counterparties and Trade Repositories (Amendment, etc, and Transitional Provision) (EU Exit) (No 2) Regulations 2019, SI 2019/1416; the International Accounting Standards, Statutory Auditors and Third Country Auditors (Amendment) (EU Exit) Regulations 2020, SI 2020/335; the Financial Services (Miscellaneous Amendments) (EU Exit) Regulations 2020, SI 2020/628; Over the Counter Derivatives, Central Counterparties and Trade Repositories (Amendment, etc, and Transitional Provision) (EU Exit) Regulations 2020, SI 2020/646; the Insolvency (Amendment) (EU Exit) Regulations 2020, SI 2020/647; the Financial Holding Companies (Approval etc) and Capital Requirements (Capital Buffers and Macro-prudential Measures) (Amendment) (EU Exit) Regulations 2020, SI 2020/1406; the European Grouping of Territorial Cooperation and Limited Liability Partnerships etc (Revocations and Amendments) (EU Exit) Regulations 2021, SI 2021/153; the Recognised Auction Platforms (Amendment and Miscellaneous Provisions) Regulations 2021, SI 2021/494; the Payment and Electronic Money Institution Insolvency Regulations 2021, SI 2021/716; the Financial Markets and Insolvency (Transitional Provision) (EU Exit) (Amendment) Regulations 2021, SI 2021/782. Note that only Regulations relevant to this Handbook are listed; the numerous other Regulations made under this section are considered outside the scope of this work.

[12.15]

[8A Supplementary power in connection with implementation period

(1) A Minister of the Crown may by regulations—

(a) provide for other modifications for the purposes of section 1B(3)(f)(i) (whether applying in all cases or particular cases or descriptions of case),

(b) provide for subsection (3) or (4) of section 1B not to apply to any extent in particular cases or descriptions of case,

(c) make different provision in particular cases or descriptions of case to that made by subsection (3) or (4) of that section,

(d) modify any enactment contained in this Act in consequence of any repeal made by section 1A(5) or 1B(6), or

(e) make such provision not falling within paragraph (a), (b), (c) or (d) as the Minister considers appropriate for any purpose of, or otherwise in connection with, Part 4 of the withdrawal agreement.

(2) The power to make regulations under subsection (1) may (among other things) be exercised by modifying any provision made by or under an enactment.

(3) In subsection (2) "enactment" does not include primary legislation passed or made after IP completion day.

(4) No regulations may be made under subsection (1) after the end of the period of two years beginning with IP completion day.]

NOTES

Commencement: 23 January 2020.

Inserted by the European Union (Withdrawal Agreement) Act 2020, s 3, as from 23 January 2020.

[12.16]

[8B Power in connection with certain other separation issues

(1) A Minister of the Crown may by regulations make such provision as the Minister considers appropriate—

(a) to implement Part 3 of the withdrawal agreement (separation provisions),

(b) to supplement the effect of section 7A in relation to that Part, or

(c) otherwise for the purposes of dealing with matters arising out of, or related to, that Part (including matters arising by virtue of section 7A and that Part).

(2) A Minister of the Crown may by regulations make such provision as the Minister considers appropriate—

(a) to implement Part 3 of the EEA EFTA separation agreement (separation provisions),

(b) to supplement the effect of section 7B in relation to that Part, or

(c) otherwise for the purposes of dealing with matters arising out of, or related to, that Part (including matters arising by virtue of section 7B and that Part).

(3) Regulations under this section may make any provision that could be made by an Act of Parliament.

(4) Regulations under this section may (among other things) restate, for the purposes of making the law clearer or more accessible, anything that forms part of domestic law by virtue of—

(a) section 7A above and Part 3 of the withdrawal agreement, or

(b) section 7B above and Part 3 of the EEA EFTA separation agreement.

(5) But regulations under this section may not—

(a) impose or increase taxation or fees,

(b) make retrospective provision,

(c) create a relevant criminal offence,

(d) establish a public authority,

(e) amend, repeal or revoke the Human Rights Act 1998 or any subordinate legislation made under it, or

(f) amend or repeal the Scotland Act 1998, the Government of Wales Act 2006 or the Northern Ireland Act 1998 (unless the regulations are made by virtue of paragraph 21(b) of Schedule 7 to this Act or are amending or repealing any provision of those Acts which modifies another enactment).

(6) In this section references to Part 3 of the withdrawal agreement or of the EEA EFTA separation agreement include references to any provision of EU law which is applied by, or referred to in, that Part (to the extent of the application or reference).]

NOTES

Commencement: 19 May 2020.

Inserted by the European Union (Withdrawal Agreement) Act 2020, s 18, as from 19 May 2020.

Regulations: the Insolvency (Amendment) (EU Exit) Regulations 2020, SI 2020/647. Other Regulations made under this section are outside the scope of this work.

[12.17]

[8C Power in connection with Ireland/Northern Ireland Protocol in withdrawal agreement

(1) A Minister of the Crown may by regulations make such provision as the Minister considers appropriate—

(a) to implement the Protocol on Ireland/Northern Ireland in the withdrawal agreement,
(b) to supplement the effect of section 7A in relation to the Protocol, or
(c) otherwise for the purposes of dealing with matters arising out of, or related to, the Protocol (including matters arising by virtue of section 7A and the Protocol).

(2) Regulations under subsection (1) may make any provision that could be made by an Act of Parliament (including modifying this Act).

(3) Regulations under subsection (1) may (among other things) make provision facilitating the access to the market within Great Britain of qualifying Northern Ireland goods.

(4) Such provision may (among other things) include provision about the recognition within Great Britain of technical regulations, assessments, registrations, certificates, approvals and authorisations issued by—
(a) the authorities of a member State, or
(b) bodies established in a member State,
in respect of qualifying Northern Ireland goods.

(5) Regulations under subsection (1) may (among other things) restate, for the purposes of making the law clearer or more accessible, anything that forms part of domestic law by virtue of section 7A and the Protocol.

[(5A) Regulations under subsection (1) may not amend, repeal or otherwise modify the operation of section 47 of the United Kingdom Internal Market Act 2020 ("the 2020 Act"), except by making—
(a) provision of the sort that is contemplated by section 47(2) of the 2020 Act (permitted checks);
(b) provision under subsection (6);
(c) provision of the sort described in paragraph 21(b) of Schedule 7 (supplementary and transitional provision etc) in connection with—
(i) provision within either of the preceding paragraphs;
(ii) Articles 5 to 10 of the Northern Ireland Protocol ceasing to apply (and the resulting operation of section 55(1) of the 2020 Act).]

(6) A Minister of the Crown may by regulations define "qualifying Northern Ireland goods" for the purposes of this Act.

(7) In this section any reference to the Protocol on Ireland/Northern Ireland includes a reference to—
(a) any other provision of the withdrawal agreement so far as applying to the Protocol, and
(b) any provision of EU law which is applied by, or referred to in, the Protocol (to the extent of the application or reference),
but does not include the second sentence of Article 11(1) of the Protocol (which provides that the United Kingdom and the Republic of Ireland may continue to make new arrangements that build on the provisions of the Belfast Agreement in other areas of North-South cooperation on the island of Ireland).]

NOTES

Commencement: 19 May 2020.

Inserted by the European Union (Withdrawal Agreement) Act 2020, s 21, as from 19 May 2020.

Sub-s (5A): inserted by the United Kingdom Internal Market Act 2020, s 55(3), as from IP completion day (as defined in the European Union (Withdrawal Agreement) Act 2020, s 39). See also s 55(1) of the 2020 Act which provides that this subsection ceases to have effect when Articles 5 to 10 of the Northern Ireland Protocol cease to apply.

Regulations: made under this section are considered to be outside the scope of this work.

9 *(Repealed by the European Union (Withdrawal Agreement) Act 2020, s 36, as from 23 January 2020.)*

Devolution

[12.18]

10 [Protection for] North-South co-operation and . . . prevention of new border arrangements

(1) In exercising any of the powers under this Act, a Minister of the Crown or devolved authority must—
(a) act in a way that is compatible with the terms of the Northern Ireland Act 1998, and
(b) have due regard to the joint report from the negotiators of the EU and the United Kingdom Government on progress during phase 1 of negotiations under Article 50 of the Treaty on European Union.

(2) Nothing in section 8 . . . or 23(1) or (6) of this Act authorises regulations which—
(a) diminish any form of North-South cooperation provided for by the Belfast Agreement . . . , or
(b) create or facilitate border arrangements between Northern Ireland and the Republic of Ireland after exit day which feature physical infrastructure, including border posts, or checks and controls, that did not exist before exit day and are not in accordance with an agreement between the United Kingdom and the EU.

[(3) A Minister of the Crown may not agree to the making of a recommendation by the Joint Committee under Article 11(2) of the Protocol on Ireland/Northern Ireland in the withdrawal agreement (recommendations as to North-South cooperation) to—
(a) alter the arrangements for North-South co-operation as provided for by the Belfast Agreement,
(b) establish a new implementation body, or
(c) alter the functions of an existing implementation body.

(4) In this section—
"the Belfast Agreement" has the meaning given by section 98 of the Northern Ireland Act 1998;
"implementation body" has the meaning given by section 55(3) of that Act.]

NOTES

Section heading: words in square brackets substituted, and word omitted repealed, by the European Union (Withdrawal Agreement) Act 2020, s 41(4), Sch 5, Pt 2, paras 38, 41(1), (2), as from IP completion day (as defined in the European Union (Withdrawal Agreement) Act 2020, s 39).

Sub-s (2) is amended as follows:

Figure omitted repealed by the European Union (Withdrawal Agreement) Act 2020, s 41(4), Sch 5, Pt 2, paras 38, 41(1), (3)(a), as from 23 January 2020.

Words omitted from para (a) repealed by the European Union (Withdrawal Agreement) Act 2020, s 41(4), Sch 5, Pt 2, paras 38, 41(1), (3)(b), as from IP completion day (as defined in the European Union (Withdrawal Agreement) Act 2020, s 39).

Sub-ss (3), (4): added by the European Union (Withdrawal Agreement) Act 2020, s 24, as from IP completion day (as defined in the European Union (Withdrawal Agreement) Act 2020, s 39).

[12.19]

11 Powers involving devolved authorities corresponding to sections 8 [to 8C]

Schedule 2 (which confers powers to make regulations involving devolved authorities which correspond to the powers conferred by sections 8 [to 8C] has effect.

NOTES

Words in square brackets substituted by the European Union (Withdrawal Agreement) Act 2020, s 41(4), Sch 5, Pt 2, paras 38, 42, as from 23 January 2020.

[12.20]

12 Retaining EU restrictions in devolution legislation etc

(1)–(6) . . .

(7) Part 1 of Schedule 3 (which makes corresponding provision in relation to executive competence to that made by subsections (1) to (6) in relation to legislative competence) has effect.

(8) . . .

(9) A Minister of the Crown may by regulations—

(a) repeal any of the following provisions—

(i) section 30A or 57(4) to (15) of the Scotland Act 1998,

(ii) section 80(8) to (8L) or 109A of the Government of Wales Act 2006, or

(iii) section 6A or 24(3) to (15) of the Northern Ireland Act 1998, or

(b) modify any enactment in consequence of any such repeal.

(10), (11) . . .

(12) Part 3 of Schedule 3 (which contains amendments of devolution legislation not dealt with elsewhere) has effect.

(13) . . .

NOTES

Commencement: this section has been brought into force as follows:

Sub-s (2): 26 June 2018 (for the purposes of making regulations under the Scotland Act 1998, s 30A).

Sub-s (4): 26 June 2018 (for the purposes of making regulations under the Government of Wales Act 2006, s 109A).

Sub-s (6): 26 June 2018 (for the purposes of making regulations under the Northern Ireland Act 1998, s 6A).

Sub-ss (7), (8), (12): 26 June 2018 (certain purposes).

Sub-ss (9)–(11), (13): 4 July 2018.

IP completion day (as defined in the European Union (Withdrawal Agreement) Act 2020, s 39) for all other purposes.

Sub-ss (1)–(6), (8), (10), (11), (13): repealed by the European Union (Withdrawal) Act 2018 (Repeal of EU Restrictions in Devolution Legislation, etc) Regulations 2022, SI 2022/357, reg 6(2), as from 31 March 2022.

Regulations: the European Union (Withdrawal) Act 2018 (Repeal of EU Restrictions in Devolution Legislation, etc) Regulations 2022, SI 2022/357.

Parliamentary [oversight of withdrawal]

NOTES

Words in square brackets in the above heading substituted by the European Union (Withdrawal Agreement) Act 2020, s 41(4), Sch 5, Pt 2, paras 38, 43, as from exit day (as defined in s 20 of this Act).

13 (*S 13 (Parliamentary approval of the outcome of negotiations with the EU) was repealed by the European Union (Withdrawal Agreement) Act 2020, s 31(1), as from 23 January 2020. S 31(2) further provides that accordingly, none of the conditions set out in paras (a)–(d) of sub-s (1) of s 13 apply in relation to the ratification of the withdrawal agreement.*)

[12.21]

[13A Review of EU legislation during implementation period

(1) Subsection (2) applies where the European Scrutiny Select Committee of the House of Commons ("the ESC") publishes a report in respect of any EU legislation made, or which may be made, during the implementation period and the report—

(a) states that, in the opinion of the ESC, the EU legislation raises a matter of vital national interest to the United Kingdom,

(b) confirms that the ESC has taken such evidence as it considers appropriate as to the effect of the EU legislation and has consulted any Departmental Select Committee of the House of Commons which the ESC considers also has an interest in the EU legislation, and

(c) sets out the wording of a motion to be moved in the House of Commons in accordance with subsection (2).

(2) A Minister of the Crown must, within the period of 14 Commons sitting days beginning with the day on which the report is published, make arrangements for the motion mentioned in subsection (1)(c) to be debated and voted on by the House of Commons.

(3) Subsection (4) applies where the EU Select Committee of the House of Lords ("the EUC") publishes a report in respect of any EU legislation made, or which may be made, during the implementation period and the report—

(a) states that, in the opinion of the EUC, the EU legislation raises a matter of vital national interest to the United Kingdom,

(b) confirms that the EUC has taken such evidence as it considers appropriate as to the effect of the EU legislation, and

(c) sets out the wording of a motion to be moved in the House of Lords in accordance with subsection (4).

(4) A Minister of the Crown must, within the period of 14 Lords sitting days beginning with the day on which the report is published, make arrangements for the motion mentioned in subsection (3)(c) to be debated and voted on by the House of Lords.

(5) In this section—

"EU legislation" means—

(a) any amendment to the Treaty on European Union, the Treaty on the Functioning of the European Union, the Euratom Treaty or the EEA agreement,

(b) any EU directive, or

(c) any EU regulation or EU decision which is not EU tertiary legislation;

"the European Scrutiny Select Committee of the House of Commons" means the Select Committee of the House of Commons known as the European Scrutiny Select Committee or any successor of that committee;

"the EU Select Committee of the House of Lords" means the Select Committee of the House of Lords known as the EU Select Committee or any successor of that committee.]

NOTES

Commencement: 23 January 2020.

Inserted by the European Union (Withdrawal Agreement) Act 2020, s 29, as from 23 January 2020.

[12.22]

[13B Certain dispute procedures under withdrawal agreement

(1) Subsection (2) applies if a request has been made under Article 170 of the withdrawal agreement to the other party in a dispute (request to establish an arbitration panel in relation to a dispute between the EU and the United Kingdom).

(2) A Minister of the Crown must, within the 14 day period beginning with the day on which the request is made, make a statement in writing to each House of Parliament that the request has been made and setting out the details of it.

(3) Subsection (4) applies if the European Court has given a ruling in response to a request by an arbitration panel under Article 174(1) of the withdrawal agreement (request for ruling by European Court on certain questions arising in a dispute submitted to arbitration).

(4) A Minister of the Crown must, within the 14 day period beginning with the publication in the Official Journal of the European Union of the ruling of the European Court, make a statement in writing to each House of Parliament that the ruling has been made and setting out the details of it contained in the Official Journal.

(5) After the end of each reporting period, a Minister of the Crown must lay before each House of Parliament a report setting out the number of times within the reporting period that the Joint Committee has been provided with notice under Article 169(1) of the withdrawal agreement (notice concerning the commencement of consultations in the Joint Committee to resolve a dispute between the EU and the United Kingdom about the interpretation and application of the withdrawal agreement).

(6) In this section—

"reporting period" means—

(a) the period of one year beginning with the day on which IP completion day falls, and

(b) each subsequent year;

"the 14 day period" means—

(a) in relation to the House of Commons, the period of 14 Commons sitting days, and

(b) in relation to the House of Lords, the period of 14 Lords sitting days.]

NOTES

Commencement: IP completion day (as defined in the European Union (Withdrawal Agreement) Act 2020, s 39).

Inserted by the European Union (Withdrawal Agreement) Act 2020, s 30, as from IP completion day (as defined in the European Union (Withdrawal Agreement) Act 2020, s 39).

Financial and other matters

[12.23]

14 Financial provision

(1) Schedule 4 (which contains powers in connection with fees and charges) has effect.

(2) A Minister of the Crown, government department or devolved authority may incur expenditure, for the purpose of, or in connection with, preparing for anything about which provision may be made under a power to make subordinate legislation conferred or modified by or under this Act, before any such provision is made.

(3) There is to be paid out of money provided by Parliament—

(a) any expenditure incurred by a Minister of the Crown, government department or other public authority by virtue of this Act, and

(b) any increase attributable to this Act in the sums payable by virtue of any other Act out of money so provided.

(4) Subsection (3) is subject to any other provision made by or under this Act or any other enactment.

[12.24]

15 Publication and rules of evidence

(1) Part 1 of Schedule 5 (which makes provision for the publication by the Queen's Printer of copies of retained direct EU legislation and related information) has effect.

(2) Part 2 of Schedule 5 (which makes provision about rules of evidence) has effect.

NOTES

Commencement: this section has been brought into force as follows:

Sub-s (1): 4 July 2018 (in so far as relating to Sch 5, para 2); 3 July 2019 (in so far as relating to Sch 5, para 1).

Sub-s (2): 4 July 2018 (in so far as relating to Sch 5, para 4); IP completion day (as defined in the European Union (Withdrawal Agreement) Act 2020, s 39) (otherwise).

[12.25]

[15A Prohibition on extending implementation period

A Minister of the Crown may not agree in the Joint Committee to an extension of the implementation period.]

NOTES

Commencement: 23 January 2020.
Inserted by the European Union (Withdrawal Agreement) Act 2020, s 33, as from 23 January 2020.

[12.26]

[15B Ministerial co-chairs of the Joint Committee

The functions of the United Kingdom's co-chair of the Joint Committee, under Annex VIII of the withdrawal agreement (rules of procedure of the Joint Committee and specialised committees), are to be exercised personally by a Minister of the Crown (and, accordingly, only a Minister of the Crown may be designated as a replacement under Rule 1(3)).]

NOTES

Commencement: 23 January 2020.
Inserted by the European Union (Withdrawal Agreement) Act 2020, s 34, as from 23 January 2020.

[12.27]

[15C No use of written procedure in the Joint Committee

(1) The United Kingdom's co-chair of the Joint Committee may not consent to the Joint Committee using the written procedure provided for in Rule 9(1) of Annex VIII of the withdrawal agreement.
(2) In subsection (1) the reference to the United Kingdom's co-chair of the Joint Committee includes a reference to any designee of the co-chair designated under Rule 1(3) of Annex VIII of the withdrawal agreement.]

NOTES

Commencement: 23 January 2020.
Inserted by the European Union (Withdrawal Agreement) Act 2020, s 35, as from 23 January 2020.

16–19 (*Ss 16, 18, 19 repealed by the European Union (Withdrawal Agreement) Act 2020, s 36, as from 23 January 2020. S 17 (Family unity for those seeking asylum or other protection in Europe) outside the scope of this work*)

General and final provision

[12.28]

20 Interpretation

(1) In this Act—

"Charter of Fundamental Rights" means the Charter of Fundamental Rights of the European Union of 7 December 2000, as adapted at Strasbourg on 12 December 2007;

["Commons sitting day" means a day on which the House of Commons is sitting (and a day is only a day on which the House of Commons is sitting if the House begins to sit on that day);"]

"devolved authority" means—
(a) the Scottish Ministers,
(b) the Welsh Ministers, or
(c) a Northern Ireland department;

"domestic law" means—
(a) in [sections 3, 7A and 7B], the law of England and Wales, Scotland and Northern Ireland, and
(b) in any other case, the law of England and Wales, Scotland or Northern Ireland;

"the EEA" means the European Economic Area;

"enactment" means an enactment whenever passed or made and includes—
(a) an enactment contained in any Order in Council, order, rules, regulations, scheme, warrant, byelaw or other instrument made under an Act,
(b) an enactment contained in any Order in Council made in exercise of Her Majesty's Prerogative,
(c) an enactment contained in, or in an instrument made under, an Act of the Scottish Parliament,
(d) an enactment contained in, or in an instrument made under, a Measure or Act of the National Assembly for Wales,
(e) an enactment contained in, or in an instrument made under, Northern Ireland legislation,
(f) an enactment contained in any instrument made by a member of the Scottish Government, the Welsh Ministers, the First Minister for Wales, the Counsel General to the Welsh Government, a Northern Ireland Minister, the First Minister in Northern Ireland, the deputy First Minister in Northern Ireland or a Northern Ireland department in exercise of prerogative or other executive functions of Her Majesty which are exercisable by such a person on behalf of Her Majesty,
(g) an enactment contained in, or in an instrument made under, a Measure of the Church Assembly or of the General Synod of the Church of England, and
(h) except in sections [1B] and 7 or where there is otherwise a contrary intention, any retained direct EU legislation;

"EU decision" means—
(a) a decision within the meaning of Article 288 of the Treaty on the Functioning of the European Union, or
(b) a decision under former Article 34(2)(c) of the Treaty on European Union;

"EU directive" means a directive within the meaning of Article 288 of the Treaty on the Functioning of the European Union;

"EU entity" means an EU institution or any office, body or agency of the EU;

"EU reference" means—
(a) any reference to the EU, an EU entity or a member State,
(b) any reference to an EU directive or any other EU law, or
(c) any other reference which relates to the EU;

"EU regulation" means a regulation within the meaning of Article 288 of the Treaty on the Functioning of the European Union;

"EU tertiary legislation" means—

(a) any provision made under—

(i) an EU regulation,

(ii) a decision within the meaning of Article 288 of the Treaty on the Functioning of the European Union, or

(iii) an EU directive,

by virtue of Article 290 or 291(2) of the Treaty on the Functioning of the European Union or former Article 202 of the Treaty establishing the European Community, or

(b) any measure adopted in accordance with former Article 34(2)(c) of the Treaty on European Union to implement decisions under former Article 34(2)(c),

but does not include any such provision or measure which is an EU directive;

"exempt EU instrument" means anything which is an exempt EU instrument by virtue of Schedule 6;

"exit day" [means [31 January 2020] at 11.00pm (and] see subsections (2) to (5));

["future relationship agreement" has the same meaning as in the European Union (Future Relationship) Act 2020 (see section 37 of that Act);]

["Joint Committee" means the Joint Committee established by Article 164(1) of the withdrawal agreement;]

["Lords sitting day" means a day on which the House of Lords is sitting (and a day is only a day on which the House of Lords is sitting if the House begins to sit on that day);]

"member State" (except in the definitions of "direct EU legislation" and "EU reference") does not include the United Kingdom;

"Minister of the Crown" has the same meaning as in the Ministers of the Crown Act 1975 and also includes the Commissioners for Her Majesty's Revenue and Customs;

"modify" includes amend, repeal or revoke (and related expressions are to be read accordingly);

"Northern Ireland devolved authority" means the First Minister and deputy First Minister in Northern Ireland acting jointly, a Northern Ireland Minister or a Northern Ireland department;

"primary legislation" means—

(a) an Act of Parliament,

(b) an Act of the Scottish Parliament,

(c) a Measure or Act of the National Assembly for Wales, or

(d) Northern Ireland legislation;

"public authority" means a public authority within the meaning of section 6 of the Human Rights Act 1998;

["ratify", whether in relation to the withdrawal agreement or otherwise, has the same meaning as it does for the purposes of Part 2 of the Constitutional Reform and Governance Act 2010 in relation to a treaty (see section 25 of that Act);]

"relevant criminal offence" means an offence for which an individual who has reached the age of 18 (or, in relation to Scotland or Northern Ireland, 21) is capable of being sentenced to imprisonment for a term of more than 2 years (ignoring any enactment prohibiting or restricting the imprisonment of individuals who have no previous convictions);

"retained direct EU legislation" means any direct EU legislation which forms part of domestic law by virtue of section 3 (as modified by or under this Act or by other domestic law from time to time, and including any instruments made under it on or after [IP completion day]);

"retrospective provision", in relation to provision made by regulations, means provision taking effect from a date earlier than the date on which the regulations are made;

"subordinate legislation" means—

(a) any Order in Council, order, rules, regulations, scheme, warrant, byelaw or other instrument made under any Act, or

(b) any instrument made under an Act of the Scottish Parliament, Northern Ireland legislation or a Measure or Act of the National Assembly for Wales,

and (except in section 7 or Schedule 2 or where there is a contrary intention) includes any Order in Council, order, rules, regulations, scheme, warrant, byelaw or other instrument made on or after [IP completion day] under any retained direct EU legislation;

"tribunal" means any tribunal in which legal proceedings may be brought;

"Wales" and "Welsh zone" have the same meaning as in the Government of Wales Act 2006 (see section 158 of that Act);

. . .

(2) In this [Act references to before, after or on exit day, or to beginning with exit day, are to be read as references to before, after or at 11.00pm on [31 January 2020] or (as the case may be) to beginning with 11.00pm on that day].

(3) Subsection (4) applies if the day or time on or at which the Treaties are to cease to apply to the United Kingdom in accordance with Article 50(3) of the Treaty on European Union is different from that specified in the definition of "exit day" in subsection (1).

(4) A Minister of the Crown [must] by regulations—

(a) amend the definition of "exit day" in subsection (1) to ensure that the day and time specified in the definition are the day and time that the Treaties are to cease to apply to the United Kingdom, and

(b) amend subsection (2) in consequence of any such amendment.

(5) In subsections (3) and (4) "the Treaties" means the Treaty on European Union and the Treaty on the Functioning of the European Union.

[(5A) In this Act references to anything which continues to be domestic law by virtue of section 1B(2) include—

(a) references to anything to which section 1B(2) applies which continues to be domestic law on or after exit day (whether or not it would have done so irrespective of that provision), and

(b) references to anything which continues to be domestic law on or after exit day by virtue of section 1B(2) (as that body of law is added to or otherwise modified by or under this Act or by other domestic law from time to time).]

(6) In this Act references to anything which continues to be domestic law by virtue of section 2 include references to anything to which subsection (1) of that section applies which continues to be domestic law on or after [IP completion day] (whether or not it would have done so irrespective of that section).

(7) In this Act references to anything which is retained EU law by virtue of section 4 include references to any modifications, made by or under this Act or by other domestic law from time to time, of the rights, powers, liabilities, obligations, restrictions, remedies or procedures concerned.

(8) References in this Act (however expressed) to a public authority in the United Kingdom include references to a public authority in any part of the United Kingdom.

(9) References in this Act to former Article 34(2)(c) of the Treaty on European Union are references to that Article as it had effect at any time before the coming into force of the Treaty of Lisbon.

(10) Any other reference in this Act to—

(a) an Article of the Treaty on European Union or the Treaty on the Functioning of the European Union, or

(b) Article 10 of Title VII of Protocol 36 to those treaties,

includes a reference to that Article as applied by Article 106a of the Euratom Treaty.

NOTES

Sub-s (1) is amended as follows:

Definition "Commons sitting day" inserted by the European Union (Withdrawal Agreement) Act 2020, s 41(4), Sch 5, Pt 2, paras 38, 44(1), (2)(a), as from 23 January 2020.

Words in square brackets in the definition "domestic law" substituted by the European Union (Withdrawal Agreement) Act 2020, s 41(4), Sch 5, Pt 2, paras 38, 44(1), (2)(b), as from exit day (as defined in sub-s (1) above).

Figure in square brackets in para (h) of the definition "enactment" substituted by the European Union (Withdrawal Agreement) Act 2020, s 41(4), Sch 5, Pt 2, paras 38, 44(1), (2)(c), as from exit day (as defined in sub-s (1) above).

Words in first (outer) pair of square brackets in the definition "exit day" substituted by the European Union (Withdrawal) Act 2018 (Exit Day) (Amendment) (No 2) Regulations 2019, SI 2019/859, reg 2(1), (2), as from 11 April 2019. Words "31 January 2020" in square brackets substituted by the European Union (Withdrawal) Act 2018 (Exit Day) (Amendment) (No 3) Regulations 2019, SI 2019/1423, reg 2(1), (2), as from 30 October 2019.

Definition "future relationship agreement" inserted by the European Union (Future Relationship) Act 2020, s 39(3), (5), Sch 6, Pt 1, para 6, as from IP completion day (as defined in the European Union (Withdrawal Agreement) Act 2020, s 39).

Definitions "Joint Committee", "Lords sitting day" and "ratify" inserted by the European Union (Withdrawal Agreement) Act 2020, s 41(4), Sch 5, Pt 2, paras 38, 44(1), (2)(d), (e), as from 23 January 2020.

Words in square brackets in the definitions "retained direct EU legislation" and "subordinate legislation" substituted by the European Union (Withdrawal Agreement) Act 2020, s 41(4), Sch 5, Pt 2, paras 38, 44(1), (2)(f), (g), as from exit day (as defined in sub-s (1) above).

Definition "withdrawal agreement" (omitted) repealed by the European Union (Withdrawal Agreement) Act 2020, s 41(4), Sch 5, Pt 2, paras 38, 44(1), (2)(h), as from exit day (as defined in sub-s (1) above).

Sub-s (2): words first (outer) pair of in square brackets substituted by SI 2019/859, reg 2(1), (3), as from 11 April 2019. Words "31 January 2020" in square brackets substituted by SI 2019/1423, reg 2(1), (3), as from 30 October 2019.

Sub-s (4): word in square brackets substituted the European Union (Withdrawal) (No 2) Act 2019, s 4(1), as from 9 September 2019.

Sub-s (5A): inserted by the European Union (Withdrawal Agreement) Act 2020, s 41(4), Sch 5, Pt 2, paras 38, 44(1), (3), as from 23 January 2020.

Sub-s (6): words in square brackets substituted by the European Union (Withdrawal Agreement) Act 2020, s 41(4), Sch 5, Pt 2, paras 38, 44(1), (4), as from exit day (as defined in sub-s (1) above).

National Assembly for Wales: see further, in relation to the renaming of the National Assembly for Wales as the Senedd Cymru or the Welsh Parliament, the Senedd and Elections (Wales) Act 2020, s 2 (with effect from 6 May 2020). See also ss 3–9 of the 2020 Act in relation to the renaming of Acts of the National Assembly for Wales, Members of the National Assembly for Wales, etc.

Regulations: the European Union (Withdrawal) Act 2018 (Exit Day) (Amendment) Regulations 2019, SI 2019/718; the European Union (Withdrawal) Act 2018 (Exit Day) (Amendment) (No 2) Regulations 2019, SI 2019/859; the European Union (Withdrawal) Act 2018 (Exit Day) (Amendment) (No 3) Regulations 2019, SI 2019/1423. Note that the amendments made by the European Union (Withdrawal) Act 2018 (Exit Day) (Amendment) (No 2) Regulations 2019, SI 2019/859 supersede the amendments made by the European Union (Withdrawal) Act 2018 (Exit Day) (Amendment) Regulations 2019, SI 2019/718.

[12.29]

21 Index of defined expressions

(1) In this Act, the expressions listed in the left-hand column have the meaning given by, or are to be interpreted in accordance with, the provisions listed in the right-hand column.

Expression	*Provision*
[Anything which continues to be domestic law by virtue of section 1B(2)	Section 20(5A)]
Anything which continues to be domestic law by virtue of section 2	Section 20(6)
Anything which is retained EU law by virtue of section 4	Section 20(7)
Article (in relation to the Treaty on European Union or the Treaty on the Functioning of the European Union)	Section 20(10)
Charter of Fundamental Rights	Section 20(1)
[Commons sitting day	Section 20(1)]
Devolved authority	Section 20(1)

Expression	*Provision*
Direct EU legislation	Section 3(2)
Domestic law	Section 20(1)
The EEA	Section 20(1)
EEA agreement	Schedule 1 to the Interpretation Act 1978
[EEA EFTA separation agreement	Section 7B(6)]
Enactment	Section 20(1)
The EU	Schedule 1 to the Interpretation Act 1978
EU decision	Section 20(1)
[EU-derived domestic legislation	Section 1B(7)]
EU directive	Section 20(1)
EU entity	Section 20(1)
EU institution	Schedule 1 to the Interpretation Act 1978
EU instrument	Schedule 1 to the Interpretation Act 1978
Euratom Treaty	Schedule 1 to the Interpretation Act 1978
EU reference	Section 20(1)
EU regulation	Section 20(1)
[European Communities Act 1972	Section 1A(7)(a)]
European Court	Schedule 1 to the Interpretation Act 1978
EU tertiary legislation	Section 20(1)
EU Treaties	Schedule 1 to the Interpretation Act 1978
Exempt EU instrument	Section 20(1)
Exit day (and related expressions)	Section 20(1) to (5)
Former Article 34(2)(c) of Treaty on European Union	Section 20(9)
[Future relationship agreement	Section 20(1)]
[Implementation period	Section 1A(6)]
[IP completion day (and related expressions)	Section 1A(6)]
[Joint Committee	Section 20(1)]
[Lords sitting day	Section 20(1)]
Member State	Section 20(1) and Schedule 1 to the Interpretation Act 1978
Minister of the Crown	Section 20(1)
Modify (and related expressions)	Section 20(1)
Northern Ireland devolved authority	Section 20(1)
Operative (in relation to direct EU legislation)	Section 3(3)
[Part (of withdrawal agreement or EEA EFTA separation agreement)	Section 1A(7)(b)]
Primary legislation	Section 20(1)
Public authority	Section 20(1)
Public authority in the United Kingdom (however expressed)	Section 20(8)
[Qualifying Northern Ireland goods	Section 8C(6)]
[Ratify	Section 20(1)]
Relevant criminal offence	Section 20(1) (and paragraph 44 of Schedule 8)
[Relevant separation agreement law	Section 7C(3)]
Retained case law	Section 6(7)
Retained direct EU legislation	Section 20(1)
Retained direct minor EU legislation	Section 7(6)
Retained direct principal EU legislation	Section 7(6)
Retained domestic case law	Section 6(7)
Retained EU case law	Section 6(7)
Retained EU law	Section 6(7)
Retained general principles of EU law	Section 6(7)
Retrospective provision	Section 20(1)
Subordinate legislation	Section 20(1)

Expression	*Provision*
[Swiss citizens' rights agreement	Section 7B(6)]
Tribunal	Section 20(1)
Wales	Section 20(1)
Welsh zone	Section 20(1)
Withdrawal agreement	[Section 1A(6)]

(2) See paragraph 22 of Schedule 8 for amendments made by this Act to Schedule 1 to the Interpretation Act 1978.

NOTES

Entry "Future relationship agreement" inserted by the European Union (Future Relationship) Act 2020, s 39(3), (5), Sch 6, Pt 1, para 7, as from IP completion day (as defined in the European Union (Withdrawal Agreement) Act 2020, s 39).

All other amendments to this section were made by the European Union (Withdrawal Agreement) Act 2020, s 41(4), Sch 5, Pt 2, paras 38, 45, as from exit day (as defined in s 20 of this Act).

[12.30]
22 Regulations

Schedule 7 (which makes provision about the scrutiny by Parliament and the devolved legislatures of regulations under this Act and contains other general provision about such regulations) has effect.

[12.31]
23 Consequential and transitional provision

(1) A Minister of the Crown may by regulations make such provision as the Minister considers appropriate in consequence of this Act.
(2) The power to make regulations under subsection (1) may (among other things) be exercised by modifying any provision made by or under an enactment.
(3) In subsection (2) "enactment" does not include primary legislation passed or made after [IP completion day].
(4) No regulations may be made under subsection (1) after the end of the period of 10 years beginning with [IP completion day].
(5) Parts 1 and 2 of Schedule 8 (which contain consequential provision) have effect.
(6) A Minister of the Crown may by regulations make such transitional, transitory or saving provision as the Minister considers appropriate in connection with the coming into force of any provision of this Act (including its operation in connection with exit day [or IP completion day]).
(7) Parts 3 and 4 of Schedule 8 (which contain transitional, transitory and saving provision) have effect.
(8) The enactments mentioned in Schedule 9 (which contains repeals not made elsewhere in this Act) are repealed to the extent specified.

NOTES

Commencement: sub-ss (1)–(4) and (6) came into force on 26 June 2018. Sub-ss (5) and (7) (which introduce Sch 8) are fully in force (for details see Sch 8 *post*). Sub-s (8) which introduces the repeals made by Sch 9 has been brought into force on 4 July 2018 and 31 December 2020 for certain purposes; but is still not in force in so far as relating to certain repeals made by Sch 9.

All amendments to this section were made by the European Union (Withdrawal Agreement) Act 2020, s 41(4), Sch 5, Pt 2, paras 38, 46, as from exit day (as defined in s 20 of this Act).

Regulations: the European Union (Withdrawal) Act 2018 (Commencement and Transitional Provisions) Regulations 2018, SI 2018/808; the European Union (Definition of Treaties Orders) (Revocation) (EU Exit) Regulations 2018, SI 2018/1012; the Accounts and Reports (Amendment) (EU Exit) Regulations 2019, SI 2019/145 at **[12.76]**; the Statutory Auditors and Third Country Auditors (Amendment) (EU Exit) Regulations 2019, SI 2019/177 at **[12.83]**; the Financial Services (Miscellaneous) (Amendment) (EU Exit) (No 3) Regulations 2019, SI 2019/1390; the European Union (Withdrawal) Act 2018 (Commencement No 5, Transitional Provisions and Amendment) Regulations 2020, SI 2020/74; the European Union (Withdrawal) Act 2018 and European Union (Withdrawal Agreement) Act 2020 (Commencement, Transitional and Savings Provisions) Regulations 2020, SI 2020/1622 at **[12.182]**;the European Grouping of Territorial Cooperation and Limited Liability Partnerships etc (Revocations and Amendments) (EU Exit) Regulations 2021, SI 2021/153. Other Regulations made under this section are outside the scope of this work.

[12.32]
24 Extent

(1) Subject to subsections (2) and (3), this Act extends to England and Wales, Scotland and Northern Ireland.
(2) Any provision of this Act which amends or repeals an enactment has the same extent as the enactment amended or repealed.
(3) Regulations under section 8(1) or 23 may make provision which extends to Gibraltar—
- (a) modifying any enactment which—
  - (i) extends to Gibraltar and relates to European Parliamentary elections, or
  - (ii) extends to Gibraltar for any purpose which is connected with Gibraltar forming part of an electoral region, under the European Parliamentary Elections Act 2002, for the purposes of such elections, or
- (b) which is supplementary, incidental, consequential, transitional, transitory or saving provision in connection with a modification within paragraph (a).

NOTES

Regulations: made under this section are considered to be outside the scope of this work.

[12.33]
25 Commencement and short title

(1) The following provisions—
- (a) sections 8 to 11 (including Schedule 2),

(b) paragraphs 4, 5, 21(2)(b), 48(b), 51(2)(c) and (d) and (4) of Schedule 3 (and section 12(8) and (12) so far as relating to those paragraphs),
(c) sections 13 and 14 (including Schedule 4),
(d) sections 16 to 18,
(e) sections 20 to 22 (including Schedules 6 and 7),
(f) section 23(1) to (4) and (6),
(g) paragraph 41(10), 43 and 44 of Schedule 8 (and section 23(7) so far as relating to those paragraphs),
(h) section 24, and
(i) this section,

come into force on the day on which this Act is passed.

(2) In section 12—

(a) subsection (2) comes into force on the day on which this Act is passed for the purposes of making regulations under section 30A of the Scotland Act 1998,
(b) subsection (4) comes into force on that day for the purposes of making regulations under section 109A of the Government of Wales Act 2006, and
(c) subsection (6) comes into force on that day for the purposes of making regulations under section 6A of the Northern Ireland Act 1998.

(3) In Schedule 3—

(a) paragraph 1(b) comes into force on the day on which this Act is passed for the purposes of making regulations under section 57(4) of the Scotland Act 1998,
(b) paragraph 2 comes into force on that day for the purposes of making regulations under section 80(8) of the Government of Wales Act 2006,
(c) paragraph 3(b) comes into force on that day for the purposes of making regulations under section 24(3) of the Northern Ireland Act 1998,
(d) paragraph 24(2) comes into force on that day for the purposes of making regulations under section 30A of the Scotland Act 1998,
(e) paragraph 24(3) comes into force on that day for the purposes of making regulations under section 57(4) of the Scotland Act 1998,
(f) paragraph 25 comes into force on that day for the purposes of making regulations under section 30A or 57(4) of the Scotland Act 1998,
(g) paragraph 43 comes into force on that day for the purposes of making regulations under section 80(8) or 109A of the Government of Wales Act 2006, and
(h) paragraphs 57 and 58 come into force on that day for the purposes of making regulations under section 6A or 24(3) of the Northern Ireland Act 1998;

and section 12(7) and (12), so far as relating to each of those paragraphs, comes into force on that day for the purposes of making the regulations mentioned above in relation to that paragraph.

(4) The provisions of this Act, so far as they are not brought into force by subsections (1) to (3), come into force on such day as a Minister of the Crown may by regulations appoint; and different days may be appointed for different purposes.

(5) This Act may be cited as the European Union (Withdrawal) Act 2018.

NOTES

Regulations: the European Union (Withdrawal) Act 2018 (Commencement and Transitional Provisions) Regulations 2018, SI 2018/808; the European Union (Withdrawal) Act 2018 (Commencement No 2) Regulations 2019, SI 2019/399; the European Union (Withdrawal) Act 2018 (Commencement No 3) Regulations 2019, SI 2019/1077; the European Union (Withdrawal) Act 2018 (Commencement No 4) Regulations 2019, SI 2019/1198; the European Union (Withdrawal) Act 2018 (Commencement No 5, Transitional Provisions and Amendment) Regulations 2020, SI 2020/74; the European Union (Withdrawal) Act 2018 and European Union (Withdrawal Agreement) Act 2020 (Commencement, Transitional and Savings Provisions) Regulations 2020, SI 2020/1622 at **[12.182]**.

SCHEDULES

SCHEDULE 1
FURTHER PROVISION ABOUT EXCEPTIONS TO SAVINGS AND INCORPORATION

Section 5(6)

Challenges to validity of retained EU law

[12.34]

1. (1) There is no right in domestic law on or after [IP completion day] to challenge any retained EU law on the basis that, immediately before [IP completion day], an EU instrument was invalid.

(2) Sub-paragraph (1) does not apply so far as—

(a) the European Court has decided before [IP completion day] that the instrument is invalid, or
(b) the challenge is of a kind described, or provided for, in regulations made by a Minister of the Crown.

(3) Regulations under sub-paragraph (2)(b) may (among other things) provide for a challenge which would otherwise have been against an EU institution to be against a public authority in the United Kingdom.

General principles of EU law

2. No general principle of EU law is part of domestic law on or after [IP completion day] if it was not recognised as a general principle of EU law by the European Court in a case decided before [IP completion day] (whether or not as an essential part of the decision in the case).

3. (1) There is no right of action in domestic law on or after [IP completion day] based on a failure to comply with any of the general principles of EU law.

(2) No court or tribunal or other public authority may, on or after [IP completion day]—

(a) disapply or quash any enactment or other rule of law, or

(b) quash any conduct or otherwise decide that it is unlawful,

because it is incompatible with any of the general principles of EU law.

Rule in Francovich

4. There is no right in domestic law on or after [IP completion day] to damages in accordance with the rule in *Francovich*.

Interpretation

5. (1) References in section 5 and this Schedule to the principle of the supremacy of EU law, the Charter of Fundamental Rights, any general principle of EU law or the rule in *Francovich* are to be read as references to that principle, Charter or rule so far as it would otherwise continue to be, or form part of, domestic law on or after [IP completion day] [by virtue of section 2, 3, 4 or 6(3) or (6) and otherwise in accordance with this Act].

(2) Accordingly (among other things) the references to the principle of the supremacy of EU law in section 5(2) and (3) do not include anything which would bring into domestic law any modification of EU law which is adopted or notified, comes into force or only applies on or after [IP completion day].

NOTES

Commencement: 4 July 2018 (para 1(2)(b) for the purpose of making regulations, and para 1(3)); IP completion day (as defined in the European Union (Withdrawal Agreement) Act 2020, s 39) (otherwise).

The words "IP completion day" in square brackets (in each place that they occur) were substituted by the European Union (Withdrawal Agreement) Act 2020, s 25(6)(a), as from exit day (as defined in s 20 of this Act) (for the purposes of s 5(6) above, and this Schedule, so far as they are in force on exit day), and as from IP completion day (as defined in the European Union (Withdrawal Agreement) Act 2020, s 39) (otherwise).

The words "by virtue of section 2, 3, 4 or 6(3) or (6) and otherwise in accordance with this Act" in square brackets were substituted by the European Union (Withdrawal Agreement) Act 2020, s 25(6)(b), as from IP completion day (as defined in the European Union (Withdrawal Agreement) Act 2020, s 39).

Regulations: the Challenges to Validity of EU Instruments (EU Exit) Regulations 2019, SI 2019/673. These Regulations make provision about the exceptions to the saving and incorporation of EU law set out in paragraph 1, which provides that, on or after IP completion day, no challenge can be brought in the UK courts to retained EU law on the basis that immediately before IP completion day, an EU instrument was invalid. Regulations 1 and 2 provide for citation, commencement and interpretation. Regulation 3 provides that this exception for claims in respect of validity will not apply in respect of a certain class of claims. They must be based on whether an EU instrument was invalid immediately before IP completion day under the grounds in Article 263 TFEU and relate to proceedings which have begun before IP completion day but are not yet decided. Regulation 4 gives jurisdiction to courts and tribunals in the UK to declare an EU instrument invalid in these cases. Regulation 5 makes provision for notice to be given to a Minister of the Crown or the devolved administrations about any proceedings under these Regulations. Regulation 6 allows for a Minister of the Crown or the devolved administrations to be able to intervene in proceedings under these Regulations.

SCHEDULE 2
CORRESPONDING POWERS INVOLVING DEVOLVED AUTHORITIES

Section 11

PART 1 DEALING WITH DEFICIENCIES ARISING FROM WITHDRAWAL

Power to deal with deficiencies

[12.35]

1. (1) A devolved authority may by regulations make such provision as the devolved authority considers appropriate to prevent, remedy or mitigate—

(a) any failure of retained EU law to operate effectively, or

(b) any other deficiency in retained EU law,

arising from the withdrawal of the United Kingdom from the EU.

(2) A Minister of the Crown acting jointly with a devolved authority may by regulations make such provision as they consider appropriate to prevent, remedy or mitigate—

(a) any failure of retained EU law to operate effectively, or

(b) any other deficiency in retained EU law,

arising from the withdrawal of the United Kingdom from the EU.

(3) Section 8(2) to (9) apply for the purposes of this Part as they apply for the purposes of section 8 (including the references to the Minister in section 8(2) and (3) (but not the reference to a Minister of the Crown in section 8(3)(b)) being read as references to the devolved authority or (as the case may be) the Minister acting jointly with the devolved authority and the references to section 8(1) being read as references to sub-paragraph (1) or (2) above).

(4) Regulations under sub-paragraph (1) above are subject to paragraphs 2 to 7.

No power to make provision outside devolved competence

2. (1) No provision may be made by a devolved authority acting alone in regulations under this Part unless the provision is within the devolved competence of the devolved authority.

(2) See paragraphs 8 to 11 for the meaning of "devolved competence" for the purposes of this Part.

. . .

3. . . .

Requirement for consultation in certain circumstances

4. No regulations may be made under this Part by a devolved authority acting alone so far as the regulations—

(a) are to come into force before [IP completion day], or

(b) remove (whether wholly or partly) reciprocal arrangements of the kind mentioned in section 8(2)(c) or (e),

unless the regulations are, to that extent, made after consulting with the Secretary of State.

Requirement for consent where it would otherwise be required

5. (1) The consent of a Minister of the Crown is required before any provision is made by the Welsh Ministers acting alone in regulations under this Part so far as that provision, if contained in an Act of the National Assembly for Wales, would require the consent of a Minister of the Crown.

(2) The consent of the Secretary of State is required before any provision is made by a Northern Ireland department acting alone in regulations under this Part so far as that provision, if contained in an Act of the Northern Ireland Assembly, would require the consent of the Secretary of State.

(3) Sub-paragraph (1) or (2) does not apply if—

(a) the provision could be contained in subordinate legislation made otherwise than under this Act by the Welsh Ministers acting alone or (as the case may be) a Northern Ireland devolved authority acting alone, and

(b) no such consent would be required in that case.

(4) The consent of a Minister of the Crown is required before any provision is made by a devolved authority acting alone in regulations under this Part so far as that provision, if contained in—

(a) subordinate legislation made otherwise than under this Act by the devolved authority, or

(b) subordinate legislation not falling within paragraph (a) and made otherwise than under this Act by (in the case of Scotland) the First Minister or Lord Advocate acting alone or (in the case of Northern Ireland) a Northern Ireland devolved authority acting alone,

would require the consent of a Minister of the Crown.

(5) Sub-paragraph (4) does not apply if—

(a) the provision could be contained in—

(i) an Act of the Scottish Parliament, an Act of the National Assembly for Wales or (as the case may be) an Act of the Northern Ireland Assembly, or

(ii) different subordinate legislation of the kind mentioned in sub-paragraph (4)(a) or (b) and of a devolved authority acting alone or (as the case may be) other person acting alone, and

(b) no such consent would be required in that case.

Requirement for joint exercise where it would otherwise be required

6. (1) No regulations may be made under this Part by the Scottish Ministers, so far as they contain provision which relates to a matter in respect of which a power to make subordinate legislation otherwise than under this Act is exercisable by—

(a) the Scottish Ministers acting jointly with a Minister of the Crown, or

(b) the First Minister or Lord Advocate acting jointly with a Minister of the Crown,

unless the regulations are, to that extent, made jointly with the Minister of the Crown.

(2) No regulations may be made under this Part by the Welsh Ministers, so far as they contain provision which relates to a matter in respect of which a power to make subordinate legislation otherwise than under this Act is exercisable by the Welsh Ministers acting jointly with a Minister of the Crown, unless the regulations are, to that extent, made jointly with the Minister of the Crown.

(3) No regulations may be made under this Part by a Northern Ireland department, so far as they contain provision which relates to a matter in respect of which a power to make subordinate legislation otherwise than under this Act is exercisable by—

(a) a Northern Ireland department acting jointly with a Minister of the Crown, or

(b) another Northern Ireland devolved authority acting jointly with a Minister of the Crown,

unless the regulations are, to that extent, made jointly with the Minister of the Crown.

(4) Sub-paragraph (1), (2) or (3) does not apply if the provision could be contained in—

(a) an Act of the Scottish Parliament, an Act of the National Assembly for Wales or (as the case may be) an Act of the Northern Ireland Assembly without the need for the consent of a Minister of the Crown, or

(b) different subordinate legislation made otherwise than under this Act by—

(i) the Scottish Ministers, the First Minister or the Lord Advocate acting alone,

(ii) the Welsh Ministers acting alone, or

(iii) (as the case may be), a Northern Ireland devolved authority acting alone.

Requirement for consultation where it would otherwise be required

7. (1) No regulations may be made under this Part by the Welsh Ministers acting alone, so far as they contain provision which, if contained in an Act of the National Assembly for Wales, would require consultation with a Minister of the Crown, unless the regulations are, to that extent, made after consulting with the Minister of the Crown.

(2) No regulations may be made under this Part by the Scottish Ministers acting alone, so far as they contain provision which relates to a matter in respect of which a power to make subordinate legislation otherwise than under this Act is exercisable by the Scottish Ministers, the First Minister or the Lord Advocate after consulting with a Minister of the Crown, unless the regulations are, to that extent, made after consulting with the Minister of the Crown.

(3) No regulations may be made under this Part by the Welsh Ministers acting alone, so far as they contain provision which relates to a matter in respect of which a power to make subordinate legislation otherwise than under this Act is exercisable by the Welsh Ministers after consulting with a Minister of the Crown, unless the regulations are, to that extent, made after consulting with the Minister of the Crown.

(4) No regulations may be made under this Part by a Northern Ireland department acting alone, so far as they contain provision which relates to a matter in respect of which a power to make subordinate legislation otherwise than under this Act is exercisable by a Northern Ireland department after consulting with a Minister of the Crown, unless the regulations are, to that extent, made after consulting with the Minister of the Crown.

(5) Sub-paragraph (2), (3) or (4) does not apply if—

(a) the provision could be contained in an Act of the Scottish Parliament, an Act of the National Assembly for Wales or (as the case may be) an Act of the Northern Ireland Assembly, and

(b) there would be no requirement for the consent of a Minister of the Crown, or for consultation with a Minister of the Crown, in that case.

(6) Sub-paragraph (2), (3) or (4) does not apply if—

(a) the provision could be contained in different subordinate legislation made otherwise than under this Act by—

(i) the Scottish Ministers, the First Minister or the Lord Advocate acting alone,

(ii) the Welsh Ministers acting alone, or

(iii) (as the case may be), a Northern Ireland devolved authority acting alone, and

(b) there would be no requirement for the consent of a Minister of the Crown, or for consultation with a Minister of the Crown, in that case.

Meaning of devolved competence: Part 1

8. (1) A provision is within the devolved competence of the Scottish Ministers for the purposes of this Part if—

(a) it would be within the legislative competence of the Scottish Parliament if it were contained in an Act of that Parliament . . . , or

(b) it meets the conditions in sub-paragraph (2).

(2) The conditions are—

(a) the provision—

(i) amends or revokes subordinate legislation made before [IP completion day] by the Scottish Ministers, the First Minister or the Lord Advocate acting alone, or

(ii) makes supplementary, incidental, consequential, transitional, transitory or saving provision in connection with any such amendment or revocation,

(b) the subject-matter of the provision does not go beyond the subject-matter of the subordinate legislation concerned,

(c) the provision only forms part of the law of Scotland,

(d) the provision does not confer or remove functions exercisable otherwise than in or as regards Scotland, and

(e) the provision does not modify any enactment so far as the enactment cannot, by virtue of paragraph 1, 4 or 5 of Schedule 4 to the Scotland Act 1998, be modified by an Act of the Scottish Parliament.

9. (1) A provision is within the devolved competence of the Welsh Ministers for the purposes of this Part if—

(a) it would be within the legislative competence of the National Assembly for Wales if it were contained in an Act of the Assembly (. . . including any provision that could be made only with the consent of a Minister of the Crown), or

(b) it meets the conditions in sub-paragraph (2).

(2) The conditions are—

(a) the provision—

(i) amends or revokes subordinate legislation made before [IP completion day] by the Welsh Ministers acting alone or the National Assembly for Wales constituted by the Government of Wales Act 1998, or

(ii) makes supplementary, incidental, consequential, transitional, transitory or saving provision in connection with any such amendment or revocation,

(b) the subject-matter of the provision does not go beyond the subject-matter of the subordinate legislation concerned,

(c) the provision only forms part of the law of England and Wales,

(d) the provision does not confer or remove functions exercisable otherwise than in relation to Wales or the Welsh zone, and

(e) the provision does not modify any enactment so far as the enactment cannot, by virtue of paragraph 5, 6 or 7 of Schedule 7B to the Government of Wales Act 2006, be modified by an Act of the National Assembly for Wales.

10. (1) A provision is within the devolved competence of a Northern Ireland department for the purposes of this Part if—

(a) the provision, if it were contained in an Act of the Northern Ireland Assembly—

(i) would be within the legislative competence of the Assembly . . . , and

(ii) would not require the consent of the Secretary of State,

(b) the provision—

(i) amends or repeals Northern Ireland legislation, and

(ii) would, if it were contained in an Act of the Northern Ireland Assembly, be within the legislative competence of the Assembly . . . and require the consent of the Secretary of State, or

(c) the provision meets the conditions in sub-paragraph (2).

(2) The conditions are—

(a) the provision—

(i) amends or revokes subordinate legislation made before [IP completion day] by a Northern Ireland devolved authority acting alone, or

(ii) makes supplementary, incidental, consequential, transitional, transitory or saving provision in connection with any such amendment or revocation,

(b) the subject-matter of the provision does not go beyond the subject-matter of the subordinate legislation concerned,

(c) the provision only forms part of the law of Northern Ireland,

(d) the provision does not confer or remove functions exercisable otherwise than in or as regards Northern Ireland,

(e) the provision does not modify any enactment so far as the enactment cannot, by virtue of section 7 of the Northern Ireland Act 1998, be modified by an Act of the Northern Ireland Assembly, and

(f) the provision does not deal with, or otherwise relate to, a matter to which paragraph 22 of Schedule 2, or paragraph 42 of Schedule 3, to the Northern Ireland Act 1998 applies.

11. References in paragraphs 8 to 10, in connection with the making of regulations under this Part, to the subject-matter of any provision or subordinate legislation are to be read as references to the subject-matter of the provision or subordinate legislation when the regulations concerned are made.

NOTES

Para 3, and the words omitted from paras 8–10, were repealed by the European Union (Withdrawal) Act 2018 (Repeal of EU Restrictions in Devolution Legislation, etc) Regulations 2022, SI 2022/357, reg 6(3)(a), as from 31 March 2022.

The words in square brackets in paras 4, 8–10 were substituted by the European Union (Withdrawal Agreement) Act 2020, s 27(7), as from exit day (as defined in s 20 of this Act).

National Assembly for Wales: as to the renaming of the National Assembly for Wales, see the note at **[12.28]**.

Regulations: Regulations made under this Part are outside the scope of this work.

[PART 1A PROVISION IN CONNECTION WITH IMPLEMENTATION PERIOD

Supplementary power in connection with implementation period

[12.36]

11A. (1) A devolved authority may by regulations—

(a) provide for other modifications for the purposes of section 1B(3)(f)(i) (whether applying in all cases or particular cases or descriptions of case),

(b) provide for subsection (3) or (4) of section 1B not to apply to any extent in particular cases or descriptions of case,

(c) make different provision in particular cases or descriptions of case to that made by subsection (3) or (4) of that section, or

(d) make such provision not falling within paragraph (a), (b) or (c) as the devolved authority considers appropriate for any purpose of, or otherwise in connection with, Part 4 of the withdrawal agreement.

(2) A Minister of the Crown acting jointly with a devolved authority may by regulations—

(a) provide for other modifications for the purposes of section 1B(3)(f)(i) (whether applying in all cases or particular cases or descriptions of case),

(b) provide for subsection (3) or (4) of section 1B not to apply to any extent in particular cases or descriptions of case,

(c) make different provision in particular cases or descriptions of case to that made by subsection (3) or (4) of that section, or

(d) make such provision not falling within paragraph (a), (b) or (c) as they consider appropriate for any purpose of, or otherwise in connection with, Part 4 of the withdrawal agreement.

(3) The power to make regulations under this Part may (among other things) be exercised by modifying any provision made by or under an enactment.

(4) In sub-paragraph (3) "enactment" does not include primary legislation passed or made after IP completion day.

(5) No regulations may be made under this Part after the end of the period of two years beginning with IP completion day.

(6) Regulations under sub-paragraph (1) are also subject to paragraphs 11B and 11C.

No power to make provision outside devolved competence

11B. (1) No provision may be made by a devolved authority acting alone in regulations under this Part unless the provision is within the devolved competence of the devolved authority.

(2) See paragraphs 11D to 11F for the meaning of "devolved competence" for the purposes of this Part.

Certain requirements for consent, joint exercise or consultation

11C. Paragraphs 5 to 7 apply for the purposes of this Part as they apply for the purposes of Part 1.

Meaning of devolved competence: Part 1A

11D. A provision is within the devolved competence of the Scottish Ministers for the purposes of this Part if—

(a) it would be within the legislative competence of the Scottish Parliament if it were contained in an Act of that Parliament (ignoring, in the case of regulations made under this Part before exit day, section 29(2)(d) of the Scotland Act 1998 so far as relating to EU law), or

(b) it is provision which could be made in other subordinate legislation by the Scottish Ministers, the First Minister or the Lord Advocate acting alone (ignoring, in the case of regulations made under this Part before exit day, section 57(2) of the Scotland Act 1998 so far as relating to EU law).

11E. A provision is within the devolved competence of the Welsh Ministers for the purposes of this Part if—

(a) it would be within the legislative competence of the National Assembly for Wales if it were contained in an Act of the Assembly (ignoring, in the case of regulations made under this Part before exit day, section 108A(2)(e) of the Government of Wales Act 2006 so far as relating to EU law but including any provision that could be made only with the consent of a Minister of the Crown), or

(b) it is provision which could be made in other subordinate legislation by the Welsh Ministers acting alone (ignoring, in the case of regulations made under this Part before exit day, section 80(8) of the Government of Wales Act 2006 so far as relating to EU law).

11F. A provision is within the devolved competence of a Northern Ireland department for the purposes of this Part if—

(a) the provision, if it were contained in an Act of the Northern Ireland Assembly—

(i) would be within the legislative competence of the Assembly (ignoring, in the case of regulations made under this Part before exit day, section 6(2)(d) of the Northern Ireland Act 1998 so far as relating to EU law), and

(ii) would not require the consent of the Secretary of State,

(b) the provision—

(i) amends or repeals Northern Ireland legislation, and

(ii) would, if it were contained in an Act of the Northern Ireland Assembly, be within the legislative competence of the Assembly (ignoring, in the case of regulations made under this Part before exit day, section 6(2)(d) of the Northern Ireland Act 1998 so far as relating to EU law) and require the consent of the Secretary of State, or

(c) the provision is provision which could be made in other subordinate legislation by any Northern Ireland devolved authority acting alone (ignoring, in the case of regulations made under this Part before exit day, section 24(1)(b) of the Northern Ireland Act 1998).]

NOTES

Commencement: 23 January 2020.

Inserted by the European Union (Withdrawal Agreement) Act 2020, s 4, as from 23 January 2020.

National Assembly for Wales: as to the renaming of the National Assembly for Wales, see the note at **[12.28]**.

[PART 1B PROVISION IN CONNECTION WITH CERTAIN OTHER SEPARATION ISSUES

Powers in connection with Part 3 of withdrawal agreement and EEA EFTA separation agreement

[12.37]

11G. (1) A devolved authority may by regulations make such provision as the devolved authority considers appropriate—

(a) to implement Part 3 of the withdrawal agreement (separation provisions),

(b) to supplement the effect of section 7A in relation to that Part, or

(c) otherwise for the purposes of dealing with matters arising out of, or related to, that Part (including matters arising by virtue of section 7A and that Part).

(2) A Minister of the Crown acting jointly with a devolved authority may by regulations make such provision as they consider appropriate—

(a) to implement Part 3 of the withdrawal agreement (separation provisions),

(b) to supplement the effect of section 7A in relation to that Part, or

(c) otherwise for the purposes of dealing with matters arising out of, or related to, that Part (including matters arising by virtue of section 7A and that Part).

(3) A devolved authority may by regulations make such provision as the devolved authority considers appropriate—

(a) to implement Part 3 of the EEA EFTA separation agreement (separation provisions),

(b) to supplement the effect of section 7B in relation to that Part, or

(c) otherwise for the purposes of dealing with matters arising out of, or related to, that Part (including matters arising by virtue of section 7B and that Part).

(4) A Minister of the Crown acting jointly with a devolved authority may by regulations make such provision as they consider appropriate—

(a) to implement Part 3 of the EEA EFTA separation agreement (separation provisions),

(b) to supplement the effect of section 7B in relation to that Part, or

(c) otherwise for the purposes of dealing with matters arising out of, or related to, that Part (including matters arising by virtue of section 7B and that Part).

(5) Regulations under this Part may make any provision that could be made by an Act of Parliament.

(6) Regulations under this Part may (among other things) restate, for the purposes of making the law clearer or more accessible, anything that forms part of domestic law by virtue of—

(a) section 7A above and Part 3 of the withdrawal agreement, or

(b) section 7B above and Part 3 of the EEA EFTA separation agreement.

(7) But regulations under this Part may not—

(a) impose or increase taxation or fees,

(b) make retrospective provision,

(c) create a relevant criminal offence,

(d) establish a public authority,

(e) amend, repeal or revoke the Human Rights Act 1998 or any subordinate legislation made under it, or

(f) amend or repeal the Scotland Act 1998, the Government of Wales Act 2006 or the Northern Ireland Act 1998 (unless the regulations are made by virtue of paragraph 21(b) of Schedule 7 to this Act or are amending or repealing any provision of those Acts which modifies another enactment).

(8) Regulations under sub-paragraph (1) or (3) are also subject to paragraphs 11H and 11I.

(9) In this paragraph references to Part 3 of the withdrawal agreement or of the EEA EFTA separation agreement include references to any provision of EU law which is applied by, or referred to in, that Part (to the extent of the application or reference).

No power to make provision outside devolved competence

11H. (1) No provision may be made by a devolved authority acting alone in regulations under this Part unless the provision is within the devolved competence of the devolved authority.

(2) See paragraphs 11J to 11L for the meaning of "devolved competence" for the purposes of this Part.

Certain requirements for consent, joint exercise or consultation

11I. Paragraphs 5 to 7 apply for the purposes of this Part as they apply for the purposes of Part 1.

Meaning of devolved competence: Part 1B

11J. A provision is within the devolved competence of the Scottish Ministers for the purposes of this Part if—

(a) it would be within the legislative competence of the Scottish Parliament if it were contained in an Act of that Parliament . . . , or

(b) it is provision which could be made in other subordinate legislation by the Scottish Ministers, the First Minister or the Lord Advocate acting alone . . .

11K. A provision is within the devolved competence of the Welsh Ministers for the purposes of this Part if—

(a) it would be within the legislative competence of the National Assembly for Wales if it were contained in an Act of the Assembly (. . . including any provision that could be made only with the consent of a Minister of the Crown), or

(b) it is provision which could be made in other subordinate legislation by the Welsh Ministers acting alone . . .

11L. A provision is within the devolved competence of a Northern Ireland department for the purposes of this Part if—

(a) the provision, if it were contained in an Act of the Northern Ireland Assembly—

(i) would be within the legislative competence of the Assembly . . . , and

(ii) would not require the consent of the Secretary of State,

(b) the provision—

(i) amends or repeals Northern Ireland legislation, and

(ii) would, if it were contained in an Act of the Northern Ireland Assembly, be within the legislative competence of the Assembly . . . and require the consent of the Secretary of State, or

(c) the provision is provision which could be made in other subordinate legislation by any Northern Ireland devolved authority acting alone . . .].

NOTES

Commencement: 19 May 2020.

Inserted by the European Union (Withdrawal Agreement) Act 2020, s 19, as from 19 May 2020.

Paras 11J, 11K, 11L: words omitted repealed by the European Union (Withdrawal) Act 2018 (Repeal of EU Restrictions in Devolution Legislation, etc) Regulations 2022, SI 2022/357, reg 6(3)(b), as from 31 March 2022.

National Assembly for Wales: as to the renaming of the National Assembly for Wales, see the note at **[12.28]**.

Regulations: the Insolvency (Amendment) (EU Exit) (Scotland) Regulations 2020, SSI 2020/337. Other Regulations made under this Part are outside the scope of this work.

[PART 1C PROVISION IN CONNECTION WITH PROTOCOL ON IRELAND/NORTHERN IRELAND

Power in connection with Protocol on Ireland/Northern Ireland

[12.38]

11M. (1) A devolved authority may by regulations make such provision as the devolved authority considers appropriate—

(a) to implement the Protocol on Ireland/Northern Ireland in the withdrawal agreement,

(b) to supplement the effect of section 7A in relation to the Protocol, or

(c) otherwise for the purposes of dealing with matters arising out of, or related to, the Protocol (including matters arising by virtue of section 7A and the Protocol).

(2) A Minister of the Crown acting jointly with a devolved authority may by regulations make such provision as they consider appropriate—

(a) to implement the Protocol on Ireland/Northern Ireland in the withdrawal agreement,

(b) to supplement the effect of section 7A in relation to the Protocol, or

(c) otherwise for the purposes of dealing with matters arising out of, or related to, the Protocol (including matters arising by virtue of section 7A and the Protocol).

(3) Regulations under this Part may make any provision that could be made by an Act of Parliament.

(4) Regulations under this Part may (among other things) make provision facilitating the access to the market within Great Britain of qualifying Northern Ireland goods.

(5) Such provision may (among other things) include provision about the recognition within Great Britain of technical regulations, assessments, registrations, certificates, approvals and authorisations issued by—

(a) the authorities of a member State, or

(b) bodies established in a member State,

in respect of qualifying Northern Ireland goods.

(6) Regulations under this Part may (among other things) restate, for the purposes of making the law clearer or more accessible, anything that forms part of domestic law by virtue of section 7A and the Protocol.

(7) Regulations under sub-paragraph (1) are also subject to paragraphs 11N and 11O.

(8) In this paragraph any reference to the Protocol on Ireland/Northern Ireland includes a reference to—

(a) any other provision of the withdrawal agreement so far as applying to the Protocol, and

(b) any provision of EU law which is applied by, or referred to in, the Protocol (to the extent of the application or reference),

but does not include the second sentence of Article 11(1) of the Protocol (which provides that the United Kingdom and the Republic of Ireland may continue to make new arrangements that build on the provisions of the Belfast Agreement in other areas of North-South cooperation on the island of Ireland).

No power to make provision outside devolved competence

11N. (1) No provision may be made by a devolved authority acting alone in regulations under this Part unless the provision is within the devolved competence of the devolved authority.

(2) See paragraphs 11P to 11R for the meaning of "devolved competence" for the purposes of this Part.

Certain requirements for consent, joint exercise or consultation

11O. Paragraphs 5 to 7 apply for the purposes of this Part as they apply for the purposes of Part 1.

Meaning of devolved competence: Part 1C

11P. A provision is within the devolved competence of the Scottish Ministers for the purposes of this Part if—

(a) it would be within the legislative competence of the Scottish Parliament if it were contained in an Act of that Parliament (ignoring section 29(2)(d) of the Scotland Act 1998 so far as relating to EU law), or

(b) it is provision which could be made in other subordinate legislation by the Scottish Ministers, the First Minister or the Lord Advocate acting alone (ignoring section 57(2) of the Scotland Act 1998 so far as relating to EU law).

11Q. A provision is within the devolved competence of the Welsh Ministers for the purposes of this Part if—

(a) it would be within the legislative competence of the National Assembly for Wales if it were contained in an Act of the Assembly (ignoring section 108A(2)(e) of the Government of Wales Act 2006 so far as relating to EU law but including any provision that could be made only with the consent of a Minister of the Crown), or

(b) it is provision which could be made in other subordinate legislation by the Welsh Ministers acting alone (ignoring section 80(8) of the Government of Wales Act 2006 so far as relating to EU law).

11R. A provision is within the devolved competence of a Northern Ireland department for the purposes of this Part if—

(a) the provision, if it were contained in an Act of the Northern Ireland Assembly—

   (i) would be within the legislative competence of the Assembly (ignoring section 6(2)(d) of the Northern Ireland Act 1998 so far as relating to EU law), and

   (ii) would not require the consent of the Secretary of State,

(b) the provision—

   (i) amends or repeals Northern Ireland legislation, and

   (ii) would, if it were contained in an Act of the Northern Ireland Assembly, be within the legislative competence of the Assembly (ignoring section 6(2)(d) of the Northern Ireland Act 1998 so far as relating to EU law) and require the consent of the Secretary of State, or

(c) the provision is provision which could be made in other subordinate legislation by any Northern Ireland devolved authority acting alone (ignoring section 24(1)(b) of the Northern Ireland Act 1998).]

NOTES

Commencement: 19 May 2020.

Inserted by the European Union (Withdrawal Agreement) Act 2020, s 22, as from 19 May 2020.

National Assembly for Wales: as to the renaming of the National Assembly for Wales, see the note at **[12.28]**.

Regulations: made under this Part are outside the scope of this work.

(Sch 2, Pt 2 (Implementing the Withdrawal Agreement) was repealed by the European Union (Withdrawal Agreement) Act 2020, s 36, as from 23 January 2020.)

SCHEDULE 3
FURTHER AMENDMENTS OF DEVOLUTION LEGISLATION AND REPORTING REQUIREMENT

(Sch 3, Pts 1 and 3 amend the Scotland Act 1998, the Government of Wales Act 2006, and the Northern Ireland Act 1998 (and were repealed in part by the European Union (Withdrawal) Act 2018 (Repeal of EU Restrictions in Devolution Legislation, etc) Regulations 2022, SI 2022/357, reg 6(4)(a), as from 31 March 2022). Sch 3, Pt 2 (Reports in Connection with Retained EU Law Restrictions) was also repealed by SI 2022/357, reg 6(4)(a), as from 31 March 2022.)

SCHEDULE 4
POWERS IN CONNECTION WITH FEES AND CHARGES

Section 14(1)

PART 1 CHARGING IN CONNECTION WITH CERTAIN NEW FUNCTIONS

Power to provide for fees or charges

[12.39]

1. (1) An appropriate authority may by regulations make provision for, or in connection with, the charging of fees or other charges in connection with the exercise of a function ("the relevant function") which a public authority has by virtue of provision made under—

(a) section 8 or Part 1 of Schedule 2 (powers to deal with deficiencies arising from withdrawal),

[(aa) section 8B or Part 1B of Schedule 2 (powers in connection with Part 3 of the withdrawal agreement and Part 3 of the EEA EFTA separation agreement),

(ab) section 8C or Part 1C of Schedule 2 (powers in connection with the Ireland/Northern Ireland Protocol in the withdrawal agreement)], . . .

(b) . . .

(2) Where there is more than one appropriate authority in relation to the relevant function, two or more of the appropriate authorities may make regulations under this paragraph jointly.

(3) Regulations under this paragraph may (among other things)—

(a) prescribe the fees or charges or make provision as to how they are to be determined;

(b) provide for the recovery or disposal of any sums payable under the regulations;

(c) confer power on the public authority to make, by subordinate legislation, any provision that the appropriate authority may make under this paragraph in relation to the relevant function.

Meaning of "appropriate authority"

2. (1) A Minister of the Crown is an "appropriate authority" for the purposes of paragraph 1.

(2) The Scottish Ministers are an "appropriate authority" for the purposes of paragraph 1—

(a) if the Scottish Ministers (whether acting jointly or alone) made the provision, as mentioned in paragraph 1(1), by virtue of which the public authority has the relevant function,

(b) if the relevant function is a function of the Scottish Ministers, the First Minister or the Lord Advocate, or

(c) if the provision by virtue of which the public authority has the relevant function, if it were included in an Act of the Scottish Parliament, would be within the legislative competence of that Parliament (ignoring section 29(2)(d) of the Scotland Act 1998 so far as relating to EU law and retained EU law).

(3) The Welsh Ministers are an "appropriate authority" for the purposes of paragraph 1—

(a) if the Welsh Ministers (whether acting jointly or alone) made the provision, as mentioned in paragraph 1(1), by virtue of which the public authority has the relevant function,

(b) if the relevant function is a function of the Welsh Ministers, or

(c) if the provision by virtue of which the public authority has the relevant function, if it were included in an Act of the National Assembly for Wales, would be within the legislative competence of that Assembly (ignoring section 108A(2)(e) of the Government of Wales Act 2006 so far as relating to EU law and retained EU law but including any provision that could be made only with consent of a Minister of the Crown).

(4) A Northern Ireland department is an "appropriate authority" for the purposes of paragraph 1—

(a) if a Northern Ireland department (whether acting jointly or alone) made the provision, as mentioned in paragraph 1(1), by virtue of which the public authority has the relevant function,

(b) if the relevant function is a function of a Northern Ireland devolved authority, or

(c) if the provision by virtue of which the public authority has the relevant function, if it were included in an Act of the Northern Ireland Assembly—

(i) would be within the legislative competence of that Assembly (ignoring section 6(2)(d) of the Northern Ireland Act 1998), and

(ii) would not require the consent of the Secretary of State.

Requirements for consent

3. (1) A Minister of the Crown may only make regulations under paragraph 1 with the consent of the Treasury.

(2) A devolved authority may only make regulations under paragraph 1 with the consent of a Minister of the Crown if—

(a) the relevant function is a function of a Minister of the Crown, or

(b) the public authority that has the relevant function—

(i) in the case of the Scottish Ministers, has any functions that can be exercised otherwise than in or as regards Scotland,

(ii) in the case of the Welsh Ministers, has any functions that can be exercised otherwise than in relation to Wales or the Welsh zone, or

(iii) in the case of a Northern Ireland department, has any functions that can be exercised otherwise than in or as regards Northern Ireland and is not an implementation body.

(3) In sub-paragraph (2)(b)(iii) "implementation body" has the same meaning as in section 55 of the Northern Ireland Act 1998 (see subsection (3) of that section).

Minister of the Crown power in relation to devolved authorities

4. A Minister of the Crown may by regulations—

(a) prescribe circumstances in which, or functions in relation to which, a devolved authority is to be regarded as being an appropriate authority for the purposes of paragraph 1;

(b) provide that a devolved authority that is regarded as being an appropriate authority under regulations made under paragraph (a) may only make regulations under paragraph 1, by virtue of being so regarded, with the consent of a Minister of the Crown;

(c) prescribe circumstances in which, or functions in relation to which, a devolved authority may, despite paragraph 3(2), make regulations under paragraph 1 without the consent of a Minister of the Crown.

Time limit for making certain provision

5. (1) Subject to [sub-paragraphs (2) and (2A)], no regulations may be made under paragraph 1 after the end of the period of two years beginning with [IP completion day].

(2) After the end of that period, regulations may be made under paragraph 1 for the purposes of—

(a) revoking any provision made under that paragraph,

(b) altering the amount of any of the fees or charges that are to be charged under any provision made under that paragraph,

(c) altering how any of the fees or charges that are to be charged under any provision made under that paragraph are to be determined, or

(d) otherwise altering the fees or charges that may be charged in relation to anything in respect of which fees or charges may be charged under any provision made under that paragraph.

[(2A) This paragraph does not apply in relation to regulations made under paragraph 1(1)(aa) or (ab).]

(3) This paragraph does not affect the continuation in force of any regulations made at or before the end of the period mentioned in sub-paragraph (1) (including the exercise after the end of that period of any power conferred by regulations made under that paragraph at or before the end of that period).

Relationship to other powers

6. This Part does not affect the powers under [sections 8 to 8C] or Schedule 2, or any other power exercisable apart from this Part, to require the payment of, or to make other provision in relation to, fees or other charges.

NOTES

Para 1: sub-paras (aa), (ab) were inserted by the European Union (Withdrawal Agreement) Act 2020, s 28, as from 19 May 2020. Sub-para (1)(b) and the preceding word were repealed by the European Union (Withdrawal Agreement) Act 2020, s 41(4), Sch 5, Pt 2, paras 38, 47(1), (2), as from 23 January 2020.

Para 5: the words in the first pair of square brackets in sub-para (1) were substituted, and sub-para (2A) was inserted, by the European Union (Withdrawal Agreement) Act 2020, s 28, as from 19 May 2020. The words in the second pair of square brackets in sub-para (1) were substituted by the European Union (Withdrawal Agreement) Act 2020, s 41(4), Sch 5, Pt 2, paras 38, 47(1), (3), as from exit day (as defined in s 20 of this Act).

Para 6: words in square brackets substituted by the European Union (Withdrawal Agreement) Act 2020, s 41(4), Sch 5, Pt 2, paras 38, 47(1), (4), as from 23 January 2020.

National Assembly for Wales: as to the renaming of the National Assembly for Wales, see the note at **[12.28]**.

Regulations: the Financial Regulators' Powers (Technical Standards etc) (Amendment etc) (EU Exit) Regulations 2018, SI 2018/1115; the EEA Passport Rights (Amendment, etc, and Transitional Provisions) (EU Exit) Regulations 2018, SI 2018/1149; the Financial Services and Markets Act 2000 (Amendment) (EU Exit) Regulations 2019, SI 2019/632 at **[12.109]**; the Uncertificated Securities (Amendment and EU Exit) Regulations 2019, SI 2019/679 at **[12.123]**; the International Accounting Standards and European Public Limited-Liability Company (Amendment etc) (EU Exit) Regulations 2019, SI 2019/685 at **[12.130]**; the Financial Services (Miscellaneous) (Amendment) (EU Exit) (No 3) Regulations 2019, SI 2019/1390. Other Regulations made under this Part are outside the scope of this work.

PART 2 MODIFYING PRE-EXIT FEES OR CHARGES

Power to modify pre-exit fees or charges

[12.40]

7. (1) Sub-paragraph (2) applies where any subordinate legislation contains provision ("the charging provision") for, or in connection with, the charging of fees or other charges that—

(a) was made under section 2(2) of the European Communities Act 1972, section 56 of the Finance Act 1973 or this Part, and

(b) forms part of retained EU law.

(2) Any appropriate authority may by regulations make provision ("the proposed modification") modifying the subordinate legislation for the purposes of—

(a) revoking the charging provision,

(b) altering the amount of any of the fees or charges that are to be charged,

(c) altering how any of the fees or charges are to be determined, or

(d) otherwise altering the fees or charges that may be charged in relation to anything in respect of which fees or charges may be charged under the charging provision.

Meaning of "appropriate authority"

8. In this Part an "appropriate authority" means a Minister of the Crown, or devolved authority, that could have made the proposed modification—

(a) under section 2(2) of the European Communities Act 1972 immediately before [IP completion day], or

(b) under section 56 of the Finance Act 1973 immediately before the amendment of that section by paragraph 17 of Schedule 8.

Restriction on exercise of power

9. (1) Where the charging provision consists solely of 1972 Act provision, regulations under this Part may not impose or increase taxation.

(2) In sub-paragraph (1) "1972 Act provision" means—

(a) provision that is made under section 2(2) of the European Communities Act 1972 and not under section 56 of the Finance Act 1973, including such provision as modified under this Part, or

(b) provision that is made under this Part and is incidental to, or supplements or replaces, provision within paragraph (a).

Requirement for consent

10. If a Minister of the Crown—

(a) is an appropriate authority, and

(b) immediately before the amendment of section 56 of the Finance Act 1973 by paragraph 17 of Schedule 8 could only have made the proposed modification under that section,

the Minister may only make that modification under this Part with the consent of the Treasury.

Relationship to other powers

11. This Part does not affect the powers under [sections 8 to 8C] or Schedule 2, or any other power exercisable apart from this Part, to require the payment of, or to make other provision in relation to, fees or other charges.

NOTES

Para 8: words in square brackets substituted by the European Union (Withdrawal Agreement) Act 2020, s 41(4), Sch 5, Pt 2, paras 38, 47(1), (5), as from exit day (as defined in s 20 of this Act).

Para 11: words in square brackets substituted by the European Union (Withdrawal Agreement) Act 2020, s 41(4), Sch 5, Pt 2, paras 38, 47(1), (6), as from 23 January 2020.

Regulations: Regulations made under this Part are outside the scope of this work.

SCHEDULE 5
PUBLICATION AND RULES OF EVIDENCE

Section 15(1) and (2)

PART 1 PUBLICATION OF RETAINED DIRECT EU LEGISLATION ETC

Things that must or may be published

[12.41]

1. (1) The Queen's Printer must make arrangements for the publication of—

(a) each relevant instrument that has been published before [IP completion day] by an EU entity, and

(b) the relevant international agreements.

(2) In this paragraph—

"relevant instrument" means—

(a) an EU regulation,

(b) an EU decision, and

(c) EU tertiary legislation;

"relevant international agreements" means—

(a) the Treaty on European Union,

(b) the Treaty on the Functioning of the European Union,

(c) the Euratom Treaty, and

(d) the EEA agreement.

(3) The Queen's Printer may make arrangements for the publication of—

(a) any decision of, or expression of opinion by, the European Court, or

(b) any other document published by an EU entity.

(4) The Queen's Printer may make arrangements for the publication of anything which the Queen's Printer considers may be useful in connection with anything published under this paragraph.

(5) This paragraph does not require the publication of—

(a) anything repealed before [IP completion day], or

(b) any modifications made on or after [IP completion day].

Exceptions from duty to publish

2. (1) A Minister of the Crown may create an exception from the duty under paragraph 1(1) in respect of a relevant instrument if satisfied that it has not become (or will not become, on [IP completion day]) retained direct EU legislation.

(2) An exception is created by giving a direction to the Queen's Printer specifying the instrument or category of instruments that are excepted.

(3) A Minister of the Crown must publish any direction under this paragraph.

(4) In this paragraph—

"instrument" includes part of an instrument;

"relevant instrument" has the meaning given by paragraph 1(2).

NOTES

Commencement: 4 July 2018 (para 2); 3 July 2019 (para 1).

All amendments to this Part were made by the European Union (Withdrawal Agreement) Act 2020, s 41(4), Sch 5, Pt 2, paras 38, 48(1), (2), as from exit day (as defined in s 20 of this Act).

PART 2 RULES OF EVIDENCE

Questions as to meaning of EU law

[12.42]

3. (1) Where it is necessary [in legal proceedings] to decide a question as to—

(a) the meaning or effect in EU law of any of the EU Treaties or any other treaty relating to the EU, or

(b) the validity, meaning or effect in EU law of any EU instrument,

the question is to be treated . . . as a question of law.

(2) In this paragraph—

. . .

"treaty" includes—

(a) any international agreement, and

(b) any protocol or annex to a treaty or international agreement.

Power to make provision about judicial notice and admissibility

4. (1) A Minister of the Crown may by regulations—

(a) make provision enabling or requiring judicial notice to be taken of a relevant matter, or

(b) provide for the admissibility in any legal proceedings of specified evidence of—

(i) a relevant matter, or

(ii) instruments or documents issued by or in the custody of an EU entity.

(2) Regulations under sub-paragraph (1)(b) may provide that evidence is admissible only where specified conditions are met (for example, conditions as to certification of documents).

(3) Regulations under this paragraph may modify any provision made by or under an enactment.

(4) In sub-paragraph (3) "enactment" does not include primary legislation passed or made after [IP completion day].

(5) For the purposes of this paragraph each of the following is a "relevant matter"—

(a) retained EU law,

(b) EU law,

(c) the EEA agreement,
[(ca) the EEA EFTA separation agreement,
(cb) the Swiss citizens' rights agreement,
(cc) the withdrawal agreement,] and
(d) anything which is specified in the regulations and which relates to a matter mentioned in paragraph (a), (b)[, (c), (ca), (cb) or (cc)].

NOTES

Commencement: 4 July 2018 (para 4); IP completion (as defined in the European Union (Withdrawal Agreement) Act 2020, s 39) (para 3).

Para 3: words in square brackets substituted, and words omitted repealed, by the European Union (Withdrawal Agreement) Act 2020, s 41(4), Sch 5, Pt 2, paras 38, 48(1), (3), as from IP completion day (as defined in the European Union (Withdrawal Agreement) Act 2020, s 39).

Para 4: all amendments to this paragraph were made by the European Union (Withdrawal Agreement) Act 2020, s 41(4), Sch 5, Pt 2, paras 38, 48(1), (4), as from exit day (as defined in s 20 of this Act).

SCHEDULE 6
INSTRUMENTS WHICH ARE EXEMPT EU INSTRUMENTS

Section 20(1)

EU decisions

[12.43]

1. (1) . . .

(2) If any decision under Title V or former Title V of the Treaty on European Union is a decision within the meaning of Article 288 of the Treaty on the Functioning of the European Union (and accordingly falls within the definition of "EU decision" in section 20(1)), it is "an exempt EU instrument".

(3) In sub-paragraph (2), the reference to former Title V of the Treaty on European Union is a reference to that Title as it had effect at any time before the coming into force of the Treaty of Lisbon.

EU regulations

2. . . .

EU tertiary legislation

3. EU tertiary legislation is "an exempt EU instrument" so far as it is made under—
(a) an EU decision . . . which is an exempt EU instrument, . . .
(b) . . .

Interpretation

4. . . .

NOTES

Words omitted repealed by the European Union (Withdrawal Agreement) Act 2020, s 41(4), Sch 5, Pt 2, paras 38, 49, as from exit day (as defined in s 20 of this Act).

SCHEDULE 7
REGULATIONS

Section 22

PART 1 SCRUTINY OF POWERS TO DEAL WITH DEFICIENCIES

Scrutiny of regulations made by Minister of the Crown or devolved authority acting alone

[12.44]

1. (1) A statutory instrument containing regulations under section 8(1) which contain provision falling within sub-paragraph (2) may not be made unless a draft of the instrument has been laid before, and approved by a resolution of, each House of Parliament.

(2) Provision falls within this sub-paragraph if it—
(a) provides for any function of an EU entity or public authority in a member State of making an instrument of a legislative character to be exercisable instead by a public authority in the United Kingdom,
(b) relates to a fee in respect of a function exercisable by a public authority in the United Kingdom,
(c) creates, or widens the scope of, a criminal offence, or
(d) creates or amends a power to legislate.

(3) Any other statutory instrument containing regulations under section 8(1) is (if a draft of the instrument has not been laid before, and approved by a resolution of, each House of Parliament) subject to annulment in pursuance of a resolution of either House of Parliament.

(4) See paragraph 3 for restrictions on the choice of procedure under sub-paragraph (3).

(5) A statutory instrument containing regulations under section 8(3)(b) (including as applied by paragraph 1(3) of Schedule 2) may not be made unless a draft of the instrument has been laid before, and approved by a resolution of, each House of Parliament.

(6) Regulations under Part 1 of Schedule 2 of the Scottish Ministers which contain provision falling within sub-paragraph (2) are subject to the affirmative procedure (see section 29 of the Interpretation and Legislative Reform (Scotland) Act 2010 (asp 10)).

(7) Any other regulations under Part 1 of Schedule 2 of the Scottish Ministers are (if they have not been subject to the affirmative procedure) subject to the negative procedure (see section 28 of the Interpretation and Legislative Reform (Scotland) Act 2010).

(8) A statutory instrument containing regulations under Part 1 of Schedule 2 of the Welsh Ministers which contain provision falling within sub-paragraph (2) may not be made unless a draft of the instrument has been laid before, and approved by a resolution of, the National Assembly for Wales.

(9) Any other statutory instrument containing regulations under Part 1 of Schedule 2 of the Welsh Ministers is (if a draft of the instrument has not been laid before, and approved by a resolution of, the National Assembly for Wales) subject to annulment in pursuance of a resolution of the Assembly.

(10) See paragraph 4 for restrictions on the choice of procedure under sub-paragraph (9).

(11) Regulations under Part 1 of Schedule 2 of a Northern Ireland department which contain provision falling within sub-paragraph (2) may not be made unless a draft of the regulations has been laid before, and approved by a resolution of, the Northern Ireland Assembly.

(12) Any other regulations under Part 1 of Schedule 2 of a Northern Ireland department are (if a draft of the regulations has not been laid before, and approved by a resolution of, the Northern Ireland Assembly) subject to negative resolution within the meaning of section 41(6) of the Interpretation Act (Northern Ireland) 1954 as if they were a statutory instrument within the meaning of that Act.

(13) This paragraph—

(a) does not apply to regulations to which paragraph 2 applies, and

(b) is subject to paragraphs 5 to 8.

Scrutiny of regulations made by Minister of the Crown and devolved authority acting jointly

2. (1) This paragraph applies to regulations under Part 1 of Schedule 2 of a Minister of the Crown acting jointly with a devolved authority.

(2) The procedure provided for by sub-paragraph (3) or (4) applies in relation to regulations to which this paragraph applies as well as any other procedure provided for by this paragraph which is applicable in relation to the regulations concerned.

(3) A statutory instrument containing regulations to which this paragraph applies which contain provision falling within paragraph 1(2) may not be made unless a draft of the instrument has been laid before, and approved by a resolution of, each House of Parliament.

(4) Any other statutory instrument containing regulations to which this paragraph applies is (if a draft of the instrument has not been laid before, and approved by a resolution of, each House of Parliament) subject to annulment in pursuance of a resolution of either House of Parliament.

(5) Regulations to which this paragraph applies which are made jointly with the Scottish Ministers and contain provision falling within paragraph 1(2) are subject to the affirmative procedure.

(6) Any other regulations to which this paragraph applies which are made jointly with the Scottish Ministers are (if they have not been subject to the affirmative procedure) subject to the negative procedure.

(7) Section 29 of the Interpretation and Legislative Reform (Scotland) Act 2010 (asp 10) (affirmative procedure) applies in relation to regulations to which sub-paragraph (5) or (6) applies and which are subject to the affirmative procedure as it applies in relation to devolved subordinate legislation (within the meaning of Part 2 of that Act) which is subject to the affirmative procedure (but as if references to a Scottish statutory instrument were references to a statutory instrument).

(8) Sections 28(2), (3) and (8) and 31 of the Interpretation and Legislative Reform (Scotland) Act 2010 (negative procedure etc) apply in relation to regulations to which sub-paragraph (6) applies and which are subject to the negative procedure as they apply in relation to devolved subordinate legislation (within the meaning of Part 2 of that Act) which is subject to the negative procedure (but as if references to a Scottish statutory instrument were references to a statutory instrument).

(9) Section 32 of the Interpretation and Legislative Reform (Scotland) Act 2010 (laying) applies in relation to the laying before the Scottish Parliament of a statutory instrument containing regulations to which sub-paragraph (5) or (6) applies as it applies in relation to the laying before that Parliament of a Scottish statutory instrument (within the meaning of Part 2 of that Act).

(10) A statutory instrument containing regulations to which this paragraph applies which are made jointly with the Welsh Ministers and contain provision falling within paragraph 1(2) may not be made unless a draft of the instrument has been laid before, and approved by a resolution of, the National Assembly for Wales.

(11) Any other statutory instrument containing regulations to which this paragraph applies which are made jointly with the Welsh Ministers is (if a draft of the instrument has not been laid before, and approved by a resolution of, the National Assembly for Wales) subject to annulment in pursuance of a resolution of the Assembly.

(12) Regulations to which this paragraph applies which are made jointly with a Northern Ireland department and contain provision falling within paragraph 1(2) may not be made unless a draft of the regulations has been laid before, and approved by a resolution of, the Northern Ireland Assembly.

(13) Any other regulations to which this paragraph applies which are made jointly with a Northern Ireland department are (if a draft of the regulations has not been laid before, and approved by a resolution of, the Northern Ireland Assembly) subject to negative resolution within the meaning of section 41(6) of the Interpretation Act (Northern Ireland) 1954 as if they were a statutory instrument within the meaning of that Act.

(14) If in accordance with sub-paragraph (4), (6), (11) or (13)—

(a) either House of Parliament resolves that an address be presented to Her Majesty praying that an instrument be annulled, or

(b) a relevant devolved legislature resolves that an instrument be annulled,

nothing further is to be done under the instrument after the date of the resolution and Her Majesty may by Order in Council revoke the instrument.

(15) In sub-paragraph (14) "relevant devolved legislature" means—

(a) in the case of regulations made jointly with the Scottish Ministers, the Scottish Parliament,

(b) in the case of regulations made jointly with the Welsh Ministers, the National Assembly for Wales, and
(c) in the case of regulations made jointly with a Northern Ireland department, the Northern Ireland Assembly.

(16) Sub-paragraph (14) does not affect the validity of anything previously done under the instrument or prevent the making of a new instrument.

(17) Sub-paragraphs (14) [to (16)] apply in place of provision made by any other enactment about the effect of such a resolution.

Parliamentary committee to sift certain deficiencies regulations of a Minister of the Crown

3. (1) Sub-paragraph (2) applies if a Minister of the Crown who is to make a statutory instrument to which paragraph 1(3) applies is of the opinion that the appropriate procedure for the instrument is for it to be subject to annulment in pursuance of a resolution of either House of Parliament.

(2) The Minister may not make the instrument so that it is subject to that procedure unless—
(a) condition 1 is met, and
(b) either condition 2 or 3 is met.

(3) Condition 1 is that a Minister of the Crown—
(a) has made a statement in writing to the effect that in the Minister's opinion the instrument should be subject to annulment in pursuance of a resolution of either House of Parliament, and
(b) has laid before each House of Parliament—
(i) a draft of the instrument, and
(ii) a memorandum setting out the statement and the reasons for the Minister's opinion.

(4) Condition 2 is that a committee of the House of Commons charged with doing so and a committee of the House of Lords charged with doing so have, within the relevant period, each made a recommendation as to the appropriate procedure for the instrument.

(5) Condition 3 is that the relevant period has ended without condition 2 being met.

(6) Sub-paragraph (7) applies if—
(a) a committee makes a recommendation as mentioned in sub-paragraph (4) within the relevant period,
(b) the recommendation is that the appropriate procedure for the instrument is for a draft of it to be laid before, and approved by a resolution of, each House of Parliament before it is made, and
(c) the Minister who is to make the instrument is nevertheless of the opinion that the appropriate procedure for the instrument is for it to be subject to annulment in pursuance of a resolution of either House of Parliament.

(7) Before the instrument is made, the Minister must make a statement explaining why the Minister does not agree with the recommendation of the committee.

(8) If the Minister fails to make a statement required by sub-paragraph (7) before the instrument is made, a Minister of the Crown must make a statement explaining why the Minister has failed to do so.

(9) A statement under sub-paragraph (7) or (8) must be made in writing and be published in such manner as the Minister making it considers appropriate.

(10) In this paragraph "the relevant period" means the period—
(a) beginning with the first day on which both Houses of Parliament are sitting after the day on which the draft instrument was laid before each House as mentioned in sub-paragraph (3)(b)(i), and
(b) ending with whichever of the following is the later—
(i) the end of the period of 10 Commons sitting days beginning with that first day, and
(ii) the end of the period of 10 Lords sitting days beginning with that first day.

(11) For the purposes of sub-paragraph (10)—
(a) where a draft of an instrument is laid before each House of Parliament on different days, the later day is to be taken as the day on which it is laid before both Houses,
(b), (c) . . .

. . .

(12) Nothing in this paragraph prevents a Minister of the Crown from deciding at any time before a statutory instrument to which paragraph 1(3) applies is made that another procedure should apply in relation to the instrument (whether under paragraph 1(3) or 5).

(13) Section 6(1) of the Statutory Instruments Act 1946 (alternative procedure for certain instruments laid in draft before Parliament) does not apply in relation to any statutory instrument to which this paragraph applies.

Committee of the National Assembly for Wales to sift certain deficiencies regulations of Welsh Ministers

4. (1) Sub-paragraph (2) applies if the Welsh Ministers are to make a statutory instrument to which paragraph 1(9) applies and are of the opinion that the appropriate procedure for the instrument is for it to be subject to annulment in pursuance of a resolution of the National Assembly for Wales.

(2) The Welsh Ministers may not make the instrument so that it is subject to that procedure unless—
(a) condition 1 is met, and
(b) either condition 2 or 3 is met.

(3) Condition 1 is that the Welsh Ministers—
(a) have made a statement in writing to the effect that in their opinion the instrument should be subject to annulment in pursuance of a resolution of the National Assembly for Wales, and
(b) have laid before the Assembly—
(i) a draft of the instrument, and
(ii) a memorandum setting out the statement and the reasons for the Welsh Ministers' opinion.

(4) Condition 2 is that a committee of the National Assembly for Wales charged with doing so has made a recommendation as to the appropriate procedure for the instrument.

(5) Condition 3 is that the period of 14 days beginning with the first day after the day on which the draft instrument was laid before the National Assembly for Wales as mentioned in sub-paragraph (3) has ended without any recommendation being made as mentioned in sub-paragraph (4).

(6) In calculating the period of 14 days, no account is to be taken of any time during which the National Assembly for Wales is—

(a) dissolved, or

(b) in recess for more than four days.

(7) Nothing in this paragraph prevents the Welsh Ministers from deciding at any time before a statutory instrument to which paragraph 1(9) applies is made that another procedure should apply to the instrument (whether under paragraph 1(9) or 7).

(8) Section 6(1) of the Statutory Instruments Act 1946 as applied by section 11A of that Act (alternative procedure for certain instruments laid in draft before the Assembly) does not apply in relation to any statutory instrument to which this paragraph applies.

(9) . . .

Scrutiny procedure in certain urgent deficiencies cases: Ministers of the Crown

5. (1) Sub-paragraph (2) applies to—

(a) a statutory instrument to which paragraph 1(1) applies, or

(b) a statutory instrument to which paragraph 1(3) applies which would not otherwise be made without a draft of the instrument being laid before, and approved by a resolution of, each House of Parliament.

(2) The instrument may be made without a draft of the instrument being laid before, and approved by a resolution of, each House of Parliament if it contains a declaration that the Minister of the Crown concerned is of the opinion that, by reason of urgency, it is necessary to make the regulations without a draft being so laid and approved.

(3) After an instrument is made in accordance with sub-paragraph (2), it must be laid before each House of Parliament.

(4) Regulations contained in an instrument made in accordance with sub-paragraph (2) cease to have effect at the end of the period of 28 days beginning with the day on which the instrument is made unless, during that period, the instrument is approved by a resolution of each House of Parliament.

(5) In calculating the period of 28 days, no account is to be taken of any time during which—

(a) Parliament is dissolved or prorogued, or

(b) either House of Parliament is adjourned for more than four days.

(6) If regulations cease to have effect as a result of sub-paragraph (4), that does not—

(a) affect the validity of anything previously done under the regulations, or

(b) prevent the making of new regulations.

(7) Sub-paragraph (8) applies to a statutory instrument to which paragraph 1(3) applies where the Minister of the Crown who is to make the instrument is of the opinion that the appropriate procedure for the instrument is for it to be subject to annulment in pursuance of a resolution of either House of Parliament.

(8) Paragraph 3 does not apply in relation to the instrument if the instrument contains a declaration that the Minister is of the opinion that, by reason of urgency, it is necessary to make the regulations without meeting the requirements of that paragraph.

Scrutiny procedure in certain urgent deficiencies cases: devolved authorities

6. (1) This paragraph applies to—

(a) regulations to which paragraph 1(6) applies, or

(b) regulations to which paragraph 1(7) applies which would not otherwise be made without being subject to the affirmative procedure.

(2) The regulations may be made without being subject to the affirmative procedure if the regulations contain a declaration that the Scottish Ministers are of the opinion that, by reason of urgency, it is necessary to make the regulations without them being subject to that procedure.

(3) After regulations are made in accordance with sub-paragraph (2), they must be laid before the Scottish Parliament.

(4) Regulations made in accordance with sub-paragraph (2) cease to have effect at the end of the period of 28 days beginning with the day on which they are made unless, during that period, the regulations are approved by resolution of the Scottish Parliament.

(5) In calculating the period of 28 days, no account is to be taken of any time during which the Scottish Parliament is—

(a) dissolved, or

(b) in recess for more than four days.

(6) If regulations cease to have effect as a result of sub-paragraph (4), that does not—

(a) affect the validity of anything previously done under the regulations, or

(b) prevent the making of new regulations.

(7) . . .

7. (1) Sub-paragraph (2) applies to—

(a) a statutory instrument to which paragraph 1(8) applies, or

(b) a statutory instrument to which paragraph 1(9) applies which would not otherwise be made without a draft of the instrument being laid before, and approved by a resolution of, the National Assembly for Wales.

(2) The instrument may be made without a draft of the instrument being laid before, and approved by a resolution of, the National Assembly for Wales if it contains a declaration that the Welsh Ministers are of the opinion that, by reason of urgency, it is necessary to make the regulations without a draft being so laid and approved.

(3) After an instrument is made in accordance with sub-paragraph (2), it must be laid before the National Assembly for Wales.

(4) Regulations contained in an instrument made in accordance with sub-paragraph (2) cease to have effect at the end of the period of 28 days beginning with the day on which the instrument is made unless, during that period, the instrument is approved by a resolution of the National Assembly for Wales.

(5) In calculating the period of 28 days, no account is to be taken of any time during which the National Assembly for Wales is—

(a) dissolved, or
(b) in recess for more than four days.

(6) If regulations cease to have effect as a result of sub-paragraph (4), that does not—

(a) affect the validity of anything previously done under the regulations, or
(b) prevent the making of new regulations.

(7) Sub-paragraph (8) applies to a statutory instrument to which paragraph 1(9) applies where the Welsh Ministers are of the opinion that the appropriate procedure for the instrument is for it to be subject to annulment in pursuance of a resolution of the National Assembly for Wales.

(8) Paragraph 4 does not apply in relation to the instrument if the instrument contains a declaration that the Welsh Ministers are of the opinion that, by reason of urgency, it is necessary to make the regulations without meeting the requirements of that paragraph.

(9) . . .

8. (1) This paragraph applies to—

(a) regulations to which paragraph 1(11) applies, or
(b) regulations to which paragraph 1(12) applies which would not otherwise be made without a draft of the regulations being laid before, and approved by a resolution of, the Northern Ireland Assembly.

(2) The regulations may be made without a draft of the regulations being laid before, and approved by a resolution of, the Northern Ireland Assembly if they contain a declaration that the Northern Ireland department concerned is of the opinion that, by reason of urgency, it is necessary to make the regulations without a draft being so laid and approved.

(3) After regulations are made in accordance with sub-paragraph (2), they must be laid before the Northern Ireland Assembly.

(4) Regulations made in accordance with sub-paragraph (2) cease to have effect at the end of the period of 28 days beginning with the day on which they are made unless, during that period, the regulations are approved by a resolution of the Northern Ireland Assembly.

(5) In calculating the period of 28 days, no account is to be taken of any time during which the Northern Ireland Assembly is—

(a) dissolved,
(b) in recess for more than four days, or
(c) adjourned for more than six days.

(6) If regulations cease to have effect as a result of sub-paragraph (4), that does not—

(a) affect the validity of anything previously done under the regulations, or
(b) prevent the making of new regulations.

(7) . . .

NOTES

All amendments to this Part were made by the European Union (Withdrawal Agreement) Act 2020, s 41(4), Sch 5, Pt 2, paras 38, 50, as from 23 January 2020.

National Assembly for Wales: as to the renaming of the National Assembly for Wales, see the note at **[12.28]**.

[PART 1A SCRUTINY OF SPECIFIC POWERS RELATING TO WITHDRAWAL AGREEMENT ETC

Powers in connection with Part 4 of the withdrawal agreement

[12.45]

8A. A statutory instrument containing regulations under section 1A(3)(a)(ii) may not be made unless a draft of the instrument has been laid before, and approved by a resolution of, each House of Parliament.

8B. (1) A statutory instrument containing regulations under section 8A which amend, repeal or revoke—

(a) primary legislation, or
(b) retained direct principal EU legislation,

may not be made unless a draft of the instrument has been laid before, and approved by a resolution of, each House of Parliament.

(2) Any other statutory instrument containing regulations under section 8A is subject to annulment in pursuance of a resolution of either House of Parliament.

(3) Regulations under Part 1A of Schedule 2 of the Scottish Ministers acting alone which amend, repeal or revoke—

(a) primary legislation, or
(b) retained direct principal EU legislation,

are subject to the affirmative procedure (see section 29 of the Interpretation and Legislative Reform (Scotland) Act 2010 (asp 10)).

(4) Any other regulations under Part 1A of Schedule 2 of the Scottish Ministers acting alone are subject to the negative procedure (see section 28 of the Interpretation and Legislative Reform (Scotland) Act 2010).

(5) A statutory instrument containing regulations under Part 1A of Schedule 2 of the Welsh Ministers acting alone which amend, repeal or revoke—

(a) primary legislation, or

(b) retained direct principal EU legislation,

may not be made unless a draft of the instrument has been laid before, and approved by a resolution of, the National Assembly for Wales.

(6) Any other statutory instrument containing regulations under Part 1A of Schedule 2 of the Welsh Ministers acting alone is subject to annulment in pursuance of a resolution of the National Assembly for Wales.

(7) Regulations under Part 1A of Schedule 2 of a Northern Ireland department acting alone which amend, repeal or revoke—

(a) primary legislation, or

(b) retained direct principal EU legislation,

may not be made unless a draft of the regulations has been laid before, and approved by a resolution of, the Northern Ireland Assembly.

(8) Any other regulations under Part 1A of Schedule 2 of a Northern Ireland department acting alone are subject to negative resolution within the meaning of section 41(6) of the Interpretation Act (Northern Ireland) 1954 as if they were a statutory instrument within the meaning of that Act.

8C. (1) This paragraph applies to regulations under Part 1A of Schedule 2 of a Minister of the Crown acting jointly with a devolved authority.

(2) The procedure provided for by sub-paragraph (3) or (4) applies in relation to regulations to which this paragraph applies as well as any other procedure provided for by this paragraph which is applicable in relation to the regulations concerned.

(3) A statutory instrument containing regulations to which this paragraph applies which amend, repeal or revoke—

(a) primary legislation, or

(b) retained direct principal EU legislation,

may not be made unless a draft of the instrument has been laid before, and approved by a resolution of, each House of Parliament.

(4) Any other statutory instrument containing regulations to which this paragraph applies is subject to annulment in pursuance of a resolution of either House of Parliament.

(5) Regulations to which this paragraph applies which are made jointly with the Scottish Ministers and amend, repeal or revoke—

(a) primary legislation, or

(b) retained direct principal EU legislation,

are subject to the affirmative procedure.

(6) Any other regulations to which this paragraph applies which are made jointly with the Scottish Ministers are subject to the negative procedure.

(7) Section 29 of the Interpretation and Legislative Reform (Scotland) Act 2010 (affirmative procedure) applies in relation to regulations to which sub-paragraph (5) applies as it applies in relation to devolved subordinate legislation (within the meaning of Part 2 of that Act) which is subject to the affirmative procedure (but as if references to a Scottish statutory instrument were references to a statutory instrument).

(8) Sections 28(2), (3) and (8) and 31 of the Interpretation and Legislative Reform (Scotland) Act 2010 (negative procedure etc) apply in relation to regulations to which sub-paragraph (6) applies as they apply in relation to devolved subordinate legislation (within the meaning of Part 2 of that Act) which is subject to the negative procedure (but as if references to a Scottish statutory instrument were references to a statutory instrument).

(9) Section 32 of the Interpretation and Legislative Reform (Scotland) Act 2010 (laying) applies in relation to the laying before the Scottish Parliament of a statutory instrument containing regulations to which sub-paragraph (5) or (6) applies as it applies in relation to the laying before that Parliament of a Scottish statutory instrument (within the meaning of Part 2 of that Act).

(10) A statutory instrument containing regulations to which this paragraph applies which are made jointly with the Welsh Ministers and amend, repeal or revoke—

(a) primary legislation, or

(b) retained direct principal EU legislation,

may not be made unless a draft of the instrument has been laid before, and approved by a resolution of, the National Assembly for Wales.

(11) Any other statutory instrument containing regulations to which this paragraph applies which are made jointly with the Welsh Ministers is subject to annulment in pursuance of a resolution of the National Assembly for Wales.

(12) Regulations to which this paragraph applies which are made jointly with a Northern Ireland department and amend, repeal or revoke—

(a) primary legislation, or

(b) retained direct principal EU legislation,

may not be made unless a draft of the regulations has been laid before, and approved by a resolution of, the Northern Ireland Assembly.

(13) Any other regulations to which this paragraph applies which are made jointly with a Northern Ireland department are subject to negative resolution within the meaning of section 41(6) of the Interpretation Act (Northern Ireland) 1954 as if they were a statutory instrument within the meaning of that Act.

(14) If in accordance with sub-paragraph (4), (6), (11) or (13)—

(a) either House of Parliament resolves that an address be presented to Her Majesty praying that an instrument be annulled, or

(b) a relevant devolved legislature resolves that an instrument be annulled,

nothing further is to be done under the instrument after the date of the resolution and Her Majesty may by Order in Council revoke the instrument.

(15) In sub-paragraph (14) "relevant devolved legislature" means—

(a) in the case of regulations made jointly with the Scottish Ministers, the Scottish Parliament,
(b) in the case of regulations made jointly with the Welsh Ministers, the National Assembly for Wales, and
(c) in the case of regulations made jointly with a Northern Ireland department, the Northern Ireland Assembly.

(16) Sub-paragraph (14) does not affect the validity of anything previously done under the instrument or prevent the making of a new instrument.

(17) Sub-paragraphs (14) to (16) apply in place of provision made by any other enactment about the effect of such a resolution.

Powers in connection with other separation issues in the withdrawal agreement etc

8D. (1) A statutory instrument containing regulations under section 8B which amend, repeal or revoke—
(a) primary legislation, or
(b) retained direct principal EU legislation,
may not be made unless a draft of the instrument has been laid before, and approved by a resolution of, each House of Parliament.

(2) Any other statutory instrument containing regulations under section 8B is subject to annulment in pursuance of a resolution of either House of Parliament.

(3) Regulations under Part 1B of Schedule 2 of the Scottish Ministers acting alone which amend, repeal or revoke—
(a) primary legislation, or
(b) retained direct principal EU legislation,
are subject to the affirmative procedure (see section 29 of the Interpretation and Legislative Reform (Scotland) Act 2010).

(4) Any other regulations under Part 1B of Schedule 2 of the Scottish Ministers acting alone are subject to the negative procedure (see section 28 of the Interpretation and Legislative Reform (Scotland) Act 2010).

(5) A statutory instrument containing regulations under Part 1B of Schedule 2 of the Welsh Ministers acting alone which amend, repeal or revoke—
(a) primary legislation, or
(b) retained direct principal EU legislation,
may not be made unless a draft of the instrument has been laid before, and approved by a resolution of, the National Assembly for Wales.

(6) Any other statutory instrument containing regulations under Part 1B of Schedule 2 of the Welsh Ministers acting alone is subject to annulment in pursuance of a resolution of the National Assembly for Wales.

(7) Regulations under Part 1B of Schedule 2 of a Northern Ireland department acting alone which amend, repeal or revoke—
(a) primary legislation, or
(b) retained direct principal EU legislation,
may not be made unless a draft of the regulations has been laid before, and approved by a resolution of, the Northern Ireland Assembly.

(8) Any other regulations under Part 1B of Schedule 2 of a Northern Ireland department acting alone are subject to negative resolution within the meaning of section 41(6) of the Interpretation Act (Northern Ireland) 1954 as if they were a statutory instrument within the meaning of that Act.

8E. (1) This paragraph applies to regulations under Part 1B of Schedule 2 of a Minister of the Crown acting jointly with a devolved authority.

(2) The procedure provided for by sub-paragraph (3) or (4) applies in relation to regulations to which this paragraph applies as well as any other procedure provided for by this paragraph which is applicable in relation to the regulations concerned.

(3) A statutory instrument containing regulations to which this paragraph applies which amend, repeal or revoke—
(a) primary legislation, or
(b) retained direct principal EU legislation,
may not be made unless a draft of the instrument has been laid before, and approved by a resolution of, each House of Parliament.

(4) Any other statutory instrument containing regulations to which this paragraph applies is subject to annulment in pursuance of a resolution of either House of Parliament.

(5) Regulations to which this paragraph applies which are made jointly with the Scottish Ministers and amend, repeal or revoke—
(a) primary legislation, or
(b) retained direct principal EU legislation,
are subject to the affirmative procedure.

(6) Any other regulations to which this paragraph applies which are made jointly with the Scottish Ministers are subject to the negative procedure.

(7) Section 29 of the Interpretation and Legislative Reform (Scotland) Act 2010 (affirmative procedure) applies in relation to regulations to which sub-paragraph (5) applies as it applies in relation to devolved subordinate legislation (within the meaning of Part 2 of that Act) which is subject to the affirmative procedure (but as if references to a Scottish statutory instrument were references to a statutory instrument).

(8) Sections 28(2), (3) and (8) and 31 of the Interpretation and Legislative Reform (Scotland) Act 2010 (negative procedure etc) apply in relation to regulations to which sub-paragraph (6) applies as they apply in relation to devolved subordinate legislation (within the meaning of Part 2 of that Act) which is subject to the negative procedure (but as if references to a Scottish statutory instrument were references to a statutory instrument).

(9) Section 32 of the Interpretation and Legislative Reform (Scotland) Act 2010 (laying) applies in relation to the laying before the Scottish Parliament of a statutory instrument containing regulations to which sub-paragraph (5) or (6) applies as it applies in relation to the laying before that Parliament of a Scottish statutory instrument (within the meaning of Part 2 of that Act).

(10) A statutory instrument containing regulations to which this paragraph applies which are made jointly with the Welsh Ministers and amend, repeal or revoke—

(a) primary legislation, or

(b) retained direct principal EU legislation,

may not be made unless a draft of the instrument has been laid before, and approved by a resolution of, the National Assembly for Wales.

(11) Any other statutory instrument containing regulations to which this paragraph applies which are made jointly with the Welsh Ministers is subject to annulment in pursuance of a resolution of the National Assembly for Wales.

(12) Regulations to which this paragraph applies which are made jointly with a Northern Ireland department and amend, repeal or revoke—

(a) primary legislation, or

(b) retained direct principal EU legislation,

may not be made unless a draft of the regulations has been laid before, and approved by a resolution of, the Northern Ireland Assembly.

(13) Any other regulations to which this paragraph applies which are made jointly with a Northern Ireland department are subject to negative resolution within the meaning of section 41(6) of the Interpretation Act (Northern Ireland) 1954 as if they were a statutory instrument within the meaning of that Act.

(14) If in accordance with sub-paragraph (4), (6), (11) or (13)—

(a) either House of Parliament resolves that an address be presented to Her Majesty praying that an instrument be annulled, or

(b) a relevant devolved legislature resolves that an instrument be annulled,

nothing further is to be done under the instrument after the date of the resolution and Her Majesty may by Order in Council revoke the instrument.

(15) In sub-paragraph (14) "relevant devolved legislature" means—

(a) in the case of regulations made jointly with the Scottish Ministers, the Scottish Parliament,

(b) in the case of regulations made jointly with the Welsh Ministers, the National Assembly for Wales, and

(c) in the case of regulations made jointly with a Northern Ireland department, the Northern Ireland Assembly.

(16) Sub-paragraph (14) does not affect the validity of anything previously done under the instrument or prevent the making of a new instrument.

(17) Sub-paragraphs (14) to (16) apply in place of provision made by any other enactment about the effect of such a resolution.

Powers in connection with the Ireland/Northern Ireland Protocol in the withdrawal agreement

8F. (1) A statutory instrument containing regulations under section 8C(1) which contain provision falling within sub-paragraph (2) may not be made unless a draft of the instrument has been laid before, and approved by a resolution of, each House of Parliament.

(2) Provision falls within this sub-paragraph if it—

(a) amends, repeals or revokes primary legislation or retained direct principal EU legislation,

(b) establishes a public authority,

(c) relates to a fee in respect of a function exercisable by a public authority in the United Kingdom,

(d) creates, or widens the scope of, a criminal offence,

(e) creates or amends a power to legislate, or

(f) facilitates the access to the market within Great Britain of qualifying Northern Ireland goods.

(3) Any other statutory instrument containing regulations under section 8C(1) is subject to annulment in pursuance of a resolution of either House of Parliament.

(4) A statutory instrument containing regulations under section 8C(6) may not be made unless a draft of the instrument has been laid before, and approved by a resolution of, each House of Parliament.

(5) Regulations under Part 1C of Schedule 2 of the Scottish Ministers acting alone which contain provision falling within sub-paragraph (2) are subject to the affirmative procedure (see section 29 of the Interpretation and Legislative Reform (Scotland) Act 2010).

(6) Any other regulations under Part 1C of Schedule 2 of the Scottish Ministers acting alone are subject to the negative procedure (see section 28 of the Interpretation and Legislative Reform (Scotland) Act 2010).

(7) A statutory instrument containing regulations under Part 1C of Schedule 2 of the Welsh Ministers acting alone which contain provision falling within sub-paragraph (2) may not be made unless a draft of the instrument has been laid before, and approved by a resolution of, the National Assembly for Wales.

(8) Any other statutory instrument containing regulations under Part 1C of Schedule 2 of the Welsh Ministers acting alone is subject to annulment in pursuance of a resolution of the National Assembly for Wales.

(9) Regulations under Part 1C of Schedule 2 of a Northern Ireland department acting alone which contain provision falling within sub-paragraph (2) may not be made unless a draft of the regulations has been laid before, and approved by a resolution of, the Northern Ireland Assembly.

(10) Any other regulations under Part 1C of Schedule 2 of a Northern Ireland department acting alone are subject to negative resolution within the meaning of section 41(6) of the Interpretation Act (Northern Ireland) 1954 as if they were a statutory instrument within the meaning of that Act.

8G. (1) This paragraph applies to regulations under Part 1C of Schedule 2 of a Minister of the Crown acting jointly with a devolved authority.

(2) The procedure provided for by sub-paragraph (3) or (4) applies in relation to regulations to which this paragraph applies as well as any other procedure provided for by this paragraph which is applicable in relation to the regulations concerned.

(3) A statutory instrument containing regulations to which this paragraph applies which contain provision falling within paragraph 8F(2) may not be made unless a draft of the instrument has been laid before, and approved by a resolution of, each House of Parliament.

(4) Any other statutory instrument containing regulations to which this paragraph applies is subject to annulment in pursuance of a resolution of either House of Parliament.

(5) Regulations to which this paragraph applies which are made jointly with the Scottish Ministers and contain provision falling within paragraph 8F(2) are subject to the affirmative procedure.

(6) Any other regulations to which this paragraph applies which are made jointly with the Scottish Ministers are subject to the negative procedure.

(7) Section 29 of the Interpretation and Legislative Reform (Scotland) Act 2010 (affirmative procedure) applies in relation to regulations to which sub-paragraph (5) applies as it applies in relation to devolved subordinate legislation (within the meaning of Part 2 of that Act) which is subject to the affirmative procedure (but as if references to a Scottish statutory instrument were references to a statutory instrument).

(8) Sections 28(2), (3) and (8) and 31 of the Interpretation and Legislative Reform (Scotland) Act 2010 (negative procedure etc) apply in relation to regulations to which sub-paragraph (6) applies as they apply in relation to devolved subordinate legislation (within the meaning of Part 2 of that Act) which is subject to the negative procedure (but as if references to a Scottish statutory instrument were references to a statutory instrument).

(9) Section 32 of the Interpretation and Legislative Reform (Scotland) Act 2010 (laying) applies in relation to the laying before the Scottish Parliament of a statutory instrument containing regulations to which sub-paragraph (5) or (6) applies as it applies in relation to the laying before that Parliament of a Scottish statutory instrument (within the meaning of Part 2 of that Act).

(10) A statutory instrument containing regulations to which this paragraph applies which are made jointly with the Welsh Ministers and contain provision falling within paragraph 8F(2) may not be made unless a draft of the instrument has been laid before, and approved by a resolution of, the National Assembly for Wales.

(11) Any other statutory instrument containing regulations to which this paragraph applies which are made jointly with the Welsh Ministers is subject to annulment in pursuance of a resolution of the National Assembly for Wales.

(12) Regulations to which this paragraph applies which are made jointly with a Northern Ireland department and contain provision falling within paragraph 8F(2) may not be made unless a draft of the regulations has been laid before, and approved by a resolution of, the Northern Ireland Assembly.

(13) Any other regulations to which this paragraph applies which are made jointly with a Northern Ireland department are subject to negative resolution within the meaning of section 41(6) of the Interpretation Act (Northern Ireland) 1954 as if they were a statutory instrument within the meaning of that Act.

(14) If in accordance with sub-paragraph (4), (6), (11) or (13)—

(a) either House of Parliament resolves that an address be presented to Her Majesty praying that an instrument be annulled, or

(b) a relevant devolved legislature resolves that an instrument be annulled,

nothing further is to be done under the instrument after the date of the resolution and Her Majesty may by Order in Council revoke the instrument.

(15) In sub-paragraph (14) "relevant devolved legislature" means—

(a) in the case of regulations made jointly with the Scottish Ministers, the Scottish Parliament,

(b) in the case of regulations made jointly with the Welsh Ministers, the National Assembly for Wales, and

(c) in the case of regulations made jointly with a Northern Ireland department, the Northern Ireland Assembly.

(16) Sub-paragraph (14) does not affect the validity of anything previously done under the instrument or prevent the making of a new instrument.

(17) Sub-paragraphs (14) to (16) apply in place of provision made by any other enactment about the effect of such a resolution.]

NOTES

Commencement: see the note below.

Inserted by the European Union (Withdrawal Agreement) Act 2020, s 41(4), Sch 5, Pt 2, paras 38, 51, as from 23 January 2020 (for the purposes of making regulations under s 8A, or Part 1A of Schedule 2), and as from exit day (as defined in s 20 of this Act) (for the purposes of making regulations under s 1A(3)(a)(ii)). This Part came into force on 19 May 2020 for all other purposes.

National Assembly for Wales: as to the renaming of the National Assembly for Wales, see the note at **[12.28]**.

PART 2 SCRUTINY OF OTHER POWERS UNDER ACT

Power to enable challenges to validity of retained EU law

[12.46]

9. (1) A statutory instrument containing regulations under paragraph 1(2)(b) of Schedule 1 may not be made unless a draft of the instrument has been laid before, and approved by a resolution of, each House of Parliament.

(2) This paragraph is subject to paragraph 19.

[Power in relation to interpretation of retained EU law

9A. A statutory instrument containing regulations under section 6(5A) may not be made unless a draft of the instrument has been laid before, and approved by a resolution of, each House of Parliament.]

10. . . .

Power to repeal provisions relating to retained EU law restrictions

11. A statutory instrument containing regulations under section 12(9) may not be made unless a draft of the instrument has been laid before, and approved by a resolution of, each House of Parliament.

Powers in connection with fees and charges

12. (1) A statutory instrument containing regulations of a Minister of the Crown under Schedule 4 which contain provision which does not relate to altering the amount of a fee or charge to reflect changes in the value of money may not be made unless a draft of the instrument has been laid before, and approved by a resolution of, each House of Parliament.

(2) Any other statutory instrument containing regulations under Schedule 4 of a Minister of the Crown is (if a draft of the instrument has not been laid before, and approved by a resolution of, each House of Parliament) subject to annulment in pursuance of a resolution of either House of Parliament.

(3) Paragraphs 1(6) to (13)(a) and 2 apply to regulations under Schedule 4 as they apply to regulations under Part 1 of Schedule 2 except that any reference to provision falling within paragraph 1(2) is to be read as a reference to any provision made under Schedule 4 which does not relate to altering the amount of a fee or charge to reflect changes in the value of money.

(4) This paragraph is subject to paragraph 19.

Power to make provision about judicial notice and admissibility

13. A statutory instrument containing regulations under paragraph 4 of Schedule 5 may not be made unless a draft of the instrument has been laid before, and approved by a resolution of, each House of Parliament.

Power to amend the definition of "exit day"

14. A statutory instrument containing regulations under section 20(4) [is subject to annulment in pursuance of a resolution of either] House of Parliament.

Power to make consequential provision

15. (1) A statutory instrument containing regulations under section 23(1) is (if a draft of the instrument has not been laid before, and approved by a resolution of, each House of Parliament) subject to annulment in pursuance of a resolution of either House of Parliament.

(2) See paragraph 17 for restrictions on the choice of procedure under sub-paragraph (1).

Power to make transitional, transitory or saving provision

16. (1) Sub-paragraph (2) applies if a Minister of the Crown who is to make regulations under section 23(6) considers that—

- (a) it is not appropriate for the statutory instrument containing them to be subject to no parliamentary procedure, and
- (b) it is appropriate for that statutory instrument to be subject to the parliamentary procedure in sub-paragraph (2).

(2) The statutory instrument containing the regulations may not be made unless a draft of the instrument has been laid before, and approved by a resolution of, each House of Parliament.

(3) Sub-paragraph (4) applies if a Minister of the Crown who is to make regulations under section 23(6) considers that—

- (a) it is not appropriate for the statutory instrument containing them to be subject to no parliamentary procedure, and
- (b) it is appropriate for that statutory instrument to be subject to the parliamentary procedure in sub-paragraph (4).

(4) The statutory instrument containing the regulations is subject to annulment in pursuance of a resolution of either House of Parliament.

Parliamentary committee to sift . . . consequential regulations of a Minister of the Crown

17. (1) Sub-paragraph (2) applies if a Minister of the Crown who is to make a statutory instrument to which paragraph . . . or 15 applies is of the opinion that the appropriate procedure for the instrument is for it to be subject to annulment in pursuance of a resolution of either House of Parliament.

(2) The Minister may not make the instrument so that it is subject to that procedure unless—

- (a) condition 1 is met, and
- (b) either condition 2 or 3 is met.

(3) Condition 1 is that a Minister of the Crown—

- (a) has made a statement in writing to the effect that in the Minister's opinion the instrument should be subject to annulment in pursuance of a resolution of either House of Parliament, and
- (b) has laid before each House of Parliament—
  - (i) a draft of the instrument, and
  - (ii) a memorandum setting out the statement and the reasons for the Minister's opinion.

(4) Condition 2 is that a committee of the House of Commons charged with doing so and a committee of the House of Lords charged with doing so have, within the relevant period, each made a recommendation as to the appropriate procedure for the instrument.

(5) Condition 3 is that the relevant period has ended without condition 2 being met.

(6) Sub-paragraph (7) applies if—

- (a) a committee makes a recommendation as mentioned in sub-paragraph (4) within the relevant period,
- (b) the recommendation is that the appropriate procedure for the instrument is for a draft of it to be laid before, and approved by a resolution of, each House of Parliament before it is made, and
- (c) the Minister who is to make the instrument is nevertheless of the opinion that the appropriate procedure for the instrument is for it to be subject to annulment in pursuance of a resolution of either House of Parliament.

(7) Before the instrument is made, the Minister must make a statement explaining why the Minister does not agree with the recommendation of the committee.

(8) If the Minister fails to make a statement required by sub-paragraph (7) before the instrument is made, a Minister of the Crown must make a statement explaining why the Minister has failed to do so.

(9) A statement under sub-paragraph (7) or (8) must be made in writing and be published in such manner as the Minister making it considers appropriate.

(10) In this paragraph "the relevant period" means the period—
- (a) beginning with the first day on which both Houses of Parliament are sitting after the day on which the draft instrument was laid before each House of Parliament as mentioned in sub-paragraph (3)(b)(i), and
- (b) ending with whichever of the following is the later—
  - (i) the end of the period of 10 Commons sitting days beginning with that first day, and
  - (ii) the end of the period of 10 Lords sitting days beginning with that first day.

(11) For the purposes of sub-paragraph (10)—
- (a) where a draft of an instrument is laid before each House of Parliament on different days, the later day is to be taken as the day on which it is laid before both Houses,
- (b), (c) . . .

. . .

(12) Nothing in this paragraph prevents a Minister of the Crown from deciding at any time before a statutory instrument to which paragraph . . . 15 applies is made that another procedure should apply in relation to the instrument (whether under that paragraph or paragraph 19).

(13) Section 6(1) of the Statutory Instruments Act 1946 (alternative procedure for certain instruments laid in draft before Parliament) does not apply in relation to any statutory instrument to which this paragraph applies.

18. . . .

Scrutiny procedure for certain powers to which this Part applies in urgent cases

19. (1) Sub-paragraph (2) applies to—
- (a) a statutory instrument to which paragraph 9(1) . . . or 12(1) applies, or
- (b) a statutory instrument to which paragraph . . . , 12(2) or 15 applies which would not otherwise be made without a draft of the instrument being laid before, and approved by a resolution of, each House of Parliament.

(2) The instrument may be made without a draft of the instrument being laid before, and approved by a resolution of, each House of Parliament if it contains a declaration that the Minister of the Crown concerned is of the opinion that, by reason of urgency, it is necessary to make the regulations without a draft being so laid and approved.

(3) After an instrument is made in accordance with sub-paragraph (2), it must be laid before each House of Parliament.

(4) Regulations contained in an instrument made in accordance with sub-paragraph (2) cease to have effect at the end of the period of 28 days beginning with the day on which the instrument is made unless, during that period, the instrument is approved by a resolution of each House of Parliament.

(5) In calculating the period of 28 days, no account is to be taken of any time during which—
- (a) Parliament is dissolved or prorogued, or
- (b) either House of Parliament is adjourned for more than four days.

(6) If regulations cease to have effect as a result of sub-paragraph (4), that does not—
- (a) affect the validity of anything previously done under the regulations, or
- (b) prevent the making of new regulations.

(7) . . .

(8) Sub-paragraph (9) applies to a statutory instrument to which paragraph . . . 15 applies where the Minister of the Crown who is to make the instrument is of the opinion that the appropriate procedure for the instrument is for it to be subject to annulment in pursuance of a resolution of either House of Parliament.

(9) Paragraph 17 does not apply in relation to the instrument if the instrument contains a declaration that the Minister is of the opinion that, by reason of urgency, it is necessary to make the regulations without meeting the requirements of that paragraph.

NOTES

Para 9A: inserted by the European Union (Withdrawal Agreement) Act 2020, s 41(4), Sch 5, Pt 2, paras 38, 52(1), (2), as from 19 May 2020.

Para 14: words in square brackets substituted by the European Union (Withdrawal) Act 2019, s 2, as from 8 April 2019.

All words omitted were repealed by the European Union (Withdrawal Agreement) Act 2020, s 41(4), Sch 5, Pt 2, paras 38, 52(1)–(7), as from 23 January 2020.

PART 3 GENERAL PROVISION ABOUT POWERS UNDER ACT

Scope and nature of powers: general

[12.47]

20. (1) Any power to make regulations under this Act—
- (a) so far as exercisable by a Minister of the Crown or by a Minister of the Crown acting jointly with a devolved authority, is exercisable by statutory instrument,
- (b) so far as exercisable by the Welsh Ministers or by the Welsh Ministers acting jointly with a Minister of the Crown, is exercisable by statutory instrument, and
- (c) so far as exercisable by a Northern Ireland department (other than when acting jointly with a Minister of the Crown), is exercisable by statutory rule for the purposes of the Statutory Rules (Northern Ireland) Order 1979 (SI 1979/1573 (NI 12)) (and not by statutory instrument).

(2) For regulations made under this Act by the Scottish Ministers, see also section 27 of the Interpretation and Legislative Reform (Scotland) Act 2010 (asp 10) (Scottish statutory instruments).

21. Any power to make regulations under this Act—

(a) may be exercised so as to—

(i) modify [anything which continues to be domestic law by virtue of section 1B(2) or any] retained EU law, or

(ii) make different provision for different cases or descriptions of case, different circumstances, different purposes or different areas, and

(b) includes power to make supplementary, incidental, consequential, transitional, transitory or saving provision (including provision re-stating [anything which continues to be domestic law by virtue of section 1B(2), or any retained EU law,] in a clearer or more accessible way).

22. The fact that a power to make regulations is conferred by this Act does not affect the extent of any other power to make regulations under this Act.

Scope of consequential and transitional powers

23. (1) The fact that anything continues to be, or forms part of, domestic law by virtue of any provision of [sections 1A] to 6 or Schedule 1 does not prevent it from being modified by regulations made under section 23(1) in consequence of any other provision made by or under this Act.

(2) Accordingly, [anything which continues to be domestic law by virtue of section 1B(2) or] any retained EU law may, for example, be modified by regulations made under section 23(1) in consequence of the repeal of any enactment contained in the European Communities Act 1972.

(3) The power to make regulations under section 23(6) includes the power to make transitional, transitory or saving provision in connection with—

(a) the repeal of any enactment contained in the European Communities Act 1972, or

(b) the withdrawal of the United Kingdom from the EU,

which is additional to that made by any provision of [sections 1A] to 6 or Schedule 1 or alters its effect in particular cases or descriptions of case.

(4) The power to make regulations under section 23(1) includes the power to make transitional, transitory or saving provision which—

(a) is in connection with any repeal or revocation made by any such regulations of an enactment in consequence of—

(i) the repeal of any enactment contained in the European Communities Act 1972, or

(ii) the withdrawal of the United Kingdom from the EU, and

(b) is additional to that made by any provision of [sections 1A] to 6 or Schedule 1 or alters its effect in particular cases or descriptions of case.

(5) Provision of the kind mentioned in sub-paragraph (3) or (4) may (among other things) include further provision treating any provision of that kind as [anything which continues to be domestic law by virtue of section 1B(2), or as retained EU law,] for particular purposes or all purposes.

[Anticipatory exercise of powers in relation to section 1B(2) saved law

23A. Any power to make regulations under this Act which modify anything which continues to be domestic law by virtue of section 1B(2) is capable of being exercised before exit day so that the regulations come into force on or after exit day.]

Anticipatory exercise of powers in relation to retained EU law

24. Any power to make regulations under this Act which modify retained direct EU legislation, anything which is retained EU law by virtue of section 4 or any other retained EU law is capable of being exercised before [IP completion day] so that the regulations come into force on or after [IP completion day].

[Anticipatory exercise of powers in relation to the withdrawal agreement etc

24A. Any power to make regulations under this Act in relation to the withdrawal agreement, the EEA EFTA separation agreement or the Swiss citizens' rights agreement, or any modification of any of them which requires ratification, is capable of being exercised before the agreement or (as the case may be) modification concerned is ratified.]

Scope of appointed day powers

25. Any power of a Minister of the Crown under this Act to appoint a day includes a power to appoint a time on that day if the Minister considers it appropriate to do so.

Effect of certain provisions in Schedule 8 on scope of powers

26. The modifications made by Part 1 of Schedule 8 and paragraphs 18 to 22 and 31 to 35 of that Schedule do not prevent or otherwise limit the making of different provision, in particular cases or descriptions of case, in regulations under section 23(1) or in any other regulations under this Act.

Disapplication of certain review provisions

27. Section 28 of the Small Business, Enterprise and Employment Act 2015 (duty to review regulatory provisions in secondary legislation) does not apply in relation to any power to make regulations conferred by this Act.

Explanatory statements for certain powers: appropriateness, equalities etc

28. (1) This paragraph applies where—

(a) a statutory instrument containing regulations under section 8(1) . . . or 23(1) or paragraph 1(2) or 12(2) of Schedule 2, or

(b) a draft of such an instrument,

is to be laid before each House of Parliament.

(2) Before the instrument or draft is laid, the relevant Minister must make a statement to the effect that in the Minister's opinion the instrument or draft does no more than is appropriate.

(3) Before the instrument or draft is laid, the relevant Minister must make a statement as to why, in the Minister's opinion—

(a) there are good reasons for the instrument or draft, and

(b) the provision made by the instrument or draft is a reasonable course of action.

(4) Before the instrument or draft is laid, the relevant Minister must make a statement—

(a) as to whether the instrument or draft amends, repeals or revokes any provision of equalities legislation, and

(b) if it does, explaining the effect of each such amendment, repeal or revocation.

(5) Before the instrument or draft is laid, the relevant Minister must make a statement to the effect that, in relation to the instrument or draft, the Minister has, so far as required to do so by equalities legislation, had due regard to the need to eliminate discrimination, harassment, victimisation and any other conduct that is prohibited by or under the Equality Act 2010.

(6) Before the instrument or draft is laid, the relevant Minister must make a statement otherwise explaining—

(a) the instrument or draft,

(b) its purpose,

(c) the law before [IP completion day] which is relevant to it, and

(d) its effect (if any) on retained EU law.

(7) Where an instrument or draft creates a criminal offence, the statement required by sub-paragraph (3) must (among other things) include an explanation of why, in the relevant Minister's opinion, there are good reasons for creating the offence and for the penalty provided in respect of it.

(8) If the relevant Minister fails to make a statement required by sub-paragraph (2), (3), (4), (5) or (6) before the instrument or draft is laid, a Minister of the Crown must make a statement explaining why the relevant Minister has failed to do so.

(9) A statement under sub-paragraph (2), (3), (4), (5), (6) or (8) must be made in writing and be published in such manner as the Minister making it considers appropriate.

(10) For the purposes of this paragraph, where an instrument or draft is laid before each House of Parliament on different days, the earlier day is to be taken as the day on which it is laid before both Houses.

(11) This paragraph does not apply in relation to any laying before each House of Parliament of an instrument or draft instrument where an equivalent draft instrument (ignoring any differences relating to procedure) has previously been laid before both Houses.

(12) In this paragraph—

"equalities legislation" means the Equality Act 2006, the Equality Act 2010 or any subordinate legislation made under either of those Acts;

"the relevant Minister" means the Minister of the Crown who makes, or is to make, the instrument.

29. (1) This paragraph applies where—

(a) a Scottish statutory instrument containing regulations under Part 1 . . . of Schedule 2, or

(b) a draft of such an instrument,

is to be laid before the Scottish Parliament.

(2) Before the instrument or draft is laid, the Scottish Ministers must make a statement to the effect that in the Scottish Ministers' opinion the instrument or draft does no more than is appropriate.

(3) Before the instrument or draft is laid, the Scottish Ministers must make a statement as to why, in the Scottish Ministers' opinion—

(a) there are good reasons for the instrument or draft, and

(b) the provision made by the instrument or draft is a reasonable course of action.

(4) Before the instrument or draft is laid, the Scottish Ministers must make a statement—

(a) as to whether the instrument or draft amends, repeals or revokes any provision of equalities legislation, and

(b) if it does, explaining the effect of each such amendment, repeal or revocation.

(5) Before the instrument or draft is laid, the Scottish Ministers must make a statement to the effect that, in relation to the instrument or draft, the Scottish Ministers have, so far as required to do so by equalities legislation, had due regard to the need to eliminate discrimination, harassment, victimisation and any other conduct that is prohibited by or under the Equality Act 2010.

(6) Before the instrument or draft is laid, the Scottish Ministers must make a statement otherwise explaining—

(a) the instrument or draft,

(b) its purpose,

(c) the law before [IP completion day] which is relevant to it, and

(d) its effect (if any) on retained EU law.

(7) Where an instrument or draft creates a criminal offence, the statement required by sub-paragraph (3) must (among other things) include an explanation of why, in the Scottish Ministers' opinion, there are good reasons for creating the offence and for the penalty provided in respect of it.

(8) If the Scottish Ministers fail to make a statement required by sub-paragraph (2), (3), (4), (5) or (6) before the instrument or draft is laid, the Scottish Ministers must make a statement explaining why they have failed to do so.

(9) A statement under sub-paragraph (2), (3), (4), (5), (6) or (8) must be made in writing and be published in such manner as the Scottish Ministers consider appropriate.

(10) In this paragraph "equalities legislation" means the Equality Act 2006, the Equality Act 2010 or any subordinate legislation made under either of those Acts.

Further explanatory statements in certain sub-delegation cases

30. (1) This paragraph applies where—

(a) a statutory instrument containing regulations under section 8(1) . . . or paragraph 1 of Schedule 4 which create a relevant sub-delegated power, or

(b) a draft of such an instrument,

is to be laid before each House of Parliament.

(2) Before the instrument or draft is laid, the relevant Minister must make a statement explaining why it is appropriate to create a relevant sub-delegated power.

(3) If the relevant Minister fails to make a statement required by sub-paragraph (2) before the instrument or draft is laid, a Minister of the Crown must make a statement explaining why the relevant Minister has failed to do so.

(4) A statement under sub-paragraph (2) or (3) must be made in writing and be published in such manner as the Minister making it considers appropriate.

(5) Sub-paragraphs (10) and (11) of paragraph 28 apply for the purposes of this paragraph as they apply for the purposes of that paragraph.

(6) For the purposes of this paragraph references to creating a relevant sub-delegated power include (among other things) references to—

(a) amending a power to legislate which is exercisable by statutory instrument by a relevant UK authority so that it becomes a relevant sub-delegated power, or

(b) providing for any function of an EU entity or public authority in a member State of making an instrument of a legislative character to be exercisable instead as a relevant sub-delegated power by a public authority in the United Kingdom.

(7) In this paragraph—

"the relevant Minister" means the Minister of the Crown who makes, or is to make, the instrument;

"relevant sub-delegated power" means a power to legislate which—

(a) is not exercisable by any of the following—

(i) statutory instrument,

(ii) Scottish statutory instrument, or

(iii) statutory rule, or

(b) is so exercisable by a public authority other than a relevant UK authority;

"relevant UK authority" means a Minister of the Crown, a member of the Scottish Government, the Welsh Ministers, the First Minister for Wales, the Counsel General to the Welsh Government or a Northern Ireland devolved authority.

31. (1) This paragraph applies where—

(a) a Scottish statutory instrument containing regulations under Part 1 . . . of Schedule 2 or paragraph 1 of Schedule 4 which create a relevant sub-delegated power, or

(b) a draft of such an instrument,

is to be laid before the Scottish Parliament.

(2) Before the instrument or draft is laid, the Scottish Ministers must make a statement explaining why it is appropriate to create a relevant sub-delegated power.

(3) If the Scottish Ministers fail to make a statement required by sub-paragraph (2) before the instrument or draft is laid, the Scottish Ministers must make a statement explaining why they have failed to do so.

(4) A statement under sub-paragraph (2) or (3) must be made in writing and be published in such manner as the Scottish Ministers consider appropriate.

(5) For the purposes of this paragraph references to creating a relevant sub-delegated power include (among other things) references to—

(a) amending a power to legislate which is exercisable by Scottish statutory instrument by a member of the Scottish Government so that it becomes a relevant sub-delegated power, or

(b) providing for any function of an EU entity or public authority in a member State of making an instrument of a legislative character to be exercisable instead as a relevant sub-delegated power by a public authority in the United Kingdom.

(6) In this paragraph "relevant sub-delegated power" means a power to legislate which—

(a) is not exercisable by Scottish statutory instrument, or

(b) is so exercisable by a public authority other than a member of the Scottish Government.

Annual reports in certain sub-delegation cases

32. (1) Each person by whom a relevant sub-delegated power is exercisable by virtue of regulations made by a Minister of the Crown under section 8(1) . . . or paragraph 1 of Schedule 4 must—

(a) if the power has been exercised during a relevant year, and

(b) as soon as practicable after the end of the year,

prepare a report on how the power has been exercised during the year.

(2) The person must—

(a) lay the report before each House of Parliament, and

(b) once laid—

(i) provide a copy of it to a Minister of the Crown, and

(ii) publish it in such manner as the person considers appropriate.

(3) In this paragraph—

"relevant sub-delegated power" has the same meaning as in paragraph 30;

"relevant year" means—

(a) in the case of a person who prepares an annual report, the year by reference to which the report is prepared, and

(b) in any other case, the calendar year.

33. (1) Each person by whom a relevant sub-delegated power is exercisable by virtue of regulations made by the Scottish Ministers by Scottish statutory instrument under Part 1 . . . of Schedule 2 or paragraph 1 of Schedule 4 must—

(a) if the power has been exercised during a relevant year, and

(b) as soon as practicable after the end of the year,

prepare a report on how the power has been exercised during the year.

(2) The person must—

(a) lay the report before the Scottish Parliament, and

(b) once laid—

(i) send a copy of it to the Scottish Ministers, and

(ii) publish it in such manner as the person considers appropriate.

(3) In this paragraph—

"relevant sub-delegated power" has the same meaning as in paragraph 31;

"relevant year" means—

(a) in the case of a person who prepares an annual report, the year by reference to which the report is prepared, and

(b) in any other case, the calendar year.

Further explanatory statements in urgency cases

34. (1) This paragraph applies where a statutory instrument containing regulations under this Act is to be made by virtue of paragraph 5(2) or 19(2).

(2) The Minister of the Crown who is to make the instrument must make a statement in writing explaining the reasons for the Minister's opinion that, by reason of urgency, it is necessary to make the regulations without a draft of the instrument containing them being laid before, and approved by a resolution of, each House of Parliament.

(3) A statement under sub-paragraph (2) must be published before, or at the same time as, the instrument as made is laid before each House of Parliament.

(4) If the Minister—

(a) fails to make the statement required by sub-paragraph (2) before the instrument is made, or

(b) fails to publish it as required by sub-paragraph (3),

a Minister of the Crown must make a statement explaining the failure.

(5) A statement under sub-paragraph (4) must be made in writing and be published in such manner as the Minister making it considers appropriate.

(6) For the purposes of this paragraph, where an instrument is laid before each House of Parliament on different days, the earlier day is to be taken as the day on which it is laid before both Houses.

35. (1) This paragraph applies where regulations are to be made by the Scottish Ministers under this Act by virtue of paragraph 6(2) . . .

(2) The Scottish Ministers must make a statement in writing explaining the reasons for the Scottish Ministers' opinion that, by reason of urgency, it is necessary to make the regulations without them being subject to the affirmative procedure.

(3) A statement under sub-paragraph (2) must be published before, or at the same time as, the regulations as made are laid before the Scottish Parliament.

(4) If the Scottish Ministers—

(a) fail to make the statement required by sub-paragraph (2) before the regulations are made, or

(b) fail to publish it as required by sub-paragraph (3),

they must make a statement explaining the failure.

(5) A statement under sub-paragraph (4) must be made in writing and be published in such manner as the Scottish Ministers consider appropriate.

Hybrid instruments

36. If an instrument, or a draft of an instrument, containing regulations under this Act would, apart from this paragraph, be treated as a hybrid instrument for the purposes of the standing orders of either House of Parliament, it is to proceed in that House as if it were not a hybrid instrument.

Procedure on re-exercise of certain powers

37. (1) A power to make regulations which, under this Schedule, is capable of being exercised subject to different procedures may (in spite of section 14 of the Interpretation Act 1978) be exercised, when revoking, amending or re-enacting an instrument made under the power, subject to a different procedure from the procedure to which the instrument was subject.

(2) For the purposes of sub-paragraph (1) in its application to regulations under section 23(6) no procedure is also a procedure.

Combinations of instruments

38. (1) Sub-paragraph (2) applies to a statutory instrument containing regulations under this Act which is subject to a procedure before Parliament for the approval of the instrument in draft before it is made or its approval after it is made.

(2) The statutory instrument may also include regulations under this Act or another enactment which are made by statutory instrument which is subject to a procedure before Parliament that provides for the annulment of the instrument after it has been made.

(3) Where regulations are included as mentioned in sub-paragraph (2), the procedure applicable to the statutory instrument is the procedure mentioned in sub-paragraph (1) and not the procedure mentioned in sub-paragraph (2).

(4) Sub-paragraphs (1) to (3) apply in relation to a statutory instrument containing regulations under this Act which is subject to a procedure before the National Assembly for Wales as they apply in relation to a statutory instrument containing regulations under this Act which is subject to a procedure before Parliament but as if the references to Parliament were references to the National Assembly for Wales.

(5) Sub-paragraphs (1) to (3) apply in relation to a statutory rule as they apply in relation to a statutory instrument but as if the references to Parliament were references to the Northern Ireland Assembly.

(6) Sub-paragraphs (1) to (3) apply in relation to a statutory instrument containing regulations under this Act which is subject to a procedure before the Scottish Parliament, the National Assembly for Wales or the Northern Ireland Assembly as well as a procedure before Parliament as they apply to a statutory instrument containing regulations under this Act which is subject to a procedure before Parliament but as if the references to Parliament were references to Parliament and the Scottish Parliament, the National Assembly for Wales or (as the case may be) the Northern Ireland Assembly.

(7) This paragraph does not prevent the inclusion of other regulations in a statutory instrument or statutory rule which contains regulations under this Act (and, accordingly, references in this Schedule to an instrument containing regulations are to be read as references to an instrument containing (whether alone or with other provision) regulations).

NOTES

All amendments to this Part were made by the European Union (Withdrawal Agreement) Act 2020, s 41(4), Sch 5, Pt 2, paras 38, 53. The substitution of the words "IP completion day" in paras 24, 28 and 29 apply from exit day (as defined in s 20 of this Act). All other amendments apply from 23 January 2020.

National Assembly for Wales: as to the renaming of the National Assembly for Wales, see the note at **[12.28]**.

SCHEDULE 8
CONSEQUENTIAL, TRANSITIONAL, TRANSITORY AND SAVING PROVISION

Section 23(5) and (7)

PART 1 GENERAL CONSEQUENTIAL PROVISION

Existing ambulatory references to retained direct EU legislation

[12.48]

1. (1) Any reference [so far as it], immediately before [IP completion day]—
- (a) exists in—
  - (i) any enactment,
  - (ii) any EU regulation, EU decision, EU tertiary legislation or provision of the EEA agreement which is to form part of domestic law by virtue of section 3, or
  - (iii) any document relating to anything falling within sub-paragraph (i) or (ii), and
- (b) is a reference to (as it has effect from time to time) any EU regulation, EU decision, EU tertiary legislation or provision of the EEA agreement which is to form part of domestic law by virtue of section 3,

is to be read, on or after [IP completion day], as a reference to the EU regulation, EU decision, EU tertiary legislation or provision of the EEA agreement as it forms part of domestic law by virtue of section 3 and, unless the contrary intention appears, as modified by domestic law from time to time.

(2) Sub-paragraph (1) does not apply to any reference [so far as it] forms part of a power to make, confirm or approve subordinate legislation so far as the power to make the subordinate legislation—
- (a) continues to be part of domestic law by virtue of section 2, and
- (b) is subject to a procedure before Parliament, the Scottish Parliament, the National Assembly for Wales or the Northern Ireland Assembly.

(3) Sub-paragraphs (1) and (2) are subject to any other provision made by or under this Act or any other enactment.

[Existing ambulatory references to relevant separation agreement law

1A. (1) Any reference which, immediately before IP completion day—
- (a) exists in—
  - (i) any enactment,
  - (ii) any EU regulation, EU decision, EU tertiary legislation or provision of the EEA agreement which is to form part of domestic law by virtue of section 3, or
  - (iii) any document relating to anything falling within sub-paragraph (i) or (ii), and
- (b) is a reference to (as it has effect from time to time) any of the EU Treaties, any EU instrument or any other document of an EU entity,

is, if the treaty, instrument or document has effect on or after IP completion day by virtue of section 7A or 7B and so far as required for the purposes of relevant separation agreement law, to be read on or after that day as, or including, a reference to the treaty, instrument or document as it so has effect (including, so far as so required, as it has effect from time to time). .

(2) In sub-paragraph (1) "treaty" includes any international agreement (and any protocol or annex to a treaty or international agreement).

(3) Sub-paragraphs (1) and (2) are subject to any other provision made by or under this Act or any other enactment.]

Other existing ambulatory references

2. (1) Any reference [so far as it]—
- (a) exists, immediately before [IP completion day], in—
  - (i) any enactment,
  - (ii) any EU regulation, EU decision, EU tertiary legislation or provision of the EEA agreement which is to form part of domestic law by virtue of section 3, or
  - (iii) any document relating to anything falling within sub-paragraph (i) or (ii),
- (b) is not a reference to which paragraph 1(1) applies, and

(c) is, immediately before [IP completion day], a reference to (as it has effect from time to time) any of the EU Treaties, any EU instrument or any other document of an EU entity,

is to be read, on or after [IP completion day], as a reference to the EU Treaty, instrument or document as it has effect immediately before [IP completion day].

(2) Sub-paragraph (1) does not apply to any reference [so far as it] forms part of a power to make, confirm or approve subordinate legislation so far as the power to make the subordinate legislation—

(a) continues to be part of domestic law by virtue of section 2, and

(b) is subject to a procedure before Parliament, the Scottish Parliament, the National Assembly for Wales or the Northern Ireland Assembly.

[(2A) Sub-paragraph (1) does not apply so far as any reference forms part of relevant separation agreement law.]

(3) Sub-paragraphs (1) [to (2A)] are subject to any other provision made by or under this Act or any other enactment.

[Existing non-ambulatory references

2A. (1) Any reference which, immediately before IP completion day—

(a) exists in—

(i) any enactment,

(ii) any EU regulation, EU decision, EU tertiary legislation or provision of the EEA agreement which is to form part of domestic law by virtue of section 3, and

(b) is a reference to any of the EU Treaties, any EU instrument or any other document of an EU entity as it has effect at a particular time which is earlier than IP completion day,

is to be read, on or after IP completion day, in accordance with one or more of subparagraphs (2) to (4).

(2) If the treaty, instrument or document has effect by virtue of section 7A or 7B on or after IP completion day and so far as required for the purposes of relevant separation agreement law, the reference is to be read on or after that day as, or as including, a reference to the treaty, instrument or document as it so has effect (including, so far as so required, as it has effect from time to time).

(3) So far as—

(a) the reference is a reference to—

(i) any EU regulation, EU decision or EU tertiary legislation,

(ii) any provision of the EEA agreement, or

(iii) any part of anything falling within sub-paragraph (i) or (ii),

(b) what has been referred to ("the subject law") is to form part of domestic law by virtue of section 3 or forms part of domestic law by virtue of section 1 of the Direct Payments to Farmers (Legislative Continuity) Act 2020, and

(c) there has been no relevant modification of the subject law after the particular time and before IP completion day (or, where the subject law forms part of domestic law by virtue of section 1 of the Direct Payments to Farmers (Legislative Continuity) Act 2020, before exit day),

the reference is to be read, on or after IP completion day, as a reference to the subject law as it forms part of domestic law by virtue of section 3 or (as the case may be) section 1 of the Direct Payments to Farmers (Legislative Continuity) Act 2020.

(4) So far as the reference is not to be read in accordance with sub-paragraphs (2) and (3), the reference is to be read, on or after IP completion day, as a reference to the treaty, instrument or document as it had effect in EU law at the particular time.

(5) Sub-paragraph (3) does not determine whether, where the subject law is modified by domestic law on or after IP completion day, the reference is to be read as a reference to the subject law as modified; but, where the subject law forms part of domestic law by virtue of section 1 of the Direct Payments to Farmers (Legislative Continuity) Act 2020 and is modified by domestic law before IP completion day, the reference is to be read by virtue of sub-paragraph (3) as a reference to the subject law as so modified.

(6) This paragraph is subject to any provision made by or under this Act or any other enactment.

(6A) This paragraph does not apply to a reference in—

(a) the Direct Payments to Farmers (Legislative Continuity) Act 2020 or any subordinate legislation made under that Act, or

(b) any retained direct EU CAP legislation (within the meaning given by section 2(10) of that Act).

(7) In this paragraph—

"relevant modification" means any modification in EU law which—

(a) is to form part of domestic law by virtue of section 3 or forms part of domestic law by virtue of section 1 of the Direct Payments to Farmers (Legislative Continuity) Act 2020, and

(b) would, if the reference were to the subject law as modified, result in an alteration to the effect of the reference (ignoring any alteration which is irrelevant in the context concerned);

"the subject law" has the meaning given by sub-paragraph (3)(b);

"treaty" includes any international agreement (and any protocol or annex to a treaty or international agreement).]

Existing powers to make subordinate legislation etc

3. (1) Any power to make, confirm or approve subordinate legislation which—

(a) was conferred before the day on which this Act is passed, and

(b) is capable of being exercised to amend or repeal (or, as the case may be, result in the amendment or repeal of) an enactment contained in primary legislation,

is to be read, so far as the context permits or requires, as being capable of being exercised to modify (or, as the case may be, result in the modification of) any retained direct EU legislation or anything which is retained EU law by virtue of section 4.

(2) But sub-paragraph (1) does not apply if the power to make, confirm or approve subordinate legislation is only capable of being exercised to amend or repeal (or, as the case may be, result in the amendment or repeal of) an enactment contained in Northern Ireland legislation which is an Order in Council.

4. (1) Any subordinate legislation which—

(a) is, or is to be, made, confirmed or approved by virtue of paragraph 3, and

(b) amends or revokes any retained direct principal EU legislation,

is to be subject to the same procedure (if any) before Parliament, the Scottish Parliament, the National Assembly for Wales or the Northern Ireland Assembly as would apply to that legislation if it were amending or repealing an enactment contained in primary legislation.

(2) Any subordinate legislation which—

(a) is, or is to be, made, confirmed or approved by virtue of paragraph 3, and

(b) either—

(i) modifies (otherwise than as a connected modification and otherwise than by way of amending or revoking it) any retained direct principal EU legislation, or

(ii) modifies (otherwise than as a connected modification) anything which is retained EU law by virtue of section 4,

is to be subject to the same procedure (if any) before Parliament, the Scottish Parliament, the National Assembly for Wales or the Northern Ireland Assembly as would apply to that legislation if it were amending or repealing an enactment contained in primary legislation.

(3) Any subordinate legislation which—

(a) is, or is to be, made, confirmed or approved by virtue of paragraph 3, and

(b) amends or revokes any retained direct minor EU legislation,

is to be subject to the same procedure (if any) before Parliament, the Scottish Parliament, the National Assembly for Wales or the Northern Ireland Assembly as would apply to that legislation if it were amending or revoking an enactment contained in subordinate legislation made under a different power.

(4) Any subordinate legislation which—

(a) is, or is to be, made, confirmed or approved by virtue of paragraph 3, and

(b) modifies (otherwise than as a connected modification and otherwise than by way of amending or revoking it) any retained direct minor EU legislation,

is to be subject to the same procedure (if any) before Parliament, the Scottish Parliament, the National Assembly for Wales or the Northern Ireland Assembly as would apply to that legislation if it were amending or revoking an enactment contained in subordinate legislation made under a different power.

(5) Any subordinate legislation which—

(a) is, or is to be, made, confirmed or approved by virtue of paragraph 3, and

(b) modifies as a connected modification any retained direct EU legislation or anything which is retained EU law by virtue of section 4,

is to be subject to the same procedure (if any) before Parliament, the Scottish Parliament, the National Assembly for Wales or the Northern Ireland Assembly as would apply to the modification to which it is connected.

(6) Any provision which may be made, confirmed or approved by virtue of paragraph 3 may be included in the same instrument as any other provision which may be so made, confirmed or approved.

(7) Where more than one procedure of a kind falling within sub-paragraph (8) would otherwise apply in the same legislature for an instrument falling within sub-paragraph (6), the higher procedure is to apply in the legislature concerned.

(8) The order of procedures is as follows (the highest first)—

(a) a procedure which requires a statement of urgency before the instrument is made and the approval of the instrument after it is made to enable it to remain in force,

(b) a procedure which requires the approval of the instrument in draft before it is made,

(c) a procedure not falling within paragraph (a) which requires the approval of the instrument after it is made to enable it to come into, or remain in, force,

(d) a procedure which provides for the annulment of the instrument after it is made,

(e) a procedure not falling within any of the above paragraphs which provides for the laying of the instrument after it is made,

(f) no procedure.

(9) The references in this paragraph to amending or repealing an enactment contained in primary legislation or amending or revoking an enactment contained in subordinate legislation do not include references to amending or repealing or (as the case may be) amending or revoking an enactment contained in any Northern Ireland legislation which is an Order in Council.

(10) In this paragraph "connected modification" means a modification which is supplementary, incidental, consequential, transitional or transitory, or a saving, in connection with—

(a) another modification under the power of retained direct EU legislation or anything which is retained EU law by virtue of section 4, or

(b) anything else done under the power.

5. (1) This paragraph applies to any power to make, confirm or approve subordinate legislation—

(a) which was conferred before the day on which this Act is passed, and

(b) is not capable of being exercised as mentioned in paragraph 3(1)(b) or is only capable of being so exercised in relation to Northern Ireland legislation which is an Order in Council.

(2) Any power to which this paragraph applies (other than a power to which sub-paragraph (4) applies) is to be read—

(a) so far as is consistent with any retained direct principal EU legislation or anything which is retained EU law by virtue of section 4, and

(b) so far as the context permits or requires,

as being capable of being exercised to modify (or, as the case may be, result in the modification of) any retained direct minor EU legislation.

(3) Any power to which this paragraph applies (other than a power to which sub-paragraph (4) applies) is to be read, so far as the context permits or requires, as being capable of being exercised to modify (or, as the case may be, result in the modification of)—

(a) any retained direct principal EU legislation, or

(b) anything which is retained EU law by virtue of section 4,

so far as the modification is supplementary, incidental or consequential in connection with any modification of any retained direct minor EU legislation by virtue of sub-paragraph (2).

(4) Any power to which this paragraph applies so far as it is a power to make, confirm or approve transitional, transitory or saving provision is to be read, so far as the context permits or requires, as being capable of being exercised to modify (or, as the case may be, result in the modification of)—

(a) any retained direct EU legislation, or

(b) anything which is retained EU law by virtue of section 4.

6. Any subordinate legislation which is, or is to be, made, confirmed or approved by virtue of paragraph 5(2), (3) or (4) is to be subject to the same procedure (if any) before Parliament, the Scottish Parliament, the National Assembly for Wales or the Northern Ireland Assembly as would apply to that legislation if it were doing anything else under the power.

[**7.** Any power to make, confirm or approve subordinate legislation which, immediately before exit day, is subject to an implied restriction that it is exercisable only compatibly with EU law is to be read—

(a) on or after exit day, without that restriction, and

(b) on or after IP completion day, without any corresponding restriction in relation to compatibility with retained EU law,

so far as the restriction concerned is not applicable to and in the United Kingdom by virtue of the withdrawal agreement.]

8. (1) Paragraphs 3 to 7 and this paragraph—

(a) do not prevent the conferral of wider powers,

(b) . . . and

(c) are subject to any other provision made by or under this Act or any other enactment.

(2) For the purposes of paragraphs 3 and 5—

(a) a power is conferred whether or not it is in force, and

(b) a power in retained direct EU legislation is not conferred before the day on which this Act is passed.

(3) A power which, by virtue of paragraph 3 or 5 or any Act of Parliament passed before, and in the same Session as, this Act, is capable of being exercised to modify any retained EU law is capable of being so exercised before [IP completion day] so as to come into force on or after [IP completion day].

Review provisions in existing subordinate legislation

9. (1) In carrying out a review of a provision of subordinate legislation on or after [IP completion day] (whether under provision made in accordance with section 28 of the Small Business, Enterprise and Employment Act 2015 or otherwise), a person is not required, by any [pre-IP completion day] enactment, to have regard to how any former EU obligation is implemented elsewhere than in the United Kingdom.

(2) In this paragraph—

"former EU obligation" means an obligation by which the United Kingdom is, as a result of the United Kingdom's withdrawal from the EU, no longer bound at the time of the review;

"[pre-IP completion day] enactment" means an Act passed, or subordinate legislation made, before [IP completion day];

"subordinate legislation" does not include an instrument made under an Act of the Scottish Parliament, Northern Ireland legislation or a Measure or Act of the National Assembly for Wales.

Future powers to make subordinate legislation

10. (1) This paragraph applies to any power to make, confirm or approve subordinate legislation which is conferred on or after the day on which this Act is passed.

(2) Any power to which this paragraph applies (other than a power to which sub-paragraph (4) applies) may—

(a) so far as is consistent with any retained direct principal EU legislation or anything which is retained EU law by virtue of section 4, and

(b) so far as applicable and unless the contrary intention appears,

be exercised to modify (or, as the case may be, result in the modification of) any retained direct minor EU legislation.

(3) Any power to which this paragraph applies (other than a power to which sub-paragraph (4) applies) may, so far as applicable and unless the contrary intention appears, be exercised to modify (or, as the case may be, result in the modification of)—

(a) any retained direct principal EU legislation, or

(b) anything which is retained EU law by virtue of section 4,

so far as the modification is supplementary, incidental or consequential in connection with any modification of any retained direct minor EU legislation by virtue of sub-paragraph (2).

(4) Any power to which this paragraph applies so far as it is a power to make, confirm or approve transitional, transitory or saving provision may, so far as applicable and unless the contrary intention appears, be exercised to modify (or, as the case may be, result in the modification of)—

(a) any retained direct EU legislation, or

(b) anything which is retained EU law by virtue of section 4.

11. (1) Sub-paragraph (2) applies to any power to make, confirm or approve subordinate legislation which—

(a) is conferred on or after the day on which this Act is passed, and
(b) is capable of being exercised to amend or revoke (or, as the case may be, result in the amendment or revocation of) any retained direct principal EU legislation.

(2) The power may, so far as applicable and unless the contrary intention appears, be exercised—
(a) to modify otherwise than by way of amendment or revocation (or, as the case may be, result in such modification of) any retained direct principal EU legislation, or
(b) to modify (or, as the case may be, result in the modification of) anything which is retained EU law by virtue of section 4.

12. (1) Paragraphs 10 and 11 and this paragraph—
(a) do not prevent the conferral of wider powers,
(b) . . . and
(c) are subject to any other provision made by or under this Act or any other enactment.

(2) For the purposes of paragraphs 10 and 11—
(a) a power is conferred whether or not it is in force,
(b) a power in retained direct EU legislation is conferred on or after the day on which this Act is passed, and
(c) the references to powers conferred include powers conferred by regulations under this Act (but not powers conferred by this Act).

(3) A power which, by virtue of paragraph 10 or 11 or any Act of Parliament passed after [this Act and before IP completion day], is capable of being exercised to modify any retained EU law is capable of being so exercised before [IP completion day] so as to come into force on or after [IP completion day].

Affirmative procedure for instruments which amend or revoke subordinate legislation made under section 2(2) of the ECA (including subordinate legislation implementing EU directives)

13. (1) A statutory instrument which—
(a) is to be made on or after [IP completion day] by a Minister of the Crown under a power conferred before the beginning of the Session in which this Act is passed,
(b) is not to be made jointly with any person who is not a Minister of the Crown,
(c) amends or revokes any subordinate legislation made under section 2(2) of the European Communities Act 1972, and
(d) would otherwise be subject to a lower procedure before each House of Parliament and no procedure before any other legislature,

may not be made unless a draft of the instrument has been laid before, and approved by a resolution of, each House of Parliament.

(2) Sub-paragraph (1) has effect instead of any other provision which would otherwise apply in relation to the procedure for such an instrument before each House of Parliament but does not affect any other requirements which apply in relation to making, confirming or approving the instrument.

(3) Any provision which—
(a) may be made under the power mentioned in sub-paragraph (1)(a),
(b) is not provision which falls within sub-paragraph (1)(c), and
(c) is subject to a lower procedure than the procedure provided for by sub-paragraph (1),

may be included in an instrument to which sub-paragraph (1) applies (and is accordingly subject to the procedure provided for by that sub-paragraph instead of the lower procedure).

(4) If a draft of a statutory instrument which—
(a) is to be made on or after [IP completion day] by a Minister of the Crown under a power conferred before the beginning of the Session in which this Act is passed,
(b) is not to be made jointly with any person who is not a Minister of the Crown,
(c) amends or revokes any provision, made otherwise than under section 2(2) of the European Communities Act 1972 (whether or not by way of amendment), of subordinate legislation made under that section, and
(d) would otherwise be subject to a lower procedure before each House of Parliament and no procedure before any other legislature,

is laid before, and approved by a resolution of, each House of Parliament, then the instrument is not subject to the lower procedure.

(5) This paragraph applies to an instrument which is subject to a procedure before the House of Commons only as it applies to an instrument which is subject to a procedure before each House of Parliament but as if the references to each House of Parliament were references to the House of Commons only.

(6) For the purposes of this paragraph, the order of procedures is as follows (the highest first)—
(a) a procedure which requires a statement of urgency before the instrument is made and the approval of the instrument after it is made to enable it to remain in force,
(b) a procedure which requires the approval of the instrument in draft before it is made,
(c) a procedure not falling within paragraph (a) which requires the approval of the instrument after it is made to enable it to come into, or remain in, force,
(d) a procedure which provides for the annulment of the instrument after it is made,
(e) a procedure not falling within any of the above paragraphs which provides for the laying of the instrument after it is made,
(f) no procedure.

(7) For the purposes of this paragraph a power is conferred whether or not it is in force.

(8) References in this paragraph, other than in sub-paragraph (4), to subordinate legislation made under section 2(2) of the European Communities Act 1972—
(a) do not include references to any provision of such legislation which is made (whether or not by way of amendment) otherwise than under section 2(2) of that Act, and

(b) do include references to subordinate legislation made otherwise than under section 2(2) of that Act so far as that legislation is amended by provision made under that section (but do not include references to any primary legislation so far as so amended).

[(8A) This paragraph does not apply where the amendment or revocation of subordinate legislation is for the purposes of—

(a) the withdrawal agreement (other than Part 4 of that agreement),
(b) the EEA EFTA separation agreement, . . .
(c) the Swiss citizens' rights agreement[, or
(d) a future relationship agreement.]]

(9) This paragraph is subject to any other provision made by or under this Act or any other enactment.

Enhanced scrutiny procedure for instruments which amend or revoke subordinate legislation under section 2(2) of the ECA (including subordinate legislation implementing EU directives)

14. (1) This paragraph applies where, on or after [IP completion day]—

(a) a statutory instrument which—
    (i) amends or revokes subordinate legislation made under section 2(2) of the European Communities Act 1972, and
    (ii) is made under a power conferred before the beginning of the Session in which this Act is passed, or
(b) a draft of such an instrument,

is to be laid before each House of Parliament and subject to no procedure before any other legislature.

(2) The relevant authority must publish, in such manner as the relevant authority considers appropriate, a draft of the instrument at least 28 days before the instrument or draft is laid.

(3) The relevant authority must make a scrutiny statement before the instrument or draft is laid.

(4) A scrutiny statement is a statement—

(a) setting out the steps which the relevant authority has taken to make the draft instrument published in accordance with sub-paragraph (2) available to each House of Parliament,
(b) containing information about the relevant authority's response to—
    (i) any recommendations made by a committee of either House of Parliament about the published draft instrument, and
    (ii) any other representations made to the relevant authority about the published draft instrument, and
(c) containing any other information that the relevant authority considers appropriate in relation to the scrutiny of the instrument or draft instrument which is to be laid.

(5) A scrutiny statement must be in writing and must be published in such manner as the relevant authority considers appropriate.

(6) Sub-paragraphs (2) to (5) do not apply if the relevant authority—

(a) makes a statement in writing to the effect that the relevant authority is of the opinion that, by reason of urgency, sub-paragraphs (2) to (5) should not apply, and
(b) publishes the statement in such manner as the relevant authority considers appropriate.

(7) This paragraph does not apply in relation to any laying before each House of Parliament of an instrument or draft instrument where an equivalent draft instrument (ignoring any differences relating to procedure) has previously been laid before both Houses.

(8) This paragraph applies to an instrument which is subject to a procedure before the House of Commons only as it applies to an instrument which is subject to a procedure before each House of Parliament but as if references to each or either House of Parliament, or both Houses, were references to the House of Commons only.

(9) For the purposes of this paragraph—

(a) a power is conferred whether or not it is in force,
(b) the draft instrument published under sub-paragraph (2) need not be identical to the final version of the instrument or draft instrument as laid,
(c) where an instrument or draft is laid before each House of Parliament on different days, the earlier day is to be taken as the day on which it is laid before both Houses, and
(d) in calculating the period of 28 days, no account is to be taken of any time during which—
    (i) Parliament is dissolved or prorogued, or
    (ii) either House of Parliament is adjourned for more than four days.

(10) Sub-paragraph (8) of paragraph 13 applies for the purposes of this paragraph as it applies for the purposes of sub-paragraph (1) of that paragraph.

(11) In this paragraph "the relevant authority" means—

(a) in the case of an Order in Council or Order of Council, the Minister of the Crown who has responsibility in relation to the instrument,
(b) in the case of any other statutory instrument which is not to be made by a Minister of the Crown, the person who is to make the instrument, and
(c) in any other case, the Minister of the Crown who is to make the instrument.

[(11A) This paragraph does not apply where the amendment or revocation of subordinate legislation is for the purposes of—

(a) the withdrawal agreement (other than Part 4 of that agreement),
(b) the EEA EFTA separation agreement, . . .
(c) the Swiss citizens' rights agreement[, or
(d) a future relationship agreement.]]

(12) This paragraph is subject to any other provision made by or under this Act or any other enactment.

Explanatory statements for instruments amending or revoking regulations etc under section 2(2) of the ECA

15. (1) This paragraph applies where, on or after [IP completion day]—

(a) a statutory instrument which amends or revokes any subordinate legislation made under section 2(2) of the European Communities Act 1972, or

(b) a draft of such an instrument,

is to be laid before each House of Parliament or before the House of Commons only.

(2) Before the instrument or draft is laid, the relevant authority must make a statement as to why, in the opinion of the relevant authority, there are good reasons for the amendment or revocation.

(3) Before the instrument or draft is laid, the relevant authority must make a statement otherwise explaining—

(a) the law which is relevant to the amendment or revocation, and

(b) the effect of the amendment or revocation on retained EU law.

(4) If the relevant authority fails to make a statement required by sub-paragraph (2) or (3) before the instrument or draft is laid—

(a) a Minister of the Crown, or

(b) where the relevant authority is not a Minister of the Crown, the relevant authority,

must make a statement explaining why the relevant authority has failed to make the statement as so required.

(5) A statement under sub-paragraph (2), (3) or (4) must be made in writing and be published in such manner as the person making it considers appropriate.

(6) For the purposes of this paragraph, where an instrument or draft is laid before each House of Parliament on different days, the earlier day is to be taken as the day on which it is laid before both Houses.

(7) This paragraph applies in relation to instruments whether the power to make them is conferred before, on or after [IP completion day] including where the power is conferred by regulations under this Act (but not where it is conferred by this Act).

(8) This paragraph does not apply in relation to any laying before each House of Parliament, or before the House of Commons only, of an instrument or draft instrument where an equivalent draft instrument (ignoring any differences relating to procedure) has previously been laid before both Houses or before the House of Commons only.

(9) Sub-paragraph (8) of paragraph 13 applies for the purposes of this paragraph as it applies for the purposes of sub-paragraph (1) of that paragraph.

(10) In this paragraph "the relevant authority" means—

(a) in the case of an Order in Council or Order of Council, the Minister of the Crown who has responsibility in relation to the instrument,

(b) in the case of any other statutory instrument which is not made by a Minister of the Crown, the person who makes, or is to make, the instrument, and

(c) in any other case, the Minister of the Crown who makes, or is to make, the instrument.

[(11) This paragraph does not apply where the amendment or revocation of subordinate legislation is for the purposes of—

(a) the withdrawal agreement (other than Part 4 of that agreement),

(b) the EEA EFTA separation agreement, . . .

(c) the Swiss citizens' rights agreement[, or

(d) a future relationship agreement.]]

16. (1) This paragraph applies where, on or after [IP completion day]—

(a) a Scottish statutory instrument which amends or revokes any subordinate legislation made under section 2(2) of the European Communities Act 1972, or

(b) a draft of such an instrument,

is to be laid before the Scottish Parliament.

(2) Before the instrument or draft is laid, the relevant authority must make a statement as to why, in the opinion of the relevant authority, there are good reasons for the amendment or revocation.

(3) Before the instrument or draft is laid, the relevant authority must make a statement otherwise explaining—

(a) the law which is relevant to the amendment or revocation, and

(b) the effect of the amendment or revocation on retained EU law.

(4) If the relevant authority fails to make a statement required by sub-paragraph (2) or (3) before the instrument or draft is laid, the relevant authority must make a statement explaining why the relevant authority has failed to make the statement as so required.

(5) A statement under sub-paragraph (2), (3) or (4) must be made in writing and be published in such manner as the relevant authority considers appropriate.

(6) This paragraph applies in relation to instruments whether the power to make them is conferred before, on or after [IP completion day] including where the power is conferred by regulations under this Act (but not where it is conferred by this Act).

(7) Sub-paragraph (8) of paragraph 13 applies for the purposes of this paragraph as it applies for the purposes of sub-paragraph (1) of that paragraph.

(8) In this paragraph "the relevant authority" means—

(a) in the case of a Scottish statutory instrument which is not made by the Scottish Ministers, other than an Order in Council, the person who makes, or is to make, the instrument, and

(b) in any other case, the Scottish Ministers.

[(9) This paragraph does not apply where the amendment or revocation of subordinate legislation is for the purposes of—

(a) the withdrawal agreement (other than Part 4 of that agreement),

(b) the EEA EFTA separation agreement, . . .

(c) the Swiss citizens' rights agreement[, or
(d) a future relationship agreement.]]

NOTES

Commencement: exit day (as defined in s 20 of this Act) (paras 7, 8, 10–12); IP completion day (as defined in the European Union (Withdrawal Agreement) Act 2020, s 39) (otherwise).

Para 1: words "so far as it" in square brackets substituted by the European Union Withdrawal (Consequential Modifications) (EU Exit) Regulations 2020, SI 2020/1447, reg 3(2)(a), as from IP completion day (as defined in the European Union (Withdrawal Agreement) Act 2020, s 39). Words "IP completion day" in square brackets substituted by the European Union (Withdrawal Agreement) Act 2020, s 41(4), Sch 5, Pt 2, paras 38, 54(1), (2), as from IP completion day (as defined in the European Union (Withdrawal Agreement) Act 2020, s 39).

Para 1A: inserted by SI 2020/1447, reg 3(2)(b), as from IP completion day (as defined in the European Union (Withdrawal Agreement) Act 2020, s 39).

Para 2: words "so far as it" in square brackets in sub-paras (1) and (2) substituted by SI 2020/1447, reg 3(2)(c), as from IP completion day (as defined in the European Union (Withdrawal Agreement) Act 2020, s 39). All other amendments to this paragraph were made by the European Union (Withdrawal Agreement) Act 2020, s 41(4), Sch 5, Pt 2, paras 38, 54(1), (3), as from IP completion day (as defined in the European Union (Withdrawal Agreement) Act 2020, s 39).

Para 2A: inserted by SI 2020/1447, reg 3(2)(d), as from IP completion day (as defined in the European Union (Withdrawal Agreement) Act 2020, s 39). Note that reg 3(2)(d) of the 2020 Regulations was amended by the Spirit Drinks, Wine and European Union Withdrawal (Consequential Modifications) (Amendment) (EU Exit) Regulations 2020, SI 2020/1636, reg 4, as from 30 December 2020 (and the effect of the amendment has been incorporated in the text set out above).

Para 7: substituted by the European Union (Withdrawal Agreement) Act 2020, s 41(4), Sch 5, Pt 2, paras 38, 54(1), (4), as from exit day (as defined in s 20 of this Act).

Para 8: words omitted repealed by the European Union (Withdrawal) Act 2018 (Repeal of EU Restrictions in Devolution Legislation, etc) Regulations 2022, SI 2022/357, reg 6(5)(a), as from 31 March 2022. Words in square brackets substituted by the European Union (Withdrawal Agreement) Act 2020, s 41(4), Sch 5, Pt 2, paras 38, 54(1), (5), as from exit day (as defined in s 20 of this Act).

Para 9: word in square brackets substituted by the European Union (Withdrawal Agreement) Act 2020, s 41(4), Sch 5, Pt 2, paras 38, 54(1), (6), as from IP completion day (as defined in the European Union (Withdrawal Agreement) Act 2020, s 39).

Para 12: words omitted repealed by SI 2022/357, reg 6(5)(a), as from 31 March 2022. Words in square brackets substituted by the European Union (Withdrawal Agreement) Act 2020, s 41(4), Sch 5, Pt 2, paras 38, 54(1), (7), as from exit day (as defined in s 20 of this Act).

Para 13: words in square brackets in sub-paras (1)(a) and (4)(a) substituted, and sub-para (8A) inserted, by the European Union (Withdrawal Agreement) Act 2020, s 41(4), Sch 5, Pt 2, paras 38, 54(1), (8), as from IP completion day (as defined in the European Union (Withdrawal Agreement) Act 2020, s 39). Word omitted from sub-para (8A)(b) repealed, and sub-para (8A)(d) and the preceding word inserted, by the European Union (Future Relationship) Act 2020, s 39(3), (5), Sch 6, Pt 1, para 8, as from IP completion day (as defined in the European Union (Withdrawal Agreement) Act 2020, s 39).

Para 14: words in square brackets in sub-para (1) substituted, and sub-para (11A) inserted, by the European Union (Withdrawal Agreement) Act 2020, s 41(4), Sch 5, Pt 2, paras 38, 54(1), (9), as from IP completion day (as defined in the European Union (Withdrawal Agreement) Act 2020, s 39). Word omitted from sub-para (11A)(b) repealed, and sub-para (11A)(d) and the preceding word inserted, by the European Union (Future Relationship) Act 2020, s 39(3), (5), Sch 6, Pt 1, para 8, as from IP completion day (as defined in the European Union (Withdrawal Agreement) Act 2020, s 39).

Para 15: words in square brackets in sub-paras (1) and (7) substituted, and sub-para (11) added, by the European Union (Withdrawal Agreement) Act 2020, s 41(4), Sch 5, Pt 2, paras 38, 54(1), (10), as from IP completion day (as defined in the European Union (Withdrawal Agreement) Act 2020, s 39). Word omitted from sub-para (11)(b) repealed, and sub-para (11)(d) and the preceding word inserted, by the European Union (Future Relationship) Act 2020, s 39(3), (5), Sch 6, Pt 1, para 8, as from IP completion day (as defined in the European Union (Withdrawal Agreement) Act 2020, s 39).

Para 16: words in square brackets in sub-paras (1) and (6) substituted, and sub-para (9) added, by the European Union (Withdrawal Agreement) Act 2020, s 41(4), Sch 5, Pt 2, paras 38, 54(1), (11), as from IP completion day (as defined in the European Union (Withdrawal Agreement) Act 2020, s 39). Word omitted from sub-para (9)(b) repealed, and sub-para (9)(d) and the preceding word inserted, by the European Union (Future Relationship) Act 2020, s 39(3), (5), Sch 6, Pt 1, para 8, as from IP completion day (as defined in the European Union (Withdrawal Agreement) Act 2020, s 39).

National Assembly for Wales: as to the renaming of the National Assembly for Wales, see the note at **[12.28]**.

PART 2 SPECIFIC CONSEQUENTIAL PROVISION

(This Part contains various amendments that are outside the scope of this work.)

PART 3 GENERAL TRANSITIONAL, TRANSITORY OR SAVING PROVISION

Continuation of existing acts etc

[12.49]

[36A. (1) Anything done—
(a) in connection with anything which continues to be domestic law by virtue of section 1A(2) or 1B(2), or
(b) for a purpose mentioned in section 2(2)(a) or (b) of the European Communities Act 1972 or otherwise related to the EU or the EEA,

if in force or effective immediately before exit day, continues to be in force or effective on and after exit day.

(2) Anything done—
(a) in connection with anything which continues to be domestic law by virtue of section 1A(2) or 1B(2), or
(b) for a purpose mentioned in section 2(2)(a) or (b) of the European Communities Act 1972 or otherwise related to the EU or the EEA,

which, immediately before exit day, is in the process of being done continues to be done on and after exit day.

(3) Sub-paragraphs (1) and (2) are subject to—
(a) sections 1 to 1B and the withdrawal of the United Kingdom from the EU,
(b) any provision made under section 23(6) of this Act or section 41(5) of the European Union (Withdrawal Agreement) Act 2020, and
(c) any other provision made by or under this Act, the European Union (Withdrawal Agreement) Act 2020 or any other enactment.

(4) References in this paragraph to anything done include references to anything omitted to be done.]

37. (1) Anything done—

(a) in connection with anything which continues to be, or forms part of, domestic law by virtue of section 2, 3, 4 or 6(3) or (6), or

(b) for a purpose mentioned in section 2(2)(a) or (b) of the European Communities Act 1972 or otherwise related to the EU or the EEA,

if in force or effective immediately before [IP completion day], continues to be in force or effective on and after [IP completion day].

(2) Anything done—

(a) in connection with anything which continues to be, or forms part of, domestic law by virtue of section 2, 3, 4 or 6(3) or (6), or

(b) for a purpose mentioned in section 2(2)(a) or (b) of the European Communities Act 1972 or otherwise related to the EU or the EEA,

which, immediately before [IP completion day], is in the process of being done continues to be done on and after [IP completion day].

(3) Sub-paragraphs (1) and (2) are subject to—

(a) [sections 1 to 1B] and the withdrawal of the United Kingdom from the EU,

(b) sections 2 to [7C] and Schedule 1,

(c) any provision made under section 23(6) [of this Act or section 41(5) of the European Union (Withdrawal Agreement) Act 2020], and

(d) any other provision made by or under this Act[, the European Union (Withdrawal Agreement) Act 2020] or any other enactment.

(4) References in this paragraph to anything done include references to anything omitted to be done.

NOTES

Commencement: IP completion day (as defined in the European Union (Withdrawal Agreement) Act 2020, s 39).

Para 36A: inserted by the European Union (Withdrawal Agreement) Act 2020, s 41(4), Sch 5, Pt 2, paras 38, 55(1), (2), as from exit day (as defined in s 20 of this Act).

Para 37: all amendments to this paragraph were made by the European Union (Withdrawal Agreement) Act 2020, s 41(4), Sch 5, Pt 2, paras 38, 55(1), (3), as from IP completion day (as defined in the European Union (Withdrawal Agreement) Act 2020, s 39).

Note that para 37(1) above does not apply to a decision by ESMA to recognise a central counterparty under Article 25 of the EMIR Regulation where that decision is in force immediately before IP completion day; see the Central Counterparties (Amendment, etc, and Transitional Provision) (EU Exit) Regulations 2018, SI 2018/1184, reg 10.

PART 4 SPECIFIC TRANSITIONAL, TRANSITORY AND SAVING PROVISION

Retention of [saved EU law at end of implementation period]

[12.50]

[37A. The repeal of section 1A(1) to (4) by section 1A(5) and the repeal of section 1B(1) to (5) by section 1B(6) do not prevent an enactment to which section 2 applies from continuing to be read, on and after IP completion day and by virtue of section 2, in accordance with section 1B(3) or (4).]"

38. Section 4(2)(b) does not apply in relation to any rights, powers, liabilities, obligations, restrictions, remedies or procedures so far as they are of a kind recognised by a court or tribunal in the United Kingdom in a case decided on or after [IP completion day] but begun before [IP completion day] (whether or not as an essential part of the decision in the case).

39. (1) Subject as follows and subject to [relevant separation agreement law (for which see section 7C) and] any provision made by regulations under section 23(6) [of this Act or section 41(5) of the European Union (Withdrawal Agreement) Act 2020], section 5(4) and paragraphs 1 to 4 of Schedule 1 apply in relation to anything occurring before [IP completion day] (as well as anything occurring on or after [IP completion day]).

(2) Section 5(4) and paragraphs 1 to 4 of Schedule 1 do not affect any decision of a court or tribunal made before [IP completion day].

(3) Section 5(4) and paragraphs 3 and 4 of Schedule 1 do not apply in relation to any proceedings begun, but not finally decided, before a court or tribunal in the United Kingdom before [IP completion day].

(4) Paragraphs 1 to 4 of Schedule 1 do not apply in relation to any conduct which occurred before [IP completion day] which gives rise to any criminal liability.

(5) Paragraph 3 of Schedule 1 does not apply in relation to any proceedings begun within the period of three years beginning with [IP completion day] so far as—

(a) the proceedings involve a challenge to anything which occurred before [IP completion day], and

(b) the challenge is not for the disapplication or quashing of—

(i) an Act of Parliament or a rule of law which is not an enactment, or

(ii) any enactment, or anything else, not falling within sub-paragraph (i) which, as a result of anything falling within that sub-paragraph, could not have been different or which gives effect to, or enforces, anything falling within that sub-paragraph.

(6) Paragraph 3(2) of Schedule 1 does not apply in relation to any decision of a court or tribunal, or other public authority, on or after [IP completion day] which is a necessary consequence of any decision of a court or tribunal made before [IP completion day] or made on or after that day by virtue of this paragraph.

(7) Paragraph 4 of Schedule 1 does not apply in relation to any proceedings begun within the period of two years beginning with [IP completion day] so far as the proceedings relate to anything which occurred before [IP completion day].

Main powers in connection with withdrawal

40. The prohibition on making regulations under section [6(5A),] 8, [8A] . . . or 23(1) or [Part 1 or 1A of] Schedule 2 after a particular time does not affect the continuation in force of regulations made at or before that time (including the exercise after that time of any power conferred by regulations made at or before that time).

Devolution

41. (1) The amendments made by section 12 and Part 1 of Schedule 3 do not affect the validity of—

(a) any provision of an Act of the Scottish Parliament, Act of the National Assembly for Wales or Act of the Northern Ireland Assembly made before [IP completion day],

(b) any subordinate legislation which is subject to confirmation or approval and is made and confirmed or approved before [IP completion day], or

(c) any other subordinate legislation made before [IP completion day].

(2) Accordingly and subject to sub-paragraphs (3) to (10), the validity of anything falling within sub-paragraph (1)(a), (b) or (c) is to be decided by reference to the law before [IP completion day].

(3) Section 29(2)(d) of the Scotland Act 1998, so far as relating to EU law, does not apply to any provision of an Act of the Scottish Parliament made before [IP completion day] if the provision—

(a) comes into force on or after [IP completion day] or comes into force before that day and is a power to make, confirm or approve subordinate legislation, and

(b) is made when there are no regulations under section 30A of the Scotland Act 1998 by virtue of which the provision would be in breach of the restriction in subsection (1) of that section when the provision comes into force (or, in the case of a provision which comes into force before [IP completion day], on or after [IP completion day]) if the provision were made and the regulations were in force at that time.

(4) Section 108A(2)(e) of the Government of Wales Act 2006, so far as relating to EU law, does not apply to any provision of an Act of the National Assembly for Wales made before [IP completion day] if the provision—

(a) comes into force on or after [IP completion day] or comes into force before that day and is a power to make, confirm or approve subordinate legislation, and

(b) is made when there are no regulations under section 109A of the Government of Wales Act 2006 by virtue of which the provision would be in breach of the restriction in subsection (1) of that section when the provision comes into force (or, in the case of a provision which comes into force before [IP completion day], on or after [IP completion day]) if the provision were made and the regulations were in force at that time.

(5) Section 6(2)(d) of the Northern Ireland Act 1998, so far as relating to EU law, does not apply to any provision of an Act of the Northern Ireland Assembly made before [IP completion day] if the provision—

(a) comes into force on or after [IP completion day] or comes into force before that day and is a power to make, confirm or approve subordinate legislation, and

(b) is made when there are no regulations under section 6A of the Northern Ireland Act 1998 by virtue of which the provision would be in breach of the restriction in subsection (1) of that section when the provision comes into force (or, in the case of a provision which comes into force before [IP completion day], on or after [IP completion day]) if the provision were made and the regulations were in force at that time.

(6) Section 57(2) of the Scotland Act 1998, so far as relating to EU law, does not apply to the making, confirming or approving before [IP completion day] of any subordinate legislation if the legislation—

(a) comes into force on or after [IP completion day], and

(b) is made, confirmed or approved when there are no regulations under subsection (4) of section 57 of the Scotland Act 1998 by virtue of which the making, confirming or approving would be in breach of the restriction in that subsection when the legislation comes into force if—

(i) the making, confirming or approving had occurred at that time,

(ii) in the case of legislation confirmed or approved, the legislation was made at that time, and

(iii) the regulations were in force at that time.

(7) Section 80(8) of the Government of Wales Act 2006, so far as relating to EU law, does not apply to the making, confirming or approving before [IP completion day] of any subordinate legislation if the legislation—

(a) comes into force on or after [IP completion day], and

(b) is made, confirmed or approved when there are no regulations under subsection (8) of section 80 of the Government of Wales Act 2006 by virtue of which the making, confirming or approving would be in breach of the restriction in that subsection, so far as relating to retained EU law, when the legislation comes into force if—

(i) the making, confirming or approving had occurred at that time,

(ii) in the case of legislation confirmed or approved, the legislation was made at that time, and

(iii) the regulations were in force at that time.

(8) Section 24(1)(b) of the Northern Ireland Act 1998, so far as relating to EU law, does not apply to the making, confirming or approving before [IP completion day] of any subordinate legislation if the legislation—

(a) comes into force on or after [IP completion day], and

(b) is made, confirmed or approved when there are no regulations under subsection (3) of section 24 of the Northern Ireland Act 1998 by virtue of which the making, confirming or approving would be in breach of the restriction in that subsection when the legislation comes into force if—

(i) the making, confirming or approving had occurred at that time,

(ii) in the case of legislation confirmed or approved, the legislation was made at that time, and

(iii) the regulations were in force at that time.

(9) For the purposes of sub-paragraphs (3) to (8) assume that the restrictions relating to retained EU law in—

(a) sections 30A(1) and 57(4) of the Scotland Act 1998,

(b) sections 80(8) and 109A(1) of the Government of Wales Act 2006, and

(c) sections 6A(1) and 24(3) of the Northern Ireland Act 1998,

come into force on [IP completion day].

(10) Section 57(2) of the Scotland Act 1998, section 80(8) of the Government of Wales Act 2006 and section 24(1)(b) of the Northern Ireland Act 1998, so far as relating to EU law, do not apply to[—

(a) the making of regulations before exit day under Part 1A of Schedule 2, or

(b) the making of regulations under—

(i) Part 1B or 1C of Schedule 2, or

(ii) Schedule 4.]

42. The amendments made by Part 1 of Schedule 3 do not affect the validity of any act (other than the making, confirming or approving of subordinate legislation) done before [IP completion day] by a member of the Scottish Government, the Welsh Ministers, the First Minister for Wales, the Counsel General to the Welsh Government, a Northern Ireland Minister, the First Minister in Northern Ireland, the deputy First Minister in Northern Ireland or a Northern Ireland department.

43. . . .

Other provision

44. (1) The definition of "relevant criminal offence" in section 20(1) is to be read, until the appointed day, as if for the words "the age of 18 (or, in relation to Scotland or Northern Ireland, 21)" there were substituted "the age of 21".

(2) In sub-paragraph (1), "the appointed day" means the day on which the amendment made to section 81(3)(a) of the Regulation of Investigatory Powers Act 2000 by paragraph 211 of Schedule 7 to the Criminal Justice and Court Services Act 2000 comes into force.

45. (1) The amendment made by paragraph 17 does not affect whether the payment of any fees or other charges may be required under section 56 of the Finance Act 1973 in connection with a service or facilities provided, or an authorisation, certificate or other document issued, before that amendment comes into force.

(2) Sub-paragraph (3) applies where—

(a) immediately before the amendment made by paragraph 17 comes into force, the payment of fees or other charges could be required, under section 56 of the Finance Act 1973, in connection with the provision of a service or facilities, or issuing an authorisation, certificate or other document, in pursuance of an EU obligation, and

(b) after the amendment made by paragraph 17 comes into force—

(i) regulations made under that section (whether or not modified under Part 2 of Schedule 4 or otherwise) prescribing the fees or charges, or under which the fees or charges are to be determined, form part of retained EU law, and

(ii) the service or facilities are provided, or the authorisation, certificate or other document is issued, under or in connection with retained EU law.

(3) Despite the amendment made by paragraph 17, the payment of fees or other charges may be required, under that section and in accordance with the regulations, in connection with the provision of the service or facilities, or the issuing of the authorisation, certificate or other document.

NOTES

Commencement: 26 June 2018 (paras 41(10), 43, 44); 4 July 2018 (para 40); 1 March 2019 para 41(3)–(9)); IP completion day (as defined in the European Union (Withdrawal Agreement) Act 2020, s 39) (otherwise).

Words in square brackets in the heading preceding para 37A substituted by the European Union (Withdrawal Agreement) Act 2020, s 41(4), Sch 5, Pt 2, paras 38, 56(1), (2), as from IP completion day (as defined in the European Union (Withdrawal Agreement) Act 2020, s 39).

Para 37A: inserted by the European Union (Withdrawal Agreement) Act 2020, s 41(4), Sch 5, Pt 2, paras 38, 56(1), (3), as from IP completion day (as defined in the European Union (Withdrawal Agreement) Act 2020, s 39).

Para 38: words in square brackets substituted by the European Union (Withdrawal Agreement) Act 2020, s 41(4), Sch 5, Pt 2, paras 38, 56(1), (4), as from IP completion day (as defined in the European Union (Withdrawal Agreement) Act 2020, s 39).

Para 39: words "IP completion day" in square brackets substituted, and other words in square brackets inserted, by the European Union (Withdrawal Agreement) Act 2020, s 41(4), Sch 5, Pt 2, paras 38, 56(1), (5), as from IP completion day (as defined in the European Union (Withdrawal Agreement) Act 2020, s 39).

Para 40: the figure "6(5A)," in square brackets was inserted by the European Union (Withdrawal Agreement) Act 2020, s 41(4), Sch 5, Pt 2, paras 38, 56(1), (6)(a), as from 19 May 2020. All other amendments to this paragraph were made by the European Union (Withdrawal Agreement) Act 2020, s 41(4), Sch 5, Pt 2, paras 38, 56(1), (6)(b)–(d), as from 23 January 2020.

Para 41 is amended as follows:

The words "IP completion day" in square brackets were substituted by the European Union (Withdrawal Agreement) Act 2020, s 41(4), Sch 5, Pt 2, paras 38, 56(1), (7)(a), as from 23 January 2020 (in so far as the words occur in sub-paras (3)–(9)), and as from IP completion day (as defined in the European Union (Withdrawal Agreement) Act 2020, s 39) (otherwise).

Words in square brackets in sub-para (10) substituted by the European Union (Withdrawal Agreement) Act 2020, s 41(4), Sch 5, Pt 2, paras 38, 56(1), (7)(b), as from exit day (as defined in s 20 of this Act) (for the purposes of making regulations under s 8A, or Part 1A of Sch 2), as from 19 May 2020 (for all other purposes except in so far as relating to the making of regulations under Part 1 of Sch 2), and as from IP completion day (otherwise).

Para 42: words in square brackets substituted by the European Union (Withdrawal Agreement) Act 2020, s 41(4), Sch 5, Pt 2, paras 38, 56(1), (8), as from IP completion day (as defined in the European Union (Withdrawal Agreement) Act 2020, s 39).

Para 43: repealed by the European Union (Withdrawal) Act 2018 (Repeal of EU Restrictions in Devolution Legislation, etc) Regulations 2022, SI 2022/357, reg 6(5)(c), as from 31 March 2022.

National Assembly for Wales: as to the renaming of the National Assembly for Wales, see the note at **[12.28]**.

SCHEDULE 9
ADDITIONAL REPEALS

(*Repeals the European Parliamentary Elections Act 2002, the European Parliament (Representation) Act 2003, the European Union (Amendment) Act 2008, the European Union Act 2011, the European Union (Approval of Treaty Amendment Decision) Act 2012, the European Union (Approvals) Act 2013, the European Union (Approvals) Act 2014, the European Union (Finance) Act 2015, the European Union (Approvals) Act 2015, and ss 82, 88(5)(c) of the*

Serious Crime Act 2015.)

EUROPEAN UNION (WITHDRAWAL AGREEMENT) ACT 2020

(2020 c 1)

An Act to implement, and make other provision in connection with, the agreement between the United Kingdom and the EU under Article 50(2) of the Treaty on European Union which sets out the arrangements for the United Kingdom's withdrawal from the EU

[23 January 2020]

NOTES

'Exit day' and 'IP completion day': 'exit day' is defined by the European Union (Withdrawal) Act 2018, s 20 (at **[12.28]**) as 31 January 2020 at 11pm. 'IP completion day' is defined by section 39 of this Act (at **[12.53]**) as 31 December 2020 at 11pm.

ARRANGEMENT OF SECTIONS

PART 1 IMPLEMENTATION PERIOD

1–4 (*Ss 1–4 insert the European Union (Withdrawal) Act 2018, ss 1A, 1B, 8A, Sch 2, Pt 1A ante.*)

PART 2 REMAINING IMPLEMENTATION OF WITHDRAWAL AGREEMENT ETC: GENERAL

5, 6 (*Ss 5, 6 insert the European Union (Withdrawal) Act 2018, ss 7A, 7B ante.*)

PART 3 CITIZENS' RIGHTS

7–11 (*Ss 7–11 (Rights in relation to entry and residence) are outside the scope of this work.*)

Professional qualifications

[12.51]

12 Recognition of professional qualifications

(1) An appropriate authority may by regulations make such provision as the authority considers appropriate—
- (a) to implement Chapter 3 of Title II of Part 2 of the withdrawal agreement (professional qualifications),
- (b) to supplement the effect of section 7A of the European Union (Withdrawal) Act 2018 in relation to that Chapter, or
- (c) otherwise for the purposes of dealing with matters arising out of, or related to, that Chapter (including matters arising by virtue of section 7A of that Act and that Chapter).

(2) An appropriate authority may by regulations make such provision as the authority considers appropriate—
- (a) to implement Chapter 3 of Title II of Part 2 of the EEA EFTA separation agreement (professional qualifications),
- (b) to supplement the effect of section 7B of the European Union (Withdrawal) Act 2018 in relation to that Chapter, or
- (c) otherwise for the purposes of dealing with matters arising out of, or related to, that Chapter (including matters arising by virtue of section 7B of that Act and that Chapter).

(3) An appropriate authority may by regulations make such provision as the authority considers appropriate—

(a) to implement professional qualification provisions of the Swiss citizens' rights agreement,

(b) to supplement the effect of section 7B of the European Union (Withdrawal) Act 2018 in relation to those provisions, or

(c) otherwise for the purposes of dealing with matters arising out of, or related to, those provisions (including matters arising by virtue of section 7B of that Act and those provisions).

(4) For the purposes of subsection (3) the following are "professional qualification provisions" of the Swiss citizens' rights agreement—

(a) Part 4 of that agreement (mutual recognition of professional qualifications);

(b) Article 23(4) of that agreement as regards the recognition of professional qualifications.

(5) If an appropriate authority considers it appropriate, regulations under subsection (1) or (2) relating to the implementation of a provision of Chapter 3 of Title II of Part 2 of the withdrawal agreement or of the EEA EFTA separation agreement may be made so as to apply both to—

(a) persons to whom the provision in question applies, and

(b) persons to whom that provision does not apply but who may be granted leave to enter or remain in the United Kingdom by virtue of residence scheme immigration rules, whether or not they have been granted such leave (see section 17).

(6) The power to make regulations under subsection (1), (2) or (3) may (among other things) be exercised by modifying any provision made by or under an enactment.

(7) In subsection (6) "enactment" does not include primary legislation passed or made after IP completion day.

(8) In this section, "appropriate authority" means—

(a) a Minister of the Crown,

(b) a devolved authority, or

(c) a Minister of the Crown acting jointly with a devolved authority.

(9) Schedule 1 contains further provision about the power of devolved authorities to make regulations under this section.

NOTES

Commencement: 19 May 2020.

Regulations: the Professional Qualifications and Services (Amendments and Miscellaneous Provisions) (EU Exit) Regulations 2020, SI 2020/1038; the Services of Lawyers and Lawyer's Practice (Revocation etc) (EU Exit) Regulations 2020, SI 2020/1342. Other Regulations made under this section are outside the scope of this work.

13–17 *(Ss 13–17 (Co-ordination of social security systems; Equal treatment etc; Independent Monitoring Authority; etc) outside the scope of this work.)*

PART 4 OTHER SUBJECT AREAS

18–37 *(Ss 18–37 amend the European Union (Withdrawal) Act 2018 ante, and are otherwise outside the scope of this work.)*

PART 5 GENERAL AND FINAL PROVISION

Parliamentary sovereignty

[12.52]

38 Parliamentary sovereignty

(1) It is recognised that the Parliament of the United Kingdom is sovereign.

(2) In particular, its sovereignty subsists notwithstanding—

(a) directly applicable or directly effective EU law continuing to be recognised and available in domestic law by virtue of section 1A or 1B of the European Union (Withdrawal) Act 2018 (savings of existing law for the implementation period),

(b) section 7A of that Act (other directly applicable or directly effective aspects of the withdrawal agreement),

(c) section 7B of that Act (deemed direct applicability or direct effect in relation to the EEA EFTA separation agreement and the Swiss citizens' rights agreement), and

(d) section 7C of that Act (interpretation of law relating to the withdrawal agreement (other than the implementation period), the EEA EFTA separation agreement and the Swiss citizens' rights agreement).

(3) Accordingly, nothing in this Act derogates from the sovereignty of the Parliament of the United Kingdom.

NOTES

Commencement: 23 January 2020.

Interpretation

[12.53]

39 Interpretation

(1) In this Act—

"devolved authority" means—

(a) the Scottish Ministers,

(b) the Welsh Ministers, or

(c) a Northern Ireland department;

"EEA EFTA separation agreement" means (as modified from time to time in accordance with any provision of it) the Agreement on arrangements between Iceland, the Principality of Liechtenstein, the Kingdom of Norway and the United Kingdom of Great Britain and Northern Ireland following the withdrawal of the United Kingdom from the European Union, the EEA Agreement and other agreements applicable between the United Kingdom and the EEA EFTA States by virtue of the United Kingdom's membership of the European Union;

"enactment" means an enactment whenever passed or made and includes—

(a) an enactment contained in any Order in Council, order, rules, regulations, scheme, warrant, byelaw or other instrument made under an Act of Parliament,

(b) an enactment contained in any Order in Council made in exercise of Her Majesty's Prerogative,

(c) an enactment contained in, or in an instrument made under, an Act of the Scottish Parliament,

(d) an enactment contained in, or in an instrument made under, a Measure or Act of the National Assembly for Wales,

(e) an enactment contained in, or in an instrument made under, Northern Ireland legislation,

(f) an enactment contained in any instrument made by a member of the Scottish Government, the Welsh Ministers, the First Minister for Wales, the Counsel General to the Welsh Government, a Northern Ireland Minister, the First Minister in Northern Ireland, the deputy First Minister in Northern Ireland or a Northern Ireland department in exercise of prerogative or other executive functions of Her Majesty which are exercisable by such a person on behalf of Her Majesty,

(g) an enactment contained in, or in an instrument made under, a Measure of the Church Assembly or of the General Synod of the Church of England, and

(h) any retained direct EU legislation;

"IP completion day" means 31 December 2020 at 11.00 p.m (and see subsections (2) to (5));

"Minister of the Crown" has the same meaning as in the Ministers of the Crown Act 1975 and also includes the Commissioners for Her Majesty's Revenue and Customs;

"modify" includes amend, repeal or revoke (and related expressions are to be read accordingly);

"primary legislation" means—

(a) an Act of Parliament,

(b) an Act of the Scottish Parliament,

(c) a Measure or Act of the National Assembly for Wales, or

(d) Northern Ireland legislation;

"subordinate legislation" means any Order in Council, order, rules, regulations, scheme, warrant, byelaw or other instrument made under any primary legislation;

"Swiss citizens' rights agreement" means (as modified from time to time in accordance with any provision of it) the Agreement signed at Bern on 25 February 2019 between the United Kingdom of Great Britain and Northern Ireland and the Swiss Confederation on citizens' rights following the withdrawal of the United Kingdom from—

(a) the European Union, and

(b) the free movement of persons agreement,

so far as the Agreement operates for the purposes of the case where "specified date" for the purposes of that Agreement has the meaning given in Article 2(b)(ii) of that Agreement;

"withdrawal agreement" means the agreement between the United Kingdom and the EU under Article 50(2) of the Treaty on European Union which sets out the arrangements for the United Kingdom's withdrawal from the EU (as that agreement is modified from time to time in accordance with any provision of it).

(2) In this Act references to before, after or on IP completion day, or to beginning with IP completion day, are to be read as references to before, after or at 11.00pm on 31 December 2020 or (as the case may be) to beginning with 11.00pm on that day.

(3) Subsection (4) applies if, by virtue of any change to EU summer-time arrangements, the transition or implementation period provided for by Part 4 of the withdrawal agreement is to end on a day or time which is different from that specified in the definition of "IP completion day" in subsection (1).

(4) A Minister of the Crown may by regulations—

(a) amend the definition of "IP completion day" in subsection (1) to ensure that the day and time specified in the definition are the day and time that the transition or implementation period provided for by Part 4 of the withdrawal agreement is to end, and

(b) amend subsection (2) in consequence of any such amendment.

(5) In subsection (3) "EU summer-time arrangements" means the arrangements provided for by Directive 2000/84/EC of the European Parliament and of the Council of 19 January 2001 on summer-time arrangements.

(6) In this Act any reference to an Article of the Treaty on European Union includes a reference to that Article as applied by Article 106a of the Euratom Treaty.

NOTES

Commencement: 23 January 2020.

National Assembly for Wales: as to the renaming of the National Assembly for Wales, see the note at **[12.28]**.

Supplementary and final

[12.54]

40 Regulations

Schedule 4 contains provision about regulations under this Act (including provision about procedure).

NOTES

Commencement: 23 January 2020.

[12.55]

41 Consequential and transitional provision etc

(1) A Minister of the Crown may by regulations make such provision as the Minister considers appropriate in consequence of this Act.

(2) The power to make regulations under subsection (1) may (among other things) be exercised by modifying any provision made by or under an enactment.

(3) In subsection (2) "enactment" does not include primary legislation passed or made after IP completion day.

(4) Parts 1 and 2 of Schedule 5 contain minor and consequential provision.

(5) A Minister of the Crown may by regulations make such transitional, transitory or saving provision as the Minister considers appropriate in connection with the coming into force of any provision of this Act (including its operation in connection with exit day or IP completion day).

(6) Part 3 of Schedule 5 contains transitional, transitory and saving provision.

NOTES

Commencement: 23 January 2020 (sub-ss (1), (3), (5), and sub-ss (4) and (6) for certain purposes); immediately before exit day (as defined in the European Union (Withdrawal) Act 2018, s 20) (sub-s (4) for certain purposes); exit day (as defined in the European Union (Withdrawal) Act 2018, s 20) (sub-ss (4) and (6) for certain purposes); 19 May 2020 (sub-ss (4) and (6) for certain purposes); 31 December 2020 (sub-s (4) for certain purposes); IP completion day (as defined in s 39 of this Act) (sub-s (4) for certain purposes); to be appointed (otherwise).

Regulations: the Financial Services (Consequential Amendments) Regulations 2020, SI 2020/56; the Companies and Statutory Auditors etc (Consequential Amendments) (EU Exit) Regulations 2020, SI 2020/523; the Financial Services and Economic and Monetary Policy (Consequential Amendments) (EU Exit) Regulations 2020, SI 2020/1301; the European Union Withdrawal (Consequential Modifications) (EU Exit) Regulations 2020, SI 2020/1447; the Challenges to Validity of EU Instruments (Amendment) (EU Exit) Regulations 2020, SI 2020/1503; the European Union (Withdrawal) Act 2018 and European Union (Withdrawal Agreement) Act 2020 (Commencement, Transitional and Savings Provisions) Regulations 2020, SI 2020/1622 at **[12.182]**. Other Regulations made under this section are outside the scope of this work.

[12.56]

42 Extent, commencement and short title

(1) Subject to subsections (2) to (5), this Act extends to England and Wales, Scotland and Northern Ireland.

(2) Any provision of this Act which amends or repeals an enactment has the same extent as the enactment amended or repealed.

(3) Accordingly, section 1 (but not section 2) also extends to the Isle of Man, the Channel Islands and Gibraltar.

(4) The power in section 36 of the Immigration Act 1971 or (as the case may be) section 60(4) of the UK Borders Act 2007 may be exercised so as to extend (with or without modifications) to the Isle of Man or any of the Channel Islands the modifications made to that Act by section 10 above.

(5) Paragraphs 1 and 2 of Schedule 5, so far as they relate to the modification of any provision in subordinate legislation which extends outside England and Wales, Scotland and Northern Ireland, also extend there.

(6) The following provisions—

- (a) sections 3 and 4,
- (b) sections 11, 16 and 17,
- (c) sections 20, 29 and 31 to 40 (including Schedule 4),
- (d) section 41(1) to (3) and (5),
- (e) the following provisions of Schedule 5—
  - (i) paragraphs 1(3) to (6) and 2,
  - (ii) paragraph 3(2) to (8),
  - (iii) paragraph 4,
  - (iv) paragraphs 5 and 7(a) and (b),
  - (v) paragraphs 8 and 12(a) and (b),
  - (vi) paragraphs 17, 20, 22, 24, 27 and 31,
  - (vii) paragraphs 32, 36(a) and (b) and 37(b) and (c),
  - (viii) paragraphs 38, 41(1) and (3)(a), 42, 44(1), (2)(a), (d) and (e) and (3), 47(1), (2), (4) and (6) and 50,
  - (ix) paragraphs 51 and 56(1) and (7)(b) for the purposes of making regulations under section 8A of, or Part 1A of Schedule 2 to, the European Union (Withdrawal) Act 2018,
  - (x) paragraphs 52(1) and (3) to (7) and 53(1) to (4), (6), (7)(a), (8)(a) and (9) to (13),
  - (xi) paragraph 56(1) and (6)(b) to (d), and
  - (xii) paragraphs 65 to 68,

  (and section 41(4) and (6) so far as relating to any provision so far as it falls within any of sub-paragraphs (i) to (xii)), and
- (f) this section,

come into force on the day on which this Act is passed.

(7) The provisions of this Act, so far as they are not brought into force by subsection (6), come into force on such day as a Minister of the Crown may by regulations appoint; and different days may be appointed for different purposes.

(8) This Act may be cited as the European Union (Withdrawal Agreement) Act 2020.

NOTES

Commencement: 23 January 2020.

Regulations: the European Union (Withdrawal Agreement) Act 2020 (Commencement No 1) Regulations 2020, SI 2020/75; the European Union (Withdrawal Agreement) Act 2020 (Commencement No 2) Regulations 2020, SI 2020/317 (note that these Regulations commence certain provisions in s 15 and Schs 2 and 3 which are outside the scope of this work); the European Union (Withdrawal Agreement) Act 2020 (Commencement No 3) Regulations 2020, SI 2020/518; the European Union (Withdrawal) Act 2018 and European Union (Withdrawal Agreement) Act 2020 (Commencement, Transitional and Savings Provisions) Regulations 2020, SI 2020/1622 at **[12.182]**.

SCHEDULES

SCHEDULES 1–3

(Schedule 1 (Powers of Devolved Authorities under Sections 12, 13 and 14); Schedule 2 (Independent Monitoring Authority for the Citizens' Rights Agreements); Schedule 3 (Protection for Certain Rights, Safeguards etc in Belfast Agreement) are outside the scope of this work.)

SCHEDULE 4
REGULATIONS UNDER THIS ACT

Section 40

PART 1 PROCEDURE

Rights in relation to entry and residence

[12.57]

1. (1) A statutory instrument containing—

(a) the first regulations under section 7(1)(b), (c), (d), (e), (f) or (g), 8(1) or 9, or
(b) regulations under section 7, 8 or 9 which amend, repeal or revoke primary legislation or retained direct principal EU legislation,

may not be made unless a draft of the instrument has been laid before, and approved by a resolution of, each House of Parliament.

(2) Any other statutory instrument containing regulations under section 7, 8 or 9 is subject to annulment in pursuance of a resolution of either House of Parliament.

2. (1) A statutory instrument containing the first regulations under section 11—

(a) must be laid before Parliament after being made, and
(b) ceases to have effect at the end of the period of 40 days beginning with the day on which the instrument is made unless, during that period, the instrument is approved by a resolution of each House of Parliament.

(2) Any other statutory instrument containing regulations under section 11 which amend, repeal or revoke—

(a) primary legislation, or
(b) retained direct principal EU legislation,

may not be made unless a draft of the instrument has been laid before, and approved by a resolution of, each House of Parliament.

(3) A statutory instrument containing regulations under section 11, other than a statutory instrument to which sub-paragraph (1) or (2) applies, is subject to annulment in pursuance of a resolution of either House of Parliament.

(4) In calculating the period of 40 days for the purposes of sub-paragraph (1) no account is to be taken of any time during which—

(a) Parliament is dissolved or prorogued, or
(b) either House of Parliament is adjourned for more than four days.

(5) If regulations cease to have effect as a result of sub-paragraph (1) that—

(a) does not affect the validity of anything previously done under the regulations, and
(b) does not prevent the making of new regulations.

Powers under sections 12, 13 and 14: sole exercise

3. (1) A statutory instrument containing regulations under section 12, 13 or 14 of a Minister of the Crown acting alone which amend, repeal or revoke—

(a) primary legislation, or
(b) retained direct principal EU legislation,

may not be made unless a draft of the instrument has been laid before, and approved by a resolution of, each House of Parliament.

(2) Any other statutory instrument containing regulations under section 12, 13 or 14 of a Minister of the Crown acting alone is subject to annulment in pursuance of a resolution of either House of Parliament.

(3) Regulations under section 12, 13 or 14 of the Scottish Ministers acting alone which amend, repeal or revoke—

(a) primary legislation, or
(b) retained direct principal EU legislation,

are subject to the affirmative procedure (see section 29 of the Interpretation and Legislative Reform (Scotland) Act 2010 (asp 10)).

(4) Any other regulations under section 12, 13 or 14 of the Scottish Ministers acting alone are subject to the negative procedure (see section 28 of the Interpretation and Legislative Reform (Scotland) Act 2010).

(5) A statutory instrument containing regulations under section 12, 13 or 14 of the Welsh Ministers acting alone which amend, repeal or revoke—

(a) primary legislation, or
(b) retained direct principal EU legislation,

may not be made unless a draft of the instrument has been laid before, and approved by a resolution of, the National Assembly for Wales.

(6) Any other statutory instrument containing regulations under section 12, 13 or 14 of the Welsh Ministers acting alone is subject to annulment in pursuance of a resolution of the National Assembly for Wales.

(7) Regulations under section 12, 13 or 14 of a Northern Ireland department acting alone which amend, repeal or revoke—

(a) primary legislation, or
(b) retained direct principal EU legislation,

may not be made unless a draft of the regulations has been laid before, and approved by a resolution of, the Northern Ireland Assembly.

(8) Any other regulations under section 12, 13 or 14 of a Northern Ireland department acting alone are subject to negative resolution within the meaning of section 41(6) of the Interpretation Act (Northern Ireland) 1954 as if they were a statutory instrument within the meaning of that Act.

Powers under sections 12, 13 and 14: joint exercise

4. (1) This paragraph applies to regulations under section 12, 13 or 14 of a Minister of the Crown acting jointly with a devolved authority.

(2) The procedure provided for by sub-paragraph (3) or (4) applies in relation to regulations to which this paragraph applies as well as any other procedure provided for by this paragraph which is applicable in relation to the regulations concerned.

(3) A statutory instrument containing regulations to which this paragraph applies which amend, repeal or revoke—

(a) primary legislation, or

(b) retained direct principal EU legislation,

may not be made unless a draft of the instrument has been laid before, and approved by a resolution of, each House of Parliament.

(4) Any other statutory instrument containing regulations to which this paragraph applies is subject to annulment in pursuance of a resolution of either House of Parliament.

(5) Regulations to which this paragraph applies which are made jointly with the Scottish Ministers and amend, repeal or revoke—

(a) primary legislation, or

(b) retained direct principal EU legislation,

are subject to the affirmative procedure.

(6) Any other regulations to which this paragraph applies which are made jointly with the Scottish Ministers are subject to the negative procedure.

(7) Section 29 of the Interpretation and Legislative Reform (Scotland) Act 2010 (affirmative procedure) applies in relation to regulations to which sub-paragraph (5) applies as it applies in relation to devolved subordinate legislation (within the meaning of Part 2 of that Act) which is subject to the affirmative procedure (but as if references to a Scottish statutory instrument were references to a statutory instrument).

(8) Sections 28(2), (3) and (8) and 31 of the Interpretation and Legislative Reform (Scotland) Act 2010 (negative procedure etc) apply in relation to regulations to which sub-paragraph (6) applies as they apply in relation to devolved subordinate legislation (within the meaning of Part 2 of that Act) which is subject to the negative procedure (but as if references to a Scottish statutory instrument were references to a statutory instrument).

(9) Section 32 of the Interpretation and Legislative Reform (Scotland) Act 2010 (laying) applies in relation to the laying before the Scottish Parliament of a statutory instrument containing regulations to which sub-paragraph (5) or (6) applies as it applies in relation to the laying before that Parliament of a Scottish statutory instrument (within the meaning of Part 2 of that Act).

(10) A statutory instrument containing regulations to which this paragraph applies which are made jointly with the Welsh Ministers and amend, repeal or revoke—

(a) primary legislation, or

(b) retained direct principal EU legislation,

may not be made unless a draft of the instrument has been laid before, and approved by a resolution of, the National Assembly for Wales.

(11) Any other statutory instrument containing regulations to which this paragraph applies which are made jointly with the Welsh Ministers is subject to annulment in pursuance of a resolution of the National Assembly for Wales.

(12) Regulations to which this paragraph applies which are made jointly with a Northern Ireland department and amend, repeal or revoke—

(a) primary legislation, or

(b) retained direct principal EU legislation,

may not be made unless a draft of the regulations has been laid before, and approved by a resolution of, the Northern Ireland Assembly.

(13) Any other regulations to which this paragraph applies which are made jointly with a Northern Ireland department are subject to negative resolution within the meaning of section 41(6) of the Interpretation Act (Northern Ireland) 1954 as if they were a statutory instrument within the meaning of that Act.

(14) If in accordance with sub-paragraph (4), (6), (11) or (13)—

(a) either House of Parliament resolves that an address be presented to Her Majesty praying that an instrument be annulled, or

(b) a relevant devolved legislature resolves that an instrument be annulled,

nothing further is to be done under the instrument after the date of the resolution and Her Majesty may by Order in Council revoke the instrument.

(15) In sub-paragraph (14) "relevant devolved legislature" means—

(a) in the case of regulations made jointly with the Scottish Ministers, the Scottish Parliament,

(b) in the case of regulations made jointly with the Welsh Ministers, the National Assembly for Wales, and

(c) in the case of regulations made jointly with a Northern Ireland department, the Northern Ireland Assembly.

(16) Sub-paragraph (14) does not affect the validity of anything previously done under the instrument or prevent the making of a new instrument.

(17) Sub-paragraphs (14) to (16) apply in place of provision made by any other enactment about the effect of such a resolution.

Power to amend definition of "IP completion day"

5. A statutory instrument containing regulations under section 39(4) is subject to annulment in pursuance of a resolution of either House of Parliament.

Consequential provision

6. A statutory instrument containing regulations under section 41(1) is subject to annulment in pursuance of a resolution of either House of Parliament.

The IMA

7. A statutory instrument containing regulations under paragraph 39 or 40 of Schedule 2 may not be made unless a draft of the instrument has been laid before, and approved by a resolution of, each House of Parliament.

Power under paragraph 1(3) of Schedule 5: sole exercise

8. (1) A statutory instrument containing regulations made by a Minister of the Crown acting alone under paragraph 1(3) of Schedule 5 on or after exit day is subject to annulment in pursuance of a resolution of either House of Parliament.

(2) Regulations made by the Scottish Ministers acting alone under paragraph 1(3) of Schedule 5 on or after exit day are subject to the negative procedure (see section 28 of the Interpretation and Legislative Reform (Scotland) Act 2010).

(3) A statutory instrument containing regulations made by the Welsh Ministers acting alone under paragraph 1(3) of Schedule 5 on or after exit day is subject to annulment in pursuance of a resolution of the National Assembly for Wales.

(4) Regulations made by a Northern Ireland department acting alone under paragraph 1(3) of Schedule 5 on or after exit day are subject to negative resolution within the meaning of section 41(6) of the Interpretation Act (Northern Ireland) 1954 as if they were a statutory instrument within the meaning of that Act.

Power under paragraph 1(3) of Schedule 5: joint exercise

9. (1) This paragraph applies to regulations under paragraph 1(3) of Schedule 5 of a Minister of the Crown acting jointly with a devolved authority.

(2) The procedure provided for by sub-paragraph (3) applies in relation to regulations to which this paragraph applies as well as any other procedure provided for by this paragraph which is applicable in relation to the regulations concerned.

(3) A statutory instrument containing regulations to which this paragraph applies which are made on or after exit day is subject to annulment in pursuance of a resolution of either House of Parliament.

(4) Regulations to which this paragraph applies which are made jointly with the Scottish Ministers on or after exit day are subject to the negative procedure.

(5) Sections 28(2), (3) and (8) and 31 of the Interpretation and Legislative Reform (Scotland) Act 2010 (negative procedure etc) apply in relation to regulations to which sub-paragraph (4) applies as they apply in relation to devolved subordinate legislation (within the meaning of Part 2 of that Act) which is subject to the negative procedure (but as if references to a Scottish statutory instrument were references to a statutory instrument).

(6) Section 32 of the Interpretation and Legislative Reform (Scotland) Act 2010 (laying) applies in relation to the laying before the Scottish Parliament of a statutory instrument containing regulations to which sub-paragraph (4) applies as it applies in relation to the laying before that Parliament of a Scottish statutory instrument (within the meaning of Part 2 of that Act).

(7) A statutory instrument containing regulations to which this paragraph applies which are made jointly with the Welsh Ministers on or after exit day is subject to annulment in pursuance of a resolution of the National Assembly for Wales.

(8) Regulations to which this paragraph applies which are made jointly with a Northern Ireland department on or after exit day are subject to negative resolution within the meaning of section 41(6) of the Interpretation Act (Northern Ireland) 1954 as if they were a statutory instrument within the meaning of that Act.

(9) If in accordance with this paragraph—

(a) either House of Parliament resolves that an address be presented to Her Majesty praying that an instrument be annulled, or

(b) a relevant devolved legislature resolves that an instrument be annulled,

nothing further is to be done under the instrument after the date of the resolution and Her Majesty may by Order in Council revoke the instrument.

(10) In sub-paragraph (9) "relevant devolved legislature" means—

(a) in the case of regulations made jointly with the Scottish Ministers, the Scottish Parliament,

(b) in the case of regulations made jointly with the Welsh Ministers, the National Assembly for Wales, and

(c) in the case of regulations made jointly with a Northern Ireland department, the Northern Ireland Assembly.

(11) Sub-paragraph (9) does not affect the validity of anything previously done under the instrument or prevent the making of a new instrument.

(12) Sub-paragraphs (9) to (11) apply in place of provision made by any other enactment about the effect of such a resolution.

Power under paragraph 3(2) of Schedule 5

10. (1) Regulations made by the Scottish Ministers under paragraph 3(2) of Schedule 5 on or after exit day are subject to the negative procedure (see section 28 of the Interpretation and Legislative Reform (Scotland) Act 2010).

(2) A statutory instrument containing regulations made by the Welsh Ministers under paragraph 3(2) of Schedule 5 on or after exit day is subject to annulment in pursuance of a resolution of the National Assembly for Wales.

(3) Regulations made by a Northern Ireland department under paragraph 3(2) of Schedule 5 on or after exit day are subject to negative resolution within the meaning of section 41(6) of the Interpretation Act (Northern Ireland) 1954 as if they were a statutory instrument within the meaning of that Act.

NOTES

Commencement: 23 January 2020.

National Assembly for Wales: as to the renaming of the National Assembly for Wales, see the note at **[12.28]**.

PART 2 GENERAL PROVISION ABOUT POWERS UNDER ACT

Scope and nature of powers: general

[12.58]

11. (1) Any power to make regulations under this Act—

(a) so far as exercisable by a Minister of the Crown or by a Minister of the Crown acting jointly with a devolved authority, is exercisable by statutory instrument,

(b) so far as exercisable by the Welsh Ministers or by the Welsh Ministers acting jointly with a Minister of the Crown, is exercisable by statutory instrument, and

(c) so far as exercisable by a Northern Ireland department (other than when acting jointly with a Minister of the Crown), is exercisable by statutory rule for the purposes of the Statutory Rules (Northern Ireland) Order 1979 (SI 1979/1573 (NI 12)) (and not by statutory instrument).

(2) For regulations made under this Act by the Scottish Ministers, see also section 27 of the Interpretation and Legislative Reform (Scotland) Act 2010 (asp 10) (Scottish statutory instruments).

12. Any power to make regulations under this Act—

(a) may be exercised so as to make different provision for different cases or descriptions of case, different circumstances, different purposes or different areas, and

(b) includes power to make supplementary, incidental, consequential, transitional, transitory or saving provision.

13. The fact that a power to make regulations is conferred by this Act does not affect the extent of any other power to make regulations under this Act.

Anticipatory exercise of powers in relation to withdrawal agreement etc

14. Any power to make regulations under this Act in relation to the withdrawal agreement, the EEA EFTA separation agreement or the Swiss citizens' rights agreement, or any modification of any of them which requires ratification, is capable of being exercised before the agreement or (as the case may be) modification concerned is ratified.

Scope of appointed day power

15. The power of a Minister of the Crown under section 42(7) to appoint a day includes a power to appoint a time on that day if the Minister considers it appropriate to do so.

Hybrid instruments

16. If an instrument, or a draft of an instrument, containing regulations under this Act would, apart from this paragraph, be treated as a hybrid instrument for the purposes of the standing orders of either House of Parliament, it is to proceed in that House as if it were not a hybrid instrument.

Combinations of instruments

17. (1) Sub-paragraph (2) applies to a statutory instrument containing regulations under this Act which is subject to a procedure before Parliament for the approval of the instrument in draft before it is made or its approval after it is made.

(2) The statutory instrument may also include regulations under this Act or another enactment which are made by statutory instrument which is subject to a procedure before Parliament that provides for the annulment of the instrument after it has been made.

(3) Where regulations are included as mentioned in sub-paragraph (2), the procedure applicable to the statutory instrument is the procedure mentioned in sub-paragraph (1) and not the procedure mentioned in sub-paragraph (2).

(4) Sub-paragraphs (1) to (3) apply in relation to a statutory instrument containing regulations under this Act which is subject to a procedure before the National Assembly for Wales as they apply in relation to a statutory instrument containing regulations under this Act which is subject to a procedure before Parliament but as if the references to Parliament were references to the National Assembly for Wales.

(5) Sub-paragraphs (1) to (3) apply in relation to a statutory rule as they apply in relation to a statutory instrument but as if the references to Parliament were references to the Northern Ireland Assembly.

(6) Sub-paragraphs (1) to (3) apply in relation to a statutory instrument containing regulations under this Act which is subject to a procedure before the Scottish Parliament, the National Assembly for Wales or the Northern Ireland Assembly as well as a procedure before Parliament as they apply to a statutory instrument containing regulations under this Act which is subject to a procedure before Parliament but as if the references to Parliament were references to Parliament and the Scottish Parliament, the National Assembly for Wales or (as the case may be) the Northern Ireland Assembly.

(7) This paragraph does not prevent the inclusion of other regulations in a statutory instrument or statutory rule which contains regulations under this Act (and, accordingly, references in this Schedule to an instrument containing regulations are to be read as references to an instrument containing (whether alone or with other provision) regulations).

NOTES

Commencement: 23 January 2020.

National Assembly for Wales: as to the renaming of the National Assembly for Wales, see the note at **[12.28]**.

SCHEDULE 5
CONSEQUENTIAL AND TRANSITIONAL PROVISION ETC

Section 41(4) and (6)

PART 1 GENERAL CONSEQUENTIAL PROVISION

Subordinate legislation with commencement by reference to exit day

[12.59]

1. (1) Any provision in subordinate legislation made before exit day under—

(a) any provision of the European Union (Withdrawal) Act 2018 (or any provision made under any such provision), or

(b) any other enactment,

which provides, by reference to exit day (however expressed), for all or part of that or any other subordinate legislation to come into force immediately before exit day, on exit day or at any time after exit day is to be read instead as providing for the subordinate legislation or (as the case may be) the part to come into force immediately before IP completion day, on IP completion day or (as the case may be) at the time concerned after IP completion day.

(2) Sub-paragraph (1) does not apply so far as it is expressly disapplied by the subordinate legislation that provides as mentioned in that sub-paragraph.

(3) An appropriate authority may by regulations—

(a) provide for sub-paragraph (1) not to apply to any extent in particular cases or descriptions of case, or

(b) make different provision in particular cases or descriptions of case to that made by sub-paragraph (1).

(4) But see paragraph 2 for further provision about the power of a devolved authority acting alone to make regulations under sub-paragraph (3).

(5) No regulations may be made under sub-paragraph (3) after the end of the period of one year beginning with IP completion day.

(6) In this paragraph "appropriate authority" means—

(a) a Minister of the Crown,

(b) a devolved authority, or

(c) a Minister of the Crown acting jointly with a devolved authority.

2. (1) No provision may be made by a devolved authority acting alone in regulations under paragraph 1(3) so far as those regulations relate to the coming into force of regulations under section 23(1) or (6) of, or paragraph 1(2)(b) of Schedule 1 to, the European Union (Withdrawal) Act 2018.

(2) Subject to this, no provision may be made by a devolved authority acting alone in regulations under paragraph 1(3) relating to the coming into force of all or part of any subordinate legislation unless—

(a) the devolved authority acting alone otherwise than under paragraph 1(3) made the provision for the coming into force of the subordinate legislation or part and either—

(i) the regulations provide for paragraph 1(1) not to apply to the subordinate legislation or part, or

(ii) the devolved authority acting alone otherwise than under paragraph 1(3) could provide for the subordinate legislation or part to come into force at the same time as is provided for by virtue of the regulations, or

(b) the devolved authority acting alone could make provision corresponding to that made by the subordinate legislation or part and could provide for that provision to come into force at the same time as is provided for by virtue of the regulations.

(3) Where the test in sub-paragraph (2)(a) or (b) is (to any extent) only met by a devolved authority acting alone with the consent of a Minister of the Crown, the consent of a Minister of the Crown is required before the regulations under paragraph 1(3) may be made by the devolved authority acting alone.

(4) Except where sub-paragraph (3) applies, no provision may be made under paragraph 1(3) by a devolved authority acting alone unless the devolved authority has consulted a Minister of the Crown.

Devolved preparatory legislation of a kind mentioned in paragraph 41(3) to (5) of Schedule 8 to EUWA 2018

3. (1) Any provision of primary legislation which—

(a) is made before exit day by virtue of any of sub-paragraphs (3) to (5) of paragraph 41 of Schedule 8 to the European Union (Withdrawal) Act 2018, and

(b) provides, by reference to exit day (however expressed), for itself or any other provision so made to come into force on exit day or at any time after exit day,

is to be read instead as providing for the provision to come into force on IP completion day or (as the case may be) at that time after IP completion day.

(2) But a relevant devolved authority may, by regulations and subject to sub-paragraphs (4) to (7)—

(a) provide for sub-paragraph (1) not to apply to any extent in particular cases or descriptions of case,

(b) make different provision in particular cases or descriptions of case to that made by sub-paragraph (1), or

(c) make such provision as the relevant devolved authority considers appropriate in consequence of sub-paragraph (1) (including provision restating the effect of that sub-paragraph).

(3) The power to make regulations under sub-paragraph (2) may (among other things) be exercised by modifying any provision made by or under an enactment.

(4) No provision may be made by the Scottish Ministers in regulations under sub-paragraph (2) unless it would be within the legislative competence of the Scottish Parliament if it were contained in an Act of that Parliament.

(5) No provision may be made by the Welsh Ministers in regulations under sub-paragraph (2) unless it would be within the legislative competence of the National Assembly for Wales if it were contained in an Act of the Assembly (including any provision that could be made only with the consent of a Minister of the Crown).

(6) No provision may be made by a Northern Ireland department in regulations under sub-paragraph (2) unless it would be within the legislative competence of the Northern Ireland Assembly if it were contained in an Act of the Assembly (including any provision that could be made only with the consent of the Secretary of State).

(7) No regulations may be made under sub-paragraph (2) after the end of the period of one year beginning with IP completion day.

(8) In this paragraph "relevant devolved authority" means—

(a) in relation to any provision of an Act of the Scottish Parliament, the Scottish Ministers,
(b) in relation to any provision of an Act of the National Assembly for Wales, the Welsh Ministers, and
(c) in relation to any provision of an Act of the Northern Ireland Assembly, a Northern Ireland department.

Power to make consequential regulations under EUWA 2018

4. (1) The power of a Minister of the Crown under section 23(1) of the European Union (Withdrawal) Act 2018 to make such provision as the Minister considers appropriate in consequence of that Act includes the power to make such provision as the Minister considers appropriate in consequence of that Act as modified, or to be modified, by or under this Act (and references in the Act of 2018 to the power under section 23(1) of that Act are to be read accordingly).

(2) Sub-paragraph (1) does not limit the power conferred by section 41(1) above.

(3) The reference in sub-paragraph (1) to any modification by or under this Act of the European Union (Withdrawal) Act 2018 includes a reference to any modification made by or under this Act of a provision of another Act which was inserted into that other Act or otherwise modified by the Act of 2018.

NOTES

Commencement: 23 January 2020 (paras 1(3)–(6), 2, 3(2)–(8), 4); immediately before exit day (as defined in the European Union (Withdrawal) Act 2018, s 20) (para 1(1), (2)); exit day (as defined in the European Union (Withdrawal) Act 2018, s 20) (para 3(1)).

National Assembly for Wales: as to the renaming of the National Assembly for Wales, see the note at **[12.28]**.

Regulations: the Financial Services (Consequential Amendments) Regulations 2020, SI 2020/56; the European Union (Withdrawal Agreement) Act 2020 (Disapplication of the Deferral of Subordinate Legislation) (Wales) (EU Exit) Regulations 2020, SI 2020/93.

(Sch 5, Pt 2 (Specific Consequential Provision etc) amends the European Union (Withdrawal) Act 2018 ante, and other enactments that are outside the scope of this work.)

PART 3 TRANSITIONAL, TRANSITORY AND SAVING PROVISION

Retention of existing grounds for deportation

[12.60]
63. (*Outside the scope of this work.*)

Certain powers of devolved authorities in relation to EU law

64. Section 57(2) of the Scotland Act 1998, section 80(8) of the Government of Wales Act 2006 and section 24(1)(b) of the Northern Ireland Act 1998, so far as relating to EU law, do not apply to the making of regulations under section 12, 13 or 14.

Savings in connection with section 36

65. Section 36(e) and (f) do not affect the continued operation of the amendments made by section 2 of the European Union (Withdrawal) Act 2019 and section 4 of the European Union (Withdrawal) (No 2) Act 2019.

Regulations under EUWA 2018 etc

66. (1) The fact that a power to make regulations is conferred by this Act in the European Union (Withdrawal) Act 2018 does not affect the extent of any other power to make regulations under that Act.

(2) The modifications made by this Act to any power to make regulations conferred by the European Union (Withdrawal) Act 2018 do not affect the validity of any regulations made under that power before the coming into force of the modifications.

(3) Sub-paragraph (2) is subject to any provision made by regulations under section 41(5) above or section 23(6) of the Act of 2018.

Time-limited powers

67. The prohibition on making regulations under paragraph 1(3) or 3(2) of this Schedule after the end of the period of one year beginning with IP completion day does not affect the continuation in force of regulations made at or before that time.

Power to make transitional, transitory or saving regulations under EUWA 2018

68. (1) The power of a Minister of the Crown under section 23(6) of the European Union (Withdrawal) Act 2018 to make such transitional, transitory or saving provision as the Minister considers appropriate in connection with the coming into force of any provision of that Act includes the power to make such transitional, transitory or saving provision as the Minister considers appropriate in connection with the coming into force (whether by virtue of this Act, this Act and that Act, or otherwise) of any provision of that Act as inserted into that Act, or modified, by or under this Act (and references in the Act of 2018 to the power under section 23(6) of that Act are to be read accordingly).

(2) Sub-paragraph (1) does not limit the power conferred by section 41(5) above; and the power of a Minister of the Crown under section 25(4) of the European Union (Withdrawal) Act 2018 does not apply to any insertions into, or other modifications of, that Act made by this Act (for which see section 42(6) and (7) above).

(3) References in this paragraph to any modification made by or under this Act of any provision of the European Union (Withdrawal) Act 2018 include references to any modification made by or under this Act of a provision of another Act which was inserted into that other Act or otherwise modified by the Act of 2018.

NOTES

Commencement: 23 January 2020 (paras 65–68); exit day (as defined in the European Union (Withdrawal) Act 2018, s 20) (para 63); 19 May 2020 (para 64).

EUROPEAN PUBLIC LIMITED-LIABILITY COMPANY (AMENDMENT ETC) (EU EXIT) REGULATIONS 2018

(SI 2018/1298)

NOTES

Made: 3 December 2018.

Authority: European Union (Withdrawal) Act 2018, s 8(1).

Commencement: IP completion day (as defined in the European Union (Withdrawal Agreement) Act 2020, s 39).

These Regulations are reproduced as amended by: the International Accounting Standards and European Public Limited-Liability Company (Amendment etc) (EU Exit) Regulations 2019, SI 2019/685; the Companies and Statutory Auditors etc (Consequential Amendments) (EU Exit) Regulations 2020, SI 2020/523.

PART 1 INTRODUCTION

[12.61]

1 Citation and commencement

These Regulations may be cited as the European Public Limited-Liability Company (Amendment etc) (EU Exit) Regulations 2018 and come into force on exit day.

NOTES

Commencement: IP completion day (as defined in the European Union (Withdrawal Agreement) Act 2020, s 39).

As to the commencement of these Regulations, see the European Union (Withdrawal Agreement) Act 2020, Sch 5, para 1 (at **[12.59]**) which gives legal effect to the implementation period by 'non-textually amending' the coming into force dates of subordinate legislation which comes into force immediately before exit day, on exit day or at any time after exit day. This subordinate legislation will instead come into force immediately before the end of the implementation period (IP completion day), on IP completion day or (as the case may be) at the time concerned after IP completion day.

PARTS 2, 3

2–139 *(Part 2 (regs 2–95) amends the European Public Limited-Liability Company Regulations 2004, SI 2004/2326, the European Public Limited-Liability Company (Employee Involvement) (Great Britain) Regulations 2009, SI 2009/2401, the Registrar of Companies (Fees) (European Economic Interest Grouping and European Public Limited-Liability Company) Regulations 2012, SI 2012/1908 at* **[4.470]***, and the European Public Limited-Liability Company (Register of People with Significant Control) Regulations 2016, SI 2016/375 (and amends the European Public Limited-Liability Company (Employee Involvement) (Northern Ireland) Regulations 2009). Part 3 (regs 96–139) amends Council Regulation 2157/2001/EC on the Statute for a European Company.)*

PART 4 TRANSITIONAL AND SAVINGS PROVISIONS

[12.62]

140 Provisions in respect of amendments made to the European Public Limited-Liability Company Regulations 2004 and Council Regulation 2157/2001/EC of 8 October 2001 on the Statute for a European Company

In regulations 141 to 145—

"the 2004 Regulations" means the European Public Limited-Liability Company Regulations 2004;

"the 2006 Act" means the Companies Act 2006;

"the EC Regulation" means Council Regulation 2157/2001/EC of 8 October 2001 on the Statute for a European Company;

"SE" means a European Public Limited-Liability Company (or Societas Europaea) within the meaning of the EC Regulation, as it had effect immediately before [IP completion day], that was registered in the United Kingdom;

"UK Societas" means a SE which on [IP completion day] converted to a UK Societas within the meaning of the EC Regulation.

NOTES

Commencement: IP completion day (as defined in the European Union (Withdrawal Agreement) Act 2020, s 39).

Words in square brackets substituted by the Companies and Statutory Auditors etc (Consequential Amendments) (EU Exit) Regulations 2020, SI 2020/523, reg 5(a), with effect from immediately before IP completion day.

[12.63]

141

Despite the amendments and revocations made by these Regulations—

(a) regulation 13 of the 2004 Regulations (documents sent to the registrar), as it applies in respect of the application and modification of section 1094 of the 2006 Act; and

(b) regulation 14 of the 2004 Regulations (application of the 2006 Act to the registration of SEs), as it applies in respect of the application and modification of section 1084 of the 2006 Act,

continue to have effect, on and after [IP completion day], in relation to an SE which dissolved before [IP completion day].

NOTES

Commencement: IP completion day (as defined in the European Union (Withdrawal Agreement) Act 2020, s 39).

Words in square brackets substituted by the Companies and Statutory Auditors etc (Consequential Amendments) (EU Exit) Regulations 2020, SI 2020/523, reg 5(a), with effect from immediately before IP completion day.

[12.64]
142

(1) To the extent that enactments or rules of law applied to a dissolved SE immediately before [IP completion day], by virtue of applying to a public limited-liability company pursuant to the EC Regulation, they continue to apply to a dissolved SE after [IP completion day].

(2) If an SE dissolved before [IP completion day], and accordingly did not convert to a UK Societas under the EC Regulation, but after [IP completion day] is restored to the register, upon restoration it is deemed to have become a UK Societas on [IP completion day].

NOTES

Commencement: IP completion day (as defined in the European Union (Withdrawal Agreement) Act 2020, s 39).

Words in square brackets substituted by the Companies and Statutory Auditors etc (Consequential Amendments) (EU Exit) Regulations 2020, SI 2020/523, reg 5(a), with effect from immediately before IP completion day.

[12.65]
143

(1) Where the amendments made by regulation 28 would (apart from this paragraph) require a UK Societas's register of supervisory organ members to contain additional particulars in respect of an existing corporate member, the UK Societas need not comply with that requirement until three months after [IP completion day].

(2) In this paragraph, "existing corporate member" means a body corporate, or a firm that is a legal person under the law by which it is governed, whose particulars were contained in the UK Societas's register of supervisory organ members immediately before [IP completion day].

NOTES

Commencement: IP completion day (as defined in the European Union (Withdrawal Agreement) Act 2020, s 39).

Words in square brackets substituted by the Companies and Statutory Auditors etc (Consequential Amendments) (EU Exit) Regulations 2020, SI 2020/523, reg 5(a), with effect from immediately before IP completion day.

[12.66]
144

Despite the amendments and revocations made by these Regulations, regulation 88 (effect of registration), together with paragraphs 2 to 9 of Schedule 4 (modifications of the Companies Acts) of the 2004 Regulations as they had effect immediately before [IP completion day], continues to have effect on and after [IP completion day], in respect of an SE that converted to a public limited-liability company in accordance with Article 66 of the EC Regulation, as it had effect immediately before [IP completion day.

NOTES

Commencement: IP completion day (as defined in the European Union (Withdrawal Agreement) Act 2020, s 39).

Words in square brackets substituted by the Companies and Statutory Auditors etc (Consequential Amendments) (EU Exit) Regulations 2020, SI 2020/523, reg 5(a), with effect from immediately before IP completion day.

[12.67]
145

Where an SE has converted on [IP completion day] to a UK Societas, that UK Societas is required to comply with the provisions in Part 6 (trading disclosures) of the Company, Limited Liability Partnership and Business (Names and Trading Disclosures) Regulations 2015 within the period of three months beginning on [IP completion day].

NOTES

Commencement: IP completion day (as defined in the European Union (Withdrawal Agreement) Act 2020, s 39).

Words in square brackets substituted by the Companies and Statutory Auditors etc (Consequential Amendments) (EU Exit) Regulations 2020, SI 2020/523, reg 5(a), with effect from immediately before IP completion day.

[12.68]
146 Provisions in Respect of Amendments Made to the European Public Limited-Liability Company (Employee Involvement) (Great Britain) Regulations 2009

(1) Despite the revocations and amendments made by these Regulations, an employee who was a member of a special negotiating body before [IP completion day]—

(a) may after [IP completion day] present a complaint to an employment tribunal under regulation 28 (right to time off: complaints to tribunals) of the European Public Limited-Liability Company (Employee Involvement) (Great Britain) Regulations 2009, and regulation 28A (extension of time limit to facilitate conciliation before institution of proceedings) applies accordingly, that the employer—
   (i) has unreasonably refused to permit the employee to take time off as required under regulation 26 (right to time off for members of special negotiating body etc), or
   (ii) has failed to pay the whole or any part of any amount to which the employee is entitled under regulation 27 (right to remuneration for time off under regulation 26),

   provided the complaint is in respect of a time off before [IP completion day];

(b) who is dismissed, is to be regarded as unfairly dismissed within the terms of regulation 29(2) and (3) (unfair dismissal), and regulation 30 (subsidiary provisions relating to unfair dismissal) applies accordingly, provided the reason (or, if more than one, the principal reason) for the dismissal occurred before [IP completion day];

(c) has the right not to be subjected to any detriment within the terms of regulation 31(2) and (3) (detriment), and regulation 32 (detriment: enforcement and subsidiary provisions) applies accordingly, provided the grounds for the detriment occurred before [IP completion day].

NOTES

Commencement: IP completion day (as defined in the European Union (Withdrawal Agreement) Act 2020, s 39).

Words in square brackets substituted by the Companies and Statutory Auditors etc (Consequential Amendments) (EU Exit) Regulations 2020, SI 2020/523, reg 5(a), with effect from immediately before IP completion day.

[12.69]
147

In regulations 148 to [152A]—

"the pre-exit 2009 GB Regulations" means the European Public Limited-Liability Company (Employee Involvement) (Great Britain) Regulations 2009, as they had effect immediately before [IP completion day];

"the 2009 GB Regulations" means the European Public Limited-Liability Company (Employee Involvement) (Great Britain) Regulations 2009;

"SE" means a European Public Limited-Liability Company (or Societas Europaea) within the meaning of the EC Regulation, as it had effect immediately before [IP completion day].

NOTES

Commencement: IP completion day (as defined in the European Union (Withdrawal Agreement) Act 2020, s 39).

Figure in square brackets substituted by the International Accounting Standards and European Public Limited-Liability Company (Amendment etc) (EU Exit) Regulations 2019, SI 2019/685, reg 21, Sch 3, Pt 2, paras 13, 14, as from IP completion day (as defined in the European Union (Withdrawal Agreement) Act 2020, s 39).

Words in square brackets substituted by the Companies and Statutory Auditors etc (Consequential Amendments) (EU Exit) Regulations 2020, SI 2020/523, reg 5(a), with effect from immediately before IP completion day.

[12.70]
148

Despite the amendments and revocations made by these Regulations, regulations 3 and 7 to 18 of the pre-exit 2009 GB Regulations continue, on and after [IP completion day], to have effect in relation to a special negotiating body reconvened under regulation 17 (decision not to open, or to terminate, negotiations) of the 2009 GB Regulations, as appropriate and practicable and subject to the modifications in regulation 149.

NOTES

Commencement: IP completion day (as defined in the European Union (Withdrawal Agreement) Act 2020, s 39).

Words in square brackets substituted by the Companies and Statutory Auditors etc (Consequential Amendments) (EU Exit) Regulations 2020, SI 2020/523, reg 5(a), with effect from immediately before IP completion day.

[12.71]
149

The modifications to the pre-exit 2009 Regulations are as follows—

(a) references to "EEA State", "an EEA State" or "EEA States" are to be read as though they were references to "Relevant State", "a Relevant State" or "Relevant States";

(b) references to "SE" or "SE's" are to be read as if they were references to "UK Societas" or "UK Societas's"—

(i) in regulation 3 (interpretation)—

(aa) in paragraph (1), in the definitions of "employee involvement agreement" and "participation";

(bb) in paragraph (2), in the definitions of "information" and "consultation";

(ii) in regulation 15(2)(g) and (3A);

(iii) in the definition of "reduction of participation rights" in regulation 16(3); and

(iv) in regulation 17(3)(b), (4)(b)(ii) and (c)(ii);

(c) otherwise, regulation 3 (interpretation) is to be read as if amended by these Regulations, save as if—

(i) in paragraph (1) the following definitions were not omitted—

(aa) "absolute majority vote";

(bb) "agency worker";

(cc) "participation";

(dd) "SE established by merger";

(ee) "SE established by formation of a holding company or subsidiary company";

(ff) "SE established by transformation";

(gg) "suitable information relating to the use of agency workers";

(hh) "two thirds majority vote";

(ii) "UK members of the special negotiating body";

(ii) the definition of "information and consultation representative" were omitted;

(iii) after "participation" there were inserted—

""Relevant State" means an EEA State or the United Kingdom;";

(iv) for the definition of "SE" there were substituted—

""SE" means a European Public Limited Liability Company (or Societas Europaea) within the meaning of the EC Regulation, as it had effect immediately before [IP completion day];";

(v) in paragraph (2), the definition of "special negotiating body" were to a special negotiating body reconvened after [IP completion day] under regulation 17 (decision not to open, or to terminate, negotiations) of these Regulations, as they have effect after [IP completion day];

(d) regulation 14 (negotiations to reach an employee involvement agreement) is to be read as if paragraphs (2) and (3) were omitted.

NOTES

Commencement: IP completion day (as defined in the European Union (Withdrawal Agreement) Act 2020, s 39).

Words in square brackets substituted by the Companies and Statutory Auditors etc (Consequential Amendments) (EU Exit) Regulations 2020, SI 2020/523, reg 5(a), with effect from immediately before IP completion day.

[12.72]

150

Regulations 146 to 149 are without prejudice to the application otherwise, in these circumstances, of the remaining regulations of the 2009 GB Regulations.

NOTES

Commencement: IP completion day (as defined in the European Union (Withdrawal Agreement) Act 2020, s 39).

[12.73]

151

If an employee involvement agreement is not agreed following the reconvening of a special negotiating body, the standard rules on employee involvement in the Schedule to the pre-exit 2009 GB Regulations do not apply.

NOTES

Commencement: IP completion day (as defined in the European Union (Withdrawal Agreement) Act 2020, s 39).

[12.74]

152

If an employee involvement agreement is agreed following the reconvening of a special negotiating body, the provisions of the 2009 GB Regulations apply thereafter.

NOTES

Commencement: IP completion day (as defined in the European Union (Withdrawal Agreement) Act 2020, s 39).

[12.75]

[152A

(1) Despite the amendments and revocations made by these Regulations, paragraph 5(1) of the Schedule to the pre-exit 2009 GB Regulations applies to a UK Societas whose representative body was established less than four years before IP completion day.

(2) Where paragraph 5(1) applies—

(a) regulations 14 to 16 and 18 of the pre-exit 2009 GB Regulations apply, to the representative body as they apply to the special negotiating body, and the date referred to in regulation 14(3) is the date of the decision;

(b) Parts 2 and 3 of the Schedule to the pre-exit 2009 GB Regulations apply, where appropriate, and

(c) the following modifications to the pre-exit 2009 GB Regulations have effect—

(i) references to "EEA State" are to be read as though they were references to "Relevant State";

(ii) references to "SE" are to be read as if they were references to "UK Societas".]

NOTES

Commencement: IP completion day (as defined in the European Union (Withdrawal Agreement) Act 2020, s 39).

Inserted by the International Accounting Standards and European Public Limited-Liability Company (Amendment etc) (EU Exit) Regulations 2019, SI 2019/685, reg 21, Sch 3, Pt 2, para 15, as from IP completion day (as defined in the European Union (Withdrawal Agreement) Act 2020, s 39). Note that Sch 3, Pt 2, para 15 to the 2019 Regulations was amended by the Companies and Statutory Auditors etc (Consequential Amendments) (EU Exit) Regulations 2020, SI 2020/523, reg 26(c), with effect from immediately before IP completion day; and that the affect of the amendment has been incorporated in the text set out above.

153–159A *(Regs 153–159A contain transitional provisions relating to the European Public Limited-Liability Company (Employee Involvement) (Northern Ireland) Regulations 2009, and are outside the scope of this work.)*

ACCOUNTS AND REPORTS (AMENDMENT) (EU EXIT) REGULATIONS 2019

(SI 2019/145)

NOTES

Made: 30 January 2019.

Authority: European Communities Act 1972, s 2(2); European Union (Withdrawal) Act 2018, ss 8(1), 23(1), Sch 7, para 21 (see also the note "Statutory Instruments made under the European Communities Act 1972" preceding paragraph **[4.1]** *ante*).

Commencement: see reg 1 *post*.

These Regulations are reproduced as amended by: the Companies and Statutory Auditors etc (Consequential Amendments) (EU Exit) Regulations 2020, SI 2020/523.

[12.76]
1 Citation, commencement and effect

(1) These Regulations may be cited as the Accounts and Reports (Amendment) (EU Exit) Regulations 2019.

(2) These Regulations come into force as follows—

(a) this regulation and Schedule 1 come into force on the seventh day after the day on which these Regulations are made;

(b) the provisions to which regulation 2 applies have effect in relation to financial years beginning on or after [IP completion day];

(c) the rest of these Regulations come into force on exit day.

NOTES

Para (2): words in square brackets substituted by the Companies and Statutory Auditors etc (Consequential Amendments) (EU Exit) Regulations 2020, SI 2020/523, reg 10, with effect from immediately before IP completion day (as defined in the European Union (Withdrawal Agreement) Act 2020, s 39).

As to the commencement of these Regulations, see the European Union (Withdrawal Agreement) Act 2020, Sch 5, para 1 (at **[12.59]**) which gives legal effect to the implementation period by 'non-textually amending' the coming into force dates of subordinate legislation which comes into force immediately before exit day, on exit day or at any time after exit day. This subordinate legislation will instead come into force immediately before the end of the implementation period (IP completion day), on IP completion day or (as the case may be) at the time concerned after IP completion day.

[12.77]
2

The provisions to which this regulation applies are—

(a) Part 1 of Schedule 2, except—

(i) paragraphs 1, 4, 15 and 18(b);

(ii) paragraph 18(a), in so far as the new definitions do not apply to enactments which operate by reference to financial years;

(b) Part 2 of Schedule 2;

(c) Schedule 3, except paragraphs 2, 3, 6, 8 to 11, 14, 18, 22 to 35, 37 and 41.

NOTES

Commencement: IP completion day (as defined in the European Union (Withdrawal Agreement) Act 2020, s 39).

[12.78]
3 Interpretation

In these Regulations, "financial year" is to be construed in relation to any amendment to an enactment made by these Regulations, as having the same meaning as in that enactment.

NOTES

Commencement: IP completion day (as defined in the European Union (Withdrawal Agreement) Act 2020, s 39).

4–6 (*Reg 4 introduces Sch 1 to these Regulations (Amendments made under section 2(2) of the European Communities Act 1972). Reg 5 introduces Sch 2 (Amendments made under the European Union (Withdrawal) Act 2018: primary legislation). Reg 6 introduces Sch 3 (Amendments made under the European Union (Withdrawal) Act 2018: Secondary Legislation).*)

[12.79]
7 Transitional provision

(1) This regulation applies in relation to financial years that begin before, but end on or after [IP completion day].

(2) The enactments amended by the provisions to which regulation 2 applies, so far as they operate by reference to financial years, as specified in regulation 2, have effect as if the United Kingdom were a member State until the end of the financial year in question.

(3) The enactments amended by paragraph 5(a) of Schedule 3 have effect as if Part 14 of the Companies Act 2006 had effect as it had effect immediately before [IP completion day] until the end of the financial year in question.

NOTES

Commencement: IP completion day (as defined in the European Union (Withdrawal Agreement) Act 2020, s 39).

Words in square brackets substituted by the Companies and Statutory Auditors etc (Consequential Amendments) (EU Exit) Regulations 2020, SI 2020/523, reg 11, with effect from immediately before IP completion day (as defined in the European Union (Withdrawal Agreement) Act 2020, s 39).

SCHEDULES

SCHEDULES 1–3

(*Sch 1 amends the Companies Act 2006, s 384B, the Large and Medium-sized Companies and Groups (Accounts and Reports) Regulations 2008, SI 2008/410, Sch 7, and the Limited Liability Partnerships (Accounts and Audit) (Application of Companies Act 2006) Regulations 2008, SI 2008/1911, reg 5A. Sch 2, Pt 1 amends Part 15 (Accounts and Reports) of the Companies Act 2006 (and contains consequential amendments). Sch 2, Pt 2 amends the Building Societies Act 1986 and the Friendly Societies Act 1992 (outside the scope of this work). Sch 3 contains various amendments to the Small Companies and Groups (Accounts and Directors' Report) Regulations 2008, SI 2008/409, the Large and Medium-sized Companies and Groups (Accounts and Reports) Regulations 2008, SI 2008/410, the Partnerships (Accounts) Regulations 2008, SI 2008/569, the Limited Liability Partnerships (Accounts and Audit) (Application of Companies Act 2006) Regulations 2008, SI 2008/1911, the Overseas Companies Regulations 2009,*

SI 2009/1801, the Supervision of Accounts and Reports (Prescribed Body) and Companies (Defective Accounts and Directors' Reports) (Authorised Person) Order 2012, SI 2012/1439, the Companies (Receipt of Accounts and Reports) Regulations 2013, SI 2013/1973, and the Reports on Payments to Governments Regulations 2014, SI 2014/3209 which, in so far as relevant to this Handbook, have been incorporated at the appropriate place.)

INSOLVENCY (AMENDMENT) (EU EXIT) REGULATIONS 2019

(SI 2019/146)

NOTES

Made: 30 January 2019.

Authority: European Communities Act 1972, s 2(2), European Union (Withdrawal) Act 2018, s 8(1) (see also the note "Statutory Instruments made under the European Communities Act 1972" preceding paragraph **[4.1]** *ante*).

Commencement: see reg 1(2), (3).

These Regulations are reproduced as amended by: the Insolvency (Amendment) (EU Exit) (No 2) Regulations 2019, SI 2019/1459; the Insolvency (Amendment) (EU Exit) Regulations 2020, SI 2020/647.

[12.80]

1 Citation and commencement

(1) These Regulations may be cited as the Insolvency (Amendment) (EU Exit) Regulations 2019.

(2) The following provisions of these Regulations come into force on the day after these Regulations are made—

(a) regulation 2 as it relates—

(i) to paragraph 177 of the Schedule, and

(ii) Part 12 of the Schedule,

(b) paragraph 177 of the Schedule, and

(c) Part 12 of the Schedule.

(3) The remainder of these Regulations come into force on exit day.

NOTES

Commencement: IP completion day (as defined in the European Union (Withdrawal Agreement) Act 2020, s 39).

As to the commencement of these Regulations, see the European Union (Withdrawal Agreement) Act 2020, Sch 5, para 1 (at **[12.59]**) which gives legal effect to the implementation period by 'non-textually amending' the coming into force dates of subordinate legislation which comes into force immediately before exit day, on exit day or at any time after exit day. This subordinate legislation will instead come into force immediately before the end of the implementation period (IP completion day), on IP completion day or (as the case may be) at the time concerned after IP completion day.

2 (*Introduces the Schedule to the Regulations.*)

[12.81]

3 Extent and application

Any provision of these Regulations amending or applying an enactment has the same extent as the enactment amended or applied, except that—

(a) . . .

(b) the amendments made to [the Insolvency Act 1986] by Part 7 of the Schedule apply to Scotland only.

NOTES

Commencement: IP completion day (as defined in the European Union (Withdrawal Agreement) Act 2020, s 39).

Para (a) revoked, and words in square brackets in para (b) substituted, by the Insolvency (Amendment) (EU Exit) (No 2) Regulations 2019, SI 2019/1459, reg 2, Schedule, para 2, as from IP completion day (as defined in the European Union (Withdrawal Agreement) Act 2020, s 39).

[12.82]

4 Temporal application and savings

(1) . . . Nothing in these Regulations affects—

(a) . . .

(b) the saving for the existing law in article 3 of the Insolvency Amendment (EU 2015/848) Regulations 2017.

[(2) The amendments made by these Regulations do not apply in respect of any insolvency proceedings and actions falling within Article 67(3)(c) of the withdrawal agreement.]

(3)–(5) . . .

NOTES

Commencement: IP completion day (as defined in the European Union (Withdrawal Agreement) Act 2020, s 39).

All words omitted were revoked, and para (2) was substituted, by the Insolvency (Amendment) (EU Exit) Regulations 2020, SI 2020/647, reg 2(a), with effect from immediately before IP completion day (as defined in the European Union (Withdrawal Agreement) Act 2020, s 39).

5 (*Revoked by the Insolvency (Amendment) (EU Exit) Regulations 2020, SI 2020/647, reg 2(b), with effect from immediately before IP completion day (as defined in the European Union (Withdrawal Agreement) Act 2020, s 39).)*)

SCHEDULE

(Paras 1–15 (Pt 1) amend European Parliament and Council Regulation 2015/848/EU on insolvency proceedings at

[11.225]. *Paras 16–44 (Pt 2) and paras 133–138 (Pt 7) amend the Insolvency Act 1986 at* **[9.136]**. *Para 45 (Pt 3) amends the Insolvency Act 1986, s 8 as it has effect (due to savings) prior to its substitution by the Enterprise Act 2002. Paras 46–107 (Pt 4) amend the Insolvency (England and Wales) Rules 2016, SI 2016/1024 at* **[10.474]**. *Pt 5 amends legislation outside the scope of this work. Paras 111–132 (Pt 6) amend the Cross-Border Insolvency Regulations 2006, SI 2006/1030 at* **[10.175]** *and legislation that is outside the scope of this work. Pts 8–12 amend Scottish and Northern Ireland legislation and other legislation that is outside the scope of this work).*

STATUTORY AUDITORS AND THIRD COUNTRY AUDITORS (AMENDMENT) (EU EXIT) REGULATIONS 2019

(SI 2019/177)

NOTES

Made: 1 February 2019.

Authority: European Union (Withdrawal) Act 2018, ss 8(1), 23(1), Sch 7, para 21; European Communities Act 1972, s 2(2); Limited Liability Partnerships Act 2000, ss 15, 17; Companies (Audit, Investigations and Community Enterprise) Act 2004, s 18A; Companies Act 2006, ss 484(1), 519A(5), 1239(1)(b), (2), (5)(d), 1241(2)(c), 1246(1), 1252(1), (4)(a), (8), 1292(1), (2) (see also the note "Statutory Instruments made under the European Communities Act 1972" preceding paragraph **[4.1]** *ante*).

Commencement: 22 February 2019 (regs 105–107); IP completion day (as defined in the European Union (Withdrawal Agreement) Act 2020, s 39) (otherwise).

These Regulations are reproduced as amended by: the Statutory Auditors, Third Country Auditors and International Accounting Standards (Amendment) (EU Exit) Regulations 2019, SI 2019/1392; the Statutory Auditors and Third Country Auditors (Amendment) (EU Exit) Regulations 2020, SI 2020/108; the International Accounting Standards, Statutory Auditors and Third Country Auditors (Amendment) (EU Exit) Regulations 2020, SI 2020/335; the Companies and Statutory Auditors etc (Consequential Amendments) (EU Exit) Regulations 2020, SI 2020/523; the Statutory Auditors and Third Country Auditors (Amendment) (EU Exit) (No 2) Regulations 2020, SI 2020/1247; the Statutory Auditors and Third Country Auditors (Amendment) Regulations 2022, SI 2022/762.

For a summary of all Orders and Regulations made under the Companies Act 2006, see Appendix 4 at **[A4]**.

PART 1 INTRODUCTION

[12.83]

1 Citation and commencement

These Regulations may be cited as the Statutory Auditors and Third Country Auditors (Amendment) (EU Exit) Regulations 2019.

NOTES

Commencement: IP completion day (as defined in the European Union (Withdrawal Agreement) Act 2020, s 39).

[12.84]

2

These Regulations come into force on exit day, except for [—

(a) regulation 14, which comes into force 21 days after the day on which the Statutory Auditors, Third Country Auditors and International Accounting Standards (Amendment) (EU Exit) Regulations 2019 are made; and

(b) Part 5, which comes into force on 22 February 2019].

NOTES

Commencement: IP completion day (as defined in the European Union (Withdrawal Agreement) Act 2020, s 39).

Words in square brackets substituted by the Statutory Auditors, Third Country Auditors and International Accounting Standards (Amendment) (EU Exit) Regulations 2019, SI 2019/1392, regs 2, 3, as from 13 November 2019.

As to the commencement of these Regulations, see the European Union (Withdrawal Agreement) Act 2020, Sch 5, para 1 (at **[12.59]**) which gives legal effect to the implementation period by 'non-textually amending' the coming into force dates of subordinate legislation which comes into force immediately before exit day, on exit day or at any time after exit day. This subordinate legislation will instead come into force immediately before the end of the implementation period (IP completion day), on IP completion day or (as the case may be) at the time concerned after IP completion day.

PARTS 2–8

3–111 *(Regs 3–9 amend the Companies Act 2006, Part 16 at* **[1.541]**. *Regs 10–26 amend Part 42 of that Act at* **[1.1380]**. *Regs 27–36 amend Schs 10–12 to that Act at* **[1.1523]** *et seq. Regs 37–45 amend various pieces of primary legislation (including the Companies (Audit, Investigations and Community Enterprise) Act 2004). Regs 46–74 amend various pieces of subordinate legislation (including the Limited Liability Partnerships (Accounts and Audit) (Application of Companies Act 2006) Regulations 2008, SI 2008/1911; the Statutory Auditors (Amendment of Companies Act 2006 and Delegation of Functions etc) Order 2012, SI 2012/1741; the Statutory Auditors and Third Country Auditors Regulations 2013, SI 2013/1672; the Companies (Bodies Concerned with Auditing Standards etc) (Exemption from Liability) Regulations 2016, SI 2016/571; and the Statutory Auditors and Third Country Auditors Regulations 2016, SI 2016/649). Regs 75–104 amend the retained Regulation 537/2014/EU of the European Parliament and of the Council on specific requirements regarding statutory audit of public-interest entities and repealing Commission Decision 2005/909/EC. Regs 105–107 amend the Statutory Auditors and Third Country Auditors Regulations 2016, SI 2016/649. Reg 108 introduces Schedule 1 (Approval of equivalent third countries and transitional third countries). Reg 109 introduces Schedule 2 (Approval of third country competent authorities). Reg 110 introduces Schedule 3 (Revocation of retained direct EU legislation). Reg 111 introduces Schedule 4 (Transitional provisions).)*

SCHEDULES

SCHEDULE 1
APPROVAL OF EQUIVALENT THIRD COUNTRIES AND TRANSITIONAL THIRD COUNTRIES

Regulation 108

Equivalent third countries

[12.85]

1. [(1) The EEA States and Gibraltar are approved as equivalent third countries for financial years beginning on or after IP completion day and are listed in column 1 of Table 1 of this Schedule.]

[(1A) The countries determined by the European Commission immediately before IP completion day as having an equivalent system of audit inspections, investigations and sanctions to those in the European Union by virtue of an instrument adopted under Article 46(2) of Directive 2006/43/EC of the European Parliament and of the Council of 17th May 2006 on statutory audits of annual accounts and consolidated accounts, amending Council Directives 78/660/EEC and 83/349/EEC and repealing Council Directive 84/253/EEC, are approved as equivalent third countries and are listed in column 1 of Table 1 of this Schedule.]

[(2) Approval is granted for an indefinite period, unless a date is recorded in column 2 of the Table against a country's name, in which case the approval ceases to apply for financial years beginning after that date.]

Transitional third countries

2. . . .

Table 1

Equivalent third country	***Date of last day of approval***
Abu Dhabi	
Australia	
[Austria]	
[Belgium]	
Brazil	
[Bulgaria]	
Canada	
China	
[Croatia]	
[Cyprus]	
[Czech Republic]	
[Denmark]	
Dubai International Financial Centre	
[Estonia]	
[Finland]	
[France]	
[Germany]	
[Gibraltar]	
[Greece]	
Guernsey	
[Hungary]	
[Iceland]	
Indonesia	
[Ireland]	
Isle of Man	
[Italy]	
Japan	
Jersey	
[Latvia]	
[Liechtenstein]	
[Lithuania]	
[Luxembourg]	
Malaysia	
[Malta]	
Mauritius	
[Netherlands]	
New Zealand	
[Norway]	

Equivalent third country	Date of last day of approval
[Poland]	
[Portugal]	
[Romania]	
Singapore	
[Slovakia]	
Slovenia	
South Africa	
South Korea	
[Spain]	
[Sweden]	
Switzerland	
Taiwan	
Thailand	
Turkey	
The United States of America	. . .

Table 2

. . .

NOTES

Commencement: IP completion day (as defined in the European Union (Withdrawal Agreement) Act 2020, s 39).

Para 1(1) was substituted, para 1(1A) was inserted, and the words omitted in the entry relating to the United States of America in the table in para 2 were revoked, by the Statutory Auditors and Third Country Auditors (Amendment) Regulations 2022, SI 2022/762, art 2(2), as from 27 July 2022.

All other amendments to this Schedule were made by the Statutory Auditors and Third Country Auditors (Amendment) (EU Exit) (No 2) Regulations 2020, SI 2020/1247, reg 2(1), (2) with effect from immediately before IP completion day.

SCHEDULE 2
APPROVAL OF THIRD COUNTRY COMPETENT AUTHORITIES

Regulation 109

Approved third country competent authorities

[12.86]

1 [(1) The competent authorities of the EEA States and Gibraltar are approved as approved third country competent authorities on IP completion day and are listed in column 1 of Table 3 of this Schedule.]

[(1A) The third country competent authorities which the European Commission has decided immediately before IP completion day are adequate to cooperate with the competent authorities of Member States on the exchange of audit working papers or other documents held by statutory auditors and audit firms under Article 47(3) of Directive 2006/43/EC of the European Parliament and of the Council of 17th May 2006 on statutory audits of annual accounts and consolidated accounts, amending Council Directives 78/660/EEC and 83/349/EEC and repealing Council Directive 84/253/EEC are approved as approved third country competent authorities and are listed in column 1 of Table 3 of this Schedule.]

(2) Approval is granted for an indefinite period, unless a date is recorded in column 2 of the Table against a third country competent authority's name, in which case the approval ceases to apply after that date.

Table 3

Approved third country competent authority	Date of last day of approval
The Australian Securities and Investments Commission	
Austrian Auditing Oversight Authority	. . .
Belgian Audit Oversight College	. . .
The Comissão de Valores Mobiliários of Brazil	
Commission for public oversight of statutory auditors Bulgaria	. . .
The Canadian Public Accountability Board	
[The Ministry of Finance of the People's Republic of China	14 November 2024]
[The Securities Regulatory Commission of the People's Republic of China	14 November 2024]
Ministry of Finance of the Republic of Croatia	. . .
Cyprus Audit Oversight Board	. . .
Public Audit Oversight Board of the Czech Republic	. . .
Danish Business Authority	. . .
The Dubai Financial Service Authority of Dubai International Financial Centre	

Approved third country competent authority	***Date of last day of approval***
Estonian Auditing Oversight Board	. . .
Finnish Patent and Registration Office—Auditor Oversight Unit	. . .
Haut Conseil du Commissariat aux Comptes France	. . .
Audit Oversight Body Germany	. . .
Gibraltar Financial Services Commission	. . .
Hellenic Accounting and Auditing Standards Oversight Board	. . .
The Registrar of Companies of Guernsey	. . .
Auditors' Public Oversight Authority—Ministry for National Economy of Hungary	. . .
Audit Oversight Board Iceland	. . .
. . .	. . .
Irish Auditing and Accounting Supervisory Authority	. . .
Isle of Man Financial Services Authority	. . .
Commissione Nazionale per le Societa e la Borsa Italy	. . .
The Financial Services Agency of Japan	. . .
The Certified Public Accountants and Auditing Oversight Board of Japan	. . .
The Jersey Financial Services Commission	. . .
Ministry of Finance of Latvia Commercial Companies Audit Policy and Oversight Unit	. . .
Financial market authority Liechtenstein	. . .
Authority of Audit, Accounting, Property Valuation and Insolvency of Lithuania	. . .
Commission de Surveillance du Secteur Financier Luxembourg	. . .
The Audit Oversight Board of Malaysia	. . .
Accountancy Board Malta	. . .
The Netherlands Authority for the Financial Markets	. . .
Finanstilsynet Norway	. . .
Audit Oversight Commission Poland	. . .
Comissão do Mercado de Valores Mobiliários Portugal	. . .
Authority for Public Oversight of the Statutory Audit Activity Romania	. . .
Auditing Oversight Authority Slovakia	. . .
Agency of Public Oversight of Auditing Slovenia	. . .
The Independent Regulatory Board for Auditors of South Africa	[30 April 2026]
The Financial Services Commission of South Korea	. . .
Financial Supervisory Service of South Korea	. . .
Instituto de Contabilidad y Auditoría de Cuentas Spain	. . .
Swedish Inspectorate of Auditors	. . .
The Federal Audit Oversight Authority of Switzerland	. . .
The Financial Supervisory Commission of Taiwan	. . .
The Securities and Exchange Commission of Thailand	. . .
The Public Company Accounting Oversight Board of the United States of America	. . .
The Securities and Exchange Commission of the United States of America	. . .

NOTES

Commencement: IP completion day (as defined in the European Union (Withdrawal Agreement) Act 2020, s 39).

Para 1(1) was substituted, para 1(1A) was inserted, by the Statutory Auditors and Third Country Auditors (Amendment) Regulations 2022, SI 2022/762, art 2(3)(a), as from 27 July 2022.

Table 3 is amended as follows:

Entries in square brackets inserted, entry "The Finance Professions Supervisory Centre of Indonesia" (omitted) revoked, and words in square brackets in the entry "The Independent Regulatory Board for Auditors of South Africa" substituted, by the Statutory Auditors and Third Country Auditors (Amendment) (EU Exit) Regulations 2020, SI 2020/108, regs 2, 3, with effect from immediately before IP completion day (as defined in the European Union (Withdrawal Agreement) Act 2020, s 39). Note that reg 3 of the 2020 Regulations was amended by the Statutory Auditors and Third Country Auditors (Amendment) (EU

Exit) (No 2) Regulations 2020, SI 2020/1247, reg 3 and that amendment comes into force immediately before reg 3 of the 2020 Regulations; and the effect of that amendment has been incorporated in the text above.

The words omitted from the final two entries of the table were revoked by SI 2022/762, art 2(3)(b), as from 27 July 2022.

All other words omitted were revoked by the Statutory Auditors and Third Country Auditors (Amendment) (EU Exit) (No 2) Regulations 2020, SI 2020/1247, reg 2(1), (3) with effect from immediately before IP completion day.

SCHEDULE 3
REVOCATION OF RETAINED DIRECT EU LEGISLATION

Regulation 110

[12.87]

1. The following instruments are revoked—

(a) Commission Decision No 2008/627/EC of 29 July 2008 concerning a transitional period for audit activities of certain third country auditors and audit entities;

(b) Commission Decision 2010/64 of 5 February 2010 on the adequacy of the competent authorities of certain third countries pursuant to Directive 2006/43/EC of the European Parliament and of the Council;

(c) Commission Decision 2010/485/EU of 1 September 2010 on the adequacy of the competent authorities of Australia and the United States pursuant to Directive 2006/43/EC of the European Parliament and of the Council;

(d) Commission Decision 2011/30/EU of 19 January 2011 on the equivalence of certain third country public oversight, quality assurance, investigation and penalty systems for auditors and audit entities and a transitional period for audit activities of certain third country auditors and audit entities in the European Union;

(e) Commission Implementing Decision 2013/281/EU of 11 June 2013 on the equivalence of the public oversight, quality assurance, investigation and penalty systems for auditors and audit entities of the United States of America pursuant to Directive 2006/43/EC of the European Parliament and the Council;

(f) Commission Implementing Decision 2013/288/EU of 13 June 2013 amending Decision 2011/30/EU on the equivalence of certain third country public oversight, quality assurance, investigation and penalty systems for auditors and audit entities and a transitional period for audit activities of certain third country auditors and audit entities in the European Union;

(g) Commission Implementing Decision (EU) 2016/1010 of 21 June 2016 on the adequacy of the competent authorities of certain third countries and territories pursuant to Directive 2006/43/EC of the European Parliament and of the Council;

(h) Commission Implementing Decision (EU) 2016/1155 of 14 July 2016 on the equivalence of the public oversight, quality assurance, investigation and penalty systems for auditors and audit entities of the United States of America pursuant to Directive 2006/43/EC of the European Parliament and the Council;

(i) Commission Implementing Decision (EU) 2016/1156 of 14 July 2016 on the adequacy of the competent authorities of the United States of America pursuant to Directive 2006/43/EC of the European Parliament and of the Council;

(j) Commission Implementing Decision (EU) 2016/1223 of 25 July 2016 amending Decision 2011/30/EU on the equivalence of certain third country public oversight, quality assurance, investigation and penalty systems for auditors and audit entities and a transitional period for audit activities of certain third country auditors and audit entities in the European Union;

[(k) Commission Implementing Decision (EU) 2019/1874 of 6 November 2019 on the adequacy of the competent authorities of the People's Republic of China pursuant to Directive 2006/43/EC of the European Parliament and of the Council.]

NOTES

Commencement: IP completion day (as defined in the European Union (Withdrawal Agreement) Act 2020, s 39).

Sub-para (k) added by the International Accounting Standards, Statutory Auditors and Third Country Auditors (Amendment) (EU Exit) Regulations 2020, SI 2020/335, regs 6, 9, with effect from immediately before IP completion day.

SCHEDULE 4
TRANSITIONAL PROVISIONS

Regulation 111

[12.88]

1. The amendments made by the following regulations do not apply in relation to audits of accounts for financial years that begin before [IP completion day]—

[(za) regulations 4 and 50(b);]

(a) regulations 8(a)(i), 53(a)(i) and 66(d)(i), in so far as they exempt public interest entities, whose transferable securities are admitted to trading on a regulated market situated or operating in an EEA State but not in the United Kingdom, from having to appoint auditors in accordance with—

  (i) Articles 16 and 17 of the Audit Regulation;

  (ii) sections 485A to 485C, 489A to 489C and 494ZA of the Companies Act 2006; and

  (iii) in relation to limited liability partnerships, sections 485A to 485C and 494ZA of the Companies Act 2006 as applied with modifications by regulations 34A and 38A of the Limited Liability Partnerships (Accounts and Audit) (Application of Companies Act 2006) Regulations 2008;

(b) regulations 32(d)(i) and 66(d)(i), in so far as they exempt statutory auditors of public interest entities, whose transferable securities are admitted to trading on a regulated market situated or operating in an EEA State but not in the United Kingdom, from being subject to—

  (i) regulations 5(1)(f) and 9(1) of the Statutory Auditors and Third Country Auditors Regulations 2016 and Articles 24(1)(a) and (c), and 26 of the Audit Regulation, on inspections of audits of public interest entities by the competent authority and any enforcement action taken following those inspections; and

(ii) paragraph 10C of Schedule 10 to the Companies Act 2006, regulations 13 and 13A of, and Schedule 1 to, the Statutory Auditors and Third Country Auditors Regulations 2016, and Articles 4 to 11, 17(7) and 18 of the Audit Regulation, on technical standards and of other standards of professional ethics and internal quality control of statutory audits of public interest entities;

(c) regulation 80(a)(iv) and (vi), and (d)(iv)—

(i) in relation to the provision of non-audit services to subsidiary undertakings in third countries which are not EEA States and parent undertakings in EEA States; and

(ii) where, for the purposes of Article 5(1) of the Audit Regulation, "within the Union" means in an EEA State or the United Kingdom.

[**1A**. In its continuing application in relation to audits of accounts for financial years that begin before IP completion day, section 479A(1)(b) of the Companies Act 2006 (including as modified by regulation 34A of the Limited Liability Partnerships (Accounts and Audit) (Application of Companies Act 2006) Regulations 2008) must be treated as if the reference to a parent undertaking being established under the law of an EEA State included a reference to a parent undertaking being established under the law of any part of the United Kingdom.]

2. In relation to audits of accounts for financial years that begin before [IP completion day]—

(a) Gibraltar, or a third country which immediately before [IP completion day] was an EEA State, is to be treated by the competent authority as if it is a [an equivalent third country];

(b) a third country which was determined by the European Commission as having an equivalent system of audit inspections, investigations and sanctions to those in the European Union by virtue of an instrument adopted under Article 46(2) of Directive 2006/43/EC of the European Parliament and of the Council on statutory audits of annual accounts and consolidated accounts, is to be treated by the competent authority as an equivalent third country for those financial years to which the instrument applied in relation to that country;

(c) a third country which was the subject of transitional arrangements in respect of its system of audit inspections, investigations and sanctions in the European Union by virtue of an instrument adopted under Article 46(2) of Directive 2006/43/EC of the European Parliament and of the Council on statutory audits of annual accounts and consolidated accounts, is to be treated by the competent authority as a transitional third country for those financial years to which the instrument applied in relation to that country.

3. For investigations under the Statutory Auditors and Third Country Auditors Regulations 2016 that begin before [IP completion day], and any enforcement action taken under those Regulations following those investigations, the amendments made by regulations 32(d)(i) and 66(d)(i) do not apply in so far as they exempt statutory auditors of public interest entities, whose transferable securities are admitted to trading on a regulated market situated or operating in an EEA State but not in the United Kingdom, from being subject to regulation 5(1)(f) and Schedule 2 to the Statutory Auditors and Third Country Auditors Regulations 2016, and Article 24(1)(b) and (c) of the Audit Regulation, on investigations of audits of public interest entities by the competent authority.

4. For the purposes of this Schedule—

(a) the definitions in Part 42 of the Companies Act 2006 apply; and

(b) Gibraltar must be treated as if it were an EEA State.

NOTES

Commencement: IP completion day (as defined in the European Union (Withdrawal Agreement) Act 2020, s 39).

Words "IP completion day" in square brackets (in each place that they occur) substituted by the Companies and Statutory Auditors etc (Consequential Amendments) (EU Exit) Regulations 2020, SI 2020/523, reg 19, with effect from immediately before IP completion day.

Sub-para (za) of para 1 and para 1A were inserted by the Statutory Auditors and Third Country Auditors (Amendment) (EU Exit) Regulations 2020, SI 2020/108, regs 2, 4, as from IP completion day (as defined in the European Union (Withdrawal Agreement) Act 2020, s 39).

Words "an equivalent third country" in square brackets in para 2 substituted by the Statutory Auditors and Third Country Auditors (Amendment) (EU Exit) (No 2) Regulations 2020, SI 2020/1247, reg 2(1), (4) with effect from immediately before IP completion day.

TAKEOVERS (AMENDMENT) (EU EXIT) REGULATIONS 2019 (NOTE)

(SI 2019/217)

[12.89]

NOTES

Made: 11 February 2019.

Authority: European Union (Withdrawal) Act 2018, s 8(1), Sch 7, para 21.

Commencement: IP completion day (as defined in the European Union (Withdrawal Agreement) Act 2020, s 39).

General purpose

The Directive of the European Parliament and of the Council 2004/25/EC on takeover bids at **[11.51]** established the legal framework through which company takeovers are regulated in the European Economic Area. It was transposed into UK domestic law by Part 28 of the Companies Act 2006.

As well as implementing the Directive, Part 28 of the 2006 Act designated the Panel on Takeovers and Mergers (the Panel) as the UK's supervisory authority for takeovers. The Directive created minimum standards on takeover supervision in the regulated markets of EEA member states. In the UK, the primary regulated market is the main market of the London Stock Exchange.

These Regulations were made to effect the changes required to Part 28 of the Act to separate the UK domestic takeover regime from the European takeover regime.

Amendments to existing legislation

These Regulations amend Part 28 of the Companies Act 2006 at **[1.1105]** (and contain consequential amendments to the 2006 Act). They also amend the Large and Medium-sized Companies and Groups (Accounts and Reports) Regulations 2008, SI 2008/410 at **[4.60]**, and the Unregistered Companies Regulations 2009, SI 2009/2436 at **[4.389]**.

The amendments remove references to EU law in order to ensure legal clarity, and to effect a freestanding domestic takeover regime. The following amendments are made to the 2006 Act:

— cross-references to Directive Articles have been updated in sections 943, 953, 968, 970 and 980;

— references to the Directive and definitions for the Directive have been removed in sections 971 and 980;

— provisions specifically for EEA member states have been removed in sections 978 and Schedule 2;

— definitions have been clarified in section 971; and

— the definition of takeover bid has been amended and consolidated in paragraph 20 of the new Schedule 1C to the 2006 Act, removing existing definitions of takeover bid throughout the Act.

Duty for the Panel to make rules giving effect to specific Directive Articles

The obligation for the Panel to make rules giving effect to specific Directive Articles was transposed by cross-referring to those Articles.

These Regulations copy the relevant Articles into the new Schedule 1C to the 2006 Act (with the exception of Article 4.2 on shared jurisdiction – as to which, see below). Corrective amendments have been made where appropriate for UK legislation. The meaning and applicability of these Articles have not changed.

Shared jurisdiction

The EU takeovers regime includes a system of shared jurisdiction for companies that have their registered offices, and their securities admitted to trading, in different EEA member states under Article 4.2 of the Directive. Article 4.2 specifies the competent authority responsible for supervising particular aspects of a takeover bid for such companies. The supervision of a takeover bid of companies captured by the shared jurisdiction regime is shared by two supervisory authorities, one in the country where the company has its registered office, and the other where the company's securities are admitted to trading on a regulated market.

The shared jurisdiction regime works on a reciprocal basis within the EU legislative and cooperative framework. This reciprocal arrangement no longer applies to the UK after exit, therefore these Regulations remove the requirement for the Panel to implement the shared jurisdiction regime from the 2006 Act.

Offers for companies that have their registered office in the UK and that satisfy the "residency test" within the *City Code on Takovers and Mergers* will be placed within the sole jurisdiction of the Panel. Offers for companies that have their registered office in an EEA member state, and their securities admitted to trading only on a regulated market in the UK, will no longer be regulated by the Panel.

Restrictions on the disclosure of confidential information

Section 948 of the 2006 Act restricts the disclosure of confidential information obtained by the Panel during the course of its duties, prescribing the conditions under which such information can be disclosed, and the persons or organisations that information can be shared with. It applies both to the Panel and to bodies with whom it shares information. Section 949 of the 2006 Act makes disclosure of information in contravention of section 948 a criminal offence. Schedule 2 to the 2006 Act lists the organisations to which the Panel can disclose information for specified purposes.

The 2006 Act provides an exemption from the section 948 restriction to EEA public bodies in particular circumstances, enabling them to disclose confidential information forwarded to them by the Panel in order to discharge an EU obligation. The Directive provides reciprocal protections for the disclosure of confidential information. The exempt EEA public bodies are bound by their national laws and EU laws to prevent inappropriate disclosure of information passed to them by the UK authorities. After exit these reciprocal obligations no longer apply to the UK.

These Regulations remove the specific exemption for EEA public bodies from the section 949 offence and thus ensure recourse for inappropriate onward disclosures of information.

Section (E) of Part 2 of Schedule 2 to the 2006 Act allows for the disclosure of information by the Panel for the purpose of assisting overseas regulatory authorities to exercise their regulatory functions. After exit the Panel will therefore continue to be able to disclose information to EEA public authorities (as it can to authorities from other countries), but onward disclosure by EEA authorities is no longer permitted.

Section (E) of Part 2 of Schedule 2 also allows disclosure of information in pursuance of any EU obligation. These Regulations remove this information gateway, as the UK is no longer part of the EU regime.

Duty of cooperation

Cooperation with overseas authorities is mutually beneficial. Section 950 of the 2006 Act places a duty on the Panel to cooperate with its counterparts and financial authorities with similar regulatory functions to the Financial Conduct Authority, the Prudential Regulation Authority, and the Bank of England in any country or territory outside the UK. The 2006 Act also places a specific duty on the Panel to cooperate with EEA member state supervisory authorities and public financial institutions. This duty is reciprocal, but after exit, EEA member states are no longer obliged by the Directive to cooperate with the UK in this way.

These Regulations therefore remove the specific obligation for the Panel to cooperate with EEA member states' supervisory authorities and public financial institutions. However, the Panel will still have a duty to cooperate with these authorities under the general duty to cooperate with overseas authorities.

Breakthrough

Article 11 of the Directive concerning breakthrough enables offerors for companies with specified restrictions (eg, concerning the transfer of securities or voting rights) in their articles of association, or with specified contractual restrictions, to overcome those restrictions during the course of a takeover bid. Article 12 of the Directive allows EEA member states to make Article 11 optional for companies, but they must provide a legal framework for companies to use these provisions if they choose to do so. The UK opted to make Article 11 optional.

The breakthrough provisions were transposed in Chapter 2 of Part 28 of the 2006 Act but used cross-references to the Directive. These Regulations transpose the text of the Directive, with drafting corrections where required, to ensure appropriate statutory interpretation.

FINANCIAL MARKETS AND INSOLVENCY (AMENDMENT AND TRANSITIONAL PROVISION) (EU EXIT) REGULATIONS 2019

(SI 2019/341)

NOTES

Made: 21 February 2019.

Authority: European Union (Withdrawal) Act 2018, s 8(1), Sch 7, para 21; European Communities Act 1972, s 2(2) (see also the note "Statutory Instruments made under the European Communities Act 1972" preceding paragraph **[4.1]** *ante*).

Commencement: 22 February 2019 (regs 1, 13–20); IP completion day (as defined in the European Union (Withdrawal Agreement) Act 2020, s 39) (otherwise).

These Regulations are reproduced as amended by: the Financial Services (Miscellaneous) (Amendment) (EU Exit) Regulations 2019, SI 2019/710; the Financial Services (Consequential Amendments) Regulations 2020, SI 2020/56; the Financial Services and Economic and Monetary Policy (Consequential Amendments) (EU Exit) Regulations 2020, SI 2020/1301; the Financial Markets and Insolvency (Transitional Provision) (EU Exit) (Amendment) Regulations 2021, SI 2021/782.

Gibraltar: as to the application of these Regulations to Gibraltar, see the Gibraltar (Miscellaneous Amendments) (EU Exit) Regulations 2019, SI 2019/680 at **[12.128]**.

ARRANGEMENT OF REGULATIONS

PART 1 INTRODUCTION

[12.90]

1 Citation, commencement and interpretation

(1) These Regulations may be cited as the Financial Markets and Insolvency (Amendment and Transitional Provision) (EU Exit) Regulations 2019.

(2) This regulation and Part 4 come into force on the day after the day on which these Regulations are made.

(3) The other provisions of these Regulations come into force on exit day.

(4) In these Regulations—

"the 2000 Act" means the Financial Services and Markets Act 2000;

"the 1999 Regulations" means the Financial Markets and Insolvency (Settlement Finality) Regulations 1999.

NOTES

As to the commencement of these Regulations, see the European Union (Withdrawal Agreement) Act 2020, Sch 5, para 1 (at **[12.59]**) which gives legal effect to the implementation period by 'non-textually amending' the coming into force dates of subordinate legislation which comes into force immediately before exit day, on exit day or at any time after exit day. This subordinate legislation will instead come into force immediately before the end of the implementation period (IP completion day), on IP completion day or (as the case may be) at the time concerned after IP completion day.

PARTS 2, 3

2–12 (*Regs 2, 3 (Part 2) amend Part 7 of the Companies Act 1989 at* **[5.135]** *and the Banking Act 2009. Regs 4–12 (Part 3) amend the Financial Markets and Insolvency (Settlement Finality) Regulations 1999, SI 1999/2979 at* **[10.61]**, *the Financial Markets and Insolvency Regulations 1991, SI 1991/880 at* **[6.8]**, *and the Financial Collateral Arrangements (No 2) Regulations 2003, SI 2003/3226.*)

PART 4 TEMPORARY DESIGNATION REGIME

[12.91]

13 Interpretation

In this Part—

"designating authority" has the same meaning as in the 1999 Regulations;

"Settlement Finality Directive" means Directive 98/26/EC of the European Parliament and of the Council of 19 May 1998 on settlement finality in payment and securities settlement systems as it has effect in EU law as amended from time to time;

"system" has the same meaning as in the 1999 Regulations;

"temporary designation" in respect of a system means that such system is taken to be the subject of a designation order under regulation 4(1) of the 1999 Regulations;

"temporary designation period" means the period determined by regulation 18.

[12.92]

14 Application of Part 4

This Part applies to a system ("S") and a body corporate or unincorporated body of persons ("P") that is the operator of S, where—

(a) immediately before [IP completion day], S is specified as a system and P is specified as the system operator in relation to S, by an EEA state (other than the United Kingdom), to be included within the scope of the Settlement Finality Directive in accordance with article 10 of that directive; and

(b) before [IP completion day], P has complied with the notification requirement in regulation 15.

NOTES

Words "IP completion day" in square brackets substituted by the Financial Services (Consequential Amendments) Regulations 2020, SI 2020/56, reg 13 (with effect from immediately before 11.00pm on 31 January 2020).

[12.93]

15 Notification requirement

(1) Where P intends S to have temporary designation, it must notify the designating authority.

(2) For the purposes of paragraph (1), the notification must—

(a) be made no later than [IP completion day];

(b) be made in such manner as the designating authority may direct; and

(c) contain, or be accompanied by, such information as the designating authority may direct.

(3) The designating authority must confirm receipt of the notification promptly to P.

NOTES

Words "IP completion day" in square brackets substituted by the Financial Services (Consequential Amendments) Regulations 2020, SI 2020/56, reg 13 (with effect from immediately before 11.00pm on 31 January 2020).

[12.94]

16 Effect of acknowledgment of notification

(1) Where P has made a notification under paragraph (1) of regulation 15, which has been acknowledged by the designating authority in accordance with paragraph (3) of regulation 15, S is a temporarily designated system.

(2) [Subject to regulation 17,] a temporarily designated system has temporary designation, from [IP completion day] to the end of the temporary designation period.

(3) Regulations 5 (fees) and 10 (provision of information by designated systems) of the 1999 Regulations do not apply to a temporarily designated system until such time as it makes an application under regulation 3 (application for designation) of the 1999 Regulations.

(4) The designating authority must publish on its website a list of temporarily designated systems.

NOTES

Para (2): words in first pair of square brackets inserted by the Financial Markets and Insolvency (Transitional Provision) (EU Exit) (Amendment) Regulations 2021, SI 2021/782, reg 2(2), as from 1 July 2021. Words "IP completion day" in square brackets substituted by the Financial Services (Consequential Amendments) Regulations 2020, SI 2020/56, reg 13 (with effect from immediately before 11.00pm on 31 January 2020).

[12.95]

17 Cessation of temporary designation

(1) A temporarily designated system ceases to be a temporarily designated system where any of the following conditions are met.

[(2) The first condition is that—

(a) P has not submitted an application under regulation 3(1) of the 1999 Regulations by the end of the period of 6 months beginning on the day after IP completion day; and

(b) a period of 2 years and 6 months has passed since IP completion day.]

(3) The second condition is that the temporarily designated system ceases to be specified as included within the scope of the Settlement Finality Directive in accordance with article 10 of that Directive.

(4) The third condition is that P has submitted an application to the designating authority under regulation 3(1) of the 1999 Regulations and—

(a) withdraws its application; or

(b) the application is determined by the designating authority.

(5) The fourth condition is that the Bank of England directs that the system is to cease to be a temporarily designated system.

(6) A direction may only be given under paragraph (5) where—

(a) the Bank of England considers that there would otherwise be an adverse effect on financial stability in the United Kingdom;

(b) P has expressly renounced the temporary designation; or

(c) P has submitted an application to the designating authority under regulation 3(1) of the 1999 Regulations, and has made false statements in relation to the application or has sought to obtain designation by any other irregular means.

NOTES

Para (2): substituted by the Financial Markets and Insolvency (Transitional Provision) (EU Exit) (Amendment) Regulations 2021, SI 2021/782, reg 2(3), as from 1 July 2021.

[12.96]

18 Temporary designation period duration

(1) The temporary designation period is the period of 3 years beginning on the day after [IP completion day].

(2) If the Treasury is satisfied that it is necessary and proportionate to avoid disruption to the financial stability of the United Kingdom, it may by regulations amend paragraph (1) to extend the temporary designation period by a period not exceeding 12 months.

(3) If the Treasury is satisfied that the conditions in paragraph (2) are met, it may exercise the power to extend the temporary designation period by regulations as described there on more than one occasion.

NOTES

Words "IP completion day" in square brackets substituted by the Financial Services (Consequential Amendments) Regulations 2020, SI 2020/56, reg 13 (with effect from immediately before 11.00pm on 31 January 2020).

[12.97]

[18A Transitional provisions: bank stabilisation

(1) A temporarily designated system is to be treated as a "designated settlement system" for the purposes of section 48B (special bail-in provision) of the Banking Act 2009.

(2) An operator of a temporarily designated system is to be treated as an "excluded person" for the purposes of sections 70A to 70C (suspension of obligations, restriction of security interests, suspension of termination rights) of the Banking Act 2009.]

NOTES

Commencement: see the note below.

Inserted by the Financial Services (Miscellaneous) (Amendment) (EU Exit) Regulations 2019, SI 2019/710, reg 20 (this amendment comes into force immediately before IP completion day (as defined in the European Union (Withdrawal Agreement) Act 2020, s 39)).

[12.98]

19 Regulations under this Part

(1) Any power to make regulations conferred on the Treasury by this Part is exercisable by statutory instrument.

(2) Such regulations may—

(a) contain incidental, supplemental, consequential and transitional provision; and

(b) make different provision for different purposes.

(3) A statutory instrument containing regulations made under this Part is subject to annulment in pursuance of a resolution of either House of Parliament.

[12.99]

20 Application of the 2000 Act to the Bank of England in relation to its functions under this Part

Section 398 (misleading FCA or PRA: residual cases) of the 2000 Act applies to information given to the Bank of England in purported compliance with a requirement that is imposed by or under this Part.

PART 5 EXISTING DESIGNATION ORDERS

[12.100]

21 Existing designation orders

(1) Nothing in these Regulations affects any designation order, or any other decision of a designating authority, made under the 1999 Regulations in relation to a designated system, which order or decision is in force immediately before [IP completion day].

(2) Expressions used in paragraph (1) have the same meanings as in the 1999 Regulations.

NOTES

Commencement: IP completion day (as defined in the European Union (Withdrawal Agreement) Act 2020, s 39).

Para (1): the words "IP completion day" in square brackets are substituted by the Financial Services and Economic and Monetary Policy (Consequential Amendments) (EU Exit) Regulations 2020, SI 2020/1301, reg 3, Schedule, para 23(b), as from 30 December 2020.

COMPANIES, LIMITED LIABILITY PARTNERSHIPS AND PARTNERSHIPS (AMENDMENT ETC) (EU EXIT) REGULATIONS 2019

(SI 2019/348)

NOTES

Made: 19 February 2019.

Authority: European Union (Withdrawal) Act 2018, s 8(1), Sch 7, para 21.

Commencement: IP completion day (as defined in the European Union (Withdrawal Agreement) Act 2020, s 39).

These Regulations are reproduced as amended by: the Companies and Statutory Auditors etc (Consequential Amendments) (EU Exit) Regulations 2020, SI 2020/523.

PART 1 INTRODUCTION

[12.101]

1 Citation, commencement and extent

These Regulations may be cited as the Companies, Limited Liability Partnerships and Partnerships (Amendment etc) (EU Exit) Regulations 2019.

NOTES

Commencement: IP completion day (as defined in the European Union (Withdrawal Agreement) Act 2020, s 39).

[12.102]

2

These Regulations come into force on exit day.

NOTES

Commencement: IP completion day (as defined in the European Union (Withdrawal Agreement) Act 2020, s 39).

As to the commencement of these Regulations, see the European Union (Withdrawal Agreement) Act 2020, Sch 5, para 1 (at **[12.59]**) which gives legal effect to the implementation period by 'non-textually amending' the coming into force dates of subordinate legislation which comes into force immediately before exit day, on exit day or at any time after exit day. This subordinate legislation will instead come into force immediately before the end of the implementation period (IP completion day), on IP completion day or (as the case may be) at the time concerned after IP completion day.

[12.103]

3

Any amendment or revocation made by these Regulations has the same extent as the enactment to which the amendment or revocation relates.

NOTES

Commencement: IP completion day (as defined in the European Union (Withdrawal Agreement) Act 2020, s 39).

4 (*Reg 4 (interpretation) provides that in these Reulations "the Act" means the Companies Act 2006.*)

PART 2 REVOCATIONS

[12.104]

5 Revocations

The following instruments are revoked to the extent specified—

(a) the Companies (Cross-Border Mergers) Regulations 2007 in their entirety;
(b) the Companies (Cross-Border Mergers) (Amendment) Regulations 2008 in their entirety;
(c) Part 4 (Amendments to the Companies (Cross-Border Mergers) Regulations 2007) of the Companies (Reporting Requirements in Mergers and Divisions) Regulations 2011;
(d) the Companies (Cross-Border Mergers) (Amendment) Regulations 2015 in their entirety; and
(e) the Commission Implementing Regulation (EU) 2015/884 of 8 June 2015 establishing technical specifications and procedures required for the system of interconnection of registers established by Directive 2009/101/EC of the European Parliament and of the Council in its entirety.

NOTES

Commencement: IP completion day (as defined in the European Union (Withdrawal Agreement) Act 2020, s 39).

PARTS 3, 4

6–9 (*Regs 6–8 (Part 3) introduce Schs 1–3 post. Reg 9 (Part 4) introduces Sch 4 post.*)

SCHEDULES

SCHEDULES 1–3

(*Sch 1 contains various amendments to the Companies Act 2006. Sch 2 contains amendments to, inter alia, the Companies (Political Expenditure Exemption) Order 2007, the Companies (Disclosure of Date of Birth Information) Regulations 2015, the Register of People with Significant Control Regulations 2016, and the Scottish Partnerships (Register of People with Significant Control) Regulations 2017. Sch 3 contains consequential amendments which, where appropriate, have been incorporated at the appropriate place.*)

SCHEDULE 4
TRANSITIONAL PROVISIONS

Regulation 9

PART 1 TRANSITIONAL PROVISIONS RELATING TO SCHEDULE 1

[12.105]

1 Section 141—subsidiary acting as authorised dealer in securities

Where the amendment made by paragraph 2 of Schedule 1 would (apart from this paragraph) mean that a subsidiary which immediately before [IP completion day] is a member of its holding company can no longer be such a member—

(a) for the period of one year beginning on [IP completion day]—
   (i) the amendment made by paragraph 2 of Schedule 1 to these Regulations does not apply to the subsidiary; and

(ii) section 141(2)(b) of the Act is to be read, in relation to the subsidiary, as—

"(b) is a member of or has access to an EU regulated market or UK regulated market"; and

(b) from the end of that period—

(i) the subsidiary may continue to be a member of the company; and

(ii) sections 137(3) and (4) of the Act apply to it with the following modifications—

(aa) for "this section", read "paragraph 1(b)(i) of Schedule 4 to the Companies, Limited Liability Partnerships and Partnerships (Amendment etc) (EU Exit) Regulations 2019"; and

(bb) in subsection (4), for "mentioned in subsection (1) above" read "held at the end of the period of one year beginning on [IP completion day]".

2 Section 164 and 278—particulars of corporate directors and secretaries

(1) Where the amendments made by paragraphs 4 and 5 of Schedule 1 would (apart from this paragraph) require a company's register of directors or register of secretaries to contain additional particulars in respect of an existing corporate director or secretary, the company need not comply with that requirement until three months after [IP completion day].

(2) Where the amendments made by paragraph 23 of Schedule 3 would (apart from this paragraph) require a limited liability partnership's register of members to contain additional particulars in respect of an existing corporate member or firm, the limited liability partnership need not comply with that requirement until three months after [IP completion day].

(3) Where the amendment made by paragraph 4 of Schedule 1 would (apart from this paragraph) require notice to be given under regulation 5(3D) of the European Economic Interest Grouping Regulations 1989 (notification of changes to the particulars of a manager of a grouping), that requirement need not be complied with until three months after [IP completion day].

(4) In this paragraph—

"existing corporate director or secretary" means a body corporate, or a firm that is a legal person under the law by which it is governed, whose particulars were contained in the company's register of directors or register of secretaries immediately before [IP completion day];

"existing corporate member or firm" means a body corporate, or a firm that is a legal person under the law by which it is governed, whose particulars were contained in the limited liability partnership's register of members immediately before [IP completion day].

3 Section 832—distributions

(1) This paragraph applies to a company that is an investment company within the meaning of section 833 of the Act immediately before [IP completion day].

(2) For the period of one year beginning on [IP completion day]—

(a) the amendment made by paragraph 12 of Schedule 1 does not apply to the company;

(b) section 832 of the Act applies to the company as if subsection (5)(a) was substituted by—

"(a) the company's shares must be shares admitted to trading on a UK regulated market or an EU regulated market".

NOTES

Commencement: IP completion day (as defined in the European Union (Withdrawal Agreement) Act 2020, s 39).

Words "IP completion day" in square brackets substituted by the Companies and Statutory Auditors etc (Consequential Amendments) (EU Exit) Regulations 2020, SI 2020/523, reg 20, with effect from immediately before IP completion day.

PART 2 TRANSITIONAL PROVISIONS RELATING TO SCHEDULE 2

[12.106]

4 Overseas Companies Regulations 2009

(1) This paragraph applies to an overseas company that has a UK establishment immediately before [IP completion day].

(2) If there are additional registrable particulars in respect of that establishment, the company must, within the period of three months beginning on [IP completion day], deliver to the registrar a return containing those particulars.

(3) The requirement in sub-paragraph (2) is to be treated, for the purposes of Part 2 of the Overseas Companies Regulations 2009, as a requirement of that Part.

(4) The amendments made by paragraph 6 of Schedule 2 do not apply to the company until three months after [IP completion day].

(5) In this paragraph—

"Additional registrable particulars" means such particulars as the company would be required to provide in a return under regulation 6 of the Overseas Companies Regulations 2009 were the company opening the establishment on the date of the return, to the extent that the company was not required already to deliver a return to the registrar containing those particulars before [IP completion day];

"UK establishment" has the same meaning as it has in the Overseas Companies Regulations 2009.

5 Permitted disclosure to credit reference agencies, credit institutions and financial institutions

(1) This paragraph applies to a credit reference agency, credit institution or financial institution that had, before [IP completion day], delivered to the registrar a statement that it met the conditions for permitted disclosure in accordance with a permitted disclosure provision.

(2) For the period of one year beginning on [IP completion day]—

(a) the amendments made by these Regulations to the permitted disclosure provisions do not affect the disclosure by the registrar of protected information to the credit reference agency, credit institution or financial institution;

(b) the permitted disclosure provisions have effect, in relation to a credit reference agency, credit institution or financial institution, as they did immediately before [IP completion day] and for the purposes of this sub-paragraph the United Kingdom must be treated as if it were an EEA State and within the European Economic Area.

(3) In this paragraph—

"the permitted disclosure provisions" are—

(a) Schedule 2 to the Overseas Companies Regulations 2009;

(b) Schedule 2 to the Companies (Disclosure of Address) Regulations 2009;

(c) Schedule 2 to the Companies (Disclosure of Date of Birth Information) Regulations 2015;

(d) Schedule 4 to the Register of People with Significant Control Regulations 2016; and

(e) Schedule 5 to the Scottish Partnerships (Register of People with Significant Control) Regulations 2017;

"credit institution", "credit reference agency" and "financial institution" have the same meanings as they have in the permitted disclosure provisions.

6 Interpretation

Except where the contrary intention appears, expressions used in this Schedule have the same meanings as they have in the Act.

NOTES

Commencement: IP completion day (as defined in the European Union (Withdrawal Agreement) Act 2020, s 39).

Words "IP completion day" in square brackets substituted by the Companies and Statutory Auditors etc (Consequential Amendments) (EU Exit) Regulations 2020, SI 2020/523, reg 20, with effect from immediately before IP completion day.

EUROPEAN UNION (WITHDRAWAL) ACT 2018 (CONSEQUENTIAL MODIFICATIONS AND REPEALS AND REVOCATIONS) (EU EXIT) REGULATIONS 2019

(SI 2019/628)

NOTES

Made: 21 March 2019.

Authority: European Union (Withdrawal) Act 2018, 8(1), 23(1), (2), Sch 7, para 21(b).

Commencement: see reg 1 below.

Note: only regs 1–3 of these Regulations are relevant to this Handbook (and reg 2 has subsequently been revoked; see below). The other provisions have been omitted and are not annotated.

These Regulations are reproduced as amended by: the Direct Payments to Farmers (Legislative Continuity) Act 2020 (Consequential Amendments) Regulations 2020, SI 2020/463; the European Union Withdrawal (Consequential Modifications) (EU Exit) Regulations 2020, SI 2020/1447.

PART 1 INTRODUCTION

[12.107]

1 Citation, commencement, extent and interpretation

(1) These Regulations may be cited as the European Union (Withdrawal) Act 2018 (Consequential Modifications and Repeals and Revocations) (EU Exit) Regulations 2019 and come into force in accordance with paragraphs (2) and (3).

(2) The following come into force on the day after the day on which these Regulations are made—

(a) this regulation and regulations 7 and 8;

(b) regulation 4(5) insofar as it relates to the following definitions (definitions relating to EU Exit)—

(i) "exit day" (and related expressions);

(ii) "retained EU law";

(iii) "retained direct minor EU legislation";

(iv) "retained direct principal EU legislation";

(v) "retained direct EU legislation";

(vi) "retained EU obligation";

(c) regulation 4(6)(d).

(3) Otherwise, these Regulations come into force on exit day.

(4) Any provision of these Regulations which amends, repeals or revokes an enactment has the same extent as the enactment amended, repealed or revoked.

(5) In these Regulations "the Act" means the European Union (Withdrawal) Act 2018.

NOTES

As to the commencement of these Regulations, see the European Union (Withdrawal Agreement) Act 2020, Sch 5, para 1 (at **[12.59]**) which gives legal effect to the implementation period by 'non-textually amending' the coming into force dates of subordinate legislation which comes into force immediately before exit day, on exit day or at any time after exit day. This subordinate legislation will instead come into force immediately before the end of the implementation period (IP completion day), on IP completion day or (as the case may be) at the time concerned after IP completion day.

PART 2 INTERPRETATION OF REFERENCES TO EU INSTRUMENTS ETC

2 (*Revoked by the European Union Withdrawal (Consequential Modifications) (EU Exit) Regulations 2020, SI 2020/1447, reg 10, with effect from immediately before IP completion day (as defined in the European Union (Withdrawal Agreement) Act 2020, s 39).*)

[12.108]

3 Interpretation of references created on or after exit day to EU regulations etc

(1) The Interpretation Act 1978 is amended as follows.

(2) In section 20 (references to other enactments), after subsection (2), insert—

"(3) Where an Act passed on or after exit day refers to any EU regulation, EU decision, EU tertiary legislation or provision of the EEA agreement, the reference, unless the contrary intention appears, is a reference to the EU regulation, EU decision, EU tertiary legislation or provision of the EEA agreement as it forms part of domestic law by virtue of section 3 of the European Union (Withdrawal) Act 2018 [or section 1 of the Direct Payments to Farmers (Legislative Continuity) Act 2020].

(4) Subsection (3) does not determine any question as to whether the reference is to be read as a reference to the EU regulation, EU decision, EU tertiary legislation or provision of the EEA agreement as modified by domestic law (and, accordingly, is without prejudice to subsection (2)).

(5) Any expression in subsection (3) or (4) which is defined in the European Union (Withdrawal) Act 2018 has the same meaning in that subsection as in that Act."

(3) *(Outside the cope of this work.)*

NOTES

Commencement: IP completion day (as defined in the European Union (Withdrawal Agreement) Act 2020, s 39).

Para (2): words in square brackets inserted by the Direct Payments to Farmers (Legislative Continuity) Act 2020 (Consequential Amendments) Regulations 2020, SI 2020/463, reg 10(1), (4), as from 30 April 2020.

FINANCIAL SERVICES AND MARKETS ACT 2000 (AMENDMENT) (EU EXIT) REGULATIONS 2019

(SI 2019/632)

NOTES

Made: 22 March 2019.

Authority: European Communities Act 1972, s 2(2); European Union (Withdrawal) Act 2018, s 8(1), Sch 4, para 1, Sch 7, para 21 (see also the note "Statutory Instruments made under the European Communities Act 1972" preceding paragraph **[4.1]** *ante*).

Commencement: 23 March 2019 (in so far as relating to the regs specified in reg 1(2) *below*); IP completion day (as defined in the European Union (Withdrawal Agreement) Act 2020, s 39) (otherwise).

These Regulations are reproduced as amended by: the Financial Services and Economic and Monetary Policy (Consequential Amendments) (EU Exit) Regulations 2020, SI 2020/1301.

Gibraltar: as to the application of these Regulations to Gibraltar, see the Gibraltar (Miscellaneous Amendments) (EU Exit) Regulations 2019, SI 2019/680 at **[12.128]**.

ARRANGEMENT OF REGULATIONS

PART 1 INTRODUCTORY

[12.109]
1 Citation, commencement and interpretation

(1) These Regulations may be cited as the Financial Services and Markets Act 2000 (Amendment) (EU Exit) Regulations 2019.

(2) This regulation, Part 7, Part 8 and the following regulations come into force on the day after the day on which these Regulations are made—

(a) regulation 49(e);
(b) regulation 85(3), (6), (8), (11) and (14);
(c) regulation 87(b);
(d) regulation 88(e);
(e) regulation 130;
(f) regulation 171;
(g) regulation 179(3);
(h) regulation 187(3), in so far as it inserts paragraph (3) in article 1 of the Financial Services and Markets Act 2000 (Qualifying EU Provisions) Order 2013; and
(i) regulation 190(3), in so far as it inserts paragraph (3) in article 1 of the Financial Services and Markets Act 2000 (Qualifying EU Provisions) (No 2) Order 2013.

(3) The other provisions of these Regulations come into force on exit day.

(4) In these Regulations, "the Act" means the Financial Services and Markets Act 2000.

NOTES

As to the commencement of these Regulations, see the European Union (Withdrawal Agreement) Act 2020, Sch 5, para 1 (at **[12.59]**) which gives legal effect to the implementation period by 'non-textually amending' the coming into force dates of subordinate legislation which comes into force immediately before exit day, on exit day or at any time after exit day. This subordinate legislation will instead come into force immediately before the end of the implementation period (IP completion day), on IP completion day or (as the case may be) at the time concerned after IP completion day.

PARTS 2–6

2–196 (*Part 2 (regs 2–119) amends FSMA 2000 at* **[7.1]**. *Part 3 (regs 120–161) amends the Regulated Activities Order at* **[8.1]**. *Part 4 (regs 162–176) amends the Financial Promotion Order at* **[8.443]** *Part 5 (regs 177–193) contains consequential amendments to other subordinate legislation made under FSMA 2000. Part 6 (regs 194–196) contains amendments to legislation that is outside the scope of this work.*)

PART 7 TRANSITIONAL POWERS OF THE FINANCIAL REGULATORS

[12.110]
197 Interpretation

(1) In this Part—

"transitional direction" means a direction under regulation 198(1);
"relevant obligation" has the meaning given by regulation 199.

(2) For the purposes of this Part, each of the following is a "regulator"—

(a) the Bank of England;
(b) the Prudential Regulation Authority;
(c) the Financial Conduct Authority.

[12.111]
198 Power of the regulators to give transitional directions

(1) A regulator may direct that a relevant obligation to which a person is subject—

(a) is not to apply to the person, or
(b) is to apply to the person with modifications specified in the direction.

(2) Power under paragraph (1) is subject to regulation 200.

(3) Power of a regulator under paragraph (1) is exercisable on the regulator's own initiative.

(4) Power of a regulator under paragraph (1), so far as it relates to rules made by the regulator, is in addition to (and does not limit) power of the regulator under section 138A of the Act.

[12.112]
199 Meaning of "relevant obligation"

(1) An obligation is a "relevant obligation", in relation to a regulator and a person, if—

(a) the obligation is imposed by or under an enactment,
(b) the obligation is not an excluded obligation,
(c) the regulator has responsibility for supervising, or has other functions relating to, the person's compliance with the obligation, and
(d) as a result of the operation of an exit instrument, the obligation—
 (i) begins to apply in the person's case, or
 (ii) applies in the person's case differently from how it would, but for the exit instrument, apply in the person's case.

(2) In this regulation—

"enactment" means—
 (a) an enactment contained in—
  (i) an Act, or
  (ii) subordinate legislation (within the meaning of the Interpretation Act 1978),

(b) an enactment which is retained direct EU legislation, or

(c) an enactment contained in, or in an instrument made under, Northern Ireland legislation;

"excluded obligation", in relation to a regulator, means—

(a) an obligation to satisfy the threshold conditions in relation to a regulated activity, or

(b) an obligation imposed by or under rules made under section 64A or 137O of the Act;

"exit instrument" means—

(a) regulations under section 8 of the European Union (Withdrawal) Act 2018, or

(b) an instrument under regulation 3 of the Financial Regulators' Powers (Technical Standards etc) (Amendment etc) (EU Exit) Regulations 2018;

"regulated activity" and "threshold conditions" have the same meaning as in the Act (see, in particular, sections 22 and 55B).

[12.113]

200 Giving, and effect, of transitional directions

(1) A transitional direction—

(a) may not be given more than 2 years after [IP completion day],

(b) may specify the period in relation to which it has effect, subject to paragraph (2),

(c) may be given subject to conditions, and

(d) may be given to a particular person or particular persons, or to persons of a description specified in the direction.

(2) A transitional direction—

(a) is of no effect in relation to times before it is given,

(b) is of no effect in relation to times before [IP completion day], and

(c) is of no effect in relation to times more than 2 years after [IP completion day] (without prejudice to any continuing effect in relation to earlier times).

(3) A regulator may not give a transitional direction, or a set of two or more transitional directions, to any person or persons unless the regulator is satisfied that the direction, or the directions viewed collectively, will prevent or mitigate disruption that could reasonably be expected to arise—

(a) for the person, or

(b) (as the case may be) for the persons viewed collectively,

from compliance with the unmodified obligation, or with the unmodified obligations viewed collectively, at times in relation to which the direction is, or the directions are, to have effect.

(4) The Financial Conduct Authority may not give a transitional direction, or a set of two or more transitional directions, unless the Authority is satisfied that doing so would not adversely affect the advancement of its key objectives viewed collectively; and here the reference to the Authority's key objectives is to its objectives set out in section 1B of the Act, read with section 1IA of the Act.

(5) The Prudential Regulation Authority may not give a transitional direction, or a set of two or more transitional directions, unless the Authority is satisfied that doing so would not adversely affect the advancement of its objectives under the Act.

(6) The Bank of England may not give a transitional direction, or a set of two or more transitional directions, unless the Bank is satisfied that doing so would not adversely affect the advancement of the Bank's financial stability objective set out in section 2A(1) of the Bank of England Act 1998.

(7) For the purposes of this regulation, two or more transitional directions given by a regulator are a "set" if the regulator declares them to be a set.

NOTES

Paras (1), (2): the words "IP completion day" in square brackets were substituted by the Financial Services and Economic and Monetary Policy (Consequential Amendments) (EU Exit) Regulations 2020, SI 2020/1301, reg 3, Schedule, para 33(y), as from 30 December 2020.

[12.114]

201 Variation of transitional directions

(1) A regulator's power under regulation 198(1) includes power to give a direction varying (or further varying) a transitional direction already given by that regulator, subject to paragraph (2).

(2) The way in which the power to vary is exercised must be such that the resulting—

(a) varied direction, or

(b) where the earlier direction was part of a set of transitional directions, set of directions as varied,

could be given by revoking existing, and giving new, transitional directions.

(3) Where a transitional direction has been given to two or more particular persons, or to persons of a description specified in the direction, the power to vary it may be exercised in relation to all, some or any one of those persons.

(4) Regulation 200(7) (meaning of "set") applies also for the purposes of paragraph (2).

[12.115]

202 Consultation

(1) A regulator, before it gives a transitional direction in which another regulator has an interest, must consult that other regulator.

(2) For the purposes of paragraph (1)—

(a) the Prudential Regulation Authority has an interest in a transitional direction if the direction—

(i) might affect the Authority's discharge of functions conferred on it by or under—

(aa) the Act, or

(bb) retained EU law, or

(ii) would apply to a PRA-authorised person, or to a person connected with a PRA-authorised person;

(b) the Financial Conduct Authority has an interest in all transitional directions;

(c) the Bank of England has an interest in a transitional direction if the direction—

(i) might affect the Bank's discharge of functions conferred on it by or under—

(aa) the Act,

(bb) the Banking Act 2009, or

(cc) retained EU law, or

(ii) would apply to—

(aa) a central counterparty or a central securities depository, or

(bb) a financial counterparty, or a non-financial counterparty, within the meaning of the EMIR regulation.

(3) A regulator, before it gives a transitional direction, must consult the Treasury on a draft of the proposed direction.

(4) Paragraphs (1) and (3) do not apply in the case of a transitional direction if the regulator assesses that the urgency of the situation is such that the direction should be given before the required consultation is begun or completed, but in that event the regulator must (as the case may be)—

(a) begin the consultation required by those paragraphs in the case of the direction as soon as the direction is given, or

(b) complete the consultation.

(5) In paragraph (2)—

"central counterparty", and "the EMIR regulation", have the same meaning as in Part 18 of the Act (see section 313(1) of the Act);

"central securities depository" has the same meaning as in the Act (see section 417(1) of the Act);

"PRA-authorised person" has the same meaning as in the Act (see section 2B(5) of the Act).

(6) For the purposes of paragraph (2), a person is connected with another person if the first person is connected with the other person for the purposes of section 165 of the Act (see subsection (11) of that section).

[12.116]

203 Notification and publication of transitional directions

(1) Where a transitional direction is given by a regulator, the regulator—

(a) must prepare—

(i) an explanation of the purpose of the direction,

(ii) such guidance in connection with the direction as the regulator considers appropriate, and

(iii) a statement to the effect that the regulator is satisfied as required by paragraph (4), or (as the case may be) paragraph (5) or (6), of regulation 200, and

(b) must publish the direction and the matters listed in sub-paragraph (a).

(2) Paragraph (1)(b) does not apply if the regulator is satisfied that it is inappropriate to publish the direction.

(3) Where a transitional direction is given by a regulator and the direction is not published on the regulator's website, the regulator must take the steps appearing to the regulator to be best calculated to bring the direction, and the matters listed in paragraph (1)(a), to the attention of—

(a) in the case of a direction given to a particular person or particular persons, that person or those persons, or

(b) in the case of a direction given to persons of a description specified in the direction, any persons who are likely to be affected by the direction.

(4) Where a regulator gives a transitional direction, the regulator must without delay provide the Treasury with a copy of the direction.

(5) Section 139A(5) of the Act (consultation) does not apply to guidance under paragraph (1)(a)(ii).

[12.117]

204 Revocation of transitional directions

(1) A regulator may revoke a transitional direction given by the regulator, either wholly or in relation to one or some of the persons to whom it was given.

(2) Power of a regulator to revoke a transitional direction is exercisable on the regulator's own initiative.

(3) Where a regulator revokes a transitional direction in relation to a particular person or particular persons, the regulator must provide the person, or each of the persons, with a copy of the revocation.

(4) Where a regulator revokes a transitional direction in relation to persons of a description specified in the revocation, the regulator must take the steps appearing to the regulator to be best calculated to bring the revocation to the attention of any persons likely to be affected by it.

(5) Where a regulator revokes a transitional direction, the regulator must without delay provide the Treasury with a copy of the revocation.

[12.118]

205 Annual reports and complaints

(1) Power to give a transitional direction is treated as a "relevant sub-delegated power" for the purposes of paragraph 32 of Schedule 7 to the European Union (Withdrawal) Act 2018.

(2) Functions under this Part are to be treated as not being "relevant functions" for the purposes of section 84 of the Financial Services Act 2012 (arrangements for the investigation of complaints relating to exercise of relevant functions of regulators).

PART 8 REGULATORS' FEES

[12.119]

206 Meaning of "qualifying functions" in this Part

(1) For the purposes of this Part, the "qualifying functions" of the Bank of England, or of the Financial Conduct Authority or the Prudential Regulation Authority, are—

(a) its functions under or as a result of a qualifying provision that is specified, or of a description specified, for the purposes of this paragraph by the Treasury by order, and

(b) its functions under or as a result of regulations made under section 8 of the European Union (Withdrawal) Act 2018.

(2) In paragraph (1)(a) "qualifying provision" has the meaning given by section 425C of the Act (as substituted by these Regulations).

(3) An order under paragraph (1) may—

(a) contain such incidental, supplemental, consequential and transitional provision as the person making it considers appropriate, and

(b) make different provision for different cases.

(4) Power to make an order under paragraph (1) is exercisable by statutory instrument.

(5) A statutory instrument containing an order under paragraph (1) is subject to annulment in pursuance of a resolution of either House of Parliament.

[12.120]

207 Fees: Bank of England

(1) The Bank of England may, in connection with the discharge of any of its qualifying functions, require recognised clearing houses, third country central counterparties, recognised CSDs or settlement internalisers to pay fees to the Bank.

(2) The power of the Bank to set fees includes power to set fees for the purpose of meeting expenses incurred by it or the Financial Conduct Authority—

(a) in preparation for the exercise by the Bank of its qualifying functions, or

(b) for the purpose of facilitating the exercise by the Bank of those functions or otherwise in connection with their exercise by it.

(3) It is irrelevant when the expenses were incurred.

(4) Any fee which is owed to the Bank under this regulation may be recovered as a debt due to the Bank.

(5) In this regulation—

"CSD regulation" has the meaning given by section 417 of the Act,

"recognised clearing house", "recognised CSD" and "third country central counterparty" have the meaning given by section 285 of the Act, and

"settlement internaliser" has the meaning given by Article 2(1)(11) of the CSD regulation.

[12.121]

208 Fees: Financial Conduct Authority

(1) The Financial Conduct Authority ("the FCA") may make rules providing for the payment to it of such fees, in connection with the discharge of any of its qualifying functions, as it considers will (taking account of its expected income from fees and charges provided for by any provision of the Act other than sections 137SA, 137SB and 333T) enable it—

(a) to meet expenses incurred in carrying out the functions conferred on it by or under the Act, other than its excepted functions, or for any incidental purpose,

(b) to repay the principal of, and pay any interest on, any relevant borrowing and to meet relevant commencement expenses, and

(c) to maintain adequate reserves.

(2) It is irrelevant when the expenses mentioned in paragraph (1)(a) were incurred.

(3) The "excepted functions" of the FCA are—

(a) its functions under sections 137SA and 137SB of the Act, and

(b) its functions under section 333T of the Act so far as relating to the collection of payments.

(4) In paragraph (1)(b) "relevant borrowing" and "relevant commencement expenses" have the meaning given by paragraph 23(3) and (5) of Schedule 1ZA to the Act.

(5) In fixing the amount of any fee which is to be payable to the FCA, no account is to be taken of any sums which the FCA receives, or expects to receive, by way of penalties imposed by it under the Act.

(6) Any fee which is owed to the FCA under any provision made under this regulation may be recovered as a debt due to the FCA.

(7) Chapter 2 of Part 9A of the Act (rules: procedural provisions etc) applies in relation to rules under this regulation as it applies in relation to rules under paragraph 23 of Schedule 1ZA to the Act.

(8) The requirements of sections 138I and 138K of the Act in so far as they apply to a proposal to make rules under this regulation may be satisfied by things done (wholly or in part) before the date on which this regulation comes into force.

[12.122]

209 Fees: Prudential Regulation Authority

(1) The Prudential Regulation Authority ("the PRA") may make rules providing for the payment to it of such fees, in connection with the discharge of any of its qualifying functions, as it considers will (taking account of its expected income from fees and charges provided for by any provision of the Act) enable it—

(a) to meet expenses incurred in carrying out the functions conferred on it by or under the Act or for any incidental purpose,

(b) to repay the principal of, and pay any interest on, any relevant borrowing and to meet relevant commencement expenses, and

(c) to maintain adequate reserves.

(2) It is irrelevant when the expenses mentioned in paragraph (1)(a) were incurred.

(3) In paragraph (1)(b) "relevant borrowing" and "relevant commencement expenses" have the meaning given by paragraph 31(3) and (5) of Schedule 1ZB to the Act.

(4) In fixing the amount of any fee which is to be payable to the PRA, no account is to be taken of any sums which the PRA receives, or expects to receive, by way of penalties imposed by it under the Act.

(5) Any fee which is owed to the PRA under any provision made under this regulation may be recovered as a debt due to the PRA.

(6) Chapter 2 of Part 9A of the Act (rules: procedural provisions etc) applies in relation to rules under this regulation as it applies in relation to rules under paragraph 31 of Schedule 1ZB to the Act.

(7) The requirements of sections 138J and 138K of the Act in so far as they apply to a proposal to make rules under this regulation may be satisfied by things done (wholly or in part) before the date on which this regulation comes into force.

UNCERTIFICATED SECURITIES (AMENDMENT AND EU EXIT) REGULATIONS 2019

(SI 2019/679)

NOTES

Made: 26 March 2019.

Authority: European Communities Act 1972, s 2(2); Companies Act 2006, ss 784(1), 785(1), 788, 1292; European Union (Withdrawal) Act 2018, s 8(1), Sch 4, para 1, Sch 7, para 21 (see also the note "Statutory Instruments made under the European Communities Act 1972" preceding paragraph **[4.1]** *ante*).

Commencement: 27 March 2019 (regs 1–13); IP completion day (as defined in the European Union (Withdrawal Agreement) Act 2020, s 39) (regs 14–16).

For a summary of all Orders and Regulations made under the Companies Act 2006, see Appendix 4 at **[A4]**.

PART 1 GENERAL

[12.123]

1 Citation and commencement

(1) These Regulations may be cited as the Uncertificated Securities (Amendment and EU Exit) Regulations 2019.

(2) Parts 1 to 4 come into force on the day after the day on which these Regulations are made.

(3) Part 5 comes into force on exit day.

NOTES

As to the commencement of these Regulations, see the European Union (Withdrawal Agreement) Act 2020, Sch 5, para 1 (at **[12.59]**) which gives legal effect to the implementation period by 'non-textually amending' the coming into force dates of subordinate legislation which comes into force immediately before exit day, on exit day or at any time after exit day. This subordinate legislation will instead come into force immediately before the end of the implementation period (IP completion day), on IP completion day or (as the case may be) at the time concerned after IP completion day.

PARTS 2, 3

2–9 *(Part 2 (regs 2, 3) amends the Companies Act 2006, Schs 2 and 11A, and the Financial Services (Banking Reform) Act 2013, ss 41, 112, 115. Part 3 (regs 4–9) amends the Uncertificated Securities Regulations 2001, SI 2001/3755, and contains consequential amendments to the Stamp Duty Reserve Tax Regulations 1986, SI 1986/1711, the Financial Services and Markets Act 2000 (Regulated Activities) Order 2001, SI 2001/544, the Financial Services and Markets Act 2000 (Exemption) Order 2001SI 2001/1201, the Financial Services and Markets Act 2000 (Disclosure of Confidential Information) Regulations 2001SI 2001/2188, and the Financial Services and Markets Act 2000 (Excluded Activities and Prohibitions) Order 2014, SI 2014/2080. All amendments have been incorporated at the appropriate place.)*

PART 4 TRANSITIONAL PROVISIONS AND REVIEW

[12.124]

10 Transitional provisions: interpretation

In this regulation and in regulations 11 and 12—

"the Act" means the Financial Services and Markets Act 2000;

"CSD Operator" means a person established in the United Kingdom who immediately before 30th March 2017—

(a) was an Operator approved under the Uncertificated Securities Regulations 2001,

(b) operated a securities settlement system referred to in point (3) of Section A of the Annex to the CSD regulation in the United Kingdom, and

(c) provided at least one other core service listed in Section A of that Annex in the United Kingdom;

"commencement" means the coming into force of this Part of these Regulations;

"CSD regulation" means Regulation (EU) No 909/2014 of the European Parliament and of the Council of 23rd July 2014 on improving securities settlement in the European Union and on central securities depositories;

"Operator register of securities" has the meaning given in regulation 3 of the Uncertificated Securities Regulations 2001;

"recognised CSD" has the meaning given in section 285 of the 2000 Act.

[12.125]

11 Transitional and saving provisions for Operators

(1) The transition period for a CSD Operator begins with commencement.

(2) The transition period for a CSD Operator ends immediately after—

(a) the Bank of England determines its application under section 288A of the 2000 Act in accordance with Article 17 of the CSD regulation and any directly applicable EU regulation made under that Article, or

(b) if the CSD Operator has not made an application under section 288A of the 2000 Act before the end of that period, the end of the six month period specified in Article 69(2) of the CSD regulation.

(3) Regulations 2 to 9 do not apply in respect of a CSD Operator during its transition period.

(4) Nothing in these Regulations affects the validity of a CSD Operator's approval as an Operator under the Uncertificated Securities Regulations 2001 during its transition period.

(5) Where—

(a) a CSD Operator has made an application under section 288A of the 2000 Act, and

(b) the Bank of England has determined that application in accordance with Article 17 of the CSD regulation and any directly applicable EU regulation made under that Article,

any previous approval as an Operator under the Uncertificated Securities Regulations 2001 shall cease to have effect.

(6) Following any decision of the Bank under paragraph (5)—

(a) such decision shall not itself invalidate or otherwise affect any act of the CSD Operator carried out in its capacity as an approved Operator before such decision, and

(b) unless the context requires otherwise, any such act shall be treated as an act of the CSD Operator in its capacity as an Operator as defined in regulation 3(1) of the Uncertificated Securities Regulations 2001.

[12.126]

12 Transitional and savings provisions for issuers

(1) Paragraphs (2) and (3) apply where—

(a) title to units of a security to which Article 49(1) of the CSD regulation applies is recorded on the Operator register of securities of a CSD Operator immediately before the transition period for that CSD Operator ends (in accordance with regulation 11(2)), and

(b) the CSD Operator is recognised as a recognised CSD.

(2) The issuer of the security is not required to make a request under Article 49(2) of the CSD regulation for recording its securities in the relevant system.

(3) The fact that the issuer of the security has not made a request as described in paragraph (2) does not prevent—

(a) title to units of that security continuing to be evidenced otherwise than by a certificate by virtue of the Uncertificated Securities Regulations 2001, and

(b) transfer of title to units of that security continuing to be subject to those Regulations.

[12.127]

13 Review

(1) The Treasury must from time to time—

(a) carry out a review of the regulatory provisions contained in regulations 3, 5, and 6 of and paragraphs 5 and 25 of Schedule 1 and paragraphs 1, 2, 5, 6, 9 and 10 of Schedule 3 to the Uncertificated Securities Regulations 2001; and

(b) publish a report setting out the conclusions of the review.

(2) The first report under this regulation must be published before the end of the period of five years beginning with the day on which these Regulations come into force.

(3) Subsequent reports must be published at intervals not exceeding five years.

(4) Section 30(3) of the Small Business, Enterprise and Employment Act 2015 requires that a report published under this regulation must, so far as is reasonable, have regard to how the obligations under Regulation (EU) No 909/2014 of the European Parliament and of the Council of 23rd July 2014 on improving securities settlement in the European Union and on central securities depositories is implemented in other member States.

(5) In this regulation, "regulatory provisions" has the same meaning as in sections 28 to 32 of the Small Business, Enterprise and Employment Act 2015 (see section 32 of that Act).

PART 5 AMENDMENTS IN CONNECTION WITH EXITING THE EUROPEAN UNION

14–16 *(Reg 14 amends the Uncertificated Securities Regulations 2001, SI 2001/3755. Reg 15 amends European Parliament and Council Regulation 236/2012/EU on short selling and certain aspects of credit default swaps (outside the scope of this work). Reg 16 inserts the Central Securities Depositories Regulations 2014, SI 2014/2879, reg 5O (outside the scope of this work))*

GIBRALTAR (MISCELLANEOUS AMENDMENTS) (EU EXIT) REGULATIONS 2019

(SI 2019/680)

NOTES

Made: 26 March 2019.

Authority: European Union (Withdrawal) Act 2018, s 8(1), Sch 7, para 21.

Commencement: IP completion day (as defined in the European Union (Withdrawal Agreement) Act 2020, s 39) (regs 2–5, 11 and Schs 1, 2); immediately before IP completion day (otherwise).

These Regulations are reproduced as amended by: the Financial Services (Electronic Money, Payment Services and Miscellaneous Amendments) (EU Exit) Regulations 2019, SI 2019/1212; the Prospectus (Amendment etc) (EU Exit) Regulations 2019, SI 2019/1234; the Financial Services (Miscellaneous Amendments) (EU Exit) Regulations 2020, SI 2020/628; the Over the Counter Derivatives, Central Counterparties and Trade Repositories (Amendment, etc, and Transitional Provision) (EU Exit) Regulations 2020, SI 2020/646; the Financial Services and Economic and Monetary Policy (Consequential Amendments) (EU Exit) Regulations 2020, SI 2020/1301.

PART 1 INTRODUCTION

[12.128]

1 Citation, commencement and interpretation

(1) These Regulations may be cited as the Gibraltar (Miscellaneous Amendments) (EU Exit) Regulations 2019.

(2) Regulations 2, 3, 4, 5, 11 and Schedules 1 and 2 come into force on exit day.

(3) The other provisions in these Regulations come into force immediately before exit day.

(4) In these Regulations—

(a) the "CIIU (EU Exit) Regulations 2019" means the Credit Institutions and Insurance Undertakings Reorganisation and Winding Up (Amendment) (EU Exit) Regulations 2019;

(b) "Gibraltarian insurer" means an undertaking pursuing the activity of direct insurance (within the meaning of Directive 2009/138/EC of the European Parliament and of the Council on the taking up and pursuit of the business of Insurance and Reinsurance ("Solvency 2 Directive") which has received authorisation under the law of Gibraltar which was relied on by Gibraltar before [IP completion day] to implement Article 14 or Article 162 of the Solvency 2 Directive from the Gibraltarian regulator.

NOTES

Commencement: immediately before IP completion day (as defined in the European Union (Withdrawal Agreement) Act 2020, s 39).

Para (4): the words "IP completion day" in square brackets were substituted by the Financial Services and Economic and Monetary Policy (Consequential Amendments) (EU Exit) Regulations 2020, SI 2020/1301, reg 3, Schedule, para 40(a), as from 30 December 2020.

As to the commencement of these Regulations, see the European Union (Withdrawal Agreement) Act 2020, Sch 5, para 1 (at **[5.87]**) which gives legal effect to the implementation period by 'non-textually amending' the coming into force dates of subordinate legislation which comes into force immediately before exit day, on exit day or at any time after exit day. This subordinate legislation will instead come into force immediately before the end of the implementation period (IP completion day), on IP completion day or (as the case may be) at the time concerned after IP completion day.

PART 2 GIBRALTAR RELATED AMENDMENTS

2–10 (*Reg 2 contains modifications to the Insurers (Reorganisation and Winding Up) Regulations 2004 in relation to the winding up or reorganisation of Gibraltarian insurers, or the determination of Gibraltarian rights in relation to the winding-up or reorganisation of UK insurers. It also introduces further modifications in Sch 1 to these Regulations (outside the scope of this work). Reg 3 provides that the Credit Institutions (Reorganisation and Winding Up) Regulations 2004 apply in relation to the winding up or reorganisation of Gibraltarian credit institutions, investment firms and group companies, or the determination of Gibraltarian rights in relation to the winding-up or reorganisation of UK credit institutions: (a) as if the amendments made by the CIIU (EU Exit) Regulations 2019 had not been made; and (b) subject to the modifications set out in Schedule 2 to these Regulations (outside the scope of this work). Reg 4 contains modifications to the Insurers (Reorganisation and Winding Up) (Lloyd's) Regulations 2005 in relation to the winding up or reorganisation of Gibraltarian insurers, or the determination of Gibraltarian rights in relation to the winding-up or reorganisation of UK insurers, and is outside the scope of this work. Reg 5 amends the Financial Services and Markets Act 2000 (Financial Promotion) Order 2005. Reg 6 amends the Credit Transfers and Direct Debits in Euro (Amendment) (EU Exit) Regulations 2018. Reg 7 amends the Friendly Societies (Amendment) (EU Exit) Regulations 2018. Reg 8 amends the Market Abuse (Amendment) (EU Exit) Regulations 2019. Reg 9 amends the Financial Services and Markets Act 2000 (Amendment) (EU Exit) Regulations 2019. Reg 10 amends the Solvency 2 and Insurance (Amendment, etc) (EU Exit) Regulations 2019. In so far as relevant to this work, all amendments made by regs 5 to 10 have been incorporated at the appropriate place.*)

PART 3 SAVING PROVISIONS FOR GIBRALTAR

[12.129]

11 Saving for certain financial services legislation relating to Gibraltar

(1) In so far as Regulations specified in paragraph (5)—

(a) are made before [IP completion day] under the European Union (Withdrawal) Act 2018, and

(b) on or after [IP completion day], amend, repeal or revoke an enactment that, before [IP completion day], applies to—

(i) activities in connection with Gibraltar of a person regulated by the Prudential Regulation Authority, the Bank of England, the Financial Conduct Authority or the Payment Systems Regulator;

(ii) Gibraltar trading venue or financial instruments admitted to trading or traded on a Gibraltar trading venue;

(iii) activities of a Gibraltar-based firm;

(iv) the charging of interchange fees (as defined by Article 2(10) of Regulation (EU) 2015/751 of the European Parliament and of the Council of 29 April 2015 on interchange fees for card-based payment transactions) in relation to transactions between the UK and Gibraltar; or

(v) functions of the Financial Services Commission of Gibraltar, the Regulations are to be read as if the amendment, repeal or revocation had not been made in relation to the matters referred to in paragraphs (i) to (v) ("the relevant matters"), and paragraph (4) applies.

(2) In so far as an enactment specified in the Schedule to the Financial Regulators' Powers (Technical Standards etc) (Amendment etc) (EU Exit) Regulations 2018—

(a) applies to the relevant matters, and

(b) has been amended, repealed or revoked under those Regulations,

unless this paragraph is disapplied (in whole or in part) in the instrument which amended, repealed or revoked the enactment, the enactment is to be read if the amendment, repeal or revocation had not been made in relation to the relevant matters, and paragraph (4) applies.

(3) In so far as an enactment specified in paragraph (6)—

(a) applies to the relevant matters, and

(b) has been amended, repealed or revoked by regulations made under the European Union (Withdrawal) Act 2018,

the enactment is to be read if the amendment, repeal or revocation had not been made in relation to the relevant matters, and paragraph (4) applies.

(4) If this paragraph applies, an enactment referred to in paragraph (1)(b), (2) or (3) is to be read with any modifications necessary to ensure that the enactment continues to apply to the relevant matters after [IP completion day] as it applied to them before [IP completion day].

(5) The Regulations are—

(a) the Trade Repositories (Amendment and Transitional Provision) (EU Exit) Regulations 2018;

(b) the Central Counterparties (Amendment, etc, and Transitional Provision) (EU Exit) Regulations 2018;

(c) the Central Securities Depositories (Amendment) (EU Exit) Regulations 2018;

(d) the Short Selling (Amendment) (EU Exit) Regulations 2018;

(e) the Capital Requirements (Amendment) (EU Exit) Regulations 2018;

(f) the Markets in Financial Instruments (Amendment) (EU Exit) Regulations 2018 (except for Part 2, Chapter 3 of Part 3, and regulations 28(10), 29(3) and 30(1));

(g) the Credit Transfers and Direct Debits in Euro (Amendment)(EU Exit) Regulations 2018 (except for regulation 6(2));

(h) the Financial Markets and Insolvency (Amendment and Transitional) (EU Exit) Regulations 2019 (except for regulations 5(7), 8(3)(a), 8(4)(b), 8(6) and 9);

(i) the Payment Accounts (Amendment) (EU Exit) Regulations 2019;

(j) the Interchange Fee (Amendment) (EU Exit) Regulations 2019;

(k) the Social Entrepreneurship Funds (Amendment) (EU Exit) Regulations 2019;

(l) the Venture Capital Funds (Amendment) (EU Exit) Regulations 2019

(m) the Long-term Investment Funds (Amendment) (EU Exit) Regulations 2019;

(n) the Collective Investment Schemes (Amendment etc) (EU Exit) Regulations 2019;

(o) the Money Market Funds (Amendment) (EU Exit) Regulations 2019;

(p) the Over the Counter Derivatives, Central Counterparties and Trade Repositories (Amendment, etc, and Transitional Provision) (EU Exit) Regulations 2019;

(q) the Investment Exchanges, Clearing Houses and Central Securities Depositories (Amendment) (EU Exit) Regulations 2019;

(r) the Financial Conglomerates and Other Financial Groups (Amendments etc) (EU Exit) Regulations 2019;

(s) the Securitisation (Amendment) (EU Exit) Regulations 2019;

(t) the Transparency of Securities Financing Transactions and of Reuse (Amendment) (EU Exit) Regulations 2019;

(u) the Benchmarks (Amendment and Transitional Provision) (EU Exit) Regulations 2019;

(v) the Money Laundering and Transfer of Funds (Information) (Amendment) (EU Exit) Regulations 2019;

(w) the Packaged Retail and Insurance-based Investment Products (Amendment) (EU Exit) Regulations 2019;

(x) the Credit Rating Agencies (Amendments etc) (EU Exit) Regulations 2019;

(y) Part 6 of the Solvency 2 and Insurance (Amendment, etc) (EU Exit) Regulations 2019;

(z) regulation 12, and Parts 3 to 6 of the Financial Services and Markets Act 2000 (Amendment) (EU Exit) Regulations 2019 (except for [regulations 126, 127, 154, 179(2), 187 and 190]);

[(z1) the Official Listing of Securities, Prospectus and Transparency (Amendment etc) (EU Exit) Regulations 2019;

(z2) the Prospectus (Amendment etc) (EU Exit) Regulations 2019];

[(z3) the Over the Counter Derivatives, Central Counterparties and Trade Repositories (Amendment, etc, and Transitional Provision) (EU Exit) (No 2) Regulations 2019 (except for regulation 34(a)(i) and (b));

(z4) regulations 18 to 21 of the Financial Services (Miscellaneous Amendments) (EU Exit) Regulations 2020];

[(z5) the Over the Counter Derivatives, Central Counterparties and Trade Repositories (Amendment, etc, and Transitional Provision) (EU Exit) Regulations 2020].

(6) The enactments are—

(a) paragraphs 15BB and 15C of Schedule 6 to the Insolvency Act 1986;

(b) sections 213(10) and (11), 214(5) and 224(4) of the Financial Services and Markets Act 2000;

(c) the Financial Services and Markets Act 2000 (Compensation Scheme: Electing Participants) Regulations 2001.

(7) For the purposes of this regulation—

(a) an "enactment" includes an instrument which is direct EU legislation;

(b) a "Gibraltar-based firm" has the same meaning as in article 1(2) of the Financial Services and Markets Act 2000 (Gibraltar) Order 2001;

(c) "Gibraltar trading venue" has the meaning given in Article 2 of Regulation (EU) 596/2014 of the European Parliament and of the Council of 16 April 2014 on market abuse as that regulation forms part of domestic law under section 3 of the European Union (Withdrawal) Act 2018;

[(d) for the purposes of the Regulations specified in sub-paragraphs (5)(a), (b), (p)[, (z4) and (z5)] (which amend Regulation (EU) No 648/2012 of the European Parliament and of the Council of 4 July 2012 on OTC derivatives, central counterparties and trade repositories ("EMIR")), "firm" in paragraph (1)(b)(iii) of this regulation is to include a "pension scheme arrangement" within the meaning given by Article 2(10) of EMIR (as it has effect in EU law and as if the United Kingdom were a Member State)].

(8) Nothing in this regulation saves any obligation of the Prudential Regulation Authority, the Bank of England, the Financial Conduct Authority or the Payment Systems Regulator after [IP completion day]—

(a) to act in accordance with, or to take any account of—

(i) guidelines, guidance, opinions, recommendations or decisions issued by any of the European Supervisory Authorities whether before or after [IP completion day];

(ii) technical standards adopted by the European Commission after [IP completion day];

(b) to provide information to, or co-operate with—

(i) a European Supervisory Authority or any other EU institution, agency or body (an "EU entity"); or

(ii) a competent authority of a member State.

(9) Where the effect of this regulation would be to make a right or obligation of any person dependent on a decision from an EU entity in circumstances where that right or obligation would after [IP completion day], apart from this regulation, be dependent on a decision from a UK regulator, any reference to the EU entity in relation to that decision is to be treated as a reference to the relevant UK regulator.

(10) For the purposes of paragraph (9)—

(a) "decision" includes any form of permission, authorisation, designation, recognition or registration required for the exercise of the right or the imposition of the obligation;

(b) "UK regulator" means the Prudential Regulation Authority, the Financial Conduct Authority, the Bank of England, the Payment Systems Regulator or HM Treasury;

(c) the "relevant UK regulator" is the UK regulator to which the functions of the EU entity in relation to the decision in question have been transferred under the European Union (Withdrawal) Act 2018.

NOTES

Commencement: IP completion day (as defined in the European Union (Withdrawal Agreement) Act 2020, s 39).

The words "IP completion day" in square brackets (in each place that they occur) were substituted by the Financial Services and Economic and Monetary Policy (Consequential Amendments) (EU Exit) Regulations 2020, SI 2020/1301, reg 3, Schedule, para 40(f), as from 30 December 2020. This regulation is also amended as follows—

Para (5): words in square brackets in sub-para (z) substituted by the Financial Services (Electronic Money, Payment Services and Miscellaneous Amendments) (EU Exit) Regulations 2019, SI 2019/1212, reg 22(1), (3), with effect from immediately before IP completion day (as defined in the European Union (Withdrawal Agreement) Act 2020, s 39). Sub-paras (z1), (z2) added by the Prospectus (Amendment etc) (EU Exit) Regulations 2019, SI 2019/1234, reg 29, with effect from immediately before IP completion day (as defined in the European Union (Withdrawal Agreement) Act 2020, s 39). Sub-paras (z3), (z4) added by the Financial Services (Miscellaneous Amendments) (EU Exit) Regulations 2020, SI 2020/628, reg 13(1), (2), with effect from immediately before IP completion day (as defined in the European Union (Withdrawal Agreement) Act 2020, s 39). Sub-para (z5) added by the Over the Counter Derivatives, Central Counterparties and Trade Repositories (Amendment, etc, and Transitional Provision) (EU Exit) Regulations 2020, SI 2020/646, reg 12(1), (2), as from 25 June 2020.

Para (7): sub-para (d) added by SI 2020/628, reg 13(1), (3), with effect from immediately before IP completion day (as defined in the European Union (Withdrawal Agreement) Act 2020, s 39). The words ", (z4) and (z5)" in square brackets in para (d) were substituted by virtue of SI 2020/646, reg 12(1), (3), as from 25 June 2020 (see further the note below).

Note that SI 2020/646, reg 12(3) actually provides as follows—

"(3) In paragraph (7)(d), for "and (z4)" substitute ", (z4) and (z5)".".

Note also that the words "and (z4)" did not occur in sub-para (d) of para (7). However, the words "and (z3)" did occur in that sub-paragraph, and it is assumed that the words ", (z4) and (z5)" are to be substituted for the words "and (z3)". The text above is reproduced accordingly.

SCHEDULES

SCHEDULES 1 & 2

(Sch 1 contains further modifications of the Insurers (Reorganisation and Winding up) Regulations 2004, as introduced by reg 2 ante, and is outside the scope of this work. Sch 2 (Modifications to the Credit Institutions (Reorganisation and Winding up) Regulations 2004) is also outside the scope of this work.)

INTERNATIONAL ACCOUNTING STANDARDS AND EUROPEAN PUBLIC LIMITED-LIABILITY COMPANY (AMENDMENT ETC) (EU EXIT) REGULATIONS 2019

(SI 2019/685)

NOTES

Made: 26 March 2019.

Authority: European Union (Withdrawal) Act 2018, s 8(1), Sch 4, para 1, Sch 7, para 21.

Commencement: IP completion day (as defined in the European Union (Withdrawal Agreement) Act 2020, s 39).

These Regulations are reproduced as amended by: the International Accounting Standards, Statutory Auditors and Third Country Auditors (Amendment) (EU Exit) Regulations 2020, SI 2020/335; the Companies and Statutory Auditors etc (Consequential Amendments) (EU Exit) Regulations 2020, SI 2020/523.

ARRANGEMENT OF REGULATIONS

PART 1
INTRODUCTORY

PART 1 INTRODUCTORY

[12.130]

1 Citation, [commencement, application and transitional provisions]

(1) These Regulations may be cited as the International Accounting Standards and European Public Limited-Liability Company (Amendment etc) (EU Exit) Regulations 2019.

(2) These Regulations come into force on exit day.

(3) Parts 1 to 3 of Schedule 1 have effect in relation to accounts for financial years beginning on or after [IP completion day].

(4) In relation to accounts for financial years which begin before but end on or after [IP completion day], the enactments amended by Parts 1 to 3 of Schedule 1 have effect as if the United Kingdom were a member State until the end of the financial year in question.

[(5) For the purposes of Part 15 of the Companies Act 2006, where accounts for a financial year within paragraph (6) are permitted to be prepared in accordance with international accounting standards (as defined in section 474 of that Act), the accounts may be prepared in accordance with international accounting standards which have been adopted for use within the United Kingdom by virtue of Chapter 3 of Part 2 of these Regulations.

(6) The financial years referred to in paragraph (5) are—

(a) a financial year which begins before but ends on or after IP completion day;

(b) a financial year which ends before IP completion day, where IP completion day occurs before the end of the period for filing the accounts.

(7) Where, in reliance on paragraph (5), accounts are prepared in accordance with international accounting standards which have been adopted for use within the United Kingdom, the notes to the accounts must include a statement to that effect.

(8) Where a statement is included in the notes to the accounts in accordance with paragraph (7), the notes need not include the statement specified under section 397(2) or section 406(2) of the Companies Act 2006 (as the case may be).]

NOTES

Commencement: IP completion day (as defined in the European Union (Withdrawal Agreement) Act 2020, s 39).

The words in square brackets in the regulation heading were substituted, and paras (5)–(8) were added, by the International Accounting Standards, Statutory Auditors and Third Country Auditors (Amendment) (EU Exit) Regulations 2020, SI 2020/335, regs 2–4, with effect from immediately before IP completion day (as defined in the European Union (Withdrawal Agreement) Act 2020, s 39).

Words in square brackets in paras (3) and (4) substituted by the Companies and Statutory Auditors etc (Consequential Amendments) (EU Exit) Regulations 2020, SI 2020/523, reg 22, with effect from immediately before IP completion day.

As to the commencement of these Regulations, see the European Union (Withdrawal Agreement) Act 2020, Sch 5, para 1 (at **[12.59]**) which gives legal effect to the implementation period by 'non-textually amending' the coming into force dates of subordinate legislation which comes into force immediately before exit day, on exit day or at any time after exit day. This subordinate legislation will instead come into force immediately before the end of the implementation period (IP completion day), on IP completion day or (as the case may be) at the time concerned after IP completion day.

[12.131]
2 Interpretation

In these Regulations, "financial year" is to be construed in relation to any amendment to an enactment made by these Regulations, as having the same meaning as in that enactment.

NOTES

Commencement: IP completion day (as defined in the European Union (Withdrawal Agreement) Act 2020, s 39).

PART 2 ADOPTION OF INTERNATIONAL ACCOUNTING STANDARDS

CHAPTER 1 INTERPRETATION

[12.132]
3 Interpretation of this Part

In this Part—

"international accounting standards" has the meaning given by Article 2 of Regulation (EC) No 1606/2002 of the European Parliament and of the Council of 19 July 2002 on the application of international accounting standards;

"publish" means to make available free of charge on a publicly accessible website;

"UK-adopted international accounting standards" has the meaning given by section 474(1) of the Companies Act 2006;

"undertaking" has the same meaning as in section 1161(1) of the Companies Act 2006.

NOTES

Commencement: IP completion day (as defined in the European Union (Withdrawal Agreement) Act 2020, s 39).

CHAPTER 2 INTERNATIONAL ACCOUNTING STANDARDS ON [IP COMPLETION DAY]

[12.133]
4 International accounting standards in the UK on [IP completion day]

The international accounting standards adopted for use within the United Kingdom on [IP completion day] are those which were contained in Commission Regulation (EC) No 1126/2008 of 3 November 2008 adopting certain international accounting standards in accordance with Regulation (EC) No 1606/2002 of the European Parliament and of the Council on the application of international accounting standards, as it had effect immediately before [IP completion day].

NOTES

Commencement: IP completion day (as defined in the European Union (Withdrawal Agreement) Act 2020, s 39).

Words "IP completion day" in square brackets (including in the heading preceding this regulation) substituted by the Companies and Statutory Auditors etc (Consequential Amendments) (EU Exit) Regulations 2020, SI 2020/523, reg 23, with effect from immediately before IP completion day.

CHAPTER 3 THE FUNCTIONS OF THE SECRETARY OF STATE

[12.134]
5 Responsibility for adoption of international accounting standards

The Secretary of State is responsible for—

(a) the adoption of international accounting standards for use within the United Kingdom, with a view to harmonising the financial information presented by the companies required by section 403(1) of the Companies Act 2006 to prepare their accounts in accordance with UK-adopted international accounting standards, in order to ensure—
  (i) a high degree of transparency and international comparability of financial statements; and
  (ii) the efficient allocation of capital, including the smooth functioning of capital markets in the United Kingdom; and

(b) participating in and contributing to the development of a single set of international accounting standards.

NOTES

Commencement: IP completion day (as defined in the European Union (Withdrawal Agreement) Act 2020, s 39).

[12.135]

6 Power of the Secretary of State to adopt international accounting standards

(1) The Secretary of State may adopt international accounting standards for use within the United Kingdom, in accordance with regulations 7 and 8.

(2) In exceptional circumstances, the Secretary of State may exercise the power to adopt international accounting standards in accordance with paragraph (3) or (4).

(3) Where the effect of regulation 7 is that an international accounting standard taken as a whole cannot be adopted, the Secretary of State may adopt an international accounting standard in part only, provided that—

(a) those parts of the standard which are not adopted are—
  (i) severable from the standard so that the rest of the standard is operational;
  (ii) severed only to the extent necessary to enable adoption of the rest of the standard for use within the United Kingdom; and

(b) adoption of that part of the standard would be in compliance with regulation 7.

(4) Where there is an option available as part of the standard, the Secretary of State may—

(a) make provision in the standard to extend the scope of undertakings eligible to use that option; and

(b) make such extension of scope subject to an undertaking meeting criteria specified by the Secretary of State.

NOTES

Commencement: IP completion day (as defined in the European Union (Withdrawal Agreement) Act 2020, s 39).

[12.136]

7 Basis for adoption of international accounting standards

(1) The Secretary of State may only adopt an international accounting standard under regulation 6 if the Secretary of State is of the view that, in relation to the form of the standard the Secretary of State intends to adopt—

(a) the standard is not contrary to either of the following principles—
  (i) an undertaking's accounts must give a true and fair view of the undertaking's assets, liabilities, financial position and profit or loss;
  (ii) consolidated accounts must give a true and fair view of the assets, liabilities, financial position and profit or loss of the undertakings included in the accounts taken as a whole, so far as concerns members of the undertaking;

(b) the use of the standard is likely to be conducive to the long term public good in the United Kingdom; and

(c) the standard meets the criteria of understandability, relevance, reliability and comparability required of the financial information needed for making economic decisions and assessing the stewardship of management.

(2) In deciding whether the use of a standard is likely to be conducive to the long term public good in the United Kingdom, the Secretary of State must have regard, in particular, to the following matters—

(a) whether the use of the standard is likely to improve the quality of financial reporting;

(b) the costs and benefits that are likely to result from the use of the standard; and

(c) whether the use of the standard is likely to have an adverse effect on the economy of the United Kingdom, including on economic growth.

(3) The Secretary of State may, by regulations made by statutory instrument, amend paragraph (2).

(4) Regulations made under paragraph (3) are subject to annulment in pursuance of a resolution of either House of Parliament.

NOTES

Commencement: IP completion day (as defined in the European Union (Withdrawal Agreement) Act 2020, s 39).

[12.137]

8 Adoption of standards: consultation

Before adopting an international accounting standard under regulation 6, the Secretary of State must consult such persons as the Secretary of State considers to be representative of those with an interest in the quality and availability of accounts, including users and preparers of accounts.

NOTES

Commencement: IP completion day (as defined in the European Union (Withdrawal Agreement) Act 2020, s 39).

[12.138]

9 Consideration of standards: publication requirements

(1) The Secretary of State must publish the final decision in relation to any standard which the Secretary of State has considered for adoption under regulation 6, giving reasons for any decision to—

(a) adopt the standard in whole;

(b) adopt the standard in part;

(c) extend the scope of undertakings eligible to use an option in the standard; or
(d) not adopt the standard.

(2) Where the Secretary of State adopts a standard under regulation 6, the Secretary of State must publish within 3 working days, beginning with the day after the day that the standard is adopted—
(a) a statement that the standard has been adopted;
(b) the wording of the adopted standard;
(c) where the scope of undertakings eligible to use an option in the standard has been extended, a statement that this has been done, setting out the full details; and
(d) a description of the financial years in respect of which that standard must be used.

(3) The Secretary of State must maintain and publish a consolidated text of UK-adopted international accounting standards, which must be kept up to date.

(4) Information required to be published under paragraphs (1), (2) and (3) must be published on the same website.

(5) In this regulation, "working day" means any day other than—
(a) Saturday or Sunday;
(b) Christmas Day or Good Friday; or
(c) a day which is a bank holiday under the Banking and Financial Dealings Act 1971 in any part of the United Kingdom.

NOTES

Commencement: IP completion day (as defined in the European Union (Withdrawal Agreement) Act 2020, s 39).

[12.139]
10 Certification

(1) The production of a printed copy of an international accounting standard purported to have been adopted by the Secretary of State on which is endorsed a certificate signed by the Secretary of State and stating—
(a) that the international accounting standard was adopted by the Secretary of State,
(b) that the copy is a true copy of the adopted standard,
is evidence (or, in Scotland, sufficient evidence) of the facts stated in the certificate.

(2) A certificate purporting to be signed as mentioned in paragraph (1) is to be deemed to have been duly signed unless the contrary is shown.

(3) Any person wishing in any legal proceedings to cite an international accounting standard adopted by the Secretary of State may require the Secretary of State to cause a copy of it to be endorsed with such a certificate as is mentioned in this regulation.

NOTES

Commencement: IP completion day (as defined in the European Union (Withdrawal Agreement) Act 2020, s 39).

[12.140]
11 Periodic review by Secretary of State of impact of adopted standard

(1) The Secretary of State must publish a statement setting out the Secretary of State's policy on what amounts to a significant change in accounting practice, and must keep this policy statement under review.

(2) Paragraphs (3) and (4) apply in relation to the adoption of any standard by the Secretary of State under regulation 6 which the Secretary of State considers likely to lead to a significant change in accounting practice.

(3) The Secretary of State must—
(a) carry out a review of the impact of the adoption of the standard; and
(b) publish a report setting out the conclusions of the review no later than 5 years after the date on which the standard takes effect (being the first day of the first financial year in respect of which it must be used).

(4) The Secretary of State may carry out subsequent reviews from time to time, and in the event of doing so the Secretary of State must publish a report setting out the conclusions of any review conducted.

NOTES

Commencement: IP completion day (as defined in the European Union (Withdrawal Agreement) Act 2020, s 39).

[12.141]
12 Secretary of State's duty to report to Parliament

The Secretary of State must lay a report before Parliament reporting on the carrying out of the Secretary of State's responsibilities under these Regulations within one year of the coming into force of these Regulations, and lay a further report for every subsequent year.

NOTES

Commencement: IP completion day (as defined in the European Union (Withdrawal Agreement) Act 2020, s 39).

CHAPTER 4 POWER FOR SECRETARY OF STATE TO DELEGATE ADOPTION FUNCTION

[12.142]
13 Delegation of the Secretary of State's functions

(1) The Secretary of State may make regulations under this regulation ("delegation regulations") for the purpose of enabling functions of the Secretary of State under Chapter 3 of this Part to be exercised by a body designated by the regulations.

(2) The body designated may be a body corporate or an unincorporated association, and must already be in existence at the time the delegation regulations are made.

(3) Delegation regulations have the effect of making the body designated by the regulations designated under section 5 of the Freedom of Information Act 2000 (further powers to designate public authorities).

(4) Delegation regulations have the effect of transferring to the body designated by them all functions of the Secretary of State under Chapter 3 of this Part subject to such exceptions and reservations as may be specified in the regulations.

(5) Delegation regulations may confer on the body designated by them such other functions supplementary or incidental to those transferred as appear to the Secretary of State to be appropriate.

(6) Delegation regulations may be amended or, if it appears to the Secretary of State that it is no longer in the public interest that the regulations should remain in force, revoked by further regulations under this regulation.

(7) Where functions are transferred or resumed, the Secretary of State may by regulations confer or, as the case may be, take away such other functions supplementary or incidental to those transferred or resumed as appear to him to be appropriate.

(8) Regulations under this regulation which have the effect of transferring or resuming any functions must not be made unless a draft has been laid before Parliament and approved by a resolution of each House of Parliament.

(9) Any other regulations made under this regulation are subject to annulment in pursuance of a resolution of either House of Parliament.

NOTES

Commencement: IP completion day (as defined in the European Union (Withdrawal Agreement) Act 2020, s 39).

Regulations: the International Accounting Standards (Delegation of Functions) (EU Exit) Regulations 2021, SI 2021/609 at **[12.191]**.

[12.143]

14

(1) The Secretary of State's power to make delegation regulations under regulation 13 is exercisable in accordance with this regulation.

(2) The Secretary of State may make delegation regulations designating a body only if it appears to him that—

(a) the body is able and willing to exercise the functions that would be transferred by the regulations, and

(b) the body has arrangements in place relating to the exercise of those functions which are such as to be likely to ensure that the conditions in paragraph (3) are met.

(3) The conditions are—

(a) that the functions in question will be exercised effectively, and

(b) where the delegation regulations are to contain any requirements or other provision specified under paragraph (4), that those functions will be exercised in accordance with any such requirements or provisions.

(4) The delegation regulations may contain such requirements or other provision relating to the exercise of the functions by the designated body as appear to the Secretary of State to be appropriate.

NOTES

Commencement: IP completion day (as defined in the European Union (Withdrawal Agreement) Act 2020, s 39).

Regulations: the International Accounting Standards (Delegation of Functions) (EU Exit) Regulations 2021, SI 2021/609 at **[12.191]**.

CHAPTER 5 SUPPLEMENTARY PROVISIONS WITH RESPECT TO DELEGATION

[12.144]

15 Operation of this Chapter

(1) This Chapter has effect in relation to a body designated by delegation regulations under regulation 13.

(2) Any power conferred by this Chapter to make provision by regulations is a power to make provision by regulations under regulation 13.

NOTES

Commencement: IP completion day (as defined in the European Union (Withdrawal Agreement) Act 2020, s 39).

[12.145]

16 Status

The body is not to be regarded as acting on behalf of the Crown and its members, officers and employees are not to be regarded as Crown servants.

NOTES

Commencement: IP completion day (as defined in the European Union (Withdrawal Agreement) Act 2020, s 39).

[12.146]

17 Reporting by the body

(1) The body must, at least once in each calendar year for which the delegation regulations are in force, make a report to the Secretary of State on—

(a) the discharge of the functions transferred to it, and

(b) such other matters as the Secretary of State may by regulations require.

(2) Delegation regulations may modify paragraph (1) as it has effect in relation to the calendar year in which the regulations come into force or are revoked.

(3) The Secretary of State must lay before Parliament copies of each report received under this paragraph.

NOTES

Commencement: IP completion day (as defined in the European Union (Withdrawal Agreement) Act 2020, s 39).

[12.147]

18 Other supplementary provisions

(1) The transfer of a function to a body designated by delegation regulations does not affect anything previously done in the exercise of the function transferred; and the resumption of a function so transferred does not affect anything previously done in exercise of the function resumed.

(2) The Secretary of State may by regulations make such transitional and other supplementary provision as the Secretary of State thinks necessary or expedient in relation to the transfer or resumption of a function.

(3) The provision that may be made in connection with the transfer of a function includes, in particular, provision—

(a) for applying to the body designated by the delegation regulations, in connection with the function transferred, any provision applying to the Secretary of State which is contained in or made under any other enactment;

(b) for the transfer of any property, rights or liabilities from the Secretary of State to that body;

(c) for the carrying on and completion by that body of anything in the process of being done by the Secretary of State when the regulations take effect;

(d) for the substitution of that body for the Secretary of State in any instrument, contract or legal proceedings.

(4) The provision that may be made in connection with the resumption of a function includes, in particular, provision—

(a) for the transfer of any property, rights or liabilities from that body to the Secretary of State;

(b) for the carrying on and completion by the Secretary of State of anything in the process of being done by that body when the regulations takes effect;

(c) for the substitution of the Secretary of State for that body in any instrument, contract or legal proceedings.

NOTES

Commencement: IP completion day (as defined in the European Union (Withdrawal Agreement) Act 2020, s 39).

CHAPTER 6 CONSEQUENTIAL AMENDMENTS, REVOCATIONS AND TRANSITIONAL PROVISION RELATING TO THE ADOPTION OF INTERNATIONAL ACCOUNTING STANDARDS

[12.148]

19 Consequential amendments and transitional provision relating to the adoption of international accounting standards

Schedule 1 has effect.

NOTES

Commencement: IP completion day (as defined in the European Union (Withdrawal Agreement) Act 2020, s 39).

[12.149]

20 Revocations and transitional provision

(1) Schedule 2 has effect and the instruments listed in that Schedule are revoked, subject to paragraph (2).

(2) Any provisions in the instruments listed in Schedule 2 concerning the application of international accounting standards adopted in accordance with Regulation (EC) No 1606/2002 of the European Parliament and of the Council on the application of international accounting standards before [IP completion day], apply to the international accounting standards adopted by virtue of [regulation 4] as they applied to the international accounting standards adopted by the Commission.

NOTES

Commencement: IP completion day (as defined in the European Union (Withdrawal Agreement) Act 2020, s 39).

Para (2): words "IP completion day" in square brackets substituted by the Companies and Statutory Auditors etc (Consequential Amendments) (EU Exit) Regulations 2020, SI 2020/523, reg 23, with effect from immediately before IP completion day. Words in second pair of square brackets substituted by the International Accounting Standards, Statutory Auditors and Third Country Auditors (Amendment) (EU Exit) Regulations 2020, SI 2020/335, regs 2, 5, with effect from immediately before IP completion day (note that this amendment corrects an error in the original Regulations).

PART 3 TRANSITIONAL AND CONSEQUENTIAL AMENDMENTS RELATING TO EUROPEAN PUBLIC LIMITED-LIABILITY COMPANIES

[12.150]

21 Transitional and consequential amendments relating to European Public Limited-Liability Companies

Schedule 3 has effect.

NOTES

Commencement: IP completion day (as defined in the European Union (Withdrawal Agreement) Act 2020, s 39).

PART 4 MISCELLANEOUS AMENDMENTS

22, 23 (*Reg 22 amends the Competition (Amendment etc) (EU Exit) Regulations 2019, SI 2019/93. Reg 23 amends the Accounts and Reports (Amendment) (EU Exit) Regulations 2019, SI 2019/145 at* **[12.76]**.)

SCHEDULES

SCHEDULE 1

CONSEQUENTIAL AMENDMENTS AND TRANSITIONAL PROVISION RELATING TO THE ADOPTION OF INTERNATIONAL ACCOUNTING STANDARDS IN THE UNITED KINGDOM

Regulation 19

(Sch 1, Pt 1 amends the Companies Act 2006 (and other Acts that are outside the scope of this work). Sch 1,

Pt 2 amends the Companies (Revision of Defective Accounts and Reports) Regulations 2008, the Small Companies and Groups (Accounts and Directors' Report) Regulations 2008, the Large and Medium-sized Companies and Groups (Accounts and Reports) Regulations 2008, the Limited Liability Partnerships (Accounts and Audit) (Application of Companies Act 2006) Regulations 2008, the Small Limited Liability Partnerships (Accounts) Regulations 2008, and the the Large and Medium-sized Limited Liability Partnerships (Accounts) Regulations 2008 (and other statutory instruments that are outside the scope of this work). Sch 1, Pt 3 repeals all of Regulation 1606/2002/EC of the European Parliament and of the Council on the application of international accounting standards (with the exception of Article 2), and amends Regulation 648/2012/EU of the European Parliament and of the Council on OTC derivatives, central counterparties and trade repositories (the EMIR Regulation) – as it forms part of retained EU law).

PART 4 TRANSITIONAL PROVISION: IAS ACCOUNTS AND FIRST IAS YEAR

Companies

[12.151]

64. (1) Where a company's individual accounts are prepared in accordance with the pre-commencement version of section 395(1)(b) of the Companies Act 2006, the accounts are to continue to be treated as "IAS individual accounts" for the purposes of that Act.

(2) Where, in the last financial year of a company to begin before [IP completion day], the company's individual accounts are prepared in accordance with the pre-commencement version of section 395(1)(b) of that Act, section 395(3) and (4) of that Act have effect in relation to the company as if the references to the first IAS year were to that financial year.

(3) Where the group accounts of a company are prepared in accordance with the pre-commencement version of section 403(2)(b) of the Companies Act 2006, the accounts are to continue to be treated as "IAS group accounts" for the purposes of that Act.

(4) Where, in the last financial year of a company to begin before [IP completion day], the group accounts of the company are prepared in accordance with the pre-commencement version of section 403(2)(b) of that Act, section 403(4) and (5) of that Act have effect in relation to the company as if the reference to the first IAS year were to that financial year.

(5) In this paragraph, references to the "pre-commencement version" of a provision of the Companies Act 2006 are to that provision as it had effect before [IP completion day] in relation to a financial year of a company that began before [IP completion day].

Limited Liability Partnerships

65. (1) Where an LLP's individual accounts are prepared in accordance with the pre-commencement version of section 395(1)(b) of the Companies Act 2006 as applied to LLPs, the accounts are to continue to be treated as "IAS individual accounts" for the purposes of that Act as applied to LLPs.

(2) Where, in the last financial year of an LLP to begin before [IP completion day], the LLP's individual accounts are prepared in accordance with the pre-commencement version of section 395(1)(b) of that Act as applied to LLPs, section 395(3) and (4) of that Act as applied to LLPs have effect in relation to the LLP as if the references to the first IAS year were to that financial year.

(3) Where the group accounts of an LLP are prepared in accordance with the pre-commencement version of section 403(1)(b) of the Companies Act 2006 as applied to LLPs, the accounts are to continue to be treated as "IAS group accounts" for the purposes of that Act as applied to LLPs.

(4) Where, in the last financial year of an LLP to begin before [IP completion day], the group accounts of the LLP are prepared in accordance with the pre-commencement version of section 403(1)(b) of that Act as applied to LLPs, section 403(2) and (3) of that Act as applied to LLPs have effect in relation to the LLP as if the reference to the first IAS year were to that financial year.

(5) In this paragraph—

(a) "LLP" means a limited liability partnership registered under the Limited Liability Partnerships Act 2000;

(b) references to a provision of the Companies Act 2006 "as applied to LLPs" means to that provision as applied to LLPs by regulation 9 of the Limited Liability Partnerships (Accounts and Audit) (Application of Companies Act 2006) Regulations 2008;

(c) references to the "pre-commencement version" of a provision of the Companies Act 2006 as applied to LLPs are to that provision as applied to LLPs, as it had effect before [IP completion day] in relation to a financial year of an LLP that began before [IP completion day].

(Paras 66 and 67 relate to building societies and friendly societies and are outside the scope of this work.)

NOTES

Commencement: IP completion day (as defined in the European Union (Withdrawal Agreement) Act 2020, s 39).

Words "IP completion day" in square brackets (in every place that they occur) substituted by the Companies and Statutory Auditors etc (Consequential Amendments) (EU Exit) Regulations 2020, SI 2020/523, reg 25, with effect from immediately before IP completion day.

SCHEDULE 2

(Repeals Commission Regulation 1126/2008/EC adopting certain international accounting standards in accordance with Regulation (EC) No 1606/2002 of the European Parliament and of the Council, and various Commission Regulations that amended the 2008 Regulation.)

SCHEDULE 3
AMENDMENTS RELATING TO EUROPEAN PUBLIC LIMITED-LIABILITY COMPANIES

Regulation 21

PART 1 APPLICATION OF THE COMPANIES ACT 2006, THE OVERSEAS COMPANIES REGULATIONS 2009 AND THE OVERSEAS COMPANIES (EXECUTION OF DOCUMENTS AND REGISTRATION OF CHARGES) REGULATIONS 2009 TO EUROPEAN PUBLIC LIMITED-LIABILITY COMPANIES

Interpretation

[12.152]

1. In this Part—

"the Overseas Companies Regulations" means the Overseas Companies Regulations 2009;

"SE" means a European Public Limited-Liability Company (or Societas Europaea), within the meaning of Council Regulation 2157/2001/EC of 8 October 2001 on the Statute for a European Company, as it has effect in EU law as amended from time to time.

Application of the Companies Act 2006

2. An SE which subsists on [IP completion day] is regarded—

(a) for the purpose of section 1044 (overseas companies) of the Companies Act 2006 as having been incorporated outside the United Kingdom, and

(b) for the purpose of section 1050 (accounts and reports: credit or financial institutions) of the Companies Act 2006 as having been incorporated outside the United Kingdom and Gibraltar.

3. In the application of Part 35 of the Companies Act (the registrar of companies) to an SE, references to "director" or "board of directors" are to be read as if they were references—

(a) in a one-tier system, to the members of the administrative organ of an SE;

(b) in a two-tier system, to the members of the supervisory and management organs of an SE.

Application of the Overseas Companies Regulations

4. Paragraphs 5 to 10 apply in the application of the Overseas Companies Regulations to an SE.

5. References to "directors" or "board of directors" are to be read as if they were references—

(a) in a one-tier system, to the members of the administrative organ of an SE;

(b) in a two-tier system, to the members of the supervisory and management organs of an SE.

6. In regulation 6 (particulars of the company), paragraph (1)(c) is to be read as if "if it is registered in the country of its incorporation," were omitted.

7. In regulation 31 (application and interpretation of Chapter), the definition of "parent law" in paragraph (2) is to be read as if for "incorporated" there were substituted "registered".

8. In regulation 60 (requirement to display name etc at business location), the words in paragraph (1) before sub-paragraph (a) are to be read as if for "incorporation" there were substituted "registration".

9. Regulation 61 (manner of display of name etc) is to be read as if for "incorporation" there were substituted "registration".

10. In regulation 63 (particulars to appear in business letters, order forms and websites)—

(a) paragraph (4)(a) is to be read as if for "incorporation" there were substituted "registration";

(b) paragraph (4)(b) is to be read as if—

(i) ", if any," were omitted; and

(ii) for "incorporation" there were substituted "registration".

Transitional provision for the application of the Overseas Companies Regulations 2009 to existing establishments of SEs

11. (1) Where—

(a) an SE has a UK establishment, within the meaning of the Overseas Companies Regulations, on [IP completion day], or

(b) an SE which is a credit or financial institution has a branch in the United Kingdom, within the meaning of Part 6 of the Overseas Companies Regulations, on [IP completion day],

the SE is treated for the purposes of the Overseas Companies Regulations as if it had opened its UK establishment or branch on [IP completion day].

(2) Sub-paragraph (1) does not apply in respect of regulation 7(1)(b) (particulars of the establishment) of the Overseas Companies Regulations.

(3) Where sub-paragraph (1) applies—

(a) regulations 4(1) and 45 are to be read as if for "one month" there were substituted "three months";

(b) the SE must comply with its obligations in Part 7 (trading disclosures) of the Overseas Companies Regulations within three months of [IP completion day].

Transitional provision for the application of the Overseas Companies (Execution of Documents and Registration of Charges) Regulations 2009

12. In the application of the Overseas Companies (Execution of Documents and Registration of Charges) Regulations 2009 to an SE—

(a) a charge subsisting on the day on which Part 3 of those Regulations applies to the SE ("the relevant day") is to be treated for the purpose of regulation 24 of those Regulations as if that charge had been created on the relevant day;

(b) where sub-paragraph (a) applies, regulation 24(1) of those Regulations is to be read as if for "21 days" there were substituted "three months".

NOTES

Commencement: IP completion day (as defined in the European Union (Withdrawal Agreement) Act 2020, s 39).

Paras 2, 11: words "IP completion day" in square brackets substituted by the Companies and Statutory Auditors etc (Consequential Amendments) (EU Exit) Regulations 2020, SI 2020/523, reg 25, with effect from immediately before IP completion day.

(Sch 3, Pt 2 amends the European Public Limited-Liability Company (Amendment etc) (EU Exit) Regulations 2018. Sch 3, Pt 3 contains minor and consequential amendments which, in so far as relevant, have been incorporated at the appropriate place.

OFFICIAL LISTING OF SECURITIES, PROSPECTUS AND TRANSPARENCY (AMENDMENT ETC) (EU EXIT) REGULATIONS 2019

(SI 2019/707)

NOTES

Made: 27 March 2019.

Authority: European Union (Withdrawal) Act 2018, s 8(1), Sch 7, para 21.

Commencement: IP completion day (as defined in the European Union (Withdrawal Agreement) Act 2020, s 39).

These Regulations are reproduced as amended by: the Prospectus (Amendment etc) (EU Exit) Regulations 2019, SI 2019/1234; the Financial Services and Economic and Monetary Policy (Consequential Amendments) (EU Exit) Regulations 2020, SI 2020/1301; the Securities Financing Transactions, Securitisation and Miscellaneous Amendments (EU Exit) Regulations 2020, SI 2020/1385.

Gibraltar: as to the application of these Regulations to Gibraltar, see the Gibraltar (Miscellaneous Amendments) (EU Exit) Regulations 2019, SI 2019/680 at **[12.128]**.

ARRANGEMENT OF REGULATIONS

PART 1 GENERAL

[12.153]

1 Citation and commencement

(1) These Regulations may be cited as the Official Listing of Securities, Prospectus and Transparency (Amendment etc) (EU Exit) Regulations 2019.

(2) These Regulations come into force on exit day.

NOTES

Commencement: IP completion day (as defined in the European Union (Withdrawal Agreement) Act 2020, s 39).

As to the commencement of these Regulations, see the European Union (Withdrawal Agreement) Act 2020, Sch 5, para 1 (at **[12.59]**) which gives legal effect to the implementation period by 'non-textually amending' the coming into force dates of subordinate legislation which comes into force immediately before exit day, on exit day or at any time after exit day. This subordinate legislation will instead come into force immediately before the end of the implementation period (IP completion day), on IP completion day or (as the case may be) at the time concerned after IP completion day.

[12.154]

2 Interpretation

In these Regulations—

"FSMA 2000" means the Financial Services and Markets Act 2000;

"the FCA" means the Financial Conduct Authority.

NOTES

Commencement: IP completion day (as defined in the European Union (Withdrawal Agreement) Act 2020, s 39).

Part 12 Exiting the EU Materials

PARTS 2, 3

3–69 *(Regs 3–39 (Part 2) amend the Financial Services and Markets Act 2000 at* **[7.1]**, *and repeal the Companies Act 2006, s 1273. Note that the following regulations were revoked by the Prospectus (Amendment etc) (EU Exit) Regulations 2019, SI 2019/1234, as from 6 September 2019: regs 4, 6, 9, 11–17. Regs 40–69 (Part 3) amend Commission Regulation 809/2004/EC implementing Directive 2003/71/EC of the European Parliament and of the Council as regards information contained in prospectuses as well as the format, incorporation by reference and publication of such prospectuses and dissemination of advertisements; Commission Regulation 1569/2007/EC establishing a mechanism for the determination of equivalence of accounting standards applied by third country issuers of securities pursuant to Directives 2003/71/EC and 2004/109/EC of the European Parliament and of the Council; Commission Decision 2008/961/EC on the use by third countries' issuers of securities of certain third country's national accounting standards and International Financial Reporting Standards to prepare their consolidated financial statements; and European Parliament and Council Regulation 2017/1129/EU on the prospectus to be published when securities are offered to the public or admitted to trading on a regulated market, and repealing Directive 2003/71/EC (as those Regulations apply in the UK). Note that Commission Regulation 809/2004/EC was repealed by Commission Delegated Regulation 2019/980/EU, as from 21 July 2019, and note also that Council Regulation 2017/1129/EU (the Prospectus Regulation) is at* **[11.320]**. *Note that regs 40–66 were revoked by the Prospectus (Amendment etc) (EU Exit) Regulations 2019, SI 2019/1234, as from 6 September 2019).*

PART 4 TRANSFER OF DIRECTIVE FUNCTIONS TO THE TREASURY OR THE FCA

[12.155]

70 Interpretation of Schedule 2

Part 1 of Schedule 2 contains interpretative provisions for the purposes of that Schedule.

NOTES

Commencement: IP completion day (as defined in the European Union (Withdrawal Agreement) Act 2020, s 39).

[12.156]

71 Transfer of directive functions to the Treasury

(1) The Treasury may make regulations for the purposes specified in Part 2 of Schedule 2.

(2) The power to make regulations conferred on the Treasury by this regulation is exercisable by statutory instrument.

(3) The regulations may—

(a) contain incidental, supplemental, consequential and transitional provision, and

(b) make different provision for different purposes.

(4) A statutory instrument containing regulations under this regulation is subject to annulment in pursuance of a resolution of either House of Parliament.

NOTES

Commencement: IP completion day (as defined in the European Union (Withdrawal Agreement) Act 2020, s 39).

[12.157]

72 Transfer of directive functions to the FCA

The FCA may make technical standards for the purposes specified in Part 3 of Schedule 2.

NOTES

Commencement: IP completion day (as defined in the European Union (Withdrawal Agreement) Act 2020, s 39).

PART 5 TRANSITIONAL PROVISION

73 *(Reg 73 (Prospectus approved before 21st July 2019 by competent authority of other EEA state) was due to come into force on IP completion day (as defined in the European Union (Withdrawal Agreement) Act 2020, s 39), but was revoked by the Securities Financing Transactions, Securitisation and Miscellaneous Amendments (EU Exit) Regulations 2020, SI 2020/1385, reg 63, with effect from immediately before IP completion day.)*

SCHEDULES

SCHEDULE 1
AMENDMENTS OF ANNEXES TO COMMISSION REGULATION (EC) NO 809/2004

(This Schedule contained amendments to Commission Regulation 809/2004/EC implementing Directive 2003/71/EC of the European Parliament and of the Council as regards information contained in prospectuses as well as the format, incorporation by reference and publication of such prospectuses and dissemination of advertisements. It was revoked by the Prospectus (Amendment etc) (EU Exit) Regulations 2019, SI 2019/1234, regs 11, 24, as from 6 September 2019. Note also that the 2004 Regulation was repealed by Commission Delegated Regulation 2019/980/EU, as from 21 July 2019.)

SCHEDULE 2
TRANSFER OF FUNCTIONS TO THE TREASURY AND THE FCA

Regulations 70 to 72

PART 1 INTERPRETATION

[12.158]

1. In this Schedule—

. . .

. . .

"the Disclosure Guidance and Transparency Rules sourcebook" means the Disclosure Guidance and Transparency Rules sourcebook made under FSMA 2000 by the FCA, as it has effect on [IP completion day].

NOTES

Commencement: IP completion day (as defined in the European Union (Withdrawal Agreement) Act 2020, s 39).

Definitions omitted revoked by the Prospectus (Amendment etc) (EU Exit) Regulations 2019, SI 2019/1234, regs 11, 25(1), (2), as from 6 September 2019.

Words in square brackets in the definition "the Disclosure Guidance and Transparency Rules sourcebook" substituted by the Financial Services and Economic and Monetary Policy (Consequential Amendments) (EU Exit) Regulations 2020, SI 2020/1301, reg 3, Schedule, para 42(b), as from 30 December 2020.

PART 2 DIRECTIVE FUNCTIONS TRANSFERRED TO THE TREASURY

[12.159]

2. The following purposes are specified for the purposes of regulation 71.

3–9 . . .

10. To establish for the purposes of transparency rules an indicative list of means that are not to be considered electronic means.

11. In order to take account of developments on financial markets, to specify the conditions under which an annual financial report, published in accordance with an obligation imposed by virtue of section 89C of FSMA 2000, including the audit report, must remain available to the public and to adapt the period referred to in rule 4.1.4 of the Disclosure Guidance and Transparency Rules sourcebook.

12. In order to take account of developments on financial markets, to specify the requirements to be met by the half-yearly financial reports required by virtue of section 89C of FSMA 2000, to specify the conditions under which such a report, including the auditors' review, must remain available to the public, to clarify the nature of the auditors' review, to specify the minimum contents of the condensed balance sheet and profit and loss accounts and explanatory notes on those accounts, and to adapt the period referred to in rule 4.2.2(3) of the Disclosure Guidance and Transparency Rules sourcebook.

13. In order to take account of developments on financial markets, to do one or more of the following—

(a) to specify requirements to be met by shareholders when giving notification to the issuer of the proportion of voting rights as a result of events changing the breakdown of voting rights, and on the basis of the information disclosed pursuant to rule 5.6.1 of the Disclosure Guidance and Transparency Rules sourcebook;

(b) to specify requirements to be complied with in order for an issuer to benefit from the exemption in rule 5.1.3 (1) or (2) of that sourcebook;

(c) to specify requirements to be complied with in order for an issuer to benefit from the exemption in rule 5.1.3(3) of that sourcebook;

(d) to specify the maximum length of the settlement cycle referred to in rule 5.1.3(1) of that sourcebook;

(e) to draw up a list of the events changing the breakdown of voting rights and giving rise to an obligation to notify the issuer in accordance with rule 5.1.2 of that sourcebook.

14. In order to take account of developments on financial markets, to do one or more of the following—

(a) to make provision for the publication by the FCA of a calendar of trading days in each regulated market;

(b) to establish in which cases the shareholder, or the person regarded by virtue of section 89F(1)(b)(ii) of FSMA 2000 as holding voting rights in respect of shares, or both, are to give any notification to the issuer that is required by virtue of section 89B of that Act;

(c) to clarify the circumstances under which the shareholder, or the person regarded by virtue of section 89F(1)(b)(ii) of that Act as holding voting rights in respect of shares, should have learned of the acquisition or disposal of voting rights.

15. To clarify the conditions of independence to be complied with by management companies and their parent undertakings or by investment firms and their parent undertakings in order to benefit from rule 5.4.1 or 5.4.2 of the Disclosure Guidance and Transparency Rules sourcebook.

16. To specify the contents of the notification to be made, the notification period, and to whom the notification is to be made, under rule 5.3.1 of the Disclosure Guidance and Transparency Rules sourcebook.

17. In order to take account of developments on financial markets, to specify the requirements that must be imposed on issuers by transparency rules made by virtue of section 89D of FSMA 2000.

18. In order to take account of developments on financial markets and developments in information and communication technology, to specify requirements that must be imposed by Section 1 of Chapter 6 of the Disclosure Guidance and Transparency Rules sourcebook, so far as relating to issuers of shares or debt securities.

19. To specify the minimum standards for—

(a) the dissemination of information in accordance with Section 3 of Chapter 6 of the Disclosure Guidance and Transparency Rules sourcebook;

(b) the central storage mechanism required by section 89W of FSMA 2000.

20. To establish general criteria for the purposes of section 89A(4A) of FSMA 2000 in relation to financial statements and information required under the law, regulations or administrative provisions of a country or territory outside the United Kingdom and to state that, by reason of its domestic law, its administrative provisions, or practices or procedures based on international standards set by international organisations, a country or territory outside the United Kingdom ensures equivalent information requirements.

NOTES

Commencement: IP completion day (as defined in the European Union (Withdrawal Agreement) Act 2020, s 39).

Paras 3–9: revoked by the Prospectus (Amendment etc) (EU Exit) Regulations 2019, SI 2019/1234, regs 11, 25(1), (3), as from 6 September 2019.

PART 3 DIRECTIVE FUNCTIONS TRANSFERRED TO FCA

[12.160]

21. The following purposes are specified for the purposes of regulation 72.

22–30 . . .

31. To specify the electronic reporting format for annual financial reports published in accordance with an obligation imposed by virtue of section 89C(2) of FSMA 2000.

32. To specify the method of calculating any percentage threshold applying for the purposes of rule 5.1.3 of the Disclosure Guidance and Transparency Rules sourcebook.

33. To establish standard forms, templates and procedures to be used when—

(a) notifying required information to the issuer under transparency rules made by virtue of section 89B of FSMA 2000, or

(b) notifying the FCA under transparency rules made by virtue of section 89B of FSMA 2000.

34. To specify for the purposes of rule 5.3.3A of the Disclosure Guidance and Transparency Rules sourcebook—

(a) the method for calculating the number of voting rights in the case of financial instruments referenced to a basket of shares or an index, and

(b) the methods for determining delta for the purposes of calculating voting rights relating to financial instruments which provide exclusively for a cash settlement.

35. To specify the cases in which the exemptions laid down in rules 5.1.3, 5.4.1, 5.4.2 and 5.8.6 of the Disclosure Guidance and Transparency Rules sourcebook apply to financial instruments held by a person fulfilling orders received from clients or responding to a client's request to trade otherwise than on a proprietary basis, or hedging positions arising out of such dealings.

NOTES

Commencement: IP completion day (as defined in the European Union (Withdrawal Agreement) Act 2020, s 39).

Paras 22–30: revoked by the Prospectus (Amendment etc) (EU Exit) Regulations 2019, SI 2019/1234, regs 11, 25(1), (4), as from 6 September 2019.

FINANCIAL SERVICES (MISCELLANEOUS) (AMENDMENT) (EU EXIT) REGULATIONS 2019

(SI 2019/710)

NOTES

Made: 27 March 2019.

Authority: European Union (Withdrawal) Act 2018, s 8(1), Sch 7, para 21.

Commencement: see reg 1 *post*.

These Regulations are reproduced as amended by: the Financial Services and Economic and Monetary Policy (Consequential Amendments) (EU Exit) Regulations 2020, SI 2020/1301; the Securities Financing Transactions, Securitisation and Miscellaneous Amendments (EU Exit) Regulations 2020, SI 2020/1385.

PART 1 INTRODUCTION

[12.161]

1 Citation and commencement

(1) These Regulations may be cited as the Financial Services (Miscellaneous) (Amendment) (EU Exit) Regulations 2019.

(2) Regulation 38 comes into force on the day before the day on which exit day falls.

(3) Regulations 1 and 13 to 24 come into force immediately before exit day.

(4) The other provisions in these Regulations come into force on exit day.

NOTES

Commencement: immediately before IP completion day (as defined in the European Union (Withdrawal Agreement) Act 2020, s 39).

As to the commencement of these Regulations, see the European Union (Withdrawal Agreement) Act 2020, Sch 5, para 1 (at **[12.59]**) which gives legal effect to the implementation period by 'non-textually amending' the coming into force dates of subordinate legislation which comes into force immediately before exit day, on exit day or at any time after exit day. This subordinate legislation will instead come into force immediately before the end of the implementation period (IP completion day), on IP completion day or (as the case may be) at the time concerned after IP completion day.

PART 2 AMENDMENT OF PRIMARY LEGISLATION

2–5 *(Part 2 (regs 2–5) amends the Insolvency Act 1986, the Financial Services and Markets Act 2000, the Income Tax Act 2007, and the Corporation Tax Act 2009. In so far as relevant to this Handbook, these amendments have been incorporated at the appropriate place.)*

PART 3 AMENDMENT AND REVOCATION OF SECONDARY LEGISLATION

6–25 *(Regs 6–25 contain amendments to the following: the Financial Services and Markets Act 2000 (Regulated Activities) Order 2001, the Building Societies Act 1986 (Modification of the Lending Limit and Funding Limit Calculations) Order 2004, the Financial Services and Markets Act 2000 (Prescribed Financial Institutions) Order 2013, the Payment to Treasury of Penalties (Enforcement Costs) Order 2013, the Small and Medium Sized Business (Credit Information) Regulations 2015, the Financial Services and Markets Act 2000 (Benchmarks) Regulations 2018, the Alternative Investment Fund Managers (Amendment etc) (EU Exit) Regulations 2019, the Bank of England (Amendment) (EU Exit) Regulations 2018, the Central Securities Depositories (Amendment) (EU Exit) Regulations 2018, the Markets in Financial Instruments (Amendment) (EU Exit) Regulations 2018, the Bank Recovery and Resolution and Miscellaneous Provisions (Amendment) (EU Exit) Regulations 2018, the Credit Institutions and Insurance Undertakings Reorganisation and Winding Up (Amendment) (EU Exit) Regulations 2019, the Financial Services and Markets Act 2000 (Amendment) (EU Exit) Regulations 2019, the Financial Markets and Insolvency (Amendment and Transitional Provision) (EU Exit) Regulations 2019, the Over the Counter Derivatives, Central Counterparties and Trade Repositories (Amendment, etc, and Transitional Provision) (EU Exit) Regulations 2019, the Solvency 2 and Insurance (Amendment etc) (EU Exit) Regulations 2019, the Credit Rating Agencies (Amendment, etc) (EU Exit) Regulations 2019, and the Equivalence Determinations for Financial Services and Miscellaneous Provisions (Amendment etc) (EU Exit) Regulations 2019. They also revoke the European Cooperative Society Regulations 2006. In so far as relevant to this Handbook, these amendments have been incorporated at the appropriate place.)*

PART 4 AMENDMENT OF RETAINED EU LAW

26–35 *(Regs 26–35 amend and repeal various EU Regulations and Decisions in their application to the UK, and are outside the scope of this work.)*

PART 5 TRANSITIONAL AND SAVING PROVISIONS

36 *(Introduces the Schedule to these Regulations.)*

[12.162]

37 Transitional provision: references to "qualifying EU provision" etc

(1) Except where the contrary intention is stated, a relevant amendment does not—

- (a) affect the previous operation of the original operative provision, or anything done under, or associated with, that provision;
- (b) affect any right, privilege, obligation or liability acquired, accrued or incurred under, or in association with, the original operative provision;
- (c) affect any penalty, punishment, or other measure incurred or imposed in respect of any infringement of, or offence committed in respect of either the original operative provision or any associated provision;
- (d) affect any investigation, legal proceeding or remedy in respect of any right, privilege, obligation, liability, penalty, punishment, or other measure associated with the original operative provision,

and any such investigation, legal proceeding, remedy or power may be instituted, continued, enforced, or exercised and any such penalty, punishment or other measure may be incurred or imposed, as if the relevant amendment had not been made.

(2) For the purposes of this regulation—

"operative provision" means a provision amended by a relevant amendment,

"original operative provision" means the operative provision as in force on the day before the relevant amendment came into force, and

"relevant amendment" means—

- (a) provision in regulations made under the European Union (Withdrawal) Act 2018 which provides that for references to "qualifying EU provision" there are substituted "qualifying provision", where those references are in the Financial Services and Markets Act 2000, or in subordinate legislation made by the Treasury under that Act, or
- (b) regulation 45 (section 168 (appointment of persons to carry out investigations in particular cases)) or 46 (section 169 (investigations etc in support of overseas regulator) of the Financial Services and Markets Act 2000 (Amendment) (EU Exit) Regulations 2019.

NOTES

Commencement: IP completion day (as defined in the European Union (Withdrawal Agreement) Act 2020, s 39).

[12.163]

38 Transitional provision: recognition of overseas investment exchanges

(1) Where an application under section 287(1) of the Financial Services and Markets Act 2000 (application by an investment exchange) is made, and the conditions in paragraph (2) are satisfied, the requirement in section 292(3)(d) of that Act (overseas investment exchanges and overseas clearing houses) does not apply to the determination of the application.

(2) The conditions in this paragraph are that the application is—

- (a) made by an EEA market operator at any time before [IP completion day], and
- (b) determined by the Financial Conduct Authority—
  - (i) on or after the day on which this regulation comes into force, and

Part 12 Exiting the EU Materials

(ii) before two years beginning with [IP completion day].

(3) Where a recognition order is made by virtue of paragraph (1), section 292(5)(c) of the Financial Services and Markets Act 2000 does not apply.

(4) Paragraph (3) ceases to have effect after the period of two years beginning with [IP completion day].

(5) In this regulation—

"EEA market operator" means a person who is authorised in accordance with Directive 2014/65/EU of the European Parliament and of the Council on markets in financial instruments (as that Directive has effect in EU law) to manage or operate the business of a regulated market, and may be the regulated market itself, whose home state is an EEA State other than the United Kingdom, and

"regulated market" has the meaning given in Article 2(13) of Regulation (EU) No 600/2014 of the European Parliament and of the Council of 15 May 2014 on markets in financial instruments and amending Regulation (EU) No 648/2012 as that Regulation forms part of domestic law under section 3 of the European Union (Withdrawal) Act 2018.

NOTES

Commencement: the day before IP completion day (as defined in the European Union (Withdrawal Agreement) Act 2020, s 39).

The words "IP completion day" in square brackets (in every place that they occur) were substituted by the Financial Services and Economic and Monetary Policy (Consequential Amendments) (EU Exit) Regulations 2020, SI 2020/1301, reg 3, Schedule, para 43(k), as from 30 December 2020.

39–41 *(Reg 39 contains transitional provisions regarding central securities depositories (outside the scope of this work). Reg 40 amends the Consumer Credit (Amendment) (EU Exit) Regulations 2018 (outside the scope of this work). Reg 41 was revoked by the Securities Financing Transactions, Securitisation and Miscellaneous Amendments (EU Exit) Regulations 2020, SI 2020/1385, reg 64, with effect from immediately before IP completion day.)*

SCHEDULE
TRANSITIONAL PROVISION: INSURANCE BUSINESS TRANSFER SCHEMES

(*Outside the scope of this work.*)

PROSPECTUS (AMENDMENT ETC) (EU EXIT) REGULATIONS 2019

(SI 2019/1234)

NOTES

Made: 9.00am on 5 September 2019.

Authority: European Union (Withdrawal) Act 2018, s 8(1), Sch 7, para 21.

Commencement: see reg 1 *post*.

These Regulations are reproduced as amended by: the Financial Services and Economic and Monetary Policy (Consequential Amendments) (EU Exit) Regulations 2020, SI 2020/1301.

Gibraltar: as to the application of these Regulations to Gibraltar, see the Gibraltar (Miscellaneous Amendments) (EU Exit) Regulations 2019, SI 2019/680 at **[12.128]**.

PART 1 GENERAL

[12.164]

1 Citation, commencement and interpretation

(1) These Regulations may be cited as the Prospectus (Amendment etc) (EU Exit) Regulations 2019.

(2) This regulation and regulations 10 to 17, 19 to 25, 27 and 28 come into force on the day after the day on which these Regulations are made.

(3) Regulations 18 and 29 come into force immediately before exit day.

(4) The remainder of these Regulations comes into force on exit day.

(5) In these Regulations—

"the 2019 Regulations" means the Official Listing of Securities, Prospectus and Transparency (Amendment etc) (EU Exit) Regulations 2019;

"the FCA" means the Financial Conduct Authority;

"FSMA" means the Financial Services and Markets Act 2000;

"the Prospectus Regulation" means Regulation (EU) No 2017/1129 of the European Parliament and of the Council of 14 June 2017 on the prospectus to be published when securities are offered to the public or admitted to trading on a regulated market, and repealing Directive 2003/71/EC.

NOTES

Commencement: 6 September 2019.

As to the commencement of these Regulations, see the European Union (Withdrawal Agreement) Act 2020, Sch 5, para 1 (at **[12.59]**) which gives legal effect to the implementation period by 'non-textually amending' the coming into force dates of subordinate legislation which comes into force immediately before exit day, on exit day or at any time after exit day. This subordinate legislation will instead come into force immediately before the end of the implementation period (IP completion day), on IP completion day or (as the case may be) at the time concerned after IP completion day.

PART 2 AMENDMENTS OF FSMA

2–9 *(Regs 2–9 amend the Financial Services and Markets Act 2000.)*

PART 3 AMENDMENTS OF THE 2019 REGULATIONS

10–25 *(Regs 10–25 amend the Official Listing of Securities, Prospectus and Transparency (Amendment etc) (EU Exit) Regulations 2019.)*

PART 4 AMENDMENTS OF SECONDARY LEGISLATION

26–30 *(Regs 26–30 amend the Financial Services and Markets Act 2000 (Amendment) (EU Exit) Regulations 2019, the Financial Services and Markets Act 2000 (Amendment) (EU Exit) Regulations 2019, the Gibraltar (Miscellaneous Amendments) (EU Exit) Regulations 2019, and the Financial Services and Markets Act 2000 (Prospectus) Regulations 2019.)*

PART 5 AMENDMENTS OF RETAINED EUROPEAN UNION LAW

CHAPTER 1 AMENDMENTS OF THE PROSPECTUS REGULATION

31–70 *(Regs 31–70 amend Regulation 2017/1129/EU of the European Parliament and of the Council on the prospectus to be published when securities are offered to the public or admitted to trading on a regulated market (the Prospectus Regulation).)*

CHAPTER 2 AMENDMENTS OF COMMISSION DELEGATED REGULATION (EU) 2019/980

71 *(Reg 71 amends Commission Delegated Regulation 2019/980/EU supplementing Regulation (EU) 2017/1129 of the European Parliament and the Council as regards the format, content, scrutiny and approval of the prospectus to be published when securities are offered to the public or admitted to trading on a regulated market, and repealing Commission Regulation (EC) No 809/2004; and introduces the Schedule to these Regulations.)*

CHAPTER 3 AMENDMENTS OF COMMISSION REGULATION (EC) 1569/2007

72 *(Amends Commission Regulation 1569/2007/EC establishing a mechanism for the determination of equivalence of accounting standards applied by third country issuers of securities pursuant to Directives 2003/71/EC and 2004/109/EC of the European Parliament and of the Council.)*

CHAPTER 4 AMENDMENTS OF THE EEA AGREEMENT

73 *(Amends Annex 9 to the EEA agreement (outside the scope of this work).)*

PART 6 TRANSITIONAL PROVISION

[12.165]

74 Transitional provision for prospectuses notified under the Prospectus Regulation before [IP completion day]

(1) Paragraphs (2) and (3) apply to a prospectus, and any supplement to that prospectus, in respect of which the FCA has received a notification of approval given in accordance with Article 25 of the Prospectus Regulation before [IP completion day].

(2) On and after [IP completion day], the prospectus and any supplement is to be treated for the purposes of the Prospectus Regulation (as it forms part of retained EU law) as if it had been approved by the FCA at the time when it was approved by the competent authority of the home Member State.

(3) Terms used in paragraphs (1) and (2) which are used in the Prospectus Regulation, in particular "approval", "competent authority" and "home Member State", have the meanings given in the Prospectus Regulation, as read with Annex 9 to the EEA Agreement, as that Regulation applied immediately before [IP completion day].

(4) Where, on or after [IP completion day], a supplement is required under Article 23 of the Prospectus Regulation to a prospectus referred to in paragraph (1), the FCA is the competent authority in relation to that supplement for the purposes of the Prospectus Regulation.

NOTES

Commencement: 6 September 2019.

The words "IP completion day" in square brackets (in every place that they occur) were substituted by the Financial Services and Economic and Monetary Policy (Consequential Amendments) (EU Exit) Regulations 2020, SI 2020/1301, reg 3, Schedule, para 48(f), as from 30 December 2020.

[12.166]

75 Transitional provision for registration documents and universal registration documents notified under the Prospectus Regulation before [IP completion day]

(1) Paragraphs (2) to (4) apply in relation to a registration document or universal registration document, and any amendment or supplement to those documents, in respect of which the FCA has received a notification of approval given in accordance with Article 26 of the Prospectus Regulation before [IP completion day].

(2) On and after [IP completion day], the registration document or universal registration document and any amendment or supplement to those documents, is to be treated for the purposes of the Prospectus Regulation (as it forms part of retained EU law) as if it had been approved by the FCA at the time when the competent authority of the Member State gave the approval in question.

(3) A registration document or universal registration document notified in accordance with paragraph (2) may be used on or after [IP completion day] as a constituent part of a prospectus submitted for approval to the FCA.

(4) Terms used in paragraphs (1) and (2) which are used in the Prospectus Regulation have the meanings given in the Prospectus Regulation, as read with Annex 9 to the EEA Agreement, as that Regulation applied immediately before [IP completion day].

(5) Where, on or after [IP completion day], a supplement is required under Article 23 of the Prospectus Regulation to a registration document or universal registration document referred to in paragraph (1), the FCA is the competent authority in relation to that supplement for the purposes of the Prospectus Regulation.

NOTES

Commencement: 6 September 2019.

The words "IP completion day" in square brackets (in every place that they occur) were substituted by the Financial Services and Economic and Monetary Policy (Consequential Amendments) (EU Exit) Regulations 2020, SI 2020/1301, reg 3, Schedule, para 48(f), as from 30 December 2020.

SCHEDULE
AMENDMENTS OF ANNEXES TO COMMISSION DELEGATED REGULATION (EU) 2019/980

(*Contains amendments to Commission Delegated Regulation 2019/980/EU supplementing Regulation (EU) 2017/1129 of the European Parliament and of the Council as regards the format, content, scrutiny and approval of the prospectus to be published when securities are offered to the public or admitted to trading on a regulated market, and repealing Commission Regulation (EC) No 809/2004.*)

FREEDOM OF ESTABLISHMENT AND FREE MOVEMENT OF SERVICES (EU EXIT) REGULATIONS 2019

(SI 2019/1401)

NOTES

Made: 28 October 2019.

Authority: European Union (Withdrawal) Act 2018, s 8(1).

Commencement: IP completion day (as defined in the European Union (Withdrawal Agreement) Act 2020, s 39).

[12.167]
1 Citation and commencement

These Regulations may be cited as the Freedom of Establishment and Free Movement of Services (EU Exit) Regulations 2019 and come into force on exit day.

NOTES

Commencement: IP completion day (as defined in the European Union (Withdrawal Agreement) Act 2020, s 39).

As to the commencement of these Regulations, see the European Union (Withdrawal Agreement) Act 2020, Sch 5, para 1 (at **[12.59]**) which gives legal effect to the implementation period by 'non-textually amending' the coming into force dates of subordinate legislation which comes into force immediately before exit day, on exit day or at any time after exit day. This subordinate legislation will instead come into force immediately before the end of the implementation period (IP completion day), on IP completion day or (as the case may be) at the time concerned after IP completion day.

[12.168]
2 Cessation of freedom of establishment

(1) Any rights, powers, liabilities, obligations, restrictions, remedies and procedures which—
- (a) continue by virtue of section 4(1) of the European Union (Withdrawal) Act 2018; and
- (b) are derived (directly or indirectly) from—
  - (i) Article 49 of the Treaty on the Functioning of the European Union;
  - (ii) Article 31 of the EEA Agreement;
  - (iii) Article 4 of the Agreement between the European Community and its Member States and the Swiss Confederation on the free movement of persons signed at Luxembourg on 21st June 1999;
  - (iv) Article 13 of the Agreement establishing an Association between the European Economic Community and Turkey signed at Ankara on 12th September 1963 and Article 41 of the additional Protocol to that Agreement signed at Brussels on 23rd November 1970,

cease to be recognised and available in domestic law (and to be enforced, allowed and followed accordingly).

(2) But the cessation of the rights, powers, liabilities, obligations, restrictions, remedies and procedures set out at paragraph (1)(b)(iii) and (iv) does not apply to any matter which falls within the interpretation, application or operation of the Immigration Acts.

NOTES

Commencement: IP completion day (as defined in the European Union (Withdrawal Agreement) Act 2020, s 39).

[12.169]
3 Cessation of free movement of services

(1) Any rights, powers, liabilities, obligations, restrictions, remedies and procedures which—
- (a) continue by virtue of section 4(1) of the European Union (Withdrawal) Act 2018; and
- (b) are derived (directly or indirectly) from—
  - (i) Articles 56 and 57 of the Treaty on the Functioning of the European Union;
  - (ii) Articles 36 and 37 of the EEA Agreement;

(iii) Article 5 of the Agreement between the European Community and its Member States and the Swiss Confederation on the free movement of persons signed at Luxembourg on 21st June 1999;

(iv) Article 14 of the Agreement establishing an Association between the European Economic Community and Turkey signed at Ankara on 12th September 1963 and Article 41 of the additional Protocol to that Agreement signed at Brussels on 23rd November 1970,

cease to be recognised and available in domestic law (and to be enforced, allowed and followed accordingly).

(2) But the cessation of the rights, powers, liabilities, obligations, restrictions, remedies and procedures set out at paragraph (1)(b)(iii) and (iv) does not apply to any matter which falls within the interpretation, application or operation of the Immigration Acts.

NOTES

Commencement: IP completion day (as defined in the European Union (Withdrawal Agreement) Act 2020, s 39).

[12.170]

4 Cessation of discrimination on the grounds of nationality

The prohibitions on the grounds of nationality which—

(a) continue by virtue of section 4(1) of the European Union (Withdrawal) Act 2018; and

(b) are derived from—

(i) Article 18 of the Treaty on the Functioning of the European Union;

(ii) Article 4 of the EEA Agreement;

(iii) Article 2 of the Agreement between the European Community and its Member States and the Swiss Confederation on the free movement of persons signed at Brussels on 21st June 1999; and

(iv) Article 9 of the Agreement establishing an Association between the European Economic Community and Turkey signed at Ankara on 12th September 1963 and Article 41 of the additional Protocol to that Agreement signed at Brussels on 23rd November 1970,

so far as they relate to the cessation effected by regulations 2(1)(b) and 3(1)(b), cease to be recognised and available in domestic law (and to be enforced, allowed and followed accordingly).

NOTES

Commencement: IP completion day (as defined in the European Union (Withdrawal Agreement) Act 2020, s 39).

STATUTORY AUDITORS AND THIRD COUNTRY AUDITORS (AMENDMENT) (EU EXIT) REGULATIONS 2020

(SI 2020/108)

NOTES

Made: 31 January 2020.

Authority: European Communities Act 1972, s 2(2); Companies Act 2006, ss 484(1), 1240A, 1240B and 1292(1); Limited Liability Partnerships Act 2000, ss 15, 17(3) (see also the note "Statutory Instruments made under the European Communities Act 1972" preceding paragraph **[4.1]** *ante*).

Commencement: see reg 1 below.

For a summary of all Orders and Regulations made under the Companies Act 2006, see Appendix 4 at **[A4]**.

ARRANGEMENT OF REGULATIONS

PART 1 INTRODUCTORY

[12.171]

1 Citation, commencement and application

(1) These Regulations may be cited as the Statutory Auditors and Third Country Auditors (Amendment) (EU Exit) Regulations 2020.

(2) These Regulations come into force—

(a) in the case of Part 2, immediately before IP completion day;

(b) otherwise on the 21st day after the day on which these Regulations are made.

(3) The amendments made by regulation 16 apply in relation to financial years beginning on or after 6th April 2020.

NOTES

Commencement: 21 February 2020.

PART 2 AMENDMENTS TO THE STATUTORY AUDITORS AND THIRD COUNTRY AUDITORS (AMENDMENT) (EU EXIT) REGULATIONS 2019

2–4 (*Amend the Statutory Auditors and Third Country Auditors (Amendment) (EU Exit) Regulations 2019 at* **[12.83]**.)

PART 3 EQUIVALENT THIRD COUNTRIES AND APPROVED THIRD COUNTRY COMPETENT AUTHORITIES

CHAPTER 1 PROCEDURES RELATING TO APPROVALS FOR EQUIVALENT THIRD COUNTRIES AND TRANSITIONAL THIRD COUNTRIES

[12.172]

5 Application and interpretation

(1) This Chapter applies in relation to the grant of—

(a) approval to a third country as an equivalent third country;

(b) provisional approval to a third country as an equivalent third country; or

(c) transitional approval to a third country as a transitional third country;

by relevant regulations.

(2) In this Chapter, "relevant regulations" means regulations under section 1240A(1) of the Companies Act 2006 made by the Secretary of State.

NOTES

Commencement: 21 February 2020.

[12.173]

6 Definition of a comparable audit regulatory regime

For the purposes of these Regulations, the audit regulatory regime of a third country is comparable to that of the United Kingdom if there are comparable requirements to those in regulations 3, 5, 6 and 9 of the Statutory Auditors and Third Country Auditors Regulations 2016 in that country's audit regulatory regime.

NOTES

Commencement: 21 February 2020.

[12.174]

7 Power of Secretary of State to take into account a report from the competent authority

(1) Before granting approval, provisional approval or transitional approval to a third country by relevant regulations, the Secretary of State may take into account a report prepared by the competent authority that assesses the extent to which the third country's audit regulatory regime is comparable to that of the United Kingdom.

(2) The report of the competent authority may take account of any assessments of the third country's audit regulatory regime carried out by or on behalf of an equivalent third country or a transitional third country.

NOTES

Commencement: 21 February 2020.

[12.175]

8 Conditions for grant of approval

(1) The Secretary of State may not grant to a third country—

(a) approval as an equivalent third country unless the Secretary of State is satisfied that condition A is met;

(b) provisional approval as an equivalent third country unless the Secretary of State is satisfied that condition B is met; or

(c) transitional approval as a transitional third country unless the Secretary of State is satisfied that condition C is met.

(2) Condition A is that the third country has an audit regulatory regime that is comparable to that of the United Kingdom.

(3) Condition B is that it is likely that—

(a) the third country has an audit regulatory regime that is comparable to that of the United Kingdom; and

(b) that comparability can reasonably be expected to have been established before the end of the period of provisional approval.

(4) Condition C is that it is likely that—

(a) the third country's audit regulatory regime will be comparable to that of the United Kingdom before the end of the period of transitional approval; or

(b) the third country will make acceptable progress towards its audit regulatory regime being so comparable before the end of the period of transitional approval.

NOTES

Commencement: 21 February 2020.

[12.176]

9 Suspension of approval

(1) If, in relation to a third country which has been granted approval, provisional approval or transitional approval by relevant regulations, the Secretary of State is no longer satisfied that condition A, B or C is met, the Secretary of State may direct that the approval, provisional approval or transitional approval is suspended with effect—

(a) from a date specified in the direction; or

(b) for financial years beginning or ending on or after a date specified in the direction;

for a period of no longer than two years beginning on the date of the direction.

(2) A suspension under paragraph (1) may be extended so that the suspension is for a total period of no longer than three years beginning on the date of the direction.

(3) The Secretary of State may revoke a direction to suspend approval, provisional approval or transitional approval.

(4) The Secretary of State must inform the competent authority of—

(a) any suspension of approval, provisional approval or transitional approval;

(b) any extension of such a suspension; and

(c) any revocation of a direction to suspend approval, provisional approval or transitional approval.

(5) The Secretary of State must make arrangements for—

(a) publication on a publicly accessible website of details of—

(i) any suspension of approval, provisional approval or transitional approval;

(ii) any extension of such a suspension; and

(iii) any revocation of a direction to suspend approval, provisional approval or transitional approval; and

(b) informing any registered third country auditors of any UK-traded third country companies incorporated or formed under the law of a third country whose approval, provisional approval or transitional approval has been suspended—

(i) of that suspension;

(ii) of any extension of that suspension; and

(iii) where there is subsequently a revocation of the direction to suspend approval, provisional approval or transitional approval, of that revocation.

(6) For the purposes of this regulation—

(a) approval granted for an indefinite period under Schedule 1 to the Statutory Auditors and Third Country Auditors (Amendment) (EU Exit) Regulations 2019 is to be treated as if it were granted under relevant regulations on the basis that condition A were met;

(b) approval granted for a finite period of time under that Schedule is to be treated as if it were granted under relevant regulations on the basis that condition B were met;

(c) transitional approval granted under that Schedule is to be treated as if it were granted under relevant regulations on the basis that condition C were met.

NOTES

Commencement: 21 February 2020.

CHAPTER 2 PROCEDURES RELATING TO APPROVALS FOR THIRD COUNTRY COMPETENT AUTHORITIES

[12.177]

10 Application and interpretation

(1) This Chapter applies in relation to the grant of—

(a) approval to a third country competent authority as an approved third country competent authority; or

(b) provisional approval to a third country competent authority as an approved third country competent authority;

by relevant regulations.

(2) In this Chapter, "relevant regulations" means regulations under section 1240B(1) of the Companies Act 2006 made by the Secretary of State.

NOTES

Commencement: 21 February 2020.

[12.178]

11 Definition of when a third country competent authority is adequate in relation to exchange of papers and reports

For the purposes of these Regulations, a third country competent authority is adequate, in relation to the authority's ability to co-operate with the competent authority on the exchange of audit working papers and investigation reports, if provisions with content comparable to that of sections 1224A, 1224B and 1253A to 1253C of, and Schedule 11A to, the Companies Act 2006, or provisions which are expected to achieve comparable outcomes, apply in the country of that competent authority.

NOTES

Commencement: 21 February 2020.

[12.179]

12 Power of Secretary of State to take into account a report from the competent authority

(1) Before granting approval or provisional approval to a third country competent authority by relevant regulations, the Secretary of State may take into account a report prepared by the competent authority that assesses the extent to which the third country competent authority is adequate in relation to that authority's ability to co-operate with the competent authority on the exchange of audit working papers and investigation reports.

(2) The report of the competent authority may take account of any assessments of the third country competent authority carried out by or on behalf of an equivalent third country or a transitional third country.

NOTES

Commencement: 21 February 2020.

[12.180]

13 Conditions for grant of approval

(1) The Secretary of State may not grant to a third country competent authority—

(a) approval as an approved third country competent authority unless the Secretary of State is satisfied that condition A is met; or

(b) provisional approval as an approved third country competent authority unless the Secretary of State is satisfied that condition B is met.

(2) Condition A is that the third country competent authority is adequate in relation to its ability to co-operate with the competent authority on the exchange of audit working papers and investigation reports.

(3) Condition B is that it is likely that—

(a) the third country competent authority is adequate in relation to its ability to co-operate with the competent authority on the exchange of audit working papers and investigation reports; and

(b) that adequacy can reasonably be expected to have been established before the end of the period of provisional approval.

NOTES

Commencement: 21 February 2020.

[12.181]

14 Suspension of approval

(1) If, in relation to a third country competent authority which has been granted approval or provisional approval by relevant regulations, the Secretary of State is no longer satisfied that condition A or B is met, the Secretary of State may direct that the approval or provisional approval is suspended with effect—

(a) from a date specified in the direction; or

(b) for financial years beginning or ending on or after a date specified in the direction;

for a period of no longer than two years beginning on the date of the direction.

(2) A suspension under paragraph (1) may be extended so that the suspension is for a total period of no longer than three years beginning on the date of the direction.

(3) The Secretary of State may revoke a direction to suspend approval or provisional approval.

(4) The Secretary of State must inform the competent authority of—

(a) any suspension of approval or provisional approval;

(b) any extension of such a suspension; and

(c) any revocation of a direction to suspend approval or provisional approval.

(5) The Secretary of State must make arrangements for—

(a) publication on a publicly accessible website of details of—

(i) any suspension of approval or provisional approval;

(ii) any extension of such a suspension; and

(iii) any revocation of a direction to suspend approval or provisional approval; and

(b) informing any statutory auditor whose audit working papers and investigation reports are due to be transferred to a third country competent authority whose approval or provisional approval has been suspended, or whose audit working papers and investigation reports have been transferred to such a third country competent authority in the three years preceding the suspension of approval or provisional approval—

(i) of the suspension of approval or provisional approval of that third country competent authority;

(ii) of any extension of that approval; and

(iii) where there is subsequently a revocation of the direction to suspend approval or provisional approval, of that revocation.

(6) For the purposes of this regulation—

(a) approval granted for an indefinite period under Schedule 2 to the Statutory Auditors and Third Country Auditors (Amendment) (EU Exit) Regulations 2019 is to be treated as if it were granted under relevant regulations on the basis that condition A were met;

(b) approval granted for a finite period of time under that Schedule is to be treated as if it were granted under relevant regulations on the basis that condition B were met.

NOTES

Commencement: 21 February 2020.

PART 4 AMENDMENTS MADE UNDER SECTION 2(2) OF THE EUROPEAN COMMUNITIES ACT 1972

15–17 *(Amend the Companies Act 2006, the Insurance Accounts Directive (Lloyd's Syndicate and Aggregate Accounts) Regulations 2008 (outside the scope of this work), and the Statutory Auditors and Third Country Auditors*

Regulations 2016.)

EUROPEAN UNION (WITHDRAWAL) ACT 2018 AND EUROPEAN UNION (WITHDRAWAL AGREEMENT) ACT 2020 (COMMENCEMENT, TRANSITIONAL AND SAVINGS PROVISIONS) REGULATIONS 2020

(SI 2020/1622)

NOTES

Made: 21 December 2020.

Authority: European Union (Withdrawal) Act 2018, ss 23(6), 25(4), Sch 7, paras 23(3), 26; European Union (Withdrawal Agreement) Act 2020, ss 41(5), 42(7), Sch 5, para 68(1).

Commencement: see reg 1 *below*.

ARRANGEMENT OF REGULATIONS

PART 1
CITATION, COMMENCEMENT AND INTERPRETATION

PART 3
TRANSITIONAL AND SAVING PROVISIONS

PART 1 CITATION, COMMENCEMENT AND INTERPRETATION

[12.182]

1 Citation, commencement and interpretation

(1) These Regulations may be cited as the European Union (Withdrawal) Act 2018 and European Union (Withdrawal Agreement) Act 2020 (Commencement, Transitional and Savings Provisions) Regulations 2020.

(2) Part 3 (transitional and saving provisions) comes into force on IP completion day.

(3) In these Regulations—

"ECA 1972" means the European Communities Act 1972;

"EU(A)A 2008" means the European Union (Amendment) Act 2008;

"EU(W)A 2018" means the European Union (Withdrawal) Act 2018;

"EU(WA)A 2020" means the European Union (Withdrawal Agreement) Act 2020;

"GOWA 2006" means the Government of Wales Act 2006;

"IA 1978" means the Interpretation Act 1978;

"ILR(S)A 2010" means the Interpretation and Legislative Reform (Scotland) Act 2010;

"NIA 1998" means the Northern Ireland Act 1998;

"SA 1998" means the Scotland Act 1998.

PART 2 PROVISIONS COMING INTO FORCE

2–5 (*Regs 2–5 bring into force various provisions of the European Union (Withdrawal) Act 2018 and the European Union (Withdrawal Agreement) Act 2020. These have been noted to the relevant provisions ante*.)

PART 3 TRANSITIONAL AND SAVING PROVISIONS

[12.183]

6 European Communities Act 1972

Despite the ECA 1972 ceasing to have effect by virtue of section 1A(5) of EU(W)A 2018, section 11(2) of ECA 1972 continues to have effect on and after IP completion day in relation to the communication, or public disclosure, of any classified information on or after IP completion day by a person who acquired, or obtained cognisance of, the classified information before IP completion day.

NOTES

Commencement: IP completion day (as defined in the European Union (Withdrawal Agreement) Act 2020, s 39).

[12.184]

7 Interpretation Act 1978

(1) The repeal by paragraph 22(a) of Schedule 8 to EU(W)A 2018 of the definitions of "the Treaties" and "the EU Treaties" (as defined by section 1(2) of ECA 1972) in Schedule 1 to IA 1978, and the insertion by paragraph 22(e) of Schedule 8 to EU(W)A 2018 of definitions of those expressions in Schedule 1 to IA 1978, do not affect the interpretation of those expressions in pre-IPCD legislation on and after IP completion day in relation to a time before IP completion day.

(2) In its application to an Act passed, or subordinate legislation made, before 19th June 2008, the definition of "the Communities" in Schedule 1 to IA 1978, as inserted by paragraph 22(e) of Schedule 8 to EU(W)A 2018, has effect on and after IP completion day, in its application in relation to a time before 19th June 2008, as if the words from "but" to the end were omitted.

(3) In this regulation—

"pre-IPCD legislation" means an Act passed, or subordinate legislation made, before IP completion day;

"subordinate legislation" has the same meaning as in IA 1978.

NOTES

Commencement: IP completion day (as defined in the European Union (Withdrawal Agreement) Act 2020, s 39).

8–16 *(Reg 8 (European Union (Amendment) Act 2008); reg 9 (Further savings in relation to the European Union (Amendment) Act 2008); reg 10 (Devolution); reg 11 (Scotland Act 1998); reg 12 (Scottish Taxpayers); reg 13 (Interpretation and Legislative Reform (Scotland) Act 2010); reg 14 (Government of Wales Act 2006); reg 15 (Welsh taxpayers); reg 16 (Northern Ireland Act 1998); outside the scope of this work.)*

[12.185]

17 Transitional provision for section 5A of EU(W)A 2018

Nothing in section 5A of EU(W)A 2018 prevents the modification on or after IP completion day of retained EU law by an enactment passed or made before IP completion day and coming into force or otherwise having effect on or after IP completion day (whether or not that enactment is itself retained EU law).

NOTES

Commencement: IP completion day (as defined in the European Union (Withdrawal Agreement) Act 2020, s 39).

[12.186]

18 Transitional provision for paragraph 14 of Schedule 8 to EU(W)A 2018

Paragraph 14 of Schedule 8 to EU(W)A 2018 does not apply to a statutory instrument which was made before IP completion day but which would otherwise be subject to that paragraph.

NOTES

Commencement: IP completion day (as defined in the European Union (Withdrawal Agreement) Act 2020, s 39).

[12.187]

19 Cross-references

(1) Paragraphs 1 and 2A(3) of Schedule 8 to EU(W)A 2018 do not apply to any reading on or after IP completion day of a reference so far as the reference relates to a time before IP completion day (unless a contrary intention appears in relation to the reference concerned).

(2) Paragraph 2 of that Schedule does not apply to any reading on or after IP completion day of a reference so far as the reference relates to a time before IP completion day which is earlier than immediately before IP completion day (unless a contrary intention appears in relation to the reference concerned).

NOTES

Commencement: IP completion day (as defined in the European Union (Withdrawal Agreement) Act 2020, s 39).

[12.188]

20 Relation to interpretation legislation

(1) Parts 3 and 4 of Schedule 8 to EU(W)A 2018, Part 3 of Schedule 5 to EU(WA)A 2020, these Regulations and other regulations made under section 23(6) of EU(W)A 2018 or section 41(5) of EU(WA)A 2020 are without prejudice (so far as it is required) to section 16 of IA 1978 or any provision of interpretation legislation which corresponds to that section.

(2) In this regulation, "interpretation legislation" means ILR(S)A 2010, the Scotland Act 1998 (Transitory and Transitional Provisions) (Publication and Interpretation etc of Acts of the Scottish Parliament) Order 1999, the Interpretation Act (Northern Ireland) 1954 or the Legislation (Wales) Act 2019.

NOTES

Commencement: IP completion day (as defined in the European Union (Withdrawal Agreement) Act 2020, s 39).

[12.189]

21 General saving provision

Any saving of a provision by Part 4 of Schedule 8 to EU(W)A 2018, these Regulations or other regulations made under section 23(6) of that Act or section 41(5) of EU(WA)A 2020 includes, so far as is required for the operation of the saved provision, the saving of any other provision relating to that provision.

NOTES

Commencement: IP completion day (as defined in the European Union (Withdrawal Agreement) Act 2020, s 39).

[12.190]

22 General provision relating to repeals

The repeal of an enactment by EU(W)A 2018 does not affect an amendment of an enactment made by the repealed enactment so far as—

(a) the enactment as amended otherwise continues to have effect (whether by virtue of transitional or saving provision or otherwise), or

(b) any other transitional or saving provision relating to the enactment as amended otherwise continues to have effect.

NOTES

Commencement: IP completion day (as defined in the European Union (Withdrawal Agreement) Act 2020, s 39).

INTERNATIONAL ACCOUNTING STANDARDS (DELEGATION OF FUNCTIONS) (EU EXIT) REGULATIONS 2021

(SI 2021/609)

NOTES

Made: 21 May 2021.

Authority: Companies (Audit, Investigations and Community Enterprise) Act 2004, s 18A(1), (3); International Accounting Standards and European Public Limited-Liability Company (Amendment etc) (EU Exit) Regulations 2019, regs 13(1), (4), 14(4).

Commencement: 22 May 2021.

[12.191]

1 Citation, commencement and interpretation

(1) These Regulations may be cited as the International Accounting Standards (Delegation of Functions) (EU Exit) Regulations 2021 and come into force on the day after the day on which these Regulations are made.

(2) In these Regulations—

(a) "the 2004 Act" means the Companies (Audit, Investigations and Community Enterprise) Act 2004;

(b) "the principal Regulations" means the International Accounting Standards and European Public Limited-Liability Company (Amendment etc) (EU Exit) Regulations 2019;

(c) "the UK Endorsement Board" means the UK Accounting Standards Endorsement Board, an unincorporated association of that name established on 26th March 2021.

NOTES

Commencement: 22 May 2021.

[12.192]

2 Delegation of the Secretary of State's functions

(1) The UK Endorsement Board is designated for the purpose of enabling it to exercise functions of the Secretary of State under Chapter 3 of Part 2 of the principal Regulations.

(2) The functions of the Secretary of State under regulations 7(3) and 12 of the principal Regulations are not transferred by these Regulations.

NOTES

Commencement: 22 May 2021.

[12.193]

3 Requirements for recording decisions

The UK Endorsement Board must have satisfactory arrangements for—

(a) recording decisions made in the exercise of the functions transferred by these Regulations, and

(b) the safekeeping of the records of those decisions.

NOTES

Commencement: 22 May 2021.

[12.194]

4 Exemption from liability

(1) The exemption from liability in subsections (3) and (4) of section 18A (power to confer exemption from liability) of the 2004 Act applies to the UK Endorsement Board in accordance with paragraph (2).

(2) The section 16(2) activity which is specified under section 18A(3) of the 2004 Act is the activity in subsection (2)(a) of section 16 of the 2004 Act.

NOTES

Commencement: 22 May 2021.

APPENDICES

Appendix 1: Companies Act 2006 Model Articles

[A1]

NOTES

These model articles are prescribed by the Secretary of State under the Companies Act 2006, s 19(1) at **[1.20]**. They are contained in Schs 1–3 to the Companies (Model Articles) Regulations 2008, SI 2008/3229 at **[4.187]** et seq, and do not affect companies formed before 1 October 2009.

By virtue of s 19(3), (4) of the 2006 Act, a company may adopt all or any of the provisions of the model articles, and any amendment of the model articles by Regulations made under s 19 does not affect a company registered before the amendment takes effect.

By s 20 of the 2006 Act (at **[1.21]**) on the formation of a limited company (a) if articles are not registered, or (b) if articles are registered, in so far as they do not exclude or modify the relevant model articles, then the relevant model articles (so far as applicable) form part of the company's articles in the same manner and to the same extent as if articles in the form of those articles had been duly registered.

Sch 1 (Model Articles for Private Companies Limited by Shares), Sch 2 (Model Articles for Private Companies Limited by Guarantee), and Sch 3 (Model Articles for Public Companies) are reproduced below at **[A1.1]**, **[A1.2]**, and **[A1.3]** respectively.

MODEL ARTICLES FOR PRIVATE COMPANIES LIMITED BY SHARES

[A1.1]

NOTES

These are set out in Schedule 1 to the Companies (Model Articles) Regulations 2008.

These Articles are reproduced as amended by: the Mental Health (Discrimination) Act 2013.

As to the effect of amendments to these Model Articles, see further the introductory notes to Appendix 1 *ante*.

INDEX TO THE ARTICLES

PART 1 INTERPRETATION AND LIMITATION OF LIABILITY

1 Defined terms

In the articles, unless the context requires otherwise—

"articles" means the company's articles of association;

"bankruptcy" includes individual insolvency proceedings in a jurisdiction other than England and Wales or Northern Ireland which have an effect similar to that of bankruptcy;

"chairman" has the meaning given in article 12;

"chairman of the meeting" has the meaning given in article 39;

"Companies Acts" means the Companies Acts (as defined in section 2 of the Companies Act 2006), in so far as they apply to the company;

"director" means a director of the company, and includes any person occupying the position of director, by whatever name called;

"distribution recipient" has the meaning given in article 31;

"document" includes, unless otherwise specified, any document sent or supplied in electronic form;

"electronic form" has the meaning given in section 1168 of the Companies Act 2006;

"fully paid" in relation to a share, means that the nominal value and any premium to be paid to the company in respect of that share have been paid to the company;

"hard copy form" has the meaning given in section 1168 of the Companies Act 2006;

"holder" in relation to shares means the person whose name is entered in the register of members as the holder of the shares;

"instrument" means a document in hard copy form;

"ordinary resolution" has the meaning given in section 282 of the Companies Act 2006;

"paid" means paid or credited as paid;

"participate", in relation to a directors' meeting, has the meaning given in article 10;

"proxy notice" has the meaning given in article 45;

"shareholder" means a person who is the holder of a share;

"shares" means shares in the company;

"special resolution" has the meaning given in section 283 of the Companies Act 2006;

"subsidiary" has the meaning given in section 1159 of the Companies Act 2006;

"transmittee" means a person entitled to a share by reason of the death or bankruptcy of a shareholder or otherwise by operation of law; and

"writing" means the representation or reproduction of words, symbols or other information in a visible form by any method or combination of methods, whether sent or supplied in electronic form or otherwise.

Unless the context otherwise requires, other words or expressions contained in these articles bear the same meaning as in the Companies Act 2006 as in force on the date when these articles become binding on the company.

2 Liability of members

The liability of the members is limited to the amount, if any, unpaid on the shares held by them.

PART 2 DIRECTORS

Directors' Powers and Responsibilities

3 Directors' general authority

Subject to the articles, the directors are responsible for the management of the company's business, for which purpose they may exercise all the powers of the company.

4 Shareholders' reserve power

(1) The shareholders may, by special resolution, direct the directors to take, or refrain from taking, specified action.

(2) No such special resolution invalidates anything which the directors have done before the passing of the resolution.

5 Directors may delegate

(1) Subject to the articles, the directors may delegate any of the powers which are conferred on them under the articles—

- (a) to such person or committee;
- (b) by such means (including by power of attorney);
- (c) to such an extent;
- (d) in relation to such matters or territories; and
- (e) on such terms and conditions;

as they think fit.

(2) If the directors so specify, any such delegation may authorise further delegation of the directors' powers by any person to whom they are delegated.

(3) The directors may revoke any delegation in whole or part, or alter its terms and conditions.

6 Committees

(1) Committees to which the directors delegate any of their powers must follow procedures which are based as far as they are applicable on those provisions of the articles which govern the taking of decisions by directors.

(2) The directors may make rules of procedure for all or any committees, which prevail over rules derived from the articles if they are not consistent with them.

Decision-Making by Directors

7 Directors to take decisions collectively

(1) The general rule about decision-making by directors is that any decision of the directors must be either a majority decision at a meeting or a decision taken in accordance with article 8.

(2) If—

- (a) the company only has one director, and
- (b) no provision of the articles requires it to have more than one director,

the general rule does not apply, and the director may take decisions without regard to any of the provisions of the articles relating to directors' decision-making.

8 Unanimous decisions

(1) A decision of the directors is taken in accordance with this article when all eligible directors indicate to each other by any means that they share a common view on a matter.

(2) Such a decision may take the form of a resolution in writing, copies of which have been signed by each eligible director or to which each eligible director has otherwise indicated agreement in writing.

(3) References in this article to eligible directors are to directors who would have been entitled to vote on the matter had it been proposed as a resolution at a directors' meeting.

(4) A decision may not be taken in accordance with this article if the eligible directors would not have formed a quorum at such a meeting.

9 Calling a directors' meeting

(1) Any director may call a directors' meeting by giving notice of the meeting to the directors or by authorising the company secretary (if any) to give such notice.

(2) Notice of any directors' meeting must indicate—

- (a) its proposed date and time;
- (b) where it is to take place; and
- (c) if it is anticipated that directors participating in the meeting will not be in the same place, how it is proposed that they should communicate with each other during the meeting.

(3) Notice of a directors' meeting must be given to each director, but need not be in writing.

(4) Notice of a directors' meeting need not be given to directors who waive their entitlement to notice of that meeting, by giving notice to that effect to the company not more than 7 days after the date on which the meeting is held. Where such notice is given after the meeting has been held, that does not affect the validity of the meeting, or of any business conducted at it.

10 Participation in directors' meetings

(1) Subject to the articles, directors participate in a directors' meeting, or part of a directors' meeting, when—

- (a) the meeting has been called and takes place in accordance with the articles, and

(b) they can each communicate to the others any information or opinions they have on any particular item of the business of the meeting.

(2) In determining whether directors are participating in a directors' meeting, it is irrelevant where any director is or how they communicate with each other.

(3) If all the directors participating in a meeting are not in the same place, they may decide that the meeting is to be treated as taking place wherever any of them is.

11 Quorum for directors' meetings

(1) At a directors' meeting, unless a quorum is participating, no proposal is to be voted on, except a proposal to call another meeting.

(2) The quorum for directors' meetings may be fixed from time to time by a decision of the directors, but it must never be less than two, and unless otherwise fixed it is two.

(3) If the total number of directors for the time being is less than the quorum required, the directors must not take any decision other than a decision—

(a) to appoint further directors, or
(b) to call a general meeting so as to enable the shareholders to appoint further directors.

12 Chairing of directors' meetings

(1) The directors may appoint a director to chair their meetings.

(2) The person so appointed for the time being is known as the chairman.

(3) The directors may terminate the chairman's appointment at any time.

(4) If the chairman is not participating in a directors' meeting within ten minutes of the time at which it was to start, the participating directors must appoint one of themselves to chair it.

13 Casting vote

(1) If the numbers of votes for and against a proposal are equal, the chairman or other director chairing the meeting has a casting vote.

(2) But this does not apply if, in accordance with the articles, the chairman or other director is not to be counted as participating in the decision-making process for quorum or voting purposes.

14 Conflicts of interest

(1) If a proposed decision of the directors is concerned with an actual or proposed transaction or arrangement with the company in which a director is interested, that director is not to be counted as participating in the decision-making process for quorum or voting purposes.

(2) But if paragraph (3) applies, a director who is interested in an actual or proposed transaction or arrangement with the company is to be counted as participating in the decision-making process for quorum and voting purposes.

(3) This paragraph applies when—

(a) the company by ordinary resolution disapplies the provision of the articles which would otherwise prevent a director from being counted as participating in the decision-making process;
(b) the director's interest cannot reasonably be regarded as likely to give rise to a conflict of interest; or
(c) the director's conflict of interest arises from a permitted cause.

(4) For the purposes of this article, the following are permitted causes—

(a) a guarantee given, or to be given, by or to a director in respect of an obligation incurred by or on behalf of the company or any of its subsidiaries;
(b) subscription, or an agreement to subscribe, for shares or other securities of the company or any of its subsidiaries, or to underwrite, sub-underwrite, or guarantee subscription for any such shares or securities; and
(c) arrangements pursuant to which benefits are made available to employees and directors or former employees and directors of the company or any of its subsidiaries which do not provide special benefits for directors or former directors.

(5) For the purposes of this article, references to proposed decisions and decision-making processes include any directors' meeting or part of a directors' meeting.

(6) Subject to paragraph (7), if a question arises at a meeting of directors or of a committee of directors as to the right of a director to participate in the meeting (or part of the meeting) for voting or quorum purposes, the question may, before the conclusion of the meeting, be referred to the chairman whose ruling in relation to any director other than the chairman is to be final and conclusive.

(7) If any question as to the right to participate in the meeting (or part of the meeting) should arise in respect of the chairman, the question is to be decided by a decision of the directors at that meeting, for which purpose the chairman is not to be counted as participating in the meeting (or that part of the meeting) for voting or quorum purposes.

15 Records of decisions to be kept

The directors must ensure that the company keeps a record, in writing, for at least 10 years from the date of the decision recorded, of every unanimous or majority decision taken by the directors.

16 Directors' discretion to make further rules

Subject to the articles, the directors may make any rule which they think fit about how they take decisions, and about how such rules are to be recorded or communicated to directors.

Appointment of Directors

17 Methods of appointing directors

(1) Any person who is willing to act as a director, and is permitted by law to do so, may be appointed to be a director—

(a) by ordinary resolution, or

(b) by a decision of the directors.

(2) In any case where, as a result of death, the company has no shareholders and no directors, the personal representatives of the last shareholder to have died have the right, by notice in writing, to appoint a person to be a director.

(3) For the purposes of paragraph (2), where 2 or more shareholders die in circumstances rendering it uncertain who was the last to die, a younger shareholder is deemed to have survived an older shareholder.

18 Termination of director's appointment

A person ceases to be a director as soon as—

(a) that person ceases to be a director by virtue of any provision of the Companies Act 2006 or is prohibited from being a director by law;
(b) a bankruptcy order is made against that person;
(c) a composition is made with that person's creditors generally in satisfaction of that person's debts;
(d) a registered medical practitioner who is treating that person gives a written opinion to the company stating that that person has become physically or mentally incapable of acting as a director and may remain so for more than three months;
(e) . . .
(f) notification is received by the company from the director that the director is resigning from office, and such resignation has taken effect in accordance with its terms.

NOTES

Para 18(e) was revoked by the Mental Health (Discrimination) Act 2013, s 3(1)(a), as from 28 April 2013.

19 Directors' remuneration

(1) Directors may undertake any services for the company that the directors decide.

(2) Directors are entitled to such remuneration as the directors determine—

(a) for their services to the company as directors, and
(b) for any other service which they undertake for the company.

(3) Subject to the articles, a director's remuneration may—

(a) take any form, and
(b) include any arrangements in connection with the payment of a pension, allowance or gratuity, or any death, sickness or disability benefits, to or in respect of that director.

(4) Unless the directors decide otherwise, directors' remuneration accrues from day to day.

(5) Unless the directors decide otherwise, directors are not accountable to the company for any remuneration which they receive as directors or other officers or employees of the company's subsidiaries or of any other body corporate in which the company is interested.

20 Directors' expenses

The company may pay any reasonable expenses which the directors properly incur in connection with their attendance at—

(a) meetings of directors or committees of directors,
(b) general meetings, or
(c) separate meetings of the holders of any class of shares or of debentures of the company,

or otherwise in connection with the exercise of their powers and the discharge of their responsibilities in relation to the company.

PART 3 SHARES AND DISTRIBUTIONS

Shares

21 All shares to be fully paid up

(1) No share is to be issued for less than the aggregate of its nominal value and any premium to be paid to the company in consideration for its issue.

(2) This does not apply to shares taken on the formation of the company by the subscribers to the company's memorandum.

22 Powers to issue different classes of share

(1) Subject to the articles, but without prejudice to the rights attached to any existing share, the company may issue shares with such rights or restrictions as may be determined by ordinary resolution.

(2) The company may issue shares which are to be redeemed, or are liable to be redeemed at the option of the company or the holder, and the directors may determine the terms, conditions and manner of redemption of any such shares.

23 Company not bound by less than absolute interests

Except as required by law, no person is to be recognised by the company as holding any share upon any trust, and except as otherwise required by law or the articles, the company is not in any way to be bound by or recognise any interest in a share other than the holder's absolute ownership of it and all the rights attaching to it.

24 Share certificates

(1) The company must issue each shareholder, free of charge, with one or more certificates in respect of the shares which that shareholder holds.

(2) Every certificate must specify—

(a) in respect of how many shares, of what class, it is issued;
(b) the nominal value of those shares;
(c) that the shares are fully paid; and

(d) any distinguishing numbers assigned to them.

(3) No certificate may be issued in respect of shares of more than one class.

(4) If more than one person holds a share, only one certificate may be issued in respect of it.

(5) Certificates must—

(a) have affixed to them the company's common seal, or
(b) be otherwise executed in accordance with the Companies Acts.

25 Replacement share certificates

(1) If a certificate issued in respect of a shareholder's shares is—

(a) damaged or defaced, or
(b) said to be lost, stolen or destroyed,

that shareholder is entitled to be issued with a replacement certificate in respect of the same shares.

(2) A shareholder exercising the right to be issued with such a replacement certificate—

(a) may at the same time exercise the right to be issued with a single certificate or separate certificates;
(b) must return the certificate which is to be replaced to the company if it is damaged or defaced; and
(c) must comply with such conditions as to evidence, indemnity and the payment of a reasonable fee as the directors decide.

26 Share transfers

(1) Shares may be transferred by means of an instrument of transfer in any usual form or any other form approved by the directors, which is executed by or on behalf of the transferor.

(2) No fee may be charged for registering any instrument of transfer or other document relating to or affecting the title to any share.

(3) The company may retain any instrument of transfer which is registered.

(4) The transferor remains the holder of a share until the transferee's name is entered in the register of members as holder of it.

(5) The directors may refuse to register the transfer of a share, and if they do so, the instrument of transfer must be returned to the transferee with the notice of refusal unless they suspect that the proposed transfer may be fraudulent.

27 Transmission of shares

(1) If title to a share passes to a transmittee, the company may only recognise the transmittee as having any title to that share.

(2) A transmittee who produces such evidence of entitlement to shares as the directors may properly require—

(a) may, subject to the articles, choose either to become the holder of those shares or to have them transferred to another person, and
(b) subject to the articles, and pending any transfer of the shares to another person, has the same rights as the holder had.

(3) But transmittees do not have the right to attend or vote at a general meeting, or agree to a proposed written resolution, in respect of shares to which they are entitled, by reason of the holder's death or bankruptcy or otherwise, unless they become the holders of those shares.

28 Exercise of transmittees' rights

(1) Transmittees who wish to become the holders of shares to which they have become entitled must notify the company in writing of that wish.

(2) If the transmittee wishes to have a share transferred to another person, the transmittee must execute an instrument of transfer in respect of it.

(3) Any transfer made or executed under this article is to be treated as if it were made or executed by the person from whom the transmittee has derived rights in respect of the share, and as if the event which gave rise to the transmission had not occurred.

29 Transmittees bound by prior notices

If a notice is given to a shareholder in respect of shares and a transmittee is entitled to those shares, the transmittee is bound by the notice if it was given to the shareholder before the transmittee's name has been entered in the register of members.

Dividends and Other Distributions

30 Procedure for declaring dividends

(1) The company may by ordinary resolution declare dividends, and the directors may decide to pay interim dividends.

(2) A dividend must not be declared unless the directors have made a recommendation as to its amount. Such a dividend must not exceed the amount recommended by the directors.

(3) No dividend may be declared or paid unless it is in accordance with shareholders' respective rights.

(4) Unless the shareholders' resolution to declare or directors' decision to pay a dividend, or the terms on which shares are issued, specify otherwise, it must be paid by reference to each shareholder's holding of shares on the date of the resolution or decision to declare or pay it.

(5) If the company's share capital is divided into different classes, no interim dividend may be paid on shares carrying deferred or non-preferred rights if, at the time of payment, any preferential dividend is in arrear.

(6) The directors may pay at intervals any dividend payable at a fixed rate if it appears to them that the profits available for distribution justify the payment.

(7) If the directors act in good faith, they do not incur any liability to the holders of shares conferring preferred rights for any loss they may suffer by the lawful payment of an interim dividend on shares with deferred or non-preferred rights.

31 Payment of dividends and other distributions

(1) Where a dividend or other sum which is a distribution is payable in respect of a share, it must be paid by one or more of the following means—

- (a) transfer to a bank or building society account specified by the distribution recipient either in writing or as the directors may otherwise decide;
- (b) sending a cheque made payable to the distribution recipient by post to the distribution recipient at the distribution recipient's registered address (if the distribution recipient is a holder of the share), or (in any other case) to an address specified by the distribution recipient either in writing or as the directors may otherwise decide;
- (c) sending a cheque made payable to such person by post to such person at such address as the distribution recipient has specified either in writing or as the directors may otherwise decide; or
- (d) any other means of payment as the directors agree with the distribution recipient either in writing or by such other means as the directors decide.

(2) In the articles, "the distribution recipient" means, in respect of a share in respect of which a dividend or other sum is payable—

- (a) the holder of the share; or
- (b) if the share has two or more joint holders, whichever of them is named first in the register of members; or
- (c) if the holder is no longer entitled to the share by reason of death or bankruptcy, or otherwise by operation of law, the transmittee.

32 No interest on distributions

The company may not pay interest on any dividend or other sum payable in respect of a share unless otherwise provided by—

- (a) the terms on which the share was issued, or
- (b) the provisions of another agreement between the holder of that share and the company.

33 Unclaimed distributions

(1) All dividends or other sums which are—

- (a) payable in respect of shares, and
- (b) unclaimed after having been declared or become payable,

may be invested or otherwise made use of by the directors for the benefit of the company until claimed.

(2) The payment of any such dividend or other sum into a separate account does not make the company a trustee in respect of it.

(3) If—

- (a) twelve years have passed from the date on which a dividend or other sum became due for payment, and
- (b) the distribution recipient has not claimed it,

the distribution recipient is no longer entitled to that dividend or other sum and it ceases to remain owing by the company.

34 Non-cash distributions

(1) Subject to the terms of issue of the share in question, the company may, by ordinary resolution on the recommendation of the directors, decide to pay all or part of a dividend or other distribution payable in respect of a share by transferring non-cash assets of equivalent value (including, without limitation, shares or other securities in any company).

(2) For the purposes of paying a non-cash distribution, the directors may make whatever arrangements they think fit, including, where any difficulty arises regarding the distribution—

- (a) fixing the value of any assets;
- (b) paying cash to any distribution recipient on the basis of that value in order to adjust the rights of recipients; and
- (c) vesting any assets in trustees.

35 Waiver of distributions

Distribution recipients may waive their entitlement to a dividend or other distribution payable in respect of a share by giving the company notice in writing to that effect, but if—

- (a) the share has more than one holder, or
- (b) more than one person is entitled to the share, whether by reason of the death or bankruptcy of one or more joint holders, or otherwise,

the notice is not effective unless it is expressed to be given, and signed, by all the holders or persons otherwise entitled to the share.

Capitalisation of Profits

36 Authority to capitalise and appropriation of capitalised sums

(1) Subject to the articles, the directors may, if they are so authorised by an ordinary resolution—

- (a) decide to capitalise any profits of the company (whether or not they are available for distribution) which are not required for paying a preferential dividend, or any sum standing to the credit of the company's share premium account or capital redemption reserve; and
- (b) appropriate any sum which they so decide to capitalise (a "capitalised sum") to the persons who would have been entitled to it if it were distributed by way of dividend (the "persons entitled") and in the same proportions.

(2) Capitalised sums must be applied—

(a) on behalf of the persons entitled, and
(b) in the same proportions as a dividend would have been distributed to them.

(3) Any capitalised sum may be applied in paying up new shares of a nominal amount equal to the capitalised sum which are then allotted credited as fully paid to the persons entitled or as they may direct.

(4) A capitalised sum which was appropriated from profits available for distribution may be applied in paying up new debentures of the company which are then allotted credited as fully paid to the persons entitled or as they may direct.

(5) Subject to the articles the directors may—

(a) apply capitalised sums in accordance with paragraphs (3) and (4) partly in one way and partly in another;
(b) make such arrangements as they think fit to deal with shares or debentures becoming distributable in fractions under this article (including the issuing of fractional certificates or the making of cash payments); and
(c) authorise any person to enter into an agreement with the company on behalf of all the persons entitled which is binding on them in respect of the allotment of shares and debentures to them under this article.

PART 4 DECISION-MAKING BY SHAREHOLDERS

Organisation of General Meetings

37 Attendance and speaking at general meetings

(1) A person is able to exercise the right to speak at a general meeting when that person is in a position to communicate to all those attending the meeting, during the meeting, any information or opinions which that person has on the business of the meeting.

(2) A person is able to exercise the right to vote at a general meeting when—

(a) that person is able to vote, during the meeting, on resolutions put to the vote at the meeting, and
(b) that person's vote can be taken into account in determining whether or not such resolutions are passed at the same time as the votes of all the other persons attending the meeting.

(3) The directors may make whatever arrangements they consider appropriate to enable those attending a general meeting to exercise their rights to speak or vote at it.

(4) In determining attendance at a general meeting, it is immaterial whether any two or more members attending it are in the same place as each other.

(5) Two or more persons who are not in the same place as each other attend a general meeting if their circumstances are such that if they have (or were to have) rights to speak and vote at that meeting, they are (or would be) able to exercise them.

38 Quorum for general meetings

No business other than the appointment of the chairman of the meeting is to be transacted at a general meeting if the persons attending it do not constitute a quorum.

39 Chairing general meetings

(1) If the directors have appointed a chairman, the chairman shall chair general meetings if present and willing to do so.

(2) If the directors have not appointed a chairman, or if the chairman is unwilling to chair the meeting or is not present within ten minutes of the time at which a meeting was due to start—

(a) the directors present, or
(b) (if no directors are present), the meeting,

must appoint a director or shareholder to chair the meeting, and the appointment of the chairman of the meeting must be the first business of the meeting.

(3) The person chairing a meeting in accordance with this article is referred to as "the chairman of the meeting".

40 Attendance and speaking by directors and non-shareholders

(1) Directors may attend and speak at general meetings, whether or not they are shareholders.

(2) The chairman of the meeting may permit other persons who are not—

(a) shareholders of the company, or
(b) otherwise entitled to exercise the rights of shareholders in relation to general meetings,

to attend and speak at a general meeting.

41 Adjournment

(1) If the persons attending a general meeting within half an hour of the time at which the meeting was due to start do not constitute a quorum, or if during a meeting a quorum ceases to be present, the chairman of the meeting must adjourn it.

(2) The chairman of the meeting may adjourn a general meeting at which a quorum is present if—

(a) the meeting consents to an adjournment, or
(b) it appears to the chairman of the meeting that an adjournment is necessary to protect the safety of any person attending the meeting or ensure that the business of the meeting is conducted in an orderly manner.

(3) The chairman of the meeting must adjourn a general meeting if directed to do so by the meeting.

(4) When adjourning a general meeting, the chairman of the meeting must—

(a) either specify the time and place to which it is adjourned or state that it is to continue at a time and place to be fixed by the directors, and
(b) have regard to any directions as to the time and place of any adjournment which have been given by the meeting.

(5) If the continuation of an adjourned meeting is to take place more than 14 days after it was adjourned, the company must give at least 7 clear days' notice of it (that is, excluding the day of the adjourned meeting and the day on which the notice is given)—

(a) to the same persons to whom notice of the company's general meetings is required to be given, and

(b) containing the same information which such notice is required to contain.

(6) No business may be transacted at an adjourned general meeting which could not properly have been transacted at the meeting if the adjournment had not taken place.

Voting at General Meetings

42 Voting: general

A resolution put to the vote of a general meeting must be decided on a show of hands unless a poll is duly demanded in accordance with the articles.

43 Errors and disputes

(1) No objection may be raised to the qualification of any person voting at a general meeting except at the meeting or adjourned meeting at which the vote objected to is tendered, and every vote not disallowed at the meeting is valid.

(2) Any such objection must be referred to the chairman of the meeting, whose decision is final.

44 Poll votes

(1) A poll on a resolution may be demanded—

(a) in advance of the general meeting where it is to be put to the vote, or

(b) at a general meeting, either before a show of hands on that resolution or immediately after the result of a show of hands on that resolution is declared.

(2) A poll may be demanded by—

(a) the chairman of the meeting;

(b) the directors;

(c) two or more persons having the right to vote on the resolution; or

(d) a person or persons representing not less than one tenth of the total voting rights of all the shareholders having the right to vote on the resolution.

(3) A demand for a poll may be withdrawn if—

(a) the poll has not yet been taken, and

(b) the chairman of the meeting consents to the withdrawal.

(4) Polls must be taken immediately and in such manner as the chairman of the meeting directs.

45 Content of proxy notices

(1) Proxies may only validly be appointed by a notice in writing (a "proxy notice") which—

(a) states the name and address of the shareholder appointing the proxy;

(b) identifies the person appointed to be that shareholder's proxy and the general meeting in relation to which that person is appointed;

(c) is signed by or on behalf of the shareholder appointing the proxy, or is authenticated in such manner as the directors may determine; and

(d) is delivered to the company in accordance with the articles and any instructions contained in the notice of the general meeting to which they relate.

(2) The company may require proxy notices to be delivered in a particular form, and may specify different forms for different purposes.

(3) Proxy notices may specify how the proxy appointed under them is to vote (or that the proxy is to abstain from voting) on one or more resolutions.

(4) Unless a proxy notice indicates otherwise, it must be treated as—

(a) allowing the person appointed under it as a proxy discretion as to how to vote on any ancillary or procedural resolutions put to the meeting, and

(b) appointing that person as a proxy in relation to any adjournment of the general meeting to which it relates as well as the meeting itself.

46 Delivery of proxy notices

(1) A person who is entitled to attend, speak or vote (either on a show of hands or on a poll) at a general meeting remains so entitled in respect of that meeting or any adjournment of it, even though a valid proxy notice has been delivered to the company by or on behalf of that person.

(2) An appointment under a proxy notice may be revoked by delivering to the company a notice in writing given by or on behalf of the person by whom or on whose behalf the proxy notice was given.

(3) A notice revoking a proxy appointment only takes effect if it is delivered before the start of the meeting or adjourned meeting to which it relates.

(4) If a proxy notice is not executed by the person appointing the proxy, it must be accompanied by written evidence of the authority of the person who executed it to execute it on the appointor's behalf.

47 Amendments to resolutions

(1) An ordinary resolution to be proposed at a general meeting may be amended by ordinary resolution if—

(a) notice of the proposed amendment is given to the company in writing by a person entitled to vote at the general meeting at which it is to be proposed not less than 48 hours before the meeting is to take place (or such later time as the chairman of the meeting may determine), and

(b) the proposed amendment does not, in the reasonable opinion of the chairman of the meeting, materially alter the scope of the resolution.

(2) A special resolution to be proposed at a general meeting may be amended by ordinary resolution, if—

(a) the chairman of the meeting proposes the amendment at the general meeting at which the resolution is to be proposed, and

(b) the amendment does not go beyond what is necessary to correct a grammatical or other non-substantive error in the resolution.

(3) If the chairman of the meeting, acting in good faith, wrongly decides that an amendment to a resolution is out of order, the chairman's error does not invalidate the vote on that resolution.

PART 5 ADMINISTRATIVE ARRANGEMENTS

48 Means of communication to be used

(1) Subject to the articles, anything sent or supplied by or to the company under the articles may be sent or supplied in any way in which the Companies Act 2006 provides for documents or information which are authorised or required by any provision of that Act to be sent or supplied by or to the company.

(2) Subject to the articles, any notice or document to be sent or supplied to a director in connection with the taking of decisions by directors may also be sent or supplied by the means by which that director has asked to be sent or supplied with such notices or documents for the time being.

(3) A director may agree with the company that notices or documents sent to that director in a particular way are to be deemed to have been received within a specified time of their being sent, and for the specified time to be less than 48 hours.

49 Company seals

(1) Any common seal may only be used by the authority of the directors.

(2) The directors may decide by what means and in what form any common seal is to be used.

(3) Unless otherwise decided by the directors, if the company has a common seal and it is affixed to a document, the document must also be signed by at least one authorised person in the presence of a witness who attests the signature.

(4) For the purposes of this article, an authorised person is—

(a) any director of the company;

(b) the company secretary (if any); or

(c) any person authorised by the directors for the purpose of signing documents to which the common seal is applied.

50 No right to inspect accounts and other records

Except as provided by law or authorised by the directors or an ordinary resolution of the company, no person is entitled to inspect any of the company's accounting or other records or documents merely by virtue of being a shareholder.

51 Provision for employees on cessation of business

The directors may decide to make provision for the benefit of persons employed or formerly employed by the company or any of its subsidiaries (other than a director or former director or shadow director) in connection with the cessation or transfer to any person of the whole or part of the undertaking of the company or that subsidiary.

Directors' Indemnity and Insurance

52 Indemnity

(1) Subject to paragraph (2), a relevant director of the company or an associated company may be indemnified out of the company's assets against—

(a) any liability incurred by that director in connection with any negligence, default, breach of duty or breach of trust in relation to the company or an associated company,

(b) any liability incurred by that director in connection with the activities of the company or an associated company in its capacity as a trustee of an occupational pension scheme (as defined in section 235(6) of the Companies Act 2006),

(c) any other liability incurred by that director as an officer of the company or an associated company.

(2) This article does not authorise any indemnity which would be prohibited or rendered void by any provision of the Companies Acts or by any other provision of law.

(3) In this article—

(a) companies are associated if one is a subsidiary of the other or both are subsidiaries of the same body corporate, and

(b) a "relevant director" means any director or former director of the company or an associated company.

53 Insurance

(1) The directors may decide to purchase and maintain insurance, at the expense of the company, for the benefit of any relevant director in respect of any relevant loss.

(2) In this article—

(a) a "relevant director" means any director or former director of the company or an associated company,

(b) a "relevant loss" means any loss or liability which has been or may be incurred by a relevant director in connection with that director's duties or powers in relation to the company, any associated company or any pension fund or employees' share scheme of the company or associated company, and

(c) companies are associated if one is a subsidiary of the other or both are subsidiaries of the same body corporate.

MODEL ARTICLES FOR PRIVATE COMPANIES LIMITED BY GUARANTEE

[A1.2]

NOTES

These are set out in Schedule 2 to the Companies (Model Articles) Regulations 2008.

These Articles are reproduced as amended by: the Mental Health (Discrimination) Act 2013.

As to the effect of amendments to these Model Articles, see further the introductory notes to Appendix 1 *ante*.

INDEX TO THE ARTICLES

Appendices

PART 1 INTERPRETATION AND LIMITATION OF LIABILITY

1 Defined terms

In the articles, unless the context requires otherwise—

"articles" means the company's articles of association;

"bankruptcy" includes individual insolvency proceedings in a jurisdiction other than England and Wales or Northern Ireland which have an effect similar to that of bankruptcy;

"chairman" has the meaning given in article 12;

"chairman of the meeting" has the meaning given in article 25;

"Companies Acts" means the Companies Acts (as defined in section 2 of the Companies Act 2006), in so far as they apply to the company;

"director" means a director of the company, and includes any person occupying the position of director, by whatever name called;

"document" includes, unless otherwise specified, any document sent or supplied in electronic form;

"electronic form" has the meaning given in section 1168 of the Companies Act 2006;

"member" has the meaning given in section 112 of the Companies Act 2006;

"ordinary resolution" has the meaning given in section 282 of the Companies Act 2006;

"participate", in relation to a directors' meeting, has the meaning given in article 10;

"proxy notice" has the meaning given in article 31;

"special resolution" has the meaning given in section 283 of the Companies Act 2006;

"subsidiary" has the meaning given in section 1159 of the Companies Act 2006; and

"writing" means the representation or reproduction of words, symbols or other information in a visible form by any method or combination of methods, whether sent or supplied in electronic form or otherwise.

Unless the context otherwise requires, other words or expressions contained in these articles bear the same meaning as in the Companies Act 2006 as in force on the date when these articles become binding on the company.

2 Liability of members

The liability of each member is limited to £1, being the amount that each member undertakes to contribute to the assets of the company in the event of its being wound up while he is a member or within one year after he ceases to be a member, for—

(a) payment of the company's debts and liabilities contracted before he ceases to be a member,
(b) payment of the costs, charges and expenses of winding up, and
(c) adjustment of the rights of the contributories among themselves.

PART 2 DIRECTORS

Directors' Powers and Responsibilities

3 Directors' general authority

Subject to the articles, the directors are responsible for the management of the company's business, for which purpose they may exercise all the powers of the company.

4 Members' reserve power

(1) The members may, by special resolution, direct the directors to take, or refrain from taking, specified action.

(2) No such special resolution invalidates anything which the directors have done before the passing of the resolution.

5 Directors may delegate

(1) Subject to the articles, the directors may delegate any of the powers which are conferred on them under the articles—

(a) to such person or committee;
(b) by such means (including by power of attorney);
(c) to such an extent;
(d) in relation to such matters or territories; and
(e) on such terms and conditions;

as they think fit.

(2) If the directors so specify, any such delegation may authorise further delegation of the directors' powers by any person to whom they are delegated.

(3) The directors may revoke any delegation in whole or part, or alter its terms and conditions.

6 Committees

(1) Committees to which the directors delegate any of their powers must follow procedures which are based as far as they are applicable on those provisions of the articles which govern the taking of decisions by directors.

(2) The directors may make rules of procedure for all or any committees, which prevail over rules derived from the articles if they are not consistent with them.

Decision-Making by Directors

7 Directors to take decisions collectively

(1) The general rule about decision-making by directors is that any decision of the directors must be either a majority decision at a meeting or a decision taken in accordance with article 8.

(2) If—

(a) the company only has one director, and
(b) no provision of the articles requires it to have more than one director,

the general rule does not apply, and the director may take decisions without regard to any of the provisions of the articles relating to directors' decision-making.

8 Unanimous decisions

(1) A decision of the directors is taken in accordance with this article when all eligible directors indicate to each other by any means that they share a common view on a matter.

(2) Such a decision may take the form of a resolution in writing, copies of which have been signed by each eligible director or to which each eligible director has otherwise indicated agreement in writing.

(3) References in this article to eligible directors are to directors who would have been entitled to vote on the matter had it been proposed as a resolution at a directors' meeting.

(4) A decision may not be taken in accordance with this article if the eligible directors would not have formed a quorum at such a meeting.

9 Calling a directors' meeting

(1) Any director may call a directors' meeting by giving notice of the meeting to the directors or by authorising the company secretary (if any) to give such notice.

(2) Notice of any directors' meeting must indicate—

- (a) its proposed date and time;
- (b) where it is to take place; and
- (c) if it is anticipated that directors participating in the meeting will not be in the same place, how it is proposed that they should communicate with each other during the meeting.

(3) Notice of a directors' meeting must be given to each director, but need not be in writing.

(4) Notice of a directors' meeting need not be given to directors who waive their entitlement to notice of that meeting, by giving notice to that effect to the company not more than 7 days after the date on which the meeting is held. Where such notice is given after the meeting has been held, that does not affect the validity of the meeting, or of any business conducted at it.

10 Participation in directors' meetings

(1) Subject to the articles, directors participate in a directors' meeting, or part of a directors' meeting, when—

- (a) the meeting has been called and takes place in accordance with the articles, and
- (b) they can each communicate to the others any information or opinions they have on any particular item of the business of the meeting.

(2) In determining whether directors are participating in a directors' meeting, it is irrelevant where any director is or how they communicate with each other.

(3) If all the directors participating in a meeting are not in the same place, they may decide that the meeting is to be treated as taking place wherever any of them is.

11 Quorum for directors' meetings

(1) At a directors' meeting, unless a quorum is participating, no proposal is to be voted on, except a proposal to call another meeting.

(2) The quorum for directors' meetings may be fixed from time to time by a decision of the directors, but it must never be less than two, and unless otherwise fixed it is two.

(3) If the total number of directors for the time being is less than the quorum required, the directors must not take any decision other than a decision—

- (a) to appoint further directors, or
- (b) to call a general meeting so as to enable the members to appoint further directors.

12 Chairing of directors' meetings

(1) The directors may appoint a director to chair their meetings.

(2) The person so appointed for the time being is known as the chairman.

(3) The directors may terminate the chairman's appointment at any time.

(4) If the chairman is not participating in a directors' meeting within ten minutes of the time at which it was to start, the participating directors must appoint one of themselves to chair it.

13 Casting vote

(1) If the numbers of votes for and against a proposal are equal, the chairman or other director chairing the meeting has a casting vote.

(2) But this does not apply if, in accordance with the articles, the chairman or other director is not to be counted as participating in the decision-making process for quorum or voting purposes.

14 Conflicts of interest

(1) If a proposed decision of the directors is concerned with an actual or proposed transaction or arrangement with the company in which a director is interested, that director is not to be counted as participating in the decision-making process for quorum or voting purposes.

(2) But if paragraph (3) applies, a director who is interested in an actual or proposed transaction or arrangement with the company is to be counted as participating in the decision-making process for quorum and voting purposes.

(3) This paragraph applies when—

- (a) the company by ordinary resolution disapplies the provision of the articles which would otherwise prevent a director from being counted as participating in the decision-making process;
- (b) the director's interest cannot reasonably be regarded as likely to give rise to a conflict of interest; or
- (c) the director's conflict of interest arises from a permitted cause.

(4) For the purposes of this article, the following are permitted causes—

- (a) a guarantee given, or to be given, by or to a director in respect of an obligation incurred by or on behalf of the company or any of its subsidiaries;

(b) subscription, or an agreement to subscribe, for securities of the company or any of its subsidiaries, or to underwrite, sub-underwrite, or guarantee subscription for any such securities; and

(c) arrangements pursuant to which benefits are made available to employees and directors or former employees and directors of the company or any of its subsidiaries which do not provide special benefits for directors or former directors.

(5) For the purposes of this article, references to proposed decisions and decision-making processes include any directors' meeting or part of a directors' meeting.

(6) Subject to paragraph (7), if a question arises at a meeting of directors or of a committee of directors as to the right of a director to participate in the meeting (or part of the meeting) for voting or quorum purposes, the question may, before the conclusion of the meeting, be referred to the chairman whose ruling in relation to any director other than the chairman is to be final and conclusive.

(7) If any question as to the right to participate in the meeting (or part of the meeting) should arise in respect of the chairman, the question is to be decided by a decision of the directors at that meeting, for which purpose the chairman is not to be counted as participating in the meeting (or that part of the meeting) for voting or quorum purposes.

15 Records of decisions to be kept

The directors must ensure that the company keeps a record, in writing, for at least 10 years from the date of the decision recorded, of every unanimous or majority decision taken by the directors.

16 Directors' discretion to make further rules

Subject to the articles, the directors may make any rule which they think fit about how they take decisions, and about how such rules are to be recorded or communicated to directors.

Appointment of Directors

17 Methods of appointing directors

(1) Any person who is willing to act as a director, and is permitted by law to do so, may be appointed to be a director—

(a) by ordinary resolution, or

(b) by a decision of the directors.

(2) In any case where, as a result of death, the company has no members and no directors, the personal representatives of the last member to have died have the right, by notice in writing, to appoint a person to be a director.

(3) For the purposes of paragraph (2), where 2 or more members die in circumstances rendering it uncertain who was the last to die, a younger member is deemed to have survived an older member.

18 Termination of director's appointment

A person ceases to be a director as soon as—

(a) that person ceases to be a director by virtue of any provision of the Companies Act 2006 or is prohibited from being a director by law;

(b) a bankruptcy order is made against that person;

(c) a composition is made with that person's creditors generally in satisfaction of that person's debts;

(d) a registered medical practitioner who is treating that person gives a written opinion to the company stating that that person has become physically or mentally incapable of acting as a director and may remain so for more than three months;

(e) . . .

(f) notification is received by the company from the director that the director is resigning from office, and such resignation has taken effect in accordance with its terms.

NOTES

Para 18(e) was revoked by the Mental Health (Discrimination) Act 2013, s 3(1)(b), as from 28 April 2013.

19 Directors' remuneration

(1) Directors may undertake any services for the company that the directors decide.

(2) Directors are entitled to such remuneration as the directors determine—

(a) for their services to the company as directors, and

(b) for any other service which they undertake for the company.

(3) Subject to the articles, a director's remuneration may—

(a) take any form, and

(b) include any arrangements in connection with the payment of a pension, allowance or gratuity, or any death, sickness or disability benefits, to or in respect of that director.

(4) Unless the directors decide otherwise, directors' remuneration accrues from day to day.

(5) Unless the directors decide otherwise, directors are not accountable to the company for any remuneration which they receive as directors or other officers or employees of the company's subsidiaries or of any other body corporate in which the company is interested.

20 Directors' expenses

The company may pay any reasonable expenses which the directors properly incur in connection with their attendance at—

(a) meetings of directors or committees of directors,

(b) general meetings, or

(c) separate meetings of the holders of debentures of the company,

or otherwise in connection with the exercise of their powers and the discharge of their responsibilities in relation to the company.

PART 3 MEMBERS

Becoming and Ceasing to be a Member

21 Applications for membership

No person shall become a member of the company unless—

(a) that person has completed an application for membership in a form approved by the directors, and

(b) the directors have approved the application.

22 Termination of membership

(1) A member may withdraw from membership of the company by giving 7 days' notice to the company in writing.

(2) Membership is not transferable.

(3) A person's membership terminates when that person dies or ceases to exist.

Organisation of General Meetings

23 Attendance and speaking at general meetings

(1) A person is able to exercise the right to speak at a general meeting when that person is in a position to communicate to all those attending the meeting, during the meeting, any information or opinions which that person has on the business of the meeting.

(2) A person is able to exercise the right to vote at a general meeting when—

(a) that person is able to vote, during the meeting, on resolutions put to the vote at the meeting, and

(b) that person's vote can be taken into account in determining whether or not such resolutions are passed at the same time as the votes of all the other persons attending the meeting.

(3) The directors may make whatever arrangements they consider appropriate to enable those attending a general meeting to exercise their rights to speak or vote at it.

(4) In determining attendance at a general meeting, it is immaterial whether any two or more members attending it are in the same place as each other.

(5) Two or more persons who are not in the same place as each other attend a general meeting if their circumstances are such that if they have (or were to have) rights to speak and vote at that meeting, they are (or would be) able to exercise them.

24 Quorum for general meetings

No business other than the appointment of the chairman of the meeting is to be transacted at a general meeting if the persons attending it do not constitute a quorum.

25 Chairing general meetings

(1) If the directors have appointed a chairman, the chairman shall chair general meetings if present and willing to do so.

(2) If the directors have not appointed a chairman, or if the chairman is unwilling to chair the meeting or is not present within ten minutes of the time at which a meeting was due to start—

(a) the directors present, or

(b) (if no directors are present), the meeting,

must appoint a director or member to chair the meeting, and the appointment of the chairman of the meeting must be the first business of the meeting.

(3) The person chairing a meeting in accordance with this article is referred to as "the chairman of the meeting".

26 Attendance and speaking by directors and non-members

(1) Directors may attend and speak at general meetings, whether or not they are members.

(2) The chairman of the meeting may permit other persons who are not members of the company to attend and speak at a general meeting.

27 Adjournment

(1) If the persons attending a general meeting within half an hour of the time at which the meeting was due to start do not constitute a quorum, or if during a meeting a quorum ceases to be present, the chairman of the meeting must adjourn it.

(2) The chairman of the meeting may adjourn a general meeting at which a quorum is present if—

(a) the meeting consents to an adjournment, or

(b) it appears to the chairman of the meeting that an adjournment is necessary to protect the safety of any person attending the meeting or ensure that the business of the meeting is conducted in an orderly manner.

(3) The chairman of the meeting must adjourn a general meeting if directed to do so by the meeting.

(4) When adjourning a general meeting, the chairman of the meeting must—

(a) either specify the time and place to which it is adjourned or state that it is to continue at a time and place to be fixed by the directors, and

(b) have regard to any directions as to the time and place of any adjournment which have been given by the meeting.

(5) If the continuation of an adjourned meeting is to take place more than 14 days after it was adjourned, the company must give at least 7 clear days' notice of it (that is, excluding the day of the adjourned meeting and the day on which the notice is given)—

(a) to the same persons to whom notice of the company's general meetings is required to be given, and

(b) containing the same information which such notice is required to contain.

(6) No business may be transacted at an adjourned general meeting which could not properly have been transacted at the meeting if the adjournment had not taken place.

Voting at General Meetings

28 Voting: general

A resolution put to the vote of a general meeting must be decided on a show of hands unless a poll is duly demanded in accordance with the articles.

29 Errors and disputes

(1) No objection may be raised to the qualification of any person voting at a general meeting except at the meeting or adjourned meeting at which the vote objected to is tendered, and every vote not disallowed at the meeting is valid.

(2) Any such objection must be referred to the chairman of the meeting whose decision is final.

30 Poll votes

(1) A poll on a resolution may be demanded—

(a) in advance of the general meeting where it is to be put to the vote, or

(b) at a general meeting, either before a show of hands on that resolution or immediately after the result of a show of hands on that resolution is declared.

(2) A poll may be demanded by—

(a) the chairman of the meeting;

(b) the directors;

(c) two or more persons having the right to vote on the resolution; or

(d) a person or persons representing not less than one tenth of the total voting rights of all the members having the right to vote on the resolution.

(3) A demand for a poll may be withdrawn if—

(a) the poll has not yet been taken, and

(b) the chairman of the meeting consents to the withdrawal.

(4) Polls must be taken immediately and in such manner as the chairman of the meeting directs.

31 Content of proxy notices

(1) Proxies may only validly be appointed by a notice in writing (a "proxy notice") which—

(a) states the name and address of the member appointing the proxy;

(b) identifies the person appointed to be that member's proxy and the general meeting in relation to which that person is appointed;

(c) is signed by or on behalf of the member appointing the proxy, or is authenticated in such manner as the directors may determine; and

(d) is delivered to the company in accordance with the articles and any instructions contained in the notice of the general meeting to which they relate.

(2) The company may require proxy notices to be delivered in a particular form, and may specify different forms for different purposes.

(3) Proxy notices may specify how the proxy appointed under them is to vote (or that the proxy is to abstain from voting) on one or more resolutions.

(4) Unless a proxy notice indicates otherwise, it must be treated as—

(a) allowing the person appointed under it as a proxy discretion as to how to vote on any ancillary or procedural resolutions put to the meeting, and

(b) appointing that person as a proxy in relation to any adjournment of the general meeting to which it relates as well as the meeting itself.

32 Delivery of proxy notices

(1) A person who is entitled to attend, speak or vote (either on a show of hands or on a poll) at a general meeting remains so entitled in respect of that meeting or any adjournment of it, even though a valid proxy notice has been delivered to the company by or on behalf of that person.

(2) An appointment under a proxy notice may be revoked by delivering to the company a notice in writing given by or on behalf of the person by whom or on whose behalf the proxy notice was given.

(3) A notice revoking a proxy appointment only takes effect if it is delivered before the start of the meeting or adjourned meeting to which it relates.

(4) If a proxy notice is not executed by the person appointing the proxy, it must be accompanied by written evidence of the authority of the person who executed it to execute it on the appointor's behalf.

33 Amendments to resolutions

(1) An ordinary resolution to be proposed at a general meeting may be amended by ordinary resolution if—

(a) notice of the proposed amendment is given to the company in writing by a person entitled to vote at the general meeting at which it is to be proposed not less than 48 hours before the meeting is to take place (or such later time as the chairman of the meeting may determine), and

(b) the proposed amendment does not, in the reasonable opinion of the chairman of the meeting, materially alter the scope of the resolution.

(2) A special resolution to be proposed at a general meeting may be amended by ordinary resolution, if—

(a) the chairman of the meeting proposes the amendment at the general meeting at which the resolution is to be proposed, and

(b) the amendment does not go beyond what is necessary to correct a grammatical or other non-substantive error in the resolution.

(3) If the chairman of the meeting, acting in good faith, wrongly decides that an amendment to a resolution is out of order, the chairman's error does not invalidate the vote on that resolution.

PART 4 ADMINISTRATIVE ARRANGEMENTS

34 Means of communication to be used

(1) Subject to the articles, anything sent or supplied by or to the company under the articles may be sent or supplied in any way in which the Companies Act 2006 provides for documents or information which are authorised or required by any provision of that Act to be sent or supplied by or to the company.

(2) Subject to the articles, any notice or document to be sent or supplied to a director in connection with the taking of decisions by directors may also be sent or supplied by the means by which that director has asked to be sent or supplied with such notices or documents for the time being.

(3) A director may agree with the company that notices or documents sent to that director in a particular way are to be deemed to have been received within a specified time of their being sent, and for the specified time to be less than 48 hours.

35 Company seals

(1) Any common seal may only be used by the authority of the directors.

(2) The directors may decide by what means and in what form any common seal is to be used.

(3) Unless otherwise decided by the directors, if the company has a common seal and it is affixed to a document, the document must also be signed by at least one authorised person in the presence of a witness who attests the signature.

(4) For the purposes of this article, an authorised person is—

(a) any director of the company;

(b) the company secretary (if any); or

(c) any person authorised by the directors for the purpose of signing documents to which the common seal is applied.

36 No right to inspect accounts and other records

Except as provided by law or authorised by the directors or an ordinary resolution of the company, no person is entitled to inspect any of the company's accounting or other records or documents merely by virtue of being a member.

37 Provision for employees on cessation of business

The directors may decide to make provision for the benefit of persons employed or formerly employed by the company or any of its subsidiaries (other than a director or former director or shadow director) in connection with the cessation or transfer to any person of the whole or part of the undertaking of the company or that subsidiary.

Directors' Indemnity and Insurance

38 Indemnity

(1) Subject to paragraph (2), a relevant director of the company or an associated company may be indemnified out of the company's assets against—

(a) any liability incurred by that director in connection with any negligence, default, breach of duty or breach of trust in relation to the company or an associated company,

(b) any liability incurred by that director in connection with the activities of the company or an associated company in its capacity as a trustee of an occupational pension scheme (as defined in section 235(6) of the Companies Act 2006),

(c) any other liability incurred by that director as an officer of the company or an associated company.

(2) This article does not authorise any indemnity which would be prohibited or rendered void by any provision of the Companies Acts or by any other provision of law.

(3) In this article—

(a) companies are associated if one is a subsidiary of the other or both are subsidiaries of the same body corporate, and

(b) a "relevant director" means any director or former director of the company or an associated company.

39 Insurance

(1) The directors may decide to purchase and maintain insurance, at the expense of the company, for the benefit of any relevant director in respect of any relevant loss.

(2) In this article—

(a) a "relevant director" means any director or former director of the company or an associated company,

(b) a "relevant loss" means any loss or liability which has been or may be incurred by a relevant director in connection with that director's duties or powers in relation to the company, any associated company or any pension fund or employees' share scheme of the company or associated company, and

(c) companies are associated if one is a subsidiary of the other or both are subsidiaries of the same body corporate.

MODEL ARTICLES FOR PUBLIC COMPANIES

[A1.3]

NOTES

These are set out in Schedule 3 to the Companies (Model Articles) Regulations 2008.

These Articles are reproduced as amended by: the Mental Health (Discrimination) Act 2013.

As to the effect of amendments to these Model Articles, see further the introductory notes to Appendix 1 *ante*.

INDEX TO THE ARTICLES

PART 1 INTERPRETATION AND LIMITATION OF LIABILITY

PART 2 DIRECTORS

Directors' Powers and Responsibilities

Decision-Making by Directors

Appointment of Directors

Alternate Directors

PART 3 DECISION-MAKING BY MEMBERS

Organisation of General Meetings

Voting at General Meetings

Restrictions on Member Rights

Application of Rules to Class Meetings

PART 4 SHARES AND DISTRIBUTIONS

PART 5 MISCELLANEOUS PROVISIONS

PART 1 INTERPRETATION AND LIMITATION OF LIABILITY

1 Defined terms

In the articles, unless the context requires otherwise—

"alternate" or "alternate director" has the meaning given in article 25;
"appointor" has the meaning given in article 25;
"articles" means the company's articles of association;
"bankruptcy" includes individual insolvency proceedings in a jurisdiction other than England and Wales or Northern Ireland which have an effect similar to that of bankruptcy;
"call" has the meaning given in article 54;
"call notice" has the meaning given in article 54;
"certificate" means a paper certificate (other than a share warrant) evidencing a person's title to specified shares or other securities;
"certificated" in relation to a share, means that it is not an uncertificated share or a share in respect of which a share warrant has been issued and is current;
"chairman" has the meaning given in article 12;
"chairman of the meeting" has the meaning given in article 31;
"Companies Acts" means the Companies Acts (as defined in section 2 of the Companies Act 2006), in so far as they apply to the company;
"company's lien" has the meaning given in article 52;
"director" means a director of the company, and includes any person occupying the position of director, by whatever name called;
"distribution recipient" has the meaning given in article 72;
"document" includes, unless otherwise specified, any document sent or supplied in electronic form;
"electronic form" has the meaning given in section 1168 of the Companies Act 2006;
"fully paid" in relation to a share, means that the nominal value and any premium to be paid to the company in respect of that share have been paid to the company;
"hard copy form" has the meaning given in section 1168 of the Companies Act 2006;
"holder" in relation to shares means the person whose name is entered in the register of members as the holder of the shares, or, in the case of a share in respect of which a share warrant has been issued (and not cancelled), the person in possession of that warrant;
"instrument" means a document in hard copy form;
"lien enforcement notice" has the meaning given in article 53;
"member" has the meaning given in section 112 of the Companies Act 2006;
"ordinary resolution" has the meaning given in section 282 of the Companies Act 2006;
"paid" means paid or credited as paid;
"participate", in relation to a directors' meeting, has the meaning given in article 9;
"partly paid" in relation to a share means that part of that share's nominal value or any premium at which it was issued has not been paid to the company;
"proxy notice" has the meaning given in article 38;
"securities seal" has the meaning given in article 47;
"shares" means shares in the company;
"special resolution" has the meaning given in section 283 of the Companies Act 2006;
"subsidiary" has the meaning given in section 1159 of the Companies Act 2006;
"transmittee" means a person entitled to a share by reason of the death or bankruptcy of a shareholder or otherwise by operation of law;
"uncertificated" in relation to a share means that, by virtue of legislation (other than section 778 of the Companies Act 2006) permitting title to shares to be evidenced and transferred without a certificate, title to that share is evidenced and may be transferred without a certificate; and
"writing" means the representation or reproduction of words, symbols or other information in a visible form by any method or combination of methods, whether sent or supplied in electronic form or otherwise.

Unless the context otherwise requires, other words or expressions contained in these articles bear the same meaning as in the Companies Act 2006 as in force on the date when these articles become binding on the company.

2 Liability of members

The liability of the members is limited to the amount, if any, unpaid on the shares held by them.

PART 2 DIRECTORS

Directors' Powers and Responsibilities

3 Directors' general authority

Subject to the articles, the directors are responsible for the management of the company's business, for which purpose they may exercise all the powers of the company.

4 Members' reserve power

(1) The members may, by special resolution, direct the directors to take, or refrain from taking, specified action.

(2) No such special resolution invalidates anything which the directors have done before the passing of the resolution.

5 Directors may delegate

(1) Subject to the articles, the directors may delegate any of the powers which are conferred on them under the articles—

(a) to such person or committee;
(b) by such means (including by power of attorney);
(c) to such an extent;

(d) in relation to such matters or territories; and
(e) on such terms and conditions;

as they think fit.

(2) If the directors so specify, any such delegation may authorise further delegation of the directors' powers by any person to whom they are delegated.

(3) The directors may revoke any delegation in whole or part, or alter its terms and conditions.

6 Committees

(1) Committees to which the directors delegate any of their powers must follow procedures which are based as far as they are applicable on those provisions of the articles which govern the taking of decisions by directors.

(2) The directors may make rules of procedure for all or any committees, which prevail over rules derived from the articles if they are not consistent with them.

Decision-Making by Directors

7 Directors to take decisions collectively

Decisions of the directors may be taken—

(a) at a directors' meeting, or
(b) in the form of a directors' written resolution.

8 Calling a directors' meeting

(1) Any director may call a directors' meeting.

(2) The company secretary must call a directors' meeting if a director so requests.

(3) A directors' meeting is called by giving notice of the meeting to the directors.

(4) Notice of any directors' meeting must indicate—

(a) its proposed date and time;
(b) where it is to take place; and
(c) if it is anticipated that directors participating in the meeting will not be in the same place, how it is proposed that they should communicate with each other during the meeting.

(5) Notice of a directors' meeting must be given to each director, but need not be in writing.

(6) Notice of a directors' meeting need not be given to directors who waive their entitlement to notice of that meeting, by giving notice to that effect to the company not more than 7 days after the date on which the meeting is held. Where such notice is given after the meeting has been held, that does not affect the validity of the meeting, or of any business conducted at it.

9 Participation in directors' meetings

(1) Subject to the articles, directors participate in a directors' meeting, or part of a directors' meeting, when—

(a) the meeting has been called and takes place in accordance with the articles, and
(b) they can each communicate to the others any information or opinions they have on any particular item of the business of the meeting.

(2) In determining whether directors are participating in a directors' meeting, it is irrelevant where any director is or how they communicate with each other.

(3) If all the directors participating in a meeting are not in the same place, they may decide that the meeting is to be treated as taking place wherever any of them is.

10 Quorum for directors' meetings

(1) At a directors' meeting, unless a quorum is participating, no proposal is to be voted on, except a proposal to call another meeting.

(2) The quorum for directors' meetings may be fixed from time to time by a decision of the directors, but it must never be less than two, and unless otherwise fixed it is two.

11 Meetings where total number of directors less than quorum

(1) This article applies where the total number of directors for the time being is less than the quorum for directors' meetings.

(2) If there is only one director, that director may appoint sufficient directors to make up a quorum or call a general meeting to do so.

(3) If there is more than one director—

(a) a directors' meeting may take place, if it is called in accordance with the articles and at least two directors participate in it, with a view to appointing sufficient directors to make up a quorum or calling a general meeting to do so, and
(b) if a directors' meeting is called but only one director attends at the appointed date and time to participate in it, that director may appoint sufficient directors to make up a quorum or call a general meeting to do so.

12 Chairing directors' meetings

(1) The directors may appoint a director to chair their meetings.

(2) The person so appointed for the time being is known as the chairman.

(3) The directors may appoint other directors as deputy or assistant chairmen to chair directors' meetings in the chairman's absence.

(4) The directors may terminate the appointment of the chairman, deputy or assistant chairman at any time.

(5) If neither the chairman nor any director appointed generally to chair directors' meetings in the chairman's absence is participating in a meeting within ten minutes of the time at which it was to start, the participating directors must appoint one of themselves to chair it.

13 Voting at directors' meetings: general rules

(1) Subject to the articles, a decision is taken at a directors' meeting by a majority of the votes of the participating directors.

(2) Subject to the articles, each director participating in a directors' meeting has one vote.

(3) Subject to the articles, if a director has an interest in an actual or proposed transaction or arrangement with the company—

(a) that director and that director's alternate may not vote on any proposal relating to it, but

(b) this does not preclude the alternate from voting in relation to that transaction or arrangement on behalf of another appointor who does not have such an interest.

14 Chairman's casting vote at directors' meetings

(1) If the numbers of votes for and against a proposal are equal, the chairman or other director chairing the meeting has a casting vote.

(2) But this does not apply if, in accordance with the articles, the chairman or other director is not to be counted as participating in the decision-making process for quorum or voting purposes.

15 Alternates voting at directors' meetings

A director who is also an alternate director has an additional vote on behalf of each appointor who is—

(a) not participating in a directors' meeting, and

(b) would have been entitled to vote if they were participating in it.

16 Conflicts of interest

(1) If a directors' meeting, or part of a directors' meeting, is concerned with an actual or proposed transaction or arrangement with the company in which a director is interested, that director is not to be counted as participating in that meeting, or part of a meeting, for quorum or voting purposes.

(2) But if paragraph (3) applies, a director who is interested in an actual or proposed transaction or arrangement with the company is to be counted as participating in a decision at a directors' meeting, or part of a directors' meeting, relating to it for quorum and voting purposes.

(3) This paragraph applies when—

(a) the company by ordinary resolution disapplies the provision of the articles which would otherwise prevent a director from being counted as participating in, or voting at, a directors' meeting;

(b) the director's interest cannot reasonably be regarded as likely to give rise to a conflict of interest; or

(c) the director's conflict of interest arises from a permitted cause.

(4) For the purposes of this article, the following are permitted causes—

(a) a guarantee given, or to be given, by or to a director in respect of an obligation incurred by or on behalf of the company or any of its subsidiaries;

(b) subscription, or an agreement to subscribe, for shares or other securities of the company or any of its subsidiaries, or to underwrite, sub-underwrite, or guarantee subscription for any such shares or securities; and

(c) arrangements pursuant to which benefits are made available to employees and directors or former employees and directors of the company or any of its subsidiaries which do not provide special benefits for directors or former directors.

(5) Subject to paragraph (6), if a question arises at a meeting of directors or of a committee of directors as to the right of a director to participate in the meeting (or part of the meeting) for voting or quorum purposes, the question may, before the conclusion of the meeting, be referred to the chairman whose ruling in relation to any director other than the chairman is to be final and conclusive.

(6) If any question as to the right to participate in the meeting (or part of the meeting) should arise in respect of the chairman, the question is to be decided by a decision of the directors at that meeting, for which purpose the chairman is not to be counted as participating in the meeting (or that part of the meeting) for voting or quorum purposes.

17 Proposing directors' written resolutions

(1) Any director may propose a directors' written resolution.

(2) The company secretary must propose a directors' written resolution if a director so requests.

(3) A directors' written resolution is proposed by giving notice of the proposed resolution to the directors.

(4) Notice of a proposed directors' written resolution must indicate—

(a) the proposed resolution, and

(b) the time by which it is proposed that the directors should adopt it.

(5) Notice of a proposed directors' written resolution must be given in writing to each director.

(6) Any decision which a person giving notice of a proposed directors' written resolution takes regarding the process of adopting that resolution must be taken reasonably in good faith.

18 Adoption of directors' written resolutions

(1) A proposed directors' written resolution is adopted when all the directors who would have been entitled to vote on the resolution at a directors' meeting have signed one or more copies of it, provided that those directors would have formed a quorum at such a meeting.

(2) It is immaterial whether any director signs the resolution before or after the time by which the notice proposed that it should be adopted.

(3) Once a directors' written resolution has been adopted, it must be treated as if it had been a decision taken at a directors' meeting in accordance with the articles.

(4) The company secretary must ensure that the company keeps a record, in writing, of all directors' written resolutions for at least ten years from the date of their adoption.

19 Directors' discretion to make further rules

Subject to the articles, the directors may make any rule which they think fit about how they take decisions, and about how such rules are to be recorded or communicated to directors.

Appointment of Directors

20 Methods of appointing directors

Any person who is willing to act as a director, and is permitted by law to do so, may be appointed to be a director—

(a) by ordinary resolution, or

(b) by a decision of the directors.

21 Retirement of directors by rotation

(1) At the first annual general meeting all the directors must retire from office.

(2) At every subsequent annual general meeting any directors—

(a) who have been appointed by the directors since the last annual general meeting, or

(b) who were not appointed or reappointed at one of the preceding two annual general meetings,

must retire from office and may offer themselves for reappointment by the members.

22 Termination of director's appointment

A person ceases to be a director as soon as—

(a) that person ceases to be a director by virtue of any provision of the Companies Act 2006 or is prohibited from being a director by law;

(b) a bankruptcy order is made against that person;

(c) a composition is made with that person's creditors generally in satisfaction of that person's debts;

(d) a registered medical practitioner who is treating that person gives a written opinion to the company stating that that person has become physically or mentally incapable of acting as a director and may remain so for more than three months;

(e) . . .

(f) notification is received by the company from the director that the director is resigning from office as director, and such resignation has taken effect in accordance with its terms.

NOTES

Para 22(e) was revoked by the Mental Health (Discrimination) Act 2013, s 3(1)(c), as from 28 April 2013.

23 Directors' remuneration

(1) Directors may undertake any services for the company that the directors decide.

(2) Directors are entitled to such remuneration as the directors determine—

(a) for their services to the company as directors, and

(b) for any other service which they undertake for the company.

(3) Subject to the articles, a director's remuneration may—

(a) take any form, and

(b) include any arrangements in connection with the payment of a pension, allowance or gratuity, or any death, sickness or disability benefits, to or in respect of that director.

(4) Unless the directors decide otherwise, directors' remuneration accrues from day to day.

(5) Unless the directors decide otherwise, directors are not accountable to the company for any remuneration which they receive as directors or other officers or employees of the company's subsidiaries or of any other body corporate in which the company is interested.

24 Directors' expenses

The company may pay any reasonable expenses which the directors properly incur in connection with their attendance at—

(a) meetings of directors or committees of directors,

(b) general meetings, or

(c) separate meetings of the holders of any class of shares or of debentures of the company,

or otherwise in connection with the exercise of their powers and the discharge of their responsibilities in relation to the company.

Alternate Directors

25 Appointment and removal of alternates

(1) Any director (the "appointor") may appoint as an alternate any other director, or any other person approved by resolution of the directors, to—

(a) exercise that director's powers, and

(b) carry out that director's responsibilities,

in relation to the taking of decisions by the directors in the absence of the alternate's appointor.

(2) Any appointment or removal of an alternate must be effected by notice in writing to the company signed by the appointor, or in any other manner approved by the directors.

(3) The notice must—

(a) identify the proposed alternate, and

(b) in the case of a notice of appointment, contain a statement signed by the proposed alternate that the proposed alternate is willing to act as the alternate of the director giving the notice.

26 Rights and responsibilities of alternate directors

(1) An alternate director has the same rights, in relation to any directors' meeting or directors' written resolution, as the alternate's appointor.

(2) Except as the articles specify otherwise, alternate directors—

(a) are deemed for all purposes to be directors;
(b) are liable for their own acts and omissions;
(c) are subject to the same restrictions as their appointors; and
(d) are not deemed to be agents of or for their appointors.

(3) A person who is an alternate director but not a director—
(a) may be counted as participating for the purposes of determining whether a quorum is participating (but only if that person's appointor is not participating), and
(b) may sign a written resolution (but only if it is not signed or to be signed by that person's appointor).

No alternate may be counted as more than one director for such purposes.

(4) An alternate director is not entitled to receive any remuneration from the company for serving as an alternate director except such part of the alternate's appointor's remuneration as the appointor may direct by notice in writing made to the company.

27 Termination of alternate directorship

An alternate director's appointment as an alternate terminates—
(a) when the alternate's appointor revokes the appointment by notice to the company in writing specifying when it is to terminate;
(b) on the occurrence in relation to the alternate of any event which, if it occurred in relation to the alternate's appointor, would result in the termination of the appointor's appointment as a director;
(c) on the death of the alternate's appointor; or
(d) when the alternate's appointor's appointment as a director terminates, except that an alternate's appointment as an alternate does not terminate when the appointor retires by rotation at a general meeting and is then re-appointed as a director at the same general meeting.

PART 3 DECISION-MAKING BY MEMBERS

Organisation of General Meetings

28 Members can call general meeting if not enough directors

If—
(a) the company has fewer than two directors, and
(b) the director (if any) is unable or unwilling to appoint sufficient directors to make up a quorum or to call a general meeting to do so,

then two or more members may call a general meeting (or instruct the company secretary to do so) for the purpose of appointing one or more directors.

29 Attendance and speaking at general meetings

(1) A person is able to exercise the right to speak at a general meeting when that person is in a position to communicate to all those attending the meeting, during the meeting, any information or opinions which that person has on the business of the meeting.

(2) A person is able to exercise the right to vote at a general meeting when—
(a) that person is able to vote, during the meeting, on resolutions put to the vote at the meeting, and
(b) that person's vote can be taken into account in determining whether or not such resolutions are passed at the same time as the votes of all the other persons attending the meeting.

(3) The directors may make whatever arrangements they consider appropriate to enable those attending a general meeting to exercise their rights to speak or vote at it.

(4) In determining attendance at a general meeting, it is immaterial whether any two or more members attending it are in the same place as each other.

(5) Two or more persons who are not in the same place as each other attend a general meeting if their circumstances are such that if they have (or were to have) rights to speak and vote at that meeting, they are (or would be) able to exercise them.

30 Quorum for general meetings

No business other than the appointment of the chairman of the meeting is to be transacted at a general meeting if the persons attending it do not constitute a quorum.

31 Chairing general meetings

(1) If the directors have appointed a chairman, the chairman shall chair general meetings if present and willing to do so.

(2) If the directors have not appointed a chairman, or if the chairman is unwilling to chair the meeting or is not present within ten minutes of the time at which a meeting was due to start—
(a) the directors present, or
(b) (if no directors are present), the meeting,

must appoint a director or member to chair the meeting, and the appointment of the chairman of the meeting must be the first business of the meeting.

(3) The person chairing a meeting in accordance with this article is referred to as "the chairman of the meeting".

32 Attendance and speaking by directors and non-members

(1) Directors may attend and speak at general meetings, whether or not they are members.

(2) The chairman of the meeting may permit other persons who are not—
(a) members of the company, or
(b) otherwise entitled to exercise the rights of members in relation to general meetings,

to attend and speak at a general meeting.

33 Adjournment

(1) If the persons attending a general meeting within half an hour of the time at which the meeting was due to start do not constitute a quorum, or if during a meeting a quorum ceases to be present, the chairman of the meeting must adjourn it.

(2) The chairman of the meeting may adjourn a general meeting at which a quorum is present if—

(a) the meeting consents to an adjournment, or

(b) it appears to the chairman of the meeting that an adjournment is necessary to protect the safety of any person attending the meeting or ensure that the business of the meeting is conducted in an orderly manner.

(3) The chairman of the meeting must adjourn a general meeting if directed to do so by the meeting.

(4) When adjourning a general meeting, the chairman of the meeting must—

(a) either specify the time and place to which it is adjourned or state that it is to continue at a time and place to be fixed by the directors, and

(b) have regard to any directions as to the time and place of any adjournment which have been given by the meeting.

(5) If the continuation of an adjourned meeting is to take place more than 14 days after it was adjourned, the company must give at least 7 clear days' notice of it (that is, excluding the day of the adjourned meeting and the day on which the notice is given)—

(a) to the same persons to whom notice of the company's general meetings is required to be given, and

(b) containing the same information which such notice is required to contain.

(6) No business may be transacted at an adjourned general meeting which could not properly have been transacted at the meeting if the adjournment had not taken place.

Voting at General Meetings

34 Voting: general

A resolution put to the vote of a general meeting must be decided on a show of hands unless a poll is duly demanded in accordance with the articles.

35 Errors and disputes

(1) No objection may be raised to the qualification of any person voting at a general meeting except at the meeting or adjourned meeting at which the vote objected to is tendered, and every vote not disallowed at the meeting is valid.

(2) Any such objection must be referred to the chairman of the meeting whose decision is final.

36 Demanding a poll

(1) A poll on a resolution may be demanded—

(a) in advance of the general meeting where it is to be put to the vote, or

(b) at a general meeting, either before a show of hands on that resolution or immediately after the result of a show of hands on that resolution is declared.

(2) A poll may be demanded by—

(a) the chairman of the meeting;

(b) the directors;

(c) two or more persons having the right to vote on the resolution; or

(d) a person or persons representing not less than one tenth of the total voting rights of all the members having the right to vote on the resolution.

(3) A demand for a poll may be withdrawn if—

(a) the poll has not yet been taken, and

(b) the chairman of the meeting consents to the withdrawal.

37 Procedure on a poll

(1) Subject to the articles, polls at general meetings must be taken when, where and in such manner as the chairman of the meeting directs.

(2) The chairman of the meeting may appoint scrutineers (who need not be members) and decide how and when the result of the poll is to be declared.

(3) The result of a poll shall be the decision of the meeting in respect of the resolution on which the poll was demanded.

(4) A poll on—

(a) the election of the chairman of the meeting, or

(b) a question of adjournment,

must be taken immediately.

(5) Other polls must be taken within 30 days of their being demanded.

(6) A demand for a poll does not prevent a general meeting from continuing, except as regards the question on which the poll was demanded.

(7) No notice need be given of a poll not taken immediately if the time and place at which it is to be taken are announced at the meeting at which it is demanded.

(8) In any other case, at least 7 days' notice must be given specifying the time and place at which the poll is to be taken.

38 Content of proxy notices

(1) Proxies may only validly be appointed by a notice in writing (a "proxy notice") which—

(a) states the name and address of the member appointing the proxy;

(b) identifies the person appointed to be that member's proxy and the general meeting in relation to which that person is appointed;

(c) is signed by or on behalf of the member appointing the proxy, or is authenticated in such manner as the directors may determine; and
(d) is delivered to the company in accordance with the articles and any instructions contained in the notice of the general meeting to which they relate.

(2) The company may require proxy notices to be delivered in a particular form, and may specify different forms for different purposes.

(3) Proxy notices may specify how the proxy appointed under them is to vote (or that the proxy is to abstain from voting) on one or more resolutions.

(4) Unless a proxy notice indicates otherwise, it must be treated as—
(a) allowing the person appointed under it as a proxy discretion as to how to vote on any ancillary or procedural resolutions put to the meeting, and
(b) appointing that person as a proxy in relation to any adjournment of the general meeting to which it relates as well as the meeting itself.

39 Delivery of proxy notices

(1) Any notice of a general meeting must specify the address or addresses ("proxy notification address") at which the company or its agents will receive proxy notices relating to that meeting, or any adjournment of it, delivered in hard copy or electronic form.

(2) A person who is entitled to attend, speak or vote (either on a show of hands or on a poll) at a general meeting remains so entitled in respect of that meeting or any adjournment of it, even though a valid proxy notice has been delivered to the company by or on behalf of that person.

(3) Subject to paragraphs (4) and (5), a proxy notice must be delivered to a proxy notification address not less than 48 hours before the general meeting or adjourned meeting to which it relates.

(4) In the case of a poll taken more than 48 hours after it is demanded, the notice must be delivered to a proxy notification address not less than 24 hours before the time appointed for the taking of the poll.

(5) In the case of a poll not taken during the meeting but taken not more than 48 hours after it was demanded, the proxy notice must be delivered—
(a) in accordance with paragraph (3), or
(b) at the meeting at which the poll was demanded to the chairman, secretary or any director.

(6) An appointment under a proxy notice may be revoked by delivering a notice in writing given by or on behalf of the person by whom or on whose behalf the proxy notice was given to a proxy notification address.

(7) A notice revoking a proxy appointment only takes effect if it is delivered before—
(a) the start of the meeting or adjourned meeting to which it relates, or
(b) (in the case of a poll not taken on the same day as the meeting or adjourned meeting) the time appointed for taking the poll to which it relates.

(8) If a proxy notice is not signed by the person appointing the proxy, it must be accompanied by written evidence of the authority of the person who executed it to execute it on the appointor's behalf.

40 Amendments to resolutions

(1) An ordinary resolution to be proposed at a general meeting may be amended by ordinary resolution if—
(a) notice of the proposed amendment is given to the company secretary in writing by a person entitled to vote at the general meeting at which it is to be proposed not less than 48 hours before the meeting is to take place (or such later time as the chairman of the meeting may determine), and
(b) the proposed amendment does not, in the reasonable opinion of the chairman of the meeting, materially alter the scope of the resolution.

(2) A special resolution to be proposed at a general meeting may be amended by ordinary resolution, if—
(a) the chairman of the meeting proposes the amendment at the general meeting at which the resolution is to be proposed, and
(b) the amendment does not go beyond what is necessary to correct a grammatical or other non-substantive error in the resolution.

(3) If the chairman of the meeting, acting in good faith, wrongly decides that an amendment to a resolution is out of order, the chairman's error does not invalidate the vote on that resolution.

Restrictions on Members' Rights

41 No voting of shares on which money owed to company

No voting rights attached to a share may be exercised at any general meeting, at any adjournment of it, or on any poll called at or in relation to it, unless all amounts payable to the company in respect of that share have been paid.

Application of Rules to Class Meetings

42 Class meetings

The provisions of the articles relating to general meetings apply, with any necessary modifications, to meetings of the holders of any class of shares.

PART 4 SHARES AND DISTRIBUTIONS

Issue of Shares

43 Powers to issue different classes of share

(1) Subject to the articles, but without prejudice to the rights attached to any existing share, the company may issue shares with such rights or restrictions as may be determined by ordinary resolution.

(2) The company may issue shares which are to be redeemed, or are liable to be redeemed at the option of the company or the holder, and the directors may determine the terms, conditions and manner of redemption of any such shares.

44 Payment of commissions on subscription for shares

(1) The company may pay any person a commission in consideration for that person—
- (a) subscribing, or agreeing to subscribe, for shares, or
- (b) procuring, or agreeing to procure, subscriptions for shares.

(2) Any such commission may be paid—
- (a) in cash, or in fully paid or partly paid shares or other securities, or partly in one way and partly in the other, and
- (b) in respect of a conditional or an absolute subscription.

Interests in Shares

45 Company not bound by less than absolute interests

Except as required by law, no person is to be recognised by the company as holding any share upon any trust, and except as otherwise required by law or the articles, the company is not in any way to be bound by or recognise any interest in a share other than the holder's absolute ownership of it and all the rights attaching to it.

Share Certificates

46 Certificates to be issued except in certain cases

(1) The company must issue each member with one or more certificates in respect of the shares which that member holds.

(2) This article does not apply to—
- (a) uncertificated shares;
- (b) shares in respect of which a share warrant has been issued; or
- (c) shares in respect of which the Companies Acts permit the company not to issue a certificate.

(3) Except as otherwise specified in the articles, all certificates must be issued free of charge.

(4) No certificate may be issued in respect of shares of more than one class.

(5) If more than one person holds a share, only one certificate may be issued in respect of it.

47 Contents and execution of share certificates

(1) Every certificate must specify—
- (a) in respect of how many shares, of what class, it is issued;
- (b) the nominal value of those shares;
- (c) the amount paid up on them; and
- (d) any distinguishing numbers assigned to them.

(2) Certificates must—
- (a) have affixed to them the company's common seal or an official seal which is a facsimile of the company's common seal with the addition on its face of the word "Securities" (a "securities seal"), or
- (b) be otherwise executed in accordance with the Companies Acts.

48 Consolidated share certificates

(1) When a member's holding of shares of a particular class increases, the company may issue that member with—
- (a) a single, consolidated certificate in respect of all the shares of a particular class which that member holds, or
- (b) a separate certificate in respect of only those shares by which that member's holding has increased.

(2) When a member's holding of shares of a particular class is reduced, the company must ensure that the member is issued with one or more certificates in respect of the number of shares held by the member after that reduction. But the company need not (in the absence of a request from the member) issue any new certificate if—
- (a) all the shares which the member no longer holds as a result of the reduction, and
- (b) none of the shares which the member retains following the reduction,

were, immediately before the reduction, represented by the same certificate.

(3) A member may request the company, in writing, to replace—
- (a) the member's separate certificates with a consolidated certificate, or
- (b) the member's consolidated certificate with two or more separate certificates representing such proportion of the shares as the member may specify.

(4) When the company complies with such a request it may charge such reasonable fee as the directors may decide for doing so.

(5) A consolidated certificate must not be issued unless any certificates which it is to replace have first been returned to the company for cancellation.

49 Replacement share certificates

(1) If a certificate issued in respect of a member's shares is—
- (a) damaged or defaced, or
- (b) said to be lost, stolen or destroyed,

that member is entitled to be issued with a replacement certificate in respect of the same shares.

(2) A member exercising the right to be issued with such a replacement certificate—
- (a) may at the same time exercise the right to be issued with a single certificate or separate certificates;
- (b) must return the certificate which is to be replaced to the company if it is damaged or defaced; and
- (c) must comply with such conditions as to evidence, indemnity and the payment of a reasonable fee as the directors decide.

Shares not Held in Certificated Form

50 Uncertificated shares

(1) In this article, "the relevant rules" means—

(a) any applicable provision of the Companies Acts about the holding, evidencing of title to, or transfer of shares other than in certificated form, and
(b) any applicable legislation, rules or other arrangements made under or by virtue of such provision.

(2) The provisions of this article have effect subject to the relevant rules.

(3) Any provision of the articles which is inconsistent with the relevant rules must be disregarded, to the extent that it is inconsistent, whenever the relevant rules apply.

(4) Any share or class of shares of the company may be issued or held on such terms, or in such a way, that—
(a) title to it or them is not, or must not be, evidenced by a certificate, or
(b) it or they may or must be transferred wholly or partly without a certificate.

(5) The directors have power to take such steps as they think fit in relation to—
(a) the evidencing of and transfer of title to uncertificated shares (including in connection with the issue of such shares);
(b) any records relating to the holding of uncertificated shares;
(c) the conversion of certificated shares into uncertificated shares; or
(d) the conversion of uncertificated shares into certificated shares.

(6) The company may by notice to the holder of a share require that share—
(a) if it is uncertificated, to be converted into certificated form, and
(b) if it is certificated, to be converted into uncertificated form,
to enable it to be dealt with in accordance with the articles.

(7) If—
(a) the articles give the directors power to take action, or require other persons to take action, in order to sell, transfer or otherwise dispose of shares, and
(b) uncertificated shares are subject to that power, but the power is expressed in terms which assume the use of a certificate or other written instrument,
the directors may take such action as is necessary or expedient to achieve the same results when exercising that power in relation to uncertificated shares.

(8) In particular, the directors may take such action as they consider appropriate to achieve the sale, transfer, disposal, forfeiture, re-allotment or surrender of an uncertificated share or otherwise to enforce a lien in respect of it.

(9) Unless the directors otherwise determine, shares which a member holds in uncertificated form must be treated as separate holdings from any shares which that member holds in certificated form.

(10) A class of shares must not be treated as two classes simply because some shares of that class are held in certificated form and others are held in uncertificated form.

51 Share warrants

(1) The directors may issue a share warrant in respect of any fully paid share.

(2) Share warrants must be—
(a) issued in such form, and
(b) executed in such manner,
as the directors decide.

(3) A share represented by a share warrant may be transferred by delivery of the warrant representing it.

(4) The directors may make provision for the payment of dividends in respect of any share represented by a share warrant.

(5) Subject to the articles, the directors may decide the conditions on which any share warrant is issued. In particular, they may—
(a) decide the conditions on which new warrants are to be issued in place of warrants which are damaged or defaced, or said to have been lost, stolen or destroyed;
(b) decide the conditions on which bearers of warrants are entitled to attend and vote at general meetings;
(c) decide the conditions subject to which bearers of warrants may surrender their warrant so as to hold their shares in certificated or uncertificated form instead; and
(d) vary the conditions of issue of any warrant from time to time,
and the bearer of a warrant is subject to the conditions and procedures in force in relation to it, whether or not they were decided or specified before the warrant was issued.

(6) Subject to the conditions on which the warrants are issued from time to time, bearers of share warrants have the same rights and privileges as they would if their names had been included in the register as holders of the shares represented by their warrants.

(7) The company must not in any way be bound by or recognise any interest in a share represented by a share warrant other than the absolute right of the bearer of that warrant to that warrant.

Partly Paid Shares

52 Company's lien over partly paid shares

(1) The company has a lien ("the company's lien") over every share which is partly paid for any part of—
(a) that share's nominal value, and
(b) any premium at which it was issued,
which has not been paid to the company, and which is payable immediately or at some time in the future, whether or not a call notice has been sent in respect of it.

(2) The company's lien over a share—
(a) takes priority over any third party's interest in that share, and
(b) extends to any dividend or other money payable by the company in respect of that share and (if the lien is enforced and the share is sold by the company) the proceeds of sale of that share.

(3) The directors may at any time decide that a share which is or would otherwise be subject to the company's lien shall not be subject to it, either wholly or in part.

53 Enforcement of the company's lien

(1) Subject to the provisions of this article, if—

(a) a lien enforcement notice has been given in respect of a share, and

(b) the person to whom the notice was given has failed to comply with it,

the company may sell that share in such manner as the directors decide.

(2) A lien enforcement notice—

(a) may only be given in respect of a share which is subject to the company's lien, in respect of which a sum is payable and the due date for payment of that sum has passed;

(b) must specify the share concerned;

(c) must require payment of the sum payable within 14 days of the notice;

(d) must be addressed either to the holder of the share or to a person entitled to it by reason of the holder's death, bankruptcy or otherwise; and

(e) must state the company's intention to sell the share if the notice is not complied with.

(3) Where shares are sold under this article—

(a) the directors may authorise any person to execute an instrument of transfer of the shares to the purchaser or a person nominated by the purchaser, and

(b) the transferee is not bound to see to the application of the consideration, and the transferee's title is not affected by any irregularity in or invalidity of the process leading to the sale.

(4) The net proceeds of any such sale (after payment of the costs of sale and any other costs of enforcing the lien) must be applied—

(a) first, in payment of so much of the sum for which the lien exists as was payable at the date of the lien enforcement notice,

(b) second, to the person entitled to the shares at the date of the sale, but only after the certificate for the shares sold has been surrendered to the company for cancellation or a suitable indemnity has been given for any lost certificates, and subject to a lien equivalent to the company's lien over the shares before the sale for any money payable in respect of the shares after the date of the lien enforcement notice.

(5) A statutory declaration by a director or the company secretary that the declarant is a director or the company secretary and that a share has been sold to satisfy the company's lien on a specified date—

(a) is conclusive evidence of the facts stated in it as against all persons claiming to be entitled to the share, and

(b) subject to compliance with any other formalities of transfer required by the articles or by law, constitutes a good title to the share.

54 Call notices

(1) Subject to the articles and the terms on which shares are allotted, the directors may send a notice (a "call notice") to a member requiring the member to pay the company a specified sum of money (a "call") which is payable in respect of shares which that member holds at the date when the directors decide to send the call notice.

(2) A call notice—

(a) may not require a member to pay a call which exceeds the total sum unpaid on that member's shares (whether as to the share's nominal value or any amount payable to the company by way of premium);

(b) must state when and how any call to which it relates it is to be paid; and

(c) may permit or require the call to be paid by instalments.

(3) A member must comply with the requirements of a call notice, but no member is obliged to pay any call before 14 days have passed since the notice was sent.

(4) Before the company has received any call due under a call notice the directors may—

(a) revoke it wholly or in part, or

(b) specify a later time for payment than is specified in the notice,

by a further notice in writing to the member in respect of whose shares the call is made.

55 Liability to pay calls

(1) Liability to pay a call is not extinguished or transferred by transferring the shares in respect of which it is required to be paid.

(2) Joint holders of a share are jointly and severally liable to pay all calls in respect of that share.

(3) Subject to the terms on which shares are allotted, the directors may, when issuing shares, provide that call notices sent to the holders of those shares may require them—

(a) to pay calls which are not the same, or

(b) to pay calls at different times.

56 When call notice need not be issued

(1) A call notice need not be issued in respect of sums which are specified, in the terms on which a share is issued, as being payable to the company in respect of that share (whether in respect of nominal value or premium)—

(a) on allotment;

(b) on the occurrence of a particular event; or

(c) on a date fixed by or in accordance with the terms of issue.

(2) But if the due date for payment of such a sum has passed and it has not been paid, the holder of the share concerned is treated in all respects as having failed to comply with a call notice in respect of that sum, and is liable to the same consequences as regards the payment of interest and forfeiture.

57 Failure to comply with call notice: automatic consequences

(1) If a person is liable to pay a call and fails to do so by the call payment date—

(a) the directors may issue a notice of intended forfeiture to that person, and

(b) until the call is paid, that person must pay the company interest on the call from the call payment date at the relevant rate.

(2) For the purposes of this article—

(a) the "call payment date" is the time when the call notice states that a call is payable, unless the directors give a notice specifying a later date, in which case the "call payment date" is that later date;

(b) the "relevant rate" is—

(i) the rate fixed by the terms on which the share in respect of which the call is due was allotted;

(ii) such other rate as was fixed in the call notice which required payment of the call, or has otherwise been determined by the directors; or

(iii) if no rate is fixed in either of these ways, 5 per cent per annum.

(3) The relevant rate must not exceed by more than 5 percentage points the base lending rate most recently set by the Monetary Policy Committee of the Bank of England in connection with its responsibilities under Part 2 of the Bank of England Act 1998.

(4) The directors may waive any obligation to pay interest on a call wholly or in part.

58 Notice of intended forfeiture

A notice of intended forfeiture—

(a) may be sent in respect of any share in respect of which a call has not been paid as required by a call notice;

(b) must be sent to the holder of that share or to a person entitled to it by reason of the holder's death, bankruptcy or otherwise;

(c) must require payment of the call and any accrued interest by a date which is not less than 14 days after the date of the notice;

(d) must state how the payment is to be made; and

(e) must state that if the notice is not complied with, the shares in respect of which the call is payable will be liable to be forfeited.

59 Directors' power to forfeit shares

If a notice of intended forfeiture is not complied with before the date by which payment of the call is required in the notice of intended forfeiture, the directors may decide that any share in respect of which it was given is forfeited, and the forfeiture is to include all dividends or other moneys payable in respect of the forfeited shares and not paid before the forfeiture.

60 Effect of forfeiture

(1) Subject to the articles, the forfeiture of a share extinguishes—

(a) all interests in that share, and all claims and demands against the company in respect of it, and

(b) all other rights and liabilities incidental to the share as between the person whose share it was prior to the forfeiture and the company.

(2) Any share which is forfeited in accordance with the articles—

(a) is deemed to have been forfeited when the directors decide that it is forfeited;

(b) is deemed to be the property of the company; and

(c) may be sold, re-allotted or otherwise disposed of as the directors think fit.

(3) If a person's shares have been forfeited—

(a) the company must send that person notice that forfeiture has occurred and record it in the register of members;

(b) that person ceases to be a member in respect of those shares;

(c) that person must surrender the certificate for the shares forfeited to the company for cancellation;

(d) that person remains liable to the company for all sums payable by that person under the articles at the date of forfeiture in respect of those shares, including any interest (whether accrued before or after the date of forfeiture); and

(e) the directors may waive payment of such sums wholly or in part or enforce payment without any allowance for the value of the shares at the time of forfeiture or for any consideration received on their disposal.

(4) At any time before the company disposes of a forfeited share, the directors may decide to cancel the forfeiture on payment of all calls and interest due in respect of it and on such other terms as they think fit.

61 Procedure following forfeiture

(1) If a forfeited share is to be disposed of by being transferred, the company may receive the consideration for the transfer and the directors may authorise any person to execute the instrument of transfer.

(2) A statutory declaration by a director or the company secretary that the declarant is a director or the company secretary and that a share has been forfeited on a specified date—

(a) is conclusive evidence of the facts stated in it as against all persons claiming to be entitled to the share, and

(b) subject to compliance with any other formalities of transfer required by the articles or by law, constitutes a good title to the share.

(3) A person to whom a forfeited share is transferred is not bound to see to the application of the consideration (if any) nor is that person's title to the share affected by any irregularity in or invalidity of the process leading to the forfeiture or transfer of the share.

(4) If the company sells a forfeited share, the person who held it prior to its forfeiture is entitled to receive from the company the proceeds of such sale, net of any commission, and excluding any amount which—

(a) was, or would have become, payable, and

(b) had not, when that share was forfeited, been paid by that person in respect of that share,

but no interest is payable to such a person in respect of such proceeds and the company is not required to account for any money earned on them.

62 Surrender of shares

(1) A member may surrender any share—

(a) in respect of which the directors may issue a notice of intended forfeiture;
(b) which the directors may forfeit; or
(c) which has been forfeited.

(2) The directors may accept the surrender of any such share.

(3) The effect of surrender on a share is the same as the effect of forfeiture on that share.

(4) A share which has been surrendered may be dealt with in the same way as a share which has been forfeited.

Transfer and Transmission of Shares

63 Transfers of certificated shares

(1) Certificated shares may be transferred by means of an instrument of transfer in any usual form or any other form approved by the directors, which is executed by or on behalf of—

(a) the transferor, and
(b) (if any of the shares is partly paid) the transferee.

(2) No fee may be charged for registering any instrument of transfer or other document relating to or affecting the title to any share.

(3) The company may retain any instrument of transfer which is registered.

(4) The transferor remains the holder of a certificated share until the transferee's name is entered in the register of members as holder of it.

(5) The directors may refuse to register the transfer of a certificated share if—

(a) the share is not fully paid;
(b) the transfer is not lodged at the company's registered office or such other place as the directors have appointed;
(c) the transfer is not accompanied by the certificate for the shares to which it relates, or such other evidence as the directors may reasonably require to show the transferor's right to make the transfer, or evidence of the right of someone other than the transferor to make the transfer on the transferor's behalf;
(d) the transfer is in respect of more than one class of share; or
(e) the transfer is in favour of more than four transferees.

(6) If the directors refuse to register the transfer of a share, the instrument of transfer must be returned to the transferee with the notice of refusal unless they suspect that the proposed transfer may be fraudulent.

64 Transfer of uncertificated shares

A transfer of an uncertificated share must not be registered if it is in favour of more than four transferees.

65 Transmission of shares

(1) If title to a share passes to a transmittee, the company may only recognise the transmittee as having any title to that share.

(2) Nothing in these articles releases the estate of a deceased member from any liability in respect of a share solely or jointly held by that member.

66 Transmittees' rights

(1) A transmittee who produces such evidence of entitlement to shares as the directors may properly require—

(a) may, subject to the articles, choose either to become the holder of those shares or to have them transferred to another person, and
(b) subject to the articles, and pending any transfer of the shares to another person, has the same rights as the holder had.

(2) But transmittees do not have the right to attend or vote at a general meeting in respect of shares to which they are entitled, by reason of the holder's death or bankruptcy or otherwise, unless they become the holders of those shares

67 Exercise of transmittees' rights

(1) Transmittees who wish to become the holders of shares to which they have become entitled must notify the company in writing of that wish.

(2) If the share is a certificated share and a transmittee wishes to have it transferred to another person, the transmittee must execute an instrument of transfer in respect of it.

(3) If the share is an uncertificated share and the transmittee wishes to have it transferred to another person, the transmittee must—

(a) procure that all appropriate instructions are given to effect the transfer, or
(b) procure that the uncertificated share is changed into certificated form and then execute an instrument of transfer in respect of it.

(4) Any transfer made or executed under this article is to be treated as if it were made or executed by the person from whom the transmittee has derived rights in respect of the share, and as if the event which gave rise to the transmission had not occurred.

68 Transmittees bound by prior notices

If a notice is given to a member in respect of shares and a transmittee is entitled to those shares, the transmittee is bound by the notice if it was given to the member before the transmittee's name has been entered in the register of members.

Consolidation of Shares

69 Procedure for disposing of fractions of shares

(1) This article applies where—

(a) there has been a consolidation or division of shares, and
(b) as a result, members are entitled to fractions of shares.

(2) The directors may—

(a) sell the shares representing the fractions to any person including the company for the best price reasonably obtainable;

(b) in the case of a certificated share, authorise any person to execute an instrument of transfer of the shares to the purchaser or a person nominated by the purchaser; and

(c) distribute the net proceeds of sale in due proportion among the holders of the shares.

(3) Where any holder's entitlement to a portion of the proceeds of sale amounts to less than a minimum figure determined by the directors, that member's portion may be distributed to an organisation which is a charity for the purposes of the law of England and Wales, Scotland or Northern Ireland.

(4) The person to whom the shares are transferred is not obliged to ensure that any purchase money is received by the person entitled to the relevant fractions.

(5) The transferee's title to the shares is not affected by any irregularity in or invalidity of the process leading to their sale.

Distributions

70 Procedure for declaring dividends

(1) The company may by ordinary resolution declare dividends, and the directors may decide to pay interim dividends.

(2) A dividend must not be declared unless the directors have made a recommendation as to its amount. Such a dividend must not exceed the amount recommended by the directors.

(3) No dividend may be declared or paid unless it is in accordance with members' respective rights.

(4) Unless the members' resolution to declare or directors' decision to pay a dividend, or the terms on which shares are issued, specify otherwise, it must be paid by reference to each member's holding of shares on the date of the resolution or decision to declare or pay it.

(5) If the company's share capital is divided into different classes, no interim dividend may be paid on shares carrying deferred or non-preferred rights if, at the time of payment, any preferential dividend is in arrear.

(6) The directors may pay at intervals any dividend payable at a fixed rate if it appears to them that the profits available for distribution justify the payment.

(7) If the directors act in good faith, they do not incur any liability to the holders of shares conferring preferred rights for any loss they may suffer by the lawful payment of an interim dividend on shares with deferred or non-preferred rights.

71 Calculation of dividends

(1) Except as otherwise provided by the articles or the rights attached to shares, all dividends must be—

(a) declared and paid according to the amounts paid up on the shares on which the dividend is paid, and

(b) apportioned and paid proportionately to the amounts paid up on the shares during any portion or portions of the period in respect of which the dividend is paid.

(2) If any share is issued on terms providing that it ranks for dividend as from a particular date, that share ranks for dividend accordingly.

(3) For the purposes of calculating dividends, no account is to be taken of any amount which has been paid up on a share in advance of the due date for payment of that amount.

72 Payment of dividends and other distributions

(1) Where a dividend or other sum which is a distribution is payable in respect of a share, it must be paid by one or more of the following means—

(a) transfer to a bank or building society account specified by the distribution recipient either in writing or as the directors may otherwise decide;

(b) sending a cheque made payable to the distribution recipient by post to the distribution recipient at the distribution recipient's registered address (if the distribution recipient is a holder of the share), or (in any other case) to an address specified by the distribution recipient either in writing or as the directors may otherwise decide;

(c) sending a cheque made payable to such person by post to such person at such address as the distribution recipient has specified either in writing or as the directors may otherwise decide; or

(d) any other means of payment as the directors agree with the distribution recipient either in writing or by such other means as the directors decide.

(2) In the articles, "the distribution recipient" means, in respect of a share in respect of which a dividend or other sum is payable—

(a) the holder of the share; or

(b) if the share has two or more joint holders, whichever of them is named first in the register of members; or

(c) if the holder is no longer entitled to the share by reason of death or bankruptcy, or otherwise by operation of law, the transmittee.

73 Deductions from distributions in respect of sums owed to the company

(1) If—

(a) a share is subject to the company's lien, and

(b) the directors are entitled to issue a lien enforcement notice in respect of it,

they may, instead of issuing a lien enforcement notice, deduct from any dividend or other sum payable in respect of the share any sum of money which is payable to the company in respect of that share to the extent that they are entitled to require payment under a lien enforcement notice.

(2) Money so deducted must be used to pay any of the sums payable in respect of that share.

(3) The company must notify the distribution recipient in writing of—

(a) the fact and amount of any such deduction;
(b) any non-payment of a dividend or other sum payable in respect of a share resulting from any such deduction; and
(c) how the money deducted has been applied.

74 No interest on distributions

The company may not pay interest on any dividend or other sum payable in respect of a share unless otherwise provided by—

(a) the terms on which the share was issued, or
(b) the provisions of another agreement between the holder of that share and the company.

75 Unclaimed distributions

(1) All dividends or other sums which are—

(a) payable in respect of shares, and
(b) unclaimed after having been declared or become payable,

may be invested or otherwise made use of by the directors for the benefit of the company until claimed.

(2) The payment of any such dividend or other sum into a separate account does not make the company a trustee in respect of it.

(3) If—

(a) twelve years have passed from the date on which a dividend or other sum became due for payment, and
(b) the distribution recipient has not claimed it,

the distribution recipient is no longer entitled to that dividend or other sum and it ceases to remain owing by the company.

76 Non-cash distributions

(1) Subject to the terms of issue of the share in question, the company may, by ordinary resolution on the recommendation of the directors, decide to pay all or part of a dividend or other distribution payable in respect of a share by transferring non-cash assets of equivalent value (including, without limitation, shares or other securities in any company).

(2) If the shares in respect of which such a non-cash distribution is paid are uncertificated, any shares in the company which are issued as a non-cash distribution in respect of them must be uncertificated.

(3) For the purposes of paying a non-cash distribution, the directors may make whatever arrangements they think fit, including, where any difficulty arises regarding the distribution—

(a) fixing the value of any assets;
(b) paying cash to any distribution recipient on the basis of that value in order to adjust the rights of recipients; and
(c) vesting any assets in trustees.

77 Waiver of distributions

Distribution recipients may waive their entitlement to a dividend or other distribution payable in respect of a share by giving the company notice in writing to that effect, but if—

(a) the share has more than one holder, or
(b) more than one person is entitled to the share, whether by reason of the death or bankruptcy of one or more joint holders, or otherwise,

the notice is not effective unless it is expressed to be given, and signed, by all the holders or persons otherwise entitled to the share.

Capitalisation of Profits

78 Authority to capitalise and appropriation of capitalised sums

(1) Subject to the articles, the directors may, if they are so authorised by an ordinary resolution—

(a) decide to capitalise any profits of the company (whether or not they are available for distribution) which are not required for paying a preferential dividend, or any sum standing to the credit of the company's share premium account or capital redemption reserve; and
(b) appropriate any sum which they so decide to capitalise (a "capitalised sum") to the persons who would have been entitled to it if it were distributed by way of dividend (the "persons entitled") and in the same proportions.

(2) Capitalised sums must be applied—

(a) on behalf of the persons entitled, and
(b) in the same proportions as a dividend would have been distributed to them.

(3) Any capitalised sum may be applied in paying up new shares of a nominal amount equal to the capitalised sum which are then allotted credited as fully paid to the persons entitled or as they may direct.

(4) A capitalised sum which was appropriated from profits available for distribution may be applied—

(a) in or towards paying up any amounts unpaid on existing shares held by the persons entitled, or
(b) in paying up new debentures of the company which are then allotted credited as fully paid to the persons entitled or as they may direct.

(5) Subject to the articles the directors may—

(a) apply capitalised sums in accordance with paragraphs (3) and (4) partly in one way and partly in another;
(b) make such arrangements as they think fit to deal with shares or debentures becoming distributable in fractions under this article (including the issuing of fractional certificates or the making of cash payments); and
(c) authorise any person to enter into an agreement with the company on behalf of all the persons entitled which is binding on them in respect of the allotment of shares and debentures to them under this article.

PART 5 MISCELLANEOUS PROVISIONS

Communications

79 Means of communication to be used

(1) Subject to the articles, anything sent or supplied by or to the company under the articles may be sent or supplied in any way in which the Companies Act 2006 provides for documents or information which are authorised or required by any provision of that Act to be sent or supplied by or to the company.

(2) Subject to the articles, any notice or document to be sent or supplied to a director in connection with the taking of decisions by directors may also be sent or supplied by the means by which that director has asked to be sent or supplied with such notices or documents for the time being.

(3) A director may agree with the company that notices or documents sent to that director in a particular way are to be deemed to have been received within a specified time of their being sent, and for the specified time to be less than 48 hours.

80 Failure to notify contact details

(1) If—

(a) the company sends two consecutive documents to a member over a period of at least 12 months, and

(b) each of those documents is returned undelivered, or the company receives notification that it has not been delivered,

that member ceases to be entitled to receive notices from the company.

(2) A member who has ceased to be entitled to receive notices from the company becomes entitled to receive such notices again by sending the company—

(a) a new address to be recorded in the register of members, or

(b) if the member has agreed that the company should use a means of communication other than sending things to such an address, the information that the company needs to use that means of communication effectively.

Administrative Arrangements

81 Company seals

(1) Any common seal may only be used by the authority of the directors.

(2) The directors may decide by what means and in what form any common seal or securities seal is to be used.

(3) Unless otherwise decided by the directors, if the company has a common seal and it is affixed to a document, the document must also be signed by at least one authorised person in the presence of a witness who attests the signature.

(4) For the purposes of this article, an authorised person is—

(a) any director of the company;

(b) the company secretary; or

(c) any person authorised by the directors for the purpose of signing documents to which the common seal is applied.

(5) If the company has an official seal for use abroad, it may only be affixed to a document if its use on that document, or documents of a class to which it belongs, has been authorised by a decision of the directors.

(6) If the company has a securities seal, it may only be affixed to securities by the company secretary or a person authorised to apply it to securities by the company secretary.

(7) For the purposes of the articles, references to the securities seal being affixed to any document include the reproduction of the image of that seal on or in a document by any mechanical or electronic means which has been approved by the directors in relation to that document or documents of a class to which it belongs.

82 Destruction of documents

(1) The company is entitled to destroy—

(a) all instruments of transfer of shares which have been registered, and all other documents on the basis of which any entries are made in the register of members, from six years after the date of registration;

(b) all dividend mandates, variations or cancellations of dividend mandates, and notifications of change of address, from two years after they have been recorded;

(c) all share certificates which have been cancelled from one year after the date of the cancellation;

(d) all paid dividend warrants and cheques from one year after the date of actual payment; and

(e) all proxy notices from one year after the end of the meeting to which the proxy notice relates.

(2) If the company destroys a document in good faith, in accordance with the articles, and without notice of any claim to which that document may be relevant, it is conclusively presumed in favour of the company that—

(a) entries in the register purporting to have been made on the basis of an instrument of transfer or other document so destroyed were duly and properly made;

(b) any instrument of transfer so destroyed was a valid and effective instrument duly and properly registered;

(c) any share certificate so destroyed was a valid and effective certificate duly and properly cancelled; and

(d) any other document so destroyed was a valid and effective document in accordance with its recorded particulars in the books or records of the company.

(3) This article does not impose on the company any liability which it would not otherwise have if it destroys any document before the time at which this article permits it to do so.

(4) In this article, references to the destruction of any document include a reference to its being disposed of in any manner.

83 No right to inspect accounts and other records

Except as provided by law or authorised by the directors or an ordinary resolution of the company, no person is entitled to inspect any of the company's accounting or other records or documents merely by virtue of being a member.

84 Provision for employees on cessation of business

The directors may decide to make provision for the benefit of persons employed or formerly employed by the company or any of its subsidiaries (other than a director or former director or shadow director) in connection with the cessation or transfer to any person of the whole or part of the undertaking of the company or that subsidiary.

Directors' Indemnity and Insurance

85 Indemnity

(1) Subject to paragraph (2), a relevant director of the company or an associated company may be indemnified out of the company's assets against—

- (a) any liability incurred by that director in connection with any negligence, default, breach of duty or breach of trust in relation to the company or an associated company,
- (b) any liability incurred by that director in connection with the activities of the company or an associated company in its capacity as a trustee of an occupational pension scheme (as defined in section 235(6) of the Companies Act 2006),
- (c) any other liability incurred by that director as an officer of the company or an associated company.

(2) This article does not authorise any indemnity which would be prohibited or rendered void by any provision of the Companies Acts or by any other provision of law.

(3) In this article—

- (a) companies are associated if one is a subsidiary of the other or both are subsidiaries of the same body corporate, and
- (b) a "relevant director" means any director or former director of the company or an associated company.

86 Insurance

(1) The directors may decide to purchase and maintain insurance, at the expense of the company, for the benefit of any relevant director in respect of any relevant loss.

(2) In this article—

- (a) a "relevant director" means any director or former director of the company or an associated company,
- (b) a "relevant loss" means any loss or liability which has been or may be incurred by a relevant director in connection with that director's duties or powers in relation to the company, any associated company or any pension fund or employees' share scheme of the company or associated company, and
- (c) companies are associated if one is a subsidiary of the other or both are subsidiaries of the same body corporate.

Appendix 2: Companies Act 1985, Table A

[A2]

NOTES

The Companies Act 1985, Table A is set out in the Schedule to the Companies (Tables A to F) Regulations 1985, SI 1985/805.

The Companies Act 1985, s 8(2), (3) (repealed by CA 2006, but see the note relating to SI 2008/2860 below) provide as follows—

"(2) In the case of a company limited by shares, if articles are not registered or, if articles are registered, in so far as they do not exclude or modify Table A, that Table (so far as applicable, and as in force at the date of the company's registration) constitutes the company's articles, in the same manner and to the same extent as if articles in the form of that Table had been duly registered.

(3) If in consequence of regulations under this section Table A is altered, the alteration does not affect a company registered before the alteration takes effect, or repeal as respects that company any portion of the Table.".

Following amendments by Regulations made under s 8 of the 1985 Act, this table is set out below both in its original form and in its form as amended at different dates.

Note also that this Table A was also amended by the Companies Act 1985 (Electronic Communications) Order 2000, SI 2000/3373. The 2000 Order was made under the powers conferred by the Electronic Communications Act 2000, ss 8, 9. It is assumed that these amendments (which do not fall within s 8(3) of the 1985 Act) are generally applicable.

Note that the Companies Act 2006 (Commencement No 8, Transitional Provisions and Savings) Order 2008, SI 2008/2860, Sch 2, para 1(1) provides that nothing in the Companies Act 2006 affects (a) the registration or re-registration of a company under the former Companies Acts, or the continued existence of a company by virtue of such registration or re-registration, or (b) the application in relation to an existing company of (i) Table B in the Joint Stock Companies Act 1856, (ii) Table A in any of the former Companies Acts, or (iii) the Companies (Tables A to F) Regulations 1985 or the Companies (Tables A to F) Regulations (Northern Ireland) 1986. See further the savings notes to the Companies (Tables A to F) Regulations 1985 preceding **[6.1]**.

TABLE A
REGULATIONS FOR MANAGEMENT OF A COMPANY LIMITED BY SHARES

INTERPRETATION

1. In these regulations—

["the Act" means the Companies Act 1985 including any statutory modification or re-enactment thereof for the time being in force and any provisions of the Companies Act 2006 for the time being in force;]

"the articles" means the articles of the company.

"clear days" in relation to the period of a notice means that period excluding the day when the notice is given or deemed to be given and the day for which it is given or on which it is to take effect.

["communication" means the same as in the Electronic Communications Act 2000.]

["electronic communication" means the same as in the Electronic Communications Act 2000.]

"executed" includes any mode of execution.

"office" means the registered office of the company.

"the holder" in relation to shares means the member whose name is entered in the register of members as the holder of the shares.

"the seal" means the common seal of the company.

"secretary" means the secretary of the company or any other person appointed to perform the duties of the secretary of the company, including a joint, assistant or deputy secretary.

"the United Kingdom" means Great Britain and Northern Ireland.

Unless the context otherwise requires, words or expressions contained in these regulations bear the same meaning as in the Act but excluding any statutory modification thereof not in force when these regulations become binding on the company.

NOTES

Definition "the Act" substituted by the Companies (Tables A to F) (Amendment) Regulations 2007, SI 2007/2541, reg 3, as from 1 October 2007; the original definition read as follows—

"the Act" means the Companies Act 1985 including any statutory modification or re-enactment thereof for the time being in force.".

Definitions "communication" and "electronic communication" inserted by the Companies Act 1985 (Electronic Communications) Order 2000, SI 2000/3373, art 32(1), Sch 1, para 1, as from 22 December 2000.

SHARE CAPITAL

2. Subject to the provisions of the Act and without prejudice to any rights attached to any existing shares, any share may be issued with such rights or restrictions as the company may by ordinary resolution determine.

3. Subject to the provisions of the Act, shares may be issued which are to be redeemed or are to be liable to be redeemed at the option of the company or the holder on such terms and in such manner as may be provided by the articles.

4. The company may exercise the powers of paying commissions conferred by the Act. Subject to the [provisions] of the Act, any such commission may be satisfied by the payment of cash or by the allotment of fully or partly paid shares or partly in one way and partly in the other.

NOTES

Word in square brackets substituted for the original word "provision" by the Companies (Tables A to F) (Amendment) Regulations 1985, SI 1985/1052, reg 2, as from 1 August 1985.

5. Except as required by law, no person shall be recognised by the company as holding any share upon any trust and (except as otherwise provided by the articles or by law) the company shall not be bound by or recognise any interest in any share except an absolute right to the entirety thereof in the holder.

SHARE CERTIFICATES

6. Every member, upon becoming the holder of any shares, shall be entitled without payment to one certificate for all the shares of each class held by him (and, upon transferring a part of his holding of shares of any class, to a certificate for the balance of such holding) or several certificates each for one or more of his shares upon payment for every certificate after the first of such reasonable sum as the directors may determine. Every certificate shall be sealed with the seal and shall specify the number, class and distinguishing numbers (if any) of the shares to which it relates and the amount or respective amounts paid up thereon. The company shall not be bound to issue more than one certificate for shares held jointly by several persons and delivery of a certificate to one joint holder shall be a sufficient delivery to all of them.

7. If a share certificate is defaced, worn-out, lost or destroyed, it may be renewed on such terms (if any) as to evidence and indemnity and payment of the expenses reasonably incurred by the company in investigating evidence as the directors may determine but otherwise free of charge, and (in the case of defacement or wearing-out) on delivery up of the old certificate.

LIEN

8. The company shall have a first and paramount lien on every share (not being a fully paid share) for all moneys (whether presently payable or not) payable at a fixed time or called in respect of that share. The directors may at any time declare any share to be wholly or in part exempt from the provisions of this regulation. The company's lien on a share shall extend to any amount payable in respect of it.

9. The company may sell in such manner as the directors determine any shares on which the company has a lien if a sum in respect of which the lien exists is presently payable and is not paid within fourteen clear days after notice has been given to the holder of the share or to the person entitled to it in consequence of the death or bankruptcy of the holder, demanding payment and stating that if the notice is not complied with the shares may be sold.

10. To give effect to a sale the directors may authorise some person to execute an instrument of transfer of the shares sold to, or in accordance with the directions of, the purchaser. The title of the transferee to the shares shall not be affected by any irregularity in or invalidity of the proceedings in reference to the sale.

11. The net proceeds of the sale, after payment of the costs, shall be applied in payment of so much of the sum for which the lien exists as is presently payable, and any residue shall (upon surrender to the company for cancellation of the certificate for the shares sold and subject to a like lien for any moneys not presently payable as existed upon the shares before the sale) be paid to the person entitled to the shares at the date of the sale.

CALLS ON SHARES AND FORFEITURE

12. Subject to the terms of allotment, the directors may make calls upon the members in respect of any moneys unpaid on their shares (whether in respect of nominal value or premium) and each member shall (subject to receiving at least fourteen clear days' notice specifying when and where payment is to be made) pay to the company as required by the notice the amount called on his shares. A call may be required to be paid by instalments. A call may, before receipt by the company of any sum due thereunder, be revoked in whole or part and payment of a call may be postponed in whole or part. A person upon whom a call is made shall remain liable for calls made upon him notwithstanding the subsequent transfer of the shares in respect whereof the call was made.

13. A call shall be deemed to have been made at the time when the resolution of the directors authorising the call was passed.

14. The joint holders of a share shall be jointly and severally liable to pay all calls in respect thereof.

15. If a call remains unpaid after it has become due and payable the person from whom it is due and payable shall pay interest on the amount unpaid from the day it became due and payable until it is paid at the rate fixed by the terms of allotment of the share or in the notice of the call or, if no rate is fixed, at the appropriate rate (as defined by the Act) but the directors may waive payment of the interest wholly or in part.

16. An amount payable in respect of a share on allotment or at any fixed date, whether in respect of nominal value or premium or as an instalment of a call, shall be deemed to be a call and if it is not paid the provisions of the articles shall apply as if that amount had become due and payable by virtue of a call.

17. Subject to the terms of allotment, the directors may make arrangements on the issue of shares for a difference between the holders in the amounts and times of payment of calls on their shares.

18. If a call remains unpaid after it has become due and payable the directors may give to the person from whom it is due not less than fourteen clear days' notice requiring payment of the amount unpaid together with any interest which may have accrued. The notice shall name the place where payment is to be made and shall state that if the notice is not complied with the shares in respect of which the call was made will be liable to be forfeited.

19. If the notice is not complied with any share in respect of which it was given may, before the payment required by the notice has been made, be forfeited by a resolution of the directors and the forfeiture shall include all dividends or other moneys payable in respect of the forfeited shares and not paid before the forfeiture.

20. Subject to the provisions of the Act, a forfeited share may be sold, re-allotted or otherwise disposed of on such terms and in such manner as the directors determine either to the person who was before the forfeiture the holder or to any other person and at any time before sale, re-allotment or other disposition, the forfeiture may be cancelled on such terms as the directors think fit. Where for the purposes of its disposal a forfeited share is to be transferred to any person the directors may authorise some person to execute an instrument of transfer of the share to that person.

21. A person any of whose shares have been forfeited shall cease to be a member in respect of them and shall surrender to the company for cancellation the certificate for the shares forfeited but shall remain liable to the company for all moneys which at the date of forfeiture were presently payable by him to the company in respect of those shares with interest at the rate at which interest was payable on those moneys before the forfeiture or, if no interest was so payable, at the appropriate rate (as defined in the Act) from the date of forfeiture until payment but the directors may waive payment wholly or in part or enforce payment without any allowance for the value of the shares at the time of forfeiture or for any consideration received on their disposal.

22. A statutory declaration by a director or the secretary that a share has been forfeited on a specified date shall be conclusive evidence of the facts stated in it as against all persons claiming to be entitled to the share and the declaration shall (subject to the execution of an instrument of transfer if necessary) constitute a good title to the share and the person to whom the share is disposed of shall not be bound to see to the application of the consideration, if any, nor shall his title to the share be affected by any irregularity in or invalidity of the proceedings in reference to the forfeiture or disposal of the share.

TRANSFER OF SHARES

23. The instrument of transfer of a share may be in any usual form or in any other form which the directors may approve and shall be executed by or on behalf of the transferor and, unless the share is fully paid, by or on behalf of the transferee.

24. The directors may refuse to register the transfer of a share which is not fully paid to a person of whom they do not approve and they may refuse to register the transfer of a share on which the company has a lien. They may also refuse to register a transfer unless—

(a) it is lodged at the office or at such other place as the directors may appoint and is accompanied by the certificate for the shares to which it relates and such other evidence as the directors may reasonably require to show the right of the transferor to make the transfer;
(b) it is in respect of only one class of shares; and
(c) it is in favour of not more than four transferees.

25. If the directors refuse to register a transfer of a share, they shall within two months after the date on which the transfer was lodged with the company send to the transferee notice of the refusal.

26. The registration of transfers of shares or of transfers of any class of shares may be suspended at such times and for such periods (not exceeding thirty days in any year) as the directors may determine.

27. No fee shall be charged for the registration of any instrument of transfer or other document relating to or affecting the title to any share.

28. The company shall be entitled to retain any instrument of transfer which is registered, but any instrument of transfer which the directors refuse to register shall be returned to the person lodging it when notice of the refusal is given.

TRANSMISSION OF SHARES

29. If a member dies the survivor or survivors where he was a joint holder, and his personal representatives where he was a sole holder or the only survivor of joint holders, shall be the only persons recognised by the company as having any title to his interest; but nothing herein contained shall release the estate of a deceased member from any liability in respect of any share which had been jointly held by him.

30. A person becoming entitled to a share in consequence of the death or bankruptcy of a member may, upon such evidence being produced as the directors may properly require, elect either to become the holder of the share or to have some person nominated by him registered as the transferee. If he elects to become the holder he shall give notice to the company to that effect. If he elects to have another person registered he shall execute an instrument of transfer of the share to that person. All the articles relating to the transfer of shares shall apply to the notice or instrument of transfer as if it were an instrument of transfer executed by the member and the death or bankruptcy of the member had not occurred.

31. A person becoming entitled to a share in consequence of the death or bankruptcy of a member shall have the rights to which he would be entitled if he were the holder of the share, except that he shall not, before being registered as the holder of the share, be entitled in respect of it to attend or vote at any meeting of the company or at any separate meeting of the holders of any class of shares in the company.

ALTERATION OF SHARE CAPITAL

32. The company may by ordinary resolution—

(a) increase its share capital by new shares of such amount as the resolution prescribes;
(b) consolidate and divide all or any of its share capital into shares of larger amount than its existing shares;
(c) subject to the provisions of the Act, sub-divide its shares, or any of them, into shares of smaller amount and the resolution may determine that, as between the shares resulting from the sub-division, any of them may have any preference or advantage as compared with the others; and
(d) cancel shares which, at the date of the passing of the resolution, have not been taken or agreed to be taken by any person and diminish the amount of its share capital by the amount of the shares so cancelled.

33. Whenever as a result of a consolidation of shares any members would become entitled to fractions of a share, the directors may, on behalf of those members, sell the shares representing the fractions for the best price reasonably obtainable to any person (including, subject to the provisions of the Act, the company) and distribute the net proceeds of sale in due proportion among those members, and the directors may authorise some person to execute an instrument of transfer of the shares to, or in accordance with the directions of, the purchaser. The transferee shall not be bound to see to the application of the purchase money nor shall his title to the shares be affected by any irregularity in or invalidity of the proceedings in reference to the sale.

34. Subject to the provisions of the Act, the company may by special resolution reduce its share capital, any capital redemption reserve and any share premium account in any way.

PURCHASE OF OWN SHARES

35. Subject to the provisions of the Act, the company may purchase its own shares (including any redeemable shares) and, if it is a private company, make a payment in respect of the redemption or purchase of its own shares otherwise than out of distributable profits of the company or the proceeds of a fresh issue of shares.

GENERAL MEETINGS

36. *All general meetings other than annual general meetings shall be called extraordinary general meetings.*

NOTES

Revoked by the Companies (Tables A to F) (Amendment) Regulations 2007, SI 2007/2541, reg 4, as from 1 October 2007.

37. The directors may call general meetings and, on the requisition of members pursuant to the provisions of the Act, shall forthwith proceed to convene [a] general meeting [in accordance with the provisions of the Act]. If there are not within the United Kingdom sufficient directors to call a general meeting, any director or any member of the company may call a general meeting.

NOTES

Words in square brackets substituted for the original words "an extraordinary" and "for a date not later than eight weeks after receipt of the requisition" respectively, by the Companies (Tables A to F) (Amendment) Regulations 2007, SI 2007/2541, reg 5, as from 1 October 2007.

NOTICE OF GENERAL MEETINGS

38. *An annual general meeting and an extraordinary general meeting called for the passing of a special resolution or a resolution appointing a person as a director shall be called by at least twenty-one clear days' notice. All other extraordinary* general meetings shall be called by at least fourteen clear days' notice but a general meeting may be called by shorter notice if it is so agreed—

(a) in the case of an annual general meeting, by all the members entitled to attend and vote thereat; and

(b) *in the case of any other meeting* by a majority in number of the members having a right to attend and vote being a majority together holding not less than ninety-*five* per cent in nominal value of the shares giving that right.

The notice shall specify the time and place of the meeting and the general nature of the business to be transacted *and, in the case of an annual general meeting, shall specify the meeting as such.*

Subject to the provisions of the articles and to any restrictions imposed on any shares, the notice shall be given to all the members, to all persons entitled to a share in consequence of the death or bankruptcy of a member and to the directors and auditors.

NOTES

The Companies (Tables A to F) (Amendment) Regulations 2007, SI 2007/2541, regs 8, 9, provide that the following amendments apply (as from 1 October 2007) in so far as this regulation relates to private companies limited by shares—

(i) Omit the words "An annual general meeting and an extraordinary general meeting called for the passing of a special resolution or a resolution appointing a person as a director shall be called by at least twenty-one clear days' notice. All other extraordinary".

(ii) Omit paragraph (a).

(iii) In paragraph (b), omit the words "in the case of any other meeting" and "-five".

(iv) Omit the words "and, in the case of an annual general meeting, shall specify the meeting as such".

Regulations 19, 20 of the 2007 Regulations further provide that the following amendments apply (as from 1 October 2007) in so far as this regulation relates to public companies limited by shares—

(i) After the words "annual general meeting" omit the words "and an extraordinary general meeting called for the passing of a special resolution or a resolution appointing a person as a director".

(ii) After the words "All other" omit the word "extraordinary".

39. The accidental omission to give notice of a meeting to, or the non-receipt of notice of a meeting by, any person entitled to receive notice shall not invalidate the proceedings at that meeting.

PROCEEDINGS AT GENERAL MEETINGS

40. No business shall be transacted at any meeting unless a quorum is present. Two persons entitled to vote upon the business to be transacted, each being a member or a proxy for a member or a duly authorised representative of a corporation, shall be a quorum.

NOTES

The Companies (Tables A to F) (Amendment) Regulations 2007, SI 2007/2541, regs 8, 10, provide that the following amendment applies (as from 1 October 2007) in so far as this regulation relates to private companies limited by shares—

At the beginning of the second sentence insert the words "Save in the case of a company with a single member".

41. If such a quorum is not present within half an hour from the time appointed for the meeting, or if during a meeting such a quorum ceases to be present, the meeting shall stand adjourned to the same day in the next week at the same time and place or [to] such time and place as the directors may determine.

NOTES

Word in square brackets inserted by the Companies (Tables A to F) (Amendment) Regulations 1985, SI 1985/1052, reg 2, as from 1 August 1985.

42. The chairman, if any, of the board of directors or in his absence some other director nominated by the directors shall preside as chairman of the meeting, but if neither the chairman nor such other director (if any) be present within fifteen minutes after the time appointed for holding the meeting and willing to act, the directors present shall elect one of their number to be chairman and, if there is only one director present and willing to act, he shall be chairman.

43. If no director is willing to act as chairman, or if no director is present within fifteen minutes after the time appointed for holding the meeting, the members present and entitled to vote shall choose one of their number to be chairman.

44. A director shall, notwithstanding that he is not a member, be entitled to attend and speak at any general meeting and at any separate meeting of the holders of any class of shares in the company.

45. The chairman may, with the consent of a meeting at which a quorum is present (and shall if so directed by the meeting), adjourn the meeting from time to time and from place to place, but no business shall be transacted at an adjourned meeting other than business which might properly have been transacted at the meeting had the adjournment not taken place. When a meeting is adjourned for fourteen days or more, at least seven clear days' notice shall be given specifying the time and place of the adjourned meeting and the general nature of the business to be transacted. Otherwise it shall not be necessary to give any such notice.

46. A resolution put to the vote of a meeting shall be decided on a show of hands unless before, or on the declaration of the result of, the show of hands a poll is duly demanded. Subject to the provisions of the Act, a poll may be demanded—

(a) by the chairman; or

(b) by at least two members having the right to vote at the meeting; or

(c) by a member or members representing not less than one-tenth of the total voting rights of all the members having the right to vote at the meeting; or

(d) by a member or members holding shares conferring a right to vote at the meeting being shares on which an aggregate sum has been paid up equal to not less than one-tenth of the total sum paid up on all the shares conferring that right;

and a demand by a person as proxy for a member shall be the same as a demand by the member.

47. Unless a poll is duly demanded a declaration by the chairman that a resolution has been carried or carried unanimously, or by a particular majority, or lost, or not carried by a particular majority and an entry to that effect in the minutes of the meeting shall be conclusive evidence of the fact without proof of the number or proportion of the votes recorded in favour of or against the resolution.

48. The demand for a poll may, before the poll is taken, be withdrawn but only with the consent of the chairman and a demand so withdrawn shall not be taken to have invalidated the result of a show of hands declared before the demand was made.

49. A poll shall be taken as the chairman directs and he may appoint scrutineers (who need not be members) and fix a time and place for declaring the result of the poll. The result of the poll shall be deemed to be the resolution of the meeting at which the poll was demanded.

50. *In the case of an equality of votes, whether on a show of hands or on a poll, the chairman shall be entitled to a casting vote in addition to any other vote he may have.*

NOTES

Revoked by the Companies (Tables A to F) (Amendment) (No 2) Regulations 2007, SI 2007/2826, reg 3, as from 1 October 2007.

51. A poll demanded on the election of a chairman or on a question of adjournment shall be taken forthwith. A poll demanded on any other question shall be taken either forthwith or at such time and place as the chairman directs not being more than thirty days after the poll is demanded. The demand for a poll shall not prevent the continuance of a meeting for the transaction of any business other than the question on which the poll was demanded. If a poll is demanded before the declaration of the result of a show of hands and the demand is duly withdrawn, the meeting shall continue as if the demand had not been made.

52. No notice need be given of a poll not taken forthwith if the time and place at which it is to be taken are announced at the meeting at which it is demanded. In any other case at least seven clear days' notice shall be given specifying the time and place at which the poll is to be taken.

53. *A resolution in writing executed by or on behalf of each member who would have been entitled to vote upon it if it had been proposed at a general meeting at which he was present shall be as effectual as if it had been passed at a general meeting duly convened and held and may consist of several instruments in the like form each executed by or on behalf of one or more members.*

NOTES

Revoked by the Companies (Tables A to F) (Amendment) Regulations 2007, SI 2007/2541, reg 6, as from 1 October 2007.

VOTES OF MEMBERS

54. Subject to any rights or restrictions attached to any shares, on a show of hands every member who (being an individual) is present in person [or by proxy] or (being a corporation) is present by a duly authorised representative [or by proxy], [unless the proxy (in either case) or the representative is] himself a member entitled to vote, shall have one vote and on a poll every member shall have one vote for every share of which he is the holder.

NOTES

Words in first and second pairs of square brackets inserted, and words in third pair of square brackets substituted for the original words "not being", by the Companies (Tables A to F) (Amendment) (No 2) Regulations 2007, SI 2007/2826, reg 4, as from 1 October 2007.

55. In the case of joint holders the vote of the senior who tenders a vote, whether in person or by proxy, shall be accepted to the exclusion of the votes of the other joint holders; and seniority shall be determined by the order in which the names of the holders stand in the register of members.

56. A member in respect of whom an order has been made by any court having jurisdiction (whether in the United Kingdom or elsewhere) in matters concerning mental disorder may vote, whether on a show of hands or on a poll, by his receiver, curator bonis or other person authorised in that behalf appointed by that court, and any such receiver, curator bonis or other person may, on a poll, vote by proxy. Evidence to the satisfaction of the directors of the authority of the person claiming to exercise the right to vote shall be deposited at the office, or at such other place as is specified in accordance with the articles for the deposit of instruments of proxy, not less than 48 hours before the time appointed for holding the meeting or adjourned meeting at which the right to vote is to be exercised and in default the right to vote shall not be exercisable.

57. No member shall vote at any general meeting or at any separate meeting of the holders of any class of shares in the company, either in person or by proxy, in respect of any share held by him unless all moneys presently payable by him in respect of that share have been paid.

58. No objection shall be raised to the qualification of any voter except at the meeting or adjourned meeting at which the vote objected to is tendered, and every vote not disallowed at the meeting shall be valid. Any objection made in due time shall be referred to the chairman whose decision shall be final and conclusive.

59. On a poll votes may be given either personally or by proxy. A member may appoint more than one proxy to attend on the same occasion.

60. [The appointment of] a proxy shall be *in writing* executed by or on behalf of the appointor and shall be in the following form (or in a form as near thereto as circumstances allow or in any other form which is usual or which the directors may approve)—

". . . . . PLC/Limited

I/We, ... of . . . .

being a member/members of the above-named company,

hereby appoint . . . . of . . . .,

or failing him, ... of . . . .,

as my/our proxy to vote in my/our name[s] and on my/our behalf at the *annual/extraordinary* general meeting of the company, to be held on

. . . . 19. . . . ., and at any adjournment thereof.

Signed on . . . . 19. . . . . "

NOTES

Words in square brackets substituted for the original words "An instrument appointing", and words "in writing" in italics revoked, by the Companies Act 1985 (Electronic Communications) Order 2000, SI 2000/3373, art 32(1), Sch 1, para 2, as from 22 December 2000.

The Companies (Tables A to F) (Amendment) Regulations 2007, SI 2007/2541, regs 8, 11, provide that the following amendment applies (as from 1 October 2007) in so far as this regulation relates to private companies limited by shares—

After the words "our behalf at the" omit the words "annual/extraordinary".

Regulations 19, 21 of the 2007 Regulations further provide that the following amendment applies (as from 1 October 2007) in so far as this regulation relates to public companies limited by shares—

After the words "our behalf at the annual/" omit the word "extraordinary" and insert the words "any other".

61. Where it is desired to afford members an opportunity of instructing the proxy how he shall act the [appointment of] a proxy shall be in the following form (or in a form as near thereto as circumstances allow or in any other form which is usual or which the directors may approve)—

". . . . . PLC/Limited

I/We, ... of . . . .

being a member/members of the above-named company,

hereby appoint . . . . of . . . .,

or failing him, ... of . . . .,

as my/our proxy to vote in my/our name[s] and on my/our behalf at the *annual/extraordinary* general meeting of the company, to be held on

. . . . 19. . . . ., and at any adjournment thereof.

This form is to be used in respect of the resolutions mentioned below as follows:

Resolution No 1 *for *against

Resolution No 2 *for *against.

* Strike out whichever is not desired.

Unless otherwise instructed, the proxy may vote as he thinks fit or abstain from voting.

Signed this . . . . day of . . . . 19. . . . ."

NOTES

Words in square brackets substituted for the original words "instrument appointing" by the Companies Act 1985 (Electronic Communications) Order 2000, SI 2000/3373, art 32(1), Sch 1, para 3, as from 22 December 2000.

The Companies (Tables A to F) (Amendment) Regulations 2007, SI 2007/2541, regs 8, 12, provide that the following amendment applies (as from 1 October 2007) in so far as this regulation relates to private companies limited by shares—

After the words "our behalf at the" omit the words "annual/extraordinary".

Regulations 19, 22 of the 2007 Regulations further provide that the following amendment applies (as from 1 October 2007) in so far as this regulation relates to public companies limited by shares—

After the words "our behalf at the annual/" omit the word "extraordinary" and insert the words "any other".

62. [The appointment of] a proxy and any authority under which it is executed or a copy of such authority certified notarially or in some other way approved by the directors may—

(a) [in the case of an instrument in writing] be deposited at the office or at such other place within the United Kingdom as is specified in the notice convening the meeting or in any instrument of proxy sent out by the company in relation to the meeting not less than 48 hours before the time for holding the meeting or adjourned meeting at which the person named in the instrument proposes to vote; or

[(aa) in the case of an appointment contained in an electronic communication, where an address has been specified for the purpose of receiving electronic communications—

(i) in the notice convening the meeting, or

(ii) in any instrument of proxy sent out by the company in relation to the meeting, or

(iii) in any invitation contained in an electronic communication to appoint a proxy issued by the company in relation to the meeting,

be received at such address not less than 48 hours before the time for holding the meeting or adjourned meeting at which the person named in the appointment proposes to vote;]

(b) in the case of a poll taken more than 48 hours after it is demanded, be deposited [or received] as aforesaid after the poll has been demanded and not less than 24 hours before the time appointed for the taking of the poll; or

(c) where the poll is not taken forthwith but is taken not more than 48 hours after it was demanded, be delivered at the meeting at which the poll was demanded to the chairman or to the secretary or to any director;

[and an appointment of proxy which is not deposited, delivered or received] in a manner so permitted shall be invalid.

[In this regulation and the next, "address", in relation to electronic communications, includes any number or address used for the purposes of such communications.]

NOTES

Words in first pair of square brackets substituted for the original words "The instrument appointing", words in fifth pair of square brackets substituted for the original words "and an instrument of proxy which is not deposited or delivered", and other words in square brackets inserted, by the Companies Act 1985 (Electronic Communications) Order 2000, SI 2000/3373, art 32(1), Sch 1, para 4, as from 22 December 2000.

63. A vote given or poll demanded by proxy or by the duly authorised representative of a corporation shall be valid notwithstanding the previous determination of the authority of the person voting or demanding a poll unless notice of the determination was received by the company at the office or at such other place at which the instrument of proxy was duly deposited [or, where the appointment of the proxy was contained in an electronic communication, at the address at which such appointment was duly received] before the commencement of the meeting or adjourned meeting at which the vote is given or the poll demanded or (in the case of a poll taken otherwise than on the same day as the meeting or adjourned meeting) the time appointed for taking the poll.

NOTES

Words in square brackets inserted by the Companies Act 1985 (Electronic Communications) Order 2000, SI 2000/3373, art 32(1), Sch 1, para 5, as from 22 December 2000.

Number of Directors

64. Unless otherwise determined by ordinary resolution, the number of directors (other than alternate directors) shall not be subject to any maximum but shall be not less than two.

Alternate Directors

65. Any director (other than an alternate director) may appoint any other director, or any other person approved by resolution of the directors and willing to act, to be an alternate director and may remove from office an alternate director so appointed by him.

66. An alternate director shall be entitled to receive notice of all meetings of directors and of all meetings of committees of directors of which his appointor is a member, to attend and vote at any such meeting at which the director appointing him is not personally present, and generally to perform all the functions of his appointor as a director in his absence but shall not be entitled to receive any remuneration from the company for his services as an alternate director. But it shall not be necessary to give notice of such a meeting to an alternate director who is absent from the United Kingdom.

67. An alternate director shall cease to be an alternate director if his appointor ceases to be a director; but, if a director retires by rotation or otherwise but is reappointed or deemed to have been reappointed at the meeting at which he retires, any appointment of an alternate director made by him which was in force immediately prior to his retirement shall continue after his reappointment.

68. Any appointment or removal of an alternate director shall be by notice to the company signed by the director making or revoking the appointment or in any other manner approved by the directors.

69. Save as otherwise provided in the articles, an alternate director shall be deemed for all purposes to be a director and shall alone be responsible for his own acts and defaults and he shall not be deemed to be the agent of the director appointing him.

POWERS OF DIRECTORS

70. Subject to the provisions of the Act, the memorandum and the articles and to any directions given by special resolution, the business of the company shall be managed by the directors who may exercise all the powers of the company. No alteration of the memorandum or articles and no such direction shall invalidate any prior act of the directors which would have been valid if that alteration had not been made or that direction had not been given. The powers given by this regulation shall not be limited by any special power given to the directors by the articles and a meeting of directors at which a quorum is present may exercise all powers exercisable by the directors.

71. The directors may, by power of attorney or otherwise, appoint any person to be the agent of the company for such purposes and on such conditions as they determine, including authority for the agent to delegate all or any of his powers.

DELEGATION OF DIRECTORS' POWERS

72. The directors may delegate any of their powers to any committee consisting of one or more directors. They may also delegate to any managing director or any director holding any other executive office such of their powers as they consider desirable to be exercised by him. Any such delegation may be made subject to any conditions the directors may impose, and either collaterally with or to the exclusion of their own powers and may be revoked or altered. Subject to any such conditions, the proceedings of a committee with two or more members shall be governed by the articles regulating the proceedings of directors so far as they are capable of applying.

APPOINTMENT AND RETIREMENT OF DIRECTORS

73. *At the first annual general meeting all the directors shall retire from office, and at every subsequent annual general meeting one-third of the directors who are subject to retirement by rotation or, if their number is not three or a multiple of three, the number nearest to one-third shall retire from office; but, if there is only one director who is subject to retirement by rotation, he shall retire.*

NOTES

The Companies (Tables A to F) (Amendment) Regulations 2007, SI 2007/2541, regs 8, 13, provide that this regulation is revoked (as from 1 October 2007) in so far as it relates to private companies limited by shares.

74. *Subject to the provisions of the Act, the directors to retire by rotation shall be those who have been longest in office since their last appointment or reappointment, but as between persons who became or were last reappointed directors on the same day those to retire shall (unless they otherwise agree among themselves) be determined by lot.*

NOTES

The Companies (Tables A to F) (Amendment) Regulations 2007, SI 2007/2541, regs 8, 13, provide that this regulation is revoked (as from 1 October 2007) in so far as it relates to private companies limited by shares.

75. *If the company, at the meeting at which a director retires by rotation, does not fill the vacancy the retiring director shall, if willing to act, be deemed to have been reappointed unless at the meeting it is resolved not to fill the vacancy or unless a resolution for the reappointment of the director is put to the meeting and lost.*

NOTES

The Companies (Tables A to F) (Amendment) Regulations 2007, SI 2007/2541, regs 8, 13, provide that this regulation is revoked (as from 1 October 2007) in so far as it relates to private companies limited by shares.

76. No person *other than a director retiring by rotation* shall be appointed or reappointed a director at any general meeting unless—

(a) he is recommended by the directors; or

(b) not less than fourteen nor more than thirty-five clear days before the date appointed for the meeting, notice executed by a member qualified to vote at the meeting has been given to the company of the intention to propose that person for appointment or reappointment stating the particulars which would, if he were so appointed or reappointed, be required to be included in the company's register of directors together with notice executed by that person of his willingness to be appointed or reappointed.

NOTES

The Companies (Tables A to F) (Amendment) Regulations 2007, SI 2007/2541, regs 8, 14, provide that the following amendment applies (as from 1 October 2007) in so far as this Regulation relates to private companies limited by shares—

After the words "No person" omit the words "other than a director retiring by rotation".

77. Not less than seven nor more than twenty-eight clear days before the date appointed for holding a general meeting notice shall be given to all who are entitled to receive notice of the meeting of any person *(other than a director retiring by rotation at the meeting)* who is recommended by the directors for appointment or reappointment as a director at the meeting or in respect of whom notice has been duly given to the company of the intention to propose him at the meeting for appointment or reappointment as a director. The notice shall give the particulars of that person which would, if he were so appointed or reappointed, be required to be included in the company's register of directors.

NOTES

The Companies (Tables A to F) (Amendment) Regulations 2007, SI 2007/2541, regs 8, 15, provide that the following amendment applies (as from 1 October 2007) in so far as this Regulation relates to private companies limited by shares—

After the words "meeting of any person" omit the words "(other than a director retiring by rotation at the meeting)".

78. *Subject as aforesaid,* the company may by ordinary resolution appoint a person who is willing to act to be a director either to fill a vacancy or as an additional director and may also determine the rotation in which any additional directors are to retire.

NOTES

The Companies (Tables A to F) (Amendment) Regulations 2007, SI 2007/2541, regs 8, 16, provide that the following amendment applies (as from 1 October 2007) in so far as this Regulation relates to private companies limited by shares—

Omit the words "Subject as aforesaid,".

79. The directors may appoint a person who is willing to act to be a director, either to fill a vacancy or as an additional director, provided that the appointment does not cause the number of directors to exceed any number fixed by or in accordance with the articles as the maximum number of directors. *A director so appointed shall hold office only until the next following annual general meeting and shall not be taken into account in determining the directors who are to retire by rotation at the meeting. If not reappointed at such annual general meeting, he shall vacate office at the conclusion thereof.*

NOTES

The Companies (Tables A to F) (Amendment) Regulations 2007, SI 2007/2541, regs 8, 17, provide that the following amendment applies (as from 1 October 2007) in so far as this Regulation relates to private companies limited by shares—

Omit the second and third sentences.

80. *Subject as aforesaid, a director who retires at an annual general meeting may, if willing to act, be reappointed. If he is not reappointed, he shall retain office until the meeting appoints someone in his place, or if it does not do so, until the end of the meeting.*

NOTES

The Companies (Tables A to F) (Amendment) Regulations 2007, SI 2007/2541, regs 8, 18, provide that this regulation is revoked (as from 1 October 2007) in so far as it relates to private companies limited by shares.

DISQUALIFICATION AND REMOVAL OF DIRECTORS

81. The office of a director shall be vacated if—

(a) he ceases to be a director by virtue of any provision of the Act or he becomes prohibited by law from being a director; or

(b) he becomes bankrupt or makes any arrangement or composition with his creditors generally; or

(c) he is, or may be, suffering from mental disorder and either—

  (i) he is admitted to hospital in pursuance of an application for admission for treatment under the Mental Health Act 1983 or, in Scotland, an application for admission under the Mental Health (Scotland) Act 1960, or

  (ii) an order is made by a court having jurisdiction (whether in the United Kingdom or elsewhere) in matters concerning mental disorder for his detention or for the appointment of a receiver, curator bonis or other person to exercise powers with respect to his property or affairs; or

(d) he resigns his office by notice to the company; or

(e) he shall for more than six consecutive months have been absent without permission of the directors from meetings of directors held during that period and the directors resolve that his office be vacated.

REMUNERATION OF DIRECTORS

82. The directors shall be entitled to such remuneration as the company may by ordinary resolution determine and, unless the resolution provides otherwise, the remuneration shall be deemed to accrue from day to day.

DIRECTORS' EXPENSES

83. The directors may be paid all travelling, hotel, and other expenses properly incurred by them in connection with their attendance at meetings of directors or committees of directors or general meetings or separate meetings of the holders of any class of shares or of debentures of the company or otherwise in connection with the discharge of their duties.

DIRECTORS' APPOINTMENTS AND INTERESTS

84. Subject to the provisions of the Act, the directors may appoint one or more of their number to the office of managing director or to any other executive office under the company and may enter into an agreement or arrangement with any director for his employment by the company or for the provision by him of any services outside the scope of the ordinary duties of a director. Any such appointment, agreement or arrangement may be made upon such terms as the directors determine and they may remunerate any such director for his services as they think fit. Any appointment of a director to an executive office shall terminate if he ceases to be a director but without prejudice to any claim to damages for breach of the contract of service between the director and the company. A managing director and a director holding any other executive office shall not be subject to retirement by rotation.

85. Subject to the provisions of the Act, and provided that he has disclosed to the directors the nature and extent of any material interest of his, a director notwithstanding his office—

(a) may be a party to, or otherwise interested in, any transaction or arrangement with the company or in which the company is otherwise interested;

(b) may be a director or other officer of, or employed by, or a party to any transaction or arrangement with, or otherwise interested in, any body corporate promoted by the company or in which the company is otherwise interested; and

(c) shall not, by reason of his office, be accountable to the company for any benefit which he derives from any such office or employment or from any such transaction or arrangement or from any interest in any such body corporate and no such transaction or arrangement shall be liable to be avoided on the ground of any such interest or benefit.

86. For the purposes of regulation 85—

(a) a general notice given to the directors that a director is to be regarded as having an interest of the nature and extent specified in the notice in any transaction or arrangement in which a specified person or class of persons is interested shall be deemed to be a disclosure that the director has an interest in any such transaction of the nature and extent so specified; and

(b) an interest of which a director has no knowledge and of which it is unreasonable to expect him to have knowledge shall not be treated as an interest of his.

DIRECTORS' GRATUITIES AND PENSIONS

87. The directors may provide benefits, whether by the payment of gratuities or pensions or by insurance or otherwise, for any director who has held but no longer holds any executive office or employment with the company or with any body corporate which is or has been a subsidiary of the company or a predecessor in business of the company or of any such subsidiary, and for any member of his family (including a spouse and a former spouse) or any person who is or was dependent on him, and may (as well before as after he ceases to hold such office or employment) contribute to any fund and pay premiums for the purchase or provision of any such benefit.

PROCEEDINGS OF DIRECTORS

88. Subject to the provisions of the articles, the directors may regulate their proceedings as they think fit. A director may, and the secretary at the request of a director shall, call a meeting of the directors. It shall not be necessary to give notice of a meeting to a director who is absent from the United Kingdom. Questions arising at a meeting shall be decided by a majority of votes. In the case of an equality of votes, the chairman shall have a second or casting vote. A director who is also an alternate director shall be entitled in the absence of his appointor to a separate vote on behalf of his appointor in addition to his own vote.

89. The quorum for the transaction of the business of the directors may be fixed by the directors and unless so fixed at any other number shall be two. A person who holds office only as an alternate director shall, if his appointor is not present, be counted in the quorum.

90. The continuing directors or a sole continuing director may act notwithstanding any vacancies in their number, but, if the number of directors is less than the number fixed as the quorum, the continuing directors or director may act only for the purpose of filling vacancies or of calling a general meeting.

91. The directors may appoint one of their number to be the chairman of the board of directors and may at any time remove him from that office. Unless he is unwilling to do so, the director so appointed shall preside at every meeting of directors at which he is present. But if there is no director holding that office, or if the director holding it is unwilling to preside or is not present within five minutes after the time appointed for the meeting, the directors present may appoint one of their number to be chairman of the meeting.

92. All acts done by a meeting of directors, or of a committee of directors, or by a person acting as a director shall, notwithstanding that it be afterwards discovered that there was a defect in the appointment of any director or that any of them were disqualified from holding office, or had vacated office, or were not entitled to vote, be as valid as if every such person had been duly appointed and was qualified and had continued to be a director and had been entitled to vote.

93. A resolution in writing signed by all the directors entitled to receive notice of a meeting of directors or of a committee of directors shall be as valid and effectual as if it had been passed at a meeting of directors or (as the case may be) a committee of directors duly convened and held and may consist of several documents in the like form each signed by one or more directors; but a resolution signed by an alternate director need not also be signed by his appointor and, if it is signed by a director who has appointed an alternate director, it need not be signed by the alternate director in that capacity.

94. Save as otherwise provided by the articles, a director shall not vote at a meeting of directors or of a committee of directors on any resolution concerning a matter in which he has, directly or indirectly, an interest or duty which is material and which conflicts or may conflict with the interests of the company unless his interest or duty arises only because the case falls within one or more of the following paragraphs—

(a) the resolution relates to the giving to him of a guarantee, security, or indemnity in respect of money lent to, or an obligation incurred by him for the benefit of, the company or any of its subsidiaries;

(b) the resolution relates to the giving to a third party of a guarantee, security, or indemnity in respect of an obligation of the company or any of its subsidiaries for which the director has assumed responsibility in whole or part and whether alone or jointly with others under a guarantee or indemnity or by the giving of security;

(c) his interest arises by virtue of his subscribing or agreeing to subscribe for any shares, debentures or other securities of the company or any of its subsidiaries, or by virtue of his being, or intending to become, a participant in the underwriting or sub-underwriting of an offer of any such shares, debentures, or other securities by the company or any of its subsidiaries for subscription, purchase or exchange;

(d) the resolution relates in any way to a retirement benefits scheme which has been approved, or is conditional upon approval, by the Board of Inland Revenue for taxation purposes.

For the purposes of this regulation, an interest of a person who is, for any purpose of the Act (excluding any statutory modification thereof not in force when this regulation becomes binding on the company), connected with a director shall be treated as an interest of the director and, in relation to an alternate director, an interest of his appointor shall be treated as an interest of the alternate director without prejudice to any interest which the alternate director has otherwise.

95. A director shall not be counted in the quorum present at a meeting in relation to a resolution on which he is not entitled to vote.

96. The company may by ordinary resolution suspend or relax to any extent, either generally or in respect of any particular matter, any provision of the articles prohibiting a director from voting at a meeting of directors or of a committee of directors.

97. Where proposals are under consideration concerning the appointment of two or more directors to offices or employments with the company or any body corporate in which the company is interested the proposals may be divided and considered in relation to each director separately and (provided he is not for another reason precluded from voting) each of the directors concerned shall be entitled to vote and be counted in the quorum in respect of each resolution except that concerning his own appointment.

98. If a question arises at a meeting of directors or of a committee of directors as to the right of a director to vote, the question may, before the conclusion of the meeting, be referred to the chairman of the meeting and his ruling in relation to any director other than himself shall be final and conclusive.

SECRETARY

99. Subject to the provisions of the Act, the secretary shall be appointed by the directors for such term, at such remuneration and upon such conditions as they may think fit; and any secretary so appointed may be removed by them.

MINUTES

100. The directors shall cause minutes to be made in books kept for the purpose—

(a) of all appointments of officers made by the directors; and

(b) of all proceedings at meetings of the company, of the holders of any class of shares in the company, and of the directors, and of committees of directors, including the names of the directors present at each such meeting.

THE SEAL

101. The seal shall only be used by the authority of the directors or of a committee of directors authorised by the directors. The directors may determine who shall sign any instrument to which the seal is affixed and unless otherwise so determined it shall be signed by a director and by the secretary or by a second director.

DIVIDENDS

102. Subject to the provisions of the Act, the company may by ordinary resolution declare dividends in accordance with the respective rights of the members, but no dividend shall exceed the amount recommended by the directors.

103. Subject to the provisions of the Act, the directors may pay interim dividends if it appears to them that they are justified by the profits of the company available for distribution. If the share capital is divided into different classes, the directors may pay interim dividends on shares which confer deferred or non-preferred rights with regard to dividend as well as on shares which confer preferential rights with regard to dividend, but no interim dividend shall be paid on shares carrying deferred or non-preferred rights if, at the time of payment, any preferential dividend is in arrear. The directors may also pay at intervals settled by them any dividend payable at a fixed rate if it appears to them that the profits available for distribution justify the payment. Provided the directors act in good faith they shall not incur any liability to the holders of shares conferring preferred rights for any loss they may suffer by the lawful payment of an interim dividend on any shares having deferred or non-preferred rights.

104. Except as otherwise provided by the rights attached to shares, all dividends shall be declared and paid according to the amounts paid up on the shares on which the dividend is paid. All dividends shall be apportioned and paid proportionately to the amounts paid up on the shares during any portion or portions of the period in respect of which the dividend is paid; but, if any share is issued on terms providing that it shall rank for dividend as from a particular date, that share shall rank for dividend accordingly.

105. A general meeting declaring a dividend may, upon the recommendation of the directors, direct that it shall be satisfied wholly or partly by the distribution of assets and, where any difficulty arises in regard to the distribution, the directors may settle the same and in particular may issue fractional certificates and fix the value for distribution of any assets and may determine that cash shall be paid to any member upon the footing of the value so fixed in order to adjust the rights of members and may vest any assets in trustees.

106. Any dividend or other moneys payable in respect of a share may be paid by cheque sent by post to the registered address of the person entitled or, if two or more persons are the holders of the share or are jointly entitled to it by reason of the death or bankruptcy of the holder, to the registered address of that one of those persons who is first named in the register of members or to such person and to such address as the person or persons entitled may in writing direct. Every cheque shall be made payable to the order of the person or persons entitled or to such other person as the person or persons entitled may in writing direct and payment of the cheque shall be a good discharge to the company. Any joint holder or other person jointly entitled to a share as aforesaid may give receipts for any dividend or other moneys payable in respect of the share.

107. No dividend or other moneys payable in respect of a share shall bear interest against the company unless otherwise provided by the rights attached to the share.

108. Any dividend which has remained unclaimed for twelve years from the date when it became due for payment shall, if the directors so resolve, be forfeited and cease to remain owing by the company.

ACCOUNTS

109. No member shall (as such) have any right of inspecting any accounting records or other book or document of the company except as conferred by statute or authorised by the directors or by ordinary resolution of the company.

CAPITALISATION OF PROFITS

110. The directors may with the authority of an ordinary resolution of the company—

(a) subject as hereinafter provided, resolve to capitalise any undivided profits of the company not required for paying any preferential dividend (whether or not they are available for distribution) or any sum standing to the credit of the company's share premium account or capital redemption reserve;

(b) appropriate the sum resolved to be capitalised to the members who would have been entitled to it if it were distributed by way of dividend and in the same proportions and apply such sum on their behalf either in or towards paying up the amounts, if any, for the time being unpaid on any shares held by them respectively, or in paying up in full unissued shares or debentures of the company of a nominal amount equal to that sum, and allot the shares or debentures credited as fully paid to those members, or as they may direct, in those proportions, or partly in one way and partly in the other: but the share premium account, the capital redemption reserve, and any profits which are not available for distribution may, for the purposes of this regulation, only be applied in paying up unissued shares to be allotted to members credited as fully paid;

(c) make such provision by the issue of fractional certificates or by payment in cash or otherwise as they determine in the case of shares or debentures becoming distributable under this regulation in fractions; and

(d) authorise any person to enter on behalf of all the members concerned into an agreement with the company providing for the allotment to them respectively, credited as fully paid, of any shares or debentures to which they are entitled upon such capitalisation, any agreement made under such authority being binding on all such members.

NOTICES

[111. Any notice to be given to or by any person pursuant to the articles (other than a notice calling a meeting of the directors) shall be in writing or shall be given using electronic communications to an address for the time being notified for that purpose to the person giving the notice.

In this regulation, "address", in relation to electronic communications, includes any number or address used for the purposes of such communications.]

NOTES

Substituted by the Companies Act 1985 (Electronic Communications) Order 2000, SI 2000/3373, art 32(1), Sch 1, para 6, as from 22 December 2000. The original reg 111 read as follows—

"111. Any notice to be given to or by any person pursuant to the articles shall be in writing except that a notice calling a meeting of the directors need not be in writing.".

112. The company may give any notice to a member either personally or by sending it by post in a prepaid envelope addressed to the member at his registered address or by leaving it at that address [or by giving it using electronic communications to an address for the time being notified to the company by the member]. In the case of joint holders of a share, all notices shall be given to the joint holder whose name stands first in the register of members in respect of the joint holding and notice so given shall be sufficient notice to all the joint holders. A member whose registered address is not within the United Kingdom and who gives to the company an address within the United Kingdom at which notices may be given to him[, or an address to which notices may be sent using electronic communications,] shall be entitled to have notices given to him at that address, but otherwise no such member shall be entitled to receive any notice from the company.

[In this regulation and the next, "address", in relation to electronic communications, includes any number or address used for the purposes of such communications.]

NOTES

Words in square brackets inserted by the Companies Act 1985 (Electronic Communications) Order 2000, SI 2000/3373, art 32(1), Sch 1, para 7, as from 22 December 2000.

113. A member present, either in person or by proxy, at any meeting of the company or of the holders of any class of shares in the company shall be deemed to have received notice of the meeting and, where requisite, of the purposes for which it was called.

114. Every person who becomes entitled to a share shall be bound by any notice in respect of that share which, before his name is entered in the register of members, has been duly given to a person from whom he derives his title.

115. Proof that an envelope containing a notice was properly addressed, prepaid and posted shall be conclusive evidence that the notice was given. [Proof that a notice contained in an electronic communication was sent in accordance with guidance issued by the Institute of Chartered Secretaries and Administrators shall be conclusive evidence that the notice was given.] A notice shall, *unless the contrary is proved,* be deemed to be given at the expiration of 48 hours after the envelope containing it was posted [or, in the case of a notice contained in an electronic communication, at the expiration of 48 hours after the time it was sent].

NOTES

Words in square brackets inserted by the Companies Act 1985 (Electronic Communications) Order 2000, SI 2000/3373, art 32(1), Sch 1, para 8, as from 22 December 2000; words in italics revoked by the Companies (Tables A to F) (Amendment) Regulations 1985, SI 1985/1052, reg 2, as from 1 August 1985.

116. A notice may be given by the company to the persons entitled to a share in consequence of the death or bankruptcy of a member by sending or delivering it, in any manner authorised by the articles for the giving of notice to a member, addressed to them by name, or by the title of representatives of the deceased, or trustee of the bankrupt or by any like description at the address, if any, within the United Kingdom supplied for that purpose by the persons claiming to be so entitled. Until such an address has been supplied, a notice may be given in any manner in which it might have been given if the death or bankruptcy had not occurred.

Winding Up

117. If the company is wound up, the liquidator may, with the sanction of [a special] resolution of the company and any other sanction required by the Act, divide among the members in specie the whole or any part of the assets of the company and may, for that purpose, value any assets and determine how the division shall be carried out as between the members or different classes of members. The liquidator may, with the like sanction, vest the whole or any part of the assets in trustees upon such trusts for the benefit of the members as he with the like sanction determines, but no member shall be compelled to accept any assets upon which there is a liability.

NOTES

Words in square brackets substituted for the original words "an extraordinary" by the Companies (Tables A to F) (Amendment) Regulations 2007, SI 2007/2541, reg 7, as from 1 October 2007.

Indemnity

118. Subject to the provisions of the Act but without prejudice to any indemnity to which a director may otherwise be entitled, every director or other officer or auditor of the company shall be indemnified out of the assets of the company against any liability incurred by him in defending any proceedings, whether civil or criminal, in which judgment is given in his favour or in which he is acquitted or in connection with any application in which relief is granted to him by the court from liability for negligence, default, breach of duty or breach of trust in relation to the affairs of the company.

Appendix 3: Companies Act 1948, Table A

[A3]

NOTES

Table A was contained in the First Schedule to the Companies Act 1948.

Generally, the Table A which applies to any company is the Table A in force at the date of the company's registration, and if Table A is altered, the alteration does not affect a company registered before the alteration takes effect; see CA 1985, s 8(2), (3) and the introductory notes to the 1985 Table A at **[A2]**. Note that CA 1985, s 8 was repealed by CA 2006, but see further the note relating to SI 2008/2860 below.

Accordingly, Table A to the 1948 Act, which was specifically preserved by the Companies Consolidation (Consequential Provisions) Act 1985, s 31(8), is set out below both in its original form and in its form as amended at different dates. Note that the Companies Consolidation (Consequential Provisions) Act 1985 was repealed by the Companies Act 2006 (Consequential Amendments and Transitional Provisions) Order 2011, SI 2011/1265, art 2, as from 12 May 2011. Article 5 of the 2011 Order (at **[4.427]**) provides, inter alia, that the repeal of the 1985 Act does not affect the operation of any saving that remains capable of having effect in relation to the repeal of an enactment by that Act.

Part I of Table A applies (subject to the savings set out in CA 1980, s 88(4)) in relation to private companies limited by shares as it applies in relation to public companies so limited (CA 1980, Sch 3, para 36(1)).

Note that the Companies Act 2006 (Commencement No 8, Transitional Provisions and Savings) Order 2008, SI 2008/2860, Sch 2, para 1(1) provides that nothing in the Companies Act 2006 affects (a) the registration or re-registration of a company under the former Companies Acts, or the continued existence of a company by virtue of such registration or re-registration, or (b) the application in relation to an existing company of (i) Table B in the Joint Stock Companies Act 1856, (ii) Table A in any of the former Companies Acts, or (iii) the Companies (Tables A to F) Regulations 1985 or the Companies (Tables A to F) Regulations (Northern Ireland) 1986.

TABLE A

PART I REGULATIONS FOR MANAGEMENT OF A COMPANY LIMITED BY SHARES, NOT BEING A PRIVATE COMPANY

Interpretation

1. In these regulations:—

"the Act" means the Companies Act, 1948.

"the seal" means the common seal of the company.

"secretary" means any person appointed to perform the duties of the secretary of the company.

"the United Kingdom" means Great Britain and Northern Ireland.

Expressions referring to writing shall, unless the contrary intention appears, be construed as including references to printing, lithography, photography, and other modes of representing or reproducing words in a visible form.

Unless the context otherwise requires, words or expressions contained in these regulations shall bear the same meaning as in the Act or any statutory modification thereof in force at the date at which these regulations become binding on the company.

Share Capital and Variation of Rights

2. Without prejudice to any special rights previously conferred on the holders of any existing shares or class of shares, any share in the company may be issued with such preferred, deferred or other special rights or such restrictions, whether in regard to dividend, voting, return of capital or otherwise as the company may from time to time by ordinary resolution determine.

3. Subject to the provisions of *section 58 of the Act, any preference shares* may, with the sanction of an ordinary resolution, be issued on the terms that they are, or at the option of the company are liable, to be redeemed on such terms and in such manner as the company before the issue of the shares may by special resolution determine.

NOTES

Reg 3: for the words in italics there are substituted the words "Part III of CA 1981, any shares" by CA 1981, Sch 3, in relation to any company registered on or after 3 December 1981.

4. If at any time the share capital is divided into different classes of shares, the rights attached to any class (*unless otherwise provided by the terms of issue of the shares of that class*) may, whether or not the company is being wound up, be varied with the consent in writing of the holders of three-fourths of the issued shares of that class, or with the sanction of an extraordinary resolution passed at a separate general meeting of the holders of the shares of the class. *To every such separate general meeting the provisions of these regulations relating to general meetings shall apply, but so that the necessary quorum shall be two persons at least holding or representing by proxy one-third of the issued shares of the class and that any holder of shares of the class present in person or by proxy may demand a poll.*

NOTES

Words in italics repealed by CA 1980, Sch 4, in relation to any company registered on or after 22 December 1980.

5. The rights conferred upon the holders of the shares of any class issued with preferred or other rights shall not, unless otherwise expressly provided by the terms of issue of the shares of that class, be deemed to be varied by the creation or issue of further shares ranking pari passu therewith.

6. The company may exercise the powers of paying commissions conferred by section 53 of the Act, provided that the rate per cent or amount of the commission paid or agreed to be paid shall be disclosed in the manner required by the said section and the rate of the commission shall not exceed the rate of 10 per cent of the price at which the shares in respect whereof the same is paid are issued or an amount equal to 10 per cent of such price (as the case may be). Such commission may be satisfied by the payment of cash or the allotment of fully or partly paid shares or partly in one way and partly in the other. The company may also on any issue of shares pay such brokerage as may be lawful.

7. Except as required by law, no person shall be recognised by the company as holding any share upon any trust, and the company shall not be bound by or be compelled in any way to recognise (even when having notice thereof) any equitable, contingent, future or partial interest in any share or any interest in any fractional part of a share or (except only as by these regulations or by law otherwise provided) any other rights in respect of any share except an absolute right to the entirety thereof in the registered holder.

8. Every person whose name is entered as a member in the register of members shall be entitled without payment to receive within two months after allotment or lodgment of transfer (or within such other period as the conditions of issue shall provide) one certificate for all his shares or several certificates each for one or more of his shares upon payment of 2s 6d for every certificate after the first or such less sum as the directors shall from time to time determine. Every certificate shall be under the seal [or under the official seal kept by the company by virtue of section 2 of the Stock Exchange (Completion of Bargains) Act 1976] and shall specify the shares to which it relates and the amount paid up thereon. Provided that in respect of a share or shares held jointly by several persons the company shall not be bound to issue more than one certificate, and delivery of a certificate for a share to one of several joint holders shall be sufficient delivery to all such holders.

NOTES

Reg 8: words in square brackets inserted by the Stock Exchange (Completion of Bargains) Act 1976, s 2(3), in relation to any company registered on or after 2 February 1979.

9. If a share certificate be defaced, lost or destroyed, it may be renewed on payment of a fee of 2s 6d or such less sum and on such terms (if any) as to evidence and indemnity and the payment of out-of-pocket expenses of the company of investigating evidence as the directors think fit.

10. *The company shall not give, whether directly or indirectly, and whether by means of a loan, guarantee, the provision of security or otherwise, any financial assistance for the purpose of or in connection with a purchase or subscription made or to be made by any person of or for any shares in the company or in its holding company nor shall the company make a loan for any purpose whatsoever on the security of its shares or those of its holding company, but nothing in this regulation shall prohibit transactions mentioned in the proviso to section 54(1) of the Act.*

NOTES

Reg 10: repealed by CA 1981, Sch 4, in relation to any company registered on or after 3 December 1981.

Lien

11. The company shall have a first and paramount lien on every share (not being a fully paid share) for all moneys (whether presently payable or not) called or payable at a fixed time in respect of that share, *and the company shall also have a first and paramount lien on all shares (other than fully paid shares) standing registered in the name of a single person for all moneys presently payable by him or his estate to the company*; but the directors may at any time declare any share to be wholly or in part exempt from the provisions of this regulation. The company's lien, if any, on a share shall extend to all dividends payable thereon.

NOTES

Words in italics repealed by CA 1980, Sch 4, in relation to any company registered on or after 22 December 1980.

12. The company may sell, in such manner as the directors think fit, any shares on which the company has a lien, but no sale shall be made unless a sum in respect of which the lien exists is presently payable, nor until the expiration of fourteen days after a notice in writing, stating and demanding payment of such part of the amount in respect of which the lien exists as is presently payable, has been given to the registered holder for the time being of the share, or the person entitled thereto by reason of his death or bankruptcy.

13. To give effect to any such sale the directors may authorise some person to transfer the shares sold to the purchaser thereof. The purchaser shall be registered as the holder of the shares comprised in any such transfer, and he shall not be bound to see to the application of the purchase money, nor shall his title to the shares be affected by any irregularity or invalidity in the proceedings in reference to the sale.

14. The proceeds of the sale shall be received by the company and applied in payment of such part of the amount in respect of which the lien exists as is presently payable, and the residue, if any, shall (subject to a like lien for sums not presently payable as existed upon the shares before the sale) be paid to the person entitled to the shares at the date of the sale.

Calls on Shares

15. The directors may from time to time make calls upon the members in respect of any moneys unpaid on their shares (whether on account of the nominal value of the shares or by way of premium) and not by the conditions of allotment thereof made payable at fixed times, provided that no call shall exceed one-fourth of the nominal value of the share or be payable at less than one month from the date fixed for the payment of the last preceding call, and each member shall (subject to receiving at least fourteen days' notice specifying the time or times and place of payment) pay to the company at the time or times and place so specified the amount called on his shares. A call may be revoked or postponed as the directors may determine.

16. A call shall be deemed to have been made at the time when the resolution of the directors authorising the call was passed and may be required to be paid by instalments.

17. The joint holders of a share shall be jointly and severally liable to pay all calls in respect thereof.

18. If a sum called in respect of a share is not paid before or on the day appointed for payment thereof, the person from whom the sum is due shall pay interest on the sum from the day appointed for payment thereof to the time of actual payment at such rate not exceeding 5 per cent per annum as the directors may determine, but the directors shall be at liberty to waive payment of such interest wholly or in part.

19. Any sum which by the terms of issue of a share becomes payable on allotment or at any fixed date, whether on account of the nominal value of the share or by way of premium, shall for the purposes of these regulations be deemed to be a call duly made and payable on the date on which by the terms of issue the same becomes payable, and in case of non-payment all the relevant provisions of these regulations as to payment of interest and expenses, forfeiture or otherwise shall apply as if such sum had become payable by virtue of a call duly made and notified.

20. The directors may, on the issue of shares, differentiate between the holders as to the amount of calls to be paid and the times of payment.

21. The directors may, if they think fit, receive from any member willing to advance the same, all or any part of the moneys uncalled and unpaid upon any shares held by him, and upon all or any of the moneys so advanced may (until the same would, but for such advance, become payable) pay interest at such rate not exceeding (unless the company in general meeting shall otherwise direct) 5 per cent per annum, as may be agreed upon between the directors and the member paying such sum in advance.

Transfer of Shares

22. The instrument of transfer of any share shall be executed by or on behalf of the transferor and transferee, and, *except as provided by sub-paragraph (a) of paragraph 2 of the Seventh Schedule to the Act*, the transferor shall be deemed to remain a holder of the share until the name of the transferee is entered in the register of members in respect thereof.

NOTES

Words in italics repealed by CA 1967, Sch 8, Pt III, in relation to any company registered on or after 27 January 1968.

23. Subject to such of the restrictions of these regulations as may be applicable, any member may transfer all or any of his shares by instrument in writing in any usual or common form or any other form which the directors may approve.

24. The directors may decline to register the transfer of a share (not being a fully paid share) to a person of whom they shall not approve, and they may also decline to register the transfer of a share on which the company has a lien.

25. The directors may also decline to recognise any instrument of transfer unless:—

(a) a fee of 2s 6d or such lesser sum as the directors may from time to time require is paid to the company in respect thereof;

(b) the instrument of transfer is accompanied by the certificate of the shares to which it relates, and such other evidence as the directors may reasonably require to show the right of the transferor to make the transfer; and

(c) the instrument of transfer is in respect of only one class of share.

26. If the directors refuse to register a transfer they shall within two months after the date on which the transfer was lodged with the company send to the transferee notice of the refusal.

27. The registration of transfers may be suspended at such times and for such periods as the directors may from time to time determine, provided always that such registration shall not be suspended for more than thirty days in any year.

28. The company shall be entitled to charge a fee not exceeding 2s 6d on the registration of every probate, letters of administration, certificate of death or marriage, power of attorney, notice in lieu of distringas, or other instrument.

Transmission of Shares

29. In case of the death of a member the survivor or survivors where the deceased was a joint holder, and the legal personal representatives of the deceased where he was a sole holder, shall be the only persons recognised by the company as having any title to his interest in the shares; but nothing herein contained shall release the estate of a deceased joint holder from any liability in respect of any share which had been jointly held by him with other persons.

30. Any person becoming entitled to a share in consequence of the death or bankruptcy of a member may, upon such evidence being produced as may from time to time properly be required by the directors and subject as hereinafter provided, elect either to be registered himself as holder of the share or to have some person nominated by him registered as the transferee thereof, but the directors shall, in either case, have the same right to decline or suspend registration as they would have had in the case of a transfer of the share by that member before his death or bankruptcy, as the case may be.

31. If the person so becoming entitled shall elect to be registered himself, he shall deliver or send to the company a notice in writing signed by him stating that he so elects. If he shall elect to have another person registered he shall testify his election by executing to that person a transfer of the share. All the limitations, restrictions and provisions of these regulations relating to the right to transfer and the registration of transfers of shares shall be applicable to any such notice or transfer as aforesaid as if the death or bankruptcy of the member had not occurred and the notice or transfer were a transfer signed by that member.

32. A person becoming entitled to a share by reason of the death or bankruptcy of the holder shall be entitled to the same dividends and other advantages to which he would be entitled if he were the registered holder of the share, except that he shall not, before being registered as a member in respect of the share, be entitled in respect of it to exercise any right conferred by membership in relation to meetings of the company:

Provided always that the directors may at any time give notice requiring any such person to elect either to be registered himself or to transfer the share, and if the notice is not complied with within ninety days the directors may thereafter withhold payment of all dividends, bonuses or other moneys payable in respect of the share until the requirements of the notice have been complied with.

Forfeiture of Shares

33. If a member fails to pay any call or instalment of a call on the day appointed for payment thereof, the directors may, at any time thereafter during such time as any part of the call or instalment remains unpaid, serve a notice on him requiring payment of so much of the call or instalment as is unpaid, together with any interest which may have accrued.

34. The notice shall name a further day (not earlier than the expiration of fourteen days from the date of service of the notice) on or before which the payment required by the notice is to be made, and shall state that in the event of non-payment at or before the time appointed the shares in respect of which the call was made will be liable to be forfeited.

35. If the requirements of any such notice as aforesaid are not complied with, any share in respect of which the notice has been given may at any time thereafter, before the payment required by the notice has been made, be forfeited by a resolution of the directors to that effect.

36. A forfeited share may be sold or otherwise disposed of on such terms and in such manner as the directors think fit, and at any time before a sale or disposition the forfeiture may be cancelled on such terms as the directors think fit.

37. A person whose shares have been forfeited shall cease to be a member in respect of the forfeited shares, but shall, notwithstanding, remain liable to pay to the company all moneys which, at the date of forfeiture, were payable by him to the company in respect of the shares, but his liability shall cease if and when the company shall have received payment in full of all such moneys in respect of the shares.

38. A statutory declaration in writing that the declarant is a director or the secretary of the company, and that a share in the company has been duly forfeited on a date stated in the declaration, shall be conclusive evidence of the facts therein stated as against all persons claiming to be entitled to the share. The company may receive the consideration, if any, given for the share on any sale or disposition thereof and may execute a transfer of the share in favour of the person to whom the share is sold or disposed of and he shall thereupon be registered as the holder of the share, and shall not be bound to see to the application of the purchase money, if any, nor shall his title to the share be affected by any irregularity or invalidity in the proceedings in reference to the forfeiture, sale or disposal of the share.

39. The provisions of these regulations as to forfeiture shall apply in the case of non-payment of any sum which, by the terms of issue of a share, becomes payable at a fixed time, whether on account of the nominal value of the share or by way of premium, as if the same had been payable by virtue of a call duly made and notified.

Conversion of Shares into Stock

40. The company may by ordinary resolution convert any paid-up shares into stock, and reconvert any stock into paid-up shares of any denomination.

41. The holders of stock may transfer the same, or any part thereof, in the same manner, and subject to the same regulations, as and subject to which the shares from which the stock arose might previously to conversion have been transferred, or as near thereto as circumstances admit; and the directors may from time to time fix the minimum amount of stock transferable but so that such minimum shall not exceed the nominal amount of the shares from which the stock arose.

42. The holders of stock shall, according to the amount of stock held by them, have the same rights, privileges and advantages as regards dividends, voting at meetings of the company and other matters as if they held the shares from which the stock arose, but no such privilege or advantage (except participation in the dividends and profits of the company and in the assets on winding up) shall be conferred by an amount of stock which would not, if existing in shares, have conferred that privilege or advantage.

43. Such of the regulations of the company as are applicable to paid-up shares shall apply to stock, and words "share" and "shareholder" therein shall include "stock" and "stockholder".

Alteration of Capital

44. The company may from time to time by ordinary resolution increase the share capital by such sum, to be divided into shares of such amount, as the resolution shall prescribe.

45. The company may by ordinary resolution—

(a) consolidate and divide all or any of its share capital to shares of larger amount than its existing shares;

(b) sub-divide its existing shares, or any of them, into shares of smaller amount than is fixed by the memorandum of association subject, nevertheless, to the provisions of section 61(1)(d) of the Act;

(c) cancel any shares which, at the date of the passing of the resolution, have not been taken or agreed to be taken by any person.

46. The company may by special resolution reduce its share capital, any capital redemption reserve fund or any share premium account in any manner and with, and subject to, any incident authorised, and consent required, by law.

General Meetings

47. The company shall in each year hold a general meeting as its annual general meeting in addition to any other meetings in that year, and shall specify the meeting as such in the notices calling it; and not more than fifteen months shall elapse between the date of one annual general meeting of the company and that of the next. Provided that so long as the company holds its first annual general meeting within eighteen months of its incorporation, it need not hold it in the year of its incorporation or in the following year. The annual general meeting shall be held at such time and place as the directors shall appoint.

48. All general meetings other than annual general meetings shall be called extraordinary general meetings.

49. The directors may, whenever they think fit, convene an extraordinary general meeting, and extraordinary general meetings shall also be convened on such requisition, or, in default, may be convened by such requisitionists, as provided by section 132 of the Act. If at any time there are not within the United Kingdom sufficient directors capable of acting to form a quorum, any director or any two members of the company may convene an extraordinary general meeting in the same manner as nearly as possible as that in which meetings may be convened by the directors.

Notice of General Meetings

50. An annual general meeting and a meeting called for the passing of a special resolution shall be called by twenty-one days' notice in writing at the least, and a meeting of the company other than an annual general meeting or a meeting for the passing of a special resolution shall be called by fourteen days' notice in writing at the least. The notice shall be exclusive of the day on which it is served or deemed to be served and of the day for which it is given, and shall specify the place, the day and the hour of meeting and, in case of special business, the general nature of that business, and shall be given, in manner hereinafter mentioned or in such other manner, if any, as may be prescribed by the company in general meeting, to such persons as are, under the regulations of the company, entitled to receive such notices from the company:

Provided that a meeting of the company shall, notwithstanding that it is called by shorter notice than that specified in this regulation, be deemed to have been duly called if it is so agreed—

(a) in the case of a meeting called as the annual general meeting, by all the members entitled to attend and vote thereat; and

(b) in the case of any other meeting, by a majority in number of the members having a right to attend and vote at the meeting, being a majority together holding not less than 95 per cent in nominal value of the shares giving that right.

51. The accidental omission to give notice of a meeting to, or the non-receipt of notice of a meeting by, any person entitled to receive notice shall not invalidate the proceedings at that meeting.

Proceedings at General Meetings

52. All business shall be deemed special that is transacted at an extraordinary general meeting, and also all that is transacted at an annual general meeting, with the exception of declaring a dividend, the consideration of the accounts, balance sheets, and the reports of the directors and auditors, the election of directors in the place of those retiring and the appointment of, and the fixing of the remuneration of, the auditors.

53. No business shall be transacted at any general meeting unless a quorum of members is present at the time when the meeting proceeds to business; save as herein otherwise provided *three members present in person shall be a quorum.*

NOTES

For the words in italics there are substituted the words "two members present in person or by proxy shall be a quorum" by CA 1980, Sch 3, in relation to any company registered on or after 22 December 1980.

54. If within half an hour from the time appointed for the meeting a quorum is not present, the meeting, if convened upon the requisition of members, shall be dissolved; in any other case it shall stand adjourned to the same day in the next week, at the same time and place or to such other day and at such other time and place as the directors may determine, *and if at the adjourned meeting a quorum is not present within half an hour from the time appointed for the meeting, the members present shall be a quorum.*

NOTES

Words in italics repealed by CA 1980, Sch 4, in relation to any company registered on or after 22 December 1980.

55. The chairman, if any, of the board of directors shall preside as chairman at every general meeting of the company, or if there is no such chairman, or if he shall not be present within fifteen minutes after the time appointed for the holding of the meeting or is unwilling to act the directors present shall elect one of their number to be chairman of the meeting.

56. If at any meeting no director is willing to act as chairman or if no director is present within fifteen minutes after the time appointed for holding the meeting, the members present shall choose one of their number to be chairman of the meeting.

57. The chairman may, with the consent of any meeting at which a quorum is present (and shall if so directed by the meeting), adjourn the meeting from time to time and from place to place, but no business shall be transacted at any adjourned meeting other than the business left unfinished at the meeting from which the adjournment took place. When a meeting is adjourned for thirty days or more, notice of the adjourned meeting shall be given as in the case of an original meeting. Save as aforesaid it shall not be necessary to give any notice of an adjournment or of the business to be transacted at an adjourned meeting.

58. At any general meeting a resolution put to the vote of the meeting shall be decided on a show of hands unless a poll is (before or on the declaration of the result of the show of hands) demanded—

(a) by the chairman; or

(b) by at least *three* members present in person or by proxy; or

(c) by any member or members present in person or by proxy and representing not less than one-tenth of the total voting rights of all the members having the right to vote at the meeting; or

(d) by a member or members holding shares in the company conferring a right to vote at the meeting being shares on which an aggregate sum has been paid up equal to not less than one-tenth of the total sum paid up on all the shares conferring that right.

Unless a poll be so demanded a declaration by the chairman that a resolution has on a show of hands been carried or carried unanimously, or by a particular majority, or lost and an entry to that effect in the book containing the minutes of the proceedings of the company shall be conclusive evidence of the fact without proof of the number or proportion of the votes recorded in favour of or against such resolution.

The demand for a poll may be withdrawn.

NOTES

For the word in italics there is substituted the word "two" by CA 1980, Sch 3, in relation to any company registered on or after 22 December 1980.

59. Except as provided in regulation 61, if a poll is duly demanded it shall be taken in such manner as the chairman directs, and the result of the poll shall be deemed to be the resolution of the meeting at which the poll was demanded.

60. In the case of an equality of votes, whether on a show of hands or on a poll, the chairman of the meeting at which the show of hands takes place or at which the poll is demanded, shall be entitled to a second or casting vote.

61. A poll demanded on the election of a chairman or on a question of adjournment shall be taken forthwith. A poll demanded on any other question shall be taken at such time as the chairman of the meeting directs, and any business other than that upon which a poll has been demanded may be proceeded with pending the taking of the poll.

Votes of Members

62. Subject to any rights or restrictions for the time being attached to any class or classes of shares, on a show of hands every member present in person shall have one vote, and on a poll every member shall have one vote for each share of which he is the holder.

63. In the case of joint holders the vote of the senior who tenders a vote, whether in person or by proxy, shall be accepted to the exclusion of the votes of the other joint holders; and for this purpose seniority shall be determined by the order in which the names stand in the register of members.

64. A member of unsound mind, or in respect of whom an order has been made by any court having jurisdiction in lunacy, may vote, whether on a show of hands or on a poll, by his committee, receiver, curator bonis, or other person in the nature of a committee, receiver or curator bonis appointed by that court, and any such committee, receiver, curator bonis or other person may, on a poll, vote by proxy.

65. No member shall be entitled to vote at any general meeting unless all calls or other sums presently payable by him in respect of shares in the company have been paid.

66. No objection shall be raised to the qualification of any voter except at the meeting or adjourned meeting at which the vote objected to is given or tendered, and every vote not disallowed at such meeting shall be valid for all purposes. Any such objection made in due time shall be referred to the chairman of the meeting whose decision shall be final and conclusive.

67. On a poll votes may be given either personally or by proxy.

68. The instrument appointing a proxy shall be in writing under the hand of the appointer or of his attorney duly authorised in writing, or, if the appointer is a corporation, either under seal, or under the hand of an officer or attorney duly authorised. A proxy need not be a member of the company.

69. The instrument appointing a proxy and the power of attorney or other authority if any, under which it is signed or a notarially certified copy of that power or authority shall be deposited at the registered office of the company or at such other place within the United Kingdom as is specified for that purpose in the notice convening the meeting, not less than 48 hours before the time for holding the meeting or adjourned meeting, at which the person named in the instrument proposes to vote, or, in the case of a poll, not less than 24 hours before the time appointed for the taking of the poll, and in default the instrument of proxy shall not be treated as valid.

70. An instrument appointing a proxy shall be in the following form or a form as near thereto as circumstances admit—

". . . . . Limited

I/We, ... of . . . .

in the county of . . . . ,

being a member/members of the above-named company,

hereby appoint . . . . of . . . . ,

or failing him, ... of . . . . ,

as my/our proxy to vote for me/us on my/our behalf at the [annual or extraordinary, as the case may be] general meeting of the company, to be held on

the . . . . day of . . . . 19. . . . . , and at any adjournment thereof.

Signed this . . . . day of . . . . 19. . . . . "

71. Where it is desired to afford members an opportunity of voting for or against a resolution the instrument appointing a proxy shall be in the following form or a form as near thereto as circumstances admit—

". . . . . Limited

I/We, ... of . . . .

in the county of . . . . ,

being a member/members of the above-named company,

hereby appoint . . . . of . . . . ,

or failing him, ... of . . . . ,

as my/our proxy to vote for me/us on my/our behalf at the [annual or extraordinary, as the case may be] general meeting of the company, to be held on

the . . . . day of . . . . 19. . . . . , and at any adjournment thereof.

Signed this . . . . day of . . . . 19. . . . ."

This form is to be used *in favour of/against the resolution. Unless otherwise instructed, the proxy will vote as he thinks fit.

* Strike out whichever is not desired."

72. The instrument appointing a proxy shall be deemed to confer authority to demand or join in demanding a poll.

73. A vote given in accordance with the terms of an instrument of proxy shall be valid notwithstanding the previous death or insanity of the principal or revocation of the proxy or of the authority under which the proxy was executed, on the transfer of the share in respect of which the proxy is given, provided that no intimation in writing of such death, insanity, revocation or transfer as aforesaid shall have been received by the company at the office before the commencement of the meeting or adjourned meeting at which the proxy is used.

[73A. Subject to the provisions of CAs 1948 to *1980* a resolution in writing signed by all the members for the time being entitled to receive notice of and to attend and vote at general meetings (or being corporations by their duly authorised representatives) shall be as valid and effective as if the same had been passed at a general meeting of the company duly convened and held.]

NOTES

Added by CA 1980, Sch 3, in relation to any company registered on or after 22 December 1980; for the year in italics there is substituted the year "1981" by CA 1981, Sch 3, in relation to any company registered on or after 3 December 1981.

Corporations acting by Representatives at Meetings

74. Any corporation which is a member of the company may by resolution of its directors or other governing body authorise such person as it thinks fit to act as its representative at any meeting of the company or of any class of members of the company, and the person so authorised shall be entitled to exercise the same powers on behalf of the corporation which he represents as that corporation could exercise if it were an individual member of the company.

Directors

75. The number of the directors and the names of the first directors shall be determined in writing by the subscribers of the memorandum of association or a majority of them.

76. The remuneration of the directors shall from time to time be determined by the company in general meeting. Such remuneration shall be deemed to accrue from day to day. The directors may also be paid all travelling, hotel and other expenses properly incurred by them in attending and returning from meetings of the directors or any committee of the directors or general meetings of the company or in connection with the business of the company.

77. The shareholding qualification for directors may be fixed by the company in general meeting, and unless and until so fixed no qualification shall be required.

78. A director of the company may be or become a director or other officer of, or otherwise interested in, any company promoted by the company or in which the company may be interested as shareholder or otherwise, and no such director shall be accountable to the company for any remuneration or other benefits received by him as a director or officer of, or from his interest in, such other company unless the company otherwise direct.

Borrowing Powers

79. The directors may exercise all the powers of the company to borrow money, and to mortgage or charge its undertaking, property and uncalled capital or any part thereof, and[, subject to section 14 of CA 1980] to issue debentures, debenture stock, and other securities whether outright or as security for any debt, liability or obligation of the company or of any third party:

Provided that the amount for the time being remaining undischarged of moneys borrowed or secured by the directors as aforesaid (apart from temporary loans obtained from the company's bankers in the ordinary course of business) shall not at any time, without the previous sanction of the company in general meeting, exceed the nominal amount of the share capital of the company for the time being issued, but nevertheless no lender or other person dealing with the company shall be concerned to see or inquire whether this limit is observed. No debt incurred or security given in excess of such limit shall be invalid or ineffectual except in the case of express notice to the lender or the recipient of the security at the time when the debt was incurred or security given that the limit hereby imposed had been or was thereby exceeded.

NOTES

Words in square brackets inserted by CA 1980, Sch 3, in relation to any company registered on or after 22 December 1980.

Powers and Duties of Directors

80. The business of the company shall be managed by the directors, who may pay all expenses incurred in promoting and registering the company, and may exercise all such powers of the company as are not, by the *Act* or by these regulations, required to be exercised by the company in general meeting, subject, nevertheless, to any of these regulations, to the provisions of the *Act* and to such regulations being not inconsistent with the aforesaid regulations or provisions, as may be prescribed by the company in general meeting; but no regulation made by the company in general meeting shall invalidate any prior act of the directors which would have been valid if that regulation had not been made.

NOTES

For the words in italics there are substituted the words "Companies Acts 1948 to 1980" in both places by CA 1980, Sch 3, in relation to companies registered on or after 22 December 1980; in the text as substituted the year "1980" is substituted by the year "1981" by CA 1981, Sch 3, in relation to companies registered on or after 3 December 1981.

81. The directors may from time to time and at any time by power of attorney appoint any company, firm or person or body of persons, whether nominated directly or indirectly by the directors, to be the attorney or attorneys of the company for such purposes and with such powers, authorities and discretions (not exceeding those vested in or exercisable by the directors under these regulations) and for such period and subject to such conditions as they may think fit, and any such powers of attorney may contain such provisions for the protection and convenience of persons dealing with any such attorney as the directors may think fit and may also authorise any such attorney to delegate all or any of the powers, authorities and discretions vested in him.

82. The company may exercise the powers conferred by section 35 of the Act with regard to having an official seal for use abroad, and such powers shall be vested in the directors.

83. The company may exercise the powers conferred upon the company by sections 119 to 123 (both inclusive) of the Act with regard to the keeping of a dominion register, and the directors may (subject to the provisions of those sections) make and vary such regulations as they may think fit respecting the keeping of any such register.

84. (1) A director who is in any way, whether directly or indirectly, interested in a contract or proposed contract with the company shall declare the nature of his interest at a meeting of the directors in accordance with section 199 of the Act.

(2) A director shall not vote in respect of any contract or arrangement in which he is interested, and if he shall do so his vote shall not be counted, nor shall he be counted in the quorum present at the meeting, but neither of these prohibitions shall apply to—

(a) any arrangement for giving any director any security or indemnity in respect of money lent by him to or obligations undertaken by him for the benefit of the company; or

(b) to any arrangement for the giving by the company of any security to a third party in respect of a debt or obligation of the company for which the director himself has assumed responsibility in whole or in part under a guarantee or indemnity or by the deposit of a security; or

(c) any contract by a director to subscribe for or underwrite shares or debentures of the company; or

(d) any contract or arrangement with any other company in which he is interested only as an officer of the company or as holder of shares or other securities;

and these prohibitions may at any time be suspended or relaxed to any extent, and either generally or in respect of any particular contract, arrangement or transaction, by the company in general meeting.

(3) A director may hold any other office or place of profit under the company (other than the office of auditor) in conjunction with his office of director for such period and on such terms (as to remuneration and otherwise) as the directors may determine and no director or intending director shall be disqualified by his office from contracting with the company either with regard to his tenure of any such other office or place of profit or as vendor, purchaser or otherwise, nor shall any such contract, or any contract or arrangement entered into by or on behalf of the company in which any director is in any way interested, be liable to be avoided, nor shall any director so contracting or being so interested be liable to account to the company for any profit realised by any such contract or arrangement by reason of such director holding that office or of the fiduciary relation thereby established.

(4) A director, notwithstanding his interest, may be counted in the quorum present at any meeting whereat he or any other director is appointed to hold any such office or place of profit under the company or whereat the terms of any such appointment are arranged, and he may vote on any such appointment or arrangement other than his own appointment or the arrangement of the terms thereof.

(5) Any director may act by himself or his firm in a professional capacity for the company, and he or his firm shall be entitled to remuneration for professional services as if he were not a director; provided that nothing herein contained shall authorise a director or his firm to act as auditor to the company.

85. All cheques, promissory notes, drafts, bills of exchange and other negotiable instruments, and all receipts for moneys paid to the company, shall be signed, drawn, accepted, endorsed, or otherwise executed, as the case may be, in such manner as the directors shall from time to time by resolution determine.

86. The directors shall cause minutes to be made in books provided for the purpose—

(a) of all appointments of officers made by the directors;

(b) of the names of the directors present at each meeting of the directors and of any committee of the directors;

(c) of all resolutions and proceedings at all meetings of the company, and of the directors, and of committees of directors;

and every director present at any meeting of directors or committee of directors shall sign his name in a book to be kept for that purpose.

87. The directors on behalf of the company may pay a gratuity or pension or allowance on retirement to any director who has held any other salaried office or place of profit with the company or to his widow or dependants and may make contributions to any fund and pay premiums for the purchase or provision of any such gratuity, pension or allowance.

Disqualification of Directors

88. The office of director shall be vacated if the director—

(a) ceases to be a director by virtue of section 182 or 185 of the Act; or

(b) becomes bankrupt or makes any arrangement or composition with his creditors generally; or

(c) becomes prohibited from being a director by reason of any order made under section 188 of the Act [*or under section 28 of CA 1976*]; or

(d) becomes of unsound mind; or

(e) resigns his office by notice in writing to the company; or

(f) shall for more than six months have been absent without permission of the directors from meetings of the directors held during that period.

NOTES

Words in square brackets inserted by CA 1976, in relation to any company registered on or after 1 June 1977, and repealed by CA 1981, Sch 4, in relation to any company registered on or after 3 December 1981.

Rotation of Directors

89. At the first annual general meeting of the company all the directors shall retire from office, and at the annual general meeting in every subsequent year one-third of the directors for the time being, or, if their number is not three or a multiple of three, then the number nearest one-third, shall retire from office.

90. The directors to retire in every year shall be those who have been longest in office since their last election, but as between persons who became directors on the same day those to retire shall (unless they otherwise agree among themselves) be determined by lot.

91. A retiring director shall be eligible for re-election.

92. The company at the meeting at which a director retires in manner aforesaid may fill the vacated office by electing a person thereto, and in default the retiring director shall if offering himself for re-election be deemed to have been re-elected, unless at such meeting it is expressly resolved not to fill such vacated office or unless a resolution for the re-election of such director shall have been put to the meeting and lost.

93. No person other than a director retiring at the meeting shall unless recommended by the directors be eligible for election to the office of director at any general meeting unless not less than three nor more than twenty-one days before the date appointed for the meeting there shall have been left at the registered office of the company notice in writing, signed by a member duly qualified to attend and vote at the meeting for which such notice is given, of his intention to propose such person for election, and also notice in writing signed by that person of his willingness to be elected.

94. The company may from time to time by ordinary resolution increase or reduce the number of directors, and may also determine in what rotation the increased or reduced number is to go out of office.

95. The directors shall have power at any time, and from time to time, to appoint any person to be a director, either to fill a casual vacancy or as an addition to the existing directors, but so that the total number of directors shall not at any time exceed the number fixed in accordance with these regulations. Any director so appointed shall hold office only until the next following annual general meeting, and shall then be eligible for re-election but shall not be taken into account in determining the directors who are to retire by rotation at such meeting.

96. The company may by ordinary resolution, of which special notice has been given in accordance with section 142 of the Act, remove any director before the expiration of his period of office notwithstanding anything in these regulations or in any agreement between the company and such director. Such removal shall be without prejudice to any claim such director may have for damages for breach of any contract of service between him and the company.

97. The company may by ordinary resolution appoint another person in place of a director removed from office under the immediately preceding regulation, and without prejudice to the powers of the directors under regulation 95 the company in general meeting may appoint any person to be a director either to fill a casual vacancy or as an additional director. A person appointed in place of a director so removed or to fill such a vacancy shall be subject to retirement at the same time as if he had become a director on the day on which the director in whose place he is appointed was last elected a director.

Proceedings of Directors

98. The directors may meet together for the despatch of business, adjourn, and otherwise regulate their meetings, as they think fit. Questions arising at any meeting shall be decided by a majority of votes. In case of an equality of votes, the chairman shall have a second or casting vote. A director may, and the secretary on the requisition of a director shall, at any time summon a meeting of the directors. It shall not be necessary to give notice of a meeting of directors to any director for the time being absent from the United Kingdom.

99. The quorum necessary for the transaction of the business of the directors may be fixed by the directors, and unless so fixed shall be two.

100. The continuing directors may act notwithstanding any vacancy in their body, but, if and so long as their number is reduced below the number fixed by or pursuant to the regulations of the company as the necessary quorum of directors, the continuing directors or director may act for the purpose of increasing the number of directors to that number, or of summoning a general meeting of the company, but for no other purpose.

101. The directors may elect a chairman of their meetings and determine the period for which he is to hold office; but if no such chairman is elected, or if at any meeting the chairman is not present within five minutes after the time appointed for holding the same, the directors present may choose one of their number to be chairman of the meeting.

102. The directors may delegate any of their powers to committees consisting of such member or members of their body as they think fit; any committee so formed shall in the exercise of the powers so delegated conform to any regulations that may be imposed on it by the directors.

103. A committee may elect a chairman of its meetings; if no such chairman is elected, or if at any meeting the chairman is not present within five minutes after the time appointed for holding the same, the members present may choose one of their number to be chairman of the meeting.

104. A committee may meet and adjourn as it thinks proper. Questions arising at any meeting shall be determined by a majority of votes of the members present, and in the case of an equality of votes the chairman shall have a second or casting vote.

105. All acts done by any meeting of the directors or of a committee of directors or by any person acting as a director shall, notwithstanding that it be afterwards discovered that there was some defect in the appointment of any such director or person acting as aforesaid, or that they or any of them were disqualified, be as valid as if every such person had been duly appointed and was qualified to be a director.

106. A resolution in writing, signed by all the directors for the time being entitled to receive notice of a meeting of the directors, shall be as valid and effectual as if it had been passed at a meeting of the directors duly convened and held.

Managing Director

107. The directors may from time to time appoint one of more of their body to the office of managing director for such period and on such terms as they think fit, and, subject to the terms of any agreement entered into in any particular case, may revoke such appointment. A director so appointed shall not, whilst holding that office, be subject to retirement by rotation or be taken into account in determining the rotation of retirement of directors, but his appointment shall be automatically determined if he cease from any cause to be a director.

108. A managing director shall receive such remuneration (whether by way of salary, commission or participation in profits, or partly in one way and partly in another) as the directors may determine.

109. The directors may entrust to and confer upon a managing director any of the powers exercisable by them upon such terms and conditions and with such restrictions as they may think fit, and either collaterally with or to the exclusion of their own powers and may from time to time revoke, withdraw, alter or vary all or any of such powers.

Secretary

110. [Subject to Section 21(5) of CA 1976] the secretary shall be appointed by the directors for such term, at such remuneration and upon such conditions as they may think fit; and any secretary so appointed may be removed by them.

NOTES

Words in square brackets inserted by CA 1976, Sch 2, in relation to any company registered on or after 18 April 1977.

111. No person shall be appointed or hold office as secretary who is—

(a) the sole director of the company; or

(b) a corporation the sole director of which is the sole director of the company; or

(c) the sole director of a corporation which is the sole director of the company.

112. A provision of the Act or these regulations requiring or authorising a thing to be done by or to a director and the secretary shall not be satisfied by its being done by or to the same person acting both as director and as, or in place of, the secretary.

The Seal

113. The directors shall provide for the safe custody of the seal, which shall only be used by the authority of the directors or of a committee of the directors authorised by the directors in that behalf, and every instrument to which the seal shall be affixed shall be signed by a director and shall be countersigned by the secretary or by a second director or by some other person appointed by the directors for the purpose.

Dividends and Reserve

114. The company in general meeting may declare dividends, but no dividend shall exceed the amount recommended by the directors.

115. The directors may from time to time pay to the members such interim dividends as appear to the directors to be justified by the profits of the company.

116. *No dividend shall be paid otherwise than out of profits.*

NOTES

Substituted by CA 1980, Sch 3, in relation to any company registered on or after 22 December 1980, as follows—

"No dividend or interim dividend shall be paid otherwise than in accordance with the provisions of Part III of CA 1980 which apply to the company.".

117. The directors may, before recommending any dividend, set aside out of the profits of the company such sums as they think proper as a reserve or reserves which shall, at the discretion of the directors, be applicable for any purpose to which the profits of the company may be properly applied, and pending such application may, at the like discretion, either be employed in the business of the company or be invested in such investments (other than shares of the company) as the directors may from time to time think fit. The directors may also without placing the same to reserve carry forward any profits which they may think prudent not to divide.

118. Subject to the rights of persons, if any, entitled to shares with special rights as to dividend, all dividends shall be declared and paid according to the amounts paid or credited as paid on the shares in respect whereof the dividend is paid, but no amount paid or credited as paid on a share in advance of calls shall be treated for the purposes of this regulation as paid on the share. All dividends shall be apportioned and paid proportionately to the amounts paid or credited as paid on the shares during any portion or portions of the period in respect of which the dividend is paid; but if any share is issued on terms providing that it shall rank for dividend as from a particular date such share shall rank for dividend accordingly.

119. The directors may deduct from any dividend payable to any member all sums of money (if any) presently payable by him to the company on account of calls or otherwise in relation to the shares of the company.

120. Any general meeting declaring a dividend or bonus may direct payment of such dividend or bonus wholly or partly by the distribution of specific assets and in particular of paid up shares, debentures or debenture stock of any other company or in any one or more of such ways, and the directors shall give effect to such resolution, and where any difficulty arises in regard to such distribution, the directors may settle the same as they think expedient, and in particular may issue fractional certificates and fix the value for distribution of such specific assets or any part thereof and may determine that cash payments shall be made to any members upon the footing of the value so fixed in order to adjust the rights of all parties, and may vest any such specific assets in trustees as may seem expedient to the directors.

121. Any dividend, interest or other moneys payable in cash in respect of shares may be paid by cheque or warrant sent through the post directed to the registered address of the holder or, in the case of joint holders, to the registered address of that one of the joint holders who is first named on the register of members or to such person and to such address as the holder or joint holders may in writing direct. Every such cheque or warrant shall be made payable to the order of the person to whom it is sent. Any one of two or more joint holders may give effectual receipts for any dividends, bonuses or other moneys payable in respect of the shares held by them as joint holders.

122. No dividend shall bear interest against the company.

Accounts

123. The directors *shall cause proper books of account to be kept with respect to—*

(a) *all sums of money received and expended by the company and the matters in respect of which the receipt and expenditure takes place;*

(b) *all sales and purchases of goods by the company; and*

(c) *the assets and liabilities of the company.*

Proper books shall not be deemed to be kept if there are not kept such books of account as are necessary to give a true and fair view of the state of the company's affairs and to explain its transactions.

NOTES

For the words in italics there are substituted the words "shall cause accounting records to be kept in accordance with section 12 of CA 1976" by CA 1976, Sch 2, in relation to any company registered on or after 1 October 1977.

124. *The books of account shall be kept at the registered office of the Company, or, subject to section 147(3) of the Act, at such other place or places as the directors think fit, and shall always be open to the inspection of the directors.*

NOTES

Substituted by CA 1976, Sch 2, in relation to any company registered on or after 1 October 1977, as follows—

"The accounting records shall be kept at the registered office of the company or, subject to section 12(6) and (7) of CA 1976, at such other place or places as the directors think fit, and shall always be open to the inspection of the officers of the company.".

125. The directors shall from time to time determine whether and to what extent and at what times and places and under what conditions or regulations the accounts and books of the company or any of them shall be open to the inspection of members not being directors, and no member (not being a director) shall have any right of inspecting any account or book or document of the company except as conferred by statute or authorised by the directors or by the company in general meeting.

126. The directors shall from time to time, in accordance with *sections 148, 150 and 157 of the Act*, cause to be prepared and to be laid before the company in general meeting such profit and loss accounts, balance sheets, group accounts (if any) and reports as are referred to in those sections.

NOTES

For the words in italics there are substituted the words "sections 150 and 157 of the Act and sections 1, 6 and 7 of CA 1976" by CA 1976, Sch 2, in relation to any company registered on or after 1 October 1977.

127. A copy of every balance sheet (including every document required by law to be annexed thereto) which is to be laid before the company in general meeting, together with a copy of the auditors' report [and directors' report], shall not less than twenty-one days before the date of the meeting be sent to every member of, and every holder of debentures of, the company and to every person registered under regulation 31. Provided that this regulation shall not require a copy of those documents to be sent to any person of whose address the company is not aware or to more than one of the joint holders of any shares or debentures.

NOTES

Words in square brackets inserted by CA 1976, Sch 2, in relation to any company registered on or after 1 October 1977.

Capitalisation of Profits

128. The company in general meeting may upon the recommendation of the directors resolve that it is desirable to capitalise any part of the amount for the time being standing to the credit of any of the company's reserve accounts or to the credit of the profit and loss account or otherwise available for distribution, and accordingly that such sum be set free for distribution amongst the members who would have been entitled thereto if distributed by way of dividend and in the same proportions on condition that the same be not paid in cash but be applied either in or towards paying up any amounts for the time being unpaid on any shares held by such members respectively or paying up in full unissued shares or debentures of the company to be allotted and distributed credited as fully paid up to and amongst such members in the proportion aforesaid, or partly in the one way and partly in the other, and the directors shall give effect to such resolution:

Provided that a share premium account and a capital redemption reserve fund may, for the purposes of this regulation, only be applied in the paying up of unissued shares to be issued to members of the company as fully paid bonus shares.

NOTES

For the word in italics there is substituted the word "allotted" by CA 1980, Sch 3, in relation to any company registered on or after 22 December 1980.

[128A. The company in general meeting may on the recommendation of the directors resolve that it is desirable to capitalise any part of the amount for the time being standing to the credit of any of the company's reserve accounts or to the credit of the profit and loss account which is not available for distribution by applying such sum in paying up in full unissued shares to be allotted as fully paid bonus shares to those members of the company who would have been entitled to that sum if it were distributed by way of dividend (and in the same proportions), and the directors shall give effect to such resolution.]

NOTES

Added by CA 1980, Sch 3, in relation to any company registered on or after 22 December 1980.

129. *Whenever such a resolution as aforesaid shall have been passed* the directors shall make all appropriations and applications of the undivided profits resolved to be capitalised thereby, and all allotments and issues of fully-paid shares or debentures, if any, and generally shall do all acts and things required to give effect thereto, with full power to the directors to make such provision by the issue of fractional certificates or by payment in cash or otherwise as they think fit for the case of shares or debentures becoming distributable in fractions, and also to authorise any person to enter on behalf of all members entitled thereto into an agreement with the company providing for the allotment to them respectively, credited as fully paid up, of any further shares or debentures to which they may be entitled upon such capitalisation, or (as the case may require) for the payment up by the company on their behalf, by the application thereto of their respective proportions of the profits resolved to be capitalised, of the amounts or any part of the amounts remaining unpaid on their existing shares, and any agreement made under such authority shall be effective and binding on all such members.

NOTES

For the words in italics there are substituted the words "Whenever a resolution is passed in pursuance of regulation 128 or 128A above" by CA 1980, Sch 3, in relation to any company registered on or after 22 December 1980.

Audit

130. Auditors shall be appointed and their duties regulated in accordance with *sections 159 to 162 of the Act.*

NOTES

The regulation set out above applies to any company registered before 27 January 1968.

For the words in italics there are substituted the words "sections 159 to 161 of the Act and section 14 of the Companies Act 1967" by CA 1967, in relation to any company registered between 27 January 1968 and 17 April 1977; for the words in italics there are substituted the words "section 161 of the Act, section 14 of CA 1967 and sections 13 to 18 of CA 1976" by CA 1976, in relation to any company registered between 18 April 1977 and 2 December 1981, and for the words in italics there are substituted the words "section 161 of the Act, sections 14 and 23A of CA 1967, sections 13 to 18 of CA 1976 and sections 7 and 12 of CA 1981" by CA 1981, in relation to any company registered between 3 December 1981 and 30 June 1985.

Notices

131. A notice may be given by the company to any member either personally or by sending it by post to him or to his registered address, or (if he has no registered address within the United Kingdom) to the address, if any, within the United Kingdom supplied by him to the company for the giving of notice to him. Where a notice is sent by post, service of the notice shall be deemed to be effected by properly addressing, prepaying, and posting a letter containing the notice, and to have been effected in the case of a notice of a meeting at the expiration of 24 hours after the letter containing the same is posted, and in any other case at the time at which the letter would be delivered in the ordinary course of post.

132. A notice may be given by the company to the joint holders of a share by giving the notice to the joint holder first named in the register of members in respect of the share.

133. A notice may be given by the company to the persons entitled to a share in consequence of the death or bankruptcy of a member by sending it through the post in a prepaid letter addressed to them by name, or by the title of representatives of the deceased, or trustee of the bankrupt, or any like description, at the address, if any, within the United Kingdom supplied for the purpose by the persons claiming to be so entitled, or (until such an address has been so supplied) by giving the notice in any manner in which the same might have been given if the death or bankruptcy had not occurred.

134. Notice of every general meeting shall be given in any manner hereinbefore authorised to—

(a) every member except those members who (having no registered address within the United Kingdom) have not supplied to the company an address within the United Kingdom for the giving of notices to them;

(b) every person upon whom the ownership of a share devolves by reason of his being a legal personal representative or a trustee in bankruptcy of a member where the member but for his death or bankruptcy would be entitled to receive notice of the meeting; and

(c) the auditor for the time being of the company.

No other person shall be entitled to receive notices of general meetings.

Winding up

135. If the company shall be wound up the liquidator may, with the sanction of an extraordinary resolution of the company and any other sanction required by the Act, divide amongst the members in specie or kind the whole or any part of the assets of the company (whether they shall consist of property of the same kind or not) and may, for such purpose set such value as he deems fair upon any property to be divided as aforesaid and may determine how such division shall be carried out as between the members or different classes of members. The liquidator may, with the like sanction, vest the whole or any part of such assets in trustees upon such trusts for the benefit of the contributories as the liquidator, with the like sanction, shall think fit, but so that no member shall be compelled to accept any shares or other securities whereon there is any liability.

Indemnity

136. Every director, managing director, agent, auditor, secretary and other officer for the time being of the company shall be indemnified out of the assets of the company against any liability incurred by him in defending any proceedings, whether civil or criminal, in which judgment is given in his favour or in which he is acquitted or in connection with any application under section 448 of the Act in which relief is granted to him by the court.

PART II REGULATIONS FOR THE MANAGEMENT OF A PRIVATE COMPANY LIMITED BY SHARES

1. The regulations contained in Part I of Table A (with the exception of regulations 24 and 53) shall apply.

2. The company is a private company and accordingly—

(a) the right to transfer shares is restricted in manner hereinafter prescribed;

(b) the number of members of the company (exclusive of persons who are in the employment of the company and of persons who having been formerly in the employment of the company were while in such employment and have continued after the determination of such employment to be members of the company) is limited to fifty. Provided that where two or more persons hold one or more shares in the company jointly they shall for the purpose of this regulation be treated as a single member;

(c) any invitation to the public to subscribe for any shares or debentures of the company is prohibited;

(d) the company shall not have power to issue share warrants to bearer.

3. The directors may, in their absolute discretion and without assigning any reason therefor, decline to register any transfer of any share, whether or not it is a fully paid share.

4. No business shall be transacted at any general meeting unless a quorum of members is present at the time when the meeting proceeds to business; save as herein otherwise provided two members present in person or by proxy shall be a quorum.

5. Subject to the provisions of the Act, a resolution in writing signed by all the members for the time being entitled to receive notice of and to attend and vote at general meetings (or being corporations by their duly authorised representatives) shall be as valid and effective as if the same had been passed at a general meeting of the company duly convened and held.

6. The directors may at any time require any person whose name is entered in the register of members of the company to furnish them with any information, supported (if the directors so require) by a statutory declaration, which they may consider necessary for the purpose of determining whether or not the company is an exempt private company within the meaning of subsection (4) of section 129 of the Act.

Note. Regulations 3 and 4 of this Part are alternative to regulations 24 and 53 respectively of Part I.

NOTES

Pt II repealed by CA 1980, Sch 3, in relation to any company registered on or after 22 December 1980.

Reg 6 repealed by CA 1967, Sch 8, Pt III, in relation to any company registered on or after 27 January 1968.

Appendices

Appendix 4: Statutory Instruments made under the Companies Act 2006

[A4]

NOTES

This Appendix lists all statutory instruments made under, or partly under, the Companies Act 2006, with the exception of statutory instruments applying to Northern Ireland only (which are not listed). Statutory instruments which are no longer in force are printed in italics.

The majority of the statutory instruments listed below are set out in Part 4 of this Handbook. Note, however, that where the substantive authority for a statutory instrument is an Act other than the Companies Act 2006 (and the 2006 Act authority is merely ancillary) the statutory instrument will be elsewhere in this Handbook.

Note that the summaries below relate to the statutory instrument as originally enacted. The summaries are not updated in cases where the statutory instrument in question has subsequently been amended.

2022 Statutory Instruments

SI 2022/870: Register of Overseas Entities (Delivery, Protection and Trust Services) Regulations 2022

Authority: Economic Crime (Transparency and Enforcement) Act 2022, ss 25(1), (3)(a)–(d), (f), (4), 67(2), (3)(a); Companies Act 2006, ss 1069(1), 1292(1)(a), (b), 1292(1)(a), (b). These Regulations make provision relating to the register of overseas entities ("the register") kept by the registrar of companies for England and Wales ("the registrar") in accordance with Part 1 of the Economic Crime (Transparency and Enforcement) Act 2022. The provisions relate to the electronic delivery of documents, the protection of information and the definition of registrable beneficial owners. Part 1 provides for citation, commencement and extent. The Regulations come into force on the day section 3 of the 2022 Act comes into force; and they apply to the UK. Part 2 makes provision under s 1069 of the Companies Act 2006 for certain specified documents which must be delivered to the registrar for the purposes of the register to be delivered by electronic means. Regulation 4 provides an exception. Part 3 makes provision under section 25 of the Economic Crime (Transparency and Enforcement) Act 2022 requiring the registrar to make information relating to a relevant individual (an individual who is or used to be a registrable beneficial owner or managing officer of an overseas entity) unavailable for public inspection and to refrain from disclosing that information except in specified circumstances. Regulations 5 and 6 set out when protected information must be made unavailable for public inspection and not disclosed by the registrar. Regulation 7 makes provision for the grounds on which an application to protect information can be made, the application process including details as to what the application must contain and determination of the application by the registrar. Regulation 8 makes further provision about the application and its determination, including the ability of the registrar to refer any question relating to the assessment of the nature or extent of any relevant risk to any other person who the registrar considers may be able to assist. Regulation 9 sets out how an application can be withdrawn before it is determined. Regulation 10 makes provision for appeals to the High Court or Court of Session when an application to protect information is unsuccessful. Regulation 10 provides that no appeal can be made without the permission of the court. Regulation 11 makes provision as to the steps the registrar must take following a determination that the application has been unsuccessful. Regulations 12 and 13 make provision for the duration of a determination that the information must be protected including provision for revocation by the registrar. Part 4 specifies that overseas trust service providers which are based where trust services are regulated are subject to its own disclosure requirements for the purposes of Schedule 2 to the Economic Crime (Transparency and Enforcement) Act 2022 (which defines "registrable beneficial owner": a legal entity must be subject to its own disclosure requirements to be a registrable beneficial owner). The Regulations are at **[10.1376]**.

SI 2022/762: Statutory Auditors and Third Country Auditors (Amendment) Regulations 2022

Authority: Companies Act 2006, ss 1240A, 1240B, 1292(1). These Regulations make amendments to the UK's audit regime by amending the Statutory Auditors and Third Country Auditors (Amendment) (EU Exit) Regulations 2019 ("the 2019 Regulations"). Regulation 1 provides for citation and commencement (the Regulations come into force on 27 July 2022). Regulation 2(1) introduces the amendments in reg 2(2) and (3). Regulation 2(2)(a) grants fresh approval to the third countries previously approved by paragraph 1 of Schedule 1 to the 2019 Regulations but not as yet by the Secretary of State under section 1240A of the Companies Act 2006. This is in order to remedy a technical problem whereby section 1262 of the Companies Act 2006 provides that an "equivalent third country" is one approved by the Secretary of State under section 1240A and does not include reference to the remaining third countries referred to in paragraph 1 of Schedule 1 to the 2019 Regulations. Regulation 2(2)(b) amends Schedule 1 to the 2019 Regulations to remove the expiry date of the current period of provisional equivalence for the United States of America in Table 1, so that full equivalence is granted indefinitely. Regulation 2(3)(a) grants fresh approval to the third country competent authorities previously approved by paragraph 1 of Schedule 2 to the 2019 Regulations but not yet by the Secretary of State under section 1240B of the Companies Act 2006. This is in order to remedy a technical problem whereby section 1262 of the Companies Act 2006 provides that an "approved third country competent authority" is one approved by the Secretary of State under section 1240B and does not include reference to the remaining third country competent authorities referred to in paragraph 1 of Schedule 2 to the 2019 Regulations. Regulation 2(3)(b) amends Schedule 2 to the 2019 Regulations to remove the expiry date of the current period of provisional adequacy for the competent authorities of the United States (the Public Company Accounting Oversight Board and the Securities and Exchange Commission) in Table 3, so that full adequacy is granted indefinitely.

SSI 2022/207: Companies Act 2006 (Scottish public sector companies to be audited by the Auditor General for Scotland) Order 2022

Authority: Companies Act 2006, s 483(1), (4). Article 1 of this Order provides for citation, commencement and interpretation (the Order comes into force on 15 June 2022). Article 2 provides that Scottish Rail Holdings Limited ("the Company"), being a company with a registered office in Scotland, is to have its accounts audited by the Auditor General for Scotland. Article 3 provides that the company will be exempt from the auditing of company accounts requirements of Part 16 of the Companies Act 2006.

SI 2022/31: Companies (Strategic Report) (Climate-related Financial Disclosure) Regulations 2022

Authority: Companies Act 2006, s 468(1), (2). These Regulations require certain companies to provide climate-related financial disclosures in their strategic report. The requirement applies to a traded company, a banking company, an authorised insurance company and a company carrying on insurance business which in each case satisfy various conditions, including that of having more than 500 employees. The companies are listed in section 414CA(1) of the Companies Act 2006 and the requirement for more than 500 employees is set out in section 414CA(4), as applied by section 414CA(1B). In addition, these Regulations require two further types of company, with more than 500 employees, to make climate-related financial disclosures. These are a company which has securities admitted to trading on the Alternative Investment Market, and a high turnover company which is a company which does not fall within another category but which has a turnover of more than £500 million (see regulation 3). Regulation 1 provides for citation and commencement. Regulation 2 makes a minor amendment to section 414C of the 2006 Act. Regulation 4, inter alia, inserts section 414CB(2A) into the 2006 Act which defines climate-related financial disclosures. Regulation 5 provides for a review of the Regulations before 6 April 2027 with subsequent reviews at intervals not exceeding five years.

2021 Statutory Instruments

SI 2021/465: Supervision of Accounts and Reports (Prescribed Body) and Companies (Defective Accounts and Reports) (Authorised Person) Order 2021

Authority: Companies (Audit, Investigations and Community Enterprise) Act 2004, ss 14(1), (5), (8), (10), 18A(1), (3); Companies Act 2006, ss 457(1), (2), (5), (6), 1292(1)(b), (c). This Order appoints and authorises the Financial Reporting Council Limited ("the FRC") for certain purposes under the Companies (Audit, Investigations and Community Enterprise) Act 2004 ("the 2004 Act") and the Companies Act 2006 ("the 2006 Act"). It also applies an exemption of liability to the FRC under s18A of the 2004 Act. The Order applies to the whole of the United Kingdom. Article 1 deal with citation, commencement and interpretation. This Order comes into force on 6 May 2021. Article 2 appoints the FRC to exercise the functions described in s 14(2) of the 2004 Act. These functions include keeping certain periodic accounts and reports under review and informing the Financial Conduct Authority of any conclusions the FRC reaches as regards those accounts and reports. Article 3 appoints the FRC to exercise the functions described in s 14(2) of the 2004 Act to periodic accounts and reports that fall within the definitions of accounts within the Disclosure Guidance and Transparency Rules Sourcebook. Article 4 authorises the FRC for the purposes of s 456 of the 2006 Act and authorises the FRC to apply to the court for a declaration in respect of defective accounts or reports. Article 5 imposes a record keeping requirement onto the FRC in relation to the functions conferred by this Order. Articles 6 and 7 make consequential amendments to the Limited Liability Partnerships (Accounts and Audit) (Application of Companies Act 2006) Regulations 2008; and to the Supervision of Accounts and Reports (Prescribed Body) and Companies (Defective Accounts and Directors' Reports) (Authorised Person) Order 2012. Article 8 amends the Companies (Bodies Concerned with Auditing Standards etc) (Exemption from Liability) Regulations 2016 to apply the exemption from liability contained in s 18A(3) and (4) of the 2004 Act to the FRC. Article 9 provides application and transitional provisions. The Order is at **[4.722]**.

SSI 2021/129: Companies Act 2006 (Scottish public sector companies to be audited by the Auditor General for Scotland) Order 2021

Authority: Companies Act 2006, s 483(1), (4). Article 1 of this Order provides for citation, commencement and interpretation. The Order comes into force on 10 March 2021. Article 2 provides that Ferguson Marine (Port Glasgow) Holdings Limited, being a company with a registered office in Scotland, is to have its accounts audited by the Auditor General for Scotland. Article 3 provides that the company will be exempt from the auditing of company accounts requirements of Part 16 of the Companies Act 2006.

2020 Statutory Instruments

SSI 2020/402: Companies Act 2006 (Scottish public sector companies to be audited by the Auditor General for Scotland) Order 2020

Authority: Companies Act 2006, s 483(1), (4). Article 1 of this Order provides for citation and commencement. The Order comes into force on 26 November 2020. Article 2 provides that Scottish National Investment Bank plc, being a company with a registered office in Scotland, is to have its accounts audited by the Auditor General for Scotland. Article 3 provides that the company will be exempt from the auditing of company accounts requirements of Part 16 of the Companies Act 2006.

SI 2020/1247: Statutory Auditors and Third Country Auditors (Amendment) (EU Exit) (No 2) Regulations 2020

Authority: Companies Act 2006, ss 1240A, 1240B, 1292(1). Regulation 1 provides for citation and commencement. Regulation 2(1) introduces the amendments made by reg 2 to the Statutory Auditors and Third Country Auditors (Amendment) (EU Exit) Regulations 2019. Regulation 2(2) grants the EEA States and Gibraltar approval as equivalent third countries, and reg 2(3) grants the competent authorities of the EEA States and Gibraltar approval as approved third country competent authorities, for the purposes of Part 42 of the Companies Act 2006 (as prospectively amended by the Statutory Auditors and Third Country Auditors (Amendment) (EU Exit) Regulations 2019 (SI 2019/177) ('the 2019 Regulations')). These changes will take effect from IP completion day. Previously, the 2019 Regulations granted these countries approval as transitional third countries until 31 December 2020, and their competent authorities provisional approval as approved third country competent authorities until 31 December 2020. Regulation 3 extends the grant of provisional approval as an approved third country competent authority to the Independent Regulatory Board of Auditors of South Africa. Approval is granted from the end of the Transition Period and previously would have applied until 31 July 2022. It will now apply until 30 April 2026. This reflects Commission Implementing Decision 2020/589/EU on the adequacy of the competent authority of the Republic of South Africa pursuant to Directive 2006/43/EC on statutory audits of annual accounts and consolidated accounts, etc.

SI 2020/990: Pension Protection Fund (Moratorium and Arrangements and Reconstructions for Companies in Financial Difficulty) (Amendment and Revocation) Regulations 2020

Authority: Insolvency Act 1986, ss A51, A55(1); Companies Act 2006, ss 901I, 1291, 1292; Corporate Insolvency and Governance Act 2020, s 43. These Regulations amend the Pension Protection Fund (Moratorium and Arrangements and Reconstructions for Companies in Financial Difficulty) Regulations 2020 (SI 2020/693) to apply those provisions to co-operative societies and community benefit societies. These Regulations, in certain circumstances, extend to the Board of the Pension Protection Fund ("the Board") rights that are normally exercised by a pension scheme's trustees or managers where they are creditors of a co-operative society or community benefit society. Where the trustees or managers lose their rights as a result the Board is required to consult with them. Regulation 1 provides for citation and commencement. Regulation 2 introduces the amendments made by regs 3 to 5. Regulation 3 adds certain definitions to reg 1 of the 2020 Regulations. Regulation 4 amends reg 2 of the 2020 Regulations. The amended reg 2 now also applies when a moratorium under Part A1 of the Insolvency Act 1986 is or has been in force in relation to a relevant co-operative society or community benefit society which is, or has been at some point while the moratorium has been in force, an employer in respect of an eligible pension scheme. It gives the Board the right, instead of the trustees or managers of the scheme, to participate in decisions as to whether to extend the moratorium and decisions in relation to a challenge to the directors' actions. The Board must consult the trustees or managers before exercising those rights. Regulation 5 amends reg 3 of the 2020 Regulations. The amended reg 3 now also applies when a restructuring plan (a compromise or arrangement) is proposed under Part 26A of the Companies Act 2006 in relation to a relevant society which is an employer in respect of an eligible pension scheme and the trustees or managers of the scheme are a creditor of that society to whom the compromise or arrangement is proposed. It gives the Board, in addition to the trustees or managers, the rights exercisable by the trustees or managers as creditors under Part 26A. It gives the Board, instead of the trustees or managers, the right to vote on a compromise or arrangement and the Board must consult the trustees or managers before exercising this right. Regulation 6 revokes the Pension Protection Fund (Moratorium and Arrangements and Reconstructions for Companies in Financial Difficulty) (Amendment) Regulations 2020 as those Regulations were defective (see below).

SI 2020/783: Pension Protection Fund (Moratorium and Arrangements and Reconstructions for Companies in Financial Difficulty) (Amendment) Regulations 2020

Authority: Insolvency Act 1986, ss A51, A55(1); Companies Act 2006, ss 901I, 1291, 1292; Corporate Insolvency and Governance Act 2020, s 43. These Regulations amend the Pension Protection Fund (Moratorium and Arrangements and Reconstructions for Companies in Financial Difficulty) Regulations 2020 (see the note below) to apply those provisions to co-operative societies and community benefit societies. They were, however, revoked by the Pension Protection Fund (Moratorium and Arrangements and Reconstructions for Companies in Financial Difficulty) (Amendment) Regulations 2020, as from 16 September 2020 (see the note above).

SI 2020/693: Pension Protection Fund (Moratorium and Arrangements and Reconstructions for Companies in Financial Difficulty) Regulations 2020

Authority: Insolvency Act 1986, ss A51, A55(1); Companies Act 2006, ss 901I, 1291, 1292; Corporate Insolvency and Governance Act 2020, s 43. These Regulations, in certain circumstances, give the Board of the Pension Protection Fund ("the Board") rights that are normally exercised by a pension scheme's trustees or managers where they are creditors. Where the trustees or managers lose their rights as a result the Board is required to consult with them. Regulation 1 provides for citation and commencement, etc (these Regulations come into force on 7 July 2020). Regulation 2 applies when a moratorium under Part A1 of the Insolvency Act 1986 is or has been in force in relation to a company, Limited Liability Partnership or Charitable Incorporated Organisation ("CIO") which is, or has been at some point while the moratorium has been in force, an employer in respect of an eligible pension scheme. It gives the Board the right, instead of the trustees or managers, to participate in decisions as to whether to extend the moratorium and decisions in relation to a challenge to the directors' actions. The Board must consult the trustees or managers before exercising those rights. Regulation 3 applies when a restructuring plan (a compromise or arrangement) is proposed under Part 26A of the Companies Act 2006 in relation to a company or LLP which is an employer in respect of an eligible pension scheme and the trustees or managers of the scheme are a creditor of that company or LLP to whom the compromise or arrangement is proposed. It gives the Board, in addition to the trustees or managers, the rights exercisable by the trustees or managers as creditors under Part 26A. It gives the Board, instead of the trustees or managers, the right to vote on a compromise or arrangement and the Board must consult the trustees or managers before exercising this right.

SI 2020/645: Companies etc (Filing Requirements) (Temporary Modifications) Regulations 2020

Authority: Companies Act 2006, ss 1049(3), 1050(5); Corporate Insolvency and Governance Act 2020, s 39(1), (4). These Regulations, which come into force on 27 June 2020, temporarily extend the period within which certain filing requirements must be met by companies and other bodies. Regulations 4 to 20 modify various provisions of the Companies Act 2006 to extend the period during which certain filing obligations must be met by companies. Regulations 22 to 36 modify the Scottish Partnerships (Register of People with Significant Control) Regulations 2017 (SI 2017/694) to extend the period during which certain filing obligations must be met by Scottish partnerships. Regulations 37 to 41 modify the Limited Partnerships Act 1907, the Companies Act 1985, the Limited Liability Partnerships Act 2000, the European Public Limited-Liability Company Regulations 2004 (SI 2004/2326), and the Overseas Companies Regulations 2009 (SI 2009/1801) to extend the period during which certain filing obligations must be met by companies, limited partnerships, limited liability partnerships, European public limited-liability companies, overseas companies and unregistered companies. Regulation 41(4) provides that regulation 41 (modifications of the Overseas Companies Regulations 2009) expires at the end of the day on 5 April 2021, subject to the saving provision provided for in that regulation. The other modifications made by these Regulations will also expire at the end of the day on 5 April 2021 by virtue of section 39(8) of the Corporate Insolvency and Governance Act 2020 (subject to the saving provision in section 39(9)). The specific modifications of the provisions detailed above are noted to the relevant provision concerned, and the Regulations are set out in full at **[4.681]**.

SI 2020/108: Statutory Auditors and Third Country Auditors (Amendment) (EU Exit) Regulations 2020

Authority: European Communities Act 1972, s 2(2); Companies Act 2006, ss 484(1), 1240A, 1240B and 1292(1); Limited Liability Partnerships Act 2000, ss 15, 17(3). These Regulations make changes to the UK's audit regime. See the Regulations at **[12.171]**. In Part 2, regulation 3 grants provisional approval to the Chinese audit competent authorities under s 1240B of the Companies Act 2006 in relation to the adequacy of their arrangements for co-operating with other national competent authorities on the exchange of audit working papers and investigation reports. Regulation 3 also removes the Indonesian competent authority from the list of competent authorities which have provisional approval, and extends the expiry date for the provisional approval for the South African competent authority. Part 3 sets out procedures for approvals by the Secretary of State granted under ss 1240A and 1240B of the 2006 Act. Chapter 1 of Part 3 (made under s 1240A) sets out procedures for the approval, provisional approval and transitional approval of third countries in relation to the comparability of their audit regulatory regime to the UK's audit regulatory regime. Chapter 2 of Part 3 (made under s 1240B) sets out procedures for the approval and provisional approval of third country competent authorities as approved third country competent authorities in relation to the exchange of audit working papers and investigation reports. The procedures in both cases provide that the Secretary of State may take into account a report prepared by the UK competent authority assessing the basis for equivalence of the third country or adequacy of the third country competent authority concerned. There is also a power for the Secretary of State to suspend the grant of an approval, but also to revoke suspension, with provisions relating to the publication of suspensions and revocations and the informing of those affected (see regs 9 and 14). Part 4 makes changes under s 2(2) of the European Communities Act 1972 to the UK's audit regulatory regime. Regulation 15 amends s 1253D of the 2006 Act in order to transpose Commission Implementing Decision (EU) 1874 of 2019 on the adequacy of the competent authorities of the People's Republic of China pursuant to Directive 2006/43/EC of the European Parliament and of the Council ("the Audit Directive"). That Decision was issued under Article 47 of the Audit Directive. This regulation also removes the competent authorities of South Africa and Indonesia from s 1253D. Regulation 15 and regulation 17 replace the definition of "key audit partner" in Schedule 10 to the 2006 Act and Schedule 1 to the Statutory Auditors and Third Country Auditors Regulations 2016 (SI 2016/649) respectively. Regulation 16 amends the Insurance Accounts Directive (Lloyd's Syndicate and Aggregate Accounts) Regulations 2008 (SI 2008/1950) to modify the specification of the services carried out by an audit firm which must be disclosed in the notes of accounts to the Lloyd's Syndicate to which the audit firm is providing audit services. Regulation 17 also makes minor and technical changes to the Statutory Auditors and Third Country Auditors Regulations 2016, to match the transposition of the Audit Directive and Regulation (EU) No 537/2014 of the European Parliament and of the Council on specific requirements regarding statutory audit of public-interest entities and repealing Commission Decision 2005/909/EC Text with EEA relevance with terms used in similar domestic legislation.

2019 Statutory Instruments

SI 2019/1392: Statutory Auditors, Third Country Auditors and International Accounting Standards (Amendment) (EU Exit) Regulations 2019

Authority: European Union (Withdrawal) Act 2018, s 8(1), Sch 7, para 21; Deregulation Act 2015, s 104(1); Companies Act 2006, ss 484(1), 1292(1); Limited Liability Partnerships Act 2000, ss 15, 17. These Regulations amend the Statutory Auditors and Third Country Auditors (Amendment) (EU Exit) Regulations 2019 (SI 2019/177) ("the Audit SI"), the Accounts and Reports (Amendment) (EU Exit) Regulations 2019 (SI 2019/145) and the International Accounting Standards and European Public Limited-Liability Company (Amendment etc) (EU Exit) Regulations 2019 (SI 2019/685) ("the Accounting Standards SI"). Regulation 1 provides for citation and commencement. Regulation 2 introduces the amendments to the Audit SI. Regulation 3 makes an amendment to the commencement provision of the Audit SI. The effect is to bring provisions concerning new powers inserted into the Companies Act 2006 by the Audit SI (ss 1240A and 1240B concerning the equivalence of third countries and the adequacy of third country competent authorities) into force 21 days after the making of these Regulations (ie, 13 November 2019). Regulations 4 and 7 remove access to exemption from audit for a subsidiary which is a company (in the case of reg 4) or a limited liability partnership (in the case of reg 7) and which has an EEA parent where the subsidiary is included in the parent's consolidated accounts and the accounts are drawn up in accordance with the EU's Accounting Directive (Directive 2013/34/EU of the European Parliament and of the Council on the annual financial statements, consolidated financial statements and related reports of certain types of undertakings) or in accordance with UK-adopted international accounting standards. This exemption will now only be available to subsidiaries which have a UK parent. Regulations 5, 6 and 10 make some minor and technical consequential amendments to the Companies Act 2006. Regulation 8 corrects an error in the Audit SI. The error was contained in a textual amendment which the Audit SI made to Regulation (EU) No 537/2014 of the European Parliament and of the Council on specific requirements regarding statutory audit of public-interest entities and repealing Commission Decision 2005/909/EC ("the Audit Regulation"). The Audit Regulation becomes domestic law on IP completion day (as defined in the European Union (Withdrawal Agreement) Act 2020, s 39) by operation of s 3 of the European Union (Withdrawal) Act 2018. The consequence of the error would have been to change the effect of part of Article 26 of the Audit Regulation, which sets the frequency of inspections of audit firms by the national competent authority for audit. The error would have affected the frequency of inspections of some auditors of public interest entities (which include banks, building societies, insurers and undertakings with transferable securities admitted to trading on a regulated market). This instrument corrects the error, so that the frequency of inspections will continue to be as it was under the Audit Regulation before the UK's exit from the EU. Regulations 11 and 12 update the list of revocations of directly applicable EU legislation concerning international accounting standards in Schedule 2 to the Accounting Standards SI.

SI 2019/970: Companies (Directors' Remuneration Policy and Directors' Remuneration Report) Regulations 2019

Authority: European Communities Act 1972, s 2(2); Companies Act 2006, ss 421(1), 468(1), (2), 1292(1). These Regulations implement Articles 9A and 9B of Directive 2007/36/EC of the European Parliament and of the Council on the exercise of certain rights of shareholders in listed companies (the Shareholders' Rights Directive). They do so by amending CA 2006, and the Large and Medium-sized Companies and Groups (Accounts and Reports) Regulations 2008 (SI 2008/410). Those enactments already provide a legal framework in the UK for approval of and voting on directors' remuneration, and the existing legislation applies to quoted companies (as defined in s 385 of the 2006 Act) which includes traded companies unless they are unquoted companies (also defined in s 385). This framework is amended by these Regulations to implement the Directive, including bringing unquoted traded companies within scope of the existing legal framework. They do so by amending the Companies Act 2006, and the Large and Medium-sized Companies and Groups (Accounts and Reports) Regulations 2008 (SI 2008/410). Those enactments already provide a legal framework in the UK for approval of and voting on directors' remuneration, and the existing legislation applies to quoted companies which includes traded companies unless they are unquoted companies. This framework is amended by these Regulations to implement the Directive, including bringing unquoted traded companies within scope of the existing legal framework. These Regulations amend Chapters 4 and 4A of Part 10 (relating to members' approval and remuneration of directors), Chapters 6 (directors' remuneration report), 7 (publication of accounts and reports), 9 (members' approval of directors' remuneration report), 10 (filing of accounts and reports) and 12 (supplementary provisions) of Part 15 (accounts and reports), and Chapter 3 (functions of the auditor) of Part 16 (audit) of the Act. They also amend reg 11 of, and Schedule 8 to the 2008 Regulations. These Regulations implement a requirement of the Directive that the remuneration of the Chief Executive Officer and any Deputy Chief Executive Officer must be reported even if they are not a director on the board of the company. Previously under UK law, only the remuneration of the directors on the board were required to be reported. See **[4.679]**.

SSI 2019/180: Companies Act 2006 (Scottish public sector companies to be audited by the Auditor General for Scotland) Order 2019

Authority: Companies Act 2006, s 483(1)–(3). This Order provides that ILF Scotland, being a company with a registered office in Scotland, is to have its accounts audited by the Auditor General for Scotland. This means that in terms of s 475 of the Companies Act 2006 this company will be exempt from the auditing of company accounts requirements of Part 16 of that Act. ILF Scotland is a non-profit making public sector company, which appears to Scottish Ministers in terms of s 483(2) of the 2006 Act to carry out functions of a public nature and is funded by bodies audited by the Auditor General for Scotland.

SI 2019/679: Uncertificated Securities (Amendment and EU Exit) Regulations 2019

Authority: European Communities Act 1972, s 2(2); Companies Act 2006, ss 784(1), 785(1), 788, 1292; European Union (Withdrawal) Act 2018, s 8(1), Sch 4, para 1, Sch 7, para 21. These Regulations amend the Uncertificated Securities Regulations 2001 (SI 2001/3755) to revoke certain provisions which overlap with requirements now the subject of the Central Securities Depositories Regulations 2017 (SI 2017/1064). They also amend the Companies Act 2006 and the Financial Services (Banking Reform) Act 2013. This reflects the change from CSDs being approved operators under the 2001 Regulations to being authorised or recognised under the 2017 Regulations and Part 18 of FSMA 2000. The Regulations also contain consequential amendments to the Stamp Duty Reserve Tax Regulations 1986, SI 1986/1711, the Financial Services and Markets Act 2000 (Regulated Activities) Order 2001SI 2001/544, the Financial Services and Markets Act 2000 (Exemption) Order 2001SI 2001/1201, the Financial Services and Markets Act 2000 (Disclosure of Confidential Information) Regulations 2001SI 2001/2188, and the Financial Services and Markets Act 2000 (Excluded Activities and Prohibitions) Order 2014, SI 2014/2080. Part 5 is made in exercise of the powers in European Union (Withdrawal) Act 2018. It also amends the Uncertificated Securities Regulations 2001 (as from IP completion day (as defined in the European Union (Withdrawal Agreement) Act 2020, s 39)) and amends the EU Short Selling Regulation (in its application to the UK after IP completion day). It also enables the Bank of England to charge fees to third country Central Securities Depositories in connection with certain of its functions in relation to them after withdrawal. The Order is at **[12.123]**.

SI 2019/567: Companies Act 2006 (Extension of Takeover Panel Provisions) (Isle of Man) Order 2019

Authority: Companies Act 2006, s 965. This Order replaces the Companies Act 2006 (Extension of Takeover Panel Provisions) (Isle of Man) Order 2008 (SI 2008/3122), partly to reflect changes in responsibility for company registration on the Isle of Man and partly to deal with the United Kingdom's withdrawal from the European Union. It applies Chapter 1 of Part 28 of the Companies Act 2006 to the Isle of Man afresh, subject to the modifications set out in the Schedule. Article 1 deals with citation and commencement. The Order comes into force on IP completion day (as defined in the European Union (Withdrawal Agreement) Act 2020, s 39). Article 2 applies Chapter 1 of Part 28 of the Companies Act 2006 to the Isle of Man afresh, subject to the modifications set out in the Schedule. Article 3 revokes the 2008 Order and the Companies Act 2006 (Extension of Takeover Panel Provisions) (Isle of Man) Order 2009 (SI 2009/1378). The Order is at **[4.675]**.

SI 2019/177: Statutory Auditors and Third Country Auditors (Amendment) (EU Exit) Regulations 2019

Authority: European Union (Withdrawal) Act 2018, ss 8(1), 23(1), Sch 7, para 21; European Communities Act 1972, s 2(2); Limited Liability Partnerships Act 2000, ss 15, 17; Companies (Audit, Investigations and Community Enterprise) Act 2004, s 18A; Companies Act 2006, ss 484(1), 519A(5), 1239(1)(b), (2), (5)(d), 1241(2)(c), 1246(1), 1252(1), (4)(a), (8), 1292(1), (2). These Regulations are primarily made in exercise of the powers conferred by s 8(1) of the European Union (Withdrawal) Act 2018 in order to address failures of retained EU law to operate effectively and other deficiencies arising from the withdrawal of the UK from the EU. They are also made under the other powers listed *ante*. They make amendments to legislation in the field of statutory auditing, in particular to the regulatory oversight and professional recognition of statutory auditors and third country auditors, and the requirements for the statutory audit of certain types of business undertakings, which may be companies, limited liability partnerships, building societies, friendly societies, or certain other types of insurance companies. Part 1 provides for citation and commencement, etc. Part 2 amends primary legislation including Parts 16 and 42 of, and Schedules 10, 11, 11A and 12 to, the Companies Act 2006. It also amends the Building Societies Act 1986, the Friendly Societies Act 1992, the Companies (Audit, Investigations and Community Enterprise) Act 2004, and the Local Audit and Accountability Act 2014. In particular, reg 14 introduces new powers contained in ss 1240A and 1240B) of the Companies Act 2006. Section 1240A confers on the Secretary of State powers to approve the audit regulatory regime of third countries as being equivalent, in this case, to the UK. Section 1240B confers on the Secretary of State powers to approve third country competent authorities as being adequate in relation to their ability to co-operate with the competent authority on the transfer of audit working papers. These powers replace powers previously exercised in respect of the EU by the European Commission under Articles 46 and 47 of Directive 2006/43/EC of the European Parliament and of the Council on statutory audits of annual accounts and consolidated accounts. Part 3 amends various pieces of secondary legislation concerning statutory audits and statutory auditors, audit reporting requirements and other requirements such as keeping a register of third country auditors. These include the Limited Liability Partnerships (Accounts and Audit) (Application of Companies Act 2006) Regulations 2008, SI 2008/1911; the Statutory Auditors (Amendment of Companies Act 2006 and Delegation of Functions etc) Order 2012, SI 2012/1741; the Statutory Auditors and Third Country Auditors Regulations 2013, SI 2013/1672; the Companies (Bodies Concerned with Auditing Standards etc) (Exemption from Liability) Regulations 2016, SI 2016/571; and the Statutory Auditors and Third Country Auditors Regulations 2016, SI 2016/649. Part 4 amends the retained Regulation 537/2014/EU of the European Parliament and of the Council on specific requirements regarding statutory audit of public-interest entities and repealing Commission Decision 2005/909/EC. Part 5 contains amendments to the Statutory Auditors and Third Country Auditors Regulation 2016 which are made under s 2(2) of the European Communities Act 1972, and which implement aspects of Article 32 of Directive 2006/43/EC of the European Parliament and of the Council on statutory audits of annual accounts and consolidated accounts. Part 6 introduces Schedule 1, which lists countries approved as equivalent third countries and transitional third countries, and Schedule 2, which lists third country competent authorities approved as adequate. Part 7 introduces Schedule 3 which revokes various pieces of retained direct EU legislation that are no longer needed. Part 8 introduces Schedule 4 which sets out the transitional provisions for some of the amendments made by these Regulations. See **[12.88]**.

2018 Statutory Instruments

SI 2018/1155: Companies (Directors' Report) and Limited Liability Partnerships (Energy and Carbon Report) Regulations 2018

Authority: CA 2006, ss 416(4), 1292(1); Limited Liability Partnerships Act 2000, ss 15, 17. These Regulations make changes to the reporting requirements in the Large and Medium-sized Companies and Groups (Accounts and Reports) Regulations 2008 (the "2008 Regulations"). They also make changes to the requirements in the Limited Liability Partnerships (Accounts and Audit) (Application of Companies Act 2006) Regulations 2008 (the "LLP Regulations"). Part 1 contains introductory provisions. These Regulations come into force on 1 April 2019, and have effect in respect of financial years beginning on or after that date. Part 2 amends regulation 10 and Part 7 of Schedule 7 to the 2008 Regulations to provide new requirements on quoted companies to make statements in the directors' report concerning the company's energy use from activities for which the company is responsible and from purchases for its own use, and action taken to increase its energy efficiency. Part 2 also inserts a new Part 7A into Schedule 7 to the 2008 Regulations to provide for new requirements on large unquoted companies to make statements in the directors' report concerning the company's greenhouse gas emissions, energy use and action taken to increase energy efficiency within the UK. Where large unquoted companies' activities consist wholly or mainly of offshore activities, the company must also include certain activities in the offshore area. Regulation 5 amends regulation 14 of the 2008 Regulations to provide that these new provisions will be subject to a review by the Secretary of State every 5 years. Regulations 6 and 7 provide that these statements are not required where making the statement would be seriously prejudicial to the interests of the company or if the company has used a small amount of energy in the financial year to which the directors' report relates. Regulations 6 and 7 also provide that, if a company's directors' report is a group directors' report, the company must make the required statements on the basis of the company's information and its subsidiaries' that are quoted companies, unquoted companies or limited liability partnerships, with provision to exclude any information which a subsidiary would not itself be required to disclose in its report. Provision is also made to the effect that a subsidiary which would itself be required to report is not so required where a parent company prepares such a group report, subject to a number of conditions. Part 3 amends the LLP Regulations which apply to limited liability partnerships certain provisions of the 2006 Act relating to accounts and auditor's reports. Regulation 10 inserts a new regulation 12B into the LLP Regulations to provide for large LLPs to prepare an equivalent report to the directors' report (the "energy and carbon report") for each financial year. The inserted regulation 12B makes provision for the content of the energy and carbon report, which must identify the members during the financial year and the name of the member signing the report. The energy and carbon report must include statements concerning the LLP's greenhouse gas emissions, energy use and action to be taken to increase its energy efficiency in the same manner as is required of unquoted companies in Part 2 to these Regulations. In particular, the inserted regulation 12B applies sections 415 and 419 of the 2006 Act, with modifications, which includes provision that it is a criminal offence to either fail to comply with a duty to prepare an energy and carbon report where the member failed to take all reasonable steps or to approve an energy and carbon report that does not comply with the statutory requirements where the member acted knowingly or recklessly and failed to take reasonable steps. The inserted regulation 12B also provides that, if an LLP's report is a group energy and carbon report, the LLP must make the required statements on the basis of the LLP's information and its subsidiaries' that are quoted companies, unquoted companies or limited liability partnerships, with provision to exclude any information which a subsidiary would not itself be required to disclose in its report. Provision is also made to the effect that a subsidiary who would themselves be required to report is not so required where a parent LLP prepares such a group report, subject to a number of conditions. Regulations 11 to 24 amend the application of the requirements of Part 15 of the 2006 Act to LLPs concerning the publication and filing with the registrar of companies of accounts and auditor's reports on them, to provide that many of those requirements extend to the energy and carbon report where the LLP is under a duty to prepare an energy and carbon report. Section 453 of the 2006 Act as it applies to LLPs is amended to provide that the civil penalties to which an LLP is liable under the Companies (Late Filing Penalties) and Limited Liability Partnerships (Filing Periods and Late Filing Penalties) Regulations 2008 (SI 2008/497) if it fails to comply with the filing requirements in section 441 of the 2006 Act apply where the failure concerns, not only the LLP's accounts and auditor's report, but also an energy and carbon report. Regulation 21 amends the application of the provisions on defective accounts in the 2006 Act and the Companies (Revision of Defective Accounts and Reports) Regulations 2008 (SI 2008/373) to include provision for a defective energy and carbon report. Regulation 22 amends the application of section 459 of the 2006 Act so that the Financial Reporting Council can require the provision of information in relation to the energy and carbon report. Regulation 24 amends the application of section 463 of the 2006 Act so that members are liable to compensate the LLP for any loss suffered, not only for false or misleading statements in a strategic report, but also in an energy and carbon report. Regulation 25 amends the review provisions in the LLP Regulations 2008 so that these provisions will be subject to a review every 5 years.

SI 2018/860: Companies (Miscellaneous Reporting) Regulations 2018

Authority: CA 2006, ss 396(3), 404(3), 416(4), 421(1)–(2A), 468, 1292(1)(a), (c); Companies (Audit, Investigations and Community Enterprise) Act 2004, ss 34(3)(a), 62(2). These Regulations make changes to the reporting requirements found in Part 15 of the Companies Act 2006 and the Large and Medium-Sized Companies and Groups (Accounts and Reports) Regulations 2008. These Regulations also amend the Community Interest Company Regulations 2005. These Regulations extend to the whole of the UK. Regulation 1 makes provision for differential commencement in relation to the provisions of these Regulations and for their application. Part 2 (regs 3 to 6) amends the Companies Act 2006, providing a new requirement to include a statement in the strategic report on how the directors have had regard to the matters set out in section 172 of that Act in the exercise of their duties. Part 3 amends the 2008 Regulations to require companies to report additional information in the directors' report. Regulation 8 makes consequential provision, and regulation 9 amends the review clause in the 2008 Regulations to require a review of the amendments made by these Regulations. Regulation 10 corrects definitions in Schedule 5 to the 2008 Regulations which refer to repealed legislation. This regulation will align the definitions in Schedule 5 with those in Schedule 8 of the 2008 Regulations which were previously amended, as well as the definitions used in the new Schedule 4A of the CIC Regulations inserted by regulations 20 to 23 of these Regulations. Regulation 12 aligns the formula provided in Schedule 7 to the 2008 Regulations for calculating the average number of employees with the formula used in the Companies Act 2006. Regulation 13 amends Part 4 of Schedule 7 of the 2008 Regulations to require additional reporting on a company's engagement with its employees, and suppliers, customers and others in a business relationship, to provide further explanation on how the directors of the company have complied with the duty to have regard in section 172. Regulation 14 inserts a new Part 8 into Schedule 7 to the 2008 Regulations requiring companies which in a financial year have more than 2000 employees, or a turnover of more than £200 million and a balance sheet total of more than £2 billion, to provide a statement of corporate governance arrangements in relation to that year. Regulations 15 to 19 amend Schedule 8 to the 2008 Regulations to require additional information in the Directors' Remuneration Report. Regulation 16 requires that the annual statement from the chair of the remuneration committee includes a summary of any discretion exercised by the remuneration committee in relation to the award of directors' remuneration. Regulation 17 requires companies to report how much of a director's pay award is attributable to share price growth, and extends the requirement to report on the exercise of discretion in relation to the award to specifically address whether discretion has been exercised due to changes in share price. It also places new requirements on companies with more than 250 UK employees to report pay ratio information comparing the remuneration of the CEO with the 25th, 50th and 75th percentile of the full time equivalent remuneration of the company's UK employees. For a parent company within the meaning of the Companies Act 2006 the information must relate to the group. Regulation 18 places a new requirement for companies to include in the remuneration policy an illustration, in relation to performance measures or targets, of the maximum remuneration of directors assuming share price growth of 50% during the performance period. Regulation 19 inserts a new definition into the interpretation provision for Schedule 8. Part 4 (regs 20 to 23) amends the CIC Regulations. These provisions remedy a gap created when Schedule 3 to the Small Companies and Groups (Accounts and Reports) Regulations 2008 ("the Small Company Regulations") was revoked by the Companies, Partnerships and Groups (Accounts and Reports) Regulations 2015. Section 34 of the Companies, Audit, Investigations and Enterprise Act 2004 requires regulations to make provision for community interest company reports to include information about the remuneration of directors. Regulation 23 amends the CIC Regulations by inserting Schedule 4A into the CIC Regulations, the content of which is a reproduction of the revoked Schedule 3, with minor amendments to definitions to include cross-references to the appropriate legislation.

SI 2018/528: Companies (Disclosure of Address) (Amendment) Regulations 2018

Authority: CA 2006, ss 243(4), (5)(b)–(d), 1088, 1292(1), (4); Limited Liability Partnerships Act 2000, ss 15(a), 17(2)(c), (3)(a). These Regulations amend the Companies (Disclosure of Address) Regulations 2009, SI 2009/214 (at **[4.191]**). The main amendments are to Part 3. Regulation 4 of these substitutes regulation 9 of the 2009 Regulations so that it now provides that an individual whose usual residential address is on the register in accordance with the listed provisions, can simply apply under the Companies Act 2006, s 1088 to the registrar to make that address unavailable for public inspection on the companies register, without having to demonstrate (as they did previously) that they have met any of the specified criteria. These amendments also remove the restriction preventing individuals from applying under s 1088 where a usual residential address was placed on the register before 1 January 2003, but require certain details to be provided with such an application. Amendments to regulations 9 and 10 also set out further instances of the circumstances in which an individual's address may have been placed on the public register. Amendments to regulation 10 (under which a company can make an application to remove usual residential address information of its members and former members) and regulation 11 (under which an individual who has registered a charge can apply to make an address unavailable) mean that the restriction preventing such applications from being made in respect of addresses placed on the register before 1 January 2003 is removed. Amendments made to regulations 12 and 14 reflect the fact that the registrar will no longer be making a determination on applications made under regulation 9. Amendments to regulation 13 provide for the registrar to make residential address information unavailable for public inspection pursuant to applications made under regulation 9. Where there remains a requirement for an applicant's current address to remain on the register, these amendments provide that the usual residential address will be replaced with a service address. Where there is no longer any such requirement, the amendments provide that the registrar will make the address unavailable for public inspection by way of partial suppression. Transitional provisions in regulation 8 of these Regulations provide that If a s 1088 application was received by the registrar before 26 April 2018, the application must be dealt with by the registrar in accordance with the 2009 Regulations as they applied before that date. Amendments have also been made to the 2009 Regulations by regulation 3 to ensure that one of the grounds on which an individual is able to make an application under the Companies Act 2006, s 243 (to prevent disclosure of their address by the registrar to credit reference agencies) is that they are or have been a constable. Consequential amendments are also made to the Limited Liability Partnerships (Application of Companies Act 2006) Regulations 2009 and the Scottish Partnerships (Register of People with Significant Control) Regulations 2017.

2017 Statutory Instruments

SI 2017/1233: Index of Company Names (Listed Bodies) Order 2017

Authority: CA 2006, s 1099(4)(a). This Order amends s 1099(3) of the Companies Act 2006 in consequence of Part 11 of the Charities Act 2011 and the Charitable Incorporated Organisations (General) Regulations 2012 (SI 2012/3012), which make provision for the formation and registration of charitable incorporated organisations (CIOs). A CIO is a legal form created specifically to meet the needs of charities under the Charities Act 2006 (the provisions have now been consolidated into the Charities Act 2011). The provisions of the Charities Act 2011 relating to the registration of CIOs extend to England and Wales only. Equivalent provision has been made for the Scottish charitable incorporated organisation in Scotland by Chapter 7 of Part 1 of the Charities and Trustee Investment (Scotland) Act 2005. Section 1099 of the Companies Act 2006 requires the registrar of companies to keep an index of the names of certain companies, but also of other bodies listed in subsection (3) of that section.

SI 2017/1164: Statutory Auditors Regulations 2017

Authority: CA 2006, ss 454(3), (4), 1292(1)(a), (c); European Communities Act 1972, s 2(2); Limited Liability Partnerships Act 2000, ss 15(a), 17. These Regulations implement obligations in Directive 2014/56/EU of the European Parliament and of the Council of 16 April 2014 amending Directive 2006/43/EC on statutory audits of annual accounts and consolidated accounts ("the Audit Directive"), and Regulation (EU) 537/2014 of the European Parliament and of the Council of 16 April 2014 on specific requirements regarding statutory audit of public-interest entities and repealing Commission Decision 2005/909/EC ("the Audit Regulation"). The Audit Regulation is directly applicable, but changes have been made to domestic law to remove inconsistencies between domestic law and the Audit Regulation. Regulations 1 and 2 deal with citation, commencement, interpretation and application. Regulation 3 and Schedule 1 make amendments in respect of the transposition for building societies, friendly societies and companies, in particular to provide an effective enforcement mechanism for the rotation and retendering for statutory auditors, and also to provide consistency between the legislative frameworks for these entities. Regulation 4 and Schedule 2 make amendments to the Insurance Accounts Directive (Miscellaneous Insurance Undertakings) Regulations 2008 (SI 2008/565) to implement requirements of the Audit Directive and the Audit Regulation in respect of miscellaneous forms of insurance undertaking. This includes insurers that are co-operative or community benefit societies (previously industrial and provident societies) in Great Britain, and industrial and provident societies in Northern Ireland. Regulation 5 and Schedule 3 make amendments to the Limited Liability Partnerships (Accounts and Audit) (Application of Companies Act 2006) Regulations 2008 (SI 2008/1911). This is to give effect to requirements of the Audit Directive and the Audit Regulation for limited liability partnerships which are public-interest entities, and otherwise to mirror the legislative framework for companies to ensure consistency of requirements for the auditing of different types of business entities. Regulations 6–13 make consequential amendments to the Companies (Revision of Defective Accounts and Reports) Regulations 2008 (SI 2008/373) to take account of the changes to the requirements in respect of audit reporting made by the Statutory Auditors and Third Country Auditors Regulations of both 2016 and 2017 and by these Regulations. Regulations 15 and 16 make consequential amendments to the Statutory Auditors and Third Country Auditors Regulations 2016 (SI 2016/649). Regulations 17 and 18 make consequential amendments to the Statutory Auditors (Amendment of Companies Act 2006 and Delegation of Functions etc) Order 2012 (SI 2012/1741). Regulation 19 and Schedule 4 give effect to a number of revocations and repeals. The Bank Accounts Directive (Miscellaneous Banks) Regulations 2008 (SI 2008/567) are revoked for accounting years beginning on or after 30 November 2018, as there will no longer be any miscellaneous banks in existence by that date. There are also consequential revocations and repeals, and the revocation of spent enactments. The Regulations are at **[4.671]**.

2016 Statutory Instruments

SI 2016/1245: Companies, Partnerships and Groups (Accounts and Non-Financial Reporting) Regulations 2016

Authority: CA 2006, ss 468(1)(a)–(c), (2), 1292(1). These Regulations implement Article 1(1) and (3) of Directive 2014/95/EU of the European Parliament and of the Council amending Directive 2013/34/EU as regards disclosure of non-financial and diversity information by certain large undertakings and groups. Article 1(1) inserts Article 19a, and Article 1(3) inserts Article 29a, into Directive 2013/34/EU of the European Parliament and of the Council on the annual financial statements, consolidated financial statements and related reports of certain types of undertakings ("the Accounting Directive"). These Regulations also make some amendments with respect to the transposition of Article 23(1) of the Accounting Directive. The Accounting Directive applies only to certain types of undertaking, which have limited liability. Regulation 1 restricts the effect of the amendments to the Companies Act 2006 to companies and qualifying partnerships. The word 'company' has the meaning given by s 1 of the 2006 Act. Qualifying partnerships are defined in reg 3 of the Partnerships (Accounts) Regulations 2008 (SI 2008/569). Regulation 2 introduces the amendments made by regs 3 and 4. Regulation 3 concerns the transposition of Article 23(1) of the Accounting Directive, to ensure that the parent company of a small group cannot benefit from an exemption from the requirement to produce group accounts if a member of the group is established under the law of an EEA state and is one of the types of entities listed in newly inserted section 399(2B). Regulation 4 inserts new ss 414CA and 414CB into the 2006 Act. By section 414A of the 2006 Act, the directors of a company must produce a strategic report for each financial year, while the directors of a company which is a parent company producing group accounts must produce a group strategic report (which is a consolidated report relating to all the undertakings included in the consolidated accounts). Section 414C sets out the required content of a strategic report. Inserted section 414CA requires companies and groups of a certain type, which are not small or medium-sized, and which have more than 500 employees in a financial year, to produce a non-financial statement as part of their strategic report. The requirement to produce a non-financial statement does not apply to a company which is a subsidiary undertaking if that company and its subsidiary undertakings (if any) are included in a group strategic report which complies with the requirements in subsection (8), or in a consolidated management report of an EEA undertaking which complies with the requirements in subsection (9). Inserted section 414CB sets out the requirements for the contents of the non-financial information statement. The statement must include such information as is necessary for an understanding of the company's development, performance and position and the impact of the company's activity, and must include information relating to certain matters. Some information requirements can be fulfilled by the company publishing the information by means of a national, EU-based or international reporting framework. Compliance with section 414CB(1)–(6) is deemed to fulfil some of the requirements for non-financial information contained in section 414C. Information about impending developments or matters in the course of negotiation which would, in the opinion of the directors, be seriously prejudicial to the commercial interests of the company can in certain circumstances be withheld.

SI 2016/649: Statutory Auditors and Third Country Auditors Regulations 2016

Authority: CA 2006, ss 494(1), (2)(b), (4)(a), 519A(5), 1241(2)(c), 1252(1), (8), 1292(1)(a), (2), (4), Sch 13, para 11(2); Companies (Audit, Investigations and Community Enterprise) Act 2004, s 18A(1), (3), (6); European Communities Act 1972, s 2(2). These Regulations implement obligations in Directive 2014/56/EU (which amended the 2006 Audit Directive). They also make amendments in consequence of the 2005 Audit Regulation to remove inconsistencies between domestic law and the Audit Regulation. Part 1 of the Regulations concerns introductory matters, including the application of the Regulations. By reg 1, some aspects of the Regulations apply only in relation to financial years beginning on or after 17 June 2016, including the requirements for all public interest entities to put their audit work out to tender at least every ten years and to change their auditor at least every twenty years as well as the extension of the controls which currently apply in relation to the sharing of audit working papers with third country competent authorities to the sharing of audit investigation reports with those competent authorities. There are transitional arrangements relating to investigations and enforcement action beginning before these Regulations come into force. This Part also contains definitions. Part 2 concerns the functions of the competent authority under these Regulations and the Audit Regulation. Ie, the Financial Reporting Council Limited. Regulation 3 sets out the responsibilities of the competent authority and permits the authority both to delegate tasks arising from its responsibilities to any recognised supervisory body, and also to subsequently reclaim tasks it has delegated. It also introduces Schedule 1, which prescribes requirements for the standards the competent authority must determine in relation to the obligations of statutory auditors in relation to professional ethics, independence, objectivity and confidentiality. Regulation 4 sets out the requirement that statutory auditors must comply with certain standards when conducting a statutory audit, which include the standards set under Schedule 1. Regulation 5 sets out the powers of the competent authority to impose sanctions on statutory auditors who breach the relevant requirements, which include the requirements in these Regulations (including the requirement in reg 4), the requirements in the Audit Regulation, and in various enactments which govern statutory audit for a range of audited persons. The competent authority is required by reg 6 to publish details of sanctions imposed under reg 5. Regulation 7 concerns the ability of the competent authority to enforce sanctions which have not been complied with by way of application to court for a court order. Regulation 8 provides that if a financial penalty is not paid when due, it will attract interest and may be recovered by the competent authority as a debt. Regulation 9 requires the competent authority to monitor the conduct of statutory audit work which relate to public interest entities (public interest entities are defined in reg 2 as an entity which issues securities which are admitted to trading on a regulated market, a credit institution or an insurance undertaking). The monitoring must take the form of a system of inspections which satisfy Article 26 of the Audit Regulation. Regulation 9 sets out the requirements for monitoring the conduct of statutory audit work for all other audited persons, which include having arrangements which operate independently of the persons being monitored, having adequate resourcing for effective monitoring, using suitably qualified and experienced persons to carry out inspections and avoiding conflicts of interest between those carrying out inspections and those being monitored. Regulation 10 gives effect to Schedule 2, which concerns powers of investigation of the competent authority. Regulation 11 concerns the performance of third country audit functions. The entities concerned are incorporated outside the EEA, but are traded in the UK or their transferable securities are admitted to a regulated market in an EEA state. Regulation 11 applies the system of requirements for audits, monitoring of audits and sanctions and enforcement in regs 4–9 and Schedule 2 to the performance of third country audit functions, with appropriate modifications. Regulation 12 in Part 3 provides that any term in a contract which, in relation to the conduct of a statutory audit of an audited person, has the effect of restricting the audited person's choice of statutory auditor to certain categories or lists of statutory auditors, has no effect (unless the audited entity is a public interest entity). Part 4 concerns miscellaneous matters. Regulation 13 gives power to the competent authority to grant to a statutory auditor, where exceptional circumstances exist, an exemption from the requirements of Article 4(2) of the Audit Regulation (which sets a limit for fees for non-audit services over a three year period of 70% in relation to the audit fees for an entity). The exemption may be granted for up to two consecutive financial years. Schedule 3 makes amendments to the Companies Act 2006. In particular, amendments are made to Part 16 of that Act in relation to rotation and retendering for statutory auditors for public interest entities. A maximum engagement period of ten years is introduced, although this can be extended to twenty years provided that there is a selection procedure at least every ten years. There are transitional arrangements in relation to the application of the maximum engagement period. Schedule 4 makes amendments to Part 8 of the Building Societies Act 1986 which mirror the amendments made to Part 16 of the Companies Act 2006 in Schedule 3. Building societies are all public interest entities. Schedule 5 makes consequential amendments to the Companies (Audit, Investigations and Community Enterprise) Act 2004. Amendments are also made to the Local Audit and Accountability Act 2014 to provide that the amendments to Part 42 of the Companies Act 2006 do not apply in relation to local audit under that Act. Regulations 14, 18, 19, 20, 22 and 23 make amendments to other secondary legislation. Regulation 21 excludes a large debt securities issuer from the definition of "UK-traded non-EEA company" for the purposes of Part 42 of the 2006 Act. Regulation 24 requires the Secretary of State to review the provisions of these Regulations, and to publish a report within five years. See **[4.650]**.

SI 2016/621: Registrar of Companies (Fees) (Amendment) Regulations 2016

Authority: CA 2006, ss 243(3), 790ZF, 1063(1)–(3), 1087B(3), 1292(1). These Regulations amend the Registrar of Companies (Fees) (Companies, Overseas Companies and Limited Liability Partnerships) Regulations 2012 (SI 2012/1907), the Registrar of Companies (Fees) (European Economic Interest Grouping and European Public Limited-Liability Company) Regulations 2012 (SI 2012/1908) and the Registrar of Companies (Fees) (Limited Partnerships and Newspaper Proprietors) Regulations 2009 (SI 2009/2392) which require payment of fees in respect of functions performed by the registrar of companies relating to companies, overseas companies, LLPs, European Economic Interest Groupings, European Public Limited-Liability Companies, limited partnerships and the register of newspaper proprietors. Amongst other things, these Regulations amend the Registrar of Companies (Fees) (Companies, Overseas Companies and Limited Liability Partnerships) Regulations 2012 to include (in addition to protected information) provision for fees for the disclosure of restricted DOB information and information within the Companies Act 2006, s 790ZF(2). The disclosure of information within s 790ZF(2) of the 2006 Act relates to people with significant control of companies or LLPs. Modifications apply to the fees set out in Schedule 3 in specified circumstances. These amendments also removes the fees for the bulk electronic transfer of protected information. These Regulations also make equivalent changes for the disclosure of restricted DOB information relating to the manager of an EEIG. These Regulations also repeal the fee payable on registration of an annual return by a company or LLP and substitutes it with the same fee payable on registration of a confirmation statement. This change is a consequence of an amendment to the 2006 Act by the Small Business, Enterprise and Employment Act 2015. They also amend the Registrar of Companies (Fees) (Limited Partnerships and Newspaper Proprietors) Regulations 2009 to remove fees concerning the register of newspaper proprietors. This is as a consequence of the repeal of the majority of the Newspaper Libel and Registration Act 1881 by the Deregulation Act 2015. Regulations 19 to 22 set out transitional and saving provisions.

SI 2016/599: Companies and Limited Liability Partnerships (Filing Requirements) Regulations 2016

Authority: CA 2006, ss 9(5A) and (5B), 243(3), 853C(3), 1042, 1043, 1087B(3), 1167 and 1292; Limited Liability Partnerships Act 2000, ss 15(a), 17(1)–(3); Small Business, Enterprise and Employment Act 2015, s 159(1), (2). These Regulations apply with modifications various company filing changes made by the Small Business, Enterprise and Employment Act 2015 to limited liability partnerships and unregistered companies, as well as making amendments to other instruments in consequence of those changes. These Regulations also prescribe the classification scheme for company type and the classification system for a company's principal business activities for the purposes of s 9(5A) and (5B) and s 853C(3) of the Companies Act 2006. Section 92 of the 2015 Act replaced the requirement in Part 24 of the 2006 Act for companies to deliver an annual return to the registrar with a requirement for companies to deliver a confirmation statement. Section 94 of and Schedule 5 to the 2015 Act also amends the 2006 Act so that companies can choose to keep information held on their register of members, register of directors and register of company secretaries at the registrar as an alternative to keeping that information on the registers at the company. Regulations 1 and 2 provide for citation, commencement and interpretation. They come into force on 30 June 2016. Regulation 3 and Sch 1 amend the Limited Liability Partnerships (Application of Companies Act 2006) Regulations 2009 (SI 2009/1804) to apply the changes made by ss 92 and 94 of, and Sch 5 to, the 2015 Act to LLPs with modifications. It also makes other consequential amendments to the 2009 Regulations to reflect the changes made by the 2015 Act. Regulation 4 and Sch 2 amend the Unregistered Companies Regulations 2009 (SI 2009/2436). It applies the requirement for companies to deliver a confirmation statement under Part 24 of the 2006 Act to unregistered companies which prior to these Regulations were required to deliver an annual return. Regulation 5 and Sch 3 contain consequential amendments to other instruments. Previously, a company's annual return was required under s 855 of the 2006 Act to contain information about the company's type and its principal business activities. Information as to the company's type was required to be given by reference to the classification scheme prescribed in the Companies Act 2006 (Annual Return and Service Addresses) Regulations 2008 (SI 2008/3000). Information as to the principal business activities was permitted to be given by reference to the classification system also prescribed in those Regulations. Under s 853C of the 2006 Act (duty to notify a change in the company's principal business activities) a company is required to notify the registrar of a change in its principal business activities at the same time as making a confirmation statement. The information as to the company's principal business activities may be given by reference to one or more categories of a prescribed system of classifying business activities. In addition, s 9 of the 2006 Act sets out the documents that must be delivered to the registrar for a new company to be incorporated. Alongside these registration documents, under s 9(5A) and (5B), information must also be delivered to the registrar as to the proposed company's type and principal business activities. This information may also be given by reference to a prescribed system. Regulation 6 and Sch 4 to these Regulations prescribe the classification scheme for company type, while reg 7 and Sch 5 prescribe the classification system for a company's principal business activities for the purposes of s 9(5A) and(5B) and s 853C(3) of the 2006 Act. The substance of these classifications is consistent with the previous system set out in SI 2008/3000 for the purpose of a company's annual return. The Regulations are at **[4.640]**.

SI 2016/575: Limited Liability Partnerships, Partnerships and Groups (Accounts and Audit) Regulations 2016

Authority: CA 2006, s 396(3); Limited Liability Partnerships Act 2000, ss 15, 17; European Communities Act 1972, s 2(2). These Regulations amend the law relating to the preparation of the annual accounts of LLPs and to related matters such as the filing of their accounts. This includes the introduction of an exemption from certain financial reporting requirements for very small LLPs ("micro-entities"). These Regulations also introduce such an exemption for very small partnerships (including limited partnerships) which are "qualifying partnerships" under the Partnerships (Accounts) Regulations 2008. As regards qualifying partnerships (but not LLPs), these Regulations implement aspects of Directive 2013/34/EU of the European Parliament and of the Council on the annual financial statements, consolidated financial statements and related reports of certain types of undertakings, amending Directive 2006/43/EC of the European Parliament and of the Council and repealing Council Directives 78/660/EEC and 83/349/EEC (the New EU Accounting Directive). Part 1 of the Regulations deals with introductory matters. Regulation 1 provides that the amended law applies in respect of financial years commencing on or after 1 January 2016, but an LLP or qualifying partnership may also choose to apply the amended law (except in one respect) to its financial year beginning on or after 1 January 2015 (but before 1 January 2016) if a copy of its accounts for that financial year has not already been delivered to the registrar of companies before the Regulations come into force. Part 2 of the Regulations amends the Limited Liability Partnerships (Accounts and Audit) (Application of Companies Act 2006) Regulations 2008 at **[10.223]**. Part 3 amends the Small Limited Liability Partnerships (Accounts) Regulations 2008 at **[10.288]**. Part 4 amends the Large and Medium-sized Limited Liability Partnerships (Accounts) Regulations 2008 at **[4.60]**. Part 5 amends the Small Companies (Micro-Entities' Accounts) Regulations 2013 and the Partnerships (Accounts) Regulations 2008 at **[10.288]**. Part 6 makes a minor correction to the Large and Medium-sized Companies and Groups (Accounts and Reports) Regulations 2008. Regulations 26, 46, 62, 64 and 67 require the Secretary of State to review the provisions amended or affected by these Regulations, and to publish a report within five years after these Regulations come into force and within every five years after that. Following a review it will fall to the Secretary of State to consider whether the provisions should remain as they are, or be revoked or be amended. A further instrument would be needed to revoke or amend the provisions.

SI 2016/441: Registrar of Companies and Applications for Striking Off (Amendment) Regulations 2016

Authority: CA 2006, ss 1095(1), (2), 1292(1). These Regulations amend the Registrar of Companies and Applications for Striking Off Regulations 2009, SI 2009/1803 at **[4.317]**. The 2009 Regulations contain provisions on the rectification of the register of companies. On receipt of an application, the registrar of companies must remove from the register material that is factually inaccurate, derived from something that is factually inaccurate or forged, or derived from anything invalid or ineffective or done without a company's authority, unless a valid objection is made within 28 days. Together with the Small Business, Enterprise and Employment Act 2015, s 102 (which amends CA 2006, s 1095), these Regulations introduce a new system for removing from the register material naming a person as a company director. Regulation 1 provides for citation and commencement. Regulation 2(1) introduces the amendments in ref 2(2), (3). Regulation 2(2) amends reg 4 of the 2009 Regulations. While a valid objection will still prevent material being removed from the register in most cases, under reg 4, as amended, an objection will no longer prevent removal of material naming the person as a director where the application is made by or on behalf of the person so named. Regulation 2(3) amends reg 5 of the 2009 Regulations to provide that a company may instead prevent the material about the director from being removed from the register by providing evidence that the person consented to act as a director of the company. It also sets out further particulars of the application process, and makes a change consequential to reg 2(2). Regulation 3 requires the Secretary of State to review the operation and effect of these Regulations and publish a report within 5 years after they come into force and within every 5 years after that. Following a review it will fall to the Secretary of State to consider whether these Regulations should remain as they are, or be revoked or be amended. A further instrument would be needed to revoke these Regulations or to amend them.

SI 2016/423: Companies (Address of Registered Office) Regulations 2016

Authority: CA 2006, s 1097A; Limited Liability Partnerships Act 2000, s 15. These Regulations make provision relating to applications to change the address of a company's registered office. The address will be changed if the registrar is satisfied that the company is not authorised to use the address. When an application is successful, the registrar must change the address of the company's registered office to an address that has previously been nominated by the registrar (otherwise known as a "default address"). Regulation 1 provides for citation, commencement and interpretation. Regulations 2–6 provide for the initial application process. Applications may be made by any person (reg 2) and must include the information specified in regulation 3. Unless the registrar dismisses the application immediately because there is no reasonable prospect of success, the registrar must give notice to the company of the application and invite the company to provide evidence that would satisfy the registrar that the company is authorised to use the address as its registered office (regs 5 and 6). Unless the company itself decides to change the address of its registered office, the company must respond with evidence that will satisfy the registrar that the company is authorised to use the address as its registered office. If the company fails to provide adequate evidence within the specified period, the registrar must change the address of the registered office to a default address (regs 7 and 8). Regulation 9 makes provision assisting the registrar in how to determine an application. This includes the ability of the registrar to refer applications or questions relating to the application to the court. The registrar may also, without further enquiry, rely on evidence listed in the Schedule, to be satisfied that the company is authorised to use the address as its registered office. This includes, for example, evidence suggesting the company or a related group undertaking has a proprietary interest at the address subject to the application. Upon determining an application, the registrar must give notice of the decision to both parties involved (reg 10). Either the applicant or the company is entitled to bring an application to the court under s 1097A(6) of the 2006 Act, but any application must be brought within 28 days (reg 16). Where the address of a registered office is changed by the registrar (after a successful application or following direction from the court), the duties specified under regs 11 and 17 (which relate to inspection of company records, or the disclosure or display of information) are temporarily suspended for 28 days or, where an appeal is brought by the company, throughout the appeal process. Where a default address is used as a registered office, regulations 12–15 provide how the default address may be administered by the registrar, and for what purposes the default address may be used. In particular, regulations 14 and 15 provide for the way in which the company may receive documents delivered to the company at the default address. When the address of the registered office has been changed to a default address, Regulation 18 enables the registrar to require evidence that a company is authorised to use an address when the company gives notice to change the address of its registered office. Regulations 19–21 amend the Limited Liability Partnerships (Application of Companies Act 2006) Regulations 2009 (SI 2009/1804) to apply, with modifications, these Regulations to LLPs. The 2009 Regulations are at **[10.319]**. Regulation 22 requires the Secretary of State to review the operation and effect of these Regulations and publish a report within 5 years after they come into force and within every 5 years after that. Following a review it will fall to the Secretary of State to consider whether the Regulations should remain as they are, or be revoked or be amended. A further instrument would be needed to revoke the Regulations or to amend them. These Regulations are reproduced in full at **[4.621]**.

SI 2016/339: Register of People with Significant Control Regulations 2016

Authority: CA 2006, ss 243, 790B(1)(b), 790C(7)(d), 790C(12), 790K(5), 790M(7), 790O(2), 790ZF, 790ZG, 1088, 1292, Sch 1A, para 25(5)(b), Sch 1B, paras 12(1), (2). These Regulations make provisions which supplement Part 21A of the Companies Act 2006 in respect of information about people with significant control of companies. They also make consequential amendments to the Companies (Disclosure of Address) Regulations 2009, SI 2009/214 at **[4.191]**. Part 1 of these Regulations makes provision with regard to citation, commencement and interpretation. Part 2 makes provision about the scope and application of Part 21A of the Companies Act 2006, and prescribes the fee to be charged by companies when supplying copies of their registers of persons with significant control. Part 3 makes provision about the particulars to be noted in a company's register of persons with significant control concerning the nature of a person's control over the company. It also specifies characteristics of foreign limited partners in connection with determining whether a person has significant control over a company. Part 4 sets out additional information to be included in a company's register of persons with significant control where there are no registrable persons, there is an unidentified registrable person, there are unconfirmed details of a registrable person, a company's investigations are ongoing and where there have been failures to comply with requirements to provide information under ss 790D and 790E of the Companies Act 2006. Part 5 sets out requirements concerning notices to be issued by companies, and matters to be taken into account, when seeking to enforce the disclosure requirements of Part 21A of the Companies Act 2006. Part 6 Regulations makes provision about the protection of a registrable person's usual residential address information. It sets out when usual address information may be disclosed by the registrar to specified public authorities and credit reference agencies, along with the process by which applications may be made to require the registrar to refrain from disclosing usual residential address information. Part 7 makes provision about the protection of a registrable person's particulars. It sets out the process by which applications may be made to require the registrar to refrain from using or disclosing those particulars, and also prescribes when companies must not use or disclose those particulars. Part 8 contains transitional provisions about applications to require the registrar to refrain from using or disclosing a registrable person's particulars and the date on which a person is deemed to have become registrable where the person was registrable on commencement of these Regulations. Part 8 of these Regulations also makes amendments to the Companies (Disclosure of Address) Regulations 2009 (reg 48 and Schedule 5) in order to more closely align the 2009 Regulation's regime for the protection of directors' residential addresses from disclosure with the related regime about the protection of a person with significant control's usual residential address information set out in Part 6 of these Regulations. The amendments also expand the grounds on which applications may be made for protection under the 2009 Regulations to include situations where a successful application has been made under Part 6 of these Regulations. Part 8 also requires the Secretary of State to review the operation and effect of these Regulations and publish a report within the period that the Secretary of State is obliged to review and report on Part 21A of the Companies Act 2006. The Regulations are at **[4.559]**.

2015 Statutory Instruments

SI 2015/1928: Reports on Payments to Governments (Amendment) Regulations 2015

Authority: CA 2006, s 1102(2), (3); European Communities Act 1972, s 2(2). These Regulations amend the Reports on Payments to Governments Regulations 2014 (SI 2014/3209). The 2014 Regulations implemented Chapter 10 of Directive 2013/34/EU on the annual financial statements, consolidated financial statements and related reports of certain types of undertakings, amending Directive 2006/43/EC and repealing Council Directives 78/660/EEC and 83/349/EEC. Regulation 1 deals with citation and commencement. Regulation 2 corrects errors in the 2014 Regulations which derive from an unduly restrictive definition in the 2014 Regulations of the term "undertaking". That definition feeds into other definitions and provisions in the 2014 Regulations. In particular, reg 8 of the 2014 Regulations (as amended by these Regulations) imposes a duty on the directors of certain UK parent undertakings to prepare a consolidated report, and regs 9–11 of the 2014 Regulations make provision about the content of such a report and provision for exemptions. The amendments made by reg 2 of these Regulations ensure (by expanding the definition of "subsidiary undertaking" in the 2014 Regulations) that the subsidiary undertakings to be included in consolidated reports are not restricted to UK entities. Regulations 3 and 4 apply (with some modifications) the provisions of Part 35 of the Companies Act 2006 listed in Tables A and B in those regulations to documents delivered to the registrar under the 2014 Regulations by partnerships or limited partnerships. The provisions applied relate to public notice of receipt of certain documents, inspection of the register and language requirements (translation) for documents delivered to the registrar.

SI 2015/1695: Companies and Limited Liability Partnerships (Filing Requirements) Regulations 2015

Authority: CA 2006, ss 1042, 1043, 1292; Limited Liability Partnerships Act 2000, ss 15(a), 17(3)(a); European Communities Act 1972, s 2(2); Interpretation Act 1978, s 14A. These Regulations introduce changes for limited liability partnerships, European Public Limited-Liability Companies ("SEs"), European Economic Interest Groupings, unregistered companies and companies authorised to register. These changes are consequent on changes made to the Companies Act 2006 by Part 8 of the Small Business, Enterprise and Employment Act 2015. Regulations 1–3 provide for citation, commencement and application. Regulations 4 and 5 amends ss 1000, 1001 and 1003 of CA 2006 as modified by regulations 50 and 51 of the Limited Liability Partnerships (Application of Companies Act 2006) Regulations 2009 to apply to LLPs. These amendments reduce timescales for striking an LLP from the register and reflect changes made to Part 1 of Chapter 31 of the CA 2006 by the 2015 Act. Regulation 6 amends s 1087 of CA 2006 (as modified by regulation 66 of the Limited Liability Partnerships (Application of Companies Act 2006) Regulations 2009) and modifies sections 1087A and 1087B of the CA 2006 so that they apply to LLPs. These amendments require the registrar to omit the 'day' of the date of birth of members of an LLP from the material on the register available for public inspection and prevent the registrar from disclosing date of birth information except in specific circumstances. Sections

1087A and 1087B CA 2006 were inserted by the 2015 Act. Regulation 8(3) and (4) amends the European Economic Interest Grouping Regulations 1989 to make equivalent provision for EEIGs, whilst regulation 9(3) amends the Unregistered Companies Regulations 2009 to make equivalent provision for unregistered companies. Regulations 7, 8(2) and 10 amend the European Public Limited-Liability Company Regulations 2004, the European Economic Interest Grouping Regulations 1989 and the Companies (Companies Authorised to Register) Regulations 2009 so that, when a notice relating to a member, manager, director or secretary acting in the relevant capacity is delivered to the registrar of companies, the notice itself will no longer need to contain a statement of that person's consent to act. Instead, the statement required will be that the person has already provided the consent. Regulation 9(2) amends the Unregistered Companies Regulations 2009 to apply the new notification requirement in s 1079B of the CA 2006 to unregistered companies. Regulation 11 requires the Secretary of State to review the operation and effect of these Regulations and publish a report within five years after they come into force and at least every five years after that.

SI 2015/1694: Companies (Disclosure of Date of Birth Information) Regulations 2015

Authority: CA 2006, ss 243(3), 1087B(2), (3), 1292(1). These Regulations specify the conditions for disclosure of date of birth information ("DOB information" in s 1087A of the Companies Act 2006) to public authorities and credit reference agencies under s 1087B of that Act. Regulation 1 deals with citation, commencement and interpretation. Regulation 2 and Schedule 1 specify the public authorities to whom the registrar may disclose DOB information in accordance with s 1087B of the Companies Act 2006. Regulations 2 and 3 and Schedule 2 specify the conditions for the disclosure of such information to a public authority or credit reference agency. The Regulations are at **[4.552]**.

SI 2015/1675: Accounting Standards (Prescribed Bodies) (United States of America and Japan) Regulations 2015

Authority: CA 2006, ss 464(1), (3), 1292(1)(a); Interpretation Act 1978, s 14A. Statements of standard accounting practice issued by a body prescribed under the Companies Act 2006, s 464 are "accounting standards" for the purposes of Part 15 of that Act (accounts and audit). The Accounting Standards (Prescribed Bodies) (United States of America and Japan) Regulations 2012 (SI 2012/2405) prescribed the Accounting Standards Board of Japan and the Financial Accounting Standards Board in respect of the group accounts of parent companies that are admitted to trading on Japanese stock exchanges and of parent companies whose securities are registered with the US Securities and Exchange Commission respectively. These bodies are only prescribed for group accounts for financial years ending on or before 31 December 2014 and the Regulations cease to have effect on 31 December 2015. Regulation 1 of these Regulations deals with citation and commencement and provides that these Regulations expire on 30 September 2022. Regulation 2–4 prescribe the Accounting Standards Board of Japan and the Financial Accounting Standards Board in respect of the group accounts of parent companies that are admitted to trading on Japanese stock exchanges and of parent companies whose securities are registered with the US Securities and Exchange Commission respectively. Regulations 5–7 limit the prescription of these bodies in relation to group accounts of parent companies. Regulations 8 and 9 require the Secretary of State to review the operation and effect of these Regulations and publish a report within five years after the Regulations come into force. Following the review it will fall to the Secretary of State to consider whether the Regulations should be allowed to expire as reg 1(3) provides, be revoked early, or continue in force with or without amendment. A further instrument would be needed to continue the Regulations in force with or without amendments or to revoke them early. The Financial Reporting Council Limited remains prescribed under Part 5 of the Statutory Auditors (Amendment of Companies Act 2006 and Delegation of Functions etc) Order 2012 (SI 2012/1741).

SI 2015/1672: Companies, Partnerships and Groups (Accounts and Reports) (No 2) Regulations 2015

Authority: CA 2006, ss 396(3), 473(2), 1292(1). These Regulations amend the law relating to the preparation of the annual accounts of companies. They extend to the whole of the UK. Regulations 1 and 2 deal with citation, commencement, interpretation and application. Regulations 3 and 4 implement the final words of Article 12(6)(d) of Directive 2013/34/EU on the annual financial statements, consolidated financial statements and related reports of certain types of undertakings, amending Directive 2006/43/EC of the European Parliament and of the Council and repealing Council Directives 78/660/EEC and 83/349/EEC. The Companies, Partnerships and Groups (Accounts and Reports) Regulations 2015 (SI 2015/980) ("the 2015 Regulations") implemented obligations in Chapters 1–9 of that Directive. Regulation 3 amends Schedule 1 to the Small Companies and Groups (Accounts and Directors' Report) Regulations 2008 (SI 2008/409), and reg 4 amends Schedules 1, 2 and 3 to the Large and Medium-sized Companies and Groups (Accounts and Reports) Regulations 2008 (SI 2008/410). The effect of these amendments is that, where provision for diminution in value has been made in respect of goodwill and the reasons for which that provision was made have ceased to apply to any extent, the provision must not be written back to any extent. The amendments made by regulations 3 and 4 apply in respect of financial years beginning on or after 1 January 2016, but a company which has chosen to apply the amendments made by the 2015 Regulations to its financial year beginning on or after 1 January 2015 (but before 1 January 2016) must also apply the amendments made by regulations 3 or 4 (as the case may be) to that financial year (reg 2(2)). The amendments made by regulations 3 and 4 do not apply in relation to limited liability partnerships (reg 2(3)). Regulation 5 makes consequential and minor amendments to regs 2 and 3 of the 2015 Regulations.

SI 2015/980: Companies, Partnerships and Groups (Accounts and Reports) Regulations 2015

Authority: CA 2006, ss 396(3), 404(3), 409(1), (2), 412(1), (2), 468(1), (2), 473(2), 484, 1292(1); European Communities Act 1972, s 2(2). These Regulations amend the law relating to the preparation of the annual accounts of companies (and partnerships all of whose members have limited liability) and related matters such as the filing of such accounts. They implement obligations in Directive 2013/34/EU of the European Parliament and of the Council on the annual financial statements, consolidated financial statements and related reports of certain types of undertakings, amending Directive 2006/43/EC of the European Parliament and of the Council and repealing Council Directives 78/660/EEC and 83/349/EEC. Part 1 of the Regulations contains introductory matters and these include the application of the Regulations. The Regulations apply in respect of financial years beginning on or after 1 January 2016, but a company may instead apply the amended law (except in one respect) to its financial year beginning on or after 1 January 2015 (but before 1 January 2016) if this is desired (regulation 2). Part 2 of the Regulations amends the Companies Act 2006. Regulation 4(3) and (4) raises the thresholds which determine when a company or group qualifies as "small" for the purposes of certain accounting and reporting exemptions, and for exemption from audit. Regulation 4(5)(b) substitutes a new section 384(2)(a) with the effect that a company that is a member of a group of companies one or more of which is admitted to trading on an EEA regulated market (such as the London Stock Exchange) does not qualify as "small". Regulation 5(6), (7) and (8) makes changes to the law in connection with the preparation by a parent of group accounts and the exemptions from that obligation. One such change is to provide that a parent company need not prepare group accounts if the only reason why it does not qualify as "small" is because it is a public company, provided that it is not a company admitted to trading on a regulated EEA market. Other changes to the law concern the exemptions from a parent company's obligation to prepare group accounts where that parent is itself included in the group accounts of a larger group. Regulation 5(13) repeals s 410 of the Act with the effect that it will no longer be possible for a company to disclose relevant information about related companies (for instance, its subsidiaries) in its annual return – such information (where required) will have to be disclosed in the annual accounts. Regulation 5(14), (15) and (16) makes changes to ss 410A, 411 and 413 of the Act as regards the information which, generally speaking, companies must provide in their annual accounts concerning "off-balance sheet arrangements", employee numbers and costs, and directors' benefits. Regulation 7 has the effect that small companies which qualify as "micro-entities" (see s 384A) are no longer required to prepare directors' reports. Regulation 8(3) amends s 444 of the Act, which concerns the filing obligations of small companies. Key changes here reflect the fact that a small company will no longer be able to file (at Companies House) annual accounts which are an abbreviated version of the accounts which it prepares and sends to shareholders – instead a small company will file the versions of the balance sheet and profit and loss account (where the profit and loss account is filed) which are prepared and sent to the shareholders. Regulation 9(2) and (3) raises the thresholds which determine when a company or group qualifies as "medium-sized" for the purposes of certain accounting and reporting exemptions. Regulation 11 substitutes new ss 496 and 497A of the Act. The substituted sections contain more detailed requirements than the current sections as to the content of an auditor's report on a company's non-financial reports – strategic reports, director's reports and (where applicable), separate corporate governance statements. Part 3 of the Regulations amends the Small Companies and Groups (Accounts and Directors' Report) Regulations 2008 (SI 2008/409). Regulation 16 makes various changes to Part 1 of Schedule 1 to SI 2008/409 and these include allowing companies which qualify as "small" to prepare abridged versions of the prescribed balance sheet and profit and loss account formats set out in Schedule 1, and allowing "small" companies to adapt the prescribed formats if conditions are satisfied. Regulation 16 also makes changes to the prescribed formats. Regulation 17 amends Part 2 of Schedule 1 to SI 2008/409 concerning accounting principles and rules applicable to the annual accounts of "small" companies. The changes are largely minor and/or technical. Regulation 18 amends Part 3 of Schedule 1 to SI 2008/409 and the effect is greatly to reduce the number of notes to the annual accounts of "small companies". Regulations 19 and 20 revoke Schedules 2 and 3 respectively to SI 2008/409. Regulations 18 to 20 reflect Article 16.3 of the Directive pursuant to which the information which Member State can compel "small" companies to provide in their accounts is limited. Regulation 21 revokes Schedule 4 to SI 2008/409 to reflect the fact that "small" companies are no longer permitted to file accounts which are different to those which they prepare and send to their shareholders. Regulations 21 and 22 amend Schedule 6 to SI 2008/409 concerning the accounts of a "small" group. Part 4 of the Regulations amends the Large and Medium-sized Companies and Groups (Accounts and Reports) Regulations 2008 (SI 2008/410). Regulation 27 makes various changes to Part 1 of Schedule 1 to SI 2008/410. These include allowing such companies to adapt the prescribed balance sheet and profit and loss account formats set out in Schedule 1 and changes to the prescribed formats. Regulation 28 amends Part 2 of Schedule 1 to SI 2008/410 concerning accounting principles and rules applicable to "medium-sized" and "large" companies. These are largely minor and/or technical and mirror the changes being made to Part 2 of Schedule 1 to SI 2008/409. Regulation 29 amends Part 3 of Schedule 1 to SI 2008/410. The effect is to make some largely minor amendments to the law relating to the notes to the annual accounts of these companies. Regulations 32 and 33 make parallel provision to regulations 28 and 29 respectively as regards "banking companies", and regulations 35 and 36 make similar provision in the case of "insurance companies". Regulations 37 and 38 amend Schedule 4 to SI 2008/410 which schedule concerns the information which all companies to which SI 2008/410 applies must provide in their annual accounts as regards "related undertakings" (including subsidiaries). Regulation 37(4) amends paragraph 7 to this Schedule with these companies must provide information regarding their membership of undertakings which have unlimited liability. Regulation 39 amends Schedule 6 to SI 2008/410 as regards the accounts of "medium-sized" and "large" groups. Part 5 of the

Regulations amends the Partnership (Accounts) Regulations 2008 (SI 2008/569). SI 2008/569 applies, with modifications and omissions, Parts 15 and 16 of the Act and SI 2008/409 and 2008/410 to "qualifying partnerships", essentially partnerships all of whose members have limited liability. Part 5 of the Regulations makes a small number of minor amendments to SI 2008/569 as a consequence of the Directive and changes being made to SI 2008/409 by regulations 18, 19 and 20 of the Regulations. See **[4.548]**.

SI 2015/842: Companies (Disclosure of Address) (Amendment) Regulations 2015

Authority: CA 2006, s 243(2). These Regulations amend the Companies (Disclosure of Address) Regulations 2009 (SI 2009/214) by including the Minister for the Cabinet Office in Schedule 1 to those Regulations. Schedule 1 (which is at **[4.207]**) specifies the public authorities to whom the registrar may disclose protected information in accordance with the Companies Act 2006, s 243. For this purpose "protected information", as defined by s 240 of the 2006 Act, means, in relation to a company director who is an individual, information as to that director's usual residential address or the information that the service address of the director is that director's usual residential address.

SI 2015/532: Companies Act 2006 (Amendment of Part 18) Regulations 2015

Authority: CA 2006, s 737. These Regulations amend Part 18 (Acquisition by limited company of its own shares) of the Companies Act 2006 (at **[1.741]** et seq). Regulations 1 and 2 provide for citation and commencement, and introduce the amendments made by regs 3–9. Regulation 3 provides that a company that buys back its own shares may finance the purchase in accordance with Chapter 5 or, without Chapter 5 applying, under s 692(1ZA) of the 2006 Act. Section 692(1ZA) specifies the maximum value of shares that may be bought back under this procedure, being the aggregate purchase price in a financial year, as the lower of £15,000 or 5% of the nominal value of the fully paid share capital as at the beginning of the financial year. Regulation 4 removes the requirement to deliver a statement of capital to the registrar when shares are cancelled under s 708(2) following a purchase by a company of its own shares for the purposes of an employees' share scheme, if the statement of capital would be identical to that delivered under s 720B(1) (registration of documents for purchase of own shares for the purpose of or pursuant to an employees' share scheme). Regulation 5 inserts a new subsection into s 709 that provides that Chapter 5 is subject to the procedure in s 692(1ZA) to ensure that there is no conflict. Regulation 6 amends s 723 so that where a company buys back its own shares under s 720A for the purposes of or pursuant to an employees' share scheme, the time limit for the return of the shares to the company such that the obligation to pay arises is specified in relation to the date the resolution approving such buy back is passed. This is to allow a company to take advantage of the option of deferred payment in s 691(3). Regulations 7, 8 and 9 ensure that shares bought back under section 692(1ZA) and those bought back under Chapter 5 of Part 18 are treated consistently in accountancy terms. In particular, regulation 7 prevents shares bought back under section 692(1ZA) from being held in treasury.

SI 2015/472: Companies Act 2006 (Amendment of Part 17) Regulations 2015

Authority: CA 2006, ss 657(3), 1290. These Regulations amend the Companies Act 2006, s 641 to prohibit a company from reducing its share capital as part of a scheme of arrangement where the purpose of the scheme is to acquire all the shares of the company, except where the acquisition amounts to a restructuring that inserts a new holding company into the group structure. See that section at **[1.724]**.

SI 2015/17: Company, Limited Liability Partnership and Business (Names and Trading Disclosures) Regulations 2015

Authority: CA 2006, ss 54(1)(c), 56(1)(a), (5), 57(1)(a), (2), (5), 60(1)(b), 65(1), (2), (4), 66(2), (3), (4), (6), 82, 84, 1193(1)(c), 1195(1)(a), (5), 1197(1), (2), (3), 1292(1), (2), 1294, 1296 and ss 54(1)(c), 56(1)(a) and 1292(1) of the 2006 Act as applied to LLPs by regs 8 and 81 of the Limited Liability Partnerships (Application of Companies Act 2006) Regulations 2009. These Regulations (which are at **[4.514]** et seq) deal with restrictions relating to the registered name of a company, a limited liability partnership and to business names, and making requirements relating to trading disclosures. Part 2 concerns company names. The characters that are permitted to be used in the name of a company registered under the Companies Act 2006 are set out in reg 2 and Sch 1. These include ligatures, accents and diacritical marks, but do not include characters in lower case. Part 3 is about the application of these regulations to the names of LLPs. Regulation 11(1) extends the application of reg 9 in Part 2 to LLPs, thereby requiring persons to obtain the approval of the Secretary of State, or seek the views of a specified Government department or other body, to register a name. Regulation 11(2) and Sch 5 make amendments to the Limited Liability Partnerships (Application of Companies Act 2006) Regulations 2009 as a consequence of these regulations. Part 4 concerns overseas companies' names. An EEA company may always register its corporate name provided that name complies with reg 2 (see s 1047(3) and (5) of the 2006 Act). Part 5 deals with restrictions on names used by any person carrying on business in the UK. Part 6 deals with trading disclosures to be made by a company. All displays and disclosures required by these Regulations are to be in characters which can be read with the naked eye. Part 7 introduces the amendments and revocations made by Sch 6. This includes the revocation of the Company and Business Names (Miscellaneous Provisions) Regulations 2009, SI 2009/1085, the Company, Limited Liability Partnership and Business Names (Miscellaneous Provisions) (Amendment) Regulations 2009,

SI 2009/2404, the Company, Limited Liability Partnership and Business Names (Public Authorities) Regulations 2009, SI 2009/2982, the Companies (Trading Disclosures) Regulations 2008, SI 2008/495, and the Companies (Trading Disclosures) (Amendment) Regulations 2009, SI 2009/218.

2014 Statutory Instruments

SI 2014/3209: Reports on Payments to Governments Regulations 2014

Authority: CA 2006, ss 468, 1069, 1105; Limited Liability Partnerships Act 2000, ss 15, 17; European Communities Act 1972, s 2(2). These Regulations come into force on 1 December 2014 and extend to the whole of the UK. They implement chapter 10 of Directive 2013/34/EU on the annual financial statements, consolidated financial statements and related reports of certain types of undertakings. Chapter 10 requires certain undertakings active in the extractive or primary logging industries to make and publish reports on payments made to governments. Regulations 1 and 3 provide for citation, commencement and interpretation. Regulation 3 provides that these Regulations will apply to all undertakings in relation to a financial year starting on or after 1 January 2015, apart from those undertakings which are subsidiaries of parent undertakings who are obliged to prepare consolidated groups accounts in member States other than the UK. These Regulations will apply in relation to financial years for these undertakings beginning on or after 1 January 2016. Regulation 4 contains the obligation on directors of undertakings which are both large or classified as public interest entities and active in the extractive or primary logging industries to produce a report on payments made to governments. Regulation 5 sets out the required content of the report. It allows undertakings to disclose payments at the entity level rather than a project level where payments are made in respect of obligations imposed at the entity level instead of at project level. For instance, if an undertaking has more than one project in a host country, and that country's government levies corporate income taxes on the undertaking with respect to the undertaking's income in the country as a whole, and not with respect to a particular project or operation within the country, the undertaking would be permitted to disclose the resulting income tax payment or payments without specifying a particular project associated with the payment. Regulations 6 and 7 contain exemptions from the requirement to prepare a report. These exemptions are for undertakings whose payments are included in a consolidated report of a parent undertaking in any member State. Regulation 8 requires directors of parent undertakings that have subsidiaries that are mining or quarrying undertakings or logging undertakings to prepare a consolidated report on payments made to governments if obliged to prepare consolidated group accounts under the 2006 Act. Regulation 9 sets out the required content of the consolidated report and reg 10 contains exemptions from the obligation to prepare a consolidated report. Regulation 11 provides that payments made by a subsidiary undertaking may be excluded from a consolidated report in certain situations, provided that those subsidiary undertakings are also excluded on the same ground from the consolidated group accounts. Regulations 12 and 13 make provision for a further exemption for undertakings from the duty to prepare a report or consolidated report under these Regulations where an undertaking has already reported its payments made to governments under equivalent reporting requirements in a third-country. Regulation 14 obliges directors of undertakings who are required to prepare a report or consolidated report to deliver such reports to the registrar of companies within 11 months after the end of the financial year of the undertaking. Regulation 15 requires directors of undertakings that produce reports in accordance with equivalent reporting requirements to deliver the information contained in such reports to the registrar within 28 days of the report being made publicly available under the third-country reporting regime. It allows for the delivery of such information to be in a language other than English if accompanied by a certified translation. Reports delivered under regulations 14 or 15 must be delivered by electronic means. Regulation 16 makes it an offence to deliver to the registrar a false, misleading or deceptive document or statement under these Regulations. Regulations 17 and 18 create an enforcement regime to secure compliance with these Regulations. Regulation 19 gives the court the power to order the directors of an undertaking in default of an obligation to deliver a report under reg 14 or information under reg 15 to make good such default. Regulation 20 makes necessary consequential amendments to the 2006 Act and the Limited Liability Partnerships (Application of Companies Act 2006) Regulations 2009 (SI 2009/1804) to ensure that documents delivered to the registrar under these Regulations are subject to the Directive disclosure requirements. Regulation 21 requires the Secretary of State to review the operation and effect of these Regulations and publish a report within three years after they come into force and within every five years after that. Following a review it will fall to the Secretary of State to consider whether these Regulations should remain as they are, or be revoked or be amended.

SI 2014/3140: Company, Limited Liability Partnership and Business Names (Sensitive Words and Expressions) Regulations 2014

Authority: CA 2006, ss 55(1), 56(1)(b), 1194(1), 1195(1)(b), 1292(1). Under ss 55(1) and 1194(1) of the Companies Act 2006 (including s 55(1) as applied to limited liability partnerships by reg 8 of the Limited Liability Partnerships (Application of Companies Act 2006) Regulations 2009, SI 2009/1804), a person must obtain the approval of the Secretary of State to register a company or LLP by a name, or carry on business in the UK under a name, that includes a word or expression that is specified in Regulations made by the Secretary of State. Part 1 of Schedule 1 to these Regulations sets out which words and expressions are specified by the Secretary of State as requiring prior approval for use in the names of companies, LLPs and businesses, and Part 2 of Schedule 1 sets out words and expressions that the Secretary of State is specifying as requiring prior approval when used in the names of companies or LLPs only. Regulations 3(1)(b) and (c) and 4(b) and (c) provide that the specified words and expressions are specified in all their plural, possessive and (where relevant) feminine forms, and, in the case of Gaelic and Welsh words, in their grammatically mutated forms. Sections 56(1) and 1195(1) of the 2006 Act (including s 56(1) as applied to LLPs) give the Secretary of State the power to require that, in connection with an application for use of a sensitive word or expression, the applicant must seek the view of a specified government department or other body. Schedule 2 lists the government departments and other bodies whose views must be sought. Part 2 of Schedule 2 identifies the relevant government department or public authority whose view must be sought where the situation of the company's or LLP's registered office is relevant. The reference in reg 6(a)(i) to a registered office which is situated in England and Wales arises because England and Wales are usually treated in the 2006 Act as a single jurisdiction for the purposes of the situation of the registered office. However, a company whose registered office is situated in Wales can require the register of companies to state that its registered office is situated in Wales. In this case, the company will be governed by reg 6(b)(i) rather than reg 6(a)(i). The position is similar for an LLP whose registered office is situated in Wales. Since overseas companies are not required by the Overseas Companies Regulations 2009 (SI 2009/1801) to register in a specified part of the UK, they are treated for the purposes of reg 6 in the same way as companies registered in England and Wales. These Regulations revoke the Company, Limited Liability Partnership and Business Names (Sensitive Words and Expressions) Regulations 2009, SI 2009/2615. See **[4.503]**.

SI 2014/2009: Local Audit (Delegation of Functions) and Statutory Audit (Delegation of Functions) Order 2014

Authority: CA 2006, ss 1252, 1253, Sch 13, paras 7(3), 11(2), (3)(a). This Order concerns the transfer of functions of the Secretary of State under Part 42 of the Companies Act 2006 (statutory auditors), as applied with modifications to local audits by the Local Audit and Accountability Act 2014, Sch 5. Local audits are audits of the accounts of relevant authorities within the meaning of that Act (listed in Schedule 2 to the 2014 Act — local authorities and certain other public bodies in England and a very limited category of authorities which exercise functions partly in England and partly in Wales). The functions are transferred to the Financial Reporting Council Limited ("the designated body"). Article 1 deals with citation, commencement and interpretation. The effect of article 2 is to transfer all of the functions under Part 42 of the Companies Act 2006 to the designated body, subject to a number of specified exceptions and reservations. Article 3 has the effect that the designated body is a public authority for the purposes of the Freedom of Information Act 2000, so far as it is exercising functions transferred or conferred by this Order. Article 4 imposes consultation requirements on the designated body. Articles 5, 6 and 7 respectively require the designated body to publish an annual work programme, to record decisions, and to notify the Secretary of State of certain matters. Article 8 provides that financial penalties received by the designated body may not be retained but (after deduction of the body's reasonable costs) must be paid over to the Secretary of State. Article 9 has the effect that references to the Secretary of State in s 1256 of the 2006 Act (time limits for prosecution of offences) are to be construed as references to either the Secretary of State or the designated body. Article 10 amends the Statutory Auditors (Amendment of Companies Act 2006 and Delegation of Functions etc) Order 2012 (SI 2012/1741) so as to reduce the period required for consultation by the designated body prior to making an order or regulations under powers relating to statutory audit of companies.

2013 Statutory Instruments

SI 2013/3008: Small Companies (Micro-Entities' Accounts) Regulations 2013

Authority: CA 2006, ss 396(3), 468, 1292; European Communities Act 1972, s 2(2). These Regulations introduce an exemption from certain financial reporting requirements ("the Micros-Exemption") for very small companies ("Micro-Entities") preparing Companies Act individual accounts. The Micros-Exemption forms part of Directive 2013/34/EU of the European Parliament and of the Council of 26 June 2013 on the annual financial statements, consolidated financial statements and related reports of certain types of undertakings, amending Directive 2006/43/EC of the European Parliament and of the Council and repealing Council Directives 78/660EEC and 83/349/EEC ("the New Accounting Directive"). These Regulations implement that part of the New Accounting Directive. Regulation 3 limits the application of these Regulations to companies formed and registered (or treated as formed and registered) under the 2006 Act. It provides that the amendments made by these Regulations to any provision of the Companies Act 2006 or the Small Companies and Groups (Accounts and Directors' Report) Regulations 2008 do not have effect in relation to the application of any such provision: (a) to qualifying partnerships by regs 4(1) and 9(1) of and Part 1 of the Schedule to the Partnerships (Accounts) Regulations 2008; (b) to limited liability partnerships by the Limited Liability Partnerships (Accounts and Audit) (Application of Companies Act 2006) Regulations 2008; (c) to limited liability partnerships by the Small Limited Liability Partnerships (Accounts) Regulations 2008; (d) to overseas companies by Chapter 3 of Part 5 or Chapter 3 of Part 6 of the Overseas Companies Regulations 2009; (e) to unregistered companies by reg 3 of, and Schedule 1 to, the Unregistered Companies Regulations 2009; (f) to companies registered pursuant to s 1040 of the 2006 Act by reg 18 of the Companies (Companies Authorised to Register) Regulations 2009. Furthermore, any new provision of the 2006 Act or the 2008 Regulations inserted by these Regulations is not, by virtue of any provision mentioned in paragraphs (a) to (f) above, applied to the entities mentioned in those paragraphs. Regulation 4 inserts new ss 384A and 384B into the 2006 Act. Section 384A prescribes the thresholds, based on turnover, balance sheet total and employee numbers, relevant to qualification as a Micro-Entity. Section 384B identifies those categories of company (including charities, those companies already excluded from the small companies' regime under Part 15 of the 2006 Act and those companies voluntarily preparing group accounts (or whose accounts are included in consolidated group accounts prepared by another company)) which are excluded from being treated as Micro-Entities. Regulation 5 amends s 393 of the 2006 Act to identify, in the case of Micro-Entities, relevant considerations for company directors, when deciding whether to approve accounts on the basis that they give a true and fair view of the financial position of the company. It amends s 396 of the 2006 Act to introduce a presumption that Micro-Entities' accounts which comply with certain minimum requirements give a true and fair view. It also prescribes the statement to appear above the signature in the balance sheet, in circumstances where accounts are prepared in accordance with provisions applicable to companies which qualify as Micro-Entities. Regulation 6 amends s 444 of the 2006 Act to provide that companies preparing abridged accounts in accordance with the exemption for Micro-Entities must file a copy of those accounts at Companies House and removes the option to file abbreviated accounts under that section. Regulation 7 amends s 469 of the 2006 Act to exempt Micro-Entities from the requirement to draw up a note relating to the exchange rate applied, when translating amounts set out in the accounts into euros. It amends s 472 of the 2006 Act to provide that minimum prescribed notes to the accounts for Micro-Entities must appear in the balance sheet and not in a separate document. It amends s 474 of the 2006 Act to insert definitions relating, first, to minimum financial reporting requirements for Micro-Entities and, second, to those provisions of Parts 15 and 16 of the 2006 Act (and of regulations under Part 15) which relate specifically to the individual accounts of Micro-Entities. The amendment made by reg 7 to s 471 of the 2006 Act does not implement an EU obligation but is made more accurately to describe the subject matter of s 408, to which s 471 cross-refers. Regulation 8 amends s 495 of the 2006 Act to identify, in the case of Micro-Entities, relevant considerations for auditors, when deciding for the purposes of the auditor's report whether the accounts give a true and fair view of the financial position of the company. Regulation 9 amends Part 2 of the Small Companies and Groups (Accounts and Directors' Report) Regulations 2008. It exempts Micro-Entities from the obligation to draw up notes to the accounts other than the prescribed minimum notes. It disapplies, in the case of Micro-Entities, provision for fair value accounting and provision for the filing of abbreviated accounts. Regulation 10 amends Part 1 of Schedule 1 to the 2008 Regulations to provide, in a new Section C, for two abridged balance sheet formats and one abridged profit and loss account format for Micro-Entities. Regulation 11 makes a number of amendments to Part 2 of Schedule 1 to the 2008 Regulations in consequence of the addition to Part 1 of that Schedule of new Section C. Regulation 11(2)(b) and (c) does not implement an EU obligation but corrects erroneous descriptions of prescribed line items in the 2008 Regulations. Regulations 12 and 13 make a number of amendments to Schedules 6 and 8 to the 2008 Regulations in consequence of the addition to Part 1 of Schedule 1 of new Section C.

SI 2013/2224: Companies (Revision of Defective Accounts and Reports) (Amendment) (No 2) Regulations 2013

Authority: CA 2006, s 454(3), (4). These Regulations revoke and replace the Companies (Revision of Defective Accounts and Reports) (Amendment) Regulations (SI 2013/1971) because of defects in the original 2013 Regulations, in particular, they correct the application date for the amendments made by the instrument. The original 2013 Regulations 2013 made amendments to the Companies (Revision of Defective Accounts and Reports) Regulations 2008 (SI 2008/373) and were made in consequence of amendments to the 2006 Act made by the Enterprise and Regulatory Reform Act 2013 (ie, the insertion of new s 422A allowing for a revised directors' remuneration policy) and the Companies Act 2006 (Strategic Report and Directors' Report) Regulations 2013 (SI 2013/1970) (ie, the insertion of new ss 414A–414E requiring the preparation of a strategic report, and amending s 426 of the 2006 Act to refer to an option to provide a copy of the strategic report with supplementary material instead of a summary financial statement). Those amendments to the Companies Act 2006 take effect in relation to reports prepared in respect of financial years ending on or after 30 September. The original 2013 Regulations 2013 erroneously applied the amendments to the 2008 Regulations to financial years commencing 1 October 2013. This instrument ensures that the amendments to the 2008 Regulations apply consistently with the relevant amendments to the Companies Act 2006.

SI 2013/2005: Companies and Partnerships (Accounts and Audit) Regulations 2013

Authority: CA 2006, ss 409(1), (2), 468, 484(1), 1292; Limited Liability Partnerships Act 2000, s 15. These Regulations amend certain accounting and auditing provisions in the Companies Act 2006 and certain provisions of the 2006 Act as they are applied to LLPs by the Limited Liability Partnerships (Accounts and Audit) (Application of Companies Act 2006) Regulations 2008 (SI 2008/1911). The Regulations also make amendments to the Partnerships (Accounts) Regulations 2008 (SI 2008/569). Regulation 1 deals with citation, commencement, application and interpretation. These Regulations apply in relation to a financial year beginning on or after 1 October 2013. Regulation 2 amends s 448 of the 2006 Act. Where certain conditions are met s 448(1) exempts the directors of an unlimited company from the obligation which would otherwise arise under Chapter 10 of Part 15 of the 2006 Act to deliver accounts and reports in relation to the company to the registrar of companies. Section 448(3) provides that this exemption is not available in relation to certain descriptions of unlimited company. The purpose of s 448(3)(b) is to ensure that the exemption is not available in relation to unlimited companies covered by Council Directive 78/660/EEC on the annual accounts of certain types of companies. However, it is drafted in such a way that the exemption is available to certain unlimited companies which are covered by that Directive. Regulation 2 remedies this defect by amending s 448(3) and replacing s 448(5). Regulation 2 also amends the definition of e-money issuers in the 2006 Act to take into account changes made to the regulation of the activity of e-money issuing under the Electronic Money Directive and applies these changes to limited liability partnerships, where this has not already been done by the Electronic Money Regulations 2011 (SI 2011/99). It ensures that e-money issuers are excluded from certain exemptions to accounting and auditing requirements under the 2006 Act. Regulation 3 amends provisions of the 2006 Act as set out in their application to LLPs in the Limited Liability Partnerships (Accounts and Audit) (Application of Companies Act 2006) Regulations 2008. Regulation 4 amends the 2008 Partnerships Regulations. It amends the UK's implementation, in respect of partnerships, of Council Directive 90/605/EEC, which amended Council Directive 78/660/EEC and Council Directive 83/349/EEC on consolidated accounts, and of Directive 2006/43/EC on statutory audits of annual accounts and consolidated accounts. Regulation 4(3) replaces reg 3 of the 2008 Regulations with new regs 3 and 3A. New reg 3 provides a new definition of "qualifying partnership", replacing the definition in reg 3(1) and (4) of the 2008 Regulations, and also re-enacts (with clarifications) the provision in existing reg 3(3) dealing with the effect of changes in the constitution of a qualifying partnership. The purpose of providing for a new definition is to ensure that the "qualifying partnerships" covered by the 2008 Regulations are those UK partnerships to which Council Directive 78/660/EEC applies. New reg 3A defines references in regulations 4–15 of the 2008 Regulations to the members of a qualifying partnership. It replaces the provision made for that purpose by existing reg 3(2) and (4) of the 2008 Regulations, read with existing reg 2(2). The new provisions correct defects in the existing provisions and clarify their effect. They do not re-enact an existing provision which includes in the concept of a member of a qualifying partnership the members of certain connected partnerships. Regulation 4(5) of these Regulations amends reg 6 of the 2008 Regulations, which imposes requirements necessary to enable the UK to take advantage of the option to derogate in Article 47(1a) of Council Directive 78/660/EEC. The amendments correct defects in existing reg 6(1)–(3), ensuring that the requirement in reg 6(3) for partnership accounts to be available for inspection applies where the Directive requires it to apply. Regulations 5 and 6 make amendments to the Small Companies and Groups (Accounts and Directors' Report) Regulations 2008 (SI 2008/409) and the Large and Medium-sized Companies and Groups (Accounts and Reports) Regulations 2008 (SI 2008/410) to take account of the changes to the 2008 Partnership Regulations. Regulation 7 corrects an oversight in the 2008 Regulations by revoking the Partnerships and Unlimited Companies (Accounts) (Amendment) Regulations 2005 (SI 2005/1987) and the Partnerships and Unlimited Companies (Accounts) (Amendment) Regulations (Northern Ireland) 2006. These are now spent as they amend instruments which have been revoked.

SI 2013/1981: Large and Medium-sized Companies and Groups (Accounts and Reports) (Amendment) Regulations 2013

Authority: CA 2006, ss 421(1)–(2A), 422A(4), 1292(1)(a), (c). These Regulations substitute Schedule 8 to the Large and Medium-sized Companies and Groups (Accounts and Reports) Regulations 2008 (SI 2008/410) and make consequential amendments to reg 11 of the 2008 Regulations. Schedule 8 specifies the information to be included in the directors' remuneration report which the directors of a quoted company are required to prepare under CA 2006, s 420. Part 1 of Sch 8 contains introductory provisions. Part 2 of Schedule 8 provides that the report shall contain a summary statement by the chair of the remuneration committee. Part 3 of Schedule 8 requires the report to contain information about the remuneration of the directors in the financial year being reported on ("the relevant financial year"), including a single total figure table of remuneration in respect of each person who was a director during the relevant financial year, payments made to directors for loss of office, a performance graph which sets out the total shareholder return of the company on the class of equity share capital, if any, which caused the company to fall within the definition of "quoted company" in s 385 of the 2006 Act, the percentage change in the remuneration of the chief executive officer, the relative importance of spend on pay, a statement of how the directors' remuneration policy of the company will be implemented in the financial year following the relevant financial year, the consideration given by directors to the matter of remuneration and a statement of the result of the voting on any resolutions in respect of the directors' remuneration report or policy at the last general meeting of the company. Part 4 of Schedule 8 sets out the requirements relating to the company's future directors' remuneration policy and requires a future remuneration policy table, an illustration of the application of that policy to the directors, the company's policy on payment for loss of office and a statement regarding consideration of the company's overall pay policy and the views of shareholders in the formulation of the policy. Part 6 of Schedule 8 sets out the requirements for a revised directors' remuneration policy, and Part 5 defines the auditable part of the report. The 2008 Regulations are at **[4.60]**.

SI 2013/1973: Companies (Receipt of Accounts and Reports) Regulations 2013

Authority: CA 2006, s 426(1), (3). These Regulations (which come into force on 1 October 2013 and apply in relation to annual accounts and reports prepared in respect of a company's financial year ending on or after 30 September 2013) concern the circumstances under which companies may send to members a copy of the company's strategic report with supplementary material in accordance with the Companies Act 2006, s 426, instead of the company's full accounts and reports. Section 426 (as originally enacted) provided that a company could prepare and send a summary financial statement to persons who were entitled to receive full copies of the company's accounts and reports. That section was amended the Companies Act 2006 (Strategic Report and Directors' Report) Regulations 2013 (SI 2013/1970) to provide that instead of an option to provide a summary financial statement the company could provide a copy of its strategic report with supplementary material. The requirement for a company to prepare a strategic report is set out in s 414A of Part 15 of the 2006 Act, and supplementary material is described in s 426A of that Act (both inserted by the 2013 Regulations). Regulations 1 and 2 of these Regulations deal with citation, commencement and interpretation. Regulation 3 revokes the Companies (Summary Financial Statement) Regulations 2008 (SI 2008/374) subject o certain savings. Regulations 4–8 provide for the conditions under which a company may provide a copy of the strategic report with supplementary material and the procedures by which it can be ascertained whether a person wishes to receive full accounts and reports. These regulations are in substantially the same form as regulations 4–8 of the revoked 2008 Regulations. These Regulations are at **[4.494]**.

SI 2013/1972: Unregistered Companies (Amendment) Regulations 2013

Authority: CA 2006, s 1043. These Regulations amend the Unregistered Companies Regulations 2009 (SI 2009/2436) which applied to unregistered companies specified provisions of the Companies Act 2006. Regulation 1 provides for citation, commencement and application. Regulation 2 amends Schedule 1 to the 2009 Regulations in consequence of amendments to the 2006 Act made by the Companies Act 2006 (Strategic Report and Directors' Report) Regulations 2013 (SI 2013/1970) and by the Enterprise and Regulatory Reform Act 2013. Regulation 2(2)(a) disapplies ss 414A to 414D of the Act for unregistered companies. SI 2013/1970 amended the 2006 Act to repeal s 417 (the business review) and to insert new ss 414A to 414D requiring companies to prepare a strategic report the contents of which are in similar terms to repealed s 417. As s 417 was not applied to unregistered companies by SI 2009/2436 these new sections are also disapplied. Regulation 2(2)(a) disapplies ss 426–429 for unregistered companies. SI 2013/1970 made changes to sections 426–429 (summary financial statements) to provide for an option for companies to provide a copy of the strategic report and supplementary material to members who elect not to receive the full accounts and report, rather than a summary financial statement. As unregistered companies will not be required to prepare a strategic report these sections are disapplied. Regulation 2(2)(a) amends the 2009 Regulations to disapply the provisions of sections 420–422A and 439–440 of the Act in respect of unregistered companies. Sections 421 and 439 were amended by the Enterprise and Regulatory Reform Act 2013 and new ss 422A and 439A were inserted in the 2006 Act in order to provide for a binding shareholder vote on a quoted company's directors remuneration policy. Section 80 of the 2013 Act inserted a new Chapter 4A into Part 10 of the 2006 Act (ss 226A–226F) to provide for restrictions resulting from the binding vote on payments by the company to directors of remuneration or loss of office. Regulation 2(2)(b) removes modifications to the 2006 Act consequential upon the above amendments. See **[4.398]**.

SI 2013/1971: Companies (Revision of Defective Accounts and Reports) (Amendment) Regulations 2013

These Regulations amended the Companies (Revision of Defective Accounts and Reports) Regulations 2008, SI 2008/373 in consequence of amendments to the 2006 Act made by (i) the Enterprise and Regulatory Reform Act 2013 (ie, the insertion of new s 422A allowing for a revised directors' remuneration policy) and (ii) the Companies Act 2006 (Strategic Report and Directors' Report) Regulations 2013, SI 2013/1970 (ie, the insertion of new ss 414A–414E requiring the preparation of a strategic report, and the amendment of s 426 of that Act (option to provide strategic report with supplementary material). These Regulations came into force on 1 October 2013, and had effect as respects a company's financial year beginning on or after that date. These Regulations were revoked by SI 2013/2224 because of defects in these Regulations. See the entry for those Regulations above.

SI 2013/1970: Companies Act 2006 (Strategic Report and Directors' Report) Regulations 2013

Authority: CA 2006, ss 416, 468, 473(2), 1292(1). These Regulations amend the Companies Act 2006 to insert new sections which provide for the preparation by companies of a strategic report. The Regulations also amend the requirements for the contents of the directors' report set out in the Large and Medium-sized Companies and Groups (Accounts and Reports) Regulations 2008, SI 2008/410, Sch 7 and in the Small Companies and Groups (Accounts and Directors' Report) Regulations 2008, SI 2008/409, Sch 5. The Regulations amend the 2006 Act to substitute for summary financial statements the strategic report and supplementary material. Regulation 1 deals with citation, commencement and application (the Regulations apply in respect of financial years ending on or after 30 September 2013). Regulation 2 introduces the amendments in reg 3–5. Regulation 3 inserts a new Chapter 4A into Part 15 of the 2006 Act (see **[1.469]** et seq). New s 414A requires companies (other than those eligible for the small companies regime for accounts (see s 414B)) to prepare a strategic report. New s 414C prescribes the content of that report, including a requirement to provide information regarding the employment of people of each sex within the company. New s 414D requires that the report shall be approved by the directors and signed by one of them. Regulation 4 amends s 415A as a consequence of new s 414B. Regulation 5 repeals s 417 (contents of directors' report: business review) of the 2006 Act. It will no longer be a requirement for a business review to be prepared as part of the directors' report. Regulation 6 amends s 416 (content of directors' report) of the 2006 Act to omit the need for a statement by the company of its principal activities in the course of the year. Regulations 7 and 8 amend the provisions of the Large and Medium-sized Companies and Groups (Accounts and Reports) Regulations 2008 and the Small Companies and Groups (Accounts and Directors' Report) Regulations 2008 which prescribe the contents of the directors' report to remove certain items of information from the report, and limit the need to provide information on a company's purchase of its own shares to public companies. The Large and Medium-sized Companies and Groups (Accounts and Reports) Regulations 2008 are amended to require quoted companies to make certain disclosures regarding greenhouse gas emissions. Regulations 9–12 amend s 426 of the 2006 Act to substitute for a summary financial statement a copy of the strategic report and supplementary material, repeal s 427 of the 2006 Act (form and contents of summary financial statement: unquoted companies) and s 428 (form and contents of summary financial statement: quoted companies), and insert a new s 426A (Supplementary material). Regulation 13 repeals s 429 of the

2006 Act (summary financial statements: offences). Regulation 14 introduces the consequential amendments contained in the Schedule to these Regulations.

SI 2013/1947: Companies and Limited Liability Partnerships (Forms, etc) Amendment Regulations 2013

Authority: Companies Act 1985, ss 6(1)(b)(i), 10, 12, 30, 43(3), 49(4), 51(4), 53(1)(b), 54(4), 88(2), (3), 117(2), (3), 169, 169A, 190(5), 224(2), 225, 228(2)(f), 242(1), 244(3), 266(1), (3), 287(3), 288(2), 288A, 318(4), 325, 353(2), 363, 364(2), (3), 391(2), 652A, 652D, 691, 692(1), 694(4)(a), (b), 701, 702(1), 703P(1), (3), (5), 703Q(1), (2), 706, 710B(3), (8), 744, Sch 9, para 6, Sch 13, para 27 (all repealed subject to savings); the Companies Act 1989, s 144(4); the CA 2006, ss 1292(2), 1296(1), (2), 1300(2); the Insolvency Act 1986, s 38(3), (4); the Water Act 1989, s 185(2)(d), Sch 25, para 71(2); the Welsh Language Act 1993, s 26(3). These Regulations amend the transitional provisions in the eighth commencement order and revoke a number of instruments relating to prescribed forms for companies and LLPs that are no longer required. The revoked instruments are as follows: the Companies (Forms) (Amendment) Regulations 1986, SI 1986/2097; the Companies (Forms) (Amendment) Regulations 1988, SI 1988/1359; the Companies Act 1985 (Modifications for Statutory Water Companies) Regulations 1989, SI 1989/1461; the Companies (Forms) (Amendment) Regulations 1990, SI 1990/572; the Definition of Subsidiary (Consequential Amendments) Regulations 1990, SI 1990/1395; the Companies (Forms Amendment No 2 and Company's Type and Principal Business Activities) Regulations 1990, SI 1990/1766; the Companies (Forms) Regulations 1991, SI 1991/879; the Companies (Forms) (No2) Regulations 1991, SI 1991/1259; the Companies (Forms) (Amendment) Regulations 1992, SI 1992/3006; the Companies (Welsh Language Forms and Documents) Regulations 1994, SI 1994/117; the Companies (Welsh Language Forms and Documents) (Amendment) Regulations 1995, SI 1995/734; the Companies (Forms) (Amendment) Regulations 1995, SI 1995/736; the Companies (Forms) (No 2) Regulations 1995, SI 1995/1479; the Companies (Welsh Language Forms and Documents) (No 2) Regulations 1995, SI 1995/1480; the Companies (Welsh Language Forms and Documents) (No 3) Regulations 1995, SI 1995/1508; the Companies (Forms) (Amendment) Regulations 1996, SI 1996/594; the Companies (Welsh Language Forms and Documents) Regulations 1996, SI 1996/595; the Companies (Principal Business Activities) (Amendment) Regulations 1996, SI 1996/1105; the Companies (Forms) (Amendment) Regulations 1998, SI 1998/1702; the Companies (Forms) (Amendment) Regulations 1999, SI 1999/2356; the Companies (Welsh Language Forms) (Amendment) Regulations 1999, SI 1999/2357; the Companies (Forms) (Amendment) (No 2) Regulations 1999, SI 1999/2678; the Companies (Welsh Language Forms) (Amendment) (No 2) Regulations 1999, SI 1999/2679; the Companies (Welsh Language Forms) (Amendment) Regulations 2000, SI 2000/2413; the Limited Liability (Welsh Language Forms) Regulations 2001, SI 2001/2917; the Limited Liability Partnerships (Forms) Regulations 2002, SI 2002/690; the Companies (Forms) (Amendment) Regulations 2002, SI 2002/691; the Companies (Principal Business Activities) (Amendment) Regulations 2002, SI 2002/3081; the Limited Liability Partnerships (Welsh Language Forms) Regulations 2003, SI 2003/61; the Companies (Welsh Language Forms) Regulations 2003, SI 2003/62; the Companies (Forms) (Amendment) Regulations 2003, SI 2003/2982; the Companies (Welsh Language Forms) (Amendment) Regulations 2005, SI 2005/2746; the Companies (Forms) (Amendment) Regulations 2005, SI 2005/2747; the Companies (Welsh Language Forms) (Amendment) Regulations 2008, SI 2008/1860; the Companies (Forms) (Amendment) Regulations 2008, SI 2008/1861.Also revoked is reg 5 of the Companies Act 1985 (Annual Return) and Companies (Principal Business Activities) (Amendment) Regulations 2008, SI 2008/1659.

SI 2013/1773: Alternative Investment Fund Managers Regulations 2013

Authority: FSMA 2000, ss 183, 188, 213(10), 214(5), 224(4), 262, 349, 428(3), Sch 3, paras 13(1)(b), 14(1)(b), 17(b), 22; Companies Act 2006, ss 784, 785; European Communities Act 1972, s 2(2). These Regulations implement (in part) Directive 2011/61/EU of the European Parliament and of the Council on Alternative Investment Fund Managers ("AIFMD"), Regulation (EU) No 231/2013 supplementing AIFMD, Regulation (EU) No 345/2013 on European venture capital funds, and Regulation (EU) No 346/2013 on European social entrepreneurship funds, and an element of Directive 2011/89/EU of the European Parliament and of the Council amending Directives 98/78/EC, 2002/87/EC, 2006/48/EC and 2009/138/EC as regards the supplementary supervision of financial entities in a financial conglomerate. The Financial Conduct Authority is responsible for implementing other parts of AIFMD. Part 1 (regs 1–4) contains introductory provisions dealing with citation, commencement and interpretation. Part 2 (regs 5–8) deals with the authorisation of full-scope UK AIFMs. Part 3 (regs 9–23) concern small AIFMs. Part 4 (regs 24–33) deals with the operating conditions for external valuers, full-scope AIFMs and depositaries. Part 5 (regs 34–44) deals with AIFs which acquire control of non-listed companies and issuers. Part 6 (regs 45–64) concerns the marketing of AIFs. Part 7 (regs 65–69) provides for the powers and duties of the FCA under these Regulations. Part 8 (regs 70, 71) deals with the application of the procedural provisions of FSMA 2000 and the application of the 2000 Act to unauthorised AIFMs. Part 9 (regs 72–78) contain transitional provisions. Part 10 (regs 79–81) imposes a duty on the Treasury to review the operation of these Regulations within five years, and introduces the amendments in Sch 1 and Sch 2 to these Regulations (amendments to primary legislation and secondary legislation respectively).

SI 2013/1672: Statutory Auditors and Third Country Auditors Regulations 2013

Authority: CA 2006, ss 1239(1)(b), (2)(a), (f), (5)(d), (6)(a), 1246(1), 1292(1); European Communities Act 1972, s 2(2). These Regulations concern third country auditors as defined in the Companies Act 2006, s 1261. Regulations 1–3 deal with citation and commencement. Regulation 4 introduces the Schedule of revocations. Regulation 5 defines terms used in the Regulations. Regulations 6–12 make provision in respect of the statutory register of third country auditors and the requirements relating to registration. Regulation 6(1) requires the Financial Reporting Council Limited to keep the register and reg 6(2) and (3) prescribes the information which the register must contain. Pursuant to reg 6(4) and (5) the register must be kept in electronic form and be available for inspection. Regulations 7 and 8 set out matters with which a third country auditor must comply in order to become registered. Application is made to the FRC and reg 9 provides for the circumstances in which the FRC may, and will not, register the applicant. Regulation 10 provides for the allocation by the FRC to a successful applicant of its "registered number". Pursuant to reg 11, a registered third country auditor has a duty to provide the FRC with updated information (eg, to ensure that information on the register concerning the third country auditor remains correct). Regulation 12 concerns the removal of third country auditors from the register. Regulations 6 to 12 consolidate (with some minor amendments) the existing law relating to the register of third country auditors and the registration process. Regulation 13 (which amends the Companies Act 2006 (Transfer of Audit Working Papers to Third Countries) Regulations 2010) delays the coming into force of amendments to ss 1253D, 1253DE and 1253E of the 2006 Act. Regulation 13 implements Commission Decision 2013/280/EU pursuant to which the Public Company Accounting Oversight Board of the USA and the Securities and Exchange Commission of the USA are to remain, until 31 July 2016, bodies to which EU Member States may allow the transfer of audit working papers. Regulations 14–17 amend the 2006 Act. These regulations re-implement obligations in Directive 2006/43/EC of the European Parliament and of the Council of 17 May 2006 on statutory audits of annual accounts and consolidated accounts or else make provision for matters which arise out of or relate to these obligations. Regulation 16 amends Schedule 10 to the 2006 Act to allow an entity carrying out inspections of "third country audit functions" performed by "statutory auditors" (see the definitions at, respectively, paragraph 13 of Schedule 10 to, and section 1210 of, the 2006 Act) to determine sanctions against such auditors where its inspections reveal breaches of the relevant rules of the auditor's professional body. In addition, it obliges the professional body to treat such sanctions as if they were sanctions which the professional body had itself imposed. Regulation 17 amends Schedule 12 to the 2006 Act. It allows the waiving of hearings in connection with disciplinary proceedings involving registered third country auditors. The Schedule revokes the Statutory Auditors and Third Country Auditors (Amendment) Regulations 2008, the Statutory Auditors and Third Country Auditors (Amendment) (No 2) Regulations 2008, and Statutory Auditors and Third Country Auditors (Amendment) Regulations 2009. The Regulations are at **[4.482]**.

SI 2013/999: Companies Act 2006 (Amendment of Part 18) Regulations 2013

Authority: CA 2006, s 737. These Regulations (which come into force on 30 April 2013) amend Part 18 of the Companies Act 2006 at **[1.741]** et seq (Acquisition by limited company of its own shares). Regulations 1 and 2 deal with citation, commencement and interpretation. Regulation 3 (which amends s 691) removes the requirement on private limited companies to pay on purchase the price of shares in full in cases where the buy back is for an employees' share scheme; this will allow a private company to pay for its shares by instalments. Regulation 4 (which amends s 692) permits private companies to use cash without having to identify it as distributable reserves to finance the buyback of its own shares, up to the value of £15,000 or 5% of the share capital of the company in each financial year. Regulation 5 (which amends ss 694, 697, 700) changes the requirements for shareholder authorisations concerning contracts for share buyback to be passed; instead of the authorisation being given by special resolution (a majority of 75% of shareholders), it may be given by ordinary resolution (being a simple majority, ie over 50% of shareholders). Regulations 6–9 amend ss 693, 694, 704 and insert s 693A to allow a company to make off-market purchases of its own shares without having each buyback contract approved by shareholder resolution, as long as the company has a resolution from the shareholders authorising this. Regulations 10–13 (which amend ss 712, 713, 723 and insert ss 720A, 720B) amend the requirements that a company must fulfil when buying back its own shares using capital in cases where the buy back is for the purposes of or pursuant to an employees' share scheme. The amendments reduce the requirement to a statement by the directors that the company is solvent and a special resolution by the shareholders. Regulations 14 and 15 (which amend ss 724, 729) allow a company limited by shares to hold its own shares in treasury and to deal with such shares as treasury shares. The change also allows shares bought back with cash to be held as treasury shares.

SI 2013/632: Uncertificated Securities (Amendment) Regulations 2013

Authority: CA 2006, ss 784, 785, 788, 1292. These Regulations amend the Uncertificated Securities Regulations 2001, SI 2001/3755 (at **[6.40]** et seq). The 2001 Regulations enable title to securities to be transferred without a written instrument and make provision in respect of the approval and regulation of operators of "relevant systems", ie, computer-based systems that allow for title for units of securities to be evidenced and transferred without a written instrument. The purpose of these Regulations is to transfer responsibility for the approval and regulation of operators of relevant systems from the Treasury to the Bank of England. These Regulations also provide the Bank of England with new powers to require reports to be produced by skilled persons in respect of operators of relevant systems and to appoint investigators for the purpose of making inquiries about operators of relevant systems in appropriate cases. These Regulations also substitute a new Sch 2 to the 2001 Regulations in order to replace provision regarding the prevention of restrictive practices with provision for the purpose of preventing operators of relevant systems from adopting and maintaining excessive regulatory provision. As a result of the substitution, operators of relevant systems will now be subject to the Competition Act 1998 without exemption and their rules and practices will be subject to the Bank of England's on-going scrutiny.

SI 2013/600: Companies Act 2006 (Amendment of Part 25) Regulations 2013

Authority: CA 2006, ss 894(1), 1292(1). Regulation 1 of these Regulations provides for citation and commencement. Regulation 2 gives effect to Sch 1 to these Regulations which creates a new Chapter A1 in Part 25 of the 2006 Act. Chapter A1 sets out a single scheme for registration of company charges that applies to any company registered in the UK. It replaces Chapter 1 of Part 25 (companies registered in England and Wales and Northern Ireland) and Chapter 2 of that Part (companies registered in Scotland). Those Chapters are repealed by reg 3 of these Regulations. Regulation 4 revokes the Companies (Particulars of Company charges) Regulations 2008 (SI 2008/2996). Regulation 5 gives effect to Sch 2 which contains minor and consequential amendments. Regulation 6 provides for application and contains transitional provisions; ie, subject to certain exceptions, these Regulations apply only to charges created on or after 6 April 2013. Chapter A1 is at **[1.982]** et seq.

SI 2013/415: Civil Courts (Amendment) Order 2013

Authority: CA 2006, s 1156(3); County Courts Act 1984, s 2(1); Matrimonial and Family Proceedings Act 1984, s 33(1); Insolvency Act 1986, ss 117, 374. This Order amends the Civil Courts Order 1983 (SI 1983/713). It provides for a new county court at Chippenham. Burton-on-Trent County Court and Trowbridge County Court are discontinued. Jurisdiction in respect of existing cases in the closing courts is transferred to courts named in directions made by the Lord Chancellor. This Order was revoked by the Crime and Courts Act 2013 (Consequential, Transitional and Saving Provisions) Order 2014, SI 2014/820, as from 22 April 2014.

2012 Statutory Instruments

SI 2012/2405: Accounting Standards (Prescribed Bodies) (United States of America and Japan) Regulations 2012

Authority: CA 2006, ss 464(1), (3), 1292(1)(a). Regulations 2(a) and 3 of these Regulations prescribe the Financial Accounting Standards Board (a body formed under the law of the USA) in respect of the group accounts of parent companies whose securities are registered with the Securities and Exchange Commission of the United States of America. Regulations 2(b) and 4 prescribe the Accounting Standards Board of Japan (a body formed under the law of Japan) in respect of the group accounts of parent companies whose securities are admitted to trading on Japanese stock exchanges. Regulation 5 provides that those bodies are not prescribed for the group accounts of parent companies with securities admitted to trading on a regulated market in an EEA State. Regulation 6 provides that those bodies are prescribed only in respect of groups accounts for financial years ending on or before 31 December 2014. The Financial Reporting Council Limited remains prescribed under Part 5 of the Statutory Auditors (Amendment of Companies Act 2006 and Delegation of Functions etc) Order 2012 (SI 2012/1741). The Regulations extend to the whole of the UK. They ceased to have effect on 31 December 2015.

SI 2012/2301: Companies and Limited Liability Partnerships (Accounts and Audit Exemptions and Change of Accounting Framework) Regulations 2012

Authority: CA 2006, ss 468, 473, 484, 1043, 1104(2)(a), 1105(2)(d), 1108(2)(b), 1292(1)(c); Limited Liability Partnerships Act 2000, ss 15, 17. These Regulations amend provisions of the Companies Act 2006 (and statutory instruments made under that Act) relating to exemption from audit, the requirements to prepare individual accounts and to deliver individual accounts to the registrar of companies and the applicable accounting framework for individual and group company accounts. The Regulations come into force on 1 October 2012 and apply to financial years ending on or after that date. The Regulations give effect to optional derogations not previously applied in Council Directive 78/660/EEC on the annual accounts of certain types of companies). Regs 1–3 deal with citation, commencement, application and interpretation. Reg 4 widens the exemption from audit for small companies to provide that a company must only meet the general small company criteria for accounts and reports to qualify for the exemption. Reg 5 widens in the same way the conditions for qualification for audit exemption of a small company which is in a small group. Regs 6 and 7 introduce an exemption from the audit of individual accounts for subsidiary companies whose parent undertaking is established under the law of an EEA state. Various conditions must be satisfied in order for the subsidiary company to qualify for the exemption, principally the parent undertaking must give a statutory guarantee of the debts and liabilities to which the subsidiary company is subject as at the last day of the financial year in which the subsidiary company is seeking an audit exemption. Various categories of company are excluded from the exemption including quoted companies, some financial services companies and trade unions and employers' associations. Regs 8–11 introduce exemptions for dormant subsidiaries from the requirement to prepare individual accounts and to deliver individual accounts to the registrar. To qualify for the exemption the dormant subsidiary must have satisfied the same conditions which subsidiaries must satisfy to qualify for the audit exemption established by regs 6 and 7. Companies excluded from the exemption include quoted companies, some financial services companies and trade unions and employers' associations. Regulations 12–14 provide that company directors who prepare a company's individual accounts in accordance with international accounting standards may switch to Companies Act accounts for a reason other than a relevant change of circumstances provided they have not switched to Companies Act accounts in the period of five years preceding the first day of the financial year in which they wish to implement the change of accounting framework. Regs 15–17 do the same in relation to a parent company's group accounts provided the parent company's accounts are not required by Article 4 of the IAS Regulation (EC) No 1606/2002 to be prepared in accordance with international accounting standards. Reg 18 amends the meaning of 'annual accounts' so that any reference to annual accounts in Part 15 of the Companies Act 2006 only includes a reference to individual accounts where a company has prepared them. Reg 19 adds to the list of documents subject to Directive disclosure requirements, the documents which a subsidiary company must deliver to the registrar in order to qualify for the exemptions established by regs 6–11. The Registrar must publish notice of having received those documents in the London Gazette. Reg 20 amends the Limited Liability Partnerships (Accounts and Audit) (Application of Companies Act 2006) Regulations 2008, SI 2008/1911 (at **[10.223]**) to apply to limited liability partnerships the same exemptions from audit and requirements to prepare individual accounts and to deliver individual accounts to the registrar, and the same change in the provisions governing the applicable accounting framework for individual and group accounts, as those introduced by these Regulations in relation to companies. Regs 21 and 22 respectively amend the Registrar of Companies and Applications for Striking Off Regulations 2009, SI 2009/1803 (at **[4.317]**) and the Limited Liability Partnerships (Application of Companies Act 2006) Regulations 2009, SI 2009/1804 (at **[10.319]**) to provide that copies of documents which must be filed with the registrar of companies in order for subsidiary companies and LLPs to take advantage of the exemptions from the audit, preparation and filing of individual accounts introduced by these Regulations can be drawn up and delivered to the registrar in Welsh or in a language other than English, accompanied by a certified translation into English. Reg 22 also amends the Limited Liability Partnerships (Application of Companies Act 2006) Regulations 2009 to require the Registrar to publish in the London Gazette, notice of having received the documents which a subsidiary LLP must file in order to qualify for the exemptions from audit, preparation or filing of individual accounts established by these Regulations. Reg 23 amends the Unregistered Companies Regulations 2009, SI 2009/2436 (at **[4.389]**) to require the Registrar to do the same with regard to unregistered companies.

SI 2012/1908: Registrar of Companies (Fees) (European Economic Interest Grouping and European Public Limited-Liability Company) Regulations 2012

Authority: CA 2006, ss 1063(1)–(3), 1292(1). These Regulations provide for the fees to be payable to the registrar of companies in respect of his functions relating to the registration of documents relating to European Economic Interest Groupings and European Public Limited-Liability Companies, and the inspection or provision of copies of documents kept by him relating to EEIGs. The Regulations come into force on 1 October 2012. They replace the Registrar of Companies (Fees) (European Economic Interest Grouping and European Public Limited Liability Company) Regulations 2009 (SI 2009/2403) which are revoked subject to transitional provisions. See the 2012 Regulations at **[4.470]**.

SI 2012/1907: Registrar of Companies (Fees) (Companies, Overseas Companies and Limited Liability Partnerships) Regulations 2012

Authority: CA 2006, ss 243(3), 1063(1)–(3), 1292(1). These Regulations provide for the fees to be payable to the registrar of companies in respect of his functions relating to the registration of documents, the inspection or provision of copies of documents kept by him and the disclosure of information protected under the Companies Act 2006 relating to companies, overseas companies and limited liability partnerships. The Regulations come into force on 1 October 2012. They replace the Registrar of Companies (Fees) (Companies, Overseas Companies and Limited Liability Partnerships) Regulations 2009 (SI 2009/2101). The amount of the fees in these Regulations has been reduced from the corresponding fees in the replaced Regulations in respect of: (a) registration of annual returns delivered by electronic means by a company or limited liability partnership, (b) registration of a company under section 14 of the Companies Act 2006, or registration of a limited liability partnership under section 3 of the Limited Liability Partnerships Act 2000, where documents are delivered by electronic means, (c) inspection and provision of a copy document by means of Companies House Direct or Extranet in respect of a company, limited liability partnership or overseas company, (d) an application by a specified public authority or credit reference agency for a directors' snapshot package, and (e) the inspection of particulars of a company director, company secretary or a member of a limited liability partnership is free in some circumstances. Regulation 3 and Schedule 1 to the Regulations provide the fees to be payable in respect of the registration of documents by the registrar. Regulation 4 and Schedule 2 to the Regulations provide the fees to be payable in respect of the inspection or provision of copies of documents kept by the registrar. Regulation 6 and Schedule 3 to the Regulations provide the fees to be payable in respect of the disclosure of protected information under the Companies Act 2006 relating to directors of companies, directors and permanent representatives of overseas companies and members of limited liability partnerships. See **[4.452]**.

SI 2012/1741: Statutory Auditors (Amendment of Companies Act 2006 and Delegation of Functions etc) Order 2012

Authority: European Communities Act 1972, s 2(2)(a), (b); CA 2006, ss 464(1), (3), 504(1)(b)(ii), 525(1)(a)(ii), 1228(1), (2), (6), 1231(4), 1239, 1252(1), (2)(b), (4)(a), (5)–(8), 1253(4), 1292(1)(b), (c), (2), Sch 13, paras 7(3), 11(2), (3)(a). This Order amends the law relating to statutory auditors as defined in the Companies Act 2006, s 1210. It extends to the whole of the UK. Part 2 of the Order (arts 4, 5) amends the 2006 Act. It re-implements obligations in Directive 2006/43/EC on statutory audits of annual accounts and consolidated accounts, and makes provision for matters which arise out of or relate to these obligations. Article 4 substitutes new ss 1225–1225G for the existing s 1225 in Part 42 of the 2006 Act.

They provide for additional types of action which may be taken against a statutory auditor's professional body (in connection with securing the body's responsibilities properly to supervise its statutory auditor members). The Secretary of State may now give a direction to a professional body (eg, directing the body to do specified things) and may now impose a financial penalty upon such a body. Article 5 amends Schedule 10 to the 2006 Act. Part 3 of the Order (arts 6–16) concerns the transfer of functions of the Secretary of State under Part 42 of the 2006 Act to the Financial Reporting Council Limited ("the designated body"). It revokes the Statutory Auditors (Delegation of Functions etc) Order 2008 (SI 2008/496) whereby functions under Part 42 were transferred to the body called the Professional Oversight Board. Part 4 (arts 17–21) concerns the appointment of the designated body as "Independent Supervisor" of the Auditors General. It revokes the Independent Supervisor Appointment Order 2007 (SI 2007/3534) whereby the Professional Oversight Body performed this supervisory function. Part 5 (arts 22–24) concerns the prescription of the designated body for the purposes of s 464 of the 2006 Act, ie, the body responsible for issuing "accounting standards". It revokes the Accounting Standards (Prescribed Body) Regulations 2008 (SI 2008/651) whereby the body known as the Accounting Standards Board performed this role. The Schedule contains minor and consequential amendments. The Order is at **[4.430]**.

SI 2012/1439: Supervision of Accounts and Reports (Prescribed Body) and Companies (Defective Accounts and Directors' Reports) (Authorised Person) Order 2012

Authority: CA 2006, ss 457(1), (2), (5), (6), 462, 1292(1)(b), (c); Companies (Audit, Investigations and Community Enterprise) Act 2004, ss 14(1), (5), (8), 15E. This Order appoints the Conduct Committee to exercise the functions described in the Companies (Audit, Investigations and Community Enterprise) Act 2004, s 14(2). These functions are keeping certain periodic accounts and reports under review, and informing the FSA of any conclusions the Committee reaches as regards those accounts and reports. Article 2 of the Order limits the appointment to accounts and reports produced by relevant corporate bodies issuing transferable securities which are admitted to trading on a regulated market. The relevant corporate bodies are those whose home Member State is the UK for the purposes of the Transparency Directive (2004/109/EC). Under article 3 the appointment only relates to annual and half-yearly reports. Article 4 authorises the Conduct Committee for the purposes of the Companies Act 2006, s 456; ie authorises the Committee to apply to the court for a declaration (or declarator in Scotland) etc in respect of defective accounts or directors' reports. Article 5 imposes a record keeping requirement in relation to the functions conferred by this Order. The Order also amends s 15D of the 2004 Act, s 461 of the 2006 Act, and the Limited Liability Partnerships (Accounts and Audit) (Application of Companies Act 2006) Regulations 2008, SI 2008/1911. It also revokes the Companies (Defective Accounts and Directors' Reports) (Authorised Person) and Supervision of Accounts and Reports (Prescribed Body) Order 2008, SI 2008/623 (subject to transitional provisions). Note that arts 2–5 and 7, 8 were revoked by the Supervision of Accounts and Reports (Prescribed Body) and Companies (Defective Accounts and Reports) (Authorised Person) Order 2021, SI 2021/465, as from 6 May 2021 (see art 9 of the 2021 Order for transitional provisions in relation to the continuity of functions, etc). The only provisions now in force are art 1 (Citation, coming into force and interpretation), and art 6 (Amendments to categories of permitted disclosure) which amends s 15D of the 2004 Act, and s 461 of the 2006 Act.

2011 Statutory Instruments

SI 2011/2198: Companies (Disclosure of Auditor Remuneration and Liability Limitation Agreements) (Amendment) Regulations 2011

Authority: CA 2006, ss 494, 1292(1)(c). These Regulations amend the Companies (Disclosure of Auditor Remuneration and Liability Limitation Agreements) Regulations 2008 SI 2008/489 at **[4.115]** et seq. The main effect of these Regulations is to replace Sch 2 to the 2008 Regulations (with a new Sch 2A). The list of types of service in respect of which disclosure has to be made, set out in the substituted Sch 2A, has been updated to correlate with the revised Ethical Standards published by the Auditing Practices Board of the Financial Reporting Council. These Regulations also make further consequential amendments, and contain transitional provisions.

SI 2011/2194: Overseas Companies (Execution of Documents and Registration of Charges) (Amendment) Regulations 2011

Authority: CA 2006, ss 1052, 1292(1)(c). These Regulations amend the Companies (Execution of Documents and Registration of Charges) Regulations 2009, SI 2009/1917 (at **[4.326]** et seq). The main effect of these Regulations is to remove the requirements in regulations 9–22 of the 2009 Regulations for the registration with the registrar of companies of charges created by registered overseas companies over property of the company situated in the UK. Those provisions are revoked (subject to transitional provisions) as from 1 October 2011.

SI 2011/2097: Civil Courts (Amendment No 3) Order 2011

Authority: County Courts Act 1984, s 2(1); Senior Courts Act 1981, s 99(1); Insolvency Act 1986, ss 117, 374; CA 2006, 1156(3). This Order amends the Civil Courts Order 1983, SI 1983/713. The county courts listed in the Schedule to the Order are discontinued. The Order also establishes a district registry of the High Court at Telford and provides that Telford County Court has jurisdiction to deal with bankruptcy matters and to wind up companies. It also clarifies that Workington County Court has winding up jurisdiction. This Order was revoked by the Crime and Courts Act 2013 (Consequential, Transitional and Saving Provisions) Order 2014, SI 2014/820, as from 22 April 2014.

SI 2011/1856: Statutory Auditors and Third Country Auditors (Amendment) Regulations 2011

Authority: CA 2006, ss 1239(1)(b), (2), (5)(d), 1246(1),1292(1)(c); European Communities Act 1972, s 2(2). These Regulations amend s 1242 of, and Sch 10 to, the Companies Act 2006, and the Statutory Auditors and Third Country Auditors Regulations 2007, SI 2007/3494. The Regulations give effect to Commission Decision 2011/30/EU of 19 January 2011 (OJ L15, 20.1.2011, p 12) on the equivalence of certain third country public oversight, quality assurance, investigation and penalty systems for auditors and audit entities and a transitional period for audit activities of certain third country auditors and audit entities in the European Union. The 2006 Act is at **[1.1]** et seq. These Regulations also amend the Companies (Audit, Investigations and Community Enterprise) Act 2004, s 16 at **[5.216]**.

SI 2011/1487: Companies Act 2006 (Annual Returns) Regulations 2011

Authority: CA 2006, ss 855(3), 857, 1167, 1292(1). These Regulations are concerned with the information which must be included in a company's annual return under Part 24 of the Companies Act 2006. They amended various provisions in the original Part 24 of the 2006 Act. A new Part 24 (ss 853A–853L) was substituted for the original Part 24 (ss 854–859) by the Small Business, Enterprise and Employment Act 2015, s 92, as from 30 June 2016. The original Part 24 is now set out in the notes to s 853A at **[1.971]**. They also make consequential amendments to Sch 8 to the 2006 Act, and amend the Companies Act 2006 (Annual Return and Service Addresses) Regulations 2008, SI 2008/3000).

SI 2011/1265: Companies Act 2006 (Consequential Amendments and Transitional Provisions) Order 2011

Authority: CA 2006, ss 1292, 1294, 1296. This Order makes amendments to primary and secondary legislation that are consequential on certain provisions of the Companies Act 2006 having been brought into force, including the replacement of references to various provisions of the Companies Act 1985 with references to the appropriate, superseding provisions of the Companies Act 2006. It also repeals the Companies Consolidation (Consequential Provisions) Act 1985 subject to savings and transitional provisions. See **[4.425]** et seq.

SI 2011/324: Registrar of Companies (Fees) (European Economic Interest Grouping) (Amendment) Regulations 2011

Authority: CA 2006, s 1063(1)–(3). These Regulations amended the Registrar of Companies (Fees) (European Economic Interest Grouping and European Public Limited-Liability Company) Regulations 2009, SI 2009/2403, as from 6 April 2011. They were revoked by the Registrar of Companies (Fees) (European Economic Interest Grouping and European Public Limited-Liability Company) Regulations 2012, SI 2012/1908, reg 6, as from 1 October 2012, subject to transitional provisions in reg 5 of the 2012 Regulations at **[4.475]**.

SI 2011/319: Registrar of Companies (Fees) (Limited Partnerships) (Amendment) Regulations 2011

Authority: CA 2006, s 1063(1)–(3). These Regulations amend the Registrar of Companies (Fees) (Limited Partnerships and Newspaper Proprietors) Regulations 2009, SI 2009/2392, as from 6 April 2011. See the 2009 Regulations at **[4.370]**.

SI 2011/309: Registrar of Companies (Fees) (Companies, Overseas Companies and Limited Liability Partnerships) (Amendment) Regulations 2011

Authority: CA 2006, ss 243(3), 1063(1)–(3). These Regulations amended the Registrar of Companies (Fees) (Companies, Overseas Companies and Limited Liability Partnerships) Regulations 2009, SI 2009/2101, as from 6 April 2011. They were revoked by the Registrar of Companies (Fees) (Companies, Overseas Companies and Limited Liability Partnerships) Regulations 2012, SI 2012/1907, reg 8, as from 1 October 2012, subject to transitional provisions in reg 7 of the 2012 Regulations at **[4.458]**

2010 Statutory Instruments

SI 2010/2156: Companies (Disclosure of Address) (Amendment) Regulations 2010

Authority: CA 2006, s 243(2), (3). These Regulations amend the Companies (Disclosure of Address) Regulations 2009 by including the Marine Management Organisation in Sch 1 to those Regulations (see at **[4.207]**). Schedule 1 to those Regulations specifies the public authorities to whom the registrar may disclose protected information in accordance with s 243 of the Companies Act 2006. For this purpose "protected information" is defined by s 240(1) of the 2006 Act.

2009 Statutory Instruments

SI 2009/3022: Companies Act 2006 (Amendment of Section 413) Regulations 2009

Authority: CA 2006, s 468(1), (2). These Regulations amend s 413(8) of the 2006 Act (at **[1.467]**) so that banking companies and the holding companies of credit institutions are only required to make aggregate disclosures of the amounts specified in s 413(5)(a) and (c) (correcting an incorrect cross-reference). This is in implementation of the Member State option in Article 40(7) of Council Directive 86/635/EEC on the annual accounts and consolidated accounts of banks and other financial institutions.

SI 2009/2982: Company, Limited Liability Partnership and Business Names (Public Authorities) Regulations 2009

Authority: CA 2006, ss 54(1)(c), 56(1)(a), 1193(1)(c), 1195(1)(a), 1292(1). Under ss 54(1)(c) and 1193(1)(c) of CA 2006 a person is required to obtain the approval of the Secretary of State to register a company by a name, or carry on business in the UK under a name, that would be likely to give the impression that the company or business is connected with a public authority specified by the Secretary of State. These Regulations (i) specified the public authorities for these purposes; (ii) set out the relevant government department or other body whose view an applicant must seek in connection with an application for approval of the Secretary of State for use of a name under section 54(1)(c) or 1193(1)(c) of the Act. The Regulations made the same provision for limited liability partnerships. They were revoked by the Company, Limited Liability Partnership and Business (Names and Trading Disclosures) Regulations 2015, SI 2015/17, reg 30, Sch 6, para 1(c), as from 31 January 2015. The 2015 Regulations are at **[4.514]**.

SI 2009/2615: Company, Limited Liability Partnership and Business Names (Sensitive Words and Expressions) Regulations 2009

Authority: CA 2006, ss 55(1), 56(1)(b), 1194(1), 1195(1)(b), 1292(1). Under ss 55(1) and 1194(1) of the Companies Act 2006 (including s 55(1) as applied to LLPs by the Limited Liability Partnerships (Application of Companies Act 2006) Regulations 2009, SI 2009/1804, reg 8), a person must obtain the approval of the Secretary of State to register a company or LLP by a name, or carry on business in the UK under a name, that includes a word or expression that is specified in regulations made by the Secretary of State. These Regulations also provide that the view of a specified Government department or other body must be obtained in relation to certain other specified words. They also provide that the specified words and expressions are specified in all their plural, possessive and (where relevant) feminine forms, and, in the case of Gaelic and Welsh words, in their grammatically mutated forms. These Regulations were revoked and replaced by the Company, Limited Liability Partnership and Business Names (Sensitive Words and Expressions) Regulations 2014, SI 2014/3140, as from 31 January 2015. The 2014 Regulations are at **[4.503]**.

SI 2009/2476: Companies Act 2006 and Limited Liability Partnerships (Transitional Provisions and Savings) (Amendment) Regulations 2009

Authority: CA 2006, ss 1292(2), 1296(1), 1300(2); Limited Liability Partnerships Act 2000, ss 15, 17. These Regulations amend the 8th Companies Act 2006 commencement order in order to prevent s 22(2) of the 2006 Act coming into force on 1 October 2009. They also (i) amend the transitional provisions in connection with the commencement of ss 1012–1023 of the 2006 Act; (ii) make corresponding amendments in relation the application of those sections to LLPs; (iii) provide for new savings in relation to the repeal of CA 1985, s 26(2) and the Business Names Act 1985 (ie, in relation to names likely to give an impression of a connection with the Welsh Assembly Government). See the note at **[4.424]**.

SI 2009/2455: Civil Courts (Amendment) Order 2009

Authority: CA 2006, s 1156(3). This Order amended the Civil Courts Order 1983 (SI 1983/713) as a consequence of the Companies Act 2006 and Regulations made under the Limited Liability Partnerships Act 2000 which applied and modified provisions of the 2006 Act in relation to LLPs. The 2006 Act and the Regulations give the power to exclude a county court from having jurisdiction to deal with matters under that Act (including as applied to LLP) and, for the purposes of those jurisdictions, assign the district of that court to another county court. A new art 10A of the Order sets out the provision to exclude specified county courts from having the jurisdiction to deal with matters under the 2006 Act and the Regulations, and assigns the district of each excluded court to another county court. A sixth column is inserted in Schedule 3 of the Order to set out those courts to which are attached the district of the county courts excluded from having jurisdiction under the 2006 Act and the Regulations. This Order was revoked by the Crime and Courts Act 2013 (Consequential, Transitional and Saving Provisions) Order 2014, SI 2014/820, as from 22 April 2014.

SI 2009/2439: Registrar of Companies (Fees) (Amendment) Regulations 2009

Authority: CA 2006, s 1063(1)–(3). These Regulations amended the Registrar of Companies (Fees) (Companies, Overseas Companies and Limited Liability Partnerships) Regulations 2009, SI 2009/2101. These amendments had two main purposes: (i) to extend their application to companies within the Companies Act 2006, s 1040 (ie, a company not formed under the Companies Acts but authorised to register), and unregistered companies under s 1043 of the 2006 Act; (ii) to disapply the subscription fee payable for Companies House Direct, Extranet and XML, which provide inspection, or provision of copies, of documents kept by the registrar, where the subscription fee is paid under Regulations relating to European Economic Interest Groupings and limited partnerships. These Regulations were revoked by the Registrar of Companies (Fees) (Companies, Overseas Companies and Limited Liability Partnerships) Regulations 2012, SI 2012/1907, reg 8, as from 1 October 2012, subject to transitional professions in reg 7 of the 2012 Regulations at **[4.458]**.

SI 2009/2437: Companies (Companies Authorised to Register) Regulations 2009

Authority: European Communities Act 1972, s 2(2); CA 2006, ss 1042, 1292(1). These Regulations make provision in connection with the registration of a company on an application under section 1040 of the Companies Act 2006 (ie, a company not formed under the Companies Acts but authorised to register). These Regulations replace the provisions made by ss 681 to 682, and 684 to 690 of and Schedule 21 to the Companies Act 1985. Part 1 of the Regulations deals with citation etc. Part 2 deals with the process of an application to register under s 1040 of the 2006 Act. Regulation 3 provides that a company may not register without the assent of a specified majority of its members. Regulation 4 sets out the requirements for the application to the registrar of companies to register under s 1040, and specifies the documents that need to be provided with that application. Regulations 5, 6, 7 and 8 make detailed provision regarding the statements which must accompany the application, namely, a statement of capital and initial shareholdings (in the case of an application by a joint stock company), a statement of guarantee (in the case of a company wishing to register as company limited by guarantee), a statement of proposed officers and a statement of compliance. Regulation 9 provides for the requirements that are to be met for a joint stock company to register as a public company. Regulation 10 sets out the circumstances in which a company may change its name on registration. Regulations 11 and 12 require the registrar to register a company which complies with the registration requirements in these Regulations and to issue the company with a certificate of incorporation. Part 3 provides for the effects of registration under the 2006 Act. Regulation 18 provides that, on registration, the provisions of the Companies Acts apply to the company which has made the application to register under s 1040 as if it had been formed and registered under the 2006 Act. Regulations 14, 15 and 21 make provision for the transfer of property, rights and liabilities and the effect on pending legal proceedings, and the capital structure of the company. Regulations 16, 17, 19, 20, and 22 make provision for matters relating to the company's constitution. See **[4.400]**.

SI 2009/2436: Unregistered Companies Regulations 2009

Authority: CA 2006, ss 1043, 1210(1)(h), 1292(2). These Regulations apply specified provisions of the 2006 Act (and also provisions of the Companies Act 1985) to unregistered companies. Regulation 3 applies the provisions of the 1985 Act and the 2006 Act that are specified in Schedule 1 (with specified modifications). Regulations 4 and 5 contain adaptations of general effect. Regulation 6 provides for a person appointed as auditor of an unregistered company to be a statutory auditor for the purposes of Part 42 of the Act. Regulation 7 revokes specified regulations (including those applying to Northern Ireland) which apply provisions of the 1985 Act and the Act to unregistered companies. Provisions in those Regulations are reproduced in these Regulations. Transitional and saving provisions are set out in Schedule 2 to the Regulations. See **[4.389]**.

SI 2009/2425: Companies (Authorised Minimum) Regulations 2009

Authority: CA 2006, ss 763(2)–(4), 766(1)(a), (2), 1292(1), (2). These Regulations relate to provisions of the Companies Act 2006 which refer to the "authorised minimum" share capital requirement for public companies. There is a definition of "the authorised minimum" in s 763(1) of the 2006 Act, ie, £50,000 or the prescribed euro equivalent. Regulation 2 prescribes, for the purposes of this definition, the amount in euros which is to be treated as equivalent to the sterling amount of the authorised minimum (€57,100). Regulations 3 and 4 provide for the application of the authorised minimum requirement for the purposes of certain provisions of the 2006 Act. The provisions in question have the effect of requiring a public company to re-register as a private company where certain events cause the nominal value of its allotted share capital to fall below the authorised minimum. The events are a reduction of share capital confirmed by court order or the mandatory cancellation of shares in particular circumstances. Regulation 5 deals with registration by the registrar of companies of court orders confirming the reduction of public companies' share capital. It enables the registrar to assume, in certain circumstances, that the authorised minimum requirement is no longer satisfied by the company. Regulation 6 enables the courts, in specified proceedings, to make a determination in certain circumstances about the exchange rates to be applied in working out whether a public company satisfies the authorised minimum requirement. Regulation 7 prevents anyone from being liable as a result of reliance, for the purposes of these Regulations, on an exchange rate published by the Financial Times. It also prevents liability arising if an erroneous exchange rate published by the Financial Times is relied on for the purposes of the Regulations. Finally, it excludes liability for acts or omissions leading to the Financial Times not publishing an exchange rate capable of being relied on for the purposes of the Regulations. Regulation 8 revokes regulation 2 of the Companies (Authorised Minimum) Regulations 2008 (SI 2008/729); and regulation 9 makes transitional provisions and savings. Those transitional provisions and savings take account of transitional provisions and savings in Schedule 2 to the Companies Act 2006 (Commencement No 8, Transitional Provisions and Savings) Order 2008 (SI 2008/2860). See **[4.381]** et seq.

SI 2009/2404: Company, Limited Liability Partnership and Business Names (Miscellaneous Provisions) (Amendment) Regulations 2009

Authority: CA 2006, ss 65, 66, 1197, 1292(1); Limited Liability Partnerships Act 2000, ss 15, 17. These Regulations corrected errors in the Company and Business Names (Miscellaneous Provisions) Regulations 2009, SI 2009/1085 (now revoked). These Regulations were revoked by the Company, Limited Liability Partnership and Business (Names and Trading Disclosures) Regulations 2015, SI 2015/17, reg 30, Sch 6, para 1(b), as from 31 January 2015. The 2015 Regulations are at **[4.514]**.

SI 2009/2403: Registrar of Companies (Fees) (European Economic Interest Grouping and European Public Limited-Liability Company) Regulations 2009

Authority: CA 2006, ss 1063(1)–(3), 1292(1). These Regulations were revoked and replaced by the Registrar of Companies (Fees) (European Economic Interest Grouping and European Public Limited-Liability Company) Regulations 2012, SI 2012/1908, as from 1 October 2012; subject to transitional provisions in relation to documents delivered to the registrar on or before 30 September 2012, and applications made or subscriptions payable to the registrar on or before that date (see reg 5 of the 2012 Regulations). These Regulations originally provided for the fees payable to the registrar of companies in respect of his functions relating to the registration of documents relating to European Economic Interest Groupings and European Public Limited-Liability Companies, and the inspection or provision of copies of documents kept by him relating to EEIGs. They came into force on 1 October 2009 and extended to the UK. They replaced (i) the European Economic Interest Grouping (Fees) Regulations 2004 (SI 2004/2643), (ii) the European Public Limited-Liability Company (Fees) Regulations 2004 (SI 2004/2407), (iii) the European Economic Interest Grouping (Fees) Regulations (Northern Ireland) 1989 (SR 1989 No 218), and (iv) the European Public Limited-Liability Company (Fees) Regulations (Northern Ireland) 2004 (SR 2004 No 418). See the 2012 Regulations at **[4.470]**.

SI 2009/2400: European Public Limited-Liability Company (Amendment) Regulations 2009

Authority: CA 2006, ss 1102(2), (3), 1108(2)(b); European Communities Act 1972, s 2(2). These Regulations, which come into force on 1 October 2009, amend the European Public Limited-Liability Company Regulations 2004 (SI 2004/2326). Some of the amendments are consequential on the extension of the 2004 Regulations to Northern Ireland, and the revocation of the equivalent Northern Ireland Regulations by s 1285 of CA 2006. Other amendments replace references to provisions of CA 1985 with references to the equivalent provisions of the 2006 Act. Other amendments are consequential on changes to UK company law and reflect changes made to company law by CA 2006. These Regulations also prescribe new forms for SEs which replace those currently contained in the 2004 Regulations. In addition, Part 3 of the 2004 Regulations, which relates to the involvement of employees in relation to the running of an SE, is omitted and is re-enacted with modifications in the European Public Limited-Liability Company (Employee Involvement) (Great Britain) Regulations 2009 (SI 2009/2401).

SI 2009/2399: European Economic Interest Grouping (Amendment) Regulations 2009

Authority: CA 2006, s 1108(2)(b); European Communities Act 1972, s 2(2). These Regulations come into force on 1 October 2009 and amend the European Economic Interest Grouping Regulations 1989 (SI 1989/638) at **[10.13]** et seq. Some of the amendments are consequential on the extension of the 1989 Regulations to Northern Ireland, and the revocation of the equivalent Northern Ireland Regulations by s 1286 of CA 2006. Other amendments replace references to provisions of CA 1985 with references to the equivalent provisions of the 2006 Act. Other amendments are consequential on changes to UK company law and reflect changes made to company law by CA 2006. The Regulations also prescribe new forms for EEIGs which replace those currently contained in the 1989 Regulations.

SI 2009/2392: Registrar of Companies (Fees) (Limited Partnerships and Newspaper Proprietors) Regulations 2009

Authority: CA 2006, ss 1063(1)–(3), 1292(1), (2), 1296. These Regulations were made on 28 August 2009. They provide for the fees to be payable to the registrar of companies in respect of his functions relating to the registration of documents relating to limited partnerships and the register of the proprietors of newspapers, and the inspection or provision of copies of documents kept by him relating to limited partnerships. See **[4.370]**.

SI 2009/2101: Registrar of Companies (Fees) (Companies, Overseas Companies and Limited Liability Partnerships) Regulations 2009

Authority: CA 2006, ss 243(3), 1063(1)–(3), 1292(1). These Regulations were made on 30 July 2009 and come into force on 1 October 2009. They were revoked and replaced by the Registrar of Companies (Fees) (Companies, Overseas Companies and Limited Liability Partnerships) Regulations 2012, SI 2012/1907, as from 1 October 2012, subject to transitional provisions in relation to documents delivered to the registrar on or before 30 September 2012, and applications made or subscriptions payable to the registrar on or before that date (see reg 7 of the 2012 Regulations). These Regulations originally provided for the fees payable to the registrar of companies in respect of his functions relating to the registration of documents, the inspection or provision of copies of documents kept by him, and the disclosure of information protected under the Companies Act 2006 relating to companies, overseas companies and limited liability partnerships. he Regulations extended to the whole of the UK. They replaced (i) the Companies (Fees) Regulations (Northern Ireland) 1995 (SR 1995 No 312), (ii) the Companies (Fees) Regulations 2004 (SI 2004/2621), (iii) the Limited Liability Partnerships (Fees) Regulations 2004 (SI 2004/2620), and (iv) the Limited Liability Partnerships (Fees) Regulations (Northern Ireland) 2004 (SR 2004 No 396), subject to the transitional provisions. They also revoked the Companies (Competent Authority) (Fees) Regulations 2002 (SI 2002/502), the Limited Liability Partnerships (Competent Authority) (Fees) Regulations 2002 (SI 2002/503) and the Limited Liability Partnerships (Records Inspection) (Fee) Regulations (Northern Ireland) 2004 (SR 2004 No 397). See the 2012 Regulations at **[4.452]**.

SI 2009/2022: Companies (Share Capital and Acquisition by Company of its Own Shares) Regulations 2009

Authority: CA 2006, ss 562(6)(a), 657, 737, 1292(1)(c). These Regulations change 3 elements of the Companies Act 2006 to: (i) reduce the minimum pre-emption rights issue subscription period set out in s 562(5) of the 2006 Act from 21 days to 14 days (this amendment will align UK and EU Company law (Directive 77/91/EEC) in this area); (ii) introduce a requirement in s 646 of the 2006 Act so that, when creditors object to a reduction in a company's capital, they should demonstrate that their claim is at risk and that the company has not provided adequate safeguards; (iii) repeal s 725 of the 2006 Act to remove the 10% limit on companies holding shares in treasury. The Regulations also amend ss 694, 697, 700 and 701 of the 2006 Act to extend the period for which authorisation may be given for the purchase by a company of its own shares from 18 months to 5 years. An option arising from Directive 2006/68/EC. See **[4.369]**.

SI 2009/1941: Companies Act 2006 (Consequential Amendments, Transitional Provisions and Savings) Order 2009

Authority: CA 2006, ss 657, 1088, 1292, 1294, 1296(1), 1300(2); European Communities Act 1972, s 2(2). This Order makes consequential amendments, repeals and revocations in connection with the coming into force of various provisions of CA 2006 on 1 October 2009. It also contains some further transitional provisions and savings. See **[4.355]**.

SI 2009/1917: Overseas Companies (Execution of Documents and Registration of Charges) Regulations 2009

Authority: CA 2006, ss 1045, 1052, 1105, 1292(1). These Regulations apply to companies incorporated outside the United Kingdom as defined in section 1044 of the Companies Act 2006. Part 2 of the Regulations makes provision in respect of overseas companies for the application (with modifications) to such companies of provisions of the Companies Act 2006 relating to company contracts and the formalities of doing business under the law of England and Wales, Northern Ireland and Scotland. Regulation 4 applies sections 43 (company contracts), 44 (execution of documents), 46 (execution of deeds) of the Companies Act 2006 to overseas companies. Regulation 5 applies section 48 (execution of documents by companies) to overseas companies under the law of Scotland. Regulation 6 applies section 51 (pre-incorporation contracts) of the Companies Act 2006. Part 3 of the Regulations makes provision for the registration of charges created by those overseas companies which have registered particulars with the registrar of companies under section 1046 of the Companies Act 2006. Regulations 8 to 13 provide for the type of charge granted by an overseas company over property situated in the United Kingdom and the particulars of the charge which must be delivered to the registrar for registration. Regulation 12 specifies the period in which the particulars must be registered, and regulation 27 provides for translations into English where the document creating the charge is not drawn up in English. Regulations 14 to 17 make particular provision for the registration of debentures. Regulation 19 provides for the consequences of the failure to register such charges. Regulation 18 requires the registrar to maintain a register of charges required to registered under these Regulations. Regulations 20, 21 and 22 require the notification to the registrar of the appointment of receivers or managers over the property the subject of the charge, of any memorandum of satisfaction and release, and of a court order for rectification of the register. Regulations 23 to 26 provide that the overseas company must make copies of registered charges available for inspection and must maintain a register of charges that is available for inspection. Regulation 28 makes transitional and saving provisions. See **[4.326]**.

SI 2009/1890: Companies Act 2006 (Consequential Amendments) (Taxes and National Insurance) Order 2009

Authority: CA 2006, s 1294. This Order makes consequential amendments to tax and national insurance legislation to take account of provisions of the Companies Act 2006 (and related secondary legislation) which are in force, or enter into force on 1 October 2009. None of the enactments amended by this Order appear in this Handbook.

SI 2009/1889: Companies Act 2006 (Consequential Amendments) (Uncertificated Securities) Order 2009

Authority: CA 2006, ss 784, 785, 788, 1292, 1294. This Order makes consequential amendments to the Uncertificated Securities Regulations 2001, SI 2001/3755 at **[6.40]** et seq to take account of provisions of the Companies Act 2006 which enter into force on 1 October 2009.

SI 2009/1804: Limited Liability Partnerships (Application of Companies Act 2006) Regulations 2009

Authority: CA 2006, ss 1101, 1292, 1294 and 1296; Limited Liability Partnerships Act 2000, ss 15, 17. These Regulations replace provisions of the Limited Liability Partnerships Regulations 2001 (SI 2001/1090) and the Limited Liability Partnerships Regulations (Northern Ireland) 2004 (SR 2004/307) which apply to LLPs provisions of the Companies Act 1985 and the Companies (Northern Ireland) Order 1986 (with modifications). They apply instead provisions of the Companies Act 2006 to LLPs (with modifications). Separate regulations (ie, the Limited Liability Partnerships (Accounts and Audit) (Application of Companies Act 2006) Regulations 2008 (SI 2008/1911), the Small Limited Liability Partnerships (Accounts) Regulations 2008 (SI 2008/1912), and the Large and Medium-sized Limited Liability Partnerships (Accounts) Regulations 2008 (SI 2008/1913)) have previously applied to LLPs provisions on accounts and audit contained in the 2006 Act and Regulations made under that Act. See **[10.319]**.

SI 2009/1803: Registrar of Companies and Applications for Striking Off Regulations 2009

Authority: CA 2006, ss 1003(2)(b), 1081(2), 1095(1), (2), 1104(2)(a), 1105(2)(d), 1108(2), 1167, 1292(1), (3), (4). These Regulations make provision relating to the functions of the registrar of companies under Part 35 of the Companies Act 2006 and the delivery of documents to the registrar under the 2006 Act and under other enactments. They also make provision relating to applications for striking a company's name off the register under Part 31 of the 2006 Act. Regulation 2 requires an application to strike a company's name off the register under s 1003 of the 2006 Act (voluntary striking off) to contain a directors' declaration. Regulation 3 authorises the registrar to annotate the register where material on the register appears to be misleading or confusing. "The register" is defined in s 1080(2) of the 2006 Act, read with s 1120, and refers to the records held by the registrar relating to companies and overseas companies. The power in regulation 3 is subject to s 1081(3) to (5) of the 2006 Act. The material to which the power applies is limited by paragraph 105 of Schedule 2 to the Companies Act 2006 (Commencement No 8, Transitional Provisions and Savings) Order 2008, as amended by the Companies Act 2006 (Part 35) (Consequential Amendments, Transitional Provisions and Savings) Order 2009. Regulation 4 provides that an application may be made to the registrar by specified persons to remove from the register particular material concerning a company's officers or registered office where the material derives from anything invalid or ineffective or from anything done without the authority of the company, or is factually inaccurate or derived from something that is factually inaccurate or forged. Regulation 4 also provides for applications to remove from the register similar material relating to overseas companies. Regulation 5 sets out further requirements for applications under regulation 4 and makes provision for objections to such applications and for notices to be sent by the registrar. The requirements for applications are in addition to those in s 1095 of the 2006 Act which, among other things, requires an application to be accompanied by a statement that the material is such that it may be the subject of an application and is required to be removed. If no objection to the application is received, the Act provides that the registrar may accept this statement as sufficient evidence that the material should be removed from the register. But if an objection is received, the Regulations provide that the registrar must reject the application. Regulations 6 and 7 are concerned with exceptions to the general rule in s 1103 of the 2006 Act that documents required to be delivered to the registrar by specified provisions of the 2006 Act, by orders or regulations made under those provisions or by other specified legislation must be drawn up and delivered to the registrar in English. This general rule is qualified by ss 1104 and 1105. Section 1104 allows documents relating to a Welsh company (as defined in s 88(1)) to be drawn up and delivered to the registrar in Welsh. Such a document must, when delivered to the registrar, be accompanied by a certified translation into English, but regulations may provide for exceptions to that requirement. Regulation 6 provides exceptions for certain documents relating to non-traded companies (as defined in the Companies Act 2006). It also revokes existing exceptions. Section 1105 allows regulations to specify documents which, by way of exception to the general rule in section 1103, may be drawn up and delivered to the registrar in a language other than English provided that, on delivery, they are accompanied by a certified translation into English. "Certified translation" is defined in s 1107. Regulation 7 specifies a number of documents for this purpose. For overseas companies, further exceptions to the rule in s 1103 are provided by regulation 78 of the Overseas Companies Regulations 2009. Section 1105 does not apply to any document relating to a Welsh company that is drawn up and delivered to the registrar in Welsh (see section 1104(5)). Section 1108 of the 2006 Act provides that names and addresses in a document delivered to the registrar under any enactment must contain only letters, characters and symbols which are permitted by regulations. The section applies to all documents delivered to the registrar on or after 1st October 2009 (see paragraph 108 of Schedule 2 to the Companies Act 2006 (Commencement No 8, Transitional Provisions and Savings) Order 2008). Regulation 8 specifies the permitted characters and symbols for this purpose. It also provides that the rule in s 1108(1) does not apply to certain documents, thereby allowing names and addresses in these documents to contain characters and symbols which would otherwise not be permitted. See **[4.317]**.

SI 2009/1802: Companies Act 2006 (Part 35) (Consequential Amendments, Transitional Provisions and Savings) Order 2009

Authority: CA 2006, ss 1290, 1292(4), 1294(6); European Communities Act 1972, s 2(2). This Order amends Part 35 of the Companies Act 2006 (at **[1.1223]** et seq) and the Companies Act 2006 (Commencement No 8, Transitional Provisions and Savings) Order 2008, SI 2008/2860. Articles 4, 6–11 and 13–16 make consequential amendments to Part 35 of the 2006 Act (the Registrar of Companies), the effect of which is to extend certain provisions of Part 35 to documents or, as the case may be, functions of the registrar relating to bodies other than companies or overseas companies. Article 3 adds to Part 35 a new section indicating how the provisions of Part 35, as amended by the Order, apply. Article 5 makes consequential amendments to s 1067 of the 2006 Act. These relate to overseas companies and are made in consequence of provision made by the Overseas Companies Regulations 2009, SI 2009/1801. References to "branches" of overseas companies in s 1067 are replaced by references to the "UK establishments" of overseas companies. Article 17 makes incidental amendments to Schedule 8 to the 2006 Act. Article 12 amends s 1087 to expand the list in that section of material which the registrar must not make available for public inspection. These amendments are made in consequence of provision made elsewhere in the 2006 Act. Article 18 and the Schedule replace a number of the transitional provisions and savings relating to Part 35 of the 2006 Act which are contained in Schedule 2 to the Eighth Commencement Order. The effect of paragraphs 98, 103, 104 and 108 is unchanged. Paragraphs 97, 99, 100, 101, 102, 105, 106 and 107 are modified so that they take account of the fact that the provisions of Part 35 to which they relate (including ss 1075 and 1076 as amended by this Order) either are not limited to documents relating to companies or are so limited but are not limited to documents delivered (or, where relevant, issued) under the 2006 Act, the Companies Act 1985 or the Companies (Northern Ireland) Order 1986. The effect of these paragraphs is also changed as they relate to documents delivered under the 2006 Act, the 1985 Act and the 1986 Order. Paragraph 109 is changed so that the offence in s 1112 of the 2006 Act applies to any document delivered or statement made, for any purpose of the Companies Acts (as defined in s 2 of the 2006 Act), on or after 1 October 2009.

SI 2009/1801: Overseas Companies Regulations 2009

Authority: CA 2006, ss 1046(1), (2), (4)–(6), 1047(1), 1049(1)–(3), 1050(3)–(5), 1051(1)–(3), 1053(2)–(5), 1054(1), (2), 1055, 1056, 1058(1)–(3), 1078(5), 1105(1), (2), 1140(2), 1292(1), (4), 1294. These Regulations impose various registration and filing requirements on companies incorporated outside the United Kingdom ("overseas companies") that open an establishment, whether a place of business or a branch, in the UK (a "UK establishment"). They replace Part 23 of, and Schedules 21A to 21D to, the Companies Act 1985 (and the equivalent Northern Ireland provisions) which, amongst other things, implemented (a) the Eleventh Company Law Directive (89/666/EEC), and (b) the Council Directive on the obligations of branches established in a Member State of credit and financial institutions having their head offices outside that Member State regarding the publication of annual accounting documents (the Bank Branches Directive) (89/117/EEC). Part 1 deals with citation, commencement and interpretation. Part 2 (regs 3 to 11) requires an overseas company to register certain particulars and documents with the registrar of companies within one month of opening a UK establishment. Part 3 (regs 12 to 17) requires an overseas company to file details of any alterations to the particulars or documents registered under Part 2. An overseas company is required (Part 4) to register particulars about the usual residential address of its directors and permanent representatives. Part 4 (regs 18 to 29) and Schedules 1 to 3 implement s 1055 of the Companies Act 2006, which requires provision to be made corresponding to that made by ss 240 to 246 of the Act (directors' residential addresses: protection from disclosure). Those provisions prescribe the circumstances in which information about a director's residential address can be used by a company and the registrar and disclosed to third parties by the registrar. Part 4 also contains provisions corresponding to provisions made by regulations under s 243(3) to (6) of the Act in the Companies (Disclosure of Address) Regulations 2009 (SI 2009/214). Part 5 concerns the delivery of accounting documents to the registrar by limited overseas companies that are not credit or financial institutions. Chapter 2 (regs 31 to 35) applies where the parent law of an overseas company requires the preparation and disclosure of accounts. In those cases the company must deliver to the registrar such accounts and accompanying reports (including any audit and directors' reports) that it files under its parent law. In certain circumstances specified in regulation 32, where an overseas company has more than one UK establishment it is not necessary for that company to file accounts in respect of each of its UK establishments. Regulation 33 also requires the company to notify the registrar of the legislation and accounting principles under which the accounts have been prepared. Chapter 3 (regs 36 to 42), together with Schedules 4 and 5, applies where the parent law of an overseas company does not require accounts to be prepared and disclosed. It applies to such companies, with modifications, certain provisions of Part 15 (accounting documents) of the Act. The Regulations set out the provisions of Part 15 that are applied as modified. There are three main obligations: (a) to prepare accounts in accordance with parent law, international accounting standards or Schedule 4 (or, if the company is a parent company, Schedule 5) to these Regulations, (b) to identify the set of accounting principles on which accounts have been prepared, (c) to file those accounts with the registrar. Part 6 (regs 43 to 57), together with Schedules 6 and 7, concerns the delivery of accounting documents to the registrar by overseas credit or financial institutions. The structure mirrors Part 5 in that different provision is made for institutions required by parent law to prepare accounts and those not so required. Part 7 (regs 58 to 67) requires overseas companies carrying on business in the UK to make certain trading disclosures. Under Part 8 (regs 68 to 74) an overseas company with a UK establishment is required to notify the registrar if it is being wound up (reg 69) or subject to insolvency proceedings (reg 71) and the liquidator of such a company is likewise subject to filing obligations (reg 70). Furthermore, an overseas company with a UK establishment must notify the registrar if a judicial factor is appointed (reg 73). Part 9 (regs 75 to 77) contains miscellaneous provisions concerning service of documents (reg 75), documents subject to Directive disclosure requirements (reg 76), the duty to give notice of ceasing to have a registrable presence (reg 77). Part 10 (regs 78 to 80) contain supplementary provisions: regulation 78 concerns the documents which may be drawn up and delivered to the registrar in a language other than English, on condition that they are accompanied by a certified translation into English. Those documents include the constitution and accounting documents delivered under these Regulations; revocation of the Oversea Companies and Credit and Financial Institutions (Branch Disclosure) Regulations 1992 (SI 1992/3179) which amended Part 23 of the 1985 Act so as to implement the two Directives mentioned *ante* (reg 79); and transitional provisions and savings (reg 80). See **[4.216]**.

SI 2009/1581: Companies Act 2006 (Accounts, Reports and Audit) Regulations 2009

Authority: CA 2006, ss 468(1), (2), 1292(1); European Communities Act 1972, s 2(2). These Regulations implement, in part, Directive 2006/46 of the European Parliament and the Council amending Council Directives 78/660/EEC on the annual accounts of certain types of companies, 83/349/EEC on consolidated accounts, 86/635/EEC on the annual accounts and consolidated accounts of banks and other financial institutions and 91/674/EEC on the annual accounts and consolidated accounts of insurance undertakings. Annex C of the Disclosure Rules and Transparency Rules Sourcebook (Corporate Governance Rules) Instrument 2008 made by the Financial Services Authority on 26 June 2008 (FSA 2008/32) requires certain publicly traded companies to prepare a corporate governance statement in implementation of Articles 1.7 and 2.2 of Directive 2006/46. Part 2 of the Regulations implements the Directive's requirements that where the corporate governance statement is a separate statement and not part of the directors' report, it must be filed with the registrar of companies and the auditor must give an opinion as to whether the information required to be shown in the statement as to internal control and risk management systems in relation to the financial reporting process and certain disclosures required by the Takeovers Directive (Directive 2004/25/EEC) is consistent with the annual accounts for the year in question. For the remaining information in the corporate governance statement, the auditor must check that the statement has been produced. Part 3 of the Regulations amends Part 15 of CA 2006 (accounts and reports) and Regulations made under that Part (ie, the Small Companies and Groups (Accounts and Directors' Report) Regulations 2008, SI 2008/409 and the Large and Medium-sized Companies and Groups (Accounts and Reports) Regulations 2008, SI 2008/410).

SI 2009/1378: Companies Act 2006 (Extension of Takeover Panel Provisions) (Isle of Man) Order 2009

Authority: CA 2006, s 965. This Order applies Sch 2 to the Companies Act 2006 (as substituted by the Companies Act 2006 (Amendment of Schedule 2) (No 2) Order 2009, SI 2008/1208) to the Isle of Man. It was revoked by the Companies Act 2006 (Extension of Takeover Panel Provisions) (Isle of Man) Order 2019, SI 2019/567, as from IP completion day (as defined in the European Union (Withdrawal Agreement) Act 2020, s 39).

SI 2009/1208: Companies Act 2006 (Amendment of Schedule 2) (No 2) Order 2009

Authority: CA 2006, ss 948(4), 1292(1)(c). This Order substitutes Sch 2 to the Companies Act 2006 and revokes the Companies Act 2006 (Amendment of Schedule 2) Order 2009, SI 2009/202. Under s 948 of the 2006 Act, information received by the Takeover Panel in connection with the exercise of its statutory functions may not be disclosed without the consent of the individual (where it concerns a person's private affairs) or business to which it relates except as permitted by that section. Schedule 2 specifies for the purposes of s 948(3) of the Act the persons to whom disclosure may be made and the descriptions of disclosures which are exempt from the prohibition in s 948(2). Schedule 2 is amended by this Order to include specified persons exercising functions of a public nature in the Isle of Man, Jersey and Guernsey, and to add descriptions of disclosures the purpose of which is to facilitate the exercise of functions of a public nature in the Isle of Man, Jersey and Guernsey.

SI 2009/1085: Company and Business Names (Miscellaneous Provisions) Regulations 2009

Authority: CA 2006, ss 57(1)(a), (2), (5), 60(1), 65, 66, 1197, 1292(1). These Regulations dealt with restrictions relating to the registered name of a company and to business names. They were revoked by the Company, Limited Liability Partnership and Business (Names and Trading Disclosures) Regulations 2015, SI 2015/17, reg 30, Sch 6, para 1(a), as from 31 January 2015. The 2015 Regulations are at **[4.514]**.

SI 2009/388: Companies (Shares and Share Capital) Order 2009

Authority: CA 2006, ss 10(2)(c)(i), 32(2)(c)(i), 108(3)(c)(i), 555(3)(a), (4)(c)(i), 556(3), 583(4), 619(3)(c)(i), 621(3)(c)(i), 625(3)(c)(i), 627(3)(c)(i), 644(2)(c)(i), 649(2)(c)(i), 663(3)(c)(i), 689(3)(c)(i), 708(3)(c)(i), 714(5), 727(3), 730(5)(c)(i), 1167. This Order makes provision in relation to shares and share capital for the purposes of various provisions of the Companies Act 2006. The Act requires companies, in various circumstances, to deliver a statement of capital to the registrar of companies. It also requires a company to send a current statement of capital to any member of the company on request. A statement of capital must (among other things) state, for each class of the company's shares, such particulars of the rights attached to shares as are prescribed by order or regulations. Article 2 prescribes these particulars. Where the company is a limited company, the shares are redeemable and the directors (duly authorised) determined the terms, conditions and manner of redemption, s 685(3)(b) of the Act also requires a statement of capital to state the terms, conditions and manner of redemption. Article 2 does not apply to the statement of capital in a company's annual return, the contents of which are regulated by s 856(2) of the Act as amended by the Companies Act 2006 (Annual Return and Service Addresses) Regulations 2008 (SI 2008/3000). Where an unlimited company allots shares of a class with rights that are not in all respects uniform with shares previously allotted, s 556 of the Act requires the company to deliver a return of the allotment to the registrar of companies for registration. The return must contain such particulars of the rights attached to the shares as are prescribed by order or regulations. Article 2 prescribes these particulars. Article 3 prescribes the information that must be included in a return of an allotment of shares delivered to the registrar of companies under s 555 of the Act by a limited company. Section 583 of the Act provides that a share in a company is deemed paid up (as to its nominal value or any premium on it) in cash, or allotted for cash, if the consideration received for the allotment or payment up is a cash consideration. "Cash consideration" is defined in sub-s (3), which lists a number of methods of payment and provides also that "cash consideration" is constituted by payment by any other means giving rise to a present or future entitlement (of the company or a person acting on the company's behalf) to a payment, or credit equivalent to payment, in cash. The definition may be supplemented by order providing that particular means of payment are to be regarded as falling into that last category. Article 4 provides that "cash consideration" includes a settlement bank's obligation to make a payment in respect of the allotment or payment up of shares under the CREST system, which is the settlement system operated by Euroclear UK & Ireland Limited. The CREST system is regulated by the Uncertificated Securities Regulations 2001. Article 4 also supplements, in the same way, the definition of "cash consideration" which applies for the purposes of s 727(1)(a). That section permits a company to sell for a cash consideration any shares which it holds as treasury shares. Section 713 of the Act provides that a payment out of capital by a private company for the redemption or purchase of its own shares is not lawful unless, among other things, the company's directors make a statement in accordance with s 714. The statement must be in the form prescribed by order or regulations and must contain (among other things) such information with respect to the nature of the company's business as may be so prescribed. Article 5 prescribes both the form of a directors' statement under s 714 and the information as to the nature of the company's business which such a statement must contain. The Order comes into force on 1 October 2009 and is at **[4.211]**.

SI 2009/218: Companies (Trading Disclosures) (Amendment) Regulations 2009

Authority: CA 2006, ss 82, 1292(1)(a). These Regulations dealt with trading disclosures to be made by a company. They amended the Companies (Trading Disclosures) Regulations 2008, SI 2008/495 (now revoked) to provide two further exceptions from the obligation on a company to display its registered name at business premises. They were revoked by the Company, Limited Liability Partnership and Business (Names and Trading Disclosures) Regulations 2015, SI 2015/17, reg 30, Sch 6, para 1(e), as from 31 January 2015. The 2015 Regulations are at **[4.514]**.

SI 2009/214: Companies (Disclosure of Address) Regulations 2009

Authority: CA 2006, ss 243(2)–(6), 1088(1)–(3), (5), 1292(1), (4). These Regulations specify the conditions for disclosure of directors' usual residential addresses to public authorities and credit reference agencies under s 243 of the Companies Act 2006, make provision for applications to the registrar of companies under s 243 of the Act to refrain from disclosing a director's usual residential address to a credit reference agency, and make provision for applications to the registrar of companies under s 1088 of the Act for addresses on the register to be made unavailable for public inspection. Part 1 of these Regulations provides for citation, commencement and interpretation. Part 2 applies to protected information as defined in s 240 of the Act. Regulation 2 and Schedule 1 specify the public authorities to whom the registrar may disclose protected information in accordance with s 243 of the Act. Regulations 2 and 3 and Schedule 2 specify the conditions for the disclosure of such information to a public authority or credit reference agency. Regulation 4 provides for the registrar to refrain from disclosing protected information to a credit reference agency in respect of a beneficiary of a successful decision under s 243 or applicant for a s 243 decision. Regulations 5, 6, 7 and 8 (a) make provision as to who may make an application to the registrar under section 243; (b) prescribe the grounds for making an application under section 243; (c) make provision for the manner of making an application; (d) make provision for the evidence to be delivered to the registrar in support of the application; and (e) empower the registrar to refer questions to other bodies for the purposes of deciding upon applications. Part 3 of the Regulations makes provision for an application under s 1088 of the Act for the registrar to make an address on the register unavailable for public inspection. Regulations 9, 10, 11, 12 and 13 make similar provision in relation to applications under s 1088 to that made in regulations 5 to 8 and make provision as to the effect of a successful application under s 1088. Part 4 of the Regulations contains provisions relating to both applications and decisions under s 243 and under s 1088. Regulation 14 provides for appeals to the court against the decision of the registrar rejecting an application. Regulation 15 determines the duration for which a decision in favour of an applicant shall continue to have effect, and reg 16 provides that the registrar may revoke a decision under s 243 or 1088 where an offence has been committed under s 1112 of the Act (general false statement offence). See **[4.191]**.

SI 2009/202: Companies Act 2006 (Amendment of Schedule 2) Order 2009

Authority: CA 2006, s 948(4). This Order amended CA 2006, Sch 2 in consequence of the enactment of the Companies Act 2006 (Extension of Takeover Panel Provisions) (Isle of Man) Order 2008 (SI 2008/3122). That Order applied the Takeover Panel provisions of Part 28 of, and Sch 2 to, CA 2006 in the Isle of Man. It was revoked by the Companies Act 2006 (Amendment of Schedule 2) (No 2) Order 2009, SI 2008/1208, as from 1 July 2009 and the amendments made by this instrument were re-enacted in the substituted Schedule contained in the No 2 Order.

2008 Statutory Instruments

SI 2008/3229: Companies (Model Articles) Regulations 2008

Authority: CA 2006, s 19. These Regulations prescribe model forms of articles of association for: (i) private companies limited by shares (reg 2 and Sch 1), (ii) private companies limited by guarantee (reg 3 and Sch 2), and (iii) public companies (reg 4 and Sch 3). These model articles will automatically form the articles of association for companies formed under the Companies Act 2006 which, on their formation, either do not register their own articles of association with the registrar of companies under that Act, or, if they do so, do not exclude the model articles in whole or in part (s 20 of the 2006 Act). Other companies are free to adopt the model articles in whole or in part. See **[4.187]**.

SI 2008/3122: Companies Act 2006 (Extension of Takeover Panel Provisions) (Isle of Man) Order 2008

Authority: CA 2006, s 965. This Order extends the provisions of Chapter 1 of Part 28 of the 2006 Act to the Isle of Man with certain modifications. Its purpose is to place on a statutory footing the role of the Panel on Takeovers and Mergers ("the Takeovers Panel") in supervising relevant takeovers involving Isle of Man companies. The modifications in the Schedule reflect differences in the legal system and governmental and regulatory structures of the Isle of Man, and make necessary consequential amendments to the Financial Services Act 2008 (an Act of Tynwald). Among other things, the modifications impose a duty on the Island's Financial Supervision Commission to co-operate with the Takeover Panel. The modifications also provide for the exchange of information about takeovers (subject to appropriate safeguards) between: (i) the Takeover Panel and those with regulatory, registry, prosecution and disciplinary functions on the Isle of Man in relation to companies and their officers; and (ii) those Manx authorities and corresponding bodies elsewhere. This Order was revoked by the Companies Act 2006 (Extension of Takeover Panel Provisions) (Isle of Man) Order 2019, SI 2019/567, as from IP completion day (as defined in the European Union (Withdrawal Agreement) Act 2020, s 39).

SI 2008/3014: Companies (Registration) Regulations 2008

Authority: CA 2006, ss 8(2), 10(3), 11(2), 103(2)(a), 110(2)(a), 1167, 1292(1)(a). The Companies Act 2006 makes changes to the form of a company's constitutional documents. The Companies Act 1985 and the Companies (Northern Ireland) Order 1986 (SI 1986/1032) both require a company to include a substantial amount of information in its memorandum of association and allow a company's constitutional rules to be divided between its memorandum and articles of association. Under the 2006 Act, all the constitutional rules will be contained in the articles of association; the memorandum of association will, therefore, be a much shorter document. Regulation 2 prescribes the form of the memorandum of association required under the 2006 Act. The forms in Schs 1 and 2 serve the limited purpose of providing evidence of the intention of each subscriber to form a company and become a member of that company and, in the case of a company that is to have a share capital on formation, to take at least one share. Regulations 3 and 4 prescribe the information required to be contained in the statement of capital and the statement of guarantee to identify each subscriber to the memorandum of association. This is the name and address of each subscriber. Regulations 5 and 6 prescribe the forms of assent for re-registration of a private limited company as an unlimited company and re-registration of a public company as a private and unlimited company. These forms are set out in Schs 3 and 4. These Regulations come into force on 1 October 2009. See **[4.179]** et seq.

SI 2008/3007: Companies (Fees for Inspection of Company Records) Regulations 2008

Authority: CA 2006, ss 162(5)(b), 275(5)(b), 877(4)(b), 892(4)(b), 1137(4), 1167, 1292(1)(c) (note that ss 877 and 892 were repealed on 6 April 2013). These Regulations (which come into force on 1 October 2009) prescribe the fees payable by a person who wishes to exercise a right under the Companies Act 2006 to inspect, in relation to a company, its register of directors, its register of secretaries or its register of charges and instruments creating those charges. See **[4.177]**.

SI 2008/3006: Companies (Company Records) Regulations 2008

Authority: CA 2006, ss 1136, 1137, 1292(1). These Regulations relate to the inspection and provision of copies of company records. Previous legislation relating to company records is revoked subject to a saving for requests to be provided with a copy of a record where the request is made before 1 October 2009 (reg 2). A company may keep company records referred to in the provisions listed in s 1136(2) of the Companies Act 2006 available for inspection at one location other than its registered office (Part 2). That location must be notified to the registrar of companies. The reference in regulation 3 to registration in a particular part of the United Kingdom is to registration by the registrar of companies for that part of the United Kingdom (see s 1060 of the Act). Part 3 sets out the obligations of companies in relation to company records in respect of which there is a right of inspection. A private company shall make its company records available for at least 2 hours between 9am and 5pm on a working day and that working day and time period must be specified by giving the required notice (reg 4(1) and (4)). The required notice is either at least 2 working days in the circumstances set out in regulation 4(2) or at least 10 working days in all other cases (reg 4(3)). A public company is required to make its company records available for inspection between 9am and 5pm on every working day (reg 5). A company is not required to present a company record in a different order, structure or form to the one set out in that record (reg 6(1)). A person may make a copy of a company record but a company is not required to assist that person in making that copy (reg 6(2)). However, nothing in these Regulations prevents a company from providing more extensive facilities than those set out in these Regulations (see s 1137(5)(a) of the Act). Part 4 deals with the obligations of companies in relation to the provision of copies of company records. "Hard copy form", "electronic copy form" and related expressions are defined in s 1168 of the Act. Company records may be kept in hard copy or electronic form provided that the information is adequately recorded (see s 1135(1) of the Act) but if kept in electronic form, they must be capable of being reproduced in hard copy form (see s 1135(2) of the Act). A person who requests a hard copy of a company record must be supplied with a hard copy (reg 7). A person who requests an electronic copy of a record must be supplied with an electronic copy unless the record is only kept in hard copy (reg 8(1) and (2)). The company can decide which electronic form in which to supply the record (reg 8(1)) (subject to s 1168(5) and (6) of the Act which imposes conditions relating to the form and legibility of the copy). Where a company provides a copy of a company record in electronic form to a company member or debenture holder, it is not then obliged to send a hard copy of that record to such a person free of charge (reg 8(3)). Regulation 8(3), in conjunction with s 1143 of the Act, disapplies s 1145 of the Act. A company is not required to present information in a copy of a company record in a different order, structure or form to the one set out in that record (reg 9). See **[4.168]**.

SI 2008/3000: Companies Act 2006 (Annual Return and Service Addresses) Regulations 2008

Authority: CA 2006, ss 857, 1141, 1167, 1292(1). These Regulations deal with the information to be provided in the annual return of a company under the Companies Act 2006. They also prescribe conditions to be met by a service address for the purposes of the Companies Acts (as defined in s 2 of the Companies Act 2006). Regulation 1 deals with citation etc. It also provides that Part 2 (regs 2 to 9) applies to annual returns made up to a date on or after 1 October 2009. Regulations 2 to 4 amend s 855 of the Companies Act 2006. The amendments specify the particulars of directors and secretaries required to be provided in the annual return. A company that keeps its records at a place specified in regulations under s 1136 of the Companies Act 2006 is required to indicate the address of that place and the records kept there. A company is also required to indicate whether its shares are admitted to trading on a regulated market. "Regulated market" is defined in s 1173 of the Companies Act 2006. Regulation 5 and Schedule 1 prescribe the classification scheme for company type. Regulation 6 and Schedule 2 prescribe the classification system for a company's principal business activities. Regulation 7 amends s 856 of the Companies Act 2006 as to the information to be given about the company's shareholders. The effect is that the information to be supplied depends on whether or not any of the company's shares were shares admitted to trading on a regulated market during the period to which the return relates. The effect of regulation 8 is that a company's annual return need not give details of any shadow directors it has. A shadow director may still be liable for failure to deliver the annual return. Regulation 9 amends the index of defined expressions in Sch 8 to the Companies Act 2006 so it lists the expressions defined in subsection (4) of s 855 inserted by regulation 4. Regulation 10 sets out the conditions with which a service address must comply. See **[4.167]**.

SI 2008/2996: Companies (Particulars of Company Charges) Regulations 2008

Authority: CA 2006, ss 860, 862, 878, 880, 1167. These Regulations were revoked by the Companies Act 2006 (Amendment of Part 25) Regulations 2013, SI 2013/600, as from 6 April 2013. Note that the 2013 Regulations repealed Chapters 1 and 2 of Part 25 of the 2006 Act (ss 860–892) and replaced them with a new Chapter 1A (ss 859A–859Q). Note also that by virtue of reg 6 of the 2013 Regulations, the insertion of Chapter 1A and the repeal of Chapters 1 and 2 applies in relation to charges created on or after 6 April 2013. They dealt with the information to be provided to the Registrar of Companies on the registration of a company charge under Part 25 of the Companies Act 2006. Regulation 2 set out the information that was to be provided when a company registered in England and Wales or Northern Ireland created a charge of a kind specified in s 860(7) of the Act. Regulation 3 made the same provision but for companies registered in Scotland which created a charge of the kind specified in s 878(7) of the Act. Regulation 4 set out the information that was to be provided when a company registered in England and Wales, Northern Ireland or Scotland acquired property which was already subject to a charge which, if it had been created by the company after the acquisition of the property, would have been required to be registered under Part 25 of the Act.

SI 2008/2860: Companies Act 2006 (Commencement No 8, Transitional Provisions and Savings) Order 2008

Authority: CA 2006, ss 1292(1), 1296(1), (2), 1300(2). This Order brings into force certain provisions of CA 2006 on various dates and contains transitional provisions and savings. For details relating to the commencement of the 2006 Act, see the Table of Commencements in Part 2 of this Handbook *ante*. Note that the commencement orders themselves were removed from Part 2 in the 2022 edition of this work in order to create space for newer legislation. Since that edition, the commencement orders have only been reproduced in the online only Appendix 10 to this Handbook.

SI 2008/2639: Statutory Auditors and Third Country Auditors (Amendment) (No 2) Regulations 2008

Authority: CA 2006, ss 1239(1)(b), (2), (5)(d), 1246(1), 1292(1)(c). These Regulations amended the Statutory Auditors and Third Country Auditors Regulations 2007, SI 2007/3494. They made provision in respect of "exempt third country auditors" and gave effect to Commission Decision 2008/627/EC of 29 July 2008 concerning a transitional period for audit activities of certain third country auditors and audit entities (OJ L202,31.7.2008, p 70). These Regulations were revoked by the Statutory Auditors and Third Country Auditors Regulations 2013, SI 2013/1672 as from 31 July 2013. The 2013 Regulations are at **[4.482]**.

SI 2008/1915: Companies (Reduction of Share Capital) Order 2008

Authority: CA 2006, ss 643(3), 654, 1167. This Order prescribes the form in which a solvency statement must be made when a private company proposes to reduce its share capital in reliance on the statement without getting a court order. The Order also provides that when a company reduces its share capital, the prohibition on distribution in s 654(1) of the 2006 Act does not apply unless, where the reduction is confirmed by court order, the court orders that it is not distributable. That, however, does not affect the operation of anything to the contrary in (i) an order of, or undertaking to, the court, (ii) the resolution for, or any other resolution relevant to, the reduction, or (iii) the company's memorandum or articles. See **[4.164]**.

SI 2008/1911: Limited Liability Partnerships (Accounts and Audit) (Application of Companies Act 2006) Regulations 2008

Authority: Limited Liability Partnerships Act 2000, ss 15, 17; CA 2006, ss 1210(1)(h), 1292(2). These Regulations replace provisions of the Limited Liability Partnerships Regulations 2001, SI 2001/1090 and the Limited Liability Partnerships Regulations (Northern Ireland) 2004 which apply provisions of the Companies Act 1985 and the Companies (Northern Ireland) Order 1986 relating to accounts and audit to LLPs. They apply to LLPs, with modifications, provisions on the accounts and audit of companies contained in the Companies Act 2006 and extend to the UK (reflecting the extent of the 2006 Act). See **[10.223]** et seq.

SI 2008/1886: Companies Act 2006 (Commencement No 7, Transitional Provisions and Savings) Order 2008

Authority: CA 2006, ss 1296(2), 1300(2). This Order brings into force certain provisions of CA 2006 on various dates and contains transitional provisions and savings. For details relating to the commencement of the 2006 Act, see the Table of Commencements in Part 2 of this Handbook *ante*. Note that the commencement orders themselves were removed from Part 2 in the 2022 edition of this work in order to create space for newer legislation. Since that edition, the commencement orders have only been reproduced in the online only Appendix 10 to this Handbook.

SI 2008/1861: Companies (Forms) (Amendment) Regulations 2008

Authority: CA 1985, s 363(2); CA 2006, s 1167. These Regulations prescribed amended form 363a for the purposes of s 363(2) of CA 1985, with effect from 1 October 2008. The Regulations also revoked the existing forms 363a and 363s (prescribed by the Companies (Forms) (Amendment) Regulations 2002) and form 363a and 363s (prescribed by Companies (Forms) (Amendment) Regulations 1999 and retained as alternatives to the forms prescribed by the 2002 Regulations). However, continued use of those revoked forms was permitted for returns made up to a date before 1 October 2008. Form 363a was amended to reflect amendments to the shareholder information provided. The amendments were made by the Companies Act 1985 (Annual Return) Regulations 2008 (SI 2008/1659) applying to annual returns made up to a date on or after 1 October 2008. See also the Companies (Welsh Language Forms) (Amendment) Regulations 2008, SI 2008/1861 (made under the same sections as extended by the Welsh language Act 1993) for the Welsh equivalents. Section 1167 of the Companies Act 2006 merely defines the term "prescribed" for the purposes of the 2006 Act and, therefore, these Regulations effectively lapsed on the repeal of s 363(2) of the 1985 Act on 1 October 2009.

SI 2008/1738: Company Names Adjudicator Rules 2008

Authority: CA 2006, s 71. These Rules regulate the proceedings before a company names adjudicator under s 69 of the 2006 Act when an application has been made objecting to a company's registered name because of its similarity to another name in which the objector has goodwill. Rules 1 and 2 contain introductory provisions, including provisions relating to forms and fees. Rules 3 to 9 contain provisions relating to proceedings before the company names adjudicator. These include provisions relating to applications for objections to a company's registered name; evidence rounds; the adjudicator's decision; the adjudicator's powers and provisions on the conduct of such proceedings. Rule 10 contains provisions on corrections of irregularities of procedure. Rules 11 and 12 contain provisions relating to costs or expenses. Rule 13 contains provisions on providing an address for service, and rules 14 and 15 set hours of business. The Schedule contains the fees which are required to accompany each form. See **[4.148]**.

SI 2008/1659: Companies Act 1985 (Annual Return) and Companies (Principal Business Activities) (Amendment) Regulations 2008

Authority: CA 1985, ss 364(3), 365(1); CA 2006, s 1167. These Regulations concerned the information to be provided about share capital and shareholders in the annual return of a company under CA 1985. The type of information to be supplied depended on whether or not any of the company's shares were shares admitted to trading on a regulated market during the period to which the return related. These Regulations amended various provisions in Chapter III of Part XI of the 1985 Act (Company Administration and Procedure) and in the Companies (Forms Amendment No 2 and Company's Type and Principal Business Activities) Regulations 1990 (SI 1990/1766). Section 1167 of the Companies Act 2006 merely defines the term "prescribed" for the purposes of the 2006 Act and, therefore, these Regulations effectively lapsed on the repeal of ss 364(3), 365(1) of the 1985 Act on 1 October 2009.

SI 2008/954: Companies Act 2006 (Consequential Amendments) (Taxes and National Insurance) Order 2008

Authority: CA 2006, ss 1292, 1294, 1296. This Order makes consequential amendments to the legislation for which Her Majesty's Revenue and Customs are responsible to take account of the provisions of the Companies Act 2006 which came into force on 6 April 2008. All of the enactments amended relate to taxation and national insurance, and none of them are included in this work.

SI 2008/948: Companies Act 2006 (Consequential Amendments etc) Order 2008

Authority: CA 2006, ss 1292, 1294, 1296. This Order makes a variety of amendments to legislation consequential on the coming into force, on 6 April 2008, of various provisions of the 2006 Act (see the Companies Act 2006 (Commencement No 5, Transitional Provisions and Savings) Order 2007 (SI 2007/3495)). It also contains savings provisions. The Order is at **[4.136]**.

SI 2008/729: Companies (Authorised Minimum) Regulations 2008

Authority: CA 2006, ss 763(2), 766(1)(a), (2), 1292(1)(a), (b). These Regulations relate to provisions of CA 1985, the Companies (Northern Ireland) Order 1986, and CA 2006 which refer to the "authorised minimum" share capital requirement for public companies. Reg 2 prescribes, for the purposes of s 763 of the 2006 Act, the amount in euros which is to be treated as equivalent to the sterling amount of the authorised minimum (ie, €65,600). Regulations 3 and 4 provide for the application of the authorised minimum requirement for the purposes of particular provisions of the 1985 Act and the 1986 Order which refer to it. Regulation 5 deals with registration by the registrar of companies of court orders confirming the reduction of public companies' share capital and with re-registration of public companies as private companies where a mandatory cancellation of shares has the effect of bringing the nominal value of the company's allotted share capital below the authorised minimum. Regulation 6 enables the courts, in specified proceedings, to make a determination in certain circumstances about the exchange rates to be applied in working out whether a public company satisfies the authorised minimum requirement. Regulation 7 prevents anyone from being liable as a result of reliance, for the purposes of these Regulations, on an exchange rate published by the Financial Times. It also prevents liability arising if an erroneous exchange rate published by the Financial Times is relied on for the purposes of the Regulations. Finally, it excludes liability for acts or omissions leading to the Financial Times not publishing an exchange rate capable of being relied on for the purposes of the Regulations. See **[4.130]**.

SI 2008/674: Companies Act 2006 (Commencement No 6, Saving and Commencement Nos 3 and 5 (Amendment)) Order 2008

Authority: CA 2006, ss 1292(1)(b), 1296(1), (2), 1300(2). This Order brings into force certain provisions of CA 2006 on various dates and contains savings provisions. For details relating to the commencement of the 2006 Act, see the Table of Commencements in Part 2 of this Handbook *ante*. Note that the commencement orders themselves were removed from Part 2 in the 2022 edition of this work in order to create space for newer legislation. Since that edition, the commencement orders have only been reproduced in the online only Appendix 10 to this Handbook.

SI 2008/651: Accounting Standards (Prescribed Body) Regulations 2008

Authority: CA 2006, s 464(1) and (3). These Regulations prescribed the Accounting Standards Board established under the articles of association of the Financial Reporting Council Limited for the purposes of the Companies Act 2006, s 464. Statements of standard accounting practice issued by a body so prescribed were "accounting standards" for the purposes of the provisions of Part 15 of the Companies Act 2006 (accounts and audit). Regulation 3 revoked the Accounting Standards (Prescribed Body) Regulations 2005 and the Accounting Standards (Prescribed Body) Regulations (Northern Ireland) 1990 under which the Accounting Standards Board as established under the articles of association of the Accounting Standards Board Limited was prescribed for the purposes of the Companies Act 1985, s 256 and Article 264 of the Companies (Northern Ireland) Order 1986. Regulation 4 made a transitional provision in relation to statements of standard accounting practice issued for the purposes of s 256 of the 1985 Act and Article 264 of the 1986 Order. These Regulations was revoked by the Statutory Auditors (Amendment of Companies Act 2006 and Delegation of Functions etc) Order 2012, SI 2012/1741, as from 2 July 2012. Article 23 of the 2012 Order appoints the Financial Reporting Council Limited for the purposes of s 464 of the 2006 Act. Article 24 of the 2012 Order provides for transitional provisions in connection with the revocation of this Order. See the 2012 Order at **[4.430]**.

SI 2008/623: Companies (Defective Accounts and Directors' Reports) (Authorised Person) and Supervision of Accounts and Reports (Prescribed Body) Order 2008

Authority: Companies (Audit, Investigations and Community Enterprise) Act 2004, s 14(1), (5), (8); CA 2006, s 457(1), (2), (5), (6). This Order authorised the Financial Reporting Review Panel established under the articles of association of the Financial Reporting Council Limited for the purposes of CA 2006, s 456 (application to court in respect of defective accounts or directors' reports). It replaced the Companies (Defective Accounts) (Authorised Person) Order 2005 (SI 2005/699) and the Companies (Defective Accounts) (Authorised Person) Order (Northern Ireland) 1991 under which the Financial Reporting Review Panel as established under the articles of association of the Financial Reporting Review Panel Limited was authorised for the purposes of s 245B of CA 1985 and Article 253B of the Companies (Northern Ireland) Order 1986. It also appointed the FRRP to exercise the functions mentioned in s 14(2) of the Companies (Audit, Investigations and Community Enterprise) Act 2004. It replaced the Supervision of Accounts and Reports (Prescribed Body) Order 2007 (SI 2007/2583). This Order was revoked by the Supervision of Accounts and Reports (Prescribed Body) and Companies (Defective Accounts and Directors' Reports) (Authorised Person) Order 2012, SI 2012/1439, as from 2 July 2012 (subject to transitional provisions). The 2012 Order is at **[4.429]**.

SI 2008/569: Partnerships (Accounts) Regulations 2008

Authority: CA 2006, ss 1210(1)(h), 1292(2); European Communities Act 1972, s 2(2). These Regulations replace the provisions of the Partnerships and Unlimited Companies (Accounts) Regulations 1993 (SI 1993/1820), and of the Partnerships and Unlimited Companies (Accounts) Regulations (Northern Ireland) 1994 (SR 1994/133). They continue the implementation of Council Directive 90/605/EEC amending Directive 78/660/EEC on annual accounts, and Directive 83/349/EEC on consolidated accounts. They also implement, in part, Directive 2006/43/EC on statutory audits of annual accounts and consolidated accounts. The Regulations come into force on 6 April 2008 and apply to financial years of qualifying partnerships beginning on or after that date, and auditors appointed in respect of those financial years. See **[10.202]** et seq.

SI 2008/499: Statutory Auditors and Third Country Auditors (Amendment) Regulations 2008

Authority: CA 2006, s 1239; European Communities Act 1972, s 2(2). These Regulations correct errors in the Statutory Auditors and Third Country Auditors Regulations 2007, SI 2007/3494. Regulation 1(3) of the 2007 Regulations purports to bring reg 38(2)(b)–(d) into force on 29 June 2008. There is no para (2)(b)–(d) of reg 38, and it is para (2)(b)–(d) of reg 40 that should have been brought into force on that date. Regulation 7(2) of the 2007 Regulations provides that the new s 1223A of the Companies Act 2006 (as inserted by reg 7(1) of the 2007 Regulations) applies only to "EEA auditors" (ie, auditors qualified elsewhere in the European Economic Area) appointed as statutory auditors for financial years beginning on or after 6 April 2008. These Regulations revoke reg 7(2) so that s 1223A also applies to EEA auditors who have not been appointed as statutory auditors at all. Regulation 15(1) of the 2007 Regulations inserts three new sections into the Companies Act 2006, about the transfer of audit working papers to countries outside the European Economic Area. Regulation 15(2) provides that one of those new sections (ie, s 1253E) applies only to working papers for audits for financial years beginning on or after 6 April 2008. These Regulations provide that another of those new sections (s 1253D) also applies only to working papers for audits for financial years beginning on or after that date. These Regulations also correct drafting errors in regs 34 and 36 of the 2007 Regulations. Note that these Regulations were revoked by the Statutory Auditors and Third Country Auditors Regulations 2013, SI 2013/1672 (at **[4.482]**) *as from 31 July 2013.*

SI 2008/497: Companies (Late Filing Penalties) and Limited Liability Partnerships (Filing Periods and Late Filing Penalties) Regulations 2008

Authority: CA 1985, s 257(1), (4)(a), (d); Limited Liability Partnerships Act 2000, s 15(a); CA 2006, ss 453, 1292(1)(a), (c). These Regulations determine the penalties which companies must pay to the registrar of companies if they file their annual accounts and reports late, and which limited liability partnerships must pay if they deliver their accounts and auditors' reports late. See **[4.125]** et seq.

SI 2008/496: Statutory Auditors (Delegation of Functions etc) Order 2008

Authority: CA 1989, s 46(4): CA 2006, ss 504(1)(b)(ii), 1252(1), (4)(a), (5), (8), 1253(4), Sch 13, paras 7(3), 11(2), (3)(a). This Order transferred most of the functions of the Secretary of State under Part 42 of the Companies Act 2006 (statutory auditors) to the Professional Oversight Board. It implemented, in part, Article 32 of Directive 2006/43 EC on statutory audits of annual accounts and consolidated accounts, amending Council Directives 78/660/EEC and 83/349/EEC and repealing Council Directive 84/253/EEC. The designation was of two successive bodies known as the Professional Oversight Board, because on 6 April 2008 the body of that name established by The Professional Oversight Board Limited was replaced by the body of that name established by The Financial Reporting Council Limited. Articles 1 and 2 of the Order dealt with citation, commencement and interpretation. Article 3 of the Order transferred certain functions conferring powers to make

Regulations on 1 March 2008. Article 4 of the Order transferred the Secretary of State's functions under Part 42 of the Companies Act 2006 on 6 April 2008, subject to the exceptions and reservations it describes. Article 5 conferred on the Professional Oversight Board the functions relating to notices of auditor resignations under ss 522–525 of the 2006 Act (also on 6 April 2008). Articles 6–9 imposed requirements on the Professional Oversight Board of consultation, publishing an annual work programme, record keeping and notification of certain matters to the Secretary of State. Article 10 modified s 1256 of the Companies Act 2006, so that references to the Secretary of State in respect of the time limits for certain prosecutions were treated as references to the Professional Oversight Board. Article 11 appointed the Auditing Practices Board on 6 April 2008 to issue guidance on the meaning of senior statutory auditor for the purposes of s 504(1)(b)(ii) of the Companies Act 2006. Article 12 revoked the Companies Act 1989 (Delegation) Order 2005. That Order transferred to the Professional Oversight Board for Accountancy the functions of the Secretary of State under Part 2 of the Companies Act 1989 (repealed by the Companies Act 2006). This Order was revoked by the Statutory Auditors (Amendment of Companies Act 2006 and Delegation of Functions etc) Order 2012, SI 2012/1741, as from 2 July 2012; see the 2012 Order at **[4.430]**. *Article 7 of the 2012 Order (at* **[4.434]***) transfers the Secretary of State's functions under Part 42 of the 2006 Act to the Financial Reporting Council Limited (again subject to certain exceptions and reservations). Article 16 of the 2012 Order provides for transitional provisions in connection with the revocation of this Order (see* **[4.443]***).*

SI 2008/495: Companies (Trading Disclosures) Regulations 2008

Authority: CA 2006, ss 82, 84, 1292(1)(a), 1294. These Regulations deal with trading disclosures to be made by a company. All displays and disclosures required by these Regulations are to be in characters which can be read with the naked eye (regulation 2). Regulation 3 specifies that a company's registered name must be displayed at the registered office and other places at which records are kept for inspection. This regulation does not apply to any company which is "dormant" as defined in section 1169 of the Companies Act 2006 ("the Act"). Regulation 4 applies to locations other than those referred to in reg 3. Regulation 4 specifies that a company's registered name must also be displayed at any location at which it carries on business. This regulation does not apply to a location which is primarily used for living accommodation. Regulation 5 sets out the manner in which a company is required to display its registered name. The name must be positioned so that it can easily be seen by any visitor to the premises (reg 5(2)). The name must also be displayed continuously unless the multiple occupation exception set out in reg 5(3) applies. Regulation 6(1) specifies the documentation on which a company's registered name should appear. A company must also display its registered name on its websites (reg 6(2)). Regulation 7 sets out the particulars, in addition to the registered name, which should appear on a company's business letters, order forms and websites. The reference to registration in a particular part of the United Kingdom is to registration by the Registrar of Companies for that part of the United Kingdom (s 1060 of the Act). Regulation 7 implements Article 4 (apart from references to a company being wound up) of Directive 2003/58/EC of the European Parliament and the Council amending Council Directive 68/151/EEC, as regards disclosure requirements in respect of certain types of companies. These requirements in Article 4 were previously implemented by regulation 6 of, and the Schedules to, the Companies (Registrar, Languages and Trading Disclosures) Regulations 2006 (SI 2006/3429) which amended provisions of the Companies Act 1985 ("the 1985 Act") and the Companies (Northern Ireland) Order 1986 ("the 1986 Order"). Those provisions of the 1985 Act and 1986 Order are repealed on 1 October 2008. Where a company's business letter includes the name of a director of that company, other than in the text or as a signatory, the letter must disclose the name of every director of that company (reg 8). Regulation 9 deals with disclosures relating to the registered office and any other place at which the company keeps records available for inspection under the Companies Acts. "Working day" is defined in s 1173(1) of the Act. It is an offence to fail to comply with a requirement of these Regulations and for these purposes a shadow director is to be treated as an officer of the company (reg 10). Regulation 11 revokes regulation 6 of, and the Schedules to, SI 2006/3429. They were revoked by the Company, Limited Liability Partnership and Business (Names and Trading Disclosures) Regulations 2015, SI 2015/17, reg 30, Sch 6, para 1(d), as from 31 January 2015. The 2015 Regulations are at **[4.514]**.

SI 2008/489: Companies (Disclosure of Auditor Remuneration and Liability Limitation Agreements) Regulations 2008

Authority: CA 2006, ss 494, 538, 1292(1)(a); European Communities Act 1972, s 2(2). These Regulations provide for companies to disclose fees receivable by their auditors and their auditors' associates' and also to disclose liability limitation agreements that they make with their auditors. Disclosure must be in a note to the company's annual accounts. Small and medium-sized companies (defined in reg 3(2)(a) and (b) in the same way as in the Companies Act 2006) must disclose the fee paid to their auditors for the audit itself (reg 4). The Secretary of State (or, if a delegation order is made under s 1252 of the Companies Act 2006, the body to whom the Secretary of State's functions are delegated) may require the auditors of a medium-sized company to give him limited information about other fees paid to them if the company does not voluntarily disclose that information itself (reg 4(4)): this provision implements Article 49.1(c) of Directive 2006/43/EC of the European Parliament and of the Council on statutory audit of annual accounts and consolidated accounts, amending Council Directives 78/660/EEC and 83/349/EEC and repealing Council Directive 84/253/EEC. Every other company must disclose both the audit fee and all other fees receivable by the auditors for services supplied by them and their associates to the company, its subsidiaries (except where its control over a subsidiary is subject to severe long-term restrictions) and associated pension schemes (reg 5(1)). Auditors' associates are defined in Sch

1; associated pension schemes are defined in reg 3(1). Each type of service specified in Sch 2 and the fee paid for it must be separately disclosed (reg 5(3)); and services to the company and its subsidiaries on the one hand and to associated pension schemes on the other must be separately disclosed (reg 5(4)). No disclosure is required of fees for non-accountancy services supplied by a distant associate of the company's auditors where the total fees for those services are not more than £10,000 or 1% of all the audit fees received by the auditors in the auditors' financial year ending not later than the company's financial year to which the accounts relate (reg 5(6) and (7)). Consolidated group accounts (except those of small or medium-sized groups which are not ineligible) must disclose the types of services specified in Sch 2 and the fees paid for them as if the group were a single company: but if that is done, the individual companies do not need to disclose them (reg 6). Auditors must supply their company's directors with the information needed to enable the company to disclose the types of services specified in Sch 2 and the fees paid for them (reg 7).A company which has made a liability limitation agreement with its auditors must disclose its principal terms and the date of the approval resolution (or resolution waiving the need for approval in the case of a private company) passed by the company's members (reg 8). The disclosure must be in a note to the accounts for the year in question or (if the agreement was entered into too late to be included in those accounts) in a note to the next year's accounts. See **[4.115]**.

SI 2008/410: Large and Medium-sized Companies and Groups (Accounts and Reports) Regulations 2008

Authority: CA 2006, ss 396(3), 404(3), 409(1)–(3), 412(1)–(3), 416(4), 421(1), (2), 445(3)(a), (b), 677(3)(a), 712(2)(b)(i), 831(3)(a), 832(4)(a), 836(1)(b)(i), 1292(1)(a), (c). These Regulations specify the form and content of the accounts and reports of companies under Part 15 of the Companies Act 2006), other than those subject to the small companies regime. They are dealt with separately in the Small Companies and Groups (Accounts and Directors' Report) Regulations 2008. The Regulations replace provisions previously contained in the Schedules to Part 7 of the Companies Act 1985 and in the Schedules to Part 8 of the Companies (Northern Ireland) Order 1986. They extend to the whole of the UK. The Regulations come into force on 6 April 2008 and, with one exception, apply to financial years beginning on or after that date (reg 2). The corresponding provisions of the 1985 Act or the 1986 Order continue to apply to accounts and reports for financial years beginning before that date. The new disclosure required by para 4 of Sch 8 to the Regulations applies in relation to financial years beginning on or after 6 April 2009 (reg 2(3)). The Regulations continue the implementation of the following Directives: Council Directive 78/660/EEC on the annual accounts of certain types of companies ("the Fourth Directive"); Council Directive 83/349/EEC on consolidated accounts ("the Seventh Directive"); Council Directive 86/635/EEC on the annual accounts and consolidated accounts of banks and other financial institutions ("the Bank Accounts Directive"); and Council Directive 91/674/EEC on the annual accounts and consolidated accounts of insurance undertakings ("the Insurance Accounts Directive"). Regulation 3(1) of, and Sch 1 to, the Regulations specify the form and content of the individual accounts of a company which is not a banking or insurance company, and the directors of which are preparing Companies Act individual accounts. The Schedule re-enacts Sch 4 to the 1985 Act and Sch 4 to the 1986 Order, with two substantive modifications. Paragraph 36(4) of Sch 1 implements Article 1.5 of Directive 2006/46 of the European Parliament and the Council amending the Fourth, Seventh, Bank Accounts and Insurance Accounts Directives. Paragraph 72 of Sch 1 implements Article 1.6(7b) of Directive 2006/46. The Directive is also to be implemented by the Small Companies and Groups (Accounts and Directors' Report) Regulations 2008, the Companies Act 2006 (Amendment) (Accounts and Reports) Regulations 2008, and by the FSA using powers under the Financial Services and Markets Act 2000. Paragraph 36(4) of Sch 1 gives companies the option of including financial instruments in the accounts at a fair value provided that they may be so included under international accounting standards adopted under the IAS Regulation (as defined in s 474(1) of the 2006 Act) on or before 5 September 2006, and provided that the disclosures required by such standards are made. Paragraph 72 requires companies to make certain disclosures about transactions with related parties. Regulation 4 specifies certain exemptions for medium-sized companies the directors of which are preparing Companies Act accounts. It re-enacts the exemptions in s 246A of the 1985 Act and in art 254A of the 1986 Order, save that medium-sized companies are required by reg 4(3) to disclose their turnover in the accounts delivered to the registrar of companies. Regulation 4(2)(b) implements the member State option in Article 1.6 of Directive 2006/46 exempting medium-sized companies from making the disclosures about related party transactions required by para 72 of Sch 1 to the Regulations. Regulation 5 of, and Sch 2 to, the Regulations specify the form and content of the individual accounts of a banking company the directors of which are preparing Companies Act accounts. The Schedule re-enacts Sch 9 to the 1985 Act and Sch 9 to the 1986 Order. Paragraph 44(4) of Sch 2 contains the equivalent provision to para 36(4) of Sch 1 and para 92 the equivalent provision to para 72 of Sch 1 (see above) in implementation of Article 3 of Directive 2006/46. Regulation 6 of, and Sch 3 to, the Regulations specify the form and content of the individual accounts of an insurance company the directors of which are preparing Companies Act accounts. The Schedule re-enacts Sch 9A to the 1985 Act and Sch 9A to the 1986 Order. Paragraph 30(4) of Sch 3 contains the equivalent provision to para 36(4) of Sch 1 and para 90 the equivalent provision to para 72 of Sch 1 (see above) in implementation of Article 4 of Directive 2006/46. Regulations 7 and 8 of, and Schedules 4 and 5 to, the Regulations specify information about related undertakings and directors' remuneration which a company must include in the notes to the individual accounts which it prepares, whether they are Companies Act individual accounts or IAS individual accounts. The Schedules re-enact Schedules 5 and 6 to the 1985 Act and Schedules 5 and 6 to the 1986 Order. Regulation 9 of, and Sch 6 to, the Regulations specify the form and content of group accounts. The Schedule re-enacts Sch 4A to the 1985 Act and Sch 4A to the 1986 Order, save that paras 9,

13 and 17 have been simplified to facilitate convergence with international accounting standards. Regulation 10 of, and Sch 7 to, the Regulations specify information to be included in the directors' report which the directors of a company are required to prepare under section 415 of the 2006 Act. The Schedule re-enacts the provisions in Sch 7 to the 1985 Act and Sch 7 to the 1986 Order, save that the thresholds for disclosure of political donations and expenditure and charitable donations have been raised from £200 to £2000 (paras 3 and 5), and that provision is now made for disclosure of donations to independent election candidates (para 3). Paragraphs 13 and 14 of Sch 7 continue the implementation of Directive 2004/25/EEC of the European Parliament and the Council on takeover bids. Regulation 11 of, and Sch 8 to, the Regulations specify information to be included in the directors' remuneration report which the directors of a quoted company are required to prepare under section 420 of the 2006 Act. The Schedule re-enacts the provisions in Sch 7A to the 1985 Act and Sch 7A to the 1986 Order, with the addition of a new requirement in para 4 that the directors' remuneration report contain a statement of how pay and employment conditions elsewhere in the company and group have been taken into account in determining directors' remuneration for the financial year in question. Regulation 12 of, and Sch 9 to, the Regulations define the term "provisions" for the purposes of the Regulations and for the purposes of sections 677(3)(a) (Companies Act accounts: relevant provisions for purposes of financial assistance), 712(2)(b)(i) (Companies Act accounts: relevant provisions to determine available profits for redemption or purchase out of capital), 831(3)(a) (Companies Act accounts: net asset restriction on public company distributions), 832(4)(a) (Companies Act accounts: investment companies distributions) and 836(1)(b)(i) (Companies Act accounts: relevant provisions for distribution purposes) of the 2006 Act. Regulation 13 of, and Sch 10 to, the Regulations contain general interpretation provisions. See **[4.60]**.

SI 2008/409: Small Companies and Groups (Accounts and Directors' Report) Regulations 2008

Authority: CA 2006, ss 396(3), 404(3), 409(1), (3), 412(1), (3), 416(4), 444(3)(a), (b), 677(3)(a), 712(2)(b)(i), 836(1)(b)(i), 1292(1)(a), (c). These Regulations specify the form and content of the accounts and directors' report of companies subject to the small companies regime under Part 15 of the Companies Act 2006. Section 381 of the 2006 Act defines what is meant by "small companies regime". The Regulations replace provisions previously contained in the Schedules to Part 7 of the Companies Act 1985 and in the Schedules to Part 8 of the Companies (Northern Ireland) Order 198. They extend to the whole of the United Kingdom. The Regulations come into force on 6 April 2008, and apply in relation to financial years beginning on or after that date (reg 2). The corresponding provisions of the 1985 Act or the 1986 Order continue to apply to accounts and directors' reports for financial years beginning before that date. The Regulations continue the implementation of the following Directives: Council Directive 78/660/EEC on the annual accounts of certain types of companies ("the Fourth Directive"), and Council Directive 83/349/EEC on consolidated accounts ("the Seventh Directive"). Regulation 3(1) of, and Sch 1 to, the Regulations specify the form and content of the individual accounts of a company which is subject to the small companies regime and which is preparing Companies Act individual accounts. Sch 1 re-enacts Sch 8 to the 1985 Act and Sch 8 to the 1986 Order, with one substantive modification. Paragraph 36(4) of Sch 1 implements article 1.5 of Directive 2006/46 of the European Parliament and the Council amending the Fourth and Seventh Directives and Council Directives 86/635/EEC on the annual accounts and consolidated accounts of banks and other financial institutions and 91/674/EEC on the annual accounts and consolidated accounts of insurance undertakings. The Directive is also to be implemented by the Large and Medium-sized Companies and Groups (Accounts and Reports) Regulations 2008, the Companies Act 2006 (Amendment) (Accounts and Reports) Regulations 2008, and by the FSA using powers under the Financial Services and Markets Act 2000. Paragraph 36(4) of Sch 1 gives companies the option of including financial instruments in the accounts at a fair value provided that they may be so included under international accounting standards adopted under the IAS Regulation (as defined in s 474(1) of the 2006 Act) on or before 5 September 2006, and provided that the disclosures required by such standards are made. Regulation 4 of, and Sch 2 to, the Regulations re-enact the requirements of Part 1 of Sch 5 to the 1985 Act and Part 1 of Sch 5 to the 1986 Order for small companies. They concern information about related undertakings which must be provided in the notes to a company's individual accounts, whether they are Companies Act accounts or IAS accounts. Regulation 5 of, and Sch 3 to, the Regulations re-enact the requirements of Part 1 of Sch 6 to the 1985 Act and Part 1 of Sch 6 to the 1986 Order as they apply to small companies. They concern information about directors' remuneration which must be provided in the notes to a company's individual accounts, whether they are Companies Act accounts or IAS accounts. Regulation 6 of, and Sch 4 to, the Regulations make provision about Companies Act individual accounts which may be delivered to the registrar of companies for a small company under section 444 of the 2006 Act. Sch 4 re-enacts Sch 8A to the 1985 Act and Sch 8A to the 1986 Order. Regulation 7 of, and Sch 5 to, the Regulations specify information to be included in the directors' report which a company's directors are required to prepare under section 415 of the 2006 Act. Schedule 5 re-enacts the provisions in Sch 7 to the 1985 Act and Sch 7 to the 1986 Order as they apply to small companies, with two modifications – the thresholds for disclosure of political donations and expenditure and charitable donations have been raised from £200 to £2000 (paragraphs 2 and 4), and provision is now made for disclosure of donations to independent election candidates (paragraph 2). Regulation 8 of, and Part 1 of Sch 6 to, the Regulations specify the form and content of Companies Act group accounts which a parent company subject to the small companies regime may choose to prepare, although not required to do so (see s 398 of the 2006 Act). The Schedule re-enacts Sch 4A to the 1985 Act and Sch 4A to the 1986 Order as they apply to small companies, save that paragraphs 9, 13 and 17 have been simplified to facilitate convergence with international accounting standards. Regulations 9 and 10 apply the provisions of Sch 3 (information in notes to accounts about directors' benefits) and Part 2 of Sch 6 (information in notes about related undertakings) to Companies

Act or IAS group accounts which the directors of a small parent company choose to prepare. Part 2 of Sch 6 re-enacts Part 2 of Sch 5 to the 1985 Act and Part 2 of Sch 5 to the 1986 Order. Regulation 11 makes provision for exemptions from Companies Act group accounts which may be delivered to the registrar of companies for a small parent company under section 444 of the 2006 Act. Regulation 12 of, and Sch 7 to, the Regulations define the term "provisions" for the purposes of the Regulations and for the purposes of sections 677(3)(a) (Companies Act accounts: relevant provisions for purposes of financial assistance), 712(2)(b)(i) (Companies Act accounts: relevant provisions to determine available profits for redemption or purchase out of capital) and 836(1)(b)(i) (Companies Act accounts: relevant provisions for distribution purposes) of the 2006 Act. Regulation 13 of, and Sch 8 to, the Regulations contain general interpretation provisions. See **[4.41]**.

SI 2008/393: Companies Act 2006 (Amendment) (Accounts and Reports) Regulations 2008

Authority: CA 2006, ss 468(1), (2), 473(2), 484, 1292(1)(a), (c). Regulation 1 provides for citation and interpretation. Regulation 2 (commencement and application) provides that the Regulations come into force on 6 April 2008 and apply in relation to financial years beginning on or after that date. It further provides that in determining whether a company or group qualifies as small or medium-sized under ss 382(2), 383(3), 465(2) or 466(3) of the 2006 Act (qualification in relation to subsequent financial year by reference to circumstances in preceding financial years) in relation to a financial year ending on or after 6 April 2008, the company or group shall be treated as having qualified as small or medium-sized (as the case may be) in any previous financial year in which it would have so qualified if amendments to the same effect as those made by these Regulations had been in force. Regulations 3–13 contain various amendments to Pts 15 and 16 of the 2006 Act (at **[1.430]** and **[1.541]** respectively).

SI 2008/374: Companies (Summary Financial Statement) Regulations 2008

Authority: CA 2006, ss 426(1), (3), 427(2), (5), 428(2), (5), 1292(1). These Regulations concern the summary financial statements which companies may send out in place of their full accounts and reports under ss 426–428 of CA 2006. They come into force on 6 April 2008 and apply in relation to companies' financial years beginning on or after that date. They revoke and replace the Companies (Summary Financial Statement) Regulations 1995, SI 1995/2092 (which were made under the corresponding provisions of CA 1985), and the Companies (Summary Financial Statement) Regulations (Northern Ireland) 1996, SR 1996/179. They are revoked by the Companies (Receipt of Accounts and Reports) Regulations 2013, SI 2013/1973, reg 3(1), as from 1 October 2013, in relation to annual accounts and reports prepared in respect of a company's financial year ending on or after 30 September 2013 (subject to transitional provisions).

SI 2008/373: Companies (Revision of Defective Accounts and Reports) Regulations 2008

Authority: CA 2006, ss 454(3), (4), 1292(1)(a), (c). These Regulations set out how the provisions of CA 2006 are to apply to revised annual accounts, directors' reports, directors' remuneration reports and summary financial statements prepared under this section. They come into force on 6 April 2008 and apply in relation to companies' financial years beginning on or after that date. They revoke and replace (subject to transitional provisions) the Companies (Revision of Defective Accounts and Report) Regulations 1990, SI 1990/2570 which were made under the Companies Act 1985, and the Companies (Revision of Defective Accounts and Report) Regulations (Northern Ireland) 1991, SR 1991/268. See **[4.21]** et seq.

SSI 2008/144: Companies Act 2006 (Scottish public sector companies to be audited by the Auditor General for Scotland) Order 2008

Authority: CA 2006, s 483(1)–(3). This Order provides that certain companies with registered offices in Scotland are to have their accounts audited by the Auditor General for Scotland. This means that in terms of s 475 of the 2006 Act, these companies will be exempt from the auditing of company accounts requirements of Part 16. The companies subject to this Order are non-profit making public sector companies, which appear to Scottish Ministers to carry out functions of a public nature or are funded by bodies audited by the Auditor General for Scotland.

2007 Statutory Instruments

SI 2007/3535: Companies (Fees for Inspection and Copying of Company Records) (No 2) Regulations 2007

Authority: CA 2006, ss 744(1)(b), (2), 749(1), 1137(1), (4), 1167, 1292(1)(a), (c). These Regulations prescribe the fees payable by a person who wishes to exercise a right under CA 2006 to inspect the register of debenture holders of a company or to receive a copy of that register or a copy of a debenture trust deed. These Regulations replace fees prescribed in the Companies (Inspection and Copying of Registers, Indices and Documents) Regulations 1991, SI 1991/1998 (and the Companies (Inspection and Copying of Registers, Indices and Documents) Regulations 1993 (Northern Ireland)) subject to transitional savings. See **[4.16]**.

SI 2007/3534: Independent Supervisor Appointment Order 2007

Authority: CA 2006, s 1228. This Order appointed the Professional Oversight Board as Independent Supervisor of the Auditors General when they carry out the functions of statutory auditors. Articles 4–7 created additional provisions and requirements for the exercise of that function, including requirements for the contents of reports by the Independent Supervisor on the exercise of its functions; and requirements for consultation and record-keeping. It was revoked by the Statutory Auditors (Amendment of Companies Act 2006 and Delegation of Functions etc) Order 2012, SI 2012/1741, as from 2 July 2012 (see the 2012 Order **[4.430]**). *Article 18 of the 2012 Order (at* **[4.445]**) *appoints the Financial Reporting Council Limited to discharge the function mentioned in s 1229(1) of the 2006 Act. Article 21 of the 2012 Order provides for transitional provisions in connection with the revocation of this Order (see* **[4.448]**).

SI 2007/3495: Companies Act 2006 (Commencement No 5, Transitional Provisions and Savings) Order 2007

Authority: CA 2006, ss 1292, 1296, 1300(2). This Order brings into force certain provisions of CA 2006 on various dates and contains transitional provisions and savings. For details relating to the commencement of the 2006 Act, see the Table of Commencements in Part 2 of this Handbook *ante*. Note that the commencement orders themselves were removed from Part 2 in the 2022 edition of this work in order to create space for newer legislation. Since that edition, the commencement orders have only been reproduced in the online only Appendix 10 to this Handbook.

SI 2007/3494: Statutory Auditors and Third Country Auditors Regulations 2007

Authority: CA 2006, ss 1239, 1241(2)(c), 1246, 1292(1)(a), (b), (2), Sch 11, para 8(1)(a); European Communities Act 1972, s 2(2). The Regulations implement in part Directive 2006/43/EC of the European Parliament and of the Council on statutory audits of annual accounts and consolidated accounts, amending Council Directives 78/660/EEC and 83/349/EEC and repealing Council Directive 84/253/EEC ("the Audit Directive"). Regulations 4 to 16 amend provisions in Part 42 of the Companies Act 2006 (statutory auditors). Regulation 4 requires supervisory bodies to extend certain of their rules to former members. Regulation 6 requires an aptitude test in connection with the recognition of the qualifications of third country auditors. Regulation 8 and the Schedule impose an obligation of confidentiality in relation to the regulatory bodies for the audit profession. Regulation 14 requires those bodies to cooperate with regulatory bodies in other EEA States, and regulation 15 imposes requirements in relation to working arrangements entered into by them for the transfer of papers to regulatory bodies outside of the EEA. Regulation 9 allows the Independent Supervisor of the Auditors General a choice as to whether to establish supervision arrangements itself, or to enter into supervision arrangements with other bodies. Regulation 16 extends the power of the Secretary of State to issue directions to comply with international obligation, so that they may be issued to the Independent Supervisor. Regulations 17 to 28 amend provisions in Schedule 10 to the Companies Act 2006, which have the effect of requiring recognised supervisory bodies to have certain rules with which their members must comply if they wish to act as statutory auditors. Regulation 17 requires an aptitude test in connection with the recognition of qualifications of EEA auditors. Regulations 19 and 21 introduce additional reporting and independence requirements, and regulation 20 requires certain technical standards in relation to group audits. Regulations 22 and 23 impose requirements as to the monitoring and enforcement of the bodies' rules. Regulation 24 regulates the transfer by statutory auditors of papers to regulatory bodies outside of the EEA. Regulations 26 to 28 require some standards to be set, and some monitoring to be conducted, by a body independent of the recognised supervisory bodies. Regulations 29–40 originally set out procedural and substantive requirements for the registration of third country auditors and make some minor amendments to the Companies Act 2006. Regulations 34–40 were subsequently revoked by SI 2013/1672. Regulation 30 extends the power in s 1239(7) of the Companies Act 2006 so that the Secretary of State may direct in writing that specified requirements of regulations concerning the register of third country auditors are not to apply to a particular registered third country auditor or a class of registered third country auditors. Regulation 42 amends s 994 of the Companies Act 2006. It allows a company member to petition a court if the company's auditor has been dismissed on improper grounds. Regulation 45 revokes the Company Auditors (Examinations) Regulations 1990, the Companies Act 1989 (Register of Auditors and Information About Audit Firms) Regulations 1991, and the equivalent Northern Ireland regulations.

SI 2007/2974: Companies (Cross-Border Mergers) Regulations 2007

Authority: CA 2006, ss 1102(2), 1105(2)(d), 1106(2); European Communities Act 1972, s 2(2). These Regulations implement Directive 2005/56/EC on cross-border mergers of limited liability companies. The Regulations provide a framework whereby companies may engage in a cross-border merger. The term "cross-border merger" is defined in reg 2 by reference to three categories: a merger by absorption, a merger by absorption of a wholly-owned subsidiary, and a merger by formation of a new company. The merger must involve at least one company formed and registered in the United Kingdom (a "UK company"), and at least one company formed and registered in an EEA State other than the United Kingdom (an "EEA company"). These Regulations were revoked by the Companies, Limited Liability Partnerships and Partnerships (Amendment etc) (EU Exit) Regulations 2019, SI 2019/348, as from IP completion day (as defined in the European Union (Withdrawal Agreement) Act 2020, s 39).

SI 2007/2612: Companies (Fees for Inspection and Copying of Company Records) Regulations 2007

Authority: CA 2006, ss 116(1)(b), (2), 229(2), 238(2), 358(4), 807(2), 811(2), 1137(1), (4), 1167, 1292(1)(a), (c). These Regulations prescribe the fees payable by a person who wishes to exercise a right under CA 2006 to inspect a company record or to receive a copy of a company record. They replace fees prescribed in the Companies (Inspection and Copying of Registers, Indices and Documents) Regulations 1991 (SI 1991/1998) subject to transitional savings. See **[4.11]**.

SI 2007/2607: Companies Act 2006 (Commencement No 4 and Commencement No 3 (Amendment)) Order 2007

Authority: CA 2006, ss 1296(1), 1300(2). This Order brings into force the power to make Regulations about fees charged by companies for inspection of company records and provision of copies. It also amends the third commencement Order (SI 2007/2194) in order to reverse the repeal of certain provisions of CA 1985. For details relating to the commencement of the 2006 Act, see the Table of Commencements in Part 2 of this Handbook *ante*. Note that the commencement orders themselves were removed from Part 2 in the 2022 edition of this work in order to create space for newer legislation. Since that edition, the commencement orders have only been reproduced in the online only Appendix 10 to this Handbook.

SI 2007/2242: Companies (Interest Rate for Unauthorised Political Donation or Expenditure) Regulations 2007

Authority: CA 2006, ss 369(5)(b), 1167. Where a company has made a political donation or incurred political expenditure without the authorisation required by CA 2006 the directors are liable to make good to the company the amount of the unauthorised donation or expenditure with interest. These Regulations set the rate of interest to be applied at 8% per annum. See **[4.10]**.

SI 2007/2194: Companies Act 2006 (Commencement No 3, Consequential Amendments, Transitional Provisions and Savings) Order 2007

Authority: CA 2006, ss 1292, 1294, 1296, 1300(2). This Order brings into force certain provisions of CA 2006 on various dates and contains transitional provisions and savings. For details relating to the commencement of the 2006 Act, see the Table of Commencements in Part 2 of this Handbook *ante*. Note that the commencement orders themselves were removed from Part 2 in the 2022 edition of this work in order to create space for newer legislation. Since that edition, the commencement orders have only been reproduced in the online only Appendix 10 to this Handbook.

SI 2007/2081: Companies (Political Expenditure Exemption) Order 2007

Authority: CA 2006, ss 377, 1292(1)(c). This Order exempts certain political expenditure incurred by news companies from the need for authorisation by the company's members under Part 14 of the Companies Act 2006. The expenditure exempted, described in art 3 of the Order, is that incurred in the preparation, publication and dissemination of news material which is capable of being reasonably regarded as intended to affect public support for a political party or other political organisation, or an independent election candidate, or to influence voters in relation to any national or regional referendum held under the law of a member State. The companies exempted, described in art 4 of the Order, are those whose ordinary course of business includes the preparation, publication or dissemination to the public, or any part of the public, of news material. This Order replaces the Companies (EU Political Expenditure) Exemption Order 2001, which was made under s 347B of the Companies Act 1985. Section 347B is repealed by CA 2006 with effect from the date on which this Order comes into force. See **[4.6]**.

SI 2007/1093: Companies Act 2006 (Commencement No 2, Consequential Amendments, Transitional Provisions and Savings) Order 2007

Authority: CA 2006, ss 1292(1), 1294(1), 1296(1), (2), 1300(2). This Order brings into force certain provisions of CA 2006 on various dates and contains transitional provisions and savings. For details relating to the commencement of the 2006 Act, see the Table of Commencements in Part 2 of this Handbook *ante*. Note that the commencement orders themselves were removed from Part 2 in the 2022 edition of this work in order to create space for newer legislation. Since that edition, the commencement orders have only been reproduced in the online only Appendix 10 to this Handbook.

SI 2007/318: Companies Acts (Unregistered Companies) Regulations 2007

Authority: CA 2006, s 1043. These Regulations applied Part 28 of CA 2006 (takeovers etc), and certain ancillary provisions, to unregistered companies. They further implemented Directive 2004/25/EC of the European Parliament and of the Council on Takeover Bids. These Regulations were revoked by the Unregistered Companies Regulations 2009, SI 2009/2436, reg 8, as from 1 October 2009, subject to transitional provisions and savings in Sch 2 to those Regulations at **[4.399]**.

2006 Statutory Instruments

SI 2006/3429: Companies (Registrar, Languages and Trading Disclosures) Regulations 2006

Authority: CA 2006, ss 1091(4), 1105(2)(d), 1106(2); European Communities Act 1972, s 2(2); Limited Liability Partnerships Act 2000, ss 15, 17. These Regulations implement provisions of Directive 2003/58/EC of the European Parliament and the Council of 15 July 2003 amending Council Directive 68/151/EEC, as regards disclosure requirements in respect of certain types of companies. They do so by amending the Companies Act 1985 and the Companies (Northern Ireland) Order 1986 so far as not yet repealed by the Companies Act 2006, and by supplementing provisions of the Companies Act 2006 brought into force on the same date as these Regulations. Regulation 1 provides for citation etc. Regulation 2 applies when the registrar of companies provides a copy in electronic form of material on the register to a person requesting that the copy be certified as a true copy. The registrar's certificate must be certified by an electronic signature which is uniquely linked to the registrar by means under his sole control and which is linked to the certificate and the copy in such a way that subsequent changes are detectable. Regulation 3 amends the 1985 Act and the 1986 Order (except in respect of limited liability partnerships) by no longer requiring copies of certain documents delivered to the registrar to be office copies (ie, hard copies). The effect of regulation 4 is that when a contract for the allotment of shares paid up other than in cash is delivered to the registrar, it need not be in English but must be accompanied by a certified translation into English. Regulation 5 enables companies to deliver to the registrar any of the documents to which Council Directive 68/151/EEC applies (listed in s 1078 of the 2006 Act) in any of the official languages of the European Union if accompanied by a certified translation into English. Regulations 6 and 7 and Schedules 1 and 2 amend the 1985 Act, the 1986 Order, the Insolvency Act 1986 and the Insolvency (Northern Ireland) Order 1989 so as to include websites and documents in electronic form in provisions requiring the company's name, registered number, registered office and other particulars, and the fact that the company is being wound up (where that is so), to appear on correspondence, publications and other documents. See **[4.1]**.

SI 2006/3428: Companies Act 2006 (Commencement No 1, Transitional Provisions and Savings) Order 2006

Authority: CA 2006, ss 1296(1), (2), 1300(2). This Order brings into force certain provisions of CA 2006 on various dates and contains transitional provisions and savings. For details relating to the commencement of the 2006 Act, see the Table of Commencements in Part 2 of this Handbook *ante*. Note that the commencement orders themselves were removed from Part 2 in the 2022 edition of this work in order to create space for newer legislation. Since that edition, the commencement orders have only been reproduced in the online only Appendix 10 to this Handbook.

Index

P

Q

R

U